THE EUROPA WORLD YEAR BOOK 2009

VOLUME II

KAZAKHSTAN–ZIMBABWE

LONDON AND NEW YORK

First published 1926

© **Routledge 2009**
Albert House, 1–4 Singer Street, London, EC2A 4BQ, United Kingdom
(Routledge is an imprint of the Taylor & Francis Group, an Informa business)

All rights reserved. No part of this
publication may be photocopied, recorded,
or otherwise reproduced, stored in a retrieval
system or transmitted in any form or by any
electronic or mechanical means without the
prior permission of the copyright owner.

ISBN13: 978-1-85743-511-5 (The Set)
978-1-85743-542-9 (Vol. II)
ISBN10: 1-85743-511-7 (The Set)
1-85743-542-7 (Vol. II)
ISSN: 0071-2302
Library of Congress Catalog Card Number 59-2942

Senior Editor: Joanne Maher

Statistics Editor: Philip McIntyre

Regional Editors: Lynn Daniel, Katie Dawson, Lucy Dean, Iain Frame,
Imogen Gladman, Dominic Heaney, Juliet Love, Jillian O'Brien, Jacqueline West

International Organizations Editors: Catriona Appeatu Holman, Helen Canton

Associate Regional Editors: David Gruar, Sianan Healy,
Meena Khan, Christopher Matthews, Anna Thomas

Assistant Editors: Kim Chamberlain, Neil Higgins, William Huckin,
Catriona Marcham, Simon Molony, Adrian Reynolds,
Janine Tenzer, Amyas Varcoe, Gareth Vaughan

Contributing Editor: Katharine Murison

Associate Editor, Directory Research: James Middleton

Editorial Director: Paul Kelly

Typeset in New Century Schoolbook

Typeset by Data Standards Limited, Frome, Somerset

Printed and bound in Great Britain by Polestar Wheatons, Exeter

FOREWORD

THE EUROPA WORLD YEAR BOOK was first published in 1926. Since 1960 it has appeared in annual two-volume editions, and has become established as an authoritative reference work, providing a wealth of detailed information on the political, economic and commercial institutions of the world.

Volume I contains a comprehensive listing of some 1,900 international organizations, commissions and specialized bodies, and the first part of the alphabetical survey of countries of the world, from Afghanistan to Jordan. Volume II contains countries from Kazakhstan to Zimbabwe. An Index of Territories covered in both volumes is to be found at the end of Volume II.

The International Organizations section gives extensive coverage to the United Nations and its related agencies and bodies. There are also detailed articles concerning other major international and regional organizations; entries for many affiliated organizations appear within these articles. In addition, the section includes briefer details of some 1,500 other international organizations. A comprehensive Index of International Organizations is included at the end of Volume I.

Each country is covered by an individual chapter, containing: an introductory survey including recent history, economic affairs, government, defence, education, and public holidays; an economic and demographic survey using the latest available statistics on area and population, health and welfare, agriculture, forestry, fishing, industry, finance, trade, transport, tourism, the media, and education; and a directory section listing names, addresses and other useful facts about organizations in the fields of government, election commissions, political parties, diplomatic representation, judiciary, religions, the media, telecommunications, banking, insurance, trade and industry, development organizations, chambers of commerce, industrial and trade associations, utilities, trade unions, transport, and tourism.

The entire content of the print edition of THE EUROPA WORLD YEAR BOOK is available online at www.europaworld.com. This prestigious resource incorporates sophisticated search and browse functions as well as specially commissioned visual and statistical content. An ongoing programme of updates of key areas of information ensures currency of content, and enhances the richness of the coverage for which THE EUROPA WORLD YEAR BOOK is renowned.

Readers are referred to the nine titles in the Europa Regional Surveys of the World series: AFRICA SOUTH OF THE SAHARA, CENTRAL AND SOUTH-EASTERN EUROPE, EASTERN EUROPE, RUSSIA AND CENTRAL ASIA, THE FAR EAST AND AUSTRALASIA, THE MIDDLE EAST AND NORTH AFRICA, SOUTH AMERICA, CENTRAL AMERICA AND THE CARIBBEAN, SOUTH ASIA, THE USA AND CANADA, and WESTERN EUROPE, available both in print and online, offer comprehensive analysis at regional, sub-regional and country level. More detailed coverage of international organizations is to be found in THE EUROPA DIRECTORY OF INTERNATIONAL ORGANIZATIONS.

The content of THE EUROPA WORLD YEAR BOOK is extensively revised and updated by a variety of methods, including direct mailing to all the institutions listed. Many other sources are used, such as national statistical offices, government departments and diplomatic missions. The editors thank the innumerable individuals and organizations world-wide whose generous co-operation in providing current information for this edition is invaluable in presenting the most accurate and up-to-date material available.

May 2009

ACKNOWLEDGEMENTS

The editors gratefully acknowledge particular indebtedness for permission to reproduce material from the following sources: the United Nations' statistical databases and *Demographic Yearbook*, *Statistical Yearbook*, *Monthly Bulletin of Statistics*, *Industrial Commodity Statistics Yearbook* and *International Trade Statistics Yearbook*; the United Nations Educational, Scientific and Cultural Organization's *Statistical Yearbook* and Institute for Statistics database; the *Human Development Report* of the United Nations Development Programme; the Food and Agriculture Organization of the United Nations' statistical database; the statistical databases of the World Health Organization; the International Labour Office's statistical database and *Yearbook of Labour Statistics*; the World Bank's *World Bank Atlas*, *Global Development Finance*, *World Development Report* and *World Development Indicators*; the International Monetary Fund's statistical database, *International Financial Statistics* and *Government Finance Statistics Yearbook*; the World Tourism Organization's *Compendium* and *Yearbook of Tourism Statistics*; the US Geological Survey; the International Telecommunication Union; and *The Military Balance 2009*, a publication of the International Institute for Strategic Studies, Arundel House, 13–15 Arundel Street, London WC2R 3DX. Statistics Canada information is used with the permission of Statistics Canada. Users are forbidden to copy this material and/or redisseminate the data, in an original or modified form, for commercial purposes, without the expressed permission of Statistics Canada. Information on the availability of the wide range of data from Statistics Canada can be obtained from Statistics Canada's Regional Offices, its website at www.statcan.ca, and its toll-free access number 1-800-263-1136.

HEALTH AND WELFARE STATISTICS: SOURCES AND DEFINITIONS

Total fertility rate Source: WHO Statistical Information System. The number of children that would be born per woman, assuming no female mortality at child-bearing ages and the age-specific fertility rates of a specified country and reference period.

Under-5 mortality rate Source: WHO Statistical Information System. Defined by WHO as the probability of a child born in a specific year or period dying before the age of five, if subject to the age-specific mortality rates of that year or period.

HIV/AIDS Source: UNAIDS. Estimated percentage of adults aged 15 to 49 years living with HIV/AIDS. < indicates 'fewer than'.

Health expenditure Source: WHO Statistical Information System.
US $ per head (PPP)
International dollar estimates, derived by dividing local currency units by an estimate of their purchasing-power parity (PPP) compared with the US dollar. PPPs are the rates of currency conversion that equalize the purchasing power of different currencies by eliminating the differences in price levels between countries.
% of GDP
GDP levels for OECD countries follow the most recent UN System of National Accounts. For non-OECD countries a value was estimated by utilizing existing UN, IMF and World Bank data.
Public expenditure
Government health-related outlays plus expenditure by social schemes compulsorily affiliated with a sizeable share of the population, and extrabudgetary funds allocated to health services. Figures include grants or loans provided by international agencies, other national authorities, and sometimes commercial banks.

Access to water and sanitation Source: WHO/UNICEF Joint Monitoring Programme on Water Supply and Sanitation (JMP) (Progress on Drinking Water and Sanitation, 2008). Defined in terms of the percentage of the population using improved facilities in terms of the type of technology and levels of service afforded. For water, this includes house connections, public standpipes, boreholes with handpumps, protected dug wells, protected spring and rainwater collection; allowance is also made for other locally defined technologies. Sanitation is defined to include connection to a sewer or septic tank system, pour-flush latrine, simple pit or ventilated improved pit latrine, again with allowance for acceptable local technologies. Access to water and sanitation does not imply that the level of service or quality of water is 'adequate' or 'safe'.

Human Development Index (HDI) Source: UNDP, *Human Development Report* (2007/08, Statistical Update). A summary of human development measured by three basic dimensions: prospects for a long and healthy life, measured by life expectancy at birth; knowledge, measured by adult literacy rate (two-thirds' weight) and the combined gross enrolment ratio in primary, secondary and tertiary education (one-third weight); and standard of living, measured by GDP per head (PPP US $). The index value obtained lies between zero and one. A value above 0.8 indicates high human development, between 0.5 and 0.8 medium human development, and below 0.5 low human development. A centralized data source for all three dimensions was not available for all countries. In some such cases other data sources were used to calculate a substitute value; however, this was excluded from the ranking. Other countries, including non-UNDP members, were excluded from the HDI altogether. In total, 179 countries were ranked for 2006.

CONTENTS

Abbreviations	Page ix	Nicaragua	Page 3408
International Telephone Codes	xiii	Niger	3428
		Nigeria	3446
Kazakhstan	2597	Norway	3472
Kenya	2617	Norwegian External Territories:	
Kiribati	2640	Svalbard	3497
The Democratic People's Republic of Korea (North Korea)	2649	Jan Mayen	3499
The Republic of Korea (South Korea)	2679	Norwegian Dependencies	3499
Kosovo	2714	Oman	3500
Kuwait	2726	Pakistan	3516
Kyrgyzstan	2747	Palau	3566
Laos	2765	Palestinian Autonomous Areas	3574
Latvia	2781	Panama	3601
Lebanon	2799	Papua New Guinea	3620
Lesotho	2830	Paraguay	3641
Liberia	2843	Peru	3659
Libya	2860	The Philippines	3683
Liechtenstein	2880	Poland	3722
Lithuania	2888	Portugal	3747
Luxembourg	2908	Qatar	3774
The former Yugoslav republic of Macedonia	2920	Romania	3792
Madagascar	2939	The Russian Federation	3816
Malawi	2957	Rwanda	3857
Malaysia	2974	Saint Christopher and Nevis	3875
The Maldives	3013	Saint Lucia	3885
Mali	3027	Saint Vincent and the Grenadines	3896
Malta	3044	Samoa	3906
The Marshall Islands	3056	San Marino	3915
Mauritania	3065	São Tomé and Príncipe	3922
Mauritius	3081	Saudi Arabia	3932
Mexico	3097	Senegal	3957
The Federated States of Micronesia	3128	Serbia	3981
Moldova	3136	Seychelles	4006
Monaco	3155	Sierra Leone	4014
Mongolia	3162	Singapore	4030
Montenegro	3186	Slovakia	4056
Morocco	3195	Slovenia	4076
Mozambique	3220	Solomon Islands	4093
Myanmar	3239	Somalia	4106
Namibia	3266	South Africa	4125
Nauru	3284	Spain	4160
Nepal	3292	Spanish External Territories:	
The Netherlands	3319	Ceuta	4203
Netherlands Dependencies:		Melilla	4208
Aruba	3345	Sri Lanka	4213
The Netherlands Antilles	3352	Sudan	4242
New Zealand	3364	Suriname	4267
New Zealand's Dependent Territories:		Swaziland	4280
Ross Dependency	3389	Sweden	4294
Tokelau	3389	Switzerland	4320
New Zealand's Associated States:		Syria	4347
The Cook Islands	3394	Taiwan (see China, Vol. I)	
Niue	3401	Tajikistan	4373

CONTENTS

Tanzania	Page 4392
Thailand	4412
Timor-Leste	4445
Togo	4464
Tonga	4482
Trinidad and Tobago	4493
Tunisia	4511
Turkey	4530
Turkmenistan	4568
Tuvalu	4585
Uganda	4592
Ukraine	4610
The United Arab Emirates	4640
The United Kingdom	4660
United Kingdom Crown Dependencies:	
The Channel Islands	4734
The Isle of Man	4741
United Kingdom Overseas Territories:	
Anguilla	4746
Bermuda	4753
The British Antarctic Territory	4760
The British Indian Ocean Territory	4761
The British Virgin Islands	4762
The Cayman Islands	4769
The Falkland Islands	4777
Gibraltar	4783
Montserrat	Page 4791
The Pitcairn Islands	4798
Saint Helena and Dependencies	4800
South Georgia and the South Sandwich Islands	4805
The Turks and Caicos Islands	4805
The United States of America	4812
United States Commonwealth Territories:	
The Northern Mariana Islands	4887
Puerto Rico	4893
United States External Territories:	
American Samoa	4906
Guam	4912
The United States Virgin Islands	4919
Other United States Territories	4925
Uruguay	4927
Uzbekistan	4945
Vanuatu	4964
The Vatican City	4976
Venezuela	4986
Viet Nam	5012
Yemen	5041
Zambia	5063
Zimbabwe	5080
Index of Territories	5104

ABBREVIATIONS

AB	Aktiebolag (Joint-Stock Company); Alberta	BSEC	(Organization of the) Black Sea Economic Co-operation	CSCE	Conference on Security and Cooperation in Europe
Abog.	Abogado (Lawyer)	bte	boîte (box)	CSTAL	Confederación Sindical de los Trabajadores de América Latina
Acad.	Academician; Academy	Bul.	Bulvar (boulevard)		
ACP	African, Caribbean and Pacific (countries)	bulv.	bulvarīs (boulevard)	CT	Connecticut
ACT	Australian Capital Territory			CTCA	Confederación de Trabajadores Centro-americanos
AD	anno Domini	C	Centigrade	Cttee	Committee
ADB	African Development Bank; Asian Development Bank	c.	circa; cuadra(s) (block(s))	cu	cubic
ADC	aide-de-camp	CA	California	cwt	hundredweight
Adm.	Admiral	CACM	Central American Common Market		
admin.	administration	Cad.	Caddesi (Street)	DC	District of Columbia; Distrito Capital; Distrito Central
AEC	African Economic Community; African Economic Conference	CAP	Common Agricultural Policy	d.d.	delniška družba, dioničko društvo (joint stock company)
AfDB	African Development Bank	cap.	capital		
AG	Aktiengesellschaft (Joint-Stock Company)	Capt.	Captain	DE	Delaware; Departamento Estatal
AH	anno Hegirae	CAR	Central African Republic	Dec.	December
a.i.	ad interim	CARICOM	Caribbean Community and Common Market	Del.	Delegación
AID	(US) Agency for International Development	CBSS	Council of Baltic Sea States	Dem.	Democrat; Democratic
AIDS	acquired immunodeficiency syndrome	CCL	Caribbean Congress of Labour	Dep.	Deputy
AK	Alaska	Cdre	Commodore	dep.	deposits
Al.	Aleja (Alley, Avenue)	CEMAC	Communauté économique et monétaire de l'Afrique centrale	Dept	Department
AL	Alabama	Cen.	Central	devt	development
ALADI	Asociación Latinoamericana de Integración	CEO	Chief Executive Officer	DF	Distrito Federal
Alt.	Alternate	CET	common external tariff	Dgo	Durango
AM	Amplitude Modulation	CFA	Communauté Financière Africaine; Coopération Financière en Afrique centrale	Diag.	Diagonal
a.m.	ante meridiem (before noon)			Dir	Director
amalg.	amalgamated			Div.	Division(al)
Apdo	Apartado (Post Box)	CFE	Treaty on Conventional Armed Forces in Europe	DM	Deutsche Mark
APEC	Asia-Pacific Economic Co-operation			DMZ	demilitarized zone
		CFP	Common Fisheries Policy; Communauté française du Pacifique; Comptoirs français du Pacifique	DNA	deoxyribonucleic acid
approx.	approximately			DN	Distrito Nacional
Apt	Apartment			Doc.	Docent
AR	Arkansas			Dott.	Dottore/essa
ARV	advanced retroviral	Chair.	Chairman/person/woman	DPRK	Democratic People's Republic of Korea
AŞ	Anonim Şirketi (Joint-Stock Company)	Chih.	Chihuahua		
		CI	Channel Islands	Dr	Doctor
A/S	Aktieselskab (Joint-Stock Company)	Cia	Companhia	Dr.	Drive
		Cía	Compañía	Dra	Doctora
ASEAN	Association of South East Asian Nations	Cie	Compagnie	Dr Hab.	Doktor Habilitowany (Assistant Professor)
		c.i.f.	cost, insurance and freight		
asscn	association	C-in-C	Commander-in-Chief	DRC	Democratic Republic of the Congo
assoc.	associate	circ.	circulation	DR-CAFTA	Dominican Republic-Central American Free Trade Agreement
ASSR	Autonomous Soviet Socialist Republic	CIS	Commonwealth of Independent States		
				Drs	Doctorandus
asst	assistant	CJD	Creutzfeldt-Jakob disease	DU	depleted uranium
AU	African Union	cm	centimetre(s)	dwt	dead weight tons
Aug.	August	cnr	corner		
auth.	authorized	CO	Colorado		
av., Ave	Avenija, Avenue	Co	Company; County	E	East; Eastern
Av., Avda	Avenida (Avenue)	c/o	care of	EBRD	European Bank for Reconstruction and Development
Avv.	Avvocato (Lawyer)	Coah.	Coahuila		
AZ	Arizona	Col	Colonel		
		Col.	Colima; Colonia	EC	European Community
		COMESA	Common Market for Eastern and Southern Africa	ECA	(United Nations) Economic Commission for Africa
b.b.	bez broja (without number)				
BC	British Columbia	Comm.	Commission; Commendatore	ECE	(United Nations) Economic Commission for Europe
BC	before Christ	Commdr	Commander		
Bd	Board	Commdt	Commandant	ECLAC	(United Nations) Economic Commission for Latin America and the Caribbean
Bd, Bld, Blv., Blvd	Boulevard	Commr	Commissioner		
		Cond.	Condiminio		
b/d	barrels per day	Confed.	Confederation	ECO	Economic Co-operation Organization
BFPO	British Forces' Post Office	Cont.	Contador (Accountant)		
Bhd	Berhad (Public Limited Company)	COO	Chief Operating Officer	Econ.	Economics; Economist
		COP	Conference of (the) Parties	ECOSOC	(United Nations) Economic and Social Council
Bldg	Building	Corp.	Corporate		
blk	block	Corpn	Corporation	ECOWAS	Economic Community of West African States
Blvr	Bulevar	CP	Case Postale, Caixa Postal, Casella Postale (Post Box); Communist Party		
BP	Boîte postale (Post Box)			ECU	European Currency Unit
br.(s)	branch(es)			Edif.	Edificio (Building)
Brig.	Brigadier	C por A	Compañía por Acciones (Joint Stock Company)	edn	edition
BSE	bovine spongiform encephalopathy			EEA	European Economic Area
		CPSU	Communist Party of the Soviet Union	EFTA	European Free Trade Association
		Cres.	Crescent		

ABBREVIATIONS

e.g.	exempli gratia (for example)	Hon.	Honorary, Honourable	kom.	komnata (room)
EIB	European Investment Bank	hp	horsepower	kor.	korpus (block)
EMS	European Monetary System	HPAI	highly pathogenic avian influenza	k'och.	k'ochasi (street)
EMU	Economic and Monetary Union			KS	Kansas
eMv	electron megavolt	HQ	Headquarters	küç	küçasi (street)
Eng.	Engineer; Engineering	HRH	His/Her Royal Highness	kv.	kvartal (apartment block); kvartira (apartment)
EP	Empresa Pública	HSC	Harmonized System Classification		
ERM	Exchange Rate Mechanism			kW	kilowatt(s)
ESACA	Emisora de Capital Abierto Sociedad Anónima	HSH	His/Her Serene Highness	kWh	kilowatt hours
		Hwy	Highway	KY	Kentucky
Esc.	Escuela; Escudos; Escritorio				
ESCAP	(United Nations) Economic and Social Commission for Asia and the Pacific	IA	Iowa	LA	Louisiana
		IBRD	International Bank for Reconstruction and Development	lauk	laukums (square)
				lb	pound(s)
ESCWA	(United Nations) Economic and Social Commission for Western Asia			LDCs	Least Developed Countries
		ICC	International Chamber of Commerce; International Criminal Court	Lic.	Licenciado
				Licda	Licenciada
esq.	esquina (corner)			LNG	liquefied natural gas
est.	established; estimate; estimated	ICRC	International Committee of the Red Cross	LPG	liquefied petroleum gas
etc.	et cetera			Lt, Lieut	Lieutenant
EU	European Union	ICT	information and communication technology	Ltd	Limited
eV	eingetragener Verein				
excl.	excluding	ICTR	International Criminal Tribunal for Rwanda		
exec.	executive				
Ext.	Extension	ICTY	International Criminal Tribunal for the former Yugoslavia	m	metre(s)
				m.	million
F	Fahrenheit	ID	Idaho	MA	Massachusetts
f.	founded	IDA	International Development Association	Maj.	Major
FAO	Food and Agriculture Organization			Man.	Manager; managing
		IDB	Inter-American Development Bank	MB	Manitoba
f.a.s.	free alongside ship			mbH	mit beschränkter Haftung (with limited liability)
Feb.	February	IDPs	internally displaced persons		
Fed.	Federal; Federation	i.e.	id est (that is to say)	MD	Maryland
feds	federations	IFC	International Finance Corporation	MDG	Millennium Development Goal
FL	Florida			MDRI	multilateral debt relief initiative
FM	frequency modulation	IGAD	Intergovernmental Authority on Development	ME	Maine
fmr(ly)	former(ly)			Me	Maître
f.o.b.	free on board	IHL	International Humanitarian Law	mem.(s)	member(s)
Fr	Father	IL	Illinois	MEP	Member of the European Parliament
Fr.	Franc	ILO	International Labour Organization/Office		
Fri.	Friday			Mercosul	Mercado Comum do Sul (Southern Common Market)
FRY	Federal Republic of Yugoslavia	IMF	International Monetary Fund		
ft	foot (feet)	IML	International Migration Law	Mercosur	Mercado Común del Sur (Southern Common Market)
FTA	free trade agreement/area	in (ins)	inch (inches)		
FYRM	former Yugoslav republic of Macedonia	IN	Indiana	Méx.	México
		Inc, Incorp.		MFN	most favoured nation
		Incd	Incorporated	mfrs	manufacturers
g	gram(s)	incl.	including	Mgr	Monseigneur; Monsignor
g.	gatve (street)	Ind.	Independent	MHz	megahertz
GA	Georgia	INF	Intermediate-Range Nuclear Forces	MI	Michigan
GATT	General Agreement on Tariffs and Trade			MIA	missing in action
		Ing.	Engineer	Mich.	Michoacán
GCC	Gulf Co-operation Council	Insp.	Inspector	MIGA	Multilateral Investment Guarantee Agency
Gdns	Gardens	Int.	International		
GDP	gross domestic product	Inzå.	Engineer	Mil.	Military
GEF	Global Environment Facility	IP	intellectual property	Mlle	Mademoiselle
Gen.	General	IPU	Inter-Parliamentary Union	mm	millimetre(s)
GeV	giga electron volts	Ir	Engineer	Mme	Madame
GM	genetically modified	IRF	International Road Federation	MN	Minnesota
GmbH	Gesellschaft mit beschränkter Haftung (Limited Liability Company)	irreg.	irregular	mnt.	mante (road)
		Is	Islands	MO	Missouri
		ISIC	International Standard Industrial Classification	Mon.	Monday
GMO(s)	genetically modified organism(s)			Mor.	Morelos
GMT	Greenwich Mean Time	IT	information technology	MOU	memorandum of understanding
GNI	gross national income	ITU	International Telecommunication Union	movt	movement
GNP	gross national product			MP	Member of Parliament
Gov.	Governor	ITUC	International Trade Union Confederation	MS	Mississippi
Govt	Government			MSS	Manuscripts
Gro	Guerrero	Iur.	Lawyer	MT	Montana
grt	gross registered tons			MW	megawatt(s); medium wave
GSM	Global System for Mobile Communications	Jal.	Jalisco	MWh	megawatt hour(s)
		Jan.	January		
Gto	Guanajuato	Jnr	Junior		
GWh	gigawatt hours	Jr	Jonkheer (Esquire); Junior		
		Jt	Joint	N	North; Northern
ha	hectares			n.a.	not available
HE	His/Her Eminence; His/Her Excellency	Kav.	Kaveling (Plot)	nab.	naberezhnaya (embankment, quai)
hf	hlutafelag (Limited Company)	kg	kilogram(s)	NAFTA	North American Free Trade Agreement
HI	Hawaii	KG	Kommandit Gesellschaft (Limited Partnership)		
HIPC	heavily indebted poor country			nám.	náměstí (square)
HIV	human immunodeficiency virus	kHz	kilohertz	Nat.	National
hl	hectolitre(s)	KK	Kaien Kaisha (Limited Company)	NATO	North Atlantic Treaty Organization
HM	His/Her Majesty	km	kilometre(s)		

ABBREVIATIONS

Nay.	Nayarit	PR	Puerto Rico	SE	South-East
NB	New Brunswick	pr.	prospekt, prospekti (avenue)	Sec.	Secretary
NC	North Carolina	Pres.	President	Secr.	Secretariat
NCD	National Capital District	PRGF	Poverty Reduction and Growth Facility	Sen.	Senior; Senator
NCO	non-commissioned officer			Sept.	September
ND	North Dakota	Prin.	Principal	SER	Sua Eccellenza Reverendissima (His Eminence)
NE	Nebraska; North-East	Prof.	Professor		
NEPAD	New Partnership for Africa's Development	Propr	Proprietor	SFRY	Socialist Federal Republic of Yugoslavia
		Prov.	Province; Provincial; Provinciale (Dutch)		
NGO	non-governmental organization			SGP	Stability and Growth Pact
NH	New Hampshire	prov.	provulok (lane)	Sin.	Sinaloa
NJ	New Jersey	PRSP	Poverty Reduction Strategy Paper	SIS	Small(er) Island States
NL	Newfoundland and Labrador, Nuevo León			SITC	Standard International Trade Classification
		pst.	puistotie (avenue)		
NM	New Mexico	PT	Perseroan Terbatas (Limited Company)	SJ	Society of Jesus
NMP	net material product			SK	Saskatchewan
no	numéro, número (number)	Pte	Private; Puente (Bridge)	Skt	Sankt (Saint)
no.	number	Pty	Proprietary	SLP	San Luis Potosí
Nov.	November	p.u.	paid up	SMEs	small and medium-sized enterprises
NPT	Non-Proliferation Treaty	publ.	publication; published		
nr	near	Publr	Publisher	s/n	sin número (without number)
nrt	net registered tons	Pue.	Puebla	Soc.	Society
NS	Nova Scotia	Pvt	Private	Sok.	Sokak (Street)
NSW	New South Wales			Son.	Sonora
NT	Northwest Territories			Șos.	Șosea (Road)
NU	Nunavut Territory	QC	Québec	SP	São Paulo
NV	Naamloze Vennootschap (Limited Company); Nevada	QIP	Quick Impact Project	SpA	Società per Azioni (Joint-Stock Company)
		Qld	Queensland		
NW	North-West	Qro	Querétaro	Sq.	Square
NY	New York	Q. Roo	Quintana Roo	sq	square (in measurements)
NZ	New Zealand	q.v.	quod vide (to which refer)	Sr	Senior; Señor
				Sra	Señora
				Srl	Società a Responsabilità Limitata (Limited Company)
OAPEC	Organization of Arab Petroleum Exporting Countries	Rag.	Ragioniere (Accountant)		
		Rd	Road	SSR	Soviet Socialist Republic
OAS	Organization of American States	R(s)	rand; rupee(s)	St	Saint, Sint; Street
OAU	Organization of African Unity	reg., regd	register; registered	Sta	Santa
Oax.	Oaxaca	reorg.	reorganized	Ste	Sainte
Oct.	October	Rep.	Republic; Republican; Representative	STI(s)	sexually transmitted infection(s)
OECD	Organisation for Economic Cooperation and Development			str.	strada, stradă (street)
		Repub.	Republic	str-la	stradelă (street)
OECS	Organisation of Eastern Caribbean States	res	reserve(s)	subs.	subscribed; subscriptions
		retd	retired	Sun.	Sunday
Of.	Oficina (Office)	Rev.	Reverend	Supt	Superintendent
OH	Ohio	RI	Rhode Island	SUV	sports utility vehicle
OIC	Organization of the Islamic Conference	RJ	Rio de Janeiro	sv.	Saint
		Rm	Room	SW	South-West
OK	Oklahoma	RN	Royal Navy		
ON	Ontario	ro-ro	roll-on roll-off		
OPEC	Organization of the Petroleum Exporting Countries	RP	Recette principale	Tab.	Tabasco
		Rp.(s)	rupiah(s)	Tamps	Tamaulipas
opp.	opposite	Rpto	Reparto (Estate)	TAȘ	Turkiye Anonim Șirketi (Turkish Joint-Stock Company)
OR	Oregon	RSFSR	Russian Soviet Federative Socialist Republic		
Org.	Organization			Tas	Tasmania
ORIT	Organización Regional Interamericana de Trabajadores	Rt	Right	TD	Teachta Dàla (Member of Parliament)
				tech., techn.	technical
OSCE	Organization for Security and Cooperation in Europe	S	South; Southern; San	tel.	telephone
		SA	Société Anonyme, Sociedad Anónima (Limited Company); South Australia	TEU	20-ft equivalent unit
				Thur.	Thursday
				TN	Tennessee
p.	page	SAARC	South Asian Association for Regional Co-operation	tř	třída (avenue)
p.a.	per annum			Treas.	Treasurer
PA	Palestinian Authority; Pennsylvania	SACN	South American Community of Nations	Tue.	Tuesday
				TV	television
Parl.	Parliament(ary)	SADC	Southern African Development Community	TX	Texas
per.	pereulok (lane, alley)				
PE	Prince Edward Island	SA de CV	Sociedad Anónima de Capital Variable (Variable Capital Company)		
Perm. Rep.	Permanent Representative				
PF	Postfach (Post Box)			u.	utca (street)
PICTs	Pacific Island countries and territories	SAECA	Sociedad Anónima Emisora de Capital Abierto	u/a	unit of account
				UAE	United Arab Emirates
PK	Posta Kutusu (Post Box)	SAR	Special Administrative Region	UEE	Unidade Económica Estatal
Pl.	Plac, Plads (square)	SARL	Sociedade Anônima de Responsabilidade Limitada (Joint-Stock Company of Limited Liability)	UEMOA	Union économique et monetaire ouest-africaine
pl.	platz; place; ploshchad (square)				
PLC	Public Limited Company			UK	United Kingdom
PLO	Palestine Liberation Organization			ul.	ulica, ulitsa (street)
		SARS	Severe Acute Respiratory Syndrome	UM	ouguiya
p.m.	post meridiem (after noon)			UN	United Nations
PMB	Private Mail Bag	Sat.	Saturday	UNAIDS	United Nations Joint Programme on HIV/AIDS
PNA	Palestinian National Authority	SC	South Carolina		
POB	Post Office Box	SD	South Dakota	UNCTAD	United Nations Conference on Trade and Development
pp.	pages	Sdn Bhd	Sendirian Berhad (Private Limited Company)		
PPP	purchasing-power parity			UNDP	United Nations Development Programme
PQ	Québec	SDR(s)	Special Drawing Right(s)		

ABBREVIATIONS

UNEP	United Nations Environment Programme	USSR	Union of Soviet Socialist Republics	W	West; Western
UNESCO	United Nations Educational, Scientific and Cultural Organization	UT	Utah	WA	Washington (State); Western Australia
				Wed.	Wednesday
				WEU	Western European Union
UNHCHR	UN High Commissioner for Human Rights			WFP	World Food Programme
				WFTU	World Federation of Trade Unions
UNHCR	United Nations High Commissioner for Refugees	VA	Virginia		
		VAT	value-added tax	WHO	World Health Organization
UNICEF	United Nations Children's Fund	VEB	Volkseigener Betrieb (Public Company)	WI	Wisconsin
Univ.	University			WSSD	World Summit on Sustainable Development
UNODC	United Nations Office on Drugs and Crime	v-CJD	new variant Creutzfeldt-Jakob disease		
				WTO	World Trade Organization
UNRWA	United Nations Relief and Works Agency for Palestine Refugees in the Near East	Ven.	Venerable	WV	West Virginia
		Ver.	Veracruz	WY	Wyoming
		VHF	Very High Frequency		
UNWTO	World Tourism Organization	VI	(US) Virgin Islands		
Urb.	Urbanización (District)	Vic	Victoria		
US	United States	Vn	Veien (Street)		
USA	United States of America	vol.(s)	volume(s)	yr	year
USAID	United States Agency for International Development	VT	Vermont	YT	Yukon Territory
		vul.	vulitsa, vulytsa (street)	Yuc.	Yucatán

xii

INTERNATIONAL TELEPHONE CODES

To make international calls to telephone and fax numbers listed in *The Europa World Year Book*, dial the international access code of the country from which you are calling, followed by the appropriate country code for the organization you wish to call (listed below), followed by the area code (if applicable) and telephone or fax number listed in the entry.

	Country code	+ or – GMT*
Afghanistan	93	+4½
Albania	355	+1
Algeria	213	+1
Andorra	376	+1
Angola	244	+1
Antigua and Barbuda	1 268	–4
Argentina	54	–3
Armenia	374	+4
Australia	61	+8 to +10
Australian External Territories:		
Australian Antarctic Territory	672	+3 to +10
Christmas Island	61	+7
Cocos (Keeling) Islands	61	+6½
Norfolk Island	672	+11½
Austria	43	+1
Azerbaijan	994	+5
Bahamas	1 242	–5
Bahrain	973	+3
Bangladesh	880	+6
Barbados	1 246	–4
Belarus	375	+2
Belgium	32	+1
Belize	501	–6
Benin	229	+1
Bhutan	975	+6
Bolivia	591	–4
Bosnia and Herzegovina	387	+1
Botswana	267	+2
Brazil	55	–3 to –4
Brunei	673	+8
Bulgaria	359	+2
Burkina Faso	226	0
Burundi	257	+2
Cambodia	855	+7
Cameroon	237	+1
Canada	1	–3 to –8
Cape Verde	238	–1
Central African Republic	236	+1
Chad	235	+1
Chile	56	–4
China, People's Republic	86	+8
Special Administrative Regions:		
Hong Kong	852	+8
Macao	853	+8
China (Taiwan)	886	+8
Colombia	57	–5
Comoros	269	+3
Congo, Democratic Republic	243	+1
Congo, Republic	242	+1
Costa Rica	506	–6
Côte d'Ivoire	225	0
Croatia	385	+1
Cuba	53	–5
Cyprus	357	+2
'Turkish Republic of Northern Cyprus'	90 392	+2
Czech Republic	420	+1
Denmark	45	+1
Danish External Territories:		
Faroe Islands	298	0
Greenland	299	–1 to –4
Djibouti	253	+3
Dominica	1 767	–4
Dominican Republic	1 809	–4
Ecuador	593	–5

	Country code	+ or – GMT*
Egypt	20	+2
El Salvador	503	–6
Equatorial Guinea	240	+1
Eritrea	291	+3
Estonia	372	+2
Ethiopia	251	+3
Fiji	679	+12
Finland	358	+2
Finnish External Territory:		
Åland Islands	358	+2
France	33	+1
French Overseas Regions and Departments:		
French Guiana	594	–3
Guadeloupe	590	–4
Martinique	596	–4
Réunion	262	+4
French Overseas Collectivities:		
French Polynesia	689	–9 to –10
Mayotte	262	+3
Saint-Barthélemy	590	–4
Saint-Martin	590	–4
Saint Pierre and Miquelon	508	–3
Wallis and Futuna Islands	681	+12
Other French Overseas Territory:		
New Caledonia	687	+11
Gabon	241	+1
Gambia	220	0
Georgia	995	+4
Germany	49	+1
Ghana	233	0
Greece	30	+2
Grenada	1 473	–4
Guatemala	502	–6
Guinea	224	0
Guinea-Bissau	245	0
Guyana	592	–4
Haiti	509	–5
Honduras	504	–6
Hungary	36	+1
Iceland	354	0
India	91	+5½
Indonesia	62	+7 to +9
Iran	98	+3½
Iraq	964	+3
Ireland	353	0
Israel	972	+2
Italy	39	+1
Jamaica	1 876	–5
Japan	81	+9
Jordan	962	+2
Kazakhstan	7	+6
Kenya	254	+3
Kiribati	686	+12 to +13
Korea, Democratic People's Republic (North Korea)	850	+9
Korea, Republic (South Korea)	82	+9
Kosovo	381†	+3
Kuwait	965	+3
Kyrgyzstan	996	+5
Laos	856	+7
Latvia	371	+2
Lebanon	961	+2
Lesotho	266	+2

INTERNATIONAL TELEPHONE CODES

	Country code	+ or − GMT*
Liberia	231	0
Libya	218	+1
Liechtenstein	423	+1
Lithuania	370	+2
Luxembourg	352	+1
Macedonia, former Yugoslav republic	389	+1
Madagascar	261	+3
Malawi	265	+2
Malaysia	60	+8
Maldives	960	+5
Mali	223	0
Malta	356	+1
Marshall Islands	692	+12
Mauritania	222	0
Mauritius	230	+4
Mexico	52	−6 to −7
Micronesia, Federated States	691	+10 to +11
Moldova	373	+2
Monaco	377	+1
Mongolia	976	+7 to +9
Montenegro	382	+1
Morocco	212	0
Mozambique	258	+2
Myanmar	95	+6½
Namibia	264	+2
Nauru	674	+12
Nepal	977	+5¾
Netherlands	31	+1
Netherlands Dependencies:		
Aruba	297	−4
Netherlands Antilles	599	−4
New Zealand	64	+12
New Zealand's Dependent and Associated Territories:		
Tokelau	690	−10
Cook Islands	682	−10
Niue	683	−11
Nicaragua	505	−6
Niger	227	+1
Nigeria	234	+1
Norway	47	+1
Norwegian External Territory:		
Svalbard	47	+1
Oman	968	+4
Pakistan	92	+5
Palau	680	+9
Palestinian Autonomous Areas	970 or 972	+2
Panama	507	−5
Papua New Guinea	675	+10
Paraguay	595	−4
Peru	51	−5
Philippines	63	+8
Poland	48	+1
Portugal	351	0
Qatar	974	+3
Romania	40	+2
Russian Federation	7	+2 to +12
Rwanda	250	+2
Saint Christopher and Nevis	1 869	−4
Saint Lucia	1 758	−4
Saint Vincent and the Grenadines	1 784	−4
Samoa	685	−11
San Marino	378	+1
São Tomé and Príncipe	239	0
Saudi Arabia	966	+3
Senegal	221	0
Serbia	381	+1
Seychelles	248	+4
Sierra Leone	232	0
Singapore	65	+8
Slovakia	421	+1
Slovenia	386	+1

	Country code	+ or − GMT*
Solomon Islands	677	+11
Somalia	252	+3
South Africa	27	+2
Spain	34	+1
Sri Lanka	94	+5½
Sudan	249	+2
Suriname	597	−3
Swaziland	268	+2
Sweden	46	+1
Switzerland	41	+1
Syria	963	+2
Tajikistan	992	+5
Tanzania	255	+3
Thailand	66	+7
Timor-Leste	670	+9
Togo	228	0
Tonga	676	+13
Trinidad and Tobago	1 868	−4
Tunisia	216	+1
Turkey	90	+2
Turkmenistan	993	+5
Tuvalu	688	+12
Uganda	256	+3
Ukraine	380	+2
United Arab Emirates	971	+4
United Kingdom	44	0
United Kingdom Crown Dependencies	44	0
United Kingdom Overseas Territories:		
Anguilla	1 264	−4
Ascension Island	247	0
Bermuda	1 441	−4
British Virgin Islands	1 284	−4
Cayman Islands	1 345	−5
Diego Garcia (British Indian Ocean Territory)	246	+5
Falkland Islands	500	−4
Gibraltar	350	+1
Montserrat	1 664	−4
Pitcairn Islands	872	−8
Saint Helena	290	0
Tristan da Cunha	290	0
Turks and Caicos Islands	1 649	−5
United States of America	1	−5 to −10
United States Commonwealth Territories:		
Northern Mariana Islands	1 670	+10
Puerto Rico	1 787	−4
United States External Territories:		
American Samoa	1 684	−11
Guam	1 671	+10
United States Virgin Islands	1 340	−4
Uruguay	598	−3
Uzbekistan	998	+5
Vanuatu	678	+11
Vatican City	39	+1
Venezuela	58	−4½
Viet Nam	84	+7
Yemen	967	+3
Zambia	260	+2
Zimbabwe	263	+2

* The times listed compare the standard (winter) times in the various countries. Some countries adopt Summer (Daylight Saving) Time—i.e. +1 hour—for part of the year.

† Mobile telephone numbers for Kosovo use either the country code for Monaco (377) or the country code for Slovenia (386).

Note: Telephone and fax numbers using the Inmarsat ocean region code 870 are listed in full. No country or area code is required, but it is necessary to precede the number with the international access code of the country from which the call is made.

Europa World *Plus*

Europa World and the Europa Regional Surveys of the World online

www.europaworld.com

Free trial available!

Europa World *Plus* enables you to subscribe to Europa World together with as many of the nine Regional Surveys of the World online as you choose, in one simple annual subscription.

The Europa Regional Surveys of the World complement and expand upon the information in Europa World with in-depth, expert analysis at regional, sub-regional and country level.

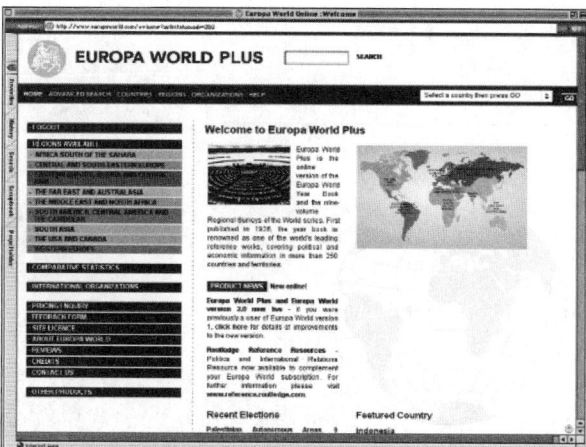

Providing:

* An interactive online library for all the countries and territories of each of the world regions
* Impartial coverage of issues of regional importance from acknowledged experts
* A vast range of up-to-date economic, political and statistical data
* Book and periodical bibliographies - direct you to further research

* Extensive directory of research institutes specializing in the region
* Ability to search by content type across regions
* Thousands of click-through web links to external sites

The nine titles that make up the series are as follows: *Africa South of the Sahara; Central and South-Eastern Europe; Eastern Europe, Russia and Central Asia; The Far East and Australasia; The Middle East and North Africa; South America, Central America and the Caribbean; South Asia; The USA and Canada; Western Europe.*

For further information and to register for a free trial please contact us at:
Tel: + 44 (0) 20 7017 6062
Fax: + 44 (0) 20 7017 6720
E-mail: reference.online@tandf.co.uk

KAZAKHSTAN

Introductory Survey

Location, Climate, Language, Religion, Flag, Capital

The Republic of Kazakhstan extends 1,900 km (1,200 miles) from the Volga river in the west to the Altai mountains in the east, and about 1,300 km (800 miles) from the Siberian plain in the north to the Central Asian deserts in the south. To the south it borders Turkmenistan, Uzbekistan and Kyrgyzstan. To the east the border is with the People's Republic of China. There is a long border in the north with Russia and a coastline of 2,320 km (1,400 miles) on the Caspian Sea in the south-west. The climate is of a strongly continental type, but there are wide variations throughout the territory. Average temperatures in January range from −18°C (0°F) in the north to −3°C (27°F) in the south. In July average temperatures are 19°C (66°F) in the north and 28°C–30°C (82°F–86°F) in the south. Average annual rainfall in mountainous regions reaches 1,600 mm (63 ins), whereas in the central desert areas it is less than 100 mm (4 ins). The state language is Kazakh; however, Russian is employed officially in state and local government bodies. The predominant religion is Islam, most ethnic Kazakhs being Sunni Muslims of the Hanafi school. Other ethnic groups have their own religious communities, notably the (Christian) Eastern Orthodox Church, which is attended mainly by Slavs. The national flag (proportions 1 by 2) consists of a light blue field, at the centre of which is a yellow sun (a disc surrounded by 32 rays), framed by the wings of a flying eagle, also in yellow, with a vertical stripe of national ornamentation in yellow near the hoist. In November 1997 the capital was moved from Almaty to Akmola (formerly Tselinograd), now known as Astana.

Recent History

After the February Revolution and the Bolshevik coup in Russia in 1917, there was civil war throughout Kazakhstan, which had come under Russian control in the first half of the 18th century. Bolshevik forces finally overcame those of the White Army, foreign interventionists and local nationalists. In 1920 the Kyrgyz Autonomous Soviet Socialist Republic (ASSR) was created within the Russian Soviet Federative Socialist Republic (the Russian Federation): the Kazakhs were known to the Russians as Kyrgyz, to distinguish them from the unrelated Cossacks. In 1925 the Kyrgyz ASSR was renamed the Kazakh ASSR; the Karakalpak region (Qoraqalpog'iston, now in Uzbekistan) was detached in 1930, and became an autonomous republic within the Uzbek Soviet Socialist Republic (SSR) in 1936. In December 1936 the Kazakh ASSR became a full Union Republic of the USSR, as the Kazakh SSR.

Under Soviet rule parts of Kazakhstan were heavily industrialized. However, more than 1m. people were estimated to have died as a result of the starvation that accompanied the campaign in the early 1930s to collectivize agriculture and settle nomadic peoples. Many of those deported from parts of the USSR during the Second World War (including Germans, Crimean Tatars, Baltic and Caucasian peoples) were sent to the Republic. During Nikita Khrushchev's period in office as Soviet leader (1953–64) large areas of previously uncultivated land in Kazakhstan were transformed into arable land. This, along with intensive industrialization, and the development of nuclear-testing sites and the Baikonur space centre brought large numbers of ethnic Russians to Kazakhstan; the proportion of Russians increased from 19.7% of the population in 1926 to 42.7% in 1959.

In June 1989 Nursultan Nazarbaev, Chairman of the republican Council of Ministers since March 1984, was appointed First Secretary of the Communist Party of Kazakhstan (CPK). Political and administrative changes were instituted in September 1989: a permanent Supreme Kenges (Supreme Council or Supreme Soviet—legislature) was to be established, and elections were to be conducted on a multi-candidate basis. The state duties hitherto held by the First Secretary of the CPK were transferred to the Chairman of the Supreme Kenges, to which post Nazarbaev was elected in February 1990. Many candidates stood unopposed at elections to the Supreme Kenges in March, and the system of reserved seats for CPK-affiliated organizations was retained, resulting in a substantial communist majority. In April the body elected Nazarbaev the first President of Kazakhstan.

On 25 October 1990 the Supreme Kenges declared its sovereignty, asserting republican control over natural resources and the economy. Nazarbaev strongly supported a redefinition of the respective all-Union and republican powers, and the Kazakhstani Government participated in discussions on the new Union Treaty in early 1991, although Nazarbaev also sought economic sovereignty for Kazakhstan, where some 90% of enterprises were under all-Union control.

In the referendum on the future of the USSR conducted in nine Soviet republics in March 1991, almost 90% of the electorate voted in Kazakhstan, of whom 94% endorsed the proposal to preserve the USSR as a 'union of sovereign states'. In June the Supreme Kenges voted, in principle, to adopt a draft union treaty. Kazakhstan was to sign the treaty in August, but the event was forestalled by an attempted coup, led by conservative communists, in Moscow, the Soviet and Russian capital. As the coup attempt collapsed, Nazarbaev resigned from the Politburo and Central Committee of the Communist Party of the Soviet Union (CPSU), in protest at the open support granted to the putschists by the CPSU leadership. The CPK was ordered to cease activities in state and government organs, and in September the party withdrew from the CPSU; elements from the party went to form the Socialist Party of Kazakhstan (SPK).

On 1 December 1991 Nazarbaev was elected unopposed as President of Kazakhstan in direct popular elections. On 8 December the leaders of Russia, Ukraine and Belarus signed an agreement establishing the Commonwealth of Independent States (CIS, see p. 225). On 16 December Kazakhstan became the last of the republics to declare independence from the USSR, as the Republic of Kazakhstan. The country became a co-founder of the CIS on 21 December, when the leaders of 11 former Soviet countries met in Almaty.

The Constitution, adopted in January 1993, invoked legislation adopted in September 1989, denoting Kazakh as the state language and Russian as a language of inter-ethnic communication. The document required that the President be fluent in Kazakh. Meanwhile, increased emigration, particularly by ethnic Germans (more than 300,000 of whom left Kazakhstan in the early 1990s) and Russians, was accompanied, albeit on a much smaller scale, by the return of ethnic Kazakhs from Kyrgyzstan, Mongolia, Tajikistan and Turkmenistan.

In June 1991 some 5,000 people demonstrated in Almaty against continued communist predominance in the Government and Supreme Kenges, demanding the formation of a new, coalition administration. In October the three most prominent nationalist opposition parties (the Freedom—Azat movement, the Republican Party and the Jeltoqsan National Democratic Party) united to form the Republican Party—Freedom (RP—F). The Union of National Unity of Kazakhstan was established in February 1993, with the declared aim of promoting social harmony and countering radical nationalism. Nazarbaev (who held no party affiliation) became Chairman of the Union, which was reorganized as a political party, the People's Unity Party (PUP), later in 1993.

In December 1993 the Supreme Kenges voted to dissolve itself and to grant Nazarbaev the power to rule by decree pending elections to a new legislature, which was to be reduced in size from 360 to 177 seats. Kazakhstan's first multi-party elections were duly held on 7 March 1994, with the participation of 74% of the electorate; a number of irregularities were reported by international observers. The PUP obtained 33 seats, which, when combined with the 42 seats won by candidates from the so-called 'President's List' (candidates nominated by Nazarbaev) and those of pro-Nazarbaev independents, ensured that Nazarbaev's supporters emerged as the strongest force in the assembly. The Confederation of Kazakhstani Trade Unions (CKTU) won 11 seats, the People's Congress Party of Kazakhstan (PCPK) nine and the SPK eight. The CPK was granted legal status in March, and in May claimed a membership of some 50,000. In that month the CKTU, the SPK and the PCPK formed an opposition bloc in the Supreme Kenges, with the stated aim of acting as a guarantor against 'dictatorship by executive bodies'.

In May 1994 some 96 members of the Supreme Kenges endorsed a motion expressing no confidence in the Government's economic, social and legal policies, and in June Nazarbaev announced a major government reorganization. The Government of Sergei Tereshchenko (premier since 1991) resigned in October 1994, admitting its failure to reform the economy. Akezhan Kazhegeldin, an economist and First Deputy Prime Minister in the outgoing Council of Ministers, was appointed premier.

In February 1995 the Constitutional Court declared the results of the 1994 general election to be invalid, owing to procedural irregularities. In March the Government was forced to tender its resignation, on the grounds that it had been approved by an unconstitutional parliament (although it was subsequently reinstated virtually unchanged). Nazarbaev was thereby effectively empowered to rule by decree pending further legislative elections. At a national referendum on 29 April more than 95% of voters endorsed the extension of Nazarbaev's five-year mandate until 1 December 2000.

In May 1995 Nazarbaev ordered the establishment of a special council to prepare (under his guidance) a new constitution. The final draft, which was approved by 89.1% of the electorate in a referendum on 30 August, preserved the President's extensive executive powers. The Supreme Kenges was replaced by a bicameral Parliament, comprising a 47-member Senat (Senate—with 40 members elected by Kazakhstan's regional administrative bodies and seven appointed by the President) and a directly elected 67-member Majlis (Assembly). The Constitutional Court was replaced by a Constitutional Council, the rulings of which were to be subject to a presidential right of veto.

Indirect elections to the Senat took place on 5 December 1995. Direct elections were held to the Majlis on 9 December, with the participation of 80.7% of the electorate; further rounds of voting took place later in the month and in February 1996, in those constituencies where no candidate had obtained the requisite 50% of the votes. Foreign observers reported procedural violations.

Popular dissatisfaction with the Government's economic and social policies became more pronounced in 1996. In April a new opposition movement, Citizen (Azamat), was established. Prolonged delays in payments of wages, owing to the insolvency of numerous state-owned enterprises, were a principal cause of strikes and unauthorized demonstrations throughout 1997 and early 1998, as was the ongoing reform of pensions legislation.

Meanwhile, in late 1996 the relocation of civil servants from Almaty to the northern city of Akmola (formerly Tselinograd) marked the beginning of the transfer of the capital city (in July 1994 the Supreme Kenges had approved a proposal by Nazarbaev to transfer the capital to Akmola by 2000). In November 1997 the new capital was officially inaugurated by Nazarbaev, and a joint session of both chambers of Parliament was held for the first time in Akmola in the following month. A ceremony was held in June 1998 to mark the official opening of the capital under the new name of Astana.

In March 1997, while Kazhegeldin was out of the country, Nazarbaev undertook a major reorganization and rationalization of the state apparatus. The Ministry of Petroleum and Natural Gas was abolished and replaced by a new state company, KazakhOil. Seven government institutions, including the Ministries of Defence and of Internal Affairs, were directly subordinated to the President, and the structure of regional government was reorganized. In October Kazhegeldin's resignation, ostensibly for health reasons, was announced; in the previous month a Russian newspaper had published an admission by Kazhegeldin of his involvement, in the late 1980s, with the former Soviet state security service (KGB). Nazarbaev appointed Nurlan Balgymbaev, hitherto head of KazakhOil, as his replacement.

In January 1998 17 political parties and movements signed a 'memorandum on mutual understanding and co-operation', pledging their support for the President. In April an opposition leader was sentenced to one year's imprisonment, having been convicted of insulting the President during an unauthorized rally in November 1997. In September 1998 Nazarbaev outlined proposals for political reforms, including amendments to electoral procedures and enhanced legislative powers. In October, however, a joint session of Parliament rejected Nazarbaev's proposed constitutional reforms, and instead voted to schedule a presidential election before the expiry of Nazarbaev's extended mandate in 2000 and to decrease the quota of votes required by parties in order to secure representation in the legislature, from 10% to 7%.

During November 1998 several opposition figures were deemed ineligible to contest the presidency by the Central Electoral Commission, in accordance with a presidential decree, enacted in May, which prevented those convicted of an administrative offence in the 12 months prior to an election from registering as a candidate. The most prominent disqualification was that of Kazhegeldin, who had been widely regarded as Nazarbaev's principal rival, after he attended a meeting of an unauthorized political organization. Kazhegeldin subsequently established a new political party, the Republican People's Party of Kazakhstan (RPPK). A number of other opposition parties were formed in late 1998 and early 1999, although many were prevented from registering. Among those to be accorded official status was the pro-presidential Fatherland party (Otan).

The Organization for Security and Co-operation in Europe (OSCE, see p. 366) was among international bodies to express serious concern at the conduct of the presidential election, contested by four candidates on 10 January 1999. Nazarbaev was elected to a further term, with 81.0% of the votes cast by 88.3% of the registered electorate. A new Government, headed by Balgymbaev, was appointed later in the month.

In August 1999 the President of KazakhOil, Nurlan Kaparov, was dismissed, having been accused by Nazarbaev of having exceeded his powers. Earlier that month the Minister of Defence, Gen. Mukhtar Altynbaev, and the Chairman of the National Security Committee (KNB), Nurtai Abykaev, had been dismissed, after admitting responsibility for the attempted illegal sale of military aircraft to the Democratic People's Republic of Korea. In September Kazhegeldin, who had been charged with tax evasion in April, was arrested at an airport in Moscow, but released following criticism of his detention by the OSCE. Owing to the outstanding charges against him, Kazhegeldin, together with two other leading members of the RPPK, was barred from registering as a candidate for the parliamentary elections in October. (Further charges were brought against him in February 2000.)

In late September 1999 the RPPK announced that it would boycott the forthcoming elections to the Majlis, in protest at the severe restrictions imposed on opposition parties by the President, although some of the party's members were to stand as independents. In early October Balgymbaev resigned the premiership and resumed his former position as President of KazakhOil. He was replaced as Prime Minister by Kasymzhomart Tokaev, a former Minister of Foreign Affairs. A government reorganization followed. Elections to the Majlis (as well as to municipal and local councils) were held on 10 October. Sixty-five candidates from nine political parties contested 10 seats allocated, for the first time, according to a party-list system, while almost 500 candidates contested the remaining 67 single-mandate constituency seats. All of the 10 party-list seats were filled at the first round (four by Fatherland, and two by each of the CPK, the Agrarian Party of Kazakhstan—APK and the Civic Party of Kazakhstan, but only 20 of the 67 directly elected seats were filled, and a second round of voting was held on 24 October. Final results indicated that Fatherland was to be the largest political grouping in the new Majlis, with 23 seats; the Civic Party held 13. Three other parties achieved representation, and 34 independent candidates were elected. The rate of participation by voters was reported to be 62.6%. Observers from the OSCE cited numerous breaches of electoral law.

In June 2000 a law (confirmed by the Constitutional Court in July) was approved awarding Nazarbaev certain lifetime guarantees and rights. In June 2001 a month-long amnesty was declared, to allow the return of capital that had been transferred abroad in violation of financial legislation; the Chairman of the National Bank of Kazakhstan (NBK) subsequently announced that US $480m. had been returned to domestic banks. In September 2001 Kazhegeldin, who had been tried *in absentia* on charges of abuse of power, tax evasion and the illegal possession of weapons, was sentenced to 10 years' imprisonment.

In November 2001 Nazarbaev approved the resignation of Rakhat Aliev as Deputy Chairman of the KNB, amid accusations of abuse of power. Persistent reports that Aliev, the husband of Nazarbaev's daughter, Darigha Nazarbaeva, controlled the majority of Kazakhstan's media outlets and influenced their output, prompted the Akim (Governor) of Pavlodar Oblast, Galymzhan Zhakiyanov, and a number of other prominent political and business figures, including the Deputy Prime Minister, criticized the small number of administrative units covered, while the conduct of the elections to the oblast posts (in which all the incumbent candidates were returned to office, and in which all candidates had been nominated by the local authorities) was also criticised.

In April 2005 a law was introduced prohibiting demonstrations both during and immediately after elections. Concern was expressed at an announcement in July that the security agencies were preparing to use force against any popular unrest that might arise around the time of the forthcoming presidential election: the Minister of Internal Affairs, Turisbekov, asserted that the country would not allow a repetition of the events that had taken place in 2003–05 in Georgia, Ukraine and Kyrgyzstan (where popular revolts, following disputed elections, had led to the collapse of the incumbent regimes). In early August 2005 the For a Just Kazakhstan coalition, led by Tuyakbai, and comprising the CPK, Forward, the Generation Pensioners' Movement and Real Bright Road, was officially registered with the Ministry of Justice.

On 19 August 2005 partial elections to the Senate, originally scheduled to be held in December, took place. Fatherland secured 10 of the 16 seats contested; three seats were won by other pro-Nazarbaev parties and three by independents. In September the Majlis confirmed that a presidential election would be held in December, one year earlier than had been anticipated. Later in September the For a Just Kazakhstan movement elected Tuyakbai to stand as its single opposition candidate in the election.

In the presidential ballot, conducted on 4 December 2005, Nazarbaev was re-elected as President, with 91.2% of the votes cast, according to official results; his candidacy was supported by an electoral bloc, the Popular Coalition, which included Fatherland, Mutual Help, the DPK, the APK and the Civic Party of Kazakhstan. Of the four other candidates, Nazarbaev's closest rival was Tuyakbai, who received 6.6% of the votes. The rate of participation was 76.8%. Monitors from the OSCE declared that the conduct of the election had not satisfied international standards of democracy. On 18 January both chambers of Parliament unanimously approved Nazarbaev's nomination of Axmetov as Prime Minister. On the following day Nazarbaev approved a new Government, which retained most members of the previous administration. New appointments included those of Kärım Mäsımov, a longstanding presidential aide and prominent economist, as Deputy Prime Minister and Natalya Korzhova as Minister of Finance.

In mid-February 2006 Altynbek Sarsenbaev, one of the leaders of Real Bright Road and a prominent supporter of Tuyakbai's presidential campaign, was shot dead in Almaty. A special commission was established to investigate the killing, which opposition representatives claimed had been politically motivated. Those detained on suspicion of involvement in the case included five KNB officials and the head of the administration of the Senat, Erzhan Utembaev. The head of the KNB, Nartai Dutbaev, subsequently resigned as a result of the investigation. An unsanctioned protest rally was held in Almaty in late February, at which demonstrators urged the authorities to end the persecution of opposition representatives and to bring the perpetrators to trial; a number of organizers of the demonstration were later imprisoned. In March Real Bright Road was granted official registration.

In April 2006 Nazarbaev appointed Mäsımov to the additional post of Minister of the Economy and Budgetary Planning. (He was replaced in this position by Aslan Musin in October.) In June the trial began of 10 suspects charged with involvement in the killing of Sarsenbaev. During the trial Utembaev pleaded not guilty to having ordered the murder, despite reportedly having earlier confessed to so doing. In June the Majlis adopted a number of controversial legislative amendments designed to enforce greater regulation over media outlets, which, despite strong criticism from the OSCE, were endorsed by the Senat on 29 June and signed into law by the President on 4 July. Also in July, at an extraordinary Fatherland party congress in Astana, the party merged with Nazarbaeva's Mutual Help party, thereby consolidating support for Nazarbaev in the Majlis prior to forthcoming legislative elections. In October President Nazarbaev appointed several new ministers in a governmental reorganization. In December the APK and Civic Party also merged with Fatherland; the new party, known as Light of the Fatherland (Nur Otan) controlled 57 seats in the Majlis.

On 8 January 2007 Axmetov tendered his resignation as Prime Minister; it was reported that Nazarbaev had continually criticized him for poor organization and budget planning. On 10 January the Majlis voted to approve the President's nomination of Mäsımov as premier. Musin was appointed as Deputy Prime Minister (retaining the portfolio of the economy and budget planning), while Axmetov became Minister of Defence. In May Parliament approved extensive constitutional amendments, proposed by President Nazarbaev, strengthening the powers of an expanded Majlis, which was henceforth to approve prime ministerial appointments. The presidential term of office was to be reduced from seven to five years with effect from 2012, while the restriction on the incumbent President to two terms in office was to be removed.

In June 2007 Rakhat Aliev, now the Kazakhstani ambassador to Austria, was arrested in that country, after the Kazakhstani Government issued an arrest warrant against him in May for his alleged involvement in the kidnapping of two banking associates; Kazakhstan officially requested his extradition. (In January 2008 one of Almaty's district courts imposed a 20-year sentence of imprisonment on Aliev, who had claimed asylum in Austria, for his involvement in the creation of an organized criminal group and the abductions of the banking officials. In March, at a second trial *in absentia*, a military court sentenced Aliev to another 20 years' imprisonment for illegal possession of armaments and ammunition, misappropriation of property and planning a coup.)

On 20 June 2007 President Nazarbaev dissolved the Majlis and announced that legislative elections were to be brought forward to 18 August (two years earlier than scheduled). At the elections the pro-presidential party, Light Of The Fatherland, won 88.4% of votes cast, securing all 98 contested seats in the enlarged 107-member Majlis. None of the other six parties participating in the poll achieved the 7% minimum of votes required to gain representation in the chamber; the newly established National Social-Democratic Party (NSDP) received 4.5% and Bright Road 3.1% of the votes cast. The leaders of the NSDP, Bright Road and the Communist People's Party refused to acknowledge the results and demanded that the poll be repeated. The OSCE announced that, despite some improvements, the poll had failed to meet international standards. In accordance with the amended Constitution, the Assembly of Nations of Kazakhstan (which represents the country's minority ethnic groups) elected the remaining nine deputies to the Majlis on 20 August. A reorganized Government was approved at the first session of the new Parliament on 2 September; most of the incumbent ministers retained their posts. Ömırzaq Şökeev, hitherto Akim of Southern Kazakhstan Oblast, became the new Deputy Prime Minister, succeeding Musin, who was elected Chairman of the Majlis. In November a new Minister of Finance, Bolat Jämışev, was appointed, while Vladımır Bojko, hitherto First Deputy Chairman of the KNB, replaced the incumbent Minister of Emergency Situations, who had been dismissed over his suspected involvement in a corrupt land agreement during his tenure as Akim of Almaty. A new Minister of Industry and Trade was appointed in February 2008. At the end of the month, during a party congress, Real Bright Road was renamed Freedom (Azat).

In April 2008 the hitherto Minister of Agriculture was replaced by his deputy and was appointed Mayor of Almaty. In June public access to the Kazakh-language website of Radio Free Europe/Radio Liberty, which had been suspended by the authorities in April, was restored, following pressure from the OSCE, the USA, and other international representatives. Elections were held to one-half of the 32 indirectly elected seats in the Senat on 4 October 2008; the Central Election Commission announced that the rate of voter participation was 97.6%.

In September 2008 it was reported that a former head of KazMunaiGaz and associate of Rakhat Aliev, Şerik Burkitbaev, had been arrested and was to be charged with embezzlement. In the same month Alnur Musaev, formerly the head of the National Security Committee and an associate of Rakhat Aliev, who had also received asylum in Austria after being sentenced *in absentia* to a 20-year term of imprisonment in the previous March, claimed there had been an abduction attempt against him. In late November the Majlis approved legislation restricting freedom of religious worship, which included provisions penalizing religious associations without registration, despite government pledges shortly beforehand that the legislation would be drafted in consultation with the OSCE. In December several journalists associated with independent publications were assaulted.

Oraz Jandosov, to form a new political movement, the Democratic Choice of Kazakhstan (DCK), in late November. The DCK, which aimed to revive democratic reform, decentralize political power and ensure the freedom of the mass media, criticized the concentration of power among members of Nazarbaev's family and a small group of leading entrepreneurs. Tokaev subsequently announced that two attempts to assassinate the President had been averted, and threatened to tender his resignation from the premiership unless the President dismissed ministers whom he denounced as disloyal, owing to their involvement in the formation of the DCK. Jandosov, Alikhan Baymenov (the Minister of Labour and Social Security) and two deputy ministers resigned shortly afterwards, announcing that they were unable to work with the Prime Minister; Nazarbaev dismissed Zhakiyanov on the same day. In early 2002 the United Democratic Party, which declared its main aim to be the creation of a parliamentary republic, was formed by the merger of the Citizen (Azamat) Democratic Party, the PCPK and the RPPK.

Meanwhile, in December 2001 Altynbaev was reappointed Minister of Defence. In January 2002 amendments to media legislation came into effect, which required 50% of all radio and television programmes to be broadcast in Kazakh, restricted the rebroadcast of foreign (mainly Russian) television programmes, and was intended to subject internet sites to the same controls as print media. In mid-January a further assassination attempt against the President was reported to have been thwarted. In late January Tokayev announced his resignation. On 31 January a new Government was sworn in, led by a former Deputy Prime Minister, Imangali Tasmagambetov; Tokaev was appointed State Secretary and Minister of Foreign Affairs. Meanwhile, divisions emerged within the DCK, prompting a number of its founding members, including Jandosov and Zhakiyanov, to form a new party, Bright Road (Ak Zhol).

Also in March 2002 a warrant was issued for the arrest of Zhakiyanov, on charges of abuse of power during his tenure as Akim of Pavlodar Oblast. He subsequently sought refuge in the French embassy until April, when agreement was reached between the Government and the ambassadors of France, Germany, the United Kingdom and the USA that Zhakiyanov would be permitted to go free until an investigation into the allegations had been carried out. However, less than one week later he was arrested and flown to the north-eastern city of Pavlodar, in contravention of the agreement. In mid-May it was reported that Zhakiyanov had been admitted to hospital following interrogation by security officials. Zhakiyanov's trial commenced in July, and he was sentenced to a seven-year term in August.

In July 2002 Nazarbaev signed into law new legislation on political parties, which required a party to demonstrate that it had at least 50,000 members (rather than the previous 3,000), representing every administrative region of the country, in order to qualify for registration. In the same month a former Minister of Energy, Industry and Trade and founding member of the DCK, Mukhtar Ablyazov, was sentenced to six years' imprisonment, having been found guilty of abuse of office. In late August Nazarbaev carried out a reorganization of the Government. On 8 October partial elections to fill 16 seats in the Senate were conducted; Fatherland remained the largest grouping in the chamber, accounting for 18 of the 47 senators.

In January 2003 it was reported that Jandosov had been appointed as an aide to President Nazarbaev, suggesting to many observers that Bright Road was in fact supportive of the incumbent leadership. In the same month the DCK's party registration was annulled by the Ministry of Justice, and in mid-January the establishment of a new opposition bloc, Democracy-Elections-Kazakhstan, was announced, with the aim of uniting those parties prevented from re-registering by the new legislation on political parties. By the end of the re-registration period in April, only seven parties had satisfied the criteria for registration.

In late January 2003 Sergei Duvanov, an independent journalist, was convicted of rape and sentenced to more than three years' imprisonment. He had been arrested in October 2002, shortly before he was due to travel to the USA to speak about press freedoms and human rights issues in Kazakhstan. Duvanov's conviction prompted the US embassy to express concern about judicial procedure during his trial. In mid-February 2003 the European Parliament adopted a resolution condemning the sentences awarded to Duvanov and the opposition politicians Ablyazov and Zhakiyanov, and demanding that an independent investigation into their trials be carried out. Ablyazov was pardoned in May, and subsequently announced his withdrawal from politics. (Duvanov was released in August 2004, and Zhakiyanov was released on parole in January 2006.) Meanwhile, in March 2003 Nazarbaev's links with US petroleum companies came under scrutiny when a US businessman was indicted in the USA for allegedly offering financial incentives to Kazakhstani officials, in an attempt to influence the award of important contracts (see below).

In May 2003 the Government defeated a parliamentary vote of no confidence, prompted by opposition to government plans to introduce legislation on land reform, which would permit the private ownership of land. However, on 9 June Tasmagambetov tendered his resignation, after it emerged that the results of the no confidence vote had been falsified by supporters of the Government. A new Government, led by Daniäl Axmetov, a former Akim of Pavlodar Oblast, was appointed in June, which included more than two-thirds of the ministers of the outgoing administration. The land reform bill was approved by Parliament on 20 June.

In September 2003 Zautbek Turisbekov was appointed as Minister of Internal Affairs, replacing Col-Gen. Kairbek Suleimonov, after Nazarbaev reportedly decreed that the heads of the law-enforcement and security bodies should be civilian appointments. Elections to local councils took place on 20 September, with further rounds of voting in October–November. The OSCE was again critical of the conduct of the electoral process.

In October 2003 a new party, Mutual Help (Asar), led by Darigha Nazarbaeva, was officially registered. In March 2004 Nurtai Abykayev was appointed as Chairman of the Senate. In early May four political parties that had not been granted official registration were declared invalid by a court ruling: Kazakh Ely, the Republican People's Party of Kazakhstan, the Azamat Party and the People's Congress of Kazakhstan. However, in mid-June the Ministry of Justice officially registered the People's Communist Party of Kazakhstan and the Democratic Party of Kazakhstan (DPK).

On 19 September 2004 elections took place to the Majlis, with 'run-off' elections held on 3 October in 22 constituencies where no candidate had received an overall majority of the votes cast. Fatherland emerged as the largest grouping, with 42 seats, giving it an absolute majority in the chamber. An electoral coalition formed by the APK and the Civic Party of Kazakhstan won 11 seats, while Mutual Help obtained four seats. Bright Road and the DPK each obtained one seat, and 18 non-partisan candidates were elected. The rate of participation by the electorate was 56.7% in the first round of voting and 45.2% in the second round. Monitors from the OSCE criticized the conduct of the polls, and in particular, the media. Alikhan Baymenov of Bright Road, who was effectively the only opposition representative elected to the new legislature, subsequently announced that he would not take up his seat in the Majlis, alleging that the results of the elections had been falsified. The Chairman of the outgoing legislature, Zharmakhan Tuyakbai, resigned from Fatherland in mid-October in order to protest against the conduct of the elections. At the inaugural session of the new Majlis, held on 3 November, Oral Muxamejanov was elected Chairman.

In January 2005, following an declaration by the DCK in the previous month that it regarded the Kazakhstani Government to be illegitimate and urged non-violent civil disobedience, a court ordered that the party be dismantled, on the grounds that it had breached national security laws. Later in the month at least 1,000 people took part in an unsanctioned rally organized by Bright Road, the DCK and the CPK to protest against the closure of the party; in October 2004 the three parties had established a Co-ordinating Council of Opposition Democratic Forces of Kazakhstan, which aimed to draft a new constitution and create a more influential democratic movement in the country. In February 2005 the Co-ordinating Council of Opposition Democratic Forces of Kazakhstan announced that it was to establish a new national movement, to be known as For a Just Kazakhstan. In late March former members of the DCK announced the establishment of a new grouping, Forward (Alga), led by Asylbek Kozhakhmetov. (However, in February 2006 the party was refused registration.) In late April 2005 another new party, Real Bright Road (Naghyz Ak Zhol), held its founding congress, following divisions within Bright Road.

Meanwhile, in early December 2004 President Nazarbaev had issued a decree allowing village akims to be elected, and providing for 'experimental' elections of akims (who had hitherto been appointed) in several oblasts. Elections were duly held in villages and in four oblasts during 2005. Opposition representatives

In January 2009, following the onset of the international financial crisis (see Economic Affairs), Nazarbaev appointed the hitherto Chairman of Halyk Bank, Grigorii Marchenko, to the post of Governor of the National Bank (which he had previously held in 1999–2004, before briefly serving as Deputy Prime Minister). Nazarbaev expressed further pledges to address endemic corruption, particularly in the law-enforcement system, after acknowledging lack of progress in that area; significant public sector salary increases were introduced at the beginning of 2009 in an effort to reduce bribery. In February plans by Freedom to organize a nationwide day of protests to demand the resignation of the Government were obstructed by refusal of the authorities to grant permission for the staging of demonstrations outwith Almaty (where a rally proceeded); leaders of the party had proposed alternative economic stabilization proposals in response to the Government's perceived failure to address the effects of the financial crisis. Also in February the Constitutional Court revoked the legislation on religion approved in November, after a report by the OSCE Office for Democratic Institutions and Human Rights criticized it as being incompatible with both democratic standards and Kazakhstan's commitments towards the OSCE (in view of its forthcoming assumption of the body's chairmanship—see below). In early March a number of significant appointments of government ministers and other public officials were effected. Şökeev received the post of First Deputy Prime Minister, while Serık Axmetov, hitherto Minister of Transport, became a Deputy Prime Minister. In early April new appointments were announced to the posts of Minister of Justice and Minister of Internal Affairs.

The issue of the legal status of the Caspian Sea—and the division of the substantial mineral resources believed to be located in the seabed—has been a source of tension between the five littoral states: Azerbaijan, Iran, Kazakhstan, Russia and Turkmenistan. In July 1998 Nazarbaev and the Russian President, Boris Yeltsin, signed a bilateral agreement on the delineation of their countries' respective boundaries of the Caspian seabed, by which Russia for the first time formally recognized Kazakhstan's claim to, and right to exploit, its offshore petroleum resources, prompting particular criticism from Iran, which continued to assert that partitioning of the seabed required the consensus of all five littoral states. In October 2000 Nazarbaev and the recently elected President of Russia, Vladimir Putin, signed an additional agreement, on the definition of the legal status of the Caspian Sea, and the 1998 agreement was further augmented in May 2002, when an accord was signed on the equal division of three oilfields in the northern Caspian. Russia and Kazakhstan have also signed a Treaty of Eternal Friendship and Co-operation, which provides for mutual military assistance in the event of aggression by a third party. In November 2001 Kazakhstan concluded a bilateral agreement with Azerbaijan on the two countries' respective mineral rights in the Caspian Sea, prompting further protests from Iran. In May 2003 Azerbaijan, Kazakhstan and Russia signed a trilateral agreement. In November representatives of Azerbaijan, Iran, Kazakhstan, Russia and Turkmenistan, meeting in Tehran, Iran, signed a UN-sponsored framework Convention for the Protection of the Marine Environment of the Caspian Sea, which sought to alleviate environmental damage in the Caspian Sea region. In mid-January 2005 Nazarbaev and Putin signed a treaty in Moscow defining the 7,500-km land border between their two countries. In May 2008 newly installed Russian President Dmitrii Medvedev made his first official international visit to Kazakhstan, where he discussed bilateral co-operation with President Nazarbaev. In September Medvedev and Nazarbaev met in the north-western town of Aktobe to discuss security issues; Nazarbaev was reported to have expressed support for Russia with regard to the military conflict in Georgia in August (see the chapter on Georgia).

In the early 1990s the issue of the formerly Soviet, subsequently Russian-controlled, nuclear warheads deployed in Kazakhstan (effectively making the country the fourth largest nuclear power in the world) was the focus of international concern. In September 1992 the Kazakhstani legislature ratified the first Strategic Arms Reduction Treaty, signed by the USA and the USSR in July 1991. In December 1993 the Kazakhstani legislature ratified the Treaty on the Non-Proliferation of Nuclear Weapons. By April 1995 all nuclear warheads had been transferred to Russia, and in September 1996 Russia and Kazakhstan signed a final protocol governing the withdrawal of military units linked to the Russian nuclear weapons facilities in Kazakhstan. In November 2001 the Kazakhstani legislature ratified the Comprehensive Nuclear Test Ban Treaty.

In May 2001 the signatories of the CIS Collective Security Treaty (Armenia, Belarus, Kazakhstan, Kyrgyzstan, Russia and Tajikistan) agreed to form a Collective Rapid Reaction Force in Bishkek, Kyrgyzstan, to combat Islamist militancy in Central Asia; in January 2002 it was announced that the force was ready to undertake combat missions. An anti-terrorism centre became operational in Bishkek in August 2001. In April 2003 the signatories of the Treaty formally inaugurated the Collective Security Treaty Organization (CSTO, see p. 438), to which Uzbekistan subsequently acceded.

In 1992 Kazakhstan joined the Economic Co-operation Organization (ECO, see p. 249), founded by Iran, Pakistan and Turkey. In 1994 Kazakhstan, Kyrgyzstan and Uzbekistan formed a trilateral economic area, and in February 1995 an Interstate Council was established to supervise its implementation. Several agreements to expand economic co-operation were signed by the three countries in 1996. In 1998 Tajikistan joined the alliance, which was renamed the Central Asian Co-operation Organization (CACO) in March 2002. Meanwhile, in January 1995 Kazakhstan established a customs union with Russia and Belarus, and in March 1996 the three members of the customs union were joined by Kyrgyzstan; Tajikistan joined the union in April 1998. In October 2000 a new economic body, the Eurasian Economic Community (EURASEC, see p. 426), was established to supersede the customs union, and this organization merged with CACO in January 2006. In October 2007 EURASEC leaders approved the legal basis for the establishment of a new customs union that was initially to comprise Belarus, Kazakhstan and Russia, with Kyrgyzstan, Tajikistan and Uzbekistan expected to join by 2011. In September 2002 President Nazarbaev and the President of Uzbekistan, Islam Karimov, signed a bilateral agreement on the delimitation of all disputed sectors of their countries' common border. A border agreement with Turkmenistan, which had been signed in July 2001, was ratified by the Senat in June 2003, and in July Nazarbaev signed a number of laws confirming the delimitation of Kazakhstan's borders with Kyrgyzstan, Turkmenistan and Uzbekistan.

In 1995 Nazarbaev made an official visit to the People's Republic of China, where an agreement was signed to improve long-term stability between the two countries, following concerns about Chinese underground nuclear tests near the border with eastern Kazakhstan. Bilateral relations were further strengthened by two accords concluded in 1997, whereby China was granted permission to exploit two of the largest oilfields in Kazakhstan. The agreements provided for the construction of a petroleum pipeline connecting the two countries, work on which commenced in September 2004. Construction, at an estimated cost of US $700m., was completed in late 2005. Meanwhile, in November 1998 Nazarbaev made a state visit to China, which resulted in the signature of a communiqué on the full settlement of outstanding border issues, and of an agreement outlining future bilateral relations. In July 2005 Nazarbaev and Chinese President Hu Jintao signed an agreement on the establishment of a strategic partnership between the two countries. China and Kazakhstan have attended annual summit meetings of the heads of state of the so-called Shanghai Five (also comprising Kyrgyzstan, Russia and Tajikistan), which aimed to promote economic co-operation and regional co-ordination on border and security issues. Members of the alliance, which became the Shanghai Co-operation Organization (SCO, see p. 440) upon the accession of Uzbekistan in 2001, signed the Shanghai Convention on Combating Terrorism, Separatism and Extremism in June 2001. In August 2003 Kazakhstan and China jointly hosted military manoeuvres involving the member states of the SCO. In July 2005, at a summit meeting in Astana, members of the SCO approved anti-terrorist measures, and signed a declaration advocating non-interference in the affairs of sovereign states. Several bilateral co-operation agreements were signed during a Chinese official visit in November 2007; a second stage in construction of the petroleum pipeline system linking Kazakhstan with China commenced in December.

Following the suicide attacks on the USA on 11 September 2001, President Nazarbaev expressed his support for US-led military action against the al-Qa'ida (Base) organization of the Saudi-born militant Islamist, Osama bin Laden, and the regime of its hosts, the Taliban, in Afghanistan (see the chapters on Afghanistan and the USA). The USA acknowledged Kazakhstan's strategic importance, and Kazakhstan offered the USA the use of airports, airspace and military bases. In February 2006 it was announced that US forces were to participate in Kazakhstani-British military exercises in Kazakhstan in September, and were to engage in the command component of the exercises for the first time. Meanwhile, Nazarbayev's links with US petroleum companies were subject to legal scrutiny from March 2003, when James H. Giffen, a US businessman and former adviser to Nazarbaev, was indicted in the USA under the 1977 Foreign Corrupt Practices Act, which prohibits US companies or individuals from offering financial inducements to foreign officials in order to secure an agreement. He was accused of offering bribes to prominent Kazakhstani politicians, including Nazarbaev, in return for securing valuable contracts for US petroleum companies. In April 2004 a US federal court indicted Giffen and an executive of the petroleum company, ExxonMobil, on charges of corrupt business practices. In October 2005 a judge allowed Giffen to use classified information in his defence as evidence that the US Government had endorsed his actions. In September 2006 Nazarbaev met US President George W. Bush during an official visit to Washington, DC. The two Presidents subsequently issued a joint statement envisaging further bilateral co-operation in the energy sector. President Bush publicly thanked Nazarbaev for his assistance in the US-led military action and announced that the USA would support the efforts of Kazakhstan (which Bush referred to as a 'free nation') to join the World Trade Organisation (WTO, see p. 410). At an OSCE meeting in Madrid, Spain, at the end of November 2007, Kazakhstan secured approval to assume the rotating chairmanship of that body in 2010, despite criticism by OSCE monitors of the conduct of elections in August and criticism issued by the organization of media censorship and legislation, approved in late 2008 but subsequently rescinded, restricting religious practice (see above) and continuing international concerns over human rights in the country. In mid-2008 Kazakhstan hosted a session of the OSCE Parliamentary Assembly.

Government

Under the terms of the 1995 Constitution (to which a number of amendments were made in October 1998 and May 2007), the President of the Republic is Head of State and commander-in-chief of the armed forces, and holds broad executive powers. The President is directly elected by universal adult suffrage. (Under the constitutional amendments of May 2007, the presidential term was reduced from seven to five years, with effect from 2012.) The Government, headed by the Prime Minister, is responsible to the President. The supreme legislative organ is the bicameral Parliament, comprising the Senat (Senate, upper chamber) and the Majlis (Assembly, lower chamber). The Senat comprises 47 members, of whom 32 are elected by regional assemblies, while the remaining 15 deputies are appointed by the President. The Majlis comprises 107 deputies, of whom 98 are directly elected; the remaining nine deputies are elected by the Assembly of Nations of Kazakhstan (a 350-member body representing the country's minority ethnic groups). The Senat's term is six years, and that of the Majlis is five years. One-half of the elected deputies in the Senat are subject to election every three years.

For administrative purposes, Kazakhstan is divided into 16 units (14 regions and the cities of Almaty and Astana). The city of Leninsk (now Turatam) serving the Baikonur space centre, and formerly one of Kazakhstan's administrative units, was transferred to Russian jurisdiction in August 1995. In January 2004 President Nazarbaev and the Russian President, Vladimir Putin, signed an agreement permitting Russia's continued use of the Baikonur space centre until 2050.

Defence

Following Kazakhstan's independence from the USSR in 1991, the armed forces were established by presidential decree in May 1992. The length of compulsory military service was reduced from two years to one year at the beginning of 2006. As assessed at November 2008, the estimated strength of the national armed forces was 49,000 (including an army of 30,000, air force of 12,000 and navy of 3,000). In addition, there were 31,500 paramilitary troops (including an estimated 20,000 troops attached to the Ministry of Internal Affairs, and an estimated 9,000 border guards). Kazakhstan participates, with Russia, Azerbaijan and Turkmenistan, in the operation of the Caspian Sea Flotilla, a former Soviet force based, under Russian command, at Astrakhan (Russia). In mid-1992 Kazakhstan signed a Collective Security Treaty with five other members of the Commonwealth of Independent States (CIS, see p. 225); in May 2001 it was announced that the signatory countries were to form a Collective Rapid Reaction Force to combat Islamist militancy in Central Asia. In April 2003 the Collective Security Treaty Organization (CSTO) was inaugurated as the successor to the CIS collective security system, with the participation of Armenia, Belarus, Kazakhstan, Kyrgyzstan, Russia and Tajikistan. A nuclear successor state to the USSR, Kazakhstan undertook to dismantle its nuclear capabilities, ratifying the first Strategic Arms Reduction Treaty in 1992 and the Treaty on the Non-Proliferation of Nuclear Weapons in 1993. All nuclear warheads had been transferred to Russia by mid-1995, and a final protocol for the withdrawal of the Russian strategic-missile troops was signed in September 1996. In May 1994 Kazakhstan joined the North Atlantic Treaty Organization's (NATO) 'Partnership for Peace' programme of military co-operation (see p. 353). Kazakhstan became a full member of the UN Conference on Disarmament in August 1999. In early 2007 the Government announced a programme to reorganize the armed forces, in co-operation with Russia, by 2015. The budget for 2007 allocated 142,000m. tenge to defence.

Economic Affairs

In 2007, according to estimates by the World Bank, Kazakhstan's gross national income (GNI), measured at average 2005–07 prices, was US $78,281m., equivalent to $5,060 per head (or $9,700 per head on an international purchasing-power parity basis). During 2000–07, it was estimated, the population decreased at an average annual rate of 0.6%, while gross domestic product (GDP) per head increased, in real terms, by an average of 9.5% per year. Overall GDP increased, in real terms, at an average annual rate of 10.1% in 2000–07. Real GDP increased by 8.5% in 2007.

Agriculture (including forestry and fishing) contributed 5.8% of GDP in 2007 and provided 33.6% of total employment in 2004. There are large areas of land suitable for agriculture, and Kazakhstan is a major producer and exporter of agricultural products. The principal crops include fruit, sugar beet, vegetables, potatoes, cotton and, most importantly, cereals. Livestock-breeding is also important, and Kazakhstan is a significant producer of karakul and astrakhan wools. According to the World Bank, the GDP of the agricultural sector increased, in real terms, by an average of 5.7% per year in 2000–07. Agricultural GDP increased by 5.0% in 2007.

Industry (including mining, manufacturing, construction, and power) contributed 38.7% of GDP in 2007, and 17.4% of total employment in 2004. The principal branches of industry include the fuel industry and metal-processing. According to World Bank figures, industrial GDP increased, in real terms, at an average annual rate of 11.6% in 2000–07. The GDP of the sector increased by 10.0% in 2007.

Mining and quarrying provided 2.6% of employment in 2004, and contributed 15.4% of GDP in 2007. Kazakhstan possesses immense mineral wealth, and large-scale mining and processing industries have been developed. There are major coalfields (in the Karaganda, Turgai, Ekibastuz and Maikuben basins), as well as substantial deposits of iron ore, lead, zinc ore, titanium, magnesium, chromium, tungsten, molybdenum, gold, silver, copper and manganese. Petroleum is extracted, and Kazakhstan possesses substantial reserves of natural gas. The discovery of major petroleum reserves at the offshore Kashagan oilfield was announced in 2000 (see below). In January 2004 the state-owned hydrocarbons company KazMunaiGaz awarded the Russian energy company LUKoil a 50% stake in a 40-year production-sharing contract for the development of the Tyub-Karagan field in the Caspian Sea, which has petroleum reserves of an estimated 100m. metric tons. In January 2005 the Kazakhstani and Russian Presidents signed an agreement confirming the equal rights of both countries to the Imashevskoye natural gas field, the second largest natural gas field in Kazakhstan, which was to be developed jointly by KazMunaiGaz and the Russian energy company Gazprom. Also in 2005 a subsidiary of KazMunaiGaz signed a production-sharing agreement with the Russian state-owned petroleum companies Zarubezhneft and Rosneft to develop the offshore Kurmanagazy oilfield, estimated to contain recoverable reserves of petroleum of between 900m. and 1,000m. metric tons. At the end of 2007 Kazakhstan's proven total reserves (on shore and off shore) of petroleum and natural gas were estimated at 39,800m. barrels and 1,900,000m. cu m, respectively.

Manufacturing provided 7.2% of employment in 2004, and contributed 11.8% of GDP in 2007. The GDP of the manufacturing sector increased at an average annual rate of 8.7% in 2000–07, according to the World Bank. This sector's GDP increased by 7.0% in 2007.

In 2005 coal-fired thermal power stations provided about 70.3% of annual domestic electricity production, while hydroelectric power stations accounted for 11.6% of production and natural gas for 10.7%. In 2007 mineral products accounted for 11.1% of total imports.

The services sector contributed some 55.6% of GDP in 2007 and provided 49.0% of employment in 2004. According to World Bank figures, the GDP of the services sector increased, in real terms, at an average annual rate of 10.7% during 2000–07. Services GDP increased by 10.0% in 2007.

In 2007 Kazakhstan recorded a visible trade surplus of US $15,091.0m., and there was a deficit of $7,333.4m. on the current account of the balance of payments. In that year the principal source of imports was Russia, which accounted for 35.5% of total imports. Other major suppliers were the People's Republic of China (10.7%) and Germany. The principal market for exports in that year was Italy, which accounted for 16.3% of total exports. Other important purchasers of exports were Switzerland-Liechtenstein (15.7%), the People's Republic of China, Russia, France and the Netherlands. The main exports were mineral products and base metals. The principal imports in that year were machinery and electrical equipment, mineral products, transportation equipment, base metals and chemical products.

In 2007 Kazakhstan recorded a budgetary surplus of some 199,091.2m. tenge (equivalent to around 1.5% of GDP). At the end of 2006 Kazakhstan's external debt amounted to US $74,148m. of which $2,136m. was long-term public debt. In that year the cost of debt-servicing was equivalent to 33.7% of the value of exports of goods and services. The annual rate of inflation averaged 7.8% during 2000–07. Consumer prices increased by 18.8% in 2007 and by 9.5% in 2008. In 2006, according to preliminary figures, 6.6% of the labour force were unemployed.

In addition to its membership of the economic bodies of the Commonwealth of Independent States (CIS, see p. 225), Kazakhstan has joined the Asian Development Bank (see p. 191), is a 'Country of Operations' of the European Bank for Reconstruction and Development (EBRD, see p. 251) and is a member of the Economic Co-operation Organization (ECO, see p. 249).

After independence in 1991, contraction was recorded annually until 1995, when signs of an economic recovery emerged. In 1996 a large-scale privatization programme was extended to include the hydrocarbons and metallurgical sectors. In 1998 the economy was severely affected by the economic crises in Russia and Asia, and the subsequent decline in prices for Kazakhstan's principal exports. However, by mid-2000 Kazakhstan had repaid all debts owed to the IMF, seven years ahead of schedule. A National Oil Fund was created in 2001, to manage the country's wealth and guard against sudden declines in petroleum prices. Meanwhile, progress in the development project at the Kashagan oilfield (which was discovered in July 2000) was delayed; in 2008, after the Government negotiated a larger share in the international oil consortium, it was announced that petroleum extraction was expected to begin in 2013. Recoverable oil reserves at the Kashagan field were estimated at 18,000m. barrels and the authorities hoped to channel profits into fiscal expenditures and economic development projects. Petroleum exports increased significantly following the official opening, in November 2001, of a new, 1,500-km petroleum pipeline, connecting the onshore Tengiz field in western Kazakhstan with Novorossiisk, on the Russian Black Sea coast. In May 2005 a pipeline constructed to transport petroleum from Baku, Azerbaijan, via Tbilisi, Georgia, to Ceyhan, Turkey, and onto Western markets (the BTC pipeline) was officially inaugurated. In December 2007 a second stage in construction of a petroleum pipeline system linking Kazakhstan with the People's Republic of China commenced. In the same month Kazakhstan, Russia and Turkmenistan signed a formal agreement for the construction of a Caspian natural gas pipeline to transport Central Asian gas supplies to Russia. In late 2008 it was reported that petroleum from Kazakhstan had for the first time been transported by the BTC pipeline to Western markets. Adverse conditions resulting from the international banking crisis, which ensued from September, required that the authorities initiate an 'anti-crisis' programme. The construction sector was notably affected by the sudden fall in investment which characterized the downturn, owing to strong levels of interdependence between the real estate market and the financial services sector. The Government subsequently pledged to assist troubled construction firms with the completion of outstanding projects, while mortgages were to be made available at lower rates of interest. It was hoped these measures would temper the devaluation of property assets held by the country's banks, and stem rising unemployment. Elsewhere, one of Kazakhstan's principal trading partners, Russia, was under increased strain as a result of the continued financial turmoil. The steep depreciation of the Russian ruble against the tenge was expected to lead to accentuate the effects of a downturn in global demand for some of Kazakhstan's principal exports, including metals and mineral products.

Education

General education (primary and secondary) is compulsory, and is fully funded by the state. Primary education begins at seven years of age and lasts for four years. Secondary education, beginning at 11 years of age, lasts for a further seven years, comprising a first cycle of five years and a second of two years. In 2004 total enrolment at primary schools included 93% of the relevant age-group, and the comparable ratio for secondary enrolment was 92%. After completing general education, pupils may continue their studies at specialized secondary schools. In 2004/05 there were a total of 181 higher schools (including universities), with a total enrolment of 747,100 students. Ethnic Kazakhs form a greater proportion (64% in 1995/96) of students in higher education than in general education, since many ethnic Russians choose to study at universities outside Kazakhstan. None the less, the majority of higher-education students (approximately 75% in 1997) are instructed in Russian. The number of private general schools in Kazakhstan increased from 18 in 1994/95 to 181 by 2005/06. In 2003/04 there were 179 private secondary vocational schools and 134 private higher schools (including universities). Government expenditure on education in 2001 was 105,024m. tenge (14.7% of total spending). In 2008 the Government announced a comprehensive reform programme of the education system, which included a rise in state expenditure from some 3.6% of GDP in 2008 to 7% of GDP, and a planned increase in the period of compulsory education from 11 to 12 years in 2010.

Public Holidays

2009: 1–2 January (New Year), 7 January (Orthodox Christmas), 8 March (International Women's Day), 21–23 March (Nauryz Meyramy, Spring Holiday), 1 May (Day of Unity of the Peoples of Kazakhstan), 9 May (Victory Day, Day of Remembrance), 30 August (Constitution Day), 27 November* (Kurban Bayram, Id al-Adha or Feast of the Sacrifice), 16 December (Independence Day).

2010: 1–2 January (New Year), 7 January (Orthodox Christmas), 8 March (International Women's Day), 21–23 March (Nauryz Meyramy, Spring Holiday), 1 May (Day of Unity of the Peoples of Kazakhstan), 9 May (Victory Day, Day of Remembrance), 30 August (Constitution Day), 16 November* (Kurban Bayram, Id al-Adha or Feast of the Sacrifice), 16 December (Independence Day).

* These holidays are dependent on the Islamic lunar calendar and may vary by one or two days from the dates given.

Weights and Measures

The metric system is in force.

KAZAKHSTAN

Statistical Survey

Source (unless otherwise stated): Statistical Agency of the Republic of Kazakhstan, 050009 Almaty, Abay kosh. 125; tel. (727) 261-13-23; fax (727) 242-08-24; e-mail stat@mail.online.kz; internet www.stat.kz.

Area and Population

AREA, POPULATION AND DENSITY

Area (sq km)	2,724,900*
Population (census results)	
12 January 1989†	16,464,464
25 February–4 March 1999	
Males	7,201,785
Females	7,751,341
Total	14,953,126
Population (official estimates at 1 January)	
2007	15,396,878
2008	15,565,647
2009	15,778,160
Density (per sq km) at 1 January 2009	5.8

* 1,049,150 sq miles.
† Figure refers to the *de jure* population. The *de facto* total was 16,536,511.

PRINCIPAL ETHNIC GROUPS
(1 January 2004, official estimates)

	Number	%
Kazakh	8,550,986	57.19
Russian	4,072,337	27.24
Ukrainian	469,397	3.14
Uzbek	409,770	2.74
German	237,643	1.59
Tatar	232,735	1.56
Uigur	223,039	1.49
Others	755,293	5.05
Total	**14,951,200**	**100.00**

ADMINISTRATIVE DIVISIONS
(1 January 2009, official estimates)

	Area (sq km)	Population	Density (per sq km)	Capital city
Oblasts				
Akmola	146,200	742,039	5.08	Kokshetau
Aktobe	300,600	711,884	2.37	Aktobe
Almaty	224,000	1,667,060	7.44	Taldykorgan
Atyrau	118,600	501,607	4.23	Atyrau
Eastern Kazakhstan	283,200	1,419,028	5.01	Ust-Kamenogorsk
Jambul	144,300	1,031,388	7.15	Taraz
Karaganda	428,000	1,346,331	3.15	Karaganda
Kostanai	196,000	889,348	4.54	Kostanai
Kyzyl-Orda	226,000	641,668	2.84	Kyzyl-Orda
Mangystau	165,600	425,657	2.57	Aktau
Northern Kazakhstan	98,000	648,343	6.62	Petropavlovsk
Pavlodar	124,800	748,909	6.00	Pavlodar
Southern Kazakhstan	117,300	2,381,896	20.31	Chimkent
Western Kazakhstan	151,300	618,868	4.09	Oral
Cities				
Almaty	700	1,364,554	1,949.36	—
Astana (capital)	300	639,580	2,131.93	—
Total	**2,724,900**	**15,778,160**	**5.79**	—

PRINCIPAL TOWNS
(population at 1999 census)

Almaty (Alma-Ata)	1,129,400	Petropavlovsk	203,500
Karaganda	436,900	Oral	195,500
Chimkent	360,100	Temirtau	170,500
Taraz*	330,100	Kyzyl-Orda	157,400
Astana† (capital)	313,000	Aktau‡	143,400
Ust-Kamenogorsk	311,000	Atyrau§	142,500
Pavlodar	300,500	Ekibastuz	127,200
Semipalatinsk	269,600	Kokchetau	123,400
Aktobe	253,100	Rudniy	109,500
Kostanai	221,400		

* Formerly Jambul.
† Formerly Akmola, and prior to that, Tselinograd.
‡ Formerly Shevchenko.
§ Formerly Guriyev.

Mid-2007 ('000, incl. suburbs, UN estimate): Almaty (Alma-Ata) 1,209 (Source: UN, *World Urbanization Prospects: The 2007 Revision*).

IMMIGRATION AND EMIGRATION

	2005	2006	2007
Immigrants	373,434	361,788	365,137
Emigrants	350,766	328,747	354,175

BIRTHS, MARRIAGES AND DEATHS

	Registered live births Number	Rate (per 1,000)	Registered marriages Number	Rate (per 1,000)	Registered deaths Number	Rate (per 1,000)
2000	222,054	14.9	90,873	6.1	149,778	10.0
2001	221,487	14.9	92,852	6.3	147,876	10.0
2002	227,171	15.3	98,986	6.7	149,381	10.1
2003	247,946	16.6	110,414	7.4	155,277	10.4
2004	273,028	18.2	114,685	7.6	152,250	10.1
2005	278,977	18.4	123,045	8.1	157,121	10.4
2006	301,756	19.7	137,204	9.0	157,210	10.3
2007	321,963	20.8	146,379	9.5	158,927	10.2

Life expectancy (years at birth, WHO estimates): 63.9 (males 58.6; females 69.5) in 2006 (Source: WHO, *World Health Statistics*).

KAZAKHSTAN

ECONOMICALLY ACTIVE POPULATION
(labour force survey, annual averages, '000 persons)

	2002	2003	2004
Agriculture, forestry and fishing	2,380.2	2,462.6	2,406.0
Mining and quarrying	167.3	181.7	186.0
Manufacturing	503.7	506.4	519.8
Electricity, gas and water supply	153.0	167.2	163.8
Construction	268.4	329.5	380.7
Wholesale and retail trade; repair of motor vehicles, motor cycles and personal and household goods	1,007.2	1,015.1	1,058.7
Hotels and restaurants	56.5	70.2	82.0
Transport, storage and communications	503.7	503.9	519.7
Financial intermediation	50.1	53.5	60.7
Real estate, renting and business activities	203.4	207.1	233.6
Public administration and defence; compulsory social security	280.4	318.2	334.7
Education	589.0	631.1	666.2
Health and social work	292.6	299.7	318.7
Community, social and personal services	186.3	196.3	201.3
Households with employed persons	66.8	42.5	49.4
Extra-territorial organizations and bodies	0.3	0.3	0.5
Total employed	6,708.9	6,985.2	7,181.8
Unemployed	690.7	672.1	658.8
Total labour force	7,399.6	7,657.3	7,840.6

Source: ILO.

2005 ('000 persons): Total employed 7,260.9 (males 3,764.4, females 3,496.5); Unemployed 640.7 (males 270.6, females 370.1); Total labour force 7,901.7 (males 4,035.0, females 3,866.7).

2006 ('000 persons): Total employed 7,403.5 (males 3,808.9, females 3,594.6); Unemployed 625.4 (males 262.5, females 362.9); Total labour force 8,028.9 (males 4,071.5, females 3,957.4).

2007 ('000 persons): Total employed 7,631.1 (males 3,922.8, females 3,708.3); Unemployed 597.2 (males 244.5, females 352.7); Total labour force 8,228.3 (males 4,167.3, females 4,061.0).

2008 ('000 persons, preliminary figures): Total employed 7,854.7; Unemployed 557.7; Total labour force 8,412.4.

Health and Welfare

KEY INDICATORS

Total fertility rate (children per woman, 2006)	2.2
Under-5 mortality rate (per 1,000 live births, 2006)	29
HIV/AIDS (% of persons aged 15–49, 2007)	0.1
Physicians (per 1,000 head, 2006)	3.9
Hospital beds (per 1,000 head, 2006)	7.8
Health expenditure (2006): US $ per head (PPP)	330
Health expenditure (2006): % of GDP	3.7
Health expenditure (2006): public (% of total)	64.6
Access to water (% of persons, 2006)	96
Access to sanitation (% of persons, 2006)	97
Human Development Index (2006): ranking	71
Human Development Index (2006): value	0.807

For sources and definitions, see explanatory note on p. vi.

Agriculture

PRINCIPAL CROPS
('000 metric tons)

	2005	2006	2007
Wheat	11,198.4	13,500.0	16,500.0
Rice, paddy	310.0*	320.0†	320.0†
Barley	1,445.0*	1,800.0†	2,600.0
Maize	494.0*	495.0†	600†
Rye	23.0*	25.0†	30.0†
Oats	120.0*	165.0†	180.0
Millet	56.0*	65.0†	82.0†
Buckwheat	58.0*	66.0†	80.0†
Potatoes	2,520.8	2,361.6	2,414.8
Sugar beet	310.8	339.0	309.4
Beans, dry	5.0*	6.5†	6.0†
Peas, dry	30.0*	38.9†	45.0†
Soybeans*	45.0	48.0	70.0
Sunflower seed	267.4	268.0	205.8
Safflower seed†	75.0	75.0	65.0
Seed cotton	465.0	435.4	441.7
Cabbages and other brassicas	341.0*	320.0†	343.0
Tomatoes	516.0*	490.0†	523.5†
Cucumbers and gherkins	275.0*	260.0†	277.5†
Aubergines (Eggplants)	50.0*	48.5†	51.5†
Chillies and peppers, green	77.0*	73.5†	78.5†
Onions, dry	345.0*	329.0†	349.0†
Carrots and turnips	250.0*	237.0†	252.0†
Watermelons†	703.5	660.0	653.0
Apples†	170.0	160.0	132.5
Pears†	15.0	16.0	13.0
Cherries†	12.0	13.0	13.0
Plums and sloes†	8.0	8.0	7.0
Grapes†	50.0	29.0	32.9
Tobacco, unmanufactured†	14.0	13.5	14.7

* Unofficial figure(s).
† FAO estimate(s).

Aggregate production ('000 metric tons, may include official, semi-official or estimated data): Total cereals 13,728.0 in 2005, 16,461.6 in 2006; 20,494.6 in 2007; Total roots and tubers 2,520.8 in 2005, 2,361.6 in 2006; 2,414.8 in 2007; Total vegetables (incl. melons) 2,897.1 in 2005, 2,731.7 in 2006; 2,864.7 in 2007; Total fruits (excl. melons) 300.1 in 2005, 252.2 in 2006; 223.6 in 2007.

Source: FAO.

LIVESTOCK
('000 head, year ending September)

	2005	2006	2007
Horses	1,120.4	1,163.5	1,235.6
Asses	31.0*	n.a.	n.a.
Cattle	5,203.9	5,457.4	5,660.4
Buffaloes*	9.0	10.0	10.0
Camels	125.7	130.5	138.6
Pigs	1,292.1	1,281.9	1,304.9
Sheep	11,518.5†	12,183.5*	13,046.8
Goats	1,890.6†	2,151.0*	2,303.5*
Chickens	25,526†	26,100*	28,100*
Turkeys	80†	100*	100*

* FAO estimate(s).
† Unofficial figure.

Source: FAO.

KAZAKHSTAN

LIVESTOCK PRODUCTS
('000 metric tons)

	2005	2006	2007
Cattle meat	345.0*	370.0†	383.8†
Sheep meat	110.0*	110.5†	114.0†
Goat meat	7.7*	10.0†	10.5†
Horse meat	55*	56†	58†
Pig meat	200.0*	210.0†	218†
Chicken meat	43.0*	50.0†	52.0†
Cows' milk	4,693.0	4,861.0†	5,006.7†
Sheeps' milk	42.0	50.0†	51.0†
Goats' milk	14.0	15.0†	15.5†
Hen eggs	139.4*	139.0†	147.7†
Wool, greasy	30.4	32.4	34.2

* Unofficial figure.
† FAO estimate.
Source: FAO.

Forestry

ROUNDWOOD REMOVALS
(unofficial figures, cubic metres, excl. bark)

	2003	2004	2005
Sawlogs, veneer logs and logs for sleepers	103,920	216,800	513,600
Pulpwood	12,990	27,100	64,200
Other industrial roundwood	12,990	27,100	64,200
Fuel wood	170,900	202,000	210,000
Total	300,800	473,000	852,000

2006–07: Figures assumed to be unchanged from 2005 (FAO estimates).
Source: FAO.

SAWNWOOD PRODUCTION
(cubic metres, incl. railway sleepers)

	2003*	2004	2005*
Coniferous (softwood)	245,791	109,600	113,275
Broadleaved (hardwood)	19,293	24,600	25,425
Total	265,084	134,200	138,700

* Unofficial figures.
2006–07: Figures assumed to be unchanged from 2005 (FAO estimates).
Source: FAO.

Fishing

('000 metric tons, live weight)

	2004	2005	2006
Capture	33.9	34.9	35.1
Freshwater bream	21.9	20.0*	17.2
Common carp	0.6	0.8	0.1
Crucian carp	1.4	2.4	2.2
Roaches	1.6	1.4	2.0
Asp	0.9	0.8*	0.8*
Northern pike	0.8	0.8	0.8
Wels (Som) catfish	0.9	1.8	1.9
Pike-perch	2.7	2.9	3.5
Aquaculture	0.6	1.1	0.5
Total catch	34.5	36.0*	35.7*

* FAO estimate.
Source: FAO.

Mining

('000 metric tons, unless otherwise indicated)

	2004	2005	2006
Hard coal }	86,875	86,617	96,231
Brown coal (incl. lignite) }			
Crude petroleum*	59,485	61,486	65,003
Natural gas (million cu m)	22,102	24,973	26,382
Iron ore (gross weight)	20,303	19,471	22,263
Bauxite	4,706	4,815	4,884
Lead ore (metal content)	33	31	48
Zinc ore (metal content)	361	364	405
Manganese ore	2,318	2,233	2,531
Chromite	3,287	516	269
Silver ore (metal content, metric tons)	773,296	883,210	806,083
Gold (metal content, kg)	28,837	27,649	30,835
Asbestos	347	306	315

* Including gas condensate.

2007 ('000 metric tons, unless otherwise indicated): Hard coal and brown coal (incl. lignite) 98,384; Crude petroleum (incl. gas condensate) 67,125; Natural gas (million cu m) 29,562; Iron ore (gross weight) 23,834; Chromite 231; Asbestos 293.

Industry

SELECTED PRODUCTS
('000 metric tons, unless otherwise indicated)

	2005	2006	2007
Wheat flour	2,756	2,850	3,080
Raw sugar	529	490	393
Wine ('000 hectolitres)	529	368	n.a.
Beer ('000 hectolitres)	3,235	3,638	n.a.
Cigarettes (million)	30,008	30,834	n.a.
Woven cotton fabrics (metric tons)	35,530	56,460	n.a.
Motor spirit (petrol)	2,359	2,345	2,633
Kerosene	249	314	385
Gas-diesel (distillate fuel) oils	3,705	3,888	4,295
Residual fuel oils (Mazout)	3,550	3,333	2,584
Cement	4,181	4,880	5,699
Crude steel	4,477	4,245	4,784
Copper (unrefined, metric tons)	418,356	427,723	406,921
Electric energy (million kWh)	67,920	71,669	76,621

Finance

CURRENCY AND EXCHANGE RATES

Monetary Units
100 tein = 1 tenge.

Sterling, Dollar and Euro Equivalents (31 December 2008)
£1 sterling = 176.088 tenge;
US $1 = 120.790 tenge;
€1 = 168.103 tenge;
1,000 tenge = £5.68 = $8.28 = €5.95.

Average Exchange Rate (tenge per US $)
2006   126.089
2007   122.554
2008   120.299

Note: The tenge was introduced on 15 November 1993, replacing the old Russian (formerly Soviet) rouble at an exchange rate of 1 tenge = 500 roubles. On 18 November the rate was adjusted to 250 roubles per tenge. In April 1999 the tenge was allowed to 'float' on foreign exchange markets.

KAZAKHSTAN

Statistical Survey

STATE BUDGET
(million tenge)

Revenue*	2005	2006	2007
Tax revenue	1,998,314.0	2,209,102.4	2,356,040.3
Other current revenue	66,036.5	54,764.3	181,102.4
Capital revenue	34,181.7	74,165.7	92,685.9
Official transfers	—	1.8	258,045.3
Total	2,098,532.2	2,338,034.2	2,887,873.9

Expenditure†	2005	2006	2007
General public services	103,786.0	124,546.1	164,743.8
Defence	78,663.5	99,991.7	166,646.3
Public order and security	152,904.3	179,871.9	240,992.8
Education	256,935.0	327,290.7	455,430.1
Health care	185,456.2	223,372.6	299,380.6
Social security and social assistance	345,356.3	422,423.3	502,381.4
Housing and communal services	118,326.1	135,010.0	199,937.0
Recreation and cultural activities	57,075.7	81,164.0	122,209.9
Agriculture, forestry, water management, fishing and environmental protection	64,578.1	77,025.4	100,955.1
Transport and communications	119,476.1	161,806.9	289,653.9
Official transfers	369,258.3	197,407.3	38.4
Total (incl. others)	1,946,146.2	2,150,559.8	2,678,280.3

* Excluding grants received (million tenge): 7,239.2 in 2005; 7,917.5 in 2006; 8,102.0 in 2007.
† Excluding net expenditure minus repayments (million tenge): 98,481.4 in 2005; 97,936.8 in 2006; 416,786.8 in 2007.

Source: Ministry of Finance, Astana.

INTERNATIONAL RESERVES
(US $ million at 31 December)

	2005	2006	2007
Gold	985.5	1,376.2	1,852.5
IMF special drawing rights	1.2	1.3	1.4
Reserve position in IMF	0.0	0.0	0.0
Foreign exchange	6,083.0	17,749.5	15,775.4
Total	7,069.7	19,127.0	17,629.3

Source: IMF, *International Financial Statistics*.

MONEY SUPPLY
(million tenge at 31 December)

	2005	2006	2007
Currency outside banks	411,813	600,832	739,687
Demand deposits at commercial banks	381,364	663,600	756,591
Total money (incl. others)	799,440	1,281,549	1,532,688

Source: IMF, *International Financial Statistics*.

COST OF LIVING
(Consumer Price Index; base: previous year = 100)

	2006	2007	2008
Food and beverages	107.3	126.6	110.8
Other consumer goods	107.1	110.5	105.7
Services	111.6	115.4	111.4
All items	108.4	118.8	109.5

NATIONAL ACCOUNTS
Expenditure on the Gross Domestic Product
(million tenge at current prices)

	2005	2006	2007
Final consumption expenditure	4,638,271.1	5,709,745.2	7,215,844.7
Households	3,685,763.3	4,547,334.5	5,641,240.9
Non-profit institutions serving households	98,677.7	122,564.8	154,197.5
General government	853,830.1	1,039,845.9	1,420,406.3
Gross capital formation	2,283,098.7	3,413,877.7	4,774,411.9
Gross fixed capital formation. Acquisitions, less disposals of valuables	2,122,679.1	3,084,388.0	3,857,191.9
Changes in inventories	160,419.6	329,489.7	917,220.0
Total domestic expenditure	6,921,369.8	9,123,622.9	11,990,256.6
Exports of goods and services (net)	669,223.7	1,090,108.3	859,537.4
GDP in market prices	7,590,593.5	10,213,731.2	12,849,794.0

Gross Domestic Product by Economic Activity

	2005	2006	2007
Agriculture, hunting, forestry and fishing	483,484.6	561,329.8	727,335.8
Mining and quarrying	1,198,887.4	1,646,628.0	1,934,762.2
Manufacturing	914,013.2	1,188,108.0	1,476,647.6
Electricity, gas and water supply	148,303.1	183,808.0	223,716.2
Construction	594,986.2	1,001,218.6	1,213,216.6
Wholesale and retail trade; repair of motor vehicles, motorcycles and personal and household goods	965,973.3	1,248,901.1	1,702,210.5
Transport, storage and communication	896,814.2	1,178,831.9	1,481,636.2
Financial intermediation	245,775.6	475,525.9	761,616.0
Real estate, renting and business activities	1,142,799.2	1,515,722.2	1,896,241.5
Public administration and defence; compulsory social security	157,851.5	190,892.5	249,746.8
Education	263,460.9	321,669.4	418,932.8
Health and social work	129,837.5	158,772.9	213,356.9
Other community, social and personal services	146,257.6	182,522.6	244,744.7
Sub-total	7,288,444.3	9,853,930.9	12,544,163.8
Less Financial intermediation services indirectly measured	165,700.7	306,033.9	613,954.8
Gross value added in basic prices	7,122,743.6	9,547,897.0	11,930,209.0
Taxes, less subsidies, on products	467,849.9	665,834.2	919,585.0
GDP in market prices	7,590,593.5	10,213,731.2	12,849,794.0

BALANCE OF PAYMENTS
(US $ million)

	2005	2006	2007
Exports of goods f.o.b.	28,300.6	38,762.1	48,351.1
Imports of goods f.o.b.	-17,978.8	-24,120.4	-33,260.2
Trade balance	10,321.8	14,641.7	15,091.0
Exports of services	2,228.4	2,818.7	3,555.0
Imports of services	-7,495.7	-8,760.4	-11,626.8
Balance on goods and services	5,054.5	8,700.1	7,019.1
Other income received	680.3	1,430.5	3,463.0
Other income paid	-6,377.2	-10,922.0	-15,656.0
Balance on goods, services and income	-642.4	-793.1	-5,173.9
Current transfers received	810.0	904.2	903.8
Current transfers paid	-1,223.5	-2,111.4	-3,063.3
Current balance	-1,055.8	-1,998.6	-7,333.4
Capital account (net)	14.0	31.9	-37.6

KAZAKHSTAN

Statistical Survey

—continued	2005	2006	2007
Direct investment abroad	145.9	384.7	-3,243.6
Direct investment from abroad	1,971.2	6,278.2	10,188.6
Portfolio investment assets	-5,157.1	-9,176.7	-4,095.3
Portfolio investment liabilities	1,204.4	4,675.4	-468.8
Financial derivatives assets	-119.7	-91.6	-614.0
Financial derivatives liabilities	7.0	23.8	247.3
Other investment assets	-4,310.4	-8,032.6	-11,815.8
Other investment liabilities	7,156.7	22,107.7	17,114.0
Net errors and omissions	-1,800.0	-3,127.7	-2,970.2
Overall balance	-1,943.8	11,074.6	-3,028.7

Source: IMF, *International Financial Statistics*.

External Trade

PRINCIPAL COMMODITIES
(distribution by SITC, US $ million)

Imports c.i.f.	2005	2006	2007
Food and live animals	987.9	1,322.7	1,737.5
Mineral fuels, lubricants and related materials	2,062.1	3,051.2	3,639.1
Petroleum and related products	1,412.5	2,378.3	3,003.5
Chemicals and related products	1,615.9	2,030.8	2,716.7
Manufactured goods classified chiefly by material	3,743.8	4,864.5	6,888.8
Iron and steel	1,709.1	1,967.7	2,731.2
Machinery and transport equipment	7,192.5	10,180.4	14,464.6
Machinery specialized for particular industries	1,447.8	1,386.0	2,228.1
General industrial machinery, equipment and parts	1,348.8	1,967.5	2,510.4
Electrical machinery, apparatus, appliances and parts	895.0	1,238.8	1,841.1
Road vehicles	1,605.1	2,587.2	4,311.2
Passenger cars and other passenger vehicles	757.6	1,407.4	2,392.1
Miscellaneous manufactured articles	1,143.6	1,520.8	2,230.7
Total (incl. others)	17,352.2	23,663.1	32,756.4

Exports f.o.b.	2005	2006	2007
Food and live animals	610.9	985.8	1,937.7
Crude materials (inedible) except fuels	1,872.9	2,305.5	2,960.4
Metalliferous ore and metal scrap	1,555.3	1,929.6	2,494.4
Mineral fuels, lubricants and related materials	19,525.4	26,279.3	31,518.6
Petroleum and related products	18,341.8	24,850.1	29,778.5
Manufactured goods classified chiefly by material	4,654.6	6,467.4	8,556.7
Iron and steel	2,022.5	2,094.1	3,502.6
Non-ferrous metals	2,242.8	3,982.1	4,537.7
Copper	1,504.8	2,620.9	2,774.8
Total (incl. others)	27,849.0	38,244.4	47,755.3

Source: UN, *International Trade Statistics Yearbook*.

PRINCIPAL TRADING PARTNERS
(distribution by SITC, US $ million)

Imports c.i.f.	2005	2006	2007
Belarus	208.0	284.4	396.0
China, People's Republic	1,251.8	1,924.9	3,507.3
Finland	197.9	235.0	307.4
France (incl. Monaco)	291.1	459.7	705.5
Germany	1,300.7	1,809.2	2,587.3
Italy	679.8	1,430.1	1,130.9
Japan	598.6	914.1	1,369.7
Korea, Republic	256.1	359.3	625.9
Netherlands	140.5	189.5	375.7
Poland	197.1	303.4	397.0
Russia	6,591.3	9,065.7	11,626.9
Sweden	261.4	298.1	311.2
Switzerland-Liechtenstein	201.3	97.3	248.5
Turkey	399.9	558.3	959.0
Ukraine	844.7	979.7	1,528.5
United Kingdom	423.3	506.2	737.1
USA	1,205.3	1,105.8	1,625.7
Uzbekistan	254.5	319.1	538.5
Total (incl. others)	17,352.2	23,663.1	32,756.4

Exports f.o.b.	2005	2006	2007
British Virgin Islands	551.5	109.8	95.0
Canada	528.1	287.3	420.5
China, People's Republic	2,423.9	3,592.5	5,639.6
France (incl. Monaco)	2,665.1	3,347.0	3,982.7
Germany	408.9	551.2	392.3
Iran	886.1	2,077.6	2,451.4
Israel	661.6	622.4	1,059.0
Italy	4,190.5	6,891.6	7,774.2
Netherlands	877.8	1,704.6	2,464.3
Poland	367.6	204.4	257.0
Portugal	317.0	298.2	394.6
Romania	460.3	747.1	686.5
Russia	2,927.2	3,730.0	4,659.1
Spain	464.5	968.4	775.9
Switzerland-Liechtenstein	5,509.5	6,721.2	7,475.9
Turkey	157.0	348.2	934.4
Ukraine	200.4	622.8	1,113.1
United Kingdom	320.5	1,143.9	1,133.2
USA	666.0	462.3	422.2
Uzbekistan	242.6	384.6	871.8
Total (incl. others)	27,849.0	38,244.4	47,755.3

Source: UN, *International Trade Statistics Yearbook*.

Transport

RAILWAYS
(estimated traffic)

	2005	2006	2007
Paying passengers (million journeys)	16.5	17.8	18.1
Passenger-km (million)	12,136	13,670	14,587
Freight carried ('000 metric tons)	222,700	246,900	260,600
Freight net ton-km (million)	171,900	191,200	200,800

ROAD TRAFFIC
(motor vehicles in use at 31 December)

	2005	2006	2007
Passenger cars	1,405,300	1,745,000	2,183,100
Lorries and vans	281,500	311,800	359,200
Buses and coaches	65,698	75,042	83,372

KAZAKHSTAN

SHIPPING

Merchant Fleet
(registered at 31 December)

	2005	2006	2007
Number of vessels	45	59	63
Total displacement (grt)	43,486	64,932	54,291

Source: Lloyd's Register-Fairplay, *World Fleet Statistics*.

CIVIL AVIATION
(traffic on scheduled services)

	2005	2006	2007
Passengers carried (million)	1.7	1.9	2.7
Passenger-km (million)	3,265	3,787	5,457
Total ton-km (million)	96.7	69.9	88.1

Tourism

FOREIGN TOURIST ARRIVALS

Country of residence	2004	2005	2006
China, People's Republic	76,806	85,696	117,279
Kyrgyzstan	1,091,923	851,568	1,018,524
Russia	1,628,823	1,405,543	1,385,964
Tajikistan	260,487	286,042	301,971
Uzbekistan	767,162	1,266,401	1,352,879
Total (incl. others)	4,291,040	4,364,949	4,706,742

Tourism receipts (US $ million, incl. passenger transport): 803 in 2004; 801 in 2005; 973 in 2006.

Source: World Tourism Organization.

Communications Media

	2005	2006	2007
Telephones ('000 main lines in use)	2,708.0	2,928.0	3,236.9
Mobile cellular telephones ('000 subscribers)	5,398.0	7,830.4	12,587.8
Internet users ('000)	609.2	1,247.0	1,900.6
Broadband subscribers ('000)	3.0	30.5	381.2

Book production (titles, incl. pamphlets): 1,223 in 1999.

Book production (copies, 1996): 21,014,000.

Daily newspapers (1996): Titles 3; Average circulation 500,000.

Radio receivers ('000 in use, 1997): 6,470.

Television receivers ('000 in use, 2001): 5,440.

Sources: UNESCO, *Statistical Yearbook*; UN, *Statistical Yearbook*; International Telecommunication Union.

Education

(state educational institutions, 2007/08)

	Institutions	Teachers	Students ('000)
Pre-primary	1,500	24,089	232.9
Primary *and* Secondary: general*	7,958	279,098	2,627.4
Secondary: vocational	460	31,560	499.5
Professional-technical schools	313	6,165	106.8
Higher	167	41,207	717.1

* Excluding 79 secondary-general evening schools with 24,000 students.

Note: There were, additionally: 155 private primary and secondary-general schools, with 20,000 students; 179 private secondary-vocational schools, with 88,700 students; and 134 non-governmental higher education institutes, with 297,900 students, in 2003/04.

Adult literacy rate (UNESCO estimates): 99.6% (males 99.8%; females 99.5%) in 2007 (Source: UNESCO Institute for Statistics).

Directory

The Constitution

The Constitution of the Republic of Kazakhstan was endorsed by 89% of the electorate voting in a national referendum on 30 August 1995, and was officially adopted on 6 September, replacing the Constitution of January 1993. A number of constitutional amendments were adopted on 8 October 1998 and on 18 May 2007. The following is a summary of the Constitution's main provisions:

GENERAL PROVISIONS

The Republic of Kazakhstan is a democratic, secular, law-based, unitary state with a presidential system of rule. The state ensures the integrity, inviolability and inalienability of its territory. State power belongs to the people, who exercise it directly through referendums and free elections, and also delegate the exercise of their power to state bodies. State power is separated into legislative, executive and judicial branches, with a system of checks and balances being applied.

Ideological and political diversity are recognized. State and private property are recognized. The state language is Kazakh. Russian is employed officially in state bodies and local government bodies on a par with Kazakh.

HUMAN AND CIVIL RIGHTS AND LIBERTIES

Citizenship of the Republic of Kazakhstan is acquired and terminated in accordance with the law. Citizenship of another state is not recognized for any citizen of Kazakhstan. The rights and liberties of the individual are recognized and guaranteed. No one may be subjected to discrimination on grounds of origin, sex, race, language, religious or other beliefs, or place of residence. No one may be subjected to torture, violence or other treatment or punishment that is cruel or degrading. Provision is made for the abolition of the death penalty. All are entitled to use their native language and practise their native culture. Freedom of speech and creativity are guaranteed. Censorship is prohibited. Citizens are entitled to assemble and to hold demonstrations peacefully and without weapons. Defence of the republic is the duty and obligation of every citizen. Human and civil rights and liberties may be restricted only by law and only to the extent that is necessary to defend the constitutional system and to safeguard public order. Any action capable of disrupting inter-ethnic accord is deemed unconstitutional.

THE PRESIDENT OF THE REPUBLIC

The President of the Republic is the Head of State, who determines the main directions of the state's domestic and foreign policy and represents Kazakhstan domestically and internationally. The President is elected for a seven-year term by secret ballot on the basis of general, equal and direct suffrage. (Under the constitutional amendments of May 2007, the presidential term was reduced to five years, with effect from 2012.) A citizen of the republic by birth, who is at least 40 years of age, has a fluent command of the state language, and has lived in Kazakhstan for no less than 15 years, may be elected President.

The President: addresses an annual message to the people; schedules regular and extraordinary elections to Parliament; signs and promulgates laws submitted by the Senat (Senate), or returns draft legislation for further discussion; appoints the Prime Minister and relieves him of office, subject to the approval of the Majlis (Assembly); with the consent of the Senat, appoints to and relieves of office the Chairman of the National Bank, the Prosecutor-General and the Chairman of the National Security Committee; appoints and recalls the heads of diplomatic missions of the republic; decides on the holding of referendums; negotiates and signs international treaties; is supreme Commander-in-Chief of the armed forces; bestows state awards and confers honours; resolves matters of citizenship and of granting political asylum; in the event of aggression against the republic, imposes martial law or announces a partial or general mobilization; forms the Security Council, the Supreme Judicial Council and other consultative and advisory bodies.

The President may be relieved of office only in the event of his having committed an act of treason or if he exhibits a consistent incapacity to carry out his duties owing to illness. A decision on the President's early dismissal is adopted at a joint sitting of the chambers of Parliament by a majority of no less than three-quarters of the total number of deputies of each chamber. The question of dismissal of the President may not be raised at the same time as he is considering early termination of the authority of Parliament.

PARLIAMENT

Parliament is the supreme representative body of the republic, exercising legislative functions. It consists of two chambers, the Senate and the Majlis. The Senate comprises 47 members, of whom 32 are elected at joint sittings of the deputies of all representative bodies of the regions and the capital city, while 15 deputies are appointed by the President. The Majlis comprises 107 deputies, of whom 98 are elected by general, equal and direct suffrage and on a basis of party-list proportional representation. The remaining nine deputies are elected by the Assembly of Nations of Kazakhstan (a 350-member body representing the country's minority ethnic groups). The Senate's term is six years, and that of the Majlis is five years. One-half of the elected deputies in the Senate are subject to election every three years.

THE GOVERNMENT

The Government exercises the executive power of the republic and is responsible to the President. The Government drafts the main areas of the state's socio-economic policy, defence capability, security and public order, and orders their implementation; presents to Parliament the republican budget and the report of its implementation, and ensures that the budget is implemented; submits draft legislation to the Majlis and provides for the implementation of laws; organizes the management of state property; formulates measures for the pursuit of Kazakhstan's foreign policy; directs the activity of Ministries, State Committees and other central and local executive bodies. The Prime Minister, who is a member of the parliamentary majority party, proposes members of the Government, subject to the approval of the Majlis, organizes and directs the activity of the Government and is personally responsible for its work. A motion of 'no confidence' in a new Government may be approved by a simple majority of votes in the Majlis.

LOCAL STATE ADMINISTRATION GOVERNMENT

Local state administration is exercised by local representative and executive bodies, which are responsible for the state of affairs on their own territory. The local representative councils (maslikhat) express the will of the population and, bearing in mind the overall state interest, define the measures necessary to realize this will and monitor their implementation. Councils are elected for a five-year term by a secret ballot on the basis of general, equal and direct suffrage. The local executive bodies (akimiyat) are part of the unified system of executive bodies of Kazakhstan, and ensure that the general state policy of the executive authority is implemented in co-ordination with the interests and development needs of the corresponding territory. Each local executive body is headed by the Akim (Governor) of the corresponding administrative-territorial unit, who is appointed by the President after the approval of the appropriate maslikhat.

The Government

HEAD OF STATE

President: NURSULTAN A. NAZARBAEV (elected indirectly 24 April 1990; elected unopposed 1 December 1991; term extended by referendum 29 April 1995; re-elected 10 January 1999; re-elected 4 December 2005; inaugurated 11 January 2006).

GOVERNMENT
(April 2009)

Prime Minister: KÄRIM Q. MÄSIMOV.
First Deputy Prime Minister: ÖMIRZAQ E. ŞÖKEEV.
Deputy Prime Minister: ERBOL T. ORINBAEV.
Deputy Prime Minister: SERIK N. AXMETOV.
Minister of Foreign Affairs: MARAT M. TÄJIN.
Minister of Defence: DANÏAL K. AXMETOV.
Minister of Internal Affairs: SERIK N. BAYMAĞANBETOV.
Minister of Health: JAQSILIQ A. DOSQALÏEV.
Minister of Industry and Trade: VLADÏMÏR S. ŞKOLNÏK.
Minister of Culture and Information: MUXTAR A. QUL-MUXAMMED.
Minister of Tourism and Sport: TEMIRXAN M. DOSMUXANBETOV.
Minister of Education and Science: JANSEYIT Q. TÜYMEBAEV.
Minister of Environmental Protection: NURĞALÏ S. ÄŞIMOV.
Minister of Agriculture: AQILBEK Q. KÜRIŞBAEV.
Minister of Transport and Communications: ÄBILĞAZI Q. QUSAYINOV.
Minister of Labour and Social Security: GÜLŞARA N. ÄBDIQALIQOVA.
Minister of Finance: BOLAT B. JÄMIŞEV.
Minister of Emergency Situations: VLADÏMÏR K. BOJKO.
Minister of the Economy and Budgetary Planning: BAQIT T. SULTANOV.
Minister of Energy and Mineral Resources: SAWAT M. MIÑBAEV.
Minister of Justice: RAŞÏD T. TÜSIPBEKOV.

MINISTRIES

Office of the President: 010000 Astana, Beibitshilik kosh. 11; tel. (7172) 32-13-99; fax (7172) 32-61-72; internet www.akorda.kz.

Office of the Prime Minister: 010000 Astana, Beibitshilik kosh. 11; tel. (7172) 32-31-04; fax (7172) 32-40-89; internet www.government.kz.

Ministry of Agriculture: 010000 Astana, Kenesary kosh. 36; tel. (7172) 32-37-63; fax (7172) 32-62-99; e-mail mailbox@minagri.kz; internet www.minagri.kz.

Ministry of Culture and Information: 010000 Astana, Solzhagau, Ministrilkter uyi, 15 kireberis, 3rd floor, office 305; tel. (7172) 74-01-07; fax (7172) 50-30-51; e-mail mkis@mininfo.katelco.kz; internet www.sana.gov.kz.

Ministry of Defence: 010000 Astana, Solzhagau, AEA, 2-ui Barlyk kukyktar korgalgan; tel. (7172) 72-15-91; internet www.mod.kz.

Ministry of the Economy and Budgetary Planning: 010000 Astana, 35 kosh. 7; tel. (7172) 74-28-09; e-mail info@minplan.kz; internet www.minplan.kz.

Ministry of Education and Science: 010000 Astana, Orynbor kosh. 8; tel. (7172) 74-24-28; fax (7172) 74-24-16; e-mail pressa@edu.gov.kz; internet www.edu.gov.kz.

Ministry of Emergency Situations: 010000 Astana, Beibitshilik kosh. 22; tel. (7172) 94-48-29; e-mail mchs@emer.kz; internet www.emer.kz.

Ministry of Energy and Mineral Resources: 010000 Astana, Kabanbay batyr kosh. 22; tel. (7172) 97-68-83; e-mail ayan@memr.kz; internet www.memr.gov.kz.

Ministry of Environmental Protection: 010000 Astana, Solzhagalau, ui. Ministrigi 35-8/14; tel. (7172) 74-00-75; fax (7172) 59-19-73; internet www.nature.kz.

Ministry of Finance: 010000 Astana, pl. Respubliki 60; tel. (7172) 28-00-65; fax (7172) 32-40-89; e-mail info@minfin.kz; internet www.minfin.kz.

Ministry of Foreign Affairs: 010000 Astana, Solzhagau, Tauelsizdik kosh. 31; tel. (7172) 72-05-18; fax (7172) 72-05-16; e-mail midrk@mid.kz; internet www.mfa.kz.

Ministry of Health: 010000 Astana, Solzhagau, Ministrilkter uyi, 5 kireberis; tel. (7172) 74-32-43; e-mail zdrav@mz.gov.kz; internet www.mz.gov.kz.

Ministry of Industry and Trade: 010000 Astana, Kabanbai batyr d-ly. 49, 'Transport Tauer'; tel. (7172) 29-90-25; fax (7172) 24-12-13; internet www.mit.kz.

Ministry of Internal Affairs: 010000 Astana, Manas kosh. 4; tel. (7172) 72-24-93; fax (7172) 34-17-38; e-mail press@mvd.kz; internet www.mvd.kz.

Ministry of Justice: 010000 Astana, Solzhagau, Orynbor kosh. 8, Ministrilkter uyi, 13 kireberis; tel. (7172) 74-07-37; fax (7172) 74-09-54; e-mail news@minjust.kz; internet www.minjust.kz.

Ministry of Labour and Social Security: 010000 Astana, Manas kosh. 2; tel. (7172) 71-28-51; fax (7172) 74-36-08; e-mail inter@enbek.kz; internet www.enbek.kz.

Ministry of Tourism and Sport: 010000 Astana, Abai d-ly 33; tel. (7172) 75-30-10; fax (7172) 75-33-28; e-mail kense@komtur.kz; internet www.mts.gov.kz.

Ministry of Transport and Communications: 010000 Astana, Kabanbai batyra d-ly 47; tel. (7172) 24-13-12; fax (7172) 24-14-19; e-mail janibek@mtc.gov.kz; internet www.mtk.gov.kz.

KAZAKHSTAN

President

Presidential Election, 4 December 2005

Candidates	Votes	%
Nursultan A. Nazarbaev	6,147,517	91.15
Zharmakhan A. Tuyakbai	445,934	6.61
Others	150,816	2.24
Total	**6,744,267**	**100.00**

Legislature

Parliament is a bicameral legislative body, comprising the Senate and the Majlis (Assembly).

Majlis

010000 Astana, Parliament House; tel. (7172) 15-30-19; fax (7172) 33-30-99; e-mail www@parlam.kz; internet www.parlam.kz.

Chairman: ORAL B. MUXAMEJANOV.

General Election, 18 August 2007

Parties	Votes	%	Seats
Light Of The Fatherland (Nur Otan)	5,247,720	88.41	98
National Social-Democratic Party	269,310	4.54	—
Bright Road—Democratic Party of Kazakhstan (Ak Zhol)	183,346	3.09	—
Village Kazakhstani Social-Democratic Party (Auyl)	89,855	1.51	—
Communist People's Party of Kazakhstan	76,799	1.29	—
Party of Patriots of Kazakhstan	46,436	0.78	—
Spirituality Party (Rukhaniyat)	22,159	0.37	—
Total (incl. others)	**5,935,625**	**100.00**	**107***

*Including nine deputies elected by the Assembly of Nations of Kazakhstan (a body representing the country's minority ethnic groups) on 20 August 2007.

Senate

010000 Astana, Abay d-ly 33, Parliament House; tel. (7172) 15-33-76; fax (7172) 33-31-18; e-mail smimazh@parlam.kz; internet www.parlam.kz.

Chairman: KASYM-ZHOMART K. TOKAEV.

The 47-member Senate is the upper chamber of Parliament. Elections are held every three years for one-half of the 32 seats elected by special colleges (comprising members of local councils) in Kazakhstan's 14 regions and two cities; the term of office for members of the Senate is six years. Under constitutional amendments adopted on 18 May 2007, the number of deputies appointed by the President increased from seven to 15; the additional eight members were officially appointed to the Senate by presidential decree in August. Partial elections to the Senate were conducted on 4 October 2008.

Election Commission

Ortalyk Sailau Komissiyasy (Central Election Commission): 010000 Astana, Beibitshilik kosh. 4; tel. (7172) 75-21-21; fax (7172) 33-33-88; e-mail info@election.kz; internet www.election.kz; Chair. KUANDYK T. TURGANKULOV.

Political Organizations

A new law was introduced in July 2002, which required all parties to have a minimum of 50,000 members from among all the country's regions in order to qualify for official registration. In 2008 the following nine parties were registered.

Bright Road Democratic Party of Kazakhstan (Ak Zhol) (Kazakstannyn 'Ak Zhol' Demokratiyalyk Partiyasy): 010000 Astana, Imanov kosh. 18/7; tel. (7172) 22-10-66; fax (7172) 22-14-50; e-mail elena_akzhol@mail.ru; internet www.akzhol.kz; f. 2002 by former members of the Democratic Choice of Kazakhstan; merged with Justice Democratic Party (Adilet) in 2007; Chair. ALIKHAN M. BAYMENOV; 175,862 mems (2007).

Communist Party of Kazakhstan (CPK) (Kazakstan Kommunistik Partiyasy): 010000 Astana, Beibitshilik kosh. 27/49; tel. and fax (7172) 21-32-97; e-mail pravdakz@list.ru; f. 1937; suspended Aug. 1991, re-registered Aug. 1998 and March 2003; contested 2004 legislative elections in alliance with Democratic Choice of Kazakhstan, as the People's Opposition Union of Communists and DVK bloc; mem. of For a Just Kazakhstan opposition bloc formed in 2005; Chair. SERIKBOLSYN A. ABDILDIN; 54,246 mems (2007).

Communist People's Party of Kazakhstan (Kazakstan Kommunistik Khalyk Partiyasy): 010000 Astana, Zheltoksan kosh. 36A/37; tel. and fax (7172) 21-32-97; e-mail knpk@rambler.ru; internet www.knpk.kz; f. 2004 by fmr mems of the Communist Party of Kazakhstan; Sec. of the Central Cttee VLADISLAV B. KOSAREV; 90,000 mems (2007).

Freedom Democratic Party of Kazakhstan (Azat) ('Azat' Kazakstannyn Demokratiyalyk Partiyasy): 050000 Almaty, Kabanai batyr kosh. 58; tel. (727) 266-49-39; fax (727) 266-36-43; e-mail nast_akjol@mail.ru; internet www.azat-party.info; f. 2004 as Real Bright Road—Democratic Party of Kazakhstan; present name adopted 2008; supports construction of a democratic, secular, social government and the rule of law, and an open society; Leader BOLAT M. ABILOV; 97,157 mems (2007).

Light Of The Fatherland People's Democratic Party (Nur Otan) ('Nur Otan' Khalyktyk Demokratiyalyk Partiyasy): 050000 Almaty, Abylai khan d-ly 79; tel. (727) 279-78-00; fax (727) 279-40-66; e-mail partyotan@nursat.kz; internet www.ndp-nurotan.kz; f. 2006 by merger of Fatherland, Civic Party of Kazakhstan and Agrarian Party of Kazakhstan; supports administration of President Nazarbaev; Chair. NURSULTAN A. NAZARBAEV; First Deputy Chair. BAKYTZHAN T. ZHUMAGULOV; 607,557 mems (2007).

National Social-Democratic Party (Zhalpyulttyk Sotsial Demokratiyalyk Partiyasy—ZhSDP): 050000 Almaty, Kabanbai batyr kosh. 58; tel. (727) 663-64-06; fax (727) 266-36-43; e-mail ocdp@mail.ru; internet www.osdp.kz; f. 2006; contested 2007 legislative elections in coalition with Real Bright Road—Democratic Party of Kazakhstan; Chair. ZHARMAKHAN A. TUYAKBAI; 140,000 mems (2007).

Party of Patriots of Kazakhstan (PPK) (Kazakstan Patriottary Partiyasy): 050000 Almaty, Zhibek-zholy kosh. 76/318; tel. and fax (7172) 22-98-34; f. 2000; Chair. GANI E. KASYMOV; 172,000 mems (2007).

Spirituality Party ('Ruxaniyat' Partiyasy): 010000 Astana, Saryarka kosh. 5; tel. and fax (7172) 97-73-80; e-mail kazayelder@nursat.kz; f. 1995 as Renaissance Party of Kazakhstan; re-registered under new name 2003; supports Govt of President Nazarbaev; Chair. ALTYNSHASH K. JAGANOVA; 72,000 mems (2007).

Village Kazakhstani Social-Democratic Party (Auyl) ('Auyl' Kazakstandyk Sotsial-Demokratiyalyk Partiyasy): 010000 Astana, Beibitshilik kosh. 46/109; tel. and fax (7172) 31-71-57; e-mail kaliev@parlam.kz; internet auyl.by.ru; registered in 2002; seeks to strengthen government support for the agricultural sector; Chair. GANI A. KALIEV; 61,043 mems (2007).

Diplomatic Representation

EMBASSIES IN KAZAKHSTAN

Afghanistan: 010000 Astana, Diplomatiyalyk kalashyk C-10; tel. (7172) 24-29-46; fax (7172) 24-30-25; e-mail af_embassyalmaty@yahoo.com; Ambassador AZIZ ARYANFAR.

Armenia: 010000 Astana, Perspektivnaya kosh. 57; tel. and fax (7172) 24-19-74; e-mail armeniaemb_kz@gmail.com; Ambassador VASILY KAZARIAN.

Austria: 010000 Astana, Kosmonavtov kosh. 62; tel. (7172) 97-78-69; fax (7172) 97-78-50; e-mail astana-ob@bmeia.gv.at; Ambassador URSULA FAHRINGER.

Azerbaijan: 010000 Astana, Diplomatiyalyk kalashyk B-6; tel. (7172) 24-15-81; fax (7172) 24-15-32; e-mail astana@azembassy.kz; internet www.azembassy.kz; Ambassador LATIF GANDILOV.

Belarus: 010000 Astana, Kenesary kosh. 35; tel. (7172) 32-48-29; fax (7172) 32-18-70; e-mail kazakhstan@belembassy.org; internet kazakhstan.belembassy.org; Ambassador VASILII I. HAPEYEV.

Belgium: 010000 Astana, Kosmonavtov kosh. 62; tel. (7172) 97-44-85; fax (7172) 97-78-49; e-mail embassy.astana@diplobel.fed.be; Ambassador CHRISTIAN MEERSCHMAN.

Brazil: 010000 Astana, Kabanbai Batyr kosh. 6/1; tel. (7172) 24-46-84; fax (7172) 24-47-43; e-mail brasembastana@mre.gov.br; Ambassador FREDERICO S. DUQUE ESTRADA MEYER.

Bulgaria: 050000 Almaty, Gornyi Gigant, 8-shi Gvardiyalyk Diviziya kosh. 128; tel. and fax (727) 262-99-56; e-mail bulgarianembassy@rambler.ru; internet www.mfa.bg/almaty; Ambassador NIKOLA F. BORISOV.

Canada: 050010 Almaty, Karasai batyr kosh. 34; tel. (727) 250-11-51; fax (727) 258-24-93; e-mail almat@international.gc.ca; internet www.dfait-maeci.gc.ca/canadaeuropa/kazakhstan; Ambassador MARGARET SKOK.

KAZAKHSTAN — Directory

China, People's Republic: 010000 Astana, Kabanbai Batyr d-ly 37, 5 blok; tel. (7172) 79-35-61; fax (7172) 79-35-65; e-mail chinaemb_kz@mfa.gov.cn; internet kz.china-embassy.org; Ambassador CHEN GOPIN.

Cuba: 010000 Astana, Kabanbai batyr d-ly 27/2; tel. and fax (7172) 24-24-67; fax (7172) 24-26-38; e-mail natembacu@mail.online.kz; internet www.cubakaz.com; Ambassador ABELARDO HERNÁNDEZ FERRER.

Czech Republic: 010000 Astana, Sary-Arka 6, Biznes-Tsentr Arman, 13th floor; tel. (7172) 66-04-72; fax (7172) 66-01-42; e-mail astana@embassy.mzv.cz; internet www.mzv.cz/astana; Ambassador BEDŘICH KOPECKÝ.

Egypt: 010000 Astana, Karaetkel sh-a 2, 109; tel. (7172) 24-12-66; fax (7172) 24-16-64; e-mail egyptianemb_kz@yahoo.com; Ambassador ABDALLAH OMAR ELARNOSI.

France: 010000 Astana, Kosmonavtov kosh. 62; tel. (7172) 97-51-00; fax (7172) 97-51-01; e-mail ambafrance@mail.kz; internet www.ambafrance-kz.kz; Ambassador ALAIN COUANON.

Georgia: 010000 Astana, Diplomatiyalyk kalashyk C-4; tel. and fax (7172) 24-34-26; e-mail astana.emb@mfa.gov.ge; Ambassador ZURAB SHURGHAIA.

Germany: 010000 Astana, Kosmonavtov kosh. 62; tel. (7172) 79-12-00; fax (7172) 79-12-13; e-mail info@astana.diplo.de; internet www.astana.diplo.de; Ambassador RAINER EUGEN SCHLAGETER.

Greece: 010000 Astana, Karaetkel sh-a 2, 109; tel. (7172) 24-12-66; fax (7172) 24-47-76; e-mail gremb.ast@mfa.gr; Ambassador EVANGELOS DENAXAS.

Holy See: 010000 Astana, Zelenaya Alleya kosh. 20; tel. (7172) 24-12-69; fax (7172) 24-16-04; e-mail nuntius_kazakhstan@lycos.com; Apostolic Nuncio Most Rev. MIGUEL MAURY BUENDÍA (Titular Archbishop of Italica).

Hungary: 050000 Almaty, Kenesary kosh. 47/40; tel. (7172) 59-15-58; fax (7172) 59-15-57; e-mail humembtse@mail.online.kz; Ambassador JÁNOS BALLA.

India: 010000 Astana, Kabanbai Batyr kosh. 6/1, Kenselik ortalygy 'Kaskad', 5th Floor; tel. (7172) 92-57-00; fax (7172) 92-57-16; e-mail aaadmn@netel.kz; internet www.indembassy.kz; Ambassador ASHOK SAJJANHAR.

Iran: 050000 Almaty, ul. Luganskii kosh. 31–33; tel. (727) 262-19-74; fax (7272) 263-26-54; e-mail iranembassy@itte.kz; Ambassador RAMIN MEHMAN PARAST.

Iraq: 010000 Astana, Riksos Prezident Otel, konakuyi 5005 belmesi; tel. (7127) 24-50-50; Chargé d'affaires a.i. HALDUN ABDULRAHMAN AL-JAMA.

Israel: 010000 Astana, ul. Auezov kosh. 8; tel. (7172) 68-87-38; fax (7172) 68-87-35; e-mail info@astana.mfa.gov.il; internet astana.mfa.gov.il; Ambassador ISRAEL MEI-AMI.

Italy: 010000 Astana, Shuba sh-a, Kosmonavtov kosh. 62; tel. (7172) 24-33-90; fax (7172) 24-36-86; e-mail ambasciata.astana@esteri.it; internet www.ambastana.esteri.it; Ambassador BRUNO ANTONIO PASQUINO.

Japan: 010000 Astana, Chubar sh-a, Kosmonavtov kosh. 62; tel. (7172) 97-78-43; fax (7172) 97-78-42; internet www.kz.emb-japan.go.jp/jp/index_r.htm; Ambassador SIGEO NATSUI.

Jordan: 010000 Astana, Novostroitel kosh. 8/2; tel. (7172) 24-52-54; fax (7172) 24-52-53; e-mail astana@fm.gov.jo; Chargé d'affaires SLAIMAN ARABIAT.

Korea, Republic: 010000 Astana, Kabanbai batyr d-ly 6/1/91–93; tel. (7172) 92-55-91; fax (7172) 92-55-96; e-mail koreaemb-kz@mofat.go.kr; internet kaz.mofat.go.kr; Ambassador KIM IL-SOO.

Kyrgyzstan: 010000 Astana, Diplomatiyalyk kalashyk B-5; tel. (7172) 24-20-24; fax (7172) 24-24-14; e-mail kz@mail.online.kz; Ambassador JANUSH. RUSTENBEKOV.

Latvia: 010000 Astana, Kabanbai Batyr d-ly 6/1/122, Kaskad Business Centre; tel. (7172) 92-53-16; fax (7172) 92-53-19; Ambassador RETS PLĒSUMS.

Lebanon: 010000 Astana, Tauelsyzdyk 2, 13th floor; tel. (7172) 79-35-15; fax (7172) 79-35-16; e-mail embassylebanon-kz@hotmail.com; Ambassador VAZKEN KAVLAKIAN.

Libya: 010000 Astana, Karaokel-2 sh-a, 110; tel. (7172) 24-18-79; fax (7172) 24-27-57; e-mail libya@nursat.kz; Chargé d'affaires a.i. AHMED EDDEB.

Lithuania: 050059 Almaty, Gornyi Gigant, Eskandir kosh. 15; tel. (727) 263-41-02; fax (727) 263-19-75; e-mail amb.kz@urm.lt; internet kz.mfa.lt; Ambassador ROMUALDAS KOZYROVIČIUS.

Malaysia: 050051 Almaty, Rubenshtein kosh. 9A; tel. (727) 333-44-83; fax (727) 387-28-25; e-mail mwalmaty@nursat.kz; Ambassador TEN SEN SAN.

Mongolia: 050000 Almaty, Musabayev kosh. 1; tel. (727) 269-35-70; fax (727) 258-17-27; e-mail info@mongemb.kz; Ambassador RAVDANGIIN KHATANBAATAR.

Netherlands: 010000 Astana, Kosmonavtov kosh. 62/801; tel. (7172) 97-44-81; fax (7172) 97-44-83; e-mail ast@minbuza.nl; Ambassador KLAAS VAN DER TEMPEL.

Oman: 010000 Astana, Chubar sh-a, Novostroitel kosh. 3; tel. (7172) 24-18-61; fax (7172) 24-18-63; Ambassador AHMED BIN NASSER AL-MAHRIZI.

Pakistan: 050004 Almaty, Tulebaev kosh. 25; tel. (727) 273-15-02; fax (727) 273-13-00; e-mail parepalmaty@hotmail.com; Ambassador IRFAN-UR-REHMAN RAJA.

Poland: 050059 Almaty, Zharkent kosh. 9/11–13; tel. (727) 258-16-17; fax (727) 258-15-50; e-mail ambpol@mail.kz; internet www.almaty.polemb.net; Ambassador PAWEŁ CIEPLAK.

Qatar: 010000 Astana, Saraishyk kosh. 20A; tel. (7172) 28-61-23; fax (7172) 28-61-35; Ambassador NASSER BIN RASHID AN-NUAIMI.

Romania: 050010 Almaty, Pushkin kosh. 97; tel. (727) 261-57-72; fax (727) 272-11-30; e-mail amb@rom.ricc.kz; Ambassador EMIL RAPCEA.

Russia: 010000 Astana, Baraev kosh. 4; tel. (7172) 22-17-14; fax (7172) 22-38-49; e-mail rfe@nursat.kz; internet www.rfembassy.kz; Ambassador MIKHAIL N. BOCHARNIKOV.

Saudi Arabia: 050000 Almaty, Gornaya kosh. 97; tel. (727) 250-28-71; fax (727) 250-28-11; e-mail kzemb@mofa.gov.sa; Ambassador HISHAM BIN ABDEL-WAHAB ZARAA.

Slovakia: 010000 Astana, Karaotkel sh-a 2, 5; tel. (7172) 24-11-91; fax (7172) 24-20-48; e-mail zuastana@post.sk; internet www.mzv.sk/astana; Ambassador Dr DUŠAN PODHORSKÝ.

South Africa: 010000 Astana, Kabanbai batyr d-ly 6/1; tel. (7172) 92-53-27; fax (7172) 92-53-26; e-mail almaty@foreign.gov.za; Ambassador BEKIZIZVE WISDOM GILA.

Spain: 010000 Astana, Kenesary kosh. 47/25; tel. (7172) 21-69-84; fax (7172) 20-03-17; e-mail emb.astana@maec.es; Ambassador ALBERTO ANTÓN CORTÉS.

Switzerland: 100000 Astana, Sary-Arka 6; tel. (7172) 66-03-40; fax (7172) 66-03-42; e-mail vertretung@alm.rep.admin.ch; Ambassador STEFAN NELLEN.

Tajikistan: 010000 Astana, Chubar sh-a, Marsovaya kosh. 15; tel. and fax (7172) 24-09-29; e-mail emb_tj@ok.kz; Ambassador BAHROM M. HOLNAZAROV.

Turkey: 010000 Astana, Kabanbai batyr d-ly 6/1/23/101; tel. (7172) 92-58-70; fax (7172) 92-58-74; e-mail astanaturkbe@gmail.com; Ambassador ATILLA GÜNAY.

Turkmenistan: 010000 Astana, Otyrar kosh. 64; tel. and fax (7172) 21-08-82; e-mail tm_emb@at.kz; Ambassador KURBANMUKHAMMED G. KASYMOV.

Ukraine: 010000 Astana, Kenesary kosh. 41; tel. (7172) 32-60-42; fax (7172) 32-68-11; e-mail embassy_ua@kepter.kz; internet www.mfa.gov.ua/kazakhstan; Ambassador MYKOLA F. SELIVON.

United Arab Emirates: 010000 Astana, Diplomatiyalyk kalashyk C-15; tel. (7172) 24-36-75; fax (7172) 24-36-76; e-mail emaratembassy_kz@yahoo.com; Ambassador IBRAHIM HASSAN SAIF.

United Kingdom: 010000 Astana, Shubar sh-a, Kosmonavtov kosh. 62; tel. (7172) 55-62-00; fax (7172) 55-62-11; e-mail britishembassy@mail.online.kz; internet www.ukinkz.fco.gov.uk; Ambassador PAUL BRUMMELL.

USA: 010010 Astana, Ak Bulak 4/23-22/3; tel. (7172) 70-21-00; fax (7172) 34-08-90; e-mail info@usembassy.kz; internet kazakhstan.usembassy.gov; Ambassador RICHARD E. HOAGLAND.

Uzbekistan: 050010 Almaty, Beribaev kosh. 36; tel. (727) 291-02-35; fax (727) 291-10-55; e-mail emb-uzbekistan@mail.ru; Ambassador FARRUH TURSUNOV.

Viet Nam: 100000 Astana, Saryarka kosh. 6; tel. (7172) 66-03-67; fax (7172) 66-03-79; Chargé d'affaires VU THE HIEP.

Judicial System

Supreme Court of the Republic of Kazakhstan (Kazakhstan Respublikasynyn Zhogargy Soty): 010000 Astana, Solzhagau, Tauelsizdik kosh. 39; tel. (7172) 74-75-00; fax (7172) 74-78-13; e-mail ms@supcourt.kz; internet www.supcourt.kz; Chair. MUSABEK T. ALIMBEKOV.

Constitutional Council of the Republic of Kazakhstan (Kazakstan Respublikasy Konstitutsiyalyk Keneci): 010000 Astana, Solzhagau, Tauelsizdik kosh. 39; tel. (7172) 74-79-56; fax (7172) 74-76-51; e-mail liaison@constcouncil.kz; internet www.constcouncil.kz; f. 1995; seven mems; Chair. IGOR I. ROGOV.

Prosecutor-General: KAYRAT A. MAMI, 010000 Astana, Seifullin kosh. 37; e-mail gp-rk@mail.online.kz; internet www.procuror.kz.

Religion

The major religion of the Kazakhs is Islam. They are almost exclusively Sunni Muslims of the Hanafi school. The Russian Orthodox Church is the dominant Christian denomination; it is attended mainly by Slavs. There are also Protestant Churches (mainly Baptists), as well as a Roman Catholic (Latin Rite) presence and a Jewish community. In mid-2005 legislation was introduced, which required all religious organizations and communities to register with the state authorities.

ISLAM

The Kazakhs were converted to Islam only in the early 19th century, and for many years elements of animist practices remained. Over the period 1985–90 the number of mosques in Kazakhstan increased from 25 to 60. By 1991 there were an estimated 230 Muslim religious communities functioning in Kazakhstan and an Islamic institute had been opened in Almaty. The Islamic revival intensified following Kazakhstan's independence from the USSR, and during 1991–94 some 4,000 mosques were reported to have been opened.

Religious Administration of Muslims of Kazakhstan (Kazakstan musylmandary dini baskarmasy): 050000 Almaty; tel. (727) 230-63-65; fax (727) 297-94-23; e-mail susaev@bk.ru; internet www.muftyat.kz; Chair. Chief Mufti ABSATTAR B. Haji DERBISALI.

CHRISTIANITY

The Roman Catholic Church

The organization of the Roman Catholic Church in Kazakhstan comprises one archdiocese, two dioceses and one apostolic administration. There were an estimated 183,600 adherents at 31 December 2006.

Archbishop of the Archdiocese of the Most Holy Virgin Mary at Astana: Rt Rev. TOMASZ PETA, 010010 Astana, Tashenov kosh.3, POB 622; tel. (7172) 37-29-35; fax (7172) 37-29-27; e-mail catholic_astana@mail.ru; internet www.catholic-kazakhstan.org.

The Russian Orthodox Church (Moscow Patriarchate)

Metropolitanate of Astana and Almaty: 050014 Almaty, mikroraion Dorozhnik 29; tel. (727) 298-94-15; e-mail office@orthodox.kz; internet www.orthodox.kz; f. 2003; three dioceses; Metropolitan MEFODII (NEMTSOV).

JUDAISM

Mitsva Association of Kazakhstan: Almaty; tel. (727) 273-54-49; fax (727) 258-34-59; e-mail contact@mitsva.kz; internet www.mitsva.kz; f. 1992; unites Jewish communities across Kazakhstan; Pres. ALEKSANDR BARON.

Rabbi of Almaty: Rabbi MENACHEM GERSHOVICH.

The Press

PRINCIPAL DAILY NEWSPAPERS

Aikyn/Liter (Travel Warrant): 050000 Almaty, Jubanov 94A; tel. (727) 295-24-52; fax (727) 295-24-53; internet www.aikyn.kz; internet www.liter.kz; f. 2004; five a week; Kazakh and Russian edns; weekly arts and information supplement, *Aikyn apta/ Liter nedelya* (Thursdays); Editor-in-Chief ERLAN X. BEKXOJIN; circ. 39,300 (Kazakh edn, *Aikyn*), 33,600 (Russian edn, *Liter*).

Almaty Herald: 050000 Almaty, ul. Rozybakiev kosh. 37; tel. (727) 241-45-69; fax (727) 241-40-78; e-mail herald@nursat.kz; Editor-in-Chief OLESSYA IVANOVA.

Egemen Kazakhstan (Sovereign Kazakhstan): 050044 Almaty, Gogol kosh. 39; tel. and fax (727) 263-25-46; tel. (7172) 34-16-41; e-mail astegemen@nursat.kz; internet www.egemen.kz; f. 1919; 6 a week; organ of the Govt; in Kazakh; Pres. SAUYTBEK ABDRAXMANOV; Editor-in-Chief ZHANBOLAT AUPBAEV.

Ekspress-K: 050044 Almaty, Abdullinykh kosh. 6; tel. (727) 259-60-00; fax (727) 259-60-39; e-mail daily@express-k.kz; internet www.express-k.kz; f. 1920; 5 a week; in Russian; Editor-in-Chief ADILXAN NUSUPOV; circ. 19,500.

Kazakhstanskaya Pravda (Kazakhstani Truth): 050044 Almaty, Gogol kosh. 39; tel. (727) 263-65-65; fax (727) 250-18-73; e-mail kpam@kaznet.kz; internet www.kazpravda.kz; f. 1920; 5 a week; publ. by the Govt; in Russian; Editor-in-Chief V. MIKHAILOV; circ. 34,115.

Vechernii Almaty (Evening Almaty): 050016 Almaty, Abylai-khana d-ly 2; tel. and fax (727) 279-28-90; e-mail vecherni_almaty@mail.ru; internet www.vechorka.kz; f. 1968; in Russian; Editor-in-Chief ELMIRA R. PASHINA.

Vremya (Time): 050000 Almaty, Raiymbek d-ly 115; tel. (727) 259-71-96; e-mail info@time.kz; internet www.time.kz; f. 1999; in Russian; general; Editor-in-Chief VADIM N. BOREIKO; circ. 250,000 (2004).

OTHER PUBLICATIONS

Akikat (Justice): 050044 Almaty, Gogol kosh. 39; tel. (727) 273-84-03; f. 1921; monthly; social and political.

Ana Tili (Native Language): 050044 Almaty, Dostyk d-ly 7; tel. (727) 233-22-21; fax (727) 233-34-73; f. 1990; weekly; in Kazakh; Editor-in-Chief ZH. BEISENBAY-ULY; circ. 11,073.

Dala Men Qala: 051200 Almaty, Maulenov kosh. 92/3; tel. (727) 267-64-04; e-mail dalamenkala@mail.ru; internet dmk.kz; f. 2003; weekly; politics, society; Editor-in-Chief SAPARBAY PARMANKULOV.

Delovaya Nedelya (Business Week): 050044 Almaty, Zhibek-zholy d-ly 64; tel. (727) 250-62-72; fax (727) 273-91-48; e-mail rikki@asdc.kz; internet www.dn.kz; f. 1992; weekly; business, politics, finance of Kazakhstan and Central Asia; in Russian; Editor-in-Chief S. A. KORZHUMBAEV; circ. 15,000.

Delovoi Kazakhstan (Business Kazakhstan): 050013 Astana, pl. Respubliki 15/553, POB 388; tel. (727) 295-23-01; fax (727) 295-23-02; e-mail dk@intelsoft.kz; internet www.dknews.kz; in Russian; weekly; f. 2006; Chief Editor SERIK KORJUMBAEV; circ. 15,000 (2009).

Druzhnye Rebyata (Friendly Chaps): 050009 Almaty, Abay d-ly 143/508; tel. (727) 242-77-89; e-mail jorken@mail.ru; f. 1933 as *Pioner Kazakhstana* (Kazakhstani Pioneer); present name adopted 1956; weekly; in Russian; for children.

Ekologicheskii Kuryer int (Ecological Courier International): 050000 Almaty, Panfilov kosh. 106A; tel. (727) 261-12-23; fax (727) 261-12-10; e-mail ecocourier@nursat.kz; every two weeks; in Russian; environmental concerns; Editor EDUARD MATSKEVICH; circ. 3,000.

Ekspert Kazakhstan: 05000 Almaty, Furmanov kosh. 122; tel. (727) 295-28-32; fax (727) 295-28-33; e-mail expert@expertkazahstan.kz; internet www.expert.ru/printissues/kazakhstan/; f. 2003; weekly; business and economics; in Russian; Chief Editor ANDREI SKIRKA.

Karavan (Caravan): 050000 Almaty, pl. Respubliki 13; tel. (727) 258-36-13; fax (727) 258-36-12; e-mail kaztag@caravan.kz; internet www.caravan.kz; f. 1991; weekly; in Russian; Editor-in-Chief ADIL IBRAEV; circ. 250,000.

Kazak Adebiety (Kazakh Literature): 050000 Almaty, Ablai-khan kosh. 105; tel. and fax (727) 269-54-62; f. 1934; weekly; organ of the Union of Writers of Kazakhstan; in Kazakh; Editor-in-Chief A. ZHAKSYBAEV; circ. 7,874.

Kazakhstan: 050044 Almaty, Zhibek-zholy d-ly 50; tel. (727) 233-13-56; f. 1992; weekly; analytical publication on the extractive industry intended for an audience of international investors; in Russian and English; Editor-in-Chief N. ORAZBEKOV.

Kazakstan Aielderi (Women of Kazakhstan): 050044 Almaty, Zhibek-zholy d-ly 50; tel. (727) 233-06-23; fax (727) 246-15-53; f. 1925; monthly; culture and housekeeping; in Kazakh; Editor-in-Chief ALTYNSHASH K. JAGANOVA; circ. 15,200.

Kazakstan Mektebi (Kazakhstani School): 050004 Almaty, Ablai-khan d-ly 34; tel. (727) 239-76-65; f. 1925; monthly; publ. by the Ministry of Education and Science; in Kazakh; Editor-in-Chief S. ABISHEVA; circ. 10,000.

Kazakstan Zaman (Kazakh Time): 050002 Almaty, Dostyk d-ly 106G; tel. (727) 265-07-39; e-mail kazakstanzaman@mail.ru; f. 1992; in Kazakh and Turkish; weekly; circ. 15,000; Gen. Dir ERSIN DEMIRCI.

Kazakstannyn zher resurstary/Zemelnye Resursy Kazakhstana (Land Resources of Kazakhstan): 010000 Astana, 35 kosh., 12 kireberis, 5th floor; tel. (7172) 74-24-62; e-mail info@zherim.kz; internet www.auzr.kz/?id=15; every two months; Kazakh and Russian edns; publication of Republican Agency for the Management of Land Resources; Chair of Editorial Bd B. S. OSPANOV.

Kontinent (Continent): 050000 Almaty, POB 271; tel. (727) 250-10-39; fax (727) 250-10-41; e-mail bzchyt@kaznet.kz; f. 1999; every two weeks; policy and society journal; Editor-in-Chief ANDREI KUKUSHKIN; circ. 10,000.

Korye Ilbo (Korean News): 050044 Almaty, Zhibek-zholy d-ly 50; tel. (727) 233-90-10; fax (727) 263-25-46; f. 1923; weekly; in Korean and Russian; Editor-in-Chief YAN WON SIK.

Kredo (Credo): 100029 Karaganda, Oktyabrskaya 25; e-mail credogazeta@topmail.kz; internet www.catholic-kazakhstan.org/Credo/index.htm; f. 1995; monthly; Catholic; in Russian; Chief Editor N. MAMAEV.

Medicina (Medicine): 050004 Almaty, Ablai-khan d-ly 63; tel. (727) 273-48-01; fax (727) 273-16-90; e-mail zdrav_kz@nursat.kz; f. 2000; monthly; in Kazakh; Editor-in-Chief A. SH. SEYSENBAEV; circ. 5,000.

KAZAKHSTAN

Megapolis (Megalopolis): 050060 Almaty, P. Tazhibaevoy kosh. 155; tel. and fax (727) 315-09-87; e-mail info@megapolis.kz; internet www.megapolis.kz; f. 2000; general; weekly; Gen. Dir RINAT ASKAROV; Chief Editor IGOR SHAXNOVICH.

Mir Yevrasii (The World of Eurasia): 050009 Almaty, Abay d-ly 153, 4th floor, office 15; tel. (727) 269-58-18; fax (727) 269-59-10; e-mail epolet@list.ru; internet www.worldeurasia.info; f. 2004; in Russian; monthly; politics, international relations; Editor EDUARD POLETAEV.

Novoye Pokoleniye (New Generation): 050091 Almaty, Bogenbai batyr kosh. 156A/505; tel. (727) 334-09-11; fax (727) 250-95-46; e-mail np@np.kz; internet www.np.kz; f. 1998; weekly; economic and political affairs of Kazakhstan and the CIS, with supplement on the arts; in Russian; Editor-in-Chief SERGEI APARIN; circ. 40,000.

Panorama: 050013 Almaty, pl. Respubliki 15/647; tel. (727) 772-87-66; fax (727) 767-25-27; e-mail panorama@intelsoft.kz; internet www.panorama.kz; f. 1992; weekly; analytical coverage of politics, economics, business and international relations; in Russian; Dir ALEKSANDR NESUKANNYI; Editor-in-Chief LERA TSOY; circ. 20,000.

Parasat (Nobility): 050000 Almaty, Aiteke bi 28; tel. (727) 293-94-71; fax (727) 293-94-74; f. 1958; monthly; socio-political, literary, illustrated; in Kazakh; Editor-in-Chief BAKKOZHA S. MUKAY; circ. 20,000.

Petroleum of Kazakhstan: 050091 Almaty, Nauryzbai-batyr kosh. 58; tel. (727) 258-28-33; fax (727) 250-50-82; e-mail office@petroleumjournal.kz; internet www.petroleumjournal.kz; every two months; in Russian and English; Editor-in-Chief OLEG C. CHERVINSKY; circ. 2,000.

Pro Sport Kazakhstan: 050008 Almaty, Abay d-ly 54/1; tel. and fax (727) 250-90-30; two a week; in Russian; sport.

Rukh-Miras (Heritage Movement): 050013 Almaty, Abay d-ly 14; tel. (727) 267-28-83; e-mail ieshua@front.ru; internet www.nlrk.kz; f. 2004; quarterly; literature, fine arts; in Kazakh and Russian; Chair of Bd of Editors MURAT AUEZOV; Chief Editor TALASBEK ASEMKULOV.

Respublika—Delovoye obozreniye (The Republic—Business Review): 050010 Almaty, Satpaev kosh. 2/17; tel. and fax (727) 53-46-71; e-mail assandy@fromru.com; internet www.respublika.kz; weekly; in Russian; Editor-in-Chief IRINA PETRUSHOVA.

Russkii Yazyk i Literatura v Kazakhskoye Shkole (Russian Language and Literature in the Kazakh School): 050091 Almaty, Abylai-khan kosh. 34; tel. (727) 239-76-68; f. 1962; every two months; in Russian; Editor-in-Chief B. S. MUKANOV.

Strana i Mir (The Country and The World): 050012 Almaty, Maulenov kosh. 92; tel. (727) 267-64-04; e-mail stranaimir@mail.ru; internet sim.kz; politics; weekly; in Russian; f. 2003; Dir-Gen. A. IBRAEV.

Turkestan: 050009 Almaty, Abay kosh. 143; tel. (727) 243-32-42; fax (727) 243-58-11; e-mail turkestan_gazeta@mail.ru; f. 1994; weekly; political; in Kazakh; Editor SH. A. PATTEYEV; circ. 10,000.

Uigur Avazi (Uigur Voice): 050044 Almaty, Zhibek-zholy d-ly 50; tel. (727) 233-84-59; f. 1957; 2 a week; publ. by the Govt; socio-political; in Uigur; Editor-in-Chief I. AZAMATOV; circ. 9,000.

Ulan (Man Alive!): 050044 Almaty, Zhibek-zholy d-ly 50; tel. (727) 233-80-03; f. 1930; weekly; in Kazakh; for children and teenagers; Editor-in-Chief S. KALIYEV; circ. 183,014.

Zerde (Intellect): 050044 Almaty, Zhibek-zholy d-ly 50; tel. (727) 233-83-81; f. 1960; monthly; popular, scientific, technical; in Kazakh; Editor-in-Chief E. RAUSHAN-ULY; circ. 68,600.

Zhas Alash (Young Generation): 050002 Almaty, M. Makatayev kosh. 22; tel. (727) 230-60-90; fax (727) 230-41-22; e-mail redaktor@zhasalash.kz; internet www.zhasalash.kz; f. 1921; publ. by the Kazakhstan Youth Union; two a week; in Kazakh; Editor-in-Chief RYSBEK SARSENBAY.

NEWS AGENCY

National Information Agency 'Kazinform': 010000 Astana, Beibitshilik kosh. 10; tel. and fax (7172) 32-75-67; e-mail product@inform.kz; internet www.inform.kz; f. 1997; 100% state-owned open jt-stock co; provides information on govt activities in Kazakhstan and abroad; Pres. ZHANAI S. OMAROV.

Publishers

Gylym (Science): 050010 Almaty, Pushkin kosh. 111–113; tel. (727) 291-18-77; fax (727) 261-88-45; f. 1946; books on natural sciences, humanities and scientific research journals; Dir S. G. BAIMENOV.

Kainar (Spring): 050009 Almaty, Abay d-ly 143; tel. (727) 242-27-96; e-mail kainar_baspasy@mail.ru; f. 1962; agriculture, history, culture, religion; Dir ORAZBEK S. SARSENBAEV.

Kazakhskaya Entsiklopediya (Kazakh Encyclopedia): 050000 Almaty; tel. (727) 262-55-66; f. 1968; Editor-in-Chief R. N. NURGALIYEV.

Directory

Kazakhstan Publishing House: 050000 Almaty, Abay d-ly 143; tel. and fax (727) 242-29-29; f. 1920; political science, economics, medicine, general and social sciences; Dir E. KH. SYZDYKOV; Editors-in-Chief M. D. SITKO, M. A. RASHEV.

Mektep: 050009 Almaty, Abay d-ly 143; tel. (727) 242-26-24; fax (727) 277-85-44; e-mail mektep@mail.ru; internet www.mektep.kz; f. 1947; mainly literature for educational institutions; dictionaries, phrase books, children's textbooks, teaching materials, reference books; publishes books in Kazakh, Russian, Uigur and Uzbek; Gen. Dir E. SATYBALDIEV.

Oner (Art): 050000 Almaty, Abay d-ly 143; tel. (727) 242-08-88; f. 1980; Dir S. S. ORAZALINOV; Editor-in-Chief A. A. ASKAROV.

Zhazushy (Writer): 050000 Almaty, Abay d-ly 143; tel. (727) 242-28-49; f. 1934; literature, literary criticism, essays and poetry; Dir D. I. ISABEKOV; Editor-in-Chief A. T. SARAEV.

Broadcasting and Communications

GOVERNMENT AGENCY

Republican Agency for Information and Communications: 010000 Astana, Ministry Bldg, Solzhagau, Ishim; tel. (7172) 74-01-35; fax (7172) 74-10-03; e-mail press@aic.gov.kz; internet www.aic.gov.kz; Chair. KUANYSHBEK B. YESEKEYEV.

TELECOMMUNICATIONS

Altel: 050000 Almaty, Jurgenev kosh. 9; tel. (727) 230-16-30; fax (727) 230-01-43; e-mail info@altel.kz; internet www.altel.kz; f. 1994; provides mobile cellular communications in Kazakhstan (as Dalacom and PAThWORD).

GSM Kazakhstan (Kcell): 050013 Almaty, Timiriyazev kosh. 2G; tel. (727) 258-11-48; fax (727) 258-89-11; e-mail info@kcell.kz; internet www.kcell.kz; f. 1998; 51% owned by TeliaSonera (Sweden), 49% by Kazakhtelecom; provides mobile cellular telecommunications services (as Kcell and Activ) in 1,449 settlements across Kazakhstan; 7.5m. subscribers (May 2009); Chief Exec. VEYSEL ARAL.

KaR-tel (K-Mobile): 050000 Almaty, Tole bi 55; tel. (727) 250-60-60; fax (727) 295-23-97; e-mail csales@kartel.kz; internet www.k-mobile.kz; f. 1999; 100% subsidiary of VympelKom-Bilain (Russia); provides mobile cellular telecommunications services (as K-Mobile, Excess and Beeline) in more than 100 settlements and along principal roads across Kazakhstan; Gen. Dir DMITRII KROMSKII; 1.6m. subscribers (mid-2005).

Kazakhtelekom: 050000 Almaty, Abylai-khana d-ly 86; tel. (727) 262-05-41; fax (727) 263-93-95; internet www.itte.kz; f. 1994; national telecommunications corpn; 60% state-owned, 40% owned by Daewoo Corpn (Republic of Korea); Pres. SERIK BURKITBAEV.

KazTransCom: 050012 Almaty, Baitursynov kosh. 46A; tel. (727) 270-13-10; fax (727) 270-13-18; e-mail ktc@kaztranscom.kz; jt-stock co; provides telecommunications services to the petroleum and natural gas sectors; won licence in 2004 to provide long-distance and international telephone calls country-wide, becoming Kazakhstan's second long-distance provider.

BROADCASTING

Private radio and television stations began operating in Kazakhstan in the 1990s. In mid-2001 there were an estimated 124 radio and television stations.

Kazakh State Television and Radio Broadcasting Corpn: 050013 Almaty, Jeltoksan kosh. 175A; tel. (727) 263-37-16; f. 1920; Pres. YERMEK TURSUNOV.

Radio

Kazakh Radio: 050013 Almaty, Jeltoksan kosh. 175A; tel. (727) 263-19-68; fax (727) 265-03-87; e-mail kazradio@astel.kz; internet www.radio.kz; f. 1921; broadcasts in Kazakh, Russian, Uigur, German and other minority languages; Gen. Dir TOREKHAN DANIYAR.

Radio 31: 050060 Almaty, Tajibayevoi kosh. 155; tel. (727) 315-29-31; e-mail radio@31.kz; internet www.31.kz; f. 1994; news and music; Dir SABIT SULEIMENOV.

Television

Khabar News Agency: 050013 Almaty, pl. Respubliki 13; tel. (727) 263-83-69; fax (727) 250-63-45; e-mail naz@khabar.almaty.kz; internet www.khabar.kz; f. 1959; international broadcasts in Kazakh, Uigur, Russian and German; two television channels; Chair. of the Bd of Dirs MAULEN ASHIMBAEV; Dir GULNAR IKSANOVA.

KTK (Kazakh Commercial Television): 050013 Almaty, pl. Respubliki 13; tel. (727) 263-44-28; fax (727) 250-66-25; e-mail ktkao@kzaira.com; f. 1990; independent; Gen. Dir ANDREI SHUKHOV; Pres. SHOKAN LAUULIN.

KAZAKHSTAN

NTK (Association of TV and Radio Broadcasters of Kazakhstan): 050013 Almaty, pl. Respubliki 13, 6th Floor; tel. (727) 270-01-83; fax (727) 270-01-85; e-mail kaztvradio@nursat.kz; f. 2000; privately owned; Pres. AIDAR ZHUMABAEV.

Finance

(cap. = capital; res = reserves; dep. = deposits; m. = million; brs = branches; amounts in tenge, unless otherwise indicated)

BANKING

Central Bank

National Bank of Kazakhstan (NBK): 050040 Almaty, Koktem-3 21; tel. (727) 270-45-91; fax (727) 250-60-90; e-mail hq@nationalbank.kz; internet www.nationalbank.kz; f. 1990; cap. 20,000.0m., res 83,734.6m., dep. 2,325,437.5m. (Dec. 2006); Gov. GRIGORII A. MARCHENKO; 19 brs.

Major Commercial Banks

Alliance Bank: 050000 Almaty, Kunayev kosh. 32; tel. (727) 258-40-40; fax (727) 259-67-87; e-mail info@alb.kz; internet www.alb.kz; f. 1999; cap. 96,380m., res 3,298m., dep. 929,386m. (Dec. 2007); Chair. DAUREN KEREIBAEV.

ATF Bank: 050000 Almaty, Furmanov kosh. 100; tel. (727) 250-30-40; fax (727) 250-19-95; e-mail info@atfbank.kz; internet www.atfbank.kz; f. 1995; present name adopted 2002; cap. 57,897.6m., res 576.0m., dep. 851,514.8m. (Dec. 2007); Chair. TIMUR ISSATAEV; 10 brs.

Bank Centercredit: 050000 Almaty, Panfilov kosh. 98; tel. (727) 259-85-98; fax (727) 258-45-10; e-mail info@centercredit.kz; internet www.centercredit.kz; f. 1988; present name adopted 1996; cap. 36,298m., res 1,448m., dep. 760,334m. (Dec. 2007); Chair. of Bd BAKHYTBEK R. BAYSEITOV; 19 brs.

BTA Bank: 050051 Almaty, Samal 2, Zholdasbekov kosh. 97; tel. (727) 250-40-70; fax (727) 250-02-24; e-mail post@bta.kz; internet www.bta.kz; f. 1997 as Bank TuranAlem; name changed as above 2008; 78% state-owned from Feb. 2009; cap. 303,427m., res −646m., dep. 2,578,698m. (Dec. 2007); Chair. ROMAN SOLODCHENKO; 23 brs.

Caspian Bank (Bank Kaspiiskii): 050012 Almaty, Adi Sharipov kosh. 90; tel. (727) 250-18-00; fax (727) 250-95-96; e-mail office@bankcaspian.kz; internet www.bc.kz; 96% owned by Caspian Group (Netherlands); cap. 17,507.4m., res 2,200.1m., dep. 212,274.6m. (Dec. 2007); Chair. MIKHEIL LOMTADZE; 17 brs.

Development Bank of Kazakhstan: 010000 Astana, pl. Respublika 32; tel. (7172) 58-02-60; fax (7172) 58-02-76; e-mail info@kdb.kz; internet www.kdb.kz; wholly state-owned; cap. 70,572.9m., res 8,424.8m., dep. 95,413.4m. (Dec. 2006); Pres. ZHANAT ZHAKANOV.

Eurasian Bank: 050002 Almaty, Kunayev kosh. 56; tel. (727) 250-86-07; fax (727) 250-86-50; e-mail info@eurasian-bank.kz; internet www.eurasian-bank.kz; f. 1994; cap. 7,999.9m., res 702.3m., dep. 129,932.7m. (Dec. 2007); Chair. ZHOMART YERTAEV; 18 brs.

Eurasian Development Bank: 050000 Almaty, Panfilov kosh. 98; tel. (727) 244-40-44; fax (727) 244-65-70; e-mail info@eabr.org; internet www.eabr.org; f. 2006; cap. US $804.8m., res $4.9m., dep. $454.7m. (Dec. 2007); Chair. IGOR FINOGENOV.

Halyk Bank: 050046 Almaty, Rozybakieva kosh. 97; tel. (727) 259-00-00; fax (727) 259-02-71; e-mail halykbank@halykbank.kz; internet www.halykbank.kz; f. 1936 as br. of Savings Bank of USSR; fully privatized in Nov. 2001; cap. 65,531m., res 94,139m., dep. 1,410,618m. (Dec. 2007); Chair of Bd of Dirs ALEKSANDR S. PAVLOV; Chair. of Managing Bd UMUT B. SHAYAKHMETOVA; 611 brs.

Kazkommertsbank (KKB): 050060 Almaty, Gagarin kosh. 135; tel. (727) 258-53-01; fax (727) 258-51-61; e-mail mailbox@kkb.kz; internet www.kkb.kz; f. 1991; cap. 6,998m., res 299,669m., dep. 2,365,932m. (Dec. 2007); Chair. NURZHAN S. SUBKHANBERDIN; Man. Dir ANDREI I. TIMCHENKO; 23 brs.

Nurbank: 050010 Almaty, Dostyk d-ly 38; tel. (727) 259-97-10; fax (727) 250-16-09; e-mail bank@nurbank.kz; internet www.nurbank.kz; f. 1992; cap. 25,036.2m., res 272.4m., dep. 159,432.9m. (Dec. 2007); Chair. NURMUKHAMED BEKTEMISSOV; 56 brs.

Temirbank: 050008 Almaty, Abay d-ly 68/74; tel. (727) 257-88-88; fax (727) 250-62-41; e-mail board@temirbank.kz; internet www.temirbank.kz; f. 1992; cap. 34,568.5m., res −107.1m., dep. 284,714.4m. (Dec. 2007); Chair. MURAT YULDASHEV; 15 brs.

Tsesnabank: 010000 Astana, Zhengis d-ly 29; tel. (7172) 77-07-70; fax (7172) 77-01-95; e-mail info@tsb.kz; internet www.tsb.kz; f. 1992; cap. 13,500.0m., res 1,738.5m., dep. 123.355.8m. (Dec. 2007); Chair. YERKEGALI YEDENBAEV; 9 brs.

Bankers' Organization

Bank Association of Kazakhstan: 010000 Almaty, Panfilov kosh. 98; tel. (727) 273-16-89; fax (727) 273-90-85; Pres. BAKHYTBEK BAISEITOV.

STOCK EXCHANGE

Kazakhstan Stock Exchange (KASE): 050000 Almaty, Dostyk 291/3a; tel. (727) 272-98-98; fax (727) 272-09-25; e-mail info@kase.kz; internet www.kase.kz; f. 1993; Pres. and Chief Exec. AZAMAT M. JOLDASBEKOV.

INSURANCE

Almaty International Insurance Group: 050000 Almaty, Kabanbai-batyr kosh. 112; tel. and fax (727) 250-12-31; internet www.aiig.escort.kz; f. 1994; Chair. SUREN AMBARTSUMIAN.

Centras Insurance: 050008 Almaty, Manas kosh. 32A; tel. (727) 259-77-55; fax (727) 259-77-66; e-mail insurance@centras.kz; internet www.cic.kz; f. 1997; non-life insurance and reinsurance; Chair. TALGAT USENOV.

Dynasty Life Insurance Co: 050000 Almaty, Seifullin kosh. 410; tel. (727) 250-73-95; e-mail dynasty@bta.nursat.kz; Chair. SERIK TEMIRGALEYEV.

Industrial Insurance Group (IIG): 050046 Almaty, Nauryzbai-batyr kosh. 65–69; tel. (727) 250-96-95; fax (727) 250-96-98; e-mail iig@kaznet.kz; f. 1998; Pres. IVAN MIKHAILOV.

KazAgroPolits Insurance Co: 050000 Almaty, Nauryzbai-batyr kosh. 49–61; tel. (727) 232-13-24; fax (727) 232-13-26; e-mail kazagropolise@mail.banknet.kz; Chair. YERMEK USPANOV.

Kazakhinstrakh (Kazakh International Insurance Co): 050044 Almaty, Zhibek-zholy d-ly 69; tel. (727) 233-73-49; fax (727) 250-74-37; e-mail kiscentr@nursat.kz; Chair. NURLAN MOLDAXMETOV.

Kazkommerts-Polits Insurance Co: 050013 Almaty, Satpaev kosh. 24; tel. (727) 258-48-08; fax (727) 292-73-97; e-mail info@kkp.kz; internet www.kkp.kz; f. 1996; non-life; Chair. MEIRAM B. SERGAZIN; Dir TALGAT K. USSENOV.

MSCA (Medical Systems of Central Asia) Interteach: 050000 Almaty, Kabanbai-batyr kosh. 122A; tel. and fax (727) 258-23-32; e-mail interteach@kaznet.kz; f. 1989; medical and travel insurance, health care, accident and employee liability insurance; 290 employees; 48 brs; Gen. Dir ERNST M. KURLEUTOV.

Trade and Industry

GOVERNMENT AGENCY

Republican Agency for the Regulation of Natural Monopolies: 010000 Astana, Bukei-khan kosh. 14; tel. (7172) 59-16-77; fax (7172) 21-54-73; e-mail info@arem.kz; internet www.regulator.kz; Chair. NURLAN SH. ALDABERGENOV.

CHAMBERS OF COMMERCE

Union of Chambers of Commerce and Industry of Kazakhstan: 050000 Almaty, Masanchi kosh. 26; tel. (727) 292-00-52; fax (727) 250-70-29; e-mail tpprkaz@online.ru; internet www.ccikaz.kz; f. 1959; Chair. ABLAI MYRZAXMETOV.

Almaty City Chamber of Commerce and Industry: 050000 Almaty, Tole bi 45; tel. (727) 262-03-01; e-mail alcci@nursat.kz; internet www.atpp.marketcenter.ru; Chair. ZULFIYA K. AKHMETZHANOVA.

Astana City Chamber of Commerce and Industry: 010000 Astana, Auezov kosh. 66, POB 1966; tel. (7172) 32-38-33; e-mail akmcci@dan.kz; internet www.chamber.kz; Chair. TATYANA I. KONONOVA.

Jambul Oblast Chamber of Commerce and Industry: 080012 Jambul obl., Taraz, Karakhana 2; tel. (7262) 43-05-98; Chair. ADILKHAN ZHAPARBEKOV.

Karaganda Oblast Chamber of Commerce and Industry: 100000 Karaganda, bulv. Mira 31; tel. (7212) 30-06-84; fax (7212) 30-05-05; e-mail karcci@mail.ru; internet www.karcci.kz; f. 1959; Chair. of Presidium NESSIP SEITOVA.

Southern Kazakhstan Oblast Chamber of Commerce and Industry: 160000 Southern Kazakhstan obl., Chimkent, Taukekhan kosh. 31; tel. (7252) 21-14-05; Chair. SYRLYBAJ ORDABEKOV.

EMPLOYERS' ORGANIZATIONS

Confederation of Employers of the Republic of Kazakhstan (KRRK): 050022 Almaty, Abay d-ly 42/44; tel. (727) 293-07-42; fax (727) 292-27-68; e-mail krrk@krrk.kz; internet www.krrk.kz; Pres. KADYR BAYIKENOV.

KAZAKHSTAN

Kazakhstan Petroleum Association: 050010 Almaty, Dostyk d-ly 43/517; tel. (727) 250-18-16; fax (727) 250-18-17; e-mail kpa@arna.kz; internet www.kpa.kz; f. 1998; Chair. NURZHAN KAMALOV; 59 mem. cos.

UTILITIES
Electricity

KEGOS—Kazakhstan Electricity Grid Operating Co (Elektr zhelilerin baskaru zhanindegi Kazakstan kompaniyasy): 050000 Almaty, Kozybayev kosh. 23; tel. (727) 271-93-59; internet www.kegoc.kz; f. 1997; technical electricity network operator; Pres. ALMASADAM M. SATKALIYEV.

Water

Almaty Vodocanal: 050057 Almaty, Zharokov kosh. 196; tel. (727) 274-84-02; fax (727) 274-98-41; e-mail vk.prm@itte.kz; internet www.almaty-vodokanal.kz; f. 1936; state-owned; responsible for water supply and sewerage in Almaty and surrounding villages; Gen. Dir VLADISLAV GALIYEV.

STATE HYDROCARBONS COMPANIES

KazMunaiGaz: 010000 Astana, Kabanbai-batyr kosh. 22; tel. (7172) 97-60-00; fax (7172) 97-60-01; e-mail info@kmg.kz; internet www.kmg.kz; f. 2002 by merger of KazakhOil and Transneftegas; national jt-stock co; subsidiaries include petroleum-transportation co KazTransOil, and gas-transportation co KazTransGas; Pres. KAIRGELDY KABYLDIN.

Munaigaz: 010000 Astana, Jeltoksan kosh. 7/1; tel. and fax (7172) 39-03-11; e-mail info@munaygas.com; internet www.munaygas.com; f. 2004; petroleum and gas prospecting and producing; Pres. YE. V. BELYAEV.

TRADE UNIONS

Confederation of Free Trade Unions of Kazakhstan: f. 1991; fmrly Independent Trade Union Centre of Kazakhstan; 9 regional brs with 2,200 mems; Chair. SERGEI BELKIN.

Confederation of Free Trade Unions of Coal and Mining Industries: 050000 Almaty; Chair. V. GAIPOV.

Federation of Trade Unions of Kazakhstan: 010000 Astana, pr. Abay 38; tel. (7172) 216-68-14; fax (7172) 21-68-35; e-mail fprkastana@fprk.kz; internet www.fprk.kz; 26 affiliated unions with 2,047,185 mems (2009); Chair. SIYAZBEK MUKASHEV.

Transport
RAILWAYS

In 2003 the total length of rail track in use was 13,601 km (3,661 km of which were electrified). The rail network is most concentrated in the north of the country, where it joins the rail lines of Russia. There are also connections with Kyrgyzstan, Uzbekistan and the People's Republic of China.

In 2009 the construction of underground railways was underway in both Almaty and Astana.

Kazakstan Temir Zholy (Kazakhstan Railways): 010011 Astana, Zhengis d-ly 98; tel. (7172) 93-44-00; fax (7172) 32-82-30; e-mail temirzhol@railways.kz; internet www.railways.kz; f. 1991; Pres. YERLAN D. ATAMKULOV.

ROADS

In 2004 Kazakhstan's total road network was 90,018 km, including 23,055 km of main roads.

INLAND WATERWAYS

Kazakhstan has an inland waterway network extending over some 4,000 km. The main navigable river is the Irtysh. The Kazakhstan River Fleet Industrial Association, comprising 11 water companies, administers river traffic.

Department of Water Transport (Ministry of Transport and Communications): 010000 Astana, Abay d-ly 49; tel. (7172) 32-03-58; fax (7172) 32-10-58; Dir JENYS M. KASYMBEK.

SHIPPING

A ferry port was inaugurated on the Caspian Sea at Aktau in 2001, with services operating to Azerbaijan, Iran and Russia. At 31 December 2007 Kazakhstan's merchant fleet comprised 63 vessels, with a combined displacement of 54,291 grt.

Aktau International Commercial Sea Port: 130000 Mangystau obl., Aktauskii akimat, Ömırzaq; tel. (7292) 51-45-49; fax (7292) 44-51-01; e-mail aktauport@aktauport.kz; internet www.portaktau.kz; f. 1963; Dir TALGAT B. ABYLGAZIN; 609 employees.

CIVIL AVIATION

There are 18 domestic airports and four airports with international services (at Aktau, Almaty, Astana and Atyrau). A new passenger terminal opened at Astana International Airport in 2005.

Department of Aviation (Ministry of Transport and Communications): 010000 Astana, Abay d-ly 49; tel. (7172) 32-63-16; fax (7172) 32-16-96; Dir S. BURANBAEV.

Air Astana: 050000 Almaty, Biznes Tsentr Samal Tauers, Joldasbekov kosh. 97; tel. (7172) 58-41-35; fax (7172) 59-87-01; e-mail hr@air-astana.kz; internet www.air-astana.kz; f. 2001 jointly by the Government (51%) and BAE Systems (United Kingdom—49%); domestic and international flights; Pres. PETER FOSTER.

Tourism

Tourism is not widely developed in Kazakhstan. In 2006 there were 4.7m. tourist arrivals in Kazakhstan. In 2005 receipts from tourism (including passenger transport) amounted to US $809m.

Kazakhstan Tourist Association (KTA): 050022 Almaty, Abay d-ly 42/44/302; tel. (727) 292-53-31; fax (727) 292-48-53; e-mail kta@mail.kz; f. 1999.

KENYA

Introductory Survey

Location, Climate, Language, Religion, Flag, Capital

The Republic of Kenya lies astride the equator on the east coast of Africa, with Somalia to the north-east, Ethiopia and Sudan to the north, Uganda to the west and Tanzania to the south. The climate varies with altitude: the coastal region is hot and humid, with temperatures averaging between 20°C and 32°C (69°F–90°F), while inland, at more than 1,500 m (5,000 ft) above sea-level, temperatures average 7°C–27°C (45°F–80°F). The highlands and western areas receive ample rainfall (an annual average of 1,000 mm–1,250 mm) but most of northern Kenya is very dry (about 250 mm). Kiswahili is the official language, while English is widely spoken and 22% and 13% of the population, respectively, speak Kikuyu and Luo as their mother tongue. Most of the country's inhabitants follow traditional beliefs. There is a sizeable Christian community, while Muslims form a smaller proportion of the population. The national flag (proportions 2 by 3) has three broad horizontal stripes, of black, red and green, separated by two narrow white stripes. Superimposed in the centre is a red shield, with black and white markings, upon crossed white spears. The capital is Nairobi.

Recent History

Kenya was formerly a British colony (inland) and protectorate (along the coast). The first significant African nationalist organization was the Kenya African Union (KAU), founded in 1944, which was supported mainly by the Kikuyu, the largest ethnic group in Kenya. In 1947 Jomo Kenyatta, a Kikuyu, became President of the KAU. Following general elections in May 1963, Kenya was granted internal self-government in June. The country became independent, within the Commonwealth, on 12 December 1963, and a republic exactly one year later. Kenyatta, then leader of the Kenya African National Union (KANU), was appointed Prime Minister in June 1963 and became the country's first President in December 1964. (He was subsequently re-elected to the presidency, unopposed, in 1969 and 1974.)

Kenyatta died in August 1978; the Vice-President, Daniel arap Moi, was proclaimed President in October, and was the sole candidate at a presidential election held (concurrently with a KANU-only general election) in November 1979. In June 1982 the National Assembly officially declared Kenya a one-party state. At a presidential election in September 1983 Moi was returned unopposed. In August 1986 KANU approved an open 'queue-voting' system to replace the secret ballot in the preliminary stage of a general election. In June 1987 it was announced that only members of the ruling party were to be entitled to vote during the preliminary stages of a general election.

In February 1988 Moi was nominated unopposed to serve a third term as President. In the same month preliminary elections under the 'queue-voting' system produced a KANU-approved list to contest 123 of the 188 elective seats in the National Assembly at a general election held in March (54 candidates received more than 70% of votes cast at the preliminary stage, and were thus deemed to have been elected, while 11 were elected unopposed).

In December 1990 KANU abolished the system of 'queue-voting' and resolved to cease expelling party members, readmitting 31 expelled members in the following month. In August six opposition leaders, including Oginga Odinga (Kenya's Vice-President in 1964–66), formed a new political movement, the Forum for the Restoration of Democracy (FORD); the Government outlawed the grouping, but it continued to operate.

In November 1991 several members of FORD were arrested prior to a planned pro-democracy rally in Nairobi, which was suppressed by the security forces. The Kenyan authorities were condemned internationally and bilateral and multilateral creditors suspended aid to Kenya indefinitely, pending the acceleration of both economic and political reforms. In December a special conference of KANU delegates acceded to the pressure for reform, resolving to introduce a multi-party political system. The National Assembly subsequently endorsed appropriate amendments to the Constitution. Former Vice-President Mwai Kibaki resigned as Minister of Health later in the month, in protest against alleged electoral malpractice by KANU, and founded the Democratic Party (DP).

During the first half of 1992 some 2,000 people were reportedly killed in tribal clashes in western Kenya. In March the Government banned all political rallies, and restrictions were placed on the activities of the press. Following a two-day general strike in April, organized by FORD, the Government ended the ban on political rallies. In August FORD split into two opposing factions, which were registered in October as separate political parties, FORD—Asili and FORD—Kenya, respectively led by Kenneth Matiba and Odinga.

At multi-party presidential and legislative elections held in December 1992 Moi was elected for a fourth term of office as President, winning 36.3% of the votes cast, ahead of Matiba (26.0%), Kibaki (19.5%) and Odinga (17.5%). Of the 188 elective seats in the National Assembly, KANU won 100 (including 16 uncontested); FORD—Asili and FORD—Kenya secured 31 seats each, and the DP took 23. Votes were cast predominantly in accordance with ethnic affiliations, with the two largest tribes, the Kikuyu and Luo, overwhelmingly rejecting KANU. An extensive reshuffle of cabinet posts was subsequently effected. In 1993 the international donor community agreed to resume the provision of aid to Kenya, in response to what it recognized as the Government's progress in implementing political and economic reforms.

In May 1995 leading opposition activists formed a new political organization, Safina. Dr Richard Leakey, a prominent white Kenyan and former Director of the Kenya Wildlife Service, was appointed as Safina's Secretary-General. The party aimed to combat corruption and human rights abuses by the Kenyan authorities and to campaign for the introduction of an electoral system of proportional representation.

During the mid-1990s Kenya's human rights record came under intense domestic and international scrutiny. In April 1995 the country's Roman Catholic bishops accused the Government of eroding judicial independence and of condoning police brutality and endemic corruption. In December the human rights organization Amnesty International alleged that the security forces were systematically torturing criminal suspects and opposition activists. In response to its critics, the Moi administration provisionally withdrew controversial draft legislation in January 1996 that would have severely restricted the freedom of the press and, in July, inaugurated a human rights committee to investigate alleged humanitarian abuses.

Divisions within opposition parties continued to undermine efforts to present a cohesive challenge to Moi and KANU prior to the 1997 elections. A renewed attempt to establish a coalition of opposition organizations, initiated in November 1995, was short-lived. Meanwhile, following an unsuccessful attempt to assume the leadership of FORD—Kenya, Raila Odinga (the son of Oginga Odinga, who died in January 1994, and a prominent opposition activist) left that party and subsequently became leader of the National Development Party (NDP). In October 1997 Matiba's faction of FORD—Asili registered as an independent party, the Forum for the Restoration of Democracy for the People (FORD—People). During the mid-1990s several opposition deputies, disaffected by these internal rivalries, defected to KANU. Within KANU itself rivalries also began to emerge, not least because the Constitution permitted Moi to stand for only one further term as President.

During the first half of 1997 Moi repeatedly refused to accede to opposition demands for a review of the Constitution prior to the forthcoming elections. Opposition organizations protested that constitutional reforms and a reorganization of the supervisory Electoral Commission were essential in order to eliminate an in-built electoral advantage for the Moi administration. In April the National Convention Executive Council (NCEC) was established as a forum embracing representatives of non-governmental organizations, religious groups and opposition parties (excluding, however, supporters of Matiba and Odinga). In mid-July Moi agreed to meet with opposition and religious leaders to discuss constitutional reform. It was subsequently announced that the opposition would henceforth be permitted to organize registered public meetings, and that a constitutional review commission would be established.

In August 1997 the IMF suspended assistance to Kenya, pending the implementation of decisive action to eliminate official corruption and to improve the system of revenue collection; the Government consequently announced the inauguration of an anti-corruption body. The NCEC organized a one-day general strike in early August, in support of its demands for constitutional reform. In late August serious unrest erupted in and around Mombasa. While the Government blamed the NCEC for orchestrating the attacks, the NCEC alleged that the Government was inciting inter-ethnic conflict with the aim of depriving opposition supporters from the predominantly Luo region of the opportunity to vote in the forthcoming elections by forcing them to flee their homes. In the following month the National Assembly approved legislation that amended the Constitution with the stated aim of ensuring free and fair democratic elections. All political parties were granted equal access to the media, and detention without trial was prohibited. In addition, the new legislation enabled the opposition to participate in selecting the 12 nominated members of the National Assembly and 10 of the 12 members of the supervisory Electoral Commission.

The presidential and legislative elections, which took place concurrently on 29 December 1997, were undermined by allegations of widespread fraud, as well as by logistical difficulties. Moi was re-elected President, winning 40.6% of the valid votes cast, while Kibaki came second, with 31.5% of the votes cast. KANU secured 107 of the 210 elected seats in the enlarged National Assembly, and the remainder were divided between nine opposition parties, with the DP taking 39 seats, the NDP 21, FORD—Kenya 17 and the Social Democratic Party 15. Safina won five seats. Moi was inaugurated for a fifth (and final) term as President in January 1998. Shortly afterwards Moi appointed a new Cabinet. However, he postponed the designation of a new Vice-President, evidently in order not to give an indication of his preferred successor to the presidency.

In early 1998 inter-ethnic violence erupted once again in the volatile Rift Valley. The Moi administration blamed the conflict on bitterness in the Kikuyu and Luo communities at the outcome of the elections, while the latter alleged persecution both by the security forces and by smaller tribal groups that had voted predominantly for Moi and KANU. In July the authorities organized a judicial inquiry into the causes of the ethnic disturbances of both 1992 and 1998. Tension between the Kikuyu and Kalenjin communities in the Rift valley remained, however, especially over disputed land vacated by the Kikuyu during the clashes.

In early August 1998 a car-bomb exploded at the US embassy in central Nairobi, concurrently with a similar attack on the US mission in Dar es Salaam, Tanzania. Some 254 people were killed in Nairobi, and more than 5,000 suffered injuries. The attacks were believed to have been co-ordinated by international Islamist terrorists, and, in mid-August, the USA retaliated by launching air strikes against targets in Afghanistan and Sudan. Four men were convicted of involvement in the bombings by a court in New York, USA, in May 2001 and were later sentenced to life imprisonment. Other suspects, including Osama bin Laden, the fugitive Saudi-born Islamist activist whom the US authorities held ultimately responsible for the bombings, were still at large.

In July 1999 Moi appointed Dr Leakey as head of the civil service and Secretary to the Cabinet, with responsibility for combating corruption in the public services. In September Moi effected a major reorganization of the Cabinet, merging several ministries and reducing the number of government ministers from 27 to 15.

In July 2000 the civil service commenced the reduction of its work-force as part of a programme of reforms to be effected over three years. Meanwhile, a parliamentary anti-graft committee sought the adoption by the National Assembly of a report in which the alleged perpetrators of corruption were named. (The Government later deleted the addendum containing the list of names, causing widespread outrage.) The committee also proposed legislation on economic crimes that would allow the anti-corruption authority (which had been established in 1997 at the insistence of the IMF) to prosecute alleged perpetrators of corruption without seeking permission from the Attorney-General. As a result of these measures, the IMF announced that it was to resume lending to Kenya. The Government agreed to a number of conditions, including the introduction of a law binding public officials to declare their wealth and liabilities and the enactment of the legislation on economic crimes. However, less than one month after the resumption of aid the High Court temporarily halted the retrenchment of civil servants, pending the final determination of a lawsuit on the issue, and ruled that all civil servants who had already been retrenched should be reinstated. In January 2001 the IMF and the World Bank expressed concern over the set-backs in the reforms, particularly the failure to approve legislation on public service ethics and economic crimes, and suspended aid to Kenya until the situation could be resolved. In August Kenyan deputies again refused to approve anti-corruption legislation, and the IMF suspended aid to Kenya indefinitely. Moi subsequently created a new police body to combat corruption.

In January 2001 Odinga, on behalf of the Luo-dominated NDP, signed a memorandum of understanding with KANU, which allowed Moi to appoint ministers from the NDP. In June Moi reorganized the Cabinet and appointed Odinga as Minister of Energy, thereby creating the first coalition Government in Kenya's history. Moi reshuffled the Cabinet again in November, introducing younger KANU ministers in an apparent attempt to provide suitable candidates for his succession; most notably Uhuru Kenyatta (son of the late President Jomo Kenyatta) and Cyrus Jirongo were appointed as Minister for Local Government and Minister for Rural Development, respectively.

The NDP was dissolved and absorbed into KANU in mid-March 2002, despite opposition from elements within both parties; Moi was elected as party Chairman, while Odinga became Secretary-General. In July some 12 opposition parties, including the DP, FORD—Kenya and the National Party of Kenya, formed an electoral alliance, the National Alliance Party of Kenya (NAK).

In August 2002 Moi publicly announced that he favoured Uhuru Kenyatta as KANU's presidential candidate. However, several senior KANU members, including the Vice-President, Prof. George Saitoti, and Odinga, subsequently announced their intention to seek the party's presidential nomination and formed the Rainbow Alliance (RA) to campaign within KANU for a democratic vote to select its candidate. Moi responded by dismissing the Vice-President. In mid-October, in protest at Moi's attempts to impose his preferred successor, members of the RA resigned from their posts in the Government and from KANU, together with some 30 KANU deputies. The RA subsequently boycotted the KANU conference, at which Kenyatta's presidential candidacy was endorsed. Later in October the RA established a new party, the Liberal Democratic Party (LDP), and joined with the NAK to form the National Rainbow Coalition (NARC), with Kibaki as its presidential candidate. The NARC proposed a vote of no confidence in Moi's Government, stating that the Government was illegally attempting to block the introduction of a new constitution. However, Moi forestalled the tabling of the motion by dissolving the National Assembly on 25 October, thereby ensuring that the elections would be held under the current Constitution.

At the presidential and legislative elections, held concurrently on 27 December 2002, the opposition secured an emphatic victory, with Kibaki winning 62.3% of the votes cast in the presidential election, and the NARC securing 125 of the 210 elected seats in the National Assembly, while Kenyatta received 31.2% of the votes cast for the presidency, and KANU won 64 seats in the legislature. The NARC were allocated a further seven appointed seats, increasing their representation to 132, and KANU a further four seats, bringing their total to 68. The electoral turn-out was 56.1%.

Following his inauguration as President on 30 December 2002, Kibaki promised reforms, including the adoption of a new constitution, under which certain powers would be transferred from the President to the legislature and the full independence of the judiciary guaranteed, the adoption of anti-corruption legislation, the privatization of state-owned companies and the dismissal of corrupt civil servants. In January 2003 Kibaki appointed a new Cabinet; however, divisions within the ruling coalition soon became apparent, as a group of 25 LDP deputies accused Kibaki of breaching a power-sharing agreement signed by the constituent parties of the NARC prior to the elections. In May the Anti-Corruption and Economic Crimes Act, which provided for the establishment of the Kenya Anti-Corruption Commission (KACC), and the Public Service (Code of Conduct and Ethics) Act, requiring elected officials and senior civil servants to declare their wealth, came into effect.

In February 2003 Kibaki appointed a commission of inquiry into the Goldenberg financial scandal, in which public funds had been paid to the company Goldenberg International in 1990–93 as subsidies for non-existent exports of gold and diamonds. Evidence presented at the inquiry indicated that Goldenberg had initially received some Ks. 13,500m. (around US $180m.) under the Government's export compensation scheme. After thousands of transfers, including dubious foreign-exchange transactions, made with the alleged complicity of officials at the central bank, the payments to Goldenberg increased to Ks. 25,000m. ($600m.), equivalent to more than 10% of Kenya's annual GDP, although it was estimated that the total amount misappropriated could reach $4,000m. The scandal had also contributed to an IMF decision to suspend the disbursement to Kenya of loans worth some $500m. in 1997. Public hearings ended in November 2004, and the commission's findings were reported to Kibaki in February 2005. It had initially been expected that prosecutions would follow from the report; however, the Minister of Justice and Constitutional Affairs, Martha Karua, stated that further investigations were necessary before any charges could be brought.

Meanwhile, a constitutional review conference opened in April 2003, but divisions persisted over the proposed post of Prime Minister. The LDP advocated an executive Prime Minister with powers to appoint the Cabinet, while Kibaki and his supporters sought to maintain a strong presidency. The ensuing tensions between the NAK and LDP factions of the NARC threatened to split the ruling coalition. In August the death of Vice-President Wamalwa, who had been regarded as a moderating influence within the Government, led to an intensification of the power struggle. President Kibaki faced demands for a successor both from Wamalwa's Luhya ethnic group and from the Luo, who proposed the appointment of Odinga to the vice-presidency. In late September Kibaki named the Minister of Home Affairs, Arthur Moody Awori (a Luhya), as Vice-President and effected a minor government reshuffle. In March 2004 the constitutional review conference voted to reduce the powers vested in the presidency and to create the new post of executive Prime Minister following the next elections, which were scheduled to be held in December 2007. Under the recommendations adopted by the conference, greater power was to be accorded to the National Assembly. The Government withdrew from the conference in protest; however, the draft constitution was successfully presented to the Attorney-General, after which it was to be considered by the National Assembly. The High Court subsequently ruled that before the document could enter into force it required the approval of a simple majority at a referendum.

The draft constitution, which was approved by the National Assembly in July 2005, confirmed the retention of the executive functions of the President, who would have the power to appoint and dismiss a non-executive Prime Minister. Devolution was to be on two levels (national and provincial), rather than the four levels originally envisaged, while the National Assembly was to remain unicameral.

There followed several months of campaigning punctuated by often violent demonstrations. Seven ministers announced their opposition to the proposed new constitution, including, most notably, Raila Odinga, whose LDP split from the NARC coalition and joined with KANU to form the Orange Democratic Movement (ODM). At the referendum, held on 21 November 2005, the draft constitution was rejected by 58.1% of voters. Some 53% of the electorate participated in the poll. Kibaki conceded defeat but ignored demands from Odinga and the ODM to hold legislative elections. Instead Kibaki moved swiftly to dismiss the entire Cabinet and in early December he unveiled a new administration, from which those ministers who had opposed the draft constitution were removed. Those NARC members who maintained their support for Kibaki subsequently formed a new coalition party, the National Rainbow Coalition—Kenya (NARC—Kenya), as a vehicle for contesting the 2007 elections. The fledgling won three of the five available parliamentary seats at by-elections held in June 2006, justifying claims that it was to be one of the main contenders in the forthcoming elections.

With a new constitution unlikely to be in place before the next general election a special review committee was established in September 2006. The committee submitted a report in November outlining proposals for a series of reforms targeting specific areas that were to be implemented prior to the elections, including reducing the number of members of the Electoral Commission from 22 to nine and the creation of 74 parliamentary seats reserved for women. However, five parties, including the ODM, rejected these proposals and the process collapsed.

In 2004 it became increasingly apparent that corruption remained endemic in Kenya, despite the NARC Government's pledge to take measures to combat it. Four senior civil servants were suspended in May following their involvement in awarding contracts to supply passport printing equipment to a fictitious British company, Anglo Leasing Ltd. In July the British High Commissioner, Sir Edward Clay, claimed that corruption had cost Kenya some Ks. 15,000m. since Kibaki took office and warned that it could lead to a reduction in donor assistance—indeed, later that month the European Union (see p. 255) withheld substantial aid. Clay subsequently produced a dossier of some 20 allegedly dubious contracts involving corruption in four ministries, and in February 2005 reiterated his criticisms, urging Kibaki to remove corrupt ministers in order that investigations could proceed unhindered.

As public resentment increased, the issue of corruption became the subject of further attention in February 2005 when the Permanent Secretary for Governance and Ethics in the Office of the President, John Githongo, resigned citing his inability to continue working for the Government. Kibaki did not appoint a replacement for Githongo, and in November disbanded the Office of Governance and Ethics. Following Githongo's resignation, the USA and Germany announced that they would withhold anti-corruption aid, and the United Kingdom imposed travel restrictions on government ministers and others implicated in corruption. Awori admitted that there was massive corruption at senior levels, and there were demands from within the Government for the resignations of corrupt ministers. Kibaki subsequently reorganized the Cabinet, dismissing several high-ranking civil servants and effectively demoting a key presidential aide, the Minister of State for Provincial Administration and National Security in the Office of the President, Christopher Murungaru, to the Ministry of Transport. Kibaki also ordered the KACC to investigate procurement procedures in the National Security department.

Meanwhile, in February 2005 the Kenya Law Society announced that it was to prosecute senior figures on corruption charges, including Awori, the Attorney-General, Amos Wako, and the Minister of Finance, David Mwiraria. It was also revealed that the four senior civil servants suspended in May 2004 had agreed to act as prosecution witnesses and to testify that they had received instructions from government ministers to pursue the transactions for which they were being prosecuted. However, Wako invoked a provision in the Constitution granting him the power to take over private prosecutions initiated by individuals or institutions and entered a *nolle prosequi* to terminate the case.

In November 2005 Githongo presented Kibaki a dossier detailing his investigations into corruption in Kenya and death threats made against him, as well as accounts of his meetings with allegedly corrupt senior officials. Awori, Mwiraria, Murungaru and Kiraitu Murungi (the Minister of Energy) were implicated by Githongo in the Anglo Leasing scandal. Githongo claimed that, in total, the four intended to defraud the exchequer of US $700m. through false military and security contracts. He further alleged that two ministers had admitted that the money was to be used for party political campaigning. Awori, Mwiraria, Murungaru and Murungi were subsequently summoned to appear before the KACC; they all denied the allegations.

In January 2006 Githongo, who considered that Kibaki had failed to act upon the information supplied, released a copy of his dossier to the British media. (Githongo remained in exile in the United Kingdom.) He also released a recording of a meeting with Murungi in which the latter allegedly attempted to impede Githongo's investigation. Following Githongo's disclosure, a delegation of deputies representing the parliamentary Public Accounts Committee (PAC) travelled to the United Kingdom and interviewed Githongo at the Kenyan High Commission in London. In early February Mwiraria resigned from the Cabinet. Pressure increased on the Government and later that month Kibaki announced the resignations of Murungi and Saitoti, the Minister of Education. (Saitoti had also been implicated in the Goldenberg scandal—see above.) All three denied any wrongdoing. Kibaki reshuffled the Cabinet following the resignations, with Amos Kimunya assuming the finance portfolio, although Awori retained his position as Vice-President despite growing demands for his resignation. The PAC began questioning Awori, Mwiraria, Murungi and Saitoti in late February. In March Saitoti was also questioned by the police about his role in the

Goldenberg affair, but the High Court of Kenya later rejected recommendations that he be charged. In a further cabinet reorganization in November, he was readmitted to the Government as Minister of Education, alongside Murungi, who resumed responsibility for the energy portfolio.

Division among the main parties intending to contest the forthcoming presidential and legislative elections emerged during 2007. In June NARC—Kenya indicated that Kibaki was to be named its presidential candidate, although this was not immediately confirmed. Dissension was also reported among ODM members and in May the party postponed for a fifth time the deadline for the submission of presidential nomination papers; however, Odinga began to emerge as the frontrunner for that party's presidential candidature. In October Minister of Health Charity Kaluki Ngilu was dismissed after she attended a rally at which Odinga launched his election campaign. Primary elections were held in November with Kibaki defecting from the ruling NARC—Kenya and choosing to contest the elections under his newly established Party of National Unity (PNU). Odinga was named the presidential candidate for the ODM. Shortly after the nominations were made an official report suggested that, despite Kibaki's renewed efforts in securing his re-election, the public was against him retaining office for a second term and Odinga held a significant lead in pre-election opinion polls.

At the legislative elections, held on 27 December 2007, the ODM secured 99 of the 210 seats in the National Assembly, the PNU won 43, the ODM—Kenya, which had broken away from the main party in August, 16 and KANU 14. Results in three constituencies were not released. The presidential election was held concurrently and the Electoral Commission of Kenya (ECK) announced that, despite indications prior to the vote that Odinga had garnered greater popular support, Kibaki had narrowly been re-elected to the presidency with 4,584,721 votes; Odinga was reported to have secured 4,352,993 votes. Official figures detailing the total number of votes cast were not immediately made available. Odinga and other opposition candidates vehemently denounced the results, while independent international observers expressed scepticism regarding the credibility of the election, which had taken place amid allegations of widespread procedural violations. The results led to an upsurge in tribal conflict between Kibaki's Kikuyu supporters and Odinga's Luo followers. Nevertheless, on 30 December Kibaki was sworn in for a second term.

By mid-January 2008 some 600 people were reported to have been killed and more than 250,000 displaced, as a result of the unrest. A mediation effort undertaken from 8 January by President John Kufuor of Ghana, in his capacity as Chairperson of the African Union (AU) Assembly, failed to bring about direct talks between Kibaki and Odinga. On that day Kibaki had announced the partial composition of his new Cabinet; despite the ODM having secured the largest number of seats in the legislature, no representatives from that party were included in the new Government. Further proposed AU-sponsored mediation was rejected by the Kenyan Government, and on 16 January the ODM, defying a ban on public demonstrations, commenced nation-wide protests scheduled to last for three days. These were violently dispersed by the security forces, resulting in additional fatalities.

On 29 January 2008 the former UN Secretary-General, Kofi Annan, formally launched a further round of negotiations, but observers believed that it would take time to resolve the deep-rooted ethnic problems that underpinned the political crisis, including the issue of land distribution. Ethnic fighting intensified and two senior ODM officials were killed. As a result Annan suspended discussions temporarily and the ODM appealed for calm. Talks resumed in early February and a proposal was made regarding the establishment of a power-sharing transitional government. Odinga had insisted that the elections be rerun, but signalled his willingness to consider this measure, which would allow for new elections to be conducted within a year. Negotiations continued haltingly throughout February with both parties reluctant to compromise. However, on 28 February Kibaki and Odinga signed an agreement on the division of power and the creation of the posts of Prime Minister and two Deputy Prime Ministers, pending a full constitutional review to be carried out within 12 months. Odinga conceded the presidency to Kibaki and accepted the role of Prime Minister. Despite the agreement, attacks were carried out in early March ahead of the opening of a new parliamentary session during which members were to debate the legislation required to legalize the power-sharing agreement. The National Accord and Reconciliation Act, which provided, *inter alia*, for the creation of the position of Prime Minister and allowed a new coalition government to begin to implement a recovery programme and assist the numerous internally displaced persons (IDPs) across the country in returning to their homes, was ratified by the National Assembly later that month. The total number of IDPs was estimated to have reached 600,000 (and over 1,000 people had been killed); in May the Government commenced 'Operation Rudi Nyumbani' which sought to return home all those IDPs dispersed throughout hundreds of refugee camps, mainly in the Rift Valley. By February 2009, however, there were still hundreds of families living in temporary accommodation, despite the closure of the vast majority of official camps.

Meanwhile, following prolonged negotiations, in mid-April 2008 Kibaki named a new coalition Government, comprising members of the PNU, the ODM and ODM—Kenya, including Uhuru Kenyatta as Deputy Prime Minister and Minister of Trade and Wycliffe Musalia Mudavadi as Deputy Prime Minister and Minister of Local Government; Stephen Kalonzo Musyoka, who had been appointed as Vice-President and Minister of Home Affairs in January, and Moses Wetangula, who assumed responsibility for the foreign affairs portfolio at the same time, retained their positions in the new 40-member Cabinet. It was agreed that a commission of inquiry to investigate the causes and perpetrators of the post-election violence should be established with immediate effect, which would be chaired by Appellate Judge Philip Waki. However, divisions soon emerged within the Cabinet as Odinga and ministers allied to the ODM sought an amnesty for all those arrested in the violence: Saitoti, who had been appointed Minister of State in the Office of the President, and Minister of Justice, National Cohesion and Constitutional Affairs Martha Karua were among the members of the Government who opposed the amnesty, and it was ultimately rejected. Waki's report, published in mid-October, recommended the establishment of a tribunal, to be known as the Special Tribunal for Kenya, to 'seek accountability against persons bearing the greatest responsibility for crimes, particularly crimes against humanity' relating to the 2007 elections. It also recommended that a comprehensive reform of the Kenya Police Service be undertaken, involving a complete audit of the current police management, structures, policies, practices and procedures. Kibaki and Odinga agreed to the establishment of the Special Tribunal in December 2008 and the following month legislation providing for its creation was introduced before the National Assembly.

On 10 June 2008 the Minister of Roads, Kipkalya Kones, and the Assistant Minister of Home Affairs, Lorna Laboso, died when the aircraft they were travelling in crashed into a hill in the Enoosupkia Forest (near the Maasai Mara game reserve) killing all those on board. The Minister of Public Works, Chris Obure assumed the roads portfolio on an acting basis. The following day by-elections were held for five seats in the National Assembly: the killings of two ODM deputies and the failure to announce the results in two Rift Valley constituencies during the unrest which followed the 2007 elections had left four seats vacant; the remaining seat was to be contested as it had previously been occupied by Kenneth Marende, who was elected speaker of the National Assembly. The by-elections were held in a largely peaceful atmosphere, despite fears of further unrest, with the ODM winning three of the seats and the PNU securing two, taking their total representations in the legislature to 102 and 45 seats, respectively.

The issue of corruption remained significant for the Government during 2008. In July Kimunya resigned from his position as Minister of Finance, owing to the commencement of an investigation into claims that he had given false information regarding the sale of a hotel to Libyan investors, although a government inquiry later cleared him of any wrongdoing. Kibabki had insisted that Kimuyu's resignation was temporary—the finance portfolio was assumed in an acting capacity by the Minister of the Environment and Mineral Resources, John Michuki—and in January 2009 Kimunya was named as Minister of Trade in a minor government reorganization. At the same time Kenyatta was appointed as the new Minister of Finance (retaining the deputy premiership), while Franklin Bett assumed the roads portfolio. Meanwhile, in August 2008 the KACC initiated the prosecution of seven deputies (both former and serving), including Minister of Information Samuel Poghisio, for accepting fraudulent allowance payments.

In September 2008 a report was published by the independent commission of inquiry, chaired by Johann Kriegler, a South

African judge and the former Chairperson of that country's Independent Electoral Commission, set up to investigate the disputed elections in December 2007. It concluded that the conduct of the elections made it 'impossible...to establish true or reliable results', and recommended that the ECK should undergo major reforms or be replaced by a new body. In December 2008 the ECK was disbanded and provision was made for its replacement by a new nine-member body, the Interim Independent Electoral Commission.

In February 2009 the UN Special Rapporteur on Extrajudicial, Summary or Arbitrary Executions, Philip Alston, issued a report in which he accused Kenya's security forces of widespread extrajudicial killings, and demanded the removal of Kenya's Police Commissioner, Hussein Ali, and Attorney-General Wako, who he described as the 'embodiment in Kenya of the phenomenon of impunity'. The report concluded that death squads had been formed on the orders of senior police officials to exterminate members of the Mungiki (an illegal religious sect allegedly responsible for a number of murders and involved in extortion), although the Kenyan Government rejected the findings. In early March Oscar Kamau Kingara, the Chief Executive of the Oscar Foundation, a civil rights advocacy group, and another senior member of the organization, John Paul Oulowere, were killed by unidentified gunmen; a government spokesman had recently accused the organization of having links with the Mungiki. Prior to the murders the Oscar Foundation had led demonstrations in the capital, expressing anger at government corruption and accusing the Kenyan police of brutality and widespread extrajudicial killings and arrests, especially of suspected Mungiki members. The deaths of the two activists precipitated further demonstrations in which one student was shot dead, and on 10 March there were violent protests in Nairobi as thousands of people, mainly students and the unemployed, took to the streets. This was regarded by many analysts as evidence of the increasing frustration with the coalition Government, which many Kenyans believed had not met expectations and had failed to implement any significant reforms; notably corruption remained a serious problem. The Government suffered a further reverse later in March when Karua announced her resignation, citing Kibaki's appointment of judges without her knowledge as the main reason for her departure.

Following the seizure of power by the National Resistance Army in Uganda in January 1986, Moi offered full co-operation to the new Ugandan President, Yoweri Museveni. After visits to Kenya by Museveni and President Ali Hassan Mwinyi of Tanzania in June, it was announced that joint commissions were to be formed to enhance co-operation between the three countries. In September, however, Ugandan authorities claimed that Kenya was harbouring anti-Museveni rebels, and stationed troops at the two countries' common border. These claims were denied, and in December, when Ugandan troops allegedly entered Kenya in pursuit of rebels, Ugandan and Kenyan armed forces exchanged fire across the border for several days; at least 15 people were reported to have been killed. Later in December Moi and Museveni agreed to withdraw troops from either side of the border. Moi visited Museveni in August 1990, indicating a renewed *détente* between Kenya and Uganda. In November 1994 Moi, Museveni and Mwinyi met in Arusha, Tanzania, and established a commission for co-operation; in March 1996 the Secretariat of the Permanent Tripartite Commission for East African Co-operation was formally inaugurated, with a view to reviving the East African Community (EAC), which had been dissolved in 1977. A treaty for the re-establishment of the EAC, providing for the promotion of free trade between the member states, the development of the region's infrastructure and economy and the creation of a regional legislative assembly and court, was ratified by the Kenyan, Tanzanian and Ugandan Heads of State in November 1999. The new EAC (see p. 425) was officially inaugurated in Arusha in January 2001. Talks on integrating the economies of the three EAC members followed, and in March 2004 Kibaki, Museveni and President Benjamin Mkapa of Tanzania signed a protocol on the creation of a customs union, eliminating most duties on goods traded within the Community, which took effect from January 2005. In May 2006 Kenya and Uganda agreed to share security information in an attempt to foster closer co-operation between the two countries.

Relations between Kenya and Sudan deteriorated in mid-1988, as the two countries made mutual accusations of aiding rebel factions. In early 1989 Sudan renewed a long-standing dispute with Kenya over the sovereignty of territory on the Kenyan side of the two countries' common border, known as the 'Elemi triangle'. During the late 1990s Kenya hosted a series of peace talks between the Sudanese Government and opposition leaders, under the auspices of the Intergovernmental Authority on Development (IGAD, see p. 321), in an attempt to resolve the conflict in southern Sudan. Further negotiations were held in Nairobi in September 2000 and June 2001, and in July 2002 the Sudanese Government and the opposition Sudan People's Liberation Movement (SPLM) signed an accord in Machakos, Kenya, which provided for the holding of a referendum on self-determination for southern Sudan after a transitional period of six years. In September 2003 Kenya and Sudan agreed to form a joint border committee. Talks aimed at achieving a final peace settlement between the Sudanese Government and the SPLM continued in Kenya throughout 2003 and 2004 (see the chapter on Sudan) and in January 2005 the Sudanese Government and southern rebels signed a peace accord in Nairobi, which officially ended the 21-year civil war.

Somalia has traditionally laid claim to part of north-eastern Kenya. During 1989 tension developed between the Kenyan authorities and ethnic Somalis from both sides of the Kenya–Somalia border, when Somalis were alleged to be largely responsible for wildlife-poaching and banditry in north-eastern Kenya. In September Moi protested strongly to the Somali Government, following an incursion into Kenya by Somali troops (reportedly pursuing Somali rebels), which resulted in the deaths of four Kenyans. In that month the Kenyan Minister of Foreign Affairs and International Co-operation stated that, while the Government supported the peace process in Somalia, it had not, as had been reported, officially declared recognition of the interim Somali President, Abdulkasim Hasan, or his Government. Moi later agreed to mediate between the interim Government and opposing rebel factions in Somalia. In July 2001 Kenya closed the border after numerous clashes were reported on the Somali side, which threatened to spill over into Kenya. However, Moi agreed to reopen the border in November. An IGAD-sponsored Somali reconciliation conference opened in the Kenyan town of Eldoret in October 2002 and was moved to Nairobi in February 2003; the talks continued throughout 2003 and early 2004, despite various disruptions, and in January 2004 representatives from more than 20 factions in attendance reached agreement on the establishment of a new Somali parliament, which was based in Nairobi until mid-2005 (see the chapter on Somalia). In early 2007 Ethiopian forces drove Islamist insurgents from the capital Mogadishu. Subsequently, Kenya closed its border to Somalia, with the aim of preventing an influx of refugees as well as insurgents fleeing from Ethiopian and Somali government forces.

Relations between the Kenyan and Ethiopian Governments became strained in 1997, owing to an increased incidence of cross-border cattle-rustling, including an attack in March during which 16 members of the Kenyan security forces were killed. A number of communiqués were subsequently signed by representatives of the two countries, agreeing to reinforce border security, to take measures to prevent the smuggling of arms and drugs, and to enhance trade. In November 1998 some 189 people (mainly Somalis) were found to have been massacred in north-eastern Kenya; Ethiopian guerrillas were widely believed to be responsible. In January 1999 the Kenyan Government protested to the Ethiopian authorities, following an incursion into Kenya by Ethiopian security forces, who were alleged to be in pursuit of Ethiopian rebels. Kenya deployed additional troops at the two countries' common frontier in May, following a series of landmine explosions in the region, which had resulted in several fatalities. Bilateral relations deteriorated further during late 2000 after it was reported that some 50 Kenyans had been killed, allegedly by Ethiopian militia forces, in cross-border clashes. In January 2001 representatives from both countries met in Nairobi and agreed to initiate measures aimed at ending border disputes. In April 2006 Kenya closed part of its border with Ethiopia when militia forces allegedly entered Kenyan territory and fighting ensued. Seven people were reported to have been killed in further fighting that broke out in August.

In October 1995, despite strong condemnation from foreign Governments, the Kenyan authorities refused to permit the international tribunal that was investigating war crimes committed in Rwanda during 1994 access to alleged Rwandan perpetrators of genocide who had fled to Kenya. In June 1996 the Moi Government closed the Rwandan embassy in Nairobi in protest at the Rwandan Government's refusal to waive diplomatic immunity for an embassy official who was suspected of plotting a murder in Kenya; the diplomat was deported. In

September, however, the first arrest in Kenya was made of a Rwandan Hutu suspected of involvement in genocide. Kenya strongly denied accusations, in November, of supplying arms to Rwandan Hutu rebels operating from within Zaire (now the Democratic Republic of the Congo). Following the *coup d'état* in Burundi in July 1996, Kenya, along with other countries of the region, imposed full economic sanctions on the administration of Maj. Pierre Buyoya; these sanctions were subsequently relaxed, and eventually withdrawn in January 1999. In November and December 1996 regional summit meetings were held in Nairobi to discuss the crisis in the Great Lakes region. Relations between the Kenyan and Rwandan Governments improved during 1997, when further Rwandan Hutus were arrested by the Kenyan security forces to stand trial on charges of genocide at the UN tribunal in Arusha, Tanzania. During a visit by Moi to Rwanda in May 2000 the two countries agreed to reopen the Kenyan embassy in Kigali and to establish a joint commission for bilateral relations.

In 1995 Kenya was reportedly sheltering about 200,000 refugees from the conflict in Somalia. The Moi Government, which claimed that the refugees placed an intolerable burden on the country's resources, repeatedly requested the UN to repatriate the total refugee population. By mid-1998 an estimated 155,000 Somalis had been repatriated from Kenya, with assistance from the office of the UN High Commissioner for Refugees. However, continuing instability in Somalia resulted in further influxes of refugees to Kenya. Kenya's total refugee population stood at 265,729 at the end of 2007, including 192,420 from Somalia and 45,261 from Sudan.

Government

Legislative power is vested in the unicameral National Assembly, with 224 members (210 elected by universal adult suffrage, the Attorney-General, the Speaker and 12 nominated members), who serve a term of five years, subject to dissolution. Executive power is held by the President, also directly elected for five years, who is assisted by an appointed Vice-President and Cabinet. There is also a Prime Minister, who has the authority to co-ordinate and supervise the execution of the Government

Defence

As assessed at November 2008, Kenya's active armed forces numbered 24,120, comprising an army of 20,000, an air force of 2,500 and a navy of 1,620; the paramilitary Police General Service Unit had a membership of 5,000. Military service is voluntary. Defence was allocated an estimated Ks. 50,800m. in the budget for 2008. Military assistance is received from the United Kingdom and from the USA, whose Rapid Deployment Force uses port and onshore facilities in Kenya.

Economic Affairs

In 2007, according to estimates by the World Bank, Kenya's gross national income (GNI), measured at average 2005–07 prices, was US $25,560m., equivalent to $680 per head (or $1,540 per head on an international purchasing-power parity basis). During 2000–07, it was estimated, the population increased at an average annual rate of 2.6%, while gross domestic product (GDP) per head increased, in real terms, by an average of 1.8% per year. Overall GDP increased, in real terms, at an average annual rate of 4.5% in 2000–07. Real GDP increased by 6.9% in 2007.

Agriculture (including forestry and fishing) contributed 25.8% of GDP and accounted for 17.8% of workers engaged in paid employment in the formal sector in that year. (According to FAO, agriculture employed 73.1% of the labour force in 2005.) The principal cash crops are tea (which contributed 17.1% of total export earnings in 2007) and coffee. Horticultural produce (Kenya is the world's fourth largest exporter of cut flowers), pyrethrum, sisal, sugar cane and cotton are also important. Maize is the principal subsistence crop. There is a significant dairy industry for domestic consumption and export. During 2000–07, according to the World Bank, agricultural GDP increased at an average annual rate of 4.2%. Agricultural GDP increased by 7.6% in 2007.

Industry (including mining, manufacturing, construction and power) contributed 17.7% of GDP and employed an estimated 19.3% of workers engaged in paid employment in the formal sector in that year. During 2000–07, according to the World Bank, industrial GDP increased at an average annual rate of 4.8%. Industrial GDP increased by 8.7% in 2007.

Mining contributed 0.8% of GDP in 2007 and employed 0.3% of those in paid formal sector employment in that year. Soda ash is the principal mineral export. Fluorspar, iron ore, salt, limestone, gold, gemstones (including rubies and sapphires), vermiculite and lead are also mined. Kenya has substantial reserves of titanium.

Manufacturing contributed an estimated 10.9% of GDP and employed 13.7% of workers engaged in paid employment in the formal sector in 2007. During 2000–07, according to the World Bank, manufacturing GDP increased at an average annual rate of 4.5%. Manufacturing GDP increased by 8.3% in 2007.

Hydroelectric power accounted for 50.4% of total electricity generated in 2005. It had accounted for an average of 81.9% during 1990–98, whereafter recurrent droughts began to affect hydroelectric production. This shortfall was taken up by petroleum, which accounted for 29.5% in 2005 (as opposed to an average of 9.2% during 1990–98). Kenya does not produce electricity from coal, natural gas or nuclear power. Energy for domestic use is derived principally from fuel wood and charcoal. The prolonged drought led to severe power shortages in 2000 and threatened to affect hydroelectric production in 2005–06. In February 2004 it was announced that the Kenyan and Tanzanian national grids were to be connected to that of Zambia under a cross-border energy project; the first phase of the project, which was to cost some US $300m., was to be commissioned in 2007, followed by a second phase in 2012. In 2007 imports of mineral fuels and lubricants (including crude petroleum intended for refining) comprised 21.3% of the value of total imports.

The services sector contributed an estimated 56.5% of GDP and employed 62.9% of workers engaged in paid employment in the formal sector in 2007. Tourism makes an important contribution to Kenya's economy and has been the country's principal source of foreign exchange since 1987. In 1998, however, a decline of 10.6% in tourist arrivals, to 894,300, was attributed partly to the effects of civil unrest in coastal areas during 1997. In 1999–2000 there was some recovery in tourism, with arrivals increasing to 1,036,628 in 2000. Following terrorist attacks in 2001, however, and subsequent warnings against travel to Kenya by the United Kingdom and the USA, the tourism industry again experienced difficulties. In 2007 tourist arrivals totalled 1,817,000, while receipts from tourism in 2006 amounted to US $1,182m. The GDP of the services sector increased at an average annual rate of 4.3% in 2000–07, according to the World Bank. Services GDP increased by 5.8% in 2007.

In 2007 Kenya recorded a visible trade deficit of US $4,258m., and there was a deficit of $1,101.8m. on the current account of the balance of payments. In 2007 the principal source of imports was the United Arab Emirates (which supplied 14.8% of total imports in that year); other major suppliers were India, the People's Republic of China, the USA, Japan and South Africa. Uganda was the principal market for Kenya's exports (purchasing 12.2%) in that year; other important purchasers were the United Kingdom, Tanzania, the Netherlands and the USA. The principal exports in 2007 were tea, vegetables and fruit, cut flowers and foliage, and chemicals and related products. The principal imports in that year were machinery and transport equipment, petroleum and petroleum products, chemicals and related products, and food and live animals.

In the financial year ending 30 June 2008 there was a budgetary deficit of Ks. 130,100m., equivalent to 7.2% of 2007 GDP. The country's external debt was US $6,534m. at the end of 2006, of which $5,807m. was long-term public debt. In that year the cost of debt-servicing was equivalent to 6.5% of the value of exports of goods and services. According to the IMF, the annual rate of inflation averaged 9.0% in 2000–07; consumer prices increased by 9.7% in 2007. Some 23% of the labour force were estimated to be unemployed in late 2000.

Kenya is a member of the Common Market for Eastern and Southern Africa (see p. 215) and, with Tanzania and Uganda, of the East African Community (see p. 425). The International Tea Promotion Association (see p. 423) is based in Kenya.

Kenya's economy is reasonably diversified, although most employment is dependent on agriculture. Development of that sector has been intermittently hindered by adverse weather conditions, resulting in sporadic food shortages, and also by rural ethnic unrest. Moreover, the country is highly vulnerable to fluctuations in international prices for its cash crops, most notably tea and coffee. Poverty is widespread, with population growth considerably higher than growth in GNI per head, and the revelation in the mid-2000s that large scale corruption remained endemic in Kenya adversely affected business confidence and investment and led international donors to withhold aid. Nevertheless, in late 2006 President Kibaki stated intentions to transform the country into a middle-income nation

KENYA

Statistical Survey

within 25 years, with a focus of the initiative being sustained annual economic growth of 10%. Outbreaks of violence that ensued following the disputed 2007 presidential election (see Recent History) precipitated temporary closures of key supply routes, disrupted the valuable tourism sector and forced many agricultural workers to abandon activities. Consequently, a severe downturn in maize production was reported in early 2008 and, as a result of many farmers being unable to plant crops for the next harvest, severe food shortages were observed. High international prices for fertilizer and fuel resulted in further pressure on the economy in general and on the primary sector in particular, and the UN World Food Programme commenced an operation in April 2009, which would result in some 2.5m. Kenyans receiving general food distributions until February 2010. Meanwhile, in late 2008 Kibaki announced that investment of US $4,500m. in the country's infrastructure was necessary to maintain economic growth, but conceded that the funds were not available in the public sector. The Government subsequently proposed a number of public private partnerships with the aim of enticing the business community to invest in public projects. Nevertheless, the global financial crisis was expected to reduce the ability of private companies to engage in such projects, while also proving detrimental to exports, remittances and capital inflows. The IMF forecast GDP growth of 6.4% in 2009, compared with 3.3% in the previous year, while inflation was projected to decline significantly having reached 25.0% in 2008.

Education

The Government provides, or assists in the provision of, schools. Primary education, which is compulsory, is provided free of charge. The education system involves eight years of primary education (beginning at six years of age), four years at secondary school and four years of university education. According to UNESCO estimates, in 2005/06 enrolment at primary schools included 75.5% of pupils in the relevant age-group (males 74.8%; females 76.1%), while enrolment at secondary schools included 42.7% of children in the relevant age-group (males 43.3%; females 42.0%). There are six state universities and seven private universities, with a total of 91,500 enrolled students in 2004/05. In 2004 spending on education represented 29.2% of total budgetary expenditure.

Public Holidays

2009: 1 January (New Year's Day), 10–13 April (Easter), 1 May (Labour Day), 1 June (Madaraka Day, anniversary of self-government), 10 October (Moi Day), 20 September* (Id al Fitr, end of Ramadan), 20 October (Kenyatta Day), 12 December (Independence Day), 25–26 December (Christmas).

2010: 1 January (New Year's Day), 2–5 April (Easter), 1 May (Labour Day), 1 June (Madaraka Day, anniversary of self-government), 10 September* (Id al Fitr, end of Ramadan), 10 October (Moi Day), 20 October (Kenyatta Day), 12 December (Independence Day), 25–26 December (Christmas).

* These holidays are determined by the Islamic lunar calendar and may vary by one or two days from the dates given.

Weights and Measures

The metric system is in use.

Statistical Survey

Source (unless otherwise stated): Central Bureau of Statistics, Ministry of Finance and Planning, POB 30266, Nairobi; tel. (20) 333971; fax (20) 333030; internet www.cbs.go.ke.

Area and Population

AREA, POPULATION AND DENSITY

Area (sq km)	
Land area	571,416
Inland water	11,230
Total	582,646*
Population (census results)†	
24 August 1989	21,443,636
24 August 1999	
Males	14,205,589
Females	14,481,018
Total	28,686,607
Population (official projected estimates at mid-year)	
2006	33,947,066
2007	34,528,249
2008	35,112,181
Density (per sq km) at mid-2008	60.3

* 224,961 sq miles.
† Excluding adjustment for underenumeration.

PRINCIPAL ETHNIC GROUPS
(census of August 1989)

African	21,163,076	European	34,560
Arab	41,595	Other*	115,220
Asian	89,185	**Total**	21,443,636

* Includes persons who did not state 'tribe' or 'race'.

POPULATION BY PROVINCE
(2008, projected estimates)

Nairobi	3,038,553	Nyanza	5,094,251
Central	3,919,100	Rift Valley	8,755,986
Coast	3,089,013	Western	4,348,746
Eastern	5,456,190	**Total**	35,112,181
North-Eastern	1,410,342		

PRINCIPAL TOWNS
(estimated population at census of August 1999)

Nairobi (capital)	2,143,020	Meru	78,100
Mombasa	660,800	Kitale	63,245
Nakuru	219,366	Malindi*	53,805
Kisumu*	194,390	Nyeri*	46,969
Eldoret*	167,016	Kericho	30,023
Thika	82,665	Kisii	29,634

* Boundaries extended between 1979 and 1989.

Mid-2007 ('000, incl. suburbs, UN estimates): Nairobi 3,010; Mombasa 882 (Source: UN, *World Urbanization Prospects: The 2007 Revision*).

BIRTHS AND DEATHS
(annual averages, UN estimates)

	1990–95	1995–2000	2000–05
Birth rate (per 1,000)	38.6	38.0	39.1
Death rate (per 1,000)	9.4	11.4	13.2

Source: UN, *World Population Prospects: The 2006 Revision*.

Life expectancy (years at birth, WHO estimates): 53.3 (males 52.3; females 54.6) in 2006 (Source: WHO, *World Health Statistics*).

KENYA

EMPLOYMENT
(labour force survey, selected urban and rural settlements, '000s)*

	2005	2006	2007†
Agriculture and forestry	327.1	334.6	339.9
Mining and quarrying	5.8	6.0	6.3
Manufacturing	248.4	254.9	261.3
Electricity and water	20.2	19.5	19.0
Construction	78.2	79.9	81.3
Wholesale and retail trade	175.4	185.9	195.8
Transport and communications	113.7	130.8	149.0
Finance, insurance, real estate and business services	88.9	92.3	95.0
Community, social and personal services	751.0	755.8	759.7
Total	**1,808.7**	**1,859.7**	**1,907.3**

* Data are for salaried employees in the formal sector only, and therefore exclude self-employed and unpaid family workers and a vast number of workers in the informal sector (almost 6.5m. in 2005, according to official estimates). According to ILO, the 1999 census recorded an employed population of 14,474,200.
† Provisional figures.

Health and Welfare

KEY INDICATORS

Total fertility rate (children per woman, 2006)	5.0
Under-5 mortality rate (per 1,000 live births, 2006)	121
HIV/AIDS (% of persons aged 15–49, 2005)	6.1
Physicians (per 1,000 head, 2004)	0.1
Hospital beds (per 1,000 head, 2006)	1.4
Health expenditure (2006): US $ per head (PPP)	105
Health expenditure (2006): % of GDP	4.6
Health expenditure (2006): public (% of total)	48.2
Access to water (% of persons, 2006)	57
Access to sanitation (% of persons, 2006)	42
Human Development Index (2006): ranking	144
Human Development Index (2006): value	0.532

For sources and definitions, see explanatory note on p. vi.

Agriculture

PRINCIPAL CROPS
('000 metric tons)

	2005	2006	2007
Wheat	368.9	358.1	265.0*
Barley	41.2	81.1	40.0
Maize	2,905.6	3,247.2	3,240.0
Millet	53.1	68.7	50.0
Sorghum	149.7	131.2	90.0
Potatoes	980.2	783.8	800.0
Sweet potatoes	230.7	808.6	800.0
Cassava (Manioc)	347.8	841.2	850.0
Sugar cane	4,800.8	4,932.8	4,950.0
Beans, dry	382.3	531.8	535.0
Cow peas, dry	36.2	87.9	80.0
Pigeon peas	96.1	1,106.6	105.0
Cashew nuts*	10.0	10.0	10.0
Coconuts*	63.0	60.0	60.0
Seed cotton*	20.0	20.5	15.0
Cottonseed*	13.0	13.0	n.a.
Cabbages and other brassicas*	600.0	550.0	550.0
Tomatoes	330.0	330.0	330.0
Onions, dry	68.0	68.0*	70.0
Carrots and turnips*	45.0	40.0	40.0
Bananas	600.0	600.0*	580.0
Plantains	600.0	600.0*	605.0
Guavas, mangoes and mangosteens*	125.0	118.0	118.0
Avocados*	75.0	70.0	70.0
Pineapples	600.0	600.0*	605.0
Papayas*	87.0	86.0	86.0

—continued

	2005	2006	2007
Coffee, green	45.2	48.3	37.5
Tea (made)	328.5	310.6	315.0
Tobacco, unmanufactured*	22.0	20.0	20.0
Sisal*	n.a.	25.0	n.a.

* FAO estimate(s).

Aggregate production ('000 metric tons, may include official, semi-official or estimated data): Total cereals 3,585.1 in 2005, 3,955.0 in 2006, 3,755.0 in 2007; Total roots and tubers 1,582.3 in 2005, 2,464.4 in 2006, 2,480.1 in 2007; Total vegetables (incl. melons) 1,736.9 in 2005, 1,661.8 in 2006, 1,663.8 in 2007; Total fruits (excl. melons) 2,411.6 in 2005, 2,266.7 in 2006, 2,254.8 in 2007.

Source: FAO.

LIVESTOCK
('000 head, year ending September)

	2005	2006	2007*
Cattle	13,019.0	12,430.3	12,500.9
Sheep	10,033.9	9,298.5	9,300.0
Goats	13,882.6	10,129.4	10,500.0
Pigs	320.0	321.1	325.0
Camels	931.3	1,057.9	1,060.0
Chickens	28,657	29,369	30,000

* FAO estimates.
Source: FAO.

LIVESTOCK PRODUCTS
('000 metric tons)

	2005	2006	2007*
Cattle meat	396.2	376.3	390.0
Sheep meat	36.7	35.0*	36.5
Goats' meat*	42.4	38.0	38.5
Pig meat	12.8	11.0	11.5
Chicken meat	18.2	16.4	16.5
Game meat*	14.0	14.0	14.0
Camel meat*	25.5	19.8	19.8
Cows' milk	2,650.0	3,500.0	3,500.0
Sheep's milk*	31.0	31.0	31.0
Goats' milk	129.0	105.0*	108.0
Camels' milk*	25.2	32.2	32.5
Hen eggs*	57.9	53.0	53.0
Honey	22.0	25.0	25.0

* FAO estimate(s).
Source: FAO.

Forestry

ROUNDWOOD REMOVALS
('000 cubic metres, excluding bark)

	2004	2005	2006
Sawlogs, veneer logs and logs for sleepers	241.0	588.0	607.0
Pulpwood	391.0	450.0	450.0
Other industrial wood	1,160.0	1,114.0	1,246.0
Fuel wood	20,369.6	25,600.0	26,400.0
Total	**22,161.6**	**27,752.0**	**28,703.0**

2007: Production as in 2006.
Source: FAO.

SAWNWOOD PRODUCTION
('000 cubic metres, including railway sleepers)

	2004	2005	2006
Coniferous (softwood)	70	116	121
Broadleaved (hardwood)	8	20	21
Total	**78**	**136**	**141**

* FAO estimates.
2007: Production as in 2006.
Source: FAO.

KENYA

Fishing

('000 metric tons, live weight)

	2004	2005	2006
Capture	126.9	147.3	158.7
Silver cyprinid	34.7	54.0	57.9
Nile tilapia	17.5	22.2	19.0
Other tilapias	3.9	1.4	3.3
Nile perch	57.2	52.4	55.7
Other freshwater fishes	4.2	4.4	9.1
Aquaculture	1.0	1.0	1.0
Total catch	127.9	148.4	159.7

Note: Figures exclude crocodiles, recorded by number rather than by weight. The number of Nile crocodiles caught was: 3,862 in 2004; 10,950 in 2005; 8,710 in 2006.

Source: FAO.

Mining

('000 metric tons, estimates)

	2004	2005	2006*
Soda ash	353.8	360.2	374.2
Fluorspar	108.0	97.3	83.0
Salt	60.0	52.0	60.0
Limestone flux	34.0	35.0	35.0

* Estimates.

Source: US Geological Survey.

Industry

SELECTED PRODUCTS
('000 metric tons, unless otherwise indicated)

	2003	2004	2005*
Wheat flour	248.6	262.3	271.6
Raw sugar	448.0	516.8	489.0
Beer ('000 hectolitres)	222.3	237.5	266.3
Cigarettes (million)	4,753.0	5,351.0	7,324.2
Cement	1,659.5	1,873.3	2,123.2
Electric energy (million kWh)	4,851.6	5,194.5	5,547.0

* Preliminary data.

2002: Kerosene and jet fuels 273; Motor spirit (petrol) 253; Gas-diesel (distillate fuel) oils 405; Residual fuel oils 533.

Finance

CURRENCY AND EXCHANGE RATES

Monetary Units
100 cents = 1 Kenya shilling (Ks.).
Ks. 20 = 1 Kenya pound (K£).

Sterling, Dollar and Euro Equivalents (30 September 2008)
£1 sterling = Ks. 131.78;
US $1 = Ks. 73.22;
€1 = Ks. 104.72;
Ks. 1,000 = £7.59 sterling = $13.66 = €9.55.

Average Exchange Rate (Ks. per US $)
2005   75.554
2006   72.101
2007   67.318

Note: The foregoing information refers to the Central Bank's mid-point exchange rate. However, with the introduction of a foreign exchange bearer certificate (FEBC) scheme in October 1991, a dual exchange rate system is in effect. In May 1994 foreign exchange transactions were liberalized and the Kenya shilling became fully convertible against other currencies.

Statistical Survey

BUDGET
(Ks. million, year ending 30 June)

Revenue	1999/2000	2000/01	2001/02*
Tax revenue	151,359.5	160,771.6	160,394.2
Taxes on income and profits	53,317.0	53,428.9	55,861.9
Taxes on goods and services	69,437.3	78,538.9	82,948.6
Value-added tax	40,944.2	50,220.9	50,871.7
Excise duties	28,493.1	28,317.9	32,076.9
Taxes on international trade	28,605.2	28,803.7	21,583.7
Import duties	28,605.2	28,803.7	21,583.7
Non-tax revenue	27,585.1	26,306.1	25,399.4
Property income	6,482.4	4,786.1	4,105.5
Administrative fees and charges	21,538.1	21,538.1	21,293.9
Total (incl. others)	184,550.9	192,221.0	187,863.8

Expenditure	1999/2000	2000/01	2001/02*
General administration	44,080.7	62,943.3	57,584.5
Defence	10,427.2	14,202.8	16,268.2
Social services	59,670.4	67,611.1	71,953.1
Education	47,726.8	49,611.3	54,653.0
Health	9,188.6	15,629.3	14,336.5
Economic services	28,481.1	39,362.3	38,069.4
General administration	5,101.3	14,085.6	12,696.2
Agriculture, forestry and fishing	8,115.4	8,269.6	7,850.1
Roads	8,848.5	9,458.4	8,856.7
Interest on public debt	28,917.8	24,425.5	29,850.9
Total	171,577.2	208,545.7	213,726.2

* Forecasts.

2005/06 (Ks. '000 million, year ending 30 June): *Revenue:* Income tax 113.9; Import duty 20.5; Value-added tax 76.3; Excise duty 50.3; Non-tax revenue 50.2; Total 311.3. *Expenditure:* Recurrent expenditure 306.5 (Interest payments 41.2; Wages and benefits 112.3; Defence 29.3); Drought relief 8.6; Net lending 67.7; Total 382.8 (Source: IMF, *Kenya: Third Review Under the Poverty Reduction and Growth Facility Arrangement and Request for Waivers of Nonobservance of Performance Criteria - Staff Report; Press Release on the Executive Board Discussion; and Statement by the Executive Director for Kenya*–January 2009).

2006/07 (Ks. '000 million, year ending 30 June): *Revenue:* Income tax 131.5; Import duty 27.5; Value-added tax 96.3; Excise duty 56.4; Non-tax revenue 61.4; Total 373.0. *Expenditure:* Recurrent expenditure 335.5 (Interest payments 42.5; Wages and benefits 127.3; Defence 28.7); Drought relief 3.7; Net lending 80.3; Total 419.5 (Source: IMF, *Kenya: Third Review Under the Poverty Reduction and Growth Facility Arrangement and Request for Waivers of Nonobservance of Performance Criteria - Staff Report; Press Release on the Executive Board Discussion; and Statement by the Executive Director for Kenya*–January 2009).

2007/08 (Ks. '000 million, year ending 30 June): *Revenue:* Income tax 151.8; Import duty 32.3; Value-added tax 112.2; Excise duty 65.6; Non-tax revenue 65.3; Total 427.2. *Expenditure:* Recurrent expenditure 403.8 (Interest payments 49.7; Wages and benefits 144.0; Defence 45.7); Civil Contingency Fund 2.0; Drought relief 3.7; Net lending 147.8; Total 557.3 (Source: IMF, *Kenya: Third Review Under the Poverty Reduction and Growth Facility Arrangement and Request for Waivers of Nonobservance of Performance Criteria - Staff Report; Press Release on the Executive Board Discussion; and Statement by the Executive Director for Kenya*–January 2009).

INTERNATIONAL RESERVES
(excl. gold, US $ million at 31 December)

	2005	2006	2007
IMF special drawing rights	0.0	0.5	0.2
Reserve position in IMF	18.2	19.2	20.2
Foreign exchange	1,780.6	2,395.3	3,334.5
Total	1,798.8	2,415.0	3,354.9

Source: IMF, *International Financial Statistics*.

MONEY SUPPLY
(Ks. million at 31 December)

	2005	2006	2007
Currency outside banks	66,327	76,479	96,124
Demand deposits at commercial banks	157,460	206,583	276,969
Total money (incl. others)	230,845	291,741	371,810

Source: IMF, *International Financial Statistics*.

KENYA

Statistical Survey

COST OF LIVING
(Consumer Price Index at December; base: October 1997 = 100)

	2000	2001	2002
Food and non-alcoholic beverages	136.3	134.8	142.5
Alcohol and tobacco	120.8	136.3	137.1
Clothing and footwear	109.9	109.8	110.7
Housing	121.6	129.3	133.9
Fuel and power	143.1	154.1	165.8
Household goods and services	117.6	119.0	120.8
Medical goods and services	134.1	152.6	158.8
Transport and communications	128.4	127.7	130.8
Recreation and education	120.2	129.6	132.8
Personal goods and services	118.2	120.5	122.8
All items (incl. others)	**129.0**	**131.1**	**136.7**

Source: IMF, *Kenya: Statistical Appendix* (July 2003).

All items (Consumer Price Index, annual averages; base 2000 = 100): 118.4 in 2003; 132.2 in 2004; 145.8 in 2005; 166.9 in 2006; 183.1 in 2007 (Source: IMF, *International Financial Statistics*).

NATIONAL ACCOUNTS

Expenditure on the Gross Domestic Product
(Ks. million at current prices)

	2003	2004	2005
Government final consumption expenditure	205,140	226,016	242,409
Private final consumption expenditure	875,154	965,528	1,077,071
Changes in inventories	7,288	10,546	−25,311
Gross fixed capital formation	179,282	206,634	263,063
Total domestic expenditure	**1,266,865**	**1,408,724**	**1,557,231**
Exports of goods and services	270,118	336,360	378,068
Less Imports of goods and services	338,394	434,234	529,749
Statistical discrepancy	−60,614	−28,345	9,605
GDP at market prices	**1,137,975**	**1,282,504**	**1,415,155**

Gross Domestic Product by Economic Activity
(Ks. million at current prices)

	2005	2006	2007*
Agriculture, forestry and fishing	343,119	385,897	418,160
Mining and quarrying	6,803	7,884	12,904
Manufacturing	149,067	166,404	176,610
Electricity, gas and water	28,766	29,027	28,105
Construction	56,121	63,927	69,279
Wholesale and retail trade, repairs	130,468	151,414	176,575
Restaurants and hotels	19,357	24,207	29,605
Transport, storage and communication	147,523	182,936	207,300
Financial services	48,364	62,922	84,871
Real estate, renting and business services	79,015	90,060	99,002
Government services	204,901	226,084	249,455
Private households	5,787	6,770	7,176
Community, social and personal service activities	53,407	58,305	63,497
Sub-total	**1,272,697**	**1,455,836**	**1,622,541**
Less Imputed bank service charge	11,514	15,376	19,365
Indirect taxes, less subsidies	156,888	180,272	211,067
GDP in market prices	**1,418,071**	**1,620,732**	**1,814,243**

*Preliminary.

BALANCE OF PAYMENTS
(US $ million)

	2005	2006	2007
Exports of goods f.o.b.	3,454.5	3,516.2	4,122.9
Imports of goods f.o.b.	−5,601.7	−6,769.5	−8,381.0
Trade balance	**−2,147.1**	**−3,253.2**	**−4,258.0**
Exports of services	1,880.1	2,461.1	2,699.0
Imports of services	−1,137.1	−1,401.5	−1,459.5
Balance on goods and services	**−1,404.2**	**−2,193.6**	**−3,018.5**
Other income received	73.3	99.4	112.8
Other income paid	−181.7	−169.5	−304.4
Balance on goods, services and income	**−1,512.6**	**−2,263.7**	**−3,210.1**
Current transfers received	1,319.2	1,832.8	2,148.8
Current transfers paid	−66.6	−47.9	−40.4
Current balance	**−259.9**	**−478.8**	**−1,101.8**
Capital account	103.3	168.4	156.8
Direct investment abroad	−9.7	−24.0	−36.0
Direct investment from abroad	21.2	50.7	727.7
Portfolio investment assets	−45.9	−23.6	−24.3
Portfolio investment liabilities	15.4	3.0	0.8
Other investment assets	−200.6	−259.6	−346.7
Other investment liabilities	730.8	927.1	1,749.4
Net errors and omissions	−237.7	218.1	−314.7
Overall balance	**117.0**	**581.3**	**811.3**

Source: IMF, *International Financial Statistics*.

External Trade

PRINCIPAL COMMODITIES
(distribution by SITC, US $ million)

Imports c.i.f.	2005	2006	2007
Food and live animals	315.4	382.2	552.5
Cereals and cereal preparations	192.4	214.8	293.5
Crude materials (inedible) except fuels	121.9	161.3	229.6
Mineral fuels, lubricants, etc.	1,340.9	1,750.3	1,917.5
Petroleum, petroleum products, etc.	1,324.4	1,719.9	1,876.6
Crude petroleum oils	682.1	763.5	731.5
Refined petroleum products	631.7	937.0	1,120.1
Animal and vegetable oils, fats and waxes	185.4	235.4	346.0
Chemicals and related products	842.1	1,005.1	1,150.8
Medicinal and pharmaceutical products	164.7	213.9	236.9
Plastics in primary forms	203.9	243.0	298.1
Basic manufactures	924.1	1,087.2	1,428.5
Iron and steel	279.2	296.1	398.9
Machinery and transport equipment	1,798.3	2,253.5	2,745.3
Power-generating machinery and equipment	69.8	96.8	142.5
Machinery specialized for particular industries	175.8	226.5	328.3
General industrial machinery, equipment and parts	174.5	180.2	233.6
Electrical machinery, apparatus, etc.	88.0	124.2	145.3
Road vehicles and parts	406.2	613.2	766.5
Passenger motor cars (excl. buses)	158.7	215.4	297.3
Motor vehicles for goods transport and special purposes	102.4	173.5	185.4
Aircraft, associated equipment and parts	603.3	589.7	499.7
Miscellaneous manufactured articles	269.8	312.0	447.9
Total (incl. others)	**5,846.2**	**7,232.9**	**8,989.3**

KENYA

Exports f.o.b.	2005	2006	2007
Food and live animals	1,173.0	1,313.9	1,517.1
Vegetables and fruit	305.7	328.1	402.0
Fresh or simply preserved vegetables	189.5	212.8	257.7
Coffee, tea, cocoa and spices	704.4	809.3	874.6
Tea	568.3	661.4	698.6
Crude materials (inedible) except fuels	392.1	481.5	568.8
Cut flowers and foliage	246.4	316.3	390.3
Mineral fuels, lubricants, etc.	626.5	254.7	174.0
Petroleum, petroleum products, etc.	624.2	251.7	170.9
Refined petroleum products	612.9	241.7	164.6
Chemicals and related products	287.0	253.2	354.3
Basic manufactures	379.0	452.4	534.6
Iron and steel	122.9	126.7	125.5
Miscellaneous manufactured articles	346.7	431.2	467.8
Total (incl. others)	3,419.9	3,501.7	4,080.8

Sources: UN, *International Trade Statistics Yearbook*.

PRINCIPAL TRADING PARTNERS
(US $ million)

Imports c.i.f.	2005	2006	2007
Bahrain	117.7	95.9	146.5
Belgium	106.7	94.4	92.6
China, People's Repub.	304.1	412.4	678.7
Egypt	83.0	114.0	165.9
France (incl. Monaco)	184.8	147.5	245.3
Germany	209.6	262.6	329.4
India	326.0	524.3	844.5
Indonesia	131.3	190.9	278.8
Ireland	12.0	218.6	54.4
Italy	104.3	168.1	196.5
Japan	305.4	408.1	611.2
Korea, Repub.	48.6	126.9	127.7
Netherlands	128.2	126.3	138.3
Pakistan	43.9	61.6	74.4
Russia	39.5	41.6	97.5
Saudi Arabia	366.8	369.1	261.4
Singapore	101.6	354.2	138.9
South Africa	564.6	470.9	525.3
Thailand	46.9	63.2	99.3
United Arab Emirates	831.2	1,075.9	1,329.0
United Kingdom	326.1	373.1	437.1
USA	563.1	343.3	661.6
Total (incl. others)	5,846.2	7,232.9	8,989.3

Exports f.o.b.	2005	2006	2007
Belgium	39.5	30.2	38.6
Burundi	49.1	30.3	36.0
Congo, Democratic Repub.	134.5	107.0	123.5
Egypt	117.1	137.1	135.4
Ethiopia	33.6	50.9	51.0
France (incl. Monaco)	72.8	64.0	63.2
Germany	69.8	65.1	88.4
India	53.1	52.2	86.7
Italy	30.4	27.9	38.3
Netherlands	243.8	277.2	325.7
Pakistan	186.2	201.7	201.0
Rwanda	96.4	66.1	86.2
Somalia	65.8	105.6	123.8
Sudan	90.4	140.5	172.3
Tanzania	264.4	253.8	331.7
Uganda	566.2	387.0	498.9
United Arab Emirates	53.9	69.2	128.2
United Kingdom	314.3	380.4	427.7
USA	228.1	291.3	285.8
Zambia	36.1	56.3	74.1
Total (incl. others)	3,419.9	3,501.7	4,080.8

Sources: UN, *International Trade Statistics Yearbook*.

Transport

RAILWAYS
(traffic)

	2000	2001	2002*
Passenger-km (million)	302	216	288
Freight ton-km (million)	1,557	1,603	1,538

* Provisional figures.

ROAD TRAFFIC
(motor vehicles in use)

	2000	2001	2002*
Motor cars	244,836	255,379	269,925
Light vans	159,450	162,603	166,811
Lorries, trucks and heavy vans	57,796	58,501	59,835
Buses and mini-buses	38,930	42,629	46,606
Motorcycles and autocycles	44,894	46,004	47,451
Other motor vehicles	31,820	32,255	32,724

* Provisional figures.

2004: Motor cars 307,772; Buses 55,705; Lorries and vans 243,612; Motorcycles 53,508.

SHIPPING

Merchant Fleet
(registered at 31 December)

	2005	2006	2007
Number of vessels	41	38	36
Total displacement ('000 grt)	19.9	17.6	15.1

Source: Lloyd's Register-Fairplay, *World Fleet Statistics*.

International Sea-borne Freight Traffic
('000 metric tons)

	1999	2000	2001*
Goods loaded	1,845	1,722	1,998
Goods unloaded	6,200	7,209	8,299

* Provisional figures.

Freight handled ('000 metric tons at Kenyan ports): 11,931 in 2003; 12,920 in 2004; 13,282 in 2005.

CIVIL AVIATION
(traffic on scheduled services)

	2002	2003	2004
Kilometres flown (million)	36	41	43
Passengers carried ('000)	1,600	1,732	2,005
Passenger-km (million)	3,939	4,245	5,310
Total ton-km (million)	465	527	674

Source: UN, *Statistical Yearbook*.

Tourism

FOREIGN TOURIST ARRIVALS
(number of visitors by country of origin)

	2001	2002	2003
Austria	19,929	20,054	22,954
France	47,802	48,101	55,057
Germany	156,414	157,394	180,156
India	23,858	24,007	27,479
Italy	53,328	53,662	61,428
Sweden	34,376	34,591	39,593
Switzerland	39,081	39,326	45,013
Tanzania	111,735	112,435	128,695
Uganda	69,781	70,218	80,373
United Kingdom	153,968	154,933	177,339
USA	65,191	65,599	75,086
Total (incl. others)	993,600	1,001,297	1,146,099

Tourism receipts (US $ million, incl. passenger transport): 799 in 2004; 969 in 2005; 1,182 in 2006.
Source: World Tourism Organization.

Total arrivals ('000): 1,361 in 2004; 1,479 in 2005; 1,601 in 2006; 1,817 in 2007.

Communications Media

	2005	2006	2007
Telephones ('000 main lines in use)	282	293	265
Mobile cellular telephones ('000 subscribers)	4,612	7,340	11,440
Personal computers ('000 in use)	300	n.a.	n.a.
Internet users ('000)	1,111	2,770	3,000
Broadband subscribers ('000)	—	17.7	n.a.

Source: International Telecommunication Union.

Television receivers ('000 in use, 2000): 768.

Radio receivers ('000 in use, 1999): 6,383.

Facsimile machines (number in use, year ending 30 June 1995): 3,800.

Daily newspapers (2000): 4 titles (average circulation 310,000 copies).

Book production (titles, 1994): 300 first editions (excl. pamphlets).

Sources: UNESCO, *Statistical Yearbook*; UN, *Statistical Yearbook*.

Education

(2003/04, unless otherwise indicated)

	Institutions	Teachers	Pupils
Pre-primary	23,977[1]	70,058	1,627,721
Primary	17,611[1]	149,893	5,926,078
Secondary:			
general secondary	3,057[1]	75,875	2,405,259
technical	36[2]	834[3]	14,597[3]
teacher training	26[4]	808[5]	18,992[6]
Higher	n.a.[7]	n.a.[7]	106,407

[1] 1998/99 figures.
[2] 1988 figure.
[3] UNESCO estimate.
[4] 1995 figure.
[5] 1985 figure.
[6] 1992 figure.
[7] In 1990 there were four universities, with 4,392 teachers.

Sources: Ministry of Education, Nairobi; UNESCO Institute for Statistics.

2005 ('000, estimates): Enrolment in primary schools 7,592; Enrolment in secondary schools 928; Enrolment in universities 90.

2006 ('000, estimates): Enrolment in primary schools 7,632; Enrolment in secondary schools 1,030; Enrolment in universities 112.

2007 ('000, estimates): Enrolment in primary schools 8,229; Enrolment in secondary schools 1,180; Enrolment in universities 118.

Adult literacy rate (UNESCO estimates): 73.6% (males 77.7%; females 70.2%) in 2000 (Source: UNESCO Institute for Statistics).

Directory

The Constitution

The Constitution was introduced at independence on 12 December 1963. Subsequent amendments, including the adoption of republican status on 12 December 1964, were consolidated in 1969. A further amendment in December 1991 permitted the establishment of a multi-party system. In September 1997 the National Assembly approved legislation which amended the Constitution with a view to ensuring free and fair democratic elections. All political parties were granted equal access to the media, and detention without trial was prohibited. In addition, the opposition was to participate in selecting the 12 nominated members of the National Assembly and 10 of the 12 members of the supervisory Electoral Commission. An amendment to the Constitution, approved by the National Assembly in November 1999, reduced the level of presidential control over the legislative process. The Constitution can be amended by the affirmative vote on Second and Third Reading of 65% of the membership of the National Assembly (excluding the Speaker and Attorney-General).

The central legislative authority is the unicameral National Assembly, in which there are 210 directly elected Representatives, 12 nominated members and two ex officio members, the Attorney-General and the Speaker. The maximum term of the National Assembly is five years from its first meeting (except in wartime). It can be dissolved by the President at any time, and the National Assembly may force its own dissolution by a vote of 'no confidence', whereupon presidential and Assembly elections have to be held within 90 days.

Executive power is vested in the President, Vice-President and Cabinet. Both the Vice-President and the Cabinet are appointed by the President, who must be a member of the Assembly and at least 35 years of age. Election of the President, for a five-year term, is by direct popular vote; the winning candidate at a presidential election must receive no less than 25% of the votes in at least five of Kenya's eight provinces. If a President dies, or a vacancy otherwise occurs during a President's period of office, the Vice-President becomes interim President for up to 90 days while a successor is elected.

In March 2008 the National Assembly adopted the National Accord and Reconciliation Act, which created the position of Prime Minister of the Government of Kenya and also provided for two Deputy Prime Ministers, who are appointed by the President. The Prime Minister is an elected member of the National Assembly who is the parliamentary leader of either the political party that has the largest number of members in the National Assembly or of a coalition of political parties, in the event that the leader of the political party that has the largest number of members in the National Assembly does not command the majority in the National Assembly. The Prime Minister has the authority to co-ordinate and supervise the execution of the Government.

The Government

HEAD OF STATE

President: Mwai Kibaki (took office 30 December 2002; re-elected 27 December 2007).

KENYA

CABINET
(May 2009)

A coalition of the Party of National Unity, the Orange Democratic Movement, and the Orange Democratic Movement—Kenya.

Prime Minister: RAILA AMOLLO ODINGA.
Vice-President and Minister of Home Affairs: STEPHEN KALONZO MUSYOKA.
Deputy Prime Minister and Minister of Finance: UHURU KENYATTA.
Deputy Prime Minister and Minister of Local Government: WYCLIFFE MUSALIA MUDAVADI.
Minister of the East African Community: AMASON KINGI JEFFAH.
Minister of Foreign Affairs: MOSES WETANGULA.
Minister of Justice, National Cohesion and Constitutional Affairs: MUTULA KILONZO.
Minister of Nairobi Metropolitan Development: NJERU GITHAE.
Minister of Public Works: CHRIS OBURE.
Minister of Transport: CHIRAU ALI MAKWERE.
Minister of Water and Irrigation: CHARITY KALUKI NGULI.
Minister of Regional Development Authorities: FREDRICK OMULO GUMO.
Minister of Information and Communications: SAMUEL LESRON POGHISIO.
Minister of Energy: KIRAITU MURUNGI.
Minister of Lands: AGGREY JAMES ORENGO.
Minister of the Environment and Mineral Resources: JOHN MICHUKI.
Minister of Forestry and Wildlife: NOAH WEKESA.
Minister of Tourism: MOHAMED NAJIB BALALA.
Minister of Agriculture: WILLIAM SAMOEI RUTO.
Minister of Livestock Development: MOHAMED ABDI KUTI.
Minister of Fisheries Development: PAUL NYONGESA OTUOMA.
Minister of the Development of Northern Kenya and Other Arid Lands: IBRAHIM ELMI MOHAMED.
Minister of Co-operatives Development: JOSEPH NYAGAH.
Minister of Industrialization: HENRY KIPRONO KOSGEY.
Minister of Housing: PETER SOITA SHITANDA.
Minister of Special Programmes: Dr NAOMI NAMSI SHABANI.
Minister of Gender and Children Affairs: ESTHER MURUGI MATHENGE.
Minister of Public Health and Sanitation: BETH WAMBUI MUGO.
Minister of Medical Services: Prof. PETER ANYANG' NYONG'O.
Minister of Labour: JOHN KIONGA MUNYES.
Minister of Youth and Sports: Dr HELEN JEPKEMOI SAMBILI.
Minister of Education: SAMSON KEGEO ONGERI.
Minister of Higher Education, Science and Technology: Dr SALLY JEPNGETICH KOSGEY.
Minister of Roads: FRANKLIN BETT.
Minister of Trade: AMOS KIMUNYA.
Ministers of State in the Office of the President: Prof. GEORGE SAITOTI (Provincial Administration and Internal Security), YUSUF MOHAMED HAJI (Defence).
Ministers of State in the Office of the Vice-President: GERALD OTIENO KAJWANG' (Immigration and Registration of Persons), WILLIAM OLE NTIMAMA (National Heritage and Culture).
Ministers of State in the Office of the Prime Minister: WYCLIFFE AMBETSA OPARANYA (Planning, National Development and Vision 2030), DALMAS ANYANGO OTIENO (Public Service).
Attorney-General: AMOS WAKO.

MINISTRIES

Office of the President: Harambee House, Harambee Ave, POB 30510, Nairobi; tel. (20) 227411; internet www.officeofthepresident.go.ke.
Office of the Vice-President and Ministry of Home Affairs: Jogoo House 'A', Taifa Rd, POB 30478, Nairobi; tel. (20) 228411; internet www.homeaffairs.go.ke.
Office of the Prime Minister: Treasury Bldg, 14th Floor, POB 74434, Harambee Ave, Nairobi; tel. (20) 252299; e-mail info@primeminister.go.ke; internet www.primeminister.go.ke.
Office of the Deputy Prime Minister and Ministry of Local Government: Jogoo House 'A', Taifa Rd, POB 30004, Nairobi; tel. (20) 217475; internet www.localgovernment.go.ke.
Office of the Deputy Prime Minister and Ministry of Trade: Teleposta Towers, Kenyatta Ave, POB 30430, Nairobi; tel. (20) 315001; fax (20) 248722; e-mail info@trade.go.ke; internet www.trade.go.ke.
Ministry of Agriculture: Kilimo House, Cathedral Rd, POB 30028, Nairobi; tel. (20) 718870; fax (20) 720586; internet www.agriculture.go.ke.
Ministry of Co-operatives Development: Social Security House (NSSF) Bldg, Eastern Wing of Block 'A', POB 30547, 00100, Nairobi; tel. (20) 2731531; internet www.co-operative.go.ke.
Ministry of the Development of Northern Kenya and Other Arid Lands: Nairobi.
Ministry of the East African Community: Co-operative House, 16th Floor, Haile Sellasie Ave, POB 8846-00200, Nairobi; tel. (20) 2245741; fax (20) 2229650; e-mail ps@meac.go.ke; internet www.meac.go.ke.
Ministry of Education: Jogoo House 'B', Harambee Ave, POB 30040, Nairobi; tel. (20) 318581; e-mail info@education.go.ke; internet www.education.go.ke.
Ministry of Energy: Nyayo House, Kenyatta Ave, POB 30582, 00100 Nairobi; tel. (20) 310112; fax (20) 228314; internet www.energy.go.ke.
Ministry of the Environment and Natural Resources: NHIF Bldg, Ragati Rd, POB 30126, Nairobi; tel. (20) 2730808; fax (20) 2710015; e-mail mec@nbnet.co.ke; internet www.environment.go.ke.
Ministry of Finance: Treasury Bldg, Harambee Ave, POB 30007, Nairobi; tel. (20) 252299; fax (20) 310833; e-mail info@treasury.go.ke; internet www.treasury.go.ke.
Ministry of Fisheries Development: Nairobi.
Ministry of Foreign Affairs: Old Treasury Bldg, Harambee Ave, POB 30551, Nairobi; tel. (20) 318888; e-mail mfapress@nbnet.co.ke; internet www.mfa.go.ke.
Ministry of Forestry and Wildlife: Utalii House, off Uhuru Highway, POB 30027, Nairobi; tel. (20) 313010.
Ministry of Gender and Children Affairs: NSSF Bldg, Block 'A', Eastern Wing, POB 16936, 00100 Nairobi; tel. (20) 2727980; fax (20) 2734417; internet www.gender.go.ke.
Ministry of Higher Education, Science and Technology: Jogoo House 'B', Harambee Ave, POB 30040, Nairobi; tel. (20) 318581; e-mail info@education.go.ke; internet www.education.go.ke.
Ministry of Housing: Ardhi House, Ngong Rd, POB 31119, 00100 Nairobi; tel. (20) 2710451; fax (20) 2721248; e-mail pro@housing.go.ke; internet www.housing.go.ke.
Ministry of Industrialization: GPO 23rd Floor, Teleposta Towers, POB 30418, 00100 Nairobi; tel. (20) 315001; e-mail info@industrialization.go.ke; internet www.tradeandindustry.go.ke.
Ministry of Information and Communications: Teleposta Towers, Kenyatta Ave, POB 30025, Nairobi; tel. (20) 251152; fax (20) 315147; internet www.information.go.ke.
Ministry of Justice, National Cohesion and Constitutional Affairs: Cooperative Bank House, Haile Selassie Ave, POB 56057-00200, Nairobi; tel. (20) 224029; e-mail ps-justice@justice.go.ke; internet www.justice.go.ke.
Ministry of Labour: Social Security House, Block 'C', Bishop Rd, POB 40326, Nairobi; tel. (20) 2729800; fax (20) 2726497; internet www.labour.go.ke.
Ministry of Lands: Ardhi House, Ngong Rd, POB 30450, 00100 Nairobi; tel. (20) 2718050; fax (20) 2724470; e-mail pslands@wananchi.com; internet www.ardhi.go.ke.
Ministry of Livestock Development: Kilimo House, Cathedral Rd, POB 34188, 00100 Nairobi; tel. (20) 2718870; fax (20) 2711149; internet www.livestock.go.ke.
Ministry of Medical Services: Afya House, Cathedral Rd, POB 30016, Nairobi; tel. (20) 717077; e-mail enquiries@health.go.ke; internet www.health.go.ke.
Ministry of Nairobi Metropolitan Development: Nairobi; internet www.nairobimetro.go.ke.
Ministry of Public Health and Sanitation: Medical HQ, Afya House, Cathedral Rd, POB 30016, Nairobi; tel. (20) 2717077; fax (20) 2725902; e-mail enquiries@health.go.ke; internet www.health.go.ke.
Ministry of Public Works: Ministry of Works Bldg, Ngong Rd, POB 30260, Nairobi; tel. (20) 2723101; e-mail info@publiworks.go.ke; internet www.works.go.ke.
Ministry of Regional Development Authorities: NSSF Bldg, 21st Floor, Eastern Wing, POB 10280, 00100 Nairobi; tel. (20) 2724646; fax 2737693; e-mail psmrd@regional-dev.go.ke; internet www.regional-dev.go.ke.
Ministry of Roads: Ministry of Works Bldg, Ngong Rd, POB 30260, Nairobi; tel. (20) 2723101; fax (20) 720044; internet www.publicworks.go.ke.

KENYA

Ministry of Special Programmes: Comcraft House, 5th Floor, Haile Selasie Ave, POB 40213, 00100 Nairobi; tel. (20) 247880; fax (20) 227622; e-mail info@sprogrammes.go.ke; internet www.sprogrammes.go.ke.

Ministry of Tourism: Utalii House, off Uhuru Highway, POB 30027, Nairobi; tel. (20) 313010; internet www.tourism.go.ke.

Ministry of Transport: Transcom House, Ngong Rd, POB 52692, Nairobi; tel. (20) 2729200; e-mail motc@insightkenya.com; internet www.transport.go.ke.

Ministry of Water: Maji House, Ngong Rd, POB 49720, 00100 Nairobi; tel. (20) 2716103; fax (20) 2727622; e-mail pro@water.go.ke; internet www.water.go.ke.

Ministry of Youth and Sports: Nairobi.

President and Legislature

PRESIDENT

Election, 27 December 2007*

Candidate	Votes
Mwai Kibaki (PNU)	4,584,721
Raila Odinga (ODM)	4,352,993
Stephen Kalonzo Musyoka (ODM—Kenya)	879,903
Others	59,411†

* Results released by the Office of the Government Spokesperson. The figure for the total number of votes cast at the election was not immediately made available.
† There were six other candidates.

NATIONAL ASSEMBLY

Speaker: KENNETH OTIATO MARENDE.

General Election, 27 December 2007

Party	Seats
ODM	99
PNU	43
ODM—Kenya	16
KANU	14
Safina	5
NARC—Kenya	4
FORD—People	3
NARC	3
New FORD—Kenya	2
CCU	2
PICK	2
DP	2
SKS	2
Others	10
Vacant	3*
Total	**210†**

* Results in three constituencies were not immediately made available and a further two seats were made vacant with the deaths of members of the National Assembly. Following by-elections in five constituencies held on 11 June 2008, the ODM held 102 seats, while the PNU held 45. All other part representations remained unchanged.
† In addition to the 210 directly elected seats, 12 are held by nominees. The Attorney-General and the Speaker are, ex officio, members of the National Assembly.

Election Commission

Interim Independent Electoral Commission (IIEC): Nairobi; f. 2009 to replace Electoral Commission of Kenya which was disbanded following disputed elections in 2007; independent.

Political Organizations

Chama Cha Uma (CCU): Nairobi; Leader DAVID NG'ETHE.

Dawa Ya Wakenya (Remedy for Kenya): f. 2007 by politicians from the North-Eastern region and the north of the Rift Valley to defend the rights of the inhabitants of those areas and to campaign for improved infrastructure, social services and security; Chair. HASSAN HAJI; Gen. Sec. MORU SHAMBARU.

Democratic Party of Kenya (DP): Gitanga Rd, POB 53695, 00200 Nairobi; tel. and fax (20) 3873595; e-mail info@democraticparty.co.ke; internet www.democraticparty.co.ke; f. 1991; Sec. (vacant); rival faction led by NGENGI MUIGAI.

Forum for the Restoration of Democracy—Asili (FORD—Asili): Anyany Estate, POB 72595, Nairobi; f. 1992; Chair. GEORGE NTHENGE; Sec. MARTIN J. SHIKUKU.

Forum for the Restoration of Democracy—Kenya (FORD—Kenya): Odinga House, POB 57449, Nairobi; tel. (20) 570361; internet www.fordkenya.com; f. 1992; predominantly Luo support; Chair. MUSIKARI KOMBO.

Forum for the Restoration of Democracy for the People (FORD—People): Nairobi; f. 1997 by fmr mems of FORD—Asili; Leader SIMEON NYACHAE.

Growth and Development Party of Kenya (GDP): Nairobi; e-mail info@gdp.co.ke; internet www.gdp.co.ke; f. 2007; Chair. AURELIO REBELO.

Kenya African National Union (KANU): KICC POB 72394, Nairobi; tel. (20) 332383; internet www.kanuonline.com; f. 1960 as KANU; sole legal party 1982–91; absorbed the National Development Party (f. 1994) in 2002; Chair. UHURU KENYATTA.

Kenya National Congress (KNC): POB 9474, Nairobi; f. 1992; Chair. Prof. KATANA MKANGI; Sec.-Gen. ONESMUS MUSYOKA MBALI.

Kenya National Democratic Alliance (KENDA): Wetithe House, Nkrumah St, POB 1851, Thika; tel. (151) 562304; f. 1991; Chair. KAMLESH PATTNI (acting); Sec.-Gen. BERNARD KALOVE.

Kenya Social Congress (KSC): POB 55318, Nairobi; f. 1992; Chair. GEORGE MOSETI ANYONA; Sec.-Gen. KASHINI MALOBA FAFNA.

Labour Party Democracy: POB 7905, Nairobi; Chair. GEOFFREY MBURU; Sec. DAVID MBURI NGACHURA.

Liberal Democratic Party (LDP): Nairobi; f. 2002 by fmr mems of KANU; Chair. DAVID MUSHA; Sec.-Gen. J. J. KAMOTHO.

Liberal Party: Chair. WANGARI MAATHAI.

Mazingira Party of Kenya (MPK): f. 2007; campaigns for the equitable sharing of wealth, sustainable use of natural resources, women's rights and the defence of Kenyan cultural values; Leader WANGARI MAATHAI; Chair. MWANGI MAKANGA.

National Party of Kenya (NPK): Nairobi; internet nationalpartyofkenya.org; f. 1992; Chair. CHARITY KALUKI NGILU; Sec.-Gen. FIDELIS MWEKE.

National Rainbow Coalition (NARC): Mwenge House, Ole Odume Rd, off Gitanga Rd and near Methodist Guest House, Nairobi; tel. (20) 571506; f. 2002; Chair. CHARITY NGILU KALUKI.

National Rainbow Coalition—Kenya (NARC—Kenya): Woodland Rd, off Lenana Rd. Kilimani; POB 34200-00100, Nairobi; tel. (20) 2726783; fax (20) 2726786; e-mail info@narckenya.co.ke; internet www.narckenya.or.ke; f. 2005 by former mems of NARC; Chair. MARTHA KARUA; Sec.-Gen. Dr MUKHISA KITUYI.

New FORD—Kenya: Nairobi; f. 2007; Chair. SOITA SHITANDA.

New Kenya African National Union (New—KANU): Nairobi; f. 2006 by former members of KANU; Pres. NICHOLAS BIWOTT.

Orange Democratic Movement (ODM): POB 2478, 00202 Nairobi; tel. (720) 360934; e-mail info@odm07.com; internet www.odm07.com; f. 2005; split in August 2007; rival faction led by STEPHEN KALONZO MUSYOKA; Leader RAILA AMOLO ODINGA.

Orange Democratic Movement—Kenya (ODM—Kenya): Nairobi; e-mail odmk2007@yahoo.com; internet odmk.org; f. 2007 following split in the ODM; Leader STEPHEN KALONZO MUSYOKA.

Party of Independent Candidates of Kenya (PICK): Plot No 299/096 Kenyatta Ave, POB 21821, Nairobi; Chair. G. N. MUSYIMI; Sec. F. NGUGI.

Party of National Unity (PNU): Nairobi; internet www.pnuparty.com; f. 2007; coalition of 14 parties including: KANU, the SPK, the SKS, Safina, NARC—Kenya, the DP, New FORD—Kenya, FORD—People, FORD—Asili, FORD—Kenya and the MPK; Chair. MWAI KIBAKI.

Patriotic Pastoralist Alliance of Kenya: f. 1997; represents the interests of northern Kenyan pastoralist communities; Leaders KHALIF ABDULLAHI, IBRAHIM WOCHE, JACKSON LAISAGOR.

People's Alliance for Change in Kenya (PACK): Nairobi; f. 1999; aims to unite diverse ethnic groups; Sec.-Gen. OLANG SANA.

Safina ('Noah's Ark'): POB 135, Nairobi; f. 1995; aims to combat corruption and human rights abuses and to introduce proportional representation; Chair. PAUL MUITE.

Shirikisho Party of Kenya (SPK): POB 70421, Nairobi; f. 1997; Sec.-Gen. YUSUF MAHMOUD ABOUBAKAR.

Sisi Kwa Sisi (SKS): Nairobi; f. 2001; Sec.-Gen. JULIUS MWANGI.

Social Democratic Party of Kenya (SDP): POB 55845, Nairobi; tel. (20) 260309; f. 1992; Chair. JUSTUS NYAGAYA; Sec.-Gen. Dr APOLLO LUGANO NJONJO.

United Agri Party of Kenya: f. 2001; Chair. GEORGE KINYUA; Sec.-Gen. SIMON MITOBIO.

KENYA

United Democratic Movement: Nairobi; Chair. KIPRUTO RONO ARAP KIRWA; Sec.-Gen. STEPHEN TARUS.

United Patriotic Party of Kenya: POB 115, Athi River; Chair. JOSEPHAT GATHUA GATHIGA; Sec. MICHAEL NJUGUNA KIGANYA.

The following organizations are banned:

February Eighteen Resistance Army: believed to operate from Uganda; Leader Brig. JOHN ODONGO (also known as STEPHEN AMOKE).

Islamic Party of Kenya (IPK): Mombasa; f. 1992; Islamic fundamentalist; Chair. Sheikh KHALIFA MUHAMMAD (acting); Sec.-Gen. ABDULRAHMAN WANDATI.

Diplomatic Representation

EMBASSIES AND HIGH COMMISSIONS IN KENYA

Algeria: 37 Muthaiga Rd, POB 53902, Nairobi; tel. (20) 310440; fax (20) 310450; e-mail algerianembassy@wananchi.com; Ambassador ALI BENZERGA.

Argentina: Posta Sacco, 6th Floor, University Way, POB 30283, 00100 Nairobi; tel. (20) 339949; fax (20) 217693; e-mail argentina@form-net.com; Ambassador DANIEL CHUBURU.

Australia: ICIPE House, Riverside Dr., off Chiromo Rd, POB 39341, Nairobi; tel. (20) 4445034; fax (20) 4444718; e-mail australian.hc.kenya@dfat.gov.au; internet www.kenya.embassy.gov.au; High Commissioner LISA FILIPETTO.

Austria: City House, 2nd Floor, Wabera St, POB 30560, 00100 Nairobi; tel. (20) 319076; fax (20) 342290; e-mail nairobi-ob@bmeia.gv.at; internet www.aussenministerium.at/nairobi; Ambassador ROLAND HAUSER.

Bangladesh: Lenana Rd, POB 41645, Nairobi; tel. (20) 8562816; fax (20) 8562817; High Commissioner A. K. M. SHAMSUDDIN.

Belgium: Muthaiga, Limuru Rd, POB 30461, Nairobi; tel. (20) 7122011; fax (20) 7123050; e-mail nairobi@diplobel.fed.be; internet www.diplomatie.be/nairobi; Ambassador LEO WILLEMS.

Brazil: Tanar Center, UN Crescent Rd, UN Close, Gigiri, Nairobi; tel. (20) 7125765; fax (20) 7125767; Ambassador JOAQUIM AUGUSTO WHITAKER SALLES.

Burundi: Coop Trust Plaza, Upper Hill, off Bunyala Rd, POB 61165, 00200 Nairobi; tel. (20) 2719200; fax (20) 2719211; e-mail embunai@yahoo.fr; Ambassador SALVATOR NTACOBAMAZE.

Canada: Limuru Rd, POB 1013, 00621 Gigiri, Nairobi; tel. (20) 3663000; fax (20) 3663900; e-mail nrobi@international.gc.ca; High Commissioner ROSS HYNES.

Chile: Riverside Dr. 66, Riverside, POB 45554, 00100 Nairobi; tel. (20) 4452950; fax (20) 4443209; e-mail echile@echile.co.ke; Ambassador GAETE VIDAL PABLO RODRIGO.

China, People's Republic: Woodlands Rd, Kilimani District, POB 30508, Nairobi; tel. (20) 2722559; fax (20) 2726402; e-mail chinaemb_ke@mfa.gov.cn; internet ke.china-embassy.org; Ambassador ZHANG MING.

Colombia: International House, 6th Floor, Mam Ngina St, POB 48494, 00100 Nairobi; tel. (20) 246770; fax (20) 246771; e-mail enairobi@cancilleria.gov.co; Ambassador MARÍA VICTORIA DÍAZ DE SUÁREZ.

Congo, Democratic Republic: Electricity House, Harambee Ave, POB 48106, 00100 Nairobi; tel. (20) 2229772; fax (20) 3754253; e-mail ambardckenyal@yahoo.com; Ambassador TADUMI ON'OKOKO.

Cuba: International House, Mama Ngina St, 13th Floor, POB 41931, Nairobi; tel. (20) 241003; fax (20) 241023; e-mail embacuba@swiftkenya.com; Ambassador JULIO CÉSAR GONZÁLEZ MARCHANTE.

Cyprus: Eagle House, 5th Floor, Kimathi St, POB 30739, 00100 Nairobi; tel. (20) 220881; fax (20) 312202; e-mail cyphc@nbnet.co.ke; High Commissioner VASSOS CHAMBERLEN.

Czech Republic: Jumia Pl., Lenana Rd, POB 48785, 00100 Nairobi; tel. (20) 2731010; fax (20) 2731013; e-mail nairobi@embassy.mzv.cz; internet www.mzv.cz/nairobi; Ambassador MARGITA FUCHSOVÁ.

Denmark: 13 Runda Dr., Runda, POB 40412, 00100 Nairobi; tel. (20) 7122848; fax (20) 7120638; e-mail nboamb@um.dk; internet www.ambnairobi.um.dk; Ambassador BO JENSEN.

Djibouti: Comcraft House, 2nd Floor, Haile Selassie Ave, POB 59528, Nairobi; tel. (20) 339640; Ambassador ADEN HOUSSEIN ABDILLAHI.

Egypt: Kingara Rd, Lavington, POB 30285, Nairobi; tel. (20) 570360; fax (20) 570383; Ambassador SAHER HASANEEN TAWFEEK HAMZA.

Eritrea: New Rehema House, 2nd Floor, Westlands, POB 38651, Nairobi; tel. (20) 443164; fax (20) 443165; e-mail eriembk@africaonline.co.ke; Ambassador SALIH OMAR ABDU.

Ethiopia: State House Ave, POB 45198, Nairobi; tel. and fax (20) 2732054; Ambassador DISSASA DIRBISSA WINSA.

Finland: International House, 2nd Floor, Mama Ngina St, POB 30379, 00100 Nairobi; tel. (20) 3750721; fax (20) 3750714; e-mail sanomat.nai@formin.fi; internet www.finland.or.ke; Ambassador HELI SIRVE.

France: Barclays Plaza, 9th Floor, Loita St, POB 41784, Nairobi; tel. (20) 2778000; fax (20) 2778180; e-mail ambafrance.nairobi@diplomatie.gouv.fr; internet www.ambafrance-ke.org; Ambassador ELIZABETH BARBIER.

Germany: Ludwig Krapf House, Riverside Dr. 113, POB 30180, Nairobi; tel. (20) 4262100; fax (20) 4262129; e-mail info@nairobi.diplo.de; internet www.nairobi.diplo.de; Ambassador WALTER JOHANNES LINDNER.

Greece: Nation Centre, 13th Floor, Kimathi St, POB 30543, Nairobi; tel. (20) 340722; fax (20) 216044; e-mail gremb.nai@mfa.gr; Ambassador POLYDOROS KOKONAS.

Holy See: Apostolic Nunciature, Manyani Rd West, Waiyaki Way, POB 14326, 00800 Nairobi; tel. (20) 4442975; fax (20) 4446789; e-mail nunciokenya@nunciokenya.org; Apostolic Nuncio Most Rev. ALAIN PAUL CHARLES LEBEAUPIN (Titular Archbishop of Vico Equense).

Hungary: Kabarsiran Ave, off James Gichuru Rd, Lavington, POB 61146, Nairobi; tel. (20) 560060; fax (20) 560114; e-mail mission.nai@kum.hu; internet www.mfa.gov.hu/kulkepviselet/KE/en/; Ambassador SÁNDOR JUHÁSZ.

India: Jeevan Bharati Bldg, 2nd Floor, Harambee Ave, POB 30074, Nairobi; tel. (20) 225104; fax (20) 316242; e-mail hcindia@kenyaweb.com; internet www.hcinairobi.co.ke; High Commissioner PARAMPREET SINGH RANDHAWA.

Indonesia: Menengai Rd, Upper Hill, POB 48868, Nairobi; tel. (20) 2714196; fax (20) 2713475; e-mail indonbi@indonesia.or.ke; internet www.indonesia.or.ke; Ambassador BUDI BOWOLEKSONO.

Iran: Dennis Pritt Rd, POB 49170, Nairobi; tel. (20) 711257; fax (20) 339936; Ambassador Dr SEYED ALI SHARIFI SADATI.

Israel: Bishop's Rd, POB 30354, Nairobi; tel. (20) 2722182; fax (20) 2715966; e-mail info@nairobi.mfa.gov.il; internet nairobi.mfa.gov.il; Ambassador JACOB KEIDAR.

Italy: International House, 9th Floor, Mama Ngina St, POB 30107, Nairobi; tel. (20) 247750; fax (20) 247086; e-mail ambasciata.nairobi@esteri.it; internet www.ambnairobi.esteri.it; Ambassador PIERANDREA MAGISTRATI.

Japan: Mara Rd, Upper Hill, POB 60202, Nairobi; tel. (20) 2898000; fax (20) 2898220; e-mail jinfocul@eojkenya.org; internet www.ke.emb-japan.go.jp; Ambassador SHIGEO IWATANI.

Korea, Republic: Anniversary Towers, 15th Floor, University Way, POB 30455-00100, Nairobi; tel. (20) 2220000; fax (20) 2217772; e-mail emb-ke@mofat.go.kr; internet ken.mofat.go.kr; Ambassador LEE HAN-GON.

Kuwait: Muthaiga Rd, POB 42353, Nairobi; tel. (20) 761614; fax (20) 762837; Chargé d'affaires a.i. JABER SALEM HUSSAIN EBRAHEEM.

Mexico: Kibagare Way, off Loresho Ridge, POB 14145, Nairobi; tel. (20) 4182593; fax (20) 4181500; e-mail mexico@embamex.co.ke; internet www.sre.gob.mx/kenia; Ambassador JUAN CARLOS CUÉ VEGA.

Morocco: Diamond Trust House, 3rd Floor, Moi Ave, POB 61098, Nairobi; tel. (20) 710647; fax (20) 222364; e-mail sifmanbi@clubinternetk.com; Ambassador ABDELILAH BENRYANE.

Mozambique: Bruce House, 3rd Floor, Standard St, POB 66923, Nairobi; tel. (20) 221979; fax (20) 222446; e-mail embamoc.quenia@minec.gov.mz; High Commissioner MARCOS NAMACHULUA; (temporarily closed in January 2008).

Netherlands: Riverside Lane, off Riverside Dr., POB 41537, Nairobi; tel. (20) 4288000; fax (20) 4447416; e-mail nlgovnai@africaonline.co.ke; internet kenia.nlambassade.org; Ambassador LAETITIA VAN DEN ASSUM.

Nigeria: Lenana Rd, Hurlingham, POB 30516, Nairobi; tel. (20) 6750310; fax (20) 3874309; e-mail ng@nigeriahighcom.org; High Commissioner CHIJIOKE WILCOX WIGWE.

Norway: Lion Pl., 1st Floor, Wayiaki Way, POB 46363, 00100 Nairobi; tel. (20) 4251000; fax (20) 4451517; e-mail emb.nairobi@mfa.no; internet www.norway.or.ke; Ambassador ELISABETH JACOBSEN.

Pakistan: St Michel Rd, Westlands Ave, POB 30045, 00100 Nairobi; tel. (20) 4443911; fax (20) 4446507; e-mail parepnairobi@iwayafrica.com; internet www.pakistanafrica.org; High Commissioner IFTIKHAR A. ARIAN.

Poland: Kabarnet Rd, off Ngong Rd, Woodley, POB 30086, 00100 Nairobi; tel. (20) 3872811; fax (20) 3872814; e-mail ambnairo@kenyaweb.com; internet www.nairobi.polemb.net; Ambassador WOJCIECH JASINSKI.

Portugal: Reinsurance Plaza, 10th Floor, Aga Khan Walk, POB 34020, 00100 Nairobi; tel. (20) 313203; fax (20) 214711; e-mail embassy.nairobi@portugal.co.ke; Ambassador LUIS LORUÁO.

Romania: Gardenia Rd, Gigiri, POB 63240, Nairobi; tel. (20) 7123109; fax (20) 7122061; e-mail secretariat@romanianembassy.co.ke; Ambassador MIHAIL CONSTANTIN COMAN.

Russia: Lenana Rd, POB 30049, Nairobi; tel. (20) 728700; fax (20) 721888; e-mail russemb@swiftkenya.com; Ambassador VALERY YEGOSHKIN.

Rwanda: International House, 12th Floor, Mama Ngina St, POB 48579, Nairobi; tel. (20) 560178; fax (20) 561932; Ambassador GEORGE WILLIAM KAYONGA.

Saudi Arabia: Muthaiga Rd, POB 58297, Nairobi; tel. (20) 762781; fax (20) 760939; Ambassador NBEEL KHALAF A. ASHOUR.

Slovakia: Milimani Rd, POB 30204, Nairobi; tel. (20) 721896; fax (20) 721898; Ambassador STEFAN MORAVEK.

Somalia: POB 30769, Nairobi; tel. (20) 580165; fax (20) 581683; Ambassador MOHAMMED ALI NUR.

South Africa: Roshanmaer Place, Lenana Rd, POB 42441, Nairobi; tel. (20) 2827100; fax (20) 2827219; e-mail nairobi@foreign.gov.za; High Commissioner TONY MSIMANGA.

Spain: CBA Bldg, Mara and Ragati Rds, Upper Hill, POB 45503, 00100 Nairobi; tel. (20) 2720222; fax (20) 2720226; e-mail emb.nairobi@maec.es; Ambassador NICOLÁS MARTÍN CINTO.

Sri Lanka: Lenana Rd, POB 48145 GPO, Nairobi; tel. (20) 572627; fax (20) 572141; e-mail slhckeny@africaonline.co.ke; High Commissioner HABEEB MOHAMMED FAROOK.

Sudan: Kabarnet Rd, off Ngong Rd, POB 48784, Nairobi; tel. (20) 720853; fax (20) 721015; Ambassador MAJOK GUANDONG.

Swaziland: Transnational Plaza, 3rd Floor, Mama Ngina St, POB 41887, Nairobi; tel. (20) 339231; fax (20) 330540; High Commissioner Prince SOLOMON MBILINI N. DLAMINI.

Sweden: Lion Pl., 3rd Floor, Waiyaki Way, Westlands, POB 30600, 00100 Nairobi; tel. (20) 4234000; fax (20) 4452008; e-mail ambassaden.nairobi@foreign.ministry.se; internet www.swedenabroad.com/nairobi; Ambassador ANNA BRANDT.

Switzerland: International House, 7th Floor, Mama Ngina St, POB 30752, Nairobi; tel. (20) 228735; fax (20) 217388; e-mail nai.vertretung@eda.admin.ch; Ambassador MARTIN GEORGES.

Tanzania: Continental House, Uhuru Highway, POB 47790, Nairobi; tel. (20) 331056; fax (20) 218269; e-mail tanzania@user.africaonline.co.ke; High Commissioner Maj.-Gen. MIRISHO SAM HAGGAI SARAKIKYA.

Thailand: Ambassador House, Rose Ave, POB 58349, Nairobi; tel. (20) 2715243; fax (20) 2715801; e-mail thainbi@thainbi.or.ke; internet www.thaiembassy.org/nairobi; Ambassador APICHIT ASATTHAWASI.

Turkey: Gigiri Rd, off Limuru Rd, POB 64748, 00620 Nairobi; tel. and fax (20) 7126929; fax (20) 7126931; e-mail tcbenair@accesskenya.co.ke; internet www.nairobi.emb.mfa.gov.tr; Ambassador LEVENT ŞAHINKAYA.

Uganda: Uganda House, 5th Floor, Kenyatta Ave, POB 60853, Nairobi; tel. (20) 4449096; fax (20) 4443772; High Commissioner Brig. (retd) MATAYO KYALIGONZA.

United Kingdom: Upper Hill Rd, POB 30465, 00100 Nairobi; tel. (20) 2844000; fax (20) 2844033; e-mail bhcinfo@jambo.co.ke; internet www.britishhighcommission.gov.uk/kenya; High Commissioner ROBERT NIGEL PAUL MACAIRE.

USA: United Nations Ave, POB 606, Village Market, 00621 Nairobi; tel. (20) 3636000; fax (20) 537810; e-mail ircnairobi@state.gov; internet nairobi.usembassy.gov; Ambassador MICHAEL E. RANNEBERGER.

Venezuela: Ngong/Kabarnet Rd, POB 34477, Nairobi; tel. (20) 574646; fax (20) 337487; e-mail embavene@africaonline.co.ke; Ambassador MARÍA JACQUELINE MENDOZA.

Yemen: cnr Ngong and Kabarnet Rds, POB 44642, Nairobi; tel. (20) 564379; fax (20) 564394; Ambassador AHMAD MAYSARI.

Zambia: Nyerere Rd, POB 48741, Nairobi; tel. (20) 724850; fax (20) 718494; High Commissioner ENESS CHISHALA CHIYENGE.

Zimbabwe: Minet-ICDC Bldg, 6th Floor, Mamlaka Rd, POB 30806, Nairobi; tel. (20) 721071; fax (20) 726503; Ambassador KELEBERT NKOMANI.

Judicial System

The Kenya Court of Appeal

POB 30187, Nairobi.

The final court of appeal for Kenya in civil and criminal process; sits at Nairobi, Mombasa, Kisumu, Nakuru and Nyeri.

Chief Justice: JOHNSON EVANS GICHERU.

Justices of Appeal: E. O. KUBASU, R. S. C. OMOLO, S. E. O. BOSIRE, D. K. AGANYANYA, J. W. ONYANGO OTIENO, EFFIE OWUOR, J. ALUOCH, E.M. GITHINJI, MOIJO M. OLE KEIWUA, PHILIP WAKI, ALNASHIR RAMAZANALI MAGAN VISRAM, JOSEPH GREGORY NYAMU.

The High Court of Kenya: Between Taifa Rd and City Hall Way, POB 30041, Nairobi; tel. (20) 221221; e-mail hck-lib@nbnet.co.ke; has unlimited criminal and civil jurisdiction at first instance, and sits as a court of appeal from subordinate courts in both criminal and civil cases. The High Court is also a court of admiralty. There are three resident puisne judges at Mombasa and at Nakuru, two resident puisne judge at Eldoret, Kisumu and Meru and one resident puisne judge at Bungoma, Embu, Kakamega, Kissi, Kitale, Machakos, Malindi and Nyeri.

Resident Magistrates' Courts: have country-wide jurisdiction, with powers of punishment by imprisonment for up to five years or by fines of up to K£500. If presided over by a chief magistrate or senior resident magistrate the court is empowered to pass any sentence authorized by law. For certain offences, a resident magistrate may pass minimum sentences authorized by law.

District Magistrates' Courts: of first, second and third class; have jurisdiction within districts and powers of punishment by imprisonment for up to five years, or by fines of up to K£500.

Kadhi's Courts: have jurisdiction within districts, to determine questions of Islamic law.

Religion

According to official government figures, Protestants, the largest religious group, represent approximately 38% of the population. Approximately 25% of the population is Roman Catholic, 7% of the population practices Islam, 1% practices Hinduism and the remainder follows various traditional indigenous religions or offshoots of Christian religions. There are very few atheists. Muslim groups dispute government estimates; most often they claim to represent 15% to 20% of the population, sometimes higher. Members of most religious groups are active throughout the country, although certain religions dominate particular regions. Muslims dominate North-Eastern Province, where the population is chiefly Somali. Muslims also dominate Coast Province, except for the western areas of the province, which are predominantly Christian. Eastern Province is approximately 50% Muslim (mostly in the north) and 50% Christian (mostly in the south). The rest of the country is largely Christian, with some persons following traditional indigenous religions. Many foreign missionary groups operate in the country, the largest of which are the African Inland Mission (Evangelical Protestant), the Southern Baptist Church, the Pentecostal Assembly of Kenya, and the Church Missionary Society of Britain (Anglican). The Government generally has permitted these missionary groups to assist the poor and to operate schools and hospitals. The missionaries openly promote their religious beliefs and have encountered little resistance.

CHRISTIANITY

National Council of Churches of Kenya: Jumuia Pl., POB 45009, 00100 Nairobi; tel. (20) 2711862; fax (20) 2724183; e-mail gsoffice@ncck.org; internet www.ncck.org; f. 1943 as Christian Council of Kenya; 24 mem. churches and 18 Christian orgs; Chair. Rev. JOSEPH WAITHONGA; Sec.-Gen. Rev. Canon PETER KARANJA MWANGI.

The Anglican Communion

Anglicans are adherents of the Church of the Province of Kenya, which was established in 1970. It comprises 28 dioceses, and has about 2.5m. members.

Archbishop of Kenya and Bishop of Nairobi: Most Rev. Dr DAVID M. GITARI, POB 40502, Nairobi; tel. (20) 2714755; fax (20) 2718442; e-mail davidgitari@insightkenya.com.

Greek Orthodox Church

Archbishop of East Africa: NICADEMUS OF IRINOUPOULIS, Nairobi; jurisdiction covers Kenya, Tanzania and Uganda.

The Roman Catholic Church

Kenya comprises four archdioceses, 20 dioceses and one Apostolic Vicariate. At 31 December 2006 an estimated 24.9% of the total population were adherents of the Roman Catholic Church.

Kenya Episcopal Conference

Kenya Catholic Secretariat, POB 13475, Nairobi; tel. (20) 443133; fax (20) 442910; e-mail csk@users.africaonline.co.ke; internet www.catholicchurch.or.ke.

f. 1976; Pres. Rt Rev. CORNELIUS K. ARAP KORIR (Bishop of Eldoret).

KENYA

Archbishop of Kisumu: Most Rev. ZACCHAEUS OKOTH, POB 1728, Kisumu; tel. (57) 2020725; fax (57) 2022203; e-mail archdiocese-ksm@net2000ke.com.

Archbishop of Mombasa: Most Rev. JOHN NJENGA, Catholic Secretariat, Nyerere Ave, POB 84425, Mombasa; tel. (41) 2311801; fax (41) 2228217; e-mail demsa@africaonline.co.ke.

Archbishop of Nairobi: Cardinal JOHN NJUE, Archbishop's House, POB 14231, 00800 Nairobi; tel. (20) 241391; fax (20) 4447027; e-mail nairobiprocure@wananchi.com.

Archbishop of Nyeri: Most Rev. NICODEMUS KIRIMA, POB 288, 10100 Nyeri; tel. (61) 2030446; fax (61) 2030435; e-mail adn@wananchi.com.

Other Christian Churches

Africa Gospel Church: Kericho; tel. (52) 20123; internet www.agckenya.org; Bishop Rev. Dr JOSEPH RONO.

African Christian Church and Schools: POB 1365, Thika; e-mail accsheadoffice@yahoo.com; f. 1948; Moderator Rt Rev. JOHN NJUNGUNA; Gen. Sec. Rev. SAMUEL MWANGI; 50,000 mems.

African Church of the Holy Spirit: POB 183, Kakamega; f. 1927; 20,000 mems.

African Israel Nineveh Church: Nineveh HQ, POB 701, Kisumu; f. 1942; High Priest Rt Rev. JOHN KIVULI, II; Gen. Sec. Rev. JOHN ARAP TONUI; 350,000 mems.

Baptist Convention of Kenya: POB 14907, Nairobi; Pres. Rev. ELIUD MUNGAI.

Church of God in East Africa: Pres. Rev. Dr BYRUM MAKOKHA.

Evangelical Fellowship of Kenya: Co-ordinator Rt Rev. ARTHUR GITONGA; Sec.-Gen. Dr WASHINGTON NG'ENG'I.

Evangelical Lutheran Church in Kenya: POB 44685, 00100 Nairobi; tel. and fax 38131231; e-mail bishopobarewa@yahoo.com; internet www.elckenya.org; Presiding Bishop Most Rev. WALTER OBARE OMWANZA; Gen. Sec. Rev. JOHN HALAKHE; 100,000 mems (2009).

Kenya Evangelical Lutheran Church: POB 54128, 00200 City Sq., Jogoo Rd, off Nile Rd, Nairobi; tel. and fax (20) 78-04-54; e-mail info@kelc.or.ke; internet www.kelc.or.ke; Bishop ZACHARIAH W. KAHUTHU; 44,000 mems (2009).

Methodist Church in Kenya: POB 47633, 00100 Nairobi; tel. (20) 2724828; fax (20) 2729790; e-mail mckconf@insightkenya.com; internet www.methodistchurchkenya.org; f. 1862; autonomous since 1967; Presiding Bishop Rev. Dr STEPHEN KANYARU M'IMPWII; 900,000 mems (2005).

Presbyterian Church of East Africa: POB 27573, 00506 Nairobi; tel. (20) 608848; fax (20) 609102; e-mail info@pcea.or.ke; internet www.pcea.or.ke; Moderator Rt Rev. Dr DAVID GITHII; Sec.-Gen. Rev. SAMUEL MURIGYH.

Other denominations active in Kenya include the African Brotherhood Church, the African Independent Pentecostal Church, Africa Inland Church in Kenya, the African Interior Church, the Episcopal Church of Kenya, the Free Pentecostal Fellowship of Kenya, the Full Gospel Churches of Kenya, the National Independent Church of Africa, the Pentecostal Assemblies of God, the Pentecostal Evangelistic Fellowship of God and the Reformed Church of East Africa.

BAHÁ'Í FAITH

National Spiritual Assembly: POB 47562, Nairobi; tel. (20) 725447; e-mail nsakenya@yahoo.com; mems resident in 9,654 localities.

ISLAM

Supreme Council of Kenyan Muslims (SUPKEM)

POB 45163, Nairobi; tel. and fax (20) 243109; Nat. Chair. Prof. ABD AL-GHAFUR AL-BUSAIDY; Sec.-Gen. MOHAMMED KHALIF.

Chief Kadhi: NASSOR NAHDI.

The Press

PRINCIPAL DAILIES

Daily Nation: POB 49010, Nairobi; tel. (20) 2221222; fax (20) 2337710; e-mail nation@africaonline.co.ke; internet www.nationaudio.com; f. 1960; English; owned by Nation Media Group; Editor-in-Chief WANGETHI MWANGI; Man. Editor JOSEPH ODINDO; circ. 195,000.

East African Standard: POB 30080, Nairobi; tel. (20) 2540280; fax (20) 2553939; e-mail online@eastandard.net; internet www.eastandard.net; f. 1902; Editor MUTUMA MATHIY; circ. 59,000.

Kenya Leo: POB 30958, Nairobi; tel. (20) 332390; f. 1983; Kiswahili; KANU party newspaper; Group Editor-in-Chief AMBOKA ANDERE; circ. 6,000.

Kenya Times: POB 30958, Nairobi; tel. (20) 2336611; fax (20) 2927348; internet www.timesnews.co.uk; f. 1983; evening; English; KANU party newspaper; Group Editor-in-Chief AMBOKA ANDERE; circ. 10,000.

The People: POB 10296, 00100 Nairobi; tel. (20) 2249686; fax (20) 2228503; e-mail info@people.co.ke; internet www.people.co.ke; f. 1993; Man. Editor MUGO THEURI; circ. 40,000.

Taifa Leo: POB 49010, Nairobi; tel. (20) 337691; Kiswahili; f. 1960; daily and weekly edns; owned by Nation Media Group; Editor ROBERT MWANGI; circ. 57,000.

Kenya has a thriving vernacular press, but titles are often short-lived. Newspapers in African languages include:

Kihooto (The Truth): Kikuyu; satirical.

Mwaria Ma (Honest Speaker): Nyeri; f. 1997; Publr Canon JAMLICK M. MIANO.

Mwihoko (Hope): POB 734, Muranga; f. 1997; Roman Catholic.

Nam Dar: Luo.

Otit Mach (Firefly): Luo.

SELECTED PERIODICALS

Weeklies and Fortnightlies

The Business Chronicle: POB 53328, Nairobi; tel. (20) 544283; fax (20) 532736; f. 1994; weekly; Man. Editor MUSYOKA KYENDO.

Coastweek: Oriental Bldg, 2nd Floor, Nkrumah Rd, POB 87270, Mombasa; tel. (41) 2230125; fax (41) 2225003; e-mail coastwk@africaonline.co.ke; internet www.coastweek.com; f. 1978; English, with German section; Friday; Editor ADRIAN GRIMWOOD; Man. Dir SHIRAZ D. ALIBHAI; circ. 54,000.

The East African: POB 49010, Nairobi; tel. (20) 221222; fax (20) 2213946; e-mail nation@africaonline.co.ke; internet www.nationaudio.com/news/eastafrican/current; f. 1994; weekly; English; owned by Nation Media Group; Editor-in-Chief JOE ODINDO; Man. Editor MBATAU WA NGAI.

The Herald: POB 30958, Nairobi; tel. (20) 332390; English; sponsored by KANU; Editor JOB MUTUNGI; circ. 8,000.

Kenrail: POB 30121, Nairobi; tel. (20) 2221211; fax (20) 2340049; quarterly; English and Kiswahili; publ. by Kenya Railways Corpn; Editor J. N. LUSENO; circ. 20,000.

Kenya Gazette: POB 30746, Nairobi; tel. (20) 334075; internet www.kenyalaw.org/KenyaGazette; f. 1898; official notices; weekly; circ. 8,000.

Post on Sunday: Nairobi; weekly; independent; Editor-in-Chief TONY GACHOKA.

Sunday Nation: POB 49010, Nairobi; f. 1960; English; owned by Nation Media Group; Man. Editor BERNARD NDERITU; circ. 170,000.

Sunday Standard: POB 30080, Nairobi; tel. (20) 552510; fax (20) 553939; English; Man. Editor DAVID MAKALI; circ. 90,000.

Sunday Times: POB 30958, Nairobi; tel. (20) 337798; Group Editor AMBOKA ANDERE.

Taifa Jumapili: POB 49010, Nairobi; f. 1987; Kiswahili; owned by Nation Media Group; Editor ROBERT K. MWANGI; circ. 56,000.

Taifa Weekly: POB 49010, Nairobi; tel. (20) 337691; f. 1960; Kiswahili; Editor ROBERT K. MWANGI; circ. 68,000.

Trans Nzoia Post: POB 34, Kitale; weekly.

The Weekly Review: Stellacom House, POB 42271, Nairobi; tel. (20) 2251473; fax (20) 2222555; f. 1975; English; Man. Dir JAINDI KISERO; circ. 16,000.

What's On: Rehema House, Nairobi; tel. (20) 27651; Editor NANCY KAIRO; circ. 10,000.

Monthlies

Africa Law Review: Tumaini House, 4th Floor, Nkrumah Ave, POB 53234, Nairobi; tel. (20) 330480; fax (20) 230173; e-mail alr@africalaw.org; f. 1987; English; Editor-in-Chief GITOBU IMANYARA.

East African Medical Journal: POB 41632, 00100 Nairobi; tel. (20) 2712010; fax (20) 2724617; e-mail eamj@ken.healthnet.org; English; f. 1923; Editor-in-Chief Prof. WILLIAM LORE; circ. 4,500.

East African Report on Trade and Industry: POB 30339, Nairobi; journal of Kenya Asscn of Mfrs; Editor GORDON BOY; circ. 3,000.

Executive: POB 47186, Nairobi; tel. (20) 530598; fax (20) 557815; e-mail spacesellers@wananchi.com; f. 1980; business; Publr SYLVIA KING; circ. 25,000.

KENYA

Kenya Farmer (Journal of the Agricultural Society of Kenya): c/o English Press, POB 30127, Nairobi; tel. (20) 20377; f. 1954; English and Kiswahili; Editor ROBERT IRUNGU; circ. 20,000.

Kenya Yetu: POB 8053, Nairobi; tel. (20) 250083; fax (20) 340659; f. 1965; Kiswahili; publ. by Ministry of Information and Communications; Editor M. NDAVI; circ. 10,000.

Nairobi Handbook: POB 30127, Accra Rd, Nairobi; Editor R. OUMA; circ. 20,000.

News from Kenya: POB 8053, Nairobi; tel. (20) 253083; fax (20) 340659; publ. by Ministry of Information and Communications.

PC World (East Africa): Gilgil House, Monrovia St, Nairobi; tel. (20) 246808; fax (20) 215643; f. 1996; Editor ANDREW KARANJA.

Presence: POB 10988, 00400 Nairobi; tel. (20) 577708; fax (20) 4948840; f. 1984; economics, law, women's issues, fiction.

Sparkle: POB 47186, Nairobi; tel. (20) 530598; fax (20) 557815; e-mail spacesellers@wananchi.com; f. 1990; children's; Editor ANNA NDILA NDUTO.

Today in Africa: POB 60, Kijabe; tel. (25) 64210; English; Man. Editor MWAURA NJOROGE; circ. 13,000.

Other Periodicals

African Ecclesiastical Review: POB 4002, 30100 Eldoret; tel. (53) 2061218; fax (53) 2062570; e-mail gabapubs@africaonline.co.ke; internet www.gabapublications.org; f. 1969; scripture, religion and devt; 4 a year; Editor and Dir Sister JUSTIN C. NABUSHAWO; circ. 2,500.

Afya: POB 30125, Nairobi; tel. (20) 501301; fax (20) 506112; e-mail amrefkco@africaonline.co.ke; journal for medical and health workers; quarterly.

Azania: POB 30710, 00100 Nairobi; tel. (20) 4343190; fax (20) 4343365; f. 1966; annual (Dec.); English and French; history, archaeology, ethnography and linguistics of East African region; circ. 650.

Busara: Nairobi; literary; 2 a year; Editor KIMANI GECAU; circ. 3,000.

Defender: AMREF, POB 30125, Nairobi; tel. (20) 201301; f. 1968; quarterly; English; health and fitness; Editor WILLIAM OKEDI; circ. 100,000.

East African Agricultural and Forestry Journal: POB 30148, Nairobi; f. 1935; English; quarterly; Editor J. O. MUGAH; circ. 1,000.

Eastern African Economic Review: POB 30022, Nairobi; f. 1954; 2 a year; Editor J. K. MAITHA.

Economic Review of Agriculture: POB 30028, Nairobi; tel. (20) 728370; f. 1968; publ. by Ministry of Agriculture; quarterly; last issue 1999; Editor OKIYA OKOITI.

Education in Eastern Africa: Nairobi; f. 1970; 2 a year; Editor JOHN C. B. BIGALA; circ. 2,000.

Finance: Nairobi; monthly; Editor-in-Chief NJEHU GATABAKI.

Inside Kenya Today: POB 8053, Nairobi; tel. (20) 340010; fax (20) 340659; English; publ. by Ministry of Tourism; quarterly; Editor M. NDAVI; circ. 10,000.

Kenya Education Journal: Nairobi; f. 1958; English; 3 a year; Editor W. G. BOWMAN; circ. 5,500.

Kenya Statistical Digest: POB 30007, Nairobi; tel. (20) 338111; fax (20) 330426; publ. by Ministry of Finance; quarterly.

Safari: Norwich Bldg, 4th Floor, Mama Ngina St, POB 30339, Nairobi; tel. (20) 2246612; fax (20) 2215127; 6 a year; English.

Target: POB 72839, Nairobi; f. 1964; English; 6 a year; religious; Editor FRANCIS MWANIKI; circ. 17,000.

NEWS AGENCY

Kenya News Agency (KNA): Information House, POB 8053, Nairobi; tel. (20) 223201; internet www.kenyanewsagency.go.ke; f. 1963; Dir S. MUSANDU.

Publishers

Academy Science Publishers: POB 24916, Nairobi; tel. (20) 884401; fax (20) 884406; e-mail asp@africaonline.co.ke; f. 1989; part of the African Academy of Sciences; Editor-in-Chief Prof. KETO E. MSHIGENI.

AMECEA Gaba Publications: Amecea Pastoral Institute, POB 4002, 30100 Eldoret; tel. (53) 2061218; fax (53) 2062570; e-mail gabapubs@africaonline.co.ke; internet www.gabapublications.org; f. 1958; anthropology, religious; owned by AMECEA Bishops; Editor and Dir Sister JUSTINE C. NABUSHAWO.

Camerapix Publishers International: POB 45048, GPO 00100, Nairobi; tel. (20) 4448923; fax (20) 4448818; e-mail rukhsana@camerapix.co.ke; internet www.camerapix.com; f. 1960; travel, topography, natural history; Man. Dir RUKHSANA HAQ.

East African Educational Publishers: cnr Mpaka Rd and Woodvale Grove, Westlands, POB 45314, 00100 Nairobi; tel. (20) 4444700; fax (20) 4448753; e-mail eaep@eastafricanpublishers.com; internet www.eastafricanpublishers.com; f. 1965 as Heinemann Kenya Ltd; present name adopted 1992; academic, educational, creative writing; some books in Kenyan languages; Chair. Dr HENRY CHAKAVA; Gen. Man. KIARIE KAMAU.

Evangel Publishing House: Lumumba Drive, off Kamiti Rd, Thika Rd, Private Bag 28963, 00200 Nairobi; tel. (20) 8560839; fax (20) 8562050; e-mail info@evangelpublishing.org; internet www.evangelpublishing.org; f. 1952; Christian literature; current backlist of about 300 titles; marriage and family, leadership, Theological Education by Extension (TEE); Gen. Man. BARINE A. KIRIMI.

Foundation Books: Nairobi; tel. (20) 765485; f. 1974; biography, poetry; Man. Dir F. O. OKWANYA.

Kenway Publications Ltd: POB 45314, Nairobi; tel. (20) 4444700; fax (20) 4451532; e-mail sales@eastafricanpublishers.com; internet www.eastafricanpublishers.com/kenway/defult.htm; f. 1981; general, regional interests; Chair. HENRY CHAKAVA.

Kenya Literature Bureau: Bellevue Area, Popo Rd, off Mombasa Rd, POB 30022, 00100 Nairobi; tel. (20) 600839; fax (20) 601474; e-mail customer@kenyaliteraturebureau.com; f. 1947 as East African Literature Bureau; name changed as above in 1980; educational and general books; CEO E. A. OBARA.

Jomo Kenyatta Foundation: Industrial Area, Enterprise Rd, POB 30533, 00100 Nairobi; tel. (20) 557222; fax (20) 531966; e-mail publish@jomokenyattaf.com; internet www.jkf.co.ke; f. 1966; primary, secondary, university textbooks; Man. Dir NANCY W. KARIMI.

Longman Kenya Ltd: Banda School, Magadi Rd, POB 24722, Nairobi; tel. (20) 891220; fax (20) 890004; f. 1966.

Macmillan Kenya Publishers Ltd: Judda Complex, Forest Rd, POB 30797, 00100 Nairobi; tel. (20) 6766962; fax (20) 6766963; e-mail info@macken.co.ke; f. 1970; atlases, children's educational, guide books, literature; Man. Dir DAVID MUITA.

Newspread International: POB 46854, Nairobi; tel. (20) 331402; fax (20) 607252; f. 1971; reference, economic devt; Exec. Editor KUL BHUSHAN.

Oxford University Press (Eastern Africa): Waiyaki Way, ABC Place, POB 72532, Nairobi; tel. (20) 440555; fax (20) 443972; f. 1954; children's, educational and general; Regional Man. ABDULLAH ISMAILY.

Paulines Publications Africa: POB 49026, 00100 Nairobi; tel. (20) 447202; fax (20) 442097; e-mail publications@paulinesafrica.org; internet www.paulinesafrica.org; f. 1985; African bible, theology, children's, educational, religious, psychology, audio cds, tapes, videos; Pres. Sister MARIA KIMANI; Dir Sister TERESA MARCAZZAN.

Transafrica Press: Kenwood House, Kimathi St, POB 48239, Nairobi; tel. (20) 331762; f. 1976; general, educational and children's; Man. Dir JOHN NOTTINGHAM.

GOVERNMENT PUBLISHING HOUSE

Government Printing Press: POB 30128, Nairobi; tel. (20) 317840.

PUBLISHERS' ORGANIZATION

Kenya Publishers' Association: POB 42767, 00100 Nairobi; tel. (20) 3752344; fax (20) 3754076; internet www.kenyabooks.org; f. 1971; organizes Nairobi International Book Fair each Sept; Chair. DAVID MUITA.

Broadcasting and Communications

TELECOMMUNICATIONS

Telkom Kenya Ltd: Teleposta Towers, Kenyatta Ave, POB 41951, Nairobi; tel. (20) 2221000; e-mail service@telkom.co.ke; internet www.telkom.co.ke; f. 1999; 51% owned by France Telecom; operates a national fixed telephone network; Man. Dir SAMMY KIRUI.

Safaricom Ltd: Safaricom House, Waiyaki Way, Westlands, POB 46350, Nairobi; tel. (20) 4273272; e-mail info@safaricom.co.ke; internet www.safaricom.co.ke; f. 1999; owned by Telkom Kenya Ltd and Vodafone Airtouch (UK); operates a national mobile cellular telephone network; Chair. NICHOLAS NG'ANG'A; CEO MICHAEL JOSEPH.

Zain: Parkside Towers, Mombasa Rd, Nairobi; tel. (20) 6910000; e-mail customercare.ke@zain.com; internet www.ke.zain.com; f. 2004; mobile cellular telephone network provider; fmrly Celtel; Man. Dir RENE MEZA.

Regulatory Authority

Communications Commission of Kenya (CCK): Waiyaki Way, POB 14448, 00800 Westlands, Nairobi; tel. (20) 4242000; fax (20)

4451866; e-mail info@cck.go.ke; internet www.cck.go.ke; f. 1999; Chair. JOSEPH NJAGI KAGAU; Dir-Gen. CHARLES J. K. NJOROGE.

BROADCASTING

Radio

Kenya Broadcasting Corpn (KBC): Broadcasting House, Harry Thuku Rd, POB 30456, Nairobi; tel. (20) 223757; fax (20) 220675; e-mail md@kbc.co.ke; internet www.kbc.co.ke; f. 1989; state corpn responsible for radio and television services; Chair. CHARLES MUSYOKI MUOKI; Man. Dir DAVID WAWERU.

Radio: National service (Kiswahili); General service (English); Vernacular services (Borana, Burji, Hindustani, Kalenjin, Kikamba, Kikuyu, Kimasai, Kimeru, Kisii, Kuria, Luo, Luhya, Rendile, Somali, Suba, Teso and Turkana).

Capital FM: Lonrho House, 19th Floor, City Sq., POB 74933, Nairobi; tel. (20) 2210020; fax (20) 340621; e-mail info@capitalfm.co.ke; internet www.capitalfm.co.ke; f. 1999; commercial station broadcasting to Nairobi and environs; Man. Dir LYNDA HOLT.

Citizen Radio: Ambank House, University Way, POB 45897, Nairobi; tel. (20) 249122; fax (20) 249126; commercial radio station broadcasting in Nairobi and its environs; Man. Dir S. K. MACHARIA.

Easy FM: Nation Centre, Kimathi St, POB 49010, Nairobi; tel. (20) 32088801; fax (20) 241892; e-mail info@nation.co.ke; internet www.nationmedia.com; f. 1999; commercial radio station broadcasting in English and Swahili; fmrly Nation FM; owned by Nation Media Group; Man. Dir IAN FERNANDES.

IQRA Broadcasting Network: Kilimani Rd, off Elgeyo Marakwet Rd, POB 21186, 00505 Nairobi; tel. (20) 3861542; fax (20) 4443978; e-mail iqrafm@swiftkenya.com; Islamic radio station broadcasting religious programmes in Nairobi; Man. Dir SHARIF HUSSEIN OMAR.

Kameme FM: Longonot Pl., Kijabe St, POB 49640, 00100 Nairobi; tel. (20) 2217963; fax (20) 2249781; e-mail info@kamemefm.com; internet www.kameme.co.ke; commercial radio station broadcasting in Kikuyu in Nairobi and its environs; Man. Dir ROSE KIMOTHO.

Kitambo Communications Ltd: Bishop's Tower, 4th Floor, Bishop's Rd, POB 56155, Nairobi; tel. (20) 4244000; commercial radio and television station broadcasting Christian programmes in Mombasa and Nairobi; Man. Dir Dr R. AYAH.

Radio Africa Ltd (KISS FM): 2nd Floor, Lion Pl., Waiyaki Way, POB 74497, 00200 Nairobi; tel. (20) 4244000; Man. Dir KIPRONO KITTONY.

Sauti ya Rehema RTV Network: Gulab Lochab Bldg, Oginga Oginga St, POB 4139, Eldoret; tel. (53) 2062252; Christian, broadcasts in Eldoret and its environs; Man. Dir Rev. ELI ROP.

Television

Kenya Broadcasting Corpn (KBC): see Radio

Television: KBC–TV; services in Kiswahili and English; operates three channels—KBC1, KBC2 and Metro TV.

Citizen TV: POB 45897, Nairobi; tel. (20) 249122; fax (20) 249126; commercial station broadcasting in Nairobi and its environs.

Family TV: Dik Dik Gardens, off Gatundu Rd, Kileleshwa, POB 2330, Nairobi; tel. (20) 4200000; fax (20) 4200100; e-mail info@familykenya.com; internet www.familykenya.com.

Kenya Television Network (KTN–TV): Nyayo House, 22nd Floor, POB 56985, Nairobi; tel. (20) 3222111; fax (20) 215400; e-mail news@ktnkenya.com; internet www.ktnkenya.tv; f. 1990; commercial station operating in Nairobi and Mombasa; Man. Dir D. J. DAVIES.

NTV: POB 49010, Nairobi; e-mail ntv@nation.co.ke; internet www.nationmedia.com/ntv; f. 1999 as Nation TV; commercial station; owned by Nation Media Group; Man. Dir IAN FERNANDES.

Stellagraphics TV (STV): NSSF Bldg, 22nd Floor, POB 42271, Nairobi; tel. (20) 218043; fax (20) 222555; f. 1998; commercial station broadcasting in Nairobi; Gen. Man. KANJA WARURU.

Finance

(cap. = capital; res = reserves; dep. = deposits; m. = million; brs = branches; amounts in Kenya shillings)

BANKING

Central Bank

Central Bank of Kenya (Banki Kuu Ya Kenya): City Sq., Haile Selassie Ave, POB 60000, 00200 Nairobi; tel. (20) 22863000; fax (20) 2250783; e-mail info@centralbank.go.ke; internet www.centralbank.go.ke; f. 1966; bank of issue; cap. 1,500m., res 10,145m., dep. 100,824m. (June 2006); Gov. Dr ANDREW KAVULYA MULLEI.

Commercial Banks

African Banking Corpn Ltd: ABC-Bank House, Mezzanine Floor, Koinange St, POB 46452, Nairobi; tel. (20) 2223922; fax (20) 2222437; e-mail headoffice@abcthebank.com; internet www.abcthebank.com; f. 1984 as Consolidated Finance Co; converted to commercial bank and adopted present name 1995; cap. 350.0m., res 6.8m., dep. 4,451.5m. (Dec. 2006); CEO SHAMAZ SAVANI; 7 brs.

Bank of Africa—Kenya: POB 69562, Re-Insurance Plaza, Taifa Rd, 00400 Nairobi; tel. (20) 3275000; fax (20) 2214166; e-mail bkofkenya@boakenya.com; internet www.boakenya.com; f. 2004; cap. 750.0m., res 69.4m., dep. 5,345.7m. (Dec. 2006); Chair. PAUL DERREUMAUX; Man. Dir PHILIPPE LEON-DUFOUR.

Barclays Bank of Kenya Ltd: 8th Barclays Plaza, Loita St, POB 30120, 00100 Nairobi; tel. (20) 2214270; fax (20) 2213915; e-mail barclays.kenya@barclays.com; f. 1978; cap. 2,037m., res 2,233m., dep. 86,215m. (Dec. 2005); Chair. SAMUEL O. J. AMBUNDO; Man. Dir ADAN MOHAMMED; 87 brs.

CFC Stanbic Bank Ltd: CFC Centre, Chiromo Rd, Westlands, POB 72833, 00200 Nairobi; tel. (20) 3752900; fax (20) 3752905; e-mail cfcstanbic@stanbic.com; internet www.cfcstanbicbank.co.ke; formed by merger of CFC Bank Ltd and Stanbic Bank Kenya Ltd in June 2008; 100% owned by CFC Stanbic Holdings Ltd; Man. Dir MICHAEL DU TOIT.

Chase Bank (Kenya) Ltd: Prudential Assurance Bldg, 6th Floor, Wabera St, POB 28987, Nairobi; tel. (20) 2252385; fax (20) 2246334; e-mail info@chasebank.co.ke; internet www.chasebankkenya.co.ke; cap. 600.0m., res 31.3m., dep. 3,369.2m. (Dec. 2006); Chair. OSMAN MURGIAN; Man. Dir and Pres. MOHAMED ZAFRULLAH KHAN.

Commercial Bank of Africa Ltd: Commercial Bank Bldg, Upper Hill, cnr Mara and Ragati Rds, POB 30437, Nairobi; tel. (20) 2228881; fax (20) 335827; e-mail cba@cba.co.ke; internet www.cba.co.ke; f. 1962; owned by Kenyan shareholders; cap. 2,257.7m., res 1,459.5m., dep. 32,667.2m. (Dec. 2006); Chair. M. H. DA GAMA-ROSE; Pres. and Man. Dir ISAAC O. AWUONDO; 12 brs.

Consolidated Bank of Kenya Ltd: Consolidated Bank House, Koinange St, POB 51133, Nairobi; tel. (20) 340208; fax (20) 340213; e-mail headoffice@consolidated-bank.com; internet www.consolidated-bank.com; f. 1989; state-owned; cap. 1,119.5m., res 206.0m., dep. 2,533.6m. (Dec. 2006); Chair. PHILIP J. NJUKI; Man. Dir DAVID K. WACHIRA.

Dubai Bank Kenya Ltd: ICEA Bldg, Kenyatta Ave, POB 11129-00400, Nairobi; tel. (20) 311109; fax (20) 2245242; e-mail info@dubaibank.co.ke; internet www.dubaibank.co.ke; 20% owned by World of Marble and Granite, Dubai (United Arab Emirates), 22.4% owned by Abdul Hassan Ahmed, 16% owned by Hassan Bin Hassan Trading Co LLC, Dubai (United Arab Emirates), 17.6% owned by Ahmed Mohamed; cap. 362m., res 41m., dep. 1,000m. (Dec. 2007); Chair. HASSAN AHMED ZUBEIDI; Man. Dir MAYANK SHARMA.

EABS Bank Ltd: Fedha Towers, 5th Floor, Muindi Mbingu St, POB 49584, 00100 Nairobi; tel. (20) 22883000; fax (20) 22883304; e-mail marketing.ho@eabsbank.com; internet www.eabsbank.com; f. 1972 as Akiba Bank Ltd, present name adopted 2005; cap. 1,362.5m., res 158.7m., dep. 7,144.8m. (Dec. 2006); Chair. N. P. G. WARREN; CEO RAJPAL ARORA; 3 brs.

Equatorial Commercial Bank Ltd: Nyerere Rd, POB 52467, Nairobi; tel. (20) 2710455; fax (20) 2710700; e-mail Customerservice@ecb.co.ke; internet www.equatorialbank.co.ke; cap. 306m. (Dec. 2001); Chair. AHMED S. NDOPE; Man. Dir K. S. KRISHNAKUMAR.

Fidelity Commercial Bank Ltd: IPS Bldg, 7th Floor, Kimathi St, POB 34886, Nairobi; tel. (20) 2242348; fax (20) 2243389; e-mail customerservice@fidelitybankkenya.com; f. 1993 as Fidelity Finance; present name adopted 1996; cap. 256.9m., res 30.2m., dep. 1,985.7m. (Dec. 2006); CEO SULTAN KHIMJI.

Fina Bank Ltd: Fina House, Kimathi St, POB 20613, 00200 Nairobi; tel. (20) 2246943; fax (20) 2247164; e-mail banking@finabank.com; internet www.finabank.com; f. 1986 as The Finance Institute of Africa Ltd; converted to commercial bank as above in 1996; cap. 504.7m., res 565.5m., dep. 8,276.5m. (Dec. 2006); Chair. DHANJI HANSRAJ CHANDARIA; Man. Dir FRANK GRIFFITHS.

Giro Commercial Bank Ltd: POB 46739, Giro House, Kimathi St, 00100 Nairobi; tel. (20) 22217776; fax (20) 22230600; e-mail info@girobankltd.com; f. 1992 as Giro Bank Ltd; name changed as above in 1999 after merging with Commerce Bank Ltd; 21.76% owned by Blandford Investments Ltd, Nairobi; cap. 309.5m., res 185.5m., dep. 4,510.5m. (Dec. 2006); Chair. CHANDAN JETHANAND GIDOOMAL; Man. Dir T. K. KRISHNAN.

Gulf African Bank (GAB): Geminia Insurance Plaza, Kilimanjaro Ave, Upper Hill, POB 43683, Nairobi; tel. (20) 2740000; e-mail info@gulfafricanbank.com; internet www.gulfafricanbank.com; f. 2007; 20% owned by Bank Muscat International (BMI), 10% owned by the International Finance Corpn (IFC); Chair. SULEIMAN SAID SHAHBAL; CEO NAJMUL HASSAN.

KENYA
Directory

Imperial Bank Ltd: POB 44905, Bunyala Rd, Upper Hill, 00100 Nairobi; tel. (20) 22719612; fax (20) 22719498; e-mail info@imperialbank.co.ke; internet www.imperialbank.co.ke; f. 1992 as Imperial Finance and Securities Company; converted to a bank and name changed as above in 1995; 100% owned by Kenyan shareholders; cap. 775.0m., res 103.8m., dep. 7,732.8m. (Dec. 2006); Chair. ALNASHIR POPAT; Man. Dir ABDULMALEK JANMOHAMED.

Kenya Commercial Bank Ltd: Kencom House, Moi Ave, POB 48400, Nairobi; tel. (20) 3270000; fax (20) 2216405; e-mail kcbhq@kcb.co.ke; internet www.kcb.co.ke; f. 1970; 23.1% state-owned; cap. 1,996.0m., res 9,811.5m., dep. 100,221.0m. (Dec. 2007); CEO MARTIN ODUOR-OTIENO; 123 brs and sub-brs.

Middle East Bank Kenya Ltd: Mebank Tower, Milimani Rd, POB 47387, 00100 Nairobi; tel. (20) 2723120; fax (20) 343776; e-mail ho@mebkenya.com; internet www.mebkenya.com; f. 1981; 25% owned by Banque Belgolaise SA (Belgium), 75% owned by Kenyan shareholders; cap. 506.8m., res 367.7m., dep. 1,880m. (Dec. 2007); Man. Dir PETER HARRIS; Exec. Dir. B. S. PAI; 2 brs.

National Bank of Kenya Ltd (Banki ya Taifa La Kenya Ltd): National Bank Bldg, Harambee Ave, POB 72866, Nairobi; tel. (20) 2226471; fax (20) 311444; e-mail info@nationalbank.co.ke; internet www.nationalbank.co.ke; f. 1968; 42% owned by National Social Security Fund, 22.5% state-owned; cap. 6,675.0m., res 1,462.2m., dep. 29,727.9m. (Dec. 2006); Chair. M. E. G. MUHINDI; Man. Dir REUBEN M. MARAMBII; 23 brs.

Oriental Commercial Bank Ltd: POB 44080, Finance House, Koinange St, 00100 Nairobi; tel. (20) 2221875; fax (20) 2219469; e-mail info@orientalbank.co.ke; f. 1991; name changed as above in 2003; Chair. GIRISH SHAH; Gen. Man. BINAY DUTTA; 4 brs.

Paramount Universal Bank Ltd: POB 14001-00800, Sound Plaza, Woodvale Grove, Westlands, Nairobi; tel. (20) 44492668; fax (20) 4449265; e-mail info@paramountbank.co.ke; internet www.paramountbank.co.ke; f. 1993 as Combined Finance Ltd; name changed as above in 2000; 25% owned by Tormount Holdings Ltd, St. Helier, 25% owned by Anwarali Merali, 25% owned by Tasneem Padamshi; Chair. ANWARALI MERALI; Man. Dir AYAZ MERALI.

Standard Chartered Bank Kenya Ltd: Stanbank House, Moi Ave, POB 30003, Nairobi; tel. (20) 32093000; fax (20) 2214086; e-mail mds.office@ke.standardchartered.com; internet www.standardchartered.com/ke; f. 1987; 74.5% owned by Standard Chartered Holdings (Africa) BV (Netherlands); cap. 1,639.8m., res 4,191.7m., dep. 67,750.5m. (Dec. 2006); Chair. HARRINGTON AWORI; CEO MICHAEL C. HART; 29 brs.

Trans-National Bank Ltd: Transnational Plaza, 2nd Floor, Mama Ngina St, POB 34353, 00100 Nairobi; tel. (20) 2224235; fax (20) 339227; e-mail info@tnbl.co.ke; internet www.tnbl.co.ke; f. 1985; cap. 583.7m., res 760.0m., dep. 1,328.6m. (Dec. 2006); Chair. MICHAEL CHERWON; CEO DHIRENDRA RANA; 9 brs.

Merchant Banks

Diamond Trust Bank Ltd: Nation Centre, 8th Floor, Kimathi St, POB 61711, 00200 Nairobi; tel. (20) 2849000; fax (20) 2245495; e-mail info@dtbkenya.co.ke; internet www.dtbafrica.com; f. 1945; cap. 559.0m., res 943.8m., dep. 16,952.5m. (Dec. 2006); Chair. MAHMOOD MANJI; Man. Dir NASIM MOHAMED DEVJI.

National Industrial Credit Bank Ltd (NIC): NIC House, Masaba Rd, POB 44599, Nairobi; tel. (20) 718200; fax (20) 718232; e-mail info@nic-bank.com; internet www.nic-bank.com; cap. 412m. (Dec. 2001); Chair. J. P. M. NDEGWA; Man. Dir JAMES MACHARIA.

Co-operative Bank

Co-operative Bank of Kenya Ltd: Co-operative Bank House, Haile Selassie Ave, POB 48231, Nairobi; tel. (20) 3276100; fax (20) 2219831; e-mail md@co-opbank.co.ke; internet www.co-opbank.co.ke; f. 1968; cap. 2,856.5m., res 1,596.9m., dep. 56,198.0m., total assets 65,708.9m. (Dec. 2007); Chair. STANLEY C. MUCHIRI; Man. Dir GIDEON MURIUKI; 29 brs.

Development Banks

Development Bank of Kenya Ltd: Finance House, 16th Floor, Loita St, POB 30483, 00100 Nairobi; tel. (20) 340426; fax (20) 2250399; e-mail dbk@devbank.com; internet www.devbank.com; f. 1963 as Development Finance Co of Kenya; current name adopted 1996; owned by Industrial and Commercial Devt Corpn (89.3%), the Commonwealth Development Corpn (10.7%); cap. 347.5m., res 725.9m., dep. 1,773.9m. (Dec. 2006); Chair. Prof. HAROUN NGENY KIPKEMBOI MENGECH; Gen. Man. VICTOR J. O. KIDIWA (acting).

East African Development Bank: Rahimtulla Tower, 2nd Floor, Upper Hill Rd, POB 47685, Nairobi; tel. (20) 340642; fax (20) 2731590; e-mail cok@eadb.org; internet www.eadb.org; Dirs J. KINYUA, F. KARUIRU.

IDB Capital Ltd: National Bank Bldg, 18th Floor, Harambee Ave, POB 44036, Nairobi; tel. (20) 247142; fax (20) 334594; e-mail idbkenya@swiftkenya.com; internet www.idbkenya.com; f. 1973 as Industrial Development Bank Ltd; adopted present name in 2005; 49% state-owned; cap. 272m., res 83m., dep. 190m. (Dec. 2002); Chair. DAVID LANGAT; Man. Dir L. A. MASAVIRU.

STOCK EXCHANGE

Nairobi Stock Exchange (NSE): Nation Centre, 1st Floor, Kimathi St, POB 43633, 00100 Nairobi; tel. (20) 2831000; fax (20) 2224200; e-mail info@nse.co.ke; internet www.nse.co.ke; f. 1954; Chair. JAMES WANGUNYU; CEO CHRIS MWEBESA.

INSURANCE

American Life Insurance Co (Kenya) Ltd: POB 30364, 00100 Nairobi; tel. (20) 2711242; fax (20) 2711378; e-mail alicolife@alico-kenya.com; internet www.alico-kenya.com; f. 1964; life and general; Man. Dir ERWIN BREWSTER.

Apollo Insurance Co Ltd: POB 30389, Nairobi; tel. (20) 223562; fax (20) 339260; f. 1977; life and general; Chair. B. M. SHAH.

Blue Shield Insurance Co Ltd: Blue Shield Towers, Upper Hill, Hospital Rd, off Mara Rd, POB 49610, Nairobi; tel. (20) 2712600; fax (20) 2712625; e-mail info@blueshield.co.ke; internet www.blueshield.co.ke; f. 1983; life and general; Chair. BETH MUIGAI; Man. Dir KULOVA WANJALA.

Cannon Assurance (Kenya) Ltd: Haile Selassie Ave, POB 30216, Nairobi; tel. (20) 335478; fax (20) 331235; e-mail info@cannon.co.ke; internet www.cannon.co.ke; f. 1964; life and general; Man. Dir I. J. TALWAR.

Fidelity Shield Insurance Ltd: 4th Floor, Rank Xerox House, Parklands Rd, Westlands, POB 47435, 00100 Nairobi; tel. (20) 4443063; fax (20) 4445699; e-mail info@fidelityshield.com; internet www.fidelityshield.com; Man. Dir SHEHNAZ SUMAR.

Heritage Insurance Co Ltd: CFC House, Mamlaka Rd, POB 30390, 00100 Nairobi; tel. (20) 2783000; fax (20) 2727800; e-mail info@heriaii.com; internet www.heritageinsurance.co.ke; f. 1976; general; Man. Dir JOHN H. D. MILNE.

Insurance Co of East Africa Ltd (ICEA): ICEA Bldg, Kenyatta Ave, POB 46143, Nairobi; tel. (20) 221652; fax (20) 338089; e-mail hof@icea.co.ke; internet www.icea.co.ke; life and general; Man. Dir J. K. NDUNGU.

Jubilee Insurance Co Ltd: POB 30376, 00100 Nairobi; tel. (20) 3281000; fax (20) 3281160; e-mail enquiry@jubileekenya.com; internet www.jubileeafrica.com; f. 1937; life, general and medical insurance and pensions; Chair. NIZAR JUMA.

Kenindia Assurance Co Ltd: Kenindia House, Loita St, POB 44372, Nairobi; tel. (20) 316099; fax (20) 218380; e-mail kenindia@kenindia.com; internet www.kenindia.co.ke; f. 1978; life and general; Man. Dir SADASIV MISHRA.

Kenya Reinsurance Corpn Ltd (KenyaRe): Reinsurance Plaza, Taifa Rd, POB 30271, Nairobi; tel. (20) 2240188; fax (20) 339161; e-mail kenyare@kenyare.co.ke; internet www.kenyare.co.ke; f. 1970; Man. Dir JOHNSON GITHAKA.

Lion of Kenya Insurance Co Ltd: POB 30190, Nairobi; tel. (20) 710400; fax (20) 711177; e-mail insurance@lionofkenya.com; f. 1978; general; CEO J. P. M. NDEGWA.

Mercantile Insurance Co Ltd: Nairobi; tel. (20) 218244; fax (20) 215528; e-mail mercantile@mercantile.co.ke; internet www.mercantile.co.ke; Man. Dir SUDHIR SATHE.

Monarch Insurance Co Ltd: Chester House, 2nd Floor, Koinange St, POB 44003, Nairobi; tel. (20) 330042; fax (20) 340691; e-mail monarch@form-net.com; f. 1975; general; Exec. Dir R. A. VADGAMA.

Pan Africa Insurance Co Ltd: POB 30065, Nairobi; tel. (20) 252168; fax (20) 217675; e-mail insure@pan-africa.com; f. 1946; life and general; Man. Dir WILLIAM OLOTCH.

Phoenix of East Africa Assurance Co Ltd: Ambank House, University Way, POB 30129-00100, Nairobi; tel. (20) 2251350; fax (20) 2211848; e-mail general@phoenix.co.ke; general; Gen. Man. KAUSHAL KUMAR.

Prudential Assurance Co of Kenya Ltd: Yaya Centre, Argwings Kodhek Rd, POB 76190, Nairobi; tel. (20) 567374; fax (20) 567433; f. 1979; general; Man. Dir JOSEPH MURAGE.

PTA Reinsurance Co (ZEP-RE): Zep-Re Pl., Longonot Rd, Upper Hill, POB 42769, Nairobi; tel. (20) 212792; fax (20) 224102; e-mail mail@zep-re.com; internet www.zep-re.com; f. 1992; Man. Dir S. M. LUBASI.

Royal Insurance Co of East Africa Ltd: Mama Ngina St, POB 40001, Nairobi; tel. (20) 717888; fax (20) 712620; f. 1979; general; CEO S. K. KAMAU.

Standard Assurance (Kenya) Ltd: POB 42996, Nairobi; tel. (20) 224721; fax (20) 224862; Man. Dir WILSON K. KAPKOTI.

KENYA

UAP Provincial Insurance Co of East Africa Ltd: Old Mutual Bldg, Kimathi St, POB 43013, Nairobi; tel. (20) 330173; fax (20) 340483; f. 1980; general; CEO E. C. BATES.

United Insurance Co Ltd: POB 30961, Nairobi; tel. (20) 227345; fax (20) 215609; Man. Dir G. KARRUIKI.

Trade and Industry

GOVERNMENT AGENCIES

Export Processing Zones Authority: Administration Bldg, Viwanda Rd, Athi River Export Processing Zone, off Nairobi-Namanga Highway, Athi River, POB 50563, Nairobi; tel. (45) 26421; fax (45) 26427; e-mail info@epzakenya.com; internet www.epzakenya.com; established by the Govt to promote investment in Export Processing Zones; Chief Exec. J. O. B. AKARA.

Export Promotion Council: Anniversary Towers, 1st and 16th Floors, University Way, POB 40247, Nairobi; tel. (20) 228534; fax (20) 218013; e-mail chiefexe@epc.or.ke; internet www.epckenya.org; f. 1992; promotes exports; Chair. Prof. PETER KIMUYU; CEO MATANDA WABUYELE.

Kenya Investment Authority: Railways HQ, Block D, 3rd Floor, Workshops Rd, POB 55704, 00200 Nairobi; tel. (20) 2221401; fax (20) 2243862; e-mail info@investmentkenya.com; internet www.investmentkenya.com; f. 1986; promotes and facilitates local and foreign investment; Man. Dir SUSAN KIKWAI.

Kenya National Trading Corpn Ltd: Yarrow Rd, off Nanyuki Rd, POB 30587, Nairobi; tel. (20) 543121; fax (20) 532800; f. 1965; promotes national control of trade in both locally produced and imported items; exports coffee and sugar; CEO S. W. O. OGESSA.

Settlement Fund Trustees: POB 30449, Nairobi; administers a land purchase programme involving over 1.2m. ha for resettlement of African farmers.

DEVELOPMENT ORGANIZATIONS

Agricultural Development Corpn: POB 47101, Nairobi; tel. (20) 250695; fax (20) 243571; f. 1965 to promote agricultural devt and reconstruction; CEO WILLIAM K. KIRWA.

Agricultural Finance Corpn: POB 30367, Nairobi; tel. (20) 317199; fax (20) 219390; e-mail info@agrifinance.org; internet www.agrifinance.org; a statutory organization providing agricultural loans; Man. Dir OMUREMBE IYADI.

Horticultural Crops Development Authority: POB 42601, Nairobi; tel. (20) 8272601; fax (20) 827264; e-mail md@hcda.or.ke; internet www.hcda.or.ke; f. 1968; invests in production, dehydration, processing and freezing of fruit and vegetables; exports of fresh fruit and vegetables; Chair. Prof. ROSALIND W. MUTUA; Man. Dir S. P. GACHANJA.

Housing Finance Co of Kenya Ltd: Rehani House, cnr Kenyatta Ave and Koinange St, POB 30088, 00100 Nairobi; tel. (20) 317474; fax (20) 340299; e-mail housing@housing.co.ke; internet www.housing.co.ke; f. 1965; Chair. KUNG'U GATABAKI; Man. Dir FRANK M. IRERI.

Industrial and Commercial Development Corpn: Uchumi House, Aga Khan Walk, POB 45519, Nairobi; tel. (20) 229213; fax (20) 333880; e-mail icdcexe@africaonline.co.ke; f. 1954; govt-financed; assists industrial and commercial devt; Chair. JOHN NGUTHU MUTIO; Exec. Dir K. ETICH ARAP BETT.

Kenya Fishing Industries Ltd: Nairobi; Man. Dir ABDALLA MBWANA.

Kenya Industrial Estates Ltd: Nairobi Industrial Estate, Likoni Rd, POB 78029, Nairobi; tel. (20) 530551; fax (20) 534625; internet www.kie.co.ke; f. 1967 to finance and develop small-scale industries.

Kenya Industrial Research and Development Institute: POB 30650, Nairobi; tel. (20) 603842; fax (20) 607023; e-mail info@kirdi.go.ke; internet www.kirdi.go.ke; f. 1942; reorg. 1979; restructured 1995; research and devt in industrial and allied technologies including engineering, agro-industrial, mining and environmental technologies; Dir Dr TOM OGADA.

Kenya Tea Development Agency: Moi Ave, POB 30213, Nairobi; tel. and fax (20) 3227000; e-mail info@ktdateas.com; internet www.ktdateas.com; f. 1964 as Kenya Tea Development Authority to develop tea growing, manufacturing and marketing among African smallholders; operates 51 factories; privatized in 2000; Chair. STEPHEN M. IMANYARA; CEO LERIONKA TIAMPATI.

CHAMBER OF COMMERCE

Kenya National Chamber of Commerce and Industry: Ufanisi House, Haile Selassie Ave, POB 47024, Nairobi; tel. (20) 220867; fax (20) 334293; internet www.kncci.org; f. 1965; 69 brs; Nat. Chair. DAVID M. GITHERE; Chief Exec. TITUS G. RUHIU.

INDUSTRIAL AND TRADE ASSOCIATIONS

Central Province Marketing Board: POB 189, Nyeri.

Coffee Board of Kenya: Coffee Plaza, Exchange Lane, off Haile Selassie Ave, POB 30566, Nairobi; tel. and fax (20) 315754; e-mail info@coffeeboard.co.ke; internet www.coffeeboard.co.ke; f. 1947; Chair. JOHN NGARI ZACHARIAH; Gen. Man. AGGREY MURUNGA.

East African Tea Trade Association: Tea Trade Centre, Nyerere Ave, POB 85174, 80100 Mombasa; tel. (41) 2220093; fax (41) 2225823; e-mail info@eatta.co.ke; internet www.eatta.com; f. 1957; organizes Mombasa weekly tea auctions; Exec. Officer HADIJA SHAKOMBO; 264 mems in 11 countries.

Fresh Produce Exporters' Association of Kenya (FPEAK): New Rehema House, 4th Floor, Rhapta Rd, Westlands, POB 40312, 00100 Nairobi; tel. (20) 4451488; fax (20) 445189; e-mail info@fpeak.org; internet www.fpeak.org; Chair. HASIT SHAH; CEO Dr STEPHEN MBITHI MWIKYA.

Kenya Association of Manufacturers: Mwanzi Rd, off Peponi Rd, Westlands, POB 30225, Nairobi; tel. (20) 3746005; fax (20) 3746028; e-mail kam@users.africaonline.co.ke; internet www.kam.co.ke; Chair. MANU CHANDARIA; Exec. Sec. LUCY MICHENI; 200 mems.

Kenya Dairy Board: NSSF Bldg, 10th Floor, Bishops Rd, POB 30406, Nairobi; tel. (20) 310559; fax (20) 244064; e-mail info@kdb.co.ke; internet www.kdb.co.ke; f. 1958; Man. Dir MACHIRA GICHOHI.

Kenya Flower Council: Muthangari Gardens, off Gitanga Rd, POB 56325, 00200 Nairobi; tel. and fax (20) 3876597; e-mail kfc@wananchi.com; internet www.kenyaflowers.com; regulates production of cut flowers; CEO JANE NGIGE.

Kenya Meat Corpn: POB 30414, Nairobi; tel. (20) 340750; f. 1953; purchasing, processing and marketing of beef livestock; Chair. H. P. BARCLAY.

Kenya Planters' Co-operative Union Ltd: Nairobi; e-mail gm@kpcu.co.ke; coffee processing and marketing; Chair. J. M. MACHARIA; Gen. Man. RUTH MWANIKI.

Kenya Sisal Board: Mutual Bldg, Kimathi St, POB 41179, Nairobi; tel. (20) 248919; fax (20) 240091; e-mail kensisa@coopkenya.com; internet www.sisalboardkenya.co.ke; f. 1946; CEO J. H. WAIRAGU; Man. Dir CHARLES K. KAGWIMI (acting).

Kenya Sugar Board: Sukari Plaza, off Waiyaki Way, POB 51500, Nairobi; tel. (20) 2023316; fax (20) 593273; e-mail Info@kenyasugar.co.ke; internet www.kenyasugar.co.ke; f. 2002 to succeed the Kenya Sugar Authority; Chair. LUKE R. OBOK; CEO F. M. CHAHONYO.

Mild Coffee Trade Association of Eastern Africa (MCTA): Nairobi; Chair. F. J. MWANGI.

National Cereals and Produce Board (NCPB): POB 30586, Nairobi; tel. (20) 536028; fax (20) 542024; e-mail cereals@africaonline.co.ke; internet www.ncpb.co.ke; f. 1995; grain marketing and handling, provides drying, weighing, storage and fumigation services to farmers and traders, stores and manages strategic national food reserves, distributes famine relief; Chair. JAMES MUTUA; Man. Dir NAFTALI MOGERE.

Pyrethrum Board of Kenya: POB 420, Nakuru; tel. (37) 211567; fax (37) 45274; e-mail pbk@pyrethrum.co.ke; internet www.kenya-pyrethrum.com; f. 1935; 14 mems; Chair. J. O. MARIARIA; CEO J. C. KIPTOON.

Tea Board of Kenya: Naivasha Rd, off Ngong Rd, POB 20064, 00200 Nairobi; tel. (20) 3874445; fax (20) 3862120; e-mail info@teaboard.or.ke; internet www.teaboard.or.ke; f. 1950; regulates tea industry on all matters of policy, licenses tea processing, carries out research on tea through **Tea Research Foundation of Kenya**, monitors tea planting and trade through registration, promotes Kenyan tea internationally; Chair. DUNSTAN M. NGUMO; Man. Dir SICILY K. KARIUKI.

EMPLOYERS' ORGANIZATIONS

Federation of Kenya Employers: Waajiri House, Argwings Kodhek Rd, POB 48311, Nairobi; tel. (20) 721929; fax (20) 721990; e-mail fkehq@fke-kenya.org; internet www.fke-kenya.org; Chair. J. P. N. SIMBA; Exec. Dir TOM DIJU OWUOR.

Association of Local Government Employers: POB 52, Muranga; Chair. S. K. ITONGU.

Distributive and Allied Industries Employers' Association: POB 30587, Nairobi; Chair. P. J. MWAURA.

Engineering and Allied Industries Employers' Association: POB 48311, Nairobi; tel. (20) 721929; Chair. D. M. NJOROGE.

Kenya Association of Building and Civil Engineering Contractors: Nairobi; Chair. G. S. HIRANI.

Kenya Association of Hotelkeepers and Caterers: Heidelberg House, Mombasa Rd, POB 9977, 00100 Nairobi; tel. (20) 604419; fax (20) 602539; e-mail info@kahc.co.ke; internet www.kahc.co.ke; f. 1944; CEO KABANDO WA KABANDO.

KENYA

Kenya Bankers' Association: POB 73100, Nairobi; tel. (20) 221792; e-mail kba@kenyaweb.com; Chair. MARTIN ODUOR-OTIENO.

Kenya Sugar Employers' Union: Kisumu; Chair. L. OKECH.

Kenya Tea Growers' Association: POB 320, Kericho; tel. (20) 21010; fax (20) 32172; Chair. M. K. A. SANG.

Kenya Vehicle Manufacturers' Association: POB 1436, Thika; Chair. C. PETERSON.

Motor Trade and Allied Industries Employers' Association: POB 48311, Nairobi; tel. (20) 721929; fax (20) 721990; Exec. Sec. G. N. KONDITI.

Sisal Growers' and Employers' Association: POB 47523, Nairobi; tel. (20) 720170; fax (20) 721990; Chair. A. G. COMBOS.

Timber Industries Employers' Association: POB 18070, Nairobi; Chair. H. S. BAMBRAH.

UTILITIES
Electricity

Energy Regulatory Commission (ERC): Integrity Centre, 1st Floor, cnr Valley and Milimani Rds, POB 42681, 00100 Nairobi; tel. (20) 2717627; fax (20) 2717603; e-mail info@erc.go.ke; internet www.erc.go.ke; f. 1997 as Energy Regulatory Board; present name assumed in 2007; govt-owned; regulates the generation, distribution, supply and use of electric power; Chair. HINDPAL SINGH JABBAL.

Kenya Electricity Generating Co Ltd (KenGen): Stima Plaza, Phase 3, Kolobot Rd, Parklands, POB 47936, Nairobi; tel. (20) 3666000; fax (20) 248848; e-mail comms@kengen.co.ke; internet www.kengen.co.ke; f. 1997 as Kenya Power Co; present name adopted 1998; generates 82% of Kenya's electricity requirements; partially privatized in 2006; Chair. TITUS KITILI MBATHI; Man. Dir and CEO EDWARD NJOROGE.

Kenya Power and Lighting Co (KPLC): Electricity House, Harambee Ave, POB 301779, Nairobi; tel. (20) 221251; fax (20) 337351; e-mail custcare@kplc.co.ke; internet www.kplc.co.ke; partially privatized in 2006; 4% owned by Transcentury Group; co-ordinates electricity transmission and distribution; Man. Dir JOSEPH K. NJOROGE.

TRADE UNIONS

Central Organization of Trade Unions (Kenya) (COTU): Solidarity Bldg, Digo Rd, POB 13000, Nairobi; tel. (20) 6761375; fax (20) 6762695; e-mail info@cotu-kenya.org; internet www.cotu-kenya.org; f. 1965 as the sole trade union fed.; Chair. RAJABU W. MWONDI; Sec.-Gen. FRANCIS ATWOLI.

Amalgamated Union of Kenya Metalworkers: POB 73651, Nairobi; tel. (20) 211060; Gen. Sec. MAERO TINDI.

Bakers', Confectionery Manufacturing and Allied Workers' Union (Kenya): POB 57751, 00200 Nairobi; Lengo House, 3rd Floor, Room 20, Tom Mboya St, opposite Gill House, Nairobi; tel. (20) 330275; fax (20) 222735; e-mail bakers@form-net.com.

Communication Workers' Union of Kenya: POB 48155, Nairobi; tel. (20) 219345; e-mail cowuk@clubinternet.com.

Dockworkers' Union: POB 98207, Mombasa; tel. (11) 491427; f. 1954; Gen. Sec. J. KHAMIS.

Kenya Airline Pilots' Association: Off Airport North Rd, POB 57505, 00200 Nairobi; tel. (20) 820354; fax (20) 820410; internet www.kalpa.co.ke.

Kenya Building, Construction, Timber, Furniture and Allied Industries Employees' Union: POB 49628, 00100 Nairobi; tel. (20) 223434; fax (20) 244779; e-mail kbctfaieu@yahoo.com; Gen. Sec. FRANCIS KARIMI MURAGE.

Kenya Chemical and Allied Workers' Union: POB 73820, Nairobi; tel. (20) 338815; Gen. Sec. WERE DIBI OGUTO.

Kenya Electrical Trades Allied Workers' Union: POB 47060, Nairobi; tel. (20) 334655.

Kenya Engineering Workers' Union: POB 73987, Nairobi; tel. (20) 333745; Gen. Sec. JUSTUS MULEI.

Kenya Game Hunting and Safari Workers' Union: Nairobi; tel. (20) 25049; Gen. Sec. J. M. NDOLO.

Kenya Jockey and Betting Workers' Union: POB 55094, Nairobi; tel. (20) 332120.

Kenya Local Government Workers' Union: POB 55827, Nairobi; tel. (20) 217213; Gen. Sec. WASIKE NDOMBI.

Kenya National Union of Fishermen: POB 83322, Nairobi; tel. (20) 227899.

Kenya Petroleum Oil Workers' Union: POB 48125, Nairobi; tel. (20) 338756; Gen. Sec. JACOB OCHINO.

Directory

Kenya Plantation and Agricultural Workers' Union: POB 1161, 20100 Nakuru; tel. and fax (51) 2212310; e-mail kpawu@africaonline.co.ke; Gen. Sec. FRANCIS ATWOLI.

Kenya Quarry and Mine Workers' Union: POB 332120, Nairobi; f. 1961; Gen. Sec. WAFULA WA MUSAMIA.

Kenya Railway Workers' Union: RAHU House, Mfangano St, POB 72029, Nairobi; tel. (20) 340302; f. 1952; Nat. Chair. FRANCIS O'LORE; Sec.-Gen. JOHN T. CHUMO.

Kenya Scientific Research, International Technical and Allied Institutions Workers' Union: Ngumba House, Tom Mboya St, POB 55094, Nairobi; tel. (20) 215713; Sec.-Gen. FRANCIS D. KIRUBI.

Kenya Shipping, Clearing and Warehouse Workers' Union: POB 84067, Mombasa; tel. (11) 312000.

Kenya Shoe and Leather Workers' Union: POB 49629, Nairobi; tel. (20) 533827; Gen. Sec. JAMES AWICH.

Kenya Union of Commercial, Food and Allied Workers: POB 2628, 00100 Nairobi; tel. (20) 245054; fax (20) 313118; e-mail kucfaw@yahoo.com.

Kenya Union of Domestic, Hotel, Educational Institutions, Hospitals and Allied Workers: POB 41763, 00100 Nairobi; tel. (20) 241509; fax (20) 243806; e-mail kudheihaworkers@hotmail.com; f. 1952; workers; Sec.-Gen. FESTUS MUTUNGA.

Kenyan Union of Entertainment and Music Industry Employees: Nairobi; tel. (20) 333745.

Kenya Union of Journalists: POB 47035, 00100 Nairobi; tel. (20) 250888; fax (20) 250880; e-mail info@kujkenya.org; f. 1962; Gen. Sec. and CEO EZEKIEL MUTUA; Chair. TERVIL OKOKO.

Kenya Union of Printing, Publishing, Paper Manufacturers and Allied Workers: POB 72358, Nairobi; tel. (20) 331387; Gen. Sec. JOHN BOSCO.

Kenya Union of Sugar Plantation Workers: POB 19019, Kisumu; tel. (57) 2021595; e-mail kuspw@swiftkisumu.com; Gen. Sec. FRANCIS BUSHURU WANGARA.

National Seamen's Union of Kenya: Mombasa; tel. (11) 312106; Gen. Sec. I. S. ABDALLAH MWARUA.

Tailors' and Textile Workers' Union: POB 72076, Nairobi; tel. (20) 338836.

Transport and Allied Workers' Union: POB 45171, Nairobi; tel. (20) 545317; Gen. Sec. JULIUS MALII.

Independent Unions

Academic Staff Association: Nairobi; e-mail dorata@uonbi.ac.ke; Interim Chair. Dr KORWA ADAR.

Kenya Medical Practitioners' and Dentists' Union: not officially registered; Nat. Chair. GIBBON ATEKA.

Kenya National Union of Teachers: POB 30407, 00100 Nairobi; tel. (20) 2220387; fax (20) 2222701; e-mail knut@nbnet.co.ke; internet www.knut.or.ke; f. 1957; Sec.-Gen. LAWRENCE KAHINDI MAJALI.

Transport

RAILWAYS

In 1999 there were some 2,700 km of track open for traffic.

Kenya Railways Corpn: POB 30121, Nairobi; tel. (20) 221211; fax (20) 224156; internet www.krc.co.ke; f. 1977; management of operations assumed by Rift Valley Railways consortium in Nov. 2006; Man. Dir A. HARIZ.

ROADS

At the end of 2004 there were an estimated 63,265 km of classified roads, of which 6,527 km were main roads and 18,885 km were secondary roads. Only an estimated 14.1% of road surfaces were paved. An all-weather road links Nairobi to Addis Ababa, in Ethiopia, and there is a 590-km road link between Kitale (Kenya) and Juba (Sudan). The rehabilitation of the important internal road link between Nairobi and Mombasa (funded by a US $165m. loan from the World Bank) was undertaken during the late 1990s.

Akamba Public Road Services: Industrial Area, POB 40322, Nairobi; tel. (20) 556062; fax (20) 559885; e-mail info@akambabus.com; internet www.akambabus.com; operates bus services from Nairobi to all major towns in Kenya and to some major towns in Uganda and Tanzania.

East African Road Services Ltd: Nairobi; tel. (20) 764622; f. 1947; operates bus services from Nairobi to all major towns in Kenya; Chair. S. H. NATHOO.

Kenya Bus Service Management Ltd: Utali Lane, View Park Towers, 10th Floor, Rm 1010, POB 41001, 00100 Nairobi; tel. (20)

2223235; fax (20) 2223110; e-mail info@kenyabus.net; internet kenyabus.net; promotes and develops transport enterprises; Man. Dir EDWINS MUKABANAH.

Kenya Roads Board: Kenya Re Towers, 3rd Floor, Ragati Rd, Upper Hill, POB 73718, Nairobi; tel. (20) 722865; internet www.krb.go.ke; f. 2000 to co-ordinate maintenance, rehabilitation and devt of the road network; Chair. ALFRED JUMA.

Speedways Trans-Africa Freighters: POB 75755, Nairobi; tel. (20) 544267; private road haulier; CEO HASSAN KANYARE.

SHIPPING

The major international seaport of Mombasa has 16 deep-water berths, with a total length of 3,044 m, and facilities for the off-loading of bulk carriers, tankers and container vessels. Kenyan ports handled some 13.3m. metric tons of cargo in 2005.

Kenya Ports Authority: POB 95009, Mombasa; tel. (41) 2112999; fax (41) 311867; internet www.kpa.co.ke; f. 1978; sole operator of coastal port facilities; also operates two inland container depots at Nairobi and Kisimu; Chair. SHUKRI BARAMADI; Man. Dir JAMES MLEWA.

Inchcape Shipping Services Kenya Ltd: Inchcape House, Archbishop Makarios Cl., off Moi Ave, POB 90194, 80100 Mombasa; tel. (41) 2314245; fax (41) 2314662; e-mail mail@iss-shipping.com; internet www.iss-shipping.com; covers all ports in Kenya and Tanzania; Man. Dir DAVID MACKAY.

Mackenzie Maritime Ltd: Maritime Centre, Archbishop Makarios Close, POB 90120, Mombasa; tel. (11) 221273; fax (11) 316260; e-mail mml@africaonline.co.ke; shipping agents; Man. Dir M. M. BROWN.

Marship Ltd: Mombasa; tel. (11) 314705; fax (11) 316654; f. 1986; shipbrokers, ship management and chartering agents; Man. Dir MICHELE ESPOSITO.

Mitchell Cotts Kenya Ltd: Voi St, Shimanzi, POB 42485, 80100 Mombasa; tel. (20) 2315780; fax (20) 2226181; e-mail sales@mitchellcotts.co.ke; internet www.mitchellcottskenya.com; f. 1926; transport and shipping agents; freight handling and distribution; warehousing; Man. Dir DANIEL TANUI.

Motaku Shipping Agencies Ltd: Motaku House, Tangana Rd, POB 80419, 80100 Mombasa; tel. (41) 2229065; fax (41) 2220777; e-mail motaku@motakushipping.com; f. 1977; ship managers and shipping agents, freight broker and charter; Man. Dir KARIM KUDRATI.

PIL (Kenya) Ltd: Liberty Plaza, Mombasa Rd, POB 40109, Nairobi; tel. (20) 825082; fax (20) 821086; e-mail admin@nbo.pilship.com; internet www.pilship.com.

Shipmarc Ltd: POB 99553, Mombasa; tel. (41) 229241; fax (41) 221390; e-mail info@shipmarckenya.com.

Southern Line Ltd: POB 90102, 80107 Mombasa; tel. (11) 229241; fax (11) 221390; e-mail shipmarc@africaonline.co.ke; operating dry cargo and tanker vessels between East African ports, Red Sea ports, the Persian (Arabian) Gulf and Indian Ocean islands.

Spanfreight Shipping Ltd: Cannon Towers, Moi Ave, POB 99760, Mombasa; tel. (11) 315623; fax (11) 312092; e-mail a23ke464@gncomtext.com; Exec. Dir DILIPKUMAR AMRITLAL SHAH.

Star East Africa Co: POB 86725, Mombasa; tel. (11) 314060; fax (11) 312818; shipping agents and brokers; Man. Dir YEUDA FISHER.

CIVIL AVIATION

Jomo Kenyatta International Airport (JKIA), in south-eastern Nairobi, and Moi International Airport, at Mombasa both service international flights. Wilson Airport, in south-western Nairobi, Eldoret Airport (which opened in 1997) and airports at Malindi and Kisumu handle internal flights. Kenya has about 150 smaller airfields. The rehabilitation and expansion of JKIA and Moi International Airport was undertaken during the late 1990s. A new cargo handling facility, The Nairobi Cargo Centre, opened at JKIA in June 1999, increasing the airport's capacity for storing horticultural exports.

Kenya Airports Authority: Jomo Kenyatta International Airport, POB 19001, Nairobi; tel. (20) 825400; fax (20) 822078; e-mail info@kenyaairports.co.ke; internet www.kenyaairports.co.ke; f. 1991; state-owned; responsible for the provision, management and operation of all airports and private airstrips; Man. Dir GEORGE MUHOHO.

Aero Kenya: Shelter Afrique House, Mamlaka Rd, Nairobi; tel. (20) 2719091; fax (20) 2719264; internet info@aerokenya.com; f. 1997; operates domestic charter and schedule services; Man. Dir Capt. CHARLES K. MUTHAMA.

African Express Airways: Airport North Rd, Jomo Kenyatta International Airport, POB 19202, 00501 Nairobi; tel. (20) 2014746; fax (20) 2049888; e-mail afex@africanexpress.co.ke; internet www.africanexpress.co.ke.

Airkenya Aviation: Wilson Airport, POB 30357, 00100 Nairobi; tel. (20) 605745; fax (20) 602951; e-mail info@airkenya.com; internet www.airkenya.com; f. 1985; operates internal scheduled and charter passenger services; CEO AMATZIA SNIR.

Blue Bird Aviation Ltd: Wilson Airport, Langata Rd, POB 52382, Nairobi; tel. (20) 602338; fax (20) 602337.

Eagle Aviation (African Eagle): POB 93926, Mombasa; tel. (11) 434502; fax (11) 434249; e-mail eaglemsa@africaonline.co.ke; f. 1986; scheduled regional and domestic passenger and cargo services; Chair. RAJA TANUJ; CEO Capt. KIRAN PATEL.

Five Forty Aviation Ltd (fly540.com): ABC Pl. Westlands, POB 10293, Nairobi; tel. (20) 4453252; fax (20) 4453257; e-mail info@fly540.com; internet www.fly540.com; f. 2006; low-cost airline operating domestic and regional flights; COO NEIL STEFFEN.

Kenya Airways Ltd (KQ): Airport North Road, Jomo Kenyatta International Airport, POB 19142, Nairobi; tel. (20) 6422000; fax (20) 823488; e-mail contact@kenya-airways.com; internet www.kenya-airways.com; f. 1977; in private sector ownership since 1996; passenger services to Africa, Asia, Europe and Middle East; freight services to Europe; internal services from Nairobi to Kisumu, Mombasa and Malindi; also operates a freight subsidiary; Chair. EVANSON MWANIKI; Man. Dir and CEO TITUS NAIKUNI.

Jetlink Express: Unit 3, Jomo Kenyatta International Airport, Nairobi; tel. (20) 827915; e-mail customercare@jetlink.co.ke; internet www.jetlink.co.ke; f. 2006; provides internal services and also operates flights to Juba (Sudan), Goma (DRC) and Kigali (Rwanda); Man. Dir and CEO Capt. ELLY ALUVALE.

CIVIL AVIATION AUTHORITY

Kenya Civil Aviation Authority: Jomo Kenyatta International Airport, POB 30163, 00100 Nairobi; tel. (20) 827470; e-mail info@kcaa.or.ke; internet www.kcaa.or.ke; f. 2002; regulatory and advisory services for air navigation; Dir Gen. C. A. KUTO.

Tourism

Kenya's main attractions for visitors are its wildlife, with 25 National Parks and 23 game reserves, the Indian Ocean coast and an equable year-round climate. In 2007 there were 1,817,000 foreign visitors. Earnings from the sector totalled US $1,182m. in 2006.

Kenya Tourism Board: Kenya-Re Towers, Ragati Rd, POB 30630, 00100 Nairobi; tel. (20) 271126; fax (20) 2719925; e-mail info@kenyatourism.org; internet www.magicalkenya.com; f. 1997; promotes Kenya as a tourist destination, monitors the standard of tourist facilities.

Kenya Tourist Development Corpn: Utalii House, 11th Floor, Uhuru Highway, POB 42013, Nairobi; tel. (20) 2229751; fax (20) 2227817; e-mail info@ktdc.co.ke; internet www.ktdc.co.ke; f. 1965; Chair. CHARLES WACHIRA NGUNDO; Man. Dir OBONDO KAJUMBI.

KIRIBATI

Introductory Survey

Location, Climate, Language, Religion, Flag, Capital

The Republic of Kiribati (pronounced 'Kir-a-bas') comprises 33 atolls, in three principal groups, scattered within an area of about 5m. sq km (2m. sq miles) in the mid-Pacific Ocean. The country extends about 3,870 km (2,400 miles) from east to west and about 2,050 km (1,275 miles) from north to south. Its nearest neighbours are Nauru, to the west, and Tuvalu and Tokelau, to the south. The climate varies between maritime equatorial in the central islands and tropical in the north and south, with daytime temperatures varying between 26°C (79°F) and 32°C (90°F). There is a season of north-westerly trade winds from March to October and a season of rains and gales from October to March. Average annual rainfall, however, varies greatly, from 3,000 mm (118 ins) in the northern islands to 1,500 mm (59 ins) in Tarawa and 700 mm (28 ins) in the Line Islands. Droughts often occur in the central and southern islands. The principal languages are I-Kiribati (Gilbertese) and English, and the islands' inhabitants are mostly Christians. The national flag (proportions 1 by 2) depicts a golden frigate bird in flight, on a red background, above a rising sun and six alternating wavy horizontal lines of blue and white, representing the sea. The capital is the island of Bairiki, in Tarawa Atoll.

Recent History

In 1892 the United Kingdom established a protectorate over the 16 atolls of the Gilbert Islands and the nine Ellice Islands (now Tuvalu). The two groups were administered together by the Western Pacific High Commission (WPHC), which was based in Fiji until its removal to the British Solomon Islands (now Solomon Islands) in 1953. The phosphate-rich Ocean Island (now Banaba), west of the Gilberts, was annexed by the United Kingdom in 1900. The Gilbert and Ellice Islands were annexed in 1915, effective from January 1916, when the protectorate became a colony. The local representative of the WPHC was the Resident Commissioner, based on Tarawa Atoll in the Gilbert group. Later in 1916 the new Gilbert and Ellice Islands Colony (GEIC) was extended to include Ocean Island and two of the Line Islands, far to the east. Christmas Island (now Kiritimati), another of the Line Islands, was added in 1919, and the eight Phoenix Islands (then uninhabited) in 1937. The Line and Phoenix Islands, south of Hawaii, were also claimed by the USA. A joint British-US administration for two of the Phoenix group, Canton (now Kanton) and Enderbury, was agreed in April 1939. During the Second World War the GEIC was invaded by Japanese forces, who occupied the Gilbert Islands in 1942–43. Tarawa Atoll was the scene of some of the fiercest fighting in the Pacific between Japan and the USA.

As part of the British Government's programme to develop its own nuclear weapons, the first test of a British hydrogen bomb was conducted near Christmas Island in May 1957. Two further tests in the same vicinity followed later that year.

In 1963, to prepare the GEIC for self-government, the first of a series of legislative and executive bodies were established. In 1972 a Governor of the GEIC was appointed to assume almost all the functions previously exercised in the colony by the High Commissioner. The five uninhabited Central and Southern Line Islands, previously administered directly by the High Commissioner, became part of the GEIC at this time. In 1974 the Legislative Council was replaced by a House of Assembly, with 28 elected members and three official members. The House elected Naboua Ratieta as Chief Minister.

In October 1975 the Ellice Islands were allowed to secede from the GEIC to form a separate territory, Tuvalu (q.v.). The remainder of the GEIC was renamed the Gilbert Islands, and the House of Assembly's membership was reduced.

In 1975 the British Government refused to recognize as legitimate a demand for independence by the people of Ocean Island (Banaba), who had been in litigation with the British Government since 1971 over revenues derived from exports of phosphate. Open-cast mining had so adversely affected the island's environment that most Banabans had been resettled on Rabi Island, 2,600 km (1,600 miles) away in the Fiji group. The Banabans rejected the British Government's argument that phosphate revenues should be distributed over the whole territory of the Gilbert Islands. In 1976 the High Court in London dismissed the Banabans' claim for unpaid royalties but upheld that for damages. An offer made by the British Government in 1977 of an *ex gratia* payment of $A10m., without admission of liability and on condition that no further judicial appeal would be made, was rejected.

The Gilbert Islands obtained internal self-government on 1 January 1977. Later in that year the number of elected members in the House of Assembly was increased to 36, and provision was subsequently made for a member appointed by the Rabi Council of Leaders. Following a general election in 1978, Ieremia Tabai, Leader of the Opposition in the previous House, was elected Chief Minister. On 12 July 1979 the Gilbert Islands became an independent republic within the Commonwealth, under the name of Kiribati. The House of Assembly was renamed the Maneaba ni Maungatabu, and Ieremia Tabai became the country's first President (Beretitenti). In September Kiribati signed a treaty of friendship with the USA, which relinquished its claim to the Line and Phoenix Islands, including Kanton and Enderbury. Kiribati did not become a member of the UN until September 1999, although it had previously joined some of the organization's agencies.

In 1981 the Banaban community on Rabi accepted the British Government's earlier *ex gratia* offer of compensation, but they continued to seek self-government. The 1979 Constitution provided for the establishment of an independent commission of inquiry to review the political status of the Banabans three years after Kiribati had achieved independence, but the inquiry was not commissioned until 1985.

The first general election since independence took place in March–April 1982. The members of the new Maneaba all sat as independents. In accordance with the 1979 Constitution, the legislature nominated from among its members candidates for the country's first presidential election, to be held on the basis of direct popular vote. President Tabai was confirmed in office at the election in May. The Government resigned in December, after the Maneaba had twice rejected proposals to increase salaries for civil servants. The legislature was dissolved, and a general election took place in January 1983. The formation of the new Maneaba necessitated a further presidential election in February, at which Tabai was re-elected for a third term of office. He was returned to office in May 1987 (following a general election in March). The May 1991 legislative election was followed by a presidential election in July, at which the former Vice-President, Teatao Teannaki, narrowly defeated Roniti Teiwaki to replace Tabai, who had served the maximum number of presidential terms permitted by the Constitution.

In 1992 the Maneaba approved an opposition motion urging the Government to seek compensation from Japan for damage caused during the Second World War. The intention to seek compensation was reiterated by President Teburoro Tito (see below) in late 1994.

In May 1994 the Government was defeated on a motion of confidence, following opposition allegations that government ministers had misused travel allowances. The Maneaba was dissolved, and at legislative elections in July five cabinet ministers lost their seats. Of the newly elected members, 13 were supporters of the Maneaban Te Mauri (Protect the Maneaba), while only eight were known to support the previously dominant National Progressive Party grouping. At the presidential election in September Teburoro Tito, of the Maneaban Te Mauri, was elected, receiving 51.1% of the total votes. The new President declared that reducing Kiribati's dependence on foreign aid would be a major objective for his Government. He also announced his intention to pursue civil and criminal action against members of the previous administration for alleged misuse of public funds while in office.

In 1995 a committee was created with the aim of assessing public opinion regarding possible amendments to the Constitution. In March 1998 more than 200 delegates attended a Constitutional Review Convention in Bairiki to consider the recommendations of a report presented to the Government in

1996, which included equalizing the status of men and women regarding the citizenship rights of foreigners marrying I-Kiribati and changes to the structure of the Council of State. Leaders of the Banaban community in Rabi, Fiji, were also consulted during 1998 as part of the review process.

A general election, held in September 1998 and contested by a record 191 candidates, failed to produce a conclusive result, necessitating a second round of voting one week later, at which the Government and opposition each lost seven seats. The new Maneaba convened in October, when it selected three presidential candidates. At a presidential election in November Tito was re-elected with 52.3% of total votes cast, defeating Dr Harry Tong, who obtained 45.8% of votes, and Ambreroti Nikora, with 1.8%.

In mid-1999 John Kum Kee, a member of the Maneaba, was sentenced to four years' imprisonment, having been convicted of bribing a customs official and evasion of customs duty. Controversy continued in 1999 regarding the renamed Millennium Island (previously Caroline Island). The island had been renamed in 1997 in an attempt to promote it as a tourist destination for the year 2000. In 1994 Kiribati had moved the international date-line to incorporate the Line and Phoenix Islands groups (including Millennium Island) in the same time zone as the Gilbert group, thus creating a large eastward anomaly in the date-line. Millennium Island's position as the first place to celebrate the New Year, however, was subsequently confirmed. In early 2000, however, opposition politicians severely criticized the Government for failing to attract the predicted numbers of tourists to the islands' millennium celebrations, despite expenditure of more than $A1m. Meanwhile, in April 1999 the Kiribati Government reiterated its desire to acquire Baker, Howland and Jarvis Islands (see US External Territories) from the USA, citing the potential economic value of their fishing resources.

In late 1999 concerns were expressed by a Pacific media organization after a New Zealand journalist working for Agence France-Presse was banned from entering Kiribati. The Kiribati Government claimed that a series of articles by the correspondent, unfavourable to Kiribati, which had been published in a regional magazine, were biased and sensationalist. In December former President Ieremia Tabai and a former member of the Maneaba, Atiera Tetoa, were fined, having been convicted of importing telecommunications equipment without a permit. They had launched Newair FM, an independent commercial radio station, 12 months previously; it had been immediately suspended and a criminal investigation was instigated by the police. Tabai subsequently established Kiribati's first private newspaper, the *Kiribati Newstar*, in an attempt to reduce the Government's control over the media in the islands.

In November 2000 the Vice-President and Minister for Home Affairs and Rural Development, Tewarika Tentoa, collapsed while addressing the Maneaba and died. The post of Vice-President was subsequently combined with the cabinet portfolio of finance and economic planning.

Campaigning for the general election during November 2002 was characterized by numerous allegations of improper conduct. Observers noted that officials from the Chinese embassy in Tarawa, accompanied by government candidates, had been donating gifts to the local community in the weeks preceding the election. (The Government had recently amended the Elections Act to allow gifts to be distributed to the public by candidates during their electoral campaigns, a practice that had been banned hitherto.) The opposition, which had stated its intention to close the Chinese satellite-tracking station (based on South Tarawa—see below) if elected, claimed that this action constituted a clear attempt to influence voters. Moreover, under a newly amended Newspaper Registration Act, President Tito ordered police to seize opposition election pamphlets in November. Further allegations that the Government was attempting to stifle freedom of expression were made by former President Ieremia Tabai, whose private radio station was finally granted a licence to broadcast in December, following delays totalling almost four years in issuing the permit.

A total of 176 candidates contested the general election on 29 November 2002. The Government suffered significant losses with 14 of its supporters (including seven ministers) failing to retain their seats. The presidential election was postponed from its original date and finally took place on 25 February 2003. At the poll Tito received 14,160 votes, while opposition candidate Taberannang Timeon secured 13,613. Tito was sworn in for his third term as President on 28 February and many of his former opponents in the legislature were expected to cross the floor to support him. However, in late March Tito was narrowly defeated on a motion of no confidence and his Government was replaced by an interim administration, the Council of State (comprising the Speaker, the Chief Justice and the Public Service Commissioner). In accordance with the Constitution, another general election was held on 9 and 14 May, when supporters of Tito secured a majority of seats. A presidential election took place in early July at which the opposition candidate, Anote Tong, narrowly defeated his brother, Harry Tong. Anote Tong's electoral campaign, which had focused on his pledge to review the lease of the Chinese satellite-tracking station on South Tarawa, had been characterized by a series of personal criticisms of his brother.

A legislative election, contested by a total of 146 candidates, was held on 22 August 2007. Decisive majorities were achieved by candidates in only 18 constituencies, thus resulting in a second round of voting on 30 August. The ministers of the incumbent Government, with the exception of Martin Tofinga, were re-elected to the Maneaba ni Maungatabu, and the Boutokan Te Koaua (Pillars of Truth) grouping of Anote Tong secured 18 seats, defeating the Maneaban Te Mauri grouping, which won seven. Anote Tong defeated three other candidates to be re-elected to the post of President on 17 October, having received almost twice as many votes as his nearest rival, Nabuti Mwemwenikarawa. Prior to the presidential election, members of the opposition grouping protested against the omission of their candidates from the contest following their failure to gain sufficient parliamentary support. Anote Tong subsequently appointed a new Cabinet, retaining Teima Onorio in the position of Vice-President with additional responsibility for commerce, industry and co-operatives, and other erstwhile ministers including Natan Teewe, who became Minister for Finance and Economic Development.

In May 2008 the Minister of Communications, Transport and Tourism, Patrick Tatireta, was forced to resign after a motion of no confidence was raised against him in the Maneaba. Controversy surrounded the Minister's dismissal of the chairman, along with members of the board of directors, of the country's shipping corporation, owing to their refusal to authorize payment for the completion of the purchase of a new ship. Deemed unseaworthy not only by the board of Kiribati Shipping Services Ltd (KSSL) but also by a maritime inspector, the vessel was to have been purchased from the WKK Shipping Line, a company owned by a close associate of Tatireta. President Tong announced that a commission of inquiry was to be established to investigate the affair. Tatireta was replaced by Temate Eriateiti.

In foreign relations, in November 2003 President Anote Tong announced the establishment of diplomatic relations with Taiwan. The Government's decision to transfer its recognition from the People's Republic of China to Taiwan caused considerable controversy within Kiribati and the region. Several hundred people staged a protest in Tarawa against the decision, claiming that it had been made in return for Taiwanese funding of Anote Tong's electoral campaign. The President strongly refuted this allegation, but did state that Taiwan had offered extensive development funds to Kiribati for adopting its position. By late November it was reported that Chinese technicians were dismantling the satellite-tracking station, which had played an important role in China's recent first manned space flight. However the Chinese embassy remained open while China requested that Kiribati reconsider its decision. Despite its efforts, which many observers believed were motivated largely by the islands' strategic importance, in late November China suspended its diplomatic relations with Kiribati. In the same week the police in Kiribati announced that they were beginning an investigation into the death threats received by President Tong, believed to be from a Chinese source. A Taiwanese embassy was opened in Tarawa in January 2004. The continued presence of mainland Chinese officials in Kiribati (three diplomats remained as caretakers of the Chinese embassy building in Tarawa in mid-2004) caused the authorities some concern. In May 2005, as part of a diplomatic tour of Pacific nations, President Chen Shui-bian of Taiwan reportedly became the first foreign head of state to visit Kiribati in an official capacity. During a reciprocal visit by President Tong to Taiwan in May 2006, President Chen described Kiribati as a 'staunch ally' and drew attention to the bilateral projects instigated since the establishment of diplomatic relations.

As a result of discussions held at the Pacific Islands Forum (see p. 393) summit meeting in Kiribati in October 2000, Japan announced that it was willing to negotiate compensation claims with the islanders for damage caused during the Second World War. Furthermore, a six-day visit by President Tito to Japan in February 2001 resulted in a number of informal agreements aimed at enhancing relations between the two countries. These included a decision to try to resolve a dispute over tuna fishing, caused by Japan's refusal to sign a convention aimed at protecting tuna stocks in the central and western Pacific Ocean, and agreements to address their differences over whaling and nuclear fuel shipments. Tito also appeared to modify his position on nuclear energy following the visit to Japan, stating that emissions of harmful 'greenhouse gases' could be reduced by replacing fossil with nuclear fuel.

In September 1995 Kiribati briefly severed relations with France, in protest at the French Government's decision to renew nuclear-weapons testing at Mururoa Atoll in French Polynesia.

Reports that Palmyra Atoll (a privately owned uninhabited US territory some 200 km north of Kiribati's northern Line Islands) was to be sold and used by a US company for the storage of nuclear waste prompted a unanimous resolution of the Maneaba, in May 1996, urging the Government to convey to the US Government the islanders' concerns over the proposals. The islanders' anxieties centred largely on Palmyra's proximity to Kiribati, coupled with the belief that the atoll's fragility and porous structure make it an unstable environment for the storage of highly toxic materials. In November 2000, however, Palmyra was purchased by The Nature Conservancy, a conservation group that planned to preserve the natural state of the atoll.

Owing to the country's high rate of population growth (about 2% per year) and, in particular, the situation of overpopulation on South Tarawa and the associated social and economic problems, it was announced in 1988 that nearly 5,000 inhabitants were to be resettled on outlying atolls, mainly in the Line Islands. In November 2004 the Government announced a major new initiative, supported by the UN Development Programme and the Asian Development Bank, to establish up to four new urban areas in the outer islands as part of ongoing efforts to ease the overcrowding on South Tarawa.

In June 2008 President Anote Tong embarked upon a state visit to New Zealand, where he attended World Environment Day celebrations. Tong met with Prime Minister Helen Clark, and the two leaders signed a declaration that envisaged increased political and economic links. Discussions focused on New Zealand's bilateral aid to Kiribati. New Zealand confirmed its support for the Marine Training Centre (see Education, below), where an expansion of facilities was planned. The Kiribati Sustainable Towns Programme was also discussed. Recently established in order to address the issue of rapid urbanization, particularly on South Tarawa, New Zealand intended to allocate to this programme the sum of $NZ15m. over a five-year period.

In 1989 a UN report on the 'greenhouse effect' (the heating of the earth's atmosphere, and a resultant rise in sea-level, as a consequence of pollution) listed Kiribati as one of the countries that would completely disappear beneath the sea in the 21st century, unless drastic action were taken. None of the land on the islands was more than 2m above sea-level, making the country extremely vulnerable to the effects of climate change. It was feared that a rise in sea-level would not only cause flooding, but would also upset the balance between sea and fresh water (below the coral sands), rendering water supplies undrinkable. In late 1997 President Tito strongly criticized the Australian Government's refusal, at the Conference of the Parties to the Framework Convention on Climate Change (under the auspices of the UN Environment Programme, see p. 65) in Kyoto, Japan, to reduce its emission of gases known to contribute to the 'greenhouse effect'. In April 2001 the USA's decision to reject the Kyoto Protocol to the UN's Framework Convention on Climate Change was widely criticized. (In December 2007, however, the new Australian Government of Kevin Rudd reversed the country's previous position, immediately signing the Kyoto Protocol.) Vice-President Teima Onorio urged the UN to work towards a co-ordinated response to the challenge of global warming.

A report released by the World Bank in 2000 listed the flooding and loss of low-lying areas, more intense cyclones and droughts, the failure of subsistence crops and coastal fisheries, the death of coral reefs and the spread of mosquito-borne diseases such as malaria and dengue fever as consequences of the 'greenhouse effect' on Pacific island nations. Meanwhile, a state of emergency was declared in Kiribati in early 1999, owing to one of the worst droughts ever recorded in the islands. In mid-1999 it was announced that two of the country's uninhabited coral reefs had been submerged as a result of the 'greenhouse effect'. Concern among the islanders intensified in early 2001 when many of the causeways linking villages on Tarawa atoll were flooded by high tides, and by the early 21st century increasingly high 'king tides' were reported to be causing regular flooding. Shortages of drinking water were also reported.

A Chinese satellite-tracking station was opened on South Tarawa in late 1997 but was dismantled in late 2003 following the suspension of diplomatic relations between the two countries (see above). Sea Launch, an international consortium led by the US Boeing Commercial Space Company, also announced plans to undertake a rocket-launching project from a converted oil-rig near the islands. A prototype satellite was launched in March 1999, and commercial operations began in late 1999. Kiribati, which, together with the South Pacific Regional Environment Programme (SPREP, see p. 436), had expressed concerns regarding the potential negative environmental impact of the site, was not expected to benefit financially from the project, as the consortium had sought to carry out its activities in international waters near the outer limits of the islands' exclusive economic zone. The US authorities dismissed environmental concerns about the negative impact of the site (particularly the dumping of large quantities of waste fuel in the islands' waters), which were expressed by both the Government of Kiribati and SPREP in 1998. These fears were compounded in March 2000 after a rocket launched from the site crashed, and, furthermore, Sea Launch refused to disclose where it had landed. In November 1999 it was announced that the Government of Kiribati and the National Space Development Agency of Japan had reached agreement on the proposed establishment of a space-vehicle launching and landing facility on Kiritimati. In the following year the Japanese organization, which was subsequently renamed the Japan Aerospace Exploration Agency, was also given permission by the Kiribati Government to use land and runway facilities on the island, free of charge, until 2020.

In March 2006 President Anote Tong announced that a large marine reserve was to be established in Kiribati. Commercial fishing was to be banned in the Phoenix Islands Protected Area (PIPA), which encompassed an area of 184,700 sq km and would afford protection to more than 120 species of coral and to 520 species of fish. The New England Aquarium, a leading US institute located in Boston, and an international conservation group were to assist in the creation of the reserve. In January 2008 the projected area of PIPA was increased by 100%.

In 2003 UNICEF established a field office in Kiribati as part of a wider strategy to increase the UN's presence in the region. In July 2007 the efforts of a team of Cuban doctors were reported to have resulted in an 80% decrease in infant mortality rates. In September 2008, furthermore, President Anote Tong became the first leader of a Pacific nation to undertake a state visit to Cuba. President Tong had discussions with Cuban President Raúl Castro concerning co-operation between their respective countries in the area of medical training and assistance. President Tong visited the I-Kiribati medical students who were enrolled at various Cuban institutions. Following the completion of the training of the I-Kiribati, who numbered more than 20, it was envisaged that the Cuban doctors would be withdrawn from Kiribati. President Tong then proceeded to Boston where, in recognition of his visionary leadership in establishing the PIPA, he received an international conservation award from the New England Aquarium. Tong also travelled to New York, to deliver an address to the UN General Assembly.

Government

Legislative power is vested in the unicameral Maneaba ni Maungatabu. It has 42 members elected by universal adult suffrage for four years (subject to dissolution), one nominated representative of the Banaban community and, if he is not an elected member, the Attorney-General as an ex-officio member. The Head of State is the Beretitenti (President), who is also Head of Government. The President is elected by direct popular vote. The President governs with the assistance of the Vice-President and Cabinet, whom he appoints from among members of the Maneaba. Executive authority is vested in the Cabinet, which is responsible to the Maneaba.

Defence

Kiribati has no defence forces: defence assistance is provided by Australia and New Zealand.

Economic Affairs

In 2007, according to estimates by the World Bank, Kiribati's gross national income (GNI), measured at average 2005–07 prices, was US $119.6m., equivalent to $1,170 per head (or $2,240 on an international purchasing-power parity basis). During 2000–07, it was estimated, the population increased at an average annual rate of 1.7% per year, while gross domestic product (GDP) per head increased, in real terms, by an estimated average of 0.3% per year. Overall GDP increased, in real terms, at an average annual rate of 2.0% in 2000–07. According to estimates by the Asian Development Bank (ADB), GDP expanded by 0.5% in 2007 and by 0.6% in 2008.

Agriculture and fishing contributed an estimated 7.0% of GDP in 2006, according to figures from the ADB. In 2005, according to official estimates, agriculture engaged less than 7.4% of the economically active population (excluding subsistence workers). The principal cash crop is coconut, yielding copra as well as coconut oil. In 2007 exports of crude coconut oil accounted for 47.5% of the country's total receipts from exports and re-exports. Export revenue from copra and copra cake reached almost $A1.7m. in 2007, accounting for 14.4 of the total. Bananas, taro, screw-pine (*Pandanus*), breadfruit and papaya are cultivated as food crops. The cultivation of seaweed began in the mid-1980s. In 2007 seaweed provided 1.9% of total export earnings. Pigs and chickens are kept. The sale of fishing licences to foreign fleets (notably from South Korea, Japan, the People's Republic of China, Taiwan and the USA) has provided an important source of income. Revenue from the sale of fishing licences reached a record $A52m. in 2001 but had declined to $A24.5m. by 2004 and continued to decrease in 2005–07. Nevertheless, in 2006 fees from fishing licences accounted for 43% of total government revenue. In September of that year a new six-year agreeement with the European Union (EU) entered into force: 16 Spanish vessels were permitted to fish for tuna in Kiribati waters, while the EU's annual financial contribution was to remain at US $0.6m. The GDP of the agricultural sector declined at an average annual rate of 4.7% in 2000–06. According to the ADB, agricultural GDP contracted by 63.3% in 2005 and by 658.4% in 2006.

Industry (including manufacturing, construction and utilities) contributed an estimated 6.5% of GDP in 2006. The sector engaged 8.7% of the economically active population in 2005. Industrial GDP contracted by an average of 1.3% per year in 2000–06. Compared with the previous year, industrial GDP was estimated by the ADB to have increased by 10.2% in 2005 and by 2.2% in 2006.

Mining of phosphate rock on the island of Banaba, which ceased in 1979, formerly provided some 80% of export earnings. Interest from a phosphate reserve fund (the Revenue Equalization Reserve Fund—RERF), established in 1956, became an important source of income (see below). The production of solar-evaporated salt for export to other islands of the Pacific (for use on fishing vessels with brine refrigeration systems) began on Kiritimati in 1985.

Manufacturing, which was estimated to have contributed just 0.8% of GDP in 2006, is confined to the small-scale production of coconut-based products, soap, foods, handicrafts, furniture, leather goods and garments. Manufacturing GDP increased by an annual average of 3.1% in 2000–06, according to ADB figures. Compared with the previous year, the GDP of the manufacturing sector decreased by 0.6% in 2005, but grew by 0.7% in 2006.

Production of electrical energy increased from 15.1m. kWh in 2001 to 21.0m. kWh in 2005. Mineral fuels accounted for an estimated 24.9% of total import costs in 2007. In 2001 the EU announced that it planned to fund the introduction of 1,500 new solar energy systems to Kiribati. Moreover, in May 2003 the Government announced the completion of a Japanese-funded programme to construct a new power station, to install two new generating units and to upgrade 16 km of power lines. The project was expected to ensure a power supply sufficient to meet Kiribati's increasing demand.

The services sector engaged 83.9% of the economically active population in 2005. Services provided 86.5% of GDP in 2006. In that year the government sector accounted for an estimated 47% of GDP, compared with 30% in 2000. Although impeded by factors such as the high costs of transport, the tourism sector makes a significant contribution to the economy. The hotel and restaurant sector provided 6.6% of GDP in 2006, according to preliminary figures. Receipts from tourism totalled $A3.0m. in 2001. An estimated 3,871 visitors arrived in Kiribati in 2008. The GDP of the services sector increased at an annual average rate of 0.9% in 2000–06. According to the ADB, the services sector's GDP increased by 5.0% in 2005 and by 5.9% in 2006.

In 2006, according to the ADB, Kiribati recorded a trade deficit of an estimated US $103.3m., and a deficit of $42.6m. on the current account of the balance of payments. The ADB estimated that the deficit on the current account was equivalent to 71.3% of GDP in 2008. Kiribati depends on imports for almost all essential commodities, and import duties are a major source of government revenue. In 2005 the principal sources of imports were Australia (32.9%) and Fiji (27.0%). The principal recipients of exports in that year were the USA and Belgium. The major imports in 2005 were food and live animals, mineral fuels, manufactures, beverages and tobacco, and chemicals. The major exports in 2007 included coconut oil, copra and copra cake, and seaweed.

Current budgetary expenditure for 2005/06 reached almost $A80.0m., while revenue totalled $A76.9m. It was anticipated that the budgetary deficit for 2006/07 would be financed wholly by a drawdown from the RERF. However, it was feared that such substantial drawdowns, which totalled $A45m. in 2007, might in the longer term jeopardize the Government's use of this source of budgetary support. In 2008, according to the ADB, the government deficit reached the equivalent of 13.0% of GDP. The country is reliant on foreign assistance for its development budget. Australia is a major provider of development assistance, with emphasis on the management of human resources, training, governance, health, education and improved customs procedures, within the framework of a new co-operation strategy. In 2008/09 aid from Australia was projected at $A18.4m. Aid from New Zealand was expected to total $NZ6.0m. in 2008/09. Through the ADB, Taiwan has provided aid to finance various development projects, as has Japan. Kiribati's total external debt was estimated by the ADB to have risen from US $47m. in 2006 to $52m. in 2007. The cost of debt-servicing was estimated to be the equivalent of 3.6% of the value of goods and services in 2006. The annual rate of inflation averaged 1.3% in 2000–06. Consumer prices rose by 4.2% in 2007 and by 11.0% in 2008. About 6.1% of the labour force were unemployed in 2005. Only around 8,600 people, equivalent to less than 20% of the working-age population, were formally employed in 2001, mainly in the public sector.

Kiribati is a member of the Pacific Community (see p. 391), the Pacific Islands Forum (see p. 393) and the Asian Development Bank (ADB, see p. 191); it is an associate member of the UN Economic and Social Commission for Asia and the Pacific (ESCAP, see p. 36), and is a signatory to the South Pacific Regional Trade and Economic Co-operation Agreement (SPARTECA, see p. 395) and to the Lomé Conventions and successor Cotonou Agreement (see p. 311) with the EU. The Council of Micronesian Government Executives, of which Kiribati was a founder member in 1996, aims to facilitate discussion of economic developments in the region and to examine possibilities for reducing the considerable cost of shipping essential goods between the islands.

Kiribati is one of the world's least developed nations. The country's export base is extremely limited, and the economy remains vulnerable to fluctuations in international copra prices. The severe drought of 2007/08 was reported to have decimated the coconut crop. With rising international prices for foodstuffs, pressure to raise levels of local food production intensified in 2008. In December Taiwan donated 200 metric tons of rice to help alleviate food shortages. Further concerns were raised regarding Kiribati's water supply; vital ground aquifers, the islands' main source, were no longer able to meet the needs of the most densely populated areas. With assistance from a team of experts from an Australian university, by early 2009 the Government had established water reserves, areas from which inhabitants and domestic animals were barred, in an attempt to ensure sustainability of water supplies. The construction of desalination plants and the purchase of water from overseas were also under consideration. In April 2009, however, it was revealed that the shortage of drinking water in the southern islands had become so serious that villagers were being forced to abandon their homes. The level of emigrants' remittances remained stable in 2008, reaching an estimated US $8m. The majority of emigrant workers are seafarers employed on foreign ships. From 2009, however, such employment opportunities were expected to be restricted by the deterioration in global economic conditions. It was hoped that this contraction might be offset by increasing seasonal demand for agricultural labourers in Australia and New Zealand, under new schemes whereby the two countries provided temporary work permits to Pacific islanders. At October 2006 the value of

KIRIBATI

the RERF was estimated at $A666m., compared with $A97m. in 1984. The Government also holds substantial offshore assets through the Kiribati Provident Fund. In addition to its efforts to assist Kiribati in the development of the outer islands, the ADB proposed to offer a loan of US $10m. to assist in the establishment of the Kiritimati Island Growth Center in 2007. The 2008–11 National Sustainable Development Strategy was expected to focus on the strategic areas of economic growth, the reduction of poverty, health and education, the environment, improved governance and the upgrading of the country's infrastructure. The ADB forecast GDP growth of 1.0% in 2009.

Education

Education is compulsory for nine years between the ages of six and 15 years, comprising six years of primary school and three years of junior secondary school, an initiative introduced in 1998. Students may then continue at secondary school for a further three years. Every atoll is provided with at least one primary and junior secondary school. In 2001/02 enrolment at primary schools reached 97.4% of pupils in the relevant age-group. In 2004/05 enrolment at secondary schools stood at 67.6% of students in the relevant age-group. In 2005 there were 91 primary schools and 35 secondary schools. In 2004/05 there were 16,133 pupils enrolled in primary school and 7,487 students enrolled in secondary school. The Government administers a technical college and training colleges for teachers, nurses and seafarers (the last, the Marine Training Centre, trains about 200 students each year for employment by overseas shipping companies). An extramural centre of the University of the South Pacific (based in Fiji) is located on South Tarawa. In 2005/06 the Government allocated $A21.9m. (equivalent to 27.4% of total budgetary expenditure) to education.

Public Holidays

2009: 1 January (New Year), 10–13 April (Easter), 18 April (National Health Day), 11 July (National Church Day), 12–16 July (National Day Celebrations), 7 August (Youth Day), 11 December (Human Rights and Peace Day), 25–26 December (Christmas).

2010: 1 January (New Year), 2–5 April (Easter), 18 April (National Health Day), 11 July (National Church Day), 12–16 July (National Day Celebrations), 7 August (Youth Day), 11 December (Human Rights and Peace Day), 25–26 December (Christmas).

Weights and Measures

The metric system is in use.

Statistical Survey

Source (unless otherwise stated): Statistics Office, Ministry of Finance and Economic Planning, POB 67, Bairiki, Tarawa; tel. 21082; fax 21307; e-mail statistics@mfep.gov.ki; internet www.spc.int/prism/country/KI/Stats.

AREA AND POPULATION

Area: 810.5 sq km (312.9 sq miles). *Principal Atolls* (sq km): Banaba (island) 6.3, Tarawa 31.0 (North 15.3, South 15.8), Abemama 27.4, Tabiteuea 37.6 (North 25.8, South 11.9), Total Gilbert group (incl. others) 285.5; Kanton (Phoenix Is) 9.2, Tabuaeran (Fanning—Line Is) 33.8, Kiritimati (Christmas—Line Is) 388.4, Total Line and Phoenix group 525.0 (Line Is 496.0, Phoenix Is 29.0).

Population: 84,494 at census of 7 November 2000; 92,533 (males 45,612, females 46,921) at census of 7 November 2005. *Principal Atolls* (2005: Banaba (island) 301; Abaiang 5,502; Tarawa 45,989 (North 5,678, South 40,311); Tabiteuea 4,898 (North 3,600, South 1,298); Total Gilbert group (incl. others) 83,683; Kanton (Phoenix Is) 41; Kiritimati 5,115; Total Line and Phoenix Group (incl. others) 8,850. *2007* (estimate at mid-year): 95,500 (Source: Asian Development Bank).

Density (mid-2007): 117.8 per sq km.

Ethnic Groups (census of 2000): Micronesians 83,452; Polynesians 641; Europeans 154; Others 247; Total 84,494.

Principal Villages: (population at 2005 census): Betio 12,509; Bikenibeu 6,170; Teaoraereke 3,939; Bairiki (capital) 2,766; Eita 2,399; Bonriki 2,119; Temwaiku 2,011. Note: All of the listed villages are in South Tarawa atoll.

Births, Marriages and Deaths: Registered live births (2005) 2,462 (birth rate 26.6 per 1,000); Marriages (registrations, 1988) 352 (marriage rate 5.2 per 1,000); Registered deaths (2005) 806 (death rate 8.7 per 1,000).

Life Expectancy (years at birth, WHO estimates): 65.3 (males 62.7; females 68.3) in 2006. Source: WHO, *World Health Statistics*.

Economically Active Population (paid employees aged 15 years and over, 2005 census): Agriculture, hunting, forestry and fishing 936; Manufacturing 305; Electricity, gas and water 293; Construction 511; Trade, restaurants and hotels 1,873; Transport, storage and communications 1,473; Financing, insurance, real estate and business services 356; Public administration 6,953; Activities not adequately defined 433; *Total employed* 13,133 (males 8,095, females 5,038); Unemployed 2,254 (males 1,130, females 1,124); *Total cash labour force* 15,387 (males 9,225, 6,162). Note: Subsistence workers (not included) numbered 21,582 (males 10,788, females 10,794).

HEALTH AND WELFARE

Key Indicators

Total Fertility Rate (children per woman, 2006): 4.2.

Under-5 Mortality Rate (per 1,000 live births, 2006): 64.

Physicians (per 1,000 head, 2004): 0.2.

Hospital Beds (per 1,000 head, 2005): 1.5.

Health Expenditure (2006): US $ per head (PPP): 290.

Health Expenditure (2006): % of GDP: 12.7.

Health Expenditure (2006): public (% of total): 92.4.

Access to Water (% of persons, 2006): 65.

Access to Sanitation (% of persons, 2006): 33.

For sources and definitions, see explanatory note on p. vi.

AGRICULTURE, ETC.

Principal Crops ('000 metric tons, 2007, FAO estimates): Taro (Cocoyam) 2.2; Other roots and tubers 8.2; Coconuts 110.0; Copra 1.9; Vegetables 6.2; Bananas 5.8.

Livestock ('000 head, year ending September 2007, FAO estimates): Pigs 12.6; Chickens 480.

Livestock Products (metric tons, 2007, FAO estimates): Pig meat 900; Poultry meat 480; Hen eggs 270.

Fishing (metric tons, live weight, 2006): Capture 31,000* (Emperors 2,900*; Mullets 2,150*; Snappers and jobfishes 3,680*; Jacks and crevalles 2,700*; Skipjack tuna 3,367; Yellowfin tuna 1,263; Other marine fishes 8,973*; Marine molluscs 5,350*); Aquaculture 10; Total catch 31,010*. Figures exclude aquatic plants (metric tons): 3,900* (all aquaculture).

*FAO estimate.

Source: FAO.

INDUSTRY

Copra Production (processed, metric tons): 10,501 in 2003; 12,334 in 2004; 6,194 in 2005.

Electric Energy (million kWh): 17.76 in 2003; 20.50 in 2004; 21.00 in 2005.

Source: Asian Development Bank, *Key Indicators of Developing Asian and Pacific Countries*.

FINANCE

Currency and Exchange Rates: Australian currency: 100 cents = 1 Australian dollar ($A). Sterling, US Dollar and Euro Equivalents (31 December 2008): £1 sterling = $A2.104; US $1 = $A1.443; €1 = $A2.001; $A100 = £47.52 = US $69.28 = €49.78. *Average Exchange Rate* (Australian dollars per US $): 1.3280 in 2006; 1.1951 in 2007; 1.1922 in 2008.

Budget (central government operations, $A '000, year ending 30 June 2006): *Revenue*: Current 76,929 (Direct taxes 27,551, Property income 45,426, Fees, etc. 3,852, Other 71; Capital receipts –6; Total 76,923. *Current Expenditure:* General public services 8,039; Public order and safety 6,987; Education 21,889; Health 13,009; Welfare and environment 2,611; Community and culture 2,575; Agriculture, etc. 1,829; Construction affairs 2,734; Communications 3,363; Commerce 1,032; Labour affairs 2,105; Others 13,794; Total 79,967.

Cost of Living (Consumer Price Index; base: 2000 = 100): All items 110.3 in 2004; 110.0 in 2005; 108.3 in 2006. Source: ILO.

Gross Domestic Product ($A '000 at constant 1991 prices): 68,311 in 2004; 63,379 in 2005 (preliminary); 62,978 in 2006 (preliminary).

Expenditure on the Gross Domestic Product ($A million at current prices, 2006): Government final consumption expenditure 36; Private final consumption expenditure 61; Gross fixed capital formation 43; *Total domestic expenditure* 140; Exports of goods and services 30; *Less* Imports of goods and services 72; *GDP in purchasers' values* 99. Source: UN Statistics Division, National Accounts Main Aggregates Database.

Gross Domestic Product by Economic Activity ($A '000 at current prices, 2006): Agriculture and fishing 5,396; Manufacturing 646; Electricity, gas and water 370; Construction 3,980; Wholesale and retail trade 7,167; Transport and communications 8,782; Financial intermediation 10,096; Government administration 38,485; Other community, social and personal service activities 2,330; *Sub-total* 77,252; *Less* Imputed bank service charge 4,385; Indirect taxes, less subsidies 17,700; *GDP in purchasers' values* 90,567. Source: Asian Development Bank, *Key Indicators of Developing Asian and Pacific Countries*.

Balance of Payments (US $ '000, 2006): Exports of goods 1,986; Imports of goods −105,243; *Trade balance* −103,257; Exports of services and income 76,322; Imports of services and income −52,965; *Balance on goods, services and income* −79,900; Current transfers received 39,780; Current transfers paid −1,538; *Current balance* −42,581 (incl. adjustments); Capital account (net) 60,180; Portfolio investment (net) −11,433; Other investments (net) 11,743; Net errors and omissions 75,774; *Overall balance* 93,683. Source: Asian Development Bank, *Key Indicators of Developing Asian and Pacific Countries*.

EXTERNAL TRADE

Principal Commodities ($A '000, 2007): *Imports:* Food and live animals 26,429; Beverages and tobacco 5,434; Crude materials (excl. fuels) 1,327; Mineral fuels, lubricants, etc. 20,849; Chemicals 3,681; Basic manufactures 10,081; Machinery and transport equipment 10,841; Miscellaneous manufactured articles 4,254; Total (incl. others) 83,632. *Exports (incl. re-exports):* Copra 769; Copra cake (meal) 904; Coconut oil (crude) 5,531; Seaweed 220; Total (incl. others) 11,655 (Re-exports 2,218).

Principal Trading Partners (US $ million, 2005): *Imports*: Australia 25.6; Fiji 21.0; Japan 14.1; New Zealand 5.3; Total (incl. others) 77.7. *Exports* (incl. re-exports): Belgium 1.1; Japan 0.7; USA 1.2; Total (incl. others) 5.2. Source: Asian Development Bank, *Key Indicators of Developing Asian and Pacific Countries*.

TRANSPORT

Road Traffic (motor vehicles registered on Tarawa, 2004): Motor cycles 634; Passenger cars 610; Buses 7; Trucks 502; Minibuses 299; Others 18; Total 2,070.

Shipping: *Merchant Fleet* (registered, at 31 December 2007): 62 vessels; total displacement 150,653 grt. (Source: Lloyd's Register-Fairplay, *World Fleet Statistics*). *International Sea-borne Freight Traffic* ('000 metric tons, 1990): Goods loaded 15; Goods unloaded 26 (Source: UN, *Monthly Bulletin of Statistics*).

Civil Aviation (traffic on scheduled services, 1998): Passengers carried 28,000; Passenger-km 11 million; Total ton-km 2 million. Source: UN, *Statistical Yearbook*.

TOURISM

Foreign Tourist Arrivals: 3,936 in 2006; 5,687 in 2007.

Tourist Arrivals by Country of Residence (by air at Tarawa, 2006): Australia 407; Fiji 284; Japan 81; Nauru 55; New Zealand 146; Solomon Islands 32; USA 20; Total (incl. others) 2,004.

Tourism Receipts ($A million): 2.1 in 1999; 2.2 in 2000; 3.0 in 2001.

COMMUNICATIONS MEDIA

Radio Receivers (1997): 17,000 in use.

Television Receivers (1997): 1,000 in use.

Telephones (main lines in use, 2007): 4,500.

Facsimile Machines (1996): 200 in use.

Mobile Cellular Telephones (subscribers, 2007): 700.

Personal Computers ('000 in use, 2005): 1.

Internet Users ('000, 2006): 2.

Non-daily Newspapers: 2 (estimated combined circulation 3,600) in 2002; 3 in 2004.

Sources: UNESCO, *Statistical Yearbook*; UN, *Statistical Yearbook*; International Telecommunication Union; Australian Press Council.

EDUCATION

Primary (2005): 91 schools; 16,133 students (males 8,167, females 7,966); 654 teachers (males 492, females 162).

Secondary (2005): 35 schools; 7,487 students (males 3,716, females 3,771); 665 teachers (males 350, females 315).

Teacher-training (2001): 198 students; 22 teachers.

Vocational (2001): 1,303 students; 17 teachers.

Adult Literacy Rate (UNESCO estimates): 92.5% (males 93%; females 92%) in 2001. Source: UNESCO, *Assessment of Resources, Best Practices and Gaps in Gender, Science and Technology in Kiribati*.

Directory

The Constitution

A new Constitution was promulgated at independence on 12 July 1979. The main provisions are as follows:

The Constitution states that Kiribati is a sovereign democratic Republic and that the Constitution is the supreme law. It guarantees protection of all fundamental rights and freedoms of the individual and provides for the determination of citizenship.

The President, known as the Beretitenti, is Head of State and Head of the Government and presides over the Cabinet which consists of the Beretitenti, the Kauoman-ni-Beretitenti (Vice-President), the Attorney-General and not more than eight other ministers appointed by the Beretitenti from an elected parliament known as the Maneaba ni Maungatabu. The Constitution stipulated that the pre-independence Chief Minister became the first Beretitenti, but that in future the Beretitenti would be elected. After each general election for the Maneaba, the chamber nominates, from among its members, three or four candidates from whom the Beretitenti is elected by universal adult suffrage. Executive authority is vested in the Cabinet, which is directly responsible to the Maneaba ni Maungatabu. The Constitution also provides for a Council of State consisting of the Chairman of the Public Services Commission, the Chief Justice and the Speaker of the Maneaba.

Legislative power resides with the single-chamber Maneaba ni Maungatabu, composed of 42 members elected by universal adult suffrage for four years (subject to dissolution), one nominated member (see below) and the Attorney-General as an ex-officio member if he is not elected. The Maneaba is presided over by the Speaker, who is elected by the Maneaba from among persons who are not members of the Maneaba.

One chapter makes special provision for Banaba and the Banabans, stating that one seat in the Maneaba is reserved for a nominated member of the Banaban community. The Banabans' inalienable right to enter and reside in Banaba is guaranteed and, where any right over or interest in land there has been acquired by the Republic of Kiribati or by the Crown before independence, the Republic is required to hand back the land on completion of phosphate extraction. A Banaba Island Council is provided for, as is an independent commission of inquiry to review the provisions relating to Banaba.

The Constitution also makes provision for finance, for a Public Service and for an independent judiciary (see Judicial System).

The Government

HEAD OF STATE

President (Beretitenti): ANOTE TONG (elected 4 July 2003; re-elected 17 October 2007).

Vice-President (Kauoman-ni-Beretitenti): TEIMA ONORIO.

KIRIBATI

CABINET
(April 2009)

President and Minister for Foreign Affairs and Immigration: ANOTE TONG.

Vice-President and Minister for Commerce, Industry and Co-operatives: TEIMA ONORIO.

Minister for Communications, Transport and Tourism Development: TEMATE ERIATEITI.

Minister for Education: JAMES TAOM.

Minister for Environment, Lands and Agricultural Development: TETABO NAKARA.

Minister for Finance and Economic Development: NATAN TEEWE.

Minister for Fisheries and Marine Resource Development: TABERANNANG TIMEON.

Minister for Health and Medical Services: Dr KAUTU TENANAUA.

Minister for Internal and Home Affairs: AMBEROTI NIKORA.

Minister for Labour and Human Resource Development: IOTEBA REDFERN.

Minister for the Line and Phoenix Islands Development: TAWITA TEMOKU.

Minister for Public Works and Utilities: KOURAITI BENIATO.

MINISTRIES

Office of the President (Beretitenti): POB 68, Bairiki, Tarawa; tel. 21183; fax 21145.

Ministry of Commerce, Industry and Co-operatives: POB 510, Betio, Tarawa; tel. 26158; fax 26233; e-mail commerce@tskl.net.ki.

Ministry of Communications, Transport and Tourism Development: POB 487, Betio, Tarawa; tel. 26003; fax 26193.

Ministry of Education, Youth and Sport Development: POB 263, Bikenibeu, Tarawa; tel. 28091; fax 28222.

Ministry of the Environment, Lands and Agricultural Development: POB 234, Bikenibeu, Tarawa; tel. 28507; fax 28334.

Ministry of Finance and Economic Development: POB 67, Bairiki, Tarawa; tel. 21816; fax 21307.

Ministry of Fisheries and Marine Resources Development: POB 64, Bairiki, Tarawa; tel. 21099; fax 21120.

Ministry of Foreign Affairs and Immigration: POB 68, Bairiki, Tarawa; tel. 21342; fax 21466; e-mail mfa@tskl.net.ki.

Ministry of Health and Medical Services: POB 268, Bikenibeu, Tarawa; tel. 28100; fax 28152.

Ministry of Internal Affairs and Social Development: POB 75, Bairiki, Tarawa; tel. 21092; fax 21133; e-mail homeaffairs@tskl.net.ki.

Ministry of Labour and Human Resource Development: POB 69, Bairiki, Tarawa; tel. 21068; fax 21452.

Ministry of Line and Phoenix Islands: Kiritimati Island; tel. 81211; fax 81278.

Ministry of Public Works and Utilities: POB 498, Betio, Tarawa; tel. 26192; fax 26172.

President and Legislature

PRESIDENT
Election, 17 October 2007

Candidate	Votes	% of votes
Anote Tong	15,676	64.3
Nabuti Mwemwenikarawa	8,151	33.4
Patrick Tatireta	356	1.5
Timon Aneri	198	0.8
Total	**24,381**	**100.0**

MANEABA NI MAUNGATABU
(House of Assembly)

This is a unicameral body comprising 42 elected members (most of whom formally present themselves for election as independent candidates), and one nominated representative of the Banaban community, along with the Attorney-General in an ex officio capacity (if the latter is not elected). An election was held on 22 August 2007, with a second round of voting conducted on 30 August.

Speaker: TAOMATI IUTA.

Election Commission

Election Commission: Tarawa; Electoral Commissioner RINE UEARA.

Political Organizations

Political organizations in Kiribati are not conventional organized bodies but loose groupings of individuals supporting similar policies. In addition to the groupings listed below, also in existence are: the National Progressive Party, led by Teatao Teannaki, and the Liberal Party, led by Tewareka Tentoa.

Boutokan Te Koaua: c/o Maneaba Ni Maungatabu, Tarawa; tel. 21880; fax 21278; mems affiliated to Anote Tong.

Maneaban Te Mauri: c/o Maneaba Ni Maungatabu, Tawara; tel. 21880; fax 21278; mems affiliated to Teburoro Tito and Harry Tong.

Maurin Kiribati Party: c/o Maneaba Ni Maungatabu, Tawara; Sec. NABUTI MWEMWENIKARAWA.

Diplomatic Representation
EMBASSY AND HIGH COMMISSIONS IN KIRIBATI

Australia: POB 77, Bairiki, Tarawa; tel. 21184; fax 21904; internet www.kiribati.embassy.gov.au; High Commissioner ANNE QUINANE.

China (Taiwan): Bairiki, Tarawa; tel. 22557; fax 22535; e-mail Kir@mofa.gov.tw; Ambassador CHEN SHIH-LIANG.

New Zealand: POB 53, Bairiki, Tarawa; tel. 21400; fax 21402; e-mail nzhc@tskl.net.ki; High Commissioner ROBERT KAIWAI.

Judicial System

There are 24 Magistrates' Courts (each consisting of one presiding magistrate and up to eight other magistrates) hearing civil, criminal and land cases. When hearing civil or criminal cases, the presiding magistrate sits with two other magistrates, and when hearing land cases with four other magistrates. A single magistrate has national jurisdiction in civil and criminal matters. Appeal from the Magistrates' Courts lies, in civil and criminal matters, to a single judge of the High Court, and, in matters concerning land, divorce and inheritance, to the High Court's Land Division, which consists of a judge and two Land Appeal Magistrates.

The High Court of Kiribati is a superior court of record and has unlimited jurisdiction. It consists of the Chief Justice and a Puisne Judge. Appeal from a single judge of the High Court, both as a Court of the First Instance and in its appellate capacity, lies to the Kiribati Court of Appeal, which is also a court of record and consists of a panel of three judges.

All judicial appointments are made by the Beretitenti (President).

High Court
POB 501, Betio, Tarawa; tel. 26007; fax 26149; e-mail robin.millhouse@gmail.com.

Chief Justice: ROBIN MILLHOUSE.

Judges of the Kiribati Court of Appeal: ROBIN MILLHOUSE (President), Sir ROBERT SMELLIE, Sir DAVID TOMPKINS, ROBERT FISHER.

Religion
CHRISTIANITY

Most of the population are Christians: 53.4% Roman Catholic and 39.2% members of the Kiribati Protestant Church, according to the 1990 census.

The Roman Catholic Church

Kiribati forms part of the diocese of Tarawa and Nauru, suffragan to the archdiocese of Suva (Fiji). At 31 December 2006 the diocese contained an estimated 60,686 adherents. The Bishop participates in the Catholic Bishops' Conference of the Pacific, based in Suva (Fiji).

Bishop of Tarawa and Nauru: Most Rev. PAUL EUSEBIUS MEA KAIUEA, Bishop's House, POB 79, Bairiki, Tarawa; tel. 21279; fax 21401; e-mail diocesetarawa@tskl.net.ki.

The Anglican Communion

Kiribati is within the diocese of Polynesia, part of the Anglican Church in Aotearoa, New Zealand and Polynesia. The Bishop in Polynesia is resident in Fiji.

Protestant Church

Kiribati Protestant Church: POB 80, Bairiki, Tarawa; tel. 21195; fax 21453; e-mail kpc@tskl.net.ki; f. 1988; Moderator Rev. BAITEKE NABETARI; Gen. Sec. Rev. TIAONTIN ARUE; 29,432 mems in 1998.

Other Churches

Seventh-day Adventist, Church of God and Assembly of God communities are also represented, as is the Church of Jesus Christ of Latter-day Saints (Mormon).

BAHÁ'Í FAITH

National Spiritual Assembly: POB 269, Bikenibeu, Tarawa; tel. and fax 28074; e-mail emi@tskl.net.ki; 2,400 mems resident in 100 localities in 1995.

The Press

Butim'aea Manin te Euangkerio: POB 80, Bairiki, Tarawa; tel. 21195; e-mail kpc@tskl.net.ki; f. 1913; Protestant Church newspaper; weekly; a monthly publication Te Kaotan te Ota is also produced; Editor Rev. TOOM TOAKAI.

Kiribati Business Link: Bairiki, Tarawa; English.

Kiribati Newstar: POB 10, Bairiki, Tarawa; tel. 21652; fax 21671; f. 2000; independent; weekly; English and I-Kiribati; Editor-in-Chief NGAUEA UATIOA.

Te Itoi ni Kiribati: POB 231, Bikenibeu, Tarawa; tel. 28138; fax 21341; f. 1914; Roman Catholic Church newsletter; monthly; circ. 2,300.

Te Mauri: Protestant Church newspaper; Editor BATIRI BATAUA.

Te Uekera: Broadcasting and Publications Authority, POB 78, Bairiki, Tarawa; tel. 21162; fax 21096; e-mail bpa_admin@tskl.net.ki; f. 1945; bi-weekly; English and I-Kiribati; Editor ROOTI TERUBEA; circ. 2,000.

Broadcasting and Communications

TELECOMMUNICATIONS

Telecom Kiribati Ltd: Bairiki, Tarawa; govt-owned; Gen. Man. ENOTA INGINTAU.

Telecom Services Kiribati Ltd: POB 72, Bairiki, Tarawa; tel. 20700; fax 21424; e-mail ceo@tskl.net.ki; internet www.tskl.net.ki; Chair. ELLIOT ALI; CEO BARANIKO TONGANIBEIA.

BROADCASTING

Regulatory Authority

Broadcasting and Publications Authority: POB 78, Bairiki, Tarawa; tel. 21187; fax 21096.

Radio

Radio Kiribati: Broadcasting and Publications Authority, POB 78, Bairiki, Tarawa; tel. 21187; fax 21096; f. 1954; statutory body; station Radio Kiribati broadcasting on SW and MW transmitters; programmes in I-Kiribati (90%) and English (10%); some advertising; Gen. Man. TANIERI TEIBUAKO.

Television

Television Kiribati Ltd: Betio, Tarawa; tel. 26036; fax 26045; internet www.tkl.com.ki.

Finance

(cap. = capital; dep. = deposits; res = reserves)

BANKING

The Bank of Kiribati Ltd: POB 66, Bairiki, Tarawa; tel. 21095; fax 21200; e-mail anzkiribati@anz.com; internet www.anz.com/kiribati; f. 1984; 75% owned by ANZ Bank, 25% by Govt of Kiribati; Chair. R. GOUDSWAARD; Pres. and Man. Dir NEVILLE OLDHAM; 3 brs.

Development Bank of Kiribati: POB 33, Bairiki, Tarawa; tel. 21345; fax 21297; e-mail dbk@tskl.net.ki; f. 1986; took over the assets of the National Loans Board; identifies, promotes and finances small-scale projects; auth. cap. $A2m.; Gen. Man. KIETAU TABWEBWEITI; 5 brs.

A network of lending entities known as 'village banks' operates throughout the islands, as do a number of credit unions under the management of the Credit Union League.

INSURANCE

Kiribati Insurance Corpn: POB 38, Bairiki, Tarawa; tel. 21260; fax 21426; e-mail kirins@tskl.net.ki; f. 1981; govt-owned; only insurance co; reinsures overseas; Gen. Man. TEAIRO TOOMA.

Trade and Industry

GOVERNMENT AGENCIES

Kiribati Copra Mill Co Ltd: POB 607, Betio, Tarawa; tel. 26831; fax 26635; e-mail kcmc@tskl.net.ki; internet www.kcmcl.ki; f. 2001.

Kiribati Housing Corporation: Bairiki, Tarawa; tel. 21092; operates the Housing Loan and Advice Centre; Chair. TOKOREAUA KAIRORO.

Kiribati Provident Fund: POB 76, Bairiki, Tarawa; tel. 21300; fax 21186; f. 1977; Gen. Man. TOKAATA NIATA.

CHAMBER OF COMMERCE

Kiribati Chamber of Commerce: POB 550, Betio, Tarawa; tel. 26351; fax 26332; Pres. WAYSANG KUM KEE; Sec.-Gen. TIARITE KWONG.

UTILITIES

Public Utilities Board: POB 443, Betio, Tarawa; tel. 26292; fax 26106; e-mail ceo.pub@tskl.net.ki; f. 1977; govt-owned; provides electricity, water and sewerage services in Tarawa; CEO TABOIA METUTERA.

Solar Energy Company (SEC): POB 493 Betio, Tarawa; tel. 26058; fax 26210; e-mail sec@tskl.net.ki; a co-operative administering and implementing solar-generated electricity projects in North Tarawa and the outer islands.

CO-OPERATIVE SOCIETIES

Co-operative societies dominate trading in Tarawa and enjoy a virtual monopoly outside the capital, except for Banaba and Kiritimati.

Bobotin Kiribati Ltd (BKL): POB 485, Betio, Tarawa; tel. 26092; fax 26224; replaced Kiribati Co-operative Wholesale Society; govt-owned; Gen. Man. AKAU TIARE.

The Kiribati Copra Co-operative Society Ltd: POB 489, Betio, Tarawa; tel. 26534; fax 26391; e-mail kccs@tskl.net.ki; f. 1976; the sole exporter of copra; seven cttee mems; 29 mem. socs; Chair. RAIMON TAAKE; CEO RUTIANO BENETITO.

TRADE UNIONS

Kiribati Trades Union Congress (KTUC): POB 166, Bairiki, Tarawa; tel. 28157; fax 28712; e-mail ktc@tskl.net.ki; f. 1982; unions and asscns affiliated to the KTUC include the Fishermen's Union, the Co-operative Workers' Union, the Seamen's Union, the Teachers' Union, the Nurses' Asscn, the Public Employees' Asscn, the Bankers' Union, Butaritari Rural Workers' Union, Christmas Island Union of Federated Workers, the Pre-School Teachers' Asscn, Makim Island Rural Workers' Org., Nanolelei Retailers' Union, the Plantation Workers' Union of Fanning Island and the Overseas Fishermen's Union (formed in 1998); 2,500 mems; Pres. TATOA KAITEIE; Gen. Sec. TAMARETI TAAU.

Transport

ROADS

Wherever practicable, roads are built on all atolls, and connecting causeways between islets are also being constructed as funds and labour permit. A programme to construct causeways between North and South Tarawa was completed in the mid-1990s. Kiribati has about 670 km of roads that are suitable for motor vehicles; all-weather roads exist in Tarawa and Kiritimati.

SHIPPING

A major project to rehabilitate the port terminal and facilities at Betio, with finance totalling some US $22m. from Japan, was completed in 2000. There are other port facilities at Banaba, Kanton and English Harbour.

Kiribati Shipping Services Ltd (KSSL): POB 495, Betio, Tarawa; tel. 26195; fax 26204; e-mail kssl@tskl.net.ki; operates three passenger/freight vessels on inter-island services and one landing craft; govt-owned; Gen. Man. Capt. ITIBWINNANG AIAIMOA.

Nikoraoi Shipping: Betio, Tarawa; tel. 26536; fax 26367.

CIVIL AVIATION

There are five international airports (Bonriki on South Tarawa, Cassidy on Kiritimati, Antekana on Butaritari, as well as others on Kanton and Tabuaeran) and several other airfields in Kiribati. Air Pacific, the Fijian carrier, operates services to Tarawa and Kiritimati, with links to Nadi (Fiji) and Honolulu (Hawaii).

Air Kiribati Ltd: POB 274, Bonriki, Tarawa; tel. 28088; fax 28216; e-mail airkiribati.admin@tsklnet.ki; internet www.kiritours.com/Travel/AirKiribati/Index; f. 1977; fmrly Air Tungaru; national airline; operates scheduled services to outer islands; Chair. TAKEI TAOABA; CEO BARANIKO BAARO.

Tourism

Kiribati's potential attractions include fishing and bird-watching opportunities, as well as the sites of Second World War battles. In 1997 Caroline Island, situated close to the recently realigned international date-line, was renamed Millennium Island in an attempt to maximize its potential for attracting visitors. However, attempts to establish tourism as a major source of revenue have been impeded by the remoteness of the islands. The number of visitor arrivals was estimated to have reached only 3,871 in 2008. In 2001 the tourism industry earned some $A3.0m.

Kiribati National Tourism Office: Ministry of Communications, Transport and Tourism Development, POB 487, Betio, Tarawa; tel. 26003; fax 26193; e-mail sto@mict.gov.ki; internet www.visit-kiribati.com; Sec. DAVID YEETING; Senior Tourist Officer TARATAAKE TEANNAKI.

THE DEMOCRATIC PEOPLE'S REPUBLIC OF KOREA

Introductory Survey

Location, Climate, Language, Religion, Flag, Capital

The Democratic People's Republic of Korea (North Korea) occupies the northern part of the Korean peninsula, bordered to the north by the People's Republic of China and, for a very short section to the north-east, by the Russian Federation, and to the south by the Republic of Korea. The climate is continental, with cold, dry winters and hot, humid summers; temperatures range from −6°C to 25°C (21°F to 77°F). The language is Korean. Buddhism, Christianity and Chundo Kyo are officially cited as the principal religions. The national flag (proportions 33 by 65) is red, with blue stripes on the upper and lower edges, each separated from the red by a narrow white stripe. Left of centre is a white disc containing a five-pointed red star. The capital is Pyongyang.

Recent History

Korea was formerly an independent monarchy. It was occupied by Japanese forces in 1905 and annexed by Japan in 1910, when the Emperor was deposed. Following Japan's surrender in August 1945, ending the Second World War, Korea was divided at latitude 38°N into military occupation zones, with Soviet forces in the North and US forces in the South. A Provisional People's Committee, led by Kim Il Sung of the Korean Communist Party (KCP), was established in the North in February 1946 and accorded government status by the Soviet occupation forces. In July the KCP merged with another group to form the North Korean Workers' Party. In 1947 a legislative body, the Choe Ko In Min Hoe Ui (Supreme People's Assembly—SPA), was established, and Kim Il Sung became Premier. A new Assembly was elected in August 1948, and the Democratic People's Republic of Korea (DPRK) was proclaimed on 9 September. In the same year the Republic of Korea (q.v.) was proclaimed in the South. Initially, the DPRK was recognized only by the USSR and other communist countries. Soviet forces withdrew from North Korea in December 1948. In the following year, as a result of a merger between communists in the North and South, the Korean Workers' Party (KWP) was formed, under the leadership of Kim Il Sung; it has held power in North Korea ever since.

The two republics each claimed to have legitimate jurisdiction over the whole Korean peninsula. North Korean forces crossed the 38th parallel in June 1950, precipitating a three-year war between North and South. The UN mounted a collective defence action in support of South Korea, and the invasion was repelled. North Korean forces were supported by the People's Republic of China from October 1950. Peace talks began in July 1951 and an armistice agreement was concluded in July 1953. The cease-fire line, which approximately follows the 38th parallel, remains the frontier between North and South Korea. A demilitarized zone (DMZ), supervised by UN forces, separates the two countries.

Through the 'personality cult' of Kim Il Sung (the 'Great Leader') and of his son Kim Jong Il (the 'Dear Leader'), and a policy of strict surveillance of the entire population, overt opposition to the KWP was effectively eliminated. The only organized opposition to the regime (albeit in exile) appeared to be the Salvation Front for the Democratic Unification of Chosun, established by former military and other officials of the DPRK in the early 1990s, with branches in Russia, Japan and China. International human rights organizations indicated that they believed there to be a number of concentration camps in North Korea, in which as many as 200,000 political prisoners were being held.

A new Constitution, adopted in December 1972, created the office of President, and Kim Il Sung was duly elected to the post. Kim Jong Il was appointed to several key positions within the KWP in 1980. In July 1984 Radio Pyongyang referred to Kim Jong Il, for the first time, as the 'sole successor' to his father, but there were reports of opposition to the President's heir, particularly among older members of the KWP.

Following elections to the eighth SPA, in November 1986 (when the 655 members were returned unopposed), Kim Il Sung was re-elected President, and a new Administration Council (cabinet) was formed. In March 1990 Kim Il Sung was returned to the post of President, and Kim Jong Il was appointed to his first state (as distinct from party) post, as First Vice-Chairman of the National Defence Commission. In February 1991 it was rumoured that there had been an unsuccessful military coup against Kim Jong Il. In December he was appointed Supreme Commander of the Korean People's Army (KPA), in place of his father, and in January 1992 he was reported to have been given control of foreign policy. In April Kim Jong Il was appointed to the rank of Marshal, while his father assumed the title of Grand Marshal.

In what was interpreted as a partial attempt to adapt to the change in international conditions following the collapse of communist regimes world-wide, the SPA (according to South Korean reports) made several amendments to the DPRK's Constitution in April 1992. Principal among these were the deletion of all references to Marxism-Leninism, and the promotion of 'economic openness' to allow limited foreign investment in the DPRK (although the KWP's guiding principle of *juche*, or self-reliance, was strongly emphasized). In September measures to address the deteriorating economic situation included a drastic devaluation of the national currency. At the fifth session of the ninth SPA in April 1993 Kim Jong Il was elected Chairman of the National Defence Commission. In July Kim Il Sung's younger brother, Kim Yong Ju, unexpectedly returned to political life after a 17-year absence, and was subsequently elevated to the position of Vice-President and to membership of the Central Committee of the KWP's (Political Bureau) Politburo.

Kim Il Sung died of heart failure on 8 July 1994. One hundred days of national mourning were observed, but, contrary to expectations, Kim Jong Il was not appointed to the leading post of President of the DPRK. Kim Jong Il did not appear in public during this period, reviving earlier speculation that he was either in poor health or that a struggle for power was taking place. It was thought that Kim Il Sung's widow, Kim Song Ae, who was the stepmother of Kim Jong Il, favoured her eldest son, Kim Pyong Il, for the presidency. In February 1995 the Minister of the People's Armed Forces, Marshal O Jin U, died; O had been a significant supporter within the military of Kim Jong Il's succession. Scheduled elections to the SPA did not take place in April 1995, and no session of the Assembly was convened in 1996.

Meanwhile, from the mid-1990s, the influence of the KPA expanded significantly, as Kim Jong Il increasingly relied upon the military to maintain his power, and the policy of *Songun* ('military first') was emphasized as the regime's central doctrine. The 50th anniversary of the establishment of the KWP in October 1995 was dominated by the military rather than the party, and several generals were promoted. However, Kim Jong Il did not assume any new posts. In February 1996 Sung Hye Rim, a former consort of Kim Jong Il and mother of his eldest son, defected to a Western European country. In February 1997 Premier Kang Song San, who had made no public appearance since early 1996, was dismissed, and replaced on an acting basis by Hong Song Nam. Deepening social unrest was indicated by an increase in the rate of defections. In February 1997 Hwang Jang Yop, a close adviser to Kim Jong Il, sought political asylum in the South Korean embassy in China while returning from an official visit to Japan, and warned that the DPRK was preparing to launch a military assault on South Korea. Hwang's defection appeared to precipitate significant changes in the KWP and military high command, as did the deaths of the Minister of the People's Armed Forces, Marshal Choe Kwang, and of his deputy, Kim Kwang Jin. Many senior officials were replaced, and some 123 generals, including many allies of Kim Jong Il, were promoted in rank in April. In August two senior North Korean diplomats, including the ambassador to Egypt, defected to the USA. There were also rumours of unrest and coup attempts, and several senior officials disappeared from public view without explanation. The official mourning period for Kim Il Sung was formally declared to be at an end in July 1997, on the third anniversary of his death. It was announced that, henceforth, the country was to use the *Juche* calendar, with 1912, the year of Kim Il Sung's birth, designated the first year of the new calendar. On 8 October 1997, in accordance with the recommendations of recent municipal and provincial conferences of the KWP (including KPA delegates), Kim Jong Il was elected General Secretary of the KWP.

Elections to the SPA finally took place in July 1998, at which the single list of candidates received 100% of the votes cast. Some two-thirds of the 687 deputies were newcomers to the Assembly, while the military reportedly doubled its representation. The first session of the 10th SPA was convened in September. However, the anticipated appointment of Kim Jong Il as President of the DPRK did not occur, as the post was effectively abolished under major amendments to the Constitution that extensively revised the structure of government. The deceased Kim Il Sung was designated 'Eternal President', thus remaining *de jure* Head of State, while Kim Jong Il, who had been re-elected Chairman of the National Defence Commission (now apparently the highest office in the state hierarchy), was reported to have assumed the role of de facto Head of State. Vice-Marshal Jo Myong Rok, the Director of the General Political Bureau of the KPA, was appointed First Vice-Chairman of the Commission, becoming the de facto second-ranking official in the DPRK. The Cabinet, as the Administration Council was redesignated, assumed many of the functions of the Central People's Committee, which was abolished. A new Presidium of the SPA was established, the President of which was to represent the State in diplomatic affairs; Kim Yong Nam, hitherto Minister of Foreign Affairs, was appointed to this position. Hong Song Nam was formally appointed Premier of the new Cabinet. Two 'technocrats', Jo Chang Dok and Kwak Pom Gi, were appointed Vice-Premiers.

Elections to the Local People's Assemblies were held in March 1999; it was reported that all candidates were fully endorsed. In October 2000 the Minister of Finance, Rim Kyong Suk, and the President of the central bank, Jong Song Thaek, were dismissed. They were replaced, respectively, by Mun Il Bong and Kim Wan Su. No reasons were given for their dismissal. The replacement of the Minister of Foreign Trade in December was also unexplained. The Minister of Agriculture was replaced in March 2001.

In January 2001 the Government urged a 'new way of thinking' to solve the country's economic and domestic problems and to complement the *Kangsong Taeguk* ('prosperous and powerful nation') philosophy adopted in the late 1990s. Meanwhile, the number of people defecting from the North to the South continued to increase, with nearly 650 such persons having settled in the latter since 1996. Several senior officials died or were replaced during 2001, including Ri Song Bok, the Secretary-General of the Party Central Committee and a senior aide to Kim Jong Il, who died in May.

In March 2002 the fifth session of the 10th SPA was held. A new land planning law was adopted with the aim of improving and intensifying land work. Premier Hong Song Nam also urged improved trade and economic co-operation, including joint ventures with other countries and international organizations. In April Kim Jong Il promoted some 55 military leaders, including Jang Song U, the elder brother of Kim's brother-in-law, Jang Song Thaek.

The question of the succession of the next generation of leadership became increasingly important following Kim Jong Il's 60th birthday in February 2002. Kim was initially believed to have been preparing his eldest son, Kim Jong Nam, to succeed him. Kim Jong Nam had served in the Ministry of Public Security and as head of the country's information technology (IT) industry since the late 1990s; however, in May 2001 he was detained in Tokyo, on charges of entering Japan with a false passport, and subsequently deported to China. The incident discredited Kim Jong Nam, and thenceforth it was reported that Kim Jong Il was preparing for leadership Kim Jong Chol, the elder son of Ko Yong Hui, described as Kim Jong Il's unofficial wife. Kim Jong Nam spent much of 2002 in Russia, where his mother, Sung Hye Rim, died in July.

In September 2002 the Government designated the city of Sinuiju a 'Special Administrative Region' designed to attract foreign investment, and appointed Yang Bin, a Chinese-born Dutch citizen, as its first governor. However, within days of his appointment, Yang was arrested by the Chinese authorities on corruption charges, and he was unable to assume his post. None the less, the creation of the region was a significant development in the country's efforts to open up the economy. Under the 'Basic Law' establishing the region, Sinuiju would have its own government and legal system for a 50-year period, without interference from the DPRK. (In late 2004 there were indications that the Sinuiju project had been abandoned, although in July 2006 it was reported that DPRK loyalists and foreign-currency management groups were being moved into the area. In mid-2007 it was further reported that some 3,000 families were being relocated from Pyongyang to Sinuiju, which had apparently been declared a special economic zone earlier in that year.) In late 2002 the Government also established a special industrial zone in Kaesong, and a special tourist zone in the region of Mount Kumgang, although these did not have the same special status as Sinuiju. Despite these developments, a meeting of senior law enforcement officials was held in Pyongyang in December during which Premier Hong urged the elimination of 'non-socialist elements'. In early 2003 it was reported that travel restrictions within the country had been reintroduced, in order to improve security.

The sixth session of the 10th SPA was held in March 2003. Unlike previous sessions, Kim Jong Il did not attend the meeting. Having disappeared from public view for 50 days, according to South Korean sources, Kim reappeared in early April, and later in that month celebrations took place in Pyongyang to mark the 10th anniversary of Kim's election as Chairman of the National Defence Commission. Further celebrations took place in July to commemorate the 50th anniversary of the Korean War truce (celebrated as a triumph for the DPRK by the country's media). In August elections were held to form the 11th SPA. Voter turnout was reported to be have been 99.9%, and all 687 candidates were elected unopposed. At the first session of the 11th SPA in September, Kim Jong Il was re-elected as Chairman of the National Defence Commission. In October Kim Yong Sun, a member of the KWP Secretariat and Chairman of the Korea Asia-Pacific Peace Committee, died, reportedly as a result of a traffic accident. Kim Yong Sun had been an important official in the area of inter-Korean relations (see below).

In early 2004 reports from defectors, as well as some documentary evidence, indicated that mistreatment of political prisoners in the DPRK had included human experimentation for the purposes of chemical weapons development. On the occasion of Kim's 62nd birthday in February 2004, there was renewed speculation on the question of his successor. It was rumoured that Kim Jong Un, younger son of Ko Yong Hui, might have emerged as the most likely candidate, having been referred to by some sources as the 'Morning Star King'.

In April 2004 more than 150 people were killed and 1,300 injured by a massive explosion on a railway line at Ryongchon, a town near the border with China. Many children were among the victims of the accident, apparently caused when electric cables ignited chemical and other materials being transported by rail, only hours after a train carrying Kim Jong Il had travelled through the area. The North Korean authorities withheld information on the accident for two days, but subsequently accepted international humanitarian aid, including a donation (made through the Red Cross) from the USA.

In July 2004 Ju Sang Song was appointed as Minister of People's Security, replacing Choe Ryong Su. Choe had been removed from his post only one year after being appointed, and the reason for his removal was unclear. Also in July the 10th anniversary of the death of Kim Il Sung was commemorated. In August Ko Yong Hui, the mother of two of Kim Jong Il's sons (see above), was reported to have died. In November there was speculation that Kim's power might be weakening, following reports that portraits of him had been removed from public locations. It was also noted that official news reports no longer referred to Kim by the honorific title of 'Dear Leader'. Some sources claimed that Kim himself was attempting to diminish the personality cult surrounding him. However, there were tentative suggestions throughout 2004 that a power struggle was taking place in Pyongyang. It was believed that in April Kim had removed his brother-in-law, Jang Song Thaek, from his position as vice-director of the KWP Central Committee and placed him under house arrest. Later in the year Jang's wife, Kim Jong Il's sister Kim Kyong Hui, was injured in a traffic incident, which was believed to have been a deliberate attack. Meanwhile, in April Kim's eldest son, Kim Jong Nam (see above), reportedly survived an assassination attempt in Austria.

In May 2005 South Korean media reported that the North Korean Minister of Post and Telecommunications, Ri Kum Bom, had been dismissed, apparently as a result of his failure to control the revelation of information earlier in the year disclosing that the DPRK was in the process of combating outbreaks of avian influenza ('bird flu'). In July it was announced that his replacement was Ryu Yong Sop. In August an unspecified number of prisoners were granted an amnesty to mark the 60th anniversary of the liberation of the Korean peninsula from Japanese rule. In October the 60th anniversary of the KWP was celebrated. North Korean citizens were reportedly granted four public holidays in honour of the event. On 9 October, the day before the anniversary, the KWP held a national meeting in Pyongyang, at which the primacy of the *Songun* ('military first') policy was reaffirmed, as was the need for economic development in order to achieve the objective of *Kangsong Taeguk* ('prosperous and powerful nation'). The anniversary itself was commemorated with a large military parade in Pyongyang. In late October it was reported that Yon Hyong Muk, a Vice-Chairman of the National Defence Commission, who was regarded as a close adviser to Kim Jong Il, had died. North Korean media reports in November indicated that Ri Kwang Nam had been replaced as Minister of Extractive Industries by Kang Min Chol, while a report in December implied that Kim Jin Song had become Minister of Culture, replacing Choe Ik Kyu. In January 2006 Jang Song Thaek made his first public appearance since 2003, prompting speculation that he had been rehabilitated following his apparent removal from favour in 2004 (see above).

While thousands took to the streets in October 2006 for mass rallies to celebrate the nuclear test (see below), in November a rare protest against the authorities occurred in a town in North Hamkyong Province. Although the number of protesters was said to be little more than 100, the demonstration was highly significant, private mass activities being forbidden by North Korean law. According to a report on *Daily NK*, a website maintained by a group campaigning for democracy in the DPRK, residents of Hoiryeong were demonstrating against 'refurbishment fees' for a local market imposed on them by the town's officials. North Korean refugees living in China also reported growing discontent towards the regime, with 90% of the 1,300 refugees questioned by the bipartisan US Committee on Human Rights in North Korea agreeing that North Koreans were expressing their concerns about persistent food shortages.

In January 2007 the Minister of Foreign Affairs, Paek Nam Sun, was reported to have died of cancer. He was replaced by Pak Ui Chun, a former ambassador to Russia, in May. At the fifth session of the 11th SPA in mid-April, Premier Pak Pong Ju was replaced by Kim Yong Il, hitherto Minister of Land and Marine Transport. Although no official explanation was given, observers suggested that the new Premier's experience in infrastructure might indicate the future direction of government policy. At the same time Vice-Marshal Kim Yong Chun, hitherto Chief of General Staff of the KPA, was appointed as a Vice-Chairman of the National Defence Commission, filling the vacancy left by the death of Yon Hyong Muk in October 2005. Gen. Kim Kyok Sik became the new KPA Chief of General Staff. The permanent staff of the National Defence Commission was expanded as part of a further reorganization of senior military officials in May 2007, with the appointment of Gen. Ri Myong Su, the former operations director of the KPA, as a standing member. The changes at the National Defence Commission were generally interpreted as an attempt to enhance its role and powers. Rumours suggesting that Kim Jong Il's health was deteriorating prompted renewed speculation regarding his successor in mid-2007. This speculation intensified in August, following reports that Kim's eldest son, Kim Jong Nam, had returned from exile to work in the organization and guidance bureau of the KWP. However, Kim dismissed reports of his ill health during the inter-Korean summit meeting held in Pyongyang in early October (see below). Thae Jong Su was appointed as a Vice-Premier of the Cabinet later in that month. In November it was reported that Jang Song Thaek had been promoted from the position of vice-director within the KWP to the directorship of the party's department responsible for state internal security, while Kim's second eldest son, Kim Jong Chol, had been appointed as a vice-director of another department of the KWP.

Several senior-level government changes were reported to have been implemented in 2008. In March Rim Kyong Man was said to have been replaced by Ri Ryong Nam in the position of Minister of Foreign Trade. It emerged in October that Chon Kil Su had been appointed as Minister of Railways, following the departure of Kim Yong Sam, while Kim Kwang Yong had succeeded Sok Kun Su as Minister of Forestry. A senior member of the KWP Politburo, Pak Song Chol, died, also in October. In January 2009 three further cabinet appointments were revealed: Ho Taek was the new Minister of Electric Power Industry, and Kim Chang Sik and Kim Thae Bong had assumed responsibility for the agriculture and metal industry portfolios, respectively. Meanwhile, elections to the new SPA, originally due to be held in August 2008, were postponed, amid increasing speculation over the health of Kim Jong Il, who had not attended a parade commemorating the country's 60th anniversary in early September. It was rumoured that he was seriously ill, a claim rejected by the Government and apparently refuted by the leader's appearance at several functions in the following months.

In January 2009 it was announced that the elections for the 12th SPA would take place on 8 March. A total of 687 candidates were duly elected unopposed; 316 deputies were reported to be entering the SPA for the first time, fewer than the number of new members elected in 2003. The level of voter participation was declared to have been 99.98%. Observers noted that the list of incoming deputies included none of Kim Jong Il's three sons, the youngest of whom, Kim Jong Un, had become the subject of increasing speculation with regard to the succession issue. Various changes to the leadership were effected at the first session of the SPA, which opened on 9 April. Notable appointments were those of Kim Wan Su as Minister of Finance and Ri Kwang Gon as President of the central bank, who exchanged responsibilities. Kim Jong Il's brother-in-law, Kim Jong Thaek, became a member of the National Defence Commission, of which O Kuk Ryok was appointed a Vice-Chairman. Also joining the National Defence Commission were U Tong Chuk and Ju Kyu Chang.

Meanwhile, the DPRK's economic difficulties and widespread food shortages were exacerbated by unusually serious flooding in 1995 and 1996, forcing the country to appeal to the UN and other international organizations for emergency food aid and flood relief. Assistance was provided by the USA, the Republic of Korea and Japan in 1995, but in early 1996 further shipments of cereals were halted, pending a positive response by the DPRK to US proposals for peace negotiations (see below). Renewed appeals for emergency aid were issued by the UN in mid-1996, to which the USA, South Korea and Japan responded on humanitarian grounds. In January 1997 it was reported that China had agreed to provide 500,000 metric tons of rice annually for five years. This was followed, in February, by an unprecedented admission from the DPRK that the country was experiencing 'temporary food problems' and that it had only one-half of the cereals necessary to feed its people.

In April and July 1997 the UN's World Food Programme (WFP, see p. 103) issued two further appeals for food and medical supplies. UN representatives sent to the DPRK to assess the extent of the crisis confirmed that chronic malnutrition was widespread, particularly among infants, and that the medical system was no longer able to provide even basic health care. The situation deteriorated in mid-1997, when severe drought devastated most of the North Korean maize crop; further damage was caused by a tidal wave on the western coast. In January 1998 WFP issued the largest appeal in the organization's history, requesting emergency aid of US $380m. Agreement was reached with the DPRK whereby additional UN staff were to be permitted to enter the country in order to monitor the distribution of aid, following allegations that previous supplies had been diverted to the army. Despite the provision of aid, severe food shortages persisted during 1998 and malnutrition was widespread among children. In December the UN issued an appeal for humanitarian aid. In mid-1999 WFP announced that increased aid had prevented starvation in the country for the time being, although poor infrastructure continued to hamper food distribution, and entry to 49 of the country's 211 counties was still forbidden. In August serious flooding destroyed large areas of farmland.

Severe weather conditions during 2000 exacerbated the situation. In February 2001 WFP agreed to provide US $93m. in aid and 810,000 tons of food, and in May South Korea began deliveries of 200,000 tons of agricultural fertilizer. In June WFP stated that the North had received 389,775 tons of food aid between January and May, but would require an additional 250,000 tons to prevent starvation later in the year. The official state media announced in June that the country had experienced 100 days of continuous drought since March. In October WFP delivered emergency food supplies to flood-stricken Kangwon Province. In November the head of the World Health Organization (WHO), Gro Harlem Brundtland, visited the DPRK and opened a permanent WHO office in Pyongyang. In December the Government launched an intensive campaign for potato and double-crop growing. In September–October 2002 representatives of FAO and WFP visited the DPRK and released a special report. Although the harvest was believed to have improved somewhat in 2002, a large cereals deficit was envisaged for 2002/03.

In November 2003 the UN made a new appeal for humanitarian assistance for the DPRK. WFP subsequently stated that in early 2004 it would be able to give food rations to only 100,000 people. A survey conducted by WFP in 2004 concluded that 37% of North Korean children aged six years and under were chronically malnourished. In November the UN stated that, despite relatively good harvests in 2004, 6.4m. people would remain in need of food aid in 2005, owing in part to a dramatic increase in food prices as a consequence of price reforms in 2002. In January 2005 it was reported that government food rations, upon which approximately two-thirds of the population were believed to depend, were to be reduced from 300g of grains per day to 250g. In June the USA pledged to supply 50,000 metric tons of food aid, its third successive annual donation. In September, however, the North Korean Government announced that it had asked humanitarian aid agencies operating in the DPRK to terminate food aid programmes and withdraw the majority of their foreign staff by the end of the year. The Government asserted that, following a harvest that year reported to be the best in a decade, it was able to feed its people without assistance, and expressed a desire to progress from humanitarian to developmental aid. (Analysts speculated that the Government of the DPRK preferred to rely on food aid from China and the Republic of Korea, as the distribution of aid from these countries was monitored less closely and the political implications of allowing Westerners access to the country were thereby avoided.) WFP terminated its operations in North Korea in January 2006, although its activities were resumed after negotiations with the Government in May.

Severe flooding in July 2006 prompted the North Korean Government to seek further humanitarian aid, and by October WFP was warning of renewed famine conditions. The shortage of food was exacerbated by the reluctance of donor nations to give aid to the DPRK following its missile tests in July and October (see below). A report published by FAO in January 2007 estimated that the number of malnourished people in the DPRK had risen to 7.9m. in the period 2001–03. The UN Development Programme (UNDP) announced that it was suspending its non-humanitarian work in the country, pending an investigation into allegations by the USA that UN funding was being misappropriated by the North Korean Government. From March 2007 all UNDP's work in the DPRK was suspended after the North Korean authorities refused to comply with certain conditions for continued operations in the country. The preliminary findings of an investigation by the UN Board of Auditors into operations in the DPRK, which were presented at the end of May, indicated that there had been some breaches of regulations but no systematic diversion of UN funds. A second phase of the audit commenced later that year, while UNDP commissioned a separate external review into other areas.

The DPRK suffered further severe flooding in August 2007, which led to some 600 deaths and left more than 100,000 people homeless, as well as causing widespread damage to infrastructure. The North Korean authorities estimated that 11% of the country's cereal crops had been destroyed. In response, the UN and the Red Cross launched international appeals for US $14m. and $5.5m., respectively, while WFP announced plans to provide emergency food aid for 215,000 people over a three-month period. South Korea, which had resumed deliveries of fertilizer to the North in March and of food aid in June, pledged aid worth $47.5m. A typhoon in September led to further flooding of farm land and the destruction of buildings. FAO estimated that the import of more than 1m. metric tons of cereals would be required during 2007/08 in order to maintain annual cereal consumption at around 160 kg per caput.

In April 2008 WFP warned of a humanitarian crisis, the food deficit for the coming year having been revised upwards to 1.66m. metric tons, more than double the shortfall of 2007. By May 2008 reports were emerging of deaths in certain provinces, prompting fears that a crisis on the scale of the famine of the 1990s was developing. The scope of WFP activities in the DPRK was to be increased under an agreement concluded with the North Korean Government in June. In September, following an appeal from the DPRK, the WFP initiated an emergency operation, envisaging expenditure of US $504m. In March 2009, however, it was revealed that WFP operations in the country had been substantially scaled down, owing to serious funding difficulties, and that aid had reached only 15% of the extent originally planned. Of the 6.2m. vulnerable people scheduled to receive WFP support, only 2m. were in fact receiving food assistance, with many rations being incomplete.

Meanwhile, the DPRK's relations with the Republic of Korea remained tense. In 1971 discussions took place for the first time between the Red Cross Societies of North and South Korea. However, negotiations were suspended in 1973, and hopes for better relations were undermined by a series of clashes between North and South Korean vessels in disputed waters during 1974. Propaganda campaigns, suspended by agreement in 1972, were resumed by both sides. In October 1978 the UN Command (UNC—under which troops were stationed in South Korea) accused the DPRK of threatening the 1953 truce, after the discovery of an underground tunnel (the third since 1974) beneath the DMZ. During the 1980s the increasing prominence of Kim Jong Il, who advocated an uncompromising policy towards the South, appeared to aggravate the situation. In 1983 some 17 South Koreans, including four government ministers, were killed in a bomb explosion in Burma (now Myanmar), in what appeared to be an assassination attempt on the South Korean President, Chun Doo-Hwan. The DPRK was held responsible for the attack, and Burma severed relations with the country. In January 1984, none the less, the DPRK suggested tripartite discussions on reunification, involving North and South Korea and the USA, but the proposal was rejected by South Korea, which favoured bilateral talks. During 1984 the DPRK's propaganda campaign was moderated, and in September North Korea provided emergency relief to flood-stricken areas of the South. In November the first discussions, on possible economic co-operation, were held, and negotiations continued in 1985. However, in February 1986, during the annual South Korean-US 'Team Spirit' military manoeuvres, North Korea suspended all negotiations with the South. The DPRK denied accusations of involvement in the explosion of a South Korean airliner over Burma in November 1987, despite the subsequent confession of an alleged North Korean agent. In August 1988 three sessions of talks were held at the 'peace village' of Panmunjom (in the DMZ) between delegates of the legislatures of North and South Korea, although the discussions (the first formal contact between the two countries since 1986) produced no conclusive results. Further negotiations in 1989 were suspended by the DPRK.

Inter-Korean discussions resumed in mid-1990, and in September the DPRK Premier visited the South Korean capital, Seoul, for discussions with his counterpart, the most senior-level bilateral contact since the end of the Korean War. Subsequent discussions culminated in the signing of an 'Agreement on Reconciliation, Non-aggression and Exchanges and Co-operation between the South and the North', in Seoul in December 1991. Both states pledged, *inter alia*, to desist from mutual slander, vilification and sabotage; to promote economic and other co-operation; to facilitate the reunion of families separated by the war; and to work towards a full peace treaty to replace the 1953 armistice agreement. In November 1992, however, the DPRK threatened a complete suspension of contacts with the South, in protest at the latter's decision to resume the 'Team Spirit' military exercises in March 1993. (The 1992 exercises had been cancelled, owing to the improvement in relations between the two states.) Relations had also been seriously impaired by the South's announcement, in October 1992, that an extensive North Korean espionage network had been discovered in South Korea, and by the North's repeated refusals to agree to simultaneous nuclear inspections in both countries (see below).

While the controversy surrounding the DPRK's suspected nuclear programme continued (see below), inter-Korean relations were strained by the DPRK's withdrawal in May 1994 of its mission to the Military Armistice Commission (the Panmunjom-based body overseeing the maintenance of the 1953 truce). Following discussions between Kim Il Sung and former US President Jimmy Carter, who visited the DPRK in June 1994, it was announced that the first summit meeting at presidential level between the two Korean states would be held in Pyongyang in July. However, the death of Kim Il Sung led to the indefinite postponement of the meeting. The signature of the US-DPRK nuclear accord in October caused South Korea to make renewed efforts to resume the inter-Korean negotiations, and in February

1995 the South announced the cancellation of the annual 'Team Spirit' manoeuvres (for the second consecutive year), as a gesture of goodwill.

Tension increased markedly in April 1996, when the DPRK announced its decision to abandon the 1953 armistice. North Korean troops subsequently made a number of incursions into the DMZ, thereby violating the provisions of the agreement. Later in the month, in an attempt to revitalize the peace process and replace the armistice agreement with a formal peace treaty, President Bill Clinton of the USA and President Kim Young-Sam of the Republic of Korea proposed four-way talks, involving the two Koreas, the USA and China. China responded positively, but the DPRK declared its willingness to hold discussions only with the USA. Relations between the two Koreas deteriorated considerably in September 1996, when a submarine from North Korea was discovered abandoned in South Korean waters. One of the two surviving crew members claimed that this was the fourth such mission undertaken by armed North Koreans. South Korea suspended all contact with the DPRK, and the UN Security Council subsequently expressed 'serious concern' at the incident. Following protracted mediation by the USA, an unprecedented apology was broadcast in South Korea by the (North) Korean Central News Agency.

In March 1997 exploratory talks between delegates from the DPRK, the Republic of Korea and the USA were held in New York to discuss the proposed quadripartite negotiations. Following the discussions, the DPRK announced that its participation in full quadripartite negotiations was conditional upon the receipt of substantial food aid. In May representatives of the Red Cross organizations of North and South Korea (in the first such meeting for five years) reached agreement on the provision of grain to the DPRK. Negotiations were concluded in October to allow foreign airlines, including those from South Korea, to use North Korean airspace.

Despite a military confrontation between North and South Korean troops in the DMZ in July 1997, full quadripartite negotiations, aimed at concluding a peace treaty between North and South Korea, finally opened in Geneva, Switzerland, in December. A second round of full discussions was held in March 1998, but proved unsuccessful, since the DPRK continued to insist on the inclusion on the agenda of the withdrawal of US troops from the Korean peninsula. In December 1997, meanwhile, negotiations in the Chinese capital of Beijing between the South and North Korean Red Cross organizations foundered, owing to North Korea's reluctance to allow South Korean officials access to the DPRK to monitor the distribution of food aid. At a subsequent meeting, in March 1998, the provision of additional food aid was agreed.

Following the inauguration of the new South Korean President, Kim Dae-Jung, in February 1998, the DPRK urged 'dialogue and negotiation' with the South Korean administration. Nevertheless, a ministerial-level meeting held in Beijing in April, to discuss the provision of fertilizer to North Korea (the first such direct contact for four years), failed when the South Koreans insisted that the DPRK enter into negotiations on the reunion of families. In that month, however, as part of Kim Dae-Jung's 'sunshine' policy of co-operation with the DPRK, the South Korean Government announced measures to encourage inter-Korean economic contacts, allowing the transfer of private funds to the North and relaxing legislation on investment. In June, in an historic development, Chung Ju-Yung, the founder of the South Korean conglomerate Hyundai, was permitted to cross the DMZ to deliver a gift of cattle to his home town; proposals for several other joint ventures were also discussed, including a plan to operate tour boats to Mount Kumgang, just north of the border. This improvement in relations seemed to be in jeopardy when, during the visit, a North Korean submarine was caught in the nets of a South Korean fishing boat; all nine crew members were found dead inside the vessel. The UNC condemned the incursion during a meeting with North Korean army officers in Panmunjom, the first such discussions to be held in seven years. A further delivery of cattle was made by Chung Ju-Yung in October, when he also met with Kim Jong Il, and in November some 800 tourists from South Korea participated in the first tour to Mount Kumgang. In December, during Chung's third visit to North Korea, a proposal for the construction of an industrial complex at Haeju was approved. Following further visits in early 1999, it was announced that these would continue on a monthly basis. In December 1998, meanwhile, South Korean naval forces sank a suspected North Korean spy boat, after pursuing it into international waters.

In June 1999 a week-long confrontation between North and South Korean naval forces in the Yellow Sea resulted in a brief gun battle, during which one North Korean torpedo boat was sunk. Two rounds of bilateral discussions in Beijing in June and July ended in failure. In September the DPRK declared invalid the Northern Limit Line (the maritime border that had separated the territorial waters of the two Koreas since 1953), in protest at the UNC's refusal to renegotiate its demarcation. Meanwhile, no discernible progress had been achieved at sessions of the quadripartite discussions held in April and August 1999. None the less, Hyundai proceeded with its plans for a number of projects in North Korea: in October the company concluded an agreement with the DPRK on the construction of the proposed industrial complex, which, it was envisaged, would comprise some 850 businesses, employing some 220,000 people, and would be capable of producing export goods worth an estimated US \$3,000m. annually. In February 2000 foreign residents in South Korea were permitted to visit Mount Kumgang for the first time. In December 1999 another major South Korean company, Samsung Electronics, announced that it had signed a contract with the DPRK for the joint development of computer software and the manufacture of electronic products. In February 2000 the construction of a motor vehicle assembly plant, in a joint venture with the Pyonghwa Motor Company of South Korea, began in Nampo, south-west of Pyongyang. According to South Korean estimates, inter-Korean trade increased by 50.2% in 1999. A number of joint North-South cultural and sporting events took place in 1999. In April 2000, following a series of senior-level bilateral contacts in Beijing, North and South Korea jointly announced that an historic summit meeting would take place between Kim Dae-Jung and Kim Jong Il in Pyongyang in June.

Following the presidential summit meeting in mid-June 2000, detailed agreements were signed pledging economic co-operation, the building of mutual trust and the resolution of reunification issues. In July ministerial-level delegations from both countries met in Seoul. This was the first visit to the South by North Korean officials since 1991. A joint communiqué was issued allowing for, inter alia, the reopening of liaison offices at Panmunjom, which had been closed in 1996, and the reconnection of the inter-Korean Kyongui railway line. The construction of a highway to run alongside the railway from North to South was subsequently agreed. In September 2000 Kim Dae-Jung formally inaugurated the project to remove thousands of landmines and rebuild the railway line and adjacent highway. Meanwhile, in August 100 North Korean families travelled to Seoul and 100 South Korean families visited Pyongyang simultaneously to meet with relatives from whom they had been separated by the Korean War. The second ministerial meeting between the two sides was held in Pyongyang later in that month. It was agreed to hold two more cross-border family reunions by the end of 2000 and to commence discussions on economic co-operation.

In a symbolic display of unity, in September 2000 the two countries marched under the same flag in the opening ceremony of the Olympic Games in Sydney, Australia. In late September the DPRK's Minister of the People's Armed Forces, Vice-Marshal Kim Il Chol, visited the South and met his counterpart, Cho Seong-Tae, the first such ministerial meeting ever held. In October Kim Dae-Jung was awarded the Nobel Peace Prize in recognition of his reunification efforts. Further sessions of interministerial, military and economic talks took place during 2000 and early 2001. However, in its annual defence policy document published in December 2000, South Korea described the North as its main enemy and alleged that the DPRK had expanded its military capacity along the DMZ. The North Korean Government was also displeased by the approval of a resolution in the South Korean legislature to demand the repatriation of prisoners of war who, it alleged, remained in detention in the North.

In early 2001 the uncompromising attitude displayed by the new US Administration towards North Korea threatened to undermine the reconciliation process. In March the DPRK unilaterally postponed scheduled cabinet-level discussions following a visit to the USA by Kim Dae-Jung, and in April North Korea denounced joint US-South Korean military exercises as a betrayal of the goodwill surrounding the June 2000 summit meeting. Ministerial discussions resumed in Seoul in September 2001, the sixth round of which was concluded in November without any agreement—the first such unsuccessful round since the presidential summit meeting.

THE DEMOCRATIC PEOPLE'S REPUBLIC OF KOREA (NORTH KOREA)   *Introductory Survey*

US President George W. Bush's reference in January 2002 to North Korea as part of an 'axis of evil' threatened seriously to damage inter-Korean relations. However, in April the North received Kim Dae-Jung's special envoy, Lim Dong-Won. Following the visit, during which Lim met Kim Jong Il, the two sides agreed to further reunions for separated families (see below) and to continuing discussions on economic co-operation. The DPRK also agreed to Lim's request that it renew dialogue with the USA and Japan. In May Park Geun-Hye, a South Korean legislator and the daughter of former President Park Chung-Hee, visited the North and met Kim Jong Il. The visit was remarkable because North Korean agents had killed Park's mother in 1974 in a bid to assassinate her father. Despite the cordial visit, North Korea cancelled economic co-operation discussions with the South in May 2002.

In May 2002 the increasing number of defectors from the North received international attention as several groups sought asylum at Canadian, Japanese and South Korean diplomatic buildings in China. They were eventually allowed to travel to the South, albeit via the Philippines. The South Korean Ministry of Unification reported in January 2003 that during 2002 some 1,141 North Koreans had defected to the South, compared with 583 in 2001.

At the end of June 2002 a gun battle between North and South Korean vessels in the Yellow Sea resulted in the sinking of a Southern patrol boat and the deaths of six crew members. South Korean military sources estimated that 30 North Korean crewmen were also killed in the confrontation, which had started when two North Korean vessels accompanying a fishing boat reportedly crossed the Northern Limit Line. Following the incident, in July South Korea suspended rice shipments to the North and economic co-operation projects, reflecting widespread public anger. None the less, Kim Dae-Jung maintained his 'sunshine' policy towards the North.

In August 2002 North and South Korea held a seventh round of ministerial discussions in Seoul, aimed at improving relations in the aftermath of the latest naval confrontation, and focusing on the issue of future family reunions, railway links (see below) and cultural exchanges. Regarding the latter, more than 300 North Korean athletes travelled to the South and participated in the Asian Games held in Busan during October. In September the first inter-Korean military 'hotline' was inaugurated to allow for improved communications during sensitive occasions.

The eighth round of ministerial talks was held in Pyongyang in October 2002 and mainly focused on economic co-operation issues, despite the fact that the USA had earlier revealed the existence of a secret nuclear weapons programme in the North (see below). At the end of that month a North Korean economic delegation began a nine-day tour of the South, including several major industrial facilities in the itinerary. Noteworthy was the fact that the delegation included Jang Song Thaek, Kim Jong Il's brother-in-law and reportedly one of his most trusted advisers, and also Kim Hi Thaek, the first deputy head of the KWP's Central Committee. At the end of December the South Korean Ministry of National Defence published a 'white paper' which, for the first time, excluded any reference to the North as its main enemy.

By late 2002 some of the goodwill generated by the historic inter-Korean summit meeting in June 2000 had been dissipated by the revelation that Kim Dae-Jung had arranged for the Korea Development Bank to give a Hyundai affiliate substantial funds to transfer to the North in order to finance the meeting. However, the election in December 2002 of Roh Moo-Hyun, the candidate of Kim's party, as President of the Republic of Korea heralded a continuation of Kim's 'sunshine' policy. In early January 2003 representatives of Roh secretly met North Korean officials in Beijing, and later in that month a ninth round of ministerial discussions was held in Seoul.

North and South Korea continued their efforts to improve bilateral relations during 2003, despite a severe deterioration in relations between the North and the USA over the issue of the former's nuclear weapons programme (see below). The DPRK hosted the 10th round of ministerial discussions at the end of April. In mid-May, however, Pyongyang announced that it no longer recognized a Joint Declaration of the Denuclearization of the Korean Pensinsula, signed with the South in 1992 (see below). Also in May 2003, at discussions between the two Koreas on economic matters, North Korea warned that the South would risk 'unspeakable disaster' if it became too confrontational in co-operating with the USA on the nuclear issue (the threat followed a summit meeting between Roh and US President George W. Bush). Attempts to develop inter-Korean relations were also complicated by confirmation in June by South Korean investigators that former President Kim Dae-Jung had made a substantial payment in order to arrange the historic inter-Korean summit meeting of 2000 (see above). In August 2003 the suicide of Hyundai official Chung Mong-Hun, who had been indicted in connection with the illegal payments to the North, further undermined the credibility of the 'sunshine' policy. Meanwhile, the 50th anniversary in July of the de facto end of the Korean War, celebrated as a triumph in North Korea, was commemorated in a sombre fashion in South Korea. Also in July, cross-border gunfire was exchanged between North and South Korean soldiers. In October the North Korean Kim Yong Sun, a leading official in inter-Korean affairs who had attended the presidential summit meeting in 2000, died, reportedly as a result of a traffic accident. In November 2003 two well-known North Korean defectors, Hwang Jang Yop (see above) and former North Korean official Kim Dok Hong, left their posts at the South Korean Institute of National Unification Policy. There was a suggestion that their resignations might have been due to fears that their criticism of the North Korean regime might be damaging to South Korean attempts to negotiate with North Korea. The resignation in January 2004 of the South Korean Minister of Foreign Affairs, Yoon Young-Kwan, was believed to have been related to tensions within the South Korean Government over the country's co-operation with the USA on the issue of North Korean weapons.

In April 2004, following a major railway accident in North Korea at Ryongchon (see above), the DPRK accepted emergency supplies and assistance from South Korea. At the end of the month a South Korean cargo plane arrived in Pyongyang carrying further emergency supplies, representing the first ever direct flight for humanitarian purposes. In May senior-level military discussions took place between the two sides, at which the establishment of a radio communication line between the North and South Korean navies was agreed. It was believed that the new communication line would reduce naval conflicts between the two sides, although later in the year there were none the less incidents of warning shots being fired by the South Korean navy at North Korean vessels considered to have intruded across the maritime border, amid accusations that in some instances South Korean navy officials had failed to report North Korean radio messages. In June, meanwhile, in a symbolic development, propaganda broadcasts across the DMZ were silenced for the first time in decades, with loudspeakers on both sides of the border being switched off. Also in June, a senior DPRK representative, the Vice-Chairman of the Korea Asia-Pacific Peace Committee, Ri Jong Hyok, made a visit to Seoul and met South Korean President Roh Moo-hyun to mark the fourth anniversary of the inter-Korean summit meeting of 2000 (see above). In July 2004 more than 450 North Korean defectors arrived in Seoul. The DPRK subsequently accused South Korean officials of kidnapping its citizens and suspended bilateral dialogue. Tensions were increased further in August following an admission by South Korea that it had in the past conducted secret nuclear experiments. It was believed that this disclosure would increase the DPRK's reluctance to dismantle its own nuclear programme. By the end of 2004 the number of North Koreans who had defected to South Korea had reportedly exceeded 6,000.

In February 2005 the South Korean Ministry of Defence urged the resumption of senior-level military talks, apparently to ease tension following North Korean accusations that Southern naval vessels had 'infiltrated' the waters of the DPRK. In April the most senior-level meeting between the two sides for five years took place when Kim Yong Nam, the President of the Presidium of the North Korean SPA, met South Korean Prime Minister Lee Hae-Chan during the course of an Asia-Africa summit meeting in Jakarta, Indonesia; the two reportedly agreed that bilateral dialogue, suspended since July of the previous year (see above), should continue. At vice-ministerial discussions in May, South Korea pledged to provide 200,000 metric tons of fertilizer to ease the DPRK's food supply problems. Three North Korean freighters reportedly docked at Ulsan in South Korea to load the fertilizer later in the month, this being the first time since 1984 that North Korean ships had docked in a South Korean port. In June 2005 South Korean Minister of Unification Chung Dong-Young visited the DPRK to mark the fifth anniversary of the inter-Korean summit of 2000, and held an unscheduled meeting with Kim Jong Il; it was speculated that the DPRK's agreement to return to the six-party talks on its nuclear programme in the following month might have been influenced by incentives offered by Chung at this meeting, including the provision of electricity (see below). In July 2005 the 15th ministerial discussions between North and South Korea, held in Seoul, concluded with a 12-point joint statement in which the two sides pledged, *inter alia*, to reopen military talks, resume reunions for separated families and hold North-South Red Cross talks to discuss the issue of 'the whereabouts of those reported missing during the Korean War' (see below). Further ministerial discussions were held in September and December. Meanwhile, a sizeable delegation from the DPRK, headed by Kim Ki Nam, a member of the KWP Politburo's Secretariat, travelled to Seoul in August to participate in celebrations commemorating the 60th anniversary of the liberation of the Korean peninsula from Japanese rule. In November it was announced that North and South Korea would present joint teams at the 2006 Asian Games in Doha, Qatar, and at the 2008 Olympic Games in Beijing, China. In March 2006 military negotiations were held between the two Koreas in the DMZ, following a break of some two years; these were reportedly the most senior-level military talks between the two sides since the 1953 armistice. In the same month, however, the Government of the DPRK postponed the scheduled 18th round of ministerial discussions between the two sides in protest at the South's conduct of joint military exercises with the USA.

Relations between the two Koreas were strained further throughout 2006, mainly as a result of the DPRK's missile tests (see below). The testing of a *Taepo Dong 2* missile on 5 July prompted the Republic of Korea to announce an indefinite suspension of food aid; however, it insisted that business co-operation, notably at Kaesong and Mount Kumgang, would not be affected. Moreover, aid was resumed after North Korea suffered severe flooding later in that month, with the South Korean Government granting US $10.5m. to the North via non-governmental organizations (NGOs) in August, followed by supplies of rice, cement, iron rods, excavators, vehicles, blankets and medical kits to the value of $200m. However, the testing of a nuclear device by the North on 9 October placed this emergency aid programme in jeopardy. While again pledging to continue its economic co-operation in Kaesong and Mount Kumgang (despite express US pleas for these links to be severed), the South Korean Government announced an indefinite suspension of humanitarian aid. (However, NGOs continued to provide relief shipments.) Although the South Korean Minister of Foreign Affairs, Ban Ki-Moon, reportedly stated that the DPRK deserved sanctions under the UN Security Council Resolution, he also urged a resumption of dialogue. Ironically, the nuclear test took place only a week after North and South Korea had conducted their first military talks since the missile tests in July. These discussions apparently ended inconclusively. However, in the weeks following the nuclear test the Republic of Korea appeared to relax its stance towards the DPRK. Significantly, the South Korean Government refused to join the US-led Proliferation Security Initiative (PSI), which provided for the stopping and searching of North Korean ships, and by early November South Korean President Roh was vowing to continue his policy of engagement with the North Korean Government. None the less, in a reversal of previous policy, in mid-November the Republic of Korea supported a UN resolution condemning the DPRK's human rights record (in previous votes it had been absent or abstained). Furthermore, a South Korean defence policy document published at the end of December described the DPRK as a 'serious threat' to the South—the most strongly worded assessment since the inception of the latter's policy of engagement in 2000. It was reported in February 2007 that the number of defectors from North to South Korea since 1953 had reached 10,000, with a record number of 1,578 arriving in 2006.

Following the progress made in mid-February 2007 at six-party talks on North Korea's nuclear programme (see below), North and South Korea held ministerial discussions later in that month, and in late March South Korea shipped 12,500 metric tons of fertilizer to the North. Inter-Korean talks on economic co-operation were held in Pyongyang in April, shortly after North Korea had failed to meet a deadline agreed in February for the closure of its nuclear rector at Yongbyon. South Korea agreed to revive its food aid programme to the North, with the provision of 400,000 metric tons of rice, but only on condition that the DPRK demonstrate some progress in complying with its commitments under the February six-party accord. Senior-level military talks at Panmunjom in mid-May resulted in agreement on a trial run of trains along reinstated cross-border rail links (see below) and, in principle, on the creation of a joint fishing zone in the disputed Yellow Sea, where naval clashes had previously occurred. However, ministerial discussions in Seoul in late May and early June ended without progress, as South Korea continued to refuse to dispatch any rice to the North while the latter's pledge to shut down the Yongbyon reactor remained unfulfilled. In late June, as inspectors of the International Atomic Energy Agency (IAEA, see p. 113) were permitted to enter North Korea for the first time since December 2002, South Korea announced the resumption of food aid to the North with a first shipment of some 3,000 tons of rice; the remainder of the promised 400,000 tons was delivered over the following six-month period. In accordance with the February agreement, a first delivery of 13,700 tons (of a promised total of 50,000 tons) of heavy fuel oil followed in July 2007. None the less, difficulties remained in inter-Korean relations. Three days of senior-level military talks ended in stalemate in late July over the disputed maritime boundary, the Northern Limit Line, which the DPRK refused to recognize, and in early August North and South Korean soldiers exchanged gunfire across the DMZ.

In early October 2007 Kim Jong Il welcomed President Roh to Pyongyang for a three-day summit meeting, which had been postponed from late August owing to severe flooding in the North. This was only the second meeting between the two countries' leaders since the Korean War. Following the meeting, Kim and Roh, who was approaching the end of his term of office, issued a declaration, in which they committed North and South Korea, *inter alia*, to working towards the replacement of the 1953 armistice agreement with a peace treaty; to making joint efforts for the smooth implementation of the six-party nuclear agreements; to creating a special 'peace zone' around Haeju; to establishing the planned joint fishing zone in the Yellow Sea; to expanding co-operation on economic and humanitarian projects; and to developing co-operation in a wide range of other areas (including education, technology, culture and sports). Several bilateral ministerial exchanges followed the meeting. A three-day visit to Seoul by Premier Kim Yong Il took place in mid-November 2007. During the first bilateral prime ministerial discussions since 1992 Kim and South Korean Prime Minister Han Duck-Soo agreed on a timetable for resuming cross-border freight rail services (see below) and on the establishment of a joint committee to advance the creation of the proposed 'peace zone' centred on Haeju, which was to involve the economic development of the city's port. Talks between the DPRK's Minister of the People's Armed Forces, Vice-Marshal Kim Il Chol, and his South Korean counterpart (the first since 2000 and only the second in more than 50 years) were held in Pyongyang later in that month to discuss the security aspects of the agreements reached by the two countries' leaders, and in early December 2007 North Korean Vice-Premier Jon Sung Hun and the South Korean Deputy Prime Minister for Finance and the Economy, Kwon O-Kyu, held discussions in Seoul on joint industrial projects. However, senior-level military talks in mid-December ended without agreement on the location of the proposed fishing zone in the Yellow Sea.

Lee Myung-Bak, of the conservative Grand National Party, who was elected President of South Korea in December 2007, advocated the adoption of a more uncompromising approach towards North Korea than that pursued over the preceding 10 years by Presidents Kim Dae-Jung and Roh Moo-Hyun: he demanded increased progress on denuclearization in return for the continuation of economic co-operation. In January 2008 President Lee announced plans to review the agreements reached at the inter-Korean summit in the previous October, and the Ministry of Unification was scaled down. None the less, humanitarian projects, such as family reunions (see below) and food and fertilizer aid, were expected to continue, and Lee proposed the creation of a 37,500m. won investment fund for the DPRK if it abandoned its nuclear weapons programme, with the aim of raising the North's per caput income to US $3,000 within 10 years. Relations between the two Governments deteriorated in March, when North Korea expelled South Korean officials from Kaesong and test-fired missiles in the Yellow Sea. The North Korean Government was reportedly dissatisfied with Lee's association of humanitarian assistance with preconditions on nuclear disarmament and human rights. Tensions rose further in July, when a female South Korean tourist was shot dead by a North Korean soldier at Mount Kumgang, having allegedly crossed into a restricted area. In response, the South Korean Government halted tours to the area, while the North refused to participate in a joint investigation into the death, warning that it would expel all 'unnecessary' South Korean nationals from the resort. Military-level talks between the two sides yielded few results in October. In November South Korea acted as the co-sponsor of a UN resolution criticizing human rights violations in the DPRK. Later in that month the North announced the suspension of non-military telephone connections with the South, as well as the closure of the border. At the beginning of March 2009, in their first, albeit brief, meeting since 2002, North Korean officials and UNC representatives had discussions at Panmunjom, in an attempt to reduce tensions.

In early March 2009 the North Korean Government again closed the border, in response to the holding of joint US-South Korean military exercises. Unable to cross the border, 80 South Korean workers were stranded at the Kaesong industrial estate. The border was then partially reopened only to be closed again without explanation. Similar, seemingly arbitrary closures of the border followed.

Meanwhile, the arrangements for further family reunions came under the auspices of the North and South Korean Red Cross organizations, which held several rounds of talks on the subject and co-ordinated the exchange of lists of potential candidates for reunion. Relations between the two sides deteriorated in late 2000, however, when North Korea accused the head of the South Korean Red Cross of defaming the former's political system. The official was replaced in January 2001. The DPRK continued to dictate terms for reunions, asking the Republic of Korea to limit the amount of money and gifts transferred during the events, which took place in November–December 2000 and in February 2001. It was subsequently reported that North Korean officials had confiscated money given to delegates for use as state funds. An historic accord between the two sides allowed 300 separated families from the North and South each to exchange letters in March. Further rounds of family reunions were held in April and September 2002 at Mount Kumgang, where officials from the two sides planned to build a centre for such meetings. In April 2004 a ninth round of reunions was delayed after a South Korean official made a joke concerning Kim Jong Il. Further rounds of reunions none the less took place during the year. As part of the reunion programme, in July 2005 the first private telephone line between North and South Korea since partition in 1945 was opened, in preparation for video conference family reunions, which took place in mid-August 2005 to coincide with the 60th anniversary of liberation from Japanese rule. Inter-Korean Red Cross discussions held later in that month at Mount Kumgang failed to resolve the question of South Korean soldiers and civilians 'abducted' to North Korea during and after the 1950–53 war: the South Korean Government estimated that more than 540 prisoners of war and some 485 abducted civilians were still alive and remained in detention in the DPRK. Further reunions were held, both in person and through video conference technology, in late 2005 and early 2006. At another Red Cross conference in February 2006, North Korea reportedly agreed to resolve the issue of South Korean prisoners of war and abductees held in the North, and a further family reunion took place in June. This reunion received particular international attention, as it involved the reuniting with his mother of Kim Young-Nam, who was said to have been abducted by North Korean security agents in 1978. However, the DPRK again suspended family reunions in July 2006, in response to the Republic's decision to suspend humanitarian aid following the North Korean missile tests. Following the test of a nuclear device in October, the prospect for further family reunions in the near future appeared uncertain. None the less, the family reunions arranged during 2006 helped to raise the total number of South Koreans visiting the North to more than 100,000 for the first time, a rise of 15.1% compared with the previous year. (Nearly 88,000 of the total of 101,708 were business people travelling to the Kaesong complex; the total figure excluded tourists visiting Mount Kumgang.) In January 2007 Choi Uk-Il, one of 33 South Korean fishermen abducted by a North Korean naval vessel in 1975, returned to the South after first fleeing to China. Inter-Korean ministerial discussions held in Pyongyang in late February and early March 2007 resulted in an agreement on the resumption of family reunions, which took place by video conference in late March and in person at Mount Kumgang in mid-May. The 16th round of 'face-to-face' reunions was held in October.

As the DPRK's financial situation worsened, economic issues played an important part in inter-Korean relations from 2000. In January 2001 it was reported that the DPRK's energy shortages had reached crisis point, and that the country was desperately researching alternative power sources. A summit meeting took place between the two Koreas in February, at which the DPRK requested immediate and substantial electricity supplies to alleviate its needs. Frustration resulted from South Korean insistence on the necessity of on-site investigations prior to the commencement of deliveries. Meanwhile, in August 2000 Hyundai agreed to establish a technologically-advanced electronic industrial compound in Kaesong in the DPRK. However, Hyundai's financial problems delayed the implementation of the project. In March 2001 the future of the Mount Kumgang tourist initiative was jeopardized by its lack of profitability, and Hyundai appealed to the South Korean Government for assistance; the Government subsequently pledged 90,000m. won to maintain the tourist cruises. Hyundai founder Chung Ju-Yung died in late March, and his funeral was attended by a delegation sent by Kim Jong Il. Progress on economic co-operation in Kaesong was made from 2002, with Kaesong being declared a special industrial zone in November of that year (see also Economic Affairs). In June 2003 the DPRK announced regulations for the development of the zone, as well as plans to develop an area of 3.3 sq km in a first phase of development extending to 2007. A South Korean company, Korea Land, was to invest around US $184m. in the project. These plans were finalized at a meeting of North and South Korean economic officials in November 2003. Although inter-Korean trade increased steadily, reportedly amounting to US $700m. in 2003, South Korea shared international concerns over North Korea's suspected illicit trade in weapons and narcotics. In June 2003 South Korean customs officials in the port of Busan seized 40 kg of methamphetamines believed to have originated in North Korea. There were also fears of very serious economic consequences for South Korea if reunification of the two Koreas were to become an imminent prospect. It was reported that in April 2004 some 1,600 South Korean companies had applied for a lease in the Kaesong special industrial zone, and in June Korea Land selected the first 15 companies that were to be permitted to conduct business in the zone. At the end of June a ceremony was held to signal the commencement of the first phase of development in Kaesong. In March 2005 the Korea Electric Power Corporation (KEPCO), of South Korea, began to supply electricity to Kaesong, representing the first cross-border flow of electricity since the peninsula's partition. In July the South Korean Minister of Unification reportedly proposed to Kim Jong Il that South Korea compensate the North with 2,000 MW of energy assistance if the latter were to abandon its nuclear weapons programme (see below). However, the DPRK rejected the offer. In October the first joint governmental office operated by both North and South Korea, to handle cross-border economic projects, was opened in Kaesong, and in December the first commercial telephone link between Kaesong and Seoul commenced operation.

The construction of the major infrastructural facilities at Kaesong, which began in June 2003, was completed in October 2007, marking the end of the development phase. The complex was scheduled to be fully operational by the end of 2010, when it was anticipated that some 450 companies, employing a total of 100,000 North Koreans, would be conducting business there. By November 2007 the number of companies from the Republic of Korea operating in Kaesong had reached 52, according to the South Korean Ministry of Unification, with more than 20,000 North Koreans working at the complex. The construction of living quarters for 15,000 North Korean workers in Kaesong was scheduled to begin in 2008; however, as a result of the deterioration in relations between the two sides, the intermittent imposition of restrictions on cross-border travel impeded the development of the facilities (see above).

In the area of infrastructural development, negotiations to re-establish the inter-Korean rail link continued during 2001. It was hoped that such a link would create a new Eurasian transport corridor that would reduce the cost and time involved in the transit of goods from North-East Asia to European markets from 25 days to about 15 days, bringing economic benefits to all participants. In February 2001 a meeting was held at the DMZ to arrange regulations for troops and workers employed to rebuild the line, and a parallel highway. However, the DPRK failed to attend a UN regional transport meeting held in Seoul in November, following the failure of the sixth round of ministerial discussions. None the less, both Koreas agreed to accelerate the reconnection following bilateral talks in April 2002. Ground-breaking ceremonies for the reconnection of the railway and road links were held on both sides of the DMZ in September, and South Korea released a loan to the North to assist the funding of the work. In February 2003 the first road reconnecting the North with the South was completed, on the eastern coast of the Korean peninsula. In June rail links between the two Koreas were officially opened, although the connections remained largely symbolic, as construction on the North Korean side to link the new railways with wider networks was yet to be completed. In December 2004 it was reported that the road link along the eastern coast of the two Koreas had been opened to traffic. By late 2005 two major rail links between North and South Korea along the west and east coasts, with adjacent roads, were believed to be complete; however, the DPRK cancelled scheduled trial runs along the cross-border rail links in May 2006, citing military security issues. South Korea had also pledged to assist the DPRK in constructing several railway stations. Following senior-level military talks at Panmunjom, in May 2007 cross-border rail links were finally trialled when, for the first time in more than 50 years, passengers were conveyed on trains travelling in each direction. However, it remained uncertain when North Korea would permit the operation of regular services. At the inter-Korean summit held in October (see above), it was decided to resume a cross-border freight rail service. A daily freight service, connecting the South with Kaesong, was duly launched in December, although North Korea continued to oppose the introduction of regular passenger services. Inter-Korean talks on improving rail links, which were held in January 2008, resulted in agreement on a reduction in the number of carriages on the freight trains (owing to lack of use) and on the need to repair the North Korean section of the reconnected railway. However, the rail service between the two sides was discontinued by the North in November 2008.

In the early 1990s there was growing international concern that the DPRK had intensified its clandestine nuclear programme at Yongbyon, north of Pyongyang, and would soon be capable of manufacturing a nuclear weapon. During 1991 pressure was increasingly applied, by the USA and Japan in particular, for the DPRK to sign the Nuclear Safeguards Agreement (NSA) with the IAEA. This was required by the DPRK's signature, in 1985, of the Treaty on the Non-Proliferation of Nuclear Weapons (the Non-Proliferation Treaty—NPT), in order that IAEA representatives might be permitted to inspect the country's nuclear facilities. However, the DPRK consistently refused to allow such inspections to take place unless there was to be a simultaneous inspection (or withdrawal) of US nuclear weapons sited in South Korea. Tension was eased considerably by the USA's decision, in October 1991, to remove all its tactical nuclear weapons from South Korea, and by South Korea's subsequent declaration that it would not manufacture, deploy or use nuclear, chemical or biological weapons. In December the South Korean Government stated that all US nuclear weapons had been withdrawn, and proposed that simultaneous inspections of military bases in the South and nuclear facilities in the North be conducted. Later in the month the two Korean states concluded an agreement 'to create a non-nuclear Korean peninsula', and in January 1992 the DPRK signed the NSA. In March delegates of North and South, meeting at Panmunjom, agreed to form a Joint Nuclear Control Commission (JNCC) to permit inter-Korean nuclear inspections to take place.

In May 1992 the DPRK submitted to the IAEA an unexpectedly detailed report on its nuclear facilities, describing, *inter alia*, the Yongbyon installation as a research laboratory. In the same month IAEA inspectors were permitted to visit North Korean nuclear facilities (the first in a series of official visits during that year). Despite the findings of the inspectors (who concluded that the Yongbyon plant was 'primitive' and far from completion, although potentially capable of producing plutonium), suspicions persisted regarding North Korean nuclear ambitions. Moreover, the DPRK repeatedly failed to agree to separate nuclear inspections by the JNCC, finally announcing in January 1993 its intention to boycott all future inter-Korean nuclear talks (in protest at the imminent resumption of the 'Team Spirit' manoeuvres). The situation became critical in February, when the DPRK refused to allow IAEA inspections of two 'undeclared' sites near Yongbyon, claiming that these were military installations unrelated to nuclear activities. In an unprecedented development, the DPRK announced in March that it was to withdraw from the NPT. In May the UN Security Council adopted a resolution urging the DPRK to reconsider its decision to withdraw from the NPT and calling on the country to allow an inspection by the IAEA of its nuclear facilities. Following negotiations with the USA, the DPRK agreed to suspend its withdrawal from the NPT; in return, the USA agreed to assist the DPRK in the development of its non-military nuclear programme. International concern regarding the North Korean weapons programme was, meanwhile, heightened by the successful testing of a medium-range missile, the *Rodong-1*, in May. In response to US pressure, the DPRK subsequently agreed to further negotiations with the IAEA: discussions at the organization's headquarters in Vienna, Austria, in September, however, were inconclusive, and further meetings were cancelled.

In February 1994, following further discussions between the DPRK and the USA, an agreement was reached whereby the IAEA would be allowed to visit all the country's declared nuclear facilities. In March, however, the inspectors were impeded in their efforts to remove samples from nuclear installations, and it was discovered that seals placed on nuclear materials by IAEA representatives during previous visits had been broken, leading the IAEA to conclude that the DPRK had, in all probability, produced more plutonium than had been admitted. In June the DPRK again threatened to withdraw from the NPT, and also to declare war against the Republic of Korea, if economic sanctions were imposed by the UN. In August the USA and the DPRK reached an agreement on the replacement of the latter's existing nuclear reactors by two light-water reactors, which were considered to be less easily adapted to the production of nuclear weaponry. The agreement also recommended the establishment of a restricted form of diplomatic representation between the two countries. Further negotiations in October led to the signing of an Agreed Framework whereby the USA undertook to establish an international consortium to finance and supply the light-water reactors, while the DPRK agreed to suspend operation of its existing reactors and halt construction at two further sites. To compensate for the DPRK's consequent shortfall in energy production until the new reactors were fully operational, the USA agreed to donate to the DPRK 500,000 metric tons annually of heavy fuel oil. IAEA inspectors subsequently travelled to Pyongyang to oversee the suspension of the country's nuclear programme.

In March 1995 several countries, led by the USA, the Republic of Korea and Japan, created the Korean Peninsula Energy Development Organization (KEDO), which insisted that the DPRK accept a South Korean-designed reactor. This demand was opposed by the DPRK. However, in August the North permitted a KEDO delegation to visit Sinpo, on the east coast of the DPRK, in order to assess its suitability as the site of the proposed nuclear power station. Finally, in December the DPRK and KEDO reached agreement on the details of implementing the October 1994 accord; this implied acceptance by the DPRK of South Korean light-water reactors. In January 1996 the DPRK announced its willingness to permit routine inspections of its nuclear installations by the IAEA. In March KEPCO was commissioned by KEDO as the principal contractor for the construction of the light-water reactors. Discussions between KEDO and the DPRK to negotiate the terms of repayment by the latter of the construction costs of the light-water reactors were successfully concluded in April 1997.

Meanwhile, US energy experts began the sealing of spent fuel rods at the DPRK's nuclear facilities. However, North Korea's continued refusal to grant IAEA inspectors access to several contentious laboratories again provoked concern that the DPRK was developing its nuclear programme. Preparation of the nuclear-reactor site at Sinpo formally began in August 1997. Negotiations held in early 1998 between the participants in KEDO (which the European Union—EU—had joined in mid-1997) concerning the financing of the light-water reactors (estimated at US $5,170m.) proved difficult, and were further complicated by South Korea's financial problems, raising fears that progress on the project would be hindered. In June 1998 the North Korean Government admitted to having sold nuclear missiles abroad, claiming that such exports were necessary, given ongoing US economic sanctions against the DPRK. Some progress was made at discussions between the USA and the DPRK in New York, USA, in September, when the DPRK agreed to resume sealing of spent fuel rods (which had been suspended earlier that year), while the USA promised to deliver the delayed shipment of heavy fuel oil. However, the US Congress was increasingly reluctant to approve financing for the purchase of fuel oil, obliging President Bill Clinton personally to authorize the disbursement of the necessary funds in October, in order to safeguard the 1994 nuclear accord.

Concerns regarding a suspected nuclear-related underground facility at Kumchang-ri, some 40 km north-west of Yongbyon, dominated a series of senior-level discussions between the USA and the DPRK in late 1998 and early 1999. The North Korean authorities were antagonized by reports that KEDO had decided, in January 1999, to delay commencing the basic construction of the light-water reactors until mid-1999. In March, following protracted negotiations in New York, agreement was finally reached permitting US access to the suspected nuclear facility. The USA announced that it would donate substantial food aid to the DPRK, in addition to agricultural assistance, although it was emphasized that the aid was being granted on purely humanitarian grounds and did not constitute compensation. The US officials who inspected the Kumchang-ri site in May found it to be incomplete and largely empty.

In May 1999 William Perry, a former US Secretary of Defense who had been appointed to review policy towards the DPRK, visited Pyongyang, where he reportedly advised the North Korean Government to abandon its nuclear ambitions in exchange for substantial economic and political benefits. Talks held during mid-1999 between the USA and the DPRK culminated in September in a decision by the USA to ease several long-standing economic sanctions (principally on non-military trade, travel and banking) against the DPRK. In return, the country agreed to suspend missile test-firing for the duration of negotiations with the USA. Earlier in the month Perry had presented a report recommending a comprehensive, long-term approach to the establishment of normal relations with the DPRK to the US President and Congress. Discussions aimed at improving US-North Korean relations were held in Beijing in November 1999 and January 2000.

Meanwhile, in November 1999 it was reported that the IAEA was supervising the final stage of the sealing of spent fuel rods at Yongbyon. After several months of delays caused by disputes over the division of the costs of the project, in December KEDO and KEPCO finally signed the contract for the construction of the two light-water reactors; in February 2000 it was reported that construction of the reactors was unlikely to be completed before 2007, some four years later than scheduled. In November 2000 North Korea, frustrated by the delay, threatened to restart missile testing unless construction of the reactors was accelerated. The DPRK denied the IAEA's claim that delays were due to the former's refusal to allow nuclear inspections.

In June 2000 the North Korean Government confirmed its moratorium on test flights of ballistic missiles. In July the USA rejected the DPRK's demand for annual payments from the USA of US $1,000m. in return for the curtailment of weapons exports. The fundamental issues of missile development and export remained unresolved. A planned visit to Pyongyang by the outgoing US President, Bill Clinton, was cancelled in December when the DPRK rejected a US proposal that the two sides prepare a draft missile accord to form a basis for talks. In early 2001 the new Administration of George W. Bush adopted a less conciliatory stance towards the DPRK, officials reportedly referring to Kim Jong Il as a 'dictator', and refusing to grant economic aid unless transparency in North Korea's missile production and export was assured and verified. Since the late 1990s elements in Bush's Republican Party had been strongly arguing in favour of a planned 'national missile defence' (NMD) system to protect the USA from long-range missile attack, and had frequently cited North Korea as a developer and exporter of such missiles. US officials feared that the DPRK had developed an intercontinental ballistic missile, the *Taepo Dong 2*, capable of striking the west coast of the USA. Bush's commitment to develop NMD was denounced by the DPRK, which responded by threatening to abandon the 1994 framework, and to resume ballistic missile testing. In March 2001 US Secretary of State Colin Powell suggested that revisions to the 1994 framework might be required. In May 2001 an EU delegation travelled to North Korea, in an effort to renew diplomatic initiatives aimed at advancing the process of détente. Kim Jong Il reportedly agreed to maintain the moratorium on the testing of missiles until at least 2003. In June 2001 President Bush sought to broaden discussions with North Korea about its missile programme to include nuclear technology and a reduction of the country's conventional forces. The North responded that discussions on the latter would take place only following the withdrawal of the 37,000 US troops from the South, and that it was also seeking financial compensation for the delay in building KEDO's two light-water reactors, which were now not expected to be completed until 2008 at the earliest. In October 2001 the North rejected suggestions by the head of the IAEA and later by US officials that inspections of its nuclear facilities were necessary; however, in December it agreed to limited international access to certain laboratories. Meanwhile, in November, a team of North Korean nuclear engineers visited power plants in the South, indicating their commitment to acquire Southern-style reactors. (See relations with the USA, below, for subsequent developments on the DPRK's nuclear weapons programme.)

The DPRK's relations with Japan have long been dominated by continuing hostility towards the latter as a result of the atrocities committed in Korea during the Japanese occupation of 1910–45. The North Korean Government had demanded thousands of millions of dollars in compensation from Japan, before normal relations could be restored. In the 1980s, following the testimony of defectors, Japan began to suspect that North Korean agents had kidnapped a number of Japanese citizens during the late 1970s and early 1980s. Japan imposed sanctions on the DPRK after its agents were accused of attempting to assassinate the South Korean President in Burma in 1983. Following the destruction of a South Korean aircraft in 1987, allegedly by North Korean agents posing as Japanese citizens (see above), Japan reimposed sanctions during 1988; the DPRK then severed diplomatic contacts with Japan, although mutual trade continued. From late 1990 there was a significant rapprochement between the DPRK and Japan, and in January 1991 a Japanese government delegation visited Pyongyang for discussions concerning the possible normalization of diplomatic relations. The Japanese delegation offered apologies, on behalf of its Government, for Japanese colonial aggression on the Korean peninsula between 1910 and 1945. Moreover, the Japanese Government expressed its willingness to make reparations for Japanese abuses of human rights in Korea during this period. However, subsequent negotiations in 1991 foundered, owing to the DPRK's demand for reparations for damage inflicted after 1945 (which the Japanese Government denied) and to Japan's insistence that North Korea's nuclear installations be opened to outside inspection; normalization talks collapsed in November 1992, as the North Korean delegation abandoned the proceedings. Relations with Japan were further strained after the DPRK's testing of the *Rodong-1* missile in the Sea of Japan (East Sea) in May 1993. The missile, according to US intelligence reports, would be capable of reaching most of Japan's major cities (and possibly of carrying either a conventional or a nuclear warhead). None the less, Japan, like the Republic of Korea, opposed the possible imposition of international economic sanctions on the DPRK in response to North Korea's refusal to allow inspections of its nuclear facilities. In March 1995 a Japanese parliamentary group visited the DPRK and reached an agreement for the resumption of normalization talks later in that year. In May Japan agreed to North Korea's request for emergency rice aid, and later in the year Japan provided aid to help the DPRK overcome the effects of serious flooding (see above). In early 1996 Japan provided a shipment of fuel oil to alleviate the DPRK's energy shortfall.

Relations were complicated in 1997 by Japanese allegations that North Korea had abducted several Japanese citizens during the 1970s. However, in August 1997, for the first time since 1992, negotiations opened on the restoration of normal bilateral relations. An agreement was signed whereby some 1,800 Japanese women married to North Koreans, who had never been permitted to leave the DPRK, were to be allowed to visit their relatives in Japan for short periods; the first such visits took place in November 1997 and January 1998. Moreover, in October 1997 the Japanese Government resumed the provision of aid to North Korea, suspended since mid-1996, donating food and medical supplies in response to the renewed appeals issued by the UN. Relations deteriorated in mid-1998, however, when the North Korean Government cancelled a third visit of the Japanese women to their homeland, following Japan's rejection of a North Korean investigation into the alleged abduction of Japanese nationals. The testing by the DPRK of a suspected *Taepo Dong* missile over Japanese territory in August prompted Japan to break off normalization talks, suspend food aid and postpone its contribution to the KEDO project. The DPRK subsequently claimed that the object launched was in fact a satellite. Tension between the two countries increased in March 1999, when Japanese naval forces pursued and opened fire on suspected North Korean spy ships that had infiltrated Japanese waters. However, relations improved following the DPRK's agreement with the USA, in September, to suspend its reported plans to test a new long-range missile. In December, following a successful visit to the DPRK by a group of Japanese parliamentarians, Japan announced an end to its ban on food aid. Later in that month intergovernmental preparatory discussions on re-establishing diplomatic relations were held in Beijing. Progress was achieved by the Japanese and North Korean Red Cross Societies at a meeting in March 2000. It was reported that the DPRK had agreed to co-operate in a further investigation into the fate of some 10 missing Japanese nationals, while Japan had agreed to a search for Korean citizens who had disappeared prior to 1945. In addition, visits to their homeland by Japanese women married to North Koreans were to resume, and Japan was to provide some 100,000 metric tons of rice to the DPRK through WFP. In late April 2000 Japanese charter flights to North Korea resumed. Following informal contacts between the North Korean and Japanese Governments, full normalization talks commenced in April; further rounds of discussions took place during the year, despite an announcement by Japan in September that relations between the two countries would not be normalized until the cases of Japanese citizens allegedly abducted by North Korean agents had been solved. In November the DPRK rejected an offer by Japan to extend economic aid rather than grant wartime compensation. Meanwhile, in September the long-delayed third visits home by the Japanese wives of North Korean men took place. In October Japan decided, on humanitarian grounds, to provide 500,000 metric tons of rice to North Korea.

In December 2000 the DPRK reiterated that normal relations with Japan could be restored only after the latter delivered an apology and compensation for its earlier colonial rule. In May 2001 Japan deported Kim Jong Nam, son of Kim Jong Il, for entering the country on a false passport (see above). In June the DPRK condemned Japan's refusal to issue visas to North Koreans planning to attend a conference on Japanese compensation for Korea, held in Japan. In August the DPRK demanded compensation for Korean victims of the atomic bombs dropped on Hiroshima and Nagasaki in 1945, and also for the collision of cargo ships from the two countries in July 2001.

The DPRK was one of several Asian countries that strongly condemned Japanese Prime Minister Junichiro Koizumi's visit to the Yasukuni Shrine in Tokyo, honouring Japan's war dead, in August 2001. In December the DPRK announced that it was abandoning efforts to locate missing Japanese nationals thought to have been abducted by North Korean agents. At the end of the month a suspected North Korean spy vessel was sunk by Japanese coastguard forces after it had been expelled from Japan's exclusive economic zone. The DPRK condemned the incident, but denied any involvement, accusing Japan of seeking to mislead world opinion. Japanese coastguard forces searched the sunken vessel in May 2002, and raised it in September of that year. In February the DPRK released a Japanese journalist who had been detained on spying charges since December 1999.

In an unexpected development, Junichiro Koizumi visited Pyongyang in September 2002, becoming the first incumbent Japanese Prime Minister to do so. His one-day visit, during which he held discussions with Kim Jong Il, was dominated by the latter's admission that North Korean agents had abducted 12 Japanese citizens in the 1970s and 1980s, of whom five were still alive. The remainder were said to have died of natural causes, although suspicions remained that they might have been executed, after the North Korean authorities failed to locate the graves. Kim apologized for the incidents, but attributed them to rogue elements within the security services. The admission led some sources to indicate that the total number of Japanese abductees might be as high as 100. The surviving captives were temporarily allowed to return to Japan in October 2002, although they had to leave behind any spouses or children. Among the abductees allowed to return was Hitomi Soga, the wife of Charles Jenkins, a US soldier who in 1965 was believed to have defected to the DPRK where he had since remained. The Japanese authorities then refused to allow the abductees to return to the DPRK. Despite this, representatives from the two countries held the first round of resumed discussions on the restoration of normal diplomatic relations in Malaysia at the end of October 2002, but failed to make any progress.

In October 2002 the alleged admission by North Korean officials to their visiting US counterparts that the DPRK was pursuing a secret nuclear weapons programme alarmed Japan. Koizumi announced that Japan would halt further economic co-operation with the DPRK until the issues of the abducted Japanese citizens and the nuclear programme were resolved. The DPRK warned Japan that it would abandon its moratorium on missile testing if normalization talks failed to make any progress. In separate incidents in February and March 2003 the DPRK test-launched two short-range ground-to-ship missiles in the Sea of Japan, and in April tested a third missile in the Yellow Sea. However, it refrained from testing longer-range ballistic missiles, which Japan considered a threat to its security. In March the DPRK was angered by Japan's launching of two spy satellites, believed to be part of a programme of intelligence-gathering on the DPRK initiated following the suspected testing of the North Korean *Taepo Dong* missile over Japan in 1998 (see above).

In June 2003 the DPRK cancelled a voyage of the *Man Gyong Bong* passenger ferry, used by ethnic Korean residents in Japan to visit relatives in North Korea, apparently owing to more stringent inspections of North Korean ships by Japan; there was speculation that illegal goods were being transported by the ferry. In August a group of 10 North Korean refugees claimed asylum at the Japanese embassy in the Thai capital of Bangkok, in what was believed to be the first incident of this kind outside China. At the end of the month Japan was one of six nations taking part in talks on the North Korean nuclear weapons programme held in Beijing. At the discussions, Japan reportedly attempted to raise the issue of Japanese citizens abducted by the DPRK (see above). In the same month, Japanese authorities seized premises owned by the General Association of Korean Residents in Japan (*Chongryon*), reportedly owing to tax evasion. Also in August, the *Man Gyong Bong* ferry arrived in the Japanese port of Niigata on its first trip to Japan in seven months. Departure of the ship from Niigata was subsequently delayed after the vessel failed safety inspections carried out by the Japanese authorities. Relatives of Japanese nationals abducted by North Korea, as well as Japanese right-wing groups, held anti-North Korean protests at the port. In October the DPRK announced that it did not wish Japan to participate in future negotiations on its nuclear weapons programme, claiming that Japan was 'an obstacle to the peaceful settlement' of the nuclear issue, and citing Japanese attempts to 'blockade' North Korea.

In January 2004 the Japanese House of Representatives approved legislation to permit the imposition of economic sanctions on the DPRK. In April legislation was approved requiring all ships entering Japanese ports from March 2005 to be insured against oil damage. This in practice amounted to a ban on entry by North Korean ships. Following a second visit by Japanese Prime Minister Koizumi to Pyongyang in May 2004, five children of the abductees who had returned to Japan in 2002 (see above) were permitted to fly to Tokyo. Their release had been secured in return for pledges of food aid and medical supplies. However, suspicions remained over the fate of other missing Japanese nationals. In July 2004 the former US soldier Charles Jenkins, husband of the Japanese abductee Hitomi Soga (see above), travelled to Indonesia with his two daughters and was reunited with his wife. (He subsequently received hospital treatment in Japan, and was then found guilty of desertion from the US army and sentenced to a short period of imprisonment.) In November the DPRK relinquished human remains which it claimed were those of Megumi Yokota, who had been kidnapped by North Korean agents in 1977. The DPRK claimed that she had committed suicide. However, subsequent DNA tests indicated that the remains were not those of Megumi Yokota. North Korea refused to accept the results of the tests. The Japanese Government subsequently suspended food aid to North Korea, and public pressure for the imposition of economic sanctions on the DPRK increased in Japan. In December 2004 the DPRK stated that it would regard the imposition of economic sanctions as tantamount to a declaration of war.

At the beginning of March 2005 legislation concerning insurance requirements for ships entering Japanese ports, which had been approved in early 2004 (see above), took effect, amounting to a ban on entry of all but 16 of an estimated 100 North Korean ships that were involved in trade with Japan. While most Japanese citizens were believed to favour the imposition of direct economic sanctions on the DPRK, the Japanese Government remained reluctant to do this, not wishing to jeopardize future negotiations concerning North Korea's nuclear weapons programme. The September 2005 six-party agreement (see below) contained a clause in which Japan and the DPRK undertook to 'take steps to normalize their relations'. Talks were held between the two countries in February 2006 to discuss issues including the alleged abductions of Japanese citizens, the development of ballistic missiles by the DPRK and the resumption of the nuclear negotiations. However, the discussions ended inconclusively, and later in that month Japan's Chief Cabinet Secretary, Shinzo Abe, announced that arrest warrants had been issued for two North Korean agents suspected of abducting four Japanese nationals in 1978.

In June 2006 the Japanese legislature enacted the North Korean Human Rights Act, which expressly linked the imposition of sanctions to issues of human rights in the DPRK. The Act stated that economic sanctions would be imposed unless the DPRK worked to resolve human rights issues; significantly, these included the abduction of Japanese nationals. When the DPRK conducted missile tests in July (see below) Japan was one of its most vehement critics, announcing unilateral sanctions against the DPRK in September. (The USA and Australia announced similar measures prior to the issuance of UN Security Council Resolution 1718 in October—see below.) The Japanese sanctions provided for the 'freezing' of transfers of funds to the DPRK by groups suspected of having links to the country's nuclear weapons or missiles programmes; this affected 15 groups and one individual. These followed more limited sanctions imposed in the immediate aftermath of the July missile tests, which included the banning of a North Korean trade ferry from Japanese ports and a moratorium on charter flights from Pyongyang.

The appointment of Shinzo Abe as Japanese Prime Minister in September 2006 signalled a firmer approach by Japan on the North Korean issue. Abe appointed a prime ministerial adviser on the issue of Japanese abductees, and also established a special government panel on the subject. Only three days after his appointment as Prime Minister, Abe met with families and supporters of abductees, a clear signal of the importance with which he regarded the issue.

Following the North Korean nuclear test on 9 October 2006, Japan was among the strongest supporters of stringent sanctions, and refused to accept the DPRK as a nuclear state. Not only did Japan support sanctions under the UN Security Council, but it also imposed firm measures of its own, banning all North Korean imports and prohibiting North Korean ships from entering Japanese waters. This stance provoked characteristic ire from the North Korean Government, which urged Japan not to attend the next round of six-party talks. In November the Japanese Government approved a ban on the export of luxury goods to the DPRK. (A similar ban was enacted by the USA in November.) However, the restoration of normal relations between the DPRK and Japan was one of the tenets of the agreement reached during six-party talks in February 2007 (see below), and a working group was established to conduct negotiations. The first bilateral discussions between the two countries for more than a year were held in Viet Nam in March, but they broke down over the issue of the Japanese abductees. In July the North Korean Ministry of Foreign Affairs issued a memorandum accusing Japan of attempting to obstruct the talks on the normalization of bilateral relations and to disrupt the six-party process with its refusal to provide energy aid and its insistence on the resolution of the abduction issue, which North Korea claimed had already been settled. The working group held its second round of bilateral discussions in Mongolia in September, reportedly in a more positive atmosphere than the March talks, although again no agreement was reached. In October Japan announced that it would not resume aid to North Korea and extended its ban on North Korean imports and the entry of North Korean ships into Japanese waters for a further six months, citing a continued lack of progress in the dispute over the abductees. Japan renewed its sanctions against the DPRK in April 2008. In June the DPRK and Japan attended bilateral talks in Beijing, with the former agreeing to carry out another investigation into the abduction issue in exchange for the withdrawal of certain Japanese sanctions, including restrictions on port visits by North Korean vessels carrying humanitarian cargo. However, in October relations suffered a further set-back when Japan sought to withhold aid for the DPRK under the six-party agreement, complaining that little progress had been made on the abduction issue. In response, the DPRK proposed the removal of Japan from the six-party process.

In March 2009, following the revelation that the DPRK was shortly to launch a satellite, Japan mobilized its missile interceptors, in the country's first deployment of this technology. The Japanese Government reiterated its warning that it would attempt to destroy any North Korean missile or debris that threatened Japanese territory.

The DPRK has considered the USA to be its main enemy since the time of the Korean War and repeatedly accused the Republic of Korea of being a US 'puppet' state. Relations deteriorated after the DPRK seized a US naval vessel, the USS Pueblo, in 1968 and detained its crew for several months. In 1969 the DPRK shot down a US reconnaissance aircraft which had apparently violated North Korean airspace, resulting in the deaths of 31 US servicemen. In 1987, in response to alleged North Korean involvement in the bombing of a South Korean airliner, the USA placed the DPRK on its list of countries supporting terrorism, and restricted contacts between US and North Korean diplomats. Relations with the USA in the 1990s were largely dominated by the DPRK's suspected nuclear ambitions (see above). In December 1994 it was announced that agreement had been reached to establish liaison offices in Washington, DC, and Pyongyang in 1995, in preparation for an eventual resumption of full diplomatic relations. However, the USA insisted that normal relations would be restored only when the DPRK ceased to export ballistic missiles and withdrew its troops from the border with South Korea; the DPRK, in turn, stated that liaison offices could only be opened when light-water nuclear reactors, in accordance with the October 1994 agreement between the DPRK and the USA, had been supplied. Relations faltered following the shooting-down of a US army helicopter which had apparently entered North Korean airspace; the DPRK initially refused to negotiate, but, after direct bilateral discussions in December, the pilot was repatriated. In January 1995 the DPRK opened its ports to US commercial shipping and removed restrictions on the import of goods from the USA. Following the severe flooding in the DPRK in 1995 and 1996, the USA provided relief aid.

The issue of four-way talks (see above) dominated relations between the USA and the DPRK in 1996, but parallel negotiations were conducted concerning the estimated 8,100 US soldiers who were listed as 'missing in action' following the Korean War. The USA agreed to provide funds to assist in locating the bodies, and it was reported that the DPRK had requested additional food aid in return for its co-operation. In December, following the issuing of a (US-brokered) apology by the DPRK for the submarine incursion into South Korean waters in September, it was reported that the USA was prepared partially to revoke its economic sanctions against North Korea, and to allow the gradual expansion of bilateral trade. In early 1997 the USA responded to a renewed appeal issued by the UN for food aid and humanitarian assistance for North Korea, as a result of which the DPRK announced its intention to take part in exploratory discussions about the proposed quadripartite talks. Bilateral discussions with the USA during 1997 focused on the establishment of liaison offices, missile non-proliferation and procedures for the exhumation of the US servicemen listed as 'missing in action'. In August, however, the defection to the USA of two North Korean diplomats (the most senior officials yet to seek asylum in North America) resulted in the suspension of the third round of missile non-proliferation talks. The DPRK was unsuccessful in attempting to make its participation in full quadripartite talks conditional upon the withdrawal of US forces from the Korean peninsula and upon the provision of food aid. None the less, the USA responded positively, on humanitarian grounds, to two further UN appeals for food aid during the year. Relations with the USA were dominated by nuclear issues and other concerns regarding the DPRK's missile development programme in 1998 and 1999 (see above). The exhumation of US soldiers listed as 'missing in action' proceeded, with 22 sets of remains returned to the USA in 1998. In October 1999 US officials visited Pyongyang to receive the remains of four soldiers, in the first such transfer to take place on North Korean territory without the involvement of the UNC. A further 15 sets of remains were returned in November 2000. Trade between the USA and the DPRK increased significantly following the partial revocation of economic sanctions against the latter in September 1999 (see above); US exports to the DPRK increased massively in 1999. Meanwhile, the USA continued to provide food aid.

In September, however, officials from the DPRK declined to attend the UN Millennium summit meeting in New York, following a confrontation between the delegation and US security officials, who suspected the North Koreans of terrorism, at Frankfurt airport in Germany. The USA subsequently apologized, describing the incident as an 'innocent mistake' and repudiating the DPRK's claim of a 'brazen plot'. In October Kim Jong Il's special envoy, Vice-Marshal Jo Myong Rok, paid a state visit to the USA, the most senior North Korean official ever to do so. Later in that month the US Secretary of State, Madeleine Albright, reciprocated the visit and met Kim Jong Il, who agreed in principle to halt his country's long-range missile-testing programme. Shortly afterwards, however, tension arose when two US fighter aircraft participating in a US-South Korean joint manoeuvre briefly crossed the military demarcation line into North Korean airspace. The DPRK protested to the UN.

Relations between the DPRK and the USA deteriorated during 2001 following the inauguration of George W. Bush as US President. Bush adopted a firmer position towards the DPRK compared with his predecessor, and this also adversely affected inter-Korean relations (see above). The DPRK condemned the joint US-South Korean military exercises held in April. In May a non-governmental delegation from the USA visited the DPRK to examine evidence of atrocities committed by US troops during the Korean War. In June Bush stated that he was willing to resume negotiations with the DPRK, albeit linking these to a reduction in North Korea's missile programme and military deployments—terms rejected by the North.

Following the terrorist attacks on the USA in September 2001, the USA paid increasing attention to North Korea's biological, chemical and nuclear weapons programmes. Although the DPRK had condemned those attacks, it subsequently opposed the US bombing of Afghanistan. By late 2001 the DPRK was drawing increasing criticism from the USA, and in October the US State Department released its annual report on religious freedom, which included the DPRK on a list of countries suppressing such beliefs. Despite signing two UN treaties against terrorism in November, the DPRK remained on the USA's list of states sponsoring terrorism.

In January 2002 the DPRK's relations with the USA deteriorated further following President Bush's reference to North Korea as forming an 'axis of evil' with Iran and Iraq. Bush's comments were believed to reflect concern that the DPRK was exporting weapons technology to countries the USA considered to be 'rogue states'. (During the 1990s the DPRK had exported missiles and related technology to countries such as Egypt, Iran, Libya, Pakistan and Syria, allegedly earning up to US $1,000m. a year.) However, when Bush visited the DMZ on a visit to the South, he urged the North to open up to the outside world. Although the USA ruled out any military action against the DPRK, in March 2002 it was revealed that the DPRK was one of seven nations considered a potential target for a US nuclear first strike, in the event of emergency circumstances. The DPRK responded by threatening to withdraw from existing agreements with the USA (see above). However, in April the North accepted a South Korean request to reopen dialogue with the USA, and invited a US envoy, Jack Pritchard, to discuss outstanding issues. At the same time the USA announced that it would release US $95m. to the DPRK in order to accelerate the building of the replacement nuclear reactors—construction of which finally began in August 2002, with a view to completion in 2008. Pritchard himself attended the ground-breaking ceremony, but stated that the DPRK must accept international inspection of its nuclear facilities, a demand that the North Korean Government stated was not mandatory until 2005.

Meanwhile, in July 2002, during the ASEAN Regional Forum (ARF) convened in Brunei, the Minister of Foreign Affairs, Paek Nam Sun, held an informal meeting with the US Secretary of State, Colin Powell, the first such meeting at this level since the inception of the Bush presidency. In August the DPRK rejected US demands for a significant reduction of its conventional military forces along its border with the South.

In October 2002 the USA revealed that senior North Korean officials had admitted to the visiting US Assistant Secretary of State for East Asian and Pacific Affairs, James Kelly, that the DPRK was pursuing a secret nuclear weapons programme in violation of the 1994 agreement. The clandestine programme was allegedly based on uranium extraction, whereas the suspended programme had been based on plutonium extraction. The admission reportedly came after Kelly presented his North Korean hosts with credible US intelligence reports about the programme, although officials of the DPRK later denied that they had made such an admission. Within days the USA declared the 1994 framework null and void and placed renewed pressure on the DPRK to halt its nuclear activities. The DPRK responded by stating that it would consider halting its nuclear programme if the USA would sign a non-aggression treaty guaranteeing it sovereignty, a demand rejected by the USA. The DPRK subsequently warned the USA of severe military measures if it continued to reject such a treaty. In mid-November 2002, however, the USA finally halted petroleum shipments to North Korea, citing the latter's violation of the 1994 framework. Further confusion over the nuclear programme emerged in November 2002 when North Korean radio reportedly admitted that the country already possessed nuclear weapons. However, the exact translation of the statement was in doubt, and most analysts concluded that the broadcast had stated that the DPRK was entitled to possess such weapons. At the same time it was widely reported that Pakistan had provided the technical expertise for North Korea's nuclear programme in exchange for ballistic missiles. Attention focused on the north-western city of Kusong, some 30 km north-west of Yongbyon, as the centre of the secret programme.

In December 2002 the DPRK announced that it would restart its nuclear reactor at Yongbyon, and the USA accused the country of narcotics-trafficking. The DPRK then removed the IAEA's monitoring and surveillance equipment from the Yongbyon facility. Security analysts, meanwhile, concluded that the DPRK already possessed between two and five nuclear devices. The IAEA reported that North Korean technicians had transferred 1,000 fuel rods (of the 8,000 necessary to reactivate it) to the Yongbyon reactor, ostensibly for the production of electricity, but probably for the production of plutonium required to manufacture nuclear devices. The DPRK expelled the two remaining IAEA inspectors at the end of the year.

In January 2003 the DPRK announced its withdrawal from the NPT, and the IAEA responded by adopting a resolution condemning the country's recent behaviour. However, President Bush indicated that the USA would resume petroleum deliveries if the DPRK abandoned its nuclear weapons programme. In February the DPRK stated that the Yongbyon reactor was operating normally, and that any US military build-up in the region could lead the North to launch a pre-emptive strike on US forces anywhere in the world. The DPRK also threatened to withdraw from the 1953 armistice if the USA imposed a blockade on the country. The USA deployed long-range bombers to its bases on the Pacific island of Guam as a precautionary measure.

In March 2003 the USA and South Korea began their annual joint military exercises amid condemnation by the North, which announced at the end of the month that it was severing military contacts with the USA at the liaison office in the DMZ. Also in early March four North Korean fighter aircraft intercepted a US reconnaissance aircraft in international airspace and closely pursued its flight, the first such incident in 32 years. Between late February and the beginning of April the DPRK also test-fired three short-range missiles, although it refrained from testing its longer-range ballistic missiles. By early April the USA had imposed new sanctions on the DPRK's Government and its Changgwang Sinyong Corporation, for exporting ballistic missiles to Pakistan. However, the sanctions were largely symbolic, since the USA had minimal economic links with the DPRK. Later in the month, the seizure by Australian authorities of the *Pong Su*, a North Korean ship carrying 50 kg of heroin, confirmed US claims that the DPRK was involved in drugs-trafficking. Also in April, the UN Security Council held discussions on the North Korean crisis for the first time. The DPRK stated prior to the discussions that the imposition of economic sanctions through the Security Council would amount to a declaration of war.

Tensions increased in late April 2003 after the North Korean media indicated that the country was preparing to reprocess, or was actually reprocessing, 8,000 spent fuel rods, a development that would enable it rapidly to produce nuclear weapons. Officials from North Korea, the USA and China held senior-level discussions in Beijing on the isse of the nuclear weapons programme. However, no agreements were reached, and US sources stated that the DPRK had, for the first time, admitted to possessing nuclear weapons and had threatened to carry out a nuclear test. In May the DPRK cited US behaviour against it as a reason for abandoning the Joint Declaration of the Denuclearization of the Korean Pensinula, a 1992 commitment with the South on a nuclear-free peninsula.

In June 2003 the DPRK for the first time publicly defended its nuclear weapons strategy, declaring that the development of nuclear weapons was a 'deterrent', and that the programme 'was not aimed at threatening or blackmailing'. In July there were new indications from US and Asian intelligence sources that the DPRK was operating a second secret nuclear facility, in addition to the plant at Yongbyon. At the end of July it was announced that the DPRK had agreed to take part in multilateral talks on its nuclear weapons programme with the USA, the Republic of Korea, Japan, China and Russia. Prior to the talks, tensions were exacerbated by the US Under-Secretary of State, John Bolton, who launched a virulent attack on Kim Jong Il in the course of a speech given in Seoul. The DPRK responded by describing Bolton as 'human scum' and refusing to negotiate with him. Furthermore, immediately in advance of the negotiations, Jack Pritchard resigned as US special envoy to North Korea. The six-party talks duly took place in Beijing in August, but little progress was achieved, the USA insisting that the DPRK unconditionally abandon its nuclear weapons programme, while the DPRK reiterated that it would continue to develop its nuclear capacity unless the USA provided a guarantee of non-aggression.

Following the six-party talks in Beijing, it was reported in September 2003 that President Bush had authorized his Assistant Secretary of State for East Asia and the Pacific, James Kelly, to abandon the USA's insistence on the full dismantling of the North Korean weapons programme before any concessions could be made. It was indicated that verifiable progress on dismantling might be sufficient. However, Kelly stated that a bilateral non-aggression treaty, as desired by the DPRK, was not a possibility, and that any guarantee would involve China, Russia, the Republic of Korea and Japan, as well as the USA. Also in October, the North Korean state news agency claimed that the DPRK had successfully completed the reprocessing of 8,000 spent fuel rods, thus generating sufficient plutonium to build a nuclear bomb. In November the Central Intelligence Agency (CIA) reported to the US Congress that it believed the DPRK had the technology to turn its nuclear fuel into functioning weapons. In early December KEDO (the international consortium established in 1995 following a 1994 agreement with the USA on assistance for energy development in the DPRK in return for nuclear non-proliferation, see above) announced that it would be suspending for one year its construction in the DPRK of two non-military nuclear reactors. Also in December 2003, the USA rejected an offer from the DPRK to 'freeze' its nuclear programme in return for concessions on security and energy aid.

In January 2004 a group of US nuclear scientists, including Siegfried Hecker, the former director of the Los Alamos nuclear research centre, was permitted to visit the Yongbyon plant in an unofficial capacity. Hecker subsequently stated that although he had seen no proof that the DPRK had produced a nuclear bomb, he had been shown radioactive plutonium metal. There was also speculation on the existence of a second nuclear programme for enriching uranium (in addition to the plutonium-reprocessing activities at Yongbyon). In February a fresh session of six-party talks took place in Beijing, but no significant resolutions were reached. In April a US expert on North Korea, Selig Harrison, visited Pyongyang and was reportedly assured that the DPRK would not transfer nuclear technology to al-Qa'ida or other 'militant' groups. At a third round of six-party talks in June little progress was achieved, with the DPRK continuing to deny the existence of a uranium enrichment programme. In July US Secretary of State Colin Powell held discussions with the North Korean Minister of Foreign Affairs, Paek Nam Sun, in Jakarta, representing the most senior-level talks between the two countries since 2002. In response to criticism of Kim Jong Il by President Bush, the Government of the DPRK issued a statement likening the US President to the Nazi leader, Adolf Hitler. Also in August 2004, it was reported that North Korea was developing a new sea-based long-range missile system, which would possibly be capable of targeting the USA. A fourth round of six-party talks scheduled for September 2004 was suspended when the DPRK refused to attend, citing US hostility. Tensions in relations with the USA increased further following the re-election of George W. Bush as US President in November. Later in that month KEDO announced its intention to suspend plans for the construction in the DPRK of two non-military nuclear reactors.

In January 2005 the North Korean Government was angered by a description of the DPRK by Condoleezza Rice, the recently appointed US Secretary of State, as an 'outpost of tyranny'. Subsequently, in a state radio broadcast in February, the DPRK for the first time explicitly stated that it possessed nuclear weapons, and that it intended to postpone its participation in six-party negotiations for an indefinite period. Subsequent suggestions by the DPRK for bilateral discussions with the USA were rejected by the latter. Early in 2005, meanwhile, Christopher Hill, hitherto the US ambassador in Seoul, replaced James Kelly as Assistant Secretary of State for East Asia and the Pacific and the USA's chief negotiator in the nuclear talks. In March Condoleezza Rice declared during a visit to Beijing that the USA would consider 'other options' if the DPRK persisted in refusing to participate in the six-party talks. In April, following a visit to the DPRK, Selig Harrison reported that the Yongbyon reactor was to be shut down in order to extract 8,000 spent fuel rods, to be reprocessed into plutonium for use in warheads. In May the DPRK announced that all 8,000 rods had been unloaded from the Yongbyon reactor 'in the shortest possible time', although there was speculation that this was unlikely to have been achieved so quickly and that the announcement might be a diplomatic ploy in advance of any resumption of discussions. Also in May tension was increased when the DPRK test-fired a ballistic missile into the Sea of Japan, while Mohammad el-Baradei, Director-General of the IAEA, stated that he believed the DPRK possessed enough weapons-grade plutonium for five or six nuclear devices. However, an apparent improvement in relations in June included a US pledge of 50,000 metric tons of food aid, and the fourth round of six-party talks began in Beijing on 26 July. On the previous day bilateral discussions were held between the representatives of the DPRK and the USA in the hope of finding a compromise between their respective opening positions. The USA continued to insist that the restoration of normal relations, removal of sanctions and guarantees of security could only follow the 'complete, verifiable and irreversible dismantling' of the DPRK's nuclear weapons programme, while the latter reiterated that only after the normalization of relations, including the signing of a peace treaty ending the Korean War, and the removal of US nuclear weapons from South Korea (the presence of which the US side denied) would the North agree to abandon its military nuclear aspirations. (The USA had indicated that, for the purpose of these talks, it was prepared to disregard the issue of the possible existence of a uranium enrichment programme in the DPRK.) The discussions went into recess in early August; their resumption was postponed until mid-September as a mark of protest by the DPRK at the annual joint military exercises performed by South Korea and the USA.

In mid-September 2005 a draft joint agreement was signed by all sides in the six-party negotiations, in which the DPRK committed itself to dismantling its nuclear weapons programme, returning to the NPT and permitting IAEA inspectors to visit its nuclear facilities. In return, the USA declared that it maintained no nuclear weapons on the Korean peninsula and had no intention of attacking the DPRK. The DPRK's right to peaceful nuclear energy was acknowledged, and it was envisaged that the provision of a civilian light-water nuclear reactor to North Korea would be discussed 'at an appropriate time'. The other five parties also pledged to provide the DPRK with energy assistance. Described in some quarters as a major breakthrough, the agreement was nevertheless vague and was compromised almost immediately when the North Korean Government insisted that it would take no steps towards dismantling its nuclear weapons programme until provided with a light-water reactor as specified in the agreement. The USA insisted that concessions such as the reactor could be expected to come into force only after the DPRK had fulfilled its dismantlement obligations. The fifth round of talks, which began in Beijing in November, was intended to discuss means of implementing the September agreement, but its opening was marred by North Korea's angry reaction to reported comments by President Bush during a visit to Brazil where he made reference to a 'tyrant in North Korea'. A five-point plan for dismantling its nuclear programme proposed at the talks by the DPRK was reportedly rejected by the USA; the discussions ended without agreement and without any setting of a date for the next round. Later in November KEDO announced that it was considering the termination of its light-water reactor construction project in the DPRK, which had been suspended since 2003. (All workers were withdrawn from KEDO's construction site in Kumho, DPRK, in January 2006, and in December KEDO's executive board signed an agreement to terminate the project. In January 2007 KEDO reportedly demanded nearly US $1,900m. in compensation.)

Meanwhile, the resumption of the six-party nuclear negotiations appeared to be jeopardized by US criticism of the alleged financial crimes of the DPRK. In September 2005 the US Government had ordered that all transactions with Banco Delta Asia in the Chinese Special Administrative Region of Macao be terminated, in relation to suspected money-laundering activities conducted with the bank by the North Korean Government, and had also 'frozen' the assets of eight North Korean companies, which it accused of proliferating weapons of mass destruction. In October the US Department of Justice accused the DPRK of having forged millions of US dollars' worth of counterfeit $100 bills since 1989, and in December 2005 Alexander Vershbow, US ambassador to the Republic of Korea, publicly described the DPRK as a 'criminal regime'. Although the US Administration insisted that the sanctions were purely a legal matter and had no political connection to the nuclear issue, the North Korean Government declared that no further six-party negotiations could be held until sanctions against it were removed. In April 2006 Christopher Hill rejected North Korean overtures for bilateral discussions in Tokyo, to coincide with a regional security forum at which all six participants in the nuclear discussions were present, insisting that communication between the two sides was only possible within the context of the six-party talks.

By mid-2006 speculation was rife that the DPRK was soon to test-launch an intercontinental ballistic missile, thus breaking the moratorium on tests imposed in 1999. In the USA, officials reportedly telephoned North Korean diplomats in the UN to warn them of the consequences of proceeding with a test, while US Secretary of State Condoleezza Rice warned that a test would be regarded as a provocative act. Japan threatened stern action should a test missile be launched. However, the DPRK continued to insist that it might be prepared to halt the planned test should the USA agree to direct bilateral talks, a request that the US Government once again rejected. Instead, the USA announced that it would deploy advanced *Patriot* missiles (capable of intercepting North Korean ballistic missiles, as well as cruise missiles and aircraft) on Japanese soil for the first time. The DPRK's decision to test seven missiles on 5 July 2006 was regarded as a deliberate attempt to provoke the USA. Of the missiles tested, at least one was a *Taepo Dong 2* missile, thought to be capable of reaching Alaska, and although the US State Department claimed that the *Taepo Dong 2* failed in mid-air after about 42 seconds of flight, the North Korean Government hailed the tests as a success, announcing that more test launches were planned.

While the international community broadly condemned the tests, harsh criticism from the USA and Japan was tempered by the more cautious stance adopted by China, Russia and the Republic of Korea. The USA and Japan urged the UN Security Council to adopt sanctions against the DPRK, while Russia and China, which as permanent members of the Council held the power of veto, emphasized the importance of the resumption of dialogue. The UN Security Council adopted Resolution 1695 on 15 July 2006, requiring member states to bar the import and export of missile-related material to and from the DPRK. By August reports indicated that the North Korean missile programme was proceeding rapidly, with the construction of new underground missile bases and silos along the east coast. According to a South Korean security expert, around 200 *Rodong* missiles with ranges of up to 2,200 km and 50 SSN-6 missiles with ranges of 2,500–4,000 km were already deployed there. The South Korean report also suggested that the DPRK had built two underground missile bases deep within the mountains of the border region with China. The South Korean Minister of Foreign Affairs warned that a North Korean nuclear test would have serious consequences.

The USA attempted once more to revive the six-party talks in September 2006, with Assistant Secretary of State Christopher Hill travelling to Beijing, Tokyo and Seoul for discussions with senior officials. However, he reiterated that the US position on the talks had not changed, and that no new incentives would be offered. (The DPRK accused the USA of threatening war by conducting a missile defence test from Alaska.) In early October 2006 the North Korean Ministry of Foreign Affairs officially announced that the DPRK would conduct a nuclear test in 'the near future'. The South Korean Government issued a 'grave warning' to the North, pointing out that such a test would violate the 1992 Joint Declaration of the Denuclearization of the Korean Peninsula.

However, in defiance of international opinion, the DPRK's nuclear test took place on 9 October 2006, reportedly from a test site near Kimchaek city in North Hampyong Province. The South Korean Minister for Unification, Lee Jong-Seok, denounced the test as a clear challenge to world peace and stability. Although the size of the nuclear device tested was thought to be very small, the detection of airborne radiation by US analysts confirmed that the device was nuclear in nature. The test prompted an emergency meeting of the UN Security Council in New York, amid strong condemnation from the international community, notably the USA and Japan.

On 14 October 2006 the UN Security Council approved a unanimous resolution imposing sanctions on the DPRK, with Russia and China unexpectedly agreeing to a range of sanctions, albeit one that was purely economic and commercial, rather than military, in nature. Resolution 1718 called on the DPRK to suspend immediately its ballistic weapons programme and further nuclear tests and to return to the six-party talks without precondition. Sanctions included provision for the inspection of cargo entering and leaving North Korean ports, a ban on weapons-related imports, a travel ban on North Korean officials thought to be involved in the weapons programme and a 'freezing' of their assets, and also a ban on the import of luxury goods. At the end of October the DPRK indicated that it would return to the six-party talks, following discussions among Chinese, US and North Korean officials. While the DPRK set no conditions for its return to the discussions, it expressed the hope that one of the topics would be the removal of financial sanctions and the release of North Korean assets. In mid-November, however, a draft UN resolution condemned the DPRK's human rights record (see above), and in the following week leaders from the Asia-Pacific Economic Co-operation (APEC, see p. 185) forum, meeting in the Vietnamese capital of Hanoi, issued a statement expressing their strong concern over the nuclear weapons test.

Discussions held in Beijing in late November 2006 between the DPRK's senior nuclear negotiator Kim Kye Gwan and US Assistant Secretary of State Christopher Hill did little to solve the impasse. Not only did the two sides fail to confirm a date for the resumption of the six-party talks, but the DPRK remained adamant that while it was ready to implement its pledge made in September 2005 to relinquish nuclear weapons, it had no intention of doing so unilaterally. Intense diplomatic activity in the following weeks resulted in the resumption of the six-nation talks on 18 December 2006. However, the DPRK stated that it would consider halting its nuclear programme only if the USA removed both its financial sanctions and the UN sanctions. The country also reiterated demands for a nuclear reactor to generate electricity. The US negotiators, meanwhile, were reported by South Korean sources to have offered a fresh programme of incentives, which would give the DPRK aid and security guarantees if it agreed to declare all its nuclear-related programmes and place them under permanent external inspection. However, the DPRK rejected the US overture, and the talks ended in deadlock.

Efforts to resume the six-party talks continued in January 2007 when, in an unprecedented development, US Assistant Secretary of State Christopher Hill held direct discussions with North Korean nuclear negotiator Kim Kye Gwan in Berlin, Germany. While the DPRK stated that an agreement had been reached, Hill denied this, none the less describing the discussions as very useful. Discreet negotiations, meanwhile, continued to take place among the main parties concerned, and by the end of January the DPRK was reported by South Korean officials to be considering ending its nuclear programme in exchange for aid. As US treasury officials met their North Korean counterparts in Beijing to discuss financial sanctions, Chinese officials announced that the six-party talks were to resume.

The six-party talks held in February 2007 resulted in an apparently significant advance: among other points, the DPRK agreed to permit IAEA inspections and to shut down its nuclear reactor at Yongbyon within 60 days in exchange for the equivalent of 50,000 metric tons of heavy fuel oil and the assurance of negotiations on the restoration of normal relations with Japan and the USA, with the latter notably agreeing to begin the process of ending the designation of the DPRK as a state sponsoring terrorism. Five working groups were to be established to address North Korean relations with both Japan and the USA, economic and energy co-operation, denuclearization of the Korean peninsula, and the establishment of a North-East Asia peace and security mechanism. The DPRK was given an incentive of a further 950,000 tons of heavy fuel oil for immobilizing its nuclear facilities and providing a complete declaration of all its nuclear programmes as part of the next phase of the agreement. Although the formal accord did not directly mention the North Korean funds in the Banco Delta Asia in Macao that had been 'frozen' by the USA in 2005 (see above), this issue was covered by a reference to 'resolving pending bilateral issues', and the USA subsequently agreed to return the funds. Mohammad el-Baradei's visit to the DPRK in mid-March 2007 was an indication of further progress, with the head of the IAEA confirming the DPRK's evident commitment to the dismantling of its nuclear programme. However, a few days later, a further round of six-party talks faltered over delays to the release of the North Korean funds in Macao, and the DPRK missed the 14 April closure deadline for the Yongbyon reactor. Meanwhile, it was reported that the DPRK had offered to return the *USS Pueblo* (seized in 1968 and now moored in Pyongyang—see above), during the visit of a US delegation collecting the remains of six US soldiers who had been killed in the Korean War. As progress on the implementation of the February 2007 agreement remained stalled, with commercial banks reportedly unwilling to transfer the Banco Delta Asia funds, North Korea test-fired three short-range missiles in late May and early June.

US Assistant Secretary of State Christopher Hill visited Pyongyang for the first time in late June 2007. Shortly afterwards North Korea confirmed that it had received the Banco Delta Asia funds, which amounted to US $25m. and had been transferred via a Russian bank, and on the following day IAEA inspectors arrived in North Korea for discussions on the closure of the Yongbyon reactor. On their first visit to the DPRK since their expulsion in December 2002, the inspectors were given unlimited access to the nuclear site. In mid-July 2007 the DPRK announced that it had shut down Yongbyon, which was subsequently verified by the IAEA. Participants in the six-party talks met in Beijing a few days later, but failed to agree upon a timetable for the second phase of the February accord, i.e. the disclosure and disablement of all North Korea's nuclear facilities. Following the discussions, Kim Kye Gwan renewed demands that North Korea should be provided with a light-water reactor in exchange for immobilizing its Yongbyon nuclear reactor. Working groups established by the six nations involved in the talks on ending North Korea's nuclear weapons programme held meetings in Panmunjom in August to discuss the technical details of the next stage of the process. Following talks between the DPRK and the USA on improving their bilateral relations, which were held in Geneva in early September, Hill announced that North Korea had agreed to declare and disable all its nuclear facilities by the end of the year. The DPRK claimed that the US delegation had agreed to its removal from the US list of countries supporting terrorism and to lift economic sanctions, but Hill denied this, stating that such action would depend on progress towards ending North Korea's nuclear programme. A group of experts from the USA, China and Russia visited the DPRK in mid-September to examine ways of disabling its nuclear facilities.

A new round of six-party talks, which was held in Beijing in late September 2007, resulted in formal agreement on a deadline of 31 December for the completion of the second phase of the February accord, under which North Korea would receive a further 900,000 metric tons of heavy fuel oil (100,000 tons having already been supplied by South Korea and China). In mid-October a US team of government officials and nuclear experts spent a week in North Korea to discuss detailed plans for disablement. Work on immobilizing the Yongbyon reactor, which was to entail the removal of 8,000 fuel rods, commenced in early November under US supervision. Following a visit to North Korea in early December, Hill reported that disablement was progressing well. Meanwhile, in a personal letter to Kim Jong Il delivered by Hill, President Bush urged the DPRK to fulfil its pledge to provide a full and complete declaration of its nuclear programmes. However, North Korea failed to meet the deadline to disclose details of its nuclear activities. The disablement of the country's nuclear facilities had also not been completed by the end of 2007, although this was attributed to technical difficulties. Hill visited Japan, South Korea, China and Russia for consultations on the denuclearization process in mid-January 2008, suggesting in South Korea that the deadline could be extended until the end of February. In late January Kim Jong Il reportedly assured a visiting Chinese diplomat that the DPRK remained committed to implementing the agreements reached at the six-party talks. Hill held discussions with Kim Kye Gwan in Beijing in mid-February, later commenting that disagreement remained over the DPRK's continued denial of US claims of the existence of a covert North Korean nuclear programme for enriching uranium; this was followed in April by the USA's contention that the DPRK had passed sensitive nuclear information to Syria. An historic concert in Pyongyang by the New York Philharmonic orchestra in February, involving the largest US presence in the country since the Korean War, was hailed as a significant act of cultural diplomacy. In May the DPRK submitted an 18,000-page report on its nuclear weapons programme to US delegates. As the six-party process apparently entered a new phase, further documentation was provided in late June, prompting President Bush to announce that the DPRK would be removed from the USA's list of state sponsors of terrorism and that US trade sanctions would be withdrawn. Soon afterwards, the cooling tower of the Yongbyon reactor was destroyed by the North Korean authorities. However, further movement on the terms of the agreement was slow, owing to disputes over the method of authentication of the North Korean progress reports and delays to the DPRK's official redesignation as a non-terrorist nation. In August these disagreements resulted in an announcement from the DPRK that it would stop dismantling its Yongbyon reactor, and, in early September, that the reactor was to be restarted. The impasse appeared to have been resolved in October, when the USA implemented the redesignation of the DPRK in return for the latter's assurance of compliance with nuclear inspections, albeit with conditions. However, the issue of the verification procedure continued to impede progress when the six-party talks resumed in Beijing in December.

Meanwhile, in May 2008 the DPRK accepted the USA's offer of substantial amounts of food aid, the bulk of which was to be delivered by WFP. In March 2009, however, following the closure of the border in response to South Korea's participation in joint military exercises with the USA, and as speculation mounted with regard to the precise nature of an imminent satellite launch announced by the DPRK (see below), the North Korean Government refused to accept any further supplies of US food aid and instructed five US aid groups to leave the country by the end of the month. In mid-March two US journalists were arrested by North Korean guards near the border with China. The North Korean authorities confirmed that the two women were being held pending an investigation into their apparent intrusion into the DPRK. It was subsequently announced that they were to be tried in June.

The DPRK's announcement of its forthcoming launch of a communications satellite aroused much concern. The US, South Korean and Japanese Governments feared that the operation might prove to be a long-range missile test of *Taepo Dong 2*. Japan began to deploy missile interceptors for the first time, reiterating that it would attempt to destroy any missile or debris that threatened Japanese territory. On 5 April 2009 the DPRK proceeded to launch its rocket, in defiance of international warnings. The rocket dropped a booster stage to the west of Japan before flying over the country towards the Pacific Ocean, where a second booster stage was released. The DPRK announced that the launch had permitted the placement of a communications satellite into orbit; however, this was contested by the US military, which asserted that the rocket's payload had landed in the Pacific Ocean. The Japanese Government requested an emergency session of the UN Security Council. The session ended without agreement after divisions emerged with regard to the response to the launch. Chinese and Russian envoys urged restraint, while the USA and Japan advocated a reinforcement of sanctions against the DPRK. However, on 13 April the Security Council released a statement condemning the rocket launch and the violation of the ban on missile tests by the DPRK. The DPRK then expelled all UN nuclear inspectors and announced its withdrawal from the six-party talks and the resumption of its nuclear programme.

The DPRK's relations with China have remained a crucial focus of North Korean foreign policy. During the years of the so-called Sino-Soviet dispute the DPRK fluctuated in its allegiance to each of its powerful northern neighbours, China and the USSR. Kim Il Sung made several official visits to China in the late 1980s, which were interpreted by some Western observers as an attempt to establish closer relations in view of the erosion of communist power in many Eastern European countries. However, the DPRK was aggrieved at China's establishment of full diplomatic relations with the Republic of Korea in August 1992. China appeared largely conciliatory with regard to North Korea's nuclear programme, and during 1993 and the first months of 1994 indicated that it would veto any attempt by the UN Security Council to impose economic sanctions on the DPRK. In 1997 China agreed to provide substantial food aid to the DPRK to alleviate the effects of flooding. Later in that year China accepted US and South Korean proposals for quadripartite negotiations with North Korea to conclude a new peace agreement with the South, and between December 1997 and August 1999 it participated in all six rounds of these negotiations. A senior North Korean delegation visited China in June 1999. During the visit China announced that it would provide the country with 150,000 metric tons of food aid and 400,000 tons of coke over the following months. In October 1999 the Chinese Minister of Foreign Affairs, Tang Jiaxuan, participated in celebrations held in Pyongyang to commemorate the 50th anniversary of the establishment of diplomatic relations between the two countries.

In late 1999 international attention was focused on the uncertain situation of the large number of North Koreans (estimated at some 30,000 by South Korean sources and at 200,000 by the voluntary organization Médecins Sans Frontières) who had crossed the border into China in recent years. In early 2000 it was reported that China had returned some 10,000 escapees to the DPRK during 1999. The number of migrants was thought to fluctuate, according to the season.

In February 2000 China permitted the DPRK to open a consulate-general in Hong Kong. In the following month Kim Jong Il attended a function at the Chinese embassy in Pyongyang. This was his first visit to the mission for 15 years. In May Kim Jong Il visited China, his first official trip abroad for 17 years. In January 2001 the North Korean leader paid a second visit to the People's Republic. During this visit, Kim held extensive discussions with Chinese leaders in Beijing, and also toured the new business zones of Shanghai and Shenzhen, where he observed joint-venture projects with foreign multinational corporations, telecommunications projects and the Shanghai Stock Exchange. In September Chinese President Jiang Zemin paid an official visit to North Korea, the first such visit since 1990. Jiang promised an additional 200,000 metric tons of food aid and 30,000 tons of diesel oil as a gesture of goodwill to alleviate North Korea's economic crisis. Jiang also reportedly urged North Korea to resume discussions with the South.

During 2002 the DPRK and China continued to seek the reconnection of the inter-Korean railway lines and their subsequent linking to China's own railway system. In May, however, China's forcible removal of North Korean refugees from South Korean embassy premises in the People's Republic again brought the issue of the refugees to international attention. Several groups of North Korean refugees had, in 2002, fled to Western, Japanese and South Korean diplomatic offices in China, embarrassing the latter, since the Chinese Government had signed a treaty with the DPRK providing for the repatriation of refugees. In June China allowed 24 North Korean refugees who had been concealed in the embassy of the Republic of Korea to leave for that country. After that incident, China began an operation against South Korean activists and missionaries who had been helping North Koreans to flee via China. It was estimated that as many as 300,000 North Korean refugees were already residing in China, with US sources stating that as many as 50,000 had fled to China in 2001 alone.

In February 2003 the President of the DPRK's SPA Presidium, Kim Yong Nam, visited Beijing and pledged to maintain strong bilateral relations. China was expected to use its influence with the DPRK to resolve the tension regarding North Korea's nuclear situation, albeit warning the UN Security Council not to involve itself in the matter. In March China cut its oil supply to the DPRK via a pipeline from Liaoning Province for three days, following North Korean missile tests in the Sea of Japan (see above).

In April 2003 China hosted and participated in senior-level meetings between the DPRK and the USA over Pyongyang's nuclear weapons programme (see above). Immediately prior to the discussions, Vice-Marshal Jo Myong Rok, the DPRK's second highest ranking official, led a military delegation to China, and held meetings with President Hu Jintao and senior military leaders. Chinese diplomatic efforts played a major role in ensuring North Korean participation in the first round of six-party talks on the nuclear issue that were held in Beijing in August (as well as in subsequent rounds—see above). In April 2004 Kim Jong Il made a secretive visit to China, where he held talks with President Hu and other officials. Topics under discussion included the nuclear issue, with China reportedly urging the DPRK to modify its stance, and economic matters. During 2004 repeated instances of defectors from the DPRK seeking refuge in foreign embassies in Beijing posed a dilemma for China, which as an official ally of the DPRK continued to refuse to grant refugee status to such persons. Many defectors were none the less able to travel to Seoul via a third country. In November, however, China forcibly repatriated a group of 70 North Korean nationals. It was believed that they would be imprisoned and possibly executed upon their return to the DPRK. Meanwhile, following the DPRK's refusal to attend a fourth round of six-party talks on the nuclear issue in September, a member of the Standing Committee of the Politburo of the Chinese Communist Party, Li Changchun, headed a delegation to Pyongyang in an attempt to persuade the DPRK to resume negotiations. In March 2005 North Korean Premier Pak Pong Ju visited Beijing and Shanghai. Chinese diplomacy received considerable credit for the achievement of the joint draft agreement at the end of the fourth round of six-party talks in September (see above). In October President Hu made his first official visit to Pyongyang, in advance of the fifth round of nuclear talks in November. In January 2006 reports emerged that Kim Jong Il had travelled incognito to the People's Republic and was visiting the special economic zone of Shenzhen, to observe the methods and results of China's economic modernization. The visit was confirmed by North Korean media following Kim's return to the DPRK.

The DPRK's relations with China deteriorated in October 2006, however, following the North Korean nuclear weapon test (see above). The test embarrassed the Chinese Government, which had repeatedly urged the DPRK to forgo its plans. Somewhat unexpectedly, China agreed to UN sanctions against the country, while ensuring that they did not contain a threat of military action. Media reports following the test suggested that China was complying with UN Security Council Resolution 1718 by inspecting vehicles bound for the DPRK and by reinforcing the border. Moreover, the Chinese Government indicated that North Korean refugees being sheltered in a US consulate in northeastern China would be allowed to travel to the Republic of Korea or the USA (a transfer that China had originally opposed), and stated that it would no longer object to Japan raising the issue of the abduction of Japanese citizens by North Korea at the six-party talks. At the same time, China Southern Airlines, the only Chinese airline offering regular flights to Pyongyang, indicated that it would suspend its operations to the North Korean capital. China reportedly threatened to cut off vital oil supplies to the DPRK should any further nuclear tests be conducted. This threat was supported by an official visit to Pyongyang by Chinese envoy Tang Jiaxuan, who returned to Beijing with assurances that no further tests were planned. China helped to broker another diplomatic advance at the end of October, when the DPRK indicated that it was willing to rejoin the six-way nuclear talks (see above). China was also reported to have permitted the release of funds from the accounts of DPRK officials held in Banco Delta Asia the following month. In September 2007 China provided North Korea with 50,000 metric tons of fuel oil, in accordance with the agreement reached in February at the six-party talks (see above), which China continued to host. Following North Korea's failure to meet the deadline for the disablement of its nuclear facilities and disclosure of its nuclear activities, in late January 2008 the head of the Chinese Communist Party's international liaison department visited Pyongyang to urge Kim Jong Il to comply with his commitments under the six-party agreement. During a visit to Beijing in late February US Secretary of State Condoleezza Rice exerted pressure on the Chinese Government to use its influence to persuade the DPRK to implement the agreement fully. The newly appointed Chinese Vice-President, Xi Jinping, who was frequently described as a potential successor to President Hu Jintao, chose North Korea as the destination for his first official visit, meeting with Kim Jong Il and other senior officials in June 2008.

In the mid-1980s the DPRK placed increased emphasis on its relations with the USSR. The DPRK's diplomatic isolation became more pronounced in the early 1990s, as former communist bloc countries attempted to foster relations with the Republic of Korea. Furthermore, the USSR announced that, from January 1991, its barter trading system with the DPRK would be abolished in favour of trade in convertible currencies at world market prices. However, an agreement was reported to have been signed in May 1993 by the DPRK and the Russian Federation (which, following the dissolution of the USSR, had assumed responsibility for many of the USSR's international undertakings) on technological and scientific co-operation. Discussions on the rescheduling of the terms of repayment of North Korea's debt to Russia took place in October 1997. In March 1999 a new bilateral treaty of friendship, good neighbourliness and co-operation was initialled in Pyongyang (to replace a 1961 bilateral treaty); a formal signing followed in February 2000, during a visit to Pyongyang by the Russian Minister of Foreign Affairs, Igor Ivanov. The treaty was ratified by the DPRK in April. In July President Vladimir Putin became the first Russian (or Soviet) leader to visit North Korea. Following Putin's visit, co-operation between Russia and the DPRK placed a strong emphasis on connecting the latter's rail system to the Trans-Siberian railway, with a view to creating a long-awaited Eurasian transport corridor, and in March 2001 the two countries signed a railway co-operation agreement.

In April 2001 the DPRK's Minister of the People's Armed Forces, Vice-Marshal Kim Il Chol, visited Moscow and reportedly negotiated the acquisition of defensive weapons such as SU-27 aircraft, anti-aircraft systems and intelligence-gathering equipment, in addition to signing a military co-operation protocol. In August Kim Jong Il undertook a 24-day visit across Russia to Moscow, where he and President Putin signed a new declaration of co-operation in politics, the economy, military matters, science and technology, and culture. However, Russia also urged the DPRK to settle the latter's outstanding bilateral debt of as much as US $5,500m. The DPRK had repaid some of this amount by sending hundreds of forced-labour woodcutters to work in Khabarovsk Krai territory—although such labour camps had reportedly been closed down by late 2002. Kim's visit suggested that the DPRK was seeking closer relations with Russia, as well as with China, to strengthen its international standing.

The DPRK continued to maintain strong relations with Russia in 2002. In April two separate Russian delegations, one led by the Mayor of St Petersburg, Vladimir Yakovlev, the other by the Russian Presidential Representative in the Far Eastern Federal Okrug (district), Konstantin Pulikovskii, visited Pyongyang to discuss co-operation in all fields, particularly business. In May the Minister of Foreign Affairs, Paek Nam Sun, visited Moscow, in the first such visit in 15 years. In July the Russian Minister of Foreign Affairs, Igor Ivanov, visited Pyongyang, and in August Kim Jong Il visited the Russian city of Vladivostok, where he held discussions with Putin, mainly focusing on the reconnection of railway links across the Korean peninsula. At the same time the DPRK and the Russian Oblast of Amur signed a co-operation agreement on agriculture and forestry. In October two North Korean military delegations visited Russia, and in December the Mayor of Moscow, Yurii Luzhkov, visited Pyongyang.

As the diplomatic crisis over the DPRK's nuclear weapons programme intensified in January 2003, Russia sought to defuse the situation by sending the Deputy Minister of Foreign Affairs, Aleksandr Losyukov, to Pyongyang, where he held discussions with Kim Jong Il. Losyukov, who had earlier visited China and subsequently the USA, urged a three-stage formula whereby the international community would accept a nuclear-free Korean peninsula, guarantees for the regime's security, and a resumption of aid. The DPRK reiterated that the crisis could be resolved only through discussions with the USA.

In March 2003 a hitherto unrealized Russian proposal to supply the DPRK with natural gas from the island of Sakhalin in return for the DPRK's abandonment of its nuclear programme was raised by the South Korean Government. In late 2003 Russia appeared to be expanding its economic links with the DPRK, with a team of Russian engineers inspecting a cargo port and petroleum refinery at Raijin, as well as assessing a stretch of railway linking the two countries across the Tumen river.

Russia supported the DPRK in early 2006; in March Glev Ivashentsov, the Russian ambassador to Seoul, was quoted by the South Korean media as stating that the use of international sanctions was not an effective measure. This stance was reiterated in July when, following the North's missile tests (see above), Russia and China ensured that attempts by the UN Security Council to impose sanctions on the DPRK were obstructed. However, Russia modified its strong anti-sanctions policy following the nuclear test of 9 October, like China using its power of veto and ensuring that UN Security Council Resolution 1718 did not include the threat of military action. The Russian authorities assisted in the process of transferring previously 'frozen' North Korean funds from the Banco Delta Asia in Macao to North Korea via a Russian bank in June 2007, thus removing the main obstacle to the implementation of the February agreement on the DPRK's nuclear programme (see above). In January 2008 Russia provided North Korea with 50,000 metric tons of fuel oil as part of its commitment under the six-party agreement on the dismantling of North Korea's nuclear facilities (see above). In April Russia and the DPRK signed an agreement to restore an existing railway line between Khasan on the Russian border and Rajin in the DPRK.

The DPRK's unilateral application for UN membership, first announced in May 1991, represented a radical departure from its earlier insistence that the two Koreas should occupy a single UN seat. This development was welcomed by the Republic of Korea, and both countries were admitted separately to the UN in September of that year. In September 1999, for the first time in seven years, the North Korean Minister of Foreign Affairs attended and addressed the annual session of the UN General Assembly, in what was perceived as an attempt to end the DPRK's diplomatic isolation. Furthermore, in January 2000 Italy became the first member of the Group of Seven (G-7) Western industrialized nations (and the sixth member of the EU) to establish diplomatic relations with the DPRK, and in May Australia restored diplomatic links with the DPRK. Diplomatic relations were established with the Philippines in July and with the United Kingdom in December. During 2001 the DPRK further expanded its range of diplomatic partners, opening relations with the Netherlands, Belgium, Canada, Spain, Germany, Luxembourg, Greece, Brazil, New Zealand, Kuwait, the EU, Bahrain, Turkey and Liechtenstein. Relations with Timor-Leste were established in late 2002. In May 2003 the DPRK opened an embassy in the United Kingdom, amid protests from human rights activists. Relations with Ireland were established in December. In March 2004 the Australian ambassador to China, Alan Thomas, was instructed to present his credentials in Pyongyang. Diplomatic relations with Myanmar were re-established in April 2007, after a hiatus of almost 25 years, and it was reported that links with six other nations were formed or restored during that year.

In April 2000 the DPRK formally applied to join the Association of South East Asian Nations (ASEAN, see p. 194). Following the DPRK's admittance to the ASEAN Regional Forum (ARF), a meeting in Thailand in July was attended for the first time by the North Korean Minister of Foreign Affairs, Paek Nam Sun, who held unprecedented meetings with his South Korean, Japanese and US counterparts. In November the APEC forum supported the DPRK's guest status in that organization. Full membership was not expected to follow until 2010 at the earliest, following the announcement by the organization in September 2007, upon the expiry of a 10-year moratorium on new members, that it was to postpone any decision on enlargement for a further three years. Meanwhile, in July 2001 the President of the Presidium of the SPA, Kim Yong Nam, visited Viet Nam, Laos and Cambodia. In March 2002 Kim visited Thailand and Malaysia, where he discussed mainly trade issues. Prime Minister Mahathir bin Mohamad of Malaysia accepted an invitation to visit the DPRK, and Indonesian President Megawati Sukarnoputri visited the country at the end of March. Kim Yong Nam reciprocated Megawati's visit in July of that year. The President of Viet Nam, Tran Duc Luong, visited the DPRK in May and signed several economic and legal co-operation agreements. In 2003 there were reports that the DPRK was selling military equipment to Pakistan, and also that military relations with Myanmar were being developed; diplomatic relations with the latter were re-established in April 2007, and in September Myanmar's Deputy Minister of Foreign Affairs reportedly visited Pyongyang for official talks with the North Korean Government. In early 2004 Pakistani nuclear scientist Abdul Qadeer Khan confessed that he had sold nuclear secrets to the DPRK. In November 2005 it was reported that the Government of Thailand was investigating claims that a Thai woman missing since 1978 had been kidnapped by North Korean agents and was now living in the DPRK. North Korea denied that its agents had abducted the woman. However, in August 2007 the Thai Minister of Foreign Affairs announced that his North Korean counterpart had agreed to co-operate on investigations into the case. In late October and early November Premier Kim Yong Il led a senior-level trip by North Korean officials to South-East Asia, visiting Cambodia, Laos, Malaysia and Viet Nam.

The DPRK has maintained close relations with a number of Middle Eastern countries, including Egypt, Libya, Syria and Iran. The President of the Presidium of the SPA, Kim Yong Nam, visited Libya and Syria in July 2002. The DPRK retained long-standing links with many African nations, and reportedly had military advisers working in some 12 of that continent's countries in 2005. In January 2004 the Vice-President of the Presidium of the SPA, Yang Hyong Sop, visited Nigeria to discuss an agreement on military technology. In May it was reported that an IAEA investigation of uranium delivered to the USA by Libya in late 2003 had revealed that the material had been supplied to Libya by the DPRK through an illicit nuclear technology procurement network operated by Pakistani nuclear scientist Abdul Qadeer Khan (see above). Further evidence concerning the transfer of nuclear material from the DPRK to Libya emerged in early 2005. In January 2007 North Korea was reported to have agreed to share its data from the October 2006 nuclear test with scientists from Iran. The alleged agreement reportedly followed a meeting between North Korean and Iranian nuclear scientists in the previous November. However, the DPRK strongly denied the allegations. In September 2007 the DPRK similarly rejected claims that it was assisting Syria to develop a nuclear weapons programme. In that month the United Arab Emirates announced that it had established diplomatic relations with North Korea at ambassadorial level. In March 2008, accompanied by the Ministers of Foreign Affairs, of Foreign Trade and of Public Health, Kim Yong Nam travelled to Namibia, where his visit prompted speculation regarding the DPRK's interest in the country's uranium resources. Kim Yong Nam and his delegation also visited Angola, the Democratic Republic of the Congo and Uganda. In September of the same year the DPRK and Kenya established diplomatic relations at ambassadorial level.

Government

The highest organ of state power is the unicameral Supreme People's Assembly (SPA), with 687 members, elected (unopposed) for five years by universal adult suffrage. The SPA elects, for its duration, the Chairman of the National Defence Commission, who, since the effective abolition of the presidency in September 1998, holds the most senior accessible office of state (although this is not formally stated in the Constitution). The SPA elects the Premier and, on the latter's recommendation, appoints other Ministers to form the Cabinet. The President of the SPA Presidium, whose members are elected by the SPA, represents the State in its relations with foreign countries.

Political power is held by the communist Korean Workers' Party (KWP), which is the most influential party in the Democratic Front for the Reunification of the Fatherland (comprising the KWP and two minor parties). The Front presents an approved list of candidates for elections to representative bodies. The KWP's highest authority is the Party Congress, which elects a Central Committee to supervise party work. The Committee elects a Political Bureau (Politburo) to direct policy. The Presidium of the Politburo is the KWP's most powerful policy-making body.

The DPRK comprises nine provinces and two cities, each with an elected Local People's Assembly.

Defence

Military service is selective: army five to eight years, navy five to 10 years, and air force three to four years. The estimated total strength of the armed forces, as assessed at November 2008, was 1,106,000: army 950,000, air force 110,000, and navy 46,000. Security and border troops numbered 189,000, and there was a workers' and peasants' militia ('Red Guards') numbering about 3.5m. The ratio of North Korea's armed forces to total population is believed to be the highest in the world. Defence expenditure for 2006 was budgeted at an estimated 5,000m. won. South Korean intelligence sources estimated the real level of defence expenditure to be more than 30% of total spending in 2004.

Economic Affairs

According to the Bank of Korea (the South Korean central bank), the gross national income (GNI) of the DPRK contracted for the second consecutive year in 2007, when it was estimated to total US $26,700m., equivalent to about $1,152 per head. According to UN estimates based on a different method of calculation, the DPRK's GNI per head increased from $577 in 2006 to $617 in 2007. During 2000–07, according to estimates by the World Bank, the population increased by an annual average of 0.5%. In 2000–07 GDP grew at an average annual rate of 1.9%, according to figures estimated by the UN. GDP was believed to have grown by 1.6% in 2007; however, South Korean sources reported that the economy had contracted by 2.3% in that year.

Agriculture (including forestry and fishing) contributed 25.0% of GDP in 2007, according to UN estimates. In mid-2005, according to FAO estimates, 26.6% of the economically active population were employed in agriculture. The principal crops are rice, maize and potatoes. The DPRK is not self-sufficient in food, and imports substantial amounts of wheat, rice and maize annually. Intermittent food shortages became a serious problem from the mid-1990s (see Recent History). According to FAO estimates, cereal production decreased from 4.7m. metric tons in 2006 to 4.2m. tons in 2007. Potato production was 2.0m. tons in 2006, approaching a similar level in 2007, according to estimates. The raising of livestock (principally cattle and pigs), forestry and fishing are important. During 2000–07, according to figures estimated by the UN, agricultural GDP increased by an average of 3.0% per year. Again according to figures from the UN, agricultural GDP declined by 2.6% in 2006, but was estimated to have expanded by 2.3% in 2007. In early 2007 the DPRK suffered its first outbreak of foot-and-mouth disease since 1960, imported livestock being cited as the source of the infection. The adverse effects of the serious floods and resultant crop losses of August 2007 (see Recent History) were subsequently compounded by the exceptionally dry weather experienced during the winter of 2007/08, followed by further heavy rains in August 2008.

In 2007, according to UN estimates, industry (including mining, manufacturing, construction and power) contributed 42.3% of GDP. During 2000–07, according to UN estimates, industrial GDP was estimated to have decreased by an average of 1.9% per year. Industrial GDP contracted by 1.2% in 2006 but increased by 1.4% in 2007.

Mining contributed 10.2% of GDP in 2006, according to South Korean estimates. The DPRK possesses considerable mineral wealth, with large deposits of coal, iron, lead, copper, zinc, tin, silver and gold. Output of hard coal was estimated to have decreased from 24.7m. metric tons in 2006 to 24.1m. tons in 2007. There are unexploited offshore deposits of petroleum and natural gas. South Korean sources estimated that the output of the mining sector increased by 1.9% in 2006 and by 0.4% in 2007.

In 2007, according to UN estimates, the manufacturing sector contributed 19.0% of GDP. In the 1990s industrial development concentrated on heavy industry (metallurgy—notably steel production, machine-building, cement and chemicals). The textiles industry has provided significant exports. According to figures from UN sources, the GDP of the manufacturing sector was estimated to have increased at an average annual rate of 1.4% in 2000–07, rising by 0.2% in 2007.

In 2005 it was estimated that 57.3% of the DPRK's energy supply was derived from hydroelectricity, followed in importance by coal (39.0%) and petroleum (3.6%). A 30-MW nuclear reactor was believed to have been inaugurated in 1987. From the 1990s the DPRK experienced increasing power shortages, as generation declined and transmission infrastructure deteriorated. Furthermore, the production of hydroelectric power was adversely affected by intermittent drought. Electricity generation in 2004 was less than 75% of the amount generated in 1990. In 2006, according to South Korean sources, the DPRK's electricity production totalled 22,500m. kWh, compared with 21,974m. kWh in 2004. Fuel oil shipments to the DPRK have been intermittently suspended owing to international concerns with regard to the country's nuclear programme (see Recent History). From the 1990s the DPRK sought greater foreign assistance in developing its offshore oilfields. Various joint ventures were established with foreign oil companies, but exploratory activities proved disappointing.

The services sector employed an estimated 30.4% of the labour force in 1990. UN sources estimated that in 2007 the DPRK's services sector accounted for 32.7% of GDP. In 2007 output in the sector was estimated to have increased by 1.0%, having risen by 1.1% in 2006 and by 1.3% in 2005.

According to South Korean sources, in 2006 total exports, excluding trade with the Republic of Korea, reached $95m. and imports totalled $205m. The DPRK's principal source of imports in 2005 (again excluding the Republic of Korea) was the People's Republic of China, which accounted for 54% of total imports, followed by Russia (11%). China was the DPRK's principal market for exports in 2005, purchasing 50% of goods, followed by Japan (13%). China was a source of crude petroleum, food and vehicles, while Japan was a destination for industrial and agricultural goods. In 2006 the value of inter-Korean trade increased by 27.8% to reach US $1,349.7m. The principal exports in 2002 were live animals and animal products (35.5% of the value of total exports, excluding trade with the Republic of Korea), textiles (16.7%) and machinery and electrical equipment (11.6%). Other export commodities in the late 1990s included tobacco and silk. The principal imports in 2002 were mineral products (15.5% of the value of total imports, excluding trade with the Republic of Korea), machinery and electrical equipment (15.4%), and textiles (10.4%). Other import items included road vehicles, chemicals and groceries.

The 2006 budget reportedly envisaged expenditure of 388,950m. won. Budget expenditure was officially stated to have exceeded the Government's target in 2007. Compared with the previous year, budget revenue increased by 6.1% in 2007. The 2008/09 budget was reported to have allocated 15.8% of total expenditure to defence. By 2008, according to one source, the DPRK's total external debt was estimated to have reached US $18,000m. Following the introduction of market-orientated reforms in 2002, the inflation rate was believed to have reached 4,000% in that year. Between mid-2007 and mid-2008 the prices of staple foods reportedly increased by 100% in Pyongyang.

The lack of reliable statistical data impedes an accurate assessment of the North Korean economy. In a report released in February 2009, the US State Department reiterated its belief that activities such as the forging of US currency and the counterfeiting of brand cigarettes remained significant sources of revenue. The establishment of a special industrial zone at Kaesong (see Recent History) contributed to a substantial increase in inter-Korean trade. The DPRK's exports to South Korea increased by almost 53% in 2006, when they reached an estimated US $519.5m. By March 2008 69 South Korean manufacturers, employing a total of 23,953 North Korean workers, were reported to be operating in the Kaesong complex. However, following the onset of the global financial crisis in the latter part of 2008 and the attendant decrease in export demand, the value of the DPRK's sales to the Republic of Korea and to China began to decline significantly. In comparison with the first month of the previous year, trade between North and South Korea declined by almost 20% in January 2009. Chinese companies were reported to have reduced the prices they were willing to pay for North Korean ores and minerals, thus depressing the production of commodities such as zinc. Meanwhile, the sharp rises in international grain prices in early 2008 exacerbated the problem of food shortages in the DPRK. In September 2008, in response to the Government's request for assistance, the World Food Programme (WFP, see p. 103) initiated an emergency operation in the DPRK. In December WFP anticipated a cereal deficit of 836,000 metric tons for the 2008/09 marketing year (November–October). In a statement released in March 2009, furthermore, WFP announced that a major funding shortfall had obliged it substantially to reduce its activities in the DPRK. Of the 6.2m. vulnerable people originally scheduled to receive WFP support, only 2m. were in fact receiving food assistance, with many rations being incomplete. Meanwhile, the five-year plan for 2008–12, announced in April 2008, accorded priority to improvements in the areas of science and technology. However, prospects for economic development remained uncertain in the context of international tension over the DPRK's nuclear weapons programme.

Education

Universal compulsory primary and secondary education were introduced in 1956 and 1958, respectively, and are provided at state expense. Free and compulsory 11-year education in state schools was introduced in 1975. Children enter kindergarten at five years of age, and people's school at the age of six. After four years, they advance to senior middle school for six years. English is compulsory as a second language at the age of 14. A report submitted to UNESCO by the North Korean Government in 2000 stated that there were 27,017 nurseries for 1,575,000 pupils, 14,167 kindergartens for 748,416 pupils, 4,886 primary schools for 1,609,865 pupils, 4,772 senior middle schools for 2,181,524 pupils, and more than 300 universities and colleges with 1.89m. students and academics. The adult literacy rate was estimated by UNESCO in 2003 to be 98%.

Public Holidays

The *Juche* calendar was introduced in the DPRK in 1997; 1912, the year of the late Kim Il Sung's birth, was designated the first year of the new calendar.

2009: 1 January (New Year), 16–17 February (Kim Jong Il's Birthday), 8 March (International Women's Day), 15 April (Day of the Sun, Kim Il Sung's Birthday), 1 May (May Day), 15 August (Anniversary of Liberation), 9 September (Independence Day), 10 October (Anniversary of the foundation of the Korean Workers' Party), 27 December (Anniversary of the Constitution).

2010: 1 January (New Year), 16–17 February (Kim Jong Il's Birthday), 8 March (International Women's Day), 15 April (Day of the Sun, Kim Il Sung's Birthday), 1 May (May Day), 15 August (Anniversary of Liberation), 9 September (Independence Day), 10 October (Anniversary of the foundation of the Korean Workers' Party), 27 December (Anniversary of the Constitution).

Weights and Measures

The metric system is in force.

Statistical Survey

Area and Population

AREA, POPULATION AND DENSITY*

Area (sq km)	122,762†
Population (census results)	
31 December 1993	
Males	10,329,699
Females	10,883,679
Total	21,213,378
Population (UN estimates at mid-year)‡	
2006	23,708,000
2007	23,790,000
2008	23,867,000
Density (per sq km) at mid-2008	194.4

* Excluding the demilitarized zone between North and South Korea, with an area of 1,262 sq km (487 sq miles).
† 47,399 sq miles.
‡ Source: UN, *World Population Prospects: The 2006 Revision*.

PRINCIPAL TOWNS
(population at 1993 census)

Pyongyang (capital)	2,741,260	Wonsan	300,148
Nampo	731,448	Pyongsong	272,934
Hamhung	709,730	Sariwon	254,146
Chongjin	582,480	Haeju	229,172
Kaesong	334,433	Kanggye	223,410
Sinuiju	326,011	Hyesan	178,020

Source: UN, *Demographic Yearbook*.

Mid-2007 ('000, incl. suburbs, UN estimates): Pyongyang 3,300; Nampo 1,127; Hamhung 773 (Source: UN, *World Urbanization Prospects: The 2007 Revision*).

BIRTHS AND DEATHS
(annual averages, UN estimates)

	1990–95	1995–2000	2000–05
Birth rate (per 1,000)	21.1	19.0	15.1
Death rate (per 1,000)	6.0	7.9	9.3

Source: UN, *World Population Prospects: The 2006 Revision*.

Life expectancy (years at birth, WHO estimates): 66.5 (males 64.4; females 68.4) in 2006 (Source: WHO, *World Health Statistics*).

ECONOMICALLY ACTIVE POPULATION
('000 persons at mid-1990, ILO estimates)

	Males	Females	Total
Agriculture, etc.	2,027	1,877	3,904
Industry	2,206	1,043	3,249
Services	1,577	1,549	3,126
Total labour force	5,810	4,469	10,279

Source: ILO, *Economically Active Population: Estimates and Projections, 1950–2010*.

Mid-2005 (estimates in '000): Agriculture, etc. 3,097; Total labour force 11,661 (Source: FAO).

THE DEMOCRATIC PEOPLE'S REPUBLIC OF KOREA (NORTH KOREA)

Statistical Survey

Health and Welfare

KEY INDICATORS

Total fertility rate (children per woman, 2006)	1.9
Under-5 mortality rate (per 1,000 live births, 2006)	55
HIV/AIDS (% of persons aged 15–49, 1994)	<0.01
Physicians (per 1,000 head, 2003)	3.3
Health expenditure (2006): US $ per head (PPP)	49
Health expenditure (2006): % of GDP	3.5
Health expenditure (2006): public (% of total)	85.6
Access to sanitation (% of persons, 2004)	59

For sources and definitions, see explanatory note on p. vi.

Agriculture

PRINCIPAL CROPS
('000 metric tons)

	2005	2006	2007*
Wheat	267*	276†	200
Rice, paddy	2,582†	2,368*	2,165
Barley	80†	90†	80
Maize	2,062†	1,836*	1,645
Rye	60†	57*	52
Oats	15†	10*	9
Millet*	60	64	61
Sorghum*	30	32	32
Potatoes*	2,070	2,000	1,900
Sweet potatoes*	360	300	290
Beans, dry*	310	280	265
Soybeans (Soya beans)	340†	345†	350
Cabbages and other brassicas*	690	680	700
Tomatoes*	71	68	65
Pumpkins, squash and gourds*	90	85	80
Cucumbers and gherkins*	67	65	66
Aubergines (Eggplants)*	47	45	46
Chillies and peppers, green*	60	58	60
Onions and shallots, green*	97	95	98
Onions, dry*	88	86	84
Garlic*	95	93	95
Apples*	668	665	635
Pears*	135	130	125
Peaches and nectarines*	124	120	120
Watermelons*	110	100	95
Cantaloupes and other melons*	121	115	110
Tobacco, unmanufactured*	65	65	63

* FAO estimate(s).
† Unofficial figure.

Aggregate production ('000 metric tons, may include official, semi-official or estimated data): Total cereals 5,156 in 2005, 4,733 in 2006, 4,244 in 2007; Total roots and tubers 2,430 in 2005, 2,300 in 2006, 2,190 in 2007; Total vegetables (incl. melons) 3,992 in 2005, 3,876 in 2006, 3,756 in 2007; Total fruits (excl. melons) 1,417 in 2005, 915 in 2006, 880 in 2007.

Source: FAO.

LIVESTOCK
('000 head, FAO estimates)

	2005	2006	2007
Horses	48	48	47
Cattle	570	575	576
Pigs	3,200	3,250	3,300
Sheep	172	172	173
Goats	2,740	2,750	2,760
Chickens	21,000	22,000	22,000
Ducks	5,500	6,000	6,000

Source: FAO.

LIVESTOCK PRODUCTS
('000 metric tons, FAO estimates)

	2005	2006	2007
Cattle meat	21.2	21.3	21.0
Goat meat	11.2	11.3	11.3
Pig meat	167.5	170.0	169.0
Chicken meat	37.4	39.0	34.0
Cows' milk	94.0	94.0	90.0
Hen eggs	140.0	143.0	142.0

Source: FAO.

Forestry

ROUNDWOOD REMOVALS
('000 cubic metres, excl. bark, FAO estimates)

	2005	2006	2007
Sawlogs, veneer logs and logs for sleepers	1,000	1,000	1,000
Other industrial wood	500	500	500
Fuel wood	5,797	5,835	5,873
Total	7,297	7,335	7,373

Sawnwood production ('000 cubic metres, incl. railway sleepers): 280 (coniferous 185, broadleaved 95) per year in 1970–2007 (FAO estimates).

Source: FAO.

Fishing

('000 metric tons, live weight, FAO estimates)

	2000	2001	2002
Capture	212.9	206.5	205.0
Freshwater fishes	8.0	4.9	5.0
Alaska pollock	60.0	60.0	60.0
Other marine fishes	112.2	109.0	107.6
Marine crustaceans	15.6	16.2	16.0
Squids	9.5	9.5	9.5
Aquaculture	66.7	63.7	63.7
Molluscs	63.0	60.0	60.0
Total catch	279.6	270.2	268.7

Note: Figures exclude aquatic plants (FAO estimates, '000 metric tons, aquaculture only): 401.0 in 2000; 391.0 in 2001; 444.3 in 2002.

2003–06: Figures assumed to be unchanged from 2002 (FAO estimates).

Source: FAO.

THE DEMOCRATIC PEOPLE'S REPUBLIC OF KOREA (NORTH KOREA)

Statistical Survey

Mining

('000 metric tons, unless otherwise indicated, estimates)

	2005	2006	2007
Hard coal	23,500	24,700	24,100
Brown coal and lignite	7,000	7,500	7,000
Iron ore: gross weight	5,000	5,040	5,130
Iron ore: metal content	1,400	1,400	1,400
Copper ore*	12	12	12
Lead ore*	13	13	13
Zinc ore*	67	67	70
Tungsten concentrates (metric tons)*	600	600	600
Silver (metric tons)*	20	20	20
Gold (kg)*	2,000	2,000	2,000
Magnesite (crude)	1,000	1,000	1,000
Phosphate rock†	300	300	300
Fluorspar‡	13	13	13
Salt (unrefined)	500	500	500
Graphite (natural)	30	30	30
Talc, soapstone and pyrophyllite	50	50	50

* Figures refer to the metal content of ores and concentrates.
† Figures refer to gross weight.
‡ Metallurgical grade.

Note: No recent data are available for the production of molybdenum ore and asbestos.

Source: US Geological Survey.

Industry

SELECTED PRODUCTS
('000 metric tons, unless otherwise indicated)

	2002	2003	2004
Nitrogenous fertilizers*	17	n.a.	n.a.
Motor spirit (petrol)	189	185	188
Kerosene	38	37	37
Gas-diesel (distillate fuel) oils	207	201	203
Residual fuel oils	119	116	117
Coke-oven coke (excl. breeze)†	2,950	n.a.	n.a.
Cement†	5,320	5,540	5,500
Pig-iron‡	800	900	900
Crude steel‡	1,030	1,090	1,070
Refined copper (primary and secondary metal)‡	15	15	15
Refined lead (primary and secondary metal)‡	6	7	9
Zinc (primary and secondary metal)	65	65	67
Electric energy (million kWh)	19,777	21,035	21,974

* Output is measured in terms of nitrogen.
† Provisional or estimated figure(s).
‡ Estimated data from the US Geological Survey.

Source: mostly UN, *Industrial Commodity Statistics Yearbook*.

2005 ('000 metric tons, estimates): Cement 5,700; Pig-iron 900; Crude steel 1,070; Refined copper (primary and secondary metal) 15; Refined lead (primary and secondary metal) 9; Refined zinc (primary and secondary metal) 72 (Source: US Geological Survey).

2006 ('000 metric tons, estimates): Cement 6,160; Pig-iron 900; Crude steel 1,180; Refined copper (primary and secondary metal) 15; Refined lead (primary and secondary metal) 9; Refined zinc (primary and secondary metal) 72; Electric energy (million kWh) 22,500 (Sources: US Geological Survey; Bank of Korea, Republic of Korea).

2007 ('000 metric tons, estimates): Cement 6,130; Pig-iron 900; Crude steel 1,230; Refined copper (primary and secondary metal) 15; Refined lead (primary and secondary metal) 9; Refined zinc (primary and secondary metal) 75 (Source: US Geological Survey).

Finance

CURRENCY AND EXCHANGE RATES

Monetary Units
100 chon (jun) = 1 won.

Sterling, Dollar and Euro Equivalents (28 November 2008)
£1 sterling = 213.170 won;
US $1 = 139.000 won;
€1 = 176.905 won;
1,000 won = £4.69 = $7.19 = €5.65.

Note: In August 2002 it was reported that a currency reform had been introduced, whereby the exchange rate was adjusted from US $1 = 2.15 won to $1 = 150 won: a devaluation of 98.6%.

BUDGET
(million won, projected)

	1992	1993	1994
Revenue	39,500.9	40,449.9	41,525.2
Expenditure	39,500.9	40,449.9	41,525.2
Economic development	26,675.1	27,423.8	28,164.0
Socio-cultural sector	7,730.6	7,751.5	8,218.3
Defence	4,582.1	4,692.2	4,816.9
Administration and management	513.1	582.4	326.0

1998 (million won, estimates): Total revenue 19,790.8; Total expenditure 20,015.2.

1999 (million won, estimates): Total revenue 19,801.0; Total expenditure 20,018.2.

2000 (million won, estimates): Total revenue 20,955.0; Total expenditure 20,903.0.

2001 (million won, projected): Total revenue 21,571.0; Total expenditure 21,571.0.

2002 (million won, projected): Total revenue 22,174.0; Total expenditure 22,174.0.

2003: Exact figures not made available following price reforms of August 2002.

2004 (million won, reported): Total revenue 337,546; Total expenditure 348,807.

2005 (million won, reported): Total expenditure 419,700.

2006 (million won, reported): Total expenditure 388,950.

NATIONAL ACCOUNTS

Gross Domestic Product by Economic Activity
('000 million won, unofficial estimates)*

	2002	2003	2004
Agriculture, forestry and fishing	6,429	5,961	6,341
Mining	1,652	1,820	2,065
Manufacturing	3,825	4,043	4,388
Electricity, gas and water	939	995	1,051
Construction	1,699	1,896	2,194
Government services	4,679	5,018	5,361
Other services	2,054	2,156	2,308
Total	21,277	21,887	23,707

* Totals may not be equal to sum of component parts, owing to rounding.

2005 (percentage distribution): Agriculture, forestry and fishing 25.0; Mining 9.9; Manufacturing 19.0; Electricity, gas and water 4.3; Construction 9.6; Government services 22.6; Other services 9.6.

2006 (percentage distribution): Agriculture, forestry and fishing 23.3; Mining 10.2; Manufacturing 19.5; Electricity, gas and water 4.5; Construction 9.0; Government services 23.7; Other services 9.8.

Source: Bank of Korea (Republic of Korea).

THE DEMOCRATIC PEOPLE'S REPUBLIC OF KOREA (NORTH KOREA) *Statistical Survey*

External Trade

PRINCIPAL COMMODITIES
(US $ million)*

Imports	2000	2001	2002
Live animals and animal products	20.3	73.9	103.4
Vegetable products	159.0	221.0	118.4
Animal or vegetable fats and oils; prepared edible fats; animal or vegetable waxes Prepared foodstuffs; beverages, spirits and vinegar; tobacco and manufactured substitutes	89.1	89.9	72.3
Mineral products	171.2	231.1	235.9
Products of chemical or allied industries	108.4	123.4	122.1
Plastics, rubber and articles thereof	67.5	66.0	66.0
Textiles and textile articles	171.9	203.9	158.5
Base metals and articles thereof	85.2	100.4	88.2
Machinery and mechanical appliances; electrical equipment; sound and television apparatus	205.1	243.8	234.7
Vehicles, aircraft, vessels and associated transport equipment	146.2	88.4	76.1
Total (incl. others)	1,406.5	1,620.3	1,525.4

Exports	2000	2001	2002
Live animals and animal products	97.9	158.4	261.1
Vegetable products	30.3	42.0	27.5
Mineral products	43.2	50.5	69.8
Products of chemical or allied industries Plastics, rubber and articles thereof	44.9	44.6	42.4
Wood, cork and articles thereof; wood charcoal; manufactures of straw, esparto, etc.	10.9	5.6	10.2
Textiles and textile articles	140.0	140.5	123.1
Natural or cultured pearls, precious or semi-precious stones, precious metals and articles thereof; imitation jewellery; coin	9.8	14.1	14.6
Base metals and articles thereof	43.9	60.2	57.4
Machinery and mechanical appliances; electrical equipment, sound and television apparatus	105.2	97.9	85.6
Total (incl. others)	565.8	650.2	735.0

* Excluding trade with the Republic of Korea (US $ million): *Imports:* 272.8 in 2000; 226.8 in 2001; 370.2 in 2002. *Exports:* 152.4 in 2000; 176.2 in 2001; 271.6 in 2002.

Source: Korea Trade-Investment Promotion Agency (KOTRA), Republic of Korea.

2005 (US $ million, unofficial estimates): *Excluding Republic of Korea:* Total imports 200; Total exports 100. *Republic of Korea only:* Total imports 715.5; Total exports 340.3 (Source: Bank of Korea, Republic of Korea).

2006 (US $ million, unofficial estimates): *Excluding Republic of Korea:* Total imports 205; Total exports 95. *Republic of Korea only:* Total imports 830.2; Total exports 519.5 (Source: Bank of Korea, Republic of Korea).

PRINCIPAL TRADING PARTNERS
(US $ million)*

Imports	2001	2002	2003
China, People's Republic	570.7	467.3	627.6
Germany	82.1	140.4	n.a.
Hong Kong	42.6	29.2	n.a.
India	154.8	186.6	157.9
Japan	249.1	135.1	91.5
Netherlands	9.1	27.6	n.a.
Russia	63.8	77.0	115.6
Singapore	112.3	83.0	n.a.
Spain	31.6	n.a.	n.a.
Thailand	106.0	172.0	203.6
United Kingdom	40.7	n.a.	n.a.
Total (incl. others)	1,620.3	1,525.4	1,614.4

Exports	2001	2002	2003
Bangladesh	38.0	32.3	n.a.
China, People's Republic	166.8	270.9	395.3
Germany	22.8	27.8	n.a.
Hong Kong	38.0	21.9	n.a.
India	3.1	4.8	1.6
Japan	225.6	234.4	173.8
Netherlands	10.4	6.4	n.a.
Russia	4.5	3.6	2.8
Spain	12.6	n.a.	n.a.
Thailand	24.9	44.6	50.7
Total (incl. others)	650.2	735.0	777.0

* Excluding trade with the Republic of Korea (US $ million): *Imports:* 226.8 in 2001; 370.2 in 2002; 435.0 in 2003. *Exports:* 176.2 in 2001; 271.6 in 2002; 289.3 in 2003.

Sources: Korea Trade-Investment Promotion Agency (KOTRA).

2004 (US $ million): *Imports:* China, People's Republic 800; Japan 89; Korea, Republic 439; Total (incl. others) 2,280. *Exports:* China, People's Republic 586; Japan 163; Korea, Republic 258; Total (incl. others) 1,280 (Source: Ministry of Unification, Republic of Korea).

Trade with Republic of Korea (US $ million, unofficial estimates): *Total imports:* 715.5 in 2005; 830.2 in 2006. *Total exports:* 340.3 in 2005; 519.5 in 2006 (Source: Bank of Korea, Republic of Korea).

Transport

SHIPPING

Merchant Fleet
(registered at 31 December)

	2005	2006	2007
Number of vessels	445	340	301
Total displacement ('000 grt)	1,257.8	1,052.6	985.6

Source: Lloyd's Register-Fairplay, *World Fleet Statistics*.

International Sea-borne Freight Traffic
(estimates, '000 metric tons)

	1988	1989	1990
Goods loaded	630	640	635
Goods unloaded	5,386	5,500	5,520

Source: UN, *Monthly Bulletin of Statistics*.

CIVIL AVIATION
(traffic on scheduled services)

	2002	2003	2004
Kilometres flown (million)	1	1	1
Passengers carried ('000)	84	75	94
Passenger-km (million)	35	32	39
Total ton-km (million)	5	5	6

Source: UN, *Statistical Yearbook*.

Tourism

	1996	1997	1998
Tourist arrivals ('000)	127	128	130

Source: World Tourism Organization.

Communications Media

	1994	1995	1996
Radio receivers ('000 in use)	2,950	3,000	3,300
Television receivers ('000 in use)	1,000	1,050	1,090
Telefax stations (number in use)	3,000*	n.a.	n.a.
Daily newspapers:			
number	11	11*	3
average circulation ('000 copies)*	5,000	5,000	4,500

* Estimate(s).

1997 ('000 in use): Radio receivers 3,360; Television receivers 1,200.

Telephones ('000 subscribers): 980 (estimate) in 2005.

Sources: UNESCO, *Statistical Yearbook*; UN, *Statistical Yearbook*.

Education

(2000)

	Institutions	Students
Kindergartens	14,167	748,416
Primary	4,886	1,609,865
Senior middle schools	4,772	2,181,524

Source: mainly Government of the Democratic People's Republic of Korea, *UNESCO Education for All Assessment Report 2000*.

Universities and Colleges: The *UNESCO Education for All Assessment Report 2000* identified more than 300 universities and colleges with 1.89m. students and academics.

Teachers (1987/88, UNESCO, *Statistical Yearbook*): Pre-primary 35,000, Primary 59,000, Secondary 111,000, Universities and colleges 23,000, Other tertiary 4,000.

Adult literacy rate (UNESCO estimate): 98.0% in 2003 (Source: UN Development Programme, *Human Development Report*).

Directory

The Constitution

A new Constitution was adopted on 27 December 1972. According to South Korean sources, several amendments were made in April 1992, including the deletion of references to Marxism-Leninism, the extension of the term of the Supreme People's Assembly from four to five years, and the promotion of limited 'economic openness'. Extensive amendments to the Constitution were approved on 5 September 1998. The main provisions of the revised Constitution are summarized below:

The Democratic People's Republic of Korea is an independent socialist state; the revolutionary traditions of the State are stressed (its ideological basis being the *juche* (self-reliance) idea of the Korean Workers' Party), as is the desire to achieve national reunification by peaceful means on the basis of national independence. The Late President Kim Il Sung is the Eternal President of the Republic.

National sovereignty rests with the working people, who exercise power through the Supreme People's Assembly and Local People's Assemblies at lower levels, which are elected by universal, equal and direct suffrage by secret ballot.

The foundation of an independent national economy, based on socialist and *juche* principles, is stressed. The means of production are owned solely by the State and socialist co-operative organizations.

Culture and education provide the working people with knowledge to advance a socialist way of life. Education is free, universal and compulsory for 11 years.

Defence is emphasized, as well as the rights of overseas nationals, the principles of friendly relations between nations based on equality, mutual respect and non-interference, proletarian internationalism, support for national liberation struggles and due observance of law.

The basic rights and duties of citizens are laid down and guaranteed. These include the right to vote and to be elected (for citizens who are more than 17 years of age), to work (the working day being eight hours), to free medical care and material assistance for the old, infirm or disabled, and to political asylum. National defence is the supreme duty of citizens.

THE STRUCTURE OF STATE

The Supreme People's Assembly

The Supreme People's Assembly is the highest organ of state power, exercises legislative power and is elected by direct, equal, universal and secret ballot for a term of five years. Its chief functions are: (i) to adopt, amend or supplement legal or constitutional enactments; (ii) to determine state policy; (iii) to elect the Chairman of the National Defence Commission; (iv) to elect the Vice-Chairmen and other members of the National Defence Commission (on the recommendation of the Chairman of the National Defence Commission); (v) to elect the President and other members of the Presidium of the Supreme People's Assembly, the Premier of the Cabinet, the President of the Central Court and other legal officials; (vi) to appoint the Vice-Premiers and other members of the Cabinet (on the recommendation of the Premier of the Cabinet); (vii) to approve the State Plan and Budget; (viii) to receive a report on the work of the Cabinet and adopt measures, if necessary; (ix) to decide on the ratification or abrogation of treaties. It holds regular and extraordinary sessions, the former being once or twice a year, the latter as necessary at the request of at least one-third of the deputies. Legislative enactments are adopted when approved by more than one-half of those deputies present. The Constitution is amended and supplemented when approved by more than two-thirds of the total number of deputies.

The National Defence Commission

The National Defence Commission, which consists of a Chairman, first Vice-Chairman, other Vice-Chairmen and members, is the highest military organ of state power, and is accountable to the Supreme People's Assembly. The National Defence Commission directs and commands the armed forces and guides defence affairs. The Chairman of the National Defence Commission serves a five-year term of office and has the most senior post in the state hierarchy.

The Presidium of the Supreme People's Assembly

The Presidium of the Supreme People's Assembly, which consists of a President, Vice-Presidents, secretaries and members, is the highest organ of power in the intervals between sessions of the Supreme People's Assembly, to which it is accountable. It exercises the following chief functions: (i) to convene sessions of the Supreme People's Assembly; (ii) to examine and approve new legislation, the State Plan and the State Budget, when the Supreme People's Assembly is in recess; (iii) to interpret the Constitution and legislative enactments; (iv) to supervise the observance of laws of State organs; (v) to organize elections to the Supreme People's Assembly and Local People's Assemblies; (vi) to form or abolish ministries or commissions of the Cabinet; (vii) to appoint or remove Vice-Premiers and other cabinet or ministry members, on the recommendation of the Premier, when the Supreme People's Assembly is not in session; (viii) to elect or transfer judges of the Central Court; (ix) to ratify or abrogate treaties concluded with other countries; (x) to appoint or recall diplomatic envoys; (xi) to confer decorations, medals, honorary titles and diplomatic ranks; (xii) to grant general amnesties or special pardons. The President of the Presidium represents the State and receives credentials and letters of recall of diplomatic representatives accredited by a foreign state.

The Cabinet

The Cabinet is the administrative and executive body of the Supreme People's Assembly and a general state management organ. It serves a five-year term and comprises the Premier, Vice-Premiers, Chairmen of Commissions and other necessary members. Its major functions are the following: (i) to adopt measures to execute state policy; (ii) to guide the work of ministries and other organs responsible to it; (iii) to establish and remove direct organs of the Cabinet and main administrative economic organizations; (iv) to draft the State Plan and adopt measures to make it effective; (v) to compile the State Budget and to implement its provisions; (vi) to organize and execute the work of all sectors of the economy, as well as education, science, culture, health and environmental protection; (vii) to adopt measures to strengthen the monetary and banking system; (viii) to adopt measures to maintain social order, protect State interests and guarantee citizens' rights; (ix) to conclude treaties; (x) to abolish decisions and directives of economic administrative organs which run counter to those of the Cabinet. The Cabinet is accountable to the Supreme People's Assembly.

Local People's Assemblies

The Local People's Assemblies and Committees of the province (or municipality directly under central authority), city (or district) and county are local organs of power. The Local People's Assemblies consist of deputies elected by direct, equal, universal and secret ballot. The Local People's Committees consist of a Chairman, Vice-Chairmen, secretaries and members. The Local People's Assemblies and Committees serve a four-year term and exercise local budgetary functions, elect local administrative and judicial personnel and carry out the decisions at local level of higher executive and administrative organs.

THE JUDICIARY

Justice is administered by the Central Court (the highest judicial organ of the State), local courts and the Special Court. Judges and other legal officials are elected by the Supreme People's Assembly. The Central Court protects state property and constitutional rights, guarantees that all state bodies and citizens observe state laws, and executes judgments. Justice is administered by the court comprising one judge and two people's assessors. The court is independent and judicially impartial. Judicial affairs are conducted by the Central Procurator's Office, which exposes and institutes criminal proceedings against accused persons. The Office of the Central Procurator is responsible to the Chairman of the National Defence Commission, the Supreme People's Assembly and the Central People's Committee.

The Government

HEAD OF STATE

President: President KIM IL SUNG died on 8 July 1994 and was declared 'Eternal President' in September 1998

Chairman of the National Defence Commission: Marshal KIM JONG IL.
Titular Head of State: KIM YONG NAM.

CABINET
(April 2009)

Premier: KIM YONG IL.
Vice-Premiers: RO TU CHOL, KWAK POM GI, JON SUNG HUN, THAE JONG SU.
Minister of Foreign Affairs: PAK UI CHUN.
Minister of People's Security: JU SANG SONG.
Minister of the People's Armed Forces: Vice-Marshal KIM YONG CHUN.
Chairman of the State Planning Commission: KIM KWANG RIN.
Minister of Electric Power Industry: HO TAEK.
Minister of Coal Industries: KIM HYONG SIK.
Minister of Extractive Industries: KANG MIN CHOL.
Minister of the Metal Industry: KIM THAE BONG.
Minister of Machine-Building Industries: JO PYONG JU.
Minister of Construction and Building Materials Industries: TONG JONG HO.
Minister of the Electronics Industry: O SU YONG.
Minister of Railways: CHON KIL SU.
Minister of Land and Marine Transport: RA TONG HUI.
Minister of Agriculture: KIM CHANG SIK.
Minister of Chemical Industry: RI MU YONG.
Minister of Light Industry: RI JU O.
Minister of Foreign Trade: RI RYONG NAM.
Minister of Forestry: KIM KWANG YONG.
Minister of Fisheries: SHIM KI YOP.
Minister of City Management: CHOE JONG GON.
Minister of Land and Environmental Protection: PAK SONG NAM.
Minister of State Construction Control: PAE TAL JUN.
Minister of Commerce: KIM BONG CHOL.
Minister of Procurement and Food Administration: CHOE NAM GYUN.
Minister of Education: KIM YONG JIN.
Minister of Post and Telecommunications: RYU YONG SOP.
Minister of Culture: KANG NUNG SU.
Minister of Finance: KIM WAN SU.
Minister of Labour: JONG YONG SU.
Minister of Public Health: CHOE CHANG SIK.
Minister of State Inspection: KIM UI SUN.
Minister of the Crude Oil Industry: KO JONG SIK.
Chairman of the Physical Culture and Sports Guidance Committee: PAK HAK SON.
President of the National Academy of Sciences: PYON YONG RIP.
President of the Central Bank: KIM WAN SU.
Director of the Central Statistics Bureau: KIM CHANG SU.
Chief Secretary of the Cabinet: KIM YONG HO.

MINISTRIES
All Ministries and Commissions are in Pyongyang.

Legislature

CHOE KO IN MIN HOE UI
(Supreme People's Assembly)

The 687 members of the 12th Supreme People's Assembly (SPA) were elected unopposed for a five-year term on 8 March 2009. The SPA's permanent body is the Presidium.
Chairman: CHOE TAE BOK.
President of the Presidium: KIM YONG NAM.
Vice-Presidents of the Presidium: YANG HYONG SOP, KIM YONG DAE.

Political Organizations

Democratic Front for the Reunification of the Fatherland: Pyongyang; f. 1946; a vanguard organization comprising political parties and mass working people's organizations seeking the unification of North and South Korea; Dir KIM YANG GON.

The component parties are:

Chondoist Chongu Party: Pyongyang; tel. (2) 334241; f. 1946; follows the guiding principle of *Innaechon* (the realization of 'heaven on earth'); satellite party of the Korean Workers' Party; Chair. RYU MI YONG.

Korean Social Democratic Party (KSDP) (Joson Sahoeminju-dang): Pyongyang; tel. (2) 5211981; fax (2) 3814410; f. 1945; advocates national independence and a democratic socialist society; satellite party of the Korean Workers' Party; Chair. KIM YONG DAE; First Vice-Chair. KANG PYONG HAK.

Korean Workers' Party (KWP): Pyongyang; f. 1945; merged with the South Korean Workers' Party in 1949; the guiding principle is the *juche* idea, based on the concept that man is the master and arbiter of all things; most significant political entity in the DPRK; 3m. mems; Gen. Sec. Marshal KIM JONG IL.

SIXTH CENTRAL COMMITTEE OF THE KWP

General Secretary: Marshal KIM JONG IL.

POLITICAL BUREAU (POLITBURO) OF THE KWP

Presidium: Marshal KIM JONG IL.
Full Members: KIM YONG NAM, KIM YONG JU, JON PYONG HO, HAN SONG RYONG.
Alternate Members: YANG HYONG SOP, CHOE TAE BOK, KIM CHOL MAN, CHOE YONG RIM, RI SON SIL.
Secretariat: Marshal KIM JONG IL, KYE UNG TAE, JON PYONG HO, HAN SONG RYONG, CHOE TAE BOK, KIM KI NAM, KIM KUK TAE, KIM JUNG RIN, JONG HA CHOL.

The component mass working people's organizations (see under Trade Unions) are:

General Federation of Trade Unions of Korea (GFTUK).
Kim Il Sung Socialist Youth League.
Korean Democratic Women's Union (KDWU).
Union of Agricultural Working People of Korea.

Diplomatic Representation

EMBASSIES IN THE DEMOCRATIC PEOPLE'S REPUBLIC OF KOREA

Cambodia: Munsudong, Taedongkang District, Pyongyang; tel. (2) 3817283; fax (2) 3817625; e-mail recpyongyang@gmail.com; Ambassador CHHORN HAY.

China, People's Republic: Kinmauldong, Moranbong District, Pyongyang; tel. (2) 3823316; fax (2) 3813425; e-mail chinaemb_kp@mfa.gov.cn; internet kp.china-embassy.org; Ambassador LIU XIAOMING.

Cuba: Munsudong, Taedongkang District, Pyongyang; tel. (2) 3827380; fax (2) 3817703; e-mail embarpdc@di.chesin.com; Ambassador JOSÉ MANUEL GALEGO MONTANO.

Czech Republic: Taedongkang Guyok 38, Taehakgori, Puksudong, Pyongyang; tel. (2) 3817021; fax (2) 3817022; e-mail pyongyang@embassy.mzv.cz; internet www.mzc.cz/pyongyang; Ambassador MARTIN TOMČO.

Egypt: 39 Munsudong, Taedongkang District, Pyongyang; tel. (2) 3817414; fax (2) 3817611; Ambassador ISMAIL ABDELRAHMAN GHONEIM HUSSEIN.

Ethiopia: POB 55, Munsudong, Taedongkang District, Pyongyang; tel. (2) 3827554; fax (2) 3827550; Chargé d'affaires FEKADE S. G. MESKEL.

Germany: Munsudong District, Pyongyang; tel. (2) 3817385; fax (2) 3817397; e-mail zreg@pjoe.auswaertiges-amt.de; Ambassador THOMAS SCHAFER.

India: Block 53, Munsudong, Taehak St, Taedongkang District, Pyongyang; tel. (2) 3817274; fax (2) 3817619; e-mail indemhoc@di.chesin.com; Ambassador ZILE SINGH.

Indonesia: 5 Foreigners' Bldg, Munsudong, Taedongkang District, Pyongyang; tel. (2) 3827439; fax (2) 3817620; e-mail kompyg2@public2.bta.net.cn; Ambassador DAULAT HOTMA AUDISON PASSARIBU.

Iran: Munhungdong, Monsu St, Taedongkang District, Pyongyang; tel. (2) 3817492; fax (2) 3817612; Ambassador MORTEZA MORADIAN.

Laos: Munhungdong, Taedongkang District, Pyongyang; tel. (2) 3827363; fax (2) 3817722; Ambassador CHALEUNE WARINTHRASAK.

Libya: Munsudong, Taedongkang District, Pyongyang; tel. (2) 3827544; fax (2) 3817267; Secretary of People's Bureau BASHIR RAMADAN KHALIFA ABU JANAH.

Malaysia: Munhungdong Diplomatic Enclave, Pyongyang; tel. (2) 3817125; fax (2) 3817845; e-mail malpygyang@kln.gov.my; Ambassador RAHIMI BIN HARUN.

Mali: Pyongyang; Ambassador NAKOUNTE DIAKITÉ.

Mongolia: Munsudong, Taedongkang District, Pyongyang; tel. (2) 3827322; fax (2) 3817323; Ambassador SODOVJAMTSYN KHÜRELBAATAR.

Nigeria: Munsudong, Taedongkang District, POB 535, Pyongyang; tel. (2) 3827558; fax (2) 3817293; Ambassador SULE BUBA.

Pakistan: 23, Block 66, Munsudong, Taedongkang District, Pyongyang; tel. (2) 3827479; fax 3817622; e-mail parep.pyongyang@kcckp.net; Ambassador NOORULLAH KHAN.

Poland: Munsudong, Taedongkang District, Pyongyang; tel. (2) 3817327; fax (2) 3817634; e-mail phenian@polemb.net; Ambassador ROMAN IWASZKIEWICZ.

Romania: Munhungdong, Taedongkang District, Pyongyang; tel. (2) 3827336; fax (2) 3817336; e-mail ambrophe@kcckp.net; Chargé d'affaires a.i. IANCU RIVIU OVIDIU.

Russia: Sinyangdong, Central District, Pyongyang; tel. (2) 3823102; fax (2) 3813427; e-mail rusembdprk@yahoo.com; Ambassador VALERY SUKHININ.

Sweden: Munsudong, Taedongkang District, Pyongyang; tel. (2) 3817485; fax (2) 3817663; e-mail ambassaden.pyongyang@foreign.ministry.se; Ambassador MATS FOYER.

Syria: Munsudong, Taedongkang District, Pyongyang; tel. (2) 3827473; fax (2) 3817635; Chargé d'affaires a.i. MUHAMMAD ADIB AL-HANI.

Thailand: Pyongyang; Ambassador NIKHOM TANTEMSAPYA.

United Kingdom: Munsudong Diplomatic Compound, Pyongyang; tel. (2) 3817980; fax (2) 3817985; e-mail postmaster.PYONX@fco.gov.uk; Ambassador PETER HUGHES.

Viet Nam: Munsudong, Taedongkang District, Pyongyang; tel. (2) 3817353; fax (2) 3817632; Ambassador LE VAN CU.

Judicial System

The judicial organs include the Central Court, the Court of the Province (or city under central authority) and the People's Court. Each court is composed of judges and people's assessors.

Procurators supervise the ordinances and regulations of all ministries and the decisions and directives of local organs of state power to ensure that they conform to the Constitution, laws and decrees, as well as to the decisions and other measures of the Cabinet. Procurators bring suits against criminals in the name of the State, and participate in civil cases to protect the interests of the State and citizens.

Central Court
Pyongyang.
The highest judicial organ; supervises the work of all courts.
President: KIM PYONG RYUL.
First Vice-President: YUN MYONG GUK.

Central Procurator's Office
Supervises work of procurator's offices in provinces, cities and counties.
Procurator-General: RI KIL SONG.

Religion

The religions that are officially reported to be practised in the DPRK are Buddhism, Christianity and Chundo Kyo, a religion peculiar to Korea combining elements of Buddhism and Christianity. Religious co-ordinating bodies are believed to be under strict state control. The exact number of religious believers is unknown.

Korean Religious Believers Council: Pyongyang; f. 1989; brings together members of religious organizations in North Korea; Chair. JANG JAE ON.

BUDDHISM
In 2002 it was reported that there were an estimated 300 Buddhist temples in the DPRK; the number of believers was estimated at about 10,000 in 2003.

Korean Buddhists Federation: POB 77, Pyongyang; tel. (2) 43698; fax (2) 3812100; f. 1945; Chair. Cen. Cttee PAK TAE HWA; Sec. SHIM SANG JIN.

CHRISTIANITY
In 2003 it was reported that there were approximately 13,000 Protestants and 3,000 Catholics in the country, many of whom worshipped in house churches (of which there were said to be about 500 in 2002). The construction of North Korea's first Russian Orthodox church was completed in August 2006.

Korean Christians Federation: Pyongyang; f. 1946; Chair. Cen. Cttee KANG YONG SOP; Sec. O KYONG U.

The Roman Catholic Church
For ecclesiastical purposes, North and South Korea are nominally under a unified jurisdiction. North Korea contains two dioceses (Hamhung and Pyongyang), both suffragan to the archdiocese of Seoul (in South Korea), and the territorial abbacy of Tokwon (Tokugen), directly responsible to the Holy See.

Diocese of Hamhung: Catholic Mission, Hamhung; 134-1 Waekwan-dong Kwan Eub, Chil kok kun, Gyeongbuk 718-800, Republic of Korea; tel. (545) 970-2000; Bishop (vacant); Apostolic Administrator of Hamhung and of the Abbacy of Tokwon Fr PLACIDUS DONG-HO RI.

Diocese of Pyongyang: Catholic Mission, Pyongyang; Bishop Rt Rev. FRANCIS HONG YONG HO (absent); Apostolic Administrator Most Rev. NICHOLAS CHEONG JIN-SUK (Archbishop of Seoul).

Korean Catholics Association: Changchung 1-dong, Songyo District, Pyongyang; tel. (2) 23492; f. 1988; Chair. Cen. Cttee JANG JAE ON; Vice-Chair. MUN CHANG HAK.

CHUNDO KYO
According to officials quoted in 2002, there were approximately 40,000 practitioners of Chundo Kyo in the DPRK.

Korean Chundoists Association: Pyongyang; tel. (2) 334241; f. 1946; Chair. of Central Guidance Cttee RYU MI YONG.

The Press

PRINCIPAL NEWSPAPERS

Choldo Sinmun: Pyongyang; f. 1947; every two days.

Joson Inmingun (Korean People's Army Daily): Pyongyang; f. 1948; daily; Editor-in-Chief Ri Tae Bong.

Kyowon Sinmun: Pyongyang; f. 1948; publ. by the Education Commission; weekly.

Minju Choson (Democratic Korea): Pyongyang; f. 1946; govt organ; 6 a week; Editor-in-Chief Kim Jong Suk; circ. 200,000.

Nongup Kunroja: Pyongyang; publ. of Cen. Cttee of the Union of Agricultural Working People of Korea.

Pyongyang Sinmun: Pyongyang; f. 1957; general news; 6 a week; Editor-in-Chief Song Rak Gyun.

Rodong Chongnyon (Working Youth): Pyongyang; f. 1946; organ of the Cen. Cttee of the Kim Il Sung Socialist Youth League; 6 a week; Editor-in-Chief Ri Jong Gi.

Rodong Sinmun (Labour Daily): Pyongyang; internet www.kcna.co.jp/today-rodong/rodong.htm; f. 1946; organ of the Cen. Cttee of the Korean Workers' Party; daily; Editor-in-Chief Choe Chil Nam; circ. 1.5m.

Rodongja Sinmun (Workers' Newspaper): Pyongyang; f. 1945; organ of the Gen. Fed. of Trade Unions of Korea; Editor-in-Chief Ri Song Ju.

Saenal (New Day): Pyongyang; f. 1971; publ. by the Kim Il Sung Socialist Youth League; 2 a week; Deputy Editor Choe Sang In.

Sonyon Sinmun: Pyongyang; f. 1946; publ. by the Kim Il Sung Socialist Youth League; 2 a week; circ. 120,000.

Tongil Sinbo: Kangan 1-dong, Youth Ave, Songyo District, Pyongyang; f. 1972; non-affiliated; weekly; Chief Editor Pak Jin Sik; circ. 300,000.

PRINCIPAL PERIODICALS

Chollima: Pyongyang; popular magazine; monthly.

Choson (Korea): Pyongyang; social, economic, political and cultural; bi-monthly.

Choson Minju Juuiinmin Gonghwaguk Palmyonggongbo (Official Report of Inventions in the DPRK): Pyongyang; 6 a year.

Choson Munhak (Korean Literature): Pyongyang; organ of the Cen. Cttee of the Korean Writers' Union; monthly.

Choson Yesul (Korean Arts): Pyongyang; organ of the Cen. Cttee of the Gen. Fed. of Unions of Literature and Arts of Korea; monthly.

Economics: POB 73, Pyongyang; fax (2) 3814410; quarterly.

History: POB 73, Pyongyang; fax (2) 3814410; quarterly.

Hwahakgwa Hwahakgoneop: Pyongyang; organ of the Hamhung br. of the Korean Acad. of Sciences; chemistry and chemical engineering; 6 a year.

Jokook Tongil: Kangan 1-dong, Youth Ave, Songyo District, Pyongyang; organ of the Cttee for the Peaceful Unification of Korea; f. 1961; monthly; Chief Editor Li Myong Gyu; circ. 70,000.

Korean Medicine: POB 73, Pyongyang; fax (2) 3814410; quarterly.

Kunroja (Workers): 1 Munshindong, Tongdaewon, Pyongyang; f. 1946; organ of the Cen. Cttee of the Korean Workers' Party; monthly; Editor-in-Chief Ryang Kyong Bok; circ. 300,000.

Kwahakwon Tongbo (Bulletins of the Academy of Science): POB 73, Pyongyang; fax (2) 3814410; organ of the Standing Cttee of the Korean Acad. of Sciences; 6 a year.

Mulri (Physics): POB 73, Pyongyang; fax (2) 3814410; quarterly.

Munhwao Haksup (Study of Korean Language): POB 73, Pyongyang; fax (2) 3814410; publ. by the Publishing House of the Acad. of Social Sciences; quarterly.

Philosophy: POB 73, Pyongyang; fax (2) 3814410; quarterly.

Punsok Hwahak (Analysis): POB 73, Pyongyang; fax (2) 3814410; organ of the Cen. Analytical Inst. of the Korean Acad. of Sciences; quarterly.

Ryoksagwahak (Historical Science): Pyongyang; publ. by the Acad. of Social Sciences; quarterly.

Saengmulhak (Biology): Pyongyang; fax (2) 3814410; publ. by the Korea Science and Encyclopedia Publishing House; quarterly.

Sahoekwahak (Social Science): Pyongyang; publ. by the Acad. of Social Sciences; 6 a year.

Suhakkwa Mulli: Pyongyang; organ of the Physics and Mathematics Cttee of the Korean Acad. of Sciences; quarterly.

FOREIGN LANGUAGE PUBLICATIONS

The Democratic People's Republic of Korea: Korea Pictorial, Pyongyang; f. 1956; illustrated news; Korean, Russian, Chinese, English, French, Arabic and Spanish edns; monthly; Editor-in-Chief Han Pom Chik.

Foreign Trade of the DPRK: Foreign Trade Publishing House, Potonggang District, Pyongyang; economic developments and export promotion; English, French, Japanese, Russian and Spanish edns; monthly.

Korea: Pyongyang; f. 1956; illustrated; Korean, Arabic, Chinese, English, French, Spanish and Russian edns; monthly.

Korea Today: Foreign Languages Publishing House, Pyongyang; current affairs; Chinese, English, French, Russian and Spanish edns; monthly; Vice-Dir and Editor-in-Chief Han Pong Chan.

Korean Women: Pyongyang; English and French edns; quarterly.

Korean Youth and Students: Pyongyang; English and French edns; monthly.

The Pyongyang Times: Sochondong, Sosong District, Pyongyang; tel. (2) 51951; English, Spanish and French edns; weekly.

NEWS AGENCY

Korean Central News Agency (KCNA): Potonggangdong 1, Potonggang District, Pyongyang; internet www.kcna.co.jp; f. 1946; sole distributing agency for news in the DPRK; publs daily bulletins in English, Russian, French and Spanish; Dir-Gen. Kim Ki Ryong.

PRESS ASSOCIATION

Korean Journalists Union: Pyongyang; tel. (2) 36897; f. 1946; assists in the ideological work of the Korean Workers' Party; Chair. Cen. Cttee Kim Song Guk.

Publishers

Academy of Sciences Publishing House: Nammundong, Central District, Pyongyang; tel. (2) 51956; f. 1953.

Academy of Social Sciences Publishing House: Pyongyang; Dir Choe Kwan Shik.

Agricultural Press: Pyongyang; labour, industrial relations; Pres. Ho Kyong Pil.

Central Science and Technology Information Agency: Pyongyang; f. 1963; Dir Ju Song Ryong.

Education Publishing House: Pyongyang; f. 1945; Pres. Kim Chang Son.

Foreign Language Press Group: Sochondong, Sosong District, Pyongyang; tel. (2) 841342; fax (2) 812100; f. 1949; Dir Choe Kyong Guk.

Foreign Language Publishing House: Oesong District, Pyongyang; Dir Kim Yong Mu.

Higher Educational Books Publishing House: Pyongyang; f. 1960; Pres. Pak Kun Song.

Kim Il Sung University Publishing House: Pyongyang; f. 1965.

Korea Science and Encyclopedia Publishing House: POB 73, Pyongyang; tel. (2) 18111; fax (2) 3814410; publishes numerous periodicals and monographs; f. 1952; Dir Gen. Kim Jung Hyop; Dir of International Co-operation Jean Bahng.

Korean People's Army Publishing House: Pyongyang; Pres. Yun Myong Do.

Korean Social Democratic Party Publishing House: Pyongyang; tel. (2) 3818038; fax (2) 3814410; f. 1946; publishes quarterly journal Joson Sahoemingjudang (in Korean) and KSDP Says (in English); Dir Kim Sok Jun.

Korean Workers' Party Publishing House: Pyongyang; f. 1945; fiction, politics; Dir Ryang Kyong Bok.

Kumsong Youth Publishing House: Pyongyang; f. 1946; Dir Han Jong Sop.

Literature and Art Publishing House: Pyongyang; f. by merger of Mass Culture Publishing House and Publishing House of the Gen. Fed. of Literary and Art Unions; Dir Gen. Ri Phyo U.

Transportation Publishing House: Namgyodong, Hyongjaesan District, Pyongyang; f. 1952; travel; Editor Paek Jong Han.

Working People's Organizations Publishing House: Pyongyang; f. 1946; fiction, government, political science; Dir Min Sang Hyon.

WRITERS' UNION

Korean Writers' Union: Pyongyang; Chair. Cen. Cttee Kim Pyong Hun.

THE DEMOCRATIC PEOPLE'S REPUBLIC OF KOREA (NORTH KOREA)

Broadcasting and Communications

North Korea established a satellite communications station in Pyongyang, through an agreement with France in 1986, which enabled North Korea to communicate by satellite with Western countries. In 1990 an agreement was reached on satellite communications for the operation of telephone, telex and telegram services between North Korea and Japan. In May the DPRK joined Intelsat (an international commercial satellite telecommunications organization). In October 2001 North Korea launched its first e-mail service provider in co-operation with China-based company Silibank.com, which was used for business and trade purposes. However, access to the internet remained severely limited, with information flow within North Korea still being conducted mainly via a closed intranet system (the Kwangmyong, meaning 'light', system). In 2002 a mobile telephone network was reportedly established in Pyongyang and surrounding areas, with mobile telephone use being permitted to approximately 1,000 government officials. However, citizens have been banned from using mobile telephones since mid-2004.

TELECOMMUNICATIONS

Korea Post and Telecommunications Co: Pyongyang; Dir KIM HYON JONG.

BROADCASTING

Regulatory Authorities

DPRK Radio and Television Broadcasting Committee: see Radio, below**Pyongyang Municipal Broadcasting Committee:** Pyongyang; Chair. KANG CHUN SHIK.

Radio

DPRK Radio and Television Broadcasting Committee: Jonsungdong, Moranbong District, Pyongyang; tel. (2) 3816035; fax (2) 3812100; programmes relayed nationally with local programmes supplied by local radio cttees; loudspeakers are installed in factories and in open spaces in all towns; home broadcasting 22 hours daily; foreign broadcasts in Russian, Chinese, English, French, German, Japanese, Spanish and Arabic; Chair. CHA SUNG SU.

Television

General Bureau of Television: Gen. Dir CHA SUNG SU.

DPRK Radio and Television Broadcasting Committee: see Radio**Kaesong Television:** Kaesong; broadcasts five hours on weekdays, 11 hours at weekends.

Korean Central Television Station: Ministry of Post and Telecommunications, Pyongyang; broadcasts five hours daily; satellite broadcasts commenced Oct. 1999.

Mansudae Television Station: Mansudae, Pyongyang; f. 1983; broadcasts nine hours of cultural programmes, music and dance, foreign films and news reports at weekends.

Finance

(cap. = capital; res = reserves; dep. = deposits; m. = million; brs = branches; amounts in won)

BANKING

During 1946–47 all banking institutions in North Korea, apart from the Central Bank and the Farmers Bank, were abolished. The Farmers Bank was merged with the Central Bank in 1959. The Foreign Trade Bank (f. 1959) conducts the international business of the Central Bank. Other banks, established in the late 1970s, are responsible for the foreign-exchange and external payment business of North Korean foreign trade enterprises.

The entry into force of the Joint-Venture Act in 1984 permitted the establishment of joint-venture banks, designed to attract investment into North Korea by Koreans resident overseas. The Foreign Investment Banking Act was approved in 1993.

Central Bank

Central Bank of the DPRK: Munsudong, Seungri St 58-1, Central District, Pyongyang; tel. (2) 3338196; fax (2) 3814624; e-mail kcb_idkb@co.chesin.com; f. 1946; bank of issue; supervisory and control bank; Pres. RI KWANG GON; 13 brs.

State Banks

Credit Bank of Korea: Chongryu 1-dong, Munsu St, Otandong, Central District, Pyongyang; tel. (2) 3818285; fax (2) 3817806; f. 1986; est. as International Credit Bank, name changed 1989; Pres. LI SUN BOK; Vice-Pres. SON YONG SUN.

Foreign Trade Bank of the DPRK: FTB Bldg, Jungsongdong, Seungri St, Central District, Pyongyang; tel. (2) 3815270; fax (2) 3814467; e-mail ftb@co.chesin.com; f. 1959; deals in international settlements and all banking business; Pres. and Chair. O KWANG CHOL; 12 brs.

International Industrial Development Bank: Jongpyong-dong, Pyongchon District, Pyongyang; tel. (2) 3818610; fax (2) 3814427; f. 2001; Pres. SHIN DOK SONG.

Korea Daesong Bank: Segoridong, Gyongheung St, Potonggang District, Pyongyang; tel. (2) 3818221; fax (2) 3814576; f. 1978; cap. 158,205.8m., res 25,917,6m., dep. 1,990,582.5m. (Dec. 2006); Pres. RI GYONG HA.

Koryo Bank: Ponghwadong, Potonggang District, Pyongyang; tel. (2) 3818168; fax (2) 3814033; e-mail krbankpy@co.chesin.com; f. 1989; est. as Koryo Finance Joint Venture Co, name changed 1994; co-operative, development, regional, savings and universal bank; Pres. PAK YONG CHIL; 10 brs.

Kumgang Bank: Jungsongdong, Central District, Pyongyang; tel. (2) 3818532; fax (2) 3814467; f. 1979; Chair. KIM JANG HO.

Private Banks

Bank of East Land: POB 32, BEL Bldg, Jonseung-dong, Moranbong District, Pyongyang; tel. (2) 3818923; fax (2) 3814410; f. 2001; commercial, investment, merchant, private and retail banking; Pres. PAK HYONG GIL.

Tanchon Commercial Bank: Saemaeul 1-dong, Pyongchon District, Pyongyang; tel. (2) 18111999; fax (2) 3814793; e-mail cbktm828@co.chesin.com; f. 1983; fmrly Changgwang Credit Bank, merged with Samchon-ri Bank and named as above Nov. 2003; cap. 50,043.9m., res 93,817.9m., dep. 875,021.9m. (Dec. 2003); Chair. KIM CHOL HWAN; Pres. KYE CHANG HO.

Joint-Venture Banks

Korea Joint Bank (KJB): Ryugyongdong, Potonggang District, Pyongyang; tel. (2) 3818151; fax (2) 3814410; f. 1989; est. with co-operation of the Federation of Korean Traders and Industrialists in Japan; 50% Korea International General Joint Venture Co, 50% General Asscn of Koreans in Japan; Gen. Man. O HO RYOL; 6 domestic brs, 1 br in Tokyo.

Korea Joint Financial Co: f. 1988; jt venture with Koreans resident in the USA.

Korea Nagwon Joint Financial Co: f. 1987; est. by Nagwon Trade Co and a Japanese co.

Korea Rakwon Joint Banking Co: Pyongyang; Man. Dir HO POK DOK.

Korea United Development Bank: Central District, Pyongyang; tel. (2) 3814165; fax (2) 3814483; e-mail kudb888@yahoo.com; f. 1991; 51% owned by Zhongce Investment Corpn (Hong Kong), 49% owned by Osandok General Bureau; Pres. KIM SE HO.

Koryo Bank: Ponghwa-dong, Potonggang District, Pyongyang; tel. (2) 18333; fax (2) 3814410; e-mail krbankpy@co.chesin.com; Pres. YONG-CHIL PAK.

Koryo Commercial Bank: tel. (2) 3812060; fax (2) 3814441; f. 1988; jt venture with Koreans resident in the USA.

Foreign Investment Banks

Daesong Credit Development Bank: Potonggang Hotel, 301 Ansan-dong, Pyongchon District, Pyongyang; tel. (2) 3814866; fax (2) 3814723; f. 1996; est. as Peregrine-Daesong Development Bank; fmrly jt venture between Oriental Commercial Holdings Ltd (Hong Kong) and Korea Daesong Bank; majority stake acquired by Global Group of Companies (UK) in May 2004; Man. NIGEL COWIE.

Golden Triangle Bank: Rajin-Sonbong Free Economic and Trade Zone; f. 1995.

INSURANCE

State Insurance Bureau: Central District, Pyongyang; tel. (2) 38196; handles all life, fire, accident, marine, hull insurance and reinsurance.

Korea Foreign Insurance Co (Chosunbohom): Central District, Pyongyang; tel. (2) 3818024; fax (2) 3814464; f. 1974; conducts marine, motor, aviation and fire insurance, reinsurance of all classes, and all foreign insurance; brs in Chongjin, Hungnam and Nampo, and agencies in foreign ports; overseas representative offices in Chile, France, Germany, Pakistan, Singapore; Pres. RI JANG SU.

Korea International Insurance Co: Pyongyang; Dir PAEK MYONG RON.

Korea Mannyon Insurance Co: Pyongyang; Pres. PAK IL HYONG.

Trade and Industry

GOVERNMENT AGENCIES

DPRK Committee for the Promotion of External Economic Co-operation: Jungsongdong, Central District, Pyongyang; tel. (2) 333974; fax (2) 3814498; Chair. PAEK HONG BONG.

DPRK Committee for the Promotion of International Trade: Central District, Pyongyang; Pres. RI SONG ROK; Chair. KIM YONG JAE.

Economic Co-operation Management Bureau: Ministry of Foreign Trade, Pyongyang; f. 1998; Dir KIM YONG SUL.

Korea International Joint Venture Promotion Committee: Pyongyang; Chair. CHAE HUI JONG.

Korean Association for the Promotion of Asian Trade: Pyongyang; Pres. RI SONG ROK.

Korean International General Joint Venture Co: Pyongyang; f. 1986; promotes jt economic ventures with foreign countries; Man. Dir RO TU CHOL.

CHAMBERS OF COMMERCE

DPRK Chamber of Commerce: POB 89, Jungsongdong, Central District, Pyongyang; tel. (2) 3815926; fax (2) 3815827; e-mail micom@co.chesin.com.

INDUSTRIAL AND TRADE ASSOCIATIONS

Korea Building Materials Trading Co: Tongdaewon District, Pyongyang; tel. (2) 18111-3818085; fax (2) 3814555; chemical building materials, woods, timbers, cement, sheet glass, etc.; Dir SHIN TONG BOM.

Korea Cereals Export and Import Corpn: Jungsongdong, Central District, Pyongyang; tel. (2) 18111-3818278; fax (2) 3813451; high-quality vegetable starches, etc.

Korea Chemicals Export and Import Corpn: Central District, Pyongyang; petroleum and petroleum products, raw materials for the chemical industry, rubber and rubber products, fertilizers, etc.

Korea Daesong General Trading Corpn: Pulgungori 1-dong, Potonggang District, Pyongyang; tel. (2) 18111; fax (2) 3814432; e-mail Daesong@silibank.com; Gen. Dir CHOE JONG SON.

Korea Daesong Jei Trading Corpn: Pulgungori 1-dong, Potonggang District, Pyongyang; tel. (2) 18111-3818213; fax (2) 3814431; machinery and equipment, chemical products, textiles, agricultural products, etc.

Korea Daesong Jesam Trading Corpn: Pulgungori 1-dong, Potonggang District, Pyongyang; tel. (2) 18111-3818562; fax (2) 3814431; remedies for diabetes, tonics, etc.

Korea Ferrous Metals Export and Import Corpn: Potonggang 2-dong, Potonggang District, Pyongyang; tel. (2) 18111-3818078; fax (2) 3814581; steel products.

Korea Film Export and Import Corpn: Daedongmundong, Central District, POB 113, Pyongyang; tel. (2) 180008034; fax (2) 3814410; f. 1956; feature films, cartoons, scientific and documentary films; Dir-Gen. CHOE HYOK U.

Korea First Equipment Export and Import Co: Central District, Pyongyang; tel. (2) 334825; f. 1960; export and import of ferrous and non-ferrous metallurgical plants, geological exploration and mining equipment, communication equipment, machine-building plant, etc.; construction of public facilities such as airports, hotels, tourist facilities, etc.; jt-venture business in similar projects; Pres. CHAE WON CHOL.

Korea Foodstuffs Export and Import Corpn: Kangan 2-dong, Songyo District, Pyongyang; tel. (2) 18111-3818289; fax (2) 3814417; cereals, wines, meat, canned foods, fruits, cigarettes, etc.

Korea Fruit and Vegetables Export Corpn: Central District, Pyongyang; tel. (2) 35117; vegetables, fruit and their products.

Korea General Corpn for External Construction (GENCO): Sungri St 25, Jungsongdong, Central District, Pyongyang; tel. (2) 18111-3818090; fax (2) 3814611; e-mail gen122@co.chesin.com; f. 1961; construction of dwelling houses, public establishments, factories, hydroelectric and thermal power stations, irrigation systems, ports, bridges, and transport services, technical services; Gen. Dir CHOE BONG SU.

Korea General Machine Co: Tongsin 3-dong, Tongdaewon, Pyongyang; tel. (2) 18555-3818102; fax (2) 3814495; Dir RA IN GYUN.

Korea Hyopdong Trading Corpn: Othan-dong, Kangan St, Central District, Pyongyang; tel. (2) 18111-3818011; fax (2) 3814454; fabrics, glass products, ceramics, chemical goods, building materials, foodstuffs, machinery, etc.

Korea Industrial Technology Co: Jungsongdong, Central District, Pyongyang; tel. (2) 18111-3818025; fax (2) 3814537; Pres. KWON YONG SON.

Korea International Chemical Joint Venture Co: Pyongyang; Chair. RYO SONG GUN.

Korea Jangsu Trading Co: Kyogudong, Central District, Pyongyang; tel. (2) 18111-3818834; fax (2) 3814410; medicinal products and clinical equipment.

Korea Jeil Equipment Export and Import Corpn: Jungsongdong, Central District, Pyongyang; tel. (2) 334825; f. 1960; ferrous and non-ferrous metallurgical plant, geological exploration and mining equipment, power plant, communications and broadcasting equipment, machine-building equipment, railway equipment, construction of public facilities; Pres. CHO JANG DOK.

Korea Koryo Trading Corpn: Jongpyongdong, Pyongchon District, Pyongyang; tel. (2) 18111-3818104; fax (2) 3814646; Dir KIM HUI DUK.

Korea Kwangmyong Trading Corpn: Jungsongdong, Central District, Pyongyang; tel. (2) 18111-3818111; fax (2) 3814410; dried herbs, dried and pickled vegetables; Dir CHOE JONG HUN.

Korea Light Industry Import-Export Co: Juchetab St, Tongdaewon District, Pyongyang; tel. (2) 37661; exports silk, cigarettes, canned goods, drinking glasses, ceramics, handbags, pens, plastic flowers, musical instruments, etc.; imports chemicals, dyestuffs, machinery, etc.; Dir CHOE PYONG HYON.

Korea Machine Tool Trading Corpn: Tongdaewon District, Pyongyang; tel. (2) 18555-381810; fax (2) 3814495; Dir KIM KWANG RYOP.

Korea Machinery and Equipment Export and Import Corpn: Potonggang District, Pyongyang; tel. (2) 333449; f. 1948; metallurgical machinery and equipment, electric machines, building machinery, farm machinery, diesel engines, etc.

Korea Mansu Trading Corpn: Chollima St, Central District, POB 250, Pyongyang; tel. (2) 43075; fax (2) 812100; f. 1974; antibiotics, pharmaceuticals, vitamin compounds, drugs, medicinal herbs; Dir KIM JANG HUN.

Korea Marine Products Export and Import Corpn: Central District, Pyongyang; canned, frozen, dried, salted and smoked fish, fishing equipment and supplies.

Korea Minerals Export and Import Corpn: Central District, Pyongyang; minerals, solid fuel, graphite, precious stones, etc.

Korea Namheung Trading Co: Sinri-dong, Tongdaewon District, Pyongyang; tel. (2) 18111-3818974; fax (2) 3814623; high-purity reagents, synthetic resins, vinyl films, essential oils, menthol and peppermint oil.

Korea Non-ferrous Metals Export and Import Corpn: Potonggang 2-dong, Potonggang District, Pyongyang; tel. (2) 18111-3818247; fax (2) 3814569.

Korea Okyru Trading Corpn: Kansongdong, Pyongchon District, Pyongyang; tel. (2) 18111-3818110; fax (2) 3814618; agricultural and marine products, household goods, clothing, chemical and light industrial products.

Korea Ponghwa Contractual Joint Venture Co: Pyongyang; Dir MUN YONG OK.

Korea Ponghwa General Trading Corpn: Jungsongdong, Central District, Pyongyang; tel. (2) 18111-3818023; fax (2) 3814444; machinery, metal products, minerals and chemicals.

Korea Publications Export and Import Corpn: Yokjondong, Yonggwang St, Central District, Pyongyang; tel. (2) 3818536; fax (2) 3814404; f. 1948; export of books, periodicals, postcards, paintings, cassettes, videos, CDs, CD-ROMs, postage stamps and records; import of books; Pres. RI YONG.

Korea Rungra Co: Sinwondong, Potonggang District, Pyongyang; tel. (2) 18111-3818112; fax (2) 3814608; Dir CHOE HENG UNG.

Korea Rungrado Trading Corpn: Segori-dong, Potonggang District, Pyongyang; tel. (2) 18111-3818022; fax (2) 3814507; food and animal products; Gen. Dir PAK KYU HONG.

Korea Ryongaksan General Trading Corpn: Pyongyang; Gen. Dir HAN YU RO.

Korea Samcholli General Corpn: Pyongyang; Dir JONG UN OP.

Korea Technology Corpn: Jungsongdong, Central District, Pyongyang; tel. (2) 18111-3818090; fax (2) 3814410; scientific and technical co-operation.

Korea Unha Trading Corpn: Rungra 1-dong, Taedonggang District, Pyongyang; tel. (2) 18111-3818236; fax (2) 3814506; clothing and fibres.

Korea Yonghung Trading Co: Tongan-dong, Central District, Pyongyang; tel. (2) 18111-3818223; fax (2) 3814527; e-mail greenlam@co.chesin.com; f. 1979; export of freight cars, vehicle parts, marine products, electronic goods, import of steel, chemical products; Pres. CHOE YONG DOK.

Pyongsu JV Co Ltd: Pyongyang; f. 2004; pharmaceutical mfr, medical products incl. analgesics; jt venture with Interpacific/Zuellig Pharma (Switzerland).

TRADE UNIONS

General Federation of Trade Unions of Korea (GFTUK): POB 333, Dongmun-dong, Daedonggang District, Pyongyang; fax (2) 3814427; f. 1945; 1.6m. mems (2003); seven affiliated unions (2003); Pres. RYOM SUN GIL.

Trade Union of Construction and Forestry Workers of Korea: Pyongyang; f. 1945; 160,000 mems (2003); Pres. WON HYONG GUK.

Trade Union of Educational and Cultural Workers: POB 333, Dongmun-dong, Daedonggang District, Pyongyang; fax (2) 3814427; f. 1946; 89,800 mems (2003); Pres. KIM YONG DO.

Trade Union of Light and Chemical Industries of Korea: Pyongyang; f. 1945; 372,500 mems (2003); Pres. RI JIN HAK.

Trade Union of Metal and Engineering Industries of Korea: Pyongyang; f. 1945; 332,800 mems (2003); Pres. CHOE GWANG HYON.

Trade Union of Mining and Power Industries of Korea: Pyongyang; f. 1945; 221,000 mems (2003); Pres. SON YONG JUN.

Trade Union of Public Employees and Service Workers of Korea: Pyongyang; f. 1945; 305,900 mems (2003); Pres. KIM GANG HO.

Trade Union of Transport and Fisheries Workers of Korea: Pyongyang; f. 1945; 119,800 mems (2003); Pres. CHOE RYONG SU.

General Federation of Agricultural and Forestry Technique of Korea: Chung Kuyuck Nammundong, Pyongyang; f. 1946; 523,000 mems.

General Federation of Unions of Literature and Arts of Korea: Pyongyang; f. 1946; seven br. unions; Chair. Cen. Cttee CHANG CHOL.

Kim Il Sung Socialist Youth League: Pyongyang; fmrly League of Socialist Working Youth of Korea; First Sec. KIM GYONG HO.

Korean Architects' Union: Pyongyang; f. 1954; 500 mems; Chair. Cen. Cttee PAE TAL JUN.

Korean Democratic Lawyers' Association: Ryonhwa 1, Central District, Pyongyang; fax (2) 3814644; f. 1954; Chair. HAM HAK SONG.

Korean Democratic Scientists' Association: Pyongyang; f. 1956.

Korean Democratic Women's Union: Jungsongdong, Central District, Pyongyang; fax (2) 3814416; f. 1945; Chief Officer RO SONG SIL.

Korean General Federation of Science and Technology: Jungsongdong, Seungri St, Central District, Pyongyang; tel. (2) 3224389; fax (2) 3814410; f. 1946; 550,000 mems; Chair. Cen. Cttee CHOE HUI JONG.

Korean Medical Association: Pyongyang; f. 1970; Chair. CHOE CHANG SHIK.

Union of Agricultural Working People of Korea: Pyongyang; f. 1965; est. to replace fmr Korean Peasants' Union; 2.4m. mems; Chair. Cen. Cttee KANG CHANG UK.

Transport

RAILWAYS

In 2005 the total length of track was estimated at 5,214 km, of which some 70% was electrified. There are international train services to Moscow (Russia) and Beijing (People's Republic of China). Construction work on the reconnection of the Kyongui (West Coast, Sinuiju–Seoul) and East Coast Line (Wonsan–Seoul) began in September 2002. The two lines were officially opened in June 2003, but were not yet open to traffic, as construction work on the Northern side remained to be completed. The lines were reportedly completed in 2005, and in May 2007 the first cross-border trial runs were conducted. Eventually the two were to be linked to the Trans-China and Trans-Siberian railways, respectively, greatly enhancing the region's transport links.

There is an underground railway system in Pyongyang, with two public lines serving 17 stations. Unspecified plans to expand the system were announced in February 2002.

ROADS

In 2006 the road network was estimated at 25,554 km. Road links between the DPRK and the Republic of Korea were reported to have opened in late 2005.

INLAND WATERWAYS

In 2005 the total length of inland waterways was estimated at 2,253 km, most of which was navigable only by small craft. The Yalu (Amnok-gang) and Taedong, Tumen and Ryesong are the most important commercial rivers. Regular passenger and freight services: Nampo–Chosan–Supung; Chungsu–Sinuiju–Dasado; Nampo–Jeudo; Pyongyang–Nampo.

SHIPPING

The principal ports are Nampo, Wonsan, Chongjin, Rajin, Hungnam, Songnim and Haeju. At 31 December 2007 North Korea's merchant fleet comprised 301 vessels, with a combined displacement of 985,561 grt.

Bochon Shipping Co: Pyongchon District, Pyongyang.

Chon Song Shipping Co Ltd: Sochang-dong, Potonggang District, Pyongyang.

Korea Ansan Shipping Co: Nampo.

Korea Chartering Corpn: Central District, Pyongyang; arranges cargo transport and chartering.

Korea Daehung Shipping Co: Ansan 1–dong, Pyongchon District, Pyongyang; tel. (2) 18111, ext. 8695; fax (2) 3814508; f. 1994; owns 6 reefers, 3 oil tankers, 1 cargo ship.

Korea East Sea Shipping Co: Pyongyang; Dir RI TUK HYON.

Korea Foreign Transportation Corpn: Central District, Pyongyang; arranges transport of cargoes for export and import (transit goods and charters).

Korea Myohyang Shipping Co: Ryonhwadong Changgoan St, Chung District, Pyongyang; tel. (3) 8160590; fax (3) 8146420.

Korea Myongsang Shipping Co: Chongpyong-dong, Pyongchon District, Pyongyang; tel. (2) 3815842; fax (2) 3815942.

Korea Tonghae Shipping Co: Changgwang St, Central District, POB 120, Pyongyang; tel. (2) 345805; fax (2) 3814583; arranges transport by Korean vessels.

Korea Undok Shipping Co Ltd: Nampo.

Korean-Polish Shipping Co Ltd: Moranbong District, Pyongyang; tel. (2) 3814384; fax (2) 3814607; f. 1967; maritime trade mainly with Polish and Far East ports.

Ocean Maritime Management Co Ltd: Tonghungdong, Central District, Pyongyang.

Ocean Shipping Agency of the DPRK: Moranbong District, POB 21, Pyongyang; tel. (2) 3818100; fax (2) 3814531; Pres. O JONG HO.

CIVIL AVIATION

The international airport is at Sunan, 24 km from Pyongyang.

Chosonminhang/General Civil Aviation Bureau of the DPRK: Sunan Airport, Sunan District, Pyongyang; tel. (2) 37917; fax (2) 3814625; f. 1954; internal services and external flights by Air Koryo to Beijing and Shenyang (People's Republic of China), Bangkok (Thailand), Macao, Nagoya (Japan), Moscow, Khabarovsk and Vladivostok (Russia), Sofia (Bulgaria) and Berlin (Germany); charter services are operated to Asia, Africa and Europe; Pres. KIM YO UNG.

Tourism

Tourism is permitted only in officially accompanied parties. In 1999 there were more than 60 international hotels (including nine in Pyongyang) with 7,500 beds. Mount Kumgang has been developed as a tourist attraction, as part of a joint venture between North Korea and Hyundai, the South Korean conglomerate. Other tourist destinations include Mount Chilbo, Mount Kuwol, Mount Jongbang and the Ryongmum Cave. In 2000 plans were announced for the development, jointly with the People's Republic of China, of the western part of Mount Paektu, Korea's highest mountain, as a tourist resort. In 2003 it was estimated that around 1,500 Western tourists visited North Korea annually. It was estimated that more than 101,700 South Koreans visited the North in 2006 (of whom about 88,000 were business travellers to Kaesong), excluding visitors to Mount Kumgang.

Korea International Tourist Bureau: Pyongyang; Pres. HAN PYONG UN.

Korean International Youth Tourist Co: Mankyongdae District, Pyongyang; tel. (2) 73406; f. 1985; Dir HWANG CHUN YONG.

Kumgangsan International Tourist Co: Central District, Pyongyang; tel. (2) 31562; fax (2) 3812100; f. 1988.

National Tourism Administration of the DPRK: Central District, Pyongyang; tel. (2) 3818901; fax (2) 3814547; e-mail nta@silibank.com; f. 1953; state-run tourism promotion organization; Dir RYO SUNG CHOL.

Ryohaengsa (Korea International Travel Company): Central District, Pyongyang; tel. (2) 3817201; fax (2) 3817607; f. 1953; has relations with more than 200 tourist companies throughout the world; Pres. CHO SONG HUN.

State General Bureau of Tourism: Pyongyang; Pres. RYO HAK SONG.

THE REPUBLIC OF KOREA

Introductory Survey

Location, Climate, Language, Religion, Flag, Capital

The Republic of Korea (South Korea) forms the southern part of the Korean peninsula, in eastern Asia. To the north, separated by a frontier which roughly follows the 38th parallel, is the country's only neighbour, the Democratic People's Republic of Korea (North Korea). To the west is the Yellow Sea, to the south is the East China Sea, and to the east is the Sea of Japan. The climate is marked by cold, dry winters, with an average temperature of −6°C (21°F), and hot, humid summers, with an average temperature of 25°C (77°F). The language is Korean. Confucianism, Mahayana Buddhism, and Chundo Kyo are the principal traditional religions. Chundo Kyo is peculiar to Korea, and combines elements of Shaman, Buddhist and Christian doctrines. There are some 17.5m. Christians, of whom about 83% are Protestants. The national flag (proportions 2 by 3) comprises, in the centre of a white field, a disc divided horizontally by an S-shaped line, red above and blue below, surrounded by four configurations of parallel, broken and unbroken black bars. The capital is Seoul.

Recent History

(For more details of the history of Korea up to 1953, including the Korean War, and subsequent bilateral relations see the chapter on the Democratic People's Republic of Korea—DPRK.)

UN-supervised elections to a new legislature, the National Assembly (Kuk Hoe), took place in May 1948. The Assembly adopted a democratic Constitution, and South Korea became the independent Republic of Korea on 15 August 1948, with Dr Syngman Rhee, leader of the Liberal Party, as the country's first President. He remained in the post until his resignation in April 1960. Elections in July were won by the Democratic Party, led by Chang Myon, but his Government was deposed in May 1961 by a military coup, led by Gen. Park Chung-Hee. Power was assumed by the Supreme Council for National Reconstruction, which dissolved the National Assembly, suspended the Constitution and disbanded all existing political parties. In January 1963 the military leadership formed the Democratic Republican Party (DRP). Under a new Constitution, Gen. Park became President of the Third Republic in December.

Opposition to Park's regime led to the imposition of martial law in October 1972. A Constitution for the Fourth Republic, giving the President greatly increased powers, was approved by national referendum in November. A new body, the National Conference for Unification (NCU), was elected in December. The NCU re-elected President Park for a six-year term, and the DRP obtained a decisive majority in elections to the new National Assembly. In May 1975 opposition to the Government was effectively banned, and political trials followed. Elections to the NCU were held in May 1978, and the President was re-elected for a further six-year term in July. In October 1979 serious rioting erupted when Kim Young-Sam, the leader of the opposition New Democratic Party (NDP), was accused of subversive activities and expelled from the National Assembly. On 26 October Park was assassinated in an alleged coup attempt, led by the head of the Korean Central Intelligence Agency. Martial law was reintroduced, and in December the Prime Minister, Choi Kyu-Hah, was elected President by the NCU. A military coup in December was led by the head of the Defence Security Command, Lt-Gen. Chun Doo-Hwan, who arrested the Army Chief of Staff and effectively took power. Nevertheless, President Choi was inaugurated on 21 December to complete his predecessor's term of office (to 1984).

Choi promised liberalizing reforms, but in May 1980 demonstrations by students and confrontation with the army led to the arrest of about 30 political leaders, including Kim Dae-Jung, former head of the NDP. Martial law was extended throughout the country, the National Assembly was suspended, and all political activity was banned. Almost 200 people were killed when troops stormed the southern city of Gwangju, which had been occupied by students and dissidents. In August Choi resigned, and Gen. Chun was elected President. Acting Prime Minister Nam Duck-Woo formed a new State Council (cabinet) in September. In the same month the sentencing to death of Kim Dae-Jung for plotting rebellion was condemned internationally. (This sentence was subsequently suspended.) In October a new Constitution was overwhelmingly approved by referendum.

Martial law was ended in January 1981, and new political parties were formed. In the following month President Chun was re-elected: the start of his new term, in March, inaugurated the Fifth Republic. Chun's Democratic Justice Party (DJP) became the majority party in the new National Assembly, which was elected shortly afterwards. Amid opposition demands for liberalization, Chun pledged that he would retire at the end of his term in 1988, thus becoming the country's first Head of State to transfer power constitutionally.

During 1984, following an escalation of student unrest, the Government adopted a more flexible attitude towards dissidents. Several thousand prisoners were released, and the political 'blacklist' was finally abolished in March 1985. In January 1985 the New Korea Democratic Party (NKDP) was established by supporters of Kim Young-Sam and Kim Dae-Jung. At the general election to the National Assembly held in February, the DJP retained its majority, but the NKDP emerged as the major opposition force, boosted by the return from exile of Kim Dae-Jung. The new party secured 67 of the Assembly's 276 seats, while the DJP won 148 seats. Chun appointed a new State Council, with Lho Shin-Yong as Prime Minister. Before the opening session of the new National Assembly many deputies defected to the NKDP.

In April 1987 internal divisions within the NKDP led to the formation of a new opposition party, the Reunification Democratic Party (RDP); Kim Young-Sam was elected to its presidency in May. In April Chun unexpectedly announced the suspension of the process of reform until after the Olympic Games (due to be held in Seoul in September 1988). While confirming that he would leave office in February 1988, Chun indicated that his successor would be elected by the existing electoral college system, precipitating violent clashes between anti-Government demonstrators and riot police.

In June 1987 Roh Tae-Woo was nominated as the DJP's presidential candidate. However, Roh subsequently informed Chun that he would relinquish both the DJP chairmanship and his presidential candidature if the principal demands of the opposition for constitutional and electoral reform were not satisfied. Under international pressure, Chun acceded, and negotiations on constitutional amendments were announced. In August the DJP and the RDP announced that a bipartisan committee had agreed a draft Constitution. Among its provisions were the reintroduction of direct presidential elections by universal suffrage, and the restriction of the presidential mandate to a single five-year term; the President's emergency powers were also to be reduced, and serving military officers were to be prohibited from taking government office. Having been approved by the National Assembly, the amendments were endorsed in a national referendum in October, and the amended Constitution was promulgated shortly thereafter.

Kim Dae-Jung joined the RDP in August 1987; however, in November he became President of a new Peace and Democracy Party (PDP), and declared himself a rival presidential candidate. At the election, in December, Roh Tae-Woo won some 36% of the votes, while Kim Dae-Jung and Kim Young-Sam each achieved about 27%. Roh Tae-Woo was inaugurated as President on 25 February 1988, whereupon the Sixth Republic was established. At the general election to the National Assembly, in April, the DJP failed to achieve an overall majority, securing 125 of the 299 seats. The PDP achieved 70 seats, thus becoming the main opposition party; the remainder went to the RDP and the New Democratic Republican Party (NDRP—the revived and renamed DRP), led by Kim Jong-Pil.

In February 1990 the DJP merged with the RDP and the NDRP to form the Democratic Liberal Party (DLP). Roh was subsequently elected President of the DLP, while Kim Young-Sam and Kim Jong-Pil were elected as two of the party's three Chairmen. The DLP thus controlled more than two-thirds of the seats in the National Assembly. The PDP, effectively isolated as the sole opposition party, condemned the merger and demanded new elections. In March a new opposition group, the Democratic Party (DP), was formed, largely comprising members of the RDP who had opposed the merger.

In July 1990 a large rally was held in Seoul to denounce the adoption by the National Assembly of several items of controversial legislation, including proposals to restructure the military leadership and to reorganize the broadcasting media. In protest, all the opposition members of the National Assembly tendered their resignations. Although the Assembly's Speaker refused to accept the resignations, the PDP deputies returned to the National Assembly only in November, following an agreement with the DLP that local council elections would take place in the first half of 1991, to be followed by gubernatorial and mayoral elections in 1992. The DLP also agreed to abandon plans for the transfer, by constitutional amendment, of executive powers to the State Council. The local elections (the first to be held in the Republic of Korea for 30 years) took place in March and June 1991, and resulted in a decisive victory for the DLP.

Meanwhile, in April 1991 the PDP merged with the smaller opposition Party for New Democratic Alliance to form the New Democratic Party (NDP). In September the NDP and the DP agreed to merge (under the latter's name) to form a stronger opposition front. A further opposition group, the Unification National Party (UNP), was established in January 1992 by Chung Ju-Yung, the founder and honorary chairman of the powerful Hyundai industrial conglomerate.

At elections to the National Assembly in March 1992 the DLP unexpectedly failed to secure an absolute majority, obtaining a total of 149 of the 299 seats. The remainder of the seats were won by the DP (97), the UNP (31) and independent candidates (21). In May Kim Young-Sam was chosen as the DLP's candidate for the presidential election, scheduled for December, and in August he replaced Roh as the party's President; divisions within the DLP led to defections from the party by opponents of Kim Young-Sam.

The presidential election, on 18 December 1992, was won by Kim Young-Sam, with some 42% of the votes cast. Kim (who was inaugurated on 25 February 1993) was the first South Korean President since 1960 without military connections. The defeated Kim Dae-Jung subsequently announced his retirement from politics. In February 1993 Chung Ju-Yung resigned as President of the United People's Party (UPP—as the UNP had been renamed), following allegations that he had embezzled Hyundai finances to fund his election campaign. Kim Young-Sam appointed Hwang In-Sung as Prime Minister, and a new State Council was formed.

Kim Young-Sam acted swiftly to honour his campaign pledge to eliminate corruption in business and politics; in all, during 1993, Kim's anti-corruption measures were reported to have resulted in the dismissal of, or disciplinary action against, some 3,000 business, government and military officials. One of Roh Tae-Woo's former Ministers of National Defence, Lee Jong-Koo, was sentenced in November 1993 to three years' imprisonment, after having been convicted of accepting bribes from defence contractors. At the same time the announcement of measures to restrict the activities of the country's industrial conglomerates (*chaebol*) was accompanied by corruption proceedings against several prominent business executives. In November Chung Ju-Yung was sentenced to three years' imprisonment, although the sentence was suspended on account of his age (78) and past contribution to South Korean economic development.

Hwang In-Sung resigned as Prime Minister in December 1993 and was succeeded by Lee Hoi-Chang, hitherto Chairman of the Board of Audit and Inspection (BAI). However, he resigned in April 1994 and was replaced by Lee Yung-Duk, latterly the Deputy Prime Minister responsible for national unification.

In July 1994 the UPP and a smaller opposition party, the New Political Reform Party, merged to form the New People's Party (NPP). In October the Government announced that its inquiry into the role played by former Presidents Chun and Roh in the 1979 coup had found that both had participated in a 'premeditated military rebellion'. Prosecution proceedings were not initiated at this stage. In December 1994 Lee Hong-Koo (hitherto the Deputy Prime Minister responsible for national unification) was appointed Prime Minister, as part of a major restructuring of the State Council.

The DLP fared badly at elections for gubernatorial, mayoral and other municipal and provincial posts in May 1995 (the first full local elections to be held in the Republic of Korea for 34 years). A contributory factor to the DLP's poor performance was the success of a new party, the United Liberal Democrats (ULD), established in March by defectors from the DLP and led by Kim Jong-Pil (who had resigned as DLP Chairman earlier in the year). In September Kim Dae-Jung returned to politics, establishing his own party, the National Congress for New Politics (NCNP). The DP was severely undermined when many of its members left to join the NCNP.

A major scandal erupted in October 1995, when Roh Tae-Woo admitted in a televised address that he had amassed a large sum of money during his term of office. He was arrested in the following month; at his trial, which opened in December, Roh confessed to having received donations from South Korean businesses, but denied that these constituted bribes. Many senior politicians and business leaders were also detained and interrogated in connection with the affair. Kim Dae-Jung, meanwhile, unexpectedly admitted that his campaign for the 1992 presidential election had been supported by a donation of money from Roh's 'slush fund'. Kim Young-Sam denied opposition allegations that he too had benefited from a similar donation. In December 1995, in an effort to distance his party from the deepening scandal, Kim Young-Sam changed the DLP's name to the New Korea Party (NKP). A major reorganization of the State Council was effected, in which Lee Hong-Koo was replaced as Prime Minister by Lee Soo-Sung, the President of Seoul National University.

In late 1995 it was announced that Roh Tae-Woo and Chun Doo-Hwan were to be prosecuted for their involvement in the 1979 coup and the 1980 Gwangju massacre. Chun was arrested in December 1995, and in the following month he was additionally accused of accumulating a huge political 'slush fund'. At the opening of his trial for corruption in February 1996 Chun denied charges that the fund had been amassed as a result of bribe-taking. Legal proceedings in connection with the events of 1979 and 1980 opened in March 1996: Chun was charged with mutiny for his organization of the 1979 coup, and with sedition in connection with the Gwangju massacre, while Roh was charged with aiding Chun. Roh and Chun were convicted as charged in August 1996. For their role in the *coup d'état* and the Gwangju massacre, Chun was sentenced to death and Roh to $22\frac{1}{2}$ years' imprisonment; each was heavily fined in the corruption cases. Several others were also convicted for their part in the events of 1979 and 1980. Following an appeal, in which their contribution to the country's impressive economic growth and to the establishment of democratic government were cited as mitigating factors, Chun's sentence was commuted to one of life imprisonment, while Roh's term of imprisonment was reduced to 17 years.

Elections to the National Assembly took place in April 1996. Contrary to widespread predictions, the NKP only narrowly failed to retain its parliamentary majority, winning a total of 139 of the 299 seats. One factor contributing to the NKP's success was believed to have been the recent incursions into the demilitarized zone (DMZ, separating North and South Korea) by North Korean troops, which, although apparently intended to destabilize the electoral proceedings, in fact caused many voters to favour the ruling party out of concern for national security. The NCNP performed less well than had been expected, taking 79 seats; moreover, the party's leader, Kim Dae-Jung, failed to win a seat. By the time the National Assembly convened in June, the NKP had secured a working majority with the support of several opposition and independent members.

The revision of the country's labour laws, to introduce greater flexibility into the employment market (a condition of the Republic of Korea's impending membership of the Organisation for Economic Co-operation and Development—OECD, see p. 358), was initiated in May 1996. Reforms proposed by the Government in early December were severely criticized by trade unions and opposition parties. Many thousands of factory workers, as well as public sector employees, participated in a strike called by the country's principal workers' confederation, the Federation of Korean Trade Unions (FKTU), after the Government convened a dawn session of the National Assembly, which approved the labour reform bill in the absence of opposition deputies. Anti-Government demonstrators in Seoul and other major cities frequently clashed with riot police, and warrants were issued for the arrest of several leaders of the Korean Confederation of Trade Unions (KCTU). Concern was expressed that President Kim might be resorting to a more authoritarian style of leadership, particularly when it was alleged that the DPRK was lending its support to the striking workers (a tactic used by the South Korean authorities in the past to justify the suppression of domestic dissent); furthermore, foreign labour officials were threatened with deportation for encouraging union action. By mid-January 1997 support for the strikes was abating;

the KCTU proposed weekly one-day stoppages, in order to minimize financial losses, and suggested that it might accept a modification of the labour law, having previously insisted on its complete annulment. OECD issued a severe rebuke to the Government for failing to honour its pledges on labour reform, and, in a significant concession, Kim agreed to meet the leaders of the opposition parties to discuss amendments to the law; warrants for the arrest of union leaders were also suspended. In March the National Assembly approved a revised version of the legislation, whereby the implementation of certain proposals was delayed for two years, while the KCTU was granted immediate official recognition.

Meanwhile, political and economic scandals persisted throughout 1996, particularly concerning allegations of bribery, which resulted in several government resignations. The infiltration of a North Korean submarine into South Korean waters in September (see below) resulted in the dismissal of the Minister of Defence, Lee Yang-Ho. He was subsequently charged with divulging classified information and with receiving bribes in connection with the procurement of helicopters for the army, and in December was sentenced to four years' imprisonment.

In January 1997 a further major scandal erupted when Hanbo, one of the country's largest steel and construction conglomerates, was declared bankrupt. Allegations were made that Hanbo had bribed the Government to exert pressure on banks to provide substantial loans to the conglomerate. The chief executives of several large Korean banks were arrested on charges of receiving bribes, and in February the Minister of Home Affairs, Kim Woo-Suk, resigned following allegations that he too had accepted payments from the company. President Kim issued an official apology for the loan scandal, and in March Lee Soo-Sung resigned as Prime Minister in a gesture of contrition. He was replaced by Goh Kun, hitherto President of Myongju University. The repercussions of the Hanbo affair widened further, implicating, among others, Kim Soo-Han, the Speaker of the National Assembly, and President Kim himself, whose 1992 election campaign was alleged to have been funded partially by the conglomerate. In June 1997 the former Chairman of Hanbo and several senior banking officials and politicians, including Kim Woo-Suk, were convicted on charges relating to the scandal.

In July 1997 Lee Hoi-Chang, former Prime Minister and Chairman of the NKP, was nominated as the ruling party's candidate for the presidential election, scheduled for December. Lee's candidacy was severely affected by various scandals surrounding the NKP and his family. Moreover, Rhee In-Je, the defeated challenger in the contest for the NKP nomination, decided to contest the presidency, subsequently forming his own political organization, the New Party by the People. In September Lee was elected President of the NKP, replacing Kim Young-Sam, who subsequently resigned from the party in order to ensure his neutrality in the forthcoming election. In October the NCNP and the ULD established an alliance, uniting behind the NCNP presidential nominee, Kim Dae-Jung. In November the NKP announced its merger with the DP, to form the Grand National Party (GNP).

However, internal party politics were overshadowed by the crisis experienced by the Korean economy in the latter half of 1997. Many of the *chaebol* reported serious financial difficulties, having amassed huge debts which they were subsequently unable to service. Measures aimed at stabilizing the financial markets, announced in October, were unsuccessful. Moreover, in an unexpected reversal of its non-interventionist policy, the Government declared that part of the Kia Group, which was close to collapse, was to be nationalized, in an attempt to prevent further bankruptcies. Following the rejection by the legislature of the Government's financial liberalization measures, President Kim dismissed Kang Kyung-Shik, the Deputy Prime Minister and Minister of Finance and the Economy, in November, replacing him with Lim Chang-Yul, latterly Minister of Trade, Industry and Energy. An extensive economic stabilization programme, announced shortly afterwards, had little effect in curbing the depreciation of the national currency, the won, and the Government was forced to request the assistance of the IMF, a decision that was condemned by opposition politicians and the media as a 'national shame'. The true extent of the country's economic crisis became apparent in December upon the conclusion of negotiations with the IMF, which agreed to allocate substantial funds to prevent the Republic of Korea from defaulting on its repayments of external debt. Provision of the loans remained conditional upon the implementation of a programme of extensive financial and economic reforms.

The presidential election, held on 18 December 1997, was narrowly won by Kim Dae-Jung. Supporters of the ruling NKP were divided between Lee Hoi-Chang and Rhee In-Je, thus assuring victory for the NCNP-ULD alliance and the first peaceful transfer of power to an opposition politician in the Republic of Korea's history. Four other candidates contested the election. In a gesture to promote a sense of national unity, former Presidents Chun Doo-Hwan and Roh Tae-Woo were granted a presidential pardon and released from prison.

Legislation for financial reforms, to comply with the terms of the IMF agreement, was approved by the National Assembly in late December 1997. Discussions with South Korea's overseas creditors to renegotiate the terms of the country's debt repayments were successfully concluded at the end of January 1998. Compulsory reform of the *chaebol*, which had been widely criticized for contributing to the debt-repayment crisis through their extensive borrowing, and legislation to allow foreign investors to acquire majority shareholdings in South Korean companies, were among reform measures promulgated in early 1998.

Kim Dae-Jung was formally inaugurated as President in late February 1998. Despite resistance from the opposition, Kim Dae-Jung designated Kim Jong-Pil, the leader of the ULD, as acting Prime Minister, and a Cabinet was formed in early March, with the ministries divided equally between the NCNP and the ULD. Various administrative reforms were implemented, including the abolition of the two posts of Deputy Prime Minister, the merger of the Ministries for Home Affairs and Government Administration and a reduction in the powers of the Ministry of Finance and the Economy. The number of cabinet ministers was reduced to 17 (excluding the Prime Minister).

At the beginning of May 1998 a large rally organized by the KCTU in protest at job losses ended in violent clashes with riot police. Later in that month a two-day strike was called to demand that the Government fully honour its pledge to improve unemployment benefits and to reform the *chaebol*; according to the KCTU, some 120,000 workers supported the first day of the strike. The NCNP and the ULD performed well in local elections in June, although the turn-out was low. As the economic recession deepened, labour unrest increased. Tens of thousands participated in strikes in July to protest against rising unemployment, the Government's privatization proposals and plans from Hyundai Motor and Daewoo Motor for mass redundancies.

In August 1998 the National Assembly formally confirmed Kim Jong-Pil as Prime Minister, following months of legislative inactivity, during which the GNP had refused to support his nomination. However, the GNP boycotted parliamentary sessions throughout September and into October, further delaying the consideration of urgent economic reforms, in protest at a government anti-corruption campaign, which it claimed was partisan and aimed at dividing the opposition. Several GNP members were placed under investigation on suspicion of illegally raising electoral campaign funds. In late October three former aides to Lee Hoi-Chang were charged in connection with an alleged attempt to bribe North Korean officials to organize a border incursion into the DMZ in December 1997, with the aim of aiding Lee's campaign for the presidency. The dispute escalated in December 1998, when a number of opposition deputies entered a room in the assembly buildings, which was being used by the intelligence agency, and removed confidential documents on 44 politicians. The GNP claimed that the agency had been carrying out surveillance of opposition deputies and subsequently boycotted legislative proceedings. In early January 1999, as the boycott continued, the ruling parties unilaterally endorsed 130 bills without debate, including legislation on banking reform and the endorsement of a controversial fishing agreement with Japan (see below). In mid-January, however, the ruling and opposition parties agreed that all issues relating to the affair be referred to the National Assembly's steering committee.

In May 1999 a major reorganization of the State Council was effected. However, in June corruption scandals led to the replacement of the new Ministers of Justice and the Environment, and were believed to have contributed to the ruling coalition's failure to retain two parliamentary seats in by-elections held in that month. In July Kim Dae-Jung and Kim Jong-Pil agreed not to seek a constitutional amendment on the adoption of a parliamentary, rather than presidential, system of government in 1999, despite protests from several senior ULD members.

THE REPUBLIC OF KOREA (SOUTH KOREA)

As the next legislative elections approached, in January 2000 Kim Jong-Pil resigned as Prime Minister to chair the ULD, nominating Park Tae-Joon, the founder of Pohang Iron and Steel Company, as his successor. Kim Dae-Jung reorganized the State Council, as a number of ministers resigned to concentrate on campaigning for parliamentary seats. Lee Hun-Jai, hitherto the Chairman of the Financial Supervisory Commission, was appointed as Minister of Finance and the Economy. Kim Dae-Jung established a new party, the Millennium Democratic Party (MDP), to succeed the ruling NCNP, having reportedly failed in attempts to effect a merger with the ULD. In February the National Assembly approved revisions to the election law, which reduced the number of legislative seats from 299 to 273 (227 directly elected and 46 allocated by proportional representation), and reversed a ban on campaigning by civic groups against candidates. A proposal by the MDP for the introduction of a two-ballot system was rejected by the National Assembly; the ULD was believed to have voted with the opposition GNP against its coalition partner. Lee Han-Dong, recently elected as President of the ULD, subsequently announced the party's withdrawal from the ruling coalition, claiming that the MDP had failed to fulfil its electoral pledges, although Prime Minister Park was to remain in the Government.

The elections to the National Assembly were held on 13 April 2000. The GNP, which won 133 of the 273 seats, retained its position as the largest party in the Assembly, but remained four seats short of a majority. The ruling MDP secured 115 seats, while the ULD suffered a serious reverse, taking only 17 seats (compared with 50 in the 1996 elections). Only two seats were won by the Democratic People's Party (DPP), which had been formed in February by defectors from the GNP who had failed to be nominated as parliamentary candidates by their former party. In mid-May Park resigned as Prime Minister, amid increasing controversy over allegations of tax evasion. The designation of Lee Han-Dong as Park's successor indicated a restoration of MDP-ULD co-operation. Amid criticism that reform of the *chaebol* was proceeding too slowly, President Kim Dae-Jung effected a major government reorganization in August, which primarily concerned the economic portfolios.

President Kim enjoyed increasing respect within the international community, in October 2000 being awarded the Nobel Peace Prize for his contribution to democracy and human rights (and particularly for his successful attempts at reconciliation with the DPRK). However, his pursuit of reunification was criticized domestically by those who felt that, with its own economic problems, the Republic of Korea could ill afford assistance to the DPRK.

In November 2000 Kim Yong-Kap, a GNP member of the National Assembly, described the ruling MDP as 'a subsidiary' of the (North) Korean Workers' Party. The comments shocked and embarrassed both the MDP and the GNP, and the National Assembly was suspended. However, shortly after the legislature reconvened on the following evening, the GNP walked out in protest at an MDP motion to dismiss Kim Yong-Kap from his seat. A few days later there was renewed tension in the National Assembly as the GNP walked out again, this time prompted by the MDP's obstruction of a motion to impeach the Prosecutor-General, Park Soon-Yong, for alleged bias in the investigation of irregularities during the April elections. The GNP returned to the session one week later.

During 2000 and early 2001 dissatisfaction with the Government manifested itself on numerous occasions in the form of industrial and agricultural unrest. Strike action by doctors over legislation depriving physicians of their right to prescribe drugs took place in June 2000 and again in October. Mounting public anger obliged the abandonment of the renewed strike. In the following month farmers held a strike to demand that their debts be cancelled and that the Government intervene on their behalf at the World Trade Organization (WTO, see p. 410). Meanwhile, as the Daewoo Motor Company had been declared bankrupt, some 15,000 workers protested in November in Seoul against government-led corporate restructuring which would result, it was feared, in large-scale retrenchment.

In January 2001 a minor reorganization of the State Council was effected, when changes included Jin Nyum's elevation to the post of Deputy Prime Minister for Finance and the Economy. Simultaneously, a government organization law came into effect that conferred the status of Deputy Prime Minister on the portfolios of Finance and Economy and of Education and Human Resources; a Ministry of Gender Equality was also created. In March there was a major reorganization of the State Council, following the resignation of the Minister of Foreign Affairs and Trade, Lee Joung-Binn, who had caused controversy by signing a joint statement with Russia criticizing the USA's planned 'national missile defence' (NMD) system. Han Seung-Soo, a member of the Democratic People's Party, replaced him. The former Minister of Culture, Park Jie-Won, who had resigned in September 2000 following allegations of corruption, was appointed chief presidential policy adviser. Park had organized the historic inter-Korean summit in June 2000 (see below).

In early April 2001 the minor opposition DPP joined the ruling MDP-led coalition, despite protests from within the MDP. Later in that month the MDP suffered a defeat in local by-elections, and by May Kim Dae-Jung's popularity had fallen sharply, as voters grew disillusioned by his failure to implement political reforms. President Kim had also received criticism for his appointment of ministers and advisers from his home region of Jeolla, in the south-west, thereby antagonizing the south-eastern Gyeongsang region.

In August 2001 the Minister of Unification, Lim Dong-Won, came under heavy criticism from the opposition after delegates from several South Korean non-governmental organizations (NGOs) travelled to the North to mark the anniversary of Korean liberation from Japanese rule, on 15 August. In September Lim was forced to resign after the National Assembly approved a motion of no confidence in him, organized by the GNP and supported by the MDP's coalition partner, the ULD. The latter's actions effectively dissolved the ruling coalition, and President Kim appointed four new ministers. Lim was immediately appointed presidential adviser on reunification, national security and foreign affairs, reaffirming Kim's confidence in him.

In October 2001 the GNP won three by-elections, increasing its seats in the National Assembly to 136—just one short of a majority. The opposition victory created new rifts within the ruling MDP between younger reformers and party veterans, and President Kim resigned from the party presidency in November, ostensibly in order to administer state affairs without being involved in party disputes. He was succeeded, on an interim basis, by Han Kwang-Ok. By early December some eight presidential candidates had emerged within the MDP.

In late January 2002 President Kim again reorganized the State Council, dismissing the Minister of Unification, Hong Soon-Young (who had been appointed only in September), and reallocating seven other posts, as well as the positions of six of the eight senior presidential secretaries and his chief of staff. Park Jie-Won returned as Kim's special aide for policy, emphasizing his close relationship with the President. The changes were intended to strengthen Kim's authority during his final year in office. Within days, the Minister of Foreign Affairs and Trade, Han Seung-Soo, was also dismissed, owing to the country's strained relations with the USA.

The contest for the MDP's presidential nomination intensified during February 2002 as putative reformist candidates sought to present a joint candidate, and opponents of the leading contender, Rhee In-Je, moved against him. The opposition GNP also experienced a power struggle, resulting in the departure of the party Vice-President, Park Geun-Hye (daughter of former military ruler Park Chung-Hee), initially with the intention of standing for the presidency as an independent candidate. In May Park established a new party, the Korean Coalition for the Future (KCF), serving as its Chairwoman.

Meanwhile, in mid-2001 and early 2002 strike action was taken by employees of several sectors, notably airline pilots, nurses, railway staff and energy workers, who were protesting against various issues including the decline in real wage levels, privatization plans and shortened working hours. Intermittent strike action continued.

By late April 2002 Roh Moo-Hyun had secured the MDP presidential nomination, while the GNP remained mired in internal disputes; the party's eight vice-presidents all resigned on 24 March in order to 'renew the face of the party', and were succeeded by a collective leadership. Meanwhile, Lee Hoi-Chang had secured the GNP's nomination for the national presidency. Also in mid-April President Kim replaced the Deputy Prime Minister for Finance and the Economy, Jin Nyum, with Jeon Yun-Churl, hitherto the chief of staff to the President.

President Kim and six of his ministers resigned from the MDP in May 2002, in order to focus on state affairs during the final months of Kim's presidency. Kim had become increasingly embarrassed by corruption scandals involving his second and third sons, Kim Hong-Up and Kim Hong-Gul respectively, and he publicly apologized for their behaviour. In June Kim Hong-

Gul was charged with bribery and tax evasion, and subsequently went on trial. Kim Hong-Up was arrested later that month, accused of receiving bribes from businessmen. Both were subsequently sentenced to prison terms, although the two-year sentence of the latter was suspended for three years. The scandals adversely affected the MDP's performance in local elections held in mid-June.

In July 2002 President Kim reorganized the cabinet, nominating Chang Sang, hitherto President of Ewha Woman's University, as the country's first female Prime Minister. At the same time, six ministers were replaced. However, at the end of the month the National Assembly rejected Chang's appointment on the grounds of dubious property dealings and the fact that her son had adopted US citizenship. In her place, President Kim nominated Chang Dae-Whan, a former newspaper proprietor, but he too was rejected by the National Assembly in late August on the grounds of questionable financial practices. A third nominee, Kim Suk-Soo, a former Supreme Court judge and previously Head of the National Election Commission, was finally accepted by the National Assembly in October, thus ending months of political paralysis.

The MDP suffered further set-backs in by-elections held in August 2002 when the GNP won 11 out of 13 seats contested, giving it an overall majority in the National Assembly. In September Chung Mong-Joon (the sixth son of Hyundai founder Chung Ju-Yung), who was President of the Korean Football Association, announced that he was standing for the country's presidency. Chung's popularity had risen sharply following the Republic of Korea's successful co-hosting of the 2002 football World Cup. In November Chung formally established his 'National Unity 21' party, receiving support from a broad political spectrum. However, later in that month Chung and Roh agreed to present a joint candidate for the presidency, namely the latter, in order to prevent Lee Hoi-Chang's election as President in December. Under the terms of the Roh-Chung partnership, there was to be a constitutional amendment whereby the powers of the presidency would be reduced in favour of those of the Prime Minister. In the final months of 2002 the ruling MDP became mired in further scandals. In October it emerged that President Kim and Chung Mong-Joon had arranged for a Hyundai subsidiary to transfer a substantial sum of money to North Korea via the (Southern) state-owned Korea Development Bank prior to the historic inter-Korean summit of June 2000 (see below), effectively 'buying' the meeting. In November Park Geun-Hye, who had left the opposition GNP earlier in the year to form the new KCF (see above), agreed with Lee Hoi-Chang to merge her party with the GNP.

None the less, the presidential election, held on 19 December 2002, was narrowly won by Roh Moo-Hyun, who received 48.9% of the votes cast, against Lee Hoi-Chang's 46.6%. The level of participation was estimated at 70.8%. Roh's victory, despite the late withdrawal of Chung Mong-Joon's support, was generally attributed to his uncompromising stance in favour of a foreign policy more independent from the USA, whereas Lee was widely seen as having very close relations with the US Government. The MDP accused the USA of supporting Lee in the election, citing a meeting between him and the US ambassador. Relations with the USA (see below) had thus become a major election issue.

In January 2003 President-elect Roh began making various appointments. Goh Kun, hitherto the president of Transparency International Korea, an anti-corruption agency, and himself a former Prime Minister, was reappointed to that post, while Moon Hee-Sang, an MDP legislator, was appointed chief of staff, and concurrently Chairman of the Civil Service Commission. Roh was inaugurated on 25 February and promptly appointed a new cabinet. President Roh also reorganized the military and intelligence services, appointing Gen. Kim Jong-Hwan as Chairman of the Joint Chiefs of Staff, and Ko Young-Koo, a human rights lawyer, as director of the National Intelligence Service (NIS). The latter appointment reflected Roh's determination to depoliticize the agency, which had been responsible for surveillance of political figures even after the transition to democracy.

President Roh confronted immediate challenges on assuming office, most notably a diplomatic crisis between the DPRK and the USA. Other issues included the ongoing scandal surrounding Hyundai and the inter-Korean summit meeting of 2000. In March 2003 Roh appointed a special counsel to investigate the alleged transfer of funds by Hyundai to the DPRK in connection with the 2000 presidential summit meeting (see below). In the longer term Roh aimed to address regional imbalances and the disparity between rich and poor, to reduce corruption in business and the economy and to improve living standards and labour management.

In April 2003 the GNP won two out of three seats in by-elections to the National Assembly, raising its total representation to 153. However, the victory of a reformist ally of the MDP, Rhyu Si-Min, was welcomed by the Government as an indication of support for the reform process. Also in April, the National Assembly voted in favour of the dispatch of South Korean troops to support US military action in Iraq in a non-combat capacity. Despite his independent stance on relations with the USA, President Roh justified the decision in terms of strengthening Korean-US relations. Several hundred South Korean military medical and engineering personnel were sent to Iraq in May, despite widespread public opposition to the deployment.

In June 2003 two aides of former President Kim Dae-Jung, former Minister of Unification Lim Dong-Won and former Minister of Culture and Tourism Park Jie-Won, were charged in connection with illegal payments made through the Hyundai group to the DPRK to arrange the 2000 presidential summit meeting (Lim received an 18-month prison sentence in September, and Park was sentenced to 12 years' imprisonment in December). Also implicated in the scandal was Hyundai heir Chung Mong-Hun, who committed suicide in August.

In September 2003 a faction of the MDP announced its intention to form a new party, owing to internal divisions over corruption and other issues. President Roh subsequently relinquished his membership of the MDP, although he did not commit himself to joining the new organization, which was named the Uri (meaning 'our') Party in October. A large number of MDP legislators, including MDP Chairman Chyung Dai-Chul, joined the Uri Party, thus leaving the MDP with only 62 seats in the National Assembly. The Uri Party was officially inaugurated in November under a temporary leadership (Chung Dong-Young was elected Uri Party Chairman in early 2004). Another development in September, meanwhile, was the resignation of the Minister of Home Affairs, Kim Doo-Kwan, following an incident in which protesters had infiltrated a US base in Pocheon. The National Assembly had approved Kim Doo-Kwan's dismissal, despite President Roh's policy of increased independence in relations with the USA. In October there was renewed public protest over the country's involvement in Iraq, which intensified in late 2003 following the killing there of two South Korean engineers.

President Roh's declining popularity was further undermined in October 2003 by the investigation and subsequent arrest of his former aide Choi Do-Sul, who was accused of having received illegal funds from the SK Group following the 2002 presidential election. In an attempt to restore his popularity, Roh announced proposals for a referendum to be held on the issue of his presidency later in the year. However, the proposed referendum prompted further political instability, with Prime Minister Goh Kun and other government ministers offering their resignations (which were rejected by President Roh). Both the GNP and the MDP dismissed the referendum proposal as unconstitutional.

Official investigations into illegal campaign funding from leading *chaebol* during the 2002 presidential election, involving both the MDP and the GNP, were instigated in October 2003. Initially focusing on donations from the SK Group, the investigation widened in November, with forcible searches taking place at the offices of other *chaebol*, including Hyundai, LG Group and Samsung. At the end of November President Roh vetoed a bill, already approved by the National Assembly, which urged an independent investigation into the funding allegations. In December the National Assembly voted to rescind the veto, in the first reversal of a presidential decision since 1954. An independent investigator was subsequently appointed. In the same month President Roh announced that he would step down if the MDP were found by the investigation to have received one-tenth of the illegal funding taken by the GNP. In a further development in December 2003, the GNP's Lee Hoi-Chang, Roh's rival in the 2002 election, publicly admitted that his party had accepted US $42m. in illegal donations.

In January 2004 the Minister of Foreign Affairs and Trade, Yoon Young-Kwan, relinquished his post, reportedly following criticism of presidential policy by his advisers. The dispute was widely reported to have been related to President Roh's policy on independence from the USA over issues such as the North Korean nuclear weapons programme, but there was also a suggestion that Yoon Young-Kwan's departure was due to unrelated internal divisions. Yoon Young-Kwan was replaced by Ban

Ki-Moon. There were further government changes in February, following the resignation of Kim Jin-Pyo, the Deputy Prime Minister for Finance and the Economy, in order to stand as a Uri Party candidate in the legislative elections scheduled for April. Kim was replaced as Deputy Prime Minister by Lee Hun-Jai, and three further new ministers were appointed in the same month. Also in February, the National Assembly approved the deployment of an additional 3,000 non-combat troops to Iraq (the deployment was later delayed owing to security concerns—see below).

Meanwhile, investigations into political corruption continued in early 2004, and both the former MDP Chairman, Chyung Dai-Chul (now of the Uri Party), and the former Secretary-General of the GNP, Kim Young-Iel, were arrested. In February there was also speculation that Park Geun-Hye, who had returned to the GNP in advance of the 2002 elections (see above), had received undeclared funds from the GNP for the purposes of a merger with her KCF. In March 2004 it was reported that President Roh's MDP election campaign had received 12,500m. won in illicit funds, amounting to one-seventh of the 84,000m. allegedly received by the GNP and thus to more than the proportion of one-tenth that Roh had previously stated would prompt his resignation. At the end of March it was confirmed that Roh's former aide Choi Do-Sul (see above) had received US $530,000 in illegal funding.

As the legislative election of April 2004 approached, there were dramatic developments in mid-March with the impeachment of President Roh over the issue of his support for the pro-Government Uri Party, whereby he had allegedly violated electoral law. A total of 193 legislators, mostly from the GNP and Roh's former party, the MDP, voted in favour of the impeachment. There were vehement protests from supporters of President Roh in the National Assembly and members of the public following the vote, with opinion polls indicating that around 70% of the population did not support the impeachment. President Roh's position was to be reviewed by the Constitutional Court within six months, with Prime Minister Goh Kun becoming acting head of state for this period.

At the elections to the National Assembly on 15 April 2004, the Uri Party won a narrow majority in the legislature, securing 152 seats of the total of 299 in the newly expanded chamber (243 of which were determined by direct election and the remainder by proportional representation). The GNP, now under the leadership of Park Geun-Hye, secured 121 seats. Roh's former party, the MDP, won only nine seats. The success of the Uri Party was seen as a victory for Roh and an expression of public disapproval of his impeachment. It was believed that the Uri Party's majority might have been greater had it not been for comments made during the election campaign by the party's leader, Chung Dong-Young, who had offended older voters by suggesting that their participation in the election was unimportant. (Chung subsequently resigned as head of the Uri Party and was replaced by Shin Ki-Nam.) In May Roh was reinstated following the decision of the Constitutional Court to dismiss the case for impeachment. He became a formal member of the Uri Party in the same month.

Following the reinstatement of President Roh, Prime Minister Goh Kun resigned from his post; Lee Hae-Chan, a former education minister, was approved by the National Assembly as Prime Minister in June. After his appointment, three new ministerial appointments were made, including that of Chung Dong-Young as Minister of Unification. Also in June, the Government announced that the deployment of 3,000 South Korean troops to Iraq, originally approved in February (see above), would take place in August. Public opposition to this decision increased dramatically a few days later when a South Korean translator, Kim Sun-Il, who had been taken hostage in Iraq, was beheaded by his captors. In July the Minister of National Defence, Cho Young-Kil, resigned, taking responsibility for an incident in which a South Korean ship had fired warning shots at a North Korean vessel believed to be intruding in South Korean waters, with naval staff reportedly having failed to report radio communication with the North Korean ship. Cho was replaced by Yoon Kwang-Woong. Meanwhile, during mid-2004 there were various instances of labour unrest, including strikes by subway workers and by employees of a major oil company. In August President Roh announced that investigations were to be held into the past conduct of politicians during the period of Japanese rule and of dictatorial governments extending into the 1980s. The first political leader to be adversely affected by these investigations was Uri Party leader Shin Ki-Nam, who was forced to resign after it was found that his father had committed human rights abuses as a policeman during the period of Japanese colonization. Shin was replaced by Lee Bu-Young. In September controversy arose over the anti-communist national security law, which dated back to the country's pre-democratic era. (The law had been invoked, for example, in the case of Korean-German scholar Song Doo-Yul, who had been charged under the law in 2003 in connection with his alleged links to North Korea.) Human rights groups, supported by President Roh, claimed that the law was outdated and subject to abuse. However, proposals to abolish the law were rejected by the Supreme Court. In October 2004 a number of reform bills submitted to the National Assembly by the Uri Party included a renewed attempt to abolish the national security law, amid strong opposition from the GNP. In November there were further instances of labour unrest in protest at government plans to reform labour legislation to prohibit strikes by public sector workers and to allow employers to hire staff on a temporary basis. In December the National Assembly approved a proposal for South Korean troops in Iraq to remain there until the end of 2005, despite continuing strong public opposition to the deployment.

A number of government changes took place in January 2005. In March the Deputy Prime Minister for Finance and the Economy, Lee Hun-Jai, resigned as a result of controversy over his wife's real-estate investments. He was replaced by Han Duck-Soo, hitherto the Minister of Government Policy Co-ordination. Further government changes took place in June, when Roh appointed Chun Jung-Bae as Minister of Justice and Lee Jae-Yong as Minister of the Environment.

In January 2005 Lee Bu-Young resigned from the leadership of the Uri Party, citing his party's failure to realize its reform aims such as the abolition of the anti-communist national security law. Moon Hee-Sang was elected party leader in April. The Uri Party had lost its majority in the National Assembly in the previous month when the Supreme Court upheld the convictions of two party legislators for malpractice in the election of April 2004, thereby depriving them of their seats and reducing the party's representation to 146. In all, six of the legislators elected in April 2004 had subsequently lost their seats as a result of malpractice convictions, temporarily reducing the National Assembly to 293 seats. At by-elections held in late April 2005 to fill these vacancies, the opposition GNP took five of the six contested seats, with the sixth being won by an independent candidate. In May it was announced that the MDP was changing its name to the Democratic Party (DP). From July President Roh repeatedly proposed that a coalition government be formed between the Uri Party and the GNP, offering in turn to relinquish some of the powers of his office. The proposal was comprehensively rejected by GNP Chairwoman Park Geun-Hye. Another round of by-elections was held in October to replace two legislators from the Uri Party and two from the GNP who had lost their seats, again owing to convictions for electoral malpractice. The GNP won all four contested seats, thereby further reducing the Uri Party's parliamentary representation to 144 and prompting the resignation of the party's senior leadership, including Chairman Moon. Chung Sye-Kyun was appointed acting Chairman pending a leadership election in February 2006. Former party Chairman Chung Dong-Young resigned as Minister of Unification in December 2005 in order to stand in the leadership election, as did Kim Geun-Tae, the Minister of Health and Welfare.

Consequently, in January 2006 President Roh effected a government reorganization. Notably, Rhyu Si-Min was appointed Minister of Health and Welfare, while Lee Jong-Seok became Minister of Unification and acting Uri Party Chairman Chung Sye-Kyun was appointed Minister of Commerce, Industry and Energy (his replacement as acting Chairman was Yoo Jay-Kun). At the Uri Party's national convention in February Chung Dong-Young was elected to the post of Chairman for a second time. Another series of ministerial nominations was announced in March, to replace government members who subsequently resigned in order to stand at the forthcoming mayoral and gubernatorial elections scheduled for May. Also in March a scandal developed concerning the conduct of the Prime Minister, Lee Hae-Chan, with regard to a game of golf that he had played on 1 March, a public holiday that coincided with the first day of a national strike. Lee was criticized for choosing to play golf rather than oversee the Government's reaction to the strike. Objections were also raised to his choice of golfing partners, who reportedly included a businessman with a criminal record for the manipulation of share prices. Lee eventually resigned in mid-March in reaction to the scandal. Roh's nomination of Han Myeong-Sook as Lee's successor was approved by a vote in the National Assembly in mid-April, and she was thus appointed as the country's first female Prime Minister.

None the less, the appointment of a new Prime Minister failed to improve the fortunes of the Uri Party. (Conversely, the resignation of the Secretary-General of the GNP, Choi Yeon-Hee, following charges of sexual harassment, did little to boost the Uri Party's popularity.) Local elections held at the end of May 2006 resulted in victory for the GNP, which garnered 54.5% of the votes cast nation-wide, compared with just 21.2% received by the Uri Party. Significantly, of the 16 provincial governor and city mayoral positions, the Uri Party took only one, while the GNP secured 12, the DP two and an independent candidate the remaining one. In June, taking responsibility for the party's disastrous election performance, Chairman Chung Dong-Young resigned and was replaced by Kim Kun-Tae. By-elections held in July further emphasized the Uri Party's declining popularity; the GNP won three of the four seats contested, while the DP took the fourth.

Also in July 2006, President Roh effected a minor cabinet reorganization, appointing Kwon O-Kyu as Deputy Prime Minister for Finance and the Economy, Chang Byoung-Wan as Deputy Prime Minister for Planning and Budget and Kim Byong-Joon as Deputy Prime Minister for Education and Human Resources Development. (However, Kim resigned just 13 days after his appointment, amid allegations of plagiarism in his university thesis; he was replaced by Kim Shin-Il.) All three of the new appointees were widely perceived as being close allies of Roh. In the following month Kim Sung-Ho, hitherto deputy head of the Commission Against Corruption, was named as Minister of Justice, replacing Chun Jung-Bae. This arrangement was regarded as a compromise; Roh had initially planned to appoint a former senior presidential secretary for civil affairs, but had withdrawn the nomination following accusations of cronyism.

The North Korean nuclear test on 9 October 2006 (see below) resulted in a further ministerial reorganization. Both the Minister of Unification, Lee Jong-Seok, and the Minister of National Defence, Yoon Kwang-Woong, resigned amid both domestic and international criticism of the South Korean Government's continuing policy of engagement with the North. The new Minister of Unification was Lee Jae-Joung, a former Uri Party legislator, while the Army Chief of Staff, Kim Jang-Soo, took the defence portfolio. Another new appointment was that of Song Min-Soon, who was nominated to the post of Minister of Foreign Affairs and Trade (a position vacated by Ban Ki-Moon, following his appointment as UN Secretary-General).

Parliamentary by-elections and local elections held in October 2006 resulted in defeat for the Uri Party's candidates, prompting debate on a possible political realignment within the party. While some members of the Uri Party remained staunch supporters of the embattled President, others began to indicate that they might establish a new party. Intra-party relations suffered a further set-back in November, when President Roh made a contentious nomination for the post of President of the Constitutional Court (the nomination was later withdrawn under pressure from the opposition and members of the ruling party). Both the nomination and a subsequent meeting with the opposition, convened without the knowledge of Uri Party leaders, revived speculation of a rift; the party's parliamentary leader, Kim Han-Gill, warned Roh to confine himself to economic and diplomatic issues rather than becoming involved in party politics.

In addition to the issue of engagement with North Korea, public dissatisfaction with President Roh's handling of the economy also increased; house prices had risen rapidly and the education system had undergone a controversial restructuring. Many South Koreans were also deeply suspicious of the Government's plans to sign a free trade agreement (FTA) with the USA, and in November 2006 thousands took to the streets to protest against the proposed deal, leading to violent clashes with the police (see below).

By late 2006 preparations for the next presidential election, due to be held in December 2007, were well under way, with three candidates having declared their intention to stand. First of these was Park Geun-Hye, the former GNP chairwoman and daughter of the late President Park Chung-Hee, said to be popular among conservative voters. Also entering the contest was her GNP colleague Lee Myung-Bak, the former mayor of Seoul and CEO of Hyundai Engineering and Construction Company. Former Prime Minister Goh Kun, meanwhile, expressed his intention to stand as an independent candidate, only to withdraw his candidacy in January 2007, owing to lack of popular support. Although the electoral rules barred President Roh from standing for re-election, in January 2007 he suggested that the law be amended to allow future Presidents to serve for a maximum of two four-year terms, as opposed to one five-year term under the present legislation; however, he later withdrew the proposal.

In January 2007 the Uri Party announced formally that it would disband and form a new party. Initial reports suggested that the party would seek an alliance with the DP (defectors from which had originally formed the Uri Party in 2003), and that a number of Uri Party legislators had already switched their party allegiance to the DP. However, in February 2007, before these plans could be implemented, 23 legislators announced their defection from the Uri Party, joining six others who had resigned in the previous fortnight. Following this mass defection, the GNP held 127 seats and the Uri Party 110 in the National Assembly. President Roh finally announced his departure from the Uri Party, in the hope of reversing its decline in popularity. This decision forced the President to engage more deeply with the GNP and other parties; without their support the Roh administration would be unable to secure the passage of important legislation.

In March 2007, after only 10 months in office, Prime Minister Han Myeong-Sook resigned. Speculation that she was seeking to contest the forthcoming presidential election was confirmed in June, when she formally declared her intention to stand, although she withdrew her candidacy in September. Meanwhile, she was succeeded as Prime Minister by Han Duck-Soo, who had been special adviser to the President on free trade affairs since being replaced as Deputy Prime Minister for Finance and the Economy in July 2006. Further government changes followed in mid-April 2007. New appointees included Kim Jong-Min as Minister of Culture and Tourism and Kang Moo-Hyun as Minister of Maritime Affairs and Fisheries.

The GNP suffered a reverse in by-elections held in late April 2007, securing only one of the three seats contested. It was defeated by the recently formed People First Party and the DP in the other two constituencies, where the Uri Party had opted not to field candidates, instead supporting the minor opposition parties, with which it hoped to form a 'grand alliance' in advance of the forthcoming presidential and legislative elections. The polls were marked by a particularly low turn-out of 27.7%. Moreover, the GNP lost five of six mayoral and gubernatorial posts being contested concurrently. The poor performance of the GNP, which some observers attributed to bribery allegations connected with the nomination of candidates, prompted the resignation of several senior officials from the party's leadership, although its Chairman, Kang Jae-Seop, remained in his post. The party was also damaged by the extreme antagonism between its two rival presidential contenders, Park Geun-Hye and Lee Myung-Bak, while the latter's reputation was also undermined by allegations that he had been involved in fraudulent business transactions. None the less, the GNP elected Lee as its presidential candidate by a narrow margin in mid-August.

Meanwhile, the disintegration of the Uri Party continued, with a series of further defections in June and July 2007, including that of former Chairman Chung Dong-Young, which left the party with only 58 seats in the National Assembly. In early August Chung and 79 other former legislators of the Uri Party joined with five defectors from the DP to form the United New Democratic Party (UNDP). Later that month the Uri Party finally disbanded and merged into the UNDP, thus making the new party the largest in the National Assembly, with 143 seats.

In early August 2007 Roh announced a minor government reorganization, in which Chung Soung-Jin, hitherto Chairman of the Commission Against Corruption, was allocated the justice portfolio, replacing Kim Sung-Ho, who had resigned following disagreements with the President. Also appointed to the State Council were Im Sang-Gyu as Minister of Agriculture and Forestry and Yoo Young-Hwan as Minister of Information and Communication.

Chung Dong-Young was elected as the UNDP's presidential candidate in October 2007. He subsequently made efforts to persuade minor parties such as the DP and the Democratic Labour Party to form an alliance with the UNDP ahead of the elections, but without success. In early November, in a development that threatened to split the conservative vote, former Prime Minister Lee Hoi-Chang unexpectedly announced that he was leaving the GNP to stand as an independent candidate;

having been defeated in the 1997 and 2002 elections, this was his third attempt to secure the country's presidency.

A major corruption scandal at Samsung arose in late October 2007, when the former head of its legal department, Kim Yong-Chul, claimed that senior executives at the *chaebol* had regularly bribed politicians, government officials and prosecutors using a 'slush fund' totalling 200,000m. won. In late November the National Assembly approved legislation authorizing an independent investigation into Kim's allegations, which Samsung vigorously denied. Also to be examined were claims that the conglomerate had made improper payments to candidates in the 2002 presidential election. (The investigation commenced in January 2008. In April, having been charged with tax evasion and breach of trust, the Chairman of Samsung, Lee Kun-Hee, resigned, and in July he was convicted on the former charge and given a three-year suspended prison sentence.) Meanwhile, the head of the National Tax Service and two of Roh's former presidential aides were also arrested on various corruption charges. These developments proved embarrassing for Roh, who had pledged to reduce corruption in business and politics when elected in 2002.

Corruption allegations against Lee Myung-Bak gained renewed momentum in mid-November 2007, when the extradition from the USA to the Republic of Korea of one of his former business partners, to answer charges of embezzlement and money-laundering, prompted speculation that Lee himself might be implicated in the case. In early December prosecutors concluded that there was no evidence to link Lee to the financial crimes with which his former associate had been charged, but later in that month, only two days before the presidential election, the National Assembly voted to appoint an independent counsel to reinvestigate fraud claims against Lee, following the emergence of a video that purported to show the presidential candidate stating that he had established the investment company at the centre of the allegations. Lee denied any involvement in the scandal.

At the presidential election, which was held on 19 December 2007, the GNP's Lee Myung-Bak achieved a decisive victory, securing 48.7% of the votes cast, despite the allegations that had overshadowed the electoral campaign. Of the nine other candidates, his nearest rivals were Chung Dong-Young, with 26.1% of the votes, and Lee Hoi-Chang, with 15.1%. However, the level of voter participation, at 62.9%, was very low. Lee's win (by the largest margin since the reintroduction of direct elections in 1987) was attributed to a combination of the electorate's dissatisfaction with the achievements of the incumbent centre-left administration and its attraction to the new President-elect's focus on the economy. During the election campaign he had pledged to improve the country's economic prospects with his so-called '7.4.7' vision: achieving annual growth of 7%, raising average annual income per caput to US $40,000 and making the Republic of Korea one of the world's seven largest economies by 2017. More controversially, Lee also proposed the construction of a 540-km inland canal, traversing the country from Seoul in the north-west to the port city of Busan in the south-east, at a cost of 14,000,000m. won, with the aim of easing road and rail congestion, creating employment and improving growth.

In mid-January 2008 President-elect Lee Myung-Bak proposed legislation to reduce the number of government ministries from 18 to 13 (through the closure or merger of the ministries responsible for unification, science and technology, information and communication, gender equality, and maritime affairs and fisheries) and to consolidate other government agencies and offices. However, the UNDP, which remained the largest party in the National Assembly pending legislative elections scheduled for 9 April, expressed strong reservations about Lee's plans for government reorganization, particularly the proposed merger of the Ministry of Unification into the Ministry of Foreign Affairs, and a compromise was reached in February whereby the Ministries of Unification and of Gender Equality would be retained. Lee's transitional team also announced its intention to divide the country into regional economic zones, which would be encouraged to undertake independent industrial projects with the aim of decentralizing development policy.

Lee Myung-Bak was inaugurated as President on 25 February 2008. Four days previously he had been exonerated by the independent counsel re-examining the accusations of financial impropriety against him. The National Assembly subsequently approved Lee's appointment as Prime Minister of Han Seung-Soo, a veteran politician and diplomat, who had previously held various cabinet positions and was currently serving as a UN special envoy on climate change. The other members of the State Council were also designated in February, although several nominees, including Lee's choice to head the Ministry of Unification, Nam Joo-Hong, withdrew following criticism of misconduct in property dealings, of tax evasion and of malpractice in other areas. Among the nominees subsequently confirmed were Kang Man-Soo as Minister for Strategy and Finance, Kim Ha-Joong as Minister of Unification and Yu Myung-Hwan as Minister of Foreign Affairs and Trade; the position of Deputy Prime Minister was terminated. Meanwhile, there was some realignment of political parties in early 2008 in advance of the forthcoming legislative election. Lee Hoi-Chang created the Liberty Forward Party, which later absorbed the People First Party, and the UNDP and the DP merged to form the United Democratic Party (UDP), which held a total of 141 seats in the National Assembly, compared with the GNP's 130.

At the legislative election conducted on 9 April 2008 the GNP secured a narrow majority, winning 153 of the 299 seats in the National Assembly. The UDP garnered 81 seats, the Liberty Forward Party 18 seats and the pro-Park coalition 14 seats. A total of 245 candidates were directly elected, with the remaining seats being determined by proportional representation. The rate of participation by voters, at some 46%, was the lowest ever recorded at a general election. The success of the GNP was expected to facilitate the passage of legislation relating to the programme of economic reform proposed by newly appointed President Lee Myung-Bak, although the party's lack of a strong majority was likely to curb its power. The presence of more than 50 supporters of Park within the GNP contingent, as well as the pro-Park coalition and independents, was another possible constraint on Lee's ambitions.

One of President Lee's first challenges emerged in April 2008, when he agreed to rescind the country's ban on beef imports from the USA, reportedly to improve bilateral relations and expedite the FTA process. The decision prompted large-scale protests in May, amid widespread public fear of bovine spongiform encephalopathy (BSE) contamination. Daily demonstrations were attended by thousands of South Koreans; although initially peaceful, the protests escalated into violence in late May and early June, prompting the Government to offer concessions, such as a restriction on imports of cattle older than 30 months. As the protests continued, the issue became symbolic of wider public dissatisfaction with major government initiatives, including Lee's plans for the transnational canal system and the privatization of several state-owned businesses. The GNP's defeat at local elections in early June, when it secured only 10 of 52 positions (in comparison with the 22 won by the UDP, now known as the DP), was a further sign of this decline in popularity. With the affair quickly becoming a national crisis, the members of the State Council offered to resign. In July President Lee responded by effecting a cabinet reorganization, replacing the Minister of Food, Agriculture, Forestry and Fisheries, Chung Woon-Chun, with Jang Tae-Pyoung. Further controversy developed in October over the allocation of rice farming subsidies to non-tenant farmers, precipitating the resignation of a vice-minister who was allegedly implicated and a parliamentary investigation into the matter.

President Lee implemented another cabinet reorganization in January 2009, appointing Hyun In-Taek to succeed Kim Ha-Joong as Minister of Unification and dismissing Kang Man-Soo as Minister for Strategy and Finance, to be replaced by Yoon Jeung-Hyun. In the same month Won Sei-Hoon, the Minister of Public Administration and Security, was transferred to a senior intelligence position; Lee Dal-Gon was nominated to replace him.

After the end of the Korean War in 1953 relations between the Republic of Korea and the DPRK continued to be characterized by mutual suspicion. Various attacks on South Korean interests were attributed to the DPRK. These included a bomb explosion in Burma (now Myanmar) in October 1983, in which four South Korean government ministers were killed. A South Korean airliner in flight over Burma was destroyed in November 1987, allegedly by a bomb that had been concealed aboard the aircraft by North Korean agents. In April 1996 the DPRK's announcement that it was abandoning the 1953 armistice agreement was followed by a series of incursions by North Korean troops into the DMZ, and in September a North Korean submarine was found abandoned near the South Korean coast. Other confrontations included a gun battle in June 2002 between North and South Korean vessels in the Yellow Sea, which resulted in the sinking of a South Korean patrol boat and the deaths of six crew members. South Korean military sources estimated that 30 North Korean crewmen had also been killed in the incident, which had started when two North Korean vessels accompanying a fishing boat reportedly crossed the Northern Limit Line (the maritime border separating the territorial waters of the two Koreas). In February 2005 North Korea made accusations that South Korean naval vessels had 'infiltrated' the waters of the DPRK.

Bilateral and multilateral discussions regarding the situation on the Korean peninsula took place intermittently. Roh Tae-Woo's appointment as South Korean President in 1988 led to an improvement in relations with the DPRK. In September 1990 the North Korean Premier travelled to Seoul for a meeting with his South Korean counterpart, the highest level of bilateral contact since the end of the Korean War in 1953. The DPRK's abandonment in 1991 of its long-standing position that the two Koreas should occupy a single seat at the UN was regarded as a significant concession. Further prime-ministerial negotiations resulted in late 1991 in the signature of an agreement on reconciliation. In the hope ultimately of concluding a peace treaty, quadripartite negotiations, involving the two Koreas, the USA and the People's Republic of China, opened in Switzerland in December 1997. In 1998 a significant improvement in relations between North and South Korea followed the newly appointed President Kim Dae-Jung's inauguration of a 'sunshine' policy of engagement with the North. In October 1999 Hyundai concluded an agreement with the DPRK on the construction of an industrial complex at Kaesong, while a resort for South Korean tourists was developed at Mount Kumgang, also located just north of the border. As the DPRK's financial situation worsened, economic issues played an increasingly important part in inter-Korean relations from 2000. Many South Koreans had begun to question the wisdom of the allocation of extensive aid without firm preconditions, regarding the process of engagement as being increasingly unbalanced to the detriment of the South. An historic summit meeting took place between Kim Dae-Jung and the North Korean leader, Kim Jong Il, in June, during a visit by the South Korean President to the North Korean capital of Pyongyang. In December a resolution was approved by the South Korean legislature demanding the repatriation of prisoners of war who it alleged continued to be held by the North, despite the DPRK's denial of the existence of these prisoners. In late 2002 it was revealed that Kim Dae-Jung had arranged for the transfer of substantial funds from a Hyundai affiliate to the DPRK in order to convene the summit meeting of 2000. Although the election in December 2002 of Roh Moo-Hyun as South Korean President heralded a continuation of the 'sunshine' policy, in August 2003 the suicide of Hyundai official Chung Mong-Hun, who had been indicted in connection with the illegal payments to the North, further undermined the credibility of the policy.

In April 2005 the Prime Minister of South Korea, Lee Hae-Chan, met Kim Yong Nam, the President of the Presidium of the North Korean Supreme People's Assembly, in the Indonesian capital of Jakarta. However, bilateral relations deteriorated sharply in 2006 when North Korea conducted two sets of missile tests: the first in July and the second (of a nuclear device) in October. The tests placed the 'sunshine' policy, which was by now coming under heavy criticism from the South Korean public, in serious jeopardy. The Uri Party continued to emphasize the importance of dialogue, and in November the Government announced that it would not take part in the Proliferation Security Initiative (PSI), a US-led scheme to stop and search suspect North Korean ships. (The South Korean Government nevertheless agreed to comply with the sanctions imposed by the UN Security Council, and announced that North Koreans thought to be involved in the weapons programme would be banned from travelling to the South.) The GNP took the opposite stance, insisting (like the USA) that the Kaesong and Mount Kumgang projects be brought to an immediate halt. In December 2006 the Republic of Korea prompted severe condemnation from the DPRK when prosecutors indicted five people, including one US citizen of Korean origin, on charges of spying for the North. According to prosecutors, the five men had passed on official secrets, including the movements of US troops in South Korea and the personal details of South Korean politicians, at the request of North Korean officials. The DPRK denounced the action as a 'calculated plot' against the North. Two of those arrested were members of the minor Democratic Labour Party. (In April 2007 the five defendants were convicted of espionage and sentenced to prison terms ranging from four to nine years.) Despite the continuing tensions, the new Minister of Unification, Lee Jae-Joung (who had been criticized by the GNP for his allegedly pro-DPRK views), described eventual unification with the North as a primary objective. None the less, the Republic of Korea remained concerned over the DPRK's military ambitions; a defence policy document published at the end of December 2006 described the DPRK as a 'serious threat' to the South—the most strongly worded assessment since the inception of the latter's policy of engagement in 2000.

In February 2007 significant progress appeared to have been made at the six-party talks (with discussions now including representatives from Japan and Russia) when the DPRK pledged to shut down its nuclear reactor in exchange for energy aid. In October President Roh and Kim Jong Il held a three-day summit meeting in Pyongyang. Following the meeting, Kim and Roh issued a declaration committing North and South Korea, *inter alia*, to working towards the replacement of the 1953 armistice agreement with a peace treaty and to making joint efforts for the smooth implementation of the six-party nuclear agreements. There was some scepticism in South Korea about Roh's motives for organizing the summit meeting, with the GNP accusing the President of attempting to enhance his own political standing towards the end of his term of office, as well as that of the UNDP in advance of the forthcoming elections. President Lee Myung-Bak, who asumed office in February 2008, adopted a firmer stance towards the DPRK than his two immediate predecessors, linking the continuation of economic co-operation to greater progress on denuclearization. Lee announced plans to review the agreements reached at the inter-Korean summit meeting in October 2007. He initially proposed merging the Ministry of Unification into the Ministry of Foreign Affairs, but he later reached a compromise with the UNDP to retain the ministry while reducing its role. None the less, Lee proposed the creation of a 37,500m. won investment fund for the DPRK if it abandoned its nuclear weapons programme.

Meanwhile, family reunions were arranged under the auspices of the North and South Korean Red Cross organizations, which co-ordinated the exchange of lists of potential candidates, separated since the Korean War. In addition to 'face-to-face' reunions, the first private telephone line between North and South Korea since partition in 1945 was opened in July 2005, in preparation for video conference family reunions. In early 2006 the DPRK reportedly agreed to resolve the issue of South Korean prisoners of war and abductees held in the North. One of the most noteworthy reunions of the year took place in June, when Kim Young-Nam, a South Korean citizen reported to have been abducted by North Korean agents in 1978, was allowed to meet his mother. Kim insisted that he had not been abducted, maintaining that he had been rescued from a boat, thus appearing to confirm the official North Korean version of events. In January 2007 Choi Uk-Il, one of 33 South Korean fishermen abducted by a North Korean naval vessel in 1975, returned home after having first fled to China. His wife accused the South Korean authorities of failing to facilitate his repatriation.

(For full details of relations between North and South Korea, see the chapter on the Democratic People's Republic of Korea.)

The foreign policy of the Republic of Korea has long been dominated by its relations with the major powers of Russia, China, the USA and Japan, owing to its geographical position. Following President Roh Tae-Woo's inauguration in 1988, relations with the communist bloc showed signs of improvement. Trade with the USSR and the People's Republic of China expanded, and in 1990 full diplomatic relations were established with the USSR. These developments were denounced by the DPRK, its diplomatic isolation being compounded by the Republic of Korea's establishment of full diplomatic relations with the People's Republic of China (hitherto the North's principal ally) in 1992. Meanwhile, in 1991 the Republic of Korea had extended a substantial loan, of some US $1,470m., to the USSR; this debt was subsequently transferred to the Russian Federation (Russia) following the disintegration of the USSR later in that year. In September 1993 it was announced that the Republic of Korea and Russia were to participate in joint naval exercises, and in 1994 it was reported that Russia was to supply 'defensive missiles' in order to repay a part of its debt to the Republic of Korea. Further arrangements were made concerning the settlement of Russia's debt, through the provision of commodities, in July 1997.

Relations were severely tested in mid-1998 by a diplomatic dispute, provoked by Russia's expulsion of a South Korean diplomat following allegations of espionage and bribery, which culminated in the resignation of the South Korean Minister of Foreign Affairs and Trade, Park Chung-Soo. During a state visit to Russia in May 1999, Kim Dae-Jung held a summit meeting with President Boris Yeltsin. Issues discussed included South Korea's engagement policy with North Korea. The Russian Minister of Defence visited Seoul in September 1999, and the two countries conducted their first joint naval exercises in April 2000. President Vladimir Putin of Russia paid a three-day state visit to the Republic of Korea in February 2001, when he agreed to proceed with a tripartite framework of co-operation between Russia and both Koreas. Arrangements were made for Russia to supply weapons to the Republic of Korea, which were to be partially paid for by the cancellation of some Soviet-era debt. The Republic of Korea and Russia also issued a joint statement supporting the 1972 Anti-Ballistic Missile (ABM) treaty; however, US displeasure with this led to the resignation of the Minister of Foreign Affairs and Trade, Lee Joung-Binn. In December 2002 the Republic of Korea agreed to receive US $534m. worth of military equipment from Russia as part of a 1995 agreement to repay Moscow's $2,000m. debt to the Republic of Korea.

There were indications that Roh Moo-Hyun would seek to improve relations with Russia during his presidency, as part of a broader policy of reducing dependency on the USA. In March 2003 Roh revived the idea of building a 4,000-km pipeline that would provide the DPRK with Russian natural gas from Sakhalin in exchange for the abandonment of its nuclear weapons programme. At a summit meeting in Bangkok, Thailand, in October 2003 Roh and Putin agreed to co-operate on the North Korean nuclear issue. In September 2004 President Roh visited Russia. A significant agreement between state-owned oil companies of the two countries (Korean National Oil Corporation—KNOC—and Russia's Rosneft) was signed. In April 2005 the Minister of Defence, Yoon Kwang-Woong, visited Russia, where he met his Russian counterpart, Sergei Ivanov, to discuss the provision of Russian 'advanced weapons technology' by way of further servicing the Russian debt to the Republic of Korea.

Relations with China were strengthened in November 1998, when President Kim Dae-Jung paid an official visit to Beijing, meeting with Chinese President Jiang Zemin and Premier Zhu Rongji. Several accords were initialled during the visit. In August 1999 the first visit of a South Korean defence minister to China took place; a reciprocal visit to the Republic of Korea by the Chinese Minister of National Defence, Chi Haotian, took place in January 2000. The South Korean Government requested Chi's assistance in resolving the issue of seven North Korean defectors, who had recently been repatriated by China, despite South Korean protests. In October 2000 relations improved further when, during a visit to Seoul by Zhu Rongji, agreement was reached on the resumption of the quadripartite conference, incorporating the two Koreas, China and the USA, with the aim of establishing a peace mechanism for the Korean Peninsula (see the chapter on the Democratic People's Republic of Korea). Later in the month, following strong opposition from China, the Republic of Korea refused to grant a visa to the Dalai Lama, Tibet's spiritual leader, on the grounds that it would be 'inappropriate'.

A diplomatic dispute arose between the Republic of Korea and China in October 2001, following the execution in China of a South Korean national and the alleged torture of another Korean prisoner, both convicted of drugs-trafficking. In November the ministers of economics, finance and foreign affairs from China, the Republic of Korea and Japan agreed to hold regular meetings to foster closer co-operation. The South Korean Minister of National Defence, Kim Dong-Shin, paid a week-long visit to China in December, where he sought closer military co-operation with his Chinese counterparts.

In mid-2002 the Chinese authorities sought to prevent North Korean refugees from seeking asylum in various diplomatic buildings in China, including the South Korean embassy in Beijing, where a group of 23 had hidden. In response, the Chinese authorities increased efforts to combat South Korean NGOs and religious groups that were seeking to support the increasing number of North Korean refugees in China. In September Lee Hoi-Chang visited China and met President Jiang Zemin. In October the Minister of Finance proposed a three-way alliance comprising the Republic of Korea, China and Japan to manage the region's development. Also in that month the Government decided to extend working visas for ethnic Koreans in China to two years, with unlimited extensions. The initiative was intended to reduce the illegal trafficking of ethnic Koreans from China and its associated problems.

The growing diplomatic crisis over North Korea's nuclear programme from late 2002 led South Korea to seek China's assistance in persuading the North to work towards a peaceful solution. Roh made a four-day state visit to Beijing in July. Chinese diplomatic efforts subseqently played a major role (see the chapter on the Democratic People's Republic of Korea). In August 2004, however, relations between the Republic of Korea and China were damaged by controversy over the issue of the historical kingdom of Koguryo, which had covered the area of modern North Korea and part of South Korea, as well as areas of northern China. Following the deletion of references to Koguryo from the Chinese Ministry of Foreign Affairs website, the South Korean Government feared that China was planning to claim Koguryo as part of Chinese, rather than Korean, history, and to use this historical 'distortion' as a basis for present-day expansionism. In September, however, the Chinese Ministry of Foreign Affairs issued a statement declaring that its reference to Koguryo as an ancient Chinese province had been a mistake. The issue of Koguryo dominated discussions between President Roh and Chinese Prime Minister Wen Jiabao held in September 2006, not least because China was in the process of applying to the UN to register Mount Paekdu (half of which belonged to North Korea, half to China, and regarded by Korean nationalists as a sacred symbol) as an historic site. Meanwhile, in August South Korean officials stated that they would seek an FTA with China, following the conclusion of negotiations on a similar agreement with the USA (see below). Several rounds of preliminary discussions aimed at examining the potential benefits and costs of a bilateral FTA were held during 2007.

Relations between the Republic of Korea and the USA were frequently strained in the late 1970s, in particular by the proposal to withdraw US ground troops from South Korea (which was abandoned in 1979) and by the trial of Kim Dae-Jung (see above). Disputes between the Republic of Korea and the USA in the late 1980s over trade issues had subsided by mid-1991. President George Bush of the USA visited the country in January 1992, and the two leaders agreed to cancel that year's 'Team Spirit' joint military exercises. In December 1991 it had been announced that all US nuclear weapons had been withdrawn from South Korean territory. The 'Team Spirit' exercises were resumed in 1993. In July, during a visit to Seoul, US President Bill Clinton affirmed his country's continuing commitment to the defence of the Republic of Korea. In January 1994 it was announced that the USA was to deploy air-defence missiles on South Korean territory. In April 1996, during a visit to Seoul, President Clinton issued a joint US-South Korean proposal for quadripartite negotiations with the DPRK and the People's Republic of China (see above). In October 1997 the US Government asked the South Korean administration to reconsider its decision to order an air-defence missile system from France. However, the Republic of Korea was seeking to reduce its dependence on the USA for military technology. Later in that year the USA pledged financial support for the Republic of Korea, following the conclusion of an agreement with the IMF.

President Kim Dae-Jung was warmly received on a state visit to the USA in June 1998, during which he outlined his 'sunshine' policy of engagement with North Korea. A reciprocal visit was made by President Clinton to Seoul in November. In March 1999 the South Korean Government welcomed a major advance in negotiations between the DPRK and the USA on US access to a suspected nuclear site in North Korea (see the chapter on the Democratic People's Republic of Korea). During a second visit by Kim Dae-Jung to the USA, in July, the US Administration reaffirmed its support for the 'sunshine' policy. Discussions with the USA were held in late 1999 and early 2000 regarding the Republic of Korea's proposed extension of its missile range, from 180 km to 300 km for military purposes, and to 500 km for research and development. (In January 2001 a revised missile accord was signed between the Republic of Korea and the USA, permitting the former to develop missiles with greatly increased ranges and payloads.) In October 1999 the US and South Korean Governments began investigations into the alleged massacre of as many as 300 Korean refugees by US troops near Nogun-ri, in the South Korean province of North Chungcheong, shortly after the beginning of the Korean War. Revelations of the use of defoliants in the DMZ in the late 1960s created further controversy in November 1999. The herbicides, which had apparently been provided by the USA but applied by South Korean troops, included Agent Orange, which had later been found to be highly toxic. The South Korean Government announced that it was prepared to compensate both soldiers and civilians adversely affected by the defoliants, but the USA reportedly refused to accept any liability. In December a lawsuit was filed against seven US chemical companies by a group of Koreans demanding compensation for damage they claimed to have suffered as a consequence of the herbicides. (In January 2006, in the first such ruling, a South Korean court ordered the US manufacturers to pay 68,000m. won in compensation to 6,800 individuals.)

In May 2000 there was further tension between the two countries when a US aircraft accidentally released several bombs close to a village south-west of Seoul, causing minor injuries and damage to property. Violent protests were held outside the US embassy in Seoul, and the USA subsequently agreed to cease using the Koon-ni range for such training missions. (Operations subsequently resumed, the USA citing a lack of suitable alternative facilities.) Following the incident, opposition politicians demanded a review of the Status of Forces Agreement (SOFA), which governed the 37,000 US troops stationed in South Korea. In August negotiations were held on the issue, and resulted in partial agreement. Further discussions held in December successfully revised the agreement, which was signed in January 2001. However, South Korean civic groups protested that the partnership between the two countries remained biased in favour of the USA. In January 2001 outgoing US President Bill Clinton made an unprecedented statement of regret for the massacre near Nogun-ri, but many South Koreans were angry that no apology was forthcoming. Later, in January 2002, a British Broadcasting Corporation (BBC) investigation revealed that US commanders had repeatedly ordered troops to fire on refugees at Nogun-ri and elsewhere during the opening months of the Korean War. Some South Korean historians were, in late 2001, also investigating the USA's possible role in the massacre by South Korean troops of 30,000 people on Jeju Island in a suppression of communist elements in late 1948 and early 1949. Meanwhile, the USA welcomed the improvement in inter-Korean relations during 2000. US Secretary of State Madeleine Albright visited Seoul in June and in October of that year to discuss developments. In March 2001 Kim Dae-Jung paid a visit to the new Bush Administration in Washington, DC, hoping to secure support for his 'sunshine' policy. However, US President George W. Bush took a firmer stance than his predecessor and declared that North Korea should prove its abandonment of its missile testing and development programme prior to any improvement in relations or release of aid.

The Republic of Korea immediately pledged support to the USA following terrorist attacks on the latter in September 2001, and in December the National Assembly endorsed the deployment of non-combat troops to assist the US-led campaign in Afghanistan, mainly in a logistical capacity. Meanwhile, in November the USA and the Republic of Korea agreed to a major 'land-swap' whereby existing US bases would relocate to other areas within the country, allowing a consolidation of bases and training facilities over the next 10 years.

In January 2002 the Republic of Korea reacted with concern to President Bush's reference to North Korea as being part of an 'axis of evil', a remark that further undermined Kim Dae-Jung's 'sunshine' policy. None the less, the South Korean military planned to purchase US $800m. worth of surface-to-surface missiles, capable of attacking most of North Korea, from US manufacturers. At the same time GNP leader Lee Hoi-Chang visited the USA and met senior US officials, his attitude to the DPRK generally being closer to that of Bush than of Kim. Lee favoured a policy of 'strategic engagement' based on reciprocity and transparency. Bush himself visited South Korea in February and urged the North to change its ways.

In March 2002 the USA announced plans to deploy a new mobile military force unit to South Korea by 2007. The USA agreed to sell a combat-radar system to the Republic of Korea, and the two countries held their biggest-ever joint military exercises, which antagonized the North. Also in that month the South Korean Government reacted angrily to Bush's imposition of new tariffs on imported steel, since the country was a major steel exporter. At the end of the month the Ministry of National Defence announced that the Boeing Company of the USA had secured a US $4,500m. contract to supply the Republic of Korea with 40 F-15K fighter aircraft.

Relations between the Republic of Korea and the USA deteriorated noticeably after an accident in June 2002 in which a US army vehicle killed two teenaged Korean girls. The US military charged two US soldiers with negligent homicide, and the South Korean authorities subsequently requested their submission for trial at a local court, but this was rejected by the US army. In November the two soldiers were acquitted by a US military court, leading to a significant increase in anti-US sentiment among the public. Although President Bush apologized for the incident, in mid-December hundreds of thousands of people attended anti-US rallies in Seoul and across the country. Although precipitated by the issue of the acquittals, the rallies became a forum of protest against the country's dependency on the USA and that country's policy towards North Korea. Meanwhile, in October a new joint base pact came into force whereby the US military would reduce the number of its bases from 41 to 23 and return 50% of the land it used to South Korea. However, there had yet to be changes to the SOFA that governed the conduct of US troops in Korea—amendments to which had long been demanded by South Koreans. Public anger towards the USA was further raised by the crash of a reconnaissance plane in January.

The election of Roh Moo-Hyun as President raised fears that the Republic of Korea's relations with the USA would be further undermined, as Roh had campaigned for a foreign policy more independent from the USA. However, in January 2003 he indicated a more conciliatory stance, but nevertheless warned the USA against attacking North Korea, instead urging the USA to resume dialogue with the DPRK. He also instructed the military to prepare contingency plans for the possible withdrawal of US troops, and in March the US Secretary of Defense, Donald Rumsfeld, stated that the troops could be reduced in number or withdrawn completely. The USA announced that it planned to remove its 15,000 troops stationed between Seoul and the DMZ and deploy them in the south of the country.

In February 2003 the commander of the United States Forces Korea, Gen. Leon LaPorte, stated that the USA and South Korea would review their 1953 Mutual Defense Treaty, with the possibility of ending provisions under the 'Combined Forces Command' for the transfer of control over South Korea's military to the USA in wartime. However, it was noted that South Korea still remained dependent on the USA for military intelligence. Despite disagreements, South Korea and the USA held their annual joint military exercises during March 2003. In April the US military announced that it would move its main base away from Seoul as part of a global redeployment of forces. The USA envisaged eventually consolidating its forces in two major hubs: the Osan-Pyeongtaek and Daegu-Busan regions. Meanwhile, Roh arranged to send 700 non-combatant troops to Iraq in support of the USA, despite domestic protests. Roh visited President Bush in Washington, DC, in mid-May, and the two leaders agreed to work towards a peaceful solution to the crisis over North Korea's nuclear programme, although differences remained between US and South Korean policies towards the DPRK.

In March 2003, meanwhile, Donald Rumsfeld stated that the USA was considering withdrawing troops from the North–South Korean border, and in June plans were confirmed to withdraw US troops to locations 120 km south of the DMZ, as part of a wider reorganization of US forces in South Korea. There was some concern in South Korea that these developments were in preparation for an attack by the USA on North Korean nuclear facilities. Also in June, some 20,000 people protested at the US embassy in Seoul to mark the anniversary of the killing of two Korean girls by a US army vehicle (see above). In November Rumsfeld visited the Republic of Korea to discuss the US military presence as well as the deployment of South Korean troops to Iraq.

In January 2004 the two countries agreed to relocate US troops out of Seoul. In May the USA announced its intention to transfer 3,600 US troops currently stationed in South Korea to Iraq. In June, furthermore, the USA outlined plans to reduce the number of troops in South Korea by about one-third by the end of 2005. Meanwhile, the deployment of 3,000 South Korean troops to Iraq, which had been approved by the National Assembly in February 2004 (see above), remained suspended, despite US requests for the troops to be sent. In August, during discussions between South Korean and US officials, South Korea expressed its desire that the proposed withdrawal of one-third of US troops be delayed until 2006. An admission by the South Korean Government that it had conducted secret experiments for uranium enrichment and plutonium extraction in 2000 and the early 1980s represented a serious threat to the country's relations with the USA, as well as to its relations with the International Atomic Energy Agency—IAEA (see p. 113), although the amounts of nuclear material involved were reported to have been small. Also in August 2004, despite public outrage at the beheading of a South Korean hostage in June (see above), the Government refused to abandon its plans for the scheduled deployment of 3,000 South Korean troops to Iraq. In September it was announced that US troops would withdraw from the DMZ by the end of October (South Korean forces duly assumed responsibility for patrolling the border zone from the beginning of November). In October an agreement for the planned withdrawal of one-third of all US troops in South Korea was reached. The withdrawal was now due to take place in three phases extending to 2008.

In December 2004, following a vote in the National Assembly, it was announced that South Korean troops in Iraq (now numbering around 3,600) would remain there throughout 2005. Joint US-South Korean military exercises were held in mid-2005 and early 2006, eliciting protest on both occasions from the DPRK (see above, and the chapter on the Democratic People's Republic of Korea). In December 2005 the National Assembly voted to reduce the number of South Korean troops in Iraq to 2,300 and to extend their deployment until the end of 2006. In January 2006, meanwhile, a court in Seoul ordered the US pharmaceutical companies responsible for producing the toxic Agent Orange to pay compensation to those South Koreans affected by the herbicide while serving alongside the US military during the Viet Nam war (see above).

In February 2006 it was announced that negotiations had commenced with regard to an important FTA between the Republic of Korea and the USA. However, as negotiations proceeded in July an estimated 30,000 demonstrators took to the streets of Seoul to protest against what they described as 'economic subjugation'. South Korean farmers, in particular, were concerned that the proposed FTA might prove detrimental to their livelihoods. Furthermore, the Government was insistent that the South Korean rice market should be exempt from the zero tariffs proposed by the USA. Major corporations expressed reservations with regard to US demands that trade-related legislation, including fair trade laws, be applied to the South Korean *chaebol*. A further obstacle was the pharmaceutical sector, owing to the USA's strong objections to a new South Korean drug pricing system intended to ensure that medicines were available at reasonable cost to those on low incomes. Another fundamental issue was the South Korean policy of engagement towards the DPRK. The USA insisted that goods produced in the North Korean industrial complex of Kaesong should be exempt from the trade pact, while the South Korean Government regarded Kaesong as a symbol of reconciliation, serving to promote peace and stability on the Korean Peninsula. As public opposition to the proposed FTA increased, in November at least 65,000 protesters took to the streets across South Korea, as part of a general strike organized by the KCTU, to demonstrate their disapproval. Further demonstrations later in the month were severely curtailed by a heavy police presence. None the less, an estimated 5,000 farmers and their supporters defied a police ban to hold a protest in early December, to coincide with the start of the fifth round of FTA negotiations, which were again dominated by the issues of pharmaceuticals and rice. The sixth round of discussions, which took place in early 2007, drew further protests, with up to 8,000 farmers and workers taking to the streets of Seoul.

In April 2007 the Republic of Korea and the USA finally reached a compromise on the terms of the FTA. The principal elements of the agreement included wider access to the US market for South Korean carmakers, a reduction of taxes payable by television and mobile phone manufacturers and the cessation of duties levied on beef imports. Critics claimed that these measures would have a drastic impact on South Korean farmers, although the agreement did not encompass rice imports, as the Republic of Korea objected to the liberalization of that particular market. The conclusion of the FTA led to renewed protests by various sections of South Korean society. Many argued that increased US imports would render local businesses uncompetitive, thus threatening numerous livelihoods. Several senior opposition politicians joined the protests when they began a hunger strike. However, the Government took a more positive view of the agreement, regarding it as the most important bilateral development since the two nations signed the military alliance in 1953. None the less, the FTA remained subject to ratification by both countries' legislatures. Several amendments to the FTA, incorporating stricter labour and environmental provisions, were agreed before it was formally signed at the end of June 2007, mainly in order to facilitate the ratification process in the US Congress. Tens of thousands of workers participated in several days of strike action organized by the Korean Metal Workers' Union in that month in protest against the agreement. The situation in the USA was also problematic, and was further complicated by US demands that the Republic of Korea remove restrictions on the import of US beef, which had been imposed in late 2003 in response to the detection of BSE at a US cattle farm. In April 2008, however, prior to a visit to the USA by the newly elected President Lee Myung-Bak, the South Korean Government agreed to relax the restrictions on imports of US beef. The decision prompted large-scale public protests in mid-2008 and, along with other factors, was responsible for a sharp decline in support for Lee (see above). In April 2009 a parliamentary committee approved a bill to allow the ratification of the FTA, which was expected to take place in June 2009.

Meanwhile, also under discussion in 2006–07 was the continuing issue of the US military presence in the Republic of Korea. By August 2006 joint studies had been conducted on the terms of a new military alliance. In February 2007, at a meeting in Washington, DC, the South Korean Minister of National Defence, Kim Jang-Soo, and the US Secretary of Defense, Robert Gates, agreed to transfer operational control of South Korean military forces from the USA to South Korea in the event of war and to disband the Combined Forces Command in April 2012 (three years later than the USA had proposed). A new 'supporting-supported command relationship' was to be established, under which the United States Forces Korea would continue to support the South Korean military. Kim and Gates also reaffirmed earlier agreements on the relocation of US forces from Seoul to the Osan-Pyeongtaek and Daegu-Busan regions and on a reduction in the number of US troops stationed in the Republic of Korea from around 30,000 to 25,000 by 2008. The election of Lee Myung-Bak as South Korean President in mid-December 2007 prompted speculation that the new administration might attempt to renegotiate the arrangement on the transfer of wartime military control. The GNP remained staunchly opposed to the agreement concluded under Roh. Lee pledged to forge closer relations with the USA, asserting that the Republic of Korea continued to require US protection. Later in that month the National Assembly voted to extend the deployment of South Korean troops in Iraq until the end of 2008, but to reduce their number from around 1,250 to 650. The South Korean Government had come under pressure from the Bush Administration to maintain its military presence in Iraq, despite continued domestic public opposition to the deployment. In December 2008 South Korea withdrew its remaining soldiers from Iraq.

Relations between the Republic of Korea and Japan, which had long been strained, were eased by President Chun's official visit to Japan in September 1984 (the first such visit undertaken by a South Korean Head of State), during which Emperor Hirohito and Prime Minister Yasuhiro Nakasone formally expressed their regret for Japanese aggression in Korea in the past. In May 1990, during President Roh's visit to Japan, Emperor Akihito offered official apologies for the cruelties of Japanese colonial rule in Korea. In January 1992 the Japanese Prime Minister, Kiichi Miyazawa, visited the Republic of Korea, where he publicly expressed regret at the enslavement during the Second World War of an estimated 100,000 Korean women, who were used by the Japanese military for sexual purposes ('comfort women'). In late 1994 the Japanese Government announced that it would not make compensation payments directly to individuals, but would finance a programme to construct vocational training centres for the women concerned. In August 1995, on the 50th anniversary of the end of the Second World War, the Japanese Prime Minister, Tomiichi Murayama, issued a statement expressing 'deep reflection and sincere apologies' for Japanese colonial aggression. At the end of a summit meeting with President Kim in June 1996, the Japanese Prime Minister, Ryutaro Hashimoto, issued a public apology to the 'comfort women'. However, the South Korean Government regarded Japanese proposals to provide compensation through private sources of funding, rather than government money, as tantamount to a denial of moral responsibility. The conclusion of new defence co-operation guidelines between Japan and the USA in September 1997 was of concern for the Republic of Korea, which feared an expansion in Japanese military capability. Negotiations for a new fisheries agreement, under way since mid-1996, were unilaterally terminated by Japan in January 1998, following the continuing disagreement regarding sovereignty of the uninhabited Dokdo islands (or 'Takeshima' in Japanese, located between South Korea and Japan in the East

Sea—also known as the Sea of Japan), to which both countries laid claim. In April 1998 the South Korean Government announced its intention to make payments itself to surviving 'comfort women'. However, a Japanese district court ordered the Government to pay compensation to three former 'comfort women' from the Republic of Korea. Another group of South Korean 'comfort women' was refused the right to recompense by the Japanese High Court in November 2000, and in March 2001 the 1998 compensation ruling was overruled by a regional High Court.

Relations with Japan improved considerably in October 1998, meanwhile, during a four-day state visit to Tokyo by President Kim Dae-Jung. A joint declaration was signed, in which Japan apologized for the suffering inflicted on the Korean people during Japanese colonial rule. In addition, the Republic of Korea agreed to revoke a ban on the import of various Japanese goods, while Japan promised financial aid to the Republic of Korea in support of its efforts to stimulate economic recovery. In November the two countries concluded negotiations on the renewal of their bilateral fisheries agreement, which came into effect in January 1999, despite the objections of the main South Korean opposition party, which protested that it failed positively to affirm the Republic of Korea's claim to sovereignty over the disputed Dokdo islands. Differences over the accord and its implementation continued to create tension in early 1999, particularly in the Republic of Korea, where protests from fishermen, who were apparently suffering heavy losses because of the revised agreement, forced the resignation of the Minister for Maritime Affairs and Fisheries. In March increasing co-operation between the two countries was highlighted during a visit to the Republic of Korea by the Japanese Prime Minister, Keizo Obuchi, despite protests against Japan's military links with the USA and failure fully to compensate the 'comfort women'. Both countries agreed to strengthen bilateral economic relations, and Japan pledged a further US $1,000m. in aid to the Republic of Korea. The Japanese Prime Minister, Yoshiro Mori, visited Seoul in May 2000 and met with Kim Dae-Jung.

During 2001 relations with Japan deteriorated owing to the publication in February of new Japanese history textbooks which sought to justify Japan's aggression towards its Asian neighbours during the Second World War, and neglected to mention the forced prostitution of Asian (mainly Korean) 'comfort women' by the Japanese army and the forcible transfer and use of Koreans as slave labour in Japan. Large-scale protests were held in Seoul, and the Japanese ambassador was summoned to the Ministry of Foreign Affairs and Trade. In April the Republic of Korea temporarily withdrew its ambassador from Japan. President Kim Dae-Jung urged Japan to adopt 'a correct understanding of history'. The South Korean Ministry of Foreign Affairs and Trade demanded 35 major revisions to the books, but in July Japan's Ministry of Education ruled out any further significant changes, prompting Kim Dae-Jung to refuse to receive a visiting Japanese delegation and the suspension of bilateral military co-operation. Protests also took place outside the Japanese embassy in Seoul. In August the Republic of Korea was further outraged by the visit of the Japanese Prime Minister, Junichiro Koizumi, to the controversial Yasukuni Shrine in Tokyo honouring Japan's war dead. Amid popular protests, Koizumi visited Seoul in October and delivered an apology for the suffering of Koreans under Japanese rule. He was forced to cancel a visit to the National Assembly owing to the hostile sentiment of some legislators.

Along with China and North Korea, South Korea condemned Koizumi's visits to the Yasukuni Shrine in April 2002 and January 2003. However, in March 2002 Koizumi and Kim Dae-Jung agreed to begin discussions on a possible bilateral FTA, and in May Koizumi attended the opening ceremony of the 2002 football World Cup being co-hosted in Seoul. Also in attendance were Prince Takamado and his wife, who were making the first official visit to the Republic of Korea by a member of the Imperial family. Any remaining mutual hostility between the two countries was outweighed in 2002 by the need for co-operation in engaging with the North, and in December Koizumi and South Korean President-elect Roh Moo-Hyun agreed to co-ordinate their policies in this regard. Koizumi subsequently attended Roh's inauguration in February 2003. In June Roh made his first state visit to Japan and had discussions with Koizumi on the issue of North Korea's nuclear weapons programme. Although both leaders opposed any development of nuclear weapons in North Korea, Roh urged dialogue with the DPRK, whereas Koizumi favoured stricter measures towards the DPRK. Japan and the Republic of Korea continued efforts towards reaching an FTA from 2003, but negotiations faltered in November 2004, reportedly over disagreement regarding the liberalization of trade in agricultural and fisheries products.

In February 2005 tensions arose over a statement by the Japanese ambassador to Seoul, Toshiyuki Takano, implying that the Dokdo islands. The issue of the Dokdo islands renewed tensions in March when the local legislature of Japan's Shimane Prefecture, which claimed the islands as part of its territory, voted to establish a 'Takeshima Day'. In response, the South Korean Minister of Foreign Affairs and Trade, Ban Ki-Moon, cancelled a scheduled visit to Japan, while protests were held outside the Japanese embassy in Seoul. Further public demonstrations took place in April in reaction to the approval for use in Japanese schools of history textbooks, including one first published in 2001 (see above), which were regarded by Koreans (and Chinese) as failing to address the true nature of Japanese wartime conduct. Another visit to the Yasukuni Shrine by Prime Minister Koizumi in October provoked condemnation from the Republic of Korea, and prompted President Roh to cancel a scheduled visit to Japan in December. Throughout 2006 the Republic of Korea's continued requests for the shrine visits to end were disregarded by the Japanese Government. On 15 August (Liberation Day in Korea) Koizumi made another visit to the shrine, and the South Korean Ministry of Foreign Affairs and Trade issued a statement declaring that the visit would strain bilateral relations and obstruct regional co-operation and friendship. This shrine visit took place just days after the Minister of Foreign Affairs and Trade, Ban Ki-Moon, embarked upon his first trip to Japan for 10 months, not only to attend the memorial service for former Japanese Prime Minister Ryutaro Hashimoto, but also to protest against Koizumi's shrine visits and to discuss the North Korean missile crisis. In the following month no progress was forthcoming during bilateral discussions in Seoul, particularly with regard to the disputed Dokdo or Takeshima islands. The Republic of Korea had antagonized the Japanese authorities in July when it had conducted a survey of the waters around the islands, against the express wishes of Japan (which, in turn, had announced plans to conduct a similar survey in April, prompting the South Korean Government to announce a five-year plan to develop facilities on the islands and to explore the area's marine and mineral resources).

Relations deteriorated further in early 2007 after remarks made by the new Japanese Prime Minister, Shinzo Abe, regarding the treatment of 'comfort women' by Japanese soldiers during the Second World War caused public outrage in the Republic of Korea. Abe inferred that there was no direct evidence to prove that South Korean women had been coerced into sexual servitude. President Roh later expressed his disappointment at what he perceived as a succession of errors on the part of the Japanese Government in relation to the fractious history of the two countries, claiming that it had repeatedly failed to apologize for any ill-treatment suffered by South Koreans during the war. In March, furthermore, the Japanese Prime Minister refused to apologize for his previous comments. However, in April he decided not to emulate his predecessor with regard to visits to the Yasukuni Shrine (despite a clandestine visit in the previous year). Instead, Abe sent a sacred plant to the shrine, thereby appeasing both South Koreans and opponents within his own Government. In early May the Republic of Korea declared its intention to seize assets secured by nine alleged collaborators during Japanese colonial rule. Land, worth some US $3.9m. and belonging to the descendants of the collaborators, would be seized in an effort to 'restore South Korean people's dignity'. The proceeds were to be used to assist former combatants, while other land was allocated for the purposes of commemorating the Korean independence movement.

Yasuo Fukuda, who succeeded Abe as Japanese Prime Minister in September 2007, identified strengthening relations with the Republic of Korea as a priority, notably pledging not to visit the controversial Yasukuni Shrine. The election of Lee Myung-Bak as South Korean President in December was also regarded as a positive development for the bilateral relationship. Fukuda attended Lee's inauguration in February 2008, following which the two leaders agreed to undertake regular reciprocal visits and to promote the resumption of negotiations on the establishment of an FTA (stalled since late 2004). Lee and Fukuda reaffirmed these intentions during Lee's official visit to Japan in April 2008. Meanwhile, in January, in a gesture of reconciliation, the relatives of 101 South Koreans who had been forced to fight for the

THE REPUBLIC OF KOREA (SOUTH KOREA)

Japanese army during the Second World War were invited to a memorial service in Tokyo to mark the return of their remains. Japan had relinquished more than 1,000 sets of remains to South Korean diplomats since 2004, but this was the first time that the families of the dead had participated in events. In July 2008 the dispute over the Dokdo islands re-emerged when the Japanese Government announced that the islands would be described as Japanese in teachers' materials. The announcement provoked severe criticism from the South Korean Government and the recall of its ambassador to Japan, in addition to demonstrations in Seoul. A defence document reiterating Japan's stance placed further strain on bilateral relations in September.

In November 2000, after eight years' suspension, the 25th Joint Conference of Korea-Taiwan Business Councils took place in Seoul. It was agreed that henceforth conferences would be held annually alternately in Seoul and Taipei. In the same month a Korean passenger aircraft flew from Seoul to Taipei for the first time since 1992, when diplomatic relations had been severed. The Republic of Korea also maintained close relations with South-East Asian countries, and Minister of Defence Kim Dong-Shin and Prime Minister Lee Han-Dong visited Viet Nam in December 2001 and April 2002 respectively. Security, economic and trade issues were the main topics of discussions. Viet Nam had already become the principal recipient of South Korean aid. In early 2003 a South Korean newspaper funded the opening of a peace park in southern Viet Nam, as a gesture of atonement for atrocities committed by South Korean soldiers, some 300,000 of whom had fought on behalf of South Viet Nam during the Viet Nam war.

An agreement on free trade in merchandise goods was reached between the Republic of Korea and nine of the 10 members of the Association of South East Asian Nations (ASEAN, see p. 194) in August 2006. Under the agreement, which was ratified by the South Korean National Assembly in May 2007 and took effect on 1 June, 97% of South Korean products exported to the nine ASEAN countries were exempt from tariffs or would carry tariffs of less than 5% by 2010. The South Korean Government thus envisaged a substantial increase in its trade surplus with the nine South-East Asian signatories. Although more commonly known as the South Korea-ASEAN FTA, the arrangement did not include Thailand, which refused to participate in protest against the Republic of Korea's insistence on the exclusion of rice from the agreement. However, several rounds of free trade negotiations were held between the two countries during 2007, and in January 2008 it was reported that an agreement had been reached whereby Thailand would be allowed more flexibility in reducing or waiving its tariffs compared with the other ASEAN nations. Meanwhile, in November 2007 the Republic of Korea and all 10 members of ASEAN signed an agreement on free trade in services; a futher accord, covering investment, was also envisaged. An FTA between South Korea and Iceland, Liechtenstein and Switzerland took effect in September 2006. In May 2007 South Korea and the European Union (EU) commenced negotiations on the establishment of an FTA; in February 2008, following a sixth round of discussions, the EU's chief negotiator reported that 70% of issues had been resolved, and in early 2009 negotiations were reported to be approaching completion. As with the South Korean FTA with the USA (see above), farmers were resolutely opposed to such an agreement. Meanwhile, negotiations aimed at concluding an FTA between South Korea and Canada, which commenced in July 2005, continued in early 2009.

Taliban militants seized a group of 23 South Korean Christians in Afghanistan in mid-July 2007. Following the killing of two of the hostages later in that month, direct talks between South Korean officials and the Taliban were held in August. By the end of August the Taliban had released the remaining 21 hostages, who claimed to have been undertaking aid work rather than missionary activities. The South Korean authorities refused to confirm or deny speculation that a ransom had been paid to the Taliban, but stated that it had agreed to withdraw its troops from Afghanistan by the end of the year, as scheduled, and to prevent missionary groups from travelling to the country. The withdrawal of South Korea's 210-strong contingent in the International Security Assistance Force in Afghanistan (comprising military medical and engineering personnel) was completed by mid-December.

In March 2009 President Lee Myung-Bak embarked upon a state visit to Australia, where he and Prime Minister Kevin Rudd signed a pact relating to closer co-operation in the area of security, including counter-terrorism strategies and the combating of transnational crime. It was also announced that formal negotiations on an FTA between the two countries were to commence.

Government

Under the Constitution of the Sixth Republic (adopted in October 1987), executive power is held by the President, who is directly elected for one term of five years by universal suffrage. The President appoints and governs with the assistance of the State Council (Cabinet), led by the Prime Minister. Legislative power is vested in the unicameral National Assembly (Kuk Hoe), popularly elected for a four-year term. The Assembly has 299 members.

Defence

Protection of the frontier separating North and South Korea is the responsibility of the UN. Military service lasts for 26 months in the South Korean army, and for 30 months in the navy and in the air force. As assessed at November 2008, the strength of the active armed forces was 687,000 (including an estimated 140,000 conscripts): army 560,000, navy 68,000, air force 64,000. Paramilitary forces included a 3.5m.-strong civilian defence corps. In November 2008 US forces stationed in South Korea comprised 17,130 army personnel, 254 navy, 7,857 air force and 133 marines. Expenditure on defence was budgeted at 28,600,000m. won for 2008.

Economic Affairs

In 2007, according to estimates by the World Bank, the Republic of Korea's gross national income (GNI), measured at average 2005–07 prices, was US $955,802m., equivalent to $19,690 per head (or $24,750 per head on an international purchasing-power parity basis). During 2000–07, it was estimated, the population increased at an average annual rate of 0.5%, while gross domestic product (GDP) per head increased, in real terms, by an average of 4.2% per year. Overall GDP increased, in real terms, at an average annual rate of 4.7% in 2000–07. According to the Asian Development Bank (ADB), GDP rose by 5.0% in 2007 and by 2.5% in 2008.

Agriculture (including forestry and fishing) contributed an estimated 3.0% of GDP and engaged 7.4% of the employed labour force in 2007. The principal crop is rice, but barley, potatoes, sweet potatoes and fruit are also important, as is the raising of livestock (principally poultry, pigs and cattle). Fishing provides food for domestic consumption, as well as a substantial surplus for export. In the early 2000s South Korea remained one of the world's leading ocean-fishing nations. During 2000–07, according to figures from the World Bank, the GDP of the agricultural sector increased by an average of 0.2% per year. Agricultural GDP increased by 1.1% in 2007 and by 3.5% in 2008, according to the ADB.

Industry (including mining and quarrying, manufacturing, utilities and construction) contributed an estimated 39.4% of GDP, and engaged 25.9% of the employed labour force in 2007. Industry is dominated by large conglomerate companies (*chaebol*), with greatly diversified interests, especially in construction and manufacturing. According to figures from the World Bank, during 2000–07 industrial GDP increased at an average annual rate of 6.0%. The sector's GDP increased by 5.5% in 2007 and by 2.5% in 2008, according to the ADB.

South Korea is not richly endowed with natural resources. Mining and quarrying contributed less than 0.4% of GDP in 2007, employing a negligible percentage of the labour force. There are deposits of coal (mainly anthracite). Other minerals include iron ore, lead, zinc, silver, gold and limestone. Substantial offshore reserves of natural gas have been discovered.

Manufacturing contributed an estimated 27.9% of GDP and engaged 17.6% of the employed labour force in 2007. The most important branches of manufacturing include electrical machinery, transport equipment (mainly road motor vehicles and shipbuilding), non-electrical machinery, chemicals, food products, iron and steel, and textiles. During 2000–07 manufacturing GDP increased by an average of 6.9% per year, according to figures from the World Bank. The manufacturing sector's GDP expanded by 6.5% in 2007.

Energy is derived principally from nuclear power, coal and petroleum. In 2005 37.8% of total electricity output was generated by nuclear power, while thermal and hydroelectric power provided 61.3% and 0.9%, respectively. At the end of 2005 there were 20 nuclear units in operation in the country. The Republic of Korea also produces liquefied natural gas for domestic and

THE REPUBLIC OF KOREA (SOUTH KOREA)

Introductory Survey

industrial consumption. Imports of mineral fuels comprised an estimated 33.4% of the value of merchandise imports in 2008.

The services sector contributed 57.6% of GDP and engaged 66.7% of the employed labour force in 2007. Receipts from tourism are significant, totalling an estimated US $8,069m. in 2006, when the number of visitor arrivals reached almost 6.2m. During 2000–07, according to figures from the World Bank, the GDP of the services sector increased at an average annual rate of 4.1%. The GDP of the sector increased by 4.8% in 2007 and by 2.3% in 2008, according to the ADB.

In 2007 the Republic of Korea recorded a visible trade surplus of US $29,409m., and there was a surplus of $5,954m. on the current account of the balance of payments. The People's Republic of China and Japan were the principal sources of imports in 2008 (accounting for, respectively, 17.7% and 14.0% of total imports in that year); other important suppliers were the USA and Saudi Arabia. The People's Republic of China was the principal market for exports in 2008 (purchasing 21.7%), followed by the USA (11.0%). Other important markets included Japan, Hong Kong and Singapore. The main exports in 2008 were electrical machinery (particularly telecommunications and sound equipment), basic manufactures, road vehicles, and chemical products. The principal imports in that year were machinery and transport equipment (especially electrical machinery), petroleum and petroleum products, basic manufactures and chemical products.

The budget for 2009 projected expenditure of 284,500,000m. won (including capital expenditure), an increase of 26% in comparison with the previous year. A budget deficit equivalent to 3.8% of GDP was envisaged. At the end of 2008, according to the ADB, the Republic of Korea's total external debt reached US $380,495m. In that year the cost of debt-servicing was equivalent to 5.3% of the value of exports of goods and services. The average annual rate of inflation was 3.1% in 2000–07. Consumer prices increased by an average of 4.7% in 2008. The average rate of unemployment was 3.2% in 2008, but by January 2009 the rate had risen to 3.6%.

The Republic of Korea is a member of the UN Economic and Social Commission for Asia and the Pacific (ESCAP, see p. 36), the Asian Development Bank (ADB, see p. 191), Asia-Pacific Economic Co-operation (APEC, see p. 185), the Colombo Plan (see p. 425), the World Trade Organization (WTO, see p. 410) and the Organisation for Economic Co-operation and Development (OECD, see p. 358).

The eventual implementation of a free trade agreement (FTA) with the USA (see Recent History) was expected to yield major benefits to the South Korean economy. Negotiations regarding an FTA with the European Union were reported to be making good progress in early 2009. Meanwhile, in response to the greater availability of credit during 2006–07, many leading financial institutions began to accumulate higher levels of loans relative to deposits. The strong growth in both domestic consumption and private investment (notably in the manufacturing sector) that prevailed until the deterioration in global economic conditions from mid-2008 was accompanied by a concomitant decline in the savings rate. In an attempt to raise levels of interbank lending, and thereby improve the availability of credit to businesses, the central bank reduced its interest rate to 2.0% in February 2009, the sixth reduction within four months. Owing to the importance of South Korea's export trade, the maintenance of a competitive exchange rate remained a principal objective of central bank policy. In 2008 the value of the South Korean won decreased substantially in relation to the US dollar, and the currency continued to depreciate in early 2009. As the global financial crisis gathered momentum from the latter part of 2008, the Bank of Korea drew on the country's substantial international reserves in an effort to mitigate this depreciation, with limited success. In comparison with the previous three months, the value of South Korean exports was estimated to have decreased by 12% in the final quarter of 2008. Following its announcement of a 14,000,000m. won stimulus plan in November 2008, in December the Government announced a further programme of fiscal stimulus, projecting expenditure of 33,000,000m. won. The latter plan provided for reductions in corporate and personal taxation, in a further effort to encourage consumer spending. Additional expenditure of 43,000,000m. won was envisaged under a programme of job creation, announced in January 2009; the Government hoped to create almost 1m. jobs within four years. GDP was reported to have contracted by 5.1% in the final three months of 2008, before expanding by just 0.1% in the first quarter of 2009. The country therefore narrowly avoided entering recession in that quarter. The Government anticipated that the economy would contract by about 2.0% in 2009 as a whole.

Education

Education, available free of charge, is compulsory between the ages of six and 15. In 2007 a total of 541,550 children were enrolled in kindergarten. Primary education begins at six years of age and lasts for six years. There were 3,829,998 childen enrolled in primary schools in 2007. In 2005 enrolment at primary schools included 99.4% of children in the appropriate age-group. Secondary education begins at 12 years of age and lasts for up to six years, comprising two cycles of three years each, the first of which is compulsory. In 2007 there were 2,063,159 pupils enrolled in middle schools, while general and vocational high school pupils totalled 1,841,374. Enrolment at secondary schools in 2005 included 90.4% of children in the appropriate age-group (males 90%; females 91%). In 2007 there were 175 university-level institutions, with a student enrolment of 1,919,504. In that year there were 1,042 graduate schools, with a student enrolment of 296,576. Expenditure on education by the central Government was projected at 28,457,000m. won for 2006.

Public Holidays

2009: 1 January (New Year's Day), 25–27 January (Lunar New Year), 1 March (Sam Il Jol, Independence Movement Day), 5 April (Arbor Day), 2 May (Buddha's Birthday), 5 May (Children's Day), 6 June (Memorial Day), 17 July (Constitution Day), 15 August (Liberation Day), 2–4 October (Juseok, Korean Thanksgiving Day), 3 October (National Foundation Day), 25 December (Christmas Day).

2010: 1 January (New Year's Day), 14 February (Lunar New Year), 1 March (Sam Il Jol, Independence Movement Day), 5 April (Arbor Day), 5 May (Children's Day), 21 May (Buddha's Birthday), 6 June (Memorial Day), 17 July (Constitution Day), 15 August (Liberation Day), 21–23 September (Juseok, Korean Thanksgiving Day), 3 October (National Foundation Day), 25 December (Christmas Day).

Weights and Measures

The metric system is in force, although a number of traditional measures are also used.

THE REPUBLIC OF KOREA (SOUTH KOREA)

Statistical Survey

Source (unless otherwise stated): National Statistical Office, Bldg III, Government Complex-Daejeon 920, Dunsan-dong, Seo-gu, Daejeon 302-701; tel. (42) 481-2001; fax (42) 481-2460; internet www.nso.go.kr.

Area and Population

AREA, POPULATION AND DENSITY*

Area (sq km)	99,646†
Population (census results)‡	
1 November 2000	46,136,101
1 November 2005	
Males	23,620,000
Females	23,634,000
Total	47,254,000
Population (mid-year estimates)	
2006	48,297,184
2007	48,456,369
2008	48,606,787
Density (per sq km) at mid-2008	487.8

* Excluding the demilitarized zone between North and South Korea, with an area of 1,262 sq km (487 sq miles).
† 38,474 sq miles. The figure indicates territory under the jurisdiction of the Republic of Korea, surveyed on the basis of land register in 2005.
‡ Excluding adjustment for underenumeration.

ADMINISTRATIVE DIVISIONS
(population at 31 December 2005, according to resident registration programme)

Province	Area (sq km)	Population	Density (per sq km)
Seoul	605.4	10,297,004	17,008.6
Busan	764.4	3,657,840	4,785.1
Daegu	884.5	2,525,836	2,855.8
Incheon	994.1	2,632,178	2,647.7
Gwangju	501.4	1,408,106	2,808.3
Daejeon	539.8	1,462,535	2,709.5
Ulsan	1,057.1	1,095,105	1,035.9
Gyeonggi-do	10,130.9	10,853,157	1,071.3
Gangwon-do	16,613.5	1,521,099	91.6
Chungcheongbuk-do	7,431.4	1,501,674	202.1
Chungcheongnam-do	8,600.5	1,982,495	230.5
Jeollabuk-do	8,054.6	1,895,500	235.3
Jeollanam-do	12,073.5	1,976,465	163.7
Gyeongsangbuk-do	19,026.0	2,711,900	142.5
Gyeongsangnam-do	10,520.8	3,187,110	302.9
Jeju-do	1,848.3	559,747	302.8
Total	99,646.2	49,267,751	494.4

PRINCIPAL TOWNS
(population at 1995 census)

Seoul (capital)	10,231,217	Jeonju (Chonju)	563,153
Busan (Pusan)	3,814,325	Jeongju (Chongju)	531,376
Daegu (Taegu)	2,449,420	Masan	441,242
Incheon (Inchon)	2,308,188	Jinju (Chinju)	329,886
Daejeon (Taejon)	1,272,121	Kunsan	266,559
Gwangju (Kwangju)	1,257,636	Jeju (Cheju)	258,511
Ulsan	967,429	Mokpo	247,452
Seongnam (Songnam)	869,094	Chuncheon (Chunchon)	234,528
Suwon	755,550		

2000 census: Seoul 9,853,972; Busan 3,655,437; Daegu 2,473,990; Incheon 2,466,338; Daejeon 1,365,961; Gwangju 1,350,948; Ulsan 1,012,110.

Mid-2007 ('000, incl. suburbs, UN estimates): Seoul 9,796; Busan 3,480; Incheon 2,550; Daegu 2,460; Daejeon 1,486; Gwangju 1,440; Suwon 1,078; Ulsan 1,061; Seongnam 942; Goyang 903 (Source: UN, *World Urbanization Prospects: The 2007 Revision*).

BIRTHS, MARRIAGES AND DEATHS*

	Registered live births Number	Rate (per 1,000)	Registered marriages Number	Rate (per 1,000)	Registered deaths Number	Rate (per 1,000)
2000	636,780	13.4	334,030	7.0	247,346	5.2
2001	557,228	11.6	320,063	6.7	242,730	5.1
2002	494,625	10.3	306,573	6.4	246,515	5.1
2003	493,471	10.2	304,932	6.3	245,817	5.1
2004	476,052	9.8	310,944	6.4	245,771	5.1
2005	438,062	9.0	316,375	6.5	245,511	5.0
2006	451,514	9.2	332,752	6.8	243,934	5.0
2007	496,710	10.1	345,592	7.0	n.a.	n.a.

* Owing to late registration, figures are subject to continuous revision.

Life expectancy (years at birth, WHO estimates): 78.8 (males 75.4; females 82.1) in 2006 (Source: WHO, *World Health Statistics*).

ECONOMICALLY ACTIVE POPULATION*
(labour force survey, '000 persons aged 15 years and over)

	2005	2006	2007
Agriculture, forestry and fishing	1,815	1,785	1,726
Mining and quarrying	17	18	18
Manufacturing	4,234	4,167	4,119
Electricity, gas and water	71	76	86
Construction	1,814	1,835	1,850
Wholesale and retail trade, repair of motor vehicles and personal and household goods	3,748	3,713	3,677
Restaurants and hotels	2,058	2,049	2,049
Transport, storage and communications	1,429	1,470	1,498
Financial intermediation	746	786	809
Real estate, renting and business activities	2,037	2,168	2,350
Public administration and defence; compulsory social security	791	801	797
Education	1,568	1,658	1,687
Health and social work	646	686	745
Other community, social and personal service activities	1,727	1,781	1,845
Households with employed persons	130	138	161
Extra-territorial organizations and bodies	24	20	15
Total employed	22,856	23,151	23,433
Unemployed	887	827	783
Total labour force	23,743	23,978	24,216
Males	13,883	13,978	14,124
Females	9,860	10,000	10,092

* Excluding armed forces.

Source: ILO.

THE REPUBLIC OF KOREA (SOUTH KOREA)

Health and Welfare

KEY INDICATORS

Total fertility rate (children per woman, 2006)	1.2
Under-5 mortality rate (per 1,000 live births, 2006)	5
HIV/AIDS (% of persons aged 15–49, 2007)	<0.1
Physicians (per 1,000 head, 2003)	1.6
Hospital beds (per 1,000 head, 2006)	8.6
Health expenditure (2006): US $ per head (PPP)	1,487
Health expenditure (2006): % of GDP	6.5
Health expenditure (2006): public (% of total)	55.1
Access to water (% of persons, 2004)	92
Access to sanitation (% of persons, 2000)	63
Human Development Index (2006): ranking	25
Human Development Index (2006): value	0.928

For sources and definitions, see explanatory note on p. vi.

Agriculture

PRINCIPAL CROPS
('000 metric tons)

	2005	2006	2007*
Rice, paddy	6,435.0	6,324.0	5,959.5
Barley	286.9	236.6	227.0
Maize	73.5	64.6	60.0
Potatoes	894.2	631.1	625.0
Sweet potatoes	282.5	285.8	260.0
Beans, dry	7.1	6.4	6.2
Chestnuts	76.4	72.0*	70.0
Soybeans (Soya beans)	183.3	156.4	152.0
Sesame seed	23.5	15.5	14.5
Cabbages and other brassicas	2,602.6	3,068.1	3,000.0
Lettuce and chicory	167.0	160.3	158.0
Spinach	109.0	103.7	100.0
Tomatoes	439.0	433.2	425.0
Pumpkins, squash and gourds	339.1	322.0	320.0
Cucumbers and gherkins	403.3	389.6	365.0
Chillies and peppers, green	395.3	353.0	345.0
Onions and shallots, green	513.2	543.0	535.0
Onions, dry	1,023.3	889.6	855.0
Garlic	375.0	331.4	325.0
Carrots and turnips	117.7	130.4	128.0
Mushrooms	28.4	29.0	28.5
Watermelons	905.9	778.4	785.0
Cantaloupes and other melons	199.8	219.7	212.0
Tangerines, mandarins, clementines and satsumas	638.0	620.3	615.0
Apples	367.5	407.6	400.0
Pears	443.3	431.5	425.0
Peaches and nectarines	223.7	193.8	190.0
Plums and sloes	76.0	64.4	65.0
Strawberries	202.0	205.3	200.0
Grapes	381.4	330.0	325.0
Persimmons	363.8	352.8	345.0
Tobacco, unmanufactured*	35.0	34.0	35.5

* FAO estimate(s).

Aggregate production ('000 metric tons, may include official, semi-official or estimated data): Total cereals 6,816 in 2005, 6,647 in 2006, 6,269 in 2007; Total vegetables (incl. melons) 11,413 in 2005, 11,244 in 2006, 11,222 in 2007; Total fruits (excl. melons) 2,778 in 2005, 2,618 in 2006, 2,578 in 2007.

Source: FAO.

LIVESTOCK
('000 head)

	2005	2006	2007*
Cattle	2,298	2,484	2,580
Pigs	8,962	9,382	9,850
Goats	523	523*	527
Chickens	109,628	119,181	121,000

* FAO estimate(s).

Source: FAO.

LIVESTOCK PRODUCTS
('000 metric tons)

	2005	2006	2007
Cattle meat	195.0	224.0*	237.0*
Pig meat	899.4	860.0†	915.0†
Chicken meat	484.0†	496.0†	525.0*
Duck meat	52.0†	67.0†	71.0*
Cows' milk	2,228.8	2,184.0†	2,140.0†
Goats' milk*	5.2	5.1	5.0
Hen eggs	514.9	555.0*	545.0*
Other poultry eggs*	28.0	28.0	28.5
Honey	23.8	24.0*	25.0*

* FAO estimate(s).
† Unofficial figure.

Source: FAO.

Forestry

ROUNDWOOD REMOVALS
('000 cubic metres, excl. bark)

	2005	2006	2007
Sawlogs, veneer logs and logs for sleepers	297	426	440
Pulpwood	1,491	1,422	1,643
Other industrial wood	562	596	597
Fuel wood*	2,465	2,469	2,472
Total	4,815	4,913	5,152

* FAO estimates.

Source: FAO.

SAWNWOOD PRODUCTION
('000 cubic metres, incl. sleepers)

	2002	2003	2004
Coniferous (softwood)	4,209	4,200	4,200*
Broadleaved (hardwood)	201	180	166†
Total	4,410	4,380	4,366*

* FAO estimate.
† Unofficial figure.

2005–07: Figures assumed to be unchanged from 2004 (FAO estimates).

Source: FAO.

Fishing

('000 metric tons, live weight)

	2004	2005	2006
Capture	1,575.5	1,639.1	1,749.9
Croakers and drums	27.3	43.5	47.0
Japanese anchovy	196.6	249.5	265.3
Skipjack tuna	162.2	171.6	206.5
Chub mackerel	185.6	135.7	101.7
Largehead hairtail	66.3	60.1	63.7
Argentine shortfin squid	20.4	42.9	138.8
Japanese flying squid	212.8	189.1	197.1
Aquaculture	405.7	436.6	513.6
Pacific cupped oyster	239.3	251.7	283.3
Total catch	1,981.2	2,075.6	2,263.5

Note: Figures exclude aquatic plants ('000 metric tons): 556.2 (capture 9.1, aquaculture 547.1) in 2004; 528.0 (capture 15.2, aquaculture 512.8) in 2005; 779.4 (capture 13.8, aquaculture 765.6) in 2006. Also excluded are aquatic mammals, recorded by number rather than by weight; the number of dolphins and whales caught was: 254 in 2004; 551 in 2005; 544 in 2006.

Source: FAO.

THE REPUBLIC OF KOREA (SOUTH KOREA)

Mining

('000 metric tons, unless otherwise indicated)

	2004	2005	2006
Hard coal (Anthracite)	3,191	2,832	2,824
Iron ore: gross weight	233	266	227
Iron ore: metal content	127	119	155
Lead ore (metric tons)*	40	50	17
Zinc ore (metric tons)*	14	77	16
Kaolin	2,780	2,767	2,399
Feldspar	541.8	508.6	427.4
Salt (unrefined)	340.8	378.9	285.6
Mica (metric tons)	59,238	36,623	30,356
Talc (metric tons)	79,313	83,471	64,118
Pyrophyllite	827.9	885.6	677.5

* Figures refer to the metal content of ores.
Source: US Geological Survey.

Industry

SELECTED PRODUCTS
('000 metric tons, unless otherwise indicated)

	2003	2004	2005
Wheat flour	1,792	1,891	1,833
Refined sugar	1,266	1,303	1,322
Beer (million litres)	17,863	18,033	17,489
Cigarettes (million)	123,166	133,206	107,247
Cotton yarn—pure and mixed	279	264	243
Plywood ('000 cu m)	827	704	651
Newsprint	1,538	1,679	n.a.
Rubber tyres ('000)*	70,921	96,499	n.a.
Caustic soda	1,365	1,508	1,455
Liquefied petroleum gas	3,613	3,717	3,612
Naphtha	17,520	19,767	20,800
Kerosene	8,397	6,599	5,791
Gas-diesel (distillate fuel oil)	27,801	29,048	31,508
Residual fuel oil	30,095	29,918	31,305
Cement	60,725	56,955	51,391
Pig-iron	27,314	27,556	27,309
Crude steel	46,310	47,521	47,820
Television receivers ('000)	7,336	6,425	5,843
Passenger cars—produced ('000 units)	2,767	3,133	3,356
Lorries and trucks—produced (number)	233,720	210,008	218,902
Electric energy (million kWh)	345,192	368,162	389,390
Carbon black†	464.9	473.8	471.7
Products of petroleum refineries ('000 barrels)†	796,000	886,415	919,627

* Tyres for passenger cars and commercial vehicles.
† Source: US Geological Survey.

Shipbuilding (merchant ships launched, '000 grt): 8,977 in 1999; 11,211 in 2000; 8,385 in 2001.

Source: mostly UN, *Industrial Commodity Statistics Yearbook*.

2006 ('000 metric tons, unless otherwise indicated): Cement 53,971; Crude steel 48,437; Pig-iron 27,548; Carbon black 484.3; Products of petroleum refineries ('000 barrels) 947,433 (Source: US Geological Survey).

Finance

CURRENCY AND EXCHANGE RATES

Monetary Units
100 chun (jeon) = 10 hwan = 1 won.

Sterling, Dollar and Euro Equivalents (31 December 2008)
£1 sterling = 1,833.18 won;
US $1 = 1,257.50 won;
€1 = 1,750.06 won;
10,000 won = £5.45 = $7.95 = €5.71.

Average Exchange Rate (won per US $)
2006   954.79
2007   929.21
2008   1,102.47

BUDGET
('000 million won)

Revenue	2004	2005	2006*
Current revenue	177,432	190,165	208,092
Tax revenue	140,643	152,371	165,359
Non-tax revenue	36,788	37,794	42,733
Capital revenue	1,329	1,281	1,482
Total	178,760	191,447	209,574

Expenditure	2004	2005	2006*
Current expenditure	145,148	160,274	173,688
General public services	11,909	14,743	17,208
Defence	19,995	21,976	23,428
Education	22,113	27,467	28,457
Social security and welfare	15,125	16,716	18,536
Economic services	30,753	28,250	30,115
Transport and communications	14,458	14,041	13,903
Capital expenditure	26,992	24,648	26,493
Net lending	1,398	3,024	5,746
Total	173,538	187,946	205,928

* Preliminary figures.

INTERNATIONAL RESERVES
(US $ million at 31 December)

	2005	2006	2007
Gold (national valuation)	73.6	74.2	74.3
IMF special drawing rights	43.7	54.1	68.7
Reserve position in IMF	305.8	440.4	310.8
Foreign exchange	209,967.7	238,387.9	261,770.7
Total	210,390.8	238,956.6	262,224.5

Source: IMF, *International Financial Statistics*.

MONEY SUPPLY
('000 million won at 31 December)

	2005	2006	2007
Currency outside banks	21,959	23,224	23,937
Demand deposits at deposit money banks	55,045	62,395	62,034
Total money (incl. others)	77,274	85,831	86,677

Source: IMF, *International Financial Statistics*.

THE REPUBLIC OF KOREA (SOUTH KOREA)

Statistical Survey

COST OF LIVING
(Consumer Price Index; base: 2005 = 100)

	2006	2007	2008
Food and non-alcoholic beverages	102.0	104.8	109.7
Alcoholic beverages and cigarettes	99.8	100.2	100.8
Housing, water and fuels	102.9	105.2	109.7
Furnishings and household goods	101.8	105.9	111.2
Clothing and footwear	102.7	105.4	108.1
Health	102.0	103.8	105.8
Education	104.9	111.2	117.2
Communication	98.7	96.7	95.3
Transport	104.6	108.4	117.9
All items (incl. others)	102.0	104.8	109.7

NATIONAL ACCOUNTS
('000 million won at current prices)

National Income and Product

	2005	2006	2007*
Compensation of employees	365,160.8	385,003.6	410,749.3
Operating surplus	237,710.9	241,763.8	255,167.8
Domestic factor incomes	602,871.7	626,767.4	665,917.1
Consumption of fixed capital	111,106.3	117,313.1	122,314.7
Gross domestic product (GDP) at factor cost	713,978.0	744,080.5	788,231.8
Indirect taxes, *less* subsidies	96,537.9	103,964.1	112,956.8
GDP in purchasers' values	810,515.9	848,044.6	901,188.6
Net factor income from abroad	−1,216.1	1,116.5	1,352.7
Gross national income	809,299.8	849,161.2	902,541.3
Less Consumption of fixed capital	111,106.3	117,313.1	122,314.7
National income in market prices	698,193.5	731,848.0	780,226.7

* Preliminary.

Expenditure on the Gross Domestic Product

	2005	2006	2007*
Final consumption expenditure	541,528.8	580,598.5	623,582.7
Households	417,425.1	444,859.7	476,528.6
Non-profit institutions serving households	9,265.5	10,096.0	10,878.5
General government	114,838.2	125,642.8	136,175.6
Gross capital formation	243,659.5	253,118.5	264,665.9
Gross fixed capital formation	237,239.5	246,298.0	259,353.4
Changes in inventories	6,420.0	6,820.5	5,312.5
Total domestic expenditure	785,188.3	833,717.0	888,248.6
Exports of goods and services	342,588.0	364,718.4	410,940.3
Less Imports of goods and services	323,466.8	356,929.9	403,418.2
Statistical discrepancy	6,206.3	6,539.1	5,417.9
GDP in market prices	810,515.9	848,044.6	901,188.6
GDP at constant 2000 prices	723,126.8	760,251.2	798,057.0

* Preliminary.

Gross Domestic Product by Economic Activity

	2005	2006	2007*
Agriculture, forestry and fishing	24,631.4	24,635.1	23,982.2
Mining and quarrying	2,626.2	2,612.4	2,839.4
Manufacturing	204,701.0	210,948.4	223,324.2
Electricity, gas and water	16,838.7	17,526.7	18,050.7
Construction	66,375.0	67,731.0	71,118.0
Wholesale and retail trade, restaurants and hotels	67,862.2	71,014.2	74,351.1
Transport, storage and communications	52,429.5	53,814.3	57,451.1
Financial intermediation	60,483.5	63,965.4	70,904.9
Real estate, renting and business activities	90,482.4	95,836.2	102,172.0
Public administration and defence, compulsory social security	45,429.4	48,794.8	51,421.8
Education	41,569.8	44,635.2	47,442.3
Health and social work	22,069.3	25,639.2	28,574.7
Other service activities	24,975.6	26,851.1	28,671.6
Gross value added at basic prices	721,474.2	754,004.1	800,304.1
Taxes, less subsidies, on products	89,041.7	94,040.6	100,884.5
Total	810,515.9	848,044.6	901,188.6

* Preliminary.

Source: Bank of Korea.

BALANCE OF PAYMENTS
(US $ million)

	2005	2006	2007
Exports of goods f.o.b.	288,971	331,842	378,982
Imports of goods f.o.b.	−256,288	−303,937	−349,573
Trade balance	32,683	27,905	29,409
Exports of services	45,129	49,891	63,034
Imports of services	−58,788	−68,851	−83,609
Balance on goods and services	19,025	8,945	8,835
Other income received	10,432	14,547	19,327
Other income paid	−11,994	−14,014	−18,558
Balance on goods, services and income	17,462	9,478	9,603
Current transfers received	10,004	9,588	10,934
Current transfers paid	−12,486	−13,680	−14,583
Current balance	14,981	5,385	5,954
Capital account (net)	−2,340	−3,126	−2,390
Direct investment abroad	−4,291	−8,127	−15,276
Direct investment from abroad	6,309	3,586	1,579
Portfolio investment assets	−14,136	−26,912	−54,602
Portfolio investment liabilities	14,114	8,056	29,974
Financial derivatives assets	3,461	4,559	12,188
Financial derivatives liabilities	−5,167	−8,449	−6,654
Other investment assets	−2,658	−7,945	−18,424
Other investment liabilities	9,473	56,330	59,836
Net errors and omissions	119	−1,267	2,922
Overall balance	19,864	22,090	15,109

Source: IMF, *International Financial Statistics*.

THE REPUBLIC OF KOREA (SOUTH KOREA)

External Trade

PRINCIPAL COMMODITIES
(distribution by SITC, US $ million)*

Imports c.i.f.	2006	2007	2008
Food and live animals	11,357.9	13,630.4	16,405.5
Crude materials (inedible) except fuels	19,664.5	24,071.8	28,272.1
Mineral fuels, lubricants, etc.	86,706.7	96,503.6	145,514.8
Petroleum, petroleum products, etc.	66,689.2	74,059.9	104,812.6
Gas (natural and manufactured)	14,699.9	15,998.6	24,892.6
Chemicals and related products	27,573.0	32,432.5	36,658.2
Organic chemicals	8,662.6	9,778.6	10,978.5
Basic manufactures	42,313.9	51,932.9	64,983.5
Iron and steel	15,890.4	21,446.4	33,554.9
Machinery and transport equipment	92,717.6	107,499.3	114,541.8
Machinery specialized for particular industries	8,423.4	13,506.7	13,336.8
General industrial machinery, equipment and parts	9,728.1	11,916.6	13,193.4
Office machines and automatic data-processing machines	8,028.2	7,920.0	7,526.5
Telecommunications and sound equipment	7,537.6	9,204.0	10,560.6
Other electrical machinery, apparatus, etc.	41,776.9	46,088.1	48,655.5
Thermionic valves and tubes, microprocessors, transistors, etc.	24,712.8	28,420.3	29,781.1
Digital monolithic integrated units	18,026.1	n.a.	n.a.
Miscellaneous manufactured articles	26,684.0	27,572.4	28,644.1
Total (incl. others)	309,382.6	356,845.7	435,274.7

Exports f.o.b.	2006	2007	2008
Mineral fuels, lubricants, etc.	20,920.4	24,630.9	38,454.7
Petroleum, petroleum products, etc.	20,788.7	24,516.1	38,311.3
Chemicals and related products	31,806.1	37,544.7	42,709.9
Organic chemicals	12,549.4	14,968.0	15,560.5
Plastics in primary forms	11,610.9	13,541.2	15,524.3
Basic manufactures	46,559.2	52,041.3	59,559.9
Textile yarn, fabrics, etc.	10,109.5	10,373.4	10,370.9
Iron and steel	15,823.6	18,802.4	25,037.8
Machinery and transport equipment	192,359.8	216,730.2	233,688.1
Office machines and automatic data-processing machines	17,884.2	13,331.2	10,688.0
Automatic data-processing machines and units, etc.	8,511.4	3,107.4	2,791.9
Parts and accessories for office machines and automatic data-processing equipment	9,011.1	8,622.7	6,161.1

Exports f.o.b.—continued	2006	2007	2008
Telecommunications and sound equipment	37,300.4	46,612.9	49,192.8
Other electrical machinery, apparatus, etc.	48,545.9	50,962.3	49,180.2
Thermionic valves and tubes, microprocessors, transistors, etc.	28,486.4	32,737.5	28,189.2
Digital monolithic integrated units	21,998.3	n.a.	n.a.
Road vehicles	42,418.4	48,958.5	48,099.2
Motor cars and other motor vehicles	30,597.2	34,482.8	31,287.5
Other transport equipment	22,290.7	27,533.6	42,170.4
Ships, boats and floating structures	21,492.9	26,632.0	40,967.6
Miscellaneous manufactured articles	26,630.2	32,239.1	37,223.3
Total (incl. others)	325,464.8	371,489.1	422,007.3

* Excluding trade with the Democratic People's Republic of Korea.

Source: Korea International Trade Association.

PRINCIPAL TRADING PARTNERS
(US $ million)*

Imports c.i.f.	2006	2007	2008
Australia	11,309.4	13,232.5	18,000.3
Brazil	2,706.9	2,793.7	4,380.5
Canada	3,091.3	3,254.5	4,403.5
China, People's Republic	48,556.7	63,027.8	76,930.3
France	3,219.4	4,043.2	4,877.4
Germany	11,364.6	13,534.3	14,769.1
Hong Kong	2,101.3	2,142.3	2,222.7
Indonesia	8,848.6	9,113.8	11,320.3
Iran	5,049.2	6,481.8	8,223.1
Italy	2,915.6	3,582.8	4,151.4
Japan	51,926.3	56,250.1	60,956.4
Kuwait	8,133.5	8,746.8	12,128.8
Malaysia	7,242.5	8,442.2	9,909.1
Oman	5,128.7	3,813.9	5,694.7
Philippines	2,186.6	2,438.3	3,099.5
Qatar	6,985.2	8,454.0	14,374.6
Russia	4,573.0	6,977.5	8,340.1
Saudi Arabia	20,552.1	21,163.5	33,781.5
Singapore	5,886.7	6,859.7	8,361.8
Taiwan	9,287.5	9,966.5	10,642.9
Thailand	3,328.4	3,769.2	4,281.7
United Arab Emirates	12,930.9	12,656.2	19,248.5
United Kingdom	2,976.5	3,580.8	3,637.1
USA	33,654.2	37,219.3	38,364.8
Total (incl. others)	309,382.6	356,845.7	435,274.7

Exports f.o.b.	2006	2007	2008
Australia	4,692.1	4,691.2	5,171.3
Brazil	3,063.4	3,487.5	5,925.9
Canada	3,620.4	3,506.4	4,057.2
China, People's Republic	69,459.2	81,985.2	91,388.9
France	3,415.5	3,478.2	3,495.5
Germany	10,056.2	11,542.5	10,522.7
Hong Kong	18,978.9	18,654.5	19,771.9
India	5,532.8	6,600.0	8,977.1
Indonesia	4,873.5	5,770.6	7,933.6
Iran	2,559.3	3,265.6	4,342.6
Italy	4,286.3	4,151.4	3,545.6
Japan	26,534.0	26,370.2	28,252.5
Malaysia	5,227.2	5,704.2	5,794.5
Mexico	6,284.6	7,482.0	9,089.9
Netherlands	3,609.4	4,488.7	6,405.6
Philippines	3,930.5	4,420.3	5,016.3
Russia	5,179.2	8,087.7	9,478.0

THE REPUBLIC OF KOREA (SOUTH KOREA)

Exports f.o.b.—continued	2006	2007	2008
Singapore	9,489.3	11,949.5	16,293.0
Spain	3,479.2	3,924.8	3,192.5
Taiwan	12,995.7	13,027.1	11,462.0
Thailand	4,246.1	4,488.4	5,779.1
Turkey	3,035.8	4,087.4	3,772.6
United Arab Emirates	2,896.0	3,704.7	5,748.5
United Kingdom	5,635.1	6,870.0	5,936.2
USA	43,183.5	45,766.1	46,376.6
Viet Nam	3,927.5	5,760.1	7,804.8
Total (incl. others)	325,464.8	371,489.1	422,007.3

* Excluding trade with the Democratic People's Republic of Korea.

Source: Korea International Trade Association.

Trade with the Democratic People's Republic of Korea (US $ million, unofficial estimates): *Total imports:* 340.3 in 2005; 519.5 in 2006. *Total exports:* 715.5 in 2005; 830.2 in 2006 (Source: Bank of Korea, Republic of Korea).

Transport

RAILWAYS
(traffic)

	2003	2004	2005
Passengers carried ('000)	894,620	921,223	950,995
Passenger-km (million)	27,228	28,459	31,004
Freight ('000 metric tons)	47,110	44,512	41,669
Freight ton-km (million)	11,057	10,641	10,108

ROAD TRAFFIC
(motor vehicles in use at 31 December)

	2002	2003	2004
Passenger cars	9,737,428	10,278,923	10,464,827
Goods vehicles	2,894,412	3,016,407	3,942,573
Buses and coaches	1,275,319	1,246,629	98,954
Motorcycles and mopeds	1,708,457	1,730,193	1,728,463

SHIPPING

Merchant Fleet
(registered at 31 December)

	2005	2006	2007
Number of vessels	2,778	2,820	2,946
Total displacement ('000 grt)	9,251.1	10,477.1	13,102.0

Source: Lloyd's Register-Fairplay, *World Fleet Statistics*.

Sea-borne Freight Traffic
('000 metric tons)*

	2002	2003	2004
Goods loaded	319,570	340,527	317,799
Goods unloaded	615,555	616,326	593,361

* Including coastwise traffic loaded and unloaded.

CIVIL AVIATION*

	2003	2004	2005
Passengers ('000)	42,839	45,824	46,841
Passenger-km (million)	82,231	96,583	101,664
Freight ('000 metric tons)	2,632	2,978	2,989
Freight ton-km (million)	11,696	13,810	13,597

* Domestic and international flights.

Tourism

FOREIGN VISITOR ARRIVALS*

Country of nationality	2004	2005	2006
China, People's Republic	627,264	709,836	893,986
Hong Kong	155,058	166,204	142,786
Japan	2,443,070	2,439,809	2,338,921
Philippines	213,434	222,622	248,262
Russia	156,890	143,850	144,611
Taiwan	304,908	351,421	338,162
Thailand	102,588	112,724	128,555
USA	511,170	530,629	555,704
Total (incl. others)	5,818,138	6,022,752	6,155,046

* Including same-day visitors (excursionists) and crew members from ships; also including Korean nationals resident abroad.

Receipts from tourism (US $ million, incl. passenger transport): 8,226 in 2004; 8,290 in 2005; 8,069 in 2006.

Source: World Tourism Organization.

Communications Media

	2005	2006	2007
Telephones ('000 main lines in use)	23,905.2	n.a.	n.a.
Mobile cellular telephones ('000 subscribers)	38,342.3	40,971.1	43,497.5
Internet users ('000)	33,010	34,120	35,590
Broadband subscribers ('000)	12,190.7	14,042.7	14,198
Registered daily newspapers (titles)	168	187	203

1996: Facsimile machines (estimate, '000 in use): 400.

1997: Radio receivers ('000 in use) 47,500.

2000: Television receivers ('000 in use) 17,229.

2004: Personal computers ('000 in use) 26,201; Book production 27,527 titles (82,097,000 copies).

Sources: mainly UNESCO, *Statistical Yearbook*; UN, *Statistical Yearbook*; International Telecommunication Union; Korean Association of Newspapers.

Education

(2007)

	Institutions	Teachers	Pupils
Kindergarten	8,294	33,504	541,550
Primary schools	5,756	167,182	3,829,998
Middle schools	3,032	107,986	2,063,159
General high schools	1,457	83,662	1,347,363
Vocational high schools	702	36,549	494,011
Junior colleges	148	11,685	795,519
Teachers' colleges	11	855	25,834
Universities and colleges	175	52,763	1,919,504
Graduate schools	1,042	2,895	296,576

Adult literacy rate (UNESCO estimates): 97.9% (males 99.2%; females 96.6%) in 2001 (Source: UN Development Programme, *Human Development Report*).

THE REPUBLIC OF KOREA (SOUTH KOREA)

Directory

Note: from 2001 the romanization of place-names in South Korea was in the process of change. Transliteration of names of people and corporations was to remain unchanged for the time being.

The Constitution

The Constitution of the Sixth Republic (Ninth Amendment) was approved by national referendum on 29 October 1987. It came into effect on 25 February 1988. The main provisions are summarized below:

THE EXECUTIVE
The President

The President shall be elected by universal, equal, direct and secret ballot of the people for one term of five years. Re-election of the President is prohibited. In times of national emergency and under certain conditions the President may issue emergency orders and take emergency action with regard to budgetary and economic matters. The President shall notify the National Assembly of these measures and obtain its concurrence, or they shall lose effect. He may, in times of war, armed conflict or similar national emergency, declare martial law in accordance with the provisions of law. He shall lift the emergency measures and martial law when the National Assembly so requests with the concurrence of a majority of the members. The President may not dissolve the National Assembly. He is authorized to take directly to the people important issues through national referendums. The President shall appoint the Prime Minister (with the consent of the National Assembly) and other public officials.

The State Council

The State Council shall be composed of the President, the Prime Minister and no more than 30 and no fewer than 15 others appointed by the President (on the recommendation of the Prime Minister), and shall deliberate on policies that fall within the power of the executive. No member of the armed forces shall be a member of the Council, unless retired from active duty.

The Board of Audit and Inspection

The Board of Audit and Inspection shall be established under the President to inspect the closing of accounts of revenue and expenditures, the accounts of the State and other organizations as prescribed by law, and to inspect the administrative functions of the executive agencies and public officials. It shall be composed of no fewer than five and no more than 11 members, including the Chairman. The Chairman shall be appointed by the President with the consent of the National Assembly, and the members by the President on the recommendation of the Chairman. Appointments shall be for four years and members may be reappointed only once.

THE NATIONAL ASSEMBLY

Legislative power shall be vested in the National Assembly. The Assembly shall be composed of not fewer than 200 members, a number determined by law, elected for four years by universal, equal, direct and secret ballot. The constituencies of members of the Assembly, proportional representation and other matters pertaining to the Assembly elections shall be determined by law. A regular session shall be held once a year and extraordinary sessions shall be convened upon requests of the President or one-quarter of the Assembly's members. The period of regular sessions shall not exceed 100 days and of extraordinary sessions 30 days. The Assembly has the power to recommend to the President the removal of the Prime Minister or any other Minister. The Assembly shall have the authority to pass a motion for the impeachment of the President or any other public official, and may inspect or investigate state affairs, under procedures to be established by law.

THE CONSTITUTIONAL COURT

The Constitutional Court shall be composed of nine members appointed by the President, three of whom shall be appointed from persons selected by the National Assembly and three from persons nominated by the Chief Justice. The term of office shall be six years. It shall pass judgment upon the constitutionality of laws upon the request of the courts, matters of impeachment and the dissolution of political parties. In these judgments the concurrence of six members or more shall be required.

THE JUDICIARY

The courts shall be composed of the Supreme Court, which is the highest court of the State, and other courts at specified levels (for further details, see section on Judicial System). The Chief Justice and justices of the Supreme Court are appointed by the President, subject to the consent of the National Assembly. When the constitutionality of a law is a prerequisite to a trial, the Court shall request a decision of the Constitutional Court. The Supreme Court shall have the power to pass judgment upon the constitutionality or legality of administrative decrees, and shall have final appellate jurisdiction over military tribunals. No judge shall be removed from office except following impeachment or a sentence of imprisonment.

ELECTION MANAGEMENT

Election Commissions shall be established for the purpose of fair management of elections and national referendums. The National Election Commission shall be composed of three members appointed by the President, three appointed by the National Assembly and three appointed by the Chief Justice of the Supreme Court. Their term of office is six years, and they may not be expelled from office except following impeachment or a sentence of imprisonment.

POLITICAL PARTIES

The establishment of political parties shall be free and the plural party system guaranteed. However, a political party whose aims or activities are contrary to the basic democratic order may be dissolved by the Constitutional Court.

AMENDMENTS

A motion to amend the Constitution shall be proposed by the President or by a majority of the total number of members of the National Assembly. Amendments extending the President's term of office or permitting the re-election of the President shall not be effective for the President in office at the time of the proposal. Proposed amendments to the Constitution shall be put before the public by the President for 20 days or more. Within 60 days of the public announcement, the National Assembly shall decide upon the proposed amendments, which require a two-thirds' majority of the National Assembly. They shall then be submitted to a national referendum not later than 30 days after passage by the National Assembly and shall be determined by more than one-half of votes cast by more than one-half of voters eligible to vote in elections for members of the National Assembly. If these conditions are fulfilled, the proposed amendments shall be finalized and the President shall promulgate them without delay.

FUNDAMENTAL RIGHTS

Under the Constitution all citizens are equal before the law. The right of habeas corpus is guaranteed. Freedom of speech, press, assembly and association are guaranteed, as are freedom of choice of residence and occupation. No state religion is to be recognized and freedom of conscience and religion is guaranteed. Citizens are protected against retrospective legislation, and may not be punished without due process of law.

Rights and freedoms may be restricted by law when this is deemed necessary for the maintenance of national security, order or public welfare. When such restrictions are imposed, no essential aspect of the right or freedom in question may be violated.

GENERAL PROVISIONS

Peaceful unification of the Korean peninsula, on the principles of liberal democracy, is the prime national aspiration. The Constitution mandates the State to establish and implement a policy of unification. The Constitution expressly stipulates that the armed forces must maintain political neutrality at all times.

The Government

HEAD OF STATE

President: LEE MYUNG-BAK (took office 25 February 2008).

STATE COUNCIL
(April 2009)

Prime Minister: HAN SEUNG-SOO.
Minister for Strategy and Finance: YOON JEUNG-HYUN.
Minister of Unification: HYUN IN-TAEK.
Minister of Foreign Affairs and Trade: YU MYUNG-HWAN.
Minister of Justice: KIM KYUNG-HAN.
Minister of National Defence: LEE SANG-HEE.

THE REPUBLIC OF KOREA (SOUTH KOREA)

Minister of Public Administration and Security: LEE DAL-GON.

Minister of Education, Science and Technology: AHN BYONG-MAN.

Minister of Culture, Sports and Tourism: YU IN-CHON.

Minister of Food, Agriculture, Forestry and Fisheries: JANG TAE-PYOUNG.

Minister of Knowledge Economy: LEE YOUN-HO.

Minister of Health, Welfare and Family Affairs: JEON JAE-HEE.

Minister of the Environment: LEE MAN-EUI.

Minister of Labour: LEE YOUNG-HEE.

Minister of Gender Equality: BYUN DO-YOON.

Minister of Land, Transport and Maritime Affairs: CHUNG JONG-HWAN.

MINISTRIES

Office of the President: Chong Wa Dae (The Blue House), 1, Sejong-no, Jongno-gu, Seoul; tel. (2) 770-0055; fax (2) 770-0344; e-mail president@cwd.go.kr; internet www.bluehouse.go.kr.

Office of the Prime Minister: 77, Sejong-no, Jongno-gu, Seoul; tel. (2) 737-0094; fax (2) 739-5830; e-mail m-opm@opm.go.kr; internet www.opm.go.kr.

Ministry of Culture, Sports and Tourism: 82-1, Sejong-no, Jongno-gu, Seoul 110-703; tel. (2) 3704-9114; fax (2) 3704-9119; e-mail webadmin@www.mct.go.kr; internet www.mcst.go.kr.

Ministry of Education, Science and Technology: 77-6, Sejong-no, Jongno-gu, Seoul 110-760; tel. (2) 2100-6570; fax (2) 2100-6579; internet www.mest.go.kr.

Ministry of Environment: 1, Jungang-dong, Gwacheon City, Gyeonggi Prov. 427-729; tel. (2) 2110-6546; fax (2) 504-9277; e-mail chanchan@me.go.kr; internet www.me.go.kr.

Ministry for Food, Agriculture, Forestry and Fisheries: 3-108, Gwacheon Government Office Bldg, 1, Jungang-dong, Gwacheon City, Gyeonggi Prov.; tel. (2) 2110-4000; fax (2) 503-7238; e-mail wmaster@maf.go.kr; internet www.mifaff.go.kr.

Ministry of Foreign Affairs and Trade: 95-1, Doryeom-dong, Jongno-gu, Seoul 110-787; tel. (2) 3703-2114; fax (2) 2100-7999; e-mail web@mofat.go.kr; internet www.mofat.go.kr.

Ministry of Gender Equality: 55, Sejong-no, 1-ga, Jongno-gu, Seoul 110-760; tel. (2) 2100-6600; fax (2) 2106-5145; e-mail webadmin@mogef.go.kr; internet www.moge.go.kr.

Ministry for Health, Welfare and Family Affairs: 1, Jungang-dong, Gwacheon City, Gyeonggi Prov. 427-721; tel. (2) 502-8272; fax (2) 2110-6453; e-mail webmaster@mohw.go.kr; internet www.mohw.go.kr.

Ministry of Justice: 1, Jungang-dong, Gwacheon City, Gyeonggi Prov.; tel. (2) 503-7023; fax (2) 504-3337; e-mail webmaster@moj.go.kr; internet www.moj.go.kr.

Ministry of Knowledge Economy: 3, Jungang-dong, Gwacheon City, Gyeonggi Prov. 427-721; tel. (2) 2110-5291; fax (2) 503-3142; internet www.mke.go.kr.

Ministry of Labour: 1, Jungang-dong, Gwacheon City, Gyeonggi Prov. 427-716; tel. (2) 503-9713; fax (2) 503-8862; e-mail m_molab@molab.go.kr; internet www.molab.go.kr.

Ministry of Land, Transport and Maritime Affairs: 1, Jungang-dong, Gwacheon City, Gyeonggi Prov. 427-712; tel. (2) 504-9114; fax (2) 503-7400; e-mail webmaster@moct.go.kr; internet www.mltm.go.kr.

Ministry of National Defence: 1, 3-ga, Yeongsan-dong, Yeongsan-gu, Seoul 140-701; tel. (2) 795-0071; fax (2) 703-3109; e-mail cyber@mnd.go.kr; internet www.mnd.go.kr.

Ministry of Public Administration and Security: Central Government Complex, 77-6, Sejong-no, 1-ga, Jongno-gu, Seoul 110-760; tel. (2) 2100-6767; fax (2) 3703-5502; e-mail hdchoi@mogaha.go.kr; internet www.mopas.go.kr.

Ministry of Strategy and Finance: Government Complex II, 88, Gwanmunro, Gwacheon City, Gyeonggi Prov. 427-725; tel. (2) 2110-2348; fax (2) 504-1335; e-mail fppr@mofe.go.kr; internet www.mofe.go.kr.

Ministry of Unification: 77-6, Sejong-no, Jongno-gu, Seoul 110-760; tel. (2) 720-2424; fax (2) 720-2149; e-mail ispark@unikorea.go.kr; internet www.unikorea.go.kr.

President and Legislature

PRESIDENT

Election, 19 December 2007

Candidate	Votes	% of total
Lee Myung-Bak (Grand National Party)	11,492,389	48.7
Chung Dong-Young (United New Democratic Party)*	6,174,681	26.1
Lee Hoi-Chang (Independent)	3,559,963	15.1
Moon Kook-Hyun (Creative Korea Party)	1,375,498	5.8
Kwon Young-Gil (Democratic Labour Party)	712,121	3.0
Rhee In-Je (Democratic Party)*	160,708	0.7
Huh Kyung-Young (Economic Republican Party)	96,756	0.4
Geum Min (Korea Socialist Party)	18,223	0.1
Chung Kun-Mo (True Owner Coalition)	15,380	0.1
Chun Kwan (Chamsaram Society Full True Act)	7,161	0.0
Total (incl. others)	23,732,854	100.0

* In 2008 the United New Democratic Party merged with the Democratic Party to form the United Democratic Party, subsequently known as the Democratic Party.

LEGISLATURE

Kuk Hoe
(National Assembly)

1 Yeouido-dong, Yeongdeungpo-gu, Seoul 150-701; tel. (2) 788-2001; fax (2) 788-3375; e-mail webmaster@assembly.go.kr; internet www.assembly.go.kr.

Speaker: LIM CHAE-JUNG.

General Election, 9 April 2008

Party	Elected	Proportional	Total
Grand National Party	131	22	153
United Democratic Party*	66	15	81
Liberty Forward Party	14	4	18
Pro-Park Coalition†	6	8	14
Democratic Labour Party	2	3	5
Creative Korea Party	1	2	3
Independents	25	—	25
Total	245	54	299

* Later renamed the Democratic Party.
† Comprising supporters of Park Geun-Hye, former Chairwoman of the GNP.

Election Commission

National Election Commission: 2-3 Junggang-dong, Gwacheon-si, Gyeonggi-do 427-727; tel. (2) 504-2761; e-mail e_nec@nec.go.kr; internet www.nec.go.kr; Chair. YANG SUNG-TAE.

Political Organizations

Centrist Reformists Democratic Party: 25-4, Yeouido-dong, Yeongdeungpo-gu, Seoul; tel. (2) 784-7007; fax (2) 780-4074; internet minjoo.org.kr; f. 2005; fmrly Millennium Democratic Party; Pres. RHEE IN-JE.

Creative Korea Party (CKP): 28-130, Yeongdeungpo 2-dong, Yeongdeungpo-gu, Seoul; tel. (2) 784-4701; fax (2) 784-4705; internet www.ckp.kr; f. 2007; Pres. MOON KOOK-HYUN.

Democratic Labour Party (DLP): 25-1, Jongdo Bldg, Moonrae-dong, Yeongdeungpo-gu, Seoul; tel. (2) 2139-7777; fax (2) 2139-7890; e-mail kdlpinter@hotmail.com; internet www.kdlp.org; f. 2000; Pres. KANG KI-GAP.

Democratic Party: 15-16, Yeouido-dong, Yeongdeungpo-gu, Seoul 150-701; e-mail help@undp.kr; internet minjoo.kr; f. 2007; Pres. SOH HAK-KYU; est. as United New Democratic Party in 2007 by defectors and mems of the Uri Party and the Democratic Party; name changed to United Democratic Party following merger with Democratic Party in Feb. 2008; name changed as above in mid-2008.

THE REPUBLIC OF KOREA (SOUTH KOREA)

Grand National Party (GNP) (Hannara Party): 247-17, Yeomchang-dong, Gangseo-gu, Seoul 157-863; tel. (2) 3786-3000; fax (2) 3786-3610; internet www.hannara.or.kr; f. 1997; est. by merger of the original Democratic Party (f. 1990) and New Korea Party; Chair. PARK HEE-TAE.

Korea Socialist Party: BS Tower, 106-7, Nogosan-dong, Mapo-gu, Seoul; tel. (2) 711-4592; fax (2) 706-4118; internet sp.or.kr; f. 1998; Pres. GEUM MIN.

Liberty Forward Party (LFP): c/o National Assembly, 1, Yeouido-dong, Yeongdeungpo-gu, Seoul 150-701 1 Seoul; tel. (2) 780-3988; e-mail master@new-party.org; internet www.jayou.or.kr; Leader LEE HOI-CHANG.

Other parties that presented candidates for the 2007 presidential election were the Economic Republican Party, the True Owner Coalition and the Chamsaram Society Full True Act.

Civic groups play an increasingly significant role in South Korean politics. These include: the People's Solidarity for Participatory Democracy (Dir JANG HASUNG); the Citizens' Coalition for Economic Justice (Sec.-Gen. PARK BYEONG-OK); and the Citizens' Alliance for Political Reform (Leader KIM SOK-SU).

Diplomatic Representation

EMBASSIES IN THE REPUBLIC OF KOREA

Afghanistan: 27-2, Hannam-dong, Yeongsan-gu, Seoul 140-210; tel. (2) 793-3535; fax (2) 795-2662; e-mail info@afghanistanembassy.or.kr; internet www.afghanistanembassy.or.kr; Ambassador MOHAMMAD KARIM RAHIMI.

Algeria: 2-6, Itaewon 2-dong, Yeongsan-gu, Seoul 140-857; tel. (2) 794-5034; fax (2) 794-5040; e-mail sifdja01@kornet.net; internet www.algerianemb.or.kr; Ambassador RABAH HADID.

Argentina: Chun Woo Bldg, 5th Floor, 534, Itaewon-dong, Yeongsan-gu, Seoul 140-861; tel. (2) 793-4062; fax (2) 792-5820; e-mail info@argentina.or.kr; internet www.argentina.or.kr; Ambassador ALFREDO A. ALCORTA.

Australia: Kyobo Bldg, 11th Floor, 1, 1-ga, Jongno-gu, Seoul 110-714; tel. (2) 2003-0100; fax (2) 722-9264; e-mail seoul-inform@dfat.gov.au; internet www.southkorea.embassy.gov.au; Ambassador PETER ROWE.

Austria: Kyobo Bldg, Rm 1913, 1-1, 1-ga, Jongno, Jongno-gu, Seoul 110-714; tel. (2) 732-9071; fax (2) 732-9486; e-mail seoul-ob@bmeia.gv.at; internet www.bmeia.gv.at/seoul; Ambassador WILHELM DONKO.

Azerbaijan: 3/F, Annex Bldg, Hannam Tower, 730, Hannam-dong, Yeongsan-gu, Seoul 140-893; tel. (2) 797-1765; fax (2) 792-1767; e-mail seoul@mission.mfa.gov.az; internet www.azembassy.co.kr; Ambassador ROVSHAN JAMSHIDOV.

Bangladesh: 7-18, Woo Sung Bldg, Dongbinggo-dong, Yeongsan-gu, Seoul; tel. (2) 796-4056; fax (2) 790-5313; Ambassador MOHAMMAD SHAHIDUL ISLAM.

Belarus: 432-1636, Sindang 2-dong, Jung-gu, Seoul; tel. (2) 2237-8171; fax (2) 2237-8174; e-mail korea@belembassy.org; internet korea.belembassy.org; Ambassador ALEKSANDR GURYANOV.

Belgium: 737-10, Hannam-dong, Yeongsan-gu, Seoul 140-895; tel. (2) 749-0381; fax (2) 797-1688; e-mail seoul@diplobel.fed.be; internet www.belgium.or.kr; Ambassador PIERRE CLÉMENT DUBUISSON.

Brazil: Ihn Gallery Bldg, 4th and 5th Floors, 141 Palpan-dong, Jongno-gu, Seoul; tel. (2) 738-4970; fax (2) 738-4974; e-mail braseul@kornet.net; internet www.brasemb.or.kr; Ambassador CELINA ASSUMPÇÃO DO VALLE PEREIRA.

Brunei: 737-11, Hannam-dong, Yeongsan-gu, Seoul 140-210; tel. (2) 790-1078; fax (2) 790-1084; e-mail kbnbd_seoul@yahoo.com; Ambassador Dato' Paduka Haji HARUN BIN HJ ISMAIL.

Bulgaria: 723-42, Hannam 2-dong, Yeongsan-gu, Seoul 140-894; tel. (2) 794-8626; fax (2) 794-8627; e-mail ebdy1990@unitel.co.kr; Ambassador ALEXANDER SAVOV.

Cambodia: 657-162, Hannam-dong, Yeongsan-gu, Seoul 140-910; tel. (2) 3785-1041; fax (2) 3785-1040; e-mail camboemb@korea.com; Ambassador LIM SAMKOL.

Canada: POB 6299, 9/F Kolon Bldg, 45, Mugyo-dong, Jung-gu, Seoul; tel. (2) 3455-6000; fax (2) 3455-6123; e-mail canada@cec.or.kr; internet www.korea.gc.ca; Ambassador TED LIPMAN.

Chile: 1801, Coryo Daeyungak Tower, 25-5 Chungmoro 1-ga, Jung-gu, Seoul 100-706; tel. (2) 779-2610; fax (2) 779-2615; e-mail echilekr@yahoo.co.kr; internet www.echilecor.or.kr; Ambassador ADOLFO CARAFÍ MELERO.

China, People's Republic: 54, Hyoja-dong, Jongno-gu, Seoul; tel. (2) 738-1038; fax (2) 738-1059; e-mail chinaemb_kr@mfa.gov.cn; internet www.chinaemb.or.kr; Ambassador CHENG YONGHUA.

Colombia: Kyobo Bldg, 13th Floor, 1-ga, Jongno, Jongno-gu, Seoul; tel. (2) 720-1369; fax (2) 725-6959; e-mail eseul@cancilleria.gov.co; Ambassador ALEJANDRO BORDA ROJAS.

Congo, Democratic Republic: 702, Daewoo Complex Bldg, 167 Naesu-dong, Jongno-gu, Seoul; tel. (2) 722-7958; fax (2) 722-7998; e-mail congokoreambassy@yahoo.com; Ambassador N. CHRISTOPHE NGWEY.

Costa Rica: Iljin Bldg, 7, 50-1, Dohwa-dong, Mapo-gu, Seoul 121-040; tel. (2) 707-9248; fax (2) 707-9255; e-mail embajadacr@ecostarica.or.kr; internet www.ecostarica.or.kr; Ambassador FERNANDO BORBÓN ARIAS.

Côte d'Ivoire: Chungam Bldg, 2nd Floor, 794-4, Hannam-dong, Yeongsan-gu, Seoul; tel. (2) 3785-0561; fax (2) 3785-0564; e-mail abenikof@hotmail.com; Ambassador HONORAT ABENI KOFFI.

Czech Republic: 1-121, 2-ga, Shinmun-ro, Jongno-gu, Seoul 110-062; tel. (2) 725-6765; fax (2) 734-6452; e-mail seoul@embassy.mzv.cz; internet www.mzv.cz/seoul; Ambassador JAROSLAV OLSA.

Denmark: Namsong Bldg, 5th Floor, 260-199, Itaewon-dong, Yeongsan-gu, Seoul 140-200; tel. (2) 795-4187; fax (2) 796-0986; e-mail selamb@um.dk; internet www.ambseoul.um.dk; Ambassador POUL O. G. HOINESS.

Dominican Republic: Taepyeong-no Bldg, 19th Floor, 2-ga, 310, Taepyeong-no, Jung-gu, Seoul; tel. (2) 756-3513; fax (2) 756-3514; e-mail embadom@kornet.net; Ambassador HÉCTOR GALUÁN.

Ecuador: Korea First Bldg, 19th Floor, 100, Gongpyeong-dong, Jongno-gu, Seoul; tel. (2) 739-2401; fax (2) 739-2355; e-mail mecuadorcor1@kornet.net; Ambassador JOSÉ ENRIQUE NÚÑEZ TAMAYO.

Egypt: POB 3734, 46-1, Hannam-dong, Yeongsan-gu, Seoul 140-210; tel. (2) 749-0787; fax (2) 795-2588; e-mail embassyegyptkorea@yahoo.com; Ambassador MOHAMED REDA KAMEL EL-TAIFY.

El Salvador: Samsung Life Insurance Bldg, 20th Floor, Taepyeong-no 2-ga, Jung-gu, Seoul 100-716; tel. (2) 753-3432; fax (2) 753-3456; e-mail koembsal@hananet.net; Ambassador ZOILA DEL CARMEN AGUIRRE DE MAY.

Finland: Rm 1602, Kyobo Bldg 16/F, Jongno 1-ga, Jongno-gu, Seoul 110-714; tel. (2) 732-6737; fax (2) 723-4969; e-mail sanomat.seo@formin.fi; internet www.finland.or.kr; Ambassador PEKKA WUORISTO.

France: 30, Hap-dong, Seodaemun-gu, Seoul 120-030; tel. (2) 3149-4300; fax (2) 3149-4328; e-mail ambafrance@korea.com; internet www.ambafrance-kr.org; Ambassador PHILIPPE THIÉBAUD.

Gabon: Yoosung Bldg, 4th Floor, 738-20, Hannam-dong, Yeongsan-gu, Seoul; tel. (2) 793-9575; fax (2) 793-9574; e-mail amgabsel@unitel.co.kr; Ambassador JEAN-PIERRE SOLE-EMANE.

Germany: 308-5, Dongbinggo-dong, Yeongsan-gu, Seoul 140-816; tel. (2) 748-4114; fax (2) 748-4161; e-mail info@seoul.diplo.de; internet www.seoul.diplo.de; Ambassador NORBERT BAAS.

Ghana: 5-4, Hannam-dong, Yeongsan-gu, Seoul (CPOB 3887); tel. (2) 3785-1427; fax (2) 3785-1428; e-mail ghana3@kornet.net; internet www.ghanaembassy.or.kr; Ambassador NANA GABRIEL NSIAH NKETIAH.

Greece: Hanwha Bldg, 27th Floor, 1, Janggyo-dong, Jung-gu, Seoul 100-797; tel. (2) 729-1401; fax (2) 729-1402; e-mail greekemb@kornet.net; Ambassador KONSTANTINOS DRAKAKIS.

Guatemala: 614, Lotte Hotel, 1, Sogong-dong, Jung-gu, Seoul 100-635; tel. (2) 771-7582; fax (2) 771-7584; e-mail embcorea@minex.gob.gt; Ambassador RAFAEL A. SALAZAR.

Holy See: POB 393, Kwang Hwa Mun, Seoul 110-603 (Apostolic Nunciature); tel. (2) 736-5725; fax (2) 739-5738; e-mail nunseoul@kornet.net; Apostolic Nuncio Most Rev. EMIL PAUL TSCHERRIG (Titular Archbishop of Voli).

Honduras: Jongno Tower Bldg, 2nd Floor, 6, Jongno 2-ga, Jongno-gu, Seoul 110-160; tel. (2) 738-8402; fax (2) 738-8403; e-mail hondseul@kornet.net; Ambassador RENE FRANCISCO UMANA CHINCHILLA.

Hungary: 1-103, Dongbinggo-dong, Yeongsan-gu, Seoul 140-230; tel. (2) 792-2105; fax (2) 792-2109; e-mail mission.sel@kum.hu; internet www.mfa.gov.hu/emb/seoul; Ambassador MIKLÓS LENGYEL.

India: 37-3, Hannam-dong, Yeongsan-gu, CPOB 3466, Seoul 140-210; tel. (2) 798-4257; fax (2) 796-9534; e-mail eoiseoul@sinbiro.com; internet www.indembassy.or.kr; Ambassador SKAND R. TAYAL.

Indonesia: 55, Yeouido-dong, Yeongdeungpo-gu, Seoul 150-010; tel. (2) 783-5675; fax (2) 780-4280; e-mail komsel@soback.kornet.nm.kr; internet www.indonesiaseoul.org; Ambassador NICHOLAS TANDI DAMMEN.

Iran: 1-93, Dongbinggo-dong, Yeongsan-gu, Seoul 140-809; tel. (2) 793-7751; fax (2) 792-7052; e-mail iranssy@chol.com; Ambassador MOHAMMAD REZA BAKHTIARI.

Iraq: 310-49, Dongbinggo-dong, Yeongsan-gu, Seoul; tel. (2) 792-6671; fax (2) 792-6674.

THE REPUBLIC OF KOREA (SOUTH KOREA)   *Directory*

Ireland: Daehan Fire and Marine Insurance Bldg, 15th Floor, 51-1, Namchang-dong, Jung-gu, Seoul; tel. (2) 774-6455; fax (2) 774-6458; e-mail irelandkor@kornet.net; internet www.irelandhouse-korea.com; Ambassador Conor Murphy.

Israel: 18th Floor, Kabool Bldg, 149, Seorin-dong, Jongno-gu, Seoul 110-726; tel. (2) 739-8666; fax (2) 739-8667; e-mail seoul@israel.org; internet seoul.mfa.gov.il; Ambassador Yigal B. Caspi.

Italy: 1-398, Hannam-dong, Yeongsan-gu, Seoul 140-210; tel. (2) 796-0491; fax (2) 797-5560; e-mail embassy.seoul@esteri.it; internet www.ambseoul.esteri.it; Ambassador Massimo Andrea Leggeri.

Japan: 18-11, Junghak-dong, Jongno-gu, Seoul; tel. (2) 2170-5200; fax (2) 734-4528; e-mail info@japanem.or.kr; internet www.kr.emb-japan.go.jp; Ambassador Toshinori Shigeie.

Kazakhstan: 484-24, Bukak Village 11, Pyeongchang-dong, Jongno-gu, Seoul; tel. (2) 379-9714; fax (2) 395-9719; e-mail kazkor@chollian.net; internet www.kazembassy.org; Ambassador Darkhan Berdaliyev.

Kuwait: 309-15, Dongbinggo-dong, Yeongsan-gu, Seoul; tel. (2) 749-3688; fax (2) 749-3687; Ambassador Mohammed Abdulrasul Al-Awadi.

Laos: 657-93, Hannam-dong, Yeongsan-gu, Seoul; tel. (2) 796-1713; fax (2) 796-1771; e-mail laoseoul@korea.com; Ambassador Soukthavone Keola.

Lebanon: 310-49, Dongbinggo-dong, Yeongsan-gu, Seoul 140-230; tel. (2) 794-6482; fax (2) 794-6485; e-mail emleb@lebanonembassy.net; internet www.lebanonembassy.net; Ambassador Issam Mustapha.

Malaysia: 4-1, Hannam-dong, Yeongsan-gu, Seoul 140-884; tel. (2) 795-9203; fax (2) 794-5480; e-mail mwseoul@kornet.net; internet www.malaysia.or.kr; Ambassador Dato' Ramlan bin Ibrahim.

Mexico: 33-6, Hannam 1-dong, Yeongsan-gu, Seoul 140-885; tel. (2) 798-1694; fax (2) 790-0939; e-mail srecor@uriel.net; internet portal.sre.gob.mx/corea; Ambassador Leandro Arellano.

Mongolia: 33-5, Hannam-dong, Yeongsan-gu, Seoul 140-885; tel. (2) 794-1350; fax (2) 794-7605; e-mail mongol5@kornet.net; internet www.mongolembassy.com; Ambassador Dorjpalamyn Gerel.

Morocco: S-15, UN Village, 270-3, Hannam-dong, Yeongsan-gu, Seoul; tel. (2) 793-6249; fax (2) 792-8178; e-mail sifamase@kornet.net; internet www.moroccoemb.or.kr; Ambassador Mohamed Chraïbi.

Myanmar: 724-1, Hannam-dong, Yeongsan-gu, Seoul 140-210; tel. (2) 792-3341; fax (2) 796-5570; e-mail myanmare@ppp.kornet.net; Ambassador U Nyo Win.

Nepal: 244-143, Huam-dong, Yeongsan-gu, Seoul; tel. (2) 3789-9770; fax (2) 736-8848; e-mail info@nepembseoul.gov.np; internet www.nepembseoul.gov.np; Ambassador Kamal Koirala.

Netherlands: Kyobo Bldg, 14th Floor, Jongno 1-ga, Jongno-gu, Seoul 110-714; tel. (2) 737-9514; fax (2) 735-1321; e-mail seo@minbuza.nl; internet southkorea.nlembassy.org; Ambassador Hans Heinsbroek.

New Zealand: Kyobo Bldg, 15th Floor, 1, 1-ga, Jongno, Jongno-gu, KPO Box 2258, Seoul 110-110; tel. (2) 3701-7700; fax (2) 3701-7701; e-mail nzembsel@kornet.net; internet www.nzembassy.com/korea; Ambassador Jane Coombs.

Nigeria: 310-19, Dongbinggo-dong, Yeongsan-gu, Seoul; tel. (2) 797-2370; fax (2) 796-1848; e-mail chancery@nigerianembassy.or.kr; internet www.nigerianembassy.or.kr; Ambassador Desmond Akawor.

Norway: 258-8, Itaewon-dong, Yeongsan-gu, Seoul 140-200; tel. (2) 795-6850; fax (2) 798-6072; e-mail emb.seoul@mfa.no; internet www.norway.or.kr; Ambassador Didrik Tønseth.

Oman: 309-3, Dongbinggo-dong, Yeongsan-gu, Seoul; tel. (2) 790-2431; fax (2) 790-2430; e-mail omanembs@ppp.kornet.nm.kr; Ambassador Moussa Hamdan at-Tae.

Pakistan: 124-13, Itaewon-dong, Yeongsan-gu, Seoul 140-200; tel. (2) 796-8252; fax (2) 796-0313; Ambassador Murad Ali.

Panama: Northgate Bldg, 6th Floor, 66, Jeokseon-dong, Jongno-gu, Seoul; tel. (2) 734-8610; fax (2) 734-8613; e-mail panaemba@kornet.net; Ambassador Juan José Amado, III.

Papua New Guinea: 36-1, Hannam 1-dong, Yeongsan-gu, Seoul; tel. (2) 798-9854; fax (2) 798-9856; e-mail pngembsl@ppp.kornet.nm.kr; Ambassador Kuma Aua.

Paraguay: Hannam Tower, Annex Bldg, 3rd Floor, 730, Hannam-dong, Yeongsan-gu, Seoul; tel. (2) 792-8335; fax (2) 792-8334; e-mail pyemc2@kornet.net; internet www.embaparcorea.org; Ambassador Ceferino Adrian Valdez Peralta.

Peru: Daeyungak Bldg, Suite 2002, 25-5, 1-ga, Jungmu-no, Jung-gu, Seoul 100-706; tel. (2) 757-1735; fax (2) 757-1738; e-mail lpruseul@uriel.net; Ambassador Doraliza López Bravo Vda de Ruíz.

Philippines: 34-44, Itaewon 1-dong, Yeongsan-gu, Seoul; tel. (2) 796-7387; fax (2) 796-0827; e-mail seoulpe@gmail.com; Ambassador Luis Teodoro Cruz.

Poland: 70, Sagan-dong, Jongno-gu, Seoul; tel. (2) 723-9681; fax (2) 723-9680; e-mail embassy@polandseoul.org; internet www.polandseoul.org; Ambassador Marek Całka.

Portugal: Wonseo Bldg, 2nd Floor, 171, Wonseo-dong, Jongno-gu, Seoul; tel. (2) 3675-2251; fax (2) 3675-2250; e-mail ambport@chollian.net; Ambassador Henrique Silveira Borges.

Qatar: 309-5, Dongbinggo-dong, Yeongsan-gu, Seoul 140-817; tel. (2) 798-2444; fax (2) 790-1027; e-mail qatarseoul@hotmail.com; Ambassador Ahmad S. al-Midhadi.

Romania: 1-42, UN Village, Hannam-dong, Yeongsan-gu, Seoul 140-210; tel. (2) 797-4924; fax (2) 794-3114; e-mail romemb@uriel.net; Chargé d'affaires a.i. Constantin Soare.

Russia: 34-16, Jeong-dong, Jung-gu, Seoul 100-120; tel. (2) 318-2116; fax (2) 754-0417; e-mail rusemb@uriel.net; internet www.russian-embassy.org; Ambassador Gleb A. Ivashentsov.

Saudi Arabia: 1-112, 2-ga, Sinmun-no, Jongno-gu, Seoul; tel. (2) 739-0631; fax (2) 732-3110; Ambassador Abdullah A. al-A'ifan.

Serbia: 730, Hannam-dong, Yeongsan-gu, Seoul; tel. (2) 797-5109; fax (2) 790-6109; e-mail emserbseul@yahoo.com; internet www.embserb.or.kr; Ambassador Zoran Veljić.

Singapore: Seoul Finance Bldg, 28th Floor, 84, 1-ga, Taepyeong-no, Jung-gu, Seoul 100-102; tel. (2) 774-2464; fax (2) 773-2465; e-mail singemb@unitel.co.kr; internet www.mfa.gov.sg/seoul; Ambassador Chua Thai Keong.

Slovakia: 389-1, Hannam-dong, Yeongsan-gu, Seoul 140-210; tel. (2) 794-3981; fax (2) 794-3982; e-mail slovakemb@yahoo.com; Ambassador Pavel Hrmo.

South Africa: 1-37, Hannam-dong, Yeongsan-gu, Seoul 140-210; tel. (2) 792-4855; fax (2) 792-4856; e-mail general@southafrica-embassy.or.kr; internet www.southafrica-embassy.or.kr; Ambassador Stefanus Johannes Schoeman.

Spain: 726-52, Hannam-dong, Yeongsan-gu, Seoul; tel. (2) 794-3581; fax (2) 796-8207; e-mail emb.seul@mae.es; internet www.mae.es/embajadas/seul/es/home; Ambassador Juan Bautista Casas.

Sri Lanka: Kyobo Bldg, Rm 2002, 1-1, 1-ga, Jongno, Jongno-gu, Seoul 110-714; tel. (2) 735-2966; fax (2) 737-9577; e-mail lankaemb@chollian.net; Ambassador John Asitha Ivon Perera.

Sudan: 653-24, Hannam-dong, Yeongsan-gu, Seoul; tel. (2) 793-8692; fax (2) 793-8693; e-mail sudansol@yahoo.com; Ambassador Mohammed Salah Eldin Abbas.

Sweden: Seoul Central Bldg, 12th Floor, 136, Seorin-dong, Jongno-gu, KPO Box 1154, Seoul 110-611; tel. (2) 3703-3700; fax (2) 3703-3701; e-mail embassy@swedemb.or.kr; internet www.swedenabroad.com/seoul; Ambassador Lars Vargö.

Switzerland: 32-10, Songwol-dong, Jongno-gu, POB 2900, Seoul 110-101; tel. (2) 739-9511; fax (2) 737-9392; e-mail swissemb@elim.net; internet www.eda.admin.ch/seoul; Ambassador Thomas Kupfer.

Thailand: 653-7, Hannam-dong, Yeongsan-gu, Seoul 140-210; tel. (2) 795-3098; fax (2) 798-3448; e-mail rteseoul@kornet.net; internet www.thaiembassy.or.kr; Ambassador Tasanawadee Miancharoen.

Tunisia: 1-17, Dongbinggo-dong, Yeongsan-gu, Seoul 140-809; tel. (2) 790-4334; fax (2) 790-4333; e-mail ambtnkor@kornet.net; Ambassador Mustapha Khammari.

Turkey: Vivien Corpn Bldg, 4th Floor, 4-52, Seobinggo-dong, Yeongsan-gu, Seoul; tel. (2) 794-0255; fax (2) 797-8546; e-mail seulbe@soback.kornet.21.nm.kr; Ambassador Deniz Ozmen.

Ukraine: 1-97, Dongbinggo-dong, Yeongsan-gu, Seoul; tel. (2) 790-5696; fax (2) 790-5697; e-mail secretary@ukrembrk.com; internet www.ukrembrk.com; Ambassador Belashov Volodymyr.

United Arab Emirates: 5-5, Hannam-dong, Yeongsan-gu, Seoul; tel. (2) 790-3235; fax (2) 790-3238; Ambassador Abdullah Muhammadd al-Maainah.

United Kingdom: Taepyeongno 40, 4, Jeong-dong, Jung-gu, Seoul 100-120; tel. (2) 3210-5500; fax (2) 725-1738; e-mail postmaster.seoul@fco.gov.uk; internet www.ukinkorea.fco.gov.uk; Ambassador Martin Uden.

USA: 32, Sejong-no, Jongno-gu, Seoul 110-710; tel. (2) 397-4114; fax (2) 735-3903; e-mail EmbassySeoulPA@state.gov; internet seoul.usembassy.gov; Ambassador Kathleen Stevens.

Uruguay: 14F LIG Kangnam Bldg, 708-6, Yeoksam-dong, Gangnam-gu, Seoul; tel. (2) 6245-3179; fax (2) 6245-3181; e-mail uruseul@embrou.or.kr; Ambassador Nelson Yemil Chaben.

Uzbekistan: Diplomatic Center, Rm. 701, 1376-1, Seocho 2-dong, Seocho-gu, Seoul; tel. (2) 574-6554; fax (2) 578-0576; Ambassador Vitali V. Fen.

THE REPUBLIC OF KOREA (SOUTH KOREA)

Venezuela: 16th Floor, SC First Bank Bldg, 100, Gongpyeong-dong, Jongno-gu, Seoul 110-702; tel. (2) 732-1546; fax (2) 732-1548; e-mail emvesel@soback.kornet.net; internet www.venezuelaemb.or.kr; Chargé d'affaires a.i. WOLFGANG GONZÁLEZ.

Viet Nam: 28-58, Samcheong-dong, Jongno-gu, Seoul 140-210; tel. (2) 738-2318; fax (2) 739-2064; e-mail vndsq@yahoo.com; Ambassador PHAM TIEN VAN.

Yemen: 11-444, Hannam-dong, Yeongsan-gu, Seoul 140-210; tel. (2) 792-9883; fax (2) 792-9885; internet www.gpc.org.ye; Ambassador YAHYA AHMAD AL-WAZIR.

Judicial System

SUPREME COURT

The Supreme Court is the highest court, consisting of 14 Justices, including the Chief Justice. The Chief Justice is appointed by the President, with the consent of the National Assembly, for a term of six years. Other Justices of the Supreme Court are appointed for six years by the President on the recommendation of the Chief Justice. However, the appointment of the Justices of the Supreme Court requires the consent of the National Assembly. The Chief Justice may not be reappointed. The court is empowered to receive and decide on appeals against decisions of the High Courts, the Patent Court, and the appellate panels of the District Courts or the Family Court in civil, criminal, administrative, patent and domestic relations cases. It is also authorized to act as the final tribunal to review decisions of courts-martial and to consider cases arising from presidential and parliamentary elections.

Chief Justice: LEE YONG-HOON, 967, Seocho-dong, Seocho-gu, Seoul; tel. (2) 3480-1002; fax (2) 533-1911; internet www.scourt.go.kr.

Justices: CHA HAN-SUNG, KIM YONG-DAM, KIM YOUNG-RAN, YANG SEUNG-TAE, YANG CHANG-SOO, PARK SI-HWAN, KIM JI-HYUNG, LEE HONG-HOON, PARK ILL-HOAN, KIM NUNG-HWAN, JEON SOO-AHN, AHN DAI-HEE.

CONSTITUTIONAL COURT

The Constitutional Court is composed of nine adjudicators appointed by the President, of whom three are chosen from among persons selected by the National Assembly and three from persons nominated by the Chief Justice. The Court adjudicates the following matters: constitutionality of a law (when requested by the other courts); impeachment; dissolution of a political party; disputes between state agencies, or between state agencies and local governments; and petitions relating to the Constitution.

President: LEE KANG-KUK, 83 Jae-dong, Jongno-gu, Seoul 110-250; tel. (2) 708-3456; fax (2) 708-3566; internet www.ccourt.go.kr.

HIGH COURTS

There are five courts, situated in Seoul, Daegu, Busan, Gwangju and Daejeon, with five chief, 78 presiding and 145 other judges. The courts have appellate jurisdiction in civil and criminal cases and can also pass judgment on administrative litigation against government decisions.

PATENT COURT

The Patent Court opened in Daejeon in March 1998, to deal with cases in which the decisions of the Intellectual Property Tribunal are challenged. The examination of the case is conducted by a judge, with the assistance of technical examiners.

DISTRICT COURTS

District Courts are established in 13 major cities; there are 13 chief, 241 presiding and 966 other judges. They exercise jurisdiction over all civil and criminal cases in the first instance.

MUNICIPAL COURTS

There are 103 Municipal Courts within the District Court system, dealing with small claims, minor criminal offences, and settlement cases.

FAMILY COURT

There is one Family Court, in Seoul, with a chief judge, four presiding judges and 16 other judges. The court has jurisdiction in domestic matters and cases of juvenile delinquency.

ADMINISTRATIVE COURT

An Administrative Court opened in Seoul in March 1998, to deal with cases that are specified in the Administrative Litigation Act. The Court has jurisdiction over cities and counties adjacent to Seoul, and deals with administrative matters, including taxes, expropriations of land, labour and other general administrative matters. District Courts will deal with administrative matters within their districts until the establishment of regional administrative courts is complete.

COURTS-MARTIAL

These exercise jurisdiction over all offences committed by armed forces personnel and civilian employees. They are also authorized to try civilians accused of military espionage or interference with the execution of military duties.

Religion

BUDDHISM

Korean Mahayana Buddhism has about 80 denominations. The Chogye-jong is the largest Buddhist order in Korea, having been introduced from China in AD 372. The Chogye Order accounts for almost two-thirds of all Korean Buddhists. Won Buddhism combines elements of Buddhism and Confucianism.

Korean United Buddhist Association (KUBA): 46-19, Soosong-dong, Jongno-gu, Seoul 110-140; tel. (2) 732-4885; 28 mem. Buddhist orders; Pres. SONG WOL-JOO.

CHRISTIANITY

National Council of Churches in Korea: Christian Bldg, Rm 706, 136-46, Yeonchi-dong, Jongno-gu, Seoul 110-736; tel. (2) 744-3717; fax (2) 744-6189; e-mail kncc@kncc.or.kr; internet www.kncc.or.kr; f. 1924; est. as National Christian Council; present name adopted 1946; eight mem. churches; Gen. Sec. Rev. PAIK DO-WOONG.

The Anglican Communion

South Korea has three Anglican dioceses, collectively forming the Anglican Church of Korea (founded as a separate province in April 1993), under its own Primate, the Bishop of Seoul.

Bishop of Pusan (Busan): Rt Rev. SOLOMON JONG-MO YOON, 455-2, Oncheon-1-dong, Dongnae-gu, Busan 607-061; tel. (51) 554-5742; fax (51) 553-9643; e-mail adbusan@yahoo.co.kr; internet www.pusan1.net.

Bishop of Seoul: Most Rev. FRANCIS KYUNG JO-PARK, 3, Jeong-dong, Jung-gu, Seoul 100-120; tel. (2) 738-6597; fax (2) 723-2640; e-mail 44kyung@hanmail.net.

Bishop of Taejon (Daejeon): Rt Rev. ANDREW SHIN, 88-1, Sonhwa 2-dong, POB 22, Daejeon 300-600; tel. (42) 256-9987; fax (42) 255-8918.

The Roman Catholic Church

For ecclesiastical purposes, North and South Korea are nominally under a unified jurisdiction. South Korea comprises three archdioceses, 12 dioceses and one military ordinate. At 31 December 2006 some 4,681,799 people were adherents of the Roman Catholic Church.

Bishops' Conference

Catholic Bishops' Conference of Korea, 643-1, Junggok-dong, Gwangjin-gu, Seoul 143-912; tel. (2) 460-7500; fax (2) 460-7505; e-mail cbck@cbck.or.kr; internet www.cbck.or.kr.

f. 1857; Pres. Most Rev. PETER KANG (Bishop of Cheju—Jeju).

Archbishop of Kwangju (Gwangju): Most Rev. ANDREAS CHOI CHANG-MOU, Archdiocesan Office, 5-32, Im-dong, Buk-gu, Gwangju 500-868; tel. (62) 510-2838; fax (62) 525-6873; e-mail biseo@kjcatholic.or.kr.

Archbishop of Seoul: Cardinal NICHOLAS CHEONG JIN-SUK, Archdiocesan Office, 1, 2-ga, Myeong-dong, Jung-gu, Seoul 100-022; tel. (2) 727-2114; fax (2) 773-1947; e-mail ao@seoul.catholic.or.kr.

Archbishop of Taegu (Daegu): Most Rev. JOHN CHOI YOUNG-SOO, Archdiocesan Office, 225-1, Namsan 3-dong, Jung-gu, Daegu 700-804; tel. (53) 253-7011; fax (53) 253-9441; e-mail taegu@tgcatholic.or.kr.

Protestant Churches

Korean Methodist Church: 64-8, 1-ga, Taepyeong-no, Jung-gu, Seoul 100-101; KPO Box 285, Seoul 110-602; tel. (2) 399-4300; fax (2) 399-4307; e-mail bishop@kmcweb.or.kr; internet www.kmcweb.or.kr; f. 1885; 1,534,504 mems (2007); Bishop Dr KO SOO-CHUL.

Presbyterian Church in the Republic of Korea (PROK): Academy House, San 76, Suyu 6-dong, Kangbuk-ku, Seoul 142-070; tel. (2) 3499-7600; fax (2) 3499-7630; e-mail prok3000@chollian.net; internet www.prok.org; f. 1953; 337,188 mems (2005); Gen. Sec. Rev. YOON KIL-SOO.

Presbyterian Church of Korea (PCK): The Korean Church Centennial Memorial Bldg, 135, Yunji-dong, Jongno-gu, Seoul 110-470; tel. (2) 741-4350; fax (2) 766-2427; e-mail thepck@pck.or

THE REPUBLIC OF KOREA (SOUTH KOREA)

.kr; internet www.pck.or.kr; 2,395,323 mems (Dec. 2003); Moderator Rev. YOUNG TAE KIM; Gen. Sec. Rev. SEONGI CHO.

There are some 160 other Protestant denominations in the country, including the Korea Baptist Convention and the Korea Evangelical Church.

OTHER RELIGIONS

Chundo Kyo, a religion indigenous and unique to Korea, combines elements of Shaman, Buddhist, and Christian doctrines. Confucianism also has a significant number of followers. Taejong Gyo is Korea's oldest religion, dating back 4,000 years, and comprising beliefs in the national foundation myth, and the triune god, Hanul. By the 15th century the religion had largely disappeared, but a revival began in the late 19th century.

The Press

NATIONAL DAILIES
(In Korean, unless otherwise indicated)

Chosun Ilbo: 61, 1-ga, Taepyeong-no, Jung-gu, Seoul 100-756; tel. (2) 724-5114; fax (2) 724-5059; e-mail webmaster@chosun.com; internet www.chosun.com; f. 1920; morning, weekly and children's edns; independent; Korean, English, Chinese and Japanese; Executive Editor BYUN YONG-SHIK; circ. 2,470,000.

Daily Sports Seoul: 25, 1-ga, Taepyeong-no, Jung-gu, Seoul; tel. (2) 721-5114; fax (2) 721-5396; internet www.seoul.co.kr; f. 1985; morning; sports and leisure; Pres. LEE HAN-SOO; Man. Editor SON CHU-WHAN.

Dong-A Ilbo: 139-1, 3-ga, Sejong-no, Jongno-gu, Seoul 100-715; tel. (2) 2020-0114; fax (2) 2020-1239; e-mail newsroom@donga.com; internet www.donga.com; f. 1920; morning; independent; Pres. KIM HAK-JOON; Editor-in-Chief LEE HYUN-NAK; circ. 2,150,000.

Han-Joong Daily News: 91-1, 2-ga, Myeong-dong, Jung-gu, Seoul; tel. (2) 776-2801; fax (2) 778-2803; Chinese.

Hankook Ilbo: 14, Junghak-dong, Jongno-gu, Seoul; tel. (2) 724-2114; fax (2) 724-2244; internet www.hankooki.com; f. 1954; morning; independent; Pres. CHANG CHAE-KEUN; Editor-in-Chief YOON KOOK-BYUNG; circ. 2,000,000.

Hankuk Kyungje Shinmun (Korea Economic Daily): 441, Junglim-dong, Jung-gu, Seoul 100-791; tel. (2) 360-4114; fax (2) 779-4447; internet www.hankyung.com; f. 1964; morning; Pres. and CEO SHIN SANG-MIN; Man. Dir and Editor-in-Chief CHOI KYU-YOUNG.

Hankyoreh Shinmun (One Nation): 116-25, Gongdeok-dong, Mapo-gu, Seoul 121-020; tel. (2) 710-0114; fax (2) 710-0210; internet www.hani.co.kr; f. 1988; centre-left; Korean, English; CEO and Publr CHUNG TAE-KI; Editor-in-Chief SUNG HAN-PYO; circ. 500,000.

Ilgan Sports (The Daily Sports): 14, Junghak-dong, Jongno-gu, Seoul 110-792; tel. (2) 724-2114; fax (2) 724-2299; internet www.dailysports.co.kr; morning; f. 1969; Pres. CHANG CHAE-KEUN; Editor KIM JIN-DONG; circ. 600,000.

Jeil Economic Daily: 146, Ssangrin-dong, Jung-gu, Seoul; tel. (2) 6325-3114; e-mail ysk@jed.co.kr; internet www.jed.co.kr; f. 1988; morning; Pres. PARK JUNG-GU; Editor-in-Chief JANG CHANG-YONG.

JoongAng Ilbo (JoongAng Daily News): 7, Soonhwa-dong, Jung-gu, 100-759 Seoul; tel. (2) 751-9215; fax (2) 751-9219; e-mail iht@joongang.co.kr; internet www.joins.com; f. 1965; morning; Korean and English; Publr KIL JEONG-WOO; Exec. Dir CHANG SUNG-HYO; circ. 2,300,000.

Kookmin Ilbo: 12, Yeouido-dong, Yeongdeungpo-gu, Seoul; tel. (2) 781-9114; fax (2) 781-9781; internet www.kukminilbo.co.kr; Pres. RO SEUNG-SOOK.

Korea Daily News: 25, 1-ga, Taepyeong-no, Jung-gu, Seoul; tel. (2) 2000-9000; fax (2) 2000-9659; e-mail webmaster@seoul.co.kr; internet www.kdaily.com; f. 1945; morning; independent; Publr and Pres. SON CHU-HWAN; Man. Editor LEE DONG-HWA; circ. 700,000.

The Korea Herald: 1-17, Jeong-dong, Jung-gu, Seoul; tel. (2) 727-0205; fax (2) 727-0670; internet www.koreaherald.co.kr; f. 1953; morning; English; independent; Pres. WOOK HONG-JUNG; Man. Editor YU KUN-HA; circ. 150,000.

The Korea Times: 14, Junghak-dong, Jongno-gu, Seoul 110-792; tel. (2) 724-2859; fax (2) 736-4061; e-mail kt@koreatimes.co.kr; internet www.koreatimes.co.kr; f. 1950; morning; English; independent; Pres. PARK MOO-JONG; Man. Editor LEE SANG-SEOK; circ. 100,000.

Kyung-hyang Shinmun: 22, Jeong-dong, Jung-gu, Seoul; tel. (2) 3701-1114; fax (2) 737-6362; internet www.khan.co.kr; f. 1946; evening; independent; Pres. HONG SUNG-MAN; Executive Editor KIM JI-YOUNG; circ. 733,000.

Directory

Maeil Business Newspaper: 51-9, 1-ga, Bil-dong, Jung-gu, Seoul 100-728; tel. (2) 2000-2114; fax (2) 2269-6200; internet www.mk.co.kr; f. 1966; evening; economics and business; Korean, English; Pres. CHANG DAE-WHAN; Editor JANG BYUNG-CHANG; circ. 235,000.

Munhwa Ilbo: 68, 1-ga, Chungjeong-no, Jung-gu, Seoul 110-170; tel. (2) 3701-5114; fax (2) 722-8328; internet www.munhwa.co.kr; f. 1991; evening; Pres. and Publr LEE BYUN-KYU; Editor-in-Chief KANG SIN-KU.

Naeway Economic Daily: 1-12, 3-ga, Hoehyon-dong, Jung-gu, Seoul 100; tel. (2) 727-0114; fax (2) 727-0661; internet www.naeway.co.kr; f. 1973; morning; Pres. KIM CHIN-OUK; Man. Editor HAN DONG-HEE; circ. 300,000.

Segye Times: 63-1, 3-ga, Hangang-no, Yeongsan-gu, Seoul; tel. (2) 799-4114; fax (2) 799-4520; internet www.segyetimes.co.kr; f. 1989; morning; Pres. SA KWANG-KEE; Editor MOK JUNG-GYUM.

Seoul Kyungje Shinmun (Seoul Economic Daily): 19, Junghak-dong, Jongno-gu, Seoul 100; tel. (2) 724-2114; fax (2) 732-2140; e-mail webmaster@hanooki.com; internet www.sed.co.kr; f. 1960; morning; Pres. LIM KONG-JON; Man. Editor LEE JONG-WHAN; circ. 500,000.

Sports Chosun: 61, 1-ga, Taepyeong-no, Jung-gu, Seoul; tel. (2) 724-6114; fax (2) 724-6979; internet www.sportschosun.com; f. 1964; Publr BANG SANG-HOON; circ. 400,000.

LOCAL DAILIES

Chungchong Daily News: 304, Sachang-dong, Hungduk-gu, Cheongju, N. Chungcheong Prov.; tel. (43) 279-5114; fax (43) 262-2000; e-mail webmaster@ccilbo.com; internet www.ccilbo.com; f. 1946; morning; Pres. SEO JEONG-OK; Editor IM BAIK-SOO.

Daegu Ilbo: 81-2, Sincheon 3-dong, Dong-gu, Daegu; tel. (42) 932-7216; fax (42) 933-6955; e-mail tgnews@tgnews.com; internet www.tgnews.co.kr; f. 1953; morning; Pres. LEE TAE-YEUL; Editor KIM KYUNG-PAL.

Daejon Ilbo: 1-135, Munhwa 1-dong, Jung-gu, Daejeon; tel. (42) 251-3311; fax (42) 253-3320; f. 1950; evening; Pres. CHO JOON-HO; Editor KWAK DAE-YEON.

Halla Ilbo: 568-1, Samdo 1-dong, Jeju; tel. (64) 750-2114; fax (64) 750-2520; internet www.hallailbo.com; f. 1989; evening; Chair. KANG YONG-SOK; Man. Editor HONG SONG-MOK.

Incheon Ilbo: 18-1, 4-ga, Hang-dong, Jung-gu, Incheon; tel. (32) 763-8811; fax (32) 763-7711; internet www.itimes.co.kr; f. 1988; evening; Chair. MUN PYONG-HA; Man. Editor LEE JAE-HO.

Jeju Daily News: 2324-6, Yeon-dong, Jeju; tel. (64) 740-6114; fax (64) 740-6500; e-mail webmaster@jejunews.com; internet www.jejunews.com; f. 1945; evening; Pres. KIM DAE-SUNG; Man. Editor KANG BYUNG-HEE.

Jeonbuk Domin Ilbo: 207-10, 2-ga, Deokjin-dong, Deokjin-gu, Jeonju, N. Jeolla Prov.; tel. (63) 251-7114; fax (63) 251-7127; internet www.domin.co.kr; f. 1988; morning; Pres. LIM BYOUNG-CHAN; Man. Editor YANG CHAE-SUK.

Jeonbuk Ilbo: 710-5, Kumam-dong, Deokjin-gu, Jeonju, N. Jeolla Prov.; tel. (63) 250-5500; fax (63) 250-5550; f. 1950; evening; Chair. SUH CHANG-HOON; Man. Editor LEE KON-WOONG.

Jeonju Ilbo: 568-132, Sonosong-dong, Deokjin-gu, Jeonju, N. Jeolla Prov.; tel. (63) 285-0114; fax (63) 285-2060; f. 1991; morning; Chair. KANG DAE-SOON; Man. Editor SO CHAE-CHOL.

Jeonnam Ilbo: 700-5, Jungheung-dong, Buk-gu, Gwangju 500-758; tel. (62) 527-0015; fax (62) 510-0436; f. 1989; morning; Pres. PARK KEE-JUNG; Editor-in-Chief KIM YONG-OK.

Joongdo Ilbo: 274-7, Galma-dong, Seo-gu, Daejeon; tel. (42) 530-4114; fax (42) 535-5334; f. 1951; morning; CEO KIM WOK-SIK; Man. Editor SONG HYOUNG-SOP.

Kangwon Ilbo: 53, 1-ga, Jungang-no, Chuncheon, Gangwon Prov.; tel. (33) 252-7228; fax (33) 252-5884; internet www.kwnews.co.kr; f. 1945; evening; Pres. CHOI SEUNG-IK; Editor-in-Chief KIM SUNG-KEE.

Kookje Daily News: 76-2, Goje-dong, Yeonje-gu, Busan 611-702; tel. (51) 500-5114; fax (51) 500-4274; e-mail jahwang@ms.kookje.co.kr; internet www.kookje.co.kr; f. 1947; morning; Pres. ROH KI-TAE; Editor-in-Chief JEONG WON-YOUNG.

Kwangju Ilbo: 1, 1-ga, Geumnam-no, Dong-gu, Gwangju; tel. (62) 222-8111; fax (62) 227-9500; e-mail webmaster@kwangju.co.kr; internet www.kwangju.co.kr; f. 1952; evening; Chair. KIM CHONG-TAE; Man. Editor CHO DONG-SU.

Kyeonggi Ilbo: 452-1, Songjuk-dong, Changan-gu, Suwon, Gyeonggi Prov.; tel. (31) 247-3333; fax (31) 247-3349; e-mail webmaster@kgib.co.kr; internet www.kgib.co.kr; f. 1988; evening; Pres. SHIN CHANG-GI; Man. Editor LEE CHIN-YONG.

Kyeongin Ilbo: 1121-11, Ingye-dong, Paldal-gu, Suwon, Gyeonggi Prov.; tel. (31) 231-5114; fax (31) 232-1231; e-mail webmaster@kyeongin.com; internet www.kyeongin.com; f. 1960; evening; Pres. WOO JE-CHAN; Man. Editor KIM HWA-YANG.

THE REPUBLIC OF KOREA (SOUTH KOREA)

Kyungnam Shinmun: 100-5, Sinwol-dong, Changwon, S. Gyeongsang Prov.; tel. (55) 283-2211; fax (55) 283-2227; internet www.knnews.co.kr; f. 1946; evening; Pres. KIM DONG-KYU; Editor PARK SUNG-KWAN.

Maeil Shinmun: 71, 2-ga, Gyesan-dong, Jung-gu, Daegu; tel. (53) 255-5001; fax (53) 255-8902; e-mail imaeil@msnet.co.kr; internet www.m2000.co.kr; f. 1946; evening; Pres. CHO HWAN-KIL; Editor LEE YONG-KEUN; circ. 300,000.

Pusan Daily News: 1-10, Sujeong-dong, Dong-gu, Busan 601-738; tel. (51) 461-4114; fax (51) 463-8880; internet www.pusanilbo.co.kr; f. 1946; Pres. JEONG HAN-SANG; Man. Editor AHN KI-HO; circ. 427,000.

Yeongnam Ilbo: 111, Sincheon-dong, Dong-gu, Daegu; tel. (53) 756-8001; fax (53) 756-9011; internet www.yeongnam.co.kr; f. 1945; morning; Chair. PARK CHANG-HO; Man. Editor KIM SANG-TAE.

SELECTED PERIODICALS

Academy News: 50, Unjung-dong, Bundang-gu, Seongnam, Gyeonggi Prov. 463-791; tel. (31) 709-8111; fax (31) 709-9945; organ of the Acad. of Korean Studies; Pres. HAN SANG-JIN.

Eumak Dong-A: 139, Sejong-no, Jongno-gu, Seoul 110-715; tel. (2) 781-0640; fax (2) 705-4547; f. 1984; monthly; music; Publr KIM BYUNG-KWAN; Editor KWON O-KIE; circ. 85,000.

Han Kuk No Chong (FKTU News): Federation of Korean Trade Unions, FKTU Bldg, 168-24 Chungam-dong, Yongsan-gu, Seoul 140-050; tel. (2) 715-3954; fax (2) 715-7790; e-mail fktuintl@fktu.co.kr; internet www.fktu.or.kr; f. 1961; labour news; circ. 20,000.

Hyundae Munhak: Seoul; tel. (2) 516-3770; fax (2) 516-5433; e-mail webmaster@hdmh.co.kr; internet www.hdmh.co.kr; f. 1955; literature; Publr KIM SUNG-SIK; circ. 200,000.

Korea Business World: Yeouido, POB 720, Seoul 150-607; tel. (2) 532-1364; fax (2) 594-7663; f. 1985; monthly; English; Publr and Pres. LEE KIE-HONG; circ. 40,200.

Korea Buyers Guide: Rm 2301, Korea World Trade Center, 159, Samseong-dong, Gangnam-gu, Seoul; tel. (2) 551-2376; fax (2) 551-2377; e-mail info@buyersguide.co.kr; internet www.buykorea21.com; f. 1973; monthly, consumer goods; quarterly, hardware; Pres. YOU YOUNG-PYO; circ. 30,000.

Korea Journal: Korean National Commission for UNESCO, CPOB 64, Seoul 100-600; tel. (2) 755-6225; fax (2) 755-7478; e-mail kj@unesco.or.kr; internet www.ekoreajournal.net; organ of the UNESCO Korean Commission; Publr SHIN JONG-BEOM; Editor-in-Chief CHUN TAEK-SOO.

Korea Newsreview: 1-12, 3-ga, Hoehyeon-dong, Jung-gu, Seoul 100-771; tel. (2) 756-7711; weekly; English; Publr and Editor PARK CHUNG-WOONG.

Korea and World Affairs: Rm 1723, Daewoo Center Bldg, 5-541, Namdaemun-no, Jung-gu, Seoul 100-714; tel. (2) 777-2628; fax (2) 319-9591; organ of the Research Center for Peace and Unification of Korea; Pres. CHANG DONG-HOON.

Korean Business Review: FKI Bldg, 28-1, Yeouido-dong, Yeongdeungpo-gu, Seoul 150-756; tel. (2) 3771-0114; fax (2) 3771-0138; monthly; publ. by Fed. of Korean Industries; Publr KIM KAK-CHOONG; Editor SOHN BYUNG-DOO.

Literature and Thought: Seoul; tel. (2) 738-0542; fax (2) 738-2997; f. 1972; monthly; Pres. LIM HONG-BIN; circ. 10,000.

Monthly Travel: Cross Bldg, 2nd Floor, 46-6, 2-ga, Namsan-dong, Jung-gu, Seoul 100-042; tel. (2) 757-6161; fax (2) 757-6089; e-mail kotfa@unitel.co.kr; Pres. SHIN JOONG-MOK; circ. 50,000.

News Maker: 22, Jung-dong, Jung-gu, Seoul 110-702; tel. (2) 3701-1114; fax (2) 739-6190; e-mail hudy@kyunghyang.com; internet www.kyunghyang.com/newsmaker; f. 1992; Pres. JANG JUN-BONG; Editor PARK MYUNG-HUN.

Reader's Digest: 295-15, Deoksan 1-dong, Geumcheon-gu, Seoul 153-011; tel. (2) 3670-5497; fax (2) 3670-5001; internet www.readersdigest.co.kr; f. 1978; monthly; general; Pres. YANG SUNG-MO; Editor PARK SOON-HWANG; circ. 115,000.

Shin Dong-A (New East Asia): 139, Chungjeong-no, Seodaemun-gu, Seoul 120-715; tel. (2) 361-0974; fax (2) 361-0988; e-mail hans@donga.com; internet shindonga.donga.com; f. 1931; monthly; general; Publr KIM HAK-JUN; Editor LEE HYUNG-SAM; circ. 150,000.

Taekwondo: Sinmun-no Bldg, 5th Floor, 238, Sinmun-no, 1-ga, Jongno-gu, Seoul 110-061; tel. (2) 566-2505; fax (2) 553-4728; e-mail wtf@unitel.co.kr; internet www.wtf.org; f. 1973; organ of the World Taekwondo Fed; Pres. Dr KIM UN-YONG.

Vantage Point: 85-1, Susong-dong, Jongno-gu, Seoul, 110-140; tel. (2) 398-3519; fax (2) 398-3539; e-mail kseungji@yna.co.kr; internet www.yna.co.kr; f. 1978; monthly; developments in North Korea; Editor KWAK SEUNG-JI.

Weekly Chosun: 61, Taepyeong-no 1, Jung-gu, Seoul; tel. (2) 724-5114; fax (2) 724-6199; weekly; Publr BANG SANG-HOON; Editor CHOI JOON-MYONG; circ. 350,000.

The Weekly Hankook: 14, Junghak-dong, Jongno-gu, Seoul; tel. (2) 732-4151; fax (2) 724-2444; f. 1964; Publr CHANG CHAE-KUK; circ. 400,000.

Wolgan Mot: 139, Sejong-no, Jongno-gu, Seoul 110-715; tel. (2) 733-5221; f. 1984; monthly; fashion; Publr KIM SEUNG-YUL; Editor KWON O-KIE; circ. 120,000.

Women's Weekly: 14, Junghak-dong, Jongno-gu, Seoul; tel. (2) 735-9216; fax (2) 732-4125.

Yosong Dong-A (Women's Far East): 139, Sejong-no, Jongno-gu, Seoul 110-715; tel. (2) 721-7621; fax (2) 721-7676; f. 1933; monthly; women's magazine; Publr KIM BYUNG-KWAN; Editor KWON O-KIE; circ. 237,000.

NEWS AGENCY

Yonhap News Agency: 85-1, Susong-dong, Jongno-gu, Seoul; tel. (2) 398-3114; fax (2) 398-3257; internet www.yonhapnews.co.kr; f. 1980; Pres. KIM KUN.

PRESS ASSOCIATIONS

Journalists Association of Korea (JAK): Korea Press Centre Bldg, 25 1-ga, Taepyeong-no, Jung-gu, Seoul; tel. (2) 737-2483; fax (2) 738-1003; internet www.journalist.or.kr; Pres. CHUNG IL-YONG.

Korean Association of Newspapers: Korea Press Center, 13th Floor, 25, 1-ga, Taepyeong-no, Jung-gu, Seoul 100-745; tel. (2) 733-2251; fax (2) 720-3291; e-mail iwelcome@presskorea.or.kr; internet www.presskorea.or.kr; f. 1962; 48 mems; Pres. CHANG DAE-WHAN; Sec.-Gen. MOON HAN-KWON.

Korean Newspaper Editors' Association: Korea Press Center, 13th Floor, 25, 1-ga, Taepyeong-no, Jung-gu, Seoul; tel. (2) 732-1726; fax (2) 739-1985; f. 1957; 416 mems; Pres. SEONG BYONG-WUK.

Seoul Foreign Correspondents' Club: Korea Press Center, 18th Floor, 25, 1-ga, Taepyeong-no, Jung-gu, Seoul; tel. (2) 734-3272; fax (2) 734-7712; f. 1956; Pres. PARK HAN-CHUN.

Publishers

Ahn Graphics Ltd: 260-288, Seongbuk-dong, Seongbuk-gu, Seoul 136-823; tel. (2) 743-8065; fax (2) 744-3251; e-mail lbr@ag.co.kr; internet www.ag.co.kr; f. 1985; computer graphics; Pres. KIM OK-CHUL.

Bak-Young Publishing Co: 13-31, Pyeong-dong, Jongno-gu, Seoul; tel. (2) 733-6771; fax (2) 736-4818; f. 1952; sociology, philosophy, literature, linguistics, social science; Pres. AHN JONG-MAN.

BIR Publishing Co Ltd: 4/F, Gangnam Publishing Culture Center, 506 Sinsa-dong, Gangnam-Gu, Seoul 135-887; tel. (2) 3443-4318; fax (2) 3442-4661; e-mail bir@bir.co.kr; internet www.bir.co.kr; children's books.

Bobmun Sa Publishing Co: Hanchung Bldg, 4th Floor, 161-7, Yomni-dong, Mapo-gu, Seoul 121-090; tel. (2) 703-6541; fax (2) 703-6594; internet www.bobmunsa.co.kr; f. 1954; law, politics, philosophy, history; Pres. BAE HYO-SEON.

Bookhouse Publishing Co Ltd: 6/F, Dongsomun Bldg, Seoul 136-034; tel. (2) 924-4736; fax (2) 924-4738; e-mail editor@bookhouse.co.kr; internet www.bookhouse.co.kr; business, foreign novels, health.

Bumwoo Publishing Co: 525-2, Paju Book City, Munbal-ri, Gyohaeup, Paju-si, Gyeonggi-do; tel. (31) 955-6900; fax (31) 955-6905; e-mail help@bumwoosa.co.kr; internet www.bumwoosa.co.kr; f. 1966; philosophy, religion, social science, technology, art, literature, history; Pres. YOON HYUNG-DOO.

Chaeksesang Publishing Co (Book World): tel. (2) 704-1251; fax (2) 719-1258; e-mail webmaster@bkworld.co.kr; internet www.bkworld.co.kr; f. 1975.

Chajaknamu: 21-1, Sangsoo-dong, Seoul 121-160; tel. (2) 3142-9150; fax (2) 3142-9160; humanities.

Changhae Publishing: 336-10, Ahyun 2-dong, Seoul 121-012; tel. (2) 313-3200; fax (2) 313-3204; e-mail nanal21@changhae.com; internet www.changhae.com.

Cheong Moon Gak Publishing Co Ltd: 486-9, Kirum 3-dong, Seongbuk-gu, Seoul 136-800; tel. (2) 985-1451; fax (2) 988-1456; e-mail cmgbook@cmgbook.co.kr; internet www.cmgbook.co.kr; f. 1974; science, technology, business; subsidiaries HanSeung Publishers, Lux Media; Pres. KIM HONG-SEOK; Man. Dir HANS KIM.

Crayon House Co Ltd: 5/F, Crayon House Bldg, Seoul; tel. (2) 3436-1711; fax (2) 3436-1410; e-mail crayong@korea.com; internet www.crayonhouse.co.kr; f. 1996; children's books.

THE REPUBLIC OF KOREA (SOUTH KOREA)

Dai Won Publishing Co: 40-456, Hangangno 3-ga, Yeongsan-gu, Seoul 140-880; tel. (2) 2071-2000; fax (2) 793-8994; e-mail int@daiwon.co.kr; internet www.daiwon.co.kr; f. 1990; comics.

Design House Publishing Co: Paradise Bldg, 186-210, Jangchung-dong, 2-ga, Jung-gu, Seoul 100-392; tel. (2) 2275-6151; fax (2) 2275-7884; internet www.design.co.kr; f. 1987; social science, art, literature, languages, children's periodicals; Pres. LEE YOUNG-HEE.

Dong-A Publishing Co Ltd: 295-15, Toksan-dong, Seoul 140-100; tel. (2) 866-8800; fax (2) 862-0410; f. 1945; children's books, arts, humanities.

Dong-Hwa Publishing Co: 130-4, 1-ga, Wonhyoro, Yeongsan-gu, Seoul 140-111; tel. (2) 713-5411; fax (2) 701-7041; f. 1968; language, literature, fine arts, history, religion, philosophy; Pres. LIM IN-KYU.

Dongmoonsun Publishing Co: 4, Kwanhum-dong, Jongno-gu, Seoul 110-300; tel. (2) 733-4901; fax (2) 723-4518; e-mail dmoonsun@netsgo.com; humanities.

Doosan Corporation Publishing BG: 14-34, Yeouido-dong, Yeongdeungpo-gu, Seoul; tel. (2) 2167-0601; fax (2) 2167-0668; e-mail dudvkf@doosan.com; internet www.bookdonga.com; f. 1951; general works, school reference, social science, periodicals; Pres. CHOI TAE-KYUNG.

E*Public Co: 923-11, Mok 1-dong, Yangcheon-gu, Seoul 158-051; tel. (2) 653-5131; fax (2) 653-2454; e-mail skliu@panmun.co.kr; internet www.panmun.co.kr; f. 1955; social science, pure science, technology, medicine, linguistics; Pres. and CEO LIU SUNG-KWON.

Ehak Publishing Co Ltd: 17-1, Anhuk-dong, Jongno-gu, Seoul 110-240; tel. (2) 720-4572; fax (2) 720-4573; e-mail legosum@dreamwiz.com.

Eulyoo Publishing Co Ltd: 46-1, Susong-dong, Jongno-gu, Seoul 110-603; tel. (2) 733-8151; fax (2) 732-9154; e-mail eulyoo@chollian.net; f. 1945; linguistics, literature, social science, history, philosophy; Pres. CHUNG CHIN-SOOK.

Gilbut Publishing Co Ltd: 380-15, Seogyo-dong, Mapo-gu, Seoul; tel. (2) 332-0931; fax (2) 323-0586; internet www.gilbut.co.kr; f. 1991.

Gimm-Young Publishers Inc: 17, Kahoe-dong, Jongno-gu, Seoul 110-260; tel. (2) 3668-3202; fax (2) 745-4827; e-mail marketing@gimmyoung.com; f. 1979; current affairs, humanities, history, religion, children's books.

Hainaim Publishing Co Ltd: 5/F, Hainaim Bldg, 368-4, Seogyo-dong, Mapo-gu, Seoul; tel. (2) 326-1600; fax (2) 326-1624; e-mail hainaim@chollian.net; internet www.hainaim.com; f. 1983; philosophy, literature, children's; Pres. SONG YOUNG-SUK.

Haksan Publishing Co: tel. (2) 828-8988; fax (2) 828-8890; internet www.haksanpub.co.kr; f. 1995; children's books, comics, magazines.

Hakwon Publishing Co Ltd: Seocho Plaza, 4th Floor, 1573-1, Seocho-dong, Seocho-gu, Seoul; tel. (2) 587-2396; fax (2) 584-9306; f. 1945; general, languages, literature, periodicals; Pres. KIM YOUNG-SU.

Hangilsa Corpn: 520-11, Paju Book City, Munbal-ri, Gyoha-eup, Paju-si, Gyeonggi-do; tel. (31) 955-2000; fax (31) 955-2005; e-mail hangilsaone@hangilsa.co.kr; internet www.hangilsa.co.kr; f. 1976; social science, history, literature; Pres. KIM EOUN-HO.

Hanul Publishing Company: 3/F Seoul Bldg, 105-90 Gongdeok-dong, Mapo-gu, Seoul 121-801; tel. (2) 336-6183; fax (2) 333-7543; internet www.hanulbooks.co.kr; f. 1980; general, philosophy, university books, periodicals; Pres. KIM CHONG-SU.

Hollym Corporation: 13-13, Gwancheol-dong, Jongno-gu, Seoul 110-111; tel. (2) 735-7551; fax (2) 730-5149; e-mail info@hollym.co.kr; internet www.hollym.co.kr; f. 1963; academic and general books on Korea in English; Pres. HAM KI-MAN.

Hyang Mun Sa Publishing Co: 645-20, Yeoksam-dong, Gangnam-gu, Seoul 135-081; tel. (2) 538-5672; fax (2) 538-5673; f. 1950; science, agriculture, history, engineering, home economics; Pres. NAH JOONG-RYOL.

Hyonam Publishing Co Ltd: 627-5, Ahyun 3-dong, Mapo-gu, Seoul 121-013; tel. (2) 365-5056; fax (2) 365-5251; e-mail lawhyun@chollian.net; f. 1951; general, children's, literature, periodicals; Pres. CHO KEUN-TAE.

Hyungseul Publishing Co: 33, Tongeui-dong, Jongno-gu, Seoul; tel. (2) 738-6052; fax (2) 736-7134; e-mail hs@hyungseul.co.kr; internet www.hyungseul.co.kr.

Il Jin Sa Publishing Co: 5-104, Hyochang-dong, Yeongsan-gu, Seoul; tel. (2) 704-1616; fax (2) 715-3536; e-mail webmaster@iljinsa.com; internet www.iljinsa.com; f. 1956; literature, social sciences, juvenile, fine arts, philosophy, linguistics, history; Pres. KIM SUNG-JAE.

Ilchokak Publishing Co Ltd: 1-335, Sinmunno 2-ga, Jongno-gu, Seoul 110-062; tel. (2) 733-5430; fax (2) 738-5857; e-mail ilchokak@hanmail.net; internet www.ilchokak.co.kr; f. 1953; history, literature, sociology, linguistics, medicine, law, engineering; Pres. KIM SI-YEON.

Jigyungsa Publishers Ltd: 790-14, Yeoksam-dong, Gangnam-gu, Seoul 135-080; tel. (2) 557-6351; fax (2) 557-6352; e-mail jigyung@uriel.net; internet www.jigyung.co.kr; f. 1979; children's, periodicals; Pres. KIM BYUNG-JOON.

Jihak Publishing Co Ltd: 180-20, Dongkyo-dong, Mapo-gu, Seoul 121-200; tel. (2) 330-5200; fax (2) 325-4488; e-mail webmaster@jihak.co.kr; internet www.jihak.co.kr; f. 1965; philosophy, language, literature; Pres. KWON BYONG-IL.

Jimoondang: 95, Waryon-dong, Jongno-gu, Seoul 110-360; tel. (2) 743-0227; fax (2) 742-4657; e-mail plan@jipmoon.co.kr; internet www.jimoon.co.kr; f. 1970; scholarly books on Korean history, society, language, literature, religion, art, folklore, politics and economy; Pres. LIM SAM-KYU.

Jisik Sanup Publications Co Ltd: 35-18, Dongui-dong, Jongno-gu, Seoul 110-040; tel. (2) 734-1978; fax (2) 720-7900; e-mail jsp@jisik.co.kr; internet www.jisik.co.kr; f. 1969; religion, social science, art, literature, history, children's; Pres. KIM KYUNG-HEE.

Joongang Publishing Co Ltd: 172-11, Yomni-dong, Mapo-gu, Seoul 121-090; tel. (2) 717-2111; fax (2) 716-1369; f. 1972; study books, children's; Pres. KIM DUCK-KI.

Kemongsa Publishing Co Ltd: 772, Yeoksam-dong, Gangnam-gu, Seoul 135-080; tel. (2) 531-5335; fax (2) 531-5520; internet www.kemongsa.co.kr; f. 1946; picture books, juvenile, encyclopaedias, history, fiction; Pres. RHU SEUNG-HEE.

Kookminbooks Co Ltd: 514-4, Paju Book City, Munbal-ri, Gyoha-eup, Paju-si, Gyeonggi-do; tel. (31) 955-7861; fax (31) 955-7855; internet www.kmbooks.com; f. 1961; children's books.

Korea Britannica Corpn: 117, 1-ga, Jungchung-dong, Seoul 100-391; tel. (2) 272-2151; fax (2) 278-9983; f. 1968; encyclopaedias, dictionaries; Pres. JANG HO-SANG, SUJAN ELEN TAPANI.

Korea University Press: 5-1, Anam-dong, 5-ga, Seongbuk-gu, Seoul 136-701; tel. (2) 3290-4231; fax (2) 923-6311; e-mail kupress@korea.ac.uk; internet www.kupress.com; f. 1956; philosophy, history, language, literature, Korean studies, education, psychology, social science, natural science, engineering, agriculture, medicine; Pres. EUH YOON-DAE.

Kum Sung Publishing Co: 242-63, Gongdeok-dong, Mapo-gu, Seoul 121-022; tel. (2) 713-9651; fax (2) 718-4362; e-mail webmaster@kumsungpub.co.kr; internet www.kumsung.co.kr; f. 1965; literature, juvenile, social sciences, history, fine arts; Pres. KIM NAK-JOON.

Kyohak-sa Publishing Co Ltd: 105-67, Gongdeok-dong, Mapo-gu, Seoul 121-020; tel. (2) 707-5110; fax (2) 707-5160; internet www.kyohak.co.kr; f. 1952; dictionaries, educational, children's; Pres. YANG CHEOL-WOO.

Kyung Hee University Press: 1, Hoeki-dong, Dongdaemun-gu, Seoul 130-701; tel. (2) 961-0106; fax (2) 962-8840; f. 1960; general, social science, technology, language, literature; Pres. CHOE YOUNG-SEEK.

Kyungnam University Press: 28-42, Samchung-dong, Jongno-gu, Seoul 110-230; tel. and fax (2) 3700-0700; e-mail ifes@kyungnam.ac.kr; internet ifes.kyungnam.ac.kr; Pres. PARK JAE-KYU.

Minumsa Publishing Co Ltd: 5/F Kangnam Publishing Culture Centre, 506, Sinsa-dong, Gangnam-gu, Seoul 135-120; tel. (2) 515-2000; fax (2) 515-2007; e-mail michellenam@minumsa.com; internet www.minumsa.com; f. 1966; literature, philosophy, linguistics, pure science; Pres. PARK MAENG-HO.

Munhakdongne Publishing Co Ltd: 513-8, Paju Book City, Munbal-ri, Gyoha-eup, Paju-si, Gyeonggi-do 413-832; tel. (31) 955-8888; fax (2) 955-8855; e-mail editor@munhak.com; internet www.munhak.com; f. 1993; art, literature, science, philosophy, non-fiction, children's, periodicals; Pres. KANG BYUNG-SUN.

Sakyejul Publishing Ltd: 1513-3, Paju Book City, Munbal-ri, Gyoha-eup, Paju-si, Gyeonggi-do; tel. (31) 955-8558; fax (31) 955-8596; e-mail kec@sakyejul.co.kr; internet www.sakyejul.co.kr; f. 1982; social sciences, art, literature, history, children's; Pres. KANG MAR-XILL.

Sam Joong Dang Publishing Co: 261-23, Soke-dong, Yeongsan-gu, Seoul 140-140; tel. (2) 704-6816; fax (2) 704-6819; f. 1931; literature, history, philosophy, social sciences, dictionaries; Pres. LEE MIN-CHUL.

Sam Seong Dang Publishing Co: 101-14, Non Hyun-dong, Gangnam-gu, Seoul 135-010; tel. (2) 3442-6767; fax (2) 3442-6768; e-mail kyk@ssdp.co.kr; f. 1968; literature, fine arts, history, philosophy; Pres. KANG MYUNG-CHAE.

Sam Seong Publishing Co Ltd: 1516-2, Seocho-dong, Seocho-gu, Seoul 137-070; tel. (2) 3470-6900; fax (2) 597-1507; f. 1951; literature, history, juvenile, philosophy, arts, religion, science, encyclopaedias; Pres. KIM JIN-YONG.

Samsung Publishing Co Ltd: Samsung Publishing Bldg, 1516-2, Seocho 3-dong, Seocho-gul 137-871; tel. (2) 3470-6900; fax (2) 521-8534; e-mail lisababy@ssbooks.com; internet www.ssbooks.com;

www.samsungbooks.com; children's books, comics, cooking, parenting, health, travel; f. 1951; Chief Editor BOSUNG KONG.

Segyesa Publishing Co Ltd: 217-1 Poi-dong, Gangnam-gu, Seoul 135-260; tel. (2) 577-2341; fax (2) 576-9853; f. 1988; general, philosophy, literature, periodicals; Pres. CHOI SUN-HO.

Se-Kwang Music Publishing Co: 232-32, Seogye-dong, Yeongsan-gu, Seoul 140-140; tel. (2) 719-2652; fax (2) 719-2656; f. 1953; music, art; Pres. PARK SEI-WON; Chair. PARK SHIN-JOON.

Seong An Dang Publishing Co: 4579, Singil-6-dong, Yeongdeungpo-gu, Seoul 150-056; tel. (2) 3142-4151; fax (2) 323-5324; f. 1972; technology, text books, university books, periodicals; Pres. LEE JONG-CHOON.

Seoul National University Press: San 56-1, Sillim-dong, Gwanak-gu, Seoul; tel. (2) 880-0434; fax (2) 888-4148; e-mail snubook@snu.ac.kr; internet www.snupress.com; f. 1961; philosophy, engineering, social science, art, literature; Pres. LEE KI-JUN.

Si-sa-young-o-sa, Inc: 55-1, 2-ga, Jongno, Jongno-gu, Seoul 110-122; tel. (2) 274-0509; fax (2) 271-3980; internet www.ybmsisa.co.kr; f. 1959; language, literature; Pres. CHUNG YOUNG-SAM.

Sogang University Press: 1, Sinsu-dong, Mapo-gu, Seoul 121-742; tel. (2) 705-8212; fax (2) 705-8612; f. 1978; philosophy, religion, science, art, history; Pres. LEE HAN-TAEK.

Sookmyung Women's University Press: 53-12, 2-ga, Jongpa-dong, Yeongsan-gu, Seoul 140-742; tel. (2) 710-9162; fax (2) 710-9090; f. 1968; general; Pres. LEE KYUNG-SOOK.

Sungkyunkwan University Press: 53, Myeongnyun-dong 3-ga, Jongno-gu, Seoul; tel. (2) 760-1252; fax (2) 762-7452; internet www7.skku.ac.kr/skkupress.

Sungshin Women's University Press: 249-1, Dongsun-dong 3-ga, Seongbuk-gu, Seoul; tel. (2) 920-7327; fax (2) 920-7326; internet www.sungshin.ac.kr/press.

Tam Gu Dang Publishing Co: 158, 1-ga, Hanggangno, Yeongsan-gu, Seoul 140-011; tel. (2) 3785-2271; fax (2) 3785-2272; f. 1950; linguistics, literature, social sciences, history, fine arts; Pres. HONG SUK-WOO.

Woongjin Think Big Co Ltd: Jongno Tower 23/F, Jongno 2-ga, Jongno-gu, Seoul; tel. (2) 3670-1832; fax (2) 766-2722; e-mail lois.kim@email.woongjin.com; internet www.woongjin.com; children's; Pres. YOON SUCK-KEUM.

Yearimdang Publishing Co Ltd: Yearim Bldg, 153-3, Samseong-dong, Gangnam-gu, Seoul 135-090; tel. (2) 566-1004; fax (2) 567-9610; e-mail yearim@yearim.co.kr; internet www.yearim.co.kr; f. 1973; children's; Pres. NA CHOON-HO.

Yonsei University Press: 134, Sincheon-dong, Seodaemun-gu, Seoul 120-749; tel. (2) 361-3380; fax (2) 393-1421; e-mail ysup@yonsei.ac.kr; f. 1955; philosophy, religion, literature, history, art, social science, pure science; Pres. KIM BYUNG-SOO.

Youl Hwa Dang: Paju Book City, 520-10, Munbal-li, Gyoha-eup, Paju-si, Gyeonggi-do 413-832; tel. (31) 955-7000; fax (31) 955-7010; e-mail yhdp@youlhwadang.co.kr; internet www.youlhwadang.co.kr; f. 1971; art; Pres. YI KI-UNG.

Younglim Cardinal Inc: Hyecheon Bldg, 831, Yeoksam-dong, Gangnam-gu, Seoul 135-792; tel. (2) 553-8516; fax (2) 552-0436; e-mail edit@ylc21.co.kr; internet www.ylc21.co.kr; f. 1987.

PUBLISHERS' ASSOCIATION

Korean Publishers' Association: 105-2, Sagan-dong, Jongno-gu, Seoul 110-190; tel. (2) 735-2702; fax (2) 738-5414; e-mail kpa@kpa21.or.kr; internet www.kpa21.or.kr; f. 1947; Pres. BAEK SOK-GHEE; Sec.-Gen. KO HUNG-SIK.

Broadcasting and Communications

TELECOMMUNICATIONS

Korea Telecom: 206 Jungja-dong, Bundang-gu, Seongnam-si, Gyeonggi Prov. 463-711; tel. (2) 727-0114; fax (2) 750-3994; internet www.kt.co.kr; domestic and international telecommunications services and broadband internet services; privatized in June 2002; CEO JOONG SOO-NAM.

Korea Telecom (KT) Freetel: Seoul; internet www.ktf.co.kr; subsidiary of Korea Telecom; 10m. subscribers (2002); CEO JOONG SOO-NAM.

LG Dacom Corpn: Dacom Bldg, 706-1, Yeoksam-dong, Gangnam-gu, Seoul 135-610; tel. (2) 6220-0220; fax (2) 6220-0702; internet www.lgdacom.net; f. 1982; domestic and international long-distance telecommunications services and broadband internet services; CEO PARK JONG-WOOK.

LG Telecom: LG Gangnam Tower, 19th Floor, 679 Yeoksam-dong, Gangnam-gu, Seoul 135-985; tel. (2) 2005-7114; fax (2) 2005-7505;

e-mail englishweb@lgtel.co.kr; internet www.lgtelecom.com; subsidiary of LG Corpn; mobile telecommunications and wireless internet services; commenced commercial CDMA2000 1x service in May 2001; 4m. subscribers (2002); CEO JUNG IL-JAE.

Onse Telecom: 192-2, Gumi-dong, Bundang-gu, Seongnam-si, Gyeonggi Prov. 463-500; tel. and fax (31) 738-6000; internet www.onse.net; domestic and international telecommunications services; Pres. and CEO HWANG KYU-BYUNG.

SK Telecom Co Ltd: 11, Euljiro, 2-ga, Jung-gu, Seoul 100-999; tel. (2) 6100-2114; fax (2) 2121-3999; e-mail webmaster@sktelecom.com; internet www.sktelecom.com; cellular mobile telecommunications and wireless internet services; merged with Shinsegi Telecom in Jan. 2002; 16m. subscribers (2002); Pres. and CEO SHIN BAE-KIM.

BROADCASTING
Regulatory Authority

Broadcasting and Communications Commission: KBS Bldg, 923-5, Mok-dong, Yangcheon-gu, Seoul 158-715; tel. (2) 3219-5117; fax (2) 3219-5371; e-mail admin@kbc.go.kr; internet www.kbc.go.kr; Chair. CHOI SI-JUNG.

Radio

Korean Broadcasting System (KBS): 18, Yeouido-dong, Yeongdeungpo-gu, Seoul 150-790; tel. (2) 781-1000; fax (2) 781-4179; internet www.kbs.co.kr; f. 1926; publicly owned corpn with 26 local broadcasting and 855 relay stations; overseas service in Korean, English, German, Indonesian, Chinese, Japanese, French, Spanish, Russian and Arabic; Pres. LEE BYUNG-SOON.

Buddhist Broadcasting System (BBS): 140, Mapo-dong, Mapo-gu, Seoul 121-050; tel. (2) 705-5114; fax (2) 705-5229; e-mail webmaster@bbsfm.co.kr; internet www.bbsfm.co.kr; f. 1990; Pres. CHO HAE-HYONG.

Christian Broadcasting System (CBS): 917-1, Mok-dong, Yangcheon-gu, Seoul 158-701; tel. (2) 650-0500; fax (2) 654-0505; e-mail changsoo@cbs.co.kr; internet www.cbs.co.kr; f. 1954; independent religious network with 14 network stations, incl. Seoul, Daegu, Busan and Gwangju; also satellite, cable and digital media broadcasting; programmes in Korean; Pres. LEE JEONG-SIK.

Educational Broadcasting System (EBS): 92-6, Umyeon-dong, Seocho-gu, Seoul 137-791; tel. (2) 526-2000; fax (2) 526-2179; e-mail hotline@ebs.co.kr; internet www.ebs.co.kr; f. 1990; Pres. Dr PARK HEUNG-SOO.

Far East Broadcasting Co (FEBC): 89, Sangsu-dong, Mapo-gu, Seoul 121-707; tel. (2) 320-0114; fax (2) 320-0229; e-mail febcadm@febc.net; internet www.febc.net; Christian programmes; nine local stations; Pres. KIM EUN-GI.

Radio Station HLAZ: MPO Box 88, Seoul 121-707; tel. (2) 320-0114; fax (2) 320-0129; e-mail febcadm@febc.net; internet www.febc.net; f. 1973; religious, educational service operated by Far East Broadcasting Co; programmes in Korean, Chinese, Russian and Japanese; Pres. Dr BILLY KIM.

Radio Station HLKX: MPO Box 88, Seoul 121-707; tel. (2) 320-0114; fax (2) 320-0129; e-mail febcadm@febc.net; internet www.febc.net; f. 1956; religious, educational service operated by Far East Broadcasting Co; programmes in Korean, Chinese and English; Pres. Dr BILLY KIM.

Munhwa Broadcasting Corpn (MBC): 31, Yeouido-dong, Yeongdeungpo-gu, Seoul 150-728; tel. (2) 784-2000; fax (2) 784-0880; e-mail mbcir@imbc.com; internet www.imbc.com; f. 1961; public; Pres. and CEO OHM KI-YOUNG.

Pyong Hwa Broadcasting Corpn (PBC): 2-3, 1-ga, Jeo-dong, Jung-gu, Seoul 100-031; tel. (2) 270-2114; fax (2) 270-2210; internet www.pbc.co.kr; f. 1990; religious and educational programmes; Pres. Rev. PARK SHIN-EON.

Seoul Broadcasting System (SBS): 10-2, Yeouido-dong, Yeongdeungpo-gu, Seoul 150-010; tel. (2) 786-0792; fax (2) 780-2530; internet www.sbs.co.kr; f. 1991; Pres. HA KUM-LOUL.

US Forces Network Korea (AFN Korea): Seoul; tel. (2) 7914-6495; fax (2) 7914-5870; e-mail info@afnkorea.net; internet afnkorea.com; f. 1950; six originating stations and 19 relay stations; 24 hours a day.

Television

Educational Broadcasting System (EBS): see Radio.

Jeonju Television Corpn (JTV): 656-3, Sonosong-dong, Deokjin-gu, Jeonju, N. Jeolla Prov.; tel. (63) 250-5231; fax (63) 250-5249; e-mail jtv@jtv.co.kr; f. 1997.

Korean Broadcasting System (KBS): 18, Yeouido-dong, Yeongdeungpo-gu, Seoul 150-790; tel. (2) 781-1000; fax (2) 781-4179; internet www.kbs.co.kr; f. 1961; publicly owned corpn with 25 local broadcasting and 770 relay stations; Pres. JUNG YUN-JOO.

THE REPUBLIC OF KOREA (SOUTH KOREA) *Directory*

Munhwa Broadcasting Corpn (MBC-R/TV): 31, Yeouido-dong, Yeongdeungpo-gu, Seoul 150-728; tel. (2) 789-2851; fax (2) 782-3094; e-mail song@mbc.co.kr; internet www.imbc.com; f. 1961; public; owned by the Foundation for Broadcast Culture (70%) and the Chung-Soo Scholarship Foundation (30%); includes terrestrial, cable and satellite TV stations, regional stations and radio stations; Pres. and CEO CHOI MOON-SOON.

Seoul Broadcasting System (SBS): see Radio.

US Forces Network Korea (AFN Korea): Seoul; tel. (2) 7914-2711; fax (2) 7914-5870; f. 1950; main transmitting station in Seoul; 19 rebroadcast transmitters and translators; 168 hours weekly.

Finance

(cap. = capital; res = reserves; dep. = deposits; m. = million; brs = branches; amounts in won, unless otherwise indicated)

REGULATORY AUTHORITIES

Financial Services Commission: 27, Yeouido-dong, Yeongdeungpo-gu, Seoul 150-743; tel. (2) 2156-8000; internet www.fsc.go.kr; f. 1998; deliberates on and resolves financial supervision issues; supervises the Financial Supervisory Service; Chair. CHIN DONG-SOO.

Financial Supervisory Service: 27, Yeouido-dong, Yeongdeungpo-gu, Seoul 150-743; tel. (2) 3771-5000; fax (2) 785-3475; internet www.fss.or.kr; f. 1999; examines and supervises financial institutions; Gov. KIM JONG-CHANG.

BANKING

In 2003 there were 59 commercial banks in South Korea, comprising eight nation-wide banks, six regional commercial banks, five specialized banks and 40 branches of foreign banks. In mid-2006 there were 32 foreign banks operating in South Korea. The Financial Supervisory Service oversees the operations of commercial banks and the financial services sector.

Central Bank

Bank of Korea: 110, 3-ga, Namdaemun-no, Jung-gu, Seoul 100-794; tel. (2) 759-4114; fax (2) 759-4139; e-mail bokdplp@bok.or.kr; internet www.bok.or.kr; f. 1950; bank of issue; res 1,997,300m., dep. 284,148,200m. (Dec. 2007); Gov. LEE SEONG-TAE; Dep. Gov. LEE SUNG-IL; 16 domestic brs, 6 overseas offices.

Commercial Banks

Citibank Korea Inc: 39, Da-dong, Jung-gu, Seoul 100-180; tel. (2) 3455-2114; fax (2) 3455-2966; e-mail shk@goodbank.com; internet www.goodbank.com; f. 1983; fmrly KorAm Bank, name changed as above 2004; acquired by Citigroup in 2004; cap. 1,309,854m., res 791,849m., dep. 31,491,886m. (Dec. 2006); CEO and Chair. HA YUNG-KU; 222 brs.

Hana Bank: 101-1, 1-ga, Ulchi-no, Jung-gu, Seoul 100-191; tel. (2) 2002-1111; fax (2) 775-7472; e-mail webmaster@hanabank.co.kr; internet www.hanabank.co.kr; f. 1991; merged with Boram Bank in Jan. 1999; merged with Seoulbank in Dec. 2002; cap. 987,161m., res 2,133,899m., dep. 78,382,599m. (Dec. 2007); Chair. and CEO KIM JUNG-TAE; 604 brs.

Kookmin Bank: 9-1, 2-ga, Namdaemun-no, Jung-gu, CPOB 815, Seoul 100-703; tel. (2) 2073-7114; fax (2) 2073-3296; e-mail corres@kookminbank.com; internet www.kookminbank.com; f. 1963; est. as Citizen's National Bank, renamed 1995; re-est. Jan. 1999, following merger with Korea Long Term Credit Bank; merged with H & CB in Nov. 2001; cap. 1,681,896m., res 7,157,839m., dep. 155,002,422m. (Dec. 2006); Chair. CHUNG DONG-SOO; Pres. and CEO KANG CHUNG-WON; 1,122 domestic brs, 6 overseas brs.

Korea Exchange Bank: 181, 2-ga, Ulchi-no, Jung-gu, Seoul 100-793; tel. (2) 729-0114; fax (2) 775-2565; internet www.keb.co.kr; f. 1967; merged with Korea International Merchant Bank in Jan. 1999; cap. 3,224,534m., res 1,108,053m., dep. 44,430,991m. (Dec. 2007); Chair. ROBERT E. FALLON; Pres. and CEO RICHARD F. WACKER; 345 domestic brs, 19 overseas brs.

Shinhan Bank: 120, 2-ga, Taepyeong-no, Jung-gu, Seoul 100-102; tel. (2) 756-0505; fax (2) 774-7013; e-mail corres@shinhan.com; internet www.shinhan.com; f. 1982; merged with Chohung Bank in April 2006; cap. 7,528,078m., res 1,576,856m., dep. 117,415,000m. (Dec. 2006); Pres. and CEO SHIN SANG-HOON; 957 domestic brs, 12 overseas brs.

Standard Chartered First Bank Korea Limited: 100, Gongpyeong-dong, Jongno-gu, Seoul 110702; tel. (2) 3702-3114; fax (2) 3702-4934; e-mail master@kfb.co.kr; internet www.kfb.co.kr; f. 1929; acquired by Standard Chartered Bank in Jan. 2005, name changed from Korea First Bank to above in Sept. 2005; cap. 1,236,604m., res 611,251m., dep. 44,697,859m. (Dec. 2006); Chair. ROBERT T. BARNUM; Pres. and CEO DAVID EDWARDS; 367 domestic brs, 2 overseas brs.

Woori Bank: 203, 1-ga, Hoehyeon-dong, Jung-gu, Seoul; tel. (2) 2002-3000; fax (2) 2002-5687; internet www.wooribank.com; f. 2002; est. by merger of Hanvit Bank and Peace Bank of Korea; 78% government-owned; privatization plans deferred in 2008; cap. 3,179,783m., res 2,177,894m., dep. 118,368,121m. (Dec. 2007); Chair. HWANG YOUNG KEY; 712 domestic brs.

Development Banks

Export-Import Bank of Korea: 16-1, Yeouido-dong, Yeongdeungpo-gu, Seoul 150-873; tel. (2) 3779-6114; fax (2) 7841-1030; e-mail kexim@koreaexim.go.kr; internet www.koreaexim.go.kr; f. 1976; cap. 3,308,755m., res 617,762m. (Dec. 2006); Chair., Pres. and CEO KIM DONG-SOO; 11 brs.

Korea Development Bank: 16-3, Yeouido-dong, Yeongdeungpo-gu, Seoul 150-973; tel. (2) 787-4000; fax (2) 787-6191; internet www.kdb.co.kr; f. 1954; cap. 8,241,861m., res 2,532,629m., dep. 62,520,429m. (Dec. 2006); Gov. MIN EUOO-SOONG; 40 domestic brs, 6 overseas brs.

Specialized Banks

Industrial Bank of Korea: 50, 2-ga, Ulchi-no, Jung-gu, Seoul 100-758; tel. (2) 729-6114; fax (2) 729-6402; e-mail ifd@ibk.co.kr; internet www.ibk.co.kr; f. 1961; est. as the Small and Medium Industry Bank; 85.5% govt-owned; cap. 2,291,385m., res 2,552,645m., dep. 69,889,445m. (Dec. 2006); Chair. and CEO YOON YONG-RO; 417 domestic brs, 5 overseas brs.

Meritz Investment Bank: 5/F Seoul Financial Center, 84 Taepyeongno 1-ga, Jung-gu, Seoul 100-768; tel. (2) 777-7711; fax (2) 318-7060; internet www.imeritzbank.com; f. 1977; fmrly known as Korean-French Banking Corpn (SogeKo).

Provincial Banks

Daegu Bank Ltd: 118, 2-ga, Susong-dong, Susong-gu, Daegu 706-712; tel. (53) 740-2543; fax (53) 756-2095; internet www.daegubank.co.kr; f. 1967; cap. 660,600m., res 14,100m., dep. 15,615,400m. (Dec. 2006); Chair. and Pres. LEE HWAH-EON; 285 brs.

Jeju Bank: 1349, Ido-1-dong, Jeju 690-021, Jeju Prov.; tel. (64) 734-1711; fax (64) 720-0183; internet www.chejubank.co.kr; f. 1969; cap. 55,500m., res. 30,700m., dep. 1,044,100m. (2002); merged with Central Banking Co in 2000, joined the Shinhan Financial Group in 2002; Chair. and Pres. KANG JOON-HONG; 29 brs.

Jeonbuk Bank Ltd: 669-2, Geumam-dong, Deokjin-gu, Jeonju 561-711, N. Jeolla Prov.; tel. (63) 250-7114; fax (63) 250-7078; internet www.jbbank.co.kr; f. 1969; cap. 170,591m., res 625m., dep. 3,898,228m. (2005); Chair. and Pres. HONG SUNG-JOO; 74 brs.

Kwangju Bank Ltd: 7-12, Daein-dong, Dong-gu, Gwangju 501-719; tel. (62) 239-5000; fax (62) 239-5199; e-mail kbjint1@nuri.net; internet www.kjbank.com; f. 1968; cap. 220,403m., res 29,486m., dep. 11,922,497m. (Dec. 2007); Chair. JEONG TAE-SEOK; 124 brs.

Kyongnam Bank: 246-1, Sokjeon-dong, Hoewon-gu, Masan 630-010, Gyeongsang Prov.; tel. (551) 290-8000; fax (551) 294-9426; internet www.knbank.co.kr; f. 1970; est. as Gyeongnam Bank Ltd, name changed 1987; cap. 259,000m., res 24,699m., dep. 10,426,712m. (Dec. 2005); Pres. and CEO MOON DONG-SUNG; 110 brs.

Banking Association

Korea Federation of Banks: 4-1, 1-ga, Myeong-dong, Jung-gu, Seoul 100-021; tel. (2) 3705-5000; fax (2) 3705-5337; internet www.kfb.or.kr; f. 1928; Chair. SHIN DONG-HYUCK; Vice-Chair. KIM KONG-JIN.

STOCK EXCHANGE

Korea Exchange (KRX): 5-50 Jungang-dong, Jung-gu, Busan 600-015; tel. (51) 662-2000; internet www.krx.co.kr; f. 2005; formed by merger of Korea Stock Exchange, Korea Futures Exchange, Kosdaq Stock Market, Korea Securities Dealers Association; Chair. and CEO YOUNG-TAK LEE.

INSURANCE

Principal Life Companies

Allianz Life Insurance Co Ltd: Allianz Tower, 45-21 Yeouido-dong, Yeongdeungpo-gu, Seoul 150-978; tel. (2) 3787-7000; e-mail webadmin@allianzlife.co.kr; internet www.allianzlife.co.kr; fmrly Allianz Jeil Life Insurance; formed in 2000 following acquisition of Jeil (First Life) by Allianz Group; renamed as above in 2002; Pres. and CEO MANUEL BAUER.

American International Assurance Korea: 9/F, Hanil Bldg, Chungmu-ro 2ga, Chung-gu, Seoul 100-012; tel. (2) 3707-4800; fax (2) 776-7109; internet www.aiglife.co.kr; f. 1977; CEO SANG LEE.

Dongbu Life Insurance Co Ltd: Dongbu Bldg, 7th Floor, 891-10, Daechi-dong, Gangnam-gu, Seoul 135-820; tel. (2) 1588-3131; fax (2) 3011-4100; internet www.dongbulife.co.kr; f. 1989; cap. 85,200m. (2003); CEO Cho Jae-Hong.

Green Cross Life Insurance Co Ltd: 395-68, Shindaebang-dong, Dongjak-gu, Seoul; tel. (2) 3284-7000; fax (2) 3284-7455; internet www.healthcare.co.kr; CEO Lee Jung-Sang.

Hana HSBC Life Insurance Ltd: 17/F, Hana Bank HQ Bldg, 101-1 Ulchiro-1ga, Jung-gu, Seoul 100-191; tel. (2) 3709-7300; fax (2) 755-0668; jt venture between HSBC Insurance (Asia-Pacific) Holdings Ltd and Hana Financial Group; CEO David Yoon.

Hungkuk Life Insurance Co Ltd: 226, Sinmun-no 1-ga, Jongno-gu, Seoul 100-061; tel. (2) 2002-7000; fax (2) 2002-7804; e-mail webmaster@hungkuk.co.kr; internet www.hungkuk.co.kr; f. 1958; CEO Jin Hun-Jin.

ING Life Insurance Co Korea Ltd: Sean Bldg, 116, Sinmun-no, Jongno-gu, Seoul 110-700; tel. (2) 3703-9500; fax (2) 734-3309; internet www.inglife.co.kr; f. 1991; cap. 64,820m. (2002); Pres. and CEO Curt Olson.

KB Life Insurance Co Ltd: 6/F, Daewoo Bldg, 167, Naesu-dong, Jongno-gu, Seoul 110-070; tel. (2) 398-6800; fax (2) 398-6843; e-mail webmaster@kbli.co.kr; internet www.kbli.co.kr.

Korea Life Insurance Co Ltd: 60, Yeouido-dong, Yeongdeungpo-gu, Seoul 150-603; tel. (2) 789-5114; fax (2) 789-8173; internet www.korealife.com; f. 1946; cap. 3,550,000m. (2002); CEO Eun Chul-Shin.

Korean Reinsurance Company: 80, Susong-dong, Jongno-gu, Seoul 110-733; tel. (2) 3702-6000; fax (2) 739-3754; internet www.koreanre.co.kr; f. 1963; Pres. Park Jong-Won.

Kumho Life Insurance Co Ltd: 57, 1-ga, Sinmun-no, Jongno-gu, Seoul 110-061; tel. (2) 1588-4040; fax (2) 771-7561; internet www.kumholife.co.kr; f. 1988; acquired Dong-Ah Life Insurance in 2000; cap. 211,249m. (2002); Pres. Choi Byeong-Gil.

Kyobo Life Insurance Co Ltd: 1, 1-ga, Jongno, Jongno-gu, Seoul 110-714; tel. (2) 721-2121; fax (2) 737-9970; internet www.kyobo.co.kr; f. 1958; cap. 92,500m.; Chair. and CEO Shin Chang-Jae; 84 main brs.

Life Insurance Association of North America: 14/F, Seoul City Tower, 581, Namdaemunro-5-ga, Jung-gu, Seoul; tel. (2) 3781-1000; fax (2) 792-6063; internet www.lina.co.kr; f. 1987; CEO Young Ho-Lee.

LIG Life Insurance Co Ltd: 3, Sujung-dong, Dong-gu, Busan 601-716; tel. (51) 461-7700; fax (51) 465-0581; internet www.liglife.com; f. 1988; fmrly Lucky Life Insurance Co Ltd; cap. 139,054m. (2002); Pres. Lee Young-Moon.

MetLife Insurance Co of Korea Ltd: Sungwon Bldg, 8th Floor, 141, Samseong-dong, Gangnam-gu, Seoul 135-716; tel. (2) 1588-9600; fax (2) 2017-6700; internet www.metlifekorea.co.kr; f. 1989; cap. 97,700m. (2002); Pres. Stuart B. Solomon.

Mirae Asset Life Insurance: 168, Kongduk-2-dong, Mapo-gu, Seoul 121-705; tel. (2) 3271-4114; fax (2) 3271-4400; internet www.miraeassetlife.com; f. 2005; CEO Park Hyeon-Joo.

New York Life Insurance Co Ltd: 10/F, Shinyoung Bldg, 68-5, Chung Dam-dong, Gangnam-gu, Seoul; tel. (2) 2107-4600; fax (2) 2107-4700; f. 1990.

PCA Life Insurance Co Ltd: 18/F, Seoul City Tower, 581, Namdaemunro-5ga, Jung-gu, Seoul 135-749; tel. (2) 2129-1700; fax (2) 2129-1640; internet www.pcakorea.co.kr; f. 1990; cap. 52,100m. (2002); Pres. Mike Bishop.

Prudential Life Insurance Co of Korea Ltd: Prudential Bldg, Yeoksam-dong, Gangnam-gu, Seoul; tel. (2) 2144-2000; fax (2) 2144-2100; internet www.prudential.co.kr; f. 1989; cap. 26,400m.; Pres. James C. Spackman.

Samsung Life Insurance Co Ltd: 150, 2-ga, Taepyeong-no, Jung-gu, Seoul 100-716; tel. (2) 751-8000; fax (2) 751-8100; internet www.samsunglife.com; f. 1957; cap. 100,000m. (2002); Pres. Lee Soo-Chang; 1,300 brs.

Shinhan Life Insurance Co Ltd: 120, 2-ga, Taepyeong-no, Jung-gu, Seoul 100-102; tel. (2) 3455-4000; fax (2) 753-9351; internet www.shinhanlife.co.kr; f. 1990; Pres. Han Dong-Woo.

Tong Yang Life Insurance Co Ltd: 185, Ulchi-no 2-ga, Jung-gu, Seoul 100-192; tel. (2) 728-9114; fax (2) 771-1347; internet www.myangel.co.kr; f. 1989; cap. 340,325m. (2002); Pres. Ku Ja-Hong.

Non-Life Companies

AIG General Insurance: 18/F, Seoul Central Bldg, 136 Seorin-dong, Jongno-gu, Seoul; tel. (2) 2260-6800; fax (2) 2260-6707; internet www.aiggeneral.co.kr; f. 1947; Pres. Brad Bennett.

Daehan Fire and Marine Insurance Co Ltd: 51-1, Namchang-dong, Jung-gu, Seoul 100-778; tel. (2) 1588-3344; fax (2) 754-5220; e-mail dhplane@daeins.co.kr; internet www.daeins.co.kr; f. 1946; cap. 19,500m.; Pres. and CEO Lee Jun-Ho.

Dongbu Insurance Co Ltd: Dongbu Financial Center, 891-10, Daechi-dong, Gangnam-gu, Seoul 135-840; tel. (2) 2262-3450; fax (2) 2273-6785; e-mail dongbu@dongbuinsurance.co.kr; internet www.idongbu.com; f. 1962; cap. 30,000m.; Pres. Kim Soon-Hwan.

First Fire and Marine Insurance Co Ltd: 12-1, Seosomun-dong, Jung-gu, CPOB 530, Seoul 100-110; tel. (2) 316-8114; fax (2) 771-7319; internet www.insumall.co.kr; f. 1949; cap. 17,200m.; Pres. Kim Woo-Hoang.

GreenFire Marine Insurance Co Ltd: Seoul City Tower, 581, 5-ga, Namdaemun-no, Jung-gu, Seoul 100-803; tel. (2) 1588-5959; fax (2) 773-1214; internet www.greenfire.co.kr; Pres. Lee Young-Doo.

Hyundai Marine and Fire Insurance Co Ltd: 178, Sejongno, Jongno-gu, Seoul 110-731; tel. (2) 3701-8000; fax (2) 732-5687; e-mail webpd@hdinsurance.co.kr; internet www.hi.co.kr; f. 1955; cap. 30,000m.; Pres. and CEO Ha Jong-Sun.

Korean Reinsurance Co: 80, Susong-dong, Jongno-gu, Seoul 100-733; tel. (2) 3702-6000; fax (2) 739-3754; e-mail service@koreanre.co.kr; internet www.koreanre.co.kr; f. 1963; cap. 34,030m.; Pres. Park Jong-Won.

Kyobo Auto Insurance Co Ltd: 76-4, Jamwon-dong, Seocho-gu, Seoul 137-909; tel. (2) 3479-4900; fax (2) 3479-4800; internet www.kyobodirect.com; Pres. Shin Yong-Kil.

LIG Insurance Co Ltd: LG Da-dong Bldg, 85, Da-dong, Jung-gu, Seoul 100-180; tel. (2) 310-2391; fax (2) 753-1002; e-mail webmaster@lginsure.com; internet www.lginsure.com; f. 1959; fmrly LG Insurance Co; Pres. Koo Cha-Hoon.

Meritz Insurance Co Ltd: 825-2, Yeoksam-dong, Gangnam-gu, Seoul 135-934; tel. (2) 1566-7711; fax (2) 1566-4922; internet www.meritzfire.com; f. 1922; Vice-Chair. and CEO Wohn Myung-Soo.

Samsung Fire and Marine Insurance Co Ltd: Samsung Insurance Bldg, 87, 1-ga, Ulchi-no, Jung-gu, Seoul 100-191; tel. (2) 758-7948; fax (2) 758-7831; internet www.samsungfire.com; f. 1952; cap. 6,566m.; Pres. Lee Soo-Chang.

Seoul Guarantee Insurance Co: 136-74, Yeonchi-dong, Jongno-gu, Seoul 110-470; tel. (2) 3671-7459; fax (2) 3671-7480; internet www.sgic.co.kr; Pres. Jung Ki-Hong.

Shindongah Fire and Marine Insurance Co Ltd: 43, 2-ga, Taepyeong-no, Jung-gu, Seoul; tel. (2) 6366-7000; fax (2) 755-8006; internet www.sdafire.com; f. 1946; cap. 60,220m.; CEO Kwon Chu-Sin.

Ssangyong Fire and Marine Insurance Co Ltd: 60, Doryeom-dong, Jongno-gu, Seoul 110-716; tel. (2) 724-9000; fax (2) 730-1628; e-mail sfmi@ssy.insurance.co.kr; internet www.insurance.co.kr; f. 1948; cap. 27,400m.; Pres. Yang In-Jip.

Insurance Associations

General Insurance Association of Korea: KRIC Bldg, 6th Floor, 80, Susong-dong, Jongno-gu, Seoul; tel. (2) 3702-8539; fax (2) 3702-8549; internet www.knia.or.kr; f. 1946; 16 corporate mems; fmrly Korea Non-Life Insurance Asscn; Chair. Lee Sang-Yong.

Korea Life Insurance Association: Kukdong Bldg, 16th Floor, 60-1, 3-ga, Jungmu-no, Jung-gu, Seoul 100-705; tel. (2) 2262-6600; fax (2) 2262-6580; internet www.klia.or.kr; f. 1950; Chair. Lee Woo-Cheol.

Trade and Industry

GOVERNMENT AGENCIES

Fair Trade Commission: 1, Jungang-dong, Gwacheon-si, Gyeonggi Prov. 427-760; internet www.ftc.go.kr; Chair. Baek Yong-Ho; Sec.-Gen. Lee Dong-Kyu.

Federation of Korean Industries: FKI Bldg, 2nd Floor, 28-1, Yeouido-dong, Yeongdeungpo-gu, Seoul 150-756; tel. (2) 3771-0114; fax (2) 3771-0110; e-mail webmaster@fki.or.kr; internet www.fki.or.kr; f. 1961; conducts research and survey work on domestic and overseas economic conditions and trends; advises the Govt and other interested parties on economic matters; exchanges economic and trade missions with other countries; sponsors business conferences; 366 corporate mems and 63 business asscns; Chair. Cho Suk-Rai.

Korea Appraisal Board: 171-2, Samseong-dong, Gangnam-gu, Seoul; tel. (2) 2189-8000; internet www.kab.co.kr; Chair. Kang Kil-Boo.

Korea Asset Management Corpn (KAMCO): 814, Yeoksam-dong, Gangnam-gu, Seoul; tel. (2) 2103-6134; fax (2) 2103-7423; e-mail irkamco@kamco.or.kr; internet www.kamco.or.kr; f. 1963; collection and foreclosure agency; appointed following Asian financial crisis as sole institution to manage and dispose of non-performing loans for financial institutions; Chair. and CEO Lee Chol-Hwi.

THE REPUBLIC OF KOREA (SOUTH KOREA)

Korea Export Industrial Corpn: 33, Seorin-dong, Jongno-gu, Seoul; tel. (2) 853-5573; f. 1964; encourages industrial exports, provides assistance and operating capital, conducts market surveys; Pres. KIM KI-BAE.

Korea Export Insurance Corpn: 136, Seorin-dong, Jongno-gu, Seoul 110-729; tel. (2) 399-6800; fax (2) 399-6679; internet www.keic.or.kr; f. 1992; official export credit agency of Korea; Chair. and Pres. RYU CHANG-MOO.

Korea Industrial Research Institutes: FKI Bldg, 28-1, Yeouido-dong, Yeongdeungpo-gu, Seoul; tel. (2) 780-7601; fax (2) 785-5771; f. 1979; analyses industrial and technological information from abroad; Pres. KIM CHAE-KYUM.

Korea Institute for Industrial Economics and Trade (KIET): 206-9, Cheongnyangni-dong, Dongdaemun-gu, Seoul; tel. (2) 3299-3114; fax (2) 963-8540; internet www.kiet.re.kr; f. 1976; economic and industrial research; Pres. OH SANG-BONG.

Korea Land Corpn: 217, Jeongja-dong, Seongnam-shi, Gyeonggi Prov.; tel. (31) 738-7114; fax (31) 717-5431; internet world.lplus.or.kr; f. 1975; land development; CEO LEE JONG-SANG.

Korea Resources Corpn (KORES): Seoul; tel. (2) 840-5682; e-mail sbchoi@kores.or.kr; internet www.kores.or.kr; f. 1967; provides technical and financial support for the national mining industry; Pres. KIM SHIN-JONG.

Korea Trade-Investment Promotion Agency (KOTRA): 300-9, Yeomgok-dong, Seocho-gu, Seoul; tel. (2) 3460-7114; fax (2) 3460-7777; e-mail digitalkotra@kotra.or.kr; internet www.kotra.or.kr; f. 1962; various trade promotion activities, market research, cross-border investment promotion, etc.; 102 overseas brs; Pres. HONG KI-WHA.

Korean Intellectual Property Office: Government Complex-Daejeon, Dunsan-dong, Seo-gu, Daejeon; tel. (42) 481-5027; fax (42) 481-3455; internet www.kipo.go.kr; Commissioner KOH JUNG-SIK.

CHAMBER OF COMMERCE

Korea Chamber of Commerce and Industry: 45, 4-ga, Namdaemun-no, Jung-gu, Seoul 100-743; tel. (2) 316-3114; fax (2) 757-9475; internet www.korcham.net; f. 1884; over 47,000 mems; 70 local chambers; promotes development of the economy and of international economic co-operation; Chair. SOHN KYUNG-SHIK; Pres. and CEO KIM SANG-YEOL.

INDUSTRIAL AND TRADE ASSOCIATIONS

Construction Association of Korea: Construction Bldg, 8th Floor, 71-2, Nonhyon-dong, Gangnam-gu, Seoul 135-701; tel. (2) 3485-0200; fax (2) 542-6264; internet www.cak.or.kr; f. 1947; national licensed contractors' asscn; 6,823 mem. firms (2006); Pres. KWON HONG-SA.

Korea Agro-Fisheries Trade Corpn (aT): AGRO-TRADE & Exhibition Center, 232 Yangjae-dong, Seocho-gu, Seoul; tel. (2) 6300-1114; fax (2) 6300-1600; e-mail ks@at.co.kr; internet www.at.co.kr; f. 1967; fmrly Agricultural and Fishery Marketing Corpn; integrated devt for secondary processing and marketing distribution for agricultural products and fisheries products; Pres. AHN KYO-DUCK; Exec. Vice-Pres. KIM JIN-KYU.

Korea Automobile Manufacturers Association: 1461-15, Seocho 3-dong, Seocho-gu, Seoul 137-720; tel. (2) 3660-1854; fax (2) 3660-1900; e-mail cwkim@kama.or.kr; internet www.kama.or.kr; f. 1988; Chair. CHO NAM-HONG.

Korea Coal Association: 80-6, Susong-dong, Jongno-gu, Seoul; tel. (2) 734-8891; fax (2) 734-7959; f. 1949; 49 corporate mems; Chair. AHN JONG-BEOM.

Korea Consumer Goods Exporters Association: KWTC Bldg, Rm 1802, 159, Samseong-dong, Gangnam-gu, Seoul; tel. (2) 551-1865; fax (2) 551-1870; f. 1986; 230 corporate mems; Pres. YONG WOONG-SHIN.

Korea Electronics Association: 648, Yeoksam-dong, Gangnam-gu, CPOB 5650, Seoul 135-080; tel. (2) 553-0941; fax (2) 555-6195; e-mail webmaster@gokorea.org; internet www.gokea.org; f. 1976; 328 mems; Chair. YUN JONG-YONG.

Korea Federation of Textile Industries: Textile Center, 16/F, 944-31, Daechi-3dong, Gangnam-gu, Seoul 135-713; tel. (2) 528-4005; fax (2) 528-4069; e-mail kofoti@kofoti.or.kr; internet www.kofoti.or.kr; f. 1980; 50 corporate mems; Chair. CHAN RO-HEE.

Korea Foods Industry Association: 1002-6, Bangbae-dong, Seocho-gu, Seoul; tel. (2) 3470-8100; fax (2) 3471-3492; internet www.kfia.or.kr; f. 1969; 104 corporate mems; Pres. CHUN MYUNG-KE.

Korea Importers Association (KOIMA): 218, Hangang-no, 2-ga, Yeongsan-gu, Seoul 140-875; tel. (2) 792-1581; fax (2) 785-4373; e-mail info@aftak.com; internet www.koima.or.kr; f. 1970; 6,804 mems; Chair. KIM WAN-HEE.

Korea International Trade Association: 159-1, Samseong-dong, Gangnam-gu, Seoul; tel. (2) 6000-5114; fax (2) 6000-5115; internet www.kita.org; f. 1946; private, non-profitmaking business org. representing all licensed traders in South Korea; provides foreign businesses with information, contacts and advice; 80,000 corporate mems; Chair. and CEO IL SAKONG.

Korea Iron and Steel Association: 19/F, Posteel Tower, 735-3, Yeoksam-dong, Gangnam-gu, Seoul; tel. (2) 559-3508; internet www.kosa.or.kr; f. 1975; 39 corporate mems; Chair. YOO SANG-BOO.

Korea Oil Association: 28-1, Yeouido-dong, Yeongdeungpo-gu, Seoul; tel. (2) 555-8322; fax (2) 555-7825; e-mail oilassn@yahoo.co.kr; internet www.koreaoil.or.kr; f. 1980; Pres. CHOI DOO-HWAN.

Korea Productivity Center: 122-1, Jeokseon-dong, Jongno-gu, Seoul 110-052; tel. (2) 724-1114; fax (2) 736-0322; internet www.kpc.or.kr; f. 1957; services to increase productivity of industries, consulting services, education and training of specialized personnel; Chair. and CEO KIM JAE-HYUN.

Korea Sericultural Association: 17-9, Yeouido-dong, Yeongdeungpo-gu, Seoul; tel. (2) 783-6072; fax (2) 780-0706; e-mail jamsa@silktopia.or.kr; internet www.silktopia.or.kr; f. 1946; improvement and promotion of silk production; 50,227 corporate mems; Pres. CHOI YON-HONG.

Korea Shipbuilders' Association: 18/F, Landmark Tower, 837-36, Yeoksam-dong, Gangnam-gu, Seoul 135-937; tel. (2) 2112-8181; fax (2) 2112-8182; internet www.koshipa.or.kr; f. 1977; 9 mems; Chair. PARK KYU-WON.

Korea Textiles Trade Association: Textile Center, 16/F, 944-31, Daechi-3dong, Gangnam-gu, Seoul 135-713; tel. (2) 528-5158; fax (2) 528-5188; e-mail keat@kotis.net; internet www.textra.or.kr; f. 1981; 947 corporate mems; Pres. KANG TAE-SEUNG.

Korean Apparel Industry Association: Textile Centre, 16/F, 944-31, Daechi-3dong, Gangnam-gu, Seoul 135-713; tel. (2) 528-0114; fax (2) 528-0120; internet www.kaia.or.kr; f. 1993; 741 corporate mems; Chair. PARK PUNGEON.

Mining Association of Korea: 35-24, Dongui-dong, Jongno-gu, Seoul 110; tel. (2) 737-7748; fax (2) 720-5592; f. 1918; 128 corporate mems; Pres. KIM SANG-BONG.

Spinners and Weavers Association of Korea: 43-8, Gwancheol-dong, Jongno-gu, Seoul 110; tel. (2) 735-5741; fax (2) 735-5749; internet www.swak.org; f. 1947; 20 corporate mems; Chair. KIM HYONG-SANG.

EMPLOYERS' ORGANIZATION

Korea Employers' Federation: KEF Bldg, 276-1, Daeheung-dong, Mapo-gu, Seoul 121-726; tel. (2) 3270-7310; fax (2) 706-1059; e-mail delee@kef.or.kr; internet www.kef.or.kr; f. 1970; advocates employers' interests with regard to labour and social affairs; 13 regional employers' asscns, 20 economic and trade asscns, and 4,000 major enterprises; Chair. LEE SOO-YOUNG.

UTILITIES

Electricity

Korea Electric Power Corpn (KEPCO): 167, Samseong-dong, Gangnam-gu, Seoul; tel. (2) 3456-3630; fax (2) 3456-3699; internet www.kepco.co.kr; f. 1961; transmission and distribution of electric power, and development of electric power sources; six power generation subsidiaries formed in 2001; CEO KIM SANG-SOO.

Oil and Gas

Daegu City Gas Co Ltd: 2268-1, Namsan 4-dong, Jung-gu, Daegu; tel. (53) 606-1000; fax (53) 606-1004; internet www.taegugas.co.kr; f. 1983; Pres. and CEO JUNG CHOONG-YUNG.

Daehan City Gas: 27-1, Daechi-dong, Kangnam-gu, Seoul; tel. (2) 3410-8000; internet www.daehancitygas.com; f. 1978; supplies liquefied natural gas (LNG) to customers in Seoul and Gyeonggi Province; Co-CEO NAH SEONG-HWA; Co-CEO KIM BOK-HWAN.

GS Caltex: 135-985, 679 Yeoksam-dong, Gangnam-gu, Seoul; tel. (2) 2005-1114; internet www.gscaltex.com; subsidiary of GS Holdings Corpn; fmrly LG Caltex Oil, renamed as above March 2005; Chair. and CEO HUR DONG-SOO.

Hanjin City Gas: 711, Sanggye 6-dong, Nowon-gu, Seoul; tel. (2) 950-5000; fax (2) 950-5001; e-mail webmaster@hjcgas.com; internet www.hjcgas.com; f. 1985; supplies natural gas to Seoul and Gyeonggi; CEO PARK JIN-DO.

Incheon City Gas Corpn: 178-24, Gajoa-dong, Seo-gu, Incheon; tel. (32) 1600-0002; fax (32) 576-2710; internet www.icgas.co.kr; f. 1983; CEO KIM JUNG-CHI.

Jungbu City Gas Co Ltd: Jungbu; fax (41) 533-6748; e-mail webmaster@jbcitygas.com; internet www.cbcitygas.co.kr; f. 1992.

Korea Gas Corpn: 215, Jeongja-dong, Bundang-gu, Seongnam, Gyeonggi Prov.; tel. (31) 710-0114; fax (31) 710-0117; e-mail

THE REPUBLIC OF KOREA (SOUTH KOREA)

kogasmaster@kogas.or.kr; internet www.kogas.or.kr; f. 1983; state-owned; privatization pending; Pres. and CEO Choo Kang-Soo.

Korea National Oil Corpn (KNOC): tel. 380-2114; fax 387-9321; e-mail webmaster@knoc.co.kr; internet www.knoc.co.kr; CEO Kang Young-Won.

KyungDong City Gas Co: 939, Jinjang-dong, Book-gu, Ulsan; tel. (52) 219-5300; internet www.kdgas.co.kr; distributes liquefied natural gas (LNG) to residential, commercial and industrial customers in Ulsan and Yangsan; CEO Song Jae-Ho.

Kyungnam Energy Co Ltd: 55-5, Ungnam-dong, Changwon, Gyeongsangnam 641-290; tel. (55) 260-4432; fax (55) 260-4435; internet www.knenergy.co.kr; f. 1972; supplies natural gas to Changwon and the surrounding area; Pres. and CEO Chung Yeun-Wook.

Samchully Co Ltd: 35-6, Yeouido-dong, Yeongdeungpo-gu, Seoul; tel. (2) 368-3300; fax (2) 783-1206; e-mail webmaster@samchully.co.kr; internet www.samchully.co.kr; f. 1966; gas supply co for Seoul metropolitan area and Gyeonggi Prov.; Chair. Lee Young-Bok.

Seoul City Gas Co: 281, Yeomchang-dong, Gangseo-gu, Seoul 157-864; tel. (2) 810-8000; fax (2) 828-6740; internet www.seoulgas.co.kr; f. 1983; distributes gas in Seoul and Gyeonggi Province; Chair. and CEO Kim Young-Min.

SK E & S: 99, Seorin-dong, Jongno-gu, Seoul; tel. (2) 2121-3114; fax (2) 2121-3198; internet www.sk-enron.com; f. 1999; jt venture between SK Corpn and Enron Corpn (USA); supplies natural gas through nine city gas cos: Chongju City Gas, Chonnam City Gas, Chungnam City Gas, Iksan City Gas, Iksan Energy, Kangwon City Gas, Kumi City Gas and Pusan City Gas; Pres. and CEO Kim Joong-Ho.

Yesco Co Ltd: 249-8, Yongdap-dong, Sungdong-gu, Seoul; tel. (2) 1644-0303; fax (2) 3390-3117; e-mail webmaster@lsyesco.com; internet www.gaspia.com; f. 1981; fmrly Kukdong City Gas Co; part of the LS Group; supplies liquefied natural gas (LNG) to the Seoul metropolitan area; CEO and Pres. Choi Kyung-Hoon.

Water

Korea Water Resources Corpn: 6-2, Yeonchuk-dong, Daedeok-gu, Daejeon; tel. (42) 629-3114; fax (42) 623-0963; internet www.kowaco.or.kr.

Office of Waterworks, Seoul Metropolitan Govt: 27-1 Hap-dong, Seodaemun-gu, Seoul; tel. (2) 390-7332; fax (2) 362-3653; f. 1908; responsible for water supply in Seoul; Head Son Jang-Ho.

Ulsan City Water and Sewerage Board: 646-4, Sin-Jung 1-dong, Nam-gu, Ulsan; tel. (52) 743-020; fax (52) 746-928; f. 1979; responsible for water supply and sewerage in Ulsan; Dir Ho Kun-Song.

CO-OPERATIVES

Korea Auto Industries Co-operative Association: 1638-3, Seocho-dong, Seocho-gu, Seoul 137-070; tel. (2) 587-0014; fax (2) 583-7340; e-mail kaica@kaica.or.kr; internet www.kaica.or.kr; f. 1962; Chair. Shin Dal-Chuk.

Korea Computers Co-operative: 14-8, Yeouido-dong, Yeongdeungpo-gu, Seoul; tel. (2) 780-0511; fax (2) 780-7509; f. 1981; Pres. Min Kyung-Hyun.

Korea Federation of Knitting Industry Co-operatives: 586-1, Sinsa-dong, Gangnam-gu, Seoul; tel. (2) 548-2131; fax (2) 3444-9929; internet www.knit.or.kr; f. 1962; Chair. Joung Man-Sub.

Korea Federation of Non-ferrous Metal Industry Co-operatives: Backsang Bldg, Rm 715, 35-2, Yeouido-dong, Yeongdeungpo-gu, Seoul; tel. (2) 780-8551; fax (2) 784-9473; f. 1962; Chair. Park Won-Sik.

Korea Federation of Plastic Industry Co-operatives: tel. (2) 2280-8200; fax (2) 2277-3915; internet www.koreaplastic.or.kr; f. 1973.

Korea Federation of Small and Medium Business (Kbiz): 16-2, Yeouido-dong, Yeongdeungpo-gu, Seoul 150-010; tel. (2) 2124-3114; fax (2) 3775-1981; e-mail webmaster@kbiz.or.kr; internet www.kbiz.or.kr; f. 1962; Chair. Kim Ki-Mun.

Korea Federation of Weaving Industry Co-operatives: tel. (2) 752-8097; fax (2) 755-6994; e-mail weaving3@hanmail.net; internet www.weaving.or.kr; f. 1964.

Korea Information and Communication Industry Co-operative: tel. (2) 711-2266; fax (2) 7111-2272; e-mail webmaster@kicic.or.kr; internet www.kicic.or.kr; f. 1962; CEO Joo Dae-Chull.

Korea Metal Industry Co-operative: tel. (2) 780-4411; fax (2) 785-5067; e-mail master@koreametal.or.kr; internet www.koreametal.or.kr; f. 1962.

Korea Mining Industry Co-operative: 35-24, Dongui-dong, Jongno-gu, Seoul; tel. (2) 735-3490; fax (2) 735-4658; f. 1966; Chair. Jeon Hyang-Sik.

Directory

Korea Steel Industry Co-operative: 915-14, Bangbae-dong, Seocho-gu, Seoul; tel. (2) 587-3121; fax (2) 588-3671; internet www.kosic.or.kr; f. 1962; Pres. Kim Duk-Nam.

National Agricultural Co-operative Federation (NACF): 75, 1-ga, Chungjeong-no, Jung-gu, Seoul; tel. (2) 2080-5114; fax (2) 1544-2100; internet www.nonghyup.com; f. 1961; international banking, marketing, co-operative trade, utilization and processing, supply, co-operative insurance, banking and credit services, education and research; Chair. Choi Wun-Byung.

National Federation of Fisheries Co-operatives: 11-6, Sincheon-dong, Songpa-gu, Seoul; tel. (2) 2240-3114; fax (2) 2240-3024; internet www.suhyup.co.kr; f. 1962; CEO Lee Jong-Koo.

TRADE UNIONS

Federation of Korean Trade Unions (FKTU): 35, Yeouido-dong, Yeongdeungpo-gu, Seoul; tel. (2) 6277-0072; fax (2) 6277-0077; e-mail fktuintl@fktu.or.kr; internet www.efktu.or.kr/~fktueng; f. 1941; Pres. Jang Seok-Chun; affiliated to ITUC; 24 union federations are affiliated, including:

Federation of Korean Chemical Workers' Unions: FKTU Bldg 802, 35, Yeouido-dong, Yeongdeungpo-gu, Seoul 150-980; tel. (2) 6299-1234; fax (2) 6299-1235; e-mail fkcu@chollian.net; internet www.fkcu.or.kr; f. 1959; Pres. Ham Kwang-Ho; 116,286 mems.

Federation of Korean Metal Workers Trade Unions: 150-980, 9/F, 35, Yeouido-dong, Yeongdeungpo-gu, Seoul; tel. (2) 6330-8400; fax (2) 6330-8415; e-mail dykim@metall.or.kr; internet www.metall.or.kr; f. 1961; Pres. Jang Soek-Chun; 130,000 mems.

Federation of Korean Public Service Unions: Sukchun Bldg, 3rd Floor, 32-100, 4-ga, Dangsan-dong, Yeongdeungpo-gu, Seoul; tel. (2) 769-1330; fax (2) 769-1332; f. 1997; Pres. Lee Kwan-Boo; 15,641 mems.

Federation of Korean Seafarers' Unions: 544, Donhwa-dong, Mapo-gu, Seoul; tel. (2) 716-2764; fax (2) 702-2271; e-mail fksu@chollian.net; internet www.fksu.or.kr; f. 1961; Pres. Park Hee-Sung; 60,037 mems.

Federation of Korean State-invested Corporation Unions: Sunwoo Bldg, 501, 350-8, Yangjae-dong, Seocho-gu, Seoul; tel. (2) 529-2268; fax (2) 529-2270; internet www.publicunion.or.kr; f. 1998; Pres. Jang Dae-Ik; 19,375 mems.

Federation of Korean Taxi & Transport Workers' Unions: 415-7, Janan 1-dong, Dongdaemun-gu, Seoul; tel. (3) 633-0099; fax (3) 638-0090; internet www.ktaxi.or.kr; f. 1988; Pres. Kwan Oh-Man; 105,118 mems.

Federation of Korean United Workers' Unions: Sukchun Bldg, 32-100, 4-ga, Dangsan-dong, Yeongdeungpo-gu, Seoul; internet www.fkuwu.or.kr; f. 1961; 51,802 mems.

Korea Automobile & Transport Workers' Federation: 678-27, Yeoksam-dong, Gangnam-gu, Seoul; tel. (2) 554-0890; fax (2) 554-1558; f. 1963; Pres. Kang Sung-Chun; 84,343 mems.

Korea Federation of Communication Trade Unions: 10th Floor, 106-6, Guro 5-dong, Guro-gu, Seoul; tel. (2) 864-0055; fax (2) 864-5519; internet www.ictu.co.kr; f. 1961; Pres. Oh Dong-In; 18,810 mems.

Korea Federation of Food Industry Workers' Unions: 106-2, 1-ga, Yanpyeong-dong, Yeongdeungpo-gu, Seoul; tel. (2) 679-6441; fax (2) 679-6444; e-mail hpunion@hanmir.com; internet food.inochong.org; f. 2000; Pres. Baek Young-Gil; 19,146 mems.

Korea Federation of Port & Transport Workers' Unions: 19th Floor, Pyouk-San Bldg, 12-5 Dongja-dong, Yeongsan-gu, Seoul; tel. (2) 727-4741; fax (2) 727-4749; e-mail kfptwu@chollian.net; f. 1980; Pres. Choi Bong-Hong; 33,347 mems.

Korean Financial Industry Union: 9F, Dong-A Bldg, Da-dong, Chung-gu, Seoul; tel. (2) 2095-0000; fax (2) 2095-0018; internet www.kfiu.org; f. 1960; Pres. Yang Byung-Min.

Korea National Electrical Workers' Union: 167, Samseong-dong, Gangnam-gu, Seoul; tel. (2) 3456-6017; fax (2) 3456-6004; internet www.knewu.or.kr; f. 1961; Pres. Kim Ju-Young; 16,741 mems.

Korea Tobacco & Ginseng Workers' Unions: 100, Pyeongchon-dong, Daedeok-gu, Daejeon; tel. (42) 932-7118; fax (42) 931-1812; e-mail ktgson35@ktng.com; internet www.ktgwu.or.kr; f. 1960; Pres. Kang Tae-Heung; 6,008 mems.

Korea Union of Teaching and Educational Workers: tel. (2) 2691-5335; fax (2) 2691-8558; e-mail leemo@korea.com; internet www.kute.or.kr; f. 1999; 18,337 mems.

Korean Postal Workers' Union: 154-1, Seorin-dong, Jongno-gu, Seoul 110-110; tel. (2) 2195-1773; fax (2) 2195-1761; e-mail cheshin@chol.com; internet www.kpwu.or.kr; f. 1958; Pres. Jung Hyun-Young; 23,500 mems.

THE REPUBLIC OF KOREA (SOUTH KOREA)

Korean Railway Workers' Union: 40, 3-ga, Hangang-no, Yeongsan-gu, Seoul; tel. (2) 3780-5980; fax (2) 3780-5971; internet www.krwu.or.kr; f. 1947; Pres. KIM JONG-WOOK; 31,041 mems.

Korean Tourist Industry Workers' Federation: 749, 5-ga, Namdaemun-no, Jung-gu, Seoul 100-095; tel. (2) 779-1297; fax (2) 779-1298; f. 1970; Pres. JEONG YOUNG-KI; 27,273 mems.

Korean Confederation of Trade Unions: 5th Daeyoung Bldg, 139, 2-ga, Yeouido-dong, Yeongdeungpo-gu, Seoul 150-032; tel. (2) 2636-0165; fax (2) 2635-1134; internet www.kctu.org; f. 1995; legalized 1999; Chair. CHO JUN-HO; 600,000 mems.

Transport

RAILWAYS

At the end of 2001 there were 3,392 km of railways in operation. The first phase of construction of a new high-speed rail system connecting Seoul to Busan (412 km) via Cheonan, Daejeon, Daegu, and Gyungju, was completed in early 2004, with services commencing operation from April. The second phase, Daejeon–Busan, was scheduled for completion in 2010. Construction work on the reconnection of the Kyongui (West Coast, Sinuiju–Seoul) and East Coast Line (Wonsan–Seoul) began in September 2002. The two lines were reportedly completed in 2005. Scheduled cross-border trial runs took place in May 2007. Eventually the two were to be linked to the Trans-China and Trans-Siberian railways respectively.

Korean National Railroad: 139 Seonsa-ro, Seo-gu, Daejon 302-701; tel. (42) 472-3001; fax (42) 472-3020; internet www.korail.com; f. 1963; operates all railways under the supervision of the Ministry of Land, Transport and Maritime Affairs; total track length of 6,819 km (2001); Pres. PARK KWANG-SEOK (acting).

City Underground Railways

Busan Subway: Busan Urban Transit Authority, 861-1, Bumchun-dong, Busan 614-021; tel. (51) 633-8783; e-mail ipsubway@buta.or.kr; internet subway.busan.kr; f. 1988; length of 71.6 km (2 lines, with a further 3rd line under construction); Pres. LEE HYANG-YEUL.

Daegu Metropolitan Subway Corpn: 1500, Sangin 1-dong, Dalseo-gu, Daegu; tel. (53) 640-2114; fax (53) 640-2229; e-mail webmaster@daegusubway.co.kr; internet www.daegusubway.co.kr; length of 28.3 km (one line, with a further five routes totalling 125.4 km planned or under construction); CEO BAE SANG-MIN.

Daejeon Metropolitan Express Transit Corpn: tel. (42) 539-3114; fax (42) 539-3119; e-mail qnsdlqkr@hanmail.net; internet www.djet.co.kr; f. 2006; operates one line, with a further four lines planned.

Gwangju Metropolitan Rapid Transit Corpn: 529, Sangmu-no, Seo-gu, Gwangju; tel. (62) 604-8000; internet www.subway.gwangju.kr; f. 2004; one line, with a further line planned; Pres. OH HAENG-WON.

Incheon Rapid Transit Corpn: 67-2, Gansok-dong, Namdong-gu, Incheon 405-233; tel. (32) 451-2114; fax (32) 451-2160; internet www.irtc.co.kr; length of 24.6 km (22 stations, 1 line), with two further lines planned; Pres. CHOUNG IN-SOUNG.

Seoul Metropolitan Rapid Transit Corporation: 133-170, Seongdong-gu, Yongdap-dong 223-3, Seoul; tel. (2) 6211-2000; e-mail webadmin@smrt.co.kr; internet www.smrt.co.kr; operates lines 5–8.

Seoul Metropolitan Subway Corpn: 447-7, Bangbae-dong, Seocho-gu, Seoul; tel. (2) 520-5020; fax (2) 520-5039; internet www.seoulsubway.co.kr; f. 1981; length of 134.9 km (115 stations, lines 1-4); Pres. KIM SANG-DON.

ROADS

At the end of 2006 there were 102,062 km of roads. A network of motorways (3,103 km) links all the principal towns, the most important being the 428-km Seoul–Busan motorway. Improvements in relations with North Korea resulted in the commencement of work on a four-lane highway to link Seoul and the North Korean capital, Pyongyang, in September 2000. In February 2003 a road link between the two countries was reportedly opened.

Korea Expressway Corpn: 293-1, Kumto-dong, Sujong-gu, Seongnam, Gyeonggi Prov.; tel. (822) 2230-4114; fax (822) 2230-4308; internet www.freeway.co.kr; f. 1969; responsible for construction, maintenance and management of toll roads; Pres. LIEU CHULLHO.

SHIPPING

In December 2007 South Korea's merchant fleet (2,946 vessels) had a total displacement of 13,101,996 grt. Major ports include Busan, Incheon, Donghae, Masan, Yeosu, Gunsan, Mokpo, Pohang, Ulsan, Jeju and Gwangyang.

Busan Port Authority: 79-9, Jungangdong 4-ga, Junggu, Busan 600-817; tel. (2) 999-3000; fax (2) 988-8878; e-mail bpmaster@busanpa.com; internet www.busanpa.com; f. 2004; Pres. KI TAE-ROH.

Korea Shipowners' Association: Sejong Bldg, 10th Floor, 100, Dangju-dong, Jongno-gu, Seoul 110-071; tel. (2) 739-1551; fax (2) 739-1564; e-mail korea@shipowners.or.kr; internet www.shipowners.co.kr; f. 1960; 145 shipping co mems (March 2008); Chair. LEE JIN-BANG.

Korea Shipping Association: 66010, Dungchon 3-dong, Gangseo-gu, Seoul 157-033; tel. (2) 6096-2024; fax (2) 6096-2029; e-mail kimny@haewoon.co.kr; internet www.haewoon.co.kr; f. 1962; management consulting and investigation, mutual insurance; 1,189 mems; Chair. PARK HONG-JIN.

Principal Companies

DooYang Line Co Ltd: 166-4, Samseong-dong, Gangnam-gu, Seoul 135-091; tel. (2) 550-1700; fax (2) 550-1777; internet www.dooyang.co.kr; f. 1984; world-wide tramping and conventional liner trade; Pres. CHO DONG-HYUN.

Hanjin Shipping Ltd: 25-11, Yeouido-dong, Yeongdeungpo-gu, Seoul; tel. (2) 3770-6114; fax (2) 3770-6740; internet www.hanjin.com; f. 1977; marine transport, harbour service, warehousing, shipping and repair, vessel sales, harbour department and cargo service; Pres. and CEO YOUNG MIN-KIM.

Hyundai Merchant Marine Co Ltd: 66, Jeokseon-dong, Jongno-gu, Seoul 110-052; tel. (2) 3706-5114; fax (2) 723-2193; internet www.hmm.co.kr; f. 1976; Chair. HYUN YUNG-WON.

Korea Line Corpn: Dae Il Bldg, 43, Insa-dong, Jongno-gu, Seoul 110-290; tel. (2) 3701-0114; fax (2) 733-1610; f. 1968; world-wide transport service and shipping agency service in Korea; Pres. JANG HAK-SE.

Pan Ocean Shipping Co Ltd: 51-1, Namchang-dong, Jung-gu, CPOB 3051, Seoul 100-060; tel. (2) 316-5114; fax (2) 316-5296; f. 1966; transport of passenger cars and trucks, chemical and petroleum products, dry bulk cargo; Pres. CHIANG JIN-WON.

CIVIL AVIATION

There are international airports at Incheon (Seoul), Gimpo (Seoul), Busan, Cheongju, Daegu, Gwangju, Jeju and Yangyang. The main gateway into Seoul is Incheon International Airport, located 52 km from Seoul, which opened for service in 2001. The second phase of construction was completed in mid-2008.

Asiana Airlines Inc: 47, Osae-dong, Gangseo-gu, Seoul; tel. (2) 758-8114; fax (2) 758-8008; e-mail asianacr@asiana.co.kr; internet www.asiana.co.kr; f. 1988; serves 14 domestic cities and 36 destinations in 16 countries; fmrly Seoul Air International; CEO PARK SAM-KOO.

Hansung Airlines: Cheongju; tel. 1599-1090; fax (43) 210-0520; internet www.gohansung.com; f. 2004; operates low-cost flights between Cheongju and Jeju City; CEO HAN WOO-BONG.

Jeju Air: tel. (64) 746-7003; fax (64) 746-7011; internet www.jejuair.net; f. 2005; 25% owned by Jeju provincial govt, 75% by the Aekyung Group; operates low-cost flights between Jeju and the mainland; CEO JOO SANG-KIL.

Korean Air: 1370, Gonghang-dong, Gangseo-gu, Seoul; tel. (2) 656-7092; fax (2) 656-7289; internet www.koreanair.com; f. 1962; est. by the Govt, privately owned since 1969; fmrly Korean Air Lines (KAL); operates domestic and regional services and routes to the Americas, Europe, the Far East and the Middle East, serving 73 cities in 26 countries; Chair. and CEO CHO YANG-HO.

Tourism

South Korea's mountain scenery and historic sites are the principal attractions for tourists. Jeju Island, located some 100 km off the southern coast, is a popular resort. In 2006 there were 6.2m. visitors to South Korea, of whom some 38% came from Japan. Receipts from tourism in 2006 amounted to US $8,069m.

Korea National Tourism Organization: KNTO Bldg, 10, Da-dong, Jung-gu, CPOB 903, Seoul 100; tel. (2) 729-9600; fax (2) 757-5997; e-mail webmaster@mail.knto.or.kr; internet english.tour2korea.com; f. 1962; as Korea Tourist Service; Pres. (vacant).

Korea Tourism Association: Saman Bldg, 11th Floor, 945, Daechi-dong, Gangnam-gu, Seoul; tel. (2) 556-2356; fax (2) 556-3818; f. 1963; Pres. CHO HANG-KYU, KIM JAE-GI.

KOSOVO

Introductory Survey

Location, Climate, Language, Religion, Flag, Capital

The Republic of Kosovo (Kosova), formerly the province officially named Kosovo and Metohija within the Republic of Serbia, is situated in the central Balkan peninsula in south-eastern Europe. There are borders with Serbia in the north-west and north-east, the former Yugoslav republic of Macedonia in the south, Albania in the south-west, and Montenegro to the west. The climate is continental. Under a new Constitution, approved in April 2008, the official languages of Kosovo are Albanian and Serbian, while the Turkish, Bosnian and Roma languages are also accorded official status at municipal level. The principal religion in Kosovo is Islam. Serbs are principally adherents of Orthodox Christianity, as represented by the Serbian Orthodox Church. The state flag (proportions 2 by 3) is blue, with an arc of six white stars above a golden map of Kosovo. The capital is Prishtina (Prishtinë—Priština).

Recent History

Kosovo was part of the Serbian state established by the Nemanja dynasty in 1166. The Serbian Orthodox Patriarchate was established in Kosovo in the 13th century, and the territory was the location of the defeat of the Serbs by the Turkish Ottoman Empire at Fushë Kosovë (Kosovo Polje—'the Field of Blackbirds') in 1389. After continued Albanian resistance to Ottoman rule, the League of Prizren was established in 1878. Kosovo remained under Ottoman rule until its annexation by Serbia during the First Balkan War in 1912. During the Second World War Kosovo was annexed by Albania (in personal union with the Italian Crown). Following the establishment of the Federative People's Republic of Yugoslavia, the 1946 Constitution provided for the establishment of autonomous regions within Serbia in Kosovo and Metohija (as the region was renamed) and in the northern territory of Vojvodina. In 1963 the autonomous region of Kosovo and Metohija was formally upgraded in status to that of an autonomous province, a status that was confirmed by the 1974 Constitution, which also renamed the territory simply as Kosovo and increased the powers of the two autonomous provinces at the federal level of the state.

From the mid-1980s increasing Serb nationalism, and the rise to power of Slobodan Milošević (President of Serbia in 1989–97), exacerbated tensions in the province. A new Serbian Constitution of 1990 revoked the autonomy of Kosovo and Vojvodina, and this was confirmed by the April 1992 Constitution that created the Federal Republic of Yugoslavia (FRY). A republic-wide referendum on a new Serbian Constitution, largely boycotted by the ethnic Albanians, was conducted on 2 July, when a majority of Serbs approved the new Constitution. It was formally promulgated on 28 September, whereupon the designation of Kosovo reverted to that of Kosovo and Metohija (although this designation continued to be unpopular with the ethnic Albanian population of Kosovo). Meanwhile, following the constitutional referendum, 114 of 180 deputies in the Kosovo Assembly (Kuvendi i Kosovës/Skupština Kosova) met and declared Kosovo independent of Serbia. On 5 July the Serbian authorities dissolved the provincial Assembly and Government. The Kosovo presidency resigned in protest, and Serbia introduced a special administration. On 7 September members of the old representative body declared the Kosovo Assembly to have been reconvened and subsequently proclaimed a basic law of a 'Republic of Kosovo'. Meanwhile, elections, which were declared illegal by the Serbian authorities, were held in the province on 24 May. The Democratic Alliance of Kosovo (DAK) secured the most seats in the 130-member Assembly, and the DAK leader, Ibrahim Rugova, was elected President of the self-proclaimed 'Republic of Kosovo'.

Throughout the mid-1990s there were reports of harassment of Kosovo Albanians by Serbian police. The situation deteriorated further in 1996 with the emergence, in February, of an ethnic Albanian militant organization, the Kosovo Liberation Army (KLA), which announced its intention to achieve independence for Kosovo through armed resistance against the Serbian authorities, and began attacks against security forces. Special Serbian security forces undertook reprisals against the Albanian population.

Negotiations regarding the implementation of a cease-fire in Kosovo and the withdrawal of Serbian forces continued throughout 1998 and in October, following a North Atlantic Treaty Organization (NATO, see p. 351) ultimatum, Milošević, President of the FRY since the previous year, agreed to the presence in Kosovo of an Organization for Security and Co-operation in Europe (OSCE, see p. 366) mission, which began deployment in early November. Nevertheless, armed clashes between Serbian forces and the KLA increased. In January 1999 the bodies of 45 Albanians were discovered in the village of Reçak (Račak), increasing international concerns of a humanitarian crisis. In February a peace conference in Rambouillet, France, attended by Serbian and ethnic Albanian delegations, including KLA representatives, commenced. Despite the reluctance of the KLA to accept conditions for disarmament, the Albanian delegation signed the peace agreement on 18 March. However, the Serbian delegation continued to present objections to the peace plan; on 23 March the Serbian legislature adopted a resolution condemning aggression against its country and opposing the deployment of NATO forces in Kosovo. On 24 March a NATO-led aerial bombardment of military and civilian installations in the FRY (Serbia and Montenegro) commenced. Serbian security forces in Kosovo subsequently conducted mass expulsions and large-scale massacres of the Albanian civilian population, resulting in the continued exodus of refugees from the province. According to the UN High Commissioner for Refugees (UNHCR), a total of 848,100 Albanians fled or were expelled from Kosovo. On 3 June 1999 a peace agreement providing for the withdrawal of Serbian forces from Kosovo and the deployment of a joint NATO-Russian peace-keeping force was approved by the Serbian legislature. On 10 June, following a Military Technical Agreement between NATO and the Federal Government, the withdrawal of Serbian forces from Kosovo commenced, and NATO officially suspended its air operations. On the same day a UN Security Council resolution was approved, authorizing the deployment of international civil and security presences in Kosovo, and providing for the establishment of the UN Interim Administration Mission in Kosovo (UNMIK) as the supreme legal and executive authority in the region. On 12 June both Russian and NATO troops entered Kosovo. By 20 June the Serb withdrawal had been completed and the multinational NATO-led Kosovo Force (KFOR), which had an authorized strength of up to 50,000 personnel, was established. Some three weeks after the end of the conflict, an estimated 600,000 Albanians had returned to Kosovo. Over the same period some 180,000 Serbs and Roma fled the province.

In February 2000 Rugova announced the dissolution of the 'Republic of Kosovo' and of the DAK. In local government election, held in Kosovo on 28 October, Rugova's Democratic League of Kosovo (DLK—a successor organization to the DAK) secured 58% of the votes cast to 30 municipal councils, while the Democratic Party of Kosovo (DPK), led by a former KLA commander, Hashim Thaçi, won 27% of the votes. Elections to 100 seats of the 120-member Kosovo Assembly were conducted on 17 November 2001, under a UNMIK programme for establishing partial and provisional self-government in the province. (The remaining 20 seats were reserved for representatives of Serbs and other minority ethnic groups.) The DLK secured 47 seats, while the DPK won 26 seats and a coalition of Serb parties 22 seats. On 4 March 2002, following protracted inter-party discussions, Rugova was elected President of Kosovo. Under the coalition agreement, a member of the DPK, Bajram Rexhepi, became Prime Minister, and a 10-member Government (in which the DLK held four portfolios and the DPK a further two) was subsequently established. In April the Serb coalition agreed to join the administration.

In March 2004 the deaths of three Albanian boys, who had allegedly been pursued by a group of Serbs into the Ibar River, precipitated rioting in Mitrovicë (Kosovska Mitrovica), which escalated into several days of clashes between the Serbian and Albanian communities throughout Kosovo. Some 2,000 KFOR reinforcements were dispatched to quell the violence. Some 19 civilians (11 Albanians and eight Serbs) were killed in the clashes, while some 4,000 Serbs and Roma were forced to flee from their residences, after being attacked by Albanian rioters. At elections to the Kosovo Assembly on 23 October, the DLK secured 45.4% of the votes cast, thereby retaining 47 seats in the 120-member legislature, while the DPK won 28.9% of the votes cast, increasing its representation to 30 seats, while the Alliance for the Future of Kosovo (AFK) obtained 8.4% of the votes cast and nine seats. The DLK negotiated a coalition agreement, whereby the leader of the AFK, Ramush Haradinaj, became the new Prime Minister on 3 December. The election of Haradinaj, a former senior KLA leader who had been under investigation by the International Criminal Tribunal for the former Yugoslavia (ICTY, see p. 19) for alleged war crimes in Kosovo, was strongly criticized by Serbian parties. While the overall rate of participation by voters in the province was recorded at some 53.6% of the registered electorate, only about 0.3% of the Serb community participated in the poll. (Serbs retained an allocation of 10 seats in the Assembly, but continued to boycott the provisional institutions.) On 8 March 2005 Haradinaj, having received an indictment from the ICTY on a total of 37 charges, resigned as Prime Minister and surrendered to the Tribunal. His indictment prompted widespread protests in the province (causing the dispatch of British military reinforcements). On 23 March a new Government, led by Bajram Kosumi, also of the AFK, was established. (In April 2008 the ICTY acquitted Haradinaj of all charges.)

Following a favourable report of the European Commission on Serbia and Montenegro (as the FRY had been reconstituted in 2003) in April 2005, the resolution of Kosovo's future status became an increasingly pressing issue. The European Commission pledged to continue support for the eventual integration of Kosovo into European institutions, provided that the Kosovo Government demonstrated commitment to reforms and democratic principles. In September delegations from the Governments of Serbia and Kosovo met in Vienna, Austria, for preliminary discussions. On 4 October a UN Special Envoy officially submitted a review to the Secretary-General of the organization, stating that the Kosovo Government had made significant progress towards establishing executive, legislative and judicial institutions. On 24 October the UN Security Council endorsed the initiation of final status negotiations on Kosovo. In November the Serbian Government adopted a resolution rejecting the independence of Kosovo, while the Kosovo Assembly approved a motion stating that it would accept only independence as the final status of the territory. Later that month the former Finnish President, Martti Ahtisaari, who had been appointed UN Special Envoy for the Future Status Process for Kosovo, commenced separate discussions with Serbian and Kosovo leaders. On 21 January 2006 Rugova died after an illness. Later that month the DLK nominated Fatmir Sejdiu to succeed Rugova; on 10 February he was elected unopposed as the new President by the Kosovo Assembly. On 1 March Kosumi resigned as Prime Minister. On 10 March the Kosovo Assembly voted to approve Agim Çeku a former KLA chief of staff, as his successor. Meanwhile, the first round of final status negotiations on Kosovo commenced in Vienna on 20–21 February. Direct high-level discussions, the first to involve the Presidents and Prime Ministers of Serbia and Kosovo since 1999, were conducted in Vienna in July; the Kosovo delegation reiterated demands for full independence for the province by the end of 2006, while the Serbian Prime Minister, Vojislav Koštunica, maintained that Serbia would not accept a loss of territory. The Kosovo delegation remained opposed to increased decentralization, owing to concern that an effectively autonomous Serb polity would be established within the province. By the end of 2006 the two delegations had failed to reach any agreement.

On 2 February 2007 Ahtisaari presented his recommendations for the future status of Kosovo to the Serbian and Kosovo authorities and invited the delegations to engage in consultations on the draft in Vienna. The discussions, which commenced later that month, ended without success in March; Ahtisaari concluded that there was no further prospect of achieving a negotiated agreement. On 26 March Ahtisaari submitted to the UN Security Council the finalized Comprehensive Proposal for the Kosovo Status Settlement, which recommended independence for the province, initially under international military and civilian supervision. Kosovo was to adopt a constitution, flag and anthem, and be granted rights to membership of international organizations; the rights of all minority groups living in the province, particularly the Kosovo Serbs, were to be protected. Under the Proposal, an International Civilian Representative, operating under a UN and European Union (EU, see p. 255) mandate, would be appointed to supervise the implementation of the Settlement, and would be empowered to veto legislation and dismiss local officials. KFOR would continue to provide security in the province, while the EU would deploy a police mission to assist in the development of institutions of law enforcement. On 3 April Koštunica, speaking in a debate at the UN Security Council, declared that Serbia rejected the Proposal, confirming the result of a vote in the Serbian legislature in February. On 5 April Ahtisaari's Proposal was approved by 100 of the 101 votes cast in the Kosovo Assembly. During a visit to Belgrade later that month, the Russian Minister of Foreign Affairs reiterated previous statements that Russia (as a permanent member of the Security Council) would not support an imposed resolution on the status of Kosovo that was not acceptable to the Serbian Government. Çeku stated that Kosovo was prepared to declare unilateral independence in the event of a protracted delay. From late April intensive discussions on Ahtisaari's Proposal continued in the UN Security Council; however, in July it was announced that it had proved impossible to secure a resolution. In August a further series of negotiations began between Serbian and Kosovo delegations, with mediation by the USA, the EU and Russia, but again failed to resolve the impasse. On 10 December the UN Secretary-General was informed that an agreement could not be concluded.

Meanwhile, amid increasing expectations of a unilateral declaration of independence, legislative elections were conducted in Kosovo on 17 November 2007. According to official results, the DPK secured the highest number of votes cast, with 34.3% of the total, taking 37 seats in the Assembly, while the DLK received some 22.6% of the votes cast and 25 seats. With a further boycott of the elections by Serb parties, a rate of participation of about 43% of the electorate was recorded. After lengthy negotiations, the DPK and the DLK reached a coalition agreement. On 9 January 2008 an 18-member, coalition Government, headed by Thaçi, and comprising an additional eight members of the DPK, six members of the DLK, two representatives of Serb groups and one representative of the ethnic Turkish community, was approved by the Assembly. With both main parties in the administration in favour of independence, Thaçi confirmed to the Assembly that a declaration of independence was imminent, and stated that such a declaration would enjoy the support of the USA and most EU member states. On the same day Sejdiu was re-elected President in a third round of voting in the Assembly for a term that was, in an amendment to the existing Constitutional Framework for Provisional Government, extended to five years. Jakup Krasniqi of the DPK was elected President of the Assembly.

On 17 February 2008 the Assembly of Kosovo endorsed a declaration establishing the province as the Republic of Kosovo (Kosova), a sovereign state independent from Serbia, the resolution adopted being based on Ahtisaari's Comprehensive Proposal for the Kosovo Status Settlement and in accordance with UN Security Council Resolution 1244 (of 1999). Serbia immediately protested that the declaration of independence contravened international law and demanded that it be annulled. An emergency meeting of the UN Security Council failed to agree on a new resolution, with Russia, in continued strong support of Serbia, and the People's Republic of China opposing Kosovo's sovereignty among the permanent members of the Council. Several countries, including Albania, France, the USA and the United Kingdom, extended recognition to Kosovo on 18 February 2008, and were rapidly followed by a number of other states. An International Steering Group appointed a Dutch diplomat, Pieter Feith, already the EU Special Representative, as an International Civilian Representative, to supervise the implementation of the Settlement. An EU Rule of Law Mission in Kosovo (EULEX), comprising some 1,900 foreign personnel, was to be deployed in Kosovo to support the authorities in maintaining public order. In March one member of UNMIK was killed in severe clashes between Serb protesters (who had seized control of a courthouse) and UNMIK and KFOR troops in Mitrovica. Serbia insisted that it intended to organize polls for its legislative and local elections (scheduled for 11 May) in the Serb-dominated municipalities in Kosovo. Also in March Serbia announced that it intended to submit a legal challenge against Kosovo's declaration of independence at the International Court of Justice (ICJ) in The Hague, Netherlands, and would apply for international support at the UN General Assembly. A new Constitution, which had been drafted by a Constitutional Commission in accordance with the principles of the Settlement, was adopted by the Assembly on 9 April, after being approved by Feith. The Constitution, which declared Kosovo to be an independent and sovereign state, was to enter into effect on 15 June, when UNMIK was officially to transfer its functions to the Kosovo authorities. However, during the transitional period it became evident that the deployment of EULEX would not proceed as envisaged, owing to the refusal of Kosovo Serbs and the Serbian Government to accept an EU mission. A report by the UN Secretary-General on developments in Kosovo, published at the beginning of April, stated that UNMIK's mandate would remain in force under Resolution 1244, pending a further decision by the UN Security Council.

The new Constitution entered into effect on 15 June 2008, as scheduled. Serbia, supported principally by Russia, continued to oppose the deployment of EULEX. Consequently, UN Secretary-General Ban Ki-Moon presented a plan to the Security Council, whereby UNMIK was to be reorganized and substantially reduced in size to allow an increased EU operational role. On 20 June an Italian diplomat, Lamberto Zannier, was appointed the new Special Representative of the UN Secretary-General and head of UNMIK, replacing Joachim Rücker, who had held that position since September 2006. The NATO Secretary-General announced that the remaining KFOR contingent was to organize the dissolution of the Kosovo Protection Corps (KPC—formed in 1999 largely on the basis of the the KLA) and the establishment of a 2,500-member multi-ethnic Kosovo Security Force. Following polls conducted among Kosovo Serbs, without the recognition of the Kosovo Government, on 11 May, a parallel legislature comprising representatives of the Serb community from 26 municipalities, the 'Assembly of the Community of Municipalities of the Autonomous Province of Kosovo and Metohija', was convened in Mitrovica on 28 June. Following discussions between Zannier and representatives of the Serbian Government on the planned reorganization of UNMIK, it was announced in August that a substantial reduction in the Mission's personnel was to begin.

In early August 2008 Thaçi appointed Fehmi Mujota as Kosovo's first Minister of Defence. In September it was announced that Kosovo had appointed its first 10 envoys to several of the countries that had recognized its statehood (Albania, Austria, Belgium, France, Germany, Italy, Switzerland, Turkey, the United Kingdom, and the USA); while a number of diplomatic missions in Prishtina had become embassies. Also in September Sejdiu established the Consultative Council for Communities, to comprise representatives of minority ethnic groups, in accordance with Ahtisaari's Comprehensive Proposal. In October the decision of Montenegro and the former Yugoslav republic of Macedonia to extend recognition to Kosovo prompted strong protests from the Serbian Government, which expelled the ambassadors of both countries. In the same month the UN General Assembly, in support of Serbia, voted in favour of referring to the ICJ the question of whether Kosovo's unilateral declaration of independence from Serbia was in accordance with international law.

Following the continued refusal of Kosovo Serbs to accept the deployment of EULEX, in early November 2008 the UN Secretary-General presented an amended six-point plan on the reconfiguration of the international presence in Kosovo, under which police, customs officers and judges in the Serb-majority areas would receive directives from UNMIK, while those in Albanian-majority areas would be the responsibility of EULEX. (This followed an agreement in late October by the US Administration to participate in EU operations in Kosovo.) Despite international pressure, the Kosovo Government remained opposed to EULEX's deployment under the compromise plan, on the grounds that it would be detrimental to the authority of its institutions and result in an effective partition of the state. Protests were staged in Prishtina by ethnic Albanian groups in opposition to the EU presence. The Serbian Government insisted, as a precondition of its acceptance of EULEX, that the plan be officially approved by the UN Security Council, that it be neutral with regard to Kosovo's status and that it would not be mandated to implement Ahtisaari's Comprehensive Proposal. On 26 November the UN Security Council unanimously endorsed the six-point plan under the stipulated terms; the Kosovo Minister of Foreign Affairs, Skender Hyseni, while pledging co-operation with the international community, reiterated objections to the plan, claiming that it would create two parallel authorities. On 9 December EULEX began deployment throughout the country, including Mitrovica, which proceeded without incidents of violence; the police component of UNMIK was subsequently reduced from 1,582 to 55 personnel. EULEX officials began to mediate discussions with some 300 Serb officers belonging to the Kosovo Police Service, who had left their units following the declaration of independence in February and demanded to remain under the authority of UNMIK. Later in December Serbian interior ministry troops arrested 10 former members of the KLA in the neighbouring Serbian region of Preševo, on suspicion of abducting and killing Serbs in 1999; they were transferred to Belgrade.

In January 2009 the KPC was officially dissolved and replaced by the Kosovo Security Force, which was to be primarily responsible for crisis management, civil protection and mine clearance. Several thousand Serbs demonstrated in Mitrovica in protest at the establishment of the new body, claiming that it threatened regional stability. In February a Security Council, comprising the Prime Minister, Deputy Prime Ministers and a number of ministers, was established as Kosovo's highest body on security matters. Celebrations for the first anniversary of Kosovo's declaration of independence took place without incident; however, 80 opposition deputies of the Serbian legislature joined the Kosovo Serb 'Assembly' in approving a declaration affirming the constitutional status of Kosovo within Serbia and rejecting the activities of the Kosovo institutions. Meanwhile, in early February the European Parliament adopted a resolution urging all EU member states to extend recognition to Kosovo; the number of countries that had officially recognized Kosovo as a sovereign state had increased to 59 UN member nations, including 22 EU members, by mid-May. The recognition of Kosovo by the Maldives in April prompted allegations that the Maldivian Government had received a sum of some US $2m. apparently as an inducement to recognize the independence of Kosovo; these reports emerged after a Serbian delegation had urged the Maldivian President and opposition parties to cancel the extension of recognition. Also in April Spain (one of the five EU member states, with Cyprus, Greece, Romania and Slovakia, that did not recognize the independence of Kosovo) unexpectedly announced the withdrawal of its KFOR contingent, numbering some 630, from Kosovo. Meanwhile, in March the Minister of Local Government announced that the process of decentralization in Kosovo was to begin with the establishment of six Serb-dominated municipalities in Mitrovica; certain executive powers were to be transferred to municipal governments after local elections due to be held in November. In late March a discussion at the UN Security Council on progress in Kosovo became acrimonious, when Hyseni accused Serbia of encouraging criminal activity in the north of the territory and presented demands by his Government for the complete withdrawal of UNMIK (which Kosovo Albanians regarded as a violation of the sovereignty of Kosovo). However, in accordance with the report of the UN Secretary-General, it was subsequently announced that a reduced UNMIK presence was to continue in the country indefinitely under Resolution 1244.

Government

A new Constitution entered into effect in Kosovo on 15 June 2008, largely supplanting the arrangements in place since the establishment of the UN Interim Administration Mission in Kosovo (UNMIK) as the supreme executive and legal authority in the territory in June 1999, the Kosovo Assembly, (Kuvendi i Kosovës/Skupština Kosova) having adopted a declaration of independence on 17 February 2008. (The Constitution of Serbia continues to refer to Kosovo and Metohija as an integral part of that state.) This declaration was based on the Comprehensive Proposal for the Kosovo Status Settlement drawn up by the UN Special Envoy of the Secretary-General for the Future Status Process for Kosovo, Martti Ahtisaari, and in accordance with UN Security Council Resolution 1244 (of 1999). An International Civilian Representative, who was also the Special Representative of the European Union (EU, see p. 255), was appointed by an International Steering Group to supervise the implementation of the Settlement. An EU Rule of Law Mission in Kosovo (EULEX) is deployed in Kosovo to maintain public order and security, and to assist in the development of legal and judicial institutions. Although it had been intended that UNMIK would transfer its functions to government institutions and to EULEX in June 2008, it was subsequently agreed, with the approval of the UN Security Council, that police and other officials in the Serb-majority areas would receive directives from UNMIK, while those in Albanian-majority areas would be the responsibility of EULEX. On 9 December EULEX became fully operational within the framework of Resolution 1244 and under the overall authority of the UN. The International Steering Group was to conduct its first review of the implementation of the Status Settlement after a period of two years.

The Kosovo Assembly comprises 120 deputies, of whom 100 are directly elected (the remaining 20 seats are reserved for the elected representatives of specified minority ethnic communities, including eight allocated to Serbs). The Assembly has a nine-member Presidency. The President of Kosovo is elected by the Assembly for a five-year term (renewable only once), and nominates a Prime Minister, who proposes a Government, for approval by the Assembly. Kosovo comprises seven regions, which are divided into 30 municipalities.

Defence

A NATO-led Kosovo Force (KFOR—with a maximum authorized strength of 50,000 personnel) was deployed in Kosovo following the conclusion of hostilities between NATO and the Federal Republic of Yugoslavia, and with the agreement of both parties, in June 1999. At January 2009 some 15,453 KFOR troops remained in Kosovo, on the basis of UN Security Council Resolution 1244 (of 1999), to maintain security and in support of the Kosovo institutions. Additionally, following Kosovo's declaration of independence in February 2008, an EU Rule of Law Mission in Kosovo (EULEX) was to be deployed in Kosovo, with a maximum authorized strength of some 1,900 foreign personnel and 1,100 local staff. Under an amended plan, approved by the UN Security Council in November, the deployment of EULEX throughout the country took place in December. At the end of January 2009 EULEX comprised a total of 2,364 personnel. Following the installation of EULEX, the UN Interim Administration Mission in Kosovo (UNMIK), established in 1999, was substantially reduced in size, and in March 2009 comprised 55 police officers and 22 military observers. At that time the Kosovo Police Service (established in 1999) totalled 7,070 personnel (comprising 5,981 Kosovo Albanians, 701 Kosovo Serbs and 388 other ethnic group members). In January 2009 a new 2,500-member Kosovo Security Force was established under civilian control and with primary responsibilities for crisis management, civil defence and mine clearance.

Economic Affairs

In 2007, according to estimates by the UN, the gross national income (GNI) of Kosovo was US $3,779m., equivalent to $1,561 per head. During 2000–07, it was estimated, the population declined by an annual average of 1.1%, when gross domestic product (GDP) per head increased, in real terms, by 14.7%. Overall GDP increased, in real terms, at an average annual rate of 3.3% in 2000–07; growth was 3.5% in 2007.

Agriculture (including hunting, forestry and fishing) contributed 10.0% of GDP in 2004. In 2007 some 14.6% of the total employed labour force were engaged in the sector. Kosovo's principal crops are wheat, potatoes, maize and peppers. According to UN figures, agricultural production decreased by an annual average of 17.9% in 2000–07, but increased by 3.0% in 2007.

Industry (including mining, manufacturing, construction and power) contributed 31.6% of GDP in 2004 and engaged 20.7% of the employed labour force in 2007. Construction engaged 6.6% of the employed labour force in that year. Industrial production decreased by an annual average of 2.6% in 2000–07, according to UN figures. Output increased by 4.4% in 2007.

The mining, manufacturing and utilities sector contributed 17.6% of GDP in 2004. In 2007 mining and quarrying engaged 1.0% of the employed labour force; manufacturing engaged 10.4% of the employed labour force in that year. One of the principal minerals extracted is halloysite, a clay mineral used to in the production of porcelain and bone china. More significantly, Kosovo has some 14.7m. metric tons of proven lignite reserves. Lead, zinc, chromium and bauxite are also mined. The mining, manufacturing and utilities sector declined at an average annual rate of 7.9% in 2000–07. However, it increased by 3.7% in 2007.

Energy in Kosovo is derived principally from coal (which contributes, on average, 97% of total electricity generated). Imports of mineral fuels accounted for 16.6% of the value of total imports to Kosovo in 2006.

Services contributed 58.4% of GDP in 2004 and engaged 68.4% of the employed labour force in 2007. Important areas of the service sector include wholesale and retail trade, education and administration (which engaged 9.6%). According to UN estimates, GDP in the services sector increased by an annual average of 15.7% in 2000–07; sectorial GDP increased by 3.9% in 2007.

In 2007 Kosovo recorded a visible trade deficit of €1,360m., and there was a deficit of €512m. on the current account of the balance of payments. In 2006 the principal source of imports to Kosovo was the former Yugoslav republic of Macedonia (FYRM), accounting for 19.7% of the total); other major sources were Serbia, Germany, Turkey and the People's Republic of China. The principal market for exports in that year was Serbia (taking 18.9% of total exports); other important purchasers were Bulgaria, Italy, Albania, the former Yugoslav republic of Macedonia and Switzerland. The main exports in 2006 were base metals and articles thereof, mineral products, machinery and mechanical products, leather and leather goods, and prepared foodstuffs, beverages, alcohol and tobacco. The principal imports in that year were mineral products, prepared foodstuffs, beverages and tobacco, machinery and mechanical products, base metals and articles thereof and chemical products.

In 2006 the overall budgetary surplus for Kosovo was €78.6m., equivalent to an estimated 2.5% of GDP. In 2007 the overall budgetary surplus was €244.1m. In 2003–08 the rate of inflation in Kosovo increased by an annual average of 2.3%. Consumer prices increased by 4.4% in 2007 and by 9.3% in 2008. The rate of unemployment in Kosovo was estimated at 43.6% in 2007.

Following Kosovo's unilateral declaration of independence on 17 February 2008, a total of 59 UN member states, including 22 of the 27 EU member states, had recognized Kosovo as an independent sovereign state by mid-May 2009. The IMF received a membership application from Kosovo on 10 July 2008; in May 2009 the Fund voted to offer membership to Kosovo, subject to a number of technical conditions.

Kosovo's economy was formerly concentrated in extractive industry, but much of the sector became inoperative as a result of the NATO bombardment in March–June 1999 (see Recent History), compounding long-term neglect and lack of investment. Post-conflict reconstruction was supported by substantial donor assistance. The UN Interim Administration Mission in Kosovo (UNMIK) introduced an external trade regime and customs administration, and extensive economic reforms were undertaken. The privatization of socially owned enterprises commenced in 2002. Following its declaration of independence in 2008, Kosovo remained one of the poorest territories in Europe and continued to be highly reliant upon remittances from abroad. At an international donor conference, held in Brussels, Belgium, in mid-2008, some 40 countries pledged around €1,200m. to finance debt and support social and economic development projects. The Government declared that efforts to combat 'grey' (semi-licit) market activity, corruption and organized crime were a priority. Meanwhile, Serbia and Bosnia and Herzegovina imposed a boycott on the import and transport of goods with the stamp of the Kosovo Customs Authority rather than that of UNMIK; in December the Kosovo Government announced a reciprocal ban on Serbian imports. In early 2009 the Government undertook a number of measures in an effort to counteract the negative impact of the international financial crisis (which was expected to affect adversely essential foreign remittances and levels of investment), including the establishment of a multi-agency financial stabilization committee. In March Kosovo became a member of the Vienna Economic Forum (an organization promoting regional investment opportunities), although the continuing inability of the Kosovo institutions to exert authority in northern Serb-dominated areas, or to obtain recognition for the independence of Kosovo from several important states internationally also presented substantial challenges to Kosovo's economic development.

Education

Responsibility for education was transferred to the Ministry of Education, Science and Technology in 2002. The system of compulsory education was extended from eight to nine years in 2003/04, henceforth comprising a five-year period of primary education, beginning at seven years, and two cycles of secondary education, lasting four years and three years, respectively. The higher education system operates through two state universities, the University of Prishtina, and the University of Mitrovica; a total of 27,274 students were enrolled in higher education in 2006/07.

Public Holidays

2009: 1–2 January (New Year's Day), 7 January (Orthodox Christmas), 17 February (Independence Day), 9 April (Constitution Day), 13 April (Catholic Easter Monday), 20 April (Ortho-

KOSOVO

dox Easter Monday), 1 May (Labour Day), 11 May (for Europe Day), 21 September* (Small Bayram, end of Ramadan), 27 November* (Great Bayram, Feast of the Sacrifice), 25 December (Catholic Christmas).
2010: 1–2 January (New Year's Day), 7 January (Orthodox Christmas), 17 February (Independence Day), 5 April (Catholic Easter Monday), 9 April (Constitution Day), 3 May (for Labour Day), 10 May (for Europe Day), 10 September* (Small Bayram, end of Ramadan), 16 November* (Great Bayram, Feast of the Sacrifice), 27 December (for Catholic Christmas).

* These holidays are dependent on the Islamic lunar calendar and may vary by one or two days from the dates given.

Statistical Survey

Source (unless otherwise indicated): Statistical Office of Kosovo, 10000 Prishtina, Rruga Zenel Salihu 4; tel. (38) 235111; fax (38) 235033; e-mail esk@ks-gov.net; internet www.ks-gov.net/esk.

Area and Population

AREA, POPULATION AND DENSITY

Area (sq km)	10,908*
Population (census results)	
31 March 1981	1,584,440
31 March 1991†	1,956,196
Population (official estimate at 31 December)‡	
2005	2,069,989
2006	2,126,728
Density (per sq km) at 31 December 2006	195.0

* 4,212 sq miles.
† Assessment of the Office of Statistics of the former Socialist Federal Republic of Yugoslavia.
‡ Assessment of the Statistical Office of Kosovo.

POPULATION BY ETHNIC GROUP
(official estimates at 31 December 2006)

Ethnic group	Population ('000)	%
Albanians	1,932	92.0
Serbs	111	5.3
Roma	24	1.1
Turks	8	0.4
Others	25	1.2
Total	**2,100**	**100.0**

1991 census ('000): Albanians 1,596 (81.6%); Serbs 194 (9.9%); Roma 46 (2.3%); Turks 10 (0.5%); Others 110 (5.6%).

BIRTHS, MARRIAGES AND DEATHS

	Registered live births		Registered marriages		Registered deaths	
	Number	Rate (per 1,000)	Number	Rate (per 1,000)	Number	Rate (per 1,000)
2002	36,136	18.2	18,280	9.2	5,654	2.8
2003	31,994	15.9	17,034	8.4	6,417	3.2
2004	35,063	17.2	16,989	8.3	6,399	3.1
2005	37,218	18.0	15,732	7.6	7,207	3.5
2006	34,187	16.3	15,825	7.5	7,479	3.6
2007	33,112	15.6	16,824	7.9	6,681	3.1

Life expectancy (years at birth, official estimates): 69 (males 67; females 71) in 2003.

EMPLOYMENT
(labour force survey, percentage distribution)

	2005	2006	2007
Agriculture, hunting, forestry and fishing	18.8	21.4	14.6
Mining and quarrying	1.6	1.5	1.0
Manufacturing	9.6	7.3	10.4
Electricity, gas and water supply	3.2	3.6	2.7
Construction	7.9	8.1	6.6
Wholesale and retail trade; repair of motor vehicles, motorcycles and personal and household goods	13.8	16.4	16.9
Hotels and restaurants	3.5	2.8	3.9
Transport, storage and communications	4.2	3.7	4.5
Financial intermediation	1.1	1.4	1.1
Real estate, renting and business activities	2.4	2.1	1.4
Public administration and defence; compulsory social security	8.2	7.8	9.6
Education	10.8	11.7	12.1
Health and social work	5.2	5.4	7.0
Other community, social and personal service activities	9.7	7.0	8.3

Note: Reliable estimates of the number of employed people were not available. According to the results of an official agricultural household survey conducted at the end of 2005, some 500,000 farm residents of working age were engaged in some level of farming activity (of which 135,000 were employed in this activity on a full-time basis). An official statistical overview of some 54,000 registered private-sector businesses at the end of 2002 recorded 186,000 employees, whilst the number of people engaged in public administration at the end of 2005 totalled 74,081.
Registered unemployed (at 31 December 2008): 335,942. Note: According to official estimates, some 43.6% of the total labour force was unemployed in 2007.

KOSOVO

Agriculture

PRINCIPAL CROPS
('000 metric tons)

	2004	2005
Wheat	196.7	273.4
Barley	6.3	11.3
Oats	5.0	9.8
Maize (incl. mixed crops)	91.7	79.9
Potatoes	55.9	87.4
Tomatoes	11.3	15.0
Peppers	39.9	55.0
Pumpkins (incl. mixed crops)	6.1	8.3
Cabbages	15.4	18.9
Onions	9.9	11.0
Beans (incl. mixed crops)	5.3	7.5
Cucumbers	5.9	6.1
Watermelons	10.0	13.5
Apples	9.1	7.1
Pears	2.8	2.8
Plums	16.1	12.0
Vine grapes	1.4	2.2
Other grapes	2.7	3.5

Note: Data exclude second crops and autumn crops; production from state-owned enterprises is also excluded.

LIVESTOCK
('000 head, October–December unless otherwise indicated)

	2004*	2005	2006
Horses	6.7†	6.2	6.7
Cattle	240.7	351.8	382.0
Pigs	35.2	47.5	68.2
Sheep	124.4	143.0	100.8
Goats	10.8	8.9	12.1
Chickens	1,660.4	2,386.5	2,337.1
Other poultry	43.7	244.6	187.4

* November–December; the methodology used in calculating data for livestock numbers in 2004 differs slightly from that employed in 2005 and 2006, and data are, therefore, not strictly comparable.
† Including donkeys.

Note: Data exclude livestock belonging to state-owned enterprises.

LIVESTOCK PRODUCTS
(value of products sold, € '000)

	2005
Meat	2,713.3
Milk	7,194.3
Fat	279.4
Other dairy products	886.0
Eggs	4,760.3
Honey	767.5
Total (incl. others)	20,267.0

Note: Data exclude production by state-owned enterprises.

Forestry

FORESTRY REMOVALS
('000 cubic metres)

	2004	2005
Fuel wood	n.a.	393.1
Total (incl. others)	434.3	400.5

Note: Data exclude removals by state-owned enterprises.

Mining

('000 metric tons)

	2005	2006	2007
Coal	6,391.1	6,532.3	6,715.4

Industry

(million kWh)

	2005	2006	2007
Electric energy	4,000	3,971	4,309

Finance

CURRENCY AND EXCHANGE RATES

Monetary Units
100 cent = 1 euro (€).

Sterling, Dollar and Euro Equivalents (31 December 2008)
£1 sterling = 1.0475 euros;
US $1 = 0.7185 euros;
€10 = £9.55 = $13.92.

Average Exchange Rate (euros per US $)
2006   0.7971
2007   0.7306
2008   0.6827

BUDGET
(consolidated accounts, € million)

Revenue	2005	2006	2007
Tax revenue	561.6	621.5	716.2
Direct taxes	82.7	119.6	132.7
Indirect taxes	478.9	501.9	583.5
Value-added tax	241.6	258.6	313.8
Excise duties	164.3	161.9	191.4
Trade duties	74.1	82.3	81.2
Non-tax revenue	74.9	91.5	108.1
Statistical discrepancy	—	—	75.0
Total	636.5	713.1	899.3

Expenditure	2005	2006	2007
Current expenditure	529.3	502.3	506.4
Wages and salaries	194.6	203.8	209.0
Goods and services	142.8	143.0	144.9
Subsidies and transfers	191.8	155.4	153.0
Capital expenditure and net lending	166.9	132.2	148.8
Total	696.1	634.5	655.2

Source: Ministry of Economy and Finance, Prishtina.

COST OF LIVING
(Consumer Price Index; base: May 2002 = 100)

	2006	2007	2008
All items	98.5	102.8	112.4

KOSOVO

Statistical Survey

NATIONAL ACCOUNTS
(€ million at current prices)

Expenditure on the Gross Domestic Product
(provisional)

	2004	2005	2006
Government final consumption expenditure	735.5	705.2	670.8
Private final consumption expenditure	2,563.0	2,729.5	2,889.5
Gross fixed capital formation	583.6	592.8	657.1
Changes in inventories	117.7	129.4	141.2
Total domestic expenditure	4,000.1	4,156.9	4,358.6
Exports of goods and services	212.4	214.7	285.6
Less Imports of goods and services	1,205.7	1,303.3	1,452.5
GDP in market prices	3,006.5	3,068.4	3,191.7

Note: Data include contributions from UNMIK operations.

Gross Domestic Product by Economic Activity

	2002	2003	2004
Agriculture, hunting, forestry and fishing	188.0	186.7	178.4
Mining, manufacturing and utilities	359.2	322.9	313.1
Construction	208.0	221.1	248.6
Wholesale and retail trade; repair of motor vehicles, motorcycles and personal and household goods	201.3	193.4	211.5
Hotels and restaurants	63.1	67.1	68.1
Transport, storage and communications	90.6	85.9	98.7
Financial intermediation	59.6	77.7	102.5
Real estate, renting and business activities	431.3	403.1	390.8
Public administration and defence; compulsory social security	90.5	107.6	123.1
Education	19.4	21.1	9.7
Health and social work	24.9	26.3	19.6
Other community, social and personal service activities	6.7	6.4	13.7
GDP at basic prices	1,742.7	1,719.3	1,777.6
Taxes, less subsidies, on products	396.6	438.0	396.8
GDP in purchasers' values	2,139.2	2,157.4	2,174.4

Note: Data exclude contributions from UNMIK operations, which were estimated at (€ million): 450.7 in 2002; 347.6 in 2003; 298.1 in 2004.

BALANCE OF PAYMENTS
(€ million)

	2005	2006	2007
Exports of goods f.o.b.	56	111	146
Imports of goods f.o.b.	−1,100	−1,252	−1,506
Trade balance	−1,044	−1,141	−1,360
Exports of services	157	175	197
Imports of services	−192	−189	−214
Balance on goods and services	−1,079	−1,155	−1,377
Income (net)	38	44	65
Balance on goods, services and income	−1,041	−1,111	−1,312
Transfers (net)	683	728	800
Current balance	−358	−383	−512

Capital and financial account: 78 in 2005 (Direct investments 82, Portfolio investments −68, Other investments 64); 12 in 2006 (Direct investments 248, Portfolio investments −128, Other investments −108); 105 in 2007 (Direct investments 420, Portfolio investments −69, Other investments −246).

Errors and omissions: 280 in 2005; 371 in 2006; 407 in 2007.

Source: Ministry of Economy and Finance, Prishtina.

External Trade

PRINCIPAL COMMODITIES
(€ '000, distribution by Harmonized System)

Imports c.i.f.	2004	2005	2006
Live animals and animal products	52,417	54,047	50,477
Vegetable products	68,147	57,248	72,991
Prepared foodstuffs, beverages, alcohol and tobacco	165,406	163,270	180,644
Beverages, spirits and vinegar	38,906	39,531	41,681
Tobacco and manufactured tobacco substitutes	34,759	26,335	32,012
Mineral products	173,072	207,323	241,667
Mineral fuels, mineral oils and products of their distillation	148,370	182,712	217,345
Chemical products	97,966	91,118	107,730
Pharmaceutical products	40,640	28,435	30,382
Plastics, rubber and articles thereof	42,500	50,958	60,677
Plastics and articles thereof	35,217	42,267	50,562
Textiles and textile articles	31,154	35,892	45,122
Articles of stone, plaster, ceramics and glass	54,948	51,480	56,994
Ceramic products	34,068	36,247	40,230
Base metals and articles thereof	77,455	90,289	122,609
Iron and steel	43,731	47,545	66,432
Machinery and mechanical appliances; electrical equipment; sound and television apparatus	116,765	129,210	153,315
Vehicles, aircraft, vessels and associated transport equipment	50,218	104,158	79,341
Total (incl. others)	1,063,347	1,157,492	1,305,879

Exports f.o.b.	2004	2005	2006
Vegetable products	2,569	2,888	5,062
Edible vegetables (incl. some roots and tubers)	2,126	2,091	2,486
Prepared foodstuffs, beverages, alcohol and tobacco	3,836	4,585	6,195
Beverages, spirits and vinegars	2,522	2,385	2,788
Mineral products	2,483	3,210	18,790
Ores, slag and ash	1,515	1,352	8,879
Mineral fuels, mineral oils and products of their distillation	638	1,743	9,099
Plastics, rubber and articles thereof	3,675	968	3,214
Leather and leather articles	5,867	6,115	7,232
Raw hides and skins (other than fur)	5,851	6,095	7,222
Base metals and articles thereof	19,723	24,789	53,119
Iron and steel	12,037	13,575	30,385
Articles of iron and steel	2,864	2,670	3,063
Copper and articles thereof	1,904	2,810	7,764
Aluminium and articles thereof	1,803	4,178	8,243
Machinery and mechanical appliances; electrical equipment; sound and television apparatus	9,164	6,548	7,658
Total (incl. others)	56,567	56,283	110,774

2007 (€ '000): Total imports 1,576,186; Total exports 165,112.

KOSOVO

PRINCIPAL TRADING PARTNERS
(€ '000)

Imports c.i.f.	2004	2005	2006
Albania	20,237	18,093	23,108
Austria	27,650	20,719	23,539
Bosnia and Herzegovina	12,845	18,450	18,465
Brazil	21,550	16,840	18,578
Bulgaria	42,096	37,791	58,498
China, People's Rep.	34,265	54,864	74,655
Croatia	25,120	24,975	28,074
France	23,076	19,468	15,834
Germany	78,247	123,763	122,652
Greece	68,515	44,027	37,614
Hungary	19,681	16,233	20,011
Italy	44,525	49,555	52,461
Japan	8,101	13,533	8,666
Macedonia, former Yugoslav republic	149,218	220,148	257,754
Montenegro	n.a.	6,411	17,800
Poland	6,304	14,836	13,796
Serbia	161,281	152,257	191,053
Slovenia	56,870	54,998	56,001
Spain	8,534	11,741	9,391
Switzerland	16,190	18,415	22,800
Turkey	86,798	85,375	97,075
Ukraine	10,884	11,969	11,978
United Kingdom	11,112	7,478	6,378
USA	16,979	17,693	11,555
Total (incl. others)	1,063,347	1,157,492	1,305,879

Exports f.o.b.	2004	2005	2006
Albania	1,793	5,784	12,645
Austria	947	1,017	1,211
Bosnia and Herzegovina	1,503	3,411	5,126
Bulgaria	362	970	13,506
Croatia	513	928	1,123
Germany	3,262	5,965	3,952
Greece	4,262	5,522	3,914
Italy	5,536	5,668	12,654
Macedonia, former Yugoslav republic	9,641	10,828	9,734
Montenegro	n.a.	743	2,207
Netherlands	71	124	1,128
Serbia	10,060	8,158	20,910
Slovenia	954	1,231	4,515
Switzerland	128	681	7,047
Turkey	2,867	1,041	1,668
United Kingdom	636	72	62
Total (incl. others)	56,567	56,283	110,774

Transport

RAILWAYS

	2005	2006
Passenger train journeys	3,427	5,662
Passenger train-kilometres	214,731	317,320
Freight train journeys	1,440	1,494
Freight train-kilometres	69,245	82,459
Total freight transported (metric tons)	297,555	354,835

Source: Kosovo Railways, *Annual Report 2006*.

ROAD TRAFFIC
(vehicles registered at 31 December)

	2004	2005	2006
Passenger cars	137,981	145,546	146,744
Buses and coaches	1,142	13,757	239
Lorries and vans	21,565	13,887	20,611
Heavy goods vehicles	7,213	4,769	6,457
Total (incl. others)	169,072	200,000	178,185

CIVIL AVIATION
(traffic at Prishtina International Airport)

	2005	2006	2007
Aircraft movements	4,983	4,093	4,321
Passengers arrivals	452,362	427,870	483,330
Passenger departures	478,258	483,330	506,962

Education

(2006/07)

	Institutions	Pupils	Teachers
Kindergarten	40	25,670	1,179
Primary	970	322,381	16,433
Secondary	115	88,974	4,864
Special	13	814	164
Primary	7	728	129
Secondary	4	86	35
University level	n.a.	27,274	1,059

Directory

The Constitution

Following Kosovo's unilateral declaration of independence on 17 February 2008, a new Constitution was adopted on 9 April, and officially entered into effect on 15 June. The Constitution defines the Republic of Kosovo as an independent, sovereign, democratic and indivisible state. The official languages are Albanian and Serbian, while the Turkish, Bosnian and Roma languages have the status of official languages at municipal level or as provided by law. The Kosovo Assembly (Kuvendi i Kosovës/Skupština Kosova) is the highest representative and legislative institution of Kosovo. The Assembly comprises 120 deputies, of whom 100 are directly elected. The remaining 20 seats are reserved for the elected representatives of specified minority ethnic communities. The President of Kosovo is elected by a two-thirds' majority of all deputies in the Assembly. The President appoints the candidate for Prime Minister, after proposal by the political party or coalition holding the majority of seats in the Assembly. The candidate for Prime Minister submits the composition of his Government for approval by the Assembly. All authorities in the Republic of Kosovo are to abide by all its obligations under the Comprehensive Proposal for the Kosovo Status Settlement of 26 March 2007, which takes precedence over all other legal provisions in Kosovo.

The Government

HEAD OF STATE

President: FATMIR SEJDIU.

GOVERNMENT
(April 2009)

An administration comprising representatives of the Democratic Party of Kosovo (DPK), the Democratic League of Kosovo (DLK), the Independent Liberal Party (ILP) and the Turkish Democratic Party of Kosovo (TDPK).

Prime Minister: HASHIM THAÇI (DPK).
Deputy Prime Minister: HAJREDIN KUÇI (DPK).
Deputy Prime Minister: RAMË MANAJ (DLK).
Minister of Foreign Affairs: SKENDER HYSENI (DLK).
Minister of the Kosovo Security Force: FEHMI MUJOTA (DPK).
Minister of the Economy and Finance: AHMET SHALA (DPK).
Minister of Public Services: ARSIM BAJRAMI (DPK).
Minister of Education, Science and Technology: ENVER HOXHAJ (DPK).

KOSOVO

Minister of Culture, Youth and Sports: VALTON BEQIRI (Independent).
Minister of Transport and Telecommunications: FATMIR LIMAJ (DPK).
Minister of Internal Affairs: ZENUN PAJAZITI (DPK).
Minister of Justice: NEKIBE KELMENDI (DLK).
Minister of Local Government: SADRI FERATI (DLK).
Minister of the Environment and Spatial Planning: MAHIR YAĞCILAR (TDPK).
Minister of Labour and Social Welfare: NENAD RAŠIĆ (ILP).
Minister of Trade and Industry: LUTFI ZHARKU (DLK).
Minister of Energy and Mining: JUSTINA SHIROKA-PULA (DPK).
Minister of Health: ALUSH GASHI (DLK).
Minister of Communities and Return: SAŠA RAŠIĆ (ILP).
Minister of Agriculture, Forestry and Rural Development: IDRIZ VEHAPI (DPK).

MINISTRIES

Office of the President: 10000 Prishtina, Rruga Nënë Terezë; tel. (38) 213222; fax (38) 211651; e-mail beqiri@president-ksgov.net; internet www.president-ksgov.net.

Office of the Prime Minister: 10000 Prishtina, Rruga Nënë Terezë; tel. (38) 20114635; e-mail info_pmo@ks-gov.net; internet www.ks-gov.net.

Ministry of Agriculture, Forestry and Rural Development: 10000 Prishtina; tel. (38) 20038473; e-mail idriz.vehapi@ks-gov.net; internet www.mbpzhr-ks.org.

Ministry of Communities and Return: 10000 Prishtina; tel. (38) 552045; e-mail sasa.rasic@ks-gov.net; internet www.ks-gov.net/mkk.

Ministry of Culture, Youth and Sports: 10000 Prishtina; tel. (38) 211064; fax (38) 211440; e-mail info@mkrs-ks.org; internet www.mkrs-ks.org.

Ministry of the Economy and Finance: 10000 Prishtina, Sheshi Nënë Terezë; tel. (38) 213115; fax (38) 213113; e-mail info@mfe-ks.org; internet www.mfe-ks.org.

Ministry of Education, Science and Technology: 10000 Prishtina, Rruga Musine Kokalari 18, Lagjja Dadania Blloku-III; tel. (38) 541035; e-mail masht@ks-gov.net; internet www.masht-gov.net.

Ministry of Energy and Mining: 10000 Prishtina, 'Toskana', Rruga Nënë Terezë 36; tel. (38) 20021305; fax (38) 20021302; e-mail mem.informimi@gmail.com; internet www.ks-gov.net/mem.

Ministry of the Environment and Spatial Planning: 10000 Prishtina, Rruga Nazim Gafurri 31; tel. (38) 517639; fax (38) 517845; e-mail webmaster.mmph@ks-gov.net; internet www.ks-gov.net/mmph.

Ministry of Foreign Affairs: 10000 Prishtina, Government Bldg, Rruga Nënë Terezë; tel. (38) 213963; tel. fax (38) 213985; e-mail mfa@ks-gov.net; internet www.ks-gov.net/mpj.

Ministry of Health: 10000 Prishtina, Rruga Zagrebi; tel. (38) 211191; fax (38) 211371; e-mail skender.berisha@ks-gov.net; internet www.mshgov-ks.org.

Ministry of Internal Affairs: 10000 Prishtina, Bulevardi Nënë Terezë, p.n. Objekti i Qeverisë; tel. (38) 213307; e-mail merita.vidishiq@ks-gov.net; internet www.mpb-ks.org.

Ministry of Justice: 10000 Prishtina, Ndërtesa e Kuvendit, Aneksi Jugor Kati II, Sheshi Nënë Terezë; tel. (38) 20018010; e-mail liridona.kozmaqi@ks-gov.net; internet www.md-ks.org.

Ministry of the Kosovo Security Force: 10000 Prishtina; internet www.mksf-ks.org.

Ministry of Labour and Social Welfare: 10000 Prishtina, Rruga UÇK-së 1; tel. (38) 213814; fax (38) 244229; e-mail feim.osmani@ks-gov.net; internet www.mpms-ks.org.

Ministry of Local Government: 10000 Prishtina, Rruga Tirana; tel. (38) 213716; e-mail lumnije.demi@ks-gov.net; internet www.mapl-ks.net.

Ministry of Public Services: 10000 Prishtina, Rruga Nënë Terezë, Zona C-213, Ndërtesa e Gërmisë; tel. (38) 20030020; e-mail info-mshp@ks-gov.net; internet www.ks-gov.net/mshp.

Ministry of Trade and Industry: 10000 Prishtina, Qyteza Pejton, Rruga Perandori Justinian 3-5; tel. (38) 20036042; fax (38) 212807; internet www.mti-ks.org.

Ministry of Transport and Telecommunications: 10000 Prishtina; tel. (38) 211504; e-mail info.mtpt@ks-gov.net; internet www.mtpt.org.

INTERNATIONAL REPRESENTATIVES

Special Representative of the Secretary-General of the UN, Head of the UN Interim Administration Mission in Kosovo (UNMIK): LAMBERTO ZANNIER.

Special Representative of the European Union and International Civilian Representative in Kosovo: PIETER CORNELIS FEITH.

International Civilian Office (ICO): 10000 Prishtina, Rruga Ahmet Krasniqi, Blue Bldg; tel. (38) 2044100; fax (38) 2044210; e-mail office@ico-kos.org; internet www.ico-kos.org.

Legislature

Kosovo Assembly
(Kuvendi i Kosovës/Skupština Kosova)

10000 Prishtina, Rruga Nënë Terezë; tel. (38) 211186; fax (38) 211188; e-mail info@assembly-kosova.org; internet www.assembly-kosova.org.

President: JAKUP KRASNIQI.

Election, 17 November 2007

Parties	Votes	% of votes	Seats
Democratic Party of Kosovo	196,207	34.32	37
Democratic League of Kosovo	129,410	22.63	25
New Kosovo Alliance	70,165	12.27	13
Democratic League of Dardania–Albanian Christian Democratic Party of Kosovo	57,002	9.97	11
Alliance for the Future of Kosovo	54,611	9.55	10
ORA Reformist Party	23,722	4.14	—
Justice Party	9,789	1.73	—
Others	30,760	5.38	4*
Reserved seats for representatives of designated minority ethnic groups†	—	—	20
Total	**571,767**	**100.00**	**120**

* The other parties to obtain representation (one seat apiece) on the basis of national proportional representation were: the Turkish Democratic Party of Kosovo; the Vakat Coalition; the Democratic Ashkali Party of Kosovo; and the Party of Democratic Action (all four of these parties additionally obtained representation among those seats reserved for representatives of minority ethnic groups, q.v.).

† The 20 seats reserved for representatives of designated minority ethnic groups (10 seats are elected by Serbs, four by a constituency comprising Roma, Ashkali and 'Egyptians'—a subset of Roma, three by Bosniaks, two by Turks and one by Gorani) were allocated as follows, following voting within each constituent group: the Civic Initiative of Gora (1 seat); the Democratic Ashkali Party of Kosovo (2 seats); the Independent Liberal Party (3 seats); New Democracy (1 seat); the New Democratic Initiative of Kosovo (1 seat); the Party of Democratic Action (1 seat); the Serb Democratic Party of Kosovo and Metohija (3 seats); the Serb Kosovo and Metohija Party (1 seat); the Serb People's Party (1 seat); the Turkish Democratic Party of Kosovo (2 seats); Union of Independent Social Democrats of Kosovo and Metohija (1 seat); the United Roma Party of Kosovo (1 seat); and the Vakat Coalition (2 seats).

Election Commission

Central Election Commission (Komisioni Qendror i Zgjedhjeve/Centralna Izborna Komisja): 10000 Prishtina, Rruga Qyteza Pejton Mujo Ulqinaku 7; tel. (38) 246599; fax (38) 246602; e-mail kqz.sekretariati@cec-ko.org; internet www.cec-ko.org; f. 2004; Chair. TIM GULDIMANN.

Political Organizations

Albanian Christian Democratic Party of Kosovo (Partia Shqiptare Demokristane e Kosovës): 10000 Prishtina, B. Pejani 3; tel. (38) 221536; internet www.pshdk.org; f. 2000; Chair. MARK KRASNIQI.

Alliance for the Future of Kosovo (AFK) (Aleanca për Ardhmërinë e Kosovës): 10000 Prishtina, Kodra e Trimave; tel. (44) 219080; f. 2001; Leader RAMUSH HARADINAJ.

Democratic League of Dardania (Lidhja Demokratike e Dardanisë): 10000 Prishtina, Rruga Isa Kastrati 117, Lagja Velania; tel. and fax (38) 248586; e-mail info@ldd-kosova.org; internet www

KOSOVO

.ldd-kosova.org; f. Jan. 2007 by fmr mems of Democratic League of Kosovo; Leader NEXHAT DAÇI.

Democratic League of Kosovo (DLK) (Lidhja Demokratike e Kosovës): 10000 Prishtina, Kompleksi Qafa; tel. (38) 242242; fax (38) 245305; e-mail ldk@ldk-kosova.eu; internet www.ldk-kosova.eu; f. 2000 as successor to the Democratic Alliance of Kosovo; Chair. FATMIR SEJDIU.

Democratic Party of Kosovo (DPK) (Partia Demokratike e Kosovës): 10000 Prishtina, Rruga Nënë Terezë 20; tel. (44) 183445; e-mail pdk@pdk-ks.org; internet www.pdk-ks.org; f. 1999; fmrly Party for the Democratic Party of Kosovo; Chair. HASHIM THAÇI.

Independent Liberal Party (Samostalna liberalna stranka): 10000 Prishtina; internet www.sls-ks.org; f. 2006; represents Serb interests; Chair. SLOBODAN PETROVIĆ.

Justice Party (Partia e Drejtësisë): 10000 Prishtina, Vellusha, Rruga Bajram Kelmendi 22; tel. and fax (44) 248920; internet www.drejtesia.org; f. 2000; Chair. FERID AGANI.

Liberal Party of Kosovo (Partia Liberale e Kosovës): 10000 Prishtina, Bulevardi i Dëshmoreve 2; tel. and fax (38) 244865; e-mail plk@ipko.org; Chair. Prof. GJERGJ DEDAJ.

New Democracy (Nova Demokratija): 10000 Prishtina; f. 2007; represents Serb interests; Leader BRANISLAV GRBIĆ.

New Kosovo Alliance (Aleanca Kosova e Re): 10000 Prishtina, Rruga UÇK 55; tel. and fax (38) 247988; e-mail info@akr-ks.com; internet www.akr-ks.info; f. 2006; Leader BEHGJET PACOLLI.

ORA Reformist Party (Partia Reformiste ORA): 10000 Prishtina; tel. (38) 246600; e-mail info@ora-kosova.org; internet www.ora-kosova.org; Chair. TEUTA SAHATQIJA.

People's Movement of Kosovo (Lëvizja Popullore e Kosovës): 10000 Prishtina, Rruga Thimi Mitko 6; tel. (44) 131832; e-mail info@lpk-kosova.com; internet www.lpk-kosova.com; f. 1982; Chair. EMRUSH XHEMAJLI.

Serb List for Kosovo and Metohija (Srpska Lista za Kosovo i Metohiju): Mitrovicë; coalition of representatives of the Serbian Renewal Movement (q.v.), the Democratic Party (q.v.) and the Social Democratic Party (q.v.) in Kosovo.

Turkish Democratic Party of Kosovo (TDPK) (Kosova Demokratik Türk Partisi): 10000 Prizren, Rruga Adem Jashari 122; e-mail kosova_dtp@hotmail.com; internet www.kdtp.org; Chair. MAHIR YAĞCILAR.

Vakat Coalition (Koalicija Vakat): Dragaš; f. 2004; coalition of representatives of the Bosniak Democratic Party, the Fatherland (Vatan) Democratic Party and the Bosniak Party of Kosovo; Leader SADIK IDRIZI.

Other political parties represented in the Kosovo Assembly (Kuvendi i Kosovës/Skupština Kosova), following elections on 17 November 2007, were: the Democratic Ashkali Party of Kosovo (Partia Demokratike e Ashkanlive të Kosovës); the Serb Democratic Party of Kosovo and Metohija (Srpska Demokratska Stranka Kosova i Metohije), led by SLAVIŠA PETKOVIĆ; the Party of Democratic Action (Stranka Demokratske Akcije); the Serb People's Party (Srpska Narodna Stranka), led by MIHAJL SĆEPANOVIĆ; the Civic Initiative of Gora (Građanska Inicijativa Gore); the Serb Kosovo and Metohija Party (Srpska Kosovsko-Metohijka Stranka), led by DRAGIŠA MIRIĆ; the New Democratic Initiative of Kosovo (Iniciativa e re Demokrarike e Kosovës), representing the 'Egyptian' Roma; the Union of Independent Social Democrats of Kosovo and Metohija (Savez Nezavisnih Socijaldemokrata Kosova i Metohije), led by NEBOJŠA ŽIVIĆ; and the United Roma Party of Kosovo (Partia Rome e Bashkuar e Kosovës).

Diplomatic Representation

EMBASSIES IN KOSOVO

Albania: 10000 Prishtina, Qyteza Pejton, Rruga Mujo Ulqinaku 18; tel. (38) 248208; fax (38) 248209; e-mail mission.kosova@mfa.gov.al; Ambassador ISLAM LAUKA.

Austria: 10000 Prishtina, Ahmet Krasniqi 22, Arbëria 1; tel. (38) 249284; fax (38) 249285; e-mail pristina-as@bmeia.gv.at; Ambassador WALTER-MARIA STOJAN.

Croatia: 10000 Prishtina, Rruga Mujo Ulqinaku 20; tel. (38) 223978; fax (38) 223979; e-mail ured.pristina@mvpei.hr; Ambassador DAVOR VIDIŠ.

Czech Republic: 10000 Prishtina, Dragodan, Rruga Ismail Qemali 31; tel. (38) 246676; fax (38) 248782; e-mail pristina@embassy.mzv.cz; Chargé d'affaires a.i. JANINA HŘEBÍČKOVÁ.

Finland: 10000 Prishtina, Arbëri, Eduard Lir 50; tel. (38) 223775; fax (38) 232863; e-mail office@fin-kos.org; Ambassador KRISTIINA HÄIKIÖ.

France: 10000 Prishtina, Dragodan, Rruga Ismail Qemali 67; tel. (38) 22458800; fax (38) 22458801; e-mail admin-etrangers.pristina-amba@diplomatie.gouv.fr; Ambassador DELPHINE BORIONE.

Germany: 10000 Prishtina, Arbëri, Rruga Azem Jashanica 17; tel. (38) 254500; fax (38) 254536; e-mail info@pris.auswaertiges-amt.de; internet www.pristina.diplo.de; Ambassador HANS-DIETER STEINBACH.

Hungary: 10000 Prishtina, Arbëri, 24 Maj 23; tel. (38) 247763; fax (38) 247764; e-mail mission.prs@kum.hu; internet www.mfa.gov.hu; Ambassador ZOLTÁN IMECS.

Italy: 10000 Prishtina, Dragodan, Rruga Azem Jashanica 5; tel. (38) 244925; fax (38) 244929; e-mail pubblico.pristina@esteri.it; Chargé d'affaires a.i. MICHAEL LOUIS GIFFONI.

Netherlands: 10000 Prishtina, Velani, Xhemajl Berisha 12; tel. (38) 516102; Ambassador HENK VOSKAMP.

Norway: 10000 Prishtina, Pejton, Sejdi Kryeziu blloku IV; tel. (38) 232111; e-mail embpri@mfa.no; Ambassador CARL SCHIØTZ WIBYE (resident in Skopje, Former Yugoslav republic of Macedonia).

Slovenia: 10000 Prishtina, Anton Ceta 6; tel. (38) 246255; fax (38) 246256; Ambassador VOJKO VOLK.

Switzerland: 10060 Prishtina, Adrian Krasniqi 11; tel. (38) 248088; fax (38) 248078; e-mail pri.vertretung@eda.admin.ch; internet www.eda.admin.ch/pristina; Ambassador LUKAS BEGLINGER.

Turkey: 10000 Prishtina, Arbëri, Ismail Qemali 59; tel. (38) 226044; Ambassador METIN HÜSREV ÜNLER.

United Kingdom: 10000 Prishtina, Arbëri, Rruga Ismail Qemali 6; tel. (38) 254700; fax (38) 249799; e-mail britishoffice.pristina@fco.gov.uk; Ambassador ANDREW SPARKES.

USA: 10000 Prishtina, Arbëri, Nazim Hikmet 30; tel. (38) 593000; fax (38) 549890; e-mail papristina@state.gov; internet pristina.usembassy.gov; Ambassador TINA S. KAIDANOW.

Judicial System

The court system comprises a Supreme Court, district courts, municipal courts and minor offences courts.

Supreme Court: 10000 Prishtina; Pres. REXHEP HAXHIMUSA.

Religion

Most of the inhabitants of Kosovo are adherents of Islam, although most Serbs are Orthodox Christians, and several sites of historic importance to Serbian Orthodoxy are located within Kosovo. A significant minority of the Kosovo Albanian population are Roman Catholics.

ISLAM

Islamic Community: 10000 Prishtina; Pres. of the Mesihat Dr REDZEP BOJE.

CHRISTIANITY

The Eastern Orthodox Church

The Patriarchate of the Serbian Orthodox Church is located at Pej (Peć), in central Kosovo.

The Roman Catholic Church

At 31 December 2006 there were an estimated 65,000 Roman Catholics within the Apostolic Administration of Prizren.

Apostolic Administrator of Prizren: GJERGJU DODË, 20000 Prizren, Rruga I. L. Ribar 7; tel. (29) 41933; fax (29) 41232; e-mail ipeshkvia_pz@yahoo.com.

The Press

PRINCIPAL DAILIES

Bota Sot (The World Today): 10000 Prishtina, Rruga Jakove Xoxa; tel. (38) 249846; fax (38) 249845; e-mail bota-sot@ipko.net; in Albanian; Editor BAJRUSH MORINA.

Gazeta Express: 10000 Prishtina, Dardania 1/1; tel. (38) 542270; e-mail info@gazetaexpress.com; internet www.gazetaexpress.com; f. 2005; in Albanian; seven a week; Chief Exec. BATON HAXHIU.

Infopress: 10000 Prishtina; popular; supportive of Democratic Party of Kosovo; Editor AVNI AZEMI.

KOSOVO

Koha Ditore: 10000 Prishtina, POB 202; tel. (38) 249104; e-mail redaksia@kohaditore.com; internet www.kohaditore.com; in Albanian; Editor-in-Chief AGRON BAJRAMI.

Kosova Sot (Kosovo Today): 10000 Prishtina, Pallati i Shtypit; tel. (38) 525049; fax (38) 545070; e-mail kosovasot2001@yahoo.com; f. 1998; in Albanian; Dir MARGARITA KADRIU.

Lajm (The News): 10000 Prishtina; tel. (38) 243009; e-mail info@gazetalajm.info; internet www.gazetalajm.info; f. 2004; in Albanian; supportive of the New Kosovo Alliance; Chief Exec. BEHGJET PACOLLI.

PERIODICALS

Fokus Kosova/Fokus Kosovo/Focus Kosovo: 10000 Prishtina, UNMIK Administrative Headquarters; e-mail focuskosovo@un.org; internet www.unmikonline.org/pio/fokus_kosovo_eng.htm; f. 2001; publ. by UNMIK; Albanian, Serbian and English edns; seven a year; Publisher ALEXANDER IVANKO; Editor MYRIAM DESSABLES (Albanian and Serbian edns), RICARDO Z. DUNN.

Official Gazette of the Republic of Kosovo (Gazeta Zyrtare e Republikës së Kosovës/Sluzbeni list Republike Kosova/Kosova Cumhuriyeti Resmi Gazetesi/Sluzbeni Novine Republike Kosova): 10000 Prishtina, Ndërtesa e re e Qeverisë; tel. (38) 20114039; e-mail gazetazyrtare@ks-gov.net; internet www.ks-gov.net/GazetaZyrtare; f. 2005; monthly; publishes official text of laws adopted by the Kosovo Assembly (Kuvendi i Kosovës/Skupština Kosova) as promulgated by the Special Representative of the Secretary-General, resolutions adopted by the Kosovo Assembly, secondary and other legislation issued by the Government and ministries of Kosovo, agreements of international character, etc.; edns in Albanian, Serbian, English, Turkish and Bosnian; administered by the Office of the Prime Minister; Editor ARBEN VESELAJ.

Zeri: 10000 Prishtina; in Albanian; Editor-in-Chief BARDH HAMZAJ.

NEWS AGENCIES

KosovaLive: Prishtina, Aneksi te Pallati i Shtypit, Kati II; tel. (38) 248321; fax (38) 248319; e-mail editor@kosovalive.com; internet www.kosovalive.com.

Kosovapress: 10000 Prishtina, Rruga Nënë Terezë 20; tel. (38) 248721; e-mail info@kosovapress.com; internet www.kosovapress.com.

Publishers

Panorama: 10000 Prishtina; f. 1994; publishes newspapers and journals in Serbian, Albanian and Turkish; Dir JORDAN RISTIĆ.

Rilindja Publishing House: 10000 Prishtina, Dom štampe pa nr; tel. (38) 23868; popular science, literature, children's fiction, travel books, textbooks in Albanian; Dir NAZMI RRAHMANI.

Broadcasting and Communications

TELECOMMUNICATIONS

Regulatory Authority

Telecommunications Regulatory Authority (Kosovo) (ART) (Autoriteti Rregullativ i Telekomunikacionit): 10000 Prishtina; tel. (38) 212345; e-mail info@art-ks.org; internet www.art-ks.org; Chair. ANTON BERISHA.

Service Provider

PTK (Posts and Telecommunications of Kosovo): 10100 Prishtina, Dardania pa nr, Kati VIII, zyra 808; tel. (38) 524583; e-mail postaekosoves@ptkonline.com; internet www.ptkonline.com; f. 1959; became jt-stock co in 2005; provides postal and telecommunications services in Kosovo, including mobile cellular telephone services operated under the brand name Vala; Chair. of Bd of Dirs ILIR SALIHU; Man. Dir ADNAN MEROVCI.

BROADCASTING

Radio Televizioni i Kosovës (RTK) (Radio-Television Kosovo): 10000 Prishtina, Rruga Xhemail 12; tel. (38) 230102; fax (38) 235336; e-mail post@rtklive.com; internet www.rtklive.com; subsidiaries include Radio Kosova and Radio Blue Sky; Chair. Dr VJOSA DOBRUNA; Dir-Gen. AGIM ZATRIQI.

RadioTelevizioni21 (RTV21): 10000 Prishtina, Pallati i Mediave, Aneks II; tel. and fax (38) 550088; e-mail lajmet@rtv21.tv; internet www.rtv21.tv; radio and television broadcaster.

Finance

(cap. = capital; res = reserves; dep. = deposits; m. = million; amounts in euros; brs = branches)

BANKING

In early 2009 there were eight registered banks operating in Kosovo.

Regulatory Authority

Central Bank of Kosovo (Banka Qendrore Republikës së Kosoves): 10000 Prishtina, Rruga Garibaldi 33; tel. (38) 222055; fax (38) 243763; e-mail publicrelations@cbak-kos.org; internet www.bqk-kos.org; f. 1999 as the Banking and Payments Authority of Kosovo; became Central Banking Authority of Kosovo 2006; total assets 1,113.2m. (Dec. 2008); Gov. HASHIM REXHEPI; Chair. GAZMEND LUBOTENI.

Selected Banks

Banka Kombëtare Tregtare: 10000 Prishtina, Qyteza Pejton, Rruga Kosta Novakoviç 9; tel. (38) 222910; fax (38) 222907; e-mail infobktkosova@bkt.com; internet www.bkt.com.al; f. 1993; total assets 18.3m. (Dec. 2008).

Bank for Business (Banka për Biznes—BpB): Prishtina, Rruga UÇK 41; tel. (38) 244666; fax (38) 243656; e-mail info@bpbbank.com; internet www.bpbbank.com; f. 2001; total assets 41.2m. (Dec. 2007); Dir-Gen. SELVINAZE SHEHOLLI.

Economic Bank: 10000 Prishtina, Rruga Migjeni 1; tel. (38) 225353; fax (38) 225454; e-mail bek@bekonomike.com; internet www.bekonomike.com; f. 2001; total assets 86.1m. (Dec. 2008); Pres. HAJRULLAH ZAITI.

Komercijalna Banka a.d. Beograd: 40000 Mitrovica, Rruga Kralja Petra Prvog 33; tel. (28) 423822; fax (28) 425295; e-mail posta@kombank.com; internet www.kombank.com; f. 1970; Chair. VLADISLAV CVETKOVIĆ.

NLB Prishtina: 10000 Prishtina, Rruga Rexhep Luci 5; tel. (38) 234111; fax (38) 246189; e-mail info@nlbprishtina-kos.com; internet www.nlbprishtina-kos.com; f. Jan. 2008 by merger of NLB Kasabank and NLB New Bank of Kosova; 80.4% owned by NLB d.d.; total assets 200m. (Dec. 2007); Gen. Man. ALBERT LUMEZI.

ProCredit Bank Kosova: 10000 Prishtina, Nënë Terezë 16; tel. (38) 555777; fax (38) 555776; e-mail info@procreditbank-kos.com; internet www.procreditbank-kos.com; f. 2000 as Micro Enterprise Bank; present name adopted 2003; cap. 10.1m., res 0.5m., dep. 91.5m. (Dec. 2006); CEO PHILIP SIGWART.

Raiffeisen Bank Kosovo: Rruga UÇK 51; tel. (38) 222222; e-mail info@raiffeisen-kosovo.com; internet www.raiffeisen-kosovo.com; fmrly American Bank of Kosovo; acquired by Raiffeisen International (Austria) and name changed in 2003; total assets 477m. (Dec. 2007); Chair. and CEO BOGDAN MERFEA; 43 brs.

TEB sh. a.: 10000 Prishtina, Rruga Agim Ramadani 15; tel. (38) 230000; fax (38) 224699; e-mail info@teb-kos.com; internet www.teb-kos.com; f. Jan. 2008; joint venture of TEB (Turkey) and BNP Paribas (France); total assets 51.1m. (Dec. 2008).

INSURANCE

In early 2009 there were 14 registered insurance companies operating in Kosovo.

Kompania e Sigurimeve Dukagjini (Dukagjini Insurance Co.): 10000 Prishtina, Sheshi Nënë Terezë 33; tel. (38) 225385; fax (38) 225384; e-mail info@insurancedukagjini.com; internet www.insurancedukagjini.com; f. 2002; Dir EKREM LLUKA.

Sigkos: 10000 Prishtina, Rruga Sylejman Vokshi, Pallati i Kuq; tel. (38) 240022; fax (38) 240222; e-mail info@sigkos.com; internet www.sigkos.com; f. 2006; Dir IBRAHIM KASTRATI.

Trade and Industry

GOVERNMENT AGENCIES

Investment Promotion Agency of Kosovo (IPAK): 10000 Prishtina, Rruga Muharrem Fejza; tel. and fax (38) 20036527; e-mail info@invest-ks.org; internet www.invest-ks.org; CEO MUSTAFË HASANI (acting).

Kosovo Privatization Agency: 10000 Prishtina, Rruga Ilir Konushevci 8; tel. (38) 500400; fax (38) 248076; e-mail info@pak-ks.org; internet www.pak-ks.org; fmrly Kosovo Trust Agency, supervised by UNMIK; restructured as above in June 2008; Chair. DINO ASANAJ.

CHAMBERS OF COMMERCE

American Chamber of Commerce: 10000 Prishtina, Gustav Majer 6; tel. (38) 246012; fax (38) 248012; e-mail info@amchamksv

KOSOVO

.org; internet www.amchamksv.org; f. 2004; Pres. LUAN DALIPI; 70 mem. cos.

Kosovo Chamber of Commerce (Oda Ekonomike e Kosovës): 10000 Prishtina, Rruga Nënë Terezë 20; tel. (38) 224741; fax (38) 224299; e-mail info@oek-kcc.org; internet www.kosovo-eicc.org; Chair. Dr BESIM BEQAJ.

UTILITIES

Korporata Energetike e Kosovës/Energetska Korporacija Kosova (KEK) (Kosovo Energy Corpn): 10000 Prishtina; tel. (38) 240245; e-mail nezir.sinani@kek-energy.com; internet www.kek-energy.com; generation and distribution of electricity.

Prishtina Regional Water Company (Kompania Ujësjellësi Rajonal 'Prishtina'): 10000 Prishtina, Rruga Tahir Zajmi; tel. (38) 551010; e-mail info@kur-prishtina.com; internet www.kur-prishtina.com; f. 2007; offers services in central Kosovo, est. 550,000 customers; Dir SKENDER BUBLAKU.

TRADE UNIONS

Union of Independent Trade Unions of Kosovo (BSPK) (Bashkimi i Sindikatave të Pavarura të Kosovës): 38000 Prishtina, Rruga Nëna Terezë 35; tel. (38) 221782; fax (38) 223175; e-mail bspk@etuc.org; internet www.bskp.org; 120,000 mems in 18 federations (2006); Chair. HAXHI ARIFI.

Transport

RAILWAYS

In 2005 there were 436 km of railways and 33 railway stations in operation in Kosovo.

Hekurudhat e Kosovës/Kosovske Železnice (Kosovo Railways): Fushë Kosovë, Sheshi i lirisë pn; tel. (38) 536355; fax (38) 536307; e-mail info@kosovorailway.com; internet www.kosovorailway.com; f. 2005 to replace UNMIK Railway; jt-stock co; operates railway services within Kosovo and international services to Skopje, former Yugoslav republic of Macedonia; Man. Dir XHEVAT RAMOSAJ.

CIVIL AVIATION

There is an international airport at Prishtina.

KUWAIT

Introductory Survey

Location, Climate, Language, Religion, Flag, Capital

The State of Kuwait lies at the north-west extreme of the Persian (Arabian) Gulf, bordered to the north-west by Iraq and to the south by Saudi Arabia. The State comprises a mainland region and nine small islands, of which the largest is Bubiyan and the most populous is Failaka. Immediately to the south of Kuwait, along the Gulf, lies a Neutral (Partitioned) Zone of 5,700 sq km, which is shared between Kuwait and Saudi Arabia. Much of Kuwait is arid desert, and the climate is generally hot and humid. Temperatures in July and August often exceed 45°C (113°F), and in the winter months are frequently above 20°C (68°F)—although there is often frost at night. Average annual rainfall is only 111 mm. The official language is Arabic, which is spoken by the majority of Kuwaiti nationals (estimated, by official definition, to have comprised 39.8% of Kuwait's population at the census of April 2005, according to preliminary results) and by many of the country's non-Kuwaiti residents. Apart from other Arabs, the non-Kuwaitis are mainly Iranians, Indians and Pakistanis. At the 1975 census 95.0% of the population were Muslims (of whom about 70% are now thought to belong to the Sunni sect), while 4.5% were Christians, Hindus or adherents of other faiths. The national flag (proportions 1 by 2) has three equal horizontal stripes, of green, white and red, with a superimposed black trapezoid at the hoist. The capital is Kuwait City.

Recent History

Kuwait became part of Turkey's Ottoman Empire in the 16th century. During the later years of Ottoman rule Kuwait became a semi-autonomous Arab monarchy, with local administration controlled by a Sheikh of the Sabah family, which is still the ruling dynasty. In 1899, fearing an extension of Turkish control, the ruler of Kuwait made a treaty with the United Kingdom, accepting British protection while surrendering control over external relations. Nominal Turkish suzerainty over Kuwait ended in 1918, with the dissolution of the Ottoman Empire.

Petroleum was first discovered in Kuwait in 1938, but exploration was interrupted by the Second World War. After 1945 drilling resumed on a large scale, and extensive deposits of petroleum were found. Sheikh Ahmad (ruler since 1921) was succeeded in 1950 by his cousin, Sheikh Abdullah as-Salim as-Sabah, who inaugurated a programme of public works and educational development, funded by petroleum revenues, which transformed Kuwait's infrastructure and introduced a comprehensive system of welfare services.

Kuwait became fully independent on 19 June 1961, when the United Kingdom and Kuwait agreed to terminate the 1899 treaty. The ruler took the title of Amir and assumed full executive power. Kuwait was admitted to the League of Arab States (the Arab League, see p. 344) despite opposition from Iraq, which claimed that Kuwait was historically part of Iraqi territory. Kuwait's first election took place in December 1961, when voters chose 20 members of a Constituent Assembly (the other members being cabinet ministers appointed by the Amir). The Assembly drafted a new Constitution, which was adopted in December 1962. A 50-member Majlis al-Umma (National Assembly) was elected, under a limited franchise (see Government, below), in January 1963. In the absence of formal political parties (which remain illegal), candidates contested the poll as independents, although some known opponents of the Government were elected. In the same month the Amir appointed his brother, Sheikh Sabah as-Salim as-Sabah (the heir apparent), to be Prime Minister. Iraq renounced its claim to Kuwait in October, and diplomatic relations were established.

In January 1965, following conflict between the paternalistic ruling family and the democratically inclined Majlis, the powers of the Council of Ministers were strengthened. The Amir died in November 1965, and Sheikh Sabah succeeded to the throne. He was replaced as Prime Minister by his cousin, Sheikh Jaber al-Ahmad as-Sabah, who was named heir apparent in May 1966. The Neutral (Partitioned) Zone between Kuwait and Saudi Arabia was formally divided between the two countries in 1969: revenues from oil production in the area are shared equally.

As Kuwait's petroleum sector expanded during the 1960s, the country became increasingly wealthy. The Government effected an extensive redistribution of income, through public expenditure and a land compensation scheme, but there was some popular discontent concerning corruption and official manipulation of the media and the Majlis. A more representative legislature was elected in January 1971 (again under a limited franchise). A further general election took place in January 1975, but in August 1976 the Amir dissolved the Majlis, on the grounds that it was acting against the best interests of the state. Sheikh Sabah died in December 1977 and was succeeded by Crown Prince Jaber. In January 1978 the new Amir appointed Sheikh Saad al-Abdullah as-Salim as-Sabah to be his heir apparent. The new Crown Prince, hitherto Minister of Defence and the Interior, became Prime Minister in the following month. In accordance with an Amiri decree of August 1980, a new Majlis was elected in February 1981, although only one-half of the eligible 6% of the population registered to vote.

The collapse of Kuwait's unofficial stock exchange, the Souk al-Manakh, in September 1982 caused a prolonged financial crisis, and eventually led to the resignations of the Ministers of Finance (in 1983) and of Justice (in 1985). The Majlis subsequently opposed several government measures, including proposed price increases for public services, educational reforms and legislation to restrict the press, and questioned the competence of certain ministers. In July 1986 the Council of Ministers submitted its resignation to the Amir, who then dissolved the Majlis and suspended some articles of the Constitution, declaring his intention to rule by decree. The Crown Prince was immediately reappointed Prime Minister. An Amiri decree accorded the Council of Ministers greater powers of censorship, including the right to suspend publication of newspapers for up to two years.

In late 1989 the Amir refused to accept a petition, signed by more than 20,000 Kuwaiti citizens, seeking the restoration of the Majlis. In January 1990 police dispersed two pro-democracy demonstrations, although later in the month the Government agreed to relax press censorship. In June 62% of eligible voters participated in a general election for 50 members of a 'provisional' National Council; a further 25 members were appointed by the Amir. The election was boycotted by pro-democracy activists, who continued to demand the full restoration of the Majlis.

Of all the Gulf states, Kuwait has been most vulnerable to regional disruption. Immediately after independence British troops (soon replaced by an Arab League force) were dispatched to support the country against the territorial claim by Iraq. The force remained until 1963, and relations between Kuwait and Iraq were stable until 1973, when Iraqi troops occupied a Kuwaiti outpost on their joint border. Kuwait none the less supplied aid to Iraq from the outbreak of the Iran–Iraq War in 1980. As a result, Kuwaiti petroleum installations and shipping in the Persian (Arabian) Gulf were targeted intermittently by Iranian forces, and by pro-Iranian groups within Kuwait, for much of the 1980s. A large number of Iranians were among 27,000 expatriates deported in 1985–86, and in 1987 the Government initiated a five-year plan to reduce the number of expatriates in the Kuwaiti work-force. Kuwait resumed diplomatic relations with Iran following the 1988 cease-fire between Iran and Iraq.

In July 1990 the Iraqi Government implicitly criticized Kuwait (among other states) for disregarding the petroleum production quotas stipulated by the Organization of the Petroleum Exporting Countries (OPEC, see p. 386). It also declared that Kuwait should cancel Iraq's war debt and compensate it for losses of revenue incurred during the war with Iran, and as a result of Kuwait's overproduction of petroleum—to which Iraq attributed a decline in international oil prices. In addition, Iraq alleged that Kuwait had established military posts and drilled oil wells on Iraqi territory. Despite regional mediation efforts, Iraq subsequently began to deploy armed forces on the Kuwait–Iraq border.

Direct negotiations in Jeddah, Saudi Arabia, at the end of the month between Kuwaiti and Iraqi officials collapsed, and on 2 August some 100,000 Iraqi troops invaded Kuwait (whose total military strength was about 20,000): Iraq stated that it had entered at the invitation of insurgents who had overthrown the Kuwaiti Government. The Amir and other government members fled to Saudi Arabia, where they established a 'Government-in-exile', while Iraq declared that a provisional Government had been formed in Kuwait comprising Iraqi-sponsored Kuwaiti dissidents. The UN Security Council immediately adopted a series of resolutions, of which the first (Resolution 660) condemned the invasion, demanded the immediate and unconditional withdrawal of Iraqi forces from Kuwait, and appealed for a negotiated settlement of the conflict. A trade embargo was then imposed on Iraq and Kuwait. Meanwhile, the USA and member states of the European Community (now European Union—EU, see p. 255) froze all Kuwait's overseas assets to prevent their repatriation. Five days after the invasion US troops and aircraft were deployed in Saudi Arabia, with the stated aim of securing that country's borders with Kuwait in the event of further Iraqi territorial expansion. A number of European governments, together with some Arab League states, agreed to provide military support for the US forces. The Iraqi Government subsequently announced the formal annexation of Kuwait, and ordered the closure of foreign diplomatic missions there. At the end of August most of Kuwait was officially declared to be the 19th Governorate of Iraq, while a northern strip was incorporated into the Basra Governorate.

In the months following the invasion apparent attempts at demographic manipulation—by settling Iraqis and Palestinians in Kuwait and by forcing Kuwaitis to assume Iraqi citizenship—were documented. The population was estimated to have decreased from approximately 2m. prior to the invasion to some 700,000, of whom Kuwaitis constituted about 300,000, Palestinians 200,000, and the remainder comprised other Arab and Asian expatriates. Many Kuwaitis, and Arab and Asian expatriates, had fled Iraq and Kuwait into Jordan, while most European and US expatriates were detained as hostages; by the end of 1990 it was claimed that all hostages had been released.

UN Security Council Resolution 678, adopted in November 1990, authorized the multinational force by now stationed in Saudi Arabia and the Gulf region to use 'all necessary means' to liberate Kuwait. It was implied that should Iraq not begin, by 15 January 1991, to implement the terms of 10 resolutions hitherto adopted regarding the invasion, military action would ensue. Renewed international diplomatic attempts failed to avert a military confrontation. On the night of 16–17 January the US-led multinational force launched an intensive aerial bombardment of Iraq. Ground forces entered Kuwait during the night of 23–24 February, encountering relatively little effective Iraqi opposition. Within three days the Iraqi Government had agreed to comply with the terms of all Security Council resolutions concerning Kuwait, and on 28 February the USA announced a suspension of military operations. Resolutions 686 and 687, adopted by the UN Security Council in March and April respectively, dictated the terms for a permanent cease-fire: Iraq was required to release all allied prisoners of war and Kuwaitis detained as hostages, repeal all laws and decrees concerning the annexation of Kuwait, and recognize the inviolability of the Iraq–Kuwait border. Iraq promptly announced its compliance with both resolutions. Resolution 689, adopted in April, provided for the establishment of a demilitarized zone, to be supervised by a UN Iraq-Kuwait Observation Mission (UNIKOM).

Meanwhile, in October 1990, at a conference in Jeddah of some 1,000 prominent Kuwaitis, the exiled Crown Prince Saad agreed to establish government advisory committees on political, social and financial matters, and pledged to restore the country's Constitution and legislature and to organize free elections after Kuwait's eventual liberation. In February 1991, however, the Government-in-exile excluded the possibility of early elections, maintaining that the need to rebuild and repopulate the country took precedence over that for political reform. Immediately following liberation an Amiri decree imposed martial law in Kuwait, and in March the formation of a state security committee was announced: its objectives included the investigation of individuals suspected of collaboration with the Iraqi authorities in Kuwait, the prevention of unofficial acts of reprisal and the identification of those civilians relocated to Kuwait by Iraq. Palestinians in Kuwait were a particular target of reprisals, and it was alleged by several human rights organizations that they were subject to torture by Kuwaiti security forces. Kuwait's Palestinian population, which had totalled around 400,000 prior to the Iraqi invasion, was estimated to have declined to less than 50,000 by early 1992.

The Amir, the Prime Minister and other members of the exiled regime returned to Kuwait in March 1991. The Council of Ministers resigned later that month, apparently in response to public discontent at the Government's failure to restore essential services. Although several specialists were appointed to strategic posts within the new Government named by Sheikh Saad in April (most notably to the finance, planning and oil portfolios), other important positions (including the foreign affairs, interior and defence ministries) were allocated to members of the as-Sabah family.

In May 1991 it was revealed that some 900 people were under investigation in Kuwait in connection with crimes committed during the Iraqi occupation; about 200 of these were accused of collaboration. The Government undertook to investigate alleged abuses documented by the human rights organization Amnesty International, which claimed that trials were being conducted without the provision of adequate defence counsel and that in some cases torture had been used to extract confessions. Martial law was ended in June, and 29 death sentences hitherto imposed on convicted collaborators were commuted to custodial terms. Outstanding trials relating to the occupation were to be referred to civilian courts, and in August a tribunal, said to guarantee defendants the right to greater legal protection as well as a right of appeal, was established to replace the martial law courts. Amid continuing international criticism of Kuwait's record on human rights, measures were subsequently taken to prevent clandestine deportations of alleged collaborators and to permit international supervision of the expulsion of foreign nationals. However, it was widely believed that Kuwait had been motivated to curb human rights abuses primarily in an attempt to procure international support for its efforts to secure the release of Kuwaiti nationals detained in Iraq.

It was announced in May 1991 that a US military presence would remain in Kuwait until September, by which time, it was envisaged, a regional defence force would be established. However, little progress was achieved in negotiations for such a force, and in August the USA announced that it would maintain 1,500 troops in Kuwait for several more months. In September the US and Kuwaiti Governments signed a 10-year military co-operation agreement, permitting the storage of US supplies and equipment in Kuwait, and providing for joint military training and exercises. (The agreement was renewed for a further 10 years in February 2001.) Defence accords were signed with both the United Kingdom and France in 1992.

In June 1993 the State Security Court was reported to have issued death sentences against 17 people who had been found guilty of collaborating with Iraq in 1990–91; Alaa Hussein Ali, the leader of the provisional Government installed by Iraq in August 1990, was convicted *in absentia*. In February 1994 Amnesty International asserted that at least 120 alleged collaborators had been convicted by trials that failed to satisfy international minimum standards. Human rights organizations therefore welcomed the endorsement by the Majlis, in August 1995, of government proposals to abolish the State Security Court. In January 1997 the Government announced the creation of a new human rights committee within the Ministry of the Interior.

Press censorship was partially relaxed in January 1992. Elections to the new Majlis, on 5 October, were contested by some 280 candidates, many of whom (although nominally independent) were affiliated to one of several quasi-political organizations. The franchise was again restricted, with only about 81,400 men eligible to vote. Anti-Government candidates, notably those representing Islamist groups, were unexpectedly successful, securing 31 of the Assembly's 50 seats. The Prime Minister subsequently formed a new Government, including six members of the Majlis, who were allocated, *inter alia*, the oil and justice portfolios; members of the ruling family retained control of foreign affairs, the interior and defence.

The Majlis voted in December 1992 to establish a commission of inquiry into the circumstances surrounding the 1990 invasion. The commission's report, published in May 1995, revealed profound negligence on the part of government and military officials, who had apparently ignored warnings of an imminent invasion. The report also claimed that the immediate flight of members of the royal family and the Council of Ministers had deprived the country of political leadership and military organization.

Meanwhile, in January 1993 legislation was enacted whereby the Majlis would have automatic access to the financial accounts of all state-owned companies and investment organizations, and stricter penalties would be imposed in cases of abuse of public funds. Demands for greater parliamentary scrutiny of the state's investments were largely prompted by revelations of the misappropriation of funds by the London (United Kingdom)-based Kuwait Investment Office (KIO), responsible for much of Kuwait's overseas investment portfolio (22 former KIO executives, including Sheikh Fahd Muhammad as-Sabah—its Chairman at the time of the Iraqi invasion—were reportedly implicated in the allegations), and also by emerging evidence of financial misconduct at the state-owned Kuwait Oil Tanker Co. In July 1996 three former executives received prison sentences of between 15 and 40 years, having been convicted of corruption by the criminal court; they were ordered to repay embezzled funds, together with fines totalling more than US $100m. In June 1999 the High Court in London ruled that Sheikh Fahd and two other former KIO senior executives were guilty, in absentia, of conspiracy and fraud involving some $460m. against the KIO's Spanish subsidiary during 1988–92.

In June 1994 the Majlis approved legislation extending the franchise to sons of naturalized Kuwaitis. In July 1995 the Assembly approved a bill reducing from 30 years to 20 the minimum period after which naturalized Kuwaitis would become eligible to vote. In July 1996 the Ministry of the Interior announced that an electorate of just over 107,000 men was entitled to vote in the forthcoming elections to the Majlis, scheduled for 7 October. Pro-Government candidates were the most successful, securing the majority of the 50 seats. Sheikh Saad was reappointed Prime Minister, and his new Council of Ministers included four newly elected deputies.

In March 1998 Sheikh Saad submitted his Government's resignation, after members of the Majlis proposed a motion of no confidence in the Minister of Information, Sheikh Sa'ud Nasir as-Sa'ud as-Sabah, who had allowed what were deemed 'un-Islamic' publications to be exhibited at a book fair in Kuwait. The Amir immediately reappointed the Crown Prince as Prime Minister, and a new Government was named at the end of the month. The promotion of Sheikh Sa'ud to the post of Minister of Oil was controversial not only because of the recent action taken against him, but also because the oil portfolio was not customarily allocated to a member of the ruling family. An institutional crisis appeared imminent in June, when the Majlis sought to cross-examine the Minister of the Interior, Sheikh Muhammad Khalid al-Hamad as-Sabah, on issues including corruption, illicit drugs and human rights. However, the ministry in question was deemed by the Government to be 'sovereign' and therefore exempt from parliamentary examination. Tensions between the Government and the Majlis were swiftly revived in July, when the Government introduced amendments to legislation enacted in 1993 (which had already been amended in 1995) regarding repayment of debts arising from the collapse of the Souk al-Manakh in 1982. Many deputies regarded new arrangements for the discharge of liabilities to be unduly favourable to debtors, many of whom were members of the ruling family, and boycotted an initial vote before reluctantly approving the amendments in August 1998.

Confrontation persisted between the Government and the Majlis. In May 1999 the Amir dissolved the legislature and ordered fresh elections, after deputies had in the previous month questioned the Minister of Justice and of Awqaf (Religious Endowments) and Islamic Affairs over errors that had appeared in copies of the Koran printed and distributed by his ministry. Some 80% of an eligible electorate of 113,000 Kuwaiti men voted in the election, which took place on 3 July. Pro-Government candidates recorded the greatest losses, taking only 12 seats; Islamist candidates won 20 seats and liberals 14, with the remaining four seats won by independents. A new Council of Ministers led by the Prime Minister, Sheikh Saad, was inaugurated in mid-July. The ruling family retained control of the strategic foreign affairs, oil, interior and defence portfolios, although a number of liberal deputies joined the Government.

During the period between the dissolution of the Majlis and the election, the Government had promulgated some 60 decrees (subject to legislative approval), most notably one proposing that women should be allowed to contest and to vote in elections from 2003. However, the law on female suffrage was defeated by a considerable majority in the new Majlis in November 1999, as liberal deputies, who supported women's enfranchisement, registered their protest at what they considered to be the unconstitutionality of legislation by decree by joining Islamist and conservative deputies in voting against the measure. Liberal deputies immediately submitted identical legislation regarding women's suffrage, but this was narrowly defeated in a vote at the end of the month. In March 2001 the Majlis rejected, on procedural grounds, draft legislation that would increase women's political rights.

In January 2000 Alaa Hussein Ali, leader of the provisional Government installed by Iraq in August 1990, who had been in self-imposed exile since Kuwait's liberation, returned to Kuwait in order to appeal against the death sentence pronounced in June 1993 (see above). In May 2000 it was announced that Hussein had lost his appeal at the Court of First Instance, and that he planned a further challenge to his sentence. The Court of Appeal upheld the previous ruling in July, but in March 2001 commuted Hussein's death sentence to one of life imprisonment.

In July 2000 unrest was reported in the Al-Jahra region, where a community of *bidoun* ('stateless' Arabs) form the majority of the population. (About 100,000 *bidoun* reside in Kuwait, but the authorities refuse to recognize their claims to Kuwaiti nationality.) The unrest followed the approval, in May, of a draft amendment to the Citizenship Law that would grant only a small number of *bidoun* the right to Kuwaiti citizenship. Some 1,000 *bidoun* obtained Kuwaiti citizenship in early 2001, leading to protests by those whose applications had been refused.

Sheikh Saad tendered his Government's resignation in January 2001. The Crown Prince denied that this constituted an attempt to prevent parliamentary scrutiny of the Minister of Justice and of Awqaf and Islamic Affairs, Saad Jasem Yousuf al-Hashil, relating to allegations of inefficiency and corruption in his ministry. The Amir immediately reappointed Sheikh Saad as Prime Minister, and a new 15-member Government was named in February. The new administration included five younger members of the ruling family, as well as four members of the Majlis. The outgoing Deputy Prime Minister and Minister of Defence, Sheikh Salim Sabah as-Salim as-Sabah, left the Government, although the defence, foreign affairs and interior portfolios remained in the hands of the as-Sabah family. Some controversy was caused by the allocation of the oil portfolio to Dr Adil Khalid as-Sabih, the minister previously responsible for the electricity, water and housing portfolios who had recently survived a parliamentary vote of no confidence in respect of his business interests.

Meanwhile, during November 2000, as the crisis in Israeli-Palestinian relations deepened, 16 suspected Islamist militants (Kuwaitis and other Arab nationals) were arrested in Kuwait, accused of involvement in plotting bomb attacks on US military installations in the Gulf region in retaliation for perceived US support for Israel. The arrests of the alleged saboteurs followed reports that a Moroccan aide to the Saudi-born leader of the militant Islamist al-Qa'ida (Base) organization, Osama bin Laden, had entered Kuwait from Afghanistan; however, the aide subsequently fled to Iran. In June 2001 a senior Kuwaiti military official was convicted of concealing weapons to be used for terrorist purposes; he received a 10-year prison sentence, but in December this was reduced to seven years. (Eight of the suspected militants were given suspended sentences and ordered to pay fines; the remainder were acquitted.)

In January 2002 four people died following a major explosion at Raudhatain, Kuwait's second largest oilfield, to the north of Kuwait City. Adil Khalid as-Sabih immediately submitted his resignation as Minister of Oil, stating that he accepted responsibility for the incident. The Minister of Information, Sheikh Ahmad al-Fahd al-Ahmad as-Sabah, was subsequently named as acting Minister of Oil. However, a political crisis ensued after it proved impossible to find a permanent replacement for Dr as-Sabih, and Sheikh Ahmad was asked to remain in charge of the oil portfolio until the general election (scheduled for mid-2003). Meanwhile, several members of the increasingly assertive Majlis demanded the resignation of the entire Government, alleging that the explosion at Raudhatain was the result of state corruption and mismanagement. In January 2003 the Amir accepted the resignation of the Minister of Finance, of Planning and Minister of State for Administrative Development Affairs, Dr Yousuf Hamad al-Ibrahim, who had been the object of severe parliamentary criticism. Dr al-Ibrahim, a leading reformist, had in July 2002 survived a vote of no confidence instigated by Islamist Majlis deputies who accused him of poor management of the Government's fiscal affairs.

After a campaign that was overshadowed by the US-led military intervention in Iraq (which was largely conducted from Kuwaiti territory), parliamentary elections were held, as scheduled, on 5 July 2003. Islamist candidates secured 21 of the 50 seats in the Majlis, while pro-Government candidates won 14 seats, independents (regarded as being aligned with the Government) 12 and liberals three. The rate of voter participation was reported to be only 45% of the 6% of the total population who formed the electorate. The results were viewed as a major setback for those seeking political reform, and were widely interpreted as signalling popular dissatisfaction with the entire political process.

Meanwhile, following the elections, in July 2003 the ailing Crown Prince relinquished the position of Prime Minister. The appointment of Sheikh Sabah as his replacement represented an unprecedented separation between the post of Prime Minister and the position of Crown Prince, and provided some encouragement to reformists after their heavy electoral losses. A new Council of Ministers, including six new appointments, was also announced in mid-July. The most significant change was the merger of the oil portfolio with the Ministry of Electricity and Water to form the Ministry of Energy, to be headed by Sheikh Ahmad al-Fahd al-Ahmad as-Sabah.

In October 2003 and May 2004 the Council of Ministers approved legislation that would permit women to vote in and contest municipal and parliamentary elections, respectively. The Majlis gave provisional approval for the former piece of legislation in April 2005, but subsequently failed to ratify the legislation at a second vote in May. Both new laws were approved later in the month; however, this was too late to allow women to participate in the June municipal elections. By early 2006 it was reported that there were already considerably more women than men registered as voters. Kuwaiti women received their first opportunity to vote and to stand in elections at a municipal by-election on 4 April 2006, where two of the eight candidates were female. Some 28 women registered to contest legislative elections in June of the same year (see below).

In March 2004 the Minister of Finance, Mahmud Abd al-Khaliq an-Nuri, narrowly survived a vote of no confidence, having been heavily criticized by the Majlis for mismanagement during the sale of state property. Citing health reasons, an-Nuri resigned shortly after the vote; Bader Mishari al-Humaidhi, formerly Director-General of the Kuwait Fund for Arab Economic Development, was appointed as his replacement on 4 April 2005. Meanwhile, in the previous month Dr Anas Muhammad Ahmad ar-Rashaid was finally appointed as Minister of Information; he replaced Muhammad Abu al-Hassan, who had resigned in January, shortly before he was to be questioned in the Majlis by Islamist members over allowing 'immoral' Western-style concerts in Kuwait. The day after the appointment of al-Humaidhi, the Minister of Health, Muhammad Ahmad al-Jarallah, resigned in advance of a parliamentary vote on a motion of no confidence, which had been lodged on 4 April, accusing him of mismanagement; he thus became the third member of the Council of Ministers to resign in connection with hostile parliamentary questioning since the elections to the Majlis in July 2003. The Prime Minister subsequently warned the Majlis that a vote of no confidence in al-Jarallah, should it be carried, could 'negatively impact on our national unity', which in some quarters was interpreted as a sign that the increasingly assertive nature of the Majlis had begun to concern the ruling as-Sabah family. Al-Jarallah's resignation was accepted by the Prime Minister on 10 April 2005, and the Minister of Energy, Sheikh Ahmad al-Fahd as-Sabah, assumed the health portfolio in an acting capacity. In June the Prime Minister appointed Dr Massouma Saleh al-Mubarak as Minister of Planning and Minister of State for Administrative Development Affairs, making her Kuwait's first female member of the Council of Ministers.

Meanwhile, in February 2005 the Majlis approved legislation giving security agencies flexible new powers to search for and seize illegal firearms, following several battles between government forces and armed militants. Some of the violence was linked to reports of hostility towards Westerners, particularly US citizens, and al-Qa'ida was believed by some to be implicated in the violence. The new legislation was to be renewed on an annual basis.

On 15 January 2006 the death of the Amir, Sheikh Jaber, was announced. He was automatically succeeded by the Crown Prince, Sheikh Saad. However, in an unprecedented development, on 24 January Sheikh Saad, who had yet to take the oath of office, was removed from the position of Amir on health grounds, following a formal request from the Council of Ministers that the Majlis debate the issue. Under the Constitution, the law of succession required a two-thirds' majority of Majlis deputies in order to dismiss an Amir; but, in the event, the vote in favour of replacing Sheikh Saad was unanimous. It was reported that Sheikh Saad and his close supporters had, after nine days of intense negotiation, reluctantly agreed to his removal from office prior to the Majlis debate; however, his abdication letter did not bear an official stamp and was disregarded by parliamentarians. In the absence of a nominated Crown Prince, the Prime Minister, Sheikh Sabah, who was in any case regarded as the de facto ruler of the emirate, assumed the powers of the Amir until the nomination of a permanent head of state by the Council of Ministers. Sheikh Sabah was duly sworn in as Amir on 29 January, after his widely predicted nomination had been unanimously approved by the Majlis. The sole controversy attached to Sheikh Sabah's accession was that, like the late Sheikh Jaber, he belonged to the al-Jaber branch of the ruling as-Sabah family, which, by tradition, alternated the position of Amir with the as-Salim branch of the family, of which Sheikh Saad was a member.

The new Amir accepted the resignation of the Council of Ministers on 30 January 2006. In early February Sheikh Sabah appointed Sheikh Nasser al-Muhammad al-Ahmad as-Sabah, a former diplomat and the Amir's nephew, as the new Prime Minister and the erstwhile Deputy Prime Minister and Minister of the Interior, Sheikh Nawwaf al-Ahmad al-Jaber as-Sabah, the Amir's brother, as Crown Prince. The appointments, which maintained the post-2003 separation between the roles of premier and Crown Prince, emphasized the channelling of power towards the al-Jaber branch of the ruling family, although both men were respected for their extensive political experience. On the following day the Amir approved Sheikh Nasser's first Council of Ministers. Although strategic portfolios (including those of foreign affairs, finance and energy) remained unaltered, a notable change was the addition of the interior portfolio to the responsibilities of the Minister of Defence, Sheikh Jaber Mubarak al-Hamad as-Sabah, who also became First Deputy Prime Minister.

A long-running campaign for electoral reform, which sought to reduce the number of electoral constituencies in Kuwait in order to diminish the opportunities for vote-buying, began to attract extensive popular support from May 2006. A proposal by the Government to reduce the number of constituencies from 25 to 10 was rejected by the opposition, which advocated a more comprehensive reduction, to just five constituencies. Following efforts by the Majlis to cross-examine the Prime Minister on the matter, the Amir dissolved parliament and called for elections to be held on 29 June, just over one year earlier than scheduled. A loose alliance of 29 pro-reform members of the outgoing legislature was formed to contest the elections, comprising candidates from across the political spectrum. Reformists made significant gains at the polls, winning 34 of the 50 seats contested. The remaining 16 seats were won by independents and pro-Government candidates; no female candidates were elected. Voter participation was reported to be 65% of those registered to vote; despite constituting 65% of the electorate, women accounted for only 35% of the total number of votes cast. A reform bill drafted by the new Majlis proposing the introduction of a five-constituency electoral system was passed into law in July. Meanwhile, in early July a new Council of Ministers was named under Prime Minister Sheikh Nasser. Although the key portfolios remained unchanged, the Minister of Energy, Sheikh Ahmad al-Fahd as-Sabah, failed to be reappointed, after he was accused by members of the opposition and pro-reformists of having interfered in the electoral process and of seeking to block reforms.

In December 2006 the Minister of Information, Muhammad Nasser as-Sanousi, resigned following a move by the increasingly confrontational Majlis to question him over allegations that he had curbed media freedom during the recent election campaign. In the following month deputies made a similar request to question the Minister of Health, Sheikh Ahmad Abdullah al-Ahmad as-Sabah, on four charges related to the mismanagement of, and deterioration in, the medical sector. Following the cross-examination of Sheikh Ahmad in February 2007, a motion of no confidence was filed against the minister; however, in early March, one day before the Majlis was due to debate the motion, the entire Council of Ministers resigned. A new cabinet, approved by the Amir in late March, excluded Sheikh Ahmad but retained most of the key ministers in the same posts. Dr al-Mubarak was awarded the health portfolio, while Nouriya

Subeeh Barrak as-Subeeh was appointed Minister of Education, increasing to two the number of female cabinet ministers. The reorganization also included the division of the recently created Ministry of Energy into the Ministry of Oil and the Ministry of Electricity and Water; the latter was to be headed by Muhammad Abdullah Hadi al-Olaim, spokesman of the Islamic Constitutional Movement. At the end of June the Minister of Oil, Sheikh Ali al-Jarrah as-Sabah, resigned; the Majlis had been scheduled to debate a motion of no confidence in the minister after having questioned him over allegations of corruption. Al-Olaim replaced Ali as-Sabah in an acting capacity. In August Minister of Health al-Mubarak also announced her resignation, after a fire at a hospital in Kuwait City had resulted in the deaths of two patients. Towards the end of October the Prime Minister, Sheikh Nasser, instigated an extensive reorganzation of the Council of Ministers, which was approved by the Amir; the cabinet changes were apparently intended to prevent an escalation of the ongoing difficulties between the Government and the Majlis. New appointments included Sheikh Jaber Khalid al-Jaber as-Sabah as Minister of the Interior, Bader Mishari al-Humaidhi as Minister of Oil and Mustafa Jassem ash-Shimali as Minister of Finance. However, in early November al-Humaidhi resigned amid continuing controversy relating to his previous role as Minister of Finance (see above).

In late January 2008 the liberal Minister of Education, Nouriya as-Subeeh, survived a no-confidence vote in the Majlis, having undergone a lengthy interrogation by Islamist and tribal deputies with regard to alleged mismanagement of the education sector, legal irregularities and a reported failure to guarantee the complete segregation of male and female students at Kuwait's universities. The fact that political infighting was increasingly damaging Kuwait's prospects for economic and social development was said to be causing growing frustration among the population. On 17 March the entire Council of Ministers tendered its resignation, stating that relations with the Majlis had become untenable, and that parliament was continuing to obstruct ministers' attempts to carry out their duties effectively. Parliamentary deputies countered this argument by claiming that the blame for the political crisis lay with the executive, in which the as-Sabah family continued to exert considerable power. The immediate cause of the latest crisis involved a dispute concerning salary increases for state employees, with deputies asserting that the Government's proposed pay rise was too low. Having cut short a visit to Morocco, on 19 March Sheikh Sabah ordered the dissolution of the Majlis in order for fresh elections to take place on 17 May. In his speech the Amir referred to the need to 'safeguard the unity of the nation', adding that he had taken the decision to suspend parliament owing to 'irresponsible behaviour'. The May elections would be the first to use the five-constituency system adopted into law in July 2006. In early April 2008 the Minister of Commerce and Industry, Dr Falah Fahd al-Hajeri, and the Minister of State for Housing Affairs and for National Assembly Affairs, Abd al-Wahid Mahmoud al-Awadhi, tendered their resignations in order to stand as candidates in the forthcoming polls. Minister of Finance Mustafa Jassem ash-Shimali and Minister of Health Abdullah Abd ar-Rahman at-Taweel assumed responsibility for their respective portfolios pending the elections.

Meanwhile, in February 2008 tensions increased between Sunni and Shi'a Muslims in the emirate after several hundred people from the minority Shi'a community had held a rally to commemorate the death of a senior commander of the militant Shi'a organization Hezbollah in Lebanon. Imad Mughniyeh, who was killed in a bomb attack in the Syrian capital, Damascus, in that month, was described by the Kuwaiti Government as a 'terrorist', who, they claimed, had been responsible for the hijacking of a Kuwait Airways plane in 1988, in which two Kuwaiti passengers were murdered. A number of prominent Shi'a politicians and clerics were questioned by the authorities over their involvement in the rally, and many arrests were reported; Kuwaiti officials claimed that all of those under investigation were members of an illegal opposition group, Hezbollah Kuwait. In October it was reported that two prominent Shi'a members of the Majlis were among seven people acquitted by a court in Kuwait for their alleged membership of Hezbollah Kuwait.

At the legislative elections held, as scheduled, on 17 May 2008, Islamist candidates performed strongly, with Sunni Islamists winning 21 of the 50 seats in the Majlis and Shi'ite Islamists (including the Popular Action Bloc) nine; liberals and their allies garnered seven and the remaining 13 seats were won by independents. Of the 27 female candidates who stood in the election, none secured a seat in the new Assembly. In spite of opposition from several members of the Majlis, the Amir subsequently reappointed Sheikh Nasser to the post of Prime Minister, with the task of forming a new Council of Ministers. On 28 May Sheikh Nasser duly appointed a new cabinet comprising 15 ministers, two of whom were women. The incumbent Ministers of Defence, Foreign Affairs, Finance and the Interior retained their posts in the new Council of Ministers, while al-Olaim, hitherto acting Minister for Oil, was appointed to the role in a permanent capacity (also retaining the electricity and water portfolios). It was immediately apparent, however, that the elections had done little to improve relations between the Majlis and the Government. At the first session of the new legislature, held on 1 June, a number of members withdrew in protest against the composition of the new Council of Ministers.

In July 2008 hundreds of Bangladeshi workers protested about low and irregular wages and poor working conditions. The demonstration, which followed several similar ones in recent months, turned violent, and the police reportedly arrested and subsequently deported some 1,000 of the workers involved in the riot. The incident reignited international discussion of Kuwait's human rights record (a US State Department report published in June, on forced labour, had placed Kuwait in the 'worst offender' category), and the Council of Ministers subsequently announced that it would introduce a minimum monthly wage of KD 40 (US $150) for workers employed by companies contracted by the Government. In September the Government also revealed that it was considering making amendments to its much-maligned employee sponsorship system (which stipulates that foreign workers must be sponsored by a Kuwaiti employer); however, in early 2009 this system remained unchanged.

Relations between the Majlis and the Council of Ministers deteriorated further in late 2008, as members of the Assembly continued to express disquiet over the Prime Minister's handling of the Government and his alleged mismanagement of public funds. In early November three Sunni Islamist members of the Majlis submitted a request to question Sheikh Nasser over the decision to allow the controversial Iranian Shi'a cleric, Muhammad Baqer al-Fali, to visit Kuwait (al-Fali had been banned from entering Kuwait after being convicted of religious slurs that had offended Sunni Muslims and of 'threatening national unity'). To avert parliamentary questioning of the Prime Minister, on 25 November the entire Council of Ministers resigned; the Amir accepted its resignation on 1 December and asked Sheikh Nasser to form a new Government—the fifth since he had assumed the premiership in February 2006. The political upheaval jeopardized Kuwait's efforts to fortify and diversify its economy, which had suffered in 2008 in the wake of a growing global financial crisis. Notably, the resignation of the Council of Ministers undermined attempts to restore investor confidence in the Kuwait Stock Exchange (the value of traded shares had declined by 30% since the beginning of 2008, provoking demonstrations by traders concerned by a lack of official intervention and the significant losses being suffered by small investors). Following the unrest, a court ordered the closure of the bourse in mid-November, prompting the Government to instruct the state's sovereign wealth fund, the Kuwait Investment Authority, to invest in the exchange, although this announcement was overshadowed days later by the political crisis. Opposition from members of the legislature also precipitated the collapse of a potentially lucrative Government-backed joint venture between the Petrochemical Industries Co and US-based Dow Chemicals in early 2009.

On 12 January 2009 the Amir approved the formation of a new Council of Ministers. Prime Minister Sheikh Nasser retained his post, as did many of the ministers from the outgoing cabinet. Al-Olaim left the Government, the Deputy Prime Minister and foreign minister, Sheikh Dr Muhammad Sabah as-Salim as-Sabah, assuming the oil portfolio in an acting capacity, while the water and electricity portfolios were transferred to Nabil Khalaf Saeed bin Salama (who also assumed responsibility for communications). The formation of a new Council of Ministers failed to ease tension between the Majlis and the Government in the first months of 2009; several members of the National Assembly walked out of the first parliamentary session of the year in protest at the lack of new faces appointed to the cabinet. The nomination of Sheikh Ahmad Abdullah as-Sabah as Minister of Oil in early February further strained relations between the legislature and the Government. Some members of the Majlis asserted that the appointment was unconstitutional, given that he had been subject to a motion of no confidence in his capacity as Minister of Health two years previously (see above).

In March 2009 five Islamist members of the legislature sought to question the Prime Minister about allegations of mismanagement, misuse of public funds and the failure to adapt economic policy to the worsening global financial climate. The continued refusal by Sheikh Nasser to submit to scrutiny precipitated the resignation of the entire Council of Ministers on 16 March 2009; two days later the Amir ordered the dissolution of parliament. The early parliamentary election was scheduled for 16 May and, on 6 April, a minor reorganization of the Government followed the resignation of the Minister of Justice and of Awqaf and Islamic Affairs, Hussein Nasser al-Huraiti, and of the Minister of Health, Roudhan Abd al-Aziz ar-Roudhan, who were to stand as candidates for the Majlis. The Minister of Information, Sheikh Sabah Khalid al-Hamad as-Sabah, and the Minister of State for Housing Affairs and for Development Affairs, Dr Moudhi Abd al-Aziz al-Homoud, assumed their respective portfolios in an interim capacity. However, there was concern that the general election, which took place on 16 May, would not break the political impasse that had produced three parliaments in as many years and delayed the introduction of economic stimulus and financial reform. Sunni Islamists retained only 11 seats in the 50-member Assembly, losing out to liberals (who won eight seats) and Shi'ite Islamists (nine seats), with the balance gained by the tribal-based independents. The main figures involved in the previous confrontations with the Government were re-elected. Four deputies (including Dr Massouma Saleh al-Mubarak, Kuwait's first female cabinet minister) elected to the new Majlis were women, the first to be elected since women were allowed to participate in electoral politics in 2005.

Friction between Kuwait and Iraq in the aftermath of the Gulf War was exacerbated by the issue of the demarcation of their joint border. The UN commission with responsibility for delineating the frontier formalized the land border as it had been defined by British administrators in 1932 (and officially agreed by Kuwait and Iraq in 1963). The boundary, the validity of which was now rejected by Iraq, was established some 570 m north of its pre-war position, dividing the Iraqi port of Umm Qasr, with the effect that Iraq retained the town and much of the harbour while Kuwait was awarded hinterland which included an abandoned Iraqi naval base; the border also situated several Iraqi oil wells on Kuwaiti territory. In January 1993 the USA led air attacks on Iraq, and more than 1,000 US troops were dispatched to Kuwait, in response to a series of incursions by Iraqi forces into Kuwaiti territory in the days immediately preceding the designated entry into force of the new border; its formal delineation was completed in March, when the UN commission defined the maritime border along the median line of the Khawr Abd Allah waterway. Allegations made by Kuwait of Iraqi violations of the border, and of attempts to impede construction of a trench along the land border, intensified during the second half of 1993, and there were sporadic reports of exchanges of fire in the border region. In November a 775-strong armed UNIKOM reinforcement was deployed in northern Kuwait, with authorization (under specific circumstances) to use its weapons to assist the unarmed force already in the demilitarized zone.

In October 1994 Iraq deployed some 70,000 troops and 700 tanks near the border with Kuwait, in an apparent attempt to force an easing of UN economic sanctions. Kuwait immediately mobilized its army reserves, and dispatched some 20,000 troops to the border region. The USA committed almost 40,000 land, naval and air forces to the region; France and the United Kingdom deployed naval vessels, and the United Kingdom dispatched about 1,200 troops. Following Russian mediation, Iraq announced its willingness to recognize Kuwait's sovereignty and borders, on condition that the UN ease sanctions against Iraq after six months. However, the UN Security Council adopted a resolution (No. 949) requiring Iraq's unconditional recognition of Kuwait's sovereignty and borders and restricting the movement of Iraqi troops in the border area. In November Iraq officially recognized Kuwait's sovereignty, territorial integrity and political independence, as well as its UN-defined borders. Most of the US and British reinforcements deployed in the region in October had been withdrawn by the end of the year. Kuwait's relations with Iraq deteriorated sharply in September 1996, after the Kuwaiti Government agreed to the deployment in Kuwait of US military aircraft and troops in support of a US operation to force the withdrawal of Iraqi armed forces from the Kurdish 'safe haven' in northern Iraq. In December the USA announced that some 4,200 US troops deployed in Kuwait during 1996 would be withdrawn by the end of the year, although the deployment of US F-117 *Stealth* fighter aircraft was to be extended.

Kuwait and Iraq made mutual accusations of territorial violations and attacks on shipping during 1997. Meanwhile, Kuwait continued to support the maintenance of international sanctions against Iraq, and to demand adherence by Iraq to all relevant UN resolutions adopted since the Gulf crisis. Furthermore, statements by the Iraqi Government that it was holding no Kuwaiti prisoners of war were refuted by Kuwait: the Kuwaiti authorities, asserting that some 600 Kuwaitis remained captive in Iraq, claimed in late 1997 to be in possession of documentation, passed by Iraq to the International Committee of the Red Cross (ICRC), relating to 126 Kuwaiti prisoners of war. As the crisis involving weapons inspections in Iraq by the UN Special Commission (see the Recent History of Iraq) deepened in February 1998, fears were expressed for Kuwait's security—in particular that an attack on Iraq might result in the use of chemical or other weapons of mass destruction against Kuwait. The USA, supported by the United Kingdom, undertook a military deployment in the Gulf region at this time: by the end of the month, when the UN Secretary-General and the Iraqi Government reached a compromise agreement regarding weapons inspections, some 6,000 US ground troops had been dispatched to Kuwait. Following a series of air-strikes against targets in Iraq by US and British forces from December 1998, Iraq accused Kuwait of collaborating in the air attacks, and frequently reiterated claims to Kuwaiti territory. In September 1999 Kuwait lodged an official protest over changes made to the final draft of an Arab League report to which, Kuwait asserted, references to the formation of a 'mechanism' to resolve the issue of Kuwaiti and other prisoners of war in Iraq had been added; Kuwait maintained that the ICRC was the only body empowered to deal with the issue. In November the Majlis established a committee to examine future relations with Iraq, and in December the Kuwaiti Government welcomed UN Security Council Resolution 1284 (establishing a new weapons inspectorate for Iraq, q.v.), which incorporated demands for: the repatriation of Kuwaiti and other prisoners from Iraq, Iraq's co-operation with the ICRC, and the return of Kuwaiti property seized during the occupation.

In September 2000 ministers responsible for foreign affairs of the Co-operation Council for the Arab States of the Gulf (Gulf Co-operation Council—GCC, see p. 229) expressed concerns after the Iraqi leadership had repeatedly denounced both Kuwait and Saudi Arabia for allowing US and British military aircraft to use their airspace in order to conduct military attacks on Iraq, and had vowed to launch a new invasion of Kuwait. Iraq also renewed its long-standing accusation that Kuwait was drilling oil wells on Iraqi territory, and accused Kuwait and Saudi Arabia of inflicting suffering on the Iraqi population through the maintenance of UN sanctions. In late 2000 Kuwait reinforced security along its border with Iraq, partly to prevent a possible influx of *bidoun*, who had reportedly entered the demilitarized zone from Iraq and who were demanding the right of return to Kuwait (from where they had been excluded since the Gulf crisis).

In March 2001 a summit meeting of Arab League heads of state, held in Amman, Jordan, was considered to have made the most comprehensive effort hitherto in addressing divisions arising from the Gulf conflict. None the less, a draft resolution presented by the Iraqi delegation urging an end to UN sanctions and a resumption of civilian flights failed to secure adoption, owing to Iraq's unwillingness—on the grounds that it had already done sufficient to make clear its recognition of Kuwait's territorial integrity—to accede to a requirement of a specific guarantee that Iraq would not repeat the invasion of 1990. In November 2001 Kuwait issued a formal complaint to the UN following an alleged violation of its territory by Iraq. In January 2002 the Kuwaiti leadership was reported to have rejected attempts by the Arab League to persuade it to accept Iraqi proposals apparently aimed at improving bilateral relations: as part of Iraq's diplomatic offensive to secure the support of the Arab world in view of the threat of US-led military action against Saddam Hussain's regime, the Iraqi leader had conveyed an appeal to Arab states to set aside their differences. Later in the month it was reported that Iraq had announced its preparedness to allow a delegation from Kuwait to visit Iraq to verify that no Kuwaiti prisoners of war were being held. At the Arab League summit held in Beirut, Lebanon, in March 2002, however, it was announced that Kuwait and Iraq had reached agreement on the resolution of outstanding differences. The summit's final communiqué welcomed Iraq's assurances that it would respect the 'independence, sovereignty and security' of Kuwait, and safeguard its 'territorial integrity'; Iraq was urged to co-operate in seeking a 'definitive solution' to issues of Kuwaiti prisoners and detainees, and of the return of property, while Kuwait was called upon to 'co-operate with what Iraq offers with respect to its nationals' reported as missing through the ICRC.

Relations with Iraq were profoundly affected by the political repercussions of the suicide attacks against New York and Washington, DC, USA, in September 2001. Kuwait, which strongly condemned the attacks, thereafter assumed an important role in persuading other Gulf states to join the US-led 'coalition against terror'. US bases in Kuwait were subsequently used to provide logistical support to the US-led campaign against al-Qa'ida (held by the USA to be principally responsible for the suicide attacks) and its Taliban hosts in Afghanistan during late 2001. Meanwhile, in October the Kuwaiti authorities revoked the citizenship of the official spokesman of al-Qa'ida, Sulayman Abu Ghaith, after remarks he had made via the Qatar-based Al-Jazeera television station. In late 2001 the Central Bank of Kuwait implemented measures designed to prevent Islamic charitable organizations from using Kuwaiti financial institutions to channel funds to al-Qa'ida.

During the course of 2002 increased speculation that the US Administration of George W. Bush intended to extend the 'war on terror' to target the regime of Saddam Hussain in Iraq threatened to fuel opposition to a continued US presence in the region and exacerbate an increasingly tense political situation in Kuwait. At the end of December some 12,000 US troops were stationed in Kuwait, and in early 2003 Kuwait's Ministry of Defence declared that the entire northern half of Kuwait would be designated a closed military zone from February. In March an emergency meeting of the Arab League, hosted by Qatar, to discuss the deepening crisis descended into a bitter exchange of insults between, primarily, a senior Iraqi official and the Kuwaiti Minister of Information. Kuwait subsequently supported a proposal made by the President of the United Arab Emirates (UAE) for Saddam Hussain to go into exile in order to prevent a US-led war to remove his regime. At the outset of military action, which commenced in late March, US-led troops in Kuwait, the base for the main ground assault on Iraq, numbered some 140,000. Iraqi armed forces launched several missiles at Kuwaiti territory, although little damage was caused in the emirate during the course of the conflict. In the aftermath of the most intense period of fighting, which President Bush declared to have ended by early May, Kuwait renewed its financial demands against Iraq, while a number of Kuwaiti firms entered into agreements with the US-led occupying powers. In October the demilitarized zone between Iraq and Kuwait was ended and, having fulfilled its mandate, UNIKOM's operations were terminated. The resumption of diplomatic relations between Iraq and Kuwait was announced in mid-2004. In 2005 Kuwait began the construction of a 200-km steel barrier along the border with Iraq, parts of which were destroyed by Iraqi militants who claimed that it was encroaching upon their land; however, in November 2006 Iraq agreed to allow the fence to be completed. In April 2007 the Kuwaiti Government expressed its hope that the two countries would open diplomatic missions in their respective capitals in the near future. This ambition was realized in July 2008, when Kuwait announced the appointment of an ambassador to Iraq—its first since the Iraqi invasion of mid-1990; Ali Muhammad al-Momen subsequently took up his post in Baghdad on 22 October. (Iraq had earlier reopened its embassy in Kuwait, which, in April 2009, continued to be headed by a chargé d'affaires.) Further evidence of an improvement in relations between Kuwait and Iraq was provided in late February 2009, when Deputy Prime Minister and Minister of Foreign Affairs, Sheikh Dr Muhammad Sabah as-Salim as-Sabah, visited Baghdad for talks with Iraqi Prime Minister Nuri Kamal (Jawad) al-Maliki. During the visit al-Maliki spoke of Iraq's desire to distance itself from the regime of Saddam Hussain, and sought to reassure Sheikh Dr Muhammad of the country's growing emphasis on 'security' and 'stability'.

Meanwhile, in May 1994 the governing body of the UN Compensation Commission (UNCC), responsible for considering claims for compensation arising from the 1990–91 Gulf crisis, approved the first disbursements (to 670 families or individuals in 16 countries), totalling US $2.7m. By late 1996 payments amounting to $3,000m. (to be financed partly by Iraqi petroleum revenues) had been endorsed by the UN, which had yet to consider claims for a further $190,000m. In December international arbitrators recommended that a payment of $610m. should be made to the Kuwait Oil Company (KOC), in compensation for the cost of extinguishing oil wells set alight by retreating Iraqi troops in early 1991. In March 1997 the Kuwaiti general committee responsible for evaluating war damages stated that it was to begin compensation payments, initially to some 4,500 citizens who had incurred losses valued at less than $100,000. The disbursement of a further $84m. to some 33,800 individuals was authorized by the UN in February 1999. In September 2000 the UN Security Council approved the payment to the Kuwait Petroleum Corporation (which controls the KOC) of $15,900m. in compensation for lost petroleum revenues arising from the Iraqi occupation. However, the Security Council decided at the same time to reduce the share of Iraqi petroleum revenues to be paid into the compensation fund from 30% to 25%. France and Russia, which increasingly opposed the maintenance of sanctions against Iraq, had delayed a decision by the UNCC on the payment, and Russia had warned of its inclination to oppose Kuwaiti claims to reparations unless the levy on Iraqi petroleum revenues was reduced. By mid-2003 the majority of individual claimants (Kuwaitis and expatriates in Kuwait and Iraq during the Gulf war) had received compensation, with total disbursements being valued at some $17,600m. Meanwhile, the UNCC was considering a claim of $86,000m. by the Kuwait Investment Agency, principally in recompense for lost earnings during the conflict. However, in a deposition issued in June 2003, the UNCC rejected all but $1,500m. of the claim. In May 2003 UN Security Council Resolution 1483 had reduced the share of Iraqi petroleum revenue to be used for compensation payments from 25% to 5%, which was expected to result in outstanding compensation payments believed to total more than $30,000m. remaining unpaid for several decades. In January 2004, following similar announcements by the Governments of the UAE and Qatar, Sheikh Sabah stated that Kuwait was prepared to waive a 'significant proportion' of the estimated $16,000m. owed by Iraq. This did not, however, include any war reparations still claimed by the Government. In March 2005 the UN panel overseeing payments to victims of the Gulf crisis approved a further disbursement of $265m. to families of those who had died in Iraqi detention. At a final session of the UNCC governing body, held in June, a further $367m. in compensation was awarded to successful claimants. In April 2008 payments worth $972.4m. were made by the UNCC, principally to Kuwaiti state-owned and private companies for losses incurred as a result of the Iraqi invasion and occupation (including losses caused by environmental damage). In August several members of the Majlis rejected proposals of the Iraqi Government that Kuwait waive a substantial proportion of the debt and war reparations still owed by Iraq.

Relations with Jordan, which had deteriorated following that country's failure openly to denounce the Iraqi invasion, gradually eased in the mid-1990s. Flights between Kuwait and Jordan by both countries' national airlines, which had been suspended in 1990, resumed in July 1997, and the normalization of relations generally continued thereafter. In March 1999 the Jordanian embassy in Kuwait, which had been closed in 1990, was reopened. In September of that year the new King Abdullah of Jordan made his first visit to Kuwait (his father, King Hussein, had not visited after 1990), where he held talks with the Amir. Jordan and Kuwait signed a bilateral free trade agreement in December.

In July 2000 Kuwait and Saudi Arabia signed an agreement finalizing the delineation of their maritime borders. Kuwait subsequently commenced negotiations with Iran on the demarcation of respective rights to the continental shelf, following complaints by the Kuwaiti and Saudi authorities over Iran's decision to begin drilling for gas in a disputed offshore area. Iraq asserted that, as a concerned party, it should be included in the Kuwaiti-Iranian discussions. Iran suspended drilling pending the conclusion of the talks. In December a defence agreement was signed by the six member states of the GCC. Kuwait opposes any military action being taken by the USA against Iran, and supports the Iranian Government's right to develop a peaceful nuclear energy programme (see the chapter on Iran). In July 2007 the US Administration unveiled a US $20,000m. package of military assistance and weapons sales to Kuwait and the other GCC member states, in an attempt to bolster security in the Gulf region and to encourage the GCC to side with the USA in its dispute with the Iranian regime regarding the latter's nuclear programme.

Government

Under the 1962 Constitution, executive power is vested in the Amir, the Head of State (who is chosen by and from members of the ruling family), and is exercised through the Council of Ministers. The Amir appoints the Prime Minister and, on the latter's recommendation, other ministers. Legislative power is vested in the unicameral Majlis al-Umma (National Assembly), with 50 elected members who serve for four years (subject to dissolution), along with some 15 government ministers who sit as ex officio members. In May 2005 legislation was approved allowing women to vote in legislative and municipal elections for the first time. The country is divided administratively into six governorates.

Defence

As assessed at November 2008, Kuwait's active armed forces numbered 15,500—a land army of 11,000, an air force of an estimated 2,500 and a navy of around 2,000—and there were reserve forces of 23,700. Paramilitary forces comprised an estimated 6,600-strong national guard and a 500-strong coastguard. Military service is voluntary. The defence budget for 2008 was estimated at KD 1,300m. A US force has been deployed in Kuwait as part of 'Operation Iraqi Freedom' launched in 2003 (see the chapter on Iraq), and there are also small contingents of troops from the United Kingdom and Japan.

Economic Affairs

In 2005, according to estimates by the World Bank, Kuwait's gross national income (GNI), measured at average 2003–05 prices, was US $77,660m., equivalent to $30,630 per head (or $29,200 on an international purchasing-power parity basis). During 2000–07, it was estimated, the population increased at an average annual rate of 2.8%, while gross domestic product (GDP) per head increased, in real terms, by an average of 1.4% per year in 1996–2005. Overall GDP was estimated to have increased, in real terms, at an average annual rate of 8.0% in 2000–06. Real GDP increased by 6.6% in 2006.

Agriculture (including hunting, forestry and fishing) contributed 0.2% of GDP in 2007. The sector engaged 2.1% of the labour force in 2005. The principal crops are potatoes, tomatoes, cucumbers, aubergines and dates. Owing to scarcity of water, little grain is produced, and the bulk of food requirements is imported. (Imports of food and live animals accounted for 12.3% of merchandise imports in 2004.) Livestock, poultry and fishing are also important. Agricultural GDP increased, in real terms, by an average annual rate of 7.5% in 2000–06. The agricultural sector grew by 3.9% in 2006.

Industry (including mining, manufacturing, construction and power) provided 59.9% of GDP in 2007, and employed 15.4% of the labour force in 2005. During 2000–07 industrial GDP increased, in real terms, at an average annual rate of 6.3%. The sector expanded by 5.0% in 2006.

Mining and quarrying contributed 52.9% of GDP in 2007, although the sector engaged only 0.5% of the labour force in 2005. The production of petroleum and its derivatives is the most important industry in Kuwait, providing an estimated 95.2% of export revenue in 2007. At the end of 2007 the country's proven recoverable reserves of petroleum were 101,500m. barrels, representing about 8.4% of world reserves. According to oil industry figures, Kuwait's petroleum production averaged 2.62m. barrels per day (b/d) in 2007; the Government aimed to increase its production capacity to 4.0m. b/d by 2020. As a member of the Organization of the Petroleum Exporting Countries (OPEC, see p. 386), Kuwait is subject to production quotas agreed by the Organization's Conference. There are significant reserves of natural gas (1,780,000m. cu m at the end of 2007) associated with the petroleum deposits. Output was 12,600m. cu m in that year. Moreover, in March 2006 a major discovery of non-associated gas in the north of the country was announced. During 2000–06 the GDP of the mining sector increased, in real terms, at an average rate of 4.8% per year. The sector's GDP increased by 2.8% in 2006.

Manufacturing provided 4.8% of GDP in 2007, and employed 6.3% of the labour force in 2005. Petroleum refineries accounted for 60.5% of manufacturing activity, measured by gross value of output, in 2004. Of the other branches of manufacturing, the most important are the production of building materials (and related activities such as aluminium extrusion), fertilizer production, food processing and the extraction of salt and chlorine. During 2000–06 manufacturing GDP increased, in real terms, at an average annual rate of 9.7%. Growth in the manufacturing sector was 5.8% in 2006.

Electrical energy is derived from Kuwait's own resources of petroleum (providing 82.1% of total electricity production in 2005) and both local and imported natural gas (17.9%).

Services contributed 39.9% of GDP in 2007, and employed 82.4% of the labour force in 2005. Kuwait's second most important source of revenue is investment abroad, both in petroleum-related ventures and in other industries, chiefly in the USA, Western Europe and Japan; many such investments are held by the Reserve Fund for Future Generations (RFFG—to which 10% of petroleum revenues must by law be contributed each year, and which is intended to provide an income after hydrocarbon resources have been exhausted) and managed by the Kuwait Investment Authority. As part of its efforts to diversify the economy, the Government plans to develop the islands of Bubiyan and Failaka into major tourist resorts. The combined GDP of the service sectors increased, in real terms, at an average rate of 10.0% per year during 2000–06. The services sector grew by 8.4% in 2006.

In 2007 Kuwait recorded a visible trade surplus of US $46,145m., and there was a surplus of $52,734m. on the current account of the balance of payments. In 2004 the principal sources of imports were Germany and the USA, which provided, respectively, 11.5% and 10.8% of total imports; other important suppliers in that year were Saudi Arabia, the People's Republic of China, Japan and Italy. Details concerning the destination of Kuwait's petroleum exports are not available for recent years; however, the major markets for non-petroleum exports in 2004 included Saudi Arabia (10.8%), the UAE (10.0%), Indonesia, Pakistan, the USA and India. The principal exports are petroleum and petroleum products. The principal imports are machinery and transport equipment, which accounted for 40.3% of total imports in 2004, basic manufactures and other manufactured goods, food and live animals, and chemicals and related products.

A budget surplus of KD 9,324.6m. was recorded for the financial year ending 30 June 2008. A deficit of KD 6,287.3m. was forecast for 2008/09, although actual revenue from Kuwait's petroleum interests would undoubtedly be far greater than the projected figure. Kuwait's total external debt in 2006 was estimated at US $26,400m., equivalent to 26.8% of GDP. The average annual rate of inflation in 2000–07 was 2.4%; consumer prices increased by an average of 5.5% in 2007. National unemployment among Kuwaitis was estimated at only 1.5% in mid-2003; however, underemployment was unofficially reported to be up to 50%. There were 24,921 unemployed people in Kuwait in 2006.

Kuwait is a member of the Co-operation Council for the Arab States of the Gulf (Gulf Co-operation Council—GCC, see p. 229); the six GCC states established a unified regional customs tariff in January 2003, and it has been agreed to create a single market and currency no later than January 2010. The economic convergence criteria for the monetary union were agreed at a GCC summit in Abu Dhabi, the UAE, in December 2005, and in January 2008 the GCC launched its common market. Kuwait also belongs to the Organization of Arab Petroleum Exporting Countries (OAPEC, see p. 379) and to OPEC. Kuwait is a major aid donor, disbursing loans to developing countries through the Kuwait Fund for Arab Economic Development (KFAED) and the Arab Fund for Economic and Social Development (AFESD, see p. 183).

Despite its significant, oil-based wealth, Kuwait has a number of fundamental weaknesses in its economic structure: instability in its relations with Iraq have necessitated a high level of defence expenditure; reliance on petroleum revenues has impeded diversification into other industries; and its constitutional commitment to provide employment for all Kuwaitis has resulted in a heavy burden on government spending. During the early years of this century plans by the Kuwait Petroleum Corpn to allow foreign participation in a development project (known as 'Project Kuwait'), valued at US $8,500m., for the northern oilfields made extremely slow progress; the project aimed to increase production from 2.5m. b/d to 4m. b/d by 2020. However, approval by the Majlis was still required, and, despite assurances that all reserves would remain Kuwaiti-owned, many Kuwaitis remained opposed to any foreign involvement in the petroleum sector. Nevertheless, in 2003 the Majlis adopted legislation that would increase foreign investment in the economy, including the limited participation of international oil companies in the petroleum sector and measures that would permit foreign banks to operate in Kuwait. The recovery in world petroleum prices from late 1999 was the principal factor contributing to budget surpluses during 1999/2000–2007/08. The main disadvantage of the huge petroleum windfalls accrued in recent years is that incentives for the Government to introduce much-needed reforms, particularly in the non-oil sector, have been further reduced.

KUWAIT

Statistical Survey

Ostensibly, the Government remained committed to its four-year action programme, which was launched in 2004 to stimulate the private sector's role in the economy and improve the fiscal position through tax and labour market reforms and privatization; however, legislative delays hindered implementation of the proposed changes and there remained high levels of opposition to any reduction in public sector employment and salaries. While the authorities had signalled that some privatization would be implemented in 2009, the poor investment climate that predominated in the aftermath of the international banking crisis (which gathered pace from September 2008) seemed certain to impede any major developments in this regard. There were some indications that a comprehensive set of financial regulations would be introduced in either 2009 or 2010, a move likely to bring the business environment toward parity with other Gulf nations. However, the forced withdrawal of Kuwaiti-owned Petrochemical Industries Co from a planned joint venture with US-based Dow Chemicals in early 2009 was regarded as demonstrating the continued vulnerability of the private sector to state interference. Moreover, the revelation, in January 2009, that Kuwait's banks had incurred a combined loss of $1,000m. through their exposure to distressed US assets undermined confidence in the financial system. Worsening global conditions in 2009 were forecast to impact upon Kuwait's economic performance in a number of ways. Lower demand for petroleum exports, together with the steep decrease in international crude prices, would likely constrain fiscal expenditure and state-led investment. Meanwhile, further difficulties were anticipated in the banking sector, following reports that some other stricken institutions would require capital assistance. The State Planning Organization subsequently projected growth of just 1.0% for 2009, compared with 5.9% in 2008.

Education

Education is compulsory for eight years between the ages of six and 14. Although private schools exist, state education is free, and is graded into pre-primary (for children between four and six years of age), primary (for children aged six to 10), intermediate (10 to 14) and secondary (14 to 18). In 2005/06 enrolment at primary schools included 83.5% of children in the relevant age-group, while in the same year secondary enrolment included 76.6% of children in the relevant age-group. There is a teacher-training college, a technical college, and a university (where some 20,000 students were enrolled in 2006). More than 4,500 Kuwaiti students receive education abroad. Expenditure on education by the central Government in 2005/06 was budgeted at KD 573.9m. (7.9% of total expenditure).

Public Holidays

2009: 1 January (New Year's Day), 25 February (Kuwaiti National Day), 26 February (Liberation Day), 9 March* (Birth of the Prophet), 19 July* (Leilat al-Meiraj, Ascension of the Prophet), 20 September* (Id al-Fitr, end of Ramadan), 27 November* (Id al-Adha, Feast of the Sacrifice), 18 December (Islamic New Year).

2010: 1 January (New Year's Day), 25 February (Kuwaiti National Day), 26 February (Liberation Day and Birth of the Prophet), 8 July* (Leilat al-Meiraj, Ascension of the Prophet), 10 September* (Id al-Fitr, end of Ramadan), 16 November* (Id al-Adha, Feast of the Sacrifice), 7 December (Islamic New Year).

* These holidays are dependent on the Islamic lunar calendar and may vary by one or two days from the dates given.

Weights and Measures

The metric system is in force.

Statistical Survey

Sources (unless otherwise stated): Economic Research Department, Central Bank of Kuwait, POB 15, 13001 Safat, Kuwait City; tel. 2403257; fax 2440887; e-mail cbk@cbk.gov.kw; internet www.cbk.gov.kw; Central Statistical Office, Ministry of Planning, POB 26188, 13122 Safat, Kuwait City; tel. 2454968; fax 2430464; e-mail salah@mop.gov.kw; internet cso.gov.kw.

Note: Unless otherwise indicated, data refer to the State of Kuwait as constituted at 1 August 1990, prior to the Iraqi invasion and annexation of the territory and its subsequent liberation. Furthermore, no account has been taken of the increase in the area of Kuwait as a result of the adjustment to the border with Iraq that came into force on 15 January 1993.

Area and Population

AREA, POPULATION AND DENSITY

Area (sq km)	17,818*
Population (census results)†‡	
20 April 1995	1,575,570
20 April 2005 (preliminary results)	
Males	1,310,067
Females	903,336
Total	2,213,403
Population (official estimate at mid-year)§	
2006	3,051,845‖
Density (per sq km) at mid-2006	171.3¶

* 6,880 sq miles.
† Figures include Kuwaiti nationals abroad. The total population at the 2005 census comprised 880,774 Kuwaiti nationals (433,977 males, 446,797 females) and 1,332,629 non-Kuwaitis (876,090 males, 456,539 females).
‡ Excluding adjustment for underenumeration.
§ Estimate based on new methodology used by the Public Authority for Civil Information.
‖ Comprising 1,008,090 Kuwaitis (493,815 males, 514,275 females) and 2,043,755 non-Kuwaitis (1,427,677 males, 616,078 females).
¶ Preliminary.

GOVERNORATES
(population at 2005 census, preliminary)

Governorate	Area (sq km)*	Population	Density (per sq km)
Capital	199.8	261,013	1,306.4
Hawalli	⎫	487,514	⎫
Mubarak al-Kabir	⎬ 368.4	176,519	⎬ 3,491.2
Farwaniya	⎭	622,523	⎭
Al-Jahra	11,230.2	272,373	24.3
Al-Ahmadi	5,119.6	393,861	76.9
Total	**16,918.0**	**2,213,403**	**130.8**

* Excluding the islands of Bubiyan and Warba (combined area 900 sq km).

PRINCIPAL TOWNS
(population at 1995 census)

Kuwait City (capital)	28,747	Subbah as-Salem	54,608
Salmiya	129,775	Sulaibiah	53,639
Jaleeb ash-Shuyukh	102,169	Farwaniya	52,928
Hawalli	82,154	Al-Kreen	50,689
South Kheetan	62,241	Subahiya	50,644

Mid-2007 ('000, incl. suburbs, UN estimate): Kuwait City 2,063 (Source: UN, *World Urbanization Prospects: The 2007 Revision*).

KUWAIT

BIRTHS, MARRIAGES AND DEATHS

	Registered live births Number	Rate (per 1,000)	Registered marriages Number	Rate (per 1,000)	Registered deaths Number	Rate (per 1,000)
1993	37,379	25.6	10,077	6.9	3,441	2.4
1994	38,868	24.0	9,550	5.9	3,464	2.1
1995	41,169	22.8	9,515	5.3	3,781	2.1
1996	44,620	23.6	9,022	4.8	3,812	2.0
1997	42,817	21.6	9,610	4.9	4,017	2.0
1998	41,424	20.4	10,335	5.1	4,216	2.1
1999	41,135	19.5	10,847	5.1	4,187	2.0
2000	41,843	19.1	10,785	4.9	4,227	1.9

2004: Total births 47,274; Total deaths 4,793; Total marriages 12,359.

2005: Total births 50,941; Total deaths 4,784; Total marriages 12,419.

2006: Total births 52,759; Total deaths 5,247; Total marriages 12,584.

2007: Total marriages 13,306.

Life expectancy (years at birth, WHO estimates): 78 (males 77; females 79) in 2006 (Source: WHO, *World Health Statistics*).

ECONOMICALLY ACTIVE POPULATION
('000 persons aged 15 years and over, mid-2006)

	Kuwaitis	Non-Kuwaitis	Total
Agriculture, hunting and fishing	0.2	34.6	34.8
Mining and quarrying	4.7	1.6	6.3
Manufacturing	9.1	97.3	106.4
Electricity, gas and water	9.2	2.5	11.7
Construction	4.4	155.4	159.8
Wholesale and retail trade	8.2	258.9	267.0
Transport, storage and communications	8.6	53.4	62.0
Finance, insurance, real estate and business services	13.7	77.9	91.6
Public administration	260.5	672.7	933.2
Activities not adequately defined	22.5	267.5	290.0
Total labour force	**341.2**	**1,621.8**	**1,963.0**
Males	198.8	1,295.2	1,494.0
Females	142.3	326.6	468.9

Source: IMF, *Kuwait: Statistical Appendix* (June 2008).

Health and Welfare

KEY INDICATORS

Total fertility rate (children per woman, 2006)	2.2
Under-5 mortality rate (per 1,000 live births, 2006)	11
HIV/AIDS (% of persons aged 15–49, 1994)	<0.2
Physicians (per 1,000 head, 2005)	1.8
Hospital beds (per 1,000 head, 2005)	1.9
Health expenditure (2006): US $ per head (PPP)	535
Health expenditure (2006): % of GDP	2.2
Health expenditure (2006): public (% of total)	78.9
Human Development Index (2006): ranking	29
Human Development Index (2006): value	0.912

For sources and definitions, see explanatory note on p. vi.

Agriculture

PRINCIPAL CROPS
('000 metric tons)

	2005	2006*	2007*
Potatoes	20.7	22.0	23.5
Cabbages and other brassicas	9.5*	8.4	8.5
Lettuce	6.4*	6.4	6.5
Tomatoes	64.0*	55.0	55.5
Cauliflowers and broccoli	7.0*	6.9	8.5
Pumpkins, squash and gourds	5.0*	5.0	5.1
Cucumbers and gherkins	34.0*	34.0	35.0
Aubergines (Eggplants)	15.0*	15.0	15.5
Chillies and peppers, green	7.0*	7.0	8.0
Onions, dry	9.6†	7.2	7.5
Dates	15.8*	14.2	14.5

* FAO estimate(s).
† Unofficial figure.

Aggregate production ('000 metric tons, may include official, semi-official or estimated data): Total cereals 3.3 in 2005, 3.6 in 2006, 3.9 in 2007; Total roots and tubers 20.7 in 2005, 22.0 in 2006, 23.5 in 2007; Total vegetables (incl. melons) 212.6 in 2005, 200.2 in 2006, 205.0 in 2007; Total fruits (excl. melons) 16.7 in 2005, 14.6 in 2006, 14.9 in 2007.

Source: FAO.

LIVESTOCK
('000 head, year ending September)

	2004*	2005	2006*
Cattle	27.5	28.0	28.0
Camels*	5.0	5.0	5.0
Sheep	900	800	900
Goats	150.0	150.0	160.0
Chickens	31,000	30,000	32,500

* FAO estimate(s).

2007: Figures assumed to be unchanged from 2005 (FAO estimates).

Source: FAO.

LIVESTOCK PRODUCTS
('000 metric tons)

	2004*	2005	2006*
Cattle meat*	1.8	1.8	1.8
Sheep meat	29.8	34.0	30.0
Chicken meat	40.0	32.4	42.0
Cows' milk	40.0	43.0	40.0
Goats' milk	4.0	4.5	4.9
Hen eggs	22.0	26.0	22.0

* FAO estimate(s).

2007: Figures assumed to be unchanged from 2006 (FAO estimates).

Source: FAO.

Fishing

(metric tons, live weight, FAO estimates)

	2004	2005	2006
Capture	4,833	4,895	5,635
Hilsa shad	135	154	136
Mullets	298	220	301
Groupers	171	152	148
Grunts and sweetlips	109	60	107
Croakers and drums	865	674	35
Yellowfin seabream	269	280	320
Indo-Pacific king mackerel	125	97	73
Carangids	121	100	124
Natantian decapods	1,666	1,890	2,245
Aquaculture	375*	327	568
Total catch	**5,208***	**5,222**	**6,203**

* FAO estimate.

Source: FAO.

KUWAIT

Mining*

	2005	2006	2007
Crude petroleum (million barrels)	939	980	960
Natural gas (million cu metres)†	11,000	12,900	12,600

* Estimates, including an equal share of production with Saudi Arabia from the Neutral/Partitioned Zone.
† On a dry basis.
Source: US Geological Survey.

Industry

SELECTED PRODUCTS
('000 metric tons, unless otherwise stated)

	2004	2005	2006
Bran and flour*	281.6	318.3	309.1
Sulphur (by-product)†	682	700	650
Chlorine*	27.2	23.1	21.9
Caustic soda (Sodium hydroxide)*	32.6	32.2	30.5
Salt*	10.2	8.1	13.2
Nitrogenous fertilizers†‡	341	365	370
Motor spirit (petrol) (million barrels)†§	17	24	22
Kerosene (million barrels)†§	53	59	58
Gas-diesel (Distillate fuel) oils (million barrels)†§	90	95	93
Residual fuel oils (million barrels)†§	60	65	64
Quicklime†	40	50	50
Cement†	2,635	2,145	2,200
Electric energy (million kWh)*§	41,300	43,700	47,600

* Source: IMF, *Kuwait: Statistical Appendix* (July 2008).
† Source: US Geological Survey.
‡ Production in terms of nitrogen.
§ Including an equal share of production with Saudi Arabia from the Neutral/Partitioned Zone.

Finance

CURRENCY AND EXCHANGE RATES

Monetary Units
1,000 fils = 10 dirhams = 1 Kuwaiti dinar (KD).

Sterling, Dollar and Euro Equivalents (31 December 2008)
£1 sterling = 402.28 fils;
US $1 = 275.95 fils;
€1 = 384.04 fils;
10 Kuwaiti dinars = £24.86 = $36.24 = €26.04.

Average Exchange Rate (fils per US $)
2006   290.2
2007   284.2
2008   268.8

From 1 January 2003 the official exchange rate was fixed within the range of US $1 = 289 fils to $1 = 310 fils (KD 1 = $3.4602 to KD 1 = $3.2258), but this 'peg' to the US dollar was abandoned in May 2007 in favour of a basket of currencies including the pound sterling, the euro and the yen.

GENERAL BUDGET
(KD million, year ending 30 June)

Revenue	2006/07	2007/08	2008/09*
Tax revenue	287.6	355.9	339.4
International trade and transactions	190.4	224.1	209.1
Non-tax revenue	15,221.7	18,666.7	12,339.3
Oil revenue	14,511.5	17,719.5	11,652.6
Total operating revenue of government enterprises	449.0	531.1	580.9
Total	15,509.3	19,022.6	12,678.7

Expenditure	2006/07	2007/08	2008/09*
Current expenditure	5,902.0	6,797.1	9,585.7
Land acquisitions	361.2	267.9	179.2
Capital expenditure	77.1	89.8	179.0
Construction expenditure	628.3	938.4	1,485.3
Other expenditure	3,337.9	1,604.7	7,536.8
Total	10,306.4	9,698.0	18,966.0

* Projections.

INTERNATIONAL RESERVES
(US $ million at 31 December)

	2005	2006	2007
Gold (national valuation)	108.7	109.8	116.3
IMF special drawing rights	183.9	207.3	231.0
Reserve position in IMF	298.5	181.1	143.5
Foreign exchange	8,380.4	12,177.6	16,285.6
Total	8,971.5	12,675.8	16,776.4

Source: IMF, *International Financial Statistics*.

MONEY SUPPLY
(KD million at 31 December)

	2005	2006	2007
Currency outside banks	578.7	656.3	641.5
Demand deposits at deposit money banks	3,007.4	2,801.7	3,441.6
Total money	3,586.1	3,458.0	4,083.1

Source: IMF, *International Financial Statistics*.

COST OF LIVING
(Consumer Price Index; base: 2000 = 100)

	2005	2006	2007
Food	119.4	124.0	129.9
Beverages and tobacco	112.2	114.3	122.3
Clothing and footwear	118.1	122.8	128.6
Housing services	105.3	108.0	116.1
All items (incl. others)	108.8	112.1	118.3

NATIONAL ACCOUNTS
(KD million at current prices)

Expenditure on the Gross Domestic Product

	2005	2006	2007
Government final consumption expenditure	3,706.6	4,094.5	4,635.1
Private final consumption expenditure	7,585.9	8,419.4	9,682.0
Increase in stocks			
Gross fixed capital formation	3,875.7	4,786.6	6,265.9
Total domestic expenditure	15,168.2	17,300.5	20,583.0
Exports of goods and services	15,094.0	19,316.0	20,838.0
Less Imports of goods and services	6,669.0	7,122.0	9,580.0
GDP in purchasers' values	23,593.2	29,494.5	31,841.0

KUWAIT   *Statistical Survey*

Gross Domestic Product by Economic Activity

	2005	2006	2007
Agriculture, hunting, forestry and fishing	71.1	69.7	69.5
Mining and quarrying	12,265.2	16,469.4	17,387.0
Manufacturing	1,712.9	1,614.5	1,584.2
Electricity, gas and water	319.1	334.8	371.5
Construction	437.0	533.8	581.8
Trade	1,017.8	1,056.6	1,088.3
Restaurants and hotels	168.0	206.4	227.0
Transport, storage and communications	1,230.7	1,935.5	2,185.5
Finance, insurance, real estate and business services	4,021.7	4,854.0	5,664.5
Community, social and personal services	3,228.2	3,573.5	4,109.4
Sub-total	24,471.7	30,648.2	33,268.7
Import duties	173.6	186.8	180.9
Less Imputed bank service charges	−1,052.1	−1,340.5	−1,608.6
GDP in purchasers' values	23,593.2	29,494.5	31,841.0

BALANCE OF PAYMENTS
(US $ million)

	2005	2006	2007
Exports of goods f.o.b.	46,971	58,633	62,845
Imports of goods f.o.b.	−14,238	−14,329	−16,700
Trade balance	32,733	44,304	46,145
Services (net)	−3,884	−3,247	−4,924
Balance on goods and services	28,849	41,057	41,221
Other income received	9,414	14,664	17,802
Other income paid	−555	−1,413	−2,215
Balance on goods, services and income	37,708	54,308	56,808
Current transfers (net)	−3,401	−3,257	−4,074
Current balance	34,308	51,050	52,734
Capital account (net)	797	881	1,186
Direct investment abroad	−5,144	−7,951	−10,395
Direct investment from abroad	250	138	110
Portfolio investment assets	−10,006	−25,756	−37,701
Portfolio investment liabilities	−542	102	402
Other investment (net)	−15,712	−14,388	−5,700
Net errors and omissions	−3,308	−439	2,653
Overall balance	643	3,638	3,290

Source: IMF, *Kuwait: Statistical Appendix* (June 2008).

External Trade

PRINCIPAL COMMODITIES
(distribution by SITC, KD million)

Imports c.i.f.	2002	2003	2004
Food and live animals	382.9	432.3	462.2
Chemicals and related products	238.6	270.6	325.2
Basic manufactures	510.5	593.3	763.8
Machinery and transport equipment	1,089.5	1,368.3	1,511.1
Miscellaneous manufactured articles	378.1	443.8	487.3
Total (incl. others)	2,735.8	3,274.1	3,722.2

Exports f.o.b.	2002	2003	2004
Mineral fuels, lubricants, etc.	4,276	n.a.	n.a.
Petroleum, petroleum products, etc.*	4,273	5,832	5,430
Chemicals and related products	248	n.a.	321
Total (incl. others)*	4,666	6,495	8,867

*Estimates by the Central Bank of Kuwait.

2005 (KD million): Total imports 4,613.9; Total exports 13,101.6 (Petroleum, petroleum products, etc. 12,392.6).

2006 (KD million): Total imports 5,000.5; Total exports 16,252.9 (Petroleum, petroleum products, etc. 15,429.7).

2007 (KD million): Total imports 5,993.4; Total exports 17,678.0 (Petroleum, petroleum products, etc. 16,780.0).

PRINCIPAL TRADING PARTNERS
(KD million)*

Imports c.i.f.	2002	2003	2004
Australia	103.3	108.6	94.4
Brazil	25.0	35.1	40.6
Canada	41.3	48.9	48.6
China, People's Repub.	142.4	187.1	252.3
France (incl. Monaco)	88.0	95.2	113.7
Germany	255.1	336.4	426.4
India	106.4	122.7	157.8
Iran	43.8	56.5	62.5
Italy	153.0	168.0	202.3
Japan	292.4	322.9	238.4
Korea, Repub.	70.0	81.4	103.9
Malaysia	36.8	40.4	47.1
Netherlands	44.1	44.9	55.9
Saudi Arabia	176.5	222.1	294.9
Spain	43.3	48.3	48.8
Switzerland-Liechtenstein	39.5	41.7	49.8
Syria	27.4	17.4	21.6
Taiwan	31.2	34.9	42.7
Thailand	33.6	35.4	42.3
Turkey	56.3	66.6	95.6
United Arab Emirates	96.5	121.7	167.1
United Kingdom	122.0	146.1	151.2
USA	299.7	380.5	400.2
Total (incl. others)	2,735.8	3,274.1	3,722.2

Exports f.o.b.†	2002	2003	2004
Bahrain	7.7	12.5	10.5
Belgium-Luxembourg	5.7	3.1	2.0
China, People's Repub.	23.9	25.0	22.5
Egypt	10.6	12.0	13.1
India	25.1	29.4	31.5
Indonesia	39.5	37.3	51.2
Iran	7.8	6.8	6.4
Japan	5.8	2.4	1.0
Jordan	9.1	11.5	13.7
Korea, Repub.	0.7	1.0	1.8
Lebanon	5.5	4.7	8.3
Malaysia	7.0	5.7	1.3
Oman	6.5	5.5	6.2
Pakistan	17.6	24.0	39.0
Philippines	8.7	7.0	4.4
Qatar	11.1	9.6	10.0
Saudi Arabia	52.4	68.3	61.1
Spain	15.7	7.7	8.2
Syria	8.3	11.1	13.9
Taiwan	4.0	3.5	4.6
Turkey	8.0	4.6	2.9
United Arab Emirates	41.9	49.7	56.5
USA	2.9	27.7	32.0
Total (incl. others)	393.4	498.5	567.0

* Imports by country of production; exports by country of last consignment.
† Excluding petroleum exports.

Transport

ROAD TRAFFIC
(motor vehicles in use at 31 December)

	1995	1996	1997
Passenger cars	662,946	701,172	747,042
Buses and coaches	11,937	12,322	13,094
Goods vehicles	116,813	121,753	127,386

1999: Buses and coaches 12,775; Goods vehicles 97,706.

2000: Buses and coaches 10,974; Goods vehicles 80,378.

2001: Passenger cars 715,000; Commercial vehicles 226,000.

2004: Passenger cars, 858,055; Buses and coaches, 37,789; Commercial vehicles, 143,151.

SHIPPING

Merchant Fleet
(registered at 31 December)

	2005	2006	2007
Number of vessels	222	220	212
Displacement ('000 grt)	2,315.7	2,156.8	2,426.8

Source: Lloyd's Register-Fairplay, *World Fleet Statistics*.

International Sea-borne Freight Traffic
('000 metric tons)*

	1988	1989	1990
Goods loaded	61,778	69,097	51,400
Goods unloaded	7,123	7,015	4,522

* Including Kuwait's share of traffic in the Neutral/Partitioned Zone.

Source: UN, *Monthly Bulletin of Statistics*.

Goods loaded ('000 metric tons): 89,945 in 1997.

Goods unloaded ('000 metric tons): 746 in 1991 (July–December only); 2,537 in 1992; 4,228 in 1993; 5,120 in 1994; 5,854 in 1995; 6,497 in 1996; 6,049 in 1997.

CIVIL AVIATION
(traffic on scheduled services)

	2001	2002	2003
Kilometres flown (million)	37	41	39
Passengers carried ('000)	2,085	2,299	2,186
Passenger-km (million)	6,010	6,706	6,311
Total ton-km (million)	777	867	795

Source: UN, *Statistical Yearbook*.

Tourism

VISITOR ARRIVALS BY COUNTRY OF ORIGIN
(incl. excursionists)

	2002	2003	2004
Bahrain	74,979	77,512	84,934
Bangladesh	75,423	90,327	111,060
Egypt	256,867	289,401	327,460
India	314,054	363,724	413,109
Iran	99,066	100,474	121,642
Lebanon	61,687	63,735	74,629
Pakistan	84,224	111,055	123,128
Philippines	56,335	60,264	73,656
Saudi Arabia	725,025	777,831	896,102
Sri Lanka	62,586	63,269	62,676
Syria	176,375	185,946	234,726
Total (incl. others)	2,315,568	2,602,300	3,056,093

Tourism receipts (US $ million, incl. passenger transport): 330 in 2003; 413 in 2004; 408 in 2005.

Source: World Tourism Organization.

Communications Media

	2004	2005	2006
Telephones ('000 main lines in use)	497.0	510.3	517.0
Mobile cellular telephones ('000 subscribers)	2,000.0	2,277.0	2,530.0
Personal computers ('000 in use)	450	600	n.a.
Internet users ('000)	600	700	800

1996: Daily newspapers 8 (average circulation 635,000 copies); Non-daily newspapers 78.

1999: Radio receivers 1,200,000 in use; Television receivers 910,000 in use; Facsimile machines 60,000 in use; Book titles published 219.

2000: Television receivers 930,000 in use.

2004: Daily newspapers 8; Non-daily newspapers 91.

Mobile cellular telephones ('000 subscribers): 2,773.7 in 2007.

Internet users ('000): 900.0 in 2007.

Broadband subscribers ('000): 25.0 in 2005.

Sources: UNESCO, *Statistical Yearbook*; UN, *Statistical Yearbook*; International Telecommunication Union.

Education

(state-controlled schools, 2000/01)

	Schools	Teachers	Males	Females	Total
Kindergarten	153	3,379	22,142	22,128	44,270
Primary	184	8,151	48,796	49,322	98,118
Intermediate	165	9,073	47,955	47,509	95,464
Secondary	117	9,234	34,868	41,353	76,221
Religious institutes	7	351	n.a.	n.a.	2,454
Special training institutes	33	756	n.a.	n.a.	543

Private education (1996/97): 63 kindergarten schools (598 teachers, 12,172 students); 80 primary schools (2,341 teachers, 47,111 students); 82 intermediate schools (1,860 teachers, 36,254 students); 66 secondary schools (1,576 teachers, 20,932 students).

2000/01 (private education): 112 schools; 7,324 teachers; 128,204 students.

2005/06: *Teaching staff:* kindergarten 5,420, primary 20,056, secondary general 24,328, secondary technical/vocational 114, tertiary 1,986; *Student enrolment:* kindergarten 67,060, primary 203,423, secondary general 231,236; secondary technical/vocational 5,174; tertiary 37,521 (Source: UNESCO Institute for Statistics).

Adult literacy rate (UNESCO estimates): 93.9% (males 94.9%; females 92.2%) in 2007 (Source: UNESCO Institute for Statistics).

Directory

The Constitution

The principal provisions of the Constitution, promulgated on 16 November 1962, are set out below. On 29 August 1976 the Amir suspended four articles of the Constitution dealing with the National Assembly, the Majlis al-Umma. On 24 August 1980 the Amir issued a decree ordering the establishment of an elected legislature before the end of February 1981. The new Majlis was elected on 23 February, and fresh legislative elections followed on 20 February 1985. The Majlis was dissolved by Amiri decree in July 1986, and some sections of the Constitution, including the stipulation that new elections should be held within two months of dissolving the legislature (see below), were suspended. A new Majlis was elected on 5 October 1992 and convened on 20 October. In 2005 the Majlis approved legislation allowing women to vote in and stand as candidates for parliamentary and local elections.

SOVEREIGNTY

Kuwait is an independent sovereign Arab State; its sovereignty may not be surrendered, and no part of its territory may be relinquished. Offensive war is prohibited by the Constitution.

Succession as Amir is restricted to heirs of the late Mubarak as-Sabah, and an Heir Apparent must be appointed within one year of the accession of a new Amir.

EXECUTIVE AUTHORITY

Executive power is vested in the Amir, who exercises it through the Council of Ministers. The Amir will appoint the Prime Minister 'after the traditional consultations', and will appoint and dismiss ministers on the recommendation of the Prime Minister. Ministers need not be members of the Majlis al-Umma, although all ministers who are not members of parliament assume membership ex officio in the legislature for the duration of office. The Amir also formulates laws, which shall not be effective unless published in the *Official Gazette*. The Amir establishes public institutions. All decrees issued in these respects shall be conveyed to the Majlis. No law is issued unless it is approved by the Majlis.

LEGISLATURE

A National Assembly, the Majlis al-Umma, of 50 members is elected for a four-year term by all natural-born Kuwaitis over the age of 21 years, except servicemen and police, who may not vote. (Unelected cabinet ministers also sit in the Majlis, bringing the total membership to around 65.) Candidates for election must possess the franchise, be over 30 years of age and literate. The Majlis will convene for at least eight months in any year, and new elections shall be held within two months of the last dissolution of the outgoing legislature.

Restrictions on the commercial activities of ministers include an injunction forbidding them to sell property to the Government.

The Amir may ask for reconsideration of a bill that has been approved by the Majlis and sent to him for ratification, but the bill would automatically become law if it were subsequently adopted by a two-thirds' majority at the next sitting, or by a simple majority at a subsequent sitting. The Amir may declare martial law, but only with the approval of the legislature.

The Majlis may adopt a vote of no confidence in a minister, in which case the minister must resign. Such a vote is not permissible in the case of the Prime Minister, but the legislature may approach the Amir on the matter, and the Amir shall then either dismiss the Prime Minister or dissolve the Majlis.

CIVIL SERVICE

Entry to the civil service is confined to Kuwaiti citizens.

PUBLIC LIBERTIES

Kuwaitis are equal before the law in prestige, rights and duties. Individual freedom is guaranteed. No one shall be seized, arrested or exiled except within the rules of law.

No punishment shall be administered except for an act or abstaining from an act considered a crime in accordance with a law applicable at the time of committing it, and no penalty shall be imposed more severe than that which could have been imposed at the time of committing the crime.

Freedom of opinion is guaranteed to everyone, and each has the right to express himself through speech, writing or other means within the limits of the law.

The press is free within the limits of the law, and it should not be suppressed except in accordance with the dictates of law.

Freedom of performing religious rites is protected by the State according to prevailing customs, provided it does not violate the public order and morality.

Trade unions will be permitted and property must be respected. An owner is not banned from managing his property except within the boundaries of law. No property should be taken from anyone, except within the prerogatives of law, unless a just compensation be given.

Houses may not be entered, except in cases provided by law. Every Kuwaiti has freedom of movement and choice of place of residence within the State. This right shall not be controlled except in cases stipulated by law.

Every person has the right to education and freedom to choose his type of work. Freedom to form peaceful societies is guaranteed within the limits of law.

The Government

HEAD OF STATE

Amir of Kuwait: His Highness Sheikh SABAH AL-AHMAD AL-JABER AS-SABAH (acceded 29 January 2006).

COUNCIL OF MINISTERS
(April 2009)

The entire Council of Ministers resigned in March 2009, following a dispute with members of the Majlis al-Umma (National Assembly—see Legislature); two days later Sheikh Sabah ordered the dissolution of parliament. The Council of Ministers remained in place pending an early election, which was conducted on 16 May.

Prime Minister: Sheikh NASSER AL-MUHAMMAD AL-AHMAD AS-SABAH.

First Deputy Prime Minister and Minister of Defence: Sheikh JABER MUBARAK AL-HAMAD AS-SABAH.

Deputy Prime Minister and Minister of Foreign Affairs: Sheikh Dr MUHAMMAD SABAH AS-SALIM AS-SABAH.

Deputy Prime Minister and Minister of State for Cabinet Affairs: FAISAL MUHAMMAD AL-HAJJI BUKHADHOUR.

Minister of the Interior: Lt-Gen. Sheikh JABER KHALID AL-JABER AS-SABAH.

Minister of Finance: MUSTAFA JASSEM ASH-SHIMALI.

Minister of Commerce and Industry and Minister of State for National Assembly Affairs: AHMAD YAQOUB BAQER AL-ABDULLAH.

Minister of Electricity and Water and of Communications: NABIL KHALAF SAEED BIN SALAMA.

Minister of Oil: Sheikh AHMAD ABDULLAH AS-SABAH.

Minister of Public Works and Minister of State for Municipal Affairs: Dr FADHIL SAFAR ALI SAFAR.

Minister of Education and Higher Education: NOURIYA SUBEEH BARRAK AS-SUBEEH.

Minister of Social Affairs and Labour: BADER FAHAD ALI AD-DUWAILA.

Minister of Information and Acting Minister of Justice and of Awqaf (Religious Endowments) and Islamic Affairs: Sheikh SABAH KHALID AL-HAMAD AS-SABAH.

Minister of State for Housing Affairs and for Development Affairs and Acting Minister of Health: Dr MOUDHI ABD AL-AZIZ AL-HOMOUD.

PROVINCIAL GOVERNORS

Al-Ahmadi: Sheikh Dr IBRAHIM AD-DUAIJ AL-IBRAHIM AS-SABAH.
Farwaniya: ABD AL-HAMID HAJJI ABD AR-RAHIM.
Mubarak al-Kabir: Sheikh ALI ABDULLAH AS-SALIM AS-SABAH.
Hawalli: ABDULLAH ABD AR-RAHMAN AL-FARIS.
Al-Jahra: Sheikh MUBARAK AL-HUMOUD AS-SABAH.
Kuwait (Capital): Sheikh ALI JABER AL-AHMAD AS-SABAH.

MINISTRIES

Diwan of the Prime Minister: POB 1397, 13014 Kuwait City; tel. 22000000; fax 22223150; e-mail info@pm.gov.kw; internet www.pm.gov.kw.

Ministry of Awqaf (Religious Endowments) and Islamic Affairs: POB 13, 13001 Safat, Kuwait City; tel. 22487225; internet www.islam.gov.kw.

Ministry of Commerce and Industry: POB 2944, 13030 Safat, Kuwait City; tel. 2248000; fax 22424411; e-mail admin@moci.gov.kw; internet www.moci.gov.kw.

Ministry of Communications: POB 15, 13001 Safat, Kuwait City; tel. 24840606; internet www.moc.kw.

KUWAIT

Ministry of Defence: POB 1170, 13012 Safat, Kuwait City; tel. 24848300; fax 24846059; e-mail it@mod.gov.kw; internet www.mod.gov.kw.

Ministry of Education: POB 7, 13001 Safat, Hilali St, Kuwait City; tel. 24839452; fax 22423676; e-mail webmaster@moe.edu.kw; internet www.moe.edu.kw.

Ministry of Electricity and Water: POB 12, 13001 Safat, Kuwait City; tel. 25371000; fax 25371420; internet www.mew.gov.kw.

Ministry of Finance: POB 9, 13001 Safat, al-Morkab St, Ministries Complex, Kuwait City; tel. 22480000; fax 22404025; e-mail webmaster@mof.gov.kw; internet www.mof.gov.kw.

Ministry of Foreign Affairs: POB 3, 13001 Safat, Gulf St, Kuwait City; tel. 22425141; fax 22420429; e-mail emad@mofa.org; internet www.mofa.gov.kw.

Ministry of Health: POB 5, 13001 Safat, Arabian Gulf St, Kuwait City; tel. 24863840; fax 24863485; e-mail health@moh.gov.kw; internet www.moh.gov.kw.

Ministry of Higher Education: tel. 24925177; fax 24925260; e-mail info_minister@mohe.edu.kw; internet www.mohe.edu.kw.

Ministry of Information: POB 193, 13002 Safat, as-Sour St, Kuwait City; tel. 22415301; fax 22419642; e-mail info@moinfo.gov.kw; internet www.moinfo.gov.kw.

Ministry of the Interior: POB 11, 13001 Safat, Kuwait City; tel. 22430500; fax 22561268; e-mail contact@moi.gov.kw; internet www.moi.gov.kw.

Ministry of Justice: POB 6, 13001 Safat, al-Morkab St, Ministries Complex, Kuwait City; tel. 22486012; fax 22442257; e-mail info@moj.gov.kw; internet www.moj.gov.kw.

Ministry of Oil: POB 5077, 13051 Safat, Kuwait City; tel. 22406990; e-mail alnaft@moo.gov.kw; internet www.moo.gov.kw.

Ministry of Planning: POB 15, 13001 Safat, Kuwait City; tel. 22428200; fax 22430403; e-mail info@mop.gov.kw; internet www.mop.gov.kw.

Ministry of Public Works: POB 8, 13001 Safat, Kuwait City; tel. 25385520; fax 25380829; e-mail undersecretary@mpw.gov.kw; internet www.mpw.gov.kw.

Ministry of Social Affairs and Labour: POB 563, 13006 Safat, Kuwait City; tel. 22480000; fax 22419877; internet www.mosal.gov.kw.

Legislature

MAJLIS AL-UMMA
(National Assembly)

Speaker: JASEM AL-KHARAFI.

Elections to the 50-seat Majlis took place three years early on 16 May 2009, following the dissolution of parliament in March by Sheikh Sabah (precipitated by a continuing dispute between the Government and parliament over the accountability of the Prime Minister). Sunni Islamists retained only 11 seats, Shi'ite Islamists took nine; liberals and their allies secured eight; and the remaining seats were won by independent candidates. Among the incoming deputies were four women, the first to win election to the Kuwaiti legislature.

Political Organizations

Political parties are not permitted in Kuwait. However, several quasi-political organizations are in existence. Among those that have been represented in the Majlis since 1992 are:

Constitutional Group: supported by merchants.

Islamic Constitutional Movement (Hadas): internet www.icmkw.org; f. 1991; Sunni Muslim; political arm of the Muslim Brotherhood; Spokesman MUHAMMAD ABDULLAH HADI AL-OLAIM.

Islamic Salafi Alliance: Sunni Muslim; Leader KHALID SULTAN BIN ESSA.

Justice and Peace Alliance: Shi'a Muslim.

Kuwait Democratic Forum: f. 1991; loose asscn of secular, liberal and Arab nationalist groups; campaigned for the extension of voting rights to women.

National Action Bloc: Liberal, nationalist.

National Democratic Alliance (NDA): f. 1997; secular, liberal; Sec.-Gen. KHALID AL-FADALAH.

National Islamic Alliance: Shi'a Muslim.

Popular Action Bloc: loose asscn of nationalists and Shi'a Muslims; Leader AHMAD AS-SAADOUN.

Salafeen (Islamic Popular Movement): Sunni Muslim.

Diplomatic Representation

EMBASSIES IN KUWAIT

Afghanistan: POB 33186, 73452 Rawdah, Block 6, Surra St, Across Surra Co-op Society House 16, Kuwait City; tel. 25329461; fax 25326274; e-mail afg_emb_kuw@hotmail.com; Ambassador YOUSUF SAMAD.

Algeria: POB 578, 13006 Safat, Istiqlal St, Kuwait City; tel. 24820791; fax 24820853; e-mail ambalgkt@qualitynet.net; Ambassador MUHAMMAD BURUBA.

Argentina: POB 3788, 40188 Mishref, Kuwait City; tel. 25379211; fax 25379212; e-mail ekuwa@mrecic.gov.ar; Ambassador RICARDO E. INSUA.

Australia: Dar al-Awadi Complex (Level 12), Ahmad al-Jaber St, Sharq, Kuwait City; tel. 22322422; fax 22322430; e-mail austemb.kuwait@dfat.go.au; internet www.kuwait.embassy.gov.au; Ambassador GLENN MILES.

Austria: POB 15013, Daiyah, Area 3, Shawki St, House 10, 35451 Kuwait City; tel. 22552532; fax 22563052; e-mail kuwait-ob@bmaa.gv.at; Ambassador MARIAN VERBA.

Azerbaijan: Al-Yarmouk, Block No. 2, St 1, Bldg 15, Kuwait City; tel. 25355247; fax 25355246; e-mail embazerbaijan@yahoo.com; internet www.azerembassy-kuwait.org; Ambassador SHAHIN ABDULLAYEV.

Bahrain: POB 196, 13002 Safat, Area 6, Surra Rd, Villa 35, Kuwait City; tel. 25318530; fax 25330882; e-mail Kuwait.mission@mofa.gov.bh; Ambassador Sheikh KHALIFA BIN HAMAD AL-KHALIFA.

Bangladesh: POB 22344, 13084 Safat, Khaldya, Block 6, Ali bin Abi Taleb St, House 361, Kuwait City; tel. 25316042; fax 25316041; e-mail bdoot@ncc.moc.kw; Ambassador ABDELLATIF ALI AL-MAWASH.

Belgium: POB 3280, 13033 Safat, Baghdad St, Block 8, House 15, Kuwait City; tel. 25722014; fax 25748389; e-mail kuwait@diplobel.org; internet www.diplomatie.be/kuwait; Ambassador GILLES HEYVAERT.

Bhutan: POB 1510, 13016 Safat, Adailiya-Block 3, Issa Abd ar-Rahman al-Assoussi St, Jadda 32, Villa 7, Kuwait City; tel. 22516640; fax 22516550; e-mail bhutankuwait@hotmail.com; Ambassador SHERUB TENZIN.

Bosnia and Herzegovina: POB 6131, 32036 Hawalli, Bayan, Block 3, St 1, House 46, Kuwait City; tel. 25392637; fax 25392106; Ambassador JASIN RAVAŚDE.

Brazil: POB 39761, 73058 Nuzha, Block 2, St 1, Jadah 1, Villa 8, Kuwait City; tel. 25328610; fax 25328613; e-mail brasemkw@qualitynet.net; internet www.brazilianembassykw.com; Ambassador MARIO DA GRAÇA ROITER.

Bulgaria: POB 12090, 71651 Shamiya, Jabriya, Block 11, St 107 and St 1, Villa 272, Kuwait City; tel. 25314458; fax 25321453; e-mail bgembkw@fasttelco.com; internet www.mfa.bg/kuwait; Ambassador ILKO SHIVACHEV.

Canada: POB 25281, 13113 Safat, Daiyah, Area 4, 24 al-Mutawakkel St, Kuwait City; tel. 22563025; fax 22560173; e-mail kwait@international.gc.ca; internet www.dfait-maeci.gc.ca/kuwait; Ambassador J. REID HENRY.

China, People's Republic: POB 2346, 13024 Safat, Yarmouk, Sheikh Ahmad al-Jaber Bldgs 4 & 5, St 1, Villa 82, Kuwait City; tel. 25333340; fax 25333341; e-mail chinaemb_kw@mfa.gov.cn; Ambassador HUANG JIEMIN.

Czech Republic: al-Nuzha, Block 3, St 34, Bldg 13, Kuwait City; tel. 22529018; fax 22529021; e-mail kuwait@embassy.mzv.cz; internet www.mzv.cz/kuwait; Ambassador MARTIN VÁVRA.

Egypt: POB 11252, 35153 Dasmah, Istiqlal St, Kuwait City; tel. 22519955; fax 22563877; e-mail egyptembkwt@yahoo.com; Ambassador TAHER AHMED FARAHAT.

Eritrea: POB 53016, 73015 Nuzha, Jabriya, Block 9, St 21, House 9, Kuwait City; tel. 25317427; fax 26631304; Ambassador MAHMOUD OMAR CHURUM.

Ethiopia: POB 939, 45710 Safat, Jabriya, Block 10, St 107, Villa 30, Kuwait City; tel. 25330128; fax 25331179; e-mail ethiokwt@qualitynet.net; Ambassador KADAFOU MUHAMMAD HANFARY.

France: POB 1037, 13011 Safat, Mansouriah, Block 1, St 13, Villa 24, Kuwait City; tel. 22582020; fax 22571058; e-mail cad.koweit-amba@diplomatie.gouv.fr; internet www.ambafrance-kwt.org; Ambassador JEAN-RENÉ GEHAN.

Georgia: Qurtoba, Block 2, Area 1, Ave 3, Villa 6, Kuwait City; tel. 25352909; fax 25354707; e-mail kuwait.emb@mfa.gov.ge; Ambassador GOCHA JAPARIDZE.

Germany: POB 805, 13009 Safat, Dahiya Abdullah as-Salem, Area 1, Ave 14, Villa 13, Kuwait City; tel. 22520827; fax 22520763; e-mail info@kuwait.diplo.de; internet www.kuwait.diplo.de; Ambassador Dr MICHAEL WORBS.

KUWAIT

Greece: POB 23812, 13099 Safat, Khaldiya, Block 4, St 44, House 4, Kuwait City; tel. 24817100; fax 24817103; e-mail gremb.kuw@mfa.gr; Ambassador KONSTANTINOS DRAKAKIS.

Hungary: POB 23955, 13100 Safat, Bayan, Block 13, St 13, Villa 381, Kuwait City; tel. 25379351; fax 25379350; e-mail huembkwi@quality.net; internet www.mfa.gov.hu/emb/kuwait; Ambassador JÁNOS HÓVÁRI.

India: POB 1450, 13015 Safat, Diplomatic Enclave, Arabian Gulf St, Kuwait City; tel. 22530600; fax 22525811; e-mail contact@indembkwt.org; internet www.indembkwt.org; Ambassador AJAI MALHOTRA.

Indonesia: POB 21500, 13076 Safat, Kaifan, Block 6, Al-Andalus St, House 29, Kuwait City; tel. 24839927; fax 24819250; e-mail unitkom@kbrikuwait.org; internet www.kbrikuwait.org; Ambassador SUDIRMAN FAISAL ISMAIL.

Iran: POB 4686, 13047 Safat, Daiyah, Embassies Area, Block B, Kuwait City; tel. 22560694; fax 22529868; e-mail iranebassy@hotmail.com; Ambassador ALI JANNATI.

Italy: POB 4453, 13045 Safat, Kuwait City; tel. 25356010; fax 25356030; e-mail ambasciata.alkuwait@esteri.it; internet www.ambalkuwait.esteri.it; Ambassador ENRICO GRANARA.

Japan: POB 2304, 13024 Safat, Jabriya, Area 9, Plot 496, St 101, Kuwait City; tel. and fax 25326168; e-mail info@embjp-kw.org; internet www.kw.emb-japan.go.jp; Ambassador MASATOSHI MUTO.

Jordan: POB 39891, 73059 Kuwait City; tel. 22533261; fax 22533270; e-mail kujor@qualitynet.net; Ambassador JUMAA AL-ABBADI.

Korea, Republic: POB 4272, 13043 Safat, Kuwait City; tel. 25339601; fax 25312459; e-mail kuwait@mofat.go.kr; internet kwt.mofat.go.kr/index.jsp; Ambassador YOUNG-HAN MOON.

Lebanon: POB 253, 13003 Safat, Da'Yiah Diplomatic Area Plot 6, Kuwait City; tel. 22562103; fax 22571682; Ambassador Dr BASSEM ABD AL-QADIR AN-NO'MANI.

Libya: POB 21460, 13075 Safat, 27 Istiqlal St, Kuwait City; tel. 22575183; fax 22575182; Chargé d'affaires ALI JAFFERE.

Malaysia: POB 4105, 13042 Safat, Daiya, Diplomatic Enclave, Area 5, Istiqlal St, Plot 5, Kuwait City; tel. 22550394; fax 22550384; e-mail malkuwait@kln.gov.my; internet www.kln.gov.my/perwakilan/kuwait; Ambassador Dato' ASHAARY BIN SANI.

Morocco: Yarmouk, Block 2, St 2, Villa 14, Kuwait City; tel. 25312980; fax 25317423; e-mail ambkow@yahoo.fr; Ambassador MUHAMMAD BELAICHE.

Netherlands: POB 21822, 13079 Safat, Jabriya, Area 9, St 1, Plot 40A, Kuwait City; tel. 25312650; fax 25326334; e-mail kwe@minbuza.nl; internet www.netherlandsembassy.gov.kw; Ambassador TON BOON VAN OCHSSÉE.

Niger: POB 44451, 32059 Hawalli, Salwa Block 12, St 6, Villa 183, Kuwait City; tel. 25652943; fax 25640478; Ambassador ASSOUMANE GUIAOURI.

Nigeria: POB 6432, 32039 Hawalli, Surra, Area 1, St 14, House 24, Kuwait City; tel. 18278813; fax 18278896; Ambassador MUHAMMAD ADAMU JUMBA.

Oman: POB 21975, 13080 Safat, al-Odeilia Block 3, St 3, Villa 25, Kuwait City; tel. 22561956; fax 22561963; Ambassador SAEED IBN ALI AL-KALBANI.

Pakistan: POB 988, 13010 Safat, Jabriya, Police Station Rd, St 101, Plot 5, Block 11, Villa 7, Kuwait City; tel. 25327649; fax 25328013; e-mail pavepkw@pakembkw.org; internet www.pakembkw.org; Chargé d'affaires a.i. SAJJAD AHMED SEEHAR.

Philippines: POB 26288, 13123 Safat, Area 7, No. 103, Villa 503 Jabriya, Kuwait City; tel. 25349099; fax 25329319; e-mail kuwaitpe@dfa.gov.ph; internet www.philembassykuwait.gov.kw; Ambassador RICARDO M. ENDAYA.

Poland: POB 5066, 13051 Safat, Jabriya, Plot 7, St 3, House 20, Kuwait City; tel. 25311571; fax 25311576; e-mail embassy@kuwejt.polemb.net; internet www.kuwejt.polemb.net; Ambassador JANUSZ SZWEDO.

Qatar: POB 1825, 13019 Safat, Diiyah, Istiqlal St, Kuwait City; tel. 22523107; fax 22513604; e-mail kuwait@mofa.gov.qa; Ambassador ABD AL-AZIZ BIN SAAD AL-FEHAID.

Romania: POB 11149, 35152 Dasmah, Keifan, Area 4, Moona St, House 34, Kuwait City; tel. 24845079; fax 24848929; e-mail ambsa@kems.net; Ambassador CONSTANTIN VOLODEA NISTOR.

Russia: POB 1765 Safat, Daya Diplomatic Area, Block 17, Kuwait City; tel. 22560427; fax 22524969; e-mail rospos@kuwait.net; Ambassador AZAMAT R. KULMUKHAMETOV.

Saudi Arabia: POB 20498, 13065 Safat, Istiqlal St, Kuwait City; tel. 22550021; fax 22420654; Ambassador ABD AL-AZIZ AL-FAYEZ.

Senegal: POB 23892, 13099 Safat, Rawdah, Block 3, St 35, House 9, Kuwait City; tel. 22573477; fax 22542044; e-mail senegal_embassy@yahoo.com; internet www.diplomatie.gouv.sn/maeuase/ambassene_koweit.htm; Ambassador ABDOU LAHAD MBACKE.

Serbia: POB 20511, 13066 Safat, Jabriya, Block 7, St 12, Villa 3, Kuwait City; tel. 25327548; fax 25327568; e-mail embrskw@qualitynet.net; internet www.mfa.gov.yu/Embassies/kuvajt/kuvajt_e.html; Chargé d'affaires a.i. ZLATAN MALTARIĆ.

Somalia: POB 22766, 13088 Safat, Bayan, St 1, Block 7, Villa 25, Kuwait City; tel. 25394795; fax 25394829; e-mail soamin1@hotmail.com; Ambassador ABDUL KHADIR AMIN SHEIKH ABUBAKER.

South Africa: POB 2262, 40173 Mishref, Salwa Block 10, St 1, Villa 91, Unit 3, Kuwait City; tel. 25617988; fax 25617917; e-mail saemb@southafricaq8.com; internet www.southafricaq8.com; Ambassador ASHRAF SULIMAN.

Spain: POB 22207, 13083 Safat, Surra, Block 3, St 14, Villa 19, Kuwait City; tel. 25325827; fax 25325826; e-mail embespkw@mail.mae.es; Ambassador MANUEL GÓMEZ DE VALENZUELA.

Sri Lanka: Jabriya, Block 10, St 107, Villa 1, Kuwait City; tel. 25339140; fax 25339154; e-mail lankaemb@qualitynet.net; internet www.slembkwt.org; Ambassador K. S. C. DISSANAYAKE.

Switzerland: POB 23954, 13100 Safat, Qortuba, Block 2, St 1, Villa 122, Kuwait City; tel. 25340172; fax 25340176; e-mail kow.vertretung@eda.admin.ch; internet www.eda.admin.ch/kuwait; Ambassador MICHEL GOTTRET.

Syria: POB 25600, 13116 Safat, Kuwait City; tel. 25396560; fax 25396509; Ambassador ALI ABD AL-KARIM.

Thailand: POB 66647, 43757 Bayan, Block 6, St 8, Villa 1, Jabriya, Kuwait City; tel. 25317530; fax 25317532; e-mail thaiemkw@kems.net; internet www.mfa.go.th/web/1319.php?depid=217; Ambassador SURAPOL KOTESRIMUANG.

Tunisia: POB 5976, 13060 Safat, Nuzha, Plot 2, Nuzha St, Villa 45, Kuwait City; tel. 2542144; fax 2528995; e-mail tunemrku@ncc.moc.kw; Ambassador HICHEM BAYOUDH.

Turkey: POB 20627, 13067 Safat, Block 16, Plot 10, Istiqlal St, Kuwait City; tel. 22531466; fax 22560653; e-mail turkish_embassy_kuwait@hotmail.com; internet kuveyt.be.fscnet.net; Ambassador ŞAKIR FAKILI.

Ukraine: POB 7588, 32096 Hawalli, Jabriya, Block 10, St 6, House 5, Kuwait City; tel. 25318507; fax 25318508; e-mail emb_kw@mfa.gov.ua; internet www.mfa.gov.ua/kuwait; Chargé d'affaires a.i. SERHIY A. PUSHARSKY.

United Arab Emirates: POB 1828, 13019 Safat, Plot 70, Istiqlal St, Kuwait City; tel. 22528544; fax 22526382; Ambassador YOUSUF A. AL-ANSARI.

United Kingdom: POB 2, 13001 Safat, Arabian Gulf St, Kuwait City; tel. 22594320; fax 22594339; e-mail kuwait.generalenquiries@fco.gov.uk; internet ukinkuwait.fco.gov.uk; Ambassador MICHAEL ARON.

USA: POB 77, 13001 Safat, Bayan, Al-Masjed al-Aqsa St, Plot 14, Block 14, Kuwait City; tel. 22591001; fax 25380282; e-mail paskuwaitm@state.gov; internet kuwait.usembassy.gov; Ambassador DEBORAH K. JONES.

Uzbekistan: Kuwait City; Ambassador ABDURAFIK A. HOSHIMOV.

Venezuela: POB 24440, 13105 Safat, Block 5, St 7, Area 356, Surra, Kuwait City; tel. 25324367; fax 25324368; e-mail embavene@qualitynet.net; Ambassador ELOY FERNÁNDEZ AZUAJE.

Yemen: POB 7182, Al-Jabriya St, Kuwait City; tel. 25349416; fax 25349415; Ambassador Dr ALI AL-AHMADI.

Zimbabwe: POB 36484, 24755 Salmiya, Kuwait City; tel. 25620845; fax 25621491; e-mail zimkuwait@hotmail.com; Ambassador MARK GREY MARONGWE.

Judicial System

SPECIAL JUDICIARY

Constitutional Court: Comprises five judges. Interprets the provisions of the Constitution; considers disputes regarding the constitutionality of legislation, decrees and rules; has jurisdiction in challenges relating to the election of members, or eligibility for election, to the Majlis al-Umma.

ORDINARY JUDICIARY

Court of Cassation: Comprises five judges. Is competent to consider the legality of verdicts of the Court of Appeal and State Security Court; Chief Justice MUHAMMAD YOUSUF AR-RIFA'I.

Court of Appeal: Comprises three judges. Considers verdicts of the Court of First Instance; Chief Justice RASHED AL-HAMMAD.

Court of First Instance: Comprises the following divisions: Civil and Commercial (one judge), Personal Status Affairs (one judge), Lease (three judges), Labour (one judge), Crime (three judges),

KUWAIT — Directory

Administrative Disputes (three judges), Appeal (three judges), Challenged Misdemeanours (three judges); Chief Justice MUHAMMAD AS-SAKHOBY.

Summary Courts: Each governorate has a Summary Court, comprising one or more divisions. The courts have jurisdiction in the following areas: Civil and Commercial, Urgent Cases, Lease, Misdemeanours. The verdict in each case is delivered by one judge.

There is also a **Traffic Court**, with one presiding judge.

Prosecutor-General: HAMED AL-OTHMAN.

Religion

ISLAM

The majority of Kuwaitis are Muslims of the Sunni or Shi'a sects. The Shi'ite community comprises about 30% of the total.

CHRISTIANITY

The Roman Catholic Church

Latin Rite

For ecclesiastical purposes, Kuwait forms an Apostolic Vicariate. At 31 December 2006 there were an estimated 300,000 adherents in the country.

Vicar Apostolic: CAMILLO BALLIN (Titular Bishop of Arna), Bishop's House, POB 266, 13003 Safat, Kuwait City; tel. 22434637; fax 22409981; e-mail vicariate_clergy@hotmail.com; internet www.catholic-church.org/kuwait.

Melkite Rite

The Greek-Melkite Patriarch of Antioch is resident in Damascus, Syria. The Patriarchal Exarchate of Kuwait had an estimated 800 adherents at 31 December 2005.

Exarch Patriarchal: Rev. BOUTROS GHARIB, Vicariat Patriarcal Greek-Melkite, POB 1205, Salwa Block 12, St No. 6, House 58, 22013 Salmiya, Kuwait City; tel. and fax 25652802.

Syrian Rite

The Syrian Catholic Patriarch of Antioch is resident in Beirut, Lebanon. The Patriarchal Exarchate of Basra and the Gulf, with an estimated 375 adherents at 31 December 2006, is based in Basra, Iraq.

The Anglican Communion

Within the Episcopal Church in Jerusalem and the Middle East, Kuwait forms part of the diocese of Cyprus and the Gulf. The Anglican congregation in Kuwait is entirely expatriate. The Bishop in Cyprus and the Gulf is resident in Cyprus, while the Archdeacon in the Gulf is resident in Bahrain.

Other Christian Churches

National Evangelical Church in Kuwait: POB 80, 13001 Safat, Kuwait City; tel. 22407195; fax 22431087; e-mail elc@ncc.moc.kw; Rev. NABIL ATTALLAH (pastor of the Arabic-language congregation), Rev. JERRY A. ZANDSTRA (senior pastor of the English-speaking congregation); an independent Protestant Church founded by the Reformed Church in America; services in Arabic, English, Korean, Malayalam and other Indian languages; combined weekly congregation of some 20,000.

The Armenian, Greek, Coptic and Syrian Orthodox Churches are also represented in Kuwait.

The Press

Freedom of the press and publishing is guaranteed in the Constitution, although press censorship was in force between mid-1986 and early 1992 (when journalists adopted a voluntary code of practice). In February 1995 a ruling by the Constitutional Court effectively endorsed the Government's right to suspend publication of newspapers; however, legislation passed in 2006 rendered this illegal without a court order. The Government provides financial support to newspapers and magazines.

DAILIES

Al-Anbaa (The News): POB 23915, 13100 Safat, Kuwait City; tel. 24830322; fax 24832647; e-mail editorial@alanba.com.kw; internet www.alanba.com.kw; f. 1976; Arabic; general; Editor-in-Chief BIBI KHALID AL-MARZOOQ; circ. 85,000.

Arab Times: POB 2270, Airport Road, Shuwaikh, 13023 Safat, Kuwait City; tel. 24849144; fax 24818267; e-mail arabtimes@arabtimesonline.com; internet www.arabtimesonline.com; f. 1977; English; political and financial; no Fri. edn; Editor-in-Chief AHMAD ABD AL-AZIZ AL-JARALLAH; Man. Editor MISHAL AL-JARALLAH; circ. 41,922.

Kuwait Times: POB 1301, 13014 Safat, Kuwait City; tel. 24833199; fax 24835621; e-mail info@kuwaittimes.net; internet www.kuwaittimes.net; f. 1961; English, Malayalam and Urdu; political; Editor-in-Chief ABD AR-RAHMAN ALYAN; circ. 32,000.

Al-Qabas (Firebrand): POB 21800, 13078 Safat, Kuwait City; tel. 24812822; fax 24834355; e-mail info@alqabas.com.kw; internet www.alqabas.com.kw; f. 1972; Arabic; independent; Gen. Man. FOUZAN AL-FARES; Editor-in-Chief WALEED ABD AL-LATIF AN-NISF; circ. 60,000.

Ar-Ra'i al-'Aam (Public Opinion): POB 761, 13008 Safat, Kuwait City; tel. 24817777; fax 24838352; e-mail editor@alraialaam.com; internet www.alraialaam.com; f. 1961; Arabic; political, social and cultural; Editor-in-Chief YOUSUF AL-JALAHMA; circ. 101,500.

As-Seyassah (Policy): POB 2270, Shuwaikh, Kuwait City; tel. 24813566; fax 24846905; internet www.al-seyassah.com; f. 1965; Arabic; political and financial; Editor-in-Chief AHMAD ABD AL-AZIZ AL-JARALLAH; circ. 70,000.

Al-Watan (The Homeland): POB 1142, 13012 Safat, Kuwait City; tel. 24840950; fax 24818481; e-mail alwatan@alwatan.com.kw; internet www.alwatan.com.kw; f. 1962; Arabic; political; Editor-in-Chief MUHAMMAD ABD AL-QADER AL-JASEM; Gen. Man. YOUSUF BIN JASEM; circ. 91,726.

WEEKLIES AND PERIODICALS

Al-Balagh (Communiqué): POB 4558, 13046 Safat, Kuwait City; tel. 24818820; fax 24812735; e-mail albalagh5@yahoo.com; internet www.al-balagh.com; f. 1969; weekly; Arabic; general, political and Islamic affairs; Editor-in-Chief ABD AR-RAHMAN RASHID AL-WALAYATI; circ. 29,000.

Byzance: Kuwait City; f. 2007; bi-monthly; Arabic and French; lifestyle magazine, incl. features on fashion, jewellery, furniture and art; Man. Editor JEAN-PIERRE GUEIRARD; Exec. Editor-in-Chief ANTOINE DAHER.

Ad-Dakhiliya (The Interior): POB 71655, 12500 Shamiah, Kuwait City; tel. 22410091; fax 22410609; e-mail moipr@qualitynet.net; monthly; Arabic; official reports, transactions and proceedings; publ. by Public Relations Dept, Ministry of the Interior; Editor-in-Chief Lt-Col AHMAD A. ASH-SHARQAWI.

Dalal Magazine: POB 6000, 13060 Safat, Kuwait City; tel. 24832098; fax 24832039; internet www.dalal-kw.com; f. 1997; monthly; Arabic; family affairs, beauty, fashion; Editor-in-Chief AHMAD YOUSUF BEHBEHANI.

Friday Times: POB 1301, 13014 Safat, Kuwait City; tel. 24833199; fax 24835619; e-mail info@kuwaittimes.net; internet www.kuwaittimes.net; f. 2005; weekend edn of *Kuwait Times*.

Al-Hadaf (The Objective): POB 2270, 13023 Safat, Kuwait City; tel. 24813566; fax 24816042; internet www.al-seyassah.com/alhadaf; f. 1964; weekly; Arabic; social and cultural; Editor-in-Chief AHMAD ABD AL-AZIZ AL-JARALLAH; circ. 268,904.

Hayatuna (Our Life): POB 26733, 13128 Safat, Kuwait City; tel. 22530120; fax 22530736; f. 1968; fortnightly; Arabic; medicine and hygiene; publ. by Al-Awadi Press Corpn; Editor-in-Chief ABD AR-RAHMAN AL-AWADI; circ. 6,000.

Al-Iqtisadi al-Kuwaiti (Kuwaiti Economist): POB 775, 13008 Safat, Kuwait City; tel. 1805580; fax 22412927; e-mail kcci@kcci.org.kw; internet www.kcci.org.kw; f. 1960; monthly; Arabic; commerce, trade and economics; publ. by Kuwait Chamber of Commerce and Industry; Editor MAJED B. JAMALUDDIN; circ. 6,000.

Journal of the Gulf and Arabian Peninsula Studies: POB 17073, 72451 Khaldiya, Kuwait University, Kuwait City; tel. 24833215; fax 24833705; e-mail jotgaaps@kuc01.kuniv.edu.kw; internet pubcouncil.kuniv.edu.kw/jgaps; f. 1975; quarterly; Arabic and English; publ. by Academic Publication Council of Kuwait Univ; Editor-in-Chief Dr FATIMA HUSSAIN AL-ABDULRAZZAQ.

Al-Khaleej Business Magazine: POB 25725, 13118 Safat, Kuwait City; tel. 22433765; e-mail aljabriya@gulfweb.com; Editor-in-Chief AHMAD ISMAIL BEHBEHANI.

Kuwait Medical Journal (KMJ): POB 1202, 13013 Safat, Kuwait City; tel. 25316023; fax 25312630; e-mail kmj@kma.org.kw; internet www.kma.org.kw/KMJ; f. 1967; quarterly; English; publ. by the Kuwait Medical Asscn; original articles, review articles, case reports, short communications, letters to the editor and book reviews; Editor-in-Chief Prof. FOUAD ABDULLAH M. HASSAN; circ. 10,000.

Kuwait al-Youm (Kuwait Today): POB 193, 13002 Safat, Kuwait City; tel. 24842167; fax 24831044; e-mail info@ipd.gov.kw; internet www.ipd.gov.kw; f. 1954; weekly; Arabic; statistics, Amiri decrees, laws, govt announcements, decisions, invitations for tenders, etc.; publ. by the Ministry of Information; circ. 5,000.

KUWAIT

Al-Kuwaiti (The Kuwaiti): Information Dept, POB 9758, 61008 Ahmadi, Kuwait City; tel. 23981076; fax 23983661; e-mail kocinfo@kockw.com; f. 1961; monthly journal of the Kuwait Oil Co; Arabic; Editor-in-Chief KHALED AL-KHAMEES; circ. 6,500.

The Kuwaiti Digest: Information Dept, POB 9758, 61008 Ahmadi, Kuwait City; tel. 23981076; fax 23983661; e-mail kocinfo@kockw.com; f. 1972; quarterly journal of Kuwait Oil Co; English; Editor-in-Chief KHALED AL-KHAMEES; circ. 7,000.

Al-Majaless (Meetings): POB 5605, 13057 Safat, Kuwait City; tel. 24841178; fax 24847126; e-mail qasem@almajaless.com; internet www.almajaless.com; weekly; Arabic; current affairs; Editor-in-Chief QASIM ABD AL-QADIR; circ. 60,206.

Mejallat al-Kuwait (Kuwait Magazine): POB 193, 13002 Safat, Kuwait City; tel. 22415300; fax 22419642; f. 1961; monthly; Arabic; illustrated magazine; science, arts and literature; publ. by the Ministry of Information.

Mirat al-Umma (Mirror of the Nation): POB 1142, 13012 Safat, Kuwait City; tel. 24837212; fax 24838671; weekly; Arabic; Editor-in-Chief MUHAMMAD AL-JASSEM; circ. 79,500.

An-Nahdha (The Renaissance): POB 695, 13007 Safat, Kuwait City; tel. 24813133; fax 24849298; f. 1967; weekly; Arabic; social and political; Editor-in-Chief THAMER AS-SALAH; circ. 170,000.

Osrati (My Family): POB 2995, 13030 Safat, Kuwait City; tel. 24813233; fax 24838933; e-mail info@osratimag.com; internet www.osratimag.com; f. 1978; weekly; Arabic; women's magazine; publ. by Fahad al-Marzouk Establishment; Editor GHANIMA F. AL-MARZOUK; circ. 10,500.

Sawt al-Khaleej (Voice of the Gulf): POB 659, Safat, Kuwait City; tel. 24815590; fax 24839261; f. 1962; politics and literature; Arabic; Editor-in-Chief CHRISTINE KHRAIBET; Owner BAKER ALI KHRAIBET; circ. 20,000.

At-Talia (The Ascendant): POB 1082, 13011 Safat, Kuwait City; tel. 24831200; fax 24840471; f. 1962; weekly; Arabic; politics and literature; Editor AHMAD YOUSUF AN-NAFISI; circ. 10,000.

Al-Yaqza (The Awakening): POB 6000, 13060 Safat, Kuwait City; tel. 24831318; fax 24832039; internet www.alyaqza.com; f. 1966; weekly; Arabic; political, economic, social and general; Editor-in-Chief AHMAD YOUSUF BEHBEHANI; circ. 91,340.

NEWS AGENCY

Kuwait News Agency (KUNA): POB 24063, 13101 Safat, Kuwait City; tel. 24834546; fax 24813424; e-mail kuna@kuna.net.kw; internet www.kuna.net.kw; f. 1979; public corporate body; independent; also publishes research digests on topics of common and special interest; Chair. and Dir-Gen. Sheikh MUBARAK AD-DUAIJ AS-SABAH.

PRESS ASSOCIATION

Kuwait Journalists Association: POB 5454, 13055 Safat, Kuwait City; tel. 24843351; fax 24842874; e-mail kja@kja-kw.com; internet www.kja-kw.com; Chair. AHMAD YOUSUF BEHBEHANI.

Publishers

Al-Abraj Translation and Publishing Co WLL: POB 26177, 13122 Safat, Kuwait City; tel. 22442310; fax 22407024; Man. Dir Dr TARIQ ABDULLAH.

Dar as-Seyassah Publishing, Printing and Distribution Co: POB 2270, 13023 Safat, Kuwait City; tel. 24813566; fax 24833628; internet www.dar-al-seyassah.com; publ. *Arab Times*, *As-Seyassah* and *Al-Hadaf*.

Gulf Centre Publishing and Publicity: POB 2722, 13028 Safat, Kuwait City; tel. 22402760; fax 22458833; Propr HAMZA ISMAIL ESSLAH.

Kuwait National Advertising and Publishing Co (KNAPCO): POB 2268, Safat 13023; tel. 25745776; fax 25745779; e-mail support@knapco.com; internet www.knapco.com; f. 1995; publ. annual commercial business directory, *Teledymag*.

Kuwait Publishing House Co: POB 1446, 13015 Safat, Kuwait City; tel. 22449686; fax 22436956; e-mail info@kuwaitpocketguide.com; f. 1970; Dir ESAM AS'AD ABU AL-FARAJ.

Kuwait United Co for Advertising, Publishing and Distribution WLL: POB 29359, 13153 Safat, Kuwait City; tel. 24817111; fax 24817797.

At-Talia Printing and Publishing Co: POB 1082, Airport Rd, Shuwaikh, 13011 Safat, Kuwait City; tel. 24840470; fax 24815611; Man. AHMAD YOUSUF AN-NAFISI.

GOVERNMENT PUBLISHING HOUSE

Ministry of Information: see Ministries.

Broadcasting and Communications

TELECOMMUNICATIONS

National Mobile Telecommunications Co KSC (Wataniya Telecom): POB 613, 13007 Safat, Kuwait City; tel. 65805555; fax 22423369; e-mail info@wataniya.com; internet www.wataniya.com; f. 1999; Chair. and Man. Dir Sheikh ABDULLAH BIN MUHAMMAD BIN SAUD ATH-THANI; CEO and Gen. Man. SCOTT GEGENHEIMER.

VIVA: Salmiya 22002, Kuwait City; e-mail info@viva.com.kw; internet www.viva.com.kw; f. 2008; mobile cellular communications; commercial brand of Kuwait Telecom Company; Chair. ADEL MUHAMMAD AR-ROUMI; CEO NAJEEB AL-AWADI.

Zain Kuwait: POB 22244, 13083 Safat, Kuwait City; tel. 24842000; fax 24818800; e-mail info.kw@zain.com; internet www.kw.zain.com; f. 1983 as Mobile Telecommunications Co; in Sept. 2007 began operating under new global brand, Zain; Chair. ASAAD AL-BANWAN; CEO Dr SAAD AL-BARRAK.

BROADCASTING

Radio

Radio of the State of Kuwait: POB 397, 13004 Safat, Kuwait City; tel. 22423774; fax 22456660; e-mail info@moinfo.gov.kw; internet www.moinfo.gov.kw; f. 1951; broadcasts daily in Arabic, Farsi, English and Urdu, some in stereo; Dir of Radio Dr ABD AL-AZIZ ALI MANSOUR; Dir of Radio Programmes ABD AR-RAHMAN HADI.

Television

Kuwait Television: POB 193, 13002 Safat, Kuwait City; tel. 22413501; fax 22438403; e-mail info@moinfo.gov.kw; internet www.moinfo.gov.kw; f. 1961; transmission began privately in Kuwait in 1957; transmits in Arabic; colour television service began in 1973; has a total of five channels; Head of News Broadcasting MUHAMMAD AL-KAHTANI.

Ar-Rai: Kuwait City; internet www.alrai.tv; f. 2004; first private satellite television station in Kuwait; admin. offices in Kuwait and transmission facilities in Dubai (United Arab Emirates); owned by the Ar-Rai Media Group.

Finance

(cap. = capital; res = reserves; dep. = deposits; m. = million; brs = branches; amounts in Kuwaiti dinars unless otherwise stated)

BANKING

Central Bank

Central Bank of Kuwait: POB 526, 13006 Safat, Abdullah as-Salem St, Kuwait City; tel. 22449200; fax 22464887; e-mail cbk@cbk.gov.kw; internet www.cbk.gov.kw; f. 1969; cap. 5.0m., res 534.0m., dep. 4,417.5m. (March 2007); Governor Sheikh SALEM ABD AL-AZIZ SA'UD AS-SABAH.

National Banks

Al-Ahli Bank of Kuwait KSC (ABK): POB 1387, 13014 Safat, Ahmad al-Jaber St, Kuwait City; tel. 22400900; fax 22424557; e-mail marketing@abkuwait.com; internet www.eahli.com/abk; f. 1967; wholly owned by private Kuwaiti interests; cap. 100.7m., res 218.4m., dep. 2,565.8m. (Dec. 2007); Chair. AHMAD YOUSUF BEHBEHANI; Dep. Chair. and Man. Dir ALI HILAL AL-MUTAIRI; 20 brs.

Bank of Kuwait and the Middle East KSC (BKME): POB 71, 13001 Safat, Joint Banking Centre, East Tower, Darwazat Abd ar-Razzak, Kuwait City; tel. 22459771; fax 22461430; e-mail hayakom@bkme.com.kw; internet www.bkme.com; f. 1971; 75% owned by Ahli United Bank (Bahrain); cap. 84.5m., res 185.4m., dep. 1,888.4m. (Dec. 2007); Chair. and Man. Dir HAMAD ABD AL-MOHSEN AL-MARZOUQ; 22 brs.

BBK: POB 24396, 13104 Safat, Ahmad al-Jaber St, Kuwait City; tel. 22417140; fax 22440937; e-mail bbkp@batelco.com.bh; internet www.bbkonline.com; f. 1971 as Bank of Bahrain and Kuwait BSC; name changed as above in 2005; cap. BD 64.0m., res BD 80.2m., dep. BD 1,493.3m. (Dec. 2006); Chair. MURAD ALI MURAD; Gen. Man. ABDUL RAHMAN AL-KHOOHEJI.

Boubyan Bank KSC: POB 25507, 13116 Safat, Kuwait City; tel. 22325000; fax 22454263; e-mail info@bankboubyan.com; internet www.bankboubyan.com; f. 2004; cap. 105.9m., res 8.9m., dep. 595.0m. (Dec. 2007); Chair. MUHAMMAD YOUSUF AR-ROUMI.

Burgan Bank SAK: POB 5389, 12170 Safat, Abd al-Haih al-Ahmad St, Kuwait City; tel. 22439000; fax 22461148; e-mail info@burgan.com; internet www.burgan.com; f. 1975; 33.9% Kuwait Projects Co (Holding), Safat; cap. 86.1m., res 195.7m., dep. 2,380.7m. (Dec. 2007);

KUWAIT

Chair. TARIQ MUHAMMAD ABD AS-SALAM; CEO JONATHAN DAVID LYON; 20 brs.

Commercial Bank of Kuwait SAK: POB 2861, 13029 Safat, Mubarak al-Kabir St, Kuwait City; tel. 22411001; fax 22450150; e-mail cbkinq@cbk.com; internet www.cbk.com; f. 1960 by Amiri decree; cap. 121.1m., res 361.5m., dep. 3,645.3m. (Dec. 2007); Chair. ABD AL-MAJID ASH-SHATTI; CEO and Gen. Man. JAMAL ABD AL-HAMID AL-MUTAWA; 50 brs.

Gulf Bank KSC: POB 3200, 13032 Safat, Mubarak al-Kabir St, Kuwait City; tel. 22449501; fax 22445212; e-mail customerservice@gulfbank.com.kw; internet www.e-gulfbank.com; f. 1960; cap. 109.0m., res 256.0m., dep. 4,422.0m. (Dec. 2007); Chair. and Man. Dir QUTAIBA AL-GHANIM; CEO and Chief Gen. Man. LOUIS MYERS; 42 brs.

Industrial Bank of Kuwait KSC (IBK): POB 3146, 13032 Safat, Joint Banking Centre, Darwazzat Abd ar-Razaq, Commercial Area 9, Kuwait City; tel. 22457661; fax 22462057; e-mail ibk@ibkuwt.com; internet www.ibkuwt.com; 31.4% state-owned; f. 1973; cap. 20.0m., res 188.1m., dep. 86.0m. (Dec. 2007); Chair. and Man. Dir ABD AL-MOHSEN YOUSUF AL-HANIF; Gen. Man. ALI ABD AN-NABI KHAJA.

Kuwait Finance House KSC (KFH): POB 24989, 13110 Safat, Abdullah al-Mubarak St, Kuwait City; tel. 22445050; fax 22455135; e-mail kfh@kfh.com; internet www.kfh.com; f. 1977; Islamic banking and investment co; 45% state-owned; cap. 177.5m., res 1,038.5m., dep. 6,547.6m. (Dec. 2007); Chair. and Man. Dir BADER ABD AL-MOHSEN AL-MUKHAISEEM; Gen. Man. MUHAMMAD SULAYMAN AL-OMAR; 44 brs.

Kuwait International Bank KSC (KIB): POB 22822, 13089 Safat, West Tower, Joint Banking Centre, Mubarak al-Kabir St, Kuwait City; tel. 22458177; fax 22462516; e-mail contact@kib.com.kw; internet www.kib.com.kw; f. 1973 as Kuwait Real Estate Bank KSC; name changed as above in 2007 (when it was converted into an Islamic bank); wholly owned by private Kuwaiti interests; cap. 85.7m., res 54.7m., dep. 771.5m. (Dec. 2007); Chair. and Man. Dir ABD AL-WAHAB MUHAMMAD AL-WAZZAN; Gen. Man. ADIL AHMAD; 9 brs.

National Bank of Kuwait SAK (NBK): POB 95, 13001 Safat, Abdullah al-Ahmad St, Kuwait City; tel. 22422011; fax 22431888; e-mail webmaster@nbk.com; internet www.nbk.com; f. 1952; cap. 245.7m., res 1,090.4m., dep. 9,619.4m. (Dec. 2007); Chair. MUHAMMAD ABD AR-RAHMAN AL-BAHAR; CEO IBRAHIM S. DABDOUB; 66 brs in Kuwait, 44 brs abroad.

INSURANCE

Al-Ahleia Insurance Co SAK: POB 1602, Ahmad al-Jaber St, 13017 Safat, Kuwait City; tel. 22240033; fax 22430308; e-mail aic@alahleia.com; internet www.alahleia.com; f. 1962; all forms of insurance; cap. 15.6m. (July 2007); Chair. and Man. Dir SULAYMAN HAMAD MUHAMMAD AD-DALALI.

Arab Commercial Enterprises WLL (Kuwait): POB 2474, 13025 Safat, Kuwait City; tel. 22413854; fax 22409450; e-mail acekwt@ace-ins.com; f. 1952; Man. SALIM ABOU HAIDER.

Gulf Insurance Co KSC: POB 1040, 13011 Safat, Ahmad al-Jaber St, Kuwait City; tel. 1802080; fax 22422320; e-mail contacts@gulfins.com.kw; internet info@gic.com.kw; f. 1962; cap. 11.3m. (2002); all forms of insurance; Chair. FARKAD ABDULLAH AS-SANEA; CEO and Man. Dir KHALED SAOUD AL-HASSAN.

Al-Ittihad al-Watani Insurance Co for the Near East SAL: POB 781, 13008 Safat, Kuwait City; tel. 24842988; fax 22432424; Man. JOSEPH ZACCOUR.

Kuwait Insurance Co SAK (KIC): POB 769, 13008 Safat, Abdullah as-Salem St, Kuwait City; tel. 1884433; fax 22428530; e-mail info@kic-kw.com; internet www.kic-kw.com; f. 1960; cap. US $64.6m.; all life and non-life insurance; Chair. MUHAMMAD SALEH BEHBEHANI; Gen. Man. Dr ALI HAMAD AL-BAHAR.

Kuwait Reinsurance Co KSCC: POB 21929, 13080 Safat, Kuwait City; tel. 22432011; fax 22427823; e-mail kuwaitre@kuwaitre.com; internet www.kuwaitre.com; f. 1972; cap. 10.0m., total assets 59.3m. (2006); Chair. FAHED AL-IBRAHIM; Gen. Man. AMIR AL-MUHANNA.

Kuwait Technical Insurance Office: POB 25349, 13114 Safat, Kuwait City; tel. 22409600; fax 22413986.

Mohd Saleh Behbehani & Co: POB 341, 13004 Safat, Kuwait City; tel. 24721670; fax 24760070; e-mail msrybco@qualitynet.net; f. 1963; Pres. MUHAMMAD SALEH YOUSUF BEHBEHANI.

New India Assurance Co: POB 370, 13004 Safat, Kuwait City; tel. 22412085; fax 22412089.

The Northern Insurance Co Ltd: POB 579, 13006 Safat, Kuwait City; tel. 22427930; fax 22462739.

The Oriental Insurance Co Ltd: POB 22431, 13085 Safat, Kuwait City; tel. 22424016; fax 22424017; Man. JUGAL KISHORE MADAAN.

Sumitomo Marine & Fire Insurance Co (Kuwait Agency): POB 3458, 13035 Safat, Kuwait City; tel. 22433087; fax 22430853; Contact ABDULLAH BOUDROS.

Warba Insurance Co SAK: POB 24282, 13103 Safat, Kuwait City; tel. 22445140; fax 22466131; e-mail warba@warbaonline.com; internet www.warbaonline.com; f. 1976; cap. 7.7m. (2002), total assets 80.1m. (Dec. 2005); all forms of insurance; Chair. Dr HAIDER HASSAN ABD AR-RASOL AL-JUMAA; 3 brs.

STOCK EXCHANGE

Kuwait Stock Exchange (KSE): POB 22235, 13083 Safat, Mubarak al-Kabir St, Kuwait City; tel. 22992000; fax 22420779; e-mail webmaster@kuwaitse.com; internet www.kuwaitse.com; f. 1983; 197 cos and one mutual fund listed in early 2008; Dir-Gen. SALEH MUBARAK AL-FALAH.

Markets Association

Kuwait Financial Markets Association (KFMA): POB 25228, 13113 Safat, Block 12, St 101, Complex 182, Villa 4, Kuwait City; tel. 25339776; fax 25339778; e-mail kfma@kfma.org.kw; internet www.kfma.org.kw; f. 1977; represents treasury, financial and capital markets and their mems; Pres. THUNAYAN AL-GHANIM; Sec.-Gen. MESHAL AL-FARAS.

Trade and Industry

GOVERNMENT AGENCY

Kuwait Investment Authority (KIA): POB 64, 13001 Safat, Kuwait City; tel. 22485600; fax 22454059; e-mail information@kia.gov.kw; internet www.kia.gov.kw; oversees the Kuwait Investment Office (London); responsible for the Kuwaiti General Reserve; Chair. MUSTAFA JASSEM ASH-SHIMALI (Minister of Finance); Exec. Dir AHMAD M. A. BASTAKI.

DEVELOPMENT ORGANIZATIONS

Arab Planning Institute (API): POB 5834, 13059 Safat, Kuwait City; tel. 24843130; fax 24842935; e-mail api@api.org.kw; internet www.arab-api.org; f. 1966; 15 Arab mem. states; publishes *Journal of Development and Economic Policies* (twice-yearly) and proceedings of seminars and discussion group meetings, offers research, training programmes and advisory services; Dir-Gen. ESSA AL-GHAZALI.

Industrial and Financial Investments Co (IFIC): POB 26019, 13121 Safat, Joint Banking Complex, 8th Floor, Industrial Bank Bldg, Derwaza Abdulrazak, Kuwait City; tel. 22429073; fax 22448850; e-mail ific@ific.net; internet www.ific.net; f. 1983; invests directly in industry; privatized in 1996; Chair. and Man. Dir Dr TALEB AHMAD ALI.

Kuwait Fund for Arab Economic Development (KFAED): POB 2921, 13030 Safat, cnr Mubarak al-Kabir St and al-Hilali St, Kuwait City; tel. 22999000; fax 22999090; e-mail info@kuwait-fund.org; internet www.kuwait-fund.org; f. 1961; cap. KD 2,000m.; state-owned; provides and administers financial and technical assistance to developing countries; Chair. Sheikh Dr MUHAMMAD SABAH AS-SALIM AS-SABAH (Minister of Foreign Affairs); Dir-Gen. ABDULWAHAB A. AL-BADER.

Kuwait International Investment Co SAK (KIIC): POB 22792, 13088 Safat, as-Salhiya Commercial Complex, Kuwait City; tel. 22438273; fax 22454931; 30% state-owned; domestic real estate and share markets; Chair. and Man. Dir JASEM MUHAMMAD AL-BAHAR.

Kuwait Investment Co SAK (KIC): POB 1005, 13011 Safat, 5th Floor, al-Manakh Bldg, Mubarak al-Kabir St, Kuwait City; tel. 65888852; fax 22444896; e-mail info@kic.com.kw; internet www.kic.com.kw; f. 1981; 88% state-owned, 12% owned by private Kuwaiti interests; cap. KD 50.0m. (2002); international banking and investment; Chair. and Man. Dir BADER NASSER AS-SUBAIEE.

Kuwait Planning Board: c/o Ministry of Planning, POB 15, 13001 Safat, Kuwait City; tel. 22428200; fax 22414734; f. 1962; supervises long-term devt plans; through its Central Statistical Office publishes information on Kuwait's economic activity; Dir-Gen. AHMAD ALI AD-DUAIJ.

Mega Projects Agency (MPA): c/o Ministry of Public Works, POB 8, 13001 Safat, Kuwait City; tel. 25385520; fax 25385234; e-mail hmansour@mpa.gov.kw; f. 2005; supervises the progress of Failaka and Bubiyan island devts; Chair. BADER AL-HUMAIDI.

National Industries Group (Holding) SAK (NIG): POB 417, 13005 Safat, Kuwait City; tel. 24845205; fax 24839582; e-mail personnel@nig.com.kw; internet www.nigroup.net; f. 1960; cap. KD 55.8m. (2002); has controlling interest in various construction enterprises; privatized in 1995; Chair. and Man. Dir SAAD MUHAMMAD AS-SAAD.

Public Authority for Industry (PAI): POB 4690, 13047 Safat, Kuwait City; POB 10033, Shuaiba; tel. 25302222; fax 25302190; e-mail indust@pai.gov.kw; internet www.pai.gov.kw; f. 1997; suc-

KUWAIT

Directory

cessor to Shuaiba Area Authority (f. 1964); develops, promotes and supervises industry in Kuwait; CEO Dr AHMAD YAQOUB BAQER AL-ABDULLAH (Minister of Commerce and Industry); Gen. Man. ALI FAHAD AL-MUDHAF.

CHAMBER OF COMMERCE

Kuwait Chamber of Commerce and Industry: POB 775, 13008 Safat, Chamber's Bldg, Abdulaziz Hamad ash-Sager St, Kuwait City; tel. 1805580; fax 22404110; e-mail kcci@kcci.org.kw; internet www.kuwaitchamber.org.kw; f. 1959; 50,000 mems; Chair. ALI MUHAMMAD THUNAYAN AL-GHANIM; Dir-Gen. AHMAD RASHED AL-HAROUN.

STATE HYDROCARBONS COMPANIES

Kuwait Petroleum Corpn (KPC): POB 26565, 13126 Safat, as-Salhiya Commercial Complex, Fahed as-Salem St, Kuwait City; tel. 22455455; fax 22467159; e-mail info@kpc.com.kw; internet www.kpc.com.kw; f. 1980; co-ordinating org. to manage the petroleum industry; controls Kuwait Aviation Fuelling Co (KAFCO), Kuwait Foreign Petroleum Exploration Co (KUFPEC), Kuwait Gulf Oil Co (KGOC), Kuwait National Petroleum Co (KNPC), Kuwait Oil Co (KOC), Kuwait Oil Tanker Co (KOTC), Kuwait Petroleum International (Q8), Petrochemical Industries Co (PIC); Chair. Sheikh AHMAD ABDULLAH AS-SABAH; CEO SAAD ASH-SHUWAYIB.

Kuwait Aviation Fuelling Co KSC (KAFCO): POB 1654, 13017 Safat, Kuwait City; tel. 24330507; fax 24330475; e-mail airfuel@kafco.com; internet www.kafco.com; f. 1963; Dep. Chair. and Gen. Man. NASSER BADER AL-MUDHAF; 70 employees.

Kuwait Foreign Petroleum Exploration Co KSC (KUFPEC): POB 5291, 13053 Safat, Kuwait City; tel. 1836000; fax 24921818; internet www.kufpec.com; f. 1981; state-owned; overseas oil and gas exploration and devt; Chair. and Man. Dir FAHED AL-AJMI; 169 employees.

Kuwait Gulf Oil Co KSC (KGOC): POB 9919, Ahmadi 61010; tel. 23980883; e-mail info@kgoc.com; internet www.kgoc.com; f. 2002 to take over Kuwait's interest in the Partitioned Zone's offshore operator, Khafji Joint Operations, and all of Kuwait's other offshore exploration and production activities; Chair. and Man. Dir BADER NASSER AL-KHASHTI.

Kuwait National Petroleum Co KSC (KNPC): POB 70, 13001 Safat, Ali as-Salem St, Kuwait City; tel. 23989900; fax 23986188; internet www.knpc.com.kw; f. 1960; oil refining, production of liquefied petroleum gas, and domestic marketing and distribution of petroleum by-products; Chair. and Man. Dir FAROUK HUSSAIN AZ-ZANKI; 5,611 employees.

Kuwait Oil Co KSC (KOC): POB 9758, 61008 Ahmadi; tel. 23983661; fax 23984971; e-mail kocinfo@kockw.com; internet www.kockw.com; f. 1934; state-owned; Chair. and Man. Dir SAMI FAHED AR-RUSHAID; 4,815 employees.

Kuwait Petroleum International (Q8): POB 26565, 13126 Safat, Kuwait City; tel. 22332800; fax 22332776; e-mail info-kuwait@q8.com; internet www.q8.com; marketing division of KPC; controls 4,000 petrol retail stations in Europe, and European refineries with capacity of 235,000 b/d; Man. Dir HUSSEIN AL-ISMAIL.

UTILITIES

The Government planned to create regulatory bodies for each of Kuwait's utilities, with a view to facilitating their privatization.

Ministry of Electricity and Water: see Ministries; provides subsidized services throughout Kuwait.

TRADE UNIONS

Federation of Petroleum and Petrochemical Workers: Kuwait City; f. 1965; Chair. JASEM ABD AL-WAHAB AT-TOURA.

KOC Workers Union: Kuwait City; f. 1964; Chair. HAMAD SAWYAN.

Kuwait Trade Union Federation (KTUF): POB 5185, 13052 Safat, Kuwait City; tel. 25636389; fax 25627159; e-mail ktuf@hotmail.com; internet www.ktuf.org; f. 1967; central authority to which all trade unions are affiliated; KHALED M. ALAZEMI; Gen. Sec. FARRAJ A. AR-RASHEDI.

Transport

RAILWAYS

There are currently no railways in Kuwait. However, it was announced in early 2008 that a national rail network and a metro system were both at the planning stages; the projects were expected to be completed by 2016.

ROADS

Roads in the towns are metalled, and the most important are motorways or dual carriageways. There are metalled roads linking Kuwait City to Ahmadi, Mina al-Ahmadi and other centres of population in Kuwait, and to the Iraqi and Saudi Arabian borders. In 2004 the total road network was estimated at 5,749 km (613 km of motorways, 5,136 km of secondary roads), of which 85% was paved. A causeway linking Kuwait City with Subahiya was under consideration in the mid-2000s; the design-and-build contract was projected to be worth some US $1,500m.

Kuwait Public Transport Co SAK (KPTC): POB 375, 13004 Safat, Murghab, Safat Sq., Kuwait City; tel. 22469420; fax 22401265; e-mail info@kptc.com.kw; internet www.kptc.com.kw; f. 1962; state-owned; provides internal bus service; regular service to Mecca, Saudi Arabia; Chair. and Man. Dir MAHMOUD A. AN-NOURI.

SHIPPING

Kuwait has three commercial seaports. The largest, Shuwaikh, situated about 3 km from Kuwait City, was built in 1960. By 1987 it comprised 21 deep-water berths, with a total length of 4 km, three shallow-water berths and three basins for small craft, each with a depth of 3.35 m. In 1988 3.6m. metric tons of cargo were imported and 133,185 tons were exported through the port. A total of 1,189 vessels passed through Shuwaikh in 1988.

Shuaiba Commercial Port, 56 km south of Kuwait City, was built in 1967 to facilitate the import of primary materials and heavy equipment, necessary for the construction of the Shuaiba Industrial Area. By 1987 the port comprised a total of 20 berths, plus two docks for small wooden boats. Four of the berths constitute a station for unloading containers. Shuaiba handled a total of 3,457,871 metric tons of dry cargo, barge cargo and containers in 1988.

Doha, the smallest port, was equipped in 1981 to receive small coastal ships carrying light goods between the Gulf states. It has 20 small berths, each 100 m long. Doha handled a total of 20,283 metric tons of dry cargo, barge cargo and containers in 1988.

The oil port at Mina al-Ahmadi, 40 km south of Kuwait City, is capable of handling the largest oil tankers afloat, and the loading of over 2m. barrels of oil per day. By 1987 the port comprised 12 tanker berths, one bitumen-carrier berth, two LPG export berths and bunkering facilities.

Plans for the privatization of Kuwait's ports were under development in the mid-2000s. A new, US $1,500m. facility at Bubiyan was scheduled for completion in 2010.

At 31 December 2007 Kuwait's merchant fleet numbered 212 vessels, with a total displacement of 2,426,799 grt.

Kuwait Ports Authority: POB 3874, 13039 Safat, Kuwait City; tel. 24812622; fax 24819714; e-mail info@kpa.gov.kw; internet www.kpa.gov.kw; f. 1977; Dir-Gen. Dr SABER JABER AL-ALI AS-SABAH.

Principal Shipping Companies

Arab Maritime Petroleum Transport Co (AMPTC): POB 22525, 13086 Safat, Kuwait City; tel. 24844500; fax 24842996; e-mail amptc.kuwait@amptc.net; internet www.amptc.net; f. 1973; four crude petroleum tankers, two LPG carriers and one product carrier; owned by Algeria, Bahrain, Egypt, Iraq, Kuwait, Libya, Qatar, Saudi Arabia and the UAE; Gen. Man. SULAYMAN I. AL-BASSAM.

Heavy Engineering Industries and Shipbuilding Co (Heisco): POB 21998, 13080 Safat, Kuwait City; tel. 24835488; fax 24830291; e-mail marine@heisco.com; internet www.heisco.com; f. 1974 as Kuwait Shipbuilding and Repairyard Co; name changed as above in 2003; ship repairs and engineering services, underwater services, maintenance of refineries, power stations and storage tanks; maintains floating dock for vessels up to 35,000 dwt; synchrolift for vessels up to 5,000 dwt with transfer yard; seven repair jetties up to 550 m in length and floating workshop for vessels lying at anchor; Chair. JUHAIL MUHAMMAD AL-JUHAIL.

KGL Ports Int. Co (KGL PI): POB 24565, 13106 Safat, Kuwait City; tel. 24827804; fax 24827806; e-mail bader.alkhaldi@kglpi.com; internet www.kglpi.com; f. 2005; subsidiary of Kuwait and Gulf Link Transport Co; port management and stevedoring; operates Shuaiba Commercial Port Container Terminal; also operations and management contracts with ports in United Arab Emirates and Saudi Arabia; Chair. and CEO MUHAMMAD AL-MAZEEDI.

Kuwait Maritime Transport Co KSC (KMTC): POB 22595, 13086 Safat, Nafisi and Khatrash Bldg, Jaber al-Mubarak St, Kuwait City; tel. 22449974; fax 22420513; f. 1981; Chair. YOUSUF AL-MAJID.

Kuwait Oil Tanker Co SAK (KOTC): POB 810, 13009 Safat, as-Salhiya Commercial Complex, Blocks 3, 5, 7 and 9, Kuwait City; tel. 22455455; fax 22401584; e-mail ysm@kotc.com.kw; internet www.kotc.com.kw; f. 1957; state-owned; operates eight crude oil tankers, 11 product tankers and five LPG vessels; sole tanker agents for Mina al-Ahmadi, Shuaiba and Mina al-Abdullah and agents for other ports; LPG filling and distribution; Chair. and Man. Dir NABIL M. BOURISLI.

KUWAIT

United Arab Shipping Co SAG (UASC): POB 3636, 13037 Safat, Shuwaikh, Airport Rd, Kuwait City; tel. 24843150; fax 24849516; e-mail info@uasc.com.kw; internet www.uasc.net; f. 1976; national shipping co of six Arabian Gulf countries; services between Europe, Far East, Mediterranean ports, Japan and east coast of USA and South America, and ports of participant states on Persian (Arabian) Gulf and Red Sea; operates 44 vessels; subsidiary cos include: United Arab Shipping Agencies Co (Kuwait), Arab Transport Co (Aratrans), United Arab Chartering Ltd (United Kingdom), Middle East Container Repair Co (UAE), Arabian Chemicals Carriers (Saudi Arabia), United Arab Agencies Inc. (USA) and United Arab Shipping Agencies Co (Saudi Arabia); Pres. and CEO KEN BLOCH SOERENSEN.

CIVIL AVIATION

Kuwait International Airport opened in 1980, and by 2007 handled 6.9m. passengers, compared with 3.8m. in 2001. The airport is undergoing a major programme of expansion: the first phase of the project was to expand the airport's annual capacity to 20m. passengers and to modernize facilities, with a further final phase of development intended to achieve passenger capacity of 55m.

Directorate-General of Civil Aviation (DGCA): POB 17, 13001 Safat, Kuwait City; tel. 24335599; fax 24713504; Pres. FAWAZ AL-FARAH; Dir-Gen. Eng. BADER BOUTAIBAN.

Jazeera Airways: POB 29288, 13153 Safat, Kuwait City; e-mail helpdesk@jazeeraairways.com; internet www.jazeeraairways.com; f. 2005; low-cost airline owned by Boodai Group; serves 26 destinations in the Middle East, North Africa, Europe and Asia; Chair. MARWAN BOODAI; CEO ANDREW COWEN.

Kuwait Airways Corpn (KAC): POB 394, Kuwait International Airport, 13004 Safat, Kuwait City; tel. 24345555; fax 24314118; e-mail info@kuwait-airways.com; internet www.kuwait-airways.com; f. 1954; scheduled and charter passenger and cargo services to the Arabian peninsula, Asia, Africa, the USA and Europe; scheduled for privatization; Chair. and Man. Dir HAMAD A. LATIF AL-FALAH.

Kuwait National Airways: Kuwait City; f. 2006; premium services by short-haul airline, Wataniya Airlines, scheduled to commence in 2009; Chair. and Man. Dir ABD AS-SALAM AL-BAHAR; CEO GEORGE COOPER.

Tourism

Attractions for visitors include the Kuwait Towers leisure and reservoir complex, the Entertainment City theme park, the Kuwait Zoological Garden in Omariya and the Khiran Resort tourist village near the border with Saudi Arabia, as well as extensive facilities for sailing and other water sports. In early 2005 there were some 4,000 rooms available for visitors; it was intended to increase this figure to around 6,000 by 2008. Foreign tourist arrivals totalled some 3.1m. in 2004, while tourism receipts of US $408m. were recorded in 2005.

Department of Tourism: Ministry of Information, Tourism Affairs, POB 193, 18th Floor, Fahad as-Salem Tower, Fahad as-Salem St, 13002 Safat, Kuwait City; tel. 22457591; fax 22401540; e-mail tourism_kw@media.gov.kw.

Touristic Enterprises Co (TEC): POB 23310, 13094 Safat, Kuwait City; tel. 24965555; fax 24965055; e-mail info@tec.com.kw; internet www.kuwaittourism.com; f. 1976; 92% state-owned; manages 23 tourist facilities; Chair. BADER AL-BAHAR; Vice-Chair. SHAKER AL-OTHMAN.

KYRGYZSTAN

Introductory Survey

Location, Climate, Language, Religion, Flag, Capital

The Kyrgyz Republic is a small, land-locked state situated in eastern Central Asia. It borders Kazakhstan to the north, Uzbekistan to the west, Tajikistan to the south and west, and the People's Republic of China to the east. There are distinct variations in climate between low-lying and high-altitude areas. In the valleys the mean July temperature is 28°C (82°F), whereas in January it falls to an average of −18°C (−0.5°F). Annual rainfall ranges from 180 mm (7 ins) in the eastern Tien Shan mountains to 750 mm–1,000 mm (30 ins–39 ins) in the Farg'ona (Fergana) mountain range. In the settled valleys the annual average varies between 100 mm and 500 mm (4 ins–20 ins). The state language is Kyrgyz; Russian additionally has the status of an official language. The major religion is Islam, with the majority of ethnic Kyrgyz being Sunni Muslims of the Hanafi school. The national flag (proportions 3 by 5) consists of a red field, at the centre of which is a yellow sun, with 40 counter-clockwise rays surrounding a red-bordered yellow disc, on which are superimposed two intersecting sets of three red, curved, narrow bands. The capital is Bishkek.

Recent History

Following the October Revolution of 1917 in Russia, Kyrgyzstan (which had been formally incorporated into the Russian Empire in 1876) experienced a period of civil war, with anti-Bolshevik forces, including the Russian White Army and local armed groups (*basmachi*), fighting against the Bolshevik Red Army. Soviet power was established in the region by 1919. In 1918 the Turkestan Autonomous Soviet Socialist Republic (ASSR) was established within the Russian Soviet Federative Socialist Republic (the Russian Federation). In 1924 the Kara-Kyrgyz Autonomous Oblast (Region) was created. (At this time the Russians used the term Kara-Kyrgyz to distinguish the Kyrgyz from the Kazakhs, then known as Kyrgyz by the Russians.) In 1925 the region was renamed the Kyrgyz Autonomous Oblast, and it became the Kyrgyz ASSR in February 1926. On 5 December 1936 the Kyrgyz Soviet Socialist Republic (SSR) was established as a full union republic of the USSR.

During the 1920s considerable economic and social developments were made in Kyrgyzstan, when land reforms resulted in the settlement of many of the nomadic Kyrgyz. The agricultural collectivization programme of the early 1930s was strongly opposed in the republic. Despite the suppression of nationalism under Stalin (Iosif V. Dzhugashvili—Soviet leader in 1924–53), many aspects of Kyrgyz national culture were retained, although many so-called 'national communists' were expelled from the Kyrgyz Communist Party (KCP) and often imprisoned or exiled, particularly during the late 1930s. Tensions with the all-Union (Soviet) authorities continued following the death of Stalin in 1953.

The election of Mikhail Gorbachev as Soviet leader in 1985, and his introduction of the policies of perestroika (restructuring) and glasnost (openness), led to the resignation of Turdakan Usubaliyev as First Secretary of the KCP and the dismissal from office of his allies by Absamat Masaliyev, his successor. The republic's Supreme Soviet (Zhogorku Kenesh or Supreme Council—legislature) adopted Kyrgyz as the official language, although Russian was retained as a language of inter-ethnic communication. However, the conservative republican leadership opposed the development of unofficial quasi-political groups, although one such group, Ashar, was partially tolerated by the authorities and soon developed a wider political role. A notable group at this time was Osh Aymaghi, based in Osh Oblast (Region) of the Farg'ona (Fergana) valley (which is shared between Kyrgyzstan, Tajikistan and Uzbekistan). Osh Aymaghi attempted to obtain land and housing provision for ethnic Kyrgyz in the ethnic Uzbek-dominated region (Osh had been incorporated into Kyrgyzstan in 1924 but ethnic Uzbeks had recently begun to demand the establishment of an Uzbek autonomous region) and in 1990 disputes over land and homes developed into violent confrontation between ethnic Kyrgyz and Uzbeks. According to official reports, more than 300 people died, and a state of emergency and a curfew were introduced in the region, the former remaining in force until 1995; the Uzbekistani–Kyrgyzstani border was also closed.

Elections to the 350-member Kyrgyzstani Supreme Soviet in February 1990 were conducted along Soviet lines, with KCP candidates winning most seats unopposed, and in April Masaliyev was elected to the new office of Chairman of the Supreme Soviet. In October an extraordinary session of the Supreme Soviet was convened to elect the President, but Masaliyev had been discredited by the conflict in Osh. Furthermore, the opposition, which had united as the Democratic Movement of Kyrgyzstan (DMK), had become a significant political force and in the first round of voting Masaliyev failed to achieve the requisite proportion of votes to be elected; in a further round a compromise candidate, Askar Akayev, the President of the Kyrgyz Academy of Sciences, was elected to the executive presidency. Akayev rapidly allied himself with reformist politicians and economists, including leaders of the DMK. In December Masaliyev resigned as Chairman of the Supreme Soviet, and was replaced by Medetkan Sherimkulov. (Masaliyev resigned as First Secretary of the KCP in April 1991). Also in December 1990, the Supreme Soviet voted to change the name of the republic from the Kyrgyz SSR to the Republic of Kyrgyzstan. In January 1991 Akayev replaced the Council of Ministers with a smaller cabinet, comprising mainly reformist politicians. In February the capital, Frunze (named after a Red Army commander), reverted to its pre-1926 name of Bishkek. However, in a referendum held in nine Soviet Union Republics in March, 87.7% of eligible voters in Kyrgyzstan approved the proposal to retain the USSR as a 'renewed federation'.

In August 1991, when the conservative communist State Committee for the State of Emergency (SCSE) announced that it had assumed power in the Russian and Soviet capital, Moscow, there was an attempt to depose Akayev in Kyrgyzstan. Akayev dismissed the Chairman of the republican Committee of State Security (KGB) and ordered interior ministry troops to guard strategic buildings in Bishkek. He publicly denounced the coup (which the KCP had supported) and issued a decree prohibiting activity by any political party in government or state bodies. After the coup had collapsed in Moscow, Akayev and republican Vice-President German Kuznetsov renounced their membership of the Communist Party of the Soviet Union, and the entire politburo and secretariat of the KCP resigned. On 31 August the Kyrgyzstani Supreme Soviet voted to declare independence from the USSR. Akayev (the sole candidate) was re-elected President of Kyrgyzstan by direct popular vote on 12 October, receiving 95% of the votes cast.

In October 1991 Akayev signed, with representatives of seven other republics, a treaty to establish a new economic community. On 21 December Kyrgyzstan was among the 11 signatories to the Almaty (Alma-Ata) Declaration, which formally established the Commonwealth of Independent States (CIS, see p. 225).

Discussions were held throughout 1992 to draft a new constitution. The Constitution, which was finally promulgated on 5 May 1993, provided for a parliamentary system of government, with the Prime Minister as head of the executive. Legislative power was to be vested in a smaller (105-member) Zhogorku Kenesh, following a general election, which was due to be held by 1995; in the mean time, the existing assembly continued to act as the republic's parliament. Russian was accorded the constitutional status of a language of inter-ethnic communication. The country's official name was changed from the Republic of Kyrgyzstan to the less ethnically neutral Kyrgyz Republic. In July Akayev's attempts to encourage non-Kyrgyz to remain in the republic suffered a serious reverse when Kuznetsov, by this time the First Deputy Prime Minister announced his decision to return to Russia. By mid-1993 it was estimated that some 145,000 Russians had left the republic since 1989.

Akayev's presidency was destabilized during 1993 by a series of corruption scandals. Two commissions of inquiry were established to investigate the business dealings of the Vice-President, Feliks Kulov, and to examine allegations that senior politicians—including the Prime Minister since February 1992, Tursunbek Chyngyshev—had been involved in unauthorized gold exports. In December 1993 Kulov resigned and the legislature subsequently held a vote of confidence in Chyngyshev's Government: the motion failed to secure the required two-thirds' majority and Akayev dismissed the entire cabinet. A new Government, headed by Apas Jumagulov (Chairman of the Council of Ministers in 1986–91), was approved later in the month. A referendum of confidence in the presidency was held (on Akayev's initiative) in January 1994, at which 96.2% of voters endorsed Akayev's leadership.

In June 1994, in an attempt to curb the rate of emigration, Akayev issued a decree promoting the use of Russian, simplifying the procedure of application for dual citizenship, and guaranteeing the equitable representation of ethnic Russians in the state administration. The Zhogorku Kenesh adopted a resolution based on the decree in March 1996.

In September 1994 more than 180 deputies demanded the dissolution of the Kenesh and the holding of fresh elections, in protest at the continuing obstruction of the economic reform process. The Government tendered its resignation, and Akayev announced that fresh parliamentary elections would be held. The Government was promptly reinstated by Akayev, who announced the holding of a referendum in October on constitutional amendments, at which the majority of the electorate endorsed proposals for a restructured Zhogorku Kenesh, comprising a 70-member El Okuldor Palatasy (People's Assembly—upper chamber) to represent regional interests at twice-yearly sessions and a permanent, 35-member Myizam Chygaru Palatasy (Legislative Assembly—lower chamber) to represent the population as a whole. Elections to the two chambers of the new Zhogorku Kenesh were held in two rounds in February 1995. The two chambers of the Zhogorku Kenesh held their inaugural sessions on 28 March. A new Government, again led by Jumagulov, was appointed in April.

In September 1995 the Myizam Chygaru Palatasy vetoed a proposal to hold a referendum on extending the President's term of office until 2000. On 24 December 1995 Akayev received a reported 71.6% of the votes cast in a direct presidential election; Masaliyev (who had recently been reinstated as the leader of the revived KCP) won 24.4% of the votes. The rate of participation by the electorate was some 82%. Akayev was inaugurated on 30 December. Following a decree issued by Akayev, a referendum was held on 10 February 1996, at which the majority of the electorate endorsed amendments to the Constitution increasing presidential powers and decreasing those of the legislature. The Government resigned later that month; Jumagulov was reinstated as Prime Minister in March and Akayev approved a new Government shortly afterwards.

In January 1998 a new criminal code was promulgated, which effectively abolished the death penalty by imposing a moratorium on its implementation. In March Jumagulov announced his retirement and the Zhogorku Kenesh endorsed the appointment of Kuvachbek Jumaliyev as the new Prime Minister. A cabinet reorganization was also effected. In July the Constitutional Court ruled that Akayev was permitted to seek a third term in the presidential election due to be held in 2000. A referendum on several constitutional amendments took place on 17 October, with the participation of about 96% of the electorate, and some 90% of voters approved the following amendments: the number of deputies in the Myizam Chygaru Palatasy was to increase to 60, and representation in the El Okuldor Palatasy was to be reduced to 45; the electoral system was to be reformed; restrictions on parliamentary immunity were to be introduced; private land ownership was to be legalized; the presentation of unbalanced or unattainable budgets was to be banned; and the adoption of any legislation restricting freedom of speech or of the press was to be prohibited. The Zhogorku Kenesh and the majority of political parties declared their opposition to the constitutional changes and, in particular, to the introduction of private land ownership, which they feared would result in the transfer of land to foreign ownership.

By mid-December 1998 some 383 government officials had been dismissed on grounds of corruption, and in late December the President dissolved the Government for its failure to address the country's economic problems. Jumabek Ibraimov was appointed Prime Minister and a new Government was formed, in which 10 ministers from the previous administration retained their portfolios. Akayev also extended the Prime Minister's mandate, empowering him to appoint and dismiss ministers and heads of departments (hitherto the exclusive right of the President). Ibraimov died in April 1999, and Amangeldy Muraliyev was appointed in his stead.

A new electoral law was introduced at the end of May 1999 whereby, henceforth, 15 seats in the Myizam Chygaru Palatasy were to be allocated on a proportional basis for those parties that secured a minimum of 5% of the votes; the legislation also banned the use of foreign and private funds in electoral campaigns. In June legislation came into effect, banning political organizations considered a threat to Kyrgyzstan's stability and ethnic harmony. In July two new opposition parties were established: the Dignity (Ar-Namys) Party, led by Kulov (by this time Mayor of Bishkek), and the Justice (Adilettuuluk) Party.

At the elections to both chambers of the Zhogorku Kenesh, held on 20 February 2000, a total of six parties passed the 5% threshold required to secure party-list seats in the Myizam Chygaru Palatasy. A number of electoral violations were reported by the Organization for Security and Co-operation in Europe (OSCE, see p. 366). In a second round of voting on 12 March, the KCP secured 27.7% of the votes cast, ahead of the Union of Democratic Forces, with 18.6%, and the Democratic Women's Party of Kyrgyzstan, with 12.7%. The Union of Democratic Forces achieved the greatest representation of any party or bloc in the combined Zhogorku Kenesh, securing a total of 12 seats, compared with the KCP's six. Nominally independent candidates took 73 of the 105 seats in the two chambers. Kulov, who contested the poll as an independent after Dignity was prohibited from participating, failed to win a seat, prompting opposition protests and allegations of official corruption. Later in March Kulov was arrested on charges of abuse of office during his tenure as Minister of National Security in 1997–98. Although Kulov was acquitted in August 2000, a retrial was ordered, and he was sentenced to seven years' imprisonment in January 2001. An appeal was rejected in March, and in May 2002 Kulov was also found guilty of embezzlement.

Meanwhile, at the presidential election, held on 29 October 2000, Akayev secured 74.5% of the votes cast. The leader of the Fatherland Socialist Party (Ata-Meken), Omurbek Tekebayev, won 13.9% and the leader of the Social Democratic Party of Kyrgyzstan, Almazbek Atambayev, obtained 6.0% of the ballot. According to the Central Commission for Elections and Referendums, 74% of the electorate participated. However, on the day of the election a criminal case opened in Bishkek following the discovery, by international observers, of several hundred ballot papers, marked in favour of Akayev, before polling had begun officially. Moreover, opposition parties claimed that they had been prevented from participating in media broadcasts. The Chairman of the Central Commission for Elections and Referendums was forced to concede that electoral violations had taken place, leading to international condemnation. Despite mass protests and demands for the election to be repeated, on 10 November the Constitutional Court formally endorsed the results.

Akayev was inaugurated for a third term on 9 December 2000 and on 21 December Kurmanbek Bakiyev, hitherto the Governor of Chui Oblast, was appointed Prime Minister; a new Government was announced at the beginning of January 2001. In April the leaders of nine opposition parties formally announced the establishment of an alliance known as the People's Patriotic Movement, the stated objectives of which were the safeguarding of democracy and of human and constitutional rights. The movement organized demonstrations against the erosion of the independent media and against the imprisonment of Kulov. In November opposition parties including Dignity, the Fatherland Socialist Party (Ata-Meken) and the Liberty (Erkindik) party announced the formation of a new People's Congress, and elected the imprisoned Kulov its Chairman. In the following month the President signed into law a constitutional amendment granting Russian the status of official language, in what was considered a further attempt to halt the emigration of ethnic Russians from Kyrgyzstan.

In January 2002 the arrest of Azimbek Beknazarov, an opposition deputy, was denounced as politically motivated (Beknazarov had publicly criticized President Akayev's signature of a Sino-Kyrgyzstani border treaty in 1999). In March 2002 six people were reported to have been killed during clashes between protesters and security forces in the southern city of Jalal-Abad, where Beknazarov's trial was being held; it was subsequently suspended. In May the Myizam Chygaru Palatasy ratified the controversial Sino-Kyrgyzstani treaty, prompting two weeks of anti-Government demonstrations, hunger strikes and acts of civil disobedience. Protesters demanded that the Government accept responsibility for the violence of March, rescind the ratification of the border treaty (which they claimed had been signed illegally by President Akayev, since he had agreed to cede land to the People's Republic of China without the consent of the legislature), and close the criminal case against Beknazarov. Nevertheless, the El Okuldor Palatasy ratified the treaty later in May, and it was duly signed into law by the President.

In May 2002 Prime Minister Bakiyev tendered his resignation. The First Deputy Prime Minister, Nikolai Tanayev, was appointed Prime Minister and a new Government was announced in June. Meanwhile, in May Beknazarov received a one-year, suspended prison sentence. Following an appeal and further large-scale demonstrations, Beknazorov's sentence was annulled (although the initial guilty verdict was upheld), enabling him to retain his parliamentary seat. In June the Myizam Chygaru Palatasy approved an amnesty, proposed by Tanayev for both protesters and law enforcement officials involved in the disturbances of March.

In January 2003 President Akayev announced that a referendum on several constitutional amendments was to be held on 2 February. The amendments, which provided for the introduction of a unicameral legislature in 2005, in which all deputies were to be elected in single-member constituencies, were duly approved by 76.6% of the electorate, while 78.7% of voters supported Akayev's remaining in office until 2005; the reported rate of participation was 86.7%. The hasty scheduling of the referendum attracted criticism from international human rights organizations, and there were also allegations of procedural violations.

A major government reorganization took place in February 2004. In April the President introduced a new law designating Kyrgyz the state language, and stipulating measures for its promotion, apparently in order to encourage bilingualism in Kyrgyz and Russian, which was to remain an official language. In May, in advance of legislative elections, opposition parties, including Dignity, the Fatherland Socialist Party (Ata-Meken) and the Social Democratic Party of Kyrgyzstan, announced the formation of an electoral bloc, the Civic Union For Fair Elections. The formation of a larger electoral bloc, known as the People's Movement of Kyrgyzstan, was announced in September, under Bakiyev's leadership.

In January 2005 Roza Otunbayeva, a former ambassador to the United Kingdom, and the leader of the recently formed opposition Fatherland Party (Ata-Jurt), was refused permission to register as a candidate in the parliamentary elections, on the grounds that she had not been resident in the country for the previous five years; several other former diplomatic representatives were also prohibited from contesting the elections. Campaigning for the elections officially began on 2 February. Protests against the exclusion of candidates and opposition rallies demanding free and fair parliamentary elections, or the impeachment of Akayev, continued throughout February. In the first round of legislative voting on 27 February, the rate of participation by the electorate was reported to be 60%. Some 31 candidates (each of whom had received an absolute majority of votes cast in their respective electoral districts) were elected to the restructured, single-chamber, 75-member Zhogorku Kenesh. The majority of those elected were nominally independent candidates, including supporters of Akayev. Forward, Kyrgyzstan (Alga, Kyrgyzstan), established in 2003 and regarded as generally sympathetic to Akayev's administration, became the largest party faction to achieve representation, with 10 members reportedly elected. OSCE monitors concluded that the elections had not fully complied with democratic standards, while opposition and independent observers asserted that large-scale electoral fraud had taken place. Protests to dispute local polling results took place in various regions in advance of the second round of elections, held on 13 March, and the suppression of media outlets supportive of the opposition or critical of the authorities was reported. Following the second round of voting, a further 37 candidates were reported to have been elected (with a participation rate of 55%); only six opposition candidates obtained representation in the new legislature.

Dissatisfaction at the conduct of the elections, and at the failure of the opposition to obtain significant representation in the legislature, resulted in large-scale protests in a number of cities, initially in the south of Kyrgyzstan. From mid-March 2005 demonstrators occupied the regional governor's office in Jalal-Abad for several weeks and later in the month, demonstrators took control of a government building in Osh. On 22 March the Central Commission for Elections and Referendums declared that the results of voting for 69 of the 75 seats were valid; investigations into the conduct of voting in the remaining six districts were to continue. The Supreme Court, however, while emphasizing that the ruling did not constitute an annulment of the poll results, revoked the mandate of the newly elected Zhogorku Kenesh, asserting that the previous bicameral legislature continued to hold authority. On 23 March Akayev dismissed the Prosecutor-General, Myktybek Abdyldayev, and the Minister of Internal Affairs, Bakirdin Subanbekov, who had declared that he would not use force to end the protests.

By 24 March 2005 demonstrations had spread to Bishkek, and protesters stormed the presidential palace and government buildings. Akayev fled the country (maintaining that he remained Kyrgyzstan's Head of State) and Tanayev resigned as Prime Minister, while protesters freed Kulov from gaol. On the same day, at an emergency session, the lower chamber of the legislature elected in 2000 named Bakiyev acting Prime Minister (he automatically became acting President in Akayev's absence). On 25 March Bakiyev announced the appointment of several senior officials in the interim Government, including Otunbayeva as Minister of Foreign Affairs, Abdyldayev as Minister of Internal Affairs, Gen. Ismail Isakov as Minister of Defence, and Beknazarov as acting Prosecutor-General. Kulov was given responsibility for overseeing the country's law enforcement agencies and armed forces. After the Central Commission for Elections and Referendums announced that the powers of the bicameral legislature elected in 2000 were terminated, the lower and upper chambers dissolved themselves on 28 and 29 March, respectively, thereby effectively confirming the legitimacy of the recently elected legislature, and apparently overturning the ruling of the Supreme Court. Meanwhile, on 28 March the new Zhogorku Kenesh voted to confirm Bakiyev as interim Prime Minister, and to elect Tekebayev as legislative Chairman. (In late April Tekebayev was also appointed as Chairman of the Constitutional Court.) On 30 March Kulov resigned his post, reportedly owing to disagreement with Bakiyev.

On 4 April 2005 Akayev, speaking at the Kyrgyzstani embassy in Moscow, announced his resignation as President (the decision was approved by the Zhogorku Kenesh on 11 April). On 8 April Parliament voted to deprive Akayev of certain privileges associated with his status as a former president, and to remove immunity from prosecution from members of his family, allowing them to be investigated on corruption charges. The Zhogorku Kenesh subsequently scheduled a presidential election for 10 July. From mid-April protests were staged outside the Supreme Court against aspects of the legislative elections, demanding, *inter alia*, the resignation of the Chairman of the Court, Kurmanbek Osmonov, who was regarded as an ally of Akayev. However, although Osmonov submitted his resignation in late April, it was rejected by Bakiyev. In mid-May Bakiyev reached an agreement with Kulov, whose convictions had been overturned by the Supreme Court in April and who was considered his strongest rival in the presidential contest, according to which Kulov agreed to withdraw his candidacy in return for a guarantee that Bakiyev would appoint him Prime Minister should he secure the presidency. Also in mid-May, Bakiyev dismissed acting Minister of Internal Affairs Abdyldayev and replaced him with Murat Sutalinov. Violent unrest in Bishkek was reported in June.

On 10 July 2005 Bakiyev won 88.7% of the votes cast in the presidential election, which was contested by six candidates. The OSCE reported some irregularities in the counting of votes. Bakiyev was inaugurated as President on 14 August, and on 1 September the Zhogorku Kenesh confirmed Kulov's appointment as Prime Minister. In mid-September Bakiyev removed Beknazarov from his position as Prosecutor-General, together with his deputy, accusing them of negligence. Busurmankul Tabaldiyev was appointed to succeed Beknazarov on an acting basis; however, he resigned in October, and was replaced by Kambaraly Kongantiyev. Meanwhile, in late September the Zhogorku Kenesh approved 10 of the 16 ministers proposed by Bakiyev. Many ministers in the outgoing interim administration retained their portfolios, notably Isakov as Minister of Defence and Akylbek Zhaparov as Minister of the Economy and Finance. Following the rejection of Otunbayeva's nomination as Minister of Foreign Affairs, Alikbek Jekshenkulov was appointed to the post. (Otunbayeva and Beknazarov subsequently became co-chairmen of the Banner—Asaba—Party of National Revival.) Adakhan Madumarov was appointed Deputy Prime Minister and Marat Kaiypov became Minister of Justice. In October the Office of the Prosecutor-General charged former Prime Minister Tanayev, who was under house arrest in Bishkek, with abuse of power and corruption. (In May 2006 it was reported that the criminal case against Tanayev had been closed.) Also in October 2005 Bakiyev appointed Daniyar Usenov, an opponent of Kulov, to the post of acting First Deputy Prime Minister, although his nomination was rejected in November, and in the following month the Zhogorku Kenesh approved the appointment, in his place, of Medetbek Kerimkulov. The Government was sworn in on 20 December.

Meanwhile, in September 2005 Bayaman Erkinbayev, a parliamentary deputy and businessman who had actively participated in Akayev's removal from power (and who was alleged to have links to criminal groups), was murdered in Bishkek; another parliamentary deputy had been assassinated in July. In October a further parliamentary deputy, Tynychbek Akmatbayev, was killed by inmates during an official visit to a gaol. Large rallies, led by Akmatbayev's brother, Ryspek, a prominent and controversial figure alleged to be involved in organized crime (see below), subsequently took place to demand the dismissal of Kulov, whom the protesters accused of having collaborated with prisoners to organize the killing of Akmatbayev.

In January 2006 President Bakiyev decreed that measures be taken to organize a referendum on the division of power between the President and parliament; Bakiyev had pledged to award the legislature increased powers following his election. Also in early January, representatives of 17 political movements and organizations agreed to establish an opposition bloc, the People's Coalition of Democratic Forces, which united those dissatisfied with the new regime. In late January Kulov demanded reform of the judicial system and the entire law enforcement system, and criticized the Chairman of the National Security Service (SNB), Tashtemir Aitbayev, for allowing criminal elements to infiltrate the organization. Although Bakiyev rejected demands by parliamentary deputies for Aitbayev's dismissal, in early February he removed the deputy head of the SNB, and accepted the resignation of the Deputy Secretary of the Security Council. Also in early February further tensions between the Zhogorku Kenesh and the President arose when Bakiyev accused the legislature of fomenting political instability and exceeding its mandate, causing Tekebayev to tender his resignation from the parliamentary chairmanship. Although the Zhogorku Kenesh initially rejected Tekebayev's resignation, leading to further strains between the legislature and the President, it was accepted in late February. Marat Sultanov was elected as the new Chairman of the Zhogorku Kenesh in early March, and pledged to attempt to resolve disagreements with the executive without recourse to confrontation. In March President Bakiyev signed a decree officially suspending the Chairman of the National Bank, Ulan Sarbanov, from office, during his trial on charges of having illegally transferred some US $420,000 to former President Akayev in 1999. Meanwhile, in early March Bakiyev had signed a decree designating 24 March, the anniversary of Akayev's effective removal from power as a result of the so-called 'tulip revolution', a national holiday, to be known as the Day of the People's Revolution.

Parliamentary by-elections, scheduled to take place in three districts in April 2006, generated considerable controversy owing to the candidacy of Rysbek Akmatbayev. Akmatbayev, convicted twice during the 1990s for, *inter alia*, assault and robbery, had been tried, but acquitted, in early 2006 for the murder of a policeman; however, his acquittal was in the process of being appealed at the time of the polls, thus rendering his candidacy illegitimate under the terms of the Constitution. In protest at Akmatbayev's participation, thousands of demonstrators amassed in the streets of the capital on the eve of the by-elections, urging the Government to adopt a tougher stance against organized crime. The by-elections proceeded as planned on 9 April, and Akmatbayev secured a comfortable victory in the constituency that he contested. Another large-scale demonstration took place in the capital in late April when several thousand people gathered to protest against widespread corruption among state officials, demanding that Bakiyev implement the reforms that he had pledged during his election campaign. In May Akmatbayev was shot dead by unknown assailants in Bishkek.

Further evidence of a rift between the executive and the legislature emerged in late April 2006, when the Zhogorku Kenesh voted to evaluate the performance of individual members of the Government: only Prime Minister Kulov, two ministers and the head of a state committee were given positive appraisals, and in early May 14 ministers resigned. Although President Bakiyev rejected their resignations and the ministers subsequently agreed to remain in their posts, Bakiyev effected a cabinet reorganization in mid-May, which included the appointment of Usenov as First Deputy Prime Minister. The nomination of Ishengul Boljurova as a Deputy Prime Minister was rejected by the Zhogorku Kenesh in the following month. Also in mid-May Bakiyev dismissed Kombaraaly Kongantiyev as Prosecutor-General and Usen Sydykov as Chief of the Presidential Administration, and replaced Tashtemir Aitbayev as Chairman of the SNB with former Prosecutor-General Busurmankul Tabaldiyev.

In November 2006 thousands of opposition supporters attended a rally in Bishkek demanding constitutional reform and the resignation of President Bakiyev. Following a week of mass protests, the Zhogorku Kenesh approved a new Constitution on 8 November, which was to diminish the power afforded to the President and to augment that of the legislature, the capacity of which was to be enlarged to 90 members; the membership of governments was henceforth to be determined by the Zhogorku Kenesh, rather than the President. President Bakiyev signed the new Constitution into effect on 9 November. In mid-December Prime Minister Kulov tendered his resignation (together with that of his Government), with the stated aim of forcing early parliamentary elections and thereby addressing the ongoing political crisis.

At the end of December 2006 the legislature voted to adopt a number of amendments to the new Constitution, including the retraction of the legislature's power to appoint the Government, which was henceforth to be appointed by the President at the suggestion of the Prime Minister, without the need for legislative approval. These amendments were signed into law on 17 January 2007. In late January the Zhogorku Kenesh formally approved President Bakiyev's nomination of Azim Isabekov, hitherto acting Minister of Agriculture, Water Resources and Processing Industry, as Prime Minister, having twice rejected the President's nomination of Kulov. In early February Isabekov formed a new Government, in which the majority of key posts were allocated to close associates of President Bakiyev, including Usenov, who retained the position of First Deputy Prime Minister, Ednan Karabayev, who was appointed Minister of Foreign Affairs, and Igor Chudinov, who was awarded the newly-created industry, energy and fuel resources portfolio. In the same month Kulov added his voice to opposition calls for the President's resignation, strongly suggesting that the appointment of a new Prime Minister and Government would do little to restore political stability to Kyrgyzstan. On 29 March Isabekov resigned as premier, after Bakiyev reversed his decision to remove five government ministers that had been taken in response to continuing mass protests in Bishkek. The appointment of Atambayev as Prime Minister, which was regarded as an attempt to satisfy opposition demands, was approved by the Zhogorku Kenesh on the following day. A subsequent government reorganization included the dismissal of Usenov as First Deputy Prime Minister. Later in April large-scale protests in Bishkek, organized by the recently established opposition grouping led by Kulov, the United Front For A Worthy Future For Kyrgyzstan, were dispersed by the security forces, and an encampment of tents established by protesters in the city centre was removed; some 100 demonstrators were arrested and two prominent opposition leaders were detained on charges of inciting unrest.

In September 2007 the Constitutional Court ruled that the adoption of the Constitutions of both November 2006 and January 2007 had been illegal, since the drafts had not been submitted to a national referendum; consequently the Constitution in place prior to November 2006 again entered into force. Bakiyev subsequently announced that a further new constitutional text was to be proposed at a referendum on 21 October. In early October Bakiyev dismissed the Minister of Economic Development and Trade for failing to address rising food prices in the country. Later that month Bakiyev established a political party, Bright Road (Ak Zhol). The Constitution proposed at the national referendum on 21 October was endorsed by 76.1% of the electorate (with a voter turnout of 81.6%); henceforth, in legislative elections single-member constituencies were to be replaced by a proportional party list system, while the number of parliamentary deputies was to increase from 75 to 90. On the following day Bakiyev dissolved the Zhorgorku Kenesh and announced that early legislative elections were to take place later in the year; these were subsequently scheduled for 16 December. The Government submitted its resignation on 24 October, but remained in office in an interim capacity.

On 29 November 2007 Bakiyev removed Atambayev from the premiership; on the same day he appointed Iskenderbek Aidaraliyev, hitherto Governor of Jalal-Abad Oblast, as First Deputy Prime Minister and also assigned him the role of acting Prime

Minister. At the elections on 16 December Bright Road won about 47.0% of votes cast, securing 71 seats in the 90-member Zhorgorku Kenesh, ahead of the Social Democratic Party of Kyrgyzstan, with 5.1% of the votes cast and 11 seats, and the Communist Party of Kyrgyzstan, with 5.1% of the votes cast and eight seats. The Fatherland Socialist Party (Ata-Meken), despite gaining 8.3% of votes overall, narrowly failed to qualify for representation, owing to the new electoral requirement that each party obtain at least 0.5% of the votes cast in each of the country's seven oblasts and two largest cities. Although the stipulation was particularly criticized by OSCE observers, who stated that the conduct of the elections failed to meet democratic standards, and was also contested by the Fatherland Socialist Party (Ata-Meken), the electoral commission upheld the results. On 25 December Chudinov was appointed Prime Minister. A new Government, which retained the principal ministers of the former administration, was approved in the Zhorgorku Kenesh on 27 December.

On 26 May 2008 the head of the pro-presidential faction in the Zhogorku Kenesh, Elmira Ibragimova, was appointed Deputy Prime Minister, succeeding Dosbol Nur uulu (who was transferred to the post of State Secretary). On the same day Bakytbek Kalyev, hitherto the head of the State Border Guard Service, was appointed Minister of Defence, succeeding Isakov, who became Secretary of the National Security Council. In early September, on the recommendation of the Prime Minister, Bakiyev dismissed the Minister of Justice, Marat Kaiyypov, and the head of the penal service, following an investigation into a prison riot, in which two officers were killed, in August. A hitherto deputy prosecutor-general, Nurlan Tursunkulov, was appointed as the new Minister of Justice. Later that month, the Chairman of the electoral commission, Klara Kabilova, fled the country, subsequently accusing Maksim Bakiyev, the son of the President, of intimidation and threats against her as part of a government-orchestrated conspiracy to suppress the participation of opposition supporters in the forthcoming local elections, set for 5 October. In these elections, held as scheduled, observers from local non-governmental organizations alleged that numerous irregularities had enabled government candidates to win most seats in municipal councils, and contested the CEC's statement of a participation rate of 61.6%. The new electoral commission Chairman, Damir Lisovsky, denied widespread allegations of electoral fraud. In November the Minister of Industry, Energy and Fuel Resources was replaced, following criticism over energy shortages. In late December an alliance of principal opposition parties, the United People's Movement (UPM), was established to demand: the resignation of Bakiyev; an end to the appointment of leading officials based on clan and family; and the cancellation of the proposed privatization of various important facilities. Severe energy shortages, and other indications of a deterioration in the economy following the onset of the international financial crisis, led to an increase in anti-Government sentiment. In January 2009 Bakiyev removed a total of 17 ministers and senior government officials, regional officials and ambassadors. Aidaraliyev was transferred to the post of Minister of Agriculture, Water Resources and Processing Industry; he was succeeded as First Deputy Prime Minister by Omurbek Babanov (who resigned from the Social Democratic Party following his appointment). Kadyrbek Sarbayev, hitherto the ambassador to Mongolia, received the post of Minister of Foreign Affairs, replacing Karabayev.

Following the announcement of his decision to close the Manas airbase (see below) in February 2009, Bakiyev indicated his intention to seek a second term in office, and was reported to favour an early presidential election; several opposition leaders had appealed to the Constitutional Court to bring forward the next poll (due to take place in October 2010). Opposition parties threatened to begin a campaign of protests to demand that the Government end repressive measures taken against opposition leaders and activists. In early March 2009, shortly after Bakiyev had agreed to negotiate with opposition leaders, former Minister of Foreign Affairs and prominent opposition member Alikbek Jekshenkulov was arrested on suspicion of involvement in the killing of a Turkish businessman in 2007, prompting immediate speculation that his arrest had been prompted by his support of Tekebayev (who was believed to be a likely presidential candidate). In the same month Medet Sadyrkulov, the head of the presidential administration until his replacement in January, was killed in an automobile collision; several opposition leaders immediately claimed that the circumstances of his death were suspicious and that he had intended to transfer support to opponents of Bakiyev. On 19 March the Constitutional Court issued a ruling that the next presidential election take place no later than 25 October of that year; on the following day the Zhorgorku Kenesh voted in favour of the poll being conducted on 23 July. In late March the UPM, led by Beknazarov, staged large anti-Government demonstrations in Bishkek and other major towns nationwide; opposition leaders warned that they would organize further protests if major demands for the replacement of one-half of the officials in principal ministries and the CEC were not met by the Government. The UPM further announced its intention to present a single candidate to contest the forthcoming presidential election.

In January 1994 Kyrgyzstan joined the economic zone newly established by Kazakhstan and Uzbekistan, and in February 1995 an Interstate Council was formed to co-ordinate economic activity in the zone. Following the admission of Tajikistan in March 1998, in May the four countries were formally constituted as the Central Asian Economic Union (known as the Central Asian Co-operation Organization—CACO—from March 2002). Meanwhile, in March 1996 Kyrgyzstan signed a treaty with Russia, Belarus and Kazakhstan to create a 'community of integrated states', in an attempt to achieve closer economic, cultural and social integration, and joined a customs union established by the three other countries. In April 1998 Tajikistan joined the union, and in October 2000 it was superseded by a new economic body, the Eurasian Economic Community (EURASEC, see p. 426), which merged with CACO in January 2006. Kyrgyzstan was not to participate in the first stage of a customs union to be established by some of the member states of EURASEC, but it was anticipated that it would join the union by 2011.

In May 2001 the signatories of the CIS Collective Security Treaty—Armenia, Belarus, Kazakhstan, Kyrgyzstan, Russia and Tajikistan—agreed to form a Collective Rapid Reaction Force in Bishkek to combat Islamist militancy in Central Asia; in January 2002 it was announced that the force was ready to undertake combat missions. In April 2003 a successor organization to the Collective Security Treaty was formed, with the inauguration of the Collective Security Treaty Organization (CSTO). In 2003 the Islamic Party of Turkestan and the clandestine, transnational, Islamist Hizb-ut-Tahrir al-Islami (Party of Islamic Liberation) continued to be considered threats to stability in Kyrgyzstan. The latter, which aimed to unite Muslim countries and establish Islamic law, apparently solely through peaceful means, had become the most widespread illegal movement in Kyrgyzstan, particularly in southern regions, despite government attempts to suppress it.

Kyrgyzstan's campaign against Islamist extremism intensified in mid-1999, when Islamist groups believed to be based in Uzbekistan and Tajikistan took hostages in separate instances near Osh. In August Kyrgyzstani and Uzbekistani forces launched airstrikes against Tajikistani militants in the Osh region, in an attempt to prevent further acts of insurgency. However, later that month a senior Kyrgyzstani military commander was among more than 25 people kidnapped by a group of rebels, which captured three villages near the Tajikistani border. The rebels were believed to be members of the Islamic Movement of Uzbekistan (IMU), which demanded the release of Islamists imprisoned in that country. The hostage crisis intensified, with Kyrgyzstani government troops engaging in a large-scale military operation in order to defeat the rebels and free the captives. It was announced in October that all of the hostages had been released. (However, it was reported in November that the body of a police officer, taken hostage in August, had been discovered.) From August 2000 Islamist militants made a further series of incursions into Kyrgyzstan from Tajikistan, leading to armed conflict with government forces. The number of insurgents amassing on the Kyrgyzstani–Tajikistani border increased, despite intensive shelling and aerial bombardment by Kyrgyzstani troops. By the end of October, however, the Government claimed that all the rebels had left Kyrgyzstan and that it had regained full control of the border regions.

In April 2001 a local government official accused the Uzbekistani authorities of laying land-mines along the border with Kyrgyzstan, and demanded the removal of Uzbekistani troops, deployed in an effort to combat the incursions of Islamist militants and drugs-traffickers, from Kyrgyzstani border territories. Meanwhile, reports in May indicated that Islamist rebels were increasingly recruiting from southern Kyrgyzstan. In July 2003 it was reported that Kyrgyzstan was to commence the unilateral removal of land-mines along the border with Uzbekistan.

Relations with Uzbekistan were further strained in mid-2005, when the Kyrgyzstani Government refused to return a large number of refugees who had fled Uzbekistan after violence broke out in the city of Andijon in May (see the chapter on Uzbekistan). Although some refugees were repatriated, most were either given refuge in Kyrgyzstan or allowed to travel on to other countries. Apparently in response to Kyrgyzstan's refusal to co-operate with its demands, in August the Government of Uzbekistan annulled a bilateral agreement to supply natural gas to Kyrgyzstan. In September Uzbekistan issued a report accusing Kyrgyzstan of having permitted religious extremists to use bases in the south of the country to prepare to foment unrest in Andijon. In August 2006 the Kyrgyzstani authorities attracted international censure for the decision to repatriate to Uzbekistani a number of refugees from Andijon. In the same month Rafiq Qori Kamoluddin, a prominent imam in Kyrgyzstan and an ethnic Uzbek, was shot dead in an operation targeting alleged Islamist extremists conducted by the Kyrgyzstani and Uzbekistani national security services.

Kyrgyzstan endeavoured to maintain good relations with the largest and most influential CIS member, Russia. In June 1992 Akayev and the Russian President, Boris Yeltsin, signed a treaty of friendship, co-operation and mutual assistance. A further declaration on friendship, alliance and partnership was signed in July 2000. Military agreements, including a treaty of non-aggression, have also been concluded. An agreement concerning the expansion of Russian-Kyrgyzstani military co-operation was concluded in October 1997, whereby Russia was to lease four military installations in Kyrgyzstan in return for training Kyrgyzstani army recruits. In October 2003 a Russian airbase became operational at Kant, some 30 km from an airbase at Manas, occupied by the US-led anti-terrorism coalition (see below); the new base was the first Russian military installation to be established outside Russia since the collapse of the USSR. In March 2005 Putin offered Akayev the opportunity to take up residence in Russia, after he fled to that country during what became known as the 'tulip revolution' (see above). In September the Russian Minister of Defence, Sergei Ivanov, declared that Russia was to provide Kyrgyzstan with several million US dollars in military aid, to be used primarily to combat terrorism. In February 2009 Russian President Dmitrii Medvedev agreed to extend funds equivalent to more than US $2,000m. to the Kyrgyzstani Government (of which some $1,700m. were designated for the development of a major hydroelectric project), thereby, it was widely believed, securing the closure of the US airbase at Manas (see below).

Kyrgyzstan reached a series of bilateral co-operation agreements with the People's Republic of China during 1996, the terms of which provided for the partial demarcation of their shared border, which was undertaken from mid-2001. A border treaty signed in August 1999 ceded almost 95,000 ha of disputed territory to China. Akayev signed the agreement without the consent of the legislature, prompting widespread protests upon its ratification in 2002 (see above). Meanwhile, an agreement signed in April 1997 with China, Russia, Kazakhstan and Tajikistan (which, together with Kyrgyzstan, constituted the so-called Shanghai Five, later known as the Shanghai Forum) aimed to improve joint border security. The alliance, renamed the Shanghai Co-operation Organization (SCO) upon the accession of Uzbekistan, signed the Shanghai Convention on Combating Terrorism, Separatism and Extremism in mid-2001. In August an associated anti-terrorism centre became operational in Bishkek. The Presidents of Kazakhstan and Kyrgyzstan signed a border agreement in December. In March 2002 China agreed to provide Kyrgyzstan with military assistance worth some US $1.2m. In August 2003 Kyrgyzstani forces participated in major anti-terrorist manoeuvres, hosted by China and Kazakhstan. In September 2004 Tanayev and the Chinese Prime Minister, Wen Jiabao, signed a 10-year co-operation agreement on combating terrorism, separatism and religious extremism, and a protocol on the demarcation of the border between the two countries. In addition, China announced that it would provide Kyrgyzstan with a $6m. grant as part of an agreement on technical and economic co-operation. In April 2006 Minister of Defence Isakov met his Chinese counterpart, Gen. Cao Gangchuan, for sideline discussions during a meeting of the SCO in the Chinese capital, Beijing. The two ministers pledged further to consolidate bilateral relations and also to improve military co-operation in order to safeguard regional security and stability. In early 2009 public discontent was reported at the increasing number of Chinese immigrants in the country, with local industries adversely affected by imports of cheaper Chinese commodities.

Following the suicide attacks on the US cities of New York and Washington, DC, on 11 September 2001, President Akayev announced that he was prepared to give US military aircraft access to Kyrgyzstani airspace for the aerial bombardment of militants of the al-Qa'ida (Base) organization (held responsible by the USA for having co-ordinated the attacks) and its Taliban hosts in Afghanistan. In late November the Government agreed to give the US-led anti-terrorism coalition access to its military bases and, later, the airbase at Manas airport. Kyrgyzstan undertook joint exercises with US troops in February 2002, which aimed to facilitate attempts to counter insurgency in the country's mountainous regions. In September Akayev met the US President, George W. Bush, and the US Secretary of State, Colin Powell, in Washington, DC, where they discussed Kyrgyzstan's human rights record, the USA's declared 'war against terrorism' and economic issues. Although Kyrgyzstan stated that it would permit the USA to use the Manas airbase until the situation in Afghanistan stabilized, in early 2006 Kyrgyzstan presented the USA with new conditions for the use of the facility, apparently proposing to increase the rent payable by the USA from US $2m. to $200m.; President Bakiyev maintained that the proposed charge was in accordance with international norms. In July Kyrgyzstan and the USA signed an agreement allowing the latter to continue using the airbase at Manas airport in exchange for 'assistance and co-operation' of some $150m. Nevertheless, in early 2008 President Bakiyev announced that the Kyrgyzstani Government planned to request the closure of the airbase. In January 2009 a senior US military commander in charge of US strategy in Afghanistan, who emphasized the importance of the Manas airbase during a visit to Bishkek, indicated that he had received assurances from the Kyrgyzstani Government that the USA would be permitted continued use of the facility. However, in early February Bakiyev announced that the airbase would be closed, owing to the inadequate levels of rent paid by the US Administration; his decision followed a visit to Moscow during which the Russian Government offered Kyrgyzstan assistance and loans equivalent to more than US $2,000m. to compensate for economic difficulties exacerbated by the onset of the international financial crisis. A number of opposition parties protested at the envisaged closure, on the grounds that the US presence contributed to security in the country, and accused Bakiyev of responding to Russian pressure. Despite subsequent discussions between the Kyrgyzstani and US authorities, on 19 February the Zhorgorku Kenesh, with 78 votes in favour, approved the government order to close the airbase, which was enacted by Bakiyev on the following day; US forces were required to withdraw from Kyrgyzstan within a period of 180 days after the US embassy received notice of the termination of the lease.

Government

Supreme legislative power in the Kyrgyz Republic is vested in the unicameral, 90-member Zhogorku Kenesh (Supreme Council). The Zhogorku Kenesh is elected by universal suffrage for a term of five years. The President of the Republic, who is directly elected for a five-year term, is Head of State and Commander-in-Chief of the Armed Forces, and also holds extensive executive powers. The Prime Minister is appointed by the President, subject to the approval of the Zhogorku Kenesh; the remaining members of the Government are appointed by the President. The Prime Minister is empowered to appoint and dismiss ministers and heads of departments. For administrative purposes, Kyrgyzstan is divided into seven oblasts (regions) and the municipality of Bishkek (the capital).

Defence

Kyrgyzstan began to raise a national army in 1992. As assessed at November 2008, Kyrgyzstan's total armed forces numbered 10,900 (army 8,500, air force 2,400). There were also an estimated 9,500 paramilitary forces (comprising 5,000 border guards, 3,500 troops attached to the Ministry of Internal Affairs and a national guard of 1,000). Military service is compulsory and lasts for 18 months. Kyrgyzstan joined the defence structures of the Commonwealth of Independent States (CIS, see p. 225) by signing, with five other member states, a collective security agreement in May 1992; in May 2001 it was announced that the signatory countries were to form a Collective Rapid Reaction Force to combat Islamist militancy in Central Asia. In April 2003 the Collective Security Treaty Organization (CSTO) was inaugurated as the successor to the CIS collective security system, with the participation of Armenia, Belarus, Kazakhstan, Kyrgyzstan, Russia and Tajikistan. In June 1994 Kyrgyzstan joined the North Atlantic Treaty Organization's (NATO) 'Partnership for Peace' (see p. 353) programme of military co-operation. In early 2009 about 400 Russian troops were deployed at the Kant airbase (established by Russia in October 2003). In February 2009 the Kyrgyzstani legislature approved a government decision for the closure of the US military base at Manas airport (where some 1,000 US forces had been stationed—see Recent History). In 2007 state expenditure on defence totalled some 1,460m. soms.

Economic Affairs

In 2007, according to estimates by the World Bank, Kyrgyzstan's gross national income (GNI), measured at average 2005–07 prices, was US $3,099m., equivalent to $590 per head (or $1,950 per head on an international purchasing-power parity basis). During 2000–07, it was estimated, the population increased by an annual average of 0.9%, while gross domestic product (GDP) per head increased, in real terms, at an average annual rate of 3.2%. Overall GDP increased, in real terms, at an estimated average annual rate of 4.1% in 2000–07. Real GDP increased by 2.7% in 2006, and by 7.4% in 2007.

Agriculture (including forestry and fishing) contributed an estimated 33.6% of GDP in 2007, according to preliminary official figures, and engaged 34.5% of the employed labour force. By tradition, the Kyrgyz are a pastoral nomadic people, and the majority of the population (some 64.2% in 2005, according to UN estimates) reside in rural areas. Livestock-rearing, once the mainstay of agricultural activity, is declining in importance. Only about 7% of the country's land area is arable; of this, some 70% depends on irrigation. The principal crops are grain, potatoes, vegetables and sugar beet. By 2002, according to government figures, collective farms accounted for only around 6% of agricultural production, while state farms accounted for just under 2%. The GDP of the agricultural sector increased, in real terms, by an average of 2.4% per year in 2000–06; according to the Asian Development Bank (ADB, see p. 191), agricultural GDP grew by 8.1% in 2006, and by 13.4% in 2007.

Industry (comprising manufacturing, mining, utilities and construction) contributed 18.9% of GDP in 2007, according to preliminary official data, and provided 20.3% of employment. Real industrial GDP declined at an average annual rate of 1.3% in 2000–06; however, according to the ADB, the GDP of the sector increased by 1.7% in 2006, and by 16.3% in 2007.

In 2007 the mining and quarrying sector provided 0.5% of GDP, according to preliminary figures. The sector engaged 0.6% of the employed work-force in 2007. Kyrgyzstan has considerable mineral deposits, including coal, gold, tin, mercury, antimony, zinc, tungsten and uranium. In May 2001 the Government announced the discovery of new deposits of petroleum, estimated to total 70m. barrels, in an oilfield in the west. Production of gold from the Kumtor mine, which is believed to contain the eighth largest deposit of gold in the world (over 200 metric tons), began in January 1997. As a result, by 2001 Kyrgyzstan had become the 10th largest extractor and seller of gold world-wide. The Kumtor mine reportedly produced almost 4.4m. ounces of gold between 1997 and the end of 2003. Production of gold from the Jeruy deposit commenced in 2002. In April 2006 an agreement was signed with a Kazakhstani company on the development of the Taldy Bulak Levoberezhny gold deposit. Gold production totalled 10.5 tons in 2006.

Manufacturing contributed 11.3% of GDP in 2007, according to preliminary figures. The manufacturing sector employed 8.4% of the work-force in 2007. In 2005 the principal branches of manufacturing, measured by gross value of output, were metallurgy (50.6% of the total) and food products, beverages and tobacco (18.2%). Real manufacturing GDP declined by an average of 2.7% per year in 2000–06, according to the World Bank; according to ADB figures, the GDP of the sector decreased by 7.4% in 2006, but grew by 20.8% in 2007.

Kyrgyzstan's principal source of domestic energy production (and a major export) is hydroelectricity (generated by the country's mountain rivers), which provided 86.9% of the country's total energy requirements in 2005. Kyrgyzstan has insufficient petroleum and natural gas to meet its needs, and substantial imports of hydrocarbons are thus required; Kyrgyzstan exports electricity to Kazakhstan and Uzbekistan in return for coal and natural gas, respectively. Imports of mineral products comprised 32.3% of the value of total recorded imports in 2007.

In 2007, according to preliminary official figures, the services sector contributed an estimated 47.5% of GDP, and the sector provided 45.2% of employment in 2007. In 2000–06 the GDP of the sector increased, in real terms, by an average of 7.3% per year; according to the ADB, services GDP increased by 10.9% in 2006 and by 10.5% in 2007.

In 2007 Kyrgyzstan recorded a visible trade deficit of US $1,298.5m., and there was a deficit of $262.7m. on the current account of the balance of payments. In 2007 the principal source of imports (accounting for 40.5% of the total) was Russia; other major suppliers were the People's Republic of China (14.7%), Kazakhstan (12.9%) and Uzbekistan (5.0%). The main market for exports in that year was Russia (which accounted for 20.7% of all exports); other principal markets were Switzerland (19.9%), Kazakhstan (18.0%) and Afghanistan (10.4%). The main exports in 2007 were mineral products, precious and semi-precious stones and metals and textiles. The principal imports in that year were mineral products (mostly petroleum and natural gas), machinery, and electrical equipment and chemicals.

In 2007 Kyrgyzstan recorded an overall budgetary surplus of 130.0m. soms, equivalent to less than 0.1% of GDP. Kyrgyzstan's total external debt was US $2,382m. at the end of 2006, of which $1860m. was long-term public debt. In that year the cost of debt-servicing was equivalent to 5.7% of the value of exports of goods and services. The annual rate of inflation averaged 5.2% in 2000–07. According to the ADB, consumer prices increased by 5.6% in 2006 and by 10.2% in 2007. The average rate of unemployment was 10.2% in 2007.

Kyrgyzstan participates in the economic bodies of the Commonwealth of Independent States (CIS, see p. 225), and has also joined the European Bank for Reconstruction and Development (EBRD, see p. 251), as a 'Country of Operations', the Economic Co-operation Organization (ECO, see p. 249) and the ADB. In 1998 Kyrgyzstan became the first CIS country to join the World Trade Organization (WTO, see p. 410).

An ambitious programme of economic reform was undertaken following independence in 1991, resulting in GDP growth in 1996–2001 and an annual rate of inflation of less than 10% in the latter year. GDP declined in 2002, largely owing to reduced industrial output after a landslide at the Kumtor gold mine, but growth resumed in 2003 and 2004, partly thanks to increased foreign trade and measures to tackle tax evasion. Political instability following the removal of President Askar Akayev in 2005, coupled with a decline in gold production, led to a contraction in GDP in that year, although the economy benefited from the announcement by the 'Paris Club' of official creditors that it was cancelling US $124m. of Kyrgyzstan's sovereign debt and rescheduling a further $431m. The new Government identified poverty reduction and combating corruption among its principal aims. Although GDP growth was recorded thereafter (reaching 8.5% in 2007), and living standards improved notably (the poverty rate declined from 46% in 2004 to 35% in 2007), the economy remained vulnerable to external shocks, as exemplified in 2008 when the dramatic rise in international commodity prices led to mid-year inflation of 32.5% and a widening of the current account deficit. The international financial crisis, moreover, was set to result in decreases in workers' remittances, domestic demand and revenue from exports, and there was concern that advances made in poverty reduction might be reversed. Meanwhile, the country increased imports of fuel and electricity after power shortages at the Toktogul hydropower station, and the Government appealed for substantial grants and loans. In early 2009, following confirmation that the Government would close the Manas airbase (used by US and other forces for offensives in Afghanistan), it was announced that Russia had pledged Kyrgyzstan $2,150m. in aid and loans, including a $150m. grant and some $1,700m. for a planned hydroelectric project. Although the funds were certain to improve economic prospects, they also would augment dependence on Russia. Kyrgyzstan's priorities remained the creation of an environment attractive to investors (not least by reducing corruption), the diversification of the economy, reforms to the pension and taxation system, and curbing the incidence of poverty.

Education

Education is officially compulsory for nine years, comprising four years of primary school (between the ages of seven and 10), followed by five years of lower secondary school (ages 11 to 15). Pupils may then continue their studies in upper secondary schools (two years' duration), specialized secondary schools (two to four years) or technical and vocational schools (from 15 years of age). In 2005/06 total enrolment at primary schools

KYRGYZSTAN

included 85.9% of the relevant age-group; enrolment at secondary-school level in that year included 80.5% of the relevant age group. In 2007/08 there were 49 institutes of higher education, providing courses lasting between four and six years, and attended by 250,460 students. In 2007 budgetary expenditure on education amounted to 9,178.0m. soms (25.6% of total spending).

Public Holidays

2009: 1 January (New Year's Day), 7 January (Christmas), 8 March (International Women's Day), 21 March (Nooruz, Spring Holiday), 24 March (Day of the People's Revolution), 1 May (International Labour Day), 5 May (Constitution Day), 9 May (Victory Day), 31 August (Independence Day), 20 September* (Orozo Ait, Id al-Fitr, end of Ramadan), 27 November* (Kurban Ait, Id al-Adha, Feast of the Sacrifice).

2010: 1 January (New Year's Day), 7 January (Christmas), 8 March (International Women's Day), 21 March (Nooruz, Spring Holiday), 24 March (Day of the People's Revolution), 1 May (International Labour Day), 5 May (Constitution Day), 9 May (Victory Day), 31 August (Independence Day), 10 September* (Orozo Ait, Id al-Fitr, end of Ramadan), 16 November* (Kurban Ait, Id al-Adha, Feast of the Sacrifice).

* These holidays are dependent on the Islamic lunar calendar and may vary by one or two days from the dates given.

Weights and Measures

The metric system is in force.

Statistical Survey

Source (unless otherwise stated): National Statistical Committee, 720033 Bishkek, Frunze 374; tel. (312) 22-63-63; fax (312) 22-07-59; e-mail zkudabaev@nsc.bishkek.su; internet www.stat.kg.

Area and Population

AREA, POPULATION AND DENSITY

Area (sq km)	199,900*
Population (census results)†	
12 January 1989	4,257,755
24 March 1999	
Males	2,380,465
Females	2,442,473
Total	4,822,938
Population (official estimates at 1 January)	
2006	5,138,669
2007	5,189,837
2008	5,224,260
Density (per sq km) at 1 January 2008	26.1

* 77,182 sq miles.
† The figures refer to *de jure* population. The *de facto* total was 4,290,442 at the 1989 census and 4,850,700 at the 1999 census.

PRINCIPAL ETHNIC GROUPS
(official estimates at 1 January 2008, rounded figures)

	Number	%
Kyrgyz	3,616,500	69.2
Uzbek	754,500	14.5
Russian	456,400	8.7
Dungan	60,300	1.2
Uighur	51,200	1.0
Tajik	48,000	0.9
Turk	36,400	0.7
Tatar	35,000	0.7
Ukrainian	25,300	0.5
Others	140,700	2.7
Total	**5,224,300**	**100.0**

ADMINISTRATIVE DIVISIONS
(1999 census)

	Area (sq km)	Population	Density (per sq km)	Principal city
Oblasts (Regions)				
Batken	17,000	382,426	22.5	Batken
Chui	20,200	770,811	38.2	Tokmok
Issyk-Kul	43,100	413,149	9.6	Karakol
Jalal-Abad	33,700	869,259	25.8	Jalal-Abad
Naryn	45,200	249,115	5.5	Naryn
Osh	29,200	1,175,998	40.3	Osh
Talas	11,400	199,872	17.5	Talas
City				
Bishkek	100	762,308	7,623.1	—
Total	**199,900**	**4,822,938**	**24.1**	

PRINCIPAL TOWNS
(population at census of March 1999)

Bishkek (capital)*	750,327	Karakol†	64,322
Osh	208,520	Tokmok	59,409
Jalal-Abad	70,401	Kara-Balta	53,887

* Known as Frunze between 1926 and 1991.
† Formerly Przhevalsk.

Mid-2007 (incl. suburbs, UN estimate): Bishkek 837,000 (Source: UN, *World Urbanization Prospects: The 2007 Revision*).

BIRTHS, MARRIAGES AND DEATHS

	Registered live births		Registered marriages		Registered deaths	
	Number	Rate (per 1,000)	Number	Rate (per 1,000)	Number	Rate (per 1,000)
2001	98,138	19.8	27,455	5.5	32,677	6.6
2002	101,012	20.2	31,240	6.3	35,235	7.1
2003	105,490	20.9	34,266	6.8	35,941	7.1
2004	109,939	21.6	34,542	6.8	35,061	6.9
2005	109,839	21.4	37,321	7.3	36,992	7.2
2006	120,737	23.3	43,760	8.4	38,566	7.4
2007	123,251	23.5	44,392	8.5	38,180	7.3
2008	127,144	24.1	44,491	8.4	37,228	7.1

Life expectancy (years at birth, official estimates): 67.8 (males 63.6; females 72.2) in 2007.

IMMIGRATION AND EMIGRATION

	2005	2006	2007
Immigrants	3,761	3,420	3,960
Emigrants	30,741	34,423	54,608

KYRGYZSTAN

ECONOMICALLY ACTIVE POPULATION
(annual averages, '000 persons)

	2005	2006	2007
Agriculture, hunting forestry and fishing	799.6	760.2	742.4
Mining and quarrying	12.4	11.8	13.1
Manufacturing	163.9	177.9	179.8
Electricity, gas and water supply	35.2	35.6	38.3
Construction	153.7	181.4	205.3
Wholesale and retail trade; repair of motor vehicles, motor cycles and personal and household goods	301.5	308.4	316.9
Hotels and restaurants	49.0	49.0	58.4
Transport, storage and communications	115.7	120.2	133.3
Financial intermediation	8.2	9.5	9.7
Real estate, renting and business activities	34.1	36.5	45.8
Public administration and defence; compulsory social security	102.3	101.0	106.8
Education	161.8	152.9	156.6
Health and social work	85.4	87.0	86.2
Other services	54.2	64.6	60.3
Total employed	2,077.1	2,096.1	2,152.7
Unemployed	183.5	188.9	191.1
Total labour force	2,260.6	2,285.0	2,343.8
Males	1,291.6	1,315.9	n.a.
Females	969.0	969.1	n.a.

2007 (annual averages, '000 persons): Total males employed 1,251.6; total females employed 901.1.

Health and Welfare

KEY INDICATORS

Total fertility rate (children per woman, 2006)	2.5
Under-5 mortality rate (per 1,000 live births, 2006)	41
HIV/AIDS (% of persons aged 15–49, 2007)	0.1
Physicians (per 1,000 head, 2006)	2.4
Hospital beds (per 1,000 head, 2006)	5.1
Health expenditure (2006): US $ per head (PPP)	127
Health expenditure (2006): % of GDP	6.4
Health expenditure (2006): public (% of total)	43.3
Access to water (% of persons, 2006)	89
Access to sanitation (% of persons, 2006)	93
Human Development Index (2006): ranking	122
Human Development Index (2006): value	0.694

For sources and definitions, see explanatory note on p. vi.

Agriculture

PRINCIPAL CROPS
('000 metric tons)

	2005	2006	2007
Wheat	950.1	840.3	708.9
Rice, paddy	17.1	18.7	17.3
Barley	213.5	204.0	227.2
Maize	437.3	438.0	460.7
Potatoes	1,141.5	1,254.9	1,373.8
Sugar beet	288.8	226.0	155.4
Sunflower seed	69.2	61.5*	59.0*
Cabbages and other brassicas	94.7	98.0*	102.0*
Tomatoes	171.2	177.0*	183.0*
Cucumbers and gherkins	62.4	64.5*	67.0*

—continued	2005	2006	2007
Onions, dry	110.0	113.5*	118.0*
Garlic	24.2	25.0*	26.0*
Carrots and turnips	144.9	150.0*	155.0*
Apples	102.4†	130.0*	125.7*
Apricots	13.0†	16.5*	16.0*
Peaches and nectarines	3.0†	3.8*	3.7*
Grapes	11.4	14.7	14.9
Watermelons	85.8	97.7	119.1
Seed cotton	118.1	117.5	95.1
Tobacco, unmanufactured	13.4	13.4	14.4

* FAO estimate.
† Unofficial figure.

Aggregate production ('000 metric tons, may include official, semi-official or estimated data): Total cereals 1,621.6 in 2005, 1,505.2 in 2006, 1,419.4 in 2007; Total roots and tubers 1,141.5 in 2005, 1,254.9 in 2006, 1,373.8 in 2007; Total vegetables (incl. melons) 822.6 in 2005, 859.0 in 2006, 908.9 in 2007; Total fruits (excl. melons) 158.1 in 2005, 190.7 in 2006, 185.1 in 2007.

Source: FAO.

LIVESTOCK
('000 head at 1 January)

	2005	2006	2007
Horses	347	350*	351*
Asses	44†	n.a.	n.a.
Cattle	1,035	1,074	1,117
Pigs	83	78	79
Sheep	2,965	3,062†	3,198*
Goats	808	814†	850*
Chickens	4,121	4,300*	4,300*
Turkeys	154	160*	160*

* FAO estimate.
† Unofficial figure.
Source: FAO.

LIVESTOCK PRODUCTS
('000 metric tons)

	2005	2006	2007
Cattle meat	90.9	91.2*	92.0*
Sheep meat	39.2	39.4*	39.5*
Goat meat	7.2	7.2*	7.3*
Pig meat	18.7	18.8*	18.9*
Horse meat	20.3	20.4*	20.5*
Chicken meat	5.4	5.4*	5.5*
Cows' milk	1,151.4	1,165.2*	1,192.0*
Hen eggs	17.7	19.1*	20.8*
Honey	1.3	1.4*	1.4*
Wool, greasy	9.9	10.6	10.6

* FAO estimate.
Source: FAO.

Forestry

ROUNDWOOD REMOVALS
('000 cubic metres, excl. bark, unofficial figures)

	2002	2003	2004
Sawlogs, veneer logs and logs for sleepers	6	6	5
Other industrial wood	6	6	5
Fuel wood	25	25	18
Total	37	37	28

2005–07: Figures assumed to be unchanged from 2004 (FAO estimates).
Source: FAO.

KYRGYZSTAN

SAWNWOOD PRODUCTION
('000 cubic metres, incl. railway sleepers)

	2002*	2003	2004
Coniferous (softwood)	2.0	8.0	6.3
Broadleaved (hardwood)	4.0	7.2	15.7
Total	6.0	15.2	22.0

* FAO estimates.

2005–07: Figures assumed to be unchanged from 2004 (FAO estimates).

Source: FAO.

Fishing
(metric tons, live weight)

	2003	2004	2005*
Capture	14	7	7
Freshwater bream	1	2	2
Common carp	1	—	—
Silver carp	2	—	—
Other cyprinids	5	1	1
Pike-perch	1	2	2
Whitefishes	3	1	1
Aquaculture	12	20	20
Common carp	7	8	8
Grass carp	1	2	2
Silver carp	4	10	10
Total catch	26	27	27

* FAO estimates.

2006: Catch assumed to be unchanged from 2005 (FAO estimates).

Source: FAO.

Mining
('000 metric tons, unless otherwise indicated)

	2005	2006	2007
Coal	335.3	321.3	353.2
Crude petroleum	77.2	70.9	68.2
Natural gas (million cu metres)	25.1	19.4	14.9

Gold (metric tons): 16.6 in 2005; 10.6 in 2006; 10.5 in 2007 (Source: Gold Fields Mineral Services, *Gold Survey 2008*).

Industry

SELECTED PRODUCTS
('000 metric tons, unless otherwise indicated)

	2005	2006	2007
Vegetable oil	15.4	16.8	17.6
Refined sugar	44.9	58.1	39.5
Vodka ('000 hectolitres)	16.2	14.6	14.0
Beer ('000 hectolitres)	12.3	11.0	14.1
Cigarettes (million)	3,179	3,086	3,053
Textile fabrics ('000 sq metres)	1,938	1,578	1,323
Motor spirit (petrol)	13.2	9.8	12.0
Gas-diesel (distillate fuel) oil	31.4	31.3	52.0
Residual fuel oils (Mazout)	41.7	42.1	54.1
Cement	972.8	1,050.9	1,358.8
Electric energy (million kWh)	14,891	14,523	14,800

Footwear ('000 pairs): 220.5 in 2005.

Finance

CURRENCY AND EXCHANGE RATES

Monetary Units
100 tyiyns = 1 som.

Sterling, Dollar and Euro Equivalents (31 December 2008)
£1 sterling = 57.464 soms;
US $1 = 39.418 soms;
€1 = 54.858 soms;
1,000 soms = £17.40 = $25.37 = €18.23.

Average Exchange Rate (soms per US $)
2006   40.153
2007   37.316
2008   36.575

Note: In May 1993 Kyrgyzstan introduced its own currency, the som, replacing the Russian (former Soviet) rouble at an exchange rate of 1 som = 200 roubles.

BUDGET
(million soms)*

Revenue†	2005	2006	2007
Taxation	16,361.4	19,981.2	26,544.8
Corporate income taxes	1,744.2	1,820.3	2,322.9
Personal income taxes	1,283.2	1,191.6	1,736.1
Value-added tax	7,088.6	9,150.6	10,701.6
Excise taxes	1,149.7	1,205.4	1,448.2
Taxes on international trade and transactions	1,664.0	2,803.3	3,789.5
Other current revenue	3,567.9	4,696.0	7,195.3
Capital revenue	46.1	138.0	465.3
Total	19,975.4	24,815.2	34,205.4

Expenditure‡	2005	2006	2007
General public services	3,039.6	3,358.4	5,154.8
Education	4,917.7	6,314.2	9,178.0
Health care	2,283.3	3,059.1	4,028.8
Social insurance and security	2,858.1	3,610.6	3,816.9
Housing and public utilities	1,040.6	1,415.5	2,657.3
Cultural and religious activity	606.9	813.0	1,239.9
Total (incl. others)	20,143.7	25,297.8	35,864.9

* Figures represent a consolidation of the budgetary transactions of the central Government and local governments. The operations of extra-budgetary accounts, including the Social Fund (formed in 1994 by an amalgamation of the Pension Fund, the Unemployment Fund and the Social Insurance Fund), are excluded.

† Excluding grants received (million soms): 392.6 in 2005; 266.1 in 2006; 1,789.5 in 2007.

‡ Including lending minus repayments.

Source: National Bank of the Kyrgyz Republic.

INTERNATIONAL RESERVES
(US $ million at 31 December)

	2005	2006	2007
Gold	42.6	52.8	69.5
IMF special drawing rights	5.3	33.3	13.8
Foreign exchange	564.5	731.1	1,093.4
Total	612.4	817.2	1,176.7

Source: IMF, *International Financial Statistics*.

MONEY SUPPLY
(million soms at 31 December)

	2004	2005	2006
Currency outside banks	11,109	13,065	19,410
Demand deposits at banking institutions	1,935	2,123	3,655
Total money	13,045	15,188	23,065

Source: IMF, *International Financial Statistics*.

KYRGYZSTAN
Statistical Survey

COST OF LIVING
(Consumer Price Index; base: previous year = 100)

	2005	2006	2007
Food and non-alcoholic drinks	109.8	106.8	131.5
Alcoholic drinks and tobacco products	102.0	102.5	109.1
Non-food products	102.0	104.6	109.8
Services	103.2	107.6	110.6
All items (incl. others)	**104.9**	**105.1**	**120.1**

NATIONAL ACCOUNTS
(million soms at current prices)

Expenditure on the Gross Domestic Product

	2006	2007
Final consumption expenditure	128,722.7	166,145.2
Households	105,799.4	138,652.0
Non-profit institutions serving households	2,453.7	2,683.7
General government	20,469.4	24,809.5
Gross capital formation	27,534.8	36,793.5
Gross fixed capital formation	26,211.6	35,226.9
Acquisitions, less disposals, of valuables	455.3	490.6
Changes in inventories	867.9	1,076.0
Total domestic expenditure	**156,257.5**	**202,938.7**
Exports of goods and services (net)	−42,457.4	−63,168.0
Statistical discrepancy	—	−21.3
GDP in purchasers' values	**113,800.1**	**139,749.4**

Gross Domestic Product by Economic Activity

	2005	2006	2007*
Agriculture, forestry and fishing	28,739.4	32,638.2	40,552.9
Mining	556.4	488.7	548.7
Manufacturing	12,968.0	12,509.0	13,687.8
Electricity, gas and water supply	3,896.7	3,937.4	3,922.8
Construction	2,725.9	3,041.9	4,711.0
Wholesale and retail trade; repair of motor vehicles, motorcycles and personal and household goods	18,001.6	20,883.9	25,484.4
Hotels and restaurants	1,350.6	1,549.0	1,870.6
Transport and communication	6,617.6	6,887.2	10,181.7
Financial intermediation	2,250.8	2,986.4	605.7†
Real estate, renting and business activities	2,814.1	3,321.7	3,777.9
Public administration and defence; compulsory social security	4,659.8	5,053.9	5,474.7
Education	3,854.4	4,561.6	5,409.8
Health and social work	2,064.9	2,588.5	2,711.7
Other community, social and personal services	1,197.9	1,531.4	1,860.4
Sub-total	**91,698.2**	**101,978.8**	**120,800.1†**
Less Financial intermediation services indirectly measured	1,735.2	2,380.7	—
Gross value added in basic prices	**89,963.0**	**99,598.1**	**120,800.1**
Taxes, less subsidies, on products	10,936.2	14,202.0	18,949.3
GDP in market prices	**100,899.2**	**113,800.1**	**139,749.4**

* Preliminary figures.
† Including financial intermediation services indirectly measured.

BALANCE OF PAYMENTS
(US $ million)

	2005	2006	2007
Exports of goods f.o.b.	686.8	906.0	1,337.0
Imports of goods f.o.b.	−1,105.5	−1,792.4	−2,635.5
Trade balance	**−418.7**	**−886.5**	**−1,298.5**
Exports of services	259.4	378.7	684.3
Imports of services	−291.3	−460.8	−582.2
Balance on goods and services	**−450.5**	**−968.5**	**−1,196.4**
Other income received	16.5	41.6	42.6
Other income paid	−101.7	−84.7	−95.0
Balance on goods, services and income	**−535.7**	**−1,011.6**	**−1,248.8**
Current transfers received	513.6	762.4	1,065.2
Current transfers paid	−37.9	−50.0	−79.0
Current balance	**−60.0**	**−299.2**	**−262.7**
Capital account (net)	−20.5	−43.9	−74.9
Direct investment abroad	—	—	0.2
Direct investment from abroad	42.6	182.0	207.9
Portfolio investment assets	2.3	−3.0	−19.2
Portfolio investment liabilities	—	—	1.5
Other investment assets	−47.5	−24.0	19.5
Other investment liabilities	88.1	182.3	144.4
Net errors and omissions	63.6	182.4	276.3
Overall balance	**68.4**	**176.7**	**293.1**

Source: IMF, *International Financial Statistics*.

External Trade

PRINCIPAL COMMODITIES
(US $ million)

Imports c.i.f.	2005	2006	2007
Vegetable products	40.6	62.6	119.1
Prepared foodstuffs, beverages and tobacco	101.3	141.6	185.6
Mineral products	334.0	527.4	781.4
Products of chemical or allied industries	130.8	145.5	222.7
Plastics, rubber and articles thereof	60.1	85.2	104.8
Textiles and fabrics	36.6	50.9	47.9
Metals and articles thereof	66.5	104.9	177.7
Machinery, electrical equipment and parts	156.1	271.9	343.7
Vehicles and transport equipment	41.4	136.6	144.2
Total (incl. others)	**1,101.3**	**1,718.2**	**2,417.0**

Exports f.o.b.	2005	2006	2007
Vegetable products	19.9	36.6	80.3
Prepared foodstuffs, beverages and tobacco	37.2	28.9	37.3
Mineral products	96.8	177.8	330.0
Products of chemical or allied industries	13.5	14.4	24.4
Raw hides and skins, leather, fur, travel articles and bags	12.2	14.3	16.0
Textiles and fabrics	77.4	96.7	122.3
Natural and cultured pearls, precious and semi-precious stones, precious metals and products, and coins	236.2	212.6	228.5
Metals and articles thereof	23.2	27.0	52.9
Machinery, electrical equipment and parts	32.1	51.1	69.9
Vehicles and transport equipment	18.5	23.7	42.3
Total (incl. others)	**672.0**	**794.2**	**1,134.2**

Source: Asian Development Bank.

KYRGYZSTAN

PRINCIPAL TRADING PARTNERS
(US $ million)

Imports c.i.f.	2005	2006	2007
Belarus	7.1	18.7	23.8
Canada	15.0	32.2	23.0
China, People's Republic (incl. Hong Kong)	102.9	245.6	355.6
France	6.1	24.8	17.6
Germany	37.6	39.9	54.2
Kazakhstan	174.4	199.8	312.4
Korea, Republic	27.8	29.1	39.1
Netherlands	18.9	27.7	36.4
Russia	378.9	652.3	978.8
Turkey	33.4	39.5	50.9
Turkmenistan	13.0	1.8	1.3
Ukraine	40.1	41.9	79.5
USA	67.2	97.5	95.8
Uzbekistan	60.1	65.0	120.9
Total (incl. others)	1,101.3	1,718.2	2,417.0

Exports f.o.b.	2005	2006	2007
Afghanistan	12.4	74.8	118.4
Belgium	3.0	5.2	11.5
Canada	22.5	0.2	0.8
China, People's Republic (incl. Hong Kong)	26.6	38.1	61.9
India	10.2	3.7	0.8
Kazakhstan	116.1	162.6	204.6
Russia	134.4	153.8	234.6
Switzerland	65.3	207.7	226.1
Tajikistan	22.9	23.9	28.1
Turkey	18.2	27.2	43.0
United Arab Emirates	173.1	8.9	14.4
Uzbekistan	17.1	27.9	85.7
Total (incl. others)	672.0	794.2	1,134.2

Transport

RAILWAYS
(traffic)

	2005	2006	2007
Paying passengers ('000 journeys)	400	400	400
Passenger-km (million)	46.1	61.5	59.9
Freight carried (million metric tons)	1.7	1.9	2.3
Freight net ton-km (million)	661.8	751.7	853.7

ROAD TRAFFIC
(vehicles in use at 31 December)

	2001	2002	2003
Passenger cars	189,796	188,711	188,900
Motorcycles and mopeds	14,319	12,288	11,221

CIVIL AVIATION
(traffic on scheduled services)

	2005	2006	2007
Passengers carried ('000)	200	200	300
Passenger-km (million)	421.2	360.2	509.3
Total ton-km (million)	42.4	34.2	44.5

Kilometres flown (million): 7 in 2004.

Tourism

FOREIGN TOURIST ARRIVALS

Country of residence	2004	2005	2006
China, People's Republic	11,822	15,747	18,681
Germany	9,724	9,128	9,148
Kazakhstan	236,712	150,904	479,119
Russia	36,540	32,001	83,438
Tajikistan	8,190	4,565	16,588
Turkey	9,032	9,362	9,981
USA	11,111	11,727	12,772
Uzbekistan	40,655	49,376	95,091
Total (incl. others)	398,078	315,290	765,850

Tourism receipts (US $ million, incl. passenger transport): 97 in 2004; 94 in 2005; 189 in 2006.

Source: World Tourism Organization.

Communications Media

	2005	2006	2007
Telephones ('000 main lines in use)	440.4	458.9	482.1
Mobile cellular telephones ('000 subscribers)	541.7	1,261.8	2,151.7
Internet users ('000)	550.0	650.0	750.0
Broadband subscribers ('000)	2.5	2.8	2.9

Sources: UNESCO and International Telecommunication Union.

Daily newspapers (2004): 2 (average circulation 21,000).
Non-daily newspapers (2004): 83 (average circulation 427,800).
Book production (2004): 703 titles; 1,600,300 copies.
Personal computers ('000 in use): 100 in 2005.

Education

(2007/08)

	Institutions	Teachers	Students
Pre-primary	474	2,520	62,823
Primary and Secondary: general	2,168	72,097	1,080,061
Secondary: vocational	193	6,715	72,248
Higher (all institutions)	49	14,400	250,460

Adult literacy rate (official estimate): 98.7% in 2006.

Directory

The Constitution

In September 2007 the Constitutional Court ruled that the adoption of two successive Constitutions in November 2006 and January 2007 had been illegal. It restored the Constitution proclaimed on 5 May 1993, which had been revised on numerous subsequent occasions. President Kurmanbek Bakiyev subsequently scheduled a referendum on the adoption of a new Constitution for 21 October 2007. The new Constitution, which was approved by 76.1% of votes cast at the national referendum, entered into effect on 23 October. The following is a summary of its main provisions.

GENERAL PROVISIONS

The Kyrgyz Republic is a sovereign, unitary, democratic republic founded on the principle of the rule of law. All state power originates from the people of Kyrgyzstan, who exercise this power through elections and referendums, and through the state bodies and bodies of local self-government, on the basis of the Constitution and laws. Matters of legislation and other issues pertaining to the state may be decided by the people by referendum. The President of the Republic, the deputies of the Zhogorku Kenesh (Supreme Council) and representatives of local administrative bodies are all elected directly by the people. Elections are held on the basis of universal, equal and direct suffrage by secret ballot. All citizens of 18 years and over are eligible to vote.

The territory of the Kyrgyz Republic is integral and inviolable. The state language is Kyrgyz, and Russian is used as an official language. The equality and free use of other languages by representatives of the national and ethnic groups that constitute the people of Kyrgyzstan are guaranteed. The rights and freedoms of citizens may not be restricted on account of ignorance of the state language. The adoption of a state religion is prohibited. Political parties may not be formed on a religious basis, and certain provisions provide for a separation of the activities of political parties from those of the organs of the State.

HUMAN RIGHTS AND CIVIL LIBERTIES

Human rights and freedoms are absolute and inalienable. All people are equal before the laws and courts of the Kyrgyz Republic.

The freedoms of movement, association, peaceful assembly, of place of residence within the territories of the Kyrgyz Republic, and of property ownership are guaranteed. The privacy of written and telephonic conversation is respected. The freedoms of religion and thought, speech and expression are guaranteed. Citizens of the Kyrgyz Republic are permitted to obtain citizenship of another state, subject to international agreements entered into by the Kyrgyz Republic.

THE PRESIDENT

The President of the Kyrgyz Republic is Head of State. The President is a symbol of the unity of the people and state power, a guarantor of the Constitution, human rights and civil liberties. The term of office is five years, and no more than two consecutive terms may be served. The President is directly elected by the people. Any citizen of the republic between the ages of 35 and 65, who has a command of the state language, and who has resided in the Republic for at least 15 years, is permitted to contest the presidency. Presidential candidates must be nominated by no less than 50,000 electors.

The President: appoints the Prime Minister and members of the Government; dismisses members of the Government either of his own accord or at the behest of the Prime Minister; appoints heads of local state administration in consultation with the Prime Minister and orders their dismissal; appoints other leading state posts; and appoints one-half of the members of the Central Commission for Elections and Referendums. With the agreement of the Zhogorku Kenesh, he appoints the Prosecutor-General, other senior judicial posts, the Chairman of the National Bank and the Chairman of the Central Commission for Elections and Referendums. The President: presents draft legislation to the Zhogorku Kenesh; signs legislation approved by the Zhogorku Kenesh or returns it for further scrutiny; signs international agreements; may call referendums on issues of state on his own initiative or in response to proposals presented by at least 300,000 electors and a majority of deputies in the Zhogorku Kenesh; and calls elections to the Zhogorku Kenesh and to local assemblies. The President declares a state of war.

The President may be removed from office only on the basis of a charge of high treason or relating to other grave crimes made by the Zhogorku Kenesh, as confirmed by the Prosecutor-General. Any ensuing demands for a vote of impeachment must be supported by no less than two-thirds of the total membership of the Zhogorku Kenesh. For the vote of impeachment to be approved it must be supported by no less than three-quarters of the total membership of the Zhogorku Kenesh; this vote must be held no more than three months after the vote to commence impeachment proceedings was taken. In the event of impeachment being approved, the executive duties of the President are assumed on an acting basis by the Chairman of the Zhogorku Kenesh; in the event that the Chairman of the Zhogorku Kenesh is unable to assume executive powers, they are transferred to the Prime Minister. Elections for a new President must be held no later than three months after the removal from office of the outgoing President.

ZHOGORKU KENESH

Supreme legislative power is vested in the Zhogorku Kenesh, which comprises one 90-member chamber. Deputies are elected for a term of five years on the basis of party lists. Any citizen of the Kyrgyz Republic aged 25 years or older, and enjoying full civil rights, may be elected to the Zhogorku Kenesh.

The Zhogorku Kenesh: adopts the Constitution; approves amendments and additions to the Constitution; enacts legislation; confirms the republican budget and supervises its execution; determines questions pertaining to the administrative and territorial structure of the republic; designates presidential elections; approves the governmental structure proposed by the Prime Minister; may approve a vote of no confidence in the Government or in individual members thereof; consents to the appointment of the Procurator-General, as nominated by the President; elects judges of the Constitutional court, judges of the Supreme Court and the Chairman of the National Bank, at the proposal of the President; and ratifies or abrogates international agreements. The Zhogorku Kenesh may be dissolved by resolution of no less than two-thirds of its deputies.

THE GOVERNMENT

The Government of the Kyrgyz Republic is the highest organ of executive power in Kyrgyzstan. A political party that receives more than 50% of the mandates in the Zhogorku Kenesh presents its candidate for the Prime Minister for presidential approval, no later than five days from the convening of a new Zhogorku Kenesh. In the event that the nominated candidate fails to obtain the approval of the Zhogorku Kenesh, the President may request a second political party to nominate a candidate as Prime Minister, and similarly from a third political party in the event that the second candidate is not approved. In the event that the third candidate for the premiership is rejected, the President shall form an interim Government pending fresh legislative elections. A vote of no confidence in the Government may be held if demanded by at least one-third of the membership of the Zhogorku Kenesh, except in the six-month period before a presidential election, when such a vote may not be held. The President is not obliged to dismiss the Government following a vote of no confidence, unless two such votes take place within a period of three months, in which case the President may either dismiss the Government and appoint a new administration or call fresh legislative elections. The President is obliged to dismiss an individual member of the Government subject to two votes of no confidence in a six-month period.

The Government: determines all questions of state administration, other than those ascribed by the Constitution to the competence of the President and the Zhogorku Kenesh; drafts the republican budget and submits it to the Zhogorku Kenesh for approval; coordinates budgetary, financial, fiscal and monetary policy; administers state property; takes measures to defend the country and state security; executes foreign policy; and strives to guarantee the rights and freedoms of the citizens and to protect property and social order.

The authorities, duties, organization and form of local territorial-administrative bodies are determined by law.

THE CENTRAL ORGANS OF STATE POWER

The central organs of state power of the Kyrgyz Republic comprise: the Office of the Prosecutor-General; the National Bank; the Central Commission for Elections and Referendums; the Audit Chamber; and the Akyikatchi (Ombudsman), which protects the observation of human rights and civil freedoms in the Republic.

JUDICIAL SYSTEM

The judicial system comprises the Constitutional Court, the Supreme Court and regional courts. Courts are independent and governed only by the Constitution and by law. Judges of all courts remain in office for as long as their behaviour is deemed to be irreproachable. Judges of the Constitutional Court and the Supreme Court are elected by the Zhogorku Kenesh, on the recommendation of the President. Judges of local courts are appointed by the President of the Republic at the proposal of the National Council for the Judiciary, for terms of five years. The Constitutional Court comprises seven judges. The Supreme Court is the highest organ of judicial power in the sphere of civil, criminal and administrative justice.

ON REFORM

The proposed introduction of amendments or additions to the existing Constitution, or the proposed adoption of a new Constitution, may be examined by the Zhogorku Kenesh in response to a request of the President or of a majority of deputies of the Zhogorku Kenesh, or in response to an initiative supported by no less than 300,000 electors. A law amending and supplementing the existing Constitution may be adopted by a majority of no less than two-thirds of the total membership of the Zhogorku Kenesh after the holding of no fewer than two readings with an interval of three months between readings. At the demand of the majority of the total membership of the Zhogorku Kenesh, a law amending and supplementing the present Constitution may be submitted to referendum.

The Government

HEAD OF STATE

President: KURMANBEK S. BAKIYEV (elected 10 July 2005; inaugurated 14 August 2005).

KYRGYZSTAN

THE GOVERNMENT
(April 2009)

Prime Minister: Igor V. Chudinov.
First Deputy Prime Minister: Omurbek T. Babanov.
Deputy Prime Minister: Uktomkhan A. Abdullayeva.
Head of the Government Staff, Minister: Nurlan T. Aitmurzayev.
Minister of Foreign Affairs: Kadyrbek T. Sarbayev.
Minister of Defence: Bakytbek T. Kalyev.
Minister of Internal Affairs: Moldomusa T. Kongantiyev.
Minister of Justice: Nurlan Zh. Tursunkulov.
Minister of Finance: Marat A. Sultanov.
Minister of Economic Development and Trade: Akylbek U. Zhaparov.
Minister of Agriculture, Water Resources and Processing Industry: Iskenderbek R. Aidaraliyev.
Minister of Transport and Communications: Nurlan Ch. Sulaimanov.
Minister of Emergency Situations: Kamchibek K. Tashiyev.
Minister of Education and Science: Abdulda I. Musayev.
Minister of Health: Marat A. Mambetov.
Minister of Culture and Information: Sultan A. Rayev.
Minister of Labour and Social Welfare: Nazgul A. Tashpayeva.
Minister of Industry, Energy and Fuel Resources: Ilyas A. Davydov.

Note: The Chairmen of the State Committees for National Security, for Migration and Labour, for the Management of State Property, for Taxes and Collections, and for Customs are also members of the Government.

MINISTRIES

Office of the President: 720003 Bishkek, Dom Pravitelstva; tel. (312) 63-85-11; fax (312) 63-86-86; e-mail office@mail.gov.kg; internet www.president.kg.

Office of the Prime Minister: 720003 Bishkek, Dom Pravitelstva; tel. (312) 66-12-20; fax (312) 66-66-58; e-mail pmoffice@mail.gov.kg; internet www.government.gov.kg.

Ministry of Agriculture, Water Resources and Processing Industry: 720040 Bishkek, Kiyevskaya 96A; tel. (312) 62-14-27; fax (312) 62-36-32; e-mail agroprod@elcat.kg; internet www.agroprod.kg.

Ministry of Culture and Information: 720040 Bishkek, Pushkina 78; tel. (312) 62-12-00; e-mail mincultkr@mail.ru; internet www.minculture.gov.kg.

Ministry of Defence: 720001 Bishkek, Logvinenko 26; tel. (312) 66-38-28; fax (312) 66-16-02; e-mail ud@bishkek.gov.kg; internet www.mil.kg.

Ministry of Economic Development and Trade: 720002 Bishkek, pr. Chui 106; tel. (312) 66-38-00; fax (312) 66-34-98; e-mail mert_kg@mail.ru; internet www.mert.kg.

Ministry of Education and Science: 720040 Bishkek, Tynystanova 257; tel. (312) 62-36-33; fax (312) 62-36-22; e-mail monk@monk.bishkek.gov.kg; internet www.minedu.kg.

Ministry of Emergency Situations: 720055 Bishkek, Toktonaliyeva 2/1; tel. (312) 54-79-86; fax (312) 54-11-79; e-mail mecd@bishkek.gov.kg; internet www.mchs.in.kg.

Ministry of Finance: 720040 Bishkek, pr. Erkindik 58; tel. (312) 66-13-50; fax (312) 66-16-45; e-mail it@minfin.kg; internet www.minfin.kg.

Ministry of Foreign Affairs: 720040 Bishkek, bul. Erkindik 57; tel. (312) 62-05-45; fax (312) 66-05-01; e-mail gendep@mfa.gov.kg; internet www.mfa.kg.

Ministry of Health: 720040 Bishkek, Moskovskaya 148; tel. (312) 62-26-80; fax (312) 66-07-17; e-mail mz@med.kg; internet www.med.kg.

Ministry of Industry, Energy and Fuel Resources: 720055 Bishkek, Akhunbayeva 119; tel. (312) 56-18-22; fax (312) 56-20-28; internet www.mpe.gov.kg.

Ministry of Internal Affairs: 720040 Bishkek, Frunze 469; tel. (312) 66-24-50; fax (312) 68-20-44; e-mail mail@mvd.bishkek.gov.kg; internet www.mvd.kg.

Ministry of Justice: 720040 Bishkek, M. Gandi 32; tel. (312) 65-64-90; fax (312) 65-65-02; e-mail admin@minjust.gov.kg; internet www.minjust.gov.kg.

Ministry of Labour and Social Welfare: 720041 Bishkek, Tynystanova 215; tel. (312) 66-34-00; fax (312) 66-57-24; e-mail mlsp@mlsp.kg; internet www.mlsp.kg.

Ministry of Transport and Communications: 720017 Bishkek, Isanova 42; tel. (312) 61-04-72; fax (312) 66-47-81; e-mail mtk@mtk.gov.kg; internet www.mtk.gov.kg.

President

Presidential Election, 10 July 2005*

Candidates	Votes	%
Kurmanbek S. Bakiyev	1,776,156	88.72
Tursunbai Bakir uulu	78,701	3.93
Akbaraly Y. Aitikeyev	72,604	3.63
Others	38,864	1.94
Total†	2,001,974	100.00

* Preliminary official results.
† Including 18,197 votes (0.91% of the total) 'against all candidates' and 17,452 invalid votes (0.87% of the total).

Legislature

Zhogorku Kenesh
(Supreme Council)
720053 Bishkek, ul. Abdymomunov 207; tel. (312) 61-16-04; fax (312) 62-50-12; e-mail zs@kenesh.gov.kg; internet www.kenesh.kg.

Chairman: Aitibai Tagayev.

General Election, 16 December 2007*

Parties	% of votes†	Seats
Bright Road People's Party (Ak Zhol)	46.90	71
Social Democratic Party of Kyrgyzstan	5.12	11
Communist Party of Kyrgyzstan	5.05	8
Fatherland Socialist Party (Ata-Meken)	8.29	—
Others	34.64	—
Total	100.00	90

* Provisional final results.
† Parties were required to obtain at least 0.5% of votes cast in each of the country's six regions and two largest cities in order to be eligible for legislative representation.

Election Commission

Kyrgyz Respublikasynyn Shailoo Zhana Referendum Otkoruu Boyuncha Borborduk Komissiyasy (Central Commission for Elections and Referendums of the Kyrgyz Republic): 720040 Bishkek, ul. Razzakova 59; tel. (312) 62-68-25; fax (312) 66-58-60; e-mail cec@shailoo.gov.kg; internet www.shailoo.gov.kg; independent govt organ; one-half of the mems are appointed by the President of the Republic, and one-half by the Zhogorku Kenesh; Chair. Damir V. Lisovsky.

Political Organizations

At December 2007 50 political organizations were registered with the Central Election Commission. The following were among the most important operating in 2008.

Agrarian Party of Kyrgyzstan: 720000 Bishkek, Kiyevskaya 96; tel. (312) 66-28-72; f. 1993; campaigns for agrarian reform, and for the protection of the rights and interests of people working in agriculture; Leader Erkin Aliyev; c. 8,000 mems (1999).

Banner Party of National Revival (Asaba): 720000 Bishkek, pr. Chui 26; tel. (312) 43-04-45; fax (312) 28-53-64; f. 1990; re-registered 2001; nationalist, pro-democracy; mem. of the People's Movement of Kyrgyzstan electoral alliance; critical of the progress made by the administration of Kurmanbek Bakiyev in tackling issues such as crime and corruption; mem. of the opposition United People's Movement formed in late 2008; Co-Chair. Azimbek Beknazarov, Roza Otunbayeva.

Bright Road People's Party (Ak Zhol) (Ak Zhol Eldik Partiyasy): 720000 Bishkek, Toktogul 175/15; tel. (312) 62-82-45; internet www.akjolnarod.kg; f. Oct. 2007; supports administration of Pres. Bakiyev; Chair. Elmira S. Ibraimova (acting).

KYRGYZSTAN

Democratic Movement of Kyrgyzstan: 720000 Bishkek, Abdymomunova 205; tel. (312) 27-14-95; f. 1990; registered as a political party in 1993, re-registered in 2000; campaigns for civil liberties, for democratic social and legal development; participated in 2005 legislative elections as mem. of People's Movement of Kyrgyzstan electoral bloc; Leader JYPAR JEKSHEYEV; Chair. of the Exec. Cttee EDILBEK SARYBAYEV; Chair. of the Political Council VIKTOR CHERNOMORETS.

Dignity (Ar-Namys): 720033 Bishkek, Togolok Moldo 60A; tel. (312) 32-52-89; e-mail ar-namys@mail.kg; internet www.ar-namys.org; f. 1999; pro-democracy; mem. of political bloc For a Worthy Future of Kyrgyzstan United Front, formed Feb. 2007; Chair. FELIKS KULOV; c. 11,000 mems.

Fatherland Socialist Party (Ata Meken) (Ata Meken Sotsialisttik Partiyasy): 720040 Bishkek, Orozbekova 110A/2; tel. (312) 66-34-92; fax (312) 66-46-38; e-mail atameken@elcat.kg; internet www.atameken.kg; f. 1992; nationalist; supports state control of the economy; participated in 2005 legislative elections as mem. of For Fair Elections electoral bloc; supports parliamentary system of govt; mem. of the opposition United People's Movement formed in late 2008; Leader OMURBEK CH. TEKEBAYEV; more than 2,000 mems.

Forward, Kyrgyzstan (Alga, Kyrgyzstan): 720000 Bishkek, Moskovskaya 217; tel. (312) 65-13-57; f. 2003 by merger of the Manas El Party of Spiritual Revival, New Time, New Movement and the Party of Co-operators; merged with Birimdik in 2003, and with the Unity Party of Kyrgyzstan in 2004; fmrly supportive of regime of President Akayev; Chair. BOLOT BEGALIYEV; c. 7,000 mems (2004).

Free Kyrgyzstan Progressive-Democratic Party (ERK) (Erkin Kyrgyzstan): 720000 Bishkek, Abdymomunova 207; tel. (312) 22-49-57; fax (312) 22-60-35; f. 1991; social-democratic; participated in 2005 legislative elections as mem. of People's Movement of Kyrgyzstan electoral alliance; Chair. BAKIR UULU TURSUNBAI.

Justice (Adilet): 720000 Bishkek, Bokonbayev 109; tel. (312) 66-48-17; fax (312) 66-50-84; f. 1999; re-registered 2003; campaigns for economic reform, modernization and investment; Hon. Chair. CHINGIZ T. AITMATOV; Co-Chair. TOICHUBEK KASYMOV, KUBANYCHBEK JUMALIYEV, ALTAI BORUBAYEV; c. 15,000 mems (2003).

Liberty (Erkindik): 720000 Bishkek; f. 2000; participated in 2005 legislative elections as mem. of People's Movement of Kyrgyzstan electoral bloc; Chair. TOPCHUBEK TURGUNALIYEV; c. 3,700 mems (June 2004).

A New Kyrgyzstan (Jany Kyrgyzstan): 720000 Bishkek, Kiyevskaya 120; tel. (312) 21-19-61; fax (312) 21-65-04; f. 1994 as Agrarian Labour Party of Kyrgyzstan; re-registered 2001; participated in 2005 legislative elections as mem. of People's Movement of Kyrgyzstan electoral bloc; mem. of the opposition United People's Movement formed in late 2008; Chair. DOSBOL NUR UULU.

Party of Communists of Kyrgyzstan (KCP): 720001 Bishkek, pr. Chui 114/206; tel. (312) 62-49-99; fax (312) 67-02-55; e-mail anashparties@mail.ru; disbanded 1991, re-established 1992, re-registered 2007; successor to the Communist Party of Kyrgyz SSR; participated in 2005 legislative elections as mem. of People's Movement of Kyrgyzstan election bloc; Chair. ISKHAK MASALIYEV; 25,000 mems.

Republican Party of Kyrgyzstan (RPK): 720000 Bishkek, Isanova 8; tel. (312) 21-14-16; registered in 1999; advocates absolute freedom of speech, full equality of all citizens before the law and environmental protection; participated in 2005 legislative elections as mem. of People's Movement of Kyrgyzstan electoral alliance; Chair. GIYAZ TOKOMBAYEV.

Social Democratic Party of Kyrgyzstan: 720000 Bishkek, Alma-Atinskaya 4B/203; tel. (312) 43-15-07; f. 1993; supports parliamentary system of govt; mem. of the opposition United People's Movement formed in late 2008; Chair. ALMAZBEK ATAMBAYEV.

Union of Democratic Forces: 720040 Bishkek, Abdumomunova 207; tel. (312) 66-19-10; fax (312) 62-50-27; e-mail smanbaeva@kenesh.kg; f. 2005; registered Dec. 2005; seeks constitutional, judicial and economic reform in order to combat corruption, stimulate the economy and establish a strong state; advocates creation of parliamentary republic and introduction of parliamentary elections by party lists; mem. of political bloc People's Coalition of Democratic Forces (led by party's leader), formed Jan. 2006 with declared aim of reforming Kyrgyzstan's constitution and introducing parliamentary system of govt; Leader KUBATBEK BAIBOLOV.

The following Islamist groups were banned by the Supreme Court in November 2003: **Hizb-ut-Tahrir al-Islami** (Party of Islamic Liberation), the **Islamic Party of Turkestan**, the **East Turkestan Islamic Party** (Sharq Turkestan Islam Partiyasy) and the **East Turkestan Liberation Organization** (Sharq azzat Turkestan).

Diplomatic Representation

EMBASSIES IN KYRGYZSTAN

Afghanistan: 720040 Bishkek, Gorkogo 210; tel. (312) 69-01-76; fax (312) 69-03-30; e-mail afghanemb_bishkek@yahoo.com; Ambassador SHAHJAHAN AHMADI.

Azerbaijan: 720040 Bishkek, Shurukova 41; tel. (312) 51-07-70; fax (312) 51-31-72; e-mail bishkek@mission.mfa.az; Ambassador ARIF AGHAYEV.

Belarus: 720040 Bishkek, Moskovskaya 210; tel. (312) 65-13-65; fax (312) 65-11-77; e-mail kyrgyzstan@belembassy.org; Ambassador VALERY A. BRYLYOV.

China, People's Republic: 720001 Bishkek, Toktogula 196; tel. (312) 61-08-58; fax (312) 66-30-14; e-mail chinaemb_kg@mfa.gov.cn; Ambassador ZHANG YANNIAN.

Germany: 720040 Bishkek, Razzakova 28; tel. (312) 90-50-00; fax (312) 66-66-30; e-mail info@bischkek.diplo.de; internet www.bischkek.diplo.de; Ambassador HOLGER GREN.

India: 720044 Bishkek, ul. Aeroportinskaya 15A; tel. (312) 54-92-14; fax (312) 54-32-45; e-mail indembas@infotel.kg; Ambassador JYOTI SWARUP PANDE.

Iran: 720026 Bishkek, Razzakova 36; tel. (312) 62-49-17; fax (312) 66-02-09; e-mail sefabish@amil.elcat.gg; Ambassador MUHAMMAD REZA SABOURI.

Japan: 720033 Bishkek, Frunze 503; tel. (312) 61-18-75; fax (312) 61-18-82; internet www.kg.emb-japan.go.jp; Ambassador SHIGEO NATSUI.

Kazakhstan: 720040 Bishkek, pr. Mira 95 A; tel. (312) 66-21-01; fax (312) 69-20-94; e-mail kaz_emb@kazemb.elcat.kg; Ambassador BAKYT S. OSPANOV.

Korea, Republic: 720040 Bishkek, Matrosova 67/8; tel. (312) 56-02-71; fax (312) 57-60-04; Chargé d'affaires a.i. LEE KENG YUL.

Pakistan: 720040 Bishkek, Serova 37; tel. (312) 62-17-11; fax (312) 66-15-50; e-mail parepbishkek@elcat.kg; Ambassador MOHAMMAD ALAM BROHI.

Russia: 720040 Bishkek, Razzakova 17; tel. (312) 62-47-38; fax (312) 62-18-23; e-mail rusemb@saimanet.kg; internet www.kyrgyz.mid.ru; Ambassador VALENTIN S. VLASOV.

Tajikistan: 720031 Bishkek, Karadarynskaya 36; tel. (312) 51-14-64; fax (312) 51-23-43; e-mail tojsaforat@exnet.kg; Ambassador MAKHMUDZHON N. SOBIROV.

Turkey: 720040 Bishkek, Moskovskaya 89; tel. (312) 62-23-54; fax (312) 66-05-19; e-mail biskbe@infotel.kg; Ambassador FATMA SERPIL ALPMAN.

Ukraine: 720040 Bishkek, bulv. Akhunbayeva 201; tel. (312) 49-04-07; fax (312) 49-10-48; e-mail emb_kg@mfa.gov.ua; internet www.mfa.gov.ua/kirgizia; Ambassador VOLODYMYR V. SOLOVEY.

USA: 720016 Bishkek, pr. Mira 171; tel. (312) 55-12-41; fax (312) 55-12-64; internet bishkek.usembassy.gov; Chargé d'affaires a.i. EARLE D. LITZENBERGER.

Uzbekistan: 720040 Bishkek, Tynystanova 213; tel. (312) 66-20-65; fax (312) 66-44-03; e-mail uzbembish@infotel.kg; Ambassador ZIYADULLA S. PULATKHOJAYEV.

Judicial System

Supreme Court: 720000 Bishkek, Orozbekova 37; tel. (312) 66-33-18; fax (312) 66-29-46; e-mail scourt@bishkek.gov.kg; Chair. JANYL ALIYEVA.

Constitutional Court: 720040 Bishkek, pr. Erkindik 39; tel. (312) 62-04-95; fax (312) 66-28-19; e-mail konsud@bishkek.gov.kg; Chair. SVETLANA SYDYKOVA.

Office of the Prosecutor-General: 720040 Bishkek; Prosecutor-General ELMURZA R. SATYBALDIYEV.

Religion

ISLAM

The majority of Kyrgyz are Sunni Muslims (Hanafi school), as are some other groups living in the republic, such as Uzbeks and Tajiks.

Chief Mufti of the Muslims of Kyrgyzstan: Haji MURATALY AJY JUMANOV, 720000 Bishkek.

International Islamic Centre of Kyrgyzstan: 714018 Osh; Pres. Haji SADYKZHAN KAMALUDDIN.

CHRISTIANITY
Roman Catholic Church
The Church is represented in Kyrgyzstan by an Apostolic Administration, established in March 2006. There were an estimated 500 adherents in the country at 31 December 2006.

Apostolic Administrator: Most Rev. NIKOLAUS MESSMER (Titular Bishop of Carmeiano), 720040 Bishkek, Muyukovskogo 25; tel. (312) 28-50-03; fax (312) 67-03-92; e-mail nikmessmer@hotmail.com; internet www.catholic-kyrgyzstan.org.

Russian Orthodox Church (Moscow Patriarchate)
The Russian Orthodox Church (Moscow Patriarchate) in Kyrgyzstan comes under the jurisdiction of the Eparchy of Tashkent and Central Asia, headed by the Metropolitan of Tashkent and Central Asia, VLADIMIR (IKIM), resident in Uzbekistan.

JUDAISM
At the 1989 census, around 6,000 Jews were enumerated as living within the Kyrgyz SSR, mostly in Bishkek. By 1993 around 3,000 Jews had emigrated from Kyrgyzstan, mostly to Israel, and emigration continued subsequently.

Chief Rabbi: Rabbi ARIYE RAICHMAN, 720000 Bishkek, Sutombayev 193, Khabad Lyubavich Synagogue; tel. and fax (312) 68-19-66; e-mail arier@mail.ru.

The Press
In 2004 there were 83 non-daily newspapers, with an average circulation of 427,800 copies. Two daily newspapers were published in that year, with an average circulation of 21,000 copies.

PRINCIPAL NEWSPAPERS
Asaba (The Standard): 720000 Bishkek; tel. (312) 26-47-39; weekly; in Kyrgyz; supplement in Russian *Asaba-Bishkek*; Editors JUMABEK MEDERALIYEV (*Asaba*), BERMET BUKASHEVA (*Asaba-Bishkek*).

Belyi Parokhod (White Steamship): 720040 Bishkek, Ibraimova 24; tel. (312) 42-24-80; e-mail parohod@list.ru; internet www.parohod.kg; f. 1997; in Russian; independent.

Bishkek Observer: 720021 Bishkek, Frunze 429; tel. (312) 28-95-96; fax (312) 68-22-61; e-mail observer@elcat.kg; f. 2000; weekly; independent; in English; Editor AVTAR SINGH.

Bishkek Taims (Bishkek Times): 720040 Bishkek, Pushkina 70; tel. (312) 62-15-68; e-mail b-times@yandex.ru; internet www.presskg.com/bt; Editor-in-Chief NURALY KAPAROV.

Chui Baayni/Chuiskiye Izvestiya (Chui News): 720300 Bishkek, Ibraimova 24; tel. (312) 42-83-31; weekly; organ of Chui Oblast administration; Kyrgyz and Russian edns; Editor (Kyrgyz edn) KURMANBEK RAMATOV; Editor (Russian edn) A. BLINDINA.

Delo N°... (Case Number...): 720000 Bishkek; tel. (312) 62-19-80; fax (312) 66-38-66; e-mail cactus@elcat.kg; internet delo.to.kg; f. 1991; weekly; in Russian; independent; politics, crime; Editor VIKTOR ZAPOLSKII; circ. 30,000.

Erkin Too (Free Mountain): 720040 Bishkek, Ibraimova 24; tel. (312) 42-03-15; fax (312) 42-22-42; f. 1991; 2 a week; organ of the Government; publishes laws, presidential, parliamentary and govt decrees, and other legal documents; Kyrgyz; Editor-in-Chief NURLAN SHAKIYEV; circ. 10,000.

Gazeta.kg: 720000 Bishkek; internet gazeta.kg; online only, in Russian and English; independent; politics and analysis of current affairs; culture; regional news; f. 2003.

Kyrgyz Madaniyaty (Kyrgyz Culture): 720301 Bishkek, Bokonbayeva 99; tel. (312) 26-14-58; f. 1967; weekly; organ of the Union of Writers; Editor NURALY KAPAROV; circ. 15,940.

Kyrgyz Rukhu: 720040 Bishkek, Abdymomunova 193; tel. and fax (312) 66-45-43; f. 1991; weekly; Kyrgyz; Editor-in-Chief BAKBYRBEK ALENOV; circ. c. 5,000.

Kyrgyz Tuusu (Flag of Kyrgyzstan): 720040 Bishkek, Abdymomunova 193; tel. (312) 62-20-18; fax (312) 62-20-25; e-mail tuusu@infotel.kg; internet www.tuusu.kg; f. 1924; fmrly *Sovettik Kyrgyzstan*; daily; organ of the Government; Kyrgyz; Editor-in-Chief ZHEDIGER I. SAALAYEV; circ. 17,000–20,000.

Limon (Lemon): 720040 Bishkek, Moskovskaya 189; tel. (312) 65-03-03; fax (312) 65-02-04; e-mail limon@akipress.org; internet www.limon.kg; f. 1994; in Russian; youth newspaper; independent; Editor-in-Chief VENERA JAMONA KULOVA.

MSN—Moya Stolitsa—Novosti (My Capital City—News): 720001 Bishkek, Turusbekova 47; tel. (312) 21-29-79; fax (312) 21-58-94; e-mail city@infotel.kg; internet www.msn.kg; f. 2001; independent; 3 a week; in Russian; Editor-in-Chief ALEXANDER KIM; circ. 5,000 (Tues. and Thurs.), 50,000 (Fri.).

Slovo Kyrgyzstana (Word of Kyrgyzstan): 720004 Bishkek, Abdymomunova 193; tel. (312) 66-60-88; fax (312) 66-59-28; e-mail slovo@infotel.kg; internet www.sk.kg; f. 1925; daily; organ of the Government; in Russian; Editor ALEKSANDR I. MALEVANY.

The Times of Central Asia: 720000 Bishkek, Abdrahmanova 175A/303–304; tel. (312) 66-17-37; fax (312) 66-50-86; e-mail edittimes@timesca.com; internet www.timesca.com; f. 1995; weekly; in English; also distributed in Kazakhstan, Turkmenistan and Uzbekistan, and internationally; Publr GIORGIO FIACCONI.

Vechernii Bishkek (Bishkek Evening News): 720021 Bishkek, Usenbayeva 2; tel. (312) 68-21-21; fax (312) 68-02-68; e-mail webmaster@vb.kg; internet www.vb.kg; f. 1974; daily; independent; in Russian; Editor-in-Chief GENNADII A. KUZMIN; circ. (Mon.–Thur.) 20,000, (Fri.) 50,000.

Zaman Kyrgyzstan (Herald of Kyrgyzstan): 720040 Bishkek, Ibraimova 24; tel. (312) 42-62-35; e-mail zamantur@elcat.kg; f. 1992; weekly; independent; in Kyrgyz, Turkish and English; Editor-in-Chief A. KUSH; circ. 15,000.

PRINCIPAL PERIODICALS
Monthly, unless otherwise indicated.

Aalam (Universe): 720000 Bishkek, Baitik Baatyra 73; tel. (312) 54-42-07; fax (312) 54-42-09; e-mail aalamga@hotmail.kg; f. 1991; independent; Kyrgyz; weekly; Editor-in-Chief ELNURA SHABDANBEKOVA; circ. 18,000.

Agym (Current): 720040 Bishkek, pr. Manasa 40; tel. (312) 66-56-70; fax (312) 66-55-48; e-mail agym@users.kyrnet.kg; internet presskg.com/agym; f. 1992; 2 a week; in Kyrgyz; political; Editor-in-Chief MELIS ESHIMKANOV.

AKIpress: 720010 Bishkek, Moskovskaya 189; tel. and fax (312) 61-18-23; fax (312) 65-02-02; e-mail admin@akipress.org; internet www.akipress.org; f. 1993; in Russian; independent; analysis of political and economic affairs; Editor-in-Chief SAMAGAN AITYMBETOV; circ. 1,000.

Kut Bilim (Good Knowledge): 720001 Bishkek, Tynystanova 257; tel. (312) 62-04-86; e-mail kutbilim@elcat.kg; internet kb.host.net.kg; f. 1953 as *Mugalimder Gazetasy*; current name adopted 1993; organ of the Ministry of Education and Science; weekly; in Kyrgyz; Editor-in-Chief KUBATBEK CHEKIROV; circ. 6,000.

Literaturnyi Kyrgyzstan (Literary Kyrgyzstan): 720301 Bishkek, Pushkina 70; tel. (312) 626-16-01; e-mail literary_kyrgyzstan@rambler.ru; internet www.lk.to.kg; f. 1955; journal of the Union of Writers; fiction, literary criticism, journalism; in Russian; Editor-in-Chief A. I. IVANOV; circ. 3,000.

Zdravookhraneniye Kyrgyzstana (Healthcare of Kyrgyzstan): 720005 Bishkek, Moskovskaya 148; tel. (312) 62-26-80; fax (312) 66-07-17; e-mail mz@med.kg; f. 1938; 4 a year; publ. by the Ministry of Health; health research; in Russian; Editor-in-Chief T. ABDRAIMOV; circ. 3,000 (2007).

NEWS AGENCY
Kabar Kyrgyz News Agency: 720011 Bishkek, Sovetskaya 175; tel. (312) 62-05-74; fax (312) 66-11-68; e-mail s1@kabar.gov.kg; internet www.kabar.kg; Dir OLEG RYABOV.

Publishers
Ilim (Science): 720071 Bishkek, pr. Chui 265A; tel. (312) 65-56-88; e-mail ilimph@mail.ru; f. 1954; state-owned; scientific and science fiction; Dir L. V. TARASOVA.

Kyrgyz-Russian Slavic University Publishing House (Izdatelstvo Kyrgyzsko-Rossiiskogo slavyanskogo universiteta): 720000 Bishkek, Kiyevskaya 44; tel. (312) 25-53-60; internet www.krsu.edu.kg/Rus/EduIzd.htm; f. 1995; academic works of university staff; textbooks; Dir LARISA V. TARASOVA.

Kyrgyzstan: 720000 Bishkek, Abdrakhmanova 170; tel. (312) 62-19-47; politics, science, economics, literature; Dir BERIK N. CHALAGYZOV.

Tsentr Gosudarstvennogo Yazyka i Kyrgyzskoi Entsiklopedii (Centre for the State Language and the Kyrgyz Encyclopedia): 720040 Bishkek, bul. Erkindik 56; tel. (312) 62-50-72; fax (312) 62-50-03; e-mail gocst.ensk@mail.ru; dictionaries and encyclopedias; Dir BAKTYGUL KALDYBAYEVA; Editor-in-Chief USEN A. ASANOV.

Broadcasting and Communications
National Communications Agency of the Kyrgyz Republic: 720005 Bishkek, Baytik Baatyra 7B; tel. (312) 54-41-03; fax (312) 54-41-05; internet www.nas.kg; f. 1997; Dir KUBAT S. KYDYRALIYEV.

TELECOMMUNICATIONS

BiMoKom: tel. (555) 50-00-00; fax (312) 90-52-40; internet www.megacom.kg; f. 2006; provides mobile cellular telecommunications services in Bishkek, Manas Airport, the shores of Lake Issyk-Kul and in Chui, Issyk-Kul, Osh, Dzalal-Abad, Naryn, Talas and Batken Oblasts under the Megacom brand name; Dir ANDREI G. SILICH; c. 600,000 subscribers (Jan. 2008).

Kyrgyztelekom: 720000 Bishkek, pr. Chui 96; tel. (312) 68-16-16; fax (312) 66-24-24; e-mail info@kt.kg; internet www.kt.kg; f. 1993, transformed into joint stock co in 1997; state telecommunications co; 77.84% state-owned; 51% scheduled for privatization; Chair. of the Bd of Dirs SALAIDIN A. AVAZOV; Mems of the Bd of Dirs MYKTARBEK JUMABAYEV, BURKAN JUMABAYEV, DUISHENBEK R. ABDYLDAYEV, MYRBEK T. BATAKANOV.

Sky Mobile: 720011 Bishkek, pr. Chui 121; tel. (312) 58-79-15; fax (312) 90-09-16; e-mail office@bitel.kg; internet www.bitel.kg; f. 1997; provides mobile cellular telecommunications services under the Bitel and Mobi brand names; Dir-Gen. D. V. SHERSHNEV; over 1m. subscribers (Jan. 2008).

BROADCASTING

Radio and Television

State National Television and Radio Broadcasting Corpn: 720010 Bishkek, Molodoi Gvardii 59; tel. (312) 65-56-77; internet www.ktr.kg; Pres. MELIS ESHIMKANOV.

Kyrgyz Public Educational Radio and Television (Kyrgyzskoye Obshchestvennoye Obrazovatelnoye Radio i Televideniye—KOORT): 720031 Bishkek, Ibraimova 24; tel. (312) 54-77-27; fax (312) 54-77-15; e-mail office@koort.kg; f. 1997; broadcasts in Kyrgyz and Russian; educational programmes and entertainment; Gen. Dir AZIMA ABDIMAMINOVA; 103 employees.

Radio

Radio Azattyk: 720000 Bishkek; tel. (312) 66-88-17; fax (312) 66-68-14; internet www.azattyk.org; Kyrgyz language news broadcasts by Radio Free Europe/Radio Liberty (USA—based in the Czech Republic); Dir TYNTCHTYKBEK TCHOROEV; Bureau Chief KUBAT OTORBAEV.

Kyrgyz Radio: 720010 Bishkek, Molodoi Gvardii 59; tel. (312) 25-79-36; fax (312) 65-10-64; internet www.ktr.kg; f. 1931; broadcasts in Kyrgyz, Russian, English, German, Ukrainian, Uzbek, Dungan and Uigur; subsidiary of State National Television and Radio Broadcasting Corpn; Dir BAIMA SUTENOVA.

Radio Television Pyramid: 720300 Bishkek, Jantosheva 70; tel. and fax (312) 51-00-15; e-mail pyramid@tom.kg; f. 1992; privately owned; broadcasts to Bishkek and neighbouring regions; Pres. MIRBEK OROZOV.

There are several other private radio stations operating in Kyrgyzstan.

Television

Kyrgyz Television: 720300 Bishkek, Molodoi Gvardii 63; tel. (312) 25-79-36; fax (312) 25-79-30; internet www.ktr.kg; subsidiary of State National Television and Radio Broadcasting Corpn; Pres. KYYAS MOLDOKASYMOV.

TV Pyramid: 720005 Bishkek; tel. and fax (312) 41-01-31; e-mail pyramid@ss5-22.kyrnet.kg; f. 1991; privately owned; broadcasts to Bishkek and neighbouring regions; Pres. ADYLBEK T. BIINAZAROV.

Finance

(cap. = capital; res = reserves; m. = million; brs = branches; amounts in soms, unless otherwise indicated)

BANKING

Central Bank

National Bank of the Kyrgyz Republic (Kyrgyz Respublikasynyn Uluttuk Banky): 720040 Bishkek, Umetaliyeva 101; tel. (312) 66-90-08; fax (312) 61-04-56; e-mail mail@nbkr.kg; internet www.nbkr.kg; f. 1991, name changed in 1992, and as above in 1993; cap. 50.0m., res 1,069.1m., dep. 14,540.7m. (Dec. 2006); Chair. MARAT O. ALAPAYEV.

Other Banks

AsiaUniversalBank: 720001 Bishkek, Toktogula 187; tel. (312) 62-02-52; fax (312) 62-02-50; e-mail reception@aub.kg; internet www.aub.kg; f. 1997; present name adopted 2000; cap. 700.0m., res 527.3m., dep. 4,929.9m. (Dec. 2007); Chair. MIKHAIL NADEL; Chief Exec. NURDIN ABDRAZAKOV; 2 brs.

ATFBank-Kyrgyzstan: 720070 Bishkek, Jibek Jolu 493; tel. and fax (312) 67-04-71; e-mail bank@atfbank.kg; internet www.atfbank.kg; f. 1992; fmrly Energobank, present name adopted 2006; cap. 500.0m., res 1.5m., dep. 1,876.0m. (Dec. 2006); Pres. BAKIRDIN E. SARTKAZIYEV; 7 brs.

BTA Bank: 720040 Bishkek, Moskovskaya 118; tel. (312) 90-50-50; fax (312) 62-45-65; e-mail info@ineximbank.com; internet www.bta.kg; f. 1996; name changed as above 2008; cap. 800.0m., res 83.2m., dep. 4,431.0m. (Dec. 2007); Chair.of Bd MURAT KUNAKUNOV; 4 brs.

Demir Kyrgyz International Bank (DKIB): 720001 Bishkek, pr. Chui 245; tel. (312) 61-06-10; fax (312) 66-64-44; e-mail demir@demirbank.kg; internet www.demirbank.kg; f. 1997; cap. US $12.0m., res $0.5m., dep. $63.8m. (Jan. 2009); Chair. ISMAIL HASAN AKCAKAYALIOGLU; Gen. Man. L. SEVKI SARILAR; 5 brs.

Kyrgyz Investment and Credit Bank: 720001 Bishkek, Ibraimova 115A, Dordoi Plaza Business Centre; tel. (312) 69-05-55; fax (312) 69-05-60; e-mail kicb@kicb.net; internet www.kicb.net; f. 2001; 21% owned by Aga Khan Fund for Economic Development, 18% by Habib Bank (Pakistan), 17% by Deutsche Investitions und Entwicklungsgesellschaft GmbH (Germany), 17% by European Bank for Reconstruction and Development (United Kingdom), 17% by International Finance Corpn; cap. US $10m., res $8.1m., dep. $36.6m. (Aug. 2008); Chief Exec. KUANG YOUNG CHOI; 8 brs.

Kyrgyzstan Bank: 720001 Bishkek, Togolok Moldo 54A; tel. (312) 21-95-98; fax (312) 61-02-20; e-mail akb@bankkg.kg; internet www.bankkg.kg; f. 1991; cap. 138.9m., res 5.1m., dep. 1,582.0m. (Dec. 2006); Chair. ABIROV NURBEK; 29 brs.

Tolubay Bank: 720040 Bishkek, Umetaliyeva 105; tel. (312) 65-88-88; fax (312) 25-63-14; e-mail tolubay@infotel.kg; internet www.tolubaybank.kg; f. 1996; cap. 63.0m., res 12.5m., dep. 293.1m. (Dec. 2006); Chair. JENISHBEK S. BAIGUTTIYEV; 1 br.

COMMODITY EXCHANGE

Kyrgyzstan Commodity and Raw Materials Exchange: 720001 Bishkek, Belinskaya 40; tel. (312) 22-13-75; fax (312) 22-27-44; f. 1990; Gen. Dir TEMIR SARIYEV.

STOCK EXCHANGE

Kyrgyz Stock Exchange (Kyrgyz Fonduk Birzhasy/ Kyrgyzskaya Fondovaya Birzha): 720010 Bishkek, Moskovskaya 172; tel. (312) 61-07-08; fax (312) 31-14-83; e-mail kse@kse.kg; internet www.kse.kg; Pres. AIBEK TOLUBAEV.

INSURANCE

At 1 July 2005 there were 12 private insurance companies operating in Kyrgyzstan, including two that were partly Russian-owned and three that were entirely British-owned. In late 2007 there were 15 insurance companies operating in the country.

Anglo-Kyrgyz Insurance Co: 720000 Bishkek, ul. Akhunbaeva 100; tel. (312) 54-90-23; fax (312) 54-90-49; e-mail anglokgz@elcat.kg.

ATN Polis: 720000 Bishkek, ul. Isanova 42/1; tel. (312) 93-79-37; fax (312) 90-32-52; e-mail info@atnpolis.kg; internet www.atnpolis.kg; f. 2001; life and non-life.

Insurance Group of Central Asia: 720000 Bishkek, Baitik Baatyra 191, Hyatt Hotel, room 103; tel. (312) 68-12-21.

Kyrgyzinstrakh: 720001 Bishkek, pr. Chui 219; tel. (312) 61-45-88; fax (312) 61-46-45; e-mail kinstrakh@infotel.kg; internet kyrgyzinstrakh.com.kg; f. 1996 by the Russian joint-stock insurance company Investstrakh and the Kyrgyz Government to insure foreign investors; brs in Karakol and Osh; insurance and reinsurance; Chair. of Bd E. M. SEIDAKHMETOVA.

Kyrgyzstan Insurance Co: 720000 Bishkek, ul. Moskovskaya 76B; tel. (312) 28-28-15; e-mail office@insurance.kg; internet www.insurance.kg; f. 1991; Dir MARIYA ADENOVA.

Trade and Industry

GOVERNMENT AGENCIES

National Institute of Standards and Metrology: 720040 Bishkek, Panfilova 197; tel. (312) 62-68-70; fax (312) 66-13-67; e-mail nism@nism.gov.kg; internet www.nism.gov.kg; f. 1927 as the Division of the Chamber of Measures and Weights; present name adopted 2005; certification, control and testing of products and services; standardization, metrology, accreditation; Dir PATIDIN ATAKHANOV.

State Agency for Geology and Mineral Resources: 720739 Bishkek, pr. Erkindik 2; tel. (312) 66-49-01; fax (312) 66-03-91;

KYRGYZSTAN

e-mail mail@geoagency.bishkek.gov.kg; internet www.kgs.bishkek.gov.kg; Chair. SHEISHENALY MURZAGAZIYEV.

State Committee for Management of State Property: 720017 Bishkek, Moskovskaya 151; tel. (312) 62-68-52; fax (312) 66-02-36; e-mail mail@spf.bishkek.gov.kg; internet www.spf.gov.kg; f. 1991; responsible for the privatization of state-owned enterprises and deals with bankruptcies; Chair. TURSUN O. TURDUMAMBETOV.

CHAMBER OF COMMERCE

Chamber of Commerce and Industry of the Kyrgyz Republic: 720001 Bishkek, Kiyevskaya 107; tel. (312) 21-05-65; fax (312) 21-05-75; e-mail cci-kr@totel.kg; internet www.ihk-kg.de; f. 1959; supports foreign economic relations and the development of small and medium-sized enterprises; Pres. BORIS V. PERFILIYEV.

TRADE ASSOCIATION

Kyrgyzvneshtorg: 720033 Bishkek, Abdymomunova 276; tel. (312) 21-39-78; fax (312) 66-08-36; e-mail kvt@infotel.kg; f. 1992; export-import org.; Gen. Dir KADYRBEK K. KALIYEV.

UTILITIES

Electricity

NES Kyrgyzstana (National Electric Grid of Kyrgyzstan) (NESK): 720070 Bishkek, pr. Jibek Zholu 326; tel. (312) 66-10-00; fax (312) 66-06-56; e-mail nesk@elcat.kg; internet www.energo.kz; f. 2001; comprises seven companies, including four regional distribution companies, Severeletro, Oshelektro, Zhalabadelektro, Vostoelektro; one heating company, Bishkekteploset; 80.5% state-owned, 13.2% by the Social Fund of the Kyrgyz Republic; reorganization and privatization pending in 2008; cap. 1,597.4m. som (June 2006); Gen. Dir AVTANDIL CH. SYDYKOV.

Gas

Kyrgyzgaz: 720661 Bishkek, Gorkogo 22; tel. (312) 53-45-10; fax (312) 53-00-33; e-mail admin@kg.elcat.kg; internet www.kyrgyzgaz.kg; state gas distributor; Chair. KENESHBAY T. MOLDOBAYEV; Dir-Gen. SALAMAT K. AYTIKEEV.

TRADE UNIONS

Kyrgyzstan Federation of Trade Unions: 720032 Bishkek, Chui 207; tel. (312) 21-49-30; fax (312) 21-76-87; affiliated with the General Confed. of Trade Unions; Chair. SAGYN BOZGUNBAYEV.

Transport

RAILWAYS

Kyrgyzstan's railway network consists of only one main line (340 km) in northern Kyrgyzstan, which connects the country, via Kazakhstan, with the railway system of Russia. Osh, Jalal-Abad and other towns in regions of Kyrgyzstan bordering Uzbekistan are linked to that country by short lengths of railway track. In 2001 the Governments of Kyrgyzstan and the People's Republic of China signed a memorandum on the construction of a rail link from Kashgar (China) to Bishkek. In 2003 Kyrgyzstan and Kazakhstan announced that a 100-km railway link was to be built between Issyk-Kul and Almaty, Kazakhstan, although by mid-2007 work had yet to commence.

Kyrgyz Railway Administration (Kyrgyz Temir Jolu): 720009 Bishkek, L. Tolstogo 83; tel. (312) 62-48-65; fax (312) 65-06-90; e-mail asoup@imfiko.bishkek.su; internet railway.aknet.kg; f. 1992; Pres. I. S. OMURKULOV.

ROADS

In 1999 Kyrgyzstan's road network totalled an estimated 18,500 km, including 140 km of motorway; in 1996 there were 3,200 km of main roads and 6,380 km of secondary roads. About 91% of roads were paved. Work on the third and final phase of a project to reconstruct the main Bishkek–Osh highway was completed in 2004.

CIVIL AVIATION

There are three international airports at Bishkek (Manas), Osh and Tamchy (in the Issyk-Kul region).

Air Kyrgyzstan (AK): 720017 Bishkek, pr. Manasa 12A; tel. (312) 31-30-26; fax (312) 31-27-42; e-mail company@air.kg; internet www.air.kg; f. 2006 by merger of Altyn Air and Kyrgyzstan Airlines; state-owned; charter passenger services; Pres. EGEMBERDI B. MYRZABEKOV.

Itek Air: Bishkek, pr. Chui 128/10; tel. (312) 66-46-79; e-mail itek@infotel.kg; internet www.itekair.kg; f. 1999; scheduled domestic flights and flights to the People's Republic of China, Iran and Russia.

Tourism

There was little tourism in Kyrgyzstan during the Soviet period. However, the Government hoped that the country's spectacular and largely unspoilt mountain scenery, as well as the great crater lake of Issyk-Kul, might attract foreign tourists and investment. In 2006 there were 765,850 tourist arrivals, compared with 398,078 in 2004. Tourism receipts (including passenger transport) amounted to US $94m. in 2005.

State Committee for Tourism, Sport and Youth Policy: 720033 Bishkek, Togolok Moldo 17; tel. (312) 62-24-99; fax (312) 21-28-45; e-mail gktsm@gks.gov.kg; Chair. TURUSBEK CH. MAMASHEV.

LAOS

Introductory Survey

Location, Climate, Language, Religion, Flag, Capital

The Lao People's Democratic Republic is a land-locked country in South-East Asia, bordered by the People's Republic of China to the north, by Viet Nam to the east, by Cambodia to the south, by Thailand to the west and by Myanmar (formerly Burma) to the north-west. The climate is tropical, with a rainy monsoon season lasting from May to September. The temperature in the capital ranges between 23°C and 38°C in the hottest month, April, and between 14°C and 28°C in the coolest month, January. Laos comprises 47 ethnic groups. The official language, Lao or Laotian, is spoken by about two-thirds of the population. French is also spoken, and there are numerous tribal languages, including Meo. The principal religion is Buddhism. There are also some Christians and followers of animist beliefs. The national flag (proportions 2 by 3) has three horizontal stripes, of red, blue (half the total depth) and red, with a white disc in the centre. The capital is Vientiane (Viangchan).

Recent History

Laos was formerly a part of French Indo-China and comprised the three principalities of Luang Prabang, Vientiane and Champasak. These were merged in 1946, when France recognized Sisavang Vong, ruler of Luang Prabang since 1904, as King of Laos. In May 1947 the King promulgated a democratic constitution (although women were not allowed to vote until 1957). The Kingdom of Laos became independent, within the French Union, in July 1949, and full sovereignty was recognized by France in October 1953. The leading royalist politician was Prince Souvanna Phouma, who was Prime Minister in 1951–54, 1956–58, 1960 and in 1962–75. King Sisavang Vong died in October 1959, and was succeeded by his son, Savang Vatthana.

From 1950 the Royal Government was opposed by the Neo Lao Haksat (Lao Patriotic Front—LPF), an insurgent movement formed by a group of former anti-French activists. The LPF's Chairman was Prince Souphanouvong, a half-brother of Prince Souvanna Phouma, but its dominant element was the communist People's Party of Laos (PPL), led by Kaysone Phomvihane. During the 1950s the LPF's armed forces, the Pathet Lao, gradually secured control of the north-east of the country with the assistance of the Vietnamese communists, the Viet Minh, who were engaged in war with the French (until 1954). Several agreements between the Royal Government and the LPF, attempting to end the guerrilla war and reunite the country, failed during the 1950s and early 1960s. By 1965 the de facto partition of Laos was established, with the LPF refusing to participate in national elections and consolidating its power over the north-eastern provinces.

During the 1960s, as the 'Ho Chi Minh Trail' (the communist supply route to South Viet Nam) ran through Pathet Lao-controlled areas, Laos remained closely involved with the war between communist forces and anti-communist troops (supported by the USA) in Viet Nam. In 1973 the Viet Nam peace negotiations included provisions for a cease-fire in Laos. A new Government was formed in April 1974 under Prince Souvanna Phouma, with royalist, neutralist and LPF participation; Prince Souphanouvong was appointed Chairman of the Joint National Political Council. However, the LPF increased its power and eventually gained effective control of the country. This was confirmed by election victories in October and November 1975. In November King Savang Vatthana abdicated, and Prince Souvanna Phouma resigned.

In December 1975 the National Congress of People's Representatives (264 delegates elected by local authorities) abolished the monarchy and elected a 45-member legislative body, the Supreme People's Council. Souphanouvong was appointed President of the renamed Lao People's Democratic Republic and President of the Supreme People's Council. Kaysone Phomvihane, who had become Secretary-General of the Phak Pasason Pativat Lao (Lao People's Revolutionary Party—LPRP, a successor to the PPL), was appointed Prime Minister. The former King, Savang Vatthana, was designated Supreme Counsellor to the President, but he refused to co-operate with the new regime and was arrested in March 1977. (He was subsequently stated to have died in a 're-education camp'.) The LPF was replaced in February 1979 by the Lao Front for National Construction (LFNC), under the leadership of the LPRP.

In October 1986 the ailing Souphanouvong announced his resignation from his duties as President of the Republic (while retaining the title) and of the Supreme People's Assembly (as the Supreme People's Council had been renamed). Phoumi Vongvichit, formerly a Vice-Chairman in the Council of Ministers, became acting President of the Republic, while Sisomphon Lovansai, a Vice-President of the Supreme People's Assembly and a member of the LPRP Political Bureau (Politburo), became acting President of the Assembly. In November Kaysone Phomvihane was re-elected Secretary-General of the LPRP. In September 1987 it was announced that Phoumi Vongvichit had also replaced Souphanouvong as Chairman of the LFNC.

In June 1988 elections (the first since the formation of the Lao People's Democratic Republic) took place to determine the members of 113 district-level People's Councils. The LFNC approved 4,462 candidates to contest 2,410 seats. Provincial prefectural elections took place in November, when 898 candidates contested 651 seats. At the legislative election of March 1989, 121 candidates contested 79 seats in the enlarged Supreme People's Assembly. At its inaugural session in May, Nouhak Phoumsavanh (a Vice-Chairman of the Council of Ministers) was elected President of the Assembly.

Armed opposition to the Government persisted during the 1980s, particularly among hill tribes. In October 1982 Gen. Phoumi Nosavan, a 'conservative' who had been living in exile since 1965, formed the anti-communist Royal Lao Democratic Government, led by former Laotian military officers. However, many prominent exiles and resistance fighters in the United Front for the National Liberation of the Lao People (UFNLLP—formed in September 1980, and reportedly led by Gen. Phoumi since mid-1981) dissociated themselves from the Royal Government, which had established itself in southern Laos. In October 1988 the Government announced the capture of the Chief of Staff of the UFNLLP.

In December 1989 the right-wing United Lao National Liberation Front (ULNLF) proclaimed the 'Revolutionary Provisional Government' of Laos. The self-styled Government, which was headed by Outhong Souvannavong (the former President of the Royal Council of King Savang Vatthana), claimed to have used military force to 'liberate' one-third of Laotian territory. Although there were reports of attacks by insurgent guerrillas in northern Laos at this time, it was widely assumed that the ULNLF's claims were exaggerated and that its proclamation was an attempt to elicit popular support. Responsibility for defence in the 'Revolutionary Provisional Government' was reportedly allocated to Gen. Vang Pao, a leader of the Hmong tribe who in the 1970s had been a commander of the Royalist army (and who had lived in exile in the USA since 1975); Somphorn Wang (also formerly a prominent Royalist) was described as secretary of state. In late 1992 Gen. Vang Pao reportedly travelled to Singapore to direct an unsuccessful military operation from Thailand. In October Gen. Vang Pao's brother, Vang Fung, and another Hmong rebel, Moua Yee Julan (who were allegedly preparing an incursion into Laos under Gen. Vang Pao's command), were arrested in Thailand. In September 1993 Thai troops launched an offensive against Gen. Vang Pao's forces, expelling 320 rebels from Thai territory.

In June 1990 a draft Constitution, enshrining free-market principles, was published, and the Supreme People's Assembly approved legislation providing for the ownership of property, for inheritance rights and contractual obligations. In October three former government officials were arrested in connection with what were termed 'activities aimed at overthrowing the regime'. It was reported in Thailand that they had formed part of a 'Social Democrat Group', which was actively seeking the introduction of multi-party democracy. In November 1992 all three were sentenced to 14 years' imprisonment.

In March 1991, at the Fifth Congress of the LPRP, Souphanouvong retired from all his party posts. Phoumi Vongvichit and Sisomphon Lovansai also retired, and the three were appointed to a newly created advisory board to the LPRP Central Committee. Kaysone Phomvihane's title was altered from General Secretary to President of the LPRP, and his power was slightly enhanced following the abolition of the party Secretariat. A new Political Bureau and (younger) Party Central Committee were elected. Gen. Sisavat Keobounphan, the military Chief of the General Staff, was not re-elected to the Political Bureau. The leadership pledged a continuance of free-market economic reforms, but denied the need for political pluralism. However, the national motto ('peace, independence, unity, socialism') was changed to 'peace, independence, democracy, unity, prosperity'.

On 14 August 1991 the Supreme People's Assembly adopted a new Constitution, which provided for a National Assembly, confirmed the leading role of the LPRP, enshrined the right to private ownership and endowed the presidency with executive powers; new electoral legislation was also promulgated. Kaysone Phomvihane was appointed President of Laos. Gen. Khamtay Siphandone, a Vice-Chairman of the Council of Ministers, Minister of National Defence and Supreme Commander of the Lao People's Army, replaced Kaysone Phomvihane as Chairman of the Council of Ministers, restyled Prime Minister.

Kaysone Phomvihane died in November 1992. He was replaced as President of the LPRP by Gen. Khamtay Siphandone, and a specially convened meeting of the Supreme People's Assembly elected Nouhak Phoumsavanh as the country's President. At elections to the new National Assembly in December, 99.33% of eligible voters participated in the polls, in which 154 LFNC-approved candidates contested 85 seats. In February 1993 the new National Assembly re-elected Nouhak Phoumsavanh as President, confirmed Khamtay Siphandone as Prime Minister, and implemented the most extensive reorganization of the Council of Ministers since the LPRP's accession to power in 1975. Phoumi Vongvichit died in January 1994, and Souphanouvong in January 1995.

Although the 20th anniversary of the beginning of communist rule was celebrated in 1995, the Laotian Government was gradually attempting to replace communist ideology with Lao nationalism, as Laos developed a market economy with increasing foreign participation. In July senior Buddhist monks were assembled in Vientiane (as Buddhism was deemed central to Laotian cultural identity) and were encouraged by the Government to lead a 'cultural renaissance'. Meanwhile, the Government urged the security forces to suppress social problems, particularly corruption and prostitution, perceived as arising from increasing external influences.

The outcome of the LPRP congress at the end of March 1996 consolidated the country's apparent progress towards a form of military-dominated authoritarian government. The armed forces gained a majority of seats on the new nine-member Political Bureau; Khamtay Siphandone was elected as its President (replacing Nouhak Phoumsavanh, who retired from this post), and the Minister of National Defence and Commander-in-Chief of the armed forces, Lt-Gen. Chouammali Saignason, was promoted to third position, after the President of the National Assembly, Lt-Gen. Saman Vignaket. The most significant development was the failure of Khamphoui Keoboualapha, a Deputy Prime Minister responsible for many of Laos's reforms, to be re-elected either to the Political Bureau or to the Central Committee. Lts-Gen. Chouammali Saignason and Saman Vignaket were widely reported to be opposed to rapid economic and political reform.

At the opening session of the National Assembly in April 1996 Nouhak Phoumsavanh was, despite his retirement from the Political Bureau, confirmed as Head of State until the end of his term of office in February 1998. Sisavat Keobounphan (who had been restored to the Political Bureau at the previous month's elections) was elected to the new office of Vice-President, in order to relieve Nouhak Phoumsavanh of a number of presidential duties. Boungnang Volachit was approved by the National Assembly as a Deputy Prime Minister, although, contrary to expectation, Khamphoui Keoboualapha also retained his posts as Deputy Prime Minister and Chairman of the State Committee for Planning and Co-operation. However, it was expected that the latter's influence would be diminished by his exclusion from the Political Bureau and also by the establishment of a new State Planning Committee, which was to assume some of the responsibilities hitherto exercised by Khamphoui's Committee.

Elections to the National Assembly took place on 21 December 1997, at which 159 LFNC-approved candidates, including 41 members of the outgoing legislature, contested 99 seats. The three members of the LPRP Political Bureau and 10 Central Committee members who stood for election were all successful; one of the four 'independent' candidates without affiliation to the LPRP was elected. The level of participation by voters was officially recorded as 99.37%. The first session of the new National Assembly was held in February 1998, when Gen. Khamtay was elected to succeed Phoumsavanh as President of Laos. The Assembly also endorsed the appointment of Sisavat Keobounphan as Prime Minister and of Oudom Khattigna in his place as Vice-President, re-elected Saman Vignaket as President of the National Assembly, and approved a redistribution of ministerial posts.

In March 2001 the Seventh Congress of the LPRP confirmed the military's control of the Political Bureau. In a further reorganization of the Council of Ministers, Oudom was replaced as the country's Vice-President by Lt-Gen. Chouammali Saignason, who had withdrawn his candidacy for the premiership owing to ill health. Prime Minister Sisavat Keobounphan was forced to resign, in order to take responsibility for the mismanagement of the economy following the Asian financial crisis of 1997/98. His successor, the former Deputy Prime Minister and Minister of Finance, Boungnang Volachit, provided a civilian balance to the entirely military executive branch. The appointment of Thongloun Sisolit to the post of Deputy Prime Minister further increased the civilian representation on the Council of Ministers.

From the mid-1990s uprisings against the Government became more frequent. In July 1995 an army unit based near Luang Prabang mutinied after its commander, a Hmong general, was passed over for promotion. Five members of the armed forces died in the rebellion, which was believed to be symptomatic of the resentment felt by hill tribes over the political and military dominance by the lowland Lao. About 2,000 troops were dispatched to Luang Prabang to restore order. In November several people were killed in an armed assault on a bus near Luang Prabang, which was attributed to disaffected Hmong tribesmen. In October a shipment of explosives, allegedly destined for Hmong insurgents, had been intercepted on the Mekong River. Several incidents in the Luang Prabang region during 1996 were ascribed to Hmong rebels. Meanwhile, fund-raising by the Hmong community in the USA was reportedly a cause for concern within the Laotian Government.

In October 1999 an anti-Government demonstration by students and teachers was held in Vientiane. The protest, which constituted an extremely rare overt demonstration of public dissatisfaction, was reportedly swiftly dispersed by police. The Government subsequently repudiated claims that about 50 people who were involved or suspected to have been involved in the protest had been arrested, and, furthermore, denied that the demonstration had taken place; in March 2000, however, it was reported that the whereabouts of one professor and at least five students arrested during the protest remained unknown.

Civil unrest intensified throughout 2000, with a spate of bomb attacks. The first occurred in a restaurant in March, immediately drawing international attention as several tourists were injured in the blast. Two further attacks took place in Vientiane in May, coinciding with the respective visits of the Thai Prime Minister, Chuan Leekpai, and his Minister of Foreign Affairs, Surin Pitsuwan. Two more attacks followed within a week of each other, bringing the total number of injured to more than 20, with at least two killed. The Government attributed the campaign to Hmong insurgents, claiming to have arrested two men (one Lao and one Hmong) carrying explosive devices in mid-June. However, the bombing operation continued unabated. A bomb was defused near the Vietnamese embassy in Vientiane at the end of July, lending credence to the suspicion that the action was part of an internal power struggle between pro-Chinese and pro-Vietnamese governmental factions. In total, at least nine bombs exploded between March 2000 and January 2001, with the penultimate detonation occurring on the eve of the meeting of the European Union and the Association of South East Asian Nations (see p. 194) (EU-ASEAN summit) in December 2000.

Although no group admitted responsibility for the bombings, a pre-dawn assault in July 2000 on immigration and customs offices in Vang Tao, opposite the Chong Mek checkpoint on the border with Thailand, indicated the involvement of royalist rebels. The Government claimed that the attack was merely a robbery, but during the incursion the former royal flag was raised over the immigration office. (In October 2004, following their extradition from Thailand, 16 Lao nationals were convicted of robbery in connection with the raid and sentenced to prison terms of between two and 12 years.) In November 2000 about 200 workers and students were reported to have staged a demonstration in the southern province of Champasak, demanding democracy. The protest was swiftly quelled, and 15 people were arrested. However, the timing of the demonstration exacerbated the increasing sense of instability, as less than two weeks previously Helen Clark, the Prime Minister of New Zealand, had confirmed that her Government had granted political asylum to Khamsay Souphanouvong, a minister attached to the Prime Minister's office and son of the first President of the Lao People's Democratic Republic.

In October 2001 five European activists, including Olivier Dupuis, a Belgian member of the European Parliament, were arrested for distributing pro-democracy leaflets at a peaceful protest in Vientiane. The protest was held to commemorate the second anniversary of the disappearance of the five students who had participated in the demonstration of October 1999. In November 2001, following expressions of concern at the conditions under which the detainees were being held, Romani Prodi, President of the European Commission, warned the Laotian authorities that the continued detention of the activists would threaten diplomatic relations with the EU. In the same month, following a swift trial, the prisoners were convicted of attempting to spread unrest and ordered to be deported. They were also fined and given two-year suspended prison terms.

In February 2002 elections took place from among 166 LFNC-approved candidates for the 109 seats available in the National Assembly. Only one of the elected members was not affiliated to the LPRP, ensuring that the ruling party secured a comprehensive victory. In April, at the opening session of the National Assembly, the existing Cabinet was almost wholly re-elected. The former Minister of the Interior, Maj.-Gen. Asang Laoli, became Deputy Prime Minister and Maj.-Gen. Soudchai Thammasith subsequently assumed the interior portfolio. In January 2003 a cabinet reorganization was announced in an apparent attempt to strengthen the national economy. The former Governor of the Central Bank, Chansy Phosikham, was appointed Minister of Finance, Onneua Phommachanh became Minister of Industry and Handicrafts and Soulivong Daravong was placed in charge of the Ministry of Commerce and Tourism.

In September 2002 a bomb exploded at the Si Muang temple in Vientiane, injuring two children. In January 2003, for the first time, national celebrations were held to commemorate the anniversary of the birth of King Fa Ngoum, accredited with incorporating the disparate Lao principalities into the Kingdom of Lan Xang in 1353; a statue was erected and a public holiday declared. In the following month a group of armed men ambushed a bus near the town of Vang Vieng; the attack resulted in the deaths of 13 people, including three foreign nationals. Fears that tourists might be deterred from visiting Laos were intensified in April when a further attack, thought to have been perpetrated by Hmong rebels, on a bus travelling between Luang Prabang and Vientiane killed at least 12 people. In August an attack on a bus in the north of the country killed five people, and in October three bombs exploded in Vientiane. A previously unknown group, the Free Democratic People's Government of Laos (FDPGL), claimed responsibility for the bombings, as well as for the spate of bomb attacks that had occurred in the capital since 2000. It was believed that the group consisted of disaffected former members of the armed forces. However, a German-based organization, the Committee for Independence and Democracy in Laos, later claimed responsibility for the bombings, including two further attacks in February 2004, one in Vientiane, which killed two people, and one in the southern town of Savannakhet, where tourism ministers from ASEAN countries had convened.

In June 2003 it was reported that two European journalists, together with their Lao-US interpreter, had been arrested on suspicion of involvement in the murder of a Lao national and for contravening the terms of their tourist visas. The journalists had allegedly been researching the Hmong insurgency, which they had found to be almost exhausted and desperate for assistance. Following a summary trial, the three were sentenced to 15-year prison terms. Three Hmong defendants were given 20-year prison sentences. However, following intense diplomatic pressure from their respective Governments, the three foreign nationals were released in the following month. In October Political Bureau member Bouasone Bouphavanh was appointed fourth Deputy Prime Minister, with responsibility for home affairs.

In March 2004 an official from the Ministry of National Defence claimed that some 700 Hmong, including five senior commanders, had recently surrendered to the authorities, having been offered amnesty. Five bomb attacks reportedly occurred in April and May, the most serious of which killed one person and injured six others in southern Laos. In September the human rights organization Amnesty International alleged that up to 40 government troops had assaulted and murdered five Hmong children in the Xaysomboun special zone in northern Laos in May; the Government denied the accusations. Security was heightened in Vientiane in November, following two minor bomb explosions near the Thai border (for which the FDPGL claimed responsibility) and warnings of further possible attacks in advance of the ASEAN summit meeting, which was held in the capital at the end of the month. Two small bombs exploded in a village outside the capital a few days before the opening of the meeting.

In February 2006 it was announced that a legislative election would be held at the end of April, almost a year ahead of schedule. President Khamtay Siphandone stated that the decision to hold elections before the expiry of the mandate of the current Assembly had been made in order to enable the new Council of Ministers and the incoming legislature to commence their respective terms of office within close proximity of one another, in order to facilitate the forging of a strong working relationship. In March the LPRP held its Eighth Party Congress, during which Gen. Khamtay tendered his resignation as party leader; he was replaced by Vice-President Lt-Gen. Choummali Saignason. Khamtay also resigned from the Political Bureau, to which two new members were elected: Deputy Prime Minister and Minister of Foreign Affairs Somsavat Lengsavat; and Phani Yathothu, the only female member of the Bureau. Elections for a new Central Committee were also held, at which 55 members were selected. On 30 April the legislative election was duly conducted; an estimated 2.7m. voters cast their ballot. The counting of ballots was hindered by torrential rain in parts of the country. When announced in mid-May, the results showed that two nominally independent candidates (of the three who had contested the election) had been elected, alongside 113 members of the LPRP. However, some 71 of the incoming deputies had not previously been members of the National Assembly, and therefore were described by some commentators as constituting a new generation of legislators. The new National Assembly convened at the beginning of June, electing Thongsing Thammavong, Politburo member and Governor of Vientiane, as its President. Lt-Gen. Choummali Saignason was chosen to succeed Gen. Khamtay as President of Laos. Boungnang Volachit became Vice-President, while Bouasong Bouphavanh was appointed to replace him as Prime Minister. Among the new members of the Council of Ministers were two women; other notable changes included the transfer of the foreign affairs portfolio from Somsavat Lengsavat to Thongloun Sisolit, both of whom remained as Deputy Prime Ministers, along with Maj.-Gen. Asong Laoli. Maj.-Gen. Douangchai Phichit retained the defence portfolio and was promoted to the position of Deputy Prime Minister. Chansy Phosikham remained Minister of Finance. In a structural reorganization, the Ministries of Commerce and of Industry were combined to form one entity, and a new Ministry of Energy and Mining was established.

In June 2007 10 Hmong resident in the USA and a former officer of the California National Guard were arrested and charged in connection with an alleged plot to overthrow the Laos Government, which had been uncovered by US federal agents. Most of the 11 defendants, including Gen. Vang Pao, who was accused of being the leader of the group, were released on bail in July.

The National Assembly approved several ministerial changes proposed by Prime Minister Bouasone Bouphavanh in early July 2007. Chansy Phosikham was replaced as Minister of Finance by his deputy, Somdy Douangdy, and three new Ministers to the Office of the Prime Minister were appointed. Chansy succeeded Somphet Phetmala as Governor of Vientiane, with the latter becoming Deputy Minister of National Defence. The Assembly also adopted new legislation on public security. Addressing the National Assembly in the previous month, Bouasone had emphasized the need to combat rising corruption among government officials. Bosaikham Vongdara, who had served as Minister for Energy and Mining since 2006, died in July 2008. He was subsequently replaced by Soulivong Dalavong.

In foreign relations, from 1975 Laos was dependent on Vietnamese economic and military assistance, permitting the stationing of Vietnamese troops (estimated in 1987 to number between 30,000 and 50,000) on its territory. In 1977 a 25-year treaty of friendship between the two countries was signed, and Laos supported the Vietnamese-led overthrow of the Khmer Rouge regime in Kampuchea (Cambodia) in January 1979. Following the outbreak of hostilities between Viet Nam and the People's Republic of China in that year, Laos allied itself with the former. Viet Nam withdrew its military presence from Laos during 1988. The two countries signed a protocol governing military co-operation in March 1994. In July 2001 Prime Minister Boungnang Volachit visited Viet Nam on his first foreign trip since assuming office in March. In May 2002 President Khamtay Siphandone paid an official friendship visit to Viet Nam, which was reciprocated in October by the Chairman of the Vietnamese National Assembly, Nguyen Van An. The visits affirmed the strength of relations between the two countries. In February 2006 a major border crossing was opened between Sekong province in Laos and Quang Nam province in Viet Nam. It was hoped that this would facilitate economic exchanges and help to control smuggling along the common border. Discussions held during an official visit to Laos by the Vietnamese President, Nguyen Minh Triet, in February 2007 also focused on the expansion of economic co-operation. Various joint activities were organized later in that year to celebrate the 45th anniversary of the establishment of diplomatic relations between Laos and Viet Nam and the 30th anniversary of the signing of the treaty of friendship. In February 2008 it was reported that Viet Nam had become the second largest foreign investor in Laos, investing some US $600m. in economic development projects since 1989, including $270m. in the energy sector.

In February 1993 Laos, Thailand, Viet Nam and Cambodia signed a joint communiqué providing for the resumption of co-operation in the development of the Mekong River. In April 1995 in Chiang Rai, Thailand, representatives of the four countries signed an agreement on the joint exploitation and development of the lower Mekong. The accord provided for the establishment of the Mekong River Commission (see p. 427) as a successor to the Committee for Co-ordination of Investigations of the Lower Mekong Basin. In February 2008 Laos, Cambodia and Viet Nam concluded a draft agreement on defining the intersection point of their borders.

In July 1992 Laos strengthened relations with members of ASEAN by signing the ASEAN Treaty of Amity and Co-operation, which provided for wider regional co-operation and was regarded as a preliminary step to full membership of the Association. Laos attended ASEAN meetings with observer status from this time, and applied for membership of the organization in March 1996. The country was formally admitted as a full member at the organization's meeting of ministers responsible for foreign affairs in July 1997. As Chair of ASEAN for 2004/05, Laos hosted the 10th summit meeting of the Association in November 2004 and the 38th Ministerial Meeting in July 2005. Despite bomb threats made to staff at the US embassy in Vientiane, apparently by groups opposed to the Laotian Government, in the period prior to the summit meeting in November 2004, both the summit meeting itself and the ministerial conference proceeded without incident and did much to raise the international profile of Laos. In February 2008 Laos ratified the new ASEAN Charter, which codified the principles and purposes of the Association and had been signed in November 2007 at the 13th summit meeting in Singapore.

Relations with China improved in December 1986, when a Chinese delegation, led by the Deputy Minister of Foreign Affairs, made the first official Chinese visit to Laos since 1978. In December 1987, after an assurance that Chinese support would be withdrawn from Laotian resistance groups operating from within China, the two countries agreed to restore full diplomatic relations and to encourage bilateral trade. Relations between the LPRP and the Chinese Communist Party were fully restored in August 1989. In October 1991 the Laotian and Chinese Prime Ministers signed a border treaty, which established a framework for meetings of a Laotian-Chinese joint border committee. In January 1992 the committee adopted a resolution providing for the demarcation of the common border, and in June an agreement on the delineation of boundaries was signed. In November 1994 Laos and China signed a reciprocal agreement on the transport of passengers and goods on each other's sections of the Mekong River. In February 1996 Laos and China opened a section of their border to highway traffic. In October 1997 Chinese Vice-Premier Wu Bangguo made a three-day visit to Laos, and in early 1999 Prime Minister Sisavat Keobounphan made an eight-day official visit to China. The first visit ever made by a Chinese head of state to Laos was by President Jiang Zemin in November 2000. As the volume of bilateral trade continued to increase, wider co-operation with China was expected to follow a state visit by President Hu Jintao to Laos in November 2006. Relations were further strengthened in August 2007 by a seven-day official visit to China by Prime Minister Bouasone Bouphavanh, during which six agreements on co-operation in a range of areas were signed. In March 2008 Chinese Premier Wen Jiabao undertook a three-day visit to Laos for discussions with Bouasone Bouphavanh. The two leaders broadly agreed to increase exchanges, to collaborate closely on important projects and to promote strategic industries. However, China's increasing involvement in the economy of Laos, mainly in infrastructural development projects, had begun to concern the citizens of Laos. Many were perturbed by the influx of Chinese workers and business entrepreneurs, who according to some estimates totalled as many as 300,000 by 2008. In particular, in return for the granting of a concession to develop a large residential and economic zone in Vientiane, thousands of Chinese labourers were engaged to work on the construction of a new sports stadium. Financed by the China Development Bank, the national stadium was to be completed prior to the holding of the South-East Asian Games in the Laotian capital in December 2009.

Relations with Thailand from 1975 were characterized by mutual suspicion. Thailand intermittently closed its border to Laotian imports and exports, causing considerable hardship. Disputed sovereignty claims in border areas were a cause of friction, and led to clashes between Laotian and Thai troops in 1984. Further hostilities began in December 1987, resulting in hundreds of casualties. In February 1988 the two sides agreed to declare a cease-fire, to withdraw their troops from the combat area and to attempt to negotiate a peaceful solution. In March 1991 (following a military coup in Thailand) representatives of the two countries signed an agreement providing for the immediate withdrawal of troops from disputed areas. The Thai Government also undertook to suppress the activities of Laotian insurgents operating from Thai territory. In December Thailand and Laos signed a border co-operation agreement.

In June 1992 the Thai Crown Prince, Maha Vajiralongkorn, visited Vientiane for the first time. On the following day, however, about 300 guerrillas from a Thai-based rebel group, the Free Democratic Lao National Salvation Force, attacked three Laotian government posts, killing two people and causing significant damage. In the same month Laos refuted allegations made by a senior Thai military officer that a Laotian government unit was receiving training in chemical warfare from Cuban and Vietnamese experts, and also dismissed previous accusations by Laotian resistance fighters and Western aid agencies of its use of chemical warfare to suppress the activities of rebel groups. Bilateral relations improved in July, when the Thai authorities announced the arrest of 11 Laotian citizens accused of planning subversive activities against the Government in Vientiane. The first bridge (over the Mekong River) linking Laos and Thailand was opened in April 1994. In September 1996 the countries' Joint Co-operation Commission agreed to establish a boundary commission, in an effort to resolve demarcation problems. Despite various diplomatic efforts to stimulate further co-operation between the two countries, such as the signing of an extradition treaty in January 2001, the relationship was strained by the July 2000 incursion launched from Thai territory by suspected royalist rebels (see above). (In July 2004, following a lengthy legal dispute, Thailand handed over to the Laotian authorities 16 Lao nationals who were allegedly involved in the incursion, despite an earlier ruling by a Thai court rejecting their extradition.) Meanwhile, the situation deteriorated further in August 2000 after Laotian troops occupied two islands in the Mekong River, evicting 65 Thai farming families. Laos claimed that under a 1926 treaty it had sovereignty over all the islands in the Mekong, while Thailand merely requested the withdrawal of the troops. Nevertheless, in April 2001 the Thai Minister of Foreign Affairs, Surakiart Sathirathai, visited Laos, affirming the beginning of a new era of friendly Lao-Thai relations based on shared cultural values. In June Thai Prime Minister Thaksin Shinawatra arrived in Vientiane on a two-day official visit intended further to consolidate relations. In late 2003, following a meeting of the Joint Co-operation Commission, the two countries pledged to resolve all outstanding border demarcation issues, as well as agreeing to work together on a variety of social development initiatives. In March 2004, for the first time, the Thai and Laotian Governments held a joint cabinet meeting to discuss bilateral co-operation. The meeting ended with Prime Ministers Thaksin Shinawatra and Boungnang Volachit presiding over a ceremony to lay the foundation stone for a second Mekong Friendship Bridge, which was officially opened in December 2006. In June 2007 China, Laos and Thailand signed an agreement on the construction of a further bridge across the Mekong River, which would provide a direct road link from the Chinese province of Yunnan, through Laos, to the Thai capital, Bangkok. Scheduled for completion in 2011, the bridge was to be financed jointly by China and Thailand. In February 2008 Laos and Thailand agreed to complete the demarcation of their land border in that year, as the area remaining under dispute covered only 12 km, followed by that of the maritime border in 2010. At the end of February 2008 the new Thai Prime Minister, Samak Sundaravej, visited Laos on his first foreign trip since taking office earlier that month.

During the 1970s and 1980s thousands of Laotian refugees fled to Thailand to escape from civil war and food shortages. In January 1989 an estimated 90,000 Laotian refugees remained in border camps in Thailand. The office of the UN High Commissioner for Refugees (UNHCR) began a programme of voluntary repatriation in 1980. By late 1990 fewer than 6,000 refugees had been repatriated under UNHCR supervision, while some 15,000 had returned independently, and others had been resettled abroad. In June 1991 UNHCR, Laos and Thailand signed an agreement guaranteeing the repatriation or resettlement in a third country of the remaining 60,000 Laotian refugees in Thailand by the end of 1994; however, this deadline was subsequently revised on several occasions. In December 1996, according to UNHCR, 3,293 Laotian refugees remained in Thailand. In December 1997 UNHCR announced that a final review of the status of the last remaining refugees at Ban Napho camp in Thailand would be completed by January 1998, whereupon they would be repatriated or resettled in a third country. Among the camp's 1,344 refugees were reportedly 964 Hmong, most of whom were unwilling to return to Laos. In December 2003 the USA agreed to accept around 15,000 Laotian Hmong refugees living in refugee camps in Thailand. The first group of refugees was resettled in the USA in June 2004, under the aegis of the International Organization for Migration.

In early 2006 tension arose between Laos and Thailand concerning 27 Hmong refugees (all but one of whom were children), who had been reported missing from a refugee camp in Phetchabun province, north-eastern Thailand, in December 2005. The group was subsequently discovered in Laos, allegedly having been forcibly repatriated by the Thai authorities. Laos and Thailand entered into negotiations regarding the possibility of reuniting the children with their parents at the Phetchabun refugee camp, although it was later reported that the children had disappeared. In June Thai police arrested some 270 Hmong migrants who had allegedly entered Thailand illegally from Laos; however, officials of the latter country denied that the migrants were necessarily Laotian citizens. In August officials from the respective Ministries of Foreign Affairs of Laos and Thailand declared that their countries were ready to co-operate in addressing the Hmong refugee issue, for which neither side took responsibility. The Laotian Deputy Prime Minister, Somsavat Lengsavat, suggested in November that Laos might allow repatriation of Hmong refugees if they were proven to be of Laotian nationality, but reiterated that the Government had not persecuted the Hmong. In the following month UNHCR urged the Thai Government to abandon its plan for the forcible repatriation of more than 150 Hmong migrants to Laos, arguing that they would be at risk if they returned. The Thai Ministry of Foreign Affairs responded that Thai and Laotian immigration officials were determining the nationality of the migrants, who, it was stated, would not be repatriated against their will. In January 2007 the Thai Government agreed to halt the deportation process after the USA, Canada, Australia and the Netherlands agreed to provide asylum to the migrants, some of whom had protested against repatriation by locking themselves inside their detention centre. In March 2009, however, the group of Hmong, now numbering 158, including 92 children, and all recognized as refugees, remained in an immigration detention centre in Thailand, according to UNHCR, which urged the Thai authorities to release them so that they could take up the previous offers of asylum in other countries.

Meanwhile, in mid-December 2006 a meeting between the Laotian Prime Minister and his Thai counterpart reportedly resulted in an agreement to repatriate the more than 7,000 Hmong living in refugee camps in Thailand's Phetchabun province, who were alleged to be economic migrants (and to whom UNHCR did not have access), following verification of their origin. In January 2007 UNHCR expressed concern about reports that Thailand had returned 16 Hmong to Laos who had apparently not been screened to ascertain if they required international protection, urging the suspension of deportations pending the introduction of procedures to allow a proper assessment of the needs and claims of the Hmong. Thai and Laotian officials held further discussions on the repatriation of the Hmong in Phetchabun province in September, later confirming that around 200 Hmong had already been resettled in Laos in that year and that the process of verifying the identity of those remaining in Phetchabun was ongoing. A site in Kaxi district, some 150 km from Vientiane, had been prepared for those who could not return to their homes in Laos. In February 2008, following a visit to Laos, the Thai Minister of Foreign Affairs announced that the Thai authorities were nearing the completion of the screening process. Later in that month Thai defence officials announced that 10 Hmong were being repatriated from Phetchabun in advance of an official visit by the Thai Prime Minister to Laos; UNHCR sought reassurance that their return was voluntary, as claimed by the officials. Following a mass protest at the Ban Huay Nam Khao camp in Phetchabun in June, when more than 5,000 refugees marched some distance from the compound before being halted by the Thai security forces, the Thai authorities promptly deported 837 Hmong refugees to Laos. Although 3,700 of the protesters returned to the camp on the following day, 1,300 refugees remained unaccounted for after the incident. The 837 repatriations were described by the Thai army as voluntary, although concerns were raised by human rights organizations, including Amnesty International and Human Rights Watch. A total of 1,809 Hmong were deported from Thailand to Laos during 2008 (see the chapter on Thailand).

From the 1990s Laos forged closer links with Myanmar and with Cambodia. In February 1992 Khamtay Siphandone was the first foreign head of government to visit Myanmar since the military coup in that country in 1988, and in June 1994 Senior Gen. Than Shwe visited Laos, his first foreign visit as Myanmar's Head of State. Bilateral contacts continued on a frequent basis. Laos signed a treaty of friendship and assistance with Cambodia in December 1995, further to which Joint Co-operation Committees were established. In November 2001 Prince Norodom Ranariddh headed a Cambodian delegation on an official goodwill visit to Laos.

From 1989 the Laotian Government sought to improve relations with non-communist countries, in order to reduce its (especially economic) dependence on the USSR and Viet Nam. Following a visit to Japan in that year by Kaysone Phomvihane (his first official visit to a non-communist country), the Japanese Government agreed to increase grant aid to Laos. In December 1995 Japan announced that it would resume the provision of official loans to Laos in 1996. In January 2000 the Japanese Prime Minister, Keizo Obuchi, undertook an official visit to Laos, and in August 2000 a bridge over the Mekong, built with a 5,460m.-yen grant from the Japanese Government, was officially opened in Paksé. In mid-2001 Prince Akishino of Japan made a 10-day unofficial visit to Laos and, in September, Japan agreed a further loan to fund the construction of the second Mekong Friendship Bridge. Bilateral relations were further strengthened in May 2007, during a visit to Japan by Laotian Prime Minister Bouasone Bouphavanh. Bouasone held a meeting with his Japanese counterpart, Shinzo Abe, who pledged to provide continued economic assistance to Laos, including approximately US $1m. for the clearance of unexploded ordnance remaining from the Viet Nam war (see below), which was impeding development. Furthermore, it was hoped that a bilateral agreement on the liberalization, promotion and protection of investment, which was signed in January 2008, would encourage the participation of Japanese businesses in the Laotian economy.

In November 2002 the Prime Minister of India, Atal Bihari Vajpayee, paid the first visit to Laos by an Indian head of government in more than 45 years. During his stay the two countries signed agreements on co-operation in defence issues and control of drugs-trafficking. The Indian Government also agreed to provide US $10m. of credit to Laos at low interest rates.

During the Viet Nam war US aircraft completed almost 600,000 bombing missions over Laos, leaving large amounts of undetonated explosives, which were estimated to be causing 50–100 fatalities per year in the 1990s. The National Unexploded Ordnance Awareness and Clearance Programme was established in Laos in May 1995, with support from the UN. Following the adoption by 107 countries in May 2008 of the Convention on Cluster Munitions, banning the use, production, stockpiling and transfer of cluster bombs, in October Laos hosted the South East Asia Regional Conference on the Convention on Cluster Munitions, and the treaty was opened for signature in December.

Relations with the USA have been dominated by the issue of the US soldiers listed as 'missing in action' in Laos during the

Viet Nam war. In 1985 Laos agreed to co-operate with the USA in tracing missing soldiers. In August 1987 a US delegation visited Vientiane to discuss 'humanitarian co-operation' and agreed to provide Laos with aid. The first remains of US soldiers were passed to the US Government in February 1988; further operations to locate the remains of US soldiers took place in the 1990s and 2000s. In November 1991, in response to continued Laotian co-operation and the implementation of limited political and economic reforms, the US Government announced that diplomatic relations with Laos were to be upgraded to ambassadorial level. Following 17 months of hearings, in January 1993 a special US Senate panel concluded that (despite considerable public speculation to the contrary) there was 'no compelling evidence' of the survival of US servicemen in the region. In May 1995 the USA announced the ending of a 20-year embargo on aid to Laos. In November 1997 the US Deputy Secretary of State, Strobe Talbott, led the most senior-level US delegation to Laos since the mid-1970s. During the visit further US support was pledged for a programme to clear unexploded ordnance from the Viet Nam war, which had been supported by the USA since 1996. In mid-1998 US officials agreed to extend financial and logistical support for the programme until September 1999. In December 2004, following its adoption by Congress, President George W. Bush of the USA signed legislation according normal trade relations (NTR) status to Laos: this status had been suspended in 1975. The US Senate had separately adopted a resolution condemning Laos's human rights record, concerns over which had delayed the approval of NTR status. A bilateral trade agreement signed by the USA and Laos in September 2003 consequently entered into force in February 2005.

Government

Under the terms of the 1991 Constitution, executive power is vested in the President of State, while legislative power resides with the National Assembly. The President is elected for five years by the National Assembly. Members of the National Assembly are elected for a period of five years by universal adult suffrage. The Lao People's Revolutionary Party remains the sole legal political party. With the approval of the National Assembly, the President appoints the Prime Minister and members of the Council of Ministers, who conduct the government of the country. The President also appoints provincial governors and mayors of municipalities, who are responsible for local administration.

Defence

As assessed at November 2008, according to Western estimates, the strength of the armed forces was 29,100 (Lao People's Army 25,600—including an army marine section of 600—and air force 3,500). Military service is compulsory for a minimum of 18 months. There is a paramilitary self-defence force numbering more than 100,000. In 2007 defence expenditure was budgeted at an estimated 140,000m. kips.

Economic Affairs

In 2007, according to estimates by the World Bank, Laos's gross national income (GNI), measured at average 2005–07 prices, was US $3,413m., equivalent to $580 per head (or $1,940 per head on an international purchasing-power parity basis). During 2000–07, it was estimated, the population increased by an annual average of 1.7%, while gross domestic product (GDP) per head increased, in real terms, by an average of 4.8% per year. Overall GDP increased, in real terms, at an average annual rate of 6.6% in 2000–07, expanding by 7.1% in 2007. The Asian Development Bank (ADB) estimated that GDP grew by 7.2% in 2008.

Agriculture (including forestry and fishing) contributed an estimated 40.9% of GDP in 2007. According to the ADB, an estimated 78.5% of the working population were employed in the sector in 2005. Rice is the staple crop. Other crops include sweet potatoes, maize, cassava, sugar cane and fruit. Coffee, production of which reached an estimated 28,000 metric tons in 2007, is grown for export. In 2000 forest covered about 55.4% of the country's total land area. Timber remained a significant export commodity in 2007, accounting for an estimated 14.9% of total export revenue in that year. The illicit cultivation of narcotic drugs has been widespread. The UN Office on Drugs and Crime (UNODC—formerly the UN Office of Drug Control and Crime Prevention) estimated that the area under opium poppy cultivation in Laos was 1,560 ha in 2008, compared with 26,800 ha in 1998. Calculated on the basis of the area under cultivation, the country's potential production of dry opium decreased from an estimated 20.0 metric tons in 2006 to 9.0 tons in 2007, before rising to 9.6 tons in 2008. During 2000–06 agricultural GDP increased at an estimated average annual rate of 2.7%, according to figures from the World Bank. The sector's rate of growth was estimated by the ADB at 8.6% in 2007 and 2.0% in 2008, the reduction being largely attributable to serious floods in August of the latter year.

Industry (including mining, manufacturing, construction and utilities) contributed an estimated 33.9% of GDP in 2007. According to the ADB, the sector employed 9.3% of the working population in 2003. During 2000–06 industrial GDP increased at an average annual rate of 13.0%. Growth in the industrial sector was estimated by the ADB at 4.4% in 2007 and 10.2% in 2008.

Mining contributed only an estimated 5.4% of GDP in 2007, although this represented a significant increase from 1.5% in 2004. Laos has considerable mineral resources: iron ore, copper, coal, tin, gold, gemstones and gypsum are among the minerals that are exploited. Other mineral deposits include zinc, nickel, potash, lead, limestone and silver. Copper production rose from an estimated 30,480 metric tons in 2005 to 60,803 tons in 2006. Exports of copper were estimated at US $446m. in 2007, when output reached 62,541 metric tons. The value of gold exports (including re-exports) totalled $93.2m. in 2007. During 2000–06 the GDP of the mining sector increased by an average of 54.5% per year. Growth in this sector was substantial from 2003, owing to the start of gold production in that year. The sector expanded by 86.9% in 2006, a result attributed to increased copper production (see above) and an associated rise in mineral exports.

Manufacturing contributed an estimated 23.3% of GDP in 2007. It is mainly confined to the processing of raw materials (chiefly sawmilling) and agricultural produce, the production of textiles and garments (a significant export, accounting for 10.5% of total exports in 2007), and the manufacture of handicrafts and basic consumer goods for the domestic market. Manufacturing GDP increased at an estimated average annual rate of 10.3% in 2000–06. Manufacturing GDP increased by an estimated 8.1% in 2006.

Electrical energy is principally derived from hydroelectric power. Electricity is exported to Thailand and Viet Nam, and is an important source of foreign exchange. Laos's total hydroelectric power potential was estimated at 25,000 MW in 2000. In 2007 the country's total hydroelectricity generation reached an estimated 3,474m. kWh. In 2002 the Government granted a concession to the Nam Theun 2 Power Company (NTPC), enabling it to assume control of the construction of a major new hydroelectric dam. The 1,088 MW project was scheduled to become fully operational in late 2009. Under an agreement reached with Thailand in 2006, annual exports of electricity from Laos were to increase to as much as 5,000 MW. Laos is dependent on imports, mainly from Thailand, for supplies of mineral fuels.

The services sector contributed an estimated 25.2% of GDP in 2007, and engaged 8.6% of the total labour force in 2003. Receipts from tourism increased from US $146m. in 2005 to $173m. in 2006. Tourist arrivals increased from nearly 1.1m. in 2005 to more than 1.2m. in 2006. The GDP of the services sector increased at an estimated average annual rate of 6.7% in 2000–06. The sector grew by 9.1% in 2007 and by 9.7% in 2008, according to the ADB.

In 2007 Laos recorded a visible trade deficit of US $142.0m., and there was a surplus of $76.2m. on the current account of the balance of payments. Remittances from relatives residing overseas are a significant source of income for many Lao. In 2007 Thailand was the principal source of imports, supplying an estimated 70.6% (including any goods in transit) of the total. The People's Republic of China was also an important source of imports (8.6%) in that year, along with Viet Nam, Singapore, Germany and Japan. The principal destination of exports from Laos in 2007 was Thailand, which purchased 36.4% (including any goods in transit) of the total. Other significant purchasers in that year were Viet Nam (11.0%) and China (6.3%). The main exports in 2007 were copper, timber, garments, gold and electricity. The principal imports were capital goods, petroleum and material for the garment industry.

In the financial year ending 30 September 2008, including grants an overall budget deficit of 1,643,000m. new kips was recorded. The ADB estimated the budget deficit (excluding grants) to be equivalent to 5.8% of GDP in 2008. At the end of 2007 the country's external debt totalled US $2,853m.; in that year the cost of debt-servicing was equivalent to 4.3% of revenue from exports of goods and services. Consumer prices increased by an annual average of 8.9% in 2000–07. According to the ADB, the average annual rate of inflation increased from 4.5% in 2007 to 7.6% in 2008. The unemployment rate was estimated by the ADB at 1.4% of the labour force in 2005.

Laos is a member of the UN Economic and Social Commission for Asia and the Pacific (ESCAP, see p. 36), of the Asian Development Bank (ADB, see p. 191), of the Association of South East Asian Nations (ASEAN, see p. 194), of the Colombo Plan (see p. 425), which promotes economic and social development in Asia and the Pacific, and of the Mekong River Commission (see p. 427).

In order to comply with the requirements of the World Trade Organization (WTO, see p. 410), which Laos hoped to join by 2010, the Government continued to implement measures to improve trade and investment conditions; various regulations were in the process of revision in 2008. The Sixth National Socio-economic Development Plan, for the period 2006–10, projected average annual growth of between 7.5% and 8.0%. The industrial sector was to undergo particularly rapid expansion. During the plan period the Government envisaged a reduction in the incidence of poverty among households to less than 15% (compared with more than 30% in 2003). The encouragement of the private sector was also envisaged. However, despite major improvements to the road network in recent years (which greatly facilitated trade with China), the limitations of the Laotian infrastructure, combined with a shortage of the requisite skills, continued to impede progress. A special economic zone was being developed in the province of Savannakhet in 2008, in an attempt to promote private enterprise. The implementation of value-added tax (VAT) in January 2009, levied at a rate of 10%, was expected to help raise the funds required to finance wider development. None the less, lower tax revenues were expected in the 2008/09 financial year, owing to reduced activity in the resource sector (attributed to decreasing investment and declining commodity prices, notably for copper). In February 2009 the minimum wage was raised by 20%, a measure that was to benefit employees of the garment industry, in particular. The rate of corporate taxation applied to manufacturers operating in this sector was to be reduced to offset the associated increase in production costs. However, a substantial decrease in export demand for Laotian garments was reported in early 2009. The sharp decline in global economic activity from the latter part of 2008 was expected to defer any further improvement in Laos's external position, while the progress of various projects in the hydropower and mineral sectors was likely to be jeopardized. Remittances from abroad, an important source of revenue, were expected to decrease. Credit facilities for small and medium-sized enterprises were to be expanded, in response to the global downturn. The ADB envisaged a reduction in GDP growth to 5.5% in 2009.

Education

Education was greatly disrupted by the civil war, causing a high illiteracy rate, but educational facilities subsequently improved significantly. Lao is the medium of instruction. A comprehensive education system is in force. In 1990 the Government issued a decree permitting the establishment of private schools, in an effort to accommodate the increasing number of students.

Primary education begins at six years of age and lasts for five years. In 2005/06 enrolment in pre-primary education included 11% of pupils in the relevant age-group (males 11%; females 11%). In 2004/05 enrolment in primary education included 83% of children in the relevant age-group (males 85%; females 80%). Secondary education, beginning at the age of 11, lasts for six years, comprising two three-year cycles. In 2005/06 enrolment in secondary education included 43% of pupils in the relevant age-group (males 48%; females 38%). In 2006/07 there were 1,087 pre-primary institutions, 8,654 primary schools, 717 secondary schools (including 47 vocational schools, at which 26,300 pupils were enrolled) and 41 tertiary institutions (including three universities, at which 30,600 students were enrolled). Government expenditure on education in 2005 was estimated at 11.7% of total projected expenditure.

Public Holidays

2009: 1 January (New Year's Day), 6 January (Pathet Lao Day), 20 January (Army Day), 26 January (Chinese New Year), 8 March (Women's Day), 22 March (People's Party Day), 13–15 April (Lao New Year), 1 May (Labour Day), 1 June (Children's Day), 13 August (Free Laos Day), 23 August (Liberation Day), 12 October (Liberation from the French Day, Vientiane only), 2 December (Independence Day).

2010: 1 January (New Year's Day), 6 January (Pathet Lao Day), 20 January (Army Day), 14 February (Chinese New Year), 8 March (Women's Day), 22 March (People's Party Day), 13–15 April (Lao New Year), 1 May (Labour Day), 1 June (Children's Day), 13 August (Free Laos Day), 23 August (Liberation Day), 12 October (Liberation from the French Day, Vientiane only), 2 December (Independence Day).

Weights and Measures

The metric system is in force.

Statistical Survey

Source (unless otherwise stated): National Statistics Centre, rue Luang Prabang, Vientiane; tel. (21) 214740; fax (21) 219129; e-mail nscp@laotel.com; internet www.nsc.gov.la.

Area and Population

AREA, POPULATION AND DENSITY

Area (sq km)	236,800*
Population (census results)	
1 March 1995	4,581,258
1 March 2005	
Males	2,800,551
Females	2,821,431
Total	5,621,982
Population (UN estimates at mid-year)†	
2006	5,983,000
2007	6,092,000
2008	6,205,000
Density (per sq km) at mid-2008	26.2

* 91,400 sq miles.
† Source: UN, *World Population Prospects: The 2008 Revision*.

LAOS

PROVINCES
(population at mid-2005, official estimates)

	Area (sq km)	Population ('000)	Density (per sq km)
Vientiane (municipality)	3,920	698	178.1
Phongsali	16,270	166	10.2
Luang Namtha	9,325	145	15.5
Oudomxay	15,370	265	17.2
Bokeo	6,196	145	23.4
Luang Prabang	16,875	407	24.1
Houaphanh	16,500	281	17.0
Sayabouri	16,389	339	20.7
Xiangkhouang	15,880	230	14.5
Vientiane	18,526	389	21.0
Bolikhamsai	14,863	225	15.1
Khammouane	16,315	337	20.7
Savannakhet	21,774	826	37.9
Saravan	10,691	324	30.3
Sekong	7,665	85	11.1
Champasak	15,415	607	39.4
Attopu	10,320	112	10.9
Xaysomboun SR	4,506	39	8.7
Total	236,800	5,622	23.7

Note: In January 2006 the Xaysomboun SR special region was dissolved, and its administrative responsibilities were transferred to Vientiane and Xiangkhouang provinces.

PRINCIPAL TOWNS
(population at 1995 census)

Viangchan (Vientiane—capital)	160,000	Xam Nua (Sam Neua)		33,500
Savannakhet (Khanthaboury)	58,500	Luang Prabang		25,500
Pakxe (Paksé)	47,000	Thakek (Khammouan)		22,500

Source: Stefan Helders, *World Gazetteer* (internet www.world-gazetteer.com).

Mid-2007 (incl. suburbs, UN estimate): Vientiane 745,000 (Source: UN, *World Urbanization Prospects: The 2007 Revision*).

BIRTHS AND DEATHS
(annual averages, UN estimates)

	1990–95	1995–2000	2000–05
Birth rate (per 1,000)	39.9	36.5	29.1
Death rate (per 1,000)	11.8	9.7	8.1

Source: UN, *World Population Prospects: The 2008 Revision*.

Life expectancy (years at birth, WHO estimates): 60 (males 59; females 61) in 2006 (Source: WHO, *World Health Statistics*).

ECONOMICALLY ACTIVE POPULATION
('000 persons in 2003)

	Total
Agriculture, etc.	2,085
Industry	235
Services	217
Total employed	2,537
Unemployed	136
Total labour force	2,673

2005: Agriculture 2,091; Total employed 2,664; Unemployed 38; Total labour force 2,701.

Source: Asian Development Bank.

Health and Welfare

KEY INDICATORS

Total fertility rate (children per woman, 2006)	3.3
Under-5 mortality rate (per 1,000 live births, 2006)	75
HIV/AIDS (% of persons aged 15–49, 2007)	0.2
Physicians (per 1,000 head, 2004)	0.4
Hospital beds (per 1,000 head, 2005)	1
Health expenditure (2006): US $ per head (PPP)	85
Health expenditure (2006): % of GDP	3.6
Health expenditure (2006): public (% of total)	20.8
Access to adequate water (% of persons, 2006)	60
Access to adequate sanitation (% of persons, 2006)	48
Human Development Index (2006): ranking	133
Human Development Index (2006): value	0.608

For sources and definitions, see explanatory note on p. vi.

Agriculture

PRINCIPAL CROPS
('000 metric tons)

	2005	2006	2007
Rice, paddy	2,568	2,664	2,870*
Maize	373	450	450†
Potatoes†	36	36	36
Sweet potatoes	130	110	120†
Cassava (Manioc)	51	174	175†
Sugar cane	196	218	220†
Watermelons†	65	65	72
Cantaloupes and other melons†	36	36	36
Bananas†	48	48	48
Oranges†	28	28	28
Tangerines, mandarins, clementines and satsumas†	25	25	25
Pineapples†	37	37	37
Coffee, green	25	27†	28†
Tobacco, unmanufactured	28	25	25

* Unofficial figure.
† FAO estimate(s).

Aggregate production ('000 metric tons, may include official, semi-official or estimated data): Total cereals 2,941 in 2005, 3,114 in 2006, 3,320 in 2007; Total vegetables (incl. melons) 859 in 2005, 775 in 2006, 782 in 2007; Total fruits (excl. melons) 206 in 2005, 168 in 2006, 168 in 2007.

Source: FAO.

LIVESTOCK
('000 head, year ending September)

	2005	2006	2007*
Horses*	31	31	31
Cattle	1,272	1,321	1,337
Buffaloes	1,096	1,108	1,120
Pigs	1,826	2,033	2,260
Goats	190	210	230
Chickens	19,801	20,803	21,900
Ducks*	3,200	3,200	3,200

* FAO estimate(s).

Source: FAO.

LIVESTOCK PRODUCTS
('000 metric tons, FAO estimates)

	2005	2006	2007
Cattle meat	22.0	22.5	23.0
Buffalo meat	18.1	18.5	18.6
Pig meat	39.0	43.0	47.0
Chicken meat	15.4	16.2	17.1
Cows' milk	6.4	6.6	6.7
Hen eggs	12.5	12.8	12.8

Source: FAO.

Forestry

ROUNDWOOD REMOVALS
('000 cubic metres, excl. bark, FAO estimates)

	2003	2004	2005
Sawlogs, veneer logs and logs for sleepers	277	148	62
Other industrial wood	132	132	132
Fuel wood	5,913	5,928	5,944
Total	6,322	6,209	6,137

2006–07: Production assumed to be unchanged from 2005 (FAO estimates).
Source: FAO.

SAWNWOOD PRODUCTION
('000 cubic metres, incl. railway sleepers)

	2003	2004	2005
Total (all broadleaved)	125	125	130

2006–07: Production assumed to be unchanged from 2005 (FAO estimate).
Source: FAO.

Fishing

('000 metric tons, live weight)

	2003*	2004*	2005
Capture*	29.8	29.8	29.8
Cyprinids*	4.5	4.5	4.5
Other freshwater fishes*	25.3	25.3	25.3
Aquaculture	64.9	64.9	78.0
Common carp	16.2	16.2	5.8
Roho labeo	2.7	2.7	5.3
Mrigal carp	2.7	2.7	4.7
Bighead carp	3.8	3.8	6.5
Silver carp	3.8	3.8	8.0
Nile tilapia	29.2	29.2	19.6
Total catch	94.7	94.7	107.8

* FAO estimates.
2006: Catch assumed to be unchanged from 2005 (FAO estimates).
Source: FAO.

Mining

('000 metric tons, unless otherwise indicated)

	2005	2006	2007*
Coal (all grades)	232.9	233.0*	620.0
Gemstones, sapphire ('000 carats)*	1,800.0	1,200.0	1,200.0
Gold (kg)	7,058	6,088	4,161
Gypsum*	774.0	775.0	775.0
Salt	34.1	35.0	35.0
Copper (metric tons)†	30,480	60,803	62,541
Tin (metric tons)*†	450	450	450

* Estimate(s).
† Figures refer to metal content.
Source: US Geological Survey.

Industry

SELECTED PRODUCTS

	2005	2006	2007
Beer ('000 hectolitres)	927	1,059	1,029
Soft drinks ('000 hectolitres)	194	n.a.	257
Cigarettes (million packs)	105	n.a.	124
Garments (million pieces)	39	68	47
Plastic products (metric tons)	6,000	7,452	7,383
Detergent (metric tons)	880	1,082	1,255
Agricultural tools ('000)	4	n.a.	n.a.
Nails (metric tons)	980	2,099	2,168
Bricks (million)	135	n.a.	244
Hydroelectric energy (million kWh)	3,492	3,606	3,474
Tobacco (metric tons)	3,080	3,836	3,991
Plywood (million sheets)	1,320	n.a.	952

Source: Ministry of Industry and Handicrafts, Vientiane.

Finance

CURRENCY AND EXCHANGE RATES

Monetary Units
100 at (cents) = 1 new kip.

Sterling, Dollar and Euro Equivalents (31 July 2008)
£1 sterling = 17,050.5 new kips;
US $1 = 8,609.2 new kips;
€1 = 13,439.84 new kips;
100,000 new kips = £5.86 = $11.62 = €7.44.

Average Exchange Rate (new kips per US $)
2005   10,655.2
2006   10,159.9
2007   9,603.2

Note: In September 1995 a policy of 'floating' exchange rates was adopted, with commercial banks permitted to set their rates.

GENERAL BUDGET
('000 million new kips, year ending 30 September)*

Revenue†	2005/06	2006/07	2007/08‡
Tax revenue	3,641	4,721	4,970
Profits tax	459	919	1,149
Income tax	234	252	214
Turnover tax	887	1,046	1,095
Excise tax	800	999	1,179
Import duties	515	573	536
Timber royalties	172	212	150
Other tax revenue	574	720	647
Non-tax revenue	625	620	792
Payment for depreciation or dividend transfers	175	157	238
Overflight	229	231	230
Other revenue	222	232	324
Total	4,266	5,341	5,762

LAOS

Expenditure	2005/06	2006/07	2007/08‡
Current expenditure	3,124	3,526	4,565
Wages and salaries	1,263	1,589	2,062
Compensation and allowances	674	722	1,111
Subsidies and transfers			
Interest	277	198	361
Other recurrent expenditure	911	1,017	1,031
Capital expenditure and net lending	2,529	2,856	2,824
Domestically-financed	403	541	750
Foreign-financed	2,126	2,314	2,074
Onlending (net)			
Debt repayment	348	586	585
Total	6,001	6,968	7,974

* Since 1992 there has been a unified budget covering the operations of the central Government, provincial administrations and state enterprises.
† Excluding grants received ('000 million new kips): 696 in 2005/06; 674 in 2006/07; 569 in 2007/08 (budget).
‡ Budget forecasts.

Source: IMF, *Lao People's Democratic Republic: Statistical Appendix* (October 2008).

INTERNATIONAL RESERVES
(US $ million at 31 December)

	2005	2006	2007
Gold (national valuation)	5.10	7.35	7.35
IMF special drawing rights	14.09	14.71	15.47
Foreign exchange	220.21	313.73	517.09
Total	239.40	335.79	539.91

Source: IMF, *International Financial Statistics*.

MONEY SUPPLY
(million new kips at 31 December*)

	2005	2006	2007
Currency outside banks	948,550	1,230,590	1,837,920
Demand deposits at commercial banks	610,260	767,660	1,226,740
Total (incl. others)	1,558,910	1,998,320	3,064,720

* Figures rounded to the nearest ten million.

Source: IMF, *International Financial Statistics*.

COST OF LIVING
(Consumer Price Index for Vientiane; base: 2000 = 100)

	2005	2006	2007
All items	163.1	174.2	182.0

Source: IMF, *International Financial Statistics*.

NATIONAL ACCOUNTS
Gross Domestic Product by Economic Activity
('000 million new kips at current prices)

	2005	2006	2007*
Agriculture, hunting, forestry and fishing	13,593	14,943	15,891
Mining and quarrying	941	1,535	2,115
Manufacturing	6,276	7,696	9,077
Electricity, gas and water	822	887	892
Construction	761	940	1,101
Wholesale and retail trade	3,178	3,672	4,139
Hotels and restaurants	691	849	967
Transport, storage and communications	1,913	2,193	2,457
Finance and insurance	110	132	158
Ownership of dwellings	750	821	871
Public administration	1,083	886	926
Non-profit institutions	16	203	216
Other services	59	68	79
GDP at factor cost	30,193	34,827	38,889
Import duties, etc.	269	339	395
GDP in purchasers' values	30,462	35,167	39,284

* Estimates.

Source: IMF, *Lao People's Democratic Republic: Statistical Appendix* (October 2008).

BALANCE OF PAYMENTS
(US $ million)

	2005	2006	2007
Exports of goods f.o.b.	553.1	882.0	922.7
Imports of goods c.i.f.	−882.0	−1,060.2	−1,064.7
Trade balance	−328.9	−178.2	−142.0
Services and other income (net)	69.2	92.9	115.9
Balance on goods, services and income	−259.7	−85.3	−26.1
Current transfers received	124.2	151.5	102.3
Current transfers paid	−57.0	−24.9	
Current balance	−192.5	41.3	76.2
Direct investment (net)	27.7	187.3	323.5
Other investments (net)	126.7	42.6	76.4
Net errors and omissions	48.8	−173.9	−283.0
Overall balance	10.8	97.3	193.2

Source: Asian Development Bank.

External Trade

PRINCIPAL COMMODITIES
(US $ million)

Imports c.i.f.	2005	2006	2007*
Petroleum	159.5	205.5	311.0
Capital goods	488.8	684.4	1,053.2
Materials for garments industry	69.9	98.7	80.3
Electricity	26.2	28.0	37.4
Total (incl. others)	1,270.2	1,589.3	2,113.8

Exports f.o.b.	2005	2006	2007*
Timber	156.2	195.6	179.0
Coffee	7.5	9.8	28.9
Garments	138.0	127.5	126.3
Electricity	125.0	122.6	114.1
Copper	112.1	409.3	446.0
Gold (incl. re-exports)	90.7	117.9	93.2
Total (incl. others)	684.0	1,143.1	1,202.6

* Estimates.

Source: IMF, *Lao People's Democratic Republic: Statistical Appendix* (October 2008).

PRINCIPAL TRADING PARTNERS
(US $ million)

Imports	2005	2006	2007
Australia	19.9	20.6	25.5
China, People's Republic	115.9	185.6	175.6
France	13.5	11.2	12.6
Germany	11.3	12.0	34.8
Hong Kong	8.3	15.5	13.5
Japan	21.3	22.6	32.5
Korea, Republic	15.3	22.5	26.8
Singapore	44.1	45.2	43.0
Thailand*	846.2	1,125.4	1,442.8
Viet Nam	76.1	94.1	112.3
Total (incl. others)	1,270.2	1,639.3	2,043.6

Exports	2005	2006	2007
Belgium	15.6	16.7	10.7
China, People's Republic	23.2	45.1	74.8
France	41.9	29.1	26.1
Germany	31.6	34.6	43.0
Italy	8.9	6.6	7.3
Malaysia	11.8	44.6	29.8
Netherlands	13.4	14.0	10.6
Thailand*	204.4	475.5	431.5
United Kingdom	8.3	1.4	6.2
Viet Nam	86.6	109.5	130.8
Total (incl. others)	696.6	1,132.6	1,185.0

* Trade with Thailand may be overestimated, as it may include goods in transit to and from other countries.

Note: Data reflect the IMF's direction of trade methodology and, as a result, the totals may not be equal to those presented for trade in commodities.

Source: Asian Development Bank.

Transport

ROAD TRAFFIC
(motor vehicles in use at 31 December, estimates)

	1994	1995	1996
Passenger cars	18,240	17,280	16,320
Buses and coaches	440	n.a.	n.a.
Lorries and vans	7,920	6,020	4,200
Motorcycles and mopeds	169,000	200,000	231,000

Source: International Road Federation, *World Road Statistics*.

SHIPPING

Inland Waterways
(traffic)

	2002	2003	2004
Freight ('000 metric tons)	770.0	893.0	939.9
Freight ton-kilometres (million)	69.9	55.5	49.6
Passengers ('000)	2,025.0	2,203.0	2,183.5
Passenger-kilometres (million)	76.9	45.3	22.4

Source: Ministry of Communications, Transport, Post and Construction.

Merchant Fleet
(registered at 31 December)

	2005	2006	2007
Number of vessels	2	2	2
Displacement ('000 grt)	2.9	2.9	2.9

Source: Lloyd's Register-Fairplay, *World Fleet Statistics*.

CIVIL AVIATION
(traffic on scheduled services)

	2002	2003	2004
Kilometres flown (million)	2	3	3
Passengers carried ('000)	220	219	272
Passenger-kilometres (million)	91	90	113
Total ton-kilometres (million)	9	9	12

Source: UN, *Statistical Yearbook*.

Tourism

FOREIGN VISITOR ARRIVALS
(incl. excursionists)

Country of nationality	2004	2005	2006
China, People's Republic	33,019	39,210	50,317
France	27,806	35,371	32,453
Japan	20,319	22,601	23,601
Thailand	489,677	603,189	675,845
United Kingdom	27,402	29,977	31,684
USA	37,181	47,427	46,829
Viet Nam	130,816	165,151	190,442
Total (incl. others)	894,806	1,095,315	1,215,107

Tourism receipts (US $ million, excl. passenger transport): 119 in 2004; 146 in 2005; 173 in 2006.

Source: World Tourism Organization.

Communications Media

	2005	2006	2007
Telephones ('000 main lines in use)	90.8	92.2	94.8
Mobile cellular telephones ('000 subscribers)	657.5	1,009.6	1,478.4
Personal computers ('000 in use)	100	n.a.	n.a.
Internet users ('000)	50.0	70.0	100.0
Broadband subscribers ('000)	0.1	0.7	3.6

Radio receivers ('000 in use): 730 in 1997.

Television receivers ('000 in use): 280 in 2001.

Facsimile machines (estimated number in use): 500 in 1994 (Source: UN, *Statistical Yearbook*).

Book production (1995): Titles 88; copies ('000) 995.

Daily newspapers (2004): 6 (average circulation 14,558).

Non-daily newspapers (1988, estimates): 18 (average circulation 34,550).

Sources (unless otherwise specified): International Telecommunication Union; UNESCO, *Statistical Yearbook*.

Education
(2006/07)

	Institutions	Teachers	Students
Pre-primary	1,087	3,000	49,000
Primary	8,654	28,000	892,000
Secondary:			
lower	642	10,000	243,000
upper	28	500	148,000
vocational	47	1,500	26,300
University level	3	1,300	30,600
Other higher	38	1,100	30,100

Note: Figures for teachers and students are rounded to the nearest 100 persons.

Source: Ministry of Education, Vientiane.

Adult literacy rate (UNESCO estimates): 73.2% (males 80.0%; females 66.6%) in 2007 (Source: UNESCO Institute for Statistics).

Directory

The Constitution

The new Constitution was unanimously endorsed by the Supreme People's Assembly on 14 August 1991. Its main provisions are summarized below:

POLITICAL SYSTEM

The Lao People's Democratic Republic (Lao PDR) is an independent, sovereign and united country and is indivisible.

The Lao PDR is a people's democratic state. The people's rights are exercised and ensured through the functioning of the political system, with the Lao People's Revolutionary Party as its leading organ. The people exercise power through the National Assembly, which functions in accordance with the principle of democratic centralism.

The State respects and protects all lawful activities of Buddhism and the followers of other religious faiths.

The Lao PDR pursues a foreign policy of peace, independence, friendship and co-operation. It adheres to the principles of peaceful co-existence with other countries, based on mutual respect for independence, sovereignty and territorial integrity.

SOCIO-ECONOMIC SYSTEM

The economy is market-orientated, with intervention by the State. The State encourages all economic sectors to compete and co-operate in the expansion of production and trade.

Private ownership of property and rights of inheritance are protected by the State.

The State authorizes the operation of private schools and medical services, while promoting the expansion of public education and health services.

FUNDAMENTAL RIGHTS AND OBLIGATIONS OF CITIZENS

Lao citizens, irrespective of their sex, social status, education, faith and ethnic group, are equal before the law.

Lao citizens aged 18 years and above have the right to vote, and those over 21 years to be candidates, in elections.

Lao citizens have freedom of religion, speech, press and assembly, and freedom to establish associations and to participate in demonstrations which do not contradict the law.

THE NATIONAL ASSEMBLY

The National Assembly is the legislative organ, which also oversees the activities of the administration and the judiciary. Members of the National Assembly are elected for a period of five years by universal adult suffrage. The National Assembly elects its own Standing Committee, which consists of the Chairman and Vice-Chairman of the National Assembly (and thus also of the National Assembly Standing Committee) and a number of other members. The National Assembly convenes its ordinary session twice annually. The National Assembly Standing Committee may convene an extraordinary session of the National Assembly if it deems this necessary. The National Assembly is empowered to amend the Constitution; to endorse, amend or abrogate laws; to elect or remove the President of State and Vice-Presidents of State, as proposed by the Standing Committee of the National Assembly; to adopt motions expressing no confidence in the Government; to elect or remove the President of the People's Supreme Court, on the recommendation of the National Assembly Standing Committee.

THE PRESIDENT OF STATE

The President of State, who is also Head of the Armed Forces, is elected by the National Assembly for a five-year tenure. Laws adopted by the National Assembly must be promulgated by the President of State not later than 30 days after their enactment. The President is empowered to appoint or dismiss the Prime Minister and members of the Government, with the approval of the National Assembly; to appoint government officials at provincial and municipal levels; and to promote military personnel, on the recommendation of the Prime Minister.

THE GOVERNMENT

The Government is the administrative organ of the State. It is composed of the Prime Minister, Deputy Prime Ministers and Ministers or Chairmen of Committees (which are equivalent to Ministries), who are appointed by the President, with the approval of the National Assembly, for a term of five years. The Government implements the Constitution, laws and resolutions adopted by the National Assembly and state decrees and acts of the President of State. The Prime Minister is empowered to appoint Deputy Ministers and Vice-Chairmen of Committees, and junior-level government officials.

LOCAL ADMINISTRATION

The Lao PDR is divided into provinces, municipalities, districts and villages. Provincial governors and mayors of municipalities are appointed by the President of State. Deputy provincial governors, deputy mayors and district chiefs are appointed by the Prime Minister. Administration at village level is conducted by village heads.

THE JUDICIARY

The people's courts comprise the People's Supreme Court, the people's provincial and municipal courts, the people's district courts and military courts. The President of the People's Supreme Court and the Public Prosecutor-General are elected by the National Assembly, on the recommendation of the National Assembly Standing Committee. The Vice-President of the People's Supreme Court and the judges of the people's courts at all levels are appointed by the National Assembly Standing Committee.

The Government

HEAD OF STATE

President of State: Lt-Gen. CHOUMMALI SAIGNASON (elected 8 June 2006).

Vice-President: BOUNGNANG VOLACHIT.

COUNCIL OF MINISTERS
(April 2009)

Prime Minister: BOUASONE BOUPHAVANH.

Deputy Prime Minister and Minister of Foreign Affairs: THONGLOUN SISOLIT.

Deputy Prime Minister and Minister of National Defence: Maj.-Gen. DOUANGCHAI PHICHIT.

Deputy Prime Ministers: Maj.-Gen. ASANG LAOLI, SOMSAVAT LENGSAVAT.

Minister of Finance: SOMDY DOUANGDY.

Minister of Security: THONGBANH SENGAPHONE.

Minister of Justice: CHALEUN YIAPAOHEU.

Minister of Agriculture and Forestry: SITAHENG LATSAPHONE.

Minister of Communications, Transport, Post and Construction: SOMMATH PHOLSENA.

Minister of Industry and Commerce: Dr NAM VIYAKET.

Minister of Information and Culture: MOUNKEO OLABUN.

Minister of Labour and Social Welfare: ONECHANH THAMMAVONG.

Minister of Education: Prof. SOMKOT MANGNOMEK.

Minister of Public Health: Dr PONEMEKH DARALOY.

Minister of Energy and Mining: SOULIVONG DALAVONG.

Minister to the Office of the President: SOUBANH SRITHIRATH.

Ministers to the Office of the Prime Minister: BOUNTIEM PHITSAMAY, ONNEUA PHOMMACHANH, KHAM-OUANE BOUPPHA, SAISENGLI TENGIACHU, KHAMLOUAT SITLAKON, CHEUANG SOMBOUNKHAN, BUNPHENG MUNGPHOSAI, SOMPHONG MONGKONVILAI, KHEMPHENG PHOLSENA, PHOUTHONG SAENGAKHOM, DOUANGSAVAT SOUPHANAOUVONG.

President of the State Planning Committee: SOULIVONG DARAVONG.

Governor of the Central Bank: PHOUPHET KHAMPHOUNVONG.

MINISTRIES

Office of the President: rue Lane Xang, Vientiane; tel. (21) 214200; fax (21) 214208.

Office of the Prime Minister: Ban Sisavat, Vientiane; tel. (21) 213653; fax (21) 213560.

Ministry of Agriculture and Forestry: Ban Phonxay, Vientiane; tel. (21) 412359; fax (21) 412344; internet www.maf.gov.la.

Ministry of Communications, Transport, Post and Construction: ave Lane Xang, Vientiane; tel. (21) 412251; fax (21) 414123.

Ministry of Education: 1 rue Lane Xang, BP 67, Vientiane; tel. (21) 216013; fax (21) 216006; e-mail esitc@moe.gov.la; internet www.moe.gov.la.

Ministry of Energy and Mining: Vientiane.

Ministry of Finance: rue That Luang, Ban Phonxay, Vientiane; tel. (21) 412401; fax (21) 412415.

LAOS

Ministry of Foreign Affairs: rue That Luang 01004, Ban Phonxay, Vientiane; tel. (21) 413148; fax (21) 414009; e-mail cabinet@mofa.gov.la; internet www.mofa.gov.la.

Ministry of Industry and Commerce: rue Phonxay, BP 4107, Vientiane; tel. (21) 412009; fax (21) 412434; e-mail citd@moic.gov.la; internet www.moic.gov.la.

Ministry of Information and Culture: rue Setthathirath, Ban Xiengnheun, Vientiane; tel. (21) 212897; fax (21) 212408; e-mail email@mic.gov.la.

Ministry of Justice: Ban Phonxay, Vientiane; tel. (21) 414105.

Ministry of Labour and Social Welfare: rue Pangkham, Ban Sisaket, Vientiane; tel. (21) 213003.

Ministry of National Defence: rue Phone Kheng, Ban Phone Kheng, Vientiane; tel. (21) 412803.

Ministry of Public Health: Ban Simeuang, Vientiane; tel. (21) 214002; fax (21) 214001; e-mail cabinet.fr@moh.gov.la.

Ministry of Security: rue Nongbone, Ban Hatsady, Vientiane; tel. (21) 212500.

Legislature

At the election held on 30 April 2006 113 candidates of the Lao People's Revolutionary Party (LPRP) and two independents were elected to the National Assembly. (All but three candidates contesting the elections were members of the LPRP.)

President of the National Assembly: THONGSING THAMMAVONG.

Vice-Presidents: PANY YATHOTU, Dr XAYSOMPHONE PHOMVIHANE.

Political Organizations

COMMUNIST PARTY

Phak Pasason Pativat Lao (Lao People's Revolutionary Party—LPRP): Vientiane; f. 1955 as the People's Party of Laos; reorg. under present name in 1972; Cen. Cttee of 55 full mems elected at Eighth Party Congress in March 2006; Gen. Sec. Lt-Gen. CHOUMMALI SAIGNASON.

Political Bureau (Politburo)

Full members: Lt-Gen. CHOUMMALI SAIGNASON, Lt-Gen. SAMAN VIGNAKET, THONGSIN THAMMAVONG, BOUNGNANG VOLACHIT, Gen. SISAVAT KEOBOUNPHAN, Maj.-Gen. ASANG LAOLI, THOUNGLONG SISOLIT, Maj.-Gen. DOUANGCHAI PHICHIT, BOUASONE BOUPHAVANH, SOMSAVAT LENGSAVAT, PHANI YATHOTHU.

OTHER POLITICAL ORGANIZATIONS

Lao Front for National Construction (LFNC): Thanon Khouvieng, Ban Sisakhet, Muang Chanthaboury, Vientiane; tel. (21) 213752; fax (21) 213752; f. 1979 to replace the Lao Liberal Front and the Lao Patriotic Front; comprises representatives of various political and social groups, of which the LPRP (see above) is the dominant force; fosters national solidarity; Chair. Gen. SISAVAT KEOBOUNPHAN; Vice-Chair. SIHO BANNAVONG, KHAMPHOUI CHANTHASOUK, TONG YEUTHOR.

Numerous factions are in armed opposition to the Government. The principal groups are:

Democratic Chao Fa Party of Laos: led by Pa Kao Her until his death in Oct. 2002; Pres. SOUA HER; Vice-Pres. TENG TANG.

Free Democratic Lao National Salvation Force: based in Thailand.

United Front for the Liberation of Laos: Leader PHOUNGPHET PHANARETH.

United Front for the National Liberation of the Lao People: f. 1980; led by Gen. PHOUMI NOSAVAN until his death in 1985.

United Lao National Liberation Front: Sayabouri Province; comprises an estimated 8,000 members, mostly Hmong (Meo) tribesmen; Sec.-Gen. VANG SHUR.

Diplomatic Representation

EMBASSIES IN LAOS

Australia: rue Pandit J. Nehru, quartier Phonxay, BP 292, Vientiane; tel. (21) 413600; fax (21) 413601; e-mail austemb.laos@dfat.gov.au; internet www.laos.embassy.gov.au; Ambassador MICHELE FORSTER.

Brunei: Unit 12, Ban Thoungkang, Lao-Thai Friendship Rd, Sisathanak, Vientiane; tel. (21) 352294; fax (21) 352291; e-mail embdlaos@laotel.com; Ambassador Hajik SIDEK ALI.

Cambodia: rue Thadeua, Km 3, BP 34, Vientiane; tel. (21) 314952; fax (21) 314951; e-mail recamlao@laotel.com; Ambassador DAN YI.

China, People's Republic: rue Wat Nak, Muang Sisattanak, BP 898, Vientiane; tel. (21) 315100; fax (21) 315104; e-mail embassyprc@laonet.net; Ambassador PAN GUANGXUE.

Cuba: Ban Saphanthong Neua 128, BP 1017, Vientiane; tel. (21) 314902; fax (21) 314901; e-mail embacuba@laonet.net; Ambassador EDUARDO VALIDO GARCÍA.

France: rue Setthathirath, BP 06, Vientiane; tel. (21) 215253; fax (21) 215250; e-mail contact@ambafrance-laos.org; internet www.ambafrance-laos.org; Ambassador FRANÇOIS SÉNÉMAUD.

Germany: rue Sok Paluang 26, Muang Sisattanak, BP 314, Vientiane; tel. (21) 312110; fax (21) 351152; e-mail info@vien.diplo.de; Ambassador PETER WIENAND.

India: 2 Ban Wat Nak, rue Thadeua, Km 3, Sisattanak District, Vientiane; tel. (21) 352301; fax (21) 352300; e-mail indiaemb@laotel.com; internet indemblao.nic.in; Ambassador Shri SURESH K. GOEL.

Indonesia: ave Phone Keng, BP 277, Vientiane; tel. (21) 413909; fax (21) 214828; e-mail kbrivte@laotel.com; Ambassador SUTJIPTORAHHARDJO DONOKUSUMO.

Japan: rue Sisangvone, Vientiane; tel. (21) 414401; fax (21) 414406; internet www.la.emb-japan.go.jp; Ambassador MASAAKI MIYASHITA.

Korea, Democratic People's Republic: quartier Wat Nak, Vientiane; tel. (21) 315261; fax (21) 315260; Ambassador PAK MYONG GU.

Korea, Republic: rue Lao-Thai Friendship, Ban Wat Nak, Sisattanak District, BP 7567, Vientiane; tel. (21) 415833; fax (21) 415831; e-mail koramb@laotel.com; internet lao.mofat.go.kr; Ambassador PARK JAE-HYUN.

Malaysia: 23 rue Singha, quartier Phonxay, BP 789, Vientiane; tel. (21) 414205; fax (21) 414201; e-mail mwvntian@laopdr.com; internet www.kln.gov.my/perwakilan/vientiane; Ambassador ZAINAL ABIDIN AHMAD.

Mongolia: rue Wat Nak, Km 3, BP 370, Vientiane; tel. (21) 315220; fax (21) 315221; e-mail embmong@laotel.com; Ambassador TOGTOKHBAYR BATBAATAR.

Myanmar: Ban Thong Kang, rue Sok Palaung, BP 11, Vientiane; tel. (21) 314910; fax (21) 314913; e-mail mev@loxinfo.co.th; Ambassador U TIN OO.

Philippines: Ban Saphanthong Kang, Sisattanak, BP 2415, Vientiane; tel. (21) 452490; fax (21) 452493; e-mail pelaopdr@laotel.com; Ambassador ELIZABETH P. BUENSUCESO.

Poland: 263 Ban Thadeua, Km 3, quartier Wat Nak, BP 1106, Vientiane; tel. (21) 312940; fax (21) 312085; e-mail polembv@yahoo.com; internet www.vientiane.polemb.net; Chargé d'affaires Dr TOMASZ GERLACH.

Russia: Ban Thadeua, quartier Thaphalanxay, BP 490, Vientiane; tel. (21) 312222; fax (21) 312210; e-mail rusemb@laotel.com; Ambassador VLADIMIR PLOTNIKOV.

Singapore: Unit 12, Ban Naxay, rue Nong Bong, Muang Sat Settha, Vientiane; tel. (21) 416860; fax (21) 416854; e-mail singemb_vte@sgmfa.gov.sg; internet www.mfa.gov.sg/vientiane; Ambassador BENJAMIN WILLIAM.

Thailand: ave Kaysone Phomvihane, Xaysettha, Vientiane; tel. (21) 214581; fax (21) 214580; e-mail thaivtn@mfa.go.th; internet www.thaiembassy.org/vientiane; Ambassador WIBOON KHUSAKUL.

USA: 19 rue Bartholonie, BP 114, That Dam, Vientiane; tel. (21) 267000; fax (21) 267190; e-mail khammanhpx@state.gov; internet vientiane.usembassy.gov; Ambassador RAVIC ROLF HUSO.

Viet Nam: 85 23 rue Singha, Phonxay, Xaysettha, Vientiane; tel. (21) 413409; fax (21) 413379; e-mail dsqvn@laotel.com; internet www.mofa.gov.vn/vnemb.la; Ambassador NGUYEN HUY QUANG.

Judicial System

President of the People's Supreme Court: KHAMMY SAYAVONG.

Vice-President: DAVON VANGVICHIT.

People's Supreme Court Judges: NOUANTHONG VONGSA, NHOTSENG LITTHIDETH, PHOUKHONG CHANTHALATH, SENGSOUVANH CHANTHALOUNNAVONG, KESON PHANLACK, KONGCHI YANGCHY, KHAMPON PHASAIGNAVONG.

Public Prosecutor-General: SOMPHANE PHENGKHAMMY.

LAOS — *Directory*

Religion

The 1991 Constitution guarantees freedom of religious belief. The principal religion of Laos is Buddhism.

BUDDHISM

Lao Unified Buddhists' Association: Maha Kudy, Wat That Luang, Vientiane; f. 1964; Pres. (vacant); Sec.-Gen. Rev. SIHO SIHAVONG.

CHRISTIANITY

The Roman Catholic Church

For ecclesiastical purposes, Laos comprises four Apostolic Vicariates. At 31 December 2006 an estimated 0.6% of the population were adherents.

Episcopal Conference of Laos and Cambodia
c/o Mgr Pierre Bach, Paris Foreign Missions, 254 Silom Rd, Bangkok 10500, Thailand.
f. 1971; Pres. Most Rev. EMILE DESTOMBES (Titular Bishop of Altava).

Vicar Apostolic of Luang Prabang: (vacant), Evêché, BP 113, Luang Prabang.

Vicar Apostolic of Paksé: Mgr LOUIS-MARIE LING MANGKHANEKHOUN (Titular Bishop of Proconsulari), Centre Catholique, BP 77, Paksé, Champasak; tel. (31) 212879; fax (31) 251439.

Vicar Apostolic of Savannakhet: Mgr JEAN SOMMENG VORACHAK (Titular Bishop of Muzuca in Proconsulari), Centre Catholique, BP 12, Thakek, Khammouane; tel. (51) 212184; fax (51) 213070.

Vicar Apostolic of Vientiane: Mgr JEAN KHAMSÉ VITHAVONG (Titular Bishop of Moglaena), Centre Catholique, BP 113, Vientiane; tel. (21) 216593; fax (21) 215085.

The Anglican Communion

Laos is within the jurisdiction of the Anglican Bishop of Singapore.

The Protestant Church

Lao Evangelical Church: BP 4200, Vientiane; tel. (21) 169136; Exec. Pres. Rev. KHAMPHONE KOUTHAPANYA.

BAHÁ'Í FAITH

National Spiritual Assembly: BP 189, Vientiane; tel. and fax (21) 216996; e-mail usme@laotel.com; f. 1956; Sec. SUSADA SENCHANTHISAY.

The Press

Aloun Mai (New Dawn): rue That Luang, Ban Nongbone, Xaysettha, Vientiane; tel. (21) 413029; fax (21) 413037; f. 1985; quarterly; theoretical and political organ of the LPRP; Editor-in-Chief SISOUK PHILAVONG.

Finance: rue That Luang, Ban Phonxay, Vientiane; tel. (21) 412401; fax (21) 412415; organ of Ministry of Finance.

Heng Ngan: 87 ave Lane Xang, BP 780, Vientiane; tel. (21) 212756; fax (21) 219750; fortnightly; organ of the Federation of Lao Trade Unions; Editor CHANSING KOKKEOBOUNMA.

Khao Tourakit (Business News): rue Sihom, Ban Sihom, Chanthaboury, Vientiane; tel. (21) 219244; fax (21) 219223; e-mail bsnews@laotel.com; f. 1999; fortnightly; organ of the Lao National Chamber of Commerce and Industry; Editor-in-Chief SOMCHIT THIPTHIENGTHAM.

Khaokila (Sports Daily News): Ban Mixay, Chanthaboury, Vientiane; tel. (21) 252908; fax (21) 252909; e-mail khaokila@hotmail.com; f. 1999; Editor-in-Chief SUKSAKHONE SIPRASEUTH.

Lao Dong (Labour): 87 ave Lane Xang, Vientiane; f. 1986; fortnightly; organ of the Federation of Lao Trade Unions; circ. 46,000.

Laos: 80 rue Setthathirath, BP 3770, Vientiane; tel. (21) 21447; fax (21) 21445; quarterly; published in Lao and English; illustrated; Editor V. PHOMCHANHEUANG; English Editor O. PHRAKHAMSAY.

Meying Lao: rue Manthatoarath, BP 59, Vientiane; e-mail chansoda@hotmail.com; f. 1980; monthly; women's magazine; organ of the Lao Women's Union; Editor-in-Chief VATSADY KHUTNGOTHA; Editor CHANSODA PHONETHIP; circ. 7,000.

Noum Lao (Lao Youth): rue Phonthan, Ban Phonthan Neua, Xaysettha, Vientiane; tel. (21) 951067; fax (21) 416727; f. 1979; fortnightly; organ of the Lao People's Revolutionary Youth Union; Editor KHANKAB BUDARAT; circ. 1,500.

Pasason Van Athit: rue Pangkham, Ban Xiengyeun Thong, Chanthaboury, Vientiane; tel. (21) 212471; fax (21) 212470; weekly; Editor THONGLITH LIEMXAYYACHAK; circ. 2,000.

Pasaxon (The People): 80 rue Setthathirath, BP 110, Vientiane; tel. (21) 212466; fax (21) 212470; e-mail infonews@pasaxon.org.la; internet www.pasaxon.org.la; f. 1940; daily; Lao; organ of the Cen. Cttee of the LPRP; Editor BOUABAN VOLAKHOUN; circ. 28,000.

Pathet Lao: 80 rue Setthathirath, Vientiane; tel. (21) 212447; f. 2001; daily; Lao and English; organ of the Lao News Agency, Khao San Pathet Lao (KPL); Editor KHEMTHONG SANOUBAN.

Sciences and Technics: Science, Technology and the Environment Agency (STEA), BP 2279, Vientiane; f. 1991; est. as Technical Science Magazine; quarterly; organ of the Dept of Science and Technology; scientific research and development.

Siang Khong Gnaovason Song Thanva (Voice of the 2nd December Youths): Vientiane; monthly; youth journal.

Sieng Khene Lao: Vientiane; monthly; organ of the Lao Writers' Association.

Suksa Mai: Vientiane; monthly; organ of the Ministry of Education.

Valasan Khosana (Propaganda Journal): Vientiane; f. 1987; organ of the Cen. Cttee of the LPRP.

Vannasinh: Vientiane; monthly; literature magazine.

Vientiane Mai (New Vientiane): 36 rue Setthathirath, BP 989, Vientiane; tel. (21) 212623; fax (21) 215989; e-mail admin@vientianemai.net; internet www.vientianemai.net; f. 1975; morning daily; organ of the LPRP Cttee of Vientiane province and city; Editor SOMPHET INTHISARATH; circ. 2,500.

Vientiane Times: rue Pangkham, BP 5723, Vientiane; tel. (21) 216364; fax (21) 216365; e-mail info@vientianetimes.gov.la; internet www.vientianetimes.org.la; f. 1994; daily; English; Editor-in-Chief SAVANKHONE RAZMOUNTRY; circ. 3,000.

Vientiane Tourakit Sangkhom (Vientiane Business-Social): 36 rue Setthathirath, Vientiane; tel. (21) 2623; fax (21) 6365; weekly; publ. in conjunction with Vientiane Mai; Editor SOMPHET INTHISARATH; circ. 2,000.

There is also a newspaper published by the Lao People's Army, and several provinces have their own newsletters.

NEWS AGENCY

Khao San Pathet Lao (Lao News Agency—KPL): 80 rue Setthathirath, BP 3770, Vientiane; tel. (21) 215090; fax (210 212446; e-mail kplnews@yahoo.com; internet www.kplnet.net; f. 1968; dept of the Ministry of Information and Culture; news service for press, radio and television broadcasting; daily bulletins in Lao, English and French; Gen. Dir KHAMSENE PHONGSA; English Editor BOUNLERT LOUANEDOUANGCHANH.

PRESS ASSOCIATION

The Journalists' Association of the Lao PDR: BP 122, Vientiane; tel. (21) 212420; fax (21) 212408; Pres. BOUABANE VORAKHOUNE; Sec.-Gen. KHAM KHONG KONGVONGSA.

Publishers

Khoualuang Kanphim: 2–6 Khoualuang Market, Vientiane.

Lao-phanit: Ministry of Education, Bureau des Manuels Scolaires, rue Lane Xang, Ban Sisavat, Vientiane; educational, cookery, art, music, fiction.

Pakpassak Kanphin: 9–11 quai Fa-Hguun, Vientiane.

State Printing Enterprise: 314/C rue Samsemthai, BP 2160, Vientiane; tel. (21) 213273; fax (21) 215901; Dir NOUPHAY KOUNLAVONG.

Broadcasting and Communications

TELECOMMUNICATIONS

Entreprises des Postes et Télécommunications de Laos: ave Lane Xang, 01000 Vientiane; tel. (21) 215767; fax (21) 212779; e-mail laoposts@laotel.com; state enterprise, responsible for the postal service and telecommunications; Dir-Gen. KIENG KHAMKETH.

Lao Télécommunications Co Ltd: ave Lane Xang, BP 5607, 0100 Vientiane; tel. (21) 216465; fax (21) 219690; e-mail marketin@laotel.com; internet www.laotel.com; f. 1996; a jt venture between a subsidiary of the Shinawatra Group of Thailand and Entreprises des Postes et Télécommunications de Laos; awarded a 25-year contract by the Government in 1996 to undertake all telecommunications projects in the country; Dir-Gen. HOUMPHANH INTHARATH.

BROADCASTING
Radio
In addition to the national radio service, there are several local stations.

Lao National Radio: rue Phangkham, Km 6, BP 310, Vientiane; tel. (21) 212468; fax (21) 212430; e-mail laonradio@lnr.org.la; internet www.lnr.org.la; f. 1960; state-owned; programmes in Lao, French, English, Thai, Khmer and Vietnamese; domestic and international services; Dir-Gen. BOUNTHANH INTHAXAY.

In 1990 resistance forces in Laos established an illegal radio station, broadcasting anti-Government propaganda: Satthani Vithayou Kachai Siang Latthaban Potpoi Sat Lao (Radio Station of the Government for the Liberation of the Lao Nation): programmes in Lao and Hmong languages; broadcasts four hours daily.

Television
A domestic television service began in December 1983. In May 1988 a second national television station commenced transmissions from Savannakhet. In December 1993 the Ministry of Information and Culture signed a 15-year joint-venture contract with a Thai firm on the development of broadcasting services in Laos. Under the resultant International Broadcasting Corporation Lao Co Ltd, IBC Channel 3 was inaugurated in 1994 (see below).

Lao National Television (TVNL): rue Chommany Neua, Km 6, BP 5635, Vientiane; tel. (21) 710617; fax (21) 710182; e-mail lntv2007@yahoo.co.th; f. 1983; colour television service; Dir-Gen. BOUMCHOM VONGPHET.

Laos Television 3: BP 860, Vientiane; tel. (21) 315449; fax (21) 215628; operated by the International Broadcasting Corpn Lao Co Ltd; f. 1994 as IBC Channel 3; 30% govt-owned, 70% owned by the International Broadcasting Corpn Co Ltd of Thailand; programmes in Lao.

Finance
(cap. = capital; dep. = deposits; br.(s) = branch(es); m. = million)

BANKING
The banking system was reorganized in 1988–89, ending the state monopoly of banking. Some commercial banking functions were transferred from the central bank and the state commercial bank to a new network of autonomous banks. The establishment of joint ventures with foreign financial institutions was permitted.

Central Bank
Banque de la RDP Lao: rue Yonnet, BP 19, Vientiane; tel. (21) 213109; fax (21) 213108; e-mail bol@pan-laos.net.la; internet www.bol.gov.la; f. 1959 as the bank of issue; became Banque Pathetlao 1968; took over the operations of Banque Nationale du Laos 1975; known as Banque d'Etat de la RDP Lao from 1982 until adoption of present name; dep. 394,017m. kips, total assets US $361m. (Dec. 2002); Gov. PHOUPHET KHAMPHOUNVONG.

Commercial Banks
Acleda Bank Lao: 372 Dongpalane Rd, Unit 21, Ponesavanh, Sisattanak, Vientiane; tel. (21) 264994; fax (21) 264995; e-mail acledabank@acledabank.com.la; internet www.acledabank.com.kh/LA; f. 2008; Chair. CHEA SOK; Pres. and CEO PHON NARIN.

Agriculture Promotion Bank: 58 rue Hengboun, Ban Haysok, BP 5456, Vientiane; tel. (21) 212024; fax (21) 213957; e-mail apblaopdr@laonet.net; Man. Dir BOUNSONG SOMMALAVONG.

Banque pour le Commerce Extérieur Lao (BCEL): 1 rue Pangkham, BP 2925, Vientiane; tel. (21) 213200; fax (21) 213202; e-mail bcelhovt@etllao.com; internet www.bcellaos.com; f. 1975; 100% state-owned; Chair. VIENGTHONG SYPHANDONE; Man. Dir SONEXAY SITPHAXAY.

International Commercial Bank: 127/07, rue Hatsady, Hatsady Tai, Chanthaboury, Vientiane; e-mail enquiry@icb-lao.com; f. 2008.

Joint Development Bank: 82 ave Lane Xang, BP 3187, Vientiane; tel. (21) 213531; fax (21) 213530; e-mail jdb@jdbbank.com; internet www.jdbbank.com; f. 1989; the first joint-venture bank between Laos and a foreign partner; 30% owned by Banque de la RDP Lao, 70% owned by Thai company, Phrom Suwan Silo and Drying Co Ltd; cap. US $4m; Dir SAROGE SINGSOMBOON.

Lao May Bank Ltd: 39 rue Pangkham, BP 2700, Vientiane; tel. (21) 213300; fax (21) 213340; f. 1999 as a result of the consolidation by the Government of ParkTai Bank, Lao May Bank and Nakornluang Bank; merged with Lane Xang Bank Ltd in 2001.

Lao-Viet Bank (LVB): 44 ave Lane Xang, Ban Hatsady, Chanthaboury, Vientiane; tel. (21) 216316; fax (21) 212197; e-mail lvbho@laotel.com; f. 1999; jt venture between BCEL and the Bank for Investment and Development of Vietnam; cap. US $15m.; Chair. PHANSANA KHOUNNOUVONG; Gen. Dir NGUYEN VAN HIEN; 3 brs.

Phongsavanh Bank: 77 Unit 09, Samsenthai Rd, Ban Anou, Chanthaboury, Vientiane; tel. (21) 212666; e-mail info@phongsavanhbank.com; internet www.phongsavanhbank.com; f. 2007; cap. US $10m. (2007).

Vientiane Commercial Bank Ltd: 33 ave Lane Xang, Ban Hatsady, Chanthaboury, Vientiane; tel. (21) 222700; fax (21) 213513; e-mail vccbank@laotel.com; f. 1993; privately owned jt venture by Laotian, Thai, Taiwanese and Australian investors; Man. Dir SOP SISOMPHOU.

INSURANCE
Assurances Générales du Laos (AGL): Vientiane Commercial Bank Bldg, 33 ave Lane Xang, BP 4223, Vientiane; tel. (21) 215903; fax (21) 215904; e-mail agl@agl-allianz.com; internet www.agl-allianz.com; f. 1990; jt venture between Lao Govt (49%) and Assurances Générales de France (51%); sole licensed insurance co in Laos; Group Chair. Dr MICHAEL DIEKMANN; Man. Dir GUY APOVY.

Trade and Industry
GOVERNMENT AGENCY
National Economic Research Institute (NERI): rue Luang Prabang, Sithanneua, Vientiane; tel. (21) 351369; fax (21) 216660; e-mail neri@pan-laos.net; govt policy development unit; Dir SOUPHAN KEOMISAY.

DEVELOPMENT ORGANIZATIONS
Department of Domestic and Foreign Investment (DDFI): rue Luang Prabang, 01001 Vientiane; tel. (21) 222690; fax (21) 215491; e-mail fimc@laotel.com; internet invest.laopdr.org; fmrly Foreign Investment Management Committee (FIMC); provides information and assistance to existing and potential investors.

Department of Livestock and Fisheries: Ministry of Agriculture and Forestry, Ban Phonxay, BP 811, Vientiane; tel. (21) 416932; fax (21) 415674; e-mail eulaodlf@laotel.com; public enterprise; imports and markets agricultural commodities; produces and distributes feed and animals; Dir-Gen. SINGKHAM PHONVISAY.

National Agriculture and Forestry Research Institute (NAFRI): Nongviengkham, BP 7170, Vientiane; tel. (21) 770084; fax (21) 770047; e-mail info@nafri.org.la; internet www.nafri.org.la; f. 1999; br. of the Ministry of Agriculture and Forestry; supports sectoral devt and the strategic formulation of policies and programmes in accordance with govt policy; Dir-Gen. Dr MONTHATHIP CHANPHENGXAY.

State Committee for State Planning: Office of the Prime Minister, Ban Sisavat, Vientiane; tel. (21) 213653; fax (21) 213560; Pres. SOULIVONG DARAVONG.

CHAMBER OF COMMERCE
Lao National Chamber of Commerce and Industry (LNCCI): ave Kaysone Phomvihane, Sat Settha District, BP 4596, Vientiane; tel. (21) 452579; fax (21) 452580; e-mail lncci@laopdr.com; internet www.lncci.laotel.com; f. 1989; 800 mems; Pres. KISSANA VONGSAY; Sec.-Gen. KHAMPANH SENGTHONGKHAM.

TRADE ASSOCIATION
Société Lao Import-Export (SOLIMPEX): 43–47 ave Lane Xang, BP 2789, Vientiane; tel. (21) 213818; fax (21) 217054; Dir KANHKEO SAYCOCIE; Dep. Dir PHONGSAMOUTH VONGKOT.

UTILITIES
Electricity
Electricité du Laos: rue Nongbone, BP 309, Vientiane; tel. (21) 451519; fax (21) 416381; e-mail edlgmo@laotel.com; internet www.edl-laos.com; responsible for production and distribution of electricity; Man. Dir KHAMMANY INTHIRATH (acting).

Lao National Grid Co: Vientiane; responsible for Mekong hydro-electricity exports.

Water
In 1998 the Government adopted a policy of decentralization with regard to water supply and sanitation in Laos. As a result, the national water supply authority, Nam Papa Lao, was divided into Nam Papa Vientiane, with jurisdiction over the capital, and a number of provincial authorities. Activities within the sector were subsequently co-ordinated by a newly established body, the Water Supply Authority.

Nam Papa Vientiane (Vientiane Water Supply Authority): rue Phone Kheng, Thatluang Neue Village, Sat Settha District, Vientiane; tel. (21) 412880; fax (21) 414378; e-mail daophet@laotel.com; f. 1962; fmrly Nam Papa Lao; authority responsible for the water supply of Vientiane; Gen. Man. DAOPHET BOUAPHA.

Water Supply Authority (WASA): Dept of Housing and Urban Planning, Ministry of Communications, Transport, Post and Construction, ave Lane Xang, Vientiane; tel. and fax (21) 451826; e-mail mctpcwwa@laotel.com; internet www.wasa.gov.la; f. 1998; Dir NOUPHEUAK VIRABOUTH.

STATE ENTERPRISES

Agricultural Forestry Development Import-Export and General Service Co: trading co of the armed forces.

Bolisat Phatthana Khet Phoudoi Import-Export Co: rue Khoun Boulom, Vientiane; tel. (21) 216234; fax (21) 215046; f. 1984; trading co of the armed forces.

Dao-Heuang Import-Export Co: Ban Thaluang, Paksé, Champasak Province; tel. (31) 213805; fax (31) 212438; e-mail info@dao-heuang.com; internet www.daoheuangcoffee.com; f. 1990; imports and distributes whisky, beer, mineral water, coffee and foodstuffs; Pres. LEUANG LITDANG.

Lao Commodities Export Co Ltd (Lacomex): Ban Wattuang, Paksé, Champasak Province; tel. (31) 212552; fax (31) 212553; e-mail sisanouk@laotel.com; f. 1994; exports coffee under the Paksong Cafe Lao brand; Man. Dir SISANOUK SISOMBAT.

Lao Houng Heuang Export-Import Co: rue Nongbone, Vientiane; tel. (21) 217344; fax (21) 212107.

Lao State Material Import-Export Co (Lasmac): 59 Ban Hatsady Tai, Chanthaboury, Vientiane; tel. (21) 216578; fax (21) 217149; e-mail lasmac@laotel.com; internet www.lasmac.laopdr.com; f. 1983; mfr of wood products and woven plastic; exports agricultural and wood products; imports construction materials.

Luen Fat Hong Lao Plywood Industry Co: BP 83, Vientiane; tel. (21) 314990; fax (21) 314992; e-mail lfhsdsj@laotel.com; internet www.luenfathongyada.laopdr.com; development and management of forests, logging and timber production.

CO-OPERATIVES

Central Leading Committee to Guide Agricultural Co-operatives: Vientiane; f. 1978; helps to organize and plan regulations and policies for co-operatives; by the end of 1986 there were some 4,000 co-operatives, employing about 74% of the agricultural labour force; Chair. (vacant).

TRADE UNION ORGANIZATION

Federation of Lao Trade Unions: 87 ave Lane Xang, BP 780, Vientiane; tel. (21) 212754; e-mail kammabanlao@pan-laos.net.la; f. 1956; 21-mem. Cen. Cttee and five-mem. Control Cttee; Pres. BOSAIKHAM VONGDALA (acting); 70,000 mems.

Transport

RAILWAYS

In 1997 the Government announced plans to develop a comprehensive railway network, and awarded the contract to a Thai company. In 2003 the Thai Government agreed to finance a 3.5-km rail link from Tha Naleng (near Vientiane) to Nong Khai, in north-eastern Thailand; construction was completed in April 2008, and the first passenger train service commenced in March 2009. Proposals to extend the track, to link Tha Naleng with Vientiane and to extend southwards and eastwards to Vinh in Viet Nam via Thakek in central Laos, were also announced.

ROADS

The Asian Development Bank has supported an extensive development programme for the road network in Laos, in order to promote integration in the Mekong region. In 2006 there were an estimated 29,811 km of roads. The main routes link Vientiane and Luang Prabang with Ho Chi Minh City in southern Viet Nam and with northern Viet Nam and the Cambodian border, Vientiane with Savannakhet, Phongsali to the Chinese border, Vientiane with Luang Prabang and the port of Ha Tinh (northern Viet Nam), and Savannakhet with the port of Da Nang (Viet Nam). Laos, Thailand and China are linked by the Kunming–Bangkok Highway, 250 km of which traverse Laos. In February 2004 construction of a 245-km national road (Route 9) was completed, linking Laos with Thailand and Viet Nam.

The first Friendship Bridge across the Mekong River, linking Laos and Thailand between Tha Naleng and Nong Khai, was opened in April 1994. In early 1998 construction work began in Paksé on another bridge across the Mekong River. The project was granted substantial funding from the Japanese Government, and was completed in August 2000. Construction commenced in December 2003 on a second Friendship Bridge, also funded by the Japanese Government, linking Savannakhet and Mukdahan, which opened in December 2006. In 2008 plans were announced to construct a new bridge linking Thailand's northern province of Chiang Rai with Huayxai in Laos. The bridge was scheduled to open in 2011.

INLAND WATERWAYS

The Mekong River, which forms the western frontier of Laos for much of its length, is the country's greatest transport artery. However, the size of river vessels is limited by rapids, and traffic is seasonal. In April 1995 Laos, Cambodia, Thailand and Viet Nam signed an agreement regarding the joint development of the lower Mekong, and established the Mekong River Commission. There are about 4,600 km of navigable waterways.

CIVIL AVIATION

Wattay airport, Vientiane, is the principal international airport. The development of Luang Prabang airport began in 1994, and in April 1998 Luang Prabang airport also gained formal approval for international flights. Construction of a new airport in Oudomxay Province was completed in the late 1990s. Savannakhet Airport was to be developed into an international facility, as part of plans for the east–west economic corridor project, a proposed transport network linking Laos with Myanmar, Thailand and Viet Nam.

Lao Civil Aviation Department: BP 119, Vientiane; tel. and fax (21) 512163; fax (21) 520237; e-mail laodca@laotel.com; Dir-Gen. YAKUA LOPANGKAO.

Lao Airlines: National Air Transport Co, 2 rue Pangkham, BP 6441, Vientiane; tel. (21) 212057; fax (21) 212065; e-mail laoairlines@laoairlines.com; internet www.laoairlines.com; f. 1975; state airline, fmrly Lao Aviation; operates internal and international passenger and cargo transport services within South-East Asia; CEO SOMPHONE DOUANGDARA.

Tourism

Laos boasts spectacular scenery and ancient pagodas. Luang Prabang was approved by UNESCO as a World Heritage site in 1995, as was the Wat Phu temple complex in southern Laos in 2001. Total visitor arrivals increased from 894,806 in 2004 to 1,215,107 in 2006. Receipts reached US $146m. in 2005 and $173m. in 2006 (excluding passenger transport).

National Tourism Administration of Lao PDR: ave Lane Xang, BP 3556, Hadsady, Chanthaboury, Vientiane; tel. (21) 212251; fax (21) 212769; e-mail tmpd_lnta@yahoo.com; internet www.tourismlaos.gov.la; 17 provincial offices; Chair. SOMPHONG MONGKHONVILAY.

LATVIA

Introductory Survey

Location, Climate, Language, Religion, Flag, Capital

The Republic of Latvia is situated in north-eastern Europe, on the east coast of the Baltic Sea. The country is bounded by Estonia to the north and by Lithuania to the south and south-west. To the east it borders Russia, and to the south-east Belarus. Owing to the influence of maritime factors, the climate is relatively temperate, but changeable. Average temperatures in January range from −2.8°C (26.6°F) in the western coastal town of Liepāja to −6.6°C (20.1°F) in the inland town of Daugavpils. Mean temperatures for July range from 16.7°C (62.1°F) in Liepāja to 17.6°C (63.7°F) in Daugavpils. Average annual rainfall in Rīga is 617 mm (24 ins). The official language is Latvian. The major religion is Christianity: most ethnic Latvians are traditionally Lutherans or Roman Catholics, whereas ethnic Russians are mainly adherents of the Russian Orthodox Church. The national flag (proportions 1 by 2) has a maroon background, with a narrow white horizontal stripe superimposed across the central part. The capital is Rīga (Riga).

Recent History

In November 1917 representatives of Latvian nationalist groups elected a provisional national council, which informed the Russian Government of its intention to establish a sovereign, independent Latvian state. On 18 November 1918 the Latvian National Council, which had been constituted on the previous day, proclaimed the independent Republic of Latvia, with Jānis Cakste as President. Independence, under the nationalist Government of Kārlis Ulmanis, was fully achieved after the expulsion of the Bolsheviks from Rīga in May 1919, with the aid of German troops, and from the eastern province of Latgale, with Polish and Estonian assistance, in January 1920. A Latvian-Soviet peace treaty was finally signed in August. Latvia's first Constitution was adopted in 1922. An electoral system based on proportional representation permitted a large number of small parties to be represented in the Saeima (Parliament). As a result, there was little administrative stability, with 18 changes of government in 1922–34. None the less, under the dominant party, the Latvian Farmers' Union (LZS, led by Ulmanis), agrarian reforms were successfully introduced and agricultural exports flourished. The world-wide economic decline of the early 1930s, together with domestic political fragmentation, prompted a (bloodless) coup d'état in May 1934, led by Ulmanis. Martial law was introduced, the Saeima was dissolved and all political parties, including the LZS, were banned. A Government of National Unity, with Ulmanis as Prime Minister, assumed the legislative functions of the Saeima. Ulmanis became President in 1936.

Under the Treaty of Non-Aggression, signed by Germany and the USSR in August 1939, the incorporation of Latvia into the Soviet 'sphere of interests' was agreed by the two powers. A Treaty of Mutual Aid between the USSR and Latvia allowed the establishment of Soviet military bases in Latvia, and in June 1940 it was occupied by Soviet forces. A 'puppet' administration, under Augusts Kirhenšteins, was installed, and the election to the Saeima of Soviet-approved candidates took place in July. In that month the legislature proclaimed the Latvian Soviet Socialist Republic, which was formally incorporated into the USSR as a constituent union republic in August.

In the first year of Soviet rule almost 33,000 Latvians were deported to Russia and Kazakhstan, and a further 1,350 were killed. Latvian language, traditions and culture were also suppressed. In July 1941 Soviet rule in Latvia was interrupted by German occupation. Most German troops had withdrawn by 1944, although the Kurzeme region, in south-western Latvia, was retained by Germany until the end of the Second World War. Soviet Latvia was re-established in 1944–45 and the process of 'sovietization' was resumed. There were further mass deportations of Latvians to Russia and Central Asia. Independent political activities were prohibited and exclusive political power was exercised by the Communist Party of Latvia (LKP). A process of industrialization encouraged significant and sustained Russian and other Soviet immigration into the republic. Under LKP First Secretary Arvīds Pelše (appointed in 1959) and his successor, Augusts Voss (1966–84), limited autonomy gained in the 1950s was reversed.

There was a revival in Latvian national culture from the late 1970s. Political groups began to be established, including the Environmental Protection Club and Helsinki-86, established to monitor Soviet observance of the Helsinki Final Act adopted in 1975 by the Conference on (now Organization for) Security and Co-operation in Europe (CSCE—now OSCE, see p. 366). In 1986 anti-Soviet demonstrations, organized by Helsinki-86, were suppressed by the police. In 1987 there were further demonstrations on the anniversaries of significant events in Latvian history. Such movements, fostered by the greater freedom of expression permitted under the new Soviet policy of *glasnost* (openness), were strongly opposed by the LKP. In 1988 opposition movements in Latvia began to unite, and in October representatives of the leading movements organized the inaugural congress of the Latvian Popular Front (LTF), at which delegates resolved to seek sovereignty for Latvia within a renewed Soviet federation. The LTF, chaired by Dainis Ivāns, rapidly became the largest and most influential political force in Latvia, with an estimated membership of 250,000 by the end of 1988.

In September 1988 Boris Pugo was replaced as First Secretary of the LKP by Jānis Vagris. The new LKP leadership came increasingly under the influence of members of the LTF. At the end of September Latvian was designated the state language. In March 1989 candidates supported by the LTF won 26 of the 34 contested seats in elections to the USSR's Congress of People's Deputies. On 28 July, following similar measures in Lithuania and Estonia, the Latvian Supreme Soviet (Supreme Council—legislature) adopted a declaration of sovereignty and economic independence. However, there was growing support within the republic for full independence, as advocated by the Latvian National Independence Movement (LNNK), formed in 1988, particularly among ethnic Latvians (who, however, were outnumbered by ethnic Slavs in Rīga and the other large cities in the republic as a result of the Soviet policy of large-scale immigration). In December 1989 candidates supported by the LTF won some 75% of seats contested in local elections.

In January 1990 the Latvian Supreme Soviet voted to abolish the constitutional provisions that guaranteed the LKP's political predominance. In the following month the Supreme Soviet adopted a declaration condemning the Latvian legislature's decision to request admission to the USSR in 1940, and the flag, state emblems and anthem of pre-1940 Latvia were restored to official use. At elections to the Supreme Soviet in March and April 1990, pro-independence candidates endorsed by the LTF won 131 of the 201 seats; the LKP and the anti-independence Interfront (International Front—dominated by members of the Russian-speaking population) together won 59 seats. The LKP subsequently split into two parties: the majority of delegates at an extraordinary congress rejected a motion to leave the Communist Party of the Soviet Union (CPSU), and elected Alfrēds Rubiks, an opponent of independence, as First Secretary.

The new Supreme Council was convened in early May 1990, and elected Anatolijs Gorbunovs of the LKP as its Chairman (*de facto* president of the Republic). On 4 May the Supreme Council adopted a resolution that declared the incorporation of Latvia into the USSR in 1940 as unlawful, and announced the beginning of a transitional period that was to lead to full political and economic independence. Four articles of the 1922 Constitution, defining Latvia as an independent democratic state and asserting the sovereignty of the Latvian people, were restored, and were to form the basis of the newly declared Republic of Latvia's legitimacy. Ivars Godmanis, the Deputy Chairman of the LTF, was elected Prime Minister in a new, LTF-dominated Government. Meanwhile, a rival body to the Supreme Soviet had been convened at the end of April 1990. This Congress of Latvia had been elected in an unofficial poll, in which some 700,000 people were reported to have participated: only citizens of the pre-1940 republic and their descendants had been entitled to vote. The Congress, in which members of the LNNK predominated, declared Latvia to be an occupied country and adopted resolutions on independence and the withdrawal of Soviet troops.

The Supreme Council's resolutions, although more cautious than independence declarations adopted in Lithuania and Estonia, severely strained relations with the Soviet authorities. On 14 May 1990 the Soviet President, Mikhail Gorbachev, issued a decree that annulled the Latvian declaration of independence, condemning it as a violation of the USSR Constitution. The declaration was also opposed within the republic by some ethnic Slavs, who organized protest strikes and demonstrations. In December the Latvian Government claimed that special units (OMON) of the Soviet Ministry of Internal Affairs had been responsible for a series of explosions in Rīga, and in January 1991 OMON troops seized the Rīga Press House, previously the property of the LKP. Later in January a 'Committee of Public Salvation', headed by Alfrēds Rubiks, declared itself as a rival Government to the Godmanis administration; on the same day five people died when OMON troops attacked the Ministry of the Interior in Rīga. (In November 1999 10 former Soviet officers were convicted of attempting to overthrow the Latvian Government in 1991; seven received suspended prison sentences of up to four years' duration.)

The attempted seizure of power by Rubiks reinforced opposition in Latvia to inclusion in the new union treaty being prepared by nine Soviet republics. Latvia refused to conduct the all-Union referendum on the future of the USSR, which was scheduled for 17 March 1991 (although some 680,000 people, mostly ethnic Russians and Ukrainians, did participate, unofficially). Instead, a referendum on Latvian independence took place on 3 March. Of those eligible to vote, 87.6% participated, of whom, according to official results, 73.7% endorsed proposals for a democratic, independent Latvian republic.

At the time of the attempted overthrow of the Gorbachev administration in the Russian and Soviet capital, Moscow, in August 1991, immediate Soviet military intervention in Latvia was widely anticipated. However, an emergency session of the Supreme Council was convened and the full independence of Latvia was proclaimed. As the coup collapsed, the Godmanis Government took prompt action to assert control in Latvia, banning the LKP and detaining Rubiks. (In July 1995 Rubiks was found guilty of involvement in the coup attempt. He was released in November 1997.) On 6 September 1991 the USSR State Council formally recognized the independent Republic of Latvia, and the country was admitted to the UN later that month. In late 1991 the Supreme Council adopted legislation guaranteeing the right of citizenship to all citizens of the pre-1940 republic (including non-ethnic Latvians) and their descendants. Other residents of Latvia were to be required to apply for naturalization after final legislation governing citizenship was determined by a restored Saeima.

The first legislative elections since the restoration of independence took place in June 1993, with the participation of about 90% of the electorate. Only citizens of pre-1940 Latvia and their descendants were entitled to vote; consequently, some 27% of the adult population (mainly ethnic Russians) were excluded from the election. A total of 23 parties, movements and alliances contested the poll, of which eight secured representation in the 100-seat Saeima. Latvian Way (LC), a broadly-based movement established earlier in the year, emerged as the strongest party, with more than 32% of the votes and 36 seats in the assembly. The results of the elections demonstrated strong popular support for the more moderate nationalist parties, and socialist-orientated parties (including the successor of the LKP, the Latvian Socialist Party—LSP) failed to win representation. The LTF also failed to secure any seats. Only 11 of the elected deputies were non-ethnic Latvians (six of whom were ethnic Russians).

The new Saeima voted to restore the Constitution of 1922, and undertook to elect the President of the Republic from among three prominent deputies. At a third round of voting on 7 July 1993 Guntis Ulmanis (great-nephew of Kārlis Ulmanis) of the revived LZS succeeded in winning a majority, with 53 votes. He was inaugurated as President the following day, whereupon he appointed Valdis Birkavs (formerly a Deputy Chairman of the Supreme Council and a leading member of LC) as Prime Minister. The Cabinet of Ministers represented a coalition agreement between LC (the majority partner) and the LZS.

The requirements for naturalization proposed by the Government's draft citizenship law included a minimum of 10 years' permanent residence, a knowledge of Latvian to conversational level and an oath of loyalty to the republic. In March 1994 the Saeima approved the establishment of the new post of State Minister for Human Rights, in an attempt to counter accusations of violations of minority rights. Following international criticism, the Saeima adopted an amended citizenship law in July. Latvia was admitted to the Council of Europe (see p. 236) in February 1995.

Meanwhile, in July 1994 the LZS announced its withdrawal from the governing coalition, following disagreements with LC over economic and agricultural policy. A new Cabinet was appointed in September. It, too, was dominated by LC members, including the Prime Minister, Māris Gailis; Birkavs became Deputy Prime Minister and Minister of Foreign Affairs.

A general election was held on 30 September–1 October 1995. Nine parties and coalitions succeeded in obtaining the 5% of the votes required for representation in the Saeima; as a result, the assembly was highly fragmented. LC's share of the 100 seats was reduced by more than one-half, to 17, while the largest number of seats (18) was won by the newly established, leftist Democratic Party Saimnieks (The Master—DPS). The People's Movement for Latvia (Zigerists' Party), an extreme nationalist party led by a German-Latvian, Joahims Zigerists who had been convinced for inciting racial hatred in Germany in 1994, won 16 seats. In December 1995 the Saeima finally endorsed a Cabinet of Ministers led by Andris Šķēle (an entrepreneur with no party affiliation). The new Government was a broad coalition of the DPS, LC, the For Fatherland and Freedom Union (TB), the Latvian National Conservative Party (as the LNNK had been renamed), the LZS and the Latvian Unity Party (LVP). Former Prime Ministers Gailis and Birkavs were appointed to the new Cabinet, as, respectively, a Deputy Prime Minister, and Minister of Foreign Affairs. In May 1996 the Deputy Prime Minister and Minister of Agriculture, Alberīs Kauls, was dismissed, after he criticized the Prime Minister's agricultural policies. The LVP (led by Kauls) temporarily withdrew its support from the coalition, but shortly afterwards rejoined the Government, having secured approval for a new candidate as Minister of Agriculture.

On 18 June 1996 the Saeima re-elected Guntis Ulmanis for a second three-year term as President. In July it was announced that the LVP was to merge with the DPS, reinforcing the latter's position as the dominant party in the coalition. None the less, instability in both the Government and the legislature continued. In January 1997 Šķēle resigned as Prime Minister, but was swiftly reappointed by Ulmanis, who indicated his support for Šķēle's economic and structural reforms, and a new, largely unaltered Cabinet was appointed in February. Local elections conducted in March demonstrated a considerable increase in support for the LZS.

By July 1997 the governing coalition had begun to disintegrate, not least because a series of corruption scandals had prompted the resignation of several ministers, and at the end of the month Šķēle announced the resignation of the Government. Ulmanis invited Guntars Krasts, the outgoing Minister of the Economy, to form a new administration. In August the Saeima approved Krasts' proposals for a new, five-party coalition, comprising his own party, formed in the previous month by the merger of the TB and the LNNK (which had reverted to its former designation), known as the TB/LNNK, the DPS, LC, the LZS and the Christian Democratic Union of Latvia. In early 1998 Krasts was accused of negligence with regard to a privatization proposal for the state power utility, Latvenergo, during his tenure as Minister of the Economy. In March Krasts formally requested that the Saeima conduct a vote of confidence in his personal integrity, in order to confirm his mandate. The refusal of any parliamentary faction to organize such a vote was interpreted by the Prime Minister as an endorsement of his leadership. In that month Šķēle announced the formation of a new political party, later named the People's Party (TP), to contest the forthcoming elections.

In April 1998 the Minister of the Economy, Atis Sausnītis, was dismissed. Anticipating the collapse of Krasts' Government, the DPS announced its withdrawal from the coalition. At the end of the month, however, Krasts survived a parliamentary vote of no confidence proposed by the LZS and LC. At the same session the Saeima approved appointments to a new coalition Government, with members of the Cabinet of Ministers drawn from the LZS, LC, and an alliance of the Latvian National Reform Party and the Latvian Green Party.

In April 1998 draft amendments to the strict legislation regulating rights to citizenship were adopted, in response to recommendations made by the OSCE. The amendments, which removed the age-related system of naturalization that allocated dates for application by age-group, granted citizenship to stateless children (permanently resident in Latvia) born after the 1991 declaration of independence and relaxed the citizenship requirements for Russian-speakers, were approved by the Saeima in June 1998. Although widely welcomed elsewhere in Europe, the amendments were deemed inadequate by Russia, and nationalist groups within the Latvian legislature secured sufficient support inside and outside the Saeima to force a delay to the enactment of the new legislation and the organization of a referendum on the subject. The referendum was duly conducted concurrently with legislative elections on 3 October; 52.5% of the votes were cast in favour of the amendments, which were promulgated later in the month.

At the legislative elections, Šķēle's TP was the most successful single party, taking 21.2% of the votes (and 24 of the 100 legislative seats), ahead of LC with 18.1% (21 seats) and TB/LNNK with 14.7% (17 seats). Only six of the 21 participating political parties secured the minimum 5% of the votes necessary for representation in the Saeima. In November 1998 the Saeima finally approved a new, three-party, minority coalition Government, headed by Vilis Krištopans of LC. The coalition, comprising LC, TB/LNNK and the New Party (which held eight legislative seats), also drew support from the Latvian Social Democratic Alliance, which controlled 14 seats in the Saeima. In early February 1999 the Social Democrats formally joined the coalition with the appointment of one of their members to the Cabinet of Ministers.

On 17 June 1999 Vaira Viķe-Freiberga was elected President at a seventh round of voting in the Saeima, with the support of 53 deputies (compared with 20 for Valdis Birkavs of LC and nine for Ingrīda Ūdre of the New Party). Born in Latvia, but resident in Canada from the end of the Second World War until 1998, Viķe-Freiberga, a non-partisan figure who had trained as a psychologist, thus became the first female President in central or eastern Europe. At her inauguration on 8 July 1999 Viķe-Freiberga identified as priorities for her presidency Latvia's entry into the European Union (EU, see p. 255) and the North Atlantic Treaty Organization (NATO, see p. 351). Three days before her inauguration, Krištopans announced his Government's resignation, apparently in response to the recent signing by TB/LNNK of a co-operation accord with the opposition TP. President Viķe-Freiberga subsequently asked Šķēle to form a new government. Šķēle thus became Prime Minister for the third time, leading a coalition of his TP, the TB/LNNK and LC.

In early July 1999 the Saeima adopted controversial new language legislation, requiring all business and state- and municipally-organized gatherings to be conducted in Latvian. Russia immediately denounced the legislation as discriminatory, and it was also condemned by the OSCE, the Council of Europe, the European Commission and, within Latvia, by groups representing ethnic Slavs. Revised legislation, approved in early December, incorporated amendments urged by the OSCE and came into effect in September 2000.

Šķēle resigned the premiership in April 2000, after LC withdrew from the governing coalition, owing to a dispute over the management of the Latvian Privatization Agency. President Viķe-Freiberga asked Andris Bērziņš, hitherto the Mayor of Rīga, to form a new government; a coalition administration, principally comprising the TP, LC and TB/LNNK, was approved by the Saeima in early May. In November 2001 Einārs Repše resigned as Governor of the Bank of Latvia, in order to found a new political party, New Era (JL). The rightist party attracted immediate popular support, and Repše was elected Chairman at its founding congress in February 2002. In May a new Christian democratic party, the Latvian First Party (LPP), was formed.

In legislative elections, held on 5 October 2002, JL won 23.9% of the votes cast, obtaining 26 seats; the leftist, pro-Russian electoral bloc For Human Rights in a United Latvia (PCTVL), which included the People's Harmony Party (TSP) and the LSP, obtained 18.9% of the votes (25 seats); and the TP received 16.7% (20 seats). Other groups to achieve representation in the Saeima were the Greens' and Farmers' Union (ZZS—an alliance of the Centre Party, the LZS and the Latvian Green Party—LZP), with 12 seats, the LPP (10 seats) and TB/LNNK (seven); LC failed to obtain a seat in the Saeima. The rate of participation by the electorate was some 72.5%. Repše formed a coalition government comprising members of JL, the LPP, the ZZS and TB/LNNK, which was approved by the Saeima on 7 November. The Minister of Defence, Ģirts Kristovskis, was the only member of the Cabinet of Ministers to have retained his previous portfolio; a new post of Deputy Prime Minister was established, to which Ainārs Šlesers of the LPP was appointed. In late November Atis Slakteris replaced Šķēle as Chairman of the TP.

In February 2003 the TSP withdrew from the PCTVL alliance, apparently in order to pursue more moderate policies. In June the LSP also announced its withdrawal; the remainder of the PCTVL coalition was officially reconstituted as a united organization later that year. On 20 June Viķe-Freiberga was re-elected unopposed to serve a second term of office as President; she was inaugurated on 8 July. In late September tensions emerged within the Government, when its constituent parties (with the exception of JL) issued a statement expressing a lack of confidence in Repše as Prime Minister, whom it accused of authoritarianism. A compromise agreement was reached, following inter-party discussions, and in mid-November the Chairmen of the four ruling parties signed a memorandum of understanding. In late January 2004 Repše dismissed Šlesers as Deputy Prime Minister; Šlesers alleged that his removal had been prompted by a proposal to establish a special investigative committee to examine the premier's property dealings. Following the withdrawal of the LPP from the Government, on 5 February Repše announced the resignation of his administration. On 20 February President Viķe-Freiberga nominated the Co-Chairman of the LZP, Indulis Emsis, as premier. In early March Emsis secured the support of the ZZS, the LPP and the TP, and a new right-of-centre coalition Government was approved by the Saeima on 9 March, with the parliamentary support of the TSP. Šlesers was re-appointed Deputy Prime Minister.

Following Latvia's official accession to the EU on 1 May 2004 (see below), elections to the European Parliament were conducted on 13 June; the opposition TB/LNNK won four of the nine seats available, while its ally JL won two, and PCTVL, the LPP and LC each won one seat. Neither of the two major parties of the ruling coalition obtained representation. The Minister of Foreign Affairs, Rihards Piks, resigned from the Cabinet in order to take his seat in the European Parliament; he was replaced by Artis Pabriks. The Government survived motions of confidence in the Saeima in June and September. However, on 28 October the draft budget was defeated in a parliamentary vote, precipitating the collapse of the ruling coalition. President Viķe-Freiberga nominated Aigars Kalvītis of the TP (which had led opposition to the proposed budget) to form a new government, and on 2 December, following prolonged negotiations, the Saeima approved the formation of a Government comprising members of the TP, JL, the ZZS and the LPP. Several members of the outgoing administration were retained in the same posts, including Pabriks and Oskars Spurdziņš (both of the TP), as Minister of Foreign Affairs and Minister of Finance, respectively. Viķe-Freiberga reportedly opposed the proposed nomination of Šķēle as Minister of Health, and consequently Gundars Bērziņš, of the TP, was appointed to that position. The new Government was able to command a majority of votes in the legislature, which approved the draft budget on 20 December.

Local elections, held on 12 March 2005, were marred by allegations of electoral malpractice in Jūrmala and Rēzekne. In early July Jānis Jurkāns resigned as leader of the TSP, in protest at the party's decision, following electoral defeats at both European and local level, to form an alliance with the New Centre, led by Sergejs Dolgopolovs, who had been expelled from the TSP in 2003. The new union, which became known as the Harmony Centre (SC) alliance, was joined by the LSP in December 2005. Jānis Urbanovičs was elected to succeed Jurkāns as leader of the TSP in November. LC and the LPP also formed a political alliance in October, in preparation for legislative elections due to take place in October 2006.

In mid-October 2005 the Minister of the Interior, Ēriks Jēkabsons, tendered his resignation, after attracting criticism for his performance in office, and for his contacts with the controversial, self-exiled Russian businessman Boris Berezovskii. In early November Jēkabsons was replaced by Dzintars Jaundzeikars of the LPP. In late December Repše resigned as Minister of Defence, following the announcement of a criminal investigation into his property investments; although Repše denied any impropriety, he resigned his parliamentary seat and withdrew from the leadership of JL. Linda Mūrniece succeeded Repše as Minister of Defence. In mid-March 2006 Kalvītis dismissed Šlesers as Minister of Transport, after evidence emerged that implicated him in electoral malpractice in the 2005 municipal elections. In April 2006 the Ministry of the Interior launched an inquiry into allegations of financial misconduct against the JL Minister of the Economy, Krišjānis Kariņš. JL accused the LPP, which held the interior portfolio, of misusing its control of the ministry and subsequently withdrew its seven representatives from the Government, after

Kalvītis (of the TP) rejected its demand that the LPP be removed from the governing coalition. On 8 April a three-party minority Government (which excluded JL) was approved by the Saeima.

At elections to the Saeima on 7 October 2006 the TP won 19.6% of the votes cast and 23 seats, the ZZS alliance 16.7% of the votes (18 seats), JL 16.4% (18 seats), the SC alliance 14.4% (17 seats), the LPP, allied with LC, 8.6% (10 seats), TB/LNNK 6.9% (eight seats) and PCTVL 6.0% (six seats). The governing coalition of the TP, the ZZS and the LPP consequently secured a narrow parliamentary majority. Around 62.3% of the electorate participated in the elections, significantly less than had done so in 2002. Kalvītis invited TB/LNNK to join the governing coalition in order to strengthen its parliamentary majority and subsequently formed a new administration, comprising representatives of those four parties, which was approved by 58 deputies in the Saeima on 7 November 2006. In early December the Supreme Court ruled that regulations on campaign financing had been contravened, notably by the TP and the LPP, on the grounds that two independent organizations had supported their party advertising prior to the October elections. In the same month a congress of the TSP approved the consolidation of the SC alliance as a merged association (although the LSP retained its separate status as an affiliated party).

In March 2007 President Vīķe-Freiberga refused to endorse new legislation, which had been approved by the Saeima, providing for an increase in the powers vested in the Prime Minister over national security, and declared that a national referendum would be conducted on the question; following the collection of the signatures of more than 10% of the electorate, the referendum was scheduled for 7 July. On 31 May the Saiema elected Valdis Zatlers, the candidate proposed by the ruling coalition, as President, to succeed Vīķe-Freiberga. Zatlers (a medical doctor without political experience) was inaugurated on 8 July. Meanwhile, the referendum on the proposed national security legislation, conducted as scheduled, was declared by the Central Election Commission to be invalid, owing to an inadequate rate of participation, estimated at only about 37%; some 95% of those participating had voted in favour of abandoning the legislation. In August the LPP officially merged with LC; the reconstituted LPP/LC was jointly chaired by Šlesers and Godmanis.

On 17 September 2007 Jurijs Strods, a member of the TB/LNNK, tendered his resignation as Minister of the Economy. On 22 September the Chairman of the Saeima, Emsis, also resigned, after he became subject to a criminal investigation on charges of having given false testimony in a case related to corruption in the city of Ventspils. He was succeeded by Gundars Daudze, a close ally of the controversial Mayor of Ventspils, Aivars Lembergs, who had been arrested on charges of corruption and abuse of public office in March. In October Kalvītis dismissed the Minister of Regional Development and Local Government, who had voted against a government motion to remove the director of the anti-corruption bureau, Aleksejs Loskutovs; Loskutovs had been suspended from his post following the discovery of irregularities in the accounts of the bureau. Later in the month Artis Pabriks resigned as Minister of Foreign Affairs in protest at the decision to replace Loskutovs, which opponents of Kalvītis claimed was motivated by the bureau's investigations into corruption allegations involving members of the ruling coalition. The crisis precipitated a mass anti-Government demonstration in Rīga; however, the administration won a motion of no confidence in the Saeima. At the end of October the Minister of Welfare, Dagnija Stake of the ZZS, resigned, following opposition to her plans to reform the state pension system. In early December Kalvītis finally tendered the resignation of his Government. Zatlers, after rejecting an attempt by the TP to propose a further candidate, nominated Godmanis (who had hitherto held the interior portfolio) to the premiership. On 20 December a new coalition Government, comprising representatives of the TP, the LPP/LC, the ZZS and the TB/LNNK, was approved by the Saeima.

In April 2008 a new centre-right political party, the Civic Union (PS), was founded by two prominent politicians, Sandra Kalniete and Valdis Kristovskis, formerly of JL and the TB/LNNK, respectively. Also in April it was announced that at least 10% of eligible voters had signed a petition in support of a constitutional amendment that would enable voters to dissolve the legislature by referendum. Consequently, in accordance with the Constitution, a national referendum was to be conducted on the proposed amendment on 2 August. In May it was announced that a further demand, for an increase in pensions' payments, had received the requisite number of petition signatures; after the proposed change to the state pension law was rejected by the Saeima, this was also referred to a national referendum, which was subsequently scheduled for 23 August. In June Loskutovs (who remained under investigation by the Government for alleged mismanagement of funds in the anti-corruption bureau) was removed from his post by a vote in the Saeima. On 2 August the proposed constitutional amendment failed to secure sufficient support (a minimum of 50% of the registered electorate) at the national referendum. However, Zatlers described the referendum result, which was equivalent to about 40.2% of the electorate voting in favour, as significant, and submitted a legal initiative to the Saeima for consideration of the amendment. The referendum on the proposed pension reform on 23 August was also declared invalid, owing to a voter turnout of less than one-half of those who voted in the most recent legislative elections. In September public sector workers staged a large demonstration to demand improved salaries and conditions.

The severe impact of the international financial crisis (see Economic Affairs) obliged the Government in November 2008 to seek a funding agreement from international institutions, necessitating tax increases and reductions in public expenditure (despite earlier assertions by the Minister of Finance that emergency assistance would not be required); following the adoption of an austerity budget, an economic stabilization programme was approved by the IMF in December. In January 2009 the opposition organized a demonstration of about 10,000 in Rīga in protest at perceived economic mismanagement by the Government and demanding early legislative elections; some 100 protesters were arrested, following rioting. On the following day Zatlers issued an ultimatum stating that the Saeima would be dissolved if it and the Government failed to fulfil by the end of March a number of political reforms (namely: the adoption of the constitutional amendment on the dissolution of the legislature by a national referendum initiated by voters; the reformation of the electoral law; the appointment of a new director of the anti-corruption bureau; and the establishment of a committee to supervise the distribution of IMF funds). In early February the Government survived a parliamentary motion of no confidence, which had been initiated by JL. However, following protests by farmers, who demanded state assistance to compensate for increasing hardship in the sector, the Minister of Agriculture resigned. Later that month the Cabinet of Ministers failed to adopt proposed measures to reduce the number of existing government ministries, prompting Zatlers to declare that he had lost confidence in Godmanis. On 20 February, after the TP and the ZZS threatened to withdraw from the governing coalition, Godmanis tendered his resignation. Zatlers nominated Valdis Dombrovskis, a member of JL and a former Minister of Finance, to the office of Prime Minister. JL subsequently invited all parties represented in the Saeima (excepting representatives of the PCTVL) to enter into consultations on the formation of a new administration. On 12 March a new coalition Government, comprising representatives of JL, the TP, the ZZS alliance, the TB/LNNK and the PS and headed by Dombrovskis (who also held the portfolio of children, the family and social integration), was approved by the Saeima; new appointments included those of Repše as Minister of Finance and of Artis Kampars of the JL as Minister of the Economy. On the same day the Saeima finally appointed a new director of the anti-corruption bureau. At the end of March Zatlers announced that he would not implement his threat to dissolve the Saeima, in response to the installation of the new Government and some perceived progress in the adoption of political and economic reforms. On 8 April the Saeima approved amendments to two articles of the Constitution, enabling voters to initiate a referendum on the dissolution of the legislature during the second and third year of its term; the changes were to enter into effect following the next parliamentary election.

Latvia's post-independence relations with Russia were troubled by two issues. The first concerned the citizenship and linguistic rights of Latvia's large Russian-speaking community (see above). Of comparable importance was the issue of the 100,000 former Soviet troops still stationed in Latvia (jurisdiction over whom had been transferred, following the dissolution of the USSR, to Russia). Following negotiations, withdrawal of the troops began in early 1992. The process was hampered by a series of disagreements, in particular over the issue of a Russian military radar station at Skrunda, in western Latvia, that the Russians wished to retain. However, in April 1994 agreements were concluded on the complete withdrawal of the remaining 10,000 Russian troops by the end of August, as well as on social guarantees for the estimated 22,000 Russian military pensioners residing in Latvia. Installations at the Skrunda base were subsequently dismantled.

Negotiations regarding the demarcation of the Latvian–Russian border, and Latvia's claim to some 1,640 sq km of land transferred from Latvia to Russia during the Soviet era, commenced in April 1996. Latvia initially insisted (as Estonia had done) that any future border agreement should include a reference to the 1920 treaty in which Russia recognized Latvia's independence. However, in February 1997 the Latvian administration abandoned this demand, and agreed that claims to property in the disputed territory should be discussed separately from the main border agreement. In March a draft treaty on the demarcation of the border was agreed by the two countries, and full agreement on a border treaty was reached in October (although it remained unratified). In January 2007 the Latvian Government agreed to remove a declaration from the draft treaty, which had been interpreted by Russia as a territorial claim on the land that had formerly constituted part of Latvia, thereby providing for the official endorsement of the treaty. In early February the Saeima approved legislation authorizing the Government to sign the border treaty with Russia. On 27 March Kalvītis and his Russian counterpart, Mikhail Fradkov, officially signed the treaty in Moscow. The treaty was endorsed by Viķe-Freiberga in May and by Russian President Vladimir Putin in October; a legal challenge against it, proposed by JL, was rejected by the Constitutional Court in November. In early July 2008 the Russian Government announced that it intended to end the shipment of petroleum products and coal through Latvian, Estonian and Lithuanian ports by 2015, and instead use port facilities in northwestern Russia. However, later that month the Russian ambassador to Latvia appeared to withdraw the previous government statement. In August 2008 Zatlers, together with the Presidents of Estonia, Lithuania and Poland, condemned a Russian military offensive in Georgia (see the chapter on Russia.)

Relations became further strained in March 1998, following the organization, in Rīga, of a rally of Latvian veterans of Nazi German *Waffen SS* units, who had fought Soviet forces during the Second World War; the participation of senior Latvian politicians and military personnel attracted particular criticism from the Russian authorities. Government officials and serving military officers were not permitted to participate in a further veterans' rally held in March 2000. Meanwhile, tensions arising from repeated Russian threats to impose economic sanctions against Latvia, if the Government did not promptly address perceived infringements of minority rights, were exacerbated by Latvia's new state language law (see above) in 1999. The revised language law, as approved by the Saeima in December, was again denounced by Russia. Economic issues threatened to raise further tensions between the two countries in early 2003, following Russia's decision to cease using the port of Ventspils for its petroleum exports, primarily owing to the opening of a new Russian petroleum terminal on the Baltic coast at Primorsk, Leningrad Oblast. Russia also condemned amendments to legislation on education, which took effect from September 2004, and in accordance with which 60% of lessons in minority schools were to be taught in the Latvian language; in February thousands of ethnic Russians had protested in Rīga against the reforms.

On 9 May 2005 President Viķe-Freiberga travelled to Moscow to attend celebrations to commemorate the 60th anniversary of the end of the Second World War in Europe. (Notably, the Heads of State of Estonia and Lithuania declined to attend.) Three days later the Saeima adopted a declaration denouncing the Soviet occupation of Latvia and urging Russia to accept moral, legal and financial responsibility for the losses incurred by the Latvian people under Soviet rule. In late May the Saeima ratified the Council of Europe's Framework Convention for the Protection of National Minorities; however, a declaration was appended, stipulating that only Latvian citizens would be regarded as members of a national minority, thereby excluding large numbers of ethnic Russians who had failed to obtain citizenship. In August a commission was established to calculate the economic damage and human loss sustained by Latvia under Soviet governance; it was estimated that the commission might take up to five years to complete its research. Latvia (together with Estonia and Lithuania) was concerned at the signature in September of an agreement between Russia and Germany on the construction of a North European Gas Pipeline, which was to carry natural gas from Russia to Germany under the Baltic Sea, bypassing the Baltic countries. In August 2006 the Latvian authorities introduced a new citizenship law provision, stipulating that applicants who failed a Latvian language test three times would be disqualified permanently from obtaining citizenship.

Latvia enjoys close relations with Estonia and Lithuania, and the three countries have established institutions to promote co-operation, including the interparliamentary Baltic Assembly and the Baltic Council of Ministers (which meets twice yearly). In 1992 Latvia became a founder member, with Estonia, Lithuania and other countries of the region, of the Council of Baltic Sea States, a principal aim of which was to assist the political and economic development of its former communist member states (which included Russia). Differences arose in the mid-1990s between Latvia and its two closest Baltic neighbours, in particular concerning the demarcation of maritime borders. However, agreement on the delimitation of the sea border with Estonia was reached in May 1996, and the document was ratified by both countries' legislatures in August. A further agreement on fishing rights was concluded in 1997, in which year the demarcation of the land border between the two countries was completed. Negotiations between Latvia and Lithuania on their maritime border were complicated in 1996 by the Saeima's ratification of an agreement with two foreign petroleum companies to explore and develop offshore oilfields in disputed areas of the Baltic Sea. Although the two countries signed an agreement on the delimitation of their territorial waters in 1999, protests from the Latvian fishing industry prevented the agreement from being ratified by the Saeima. In 2000 a protocol was signed on the re-demarcation of the land border between the two countries. In early 2006 the leaders of all three Baltic countries reached agreement on the construction of a new nuclear power plant to replace that at Ignalina, Lithuania, and various other co-operative measures aimed at reducing Russian dominance in the supply of regional energy.

A priority of Latvian foreign policy was attaining full membership of the EU. Latvia applied for membership in October 1995, and formal negotiations on accession commenced in February 2000. In December 2002 Latvia, together with nine other countries, was formally invited to become a full member of the EU in 2004. A referendum on EU membership was held in Latvia on 20 September 2003. Of the 72.5% of the electorate who participated in the plebiscite, 66.8% voted in support of Latvia's accession to the EU, although in certain areas of the country, particularly in the predominantly Russian-speaking, south-eastern regions around the second city of Daugavpils, a majority of votes were cast against EU membership. The country became a full member on 1 May 2004. In December 2007 Latvia, together with eight other nations, implemented the EU's Schengen Agreement, enabling its citizens to travel to and from other member states, without border controls. On 8 May 2008 the Saeima voted overwhelmingly to ratify the EU's Lisbon Treaty.

In February 2002 the Secretary-General of NATO warned the Latvian Government that its existing language requirements, which demanded that candidates standing in regional and national elections be fluent in Latvian, threatened to affect adversely the likelihood of the country being admitted to the Alliance; amendments to the electoral law were duly passed in May. At a summit meeting held in Prague, Czech Republic, in November, Latvia was one of seven countries invited to join NATO in 2004. Latvia became a full member of the Alliance on 29 March 2004.

Government

Under the terms of the 1922 Constitution, which was restored in July 1993 (and amended in December 1997), Latvia is an independent democratic parliamentary republic. The supreme legislative body is the Saeima (Parliament), the 100 members of which are elected by universal adult suffrage for a four-year term. The President of the Republic, who is Head of State, is elected by a secret ballot of the Saeima, also for a period of four years. The President, who is also Head of the Armed Forces, may not serve for more than two consecutive terms. Executive power is held by the Cabinet of Ministers, which is headed by the Prime Minister. The Prime Minister is appointed by the President; the remaining members of the Cabinet are nominated by the Prime Minister. For administrative purposes, Latvia is divided into 26 districts and seven towns (including the capital, Rīga).

Defence

Until independence in August 1991, Latvia had no armed forces separate from those of the USSR. A Ministry of Defence was established in November of that year. As assessed at November 2008, Latvia's total armed forces numbered 5,187, including an army of 1,526, a navy of 700 and an air force of 480. The remainder comprised administration and command staff, central support staff and other forces. Reserve forces in the national guard numbered 11,034. Military service is compulsory from 19 years of age and lasts for 12 months. In August 1994 the withdrawal from Latvia of all former Soviet forces was completed. Latvia joined the North Atlantic Treaty Organization's (NATO) 'Partnership for Peace' programme (see p. 353) in February 1994, and became a full member of the Alliance on 29 March 2004. The budget for 2008 allocated 267m. lats to defence.

Economic Affairs

In 2007, according to estimates by the World Bank, Latvia's gross national income (GNI), measured at average 2005–07 prices, was US $22,595m., equivalent to $9,930 per head (or $16,890 per head on an international purchasing-power parity basis). During 2000–07, it was estimated, the population decreased by an annual average of 0.6%, while gross domestic product (GDP) per head increased at an average annual rate of 9.7%, in real terms. Overall GDP increased, in real terms, by an average annual rate of 7.2% in 2000–08; according to official figures, real GDP increased by 10.0% in 2007 but declined by 4.6% in 2008.

Agriculture (including hunting, forestry and fishing) contributed 3.1% of GDP in 2008, and provided 9.9% of employment in 2007. The principal sectors are dairy farming and pig-breeding. Cereals, sugar beet, potatoes and fodder crops are the main crops grown. As part of the process of land reform and privatization, the dissolution of collective and state farms was undertaken in the early 1990s. In 2003 Latvia approved a seven-year ban on the sale of rural land to foreign purchasers. Fishing makes an important contribution to the economy (an estimated 70% of the total annual catch is exported). Output of the forestry industry increased from 1996. Agricultural GDP increased, in real terms, by an average of 2.8% per year in 2000–08; the real GDP of the sector declined by 0.3% in 2008.

Industry (comprising mining and quarrying, manufacturing, construction and utilities) contributed 22.7% of GDP in 2008, and provided 28.4% of employment in 2007. Industrial GDP increased, in real terms, at an average annual rate of 6.7% in 2000–08. The GDP of the industrial sector decreased, in real terms, by 4.5% in 2008.

Mining and quarrying contributed just 0.4% of GDP in 2008, and employed 0.6% of workers in 2007. Latvia has limited mineral resources, the most important being peat, dolomite, limestone, gypsum, amber, gravel and sand. Offshore and onshore petroleum reserves have been located. According to official figures, the GDP of the mining sector increased by 2.5% in 2008.

The manufacturing sector contributed 10.6% of GDP in 2008, and provided 14.7% of employment in 2007. Real manufacturing GDP increased by an average of 4.6% per year in 2000–08. The GDP of the sector increased, in real terms, by 0.5% in 2007, but declined by 6.5% in 2008.

Latvia is highly dependent on imported fuels to provide energy. In 2007 mineral products represented 11.6% of the total value of Latvia's imports. Electric energy is supplied primarily by Estonia and Lithuania, and petroleum products are supplied by Russia and Lithuania. In 2005 hydroelectric plants provided some 67.8% of annual domestic electricity production in Latvia; a further 30.3% was derived from natural gas.

The services sector has increased in importance; the sector contributed 74.2% of GDP in 2008, and accounted for 61.7% of employment in 2007. The GDP of the sector increased, in real terms, by an annual average of 7.8% in 2000–08; however, real services GDP decreased by 2.5% in 2008. The tourism sector expanded markedly in the mid-2000s, following a significant expansion in air services between Rīga and cities in central and western Europe. Total visitor arrivals numbered 844,828 in 2007, compared with 545,366 in 2004.

In 2007 Latvia recorded a visible trade deficit of US $6,899m., and there was a deficit of $6,485m. on the current account of the balance of payments. The principal source of imports in 2007 was Germany, which accounted for 15.2% of total imports; other major sources were Lithuania, Russia, Estonia, Poland and Finland. The main market for exports in that year was Lithuania, which accounted for 15.8% of the total; other significant purchasers were Estonia, Russia, Germany, Sweden and the United Kingdom. The principal exports in 2007 were wood and wood articles, followed by base metals and manufactures, machinery and electrical equipment, chemicals, foodstuffs, beverages and tobacco and textiles. The principal imports in that year were machinery and electrical equipment, vehicles and transport equipment, mineral products, base metals, chemicals, and foodstuffs and beverages.

In 2007 the consolidated state budget recorded a surplus of 8.6m. lats (equivalent to 0.1% of GDP). At the end of 2006 Latvia's external debt totalled US $22,795m., of which $1,555m. was long-term public debt. In that year the cost of debt-servicing was equivalent to 33.3% of the value of exports of goods and services. Annual consumer-price inflation averaged 5.2% in 2000–2007. However, consumer prices increased by 10.1% in 2007. According to official statistics, some 6.1% of the population were registered as unemployed in 2007.

Latvia became a member of the World Trade Organization (WTO, see p. 410) in February 1999. In May 2004 Latvia acceded to the European Union (EU, see p. 255).

Latvia's external trade underwent a significant reorientation in the 1990s, towards the markets of central and western Europe. Conversely, in the early 2000s Latvia was able to reorientate its trade eastwards, to capitalize on rapid growth in the Russian economy. Strong growth increased employment levels significantly, but also led to price and wage inflation and a large deficit on the current account of the balance of payments. Latvia was admitted to the EU's exchange rate mechanism (ERM II) in May 2005, in advance of its eventual adoption of the common European currency, the euro. In 2007 growth began to slow, and in late 2008 the international financial crisis had an immediate negative impact on the Latvian economy. In November the Government intervened to prevent the collapse of the country's largest privately-owned financial institution, Parex Banka, acquiring a majority share thereof (by way of the state-owned Latvijas Hipotēku un Zemes Bank). In December, after the legislature adopted a revised budget providing for extensive austerity measures (based on a projected 5% annual contraction of GDP in 2009), the IMF approved an economic stabilization programme for Latvia, which was to be funded by a loan of €7,500m.; of this amount, the Fund was to contribute €1,680m. under a 27-month standby arrangement, the EU €3,100m., and Sweden, Denmark and Norway €1,800m. However, the planned austerity measures increased public discontent with the Government's perceived economic mismanagement and precipitated substantial protests in January 2009, while disputes within the governing coalition resulted in the resignation of the Prime Minister in February and the installation of a new administration in March. Meanwhile, a revised projection of the decline in GDP for 2009, to some 12%, raised the prospect that the Government would be obliged to renegotiate the stabilization agreement with the IMF, to adopt more stringent spending reductions, and to seek additional funding from the EU. In April the IMF suspended disbursements to Latvia until the Government demonstrated progress in implementing the stipulated austerity measures, emphasizing the necessity of achieving sustained reductions in the budget deficit in order to meet the criteria for Latvia's long-term objective of adopting the euro.

Education

Primary education begins at seven years of age and lasts for four years. Secondary education, beginning at the age of 11, comprises a first cycle of five years and a second of three years. Only the first nine years of education are officially compulsory. In 2005 enrolment at primary schools included 87.8% of pupils in the relevant age-group; in that year enrolment at secondary schools was equivalent to 98.2% of pupils in the relevant age–group. In the 2004/05 academic year some 65% of school-age pupils were taught in Latvian-language schools and some 25% were taught in Russian-language schools; 10% were taught in schools offering instruction in both Latvian and Russian. In 2005 higher education was offered at 57 institutions. Enrolment totalled 129,503 students in 2006/07. According to official figures, in 2006 consolidated central government expenditure on education amounted to 626.3m. lats (representing 15.5% of expenditure).

Public Holidays

2009: 1 January (New Year's Day), 10–13 April (Easter), 1 May (Labour Day), 4 May (Declaration of Independence Day), 23–24 June (Midsummer Festival), 18 November (National Day, proclamation of the Republic), 25–26 December (Christmas), 31 December (New Year's Eve).

2010: 1 January (New Year's Day), 2–5 April (Easter), 1 May (Labour Day), 4 May (Declaration of Independence Day), 23–24 June (Midsummer Festival), 18 November (National Day, proclamation of the Republic), 25–26 December (Christmas), 31 December (New Year's Eve).

Weights and Measures

The metric system is in force.

Statistical Survey

Source (unless otherwise stated): Central Statistical Bureau of Latvia, Lāčplēša iela 1, Rīga 1301; tel. 6736-6850; fax 6783-0137; e-mail csb@csb.lv; internet www.csb.lv.

Area and Population

AREA, POPULATION AND DENSITY

Area (sq km)	64,589*
Population (census results)†	
12 January 1989	2,666,567
31 March 2000	
Males	1,094,964
Females	1,282,419
Total	2,377,383
Population (official estimates at 1 January)‡	
2006	2,294,590
2007	2,281,305
2008	2,270,894
Density (per sq km) at 1 January 2008	35.2

* 24,938 sq miles.
† Figures refer to the resident population.
‡ Figures are rounded to the nearest 100 persons.

POPULATION BY ETHNIC GROUP
(official estimates, 1 January 2008)

	Number	%
Latvian	1,343,439	59.2
Russian	636,805	28.0
Belarusian	83,520	3.7
Ukrainian	56,740	2.5
Polish	54,024	2.4
Lithuanian	30,743	1.3
Others	65,623	2.9
Total	**2,270,894**	**100.0**

PRINCIPAL TOWNS
(population at 1 January 2008, official estimates)

Rīga (Riga, capital)	717,371	Jūrmala	55,580
Daugavpils	105,958	Ventspils	43,299
Liepāja	85,050	Rēzekne	35,883
Jelgava	65,635		

BIRTHS, MARRIAGES AND DEATHS

	Registered live births		Registered marriages		Registered deaths	
	Number	Rate (per 1,000)	Number	Rate (per 1,000)	Number	Rate (per 1,000)
2000	20,248	8.5	9,211	3.9	32,205	13.6
2001	19,664	8.3	9,258	3.9	32,991	14.0
2002	20,044	8.6	9,738	4.2	32,498	13.9
2003	21,006	9.0	9,989	4.3	32,437	13.9
2004	20,334	8.8	10,370	4.5	32,024	13.8
2005	21,497	9.3	12,554	5.5	32,777	14.2
2006	22,264	9.7	14,616	6.4	33,087	14.4
2007	23,070	10.1	15,451	6.8	32,940	14.4

Life expectancy (years at birth, WHO estimates): 70.9 (males 65.3; females 76.3) in 2006 (Source: WHO, *World Health Statistics*).

IMMIGRATION AND EMIGRATION

	2005	2006	2007
Immigrants	1,886	2,801	3,252
Emigrants	2,450	5,252	5,085

ECONOMICALLY ACTIVE POPULATION
(annual averages, '000 persons aged 15–74 years)

	2005	2006	2007
Agriculture, hunting and forestry	122.3	117.8	107.5
Fishing	2.9	2.4	2.8
Mining and quarrying	2.0	3.8	6.6
Manufacturing	154.1	169.6	164.8
Electricity, gas and water	23.1	22.3	20.7
Construction	90.5	103.9	125.6
Wholesale and retail trade; repair of motor vehicles, motorcycles and personal and household goods	157.7	170.2	184.6
Hotels and restaurants	27.6	29.2	31.2
Transport, storage and communications	94.6	100.8	104.0
Financial intermediation	20.1	25.1	22.0
Real estate, renting and business activities	49.2	60.7	74.0
Public administration and defence, compulsory social security	81.8	88.2	83.9
Education	90.5	87.8	81.8
Health and social work	57.9	51.0	50.1
Other community, social and personal service activities	57.6	49.5	53.7
Total employed (incl. others)	1,035.9	1,087.6	1,119.0
Males	534.1	559.2	573.5
Females	501.8	528.5	545.5
Unemployed	99.1	79.9	72.1
Total labour force	1,135.0	1,167.5	1,191.1

Health and Welfare

KEY INDICATORS

Total fertility rate (children per woman, 2006)	1.3
Under-5 mortality rate (per 1,000 live births, 2006)	9
HIV/AIDS (% of persons aged 15–49, 2007)	0.8
Physicians (per 1,000 head, 2006)	3.1
Hospital beds (per 1,000 head, 2006)	7.6
Health expenditure (2006): US $ per head (PPP)	974
Health expenditure (2006): % of GDP	6.0
Health expenditure (2006): public (% of total)	63.2
Human Development Index (2006): ranking	44
Human Development Index (2006): value	0.863

For sources and definitions, see explanatory note on p. vi.

Agriculture

PRINCIPAL CROPS
('000 metric tons)

	2005	2006	2007
Wheat	676.5	598.3	807.3
Barley	365.8	307.0	363.2*
Rye	87.2	116.8	181.1
Oats	122.0	91.6	130.2
Triticale (wheat-rye hybrid)	31.8	22.2	26.3*
Potatoes	658.2	550.9	642.0
Sugar beet	519.9	473.9	10.8
Peas, dry	2.5	0.8	1.8
Rapeseed	145.7	120.6	211.7
Cabbages and other brassicas	64.4	63.3	56.6*
Cucumbers and gherkins	12.3	6.4	5.7*
Onions, dry	15.9	13.6	12.0*
Carrots and turnips	34.7	31.6	28.3*
Apples	37.5	31.5*	25.2*
Currants	5.2	4.4*	3.5*

* FAO estimate.

Aggregate production ('000 metric tons, may include official, semi-official or estimated data): Total cereals 1,314.3 in 2005, 1,158.7 in 2006, 1,535.1 in 2007; Total roots and tubers 658.2 in 2005, 550.9 in 2006, 642.0 in 2007; Total vegetables (incl. melons) 172.3 in 2005, 175.0 in 2006, 156.5 in 2007; Total fruits (excl. melons) 57.7 in 2005, 45.7 in 2006, 36.6 in 2007.

Source: FAO.

LIVESTOCK
('000 head at 1 January)

	2005	2006	2007
Cattle	371	385	377
Pigs	436	428	419
Sheep	39	42	41
Goats	15	15	14
Horses	16	14	14
Chickens	3,450*	3,480†	3,830†

* Unofficial figure.
† FAO estimate.
Source: FAO.

LIVESTOCK PRODUCTS
('000 metric tons, unless otherwise indicated)

	2005	2006	2007
Cattle meat	20.4	20.7	22.8
Pig meat	38.5	37.8	40.4
Chicken meat	17.2	20.6	20.6
Cows' milk	806.8	812.1	838.6*
Hen eggs	32.3	33.1	39.0*

* FAO estimate.
Source: FAO.

Forestry

ROUNDWOOD REMOVALS
('000 cubic metres, excl. bark)

	2005	2006	2007
Sawlogs, veneer logs and logs for sleepers	7,951	8,372	6,717
Pulpwood	3,318	2,659	3,268
Other industrial wood	624	835	1,160
Fuel wood	950	979	1,028
Total	12,843	12,845	12,173

Source: FAO.

SAWNWOOD PRODUCTION
('000 cubic metres, incl. railway sleepers)

	2005	2006	2007
Coniferous (softwood)	3,225	3,296	2,421
Broadleaved (hardwood)	1,002	1,024	1,038
Total	4,227	4,320	3,459

Source: FAO.

Fishing

('000 metric tons, live weight)

	2004	2005	2006
Capture	125.4	150.6	140.4
Atlantic cod	5.0	4.0	4.6
Jack and horse mackerels	13.8	25.7	17.8
Atlantic herring	23.6	22.2	21.8
Sardinellas	7.0	9.7	15.6
European sprat	52.4	64.6	54.6
Chub mackerel	9.0	4.6	3.6
Northern prawn	3.2	2.4	1.6
Aquaculture	0.5	0.5	0.6
Total catch	125.9	151.2	141.0

Source: FAO.

Mining

('000 metric tons)

	2005	2006	2007
Peat	791.0	1,000.0	541.2
Gypsum	273.9	235.7	346.1
Limestone	377.3	468.1	388.1

Industry

SELECTED PRODUCTS
('000 metric tons, unless otherwise indicated)

	2002	2003	2004
Sausages	30	33	38
Preserved fish	88	70	62
Whole milk (million litres)	22.3	15.9	26.4
Yoghurt	51	54	58
Ice-cream (million litres)	12.4	14.8	13.1
Mayonnaise	7.3	7.4	8.2
Beer ('000 hectolitres)	1,199	1,364	1,315
Woven fabrics (million sq metres)	38	44	47
Leather footwear ('000 pairs)	99	169	90
Plywood ('000 cu metres)	236	237	268
Paper	21	n.a.	n.a.
Crude steel	520	n.a.	n.a.
Electric energy (million kWh)	3,975	3,975	4,689

Source: partly UN, *Industrial Commodity Statistics Yearbook*.

LATVIA

Statistical Survey

Finance

CURRENCY AND EXCHANGE RATES

Monetary Units
100 santimi = 1 lats.

Sterling, Dollar and Euro Equivalents (31 December 2008)
£1 sterling = 72.16 santimi;
US $1 = 49.50 santimi;
€1 = 68.89 santimi;
10 lats = £13.86 = $20.20 = €14.52.

Average Exchange Rate (lats per US $)
2006   0.560
2007   0.514
2008   0.4808

GOVERNMENT FINANCE
(general government operations, million lats)

Summary of Balances

	2004	2005	2006
Revenue	2,522.2	3,200.0	4,002.3
Less Expense	2,461.9	3,109.6	3,786.7
Net operating balance	60.3	90.4	215.6
Less Net acquisition of non-financial assets	137.6	188.0	245.9
Net lending/borrowing	−77.3	−97.6	−30.3

Revenue

	2004	2005	2006
Tax revenue	1,385.3	1,802.5	2,340.5
Taxes on income, profits and capital gains	563.3	689.8	911.0
Taxes on goods and services	739.8	1,021.6	1,331.4
Taxes on property	56.8	61.6	66.4
Social contributions	641.2	751.1	958.5
Grants	154.4	255.0	267.9
Other revenue	341.3	391.4	435.4
Total	2,522.2	3,200.0	4,002.3

Expense/Outlays

Expense by economic type	2004	2005	2006
Compensation of employees	654.4	778.7	970.4
Use of goods and services	433.3	539.0	664.0
Interest	54.6	52.6	57.6
Subsidies	38.5	44.0	72.2
Social benefits	681.6	778.7	927.7
Other expense	599.5	916.6	1,094.8
Total	2,461.9	3,109.6	3,786.7

Outlays by function of government	2004	2005	2006
General public services	406.6	506.9	599.2
Defence	90.1	107.7	168.4
Public order and safety	163.7	192.4	247.7
Education	429.9	510.1	626.3
Health care	245.7	306.7	421.0
Social security and social welfare	730.4	841.9	1,010.6
Housing and community amenities	135.0	191.5	205.2
Recreation, sport, cultural and religious affairs	95.1	108.7	149.5
Economic affairs	303.0	531.7	604.7
Total	2,599.5	3,297.6	4,032.6

Source: IMF, *Government Finance Statistics Yearbook*.

2007 (general government operations, million lats): Total revenue 5,251.1; Total expenditure 5,242.5.

INTERNATIONAL RESERVES
(US $ million at 31 December)

	2005	2006	2007
Gold (national valuation)	128.45	156.10	204.81
IMF special drawing rights	0.14	0.16	0.17
Reserve position in IMF	0.08	0.08	0.09
Foreign exchange	2,231.91	4,353.13	5,553.11
Total	2,360.58	4,509.47	5,758.18

Source: IMF, *International Financial Statistics*.

MONEY SUPPLY
(million lats at 31 December)

	2005	2006	2007
Currency outside banks	786	969	900
Demand deposits	2,082	3,089	3,029
Total money (incl. others)	2,870	4,064	3,934

Source: IMF, *International Financial Statistics*.

COST OF LIVING
(Consumer Price Index; base: 2000 = 100)

	2005	2006	2007
Food and non-alcoholic beverages	130.5	141.1	160.1
Fuel and light	121.0	139.6	158.4
Clothing (incl. footwear)	106.2	106.2	108.7
Rent	126.5	141.0	167.3
All items (incl. others)	121.9	129.9	143.0

NATIONAL ACCOUNTS
(million lats at current prices)*

Expenditure on the Gross Domestic Product

	2006	2007	2008
Government final consumption expenditure	1,855.2	2,574.9	3,246.4
Private final consumption expenditure	7,280.5	9,213.2	9,481.5
Gross fixed capital formation	3,644.1	4,975.1	4,911.4
Changes in inventories	789.9	994.7	732.4
Total domestic expenditure	13,569.7	17,757.9	18,371.7
Exports of goods and services	5,014.3	6,241.4	6,792.2
Less Imports of goods and services	7,412.3	9,219.5	8,920.7
GDP in market prices	11,171.7	14,779.8	16,243.2
GDP at constant 2000 prices	7,903.1	8,691.7	8,293.4

LATVIA

Gross Domestic Product by Economic Activity

	2006	2007	2008
Agriculture, hunting and forestry	333.8	456.4	440.8
Fishing	11.2	11.2	12.9
Mining and quarrying	34.0	53.5	59.5
Manufacturing	1,159.4	1,487.3	1,538.7
Electricity, gas and water supply	235.0	319.2	411.1
Construction	726.1	1,176.9	1,298.4
Wholesale and retail trade; repair of motor vehicles, motorcycles and personal and household goods	2,050.5	2,577.7	2,525.9
Hotels and restaurants	186.5	239.6	240.4
Transport, storage and communications	1,126.0	1,334.4	1,567.7
Financial intermediation	667.8	804.5	923.9
Real estate, renting and business activities	1,466.9	2,108.2	2,560.3
Public administration and defence; compulsory social security	718.7	983.1	1,128.0
Education	441.3	611.2	752.0
Health and social work	284.3	361.0	414.0
Other community, social and personal service activities	394.4	535.6	693.6
GDP at basic prices	9,835.8	13,059.7	14,567.0
Taxes *less* subsidies on products	1,335.9	1,720.1	1,676.1
GDP in purchasers' values	11,171.7	14,779.8	16,243.2

* Figures revised in accordance with standard EU classification.

BALANCE OF PAYMENTS
(US $ million)

	2005	2006	2007
Exports of goods f.o.b.	5,361	6,140	8,227
Imports of goods f.o.b.	−8,379	−11,271	−15,125
Trade balance	−3,018	−5,131	−6,899
Exports of services	2,163	2,642	3,671
Imports of services	−1,557	−1,980	−2,702
Balance on goods and services	−2,413	−4,469	−5,930
Other income received	772	1,078	1,488
Other income paid	−948	−1,610	−2,425
Balance on goods, services and income	−2,589	−5,001	−6,867
Current transfers received	1,373	1,789	2,035
Current transfers paid	−776	−1,310	−1,654
Current balance	−1,992	−4,522	−6,485
Capital account (net)	212	239	578
Direct investment abroad	−128	−173	−335
Direct investment from abroad	714	1,664	2,247
Portfolio investment assets	−270	−246	−607
Portfolio investment liabilities	131	294	−50
Financial derivatives assets	58	130	334
Financial derivatives liabilities	−134	−70	−105
Other investment assets	−398	−1,953	−6,135
Other investment liabilities	2,626	6,495	11,714
Net errors and omissions	−296	120	−173
Overall balance	524	1,979	982

Source: IMF, *International Financial Statistics*.

External Trade

PRINCIPAL COMMODITIES
(million lats)

Imports c.i.f.	2005	2006	2007
Prepared foodstuffs; beverages spirits and vinegar; tobacco and manufactured substitutes	293.7	379.2	475.5
Mineral products	752.8	854.8	896.7
Products of chemical or allied industries	409.2	530.4	631.5
Plastics, rubber and articles thereof	250.3	322.6	371.9
Paper-making material; paper and paperboard and articles thereof	143.7	135.5	154.8
Textiles and textile articles	236.6	297.0	335.6
Base metals and articles thereof	447.6	606.7	747.8
Machinery and mechanical appliances; electrical equipment; sound and television apparatus	967.7	1,257.0	1,618.6
Vehicles, aircraft, vessels and associated transport equipment	523.1	868.3	1,136.2
Total (incl. others)	4,866.9	6,378.5	7,782.1

Exports f.o.b.	2005	2006	2007
Prepared foodstuffs; beverages spirits and vinegar; tobacco and manufactured substitutes	200.1	245.2	314.1
Mineral products	265.2	182.2	165.4
Products of chemical or allied industries	160.3	222.6	300.3
Wood, cork and articles thereof; wood charcoal; manufactures of straw, esparto, etc.	717.6	739.5	908.5
Textiles and textile articles	249.0	269.3	271.0
Base metals and articles thereof	379.3	488.1	589.7
Machinery and mechanical appliances; electrical equipment; sound and television apparatus	269.4	324.0	444.0
Miscellaneous manufactured articles	128.1	149.3	157.8
Total (incl. others)	2,888.2	3,293.2	4,040.3

PRINCIPAL TRADING PARTNERS
(million lats)*

Imports c.i.f.	2005	2006	2007
Austria	78.8	98.4	115.1
Belarus	281.5	297.7	256.7
Belgium	79.4	108.7	148.8
China, People's Rep.	73.4	106.3	179.2
Czech Republic	68.4	112.1	144.9
Denmark	141.3	173.3	207.7
Estonia	383.3	494.1	629.9
Finland	284.9	363.0	397.3
France	100.2	156.4	179.8
Germany	679.0	988.5	1,180.6
Hungary	56.2	63.8	83.7
Italy	163.5	216.8	285.9
Lithuania	665.5	827.7	1,082.5
Netherlands	171.2	206.1	250.6
Norway	57.7	128.5	80.8
Poland	309.9	459.4	544.0
Russia	413.8	499.1	653.5
Spain	59.6	59.9	108.1
Sweden	248.5	321.0	379.8
Switzerland	50.9	69.5	80.9
Ukraine	92.9	67.1	77.8
United Kingdom	88.6	124.6	126.9
USA	51.7	58.6	88.8
Total (incl. others)	4,866.9	6,378.5	7,782.1

LATVIA

Statistical Survey

Exports f.o.b.	2005	2006	2007
Belarus	57.6	75.9	92.6
Belgium	20.4	46.4	41.8
Denmark	153.5	164.8	161.1
Estonia	312.3	419.1	581.8
Finland	101.7	96.2	127.0
France	51.8	57.3	63.3
Germany	295.9	332.3	353.1
Ireland	43.8	48.1	44.3
Italy	47.0	67.7	61.9
Lithuania	317.8	483.0	638.6
Netherlands	61.3	77.4	85.5
Norway	57.1	78.0	101.5
Poland	150.7	79.7	146.0
Russia	228.3	291.9	386.2
Spain	37.2	38.1	56.8
Sweden	225.0	212.9	313.0
Switzerland	46.7	40.2	27.6
Ukraine	39.8	57.7	59.8
United Kingdom	291.7	257.2	277.1
USA	78.6	61.8	55.5
Total (incl. others)	2,888.2	3,293.2	4,040.3

*Imports by country of origin; exports by country of destination.

Transport

RAILWAYS
(traffic)*

	2005	2006	2007
Passenger journeys (million)	25.9	27.4	27.4
Passenger-kilometres (million)	894	992	983
Freight transported (million metric tons)	60.1	48.7	52.2
Freight ton-kilometres (million)	19,779	16,831	18,313

* Data relating to passengers include railway personnel, and data on freight include passengers' baggage, parcel post and mail.

ROAD TRAFFIC
(motor vehicles in use at 31 December)

	2006	2007	2008
Passenger cars	822,011	904,869	932,828
Buses and coaches	10,628	10,624	10,543
Lorries and vans	121,120	129,614	129,805

SHIPPING
Merchant Fleet
(registered at 31 December)

	2005	2006	2007
Number of vessels	164	153	153
Total displacement ('000 grt)	304.8	333.3	261.8

Source: Lloyd's Register-Fairplay, *World Fleet Statistics*.

International Sea-borne Freight Traffic
('000 metric tons)

	2006	2007	2008
Goods loaded	53,069	55,178	57,654
Goods unloaded	6,428	7,256	5,995

CIVIL AVIATION
(traffic)

	2003	2004	2005
Passengers carried ('000)	408.3	674.2	1,150.7
Passenger-kilometres (million)	424.0	825.1	1,478.1
Cargo ton-kilometres (million)	21.1	40.1	9.9

Source: Ministry of Transport, Rīga.

Tourism

FOREIGN TOURIST ARRIVALS*

Country of residence	2005	2006	2007
Denmark	15,325	14,739	15,986
Estonia	64,103	82,074	76,410
Finland	90,845	88,533	75,286
Germany	123,981	108,716	111,439
Italy	25,394	25,551	27,551
Lithuania	62,279	72,790	82,703
Norway	20,894	43,687	59,017
Poland	23,732	23,030	26,353
Russia	40,488	50,040	60,055
Sweden	45,021	52,115	58,823
United Kingdom	56,370	73,760	62,699
USA	17,377	n.a.	n.a.
Total (incl. others)	730,146	816,297	844,828

* Figures refer to arrivals at accommodation establishments.

Tourism receipts (US $ million): 343 in 2004; 446 in 2005; 622 in 2006 (Source: World Tourism Organization).

Communications Media

	2005	2006	2007
Telephones ('000 main lines in use)*	731	657	644
Mobile cellular telephones ('000 subscribers)	1,871.6	2,183.7	2,217.0
Personal computers ('000 in use)	501	n.a.	n.a.
Internet users ('000)	1,030	1,071	1,177
Broadband subscribers ('000)	61	110	146
Book production: titles	2,371	2,427	2,767
Book production: copies ('000)	4,822	4,700	5,300
Newspapers: number	261	248	259
Newspapers: average annual circulation (million copies)	206	224	211
Other periodicals: number	366	387	412
Other periodicals: average annual circulation (million copies)	45.0	45.4	46.3

* At 31 December.

Radio receivers ('000 in use): 1,760 in 1997.
Television receivers ('000 in use): 1,220 in 1997.
Facsimile machines (number in use): 900 in 1996.

Sources: partly UNESCO, *Statistical Yearbook*; UN, *Statistical Yearbook*; and International Telecommunication Union.

Education

	Institutions*	Students†
Pre-primary	551*	77,278
Schools*‡	1,017	279,872
Primary (Grades 1–4)	58	n.a.
Basic (Grades 1–9)	483	n.a.
Secondary (Grades 10–12)	378	n.a.
Special	64	9,793
Vocational schools	96‖	40,439
Higher education institutions	57‖	129,503

* 2005/06 figures unless otherwise indicated.
† 2006/07 figures.
‡ Figures are for full-time general schools.
‖ Figure at 1 January 2005.

Teachers (2002): Pre-primary 7,996 (2004); Primary (including basic schools) 9,252; Secondary 16,495; Special schools 1,837; Vocational 5,639; Higher 4,535 (2004).

Adult literacy rate (UNESCO estimates): 99.8% (males 99.8%; females 99.8%) in 2007 (Source: UNESCO Institute for Statistics).

Directory

The Constitution

The Constitution of the Republic of Latvia, which had been adopted on 15 February 1922, was annulled at the time of the Soviet annexation in 1940. Latvia became a Union Republic of the USSR and a new Soviet-style Constitution became the legal basis for the governmental system of the republic. The constitutional authority for Latvian membership of the USSR, the Resolution on Latvian Entry into the USSR of 21 July 1940, was declared null and void on 4 May 1990. In the same declaration the Latvian Supreme Council announced the restoration of Articles 1, 2 and 3 of the 1922 Constitution, which describe Latvia as an independent and sovereign state, and Article 6, which states that the legislature (the Saeima) is elected by universal, equal, direct and secret vote, on the basis of proportional representation. On 6 July 1993 the 1922 Constitution was fully restored by the Saeima, following its election on 5 and 6 June. A summary of the Constitution's main provisions (including amendments adopted since its restoration) is given below.

BASIC PROVISIONS

Latvia is an independent, democratic republic, in which the sovereign power of the State belongs to the people. The territory of the Republic of Latvia comprises the provinces of Vidzeme, Latgale, Kurzeme and Zemgale, within the boundaries stipulated by international treaties.

THE SAEIMA

The Saeima (Parliament) comprises 100 representatives of the people and, according to a constitutional amendment adopted in December 1997, is elected by universal, equal, direct and secret vote, on the basis of proportional representation, for a period of four years. All Latvian citizens who have attained 18 years of age are entitled to vote and are eligible for election to the Saeima.

The Saeima elects a Board, which consists of the Chairperson, two Deputies, and Secretaries. The Board convenes the sessions of the Saeima and decrees regular and extraordinary sittings. The sessions of the Saeima are public (sittings *in camera* are held only by special request).

The right of legislation belongs to both the Saeima and the people. Draft laws may be presented to the Saeima by the President of the Republic, the Cabinet of Ministers, the Committees of the Saeima, no fewer than five members of the Saeima, or, in special cases, by one-tenth of the electorate. Before the commencement of each financial year, the Saeima approves the state budget, the draft of which is submitted by the Cabinet of Ministers. The Saeima decides on the strength of the armed forces during peacetime. The ratification of the Saeima is indispensable to all international agreements dealing with issues resolved by legislation.

THE PRESIDENT OF THE REPUBLIC

According to a constitutional amendment adopted by the Saeima in December 1997, the President of the Republic is elected by a secret ballot of the Saeima for a period of four years. At least 51 deputies must vote for the winning candidate. No person of less than 40 years of age may be elected President of the Republic. The office of President is not compatible with any other office, and the President may serve for no longer than two consecutive terms.

The President represents the State in an international capacity; he or she appoints Latvian representatives abroad, and receives representatives of foreign states accredited to Latvia; implements the decisions of the Saeima concerning the ratification of international treaties; is Head of the Armed Forces; appoints a Commander-in-Chief in time of war; and has the power to declare war on the basis of a decision of the Saeima.

The President has the right to pardon criminals serving penal sentences; to convene extraordinary meetings of the Cabinet of Ministers for the discussion of an agenda prepared by him or her, and to preside over such meetings; and to propose the dissolution of the Saeima.

The President may be held criminally accountable with the agreement of the Saeima by a majority vote of no fewer than two-thirds of its members.

THE CABINET OF MINISTERS

The Cabinet comprises the Prime Minister and the ministers nominated by him/her. This task is entrusted to the Prime Minister by the President of the Republic. All state administrative institutions are subordinate to the Cabinet, which, in turn, is accountable to the Saeima. If the Saeima adopts a vote expressing 'no confidence' in the Prime Minister, the entire Cabinet must resign. The Cabinet discusses all draft laws presented by the ministries as well as issues concerning the activities of the ministries. If the State is threatened by foreign invasion or if events endangering the existing order of the State arise, the Cabinet has the right to proclaim a state of emergency.

THE JUDICIARY

All citizens are equal before the law and the courts. Judges are independent and bound only by law. The appointment of judges is confirmed by the Saeima. Judges may be dismissed from office against their will only by a decision of the Supreme Court. The retiring age for judges is stipulated by law. Judgment may be passed solely by institutions that have been so empowered by law and in such a manner as specified by law. A Constitutional Court was established in 1996 to examine the legality of legislation.

The Government

HEAD OF STATE

President: VALDIS ZATLERS (inaugurated 8 July 2007).

CABINET OF MINISTERS
(April 2009)

A coalition of New Era (JL), the People's Party (TP), the Greens' and Farmers' Union (ZZS), the For Fatherland and Freedom Union/Latvian National Independence Movement (TB/LNNK) and the Civic Union (PS).

Prime Minister, Minister of Children, the Family and Social Integration: VALDIS DOMBROVSKIS (JL).
Minister of Defence: IMANTS VIESTURS LIEĢIS (Independent).
Minister of Foreign Affairs: MĀRIS RIEKSTIŅŠ (TP).
Minister of the Economy: ARTIS KAMPARS (JL).
Minister of Finance: EINARS REPŠE (JL).
Minister of the Interior: LINDA MŪRNIECE (JL).
Minister of Education and Science: TATJANA KOĶE (ZZS).
Minister of Culture: INTS DĀLDERIS (Independent).
Minister of Welfare: ULDIS AUGULIS (ZZS).
Minister of Regional Development and Local Government: EDGARS ZALĀNS (TP).
Minister of Transport: KASPARS GERHARDS (TB/LNNK).
Minister of Justice: MAREKS SEGLIŅŠ (TP).
Minister of Health: IVARS EGLĪTIS (TP).
Minister of the Environment: RAIMONDS VĒJONIS (ZZS).
Minister of Agriculture: JĀNIS DŪKLAVS (Independent).

MINISTRIES

Chancery of the President: Pils lauk. 3, Rīga 1900; tel. 6709-2106; fax 6709-2157; e-mail chancery@president.lv; internet www.president.lv.

Office of the Cabinet of Ministers: Brīvības bulv. 36, Rīga 1520; tel. 6708-2800; fax 6728-0469; e-mail vk@mk.gov.lv; internet www.mk.gov.lv.

Ministry of Agriculture: Republikas lauk. 2, Rīga 1981; tel. 6702-7010; fax 6702-7512; e-mail zm@zm.gov.lv; internet www.zm.gov.lv.

Ministry of Children, the Family and Social Integration: Zigfrida Annas Meierovica bulv. 14, Rīga 1050; tel. 6735-6497; fax 6735-6464; e-mail pasts@bm.gov.lv; internet www.bm.gov.lv.

Ministry of Culture: K. Valdemāra iela 11A, Rīga 1364; tel. 6707-8110; fax 6707-8107; e-mail info@km.gov.lv; internet www.km.gov.lv.

Ministry of Defence: K. Valdemāra iela 10–12, Rīga 1473; tel. 6721-0124; fax 6721-2307; e-mail kanceleja@mod.gov.lv; internet www.mod.gov.lv.

Ministry of the Economy: Brīvības iela 55, Rīga 1519; tel. 6701-3101; fax 6728-0882; e-mail pasts@em.gov.lv; internet www.em.gov.lv.

Ministry of Education and Science: Vaļņu iela 2, Rīga 1050; tel. 6704-7810; fax 6722-3905; e-mail tatjana.koke@izm.gov.lv; internet www.izm.gov.lv.

Ministry of the Environment: Peldu iela 25, Rīga 1494; tel. 6702-6448; fax 6782-0442; e-mail pasts@vidm.gov.lv; internet www.vidm.gov.lv.

Ministry of Finance: Smilšu iela 1, Rīga 1919; tel. 6709-5405; fax 6709-5503; e-mail info@fm.gov.lv; internet www.fm.gov.lv.

LATVIA

Ministry of Foreign Affairs: K. Valdemāra iela 3, Rīga 1395; tel. 6701-6201; fax 6782-8121; e-mail mfa.cha@mfa.gov.lv; internet www.mfa.gov.lv.

Ministry of Health: Brīvības iela 72, Rīga 1011; tel. 6787-6000; fax 6787-6002; e-mail vm@vm.gov.lv; internet www.vm.gov.lv.

Ministry of the Interior: Čiekurkalna 1, līnija 1, korp. 2, Rīga 1026; tel. 6721-9263; fax 6782-9686; e-mail kanceleja@iem.gov.lv; internet www.iem.gov.lv.

Ministry of Justice: Brīvības bulv. 36, Rīga 1536; tel. 6703-6801; fax 6728-5575; e-mail info@tm.gov.lv; internet www.tm.gov.lv.

Ministry of Regional Development and Local Government: Lāčplēša iela 27, Rīga 1011; tel. 6777-0401; fax 6777-0479; e-mail pasts@raplm.gov.lv; internet www.raplm.gov.lv.

Ministry of Transport: Gogoļa iela 3, Rīga 1743; tel. 6702-8205; fax 6721-7180; e-mail sat_m@sam.gov.lv; internet www.sam.gov.lv.

Ministry of Welfare: Skolas iela 28, Rīga 1331; tel. 6702-1600; fax 6727-6445; e-mail lm@lm.gov.lv; internet www.lm.gov.lv.

President

In voting by members of the Saiema (Parliament), conducted on 31 May 2007, VALDIS ZATLERS was elected President, obtaining 58 votes, defeating AIVARS ENDZIŅŠ, who received 39 votes.

Legislature

Saeima
(Parliament)

Jekaba iela 11, Rīga 1811; tel. 6708-7111; fax 6708-7100; e-mail web@saeima.lv; internet www.saeima.lv.

Chairman: GUNDARS DAUDZE.

General Election, 7 October 2006

Parties and coalitions	Votes	%	Seats
People's Party	177,481	19.55	23
Greens' and Farmers' Union*	151,595	16.70	18
New Era	148,602	16.37	18
Harmony Centre†	130,887	14.42	17
Latvian First Party and Latvian Way	77,869	8.58	10
For Fatherland and Freedom Union/ Latvian National Independence Movement	62,989	6.94	8
For Human Rights in a United Latvia	54,684	6.02	6
Others	97,558	10.75	—
Total‡	907,640	100.00	100

* Comprising the Latvian Green Party and the Centre Party Latvian Farmers' Union.
† Coalition comprising the People's Harmony Party and the New Centre.
‡ Including 5,975 invalid votes (0.66% of the total).

Election Commission

Central Election Commission (Centrālā vēlēšanu komisija—CVK): Smilšu iela 4, Rīga 1050; tel. 6732-2688; fax 6732-5251; e-mail cvk@cvk.lv; internet web.cvk.lv; Chair. ARNIS CIMDARS.

Political Organizations

There were some 69 political organizations registered in Latvia in January 2005. The following were among the most influential in mid-2008:

Centre Party Latvian Farmers' Union (CP LZS) (Centriskā partija Latvijas Zemnieku savienība): Republikas lauk. 2, Rīga 1010; tel. 6702-7163; fax 6702-7467; e-mail lzs@latnet.lv; internet www.lzs.lv; f. 1990; rural, centrist; contested 2002 and 2006 legislative elections as mem. of Greens' and Farmers' Union; Chair. AUGUSTS BRIGMANIS.

Civic Union (PS) (Pilsoniskā savienība): Arsenāla ielā 3, Rīga 1050; tel. 2928-9491; e-mail birojs@pilsoniska-savieniba.lv; internet pilsoniska-savieniba.lv; f. 2008; Chair. SANDRA KALNIETE.

For Fatherland and Freedom Union/Latvian National Independence Movement (TB/LNNK) (Apvienība 'Tēvzemei un Brīvībai'/Latvijas Nacionālās Neatkarības Kustība): Jēkaba iela 20/22–9, Rīga 1050; tel. and fax 6721-6762; e-mail tb@tb.lv; internet www.tb.lv; f. 1997 by merger; Chair. ROBERTS ZĪLE.

For Human Rights in a United Latvia (PCTVL/ZaPChEL) (Par cilvēka tiesībām vienotā Latvijā/ Za prava cheloveka v yedinoi Latvii): Rūpniecības iela 9, Rīga 1010; tel. and fax 6732-0290; e-mail info@zapchel.lv; internet www.pctvl.lv; f. 1998 as electoral alliance; became united party Nov. 2003; represents interests of Russian-speaking communities in Latvia; opposed to Latvian membership of NATO; Leaders TATJANA ŽDANOKA, JAKOVS PLINERS, JURIS SOKOLOVSKIS.

Harmony Centre (SC) (Saskaņas Centrs/ Tsentr soglasiya): Rīga; tel. 6921-8855; internet www.saskanascentrs.lv; f. 2005 as electoral alliance of the National Harmony Party, Latvian Socialist Party (LSP), New Centre and Daugavpils City Party; officially merged Dec. 2006 (excl. LSP, which remained affil.); Chair. NILS UŠAKOVS.

Latvian First Party/Latvian Way (LPP/LC) (Latvijas Pirmā Partija/Latvijas ceļš): Elizabetes iela 2, Rīga 1050; tel. 6722-6070; fax 6722-6831; e-mail info@lpplc.lv; internet www.lpplc.lv; f. Aug. 2007 by merger of Latvian First Party (f. 2002) and Latvian Way (f. 1993); contested Oct. 2006 elections as a political union; Christian democratic; Co-Chair. AINĀRS ŠLESERS, IVARS GODMANIS.

Latvian Green Party (LZP) (Latvijas Zaļā partija): Kalnciema iela 30, Rīga 1046; tel. and fax 6761-4272; e-mail birojs@zp.lv; internet www.zp.lv; f. 1990; forms part of the Greens' and Farmers' Union; Co-Chair. VIESTURS SILENIEKS, RAIMONDS VĒJONIS.

Latvian Social Democratic Workers' Party (LSDSP) (Latvijas Sociāl-demokrātiskā strādnieku partija): Aldaru iela 8, Rīga 1050; tel. 6735-6585; fax 6735-6588; e-mail lsdsp@lis.lv; internet www.lsdsp.lv; f. 1904; Chair. JĀNIS DINEVIČS.

Latvian Socialist Party (LSP) (Latvijas Sociālistiskā partija/ Sotsialisticheskaya partiya Latvii): Burtnieku iela 23, Rīga; tel. and fax 6755-5535; internet www.latsocpartija.lv; f. 1994; mem. of the For Human Rights in a United Latvia bloc in 1998–2003; joined the Harmony Centre alliance in Dec. 2005, remained affil. to Harmony Centre; Chair. ALFRĒDS RUBIKS.

New Era (JL) (Jaunais laiks): Jēkaba Kazarmās, Torņa iela 4/3B, Rīga 1050; tel. 6720-5472; fax 6720-5473; e-mail birojs@jaunaislaiks.lv; internet www.jaunaislaiks.lv; f. 2002; right-wing; Leaders SOLVITA ĀBOLTIŅA, ARTIS KAMPARS; Sec.-Gen. ĒRIKS ŠKAPARS.

People's Party (TP) (Tautas partija): Dzirnavu iela 68, Rīga; tel. 6728-6441; fax 6728-6405; e-mail info@tautaspartija.lv; internet www.tautaspartija.lv; f. 1998; Chair. ATIS SLAKTERIS.

Diplomatic Representation

EMBASSIES IN LATVIA

Austria: Elizabetes iela 15, Rīga 1010; tel. 6721-6125; fax 6721-6126; e-mail riga-ob@bmeia.gv.at; Ambassador HERMINE POPPELLER.

Azerbaijan: Raiņa bulv. 2–5, Rīga 1050; tel. 6714-2889; fax 6714-2896; e-mail office@azembassy.lv; f. 2005; Ambassador TOFIQ N. ZULFUGAROV.

Belarus: Jēzusbaznīcas iela 12, Rīga 1050; tel. 6722-2560; fax 6732-2891; e-mail latvia@belembassy.org; internet belembassy.org/latvia; Ambassador ALYAKSANDR GERASIMENKA.

Belgium: Alberta iela 13, Rīga 1010; tel. 6711-4852; fax 6711-4855; e-mail riga@diplobel.be; internet www.diplomatie.be/riga; f. 2004; Ambassador LEOPOLD MERCKX.

Canada: Baznicas iela 20–22, Rīga 1010; tel. 6781-3945; fax 6781-3960; e-mail rigag@international.gc.ca; internet www.latvia.gc.ca; Ambassador SCOTT HEATHERINGTON.

China, People's Republic: Ganību dambis 5, Rīga 1045; tel. 6735-7023; fax 6735-7025; e-mail chinaemb_lv@mfa.gov.cn; internet lv.chineseembassy.org; Ambassador CHENG WENJU.

Czech Republic: Elizabetes iela 29A, Rīga 1010; tel. 6721-7814; fax 6721-7821; e-mail riga@embassy.mzv.cz; internet www.mfa.cz/riga; Ambassador TOMÁŠ PŠTROSS.

Denmark: Pils iela 11, Rīga 1863; tel. 6722-6210; fax 6722-9218; e-mail rixamb@um.dk; internet www.ambriga.um.dk; Ambassador UFFE OTTO WOLFFHECHEL.

Estonia: Skolas iela 13, Rīga 1010; tel. 6781-2020; fax 6781-2029; e-mail embassy.riga@mfa.ee; internet www.estemb.lv; Ambassador JAAK JÕERÜÜT.

Finland: Kalpaka bulv. 1, Rīga 1605; tel. 6707-8800; fax 6707-8814; e-mail sanomat.rii@formin.fi; internet www.finland.lv; Ambassador MARIA SERENIUS.

France: Raiņa bulv. 9, Rīga 1050; tel. 6703-6600; fax 6703-6615; e-mail webmastre.ambafrance-lv@diplomatie.gouv.fr; internet www.ambafrance-lv.org; Ambassador PASCAL FIESCHI.

LATVIA

Georgia: Raiņa bulv. 3/2, Rīga 1050; tel. and fax 6721-3136; e-mail riga.emb@mfa.gov.ge; internet www.latvia.mfa.gov.ge; Ambassador KONSTANTIN KORKELIA.

Germany: Raiņa bulv. 13, Rīga 1050; tel. 6708-5100; fax 6708-5149; e-mail info@riga.diplo.de; internet www.riga.diplo.de; Ambassador DETLEF WEIGEL.

Greece: Elizabetes iela 11/5, Rīga 1010; tel. 6735-6345; fax 6735-6351; e-mail greekemb-riga@mfa.gr; Ambassador CHRYSANTHIE PANAYOTOPOULOU.

Hungary: Alberta iela 4, Rīga 1010; tel. 6721-7500; fax 6721-7878; e-mail mission.rix@kum.hu; internet www.mfa.gov.hu/emb/riga; Ambassador Dr ISTVÁN MOHÁCSI.

Ireland: Alberta iela 13, Rīga 1010; tel. 6703-9370; fax 6703-9371; e-mail rigaembassy@dfa.ie; internet www.embassyofireland.lv; Ambassador TIM MAWE.

Israel: Elizabetes iela 2, Rīga 1010; tel. 6732-0739; fax 6783-0170; e-mail press@rig.mfa.gov.il; internet riga.mfa.gov.il; Ambassador CHEN IVRI APTER.

Italy: Teātra iela 9, Rīga 1050; tel. 6721-6069; fax 6721-6084; e-mail ambitalia.riga@apollo.lv; internet www.ambriga.esteri.it; Ambassador FRANCESCO PUCCIO.

Japan: K. Valdemāra iela 21, Rīga 1010; tel. 6781-2001; fax 6781-2004; e-mail eoj@latnet.lv; Ambassador TAKASHI OSANAI.

Lithuania: Rūpniecības iela 24, Rīga 1010; tel. 6732-1519; fax 6732-1589; e-mail lt@apollo.lv; internet lv.mfa.lt; Ambassador ANTANAS VALIONIS.

Moldova: Zigfrīda Annas Meierovica bulv. 14, Rīga 1050; tel. 6735-9160; fax 6735-9165; e-mail riga@moldovaembassy.lv; Ambassador EDUARD MELNIC.

Netherlands: Torņu iela 4, Jēkaba Kazarmas 1A, Rīga 1050; tel. 6732-6147; fax 6732-6151; e-mail nedamb@apollo.lv; internet www.netherlandsembassy.lv; Ambassador JURRIAAN KRAAK.

Norway: Zirgu iela 14, POB 181, Rīga 1050; tel. 6781-4100; fax 6781-4108; e-mail emb.riga@mfa.no; internet www.norvegija.lv; Ambassador NILS OLAV STAVA.

Poland: Mednieku iela 6B, Rīga 1010; tel. 6703-1500; fax 6703-1549; e-mail ambpol@apollo.lv; internet www.ryga.polemb.net; Ambassador MACIEJ KLIMCZAK.

Portugal: Balasta Dambis 60, Oglu iela, Ķīpsala, Rīga 1048; tel. 6782-1926; fax 6767-1626; e-mail embporturiga@gmail.com; Ambassador JOÃO LUIS NIZA PINHEIRO.

Russia: Antonijas iela 2, Rīga 1010; tel. 6733-2151; fax 6783-0209; e-mail rusembas@delfi.lv; internet www.latvia.mid.ru; Ambassador ALEKSANDR A. VESHNYAKOV.

Slovakia: Smilšu iela 8, Rīga 1050; tel. 6781-4280; fax 6781-4290; e-mail embassy@riga.mfa.sk; internet www.mzv.sk/riga; Ambassador IVAN ŠPILDA.

Spain: Elizabetes iela 11, 3rd Floor, Rīga 1010; tel. 6732-0281; fax 6732-5005; e-mail emb.riga@maec.es; internet www.maec.es/Embajadas/Riga; Ambassador PAULINO GONZÁLEZ FERNÁNDEZ-CORUGEDO.

Sweden: A. Pumpura iela 8, Rīga 1010; tel. 6768-6600; fax 6768-6601; e-mail ambassaden.riga@foreign.ministry.se; internet www.swedenemb.lv; Ambassador MATS STAFFANSSON.

Switzerland: World Trade Centre, Elizabetes iela 2, Rīga 1340; tel. 6733-8351; fax 6733-8354; e-mail rig.vertretung@eda.admin.ch; internet www.eda.admin.ch/riga; Ambassador GABRIELA NÜTZI SULPIZIO.

Turkey: A. Pumpura iela 2, Rīga 1010; tel. 6782-1600; fax 6732-0334; e-mail turkishembassy.riga@gmail.com; Ambassador DURAY POLAT.

Ukraine: Kalpaka bulv. 3, Rīga 1010; tel. 6724-3082; fax 6732-5583; e-mail emb_lv@mfa.gov.ua; internet www.mfa.gov.ua/latvia; Ambassador RAUL SH. CHILACHAVA.

United Kingdom: J. Alunāna iela 5, Rīga 1010; tel. 6777-4700; fax 6777-4707; e-mail british.embassy@apollo.lv; internet ukinlatvia.fco.gov.uk; Ambassador RICHARD MOON.

USA: Raiņa bulv. 7, Rīga 1510; tel. 6703-6200; fax 6782-0047; e-mail pas@usembassy.lv; internet riga.usembassy.gov; Chargé d'affaires BRUCE DAVID ROGERS.

Uzbekistan: Elizabetes iela 11/11, Rīga 1010; tel. 6732-2424; fax 6732-2306; e-mail posoluz@apollo.lv; Ambassador KOBILJON S. NAZAROV.

Judicial System

Constitutional Court (Latvijas Republikas Satversmes tiesa): J. Alunāna iela 1, Rīga 1010; tel. 6721-0274; fax 6783-0770; e-mail tiesa@satv.tiesa.gov.lv; internet www.satv.tiesa.gov.lv; f. 1996; comprises seven judges, appointed by the Saeima for a term of 10 years; Chair. GUNĀRS KŪTRIS.

Supreme Court (Latvijas Republikas Augstākā tiesa): Brīvības bulv. 36, Rīga 1511; tel. 6702-0350; fax 6702-0351; e-mail at@at.gov.lv; internet www.at.gov.lv; Chair. IVARS BIČKOVIČS.

Office of the Prosecutor-General: Kalpaka bulv. 6, Rīga 1801; tel. 6704-4400; fax 6704-4449; e-mail una.brenca@lrp.gov.lv; internet www.lrp.gov.lv; Prosecutor-General JĀNIS MAIZĪTIS.

Religion

From the 16th century the traditional religion of the Latvians was Lutheran Christian, although there remained a substantial Roman Catholic population. Russian Orthodoxy is the religion of much of the Slavic population. During the period of Soviet rule many places of religious worship were closed. Following the restoration of independence in 1991, religious organizations regained their legal rights and property. In 2004 the statutes of 1,122 religious congregations were registered, of which 304 were Lutheran, 251 Roman Catholic, 118 Orthodox, 93 Baptist, 48 Pentecostal, 67 Old Believer, 50 Adventist, 34 evangelical Christian, 12 Methodist, 13 Jewish and 13 Muslim.

Board of Religious Affairs: Pils lauk. 4, Rīga 1050; tel. 6722-0585; e-mail zlp@zlp.gov.lv; f. 2000; govt agency, attached to the Ministry of Justice; Principal IRETA ROMANOVSKA.

CHRISTIANITY
Protestant Churches

Evangelical Lutheran Church of Latvia: M. Pils iela 4, Rīga 1050; tel. 6722-6057; fax 6782-0041; e-mail konsistorija@lutheran.lv; internet www.lutheran.lv; f. 1922; Archbishop JĀNIS VANAGS.

Latvian Conference of Seventh-day Adventists in Latvia: Baznīcas iela 12A, Rīga 1010; tel. and fax 6724-0013; e-mail viesturs@baznica.lv; internet www.adventistu.baznica.lv; f. 1920; Pres. of Council VIESTURS REĶIS.

Latvian Pentecostal Union: J. Asara iela 8, Jelgava 3001; tel. 6308-1401; fax 6308-1407; e-mail lvdaddf@hotmail.com; f. 1989; Bishop JĀNIS OZOLINKEVIČS.

Union of Baptist Churches in Latvia: Lāčplēša iela 37, Rīga 1011; tel. and fax 6722-3379; internet www.lbds.lv; f. 1860; Bishop Dr PĒTERIS SPROĢIS.

United Methodist Church in Latvia: Klaipēdas iela 56, Liepāja 3401; tel. 6343-2161; fax 6346-9848; re-est. 1991; Supt ĀRIJS VĪKSNA.

The Roman Catholic Church

Latvia comprises one archdiocese and three dioceses. At 31 December 2006 there were an estimated 435,107 adherents in the country (equivalent to 18.9% of the population).

Bishops' Conference

M. Pils iela 2A, Rīga 1050; tel. 6722-7266; fax 6722-0775; Pres. Cardinal JĀNIS PUJATS.

Archbishop of Rīga: Cardinal JĀNIS PUJATS, M. Pils iela 2A, Rīga 1050; tel. 6722-7266; fax 6722-0775; e-mail curia@e-apollo.lv; internet www.catholic.lv.

The Orthodox Church

Although the Latvian Orthodox Church has close ties with the Moscow Patriarchate, it has administrative independence.

Latvian Orthodox Church (Moscow Patriarchate): Pils iela 14, Rīga 1050; tel. 6722-5855; fax 6722-4345; e-mail sinode@orthodoxy.lv; internet www.pareizticiba.lv; f. 1850; Metropolitan of Rīga and all Latvia ALEKSANDR (KUDRJASHOV).

Latvian Old Believer (Old Ritualist) Pomor Church: Krasta iela 73, Rīga 1003; tel. 6711-3083; fax 6714-4513; e-mail oldbel@junik.lv; f. 1760 in split from Moscow Patriarchate; Head of Central Council IVANS MIZOĻUBOVS.

JUDAISM

Jewish Religious Community of Rīga: Peitavas iela 6/8, Rīga 1050; tel. 6722-4549; f. 1764; Rabbi NATAN BARKAN.

The Press

The joint-stock company Preses nams (Press House—q.v.) is the leading publisher of newspapers and magazines in Latvia. In 2002 there were eight daily newspapers, with an average circulation of 183,000. In 2006 a total of 248 daily and non-daily newspapers and

LATVIA

387 other periodicals were published. The publications listed below are in Latvian, unless otherwise indicated.

DAILIES

Bizness & Baltiya (Business and the Baltics): K. Valdemāra iela 149, Rīga 1013; tel. 6703-3011; fax 6703-3010; e-mail media@bb.lv; internet www.bb.lv; f. 1991; 5 a week; in Russian; Editor-in-Chief YURII ALEKSEYEV; circ. 12,000 (2007).

Chas (Hour): Peldu iela 15, Rīga 1050; tel. 6708-8712; fax 6721-1067; internet www.chas-daily.com; f. 1997; in Russian; Editor-in-Chief VALERY ZAITSEV; circ. 16,050 (weekdays), 22,000 (Saturdays).

Diena (Day): Mūkusalas iela 15, Rīga 1004; tel. 6706-3100; fax 6706-3169; e-mail diena@diena.lv; internet www.diena.lv; f. 1990; social and political issues; associated with free newspaper *5min*, launched in Sept. 2005; Editor-in-Chief SARMĪTE ĒLERTE; circ. 62,000.

Jaunā Avīze: Rīga; tel. 6724-2437; e-mail ja@parks.lv.

Neatkarīgā Rīta Avīze (Independent Morning Paper): Balasta dambis 3, Rīga 1081; tel. 6706-2462; fax 6706-2465; e-mail redakcija@nra.lv; internet www.nra.lv; f. 1990; Editor-in-Chief ALDIS BĒRZIŅŠ; circ. 40,000.

Rīgas Balss (RB) (Voice of Rīga): Rīga; tel. 6706-2420; fax 6706-2400; e-mail balss@rb.lv; internet www.rigasbalss.lv; f. 1957; city evening newspaper; Editor-in-Chief IVETA MEDIŅA; circ. 18,100 (Mon.–Thur.), 42,700 (Fri.).

Vakara Ziņas (The Evening News): Bezdelīgas iela 12, Rīga 1007; tel. 6761-7595; fax 6761-2383; e-mail vakara.zinas@vz.lv; internet www.vz.lv; f. 1993; popular; Editor-in-Chief AINĀRS VLADIMIROVS; circ. 53,000.

Vesti Segodnya (News Today): Mūkusalas iela 41, Rīga 1004; tel. 6706-3230; fax 6706-3232; e-mail sm@fenster.lv; in Russian; Editor-in-Chief ALEKSANDRS BĻINOVS; circ. 24,000.

OTHER NEWSPAPERS

The Baltic Times: Rupniecības iela 1–5, Rīga 1010; tel. 6722-9978; fax 6722-6041; e-mail office@baltictimes.com; internet www.baltictimes.com; f. 1996; news from Estonia, Latvia and Lithuania; in English; Man. Dir VERA ĻIOLE; Editor-in-Chief STEVE ROMAN; circ. 12,000 (2007).

Dienas Bizness (Daily Business): Balasta dambis 3, POB 2, Rīga 1081; tel. 6706-2622; fax 6706-2309; e-mail nberch@db.lv; internet www.db.lv; f. 1992; Editor-in-Chief JURIS PAIDERS; circ. 17,000.

Ieva (Eve): Stabu iela 34, Rīga 1011; tel. 6700-6102; fax 6700-6111; e-mail ieva@santa.lv; f. 1997; weekly; illustrated journal for women; Editor-in-Chief INGA GORBUNOVA; circ. 73,650.

Izglītība un Kultūra (Education and Culture): Palasta iela 10, Rīga 1502; tel. 6735-7585; fax 6735-7584; e-mail info@izglitiba-kultura.lv; internet www.izglitiba-kultura.lv; f. 1948; Editor ANITA KALMANE.

Latvijas Avīze (Latvian Newspaper): Dzirnavu iela 21, Rīga 1010; tel. 6709-6600; fax 6709-6645; e-mail mlredaktors@la.lv; internet www.la.lv; f. 1988; fmrly *Lauku Avīze* (Country Newspaper); present name adopted 2004; 3 a week; popular; agriculture, politics and sport; Editor-in-Chief LINDA RASA; circ. 59,500.

Latvijas Vēstnesis (Latvian Herald): Bruņinieku iela 36/2, Rīga 1011; tel. 6729-8833; fax 6729-9410; e-mail redakcija@lv.lv; internet www.lza.lv.htm; f. 1993; official newspaper; 4 a week; Editor-in-Chief OSKARS GERTS; circ. 3,500.

Privātā Dzīve (Private Life): Stabu iela 34, Rīga 1011; tel. 6700-6104; fax 6700-6111; e-mail pdz@santa.lv; weekly; Editor-in-Chief SANDIJA ŠĶĒLE; circ. 76,000.

Rīgas Viļņi (Riga Waves): Bruņinieku iela 49, korp. 3, Rīga 1011; tel. 6784-2577; fax 6784-2578; e-mail info@rigasvilni.lv; internet www.rigasvilni.lv; weekly.

PRINCIPAL PERIODICALS

Baltiskii Kurs/The Baltic Course: Rīga; tel. 6738-9694; fax 6738-9696; e-mail baltkurs@baltkurs.com; internet www.baltkurs.com; f. 1996; quarterly; business; in Russian and English; Int. Editor EUGENE ETERIS; Editor-in-Chief OLGA PAVUK.

Daugava: Rīga; tel. 6728-0290; e-mail ravdin@mailbox.riga.lv; f. 1977; 6 a year; literary journal; Editor-in-Chief ZHANNA EZIT; circ. 500.

Karogs (Banner): Kuršu iela 24, Rīga 1006; tel. 6755-4145; fax 6755-4146; e-mail karogs@apollo.lv; f. 1940; literary monthly; Editor-in-Chief IEVA KOLMANE; circ. 1,500.

Klubs (Club): Rīga; tel. 6746-4420; fax 6746-1438; e-mail klubs@santa.lv; f. 1994; monthly; politics, business, fashion; Editor-in-Chief JURIS SLEIERS; circ. 18,000.

Latvijas Ekonomists: Ieriķu ielā 67A, Rīga 1084; tel. 6703-1090; e-mail birojs@ekonomists.lv; internet www.ekonomists.lv; f. 1992; monthly; in Latvian and Russian; Dir INESE LAPIŅA.

Māksla Plus (M+): Akadēmijas lauk. 1, a.k. 41, Rīga 1027; tel. 6722-0722; fax 6782-0608; e-mail makslaplus@inbox.com; internet www.makslaplus.lv; cultural magazine (cinema, music, theatre, photography); Editor-in-Chief SANITA BUČINIECE.

Mans Mazais: Balasta dambis 3, Rīga 1081; tel. 6762-8274; fax 6246-5450; e-mail mansmazais@santa.lv; f. 1994; monthly; illustrated journal for young parents; Editor-in-Chief VITA BEĻAUNIECE; circ. 20,000.

Mūsmājas (Our Home): Rīga; tel. 6727-3311; fax 6729-2701; e-mail pasts@mgtops.lv; internet www.musmajas.lv; f. 1993; monthly; home and family magazine; Editor-in-Chief ILZE STRAUTIŅA; circ. 50,000.

Mūzikas Saule (Musical Sun): Arhitektu 1–305, Rīga 1050; tel. 6722-0161; fax 6957-7765; internet www.m-saule.lv; music; Editor-in-Chief IEVA ROZENTĀLE.

Rīgas Laiks (Rīga Times): Lāčplēša iela 25, Rīga 1011; tel. 6728-7922; fax 6783-0542; e-mail pasts@rigaslaiks.lv; internet www.rigaslaiks.lv; f. 1993; monthly; Editor-in-Chief INESE ZANDERE; circ. 10,000.

Santa: Balasta dambis 3, POB 32, Rīga 1081; tel. 6762-8274; fax 6246-5450; e-mail santa@santa.lv; f. 1991; monthly; illustrated journal for women; Editor-in-Chief SANTA ANCHA; circ. 42,000.

Zinātnes Vēstnesis (Scientific Herald): Akadēmijas lauk. 1, Rīga 1524; tel. 6721-2706; fax 6782-1153; e-mail lza@lza.lv; internet www.lza.lv/zv00.htm; f. 1989; published by the Latvian Scientific Council, the Latvian Academy of Science and the Latvian Society of Scientists; two a month; Editor-in-Chief ZAIGA KIPERE.

NEWS AGENCIES

Baltic News Service: Dzirnavu iela 57A, Rīga 1010; tel. 6708-8600; fax 6708-8601; internet www.bns.lv; f. 1990; news from Latvia, Lithuania, Estonia and the CIS; in English, Russian and the Baltic languages; Dir SIGITA KIRILKA.

LETA Latvian News Agency: Palasta iela 10, Rīga 1502; tel. 6722-2509; fax 6722-3850; e-mail leta.marketing@leta.lv; internet www.leta.lv; independent; Chair. MĀRTIŅŠ BARKĀNS.

PRESS ASSOCIATION

Latvian Journalists' Union (Latvijas Žurnālistu savienība): K. Valdemāra iela 118–211, Rīga 1013; tel. and fax 6721-1433; e-mail zurnalistusavieniba@e-apollo.lv; internet www.zurnalistusavieniba.lv; f. 1992; 600 mems; Pres. JURIS PAIDERS.

Publishers

Izdevniecība AGB (AGB Publishing House): K. Barona iela 31, Rīga 1011; tel. 6728-0464; fax 6728-0356; e-mail info@izdevnieciba.com; internet www.izdevnieciba.com.

Avots (Spring): Puskina iela 1A, Rīga 1050; tel. 6721-1394; fax 6722-5824; e-mail avots@apollo.lv; f. 1980; non-fiction, dictionaries, crafts, hobbies, etc.; Pres. JĀNIS LEJA.

Elpa (Breath): Doma lauk. 1, Rīga 1050; tel. 6721-1776; fax 6722-6497; e-mail elpa@apollo.lv; f. 1990; books and newspapers; Pres. MAIRITA SOLIMA.

Jāņa sēta: Elizabetes iela 83–85, Rīga 1050; tel. 6709-2290; fax 6709-2292; e-mail janaseta@janaseta.lv; internet www.janaseta.lv; f. 1991; travel and culinary books; Dir AIVARS ZVIRBULIS.

Jumava: Dzirnavu iela 73, Rīga 1011; tel. and fax 6728-0314; e-mail jumava@parks.lv; internet www.jumava.lv; f. 1994; translations, dictionaries, fiction, etc.; Pres. JURIS VISOCKIS.

Kontinents: Elijas iela 17, Rīga 1050; tel. 6720-4130; fax 6720-4129; e-mail kontinent@ml.lv; internet www.kontinents.lv; f. 1991; translated fiction, non-fiction and colour children's books; Chair. of Bd OLEG MIHALEVICH.

Nordik: Daugavgrīvas 36–9, Rīga 1048; tel. 6760-2672; fax 6760-2818; e-mail nordik@nordik.lv; internet www.nordik.lv; f. 1992; sister co, Tapals, at same address; Dir JĀNIS JUŠKA; Editor-in-Chief IEVA JANAITE.

Preses nams (Press House): Balasta dambis 3, Rīga 1081; tel. 6246-5732; internet www.presesnams.lv; f. 1990; newspapers, magazines, encyclopedias and scientific literature; controlling interest owned by Ventspils Nafta; Dir EGONS LAPIŅŠ.

Smaile (Peak): Rīga; tel. 6731-5137; f. 1999; fiction, poetry, fine arts; Dir ANDREJS BRIMERBERGS.

Zinātne Publishers Ltd (Science): Akadēmijas lauk. 1, Rīga 1050; tel. 6721-2797; fax 6722-7825; e-mail zinatne@navigator.lv; f. 1951; non-fiction, text books, dictionaries, reference books; Dir INGRĪDA SEGLINA.

Zvaigzne ABC: K. Valdemāra iela 6, Rīga 1010; tel. 6750-8799; fax 6750-8798; e-mail info@zvaigzne.lv; internet www.zvaigzne.lv;

f. 1966; privately owned; educational literature, textbooks, dictionaries, non-fiction for children and adults, fiction; Head of Bd VIJA KILBLOKA.

PUBLISHERS' ASSOCIATION

Latvian Publishers' Asscn (Latvijas Grāmatizdevēju asociācija): Rīga; tel. 6728-2392; fax 6728-0549; e-mail lga@gramatizdeveji.lv; internet www.gramatizdeveji.lv; f. 1993; 40 mems; Pres. JĀNIS LEJA.

Broadcasting and Communications

TELECOMMUNICATIONS

In 2006 there were 657,000 main telephone lines in use; 69% of lines were digital in 2001. In 2005 there were four providers of mobile telecommunications services.

Regulatory Organizations

Dept of Communications (Ministry of Transport): Gogoļa iela 3, Rīga 1190; tel. 6724-2321; fax 6782-0636; e-mail diana.ainep@sam.gov.lv; f. 1991; Dir INĀRA RUDAKA.

Public Utilities Regulatory Commission (Sabiedrisko Pakalpojumu Regulēšanas Komisija): see Trade and Industry (Utilities) section.

Major Service Providers

Lattelecom SIA: Dzirnavu iela 105, Rīga 1011; tel. 6705-5222; fax 6705-5001; e-mail nils.melngailis@lattelecom.lv; internet www.lattelecom.lv; f. 1992; 49% owned by TeliaSonera AB (Sweden); CEO NILS MELNGAILIS; 3,000 employees.

Latvian Mobile Telephone Co (Latvijas Mobilais Telefons SIA—LMT): Ropazu iela 6, Rīga 1039; tel. 6777-3200; fax 6753-5353; e-mail info@lmt.lv; internet www.lmt.lv; f. 1992; 24.5% owned by Sonera Holding BV (Finland), 24.5% owned by TeliaSonera AB (Sweden), 23.0% owned by SIA Lattelekom, 23.0% owned by Digitālais Latvijas radio un televīzijas centrs; Gen. Man. JURIS BINDE.

SIA Radiokoms: Elizabetes iela 45–47, Rīga 1010; tel. 6733-3355; e-mail radiokoms@radiokoms.lv; internet www.radiokoms.lv; Dir JANA BALODE.

Tele2: Rīga; tel. 6706-0069; fax 6706-0176; internet www.tele2.lv; f. 1991; owned by Tele2 AB (Sweden); fmrly Baltkom GSM; Pres. BILL BUTLER; 110 employees.

BROADCASTING

Regulatory Organization

National Broadcasting Council of Latvia (Nacionālā Radio un Televizijas padome): Smilšu iela 1/3, Rīga 1939; tel. 6722-1848; fax 6722-0448; e-mail Zita.Janitena@nrtp.lv; internet www.nrtp.lv; f. 1995; Chair. AIVARS BERKIS.

Radio

Latvijas Radio (Latvian Radio): Doma lauk. 8, Rīga 1505; tel. 6720-6722; fax 6720-6709; e-mail radio@radio.org.lv; internet www.latvijasradio.lv; f. 1925; state-operated service; broadcasts in Latvian and Russian; Dir-Gen. AIGARS SEMEVICS (acting).

Alise Plus: Raiņa iela 28, Daugavpils 5403; e-mail radio@aliseplus.eu; internet www.aliseplus.eu; 24-hour transmissions in Russian and Latvian.

European Hit Radio: Elijas iela 17, Rīga 1050; tel. 6957-5757; fax 6720-4407; e-mail radio@superfm.lv; internet www.europeanhitradio.com; f. 1994; 24-hour transmissions in Latvian, Russian, Estonian, Lithuanian and English; Pres. UGIS POLIS; Dir RICHARD ZAKSS.

Latvijas Kristīgais Radio (Latvian Christian Radio): Lāčplēša iela 37, Rīga 1011; tel. 6721-3704; fax 6782-0633; e-mail lkr@lkr.lv; internet www.lkr.lv; f. 1993; 24-hour transmissions in Latvian and Russian.

Radio Ef-Ei: Atbrvōsanas aleja 98, Rēzekne 4600; e-mail efei@mailbox.riga.lv; 24-hour transmissions in Russian and Latvian.

Radio Imanta: Tērbatas iela 1, Valmiera 4201; tel. 6420-7349; fax 6420-7350; e-mail radio.imanta@tl.lv; internet www.radioimanta.lv; 24-hour transmissions in Russian and Latvian; Chief Editor NILS INTERBERGS.

Radio Mix FM: L. Nometņu iela 62, Rīga 1002; 24-hour transmissions in Russian.

Radio Sigulda: L. Paegles iela 3, Sigulda 2150; tel. 6797-2678; fax 6797-3786; e-mail mail@radiosigulda.lv; internet www.radiosigulda.lv; f. 1991; 24-hour transmissions in Latvian; music radio; Dir AIVARS PLUCIS.

Radio SWH: Skanstes iela 13, Rīga 1013; tel. 6737-0067; fax 6782-8283; e-mail radio@radioswh.lv; internet www.radioswh.lv; Pres. ZITMARS LIEPINSCH.

Radio Trīs: Vaļņu iela 5, Cēsis 4101; tel. 6412-4566; fax 6412-7041; e-mail radio@radio3.lv; internet www.radio3.lv; f. 1994; Di EGILS VISKRINTS.

Radio Zemgale: Grāfa lauk. 6, Lecava 3913; e-mail rz@apollo.lv; internet www.radiozemgalei.lv; f. 2000; 24-hour transmissions in Latvian; Dir DACE DUBKEVIČA.

Television

Latvijas Televīzija (Latvian Television): Zaķusalas krastmala 3, Rīga 1509; tel. 6720-0315; fax 6720-0025; internet www.ltv.lv; f. 1954; state-operated service; two channels in Latvian, LTV1 and LTV7 (LTV7 also includes programmes in Russian, English and French); Dir-Gen. EDGARS KOTS.

Latvijas Neatkariga Televizija (Latvian Independent Television—LNT): Elijas iela 17, Rīga 1050; tel. 6707-0200; fax 6782-1128; e-mail lnt@lnt.lv; internet www.lnt.lv; f. 1996; entertainment, news reports; Dir-Gen. ANDREJS ĒĶIS.

TV3 Latvia: Mūkusalas iela 72B, Rīga 1004; tel. 6762-9366; fax 6760-0599; e-mail tv3@tv3.lv; internet www.tv3.lv; owned by Modern Times Group–MTG (Sweden); affiliated with channel 3+, targeted at a Russian-speaking audience; Dir KASPARS OZOLINS.

Finance

(cap. = capital; res = reserves; dep. = deposits; m. = million; brs = branches; amounts in lats)

BANKING

Central Bank

Bank of Latvia (Latvijas Banka): K. Valdemāra iela 2A, Rīga 1050; tel. 6702-2300; fax 6702-2420; e-mail info@bank.lv; internet www.bank.lv; f. 1990; cap. 25.0m., res 94.0m., dep. 1,623.5m. (Dec. 2007); Gov. and Chair. of Council ILMĀRS RIMŠĒVIČS.

Commercial Banks

Aizkraukles Banka: Elizabetes iela 23, Rīga 1010; tel. 6777-5222; fax 6777-5200; e-mail bank@ab.lv; internet www.ab.lv; f. 1993; cap. 15.0m., res 43.1m., dep. 990.3m. (Dec. 2007); Chair. of Bd ALEKSANDRS BERGMANIS.

DnB Nord Banka Latvija: Smilšu iela 6, Rīga 1050; tel. 6701-5204; fax 6732-3449; e-mail office@dnbnord.lv; internet www.dnbnord.lv; f. 1989; fmrly Rīgas Komercbanka PLC and AS NORD/LB Latvija; 99.76% owned by Bank DnB NORD (Denmark); cap. 99.2m., res 24.3m., dep. 1,604.0m. (Dec. 2007); Pres. and Chair. of Bd ANDRIS OZOLINS; 10 brs.

GE Money Bank: 13 Janvāra iela 3, Rīga 1050; tel. 6702-4747; fax 6721-1985; e-mail info@gemoneybank.lv; internet www.gemoneybank.lv; f. 2008 by merger of Baltic Trust Bank—BTB and GE Money; 99.48% owned by Finstar Baltic Investments; cap. 15.6m., res 11.2m., dep. 238.7m. (Dec. 2007); Chair. IEVA RĀCENĀJA; 31 brs.

Latvijas Biznesa Banka (Latvian Business Bank): 3 Antonijas iela, Rīga 1010; tel. 6777-5888; fax 6777-5849; e-mail info@lbb.lv; internet www.lbb.lv; f. 1992; present name adopted 2004; 99.87% owned by Bank of Moscow (Russia); cap. 10.8m., res 2.5m., dep. 103.2m. (Dec. 2007); Chair. and Pres. ARTIS BIRKMANIS.

Latvijas Hipotēku un Zemes Banka (Hipotēku Banka) (Mortgage and Land Bank of Latvia): Doma lauk. 4, Rīga 1977; tel. 6800-0100; fax 6777-4152; e-mail banka@hipo.lv; internet www.hipo.lv; f. 1993; present name adopted in 2000; state-owned; cap. 48.5m., res 0.5m., dep. 826.5m. (Dec. 2007); Pres. and Chair. of Bd INESIS FEIFERIS; 32 brs.

Latvijas Tirdzniecības banka (Latvian Trade Bank): Grēcinieku iela 22, Rīga 1050; tel. 6704-3500; fax 6704-3511; e-mail ltb@ltblv.com; internet www.ltblv.com; f. 1991; owned by MDM Bank (Russian Federation); cap. 8.2m., res 16.7m., dep. 547.5m. (Dec. 2007); Chair. ARMANDS STEINBERGS.

Norvik Banka: E. Birznieka-Upiša iela 21, Rīga 1011; tel. 6704-1100; fax 6704-1111; e-mail welcome@norvik.lv; internet www.norvik.lv; f. 1992; fmrly Lateko Bank; present name adopted 2006; cap. 40.5m., res 8.9m., dep. 551.0m. (Dec. 2007); Chair. of Bd ANDREJS SVIRČENKOVS; 15 brs.

Parex Banka: Smilšu iela 3, Rīga 1522; tel. 6701-0000; fax 6701-0001; e-mail info@parex.lv; internet www.parex.lv; f. 1992; cap. 65.0m., res −4.9m., dep. 2,885.7m. (Dec. 2007); 85.14% acquired by Latvijas Hipotēku un Zemes Banka in Dec. 2008; Pres. and Chair. of Bd NILS MELNGAILIS; 72 brs.

LATVIA

PrivatBank: Terbatas iela 4, Rīga 1134; tel. 6704-1300; fax 6728-2981; e-mail info@privatbank.lv; internet www.privatbank.lv; f. 1992; fmrly Paritate Banka; present name adopted 2007; cap. 10.7m., res 1.2m., dep. 89.2m. (Dec. 2007); Chair. of Bd OLEKSANDR TRUBAKOV.

Rietumu Banka: Vesetas iela 7, Rīga 1013; tel. 6702-5555; fax 6702-5588; e-mail info@rietumu.lv; internet www.rietumu.lv; f. 1992; cap. 22.5m., res 8.1m., dep. 1,096.9m. (Dec. 2007); Pres. and Chair. of Exec. Bd ALEXANDER KALINOVSKI.

SEB Latvijas Unibanka: Unicentrs, Kekavas pagasts, Rīga 1076; tel. 6721-5535; fax 6721-5335; e-mail sekretars@seb.lv; internet www.seb.lv; f. 1993; present name adopted 2005; owned by Skandinaviska Enskilda Banken AB (Sweden); cap. 37.1m., res 0.1m., dep. 2,737.6m. (Dec. 2007); Pres. AINĀRS OZOLS; 68 brs.

Svedbank: Balasta dambis 1A, Rīga 1048; tel. 6744-4444; fax 6744-4344; e-mail info@swedbank.lv; internet www.swedbank.lv; f. 1992; present name adopted 2008, following merger between Hansabank and Swedbank; cap. 406.0m., res 0.1m., dep. 4,107.4m. (Dec. 2007); Pres. and CEO MICHAEL WOLF; 86 brs.

Trasta komercbanka—TKB (Trust Commercial Bank): Miesnieku iela 9, Rīga 1050; tel. 6702-7777; fax 6702-7700; e-mail info@tkb.lv; internet www.tkb.lv; f. 1989; present name adopted 1996; cap. 6.3m., res 3.9m., dep. 252.8m. (Dec. 2007); Pres. and Chair. GUNDARS GRIEZE.

UniCredit Bank: Elizabetes iela 63, Rīga 1050; tel. 6708-5500; fax 6708-5507; e-mail info@unicreditbank.lv; internet www.unicreditbank.lv; f. 1997; fmrly Vereinsbank Rīga; present name adopted 2005; 100% owned by Bank Austria Creditanstalt AG (Austria); cap. 41.7m., res 0.0m., dep. 678.7m. (Dec. 2007); Chair. of Bd JURIS JAKOBSONS.

Savings Bank

Latvijas Krājbanka (Latvian Savings Bank): Dalina iela 15, Rīga 1013; tel. 6709-2001; fax 6721-2000; e-mail info@lkb.lv; internet www.krajbanka.lv; f. 1924; present name adopted 1998; 76.65% owned by Snoras Bankas (Lithuania); cap. 12.1m., res 18.3m., dep. 617.3m. (Dec. 2007); Pres. MARTINS BONDARS; 10 brs.

Regulatory Authority

Financial and Capital Markets Commission (Finanšu un kapitāla tirgus komisija—FKTK): Kungu iela 1, Rīga 1050; tel. 6777-4800; fax 6722-5755; e-mail fktk@fktk.lv; internet www.fktk.lv; f. 2001; Chair. ULDIS CĒRPS.

Banking Association

Association of Latvian Commercial Banks (Latvijas Komercbanku asociācija): Pērses iela 9–11, Rīga 1011; tel. 6728-4528; fax 6782-8170; e-mail asoc@bankasoc.lv; internet www.bankasoc.lv; f. 1992; 23 mems; Pres. TEODORS TVERIJONS.

INSURANCE

At September 2004 there were 18 insurance companies in Latvia, of which six were involved in life insurance and 12 in non-life insurance operations.

Balta Insurance Co: Raunas iela 10/12, Rīga 1039; tel. 6708-2233; fax 6708-2345; internet www.balta.lv; f. 1992; automobile, property, freight, travel, agricultural insurance; Pres. JANIS ABASINS.

Balva: K. Valdemāra iela 36, Rīga 1010; tel. 6750-6955; fax 6750-6956; e-mail balva@balva.lv; internet www.balva.lv; f. 1992; partly owned by Ingosstrakh (Russia); non-life insurance; Chair. of Bd ANDREW SHAKHMATOV; 31 brs.

BTA Apdrošināšana: K. Valdemāra iela 63, Rīga 1142; tel. 6702-5100; fax 6702-5190; e-mail bta@bta.lv; internet www.bta.lv; f. 1993.

Colemont FKB Latvia: Dārzauglu iela 1–50, Rīga 1012; tel. 6724-0066; fax 6720-1737; e-mail info@colemont.lv; internet www.colemont.lv; f. 2000; 60% owned by Colemont Insurance Brokers (USA); fmrly Finansu Konsultanti Un Brokeri (FKB); name changed in 2006; Chair. of Bd BEERH SURINDER KUMAR.

ERGO Latvija: Ūnijas iela 45, Rīga 1039; tel. 6708-1700; fax 6784-0102; e-mail info@ergo.lv; internet www.ergo.lv; owned by Alte Leipziger (Germany); life and non-life; Pres. of Bd ILMARS VEIDE.

Estora Reinsurance Co: Elizabetes iela 14, Rīga 1010; tel. 6733-3335; fax 6733-3898; e-mail estora@estora.com; internet www.estora.com; f. 1992; reinsurance; Dir-Gen. JERGENIJS TOLOČKOVS.

SEB Dzīvības Apdrošināšana (SEB Life Insurance): Antonijas iela 9, Rīga 1010; tel. 6707-9800; fax 6707-9808; e-mail dziviba@seb.lv; internet www.seb.lv; f. 1940; present name adopted 2005; Chair. of Bd UĢIS VORONS.

Seesam Latvia: Vienības gatve 87H, Rīga 1004; tel. 6706-1000; fax 6706-1022; e-mail seesam@seesam.lv; internet www.seesam.lv; f. 1993; owned by Pohjola Group Plc (Finland).

COMMODITY AND STOCK EXCHANGES

Rīga Stock Exchange (Rīgas Fondu birža): Vaļņu iela 1, Rīga 1050; tel. 721-2431; fax 722-9411; e-mail riga@nasdaqomxgroup.com; internet www.omxgroup.com/riga; f. 1993; owned by the NASDAQ OMX Group (USA); Chair. of Managing Bd DAIGA AUZIŅA-MELALKSNE.

Trade and Industry

GOVERNMENT AGENCY

Latvian Privatization Agency (Latvijas Privatizācijas aģentūra): K. Valdemāra iela 31, Rīga 1887; tel. 6702-1358; fax 6783-0363; e-mail lpa@mail.bkc.lv; internet www.lpa.bkc.lv; f. 1994; became state joint-stock co in 2004; Dir-Gen. ARTURS GRANTS.

DEVELOPMENT ORGANIZATIONS

Investment and Development Agency of Latvia (Latvijas Investīciju un Attīstības Aģentūra—LIAA): Pērses iela 2, Rīga 1442; tel. 6703-9400; fax 6703-9401; e-mail invest@liaa.gov.lv; internet www.liaa.gov.lv; f. 1993; promotion of business development in Latvia and foreign markets; Dir ANDRIS OZOLS.

CHAMBER OF COMMERCE

Latvian Chamber of Commerce and Industry (Latvijas Tirdzniecības un rūpniecības kamera): K. Valdemāra iela 35, Rīga 1010; tel. 6722-5595; fax 6782-0092; e-mail info@chamber.lv; internet www.chamber.lv; f. 1934; re-est. 1990; Pres. ANDRIS BĒRZIŅŠ; Dir-Gen. ANDRIS GŪTMANIS.

INDUSTRIAL AND TRADE ASSOCIATIONS

Latvian Employers' Confederation: Vilandes iela 12–1, Rīga 1010; tel. 6722-5162; fax 6722-4469; e-mail lddk@lddk.lv; internet www.lddk.lv; f. 1993 by merger of Latvian Employers' Central Assocn and Latvian Private Entrepreneurs' (Employers') Union; Pres. VITĀLIJS GAVRILOVS.

Latvian Construction Contractors' Association (LCCA) (Latvijas būvnieku asociācija—LBA): Grēcinieku ielā 22/24, kab. 201, Rīga 1050; tel. 6722-8584; fax 6721-0023; e-mail lba@latnet.lv; internet www.building.lv/lba; f. 1996; Pres. VIKTORS PURIŅŠ; 6 brs.

Latvian Electrical Engineering and Electronics Industry Association (LETERA): Dzirnavu iela 93, Rīga 1011; tel. and fax 6728-8360; e-mail letera@latnet.lv; internet www.letera.lv; f. 1995; 50 mems (enterprises and education institutions); Pres. NORMUNDS BERGS.

Latvian Fuel Traders' Association (Latvijas Degvielas Tirgotāju Asociācija): Citadeles iela 7/43, Rīga 1010; tel. 6732-0229; fax 6732-0228; e-mail birojs@ldta.lv; internet www.ldta.lv; Chair. of Bd O. KARČEVSKIS; Exec. Dir U. SAKNE.

Latvian Information Technology and Telecommunications Association (LITTA): Stabu iela 47–1, Rīga 1011; tel. 6731-1821; fax 6731-5567; e-mail litta@dtmedia.lv; internet www.litta.lv; f. 1998; Pres. IMANTS FREIBERGS.

Latvian Timber Exporters' Association (LTEA) (Latvijas Kokmateriālu Eksportētāju Asociācija): Skaistkalnes iela 1, Rīga 1004; tel. 6706-7369; fax 6786-0268; e-mail ltea@latvianwood.lv; internet www.latviantimber.lv; f. 1998; Pres. JANIS APSITIS.

UTILITIES

Regulatory Authority

Public Utilities Commission of Latvia (PUC) (Sabiedrisko Pakalpojumu Regulēšanas Komisija): Brīvības iela 55, Rīga 1010; tel. 6709-7200; fax 6709-7277; e-mail sprk@sprk.gov.lv; internet www.sprk.gov.lv; f. 2001; multi-sector regulator overseeing electricity, gas, telecommunications, post and railway sectors; Chair. VALENTĪNA ANDRĒJEVA.

Electricity

Latvenergo: Pulkveža Brieža iela 12, Rīga 1230; tel. 6772-8309; fax 6772-8811; e-mail latvenergo@latvenergo.lv; internet www.latvenergo.lv; state-owned joint-stock co; transmits and distributes electricity and heat; seven regional subsidiary cos; Chair. of Bd KĀRLIS MIĶELSONS.

Gas

Latvian Gas (Latvijas gāze): A. Briana iela 6, Rīga 1001; tel. 6736-9132; fax 6782-1406; e-mail latvijas_gaze@lg.lv; internet www.lg.lv; partially privatized in 2000–01; 8% state-owned; Chair. MĀRIS GAILIS; 2,817 employees.

Water

Major suppliers include:

Aizkraukle Water Co (Aizkraukles ūdens): Torņu iela 1, Aizkraukle 5101; fax 6512-2150; e-mail udensall@inbox.lv.

Bauska Water Co (Bauskas ūdens): Birzu iela 8A, Bauska 3901; tel. 6396-0565; fax 6396-0566; e-mail baude@apollo.lv.

Daugavpils Water Co (Daugavpils ūdens): Ūdensvada iela 3, Daugavpils 5403; tel. 6544-4565; fax 6542-5547; e-mail kontakti@daugavpils.udens.lv; internet www.daugavpils.udens.lv; f. 1889.

Liepāja Water Co (Liepājas ūdens): K. Valdemāra iela 12, Liepāja 3401; tel. 6541-1416; fax 6541-0769; e-mail dmeu@dpu.lv.

Rīga Water Co (Rīgas ūdens): Basteja bulv. l/5, Rīga 1495; tel. 6708-8555; fax 6722-2660; e-mail office@ru.lv; internet www.rw.lv; water supply and sewage treatment.

TRADE UNIONS

Free Trade Union Confederation of Latvia (Latvijas Brīvo Arodbiedrību Savienība—LBAS): Bruņinieku iela 29–31, Rīga 1001; tel. 6727-0351; fax 6727-6649; e-mail lbas@lbas.lv; internet www.lbas.lv; f. 1990; 24 branch or professional affiliated unions; Pres. PETERIS KRIGERS; 134,422 mems (2007).

Transport

RAILWAYS

In 2005 there were 2,270 km of railways on the territory of Latvia, of which 257 km were electrified. In 2007 Latvian railways carried 27.4m. passengers and 52.2m. metric tons of freight.

Latvian Railways (Latvijas Dzelzceļš): Gogoļa iela 3, Rīga 1547; tel. 6723-4940; fax 6782-0231; e-mail biruta.sakse@ldz.lv; internet www.ldz.lv; f. 1993; state joint-stock co; Chair. of Bd UGIS MAGONIS.

ROADS

In 2004 Latvia's total road network was 69,532 km, of which 6,963 km were main roads.

Latvian State Roads (Latvijas Valsts Ceļi): Gogoļa iela 3, Rīga 1050; tel. 6702-8169; fax 6702-8171; e-mail lad@lvceli.lv; internet www.lvceli.lv; f. 2004 to replace Latvian Road Administration; state joint-stock co; manages state road network, administers State Road Fund; Chair. TĀLIS STRAUME.

SHIPPING

At 31 December 2007 the Latvian-registered merchant fleet numbered 153 vessels, with a combined total displacement of 261,800 grt. In 2008 some 63.6m. metric tons of sea-borne freight were transported through the country's three main (Ventspils, Rīga and Liepāja) and seven smaller ports.

Maritime Department (Ministry of Transport): Gogoļa iela 3, Rīga 1743; tel. 6702-8198; fax 6733-1406; e-mail aigars.krastins@sam.gov.lv; internet www.sam.gov.lv; Dir AIGARS KRASTIŅŠ.

Port Authorities

Liepāja Port Authority: Liepāja Special Economic Zone, Feniksa iela 4, Liepāja 3401; tel. 6342-7605; fax 6348-0252; e-mail authority@lsez.lv; internet www.lsez.lv; Man. Dir AIVARS BOJA.

Rīga Commercial Free Port SSC: Katrinas iela 5A, Rīga 1227; tel. 6732-9224; fax 6783-0215; e-mail rto@mail.bkc.lv; internet www.rto.lv; f. 1996.

Rīga Free Port Authority (Rīgas Brīvostas Pārvalde): Kalpaka bulv. 12, Rīga 1050; tel. 6703-0800; fax 6703-0835; e-mail rop@mail.rop.lv; internet www.rop.lv; f. 1994; Chief Exec. LEONIDS LOGINOVS; Chair. of Bd ANDRIS ARGALIS.

Ventspils Free Port Authority (Ventspils brīvostas pārvalde): Jāņa iela 19, Ventspils 3601; tel. 6362-2586; fax 6362-1297; e-mail info@vbp.lv; internet portofventspils.lv; f. 1991; Chief Exec. IMANTS SARMULIS.

Ventspils Commercial Port (Ventspils Tirdzniecības Ostā): Dzintaru iela 22, Ventspils 3602; tel. 6366-8706; fax 6366-8860; e-mail vcp@vto.lv; internet www.vcp.lv; Chair. of Bd VALERIJ PASHUTA.

Shipping Company

Latvijas kugniecība (LASCO) (Latvian Shipping Co): Elizabetes iela 1, Rīga 1807; tel. 6702-0111; fax 6782-8106; e-mail lsc@lscgroup.lv; internet www.lk.lv; f. 1991; tanker, reefer, liquid petroleum gas and dry-cargo transportation; 49.94% owned by Ventspils Nafta; Pres. IMANTS SARMULIS.

CIVIL AVIATION

There is an international airport at Rīga.

Civil Aviation Agency of Latvia (Latvijas Civilās Aviācijas Administrācija): Rīga Airport 1011, Rīga 1053; tel. 6783-0936; fax 6783-0967; internet www.caa.lv; Dir MĀRIS GORODCOVS.

airBaltic Corpn: Rīga Airport, Rīga 1053; tel. 6720-7069; fax 6720-7369; e-mail info@airbaltic.lv; internet www.airbaltic.com; f. 1995; 52.6% govt-owned; Pres. and Chief Exec. BERTOLT FLICK.

Tourism

Among Latvia's principal tourist attractions are the historic centre of Rīga, with its medieval and art nouveau buildings, the extensive beaches of the Baltic coastline, and Gauja National Park, which stretches east of the historic town of Sigulda for nearly 100 km. Revenue from tourism in 2006 was some US $622m. Foreign tourist arrivals at accommodation establishments in 2007 numbered 844,828.

Latvian Tourism Development Agency: Pils lauk. 4, Rīga 1050; tel. and fax 6722-9945; fax 6735-8128; e-mail tda@latviatourism.lv; internet www.latviatourism.lv; f. 1993; Dir ULDIS VITOLINS.

LEBANON

Introductory Survey

Location, Climate, Language, Religion, Flag, Capital

The Republic of Lebanon lies in western Asia, bordered by Syria to the north and east, and by Israel and the Palestinian Autonomous Areas to the south. The country has a coastline of about 220 km (135 miles) on the eastern shore of the Mediterranean Sea. The climate varies widely with altitude. The coastal lowlands are hot and humid in summer, becoming mild (cool and damp) in winter. In the mountains, which occupy much of Lebanon, the weather is cool in summer, with heavy snowfalls in winter. Rainfall is generally abundant. The official language is Arabic, which is spoken by almost all of the inhabitants. French is widely used as a second language, while Kurdish and Armenian are spoken by small ethnic minorities. According to the UN Relief and Works Agency for Palestine Refugees in the Near East (UNRWA), at December 2008 there were 422,188 Palestinian refugees registered in Lebanon. The major religions are Islam and Christianity, and there is a very small Jewish community. In the early 1980s it was estimated that 57% of Lebanon's inhabitants were Muslims, with about 43% Christians; these figures were believed to have changed to 63% and 37%, respectively, by 1994. The principal Muslim sects are Shi'a and Sunni, while there is also a significant Druze community. By the 1980s it was generally considered that Shi'a Muslims, totalling an estimated 1.2m., constituted Lebanon's largest single community. Most Christians adhere to the Roman Catholic Church, principally the Maronite rite. In 1994 it was estimated that 29%–32% of the population of Lebanon were Shi'a Muslims, 25%–28% Maronites, 16%–20% Sunni Muslims and 3.5% Druzes. There are also Armenian, Greek and Syrian sects (both Catholic and Eastern Orthodox) and small groups of Protestants. The national flag (proportions 2 by 3) has three horizontal stripes, of red, white (half the depth) and red, with a representation of a cedar tree (in green and brown) in the centre of the white stripe. The capital is Beirut.

Recent History

Lebanon, the homeland of the ancient Phoenicians, became part of the Turkish Ottoman Empire in the 16th century, and following the dissolution of the Ottoman Empire after the First World War (1914–18), a Greater Lebanese state was created by the Allied powers. The new state was formed in order to meet the nationalist aspirations of the area's predominantly Christian population, but it also included largely Muslim-populated territories traditionally considered to be part of Syria. Lebanon was administered by France, under a League of Nations mandate, from 1920 until independence was declared on 26 November 1941. A republic was established in 1943, and full autonomy was granted in January 1944.

Religious and cultural diversity is Lebanon's defining feature. At the time of independence Christians formed a slight majority of the population, the largest single community (nearly 30% of the total) being the Maronite Christians, who mostly inhabited the north of the country and the capital, Beirut. Other Christian groups included Greek Orthodox communities, Greek Catholics and Armenians. The Muslim groups were the Sunnis, living mainly in the coastal towns of Sur (Tyre), Saida (Sidon) and Beirut, the Shi'ites, a predominantly rural community in southern Lebanon and the northern Beka'a valley, and, in much smaller numbers, the Druzes, an ancient community in central Lebanon. The relative size of the various communities provided the basis for the unwritten 'national pact' of 1943, whereby executive and legislative posts were to be shared in the ratio of six Christians to five Muslims, and seats in the Chamber of Deputies (renamed the National Assembly in March 1979) were distributed on a religious, rather than a politico-ideological, basis. The convention according to this 'confessional' arrangement was that the President was a Maronite Christian, the Prime Minister a Sunni Muslim, and the President of the National Assembly a Shi'a Muslim.

Lebanon's first President, from 1943 until 1952, was Sheikh Bishara el-Khoury. His successor was Camille Chamoun, whose reforms included the enfranchisement of women. Following elections to the Chamber of Deputies in 1957 there was considerable unrest, mainly among Muslims who mistrusted Chamoun's pro-Western foreign policy and advocated Lebanon's closer alignment with Syria and Egypt. In July 1958 Chamoun appealed to the USA for military assistance; US forces remained in Beirut until October, by which time peace had been restored. Meanwhile, Chamoun was persuaded not to seek a further presidential term, and the Chamber elected Gen. Fouad Chehab as his successor. Chehab, who took office in September 1958, adopted a foreign policy of non-alignment, and introduced state provision of health, education and other services. In 1964 he was succeeded by Charles Hélou, who continued many of Chehab's policies but was faced by increasing controversy over the status of Palestinians in Lebanon.

After the establishment of Israel in 1948, and during the subsequent Arab–Israeli wars, thousands of Palestinians fled to Lebanon, where most were housed in refugee camps in the south of the country. Following the creation of the Palestine Liberation Organization (PLO) in 1964, military training centres for Palestinian guerrilla fighters were established in the camps. From 1968 these self-styled *fedayeen* ('martyrs') began making raids into Israel, provoking retaliatory attacks by Israeli forces. In 1969 there were clashes between Lebanese security forces and the *fedayeen*. Many Christians, particularly the Maronites, advocated strict government control over the Palestinians' activities, but the majority of Muslims strongly supported Palestinian operations against Israel.

Hélou's successor, Sulayman Franjiya, took office in 1970. During his presidency the Palestinian issue was exacerbated by an influx of Palestinian fighters expelled from Jordan in July 1971. Conflict between Israeli forces and Palestinians based in Lebanon intensified, while Christian groups began their own armed campaign against the *fedayeen*. In July 1974 Palestinian forces clashed with militia of the Phalangist Party (the Phalanges libanaises or al-Kataeb, a militant right-wing Maronite Christian group now also known as the Lebanese Social Democratic Party). From April 1975 the conflict between the Palestinians and Phalangists quickly descended into full-scale civil war between the Lebanese National Movement (LNM) of left-wing Muslims (including Palestinians), led by Kamal Joumblatt of the Parti socialiste progressiste (PSP, a mainly Druze-supported group), and conservative Christian groups, mainly the Phalangist militia. Constitutional matters overtook the status of Palestinians as the main divisive issue, with the LNM advocating an end to the 'confessional' system, claiming that this unduly favoured Christians (who by now were generally accepted as no longer forming a majority of the population). Despite diplomatic efforts by Arab and Western countries, no durable cease-fire was achieved until October 1976, largely as a result of intervention in the conflict (in order to prevent an outright LNM victory) by Syrian forces in mid-1976. Under the terms of the cease-fire a 30,000-strong Arab Deterrent Force (ADF), composed mainly of Syrian troops, entered Lebanon.

President Franjiya was succeeded by Elias Sarkis in September 1976, and Prime Minister Rashid Karami by Selim al-Hoss in December. Legislative elections, due in April 1976, were postponed for an initial period of 26 months—the term of the Chamber of Deputies was subsequently extended further. Although the constitutional status quo remained intact, more than 30,000 people had already died in the civil war and the militias of the various warring factions controlled most of the country. East Beirut and much of northern Lebanon was controlled by the Lebanese Forces (LF), a coalition of Maronite militias formed in September 1976; west Beirut was controlled by Muslim groups; and Palestinians dominated much of south-west Lebanon.

In March 1978 Israeli forces advanced into southern Lebanon in a counter-attack against forces of Fatah (the Palestine National Liberation Movement), the main guerrilla group within the PLO. UN Security Council Resolution 425, adopted on 17 March, demanded an Israeli withdrawal from Lebanon (thereby respecting its territorial integrity, sovereignty and independence) and also established a UN Interim Force in Lebanon (UNIFIL, see p. 84), initially of 4,000 troops. Israeli forces withdrew in June, but transferred control of a border strip to the pro-Israeli Christian militias of Maj. Saad Haddad. In October, following several months of renewed fighting in Beirut between Syrian troops of the ADF and right-wing Christian militias, the ADF states agreed on a peace plan (the Beiteddin Declaration), which aimed to restore the authority of the Lebanese Government and army. Attempts to implement the plan were unsuccessful, however, and Lebanon's fragmentation deepened.

Al-Hoss resigned the premiership in June 1980 and was replaced in October by Chafic al-Wazzan. In August 1982, in an election boycotted by most Muslim deputies, the renamed National Assembly designated Bachir Gemayel (the younger son of the founder of the Phalangist Party and commander of the LF) to succeed President Sarkis. The President-elect was assassinated in September, and his brother, Amin, was elected in his place. Following the assassination, Phalangist forces (with the apparent complicity of occupying Israeli forces) entered the Palestinian refugee camps of Sabra and Chatila, in west Beirut, killing some 2,000 refugees. Israeli forces had re-entered Lebanon in June 1982, with the declared aim of finally eliminating the PLO's military threat to Israel's northern border; they quickly defeated Palestinian forces in south-west Lebanon and surrounded the western sector of Beirut, trapping more than 6,000 Palestinian fighters. A US-led diplomatic initiative resulted in an agreement enabling the PLO fighters to disperse among several Arab states, and a multinational peace-keeping force was deployed in Beirut. (In September 1983 intense fighting between rival factions of Fatah resulted in a truce agreement, brokered by Saudi Arabia and Syria, which led to a second evacuation of some 4,000 Palestinian fighters, most notably of the PLO Chairman, Yasser Arafat, who was exiled to Tunisia.) Negotiations between Lebanon and Israel began in December 1982, culminating in May 1983 in an agreement to end all hostilities (including the theoretical state of war that had existed between the two countries since 1948) and to withdraw all foreign troops from Lebanon. However, Syria did not recognize the accord, leaving 40,000 of its own troops and 7,000 PLO fighters in the Beka'a valley and northern Lebanon. Israel, meanwhile, redeployed a reduced force of 10,000 troops along the Awali river, south of Beirut. Maj. Haddad's South Lebanon Army (SLA) was to police southern areas as Israel's role lessened. Meanwhile, the multinational force in Beirut (comprising some 5,800 mainly French, Italian and US personnel) was drawn increasingly into the fighting, coming under frequent attack from Muslim militias who opposed its tantamount support for the Christian-led Government. In October 241 US and 58 French marines were killed in suicide bombings by Muslim groups.

The failure to conclude a peaceful settlement, and in particular the resumption of heavy fighting in February 1984 (which the reconstituted, US-trained Lebanese army was unable to suppress), led to the resignation of Prime Minister al-Wazzan, followed shortly afterwards by the withdrawal of the USA, Italy and the United Kingdom from the peace-keeping force. French troops were withdrawn in March. By this time successive defeats had left Gemayel's forces with effective control only in the mainly Christian-populated east Beirut. In March President Gemayel abrogated the May 1983 agreement with Israel, and in April 1984, with Syrian support, he formed a Government of national unity under former premier Rashid Karami. The Lebanese army failed to gain control of Beirut, and Gemayel's efforts to obtain approval for constitutional reform, already constrained by his fear of alienating his Christian supporters, were further undermined by divisions within the Cabinet.

The Israeli Government formed by Shimon Peres in September 1984 pledged to withdraw Israeli forces from Lebanon. However, while the Lebanese authorities demanded that UNIFIL police the Israeli–Lebanese border, by the time the Israeli withdrawal was completed, in June 1985, Israel had ensured that a narrow buffer zone, policed by the SLA (now commanded by Gen. Antoine Lahad), was in place along the border. With the Israeli presence in Lebanon reduced to a token force, Syria withdrew about one-third of its troops from the Beka'a valley in July, leaving some 25,000 in position.

In December 1985 the leaders of the three main Lebanese militias (the Druze forces, Amal and the LF) signed an accord in the Syrian capital, Damascus, providing for an immediate cease-fire and for the cessation of the civil war within one year. The militias were to be disarmed and disbanded, and a new constitutional regime was to be introduced within three years. However, the militias of the Sunni Murabitoun and the Iranian-backed Shi'ite Hezbollah were not parties to the agreement, which was also opposed by influential Christian elements. Furthermore, there were clashes later in December between supporters of the agreement within the LF and those who resented the concessions made by their leader, Elie Hobeika. In January 1986 Hobeika was forced into exile and replaced as LF leader by Samir Geagea, who urged renegotiation of the Damascus accord.

During 1986 Palestinian guerrillas resumed rocket attacks on settlements in northern Israel, provoking retaliatory air attacks by Israel on targets in the Beka'a valley and southern Lebanon. Meanwhile, Hezbollah escalated its attacks on SLA positions within the Israeli buffer zone, and also clashed with UNIFIL. Fighting between Palestinian guerrillas and Shi'ite Amal militiamen for control of the refugee camps in south Beirut escalated in May, before a cease-fire was imposed around the camps in June, as part of a Syrian-sponsored peace plan for Muslim west Beirut. The activities of the Amal, Druze and Sunni militias in west Beirut were temporarily curtailed by the deployment of Lebanese and Syrian troops, but fighting across the so-called 'Green Line', which had effectively divided the area from Christian east Beirut since early 1984, continued. By the time Amal and the PLO agreed in September 1987 to end hostilities, more than 2,500 people had died in the 'war of the camps'. Despite renewed fighting near Sidon in October, the Amal leader, Nabih Berri, in January 1988 announced an end to the siege of the Palestinian refugee camps in Beirut and southern Lebanon, avowedly as a gesture of support for the *intifada* (uprising) by Palestinians in the Israeli-occupied territories.

After Prime Minister Karami was killed in a bomb explosion in June 1987, Selim al-Hoss (Prime Minister in 1976–80) was appointed acting premier. In 1988 a political crisis developed as it proved impossible to find a successor to President Gemayel that was acceptable to all the warring factions. The three leading contenders for the presidency were Gen. Michel Aoun (Commander-in-Chief of the Lebanese army), Raymond Eddé (leader of the Maronite Bloc National) and Sulayman Franjiya (President in 1970–76). Franjiya was Syria's preferred candidate but was notably opposed by Geagea, who apparently ensured that the National Assembly was inquorate when it convened for the presidential election in August 1988. In September the USA and Syria agreed to support another candidate, Mikhail ad-Daher, but Christian army and LF leaders remained opposed to the imposition of any candidate by foreign powers. Gemayel's term of office expired later in the month, when a further attempt by the National Assembly to hold an election was inquorate. The outgoing President appointed an interim military administration, comprising three Christians and three Muslims, with Aoun as Prime Minister. However, the three nominated Muslim officers immediately refused to serve in the new administration, while two Christian members of the al-Hoss Government resigned, signalling their recognition of the interim military administration. The constitutional crisis, with two Governments claiming legitimacy, was further complicated in November, when the Minister of Defence in the al-Hoss Government dismissed Aoun as Commander-in-Chief of the Lebanese army; however, Aoun retained the loyalty of large sections of the military and thus remained its de facto leader.

In September 1989, following six months of fighting in Beirut between Aoun's Lebanese army and Syrian forces, a Tripartite Arab Committee—formed in May by an emergency session of Arab leaders, and comprising King Hassan of Morocco, King Fahd of Saudi Arabia and President Chadli of Algeria—announced a peace plan whereby, most notably, the Lebanese National Assembly would meet to discuss a draft charter of national reconciliation. The Committee's charter was approved by the Syrian Government and the leaders of Lebanon's Muslim militias. Aoun initially rejected its terms, on the grounds that it did not provide for the withdrawal of Syrian forces, but he was forced to relent, in view of support for the charter by almost every Arab country, as well as the USA, the USSR, the United Kingdom and France; a cease-fire accordingly took effect. The National Assembly subsequently met in Ta'if, Saudi Arabia, to discuss the charter, which was finally approved (with some amendments) in October by 58 of the 62 attending deputies (of the 99 deputies elected in May 1972, only 73 survived); it became known as the 'Ta'if agreement'. The charter provided for the transfer of executive power from the presidency to a cabinet, with portfolios divided equally between Christian and Muslim ministers. The number of seats in the National Assembly was to be increased to 108, comprising equal numbers of Christian and Muslim deputies. Following the election of a President and the formation of a new government, all militias involved in the Lebanese conflict were to be disbanded within six months, while the internal security forces would be strengthened; the Syrian armed forces would assist the new Government in implementing the security plan for a maximum of two years.

The National Assembly elected René Mouawad, a Maronite Christian deputy and a former Minister of Education and Arts, as President in early November 1989. The Assembly also unanimously endorsed the Ta'if agreement. However, Aoun, who denounced the agreement as a betrayal of Lebanese sovereignty, declared the presidential election unconstitutional and its result null and void, proclaiming himself President. Mouawad was assassinated only 17 days after his election. The National Assembly again convened and elected Elias Hrawi as the new President; the legislature also voted to extend its own term until 1994. A new Cabinet was formed by Selim al-Hoss in late November 1989.

The Christian communities were divided over the Ta'if agreement, and Geagea's refusal to reject the agreement precipitated violent clashes between his LF and Aoun's forces in January 1990: by March more than 800 people had been killed in inter-Christian fighting. (Geagea eventually announced the LF's recognition of the al-Hoss Government, and hence the Ta'if agreement, in April.) In August the National Assembly duly approved amendments to the Constitution, increasing the number of seats in the National Assembly to 108, to be divided equally between Muslims and Christians. On 21 September the Second Lebanese Republic was officially inaugurated when President Hrawi formally endorsed the amendments. In October Aoun and his forces (who continued to reject the Ta'if agreement) were expelled from east Beirut by Syrian forces and units of the Lebanese army loyal to Hrawi. The Lebanese army began to deploy in Beirut in December, by which time all militia forces had withdrawn from the city. In the same month al-Hoss submitted his Government's resignation, and Hrawi invited Omar Karami (Minister of Education and Arts in the outgoing administration) to form a government of national unity, as stipulated by the Ta'if agreement. By early 1991 the Lebanese army was established in most major southern Lebanese towns; by September the militias had been largely disbanded (although Hezbollah maintained armaments in southern Lebanon and the Beka'a valley). In May the National Assembly approved amendments to the electoral law, and in June the Cabinet appointed 40 deputies to fill the seats that had become vacant since the 1972 election as well as the nine new seats created under the Ta'if agreement. In August 1991 the National Assembly approved a general amnesty for crimes perpetrated during the civil war, although its terms excluded several specified crimes committed during 1975–90. Under a presidential pardon, Aoun was allowed to leave the French embassy compound (where he had been sheltering since his defeat in 1990) and to depart for exile in France.

In May 1991 Lebanon and Syria signed a bilateral treaty establishing formal relations in political, military and economic affairs, and confirming the role of the Syrian army as guarantor of the security plans enshrined in the Ta'if agreement. Israel immediately condemned the treaty as a further step towards the formal transformation of Lebanon into a Syrian protectorate, while its opponents within Lebanon denounced it as a threat to the country's independence. In September Lebanon and Syria concluded a mutual security agreement. Syrian forces began to withdraw from Beirut in March 1992, in preparation for their scheduled withdrawal to eastern Lebanon by September. Israel, meanwhile, reasserted its intention of maintaining a military presence in the buffer zone, and its support for the SLA, by launching severe attacks on Palestinian bases in southern Lebanon in June 1991. Lebanese forces began to take up positions in Sidon in July. Initial resistance from Palestinians loyal to Arafat was swiftly overcome, and an agreement was concluded with the PLO to allow the Lebanese army to assume control of the area. The conflict escalated further in February 1992, following the assassination by the Israeli air force of the Secretary-General of Hezbollah, Sheikh Abbas Moussawi.

The deteriorating economic situation in early 1992, combined with allegations of government corruption and incompetence, and a series of general strikes, provoked the resignation of Karami and his Cabinet in May. Subsequent talks in Damascus between President Hrawi and the Syrian leadership led to the reappointment of Rashid Solh as Prime Minister (a position that he had previously held in 1974–75). In July 1992 the National Assembly approved a new electoral law whereby the number of seats in the Assembly was raised from 108 to 128, to be divided equally between Christian and Muslim deputies. The Government's intention to conduct legislative elections in mid-1992 had prompted Christian groups to threaten a boycott of the polls, since it was not certain that Syrian forces would have withdrawn to the eastern area of the Beka'a valley by that time, in accordance with the Ta'if agreement. The Government, for its part, stated that the Lebanese army was not yet able to guarantee the country's security in the absence of Syrian troops.

Lebanon's first legislative elections for 20 years were held in three rounds, on 23 August (in the governorates of the North and the Beka'a valley), 30 August (Beirut and Mount Lebanon) and 6 September 1992 (South and An-Nabatiyah). Electoral turn-out was low (averaging 32%), especially in Maronite districts where leaders had urged a boycott. Hezbollah, contesting the elections for the first time as a political party, enjoyed considerable success in southern constituencies. The Amal leader, Nabih Berri, was appointed President of the new National Assembly in October, and Hrawi invited Rafik Hariri, a Lebanese-born Saudi Arabian business executive, to form a new government, amid hopes that he would restore some confidence in the Lebanese economy and oversee the country's reconstruction. Hariri's Cabinet was dominated by technocrats, and the system of distributing portfolios on an entirely 'confessional' basis was somewhat diluted.

In December 1992 the Lebanese army took up positions in southern suburbs of Beirut for the first time in eight years, apparently meeting no resistance from Hezbollah, which had hitherto effectively controlled the areas. From mid-1993 the Lebanese Government was said to be attempting to curtail the activities of the Damascus-based Popular Front for the Liberation of Palestine—General Command (PFLP—GC), which had begun to mount guerrilla attacks on Israeli military positions from bases in southern Lebanon. In July Israeli armed forces launched their heaviest artillery and air attacks on targets in southern Lebanon since 1982. The declared aim of 'Operation Accountability' was to eradicate the threat posed by Hezbollah and Palestinian guerrillas, and to create a flow of refugees so as to compel the Lebanese and Syrian authorities to take action against these groups. According to Lebanese sources, the week-long offensive displaced some 300,000 civilians towards the north and resulted in 128 (mainly civilian) deaths. Although a US-brokered cease-fire 'understanding' entered effect at the end of July 1993, hostilities continued in subsequent months.

In June 1994 Hezbollah reported that 26 of its fighters had been killed in an Israeli air-strike on one of its training camps in the Beka'a valley; Hezbollah responded with rocket attacks into the security zone and northern Israel. In October an Israeli attack on the town of An-Nabatiyah at-Tahta (Nabatiyah), in which seven civilians died, was apparently provoked by the deaths of 22 people in a bomb attack, attributed to Palestinian militants of the Islamic Resistance Movement (Hamas), in the Israeli city of Tel-Aviv: hitherto, Israeli operations in Lebanon had tended to be in reprisal for terrorist activity in the security zone. Clashes in southern Lebanon in December reportedly resulted in the killing by Hezbollah of several members of the Israeli military and SLA.

In March 1994, meanwhile, the National Assembly approved legislation instituting the death penalty for 'politically motivated' murders. Shortly afterwards the Maronite LF was proscribed (on the grounds that it had sought the country's partition) and its leader, Samir Geagea, was arrested and charged, along with several of his associates, in connection with the murder, in October 1990, of Dany Chamoun, son of former President Camille Chamoun and the leader of the right-wing Maronite Parti national libéral (PNL), and with the bombing of a Maronite church outside Beirut in January 1994. In September Geagea was reportedly relieved of the organization's leadership and his recognition of the Ta'if agreement revoked; the LF command had also reportedly countermanded Geagea's formal dissolution, under the Ta'if agreement, of the organization's militia status. (A successor political organization, the Lebanese Forces Party, had been created in September 1990.) In June 1995 Geagea and a co-defendant were convicted of instigating the murder of Chamoun, and were (together with seven others convicted *in absentia*) sentenced to death; the sentences were immediately commuted to life imprisonment with hard labour. In July 1996 Geagea was acquitted of involvement in the Maronite church bombing. However, by mid-1997 Geagea had received another two death sentences (one for ordering the assassination of another Maronite rival in 1990, and the other for attempting to assassinate the Minister of Defence, Michel Murr, in 1991—both of which were later commuted to life imprisonment); another sentence of life imprisonment for orchestrating the death of Prime Minister Rashid Karami in 1987; and a 10-year gaol term for attempting to recruit and arm militiamen after 1991 (when all militias had been banned).

In October 1995 the National Assembly voted to amend the Constitution to extend President Hrawi's mandate for a further three years. Prime Minister Hariri had sought an extension of the presidential term in the stated interest of promoting stability in the economic reconstruction process, and the amendment had been facilitated following intervention by Syria to resolve a procedural dispute between Hariri and the President of the National Assembly, Nabih Berri.

Elections to the National Assembly took place, in five rounds, in August–September 1996. Pro-Hariri candidates enjoyed considerable success in the first three rounds of voting (in Mount Lebanon, North Lebanon and Beirut governorates), with the Prime Minister himself winning the largest number of votes at the third round; there were, however, allegations of vote-buying involving Hariri's supporters in Beirut. In the fourth and fifth rounds (in the South and An-Nabatiyah, and in the Beka'a valley) an electoral alliance led by Amal and Hezbollah was reported to have won all but one of the 46 seats. Prior to the fifth round Syria had redeployed some 12,000 of its estimated 30,000 troops in Lebanon to the eastern part of the Beka'a valley. (Under the terms of the Ta'if agreement, the redeployment should have been completed in 1992.) The overall rate of participation averaged about 45%, suggesting that many voters had disregarded demands particularly by Aoun, Gemayel and other exiled figures for a boycott of the polls. Berri was re-elected President of the National Assembly when the new legislature convened in October 1996, and in the following month a new Government was formed under Hariri.

In April 1996 Israel commenced a sustained military offensive (code-named 'Operation Grapes of Wrath') in southern Lebanon and suburbs to the south of Beirut, aimed at preventing rocket attacks by Hezbollah on settlements in northern Israel. Some 400,000 Lebanese were displaced northwards, and the shelling by Israeli forces of a UNIFIL base at Qana, which resulted in the deaths of more than 100 Lebanese civilians who had been sheltering there, and of four UNIFIL soldiers, provoked international condemnation. After more than two weeks of hostilities a cease-fire 'understanding' took effect in late April. As in 1993, this was effectively a compromise confining the conflict to the area of the security zone, recognizing both Hezbollah's right to resist Israeli occupation and Israel's right to self-defence; the 'understanding' also envisaged the establishment of an Israel-Lebanon Monitoring Group (ILMG), comprising representatives of Israel, Lebanon, Syria, France and the USA, to supervise the cease-fire. According to the Israeli authorities, Operation Grapes of Wrath resulted in no Israeli deaths, while 170–200 Lebanese civilians, in addition to some 50 fighters, were killed. Hezbollah claimed to have sustained minimal casualties, and its military capacity appeared largely undiminished.

A subsequent UN report on the killing of Lebanese civilians at Qana concluded that it was 'unlikely' that the shelling of the UNIFIL base had, as claimed by the Israelis, been the result of 'gross technical and/or procedural errors'. Prior to the first meeting of the ILMG, in July 1996, Israel and Hezbollah reportedly exchanged prisoners and bodies of members of their armed forces for the first time since 1991. However, despite the April 1996 cease-fire 'understanding', sporadic clashes continued during 1997–98. The extent of Israeli casualties as a result of the occupation of southern Lebanon prompted a vocal campaign within Israel for a unilateral withdrawal from the security zone. In April 1998 Israel's 'inner' Security Cabinet voted to adopt UN Security Council Resolution 425, but with the stipulation that Lebanon provide guarantees of the security of Israel's northern border. Lebanon, however, emphasized that Resolution 425 demanded an unconditional withdrawal, and stated that neither would it be able to guarantee Israel's immunity from attack, nor would it be prepared to deploy the Lebanese army in southern Lebanon for this purpose; furthermore, Lebanon could not support the continued presence there of the SLA. Concern was also expressed that a unilateral withdrawal from Lebanon in the absence of a comprehensive Middle East peace settlement might foment regional instability.

Meanwhile, in late 1996 the Government had ordered the closure of about 150 radio and 50 television stations; licences to broadcast political items had been granted to only a limited number of stations, most of which were owned by prominent political figures. In September 1997 the authorities began to close down unlicensed broadcasters, and in December the Minister of the Interior, deputy premier Michel Murr, prohibited a televised satellite broadcast, from France, by Gen. Michel Aoun, on the grounds that such transmissions were undermining national security. The ban provoked a violent demonstration in Beirut, which resulted in a number of protesters being arrested and tried on charges of defying restrictions on public demonstrations imposed in 1993. (Aoun's interview was eventually broadcast in January 1998 by a private terrestrial channel.)

Voting in Lebanon's first municipal elections since 1963 took place, in four rounds, in May–June 1998. At the first round (in Mount Lebanon governorate), Hezbollah won convincing victories in Beirut's southern suburbs, while right-wing organizations opposed to the Government also took control of several councils. At the second round (in North Lebanon), efforts failed to achieve an inter-community balance in Tripoli, where a council comprising 23 Muslims and only one Christian was elected; elsewhere in the governorate there was notable success for candidates loyal to Samir Geagea. However, a joint list of candidates supported by Hariri and Berri won control of the Beirut council at the third round, while Berri's Amal gained overall control in Tyre. At the final round of voting (in the Beka'a valley), Hezbollah candidates were largely defeated by their pro-Syrian secular rivals and by members of the governorate's leading families. Other than in Beirut, the rate of voter participation was high (about 70%). (Municipal elections did not take place in southern Lebanon until September 2001, following the withdrawal of Israeli troops in 2000.)

As President Hrawi's mandate neared completion in 1998, the Commander-in-Chief of the Army, Gen. Emile Lahoud, emerged as a suitable successor: his strong leadership, firm stance on corruption and success in having reconstructed the army following the civil war were thought likely to assist the process of political reform and economic regeneration. Moreover, Syria, which remained a major influence on Lebanese politics, endorsed Lahoud's candidacy, despite his strong nationalist tendency. To enable Lahoud's appointment, the National Assembly overwhelmingly adopted an exceptional amendment to Article 49 of the Constitution—which requires that senior civil servants resign their post two years prior to seeking political office—and Lahoud was duly elected President on 15 October, with the approval of all 118 National Assembly deputies present (the vote was boycotted by the Druze leader, Walid Joumblatt, and his supporters). Lahoud took office on 24 November. Hariri unexpectedly declined an invitation from him to form a new government, and at the beginning of December Selim al-Hoss (who had headed four administrations during the civil war) was designated Prime Minister. His new Cabinet, which was almost halved in size (to 16 members), included only two ministers from the previous administration—Michel Murr notably retained the post of deputy premier as well as the interior portfolio. Several reformists were appointed to the Cabinet, which excluded representatives of the various 'confessional' blocs and former militia leaders whose rivalries had frequently undermined previous governments. Hezbollah declined to participate in the new Government. At the Cabinet's first session, held later in December, Gen. Michel Suleiman was appointed to succeed Lahoud as head of the armed forces. The al-Hoss Government's programme emphasized anti-corruption measures, economic liberalization and reduction of the public debt, as well as accelerated electoral reform. To that effect the judiciary was granted powers to investigate a number of political scandals and bring former high-ranking officials to trial. The incoming Government also revoked the five-year ban on the holding of public demonstrations.

Clashes persisted in southern Lebanon following Israel's 'adoption' of Resolution 425, amid continuing protests of violations of the April 1996 cease-fire 'understanding'. In May 1998 at least 10 people were killed in an Israeli air raid on a Fatah training camp in the central Beka'a valley; in two separate incidents in November, seven Israeli soldiers were killed as a result of attacks by Hezbollah on Israeli patrols in the occupied zone. Following further serious exchanges in December, in January 1999 Israel's Security Cabinet voted to respond to future Hezbollah offensives by targeting infrastructure in central and northern Lebanon (thereby extending the conflict beyond suspected guerrilla bases in the south). Hostilities escalated in February, when Israeli forces annexed the village of Arnoun, just outside the occupied zone; Israel also launched a peace agreement with Israel, and to establish normal relations with Israel within this comprehensive peace framework. The initiative was, however, rejected by Israel, which maintained that it would lead to the destruction of the State of Israel. During a visit to Lebanon by the US Secretary of State, Colin Powell, in April 2002, the Lebanese leadership maintained its stance that its obligation to respect the Blue Line did not exclude resistance (by Hezbollah) to 'liberate' Shebaa Farms, while President Assad gave no indication that he would exert his influence to halt Hezbollah offensives from southern Lebanon against Israel.

Jihad Jibril, the head of the PFLP—GC's military operations and son of the group's leader, was killed by a car bomb in west Beirut in May 2002. The Lebanese security forces blamed intra-Palestinian rivalries for the assassination, although many PFLP—GC officials held the Israeli intelligence services responsible. In August two people were killed in the worst factional fighting at the Ain al-Hilweh Palestinian refugee camp for several years. Tensions had escalated following the arrest of an Islamist militant in the previous month by the Lebanese army, aided by Fatah. (The Israeli daily *Ha'aretz* subsequently alleged that the violence at Ain al-Hilweh was linked to the presence there of up to 200 al-Qa'ida militants who had returned from the war in Afghanistan.) In September clashes between the Lebanese army and Palestinian militants at the al-Jalil refugee camp, near Ba'albak (Ba'albek), left one soldier and three Palestinians dead.

The Lebanese Government closed down a Christian opposition-controlled television station, Murr Television, and its sister radio station, Radio Mount Lebanon, in September 2002, claiming that they had undermined relations with Syria and violated electoral legislation banning party political broadcasts during a recent by-election in the Metn district, where one of the stations' owners, the nephew of Minister of the Interior Elias Murr, had won the seat. The ruling against Murr Television was upheld in December and a final appeal was rejected in April 2003, resulting in the station's permanent closure.

In November 2002 international donors attending a conference in Paris, France, agreed to provide Lebanon with an aid package worth some US $4,300m. to assist the country with its heavy burden of debt and to finance development projects. In April 2003, following weeks of reported disagreements between members of the Cabinet over economic and other domestic policies, the Prime Minister, Rafik Hariri, tendered his resignation and that of his Government. However, after his premiership was endorsed by the Lebanese parliament, Hariri was asked by President Lahoud to form a new 30-member cabinet. The new Government, announced two days after Hariri's resignation, brought in 11 new ministers, including Jean Obeid, who replaced Mahmoud Hammoud as Minister of Foreign Affairs and Emigrants; Hammoud was named as the new Minister of National Defence. The new Cabinet was widely considered to be the most pro-Syrian for more than a decade; it contained no members of the Christian opposition, nor of Hezbollah. Syria was still believed to be exerting considerable influence over Lebanese domestic affairs, despite the decreasing Syrian military presence in the country: in February 2003 Syria had commenced the redeployment of more than 4,000 troops stationed in northern Lebanon, under the terms of the Ta'if agreement; the withdrawal was reportedly carried out over several months.

It was reported in May 2003 that Lebanese security forces had arrested at least nine suspected al-Qa'ida operatives in Sidon. The suspects were accused of plotting to attack the US embassy in Beirut and to kidnap members of the Lebanese Cabinet. Moreover, they were believed to be linked to the al-Qa'ida militants thought to be in hiding in the Ain al-Hilweh refugee camp. In December 27 Lebanese were found guilty, and given varying prison sentences, on charges of carrying out bomb attacks against mostly US and British businesses in Lebanon between the end of 2002 and April 2003. However, a military court in Beirut acquitted three defendants of plotting to assassinate the US ambassador to Lebanon.

The Israeli Cabinet agreed in November 2003 to release more than 400 Palestinian, Lebanese (mostly Hezbollah) and other Arab prisoners in exchange for the remains of three soldiers kidnapped by Hezbollah in Shebaa Farms in 2000, as well as the return of the abducted Israeli businessman, Elhanan Tannenbaum. Israel also hoped to receive information on the fate of a missing Israeli airman, Ron Arad, who had been shot down over Lebanon in 1986, and was still believed to be held in Lebanese detention. Germany, which had mediated the negotiations between Israel and Hezbollah, oversaw the exchange, and in January 2004 the first 30 Lebanese and other Arab prisoners to be released by Israel were flown to the airport at Cologne, Germany, where they were exchanged for Tannenbaum and the remains of the Israeli soldiers. The remaining Palestinian prisoners, and the remains of 59 Lebanese militants held by Israel, were later released at Israeli border posts.

In January 2005 at least one Israeli officer and two UN observers were killed when Israeli soldiers retaliated against Hezbollah guerrilla attacks on an Israeli military vehicle patrolling Shebaa Farms. UN Secretary-General Kofi Annan criticized Israel's persistent violations of Lebanese airspace and also Hezbollah's recent launching of a drone over Israel, both of which he considered to be provocative acts; moreover, he urged Lebanon to respect the Blue Line. On 28 January the mandate of the UNIFIL observer mission (see above), already extended four times since July 2002, was extended until 31 July 2005; the UN Security Council expressed grave concern at the persistent violence along the Blue Line. The mission's mandate was extended again in July 2005 and February 2006. Meanwhile, in November 2005 Hezbollah launched what was apparently its heaviest attack on Israeli troops in the Shebaa Farms area since October 2000. Four Hezbollah militants were killed and 11 Israeli soldiers injured in the ensuing violence, in which the two sides exchanged heavy artillery fire across the border.

Meanwhile, four rounds of voting took place in municipal elections held in May 2004. At the first round (in Mount Lebanon governorate), Hezbollah and other pro-Syrian groups, such as the PSP and independent Christian candidates, defeated the primarily Christian opposition, which was reportedly suffering from internal divisions. At the second round, a list of candidates supported by Hariri won in Beirut (where turn-out was reportedly only 23%) against lists connected to the Parti communiste libanais (PCL) and the opposition Christian Free Patriotic Movement; in the Beka'a valley Hezbollah took the majority of municipalities that it contested, again securing victory over its opposition, Amal. At the third round, Hezbollah achieved further success, particularly in the mostly Shi'a villages on the Israeli border, where elections took place for the first time since the withdrawal of Israeli troops. The list supported by Hariri suffered an overwhelming defeat in the region's capital and the Prime Minister's home town, Sidon, while Amal secured an unexpected victory over Hezbollah in some mainly Shi'a villages. At the final round of elections in north Lebanon, a candidate considered to be a potential rival to Hariri as Prime Minister, Najib Mikati (also the Minister of Public Works and Transport and a close friend of Syrian President Assad), achieved success.

In August 2004, in advance of the expiry of President Lahoud's six-year term of office in November, the Cabinet voted to amend the Constitution, which prevented Lahoud from seeking a second term, to extend Lahoud's mandate by three years. Both Muslim and Christian politicians and Hariri protested against the decision, but Hariri eventually offered his support for the amendment after a meeting with Syrian politicians, including President Assad. The USA and France expressed their opposition to the move, and presented a resolution to the UN in early September in an attempt to forestall it. The UN subsequently adopted Resolution 1559, demanding that: Lebanon's sovereignty be respected; a 'free and fair' presidential election be held; the Government assert its power throughout the whole country; all foreign forces leave Lebanon; and all militias in the country, both Lebanese and non-Lebanese, disband and disarm. The resolution did not explicitly refer to Syria or its forces and agents, however. The Security Council gave Lebanon 30 days to comply with the resolution's demands, threatening to take measures against the country if it failed to meet them. Nevertheless, the National Assembly approved the constitutional amendment by 96 votes to 29, prompting the resignation of four cabinet ministers in protest.

The Syrian army responded to Resolution 1559 by redeploying about 3,000 special forces from positions to the south of Beirut, although some 14,000 Syrian troops remained in Lebanon. (Further redeployments of Syrian troops took place in December 2004, from the northern town of Batrun and from Beirut's southern suburbs and the airport to the Beka'a valley.) In October 2004, after UN Secretary-General Kofi Annan had reported Lebanon's non-compliance with the resolution, the Security Council ordered Annan to provide a report every six months detailing steps towards its fulfilment. Hariri dissolved his Cabinet a day after the release of the statement, declaring that he would not attempt to head the next government. The following day he was replaced by Omar Karami, who revealed the composition of his Cabinet five days later (which for the first time included two women). The former Minister of Public Health, Sulayman Franjiya, assumed the post of Minister of the Interior and Municipalities, while Mahmoud Hammoud became Minister of Foreign Affairs and Emigrants; Hammoud's former national defence portfolio was allocated to Abd ar-Rahim Mrad. The new Government, which received legislative approval in November, was considered to be still more favourable than its predecessor to continued Syrian influence in Lebanese affairs. The new Prime Minister criticized the recent UN Security Council resolution, asserting that: the fulfilment of its demands would lead to crises of security and stability in Lebanon; the resolution constituted external pressure on Syria and Lebanon; and the presence of Syrian troops in Lebanon was a matter only for the two countries involved. The USA exerted further pressure on Lebanon in January 2005, when it vowed to include Lebanon among its list of states deemed to sponsor terrorism if the country did not end its support for Hezbollah.

On 22 November 2004 (Independence Day) some 3,000 students from several universities and right-wing Christian activists demonstrated in Beirut against what they perceived to be Syria's dominance in Lebanon, in defiance of a government ban. At the end of the month the Government supported a march by over 100,000 demonstrators in Beirut in praise of Syria's influence in the country and rejecting the terms of UN Resolution 1559. In December parties opposed to the Lebanese Government's support of Syrian involvement in Lebanese affairs, including the main Christian opposition group, the Qornet Shehwan Gathering, Kamal Joumblatt's mainly Druze-supported PSP and the proscribed Lebanese Forces Party, issued a joint statement demanding a cessation of foreign interference in Lebanon and calling for the release of Lebanese Forces Party leader Samir Geagea, who had been imprisoned on murder charges in 1994. They also demanded an electoral law that would allow people of all political sensibilities to participate in governing the country.

On 14 February 2005 a car bombing in Beirut killed Rafik Hariri, the former Prime Minister and business executive, and 22 other people; at least 100 were injured in the blast. The attack provoked condemnation from Syrian President Assad. However, the USA, emphasizing the problems caused by the Syrian military presence in Lebanon and the inability of the Syrian-dominated intelligence services to forestall the attack, removed its ambassador to Syria for consultations, and later demanded that all Syrian troops withdraw from Lebanon. Later in the month Syria announced that it would redeploy its troops in Lebanon to the Beka'a valley. On 28 February, following a general strike and mass protests in Beirut advocated by opposition parties, at which demonstrators demanded the complete withdrawal of Syrian troops from Lebanon and an end to Syrian influence in Lebanese politics, Karami dissolved his Cabinet and resigned as premier. Nevertheless, Lahoud requested that Karami and his ministers remain in office in an interim capacity pending the appointment of a new government.

Lebanese opposition groups demanded in March 2005 that President Assad and the public prosecutor and senior security officials in Lebanon resign their posts in order to ensure that the investigation into Hariri's death be conducted legitimately and with integrity. They also announced their refusal to participate in any discussions on the formation of a new government until their demands were met. Also in March US Secretary of State Condoleezza Rice reiterated demands by President George W. Bush, the Lebanese opposition and several other countries that Syria withdraw its troops and security forces from Lebanon. Assad and Lahoud agreed at a summit meeting to the withdrawal of Syrian troops to the Beka'a valley by the end of the month; Syria later pledged to withdraw all troops prior to Lebanon's general election, scheduled to begin in May, and to provide the UN with a timetable for the withdrawal. Meanwhile, protests took place in Beirut in support of the Syrian influence and military presence in Lebanon. Syria reportedly withdrew 4,000–6,000 of its soldiers and intelligence agents from Lebanon to Syria in mid-March; 8,000–10,000 troops remained in the Beka'a valley. A UN report released later that month accused Syria of allowing political tension in Lebanon to be heightened before the murder of Hariri, and criticized Lebanon's initial attempts to investigate the incident. In April the UN Security Council approved Resolution 1595, establishing an International Independent Investigation Commission (UNIIIC) to investigate Hariri's murder. The German prosecutor appointed to head the commission, Detlev Mehlis, arrived in Lebanon in May. In April Syria had declared that it had fulfilled its promise to withdraw all troops, military assets and intelligence apparatus, and in May a UN team dispatched to Lebanon to confirm the withdrawal announced that thus far it had not found a single Syrian soldier in areas that it had inspected. However, it reported that an armed guard had blocked the road and fired shots in the air when members of the team had attempted to approach a base in Qussaya, a border village in which the PFLP—GC (which attributed the incident to a misunderstanding) had positions.

President Lahoud reappointed Karami to the post of Prime Minister on 10 March 2005. Yet in the following month Karami, having failed to form a new administration, tendered his resignation for a second time, and Najib Mikati was appointed to the post of caretaker Prime Minister. Mikati named a new Cabinet (approved by the National Assembly on 27 April), which was to be responsible for the implementation of legislation facilitating a general election. Elias Murr was appointed Deputy Prime Minister and Minister of National Defence, while Mahmoud Hammoud retained responsibility for foreign affairs and emigrants. In late April three senior Lebanese security officials with close ties to Syria announced their resignations, and by mid-May a number of other pro-Syrian security officials, whose replacement had been demanded by the opposition, had been dismissed from their posts.

Elections to the National Assembly were held in four rounds between 29 May and 19 June 2005. The first round of voting took place in the Beirut region, where turn-out was a reported 28%. The anti-Syrian Rafik Hariri Martyr List, headed by the Future Movement (Tayar al-Mustaqbal) of Rafik Hariri's son, Saad ed-Din Hariri, and including the PSP, the Lebanese Forces Party and the Qornet Shehwan Gathering, won all 19 seats. Four days later the prominent anti-Syrian journalist Dr Samir Kassir was killed in a car bombing in a Christian district of Beirut. The anti-Syrian opposition accused remaining Syrian intelligence agents of involvement in the murder, and again called on President Lahoud to resign. An estimated 45% of registered voters participated in the second round of elections conducted on 5 June in southern Lebanon; as in the first round, turn-out was reportedly lower in Christian than in Muslim districts. The Resistance and Development Bloc, consisting of the pro-Syrian Shi'a organizations Amal and Hezbollah and their allies, secured all 23 seats. The third round was held on 12 June in Mount Lebanon, where candidates contested 35 seats and turn-out was unofficially estimated at 54%, and the Beka'a Valley, where an estimated 49% of registered voters elected deputies to 23 seats. Immediately prior to the poll, Gen. Michel Aoun allied himself with pro-Syrian factions as the Free Patriotic Movement (Tayar al-Watani al-Horr), declaring that he was no longer hostile to Syria now that it had withdrawn its troops from Lebanon. Aoun's alliance took 21 seats, while Hariri's list secured 25. However, in the final round in north Lebanon on 19 June, at which turn-out was officially estimated at 49%, Hariri's list won all 28 seats. Consequently, according to final results, the Rafik Hariri Martyr List secured 72 of the National Assembly's 128 seats, allowing the officially prohibited Lebanese Forces Party to achieve parliamentary representation for the first time; the Resistance and Development Bloc won 35 seats; and the Free Patriotic Movement took 21.

In June 2005 George Hawi, the former Secretary-General of the PCL and an outspoken critic of Syrian interference in Lebanese politics, was killed by a car bomb in Beirut. The anti-Syrian opposition attributed the attack to Syrian agents and their allies in the Lebanese security services. Further bomb explosions took place in the capital throughout 2005, causing a number of fatalities. In July two people were killed in an explosion that injured pro-Syrian Deputy Prime Minister Murr, and in December the anti-Syrian publisher of the daily newspaper An-Nahar, Gebran Tueni, and three others were killed in a car bombing.

Meanwhile, pro-Syrian Nabih Berri was re-elected President of the National Assembly in June 2005. Two days later President Lahoud appointed Fouad Siniora of the Future Movement, a close ally of Rafik Hariri, as Prime Minister, and asked him to form a new government. In July Siniora announced the composition of a new Cabinet: Fawzi Salloukh was appointed Minister of Foreign Affairs and Emigrants, while Muhammad Fneish became the first representative of Hezbollah to hold cabinet office, assuming responsibility for energy and water. In the same month the National Assembly passed a law pardoning Lebanese Forces Party leader Samir Geagea, as demanded by some of the opposition (see above). Almost 40 Islamist militants, some of whom were allegedly linked to al-Qa'ida, were also released by parliamentary approval. Prime Minister Siniora met Syrian President Assad and Prime Minister Otari in Syria in August. The two states reportedly agreed to improve relations based on mutual respect, and Siniora emphasized Lebanon's support of Syria and its commitment to bilateral agreements.

Following reports that Syrian intelligence agents might not have completely withdrawn from Lebanon, the UN announced in June 2005 that it was considering sending a commission to the country to investigate the claims; Syria continued to insist that it had removed all its security personnel. UNIIIC began its inquiry into Rafik Hariri's assassination in mid-June, with a three-month mandate. In August UNIIIC arrested the three former security officials who had tendered their resignations in April (see above) for questioning regarding the assassination. A fourth security chief, who had retained his post after Hariri's murder, was also sought, and subsequently handed himself in to the organization; a former pro-Syrian parliamentary deputy was also detained. In October, shortly before UNIIIC issued its first report on the investigation, the Syrian Minister of the Interior, Maj.-Gen. Ghazi Kanaan, was found shot dead in his office. The official Syrian Arab News Agency announced that he had committed suicide. A former head of Syrian military intelligence in Lebanon, Kanaan had become Chief of Political Intelligence in Syria in 2002, and had been appointed Minister of the Interior in October 2004. Shortly before his apparent suicide, Kanaan had told a Lebanese radio station that he had been questioned by UNIIIC, but had not given any evidence against Syria. According to its report, issued in October 2005, UNIIIC had found evidence that Lebanese and Syrian intelligence and security services were directly involved in Hariri's assassination. Moreover, the report reasoned, the act was too complex and too well planned to have taken place without the approval of senior Syrian security officials and their Lebanese counterparts. UNIIIC expressed its extreme concern at the lack of co-operation by the Syrian authorities. Lebanon and Syria, which denounced the investigation's findings as politically motivated, rejected the report, and Syria announced that it had established a special judicial commission to deal with all matters relating to UNIIIC's mission. The commission was granted an extension to its mandate until December.

The UN Security Council responded to the first UNIIIC report by adopting in October 2005 a resolution, sponsored by the USA, France and the United Kingdom, establishing measures against suspects in the assassination, including prohibitions on travel and the freezing of assets. The Security Council urged Syria to co-operate fully with the investigation commission and detain suspects identified by the inquiry, threatening unspecified 'further action' should Syria fail to comply with the resolution's demands by the stipulated deadline of 15 December. Syria reported in November that it had arrested six government officials for questioning. Meanwhile, in October the UN Special Envoy, Terje Roed-Larsen, issued his report on the implementation of UN Security Council Resolution 1559, in which he praised the withdrawal of Syrian troops from Lebanon, but noted that Lebanon had still not complied with the demands that Lebanese and non-Lebanese militias disarm and disband, and that government authority be extended throughout the country. Lebanon rejected the report, asserting that the Government would deal with armed groups through national dialogue.

In December 2005 UNIIIC began questioning five Syrian officials suspected of involvement in Hariri's assassination in Vienna, Austria. Detlev Mehlis presented his second report on the investigating body's work to the UN Security Council later in the month. While noting that Syria had presented the five officials to the commission for interrogation, the report again accused Syria of reluctance to co-operate with the investigating body and of hindering the investigation. It stated that UNIIIC had found further evidence that the Lebanese and Syrian intelligence and security services had been involved in the assassination, and revealed that Mehlis had identified 19 suspects, six of whom were Syrian (including the five being questioned in Vienna). Mehlis resigned as the head of UNIIIC shortly afterwards, citing personal and professional reasons; he was replaced by Serge Brammertz, and UNIIIC's mandate was extended to 15 June 2006.

In January 2006 UNIIIC investigators declared that they wished to question Syrian President Assad and Minister of Foreign Affairs Farouk ash-Shara' in relation to Hariri's murder. (A few days earlier the Vice-President of Syria, Abd al-Halim Khaddam, who had been living in exile in Paris, having resigned his post in June 2005, had accused Assad of personally threatening Hariri. He subsequently declared that, in his view, Assad had ordered Hariri's assassination, although he awaited the final decision of the investigating commission.) However, the following day the Syrian Minister of Information announced that Syria would not permit UNIIIC to interview Assad. Ash-Shara' announced in March 2006 that he had reached an agreement with UNIIIC that provided for full Syrian co-operation with the investigation, while preserving the country's 'sovereignty and dignity'.

Ministers from Hezbollah and Amal announced in February 2006 that they were ending a boycott of cabinet meetings begun in December in protest against the Government's decision to allow an international investigation into Hariri's assassination. The announcement came shortly after Prime Minister Fouad Siniora declared to the National Assembly that the Government had always considered Hezbollah to be a movement of national resistance rather than a militia (a further demand of the ministers). Meanwhile, protests were taking place in Beirut and throughout the world against caricatures of the Prophet Muhammad (portrayal of whom is considered blasphemous in Islam), originally published in a Danish newspaper in September 2005, but subsequently reprinted in newspapers in various countries. In Beirut the protests, which had apparently been infiltrated by Islamist extremists, culminated in February 2006 in riots during which the Danish embassy was attacked and around 200 people were arrested. Apparently in response to this outbreak of disorder, the Minister of the Interior and Municipalities, Hassan as-Sabaa, resigned. The Minister of Youth and Sports, Ahmad Fatfat, assumed his responsibilities in an acting capacity.

Lebanese army sources claimed in May 2006 that four Israeli aircraft had violated southern Lebanese airspace. In the following month UNIIIC published its latest findings in its investigation into the assassination of Rafik Hariri. While maintaining that progress had been made in terms of the investigators' understanding of the links between those who had orchestrated and those who had executed the attack, the report acknowledged that it was not immediately feasible to reach any conclusions concerning possible connections between Hariri's murder and the killing of several other anti-Syrian personalities since October 2004. UNIIIC's mandate was duly extended until 15 June 2007.

On 12 July 2006 Hezbollah soldiers conducted a cross-border raid in which three Israeli troops were killed and two were captured; five more Israeli soldiers were killed during an attempt to rescue the kidnapped men. Prime Minister Siniora denied Israeli claims that his Government had organized the soldiers' abduction, and insisted that he did not condone the raid. Later that same day Israel launched a series of air raids on a number of suspected Hezbollah positions across southern Lebanon. Further strikes during the night caused extensive damage to civilian infrastructure in the area. Hezbollah declared 'open war' on 14 July, firing barrages of rockets into northern Israel in response to Israeli air-strikes. On the same day the UN Security Council held an emergency meeting, which was reported to have been called by Lebanon and at which Lebanon accused Israel of instigating the violence.

Numerous strikes were exchanged between the two warring factions on a daily basis and, despite claims to the contrary from both sides, who insisted that they were targeting political and military targets exclusively, many civilians were killed or injured in the conflict and thousands of homes were destroyed. Israel systematically targeted Lebanese infrastructure—roads and bridges were destroyed, seaports were blockaded and Beirut International Airport was bombed, forcing all international flights to be diverted to Cyprus. An estimated 70% of civilians living in southern Lebanon fled to the north of the country to escape the worst of the violence. In late July 2006 at least 28 civilians, including 19 children, were reported to have been killed when a residential building in the Lebanese village of Qana was struck by missiles during an Israeli air raid. At an emergency session of the UN Security Council, convened on the following day, members issued a statement expressing 'extreme shock and distress' at the attack; UN Secretary-General Kofi Annan, while apportioning blame for the initial outbreak of the conflict to Hezbollah, denounced the Israeli response as excessive and as being responsible for 'death and suffering on a wholly unacceptable scale'. Nevertheless, in early August the Israeli Cabinet approved a plan to send a large number of ground troops further into Lebanon, as far as the Litani river (approximately 30 km north of the Israeli–Lebanese border).

The USA and France agreed at the beginning of August 2006 upon the content of a draft resolution to be submitted to the UN Security Council, which duly convened to discuss the proposed terms. (The USA had come under criticism for apparently blocking earlier attempts to impose a cease-fire, which had led to allegations that the Bush Administration was implicitly encouraging Israel to wreak damage upon Hezbollah.) On 11 August the Security Council adopted Resolution 1701, which had been unanimously approved and which called for: an immediate and full cessation of hostilities; the extension of the Lebanese Government's authority over the whole country; and the delineation of Lebanese international boundaries, with particular regard to disputed sectors such as Shebaa Farms. The resolution was endorsed by the Lebanese Government on 12 August, and Sheikh Nasrallah announced that Hezbollah would honour the call for a cease-fire; however, 24 Israeli soldiers were killed on that same day—the greatest loss of life on any single day since the conflict began. Similarly, despite Israel's Cabinet approving the resolution on 13 August, on the following day Israeli troops launched an attack on a refugee camp in Sidon, killing an UNRWA staff member approximately one hour before the cease-fire was scheduled to take effect.

In late August 2006 Sheikh Nasrallah acknowledged that Hezbollah's kidnapping of the two Israeli soldiers that had triggered the conflict had, with hindsight, been deeply regrettable and that talks concerning their possible return, in exchange for Lebanese nationals detained by Israel, were ongoing. However, he remained defiant, claiming during a rally staged in Beirut in September that Hezbollah was stronger than it had been prior to the conflict and that the organization possessed in excess of 20,000 rockets in its arsenal. Earlier that month Israel had lifted its naval blockade of Lebanon and rescinded its restrictions on air travel to and from Lebanon, thereby formalizing the end of the conflict. However, much of southern Lebanon remained uninhabitable owing to the presence of unexploded cluster bombs. According to figures released by Lebanon's Higher Relief Council, an estimated 1,191 Lebanese civilians were killed during the conflict, and a further 4,410 were thought to have been injured. According to the Israeli Ministry of Foreign Affairs, 119 Israeli troops and 44 Israeli civilians had died in the fighting, and more than 530 Hezbollah members had also been killed. In November the findings of an official UN investigation into the conflict determined that Israel had fired artillery shells containing white phosphorus, an incendiary substance the use of which against civilians, or against legitimate military targets within residential areas, is banned under the terms of the Geneva Convention. However, the Israeli Government refuted the claim, insisting that the shells had been aimed solely at military targets in open ground. Meanwhile, in September 2006 the human rights group Amnesty International accused Hezbollah of having committed war crimes by deliberately targeting Israeli civilians in its air-strikes during the recent conflict.

In October 2006 Sheikh Nasrallah demanded that Hezbollah be allocated one-third of the seats in an expanded national unity government, prompting accusations that he was attempting to attain the right of veto in order to protect the Syrian Government from prosecution in the ongoing investigation into the assassination of Rafik Hariri. Nasrallah's demands were ignored, however, and in the following month five ministers—two members of Hezbollah and three from its ally, Amal—resigned from the Cabinet, thereby removing any Shi'a presence from the Government. A sixth resignation, that of a Christian pro-Syrian minister, followed soon afterwards. The assassination later in November of Pierre Gemayel, the Minister of Industry since 2005, rendered the political situation even more unstable. Gemayel was shot dead in his car in a suburb of Beirut, and many Lebanese leaders were quick to blame Syria for his murder. Since the Lebanese Constitution decrees that any government in which one-third of the ministers have vacated their posts must automatically be dissolved and a new government appointed, Gemayel's assassination meant that, should just one further minister leave the Cabinet for any reason, it would force the collapse of the Government.

In December 2006 thousands of demonstrators gathered in Beirut and erected tents in the capital's main square, besieging government buildings and proclaiming that the Cabinet was now constitutionally invalid. When the protests, aimed at pressurizing the Government into resigning, had failed to achieve any tangible results by late January 2007, the opposition intensified its efforts and called for a general strike, which brought commercial districts of the capital to a virtual standstill; at least three people were killed during clashes between protesters and the authorities. The security forces appeared to do little to remove the road blockades that were in place, leading to allegations that the police and the army were colluding with the opposition to bring about the Government's collapse. Nevertheless, the strike had a minimal effect on the resolve of the Government, which remained in place in early May 2008, despite the continuing efforts of those participating in the sit-in protest and the rapid intensification of sectarian violence (see below). Yet, despite the Government's refusal to submit to the wishes of the opposition, the presence of two separate Lebanese delegations at the annual summit meeting of the Arab League, held in Saudi Arabia in March 2007, aptly symbolized the endemic divisions threatening the country's future stability.

Meanwhile, a disagreement between pro-Government Sunni and anti-Government Shi'a students at Beirut Arab University in January 2007 escalated into violent clashes that spilled out onto the streets; up to four people were killed and more than 150 were injured. The incident further fuelled concerns that Lebanon was about to spiral into full-scale sectarian conflict again, fears that appeared to be shared by the Government, which responded to the latest violence by imposing an overnight curfew in Beirut—the first of its kind in a decade. In February two bombs were detonated on commuter buses travelling through Ein Alaq, a village to the north-east of Beirut, killing three people. The attacks, which took place on the eve of the second anniversary of Hariri's assassination, were widely considered to have been timed so as to deter people from travelling to Beirut to attend a rally to mark the occasion; however, amid tight security, tens of thousands of people congregated on the following day to honour their former leader. In March Hassan as-Sabaa, who had retracted his resignation as Minister of the Interior and Municipalities in November 2006, announced that four Syrian members of Fatah al-Islam—a militant Islamist Palestinian group, inspired by al-Qa'ida and alleged by the Lebanese authorities to be supported by Syria—had been arrested on suspicion of involvement in the bus explosions in Ein Alaq.

In March 2007 UNIIIC released its latest report into the assassination of Rafik Hariri, in which again it claimed to have made considerable progress in acquiring further evidence, but declined to give specific details. Brammertz did, however, state that UNIIIC had identified 250 individuals whom it wanted to question; 50 of these were to be interviewed within the next three months. UNIIIC's mandate was extended to 15 June 2008. Also in March 2007 recently appointed UN Secretary-General Ban Ki-Moon issued his report on the implementation of UN Security Council Resolution 1701, in which he rebuked both Israel and Lebanon for failing to adhere to all of its terms. However, he praised both sides' overall commitment to maintaining the cease-fire, and proposed the establishment of an independent assessment mission to assist with the monitoring of the Israeli–Lebanese border and thereby to facilitate the full implementation of the resolution.

A copy of the interim report of Israel's Winograd Commission, a government-appointed commission of inquiry into Israel's military campaign in Lebanon, was made public at the end of April 2007. This preliminary report, which focused specifically on the period between Israel's withdrawal from southern Lebanon in 2000 to mid-July 2006, contained severe criticism of prominent Israeli government officials, notably Prime Minister Olmert, Minister of Defence Amir Peretz and the Chief of Staff of the Armed Forces during the conflict, Lt-Gen. Dan Halutz (who had resigned in January 2007). Olmert was accused of having initiated the military action against Hezbollah 'hastily' and without due consideration for the likely outcome and repercussions of such action, while Halutz was deemed to have provided inadequate information to the Prime Minister and Minister of Defence regarding the shortcomings of the Israeli armed forces. Sheikh Nasrallah welcomed the findings of the Commission (for further details, see the chapter on Israel) and acknowledged the level of self-criticism that Israel had demonstrated, conceding that this was worthy of 'respect'.

At the end of May 2007 the UN Security Council adopted Resolution 1757, authorizing the formation of an international tribunal to try suspects in Hariri's assassination. The Special Tribunal for Lebanon (STL) was to comprise 11 independent judges (or 14, should a second trial chamber be created), of whom seven were to be international judges and four were to be

Lebanese; should a second trial chamber be created, there were to be nine international and five Lebanese judges. For security reasons, the tribunal would not be based in Lebanon itself, and in August it was reported that the Netherlands was close to reaching an agreement with the UN to allow it to be hosted by The Hague. While the creation of the STL was welcomed by the Siniora Government, the Hezbollah-led opposition was quick to challenge its validity. Sheikh Nasrallah insisted that any such tribunal not approved by the Lebanese legislature was illegitimate, suggesting that the new body would be unable to rely on the co-operation of Hezbollah should no agreement concerning its establishment be reached between the opposition and the Government.

In mid-June 2007 Walid Eido, a revered anti-Syrian legislator and member of Saad ed-Din Hariri's Future Movement, was killed along with nine other people, including Eido's son, in a car bombing in Beirut. Once again, suspicions were immediately raised regarding Syria's involvement; however, Syrian officials vehemently denied the allegations. A few days later, following a request by Prime Minister Siniora, the UN Security Council announced that UNIIIC was to assist with the investigation into Eido's assassination. By-elections to select replacements for Eido, in Beirut's second district, and for Pierre Gemayel, in the Metn district, were held in August. The former seat was won comfortably by the pro-Government Muhammad Amin Itani, of the Future Movement, while the latter was secured by pro-Syrian Camille Khoury, of the Free Patriotic Movement, in a very tight contest against his closest rival, former President Amin Gemayel. Khoury's victory was a considerable reverse for the Lebanese leadership, which had hoped to fill both seats with supporters of Siniora; since the assassination of Eido had reduced the number of pro-Government legislators to 68, the loss of just three more seats, for whatever reason, would result in the loss of the Siniora administration's majority quorum.

The latest UNIIIC report (the sixth compiled during the tenure of Serge Brammertz) was released in mid-July 2007. The report asserted that a 'number of persons' had now been identified who might have been involved in Hariri's assassination, and stated that Syria and other states had continued to provide a 'mostly positive response' to UNIIIC's requests for co-operation and information. Also in July Lebanese investigators concluded that Fatah al-Islam had been responsible for the killing of Pierre Gemayel. In the previous month two UN armoured vehicles travelling between the villages of Marjayoun and Khaim, close to the Israeli border, were hit by a roadside bomb; three Spanish and three Colombian UN personnel were killed in the incident. In August the UN Security Council voted to extend the mandate of UNIFIL by another year. Its mandate was extended again, until 31 August 2009, by a UN Security Council vote in late August 2008; at March 2009 UNIFIL military personnel numbered 12,261, supported by 988 international and local civilian personnel. Meanwhile, the 10th UNIIIC report, and the first to be published since the appointment in early 2008 of Daniel Bellemare in place of Brammertz, was issued in March of that year. In the report, the UN body revealed that the evidence it had examined thus far indicated that a network of people was behind Hariri's murder, without mentioning specific individuals. In early April Bellemare asked the UN Security Council for a further six months to investigate the crime. A UN Security Council resolution issued in early June extended UNI-IIC's mandate until 31 December.

At the beginning of September 2007 a 105-day siege of the Nahr al-Bared refugee camp in Tripoli was finally concluded when the Lebanese army seized control from Islamist militants. The siege had begun in late May, after members of Fatah al-Islam had fled to the camp having conducted a bank robbery in the town of Amioun, south of Tripoli. In the ensuing weeks more than 300 people were believed to have been killed in fierce clashes between the army and militants within the camp, which forced an estimated 40,000 Palestinian refugees to flee in order escape the violence. Fatah al-Islam's leader—Shaker al-Abassi, who had been sentenced to death *in absentia* in April 2004 for the murder in 2002 of a US diplomat, Laurence Foley (see the chapter on Jordan)—was reported to have been killed in the closing stages of the fighting; however, subsequent DNA tests carried out on the body thought to have been that of al-Abassi proved negative, suggesting that the militant leader might have fled the camp before the siege was concluded. The Syrian Government commended the efforts of the Lebanese army in ending the siege, and continued to deny ongoing claims that it in any way supported or condoned the activities of Fatah al-Islam. In mid-March 2008 al-Abassi was charged with incitement to murder, in connection with the bus explosions at Ein Alaq in February 2007.

With the scheduled expiry, in November 2007, of Lahoud's presidential term, the attention of the Government and the opposition in the preceding months came increasingly to focus on the election of his successor. The first session of the National Assembly to elect a new president was duly arranged for 25 September 2007—the first time that the legislature was to have met since October 2006. In a conciliatory overture, the President of the Assembly, Nabih Berri, proposed an initiative whereby the opposition would relinquish its long-standing demand for a national unity government if the rival factions could agree on a presidential candidate, although the response from Siniora and his supporters to the proposal was muted. The ambiguity of the Lebanese Constitution meant that, in the event of political divisions between the two camps preventing agreement on a common candidate, the likely eventuality remained deeply uncertain. According to the Constitution, if a new president was not elected by 23 November 2007, then Siniora and his Cabinet would automatically assume executive control. However, the Constitution also authorizes the President to decree the resignation of the Cabinet, allowing Lahoud, should he have chosen, to appoint a new, opposition cabinet, which would almost certainly have elected a pro-Syrian, anti-Government president. Lebanon experienced a further political assassination in late September, just six days before the scheduled presidential election, when Antoine Ghanem, a Christian Phalangist legislator, was killed in a car bombing in a predominantly Christian district of Beirut. Five others died in the explosion, for which Syrian officials were again obliged to deny claims of involvement by certain Lebanese leaders. Since the Government and opposition demonstrated an unwillingness to co-operate in order to elect a new president, the National Assembly failed to achieve the requisite two-thirds' quorum of members on 25 September owing to an opposition boycott; a second vote was thus scheduled for 23 October. Speculation increased at this time about the possibility of a return to a dual-government system, effectively formalizing the intense divisions in Lebanon.

Following mediation by German diplomats and representatives of the International Committee of the Red Cross, Hezbollah and Israel carried out a limited exchange of prisoners and bodies in mid-October 2007—the first such exchange between the two sides since their conflict of the previous year. However, the two Israeli soldiers whose abduction by Hezbollah militants in July 2006 had apparently provoked the conflict were not included in the arrangement. In late January 2008 Sheikh Nasrallah alleged that Hezbollah was holding the remains of a number of Israeli troops killed during the 2006 conflict. Indeed, the remains of several Israeli soldiers were handed over to Israel at the start of June 2008, when the Israeli authorities returned a Lebanese civilian who had served a six-year prison term for espionage. At the end of June the Israeli Cabinet controversially voted to exchange the bodies of the two soldiers abducted by Hezbollah in July 2006 (who it now transpired were certainly dead) for five Lebanese detainees. The exchange occurred in mid-July 2008, with a large crowd welcoming the prisoners back to Lebanon. (One of the detainees, Samir Kuntar, was a militant of the Palestine Liberation Front, who had been handed down multiple life sentences for an attack on the Israeli town of Nahariya in April 1979.) Meanwhile, in mid-June 2008, at which time indirect, bilateral talks were said to be ongoing between Israel and Syria, the Israeli Government was reported to have offered to initiate direct peace discussions with the Lebanese Government, which could include efforts to resolve the issue of the disputed Shebaa Farms area.

The second postponement of the scheduled ballot to elect a successor to President Lahoud was announced by Berri on 22 October 2007, the day before the vote was to take place; a new date of 12 November was declared. In early October US President Bush had warned the Syrian Government not to interfere in Lebanon's internal affairs, since it was a boycott of the National Assembly by pro-Syrian opposition members that had rendered the parliament inquorate. Thus began a seven-month period during which no fewer than 17 further postponements of the presidential election were ordered, owing to a failure by the opposing factions to agree first on a mutually acceptable candidate, and then on the exact nature of administration to be formed after a new president had been elected. When the parliamentary session scheduled for 23 November—at the end of which Lahoud's term of office expired—was postponed until 30 November, it meant that Lahoud was obliged to leave office without a successor having been appointed. Under the terms of the Constitution, therefore, presidential duties were assumed by the Siniora Government in an acting capacity, although, shortly before the expiry of his mandate, Lahoud had issued a statement asserting that, owing to conditions being present for a 'state of emergency', he would hand over responsibility for the country's security to the armed forces. (He and other representatives of the pro-Syrian opposition refused to recognize the legitimacy of the Government following the ministerial resignations of November 2006.) Yet Lahoud's stance was firmly rejected by the Prime Minister, who insisted that no Head of State could call a state of emergency without the approval of the Cabinet. This represented the first time that Lebanon had been without a president since the civil war ended in 1990.

Although the Commander-in-Chief of the Army, Gen. Michel Suleiman (a Maronite Christian), was chosen as a 'compromise candidate' acceptable to both pro-Government and pro-opposition politicians towards the end of November 2007, disagreements remained as to how to amend the Constitution in order to permit Suleiman, as a serving senior state official, to assume the office of Head of State. Amid a flurry of international and regional diplomatic meetings, the ministers responsible for the foreign affairs of Arab League member states, meeting in Cairo, Egypt, in early January 2008, approved details of a plan intended to bring to an end Lebanon's presidential vacuum. The three-phase proposals included the election of Suleiman as president, establishment of a Lebanese government of national unity (where Suleiman would have the deciding vote in any dispute) and approval of new electoral legislation. It was reported that the Arab League plan had received the support of both the Lebanese and Syrian administrations, but that Hezbollah and its principal allies continued to demand that they receive at least one-third of government portfolios in any new cabinet, thus granting them the right to veto important decisions. A National Assembly session to elect a president was postponed (for the 19th time) on 13 May. In early April, meanwhile, Suleiman had announced his intention to retire from his military post in August, three months in advance of the scheduled date.

In mid-December 2007 Brig.-Gen. François al-Hajj, the army's head of operations, was killed, along with three other people, in a car bomb attack in east Beirut. Observers noted the significance of the fact that al-Hajj had been widely expected to be promoted to Commander-in-Chief of the Army should Suleiman be elected as Lahoud's successor. It was, however, unclear as to which group had carried out the assassination, with Syria, Israel and Fatah al-Islam all being accused by various parties of responsibility for the blast. An explosion apparently aimed at US embassy officials in mid-January 2008 resulted in the deaths of four Lebanese bystanders. There was a further wave of unrest in the principally Shi'ite suburbs of southern Beirut in late January, which had been precipitated by popular frustration over power shortages; seven protesters were reported to have died in the ensuing clashes with security forces. A group of army officers was detained and charged by the authorities in February, amid criticism of the military's handling of the protests. Towards the end of January, meanwhile, Capt. Wissam Eid, a senior member of the police team charged with investigating the recent bombings and assassinations, was himself killed in another car bomb attack in a suburb of the capital; Eid's driver and up to 10 others also died in the explosion. In mid-February Imad Mughniyeh, one of Hezbollah's most senior militants, was killed in a car bombing in the Syrian capital. Hezbollah representatives immediately blamed Israel for Mughniyeh's death; however, Israeli officials rejected such claims. Mughniyeh had been implicated in a number of high-profile kidnappings of Western journalists, military personnel and religious envoys in Lebanon during the 1980s, as well as in several bomb attacks against principally US interests in the 1980s and 1990s; his funeral in Beirut attracted significant levels of support from Hezbollah members.

The Winograd Commission published the final results of its investigation into Israel's military campaign in Lebanon of July–August 2006 on 30 January 2008. Although the Commission described Israel's ground offensive in Lebanon as a 'serious failure' in both military and political terms—a large-scale offensive, in which 33 Israeli soldiers died, notably having been ordered in southern Lebanon only hours before an agreed cease-fire was scheduled to take effect—Prime Minister Olmert was judged to have acted 'in the sincere interest of Israel' in ordering the military action.

Lebanon's political situation deteriorated rapidly in early May 2008, when a decision taken by the Government to shut down a private telecommunications network controlled by Hezbollah and to close Beirut International Airport (where Hezbollah was accused of using surveillance equipment to spy on pro-Government politicians) prompted fierce clashes between members of the Shi'a opposition group and government loyalists. Moreover, a general strike called by the opposition in protest against price increases and to demand higher salaries descended into violence. As Sheikh Nasrallah called the Government's actions against his organization a 'declaration of war', gunmen from Hezbollah and its allies besieged the Beirut offices of the media controlled by the Future Movement's Saad ed-Din Hariri, while major roads were blocked. Observers noted that west Beirut was now effectively controlled by militants of the Hezbollah-led opposition. After several days of violent clashes, which spread to other cities such as Tripoli, at least 81 people had been killed, and up to 250 wounded, in Lebanon's worst period of unrest since the civil war. However, by mid-May the Government and army claimed to have regained control, and, following mediation by the Arab League, the Cabinet voted to revoke the measures that had provoked the recent violence—an outcome widely viewed as a demonstration of Hezbollah's growing military strength and influence. This positive development meant that the lengthy sit-in by demonstrators in the centre of Beirut came to an end and businesses that had been closed during the months of paralysis began to resume trading.

On 21 May 2008 18 months of conflict between the Lebanese Government on one side and Hezbollah and its allies on the other was apparently bought to an end through the signing of the Doha Agreement. The agreement was named after the Qatari capital, where—following effective mediation by the Qatari leadership under the auspices of the Arab League—the two sides finally agreed to seek to put aside their differences in order to restore national unity. The Doha Agreement encompassed: the election of a new president; formation of a national unity government, which would involve power-sharing with Hezbollah; and introduction of a new electoral law. A few days after the signing of the unity accord, Fouad Siniora was chosen by the National Assembly to remain as Prime Minister. Yet, notwithstanding the election of a new President (see below) and formation of a 30-member national unity Cabinet on 11 July (the administration consisted of 16 ministers of the Western-supported majority coalition, 11 linked to Hezbollah and its allies, and three appointed by President Suleiman), the security situation in Lebanon remained uneasy as the summer of 2008 progressed. Heavy fighting between supporters of the Government and pro-opposition activists was reported in the eastern Beka'a Valley and Tripoli, resulting in dozens of fatalities. Michel Suleiman had been sworn in as President on 25 May 2008, having finally been elected by the National Assembly. Prior to Suleiman's election, the President of the National Assembly, Nabih Berri, rejected the demands of some deputies that the Constitution needed to be amended to permit a serving official to become President; this occasion was deemed exceptional since the presidency was actually vacant. The new Siniora Government secured a vote of confidence in the National Assembly on 12 August, and thus would administer the country until the holding of fresh legislative elections in 2009. Elias Murr remained as Deputy Prime Minister and Minister of National Defence, Issam Abou Jamra was appointed as a second Deputy Prime Minister, Fawzi Salloukh returned to the Cabinet as Minister of Foreign Affairs and Emigrants (having resigned the post in November 2006) and Ziad Baroud was named as Minister of the Interior and Municipalities. At the end of August 2008 Brig.-Gen. Jean Kahwaji was chosen as Suleiman's successor as Commander-in-Chief of the Army.

A landmark agreement was reached between Lebanon and Syria in mid-July 2008, when the two countries announced that they were to enter into diplomatic relations and open embassies in one another's capitals for the first time since they had achieved independence in 1943 and 1945, respectively. The announcement was made by the French President, Nicolas Sarkozy, who welcomed Syria's President Assad and President Suleiman to Paris in advance of the summit convened to launch his Union for the Mediterranean initiative. Following the agreement to resume ties, it was revealed that the work of a committee to demarcate the Lebanese–Syrian border and to investigate the issue of missing persons since Lebanon's civil war would be resumed. Suleiman undertook an official visit to Damascus on 13–14 August 2008 for discussions with Assad, and the Lebanese

Cabinet formally adopted a resolution to establish diplomatic relations with Syria on 22 August.

However, the deployment of some 10,000 Syrian special forces along the border with northern Lebanon in late September 2008 caused concern among many Lebanese who were uneasy about Syria's long-term intentions towards their country and its sovereignty. The Syrian Government insisted that the presence of the troops merely constituted a campaign to prevent cross-border smuggling. Within Lebanon, meanwhile, there was a continuation of the violence being witnessed in Tripoli: in mid-August 18 people—including at least nine soldiers—died, and 45 were wounded, in a bomb explosion which targeted a military bus stop. At the end of September a second attack against a military bus in Tripoli resulted in seven deaths—up to five of them soldiers.

On 30 September 2008 the National Assembly adopted new electoral legislation as required under the terms of the Doha Agreement, in preparation for the general election subsequently scheduled for 7 June 2009. The new law involved the redrawing of electoral boundaries and the staging of elections on one day, rather than over several days (as had previously been the case). In late October Sheikh Nasrallah and Saad el-Hariri held their first meeting since 2006, in advance of a second round of discussions between Lebanon's rival political factions as part of the national dialogue which had begun on 16 September 2008. The talks were held in early November and hosted by President Suleiman; however, they failed to achieve a breakthrough regarding the drafting of a national defence strategy, largely owing to a failure by the 14 participants (who represented each of Lebanon's parliamentary blocs) to agree on the issue of how to deal with Hezbollah's military arsenal. It was agreed that a third round of talks would be held on 22 December, at which the focus was on the formation of a commitee of experts to examine the exact details of a potential national defence strategy. Further national reconciliation discussions were held during late January and early March 2009.

Meanwhile, the UN Secretary-General, Ban Ki-Moon, announced in late November 2008 that the STL established to try those charged with the assassination of former premier Rafik Hariri in February 2005 would commence proceedings in The Hague on 1 March 2009. The 11 judges—four of whom were to be Lebanese—would be led by the Canadian general prosecutor, Daniel Bellemare, with a Lebanese deputy. In the 11th UNIIIC report, issued at the start of December 2008, the Commission asserted that it had discovered evidence of links between Hariri's assassination and other political attacks that had taken place in Lebanon. On 16 December the UN Security Council approved a resolution extending UNIIIC's mandate until 28 February 2009, although Bellemare pledged that the investigation would continue after the STL began operating in March. On 29 February three of the seven suspects being detained on suspicion of withholding information and misleading the investigation of Hariri's murder were released on bail. Four pro-Syrian army generals suspected of involvement in that crime and other terrorist attacks in Lebanon remained in custody, although they had not been formally charged. The four were: Maj.-Gen. Jamil Sayyed, former head of the General Security Directorate; Maj.-Gen. Ali Hajj, former Director of the Internal Security Forces; Brig.-Gen. Raymond Azar, formerly head of military intelligence; and Mustafa Hamdan, former commander of the Presidential Guard.

The UN-sponsored STL formally opened on 1 March 2009, with general prosecutor Daniel Bellemare emphasizing that the work of the tribunal 'must and will be above politics'. The STL had a renewable three-year mandate and there was a 60-day period during which Bellemare could request that the Lebanese Government hand over to The Hague the four generals in Lebanese custody. However, it was unclear when exactly the tribunal proceedings would begin. In late March an Italian judge, Antonio Cassese, was named as President of the STL. There were reports in late April that a principal suspect in Hariri's murder, Muhammad Zuhair Siddiq (who was alleged to be a Syrian intelligence officer), had been arrested in Dubai, United Arab Emirates. The arrest was not confirmed by the UAE authorities; however, there were reports that Syrian officials had demanded Siddiq's extradition. (He had reportedly fled from house arrest in France in March 2008, having originally been detained there in October 2005.) Towards the end of April 2009 the four pro-Syrian Lebanese generals held over Hariri's assassination were unexpectedly released from custody. This followed a ruling by the STL that there was insufficient evidence to charge them, and meant that no suspects were currently being held over their alleged involvement in Hariri's murder.

On 19 March 2009 the National Assembly approved a bill which reduced the voter eligibility age in Lebanese parliamentary elections from 21 to 18; the new legislation would not, however, take effect until after the general election due to be held on 7 June 2009 as, under the terms of the Constitution, the Cabinet had four months during which to endorse it. The change in electoral law satisfied a long-standing demand of Hezbollah and its ally, Amal, since it would affect the eligibility to vote of a number of young Shi'a voters.

In late March 2009 Maj.-Gen. Kamal Naji (also known as Kamal Medhat), the deputy leader of the PLO in Lebanon, was killed, along with at least two of his bodyguards and another Palestinian official, in a roadside explosion at a Palestinian refugee camp near Sidon. Palestinian sources claimed that the bombing was in fact targeted at the head of the PLO in Lebanon, Abbas Zaki, who had also attended the camp on that day. Some Palestinian officials, as well as members of Hamas and Hezbollah, believed that Israel was responsible for Naji's death.

Government

Under the 1926 Constitution (as subsequently amended), legislative power is held by the National Assembly (called the Chamber of Deputies until 1979), with 128 members elected by universal adult suffrage for four years (subject to dissolution), on the basis of proportional representation. Seats are allocated on a religious or 'confessional' basis (divided equally between Christians and Muslims). The President of the Republic (who must be a Maronite Christian) is elected for six years by the National Assembly. The President, in consultation with deputies and the President of the National Assembly, appoints the Prime Minister (a Sunni Muslim) and other ministers to form the Cabinet, in which executive power is vested. The Ta'if agreement of October 1989, which was incorporated into the Constitution in August 1990, stated that cabinet portfolios must be distributed equally between Christian and Muslim ministers.

Defence

As assessed at November 2008, the Lebanese armed forces numbered 56,000 (army 53,900, navy 1,100, air force 1,000). Paramilitary forces included an estimated 20,000 members of the Internal Security Force, which was attached to the Ministry of the Interior and Municipalities. Compulsory military service was formally abolished in February 2007. Hezbollah's active members numbered some 2,000, as assessed at November 2008. In August 2004 there were an estimated 16,000 Syrian troops in Lebanon; however, following several redeployments, it was reported in April 2005 that Syria had withdrawn all of its forces from the country (see Recent History). Israeli armed forces and the Israeli-backed South Lebanon Army (SLA) withdrew from Lebanon in May 2000. Government expenditure on defence was budgeted at £L1,130,000m. in 2008.

The UN Interim Force in Lebanon (UNIFIL, see p. 84) observer mission numbered 1,980 troops in January 2006, assisted by about 50 military observers of the UN Truce Supervision Organization (UNTSO). At March 2009, following the adoption in August 2006 of UN Resolution 1701, which authorized an expansion of UNIFIL's capacity up to a maximum of 15,000 personnel, UNIFIL military personnel numbered 12,261, and were supported by 988 international and local civilian personnel.

Economic Affairs

In 2007, according to estimates by the World Bank, Lebanon's gross national income (GNI), measured at average 2005–07 prices, was US $23,651m., equivalent to $5,770 per head (or $10,050 per head on an international purchasing-power parity basis). During 2000–07, it was estimated, the population increased at an average annual rate of 1.2%, while gross domestic product (GDP) per head increased, in real terms, by an average of 2.0% per year. Overall GDP increased, in real terms, at an average annual rate of 3.2% in 2000–07; GDP growth of some 2.0% was recorded in 2007, following zero growth in 2006.

Agriculture (including hunting, forestry and fishing) contributed an estimated 6.1% of GDP in 2007. Some 5.1% of the employed labour force were engaged in the sector in that year. The principal crops are potatoes, tomatoes, cucumbers, citrus fruits and grapes. Viticulture is also significant. The cultivation of hashish is a notable, albeit illegal, activity in the Beka'a valley, despite official efforts to eradicate crops and switch land to other production. The GDP of the agricultural sector increased at an average annual rate of 0.1% in 2000–07; following a decline of 6.0% in 2006, agricultural GDP grew by 1.0% in 2007.

The industrial sector (including manufacturing, construction and power) contributed an estimated 23.0% of GDP in 2007. Some 25.9% of the labour force were employed in industry in 1997. Lebanon's only mineral resources consist of small reserves of lignite and iron ore, and their contribution to GDP is insignificant. The GDP of the industrial sector increased by an annual average of 3.2% per year in 2000–07; industrial GDP declined by 1.0% in 2006, but expanded by 0.5% in 2007.

Manufacturing contributed an estimated 19.2% of GDP in 2007. The sector employed about 10% of the labour force in 1985. The most important branches have traditionally been food-processing, petroleum-refining, textiles, and furniture and woodworking. Manufacturing GDP was estimated to have increased at an average annual rate of 2.4% in 2000–07; having declined by 8.6% in 2006, the GDP of the sector increased by 0.5% in 2007.

Energy is derived principally from thermal power stations, mainly using imported petroleum (which accounted for 89.7% of total electricity production in 2005). Generating capacity is inadequate to meet Lebanon's peak requirements, and interruptions to supply are frequent. From 2009, following an agreement reached with Egypt in August 2008, Lebanon was to receive a supply of electricity from the regional power grid; it was also planned that Lebanon would import natural gas from Egypt to enable a switch from fuel oil as a feedstock at one power unit. Imports of mineral products accounted for 22.8% of the value of total imports in 2007.

The services sector contributed an estimated 70.9% of GDP in 2007. In 1997 some 65.1% of the working population were employed in the sector. Financial services, particularly banking, withstood many of the disruptions inflicted on the economy by the civil conflict during 1975–90 (although trading on the Beirut Stock Exchange was suspended in 1983–96). The revival of tourism, which was of considerable importance prior to the civil conflict, remains vulnerable to the political and security situation. None the less, the sector experienced particularly strong growth in the second half of 2008: arrivals of foreign tourists in that year reached an estimated 1.3m. (an increase of more than 30% compared with 2007). The GDP of the services sector increased at an average annual rate of 2.5% in 2000–07; following an increase of 4.7% in 2006, the sector's GDP declined by 0.9% in 2007.

In 2007 Lebanon recorded a trade deficit of US $7,850m., and there was a deficit of $2,046m. on the current account of the balance of payments. The principal market for exports in 2007 was Switzerland (which took 10.9% of Lebanese exports); other significant purchasers included the United Arab Emirates, Syria and Saudi Arabia. The principal supplier of imports in the same year was the USA (9.6%); Italy, the People's Republic of China, France and Germany were also important suppliers. The principal exports in 2007 were base metal and base metal products, jewellery, machinery and electrical equipment, food, beverages and tobacco, chemical products, and paper and paper products. The principal imports in that year were mineral products, machinery and electrical equipment, chemical products, vehicles and transport equipment, base metals and base metal products, and food, beverages and tobacco.

In 2008, according to data published by the IMF, Lebanon recorded an overall budget deficit equivalent to an estimated 9.9% of GDP. At the end of 2006 Lebanon's total external debt was US $23,963m., of which $18,958m. was long-term public debt. The cost of debt-servicing in that year was equivalent to 21.0% of the value of exports of goods and services. The annual rate of inflation (year to December) averaged 3.2% in 2000–07; consumer prices increased by 9.3% in the year to December 2007. Some 9.2% of the adult labour force were unemployed in 2007.

Lebanon is a member of the Arab Fund for Economic and Social Development (see p. 183), the Arab Monetary Fund (see p. 184) and the Islamic Development Bank (see p. 340). Lebanon participates in the Greater Arab Free Trade Area (GAFTA), implemented from January 2005 under the auspices of the League of Arab States (see p. 344). A Euro-Mediterranean Association Agreement was signed with the European Union (EU, see p. 255) in 2002. Lebanon has observer status at the World Trade Organization (see p. 410), membership of which organization was applied for in 1999.

Assessments at early 2009 suggested that Lebanon's economy had performed strongly following the Doha Agreement of May 2008, and that it was demonstrating resilience to the impact of the global financial crisis. The Lebanese banking sector, in which traditionally conservative management and a deposit-led finance structure had limited exposure to the turbulence affecting the sector internationally, was particularly well placed. Tourism had recovered strongly from mid-2008, and the construction and real estate sectors had hitherto not undergone the downturn being experienced elsewhere in the region. The IMF, which in November 2008 approved some US $37.6m. in Emergency Post-Conflict Assistance (EPCA) in support of the economic programme for 2008–09, commented on the Lebanese authorities' success in, inter alia, the strengthening of international reserves, achievement of a primary budgetary surplus (excluding grants, equivalent to an estimated 0.7% of GDP in 2008), reduction of the debt-to-GDP ratio (to an estimated 162% of GDP in 2008, from 180% two years earlier) and the sustained growth and 'dedollarization' of deposits. High international prices for fuel and food during 2008, in conjunction with increases in public sector pay and pensions (for the first time since 1998) and in the minimum wage in the private sector (the first increase since 1996), had placed upward pressure on consumer prices, but the rate of inflation was expected to slow in 2009. The new funding was in addition to EPCA of $76.7m. made available by the IMF in April 2007 as part of international assistance efforts following the conflict between Israel and Hezbollah in 2006, and the IMF commented that this new disbursement was expected to help sustain the support of the international financial community for Lebanon's economic reconstruction and reform efforts: disbursements of assistance pledged at the January 2007 Paris III International Conference for Support to Lebanon had hitherto fallen short of expectations, not least because the political instability and institutional stalemate that had prevailed until mid-2008 had impeded the progress of many projects. While efforts to reduce the debt-to-GDP ratio had, to late 2008, proceeded at a faster rate than envisaged under the Paris III programme, the ratio remained one of the highest in the world. The decline in international oil prices from the latter part of 2008 was expected partially to relieve pressure on government finances represented by the state subsidy on electricity tariffs (transfers to Electricité du Liban were estimated to be equivalent to 4% of GDP in 2007). However, the subsidy, as well as Lebanon's reliance on imported energy, still represented a substantial drain on government finances, and the IMF emphasized the importance of reform of the energy sector in order to increase both capacity and efficiency and to reduce public debt. The planned sale of the two state-owned mobile telephone networks was deferred until after the legislative elections due in June 2009; meanwhile, new contracts took effect from February 2009 for the operation of the networks to April 2010. In advance of the elections there was some uncertainty regarding the likely impact of any deterioration in the security situation. Furthermore, there was concern that the deterioration of external economic conditions, particularly in the Gulf states, could result in a reduction in remittances from Lebanese expatriates, and also stem the recent recovery in sectors such as tourism.

Education

There are state-controlled primary and secondary schools, but private institutions provide the main facilities for secondary and higher education. Education is not compulsory, but state education is provided free of charge. Primary education begins at six years of age and lasts for five years. Secondary education, beginning at the age of 11, lasts for a further seven years, comprising a first cycle of four years and a second of three years. In 2006/07 enrolment at primary schools included 82.9% of the relevant age-group, while enrolment at secondary schools included 73.2% of the relevant age-group. Some 187,055 Lebanese students were enrolled in higher education in the 2006/07 academic year. In 1998 Lebanon secured a loan of US $60m. from the World Bank, in order to restructure the country's system of technical and vocational education. Expenditure on education by the central Government in 2003 was some £L810,000m. (9.4% of total budgetary expenditure).

Public Holidays

2009: 1 January (New Year's Day), 7 January*† (Ashoura), 9 February (Feast of St Maron), 9 March* (Mouloud/Yum an-Nabi, birth of Muhammad), 22 March (Arab League Anniversary), 25 March (Feast of the Annunciation), 13 April (Easter, Western Church), 17–20 April (Greek Orthodox Easter), 21 May (Ascension Day, Western Church), 19 July* (Leilat al-Meiraj, ascension of Muhammad), 15 August (Assumption), 20 September* (Id al-Fitr, end of Ramadan), 1 November (All

Saints' Day), 22 November (Independence Day), 27 November* (Id al-Adha, Feast of the Sacrifice), 18 December* (Muharram, Islamic New Year), 25 December (Christmas Day), 27 December*† (Ashoura).

2010: 1 January (New Year's Day), 9 February (Feast of St Maron), 26 February* (Mouloud/Yum an-Nabi, birth of Muhammad), 22 March (Arab League Anniversary), 25 March (Feast of the Annunciation), 2–5 April (Greek Orthodox Easter), 5 April (Easter, Western Church), 13 May (Ascension Day, Western Church), 8 July* (Leilat al-Meiraj, ascension of Muhammad), 15 August (Assumption), 10 September* (Id al-Fitr, end of Ramadan), 1 November (All Saints' Day), 16 November* (Id al-Adha, Feast of the Sacrifice), 22 November (Independence Day), 7 December* (Muharram, Islamic New Year), 16 December* (Ashoura), 25 December (Christmas Day).

* These holidays are determined by the Islamic lunar calendar and may vary by one or two days from the dates given.

† This festival occurs twice (in the Islamic years AH 1430 and 1431) within the same Gregorian year.

Weights and Measures

The metric system is in force.

Statistical Survey

Sources (unless otherwise stated): Central Administration for Statistics, Beirut; internet www.cas.gov.lb; Direction Générale des Douanes, Beirut.

Area and Population

AREA, POPULATION AND DENSITY

Area (sq km)	10,452*
Population (official estimate) 15 November 1970†	
Males	1,080,015
Females	1,046,310
Total	2,126,325
Population (UN estimates at mid-year)‡	
2006	4,126,000
2007	4,162,000
2008	4,194,000
Density (per sq km) at mid-2008	401.3

* 4,036 sq miles.

† Figures are based on the results of a sample survey, excluding Palestinian refugees in camps. The total number of registered Palestinian refugees in Lebanon was 416,608 at 30 June 2008.

‡ Source: UN, *World Population Prospects: The 2008 Revision*.

2007 (official estimate): Total resident population 3,759,137 (males 1,857,662, females 1,901,475).

PRINCIPAL TOWNS

(population in 2003)*

Beirut (capital)	1,171,000	Jounieh	79,800
Tarabulus (Tripoli)	212,900	Zahle	76,600
Saida (Sidon)	149,000	Baabda	58,500
Sur (Tyre)	117,100	Ba'albak (Ba'albek)	29,800
An-Nabatiyah at-Tahta (Nabatiyah)	89,400	Alayh	26,700

* Figures are rounded.

Source: Stefan Helders, *World Gazetteer* (internet www.world-gazetteer.com).

Mid-2007: Beirut 1,846,000 (Source: UN, *World Urbanization Prospects: The 2007 Revision*).

BIRTHS, MARRIAGES AND DEATHS

(annual averages, UN estimates)

	1990–95	1995–2000	2000–05
Birth rate (per 1,000)	24.9	22.6	17.6
Death rate (per 1,000)	7.1	7.1	7.0

Source: UN, *World Population Prospects: The 2008 Revision*.

2004 (numbers registered, official estimates): Live births 73,900; Marriages 30,014; Deaths 17,774.

2005 (numbers registered, official estimates): Live births 73,770; Marriages 29,705; Deaths 18,012.

2006 (numbers registered, official estimates): Live births 72,790; Marriages 29,078; Deaths 18,787.

2007 (numbers registered, official estimates): Live births 78,944; Marriages 35,068; Deaths 19,399.

Life expectancy (years at birth, WHO estimates): 70.2 (males 68.0; females 72.5) in 2006 (Source: WHO, *World Health Statistics*).

EMPLOYMENT

(ISIC major divisions)

	1975	1985*
Agriculture, hunting, forestry and fishing	147,724	103,400
Manufacturing	139,471	45,000
Electricity, gas and water	6,381	10,000
Construction	47,356	25,000
Trade, restaurants and hotels	129,716	78,000
Transport, storage and communications	45,529	20,500
Other services	227,921	171,000
Total	**744,098**	**452,900**

* Estimates.

1997 (provisional estimates at mid-year): Total employed 1,246,000; Unemployed 116,000; Total labour force 1,362,000.

2007 (household survey, persons aged 15 years and over): Total employed 1,033,572 (Agriculture and fishing 52,528, Unskilled 126,684, Skilled 188,168, Intermediate professions 108,051, Specialists 115,420, Office employees 84,269, Service sector workers and salespersons 131,950, General and corporate managers 132,761, Drivers 93,741). Note: Figures exclude members of the armed forces (84,224) and non-respondents (585).

Source: partly National Employment Office.

Health and Welfare

KEY INDICATORS

Total fertility rate (children per woman, 2006)	2.2
Under-5 mortality rate (per 1,000 live births, 2006)	31
HIV/AIDS (% of persons aged 15–49, 2007)	0.1
Physicians (per 1,000 head, 2005)	2.4
Hospital beds (per 1,000 head, 2005)	3.6
Health expenditure (2006): US $ per head (PPP)	608
Health expenditure (2006): % of GDP	8.9
Health expenditure (2006): public (% of total)	46.8
Access to sanitation (% of persons, 2006)	97
Human Development Index (2006): ranking	78
Human Development Index (2006): value	0.796

For sources and definitions, see explanatory note on p. vi.

LEBANON

Agriculture

PRINCIPAL CROPS
('000 metric tons)

	2005	2006*	2007*
Wheat	144	144	135
Barley	29	29	28
Potatoes	511	505	490
Almonds, with shell	28	28	27
Olives	77	85	83
Cabbages and other brassicas	80	79	77
Lettuce and chicory	29	28	27
Tomatoes	277	277	256
Cauliflowers and broccoli	31	31	30
Pumpkins, squash and gourds	24	23	21
Cucumbers and gherkins	131	130	125
Aubergines (Eggplants)	20	20	19
Onions, dry	51	51	49
Garlic	3	3	3
Beans, green	13	12	12
Carrots and turnips	11	11	10
Watermelons	74	74	65
Cantaloupes and other melons	6	6	6
Bananas	81	80	56
Oranges	236	200	195
Tangerines, mandarins, clementines and satsumas	32	31	29
Lemons and limes	113	110	110
Grapefruit and pomelos	12	12	9
Apples	115	110	98
Pears	37	36	35
Apricots	32	31	29
Sweet cherries	30	29	24
Peaches and nectarines	34	33	31
Plums and sloes	26	24	22
Strawberries	3	3	3
Grapes	111	105	100
Figs	7	6	5

* FAO estimates.

Aggregate production ('000 metric tons, may include official, semi-official or estimated data): Total cereals 177 in 2005, 174 in 2006, 168 in 2007; Total roots and tubers 512 in 2005, 506 in 2006, 491 in 2007; Total vegetables (incl. melons) 811 in 2005, 797 in 2006, 753 in 2007; Total fruits (excl. melons) 946 in 2005, 817 in 2006, 753 in 2007.

Source: FAO.

LIVESTOCK
('000 head, year ending September)

	2005	2006	2007
Horses*	6	6	6
Asses, mules or hinnies*	31	n.a.	n.a.
Cattle	77	77*	77*
Pigs	11	15*	15*
Sheep	337	337*	340*
Goats	495	495*	495*
Chickens*	36,000	35,000	35,000

* FAO estimate(s).
Source: FAO.

LIVESTOCK PRODUCTS
('000 metric tons)

	2005	2006*	2007*
Cattle meat*	69.2	53.0	53.0
Sheep meat*	7.7	14.5	14.5
Goat meat*	3.3	2.6	2.6
Pig meat*	1.1	1.3	1.3
Chicken meat	130.4	130.0	130.0
Cows' milk	189.8	180.0	180.0
Sheep's milk	22.8	22.0	22.0
Goats' milk	39.3	39.0	39.0
Hen eggs	45.5	47.0	47.0
Wool, greasy*	2.0	1.9	1.9

* FAO estimates.
Source: FAO.

Forestry

ROUNDWOOD REMOVALS
('000 cubic metres, excluding bark, FAO estimates)

	2005	2006	2007
Sawlogs, veneer logs and logs for sleepers*	7.2	7.2	7.2
Fuel wood	81.4	80.6	80.1
Total	88.5	87.8	87.3

* Assumed to be unchanged since 1992.
Source: FAO.

SAWNWOOD PRODUCTION
('000 cubic metres, including railway sleepers)

	1991	1992	1993
Total (all broadleaved)	10.9	9.1	9.1*

* FAO estimate.
1994–2007: Figures assumed to be unchanged from 1993 (FAO estimates).
Source: FAO.

Fishing

(metric tons, live weight)

	2004	2005	2006
Capture	3,866	3,798	3,811
Groupers and seabasses	245	250	252
Porgies and seabreams	365	370	371
Surmullets (Red mullets)	200	190	190
Barracudas	250	240	240
Mullets	360	365	360
Scorpionfishes	125	110	115
Carangids	400	380	383
Clupeoids	600	580	580
Tuna-like fishes	400	385	389
Mackerel-like fishes	300	320	322
Marine crustaceans	60	55	57
Aquaculture	790	803	803
Rainbow trout	700	708	708
Total catch	4,656	4,601	4,614

Source: FAO.

Mining

('000 metric tons)

	2005	2006	2007
Gypsum	30	30	30
Salt (unrefined)	3.5	3.5	3.5
Phosphoric acid	180	180	180

Source: US Geological Survey.

Industry

SELECTED PRODUCTS
('000 metric tons, unless otherwise indicated)

	2005	2006	2007
Flour and derivatives thereof	341	650	379
Cigarettes (metric tons)	n.a.	554.9	n.a.
Cement	n.a.	2,297	4,771
Bottled water and soda (million litres)	252	261*	497
Wine†	15	15	15
Electric energy (million kWh)	9,183	8,694	9,072

* Year to November.
† FAO estimates (Source: FAO).
Source: US Geological Survey.

LEBANON

Statistical Survey

Finance

CURRENCY AND EXCHANGE RATES

Monetary Units
100 piastres = 1 Lebanese pound (£L).

Sterling, Dollar and Euro Equivalents (31 December 2008)
£1 sterling = £L2,197.6;
US $1 = £L1,507.5;
€1 = £L2,908.0;
£L10,000 = £4.55 sterling = $6.63 = €4.77.

Exchange Rate: The official exchange rate has been maintained at US $1 = £L1,507.5 since September 1999.

BUDGET
(£L '000 million)*

Revenue	2006	2007	2008†
Tax revenue	4,922	5,347	6,434
Taxes on income, profits and capital gains	1,166	1,200	1,492
Taxes on property	579	441	535
Domestic taxes on goods and services	2,457	2,942	3,579
Taxes on international trade and transactions	461	493	540
Other taxes	259	271	288
Other current revenue	1,945	2,328	1,934
Income from public enterprises	1,428	1,843	1,311
Administrative fees and charges	426	393	426
Fines and confiscations	4	4	5
Other	87	88	192
Total	6,867	7,675	8,368

Expenditure	2006	2007	2008†
Personnel costs	3,499	3,803	3,783
Salaries and wages	2,346	2,588	2,524
Interest payments and financial charges	4,653	4,900	4,650
Materials and supplies	237	315	350
External services	115	120	129
Subsidies and transfers	1,553	1,664	1,773
Reserves	165	162	162
Acquisitions of land, buildings, for the construction of roads, ports, airports and water networks	5	9	11
Equipment	39	45	70
Construction in progress	440	412	370
Maintenance	86	92	101
Other expenditures related to fixed capital assets	77	44	66
Total	10,869	11,566	11,465
Current	10,220	10,964	10,848
Capital	649	601	617

* Figures, which are rounded, represent the consolidated operations of the central Government's General Budget and the Council for Development and Reconstruction. The accounts of other central government units with individual budgets (including the general social security scheme) are excluded.
† Budget proposals.
Source: Ministry of Finance.

INTERNATIONAL RESERVES
(US $ million at 31 December)

	2005	2006	2007
Gold (national valuation)	4,736.4	5,807.3	7,639.8
IMF special drawing rights	31.4	34.9	36.1
Reserve position in IMF	26.9	28.3	29.8
Foreign exchange	11,828.7	13,313.3	12,844.1
Total	16,623.4	19,183.8	20,549.8

Source: IMF, *International Financial Statistics*.

MONEY SUPPLY
(£L '000 million at 31 December)

	2005	2006	2007
Currency outside banks	1,534.7	1,809.2	1,929.2
Demand deposits at commercial banks	1,358.5	1,450.0	1,601.8
Total money (incl. others)	2,893.2	3,321.7	3,578.1

Sources: IMF, *International Financial Statistics*.

COST OF LIVING
(Consumer Price Index for Beirut; December of each year; base: December 1998 = 100)

	2005	2006	2007
Food and beverages	97.8	109.5	125.7
Water, electricity and gas	124.7	121.6	147.0
Clothing and footwear	124.9	126.5	127.6
Transport and communications	140.4	148.7	153.8
All items (incl. others)	107.5	113.5	124.1

NATIONAL ACCOUNTS
(£L '000 million)

Expenditure on the Gross Domestic Product

	2003	2004	2005
Government final consumption expenditure	31,116	33,581	33,677
Private final consumption expenditure			
Gross fixed capital formation	5,862	6,674	7,137
Changes in stocks	−129	400	−56
Total domestic expenditure	36,849	40,654	40,758
Exports of goods and services	3,788	4,878	5,335
Less Imports of goods and services	10,851	13,173	13,594
Statistical discrepancy	66	−1	—
GDP in purchasers' values	29,852	32,359	32,499

Gross Domestic Product by Economic Activity

	2003	2004	2005
Agriculture, hunting, forestry and fishing	1,639	1,705	1,690
Manufacturing	3,514	3,783	3,786
Electricity, gas and water	178	73	−188
Construction	2,213	2,404	2,669
Trade, restaurants and hotels	6,702	7,756	7,534
Transport, storage and communications	2,092	2,404	2,360
Government services	3,538	3,612	3,722
Other services	9,976	10,622	10,925
GDP in purchasers' values	29,852	32,359	32,499

Source: Ministry of Economy and Trade.

GDP at constant 2000 prices (US $ million, ESCWA estimates): 19,982 in 2004; 19,982 in 2005; 18,983 in 2006 (Source: UN Economic and Social Commission for Western Asia, *National Accounts Studies of the ESCWA Region*).

BALANCE OF PAYMENTS
(US $ million)

	2005	2006	2007
Exports of goods f.o.b.	2,652	3,207	4,077
Imports of goods f.o.b.	−9,239	−9,345	−11,926
Trade balance	−6,588	−6,138	−7,850
Exports of services	10,858	11,565	12,527
Imports of services	−7,895	−8,734	−9,986
Balance on goods and services	−3,624	−3,307	−5,309
Other income received	1,733	2,440	2,663
Other income paid	−1,919	−2,145	−2,286
Balance on goods, services and income	−3,811	−3,013	−4,932

LEBANON

—continued	2005	2006	2007
Current transfers received	4,399	5,053	5,219
Current transfers paid	-3,337	-3,242	-2,333
Current balance	-2,748	-1,202	-2,046
Capital account (net)	27	1,940	590
Direct investment abroad	-122	-70	233
Direct investment from abroad	2,791	2,739	2,845
Portfolio investment assets	-110	-355	-992
Portfolio investment liabilities	648	1,308	1,695
Other investment assets	3,658	-1,494	1,962
Other investment liabilities	32	854	2,029
Net errors and omissions	-3,719	-3,575	-6,981
Overall balance	458	146	-665

Source: IMF, *International Financial Statistics*.

External Trade

PRINCIPAL COMMODITIES
(£L '000 million)

Imports c.i.f.	2005	2006	2007
Live animals and animal products	644.9	669.1	752.5
Vegetable products	578.7	551.6	843.5
Prepared foodstuffs; beverages, spirits and vinegar; tobacco and manufactured substitutes	799.5	805.5	1,139.6
Mineral products	3,357.0	3,638.2	4,061.8
Products of chemical or allied industries	1,236.2	1,337.2	1,660.4
Plastics, rubber and articles thereof	537.8	543.8	721.6
Textiles and textile articles	733.0	700.2	777.4
Natural or cultured pearls, precious or semi-precious stones, precious metals and articles thereof; imitation jewellery; coin	741.1	438.7	727.9
Base metals and articles thereof	981.3	1,028.8	1,452.9
Machinery and mechanical appliances; electrical equipment; sound and television apparatus	1,599.3	1,693.9	2,148.5
Vehicles, aircraft, vessels and associated transport equipment	1,220.4	1,152.6	1,497.9
Total (incl. others)	14,084.5	14,171.6	17,817.4

Exports f.o.b.	2005	2006	2007
Vegetable products	115.4	121.0	158.4
Prepared foodstuffs; beverages, spirits and vinegar; tobacco and manufactured substitutes	288.2	282.1	359.5
Mineral products	189.6	129.0	135.8
Products of chemical or allied industries	245.3	244.9	352.2
Plastics, rubber and articles thereof	117.0	127.6	177.8
Paper and paperboard and articles thereof	175.1	201.6	262.0
Textiles and textile articles	122.9	131.6	154.7
Natural or cultured pearls, precious or semi-precious stones, precious metals and articles thereof; imitation jewellery; coin	337.3	836.3	735.6
Base metals and articles thereof	415.9	483.8	745.1
Machinery and mechanical appliances; electrical equipment; sound and television apparatus	474.0	503.0	693.2
Total (incl. others)	2,834.7	3,442.1	4,246.8

PRINCIPAL TRADING PARTNERS
(£L '000 million)

Imports c.i.f.	2005	2006	2007
Belgium	264.1	231.6	274.8
Brazil	241.2	342.4	433.7
China, People's Republic	1,107.5	1,133.4	1,535.0
Egypt	457.6	571.7	789.7
France	1,188.5	1,147.8	1,331.7
Germany	991.2	995.1	1,130.9
Greece	146.9	172.1	216.1
Italy	1,471.3	1,070.6	1,597.2
Japan	462.9	429.8	595.0
Korea, Republic	11.4	199.6	217.3
Kuwait	157.1	280.1	445.4
Netherlands	229.3	226.3	228.2
Romania	264.0	242.6	194.2
Russia	767.7	393.1	531.3
Saudi Arabia	496.1	446.9	425.8
Spain	252.9	224.5	322.5
Switzerland	636.8	319.7	524.6
Syria	296.9	268.4	311.4
Turkey	301.1	388.8	610.9
Ukraine	200.1	115.0	181.0
United Arab Emirates	206.3	199.2	329.2
United Kingdom	487.4	613.2	678.4
USA	825.9	1,532.1	1,718.2
Total (incl. others)	14,084.5	14,171.6	17,817.4

Exports f.o.b.	2005	2006	2007
Belgium	34.7	70.5	131.1
Egypt	82.3	72.2	171.3
France	48.5	59.0	77.0
Germany	27.6	33.5	55.6
Greece	20.1	33.6	68.3
Iran	38.9	54.4	58.9
Italy	25.9	40.9	51.4
Jordan	113.4	127.0	149.8
Korea, Republic	0.0	26.8	46.8
Kuwait	122.4	124.3	160.4
Netherlands	24.2	41.6	40.0
Nigeria	40.7	51.0	64.6
Qatar	54.6	96.2	114.2
Saudi Arabia	210.8	220.5	282.4
Spain	20.6	15.5	61.2
Switzerland	188.6	680.1	464.7
Syria	282.7	265.0	316.6
Turkey	183.4	154.3	165.2
United Arab Emirates	233.7	265.7	367.6
United Kingdom	43.5	47.6	111.4
USA	86.9	79.4	102.1
Total (incl. others)	2,834.7	3,442.1	4,246.8

Transport

ROAD TRAFFIC
(motor vehicles in use)

	1995	1996*	1997*
Passenger cars (incl. taxis)	1,197,521	1,217,000	1,299,398
Buses and coaches	5,514	5,640	6,833
Lorries and vans	79,222	81,000	85,242
Motorcycles and mopeds	53,317	54,450	61,471

* Estimates.

Source: International Road Federation, *World Road Statistics*.

Passenger cars ('000, incl. taxis): 1,370.6 in 1999; 1,370.8 in 2000; 1,370.9 in 2001 (Source: UN, *Statistical Yearbook*).

LEBANON

SHIPPING

Merchant Fleet
(registered at 31 December)

	2005	2006	2007
Number of vessels	76	65	58
Total displacement ('000 grt)	399.5	157.0	135.9

Source: Lloyd's Register-Fairplay, *World Fleet Statistics*.

International Sea-borne Freight Traffic
('000 metric tons)

	1988	1989	1990
Goods loaded	148	150	152
Goods unloaded	1,120	1,140	1,150

Source: UN, *Monthly Bulletin of Statistics*.

2002 ('000 metric tons, Beirut port only): Goods loaded 393; Goods unloaded 4,827.

2003 ('000 metric tons, Beirut port only): Goods loaded 499; Goods unloaded 4,306.

2004 ('000 metric tons, Beirut port only): Goods loaded 727; Goods unloaded 4,334.

CIVIL AVIATION
(traffic on scheduled services)

	2002	2003	2004
Kilometres flown (million)	20	20	22
Passengers carried ('000)	874	935	1,087
Passenger-km (million)	1,749	1,905	2,197
Total ton-km (million)	244	253	292

Source: UN, *Statistical Yearbook*.

Tourism

FOREIGN TOURIST ARRIVALS
('000)*

Country of nationality	2004	2005	2006
Australia	45.9	38.6	31.9
Canada	52.4	48.5	48.3
Egypt	46.1	34.3	38.7
France	94.3	80.5	66.8
Germany	48.4	51.9	39.3
Iran	89.8	92.9	86.4
Iraq	17.2	20.7	60.4
Jordan	92.8	135.2	144.2
Kuwait	79.8	64.2	50.1
Philippines	25.3	30.7	26.1
Saudi Arabia	200.9	124.7	93.6
United Kingdom	34.5	35.5	29.9
USA	78.8	68.4	64.1
Total (incl. others)	1,278.5	1,139.5	1,062.6

* Figures exclude arrivals of Syrian nationals, Palestinians and students.

Tourism receipts (US $ million, incl. passenger transport): 5,931 in 2004; 5,969 in 2005; 5,491 in 2006.

Source: World Tourism Organization.

Communications Media

	2004	2005	2006
Telephones ('000 main lines in use)	630.0	634.7	681.4
Mobile cellular telephones ('000 subscribers)	888.0	993.6	1,106.4
Personal computers ('000 in use)	400	409	n.a.
Internet users ('000)	600	700	950
Broadband subscribers ('000)	80	130	190

Radio receivers ('000 in use): 2,850 in 1997.
Facsimile machines (number in use): 3,000 in 1992.
Television receivers ('000 in use): 1,170 in 2000.
Daily newspapers (number of titles): 13 in 2000.
Daily newspapers (total average circulation, estimates, '000 copies): 220 in 2000.
Non-daily newspapers (number of titles): 7 in 2000.
Book production (number of titles): 289 in 1998.

Sources: UNESCO Institute for Statistics; UNESCO, *Statistical Yearbook*; UN, *Statistical Yearbook*; and International Telecommunication Union.

Education

(2006/07, unless otherwise indicated)

	Institutions	Teachers	Students
Pre-primary	1,938*	9,543	150,872
Primary	2,160*	32,412	450,566
Secondary:			
general	n.a.	30,475	316,439
vocational	275†	10,444	51,920
Higher	n.a.	21,778	187,055

* 1996/97 figure.
† 1994 figure.

Sources: UNESCO Institute for Statistics; Banque du Liban, *Annual Report*.

Adult literacy rate (UNESCO estimates): 86.5% (males 92.4%; females 81.0%) in 2001 (Source: UN Development Programme, *Human Development Report*).

Directory

The Constitution

The Constitution was promulgated on 23 May 1926 and amended by the Constitutional Laws of 1927, 1929, 1943, 1947 and 1990.

According to the Constitution, the Republic of Lebanon is an independent and sovereign state, and no part of the territory may be alienated or ceded. Lebanon has no state religion. Arabic is the official language. Beirut is the capital.

All Lebanese are equal in the eyes of the law. Personal freedom and freedom of the press are guaranteed and protected. The religious communities are entitled to maintain their own schools, on condition that they conform to the general requirements relating to public instruction, as defined by the state. Dwellings are inviolable; rights of ownership are protected by law. Every Lebanese citizen over 21 is an elector and qualifies for the franchise.

LEGISLATIVE POWER

Legislative power is exercised by one house, the National Assembly, with 108 seats (raised, without amendment of the Constitution, to

128 in 1992), which are divided equally between Christians and Muslims. Members of the National Assembly must be over 25 years of age, in possession of their full political and civil rights, and literate. They are considered representative of the whole nation, and are not bound to follow directives from their constituencies. They can be suspended only by a two-thirds' majority of their fellow members. Secret ballot was introduced in a new election law of April 1960.

The National Assembly holds two sessions yearly, from the first Tuesday after 15 March to the end of May, and from the first Tuesday after 15 October to the end of the year. The normal term of the National Assembly is four years; general elections take place within 60 days before the end of this period. If the Assembly is dissolved before the end of its term, elections are held within three months of dissolution.

Voting in the Assembly is public—by acclamation, or by standing and sitting. A quorum of two-thirds and a majority vote is required for constitutional issues. The only exceptions to this occur when the Assembly becomes an electoral college, and chooses the President of the Republic or Secretaries to the National Assembly, or when the President is accused of treason or of violating the Constitution. In such cases voting is secret, and a two-thirds' majority is needed for a proposal to be adopted.

EXECUTIVE POWER

With the incorporation of the Ta'if agreement into the Lebanese Constitution in August 1990, executive power was effectively transferred from the presidency to the Cabinet. The President is elected for a term of six years and is not immediately re-eligible. He is responsible for the promulgation and execution of laws enacted by the National Assembly, but all presidential decisions (with the exception of those to appoint a Prime Minister or to accept the resignation of a government) require the co-signature of the Prime Minister, who is head of the Government, implementing its policies and speaking in its name. The President must receive the approval of the Cabinet before dismissing a minister or ratifying an international treaty. The ministers and the Prime Minister are chosen by the President of the Republic in consultation with the members and President of the National Assembly. They are not necessarily members of the National Assembly, although they are responsible to it and have access to its debates. The President of the Republic must be a Maronite Christian, and the Prime Minister a Sunni Muslim; the choice of the other ministers must reflect the level of representation of the communities in the Assembly.

Note: In October 1998 the National Assembly endorsed an exceptional amendment to Article 49 of the Constitution to enable the election of Gen. Emile Lahoud, then Commander-in-Chief of the Army, as President of the Republic: the Constitution requires that senior state officials relinquish their responsibilities two years prior to seeking public office. In September 2004 the National Assembly voted in favour of a constitutional amendment extending President Lahoud's term of office for a further three years. In March 2009 the National Assembly adopted a bill lowering the age of voter eligibility from 21 to 18; however, the legislation still awaited cabinet approval and was thus not expected to enter effect until after the general election scheduled for 7 June.

The Government

HEAD OF STATE

President: Gen. MICHEL SULEIMAN (inaugurated 25 May 2008).

CABINET
(April 2009)

Prime Minister: FOUAD SINIORA.
Deputy Prime Minister and Minister of National Defence: ELIAS MURR.
Deputy Prime Minister: ISSAM ABOU JAMRA.
Minister of the Interior and Municipalities: ZIAD BAROUD.
Minister of Foreign Affairs and Emigrants: FAWZI SALLOUKH.
Minister of Justice: IBRAHIM NAJJAR.
Minister of Industry: GHAZI ZOAYTER.
Minister of Energy and Water: ALAIN TABOURIAN.
Minister of Public Works and Transport: GHAZI ARIDI.
Minister of Finance: MUHAMMAD CHATAH.
Minister of Economy and Trade: MUHAMMAD SAFADI.
Minister of Education and Higher Education: BAHIA HARIRI.
Minister of Culture: TAMMAM SALAM.
Minister of Information: TARIQ MITRI.
Minister of Tourism: ELIE MAROUNI.
Minister of Telecommunications: GEBRAN BASSIL.
Minister of Labour: MUHAMMAD FNEISH.
Minister of Agriculture: ELIAS SKAFF.
Minister of the Environment: ANTOINE KARAM.
Minister of Public Health: MUHAMMAD JAWAD KHALIFA.
Minister of Social Affairs: Dr MARIO AOUN.
Minister of the Displaced: RAYMOND AUDI.
Minister of Youth and Sports: TALAL ARSLAN.
Minister of Administrative Reform: IBRAHIM SHAMSEDDINE.
Ministers of State: WAEL ABU FAOUR, NASSIB LAHOUD, JEAN OGHASSABIAN, KHALID QABBANI, ALI QANSO, YOUSSEF TAKLA.

MINISTRIES

Presidency of the Republic of Lebanon: Presidential Palace, Baabda, Beirut; tel. (5) 920900; fax (5) 922400; e-mail president_office@presidency.gov.lb; internet www.presidency.gov.lb.

Office of the President of the Council of Ministers: Grand Sérail, place Riad es-Solh, Beirut; tel. (1) 746800; fax (1) 865630; internet www.pcm.gov.lb.

Ministry of Agriculture: Embassies St, Bir Hassan, Beirut; tel. (1) 849600; fax (1) 849620; e-mail ministry@agriculture.gov.lb; internet www.agriculture.gov.lb.

Ministry of Culture: Immeuble Hatab, rue Madame Curie, Verdun, Beirut; tel. (1) 744250; fax (1) 756303; e-mail omarhala_48@hotmail.com; internet www.culture.gov.lb.

Ministry of the Displaced: Minet el-Hosn, Starco Centre, Beirut; tel. (1) 366373; fax (1) 503040; e-mail mod@dm.net.lb.

Ministry of Economy and Trade: rue Artois, Hamra, Beirut; tel. (1) 982292; fax (1) 982293; e-mail sdabaghy@economy.gov.lb; internet www.economy.gov.lb.

Ministry of Education and Higher Education: Unesco Quarter, Habib Abi Chahla, Beirut; tel. (1) 789611; fax (1) 789606; e-mail info@higher-edu.gov.lb; internet www.higher-edu.gov.lb.

Ministry of Energy and Water: Beirut River Highway, Beirut; tel. (1) 565100; e-mail mew@terra.net.lb; internet www.energyandwater.gov.lb.

Ministry of the Environment: POB 11-2727, 7th and 8th Floors, Lazarieh Centre, Beirut; tel. (1) 976555; fax (1) 976530; e-mail webmaster@moe.gov.lb; internet www.moe.gov.lb.

Ministry of Finance: MOF Bldg, place Riad es-Solh, Beirut; tel. (1) 981001; fax (1) 981059; e-mail infocenter@finance.gov.lb; internet www.finance.gov.lb.

Ministry of Foreign Affairs and Emigrants: As-Sultana Bldg, Al Jnah, Sultan Ibrahim, Beirut; tel. (1) 8470767; fax (1) 840924; e-mail director@emigrants.gov.lb; internet www.emigrants.gov.lb.

  General Directorate of Emigrants: As-Sultana Bldg, Al Jnah, Sultan Ibrahim, Beirut; tel. (1) 840921; fax (1) 840924; e-mail director@emigrants.gov.lb; internet www.emigrants.gov.lb.

Ministry of Industry: Ministry of Industry and Petroleum Bldg, ave Sami Solh, Beirut; tel. (1) 423338; fax (1) 427112; e-mail ministry@industry.gov.lb; internet www.industry.gov.lb.

Ministry of Information: rue Hamra, Beirut; tel. (1) 754400; fax (1) 754776.

Ministry of the Interior and Municipalities: Grand Sérail, place Riad es-Solh, Beirut; tel. (1) 751601; fax (1) 750084; e-mail ministry@interior.gov.lb; internet www.moim.gov.lb.

Ministry of Justice: rue Sami Solh, Beirut; tel. (1) 422112; fax (1) 427957; e-mail info@justice.gov.lb; internet www.justice.gov.lb.

Ministry of Labour: Shiah, Beirut; tel. (1) 556804; fax (1) 556806; internet www.labor.gov.lb.

Ministry of National Defence: Yarze, Beirut; tel. (5) 420000; fax (5) 951035; e-mail cmdarm@lebarmy.gov.lb; internet www.lebarmy.gov.lb.

Ministry of Public Health: Hussein Mansour Bldg, Museum St, Beirut; tel. (1) 615020; fax (1) 615771; e-mail ministry@public-health.gov.lb; internet www.public-health.gov.lb.

Ministry of Public Works and Transport: Shiah, Beirut; tel. (5) 456482; fax (5) 455840.

Ministry of State for Administrative Reform: Immeuble Starco, rue Omar Daouk, Beirut; tel. (1) 371510; fax (1) 371599; e-mail webmaster@omsar.gov.lb; internet www.omsar.gov.lb.

Ministry of Telecommunications: 1st Floor, Ministry of Telecom Bldg, place Riad es-Solh, Beirut; tel. (1) 979161; fax (1) 979164; e-mail webmaster@mpt.gov.lb; internet www.mpt.gov.lb.

Ministry of Tourism: POB 11-5344, rue Banque du Liban 550, Beirut; tel. (1) 340940; fax (1) 340945; e-mail mot@inco.com.lb; internet www.destinationlebanon.gov.lb.

LEBANON *Directory*

Ministry of Youth and Sports: rue Sami Solh, Beirut; tel. (1) 425770; fax (1) 424387; e-mail minijes@cyberia.net.lb.

Legislature

MAJLIS AN-NUAB
(National Assembly)

The equal distribution of seats among Christians and Muslims is determined by law, and the Cabinet must reflect the level of representation achieved by the various religious denominations within that principal division. Deputies of the same religious denomination do not necessarily share the same political or party allegiances. The distribution of seats is as follows: Maronite Catholics 34; Sunni Muslims 27; Shi'a Muslims 27; Greek Orthodox 14; Druzes 8; Greek-Melkite Catholics 8; Armenian Orthodox 5; Alawites 2; Armenian Catholics 1; Protestants 1; Others 1.

President: NABIH BERRI.

General election, 29 May–19 June 2005

Party list	Seats
Rafik Hariri Martyr List*	72
Resistance and Development Bloc†	35
Free Patriotic Movement‡	21
Total	**128**

* Electoral list comprising the Future Movement (which won 36 seats), Parti socialiste progressiste (16), Lebanese Forces Party (6), Qornet Shehwan Gathering (6), Tripoli Bloc (3), Democratic Renewal (1), Democratic Left (1) and independents (3).
† Election list comprising Amal (which won 15 seats), Hezbollah (14), the Syrian Social Nationalist Party (2) and others (4).
‡ Election list comprising the Free Patriotic Movement itself (which won 14 seats), the Skaff bloc (5) and the Murr bloc (2).

Political Organizations

Amal (Hope—Afwaj al-Muqawamah al-Lubnaniyyah—Lebanese Resistance Detachments): e-mail post@amal-movement.com; internet www.amal-movement.com; f. 1975 as a politico-military organization; Shi'ite political party; contested 2005 legislative elections with Hezbollah as Resistance and Development Bloc; Leader NABIH BERRI.

Armenian Revolutionary Federation (ARF) (Tashnag): rue Spears, Beirut; e-mail www.arfd.am; f. 1890; principal Armenian party; historically the dominant nationalist party in the independent Armenian Republic of Yerevan of 1917–21, prior to its becoming part of the USSR; socialist ideology; Leader HRANT MARKARIAN.

Al-Baath (Baath Arab Socialist Party): Beirut; f. 1948; local branch of secular pro-Syrian party with policy of Arab union; Leader FAYEZ SHUKER.

Al-Baath (Baath Arab Socialist Party): f. 1966, following split in Syrian branch of Al-Baath; part of pro-Iraqi faction of Al-Baath; Sec.-Gen. ABD AL-MAJID RAFEI.

Bloc national libanais (National Bloc): rue Pasteur, Gemmayze, Beirut; tel. (1) 584585; fax (1) 584591; f. 1943; right-wing Lebanese party with policy of power-sharing between Christians and Muslims and the exclusion of the military from politics; Pres. CARLOS EDDÉ.

Free Patriotic Movement (Tayar al-Watani al-Horr): Beirut; tel. (3) 122858; e-mail info@tayyar.org; internet www.tayyar.org; aims to recover sovereignty and complete independence for Lebanon; majority of leaders and supporters are from the Christian community, although is officially secular; contested 2005 legislative elections in alliance with the Skaff and Murr blocs; Leader Gen. MICHEL AOUN.

Future Movement (Tayar al-Mustaqbal): POB 123, Koraytem, Hamra, Beirut; tel. (3) 375442; fax (1) 375442; e-mail info@almustaqbal.org; internet www.almustaqbal.org; opposed to Syrian influence in Lebanese affairs; contested 2005 legislative elections on the Rafik Hariri Martyr List with the Qornet Shehwan Gathering, Lebanese Forces Party and Parti socialiste progressiste; Leader SAAD ED-DIN HARIRI.

Hezbollah (Party of God): Beirut; e-mail moqawama@moqawama.org; internet www.hizbollah.tv; f. 1982 by Iranian Revolutionary Guards who were sent to Lebanon; militant Shi'ite faction, which has become the leading organization of Lebanon's Shi'a community and a recognized political party; demands the withdrawal of Israeli forces from the occupied Shebaa Farms area of what it considers to be southern Lebanon (but which is designated by the UN as being part of Syria) and the release of all Lebanese prisoners from Israeli detention; contested 2005 legislative elections with Amal as Resistance and Development Bloc, and achieved parliamentary and govt representation; Chair. MUHAMMAD RA'D; Leader and Sec.-Gen. Sheikh HASAN NASRALLAH; Spiritual Leader Ayatollah MUHAMMAD HUSSAIN FADLALLAH.

Hizb-ut-Tahrir al-Islami (Party of Islamic Liberation): e-mail info@hizb-ut-tahrir.org; internet www.hizb-ut-tahrir.org; f. 1953; transnational org. granted a political parties licence in Lebanon in 2006; aims to establish Islamic caliphate throughout the world; denies claims that it is a militant group; Global Leader Sheikh ABU YASIN ATA IBN KHALIL ABU RASHTA (Sheikh Ata Abu Rashta).

Al-Kataeb (Lebanese Social Democratic Party): POB 992, place Charles Hélou, Beirut; tel. (1) 584107; internet www.kataeb.org; f. 1936 as the Phalangist Party (Phalanges libanaises) by the late Pierre Gemayel; nationalist, reformist, democratic social party; largest Maronite party, although is officially secular; mem. of the Qornet Shehwan Gathering; 100,000 mems; Pres. AMIN GEMAYEL.

Lebanese Option Gathering: Beirut; f. 2007; aims to contest Hezbollah's monopoly over Shi'ite political representation in Lebanon, and to reform and develop the south of the country; Leader AHMAD AL-ASSAD.

El-Marada Movement: Zgharta; internet el-marada.net; f. as the Marada Brigade, relaunched in 1996 as a political party; advocates Lebanese unity, sovereignty and independence; Leader SULAYMAN FRANJIYA.

National Dialogue Party: POB 15-5060, First Floor, Marj ez-Zouhour Bldg, Dona Maria St, Ras en-Nabeh, Beirut; tel. (1) 637000; fax (1) 631234; e-mail info@alhiwar.com; internet www.alhiwar.com; f. 2004; advocates a comprehensive national dialogue to bring about political, social and judicial reforms; also seeks to target corruption and to ensure that the state has authority over the whole of Lebanon; Founder and Chair. FOUAD MAKHZOUMI.

Parti communiste libanais (Lebanese Communist Party—PCL): rue Al-Bahatri, Al-Watuat, Beirut; tel. and fax (1) 739615; e-mail lcparty@lcparty.org; internet www.lcparty.org; f. 1924; officially dissolved 1948–71; Marxist, with much support among intellectuals; Pres. MAURICE NOHRA; Sec.-Gen. KHALID HADDADEH.

Parti socialiste progressiste (At-Takadumi al-Ishteraki—PSP): POB 11-2893, Beirut 1107 2120; tel. (1) 303455; fax (1) 301231; e-mail internationalrelation@psp.org.lb; internet www.psp.org.lb; f. 1949; progressive party, advocates constitutional road to socialism and democracy; over 25,000 mems; mainly Druze support; contested 2005 legislative elections as part of the Rafik Hariri Martyr List; Pres. WALID JOUMBLATT; Sec.-Gen. SHARIF FAYAD.

Qornet Shehwan Gathering: f. 2001; Christian coalition of parties of diverse political persuasions and incorporating Maronite (incl. Al-Kataeb), Orthodox and Greek Catholic mems; advocates full national sovereignty for Lebanon; supports the establishment of a Palestinian state; rejects violence as a means of solving disputes; contested 2005 legislative elections as part of the Rafik Hariri Martyr List; Maronite Christian Patriarch Cardinal NASRALLAH BOUTROS (PIERRE) SFEIR is the group's unofficial patron.

Resistance and Development Bloc: electoral bloc consisting principally of Amal and Hezbollah; the two parties contested the 2000 and, with the Syrian Social Nationalist Party, 2005 legislative elections as this alliance; Leader NABIH BERRI.

Syrian Social Nationalist Party (al-Hizb as-Suri al-Qawmi al-Ijtima'i): internet www.ssnp.net; f. 1932 in Beirut; banned 1962–69; seeks creation of a 'Greater Syrian' state, incl. Lebanon, Syria, Iraq, Jordan, the Palestinian territories, Kuwait, Cyprus and parts of Egypt, Iran and Turkey; advocates separation of church and state, the redistribution of wealth and a strong military; supports Syrian involvement in Lebanese affairs; contested 2005 legislative elections as mem. of the Resistance and Development Bloc (consisting principally of Amal and Hezbollah); Leader ASSAD HARDANE.

Al-Wa'ad (National Secular Democratic Party—Pledge): Beirut; f. 1986 by the late Elie Hobeika; pro-Syrian splinter group of Lebanese Forces (see below).

Other parties include the **Independent Nasserite Movement** (Murabitoun; Sunni Muslim Militia; Leader IBRAHIM QULAYAT) and the **Lebanese Popular Congress** (Pres. KAMAL SHATILA). The **Nasserite Popular Organization** and the **Arab Socialist Union** merged in January 1987, retaining the name of the former. The **Islamic Amal** is a breakaway group from Amal, based in Ba'albak (Ba'albek) (Leader HUSSEIN MOUSSAVI). **Islamic Jihad** (Islamic Holy War) is a pro-Iranian fundamentalist guerrilla group. The **Popular Liberation Army** (f. 1985 by the late MUSTAFA SAAD) is a Sunni Muslim faction, active in the south of Lebanon. **Tawhid Islami** (the Islamic Unification Movement; f. 1982; Sunni Muslim) and the **Arab Democratic Party** (or the Red Knights; Alawites; pro-Syrian; Leader ALI EID) are based in Tripoli.

The **Lebanese Forces Party** (www.lebanese-forces.org, f. 1990), the political successor to the **Lebanese Forces** (f. 1976; coalition of Maronite militias), is still active in Lebanon, despite proscription by

LEBANON

the Government in 1994. Its leader, SAMIR GEAGEA, was imprisoned in 1995 on murder charges, but was pardoned and released in 2005.

Diplomatic Representation

EMBASSIES IN LEBANON

Algeria: POB 4794, face Hôtel Summerland, rue Jnah, Beirut; tel. (1) 826712; fax (1) 826711; Ambassador AHMAD BOUTEHRI.

Argentina: 2nd Floor, Residence des Jardins, Immeuble Moutran, 161 rue Sursock, Achrafieh, Beirut; tel. (1) 210800; fax (1) 210802; e-mail embarg@cyberia.net.lb; Chargé d'affaires a.i. MARIANO HERNÁN MUJICA.

Armenia: POB 70607, rue Jasmin, Rabieh, Mtaileb, Beirut; tel. (4) 402952; fax (4) 418860; e-mail armenia@dm.net.lb; Ambassador VAHAN TER-GHEVONDYAN.

Australia: Embassy Complex, Sérail Hill, Beirut; tel. (1) 974030; fax (1) 974029; e-mail austemle@dfat.gov.au; internet www.lebanon.embassy.gov.au; Ambassador LYNDALL SACHS.

Austria: POB 11-3942, 8th Floor, Immeuble Tabaris, 812 ave Charles Malek, Achrafieh, Beirut; tel. (1) 217360; fax (1) 217772; e-mail beirut-ob@bmeia.gv.at; Ambassador EVA MARIA ZIEGLER.

Bahrain: Beirut; Ambassador (vacant).

Belgium: Bloc A, 10e étage, Immeuble Lazarie, rue Emir Béchir, Beirut; tel. (1) 976001; fax (1) 976007; e-mail beirut@diplobel.fed.be; internet www.diplomatie.be/beirut; Ambassador JOHAN VERKAMMEN.

Brazil: POB 40242, Baabda, Beirut; tel. (5) 921255; fax (5) 923001; e-mail braemlib@terra.net.lb; Ambassador EDUARDO AUGUSTO IBIAPINA DE SEIXAS.

Bulgaria: POB 11-6544, Sector 6, Mar-Takla, Hazmieh, Beirut; tel. (5) 452883; fax (5) 452892; e-mail bg_emblb@yahoo.com; internet www.mfa.bg/beirut; Ambassador VANELIN DIMITROV LAZAROV.

Canada: POB 60163, 1e étage, Immeuble Coolrite, Autostrade Jal ed-Dib 43, Beirut; tel. (4) 713900; fax (4) 710595; e-mail berut@international.gc.ca; internet www.dfait-maeci.gc.ca/beirut; Ambassador LOUIS DE LORIMIER.

Chile: Nouvelle Naccache, 21 Bifurcation après La Belle Antique avant Carpacio, Beirut; tel. (4) 418670; fax (4) 418672; e-mail echilelb@dm.net.lb; Ambassador FELIPE DU MONCEAU DE BERGENDAL.

China, People's Republic: POB 11-8227, 72 rue Nicolas Ibrahim Sursock, Ramletbaida, Beirut 1107 2260; tel. (1) 850314; fax (1) 822492; e-mail chinaemb_lb@mfa.gov.cn; internet lb.china-embassy.org; Ambassador LIU ZHIMING.

Colombia: 5th Floor, Mazda Centre, Jal ed-Dib, Beirut; tel. (4) 712646; fax (4) 712656; e-mail ebeirut@minrelext.gov.co; Ambassador GEORGINE MALLAT.

Cuba: Center Farrania, Saïd Freiha St, Mar-Takla, Hazmieh, Beirut 2901 6727; tel. (1) 459925; fax (1) 950070; e-mail libancub@cyberia.net.lb; internet www.embacubalebanon.com; Ambassador DARÍO DE URRA TORRIENTE.

Czech Republic: POB 40195, Baabda, Beirut; tel. (5) 929010; fax (5) 922120; e-mail beirut@embassy.mzv.cz; internet www.mzv.cz/beirut; Ambassador JAN ČÍŽEK.

Denmark: POB 11-5190, Army St, Sérail Hill, Beirut; tel. (1) 991001; fax (1) 991006; e-mail beyamb@um.dk; internet www.ambbeirut.um.dk; Ambassador JAN TOP CHRISTENSEN.

Egypt: POB 5037, rue Thomas Eddison, ar-Ramla el-Baida, Beirut; tel. (1) 862917; fax (1) 863751; Ambassador AHMAD AL-BIDYAWI.

France: rue de Damas, Beirut; tel. (1) 420000; fax (1) 420013; e-mail ambafr@ciberia.net.lb; internet www.ambafrance-lb.org; Ambassador ANDRÉ PARANT.

Gabon: POB 11-1252, Riad es-Solh, Hadath, Beirut 1107 2080; tel. (5) 924649; fax (5) 924643; Ambassador SIMON NTOUTOUME EMANE.

Germany: POB 11-2820, Riad es-Solh, Beirut 1102 2110; tel. (4) 929600; fax (4) 929616; e-mail info@beirut.diplo.de; internet www.beirut.diplo.de; Ambassador HANSJOERG HABER.

Greece: POB 11-0309, Immeuble Boukhater, rue des Ambassades, Nouvelle Naccache, Beirut; tel. (4) 418772; fax (4) 418774; e-mail hellas.emb@embassyofgreecebeirut.net; internet www.embassyofgreecebeirut.net; Ambassador NIKOLAOS VAMVOUNAKIS.

Holy See: POB 1061, Jounieh (Apostolic Nunciature); tel. (9) 263102; fax (9) 264488; e-mail naliban@terra.net.lb; Apostolic Nuncio Most Rev. LUIGI GATTI (Titular Archbishop of Santa Giusta).

Hungary: POB 113-5259, 9th Floor, BAC Bldg, Justinien St, Sanayeh, Beirut; tel. (1) 730083; fax (1) 741261; e-mail mission.bej@kum.hu; internet www.mfa.gov.hu/kulkepviselet/LB; Ambassador LAJOS TAMÁS.

India: POB 113-5240, Immeuble Sahmarani, rue Kantari 31, Hamra, Beirut; tel. (1) 373539; fax (1) 373538; e-mail indembei@dm.net.lb; Ambassador NANTU SARKAR.

Indonesia: POB 40007, ave Palais Presidential, rue 68, Secteur 3, Baabda, Beirut; tel. (5) 924682; fax (5) 924678; e-mail kbri@kbri-beirut.org; internet kbri-beirut.org; Ambassador R. BAGAS HAPSORO.

Iran: POB 5030, Bir Hassan, Beirut; tel. (1) 821224; fax (1) 821230; Ambassador MUHAMMAD-REZA RAOUF SHEIBANI.

Iraq: Beirut; tel. (1) 453209; fax (1) 459850; e-mail brtemb@iraqmofamail.net; Ambassador OMAR AL-BARZENJI.

Italy: rue du Palais Présidentiel, Baabda, Beirut; tel. (5) 954955; fax (5) 959616; e-mail amba.beirut@esteri.it; internet www.ambbeirut.esteri.it; Ambassador GABRIELE CHECCHIA.

Japan: POB 11-3360, Army St, Zkak al-Blat, Serail Hill, Beirut; tel. (1) 989751; fax (1) 989754; e-mail japanemb@japanemb.org.lb; internet www.lb.emb-japan.go.jp; Ambassador YOSHIHISA KURODA.

Jordan: POB 109, Beirut 5113; tel. (5) 922500; fax (5) 922502; e-mail joremb@dm.net.lb; Ambassador ZIYAD MAJALI.

Korea, Republic: POB 40-290, Baabda, Beirut; tel. (5) 953167; fax (5) 953170; e-mail lbkor@hanmail.net; internet lbn.mofat.go.kr/eng/af/lbn/main/index.jsp; Ambassador YOUNG-HA LEE.

Kuwait: POB 4530, Rond-point du Stade, Bir Hassan, Beirut; tel. (1) 822515; fax (1) 842220; e-mail info@kuwaitinfo.net; internet www.kuwaitinfo.net; Ambassador ABD AL-AAL AL-QINAI.

Mexico: POB 70-1150, Antélias; tel. (4) 418871; fax (4) 418873; e-mail mail@embassyofmexicoinlebanon.org; internet www.embassyofmexicoinlebanon.org; Ambassador JORGE ÁLVAREZ FUENTES.

Morocco: Bir Hassan, Beirut; tel. (1) 859829; fax (1) 859839; e-mail sifmar@cyberia.net.lb; Ambassador ALI OUMLIL.

Netherlands: POB 167190, Netherlands Tower, ave Charles Malek, Achrafieh, Beirut; tel. (1) 204663; fax (1) 204664; e-mail nlgovbei@sodetel.net.lb; internet www.netherlandsembassy.org.lb; Ambassador ROBERT ZELDENRUST.

Norway: POB 113-7001, Immeuble Dimashki, rue Bliss, Ras Beirut, Hamra, Beirut 1103 2150; tel. (1) 372977; fax (1) 372979; e-mail norleb@cyberia.net.lb; internet www.norway-lebanon.org; Ambassador AUD LISE NORHEIM.

Pakistan: POB 135506, Immeuble Shell, 11e étage, Raoucheh, Beirut; tel. (1) 863041; fax (1) 864583; e-mail pakemblb@cyberia.net.lb; Ambassador NAWABZADA AMIN ULLAH KHAN RAISANI.

Paraguay: 1er étage, Immeuble Kormali, rue Ambassade de France, Hazmieh, Beirut; tel. and fax (1) 5458502; e-mail embaparlibano@hotmail.com; Chargé d'affaires FERNANDO PARISI.

Philippines: POB 136631, ave Charles Malek, Achrafieh, Beirut; tel. (1) 212001; fax (1) 212004; e-mail beirutpe@dfa.gov.ph; Ambassador GILBERTO G. B. ASUQUE.

Poland: POB 40-215, Immeuble Khalifa, ave Président Sulayman Franjiya 52, Baabda, Beirut; tel. (5) 924881; fax (5) 924882; e-mail polamb@cyberia.net.lb; internet www.polambeirut.org; Ambassador TOMASZ NIEGODZISZ.

Qatar: POB 11-6717, 1er étage, Immeuble Deebs, Shouran, Beirut; tel. (1) 865271; fax (1) 810460; e-mail beirut@mofa.gov.qa; Ambassador SAAD BIN ALI AL-MUHANNADI.

Romania: Route du Palais Presidentiel, Baabda, Beirut; tel. (5) 924848; fax (5) 924747; e-mail romembey@inco.com.lb; internet beirut.mae.ro; Ambassador DANIEL TANASE.

Russia: POB 5220, rue Mar Elias et-Tineh, Wata Mseitbeh, Beirut; tel. (1) 300041; fax (1) 303837; e-mail rusembei@cyberia.net.lb; internet www.lebanon.mid.ru; Ambassador SERGEI NIKOLAYEVICH BUKIN.

Saudi Arabia: POB 136144, Kuraitem, Beirut; tel. (1) 860351; fax (1) 861524; e-mail lbemb@mofa.gov.sa; Ambassador ALI BIN AWADH ASSERI.

Spain: POB 11-3039, Palais Chehab, Hadath Antounie, Beirut; tel. (5) 464120; fax (5) 464030; e-mail emb.beruit@mae.es; Ambassador JUAN CARLOS GAFO ACEVEDO.

Sri Lanka: POB 175, Mar-Takla, Hazmieh, Beirut; tel. (5) 924765; fax (5) 924763; e-mail slemblbn@cyberia.net.lb; Ambassador MEER SAHIB MAHROOF.

Sudan: POB 2504, Hamra, Beirut; tel. (1) 350057; fax (1) 353271; Ambassador JAMAL MUHAMMAD IBRAHIM.

Switzerland: POB 11-172, Immeuble Bourj al-Ghazal, ave Fouad Chehab, Achrafieh, Beirut; tel. (1) 324129; fax (1) 324167; e-mail bey.vertretung@eda.admin.ch; internet www.eda.admin.ch/beirut; Ambassador FRANÇOIS BARRAS.

Syria: Hamra, Beirut; Ambassador ALI ABD AL-KARIM ALI (designate).

LEBANON

Tunisia: Mar-Takla, Hazmieh, Beirut; tel. (5) 457431; fax (5) 950434; Ambassador MUHAMMAD SAMIR ABDULLAH.

Turkey: POB 70-666, zone II, rue 1, Rabieh, Beirut; tel. (4) 520929; fax (4) 407557; e-mail trbebeyr@intracom.net.lb; internet www.turkishembassy.org.lb; Ambassador SERDAR KILIÇ.

Ukraine: POB 431, Jardin al-Bacha, Jisr al-Bacha, Sin el-Fil, Beirut; tel. (1) 510527; fax (1) 510531; e-mail ukrembassy@inco.com.lb; internet www.mfa.gov.ua/lebanon; Ambassador BORIS ZHARSHOK.

United Arab Emirates: Immeuble Wafic Tanbara, Jnah, Beirut; tel. (1) 857000; fax (1) 857009; e-mail eembassy@uae.org.lb; Ambassador RAHMAN HUSSAIN AZ-ZA'ABI.

United Kingdom: POB 11-471, Serail Hill, Beirut Central District, Beirut; tel. (1) 960800; fax (1) 990420; e-mail chancery@cyberia.net.lb; internet ukinlebanon.fco.gov.uk; Ambassador FRANCES GUY.

USA: POB 70-840, Antélias; tel. (4) 542600; fax (4) 544136; e-mail pasbeirut@state.gov; internet lebanon.usembassy.gov; Ambassador MICHELE J. SISON.

Uruguay: POB 2051, Centre Stella Marris, 7e étage, rue Banque du Liban, Jounieh; tel. (9) 636529; fax (9) 636531; e-mail uruliban@dm.net.lb; internet www.embauruguaybeirut.org; Ambassador JORGE LUIS JURE.

Venezuela: POB 11-603, Immeuble Baezevale House, 5e étage, Zalka, Beirut; tel. (1) 888701; fax (1) 900757; e-mail embajadora@embavenelibano.com; internet www.embavenelibano.com; Ambassador ZOED KARAM.

Yemen: Bir Hassan, Beirut; tel. (1) 852688; fax (1) 821610; Ambassador FAISAL ABU RAS.

Judicial System

Law and justice in Lebanon are administered in accordance with the following codes, which are based upon modern theories of civil and criminal legislation:

Code de la Propriété (1930).

Code des Obligations et des Contrats (1932).

Code de Procédure Civile (1933).

Code Maritime (1947).

Code de Procédure Pénale (Code Ottoman Modifié).

Code Pénal (1943).

Code Pénal Militaire (1946).

Code d'Instruction Criminelle.

The following courts are now established:

(a) Fifty-six **'Single-Judge Courts'**, each consisting of a single judge, and dealing in the first instance with both civil and criminal cases; there are 17 such courts in Beirut and seven in Tripoli.

(b) Eleven **Courts of Appeal**, each consisting of three judges, including a President and a Public Prosecutor, and dealing with civil and criminal cases; there are five such courts in Beirut.

First President of the Courts of Appeal of Beirut: TANIOS EL-KHOURY.

(c) Four **Courts of Cassation**, three dealing with civil and commercial cases and the fourth with criminal cases. A Court of Cassation, to be properly constituted, must have at least three judges, one being the President and the other two Councillors. If the Court of Cassation reverses the judgment of a lower court, it does not refer the case back but retries it itself.

General Prosecutor of Cassation: SAID MIRZA.

(d) **State Consultative Council**, which deals with administrative cases.

President of the State Consultative Council: GHALEB GHANEM.

(e) **The Court of Justice**, which is a special court consisting of a President and four judges, deals with matters affecting the security of the State; there is no appeal against its verdicts.

In addition to the above, the Constitutional Council considers matters pertaining to the constitutionality of legislation. Military courts are competent to try crimes and misdemeanours involving the armed and security forces. Islamic (*Shari'a*), Christian and Jewish religious courts deal with affairs of personal status (marriage, death, inheritance, etc.).

President of the Constitutional Council: AMIN FARIS NASSER.

Chief of the Military Court: Brig.-Gen. MAHER SAFI ED-DIN.

Religion

Of all the regions of the Middle East, Lebanon probably presents the closest juxtaposition of sects and peoples within a small territory. Estimates for 1983 assessed the sizes of communities as: Shi'a Muslims 1.2m., Maronites 900,000, Sunni Muslims 750,000, Greek Orthodox 250,000, Druzes 250,000, Armenians 175,000. There is also a small Jewish community. In 1994 it was estimated that 29%–32% of the population of Lebanon were Shi'a Muslims, 25%–28% Maronites, 16%–20% Sunni Muslims and 3.5% Druzes. The Maronites, a uniate sect of the Roman Catholic Church, inhabited the old territory of Mount Lebanon, i.e. immediately east of Beirut. In the south, towards the Israeli frontier, Shi'a villages are most common, while between the Shi'a and the Maronites live the Druzes (divided between the Yazbakis and the Joumblatis). The Beka'a valley has many Greek Christians (both Roman Catholic and Orthodox), while the Tripoli area is mainly Sunni Muslim.

CHRISTIANITY

The Roman Catholic Church

Armenian Rite

Patriarchate of Cilicia: Patriarcat Arménien Catholique, rue de l'Hôpital orthodoxe, Jeitawi, Beirut 2078 5605; tel. (1) 570555; fax (1) 570563; e-mail nerbed19@magnarama.com; f. 1742; established in Beirut since 1929; includes patriarchal diocese of Beirut, with an estimated 14,000 adherents (31 December 2007); Patriarch Most Rev. NERSES BEDROS XIX TARMOUNI; Protosyncellus Rt Rev. VARTAN ACHKARIAN (Titular Bishop of Tokat—Armenian Rite).

Chaldean Rite

Diocese of Beirut: Evêché Chaldéen de Beyrouth, POB 373, Hazmieh, Beirut; tel. (5) 457732; fax (5) 457731; e-mail chaldepiscopus@hotmail.com; an estimated 10,000 adherents (31 December 2006); Bishop of Beirut MICHEL KASSARJI.

Latin Rite

Apostolic Vicariate of Beirut: Vicariat Apostolique, POB 11-4224, Riad es-Solh, Beirut 1107 2160; tel. (9) 236101; fax (9) 236102; e-mail vicariatlat@hotmail.com; an estimated 15,000 adherents (31 December 2006); Vicar Apostolic PAUL DAHDAH (Titular Archbishop of Arae in Numidia).

Maronite Rite

Patriarchate of Antioch and all the East: Patriarcat Maronite, Bkerké; tel. (9) 915441; fax (9) 938844; e-mail jtawk@bkerke.org.lb; includes patriarchal dioceses of Jounieh, Sarba and Jobbé; the Maronite Church in Lebanon comprises four archdioceses and six dioceses, with an estimated 1,394,516 adherents (31 December 2006); Patriarch Cardinal NASRALLAH BOUTROS (PIERRE) SFEIR.

Archbishop of Antélias: Most Rev. JOSEPH MOHSEN BÉCHARA, Archevêché Maronite, POB 70400, Antélias; tel. (4) 410020; fax (4) 415872.

Archbishop of Beirut: Most Rev. PAUL YOUSSEF MATAR, Archevêché Maronite, 10 rue Collège de la Sagesse, Achrafieh, Beirut; tel. (1) 561980; fax (1) 561930; e-mail maronitebeyrouth@yahoo.fr; also representative of the Holy See for Roman Catholics of the Coptic Rite in Lebanon.

Archbishop of Tripoli: Most Rev. GEORGES BOU-JAOUDÉ, Archevêché Maronite, POB 104, rue al-Moutran, Karm Sada, Tripoli; tel. (6) 624324; fax (6) 629393; e-mail rahmat@inco.com.lb.

Archbishop of Tyre: Most Rev. CHUCRALLAH-NABIL HAGE, Archevêché Maronite, Tyre; tel. (7) 740059; fax (7) 344891; e-mail abounacharbel@cyberia.net.lb.

Melkite Rite

Patriarch of Antioch: Patriarcat Grec-Melkite Catholique, POB 22249, 12 ave az-Zeitoon, Bab Charki, Damascus, Syria; tel. (1) 5441030; fax (1) 5417900; e-mail pat.melk@aloola.sy; internet www.pgc-lb.org; f. 1724; the Melkite Church in Lebanon comprises seven archdioceses, with an estimated 389,700 adherents (31 December 2006); Patriarch of Antioch and all the East, of Alexandria and of Jerusalem Most Rev. GRÉGOIRE III LAHAM.

Archbishop of Ba'albek: Most Rev. ELIAS RAHAL, Archevêché Grec-Catholique, Ba'albek; tel. (8) 370200; fax (8) 373986.

Archbishop of Baniyas: Most Rev. GEORGES NICOLAS HADDAD, Archevêché de Panéas, Jdeidet Marjeyoun; tel. and fax (3) 830007.

Archbishop of Beirut and Gibail: JOSEPH KALLAS, Archevêché Grec-Melkite-Catholique, POB 11-901, 655 rue de Damas, Beirut; tel. (1) 616104; fax (1) 616109; e-mail agmcb@terra.net.lb.

Archbishop of Saida (Sidon): Most Rev. ELIE BÉCHARA HADDAD, Archevêché Grec-Melkite-Catholique, POB 247, rue el-Moutran,

Sidon; tel. (7) 720100; fax (7) 722055; e-mail mhaddad.saida@hotmail.com.

Archbishop of Tripoli: Most Rev. GEORGE RIASHI, Archevêché Grec-Catholique, rue al-Kanaess, Tripoli; tel. (6) 431602; fax (6) 441716.

Archbishop of Tyre: Most Rev. GEORGES BAKOUNY, Archevêché Grec-Melkite-Catholique, POB 257, Tyre; tel. (7) 740015; fax (7) 349180; e-mail pbacouni@yahoo.com.

Archbishop of Zahleh and Furzol: Most Rev. ANDRÉ HADDAD, Archevêché Grec-Melkite-Catholique, Saidat en-Najat, Zahleh; tel. (8) 800333; fax (8) 822406; e-mail arch_zahle@hotmail.com.

Syrian Rite

Patriarchate of Antioch: Patriarcat Syrien Catholique d'Antioche, rue de Damas, POB 116/5087, Beirut 1106 2010; tel. (1) 615892; fax (1) 616573; e-mail psc_lb@yahoo.com; jurisdiction over about 150,000 Syrian Catholics in the Middle East, incl. (at 31 December 2006) 14,700 in the diocese of Beirut; Patriarch Most Rev. IGNACE JOSEPH III YOUNAN; Protosyncellus Mgr GEORGES MASRI.

The Anglican Communion

Within the Episcopal Church in Jerusalem and the Middle East, Lebanon forms part of the diocese of Jerusalem (see the chapter on Israel).

Other Christian Groups

Armenian Apostolic Orthodox Church: Armenian Catholicosate of Cilicia, POB 70317, Antélias; tel. (4) 410001; fax (4) 419724; e-mail info@armenianorthodoxchurch.org; internet www.armenianorthodoxchurch.org; f. 301 in Armenia, re-established in 1293 in Cilicia (now in Turkey), transferred to Antélias, Lebanon, 1930; Leader His Holiness ARAM KESHISHIAN I (Catholicos of Cilicia); jurisdiction over an estimated 3.5m. adherents in Lebanon, Syria, Cyprus, Kuwait, Greece, Iran, Qatar, the United Arab Emirates, South America, the USA and Canada.

National Evangelical Synod of Syria and Lebanon: POB 70890, Antélias; tel. (4) 525030; fax (4) 411184; e-mail nessl@synod-sl.org; internet www.synod-sl.org; f. 1959; 20,000 adherents (2009); Gen. Sec. Rev. FADI DAGHER.

Patriarchate of Antioch and all the East (Greek Orthodox): Patriarcat Grec-Orthodoxe, POB 9, Damascus, Syria; tel. (11) 5424400; fax (11) 5424404; e-mail info@antiochpat.org; internet www.antiochpat.org; Patriarch His Beatitude IGNATIUS (HAZIM) IV.

Patriarchate of Antioch and all the East (Syrian Orthodox): Patriarcat Syrien Orthodoxe, Bab Toma, POB 22260, Damascus, Syria; tel. 5432401; fax 5432400; Patriarch IGNATIUS ZAKKA I IWAS.

Supreme Council of the Evangelical Community in Syria and Lebanon: POB 70/1065, rue Rabieh 34, Antélias; tel. (4) 525036; fax (4) 405490; e-mail suprcoun@minero.net; Pres. Rev. Dr SALIM SAHIOUNY.

Union of the Armenian Evangelical Churches in the Near East: POB 11-377, Beirut; tel. (1) 565628; fax (1) 565629; e-mail uaecne@cyberia.net.lb; f. 1846 in Turkey; comprises about 30 Armenian Evangelical Churches in Syria, Lebanon, Egypt, Cyprus, Greece, Iran, Turkey and Australia; 7,500 mems (1990); Pres. Rev. MEGRDICH KARAGOEZIAN; Gen. Sec. SEBOUH TERZIAN.

ISLAM

Shi'a Muslims: Leader Imam Sheikh SAYED MOUSSA AS-SADR (went missing during visit to Libya in August 1978); President of the Supreme Islamic Council of the Shi'a Community of Lebanon ABD AL-AMIR QABALAN; Beirut.

Sunni Muslims: Grand Mufti of Lebanon, Dar el-Fatwa, rue Ilewi Rushed, Beirut; tel. (1) 422340; Leader Sheikh Dr MUHAMMAD RASHID QABBANI.

Druzes: Supreme Spiritual Leader of the Druze Community, Beirut; tel. (1) 341116; Supreme Spiritual Leader Sheikh AL-AQL BAHJAT GHAITH; Political Leader WALID JOUMBLATT.

Alawites: a schism of Shi'ite Islam; there are an estimated 50,000 Alawites in northern Lebanon, in and around Tripoli.

JUDAISM

Jews: Leader CHAHOUD CHREIM (Beirut).

The Press

DAILIES

Al-Akhbar (The News): POB 5963-113, 6th Floor, Concorde Centre, rue Verdun, Beirut; tel. (1) 759500; fax (1) 759597; internet www.al-akhbar.com; f. 2006; Arabic; independent; Editor KHALID SAGHIEH.

Al-Amal (Hope): POB 992, place Charles Hélou, Beirut; tel. (1) 382992; f. 1939; Arabic; organ of Al-Kataeb (Lebanese Social Democratic Party); Chief Editor ELIAS RABABI; circ. 35,000.

Al-Anwar (Lights): c/o Dar Assayad, POB 11-1038, Hazmieh, Beirut; tel. (5) 456374; fax (5) 452700; e-mail info@alanwar.com; internet www.alanwar-leb.com; f. 1959; Arabic; independent; supplement, Sunday; cultural and social; publ. by Dar Assayad SAL; Editors-in-Chief MICHEL RAAD, RAFIK KHOURY; circ. 14,419.

Aztag: POB 80-860, Shaghzoyan Cultural Centre, Bourj Hammoud; tel. (1) 258526; fax (1) 258529; e-mail info@aztagdaily.com; internet www.aztagdaily.com; f. 1927; Armenian; Editor-in-Chief SHAHAN KANDAHARIAN; circ. 6,500.

Al-Balad: Beirut; tel. (1) 494694; fax (1) 494894; e-mail crm@albaladonline.com; internet albaladonline.com; Arabic; Chair. AHMAD BADRANI; Man. Editor GEORGE JABARA.

Al-Bayrak (The Standard): Immeuble Dimitri Trad, rue Issa Maalouf, Achrafieh, Beirut; tel. (1) 216393; fax (1) 338928; e-mail dalwl@dm.net.lb; internet www.albayrakonline.com; f. 1913; Arabic; publ. by Dar Alf Leila wa Leila Publishing House; politics and society; Editor-in-Chief MELHEM KARAM; circ. 10,000.

Ach-Chaab (The People): POB 5140, Beirut; f. 1961; Arabic; Nationalist; Propr and Editor MUHAMMAD AMIN DUGHAN; circ. 7,000.

Ach-Charq (The East): POB 11-0838, rue Verdun, Riad es-Solh, Beirut; tel. (1) 810820; fax (1) 866105; e-mail info@elshark.com; internet www.elshark.com; f. 1926; Arabic; Gen. Dir and Editor-in-Chief AOUNI AL-KAAKI.

Daily Star: 6th Floor, Marine Tower, rue de la Sainte Famille, Achrafieh, Beirut; tel. (1) 587277; fax (1) 561333; e-mail editorial@dailystar.com.lb; internet www.dailystar.com.lb; f. 1952; English; Publr and Editor-in-Chief JAMIL K. MROUE; circ. 10,550.

Ad-Diyar (The Homeland): an-Nahda Bldg, Yarze, Beirut; tel. (5) 923830; fax (5) 923773; e-mail aldiyar2002@yahoo.com; internet www.addiyaronline.com; f. 1987; Arabic; Propr and Editor-in-Chief CHARLES AYYUB.

Ad-Dunya (The World): Beirut; f. 1943; Arabic; political; Chief Editor SULIMAN ABOU ZAID; circ. 25,000.

Al-Hayat (Life): POB 11-1242, rue Maarad, place Riad es-Solh, Beirut; tel. (1) 987990; fax (1) 983921; e-mail information@alhayat.com; internet www.alhayat.com; f. 1946; Arabic; independent; Editor-in-Chief GHASSAN CHARBEL; circ. 196,800.

Journal al-Haddis: POB 300, Jounieh; f. 1927; Arabic; political; Owner GEORGES ARÈGE-SAADÉ.

Lisan ul-Hal (The Organ): rue Châteaubriand, Beirut; e-mail lebanon@lissan-ul-hal.com; internet www.lissan-ul-hal.com; f. 1877; Arabic; Editor GEBRAN HAYEK; circ. 33,000.

Al-Liwa' (The Standard): POB 11-2402, Beirut; tel. (1) 735745; fax (1) 735749; e-mail events@aliwaa.com.lb; internet www.aliwaa.com; f. 1963; Arabic; Propr ABD AL-GHANI SALAM; Editor SALAH SALAM; circ. 26,000.

Al-Mustaqbal: POB 14-5426, Beirut; tel. (1) 797770; fax (1) 869264; e-mail rnakib@almustaqbal.com.lb; internet www.almustaqbal.com.lb; f. 1999; Dir TOUFIK KHATTAB; Editor HANI HAMMOUD; circ. 20,000.

An-Nahar (The Day): Immeuble An-Nahar, place des Martyrs, Marfa', Beirut 2014 5401; tel. (1) 994888; fax (1) 996777; e-mail webmaster@annahar.com.lb; internet www.annahar.com; f. 1933; Arabic; independent; publ. by Editions Dar an-Nahar SAL; Chair. GHASSAN TUÉNI; Exec. Editor-in-Chief EDMOND SAAB; circ. 50,000.

An-Nida (The Appeal): Beirut; f. 1959; Arabic; publ. by the Lebanese Communist Party; Editor KARIM MROUÉ; circ. 10,000.

L'Orient-Le Jour: POB 11-2488, Kantari, Immeuble Kantari Corner, Beirut; tel. (1) 365365; fax (1) 375888; e-mail administration@lorientlejour.com; internet www.lorientlejour.com; f. 1942; French; independent; Pres. Dir MICHEL EDDÉ; Editor-in-Chief NAJUIB AOUN; circ. 23,000.

Le Réveil: Beirut; tel. (1) 890700; f. 1977; French; Editor-in-Chief JEAN SHAMI; Dir RAYMOND DAOU; circ. 10,000.

Sada Lubnan (Echo of Lebanon): Beirut; f. 1951; Arabic; pan-Arab; Editor MUHAMMAD BAALBAKI; circ. 25,000.

As-Safir: POB 113/5015, Immeuble as-Safir, rue Monimina, Hamra, Beirut 1103-2010; tel. (1) 350001; fax (1) 743602; e-mail mail@assafir.com; internet www.assafir.com; f. 1974; Arabic; political; Publr and Editor-in-Chief TALAL SALMAN; circ. 45,000.

Sawt al-Uruba (The Voice of Europe): POB 3537, Beirut; f. 1959; Arabic; organ of the An-Najadeh Party.

Le Soir: POB 1470, rue de Syrie, Beirut; f. 1947; French; independent; Dir DIKRAN TOSBATH; Editor ANDRÉ KECATI; circ. 16,500.

Telegraf—Bairut: rue Béchara el-Khoury, Beirut; f. 1930; Arabic; political, economic and social; Editor TOUFIC ASSAD MATNI; circ. 15,500 (5,000 outside Lebanon).

LEBANON

Directory

Al-Yaum (Today): Beirut; f. 1937; Arabic; Editor WAFIC MUHAMMAD CHAKER AT-TIBY.

Zartonk: POB 11-617, rue Nahr Ibrahim, Beirut; tel. and fax (1) 566709; e-mail info@zartonkdaily.com; internet www.zartonkdaily.com; f. 1937; Armenian, Arabic and English; official organ of Armenian Liberal Democratic Party; Man. Editor BAROUYR H. AGHBASHIAN.

WEEKLIES

Achabaka (The Net): c/o Dar Assayad SAL, POB 11-1038, Hazmieh, Beirut; tel. (5) 456373; fax (5) 452700; e-mail achabaka@achabaka.com; internet www.achabaka.com; f. 1956; Arabic; society and features; Founder SAID FREIHA; Editor ELHAM FREIHA; circ. 139,775.

Al-Alam al-Lubnani (The Lebanese World): POB 462, Beirut; f. 1964; Arabic, English, Spanish, French; politics, literature and social economy; Editor-in-Chief FAYEK KHOURY; Gen. Editor CHEIKH FADI GEMAYEL; circ. 45,000.

Al-Anwar Supplement: c/o Dar Assayad, POB 11-1038, Hazmieh, Beirut; tel. (5) 450406; fax (5) 452700; e-mail info@alanwar.com; internet www.alanwar.com; cultural and social; every Sun.; supplement to daily Al-Anwar; Editor ISSAM FREIHA; circ. 90,000.

Assayad (The Hunter): c/o Dar Assayad, POB 11-1038, Hazmieh, Beirut; tel. (5) 450933; fax (5) 452700; e-mail assayad@inco.com.lb; internet www.al-sayad.com; f. 1943; Arabic; political and social; Editor-in-Chief MOUNIR NAJJAR; circ. 76,192.

Al-Bayan: Karim Centre, Tripoli; tel. and fax (6) 425555; e-mail info@albayanlebanon.com; internet albayanlebanon.com; political.

Dabbour: place du Musée, Beirut; tel. and fax (1) 616770; e-mail addabbour@yahoo.com; internet www.addabbour.com; f. 1922; Arabic; CEO JOSEPH RICHARD MOUKARZEL; circ. 12,000.

Al-Hadaf (The Target): Beirut; tel. (1) 420554; f. 1969; organ of Popular Front for the Liberation of Palestine; Arabic; Editor-in-Chief SABER MOHI ED-DIN; circ. 40,000.

Al-Hawadeth (Events): POB 1281, rue Clémenceau, Beirut; tel. (1) 216393; fax (1) 200961; e-mail info@al-hawadeth.com; internet www.al-hawadeth.com; publ. from London, United Kingdom (183–185 Askew Rd, W12 9AX; tel. (20) 8740-4500; fax. (20) 8749-9781); f. 1911; Arabic; news; Editor-in-Chief MELHEM KARAM; circ. 120,000.

L'Hebdo Magazine: POB 11-1404, Immeuble Sayegh, rue Sursock, Beirut; tel. (1) 202070; fax (1) 202663; e-mail info@ediori.com.lb; internet www.magazine.com.lb; f. 1956; French; political, economic and social; published by Editions Orientales SAL; Pres. CHARLES ABOU ADAL; Editor-in-Chief PAUL KHALIFEH; circ. 18,000.

Al-Hiwar (Dialogue): rue Donna Maria, Beirut; tel. (1) 637000; fax (1) 631282; e-mail info@alhiwar.info; internet www.alhiwar.info; f. 2000; Arabic; publ. by the National Dialogue Party; Chair. FOUAD MAKHZOUMI; Editor-in-Chief SAM MOUNASSA.

Al-Hurriya (Freedom): Beirut; e-mail alhouriaa@hotmail.com; internet www.alhourriah.org; f. 1960; Arabic; organ of the Democratic Front for the Liberation of Palestine; Editor DAOUD TALHAME; circ. 30,000.

Al-Intiqad: internet www.alintiqad.com; Arabic; political; organ of Hezbollah; Editor IBRAHIM MOUSSAWI.

Al-Iza'a (Broadcasting): POB 462, rue Selim Jazaerly, Beirut; f. 1938; Arabic; politics, art, literature and broadcasting; Editor FAYEK KHOURY; circ. 11,000.

Al-Jumhur (The Public): POB 1834, Moussaitbé, Beirut; f. 1936; Arabic; illustrated weekly news magazine; Editor FARID ABU SHAHLA; circ. 45,000, of which over 20,000 outside Lebanon.

Al-Kifah al-Arabi (The Arab Struggle): POB 5158-14, Immeuble Rouche-Shams, Beirut; tel. (1) 809300; fax (1) 808281; e-mail editor@kifaharabi.com; internet www.kifaharabi.com; f. 1974; Arabic; political, socialist, pan-Arab; Publr and Chief Editor WALID HUSSEINI.

Massis: Immeuble Eglise Ste Croix des Arméniens Catholiques, rue Zoghbi, Zalka, Beirut; tel. (4) 715263; e-mail hebdomassis@sodetel.net.lb; internet www.armeniancatholic.org; f. 1947; Armenian; Catholic; Editor-in-Chief Fr ANTRANIK GRANIAN; Dir SARKIS NADJARIAN; circ. 2,500.

Al-Moharrer (The Liberator): POB 136702, rue Hamra, Beirut; tel. (1) 750516; fax (1) 750515; e-mail almoharrer@almoharrer.net; internet www.almoharrer.net; f. 1962; Arabic; circ. 87,000; Gen. Man. WALID ABOU ZAHR.

Monday Morning: POB 165612, Immeuble Dimitri Trad, rue Issa Maalouf, Achrafieh, Beirut; tel. (1) 200961; fax (1) 335079; e-mail info@mmorning.com; internet www.mmorning.com; f. 1971; political and social affairs; publ. by Dar Alf Leila wa Leila; circ. 15,000; Editor-in-Chief MELHEM KARAM.

An-Nass (The People): POB 4886, ave Fouad Chehab, Beirut; tel. (3) 376185; fax (8) 376610; f. 1959; Arabic; weekly news magazine; Editor-in-Chief HASSAN YAGHI; circ. 22,000.

Al-Ousbou' al-Arabi (Arab Week): POB 11-1404, Immeuble Sayegh, rue Sursock, Beirut; tel. (1) 202070; fax (1) 202663; e-mail info@arabweek.com.lb; internet www.arabweek.com.lb; f. 1959; Arabic; political and social; publ. by Editions Orientales SAL; Chair. and Editor-in-Chief CHARLES ABOU ADAL; circ. 88,407 (circulates throughout the Arab world).

Phoenix: POB 113222, Beirut; tel. (1) 363133; fax (1) 371186; e-mail dolfins@cyberia.net.lb; for women; publ. by Al-Khal.

La Revue du Liban (Lebanon Review): POB 165612, Immeuble Dimitri Trad, rue Issa Maalouf, Achrafieh, Beirut; tel. (1) 200961; fax (1) 338929; e-mail rdl@rdl.com.lb; internet www.rdl.com.lb; f. 1928; French; political, social, cultural; publ. by Dar Alf Leila wa Leila; Publr MELHEM KARAM; Gen. Man. MICHEL MISK; circ. 22,000.

Sabah al-Khair (Good Morning): Beirut; Arabic; publ. by the Syrian Nationalist Party.

Sahar: c/o Dar Assayad, POB 11-1038, Hazmieh, Beirut; tel. (5) 452700; fax (5) 452957; Arabic; for teenagers; publ. by Dar Assayad SAL.

Ash-Shira' (The Sail): POB 13-5250, Beirut; tel. (1) 703000; fax (1) 866050; internet www.alshiraa.com; Arabic; Editor HASSAN SABRA; circ. 40,000.

At-Tamaddon: POB 90, Tripoli; tel. (6) 441164; fax (6) 435252; e-mail info@attamaddon.com; internet www.attamaddon.com; f. 1972; political.

OTHER SELECTED PERIODICALS

Alam at-Tijarat (Business World): Immeuble Strand, rue Hamra, Beirut; f. 1965; monthly; commercial; Editor NADIM MAKDISI; international circ. 17,500.

Al Computer, Communications and Electronics (ACCE): c/o Dar Assayad, POB 1038, Hazmieh, Beirut; tel. (5) 450935; fax (5) 452700; e-mail assayad@inco.com.lb; internet www.darassayad.net; f. 1984; monthly; computer technology; publ. by Dar Assayad International; Chief Editor ANTOINE BOUTROS; circ. 31,912 (Jan.–June 2006).

Arab Construction World: POB 13-5121, Chouran, Beirut 1102 2802; tel. (1) 352413; fax (1) 352419; e-mail info@acwmag.com; internet www.acwmag.com; f. 1985; monthly; English and Arabic; publ. by Chatila Publishing House; Pres. and Publr FATHI CHATILA; Editor-in-Chief MUHAMMAD RABIH CHATILA; circ. 10,100.

Arab Defence Journal: c/o Dar Assayad, POB 11-1038, Hazmieh, Beirut; tel. (5) 456374; fax (5) 450609; e-mail adj2004a@yahoo.com; internet www.arabdefencejournal.com; f. 1976; monthly; military; publ. by Dar Assayad International; Chief Editor FAWZI ABOU FARHAT; circ. 24,831 (July–Dec. 2005).

Arab Economist: POB 11-6068, Beirut; monthly; publ. by Centre for Economic, Financial and Social Research and Documentation SAL; Chair. HEKMAT KASSIR.

Arab Water World: POB 13-5121, Chouran, Beirut 1102-2802; tel. (1) 748333; fax (1) 352419; e-mail editorial@awwmag.com; internet www.awwmag.com; f. 1977; monthly; English and Arabic; publ. by Chatila Publishing House; Pres., Publr and Editor-in-Chief FATHI CHATILA; circ. 8,400.

The Arab World: POB 567, Jounieh; tel. and fax (9) 935096; e-mail naamanculture@lynx.net.lb; internet www.naamanculture.com; f. 1985; 24 a yr; publ. by Dar Naamān lith-Thaqāfa (Maison Naaman pour la Culture); Editor NAJI NAAMAN.

Argus: POB 16-5403, 6 rue Arguse Sodeco, Beirut; tel. (1) 219113; fax (1) 219955; e-mail argus@cyberia.net.lb; monthly; Arabic, French and English; economics and law; circ. 1,000.

Le Commerce du Levant: Kantari, Immeuble Kantari Corner, 11e étage, Beirut 2021 2502; tel. (1) 362361; fax (1) 360379; e-mail lecommerce@inco.com.lb; internet www.lecommercedulevant.com; f. 1929; monthly; French; commercial and financial; publ. by Société de la Presse Economique; Chief Editor SIBYLLE RIZK; circ. 15,000.

Déco: POB 11-1404, Immeuble Sayegh, rue Sursock, Beirut; tel. (1) 202070; fax (1) 202663; e-mail info@decomag.com.lb; internet www.decomag.com.lb; f. 2000; quarterly; French; architecture and interior design; publ. by Editions Orientales SAL; Pres. CHARLES ABOU ADAL; circ. 14,000.

Fairuz International: Dar Assayad, POB 11-1038, Hazmieh, Beirut; tel. (5) 456373; fax (5) 450609; e-mail assayad@inco.com.lb; internet www.darassayad.net; f. 1982; monthly; Arabic; for women; publ. by Dar Assayad International; Chief Editor ELHAM FREIHA; circ. 93,892 (July–Dec. 2005).

Fann at-Tasswir: POB 16-5947, Beirut; tel. (1) 498950; monthly; Arabic; photography.

Al Fares: c/o Dar Assayad, POB 11-1038, Hazmieh, Beirut; tel. (5) 450406; fax (5) 450609; e-mail assayad@inco.com.lb; internet www.darassayad.net; f. 1991; monthly; Arabic; men's interest; publ. by Dar Assayad International; Chief Editor ELHAM FREIHA; circ. 79,237 (July–Dec. 2005).

LEBANON

Al-Idari (The Manager): c/o Dar Assayad, POB 11-1038, Hamzieh, Beirut; tel. (5) 450406; fax (5) 450609; e-mail assayad@inco.com.lb; internet www.darassayad.net; f. 1975; monthly; Arabic; business management, economics, finance and investment; publ. by Dar Assayad International; Pres. BASSAM FREIHA; Gen. Man. ELHAM FREIHA; circ. 31,867.

Al-Intilak (Outbreak): Al-Intilak Printing and Publishing House, POB 4958, Beirut; tel. (1) 302018; e-mail tonehnme@cyberia.net.lb; f. 1960; monthly; Arabic; literary; Chief Editor MICHEL NEHME.

Al-Khalij Business Magazine: POB 11-8440, Beirut; tel. (1) 345568; fax (1) 602089; e-mail massaref@dm.net.lb; f. 1981; fmrly based in Kuwait; 6 a year; Arabic; Editor-in-Chief ZULFICAR KOBEISSI; circ. 16,325.

Lebanese and Arab Economy: POB 11-1801, Sanayeh, Beirut; tel. (1) 744160; fax (1) 353395; e-mail info@ccib.org.lb; internet www.ccib.org.lb; f. 1951; monthly; Arabic, English and French; publ. by Chamber of Commerce, Industry and Agriculture of Beirut and Mount Lebanon.

Majallat al-Iza'at al-Lubnaniat (Lebanese Broadcasting Magazine): c/o Radio Lebanon, rue des Arts et Métiers, Beirut; tel. (1) 863016; f. 1959; monthly; Arabic; broadcasting affairs.

Al-Mar'a: POB 11-1404, Immeuble Sayegh, rue Sursock, Beirut; tel. (1) 202070; fax (1) 202663; e-mail info@almara.com.lb; internet www.almara.com.lb; f. 2000; monthly; Arabic; for women; publ. by Editions Orientales SAL; Pres. CHARLES ABOU ADAL; circ. 20,000.

MENA Health World: POB 13-5121, Chouran, Beirut 1102 2802; tel. (1) 748333; fax (1) 352419; e-mail editorial@mhwmag.net; internet www.mhwmag.net; f. 1986 as Arab Health World magazine, but publ. suspended in 1993; relaunched as above 2006; bi-monthly; English and Arabic; publ. by Chatila Publishing House; Pres. and Publr FATHI CHATILA; Editor-in-Chief Dr RAJAA CHATILA ALAYLI.

Middle East Food: POB 13-5121, Chouran, Beirut 1102 2802; tel. (1) 352413; fax (1) 352419; e-mail info@mefmag.com; internet www.mefmag.com; f. 1985; 9 a yr; publ. by Chatila Publishing House; Editor-in-Chief ROULA HAMDAN; circ. 8,650.

Qitāboul A'lamil A'rabi (The Arab World Book): POB 567, Jounieh; tel. and fax (9) 935096; e-mail naaman@lynx.net.lb; internet www.naamanculture.com; f. 1991; 6 a yr; Arabic; publ. by Dar Naamān lith-Thaqāfa (Maison Naaman pour la Culture); Editor NAJI NAAMAN.

Rijal al-Amal (Businessmen): Beirut; f. 1966; monthly; Arabic; business; Publr and Editor-in-Chief MAHIBA AL-MALKI; circ. 16,250.

Scoop: POB 165612, rue Issa Maalouf, Sioufi, Beirut; tel. (1) 482185; fax (1) 490307; weekly; general interest; publ. by La Régie Libanaise de Publicité; circ. 100,000.

As-Sihāfa wal I'lām (Press and Information): POB 567, Jounieh; tel. and fax (9) 935096; e-mail naamanculture@lynx.net.lb; internet www.naamanculture.com; f. 1987; 12 a yr; Arabic; publ. by Dar Naaman lith-Thaqafa; Owner NAJI NAAMAN.

Siyassa was Strategia (Politics and Strategy): POB 567, Jounieh; tel. and fax (9) 935096; e-mail naamanculture@lynx.net.lb; internet www.naamanculture.com; f. 1981; 36 a year; Arabic; publ. by Dar Naaman lith-Thaqafa (Maison Naaman pour la Culture); Editor NAJI NAAMAN.

Tabibok (Your Doctor): POB 90434, Beirut; tel. (3) 604159; fax in Syria (963-11) 3738901; e-mail tabibokmag@mail.sy; internet www.tabibokmag.com; f. 1956; monthly; Arabic; medical, social, scientific; Editor Dr SAMI KABBANI; circ. 90,000.

Takarir Wa Khalfiyat (Background Reports): c/o Dar Assayad, POB 11-1038, Hamzieh, Beirut; tel. (5) 456374; fax (5) 450270; internet www.darassayad.net; f. 1976; monthly; Arabic; political and economic bulletin; publ. by Dar Assayad SAL; Editor-in-Chief HASSAN EL-KHOURY.

At-Tarik (The Road): Beirut; monthly; Arabic; cultural and theoretical; publ. by the Parti communiste libanais; circ. 5,000.

Travaux et Jours (Works and Days): Rectorat de l'Université Saint-Joseph, rue de Damas, Beirut; tel. (1) 421157; fax (1) 421005; e-mail travauxetjours@usj.edu.lb; internet www.usj.edu.lb; f. 1961; publ. twice a year; French; political, social and cultural; Editor MOUNIR CHAMOUN.

Welcome to Lebanon and the Middle East: Beirut; f. 1959; monthly; English; entertainment, touring and travel; Editor SOUHAIL TOUFIK ABOU JAMRA; circ. 6,000.

NEWS AGENCY

National News Agency (NNA): Hamra, Beirut; tel. (1) 754400; fax (1) 745776; e-mail akassas@nna-leb.gov.lb; internet www.nna-leb.gov.lb; state-owned; Dir LAURE SLEIMAN; Chief Editor ALI LAHHAM.

PRESS ASSOCIATION

Lebanese Press Order: POB 3084, ave Saeb Salam, Beirut; tel. (1) 865519; fax (1) 865516; e-mail mail@pressorder.org; internet www.pressorder.org; f. 1911; 18 mems; Pres. MUHAMMAD AL-BAALBAKI; Vice-Pres. GEORGES SKAFF; Sec. ABD AL-KARIM EL-KHALIL.

Publishers

Dar al-Adab: POB 11-4123, Beirut; tel. (1) 795135; fax (1) 861633; e-mail d_aladab@cyberia.net.lb; internet www.adabmag.com; f. 1953; dictionaries, literary and general; Man. RANA IDRISS; Editor-in-Chief SAMAH IDRISS.

Arab Institute for Research and Publishing (Al-Mouasasah al-Arabiyah Lildirasat Walnashr): POB 11-5760, Beirut; tel. and fax (1) 751438; e-mail mkayyali@nets.com.jo; internet www.airpbooks.com; f. 1969; Dir MAHER KAYYALI; works in Arabic and English.

Arab Scientific Publishers BP: POB 13-5574, Immeuble Ein at-Tenah Reem, rue Sakiet al-Janzir, Beirut; tel. (1) 786233; fax (1) 786230; e-mail asp@asp.com.lb; internet www.asp.com.lb; computer science, biological sciences, cookery, travel, politics, fiction, children's; Pres. BASSAM CHEBARO.

Dar Assayad Group (SAL and International): POB 11-1038, Hazmieh, Beirut; tel. (5) 450406; fax (5) 452700; e-mail assayad@inco.com.lb; internet www.darassayad.net; Dar Assayad SAL founded in 1943; Dar Assayad International founded in 1983 and provides publishing, advertising and distribution services; publishes in Arabic Al-Anwar (daily), Assayad (weekly), Achabaka (weekly), Background Reports, Arab Defense Journal (monthly), Fairuz (international monthly edition), Al-Idari (monthly), Al Computer, Communications and Electronics (monthly), Al-Fares (monthly); also publishes monthly background reports; has offices and correspondents in Arab countries and most parts of the world; CEO BASSAM FREIHA; Gen. Man. ELHAM FREIHA.

Chatila Publishing House: POB 13-5121, Chouran, Beirut 1102 2802; tel. (1) 352413; fax (1) 352419; e-mail info@cph.com.lb; internet www.chatilapublishing.com; f. 1977; publishes Arab Construction World (monthly), Arab Health World (monthly), Arab Water World (nine per year), Middle East Food (every 2 months), Middle East and World Construction Directory (bi-annual), Middle East and World Food Directory (bi-annual), Middle East and World Health Directory (bi-annual), Middle East and World Water Directory (bi-annual); Pres. and Publr FATHI CHATILA; Gen. Man. MUHAMMAD RABIH CHATILA.

Edition Française pour le Monde Arabe (EDIFRAMO): POB 113-6140, Immeuble Elissar, rue Bliss, Beirut; tel. (1) 862437; Man. TAHSEEN S. KHAYAT.

Editions Orientales SAL: POB 11-1404, Immeuble Sayegh, rue Sursock, Beirut; tel. (1) 202070; fax (1) 202663; e-mail info@ediori.com.lb; internet www.ediori.com.lb; political and social newspapers and magazines; Pres. and Editor-in-Chief CHARLES ABOU ADAL.

GeoProjects SARL: POB 113-5294, Immeuble Barakat, 13 rue Jeanne d'Arc, Beirut; tel. (1) 344236; fax (1) 342005; e-mail geproj@cyberia.net.lb; internet www.geoprojects.net; f. 1978; cartographers, researchers, school textbook publrs; Dir-Gen. RIDA ISMAIL.

Dar el-Ilm Lilmalayin: POB 1085, Centre Metco, rue Mar Elias, Beirut 2045 8402; tel. (1) 306660; fax (1) 701657; e-mail info@malayin.com; internet www.malayin.com; f. 1945; dictionaries, encyclopaedias, reference books, textbooks, Islamic cultural books; CEO TAREF OSMAN.

Institute for Palestine Studies, Publishing and Research Organization (IPS): POB 11-7164, rue Anis Nsouli, off Verdun, Beirut 1107 2230; tel. (1) 868387; fax (1) 814193; e-mail ipsbrt@palestine-studies.org; internet palestine-studies.org; f. 1963; independent non-profit Arab research org., which promotes better understanding of the Palestine problem and the Arab–Israeli conflict; publishes books, reprints, research papers, etc.; Chair. Dr HISHAM NASHABE; Dir MAHMOUD SOUEID.

The International Documentary Center of Arab Manuscripts: POB 2668, Immeuble Hanna, Ras Beirut, Beirut; e-mail alafaq@cyberia.net.lb; f. 1965; publishes and reproduces ancient and rare Arabic texts; Propr ZOUHAIR BAALBAKI.

Dar al-Kashaf: POB 11-2091, rue Assad Malhamee, Beirut; tel. (1) 249952; e-mail dakashaf4@yahoo.com; f. 1930; publrs of Al-Kashaf (Arab Youth Magazine), maps, atlases and business books; printers and distributors; Propr M. A. FATHALLAH.

Dar al-Kitab al-Lubnani: POB 11-8330, Beirut; tel. (1) 735731; fax (1) 351433; e-mail info@daralkitabalmasri.com; internet www.daralkitabalmasri.com; f. 1929; publr of books on Islamic studies, history, sciences and literature; Man. Dir HASSAN EZ-ZEIN.

Dar Alf Leila wa Leila: rue Issa Maalouf, Immeuble Dimitri Trad, Achrafieh, Beirut; tel. (1) 200961; fax (1) 334116; e-mail rdl@rdl.com.lb; internet www.rdl.com.lb; publishes Al-Bairaq (Arabic, daily), Al-Hawadeth (Arabic, weekly), La Revue du Liban (French, weekly), Monday Morning (English, weekly); Editor-in-Chief MELHEM KARAM.

LEBANON

Librairie du Liban Publishers: POB 11-9232, Beirut; tel. (9) 217735; fax (9) 217734; e-mail info@ldlp.com; internet www.ldlp.com; f. 1944; publr of children's books, dictionaries and reference books; distributor of books in English and French; Man. Dirs HABIB SAYEGH, PIERRE SAYEGH.

Dar al-Maaref Liban SARL: POB 2320, Riad es-Solh, Beirut; tel. (1) 931243; f. 1959; children's books and textbooks in Arabic; Man. Dir Dr FOUAD IBRAHIM; Gen. Man. JOSEPH NACHOU.

Dar al-Machreq SARL: POB 11-946, Beirut 1107 2060; tel. (1) 202423; e-mail machreq@cyberia.net.lb; internet www.darelmachreq.com; f. 1848; religion, art, Arabic and Islamic literature, history, languages, science, philosophy, school books, dictionaries and periodicals; Man. Dir SALAH ABOUJAOUDE.

Dar Naamān lith-Thaqāfa (Maison Naaman pour la Culture): POB 567, Jounieh; tel. and fax (9) 935096; e-mail naamanculture@lynx.net.lb; internet www.naamanculture.com; f. 1979; publishes Mawsou'atul 'Alamil 'Arabiyyil Mu'asser (Encyclopaedia of the Contemporary Arab World), Mawsou'atul Waqa'e'il 'Arabiyya (Encyclopaedia of Arab Events), Qitāboul A'lamil A'rabi, Siyassa was Strategia, As-Sahafa wal I'lam in Arabic, and The Arab World in English; Propr NAJI NAAMAN; Exec. Man. MARCELLE AL-ASHKAR.

Editions Dar an-Nahar SAL: BP 11-226, 36 rue Andraos, Immeuble Media Centre, Beirut; tel. (1) 561687; fax (1) 561693; e-mail darannahar@darannahar.com; internet www.darannahar.com; f. 1967; pan-Arab publishing house; Pres. GHASSAN TUÉNI; Gen. Man. SAMIA SHAMI.

Naufal Group SARL: POB 11-2161, Immeuble Naufal, rue Sourati, Beirut; tel. (1) 354898; fax (1) 354394; e-mail naufalgroup@terra.net.lb; f. 1970; subsidiary cos Macdonald Middle East Sarl, Les Editions Arabes; encyclopaedias, fiction, children's books, history, law and literature; Man. Dir TONY NAUFAL.

Publitec Publications: POB 16-6142, Beirut; tel. (1) 495401; fax (1) 493330; e-mail info@whoswhointhearabworld.info; internet www.whoswhointhearabworld.info; f. 1965; publishes Who's Who in Lebanon and Who's Who in the Arab World (both bi-annual); Pres. CHARLES GEDEON; Man. KRIKOR AYVAZIAN.

Dar ar-Raed al-Lubnani: 11-6585, Beirut; tel. (1) 663109; e-mail info@al-raed.com; f. 1971; CEO RAYED SAMMOURI.

Rihani Printing and Publishing House: Beirut; tel. (1) 868380; f. 1963; Propr ALBERT RIHANI; Man. DAOUD STEPHAN.

Sader Publishers: POB 55530, Immeuble Sader, Dekwaneh, Beirut; tel. (1) 488776; e-mail sader@saderpublishers.com; internet www.saderpublishers.com; f. 1863; legal publr; Chair. JOSEPH SADER.

Samir Éditeur: POB 55542, Jisr al-Waty, Sin el-Fil, Beirut; tel. (1) 489464; fax (1) 482541; e-mail samir@samirediteur.com; internet www.samirediteur.com; children's books in Arabic, English and French.

World Book Publishing: POB 11-3176, 282 rue Emile Eddé, Sanayeh, Beirut; tel. (1) 349370; fax (1) 351226; e-mail info@wbpbooks.com; internet www.wbpbooks.com; f. 1926; literature, education, philosophy, current affairs, self-help, children's books; Chair. M. SAID EZ-ZEIN; Man. Dir RAFIK EZ-ZEIN.

Broadcasting and Communications

TELECOMMUNICATIONS

Regulatory Authority

Telecommunications Regulatory Authority (TRA): POB 11-1226, Beirut; tel. (1) 964300; fax (1) 964341; e-mail info@tra.gov.lb; internet www.tra.gov.lb; f. 1972; f. 2007; Chair. and CEO Dr KAMAL SHEHADI.

Service Providers

OGERO (Organisme de Gestion et d'Exploitation de l'ex Radio Orient): POB 11-1226, Bir Hassan, Beirut 1107 2070; tel. (1) 840000; fax (1) 826823; internet www.ogero.gov.lb; f. 1972; 100% state-owned; plans for the incorporation of OGERO and two depts of the Ministry of Telecommunications into a single operator, Liban Télécom, were announced in 2005; preparations were stalled as a result of the conflict between Hezbollah and Israel in mid-2006, but have subsequently resumed; fixed-line operator.

In late 2008 it was announced that the planned privatization of Lebanon's two state-owned mobile telephone networks would be deferred until after the 2009 legislative elections. New management contracts to operate the Mobile Interim Company (MIC) networks until April 2010 were awarded with effect from February 2009 to Orascom Telecom Holding of Egypt (which was to operate the MIC1 network) and Zain Group of Kuwait (MIC2).

Alfa: Palm Center, rond-point Chevrolet, Beirut; tel. (3) 391111; fax (3) 391109; e-mail customercare@alfamobile.com.lb; internet www.alfa.com.lb; managed by Orascom Telecom Holding (Egypt); operates the state-owned MIC1 mobile telephone network under licence to April 2010; CEO SAMIR SALAMEH.

MTC Touch: POB 17-5051, Immeuble MTC Touch, ave Charles Helou, Beirut; tel. (3) 792000; e-mail info@mtc.com.lb; internet www.mtctouch.com.lb; managed by Zain Group (fmrly Mobile Telecommunications Co—Kuwait); operates the state-owned MIC2 mobile telephone network under licence to April 2010; Gen. Man. CLAUDE BASSIL.

BROADCASTING

Radio

Radio Liban: rue Arts et Métiers, Beirut; tel. (1) 343217; fax (1) 347489; internet www.96-2.com; run by the Ministry of Information in conjunction with Radio France International; f. 1937; Arabic programmes broadcast on 98.1 FM and 98.5 FM; scheduled for privatization; Dir-Gen. FOUAD KABALAN HAMDAN; Dir of Programmes MICHÈLE DE FREIGE.

The Home Service broadcasts in Arabic on short wave, and the Foreign Service broadcasts in Portuguese, Armenian, Arabic, Spanish, French and English.

Television

Lebanese Broadcasting Corpn (LBC) Sat Ltd: POB 111, Zouk, Beirut 165853; tel. (9) 850850; fax (9) 850916; e-mail lbcsat@lbcsat.com.lb; internet www.lbcgroup.tv; f. 1985 as Lebanese Broadcasting Corpn International SAL; name changed 1996; operates satellite channel on Arabsat 2C, Arabsat 3A and Nilesat 102; programmes in Arabic, French and English; broadcasts to Lebanon, the Middle East, Europe, the USA and Australia; Chair. Sheikh PIERRE ED-DAHER.

Future Television (Al-Mustaqbal): POB 13-6052, White House, rue Spears, Sanayeh, Beirut; tel. (1) 355355; fax (1) 753434; e-mail future@future.com.lb; internet www.future.com.lb; commercial; f. 1993; privately owned; Gen. Man. NADIM AL-MONLA.

Al-Manar (Lighthouse): Bir Hassan, Beirut; tel. (1) 540440; fax (1) 553138; e-mail info@manartv.com.lb; internet www.manartv.com.lb; f. 1991; television station owned by Lebanese Communication Group; broadcasts to Arab and Muslim audiences worldwide; operates satellite channel since May 2000; partially controlled by Hezbollah; Chair. of Bd ABDALLAH KASSIR.

Finance

(cap. = capital; dep. = deposits; res = reserves; m. = million; brs = branches; amounts in Lebanese pounds unless otherwise stated)

BANKING

Beirut was, for many years, the leading financial and commercial centre in the Middle East, but this role was destroyed by the civil conflict during 1975–90. To restore the city as a regional focus for investment banking has been a key element of the Government's reconstruction plans.

Central Bank

Banque du Liban: POB 11-5544, rue Masraf Loubnane, Beirut; tel. (1) 750000; fax (1) 747600; e-mail bdlfx@bdl.gov.lb; internet www.bdl.gov.lb; f. 1964 as successor in Lebanon to the Banque de Syrie et du Liban; cap. and res 1,974,363m., dep. 33,888,223m. (Dec. 2006); Gov. RIAD T. SALAMEH; 9 brs.

Principal Commercial Banks

Al-Ahli International Bank SAL: POB 11-5556, Immeuble International, Bab Idris, rue Omar Daouk, Beirut; tel. (1) 970921; fax (1) 970935; e-mail info@ahli.com.lb; f. 1964 as Bank of Lebanon and Kuwait SAL; merged with Lebanon brs of Jordan National (now Ahli) Bank and name changed as above 2001; subsidiary of Jordan Ahli Bank (97.9%); Pres. and Chair. Dr RAJAJ AL-MOUASHER; 8 brs.

Arab Finance House SAL (Islamic Bank) (AFH): POB 11-273, Riad es-Solh, Beirut 1107 2020; tel. (1) 706680; fax (1) 706684; e-mail info@arabfinancehouse.com; internet www.arabfinancehouse.com; f. 2003 as Arab Finance House SAL; merged into Arab Finance Investment House SAL in 2005, when name changed as above; commercial and investment banking; commercial and investment banking; cap. 30.0m., res 59.3m., dep. 37.0m. (Dec. 2006); Chair. and Gen. Man. MUHAMMAD ABD AL-LATIF AL-MANEH.

Audi Saradar Private Bank SAL: Immeuble Clover, ave Charles Malek, Achrafieh, Beirut 1107 2805; tel. (1) 205400; fax (1) 205480; e-mail contactus@audisaradarpb.com; internet www.audisaradarpb.com; f. 1948 as Banque Marius Saradar; succeeded by Banque Saradar SAL 1956; became part of Audi Saradar Group in 2004; name changed as above 2005; cap. 40,000m., res 74,638m., dep.

1,451,779m. (Dec. 2006); Chair. and Gen. Man. Mario Joseph Saradar; 3 brs.

Bank Audi SAL—Audi Saradar Group: POB 11-2560, Riad es-Solh, Beirut 1107 2808; tel. (1) 994000; fax (1) 990555; e-mail contactus@banqueaudi.com; internet www.banqueaudi.com; f. 1962 as Bank Audi; acquired Orient Credit Bank 1997 and Banque Nasr 1998; absorbed into Audi Saradar Group in 2004; cap. 492,261m., res 1,827,555m., dep. 22,665,129m. (Dec. 2007); Chair. and Gen. Man. Georges A. Achi; CEO Samir Hanna; 75 brs in Lebanon, 7 brs in Jordan.

Bank of Beirut SAL: POB 11-7354, Bank of Beirut SAL Bldg, Foch St, Beirut Central District, Beirut; tel. and fax (1) 983999; fax (1) 972972; e-mail contactus@bankofbeirut.com; internet www.bankofbeirut.com.lb; f. 1973; acquired Transorient Bank 1999, Beirut Riyad Bank 2002; cap. 158,648m., res 223,245m., dep. 5,209,233m. (Dec. 2006); Chair. and Gen. Man. Salim G. Sfeir; 44 brs in Lebanon, 6 offices abroad.

Bank of Kuwait and the Arab World SAL: POB 113-6248, Bellevue Bldg, Ain at-Tineh, Verdun, Beirut 1103 2110; tel. (1) 866306; fax (1) 865299; e-mail info@bkawbank.com; internet www.bkawbank.com; f. 1959; 74% owned by Achour Group, 15% by Maacaron Group, 10% by Merhi Group and 1% by Dr Cheaib; cap. 50,000m., res 15,636m., dep. 888,233m. (Dec. 2007); Chair. and Gen. Man. Abd ar-Razzak Achour; 14 brs in Lebanon.

BankMed SAL: POB 11-0348, Centre Groupe Méditerranée, 482 rue Clémenceau, Beirut 2022 9302; tel. (1) 373937; fax (1) 362706; internet www.bankmed.com.lb; f. 1944 as Banque Naaman et Soussou; name changed to Eastern Commercial Bank 1955, Banque de la Méditerranée SAL 1970 and as above 2006; acquired Allied Bank SAL in 2006; cap. 530,000m., res 438,799m., dep. 12,400,230m. (Dec. 2007); Chair. and Gen. Man. Muhammad Hariri; Exec. Gen. Man. Nemeh Sabbagh; 46 brs.

Banque Bemo SAL: POB 16-6353, Immeuble Bemo, place Sassine, ave Elias Sarkis, Achrafieh, Beirut 1100 2120; tel. (1) 200505; fax (1) 217860; e-mail bemosal@dm.net.lb; internet www.bemobank.com; f. 1964 as Future Bank SAL; name changed to BEMO (Banque Européenne pour le Moyen-Orient) SAL 1994 and as above 2006; cap. 43,205m., res 54,532m. (Dec. 2006), dep. 939,572m. (Dec. 2007); Chair. Henry Yordan Obegi; Gen. Man. Samih H. Saadeh; 8 brs in Lebanon, 1 br. in Cyprus.

Banque de Crédit National SAL: POB 110-204, Immeuble Marfaa, 157 rue Saad Zaghloul, Beirut; tel. (1) 990808; fax (1) 975140; e-mail bncrena@dm.net.lb; f. 1920; cap. 118,092m., res 2,024m., dep. 27,440m. (Dec. 2006); Pres. and Chair. Abdullah Tamari; Vice-Chair. and Gen. Man. Andre Boulos.

Banque de l'Industrie et du Travail SAL (BIT Bank): POB 11-3948, Immeuble BIT, 89 Riad es-Solh, Beirut 1107 2150; tel. (1) 985680; fax (1) 985681; e-mail info@bitbank.com.lb; internet www.bitbank.com.lb; f. 1960; cap. 25,444m., res 26,217m., dep. 538,599m. (Dec. 2005); Chair. and Gen. Man. Sheikh Fouad Jamil el-Khazen; Exec. Dir and Gen. Man. Nabil N. Khairallah; 12 brs.

Banque Libano-Française SAL: POB 11-0808, Tour Liberty, rue de Rome, Beirut 1107 2804; tel. and fax (1) 791332; e-mail info@eblf.com; internet www.eblf.com; f. 1967; cap. 200,000m., res 425,327m., dep. 8,034,363m. (Dec. 2007); Pres., Chair. and Gen. Man. Farid Raphaël; 32 brs.

Banque Misr-Liban SAL: rue Riad es-Solh, Beirut 2011 9301; tel. (1) 986666; fax (1) 964296; e-mail mail@bml.com.lb; internet www.bml.com.lb; f. 1929 as Banque Misr Syrie Liban; name changed as above 1958; cap. 27,000m., res 24,673m., dep. 624,321m. (Dec. 2007); Chair. Muhammad Kamal ed-Din Barakat; Gen. Man. Hadi Naffi; 14 brs.

Al-Baraka Bank Lebanon SAL: POB 113-5683, 2nd Floor, Verdun 2000 Centre, Rashid Karameh St, Beirut; tel. (1) 808008; fax (1) 806499; e-mail info@al-baraka.com; internet www.al-baraka.com; f. 1992; Islamic banking; Chair. Adnan Ahmad Youssef; Gen. Man. Mutasim Mahmassani; 6 brs.

BBAC (Bank of Beirut and the Arab Countries) SAL: POB 11-1536, Immeuble de la Banque, 250 rue Clémenceau, Riad es-Solh, Beirut 1107 2080; tel. (1) 366630; fax (1) 365200; e-mail marketing@bbac.com.lb; internet www.bbacbank.com; f. 1956; cap. 119,120m., res 137,227m., dep. 3,641,869m. (Dec. 2006); Chair. and Gen. Man. Ghassan T. Assaf; 34 brs.

BLC Bank SAL: POB 11-1126, BLC Bldg, Adlieh Intersection, Beirut 2064 5809; tel. and fax (1) 429000; e-mail info@blcbank.com; internet www.blcbank.com; f. 1950; owned by Fransabank SAL 97.51%; cap. 152,700m., res 24,939m., dep. 2,230,416m. (Dec. 2007); Chair. and Gen. Man. Maurice Sehnaoui; 35 brs.

BLOM Bank SAL: POB 11-1912, Immeuble BLOM Bank, rue Rachid Karameh, Verdun, Beirut 1107 2807; tel. (1) 743300; fax (1) 738946; e-mail blommail@blom.com.lb; internet www.blom.com.lb; f. 1951 as Banque du Liban et d'Outre-Mer; name changed as above 2000; cap. 240,000m., res 1,460,863m., dep. 22,264,430m. (Dec. 2007); Chair. and Gen. Man. Saad Azhari; 55 brs in Lebanon, 59 brs abroad.

Byblos Bank SAL: POB 11-5605, ave Elias Sarkis, Achrafieh, Beirut 1107 2811; tel. (1) 335200; fax (1) 339436; e-mail byblosbk@byblosbank.com.lb; internet www.byblosbank.com; f. 1959; merged with Banque Beyrouth pour le Commerce SAL 1997; acquired Byblos Bank Europe SA 1998, Wedge Bank Middle East SAL 2001 and ABN AMRO Bank Lebanon 2002; cap. 494,456m., res 415,286m., dep. 10,691,471m. (Dec. 2006); Pres., Chair. and Gen. Man. Dr François S. Bassil; 73 brs in Lebanon, 7 brs abroad.

Creditbank SAL: POB 16-5795, Immeuble Crédit Bancaire SAL, 680 blvd Bachir Gemayel, Achrafieh, Beirut 1100 2802; tel. (1) 485148; fax (1) 485245; e-mail info@creditbank.com.lb; internet www.creditbank.com.lb; f. 1981 as Crédit Bancaire SAL; name changed as above following merger with Crédit Lyonnais Liban SAL 2002; cap. 59,360m., res 22,863m., dep. 1,019,715m. (Dec. 2007); Chair. and Gen. Man. Tarek Joseph Khalifé; Vice-Chair. Salah Fouad Zoghby; 15 brs.

Crédit Libanais SAL: POB 16-6729, Centre Sofil, 5e étage, ave Charles Malek, Beirut 1100 2811; tel. (1) 200028; fax (1) 325713; e-mail info@creditlibanais.com.lb; internet www.creditlibanais.com.lb; f. 1961; cap. 250,000m., res 290,845m., dep. 4,509,643m. (Dec. 2006); Pres., Chair. and Gen. Man. Dr Joseph M. Torbey; 59 brs in Lebanon, 3 brs abroad.

Federal Bank of Lebanon SAL: POB 11-2209, Immeuble Renno, ave Charles Malek, St Nicolas, Beirut; tel. (1) 212307; fax (1) 215837; e-mail fedliban@cyberia.net.lb; internet www.fbl.com.lb; f. 1952; cap. 13,019m., res 7,672m., dep. 357,779m. (Dec. 2005); Chair. and Gen. Man. Ayoub Farid Michel Saab; Gen. Man. Muhammad Yasser Mortada; 8 brs.

First National Bank SAL: POB 11-0435, Immeuble 147, rue Allenby, Riad es-Solh, Beirut 2012 6004; tel. (1) 963000; fax (1) 973090; e-mail info@fnb.com.lb; internet www.fnb.com.lb; f. 1996; acquired Société Bancaire du Liban SAL 2002; cap. 40,600m., res 22,171m., dep. 1,890,201m. (Dec. 2006); Chair. and Gen. Man. Rami Refaat en-Nimer; Exec. Dir Elias Salim Baz; 18 brs.

Fransabank SAL: POB 11-0393, Riad es-Solh, Beirut 1107 2803; tel. (1) 745761; fax (1) 354572; e-mail fsb@fransabank.com; internet www.fransabank.com; f. 1978 as a result of merger between Banque Sabbag SAL and Banque Française por le Moyen Orient SAL; acquired Banque Tohmé SAL 1993, Universal Bank SAL 1999, United Bank of Saudi and Lebanon SAL 2001 and Banque de la Beka'a SAL 2003; Banque de la Beka'a was subsequently sold to Bank of Sharjah Ltd (United Arab Emirates) in July 2007; cap. 420,000m., res 240,495m., dep. 9,459,750m. (Dec. 2007); Chair. and Gen. Man. Adnan Kassar; Vice-Chair. and Gen. Man. Adel Kassar; 63 brs.

IBL Bank SAL: POB 11-5292, Immeuble Ittihadiah, ave Charles Malek, Beirut 1107 2190; tel. (1) 200350; fax (1) 204505; e-mail ibl@ibl.com.lb; internet www.ibl.com.lb; f. 1961 as Intercontinental Bank of Lebanon SAL; cap. 84,000m., res 47,249m., dep. 2,647,927m. (Dec. 2007); Chair. and Gen. Man. Salim Y. Habib; 14 brs.

Jammal Trust Bank SAL: POB 11-5640, Immeuble Jammal, rue Verdun, Beirut; tel. (1) 805702; fax (1) 864170; e-mail services@jammalbank.com.lb; internet www.jammalbank.com.lb/home.html; f. 1963 as Investment Bank SAL; cap. 58,000m., res 8,165m., dep. 442,289m. (Dec. 2006); Chair. and Gen. Man. Anwar A. al-Jammal; 22 brs in Lebanon, 4 brs in Egypt, 3 rep. offices abroad.

Lebanese Canadian Bank: POB 11-2520, Immeuble Ghantous, blvd Dora, Riad es-Solh, Beirut 1107 2110; tel. and fax (1) 379922; e-mail lebcan@lebcanbank.com; internet www.lebcanbank.com; f. 1960 as Banque des Activités Economiques; name changed to The Royal Bank of Canada (Middle East) SAL 1970 and as above 1988; cap. 110,700.0m., res 32,727.4m., dep. 4,524,666.3m. (Dec. 2007); Chair. and Gen. Man. Georges Zard Abou Jaoudé; 35 brs in Lebanon, 1 rep. office in Canada.

Lebanese Swiss Bank SAL: POB 11-9552, Immeuble Hoss, 6e étage, rue Emile Eddé, place Hamra, Ras Beirut, Beirut; tel. (1) 354501; fax (1) 346242; e-mail lbs@t-net.com.lb; f. 1962; cap. 40,000m., res 20,882m., dep. 552,866m. (Dec. 2006); Pres., Chair. and Gen. Man. Dr Tanal Sabbah; 10 brs.

Lebanon and Gulf Bank SAL: POB 11-3360, 124 Allenby St, Beirut Central District, Beirut; tel. (1) 965000; fax (1) 965999; e-mail info@lgb.com.lb; internet www.lgb.com.lb; f. 1963 as Banque de Crédit Agricole; name changed as above 1980; cap. 50,000m., res 11,218m., dep. 1,351,804m. (Dec. 2006); Pres., Chair. and Gen. Man. Abd al-Hafiz Mahmoud Itani; 11 brs.

MEAB SAL: POB 14-5958, Hejeij Bldg, Adnan al-Hakim Ave, Beirut 1105 2080; tel. (1) 826740; fax (1) 841190; e-mail meab@meabank.com; internet www.meabank.com; f. 1991 as Middle East and Africa Bank SAL; name changed as above 2003; cap. 24,000m., res 8,739m., dep. 556,717m. (Dec. 2006); Chair. Hassan M. Hejeij; Man. Dir Kassem Hejeij; Gen. Man. Hassan Hejeij; 5 brs.

LEBANON

Directory

National Bank of Kuwait (Lebanon) SAL: POB 11-5727, BAC Bldg, Sanayeh Sq., Justinien St, Riad es-Solh, Beirut 1107 2200; tel. (1) 741111; fax (1) 747846; e-mail info@nbk.com.lb; internet www.nbk.com.lb; f. 1963 as Rifbank; name changed as above 1996; cap. 40,020m., res 6,425m., dep. 320,859m. (Dec. 2006); Chair. IBRAHIM DABDOUB; Gen. Man. HANY SHERIF; 10 brs.

Near East Commercial Bank SAL: POB 16-5766, SNA Bldg, Said Akl St, Tabaris, Achrafieh, Beirut 1100 2070; tel. and fax (1) 200770; fax (1) 339000; e-mail info@necbbank.com; internet www.necbbank.com; f. 1978; cap. 26,575m., res 670m., dep. 191,883m. (June 2008); Chair. DOMINIQUE LANG; Gen. Man. FOUAD BAÏDA; 5 brs.

North Africa Commercial Bank SAL: POB 11-9575, Centre Aresco, rue Justinian, Beirut; tel. (1) 759000; fax (1) 346322; e-mail info@nacb.com.lb; internet www.nacb.com.lb; f. 1973; 99% owned by Libyan Foreign Bank; cap. 128,599m., res 14m., dep. 827,241m. (Dec. 2007); Pres. and Chair. ABOUBAKER ALI ASH-SHARIF; Gen. Man. NAJIB ABD AL-HAMID LATRASH; 2 brs.

Société Générale de Banque au Liban (SGBL): POB 11-2955, rond-point Salomé, Sin el-Fil, Beirut; tel. (1) 499813; fax (1) 502820; e-mail sgbl@sgbl.com.lb; internet www.sgbl.com.lb; f. 1953 as Banque Belgo-Libanaise; name changed to Société Générale Libano Européenne de Banque SAL in 1969; present name adopted in 2001; cap. 10,600m., res 12,600m. (Dec. 2006); CEO ANTOUN SEHNAOUI; 41 brs in Lebanon, 23 abroad.

Société Nouvelle de la Banque de Syrie et du Liban SAL (SNBSL): POB 11-957, rue Riad es-Solh, Beirut; tel. (1) 980080; fax (1) 980991; e-mail snbsl@snbsl.com.lb; f. 1963; cap. 36,225m., res 15,619m., dep. 907,362m. (Dec. 2006); Chair. RAMSAY A. EL-KHOURY; Gen. Man. SÉLIM STÉPHAN; 17 brs.

Standard Chartered Bank SAL: POB 70216, Dbayeh 509 Bldg, Dbayeh Highway, Antélias; tel. (4) 542474; fax (4) 542494; e-mail aamir.hussain@standardchartered.com; internet www.standardchartered.com/lb; f. 1979 as Metropolitan Bank SAL; acquired by Standard Chartered Bank 2000; cap. 12,000m., res 603m., dep. 150,902m. (Dec. 2005); Chair. MARTIN FISH; CEO AAMIR HUSSEIN; 5 brs.

Syrian Lebanese Commercial Bank SAL: SLCB Bldg, Makdessi St, Beirut; tel. (1) 741666; fax (1) 736629; e-mail hamra@slcbk.com; internet www.slcb.com.lb; f. 1974; cap. 100,000m., res 17,331m., dep. 120,209m. (Dec. 2007); Chair. and Gen. Man. Dr DOURAID AHMAD DERGHAM; Vice-Chair. MARCEL EL-KHOURY; 3 brs in Lebanon, 2 offices in Syria.

Development Bank

Audi Saradar Investment Bank SAL: POB 16-5110, Bank Audi Plaza, Omar ad-Daouk St, Beirut; tel. (1) 994000; fax (1) 999406; e-mail contactus@asib.com; internet www.asib.com; f. 1974 as Investment and Finance Bank; name changed to Audi Investment Bank SAL 1996 and as above 2004; medium- and long-term loans, 100% from Lebanese sources; owned by Bank Audi SAL—Audi Saradar Group; cap. 25,075m., res 92,635m., dep. 983,104m. (Dec. 2006); Chair. Dr MARWAN M. GHANDOUR; Gen. Man. RAMZI N. SALIBA.

Supervisory Body

Banking Control Commission of Lebanon: POB 11-5544, rue Masraf Loubnane, Beirut; tel. (1) 350167; fax (1) 750040; internet www.bccl.gov.lb; f. 1967; Chair. WALID R. ALAMEDDINE.

Banking Association

Association of Banks in Lebanon: POB 976, Association of Banks in Lebanon Bldg, Gouraud St, Saifi, Beirut; tel. (1) 970500; fax (1) 970501; e-mail abl@abl.org.lb; internet www.abl.org.lb; f. 1959; serves and promotes the interests of the banking community in Lebanon; mems: 64 banks and 7 foreign rep. offices; Pres. and Chair. Dr FRANÇOIS S. BASSIL; Sec.-Gen. Dr MAKRAM SADER.

STOCK EXCHANGE

Beirut Stock Exchange (BSE): POB 11-3552, 4e étage, Bloc A3, Immeuble Azareih, Beirut; tel. (1) 993555; fax (1) 993444; e-mail bse@bse.com.lb; internet www.bse.com.lb; f. 1920; recommenced trading in Jan. 1996; 10 cttee mems; Chair. Dr FADI KHALAF.

INSURANCE

About 80 insurance companies were registered in Lebanon in the late 1990s, although fewer than one-half of these were operational. An insurance law enacted in 1999 increased the required capital base for insurance firms and provided tax incentives for mergers within the sector.

Allianz SNA SAL: POB 16-6528, Immeuble Allianz SNA, Hazmieh, Beirut 1100 2130; tel. (1) 956600; fax (1) 956624; e-mail info@allianzsna.com; internet www.sna.com.lb; f. 1963 as Société Nationale d'Assurances SAL; renamed as above 2008; part of Allianz Group; cap. 13,264m. (2007); Chair. ANTOINE WAKIM; CEO XAVIER DENYS.

Arabia Insurance Co SAL: POB 11-2172, Arabia House, rue de Phénicie, Beirut; tel. (1) 363610; fax (1) 365139; e-mail arabia@arabia-ins.com.lb; internet www.arabiainsurance.com; f. 1944; cap. 51,000m.; Chair. WAHBÉ A. TAMARI; CEO FADY SHAMMAS.

Bankers Assurance SAL: POB 11-4293, Immeuble Capitole, rue Riad es-Solh, Beirut; tel. (1) 988777; fax (1) 984004; e-mail mail@bankers-assurance.com; internet www.bankers-assurance.com; f. 1972; Chair. SABA NADER; Gen. Man. EUGÈNE NADER.

Commercial Insurance Co (Lebanon) SAL: POB 11-4351, Centre Starco, North Block, 9th Floor, Beirut; tel. (1) 373070; fax (1) 373071; e-mail comins@commercialinsurance.com.lb; internet www.commercialinsurance.com.lb; f. 1962; cap. 6,000m. (March 2006); Chair. MAX R. ZACCAR; 2 brs.

Compagnie Libanaise d'Assurances SAL: POB 3685, rue Riad es-Solh, Beirut; tel. (1) 868988; e-mail lebanese@sodetel.net.lb; internet www.lebaneseinsurance.com; f. 1951; cap. 22,500m.; Chair. PEDRO ABOUJAOUDÉ; Gen. Man. JIHAD SHAKER.

Al-Ittihad al-Watani: POB 11-1270, Jisr al-Wati, Immeuble Al-Ittihad al-Watani, Beirut; tel. (1) 426480; fax (1) 426486; e-mail webmaster@alittihadalwatani.com.lb; internet www.alittihadalwatani.com.lb; f. 1947; cap. 20.6m. (2005); Chair. and Gen. Man. TANNOUS FEGHALI.

Libano-Suisse Insurance Co SAL: POB 11-3821, Commerce and Finance Bldg, Beirut 1107 2150; tel. (1) 364461; fax (1) 368724; e-mail libano-suisse@libano-suisse.com; internet www.libano-suisse.com; f. 1959; cap. 4,050m. (2000); Chair. MICHEL PIERRE PHARAON; Gen. Man. LUCIEN LETAYEF, Jr.

Al-Mashrek Insurance and Reinsurance SAL: POB 16-6154, Al-Mashrek Bldg, 65 Aabrine St, Achrafieh, Beirut 1100 2100; tel. (1) 204666; fax (1) 337625; e-mail almashrek@almashrek.com.lb; internet www.almashrek.com.lb; f. 1962; Chair. and CEO ABRAHAM MATOSSIAN.

'La Phénicienne' SAL: POB 11-5652, Immeuble Hanna Haddad, rue Amine Gemayel, Sioufi, Beirut; tel. (1) 425484; fax (1) 424532; e-mail phenicienne@sodetel.net.lb; f. 1964; cap. 3,167m.; Chair. and Gen. Man. CAROLE FÉGHALI CHAMOUN.

Trade and Industry

DEVELOPMENT ORGANIZATIONS

Council for Development and Reconstruction (CDR): POB 116-5351, Tallet es-Serail, Beirut; tel. (1) 980096; fax (1) 981252; e-mail general@cdr.gov.lb; internet www.cdr.gov.lb; f. 1977; an autonomous public institution reporting to the Cabinet, the CDR is charged with the co-ordination, planning and execution of Lebanon's public reconstruction programme; it plays a major role in attracting foreign funds; Pres. NABIL ADNAN EL-JISR.

Investment Development Authority of Lebanon (IDAL): POB 113-7251, Azarieh Tower, 4th Floor, Emir Bechir St, Riad es-Solh, Beirut; tel. (1) 983306; fax (1) 983302; e-mail invest@idal.com.lb; internet www.idal.com.lb; f. 1994; state-owned; Chair. and Gen. Man. NABIL ITANI.

Société Libanaise pour le Développement et la Reconstruction de Beyrouth (SOLIDERE): POB 11-9493, 149 rue Saad Zaghoul, Beirut 2012 7305; tel. (1) 980650; fax (1) 980662; e-mail solidere@solidere.com.lb; internet www.solidere.com.lb; f. 1994; real estate co responsible for reconstruction of Beirut Central District after the civil war; Chair. NASSER CHAMMAA; Gen. Man. MOUNIR DOUAIDY.

CHAMBERS OF COMMERCE AND INDUSTRY

Federation of the Chambers of Commerce, Industry and Agriculture in Lebanon: POB 11-1801, Immeuble CCIAB, rue Justinian, Sanayeh, Beirut; tel. (1) 744702; fax (1) 349614; e-mail fccial@cci-fed.org.lb; internet www.cci-fed.org.lb; f. 1996; Pres. GHAZI KRAYTEM.

Chamber of Commerce, Industry and Agriculture of Beirut and Mount Lebanon: POB 11-1801, rue Justinian, Sanayeh, Beirut; tel. (1) 353390; fax (1) 353395; e-mail information@ccib.org.lb; internet www.ccib.org.lb; f. 1898; 32,000 mems; Pres. GHAZI KRAYTEM.

Chamber of Commerce, Industry and Agriculture of Tripoli and North Lebanon: POB 47, rue Bechara Khoury, Tripoli; tel. (6) 627162; fax (6) 442042; e-mail abdallahg@cciat.org.lb; internet www.cciat.org.lb; Chair. ABDALLAH GHANDOUR.

Chamber of Commerce, Industry and Agriculture in Sidon and South Lebanon: POB 41, rue Maarouf Saad, Sidon; tel. (7) 720123; fax (7) 722986; e-mail chamber@ccias.org.lb; internet www.ccias.org.lb; f. 1933; Pres. MUHAMMAD ZAATARI.

LEBANON

Chamber of Commerce, Industry and Agriculture of Zahleh and Beka'a: POB 100, Zahleh; tel. (8) 802602; fax (8) 800050; e-mail info@cciaz.org.lb; internet www.cciaz.org.lb; f. 1939; 2,500 mems; Pres. EDMOND JREISSATI.

EMPLOYERS' ASSOCIATION

Association of Lebanese Industrialists: POB 11-1520, Chamber of Commerce and Industry Bldg, 5e étage, rue Justinien, Sanayeh, Beirut; tel. (1) 350280; fax (1) 351167; e-mail ali@ali.org.lb; internet www.ali.org.lb; Pres. FADY ABBOUD; Gen. Man. SAAD S. OUEINI.

UTILITIES
Electricity

Electricité du Liban (EdL): POB 131, Immeuble de l'Electricité du Liban, 22 rue du Fleuve, Beirut; tel. (1) 442720; fax (1) 443828; e-mail info@edl.gov.lb; internet www.edl.gov.lb; f. 1954; state-owned; scheduled for privatization; Chair. and Dir-Gen. KAMAL F. HAYEK.

Water

Legislation introduced in 2000 allowed for the merging of 21 water authorities into four new regional establishments for water exploitation—Beirut and the Mount of Lebanon; North Lebanon; South Lebanon; and the Beka'a. Under the reorganization the new authorities were to operate under the supervision of the Ministry of Energy and Water.

North Lebanon Water Authority: Chair. and Gen. Man. JAMAL ABD AL-LATIF KARIM.

South Lebanon Water Authority: Chair. and Gen. Man. AHMAD HASSAN NIZAM.

Litani River Authority: rue Bechara el-Khoury, Beirut; tel. (1) 666662; fax (1) 660476; e-mail litani@litani.gov.lb; internet www.litani.gov.lb; f. 1954; responsible for water resources management, irrigation, and the devt of dams and hydroelectric facilities.

TRADE UNION FEDERATION

Confédération Générale des Travailleurs du Liban (CGTL): POB 4381, Beirut; f. 1958; 300,000 mems; only national labour centre in Lebanon and sole rep. of working classes; comprises 18 affiliated feds incl. all 150 unions in Lebanon; Pres. GHASSAN GHOSN.

Transport

RAILWAYS

Office des Chemins de Fer et des Transports en Commun (OCFTC): POB 11-109, Gare St Michel, Nahr, Beirut; tel. (1) 587211; fax (1) 447007; since 1961 all railways in Lebanon have been state-owned. The original network of some 412 km is no longer functioning. However, in 2004 work began on a project to reconstruct a section of the railway network between Tripoli and the Syrian border; Dir-Gen. and Pres. RADWAN BOU NASSER ED-DIN.

ROADS

In 2005 Lebanon had an estimated 6,970 km of roads, of which some 170 km were motorways. The two international motorways are the north–south coastal road and the road connecting Beirut with Damascus in Syria. Among the major roads are those crossing the Beka'a and continuing south to Bent-Jbail and the Shtaura–Ba'albek road. Hard-surfaced roads connect Jezzine with Moukhtara, Bzebdine with Metn, Meyroub with Afka and Tannourine. A road construction project, costing some US $100m., was planned for Beirut in the late 1990s. A new, 8-km highway, linking around 26 villages in southern Lebanon, was inaugurated in August 2000. It was reported in late July 2006 that up to 80% of Lebanon's major roads, and almost all of its bridges, had been destroyed as a result of the Israeli military offensive against infrastructural targets alleged to be in use by Hezbollah militants during Israel's conflict with the organization from early July.

SHIPPING

In the 1990s a two-phase programme to rehabilitate and expand the port of Beirut commenced, involving the construction of an industrial free zone, a fifth basin and a major container terminal, at an estimated cost of US $1,000m.; the container terminal became operational in February 2005. Tripoli, the northern Mediterranean terminus of the oil pipeline from Iraq (the other is Haifa, Israel—not in use since 1948), is also a busy port, with good equipment and facilities. Jounieh, north of Beirut, is Lebanon's third most important port. A new deep-water sea port is to be constructed south of Sidon. The reconstructed port of an-Naqoura, in what was then the 'security zone' along the border with Israel, was inaugurated in June 1987. Several ports were bombed by Israeli forces during the conflict of July–August 2006, and a complete sea blockade of Lebanon was imposed by Israel at this time.

Port Authorities

Gestion et Exploitation du Port de Beyrouth: POB 1490, Beirut; tel. (1) 580211; fax (1) 585835; e-mail info@portdebeyrouth.com; internet www.portdebeyrouth.com; Pres., Dir-Gen. and Man. Dir HASSAN KAMEL KRAYTEM; Harbour Master MAROUN KHOURY.

Service d'Exploitation du Port de Tripoli: El Mina, Tripoli; tel. (6) 601225; fax (6) 220180; e-mail tport@terra.net.lb; f. 1959; Harbour Master MARWAN BAROUDI.

Principal Shipping Companies

Ets Paul Adem: Centre Moucarri, 6e étage, autostrade Dora, Bourj Hammoud, Beirut; tel. (1) 244610; fax (1) 244612; e-mail padco@inco.com.lb; f. 1971; ship owners, operators, maritime agents, brokers, consultants; Gen. Man. PAUL ADEM.

Ademar Shipping Lines: POB 175-231, rue Shafaka, Al-Medawar, Beirut; tel. and fax (1) 444100; fax (1) 444101; e-mail ademar@ademarlb.com; internet www.ademarlb.com; f. 1982.

Agence Générale Maritime (AGEMAR) SARL: POB 9255, Centre Burotec, 7e étage, rue Pasteur, Beirut; tel. (1) 583885; fax (1) 583884; Dirs S. MEDLEJ, N. MEDLEJ.

Amin Kawar & Sons (Jordan): POB 11-4230, Beirut; tel. (1) 352525; fax (1) 353802; e-mail amkawar@@travelkawar.com; internet www.kawar.com; f. 1963; Chair. TAWFIQ AMIN KAWAR; CEO RUDAIN KAWAR.

Arab Shipping and Chartering Co: POB 1084, Immeuble Ghandour, ave des Français, Beirut; tel. (1) 371044; fax (1) 373370; e-mail arabship@dm.net.lb; agents for China Ocean Shipping Co; Dir ATEF BAADARANI.

Associated Levant Lines SAL: POB 110371, Immeuble Mercedes, autostrade Dora, Beirut; tel. (1) 255366; fax (1) 255362; e-mail tgf-all@dm.net.lb; Dirs T. GARGOUR, N. GARGOUR, H. GARGOUR.

Beirut Cargo Center: Kurban Bldg, Corniche an-Nahr, Beirut; tel. (1) 585582; fax (1) 585580; e-mail bcc@bcc.com.lb; internet www.bcc.com.lb; f. 1993; air, sea and land freight forwarder; Pres. JOSEPH HARB.

Consolidated Bulk Inc: POB 70-152, Centre St Elie, Bloc A, 6e étage, Antélias, Beirut; tel. (4) 410724; fax (4) 402842; e-mail info@bulkgroup.com; internet www.bulkgroup.com; f. 1978; Gen. Man. SAMI P. ZACCA.

Continental Ship Management SARL: POB 90-1413, Centre Dora Moucarri, 8e étage, appt 804, Beirut; tel. (1) 583654; fax (1) 584440.

Continental Shipping Agencies: POB 175039, Saifi Habib Medawar Bldg, Pasteur St, Beirut; tel. (1) 567130; fax (1) 567132; e-mail info@csa-continental.com; internet www.csa-continental.com; f. 1991.

O. D. Debbas & Sons: POB 16-6678, Immeuble Debbas, 530 blvd Corniche du Fleuve, Beirut; tel. (1) 585253; fax (1) 587135; e-mail oddebbas@oddebbas.com; internet www.oddebbas.com; f. 1892; Man. Dir OIDIH ELIE DEBBAS.

Diana K Shipping Co: POB 113-5125, Immeuble Ajouz, rue Kenedi, Ein Mreisseh, Beirut; tel. (1) 363314; fax (1) 369712; e-mail dianak@cyberia.net.lb; Marine Dept Man. Capt. AMIN HABBAL.

Fauzi Jemil Ghandour: POB 1084, Beirut 1107 2070; tel. (1) 373376; fax (1) 360048; e-mail ali@seahorsenet.com; agents for Ecuadorian Line.

Freight Leader SARL: POB 175-530, 5th Floor, Pasteur St, Medawar Centre, Saifi, Beirut; tel. (1) 581870; fax (1) 564387; e-mail info@freightleader.com; internet www.freightleader.com; f. 2001; transportation services and logistics; Exec. Man. MOUSSA SALAMOUN.

Gezairi Chartering and Shipping Co (GEZACHART): POB 11-1402, Immeuble Gezairi, place Gezairi, Ras Beirut 2034 0716; tel. (1) 783783; fax (1) 784784; e-mail gezairi@gezairi.com; internet www.gezairi.com; f. 1945; ship management, chartering, brokerage; Pres. and CEO MONA BOUAZZA BAWARSHI.

Gulf Agency Co (Lebanon) Ltd: POB 11-4392, Riad es-Solh, Beirut 1107 2160; tel. (1) 446189; fax (1) 446097; e-mail lebanon@gacworld.com; internet www.gacworld.com/lebanon; f. 1969; Gen. Man. SIMON G. BEJJANI.

Lebanese Navigators Co SARL: POB 175179, Immeuble Aleddine, blvd Ghobeiry, Beirut; tel. (3) 996789; e-mail navigators@navigators-lb.com; internet www.navigators-lb.com.

Mediterranean Feedering Co SARL: POB 70-1187, Immeuble Akak, autostrade Dbayeh, Beirut; tel. (1) 403056; fax (1) 406444; e-mail mfcbeirut@attmail.com; Man. Dir EMILE AKEF EL-KHOURY.

Orient Shipping and Trading Co SARL: POB 11-2561, Immeuble Moumneh, no 72, rue Ain al-Mraisseh 54, Beirut; tel. (1) 364455; fax (1) 365570; e-mail ortship@inco.com.lb; internet orientgroup.net; Dirs ELIE ZAROUBY, EMILE ZAROUBY.

Rassem Shipping Agency: POB 11-8460, Immeuble Agha, Raoucheh, Beirut; tel. (1) 866372; fax (1) 805593.

Riga Brothers: POB 17-5134, Immeuble Mitri Haddad, rue du Port, Beirut; tel. (1) 406882.

G. Sahyouni & Co SARL: POB 17-5452, Mar Mikhael, Beirut 1104 2040; tel. (1) 257046; fax (1) 241317; e-mail lloydsbey@inco.com.lb; internet www.georgesahyouni.com; f. 1989; agents for Baltic Control Lebanon Ltd, SARL, and Lloyds; Man. Dir GEORGE SAHYOUNI.

Sinno Trading and Navigation Agency: POB 113-6977, 4e étage, Immeuble Rebeiz, Beirut; tel. and fax (1) 446707; Chair. MUHIEDDINE F. SINNO; Man. Dir AHMED JABBOURY.

Union Shipping and Chartering Agency SAL: POB 2856, Immeuble Ghandour, ave des Français, Beirut 1107 2120; tel. (1) 373376; fax (1) 360048; e-mail ucsa@seahorsenet.com; agents for Jadroslobodna, Jugo Oceania, Atlanska Plovidba, Jadroplov and Maruba.

CIVIL AVIATION

In late 2001 a major expansion project at Beirut International Airport was completed, at an estimated cost of US $600m.; facilities included a new terminal building and two new runways, increasing handling capacity to 6m. passengers a year. In 2006 some 2.9m. passengers used the airport, which in May 2005 was renamed Beirut Rafik Hariri International Airport in honour of the former Prime Minister who had been killed in February. However, the airport was targeted by Israeli armed forces in July 2006, and was closed to commercial flights during the conflict between Israel and Hezbollah. Following extensive repairs to damaged runways and other infrastructure, the airport reopened to commercial operations in August.

MEA (Middle East Airlines, Air Liban SAL): POB 11-206, blvd de l'Aéroport, Beirut 1107 2801; tel. (1) 628888; fax (1) 629260; e-mail mikaouir@mea.com.lb; internet www.mea.com.lb; f. 1945; acquired Lebanese International Airways in 1969; privatization pending; regular services throughout Europe, the Middle East, North and West Africa, and the Far East; Chair. and Dir-Gen. MUHAMMAD A. EL-HOUT; Commercial Man. NIZAR KHOURY.

Trans-Mediterranean Airways SAL (TMA): POB 30-1001, Beirut International Airport, Beirut; tel. (1) 629210; fax (1) 629219; e-mail cargo@tmacargo.com; internet www.tma.com.lb; f. 1953; scheduled services, charter activities and aircraft lease operations covering Europe, the Middle East, Africa and the Far East; also provides handling, storage and maintenance services; Chair. and Pres. MAZEN BISSAT.

Tourism

Since the end of the civil conflict in 1990 Lebanon's scenic beauty, sunny climate and historic sites have once again attracted foreign visitors. The Government has chosen to concentrate its efforts on the promotion of cultural as well as conference and exhibition-based tourism, while the country is also being promoted as an 'eco-tourism' destination. Excluding Syrian visitors, the annual total of tourist arrivals increased from 177,503 in 1992 to some 1.28m. in 2004; arrivals declined to 1.14m. in 2005. The Lebanese tourism industry experienced a significant downturn in the aftermath of the conflict between Israel and Hezbollah in mid-2006; tourist arrivals in that year numbered 1.06m. and receipts totalled US $5,491m. However, there was a marked revival in the sector following the Doha agreement of May 2008 (see Recent History), with the number of foreign tourist arrivals in that year reaching some 1.3m. (an estimated 31% increase compared with the number in 2007).

Ministry of Tourism: see section on The Government (Ministries).

LESOTHO

Introductory Survey

Location, Climate, Language, Religion, Flag, Capital

The Kingdom of Lesotho is a land-locked country, entirely surrounded by South Africa. The climate is generally mild, although cooler in the highlands: lowland temperatures range from a maximum of 32°C (90°F) in summer (October to April) to a minimum of −7°C (20°F) in winter. Rainfall averages about 725 mm (29 ins) per year, mostly falling in summer. The official languages are English and Sesotho; other languages spoken include Zulu and Xhosa. About 90% of the population are Christians. The largest denominations are the Roman Catholic, Lesotho Evangelical and Anglican Churches. The national flag (official proportions 2 by 3) has three horizontal stripes from top to bottom of blue, white and green, with a black traditional Basotho hat in the centre of the white stripe. The capital is Maseru.

Recent History

Lesotho was formerly Basutoland, which became a separate British colony in 1884 and was administered as one of the High Commission Territories in southern Africa (the others being the protectorates of Bechuanaland, now Botswana, and Swaziland). The British Act of Parliament that established the Union of South Africa in 1910 also provided for the possible inclusion in South Africa of the three High Commission Territories, subject to local consent: the native chiefs opposed requests by successive South African Governments for the transfer of the three territories.

Within Basutoland a revised Constitution, which established the colony's first Legislative Council, was introduced in 1956. A new document, granting limited powers of self-government, was adopted in September 1959. Basutoland's first general election, on the basis of universal adult suffrage, took place on 29 April 1965, and full internal self-government was achieved the following day. Moshoeshoe II, Paramount Chief since 1960, was recognized as King. The Basutoland National Party (BNP), a conservative group supporting limited co-operation with South Africa, narrowly won a majority of the seats in the new Legislative Assembly. The BNP's leader, Chief Leabua Jonathan, was appointed Prime Minister in July 1965. Basutoland became independent, as Lesotho, on 4 October 1966. The new Constitution provided for a bicameral legislature, comprising the 60-seat National Assembly and the 33-member Senate; executive power was vested in the Cabinet, which was presided over by the Prime Minister. The King was designated Head of State.

The BNP, restyled the Basotho National Party, remained in power at independence. A general election was held in January 1970, at which the opposition Basotho Congress Party (BCP), a pan-Africanist group led by Dr Ntsu Mokhehle, appeared to have won a majority of seats in the National Assembly. Chief Jonathan declared a state of emergency, suspended the Constitution and arrested several BCP organizers. The election was annulled, and the legislature prorogued. King Moshoeshoe II was placed under house arrest and subsequently exiled, although he returned in December after accepting a government order banning him from participating in politics. The country was thus effectively under the Prime Minister's personal control. An interim National Assembly, comprising the former Senate (mainly chiefs) and 60 members nominated by the Cabinet, was inaugurated in April 1973. The state of emergency was revoked in July. However, following a failed coup attempt in January 1974 by alleged supporters of the BCP, Chief Jonathan introduced stringent security laws. Mokhehle and other prominent members of the BCP went into exile abroad, and the party split into two factions, internal and external, the latter led by Mokhehle.

Although Lesotho was economically dependent on South Africa, and the Government's official policy during the 1970s was one of 'dialogue' with its neighbour, Chief Jonathan repeatedly criticized the apartheid regime, and supported the then banned African National Congress of South Africa (ANC). In December 1982 South African forces launched a major assault on the homes of ANC members in Maseru, killing more than 40 people. Lesotho's persistent refusal to sign a joint non-aggression pact led South Africa to impound consignments of armaments destined for Lesotho, and the imposition of a blockade on the common border from early 1986.

On 20 January 1986 Chief Jonathan's Government was overthrown in a coup led by Maj.-Gen. Justin Lekhanya, the head of the armed forces. A Military Council, chaired by Lekhanya, was established and executive and legislative powers were to be vested in King Moshoeshoe, assisted by the Military Council and a (mainly civilian) Council of Ministers. In March 1986 the Military Council suspended all formal political activity. In September the Council of Ministers was restructured, giving increased responsibility to Lekhanya, and the Military Council held discussions with the leaders of the five main opposition parties.

Although the South African Government denied having any part in the coup, the Lekhanya regime proved to be more amenable to South Africa's regional security policy. In March 1986 it was announced that the two countries had reached an informal agreement whereby neither would allow its territory to be used for attacks against the other. Moreover, the Lesotho Government did not join other African states in pressing for international economic sanctions against South Africa. In March 1988 Lesotho and South Africa reached final agreement on the Lesotho Highlands Water Project (LHWP), a major scheme to supply water to South Africa.

In May 1988 Mokhehle was allowed to return to Lesotho after 14 years of exile and by 1990 the two factions of the BCP had apparently reunited under Mokhehle's leadership.

In February 1990 Lekhanya dismissed three members of the Military Council and one member of the Council of Ministers, accusing them of 'insubordination'. When Moshoeshoe refused to approve new appointments to the Military Council, Lekhanya suspended the monarch's executive and legislative powers, which were assumed by the Military Council in March. Moshoeshoe (who remained Head of State) was exiled in the United Kingdom. Lekhanya announced that a general election would take place during 1992; however, party political activity remained outlawed. In June 1990 a National Constituent Assembly (including Lekhanya, members of the Council of Ministers, representatives of banned political parties, traditional chiefs and business leaders) was inaugurated to draft a new constitution. In October Lekhanya invited the King to return from exile. Moshoeshoe responded that his return would be conditional upon the ending of military rule and the establishment of an interim government, pending the readoption of the 1966 Constitution. On 6 November 1990 Lekhanya promulgated an order dethroning the King with immediate effect. Lesotho's 22 principal chiefs elected Moshoeshoe's elder son, Prince David Mohato Bereng Seeiso, as the new King; on 12 November he acceded to the throne, as King Letsie III, having undertaken to remain detached from politics.

On 30 April 1991 Lekhanya was deposed in a coup organized by disaffected army officers. Col (later Maj.-Gen.) Elias Phitsoane Ramaema succeeded Lekhanya as Chairman of the Military Council. Ramaema repealed the ban on party political activity, and by July the National Constituent Assembly had completed the draft Constitution. In May 1992 Lesotho and South Africa agreed to establish diplomatic relations at ambassadorial level. Following talks in the United Kingdom with Ramaema, former King Moshoeshoe returned from exile in July.

The general election was eventually held in March 1993. The BCP secured all 65 seats in the new National Assembly, winning 54% of the votes cast. In April Mokhehle was inaugurated as Prime Minister, and King Letsie swore allegiance to the new Constitution, under the terms of which he remained Head of State with no executive or legislative powers; executive authority was vested in the Cabinet.

A mutiny by the Royal Lesotho Defence Force (RLDF) took place in November 1993 following which four senior army officers were reported to have resigned their posts. Skirmishes near Maseru in January 1994 escalated into more serious fighting between some 600 rebel troops and a 150-strong contingent of forces loyal to the Government, reportedly resulting in the deaths of at least five soldiers and three civilians. Following mediation efforts involving representatives of Botswana, South Africa, Zimbabwe, the Commonwealth (see p. 217), the Organization of African Unity (OAU, now the African Union, see p. 172—AU) and the UN, a truce entered into force, and at the beginning of February the rival factions surrendered their weapons and returned to barracks. In April, however, the Deputy Prime Minister, Selometsi Baholo (who also held the finance portfolio), was killed during an abduction attempt by disaffected troops.

A commission to investigate the armed forces unrest of January and April 1994 began work in July. In that month Mokhehle appointed a commission of inquiry into the dethronement of King Moshoeshoe II. On 17 August Letsie announced that he had dissolved the National Assembly, dismissed the Government and suspended sections of the Constitution, citing 'popular dissatisfaction' with the BCP administration. Although several thousand people gathered outside the royal palace in Maseru in support of the deposed Government, army and police support for Letsie's 'royal coup' was evident, and subsequent clashes between demonstrators and the security forces reportedly resulted in five deaths. A well-known human rights lawyer, Hae Phoofolo, was appointed Chairman of a transitional Council of Ministers, and the Secretary-General of the BNP, Evaristus Retselisitsoe Sekhonyana, was appointed Minister of Foreign Affairs. Phoofolo identified as a priority for his administration the amendment of the Constitution to facilitate the restoration of Moshoeshoe; in the mean time, King Letsie was to act as executive and legislative Head of State.

The suspension of constitutional government was widely condemned outside Lesotho. The Presidents of Botswana, South Africa and Zimbabwe led diplomatic efforts to restore the elected Government, supported by the OAU and the Commonwealth. The USA withdrew financial assistance, and several other countries threatened sanctions. Following negotiations in South Africa, in September 1994 King Letsie and Mokhehle signed an agreement, guaranteed by Botswana, South Africa and Zimbabwe, providing for the restoration of Moshoeshoe II as reigning monarch and for the restitution of the elected organs of government; the commission of inquiry into Moshoeshoe's dethronement was to be abandoned; all those involved in the 'royal coup' were to be immune from prosecution; the political neutrality of the armed forces and public service was to be guaranteed, and consultations were to be undertaken with the aim of broadening the democratic process. Moshoeshoe was restored to the throne on 25 January 1995, undertaking not to interfere in politics. Letsie took the title of Crown Prince.

King Moshoeshoe was killed in a motor accident on 15 January 1996. The College of Chiefs subsequently elected Crown Prince David to succeed his father, and the prince was restored to the throne, resuming the title King Letsie III, on 7 February. Letsie undertook not to involve the monarchy in any aspect of political life.

In June 1997, following a protracted struggle between rival factions for control of the party, Mokhehle resigned from the BCP and formed the Lesotho Congress for Democracy (LCD), to which he transferred executive power. Some 38 members of the National Assembly joined the LCD. In July Molapo Qhobela was elected leader of the BCP. There was further controversy in August, when the Speaker of the National Assembly designated the BCP as the official opposition party. In October members of the Senate (most of whom apparently refused to recognize the legitimacy of Mokhehle's Government) voted to suspend discussion of proposed legislation, pending the King's response to appeals for the dissolution of the National Assembly. At the first annual conference of the LCD, held in January 1998, Mokhehle resigned as leader, and was made Honorary Life President of the party. In February Deputy Prime Minister Bethuel Pakalitha Mosisili was elected to succeed him as party leader. (Mokhehle died in January 1999.)

Elections to an expanded National Assembly took place on 23 May 1998, at which the LCD secured an overwhelming victory, winning 78 of the Assembly's 80 seats; the BNP was the only other party to win representation. Voting for one seat was postponed, owing to the death of a candidate. The Independent Electoral Commission (IEC) and observers representing the Southern African Development Community (SADC, see p. 400) and the Commonwealth concluded that the polls had been generally free and fair. Mosisili was elected Prime Minister by the National Assembly in late May, and a new Government was appointed in June. However, later that month the BCP, the BNP and the Marematlou Freedom Party appealed to the High Court to annul the election results; in the following month the Court ordered the IEC to permit the opposition parties to inspect election documents.

In August 1998 opposition activists began a mass vigil outside the royal palace; within one week some 2,000 people were reported to have joined the protest against the outcome of the poll. Tensions escalated as LCD militants blocked access roads to the capital, in a stated attempt to prevent supplies of weapons to the protesters. Following consultations involving the Lesotho Government and the main opposition parties, with mediation by the Government of South Africa, Mosisili announced the establishment of an independent commission, comprising representatives of the SADC 'troika' of Botswana, South Africa and Zimbabwe, to investigate the conduct and results of the May election. The commission was to be chaired by Pius Langa, the Deputy President of South Africa's Constitutional Court.

Meanwhile, revelations that state funds had been used to purchase farmland for the Commander of the Lesotho Defence Force (LDF, as the RLDF had been redesignated), Lt-Gen. Makhula Mosakeng, fuelled opposition allegations of the Commander's complicity in corruption and vote-rigging. (Mosakeng stated that the land had been acquired for army, rather than personal, use.) However, Mosakeng later announced his resignation and stated that 26 members of the military command had been dismissed.

The Langa Commission's report, which was finally released on 17 September 1998, expressed serious concerns at apparent irregularities and discrepancies in the conduct of the May general election, but the Commission was 'unable to state that the invalidity of the elections had been conclusively established'. On 22 September an SADC peace-keeping force, initially comprising 600 South African troops and 200 from Botswana, entered Lesotho. In response to criticism that he had not consulted King Letsie prior to requesting external military assistance, Mosisili stated that the monarch had, by harbouring opposition protesters in the palace grounds, contributed to the instability that had necessitated SADC intervention. (It was subsequently reported that the King had been prevented from making a broadcast to the nation.) Within Lesotho, there was widespread outrage at what was perceived as an effective 'invasion' by South Africa, and the SADC force encountered unexpectedly strong resistance. There was sustained fighting between the intervention force and rebel units of the LDF before strategic points, including military bases and the Katse Dam (part of the LHWP essential to the supply of water to South Africa), were secured, while rioting in Maseru and other towns targeted in particular South African interests and caused widespread destruction. Mosakeng and his officers, who had fled to South Africa earlier in the month, returned to resume the army command on 24 September: Mosakeng stated that his resignation had been exacted under duress and, since it had not been approved by the King, was invalid.

Following meetings with representatives of the SADC 'troika', in early October 1998 it was reported that the LCD and the main opposition parties had agreed in principle that fresh elections should be held within 15–18 months. In the mean time, the IEC was to be restructured, and the electoral system was to be reviewed, with the aim of ensuring wider inclusion in political affairs (many parties felt that the simple majority voting system was incompatible with the nature of Lesotho's political evolution). In mid-October agreement was reached on a transitional structure, designated the Interim Political Authority (IPA), to comprise representatives of 12 political parties, as well as government and parliamentary delegates, to oversee preparations for fresh elections to the National Assembly.

Multi-party talks took place in Pretoria, South Africa, during November 1998, but progress towards the establishment of the IPA was impeded after warrants were issued for the arrest, on murder charges, of several opposition activists, including two leading members of the BCP and BNP youth wings. The opposition parties stated that they would not co-operate in arrangements for the IPA until outstanding security matters, including the release of all rebel soldiers, had been expedited. A court martial in October 1999 ruled against the discharge of a total of 38 members of the LDF accused of mutiny.

The withdrawal of the SADC intervention force was completed in May 1999. This force was immediately succeeded by a new SADC mission, comprising some 300 military personnel from South Africa, Botswana and (subsequently) Zimbabwe, which remained until May 2000, assisting in the retraining and restructuring of the LDF.

Meanwhile, the 24-member IPA was inaugurated on 9 December 1998. After protracted consultations, it was announced that the number of seats in the National Assembly was to be increased by 50, to 130, effective from the elections scheduled for April 2000, with 80 seats to be allocated on the basis of simple majority in single-member constituencies, and 50 by proportional representation. The mandate of the IPA was to be extended until elections took place. In the mean time, the Presidents of South Africa, Botswana, Mozambique and Zimbabwe, together with the UN, OAU and Commonwealth Secretaries-General, were to act as guarantors to ensure the implementation of the accord. In July 1999 the IEC identified 26 May 2001 as the provisional date for the elections; however, delays in enacting legislation concerning voter registration and the electoral model caused the abandonment of this date.

In April 2000 the establishment of a commission of inquiry to investigate political events during July–November 1998 was announced. The commission, comprising three senior judges and chaired by Nigel Leon, met for the first time in June 2000 and heard evidence from several public figures. However, a number of opposition politicians criticized the commission, expressing doubts as to its impartiality. In August three LDF members were convicted by a court martial of participation in the mutiny of September 1998 and sentenced to a combined 29 years' imprisonment; a further 33 LDF members were convicted in November. The Leon commission of inquiry, which submitted its report to Prime Minister Mosisili in October 2001, rejected demands for a general amnesty to be granted to perpetrators of violence during the period under review, recommending the indictment of a number of opposition politicians and members of the armed forces.

In January 2001 a congress of the LCD re-elected Mosisili as leader of the party, for a five-year term. Shakhane Mokhehle, the incumbent and brother of the party's founder, was defeated in the election to the post of Secretary-General of the LCD by the Minister in the Prime Minister's Office, Sephiri Motanyane. In a minor cabinet reshuffle in July Mokhehle, who had disputed the results of the LCD elections, was dismissed as Minister of Justice, Human Rights and Rehabilitation, Law and Constitutional Affairs. Deputy Prime Minister Kelebone Maope resigned from the Government in September and broke away from the LCD, together with Mokhehle, to form a new opposition party, the Lesotho People's Congress (LPC), to prepare for forthcoming elections. By mid-October a total of 27 deputies had defected from the LCD to join the LPC, which was declared the main opposition party. Mosisili made new cabinet appointments in October, in an effort to consolidate his position ahead of the elections.

In mid-January 2002 a protracted dispute over the leadership of the BCP, which had been ongoing since the late 1990s, also appeared to be resolved, when the High Court ruled in favour of Tseliso Makhakhe's leadership of the party. Qhobela subsequently formed a new party, known as the Basutoland African Congress (BAC), which had been the name of the BCP in 1952–59.

Meanwhile, divisions over the electoral model, notably regarding the number of seats to be allocated by proportional representation, had continued to impede progress towards the elections. In January 2002 Parliament finally approved amendments to the electoral legislation, providing for the expansion of the National Assembly to 120 members, with 80 to be elected on a constituency basis and 40 selected by proportional representation.

The LCD won a resounding victory at the general election, which took place on 25 May 2002, retaining 77 of the 78 contested constituency seats, with 54.9% of the valid votes cast. The BNP became the second largest legislative party, securing 21 of the 40 seats allocated by proportional representation (known as compensatory seats), with 22.4% of the votes cast; the LPC won one constituency seat and four compensatory seats. Voting in two constituencies was postponed, owing to the deaths of candidates. Of the remaining 15 compensatory seats, the National Independent Party secured five, the BAC and the BCP both won three, while four smaller parties each took one seat. Mosisili was re-elected Prime Minister by the National Assembly in early June and a new Cabinet was subsequently appointed.

In mid-October 2004 a 30-member committee was established to direct a parliamentary reform programme; the committee was chaired by the leader of the Popular Front for Democracy, Lekhetho Rakuoane, and comprised government ministers and members of the National Assembly and the Senate. In mid-November the Cabinet was reorganized: Monyane Moleleki was appointed Minister of Foreign Affairs and was replaced as Minister of Natural Resources by Dr 'Mamphono Khaketla, while the Deputy Prime Minister, Lesao Lehohola, also assumed the home affairs portfolio; the former Minister of Home Affairs, Thomas Thabane, became Minister of Communications, Science and Technology. Other notable changes included the appointment of Mothejoa Metsing as the Minister of Justice, Human Rights and Rehabilitation, Law and Constitutional Affairs, and the appointment of Mpeo Mahase-Moiloa as Minister of Employment and Labour.

In mid-February 2005, following an amendment to the Local Government Act in September 2004, the IEC announced that elections to local councils were to be held, for the first time, on 30 April 2005; the elections had initially been scheduled for 1998. Voting took place in 1,272 electoral divisions, of which some 390 were reserved for women candidates, in accordance with SADC guidelines. Over 1,000 new councillors were elected to 129 councils replacing previous councils comprising traditional leaders and government officials. The ruling LCD won over three-quarters of the seats; the rate of voter participation, recorded by the IEC at less than 30%, was officially attributed to the fact that it was the first such election to be held.

In late January 2006 Khauhelo Raditapole and Kelebone Maope, the leaders of the BAC and the LPC, respectively, announced that their parties would form an alliance, following appeals by the BCP for reconciliation between political parties. Legislative elections took place on 17 February 2007, at which the LCD retained its parliamentary majority, although the party's total number of seats in the National Assembly was reduced from 77 to 61. The National Independent Party (NIP) took 21 of the 40 compensatory seats, thus becoming the second largest legislative party, while the All Basotho Convention (ABC) secured 17 constituency seats and the Lesotho Workers' Party (LWP) 10 compensatory seats. Voting in one constituency was postponed, owing to the death of a candidate. The Alliance of Congress Parties won one constituency seat and one compensatory seat, while five other parties each secured one compensatory seat. Observers from SADC and the AU declared the elections to have been free and fair. It emerged that an alliance had formed between the LCD and the NIP and that the NIP had fielded candidates from the LCD at the elections, giving the coalition a total of 82 seats in the National Assembly; a similar arrangement was made between the ABC and the LWP, resulting in that alliance securing 27 seats in total. Mosisili was reappointed Prime Minister later that month and in early March a new Cabinet was sworn in. Most notably, Mohlabi Tsekoa, hitherto Minister of Education and Training, was appointed Minister of Foreign Affairs; Mahase-Moiloa became Minister of Law and Constitutional Affairs.

During 2008 tensions had been building between the ruling and opposition parties over the formation of alliances for the 2007 legislative elections and in January 2009 the ABC claimed that the coalition formed by the LCD and the NIP contravened the Constitution. If inquiries proved this to be the case, the Prime Minister would be obliged to dissolve the National Assembly and hold new elections. In April Mosisili's residence was attacked by gunmen in an apparent assassination attempt. Three of the attackers were reported to have been killed and two men suspected of involvement in the incident were detained in South Africa; the Prime Minister escaped unharmed. Despite recent tensions, observers maintained that the prevailing situation in Lesotho was one of stability and a motive for the attack was not immediately clear.

As exemplified by South Africa's prominent role in the resolution of the 1994 constitutional crisis and by its intervention in the political crisis of September 1998, Lesotho's internal affairs continue to be strongly influenced by South Africa. Long-standing problems of border security and, in particular, the issue of disputed land in South Africa's Free State (formerly Orange Free State) have periodically caused friction between the two countries. During a two-day state visit to Lesotho in July 1995, President Nelson Mandela of South Africa advocated the pursuit of mutually beneficial policies of regional integration, and he and Prime Minister Mokhehle agreed that the issue of sovereignty in Free State should be discussed by 'appropriate' authorities. Relations between the two countries were strained in August 2000 when Lesotho withdrew its support shortly before the scheduled signing of an agreement with Botswana, Namibia and South Africa on the management of water resources from the

LESOTHO

Orange river. In September an official at the South African High Commission was killed in Maseru. Representatives of both countries met in Pretoria in November and recommended increased co-operation in areas including education and criminal justice. During a visit to Lesotho by President Thabo Mbeki of South Africa in April 2001, it was agreed to replace an intergovernmental liaison committee that had been established following SADC intervention in 1998 (see above) with a joint binational commission at ministerial level, with the aim of enhancing bilateral relations. Relations between Lesotho and South Africa were further enhanced in May 2002, when their ministers of foreign affairs signed the Joint Bilateral Commission of Cooperation programme, which aimed to raise Lesotho from its current status as a 'least developed country'.

Government

Lesotho is an hereditary monarchy. Under the terms of the Constitution, which came into effect following the March 1993 election, the King, who is Head of State, has no executive or legislative powers. The College of Chiefs is theoretically empowered, under traditional law, to elect and depose the King by a majority vote. Executive power is vested in the Cabinet, which is headed by the Prime Minister. Legislative power is exercised by the National Assembly, which is elected, at intervals of no more than five years, by universal adult suffrage in the context of a multi-party political system. A system of mixed member proportional representation was introduced at the general election of May 2002, when the National Assembly was expanded to 120 members (80 elected by simple majority in single-member constituencies and 40 selected from party lists). The upper house, the Senate, comprises traditional chiefs and 11 nominated members. Lesotho comprises 10 administrative districts, each with an appointed district co-ordinator.

Defence

Military service is voluntary. As assessed at November 2008, the Lesotho Defence Force (LDF, formerly the Royal Lesotho Defence Force) comprised 2,000 men, including an air wing of 110 men. The creation of a new commando force unit, the first professional unit in the LDF, was announced in October 2001, as part of ongoing efforts to restructure the armed forces. Budgetary expenditure on defence for 2007 was M281m.

Economic Affairs

In 2007, according to estimates by the World Bank, Lesotho's gross national income (GNI), measured at average 2005–07 prices, was US $2,007m., equivalent to $1,000 per head (or $1,890 per head on an international purchasing-power parity basis). During 2000–07, it was estimated, the population increased at an average annual rate of 0.9%, while gross domestic product (GDP) per head increased, in real terms, by an average of 2.8% per year. Overall GDP increased, in real terms, at an average annual rate of 3.8% in 2000–07; growth in 2007 was 4.9%.

Agriculture, forestry and fishing contributed just 7.1% of GDP in 2007 but employed some 94.3% of the labour force at mid-2005, according to FAO estimates. The principal agricultural export is tobacco. The main subsistence crops are potatoes, maize, sorghum and wheat. Lesotho remains a net importer of staple foodstuffs, largely owing to its vulnerability to adverse climatic conditions, especially drought. According to the World Food Programme, less than 10% of land is arable and there is no irrigation. During 2000–07 agricultural GDP declined at an average annual rate of 6.1%. According to the World Bank, agricultural GDP increased by 1.8% in 2006, but declined by 23.0% in 2007.

Industry (including mining, manufacturing, construction and power) provided 34.5% of GDP in 2007, and engaged 9.3% of the labour force in 1999. According to the World Bank, during 2000–07 industrial GDP increased by an average of 6.7% per year. Industrial GDP increased by 12.7% in 2007.

Mining contributed 6.8% of GDP in 2007. Lesotho has reserves of diamonds, which during the late 1970s provided more than 50% of visible export earnings, but large-scale exploitation of these ceased in 1982. The Lets'eng-la-Terae diamond mine reopened in April 2004 and by the time of its official inauguration in November gems with an estimated value of US $28m. had been recovered. Industrial mining at other sites was also envisaged, including a second diamond mine at Liqhobong. Lesotho also possesses deposits of uranium, lead and iron ore, and is believed to have petroleum deposits. The GDP of the mining sector

Introductory Survey

increased by an average of 70.3% per year in 2000–07; growth in 2006 was 81.3% and growth in 2007 was 33.9%.

Manufacturing contributed an estimated 18.0% of GDP in 2007. During 2000–07 manufacturing GDP increased by an average of 4.9% per year, according to the World Bank; it increased by 11.0% in 2007.

The Lesotho Highlands Water Project (LHWP) provides hydroelectricity sufficient for all Lesotho's needs and for export to South Africa; phases 1A and 1B were inaugurated in 1998 and 2004, respectively. In late September 2005 an agreement was signed for a feasibility study concerning the location of the second phase of the project. The scheme was expected to be completed by about 2030. The R200m. (US $30m.) that Lesotho receives annually in royalties from South Africa for the LHWP represents the country's largest single source of foreign exchange. Prior to the LHWP more than 90% of Lesotho's energy requirements were imported from South Africa. Imports of mineral fuels and lubricants comprised 6.4% of the total value of imports in 2004.

The services sector contributed 58.5% of GDP in 2007. During 2000–07 the GDP of the services sector increased at an average annual rate of 4.2%, according to the World Bank. Services GDP increased by 5.7% in 2007.

In 2007 Lesotho recorded a visible trade deficit of US $799.4m., but there was a surplus of $211.8m. on the current account of the balance of payments. In 2006 the principal source of imports (83.9%) was the Southern African Customs Union (SACU—i.e. chiefly South Africa—see below), which was also the second largest market for exports (17.3%), behind the USA (61.5%); the European Union was also a significant market for exports (17.2%). The principal export in that year was clothing. The principal imports in 2004 were manufactured goods, food and live animals, machinery and transport equipment and mineral fuels and lubricants.

In the financial year ending 31 March 2006 there was an overall budgetary surplus of M266.7m. The 2006/07 budget projected a surplus of M1,637.5m. Lesotho's external debt totalled US $669.9m. at the end of 2006, of which $633.4m. was long-term public debt. In that year the cost of debt-servicing was equivalent to 4.0% of revenue from exports of goods and services. The annual rate of inflation averaged 7.0% in 2000–07; consumer prices increased by 8.2% in 2007. In 1999 231,742 people were registered as unemployed, equivalent to 27.3% of the labour force. In 2006 51,595 Basotho were employed as miners in South Africa compared with 129,000 in 1989. The number was expected to continue to decrease in the coming years. According to the Central Bank of Lesotho, in 2004 Basotho miners' remittances amounted to M1,795.0m. and accounted for more than 70% of total earnings during the period 1997–2004. South African officials estimated that around 300,000 Basotho were employed in South Africa at any given time.

Lesotho is a member of the Common Monetary Area (with Namibia, South Africa and Swaziland), and a member of SACU (with Botswana, Namibia, South Africa and Swaziland). Lesotho also belongs to the Southern African Development Community (SADC, see p. 400).

Impediments to economic development in Lesotho include vulnerability to drought and serious land shortages, combined with the country's dependence on South Africa (the Lesotho currency, the loti, is fixed at par with the South African rand, exposing Lesotho to fluctuations within the South African economy). By the late 1990s the strong growth that had prevailed for most of the decade was being eroded, while retrenchment in the South African gold-mining sector resulted in a marked decline in remittances from Basotho working abroad. The textile industry benefited considerably from the USA's African Growth and Opportunities Act (AGOA), for which Lesotho was first declared eligible in April 2001; under its terms, textiles and clothing made in Lesotho had unlimited access to the US market, and by early 2002 exports of these products to the USA had increased by nearly 40%. Lesotho's qualification for the benefits of the AGOA attracted interest from foreign investors in Lesotho, notably Taiwanese textile manufacturers. However, faced with increasing competition from producers in Asia, between mid-2004 and January 2005 eight textile factories closed with the loss of more than 23,000 jobs. The textile and garment sector improved markedly in 2007, owing to a depreciation of the rand and the reduction in 2006 of rates of company tax and taxes paid by manufacturers. These had been lowered as an incentive to attract investors and the decision to exempt exporters from company tax entirely was seen as a measure favouring textile producers in particular. In 2006 the Government had also stated

LESOTHO

that it would seek to diversify Lesotho's economy, promoting agriculture and 'agroprocessing', diamond and sandstone mining and tourism as possible alternatives. Nevertheless, the country faced ongoing difficulties as a result of the high level of HIV/AIDS infection among the population. In 2007 Lesotho had the third highest prevalence of HIV/AIDS in the world, affecting some 23% of adults in the country, and some 100,000 children had been orphaned as a result of the pandemic. In late 2008 it was announced that US President George W. Bush's Millennium Challenge Corporation would grant Lesotho some US $363m., much of which was to finance health and welfare development projects. The IMF estimated GDP growth of 5.2% in 2008, and forecast growth of 5.4% in 2009.

Education

As part of an initiative begun in 2000, all primary education is available free of charge, provided mainly by the three main Christian missions (Lesotho Evangelical, Roman Catholic and Anglican), under the direction of the Ministry of Education. Officially, primary education is compulsory for seven years between six and 13 years of age. Secondary education, beginning at the age of 13, lasts for up to five years, comprising a first cycle of three years and a second of two years. According to UNESCO estimates, in 2005/06 total enrolment at primary schools included 72.4% of children in the appropriate age-group (70.8% of boys; 73.9% of girls); in that year enrolment at secondary schools included 23.9% of children in the relevant age-group (18.8% of boys; 29.0% of girls). Some 3,266 students were enrolled at the National University of Lesotho, at Roma, in 2002. Proposed expenditure on education under the 2006/07 budget was M927.4m. (representing more than 20% of total government expenditure). In January 2006 17 new schools constructed with the assistance of the Government of Japan were opened; they were expected to accommodate some 14,000 pupils.

Public Holidays

2009: 1 January (New Year's Day), 11 March (Moshoeshoe Day), 10–13 April (Easter), 1 May (Workers' Day), 21 May (Ascension Day), 25 May (Africa Day and Heroes' Day), 17 July (King's Birthday), 4 October (National Independence Day), 25 December (Christmas Day), 26 December (Boxing Day).

2010: 1 January (New Year's Day), 11 March (Moshoeshoe Day), 2–5 April (Easter), 1 May (Workers' Day), 13 May (Ascension Day), 25 May (Africa Day and Heroes' Day), 17 July (King's Birthday), 4 October (National Independence Day), 25 December (Christmas Day), 26 December (Boxing Day).

Weights and Measures

The metric system of weights and measures is in force.

Statistical Survey

Sources (unless otherwise stated): Bureau of Statistics, POB 455, Maseru 100; tel. 22323852; fax 22310177; internet www.bos.gov.ls; Central Bank of Lesotho, POB 1184, Maseru 100; tel. 22314281; fax 22310051; e-mail cbl@centralbank.org.ls; internet www.centralbank.org.ls.

Area and Population

AREA, POPULATION AND DENSITY

Area (sq km)	30,355*
Population (*de jure* census results)	
14 April 1996	1,841,967
9 April 2006	
Males	911,848
Females	960,873
Total	1,872,721
Population (UN estimates at mid-year)	
2007	2,008,000
2008	2,020,000
Density (per sq km) at mid-2008	66.5

* 11,720 sq miles.

DISTRICTS
(*de jure* population at 2006 census, preliminary figures)

District	Population
Berea	248,225
Butha-Buthe	109,139
Leribe	296,673
Mafeteng	192,795
Maseru	436,399
Mohale's Hoek	173,706
Mokhotlong	95,332
Qacha's Nek	71,756
Quthing	119,811
Thaba-Tseka	128,885
Total	**1,872,721**

PRINCIPAL TOWNS
(population at 1986 census)

Maseru (capital)	109,400	Hlotse	9,600
Maputsoa	20,000	Mohale's Hoek	8,500
Teyateyaneng	14,300	Quthing	6,000
Mafeteng	12,700		

Source: Stefan Helders, *World Gazetteer* (www.world-gazetteer.com).

Mid-2007 (including suburbs, UN estimate): Maseru 210,000 (Source: UN, *World Urbanization Prospects: The 2007 Revision*).

BIRTHS AND DEATHS
(annual averages, UN estimates)

	1990–95	1995–2000	2000–05
Birth rate (per 1,000)	35.0	34.0	31.3
Death rate (per 1,000)	10.3	11.9	17.7

Source: UN, *World Population Prospects: The 2006 Revision*.

Life expectancy (years at birth, WHO estimates): 42.2 (males 39.7; females 44.3) in 2006 (Source: WHO, *World Health Statistics*).

ECONOMICALLY ACTIVE POPULATION
(household survey, persons aged 10 years and over, 1999)

	Males	Females	Total
Agriculture	270,919	175,760	446,679
Fishing	125	—	125
Mining and quarrying	2,392	611	3,003
Manufacturing	7,957	13,839	21,795
Electricity, gas and water supply	1,722	1,541	3,263
Construction	18,947	10,548	29,495
Wholesale and retail trade; repair of motor vehicles, motorcycles and household goods	11,099	17,915	29,014
Hotels and restaurants	918	3,529	4,447
Transport, storage and communications	9,307	1,363	10,670
Financial intermediation	1,041	810	1,851
Real estate, renting and business activities	3,405	2,032	5,437
Public administration and defence; compulsory social security	5,181	2,395	7,576
Education	5,125	8,099	13,224
Health and social work	2,070	2,895	4,965
Other community, social and personal service activities	1,765	7,686	9,451
Households with employed persons	4,474	21,970	26,444
Extra-territorial organizations and bodies	126	—	126
Total employed	346,573	270,993	617,566
Unemployed	90,964	140,778	231,742
Total labour force	437,537	411,771	849,308

Source: ILO.

Mid-2005 (estimates in '000): Agriculture, etc. 684; Total 725 (Source: FAO).

Health and Welfare

KEY INDICATORS

Total fertility rate (children per woman, 2006)	3.5
Under-5 mortality rate (per 1,000 live births, 2006)	132
HIV/AIDS (% of persons aged 15–49, 2007)	23.2
Physicians (per 1,000 head, 2003)	0.05
Hospital beds (per 1,000 head, 2006)	1.30
Health expenditure (2006): US $ per head (PPP)	143
Health expenditure (2006): % of GDP	6.7
Health expenditure (2006): public (% of total)	61.6
Access to water (% of persons, 2006)	78
Access to sanitation (% of persons, 2006)	36
Human Development Index (2006): ranking	155
Human Development Index (2006): value	0.496

For sources and definitions, see explanatory note on p. vi.

Agriculture

PRINCIPAL CROPS
('000 metric tons)

	2005	2006	2007*
Wheat	10.4	7.5*	10.4
Maize	75.0	75.4	50.8
Sorghum	15.8	5.5	11.2
Potatoes*	90	90	96
Beans, dry	5.2	5.0*	5.5
Peas, dry	1.4	2.0*	2.2
Vegetables*	32	18	20

* FAO estimate(s).

Source: FAO.

LIVESTOCK
('000 head, year ending September)

	2005	2006*	2007*
Cattle	729	685	695
Sheep	1,041.3	1,000.0	1,025.0
Goats	821.2	710.0	715.0
Pigs	135.3	65.0	66.0
Horses*	45.0	50.0	55.0
Asses	84.3	n.a.	n.a.
Chickens*	2,100	1,800	1,850

* FAO estimates.

Source: FAO.

LIVESTOCK PRODUCTS
('000 metric tons, FAO estimates)

	2005	2006	2007
Cattle meat	10.1	10.2	10.5
Cows' milk	35.0	24.0	25.0
Pig meat	5.7	2.8	2.9
Chicken meat	2.1	1.8	1.9
Game meat	3.9	3.9	3.9
Hen eggs	1.6	1.5	1.6
Wool, greasy	2.6	2.6	2.6

Source: FAO.

Forestry

ROUNDWOOD REMOVALS
('000 cubic metres, excluding bark, FAO estimates)

	2005	2006	2007
Total (all fuel wood)	2,052.8	2,060.5	2,068.3

Source: FAO.

Fishing

(metric tons, live weight)

	2004	2005	2006
Capture	45	45	45
Common carp	15	15	12
North African catfish	5	5	3
Other freshwater fishes	25	25	30
Aquaculture	2	1	2
Common carp	2	1	2
Total catch	47	46	47

Source: FAO.

Mining

(cubic metres, unless otherwise indicated)

	2005	2006	2007
Fire clay*	15,000	15,000	15,000
Diamond (carats)	52,036	112,408	114,000*
Gravel and crushed rock*	300,000	300,000	300,000

* Estimated production.

Source: US Geological Survey.

Finance

CURRENCY AND EXCHANGE RATES

Monetary Units
100 lisente (singular: sente) = 1 loti (plural: maloti).

Sterling, Dollar and Euro Equivalents (31 December 2008)
£1 sterling = 13.565 maloti;
US $1 = 9.305 maloti;
€1 = 12.950 maloti;
100 maloti = £7.37 = $10.75 = €7.72.

Average Exchange Rate (maloti per US $)
2006   6.7716
2007   7.0454
2008   8.2612

Note: The loti is fixed at par with the South African rand.

BUDGET
(million maloti, year ending 31 March)

Revenue*	2004/05	2005/06	2006/07†
Tax revenue	3,678.3	4,003.1	6,008.0
Taxes on net income and profits	901.9	924.6	994.5
Company tax	219.2	194.9	203.7
Individual income tax	567.4	612.0	654.7
Other income and profit taxes	115.3	117.8	136.1
Taxes on goods and services	749.8	723.0	734.7
Customs duties	2,012.4	2,306.0	4,208.3
Other taxes	14.2	49.4	70.4
Non-tax revenue	452.1	473.3	510.0
Water royalties	194.7	235.9	268.4
Total	4,130.4	4,476.3	6,517.9

Expenditure and net lending	2004/05	2005/06	2006/07†
Wages and salaries	1,174.3	1,263.7	1,391.6
Goods and services	828.2	1,114.8	1,285.8
Subsidies and transfers	765.0	988.5	1,360.5
Interest payments	152.2	223.9	124.5
Capital expenditure (incl. lending minus repayments)	693.8	702.3	793.6
Total	3,613.5	4,293.2	4,955.9

* Excluding grants received (million maloti): 231.4 in 2004/05; 83.6 in 2005/06; 75.5 in 2006/07.

† Projections.

LESOTHO

Statistical Survey

INTERNATIONAL RESERVES
(US $ million at 31 December)

	2004	2005	2006
IMF special drawing rights	0.62	0.44	0.22
Reserve position in IMF	5.53	5.15	5.45
Foreign exchange	495.35	513.42	652.74
Total	**501.50**	**519.01**	**658.41**

2007 (US $ million at 31 December): IMF special drawing rights 6.28; Reserve position in IMF 5.71.

Source: IMF, *International Financial Statistics*.

MONEY SUPPLY
(million maloti at 31 December)

	2005	2006	2007
Currency outside banks	212.78	309.42	339.31
Demand deposits at commercial banks	1,427.86	2,187.20	2,496.89
Total money (incl. others)	**1,829.48**	**2,688.81**	**2,990.67**

Source: IMF, *International Financial Statistics*.

COST OF LIVING
(Consumer Price Index; base: April 1997 = 100)

	2005	2006	2007
Food (incl. non-alcoholic beverages)	186.0	202.8	231.5
Alcoholic beverages and tobacco	200.4	212.8	224.5
Housing, water, electricity, and other fuels	175.8	191.8	207.3
Clothing (incl. footwear)	153.1	157.4	162.0
All items (incl. others)	**175.3**	**185.9**	**200.8**

NATIONAL ACCOUNTS
(million maloti at current prices)

Expenditure on the Gross Domestic Product

	2005	2006	2007
Government final consumption expenditure	3,130	3,465	3,985
Private final consumption expenditure	9,323	10,255	11,660
Increase in stocks	20	115	−7
Gross fixed capital formation	2,146	2,380	2,870
Statistical discrepancy	308	103	448
Total domestic expenditure	**14,927**	**16,318**	**18,956**
Exports of goods and services	4,255	5,141	6,106
Less Imports of goods and services	10,431	11,189	13,283
GDP in purchasers' values	**8,750**	**10,269**	**11,778**
GDP at constant 2004 prices	**8,389**	**9,068**	**9,528**

Gross Domestic Product by Economic Activity

	2005	2006	2007
Agriculture	629	801	789
Mining and quarrying	235	517	764
Manufacturing	1,482	1,732	2,015
Electricity and water	394	447	497
Construction	411	465	575
Wholesale and retail trade	1,097	1,284	1,449
Restaurants and hotels	110	128	142
Transport and communication	507	546	593
Financial intermediation and insurance	303	387	441
Real estate and business services	1,185	1,337	1,517
Public administration	926	1,039	1,153
Education	705	765	955
Health and social work	158	172	186
Other services	83	88	97
Sub-total	**8,226**	**9,708**	**11,173**
Less Imputed bank service charge	−38	−49	−74
GDP at factor cost	**8,188**	**9,659**	**11,099**
Indirect taxes, less subsidies	563	610	679
GDP at market prices	**8,750**	**10,269**	**11,778**

BALANCE OF PAYMENTS
(US $ million)

	2005	2006	2007
Exports of goods f.o.b.	650.0	693.6	805.0
Imports of goods f.o.b.	−1,306.3	−1,361.3	−1,604.4
Trade balance	**−656.3**	**−667.7**	**−799.4**
Exports of services	52.2	59.1	76.2
Imports of services	−103.3	−95.2	−110.2
Balance on goods and services	**−707.4**	**−703.8**	**−833.4**
Other income received	370.0	412.7	517.3
Other income paid	−65.2	−32.1	−97.1
Balance on goods, services and income	**−402.6**	**−323.2**	**−413.2**
Current transfers received	303.8	392.0	628.7
Current transfers paid	−3.2	−2.6	−3.6
Current balance	**−102.0**	**66.3**	**211.8**
Capital account (net)	21.3	11.0	32.0
Direct investment from abroad	92.6	113.0	130.3
Other investment assets	−0.1	−87.8	−62.2
Other investment liabilities	34.5	−21.7	16.4
Net errors and omissions	−2.7	109.9	−58.6
Overall balance	**43.7**	**190.8**	**269.9**

Source: IMF, *International Financial Statistics*.

External Trade

PRINCIPAL COMMODITIES

Imports c.i.f. (US $ million)*	2002	2003	2004
Food and live animals	142.7	179.1	183.1
Beverages and tobacco	32.3	28.2	26.2
Crude materials, inedible except fuels	13.2	18.5	18.2
Mineral fuels and lubricants	61.7	71.7	89.0
Animal and vegetable oils, fats and waxes	9.8	7.7	8.3
Chemicals and related products	99.2	83.3	66.8
Manufactured goods	186.1	283.4	287.5
Machinery and transport equipment	98.3	135.6	146.2
Miscellaneous manufactured articles	115.8	188.8	143.5
Total (incl. others)	**799.6**	**1,115.0**	**1,399.4**

* Preliminary figures.

Exports (million maloti)	2004	2005	2006
Foodstuffs, etc.	185.5	61.4	72.9
Cereals	65.2	6.2	6.8
Beverages and tobacco	98.5	50.4	61.2
Live animals	16.8	3.3	1.3
Livestock materials	22.0	12.1	7.9
Wool	12.9	10.3	6.1
Manufactures	3,654.1	3,565.7	4,039.7
Chemicals and petroleum	32.6	13.2	15.6
Telecommunication equipment	133.6	70.5	72.3
Machinery	50.1	12.3	8.8
Furniture and parts	25.6	2.3	5.6
Clothing, etc.	3,238.0	3,355.5	3,841.1
Footwear	92.3	65.8	60.2
Other manufactures	38.7	12.9	13.3
Total (incl. others)	4,263.2	4,138.1	4,736.7

Sources: UN, *International Trade Statistics Yearbook*; IMF, *Kingdom of Lesotho: Selected Issues and Statistical Appendix* (April 2008).

PRINCIPAL TRADING PARTNERS
(million maloti)

Imports c.i.f.*	2004	2005	2006
Africa	6,628.5	7,709.9	8,574.3
SACU†	6,583.8	7,665.2	8,524.6
Asia	2,183.4	1,315.3	1,462.8
China, People's Repub.	457.4	238.9	265.7
Hong Kong	623.9	386.3	429.6
Taiwan	670.4	448.4	498.7
European Union	70.3	61.5	68.4
North America	97.5	38.1	42.3
USA	97.5	31.8	35.4
Total (incl. others)	9,036.2	9,135.7	10,160.0

Exports f.o.b.	2004	2005	2006
Africa	618.3	813.3	930.9
SACU†	585.1	714.2	817.5
European Union	650.8	711.0	813.8
North America	2,979.8	2,600.0	2,976.1
Canada	45.4	56.1	64.3
USA	2,934.4	2,543.8	2,911.8
Total (incl. others)	4,263.2	4,138.1	4,736.7

*Valuation exclusive of import duties. Figures also exclude donated food.
† Southern African Customs Union, of which Lesotho is a member; also including Botswana, Namibia, South Africa and Swaziland.

Source: IMF, *Kingdom of Lesotho: Selected Issues and Statistical Appendix* (April 2008).

Transport

ROAD TRAFFIC
(motor vehicles in use at 31 December, estimates)

	1994	1995	1996
Passenger cars	9,900	11,160	12,610
Lorries and vans	20,790	22,310	25,000

Source: International Road Federation, *World Road Statistics*.

CIVIL AVIATION
(traffic on scheduled services)

	1997	1998	1999
Kilometres flown (million)	0	1	0
Passengers carried ('000)	10	28	1
Passenger-km (million)	3	9	0
Total ton-km (million)	0	1	0

Source: UN, *Statistical Yearbook*.

Tourism

FOREIGN TOURIST ARRIVALS BY COUNTRY OF RESIDENCE

	2004	2005	2006
Botswana	1,973	2,129	1,903
Germany	1,687	1,775	1,775
South Africa	282,070	280,399	318,458
Swaziland	1,408	1,481	1,506
United Kingdom	1,970	1,950	4,937
USA	955	1,054	1,878
Zimbabwe	1,963	2,088	3,899
Total (incl. others)	303,530	303,578	356,913

Tourism receipts (US $ million, excl. passenger transport): 34 in 2004; 30 in 2005; 28 in 2006.

Source: World Tourism Organization.

Communications Media

	2005	2006	2007
Telephones ('000 main lines in use)	48.0	53.1	n.a.
Mobile cellular telephones ('000 subscribers)	249.8	357.9	456.0
Internet users ('000)	52	60	70

2006: 37,200 main telephone lines in use.

Facsimile machines (number in use, year ending 31 March 1996): 569.
Radio receivers ('000 in use): 104 in 1997.
Television receivers ('000 in use): 70 in 2001.
Non-daily newspapers (1996): 7 (average circulation 74,000 copies).

Sources: UNESCO Institute for Statistics; International Telecommunication Union.

Education

(2005/06, unless otherwise indicated)

	Institutions*	Teachers	Males	Females	Total
Primary	1,355	10,513	214,123	210,732	424,855
Secondary:					
general	228	3,527	40,661	51,807	92,468
technical and vocational	8	198	724	804	1,528
teacher training	1	n.a.	n.a.	n.a.	1,855*
University	1	n.a.	n.a.	n.a.	4,195*

* 2002/03.

Source: partly UNESCO Institute for Statistics.

Adult literacy rate (UNESCO estimates): 82.2% (males 73.7%; females 90.3%) in 2001 (Source: UNESCO Institute for Statistics).

Directory

The Constitution

The Constitution of the Kingdom of Lesotho, which took effect at independence in October 1966, was suspended in January 1970. A new Constitution was promulgated following the March 1993 general election. Its main provisions, with subsequent amendments, are summarized below:

Lesotho is an hereditary monarchy. The King, who is Head of State, has no executive or legislative powers. Executive authority is vested in the Cabinet, which is headed by the Prime Minister, while legislative power is exercised by the 120-member National Assembly, which comprises 80 members elected on a single-member constituency basis and 40 selected by a system of proportional representation. The National Assembly is elected, at intervals of no more than five years, by universal adult suffrage in the context of a multi-party political system. There is also a Senate, comprising 22 traditional chiefs and 11 nominated members. The Prime Minister is the official head of the armed forces.

The Government

HEAD OF STATE

King: HM King LETSIE III (acceded to the throne 7 February 1996).

CABINET
(April 2009)

Prime Minister and Minister of Defence and National Security: BETHUEL PAKALITHA MOSISILI.
Deputy Prime Minister and Minister of Home Affairs and Public Safety and Parliamentary Affairs: ARCHIBALD LESAO LEHOHLA.
Minister of Natural Resources (Water, Lesotho Water Highlands Project, Energy and Mining): MONYANE MOLELEKI.
Minister of Gender, Youth, Sports and Recreation: 'MATHABISO LEPONO.
Minister of Foreign Affairs and International Relations: MOHLABI TSEKOA.
Minister of Local Government and Chieftainship: Dr PONTŠO SUZAN 'MATUMELO SEKATLE.
Minister in the Prime Minister's Office: Dr MOTLOHELOA PHOOKO.
Minister of Employment and Labour: REFILOE MASAMENE.
Minister of Finance and Development Planning: Dr TIMOTHY THAHANE.
Minister of Tourism, Environment and Culture: LEBOHANG NTŠINYI.
Minister of Education and Training: Dr 'MAMPHONO KHAKETLA.
Minister of Forestry and Land Reclamation: LINCOLN RALECHATE 'MOKOSE.
Minister of Trade, Industry, Co-operatives and Marketing: POPANE LEBESA.
Minister of Justice, Human Rights and Correctional Services, Law and Constitutional Affairs: MPEO MAHASE-MOILOA.
Minister of Communications, Science and Technology: MOTHEJOA METSING.
Minister of Public Service: SEMANO SEKATLE.
Minister of Agriculture and Food Security: LESOLE MOKOMA.
Minister of Health and Social Welfare: Dr MPHU RAMATLAPENG.
Minister of Public Works and Transport: TS'ELE CHAKELA.

There were also five assistant ministers.

MINISTRIES

Office of the Prime Minister: POB 527, Maseru 100; tel. 22311000; fax 22310578; internet www.lesotho.gov.ls.
Ministry of Agriculture and Food Security: POB 24, Maseru 100; tel. 22316407; fax 22310906; e-mail tvmofilikoane@yahoo.com.
Ministry of Communications, Science and Technology: POB 36, Maseru 100; tel. 22323864; fax 22325682; e-mail m.makhorole@mcst.gov.ls.
Ministry of Defence and National Security: POB 527, Maseru 100; tel. 22316570; fax 22310518; e-mail nmokatsa@yahoo.co.uk.
Ministry of Education and Training: POB 47, Maseru 100; tel. 22313045; fax 22310562; e-mail semakaleM@education.gov.ls; internet www.education.gov.ls.
Ministry of Employment and Labour: Private Bag A116, Maseru 100; tel. 22322602; fax 22325163; e-mail privatesecemployment@leo.co.ls.
Ministry of Finance and Development Planning: POB 395, Maseru 100; tel. 22311101; fax 22310964; e-mail ps@finance.gov.ls; internet www.finance.gov.ls.
Ministry of Foreign Affairs and International Relations: POB 1387, Maseru 100; tel. 22311150; fax 22310178; e-mail information@foreign.gov.ls; internet www.foreign.gov.ls.
Ministry of Forestry and Land Reclamation: POB 92, Maseru 100; tel. 22310515; fax 22313057; e-mail lincmox@ilesotho.com.
Ministry of Gender, Youth, Sports and Recreation: POB 729, Maseru 100; tel. and fax 22311006; e-mail honsec@mgysr.gov.ls.
Ministry of Health and Social Welfare: POB 514, Maseru 100; tel. 22317707; fax 22321014; e-mail lesenyehom@health.gov.ls; internet www.health.gov.ls.
Ministry of Home Affairs and Public Safety and Parliamentary Affairs: POB 174, Maseru 100; tel. 22320017; fax 22310013; e-mail mohonoel@homeaffairs.gov.ls.
Ministry of Justice, Human Rights and Correctional Services, Law and Constitutional Affairs: POB 402, Maseru 100; tel. 22322683; fax 22311092; e-mail dps@justice.gov.ls; internet www.justice.gov.ls.
Ministry of Local Government and Chieftainship: POB 666, Maseru 100; tel. 22325331; fax 22311124; e-mail lesedi_ntho@hotmail.com; internet www.localgovt.gov.ls.
Ministry of Natural Resources: POB 772, Maseru 100; tel. 22323163; fax 22310520.
Ministry of Public Service: POB 527, Maseru 100; tel. 22311000; e-mail m.leteketa@mps.gov.ls; internet www.publicservice.gov.ls.
Ministry of Public Works and Transport: POB 20, Maseru 100; tel. 22311362; fax 22310125; e-mail cio@mopwt.gov.ls.
Ministry of Tourism, Environment and Culture: POB 52, Maseru 100; tel. 22313034; fax 22310194; e-mail pmasita.mohale@mtec.gov.ls; internet www.mtec.gov.ls.
Ministry of Trade, Industry, Co-operatives and Marketing: POB 747, Maseru 100; tel. 22312938; fax 22310644; e-mail nkaotal@mticm.gov.ls.

Legislature

PARLIAMENT

National Assembly

POB 190, Maseru; tel. 22323035; fax 22310023; internet www.parliament.ls/TheNationalAssembly/About.aspx.

Speaker: NTLHOI MOTSAMAI.

General Election, 17 February 2007

Party	Constituency seats	Compensatory seats*	Total seats
Lesotho Congress for Democracy	61	—	61
National Independent Party	—	21	21
All Basotho Convention	17	—	17
Lesotho Workers' Party	—	10	10
Basotho National Party	—	3	3
Alliance of Congress Parties	1	1	2
Basotho Batho Democratic Party	—	1	1
Basotho Congress Party	—	1	1
Basotho Democratic National Party	—	1	1
Maremathou Freedom Party	—	1	1
Popular Front for Democracy	—	1	1
Total	**79†**	**40**	**119†**

* Allocated by proportional representation.
† Voting in Makhaleng constituency was postponed, owing to the death of a candidate. The Lesotho Congress for Democracy secured the seat at a by-election held on 30 June 2007.

Senate

POB 553, Maseru 100; tel. 22315338; fax 22310023; internet www.parliament.ls/Senate/AboutSenate.aspx.

Speaker: Chief SEMPE LEJAHA.

The Senate is an advisory chamber, comprising 22 traditional chiefs and 11 members appointed by the monarch.

Election Commission

Independent Electoral Commission (IEC): Moposo House, 7th Floor, POB 12698, Kingsway 100, Maseru; tel. 22314991; fax 22310398; internet www.iec.org.ls; f. 1997 as successor to the Constituency Delimitation Commission; Chair. (vacant).

Political Organizations

All Basotho Convention (ABC): Maseru; f. 2006 by fmr mems of the Lesotho Congress for Democracy; Pres. MOTSOAHAE TOM THABANE.

Basotho Batho Democratic Party: f. 2006.

Basotho Congress Party (BCP): POB 111, Maseru 100; tel. 8737076; f. 1952; Leader NTSUKUNYANE MPHANYA.

Basotho Democratic Alliance (BDA): Maseru; f. 1984; Pres. S. C. NKOJANE.

Basotho Democratic National Party: internet bdnp.blogspot.com; f. 2006; Leader THABANG NYEOE.

Basotho National Party (BNP): POB 124, Maseru 100; f. 1958; Leader Maj.-Gen. JUSTIN METSING LEKHANYA; Sec.-Gen. RANTHOMENG MATETE; 280,000 mems.

Basutoland African Congress (BAC): Maseru; f. 2002 following split in the BCP; Leader Dr KHAUHELO RADITAPOLE; Sec.-Gen. MAHOLELA MANDORO.

Khokanyana-Phiri Democratic Alliance: Maseru; f. 1999; alliance of opposition parties comprising:

Christian Democratic Party: Maseru.

Communist Party of Lesotho (CPL): Maseru; f. 1962; banned 1970–91; supported mainly by migrant workers employed in South Africa; Sec.-Gen. MOKHAFISI KENA.

Kopanang Basotho Party (KBP): Maseru; f. 1992; campaigns for women's rights; Leader LIMAKATSO NTAKATSANE.

National Independent Party (NIP): Maseru; f. 1984; Pres. ANTHONY CLOVIS MANYELI.

National Progressive Party (NPP): Maseru; f. 1995 following split in the BNP; Leader Chief PEETE NKOEBE PEETE.

Popular Front for Democracy (PFD): Maseru; f. 1991; left-wing; Leader LEKHETHO RAKUOANE.

Social Democratic Party: Maseru; Leader MASITISE SELESO.

Lesotho Congress for Democracy (LCD): POB 7, Mohole's Hoek; tel. 785207; f. 1997 as a result of divisions within the BCP; Leader BETHUEL PAKALITHA MOSISILI; Chair. MOEKETSI MOLETSANE; Sec.-Gen. MPHO MALIE; 200,000 mems.

Lesotho Labour Party (LLP): Maseru; f. 1991; Leader MUTHUTHULEZI TYHALI.

Lesotho People's Congress (LPC): f. 2001 following split in the LCD; Leader KELEBONE ALBERT MAOPE; Sec.-Gen. SHAKHANE MOKHEHLE.

Lesotho Workers' Party (LWP): Maseru; f. 2001; Leader MACAEFA BILLY.

Marematlou Freedom Party (MFP): POB 0443, Maseru 105; tel. 315804; f. 1962 following merger between the Marema Tlou Party and Basutoland Freedom Party; Leader (vacant); Dep. Leader THABO LEANYA; 300,000 mems.

Sefate Democratic Union (SDU): Maseru; Leader BOFIHLA NKUEBE.

United Democratic Party (UDP): POB 776, Maseru 100; f. 1967; Chair. BEN L. SHEA; Leader CHARLES DABENDE MOFELI; Sec.-Gen. MOLOMO NKUEBE; 26,000 mems.

United Party (UP): Maseru; Pres. MAKARA SEKAUTU.

Diplomatic Representation

EMBASSIES AND HIGH COMMISSIONS IN LESOTHO

China, People's Republic: POB 380, Maseru 100; tel. 22316521; fax 22310489; e-mail chinaemb_ls@mfa.gov.cn; internet ls.china-embassy.org; Ambassador GAO DEYI.

Ireland: Tona-Kholo Rd, Private Bag A67, Maseru; tel. 22314068; fax 22310028; e-mail maseruembassy@dfa.ie; internet www.embassyofireland.org.ls; Ambassador PADDY FAY.

Libya: 173 Tona-Kholo Rd, Maseru West, POB 432, Maseru 100; tel. 22320148; fax 22327750; Ambassador Dr YOUSEF ALGOWIZY.

South Africa: Lesotho Bank Tower, 10th Floor, Kingsway, Private Bag A266, Maseru 100; tel. 22315758; fax 22325228; e-mail sahcmas@lesoff.co.ls; High Commissioner HAPPY MAHLANGU.

USA: 254 Kingsway, POB 333, Maseru 100; tel. 22312666; fax 22310116; e-mail infomaseru@state.gov; internet maseru.usembassy.gov; Ambassador ROBERT NOLAN.

Judicial System

HIGH COURT

The High Court is a superior court of record, and in addition to any other jurisdiction conferred by statute it is vested with unlimited original jurisdiction to determine any civil or criminal matter. It also has appellate jurisdiction to hear appeals and reviews from the subordinate courts. Appeals may be made to the Court of Appeal.

POB 90, Maseru; tel. 22312188; internet www.justice.gov.ls/judiciary/high_court.html.

Chief Justice: KELELLO GUNI (acting).

Judges: T. NOMNGCONGO, W. C. M. MAQUTU, T. E. MONAPATHI, K. MAFOSO-GUNI, G. MOFOLO, S. PEETE, M. HLAJOANE, N. MAJARA.

COURT OF APPEAL

POB 90, Maseru; tel. 22312188; internet www.justice.gov.ls/judiciary/appeal.html.

President: MATHEALIRA RAMODIBEDI.

Judges: M. E. KUMBLEBEN, H. GROSSKOPF, C. PLEWMAN, J. J. GAUNTLETT, L. S. MELUNSKY (acting).

SUBORDINATE COURTS

Each of the 10 districts possesses subordinate courts, presided over by magistrates.

Chief Magistrate: MOLEFI MAKARA.

JUDICIAL COMMISSIONERS' COURTS

These courts hear civil and criminal appeals from central and local courts. Further appeal may be made to the High Court and finally to the Court of Appeal.

CENTRAL AND LOCAL COURTS

There are 71 such courts, of which 58 are local courts and 13 are central courts which also serve as courts of appeal from the local courts. They have limited civil and criminal jurisdiction.

Religion

About 90% of the population profess Christianity.

CHRISTIANITY

African Federal Church Council (AFCC): POB 70, Peka 340; f. 1927; co-ordinating org. for 48 African independent churches.

Christian Council of Lesotho (CCL): POB 547, Maseru 100; tel. 22313639; fax 22310310; f. 1833; 112 congregations; 261,350 mems (2003); Chair. Rev. M. MOKHOSI; Sec. CATHERINE RAMOKHELE.

The Anglican Communion

Anglicans in Lesotho are adherents of the Anglican Church of Southern Africa (formerly the Church of the Province of Southern Africa). The Metropolitan of the Province is the Archbishop of Cape Town, South Africa. Lesotho forms a single diocese, with an estimated 200,000 members.

Bishop of Lesotho: (vacant), Bishop's House, POB 87, Maseru 100; tel. 22311974; fax 22310161; e-mail diocese@ilesotho.com.

The Roman Catholic Church

Lesotho comprises one archdiocese and three dioceses. At 31 December 2006 there were some 1,115,830 adherents of the Roman Catholic Church, equivalent to an estimated 48.7% of the total population.

Lesotho Catholic Bishops' Conference

Catholic Secretariat, POB 200, Maseru 100; tel. 22312525; fax 22310294.

f. 1972; Pres. Rt Rev. EVARISTUS THATHO BITSOANE (Bishop of Qacha's Nek).

Archbishop of Maseru: Most Rev. BERNARD MOHLALISI, Archbishop's House, 19 Orpen Rd, POB 267, Maseru 100; tel. 22312565; fax 22310425; e-mail archmase@lesoff.co.za.

LESOTHO — Directory

Other Christian Churches

At mid-2000 there were an estimated 279,000 Protestants and 257,000 adherents professing other forms of Christianity.

African Methodist Episcopal Church: POB 223, Maseru 100; tel. 22311801; fax 22310548; e-mail bishopsarah@leo.co.ls; f. 1903; Presiding Prelate Rt Rev. SARAH F. DAVIS; 15,000 mems.

Lesotho Evangelical Church: POB 260, Maseru 100; tel. 22323942; f. 1833; independent since 1964; Pres. Rev. JOHN RAPELANG MOKHAHLANE; Exec. Sec. Rev. A. M. THEBE; 230,000 mems (2003).

Other denominations active in Lesotho include the Apostolic Faith Mission, the Assemblies of God, the Dutch Reformed Church in Africa, the Full Gospel Church of God, Methodist Church of Southern Africa and the Seventh-day Adventists. There are also numerous African independent churches.

BAHÁ'Í FAITH

National Spiritual Assembly: POB 508, Maseru 100; tel. 22312346; fax 22310092; e-mail bahailesotho@leo.co.ls; mems resident in 444 localities.

The Press

Lesotho does not have a daily newspaper.

Leseli ka Sepolesa (The Police Witness): Press Dept, Police Headquarters, Maseru CBD, POB 13, Maseru 100; tel. 22317262; fax 22310045; fortnightly; Sesotho; publ. by the Lesotho Mounted Police Services; Editor-in-Chief CLIFFORD MOLEFE.

Leselinyana la Lesotho (Light of Lesotho): Morija Printing Works, POB 7, Morija 190; tel. 22360244; fax 22360005; e-mail mpw@lesoff.co.ls; f. 1863; fortnightly; Sesotho, with occasional articles in English; publ. by the Lesotho Evangelical Church; Editor SELBORNE MOTLATSI MOHLALISI; circ. 10,000.

Lesotho Times: Maseru; internet www.lestimes.com.

Lesotho Today/Lentsoe la Basotho (Voice of the Lesotho Nation): POB 353, Maseru 100; tel. 22323561; fax 22322764; internet www.lesothotoday.co.ls; f. 1974; weekly; Sesotho; publ. by Ministry of Communications, Science and Technology; Editor KAHLISO LESENYANE; circ. 14,000.

Makatolle: POB 111, Maseru 100; tel. 22850990; f. 1963; weekly; Sesotho; Editor M. RAMANGOEI; circ. 2,000.

MoAfrika: MoAfrika Broadcasting and Publishing Services, Carlton Centre Bldg, 1st Floor, POB 7234, Maseru 100; tel. 22321854; fax 22321956; f. 1990 as *The African*; weekly; Sesotho and English; Editor-in-Chief Prof. SEBONONOLA R. K. RAMAINOANE; circ. 5,000.

Moeletsi oa Basotho: Mazenod Institute, POB 18, Mazenod 160; tel. 22350465; fax 22350010; e-mail mzpwrks@lesoff.co.ls; f. 1933; weekly; Sesotho; publ. by the Roman Catholic Church; Editor FRANCIS KHOARIPE; circ. 20,000.

Mohahlaula: Allied Bldg, 1st Floor, Manonyane Centre, POB 14430, Maseru 100; tel. 22312777; fax 22320941; weekly; Sesotho; publ. by Makaung Printers and Publrs; Editor WILLY MOLLUNGOA.

Mololi: Cooperatives Bldg, Main North 1 Rd, POB 9933, Maseru 100; tel. 22312287; fax 22327912; f. 1997; Sesotho; organ of the Lesotho Congress for Democracy; Editor (vacant).

Mopheme (The Survivor): Allied Bldg, 1st Floor, Manonyane Centre, POB 14184, Maseru; tel. and fax 22311670; e-mail mopheme@lesoff.co.za; weekly; English and Sesotho; publ. by Newsshare Foundation; Owner and Editor LAWRENCE KEKETSO; circ. 2,500.

Public Eye/Mosotho: House No. 14A3, Princess Margaret Rd, POB 14129, Old Europa, Maseru 100; tel. 22321414; fax 22310614; e-mail editor@publiceye.co.ls; internet www.publiceye.co.ls; f. 1997; weekly; 80% English, 20% Sesotho; publ. by Voice Multimedia; also publ. *Eye on Tourism* and *Family Mirror* magazines; Editor-in-Chief BETHUEL THAI; circ. 20,000 (Lesotho and South Africa).

Southern Star: POB 7590, Maseru; tel. 22312269; fax 22310167; e-mail ba-holdings@ilesotho.com; weekly; English; Editor FRANK BOFFOE; circ. 1,500.

PERIODICALS

Justice and Peace: Catholic Bishops' Conference, Our Lady of Victories Cathedral Catholic Centre, POB 200, Maseru 100; tel. 22312750; fax 22312751; quarterly; publ. by the Roman Catholic Church.

Moqolotsi (The Journalist): House No. 1B, Happy Villa, POB 14139, Maseru 100; tel. and fax 22320941; e-mail medinles@lesoff.co.za; monthly newsletter; English; publ. by the Media Institute of Lesotho (MILES).

NGO Web: 544 Hoohlo Extension, Florida, Maseru 100; tel. 22325798; fax 22317205; e-mail lecongo@lecongo.org.ls; quarterly; English and Sesotho; publ. of the Lesotho Council of NGOs; circ. 2,000.

Review of Southern African Studies: Institute of Southern African Studies, National University of Lesotho, PO Roma 180; tel. 22340247; fax 22340601; 2 a year; arts, social and behavioural sciences; Editor TANKIE KHALANYANE.

Shoeshoe: POB 36, Maseru 100; tel. 22323561; fax 22310003; quarterly; women's interest; publ. by Ministry of Communications, Science and Technology.

Other publications include *Mara LDF Airwing/Airsquadron* and *The Sun/Thebe*.

NEWS AGENCY

Lesotho News Agency (LENA): Lesotho News Agency Complex, Lerotholi St, opp. Royal Palace, POB 36, Maseru 100; tel. 22325317; fax 22324608; e-mail l_lenanews@hotmail.com; internet www.lena.gov.ls; f. 1985; Dir NKOE THAKALI; Editor VIOLET MARAISANE.

Publishers

Longman Lesotho (Pty) Ltd: 104 Christie House, 1st Floor, Orpen Rd, Old Europa, POB 1174, Maseru 100; tel. 22314254; fax 22310118; e-mail connie.burford@pearsoned.com; Man. Dir SEYMOUR R. KIKINE.

Macmillan Boleswa Publishers Lesotho (Pty) Ltd: 523 Sun Cabanas Hotel, POB 7545, Maseru 100; tel. 22317340; fax 22310047; e-mail macmillan@lesoff.co.ls; Man. Dir PAUL MOROLONG.

Mazenod Institute: POB 39, Mazenod 160; tel. 22350224; f. 1933; Roman Catholic; Man. Fr B. MOHLALISI.

Morija Sesuto Book Depot: POB 4, Morija 190; tel. and fax 22360204; f. 1862; owned by the Lesotho Evangelical Church; religious, educational and Sesotho language and literature.

St Michael's Mission: The Social Centre, POB 25, Roma; tel. 22316234; f. 1968; religious and educational; Man. Dir Fr M. FERRANGE.

GOVERNMENT PUBLISHING HOUSE

Government Printer: POB 268, Maseru; tel. 22313023.

Broadcasting and Communications

TELECOMMUNICATIONS

Lesotho Telecommunications Authority (LTA): Moposo House, 6th Floor, Kingsway Rd, POB 15896, Maseru 100; tel. 22224300; fax 22310984; e-mail lta@lta.org.ls; internet www.lta.org.ls; f. 2000; regulates telecommunications and broadcasting; Chief Exec. MONEHELA POSHOLI.

Telecom Lesotho: POB 1037, Maseru 100; tel. 22211000; fax 22310600; e-mail enquiries@telecom.co.ls; internet www.telecom.co.ls; 70% holding acquired by the Econet Wireless Group in 2007; 30% state-owned; Chair. PAKO PETLANE; CEO ANTHONY CARTER.

Vodacom Lesotho (Pty) Ltd: Block B, Development House, Kingsway Rd, POB 7387, Maseru 100; tel. 52212201; fax 22311079; internet www.vodacom.co.ls; f. 1996; jt venture between Telecom Lesotho and Vodacom (Pty) Ltd; fmrly VCL Communications; mobile cellular telecommunications provider; CEO PIETER UYS.

BROADCASTING

RADIO

The first licences for private radio stations were issued in 1998. Licences are issued by the Lesotho Telecommunications Authority. Radio Lesotho is the only station to broadcast nationwide; all the other stations are restricted to urban areas and their peripheries.

Catholic Radio FM: Our Lady of Victories Cathedral, Catholic Centre POB 200, Maseru 100; tel. 22323247; fax 22310294; f. 1999.

Joy FM: Lesotho Sun Hotel, Suites 2204–2206, Private Bag A457, Maseru 100; tel. 22310920; fax 22310104; internet www.joyfm.co.ls; f. 2001; Sesotho and English; relays Voice of America broadcasts.

Khotso FM: Institute of Extramural Studies, National University of Lesotho POB 180, Roma; Private Bag A47, Maseru 100; tel. 22322038; fax 22340000; community radio station; sister station of DOPE FM (f. 2004).

MoAfrika FM: Carlton Centre, 2nd Floor, Kingsway, POB 7234, Maseru 100; tel. and fax 22321956; e-mail info@moafrika.co.ls; internet www.moafrika.co.ls; affiliated to the *MoAfrika* newspaper; Sesotho, Xhosa and Mandarin; news and entertainment; Man. and Editor-in-Chief Prof. SEBONONOLA R. K. RAMAINOANE.

LESOTHO

People's Choice Radio (PCFM): LNDC Centre, Development House, Level 9, Block D, POB 8800, Maseru 100; tel. 22322122; fax 22310888; internet www.pcfm.co.ls; f. 1998; news and entertainment; Man. Dir MOTLATSI MAJARA.

Radio Lesotho: Lesotho News Agency Complex, Lerotholi St, opp. Royal Palace, POB 552, Maseru 100; tel. and fax 22323371; e-mail enquiries@africanextension.com; internet www.radiolesotho.co.ls; f. 1964; state-owned; part of Lesotho Nat. Broadcasting Services; Sesotho and English; Dir of Broadcasting LEBOHANG DADA MOQASA.

TELEVISION

Lesotho Television (LTV): Lesotho News Agency Complex, Lerotholi St, opp. Royal Palace, POB 36, Maseru 100; tel. 22324735; fax 22310149; e-mail mfalatsa@yahoo.com; f. 1988 in association with M-Net, South Africa; state-owned; part of Lesotho Nat. Broadcasting Services; Sesotho and English.

Finance

(cap. = capital; res = reserves; dep. = deposits; m. = million; brs = branches; amounts in maloti)

BANKING

Central Bank

Central Bank of Lesotho: cnr Airport and Moshoeshoe Rds, POB 1184, Maseru 100; tel. 22314281; fax 22310051; e-mail cbl@centralbank.org.ls; internet www.centralbank.org.ls; f. 1978 as the Lesotho Monetary Authority; present name adopted in 1982; bank of issue; cap. 25.0m., res 1,294.4m., dep. 2,585.1m. (Dec. 2006); Gov. and Chair. Dr M. SENAOANA.

Commercial Banks

Nedbank (Lesotho) Ltd: Nedbank Building, 361 Kingsway, POB 1001, Maseru 100; tel. 22312696; fax 22310025; e-mail georgego@nedcor.co.za; f. 1997; fmrly Standard Chartered Bank Lesotho Ltd; 100% owned by Nedbank Ltd (South Africa); cap. 20m., res 33.0m., dep. 1,319.5m. (Dec. 2006); Chair. SOPHIA MOHAPI; Man. Dir KEVIN REID; 3 brs and 7 agencies.

Standard Lesotho Bank: Banking Bldg, 1st Floor, Kingsway Rd, Kingsway Town Centre, POB 1053, Maseru 100; tel. 22315737; fax 22317321; internet www.standardbank.co.ls; f. 2006 following merger between Lesotho Bank (1999) Ltd (f. 1972) and Standard Bank Lesotho Ltd (fmrly Stanbic Bank Lesotho Ltd); Chair. THABO MAKEBA; Man. Dir COLIN ADDIS; 11 brs.

INSURANCE

Alliance Insurance Co Ltd: Alliance House, 4 Bowker Rd, POB 01118, Maseru West 105; tel. 22312357; fax 22310313; e-mail alliance@alliance.co.ls; internet www.alliance.co.ls; f. 1993; life and short-term insurance; Man. Dir JOHANN PIENAAR; Gen. Mans MOK'HAPHEK'HA LAZARO, THABISO MADIBA.

Customer Protection Insurance Co Ltd: POB 201, Maseru 100; tel. 22312643; e-mail craigb@relyant.co.za; wholly owned subsidiary of Ellerine Holdings Ltd, South Africa; general short-term insurance; Chair. DENZIL MCGLASHAN.

Lesotho National General Insurance Co Ltd (LNIG): Lesotho Insurance House, Kingsway, Private Bag A65, Maseru 100; tel. 22313031; fax 22310007; e-mail manager@lngic.com; f. 1977 as Lesotho National Insurance Group; 60% owned by Regent Insurance Co Ltd (South Africa), 20% state-owned, 20% owned by Molepe Investment Holdings (Pty) Ltd; part-privatized in 1995; incorporating subsidiaries specializing in life and short-term insurance; Chair. Dr TIMOTHY THAHANE; Man. Dir R. J. LETSOELA.

Metropolitan Lesotho Ltd: Metropolitan Bldg, Kingsway St, POB 645, Maseru; tel. 22222300; fax 22317278; internet www.metropolitan.co.ls; f. 2003; subsidiary of Metropolitan Holdings Ltd, South Africa; Man. Dir NKAU MATETE.

Trade and Industry

GOVERNMENT AGENCIES

Privatisation Unit: Privatisation Project, Lesotho Utilities Sector Reform Project, Ministry of Finance and Development Planning, Lesotho Bank Mortgage Division Bldg, 2nd Floor, Kingsway St, Private Bag A249, Maseru 100; tel. 22317902; fax 22317551; e-mail mntsasa@privatisation.gov.ls; internet www.privatisation.gov.ls; CEO MOSITO KHETHISA.

Trade Promotion Unit: c/o Ministry of Trade, Industry, Co-operatives and Marketing, POB 747, Maseru 100; tel. 322138; fax 310121; e-mail tradepu@lesoff.co.za.

DEVELOPMENT ORGANIZATIONS

Basotho Enterprises Development Corpn (BEDCO): POB 1216, Maseru 100; tel. 22312094; fax 22310455; e-mail admin@bedco.org.ls; internet www.bedco.org.ls; f. 1980; promotes and assists in the establishment and devt of Basotho-owned enterprises, with emphasis on small- and medium-scale; Chair. MOHLOMI D. RANTEKOA.

Lesotho Council of Non-Governmental Organizations: House 544, Hoohlo Extension, Private Bag A445, Maseru 100; tel. 22317205; fax 22310412; e-mail lecongo@lecongo.org.ls; internet www.lecongo.org.ls; f. 1990; promotes sustainable management of natural resources, socio-economic devt and social justice; Exec. Dir SEABATA MOTSAMAI.

Lesotho Highlands Development Authority (LHDA): Lesotho Bank Tower, 3rd Floor, Kingsway, POB 7332, Maseru 100; tel. 22311280; fax 22310665; e-mail lhwp@lhda.org.ls; internet www.lhda.org.ls; f. 1986 to implement the Lesotho Highlands Water Project, being undertaken jtly with South Africa; Chair. TEBOHO NKHAHLE; CEO MASILO PHAKOE (acting).

Lesotho National Development Corpn (LNDC): Development House, Block A, Kingsway, Private Bag A96, Maseru 100; tel. 22312012; fax 22310038; e-mail info@lndc.org.ls; internet www.lndc.org.ls; f. 1967; state-owned; total assets M477.5m. (March 2006); interests in manufacturing, mining, food-processing and leisure; Chair. MOHLOMI RANTEKOA; CEO PEETE MOLAPO.

Lesotho Co-operative Handicrafts: Basotho Hat Bldg, Kingsway, PO Box 148, Maseru; tel. 22322523; e-mail lch@ilesotho.com; internet www.basothohat.co.ls; f. 1978; marketing and distribution of handicrafts; Gen. Man. KHOTSO MATLA.

CHAMBER OF COMMERCE

Lesotho Chamber of Commerce and Industry: Kingsway Ave, POB 79, Maseru 100; tel. 22316937; fax 22322794; Pres. SIMON PHAFANE.

INDUSTRIAL AND TRADE ASSOCIATIONS

Livestock Marketing Corpn: POB 800, Maseru 100; tel. 22322444; f. 1973; sole org. for marketing livestock and livestock products; liaises with marketing boards in South Africa; projects incl. an abattoir, tannery, poultry and wool and mohair scouring plants; Gen. Man. S. R. MATLANYANE.

EMPLOYERS' ORGANIZATION

Association of Lesotho Employers: 18 Bowker Rd, POB 1509, Maseru 100; tel. 22315736; fax 22325384; e-mail makeka@leo.co.ls; f. 1961; represents mems in industrial relations and on govt bodies, and advises the Govt on employers' concerns; Pres. R. LETSOELA; Exec. Dir THABO MAKEKA.

UTILITIES

Lesotho Electricity Authority (LEA): Moposo House, 6th Floor, Kingsway, Private Bag A315, Maseru; tel. 22312479; fax 22315094; e-mail secretary@lea.org.ls; internet www.lea.org.ls; f. 2004; Chief Exec. BATALATSANG KANETSI.

Lesotho Electricity Corpn (LEC): 53 Moshoeshoe Rd, POB 423, Maseru 100; tel. 22312236; fax 22310093; e-mail info@lec.co.ls; internet www.lec.co.ls; f. 1969; 100% state-owned; Man. Dir F. M. HLOAELE.

Lesotho Water and Sewerage Authority (WASA): POB 426, Maseru 100; tel. 22312449; fax 22312006; internet www.wasa.co.ls; Chair. REFILOE TLALI.

TRADE UNIONS

Congress of Lesotho Trade Unions (COLETU): POB 13282, Maseru 100; tel. 22320958; fax 22310081; f. 1998; Sec.-Gen. JUSTICE TSÍUKULU; 15,587 mems.

Construction and Allied Workers' Union of Lesotho (CAWULE): Manonyana Centre, 2nd Floor, Room 24, POB 132282, Maseru 100; tel. 63023484; fax 22321951; f. 1967; affiliated to the Building and Wood Workers Int.; Pres. L. PUTSOANE; Sec. T. TLALE.

Factory Workers' Union (FAWU): Maseru; f. 2003 following split from the Lesotho Clothing and Allied Workers' Union; Pres. KHABILE TSILO; Sec.-Gen. BILLY MACAEFA.

Lesotho Association of Teachers (LAT): POB 12528, Maseru 100; tel. and fax 22317463; affiliated to the Education Int.; Exec. Sec. PAUL P. SEMATLANE.

Lesotho Clothing and Allied Workers' Union (LECAWU): LNDC Centre, 2nd Floor, Rm 12–14, Kingsway Rd, POB 11767, Maseru 100; tel. 22324296; fax 22320958; e-mail lecawu@lesoff.co.ls;

LESOTHO

affiliated to the Int. Textile, Garment and Leather Workers' Fed.; Sec.-Gen. DANIEL MARAISANE; 6,000 mems.

Lesotho General Workers' Union: POB 322, Maseru 100; f. 1954; Chair. J. M. RAMAROTHOLE; Sec. T. MOTLOHI.

Lesotho Congress of Democratic Unions (LECODU): POB 15851, Maseru 100; tel. and fax 22323559; f. 2004; Sec.-Gen. E. T. RAMOCHELA; 15,279 mems (2005).

Lesotho Teachers' Trade Union (LTTU): POB 0509, Maseru West 105; tel. 22322774; fax 22311673; e-mail lttu@leo.co.ls; affiliated to the Education Int.; Gen. Sec. MALIMABE JOAKIM MOTOPELA.

Lesotho Transport and Allied Workers' Union: Maseru 100; f. 1959; Pres. M. BERENG; Gen. Sec. TSEKO KAPA.

Lesotho University Teachers' and Researchers' Union (LUTARU): Maseru; Pres. Dr FRANCIS MAKOA.

Transport

RAILWAYS

Lesotho is linked with the South African railway system by a short line (2.6 km in length) from Maseru to Marseilles, on the Bloemfontein–Natal main line.

ROADS

In 2000 Lesotho's road network totalled 5,940 km, of which 1,084 km were main roads and 1,950 km were secondary roads. About 18.3% of roads were paved. In 1996 the International Development Association granted US $40m. towards the Government's rolling five-year road programme. From 1996/97 an extra-budgetary Road Fund was to finance road maintenance. In March 2000 a major road network was opened, linking Maseru with the Mohale Dam.

CIVIL AVIATION

King Moshoeshoe I International Airport is at Thota-Moli, some 20 km from Maseru; in January 2002 the Government announced plans for its expansion. International services between Maseru and Johannesburg are operated by South African Airlink. The national airline company, Lesotho Airways, was sold to a South African company in 1997 as part of the Government's ongoing privatization programme; however, after two years of losses the company was liquidated in 1999.

Tourism

Spectacular mountain scenery is the principal tourist attraction, and a new ski resort was opened in 2003. Tourist arrivals totalled 356,913 in 2006. In that year receipts from tourism amounted to an estimated US $28m.

Lesotho Tourism Development Corpn (LTDC): cnr Linare and Parliament Rds, POB 1378, Maseru 100; tel. 22312238; fax 22310189; e-mail ltdc@ltdc.org.ls; internet www.ltdc.org.ls; f. 2000; successor to the Lesotho Tourist Board; Chair. MAMORUTI MALIE.

LIBERIA

Introductory Survey

Location, Climate, Language, Religion, Flag, Capital

The Republic of Liberia lies on the west coast of Africa, with Sierra Leone and Guinea to the north, and Côte d'Ivoire to the east. The climate is tropical, with temperatures ranging from 18°C (65°F) to 49°C (120°F). English is the official language but the 16 major ethnic groups speak their own languages and dialects. Liberia is officially a Christian state, although some Liberians hold traditional beliefs. There are about 670,000 Muslims. The national flag (proportions 10 by 19) has 11 horizontal stripes, alternately of red and white, with a dark blue square canton, containing a five-pointed white star, in the upper hoist. The capital is Monrovia.

Recent History

Founded by liberated black slaves from the southern USA, Liberia became an independent republic in 1847. The leader of the True Whig Party (TWP), William Tubman, who had been President of Liberia since 1944, died in July 1971 and was succeeded by his Vice-President, William R. Tolbert, who was re-elected in October 1975.

In April 1980 Tolbert was assassinated in a military coup, led by Master Sgt (later Commander-in-Chief) Samuel Doe, who assumed power as Chairman of the newly established People's Redemption Council (PRC), suspending the Constitution and proscribing all political parties. The new regime attracted international criticism for its summary execution of 13 former senior government officials who had been accused of corruption and mismanagement. In July 1981 all civilian ministers received commissions, thus installing total military rule.

A draft Constitution was approved by 78.3% of registered voters in a national referendum in July 1984. In the same month Doe dissolved the PRC and appointed a 58-member Interim National Assembly. The ban on political organizations was repealed in the same month, to enable parties to secure registration prior to presidential and legislative elections, which were due to take place in October 1985. In August 1984 Doe established the National Democratic Party of Liberia (NDPL) and formally announced his candidacy for the presidency. By early 1985 a total of 11 political associations had been formed; however, two influential parties, the Liberian People's Party (LPP) and the United People's Party (UPP), were proscribed, and apart from the NDPL only three parties—the Liberian Action Party (LAP), the Liberia Unification Party (LUP) and the Unity Party (UP)—were eventually permitted to participate in the elections. Doe won the presidential election, receiving 50.9% of the votes. At the concurrent elections to the bicameral National Assembly, the NDPL won 22 of the 26 seats in the Senate and 51 of the 64 seats in the House of Representatives. On 6 January 1986 Doe was inaugurated as President. He appointed a new Cabinet (which largely comprised members of the previous administration).

In December 1989 an armed insurrection by rebel forces began in the north-eastern border region of Nimba County. In early 1990 several hundred deaths ensued in fighting between the Liberian army (the Armed Forces of Liberia—AFL) and the rebels, who claimed to be members of a hitherto unknown opposition group, the National Patriotic Front of Liberia (NPFL), led by a former government official, Charles Taylor. The fighting swiftly degenerated into a war between Doe's ethnic group, the Krahn, and the local Gio and Mano tribes, and many thousands of people took refuge in neighbouring Guinea and Côte d'Ivoire. Taylor's authority as self-proclaimed President of his own interim administration, known as the National Patriotic Reconstruction Assembly, was challenged by a faction of the NPFL, led by Prince Yormie Johnson, which rapidly secured control of parts of Monrovia in July. In the subsequent conflict both government and rebel forces were responsible for numerous atrocities against civilians. The Economic Community of West African States (ECOWAS, see p. 243) repeatedly failed to negotiate a cease-fire, and in late August it dispatched a military force to restore peace in the region. Doe and Johnson accepted this Monitoring Group (ECOMOG, see p. 246), but its initial occupation of the port area of Monrovia encountered armed opposition by Taylor's forces.

On 30 August 1990 exiled representatives of Liberia's principal political parties and other influential groups met at a conference convened by ECOWAS in the Gambian capital, Banjul, where they elected Dr Amos Sawyer, the leader of the LPP, as President of an Interim Government of National Unity (IGNU). Doe was taken prisoner by Johnson's rebel Independent National Patriotic Front of Liberia (INPFL) on 9 September, and was killed on the following day. In early October, following Taylor's rejection of a proposed peace settlement, ECOMOG began an offensive aimed at establishing a neutral zone in Monrovia separating the three warring factions. By mid-October ECOMOG had gained control of central Monrovia. On 22 November Sawyer was inaugurated as Interim President, under the auspices of ECOWAS, in Monrovia. By January 1991 all rebel forces had withdrawn from Monrovia, and in that month Sawyer nominated ministers to the IGNU. Legislative power was vested in a 28-member Interim National Assembly, which represented the principal political factions, including the INPFL; however, the NPFL refused to participate. On 19 April a national conference re-elected Sawyer as Interim President and appointed a member of the INPFL, Peter Naigow (a former minister in Doe's administration), as Vice-President. In June Sawyer nominated a new Council of Ministers, which was subsequently approved by the Interim National Assembly. In August, however, the INPFL representatives, including Naigow, resigned from the IGNU, after Sawyer denounced the execution, apparently at Johnson's instigation, of four members of the INPFL who had reportedly complied with arrangements to relinquish weapons to ECOMOG.

In April 1991, after members of the NPFL perpetrated several incursions into Sierra Leone, Sierra Leonean forces entered Liberian territory and launched retaliatory attacks, while the NPFL reportedly advanced within Sierra Leone. It was claimed that NPFL forces were supporting a Sierra Leonean resistance movement, the Revolutionary United Front (RUF), in hostilities against government forces of that country (see the chapter on Sierra Leone). In September members of a newly emerged rebel movement, comprising former supporters of Doe, the United Liberation Movement of Liberia for Democracy (ULIMO), began attacks from Sierra Leone against NPFL forces in north-western Liberia.

At the end of October 1991 a summit meeting between Sawyer and Taylor, which took place in Yamoussoukro, Côte d'Ivoire, resulted in a peace agreement whereby the troops of all warring factions were to be disarmed and restricted to camps, while the NPFL was to relinquish the territory under its control to ECOMOG. It was also agreed that all Liberian forces would be withdrawn from Sierra Leone, and that a demilitarized zone, under the control of ECOMOG, would be created along Liberia's border with Sierra Leone. In January 1992 the Interim Election Commission and Supreme Court were established, in accordance with the peace accord. At the end of April, in response to pressure from within the NPFL, Taylor agreed to withdraw NPFL troops from the border with Sierra Leone. In May ECOMOG began to disarm the rebel factions and to deploy troops in NPFL-controlled territory, and, despite continued fighting between ULIMO and NPFL forces, established a demilitarized zone along the border with Sierra Leone.

In August 1992 ULIMO launched a renewed offensive in western Liberia, gaining control of Bomi and Grand Cape Mount Counties. In October the NPFL claimed that Nigerian aircraft under ECOMOG command had bombed its bases at Kakata and Harbel (the site of the Robertsfield International Airport and the country's principal rubber plantation), and at Buchanan, following an NPFL attack on ECOMOG forces stationed near Monrovia. The NPFL subsequently seized a number of strategic areas on the outskirts of Monrovia. ECOMOG forces (who were supported by members of the AFL and militia loyal to the IGNU) began retaliatory attacks against NPFL positions around the capital. In late October ECOMOG units succeeded in capturing the INPFL base at Caldwell, near Monrovia, and forcing Johnson to surrender. (The INPFL was subsequently disbanded.) In November the UN Security Council adopted a resolution imposing a mandatory embargo on the supply of armaments to Liberia, and authorized the UN Secretary-General to send a special representative to the country. In December ECOMOG announced that it had regained control of the area surrounding Monrovia, and in early 1993 began to advance in south-eastern Liberia, recapturing Harbel, while ULIMO was reported to have gained control of Lofa County in the west. In March ULIMO accepted an invitation from Sawyer to join the IGNU; ULIMO forces in Monrovia were subsequently disarmed. Following a major offensive, ECOMOG announced in April that it had gained control of Buchanan (which was reopened to shipping later that year).

In July 1993 a conference, attended by the factions involved in the hostilities, was convened (under the auspices of the UN and ECOWAS) in Geneva, Switzerland. Following several days of negotiations, the IGNU, the NPFL and ULIMO agreed to a cease-fire (to be monitored by a joint committee of the three factions, pending the deployment of UN observers and a reconstituted peace-keeping force), and to the establishment of a transitional administration. The peace accord was formally signed in Cotonou on 25 July. Under its terms, the IGNU was to be replaced by the Liberian National Transitional Government (LNTG), with a five-member transitional Council of State and a 35-member Transitional Legislative Assembly (comprising 13 representatives of the IGNU, 13 of the NPFL and nine of ULIMO), pending elections. In response to demands by Taylor, the dominance in ECOMOG of the Nigerian contingent was to be reduced.

The cease-fire came into effect at the end of July 1993; however, ECOMOG subsequently accused the NPFL of violating the Cotonou accord by repeatedly entering territory under its control. In August the IGNU, the NPFL and ULIMO each appointed a representative to the Council of State, while a list of nine candidates, nominated by the three factions, elected the two remaining members (who were representatives of the IGNU and ULIMO, respectively) from among their number. Dr Bismark Kuyon, a member of the IGNU, was subsequently elected Chairman of the Council of State. Shortly afterwards, however, Kuyon announced that the inauguration of the Council of State (originally scheduled to take place on 24 August) was to be postponed, pending the clear implementation of the process of disarmament.

In September 1993 the UN Security Council approved the establishment of a 300-member UN Observer Mission in Liberia (UNOMIL), which was to co-operate with ECOMOG and the Organization of African Unity (now the African Union, see p. 172) in monitoring the transitional process. In October the Transitional Legislative Assembly was established, in accordance with the peace agreement. Sawyer dismissed Kuyon (who had reportedly dissociated himself from the IGNU's refusal to relinquish power prior to disarmament) and appointed Philip Banks, hitherto Minister of Justice, in his place.

Meanwhile, it was feared that renewed hostilities in several areas of the country would jeopardize the peace accord. An armed faction styling itself the Liberia Peace Council (LPC), which reportedly comprised members of the Krahn ethnic group from Grand Gedeh County, joined by a number of disaffected AFL troops, emerged in September 1993 and subsequently entered into conflict with the NPFL in south-eastern Liberia. In December fighting between ULIMO and a newly formed movement, the Lofa Defence Force (LDF), was also reported in Lofa County. The NPFL denied involvement with the LDF, which occupied territory previously controlled by ULIMO in the north-west.

In February 1994 the Council of State elected David Kpomakpor, a representative of the IGNU, as its Chairman. In early March units belonging to UNOMIL and the new ECOMOG force (which had been reinforced by contingents from Tanzania and Uganda) were deployed, and the disarmament of all factions commenced. On 7 March the Council of State was inaugurated; it was envisaged that the presidential and legislative elections (originally scheduled for February) would take place in September. However, the disarmament process was subsequently impeded by an increase in rebel activity: in addition to continuing clashes involving the LDF and the LPC, more than 200 people were killed in fighting within ULIMO between members of the Krahn and Mandingo ethnic groups, particularly in the region of Tubmanburg (in Bomi County, where the movement was officially based). The hostilities were prompted by resentment among the Krahn at the predominance of the Mandingo in ULIMO's representation in the transitional institutions.

UNOMIL's mandate was renewed in April 1994. In May, following prolonged controversy over the allocation of principal portfolios, a 19-member Cabinet was installed, comprising seven representatives of the NPFL, seven of ULIMO and five of the former IGNU. In July, however, a faction known as ULIMO—K (led by Alhaji G. V. Kromah) launched an offensive to recapture Tubmanburg, which was under the control of Maj.-Gen. Roosevelt Johnson's forces (ULIMO—J). In early September (when the original mandate of the LNTG was due to expire) a meeting of the NPFL, the AFL and ULIMO—K took place in Akosombo, Ghana. On 12 September Taylor, Kromah and the Chief of Staff of the AFL, Lt-Gen. Hezekiah Bowen, signed a peace accord providing for the immediate cessation of hostilities and for the establishment later that month of a reconstituted Council of State, in which four of the five members were to be nominated, respectively, by the three factions and a civilian Liberian National Conference (LNC—which had been convened in Monrovia at the end of August). Meanwhile, following clashes between dissident members of the NPFL and troops loyal to Taylor, the dissidents' Central Revolutionary Council (CRC) announced that Taylor had been deposed and replaced by the Minister of Labour in the LNTG, Thomas Woewiyu, who indicated that he was not prepared to accept the Akosombo agreement. In mid-September disaffected members of the AFL, led by a former officer who had served in the Doe administration, Gen. Charles Julu, seized the presidential mansion, but were subsequently overpowered by ECOMOG forces. (Almost 80 members of the AFL, including Julu, were later arrested, and a further 2,000 troops were disarmed by ECOMOG.) Later that month the CRC, apparently in alliance with elements of the AFL, ULIMO, the LPC and the LDF, took control of Taylor's base at Gbarnga (in central Bong County); Taylor was reported to have fled to Côte d'Ivoire.

In October 1994 both the ECOMOG and UNOMIL contingents were reduced in size, in view of the lack of progress achieved in the peace process. Meanwhile, the NPFL had regained control of much of the territory, including Gbarnga, that the CRC had captured in September. In December a cease-fire entered into force and reaffirmed the terms of the Akosombo agreement, including provisions for the establishment of demilitarized zones throughout Liberia and for the installation of a reconstituted Council of State, to comprise a single representative of each of the NPFL, ULIMO, the 'Coalition Forces' (a loose alliance comprising the CRC, the LPC, the LDF and elements of the AFL), and the LNC, with a fifth member elected jointly by the NPFL and ULIMO from traditional rulers. At the end of December the UN Security Council extended the mandate of UNOMIL (now comprising some 90 observers) until April 1995, while the Nigerian Government reduced its ECOMOG contingent to 6,000 (from about 10,000).

Negotiations regarding the composition of the Council of State were impeded by Taylor's persistent demand to be granted its chairmanship. On 19 August 1995, following a further ECOWAS summit meeting in Abuja, the armed factions (the NPFL, ULIMO—K, the LPC, the CRC, the LDF, ULIMO—J and the AFL) finally signed a compromise agreement providing for the installation of a reconstituted Council of State, which was to remain in power, pending elections, for one year. An academic with no factional affiliations, Prof. Wilton Sankawulo, was to assume the office of Chairman, while the other seats were to be allocated to Taylor, Kromah, Boley, the LNC representative, Oscar Quiah, and a traditional ruler who had been nominated by ULIMO and the NPFL, Chief Tamba Taylor. Later that month a cease-fire entered into force, in compliance with the terms of the peace accord. The Council of State was formally installed on 1 September, and was to remain in place pending elections, scheduled for 20 August 1996. The Council of State subsequently appointed a transitional Council of Ministers, comprising members of the seven factions that had signed the Abuja agreement. Later in September the UN Security Council extended UNOMIL's mandate until the end of January 1996.

In November 1995 a demilitarized zone was established between NPFL and ULIMO—K forces in the region of St Paul River (between Bong and Lofa Counties). Deployment of ECOMOG forces commenced, in accordance with the Abuja peace terms, in December. Following continued clashes between the ULIMO factions, however, ULIMO—J attacked ECOMOG troops near Tubmanburg. ECOMOG suspended deployment of its forces, and launched a counter-offensive in an attempt to restore order. Hostilities continued in early 1996, with large numbers of civilians killed or displaced.

In February 1996 ULIMO—J officials stated that Johnson had been replaced as leader of the movement in the interests of the peace process. In March the Council of State announced his removal from the Council of Ministers. In subsequent clashes between the two factions of ULIMO—J, forces loyal to Johnson allegedly killed a supporter of the new leadership, prompting the Council of State to order that he be arrested on charges of murder. Johnson, however, refused to surrender to the authorities, and became effectively besieged in his private residence in Monrovia. In April government forces, led by Charles Taylor, engaged in hostilities with Johnson's supporters, in an effort to force him to surrender. The principal factions represented in the transitional authorities thus became involved in the conflict: elements of the LPC and AFL (which were predominantly Krahn) supported Johnson's forces, while the NPFL and ULIMO—K opposed them. Fighting rapidly intensified in central Monrovia and ECOMOG (which had refrained from military intervention) deployed its forces in the region, with the aim of negotiating between the warring factions. Following a lull in the fighting, however, some of Johnson's supporters launched attacks in the residential area of Mamba Point (where embassies and offices of humanitarian organizations were situated) and seized a number of civilians as hostages. Later in April a further cease-fire agreement was negotiated under the aegis of the US Government, the UN and ECOWAS, allowing the deployment of ECOMOG troops throughout Monrovia, while most of the remaining hostages were released by Johnson's supporters.

In May 1996, during the absence of Johnson (who had left the country under US protection, to attend a planned ECOWAS summit meeting), the NPFL launched a further attack against the Barclay Training Centre, prompting large numbers of civilians to flee to Monrovia Freeport. At the end of May the UN Security Council renewed the mandate of UNOMIL for a further three months, but warned the armed factions that international support would be withdrawn if fighting continued; UNOMIL was henceforth to comprise only the remaining five military and 20 civilian personnel, following the evacuation of the main mission of about 90 observers in April. In June Johnson's supporters agreed to disarm, while an ECOWAS arbitration mission commenced discussions with the faction leaders in an effort to restore the peace process.

In August 1996, at an ECOWAS conference in Abuja, the principal faction leaders (apart from Johnson, who remained abroad) signed a further peace agreement, whereby a reconstituted Council of State was to be installed by the end of that month, with a former senator, Ruth Perry, replacing Sankawulo as Chairman; Taylor and Boley were to remain members of the new administration. Under a revised schedule, elections were to take place at the end of May 1997, and power was to be transferred to an elected government by mid-June, following the dissolution of the armed factions by the end of January of that year. In order to implement the new timetable, ECOMOG (which then numbered 8,500) was to be reinforced by personnel from several West African states. At the end of August 1996 the mandate of UNOMIL was again extended.

Perry was inaugurated as Chairman of the Council of State in early September 1996; Johnson was again allocated a ministerial portfolio in a subsequent reorganization of the Cabinet. Following the expiry of the deadline for the completion of the disarmament process, which had been extended to early February 1997, ECOMOG announced that about 91% of the rebel forces (who numbered 30,000–35,000, according to revised estimates) had relinquished their armaments.

In January 1997 Taylor announced that the NPFL had been officially dissolved, in accordance with the peace agreement; the movement was subsequently reconstituted as a political organization, the National Patriotic Party (NPP). In the same month Kromah declared that ULIMO—K had also ceased to exist as a military organization, and was to be reconstituted as the All Liberian Coalition Party (ALCOP). In March Taylor, Kromah and Boley resigned from the Council of State, in compliance with the peace agreement, to allow their candidacy in the forthcoming elections. From March a number of West African countries began to dispatch additional contingents to reinforce ECOMOG (which was expected to be increased in size to about 16,000 personnel prior to the elections), with the USA providing logistical and financial assistance. In May, however, following a request by several political parties, the elections were postponed until 19 July to allow all the newly registered organizations sufficient time for preparation.

A 10-day voter registration process commenced at the end of June 1997. A total of 13 presidential candidates had emerged by this time, among them Ellen Johnson-Sirleaf (a former minister in the Tolbert administration and subsequently a World Bank official, who was to contest the election on behalf of the UP). Despite demands for a further postponement, the elections proceeded on 19 July. The elections commission announced on 23 July that Taylor had been elected President, with 75.3% of votes cast; Johnson-Sirleaf (who had been widely expected to be Taylor's strongest opponent) received only 9.6% of the votes. In the concurrent elections to the bicameral legislature (at which seats were allocated on a proportionate basis), the NPP secured 49 seats in the 64-member House of Representatives and 21 seats in the 26-member Senate, the UP won seven seats in the House of Representatives and three in the Senate, while ALCOP obtained three seats in the House of Representatives and two in the Senate. Kromah (who had won only 4.0% of the votes) subsequently declared that serious irregularities had occurred, but international observers declared the conduct of the elections to have been 'free and fair'. Taylor's overwhelming victory was generally ascribed to the widely held perception that he was the candidate most likely to achieve long-term stability in the country.

Taylor was inaugurated as President on 2 August 1997, and subsequently nominated a 19-member Cabinet, which was approved by the Senate. The new Government retained several members of the previous transitional administration, including Johnson and Woewiyu. A nine-member National Security Council, comprising several government ministers, the Chief of Staff of the Armed Forces and the Commander of ECOMOG, was established with the aim of ensuring the maintenance of civil order.

At an ECOWAS summit meeting, convened in Abuja, at the end of August 1997, it was agreed that ECOMOG was to be reconstituted and would henceforth assist in the process of national reconstruction, including the restructuring of the armed and security forces, and the maintenance of security; it was further envisaged that the contingent's mandate (officially due to expire on 2 February 1998) would be extended in agreement with the Liberian Government. Following the military coup in Sierra Leone in May 1997, ECOMOG was authorized to enforce international sanctions against the new junta led by Maj. Johnny Paul Koroma (see the chapter on Sierra Leone). In October, however, Taylor announced that he opposed the use of military force to oust the Koroma regime, and that ECOMOG would no longer be permitted to launch offensives against Sierra Leone from Liberian territory. Taylor ordered the closure of Liberia's border with Sierra Leone in response to civil disorder within that country. At the end of October Taylor established a National Human Rights Commission, which was empowered to investigate complaints of human rights violations.

In November 1997 it was reported that some 30 members of ULIMO had been arrested in southern Guinea. The alleged presence of former Liberian factions in Guinea was discussed at a meeting between Taylor and the Guinean President, Gen. Lansana Conté, in December. Taylor subsequently appointed Kromah (who had taken up residence in Guinea following his electoral defeat in July) to the post of Chairman of a National Commission on Reconciliation.

By early 1998 the ECOMOG contingent had been reduced to about 5,000 and the Government had notified ECOWAS of its desire for ECOMOG to withdraw formally by 2 February, but had also requested that Nigeria, Ghana, Burkina Faso and Niger continue to provide military assistance. Following the seizure of the Sierra Leonean capital, Freetown, by ECOMOG troops, Taylor protested that the arrest by ECOMOG of about 25 senior members of Sierra Leone's ousted junta at James Spriggs Payne Airport was an infringement of Liberian territory. The Liberian Government recalled its ambassador in Nigeria for consultations, and subsequently submitted a formal complaint to ECOWAS.

In March 1998 violent clashes erupted in Monrovia between the security forces and Johnson's supporters; Johnson subsequently claimed that members of Taylor's special security forces had attacked his private residence. ECOMOG troops were deployed to prevent further violence, and, in an attempt to ease tension in the capital, Johnson was removed from the Cabinet and appointed ambassador to India. In the same month Kromah, who had expressed concern regarding his own safety, was removed from his position as Chairman of the National Commission on Reconciliation. Later that month the Government and ECOWAS signed an agreement revising ECOMOG's mandate in the country; the contingent was henceforth banned from intervening in civil disputes.

In September 1998 security forces attempted to arrest Johnson (who had not yet assumed his ambassadorial post), pursuing him to the US embassy compound, where he and a number of his supporters had taken refuge. The Government subsequently announced that Johnson, Kromah and 21 of their associates had been charged with treason, following an abortive coup attempt, and demanded that US embassy officials relinquish Johnson to Liberian authority. After discussions with the Liberian authorities, however, US officials transported Johnson to Sierra Leone. In response to an incursion by Liberian security forces into the US embassy compound during the fighting, the US Government temporarily closed the embassy and deployed a naval vessel near the Liberian coast to facilitate the evacuation of US nationals in the event of an escalation of violence in Monrovia. The Liberian Government subsequently issued a formal apology to the USA and announced that an investigation would be conducted into the incident, in co-operation with the US authorities. In October 32 people (several, including Johnson, *in absentia*) were formally charged with treason; their trial commenced in November.

By November 1998 most of the ECOMOG forces in Liberia had been redeployed in Sierra Leone, owing to increased rebel activity in that country, and to continued tension between the Liberian Government and ECOMOG officials. In December the Government closed Liberia's border with Sierra Leone, in response to the escalation in civil conflict in the neighbouring country, and pledged support for the administration of President Ahmed Kabbah. In January 1999 it was announced that further ECOMOG troops in Liberia were to be relocated to Sierra Leone, following a major offensive by RUF forces against Freetown. A small number of ECOMOG forces remained in Liberia to provide military assistance to the armed forces. In April 13 of the defendants on trial for treason were convicted and sentenced to 10 years' imprisonment.

In August 1999 members of a rebel movement reported to comprise former members of ULIMO—K, known as the Joint Forces for the Liberation of Liberia (JFLL), attacked principal towns in Lofa County from Guinea. Some 80 aid workers, including six foreign nationals, were taken hostage by the JFLL, but were released a few days later, following negotiations by humanitarian relief officials. Taylor ordered the closure of the border with Guinea and declared a temporary state of emergency in Lofa County. At an ECOWAS meeting on relations between Liberia and Guinea, which took place in Abuja in September, it was agreed that a commission would be established to address the issue of security at the border between Liberia, Guinea and Sierra Leone. The border was reopened in February 2000.

Reports of increased activity by Liberian dissidents in Sierra Leone, where rebels had allied with Kamajor militia, and in Guinea, resulted in a further deterioration in relations between the Liberian authorities and the Governments of those countries. In July 2000 rebel forces again launched an offensive from Guinean territory against Voinjama. Another hitherto unknown movement, Liberians United for Reconciliation and Democracy (LURD), believed to be a grouping of former members of the armed factions (particularly ULIMO–K), claimed responsibility for the attacks. Taylor and Conté subsequently conducted further discussions, with mediation from the Malian President, Alpha Oumar Konaré. In August Johnson-Sirleaf and a further 14 prominent opposition leaders (many of whom were abroad) were charged with alleged involvement with the LURD dissidents.

In January 2001 the Liberian Government withdrew its ambassador in Guinea, following further Guinean bombardment of towns in the Foya district of northern Liberia. In the same month a committee of the UN Security Council reported that the Liberian Government actively supported the RUF and proposed the imposition of UN sanctions against Liberia. In February the authorities announced that the Commander of the RUF, Sam Bockarie, had left the country, and that the rebels' liaison office had been closed. In March the UN Security Council renewed the embargo on the supply of armaments to Liberia and voted in favour of a 12-month ban on diamond exports from Liberia and restrictions on the foreign travel of senior government and military officials; these latter measures were, however, deferred for a period of two months to allow the Government time to comply with demands that it expel RUF members from Liberia and end financial and military aid to the rebels. (In October 2000 the US Government had announced the imposition of diplomatic sanctions against Taylor, his relatives and close associates, prohibiting them from entering the USA until Liberia withdrew support for the RUF.) In late March 2001 Taylor expelled the ambassadors of Guinea and Sierra Leone from Liberia, claiming that they had been engaged in activity incompatible with their office, and announced the closure of the border with Sierra Leone. The Sierra Leonean authorities subsequently retaliated by ordering the Liberian chargé d'affaires to leave the country.

In April 2001 François Massaquoi, the former leader of the LDF, and Minister of Youth and Sport since 1997, was killed, after LURD forces fired on the helicopter transporting him to Voinjama. The Government subsequently intensified operations to suppress the continuing insurgency in northern Lofa County, near the border with Guinea. In May, in response to Taylor's perceived failure to comply with UN demands, the embargo on exports of diamonds from Liberia, together with the travel restrictions on senior government and military officials, entered into effect. Taylor condemned the imposition of UN sanctions, claiming that he had ended all connections with the RUF, while a large demonstration was staged in Monrovia in protest at the measures.

In July 2001 Taylor offered a general amnesty to active rebel supporters and to opposition members in exile who had been charged with treason or associated crimes. In August the Government announced that its order of expulsion against the ambassadors of Guinea and Sierra Leone accredited to Liberia had been formally withdrawn, following a request by ECOWAS. In September Johnson-Sirleaf (who had been charged with supporting anti-Government activities) returned to Monrovia under the terms of the general amnesty. In October a five-member UN commission issued a report recommending the extension of the existing sanctions against Liberia. The UN report also stated that the Liberian Government continued to use revenue generated by the timber industry and maritime activities to finance illicit trade in armaments with the RUF, and proposed the imposition of additional sanctions on timber exports.

By early 2002 LURD forces had gained considerable territory from government troops, and continued to advance southwards towards Monrovia. In response, Taylor declared a national state of emergency on 8 February (which was subsequently ratified by the legislature, and was to be revised after three months). Later that month the Government announced that it was to establish a permanent security presence at the country's northern border with Sierra Leone and Guinea. At the beginning of March the leader of LURD, Sekou Damate Conneh, announced that his forces aimed to depose Taylor and install a transitional administration in Monrovia. The rebels declared a few days later that they were prepared to enter into dialogue with government officials, but demanded that Taylor be excluded from discussions, on the grounds that he was not the legitimate Head of State of Liberia. The Government insisted that it would not contemplate the negotiation of a power-sharing agreement with the movement. Later that month a meeting of representatives of the Liberian authorities and opposition was convened at Abuja, under the aegis of ECOWAS; however, representatives of LURD failed to attend the negotiations, purportedly owing to the logistical difficulties in travelling to Abuja. At the conclusion of the discussions delegates representing 29 political and civil society associations, including major opposition leaders, urged the Government and LURD forces to declare a cease-fire. Nevertheless, fighting continued, particularly at Liberia's northern border with Guinea. At the end of March ECOWAS imposed travel restrictions on the LURD leadership, on the grounds that the movement had renewed hostilities against the Government.

On 6 May 2002 the UN Security Council adopted a resolution extending the armaments and diamond embargoes, and the travel ban, for a further 12 months. Also in May the Liberian legislature extended for a further six months the national state of emergency, after LURD forces gained further territory, seizing control of Gbarnga, in Bong County. In September Taylor ended the national state of emergency and the ban on political demonstrations, announcing that government forces had regained control of much of the territory captured by the LURD, including the significant town of Bopolu, 100 km north-west of Monrovia.

During early 2003 hostilities frequently crossed into the territory of Côte d'Ivoire, and reports emerged that Ivorian rebel groups, notably the Mouvement pour la justice et la paix (MJP) and the Mouvement populaire ivoirien du grand ouest (MPIGO), had become allied with LURD. In March LURD occupied Klay, followed by the Ricks Institute Camp for internally displaced civilians, only 20 km from Monrovia, causing large numbers of civilians to take refuge in the capital. Simultaneous heavy fighting for control of Gbarnga was reported; LURD forces had recaptured the town by April. Meanwhile, a new rebel faction, the Movement for Democracy in Liberia (MODEL), attacked and secured Zwedru in Grand Geddeh County. MODEL was believed to comprise former members of the AFL and Doe loyalists, who were mainly based in Côte d'Ivoire (and reportedly supported by the Ivorian Government). At the end of April Taylor and President Laurent Gbagbo of Côte d'Ivoire agreed to deploy joint border patrols. On 6 May the UN Security Council renewed the existing embargoes in force against Liberia for a further year, and imposed an additional ban on timber exports (which entered into effect in early July). Also in early May the Liberian authorities announced that Bockarie (who had been indicted by the Special Court established in Sierra Leone to try suspects of war crimes committed during the 10-year conflict in the country) had been killed in Liberia during an attempt to arrest him. (It was reported that he had been leading former RUF elements involved in the conflict in Liberia.) Subsequently, however, officials at the Special Court claimed that Bockarie and his immediate family had been captured and murdered by Liberian security forces to prevent him from testifying against prominent regional leaders.

The international community repeatedly urged unconditional negotiations within the framework of a mediation process led by ECOWAS, and in March 2003 LURD finally agreed, in principle, to enter into dialogue with Taylor. LURD and MODEL halted their advances on Monrovia and Buchanan at the end of May and pledged to observe a cease-fire, provided that the Government also suspended attacks. Peace discussions, attended by Taylor and LURD, commenced in Accra on 4 June, but were disrupted by the announcement of Taylor's indictment for war crimes by the Special Court, in connection with his alleged longstanding involvement with the RUF. On the following day Taylor returned to Monrovia, where he immediately announced that the authorities had suppressed an attempted coup. On the same day LURD forces launched a major attack on Monrovia from the movement's base in Tubmanburg, and rapidly reached the capital's western outskirts, causing an exodus from refugee camps towards the city centre. LURD's political leadership issued an ultimatum demanding Taylor's resignation, and French military forces commenced the evacuation of foreign nationals in response to the increasingly critical situation. Following the arrival of a MODEL delegation, the peace discussions in Ghana resumed on 9 June. Repeated demands by LURD for Taylor's resignation as a precondition to the suspension of hostilities, and Taylor's insistence that his indictment by the Sierra Leone Special Court be withdrawn, impeded progress. On 17 June, however, a cease-fire agreement was signed by the LURD and MODEL leaders, and by the Minister of Defence, Daniel Chea, on behalf of the Liberian Government. Immediately beforehand, government troops recaptured Greenville, forcing LURD to withdraw to positions some 35 km from Monrovia. The cease-fire agreement required the deployment of a multinational stabilization force and a 30-day period of discussions to resolve outstanding issues, prior to the adoption of a comprehensive peace accord.

Shortly after the cease-fire agreement was signed in Accra, however, Taylor declared that he would remain in office at least until the end of his presidential term in January 2004, and rejected the Special Court indictment against him. Serious breaches of the cease-fire were reported, and on 26 June 2003, after the resumption of heavy fighting between government and rebel forces in and around Monrovia, in which about 300 civilians were killed, US President George W. Bush urged Taylor to resign. On the following day the rebel leadership declared a unilateral cease-fire (which was, however, rapidly abandoned). At the end of June the UN Secretary-General recommended to the Security Council that a multinational peace-keeping force be deployed in Liberia in response to the critical humanitarian situation, and urged US military intervention. On 6 July Taylor announced that he had accepted, in principle, an offer of asylum from the Nigerian Head of State, Olusegun Obasanjo, but stipulated that he would not leave the country until a peace-keeping operation was installed. Following continued appeals from Liberian civilians for foreign intervention to prevent the humanitarian disaster, a US mission of military observers was dispatched to Liberia. However, Bush indicated that he would only deploy peace-keeping troops in Liberia after Taylor had left the country and a West African mission had restored order. Later in July, after the rebel offensive to oust Taylor had reached the centre of the capital, the US embassy compound (in which some 10,000 Liberian civilians had taken refuge) was repeatedly bombarded. Some 100 US marines were flown in to defend the building, while US naval vessels were stationed off the Liberian coast. Meanwhile, following the resumption of discussions between the government, LURD and MODEL delegations in Accra, it was announced that a peace accord, based on the terms of the failed cease-fire agreement, had been drafted.

On 22 July 2003 a summit meeting of ECOWAS Heads of State was convened in the Senegalese capital, Dakar. Following pressure from the UN Secretary-General, the West African delegates agreed to dispatch an initial 1,300 Nigerian peace-keeping troops (including a battalion redeployed from neighbouring Sierra Leone) to Liberia. On 1 August the UN Security Council officially authorized the establishment of a multinational force with a maximum strength of 3,250 troops, to be known as the ECOWAS Mission in Liberia (ECOMIL), which was to restore security to allow the distribution of emergency humanitarian assistance, and prepare for the deployment of a longer-term UN stabilization force. On 11 August, following continued pressure from West African Governments and the international community, Taylor relinquished power to the Vice-President, Moses Zeh Blah, before leaving Liberia for exile in the town of Calabar, in south-eastern Nigeria. Blah was inaugurated as interim Head of State, pending the installation of a government of national unity, which was the subject of continuing negotiations between the government and rebel delegations in Accra. Taylor's departure fulfilled the main demand of the rebel leadership, who ceded control of Monrovia Freeport to ECOMIL, and a further 200 US military personnel arrived in Liberia to support the peace operation. On 18 August delegates of the incumbent Government, rebel factions, political opposition and civil organizations, under the aegis of the UN, reached a comprehensive peace agreement, which provided for the establishment of a transitional power-sharing government and legislature, to comprise representatives of the participating groupings. Under the accord, Blah was to transfer power to the new administration on 14 October, all armed militia were to be disbanded, and democratic elections were to be conducted by October 2005. On 21 August 2003 the delegations elected Gyude Bryant, a prominent church figure and leader of the LAP, as Chairman of the transitional administration. Perceived as being most neutral, Bryant defeated a further two candidates for the office, Johnson-Sirleaf and Rudolph Sherman of the TWP. By the end of August a UN Joint Monitoring Committee had been dispatched to Monrovia, and ECOMIL troops (then numbering 1,500) were slowly taking control of rebel-held territory.

On 19 September 2003 the UN Security Council formally established the UN Mission in Liberia (UNMIL, see p. 86), which was mandated to support the transitional authorities and the implementation of the August peace agreement; the first contingent, of about 4,000, commenced deployment in the country (replacing ECOMIL) on 1 October. On 14 October, under the terms of the peace agreement, Bryant was officially inaugurated as Chairman of the two-year power-sharing administration, the National Transitional Government, while the leader of the UPP, Wesley Johnson, became Vice-Chairman. At the same time a 76-member unicameral legislature, the National Transitional Legislative Assembly (NTLA), comprising representatives of the groupings signatory to the August agreement and 15 deputies nominated by the counties, was installed. A prominent member of LURD, George Dweh, was subsequently elected Speaker of the new Assembly. Shortly before his inauguration, Bryant had signed an agreement for the resumption of diplomatic relations with the People's Republic of China (thereby ending links with Taiwan); the Chinese Government was expected to finance substantially reconstruction projects in the country. Later in October LURD and MODEL (which were each allocated five ministries in the National Transitional Government) submitted ministerial nominees for approval by the legislature. Of the former Taylor loyalists, Chea retained the post of Minister of Defence, while LURD representatives were awarded the portfolios of justice and finance, and the leader of MODEL, Thomas Nimely Yaya, became Minister of Foreign Affairs. (However, the political opposition and civil society groups failed to agree on representatives for the remaining six portfolios divided between them.) In early December the International Criminal Police Organization (INTERPOL) issued an arrest notice against Taylor (who remained in Nigeria) for suspected war crimes.

On 22 December 2003 the UN Security Council adopted a resolution maintaining the embargoes on imports of armaments and on exports of timber and diamonds for a minimum of one year, but envisaged that these would be ended in response to progress in the peace process and in efforts by the National Transitional Government to prevent the illicit exploitation of resources. In January 2004 it was reported that Conneh's wife, Aisha, had ousted him from the leadership of LURD, with the support of other military commanders, resulting in the division of the movement. LURD and MODEL continued to demand Bryant's resignation from the chairmanship of the interim administration as a precondition to disarmament. On 23 March, after the remaining ministerial portfolios were finally designated, Bryant finally inaugurated the National Transitional Government. In mid-April UNMIL resumed the disarmament programme.

In May 2004 the Civil Society Organizations of Liberia, a grouping of pro-democracy and human rights organizations, presented a petition to the NTLA in support of the extradition of Taylor by the Nigerian Government. (Legal representatives of Taylor continued to plead at the Special Court in Sierra Leone that, as serving President at the time of his indictment, he was immune from prosecution.) In June, in a further struggle for leadership within LURD, the national executive council announced the removal of Sekou Conneh and his replacement by Chayee Doe (a brother of the former President). Conneh refused to acknowledge the statement, and continued to reject demands by his opponents within the movement for the replacement of the LURD Minister of Finance, Lusine Kamara. In September the International Criminal Court (ICC, see p. 324) announced that Liberia had ratified the signatory treaty, thereby allowing the Court jurisdiction to prosecute crimes committed during the civil conflict. On 17 September the UN Security Council adopted a resolution extending the mandate of UNMIL for a further year (while welcoming the progress made in the peace process).

The disarmament process, under which a total of some 96,000 former combatants had relinquished armaments, officially ended on 31 October 2004, with a ceremony at which the three former armed factions were also officially dissolved (although operations continued after that date). In December the UN Security Council conducted a review of the sanctions in force on Liberia and concluded that, following the report of an assessment mission to the country, the National Transitional Government had not met the requisite conditions. The sanctions on armaments, timber and travel were consequently renewed for a further year, while, in view of preparations by the authorities to introduce a certification system, the embargo on the export of diamonds was extended for six months (and again extended in mid-2005).

Electoral reform legislation, which had been submitted to the NTLA at the end of August 2004, became an issue of contention, following attempts by the NTLA to add an amendment requiring a prior population census to be conducted, which would effectively prevent the elections from taking place in October 2005 (as specified in the comprehensive peace agreement). Ensuing disputes over the legislation between the NTLA and the Government were resolved only by sustained pressure from Bryant and the US Ambassador, thereby delaying the adoption of the legislation until December 2004. Nevertheless, in February 2005 the National Elections Commission (NEC) announced that the presidential and legislative elections would be conducted on 11 October. Some 40 prospective presidential candidates had emerged, notably including George Manneh Weah, a Liberian national who had gained international renown as an association footballer. In mid-March NTLA Speaker Dweh, together with the Deputy Speaker and two parliamentary deputies, were suspended from office on suspicion of corruption, following a report by a parliamentary committee that they had spent government funds without authorization. Dweh denied the charges against him, insisting that his suspension was not legitimate, and the UNMIL presence in Monrovia was reinforced, amid concerns of renewed unrest.

At the first round of presidential voting on 11 October 2005, which was contested by a total of 22 candidates, Weah secured 28.3% of votes cast, while Johnson-Sirleaf won 19.8% of votes and Charles Brumskine of the Liberty Party (LP) 13.9% of votes. At the elections to the 64-member lower House of Representatives Weah's party, the Congress of Democratic Change (CDC), won 15 seats, the LP nine seats, an alliance known as the Coalition for the Transformation of Liberia (COTOL) eight seats and the UP eight seats. At the elections to the 30-member Senate the COTOL secured seven seats, while the CDC, the UP and the LP each received three seats. Some 74.9% of the registered electorate voted in the presidential ballot and 76.5% in the legislative elections. Since no presidential candidate had secured an absolute majority, a second round was conducted on 8 November: Johnson-Sirleaf defeated Weah by securing 59.4% of votes cast (with 61.0% of the electorate participating). On 23 November, despite claims of electoral malpractice, the NEC officially declared that Johnson-Sirleaf had won the presidential election. Violent demonstrations by Weah's supporters in Monrovia resulted in clashes with security forces and the arrest of some 40 protesters. In mid-December, following international pressure, however, Weah agreed to suspend his legal challenge to Johnson-Sirleaf's election at the Supreme Court, and subsequently announced that he would abandon his claim to the presidency in the interests of national reconciliation. Later that month the UN Security Council again extended the sanctions on armaments and travel for a further year and those on diamonds and timber for six months, and urged the establishment of a panel of experts to assess the authorities' compliance with requirements.

Johnson-Sirleaf was inaugurated as President on 16 January 2006, thereby becoming the first woman to be elected Head of State in Africa. The two legislative chambers were officially installed on the same day. The election of a close former associate of Taylor, Edwin Snowe, as Speaker of the House of Representatives attracted controversy. Johnson-Sirleaf subsequently began to nominate ministers, who, in accordance with the Constitution, were to be approved by the Senate. In February Johnson-Sirleaf established a seven-member Truth and Reconciliation Commission, which was to investigate human rights abuses perpetrated during the civil conflict. Johnson-Sirleaf (despite having previously indicated that national reconstruction was the greatest priority for the new Government) pledged commitment to bringing Taylor to trial. In the same month the Nigerian Government announced that it had received an official request from Liberia for Taylor's extradition. (In early November 2005 the UN Security Council had extended the mandate of UNMIL to authorize Taylor's arrest and dispatch to the Special Court in Sierra Leone, in the event that he return to Liberia.) In response to Johnson-Sirleaf's request, President Obasanjo declared that he would engage in consultations with other regional leaders. Later in March 2006 Taylor fled from his residence in Calabar, but was apprehended two days later in Borno State, near the border with Cameroon, and dispatched to Liberia, from where he was immediately extradited by UNMIL peace-keepers to the Special Court. In early April Taylor pleaded 'not guilty' to all charges at the Special Court. Tribunal officials subsequently requested that his trial be transferred to the ICC at The Hague, Netherlands, (while remaining under the jurisdiction of the Special Court), in the interests of regional stability. The Dutch authorities acceded to that request on the condition that any sentence handed down to Taylor was served in another country. The United Kingdom subsequently agreed to host Taylor should he be imprisoned and, following the unanimous approval of the UN Security Council, on 20 June Taylor was transferred to The Hague where his trial commenced on 4 June 2007. Proceedings were subsequently postponed until January 2008 to allow his legal representatives additional time to prepare his case.

Meanwhile, in May 2006 ethnic tensions re-emerged as Liberians returned to Nimba County from refugee camps across West Africa to find their homes occupied by the local Gio and Mano tribes who had driven them out of the region during the 1990s (see above). UN peace-keeping forces were mobilized when rumours of an imminent attack by Liberian refugees from Guinea brought people of the Gio and Mano tribes into the streets armed with machetes. Negotiations mediated by local government officials failed to secure the return of land and property, and they called for the central Government to intervene before the situation degenerated into violent conflict.

In November 2006 the Minister of Information, Culture and Tourism, Johnny McClain, resigned from office citing insufficient funding and a lack of support from the Government. He was replaced by Rev. Dr Lawrence Bropleh. In February 2007 Willis Knuckles, the Minister of State for Presidential Affairs, resigned after allegations were published in the press of inappropriate behaviour and the sexual exploitation of young women. Johnson-Sirleaf announced in March that Dr Edward McClain would assume Knuckles' vacated portfolio on a temporary basis,

LIBERIA

Introductory Survey

pending the appointment of a new minister. In August Johnson-Sirleaf implemented a major reorganization of the Government in which Bankie King Akerele replaced George W. Wallace as Minister of Foreign Affairs. Philip Banks became Minister of Justice, replacing Frances Johnson-Morris, who assumed the commerce and industry portfolio.

In July 2007 former armed forces leader Julu was arrested, along with a number of other senior military officials, and charged with attempting a coup; they remained in custody pending trial. In December, during the trial, Julu insisted that he had no involvement in a plot to depose Johnson-Sirleaf. Meanwhile, Former President Bryant, who had been arrested and charged with embezzlement in February, was ordered to organize a new defence team, having earlier dismissed two of his lawyers. Bryant continued to plead his innocence. In January 2008 Taylor's trial resumed in The Hague as scheduled.

In July 2008 the House of Representatives approved new defence legislation following several amendments to the original draft, including awarding military responsibility to the Chief of Staff of the Armed Forces of Liberia. The new Act also provided for the professionalization of the national armed forces and forbade citizens with a record of human rights violations from enlisting in the military. Meanwhile, in June Peter B. Jallah was named Minister of National Security after the earlier nomination of Anthony B. Kromah to that post was rejected by the Senate. In August Isaac Nyenabo, the President of the Senate, was suspended for six months amid claims of 'administrative ineptitude'. In mid-March 2009, following a sustained boycott of the Senate by many of its members and the adoption of a vote of no confidence in him, Nyenabo announced his resignation. Nyenabo had been reinstated to the Senate presidency in January, after the Supreme Court ruled that his removal from that position had been illegal.

In November 2008 Charles 'Chuckie' Taylor Jr, son of the former President, was found guilty of torture and executions committed while he was head of an anti-terrorist unit during the civil conflict. He had been apprehended in Miami, USA, and taken into custody in 2006 under legislation allowing for the prosecution of such crimes committed abroad. In January 2009 he was sentenced to 97 years' imprisonment. Meanwhile, his father's trial continued at The Hague with the counsel for Taylor's defence scheduled to present its submissions in April.

Government

Under the Constitution of January 1986, legislative power is vested in the bicameral National Assembly, comprising the 64-member House of Representatives and the 30-member Senate. Members of the House of Representatives are elected by legislative constituency for a term of six years, while each county elects two members of the Senate (one for a term of nine years and one for six years). Executive power is vested in the President, who is elected to office for a six-year term (renewable only once), and who appoints the Government (subject to the approval of the Senate). Following a peace agreement in August 2003, a democratically elected administration was installed in January 2006 (replacing the power-sharing National Transitional Government). The country comprises 15 counties, which are divided into 64 districts.

Defence

Following a major rebel offensive against the capital in June 2003, the UN Security Council on 1 August authorized the establishment of an Economic Community of West African States (ECOWAS) peace-keeping contingent, the ECOWAS Mission in Liberia (ECOMIL), which was to restore security and prepare for the deployment of a longer-term UN stabilization force. The UN Mission in Liberia (UNMIL, see p. 86), which was officially established on 19 September and replaced ECOMIL on 1 October, was mandated to support the implementation of a comprehensive peace agreement, and a two-year transitional administration. With a total authorized strength of up to 15,000, at the end of January 2009 UNMIL numbered 10,595 troops, 167 military observers and 1,201 civilian police, supported by 489 international civilian personnel, 975 local staff and 206 UN volunteers. Following the completion of the disarmament programme, in January 2005 a US military commission arrived in Liberia to assist in the restructuring of the armed forces, which was ongoing in 2009. In June 2006 the armed forces began recruiting women as part of the reform process. A 3,500-member Liberia National Police force, trained by UNMIL, was also established, although by early 2009 the force remained generally ineffective with little equipment. As assessed at November 2008, the total strength of the Liberian armed forces was 2,400. In 2007 defence expenditure was estimated at US $58m. (equivalent to 6.0% of GDP).

Economic Affairs

In 2007, according to the World Bank, Liberia's gross domestic product (GDP) was US $554m., equivalent to $150 per head (or $290 per head on an international purchasing-power parity basis). During 2000–07, it was estimated, the population increased at an average annual rate of 2.9%, while GDP per head declined by 3.8%. Overall GDP decreased, in real terms, at an average annual rate of 1.0% in 2000–07; however, real GDP increased by 7.8% in 2006 and by 9.4% in 2007.

Agriculture and forestry, measured at constant 1992 prices, contributed an estimated 61.4% of GDP in 2008. An estimated 59.7% of the formal labour force were employed in the sector in that year, although FAO estimated that in mid-2005 65.0% of the total labour force were employed in the sector. The principal cash crops are rubber (which accounted for an estimated 91.9% of export earnings in 2007), cocoa beans and coffee. The principal food crops are cassava, rice, bananas, plantains, yams and sweet potatoes. Timber production has traditionally represented an important source of export revenue, providing an estimated 50.1% of export earnings in 2003 (when, however, sanctions on timber exports were imposed). According to African Development Bank (AfDB) figures, agricultural GDP declined at an average annual rate of 4.0% in 2000–07; however, the GDP of the agricultural sector increased by 7.0% in 2006, and by 5.0% in 2007.

Industry (including mining, manufacturing, construction and power), measured at constant 1992 prices, contributed an estimated 16.8% of GDP in 2008, and employed an estimated 3.2% of the formal labour force in the same year. Industrial GDP, according to AfDB figures, increased at an average annual rate of 5.2% in 2000–07; the GDP of the industrial sector increased by 8.0% in 2007.

The mining sector, measured at constant 1992 prices, contributed an estimated 0.2% of GDP in 2008, and engaged 0.8% of the formal labour force in the same year. Gold and diamonds are mined, and Liberia possesses significant amounts of barytes and kyanite. The production and export of mineral products were severely disrupted from 1990, as a result of the civil conflict. In 1997 total mineral reserves were estimated to include more than 10m. carats of diamonds and 3m. troy oz of gold. In January 2005 the Government prohibited diamond mining in order to support the enforcement of UN sanctions on the export of diamonds (imposed in 2001). However, mineral exports recommenced in 2007 (see below) and, in that year, foreign sales of gold accounted for 2.7% of total export revenue; diamonds contributed 1.3%. The GDP of the mining sector, according to the IMF, declined at an average annual rate of 40.1% in 1988–2002; mining GDP increased by 49.8% in 2000, but declined by 74.9% in 2001 and by an estimated 69.9% in 2002.

Manufacturing, measured at constant 1992 prices, provided an estimated 12.7% of GDP in 2008, and engaged an estimated 0.9% of the formal labour force in the same year. Manufacturing GDP, according to AfDB figures, increased at an average annual rate of 4.6% in 2000–06; the GDP of the manufacturing sector increased by 7.8% in 2006.

Energy is derived from the consumption of fossil fuels (62.2%) and from hydroelectric power (37.8%). In 2003 the authorities announced plans to restore power throughout the country by a programme to rehabilitate a major hydroelectric power installation, which had been damaged in the civil conflict. Liberia is dependent on imports of petroleum, which comprised an estimated 21.1% of the value of total imports in 2007.

The services sector, measured at constant 1992 prices, contributed an estimated 21.9% of GDP in 2008, and employed 37.1% of the formal labour force in that year. The GDP of the services sector, according to AfDB figures, increased at an average annual rate of 2.3% in 2000–06; the GDP of the sector increased by 10.1% in 2006.

Liberia's large open-registry ('flag of convenience') merchant shipping fleet has become an increasingly significant source of foreign exchange. In 2006 revenue from Liberia's maritime programme accounted for an estimated 8.0% of total revenue.

In 2007 Liberia recorded an estimated visible trade deficit of US $511m., and there was a deficit of $529m. on the current account of the balance of payments. In 2004 the principal source of imports (37.8%) was the Republic of Korea. The principal market for exports in 2006 was the USA (73.7%); the other major purchaser was Belgium. The principal export in 2007 was rubber. The principal imports in that year were petroleum, food (particularly rice) and live animals, and machinery and transport equipment.

Liberia's overall budgetary deficit was projected at US $3m. in 2007/08, according to IMF figures. The country's external debt totalled $2,674m. at the end of 2006, of which $1,115m. was long-term public debt. The annual rate of inflation averaged 8.8% in 2000–07; consumer prices increased by 8.0% in 2007. In 2006 unemployment was estimated at about 85.0% of the labour force.

Liberia is a member of the Economic Community of West African States (ECOWAS, see p. 243) and the Mano River Union (see p. 427), both of which aim to promote closer economic co-operation in the region.

The inauguration of Ellen Johnson-Sirleaf, a former World Bank economist, as President in January 2006 marked a turning point in Liberia's economy, which had been ravaged by the civil conflict. She appealed for international support for reconstruction, and announced measures to end endemic corruption, including the organization of a comprehensive financial audit of government institutions. UN sanctions on the export of timber were lifted in September and those on diamond exports in April 2007; shortly afterwards Liberia joined the Extractive Industries Transparency Initiative, intent on ensuring that part of the proceeds of extractive industries, including timber, would be used to improve living conditions for Liberians. In December the AfDB cancelled US $255.2m. of Liberia's debt, and in March 2008 the country cleared its long-standing overdue obligations with the IMF and reached decision point under the initiative for heavily indebted poor countries. The Government instigated a three-year poverty reduction strategy, supported by the IMF, based on consolidating peace and security, revitalizing the economy, strengthening governance and the rule of law, and rehabilitating infrastructure and delivering basic services. Notable advances were made in re-establishing the public financial management system, and the prospects for job creation seemed good; however, sharp increases in food and fuel prices in early 2008 led to elevated inflation and the widening of the trade deficit. The dramatic rise in the price of rice, moreover, led the Government to adopt a range of measures, including the temporary suspension of import duties on that commodity. The global financial crisis threatened to result in reduced remittances and donor inflows, and there were fears that a decline in world commodity prices could adversely affect Liberia's exports. Nevertheless, the IMF estimated real GDP growth of 7.1% in 2008, and forecast 12.7% growth for 2009. In early 2009 the Government declared a state of emergency and requested $1,200m. in international aid to combat a serious caterpillar infestation that affected some 500,000 people, devastated crops (particularly cocoa and coffee) and contaminated waterways.

Education

Education is provided by a mixture of government, private, church and mosque schools. The civil conflicts of 1989–96 and 1999–2003 devastated the education system as buildings and equipment were damaged and looted, and teachers, parents and children became refugees or internally displaced. By September 2005 3,817 of the country's 4,500 schools were reported to be functioning again. Education in Liberia is officially compulsory for 10 years, between six and 16 years of age. Primary education begins theoretically at six years of age and lasts for six years (grades 1–6). Secondary education, beginning theoretically at 12 years of age, lasts for a further six years, and is divided into two three-year cycles, known in Liberia as 'junior high school' (grades 7–9) and 'senior high school' (grades 10–12). Pre-primary education is undertaken from the age of five or younger and is important for those students whose mother language is not English, since English is the language of instruction throughout the school system. School attendance is not enforced and in 2006 an estimated 61% of primary school age children were out of school (60% of boys and 61% of girls). Although the 1984 Liberian Constitution includes the aspiration to provide universal free education, school attendance is discouraged by the poor quality of education offered and by official and unofficial school fees, charges and the cost of uniforms and travel. In 2006 UNESCO estimated the adult literacy rate at 54% (60% male and 49% female). The higher education sector consists of the University of Liberia in Monrovia, Cuttington University College in Bong County, the Booker Washington Institute in Kakata, Margibi County, and the William V. S. Tubman College in Maryland County. According to UNESCO, a total of 44,107 students were enrolled in tertiary education in 2000.

Public Holidays

2009: 1 January (New Year's Day), 11 February (Armed Forces Day), 11 March (Decoration Day), 15 March (J. J. Robert's Birthday), 10 April (Good Friday), 10 April (Fast and Prayer Day), 14 May (National Unification Day), 25 May (Africa Day), 26 July (Independence Day), 24 August (Flag Day), 1 November (All Saints' Day), 12 November (National Memorial Day), 29 November (President Tubman's Birthday), 25 December (Christmas Day).

2010: 1 January (New Year's Day), 11 February (Armed Forces Day), 10 March (Decoration Day), 15 March (J. J. Robert's Birthday), 2 April (Good Friday), 9 April (Fast and Prayer Day), 14 May (National Unification Day), 25 May (Africa Day), 26 July (Independence Day), 24 August (Flag Day), 1 November (All Saints' Day), 12 November (National Memorial Day), 29 November (President Tubman's Birthday), 25 December (Christmas Day).

Weights and Measures

Imperial weights and measures, modified by US usage, are in force.

LIBERIA

Statistical Survey

Sources (unless otherwise stated): the former Ministry of Planning and Economic Affairs, POB 9016, Broad St, Monrovia; the Central Bank of Liberia, POB 2048, Corner of Warren and Carey St, Monrovia; tel. 22-669-91; fax 22-61-14; internet www.cbl.org.lr/index.php.

Area and Population

AREA, POPULATION AND DENSITY

Area (sq km)	97,754*
Population (census results)	
1 February 1974	1,503,368
1 February 1984 (provisional)	
Males	1,063,127
Females	1,038,501
Total	2,101,628
Population (UN estimates at mid-year)†	
2006	3,579,000
2007	3,750,000
2008	3,942,000
Density (per sq km) at mid-2008	40.3

* 37,743 sq miles.
† Source: UN, *World Population Prospects: The 2006 Revision*.

ADMINISTRATIVE DIVISIONS
(population at 1984 census)

Counties:					
Bomi	66,420		Nimba		313,050
Bong	255,813		Rivercess		37,849
Grand Bassa	159,648		Sinoe		64,147
Grand Cape Mount	79,322		*Territories:*		
Grand Gedeh	102,810		Gibi		66,802
Lofa	247,641		Kru Coast		35,267
Maryland	85,267		Marshall		31,190
Montserrado	544,878		Sasstown		11,524
			Total		**2,101,628**

Note: The counties of Grand Kru and Margibi were subsequently established. Two further counties, River Gee and Gbarpolu, were created in 1998 and 2001, respectively.

PRINCIPAL TOWNS
(2003)

Monrovia (capital)	550,200		Harbel	17,700
Zwedru	35,300		Tubmanburg	16,700
Buchanan	27,300		Gbarnga	14,200
Yekepa	22,900		Greenville	13,500
Harper	20,000		Ganta	11,200
Bensonville	19,600			

Source: Stefan Helders, *World Gazetteer* (internet www.world-gazetteer.com).

BIRTHS AND DEATHS
(annual averages, UN estimates)

	1990–95	1995–2000	2000–05
Birth rate (per 1,000)	50.0	49.7	49.9
Death rate (per 1,000)	23.0	21.2	19.8

Source: UN, *World Population Prospects: The 2006 Revision*.

Life expectancy (years at birth, WHO estimates): 44.2 (males 42.5; females 46.0) in 2006 (Source: WHO, *World Health Statistics*).

ECONOMICALLY ACTIVE POPULATION
(formal sector)

	2006	2007	2008*
Agriculture and forestry	12,200	33,672	176,326
Mining	1,009	3,290	2,508
Manufacturing	1,045	5,813	2,785
Construction	535	987	4,300
Wholesale and retail trade	43,500	36,633	18,928
Transport	1,540	2,194	11,178
Banking and insurance	—	1,645	8,206
Business services	2,475	9,872	10,115
Social and community services	12,470	15,575	13,327
Government	58,500	31,900	47,681
Total	**133,274**	**141,581**	**295,354**

* Estimates.

Total employed in informal sector: 470,000 in 2006; 480,000 in 2007; 487,000 in 2008 (estimate).

Mid-2005 (estimates in '000): Agriculture, etc. 796; Total labour force 1,225 (Source: FAO).

Health and Welfare

KEY INDICATORS

Total fertility rate (children per woman, 2006)	6.8
Under-5 mortality rate (per 1,000 live births, 2006)	235
HIV/AIDS (% of persons aged 15–49, 2007)	1.7
Physicians (per 1,000 head, 2004)	0.03
Health expenditure (2006): US $ per head (PPP)	39
Health expenditure (2006): % of GDP	5.6
Health expenditure (2006): public (% of total)	63.9
Access to water (% of persons, 2006)	64
Access to sanitation (% of persons, 2006)	32
Human Development Index (2006): ranking	176
Human Development Index (2006): value	0.364

For sources and definitions, see explanatory note on p. vi.

Agriculture

PRINCIPAL CROPS
('000 metric tons)

	2005	2006	2007
Rice, paddy*	155	107	155
Sweet potatoes†	19	20	19
Cassava (Manioc)†	490	635	550
Taro (Cocoyam)†	26	26	25
Yams†	20	20	19
Sugar cane†	255	255	265
Oil palm fruit	183†	183*	183†
Bananas†	110	116	120
Plantains†	42	42	43
Natural rubber*	111	101	100

* Unofficial figure(s).
† FAO estimate(s).

Aggregate production ('000 metric tons, may include official, semi-official or estimated data): Total cereals 155 in 2005, 107 in 2006, 155 in 2007; Total roots and tubers 155 in 2005, 107 in 2006, 613 in 2007; Total vegetables (incl. melons) 76 in 2005, 84 in 2006, 89 in 2007; Total fruits (excl. melons) 169 in 2005, 172 in 2006, 178 in 2007.

Source: FAO.

LIBERIA

LIVESTOCK

('000 head, year ending September, FAO estimates)

	2005	2006	2007
Cattle	36	37	38
Pigs	130	150	173
Sheep	210	220	230
Goats	220	240	262
Chickens	5,300	5,600	5,920
Ducks	200	250	315

Source: FAO.

LIVESTOCK PRODUCTS

(metric tons, FAO estimates)

	2005	2006	2007
Pig meat	4,400	5,100	5,880
Chicken meat	8,480	8,960	9,480
Game meat	6,500	6,500	6,600
Cows' milk	715	735	745
Hen eggs	4,150	4,500	4,750

Source: FAO.

Forestry

ROUNDWOOD REMOVALS

('000 cubic metres, excluding bark)

	2005	2006	2007
Sawlogs, veneer logs and logs for sleepers	100	180	180
Other industrial wood*	180	180	180
Fuel wood*	5,811	6,033	6,263
Total	6,091	6,393	6,623

* FAO estimates.
Source: FAO.

SAWNWOOD PRODUCTION

('000 cubic metres, including railway sleepers)

	2005	2006	2007
Total (all broadleaved)	50	60	60

Source: FAO.

Fishing

(metric tons, live weight, capture)

	2004	2005	2006
Freshwater fishes*	4,000	4,000	4,000
African sicklefish	256	573	98
Barracudas	432	372	419
Blue butterfish	573	138	159
Bobo croaker	535	107	300
Cassava croaker	490	95	369
Clupeoids	386	216	364
Mantas, devil rays	802	435	23
Marlins, sailfishes, etc.	513	8	48
Sardinellas	1,355	386	508
Sharks, rays, skates, etc.	303	256	349
Snappers	365	458	1,194
Total catch (incl. others)*	14,525	13,347	10,424

* FAO estimates.
Source: FAO.

Mining

	2004	2005	2006
Diamonds ('000 carats)	40	n.a.	n.a.
Gold (kilograms)	110	27	11

Note: In addition to the commodities listed, Liberia produced significant quantities of a variety of industrial minerals and construction materials (clays, gypsum, sand and gravel, and stone), but insufficient information is available to make reliable estimates of output levels.
Source: US Geological Survey.

Industry

SELECTED PRODUCTS

(litres, unless otherwise indicated)

	2006	2007	2008*
Beverages	17,275,820	19,911,496	17,595,586
Cement (metric tons)	135,486	157,200	94,037
Paint (gallons)	88,998	77,890	119,540
Candles (kilograms)	579,233	473,239	289,041
Bleach	713,776	526,153	456,534
Rubbing alcohol	210,127	297,105	118,964
Mattresses (number)	n.a.	102,802	108,596
Water			
Deep well (gallons)	54,720,361	54,786,474	n.a.
Treatment plant (gallons)	643,436,265	782,711,379	n.a.

* Estimates.

Electrical energy (million kWh): 320 in 2003; 330 in 2004; 335 in 2005 (Source: UN, *Industrial Commodity Statistics Yearbook*).

Finance

CURRENCY AND EXCHANGE RATES

Monetary Units
100 cents = 1 Liberian dollar (L $).

Sterling, Dollar and Euro Equivalents (30 April 2008)
£1 sterling = L $123.908;
US $1 = L $63.000;
€1 = L $97.902;
L $1,000 = £8.07 = US $15.87 = €10.21.

Average Exchange Rate (L $ per US $)
2005   57.0958
2006   57.0133
2007   61.2722

Note: The aforementioned data are based on market-determined rates of exchange. Prior to January 1998 the exchange rate was a fixed parity with the US dollar (L $1 = US $1).

BUDGET

(US $ million)

Revenue*	2005/06	2006/07	2007/08†
Tax revenue	81.0	140.0	149.5
Taxes on income and profits	25.1	42.5	48.6
Taxes on goods and services	20.3	26.1	26.9
Maritime revenue	12.1	11.8	13.0
Taxes on international trade and transactions	35.3	69.9	70.1
Other taxes	0.3	1.4	3.8
Non-tax revenue	3.6	6.9	36.2
Stumpage fees and land rental	0.0	0.1	2.2
Total	84.6	146.8	185.7

LIBERIA

Statistical Survey

Expenditure‡	2005/06	2006/07	2007/08†
Current expenditure	67.2	106.4	167.6
Wages and salaries	32.5	40.6	67.5
Other goods and services	22.0	46.1	59.8
Subsidies, transfers and net lending	11.2	19.1	32.7
Interest on debt	1.4	0.5	7.6
Capital expenditure	6.3	16.6	21.1
Total	73.5	123.0	188.7

* Excluding grants received (US $ million): 1.0 in 2005/06; 1.5 in 2006/07; 0.0 in 2007/08 (budget projection).
† Budget projection.
‡ Includes net lending.

Source: IMF, *Liberia: Fourth Review of Performance Under the Staff-Monitored Program and Request for Three-Year Arrangement Under the Poverty Reduction and Growth Facility and the Extended Fund Facility—Staff Report; Press Release on the Executive Board Discussion* (March 2008).

INTERNATIONAL RESERVES
(US $ million at 31 December)

	2005	2006	2007
Reserve position in IMF	0.04	0.05	0.05
Foreign exchange	25.35	71.94	119.31
Total	25.40	71.99	119.36

Source: IMF, *International Financial Statistics*.

MONEY SUPPLY
(L $ million at 31 December)

	2005	2006	2007
Currency outside banks*	2,168.9	2,647.6	3,317.4
Demand deposits at commercial banks	2,701.9	3,973.2	5,541.7
Total money (incl. others)	4,871.6	6,663.5	9,099.9

* Figures refer only to amounts of Liberian coin in circulation. US notes and coin also circulate, but the amount of these in private holdings is unknown. The amount of Liberian coin in circulation is small in comparison to US currency.

Source: IMF, *International Financial Statistics*.

COST OF LIVING
(Consumer Price Index; base: May 1998 = 100)

	2003	2004	2005
Food	140.9	153.8	167.0
Fuel and light	154.4	217.6	342.1
Clothing	121.2	128.7	137.3
Rent	131.8	156.1	180.9
All items (incl. others)	157.0	169.3	187.6

Source: IMF, *Liberia: Selected Issues and Statistical Appendix* (May 2006).

All items (Consumer Price Index; base 2000 = 100): 158.4 in 2005; 167.6 in 2006; 181.0 in 2007 (Source: African Development Bank).

NATIONAL ACCOUNTS
Expenditure on the Gross Domestic Product
(US $ million at current prices)

	2005	2006	2007
Government final consumption expenditure	59	58	73
Private final consumption expenditure	476	558	656
Gross fixed capital formation	87	76	99
Total domestic expenditure	622	692	828
Exports of goods and services	201	208	256
Less Imports of goods and services	275	286	352
GDP in purchasers' values	548	612	730
GDP at constant 1990 prices	380	410	448

Note: Totals may not be equal to the sum of components, owing to rounding.
Source: UN Statistics Division, National Accounts Main Aggregates Database.

Gross Domestic Product by Economic Activity
(US $ million, at constant 1992 prices)

	2006	2007	2008*
Agriculture	192.3	210.4	213.8
Forestry	74.1	81.1	97.5
Mining and quarrying	0.7	0.8	0.8
Manufacturing	55.5	60.7	64.3
Electricity and water	3.0	3.3	3.8
Construction	11.3	12.3	16.1
Trade, restaurants and hotels	29.2	31.9	36.7
Transport and communications	30.9	33.8	34.8
Financial institutions	10.8	11.8	11.9
Government services	10.4	11.4	11.3
Other services	14.9	16.3	16.2
GDP in purchasers' values	433.2	473.9	507.1

* Estimates.

BALANCE OF PAYMENTS
(US $ million)

	2006*	2007*	2008†
Exports of goods f.o.b.	158	227	333
Imports of goods c.i.f.	−401	−487	−844
Trade balance	−243	−260	−511
Services (net)	−91	−111	−152
Balance on goods and services	−334	−371	−663
Income (net)	−168	−175	−165
Balance on goods, services and income	−502	−546	−828
Current transfers (net)	274	291	298
Current balance	−228	−255	−529
Capital and financial account (incl. net errors and omissions)	96	117	442
Overall balance	−133	−138	−87

* Estimates.
† Projections.

Source: IMF, *Liberia: Fourth Review of Performance Under the Staff-Monitored Program and Request for Three-Year Arrangement Under the Poverty Reduction and Growth Facility and the Extended Fund Facility—Staff Report; Press Release on the Executive Board Discussion* (March 2008).

External Trade

PRINCIPAL COMMODITIES
(US $ million, estimates)

Imports c.i.f.	2005	2006	2007*
Food and live animals	68.2	117.0	130.9
Rice	17.2	62.4	60.0
Beverages and tobacco	8.4	13.7	15.7
Mineral fuels and lubricants	28.9	10.6	5.7
Petroleum	91.0	122.0	105.9
Chemicals and related products	9.2	23.6	20.4
Basic manufactures	27.3	48.7	70.7
Machinery and transport equipment	32.6	57.3	97.4
Miscellaneous manufactured articles	30.3	54.4	40.6
Total (incl. others)	309.9	466.7	501.5

Exports f.o.b.	2005	2006	2007*
Rubber	126.7	150.1	183.9
Cocoa beans and coffee	0.3	0.2	2.2
Diamonds	—	—	2.7
Gold	—	0.1	5.5
Iron ore	—	1.0	0.5
Total (incl. others)	131.3	157.9	200.2

* Provisional.

LIBERIA

PRINCIPAL TRADING PARTNERS
(US $ million)

Imports c.i.f.	1986	1987	1988
Belgium-Luxembourg	8.5	11.2	15.0
China, People's Repub.	7.1	14.7	4.8
Denmark	10.6	7.6	5.9
France (incl. Monaco)	6.5	6.4	4.7
Germany, Fed. Repub.	32.7	52.3	39.5
Italy	2.5	2.2	7.3
Japan	20.1	15.0	12.0
Netherlands	20.6	26.8	14.4
Spain	2.5	6.6	3.1
Sweden	2.4	0.6	4.6
United Kingdom	24.2	18.4	12.7
USA	42.5	58.0	57.7
Total (incl. others)	259.0	307.6	272.3

Source: UN, *International Trade Statistics Yearbook*.

Exports f.o.b.	2004	2005	2006*
Belgium	30.6	28.5	39.2
China, People's Repub.	5.5	1.2	n.a.
France	1.7	n.a.	n.a.
USA	63.7	96.8	133.3
Total (incl. others)	103.8	131.8	180.8

* Estimates.

Transport

RAILWAYS
(estimated traffic)

	1991	1992	1993
Passenger-km (million)	406	417	421
Freight ton-km (million)	200	200	200

Source: UN Economic Commission for Africa, *African Statistical Yearbook*.

ROAD TRAFFIC
(estimates, '000 vehicles in use at 31 December)

	1999	2000	2001
Passenger cars	15.3	17.1	17.1
Commercial vehicles	11.9	12.8	12.8

2002: Figures assumed to be unchanged from 2001.
Source: UN, *Statistical Yearbook*.

SHIPPING
Merchant Fleet
(registered at 31 December)

	2005	2006	2007
Number of vessels	1,653	1,907	2,171
Displacement ('000 gross registered tons)	59,600.2	68,405.1	76,572.6

Source: Lloyd's Register-Fairplay, *World Fleet Statistics*.

International Sea-borne Freight Traffic
(estimates, '000 metric tons)

	1991	1992	1993
Goods loaded	16,706	17,338	21,653
Goods unloaded	1,570	1,597	1,608

Source: UN Economic Commission for Africa, *African Statistical Yearbook*.

CIVIL AVIATION
(traffic on scheduled services)

	1990	1991	1992
Passengers carried ('000)	32	32	32
Passenger-km (million)	7	7	7
Total ton-km (million)	1	1	1

Source: UN, *Statistical Yearbook*.

Communications Media

	1995	1996	1997
Radio receivers ('000 in use)	675	715	790
Television receivers ('000 in use)	56	60	70
Telephones ('000 main lines in use)	5	5	6
Daily newspapers:			
number	8	6	6
average circulation ('000 copies, estimates)	35	35	36

Sources: UNESCO Institute for Statistics; UN, *Statistical Yearbook*.

Telephones ('000 main lines in use): 6.7 in 2000; 6.8 in 2001; 6.9 in 2002 (Source: International Telecommunication Union).

Mobile cellular telephones ('000 subscribers): 160.0 in 2005; 280.0 in 2006; 563.0 in 2007 (Source: International Telecommunication Union).

Internet users ('000): 0.3 in 1999; 0.5 in 2000; 1.0 in 2001 (Source: UN, *Statistical Yearbook*).

Daily newspapers: 6 in 1998 (estimated average circulation 36,600); 3 in 2004 (Source: UNESCO Institute for Statistics).

Education

(2007/08, unless otherwise indicated)

	Teachers	Males	Females	Total
Pre-primary	25,406*	250,866	240,282	491,148
Primary	27,945*	286,028	252,814	538,842
Secondary:				
general	17,921*	91,121	68,281	159,402
technical and vocational†	603	26,988	18,079	45,067
Post-secondary technical and vocational†	430	8,842	6,789	15,631
University	772‡	25,236†	18,871†	44,107†

* 2005/06.
† 1999/2000.
‡ 2000/01.

Source: UNESCO Institute for Statistics.

Adult literacy rate (UNESCO estimates): 55.5% (males 60.2%; females 50.9%) in 2007 (Source: UNESCO Institute for Statistics).

Directory

The Constitution

The Constitution of the Republic of Liberia entered into effect on 6 January 1986, following its approval by national referendum in July 1984. Its main provisions are summarized below:

PREAMBLE

The Republic of Liberia is a unitary sovereign state, which is divided into counties for administrative purposes. There are three separate branches of government: the legislative, the executive and the judiciary. No person is permitted to hold office or executive power in more than one branch of government. The fundamental human rights of the individual are guaranteed.

LEGISLATURE

Legislative power is vested in the bicameral National Assembly, comprising a Senate and a House of Representatives. Deputies of both chambers are elected by universal adult suffrage. Each county elects two members of the Senate (one for a term of nine years and one for six years), while members of the House of Representatives are elected by legislative constituency for a term of six years. Legislation requires the approval of two-thirds of the members of both chambers, and is subsequently submitted to the President for endorsement. The Constitution may be amended by two-thirds of the members of both chambers.

EXECUTIVE

Executive power is vested in the President, who is Head of State and Commander-in-Chief of the armed forces. The President is elected by universal adult suffrage for a term of six years, and is restricted to a maximum of two terms in office. A Vice-President is elected at the same time as the President. The President appoints a Cabinet, and members of the judiciary and armed forces, with the approval of the Senate. The President is empowered to declare a state of emergency.

JUDICIARY

Judicial power is vested in the Supreme Court and any subordinate courts, which apply both statutory and customary laws in accordance with standards enacted by the legislature. The judgments of the Supreme Court are final and not subject to appeal or review by any other branch of government. The Supreme Court comprises one Chief Justice and five Associate Justices. Justices are appointed by the President, with the approval of the Senate.

POLITICAL PARTIES AND ELECTIONS

Political associations are obliged to comply with the minimum registration requirements imposed by the Elections Commission. Organizations that endanger free democratic society, or that organize, train or equip groups of supporters, are to be denied registration. Prior to elections, each political party and independent candidate is required to submit statements of assets and liabilities to the Elections Commission. All elections of public officials are determined by an absolute majority of the votes cast. If no candidate obtains an absolute majority in the first ballot, a second ballot is conducted between the two candidates with the highest number of votes. Complaints by parties or candidates must be submitted to the Elections Commission within seven days of the announcement of election results. The Supreme Court has final jurisdiction over challenges to election results.

The Government

HEAD OF STATE

President: ELLEN JOHNSON-SIRLEAF (inaugurated 16 January 2006).

THE CABINET
(April 2009)

Vice-President: JOSEPH NYUMAH BOAKAI.
Minister of Agriculture: J. CHRISTOPHER TOE.
Minister of Commerce and Industry: FRANCES JOHNSON-MORRIS.
Minister of Defence: BROWNIE SAMUKAI.
Minister of Education: JOSEPH KORTO.
Minister of Finance: AUGUSTINE NGANFUAN.
Minister of Foreign Affairs: OLUBANKE KING AKERELE.
Minister of Gender and Development: VARBAH GAYFLOR.
Minister of Health and Social Welfare: WALTER GWENIGALE.
Minister of Information, Culture and Tourism: Rev. Dr LAWRENCE K. BROPLEH.
Minister of Internal Affairs: AMBULLAI JOHNSON.
Minister of Justice: PHILLIP BANKS.
Minister of Labour: SAMUEL KOFI WOODS.
Minister of Lands, Mines and Energy: Dr EUGENE SHANNON.
Minister of Planning and Economic Affairs: AMARA KONNEH.
Minister of Posts and Telecommunications: JEREMIAH SULUNTEH.
Minister of Public Works: LUSENI DONZO.
Minister of National Security: PETER B. JALLAH.
Minister of Transport: JACKSON E. DOE.
Minister of Youth and Sport: ETMONIA TARPEH.
Minister of State for Presidential Affairs: Dr EDWARD MCCLAIN.
Minister of State for Finance, Economic and Legal Affairs: MORRIS SAYTUMAH.
Minister of State without Portfolio: NATTY DAVIS.

MINISTRIES

Office of the President: Executive Mansion, POB 10-9001, Capitol Hill, 1000 Monrovia 10; e-mail rpailey@emansion.gov.lr; internet www.emansion.gov.lr.

Ministry of Agriculture: Tubman Blvd, POB 10-9010, 1000 Monrovia 10; tel. 226399; internet www.moa.gov.lr.

Ministry of Commerce and Industry: Ashmun St, POB 10-9014, 1000 Monrovia 10; tel. 226283; internet www.moci.gov.lr.

Ministry of Defence: Benson St, POB 10-9007, 1000 Monrovia 10; tel. 226077; internet www.mod.gov.lr.

Ministry of Education: E. G. N. King Plaza, Broad St, POB 10-1545, 1000 Monrovia 10; tel. and fax 226216; internet www.moe.gov.lr.

Ministry of Finance: Broad St, POB 10-9013, 1000 Monrovia 10; tel. 47510680; internet www.mof.gov.lr.

Ministry of Foreign Affairs: Mamba Point, POB 10-9002, 1000 Monrovia 10; tel. 226763; internet www.mofa.gov.lr.

Ministry of Gender and Development: Monrovia; internet www.mogd.gov.lr.

Ministry of Health and Social Welfare: Sinkor, POB 10-9004, 1000 Monrovia 10; tel. 226317; internet www.moh.gov.lr.

Ministry of Information, Culture and Tourism: Capitol Hill, POB 10-9021, 1000 Monrovia 10; tel. and fax 226269; internet www.micat.gov.lr.

Ministry of Internal Affairs: cnr Warren and Benson Sts, POB 10-9008, 1000 Monrovia 10; tel. 226346; internet www.moia.gov.lr.

Ministry of Justice: Ashmun St, POB 10-9006, 1000 Monrovia 10; tel. 227872; internet www.moia.gov.lr.

Ministry of Labour: Mechlin St, POB 10-9040, 1000 Monrovia 10; tel. 226291; internet www.mol.gov.lr.

Ministry of Lands, Mines and Energy: Capitol Hill, POB 10-9024, 1000 Monrovia 10; tel. 226281; internet www.molme.gov.lr.

Ministry of Planning and Economic Affairs: Broad St, POB 10-9016, 1000 Monrovia 10; tel. 226962; internet www.mopea.gov.lr.

Ministry of Posts and Telecommunications: Carey St, 1000 Monrovia 10; tel. 6433715; e-mail ministryofposttelecommunication@yahoo.com.

Ministry of Presidential Affairs: Executive Mansion, Capitol Hill, 1000 Monrovia 10; tel. 228026; internet www.emansion.gov.lr.

Ministry of Public Works: Lynch St, POB 10-9011, 1000 Monrovia 10; tel. 227972; internet www.mopw.gov.lr.

Ministry of Transport: 1000 Monrovia 10; internet www.mopt.gov.lr.

Ministry of Youth and Sports: Monrovia; internet www.lys.gov.lr.

LIBERIA

President and Legislature

PRESIDENT

Presidential Election, First Round, 11 October 2005

Candidate	Votes	% of votes
George Manneh Weah (Congress for Democratic Change)	275,265	28.26
Ellen Johnson-Sirleaf (Unity Party)	192,326	19.75
Charles Walker Brumskine (Liberty Party)	135,093	13.87
Winston A. Tubman (National Democratic Party of Liberia)	89,623	9.20
Harry Varney Gboto-Nambi Sherman (Coalition for the Transformation of Liberia)	76,403	7.85
Roland Chris Yarkpah Massaquoi (National Patriotic Party)	40,361	4.14
Joseph D. Z. Korto (Liberia Equal Rights Party)	31,814	3.27
Alhaji G. V. Kromah (All Liberian Coalition Party)	27,141	2.79
Togba-Nah Tipoteh (Alliance for Peace and Democracy)	22,766	2.34
Others	82,998	8.52
Total	**973,790**	**100.00**

Presidential Election, Second Round, 8 November 2005

Candidate	Votes	% of votes
Ellen Johnson-Sirleaf (Unity Party)	478,526	59.40
George Manneh Weah (Congress for Democratic Change)	327,046	40.60
Total	**805,572**	**100.00**

LEGISLATURE

House of Representatives

Speaker: ALEX JANEKAI TYLER.

General Election, 11 October 2005

Party	% of votes	Seats
Congress for Democratic Change	23.4	15
Liberty Party	14.1	9
Unity Party	12.5	8
Coalition for the Transformation of Liberia	12.5	8
Independents	10.9	7
Alliance for Peace and Democracy	7.8	5
National Patriotic Party	6.3	4
New Deal Movement	4.7	3
All Liberian Coalition Party	3.1	2
National Democratic Party of Liberia	1.6	1
United Democratic Alliance	1.6	1
National Reformation Party	1.6	1
Total	**100.0**	**64**

Senate

President: (vacant).

General Election, 11 October 2005

Party	% of votes	Seats
Coalition for the Transformation of Liberia	23.3	7
Congress for Democratic Change	10.0	3
Unity Party	10.0	3
Liberty Party	10.0	3
Alliance for Peace and Democracy	10.0	3
National Patriotic Party	10.0	3
Independents	10.0	3
National Democratic Party of Liberia	6.7	2
National Reformation Party	3.3	1
All Liberian Coalition Party	3.3	1
United Democratic Alliance	3.3	1
Total	**100.0**	**30**

Election Commission

National Elections Commission: Tubman Blvd, 16th St, Sinkor, Monrovia; internet www.necliberia.org; independent; Chair. JAMES M. FROMAYAN.

Political Organizations

A total of 30 political parties were granted registration prior to presidential and legislative elections in October and November 2005.

Alliance for Peace and Democracy (APD): Benson St, Monrovia; tel. 6547710; e-mail karwease@go.metrostate.edu; internet www.members.tripod.com/tipoteh12/index.html; f. 2005; Leader TOGBA-NAH TIPOTEH; Chair. DUSTY WOLOKOLIE.

Liberian People's Party (LPP): Monrovia; f. 1984 by fmr mems of the Movement for Justice in Africa; Leader DUSTY WOLOKOLIE.

United People's Party (UPP): Monrovia; f. 1984 by fmr mems of the Progressive People's Party, which led opposition prior to April 1980 coup; Leader WESLEY JOHNSON.

All Liberian Coalition Party (ALCOP): Broad St, Monrovia; tel. 6524735; f. 1997 from elements of fmr armed faction the United Liberation Movement of Liberia for Democracy; Leader Alhaji G. V. KROMAH; Chair. JOHNSTON P. FANNEBRDE.

Coalition for the Transformation of Liberia (COTOL): Monrovia; f. 2005; Leader HARRY VARNEY GBOTO-NAMBI SHERMAN.

Liberian Action Party (LAP): Monrovia; f. 1984; Leader GYUDE BRYANT.

Liberian Unification Party (LUP): Monrovia; f. 1984; Leader LAVELI SUPUWOOD.

People's Democratic Party of Liberia (PDPL): Monrovia; Leader FIYAH GBOLIE.

True Whig Party (TWP): Monrovia; Leader RUDOLPH SHERMAN.

Congress for Democratic Change: Bernard Beach Compound, Monrovia; tel. 6513469; internet www.cdcforliberia.org; f. 2004; Leader GEORGE MANNEH WEAH; Chair. J. BANGULA COLE.

Free Democratic Party (FDP): Center St, Monrovia; tel. 6582291; Leader DAVID M. FARHAT; Chair. S. CIAPHA GBOLLIE.

Liberia Equal Rights Party (LERP): Duala Gas Station, Bushrod Island, Opposite Duala Market, Monrovia; f. 2005; Leader JOSEPH D. Z. KORTO; Chair. SOLOMON KING.

Liberia Destiny Party (LDP): Congo Town Back Rd, Monrovia; tel. 6511531; f. 2005; Leader MILTON NATHANIEL BARNES; Sec.-Gen. BORBOR B. KROMAH.

Liberty Party (LP): Old Rd, Sinkor Opposite Haywood Mission, POB 1340, Monrovia; tel. 6547921; f. 2005; Leader CHARLES WALKER BRUMSKINE; Chair. ISRAEL AKINSANYA.

National Democratic Party of Liberia (NDPL): Capital Bye Pass, Monrovia; f. 1997 from the fmr armed faction the Liberia Peace Council; Leader WINSTON A. TUBMAN; Chair. NYANDEH SIEH.

National Patriotic Party (NPP): Sinkor, Tubman Bldg, Monrovia; tel. 6515312; f. 1997 from the fmr armed faction the National Patriotic Front of Liberia; won the majority of seats in legislative elections in July 1997; Leader ROLAND CHRIS YARKPAH MASSAQUOI; Chair. LAWRENCE A. GEORGE.

National Reformation Party (NRP): Duala Market, Monrovia; tel. 6511531; Leader Bishop ALFRED GARPEE REEVES; Chair. Rev. SAMUEL TORMETIEE.

New Deal Movement (NDM): Randall St, Monrovia; tel. 6567470; e-mail info@newdealmovement.com; internet newdealmovement.com; f. 2002; Leader Prof. GEORGE KLAY KIEH, Jr; Chair. MOSES B. MADY-YUU (acting).

Progressive Democratic Party (PRODEM): McDonald St, Monrovia; tel. 6521091; f. early 2005 by mems of fmr rebel movement, Liberians United for Reconciliation and Democracy (emerged 1999); Leader SEKOU DAMATE CONNEH.

Reformed United Liberia Party (RULP): 70 Ashmun St, POB 1000, Monrovia; tel. 571212; f. 2005; Leader WILLIAM VACANARAT SHADRACH TUBMAN.

United Democratic Alliance (UDA): Monrovia; f. 2005 by the **Liberia National Union (LINU);** led by HENRY MONIBA; the **Liberia Education and Development Party (LEAD);** and the **Reformation Alliance Party (RAP),** led by HENRY BOIMAH FAHNBULLEH; Leader JOHN SEMBE MORLU.

Unity Party (UP): 86 Broad St, Monrovia; tel. 6512528; e-mail info@theunityparty.org; f. 1984; Leader ELLEN JOHNSON-SIRLEAF; Chair. Dr CHARLES CLARKE.

LIBERIA *Directory*

Diplomatic Representation

EMBASSIES IN LIBERIA

Algeria: Capitol By-Pass, POB 2032, Monrovia; tel. 224311; Chargé d'affaires a.i. MUHAMMAD AZZEDINE AZZOUZ.

Cameroon: 18th St and Payne Ave, Sinkor, POB 414, Monrovia; tel. 261374; Ambassador BENG'YELA AUGUSTINE GANG.

China, People's Republic: Tubman Blvd, Congotown, POB 5970, Monrovia; tel. 228024; fax 226740; e-mail Chinaemb_lr@mfa.gov.cn; internet lr.china-embassy.org; Ambassador ZHOU YUXIAO.

Congo, Democratic Republic: Spriggs Payne Airport, Sinkor, POB 1038, Monrovia; tel. 261326; Ambassador (vacant).

Côte d'Ivoire: Tubman Blvd, Sinkor, POB 126, Monrovia; tel. 261123; Ambassador CLÉMENT KAUL MELEDJE.

Cuba: 17 Kennedy Ave, Congotown, POB 3579, Monrovia; tel. 262600; Ambassador Dr MIGUEL GUSTAVO PÉREZ CRUZ.

Egypt: Coconut Plantation, Randal St, Mamba Point, POB 462, Monrovia; tel. 226226; fax 226122; Ambassador OMAR ABD EL AZIZ ESH-SHEEMY.

Ghana: cnr 11th St and Gardiner Ave, Sinkor, POB 471, Monrovia; tel. 261477; Ambassador Maj.-Gen. FRANCIS ADU-AMANFOH.

Guinea: Monrovia; Ambassador ABDOULAYE DORÉ.

Lebanon: 12th St, Monrovia; tel. 262537; Ambassador MANSOUR ABDALLAH.

Libya: Monrovia; Ambassador MUHAMMAD UMARAT-TABI.

Morocco: Tubman Blvd, Congotown, Monrovia; tel. 262767; Ambassador MOHAMED LASFAR.

Nigeria: Congotown, POB 366, Monrovia; tel. 227345; fax 226135; Ambassador EBENEZER AYOLODELE ADIGUN.

Russia: Payne Ave, Sinkor, POB 2010, Monrovia; tel. 261304; Ambassador ANDREY V. POKROVSKII.

Senegal: Monrovia; Ambassador MOCTAR TRAORÉ.

Sierra Leone: Tubman Blvd, POB 575, Monrovia; tel. 261301; Ambassador Rev. MARIE J. BARNETT.

USA: 111 United Nations Dr., Mamba Point, POB 10-0098, Monrovia; tel. 77054826; fax 7710370; e-mail ConsularMonrovia@state.gov; internet monrovia.usembassy.gov; Ambassador LINDA THOMAS-GREENFIELD.

Judicial System

In February 1982 the People's Supreme Tribunal (which had been established following the April 1980 coup) was renamed the People's Supreme Court, and its Chairman and members became the Chief Justice and Associate Justices of the People's Supreme Court. The judicial system also comprised People's Circuit and Magistrate Courts. The five-member Supreme Court was established in January 1992 to adjudicate in electoral disputes.

Chief Justice of the Supreme Court of Liberia: JOHNNIE LEWIS.

Justices: KABINEH JA'NEH, FRANCIS KORPKPOR, GLADYS JOHNSON.

Religion

Liberia is officially a Christian state, although complete religious freedom is guaranteed. Christianity and Islam are the two main religions. There are numerous religious sects, and many Liberians hold traditional beliefs.

CHRISTIANITY

Liberian Council of Churches: 15 St, Sinkor, POB 10-2191, 1000 Monrovia; tel. 6517879; e-mail liberiancouncil@yahoo.com; internet www.liberiancouncilofchurches.org; f. 1982; 11 mems, two assoc. mems, one fraternal mem.; Pres. Rev. Dr JOHN G. INNIS.

The Anglican Communion

The diocese of Liberia forms part of the Church of the Province of West Africa, incorporating the local Episcopal Church. Anglicanism was established in Liberia in 1836, and the diocese of Liberia was admitted into full membership of the Province in 1982. In 1985 the Church had 125 congregations, 39 clergy, 26 schools and about 20,000 adherents in the country. The Metropolitan of the Province is the Bishop of Koforidua, Ghana.

Bishop of Liberia: Rt Rev. JONATHAN BAU-BAU BONAPARTE HART, POB 10-0277, 1000 Monrovia; tel. 224760; fax 227519; e-mail bishop@liberia.net.

The Roman Catholic Church

Liberia comprises the archdiocese of Monrovia and the dioceses of Cape Palmas and Gbarnga. At 31 December 2006 there were an estimated 307,446 adherents in the country, equivalent to 8.9% of the total population.

Catholic Bishops' Conference of Liberia POB 10-2078, 1000 Monrovia 10; tel. 227245; fax 226175.

f. 1998; Pres. Rt Rev. LEWIS ZEIGLER (Bishop of Gbarnga).

Archbishop of Monrovia: Most Rev. MICHAEL KPAKALA FRANCIS, Archbishop's Office, POB 10-2078, 1000 Monrovia 10; tel. 6519766; fax 77003719; e-mail apostolic_adm@yahoo.com.

Other Christian Churches

Assemblies of God in Liberia: POB 1297, Monrovia; f. 1908; 14,578 adherents, 287 churches; Gen. Supt JIMMIE K. DUGBE, Sr.

Lutheran Church in Liberia (LCL): POB 10-1046, 13th St, Payne Ave, Sinkor, 1000 Monrovia 10; tel. 226262; e-mail lutheranchurchinliberia@yahoo.com; f. 1947 as Evangelical Lutheran Church, reorg. in 1965 under indigenous leadership as LCL; Pres. Bishop SUMOWARD E. HARRIS; 72,000 mems (2009).

Providence Baptist Church: cnr Broad and Center Sts, Monrovia; tel. 6533941; e-mail admin@providencebc.net; internet www.providencebc.net; f. 1821; 2,500 adherents, 300 congregations, 6 ministers, 8 schools; Pastor Rev. A. MOMOLUE DIGGS.

Liberia Baptist Missionary and Educational Convention, Inc: POB 390, Monrovia; tel. 222661; f. 1880; 72,000 adherents, 270 churches (2007); Pres. Rev. J. K. LEVEE MOULTON; Nat. Vice-Pres. Rev. J. GBANA HALL; Gen. Sec. CHARLES W. BLAKE.

United Methodist Church in Liberia: cnr 12th St and Tubman Blvd, POB 1010, 1000 Monrovia 10; tel. 223343; e-mail bishop.jinnis@liberiaumc.org; internet www.umcliberia.org; f. 1833; c. 168,300 adherents, 600 congregations, 700 ministers, 394 lay pastors; Resident Bishop Rev. Dr JOHN G. INNIS.

Other active denominations include the National Baptist Mission, the Pentecostal Church, the Presbyterian Church in Liberia, the Prayer Band and the Church of the Lord Aladura.

ISLAM

The total community numbers about 670,000.

National Muslim Council of Liberia: Monrovia; Leader Shaykh KAFUMBA KONNAH.

The Press

NEWSPAPERS

Daily Observer: POB 1858, Monrovia; tel. 6513788; e-mail editor@liberianobserver.com; internet www.liberianobserver.com; f. 1981; independent; daily; Dir KENNETH Y. BEST.

The Inquirer: POB 3600, Monrovia; tel. 6538573; fax 227036; e-mail theinquirernews@yahoo.com; internet www.theinquirer.com.lr; New Era Publications, Ltd; daily; Man. Editor PHILIP WESSEH.

Monrovia Guardian: 58 Broad Street, POB 2131, Monrovia; weekly; independent; Editor B. IGNATIUS GEORGE.

News: ACDB Bldg, POB 10-3137, Carey Warren St, Monrovia; tel. 227820; independent; weekly; Chair. WILSON TARPEH; Editor-in-Chief JEROME DALIEH.

PERIODICALS

The Kpelle Messenger: Kpelle Literacy Center, Lutheran Church, POB 1046, Monrovia; Kpelle-English; monthly; Editor Rev. JOHN J. MANAWU.

Liberia Orbit: Voinjama; e-mail orbit@tekmail.com; internet www.liberiaorbit.org; national current affairs; Editor LLOYD SCOTT.

Liberian Post: e-mail info@liberian.org; internet www.liberian.org; f. 1998; independent internet magazine; tourist information; Publr WILLEM TIJSSEN.

New Democrat: Monrovia; e-mail newdemnews@yahoo.com; internet www.newdemocratnews.com; national news and current affairs.

Patriot: Congotown 1000, Monrovia; internet www.allaboutliberia.com/patriot.htm.

The People Magazine: Bank of Liberia Bldg, Suite 214, Carey and Warren Sts, POB 3501, Monrovia; tel. 222743; f. 1985; monthly; Editor and Publr CHARLES A. SNETTER.

PRESS ORGANIZATIONS

Liberia Institute of Journalism: Kashour Bldg, 2nd Floor, cnr Broad and Johnson Sts, POB 2314, Monrovia; tel. 227327; Dir VINICIUS HODGES.

Press Union of Liberia: Benson St, POB 20-4209, Monrovia; tel. and fax 227105; f. 1985; Pres. ELIZABETH HOFF.

NEWS AGENCIES

Liberian News Agency (LINA): POB 9021, Capitol Hill, Monrovia; tel. 222229; Dir-Gen. ERNEST KIAZOLY (acting).

Broadcasting and Communications

TELECOMMUNICATIONS

Cellcom: Haile Selassie Ave, Capitol Bye-Pass, Monrovia; tel. 77777008; fax 77000101; e-mail info@cellcomgsm.com; internet www.lrcellcomgsm.com; mobile cellular telephone provider.

Comium: Comium Bldg, Congo Town, Monrovia; tel. 5600600; fax 5600611; e-mail info@comium.com.lr; internet www.comium.com.lr; mobile cellular telephone provider; Exec. Chair. MONIE R. CAPTAN.

LiberCell: Monrovia; e-mail info@awli.net; internet www.libercell.info; f. 2004; mobile cellular telephone provider; CEO AZZAM SBAITY; Gen. Man. MOHAMMED ALAWIE.

Liberia Telecommunications Corpn: Monrovia; tel. 25553000; e-mail info@libtelco.com.lr; internet www.libtelco.com.lr; Man. Dir JOE GBALAH.

Lonestar Cell: LBDI Building, Congo Town, Monrovia; tel. 6500000; fax 6501101; internet www.lonestarcell.com; mobile cellular telephone provider; f. 2001; Gen. Man. KHALED MIKKAWI.

BROADCASTING

Radio

Liberia Communications Network: Congotown 1000, Monrovia; govt-operated; broadcasts information, education and entertainment 24 hours daily in English, French and several African languages; short-wave service.

Liberia Rural Communications Network: POB 10-02176, 1000 Monrovia 10; tel. 271368; f. 1981; govt-operated; rural devt and entertainment programmes; Dir J. RUFUS KAINE (acting).

Radio Veritas: POB 3569, Monrovia; tel. 4712834; e-mail radioveritas@hotmail.com; internet radioveritas.org; f. 1981; Catholic; independent; nation-wide shortwave broadcasts; Dirs Fr ANTHONY BOWAH, LEDGERHOOD RENNIE.

Star Radio: 12 Broad St, Snapper Hill, Monrovia; tel. 77104411; e-mail star@liberia.net; internet www.starradio.org.lr; independent news and information station; f. July 1997 by Fondation Hirondelle, Switzerland, with funds from the US Agency for International Development; broadcasts in English, French and 14 African languages; Man. JAMES K. MORLU.

Television

Liberia Broadcasting System: POB 594, Monrovia; tel. 224984; internet www.liberiabroadcastingsystem.com; govt-owned; Dir-Gen. CHARLES SNETTER.

Finance

(cap. = capital; res = reserves; dep. = deposits; m. = million; br. = branch; amounts in Liberian dollars, unless otherwise indicated)

BANKING

Following intensive fighting between government and rebel forces in the capital in mid-2003, it was reported that commercial banks had resumed operations at the end of August. At that time, however, only four (of a total of 18 deposit banks established since 1954) were active, the remainder having been closed as a result of poor bank management or the 1989–96 civil conflict. The Liberian Bank for Development and Investment is the only locally owned bank.

Central Bank

Central Bank of Liberia: cnr Warren and Carey Sts, POB 2048, 1000 Monrovia; tel. 6225685; fax 6226114; e-mail webmaster@cbl.org.lr; internet www.cbl.org.lr; f. 1974 as National Bank of Liberia; name changed March 1999; bank of issue; cap. 7,133.9m., res 4,008m., dep. 4,650m. (Dec. 2006); Gov. JOSEPH MILLS JONES.

Other Banks

Ecobank Liberia Ltd: Ashmun and Randall Sts, POB 4825, Monrovia; tel. 4788834; fax 227029; e-mail ecobanklr@ecobank.com; internet www.ecobank.com; commenced operations Aug. 1999; cap. and res US $2.1m., total assets US $10.2m. (Dec. 2001); Chair. EUGENE H. COOPER; Man. Dir ESIJOLONE OKORODUDU.

First International Bank (Liberia) Ltd: Luke Bldg, Broad St, Monrovia; tel. 77026241; e-mail info@fib-lib.com; internet www.fib-lib.com; f. April 2005; Chair. FRANCIS L. M. HORTON; Exec. Dir. ARISA AWA.

Global Bank Liberia Ltd (GBLL): Ashmun and Mechlin Sts, POB 2053, Monrovia; tel. 6425760; e-mail mail@globalbankliberia.com; internet www.globalbankliberia.com; f. 2005; Italian-owned; Pres. Dr RICCARDO SEMBIANTE.

International Bank (Liberia) Ltd: 64 Broad St, POB 10292, 1000 Monrovia; tel. 6557473; fax 4074245; e-mail tjeffrey@ibliberia.com; internet www.ibliberia.com; f. 1948 as International Trust Co of Liberia; name changed April 2000; 75.5% owned by Liberian Financial Holdings; 19.1% Trust Bank Ltd (The Gambia); cap. 2m. (1989), dep. 96.4m. (Dec. 1996); CEO PATRICK ANUMEL (acting); Gen. Man. HENRY SAAMOI; 3 brs.

Liberian Bank for Development and Investment (LBDI): Ashmun and Randall Sts, POB 547, Monrovia; tel. 227140; fax 226359; e-mail lbdi@lbdi.net; internet www.lbdi.net; f. 1961; 18.7% govt-owned; cap. and res US $12.5m., total assets US $26.8m. (Dec. 2001); Chair. NATHANIEL BARNES; Pres. FRANCIS A. DENNIS, Jr.

Banking Association

Liberia Bankers' Association: POB 292, Monrovia; mems include commercial and devt banks; Pres. FRANCIS A. DENNIS, Jr.

INSURANCE

American National Underwriters, Inc: Carter Bldg, 39 Broad St, POB 180, Monrovia; tel. 114921; general; Gen. Man. S. B. MENSAH.

American Life Insurance Co: Carter Bldg, 39 Broad St, POB 60, Monrovia; f. 1969; life and general; Vice-Pres. ALLEN BROWN.

Insurance Co of Africa: 2nd Floor, International Bank Building, 64 Broad St Monrovia; tel. 6513281; internet icaliberia.com; f. 1969; life and general; Pres. SAMUEL OWAREE MINTAH.

National Insurance Corpn of Liberia (NICOL): LBDI Bldg Complex, POB 1528, Sinkor, Monrovia; tel. 262429; f. 1983; state-owned; sole insurer for Govt and parastatal bodies; also provides insurance for the Liberian-registered merchant shipping fleet; Man. Dir MIATTA EDITH SHERMAN.

Royal Exchange Assurance: Ashmun and Randall Sts, POB 666, Monrovia; all types of insurance; Man. RONALD WOODS.

United Security Insurance Agencies Inc: Randall St, POB 2071, Monrovia; life, personal accident and medical; Dir EPHRAIM O. OKORO.

Trade and Industry

GOVERNMENT AGENCIES

Budget Bureau: Capitol Hill, POB 1518, Monrovia; tel. 226340; Dir-Gen. AUGUSTINE K. NGAFUAN.

General Services Agency (GSA): Old USTC Compound, UN Dr., POB 10-9027, Monrovia; tel. 6901333; e-mail info@gsa.gov.lr; internet www.gsa.gov.lr; Dir-Gen. WILLIARD RUSSELL.

DEVELOPMENT ORGANIZATIONS

Forestry Development Authority: POB 10-3010, Kappa House, Eli Saleby Compound, Monrovia; tel. 224940; fax 226000; e-mail john.woods@fda.gov.lr; internet www.fda.gov.lr; f. 1976; responsible for forest management and conservation; Chair. EDWIN ZELEE; Man. Dir JOHN T. WOODS.

Liberia Industrial Free Zone Authority (LIFZA): One Free Zone, Monrovia; tel. 533671; e-mail mskromah@lifza.com; internet www.lifza.com; f. 1975; 98 mems; Man. Dir MOHAMMED S. KROMAH.

National Investment Commission (NIC): Fmr Executive Mansion Bldg, POB 9043, Monrovia; tel. 7873001; internet www.nic.gov.lr; f. 1979; autonomous body negotiating investment incentives agreements on behalf of Govt; promotes agro-based and industrial devt; Chair. RICHARD TOLBERT.

CHAMBER OF COMMERCE

Liberia Chamber of Commerce: Warren St, POB 92, Monrovia; tel. 223738; e-mail liberiachamber2006@yahoo.com; f. 1951; Pres. HENRY REED COOPER; Sec.-Gen. EMMETT C. A. GOODING.

LIBERIA   Directory

INDUSTRIAL AND TRADE ASSOCIATIONS

Liberian Produce Marketing Corpn: POB 662, Monrovia; tel. 222447; f. 1961; govt-owned; exports Liberian produce, provides industrial facilities for processing of agricultural products and participates in agricultural devt programmes; Man. Dir NYAH MARTEIN.

Liberian Resources Corpn (LIBRESCO): controls Liberia's mineral resources; 60% govt-owned; 40% owned by South African co, Amalia Gold.

EMPLOYERS' ASSOCIATION

National Enterprises Corpn: POB 518, Monrovia; tel. 261370; importer, wholesaler and distributor of foodstuffs, and wire and metal products for local industries; Pres. EMMANUEL SHAW, Sr.

UTILITIES

Electricity

Liberia Electricity Corpn (LEC): Waterside, UN Dr., Monrovia; tel. 6653650; e-mail mlackay@libelcorp.com; internet www.libelcorp.com; Chair. DUNSTAN MACAULEY; Man. Dir HARRY YUAN.

National Oil Co of Liberia (NOCAL): Episcopal Church Plaza, Ashmun and Randall Sts, 1000 Monrovia; internet www.nocal-lr.com; Chair. CLEMENCEAU B. UREY; Pres. and CEO FODEE KROMAH.

TRADE UNION

Liberian Labor Congress: J. B. McGill Labor Center, Gardnersville Freeway, POB 415, Monrovia; f. 2008 following merger of Liberian Federation of Labor Unions and Congress of National Trade Unions; Pres. MOSES P. BARWROR, Jr; Sec.-Gen. JERRY DUPLAYE.

Transport

RAILWAYS

Railway operations were suspended in 1990, owing to the civil conflict. Large sections of the 480-km rail network were subsequently dismantled.

Bong Mining Co Ltd: POB 538, Monrovia; tel. 225222; fax 225770; f. 1958; Gen. Man. HANS-GEORG SCHNEIDER.

Liberian Mining Co: Monrovia; tel. 221190; govt-owned; assumed control of LAMCO JV Operating Co in 1989.

National Iron Ore Co Ltd: POB 548, Monrovia; f. 1951; Gen. Man. S. K. DATTA RAY.

ROADS

In 2000 the road network in Liberia totalled an estimated 10,600 km, of which about 657 km were paved. The main trunk road is the Monrovia–Sanniquellie motor road, extending north-east from the capital to the border with Guinea, near Ganta, and eastward through the hinterland to the border with Côte d'Ivoire. Trunk roads run through Tapita, in Nimba County, to Grand Gedeh County and from Monrovia to Buchanan. A bridge over the Mano river connects with the Sierra Leone road network, while a main road links Monrovia and Freetown (Sierra Leone). Although principal roads were officially reopened to commercial traffic in early 1997, following the 1989–96 armed conflict, much of the infrastructure remained severely damaged. In late 2003 the Liberian authorities announced plans for the extensive rehabilitation of the road network, including a highway linking Monrovia with Harper, which was to be funded by the People's Republic of China.

SHIPPING

In December 2007 Liberia's open-registry fleet (2,171 vessels), the second largest in the world (after Panama) in terms of gross tonnage, had a total displacement of 76.6m. grt. Commercial port activity in Liberia was frequently suspended from 1990, as a result of hostilities. At September 2004 only Monrovia Free Port had fully resumed operations and (compared with the corresponding period in 2003) experienced a rise in vessel traffic of 95.2%, owing to increasing commercial and humanitarian activities.

Bureau of Maritime Affairs: Tubman Blvd, POB 10-9042, 1000 Monrovia 10; tel. and fax 226069; internet www.bma.gov.lr; Commissioner BINYAH C. KESSELLY.

Liberia National Shipping Line (LNSL): Monrovia; f. 1987; jt venture by the Liberian Govt and private German interests; routes to Europe, incl. the United Kingdom and Scandinavia.

National Port Authority: Freeport of Monrovia, Bushrod Island, Monrovia; tel. 6402906; fax 77861997; e-mail natportliberia@yahoo.com; internet www.nationalportauthorityliberia.org; f. 1967; administers Monrovia Free Port and the ports of Buchanan, Greenville and Harper; Chair. Dr C. WILLIAM ALLEN; Man. Dir GEORGE TUBMAN.

CIVIL AVIATION

Liberia's principal airports are Robertsfield International Airport, at Harbel, 56 km east of Monrovia, and James Spriggs Payne Airport, at Monrovia.

ADC Liberia Inc: Monrovia; f. 1993; services to the United Kingdom, the USA and destinations in West Africa.

Air Liberia: POB 2076, Monrovia; f. 1974; state-owned; scheduled passenger and cargo services; Man. Dir JAMES K. KOFA.

Tourism

Liberia's natural assets, especially its beaches and the Sapo National Park and other areas of primary tropical rainforest, have the potential to support both a beach-based and an eco-tourism industry. However, no such industry has ever been developed in Liberia and tourism has been entirely in abeyance since 1990 because of the almost continuous civil conflict since that time. The development of the country's tourist potential will be limited by high levels of violent crime and a tourism infrastructure which remains meagre or absent.

LIBYA

Introductory Survey

Location, Climate, Language, Religion, Flag, Capital

The Great Socialist People's Libyan Arab Jamahiriya extends along the Mediterranean coast of North Africa. Its neighbours are Tunisia and Algeria to the west, Niger and Chad to the south, Egypt to the east, and Sudan to the south-east. The climate is very hot and dry. Most of the country is part of the Sahara, an arid desert, but the coastal regions are cooler. Average temperatures range from 13°C (55°F) to 38°C (100°F), but a maximum of 57.3°C (135°F) has been recorded in the interior. Arabic is the official language, although English and Italian are also used in trade. Almost all of the population are Sunni Muslims. The national flag (proportions 2 by 3) is plain green. The administrative capital was formerly Tripoli (Tarabulus), but under a decentralization programme announced in September 1988 most government departments and the legislature were relocated to Sirte (Surt), while some departments were transferred to other principal towns.

Recent History

Libya, formerly an Italian colony and occupied by British and French troops in 1942, attained independence as the United Kingdom of Libya on 24 December 1951. Muhammad Idris as-Sanusi, Amir of Cyrenaica, became King Idris of Libya. British and US forces maintained bases in Libya in return for economic assistance; however, the discovery of petroleum reserves in 1959 greatly increased the country's potential for financial autonomy.

King Idris was deposed in September 1969, in a bloodless revolution led by a group of young nationalist army officers. A Revolution Command Council (RCC) was established, with Col Muammar al-Qaddafi as Chairman, and a Libyan Arab Republic was proclaimed. British and US military personnel withdrew from Libya in 1970, and in 1972 British oil interests in Libya were nationalized.

The Arab Socialist Union (ASU) was established in June 1971 as the country's sole political party. People's Congresses and Popular Committees were formed, and an undertaking was made to administer the country in accordance with Islamic principles. The General National Congress of the ASU (which comprised members of the RCC, leaders of the People's Congresses and Popular Committees and of trade unions and professional organizations) held its first session in January 1976; it was subsequently restyled the General People's Congress (GPC).

In March 1977 the GPC endorsed constitutional changes, recommended by Qaddafi, whereby the official name of the country was changed to the Socialist People's Libyan Arab Jamahiriya. Power was vested in the people through the GPC and its constituent parts. The RCC was dissolved, and a General Secretariat of the GPC (with Qaddafi as Secretary-General) was established. The GPC elected Qaddafi as Revolutionary Leader of the new state. The Council of Ministers was replaced by a General People's Committee, initially with 26 members—each a secretary of a department.

In March 1979 Qaddafi resigned from the post of Secretary-General of the General Secretariat of the GPC to devote more time to 'preserving the revolution'. The creation in early 1984 of the post of Secretary for External Security and of an office, attached to the Secretariat for Foreign Liaison, to 'combat international terrorism', combined with repressive measures to curb the activity of dissidents, apparently reflected Qaddafi's increasing sensitivity to the growth of opposition groups—principally the National Front for the Salvation of Libya (NFSL), which he accused foreign governments of fostering. In 1986 the country's official name was changed to the Great Socialist People's Libyan Arab Jamahiriya.

From 1988, in an apparent attempt to allay domestic dissatisfaction and international criticism, Qaddafi initiated a series of liberalizing economic and political reforms. In foreign policy he adopted a more pragmatic approach to his ambition of achieving Maghreb union (see below), and to his relations with other Arab and African countries. Within Libya he accused the 'revolutionary committees' (young, pro-Qaddafi activists) of murdering political opponents of his regime. Qaddafi encouraged the reopening of private businesses, in recognition of the inadequacy of state-sponsored supermarkets, and declared an amnesty for all prisoners, other than those convicted of violent crimes or of conspiring with foreign powers. Libyan citizens were guaranteed freedom to travel abroad, and the powers of the revolutionary committees were curbed. The GPC created a People's Court and People's Prosecution Bureau to replace the revolutionary courts, and approved a charter of human rights. In August Qaddafi announced that the army was to be replaced by a force of 'Jamahiri Guards', which would be supervised by 'people's defence committees'. In September it was decided to relocate all but two of the secretariats of the GPC, mostly to the town of Sirte (Surt), 400 km east of Tripoli, and in January 1989 Qaddafi announced that all state institutions, including the state intelligence service and the official Libyan news agency, were to be abolished.

In October 1990 the GPC implemented extensive changes to the General People's Committee, creating three new secretariats and electing a new Secretary-General, Abu Sa'id Omar Durdah, as well as 11 new secretaries. Three of the five-member General Secretariat of the GPC were replaced, and Abd ar-Raziq as-Sawsa was appointed Secretary-General of the GPC; in November 1992 as-Sawsa was replaced by Muhammad az-Zanati. In the same month there was a further reorganization of the General People's Committee; the former Secretary for Economic Planning, Omar al-Muntasir, was named Secretary for Foreign Liaison and International Co-operation. Regarded as a moderate, al-Muntasir's appointment was viewed by some observers as a sign of Libya's willingness to resume dialogue with the West over the Lockerbie issue (see below).

Western media reported in October 1993 that elements loyal to Qaddafi had suppressed an attempted military *coup d'état*, and that Libya's second-in-command, Maj. Abd as-Salam Jalloud, was among many placed under house arrest. Qaddafi denied that a coup had been attempted, but the appointment of known loyalists to senior positions in the General People's Committee was announced in January 1994. Most notably, Abd al-Majid al-Aoud, a member of Qaddafi's closest personal entourage, replaced Durdah, a close associate of Jalloud, as Secretary-General.

At its annual convention in March 1997 the GPC made changes to the composition and structure of the General People's Committee. Muhammad Ahmad al-Manqush was appointed Secretary-General of the Committee in December, as part of a further reorganization. The Secretariat for Arab Unity was abolished in a restructuring of the General People's Committee in December 1998, in accordance with Qaddafi's recently stated intention to forge closer relations with African rather than Arab countries.

In January 2000 Qaddafi unexpectedly attended the opening session of the GPC, at the end of which he demanded that the budget for 2000 be redrafted, with a view to channelling petroleum revenues into education, health and public services. Furthermore, he urged that the current administrative system, based on General People's Committees, be abandoned in favour of an alternative form of government. Accordingly, a radical decentralization of the Government was announced in March, whereby almost all of the People's Committees were dissolved and their responsibilities devolved mainly to local level: only those areas described as 'sovereign' were to remain under the control of the General People's Committee, now led by Mubarak Abdallah ash-Shamikh. Most notably, Ali Abd as-Salam at-Turayki was allocated the new post of Secretary for African Unity, being replaced as Secretary for Foreign Liaison and International Co-operation by Abd ar-Rahman Muhammad Shalgam. Al-Ujayli Abd as-Salam Burayni replaced Muhammad Abdullah Bait al-Mal as Secretary for Finance in October, when a further restructuring of the General People's Committees was announced; it had been reported in July that Bait al-Mal, along with the President of the Central Bank of Libya and a further 22 senior Libyan bankers, had been implicated in allegations of financial impropriety.

In September 2000 clashes occurred throughout the country between Libyans and nationals of several other African countries. The confrontations were believed to reflect resentment within Libya at the increasing numbers of black African migrants entering the country. A large number of Chadians and Sudanese were reportedly killed in incidents in the town of Az-Zawiyah, some 30 km west of Tripoli, and thousands more were interned in military camps. The Nigerian embassy in Tripoli was ransacked, and Libyan youths were also held responsible for an attack on a camp which was razed to the ground. The GPC announced its intention formally to investigate the incidents, and in October the evacuation and deportation of migrant workers from Nigeria, Chad, Niger, Sudan and Ghana commenced. It was estimated that as a result of the clashes more than 100 Africans had been killed and as many as 30,000 migrants had left Libya. Qaddafi subsequently apportioned blame for the incidents on 'foreign hostile hands' opposed to his plans to create an African Union. In May 2001 two Libyans, four Nigerians and one Ghanaian were sentenced to death for their roles in the violence. A further 12 defendants were sentenced to life imprisonment.

A minor reorganization of the General People's Committee was announced in September 2001, including the creation of a new Secretariat for Infrastructure, Urban Planning and Environment. In November it was announced that more than 40 government and bank officials had been sentenced to varying terms of imprisonment for corruption and embezzlement; reportedly among those convicted was Secretary for Finance Burayni, who received a one-year prison sentence for negligence.

In January 2003 Libya was elected to chair the session of the UN Human Rights Commission scheduled to be held in March. It was the first time since the formation of the Commission in 1947 that the decision had been voted upon, with Libya securing 33 of the 53 votes, and 17 countries, including the United Kingdom, abstaining; the USA, Canada and Guatemala opposed the proposal. Libya's election was widely criticized by a number of international human rights organizations.

In June 2003 Qaddafi dismissed ash-Shamikh from the post of Secretary of the General People's Committee, replacing him with Shukri Muhammad Ghanem, who was succeeded as Secretary for the Economy and Trade by Abd al-Qadir Balkheir. It was also announced that the Secretariat for African Unity had been merged with the Secretariat for Foreign Liaison and International Co-operation; Shalgam assumed responsibility for both portfolios. In March 2004 Qaddafi announced a further reorganization of the General People's Committee, which included the creation of four new secretariats (for national security, youth and sport, training and labour, and culture) and the restoration of the Secretariat for Energy, which had been abolished in 2000.

It was announced in October 2005 that 84 members of banned opposition group the Muslim Brotherhood, originally convicted and imprisoned in 2002, were to be retried, following the abolition in January 2005 of the unpopular People's Court, which had passed the original verdicts; the prisoners were subsequently released in March 2006. An extensive reorganization of the General People's Committee was announced that same month, including the creation of seven new secretariats. Ghanem was replaced as Secretary of the General People's Committee by the former Deputy Secretary for Production, Dr al-Baghdadi Ali al-Mahmoudi, and was handed the role of Chairman of the National Oil Corporation, while Muhammad Ali al-Houeiz, hitherto Secretary for Finance, was promoted to Deputy Secretary. The Secretariat for Energy, only reinstated in March 2004, was restructured and renamed the Secretariat for Industry, Electricity and Mines.

In May 2006 the US-based organization Human Rights Watch (HRW) called for the immediate release of Fathi al-Jahmi, a political dissident detained since March 2004 for criticizing Qaddafi. The Libyan Government avowed that the trial of al-Jahmi, who faced the death sentence if convicted, had commenced in 2005; however, no details of the specific charges were made available. HRW urged the Libyan Government to build upon its recent renunciation of terrorism by allowing peaceful opponents protesting against poor living conditions. In September 2006 HRW released a report in which it claimed that the Libyan Government routinely subjected refugees and asylum-seekers to violence, arrest without due cause and forcible deportation; the report urged members of the European Union (EU, see p. 255) to apply pressure on Libya to protect the rights of the hundreds of thousands of foreigners residing therein.

In October 2006 Abu Salim prison was again the scene of controversy when one inmate was killed and a further 17 people were injured in clashes between prisoners and guards. The disturbance, reported predominantly to have involved detainees who were members of the Libyan Islamic Fighting Group (LIFG), followed the decision by a Tripoli court earlier that same day to uphold the convictions, on charges of having links with the LIFG, of 190 inmates housed at the prison. The Libyan People's Prosecution Bureau, however, indicated that the violence had erupted when guards moved to end a sit-in protest against delays in legal proceedings. Amnesty International appealed for a thorough independent investigation into the incident.

Meanwhile, in July 2006 Qaddafi claimed that Libya had come close to building a nuclear bomb before abandoning in December 2003 its programmes to produce weapons of mass destruction (see below). In November 2006 an official source in Tripoli announced that Qaddafi's second son, Seif al-Islam, a popular figure among Libyans on account of his ongoing efforts to effect political and economic change, was to leave the country to take up employment with an international economic institution. His departure from Libya, which many feared would severely lessen hopes of genuine, lasting reform, was widely perceived to have been orchestrated by the Government in reaction to his outspoken criticism of the regime during a speech at a youth activist rally in Sirte in August.

In a speech broadcast live on state television in August 2007, Seif al-Islam Qaddafi urged the drafting of a new constitution or 'social contract' that would establish, *inter alia*, an independent central bank and a free media and judiciary. He also criticized the Libyan political system for its lack of a freely elected legislature, its refusal to allow the creation of political parties and its ongoing intolerance of political dissent, and called for political power to be more widely distributed, beyond the GPC and the General People's Committee. While few observers questioned Seif al-Islam's commitment to these proposals, it was widely believed that his father would never allow such radical reforms to be implemented.

Meanwhile, a reorganization of the General People's Committee was announced in January 2007, including five new appointments. Notable changes included the appointment of Dr Abd al-Hafid Mahmud Zalitni as Deputy Secretary and the modification of the recently restructured Secretariat for Industry, Electricity and Mines, its responsibilities to be shared henceforth between the newly created Secretariats for Industry and Mineral Resources and for Electricity, Water and Gas.

In November 2007 an audio tape purporting to be from Dr Ayman az-Zawahiri, the deputy leader of the militant Islamist organization al-Qa'ida (Base), was released; it included a message from Abu Laith al-Libi, the leader of al-Qa'ida in Afghanistan, who identified himself on the tape as also being a member of the LIFG. Al-Libi declared that the LIFG had pledged allegiance to al-Qa'ida Az-Zawahiri's own message urged the overthrow of the Libyan, Algerian, Moroccan and Tunisian Governments, and criticized Qaddafi for surrendering Libya's nuclear weapons materials to 'crusader masters'. In early April 2008 it was reported that around 90 members of the LIFG had been released from a prison in Tripoli, after they had renounced violence.

Qaddafi effected a reorganization of the General Secretariat of the GPC and of the General People's Committee in March 2008. Changes to the former included the replacement of az-Zanati as Secretary by Muftah Muhammad Kaiba, and the appointment of Huda Fathi ben Amer to the position of Secretary for Women's Affairs; changes to the latter included the appointment of former General People's Committee Secretary Mubarak Abdallah ash-Shamikh to the position of Deputy Secretary, and that of Gen. Abd al-Fattah Yunis al-Abaidi as the new Secretary for National Security. At the same time Qaddafi announced that he intended to abolish the majority of secretariats within the General People's Committee by the end of that year, in an effort to eliminate corruption and maladministration in what he termed the 'labyrinthine bureaucracy' of the Committee. Through a Wealth Distribution Programme (WDP), oil wealth would be redistributed by transferring the secretariats' powers to the people to enable them to manage their own affairs, requiring privatization of many sectors of Libyan society; only the secretariats for defence, internal security and foreign affairs would be retained, along with those responsible for strategic infrastructural projects, such as the Great Man-made River Project (see

Economic Affairs). At the beginning of September Qaddafi reiterated his plans to dismantle most of the secretariats and redistribute oil revenues, asserting that the reforms would come into effect in early 2009. Meanwhile, in August 2008 Seif al-Islam, for some time considered to be Qaddafi's probable successor, announced his intention to withdraw from politics. In the months that followed public demonstrations took place in several locations across the country to demand his return.

In November 2008, meanwhile, there were protests by members of the Tebu tribe in the southern town of Kufra against what they claimed was discrimination practised by the Qaddafi Government against indigenous peoples (including a restriction of access to health and education services). Dozens of people were reported to have been killed in violent controntations between the Libyan security forces and members of Tebu tribe.

At a meeting of the General People's Congress held in Sirte at the beginning of March 2009, it was announced the country's Basic People's Congresses had voted in the previous month to defer implementation of the WDP. At the Sirte meeting Qaddafi implemented a reorganization of the General Peoples's Committee. Notable changes included the appointment of Musa Kusa, hitherto head of Libya's foreign intelligence service, to replace Abd ar-Rahman Muhammad Shalgam as Secretary for Foreign Liaison and International Co-operation, and the appointment of Abd al-Hafid Mahmoud Zlitni, the head of the Libyan Investment Authority, to the position of Secretary for Finance and Planning. The finance and planning secretariats were among several to be merged, and the position of Secretary for Manpower, Training and Employment was abolished. The changes fell far short of the large-scale dismantling of secretariats that Qaddafi had previously outlined, but were none the less indicative of the ongoing programme of administrative retrenchment.

Various plans for pan-Arab unity led to the formation, in January 1972, of the Federation of Arab Republics, comprising Libya, Egypt and Syria. In 1972 Libya concluded an agreement with Egypt to merge the two countries in 1973. Neither union was effective, and proposals for union with Tunisia in 1974, Syria in 1980, Chad in 1981, Morocco in 1984, Algeria in 1987 and Sudan in 1990 also proved abortive.

Relations with Egypt, already tense following the failure of the Libya-Egypt union, deteriorated further when President Anwar Sadat launched the October 1973 war against Israel without consulting Qaddafi. In common with the other members of the League of Arab States (the Arab League, see p. 344), Libya strongly objected to Sadat's peace initiative with Israel, which culminated in the signing of the Camp David accords in 1978, and Libya also condemned the proposals for Middle East peace that were agreed by other Arab states in Fez, Morocco, in 1982. From the late 1980s, none the less, Egypt and Libya forged a close relationship, with Egypt acting as an intermediary between Libya and Western nations (particularly in negotiations resulting from the Lockerbie bombing—see below). Following the suspension of UN sanctions against Libya in April 1999 (see below), EgyptAir resumed regular flights to Tripoli in July 2000, and Libyan flights to Egypt recommenced later that month.

In 1973 Libyan forces occupied the 'Aozou strip', a reputedly mineral-rich region of 114,000 sq km in the extreme north of Chad, to which it laid claim on the basis of an unratified border treaty concluded by Italy and France in 1935. Thereafter, Libya became embroiled in the lengthy struggle for political control between rival forces in Chad (q.v.). During 1987 intense fighting took place for control of north-western Chad, and in August President Hissène Habré's forces advanced into the 'Aozou strip', occupying the town of Aozou. Libya responded by bombing towns in northern Chad, and recaptured Aozou. In September Chadian forces destroyed an airbase 100 km inside Libya. Later in September, however, the two countries agreed to observe a cease-fire sponsored by the Organization of African Unity (OAU, now African Union—AU, see p. 172), and in October 1988 Libya and Chad restored diplomatic relations. In August 1989, with Algerian mediation, Chad and Libya concluded an agreement to attempt to resolve the dispute over sovereignty of the 'Aozou strip' through a political settlement. Accordingly, the issue was submitted to the International Court of Justice in The Hague, Netherlands, which in February 1994 ruled against Libya's claim. All Libyan troops remaining in the 'Aozou strip' were withdrawn in May. In June Libya and Chad concluded a treaty of friendship, neighbourly terms and co-operation. In May 1998 Qaddafi made his first visit to Chad for 17 years, and in November the two countries officially opened two of their common border posts. In January 2002 Libyan mediation resulted in the brokering of a peace agreement between the Chadian Government and the rebel Mouvement pour la démocratie et la justice au Tchad, which had been in conflict since late 1998. Libya hosted talks between Chad and Sudan in February 2005, attended by Deby and President Omar Hassan Ahmad al-Bashir of Sudan, which aimed to reduce tensions between the two countries.

Libya's outspoken criticism of other Arab regimes, and perceived interference in the internal affairs of other countries, led to years of relative political isolation. However, in 1987 Qaddafi sought to realign Libyan policy with that of the majority of Arab states. Qaddafi was reconciled in March with Yasser Arafat's Fatah wing of the Palestine Liberation Organization (PLO—against which he had previously advocated revolt, owing to its more moderate policies) and attempted to reunite the opposing factions of the Palestinian movement. In September Libya re-established 'fraternal' links with Iraq, modifying its support for Iran in the Iran–Iraq War.

A summit meeting of North African heads of state, held in Morocco in February 1989, concluded a treaty proclaiming the Union du Maghreb arabe (UMA—Union of the Arab Maghreb, see p. 429), comprising Algeria, Libya, Mauritania, Morocco and Tunisia. The treaty envisaged: the establishment of a council of heads of state; regular meetings of ministers of foreign affairs; and the eventual free movement of goods, people, services and capital throughout the countries of the region. During 1989–92 the member states formulated 15 regional co-operation conventions. In February 1993, however, it was announced that, in view of the differing economic orientations of each signatory, no convention had actually been implemented, and the UMA's activities were to be limited. UMA leaders met in April 1994 (and subsequently on an annual basis). In the same year Libya threatened to leave the UMA unless member states ceased to comply with UN sanctions imposed on Libya (see below), and in 1995 it refused to assume the chairmanship of the organization, owing to their continuing compliance.

In February 1997, at a meeting hosted by Libya and attended by the Presidents of Sudan, Chad, Mali and Niger, and government ministers from Egypt, Burkina Faso and Tunisia, a treaty establishing the Community of Sahel-Saharan States (COMESSA, now CEN-SAD, see p. 425) was signed. CEN-SAD's general secretariat was temporarily located in Tripoli, and provisions were made for the establishment of a development bank, a council of heads of state and an executive council.

Libya's relations with the USA, which had been strained for many years, deteriorated significantly under the presidency of Ronald Reagan (1981–89), who accused the Libyan Government of sponsoring international terrorism. In January 1986 Reagan severed all economic and commercial relations with Libya, and in March Libyan forces fired missiles at US fighter aircraft, which were challenging Libya's attempts to enforce recognition of the whole of the Gulf of Sirte as its territorial waters. In retaliatory attacks in April US military aircraft bombed military installations, airports and official buildings, as well as alleged terrorist training camps and communication centres, in Tripoli and Benghazi. A total of 101 people, including many civilians, were reported to have died in the raids. The US Administration claimed in justification to have irrefutable proof of Libyan involvement in terrorist attacks and plots against US targets in Europe and the Middle East (including the recent bombing of a discothèque in Berlin, Germany—see below).

In November 1991 the US and British Governments announced that they would seek to extradite two Libyan citizens, Abd al-Baset Ali Muhammad al-Megrahi (a former head of security at Libyan Arab Airlines) and Al-Amin Khalifa Fhimah (an employee of the airline), alleged to have been responsible for an explosion that destroyed a Pan American World Airways (Pan Am) passenger aircraft over Lockerbie, Scotland, in December 1988, resulting in the deaths of 270 people. The Libyan Government denied any involvement in the bombing, and recommended that the allegations be investigated by a neutral body. In January 1992 the UN Security Council adopted a resolution (No. 731) demanding Libya's compliance with requests for the extradition of its two nationals and its co-operation with a French inquiry into the bombing over Niger, in September 1989, of a UTA passenger airline, in which all 171 passengers and crew had been killed. Libya's offer to try on its own territory the two men accused of the Lockerbie bombing was rejected by the USA, the United Kingdom and France, which urged the UN to impose sanctions on Libya. On 31 March 1992 the UN Security Council adopted a resolution (No. 748) providing for the imposition of economic sanctions against Libya if it refused to comply with Resolution 731, and to commit itself to a renunciation of international terrorism, by 15 April. Sanctions, including the severance of international air links, the prohibition of trade in arms and the reduction of Libya's diplomatic representation abroad, were duly imposed on the specified date. In May, at Qaddafi's instigation, 1,500 People's Congresses were convened in Libya and abroad, to enable the country's citizens to decide the fate of the two Lockerbie suspects and their response to the UN sanctions. The GPC announced in the following month its decision to allow the two Lockerbie suspects to be tried abroad, provided that the proceedings were 'fair and just'.

In August 1993 the USA, the United Kingdom and France announced that they would request the UN Security Council to strengthen the sanctions in force against Libya if, by 1 October, Libya had still not complied with Resolutions 731 and 748. The Libyan Government rejected this ultimatum, but stated its willingness to commence discussions with those three countries on an appropriate venue for the trial of the two Lockerbie suspects. In October the UN Secretary-General, Dr Boutros Boutros-Ghali, met the Libyan Secretary for Foreign Liaison and International Co-operation, but failed to secure agreement on a timetable for the surrender of the two suspects to either the USA or the United Kingdom. (US and British officials remained convinced that there was sufficient evidence of Libyan involvement to continue to seek the suspects' extradition, despite various reports issued in the early 1990s which alleged that Iranian, Syrian and Palestinian agents—sometimes separately, sometimes in collaboration—had been responsible for the bombing.) In November the Security Council adopted a resolution (No. 883) providing for the strengthening of the economic sanctions in force against Libya in the event of the country's failure fully to comply with Resolutions 731 and 748 by 1 December. The sanctions, which were duly applied, included: the closure of all Libyan Arab Airlines' offices abroad; a ban on the sale of equipment and services for the civil aviation sector; the sequestration of all Libyan financial resources overseas; and a ban on the sale to Libya of specified items for use in the petroleum and gas industries.

In January 1994 the Scottish lawyer representing the two Lockerbie suspects stated that they might be willing to stand trial in The Hague; this was subsequently endorsed as an appropriate venue by Qaddafi. In February, however, US President Bill Clinton recommended that an embargo be imposed on Libya's sales of petroleum (which accounted for some 98% of its export earnings) if the country continued to defy the international community. In mid-1996, following its repeated failure to persuade the UN to agree yet more stringent sanctions against Libya, the US Congress approved unilateral 'secondary' sanctions against Libya (and Iran). The Iran-Libya Sanctions Act (ILSA) sought to penalize companies operating in US markets that were investing more than US $40m. (later amended to $20m.) in Libya's oil and gas industries.

In July 1997 the Arab League, which had been criticized by Qaddafi for its lack of support, formally proposed that the two Libyan suspects in the Lockerbie case be tried by Scottish judges under Scottish law in a neutral country. In September the members of the League urged a relaxation of the air embargo on Libya and voted to defy UN sanctions by permitting aircraft carrying Qaddafi, and other flights for religious or humanitarian purposes, to land on their territory.

In August 1998 the United Kingdom and the USA proposed that the trial of the two Lockerbie suspects be held in the Netherlands under Scottish law and presided over by Scottish judges. The UN Security Council adopted a resolution (No. 1192) welcoming the initiative and providing for the suspension of sanctions upon the arrival in the Netherlands of the two suspects; additional sanctions were threatened if the Libyan authorities did not comply with the resolution.

In December 1998 the UN Secretary-General, Kofi Annan, held a meeting with Qaddafi in Libya in an attempt to expedite a trial of the Lockerbie suspects. Shortly afterwards the GPC endorsed the principle of a trial, but requested that the USA and the United Kingdom remove 'all remaining obstacles'. In a bid to break the impasse arising from Qaddafi's demand that the trial include a panel of international judges, envoys from Saudi Arabia and South Africa were dispatched to Libya in January 1999 to negotiate with Qaddafi. In February it was reported that the envoys had reached an understanding with the Libyan leader whereby UN observers would be allowed to monitor the two Libyan suspects during the trial, to ensure that they were not questioned by US and British agents, and afterwards, if they were convicted and imprisoned in Scotland. The diplomatic initiative culminated in March with a visit by President Nelson Mandela of South Africa to Libya, during which Qaddafi undertook to surrender the suspects by 6 April. The two Libyans duly arrived for trial in the Netherlands on 5 April and were transferred to Camp Zeist, a former US airbase near Utrecht, designated Scottish territory for the purposes of the trial, where they were formally arrested and charged with murder, conspiracy to murder and contravention of the 1982 Aviation Security Act. The UN Security Council immediately voted to suspend sanctions against Libya indefinitely, although they were not to be permanently revoked until Libya had complied with other conditions stipulated in Resolution 1192 (including the payment of compensation to the families of victims of the Lockerbie bombing). The USA refused to remove the 'secondary' sanctions against Libya, but subsequently announced that it would permit the sale of food and medical items to Libya on a 'case-by-case' basis. In June 1999 the US and Libyan ambassadors to the UN took part in what represented the first official contact between the two countries in 18 years. During the talks the USA informed Libya that it could not support a permanent end to UN sanctions until Libya had fully complied with Resolution 1192.

The two Libyan suspects appeared before the Scottish court in the Netherlands for the first time in December 1999, at a pre-trial hearing to decide on the court's jurisdiction. The presiding Scottish judge ruled that the two suspects could be tried on all three charges, and that they could be described as members of the Libyan intelligence services. The trial of al-Megrahi and Fhimah eventually commenced on 3 May 2000; both pleaded not guilty to the charges brought against them, and defence lawyers accused a number of organizations, including militant Palestinian resistance groups, of perpetrating the bombing.

In January 2001 prosecution lawyers unexpectedly announced that they would no longer pursue charges of conspiracy to murder and contravention of the 1982 Aviation Security Act. Accordingly, the trial proceeded on the sole charge of murder. On 31 January 2001 the judges announced that they had unanimously found al-Megrahi guilty of the murder of 270 people and sentenced him to life imprisonment, with the recommendation that he serve a minimum of 20 years. The judges accepted that al-Megrahi was a member of the Libyan intelligence services, and although they acknowledged their awareness of what they termed 'uncertainties and qualifications' in the case, they concluded that the evidence against him combined to form 'a real and convincing pattern' which left them with no reasonable doubt as to his guilt. Fhimah, however, was unanimously acquitted, owing to lack of proof, and freed to return to Libya. Despite mounting pressure from Arab League states, the British Government asserted that sanctions against Libya would not be permanently revoked until Libya accepted responsibility for the bombing and paid 'substantial' compensation. The newly inaugurated US President, George W. Bush, also indicated his support for this stance, and in July 2001 ILSA was extended for a further five-year term.

Meanwhile, demands for further investigation into the bombing, and Qaddafi's role in it, were rejected by senior Scottish legal officials, who stated that there was insufficient evidence to justify any further proceedings against those alleged to have abetted al-Megrahi, despite the fact that he had apparently not acted alone. Lawyers for al-Megrahi subsequently lodged an appeal against his conviction; the hearing, before five Scottish judges, began at Camp Zeist in January 2002. Al-Megrahi's lawyers based their case on what they termed new 'strong circumstantial evidence', which raised the possibility that the bomb had been placed on the aircraft at London, United Kingdom, and not in Malta, as the trial judges had concluded. In February Seif al-Islam Qaddafi indicated that Libya would pay compensation to the families of those killed in the Lockerbie bombing, regardless of the outcome of the appeal. In March the appeal was unanimously rejected, and al-Megrahi was transferred to a prison in Scotland to begin his sentence. Nevertheless, in late April 2009 lawyers for al-Megrahi began a second appeal against his conviction in a Scottish court.

In July 1999 Libya and the United Kingdom reached agreement on the full restoration of diplomatic relations after Qaddafi issued a statement in which he accepted Libya's 'general responsibility' for the death of Yvonne Fletcher, a British policewoman who was shot outside the Libyan People's Bureau in London in 1984, and agreed to co-operate with the investigation into the killing. The payment by Libya, in November 1999, of compensation to the victim's family facilitated the reopening of the British embassy in Tripoli the following month. The normalization of relations between the United Kingdom and Libya continued to progress and, in March 2001 Libya appointed an ambassador to the United Kingdom for the first time in 17 years. In August 2002 a minister of the British Foreign and Commonwealth Office visited Libya for talks with Qaddafi.

In April 2003 it was confirmed that, following negotiations in London between senior British, US and Libyan representatives, Libya had agreed to accept civil responsibility for the actions of its officials in the Lockerbie case and would pay US $10m. in compensation to the families of the victims. Payment of the compensation was to be a three-stage process: $4m. would be paid to each family on the permanent lifting of UN sanctions; a further $4m. would follow upon the removal of unilateral US sanctions; and a final payment of $2m. would be made when Libya was removed from the list of countries that the USA deemed to support international terrorism. However, Libya would pay only an additional $1m. to each family if the USA did not complete the second and third stages.

After further negotiations, on 16 August 2003 Libya delivered a letter to the President of the UN Security Council stating that it: accepted 'responsibility for the actions of its officials' in the Lockerbie bombing; agreed to pay compensation to the families of the victims; pledged co-operation in any further Lockerbie inquiry; agreed to continue its co-operation in the 'war on terror'; and to take practical measures to ensure that such co-operation was effective. Following the transfer of US $2,700m. in compensation to the International Bank of Settlements, the United Kingdom submitted a draft resolution to the Security Council requesting the formal lifting of UN sanctions against Libya. It was feared, however, that France, which had demanded a similar amount of compensation for families of victims of the UTA bombing in 1989 (see above), would veto the resolution unless Libyan officials agreed to an additional payment. The United Kingdom, France and the USA eventually agreed to postpone the vote on the draft resolution to allow more time for such an agreement to be reached. On 12 September 2003 13 of the 15 members of the UN Security Council approved the lifting of the sanctions imposed against Libya; France and the USA abstained from the vote. Later that month Libya announced its intention to commence dialogue with the USA aimed at normalizing bilateral relations. Nevertheless, the US Administration continued to insist that unilateral sanctions would remain in place until the Libyan Government addressed ongoing US concerns such as the infringement of human rights in the country and the pursuit of weapons of mass destruction.

In September 2003, following an intervention by the French President, Jacques Chirac, the Libyan Government and the families of the UTA bombing had reached partial agreement on the payment of additional compensation to the victims' relatives. Talks between Libya and France in October aimed at reaching a final settlement regarding the issue of compensation for the UTA bombing were suspended following a number of disagreements between the two sides. However, in January 2004 Libya agreed to pay an additional US $170m. to the relatives of the victims; the payment was to be made in four equal instalments, resulting in the families of each victim receiving an additional $1m.

Meanwhile, in October 2003 an official of the US Department of State accused Libya of having increased its efforts to purchase components for biological and chemical weapons since the lifting of UN sanctions the previous month, and warned that Libya would be added to the group of countries described by President Bush as forming an 'axis of evil'—comprising Iran, Iraq and the Democratic People's Republic of Korea (North Korea). In mid-December, however, in an unexpected development, the British Prime Minister, Tony Blair, announced that Libya had agreed to disclose and dismantle its programme to develop weapons of mass destruction and long-range ballistic missiles. The statement was the culmination of nine months of clandestine negotiations between Qaddafi and British and US diplomats, during which the Libyan authorities had reportedly shown evidence of a 'well advanced' nuclear weapons programme, as well as the existence of large quantities of chemical weapons and bombs designed to carry poisonous gas. Libya also agreed to adhere to the Chemical Weapons Convention and to sign an additional protocol allowing the International Atomic Energy Agency (IAEA) to carry out random inspections of its facilities. Upon visiting a number of sites in Tripoli in late December, in order to commence the process of dismantling Libya's weapons development projects, the Director-General of the IAEA, Dr Muhammad el-Baradei, insisted that these projects had been in the initial stages of development, contradicting the assessment given by the United Kingdom and the USA. In January 2004 the US Department of State confirmed that British and US intelligence agents had, in October 2003, intercepted a shipment of centrifuges capable of developing weapons-grade uranium destined for Tripoli. Also in January 2004 it was announced that Libya had ratified the IAEA's Comprehensive Nuclear Test Ban Treaty.

Further disagreements in January 2004 between the USA, the United Kingdom and the IAEA concerning their respective roles in the process of dismantling Libya's weapons facilities were finally resolved late that month: it was agreed that US and British officials would be responsible for destroying and removing the nuclear material and that the IAEA would verify that the dismantling process was complete. In February it was confirmed that an American diplomat had been stationed in the US interests section of the Belgian embassy in Tripoli, providing the USA with its first permanent diplomatic presence in Libya for 25 years. Also in February the Libyan Secretary for Foreign Liaison and International Co-operation, Abd ar-Rahman Muhammad Shalgam, visited London for talks with his British counterpart and Prime Minister Blair; this represented the first meeting between cabinet-level ministers of the two countries in more than 20 years.

The Secretary of the General People's Committee, Shukri Muhammad Ghanem, caused controversy in late February 2004 when he claimed that compensation was being paid to the families of the Lockerbie victims in order to 'buy peace' and avoid sanctions, and that the country did not accept responsibility for the Lockerbie bombing; he also denied any Libyan involvement in the murder of Yvonne Fletcher. The following day, however, Shalgam issued a statement in which he announced his regret at Ghanem's comments and reiterated that Libya stood by its acceptance of responsibility for the Lockerbie bombing. The USA subsequently lifted the restrictions on its citizens travelling to Libya. In March Libya signed an additional IAEA protocol allowing the agency to carry out random inspections of its nuclear facilities; moreover, Libya commenced the destruction of its supplies of chemical weapons and transported all of its remaining nuclear weapons-related equipment to the USA. Later that month the Organisation for the Prohibition of Chemical Weapons verified that Libya's declaration of its chemical weapons inventory (submitted to the UN in early March) had been accurate, after a series of inspections carried out by the agency's officials. In May it was announced that Libya would no longer conduct military trade with those countries that it believed to be involved in the proliferation of weapons of mass destruction.

Meanwhile, in late March 2004 William Burns, the US Assistant Secretary of the Bureau of Near Eastern Affairs, became the highest-ranking US official to visit Libya in more than 30 years; the principal issues under discussion were further moves towards the lifting of US sanctions on Libya and the restoration of normal bilateral relations. In April the USA announced that it would remove the restrictions that prevented US petroleum companies and banks from conducting commercial activities in Libya; however, it also declared that all Libyan assets held in the USA would remain frozen. In June it was revealed that Libya had resumed exports of petroleum to the USA. At the end of the month formal diplomatic relations were re-established between the two countries when a US liaison office was opened in Tripoli, and it was reported that Libya was preparing to establish diplomatic representation in Washington, DC. In September President Bush lifted all travel restrictions for charter and commercial flights between Libya and the USA. He also announced that the US $1,300m. of Libyan assets held in the USA or in US banks abroad would be unfrozen. In February 2005 the US authorities lifted all restrictions on Libyan diplomats travelling within the USA.

Relations between Libya and the United Kingdom continued to improve in 2004. In March Blair visited Tripoli and held talks with Qaddafi, after which the British Prime Minister stated that there was genuine hope for a 'new relationship', while Qaddafi insisted that he was willing to join the international 'war on terror'. It was also announced that British police officers would travel to Libya in April to continue investigations into the murder of Fletcher. In October 2005 Libya signed a memorandum of understanding with the British Government, which allowed for the deportation from the United Kingdom of Libyans suspected of involvement in terrorist activities. (The United

Kingdom is legally prevented from deporting foreign nationals to countries that it suspects of using inhumane or degrading treatment.) In May 2007 the British oil company BP (formerly British Petroleum) announced that it was to return to Libya, more than three decades after its expulsion from the country when Qaddafi had nationalized the oil industry in 1974; BP was granted onshore and offshore exploratory rights in a deal worth an estimated US $900m., a development welcomed by Blair as evidence of a 'transformed' bilateral relationship.

Meanwhile, in December 2004, with the unilateral sanctions imposed upon Libya by the USA having been lifted, Libya paid the second instalment of its compensation to the families of those killed in the Lockerbie explosion. In August 2005 the head of the Senate Foreign Relations Committee, Senator Richard Lugar, visited Libya to hold talks with Qaddafi; two months previously officials from the US State Department had praised Libya for its co-operation in the fight against international terrorism. In May 2006 the US Secretary of State, Condoleezza Rice, announced the US Administration's intention to restore full diplomatic relations between the two countries in recognition of Libya's 'continued commitment to its renunciation of terrorism', a development regarded by observers as the natural culmination of a process initiated in 2003 by Qaddafi's decision to abandon Libya's nuclear weapons programme; the US liaison office in Tripoli was formally upgraded to an embassy at the end of that month. In June 2006 Libya was removed from the US Department of State's list of countries deemed to support international terrorism. The renewal of full ties was expected significantly to boost both political and economic co-operation between the two nations, and was extended by the Bush Administration as an implicit incentive to the Iranian and North Korean Governments to dismantle their respective nuclear programmes.

In June 2006 tensions arose when Libyan lawyers in the USA insisted that, as a result of the expiration in December 2004 of an agreement concerning the transfer of the final portion of compensation for families of the victims of the Lockerbie bombing, the Libyan Government was no longer obligated to pay the final US $2m. promised to each family. Nevertheless, in July the USA lifted all air transport sanctions against Libya. In March 2007 the Libyan Government announced that it had reached an agreement with the USA that would aid the development of Libya's programme of nuclear energy generation; US officials contested that negotiations had been restricted to the possible establishment of a nuclear medicine centre in Libya. In further evidence of the improving relationship between the two countries, Shalgam made an official visit to Washington, DC, in January 2008, and held discussions with Condoleezza Rice—the first State Department visit by a Libyan foreign secretary in almost four decades. Rice called on Libya to improve its human rights record and to resolve the problem of outstanding compensation payments to families of victims of the Lockerbie bombing. Following discussions between Libyan and US officials in London in May 2008, a statement was issued reiterating the commitment of both parties to resolving all outstanding compensation claims. In mid-August representatives of both countries, meeting in Tripoli, signed a joint agreement on the full and final settlement of mutual claims by victims or their relatives in respect of bombings involving the two countries. (In the USA, the Libyan Claims Resolution Act had been signed into law earlier in the month.) Visiting Libya in early September, Rice—the first US Secretary of State to visit the country since 1953—stated that the two countries had entered a new phase in their relations, although differences remained. In October Libya paid US $1,500m. into an agreed compensation fund for the compensation of relatives of US victims of bombings covered by the agreement. In December, following Senate approval in the previous month, Gene A. Cretz was sworn in as the first US ambassador to Libya since 1972 (having been nominated to this post in July 2007). These developments in Libyan-US relations were expected to facilitate greater engagement by US investors in the Libyan economy and a growth in bilateral trade.

In January 2000 (shortly after the revelation of the seizure of missile parts by the United Kingdom) the EU withdrew an invitation to Qaddafi, issued by the Commission President, Romano Prodi, to visit the European Commission headquarters in Brussels, Belgium, on the grounds that Libya had not accepted EU conditions regarding commitment to human rights, democracy, free trade and support for the Middle East peace process. Apparently in reprisal, Libya immediately announced major commercial contracts with Russia and the People's Republic of China. Qaddafi none the less attended the EU-Africa summit meeting in Cairo, Egypt, in April, at which talks with Prodi and other European officials were described as 'positive'. Relations with the EU, and particularly with France, generally improved following talks in early 1996 between Libyan and EU representatives in Belgium. In July Qaddafi granted the French authorities investigating the 1989 bombing of the UTA passenger aircraft unprecedented access to Libyan evidence. This resulted in February 1998 in a judge's decision to try in absentia six Libyans suspected of involvement in the attack, and in March 1999 a French court sentenced the six suspects to life imprisonment. The French authorities issued international arrest warrants for the Libyans, and threatened to intensify sanctions against Libya if it did not impose the verdicts on the accused. In July Libya began payment of some US $31m. in compensation to the families of those killed in the bomb attack, although attempts by French lawyers on behalf of the victims' families to prosecute Qaddafi for complicity in the bombing of the aircraft were unsuccessful. Nevertheless, it was announced in January 2004 that Libya had agreed to pay an additional $170m. to the relatives of the victims (see above). During an official visit to Libya in November, French President Jacques Chirac affirmed his commitment to rebuilding diplomatic ties with Libya. In December 2005 the Libyan Government was ordered by a French court to pay an additional $4m. in compensation to families of victims of the 1989 bombing not included in the previous agreement. Despite the ongoing process of reparation, relations between the French and Libyan Governments improved in 2005 after France expressed its interest in assisting the development of civil nuclear technology in Libya. In March 2006 a deal on co-operation regarding the development of nuclear energy in Libya was signed by representatives of the two countries during a visit to Tripoli by the Director of France's Commissariat à l'Energie Atomique. In October 2006 it was reported that Libya and France were conducting negotiations about further possible military accords. Meanwhile, in April 2004 Qaddafi, who was visiting Europe for the first time in 15 years, met with several senior EU politicians in Brussels and addressed the European Commission. The ending of economic sanctions and an arms embargo imposed on Libya by the EU in 1986 was ratified by EU ministers in October 2004.

In October 1996, meanwhile, the German authorities announced that evidence existed to prove the Libyan Government's direct involvement in a bomb attack on a discothèque in Berlin in 1986. Arrest warrants were subsequently issued for the four Libyans suspected of carrying out the bombing, but in March 1997 a German parliamentary delegation recommended that regular contact between the German Parliament and the GPC should continue. In April 1998 Libya resolved to allow the German authorities to question the Libyan suspects. In May the two countries signed an agreement on economic co-operation. Following a lengthy trial, in November 2001 a court in Berlin sentenced four people, including a Libyan national, to between 12 and 14 years' imprisonment for their involvement in the bomb attack. Although Qaddafi's personal complicity in the incident could not be proven, the presiding judge stated that there was sufficient evidence to ascertain that the bombing had been carried out by members of the Libyan secret service and employees of the Libyan People's Bureau in the former East Germany.

In August 2003 the Qaddafi International Foundation for Charitable Associations (now the Qaddafi Development Foundation), a charity run by Seif al-Islam Qaddafi, offered to compensate the relatives of the three victims of the Berlin bomb attack. While negotiations between the USA and Libya regarding this compensation continued, a new round of talks between Germany and Libya began in July 2004 to decide upon compensation payments for the non-US citizens injured in the attack. The talks were finalized in the following month, and the Libyan authorities signed a deal in September agreeing to pay US $35m. to compensate some 160 non-US victims. The agreement signalled the start of improved relations between Germany and Libya, and in October Chancellor Gerhard Schröder paid an official visit to Libya. In talks with Schröder, Qaddafi requested compensation for the millions of landmines left behind by the Nazi German forces during the Second World War. While no compensation was offered, the German Chancellor agreed to provide assistance with mine detection and medical aid for victims. In November 2006 the German Minister of Foreign Affairs, Frank-Walter Steinmeier, visited Tripoli during a tour of North Africa. Steinmeier praised the progress made by the Libyan Government in renouncing terrorism and its nuclear weapons programme, and urged Libya to continue its gradual return to the international fold.

In February 1998 a Spanish minister visited Tripoli, following an announcement of Spain's intention to renew political and economic ties with Libya. However, the decision by France, Spain, Italy and Portugal to create a rapid reaction force in the Mediterranean was strongly condemned by Qaddafi. In July Italy formally apologized for its colonial rule of Libya, and commitments were made to improve bilateral relations. Following the suspension of international sanctions in April 1999, Italy's Prime Minister, Massimo D'Alema, travelled to Libya in December, thus becoming the first EU premier to visit the country since 1992. In December 2000 officials from the two countries signed accords regarding political consultation, visas and the removal of landmines during talks in Rome. In September 2003, just days after the ending of UN sanctions against Libya, the Spanish Prime Minister, José María Aznar López, visited Tripoli for talks with Qaddafi. In February 2004 the Italian Prime Minister, Silvio Berlusconi, became the first Western leader to meet with Qaddafi following the Libyan renouncement of its nuclear weapons programme. In August Berlusconi exerted pressure on Qaddafi to place stricter border controls on the country's northern coastline following an influx of illegal immigrants into the Italian island of Lampedusa from Libya. In October, as a result of a sudden increase in the number of illegal immigrants arriving from North Africa (up to 1,700 a week), the Italian Government began a mass expulsion of illegal immigrants to Libya. Having agreed to assist with the immigration problem, Libya returned some 1,000 of these people to Egypt. Also in October Qaddafi agreed to revoke a ban that prohibited some 20,000 Italian settlers who had been expelled from Libya in 1970 (following Qaddafi's rise to power) from visiting the country.

Diplomatic relations between Libya and Italy briefly soured, however, in early 2006. In February the Italian consulate in Benghazi and the residence of the consul were attacked and set alight by protesters, following the publication in numerous countries, including Italy, of cartoons originally printed in a Danish newspaper depicting the Prophet Muhammad, which were deemed to be offensive towards Islam. A day prior to the protests, an Italian government minister had appeared on Italian television wearing an item of clothing bearing one of the cartoons; it was claimed that the television appearance had provoked the disturbances in Benghazi, during which 11 people were killed. Libyan Secretary for National Security Nasser al-Mabrouk was suspended and referred for investigation over the conduct of security forces during the protests.

There was a significant development in relations between Libya and Italy in late August 2008 when, during a meeting with Qaddafi in Benghazi, Berlusconi issued an apology for the 'damage inflicted on Libya by Italy during the colonial era'. The two heads of state also signed a treaty of 'friendship, partnership and co-operation' (which was subsequently ratified in Sirte in February 2009), committing Italy to annual payments of US $200m. to Libya, over a period of 25 years, via investment and infrastructure projects in country. For its part, Libya agreed to co-operate more fully in efforts to combat illegal immigration, principally through the establishment of joint marine patrols of the Libyan coastline (due to commence in May 2009). This issue became particularly salient in early 2009, after a report published by the office of the United Nations High Commissioner for Refugees stated that the number of migrants arriving in Italy from Libya had risen to 33,000 in 2008 (from 20,000 in 2007). At the end of March 2009 more than 200 migrants were reported to have drowned after their boat, destined for Italy, capsized 30 miles off the Libyan coast. In an unprecedented move, Libya agreed in early May to take back more than 200 migrants discovered off the Libyan coastline by Italian marine patrols.

Meanwhile, Libya came under heavy criticism from EU officials in May 2004 after five Bulgarian nurses and a Palestinian doctor were sentenced to death for deliberately infecting more than 400 children at a Benghazi hospital in 1999 with blood containing the HIV virus. The trials were also criticized by international human rights associations as being unfair, and the nurses stated that their confessions had been extracted through torture. In December 2004 it was announced that Libya would review the sentences and later in the month Seif al-Islam Qaddafi reportedly stated that the medical workers would not be executed. By March 2005, however, the sentences remained in place and the six launched an official appeal. The judgment regarding the medical workers' appeal, which was expected in May, was delayed until November. Meanwhile, Libya continued to reject calls from Bulgaria, the USA and the EU to release the detainees, and demanded compensation from Bulgaria for the families affected by the case. The Bulgarian Government refused, stating that any payment would constitute an admission of the medical workers' guilt. In November the Supreme Court rescheduled the ruling for January 2006. However, in December 2005 the previous sentences were overturned by the Supreme Court and a retrial was ordered.

The retrial began in May 2006 but, following a brief initial hearing, was adjourned for procedural reasons until 13 June. Despite calls from the presiding judge to accelerate the pace of legal proceedings, the trial was beset by numerous subsequent delays and adjournments. Eventually, however, in December 2006, notwithstanding data arising from genetic analysis that strongly suggested that the children had been infected with HIV prior to the defendants' arrival in Libya in 1998, the original verdict was upheld and the six death sentences were reinstated. The EU Commissioner for Justice, Franco Frattini, called for the ruling to be reviewed, branding it an 'obstacle' to comfortable EU-Libyan relations, while the office of the UN High Commissioner for Human Rights urged the Libyan Government to intervene, citing 'serious and credible concerns' about the legitimacy of the trial. A few days after the ruling, the Government declared that it would not succumb to international pressure to invalidate the verdict, insisting that the Supreme Court had sole jurisdiction in the matter.

In January 2007 Qaddafi denounced 'Western intervention and pressure', reiterating the Government's argument that the outcome of the trial was a strictly juridical matter. However, it was reported later that month that the Libyan Government had extended an offer to free the six medical staff in exchange for the release of al-Megrahi, convicted for his part in the Lockerbie bombing (see above). Qaddafi, who claimed that the infections had arisen as a result of illicit experiments conducted on the children at the hospital by either the US or Israeli state intelligence agencies, linked the HIV case with the Lockerbie attack on numerous occasions, and demanded compensation of US $2,700m. to be paid to the affected families—the same amount tendered by the Libyan Government to the families of Lockerbie victims. In early 2007 the six defendants were also charged with slandering the Libyan police service, owing to their allegations of having been tortured during official interrogations; In February the defence filed an appeal against the verdict reached in December 2006, but this was rejected in July 2007 and the death sentences were upheld. A few days later, however, the High Judicial Court commuted the sentences to terms of life imprisonment, following the successful brokerage of a compensation deal, according to which the victims' families would receive a reported US $1m. for each child infected. The Bulgarian Government urged Libya to allow the medical workers to complete their sentences in Bulgaria, and Benita Ferrero-Waldner, the EU Commissioner responsible for External Relations and European Neighbourhood Policy, and Cécilia Sarkozy, then the wife of the French President Nicolas Sarkozy, both travelled to Tripoli to lobby the Libyan Government to this end. Libya finally acquiesced to the Bulgarian request, and the medical workers were duly released from Libyan custody on 24 July. Upon their return to Bulgaria, they were immediately pardoned by that country's President. A lawyer for the medical workers announced in July 2008 that the six were seeking compensation from Libya for their 'wrongful detention' and alleged mistreatment by the Libyan police.

In December 2007 Qaddafi made an official visit to the French capital at the invitation of President Nicolas Sarkozy—the first such invitation from a Western country since Libya had abandoned its nuclear weapons programme in 2003, and interpreted by some as a reward for the Libyan leader's decision to release the Bulgarian medical workers earlier in 2007 (see above). The visit provoked strong censure from both French and Libyan opposition politicians, as well as international human rights groups, owing to Libya's questionable human rights record. While Sarkozy insisted that he had broached the issue of human rights with the Libyan leader, Qaddafi was reported as saying that human rights had not in fact been discussed. During Qaddafi's visit deals worth an estimated €10,000m. were signed between the two countries, including plans for a joint-venture nuclear-powered water desalination plant and the sale of French Airbus aircraft; Libya also expressed a keen interest in the future purchase of military equipment, including fighter jets, helicopters and an air-defence radar system. Franco-Libyan relations were, however, once more strained in mid-2008 when Qaddafi criticized President Sarkozy's project to create a Union for the Mediterranean. Qaddafi, who had expressed concerns that French promotion of Mediterranean co-operation represented a reassertion of colonial dominance over former North African colonies, and also that the initiative would undermine the role of the AU, refused to attend the official inauguration of the union on in July.

In the context of progress towards the full normalization of relations between Libya and the USA, and the release from prison of the six Bulgarian medical workers, in mid-November 2008 formal negotiations on an EU-Libya Framework Agreement were inaugurated. The agreement, intended to encompass economic, political, social and cultural co-operation, would represent the first such partnership between the EU and Libya. It was also aimed to achieve greater consensus regarding the issue of illegal immigration to EU countries via Libya: during a second round of negotiations held in Tripoli in February 2009, Libya was offered some €20m. in assistance to address illegal migration.

During a visit to Libya in April 2008 by the Russian President, Vladimir Putin, several agreements were signed on co-operation in energy, military and infrastructure projects. Putin agreed to cancel Libya debts amounting to some US 4,500m. Qaddafi began his first visit to Russia in late October: the principal issues discussed during the visit were collaboration in energy projects, including Russian assistance for Libya's civilian nuclear programme, and military co-operation.

During the late 1990s and 2000s Qaddafi oscillated between identifying Libya as an African nation on the one hand, and emphasizing Libya's links with the Arab world on the other, often to suit his own political aims. In mid-1998 Qaddafi announced his intention to ally Libya more closely with African rather than Arab countries. In October, as further evidence of his dissatisfaction with Arab states, Qaddafi changed the name of Libya's mission to the Arab League from 'permanent' to 'resident'. In September 1999, on the 30th anniversary of his seizure of power, Qaddafi hosted an extraordinary OAU summit in Sirte, at which he presented his vision of a United States of Africa and demanded that Africa be given veto power on the UN Security Council. The 'Sirte Declaration', a final document adopted by the 43 attending heads of state and government, called for the strengthening of the OAU, the establishment of a pan-African parliament, African monetary union and an African court of justice. At a further extraordinary summit of the OAU in Sirte in March 2001 it was announced that the organization's member states had overwhelmingly endorsed the proposals to declare the formation of the AU. In July 2002 Qaddafi travelled to Durban, South Africa, for the 38th and final summit of the OAU, which saw the formal creation of the new AU, chaired by South African President Thabo Mbeki. During the summit Mbeki and numerous other African heads of state attempted to persuade Qaddafi to abandon his hostility towards the New Partnership for Africa's Development, a contract between Africa and the international community under which, in exchange for aid and investment, the African states agreed to strive towards democracy and good governance. In October Libya notified the Arab League of its intention to withdraw from the organization. Although no official reason for the withdrawal was given, reports indicated that senior Libyan officials had cited the Arab League's 'inefficiency' in dealing with the crises in Iraq and the Palestinian territories as its motives. In March 2003 Libyan officials confirmed that the threat of withdrawal was 'serious and official'.

Meanwhile, Qaddafi's growing influence in Africa was somewhat checked in January 2003 following the removal of some 300 Libyan troops from the Central African Republic, to whose Government they had been providing protection. In the previous month an agreement between Libya and Zimbabwe that would have resulted in the exchange of Libyan fuel for Zimbabwean beef, sugar and tobacco was abandoned. Attempts to revive the trade pact in mid-2003, which would have resulted in Zimbabwe mortgaging its petroleum assets to Libya, proved unsuccessful, and the abolition of the Secretariat for African Unity was widely interpreted as evidence of the failure of Qaddafi's African policy. In June 2004 allegations were made that in mid-2003 Qaddafi had ordered the assassination of Crown Prince Abdullah of Saudi Arabia, the kingdom's de facto leader, following a dispute between the two leaders at the Arab League summit held in March. (Libya also reportedly accused Saudi Arabia of financing Libyan opposition groups that had attempted to assassinate Qaddafi.) Libyan officials strongly refuted these allegations; however, in December 2004 Saudi Arabia recalled its ambassador from Tripoli and dismissed the Libyan ambassador in the Saudi capital, Riyadh. In the same month Libya announced that it had decided to relinquish its chairmanship of the UMA, assumed in December 2003, citing the failure of the organization to achieve regional co-operation.

In May 2006 Sudanese President Omar Hassan Ahmad al-Bashir expressed gratitude to Qaddafi for the latter's role in finding a resolution to the crisis in Darfur and proposed the establishment of a tripartite committee, comprising representatives of the Libyan and Sudanese Governments and the Sudan Liberation Movement, to oversee the implementation of the peace agreement signed between the two latter parties on 5 May (see the chapter on Sudan). In October Qaddafi and Egyptian President Muhammad Hosni Mubarak met in Tripoli to discuss the situation in Darfur, whereupon they concurred on the importance of the AU in resolving the crisis, and urged a rejection of foreign intervention. In November Qaddafi accused the USA and other Western countries of involving themselves in the Darfur crisis not because of genuine compassion but in order to secure oil, and, by means of the deployment of UN troops, to effect the return of colonialism to Africa. In July 2007 Libya hosted an international conference on Darfur, co-chaired by the AU and the UN.

In June 2006 ministers responsible for foreign affairs from Algeria, Libya, Mauritania, Morocco and Tunisia convened in Tripoli to discuss a potential revivification of the five-nation UMA, which had remained dormant for more than a decade predominately owing to Algerian–Moroccan disagreements concerning Western Sahara (see the chapters on Algeria and Morocco). This will to relaunch the UMA was restated in April 2008 during celebrations held in Morocco to mark the 50th anniversary of the summit at which the idea of a union of Arab Maghreb states was initially put forth. A year later delegates responsible for foreign affairs from the UMA member states again met in Tripoli, where they reiterated their commitment to improving political and economic co-operation among the countries of North Africa.

In March 2007 Qaddafi announced his decision to boycott the Arab League summit meeting in Riyadh, insisting that Libya was an African nation and had 'turned its back to Arabs'. Later that year Qaddafi embarked upon a tour of West Africa, including visits to Côte d'Ivoire, Guinea, Mali and Sierra Leone, and culminating with his attendance in July at an AU summit meeting, held in the Ghanaian capital, Accra, which focused predominantly on proposals to establish a pan-African government. However, Qaddafi was reported to have left the session abruptly when the majority of those present rejected his call for the immediate creation of a United States of Africa, and in February 2008 he threatened to sever Libyan ties with Africa, pledging to transfer Libya's African investments to alternative destinations in Arab and European countries if his vision for African unity continued to be ignored. In February 2009 Qaddafi was, none the less, appointed to the chairmanship of the AU. Qaddafi immediately used this role once more to promote the concept of a United States of Africa.

Meanwhile, in January 2004 it was reported that a senior Israeli diplomat had held talks in Paris, France, in December 2003 with Libyan representatives, with the aim of establishing diplomatic relations between the two countries. While an Israeli official confirmed that a meeting had taken place, the Libyan Government denied that any contact had been made.

Government

Power is vested in the people through People's Congresses, Popular Committees, Trade Unions, Vocational Syndicates, and with the General People's Congress (GPC) and its General Secretariat. The Head of State is the Revolutionary Leader, elected by the GPC; however, Col Muammar al-Qaddafi himself rejects this nomenclature and all other titles. Executive power is exercised by the General People's Committee. The country is divided into three provinces, 10 governorates and 1,500 administrative communes.

Defence

As assessed at November 2008, Libya's active armed forces totalled 76,000 (including an estimated 25,000 conscripts): army an estimated 50,000; air force 18,000; navy 8,000. Military service is by selective conscription, lasting up to two years. There was additionally a People's Militia of some 40,000 reserves. Libya's defence budget for 2007 was LD 807m.

Economic Affairs

In 2007, according to estimates by the World Bank, Libya's gross national income (GNI), measured at average 2005–07 prices, was US $55,473m., equivalent to $9,010 per head (or $14,710 on an international purchasing-power parity basis). During 2000–07, it was estimated, the population increased at an average annual rate of 2.0%, while gross domestic product (GDP) per head increased, in real terms, by an average of 1.9% per year. According to World Bank estimates, overall GDP increased, in real terms, at an average annual rate of 4.0% in 2000–07. Preliminary official data for 2002–07 indicated that real GDP increased by an average of 8.0% per year, with growth of 5.6% being recorded in 2007.

Agriculture (including forestry and fishing) contributed 2.1% of GDP in 2007, according to preliminary official figures, and engaged 7.6% of the employed labour force in the same year. The principal subsistence crops are wheat and barley; other crops include potatoes, olives, tomatoes, onions, watermelons, dates and citrus fruits. An aim of the Great Man-made River Project (GMR), in progress since 1984, is to reclaim some 130,000 ha of arable land; more than 70% of water to be delivered by the GMR is intended for agricultural use. The main agricultural activity is animal husbandry, with sheep and goats being the principal livestock. During 2002–07, according to preliminary official data, agricultural GDP increased at an average annual rate of 5.9%; the sector's GDP increased by 4.0% in 2007.

Industry (including mining, manufacturing, construction and power) contributed 75.9% of GDP in 2007, according to preliminary official figures, and engaged 16.6% of the employed labour force in the same year. Preliminary official data indicated that the GDP of the industrial sector increased at an average annual rate of 7.9% in 2002–07; industrial GDP increased by 4.5% in 2007.

Mining contributed 65.6% of GDP in 2007, according to preliminary official figures, although the sector engaged just 3.1% of the employed labour force in that year. Libya's economy is overwhelmingly reliant on its petroleum and natural gas resources. Hydrocarbons contributed 91.1% of total government revenue in 2007. At the end of 2007 proven recoverable reserves of petroleum were estimated at 41,500m. barrels, the largest proven reserves in Africa and sufficient to enable production to be maintained—at that year's levels, averaging 1.85m. barrels per day (b/d)—for 61 years. As a member of the Organization of the Petroleum Exporting Countries (OPEC, see p. 386), Libya is subject to production quotas agreed by the Organization's Conference. Libya's natural gas reserves are extensive (estimated at 1,500,000m. cu m at the end of 2007). Libya also has reserves of iron ore, salt, limestone, clay, sulphur and gypsum. According to preliminary official figures, the GDP of the mining sector increased, in real terms, at an average annual rate of 7.6% in 2002–07; mining GDP increased by 1.7% in 2007.

Manufacturing contributed 4.5% of GDP in 2007, according to preliminary official figures, and engaged 7.9% of the employed labour force in the same year. The principal manufacturing activity is petroleum refining. Other important activities include the production of iron, steel and cement, chemicals manufacturing and the processing of agricultural products. Preliminary official figures indicated that the GDP of the manufacturing sector increased at an average annual rate of 7.9% during 2002–07; the sector's GDP increased by 7.6% in 2007.

Energy is derived principally from petroleum, which contributed 71.8% of total electricity output in 2005, and natural gas (28.2%). Libya is a net exporter of fuels.

Services contributed 22.0% of GDP in 2007, according to preliminary official figures, and engaged 75.9% of the employed labour force in the same year. Efforts to reform the financial sector, hitherto highly state-controlled, have notably included the sale, in 2007–08, of minority stakes in two banks to foreign interests. A stock exchange was established in 2007. The Government has invested heavily in recent years to expand and rehabilitate the Libya's tourism infrastructure. Visitor arrivals neared 1m. in 2004. During 2002–07, according to preliminary official data, the GDP of the services sector increased at an average annual rate of 8.3%; services GDP increased by 7.9% in 2007.

In 2007 Libya recorded a visible trade surplus of US $29,269m., and there was a surplus of $28,454m. on the current account of the balance of payments. In 2004 the principal source of imports was Italy (which provided 18.3% of total imports); Germany, Japan and the Republic of Korea were also important suppliers. The principal market for exports in 2000 was Italy (42.6%); Germany, Spain, Turkey and France were also significant purchasers. The petroleum sector is overwhelmingly Libya's principal generator of exports revenue: according to balance of payments data published by the IMF, hydrocarbons (including foreign partners' share) accounted for some 97.5% of the value of merchandise exports in 2007. The principal imports in 2005 were plant and equipment, basic manufactures, and food and live animals.

An overall budgetary surplus of LD 23,096m. was recorded in 2007, equivalent to 26.2% of GDP. According to the Central Bank of Libya, the annual rate of inflation averaged 2.9% in 2003–07; consumer prices increased by an average of 6.2% in 2007, compared with an increase of 1.4% in 2006.

Libya is a member of the Arab Monetary Fund (see p. 184), the Council of Arab Economic Unity (see p. 233), the Islamic Development Bank (see p. 340), the Organization of Arab Petroleum Exporting Countries (OAPEC, see p. 379), OPEC (see p. 386) and the Union du Maghreb arabe (UMA—Union of the Arab Maghreb, see p. 429) In 2004 the World Trade Organization (WTO, see p. 410) agreed to commence accession negotiations with Libya, which had applied to join the organization in 2001.

Strong GDP growth and robust budgetary and balance of payments surpluses in 2003–07 were achieved in the context of high international oil prices, in conjunction with the ending of international sanctions and the 'normalization' of Libya's external relations. The growth of the non-hydrocarbons sector was notably strong during this period, with the construction, transport and trade sectors registering particular expansion. (Efforts to expand and upgrade infrastructure were reflected in growth in the construction sector averaging more than 14% per year in 2003–07.) A new sovereign wealth fund, the Libyan Investment Authority, which became operational in 2007, was established to manage state-allocated assets, including the Oil Reserve Fund, with the intention of creating a diversified investment portfolio (the bulk of investments were to be made overseas) as part of efforts to achieve diversification from the country's overwhelming reliance on the oil sector. With the ending of international sanctions, Libya rapidly became a major centre for hydrocarbons exploration, and output of both oil and natural gas expanded rapidly. (Libya's geographical location, close to Europe and with access to the Atlantic via the Mediterranean, together with the optimum refining-quality of its oil reserves, have made it particularly attractive to foreign oil companies.) Furthermore, since large areas of Libyan territory remained hitherto undrilled, it was believed that reserves could be significantly higher than currently estimated. However, industry analysts considered that Libya's target of oil production of 3m. b/d by the mid-2010s was unlikely to be achieved. While an expansion of output, and thus the volume of sales, of oil and natural gas was expected partially to offset the impact of lower international oil prices from the latter part of 2008, a marked contraction was expected to be recorded in the budgetary and trade supluses, while public spending requirements were expected to remain high. In an assessment of the economy issued in September 2008, the IMF noted that despite the Government's commitment to the diversification and liberalization of the economy, in the context of what was termed 'people's capitalism', the economy remained heavily state-controlled and overwhelmingly dependent on hydrocarbons. Further rationalization of public expenditure was urged in the absence of a significant decline in inflation. Moreover, the IMF expressed caution regarding implementation of the Wealth Distribution Programme (WDP), announced by Col Qaddafi in March of that year, which was intended to redistribute oil wealth by transferring effective control of the delivery of public services among the population while radically reducing the number of government ministries. (In early 2009 the country's Basic People's Congresses voted to defer implementation of the WDP.)

Education

Education is compulsory for children between six and 15 years of age. Primary education begins at the age of six and lasts for six years. Secondary education, from the age of 12, is divided into two three-year periods: an intermediate and vocational stage, and a further secondary and advanced vocational stage. In 2004/05 enrolment at the secondary level was equivalent to 98.4% of the relevant age-group. Libya also has institutes for agricultural, technical and vocational training, of which there were 84 in 2004. In 1995 the number of public universities had reached 13, but subsequent policy changes resulted in a reduction of this number, to nine, by the mid-2000s. In 1992 enrolment at the tertiary level was equivalent to 18.4% of the relevant age-group; in 2004

LIBYA

there were an estimated 196,500 students enrolled in tertiary education.

Public Holidays

2009: 7 January*† (Ashoura), 9 March* (Mouloud, Birth of Muhammad), 28 March (Evacuation Day), 11 June (Evacuation Day), 19 July* (Leilat al-Meiraj, Ascension of Muhammad), 1 September (Revolution Day), 20 September* (Id al-Fitr, end of Ramadan), 7 October (Evacuation Day), 27 November* (Id al-Adha, Feast of the Sacrifice), 18 December* (Muharram, Islamic New Year), 27 December*† (Ashoura).
2010: 26 February* (Mouloud, Birth of Muhammad), 28 March (Evacuation Day), 11 June (Evacuation Day), 8 July* (Leilat al-Meiraj, Ascension of Muhammad), 1 September (Revolution Day), 10 September* (Id al-Fitr, end of Ramadan), 7 October (Evacuation Day), 16 November* (Id al-Adha, Feast of the Sacrifice), 7 December* (Muharram, Islamic New Year), 16 December* (Ashoura).

* These holidays are dependent on the Islamic lunar calendar and may vary by one or two days from the dates given.
† This festival occurs twice (in the Islamic years AH 1430 and 1431) within the same Gregorian year.

Weights and Measures

The metric system is in force.

Statistical Survey

Sources (unless otherwise stated): National Corporation for Information and Documentation; Census and Statistical Dept, Secretariat of Planning, Sharia Damascus 40, 2nd Floor, Tripoli; tel. (21) 3331731; Central Bank of Libya, POB 1103, Sharia al-Malik Seoud, Tripoli; tel. (21) 3333591; fax (21) 4441488; e-mail info@cbl.gov.ly; internet www.cbl.gov.ly.

Area and Population

AREA, POPULATION AND DENSITY

Area (sq km)	1,775,500*
Population (census results)	
August 1995 (provisional)	
Males	2,236,943
Females	2,168,043
Total	4,404,986†
2003 (provisional)	5,678,484
Population (official estimates at 30 September)	
2007	5,735,000
2008	6,000,000
Density (per sq km) at 30 September 2008	3.4

* 685,524 sq miles.
† Excluding 406,916 non-Libyans.

Source: partly National Authority for Information and Authentication.

POPULATION BY REGION
(1995 census, provisional figures)

Al-Batnan	151,240	Misratah (Misurata)	488,573
Jebel Akhdar	381,165	Najghaza	244,553
Banghazi (Benghazi)	665,615	Tarabulus (Tripoli)	1,313,996
Al-Wosta	240,574	Az-Zawiyah (Zawia)	517,395
Al-Wahat	62,056	Jebel Gharbi	316,970
Al-Jufra	39,335	Fazzan (Fezzan)	314,029
Sofuljin	76,401	**Total**	**4,811,902**

PRINCIPAL TOWNS
(population at census of 2003)

Tarabulus (Tripoli, the capital)	1,149,957	Az-Zawiyah (Zawia)	197,177
Banghazi (Benghazi)	636,992	Al-Jabal al-Akhader	194,185
Misratah (Misurata)	360,521	Ajdabiya (Ejdabia)	165,839
Almirqeb	328,292	Garyan (Ghryan)	161,408
Turhona and Misllatah	296,092	Sirte (Surt)	156,839
Al-Jfara	289,340	Surman and Subratha	152,521
An-Niikat al-Ghames	208,954		

Source: National Authority for Information and Authentication.

BIRTHS, MARRIAGES AND DEATHS

	Registered live births		Registered marriages*		Registered deaths*	
	Number	Rate (per 1,000)	Number	Rate (per 1,000)	Number	Rate (per 1,000)
1994	98,423	20.1	19,190	3.9	14,036	2.9
1995	88,779	17.9	21,358	4.3	13,538	4.6
1996	90,428	17.8	18,743	3.7	12,281	2.4

Source: UN, *Demographic Yearbook*.

2002*: Registered live births 111,053 (rate per 1,000 20.2); Registered marriages 33,323; Registered deaths 19,362 (Source: mostly UN, *Population and Vital Statistics Report*).

* Registration is incomplete.

Life expectancy (years at birth, WHO estimates): 72.3 (males 70.2; females 74.9) in 2006 (Source: WHO, *World Health Statistics*).

EMPLOYMENT
('000 persons)

	2005	2006	2007
Agriculture, forestry and fishing	117.0	125.8	135.7
Oil and gas extraction	29.3	31.0	32.8
Mining and quarrying	21.1	22.4	23.7
Manufacturing	131.1	136.3	141.8
Electricity, gas and water	50.4	53.3	56.4
Construction	47.0	44.6	42.4
Trade, restaurants and hotels	190.1	192.6	195.1
Transport and communications	121.9	130.5	140.8
Financing, insurance and real estate	35.8	38.4	41.2
Public administration	271.8	280.9	290.4
Education	453.2	468.4	484.2
Health services	196.3	202.9	209.7
Other services	0.1	0.2	0.3
Total	**1,665.2**	**1,727.2**	**1,794.5**
Libyans	1,479.1	1,543.3	1,613.6
Non-Libyans	186.1	183.9	180.9

Source: IMF, *Socialist People's Libyan Arab Jamahiriya: Statistical Appendix* (September 2008).

LIBYA

Health and Welfare

KEY INDICATORS

Total fertility rate (children per woman, 2006)	2.8
Under-5 mortality rate (per 1,000 live births, 2006)	18
HIV/AIDS (% of persons aged 15–49, 2003)	0.30
Physicians (per 1,000 head, 2004)	1.30
Hospital beds (per 1,000 head, 2006)	3.7
Health expenditure (2006): US $ per head (PPP)	270
Health expenditure (2006): % of GDP	2.9
Health expenditure (2006): public (% of total)	70.2
Access to water (% of persons, 2002)	72
Access to sanitation (% of persons, 2004)	97
Human Development Index (2006): ranking	52
Human Development Index (2006): value	0.840

For sources and definitions, see explanatory note on p. vi.

Agriculture

PRINCIPAL CROPS
('000 metric tons)

	2005	2006	2007†
Wheat	125*	100*	100
Barley	100*	100*	100
Potatoes	195*	200*	196
Broad beans, horse beans, dry†	13	13	13
Almonds, with shell†	25	25	25
Groundnuts, with shell†	23	22	23
Olives†	180	160	165
Tomatoes†	190	184	190
Pumpkins, squash and gourds†	30	30	30
Cucumbers and gherkins†	22	17	19
Chillies and peppers, green†	15	15	15
Onions and shallots, green†	53	53	53
Onions, dry†	182	181	181
Peas, green†	5	5	5
Carrots and turnips†	25	25	25
Watermelons†	240	260	268
Cantaloupes and other melons†	26	25	26
Oranges†	44	43	45
Tangerines, mandarins, etc.†	10	10	10
Lemons and limes†	17	16	16
Apples†	20	17	19
Apricots†	18	17	17
Peaches and nectarines†	10	10	10
Plums and sloes†	32	33	33
Grapes†	30	32	30
Figs†	10	9	10
Dates†	150	170	175

* Unofficial figure.
† FAO estimates.

Aggregate production ('000 metric tons, may include official, semi-official or estimated data): Total cereals 234 in 2005, 210 in 2006, 209 in 2007; Total roots and tubers 195 in 2005, 200 in 2006, 196 in 2007; Total vegetables (incl. melons) 882 in 2005, 889 in 2006, 906 in 2007; Total fruits (excl. melons) 346 in 2005, 358 in 2006, 366 in 2007.

Source: FAO.

LIVESTOCK
('000 head, year ending September, FAO estimates)

	2002	2003	2004
Horses	45	45	45
Asses, mules or hinnies	30	30	30
Cattle	130	130	130
Camels	46	47	47
Sheep	4,500	4,500	4,500
Goats	1,265	1,265	1,265
Poultry	25	25	25

2005–07: Figures assumed to be unchanged from 2004 (FAO estimates).
Source: FAO.

LIVESTOCK PRODUCTS
('000 metric tons)

	2005	2006*	2007*
Cattle meat*	6	6	6
Sheep meat*	24	28	28
Goat meat*	6	6	6
Chicken meat*	99	99	100
Cows' milk*	130	130	130
Sheep's milk*	56	56	56
Goats' milk	15	15	15
Hen eggs*	60	60	60
Wool, greasy*	10	9	9

* FAO estimates.
Source: FAO.

Forestry

ROUNDWOOD REMOVALS
('000 cubic metres, excl. bark, FAO estimates)

	2005	2006	2007
Sawlogs, veneer logs and logs for sleepers*	63	63	63
Other industrial wood	53	53	53
Fuel wood	536	901	914
Total	652	1,017	1,030

* Annual output assumed to be unchanged since 1978.
Source: FAO.

SAWNWOOD PRODUCTION
('000 cubic metres, incl. railway sleepers, FAO estimates)

	1976	1977	1978
Total (all broadleaved)*	9	21	31

* Annual output to 2007 assumed to be unchanged since 1978 (FAO estimates).
Source: FAO.

Fishing

(metric tons, live weight, FAO estimates)

	2004	2005	2006
Capture	39,971	40,164	40,347
Groupers	2,500	2,500	2,500
Bogue	2,600	2,700	2,700
Porgies and seabreams	3,900	4,000	4,000
Surmullet	3,700	3,800	3,800
Jack and horse mackerels	4,300	4,400	4,400
Sardinellas	7,800	8,000	8,000
'Scomber' mackerels	3,500	3,600	3,600
Aquaculture	316	481	480
Total catch (incl. others)	40,287	40,645	40,827

Source: FAO.

Mining

('000 metric tons unless otherwise indicated)

	2005	2006	2007
Crude petroleum ('000 barrels)	618,000	642,800	653,800
Natural gas (million cu ft)	765,400	948,100	1,024,400
Salt*	40	40	n.a.
Gypsum (crude)*	175	175	n.a.

* Source: US Geological Survey.

LIBYA

Industry

SELECTED PRODUCTS
('000 metric tons)

	2005	2006	2007
Jet fuels (incl. kerosene)	1,495.2	1,396.2	1,470.4
Motor spirit (petrol)	800.0	757.9	812.6
Naphthas (raw)	2,769.8	2,725.3	2,676.5
Gas-diesel (distillate fuel) oil	4,103.6	4,103.7	4,137.1
Residual fuel oils	7,083.8	7,053.1	7,004.3

Cement (hydraulic, '000 metric tons): 3,600 in 2004 (estimate); 3,621 in 2005; 3,600 in 2006 (estimate) (Source: US Geological Survey).

Electric energy (million kWh): 18,943 in 2003; 20,202 in 2004; 22,500 in 2005 (Source: UN, *Industrial Commodity Statistics Yearbook*).

Finance

CURRENCY AND EXCHANGE RATES

Monetary Units
1,000 dirhams = 1 Libyan dinar (LD).

Sterling, Dollar and Euro Equivalents (31 October 2008)
£1 sterling = 2.1000 dinars;
US $1 = 1.2984 dinars;
€1 = 1.6563 dinars;
100 Libyan dinars = £47.62 = $77.02 = €60.37.

Average Exchange Rate (Libyan dinar per US $)
2005 1.3084
2006 1.3136
2007 1.2626

BUDGET
(LD million)

Revenue	2005	2006	2007
Hydrocarbon budget allocation	34,764	43,566	48,639
Non-hydrocarbon	2,650	3,523	5,475
Non-hydrocarbon tax revenue	1,526	1,768	2,531
Taxes on income and profits	397	691	1,376
Taxes on international trade	517	527	528
Other tax revenue	611	569	627
Non-hydrocarbon non-tax revenue	1,124	1,736	2,944
Total	37,413	47,088	54,114

Expenditure	2005	2006	2007
Current	8,245	9,693	12,511
Administrative budget	8,146	8,988	12,511
Expenditure on goods and services	6,649	7,424	10,414
Wages and salaries	4,258	4,772	7,286
Subsidies and other current transfers	1,497	1,564	2,097
Extrabudgetary current expenditure	99	705	—
Capital	10,815	11,685	18,506
Development budget	7,570	10,079	12,137
Extrabudgetary capital expenditure	825	1,026	4,134
Total*	19,060	21,377	31,018

*Including net lending (LD million): 2,420 in 2005; 580 in 2006; 2,235 in 2007.

Source: IMF, *The Socialist People's Libyan Arab Jamahiriya: Statistical Appendix* (September 2008).

INTERNATIONAL RESERVES
(US $ million at 31 December)

	2006	2007	2008
Gold (national valuation)	194	194	194
IMF special drawing rights	787	882	901
Reserve position in IMF	595	625	609
Foreign exchange	57,907	77,897	90,803
Total	59,483	79,598	92,507

Source: IMF, *International Financial Statistics*.

MONEY SUPPLY
(LD million at 31 December)

	2006	2007	2008
Currency outside banks	3,932.9	4,581.2	5,608.3
Private-sector deposits at Central Bank	537.5	582.6	11.3
Demand deposits at commercial banks	10,506.9	16,375.1	27,055.8
Total money (incl. others)	15,455.3	22,013.8	33,323.1

Source: IMF, *International Financial Statistics*.

COST OF LIVING
(Consumer Price Index; base: 1999 = 100)

	2005	2006	2007
Personal services and others	77.5	80.2	80.6
Medical care	107.6	115.7	121.3
Recreation and education	82.4	81.0	82.8
Transport and communication	98.3	100.1	102.8
Clothing and shoes	61.3	61.6	60.9
Furniture	71.2	71.1	69.9
Housing	86.9	99.1	106.5
Food, beverages and tobacco	77.4	78.8	88.2
All items	77.9	80.4	85.9

NATIONAL ACCOUNTS
(LD million at current prices)

Expenditure on the Gross Domestic Product

	2003	2004	2005*
Government final consumption expenditure	4,643.3	5,132.4	6,712.5
Private final consumption expenditure	14,061.8	15,669.3	18,148.6
Gross fixed capital formation	3,330.7	3,987.5	4,807.0
Changes in inventories	138.0	167.0	202.1
Total domestic expenditure	22,173.8	24,956.2	29,870.2
Exports of goods and services	18,770.0	27,928.0	40,613.0
Less Imports of goods and services	9,212.0	11,398.0	14,458.0
GDP in purchasers' values	31,731.8	41,486.2	56,025.2
GDP at constant 1997 prices	16,160.6	17,025.7	17,971.2

LIBYA

Gross Domestic Product by Economic Activity

	2005	2006	2007*
Agriculture, forestry and fishing	1,447.5	1,643.1	1,905.3
Mining and quarrying (incl. hydrocarbons)	43,946.7	55,649.0	58,963.8
Manufacturing	3,131.7	3,606.9	4,032.1
Electricity, gas and water	876.6	972.7	1,019.1
Construction	2,683.5	3,129.3	4,198.4
Trade, restaurants and hotels	2,657.5	2,863.3	3,396.3
Transport, storage and communications	2,412.6	2,724.2	3,299.5
Financial intermediation	717.1	816.5	980.8
Real estate, renting and business activities	4,324.2	4,643.5	5,218.9
Education and health, etc.†	4,556.5	5,020.0	6,606.3
Other services	166.8	194.3	223.1
Sub-total	66,920.8	81,262.9	89,843.6
Less Financial intermediation services indirectly measured	470.0	533.0	583.3
Total	66,450.7	80,729.9	89,260.3

* Preliminary figures.
† Private sector only.

BALANCE OF PAYMENTS
(US $ million)

	2005	2006	2007
Exports of goods f.o.b.	28,849	37,473	46,970
Imports of goods f.o.b.	−11,174	−13,219	−17,701
Trade balance	17,675	24,254	29,269
Exports of services	534	489	99
Imports of services	−2,349	−2,564	−2,666
Balance on goods and services	15,860	22,179	26,702
Other income received	1,837	2,180	4,471
Other income paid	−2,118	−2,775	−2,500
Balance on goods, services and income	15,579	21,584	28,673
Current transfers received	418	1,646	598
Current transfers paid	−1,052	−1,060	−817
Current balance	14,945	22,170	28,454
Direct investment abroad	−128	−474	−767
Direct investment from abroad	1,038	2,064	4,689
Portfolio investment assets	−393	−5,198	−1,409
Other investment assets	−416	−1,194	−8,970
Other investment liabilities	291	71	49
Net errors and omissions	−1,497	2,008	−1,183
Overall balance	13,840	19,447	20,862

Source: IMF, *International Financial Statistics*.

External Trade

PRINCIPAL COMMODITIES
(LD million)

Imports c.i.f.	2004	2005
Food and live animals	1,159.8	1,177.4
Beverages and tobacco	15.1	30.2
Animal and vegetable oils and fats	156.5	111.6
Crude materials (inedible) except fuels	118.1	145.8
Mineral fuels and related materials	56.4	30.0
Chemical materials	334.4	458.1
Basic manufactures	1,646.7	1,650.0
Plant and equipment	3,960.3	3,787.0
Miscellaneous products	807.9	563.1
Total	8,255.2	7,953.5

Exports f.o.b.*	2004	2005
Food and live animals	3.2	2.3
Mineral fuels and related products	20,085.6	30,312.2
Chemicals and related products	675.9	825.2
Basic manufactures	73.2	2.3
Machinery and transport equipment	8.9	2.5
Total (incl. others)	20,848.3	31,148.0

* Including re-exports.

2006 (LD million): Total imports c.i.f. 7,934.7; Total exports (incl. re-exports) 36,336.3.

PRINCIPAL TRADING PARTNERS
(US $ million)*

Imports c.i.f.	2003	2004
Argentina	25.7	99.6
Belgium	101.3	118.3
Brazil	50.7	81.2
Canada	37.2	114.4
China, People's Republic	85.1	207.3
Egypt	129.7	131.6
France (incl. Monaco)	274.3	255.4
Germany	486.2	760.8
Greece	47.7	40.9
India	12.8	162.6
Italy	925.3	1,156.7
Japan	321.9	525.4
Korea, Republic	96.5	471.2
Malta	160.6	78.0
Netherlands	69.9	72.0
Spain	64.4	92.7
Sweden	22.6	68.3
Switzerland-Liechtenstein	93.9	41.9
Tunisia	135.8	145.6
Turkey	92.1	111.3
United Arab Emirates	99.1	23.8
United Kingdom	300.8	260.2
USA	20.3	157.0
Total (incl. others)	4,322.5	6,317.6

Exports f.o.b.	1998	1999	2000
Austria	125.2	87.0	18.9
Egypt	97.6	94.1	57.1
France (incl. Monaco)	236.8	509.8	574.4
Germany	1,002.9	1,507.1	1,556.2
Greece	161.6	186.1	270.7
Italy	2,449.9	2,987.0	4,343.8
Netherlands	141.0	81.8	70.0
Portugal	29.6	20.6	49.9
Spain	685.9	1,084.5	1,555.0
Switzerland-Liechtenstein	0.9	105.2	18.4
Tunisia	303.6	320.6	423.2
Turkey	394.4	5.7	769.3
United Kingdom	158.0	104.4	233.6
Total (incl. others)	6,131.4	7,905.1	10,194.9

* Imports by country of origin; exports by country of destination. Figures exclude trade in gold.

Source: UN, *International Trade Statistics Yearbook*.

Transport

ROAD TRAFFIC
(motor vehicles in use at 31 December)

	2000	2001
Passenger cars	549,600	552,700
Commercial vehicles	177,400	195,500

Buses and coaches: 1,424 in 1995; 1,490 in 1996.

Motorcycles and mopeds: 1,078 in 1995; 1,112 in 1996.

Sources: IRF, *World Road Statistics*; UN, *Statistical Yearbook*.

SHIPPING

Merchant Fleet
(registered at 31 December)

	2005	2006	2007
Number of vessels	140	139	141
Total displacement ('000 grt)	117.3	105.4	97.9

Source: Lloyd's Register-Fairplay, *World Fleet Statistics*.

International Sea-borne Freight Traffic
(estimates, '000 metric tons)

	1991	1992	1993
Goods loaded	57,243	59,894	62,491
Goods unloaded	7,630	7,710	7,808

Source: UN Economic Commission for Africa, *African Statistical Yearbook*.

CIVIL AVIATION
(traffic on scheduled services)

	2002	2003	2004
Kilometres flown (million)	4	8	9
Passengers carried ('000)	559	742	850
Passenger-km (million)	409	825	985
Total ton-km (million)	33	69	82

Source: UN, *Statistical Yearbook*.

Tourism

VISITOR ARRIVALS*

Country of origin	2002	2003	2004
Algeria	70,416	71,657	73,459
Egypt	354,189	429,220	441,230
Morocco	19,076	19,120	20,803
Tunisia	329,145	346,331	366,871
Total (incl. others)	857,952	957,896	999,343

* Including same-day visitors (excursionists).

Tourism receipts (US $ million, incl. passenger transport): 261 in 2004; 301 in 2005; 244 in 2006.

Source: World Tourism Organization.

Communications Media

	2004	2005	2006
Telephones ('000 main lines in use)	799.5	852.3	n.a.
Mobile cellular telephones ('000 subscribers)	500.0	2,000.0	3,927.6
Broadband subscribers ('000)	—	—	9.6
Internet users ('000)	205	232	260

Book production (titles): 26 in 1994.

Radio receivers ('000 in use): 1,350 in 1997.

Television receivers ('000 in use): 730 in 1997.

Daily newspapers: 4 in 1998 (estimated average circulation 71,100).

Personal computers ('000 in use): 130 in 2005.

2007: Mobile cellular telephones ('000 subscribers) 4,500.0.

Sources: UNESCO, *Statistical Yearbook*; International Telecommunication Union.

Education

(1995/96, unless otherwise indicated)

	Institutions	Teachers	Students
Primary and preparatory: general	2,733*	122,020	1,333,679
Primary and preparatory: vocational	168	n.a.	22,490
Secondary: general	n.a.	17,668	170,573
Secondary: teacher training	n.a.	2,760†	23,919
Secondary: vocational	312	n.a.	109,074
Universities	13	n.a.	126,348

* 1993/94.
† 1992/93.

Source: partly UNESCO, *Statistical Yearbook*.

1998: 1,160,315 primary school students (Source: World Bank).

Students (UNESCO estimates, 2005/06 unless otherwise indicated): Pre-primary 22,246; Primary 755,338; Secondary 732,614; Tertiary 375,028 (2002/03) (Source: UNESCO Institute for Statistics).

Teachers (UNESCO estimates, 2005/06 unless otherwise indicated): Pre-primary 2,486; Primary 148,476; Secondary 152,338; Tertiary 15,711 (2002/03) (Source: UNESCO Institute for Statistics).

Adult literacy rate (UNESCO estimates): 86.8% (males 94.5%; females 78.4%) in 2007 (Source: UNESCO Institute for Statistics).

Directory

The Constitution

The Libyan Arab People, meeting in the General People's Congress in Sebha from 2–28 March 1977, proclaimed its adherence to freedom and its readiness to defend it on its own land and anywhere else in the world. It also announced: its adherence to socialism and its commitment to achieving total Arab Unity; its adherence to the moral human values; and confirmation of the march of the revolution led by Col Muammar al-Qaddafi, the Revolutionary Leader, towards complete People's Authority.

The Libyan Arab People announced the following:

(i) The official name of Libya is henceforth the Socialist People's Libyan Arab Jamahiriya.

(ii) The Holy Koran is the social code in the Socialist People's Libyan Arab Jamahiriya.

(iii) The Direct People's Authority is the basis for the political order in the Socialist People's Libyan Arab Jamahiriya. The People shall practise its authority through People's Congresses, Popular Committees, Trade Unions, Vocational Syndicates and the General People's Congress, in the presence of the law.

(iv) The defence of our homeland is the responsibility of every citizen. The whole people shall be trained militarily and armed by

LIBYA

general military training, the preparation of which shall be specified by the law.

The General People's Congress in its extraordinary session held in Sebha issued four decrees:

The first decree announced the establishment of the People's Authority in compliance with the resolutions and recommendations of the People's Congresses and Trade Unions.

The second decree stipulated the choice of Col Muammar al-Qaddafi, the Revolutionary Leader, as Secretary-General of the General People's Congress.

The third decree stipulated the formation of the General Secretariat of the General People's Congress (see The Government, below).

The fourth decree stipulated the formation of the General People's Committee to carry out the tasks of the various former ministries (see The Government, below).

In 1986 it was announced that the country's official name was to be the Great Socialist People's Libyan Arab Jamahiriya.

The Government

HEAD OF STATE*

Revolutionary Leader: Col MUAMMAR AL-QADDAFI (took office as Chairman of the Revolution Command Council 8 September 1969).

GENERAL SECRETARIAT OF THE GENERAL PEOPLE'S CONGRESS
(April 2009)

During 2008 Qaddafi announced his intention to dismantle the executive arm of government, retaining only a limited number of secretariats (ministries).

Secretary: MUFTAH MUHAMMAD KAIBA.
Assistant Secretary for Popular Congresses: (vacant).
Secretary for Culture and Mass Mobilization: ABD AL-HAMID AS-SID ZINTANI.
Secretary for Trade Unions, Leagues and Professional Unions: ABDALLAH IDRIS IBRAHIM.
Secretary for Social Affairs: SALIMA SHAIBAN ABD AL-JABAR.
Secretary for Infrastructure, Urban Planning and Environment: Dr SALIM AHMAD FUNAYT.
Secretary for Human Resources: Dr AL-BAGHDADI ALI AL-MAHMOUDI.
Secretary for Foreign Affairs: SULEIMAN SASI ASH-SHAHOUMI.
Secretary for Economy: ABD AS-SALAM AHMAD NUWEIR.
Secretary for Legal Affairs and Human Rights: HUSSEIN AL-WAHISHI AS-SADIQ.
Secretary for Security Affairs: MUFTAH ABD AS-SALAM BUKAR.
Secretary for Women's Affairs: HUDA FATHI BEN AMER.
Secretary for Union Syndicates and Vocational Association Affairs: Dr MUHAMMAD BIN HUSSEIN JABRAIL.

GENERAL PEOPLE'S COMMITTEE
(April 2009)

During 2008 Qaddafi announced his intention to dismantle the executive arm of government, retaining only a limited number of secretariats (ministries).

Secretary: Dr AL-BAGHDADI ALI AL-MAHMOUDI.
Deputy Secretary: MUBARAK ABDALLAH ASH-SHAMIKH.
Secretary for Foreign Liaison and International Co-operation: MUSA KUSA.
Secretary for Justice: MOUSTAFA MUHAMMAD ABU AL-JELIL.
Secretary for Finance and Planning: Dr ABD AL-HAFID MAHMOUD ZLITNI.
Secretary for the Treasury: ALI AL-HESNAWI.
Secretary for Industry, the Economy and Trade: MUHAMMAD ALI AL-HOUEIJ.
Secretary for Health and Environment: MAHMOUD MUHAMMAD HIJAZI.
Secretary for Public Utilities: MAATUK MUHAMMAD MAATUK.
Secretary for National Planning: Dr BASHIR ALI ZENBIL.
Secretary for Agriculture, Animal Wealth and Marine Resources: ABU BAKR MABROUK AL-MANSOURI.

*Qaddafi himself rejects this nomenclature and all other titles.

Secretary for Public Security: Gen. ABD AL-FATTAH YUNIS AL-ABAIDI.
Secretary for Social Affairs: Dr IBRAHIM AZ-ZARRUQ ASH-SHARIF.
Secretary for Transport and Telecommunications: MUHAMMAD ALI ZIDANE.
Secretary for Education and Research: ABD-AL KARIM AL-FAKHRI.

Legislature

GENERAL PEOPLE'S CONGRESS

The Senate and House of Representatives were dissolved after the *coup d'état* of September 1969, and the provisional Constitution issued in December 1969 made no mention of elections or a return to parliamentary procedure. However, in January 1971 Col Qaddafi announced that a new legislature would be appointed, not elected; no date was mentioned. All political parties other than the Arab Socialist Union were banned. In November 1975 provision was made for the creation of the 1,112-member General National Congress of the Arab Socialist Union, which met officially in January 1976. This later became the General People's Congress, which met for the first time in November 1976 and in March 1977 began introducing the wide-ranging changes outlined in the Constitution (above).

Secretary-General: MUFTAH MUHAMMAD KAIBA.

Political Organizations

In June 1971 the Arab Socialist Union (ASU) was established as the country's sole authorized political party. The General National Congress of the ASU held its first session in January 1976 and later became the General People's Congress (see Legislature).

The following groups are in opposition to the Government:

Ansarollah (Followers of God): f. 1996.
Islamic Martyrs' Movement (IMM): seeks to establish an Islamic republic; Leader ABU SHALTILAH; Spokesman ABDALLAH AHMAD.
Libyan Baathist Party.
Libyan Change and Reform Movement: breakaway group from NFSL.
Libyan Conservatives' Party: f. 1996.
Libyan Constitutional Grouping.
Libyan Democratic Authority: f. 1993.
Libyan Democratic Conference: f. 1992.
Libyan Democratic Movement: f. 1977; external group.
Libyan Islamic Fighting Group (LIFG): f. 1995; seeks to establish an Islamic regime; claimed responsibility for subversive activities in early 1996, and engaged in armed clashes with security forces in mid- to late 1990s; Leader ANAS SEBAI.
Libyan Movement for Change and Reform: POB 3423, London, NW6 7TZ, United Kingdom; f. 1994.
Libyan National Alliance: f. 1980 in Cairo, Egypt.
Libyan National Democratic Grouping: Leader MAHMOUD SULAYMAN AL-MAGHRABI.
Movement of Patriotic Libyans: f. 1997; aims to establish a 'free Libyan state' based on a market economy.
National Front for the Salvation of Libya (NFSL): e-mail info@libya-nfsl.org; internet www.libya-nfsl.org; f. 1981 in Khartoum, Sudan; aims to replace the existing regime by a democratically elected govt; Leader MUHAMMAD MEGARIEF.

Diplomatic Representation

EMBASSIES IN LIBYA

Afghanistan: POB 4245, Sharia Mozhar al-Aftes, Tripoli; tel. (21) 4841441; fax (21) 4841443; e-mail tripoli@afghanistan.mfa.net; Ambassador MUHAMMAD ALLAH HAYDARI.
Algeria: Sharia Kairouan 12, Tripoli; tel. (21) 4440025; fax (21) 3334631; Ambassador MENOUER RABIE.
Argentina: POB 932, Gargaresh, Madina Syahia, Tripoli; tel. (21) 4781148; fax (21) 4782105; e-mail embartrip@hotmail.com; Ambassador JUAN CARLOS VALLE RALEIGH.
Austria: POB 3207, Sharia Khalid ibn al-Walid, Garden City, Tripoli; tel. (21) 4443379; fax (21) 4440838; e-mail tripolis-ob@bmeia.gv.at; Ambassador Dr DOROTHEA AUER.

LIBYA

Bangladesh: POB 5086, Hi Damasq, Tripoli; tel. (21) 4911198; fax (21) 4906616; e-mail bdtripoli@bsisp.net; Ambassador JAMILUDDIN AHSAN.

Belarus: POB 1530, Tripoli; tel. (21) 3612555; fax (21) 3614298; e-mail libya@belembassy.org; Ambassador ANATOLIY STEPIEN.

Belgium: POB 91650, Jasmin St, Hay Andalus, Tripoli; tel. (21) 4782044; fax (21) 4782046; e-mail tripoli@diplobel.be; internet www.diplomatie.be/tripoli; Ambassador ALPHONSE CREUSEN.

Benin: POB 6676, Sharia Ghout ash-Shaal, Tripoli; tel. (21) 4837663; fax (21) 834569; Ambassador LAFIA CHABI.

Bosnia and Herzegovina: POB 6946, Sharia Abd al-Melik bin Kutn, Tripoli; tel. (21) 4774327; fax (21) 4770652; Ambassador ŽELJKO GRBIĆ.

Brazil: POB 2270, Sharia ben Ashour, Tripoli; tel. (21) 3614894; fax (21) 3614895; e-mail brcastripoli@lttnet.net; Ambassador LUCIANO AROZA.

Bulgaria: POB 2945, Sharia Selma ben Al-Ukua, Ben Ashour Area No. 58-6, Tripoli; tel. (21) 3605625; fax (21) 3609990; e-mail tripoli@embassy.transat.bg; internet www.mfa.bg/tripoli; Ambassador ALEXANDER OLSHEVSKI.

Burkina Faso: POB 81902, Route de Gargeresh, Tripoli; tel. (21) 4771221; fax (21) 4778037; e-mail ambafasolibye@yahoo.fr; Ambassador YOUSSOUF SANGARE.

Burundi: POB 2817, Sharia Ras Hassan, Tripoli; tel. (21) 608848; Ambassador RAPHAËL BITARIHO.

Canada: POB 93392, Al-Fateh Tower Post Office, Tripoli; tel. (21) 3351633; fax (21) 3351630; e-mail trpli@international.gc.ca; internet www.dfait-maeci.gc.ca/libya; Ambassador HAIG SARAFIAN.

Chad: POB 1078, Sharia Muhammad Mussadeq 25, Tripoli; tel. (21) 4443955; Ambassador IBRAHIM MAHAMAT TIDEI.

China, People's Republic: POB 5329, Sharia Menstir, Andalus, Gargaresh, Tripoli; tel. (21) 4832914; fax (21) 4831877; e-mail chinaemb_ly@mfa.gov.cn; Ambassador WANG WANGSHENG.

Croatia: Great al-Fatah Towers, Tower 2, Floor 16, Room 166, Tripoli; tel. (21) 3351097; fax (21) 3351486; e-mail croemb.tripoli@mvpei.hr; Ambassador JOVAN VEJNOVIĆ.

Cuba: POB 83738, Sharia ibn al-Youmin, Ahmed al-Mahzumi, Tripoli; tel. (21) 4775216; fax (21) 4776294; e-mail embacuba.libia@lttnet.net; internet emba.cubaminrex.cu/libia; Ambassador PABLO ÁNGEL REYES DOMÍNGUEZ.

Cyprus: POB 3284, Sharia adh-Dhul 60, Ben Ashour, Tripoli; tel. (21) 3351400; fax (21) 3351402; e-mail cyprusembassy@lttnet.net; Ambassador CHARALAMBOS HADGISAVVAS.

Czech Republic: POB 1097, Sharia Ahmad Lutfi Sayed, Sharia ben Ashour, Tripoli; tel. (21) 3615436; fax (21) 3615437; e-mail tripoli@embassy.mzv.cz; internet www.mzv.cz/tripoli; Ambassador DUŠAN STRAUCH.

Egypt: POB 1105, The Grand Hotel, Tripoli; tel. (21) 4448909; fax (21) 4449262; e-mail egyemblib@hotmail.com; internet www.mfa.gov.eg/missions/libya/tripoli/embassy/en-gb; Ambassador MUHAMMAD FATIHY REFA'A ET-TAHTAWI.

Equatorial Guinea: Tripoli.

Eritrea: POB 91279, Tripoli; tel. (21) 4773568; fax (21) 4780152; Ambassador ABDALLAH MUSSA.

France: POB 312, Sharia Beni al-Amar, Hay Andalus, Tripoli; tel. (21) 4774891; fax (21) 4778266; e-mail info@ambafrance-ly.org; internet www.ambafrance-ly.org; Ambassador FRANÇOIS GOUYETTE.

Germany: POB 302, Sharia Hassan al-Mashai, Tripoli; tel. (21) 3330554; fax (21) 4448968; e-mail info@tripolis.diplo.de; internet www.tripolis.diplo.de; Ambassador BERND WESTPHAL.

Ghana: POB 4169, Andalus 21/A, nr Funduk Shati Gargaresh, Tripoli; tel. (21) 4772534; fax (21) 4773557; e-mail ghaemb@all-computers.com; Ambassador GEORGE KUMI.

Greece: POB 5147, Sharia Jalal Bayar 18, Tripoli; tel. (21) 3338563; fax (21) 4441907; e-mail gremb.tri@mfa.gr; Ambassador CHRYSANTHI PANAGIOTOPOULOU.

Guinea: POB 10657, Hay Andalus, Tripoli; tel. (21) 4772793; fax (21) 4773441; e-mail magatte@lttnet.net; Ambassador ABDUL AZIZ SOUMAH.

Holy See: Tripoli; Apostolic Nuncio Most Rev. CAPUTO TOMMASO (Titular Archbishop of Otricoli).

Hungary: POB 4010, Sharia Talha ben Abdullah, Tripoli; tel. (21) 3618218; fax (21) 3618220; e-mail missions.tpi@kum.hu; Ambassador Dr ISTVÁN CSEJTEI.

India: POB 3150, 16 Sharia Mahmud Shaltut, Tripoli; tel. (21) 4441835; fax (21) 3337560; e-mail indembtrip@hotmail.com; Ambassador MORUGESAN MINMEKLAY.

Indonesia: POB 5921, Tripoli; tel. (21) 4842067; fax (21) 4842069; e-mail indonesia@bsisp.net.

Iran: POB 6185, Tripoli; tel. (21) 3609552; fax (21) 3611674; e-mail iran_em_tripoli@hotmail.com; Ambassador MUHAMMAD MENHAJ.

Italy: POB 912, Sharia Vahran 1, Tripoli; tel. (21) 3334133; fax (21) 3331673; e-mail ambasciata.tripoli@esteri.it; internet www.ambtripoli.esteri.it; Ambassador FRANCESCO PAULO TRUPIANO.

Japan: POB 3265, Sharia Jamal ad-Din al-Waeli, Hay Andalus, Tripoli; tel. (21) 4781041; fax (21) 4781044; Ambassador AKIRA WATANABE.

Korea, Democratic People's Republic: Tripoli; Ambassador KIM TONG JE.

Korea, Republic: POB 4781, Gargaresh, Tripoli; tel. (21) 4831322; fax (21) 4831324; e-mail lbkor@hanmail.net; Ambassador KIM JOONG-JAE.

Kuwait: POB 2225, Beit al-Mal Beach, Tripoli; tel. (21) 4440281; fax (21) 607053; Chargé d'affaires (vacant).

Lebanon: POB 927, Auss bin al-Arkam, Ben Achour 10, Tripoli; tel. (21) 3615744; fax (21) 3611740; e-mail emblebanon_ly@hotmail.com; Chargé d'affaires a.i. NAZIH ACHOUR.

Lesotho: POB 771, Hay Andalus, Tripoli; tel. (21) 4840900; fax (21) 4840901; e-mail motholok@foreign.gov.ls; Ambassador PAUL KHOASHANE MOTHOLO.

Madagascar: POB 652, Maidane az-Zajeir, Tripoli; tel. (21) 3408257; fax (21) 3408256; e-mail ambamtri@yahoo.fr; Ambassador DIEUDONNÉ MARIE MICHEL RAZAFINDRANDRIATSIMANIRY.

Malaysia: POB 6309, Hay Andalus, Tripoli; tel. (21) 4830854; fax (21) 4831496; e-mail mwtripoli@lttnet.net; Ambassador MOHD ZULKEPHLI MOHD NOOR.

Mali: POB 2008, Sharia Jaraba Saniet Zarrouk, Tripoli; tel. (21) 4444924; Ambassador OUSMANE TANDJA.

Malta: POB 2534, Sharia Ubei ben Ka'ab, Tripoli; tel. (21) 3611181; fax (21) 3611180; e-mail maltaembassy.tripoli@gov.mt; Ambassador (vacant).

Mauritania: Sharia Aïssa el-Wakwak, Tripoli; tel. (21) 4443223; Ambassador YAHIA MUHAMMAD EL-HADI.

Morocco: POB 908, Ave 7 Avril, Tripoli; tel. (21) 3617809; fax (21) 3614752; e-mail sifmatripo@hotmail.com; Ambassador DRISS ALAOUI.

Netherlands: POB 3801, Sharia Jalal Bayar 20, Tripoli; tel. (21) 4441549; fax (21) 4440386; e-mail tri@minbuza.nl; internet www.mfa.nl/tri-uk; Ambassador BART VON BARTHELD.

Niger: POB 2251, Fachloun Area, Tripoli; tel. (21) 4443104; Ambassador AMADOU TIDJANI ALI.

Nigeria: POB 4417, Sharia Bashir al-Ibrahim, Tripoli; tel. (21) 4443038; e-mail ambassador@nigeriantripoli.org; internet www.nigeriantripoli.org; Ambassador MUHAMMAD K. IBRAHIM.

Oman: Tripoli; tel. (21) 4772879; fax (21) 4773849; Ambassador Dr QASIM BIN MUHAMMAD BIN SALEM AS-SALEHI.

Pakistan: POB 2169, Sharia Huzayfa bin al-Yaman, Manshiya bin Ashour, Tripoli; tel. (21) 3610937; fax (21) 3600412; e-mail pareptripoli@hotmail.com; Ambassador JAMIL AHMED KHAN (designate).

Philippines: POB 12508, Km 7 Abu Nawas, Hay Andalus, Gargaresh, Tripoli; tel. (21) 4833966; fax (21) 4836158; e-mail tripoli_pe76@lttnet.net; Ambassador BAYANI V. MANGIBIN.

Poland: POB 519, Sharia ben Ashour 61, Tripoli; tel. (21) 3608569; fax (21) 3615199; e-mail poland@trypolis.polemb.net; internet www.trypolis.polemb.net; Ambassador JÓSEF OSAS.

Portugal: Zaid Bem Thabet, Bem Ashur St, Tripoli; tel. (21) 3621351; Ambassador RUI NOGUEIRA LOPES ALEIXO.

Qatar: POB 6312, Libay, Tripoli; tel. (21) 4832431; fax (21) 4836660; e-mail tripoli@mofa.gov.qa; Ambassador SAAD BEN ALI AL-MAHANDY.

Romania: POB 5085, Sharia Ali bin Talib, Ben Ashour, Tripoli; tel. (21) 3615295; fax (21) 3607597; e-mail ambaromatrip@hotmail.com; Ambassador STAN NICULAE.

Russia: POB 4792, Sharia Mustapha Kamel, Tripoli; tel. (21) 3330545; fax (21) 4446673; Ambassador (vacant).

Rwanda: POB 6677, Villa Ibrahim Musbah Missalati, Andalus, Tripoli; tel. (21) 72864; fax (21) 70317; Chargé d'affaires CHRISTOPHE HABIMANA.

Saudi Arabia: Sharia Kairouan 2, Tripoli; tel. (21) 30485; Chargé d'affaires MUHAMMAD HASSAN BANDAH.

Senegal: POB 6392, El-Arabia Gotchalle 246/5, Gargaresh, Tripoli; tel. (21) 4836090; fax (21) 4838955; e-mail ambassene.tripoli@stcc.presidence.sn; Chargé d'affaires a.i. MAMADOU DIOP.

Serbia: POB 1087, 14–16 Sharia Turkia, Tripoli; tel. (21) 3330819; fax (21) 3334114; e-mail serbianembassy_tripoli@yahoo.com; Ambassador Dr DUŠAN SIMEONOVIĆ.

Sierra Leone: Tripoli; Ambassador el Hadj MOHAMMED SAMURA.

Slovakia: POB 5721, Gargaresh 3 Km, Hay Andalus, Tripoli; tel. (21) 4781388; fax (21) 4781387; e-mail slovembtrp@slovembtrp.com; Ambassador BAN YURY.

Spain: POB 2302, Sharia el-Amir Abd al-Kader al-Jazairi 36, Tripoli; tel. (21) 3620051; fax (21) 3620061; e-mail emb.tripoli@maec.es; Ambassador LUIS FRANCISCO GARCÍA CEREZO.

Sudan: POB 1076, Sharia Gargaresh, Tripoli; tel. (21) 4775387; fax (21) 4774781; e-mail sudtripoli@hotmail.com; Ambassador OSMAN M. O. DIRAR.

Switzerland: POB 439, Sharia al-Moussawer ben Maghzamah, off Sharia ben Ashour, Tripoli; tel. (21) 3614118; fax (21) 3614238; e-mail tri.vertretung@eda.admin.ch; internet www.eda.admin.ch/tripoli; Ambassador DANIEL VON MURALT.

Syria: POB 4219, Sharia Muhammad Rashid Reda 4, Tripoli (Relations Office); tel. (21) 3331783; Head MUNIR BORKHAN.

Togo: POB 3420, Sharia Khaled ibn al-Walid, Tripoli; tel. (21) 4449565; fax (21) 3332423.

Tunisia: POB 613, Sharia Bashir al-Ibrahim, Tripoli; tel. (21) 3331051; fax (21) 4447600; High Representative MUHAMMAD B'RAHEM.

Turkey: POB 947, Sharia Zaviya Dahmani, Tripoli; tel. (21) 3401140; fax (21) 3401146; e-mail trablusbe@yahoo.com; Ambassador RIZA ERKMENOĞLU.

Uganda: POB 80215, Sharia Jaraba, Tripoli; tel. and fax (21) 3603083; fax (21) 3634471; e-mail info@ugembassylibya.org; internet www.ugembassylibya.org; Ambassador MOSES KIWA SEBUNYA.

Ukraine: POB 4544, Sharia Dhil, Tripoli; tel. (21) 3608665; fax (21) 3608666; e-mail emb_ly@mfa.gov.ua; internet www.mfa.gov.ua/libya; Ambassador HENNADIY LATIY.

United Kingdom: POB 4206, Tripoli; tel. (21) 3403644; fax (21) 3403648; e-mail tripoli.press@fco.gov.uk; internet ukinlibya.fco.gov.uk; Ambassador Sir VINCENT FEAN.

USA: Serraj Area, Tripoli; tel. (21) 2200125; e-mail paotripoli@state.gov; internet libya.usembassy.gov; Ambassador GENE A. CRETZ.

Venezuela: POB 2584, Sharia ben Ashour, Jamaa as-Sagaa Bridge, Tripoli; tel. (21) 3600408; fax (21) 3600407; e-mail embavenezlibia@hotmail.com; Ambassador WALID YORDI.

Viet Nam: POB 587, Sharia Gargaresh, Tripoli; tel. (21) 4835587; fax (21) 4836962; e-mail dsqvnlib@yahoo.com; Ambassador DO BA KHOA.

Yemen: POB 4839, Sharia Ubei ben Ka'ab 36, Tripoli; tel. (21) 607472; Ambassador HUSSEIN ALI HASSAN SABAH.

Judicial System

The judicial system is composed, in order of seniority, of the Supreme Court, Courts of Appeal, and Courts of First Instance and Summary Courts.

All courts convene in open session, unless public morals or public order require a closed session; all judgments, however, are delivered in open session. Cases are heard in Arabic, with interpreters provided for aliens.

The courts apply the Libyan codes, which include all the traditional branches of law, such as civil, commercial and penal codes, etc. Committees were formed in 1971 to examine Libyan law and ensure that it coincides with the rules of Islamic *Shari'a*. The proclamation of People's Authority in the Jamahiriya provides that the Holy Koran is the law of society.

Attorney-General: SALIM MUHAMMAD SALIM.

SUPREME COURT

The judgments of the Supreme Court are final. It is composed of the President and several Justices. Its judgments are issued by circuits of at least three Justices (the quorum is three). The Court hears appeals from the Courts of Appeal in civil, penal, administrative and civil status matters.

President: ABD AR-RAHMAN MUHAMMAD ABU TOTAH.

COURTS OF APPEAL

These courts settle appeals from Courts of First Instance; the quorum is three Justices. Each court of appeal has a court of assize.

COURTS OF FIRST INSTANCE AND SUMMARY COURTS

These courts are first-stage courts in the Jamahiriya, and the cases heard in them are heard by one judge. Appeals against summary judgments are heard by the appellate court attached to the court of first instance, whose quorum is three judges.

PEOPLE'S PROSECUTION BUREAU

Established by order of the General People's Congress in March 1988.

Secretary: MUHAMMAD ALI AL-MISURATI.

Religion

ISLAM

The vast majority of Libyan Arabs follow Sunni Muslim rites, although Col Qaddafi has rejected the Sunnah (i.e. the practice, course, way, manner or conduct of the Prophet Muhammad, as followed by Sunnis) as a basis for legislation.

Chief Mufti of Libya: Sheikh TAHIR AHMAD AZ-ZAWI.

CHRISTIANITY

The Roman Catholic Church

Libya comprises three Apostolic Vicariates and one Apostolic Prefecture. At 31 December 2006 there were an estimated 105,000 adherents in the country.

Apostolic Vicariate of Benghazi: POB 248, Benghazi; tel. and fax (91) 9081599; e-mail apostvicar@yahoo.com; Vicar Apostolic Mgr SYLVESTER CARMEL MAGRO (Titular Bishop of Saldae).

Apostolic Vicariate of Derna: c/o POB 248, Benghazi; Vicar Apostolic (vacant).

Apostolic Vicariate of Tripoli: POB 365, Dahra, Tripoli; tel. (21) 3331863; fax (21) 3334696; e-mail bishoptripolibya@hotmail.com; internet www.catholicinlibya.com; Vicar Apostolic Mgr GIOVANNI INNOCENZO MARTINELLI (Titular Bishop of Tabuda).

The Anglican Communion

Within the Episcopal Church in Jerusalem and the Middle East, Libya forms part of the diocese of Egypt (q.v.).

Other Christian Churches

The Coptic Orthodox Church is represented in Libya.

The Press

Most newspapers and periodicals are published either by the Jamahiriya News Agency (JANA), by government secretariats, by the Press Service or by trade unions.

DAILIES

Al-Fajr al-Jadid (The New Dawn): POB 91291, Press Bldg, Sharia al-Jamahiriya, Tripoli; tel. (21) 3606393; fax (21) 3605728; e-mail madi@alfajraljadeed.com; internet www.alfajraljadeed.com; f. 1969; publ. by JANA; also publishes bi-monthly English version; Editor AOUN ABDULLAH MADI.

Ash-Shams: POB 82331, As-Sahafa Bldg, Sharia al-Jamhouria, Tripoli; tel. (21) 4442524; fax (21) 609315; e-mail ebrahim@alshames.com; internet www.alshames.com; Editor MUHAMMAD M. IBRAHIM.

Az-Zahf al-Akhdar (The Green March): POB 14273, As-Sahafa Bldg, Sharia al-Jamhouria, Tripoli; tel. (21) 4776890; fax (21) 4772502; e-mail info@azzahfalakhder.com; internet www.azzahfalakhder.com; f. 1980; ideological journal of the revolutionary cttees; Editor-in-Chief HAMID ABU SALIM.

PERIODICALS

Al-Amal (Hope): POB 4845, Tripoli; e-mail info@alamalmag.com; internet www.alamalmag.com; monthly; social, for children; publ. by the Press Service.

Ad-Daawa al-Islamia (Islamic Call): POB 2682, Sharia Sawani, km 5, Tripoli; tel. (21) 4800294; fax (21) 4800293; f. 1980; weekly (Wed.); Arabic, English, French; cultural; publ. by the World Islamic Call Society; Eds MUHAMMAD IMHEMED AL-BALOUSHI, ABDULAHI MUHAMMAD ABD AL-JALEEL.

Economic Bulletin: POB 2303, Tripoli; tel. (21) 3337106; monthly; publ. by JANA.

Al-Jamahiriya: POB 4814, Tripoli; tel. (21) 4449294; e-mail info@aljamahiria.com; internet www.aljamahiria.com; f. 1980; weekly; Arabic; political; publ. by the revolutionary cttees.

Al-Jarida ar-Rasmiya (The Official Newspaper): Tripoli; irregular; official state gazette.

Libyan Arab Republic Gazette: Secretariat of Justice, NA, Tripoli; weekly; English; publ. by the Secretariat of Justice.

Risalat al-Jihad (Holy War Letter): POB 2682, Tripoli; tel. (21) 3331021; f. 1983; monthly; Arabic, English, French; publ. by the World Islamic Call Society.

Scientific Bulletin: POB 2303, Tripoli; tel. (21) 3337106; monthly; publ. by JANA.

Ath-Thaqafa al-Arabiya (Arab Culture): POB 4587, Tripoli; f. 1973; weekly; cultural; circ. 25,000.

The Tripoli Post: POB 1159, Al-Fateh Tower, 1st Floor, Office No. 74, Tripoli; tel. (21) 3337422; fax (21) 3351740; e-mail editor@tripolipost.com; internet www.tripolipost.com; f. 1999; weekly; English; privately owned; Editor-in-Chief Dr SAID LASWAD.

Al-Usbu ath-Thaqafi (The Cultural Week): POB 4845, Tripoli; weekly.

Al-Watan al-Arabi al-Kabir (The Greater Arab Homeland): Tripoli; f. 1987.

NEWS AGENCY

Jamahiriya News Agency (JANA): POB 2303, Sharia al-Fatah, Tripoli; tel. (21) 3402606; fax (21) 3402421; e-mail info@jananews.ly; internet www.jananews.ly; f. 1964; brs and correspondents throughout Libya and abroad; provides Arabic, English and French news services.

Publishers

Ad-Dar al-Arabia Lilkitab (Maison Arabe du Livre): POB 3185, Tripoli; tel. (21) 4447287; f. 1973 by Libya and Tunisia.

Ad-Dar al-Hikma Publishing House: Tripoli; tel. (21) 3606571; fax (21) 3606610; e-mail info@elgabooks.com.

Al-Fatah University, General Administration of Libraries, Printing and Publications: POB 13543, Tripoli; tel. (21) 4628034; fax (21) 4625045; e-mail m.alfituri@hotmail.com; f. 1955; academic books.

General Co for Publishing, Advertising and Distribution: POB 921, Sirte (Surt); tel. (54) 63170; fax (54) 62100; general, educational and academic books in Arabic and other languages; makes and distributes advertisements throughout Libya.

Ghouma Publishing: POB 80092, Tripoli; tel. (21) 3630864; e-mail ghoumapub@hotmail.com; f. 1993; book publishing, distribution and art production; Gen. Man. MUSTAFA FETOURI.

Broadcasting and Communications

TELECOMMUNICATIONS

Communications General Authority: Tripoli; f. 2006; supervisory body reporting directly to the General People's Committee.

General Directorate of Posts and Telecommunications: POB 81686, Tripoli; tel. (21) 3604101; fax (21) 3604102; Dir-Gen. ABU ZAID JUMA AL-MANSURI.

General Post and Telecommunications Co: POB 886, Sharia Zawia, Tripoli; tel. (21) 3617945; fax (21) 3619011; f. 1985; Chair. FARAJ AMARI.

BROADCASTING

Radio

Great Socialist People's Libyan Arab Jamahiriya Broadcasting Corporation: POB 80237, Tripoli; tel. (21) 3402107; fax (21) 3403468; e-mail info@en.ljbc.net; internet www.ljbc.net; f. 1968; broadcasts in Arabic; additional satellite channel broadcast for 18 hours a day from 1982; Sec.-Gen. ABDULLAH MANSOUR.

Voice of Africa: POB 4677, Sharia al-Fateh, Tripoli; tel. (21) 4449209; fax (21) 4449876; f. 1973 as Voice of the Greater Arab Homeland; adopted current name in 1998; broadcasts in Arabic, French, English, Swahili and Hausa; Dir-Gen. ABDULLAH AL-MEGRI.

Television

People's Revolution Broadcasting TV: POB 80237, Tripoli; tel. (21) 3402107; fax (21) 3403468; e-mail info@en.ljbc.net; internet www.ljbc.net; f. 1957; broadcasts in Arabic; additional satellite channels broadcast for limited hours in English; Dir ABDULLAH MANSOUR.

Finance

(cap. = capital; res = reserves; dep. = deposits; m. = million; brs = branches; amounts in Libyan dinars)

BANKING

The Libyan banking sector, hitherto highly state-controlled, was undergoing restructure in the late 2000s. Minority stakes in two state-owned commercial banks were sold to foreign banking interests in 2007–08. It was planned to sell a minority of shares in a further state-owned bank via the Libyan stock exchange in 2009.

Central Bank

Central Bank of Libya: POB 1103, Sharia al-Malik Seoud, Tripoli; tel. (21) 3333591; fax (21) 4441488; e-mail info@cbl.gov.ly; internet www.cbl.gov.ly; f. 1955 as National Bank of Libya; name changed to Bank of Libya 1963, to Central Bank of Libya 1977; state-owned; bank of issue and central bank carrying govt accounts and operating exchange control; commercial operations transferred to National Commercial Bank 1970; cap. 500.0m., res 250.0m., dep. 65,484.9m. (Dec. 2006); Gov. and Chair. FARHAT OMAR BENGDARA.

Other Banks

Alwafa Bank: POB 84212, Sharia Alfallah, Tripoli; tel. (21) 4815123; fax (21) 4801247; e-mail info@alwafabank.com; internet www.alwafabank.com; f. 2003; private bank; Chair. and Gen. Man. HADI M. GITELI.

Gumhouria Bank: POB 3224, Tripoli; tel. (21) 4440848; fax (21) 3333793; e-mail gm@gumhouriabank.com.ly; internet www.gumhouria-bank.com.ly; f. 1969 as successor to Barclays Bank International in Libya; known as Masraf al-Jumhuriya until March 1977, and as Jamahiriya Bank until Dec. 2000; merger with Umma Bank SAL completed mid-2008; wholly owned subsidiary of the Central Bank; sale of minority stake pending 2009; cap. 100.0m., res 74.0m., dep. 4,429.1m. (Dec. 2006); Chair. HAMED ARABI AL-HOUDERI; Gen. Man. MELLAD MUHAMMAD ELGHOOL; 122 brs.

Libyan Foreign Bank: POB 2542, Tower 2, Dat al-Imad Complex, Tripoli; tel. (21) 3350155; fax (21) 3350164; e-mail it@lafbank.com; internet www.lafbank.com; f. 1972 under the name Libyan Arab Foreign Bank; present name adopted 2005; offshore bank wholly owned by Central Bank of Libya; cap. 1,000.0m., res 298.9m., dep. 14,828.4m. (Dec. 2006); Chair. Dr MUHAMMAD A. BEIT EL-MAL.

National Commercial Bank SAL: POB 543, Aruba Ave, al-Baida; tel. (21) 3610306; fax (21) 3612267; e-mail ncbly@lttnet.net; internet www.ncb.ly; f. 1970 to take over commercial banking division of Central Bank (then Bank of Libya) and brs of Aruba Bank and Istiklal Bank; wholly owned by Central Bank of Libya; cap. 35m., res 83.8m., dep. 2,637.0m. (Dec. 2005); Chair. BADER A. ABU AZIZA; Gen. Man. AHMAD F. BELKHEIR; 51 brs.

Sahara Bank SPI: POB 70, Sharia 1 September 10, Tripoli; tel. (21) 3330724; fax (21) 3337922; e-mail sahbankgm1@lttnet.net; f. 1964 to take over br. of Banco di Sicilia; the Govt sold a 19% stake to BNP Paribas (France) in July 2007; cap. and res 208.2m., total assets 1,951.8m. (March 2003); Chair. and Gen. Man. Dr SALEM MUFTAH EL-GHAMATI; 20 brs.

Wahda Bank: POB 452, Fadiel Abu Omar Sq., El-Berkah, Benghazi; tel. (61) 2224256; fax (21) 2224122; e-mail wahda@wahdabank.com; internet www.wahdabank.com; f. 1970 to take over Bank of North Africa, Commercial Bank SAL, Nahda Arabia Bank, Société Africaine de Banque SAL, Kafila al-Ahly Bank; 19% stake acquired by Arab Bank PLC (Jordan) in April 2008; remainder owned by Central Bank of Libya; cap. 108m., res 94.1m., dep. 2,396.5m. (Dec. 2007); Chair. Dr ANTOINE SREIH; Gen. Man. MAHDI ALAWI; 76 brs.

STOCK EXCHANGE

Libyan Stock Market: Sharia Omar Maukhtar, Tripoli; tel. (21) 3365026; e-mail info@lsm.gov.ly; internet www.lsm.gov.ly; f. 2007; Gen. Dir SULIMAN SALEM ASH-SHOHOMIY.

INSURANCE

Libya Insurance Co: POB 80087, Aman Bldg, Sharia At-Taha, Tripoli; tel. (21) 4444174; fax (21) 4444176; e-mail infolt@libtamin.com; internet www.libtamin.com; f. 1964; merged with Al-Mukhtar Insurance Co in 1981; all classes of insurance; Man. ALI AMAR AR-RAGAYEE.

Trade and Industry

There are state trade and industrial organizations responsible for the running of industries at all levels, which supervise production, distribution and sales. There are also central bodies responsible for the power generation industry, agriculture, land reclamation and transport.

GOVERNMENT AGENCIES

Council for Oil and Gas Affairs: Tripoli; f. 2006; reports to the General People's Committee; holds ultimate responsibility for all matters involving oil, gas and their by-products; Chair. Dr AL-BAGHDADI ALI AL-MAHMOUDI.

Great Man-made River Water Utilization Authority (GMRA): POB 7217, Benghazi; tel. (61) 2230392; fax (61) 2230393; e-mail info@gmrwua.com; internet www.gmrwua.com; supervises construction of pipeline carrying water to the Libyan coast from beneath the

Sahara desert, to provide irrigation for agricultural projects; Sec. for the Great Man-made River Project ABD AL-MAJID AL-AOUD.

Libyan Economic Development Board (LEDB): Tripoli; f. 2007; charged with the drafting and execution of reform campaigns, and the facilitation of decision-making and action on critical economic issues; Chair. OMRAN BUKHRES.

Libyan Investment Authority (LIA): Tripoli; e-mail info@lia.ly; internet www.lia.ly; f. 2006, operations commenced 2007; sovereign wealth fund managing state-allocated assests, including Oil Reserve Fund; Chair. Dr ABD AL-HAFID MAHMOUD ZLITNI.

DEVELOPMENT ORGANIZATIONS

Arab Organization for Agricultural Development: POB 12898, Zohra, Tripoli; tel. and fax (21) 3619275; e-mail arabagri@lycos.com; internet www.aoad.org; responsible for agricultural devt projects.

General National Organization for Industrialization: Sharia San'a, Tripoli; tel. (21) 3334995; f. 1970; public org. responsible for the devt of industry.

Kufra and Sarir Authority: Council of Agricultural Development, Benghazi; f. 1972 to develop the Kufra oasis and Sarir area in south-east Libya.

CHAMBERS OF COMMERCE

Benghazi Chamber of Commerce, Trade, Industry and Agriculture: POB 208 and 1286, Benghazi; tel. (61) 3372319; fax (61) 3380761; f. 1956; Pres. Dr BADIA; Gen. Man. Dr TAREK TARBAGHIA; 150,000 mems.

Tripoli Chamber of Commerce and Industry: POB 2321, Sharia Najed 6–8, Tripoli; tel. (21) 3336855; fax (21) 3332655; f. 1952; Chair. MUHAMMAD KANOON; Dir-Gen. ABDULMONEM H. BURAWI; 30,000 mems.

UTILITIES

Electricity

General Electricity Company of Libya (GECOL): POB 668, Tripoli; tel. (21) 4445068; fax (21) 4447023; e-mail gecol@gecol.net; internet www.gecol.ly; Sec. of People's Cttee Eng. OMRAN IBRAHIM ABU KRAA.

STATE HYDROCARBONS COMPANIES

Until 1986 petroleum affairs in Libya were dealt with primarily by the Secretariat of the General People's Committee for Petroleum. This body was abolished in March 1986, and sole responsibility for the administration of the petroleum industry passed to the national companies that were already in existence. The Secretariat of the General People's Committee for Petroleum was re-established in March 1989 and incorporated into the new Secretariat for the General People's Committee for Energy in October 1992. This was dissolved in March 2000, and responsibility for local oil policy was transferred to the National Oil Corporation, under the supervision of the General People's Committee. Since 1973 the Libyan Government has entered into participation agreements with some of the foreign oil companies (concession holders), and nationalized others. It has concluded 85%:15% production-sharing agreements with various oil companies.

National Oil Corporation (NOC): POB 2655, Sharia Bashier Sadawi, Tripoli; tel. (21) 4446181; fax (21) 3331390; e-mail info@noclibya.com; internet en.noclibya.com.ly; f. 1970 to: undertake jt ventures with foreign cos; build and operate refineries, storage tanks, petrochemical facilities, pipelines and tankers; take part in arranging specifications for local and imported petroleum products; participate in general planning of oil installations in Libya; market crude and refined petroleum and petrochemical products; and establish and operate oil terminals; from 2000 responsible for deciding local oil policy, under supervision of General People's Committee; Chair. Dr SHOKRI MUHAMMAD GHANEM.

    Arabian Gulf Oil Co (AGOCO): POB 263, Benghazi; tel. (61) 28931; fax (21) 49031; wholly owned subsidiary of the NOC; Chair. TAWSIG MESMARI.

    Oilinvest International NV: Tripoli; f. 1988; wholly owned subsidiary of the NOC; Libya's foreign oil investment arm; Chair. and Gen. Man. AHMAD ABD AL-KARIM AHMAD.

    Agip North Africa and Middle East Ltd—Libyan Branch: POB 346, Tripoli; tel. and fax (21) 3335135; Sec. of People's Cttee OMAR AS-SWEIFI.

    Azzawiya Oil Refining Co (ARC): POB 6451, Tripoli; tel. (23) 610539; fax (23) 610543; e-mail infoazzawiya@azzawiyaoil.com; internet www.azzawiyaoil.com; f. 1976; Gen. Man. AL-MOAMARE A. SWEDAN.

    Brega Oil Marketing Co: POB 402, Sharia Bashir as-Saidawi, Tripoli; tel. (21) 4440830; f. 1971; Chair. Dr DOKALI B. AL-MEGHARIEF.

    International Oil Investments Co: Tripoli; f. 1988, with initial capital of US $500m. to acquire 'downstream' facilities abroad; Chair. MUHAMMAD AL-JAWAD.

    National Drilling and Workover Co: POB 1454, 208 Sharia Omar Mukhtar, Tripoli; tel. (21) 3332411; f. 1986; Chair. IBRAHIM BAHI.

    Ras Lanouf Oil and Gas Processing Co (RASCO): POB 1971, Ras Lanouf, Benghazi; tel. (21) 3605177; fax (21) 607924; f. 1978; Chair. ABULKASIM M. A. ZWARY.

    Sirte Oil Co: POB 385, Marsa el-Brega, Tripoli; tel. (21) 607261; fax (21) 601487; internet www.soc.com.ly; f. 1955 as Esso Standard Libya, taken over by Sirte Oil Co 1982; absorbed the National Petrochemicals Co in October 1990; exploration, production of crude oil, gas and petrochemicals, liquefaction of natural gas; Pres. MUHAMMAD SALEH.

    Umm al-Jawaby Petroleum Co: POB 693, Tripoli; Chair. and Gen. Man. MUHAMMAD TENTTOUSH.

    Waha Oil Co: POB 395, Tripoli; tel. (21) 3331116; fax (21) 3337169; e-mail infowaha@wahaoil.com; internet www.wahaoil.com; Chair. SALEH M. KAABAR.

    Zueitina Oil Co (ZOC): POB 2134, Tripoli; tel. (21) 3338011; fax (21) 3339109; f. 1986; Chair. of Management Cttee BASHIR BAZAZI.

TRADE UNIONS

General Federation of Producers' Trade Unions: POB 734, Sharia Istanbul 2, Tripoli; tel. (21) 4446011; f. 1952; affiliated to ITUC; Sec.-Gen. BASHIR IHWIJ; 17 trade unions with 700,000 mems.

General Union for Oil and Petrochemicals: Tripoli; Chair. MUHAMMAD MITHNANI.

Pan-African Federation of Petroleum Energy and Allied Workers: Tripoli; affiliated to the Organisation of African Trade Union Unity.

Transport

Department of Road Transport and Railways: POB 14527, Sharia az-Zawiyah, Tripoli; tel. and fax (21) 3605808; Dir-Gen. (Projects and Research) MUHAMMAD ABU ZIAN.

RAILWAYS

There are, at present, no railways in Libya. In mid-1998, however, the Government invited bids for the construction of a 3,170-km railway, comprising one branch, 2,178 km in length, running from north to south, and another, 992 km in length, running from east to west along the north coast. The railway may eventually be linked to other North African rail networks. In April 2008 Russia signed a US $3,480m. agreement with Libya regarding the construction of a rail link between Sirte and Benghazi. Later in the year the Libyan Government invited bids for the design of a 450-km high-speed railway between Benghazi and Tobruk.

Railway Executive Board: Tripoli; tel. (21) 3609486; fax (21) 626054; e-mail info@libyanrailways.com; oversees the planning and construction of railways.

ROADS

The most important road is the 1,822-km national coast road from the Tunisian to the Egyptian border, passing through Tripoli and Benghazi. It has a second link between Barce and Lamluda, 141 km long. Another national road runs from a point on the coastal road 120 km south of Misurata through Sebha to Ghat near the Algerian border (total length 1,250 km). There is a branch 247 km long running from Vaddan to Sirte (Surt). A 690-km road, connecting Tripoli and Sebha, and another 626 km long, from Ajdabiya in the north to Kufra in the south-east, were opened in 1983. The Tripoli–Ghat section (941 km) of the third, 1,352-km national road was opened in September 1984. There is a road crossing the desert from Sebha to the frontiers of Chad and Niger. As part of a wide-ranging agreement signed by Libya and Italy in August 2008, the latter was to fund construction of a new coastal motorway between the Tunisian and Egyptian borders.

In addition to the national highways, the west of Libya has about 1,200 km of paved and macadamized roads and the east about 500 km. All the towns and villages of Libya, including the desert oases, are accessible by motor vehicle. In 1999 Libya had an estimated total road network of 83,200 km, of which 47,590 km was paved.

SHIPPING

The principal ports are Tripoli, Benghazi, Mersa Brega, Misurata and as-Sider. Zueitina, Ras Lanouf, Mersa Hariga, Mersa Brega and as-Sider are mainly oil ports. A pipeline connects the Zelten oilfields with Mersa Brega. Another pipeline joins the Sarir oilfield with Mersa Hariga, the port of Tobruk, and a pipeline from the Sarir field to Zueitina was opened in 1968. A port is being developed at Darnah, and work on the expansion of the port of Sirte was scheduled to begin in 2010. Libya also has the use of Tunisian port facilities at Sand Gabès, to alleviate congestion at Tripoli. At 31 December 2007 Libya's merchant fleet consisted of 141 vessels, with a combined displacement of 97,944 grt.

General National Maritime Transport Co (GNMTC): POB 80173, esh-Shaab Terminal, Tripoli; tel. and fax (21) 4808094; e-mail info@gnmtc.com; internet www.gnmtc.com; f. 1975 to handle all projects dealing with maritime trade; state-owned; Chair. Capt. ALI BELHAG AHMED.

Libya Shipping Agency: POB 4288, Tripoli; tel. (21) 3402528; fax (21) 3401928; e-mail info@libyashipping.com; internet www.libyashipping.com; provides chartering, land transportation and customs clearance services; Gen. Man. IMAD FELLAH.

CIVIL AVIATION

There are four international airports: Tripoli International Airport, situated at ben Gashir, 34 km (21 miles) from Tripoli; Benina Airport 19 km (12 miles) from Benghazi; Sebha Airport; and Misurata Airport. There are a further 10 regional airports. A US $800m. programme to improve the airport infrastructure and air traffic control network was approved in mid-2001. In the mid-2000s plans were announced for the upgrade and expansion of Tripoli International Airport, which were to include the construction of two new terminals, following which the airport's annual passenger capacity was expected to increase to some 20m., compared with 3m. in 2007. Work on the project was scheduled to commence in August 2008. Meanwhile, in August 2007 a Canadian company was awarded a $541m. contract for the construction of a new international airport at Benghazi.

Afriqiyah Airways: 1st Floor, Waha Bldg, Sharia Omar al-Mokhtar, Tripoli; tel. (21) 4449734; fax (21) 3341181; e-mail customerservice@afriqiyah.aero; internet www.afriqiyah.aero; f. 2001; state-owned; flights to 23 destinations in Africa, Europe and Saudi Arabia; Chair. Capt. SABRI S. ABDALLA.

Buraq Air: Tripoli International Airport, Tripoli; e-mail lias@buraqair.com; internet www.buraqair.com; f. 2001; first privately owned Libyan airline; scheduled international passenger and cargo flights to Morocco, Syria and Turkey; domestic flights from Tripoli, Benghazi and Misurata; Chair. and Man. Dir Capt. MUHAMMAD A. BUBEIDA.

Libyan Arab Airlines (LAA): POB 2555, ben Fernas Bldg, Sharia Haiti, Tripoli; tel. (21) 3614102; fax (21) 3614815; e-mail i.alwani@ln.aero; internet www.ln.aero; f. 1989 by merger of Jamahiriya Air Transport (which in 1983 took over operations of United African Airlines) and Libyan Arab Airlines (f. 1964 as Kingdom of Libya Airlines; renamed 1969); passenger and cargo services from Tripoli, Benghazi and Sebha to destinations in Europe, North Africa, the Middle East and Asia; domestic services throughout Libya; Chair. and CEO Eng. TARIK AREBI.

Tourism

The principal attractions for visitors to Libya are Tripoli, with its beaches and annual International Fair, the ancient Roman towns of Sabratha, Leptis Magna and Cyrene, and historic oases. There were 999,343 visitor arrivals in 2004; in 2006 receipts from tourism totalled some US $244m.

General Board of Fairs: POB 891, Sharia Omar Mukhtar, Tripoli; tel. (21) 3332255; fax (21) 4448385; e-mail info@gbf.com.ly; internet gbf.com.ly; Head of Fairs GAMAL N. A. AL-AMOUSHI.

General Board of Tourism and Traditional Industries: POB 82063, Tripoli; tel. (21) 3334673; fax (21) 4445336; e-mail info@libyan-tourism.net; internet www.libyan-tourism.org; Chair. MUHAMMAD SEALNA.

LIECHTENSTEIN

Introductory Survey

Location, Climate, Language, Religion, Flag, Capital

The Principality of Liechtenstein is in central Europe. The country lies on the east bank of the Upper Rhine river, bordered by Switzerland to the west and south, and by Austria to the north and east. Liechtenstein has an Alpine climate, with mild winters. The average annual temperature is about 10°C, while average annual rainfall is about 1,000 mm. The official language is German, of which a dialect—Alemannish—is spoken. Almost all of the inhabitants profess Christianity, and about 79% are adherents of the Roman Catholic Church. The national flag (proportions 3 by 5) consists of two equal horizontal stripes, of royal blue and red, with a golden princely crown, outlined in black, in the upper hoist. The capital is Vaduz.

Recent History

Liechtenstein has been an independent state since 1719, except while under French domination briefly in the early 19th century. In 1919 Switzerland assumed responsibility for Liechtenstein's diplomatic representation, replacing Austria. In 1920 a postal union with Switzerland was agreed, and in 1924 a treaty was concluded with Switzerland whereby Liechtenstein was incorporated in a joint customs union. Franz Josef II succeeded as Reigning Prince in 1938. In 1950 Liechtenstein became a party to the Statute of the International Court of Justice (ICJ, see p. 22), in 1973 it joined the Organization for Security and Co-operation in Europe (see p. 366) and in 1978 it was admitted to the Council of Europe (see p. 236). Liechtenstein became a member of the UN in September 1990 (hitherto the country had been a member of some UN specialized agencies). In the following year Liechtenstein became a full member of the European Free Trade Association (EFTA, see p. 426).

After 42 years as the dominant party in government, the Fortschrittliche Bürgerpartei (FBP—Progressive Citizens' Party) was defeated by the Vaterländische Union (VU—Patriotic Union) at a general election to the Landtag (parliament) in February 1970. Four years later the FBP regained its majority. At the general election to the Landtag in February 1978, the VU, led by Hans Brunhart, won eight of the 15 seats, although with a minority of the votes cast, while the remaining seats were taken by the FBP, led by Dr Walter Kieber, the Head of Government since March 1974. After protracted negotiations, Brunhart replaced Kieber in April 1978. At the general election in February 1982, the distribution of seats remained unchanged, although the VU gained a majority of votes. Following a referendum in July 1984, women were granted the right to vote on a national basis. However, women were still not permitted to vote on communal affairs in three of Liechtenstein's 11 communes until April 1986, when they were finally accorded full voting rights. (An amendment to the Constitution, declaring equality between men and women, took effect in 1992.) In August 1984 Prince Franz Josef transferred executive power to his son, Prince Hans-Adam, although he remained titular Head of State until his death in November 1989, when he was succeeded by Hans-Adam (Hans-Adam II).

The composition of the Landtag remained unchanged following a general election in February 1986, when women voted for the first time in a national poll. In January 1989 the Landtag was dissolved by Prince Hans-Adam, following a dispute between the VU and the FBP regarding the construction of a new museum to accommodate the royal art collection. At the subsequent general election, which took place in March, the number of seats in the Landtag was increased from 15 to 25; the VU retained its majority, securing 13 seats, while the FBP took the remaining 12 seats.

At the next general election, which took place in February 1993, the VU lost its majority, taking only 11 of the Landtag's 25 seats. The FBP retained 12 seats, and two seats were won by an environmentalist party, the Freie Liste (FL—Free List). Lengthy negotiations resulted in the formation of a new coalition between the FBP and the VU, in which the FBP was the dominant party, and Markus Büchel of the FBP became Head of Government. In September, however, following a unanimous vote in the Landtag expressing no confidence in his leadership, Büchel was dismissed from his post, and Prince Hans-Adam dissolved the legislature. At a further general election, which was held in October, the VU regained its majority, winning 13 seats, while the FBP took 11 and the FL one. The VU became the dominant party in a new coalition with the FBP, with Mario Frick of the VU as Head of Government.

In October 1992 almost 2,000 people demonstrated in Vaduz to protest against a threat by Prince Hans-Adam that he would dissolve the Landtag if deputies did not submit to his wish to hold a proposed referendum to endorse Liechtenstein's entry to the nascent European Economic Area (EEA) shortly in advance of a similar vote in Switzerland. The Prince believed that the outcome of the Swiss poll might be prejudicial to that of the Liechtenstein vote, and that, in the event of voters' rejecting EEA membership at an early referendum, Liechtenstein might still be able to join other EFTA members in applying for admission to the European Community (EC, now European Union—EU, see p. 255). A compromise was reached, whereby the referendum was scheduled to take place shortly after the Swiss vote, while the Government agreed actively to promote a vote in favour of the EEA and to explore the possibility of applying to the EC should EEA membership be rejected. (The authorities subsequently decided that admission to the EU would not be beneficial to the Principality.) At the referendum in December, although Switzerland's voters had rejected accession to the EEA, Liechtenstein's membership was approved by 55.8% of those who voted (about 87% of the Principality's electorate); consequently, the two countries' joint customs union was renegotiated. In April 1995 a further national referendum was held, at which 55.9% of those who voted (around 82% of the electorate) approved the revised customs arrangements. Liechtenstein joined the EEA in May.

In March 1996 the Landtag adopted a unanimous motion of loyalty to the hereditary monarchy, after Prince Hans-Adam offered to resign (following tension between the Prince and the legislature—see above). At the next general election, which took place in February 1997, the VU retained its majority with 13 seats, while the FBP secured 10 and the FL two. Frick remained Head of Government. In April the FBP withdrew from the ruling coalition, leaving a single party (the VU) to govern alone for the first time since 1938. The constitutional role of the Reigning Prince came under renewed scrutiny in 1997, when, against the wishes of the Landtag, Prince Hans-Adam refused to reappoint Dr Herbert Wille, a senior judge who had advocated that constitutional issues should be decided by the Supreme Court rather than the Monarch. Dr Wille subsequently presented a formal complaint to the European Court of Human Rights, which ruled, in November 1999, that Prince Hans-Adam had restricted Wille's right to free speech; the Prince was required to pay 100,000 Swiss francs in costs.

In December 1999 Prince Hans-Adam requested an Austrian prosecutor, Kurt Spitzer, to investigate allegations in the German press based on an unpublished report of April 1999 by the German secret service that international criminals were using financial institutions in Liechtenstein to launder the proceeds of organized crime. As a result, five people were placed under investigative arrest in May 2000, including the brother of one of the Principality's most senior judges; all five were later released without charge. In his final report, which was released in August, Spitzer concluded that Liechtenstein was no more culpable of money-laundering than other countries in Europe. He blamed the current problems on the Principality's over-bureaucratic and inefficient banking system and the poor application of existing legislation designed to combat economic crimes. Spitzer also revealed that a money-laundering investigation was under way against Herbert Batliner, a lawyer who had been implicated in the party-funding scandal involving the former Federal Chancellor of Germany, Helmut Kohl, and his party, the Christlich-Demokratische Union Deutschlands (CDU—Christian Democratic Union), and in another case involving proceeds from drugs-trafficking in Colombia. In June the Financial Action Task Force on Money Laundering (FATF), a commission of the Organisation for Economic Co-operation and Development (OECD, see p. 358), included Liechtenstein on a list of countries considered uncooperative in international attempts to combat money-laundering. In an effort to improve the country's international reputation, the Liechtenstein Bankers' Association announced in July that anonymous accounts would be abolished. In the same month the Government approved the establishment of a new financial investigative unit within the police force and measures to accelerate legal assistance to foreign countries in money-laundering investigations. Legislation was promulgated in December requiring financial institutions to maintain tighter controls over accounts and transactions, including the abolition of anonymous accounts. Liechtenstein was removed from the FATF's list of unco-operative countries in 2001, and, in October of that year, the Government appointed the former head of the Swiss anti-money-laundering authority, Daniel Thelesklaf, to administer a new financial surveillance unit, which was to enforce new regulations requiring banks and lawyers to be able to verify the identity of their clients. However, Liechtenstein was among seven jurisdictions identified by OECD as 'unco-operative tax havens' lacking financial transparency in April 2002, under its initiative to abolish 'harmful tax practices'. Although four jurisdictions were subsequently removed from the list, Liechtenstein remained one of three countries so designated until May 2009 (see below).

In the general election that took place in February 2001 the VU lost its parliamentary majority, securing only 11 of the 25 seats in the Landtag, while the FBP won 13 seats and the FL obtained one. The VU administration's popularity had been adversely affected by an unresolved dispute with Prince Hans-Adam over his demands for constitutional changes, notably with regard to appointments in the judiciary (the Prince advocated that judges be nominated by the reigning Monarch rather than by parliamentary deputies); the Prince claimed that these amendments would benefit the people, while the VU regarded them as an attempt to extend the royal prerogative. A new Government comprising solely the FBP, under the leadership of Otmar Hasler, took office in April. The Prince had previously announced that if he failed to secure the support of the new Government for his proposed constitutional reforms, he would seek a national referendum; in December he also threatened to leave the Principality and take up residence in Austria.

The issue of constitutional reform was finally resolved by a national referendum, held on 14 and 16 March 2003, in which 64.3% of the votes cast were in favour of granting the Prince new powers; the voter participation rate was 87.7%. As a result of the referendum, the Prince gained the right to dismiss a government even if it retained parliamentary confidence, to appoint an interim administration pending elections, to preside over a panel to select judges, to veto laws by not signing them within a six-month period and to adopt emergency legislation. Conversely, citizens could now force a referendum on any subject by collecting a minimum of 1,500 signatures. A compromise proposal put forward by a cross-party group that included former premier Frick (the Volksinitiative für Verfassungsfrieden—People's Initiative for Constitutional Peace), which suggested that a princely veto could be overruled by a referendum and sought to limit the Prince's use of emergency legislation to times of war, received the support of only 16.5% of the voters. The overwhelming support for the Prince's proposed changes was partially attributed to widespread fear that, if fulfilled, his threat of self-imposed exile as a symbolic monarch would cause economic decline and social upheaval. Prince Hans-Adam dismissed the findings of a commission established by the Council of Europe, which stated that the constitutional amendments would constitute a retrograde step for democracy and could lead to the isolation of Liechtenstein in Europe. On 15 August 2004 Prince Hans-Adam transferred his sovereign powers to his son, Prince Alois, in accordance with an announcement that he had made in August 2003. Prince Hans-Adam, however, remained Head of State.

At the general election held on 11 and 13 March 2005 the FBP failed to retain an absolute majority, winning 12 of the 25 seats, with 48.7% of the votes cast; voter participation was 86.5%. The VU won 10 seats (38.2% of the votes), while the FL increased its representation from one seat to three (with 13.0% of the votes). In April the FBP and the VU formed a coalition Government, which comprised three representatives of the FBP, including Hasler, who remained as Prime Minister, and two of the VU, with Dr Klaus Tschütscher becoming Deputy Prime Minister.

In August 2005 a conservative group known as the Volksinitiative für das Leben (People's Initiative For Life) submitted 1,889 signatures to the Government in support of its demands for a national referendum to be held on constitutional revisions. The group hoped to amend Article 14 of the Constitution so that the highest responsibility of the state would be 'to protect human life from conception until natural death' and also aimed to insert a reference to the state's responsibility to protect human dignity. The initiative was intended to address the potential legalization of abortion and, indirectly, the issues of euthanasia, genetic technology and stem-cell research. Having failed to secure sufficient support in the Landtag, the proposals were to be subject to a national referendum. Considering the initiative to be too restrictive, the FBP and VU jointly drafted a counterproposal to make the protection of life and human dignity a right for Liechtenstein citizens rather than a duty of the state. A further amendment was added explicitly prohibiting the death penalty (which had already been abolished by a revision of the criminal code in 1985). Following its approval by the Landtag in September, the counterproposal was presented to the referendum concurrently with the People's Initiative For Life. At the referendum, held on 25 and 27 November, the initiative, which opponents claimed would prevent abortion, birth control and assisted suicide, was rejected by 80.9% of the votes cast, while the counterproposal was adopted, with the support of 79.4% of voters.

At the general election that took place on 8 February 2009 the VU won an absolute majority, securing 13 of the 25 seats (47.6% of the votes cast) and replacing the FBP as the largest party in the Landtag; the rate of participation by eligible voters was 84.6%. The FBP won 11 seats (a loss of one) and 43.5% of the votes, while the FL's representation declined from three seats to just one (8.9% of the vote). Dr Klaus Tschütscher of the VU, hitherto Deputy Prime Minister and Minister of Economic Affairs, of Justice and of Sports, was sworn in as Prime Minister on 25 March. Prior to the election, the FBP and the VU had announced their intention to despite the VU's abolute majority, the VU and FBP continued to co-operate in a coalition Government; the new administration comprised three members of the VU (including Tschütscher, who also assumed the portfolios for general government affairs, finance, and family and equal opportunity) and two representatives of the FBP.

In February 2008, following a meeting of EU ministers responsible for justice and home affairs in Brussels, Belgium, Liechtenstein became an associate member of the EU's Schengen Agreement (which binds signatories to the abolition of border controls) and the Dublin Convention on Asylum (relating to common formal arrangements on asylum). Although the Landtag ratified the agreement in June, the EU process of ratification remained incomplete, owing to ongoing negotiations between Liechtenstein and the EU on an anti-fraud agreement. Liechtenstein was expected to accede to the Schengen Agreement by November 2009. Meanwhile, an interim solution to the issue of border control between Liechtenstein and Switzerland was put in place after the latter acceded to the Schengen Agreement in December 2008.

In the latter half of the 20th century Liechtenstein's relations with the Czech Republic and Slovakia were strained. This stemmed from the expulsion of ethnic Germans from Czechoslovakia and the confiscation of their land (without compensation) following the Second World War, under the controversial Beneš Decrees. The Liechtenstein royal family lost a large part of its estates during this time—including the castles of Feldsberg and Eisgrub, now estimated to be worth some €100m. Liechtenstein, which was a sovereign, neutral state throughout both the First and Second World Wars, claimed that it was unfairly grouped together with Germany under the terms of the Decrees. Czechoslovakia, however, considered the Liechtenstein royal family to have been collaborators with the Nazi regime in Germany during the Second World War, and that its action was thus legitimate. Liechtenstein also sought damages from Germany for assets that it claimed Germany had improperly awarded to Czechoslovakia after the Second World War as reparations. The German position was that the assets were seized by Czechoslovakia and that Germany was not responsible. In February 2005, however, the ICJ ruled that it was not competent to make a decision on the claim as it predated the 1980 agreement between the two countries that disputes between them should be settled by the ICJ.

At the beginning of the 21st century the Czech Republic and Slovakia still refused to recognize Liechtenstein as a sovereign state. In October 2003 Prince Hans-Adam blocked the entry of the Czech Republic and Slovakia (along with that of the eight other EU accession states) into the EEA; the 10 countries were due to become members of the EU on 1 May 2004 and would, under normal circumstances, have automatically joined the EEA. Their accession to the EEA was delayed until November 2003, when Liechtenstein agreed to sign the enlargement treaty

LIECHTENSTEIN

on the EEA; Slovakia subsequently agreed immediately to establish diplomatic relations with Liechtenstein. Liechtenstein reiterated its demand that the Czech Republic and Slovakia acknowledge that the Principality was a sovereign, neutral state through both World Wars. To do so, however, would expose these two countries to the possibility of legal action being brought against them by Liechtenstein for the illegal seizure of land.

Following a four-year investigation, in April 2005 an Independent Commission of Historians charged with examining Liechtenstein's role in the Second World War reported that no Jewish assets were confiscated and no forced labour was used during the War, and that while 165 refugees from Nazi-controlled Austria were turned away by Liechtenstein between 1933 and 1945, 400 others were taken in and thousands more allowed safe passage to Switzerland. The Commission was appointed by the Government in 2001 after the World Jewish Congress accused the Principality's financial institutions of having hidden plundered Jewish assets for the Nazis during the War.

Relations with Germany were strained in early 2008, following the revelation that the German Federal Intelligence Service had paid some €4m. to a former employee of Liechtenstein's LGT Bank for access to records detailing accounts held by German nationals. In the aftermath of the revelations, senior members of the German Government, including the Federal Chancellor, Angela Merkel, criticized Liechtenstein's banking system and called for greater financial transparency in that country, as well as greater co-operation regarding tax evasion. Merkel's comments were strongly rejected by Prince Alois, who accused Germany of attempting to undermine Liechtenstein's sovereignty. In late February the Prime Minister, Hasler, travelled to the German capital, Berlin, for talks with Merkel, during which the Federal Chancellor urged Hasler to begin co-operation with other countries regarding fiscal data. Nonetheless, in the following months, several further countries (including the USA and the United Kingdom) began investigations into allegations of tax evasion through secret bank accounts held in Liechtenstein. In response to growing international criticism, Prince Alois announced in mid-August that the country would endeavour to co-operate more fully on matters pertaining to tax in the future, but that this should not be at the expense of the country's 'culture of privacy'. A bilateral agreement was reached with the USA in December 2008, whereby Liechtenstein would co-operate with investigations into suspected tax evasion, while Liechtenstein banks would benefit from increased access to US financial markets. Prior to the meeting in April 2009 of the Group of 20 leading industrialized and developing nations (G20) in London, United Kingdom, Liechtenstein agreed in March to amend its secrecy laws to allow for greater transparency and to comply with rules on the sharing of bank data set by OECD to combat tax evasion. As a consequence of this commitment, in May Liechtenstein, Andorra and Monaco were removed from the OECD list of 'unco-operative tax havens'.

Government

The Constitution of the hereditary Principality provides for a unicameral Landtag (parliament), comprising 25 members, who are elected by universal adult suffrage for a term of four years (subject to dissolution), on the basis of proportional representation. The country is divided into the two election districts of Oberland (Upper Country) and Unterland (Lower Country), in which the seats are allocated separately. The Oberland district has 15 seats, the smaller Unterland district has 10 seats. A five-member Government is nominated by the Reigning Prince, on the recommendation of the Landtag, for four years. In March 2003 constitutional changes that extended the powers of the monarch were approved by a referendum; he was empowered to dismiss governments (even if they retained parliamentary confidence), appoint an interim administration pending an election, approve judicial nominees, veto laws and invoke emergency legislation. Citizens could force a referendum on any subject, including the future of the monarchy, by collecting 1,500 signatures. On 15 August 2004 the sovereign rights pertaining to the Reigning Prince were transferred to the Hereditary (Crown) Prince, who was to exercise them as the representative of the Reigning Prince, who remained Head of State.

Defence

Although Liechtensteiners under the age of 60 years are liable to military service in an emergency, there has been no standing army since 1868 and there is only a small police force, with 63 members.

Economic Affairs

In 2005, according to official estimates, Liechtenstein's gross national income (GNI) was 3,892m. Swiss francs, equivalent to 111,990 Swiss francs per head (establishing Liechtenstein among the world's most affluent nations, as measured per head of population). During 2003–07 the population increased at an average annual rate of 0.8%. According to UN estimates, during 1996–2006, gross domestic product (GDP) grew, in real terms, at an average annual rate of 3.2%; the UN estimated that GDP increased by 2.7% in 2006.

Following the Second World War, the importance of agriculture declined in favour of industry. According to official provisional estimates, in 2006 the agricultural sector (together with household producers) accounted for 7% of GDP. Within the agricultural sector the emphasis is on cattle-breeding, dairy-farming and market gardening. The principal crops are maize and potatoes. In addition, wine is produced, and forestry is a significant activity. In 2007 1.1% of those employed in Liechtenstein worked in agriculture (including forestry).

In 2006, according to official provisional estimates, industry (including production of goods) contributed some 40% of GDP, while 43.5% of those employed in Liechtenstein worked in industrial activity (including mining and quarrying, processing industries, energy and water supply, and construction) in 2007. The metal, machinery and precision instruments industry is by far the most prominent sector. Other important areas are the pharmaceutical, textiles and ceramics industries.

In 2006 more than 90% of energy requirements were imported from other countries. In that year natural gas supplied 28.8% of energy requirements, electricity 26.3%, fuel oil 20.5%, motor fuel (petrol) 14.3%, and diesel 7.9%.

According to official provisional estimates, in 2005 54% of GDP was generated by the services sector, while in 2007 the sector engaged 55.4% of those employed in Liechtenstein. Financial services are of great importance. Numerous foreign corporations, holding companies and foundations (estimated to number about 75,000) have nominal offices in Liechtenstein, benefiting from the Principality's stable political situation, tradition of bank secrecy (although stricter banking legislation was introduced in 1997 and in 2000–02, partly to increase the transparency of the sector) and low fiscal charges. Such enterprises pay no tax on profit or income, contributing instead an annual levy on capital or net worth. These levies account for about 20% of the Principality's annual direct revenue. In 1980 Liechtenstein adopted legislation to increase controls on foreign firms, many of which were thereafter subject to audit and entered in the public register. Following the Principality's accession to the European Economic Area (EEA) in 1995, the registration of foreign banks was permitted. New legislation governing insurance companies was approved in 1996, and during the late 1990s the insurance sector expanded rapidly. In December 2004 the Government and the European Union (EU, see p. 255) signed an accord on savings tax, which entered into force on 1 July 2005. Under the agreement, savings income, in the form of interest payments made in Liechtenstein to residents of the EU, became subject to a withholding tax. The building and hotel trades and other service industries are also highly developed. The Government initiated a publicity campaign in 2004 to promote Liechtenstein, with the launch of a national logo (a 'democratic crown' on an aubergine background). The objective was to increase tourism and investment and further to develop the Principality as a business centre. The new coalition Government formed in March 2009 announced its commitment to pursuing this aim.

With a very limited domestic market, Liechtenstein's industry is export-orientated. In 2007, according to preliminary figures, total exports amounted to 4,182.0m. Swiss francs (with imports totalling 2,416.4m. Swiss francs). Switzerland is the principal trading partner. In 2005 Switzerland purchased 11.7% of total exports of members of the Liechtenstein Chamber of Commerce and Industry and the EEA accounted for 44.1%. Specialized machinery, dental technology, vehicle components and frozen food are important exports.

In 2007 there was a fiscal surplus of 32.9m. Swiss francs. The annual average rate of inflation decreased gradually from 5.4% in 1990 to 0.6% in 2003. Consumer prices increased by an average of 1.1% in 2006, 0.7% in 2007 and 2.5% in 2008. Traditionally the unemployment rate has been negligible; in 2007 the rate of unemployment (as a percentage of those employed) was 1.8%. More than one-third of Liechtenstein's population are resident foreigners, many of whom provide the labour for industry, while

LIECHTENSTEIN

in December 2006 14,604 workers crossed the borders from Austria and Switzerland each day to work in the Principality.

Liechtenstein has important economic links with neighbouring Switzerland. It is incorporated in a customs union with that country, and uses the Swiss franc as its currency. Liechtenstein became a member of the European Free Trade Association (EFTA, see p. 426) in May 1991 and the EEA in May 1995. The Principality is also a member of the European Bank for Reconstruction and Development (EBRD, see p. 251).

Following the revelation of a high profile tax evasion scandal in Germany in February 2008, where it transpired that members of Germany's business elite had avoided tax by channelling up to €4,000m. into secret foundations established by banks in Liechtenstein, international pressure mounted on the Government to reform the Principality's strict banking secrecy rules.

In December 2008 Liechtenstein signed an agreement with the USA to facilitate the bilateral exchange of information on tax matters. In providing US authorities with greater access to information held by its banks in cases of suspected tax evasion, the Tax Information Exchange Agreement (TIEA) signalled Liechtenstein's increasing willingness to co-operate with other states in their investigations into tax evasion. (Prior to the signing of the agreement, Liechtenstein had distinguished between tax fraud and tax evasion, considering only the former to be a criminal offence, and thus, deserving of the state's co-operation.) The TIEA was scheduled to come into effect at the beginning of 2010. The new Government formed in March 2009 pledged to remain pursuant of a 'suitable solution for international tax co-operation', and in mid-March it was announced that Liechtenstein, along with Andorra and Monaco, had agreed to comply with OECD standards on transparency and information exchange with regard to tax concerns. In turn, Liechtenstein intended to commence negotiations on bilateral tax agreements (similar to the TIEA signed with the USA) with interested states. OECD subsequently removed Liechtenstein (and Andorra and Monaco) from a list of 'unco-operative tax havens', placing it instead on a list comprising countries that have yet to implement their commitment to accepting new international standards of financial information exchange.

Education

Compulsory education begins at seven years of age. Basic instruction is given for five years at a primary school (*Primarschule*), after which a pupil may transfer to a lower secondary school (*Oberschule*) or secondary school (*Realschule*) for four years, with the option of an additional year, or to the *Liechtensteinisches Gymnasium* (grammar school) for eight years. There is no university. Many Liechtensteiners continue their studies at universities in Austria and Switzerland. Liechtenstein has a further education college for the study of philosophy, a technical college (*Fachhochschule*), a music school, an art school, an adult education centre and a school for mentally disabled children. Government expenditure on education totalled 136.2m. Swiss francs in 2006 (18.7% of total expenditure).

Public Holidays

2009: 1 January (New Year's Day), 2 January (St Berchtold's Day), 6 January (Epiphany), 2 February (Candlemas), 24 February (Shrove Tuesday), 19 March (St Joseph's Day), 10 April (Good Friday), 13 April (Easter Monday), 1 May (Labour Day), 21 May (Ascension Day), 1 June (Whit Monday), 11 June (Corpus Christi), 15 August (National Holiday and Assumption), 8 September (Nativity of the Virgin Mary), 1 November (All Saints' Day), 8 December (Immaculate Conception), 25 December (Christmas), 26 December (St Stephen's Day).

2010: 1 January (New Year's Day), 2 January (St Berchtold's Day), 6 January (Epiphany), 2 February (Candlemas), 16 February (Shrove Tuesday), 19 March (St Joseph's Day), 2 April (Good Friday), 5 April (Easter Monday), 1 May (Labour Day), 13 May (Ascension Day), 24 May (Whit Monday), 3 June (Corpus Christi), 15 August (National Holiday and Assumption), 8 September (Nativity of the Virgin Mary), 1 November (All Saints' Day), 8 December (Immaculate Conception), 25 December (Christmas), 26 December (St Stephen's Day).

Weights and Measures

The metric system is in force.

Statistical Survey

Source: Amt für Volkswirtschaft, Gerberweg 5, 9490 Vaduz; tel. 2366111; fax 2366895; e-mail info.statistik@avw.llv.li; internet www.avw.llv.li.

AREA AND POPULATION

Area: 160.0 sq km (61.8 sq miles).

Population: 35,446, incl. 11,797 resident aliens at 30 June 2008.

Density (at 30 June 2008): 221.5 per sq km.

Municipalities (population at 30 June 2008): Schaan 5,718; Vaduz (capital) 5,091; Triesen 4,739; Balzers 4,512; Eschen 4,093; Mauren 3,815; Triesenberg 2,557; Ruggell 1,928; Gamprin 1,531; Schellenberg 1,049; Planken 413; Total 35,446.

Births, Marriages and Deaths (2007, provisional): Live births 351 (9.9 per 1,000); Marriages 114 (3.2 per 1,000); Deaths 227 (6.4 per 1,000). Source: UN, *Population and Vital Statistics Report*.

Economically Active Population (2007): Agriculture and forestry 372; Industry and skilled trades 14,096 (Mining and quarrying 47, Processing industries 11,432, Energy and water supply 196, Construction 2,421); Services 17,967 (Retail, repairs, etc. 2,343, Hotels and restaurants 899, Transport and communications 1,214, Banking and insurance 2,671, Real estate, business services, etc. 2,928, Legal consultancy and trust management 2,525, Public administration 1,504, Education 956, Health and social services 1,703, Other services 1,224); Total employed 32,435; Unemployed 593; Total labour force 33,028.

HEALTH AND WELFARE

Key Indicators

Under-5 Mortality Rate (per 1,000 live births, 2004): 5.

Physicians (per 1,000 head, 1997): 1.31 (Source: Statistik des Fürstentums Liechtenstein, *Statistisches Jahrbuch (1998)*).

For sources (unless specified) and definitions, see explanatory note on p. vi.

AGRICULTURE, ETC.

Note: Figures are for farms with a minimum of either 1 ha of arable land, 30 acres of specialized cultivation, 10 acres of protected cultivation, 8 sows, 80 porkers (or capacity for 80 porkers) or 300 head of poultry, and where livestock owners are covered by the *Tierseuchenfond* (insurance against epidemics).

Principal Crops (metric tons, 1987): Wheat 460; Oats 4; Barley 416; Silo-maize 27,880; Potatoes 1,040. *2007:* Grapes 200 metric tons (FAO estimate) (Source: partly FAO).

Livestock (2007): Cattle 6,037; Pigs 1,735; Horses 441; Sheep 3,683; Goats 319; Hens 12,224.

Dairy Produce (2006, metric tons): Milk delivered to dairies 13,225; Milk for consumption and pasteurization 905; Milk for processing 5,270; Cream 1,759; Yoghurt 198. *2007:* Milk delivered to dairies 13,137 metric tons.

Forestry ('000 cubic metres, 2007, FAO estimates): Roundwood removals (excl. bark) 22.2 (Sawlogs, veneer logs and logs for sleepers 18, Fuel wood 4.2). Source: FAO.

FINANCE

Currency and Exchange Rates: Swiss currency: 100 Rappen (centimes) = 1 Franken (Swiss franc). *Sterling, Dollar and Euro Equivalents* (31 December 2008): £1 sterling = 1.551 Franken; US $1 = 1.064 Franken; €1 = 1.480 Franken; 10 Franken = £6.45 = $9.40 = €6.76. For average exchange rate, see chapter on Switzerland.

Budget (million Swiss francs, 2007): *Revenue:* Current 992.3 (Taxes and duties 764.8; Revenues from assets 167.4); Capital 18.0; Total 1,010.3. *Expenditure:* Current 853.0 (Personnel 187.5; Regular contributions 323.9; Financial allocations 175.8); Capital 106.4; Total 959.4.

Cost of Living (Consumer Price Index; base: May 2000 = 100, annual averages): All items 105.8 in 2006; 106.5 in 2007; 109.1 in 2008.

National Income and Product (million Swiss francs at current prices, 2006, preliminary): Compensation of employees 2,675.1; Gross operating surplus 1,671.4; Gross mixed income 404.7; *GDP at* *factor cost* 4,751.2; Taxes on production and imports 347.1; Subsidies –96.9; *GDP in market prices* 5,001.3.

Production Account for GDP (million Swiss francs at current prices, 2006, preliminary): Total output 12,891.1; Financial intermediation services indirectly measured –382.3; *Gross value added in basic prices* 12,508.8; Taxes, less subsidies, on products 200.9; Intermediate consumption at purchasers' prices –7,708.5; *GDP in market prices* 5,001.3.

Gross Value Added by Economic Activity (percentage, 2006, preliminary): Agriculture and households 7; Industry and production of goods 40; Financial services 29; General services 24.

EXTERNAL TRADE

Note: Imports and exports to and from Liechtenstein presented at Swiss customs, not including trade with Switzerland and goods traffic via Switzerland.

Principal Commodities ('000 Swiss francs, 2007): *Imports:* Food, animals and other products of agriculture 85,887; Raw materials, metals, construction and chemical products 427,290; Vehicles and transport equipment 94,047; Machinery and electrical products 936,203; Metal manufactures and other finished and semi-finished goods 668,461; Glass, ceramic and textile manufactures 204,584; Total 2,416,472. *Exports:* Food, animals and other products of agriculture 286,241; Raw materials, metals, construction and chemical products 276,246; Vehicles and transport equipment 363,674; Machinery and electrical products 1,973,770; Metal manufactures and other finished and semi-finished goods 968,184; Glass, ceramic and textile manufactures 313,601; Total (incl. others) 4,181,716.

Principal Trading Partners ('000 Swiss francs, 2007): *Imports:* Austria 892,673; China, People's Republic 35,803; France 43,469; Germany 972,245; Italy 125,149; Netherlands 28,579; Poland 37,141; United Kingdom 34,326; USA 44,329; Total (incl. others) 2,416,472. *Exports:* Austria 479,272; China, People's Republic 85,179; France 413,314; Germany 834,723; Hong Kong 39,695; Italy 264,367; Japan 75,586; Mexico 41,441; Poland 54,104; Russia 78,842; Singapore 73,298; Spain 162,778; Sweden 69,902; United Arab Emirates 55,736; United Kingdom 160,011; USA 596,549; Total (incl. others) 4,181,716.

TRANSPORT

Road Traffic (registered motor vehicles, 1 July 2007): Passenger cars 24,368; Commercial vehicles 2,566; Motorcycles 3,256; Total (incl. others) 31,900.

TOURISM

Arrivals by Country of Residence (2007): Austria 3,047; France 1,316; Germany 18,819; Italy 2,143; Netherlands 1,326; Switzerland 15,947; United Kingdom 2,644; USA 2,363; Total (incl. others) 59,603.

COMMUNICATIONS MEDIA

Daily Newspapers (2004): 2 (total circulation 18,387 copies). Source: UNESCO Institute for Statistics.

Radio Receivers (1998): 12,451 in use.

Television Receivers (1998): 12,089 in use.

Telephones (2006): 20,100 main lines in use. Source: International Telecommunication Union.

Mobile Cellular Telephones (2006): 28,800 subscribers. Source: International Telecommunication Union.

Internet Users (2006): 22,000. Source: International Telecommunication Union.

Broadband Subscribers (2006): 10,000. Source: International Telecommunication Union.

EDUCATION

(2007/08, unless otherwise indicated*)

Kindergarten: 49 classrooms; 79 teachers (males 1, females 78); 711 pupils (males 371, females 340).

Primary†: 138 classrooms; 262 teachers (males 63, females 199); 2,073 pupils (males 1,035, females 1,038).

High School: 34 classrooms; 101 teachers (males 45, females 56); 412 pupils (males 221, females 191).

Secondary: 45 classrooms; 127 teachers (males 60, females 67); 732 pupils (males 380, females 352).

Optional 10th School Year: 5 classrooms; 19 teachers (males 10, females 9); 78 pupils (males 32, females 46).

Vocational Training: 8 classrooms; 16 teachers (males 8, females 8); 124 pupils (males 84, females 40).

Grammar Schools (2004/05, unless otherwise indicated): 38 classrooms (2001/02); 103 teachers; 744 pupils.

Music (2004/05): 91 teachers; 2,519 pupils.

Higher Education (2004/05)‡: 527 students.

* Excluding private institutions.
† Including pre-school and reception classes.
‡ Those studying in Liechtenstein only (931 students attended institutions abroad).

Directory

The Constitution

Under the Constitution of 5 October 1921 (as amended in 1969, 1984, 2003 and 2005), the monarchy is hereditary in the male line. The Reigning Prince, who is constitutionally responsible for foreign affairs, exercises legislative power jointly with the Landtag (parliament). The Landtag comprises 25 members, who are elected for a term of four years (subject to dissolution) by universal adult suffrage, on a basis of proportional representation. Of those 25 members, 15 are elected by voters in the Oberland (Upper Country) and 10 by voters in the Unterland (Lower Country). Under the Constitution, all citizens of over 18 years of age are eligible to vote. The voters participate directly in legislation through referendums.

The Government is a collegial body consisting of five Ministers, including the Prime Minister. Each Minister has an Alternate who takes part in the meetings of the collegial Government if the Minister is unavailable. The Prime Minister, the other Ministers and their Alternates are appointed by the Reigning Prince on the recommendation of the Landtag. On the recommendation of the Landtag, the Reigning Prince appoints one of the Ministers as Deputy Prime Minister. Only native Liechtenstein citizens who meet the requirements for election to the Landtag are eligible for appointment to the Government. Each of the two regions of Liechtenstein, the Upper Country and the Lower Country, is entitled to at least two Ministers. Their respective Alternates must come from the same region. The term of office is four years (subject to dissolution).

In a referendum on 14 and 16 March 2003 the electorate approved constitutional amendments extending the powers of the monarch. He was awarded the right to dismiss governments (even if they retained parliamentary confidence), to appoint an interim administration pending fresh elections, to veto laws by not signing them within a six-month period, to dismiss individual Ministers, subject to approval by the Landtag, to preside over a panel to select judges (with a casting vote) and to invoke emergency legislation. Citizens were accorded the right to force a referendum on any subject, including the future of the monarchy, by collecting 1,500 signatures.

In a referendum on 25 and 27 November 2005 the electorate approved constitutional amendments on the protection of human dignity and the right to life. The death penalty (abolished by a revision of the criminal code in 1985) was explicitly prohibited, as was the inhumane or degrading treatment of individuals.

In accordance with a treaty concluded with Switzerland in 1924, Liechtenstein is incorporated in Swiss customs territory, and uses Swiss currency, customs and postal administration.

The Government

HEAD OF STATE

Reigning Prince: HSH Prince HANS-ADAM II (Prince of Liechtenstein, Duke of Troppau and Jägerndorf, Count of Rietberg—succeeded 13 November 1989).

On 15 August 2004 Prince Hans-Adam II transferred the execution of his sovereign powers to his son, Hereditary Prince Alois.

LIECHTENSTEIN

GOVERNMENT
(April 2009)

A coalition of the Vaterländische Union (VU—Patriotic Union) and the Fortschrittliche Bürgerpartei (FBP—Progressive Citizens' Party).

Prime Minister and Minister of General Government Affairs, of Finance and of Family and Equal Opportunity: Dr KLAUS TSCHÜTSCHER (VU).

Deputy Prime Minister and Minister of Economic Affairs, of Transport and of Construction and Public Works: Dr MARTIN MEYER (FBP).

Minister of Public Health, of Social Affairs and of Environmental Affairs, Land Use Planning, Agriculture and Forestry: RENATE MÜSSNER (VU).

Minister of Home Affairs, of Education and of Sports: HUGO QUADERER (VU).

Minister of Foreign Affairs, of Justice and of Cultural Affairs: Dr AURELIA FRICK (FBP).

Alternate Ministers: ROLAND MOSER (VU), ANDREA KLEIN (VU), Dr MAURO PEDRAZZINI (FBP), Dr PATRICK SCHÜRMANN (FBP), HUBERT BÜCHEL (VU).

GOVERNMENT OFFICES

Regierungsgebäude: Postfach 684, 9490 Vaduz; tel. 2366111; fax 2366022; e-mail office@liechtenstein.li; internet www.liechtenstein.li.

Legislature

LANDTAG

Landtagssekretariat des Fürstentums Liechtenstein: Städtle 47, 9490 Vaduz; tel. 2366576; fax 2366580; e-mail info@landtag.li; internet www.landtag.li.

President: ARTHUR BRUNHART.
Vice-President: RENATE WOHLWEND.

General Election, 8 February 2009

Party	Votes	% of votes	Seats
VU	95,219	47.60	13
FBP	86,951	43.47	11
FL	17,835	8.92	1
Total	200,005	100.00	25

Election Commissions

Hauptwahl- oder Hauptabstimmungskommission Oberland: c/o Heiligkreuz 18, Postfach 684, 9490 Vaduz; tel. 2322202; fax 2361961; e-mail nv@viv.li; independent; Chair. NORBERT VOGT (Vaduz).

Hauptwahl- oder Hauptabstimmungskommission Unterland: c/o Postfach 684, 9490 Vaduz; independent; Chair. ALOIS ALLGÄUER (Eschen).

Political Organizations

Fortschrittliche Bürgerpartei (FBP) (Progressive Citizens' Party): Aeulestr. 56, Postfach 1213, 9490 Vaduz; tel. 2377940; fax 2377949; e-mail marcus.vogt@fbp.li; internet www.fbp.li; f. 1918; Pres. MARCUS VOGT.

Freie Liste (FL) (Free List): Postfach 254, 9494 Schaan; tel. 3732042; e-mail info@freieliste.li; internet www.freieliste.li; f. 1985; social democratic and ecological party; Pres CLAUDIA HEEB-FLECK, EGON MATT.

Vaterländische Union (VU) (Patriotic Union): Fürst-Franz-Josef-Str. 13, 9490 Vaduz; tel. 2398282; fax 2398289; e-mail vu@vu-online.li; internet www.vu-online.li; f. 1936 by merger of the People's Party (f. 1918) and the Heimatdienst movement; Pres. ADOLF HEEB; Sec.-Gen. HANS-JÖRG GOOP.

Diplomatic Representation

According to an arrangement concluded in 1919, Switzerland has agreed to represent Liechtenstein's interests in countries where it has diplomatic missions and where Liechtenstein is not represented in its own right. In so doing, Switzerland always acts only on the basis of mandates of a general or specific nature, which it may either refuse or accept, while Liechtenstein is free to enter into direct relations with foreign states or to establish its own additional missions. Liechtenstein has nine diplomatic missions abroad, comprising embassies in Berlin (Germany), Bern (Switzerland), Brussels (Belgium, including a permanent mission to the European Union), Washington, DC (USA), Vienna (Austria, including permanent missions to the Organization for Security and Co-operation in Europe and the UN), as well as a permanent representative to the Council of Europe in Strasbourg (France), a permanent mission to the UN in New York (USA) and a permanent mission in Geneva (Switzerland). Liechtenstein also has a non-resident ambassador to the Holy See. There are 41 consular representatives accredited to Liechtenstein, of which 22 have offices in the Principality (representing Austria, the Central African Republic, Chad, Cyprus, Denmark, Ecuador, France, Germany, Hungary, Iceland, the Republic of Korea, Lithuania, Luxembourg, the former Yugoslav republic of Macedonia, Malta, Monaco, the Netherlands, Poland, Romania, Russia, Saint Vincent and the Grenadines, Spain, Sweden and Ukraine).

Judicial System

CIVIL AND CRIMINAL COURTS

Landgericht (County Court): Spaniagasse 1, 9490 Vaduz; tel. 2366111; fax 2366539; e-mail benedikt.marxer@lg.liv.li; Court of First Instance; one presiding judge, and 13 other judges; Presiding Judge Dr BENEDIKT MARXER.

Kriminalgericht (Criminal Court): 9490 Vaduz; bench of five judges; Presiding Judge Lic. Iur. UWE ÖHRI.

Schöffengericht (Court of Assizes): 9490 Vaduz; for minor misdemeanours; bench of three judges; Presiding Judge Dr BENEDIKT MARXER.

Jugendgericht (Juvenile Court): 9490 Vaduz; bench of three judges; Presiding Judge Lic. Iur. UWE ÖHRI.

Obergericht (Superior Court): 9490 Vaduz; Court of Second Instance; divided into three senates, each with bench of five judges; Presiding Judge and Chair. of First Senate Lic. Iur. MAX BIZOZZERO; Chair. of Second Senate Lic. Iur. RUDOLF FEHR; Chair. of Third Senate Dr GERHARD MISLIK.

Oberster Gerichtshof (Supreme Court): 9490 Vaduz; Court of Third Instance; bench of five judges; Presiding Judge Dr HANSJÖRG RÜCK.

ADMINISTRATIVE COURTS

Verwaltungsgerichtshof (Administrative Court of Appeal): Städtle 49, Postfach 804, 9490 Vaduz; tel. 2366111; appeal against decrees and decisions of the Government may be made to this court; five members; Presiding Judge Lic. Iur. ANDREAS BATLINER.

Staatsgerichtshof (State Court): Geschäftsstelle, Städtle 36, Postfach 729, 9490 Vaduz; tel. 2391010; fax 2391039; e-mail kontakt@stgh.li; internet www.stgh.li; five members; exists for the protection of Public Law; Presiding Judge Lic. Iur. MARZELL BECK.

Religion

CHRISTIANITY

The Principality comprises a single archdiocese, Vaduz, created in 1997, which is directly responsible to the Holy See. At 31 December 2006 there were an estimated 26,800 adherents of the Roman Catholic Church (some 78.8% of the population). The few Protestants (7.3%) belong to the parish of Vaduz.

Archdiocese of Vaduz: Erzbischöfliche Kanzlei, Fürst-Franz-Josef-Str. 112, Postfach 103, 9490 Vaduz; tel. 2332311; fax 2332324; e-mail erzbistum@powersurf.li; internet www.erzbistum-vaduz.li; Archbishop Most Rev. WOLFGANG HAAS.

The Press

Exclusiv: Aubündt 28, 9490 Vaduz; tel. 2328080; fax 2328081; e-mail info@exclusiv.li; internet www.exclusiv.li; f. 1996; monthly; Publr ALBERT MENNEL.

Liechtensteiner Vaterland: Austr. 81, 9490 Vaduz; tel. 2361616; fax 2361617; e-mail redaktion@vaterland.li; internet www.vaterland.li; f. 1913; publ. by Vaduzer Medienhaus AG; daily (Mon.–Sat.); organ of the VU; Editor-in-Chief GÜNTHER FRITZ; circ. 10,295.

Liechtensteiner Volksblatt: Im alten Riet 103, 9494 Schaan; tel. and fax 2375151; fax 2375155; e-mail redaktion@volksblatt.li;

internet www.volksblatt.li; f. 1878; daily (Mon.–Sat.); organ of the FBP; Editor-in-Chief Heinz Zoechbauer; circ. 9,000.

Liewo Sonntagszeitung: Austr. 81, 9490 Vaduz; tel. 2361616; fax 2361617; e-mail redaktion@liewo.li; internet www.liewo.li; f. 1993 as *Liechtensteiner Wochenzeitung*; publ. by Vaduzer Medienhaus AG; weekly (Sun.); Editor-in-Chief Corinna Beck; circ. 32,000.

Wirtschaft Regional: Austr. 81, 9490 Vaduz; tel. 2361616; fax 2361617; e-mail info@wirtschaftregional.li; internet www.wirtschaftregional.li; f. 2001; publ. by Vaduzer Medienhaus AG; weekly; Editor-in-Chief Matthias Hassler.

PRESS AGENCY

Presse- und Informationsamt (PIA) (Press and Information Office): St Florinsgasse 3, Postfach 684, 9490 Vaduz; tel. 2366721; fax 2366460; e-mail info@pia.llv.li; internet www.pia.llv.li; f. 1962; Dir Daniela Clavadetscher.

Publishers

Alpenland Verlag AG: Feldkircher Str. 13, 9494 Schaan; tel. 2395030; fax 2395031; e-mail office@buchzentrum.li; internet www.buchzentrum.li; Man. Dir Marco Nescher.

BONAFIDES Verlags-Anstalt: Pflugstr. 20, Postfach 82, 9490 Vaduz; tel. 2654680; fax 3900594; e-mail bva-fl@adon.li.

BVD Druck+Verlag AG: Landstr. 153, 9494 Schaan; tel. 2361836; fax 2361840; e-mail bvd@bvd.li; internet www.bvd.li; Pres. Kurt Göppel.

van Eck Verlag: Haldenweg 8, 9495 Triesen; tel. 3923000; fax 3922277; e-mail info@vaneckverlag.li; internet www.vaneckverlag.li; f. 1982; art, local interest, juvenile, golf, crime fiction; Man. Dirs Frank P. van Eck, Peter Göppel.

Ex Jure Verlagsanstalt: Aeulestr. 74, Postfach 86, 9490 Vaduz; tel. 2360404; fax 2360481; e-mail service@exjure.li; internet www.exjure.net; f. 1968; legal.

A. R. Gantner Verlag KG: Industriestr. 105A, Postfach 26, 9491 Ruggell; tel. 3771808; fax 3771802; e-mail bgc@adon.li; internet www.gantner-verlag.com; f. 1966; botany; Dir Bruni Gantner-Caplan.

GMG Verlag AG: Landstr. 30, 9494 Schaan; tel. 2381166; fax 2381160; e-mail verlag@gmg.biz; internet www.gmg.biz/verlag; f. 1990; Man. Dir Arthur Gassner.

Lehrmittelverlag: Pflugstr. 30, 9490 Vaduz; tel. 2366390.

Liechtenstein-Verlag AG: Landstr. 30, 9494 Schaan; tel. 2396010; fax 2396019; e-mail books@liechtensteinverlag.com; internet www.liechtensteinverlag.com; f. 1947; belles-lettres, legal and scientific books; agents for international literature; Man. Arthur Gassner.

Litag Anstalt—Literarische, Medien und Künstler Agentur: Industriestr. 26A, Postfach 131, 9491 Ruggell; tel. 3771808; fax 3771802; e-mail bgc@adon.li; f. 1956; Dir Bruni Gantner-Caplan.

MM-Verlag Buchhandlung Irmgard Meier: Pradafant 20, 9490 Vaduz; tel. 2329448; fax 2329449; e-mail mm.verlag@buchhandlung.li.

Neue Verlagsanstalt: In der Fina 18, Postfach 29, 9494 Schaan; tel. 2334381; fax 2334382; e-mail info@neue-verlagsanstalt.li; internet www.neue-verlagsanstalt.li; magazine publisher; Dir Janine Hillert.

Sändig Reprint Verlag Wohlwend: Am Schrägen Weg 12, 9490 Vaduz; tel. 2323627; fax 2323649; e-mail saendig@adon.li; internet www.saendig.com; f. 1981; natural sciences, linguistics, freemasonry, fiction, folklore, music, history; Dir Christian Wohlwend.

Topos Verlag AG: Industriestr. 26, Postfach 551, 9491 Ruggell; tel. 3771111; fax 3771119; e-mail topos@supra.net; internet www.topos.li; f. 1977; law, politics, literature, social science, periodicals; Dir Graham A. P. Smith.

Verlag der Liechtensteinischen Akademischen Gesellschaft (LAG): In der Fina 26, Postfach 829, 9494 Schaan; tel. 2323028; fax 2331449; e-mail info@verlag-lag.li; internet www.verlag-lag.li; f. 1972; Dir Norbert Jansen.

Broadcasting and Communications

TELECOMMUNICATIONS
REGULATORY AUTHORITY

Amt für Kommunikation: Kirchstr. 10, Postfach 684, 9490 Vaduz; tel. 2366488; fax 2366489; e-mail info@ak.llv.li; internet www.ak.llv.li; national regulatory authority; Dir Kurt Bühler.

MAJOR SERVICE PROVIDERS

Mobilkom Liechtenstein AG: Äulestras. 20, Postfach 1514, 9490 Vaduz; tel. 7970077; fax 7970099; internet www.mobilkom.li; f. 2000; subsidiary of Mobilkom Austria AG; mobile cellular telephone operator; Dir Michael Amman.

Telecom Liechtenstein AG: Schaanerstr. 1, 9490 Vaduz; tel. 2377400; fax 2377499; e-mail telecom@telecom.li; internet www.telecom.li; f. 1999; fixed-line and mobile cellular telecommunications, broadband internet access, digital television; Pres. Oliver Gerstgrasser.

BROADCASTING

Radio Liechtenstein: Dorfstr. 24, 9495 Triesen; tel. 3991313; fax 3991366; e-mail admin@radio.li; internet www.radio.li; f. 1995; Pres. Clemens Laternser; Editor-in-Chief Martin Frommelt.

Finance

(cap. = capital; res = reserves; dep. = deposits; m. = million; brs = branches; amounts in Swiss francs)

REGULATORY AUTHORITY

Finanzmarktaufsicht Liechtenstein (FMA) (Financial Market Authority of Liechtenstein): Heiligkreuz 8, Postfach 279, 9490 Vaduz; tel. 2367373; fax 2367374; e-mail info@fma-li.li; internet www.fma-li.li; f. 2005; independent authority under the auspices of the Landtag; regulates banks and credit institutions, insurance cos and Liechtensteinische Post AG (Liechtenstein Postal Service); Chair. René H. Melliger; CEO Mario Gassner.

BANKING

In early 2008 there were 15 banks in Liechtenstein.

Bank Alpinum AG: Städtle 17, 9490 Vaduz; tel. 2396211; fax 2396221; e-mail info@bankalpinum.com; internet www.bankalpinum.com; fmrly NewCenturyBank, renamed as above April 2006; Chair. Wolfgang Seeger; CEO Urban B. Eberle.

Bank von Ernst (Liechtenstein) AG: Egerastr. 10, Postfach 112, 9490 Vaduz; tel. 2655353; fax 2655363; e-mail info@bve.li; internet www.bve.li; wholly owned by EFG Bank (Switzerland); cap. 25m., res 10m., dep. 266m. (Dec. 2006); Chair. Jean-Pierre Cuoni; CEO Ernst Weder.

Bank Frick & Co. AG: Landstr. 14, Postfach 43, 9496 Balzers; tel. 3882121; fax 3882122; e-mail bank@bfc.li; internet www.bfc.li; Chair. Mario Frick, Sr; CEO Jürgen Frick.

Bank Vontobel (Liechtenstein) AG: Pflugstr. 20, Postfach 786, 9490 Vaduz; tel. 2364141; fax 2364142; e-mail postmaster@vontobel.li; internet www.vontobel.li; f. 2000; Chair. Dr Urs Widmer; CEO Herbert J. Scheidt.

Banque Pasche (Liechtenstein) SA: Austr. 61, Postfach 832, 9490 Vaduz; tel. 2393333; fax 2393300; e-mail pasche.liechtenstein@pasche.li; internet www.pasche.li; fmrly Swissfirst Bank (Liechtenstein) AG; 52.5% owned by Banque Pasche CM-CIC Private Banking (Switzerland); Chair. Jean-François Kurz; CEO Daniel Brühwiler.

Centrum Bank AG: Kirchstr. 3, Postfach 1168, 9490 Vaduz; tel. 2383838; fax 2383839; e-mail info@centrumbank.com; internet www.centrumbank.com; f. 1993; cap. 20m., res 131m., dep. 838m. (Dec. 2006); Chair. Dr Peter Marxer; CEO Stephan Häberle.

Hypo Investment Bank (Liechtenstein) AG: Austr. 59, Postfach 23, 9490 Vaduz; tel. 2655656; fax 2655699; e-mail info@hypo.li; internet www.hypo.li; f. 1998; CEO, Management Bd Dr Andreas Insam.

Kaiser Ritter Partner Privatbank AG: Pflugstr. 16, Postfach 725, 9490 Vaduz; tel. 2378000; fax 2378001; e-mail bank@serica.com; internet www.kaiserritterpartner.com; f. 1999; cap. 10m., res 23m., dep. 424m. (Dec. 2007); Chair. Dr Peter Ritter; CEO Dr Thomas Trauth.

LGT Bank in Liechtenstein Ltd (LGT): Herrengasse 12, Postfach 85, 9490 Vaduz; tel. 2351122; fax 2351522; e-mail info@lgt.com; internet www.lgt.com; f. 1920; present name adopted 1996; cap. 291m., res 1,042m., dep. 13,269m. (Dec. 2006); Group CEO Prince Maximilian.

Liechtensteinische Landesbank AG (State Bank): Städtle 44, Postfach 384, 9490 Vaduz; tel. 2368811; fax 2368822; e-mail llb@llb.li; internet www.llb.li; f. 1861; present name adopted 1955; cap. 1654m., res –148m., dep. 19,502m. (Dec. 2007); Chair., Bd of Dirs Dr Hans-Werner Gassner; Chair., Management Bd Dr Josef Fehr; 4 brs.

Neue Bank AG: Marktgass 20, Postfach 1533, 9490 Vaduz; tel. 2360808; fax 2329260; e-mail info@neuebankag.li; internet www.neuebankag.li; f. 1992; cap. 40m., res 42m., total assets 1,257m. (Dec. 2007); Chair. Georg Vogt.

Raiffeisen Bank (Liechtenstein) AG: Austr. 51, Postfach 1621, 9490 Vaduz; tel. 2370707; fax 2370777; e-mail info@raiffeisen.li; internet www.raiffeisen.li; f. 1998; total assets 252m. (Dec. 2006); Chair. GÜNTHER DAPUNT.

Verwaltungs- und Privat-Bank AG (VP Bank): Aeulestr. 6, 9490 Vaduz; tel. 2356655; fax 2356500; e-mail info@vpbank.com; internet www.vpbank.com; f. 1956; cap. 59m., res 496m., dep. 7,220m. (Dec. 2007); Chair. HANS BRUNHART; CEO ADOLF E. REAL; 9 brs.

Volksbank AG: Feldkircher Str. 2, 9494 Schaan; tel. 2390404; fax 2390405; e-mail info@volksbank.li; internet www.volksbank.li; f. 1997; Man. Dir GERHARD HAMEL.

Bankers' Association

Liechtensteinischer Bankverband: Pflugstr. 20, Postfach 254, 9490 Vaduz; tel. 2301323; fax 2301324; e-mail info@bankenverband.li; internet www.bankenverband.li; f. 1969; Pres. ADOLF E. REAL; Dir MICHAEL LAUBER; 15 mems.

INSURANCE

In early 2008 there were 37 insurance companies in Liechtenstein.

Fortuna Lebens-Versicherungs-AG: Städtle 35, 9490 Vaduz; tel. 2361545; fax 2361546; e-mail fl.service@fortuna.li; internet www.fortuna.li; f. 1996; Man. Dir HEINER KEIL.

Liechtensteinische AHV-IV-FAK: Gerberweg 2, Postfach 84, 9490 Vaduz; tel. 2381616; fax 2381600; e-mail ahv@ahv.li; internet www.ahv.li; state-owned; Chair. PETER WOLFF; Dir WALTER KAUFMANN.

Swisscom Re AG: Kirchstr. 12, 9490 Vaduz; tel. 2301665; fax 2301666; Man. Dirs BERNHARD LAMPERT, URS LUGINBÜHL, MARCEL VON VIVIS, THOMAS WITTBJER.

Swiss Life (Liechtenstein) AG: In der Specki 3, 9494 Schaan; tel. 3777000; fax 3777099; e-mail office@swisslife.li; internet www.swisslife.li; absorbed CapitalLeben Versicherung AG in 2007; life insurance; Chair. BRUNO GEHRIG.

Transmarine Insurance Co Ltd: Aeulestr. 38, 9490 Vaduz; tel. 2334488; fax 2334489; f. 1996.

Valorlife Lebensversicherungs-AG: Heiligkreuz 43, 9490 Vaduz; tel. 3992950; fax 3992959; e-mail info@valorlife.com; internet www.valorlife.com; f. 1998; subsidiary of Vaudoise Versicherungsgruppe (Switzerland); Pres. ROLF MEHR; Dir SERGE HEDIGER.

Insurance Association

Liechtensteinischer Versicherungsverband eV (LVV): c/o Fortuna Lebens-Versicherungs AG, Städtle 35, 9490 Vaduz; tel. 2361549; fax 2361548; e-mail office@versicherungsverband.li; internet www.versicherungsverband.li; f. 1998; Pres. HEINER KEIL; 25 mems.

Trade and Industry

CHAMBER OF COMMERCE

Liechtensteinische Industrie- und Handelskammer (Liechtenstein Chamber of Commerce and Industry): Altenbach 8, 9490 Vaduz; tel. 2375511; fax 2375512; e-mail info@lihk.li; internet www.lihk.li; f. 1947; Pres. KLAUS RISCH; Gen. Man. JOSEF BECK; 40 mems.

INDUSTRIAL ASSOCIATION

Vereinigung Bäuerlicher Organisationen im Fürstentum Liechtenstein (VBO) (Agricultural Union): Duxweg 14, Postfach 351, 9494 Mauren; tel. 3759050; fax 3759051; e-mail vbo@kba.li; Pres. THOMAS BÜCHEL.

UTILITIES

Electricity

Liechtenstein imported some 93% of its electricity in 2006, mainly from Switzerland.

Liechtensteinische Kraftwerke (LKW): Im alten Riet 17, 9494 Schaan; tel. 2360111; fax 2360112; e-mail lkw@lkw.li; internet www.lkw.li; Pres. PATRIK OEHRI; Dir-Gen. GERALD MARXER.

Gas

Liechtensteinische Gasversorgung (LGV): Im Rietacker 4, 9494 Schaan; tel. 2361555; fax 2361566; e-mail lgv@lgv.li; internet www.lgv.li; f. 1985; Dir ROLAND RISCH.

Water

Wasserversorgung Liechtensteiner Unterland (WLU): Industriestr. 36, 9487 Gamprin-Bendern; tel. 3732555; fax 3735136; e-mail info@wlu.li; supplies water to Eschen, Gamprin, Mauren, Ruggell, and Schellenberg.

Gruppenwasserversorgung Liechtensteiner Oberland (GWO): supplies water to Balzers, Planken, Schaan, Triesen, Triesenberg and Vaduz.

TRADE UNIONS

Liechtensteiner ArbeitnehmerInnenverband (LANV) (Employees' Asscn): Dorfstr. 24, 9495 Triesen; tel. 3993838; fax 3993839; e-mail info@lanv.li; internet www.lanv.li; Pres. SIGI LANGENBAHN; Sec. JÜRGEN SCHÄDLER; 1,200 mems.

Liechtensteinische Ingenieur- und Architektenvereinigung (Engineers' and Architects' Asscn): Im Oberfeld 9, 9490 Vaduz; tel. 2311320; fax 2311321; e-mail office@lia.li; internet www.lia.li; Pres. SIEGBERT KRANZ; 153 mems.

Wirtschaftskammer Liechtenstein: Zollstr. 23, 9494 Schaan; tel. 2377788; fax 2377789; e-mail info@wirtschaftskammer.li; internet www.wirtschaftskammer.li; f. 1936; aims to protect the interests of Liechtenstein artisans and tradespeople; Pres. MATT ARNOLD; Gen. Man. JÜRGEN NIGG; 3,000 mems.

Transport

RAILWAYS

Liechtenstein is traversed by some 18.5 km of railway track, which is administered by Austrian Federal Railways. There is a station at Nendeln, as well as two halts at Schaan and Schaanwald. A local service connects Feldkirch in Austria and Buchs in Switzerland via Liechtenstein, and the Arlberg Express (Paris, France, to Vienna, Austria) passes through the Principality.

ROADS

Modern roads connect the capital, Vaduz, with all the towns and villages in the Principality. There are approximately 250 km of roads, all of which are paved. The Rhine and Samina valleys are connected by a tunnel 740 m long. Public transport is provided by a well-developed network of postal buses.

Liechtenstein Bus Anstalt (LBA): Städtle 38, 9490 Vaduz; tel. 2366310; fax 2366311; e-mail info.lba@tba.llv.li; internet www.lba.li; operates 42 buses on 13 routes over 105 km; Man. Dir ULRICH FEISST.

INLAND WATERWAYS

A canal of 26 km, irrigating the Rhine valley, was opened in 1943.

Tourism

Liechtenstein has an Alpine setting in the Upper Rhine area. The principal tourist attractions include a renowned postal museum, a National Museum and the Liechtenstein State Art Collection at Vaduz, as well as the Prince's castle (although this is closed to the public) and two ruined medieval fortresses at Schellenberg. Annually about two-fifths of foreign tourists visit the winter sports resort at Malbun, in the south-east of the Principality. For summer visitors there are some 400 km of hiking trails and an extensive network of cycling paths. In 2007 Liechtenstein received 59,603 foreign visitors.

Liechtenstein Tourismus: Postfach 139, Städtle 37, 9490 Vaduz; tel. 2396300; fax 2396301; e-mail info@tourismus.li; internet www.tourismus.li; Dir ROLAND BÜCHEL.

LITHUANIA

Introductory Survey

Location, Climate, Language, Religion, Flag, Capital

The Republic of Lithuania (formerly the Lithuanian Soviet Socialist Republic) is situated on the eastern coast of the Baltic Sea, in north-eastern Europe. It is bounded by Latvia to the north, by Belarus to the south-east, by Poland to the south-west and by the Russian exclave, Kaliningrad Oblast, to the west. Lithuania's maritime position moderates an otherwise continental-type climate. Temperatures range from an average of −4.9°C (23.2°F) in January to a July mean of 17.0°C (62.6°F). Rainfall levels vary considerably from region to region: in the far west the annual average is 700 mm–850 mm (28 ins–33 ins), but in the central plain it is about 600 mm (24 ins). The official language is Lithuanian. The predominant religion is Christianity. Most ethnic Lithuanians are Roman Catholics by belief or tradition, but there are small communities of Lutherans and Calvinists, as well as a growing number of modern Protestant denominations. Adherents of Russian Orthodoxy are almost exclusively ethnic Slavs, while most Tatars have retained an adherence to Islam. The national flag (proportions 3 by 5) consists of three equal horizontal stripes of yellow (top), green and red (bottom). The capital is Vilnius.

Recent History

Prior to annexation by the Russian Empire in 1795, Lithuania was united in a Commonwealth with Poland. In 1915, after the outbreak of the First World War, it was occupied by German troops. A 'Lithuanian Conference' was convened in September 1917, which demanded the re-establishment of an independent Lithuanian state and elected a 'Lithuanian Council', headed by Antanas Smetona; it proceeded to declare independence on 16 February 1918. The new state survived both a Soviet attempt to create a Lithuanian-Belarusian Soviet republic and a Polish campaign aimed at reincorporating Lithuania. In October 1920 Poland annexed the region of Vilnius, but was forced to recognize the rest of Lithuania as an independent state (with its provisional capital at Kaunas). Soviet Russia had recognized Lithuanian independence in the Treaty of Moscow, signed in July. Lithuania's first Constitution, which declared Lithuania a parliamentary democracy, was adopted in August 1922. In December 1926 Smetona seized power in a military *coup d'état* and established an authoritarian regime, which endured until 1940.

According to the 'Secret Protocols' to the Treaty of Non-Aggression (the Molotov-Ribbentrop Pact), signed on 23 August 1939 by the USSR and Germany, Lithuania was to be part of the German sphere of influence. However, the Nazi-Soviet Treaty on Friendship and Existing Borders, agreed in September (following the outbreak of the Second World War), permitted the USSR to take control of Lithuania. In October Lithuania was compelled to agree to the stationing of 20,000 Soviet troops on its territory. In return, the USSR granted the city and region of Vilnius (which had been seized by Soviet troops in September) to Lithuania. In June 1940 the USSR dispatched a further 100,000 troops to Lithuania and forced the Lithuanian Government to resign. A Soviet-approved People's Government was formed. Elections to a People's Seim (parliament), which only pro-Soviet candidates were permitted to contest, took place in July. The Seim proclaimed the Lithuanian Soviet Socialist Republic on 21 July, and on 3 August Lithuania formally became a Union Republic of the USSR. The establishment of Soviet rule was followed by the arrest and imprisonment of many Lithuanian politicians and government officials.

Some 210,000 people, mainly Jews, were killed during the Nazi occupation of Lithuania (1941–44). The return of the Soviet Army, in 1944, was not welcomed by most Lithuanians, and anti-Soviet partisan warfare continued until 1952. Lithuanian agriculture was forcibly collectivized and rapid industrialization was implemented. Meanwhile, some 150,000 people were deported, many to Kazakhstan or to Russian Siberia and the Far East, and leaders and members of the Roman Catholic Church were persecuted and imprisoned. Lithuanian political parties were disbanded, and political power became the exclusive preserve of the Communist Party of Lithuania (CPL), the local branch of the Communist Party of the Soviet Union (CPSU). The leader (First Secretary) of the CPL in 1940–74 was Antanas Sniečkus.

A significant dissident movement was established during the 1960s and 1970s. With the introduction of the policy of *glasnost* (openness) by the Soviet leader, Mikhail Gorbachev, in the mid-1980s, a limited discussion of previously censored aspects of Lithuanian history appeared in the press. Dissident groups took advantage of a more tolerant attitude to political protests, organizing a demonstration in August 1987 to denounce the Nazi-Soviet Pact. However, in February 1988 security forces were deployed to prevent the public celebration of the 70th anniversary of Lithuanian independence. This, together with frustration among the intelligentsia at the slow pace of reform in the republic, led to the establishment in June of the Lithuanian Movement for Reconstruction (Sąjūdis). Sąjūdis organized mass demonstrations to protest against environmental pollution, the suppression of national culture and 'russification', and to condemn the signing of the Molotov-Ribbentrop Pact. The movement appealed to the CPL to support a declaration of independence and the recognition of Lithuanian as the state language. The latter demand was adopted by the Lithuanian Supreme Soviet (Supreme Council—legislature) in November, and traditional Lithuanian state symbols were restored. Other concessions made by the CPL during 1988 included the restoration of Independence Day as a public holiday and the return of buildings to the Roman Catholic Church.

Sąjūdis won 36 of the 42 popularly elected Lithuanian seats at elections to the all-Union Congress of People's Deputies in March 1989. Thereafter, the CPL began to adopt a more radical position, in an attempt to retain some measure of popular support. On 18 May the CPL-dominated Supreme Soviet approved a declaration of Lithuanian sovereignty, which asserted the supremacy of Lithuania's laws over all-Union legislation. Public debate concerning the legitimacy of Soviet rule in Lithuania intensified: a commission of the Lithuanian Supreme Soviet declared the establishment of Soviet power in 1940 to have been unconstitutional and, in August, on the 50th anniversary of the signing of the Pact with Nazi Germany, more than 1m. people participated in a 'human chain' extending from Tallinn in Estonia, through Latvia, to Vilnius.

Despite denunciations of Baltic nationalism by the all-Union authorities, the Lithuanian Supreme Soviet continued to adopt reformist legislation, including the establishment of freedom of religion and the legalization of a multi-party system. In December 1989 the CPL declared itself an independent party, no longer subordinate to the CPSU, adopting a new programme and declaring support for multi-party democracy and independent statehood. Shortly afterwards a group of former CPL members who were opposed to independence formed a separate movement, the Lithuanian Communist Party on the CPSU Platform (LCP). Meanwhile, Algirdas Brazauskas, First Secretary of the CPL since October 1988, was elected Chairman of the Presidium of the Lithuanian Supreme Soviet, defeating three other candidates, including Romualdas Ozolas, a leading member of Sąjūdis. None the less, Sąjūdis remained the dominant political force in the republic, and its supporters won an overall majority in the elections to the Lithuanian Supreme Soviet in February–March 1990. This new, pro-independence parliament elected Vytautas Landsbergis, the Chairman of Sąjūdis, to replace Brazauskas as its Chairman (de facto President of Lithuania), and on 11 March declared the restoration of Lithuanian independence: Lithuania thus became the first of the Soviet republics to make such a declaration. The Supreme Council also restored the pre-1940 name of the country (the Republic of Lithuania) and suspended the USSR Constitution on Lithuanian territory. Kazimiera Danutė Prunskienė, a member of the CPL and hitherto a Deputy Chairman of the Council of Ministers, was appointed to be the first Prime Minister of the restored republic.

The Lithuanian declarations were condemned by a special session of the all-Union Congress of People's Deputies as unconstitutional, and Soviet forces occupied CPL buildings in Vilnius. An economic embargo was imposed on Lithuania in April 1990, and vital fuel supplies were suspended; the embargo remained in force for more than two months, until Lithuania agreed to a six-month moratorium on the independence declaration, pending formal negotiations. However, talks, which began in August, were soon terminated by the Soviet Government, and in January 1991 Landsbergis revoked the suspension of the declaration of independence, since negotiations on Lithuania's status had not resumed. Tension increased in the republic when the Soviet authorities dispatched to Vilnius troops (led by the special OMON units of the Soviet Ministry of Internal Affairs), who occupied former CPSU properties that had been nationalized by the Lithuanian Government. Landsbergis mobilized popular support to help defend the parliament building, which he believed to be under threat. In mid-January 13 people were killed and about 500 injured, when Soviet troops seized the broadcasting centre in Vilnius. (In August 1999 six former officers of the LCP were convicted of complicity in attempts to overthrow the Lithuanian Government in January 1991, and sentenced to between three and 12 years' imprisonment.)

Meanwhile, policy differences had arisen within the Lithuanian leadership, and earlier in January 1991 Prunskienė and her Council of Ministers had resigned after the Supreme Council refused to sanction proposed price increases. Gediminas Vagnorius, a member of the Supreme Council, was appointed Prime Minister. At a referendum on 9 February, 90.5% of voters expressed support for the re-establishment of an independent Lithuania and for the withdrawal of the Soviet army from the republic. In common with five other Soviet republics, Lithuania refused to conduct the all-Union referendum on the future of the USSR, which was held in March. (Voting did take place unofficially in predominantly Russian- and Polish-populated areas of Lithuania, where the majority endorsed the preservation of the USSR.)

A series of attacks by OMON forces on members of the nascent Lithuanian defence force and on the customs posts on the border with Belarus, combined with the seizure of power in Moscow by the conservative communist 'State Committee for the State of Emergency' (SCSE) in August 1991, led to fears in Lithuania that there would be a renewed attempt to overthrow the Landsbergis administration and reimpose Soviet rule. Soviet military vehicles entered Vilnius, but did not prevent the convening of an emergency session of the Supreme Council, which condemned the SCSE and issued a statement supporting Boris Yeltsin, President of the Russian Federation. As the coup collapsed, the Lithuanian Government ordered the withdrawal of Soviet forces from the republic and banned the LCP. (The successor party to the CPL, the Lithuanian Democratic Labour Party—LDLP, was not banned.) The Government also began to assume effective control of the country's borders. The failed coup prompted the recognition of Lithuanian independence by other states, and on 6 September the USSR State Council recognized the independence of Lithuania and the other Baltic republics (Estonia and Latvia), all three of which were admitted to the UN and the Conference on (now Organization for) Security and Co-operation in Europe (OSCE, see p. 366) later in the month.

During the first half of 1992 there was an increasing polarity within the Supreme Council between Sąjūdis deputies and those of the mainly left-wing opposition parties, most prominently the LDLP, led by Brazauskas. In April 10 members of the Council of Ministers criticized Vagnorius's 'dictatorial' methods, and two ministers subsequently resigned. Vagnorius tendered his resignation as Prime Minister in May, but remained in the post until July, when the legislature approved a motion of no confidence in his leadership. The Seimas (Parliament—as the Supreme Council had been renamed) appointed Aleksandras Abišala, a close associate of Landsbergis, as Prime Minister; a new Council of Ministers was named shortly afterwards. Meanwhile, the growing division within the legislature had led to a boycott by pro-Sąjūdis deputies, rendering it frequently inquorate. In July, however, the Seimas approved a new electoral law, whereby Lithuania's first post-Soviet legislative elections, scheduled for late 1992, would be held under a mixed system of majority voting (for 71 seats) and proportional representation on the basis of party lists (70 seats).

The LDLP emerged as the leading party in the elections to the Seimas, which took place on 25 October and 15 November 1992, winning a total of 73 of the 141 seats. The defeat of Sąjūdis (which, in alliance with the Citizens' Charter of Lithuania, secured 30 seats) was largely attributed to popular disenchantment with its management of economic reform. The Christian Democratic Party of Lithuania (CDPL), which was closely aligned with Sąjūdis, won 16 seats. Also on 25 October a referendum approved a new Constitution, which was adopted by the Seimas on 6 November. Pending an election to the new post of President of the Republic, Brazauskas was elected by the Seimas to be its Chairman and acting Head of State. In December Brazauskas appointed Bronislovas Lubys (hitherto a Deputy Prime Minister) as Prime Minister. Lubys formed a new coalition Council of Ministers, retaining six members of the previous Government and including only three representatives of the LDLP.

The presidential election on 14 February 1993 was won by Brazauskas, with some 60% of the votes cast. His only rival was Stasys Lozoraitis, Lithuania's ambassador to the USA. Brazauskas subsequently resigned from the LDLP. Adolfas Šleževičius replaced Lubys as Prime Minister in March, and was appointed Chairman of the LDLP in April. In May a new political organization, the Conservative Party of Lithuania (CP), also known as the Homeland Union (Lithuanian Conservatives), was formed. Mainly comprising former members of Sąjūdis, and chaired by Landsbergis, the CP rapidly established itself as the principal opposition party.

The Minister of the Economy resigned in October 1995, following the collapse of several small commercial banks and in view of the slow progress achieved in the privatization programme. In November the Government survived its second vote of no confidence, initiated by the conservative opposition, which accused the LDLP of economic mismanagement. The banking crisis culminated in December with the suspension of the operations of the country's two largest commercial banks, owing to insolvency; senior officials of both institutions were arrested on charges of fraud. In January 1996 it was revealed that Šleževičius had withdrawn funds from the Lithuanian Joint Stock Innovation Bank (LJIB) only two days before the bank's suspension. Later in January Romasis Vaitekūnas, who had also withdrawn funds from the LJIB before its closure, resigned as Minister of the Interior, following public criticism of his handling of the crisis. Kazys Ratkevičius, the Chairman of the Bank of Lithuania (the central bank), also resigned. Šleževičius initially disregarded a presidential decree that he should leave office, which was upheld by the Seimas in February. He was replaced as Prime Minister by Laurynas Mindaugas Stankevičius, hitherto Minister of Government Reforms and Local Governments. Šleževičius also resigned as Chairman of the LDLP, and was succeeded by Česlovas Juršėnas, the Chairman of the Seimas.

A general election took place in two rounds on 20 October and 10 November 1996. The results confirmed the substantial loss of popular support for the LDLP, which retained only 12 seats in the Seimas. The CP obtained 70 seats, and the CDPL 16. The right-wing Lithuanian Centre Union won 13 seats and the Lithuanian Social Democratic Party (LSDP) 12. Some 53% of eligible voters participated in the first round, and about 40% took part in the second. Following the election, a coalition agreement was signed by the leaders of the CP and the CDPL. Landsbergis was elected Chairman of the Seimas in late November, and shortly afterwards the Seimas approved the appointment of Vagnorius as Prime Minister. His Government was dominated by members of the CP, with three representatives of the CDPL and two of the Centre Union. In January 1997 the Minister of Finance, Rolandas Matiliauskas, resigned, amid allegations of financial impropriety.

Brazauskas did not contest a further term of office in the presidential election held on 21 December 1997, and in the first round of voting none of the seven candidates won the overall majority of votes required to secure the presidency. In a second round of voting on 4 January 1998 the second-placed candidate after the first round, Valdas Adamkus (a former environmental protection executive, who had been naturalized in the USA), narrowly defeated Artūras Paulauskas (a prominent lawyer and deputy Prosecutor-General, supported by the Lithuanian Liberal Union), with 50.4% of the votes. The new President immediately endorsed the mandate of the incumbent Government, and in March Vagnorius was confirmed as Prime Minister by the Seimas. In April Paulauskas announced the formation of a new, centre-left political party, the New Union (Social Liberals—NU).

A serious conflict of interests between Adamkus and Vagnorius intensified in April 1999, following the President's public criticism of what he regarded as the Government's inadequate attempts to eradicate corruption in the public sector. Although Vagnorius secured the confidence of the Seimas in a non-binding vote, at the end of the month he announced his intention to resign. In mid-May Adamkus invited the Mayor of Vilnius, Rolandas Paksas (a member of the CP), to form a new government. His Council of Ministers, announced at the beginning of June, was again formed from a coalition led by the CP and the CDPL. In October Paksas indicated that he would not endorse an agreement to sell a one-third stake in the state-owned Mažeikiai Nafta petroleum refinery to a US oil company, Williams International, under the terms of which Lithuania would be required to provide long-term financing equivalent to more than twice the price paid by the US company, in order to offset the refinery's debts. None the less, the Council of Ministers endorsed the sale, which was strongly supported by Adamkus and the majority of the CP, prompting the resignations of the Ministers of National Economy and of Finance, and, in late October, of Paksas.

At the end of October 1999 Adamkus nominated Andrius Kubilius, the First Deputy Chairman of the Seimas, as Prime Minister. Kubilius's Council of Ministers, approved by the legislature in November, retained largely the same membership as the previous administration. Following the appointment of the new Government, the Lithuanian Centre Union announced that it was to become an opposition party, its leader, Ozolas, having resigned as a Deputy Chairman of the Seimas after criticizing Landsbergis (who chaired both the CP and the legislature). Paksas resigned from the CP in November, and was elected Chairman of the Lithuanian Liberal Union in December. Local elections in March 2000 resulted in considerable successes for parties of the left, most notably the NU, which had campaigned against the sale of principal state properties to foreign interests. A lack of support for the CP apparently precipitated a split in the party, as several deputies established a 'moderate' faction in the Seimas, thus depriving the CP-CDPL coalition of an automatic majority in the legislature. In May the country's two largest left-wing parties, the LSDP and the LDLP, agreed to contest forthcoming legislative elections in alliance. The New Democracy Party and the Lithuanian Russians' Union subsequently joined the alliance, named the A. Brazauskas Social Democratic Coalition, after the former President, who had been elected Honorary Chairman.

Some 56.2% of eligible voters participated in legislative elections held on 8 October 2000, at which the CP won only nine seats (compared with 70 in 1996). The A. Brazauskas Social Democratic Coalition obtained the largest representation, with 51 seats. However, the Lithuanian Liberal Union (with 34 seats) and the NU (with 29), which had formed an informal alliance prior to the elections, subsequently signed a coalition agreement and were able to form a parliamentary majority with partners that included the Lithuanian Centre Union and the Modern Christian-Democratic Union. In late October the legislature approved the appointment of Paksas as Prime Minister; Paulauskas was elected Chairman of the Seimas. The new Council of Ministers was approved at the end of the month. However, in subsequent months a number of ministers resigned from the cabinet, including the Minister of the Economy, Eugenijus Maldeikis, who was replaced by Eugenijus Gentvilas. Formalizing their electoral alliance, the LDLP merged with the LSDP at a joint congress held in January 2001; the LSDP thereby became the largest single party in the Seimas, and Brazauskas was elected its Chairman. Further political consolidation took place in May, when the CDPL merged with the Christian Democratic Union to form the Lithuanian Christian Democrats (LCD).

In mid-June 2001 the six NU members of the Council of Ministers resigned their portfolios, following disagreements with the Lithuanian Liberal Union over privatization of the energy sector and economic reform, and criticism of the Prime Minister's style of leadership. Paksas was subsequently unable to form an alternative coalition government and, despite surviving a vote of no confidence, resigned on 20 June. The NU sought a new alliance with the LSDP, and at the end of the month President Adamkus offered the post of Prime Minister to Brazauskas, who was confirmed on 3 July. The LSDP did not, however, offer the NU a formal coalition agreement, but instead agreed to an informal accord, which granted the NU the same six ministerial positions from which it had withdrawn in June (including the foreign affairs portfolio). In September Paksas resigned as Chairman of the Lithuanian Liberal Union, in compliance with intra-party demands; he was replaced by Gentvilas. In December Paksas and 10 other deputies left the parliamentary faction of the Lithuanian Liberal Union, owing, in part, to its failure to nominate Paksas as First Deputy Chairman of the Seimas; they were formally expelled from the party in January 2002, and founded the rightist Liberal Democratic Party (LDP) in March, with Paksas as its Chairman.

The results of the first round of voting in the presidential election, held on 22 December 2002, were inconclusive. A second round took place on 5 January 2003, in which Paksas obtained 54.7% of the votes cast, defeating Adamkus, with 45.3%, despite the fact that most major political parties had expressed support for the latter candidate. (However, observers noted that Adamkus appeared to have lost popularity through his implementation of market economic reforms.) Paksas was inaugurated as President on 26 February. In early March Brazauskas was reappointed as Prime Minister; he nominated a Council of Ministers that was substantially unchanged from the outgoing administration. Following the presidential election, Paksas resigned as Chairman of the LDP; Valentinas Mazuronis was elected as his successor. In May Kubilius was elected as Chairman of the CP, in succession to Landsbergis. In the same month the Lithuanian Centre Union, the Lithuanian Liberal Union and the Modern Christian-Democratic Union merged to form the Lithuanian Liberal and Centre Union, with Artūras Zuokas as Chairman. In June a faction of the Lithuanian Centre Union that did not support the merger founded the National Centre Party, and elected Ozolas its Chairman. In February 2004 the CP merged with the Lithuanian Union of Political Prisoners and Deportees to form the Homeland Union—Conservatives, Political Prisoners and Deportees, Christian Democrats (HU).

Meanwhile, following the nomination by President Paksas of a new Director-General of the State Security Department, in October 2003 a classified departmental report was disclosed, which claimed to provide evidence of links between the presidential adviser on national security, Remigijus Acas, and Yurii Borisov, an ethnic Russian with alleged connections with organized crime groups, who had contributed significant funds to Paksas's presidential election campaign. It was revealed that in April Paksas had signed a presidential decree permitting Borisov to hold dual citizenship, despite warnings from the State Security Department that he was suspected of involvement in the illegal trading of weapons. In November an emergency session of the Seimas established a special parliamentary commission to investigate Paksas's alleged links with Russian organized crime and the associated threat to national security, and the Prosecutor-General launched a criminal investigation into Borisov. Paksas subsequently dismissed a number of his senior advisers, but refused to appear before the commission. In December the Seimas approved the commission's conclusion that the President's conduct had jeopardized national security, and the following day both Brazauskas and Paulauskas appealed for the President's resignation. On 18 December the Seimas approved a draft resolution to initiate impeachment proceedings against Paksas, and an investigative commission was subsequently established to consider the charges.

On 18 February 2004 the investigative commission endorsed six charges, which were to form the basis for the impeachment of the President: that Paksas represented a threat to national security; that he had failed to protect classified information; that he had attempted illegally to influence the operations of private companies; that he was unable to reconcile his public and private interests; that he had hindered the operations of state institutions; and that he had failed to prevent his advisers from abusing their positions. On the following day the Seimas voted to initiate formal impeachment proceedings and, in the mean time, agreed to seek a ruling from the Constitutional Court as to whether the charges technically constituted a breach of the Constitution. Paksas continued to deny the charges against him, and in late February he demanded that the Seimas initiate impeachment proceedings against the parliamentary Chairman, Paulauskas, whom he accused of the unauthorized disclosure of the confidential report that had been made public in October 2003 (the request was rejected, on the grounds that the Constitution provided only for the impeachment of deputies, and not of the parliamentary Chairman). On 24 March 2004 Paksas unexpectedly announced the nomination of Borisov as a presidential adviser, but he subsequently retracted the nomination, alleging that it had been prompted by a blackmail attempt. In response to this development, on the following day the Seimas adopted a resolution urging Paksas to resign; Borisov was placed under house arrest for having violated a pledge to avoid contact with the President. On 31 March the Constitutional Court ruled that the President had severely violated the Constitution by: granting Borisov dual citizenship in exchange for financial support; failing to protect state secrets; and using his presidential office illegally to influence the actions of a company's share-holders. The ruling was followed by a parliamentary vote on Paksas's impeachment, which took place on 6 April. Paksas was removed from office, after the necessary three-fifths' majority in the Seimas supported impeachment on the three charges confirmed by the Constitutional Court. Paulauskas immediately assumed the presidency, in an acting capacity, pending a presidential election, and subsequently suspended his membership of the NU, in compliance with the Constitution. In May the Constitutional Court ruled that legislation recently passed by the Seimas, preventing an impeached head of state from seeking presidential office again, was in accordance with the Constitution, and Paksas was obliged to withdraw his candidacy from the forthcoming presidential election.

The first round of the presidential election, held on 13 June 2004 and contested by five candidates, proved inconclusive. In the second round, held on 27 June, Adamkus was narrowly elected, receiving 52.6% of the votes cast, and defeating Prunskienė. Meanwhile, Lithuania's first elections to the European Parliament, following the accession of the country to full membership of the European Union (EU, see p. 255) on 1 May (see below), were held concurrently with the first round of presidential voting, with the participation of 46% of the electorate. The recently founded Labour Party (LP), headed by a controversial, ethnically Russian business executive, Viktor Uspaskikh, won five of the 13 mandates allocated to Lithuania; the governing LSDP, the Lithuanian Liberal and Centre Union and the HU each obtained two seats, while the LDP and the Peasants' and New Democracy Union (PNDU—led by Prunskienė) each won one seat. Adamkus was inaugurated on 12 July, and on the following day the Seimas approved his nomination of Brazauskas as Prime Minister.

Elections to the Seimas, held in two rounds on 10 and 24 October 2004, demonstrated that the LP had further consolidated its support. It became the largest single party in the Seimas, receiving 28.4% of the votes cast on the basis of party lists, and obtaining 39 of the 141 elective seats. A coalition of the LSDP and the NU, known as Working for Lithuania, received 20.7% of the votes cast on the basis of party lists, and 31 seats. The HU obtained 25 seats, and the Liberal and Centre Union 18. The Order and Justice coalition, comprising the LDP and the Lithuanian People's Union for a Free Lithuania, received 11 seats, while the PNDU obtained 10.

In October 2004 the Vilnius District Court effectively cleared Paksas of disclosing state secrets by ruling that there was no indisputable evidence that Borisov had learnt from Paksas that his telephones were being monitored by the State Security Department. (However, this decision was overturned by the Court of Appeal in March 2005, when Paksas was ordered to pay a fine of 9,735 litai.) In December 2004 a congress of the LDP re-elected Paksas as the party's Chairman.

Meanwhile, following prolonged negotiations, a coalition government of the LP, the LSDP, the NU and the PNDU was presented for presidential approval in November 2004. Brazauskas was to remain as Prime Minister, while several prominent members of the LSDP and the NU were to retain the posts they had held in the outgoing administration. Uspaskikh was nominated as Minister of the Economy and Prunskienė as Minister of Agriculture. The Seimas approved the new Government in the following month.

It emerged in January 2005 that the Minister of Foreign Affairs, Antanas Valionis, a member of the NU, had previously served as a reservist in the Committee for State Security (KGB), the Soviet security service. However, although this revelation proved controversial, reservists were exempt from a law stating that all former KGB agents must formally declare their association with the organization. Later that month a Deputy Chairman of the Seimas and Chairman of the parliamentary Committee on European Affairs, Alfredas Pekeliunas, also came under investigation for membership of the KGB, a charge he denied; Pekeliunas resisted demands for his resignation. In April Algirdas Butkevičius submitted his resignation as Minister of Finance, after the governing coalition rejected a proposed tax reform programme. He was replaced by Zigmantas Balčytis, hitherto the Minister of Transport, in May. In mid-June Uspaskikh resigned from both the Government and the Seimas after an ad hoc parliamentary ethics commission concluded that he had violated the principle of the separation of public and private interests; Kęstutis Daukšys replaced him as Minister of the Economy. Meanwhile, in early June the Mayor of Vilnius, Artūras Zuokas, temporarily resigned as Chairman of the Liberal and Centre Union, pending an investigation into corruption allegations; Zuokas had been involved in a public dispute with Uspaskikh, with each accusing the other of corruption, which had led President Adamkus to appeal for their resignations. In December a parliamentary commission concluded that it was likely that Zuokas had received unauthorized financial inducements in his role as Mayor; nevertheless, in February 2006 he survived a vote of no confidence.

Meanwhile, in December 2005 the Supreme Court ruled that Paksas was not guilty of divulging confidential state information, while Borisov was granted permission to remain resident in Lithuania. In January 2006 an investigation into Brazauskas' business affairs was closed, after no evidence was found to substantiate allegations of financial impropriety relating to the privatization of a Soviet-era hotel owned by his wife.

In mid-April 2006 Paulauskas, the Chairman of the NU, was removed from his position as parliamentary speaker, following a secret ballot in the Seimas, amid accusations that he had been aware of a scandal involving the unauthorized use of official vehicles by government employees. The NU immediately announced its intention to withdraw from the governing coalition. The remaining members of the coalition, the LSDP, the LP and the PNDU, signed a new agreement on the following day, and Viktoras Muntianas of the LP was subsequently elected as the new Chairman of the Seimas. At the end of April Paulauskas was re-elected as Chairman of the NU, which in early May declared itself to be in opposition to the Government. Later that month President Adamkus expressed a lack of confidence in the Minister of Culture, Vladimiras Prudnikovas, and the Minister of Health Care, Žilvinas Padaiga, amid allegations that both LP ministers had been involved in severe financial impropriety.

In early May 2006 seven LP deputies renounced their party membership and defected to the newly reconstituted Civil Democracy Party (formerly the Citizens' Union), citing dissatisfaction with the LP leadership, in particular its Chairman, Uspaskikh, as the primary reason for their departure. The ruling coalition's number of seats in the 141-member Seimas was thereby reduced to just 62. Uspaskikh, the subject of ongoing corruption allegations, tendered his resignation as party Chairman later that month. At the end of May the LP withdrew from the ruling coalition, effectively forcing the resignation of Prime Minister Brazauskas and of the Council of Ministers. Minister of Finance Balčytis was appointed Prime Minister in an acting capacity, but in July the Seimas approved the nomination of Gediminas Kirkilas, Vice-Chairman of the LSDP, as premier. The new Council of Ministers comprised six members of the LSDP, three members of the Lithuanian Peasant Nationalists' Union (LPNU), and two members each of the Civil Democracy Party and of the Liberal and Centre Union. Balčytis retained the finance portfolio, while Petras Vaitiekūnas of the LPNU was appointed Minister of Foreign Affairs.

Kęstutis Dauksys was elected Chairman of the LP in August 2006. Uspaskikh, meanwhile, had fled to Russia, but was detained there in September, following the issuing of a European warrant for his arrest by the Lithuanian Office of the Prosecutor-General; he was subsequently released without charge. In January 2007 it was reported that Uspaskikh had registered as an LP candidate to contest the municipal elections scheduled to take place in February (see below). Meanwhile, in September 2006 the Order and Justice Party (as the LDP had been renamed) initiated a motion of no confidence against Muntianas, claiming that comments made by him concerning a recent court decision not to deport Jurijus Borisovas (a close associate of Paksas) had breached the terms of the Constitution. Muntianas comfortably survived the ensuing vote, which was supported by only 36 deputies.

From August 2006 pressure mounted on Balčytis to resign from the Council of Ministers, amid claims that his son had abused office while an employee of the Lithuanian Business Support Agency, which was responsible for the distribution of EU funding. Balčytis refused to relinquish his post until legal proceedings against his son had been concluded. In the event, however, Balčytis announced his resignation the day after his son was cleared of the charges against him.

The rate of participation at the municipal elections held on 25 February 2007 failed for the first time in the country's history to exceed 40% of the electorate. The HU was placed first, with 17.1% of the votes cast, while the LSDP came a close second, with 16.3%; the LP ranked sixth, with 6.4% of the ballot. Uspaskikh and Paksas won seats in Kedainiai and Vilnius, respectively. In May Prime Minister Kirkilas was elected Chairman of the LSDP, following the resignation of the incumbent, Brazauskas. Uspaskikh returned to Lithuania from Russia in September, despite the outstanding charges against him, and was subsequently placed under house arrest. Having failed in an attempt to secure a seat in the Seimas at a by-election in October (losing to the HU candidate), Uspaskikh was re-elected Chairman of the LP in November; he was released from house arrest, on bail, in April 2008.

In November 2007 the Minister of the Interior and the head of the police service resigned from their posts, after a police official under the influence of alcohol fatally injured three children in an automobile accident. In January 2008 an agreement was signed on the expansion of the ruling coalition to include the NU, thereby giving it a majority in the Seimas, with 73 seats. Later that month NU Chairman Paulauskas joined the Government as Minister of the Environment; representatives of the NU were also offered posts at the head of parliamentary commissions.

In February 2008 the Seimas approved a controversial agreement signed between the Government and a private investor, NDX Energija, on the establishment of the Lithuanian Electricity Organization (LEO LT), which was to be responsible for projects in the energy sector, including the construction of a new nuclear power plant. Kirkilas narrowly survived a motion of no confidence in the Seimas in April, with the support of 68 deputies; the Prime Minister's removal from office had been favoured by 63 deputies, many of whom were opposed to the creation of LEO LT, claiming that the terms agreed with NDX Energija were unfavourable to the state.

Ceslovas Juršėnas of the LSDP was elected Chairman of the Seimas at the beginning of April 2008, following the resignation of Muntianas in response to media allegations of corruption. Also in early April the Minister of Education and Science, Roma Žakaitienė, tendered her resignation, following a series of strikes by teachers; she was replaced by Algirdas Monkevičius of the NU, a previous incumbent of the post, in late May. The HU merged with the LCD in May, to form the HU—LCD. Also that month a new political organization, the National Resurrection Party (NRP), was established by television presenter Arūnas Valinskas. The Minister of Health, Rimvydas Turčinskas, resigned from the Government in mid-June, following criticism from the President; he was replaced in July by Gediminas Cerniauskas.

The HU—LCD became the largest party in the Seimas as a result of legislative elections held in two rounds on 12 and 26 October 2008, winning 19.7% of the votes cast on the basis of party lists and a total of 45 of the 141 seats. In second place, with a total of 25 seats, was Prime Minister Kirkilas's LSDP (which received 11.7% of the votes cast on the basis of party lists), followed by the NRP, with 16 seats, and the Order and Justice Party, with 15. The Liberal Movement of the Republic of Lithuania (which had been formed by a splinter group of the Liberal and Centre Union in 2006) secured 11 seats, while a coalition of the LP and the Youth party took 10 and the Liberal and Centre Union itself won eight; three other parties and four independents also obtained representation. In late October President Adamkus invited the Chairman of the HU—LCD, Andrius Kubilius, to form a government. The poor performance of the parties in the outgoing administration was attributed, in part, to a recent downturn in the economy, particularly a sharp rise in consumer prices (the inflation rate having reached 12.1% in the second quarter of the year). The electoral turn-out was 48.6% in the first round, reportedly declining to only 32.4% in the second. Uspaskikh notably secured one of the LP's seats in the Seimas, thus gaining immunity from prosecution, but in December the legislature voted to remove his immunity, as well as that of two other deputies who were standing trial at the time of their election. In a referendum held concurrently with the first round of the legislative elections on 12 October, 91.4% of the valid votes cast were in favour of the Ignalina nuclear power plant remaining in operation pending the construction of a replacement (rather than being closed in 2009, as agreed with the EU—see below), but the result was deemed invalid because, at 48.4%, the turn-out was below the required 50% of voters. Arūnas Valinskas, the leader of the NRP, was elected as Chairman of the Seimas in mid-November.

In late November 2008 the Seimas approved the nomination of Kubilius as Prime Minister, to head a four-party coalition Government controlling 80 seats in the Seimas. The new Council of Ministers, which took office in December, comprised six members of the HU—LCD, three members of the Liberal Movement of the Republic of Lithuania, two members each of the Liberal and Centre Union and of the NRP, and one independent. The HU—LCD assumed responsibility for the economy, finance and national defence portfolios, while the unaffiliated Vygaudas Ušackas, hitherto ambassador to the United Kingdom, was appointed Minister of Foreign Affairs. Addressing the country's economic difficulties was identified as the Government's main priority by Kubilius, who proposed to reform the taxation system, to restructure public finances and to reduce levels of corruption. However, the introduction of austerity measures in January 2009 (see Economic Affairs) aroused public discontent, and a protest organized that month by trade union leaders in Vilnius became violent, with police reportedly using tear gas and rubber bullets to disperse demonstrators. In February Arvydas Sekmokas was appointed to the newly created post of Minister of Energy. He encountered his first challenge in the following month, when the Constitutional Court ruled that legislation providing for the establishment of LEO LT violated the Constitution. The Government pledged to restructure LEO LT and to ensure that the state's interests were properly represented in the management of the company.

The first round of the presidential election was scheduled to be held on 17 May 2009, with a second round to take place on 7 June, if required, concurrently with elections to the European Parliament. An opinion poll in March indicated strong support for the presidential candidacy of Dalia Grybauskaitė, the European Commissioner responsible for Financial Programming and the Budget, while other prominent contenders included Algirdas Butkevičius, who had succeeded Kirkilas as Chairman of the LSDP, former Prime Minister Prunskienė, Seimas Chairman Valinskas and Valentinas Mazuronis, representing the Order and Justice Party. Grybauskaitė was elected by an overwhelming majority at the first round of voting, receiving 69.1% of valid votes cast, according to preliminary data.

Whereas Lithuania's Baltic neighbours, Estonia and Latvia, have large national minorities, ethnic Lithuanians constitute much of the republic's population: in the 2001 census ethnic Lithuanians represented some 84% of the total population, while the two largest minority groups, Poles and Russians, represented 7% and 6%, respectively. As a result, the requirements for the naturalization of non-ethnic Lithuanians were less stringent than in the neighbouring Baltic republics, where national identity was perceived in some quarters as being under threat. Under citizenship laws adopted in late 1989, all residents, regardless of ethnic origin, were eligible to apply for naturalization; by early 1993 more than 90% of the country's non-ethnic Lithuanian residents had been granted citizenship. None the less, the population of Lithuania declined by some 191,000 between 1989 and 2001. In an attempt to counter emigration (in particular to the USA), in September 2002 the Seimas approved legislation permitting Lithuanian citizens to hold dual citizenship, thereby facilitating the eventual return of Lithuanian nationals to the country. However, in November 2006 the Constitutional Court ruled that several provisions of this legislation contravened the Constitution, which only allowed dual citizenship to be held in very exceptional cases. In July 2008 the Seimas adopted an amended law on citizenship (due to expire in 2010), which notably permitted dual citizenship to be held by Lithuanian citizens who had left the country during the occupations of June 1940–March 1990, as well as their children and grandchildren. A proposal further to extend the right to dual citizenship, which had been drafted by a group of legal experts appointed by the President, was under consideration in early 2009 and was expected to require constitutional reform.

Mainly because of its citizenship laws, Lithuania's relations with Russia have generally been less strained than have those of Estonia and Latvia. During 1992 negotiations took place between Lithuania and Russia for the withdrawal of the estimated 38,000 former Soviet troops remaining in Lithuania. Agreement was reached in September, and the final troops left, as scheduled, on 31 August 1993, whereupon full state sovereignty was perceived as having been restored in Lithuania.

In November 1993 Lithuania and Russia signed several agreements, including an accord on most-favoured nation status in bilateral trade, and another concerning the transportation, via Lithuania, of Russian military equipment and troops from the Russian exclave of Kaliningrad Oblast, on the Baltic coast. However, there was disagreement between the two countries during 1994, following Lithuania's decision to introduce new regulations governing military transits. A compromise appeared to have been reached in January 1995, when the Lithuanian Government extended until December the existing procedure for military transits; Russia duly indicated that the agreement on bilateral trade would enter into force immediately. In October

1997 President Brazauskas undertook the first official visit to Russia by a Baltic head of state since the disintegration of the former USSR. During the visit a state border delimitation treaty was signed by both sides, and bilateral co-operation agreements on joint economic zones, and on the Baltic continental shelf, were also concluded. The border treaty was ratified by the Seimas in October 1999, but was not ratified by the Russian side until May 2003. Lithuania expressed support for an agreement between the EU and Russia in late 2002, which proposed simplified visa arrangements for Russian citizens traversing Lithuania to reach the exclave of Kaliningrad. New transit arrangements were implemented in Lithuania at the beginning of February 2003, in advance of Lithuania's accession to the EU in the following year.

Tensions between Lithuania and Russia were reported in the first half of 2005, following the refusal of President Adamkus to attend a commemoration held in Moscow in May to mark the 60th anniversary of the end of the Second World War in Europe. All three Baltic Governments were concerned at an agreement signed between Russia and Germany, in September, on the construction of a North European Gas Pipeline, which was to carry natural gas from Russia to Germany under the Baltic Sea, bypassing the Baltic countries, which would allow Russia to interrupt the supply of gas to the Baltic states without having to compromise supplies to Western Europe. In June 2006 Russian petroleum supplies to the Mažeikiai Nafta petroleum refinery were indefinitely suspended, on the grounds that its pipeline link had been damaged; Russia subsequently refused assistance to repair the pipeline, prompting speculation that the halt in pipeline exports was in reprisal for the majority acquisition in that year of the refinery by Polish enterprise PKN Orlen, rather than by a Russian company. In May 2008 Lithuania withdrew its earlier objections to the initiation of long-delayed talks between the EU and Russia on a new partnership agreement, after being assured that its concerns regarding the continued closure of the pipeline link to the Mažeikiai Nafta refinery and Russian policy towards Georgia and Moldova would be addressed. Following the postponement of negotiations in September, in response to Russia's failure to withdraw its troops from territory in Georgia that had been occupied in the previous month (see the chapter on Georgia), Lithuania opposed the resumption of talks, but was overruled in November by the other EU member states. Meanwhile, relations between Lithuania and Russia were further strained in June when the Seimas adopted legislation prohibiting the public display of Soviet and Nazi symbols. In late June several hundred Lithuanian websites were subject to pro-Russian attacks, their content being replaced by the Soviet flag and anti-Lithuanian propaganda. President Admakus criticized a threat by his Russian counterpart, Dmitrii Medvedev, in November to deploy short-range missiles in Kaliningrad if the USA continued to pursue its plan to install military bases in the Czech Republic and Poland as part of its missile defence system.

Lithuania's relations with neighbouring Poland were largely concerned with the status of the Polish minority in Lithuania. Following the failed coup attempt of August 1991 in Moscow, leaders of councils in Polish-populated regions of Lithuania were dismissed, in response to their alleged support for the coup, and direct rule was introduced. However, in January 1992 Lithuania and Poland signed a 'Declaration on Friendly Relations and Neighbourly Co-operation', which guaranteed the rights of the respective ethnic minorities and also recognized the existing border between the two countries. A full treaty of friendship and co-operation was signed by the respective Heads of State in April 1994. The treaty, notably, did not include a condemnatory reference to Poland's occupation of the region of Vilnius in 1920–39 (a provision that had originally been demanded by Lithuania). An agreement on free trade was signed by the two countries in June 1996, and during 1997 the Lithuanian and Polish Governments established regular forums for inter-presidential and inter-parliamentary discussion. In May 2005 the Chairmen of the national legislatures of Lithuania, Poland and Ukraine, meeting in Lutsk, Ukraine, signed a declaration establishing a new Inter-Parliamentary Assembly, which aimed to help fulfil Ukraine's objective of attaining membership of the EU and the North Atlantic Treaty Organization (NATO, see p. 351), by sharing the successful reform measures undertaken in Lithuania and Poland. In September 2006 President Adamkus made an official visit to the Polish capital, Warsaw, where he signed a joint declaration with President Lech Kaczyński on a plan to connect the electricity grids of Lithuania and Poland. A joint company to manage the project was formed in May 2008, in accordance with an agreement signed by the two Presidents in February of that year. Meanwhile, in March 2007 the Prime Ministers of the two countries signed a communiqué on Poland's involvement in the Baltic project to construct a new nuclear plant in Lithuania (see below).

Lithuania enjoys close relations with Estonia and Latvia. Relations between the three states are co-ordinated through the consultative inter-parliamentary Baltic Assembly, the Council of Baltic Sea States (see p. 235) and the Baltic Council (see p. 437). However, in the mid-1990s Lithuania's relations with Latvia came under strain, as a result of disagreement over the demarcation of the countries' maritime border. In October 1995 the Lithuanian Government protested at Latvia's signature of a preliminary agreement with two foreign petroleum companies to explore oilfields in the disputed waters. Tension increased following the ratification of the agreement by the Latvian parliament in October 1996, although in July 1999 the two countries signed an agreement on the Delimitation of the Territorial Sea, Exclusive Economic Zone and Continental Shelf in the Baltic Sea. However, protests from the Latvian fishing industry prevented the agreement from being ratified by the Latvian parliament. In December 2000 a protocol was signed for the re-demarcation of the land border between the two countries. In early 2008 Prime Minister Kirkilas welcomed a decision by the Latvian Government that ratification of the maritime border treaty would proceed separately to the signing of an economic co-operation agreement between the two countries. Meanwhile, in early 2006 the leaders of all three Baltic states had reached agreement on the construction of a new nuclear power plant to replace that at Ignalina (see below) and various other co-operative measures aimed at reducing Russian dominance in the supply of regional energy.

Lithuania pursued close co-operation with, and eventual integration into, the political, economic and defence systems of Western Europe, notably NATO and the EU. In December 1999 a summit meeting of EU Heads of State and Government in Helsinki, Finland, endorsed proposals to begin accession talks with a number of countries, including Lithuania; formal negotiations commenced in February 2000. As a concession to achieve EU membership, the Government approved a draft national energy strategy in September 1999, which provided for the decommissioning of the first unit of the Ignalina nuclear power plant by 2005. In June 2002 Lithuania agreed to decommission the plant's remaining unit in 2009, in return for a significant contribution from the EU towards the cost of the endeavour. In December 2002 Lithuania, and nine other countries, were formally invited to join the EU on 1 May 2004; at a national referendum, held on 10–11 May 2003, 90.0% of participants voted in favour of membership, and Lithuania duly acceded to the EU as scheduled. In December 2007 Lithuania, together with eight other nations, implemented the EU's Schengen Agreement, enabling its citizens to travel to and from other member states without border controls. In May 2008 the Seimas approved the ratification of the EU's Lisbon Treaty, which was designed to reform the Union's institutions. Meanwhile, in November 2002 Lithuania was one of seven countries invited to join NATO in 2004. Lithuania became a full member of the Alliance on 29 March 2004.

Government

Under the terms of the Constitution that was approved in a national referendum on 25 October 1992, supreme legislative authority resides with the Seimas (Parliament), which has 141 members, elected by universal adult suffrage for a four-year term (71 deputies are directly elected by majority vote, with 70 being elected from party lists on the basis of proportional representation). The President of the Republic (who is Head of State) is elected by direct popular vote for a period of five years (and a maximum of two consecutive terms). Executive power is vested in the Council of Ministers. This is headed by the Prime Minister, who is appointed by the President with the approval of the Seimas. For administrative purposes, Lithuania is divided into 10 counties.

Defence

Until independence Lithuania had no armed forces separate from those of the USSR. The Department of State Defence (established in April 1990) was reorganized as the Ministry of Defence in October 1991. As assessed at November 2008, Lithuania's active armed forces totalled an estimated 8,850:

army 7,380 (including 220 conscripts), navy 470 (including 120 conscripts) and air force 1,000 (including 140 conscripts). There was also a paramilitary force of 14,600 (including a border guard of 5,000) and a total of 6,700 reserves. Military service is compulsory and lasts for 12 months. The budget for 2008 allocated 1,280m. litai to defence. Lithuania became a full member of the North Atlantic Treaty Organization (NATO, see p. 351) on 29 March 2004.

Economic Affairs

In 2007, according to estimates by the World Bank, Lithuania's gross national income (GNI), measured at average 2005–07 prices, was US $33,472m., equivalent to $9,920 per head (or $17,180 per head on an international purchasing-power parity basis). During 2000–07 the population decreased at an average annual rate of 0.5%, while gross domestic product (GDP) per head increased, in real terms, by an average of 8.5% per year. Overall GDP increased, in real terms, by an average of 7.9% annually during 2000–07. Real GDP increased by 8.9% in 2007 and by 3.0% in 2008.

Agriculture (including hunting, forestry and fishing) contributed 5.5% of GDP and engaged an estimated 10.4% of the employed population in 2007. The principal crops are cereals, sugar beet, potatoes and vegetables. Legislation approved in January 2003 authorized the sale of agricultural land to foreign owners, although its implementation was to be subject to a seven-year transition period. Agricultural GDP increased, in real terms, at an average annual rate of 1.9% during 2000–07. The GDP of the sector declined by 10.7% in 2006, but recovered in 2007, increasing by 13.4%.

Industry (including mining, manufacturing, construction and power) contributed 33.7% of GDP and engaged an estimated 30.7% of the employed population in 2007. Industrial GDP increased by an average of 10.2% per year during 2000–07; the GDP of the sector increased by 7.3% in 2007.

Mining and quarrying contributed 0.5% of GDP in 2006, and provided only an estimated 0.3% of employment in 2007. Lithuania has significant reserves of peat and materials used in construction (limestone, clay, dolomite, chalk, and sand and gravel), as well as small deposits of petroleum and natural gas. In terms of gross value added, the sector registered growth of 3.0% in 2004, according to official data.

The manufacturing sector contributed 20.5% of GDP in 2006, and engaged 17.5% of the employed labour force in 2007. Based on the value of sales (excluding refined petroleum products), in 2005 the principal branches of manufacturing were food products (particularly dairy products), wood products (particularly furniture), chemicals (including fertilizers) and clothing. Manufacturing GDP increased, in real terms, at an average annual rate of 9.6% during 2000–07. Sectoral GDP increased by 5.1% in 2007.

In 2005 nuclear power accounted for 71.7% of gross electricity production, and natural gas accounted for 20.9%. Lithuania has substantial petroleum-refining and electricity-generating capacities, which enable it to export refined petroleum products and electricity. Lithuania has been a net exporter of electricity, although in June 2002 formal agreement was reached with the European Union (EU, see p. 255) on the closure of the Ignalina nuclear power plant. The first of the plant's reactors was decommissioned in 2004, with the second to follow in 2009, in return for substantial financial compensation from the EU. In February 2006 the Prime Ministers of Estonia, Latvia and Lithuania reached agreement on the construction of a new nuclear plant in Lithuania by 2015, and Poland became involved in the project in 2007. The connection of the Lithuanian electricity grid to those of Poland and Sweden was also planned. In 2007 imports of mineral fuels accounted for 16.3% of the total value of merchandise imports.

The services sector contributed 60.8% of GDP and provided 59.0% of total employment in 2007. The Baltic port of Klaipėda (Memel) is a significant entrepôt for regional trade. The GDP of the services sector increased, in real terms, by an average of 6.0% per year in 2000–07. Real services GDP increased by 4.5% in 2007.

In 2007 Lithuania recorded a visible trade deficit of US $5,873.8m., and there was a deficit of $5,692.4m. on the current account of the balance of payments. In 2007 the principal source of imports was Russia (accounting for 18.2% of the total); other major sources were Germany, Poland and Latvia. Russia was also the main market for exports in that year (accounting for 15.0% of the total); other principal markets were Latvia, Germany, Poland and Estonia. In 2007 the principal exports were mineral products, machinery and electrical equipment, vehicles and transportation equipment, chemical products, plastics and rubber, textiles, and miscellaneous manufactured articles. The principal imports were machinery and electrical equipment (particularly nuclear reactors and boilers), mineral products, vehicles and transportation equipment, chemical products, base metals, and plastics and rubber.

In 2008 there was a budgetary deficit of 3,589.7m. litai (equivalent to 3.2% of GDP). Lithuania's total external debt was US $18,955m. at the end of 2006, of which $3,244m. was long-term public debt. In that year the cost of debt-servicing was equivalent to 22.1% of the value of exports of goods and services. Annual inflation averaged 1.9% in 2000–07. The rate of inflation was 5.7% in 2007 and 10.9% in 2008. The average rate of unemployment was 4.3% in 2007, compared with 11.4% in 2004, but increased to 5.8% in 2008.

In December 2000 Lithuania became a member of the World Trade Organization (WTO, see p. 410). Lithuania acceded to full membership of the EU on 1 May 2004.

In an effort to facilitate increased integration with EU economies and further reorientate foreign trade, from February 2002 the national currency's fixed rate of exchange was linked to the common European currency, the euro, instead of the US dollar. Lithuania was one of three new member states of the EU (along with Estonia and Slovenia) to be admitted to the EU's exchange rate mechanism (ERM II) in June 2004, ahead of the country's planned adoption of the euro. In March 2006 Lithuania formally applied to become a member of the euro zone from 1 January 2007. However, in May 2006 the European Commission concluded that Lithuania would not be ready to adopt the euro in 2007, owing to its rate of consumer price inflation; in October 2006 the Government announced a new target date of 2010. Lithuania encountered further difficulties in 2008, largely owing to adverse economic conditions resulting from the onset of the international financial crisis. The real estate market, which had been subject to considerable inflation and provided a significant portion of the assets underwriting loans, experienced a sharp correction as investment activity declined. The fall in the value of real estate and other assets was projected to erode real incomes and, thus, precipitate a decline in consumption, which had been a principal source of economic growth. Moreover, the rate of consumer price inflation rose to a peak of 12.5% in June 2008, although it began to ease thereafter, as global fuel prices declined. In January 2009 the Government introduced a number of austerity measures, which included a 15% reduction in public sector salaries, pension reforms and an increase in value-added tax. These reforms aimed to reduce the Lithuanian budget deficit to below the 3% of GDP permitted for euro adoption, this limit having been exceeded in 2008, while allowing for increased spending during the coming recession (real GDP began to decline in the last quarter of 2008, and was forecast by the Ministry of Finance to contract by 10.5% in 2009). In February 2009 an economic stimulus plan, worth €1,470m., was approved. The programme included measures to support the ailing construction sector and to improve the provision of credit to businesses affected by the financial crisis.

Education

Education, beginning at six years of age, is free and compulsory until the age of 16. Pre-school education is available for children aged between one and six years. Children spend four years at primary school (Grades 1–4), followed by six years at lower secondary school (basic education, Grades 5–10) and two years at upper secondary school or gymnasium (Grades 10–12). Vocational training is available. From 2003 a uniform tuition fee was introduced for students in higher education, although there were exemptions for the highest achievers. In 2007/08 92.8% of children in the relevant age-group were enrolled in primary education, while the comparable rates of enrolment in lower secondary education and in upper secondary education were 94.9% and 78.4%, respectively. In the 2007/08 academic year 531,033 students were enrolled in 1,552 general and vocational schools. In that year there were 28 colleges and 22 universities; total enrolment in institutions of higher education was 204,432. In 1991 the first private schools were opened; by 2007/08 there were 26 private schools, 12 private colleges and seven private universities. Lithuanian is the main language of instruction, although in 2007/08 4.2% of students at general schools were taught in Russian and 3.4% were taught in Polish. Central government expenditure on educa-

LITHUANIA

tion in 2007 amounted to 2,027.1m. litai (9.9% of total expenditure).

Public Holidays

2009: 1–2 January (New Year's Day), 16 February (National Day), 11 March (Day of the Re-establishment of Independence), 13 April (Easter Monday), 1 May (Labour Day), 24 June (St John's Day), 6 July (Anniversary of the Coronation of Grand Duke Mindaugas), 15 August (Assumption), 1 November (All Saints' Day), 25–26 December (Christmas).

2010: 1 January (New Year's Day), 16 February (National Day), 11 March (Day of the Re-establishment of Independence), 5 April (Easter Monday), 1 May (Labour Day), 24 June (St John's Day), 6 July (Anniversary of the Coronation of Grand Duke Mindaugas), 15 August (Assumption), 1 November (All Saints' Day), 25–26 December (Christmas).

Weights and Measures

The metric system is in force.

Statistical Survey

Source (unless otherwise indicated): Department of Statistics to the Government of Lithuania (Statistics Lithuania), Gedimino pr. 29, Vilnius 01500; tel. (52) 236-4800; fax (5) 236-4845; e-mail statistika@stat.gov.lt; internet www.stat.gov.lt.

Area and Population

AREA, POPULATION AND DENSITY

Area (sq km)	65,300*
Population (census results)	
12 January 1989†	3,674,802
6 April 2001	
Males	1,629,148
Females	1,854,824
Total	3,483,972
Population (official estimates at 1 January)	
2007	3,384,879
2008	3,366,357
2009‡	3,350,100
Density (per sq km) at 1 January 2009‡	51.3

* 25,212 sq miles.
† Figure refers to the *de jure* population. The *de facto* total was 3,689,779.
‡ Provisional.

POPULATION BY ETHNIC GROUP
(permanent inhabitants at 2001 census)

	Number	%
Lithuanian	2,907,293	84.5
Polish	234,989	6.8
Russian	219,789	6.4
Belarusian	42,866	1.2
Others	34,035	1.0
Total	**3,483,972**	**100.0**

ADMINISTRATIVE DIVISIONS
(at 1 January 2008)

County	Area (sq km)	Population	Density (per sq km)
Alytus	5,425	177,040	32.6
Kaunas	8,089	673,706	83.3
Klaipėda	5,209	378,843	72.7
Marijampolė	4,463	181,219	40.6
Panevėžys	7,881	284,235	36.1
Šiauliai	8,540	349,876	41.0
Tauragė	4,411	127,378	28.9
Telšiai	4,350	173,383	39.9
Utena	7,201	172,580	24.0
Vilnius	9,731	848,097	87.2
Total	**65,300**	**3,366,357**	**51.6**

PRINCIPAL TOWNS
(at 1 January 2008, provisional figures)

Vilnius (capital)	544,091	Šiauliai	127,043
Kaunas	355,550	Panevėžys	113,668
Klaipėda	184,684	Alytus	68,315

BIRTHS, MARRIAGES AND DEATHS

	Registered live births		Registered marriages		Registered deaths	
	Number	Rate (per 1,000)	Number	Rate (per 1,000)	Number	Rate (per 1,000)
2000	34,149	9.8	16,906	4.8	38,919	11.1
2001	31,546	9.1	15,764	4.5	40,399	11.6
2002	30,014	8.6	16,151	4.7	41,072	11.8
2003	30,598	8.9	16,975	4.9	40,990	11.9
2004	30,419	8.8	19,130	5.6	41,340	12.0
2005	30,541	8.9	19,938	5.8	43,799	12.8
2006	31,265	9.2	21,246	6.3	44,813	13.2
2007*	32,154	9.5	23,073	6.8	45,589	13.5

* Provisional.

Life expectancy (years at birth, WHO estimates): 71.1 (males 65.3; females 77.1) in 2006 (Source: WHO, *World Health Statistics*).

IMMIGRATION AND EMIGRATION

	2005	2006	2007
Immigrants	6,789	7,745	8,609
Emigrants	15,571	12,602	13,853

ECONOMICALLY ACTIVE POPULATION
(annual averages, '000 persons)*

	2005	2006	2007
Agriculture, hunting and forestry	204.2	183.9	156.9
Fishing	2.8	2.7	2.6
Mining and quarrying	3.3	4.3	5.3
Manufacturing	266.5	264.6	267.9
Electricity, gas and water	26.5	27.1	26.2
Construction	132.5	148.7	170.9
Wholesale and retail trade; repair of motor vehicles, motorcycles and personal and household goods	233.3	254.6	262.4
Hotels and restaurants	33.1	39.0	33.5
Transport, storage and communications	93.9	98.9	111.4
Financial intermediation	16.3	16.6	22.3
Real estate, renting and business activities	81.7	75.7	83.5
Public administration and defence; compulsory social security	62.3	78.3	75.4

LITHUANIA

—continued	2005	2006	2007
Education	148.0	131.5	144.3
Health and social work	98.6	105.7	100.7
Other community, social and personal service activities	63.7	63.7	67.1
Private households with employed persons	7.1	3.6	3.9
Extra-territorial organizations and bodies	0.2	0.1	—
Total	1,473.9	1,499.0	1,534.2
Unemployed	132.9	89.3	69.0
Total labour force	1,606.8	1,588.3	1,603.2
Males	818.0	802.5	812.3
Females	788.8	785.8	790.8

* Official estimates based on results of 2001 census.

Health and Welfare

KEY INDICATORS

Total fertility rate (children per woman, 2006)	1.3
Under-5 mortality rate (per 1,000 live births, 2006)	9
HIV/AIDS (% of persons aged 15–49, 2007)	0.1
Physicians (per 1,000 head, 2006)	4.0
Hospital beds (per 1,000 head, 2006)	8.0
Health expenditure (2006): US $ per head (PPP)	1,041
Health expenditure (2006): % of GDP	6.2
Health expenditure (2006): public (% of total)	70.0
Human Development Index (2006): ranking	43
Human Development Index (2006): value	0.869

For sources and definitions, see explanatory note on p. vi.

Agriculture

PRINCIPAL CROPS
('000 metric tons)

	2005	2006	2007
Wheat	1,379.4	809.8	1,390.7
Barley	948.3	743.8	1,013.7
Rye	108.3	90.0	165.2
Oats	114.1	62.8	119.5
Triticale (wheat-rye hybrid)	201.1	110.4	227.6
Potatoes	894.7	457.1	576.1
Sugar beet	798.5	717.1	799.9
Peas, dry	21.1	15.8	24.2
Rapeseed	201.2	169.6	311.9
Cabbages and other brassicas	141.4	72.7	92.8
Onions, dry	22.3	11.5	17.6
Carrots and turnips	82.6	41.2	62.7
Apples	96.5	99.5	40.6

Aggregate production ('000 metric tons, may include official, semi-official or estimated data): Total cereals 2,811.1 in 2005, 1,857.8 in 2006, 3,017.0 in 2007; Total roots and tubers 894.7 in 2005, 457.1 in 2006, 576.1 in 2007; Total vegetables (incl. melons) 338.0 in 2005, 184.0 in 2006, 250.1 in 2007; Total fruits (excl. melons) 128.6 in 2005, 125.1 in 2006, 54.7 in 2007.

Source: FAO.

LIVESTOCK
('000 head at 1 January)

	2005	2006	2007
Horses	64	63	61
Cattle	792	800	839
Pigs	1,073	1,115	1,127
Sheep	22	29	37
Goats	27	22	21
Chickens	8,227	9,201	9,243
Turkeys	93	103	117
Rabbits and hares	96	99	n.a.

Source: FAO.

LIVESTOCK PRODUCTS
('000 metric tons)

	2005	2006	2007
Cattle meat	52.9	55.7	60.0*
Pig meat	105.6	121.8	114.0
Chicken meat	56.5	64.1	68.0*
Cows' milk	1,853.6	1,884.6	1,997.0*
Hen eggs	50.9	53.4	52.9*
Honey	1.3	1.4	1.3*

* FAO estimate.
Source: FAO.

Forestry

ROUNDWOOD REMOVALS
('000 cubic metres, excl. bark)

	2005	2006	2007
Sawlogs, veneer logs and logs for sleepers	3,520	3,285	3,320
Pulpwood	1,390	1,065	1,210
Other industrial wood	10	10	10
Fuel wood	1,130	1,230	1,315
Total	6,050	5,590	5,855

Source: FAO.

SAWNWOOD PRODUCTION
('000 cubic metres, incl. railway sleepers)

	2005	2006	2007
Coniferous (softwood)	1,025	996	905
Broadleaved (hardwood)	420	470	475
Total	1,445	1,466	1,380

Source: FAO.

Fishing

(metric tons, live weight)

	2004	2005	2006
Capture	161,988	139,785	154,548
Largehead hairtail	601	556	n.a.
Atlantic redfishes	7,136	2,359	3,002
Jack and horse mackerels	49,312	55,831	47,064
Sardinellas	35,372	19,328	24,846
European sprat	6,185	8,635	10,814
European anchovy	27,584	20,500	25,791
Chub mackerel	15,868	14,962	6,681
Northern prawn	7,057	5,860	3,082
Aquaculture	2,697	2,013	2,224
Total catch	164,685	141,798	156,772

Source: FAO.

Mining

('000 metric tons, unless otherwise indicated)

	2004	2005	2006
Crude petroleum	302	217	181
Dolomite ('000 cubic metres)	796	1,016	1,300
Limestone	960	1,178	1,279
Clay ('000 cubic metres)	200	261	281
Peat	368	536	471

LITHUANIA

Industry

SELECTED PRODUCTS
('000 metric tons, unless otherwise indicated)

	2004	2005	2006
Sausages and smoked meat products	73.5	76.3	76.7
Flour	239.1	223.6	214.4
Refined sugar	132.9	124.7	96.6
Beer ('000 hectolitres)	269.0	289.5	293.4
Wine ('000 hectolitres)	516	785	797
Cotton fabrics (million sq m)	21.9	22.0	20.4
Woollen fabrics (million sq m)	21.5	20.2	22.5
Fabrics of man-made fibres	21.2	19.9	19.4
Footwear—excl. rubber and plastic ('000 pairs)*	1,200	1,100	1,000
Plywood ('000 cubic metres)	49.9	46.6	47.1
Particle board ('000 cubic metres)	422.5	440.1	433.4
Paper and paperboard	98.2	112.6	119.2
Sulphuric acid	1,019	1,091	1,117
Nitrogenous fertilizers	612	n.a.	n.a.
Cement*	800	800	1,100
Cast iron	14.7	11.3	10.0
Television sets ('000)	1,201.7	1,152.4	711.3
Refrigerators and freezers ('000)	456.8	443.8	434.9
Bicycles ('000)	348	418	330
Electric energy (million kWh)*	19,100	14,900	11,900

* Figures are rounded.

Finance

CURRENCY AND EXCHANGE RATES

Monetary Units
100 centas = 1 litas (plural: litai).

Sterling, Dollar and Euro Equivalents (31 December 2008)
£1 sterling = 3.5726 litai;
US $1 = 2.4507 litai;
€1 = 3.4528 litai;
100 litai = £27.99 = $40.80 = €28.96.

Average Exchange Rate (litai per US $)
2006   2.7522
2007   2.5237
2008   2.3571

Note: An official mid-point exchange rate of US $1 = 4.00 litai was in operation from 1 April 1994 until 1 February 2002. From 2 February 2002 the litas was linked to the euro, with the exchange rate set at €1 = 3.4528 litai.

GOVERNMENT FINANCE
(general government transactions, million litai)

Revenue	2005	2006	2007
Taxes	14,439.1	17,138.6	20,517.8
Indirect taxes	7,950.7	9,194.8	11,418.0
Direct taxes	6,486.0	7,939.6	9,093.6
Capital taxes	2.3	4.2	6.3
Social contributions	6,080.3	7,226.3	8,775.4
Sales	1,174.7	991.4	1,113.1
Other current revenue	1,374.2	1,192.9	1,359.9
Grants and other capital transfers	583.0	847.7	1,447.7
Total	23,651.2	27,396.9	33,213.9

Expenditure	2005	2006	2007
Compensation of employees	7,430.7	8,625.8	9,763.4
Intermediate consumption	4,112.0	4,928.6	5,236.5
Interest	585.7	610.3	691.4
Subsidies	489.5	584.7	877.4
Social benefits	7,119.5	8,158.2	10,259.9
Other current expenditure	1,581.7	1,152.3	1,613.7
Capital transfers	320.3	370.7	927.0
Capital investments	2,373.8	3,338.8	5,036.5
Total	24,013.2	27,769.4	34,405.9

INTERNATIONAL RESERVES
(US $ million at 31 December)

	2005	2006	2007
Gold (national valuation)	95.34	118.14	155.36
IMF special drawing rights	0.08	0.10	0.11
Reserve position in IMF	0.02	0.05	0.05
Foreign exchange	3,720.14	5,654.26	7,565.61
Total	3,815.58	5,772.55	7,721.13

* National valuation.

Source: IMF, *International Financial Statistics*.

MONEY SUPPLY
(million litai at 31 December)

	2005	2006	2007
Currency outside banks	6,118	7,245	8,108
Demand deposits at banking institutions	14,770	17,578	15,168
Total money (incl. others)	20,901	24,835	27,940

Source: IMF, *International Financial Statistics*.

COST OF LIVING
(Consumer Price Index; base: 2000 = 100)

	2005	2006	2007
Food (incl. beverages)	105.3	111.7	124.3
Fuel and light	109.7	117.1	130.0
Clothing	87.5	83.7	81.2
Rent	115.0	123.1	138.8
All items (incl. others)	104.3	108.2	114.4

Source: ILO.

NATIONAL ACCOUNTS
(million litai at current prices)

National Income and Profit

	2005	2006	2007
Compensation of employees	29,415.1	34,966.8	41,784.9
Operating surplus and mixed income	26,745.8	29,370.3	34,080.6
Domestic primary incomes	56,160.9	64,337.1	75,865.5
Consumption of fixed capital	8,341.5	9,492.4	10,823.5
Gross domestic product (GDP) at factor cost	64,502.4	73,829.5	86,689.0
Taxes on production and imports	8,221.9	9,477.6	11,653.8
Less Subsidies	1,334.9	1,401.9	1,570.1
Statistical discrepancy	−9.0	—	—
GDP in market prices	71,380.4	81,905.2	96,772.5
Primary incomes received from abroad	2,112.8	2,429.6	2,954.6
Less Primary incomes paid abroad	3,251.4	4,193.6	6,656.2
Gross national income (GNI)	70,241.8	80,141.3	93,071.0
Less Consumption of fixed capital	8,341.5	9,492.4	10,823.5
Net national income	61,900.3	70,648.9	82,247.6
Current transfers from abroad	1,786.0	3,327.1	4,290.4
Less Current transfers paid abroad	536.2	1,642.7	1,936.2
Net national disposable income	63,150.2	72,333.3	84,601.7

LITHUANIA

Expenditure on the Gross Domestic Product

	2005	2006	2007
Final consumption expenditure	58,683.9	68,272.9	79,826.9
Households	46,308.8	53,309.8	63,170.1
Non-profit institutions serving households	144.5	183.5	244.4
General government	12,230.6	14,779.5	16,412.3
Gross capital formation	17,923.8	22,137.6	28,246.4
Gross fixed capital formation	16,302.2	20,290.8	25,648.1
Changes in inventories	1,590.8	1,794.2	2,522.5
Acquisitions, less disposals, of valuables	30.8	52.7	75.8
Total domestic expenditure	76,607.7	90,410.5	108,073.3
Exports of goods and services	41,440.1	48,892.6	53,581.4
Less Imports of goods and services	46,667.4	57,397.9	64,882.2
GDP in market prices	71,380.4	81,905.2	96,772.5
GDP at chain-linked 2000 prices	66,549.5	71,649.1	77,935.2

Gross Domestic Product by Economic Activity

	2004	2005	2006
Agriculture, hunting and forestry	3,262.5	3,601.1	3,753.3
Fishing	45.6	51.6	53.7
Mining and quarrying	301.9	344.6	393.4
Manufacturing	11,838.4	13,475.0	15,165.7
Electricity, gas and water supply	2,497.9	2,584.1	2,791.5
Construction	4,102.1	4,916.6	6,515.7
Wholesale and retail trade; repair of motor vehicles, motorcycles and personal and household goods	9,940.7	11,321.1	12,568.5
Hotels and restaurants	835.6	906.2	1,008.0
Transport, storage and communication	7,181.5	8,281.9	9,409.7
Financial intermediation	1,202.8	1,308.0	1,821.0
Real estate, renting and business activities	3,062.8	3,309.6	3,846.4
Public administration and defence; compulsory social security	5,897.3	7,425.4	8,716.3
Education	3,050.2	3,164.9	3,495.5
Health and social work	1,667.2	1,948.5	2,306.3
Other community, social and personal service activities	1,610.5	1,729.2	1,885.1
Private households with employed persons	74.4	106.7	85.5
Statistical discrepancy	—	9.1	—
Gross value added at basic prices	56,571.5	64,483.6	73,815.6
Taxes on products	6,671.1	7,832.9	9,037.6
Less Subsidies on products	655.9	936.1	948.0
GDP in market prices	62,586.7	71,380.4	81,905.2

2007 (million litai at current prices): Agriculture, hunting, forestry and fishing 4,727.2; Industry 29,229.3 (Construction 8,628.7); Services 52,742.2 (Public administration, social services and community activities 27,278.4, Trade, hotels and restaurants, and transport, storage and communication 12,442.7, Financial intermediation, real estate, and renting and business activities 13,021.1); *Gross value added at basic prices* 86,698.7; Taxes on products 11,128.1; *Less* Subsidies on products –1,054.3; *GDP in market prices* 96,772.5.

BALANCE OF PAYMENTS
(US $ million)

	2005	2006	2007
Exports of goods f.o.b.	11,774.4	14,150.6	17,162.0
Imports of goods f.o.b.	–14,690.4	–18,359.8	–23,035.8
Trade balance	–2,916.0	–4,209.3	–5,873.8
Exports of services	3,104.3	3,623.2	4,025.0
Imports of services	–2,054.6	–2,540.0	–3,392.7
Balance on goods and services	–1,866.3	–3,126.0	–5,241.6
Other income received	448.3	589.9	793.5
Other income paid	–1,075.4	–1,406.9	–2,407.2
Balance on goods, services and income	–2,493.4	–3,943.0	–6,855.3
Current transfers received	951.3	1,425.1	2,071.2
Current transfers paid	–289.1	–700.2	–908.3
Current balance	–1,831.2	–3,218.1	–5,692.4

—continued	2005	2006	2007
Capital account (net)	331.1	351.4	690.1
Direct investment abroad	–343.0	–289.5	–608.4
Direct investment from abroad	1,031.8	1,840.2	2,017.0
Portfolio investment assets	–778.5	–1,105.8	–838.0
Portfolio investment liabilities	541.6	852.1	608.8
Financial derivatives assets	27.4	9.5	4.8
Financial derivatives liabilities	–14.5	–20.5	–7.1
Other investment assets	–785.6	–475.7	–1,561.1
Other investment liabilities	2,582.6	3,852.4	6,656.0
Net errors and omissions	–49.4	–289.1	–53.9
Overall balance	712.3	1,506.7	1,215.7

Source: IMF, *International Financial Statistics*.

External Trade

PRINCIPAL COMMODITIES
(million litai)

Imports c.i.f.	2005	2006	2007
Prepared foodstuffs; beverages, spirits and vinegar; tobacco and manufactured substitutes	1,597.4	2,140.4	2,543.1
Mineral products	10,996.5	12,481.0	10,549.1
Mineral fuels	10,572.3	11,980.1	9,965.0
Products of the chemical or allied industries	3,360.5	4,497.5	5,920.5
Plastics, rubber and articles thereof	2,419.3	2,745.0	3,144.3
Textiles and textile articles	2,418.6	2,679.9	2,954.7
Base metals and articles thereof	2,990.8	3,756.1	4,781.4
Machinery and mechanical appliances; electrical equipment; sound and television apparatus	7,737.1	9,402.8	10,695.6
Nuclear reactors, boilers, etc.	4,584.7	5,491.8	5,996.1
Electrical machinery, sound and television recorders and parts thereof	3,152.4	3,910.9	4,699.4
Vehicles, aircraft, vessels and associated transport equipment	5,068.8	7,383.5	9,981.4
Total (incl. others)	43,151.9	53,274.6	60,987.4

Exports f.o.b.	2005	2006	2007
Live animals and animal products	1,468.9	1,769.6	2,374.9
Vegetable products	978.9	1,314.3	2,193.8
Prepared foodstuffs; beverages, spirits and vinegar; manufactured substitutes	1,691.5	2,234.4	2,653.6
Mineral products	8,939.8	9,292.4	5,976.6
Mineral fuels	8,859.7	9,192.6	5,865.4
Products of the chemical or allied industries	2,389.7	2,514.7	3,480.0
Fertilizers	1,453.0	1,433.5	2,134.9
Plastics, rubber and articles thereof	1,186.5	1,999.6	3,431.2
Wood, cork and articles thereof; wood charcoal; manufactures of straw, esparto, etc.	1,494.9	1,584.2	1,993.1
Textiles and textile articles	3,043.0	3,228.3	3,261.4
Articles of apparel and clothing accessories, not knitted	1,236.5	1,252.2	1,148.0
Base metals and articles thereof	1,434.2	1,779.7	2,259.4
Machinery and mechanical appliances; electrical equipment; sound and television apparatus	4,079.0	4,885.8	5,561.5
Vehicles, aircraft, vessels and associated transport equipment	2,707.4	3,948.4	4,540.3
Miscellaneous manufactured articles	1,950.5	2,425.2	2,955.8
Total (incl. others)	32,767.3	38,888.3	43,234.2

LITHUANIA

PRINCIPAL TRADING PARTNERS
(million litai)

Imports c.i.f.	2005	2006	2007
Austria	441.0	586.0	699.1
Belarus	753.6	944.7	1,218.1
Belgium	962.6	1,321.3	1,766.8
China, People's Republic	1,005.5	1,275.8	1,719.3
Czech Republic	643.0	760.4	957.2
Denmark	1,300.3	1,533.9	1,675.2
Estonia	1,222.8	1,639.3	2,189.3
Finland	1,325.1	1,547.8	1,693.9
France	1,209.7	1,679.3	2,123.7
Germany	6,538.4	7,916.2	9,108.4
Italy	1,277.2	1,798.8	2,407.8
Latvia	1,707.9	2,541.8	3,326.1
Netherlands	1,601.5	1,988.0	2,586.8
Poland	3,585.0	5,070.1	6,479.3
Russia	12,006.3	12,975.4	11,070.6
Spain	438.8	625.3	968.0
Sweden	1,481.8	1,777.1	2,296.5
Ukraine	511.1	721.6	847.4
United Kingdom	955.1	1,417.8	1,712.2
USA	843.0	859.3	1,356.1
Total (incl. others)	43,151.9	53,274.6	60,987.4

Exports f.o.b.	2005	2006	2007
Belarus	1,063.0	1,472.8	1,733.4
Belgium	617.5	482.4	729.4
Canada	939.5	765.7	192.0
Denmark	1,420.1	1,634.4	1,752.4
Estonia	1,937.0	2,515.4	2,509.9
France	2,301.8	1,626.8	1,575.8
Germany	3,075.5	3,344.9	4,531.8
Italy	631.5	822.8	980.2
Latvia	3,362.7	4,303.9	5,551.3
Netherlands	1,005.7	1,885.4	1,287.9
Norway	524.8	724.0	993.4
Poland	1,812.3	2,361.4	2,711.3
Russia	3,422.1	4,956.1	6,472.9
Singapore	918.2	901.5	197.5
Spain	833.1	740.6	607.2
Sweden	1,633.1	1,749.0	1,627.3
Ukraine	743.5	1,005.5	1,176.3
United Kingdom	1,542.1	1,714.0	1,970.5
USA	1,543.4	1,681.9	1,109.2
Total (incl. others)	32,767.3	38,888.3	43,234.2

Transport

RAILWAYS
(traffic)

	2004	2005	2006
Passenger journeys ('000)	6,983.2	6,719.9	6,193.8
Passenger-km (million)	443	428	431
Freight transported ('000 metric tons)	45,554.8	49,287.3	50,224.8
Freight ton-km (million)	11,637	12,457	12,896

ROAD TRAFFIC
(public transport and freight)

	2004	2005	2006
Passenger journeys ('000)	430,073.9	443,418.7	445,484.9
Passenger-km (million)	3,548	3,691	3,695
Freight transported ('000 metric tons)	51,456.1	55,333.5	56,026.0
Freight ton-km (million)	12,279	15,908	18,134

ROAD TRAFFIC
(motor vehicles in use at 31 December)

	2005	2006	2007
Passenger cars	1,455,276	1,592,238	1,587,903
Buses and coaches	14,839	15,134	13,997
Lorries and vans	106,247	117,427	126,507
Motorcycles and mopeds	24,027	25,478	28,826

INLAND WATERWAYS

	2004	2005	2006
Passenger journeys ('000)	1,973.9	2,122.8	2,248.1
Passenger-km (million)	2	3	3
Freight transported ('000 metric tons)	621.0	745.4	879.5
Freight ton-km (million)	1	1	2

SHIPPING

Merchant Fleet
(registered at 31 December)

	2005	2006	2007
Number of vessels	164	132	127
Total displacement ('000 grt)	476.7	448.6	425.8

Source: Lloyd's Register-Fairplay, *World Fleet Statistics*.

International Sea-borne Freight Traffic
('000 metric tons)

	1999	2000	2001
Goods loaded	12,864	18,552	18,144
Goods unloaded	2,796	4,296	4,224

Source: UN, *Monthly Bulletin of Statistics*.

CIVIL AVIATION
(traffic on scheduled services)

	2004	2005	2006
Passengers carried ('000)	591.5	674.6	729.7
Passenger-km (million)	896	1,099	1,200
Freight transported (million metric tons)	6.6	7.6	5.6
Freight ton-km (million)	9	10	5

Tourism

FOREIGN VISITORS BY COUNTRY OF ORIGIN
(arrivals at accommodation establishments)

	2004	2005	2006
Belarus	22,039	29,977	37,517
Denmark	16,438	15,337	15,817
Estonia	23,456	27,834	32,212
Finland	27,303	32,996	34,898
Germany	113,974	137,317	132,540
Italy	23,475	26,518	27,071
Latvia	35,769	43,660	56,299
Norway	11,492	14,385	19,424
Poland	85,457	94,881	102,539
Russia	49,240	50,829	59,743
Sweden	17,687	20,133	23,410
United Kingdom	22,751	32,941	39,926
USA	19,419	19,980	21,652
Total (incl. others)	590,043	681,487	756,855

Receipts from tourism (US $ million, incl. passenger transport): 834 in 2004; 975 in 2005; 1,077 in 2006.

Source: World Tourism Organization.

LITHUANIA

Communications Media

	2005	2006	2007
Telephones ('000 main lines in use)	801.1	792.4	799.4
Mobile cellular telephones ('000 subscribers)	4,353.4	4,718.2	4,912.1
Internet users ('000)	882.9	1,083.0	1,333.2
Broadband subscribers ('000)	234.1	368.7	507.6
Book titles (incl. brochures)	4,223	4,548	4,567
Newspapers: number	325	334	328
Newspapers: average circulation (million copies)	218.2	258.3	269.6
Other periodicals	543	566	581

1997: Radio receivers ('000 in use) 1,900; Facsimile machines (number in use) 6,200.

Sources: International Telecommunication Union; UNESCO, *Statistical Yearbook*; UN, *Statistical Yearbook* and Ministry of Education and Science, Vilnius.

Education

(2007/08, unless otherwise indicated)

	Institutions	Teachers	Students
General schools	1,472	41,591	489,442
Vocational schools	80	4,587	43,880
Professional college	1*	120†	20*
Colleges	28	4,791	60,096
Universities	22	10,004	144,336

* 2006/07.
† 2005/06.

Adult literacy rate (UNESCO estimates): 99.7% (males 99.7%; females 99.7%) in 2007 (Source: UNESCO Institute for Statistics).

Directory

The Constitution

The Constitution was approved in a national referendum on 25 October 1992 and adopted by the Seimas on 6 November. The following is a summary of its main provisions:

THE STATE

The Republic of Lithuania is an independent and democratic republic; its sovereignty is vested in the people, who exercise their supreme power either directly or through their democratically elected representatives. The powers of the State are exercised by the Seimas (Parliament), the President of the Republic, the Government and the Judiciary. The most significant issues concerning the State and the people are decided by referendum.

The territory of the republic is integral. Citizenship is acquired by birth or on other grounds determined by law. With certain exceptions established by law, no person may be a citizen of Lithuania and of another state at the same time. Lithuanian is the state language.

THE INDIVIDUAL AND THE STATE

The rights and freedoms of individuals are inviolable. Property is inviolable, and the rights of ownership are protected by law. Freedom of thought, conscience and religion are guaranteed. All persons are equal before the law. No one may be discriminated against on the basis of sex, race, nationality, language, origin, social status, religion or opinion. Citizens may choose their place of residence in Lithuania freely, and may leave the country at their own will. Citizens are guaranteed the right to form societies, political parties and associations. Citizens who belong to ethnic communities have the right to foster their language, culture and customs.

SOCIETY AND THE STATE

The family is the basis of society and the State. Education is compulsory until the age of 16. Education at state and local government institutions is free of charge at all levels. State and local government establishments of education are secular, although, at the request of parents, they may offer classes in religious instruction. The State recognizes traditional Lithuanian and other churches and religious organizations, but there is no state religion. Censorship of mass media is prohibited. Ethnic communities may independently administer the affairs of their ethnic culture, education, organizations, etc. The State supports ethnic communities.

NATIONAL ECONOMY AND LABOUR

Lithuania's economy is based on the right to private ownership and freedom of individual economic activity. Every person may freely choose an occupation, and has the right to adequate, safe and healthy working conditions, adequate compensation for work, and social security in the event of unemployment. Trade unions may be freely established and may function independently. Employees have the right to strike in order to protect their economic and social interests. The state guarantees the right of citizens to old-age and disability pensions, as well as to social assistance in the event of unemployment, sickness, widowhood, etc.

THE SEIMAS

Legislative power rests with the Seimas. It comprises 141 members, elected for a four-year term on the basis of universal, equal and direct suffrage by secret ballot. Any citizen who has attained 25 years of age may be a candidate for the Seimas. Members of the Seimas may not be found criminally responsible, may not be arrested, and may not be subjected to any other restrictions of personal freedom, without the consent of the Seimas. The Seimas convenes for two regular four-month sessions every year.

The Seimas considers and enacts amendments to the Constitution; enacts laws; adopts resolutions for the organization of referendums; announces presidential elections; approves or rejects the candidature of the Prime Minister, as proposed by the President of the Republic; establishes or abolishes government ministries, upon the recommendation of the Government; supervises the activities of the Government, with the power to express a vote of 'no confidence' in the Prime Minister or individual ministers; appoints judges to the Constitutional Court and the Supreme Court; approves the state budget and supervises the implementation thereof; establishes state taxes and other obligatory payments; ratifies or denounces international treaties whereto the republic is a party, and considers other issues of foreign policy; establishes administrative divisions of the republic; issues acts of amnesty; imposes direct administration and martial law, declares states of emergency, announces mobilization, and adopts decisions to use the armed forces.

THE PRESIDENT OF THE REPUBLIC

The President of the Republic is the Head of State. Any Lithuanian citizen by birth, who has lived in Lithuania for at least the three preceding years, who has reached 40 years of age and who is eligible for election to the Seimas, may be elected President of the Republic. The President is elected by the citizens of the republic, on the basis of universal, equal and direct suffrage by secret ballot, for a term of five years. No person may be elected to the office for more than two consecutive terms.

The President resolves basic issues of foreign policy and, in conjunction with the Government, implements foreign policy; signs international treaties and submits them to the Seimas for ratification; appoints or recalls, upon the recommendation of the Government, diplomatic representatives of Lithuania in foreign states and international organizations; appoints, upon the approval of the Seimas, the Prime Minister, and charges him or her with forming the Government, and approves its composition; removes, upon the approval of the Seimas, the Prime Minister from office; appoints or dismisses individual ministers, upon the recommendation of the Prime Minister; appoints or dismisses, upon the approval of the Seimas, the Commander-in-Chief of the armed forces and the head of the Security Service.

THE GOVERNMENT

Executive power is held by the Government of the Republic (Council of Ministers), which consists of the Prime Minister and other ministers. The Prime Minister is appointed and dismissed by the President of the Republic, with the approval of the Seimas. Ministers are appointed by the President, on the nomination of the Prime Minister.

LITHUANIA

The Government administers the affairs of the country, protects the inviolability of the territory of Lithuania, and ensures state security and public order; implements laws and resolutions of the Seimas as well as presidential decrees; co-ordinates the activities of the ministries and other governmental institutions; prepares the draft state budget and submits it to the Seimas; executes the state budget and reports to the Seimas on its fulfilment; drafts legislative proposals and submits them to the Seimas for consideration; establishes and maintains diplomatic representation with foreign countries and international organizations.

JUDICIAL SYSTEM

The judicial system is independent of the authority of the legislative and executive branches of government. It consists of a Constitutional Court, a Supreme Court, a Court of Appeal, and district and local courts (for details, see section on Judicial System below).

The Government

HEAD OF STATE

President: VALDAS ADAMKUS (inaugurated 12 July 2004).

Note: DALIA GRYBAUSKAITĖ was elected to succeed VALDAS ADAMKUS on 17 May 2009. Her inauguration as President was scheduled for 12 July.

COUNCIL OF MINISTERS
(April 2009)

A coalition comprising representatives of the Homeland Union—Lithuanian Christian Democrats (HU—LCD), the Liberal Movement of the Republic of Lithuania (LM), the Liberal and Centre Union (LCU) and the National Resurrection Party (NRP).

Prime Minister: ANDRIUS KUBILIUS (HU—LCD).
Minister of the Economy: DAINIUS KREIVYS (HU—LCD).
Minister of Finance: ALGIRDAS GEDIMINAS ŠEMETA (HU—LCD).
Minister of National Defence: RASA JUKNEVIČIENĖ (HU—LCD).
Minister of Energy: ARVYDAS SEKMOKAS (HU—LCD).
Minister of Culture: REMIGIJUS VILKAITIS (NRP).
Minister of Social Security and Labour: RIMANTAS JONAS DAGYS (HU—LCD).
Minister of Justice: REMIGIJUS ŠIMAŠIUS (LM).
Minister of Transport and Communications: ELIGIJUS MASIULIS (LM).
Minister of Health: ALGIS ČAPLIKAS (LCU).
Minister of Foreign Affairs: VYGAUDAS UŠACKAS (Independent).
Minister of the Interior: RAIMUNDAS PALAITIS (LCU).
Minister of Agriculture: KAZIMIERAS STARKEVIČIUS (HU—LCD).
Minister of Education and Science: GINTARAS STEPONAVIČIUS (LM).
Minister of the Environment: GEDIMINAS KAZLAUSKAS (NRP).

MINISTRIES

Office of the President: S. Daukanto 3/8, Vilnius 01021; tel. (5) 266-4154; fax (5) 266-4145; e-mail info@president.lt; internet www.president.lt.

Office of the Prime Minister: Gedimino pr. 11, Vilnius 01103; tel. (5) 266-3711; fax (5) 266-3895; e-mail kanceliarija@lrvk.lt; internet www.lrv.lt.

Ministry of Agriculture: Gedimino pr. 19, Vilnius 01103; tel. (5) 239-1032; fax (5) 239-1212; e-mail zum@zum.lt; internet www.zum.lt.

Ministry of Culture: J. Basanavičiaus 5, Vilnius 01118; tel. (5) 219-3400; fax (5) 262-3120; e-mail culture@lrkm.lt; internet www.lrkm.lt.

Ministry of the Economy: Gedimino pr. 38/2, Vilnius 01104; tel. (5) 262-3863; fax (5) 262-3974; e-mail kanc@ukmin.lt; internet www.ukmin.lt.

Ministry of Education and Science: A. Volano 2/7, Vilnius 01516; tel. (5) 219-1190; fax (5) 261-2077; e-mail smmin@smm.lt; internet www.smm.lt.

Ministry of Energy: Gedimino pr. 38/2, Vilnius 01104; tel. (5) 262-6415; e-mail a.sekmokas@enmin.lt.

Ministry of the Environment: A. Jakšto 4/9, Vilnius 01105; tel. (5) 266-3659; fax (5) 266-3663; e-mail info@am.lt; internet www.am.lt.

Ministry of Finance: J. Tumo-Vaižganto 8 A/2, Vilnius 01512; tel. (5) 239-0005; fax (5) 212-6387; e-mail finmin@finmin.lt; internet www.finmin.lt.

Ministry of Foreign Affairs: J. Tumo-Vaižganto g. 2, Vilnius 01511; tel. (5) 236-2444; fax (5) 231-3090; e-mail urm@urm.lt; internet www.urm.lt.

Ministry of Health: Vilniaus g. 33, Vilnius 01119; tel. (5) 268-5110; fax (5) 266-1402; e-mail ministerija@sam.lt; internet www.sam.lt.

Ministry of the Interior: Šventaragio 2, Vilnius 01510; tel. (5) 271-7130; fax (5) 271-8551; e-mail korespondencija@vrm.lt; internet www.vrm.lt.

Ministry of Justice: Gedimino pr. 30/1, Vilnius 01104; tel. (5) 266-2980; fax (5) 262-5940; e-mail tminfo@tm.lt; internet www.tm.lt.

Ministry of National Defence: Totorių 25/3, Vilnius 01121; tel. (5) 262-4821; fax (5) 212-6082; e-mail vis@kam.lt; internet www.kam.lt.

Ministry of Social Security and Labour: A. Vivulskio 11, Vilnius 03610; tel. (5) 266-4201; fax (5) 266-4209; e-mail post@socmin.lt; internet www.socmin.lt.

Ministry of Transport and Communications: Gedimino pr. 17, Vilnius 01505; tel. (5) 239-3938; fax (5) 212-4335; e-mail transp@transp.lt; internet www.transp.lt.

President

Presidential Election, 17 May 2009*

Candidates	Valid votes cast	% of valid votes cast
Dalia Grybauskaitė	949,426	69.08
Algirdas Butkevičius	162,561	11.83
Valentinas Mazuronis	84,635	6.16
Valdemar Tomaševski	65,161	4.74
Kazimiera Danutė Prunskienė	53,691	3.91
Loreta Graužinienė	49,669	3.61
Česlovas Jezerskas	9,176	0.67
Total	**1,374,319**	**100.00**

* Provisional results.

Legislature

Seimas
(Parliament)

Gedimino pr. 53, Vilnius 01109; tel. (5) 239-6212; fax (5) 239-6330; e-mail priim@lrs.lt; internet www.lrs.lt.

Chairman: ARŪNAS VALINSKAS.

General Election, 12 and 26 October 2008

Parties and blocs	A*	B*	Total
Homeland Union—Lithuanian Christian Democrats	18	27	45
Lithuanian Social Democratic Party	10	15	25
National Resurrection Party	13	3	16
Order and Justice Party	11	4	15
Liberal Movement of the Republic of Lithuania	5	6	11
Labour Party–Youth	8	2	10
Liberal and Centre Union	5	3	8
Lithuanian Polish Electoral Action	—	3	3
Lithuanian Peasant Nationalists' Union	—	3	3
New Union (Social Liberals)	—	1	1
Independent candidates	—	4	4
Total	**70**	**71**	**141**

* Of the 141 seats in the Seimas, 70 (A) are awarded according to proportional representation on the basis of party lists, and 71 (B) are elected in single-mandate constituencies.

Election Commission

Lietuvos Respublikos Vyriausioji rinkimų komisija (Central Electoral Committee of the Republic of Lithuania): Gedimino pr. 53, Vilnius 8860715; tel. (5) 239-6969; fax (5) 239-6960; e-mail rinkim@vrk.lt; internet www.vrk.lt; Chair. ZENONAS VAIGAUSKAS.

Political Organizations

In 2008 38 political parties were officially registered. The following were among the most significant:

Civil Democracy Party (Pilietinės Demokratijos Partija): Kaštonų g. 4, Vilnius 01107; tel. (5) 204-0204; fax (5) 204-0205; e-mail pdpsekretoriatas@gmail.com; internet www.pdp.lt; f. 2006; fmrly Civic Union; joined by fmr members of the Labour Party and the Liberal Democratic Party in 2006; Chair. ALGIMANTAS MATULEVIČIUS.

Christian-Conservative Social Union (Krikščionių Konservatorių Socialinė Sąjunga): Odminių g. 5, Vilnius 01122; tel. and fax (5) 212-6874; e-mail sekretoriatas@nks.lt; internet www.nks.lt; f. 2000; centre-right; Chair. GEDIMINAS VAGNORIUS.

Homeland Union—Lithuanian Christian Democrats (HU—LCD) (Tėvynės Sąjunga—Lietuvos Krikščionys Demokratai—TS—LKD): L. Stuokos-Gucevičiaus g. 11, Vilnius 01122; tel. (5) 212-1657; fax (5) 278-4722; e-mail sekretoriatas@tsajunga.lt; internet www.tsajunga.lt; f. 1993 as the Conservative Party of Lithuania (Homeland Union); absorbed the Lithuanian Rightist Union in Nov. 2003; merger with the Lithuanian Union of Political Prisoners and Deportees in Feb. 2004; merged with the Lithuanian Christian Democrats in May 2008, and name changed as above; Chair. ANDRIUS KUBILIUS; some 18,000 mems.

Labour Party (LP) (Darbo Partija): Ankštoji 3, Vilnius 01109; tel. (5) 210-7152; fax (5) 210-7153; e-mail info@darbopartija.lt; internet www.darbopartija.lt; f. 2003; Chair. VIKTOR USPASKIKH.

Liberal and Centre Union (Liberalų Centro Sąjunga): Vilniaus g. 22/1, Vilnius 01119; tel. (5) 231-3264; fax (5) 261-9363; e-mail info@lics.lt; internet www.lics.lt; f. 2003 by a merger of the Lithuanian Centre Union, the Lithuanian Liberal Union and the Modern Christian-Democratic Union; Chair. ARTŪRAS ZUOKAS; over 5,000 mems.

Liberal Movement of the Republic of Lithuania (Lietuvos Respublikos liberalų sąjūdis): Sėlių g. 48, Vilnius 08125; tel. and fax (5) 249-6959; e-mail info@liberalusajudis.lt; internet www.liberalusajudis.lt; f. 2006; formed by a splinter group of the Liberal and Centre Union; Chair. ELIGIJUS MASIULIS.

Lithuanian Peasant Nationalists' Union (Lietuvos Valstiečių Liaudininkų Sąjunga—LVLS): Pamėnkalnio g. 26, Vilnius 01114; tel. (5) 212-0821; fax (5) 212-0822; e-mail info@lvls.lt; internet www.lvls.lt; f. 2001 by the merger of the New Democracy Party and the Lithuanian Peasants' (Farmers') Party; fmrly Peasants' (Farmers') and New Democratic Party Union (VNDS); present name adopted Feb. 2006; Chair. RAMŪNAS KARBAUSKIS; 1,500 mems.

Lithuanian Polish Electoral Action (Akcja Wyborcza Polaków na Litwie—LLRA): Pilies g. 16, Vilnius 01123; tel. (5) 279-1887; fax (5) 233-1266; e-mail info@awpl.lt; internet www.awpl.lt; f. 1994; Chair. WALDEMAR TOMASZEWSKI.

Lithuanian Polish People's Party (Lietuvos Lenkų Liaudies Partija/Polska Partia Ludowa): Kauno g. 1A, Vilnius 03212; tel. (5) 216-2874; fax (5) 233-5467; e-mail lllp@zebra.lt; internet www.lllp.lt; f. 2002; Chair. ANTONINA POŁTAWIEC.

Lithuanian Russians' Union (Lietuvos rusų sąjunga/Soyuz Russkikh Litvy): Pamėnkalnio g. 3–27, Vilnius 01116; tel. (5) 262-4248; e-mail sojuzru@tts.lt; internet sojuzru.tts.lt; f. 1995; Chair. SERGEI DMITRIYEV.

Lithuanian Social Democratic Party (LSDP) (Lietuvos Socialdemokratų Partija): Barboros Radvilaites g. 1, Vilnius 01124; tel. (5) 261-3907; fax (5) 261-5420; e-mail info@lsdp.lt; internet www.lsdp.lt; absorbed the Lithuanian Democratic Labour Party in 2001; Chair. ALGIRDAS BUTKEVIČIUS; 11,000 mems.

National Resurrection Party (NRP) (Tautos prisikėlimo partija): Pranciškonų g. 4A/ 10, Vilnius; tel. (6) 788-2816; fax (5) 240-0493; e-mail bustine@prisikelimopartija.lt; internet www.prisikelimopartija.lt; f. 2008; Leader ARŪNAS VALINSKAS.

New Union (Social Liberals) (NU) (Naujoji sąjunga—Socialliberalai): Gedimino pr. 10/1, Vilnius 01103; tel. (5) 210-7600; fax (5) 210-7602; e-mail centras@nsajunga.lt; internet www.nsajunga.lt; f. 1998; centre-left; Chair. ARTŪRAS PAULAUSKAS.

Order and Justice Party (Partijos Tvarka ir teisingumas): Gedimino pr. 10/1, Vilnius 01103; tel. and fax (5) 269-1618; e-mail tt@tvarka.lt; internet www.ldp.lt; f. 2002; fmrly Liberal Democratic Party (LDP), renamed as above May 2006; right-wing; Chair. ROLANDAS PAKSAS; 6,500 mems (2007).

Diplomatic Representation

EMBASSIES IN LITHUANIA

Austria: Gaono g. 6, Vilnius 01131; tel. (5) 266-0580; fax (5) 279-1363; e-mail wilna-ob@bmaa.gv.at; internet www.bmeia.gv.at/wilna; Ambassador ANDREA WICKE.

Azerbaijan: Olimpiečių g. 5-7, Vilnius 02051; tel. (5) 219-0042; fax (5) 279-1504; e-mail info@azembassy.lt; Ambassador NAIRA SHAKHTAKHTINSKAYA.

Belarus: Mindaugo g. 13, Vilnius 03225; tel. (5) 266-2200; fax (5) 266-2212; e-mail emb@belarus.lt; internet www.belarus.lt; Ambassador ULADZIMIR DRAZHIN.

Belgium: Kalinausko g. 2B, Vilnius 03107; tel. (5) 266-0820; fax (5) 212-6444; e-mail vilnius@diplobel.org; internet www.diplomatie.be/vilnius; Ambassador FILIP CUMPS.

Bulgaria: Pylimo 8, Palangos 2, Vilnius 01118; tel. (5) 249-9274; fax (5) 261-9174; e-mail vilnius@bgembassy.lt; internet www.mfa.bg/vilnius; Ambassador IVAN P. DANTCHEV.

China, People's Republic: Algirdo g. 36, Vilnius 03218; tel. (5) 216-2861; fax (5) 216-2682; e-mail chinaemb_lithuania@mfa.gov.cn; internet www.chinaembassy.lt; Ambassador TONG MINGTAO.

Czech Republic: Birutės g. 16, Vilnius 08117; tel. (5) 266-1040; fax (5) 266-1066; e-mail vilnius@embassy.mzv.cz; internet www.mzv.cz/vilnius; Ambassador ALOIS BUCHTA.

Denmark: Kosciuškos g. 36, Vilnius 01100; tel. (5) 264-8760; fax (5) 231-2300; e-mail vnoamb@um.dk; internet www.ambvilnius.um.dk; Ambassador LAURIDS MIKAELSEN.

Estonia: A. Mickevičiaus g. 4A, Vilnius 08119; tel. (5) 278-0200; fax (5) 278-0201; e-mail sekretar@estemb.lt; internet www.estemb.lt; Ambassador TIIT NABER.

Finland: Klaipėdos g. 6, Vilnius 01117; tel. (5) 212-1621; fax (5) 212-2463; e-mail sanomat.vil@formin.fi; internet www.finland.lt; Ambassador MARJA-LIISA KILJUNEN.

France: Švarco g. 1, Vilnius 01131; tel. (5) 212-2979; fax (5) 212-4211; e-mail ambafrance.vilnius@diplomatie.gouv.fr; internet www.ambafrance-lt.org; Ambassador FRANÇOIS LAUMONIER.

Georgia: Poškos g. 13, Vilnius 08123; tel. (5) 273-6959; fax (5) 272-3623; e-mail embassy@georgia.w3.lt; internet www.lithuania.mfa.gov.ge; Ambassador GEORGI KERDIKOSHVILI.

Germany: Z. Sierakausko g. 24/8, Vilnius 03105; tel. (5) 210-6400; fax (5) 210-6446; e-mail info@wilna.diplo.de; internet www.deutschebotschaft-wilna.lt; Ambassador HANS PETER ANNEN.

Greece: Didžioji 33/ Rūdininkų 2; tel. (5) 261-0526; fax (5) 261-0536; e-mail embassy@grembvil.w3.lt; Ambassador CONSTANTINE CATSAMBIS.

Holy See: Kosciuškos g. 28, Vilnius 01100; tel. (5) 212-3696; fax (5) 212-4228; e-mail nuntiusbalt@aiva.lt; Apostolic Nuncio Most Rev. PETER STEPHAN ZURBRIGGEN (Titular Archbishop of Glastonia).

Hungary: Jojailos g. 4, Vilnius 01116; tel. (5) 269-0038; fax (5) 269-0039; e-mail vilnius@kum.hu; Ambassador PÉTER NOSZKÓ-HORVATH.

Ireland: Gedimino pr. 1, Vilnius 01103; tel. (5) 262-9460; fax (5) 262-9462; e-mail vilniusembassy@dfa.ie; internet www.embassyofireland.lt; f. 2005; Ambassador DÓNAL DENHAM.

Italy: Vytauto g. 1, Vilnius 08118; tel. (5) 212-0620; fax (5) 212-0405; e-mail ambasciata.vilnius@esteri.it; internet www.ambvilnius.esteri.it; Ambassador RENATO MARIA RICCI.

Japan: M. K. Čiurlionio g. 82B, Vilnius 03100; tel. (5) 231-0462; fax (5) 231-0461; Ambassador MIYOKO AKASHI.

Kazakhstan: Birutės g. 20A/35, Vilnius 08117; tel. (5) 212-2123; fax (5) 231-3580; e-mail kazemb@iti.lt; internet kazakhstan.embassy.lt; Ambassador GALYMZHAN KOISHYBAEV.

Latvia: M. K. Čiurlionio g. 76, Vilnius 03100; tel. (5) 213-1260; fax (5) 213-1130; e-mail embassy.lithuania@mfa.gov.lv; internet www.latvia.lt; Ambassador HARDIJS BAUMANIS.

Moldova: Miglos g. 61A, Vilnius 08101; tel. (5) 260-7914; fax (5) 260-7915; e-mail ambasada.vilnius@gmail.com; internet www.lituania.mfa.gov.md; Ambassador ION CIORNII.

Netherlands: Business Centre 2000, 4th Floor, Jogailos g. 4, Vilnius 01116; tel. (5) 269-0072; fax (5) 269-0073; e-mail vil@minbuza.nk; internet www.netherlandsembassy.lt; Ambassador JOHANNA GERARDA MARIA RUIGROK.

Norway: Mėsinių g. 5/2, Vilnius 01133; tel. (5) 261-0000; fax (5) 261-0100; e-mail emb.vilnius@mfa.no; internet www.norvegija.lt; Ambassador STEINAR GIL.

Poland: Smėlio g. 20A, Vilnius 10323; tel. (5) 270-9001; fax (5) 270-9007; e-mail ampol@tdd.lt; internet www.wilno.polemb.net; Ambassador JANUSZ SKOLIMOWSKI.

Portugal: Gedimino pr. 5, Vilnius 01103; tel. (5) 262-0511; fax (5) 262-0512; e-mail vilnius@embportugal.lt; Ambassador JOÃO MANUEL DA CRUZ DA SILVA LEITÃO.

Romania: Vivulskio g. 19, Vilnius 03115; tel. (5) 231-0527; fax (5) 231-0652; e-mail ambromania@romania.lt; internet www.romania.lt; Ambassador GHEORGHE TOKAY.

Russia: Latvių g. 53/54, Vilnius 08113; tel. (5) 272-1763; fax (5) 272-3877; e-mail post@rusemb.lt; internet www.rusemb.lt; Ambassador VLADIMIR V. CHKHIKVADZE.

LITHUANIA
Directory

Spain: Algirdo g. 4, Vilnius 03220; tel. (5) 231-3961; fax (5) 231-3962; e-mail emb.vilnius@mae.es; f. 2004; Ambassador JOSÉ LUÍS SOLANO GADEA.

Sweden: Didžioji g. 16, Vilnius 01128; tel. (5) 268-5010; fax (5) 268-5030; e-mail ambassaden.vilnius@foreign.ministry.se; internet www.swedenabroad.com/vilnius; Ambassador ULRIKA EVA MARIA CRONENBERG-MOSSBERG.

Turkey: Didžioji g. 37, Vilnius 01128; tel. (5) 264-9570; fax (5) 212-3277; e-mail turkemb.vilnius@mfa.gov.tr; Ambassador OGUZ ÖZGE.

Ukraine: Teatro g. 4, Vilnius 03107; tel. (5) 212-1536; fax (5) 212-0475; e-mail ukrembassy@post.5ci.lt; internet www.mfa.gov.ua/lithuania; Ambasasador IHOR V. PROKOPCHUK.

United Kingdom: Antakalnio g. 2, Vilnius 10308; tel. (5) 246-2900; fax (5) 246-2901; e-mail be-vilnius@britain.lt; internet ukinlithuania.fco.gov; Ambassador SIMON JOHN BUTT.

USA: Akmenų g. 6, Vilnius 03106; tel. (5) 266-5300; fax (5) 266-5310; e-mail webemailvilnius@state.gov; internet vilnius.usembassy.gov; Ambassador JOHN ALBERT CLOUD, , Jr.

Judicial System

The organs of justice are the Supreme Court, the Court of Appeal, district courts, local courts of administrative areas and a special court—the Commercial Court. The Seimas (Parliament) appoints and dismisses from office the judges of the Supreme Court in response to representations made by the President of the Republic (based upon the recommendation of the chairman of the Supreme Court). Judges of the Court of Appeal are appointed by the President with the approval of the Seimas (on the recommendation of the Minister of Justice), while judges of district and local courts are appointed and dismissed by the President. The Council of Judges submits recommendations to the President of the Republic concerning the appointment of judges, as well as their promotion, transfer or dismissal from office.

The Constitutional Court decides on the constitutionality of acts of the Seimas, as well as of the President and the Government. It consists of nine judges, who are appointed by the Seimas for a single term of nine years; one-third of the Court's members are replaced every three years.

The Office of the Prosecutor-General is an autonomous institution of the judiciary, comprising the Prosecutor-General and local and district prosecutors' offices which are subordinate to him. The Prosecutor-General and his deputies are appointed for terms of seven years by the President, subject to approval by the Seimas, while the prosecutors are appointed by the Prosecutor-General. The Office of the Prosecutor-General incorporates the Department for Crime Investigation. The State Arbitration decides cases of business litigation. A six-volume Civil Code, in accordance with European Union and international law, came into effect in 2001, replacing the Soviet civil legal system, which had, hitherto, remained in operation.

Constitutional Court (Lietuvos Respublikos Konstitucinis Teismas): Gedimino pr. 36, Vilnius 01104; tel. (5) 261-1466; fax (5) 212-7975; e-mail mailbox@lrkt.lt; internet www.lrkt.lt; f. 1993; Chair. KĘSTUTIS LAPINSKAS.

Court of Appeal: Gedimino pr. 40/1, Vilnius 01503; tel. (5) 266-3685; fax (5) 266-3060; e-mail apeliacinis@vtr.lt; internet www.apeliacinis.lt; Chair. VYTAS MILIUS.

Supreme Court (Lietuvos Aukščiausiasis Teismas): Gynėjų g. 6, Vilnius 01109; tel. (5) 261-0560; fax (5) 261-6813; e-mail lat@lat.lt; internet www.lat.lt; Chair. VYTAUTAS GREIČIUS.

Office of the Prosecutor-General: Rinktinės g. 5A, Vilnius 01515; tel. (5) 266-2305; fax (5) 266-2317; e-mail info@prokuraturos.lt; internet www.prokuraturos.lt; Prosecutor-General ALGIMANTAS VALANTINAS.

Religion

CHRISTIANITY

The Roman Catholic Church

Catholicism has been the principal religious affiliation in Lithuania since its adoption by the Lithuanian State in 1387. The Roman Catholic Church in Lithuania comprises two archdioceses and five dioceses. At 31 December 2006 there were an estimated 2.8m. adherents in Lithuania (equivalent to some 81.5% of the population).

Bishops' Conference: Skapo 4, Vilnius 01122; tel. (5) 212-5455; fax (5) 212-0972; e-mail lvk@lcnl.lt; internet lvk.lcn.lt; f. 2002; Pres. Most Rev. SIGITUS TAMKEVIČIUS (Archbishop of Kaunas).

Archbishop of Kaunas: Most Rev. SIGITAS TAMKEVIČIUS, Rotušės 14A, Kaunas 44279; tel. (37) 409026; fax (37) 320090; e-mail kurija@kn.lcn.lt; internet www.kaunas.lcn.lt.

Archbishop of Vilnius: Cardinal AUDRYS JUOZAS BAČKIS, Šventaragio 4, Vilnius 01122; tel. (5) 262-7098; fax (5) 212-2807; e-mail curia@vilnensis.lt; internet vilnius.lcn.lt.

Orthodox Churches

Russian Orthodox Church (Moscow Patriarchate)

The first Orthodox communities in Lithuania appeared during the 12th century. While Lithuania formed part of the Russian Empire (1795–1915), Orthodoxy was considered the state religion. There were an estimated 180,000 adherents in 2001.

Lithuanian Orthodox Church (Moscow Patriarchate): Aušros Vartų 10/3, Vilnius 01129; tel. (5) 212-7765; internet www.orthodoxy.lt; Metropolitan of Vilnius and Lithuania CHRYZOSTOM (MARTISHKIN).

Lithuanian Old Believers Pomor Church

The first communities settled in Lithuania in 1679 and the Church was established in 1709. In 1996 there were approximately 34,000 adherents.

Supreme Council of the Old Believers Pomor Church in Lithuania: Naujininkų g. 20, Vilnius 02109; tel. (5) 269-5271; f. 1925; Chair. MARK SEMIONOV (acting).

Protestant Churches

Lithuanian Evangelical Lutheran Church

The first parishes were established in 1539–69. The Lithuanian Evangelical Lutheran Church comprises one diocese. In 1998 there were approximately 30,000 adherents.

Consistory of the Lithuanian Evangelical Lutheran Church (Lietuvos Evangeliku-Liuteronu Bažnycia): Tumo-Vaižganto 50, Tauragė 72263; tel. and fax (446) 61145; e-mail redakcija@liuteronai.lt; internet www.liuteronai.lt; Bishop MINDAUGAS SABUTIS.

Lithuanian Evangelical Reformed Church

The first parishes were established after 1563. At 1 January 1996 there were approximately 12,000 adherents.

Lithuanian Evangelical Reformed Church: POB 661, Vilnius 04008; tel. and fax (5) 245-0656; Pres. of Synodie Collegium POVILAS A. JAŠINSKAS.

ISLAM

Sunni Islam is the religion of the ethnic Tatars of Lithuania. The first Tatar communities settled there in the 14th century. The first mosque in Vilnius was erected in 1558. In 2001 there were an estimated 5,000 adherents.

JUDAISM

The first Jewish communities appeared in Lithuania in the 15th century. In the 15th–17th centuries Vilnius was an important centre of Jewish culture and religion. Before the Second World War approximately 200,000 Jews lived in Lithuania; an estimated 90% were murdered during the German occupation (1941–44). At 1 January 1996 there were five religious communities, with two synagogues (in Vilnius and Kaunas). There were an estimated 5,000 adherents in Lithuania in 2001. There is a small number of Karaites (Karaim), who originate from Crimea (now in Ukraine), and who speak a Turkic language and follow a form of Judaism, resident in Lithuania.

The Press

In 2007 there were 328 newspapers and 474 periodicals published in Lithuania.

The publications listed below are in Lithuanian, except where otherwise indicated.

PRINCIPAL NEWSPAPERS

Kauno diena (Kaunas Daily): Kęstučio g. 86, Kaunas 44296; tel. (37) 302250; fax (37) 423404; e-mail redakcija@kaunodiena.lt; internet www.kaunodiena.lt; f. 1945; 6 a week; Editor-in-Chief OVIDIJUS LUKOŠIUS; circ. 50,000.

Klaipėda: Šaulių g. 21, Klaipėda 92233; tel. (46) 397750; fax (46) 397700; e-mail office@klaipeda.daily.lt; internet www.klaipeda.daily.lt; Editor VALDEMARAS PUODŽIŪNAS.

Kurier Wileński (Vilnius Courier): Birbynių g. 4A, Vilnius 02121; tel. and fax (5) 260-8444; e-mail info@kurierwilenski.lt; internet www.kurierwilenski.lt; f. 1953; 5 a week; in Polish; Editor-in-Chief ROBERT MICKIEWICZ; circ. 8,000.

Lietuvos aidas (Lithuanian Echo): Gedimino pr. 2, Vilnius 02000; tel. (52) 261-0544; fax (5) 212-4876; e-mail centr@aidas.lt; internet

LITHUANIA

www.aidas.lt; f. 1917; re-est. 1990; 5 a week; Editor-in-Chief ALGIRDAS PILVELIS; circ. 20,000.

Lietuvos rytas (Lithuanian Morning): Gedimino pr. 12A, Vilnius 01103; tel. (5) 274-3600; fax (5) 274-3700; e-mail news@lrytas.lt; internet www.lrytas.lt; f. 1990; 6 a week, with 3 supplements per week; Editor-in-Chief RIMVYDAS VALATKA; circ. 65,000 (Mon.–Fri.), 200,000 (Sat.).

Lietuvos žinios (Lithuanian News): Kęstučio g. 4/14, Vilnius 08117; tel. (5) 249-2152; fax (5) 275-3131; e-mail red@lzinios.lt; internet www.lzinios.lt; 6 a week; Gen. Dir and Editor-in-Chief VASILIAUSKAS VASILIAUSKAS.

Respublika (Republic): A. Smetonos g. 2, Vilnius 01115; tel. (5) 212-3112; fax (5) 212-3538; e-mail press@respublika.lt; f. 1989; 6 a week in Lithuanian, with 5 Russian editions per week; Editor-in-Chief VITAS TOMKUS; circ. 55,000.

Šiaulių kraštas: P. Višinskio g. 26, Šiauliai 77155; tel. (41) 591555; fax (41) 524581; e-mail redakcija@skrastas.lt; internet www.skrastas.lt.

Vakaro žinios (Evening News): Jogailos g. 11/2-11, Vilnius 01116; tel. and fax (5) 261-6875; e-mail vakarozinios@takas.lt; daily; circ. 70,000.

Vakarų ekspresas (Western Express): M. Mažvydo 3, Klaipėda 92131; tel. (46) 411308; fax (46) 310102; e-mail sekretore@ve.lt; internet www.ve.lt; f. 1990; 6 a week; Editor-in-Chief GINTARAS TOMKUS; circ. 16,000–22,000.

Verslo žinios (Business News): J. Jasinskio 16A, Vilnius 01112; tel. (5) 252-6300; fax (5) 252-6313; e-mail info@vz.lt; internet vz.lt; f. 1994; 5 a week; circ. 9,000; Editor LINAS KMIELIAUSKAS.

PRINCIPAL PERIODICALS

Artuma (Presence): Rotušės a. 23, Kaunas 44279; tel. and fax (37) 209683; e-mail redakcija@artuma.lt; internet www.artuma.lt; f. 1989 as *Caritas*; name changed as above in 1997; monthly; Catholic family magazine; Editor-in-Chief DARIUS CHMIELIAUSKAS; circ. 12,500.

Kultūros barai (Domains of Culture): Latako g. 3, Vilnius 01125; tel. (5) 261-6696; fax (5) 261-0538; e-mail kulturosbarai@takas.lt; internet www.eurozine.com; f. 1965; monthly; independent cultural magazine; Editor-in-Chief BRONYS SAVUKYNAS; circ. 3,000.

Laima: K. Donelaičio g. 70–10, Kaunas 44248; tel. (5) 272-8083; fax (5) 272-1614; e-mail laima@redakcija.lt; f. 1993; monthly; lifestyle and feature magazine for women; Editor-in-Chief GITANA BUKAUSKIENĖ; circ. 30,000.

Liaudies kultūra (Ethnic Culture): Barboros Radvilaitės 8, Vilnius 01124; tel. (5) 261-3412; fax (5) 212-4033; e-mail lkredaktore@llkc.lt; internet www.llkc.lt; f. 1988; 6 a year; Gen. Editor DALIA ANTANINA RASTENIENĖ; circ. 800.

Literatūra ir menas (Literature and Art): Mesiniu 4, Vilnius 01133; tel. (5) 269-1977; fax (5) 212-6556; e-mail lmenas@takas.lt; internet www.culture.lt/lmenas; f. 1946; weekly; publ. by the Lithuanian Writers' Union; Editor-in-Chief KORNELIJUS PLATELIS; circ. 2,000.

Lithuania in the World: J. Basanavičiaus g. 7, Vilnius 01118; tel. (5) 261-4432; fax (5) 212-5560; e-mail info@liw.lt; internet www.liw.lt; f. 1993; 6 a year; in English and Lithuanian; Exec. Editor JOLANTA LAUMENSKAITĖ; circ. 10,000.

Magazyn Wileński (Vilnius Journal): Laisvės pr. 60, Vilnius 05120; tel. (5) 242-7718; fax (5) 242-9065; e-mail magazyn@magwil.lt; internet www.magwil.lt; f. 1990; monthly; political, cultural; in Polish; Editor-in-Chief MICHAŁ MACKIEWICZ; circ. 5,000.

Mano Namai: Ozo g. 10A, Vilnius; tel. (5) 247-7714; e-mail dalia@manomai.lt; internet www.mano-namai.lt; household, interiors and food; Editor DALIA DAUGIRDIENĖ.

Metai (Year): K. Sirvydo g. 6, Vilnius 01101; tel. (5) 261-7344; e-mail metai@takas.lt; f. 1991; monthly; journal of the Lithuanian Writers' Union; Editor-in-Chief DANIELIUS MUŠINSKAS; circ. 2,000.

Mokslas ir gyvenimas (Science and Life): Antakalnio g. 36, Vilnius 10305; tel. and fax (5) 234-1572; e-mail mgredacija@takas.lt; internet ausis.gf.vu.lt/mg; f. 1957; monthly; popular and historical science; Editor-in-Chief JUOZAS BALDAUSKAS; circ. 3,500.

Moteris (Woman): P. Smuglevičiaus g. 21, Vilnius 08311; tel. and fax (5) 247-7711; e-mail info@moteris.lt; internet www.moteris.lt; f. 1952; monthly; popular, for women; Editor-in-Chief EGLE STRIAUKIENE; circ. 20,000.

Naujasis Židinys-Aidai (New Hearth–Echoes): Didžioji g. 34, Vilnius 01128; tel. (5) 212-0311; fax (5) 212-2363; e-mail aidai@aidai.lt; f. 1991; monthly; religion, culture and social affairs; Editor-in-Chief LINA KAMINSKAITĖ; circ. 1,000.

Nemunas: Gedimino g. 45, Kaunas 44239; tel. and fax (37) 322244; e-mail nemunas.redakcija@centras.lt; f. 1967; weekly; journal of the Lithuanian Writers' Union; Editor-in-Chief VIKTORAS RUDZIANSKAS; circ. 1,500.

Panelė (Young Miss): P. Smuglevičiaus g. 23, Vilnius 08311; tel. (5) 247-7716; fax (5) 247-7715; e-mail magazine@panele.lt; internet www.panele.lt; f. 1994; monthly; popular, for ages 12–25; Editor-in-Chief JURGA BALTRUKONYTĖ; circ. 66,000.

Psihologija Tau: Vilnius; e-mail redakcija@psichologijatau.lt; internet www.psichologijatau.lt; popular psychology; Editor RŪTA CHOMENTAUSKAITĖ.

Septynios meno dienos (7 meno dienos) (Seven Days of Art): Bernardinų g. 10, Vilnius 01124; tel. (5) 261-3039; fax (5) 261-1926; e-mail 7md@takas.lt; internet www.culture.lt/7menodienos; f. 1992; weekly; Editor-in-Chief LINAS VILDŽIŪNAS; circ. 1,500.

Tremtinys (Deportee): Laisvės al. 39, Kaunas 44282; tel. (37) 323204; e-mail tremtinys@erdvas.lt; internet www.lpkts.lt/tremtinys.htm; f. 1988; weekly; publ. of fmr Lithuanian Union of Political Prisoners and Deportees (now part of Homeland Union); Editor-in-Chief AUDRONĖ KAMINSKIENĖ; circ. 4,500.

Valstiečių laikraštis (Farmer's Newspaper): Laisvės pr. 60, Vilnius 05120; tel. and fax (5) 242-1281; e-mail redakcija@valstietis.lt; internet www.valstietis.lt; f. 1940; 2 a week; Editor-in-Chief JONAS ŠVOBA; circ. 68,000.

Vasario 16 (16 February): J. Gruodžio g. 9/404, Kaunas 44293; tel. (37) 225219; f. 1988; fortnightly; journal of Order and Justice—Liberal Democrats; Sec. PRIMAS NOREIKA; circ. 1,600.

NEWS AGENCIES

Baltic News Service (BNS): Jogailos g. 9/1, Vilnius 01116; tel. (5) 231-2410; fax (5) 268-1515; e-mail bns@bns.lt; f. 1991; Dir JURGITA LITVINIENĖ (acting).

ELTA Lithuanian News Agency (ELTA Lietuvos Naujienų Agentūra): Gedimino pr. 21/2, Vilnius 01103; tel. (5) 262-8864; fax (5) 261-9507; e-mail zinios@elta.lt; internet www.elta.lt; f. 1920; 18.4% owned by Ziniu Partneriai; 39.5% owned by Respublikos Investicija (both cos controlled by Respublika Gp); Dir GRAZINA RAMANAUSKAITĖ-TIUMENEVIENĖ.

Publishers

Alma littera: A. Juozapavičiaus 6/2, Vilnius 09310; tel. (5) 263-8877; fax (5) 272-8026; e-mail post@almali.lt; internet www.almali.lt; f. 1990; fiction, children's books, textbooks; Dir-Gen. ARVYDAS ANDRIJAUSKAS.

Baltos lankos leidykla (White Meadows Publishing House): Aušros Vartų g. 29/1, Vilnius 01129; tel. (5) 240-8673; fax (5) 240-7446; e-mail leidykla@baltoslankos.lt; internet www.baltoslankos.lt; f. 1992; literature, humanities, social sciences, fiction and textbooks; Dir SAULIUS ŽUKAS.

Eugrimas: Kalvariju 98/36, Vilnius 08211; tel. and fax (5) 273-3955; e-mail info@eugrimas.lt; internet www.eugrimas.lt; f. 1995; academic and professional literature, incl. economics, business, law and politics; Dir EUGENIJA PETRULIENĖ.

Katalikų pasaulio leidiniai (Editions of the Catholic World): Pylimo 27/14, Vilnius 01141; tel. (5) 212-2422; fax (5) 212-0375; internet www.katalikuleidiniai.lt; f. 1990; Dir BIRUTĖ BARTASŪNAITE.

Lietuvos rašytojų sąjungos leidykla (Lithuanian Writers' Union Publishers): K. Sirvydo 6, Vilnius 01101; tel. and fax (5) 262-8945; e-mail info@rsleidykla.lt; internet www.rsleidykla.lt; f. 1990; fiction, essays, literary heritage, children's books; Dir GIEDRE SORIENE.

Mintis leidykla (Mintis Publishing House): Z. Sierakausko g. 15, Vilnius 03105; tel. (5) 233-2943; fax (5) 216-3157; e-mail redakcija@mintis.org; internet www.mintis.org; f. 1949; philosophy, politics, history, law, mythology, textbooks, encyclopedias, biographies, fiction; also book distributor, bookshop; Dir LEONARDAS ARMONAS.

Mokslo ir enciklopedijų leidybos institutas (Science and Encyclopedia Publishing Institute): L. Asanavičiūtės 23, Vilnius 04315; tel. (5) 245-8526; fax (5) 245-8537; e-mail meli@meli.lt; internet www.meli.lt; f. 1992; encyclopedias, science and reference books, dictionaries, higher education textbooks, books for the general reader; Dir RIMANTAS KARECKAS.

Presvika: Kauno g. 28, Vilnius 03202; tel. (5) 262-3182; fax (5) 262-3110; e-mail presvika@vilnius.balt.net; internet www.presvika.lt; f. 1996; psychological and educational literature, textbooks and fiction; Dir VIOLETA BILAIŠYTĖ.

Šviesa (Light): E. Ožeškienės g. 10, Kaunas 44252; tel. (37) 409126; fax (37) 342032; e-mail mail@sviesa.lt; internet www.sviesa.lt; f. 1945; textbooks and pedagogical literature; Dir ARŪNAS BUTKUS.

Tyto alba: J. Jasinskio 10, Vilnius 01112; tel. (5) 249-7453; fax (5) 298-8602; internet www.tytoalba.lt; f. 1993; contemporary Lithu-

LITHUANIA

anian literary fiction and non-fiction, fiction in translation; Dir LOLITA VARANAVIČIENĖ.

UAB Leidykla Vaga (Furrow Publishing House Ltd): Gedimino pr. 50, Vilnius 01110; tel. (5) 249-8121; fax (5) 249-8122; e-mail info@vaga.lt; internet www.vaga.lt; f. 1945 as Lithuanian State Publishing House of Fiction; privatized and restructured in 1994; fiction, non-fiction, art, children's books; Dir VYTAS V. PETROŠIUS.

UAB Versus Aureus leidykla: Rūdninkų g. 10, Vilnius 01135; tel. and fax (5) 265-2730; e-mail versus@versus.lt; internet www.versus.lt; f. 2003; fiction, non-fiction and educational literature.

PUBLISHERS' ASSOCIATION

Lietuvos Leidėjų Asociacija (Lithuanian Publishers' Association): A. Jakšto 22–13, Vilnius 01105; tel. and fax (5) 261-7740; e-mail lla@centras.lt; internet www.lla.lt; f. 1989; Pres. EUGENIJUS KAZILIŪNAS.

Broadcasting and Communications

TELECOMMUNICATIONS
Regulatory Authority

Communications Regulatory Authority (Ryšių reguliavimo tarnyba): Algirdo 27, Vilnius 03219; tel. (5) 210-5633; fax (5) 216-1564; e-mail rrt@rrt.lt; internet www.rrt.lt; f. 2001; Dir TOMAS BARAKAUSKAS.

Service Providers

UAB BITĖ Lietuva: Žemaitės 15, Vilnius 03118; tel. (6) 560-0656; fax (6) 990-0111; e-mail info@bite.lt; internet www.bite.lt; mobile telecommunications service provider; 1.8m. subscribers (Dec. 2006); CEO MARTIN AMTOFT-CHRISTENSEN.

UAB Eurocom: Ozo g. 25, Vilnius 07150; tel. (5) 274-4699; fax (5) 274-4612; e-mail eurocom@eurocom.lt; internet www.eurocom.lt; f. 2001; fixed line and mobile telecommunications service provider; a subsidiary of VP Market; Dir SEDIMINAS JOVAIŠA.

Omnitel UAB: T. Ševčenkos 25, Vilnius 03503; tel. (698) 63333; fax (5) 274-5574; e-mail info@omnitel.net; internet www.omnitel.lt; f. 1991 as Litcom; owned by Telia Sonera (Sweden); largest mobile GSM communications provider in Lithuania; Pres. ANTANAS JUOZAS ZABULIS.

UAB Tele2: POB 147, Vilnius 01003; tel. (684) 00212; fax (5) 236-6301; e-mail tele2@tele2.lt; internet www.tele2.lt; f. 1999; owned by Tele2 AB (Sweden); provider of GSM, internet and fixed-line telecommunications services; Chief Exec. PETRAS MASIULIS.

Teo LT AB: Savanorių pr. 28, Vilnius 03116; tel. (5) 262-1511; fax (5) 212-6655; internet www.teo.lt; f. 1992 under the name Lietuvos Telekomas AB; present name adopted 2006; privatized 1998; operates public telecommunications network, repairs telecommunications equipment; monopoly withdrawn in 2003; Chair. ERIK HALLBERG; Gen. Man. ARŪNAS ŠIKŠTA; 3,200 employees.

BROADCASTING
Regulatory Authority

Lietuvos radijo ir televizijos komisija (Radio and Television Commission of Lithuania): Vytenio g. 6/23, Vilnius 03113; tel. (5) 233-0660; fax (5) 264-7125; e-mail lrtk@rtk.lt; internet www.rtk.lt; f. 1996; licensing and licence compliance; Chair. JONAS LINIAUSKAS.

Radio

Lietuvos radijas ir televizija (LRT) (Lithuanian Radio and Television): S. Konarskio 49, Vilnius 03123; tel. (5) 236-3209; fax (5) 236-3208; e-mail lrt@lrt.lt; internet www.lrt.lt; f. 1926; govt-owned; non-profit public broadcasting co; operates three national radio channels and two national television channels; Chair. of Bd GEDIMINAS ILGŪNAS; Dir-Gen. AUDRIUS SIAURUSEVIČIUS; 650 employees.

Lietuvos radijas (Lithuanian Radio): S. Konarskio 49, Vilnius 03123; tel. (5) 236-3000; fax (5) 213-5333; e-mail rimgel@lrt.lt; internet www.lrt.lt; f. 1926; broadcasts in Lithuanian, Russian, Polish, Yiddish, Belarusian and Ukrainian; Dir JURGITA LITVINIENĖ.

A2 Radijo Stotis: Laisvės pr. 3, Vilnius 04215; tel. (5) 245-4922; e-mail a2@a2.lt; internet www.a2.lt; private, commercial; Dir VYDAS IVANAUSKAS.

UAB Aukštaitijos radijas (AR): Laisvės a. 1, Panevėžys 35175; tel. and fax (45) 596969; e-mail ar@laineta.lt; private, commercial; Dir ALGIRDAS ŠATAS.

FM 99: Rotušės a. 2, POB 119, Alytus 62141; tel. (315) 76120; fax (315) 74646; e-mail fm99@fm99.lt; internet www.fm99.lt; private, commercial; broadcast by UAB Alytaus radijas; Dir LIUDAS RAMANAUSKAS.

Kauno fonas 105.4: Savanorių pr. 192–802, Kaunas 44151; tel. (37) 327427; fax (37) 327447; internet www.kf.lt; private, commercial; Dir ŪDRYS STASELKA.

UAB Laisvoji banga: Lvovo g. 25, Vilnius 09320; tel. and fax (5) 233-3121; e-mail info@laisvojibanga.lt; internet www.europeanhitradio.lt; private, commercial; broadcasts news and music; Dir JŪRATĖ OVERLINGIENĖ.

Laluna: Taikos pr. 81, Klaipėda 94114; tel. (46) 390808; fax (46) 390805; e-mail laluna@laluna.lt; internet www.laluna.lt; private, commercial; Dir TADAS ŽEMAITIS.

M-1: Laisvės pr. 60, Vilnius 05120; tel. (5) 236-0360; fax (5) 236-0366; e-mail m-1@m-1.fm; internet www.m-1.fm; f. 1989; private, commercial; Gen. Man. RŪTA GRUŠNIENĖ.

Mažeikių aidas (MA): POB 17, Ventos g. 49, Mažeikiai 89103; tel. (443) 65055; fax (443) 65600; e-mail info@mazeikiuaidas.lt; internet www.mazeikiuaidas.lt; f. 1996; private, commercial; Dir TOMAS RUGINIS.

Pūkas, UAB: Ringuvos g. 61, Kaunas 45242; tel. (37) 342424; fax (37) 342434; e-mail pukas@pukas.lt; internet www.pukas.lt; f. 1991; private, commercial; operates two radio stations and a television station; Dir KĘSTUTIS PŪKAS.

Radiocentras, UAB: Laisvės pr. 60, Vilnius 05120; tel. (5) 212-8706; fax (5) 242-9073; e-mail biuras@rc.lt; internet www.rc.lt; f. 1991; private, commercial; Gen. Man. ARTŪRAS MIRONCIKAS.

Saulės radijas, UAB: Aušros al. 64, Šiauliai 76235; tel. (41) 525141; fax (41) 424404; e-mail info@saulesradijas.lt; internet www.saulesradijas.lt; private, commercial; Dir RASA AKUČKIENĖ.

Tau: Draugystės g. 19–357, Kaunas 51230; tel. (37) 352790; fax (37) 352128; e-mail info@tau.lt; internet www.tau.lt; private, commercial; Dir GIEDRIUS GIPAS.

VšĮ Kauno radijas ir televizija: S. Daukanto 28A, Kaunas 44246; tel. (37) 321010; fax (37) 322570; e-mail kaunas@lrtv.lt; Dir P. GARNYS.

Znad Wilii, UAB: Laisvės pr. 60, Vilnius 05120; tel. (5) 249-0870; fax (5) 278-4446; e-mail radio@znadwilii.lt; internet www.znadwilii.lt; f. 1992; private, commercial; Dir-Gen. MIROSLAVAS JUCHNEVIČIUS.

Television

Lietuvos televizija (LTV): S. Konarskio 49, Vilnius 03123; tel. (5) 236-3100; fax (5) 216-3282; e-mail lrt@lrt.lt; internet www.lrt.lt; f. 1957; subsidiary of LRT (see Radio); programmes in Lithuanian, Russian, Polish, Ukrainian and Belarusian; Dir RIMVYDAS PALECKIS.

Aidas, UAB (Echo): Birutės skg. 42, Trakai 21114; tel. (528) 52480; fax (528) 55656; e-mail tvaidas@uab.lt; mainly relays German programmes; private, commercial; Dir ČESLOVAS RULEVIČIUS.

Baltijos televizija (BTV): Laisvės pr. 60, Vilnius 05120; tel. (5) 278-0805; fax (5) 278-0804; internet www.btv.lt; f. 1993; broadcasts own programmes and relays German, Polish and US broadcasts; private, commercial; Dir-Gen. GINTARAS SONGAILA.

KTV plius: Nemuno g. 79, Panevėžys 37355; tel. (45) 514103; fax (45) 443561; e-mail pictura@kateka.lt; internet www.ktvplius.lt; private, commercial; Pres. ROLANDAS MEILIŪNAS.

LNK TV (UAB Laisvas ir nepriklausomas kanalas): Šeškinės g. 20, Vilnius 07156; tel. (5) 212-4061; fax (5) 278-4530; e-mail info@lnk.lt; internet www.lnk.lt; private, commercial; broadcasts TV1; Dir PAULIUS KOVAS.

PAN-TV: Respublikos g. 19–8, Panevėžys 35185; tel. (45) 464267; e-mail pantv@takas.lt; private, commercial; Dir SAULIUS BUKELIS.

Raseiniu TV: Vytauto Vilniaus 1A, Raseiniai 60187; tel. (428) 54433; fax (428) 70422; e-mail office@mirkliai.lt; broadcast by VšĮ Raseinių televizijos ir radijo centras; Dir KĘSTUTIS SKAMARAKAS.

Šiaulių TV: Liejyklos g. 10, Šiauliai 78147; tel. and fax (41) 523809; internet www.stv.lt; private; Dir ANDRIUS SEDŽIUS.

TV3: Nemenčinės pl. 4, Vilnius 10102; tel. (5) 276-4264; fax (5) 276-4253; e-mail postmaster@tv3.lt; internet www.tv3.lt; broadcasts own programmes (20% of schedule) in Lithuanian and English, and relays international satellite channels; private, commercial; Dir RAMŪNAS ŠAUČIKOVAS.

Finance

(cap. = capital; res = reserves; dep. = deposits; m. = million; brs = branches; amounts in litai)

BANKING
Central Bank

Bank of Lithuania (Lietuvos bankas): Gedimino pr. 6, Vilnius 01103; tel. (5) 268-0029; fax (5) 262-8124; e-mail info@lb.lt; internet www.lb.lt; f. 1922; re-est. 1990; central bank, responsible for bank supervision; cap. 200.0m., res 632.2m., dep. 7,051.2m. (Dec. 2007); Chair. of Bd REINOLDIJUS ŠARKINAS; 2 brs.

Commercial Banks

Bankas Hansabankas: Savanorių pr. 19, Vilnius 03502; tel. (5) 268-4444; fax (52) 268-4700; e-mail info@hansa.lt; internet www.hansa.lt; f. 1919; as Lietuvos Taupomasis Bankas; present name adopted 2003; 99.5% owned by AS Hansapank (Estonia); cap. 569.7m., res 150.3m., dep. 12,394.9m. (Dec. 2006); Chair. of Bd GIEDRIUS DUSEVIČIUS.

Bankas Snoras: A. Vivulskio g. 7, Vilnius 03221; tel. (5) 239-2239; fax (5) 232-7300; e-mail info@snoras.com; internet www.snoras.com; f. 1992; cap. 504.5m., dep. 3,627m., total assets 5,754m. (Dec. 2007); Chair. of Supervisory Bd VLADIMIR ANTONOV; Chair. of Management Bd RAIMONDAS BARANAUSKAS.

DnB NORD Bankas: J. Basanavičiaus g. 26, Vilnius 03601; tel. (5) 239-3444; fax (5) 213-9056; e-mail info@dnbnord.lt; internet www.dnbnord.lt; f. 1924; registered as AB Lietuvos Žemės Ūkio Bankas in 1993; privatized in March 2002; present name adopted 2006; 93.1% obtained by Bank DnB Nord A/S (Denmark) in Dec. 2005; cap. 404.5m., res 4.4m., dep. 6,769.5m. (Dec. 2006); Chair. of Management Bd, Pres. and CEO WERNER SCHILLI; 77 brs.

Medicinos Bankas (Medical Bank): Pamėnkalnio g. 40, Vilnius 01114; tel. (5) 264-4800; fax (5) 264-4801; e-mail info@medbank.lt; internet www.medbank.lt; f. 1992; cap. 34.3m., res 9.3m., dep. 337.8m. (Dec. 2006); Chair. of Bd KĘSTUTIS OLŠAUSKAS; 7 brs.

Parex Bankas: K. Kalinausko g. 13, Vilnius 03107; tel. (5) 266-4600; fax (5) 266-4601; e-mail info@parex.lt; internet www.parex.lt; f. 1996; owned by Parex Group (Latvia); cap. 115.0m., res 0.5m., dep. 445.9m. (June 2007); Chair. and Chief Exec. ALMA VAITKUNSKIENE; 6 brs.

Sampo Bankas: Geležinio Vilko g. 18, Vilnius 08500; tel. (5) 210-9400; fax (5) 210-9409; e-mail bankas@sampo.lt; internet www.sampo.lt; f. 1994; fmrly Lithuanian Development Bank; present name adopted 2004; 100% owned by Danske Bank A/S (Denmark); cap. 234.9m., res 3.7m., dep. 3,781.9m. (Dec. 2006); Chair. of Bd GINTAUTAS GALVANAUSKAS.

SEB Bankas (SEB Bank): Gedimino pr. 12, Vilnius 01103; tel. (5) 268-2800; fax (5) 268-2333; e-mail info@seb.lt; internet www.seb.lt; f. 1990 as Spaudos Bankas; present name adopted 2008; 99.7% owned by Skandinaviska Enskilda Banken AB (Sweden); cap. 1,034.6m., res 24.0m., dep. 16,950.1m. (Dec. 2006); Pres. and Chief Exec. AUDRIUS ŽIUGŽDA.

Šiaulių Bankas: Tilžės str. 149, Šiauliai 76348; tel. (41) 595607; fax (41) 430774; internet www.sb.lt; f. 1992; cap. 180.3m., res 281.2m., dep. 1,350.0m. (July 2008); Chair. of Bd ALGIRDAS BUTKUS; 60 brs and client service centres (2007).

Ūkio Bankas: Maironio g. 25, Kaunas 44250; tel. (37) 301301; fax (37) 323188; e-mail ub@ub.lt; internet www.ub.lt; f. 1989; cap. 176.7m., res 180.0m., dep. 2,695.6m. (Dec. 2006); Chair. of Bd EDITA KARPAVIČIENE; Chief Exec. GINTARAS UGIANSKIS; 12 brs.

Property Bank

Turto Bankas AB: Kęstučio g. 45, Vilnius 08124; tel. (5) 278-0900; fax (5) 275-1155; e-mail info@turtas.lt; internet www.turtas.lt; f. 1996; cap. and res 9.7m., total assets 69.5m. (Dec. 2003); recovery of non-performing loans, administration of loans of the Ministry of Finance; Chair. of Bd JONAS BUDREVIČIUS; 6 brs.

Banking Association

Association of Lithuanian Banks (Lietuvos Bankų Asociacija): Ankštoji g. 5/3, Vilnius 01109; tel. (5) 249-6669; fax (5) 249-6139; e-mail info@lba.lt; internet www.lba.lt; f. 1991; Pres. STASYS KROPAS; 11 mems.

STOCK EXCHANGE

Vilnius Stock Exchange (VSE) (Vilniaus vertybinių popierių birža): Konstitucijos pr. 7, Vilnius 08501; tel. (5) 272-3871; fax (5) 272-4894; e-mail vilnius@nasdaqomxgroup.com; internet www.nasdaqomxbaltic.com; f. 1993; 93.1% owned by the NASDAQ OMX Group (USA); Chair. of Bd ARMINTA SALADŽIENĖ.

INSURANCE

Principal Insurance Companies

Commercial Union Lietuva Gyvybės draudimas: Jogailos g. 4, Vilnius 01116; tel. (5) 269-0169; fax (5) 269-0269; internet www.commercialunion.lt; f. 2001; owned by Commercial Union Polska—Towarzystwo Ubezpieczeń na Życie SA (Poland), part of the Aviva Group (United Kingdom); Dir A. UNGULAITIENĖ.

Ergo Lietuva: Geležinio vilko g. 6A, Vilnius 03507; tel. (5) 268-3000; fax (5) 268-3005; e-mail info@ergo.lt; internet www.ergo.lt; f. 1991; owned by Ergo International AG (Germany); formerly Drauda UAB; name changed as above in 2000; in 2002 merged with Preventa; Dir S. JOKUBAITIS.

Hansa Gyvybės draudimas UAB: J. Basanavičiaus g. 8/Vingrių g. 1, Vilnius 01118; tel. (5) 266-5966; fax (5) 268-5866; e-mail info@hansa.lt; internet www.hansadraudimas.lt; f. 1995; owned by Hansabankas AB (Estonia); formerly Lietuvos Draudimo Gyvybės draudimas; Lithuania's leading life insurer; Dir D. VALENTUKEVIČIUS.

Lietuvos draudimas AB (Lithuanian Insurance): J. Basanavičiaus g. 12, Vilnius 03600; tel. (5) 243-1167; fax (5) 231-4138; e-mail info@ldr.lt; internet www.ld.lt; f. 1921; privatized in 1999; part of RSA group (United Kingdom); principal non-life insurance co in Lithuania; CEO KĘSTUTIS ŠERPYTIS.

PZU Lietuva UAB: Konstitucijos pr. 7, Vilnius 09308; tel. (5) 279-0007; fax (5) 279-0019; e-mail info@pzu.lt; internet www.pzu.lt; f. 1993; owned by Powszechny Zaklad Ubezpieczen (PZU) SA (Poland); Dir G. MAŽEIKA.

SEB VB Gyvybės Draudimas UAB: Gedimino pr. 12, Vilnius 01103; tel. (5) 268-1555; fax (5) 268-1556; e-mail draudimas@seb.lt; internet www.vbgd.lt; f. 1999; owned by SEB Vilniaus bankas AB; Dir B. KAMUNTAVIČIENĖ.

Insurance Association

Association of Lithuanian Insurers: Vytenio g. 50, Vilnius 03229; tel. (5) 231-0381; e-mail asociacija@draudikai.lt; internet www.draudikai.lt; f. 1992; Dir ANDRIUS ROMANOVSKIS.

Supervisory Body

Insurance Supervisory Commission: Ukmergės g. 222, Vilnius 07157; tel. (5) 243-1370; fax (5) 272-3689; e-mail dpk@dpk.lt; internet www.dpk.lt; Chair. MINDAUGAS ŠALČIUS.

Trade and Industry

GOVERNMENT AGENCY

State Property Fund (Valstybės Turto Fondas—VTS): Vilniaus g. 16, Vilnius 01507; tel. (5) 268-4999; fax (5) 268-4997; e-mail info@vtf.lt; internet www.vtf.lt; f. 1995; privatization and management of state-owned and municipal property; Chair. GEDIMINAS RAINYS; Dir-Gen. AUDRIUS RUDYS.

DEVELOPMENT AGENCY

National Regional Development Agency (Nacionalinė Regionų Plėtros Agentūra): Lukiskių g. 5/502, Vilnius 01108; tel. and fax (5) 233-4151; e-mail nrda@nrda.lt; internet www.nrda.lt; f. 1999 by the Asscn of Lithuanian Chambers of Commerce, Industry and Crafts; Dir VAIDAS KAZAKEVIČIUS.

CHAMBERS OF COMMERCE

Association of Lithuanian Chambers of Commerce, Industry and Crafts (Lietuvos prekybos, pramonės ir amatų rūmų asociacija): J. Tumo-Vaižganto g. 9/1–63A, Vilnius 01108; tel. (5) 261-2102; fax (5) 261-2112; e-mail info@chambers.lt; internet www.chambers.lt; f. 1992; mem. of International Chamber of Commerce and of Asscn of European Chambers of Commerce and Industry; Pres. DARIUS MOCKUS.

Kaunas Chamber of Commerce, Industry and Crafts: K. Donelaičio g. 8, POB 2111, Kaunas 44213; tel. (37) 229212; fax (37) 208330; e-mail chamber@chamber.lt; internet www.chamber.lt; f. 1925; re-est. 1991; br. at Marijampolė; Pres. Prof. M. RONDOMANSKAS.

Klaipėda Chamber of Commerce, Industry and Crafts: Danės g. 17, POB 148, Klaipėda 92117; tel. (46) 390861; fax (46) 410626; internet www.kcci.lt; Pres. SIGITAS PAULAUSKAS; Dir VIKTORAS KROLIS; 250 mems.

Panevėžys Chamber of Commerce, Industry and Crafts: Respublikos g. 34, Panevėžys 35173; tel. (45) 463687; fax (45) 462227; e-mail panevezys@chambers.lt; internet www.ccic.lt; f. 1991; Pres. VYTAUTAS ŠIDLAUSKAS; Gen. Dir VYTAUTAS KAZAKEVIČIUS.

Šiauliai Chamber of Commerce, Industry and Crafts: Vilniaus g. 88, Šiauliai 76285; tel. (41) 523224; fax (41) 523903; e-mail siauliai@chambers.lt; internet www.rumai.lt; f. 1993; Dir-Gen. RIMUNDAS DOMARKAS.

Vilnius Chamber of Commerce, Industry and Crafts: Algirdo g. 31, Vilnius 03219; tel. (5) 213-5550; fax (5) 213-5542; e-mail vilnius@cci.lt; internet www.cci.lt; f. 1991; Dir-Gen. BORISAS ZAUBIDOVAS; 480 mems.

LITHUANIA   *Directory*

INDUSTRIAL ASSOCIATION

Lithuanian Confederation of Industrialists (Lietuvos pramonininkų konfederacija—LPK): A. Vienuolio g. 8, Vilnius 01104; tel. (5) 212-5217; fax (5) 212-5209; e-mail sekretoriatas@lpk.lt; internet www.lpk.lt; f. 1989; Pres. BRONISLOVAS LUBYS.

EMPLOYERS' ORGANIZATION

Lithuanian Business Employers' Confederation (Lietuvos verslo darbdavių konfederacija—LVDK): Algirdo g. 31, Vilnius 03219; tel. (5) 249-8345; fax (5) 249-6448; e-mail info@lvdk.w3.lt; internet www.ldkonfederacija.lt; f. 1999; Gen. Dir DANAS ARLAUSKAS.

UTILITIES

Energy Agency (Energetikos agentūra): Gedimino pr. 38/Vasario 16-osios g. 2, Vilnius 01104; tel. (5) 261-9225; fax (5) 262-6845; e-mail eainfo@ukmin.lt; internet www.ena.lt; f. 1993; state enterprise; attached to the Ministry of the Economy; Dir MARIJUS FRANCKEVIČIUS.

Electricity

Ignalina Nuclear Power Plant (Ignalinos Atominė Elektrinė): Karklų k., Visaginas 31500; tel. (386) 28350; fax (386) 29350; e-mail info@mail.iae.lt; internet www.iae.lt; f. 1985; first unit decommissioned in 2004; remaining unit due to be decommissioned in 2009; Dir VIKTOR SHEVALDIN.

Lietuvos Elektros Organizaciją (LEO LT AB) (Lithuanian Electricity Organization): Žvejų g. 14, Vilnius 09310; tel. (5) 278-2700; fax (5) 278-2750; e-mail info@leolt.lt; internet www.leolt.lt; holding co; owns controlling shares in three main power production and distribution cos; aims to invest in the construction of a new nuclear power plant to replace that at Ignalina (q.v.), and in planned electricity links with Poland and Sweden; 61.7% owned by the Republic of Lithuania and 38.3% by NDX Energija; f. 2008; Chair. of Supervisory Council VIRGILIJUS PODERYS; Chair. of Management Bd and CEO (vacant).

  Lietuvos Energija AB (Lithuanian Power): Žvejų g. 14, Vilnius 09310; tel. (5) 262-6822; fax (5) 212-6736; e-mail info@lietuvosenergija.lt; internet www.lpc.lt; f. 1995; restructured in 2000; 96.5% owned by LEO LT AB; Chair. of Bd and Gen. Dir DARIUS MASIONIS.

  Rytų Skirstomieji Tinklai AB (RST) (Eastern Distribution Networks): P. Lukšio g. 5B, Vilnius 08221; tel. (5) 277-7524; fax (5) 277-7514; e-mail info@rst.lt; internet www.rst.lt; f. 2001 following the reorganization of Lietuvos Energija AB; distribution network operator and public supplier of four regions; 156,000 customers (Dec. 2002); Dir RIMANTAS MILIŠAUSKAS.

  Vakarų Skirstomieji Tinklai AB (VST): Jasinskio g. 16C, Vilnius 01112; tel. (5) 2781204; fax (5) 2781269; e-mail ir@vst.lt; internet www.vst.lt; f. 2001; distribution in central and western Lithuania; 97.1% owned by LEO LT AB; Chief Exec. AIDAS IGNATAVIČIUS; 2,000 employees.

Gas

Lietuvos Dujos AB (Lithuanian Gas): Aguonų g. 24, Vilnius 03212; tel. (5) 236-0210; fax (5) 236-0200; e-mail ld@lietuvosdujos.lt; internet www.dujos.lt; f. 1995; natural gas import, sale and transportation; 17.7% state-owned; 38.9% owned by E.ON Ruhrgas International AG (Germany); 37.1% owned by OAO Gazprom (Russia); Chair. Dr ACHIM SAUL; Gen. Man. VIKTORAS VALENTUKEVIČIUS; 1,900 employees.

TRADE UNIONS

Lithuanian Labour Federation (Lietuvos Darbo Federacija): Vytauto g. 14, Vilnius 03106; tel. and fax (5) 231-2029; e-mail ldforg@ldf.lt; internet www.ldf.lt; f. 1919 as a Christian trade-union org.; re-est. 1991; 20,000 mems; Chair. VYDAS PUSKEPALIS; Sec.-Gen. JANINA ŠVEDIENĖ.

Lithuanian Trade Union Confederation (Lietuvos profesinių sąjungų konfederacija—LPSK): J. Jasinskio g. 9–213, Vilnius 01111; tel. (5) 249-6921; fax (5) 249-8078; e-mail lpsk@lpsk.lt; internet www.lpsk.lt; f. 2002 by merger of Lithuanian Union of Trade Unions (LPSS) and Lithuanian Trade Union Centre (LPSC); 25 branch trade unions with 120,000 mems; Pres. ARTŪRAS ČERNIAUSKAS.

Lithuanian Trade Union: Solidarumas (Lietuvos profesinė sąjunga 'Solidarumas'): K. Kalinausko 2, Vilnius; tel. (5) 262-1743; fax (5) 213-3295; e-mail info@lps.lt; internet www.lps.lt; f. 2002; fmrly the Lithuanian Workers' Union: Labora (f. 1989); Pres. ALDONA JAŠINSKIENĖ; 52,000 mems.

Transport

RAILWAYS

In 2008 there were 1,765 km of railway track in use in Lithuania, of which 122 km were electrified. Main lines link Vilnius with Minsk (Belarus), Kaliningrad (Russia) and Warsaw (Poland), in the latter case by way of the Belarusian town of Grodno (Horadnia).

Lithuanian Railways (Lietuvos geležinkeliai): Mindaugo g. 12–14, Vilnius 03603; tel. (5) 269-2038; fax (5) 269-2028; e-mail lgkanc@litrail.lt; internet www.litrail.lt; f. 1991; Dir-Gen. STASYS DAILYDKA; 10,392 employees.

ROADS

In 2007 the total length of the road network was estimated at 80,715 km, 88% of which were paved; the motorway network totalled 309 km.

Lithuanian Road Administration (Lietuvos automobilių kelių direkcija—LAKD): J. Basanavičiaus g. 36/2, Vilnius 03109; tel. (5) 232-9600; fax (5) 232-9609; e-mail lra@lra.lt; internet www.lra.lt; Dir-Gen. VIRGAUDAS PUODŽIUKAS.

SHIPPING

The main port is at Klaipėda. In 2007 there were 441 km of inland navigable waterways.

Port Authority

Klaipėda State Seaport Authority: J. Janonio g. 24, Klaipėda 92251; tel. (46) 499799; fax (46) 499777; e-mail info@port.lt; internet www.port.lt; multi-purpose, deep-water universal port; connects sea, land and rail routes from east and west; Dir-Gen. ALGIRDAS KAMARAUSKAS (acting).

Shipowning Company

Lithuanian Shipping Company (AB Lietuvos Jūrų Laivininkystė): Malunininku g. 3, Klaipėda 92264; tel. (46) 393105; fax (46) 393119; e-mail gp@ljl.lt; internet www.ljl.lt; f. 1969 as LISCO; partially privatized and renamed as above in June 2001; 73.24% state-owned; transportation of cargo; owns 18 vessels; Gen. Dir VYTAUTAS VISMANTAS.

CIVIL AVIATION

There are international airports at Vilnius, Kaunas, Palanga and Šiauliai.

Directorate of Civil Aviation (Oro Navigacija): Rodūnios kelias 2, Vilnius 02188; tel. (5) 273-9102; fax (5) 273-9161; e-mail info@ans.lt; internet www.ans.lt; Dir-Gen. ALGIMANTAS RAŠČIUS.

flyLAL Charters UAB: A. Gustaičio g. 4, Vilnius 02512; tel. (5) 252-5660; fax (5) 252-5661; e-mail info@flylalcharters.com; internet www.flylalcharters.com; f. 2007; owned by flyLAL Group Services AB; operates passenger and cargo charter flights; CEO ERIKAS ZUBRUS.

Tourism

Tourist attractions in Lithuania include the historic cities of Vilnius, Kaunas, Kėdainiai, Trakai and Klaipėda, coastal resorts, such as Palanga and Kuršių Nerija, and picturesque countryside. Some 756,855 tourists visited the country in 2006; tourist receipts totalled US $1,077m. (including passenger transport).

Lithuanian State Department of Tourism: Švitrigailos 11M, Vilnius 03228; tel. (5) 210-8796; fax (5) 210-8753; e-mail vtd@tourism.lt; internet www.tourism.lt; Dir NIJOLĖ KLIOKIENĖ.

LUXEMBOURG

Introductory Survey

Location, Climate, Language, Religion, Flag, Capital

The Grand Duchy of Luxembourg is a land-locked country in western Europe. It is bordered by Belgium to the west and north, by Germany to the east and by France to the south. The climate is temperate, with cool summers and mild winters. In Luxembourg-Ville the average temperature ranges from 1°C (33°F) in January to 18°C (64°F) in July, while annual rainfall averages 782 mm. Lëtzebuergesch (Luxembourgish), a German-Moselle-Frankish dialect, is the spoken language and became the official language in 1984. French is generally used for administrative purposes, while German is the principal written language of commerce and the press. Almost all of the inhabitants profess Christianity: about 87% are Roman Catholics and a small minority are Protestants. The national flag (proportions 3 by 5) consists of three equal horizontal stripes, of red, white and blue. The capital is Luxembourg-Ville (Lützelburg).

Recent History

As a founder member of the European Community (EC, now European Union—EU, see p. 255), of which Luxembourg-Ville is one of the main bases, Luxembourg has played a significant role in progress towards European integration since the Second World War. Luxembourg's commitment to such integration was exemplified by its status as one of the original signatories to the Schengen Agreement (named after the town in Luxembourg where the accord was signed by a number of EC member countries in June 1990), which binds signatories to the abolition of internal border controls.

The Belgo-Luxembourg Economic Union (BLEU) has existed since 1921, except for the period from 1940–44, when the Grand Duchy was subject to wartime occupation by Germany. In 1948 the Benelux Economic Union (see p. 425) was inaugurated between Belgium, Luxembourg and the Netherlands, becoming effective in 1960, and establishing the three countries as a single customs area in 1970.

In November 1964 Grand Duchess Charlotte abdicated, after a reign of 45 years, and was succeeded by her son, Prince Jean.

Pierre Werner, leader of the Chrëschtlech Sozial Vollekspartei (CSV—Christian Social Party), became Prime Minister in February 1959 and, during 1959–74, led successive coalition governments in which the CSV was the dominant partner, along with either the Demokratesch Partei (DP—Democratic Party) or the Lëtzebuerger Sozialistesch Arbechterpartei (LSAP—Socialist Workers' Party of Luxembourg). However, at a general election in May 1974 the CSV suffered a decrease in popularity, and, for the first time since 1919, entered into opposition. In the following month a centre-left coalition between the DP and the LSAP was formed under the premiership of the leader of the DP, Gaston Thorn. At the next general election, which took place in June 1979, the CSV increased its representation in the 59-member Chamber of Deputies (Chambre des Députés) from 18 to 24 seats. In July Werner again formed a coalition Government, comprising the CSV and the DP, which held 15 seats.

At a general election in June 1984 the CSV secured the largest number of seats (25) in the enlarged 64-member legislature. However, the success of the LSAP, which took 21 seats (compared with 14 in the previous election), was widely attributed to general dissatisfaction with an economic austerity programme, which had been introduced during the early 1980s, and with the rising level of unemployment. A centre-left coalition was formed in July 1984 between the CSV and the LSAP, with Jacques Santer of the CSV (hitherto Minister of Finance, Labour and Social Security) as Prime Minister. Elections to the Chamber of Deputies (whose membership had been reduced to 60 in January 1989) took place in June 1989. The CSV, the LSAP and the DP each lost three seats (obtaining 22, 18 and 11 seats, respectively). In the following month Santer renewed the outgoing coalition. At the next general election, in June 1994, the CSV and the LSAP each lost one representative in the legislature, winning 21 and 17 seats, respectively; the DP secured 12 seats. The CSV-LSAP coalition was again renewed, with Santer as Prime Minister. In January 1995 Santer took office as President of the Commission of the EU. He was succeeded as Prime Minister by Jean-Claude Juncker of the CSV, hitherto Minister of the Budget, of Finance and of Labour.

The two coalition partners both recorded losses at the general election held concurrently with elections to the European Parliament on 13 June 1999, the CSV winning 19 seats and the LSAP 13. The DP increased its representation from 12 to 15 seats, while the conservative Aktiounskomitee fir Demokratie a Rentegerechtegkeet (ADR—Action Committee for Democracy and Pensions Justice) took seven seats (an increase of two). The environmentalist party, Déi Gréng (The Greens), retained its five seats in the legislature. Juncker, who remained as Prime Minister, subsequently formed a new centre-right coalition of the CSV and the DP, which took office in early August.

In March 1998 Grand Duke Jean conferred broad constitutional powers upon his eldest son and heir, Prince Henri, permitting him to deputize for the Grand Duke in all official capacities. On 7 October 2000 Prince Henri succeeded his father as Head of State.

Luxembourg's banking secrecy laws have for many years been a cause of concern. In April 1993 legislation was introduced that permitted the confiscation of deposits in Luxembourg banks accruing from suspected illegal drugs-related activities and in 1997 the powers of confiscation were extended to include other illegal activities, including arms-smuggling. During 1997 the country's financial sector came under renewed scrutiny when the Belgian authorities conducted an investigation into alleged widespread tax evasion by Belgian citizens and companies based in Luxembourg. The German authorities also launched a similar investigation. Luxembourg was further criticized for refusing, as did Switzerland, to endorse the code of conduct with respect to tax havens drafted by the Organisation for Economic Co-operation and Development (OECD, see p. 358) in April 1998. During 1998 Luxembourg also opposed European Commission proposals for European taxation harmonization, which would oblige Luxembourg to impose tax on non-residents' interest and dividend income for the first time, thereby reducing the attraction of Luxembourg as a financial centre. It was in May 2000, however, that Luxembourg first endorsed OECD proposals aimed at limiting the use of bank secrecy laws for the purpose of tax evasion. In October the Chamber of Deputies approved a relaxation of bank secrecy laws to facilitate co-operation with the US Internal Revenue Service in its attempts to halt tax evasion. Luxembourg was exempted for at least six years from a requirement for EU member states to exchange banking information from 2005 under new EU taxation rules concerning overseas investments agreed in early 2003 (see Economic Affairs).

In December 2000 the Government was prominent during negotiations regarding the Treaty of Nice, which aimed to reform the institutions of the EU in light of its forthcoming enlargements. The terms of the Treaty substantially safeguarded Luxembourg's privileged position in the EU: Luxembourg was to continue to have a European Commissioner, to maintain its six seats in the European Parliament and to continue to enjoy a voting weight in the Council of the European Union out of proportion to its size. In July 2001 the Chamber of Deputies ratified the Treaty by a large majority. At the same time, Luxembourg continued, much to the frustration of most of its EU partners, to oppose the removal of the Secretariat of the European Parliament from Luxembourg-Ville, together with its 1,500 staff, whose continued presence was considered by the Luxembourg Government to be vital to the local economy.

At the general election held on 13 June 2004 the CSV increased its representation in the legislature from 19 to 24 seats. The LSAP secured 14 seats, while the DP took 10, five fewer than in 1999. Déi Gréng won seven seats and the ADR secured five. A new coalition Government comprising members of the CSV and the LSAP was sworn in on 31 July, again under the leadership of Juncker. The CSV assumed nine of the 15 ministerial posts, retaining the finance and justice portfolios and gaining the Ministry of the Interior and Spatial Planning. Jean Asselborn of the LSAP was appointed as Deputy Prime Minister and Minister of Foreign Affairs and Immigration.

A minor reorganization of the CSV government portfolios, which took effect in February 2006, was designed to enable the ministers concerned to focus on the areas of employment and the budget. Jean-Louis Schiltz, hitherto Minister of Co-operation and Humanitarian Action and Minister-delegate of Communications, assumed full ministerial responsibility for communications from Juncker and was also allocated the defence portfolio, becoming Minister of Co-operation and Humanitarian Action, of Communications and of Defence. The former Minister of Defence, Luc Frieden, retained his responsibilities as Minister of Justice and of the Treasury and Budget.

In April 2006 the ADR adopted a new name, Alternativ Demokratesch Reformpartei (Alternative Democratic Reform Party), in an attempt to broaden its appeal. However, the concurrent redesign of the party's logo to incorporate the colours of the national flag provoked criticism that it was adopting a more right-wing, nationalist stance. Several members of the ADR subsequently resigned from the party, including one of its five deputies, who remained in the legislature as an independent; the ADR consequently lost its status as an official parliamentary group.

In January 2008 two former police officers were arrested in connection with a bombing campaign that targeted a number of public buildings in 1985. Later that month both the General Director and the Secretary-General of the police force, Pierre Reuland and Guy Stebens, were suspended from office, following the publication of an open letter by the Attorney-General, Robert Biever, in which he expressed doubts over the credibility of public statements made by the two officials regarding the original investigation into the attacks; Reuland and Stebens were dismissed in September.

In February 2008 Luxembourg became the third EU member state (along with Belgium and the Netherlands) to approve legislation decriminalizing euthanasia and assisted suicide, despite opposition from the governing CSV. However, in early December Grand Duke Henri precipitated a constitutional crisis by indicating that he would refuse to ratify the legislation, citing his religious convictions. Despite his own party's opposition to the bill, Juncker criticized the Grand Duke for disregarding the expressed will of parliament and announced a proposal to amend Article 34 of the Constitution, thereby removing the Grand Duke's powers to veto legislation adopted by the legislature. The amendment was approved by the Chamber of Deputies in December and received final approval at a second reading in March 2009. Meanwhile, in December 2008 the legislation decriminalizing euthanasia and assisted suicide was approved, by 31 votes to 26, at a second reading in the Chamber of Deputies and was promulgated by Grand Duke Henri in March 2009.

Popular opposition in Luxembourg to a potential US-led military campaign in Iraq to remove the regime of Saddam Hussain culminated in nation-wide demonstrations on 15 February 2003. The Government's opposition to the military intervention (which was undertaken the following month without the support of a UN resolution), although muted, adversely affected relations with the USA. Following the swift removal of the Iraqi regime, however, the Luxembourg Government announced the allocation of €3.5m. for the financing of a humanitarian aid programme for Iraq. In March Parliament approved the secondment of 10 officers and men to the International Security Assistance Force in Afghanistan (ISAF), and, as part of the EU's first ever military operation, that of one officer to the Union's peace-keeping mission to the former Yugoslav republic of Macedonia. Four EU countries—Luxembourg, Belgium, France and Germany—all of which had opposed the US-led military campaign in Iraq, held a special summit in April to discuss defence matters, at which it was agreed to establish an autonomous European military command headquarters near Brussels, Belgium. The plan, which provoked protests from the USA and the United Kingdom, was superseded in December by a compromise agreement between France, Germany and the United Kingdom to create an EU 'planning cell' within existing defence structures.

On 1 January 2005 Juncker commenced a two-year appointment as Chairman of the Eurogroup (comprising the EU member states that belong to the euro zone). In this capacity Juncker would represent the members of the euro zone at global financial summits and would be instrumental in shaping European economic policy. Also in January Luxembourg assumed the rotating six-month presidency of the Council of the European Union. During the Luxembourg presidency the reform of the Stability and Growth Pact was successfully negotiated, the Lisbon Agenda, which aimed to create sustainable economic prosperity and full employment, was relaunched, and a new framework for relations with Russia was adopted. On 10 July Luxembourg held a national referendum (the first since 1936) on the EU constitutional treaty, which had finally been approved by the EU in mid-2004. Although there were concerns that the proposed constitution was not wholly advantageous for the smaller member states of the EU, the vast majority of political parties in Luxembourg supported the document and Juncker threatened to resign if the electorate rejected the treaty. Opposition to the treaty increased when the French and Dutch, at respective referendums in May and June, voted against its ratification. None the less, the draft treaty was approved by some 56.5% of the Luxembourg electorate. In June 2007, at a summit meeting of EU heads of state and of government in Brussels, a preliminary agreement was reached over a reform treaty to replace the constitutional treaty rejected by French and Dutch voters in 2005. On 13 December 2007 the reform treaty was signed by EU leaders, including Juncker, following a summit meeting in Lisbon, Portugal. The so-called Treaty of Lisbon was ratified by the Chamber of Deputies in late May 2008, but its future remained uncertain following its rejection at a referendum in Ireland in June.

In June 2008, at a summit meeting in The Hague, Netherlands, Juncker and his counterparts from Belgium and the Netherlands signed a new Benelux Treaty on political and economic co-operation. The document expanded the scope of the previous treaty, signed in 1958, to provide for greater co-operation between the three Governments on justice and home affairs, as well as customs and cross-border trade. In recognition of this, the official title was to change from the Benelux Economic Union to the Benelux Union. The treaty was expected to be ratified by all three countries during 2009 and to enter into effect on 1 January 2010.

Government

Luxembourg is an hereditary and constitutional monarchy. Legislative power is exercised by the unicameral Chamber of Deputies (Chambre des Députés), with 60 members elected by universal adult suffrage for five years (subject to dissolution) on the basis of proportional representation. Some legislative functions are also entrusted to the advisory State Council (Conseil d'Etat), with 21 members appointed for life by the Grand Duke, but decisions made by this body can be overruled by the legislature.

Executive power is vested in the Grand Duke, but is normally exercised by the Council of Ministers, led by the President of the Government (Prime Minister). The Grand Duke appoints ministers, but they are responsible to the legislature. Luxembourg is divided into three districts (Luxembourg, Diekirch, Grevenmacher), 12 cantons and 118 municipalities.

Defence

Luxembourg was a founder member of the North Atlantic Treaty Organization (NATO, see p. 351) in 1949. Compulsory military service was abolished in 1967, but Luxembourg maintains an army of volunteers, totalling 900, and a gendarmerie numbering 612 (as at November 2008). Expenditure of some €263m. was allocated to defence in the budget for 2007. In March 1987 the country became a signatory of the Benelux military convention, together with Belgium and the Netherlands, which was intended to standardize training methods and military equipment in the three countries. In November 2004 the European Union (EU, see p. 255) ministers responsible for defence agreed to create a number of 'battlegroups' (each comprising 1,000–1,500 troops), which could be deployed at short notice to crisis areas around the world. The EU battlegroups, two of which were to be ready for deployment at any one time, following a rotational schedule, reached full operational capacity from 1 January 2007. Luxembourg participated in a battlegroup with France, Germany and Belgium.

Economic Affairs

In 2007, according to estimates by the World Bank, Luxembourg's gross national income (GNI), measured at average 2005–07 prices, was US $36,419.6m., equivalent to $75,880 per head (or $63,590 per head on an international purchasing-power parity basis). During 2000–07, it was estimated, the population increased at an average rate of 1.3% per year, while gross domestic product (GDP) per head grew, in real terms, by an average of 2.4% per year during the same period. Overall GDP increased, in real terms, at an average annual rate of 3.7% in 2000–07; growth was 4.5% in 2007.

Agriculture (including forestry and fishing) contributed 0.3% of GDP in 2007. In the same year 1.4% of the employed labour force were engaged in the agricultural sector. The principal crops are cereals, potatoes and wine grapes. Livestock-rearing is also of some importance. Agricultural GDP decreased at an average annual rate of 3.3% in 2000–06. Real agricultural GDP declined by 0.1% in 2007.

Industry (including mining, manufacturing, construction and power) provided 15.6% of GDP in 2007, and engaged 21.3% of the employed labour force in 2007. Industrial GDP increased, in real terms, at an average annual rate of 2.3% in 2000–06, and rose by 2.6% in 2007.

Manufacturing activities constitute the most important industrial sector, contributing 8.6% of GDP in 2007 and engaging 10.6% of the employed work-force in 2005. Although the country's deposits of iron ore are no longer exploited, the iron and steel industry remains one of the most important sectors of the Luxembourg economy; metal manufactures accounted for 33.2% of total exports in 2007. The Luxembourg steel industry is dominated by Arcelor Mittal, which was formed from a merger of Arcelor and Mittal Steel in 2006. Machinery and other equipment provided 18.1% of total exports in 2007. Other important branches of manufacturing are basic manufactures and chemicals and related products. Real manufacturing GDP increased by an average of 0.3% per year in 2000–06; it grew by 2.2% in 2007.

In 2005 66.1% of net electricity production was thermal, while 20.9% was from hydroelectric installations. Imports of mineral fuels and lubricants comprised 12.8% of the value of total imports in 2007.

The services sector contributed 84.0% of GDP in 2007, and engaged 77.2% of the employed labour force in 2007. Favourable laws governing banking secrecy and taxation encouraged the development of Luxembourg as a major international financial centre. Financial services contributed 25.8% of GDP in 2007. In January 2009 there were 152 banks in Luxembourg, most of which are foreign-owned. In 2005 there were 12,600 holding companies registered in Luxembourg. In accordance with the demands of the European Commission, however, Luxembourg abolished its preferential tax regime for holding companies from 1 January 2007, although existing companies were permitted to retain their tax benefits until 2010. The replacement regime, the Family Private Assets Management Company, which was aimed at the wealth management sector, was introduced in 2007. Stock exchange activities (notably the 'Eurobond' market and investment portfolio management) are also prominent. From the mid-1990s Luxembourg has had the largest investment fund sector in Europe: in 2005 investment funds accounted for 8% of GDP. In 2007 there were 94 approved insurance companies in Luxembourg, as well as 262 reinsurance companies. The GDP of the services sector increased, in real terms, at an average annual rate of 4.1% in 2000–06; it rose by 5.9% in 2007.

In 2007, according to IMF figures, Luxembourg recorded a visible trade deficit of US $4,809.7m., but there was a surplus of $4,928.2m. on the current account of the balance of payments. Other members of the European Union (EU, see p. 255) account for much of Luxembourg's foreign trade. In 2007 the principal source of imports (33.8%) was Belgium; other major providers were Germany (29.3%), France (11.6%) and the Netherlands (6.2%). The principal market for exports in that year was Germany (26.4%); other major purchasers were France (16.6%), Belgium (12.5%) and Italy (5.4%). The principal exports in 2007 were manufactured goods, particularly metal manufactures, and machinery. The principal imports were machinery, transport equipment, manufactured articles, notably metal manufactures, and mineral fuels and lubricants.

In 2007 a budgetary surplus of €287,900, equivalent to 0.8% of GDP, was recorded. Government debt was equivalent to 6.9% of GDP in 2007. The annual rate of inflation averaged 2.5% in 2000–07; consumer prices rose by 2.3% in 2007. The rate of unemployment averaged 2.8% in 2007. In 2006 cross-border commuters from neighbouring states totalled 143,858, constituting more than one-third of the total employed in Luxembourg.

Luxembourg was a founder member of the EU, and participated in the introduction of the European single currency, the euro, on 1 January 1999. It also belongs to the Benelux Economic Union (see p. 425), which was to be renamed the Benelux Union.

Luxembourg's economy expanded at an average annual rate of more than 5% during 1985–2000, recording increases in GDP even in the early 1990s when neighbouring countries were in recession. The country's economic success was based on its development as an international financial centre, following the decline in the importance of the country's previously dominant iron and steel industry. By 2008 the country was the third largest centre in the world for private banking, after Switzerland and the Caribbean islands; approximately 25% of all investment funds in Europe were registered in Luxembourg and the financial sector accounted for nearly 30% of GDP. The rapid economic expansion of the late 1990s slowed significantly in 2000–03, when GDP growth averaged only 2.9% per year. A recovery followed, however, with GDP growth rising to 5.0% in 2005 and 6.1% in 2006 before declining again slightly to 4.5% in 2007. This strong growth was largely attributed to innovation within the banking and insurance sectors, and to the expansion of international financial markets, which stimulated Luxembourg's financial intermediation and business services. The banking sector was adversely affected by the global financial crisis from mid-2008. In late September Luxembourg contributed €2,500m. to a €11,200m. deal to rescue the European bank Fortis, and a further €400m. to a €6,400m. package to save the Belgian-French bank, Dexia; it also intervened to support three other insolvent banks. The IMF predicted a slowing in GDP growth to 0.7% in 2008 and a contraction in GDP of 4.8% in 2009, as exports of goods and services were affected by the decline in demand from external markets. Luxembourg was, however, better placed to withstand the downturn than many of its neighbours, owing to its low levels of public debt and a government surplus, which had declined from the equivalent of 3.2% of GDP in 2007 to an estimated 1.4% in 2008. The stimulus measures introduced to address the downturn, including tax cuts and rises in expenditure (with subsidies to protect employment), were nevertheless expected to lead to a government deficit of 3.2% in 2009 and public debt was expected to double. The future profitability of Luxembourg's financial sector was uncertain, not only as a result of this global crisis, but also because of the effects of EU integration, including the harmonization of taxation and regulatory structures, which threatened the banking secrecy and tax advantages that made the country attractive to investors. Under EU rules Luxembourg (along with Austria and Belgium) was allowed to retain banking secrecy until at least 2011, levying a withholding tax on non-residents' savings instead, which was to rise incrementally from 15% in 2005 to 35% in 2011. In March 2009, in response to international pressure, Luxembourg agreed to comply with OECD rules on information-sharing to combat tax evasion.

Education

Education in Luxembourg is compulsory from the age of four to 15 years. Primary education begins at six years of age and lasts for six years. German is the initial language of instruction at primary level. French is added to the programme in the second year, and replaces German as the language of instruction at higher secondary level. In 2005 enrolment in primary education included 97% of children in the relevant age-group (males 96%; females 97%).

At the age of 12, pupils can choose between secondary school (*lycée*) and technical education (*lycée technique*). The first year of secondary school is a general orientation course on comprehensive lines, which is then followed by a choice between two sections: the Classical Section, with an emphasis on Latin, and the Modern Section, which stresses English and other modern languages. The completed secondary course lasts seven years, and leads to the *Certificat de Fin d'Etudes Secondaires*, which qualifies for university entrance. The technical education course (six to eight years) leads either to a vocational diploma, a technician's diploma (*diplôme de technicien*) or a technical baccalaureate diploma (*bac technique*) and is devised in three parts: an orientation and observation course, an intermediate course and an upper course. In 2005 enrolment in secondary education included 83% of children in the relevant age-group (males 81%; females 86%).

The *Centre Universitaire* was established in 1969, offering one-year or two-year courses in the humanities, sciences and law and economics, as well as training courses for lawyers and teachers, following which the students generally attended other European universities. The *Institut Supérieur de Technologies* (IST) is an institute for higher education at university level in civil engineering, electrical engineering, applied computer sciences and mechanical engineering. In 2003 the Government founded the University of Luxembourg, operating from three campuses, Kirchberg, Limpertsberg and Walferdange, and offering a full range of degrees and post-graduate qualifications

LUXEMBOURG

taught in French, German and English. In 2005 the Government announced that a single site was to be developed at Belval-Ouest, near Esch-sur-Alzette, to accommodate all university faculties and services; the first university buildings at Belval-Ouest were expected to be completed by 2012.

General government expenditure on national education and vocational training was budgeted at €905.8m. in 2008 (equivalent to 11.9% of total expenditure).

Public Holidays

2009: 1 January (New Year's Day), 13 April (Easter Monday), 1 May (Labour Day), 21 May (Ascension Day), 1 June (Whit Monday), 23 June (National Day), 15 August (Assumption), 1 November (All Saints' Day), 25 December (Christmas), 26 December (St Stephen's Day).

2010: 1 January (New Year's Day), 5 April (Easter Monday), 1 May (Labour Day), 13 May (Ascension Day), 24 May (Whit Monday), 23 June (National Day), 15 August (Assumption), 1 November (All Saints' Day), 25 December (Christmas), 26 December (St Stephen's Day).

Weights and Measures

The metric system is in force.

Statistical Survey

Source (unless otherwise stated): Service Central de la Statistique et des Etudes Economiques (STATEC), Centre Administratif Pierre Werner, 13 rue Erasme, 1468 Luxembourg; tel. 478-42-52; fax 46-42-89; e-mail statec.post@statec.etat.lu; internet www.statec.lu.

AREA AND POPULATION

Area: 2,586 sq km (999 sq miles).

Population: 384,634 at census of 1 March 1991; 439,539 (males 216,540, females 222,999) at census of 15 February 2001; 483,800 (males 239,600, females 244,200) official estimate at 1 January 2008.

Density (January 2008): 187.1 per sq km.

Principal Towns ('000, 2008): Luxembourg-Ville (capital) 85.5; Esch-sur-Alzette 29.5; Differdange 20.4; Dudelange 18.1; Pétange 15.2; Sanem 14.2; Hesperange 12.4.

Births, Marriages and Deaths (2007): Live births 5,477 (birth rate 11.5 per 1,000); Marriages 1,969 (marriage rate 3.6 per 1,000); Deaths 3,866 (death rate 8.1 per 1,000).

Life Expectancy (years at birth, WHO estimates): 79.8 (males 76.8; females 82.6) in 2006. Source: WHO, *World Health Report*.

Immigration and Emigration (2007): Arrivals 16,675; Departures 10,674.

Employment ('000 persons, incl. armed forces, 2005): Agriculture, hunting, forestry and fishing 3.9; Mining and quarrying 0.3; Manufacturing 32.6; Electricity, gas and water supply 1.8; Construction 30.3; Wholesale and retail trade, repair of motor vehicles, motorcycles and personal and household goods 42.8; Hotels and restaurants 14.2; Transport, storage and communications 22.9; Financial intermediation 34.1; Real estate, renting and business activities 52.0; Public administration and defence and compulsory social security 16.7; Education 14.4; Health and social work 22.8; Other community, social and personal service activities 10.6; Private households with employed persons 8.2; *Total employed* 307.3. *2006:* Total employed 319,100. *2007* ('000): Agriculture 4.7; Construction 35.3; Other industry 35.7; Trade 85.2; Financial, real estate, renting and business activities 97.5; Other service activities 74.0; Total employed 332.5; Unemployed 9.6; Total labour force 342.1.

HEALTH AND WELFARE
Key Indicators

Total Fertility Rate (children per woman, 2006): 1.7.

Under-5 Mortality Rate (per 1,000 live births, 2006): 4.9.

HIV/AIDS (% of persons aged 15–49, 2007): 0.2.

Physicians (per 1,000 head, 2004): 2.7.

Hospital Beds (per 1,000 head, 2004): 6.3.

Health Expenditure (2006): US $ per head (PPP): 5,773.

Health Expenditure (2006): % of GDP: 7.2.

Health Expenditure (2006): public (% of total): 90.6.

Human Development Index (2006): ranking: 9.

Human Development Index (2006): value: 0.956.

For sources and definitions, see explanatory note on p. vi.

AGRICULTURE, ETC.

Principal Crops ('000 metric tons unless otherwise indicated, 2007, FAO estimates): Wheat 70.4; Rye 6.8; Barley 44.6; Oats 5.6; Triticale (wheat-rye hybrid) 20.6; Potatoes 20.2; Rapeseed 18.4; Mushrooms 5.0 (metric tons); Apples 4.0; Grapes 16.9.

Livestock ('000 head, year ending September 2007): Cattle 191.5; Horses 4.5; Pigs 96.9; Sheep 9.5; Poultry 79.2.

Livestock Products (metric tons, 2007, FAO estimates): Cattle meat 17,700; Pig meat 8,900; Chicken meat 120; Milk 312,500.

Forestry ('000 cubic metres, 2007, FAO estimates): *Roundwood Removals:* 290.8 (Sawlogs, veneer logs and logs for sleepers 152.6, Fuel wood 20.6, Pulpwood 115.5, Other 2.1); *Sawnwood Production* (incl. railway sleepers) 133.4 (Coniferous 113.4, Broadleaved 20).

Source: FAO.

INDUSTRY

Selected Products ('000 metric tons, 2007, unless otherwise indicated): Crude steel 2,858; Rolled steel products 2,800; Wine ('000 hl) 141.9; Beer ('000 hl) 373.7 (2005); Electric energy (million kWh) 4001.4.

FINANCE

Currency and Exchange Rates: 100 cent = 1 euro (€). *Sterling and Dollar Equivalents* (31 December 2008): £1 sterling = 1.047 euros; US $1 = 0.719 euros; €10 = £9.55 = $13.92. *Average Exchange Rate* (euros per US dollar): 0.7971 in 2006; 0.7306 in 2007; 0.6827 in 2008. Note: The national currency was formerly the Luxembourg franc. From the introduction of the euro, with Luxembourg's participation, on 1 January 1999, a fixed exchange rate of €1 = 40.3399 Luxembourg francs was in operation. Euro notes and coins were introduced on 1 January 2002. The euro and local currency circulated alongside each other until 28 February, after which the euro became the sole legal tender.

Central Budget (€ million): *Revenue:* 8,499.1 in 2005; 9,212.5 in 2006; 10,015.1 in 2007. *Expenditure:* 8,883.2 in 2005; 9,455.0 in 2006; 9,727.2 in 2007.

International Reserves (US $ million at 31 December 2007): Gold 61.90; IMF special drawing rights 20.16; Reserve position in IMF 29.59; Foreign exchange 93.81; Total 205.46. Source: IMF, *International Financial Statistics*.

Money Supply (€ million at 31 December 2007): Currency issued 1,576*; Demand deposits at banking institutions 83,210. Source: IMF, *International Financial Statistics*.

*Currency put into circulation by the Banque Centrale du Luxembourg was €46,361m.

Cost of Living (Consumer Price Index; base: 2000 = 100): All items 112.0 in 2005; 115.0 in 2006; 117.7 in 2007. Source: IMF, *International Financial Statistics*.

Gross Domestic Product (€ million at constant 2000 prices): 25,141.5 in 2004; 26,404.2 in 2005; 28,019.7 in 2006; 29,361.7 in 2007.

National Income and Product (€ million at current prices, 2007): Compensation of employees 16,239.6; Operating surplus and mixed income (incl. consumption of fixed capital) 15,914.3; *Gross domestic product (GDP) at factor cost* 32,153.9; Taxes, less subsidies, on production and imports 4,123.7; *GDP in market prices* 36,277.7; Primary incomes received from abroad 134,572.4; *Less* Primary incomes paid abroad –140,575.2; *Gross national income* 30,274.9; *Less* Consumption of fixed capital 3,988.5; *Net national income* 26,286.4.

Expenditure on the Gross Domestic Product (€ million at current prices, 2007): Final consumption expenditure 17,300.5 (Households 11,127.1, Non-profit institutions serving households 601.0, General government 5,572.5); Gross capital formation 7,304.3; *Total domestic expenditure* 24,604.8; Exports of goods and services 65,381.0; *Less* Imports of goods and services 53,709.7; Statistical discrepancy 1.6; *GDP in market prices* 36,277.7.

LUXEMBOURG

Gross Domestic Product by Economic Activity (€ million at current prices, 2007): Agriculture, hunting, forestry and fishing 137.5; Construction 1,915.0; Other industry 3,196.2; Wholesale and retail trade, repair of motor vehicles, motorcycles and personal and household goods; hotels and restaurants and transport and communications 6,671.6; Financial services 8,927.0; Real estate, renting and business activities 6,522.4; Other community, social and personal service activities 5,277.7; *Gross value added in basic prices* 32,647.5; Taxes, less subsidies, on products 3,630.1; *GDP in market prices* 36,277.7.

Balance of Payments (US $ million, 2007): Exports of goods f.o.b. 18,257; Imports of goods f.o.b. −23,066; *Trade balance* −4,810; Exports of services 64,524; Imports of services −37,453; *Balance on goods and services* 22,261; Other income received 162,971; Other income paid −177,946; *Balance on goods, services and income* 7,286; Current transfers received 6,134; Current transfers paid −8,492; *Current balance* 4,928; Capital account (net) −166; Direct investment abroad −250,036; Direct investment from abroad 188,119; Portfolio investment assets −174,516; Portfolio investment liabilities 309,874; Financial derivatives (net) 15,755; Other investment assets −250,140; Other investment liabilities 155,847; Net errors and omissions 247; *Overall balance* −89. Source: IMF, *International Financial Statistics*.

EXTERNAL TRADE

Principal Commodities (€ million, 2007): *Imports:* Food and live animals 1,120.7; Beverages and tobacco 425.3; Crude materials (inedible) except fuels 1,297.9; Mineral fuels, lubricants, etc. 2,076.4; Chemicals and related products 1,568.2; Metal manufactures 1,789.4; Other basic manufactures 1,250.8; Machinery and other equipment 2,547.1; Transport equipment 2,602.4; Miscellaneous manufactured articles 1,583.9; Total 16,262.2. *Exports:* Food and live animals 539.2; Chemicals and related products 798.7; Metal manufactures 3,928.5; Other basic manufactures 1,821.1; Machinery and other equipment 2,136.0; Transport equipment 885.7; Miscellaneous manufactured articles 1,175.6; Total (incl. others) 11,823.0.

Principal Trading Partners (€ million, 2007): *Imports:* Belgium 5,496.3; France 1,899.8; Germany 4,800.0; Italy 356.6; Netherlands 1,002.6; Switzerland 144.7; United Kingdom 282.1; USA 623.2; Total (incl. others) 16,262.2. *Exports:* Austria 243.1; Belgium 1,481.2; France 1,993.0; Germany 3,124.1; Italy 641.7; Netherlands 644.9; Spain 413.5; Sweden 172.7; Switzerland 152.2; United Kingdom 553.7; USA 298.6; Total (incl. others) 11,823.0.

TRANSPORT

Railways (traffic, million, 2006): Passenger-km 298; Freight ton-km 466.

Road Traffic (motor vehicles in use at 1 January 2007): Cars 314,718; Motorcycles 14,609; Buses and coaches 1,380; Goods vehicles 25,755; Tractors 29,169; Total 385,631.

Shipping: *River Traffic* (Port of Mertert, '000 metric tons, 2007): Goods loaded 135.4, Goods unloaded 976.9. *Merchant Fleet* (vessels registered at 31 December 2007): Number of vessels 75; Total displacement 883,524 grt (Source: Lloyd's Register-Fairplay, *World Fleet Statistics*).

Civil Aviation (traffic on scheduled services, 2007): Passengers carried 1,642,848; Freight (metric tons) 856,740.

TOURISM

Tourist Arrivals (at accommodation establishments): 912,798 in 2005; 908,171 in 2006; 981,262 in 2007.

Arrivals by Country (2007): Belgium 190,819; France 107,157; Germany 134,655; Italy 23,490; Netherlands 202,639; Spain 16,245; United Kingdom 61,894; USA 22,522; Total (incl. others) 981,262.

Tourism Receipts (US $ million): 2,577 in 2002; 3,134 in 2003; 3,889 in 2004.

COMMUNICATIONS MEDIA

Facsimile Machines: 20,000 in use (1998).

Mobile Cellular Telephones: 604,200 in 2007.

Telephones: 248,200 main lines in use in 2007.

Personal Computers ('000 in use): 290 in 2005.

Internet Users ('000): 363.9 in 2007.

Broadband Subscribers ('000): 128.5 in 2007.

Daily Newspapers: 6 (2005).

Book Production: 513 titles (1997).

Radio Receivers: 285,000 in use (1997).

Television Receivers: 260,000 in use (2000).

Sources: partly UNESCO, *Statistical Yearbook*; International Telecommunication Union.

EDUCATION

(2006/07, unless otherwise indicated)

Nursery: 858 teachers; 10,001 pupils.

Primary: 3,755 teachers; 34,970 pupils (males 17,509, females 17,461).

Secondary and Technical Secondary: 3,667 teachers (state sector only) (2005/06); 11,693 pupils (secondary) (males 5,230, females 6,463), 23,277 pupils (technical secondary) (males 12,279, females 10,998).

University-level: 9,227 students, incl. 6,063 studying abroad (2005/06).

Schools (2004/05): 375 offering a combination of nursery and primary education; 32 secondary (5 private).

Directory

The Constitution

The Constitution now in force dates back to 17 October 1868, but in 1919 a constituent assembly introduced some important changes, declaring that the sovereign power resided in the nation, that all secret treaties were denounced and that deputies were to be elected by a list system by means of proportional representation, on the basis of universal adult suffrage. Electors must be citizens of Luxembourg and must have attained 18 years of age. Candidates for election must have attained 18 years of age. The Grand Duke, who is Sovereign, chooses government ministers, may intervene in legislative questions and has certain judicial powers. There is a single-chamber legislature, the Chamber of Deputies (Chambre des Députés), with 60 members elected for five years. There are four electoral districts: the North, the Centre, the South and the East. By the law of 9 October 1956 the Constitution was further revised to the effect that: 'The exercise of prerogatives granted by the Constitution to the legislative, executive and judiciary powers, can, by treaty, be temporarily vested in institutions of international law.' The Constitution was further amended on 12 December 1994, 12 July 1996 (introducing a Constitutional Court), 12 January 1998 and 18 February 2003. A proposal to further amend the Constitution, ending the power of the Grand Duke to veto legislation adopted by parliament, was approved by the Chamber of Deputies on 12 March 2009. In addition to the Council of Ministers, which consists of the President of the Government (Prime Minister) and at least three other ministers, the State Council (Conseil d'Etat—which is the supreme administrative tribunal and which also fulfils certain legislative functions) comprises 21 members nominated by the Sovereign who serve for 15 years (not necessarily continuous) or until the age of 72.

The Government

HEAD OF STATE

Grand Duke: HRH Henri Albert Félix Marie Guillaume (succeeded to the throne 7 October 2000).

Marshal of the Court: Jean-Jacques Kasel.

COUNCIL OF MINISTERS

(April 2009)

A coalition of the Chrëschtlech Sozial Vollekspartei (CSV) and the Lëtzebuerger Sozialistesch Arbechterpartei (LSAP).

Prime Minister and Minister of State and of Finance: Jean-Claude Juncker (CSV).

Deputy Prime Minister and Minister of Foreign Affairs and Immigration: Jean Asselborn (LSAP).

LUXEMBOURG

Minister of Agriculture, Viticulture and Rural Development and of Small Business, Tourism and Housing: FERNAND BODEN (CSV).

Minister of Family Affairs and Integration and of Equal Opportunities: MARIE-JOSÉE JACOBS (CSV).

Minister of National Education and Vocational Training: MADY DELVAUX-STEHRES (LSAP).

Minister of Justice and of the Treasury and the Budget: LUC FRIEDEN (CSV).

Minister of Labour and Employment, of Culture, Higher Education and Research and of Religious Affairs: FRANÇOIS BILTGEN (CSV).

Minister of the Economy and External Trade and of Sport: JEANNOT KRECKÉ (LSAP).

Minister of Health and of Social Security: MARS DI BARTOLOMEO (LSAP).

Minister of the Environment and of Transport: LUCIEN LUX (LSAP).

Minister of the Interior and Land Management: JEAN-MARIE HALSDORF (CSV).

Minister of the Civil Service and Administrative Reform and of Public Works: CLAUDE WISELER (CSV).

Minister of Co-operation and Humanitarian Action, of Communications and of Defence: JEAN-LOUIS SCHILTZ (CSV).

Minister-delegate of Foreign Affairs and Immigration: NICOLAS SCHMIT (LSAP).

Secretary of State for Parliamentary Relations, for Agriculture, Viticulture and Rural Development and for Culture, Higher Education and Research: OCTAVIE MODERT (CSV).

MINISTRIES

Office of the Prime Minister: Hôtel de Bourgogne, 4 rue de la Congrégation, 1352 Luxembourg; tel. 478-21-00; fax 46-17-20; e-mail info@sip.etat.lu; internet www.gouvernement.lu.

Ministry of Agriculture, Viticulture and Rural Development: 1 rue de la Congrégation, 1352 Luxembourg; tel. 478-24-78; fax 46-40-27; e-mail info@ma.public.lu; internet www.ma.public.lu.

Ministry of the Civil Service and Administrative Reform: 63 ave de la Liberté, BP 1807, 1931 Luxembourg; tel. 478-31-00; fax 26-48-36-21; e-mail info@mfpra.public.lu; internet www.mfpra.public.lu.

Ministry of Culture, Higher Education and Research: 20 montée de la Pétrusse, 2273 Luxembourg; tel. 478-1; fax 29-21-86; e-mail info@mcesr.public.lu; internet www.mcesr.public.lu.

Ministry of the Economy and External Trade: 19–21 blvd Royal, 2449 Luxembourg; tel. 478-24-78; fax 46-04-48; e-mail info@eco.public.lu; internet www.eco.public.lu.

Ministry of the Environment: 18 montée de la Pétrusse, 2327 Luxembourg; tel. 478-68-24; fax 40-04-10; e-mail info@environnement.public.lu; internet www.environnement.public.lu.

Ministry of Equal Opportunities: 12–14 ave Emile Reuter, 2921 Luxembourg; tel. 478-58-14; fax 24-18-86; e-mail info@mega.public.lu; internet www.mega.public.lu.

Ministry of Family Affairs and Integration: 12–14 ave Emile Reuter, 2919 Luxembourg; tel. 478-65-00; fax 478-65-70; e-mail info@mfi.public.lu; internet www.mfi.public.lu.

Ministry of Finance: 3 rue de la Congrégation, 1352 Luxembourg; tel. 478-1; fax 47-52-41; internet www.mf.public.lu.

Ministry of Foreign Affairs and Immigration: Hôtel St Maximin, 5 rue Notre-Dame, 2240 Luxembourg; tel. 478-24-78; fax 22-31-44; e-mail webadmin@mae.etat.lu; internet www.mae.lu.

Ministry of Health: Villa Louvigny, allée Marconi, 2120 Luxembourg; tel. 478-24-78; fax 46-79-62; e-mail ministere-sante@ms.etat.lu; internet www.ms.etat.lu.

Ministry of the Interior and Land Management: 19 rue Beaumont, 1219 Luxembourg; tel. 478-46-00; fax 22-11-25; e-mail info@miat.public.lu; internet www.miat.public.lu.

Ministry of Justice: Centre Administratif Pierre Werner, 13 rue Erasme, 2934 Luxembourg; tel. 478-45-37; fax 26-68-48-61; e-mail info@mj.public.lu; internet www.mj.public.lu.

Ministry of Labour and Employment: 26 rue Zithe, 2763 Luxembourg; tel. 478-61-00; fax 478-61-08; e-mail info@mte.public.lu; internet www.mte.public.lu.

Ministry of National Education and Vocational Training: 29 rue Aldringen, 2926 Luxembourg; tel. 478-51-00; fax 478-51-13; e-mail info@men.public.lu; internet www.men.public.lu.

Ministry of Public Works: 4 blvd F. D. Roosevelt, 2450 Luxembourg; tel. 478-33-00; fax 46-27-09; e-mail info@mtp.public.lu; internet www.mtp.public.lu.

Ministry of Small Business, Tourism and Housing: 6 blvd Royal, 2449 Luxembourg; tel. 478-47-00; fax 46-11-87; internet www.mcm.public.lu (small business), www.mdt.public.lu (tourism), www.logement.lu (housing).

Ministry of Social Security: 26 rue Sainte Zithe, 2936 Luxembourg; tel. 478-63-11; fax 478-63-28; e-mail info@mss.public.lu; internet www.mss.public.lu.

Ministry of State: 4 rue de la Congrégation, 1352 Luxembourg; tel. 478-21-00; fax 46-17-20; e-mail ministere.etat@me.etat.lu; internet www.etat.lu; (incorporating Ministry of Religious Affairs).

Ministry of Transport: 19–21 blvd Royal, 2449 Luxembourg; tel. 478-44-00; fax 22-85-68; e-mail transports@tr.etat.lu; internet www.mt.public.lu.

Legislature

CHAMBER OF DEPUTIES

Chambre des Députés: Hôtel de la Chambre des Députés, 19 rue du Marché-aux-Herbes, 1728 Luxembourg; tel. 966-1; fax 22-02-30; e-mail info@chd.lu; internet www.chd.lu.

President: LUCIEN WEILER.

General Election, 13 June 2004

Party	% of votes	Seats
Chrëschtlech Sozial Vollekspartei	36.11	24
Lëtzebuerger Sozialistesch Arbechterpartei	23.37	14
Demokratesch Partei	16.09	10
Déi Gréng	11.58	7
Aktiounskomitee fir Demokratie a Rentegerechtegkeet*	9.95	5
Déi Lénk	1.90	—
Kommunistesch Partei Lëtzebuerg	0.92	—
Frai Partei Lëtzebuerg	0.12	—
Total	**100.00**	**60**

* Changed its name to Alternativ Demokratesch Reformpartei in April 2006, prompting one of its deputies to leave the party to sit as an independent.

Advisory Councils

Conseil Economique et Social: Centre Administratif Pierre Werner, 13 rue Erasme, BP 1306, 1468 Luxembourg; tel. 43-58-51; fax 42-27-29; e-mail ces@ces.etat.lu; internet www.ces.etat.lu; f. 1966; consultative body on economics and social affairs; 39 mems; Pres. SERGE ALLEGREZZA; Sec.-Gen. MARIANNE NATI-STOFFEL.

Conseil d'Etat: 5 rue Sigefroi, 2536 Luxembourg; tel. 47-30-71; fax 46-43-22; e-mail info@conseil-etat.public.lu; internet www.conseil-etat.public.lu; 21 mems nominated by the Sovereign; Pres. ALAIN MEYER; Sec.-Gen. MARC BESCH.

Political Organizations

Alternativ Demokratesch Reformpartei (ADR) (Alternative Democratic Reform Party): 4 rue de l'Eau, 1449 Luxembourg; tel. 26-20-37-06; fax 26-20-37-36; e-mail adr@chd.lu; internet www.adr.lu; f. 1987 as Aktiounskomitee 5/6 Pensioun fir jiddfereen (Action Committee 5/6 Pensions for Everyone); name changed to Aktiounskomitee fir Demokratie a Rentegerechtegkeet (Action Committee for Democracy and Pensions Justice) in 1994; present name adopted 2006; conservative; established to campaign for improved pension rights for private sector employees, but subsequently sought to broaden its concerns; Pres. ROBERT (ROBY) MEHLEN.

Chrëschtlech Sozial Vollekspartei (CSV) (Christian Social Party): 4 rue de l'Eau, BP 826, 2018 Luxembourg; tel. 22-57-31-1; fax 47-27-16; e-mail csv@csv.lu; internet www.csv.lu; f. 1914; advocates political stability, sustained economic expansion, ecological and social progress; 9,500 mems; Pres. FRANÇOIS BILTGEN; Sec.-Gen. MARCO SCHANK.

Déi Gréng (The Greens): 1 rue de Fort Elisabeth, 1463 Luxembourg; tel. 27-48-27-1; fax 27-48-27-22; e-mail greng@greng.lu; internet www.greng.lu; f. 1983; fmrly Déi Gréng Alternativ (Green Alternative Party); merged with the Gréng Lëscht Ekologesch Initiativ (Green List Ecological Initiative) in 1995; advocates 'grass-roots' democracy, environmental protection, social concern and increased aid to developing countries; Spokespersons TILLY METZ, CARLO DE TOFFOLI.

Déi Lénk (The Left): BP 817, 2018 Luxembourg; tel. 26-20-20-72; fax 26-20-20-73; e-mail sekretariat@dei-lenk.lu; internet www.dei-lenk.lu; f. 1999; individual membership; no formal leadership.

Demokratesch Partei (DP) (Democratic Party): 5 rue du St Esprit, BP 510, 2015 Luxembourg; tel. 22-10-21; fax 22-10-13; e-mail secretariat@dp.lu; internet www.dp.lu; liberal; Leader CLAUDE MEISCH; Gen. Sec. GEORGES GUDENBURG.

Kommunistesch Partei Lëtzebuerg (KPL) (Communist Party of Luxembourg): 3 rue Zénon Bernard, 4030 Esch-sur-Alzette; tel. 44-60-66-21; fax 44-60-66-66; e-mail kpl@zlv.lu; internet www.kp-l.org; f. 1921; Pres. ALI RUCKERT.

Lëtzebuerger Sozialistesch Arbechterpartei (LSAP d'Sozialisten) (Socialist Workers' Party of Luxembourg): 68 rue de Gasperich, 1617 Luxembourg; tel. 45-65-73-1; fax 45-65-75; e-mail info@lsap.lu; internet www.lsap.lu; f. 1902; social democrat; 6,000 mems; Pres. ALEX BODRY; Secs ROMAIN SCHNEIDER, CHANTAL BOLY.

Diplomatic Representation
EMBASSIES IN LUXEMBOURG

Austria: 3 rue des Bains, 1212 Luxembourg; tel. 47-11-88; fax 46-39-74; e-mail luxemburg-ob@bmeia.gv.at; internet www.bmeia.gv.at/luxemburg; Ambassador Dr CHRISTINE STIX-HACKL.

Belgium: 4 rue des Girondins, 1626 Luxembourg; tel. 44-27-46-1; fax 45-42-82; e-mail luxembourg@diplobel.fed.be; internet www.diplomatie.be/luxembourg; Ambassador ALAIN KUNDYCKI.

Cape Verde: 117 val de Ste Croix, 1371 Luxembourg; tel. 26-48-09-48; fax 26-48-09-49; e-mail ambcvlux@pt.lu; Chargé d'affaires CLARA MANUELA DA LUZ DELGADO.

China, People's Republic: 2 rue Van der Meulen, Dommeldange, 2152 Luxembourg; tel. 43-69-91-1; fax 42-24-23; e-mail chianemb_lu@mfa.gov.cn; internet lu.china-embassy.org; Ambassador MA ZHIXUE.

Czech Republic: 2 rond-point Robert Schuman, 2525 Luxembourg; tel. 26-47-78-11; fax 26-47-78-20; e-mail luxembourg@embassy.mzv.cz; internet www.mzv.cz/luxembourg; Ambassador KATEŘINA LUKEŠOVÁ.

Denmark: 4 rue des Girondins, 1626 Luxembourg; tel. 22-21-22-1; fax 22-21-24; e-mail luxamb@um.dk; internet www.ambluxembourg.um.dk; Ambassador OLE LISBORG.

Finland: 2 rue Heine, 1720 Luxembourg; tel. 49-55-51; fax 49-46-40; e-mail sanomat.lux@formin.fi; internet www.finlande.lu; Ambassador TARJA LAITIAINEN.

France: 8B blvd Joseph II, BP 359, 2013 Luxembourg; tel. 45-72-71; fax 45-72-71-227; e-mail ambassade@ambafrance-lu.org; internet www.ambafrance-lu.org; Ambassador CHARLES-HENRI D'ARAGON.

Germany: 20–22 ave Emile Reuter, BP 95, 2010 Luxembourg; tel. 45-34-45-1; fax 45-56-04; internet www.luxemburg.diplo.de; Ambassador Dr HUBERTUS VON MORR.

Greece: 27 rue Marie-Adélaïde, 2128 Luxembourg; tel. 44-51-93; fax 45-01-64; e-mail ambgrec@pt.lu; Ambassador DIONYSIOS KODELAS.

Hungary: 36 rue Marie-Adélaïde, 2128 Luxembourg; tel. 45-91-77; fax 45-82-89; e-mail ambhongr@pt.lu; internet www.mfa.gov.hu/kulkepviselet/lu; Ambassador TIBOR KECSKÉS.

Ireland: Résidence Christina, 2nd Floor, 28 route d'Arlon, 1140 Luxembourg; tel. 45-06-10-1; fax 45-88-20; e-mail luxembourg@dfa.ie; internet www.embassyofireland.lu; Ambassador MARTIN BURKE.

Italy: 5–7 rue Marie-Adélaïde, 2128 Luxembourg; tel. 44-36-44-1; fax 45-55-23; e-mail ambasciata.lussemburgo@esteri.it; internet www.amblussemburgo.esteri.it; Ambassador ROBERTO BETTARINI.

Japan: 62 ave de la Faïencerie, BP 92, 2010 Luxembourg; tel. 46-41-51-1; fax 46-41-76; e-mail embjapan@pt.lu; internet www.lu.emb-japan.go.jp; Ambassador KAZUHITO TATEBE.

Netherlands: 6 rue Ste Zithe, 2763 Luxembourg; tel. 22-75-70; fax 40-30-16; e-mail lux@minbuza.nl; internet www.paysbas.lu; Ambassador EDUARD HOEKS.

Poland: 2 rue de Pulvermühl, 2356 Luxembourg; tel. 26-00-32; fax 26-68-75-54; e-mail ambapol@pt.lu; internet www.luksemburg.polemb.net; Ambassador BARBARA LABUDA.

Portugal: 24 rue Guillaume Schneider, 2522 Luxembourg; tel. 46-61-90-1; fax 46-51-69; e-mail embport@pt.lu; Ambassador JOSÉ MANUEL DA ENCARNAÇÃO PESSANHA VIEGAS.

Romania: 41 blvd de la Pétrusse, 2320 Luxembourg; tel. 45-51-51; fax 45-51-63; e-mail ambroum@pt.lu; internet luxembourg.mae.ro; Ambassador VLAD TUDOR ALEXANDRESCU.

Russia: Château de Beggen, 1719 Luxembourg; tel. 42-23-33; fax 42-23-34; e-mail ambruslu@pt.lu; internet www.ruslux.mid.ru; Ambassador EDUARD R. MALAYAN.

Spain: 4–6 blvd Emmanuel Servais, BP 290, 2012 Luxembourg; tel. 46-02-55; fax 46-12-88; e-mail emb.luxemburgo@mae.es; internet www.maec.es/embajadas/luxemburgo; Ambassador MIGUEL BENZO PEREA.

Sweden: 2 rue Heinrich Heine, 1720 Luxembourg; tel. 26-64-61; fax 29-69-09; e-mail ambassaden.luxembourg@foreign.ministry.se; internet www.swedenabroad.com/luxembourg; Ambassador AGNETA SÖDERMAN.

Switzerland: Immeuble Forum Royal, 25A blvd Royal, 3e étage, 2449 Luxembourg; tel. 22-74-74-1; fax 22-74-74-20; e-mail lux.vertretung@eda.admin.ch; internet www.eda.admin.ch/luxembourg; Ambassador PHILIPPE GUEX.

Turkey: 49 rue Siggy vu Lëtzebuerg, 1933 Luxembourg; tel. 44-32-81; fax 44-32-81-34; e-mail ambtrlux@pt.lu; Ambassador AYSE AYHAN ASYA.

United Kingdom: 5 blvd Joseph II, 1840 Luxembourg; tel. 22-98-64; fax 22-98-67; e-mail britemb@internet.lu; internet www.britain.lu; Ambassador PETER BATEMAN.

USA: 22 blvd Emmanuel Servais, 2535 Luxembourg; tel. 46-01-23; fax 46-14-01; internet luxembourg.usembassy.gov; Ambassador ANN LOUISE WAGNER.

Judicial System

The lowest courts in Luxembourg are those of the Justices of the Peace, of which there are three, at Luxembourg-Ville, Esch-sur-Alzette and Diekirch. These are competent to deal with civil, commercial and criminal cases of minor importance. Above these are the two District Courts, Luxembourg being divided into the judicial districts of Luxembourg and Diekirch. These are competent to deal with civil, commercial and criminal cases. The Superior Court of Justice includes both a court of appeal, hearing decisions made by District Courts, and the Cour de Cassation. As the judicial system of the Grand Duchy does not employ the jury system, a defendant is acquitted if a minority of the presiding judges find him or her guilty. The highest administrative court is the Comité du Contentieux du Conseil d'Etat. Special tribunals exist to adjudicate upon various matters of social administration such as social insurance. The department of the Procureur Général (Attorney-General) is responsible for the administration of the judiciary and the supervision of judicial police investigations. In July 1996 an amendment to the Constitution introduced a Constitutional Court.

Judges are appointed for life by the Grand Duke, and are not removable except by judicial sentence.

Superior Court of Justice: Cité Judiciaire, Bâtiment CR, 2080 Luxembourg; tel. 47-59-81-1; fax 47-59-81-39-6.

President of the Superior Court of Justice: MARC SCHLUNGS.

Attorney-General: ROBERT BIEVER.

Religion
CHRISTIANITY
The Roman Catholic Church

For ecclesiastical purposes, Luxembourg comprises a single archdiocese, directly responsible to the Holy See. At 31 December 2006 adherents numbered 393,800 (around 86.5% of the total population).

Archbishop of Luxembourg: Most Rev. FERNAND FRANCK, Archevêché, 4 rue Génistre, BP 419, 2014 Luxembourg; tel. 46-20-23; fax 47-53-81; e-mail archeveche@cathol.lu; internet www.cathol.lu.

The Anglican Communion

Within the Church of England, Luxembourg forms part of the diocese of Gibraltar in Europe.

Chaplain: Rev. CHRISTOPHER LYON, 89 rue de Muhlenbach, 2168 Luxembourg; tel. and fax 43-95-93; e-mail chris.lyon@anglican.lu; internet www.anglican.lu; English-speaking church (Anglican Chaplaincy).

Protestant Churches

Protestant Church of Luxembourg: 5 rue de la Congrégation, 1352 Luxembourg; tel. 22-96-70; fax 22-96-70-70; e-mail mail@protestant.lu; internet www.protestant.lu; f. 1818 as Protestant Garnison Church, 1868 as multiconfessional community for the Grand Duchy; there are about 1,500 Evangelicals; Pres. Pastor MICHEL FAULLIMMEL.

Protestant Reformed Church of Luxembourg: 11 rue de la Libération, BP 295, 4210 Esch-sur-Alzette; tel. 54-03-45; fax 54-03-46; e-mail eglrefki@pt.lu; internet www.reformiert.lu; f. 1982; 3,500 mems in 4 parishes (2006); Pastor KARL GEORG MARHOFFER.

LUXEMBOURG   Directory

ISLAM

Centre Culturel Islamique de Luxembourg: 2 route d'Arlon, 8210 Mamer; tel. 31-00-60; fax 31-04-26; internet www.islam.lu; Imam HALIL AHMETSPAHIC.

JUDAISM

Chief Rabbi: JOSEPH SAYAGH, 34 rue Alphouse Munchen, 2172 Luxembourg; tel. 45-23-66; fax 25-04-30.

Communauté Israélite de Luxembourg (Jewish Community of Luxembourg): 45 ave Monterey, 2018 Luxembourg; tel. 45-29-14-20; fax 25-05-30; e-mail info@synagogue.lu; internet www.synagogue.lu; Pres. GUY AACH.

The Press

DAILIES

L'Essentiel: 38 ave Charlotte, 4530 Differdange; tel. 26-58-66-1; fax 26-58-66-628; e-mail denis.berche@lessentiel.lu; internet www.lessentiel.lu; f. 2007; Mon.–Fri.; French; distributed free of charge; publ. by Edita SA; Editor-in-Chief DENIS BERCHE; circ. 57,666 (2007).

Lëtzebuerger Journal: Résidence de Beauvoir, 51 rue de Strasbourg, BP 2101, 1021 Luxembourg; tel. 49-30-33-1; fax 49-20-65; e-mail journal@journal.lu; internet www.journal.lu; f. 1948; organ of the Democratic Party; Editor-in-Chief CLAUDE KARGER.

Luxemburger Wort: 2 rue Christophe Plantin, 2988 Luxembourg; tel. 49-93-1; fax 49-93-384; e-mail wort@wort.lu; internet www.wort.lu; f. 1848; German; Catholic; Christian Democrat; Editor-in-Chief LÉON ZECHES; circ. 72,222 (2007).

Le Quotidien: 44 rue du Canal, 4050 Esch-sur-Alzette; tel. 54-71-311; fax 54-71-30; e-mail redaction@lequotidien.lu; internet www.lequotidien.lu; French; circ. 6,818 (2007).

Tageblatt/Zeitung fir Lëtzebuerg: 44 rue du Canal, 4050 Esch-sur-Alzette; tel. 54-71-31-1; fax 54-71-30; e-mail redaktion@tageblatt.lu; internet www.tageblatt.lu; f. 1913; French and German; Editors-in-Chief DANIÈLE FONCK, ALVIN SOLD; circ. 20,046 (2007).

La Voix du Luxembourg: 2 rue Christophe Plantin, 2988 Luxembourg; tel. 49-93-94-00; fax 49-93-773; e-mail voix@voix.lu; internet www.voix.lu; Editor LAURENT MOYSE; circ. 6,573 (2007).

Zeitung vum Lëtzebuerger Vollek: 3 rue Zénon Bernard, 4030 Esch-sur-Alzette; tel. 44-60-66-1; fax 44-60-66-66; e-mail zeiluvol@pt.lu; internet www.zlv.lu; f. 1946; organ of the Communist Party; Editor-in-Chief ALI RUCKERT.

PERIODICALS

Aktuell: 60 blvd Kennedy, BP 149, 4002 Esch-sur-Alzette; tel. 54-05-45-1; fax 54-16-20; e-mail ogbl@ogbl.lu; internet www.ogbl.lu; f. 1919; articles in both French and German; monthly; journal of the Luxembourg General Confederation of Labour; Editor-in-Chief DANIÈLE NIELES; circ. 43,000.

Auto Moto: Inter Editions SA, 7 rue Robert Stumper, 2557 Luxembourg; tel. 49-50-10-1; fax 49-50-11; monthly; motoring; circ. 72,345 (2007).

Carrière: BP 2535, 1025 Luxembourg; tel. and fax 85-89-19; e-mail carrieremag@logic.lu; internet www.logic.lu/carriere; f. 1988; women's interest; French and German; Editor MONIQUE MATHIEU; circ. 8,000.

Contacto: 2 rue Christophe Plantin, 2988 Luxembourg; tel. 49-93-470; fax 49-93-448; e-mail contacto@saint-paul.lu; internet www.jornal-contacto.lu; Portuguese; weekly; Editor-in-Chief JOSÉ CORREIA; circ. 22,800.

Correio: Villa Hadir, 51 rue Emile Mark, 4620 Differdange; tel. 44-44-33-1; fax 44-44-33-55-5; e-mail correio@correio.lu; Portuguese; Editor-in-Chief ALEXANDRA SERRANO ARAÚJO; circ. 10,000.

Echo des entreprises: 7 rue Alcide de Gasperi, BP 1304, 1013 Luxembourg; tel. 43-53-66-1; fax 43-23-28; e-mail echo@fedil.lu; internet www.fedil.lu/echo; f. 1920; 6 a year; industry, commerce; publ. by FEDIL—Business Federation Luxembourg; Dir NICOLAS SOISSON.

Femmes Magazine: 74 rue Ermesinde, 1469 Luxembourg; tel. 26-45-85-86; fax 26-45-84-94; e-mail redaction@femmesmagazine.lu; internet www.femmesmagazine.lu; 11 a year; women's interest; Dirs MARIA PIETRANGELI, PATRICIA SCIOTTI; circ. 20,128 (2007).

D'Handwierk: 2 circuit de la Foire Internationale, BP 1604, 1016 Luxembourg; tel. 42-45-11-1; fax 42-45-25; e-mail info@fda.lu; internet www.fda.lu; monthly; organ of the Fédération des Artisans and the Chambre des Métiers; Editor CHRISTIAN REUTER.

Horesca: 7 rue Alcide de Gasperi, BP 2524, 1025 Luxembourg; tel. 42-13-55-1; fax 42-13-55-299; e-mail info@horesca.lu; internet www.horesca.lu; monthly; hotel trade, tourism, gastronomy; Editor DAVE GIANNANDREA; circ. 6,000.

Le Jeudi: 44 rue du Canal, 4050 Esch-sur-Alzette; tel. 22-05-50; fax 22-05-44; e-mail redaction@le-jeudi.lu; internet www.lejeudi.lu; f. 1997; weekly; French; Dir DANIÈLE FONCK; circ. 9,965 (2007).

De Konsument: 55 rue des Bruyères, 1274 Howald; tel. 49-60-22-1; fax 49-49-57; e-mail ulc@pt.lu; internet www.ulc.lu; 12 a year; consumer affairs; Man. GUY GOEDERT.

De Lëtzeburger Bauer: 16 blvd d'Avranches, 2980 Luxembourg; tel. 48-81-61-1; fax 40-03-75; e-mail letzeburger.bauer@netline.lu; f. 1944; weekly; journal of Luxembourg farming; circ. 7,500.

D'Lëtzeburger Land: 59 rue Glesener, BP 2083, 1020 Luxembourg; tel. 48-57-57; fax 49-63-09; e-mail land@land.lu; internet www.land.lu; f. 1954; weekly (Fri.); political, economic, cultural affairs; Man. Editor ROMAIN HILGERT; circ. 7,500.

Lux-Post: Editions Saphir, 23 rue des Gênets, 1621 Luxembourg; tel. 49-53-63; fax 48-53-70; local news; 4 regional edns; French and German; circ. 135,283 (2007).

Muselzeidung: 30 rue de Trèves, POB 36, 6701 Grevenmacher; tel. 75-87-47; fax 75-84-32; e-mail burton@pt.lu; internet www.muselzeidung.lu; f. 1981; regional magazine; monthly; German; Editor TANIA USELDINGER.

Revue: 2 rue Dicks, BP 2755, 1027 Luxembourg; tel. 49-81-81-1; fax 48-77-22; e-mail revue@revue.lu; internet www.revue.lu; f. 1945; weekly; illustrated; Editor-in-Chief ROMAIN MEYER; circ. 22,220 (2007).

Revue Technique Luxembourgeoise: 4 blvd Grande-Duchesse Charlotte, 1330 Luxembourg; tel. 45-13-54; fax 45-09-32; e-mail aliasbl@pt.lu; internet www.aliai.lu; f. 1908; quarterly; technology.

Sauerzeidung: 30 rue de Trèves, BP 36, 6701 Grevenmacher; tel. 75-87-47; fax 75-84-32; e-mail burton@pt.lu; internet www.muselzeidung.lu; f. 1988; regional newspaper; monthly; German; Publr EUGENE BURTON; circ. 10,000.

Soziale Fortschrett/Progrès Social: 11 rue du Commerce, BP 1208, Luxembourg; tel. 49-94-24-1; fax 49-94-24-49; e-mail info@lcgb.lu; internet www.lcgb.lu; f. 1921; monthly; journal of the Confed. of Christian Trade Unions of Luxembourg; Editor CHRISTIAN WELTER; circ. 36,000.

Télécran: 2 rue Christophe Plantin, BP 1008, 1010 Luxembourg; tel. 49-93-50-0; fax 49-93-59-0; e-mail telecran@telecran.lu; internet www.telecran.lu; f. 1978; TV and family weekly; illustrated; Editor-in-Chief CLAUDE FRANÇOIS; circ. 36,431 (2007).

Transport: 13 rue du Commerce, BP 2615, 1026 Luxembourg; tel. 22-67-86-1; fax 22-67-09; e-mail syprolux@pt.lu; internet www.fcpt-syprolux.lu; fortnightly; circ. 3,800.

Woxx: 51 ave de la Liberté, 2e étage, BP 684, 2016 Luxembourg; tel. 29-79-99-0; fax 29-79-79; e-mail woxx@woxx.lu; internet www.woxx.lu; f. 1988 as GréngeSpoun; weekly; social, ecological, environmental and general issues; circ. 3,000.

NEWS AGENCY

Agence Europe SA: BP 428, 2014 Luxembourg; tel. 22-00-32; fax 46-22-77; e-mail info@agenceurope.eu; internet www.agenceurope.eu; f. 1952.

PRESS ASSOCIATIONS

Association Luxembourgeoise des Editeurs de Journaux: 44 rue du Canal, 4050 Esch-sur-Alzette; tel. 54-71-31; fax 53-05-87; e-mail asold@tageblatt.lu; Pres. ALVIN SOLD.

Association Luxembourgeoise des Journalistes: BP 1732, 1017 Luxembourg; tel. 44-00-44; fax 85-88-40; e-mail rinfalt@tageblatt.lu; Pres. ROGER INFALT.

Publishers

Editions Guy Binsfeld: 14 place du Parc, 2313 Luxembourg; tel. 49-68-68; fax 40-76-09; e-mail editions@binsfeld.lu; internet www.editionsguybinsfeld.lu; f. 1979; literature, reference, children's; Dir and Chief Editor ROB KIEFFER.

Editions Mike Koedinger SA: 10 rue des Gaulois, BP 728, 2017 Luxembourg; tel. 29-66-181; e-mail sylvia@mikekoedinger.com; internet www.mikekoedinger.com; trade and customer magazines, business directories, guidebooks; CEO MIKE KOEDINGER.

Editions Phi: Villa Hadir, 51 rue Emile Mark, 4620 Differdange; tel. 44-44-33-40-1; fax 44-44-33-55-5; e-mail editions.phi@editpress.lu; internet www.phi.lu; f. 1980; literature, art; owned by Editpress SA; Dir CHRISTINE KREMER.

Editions Schortgen: 108 rue d'Alzette, BP 367, 4004 Esch-sur-Alzette; tel. 54-64-87; fax 53-05-34; e-mail editions@schortgen.lu;

internet www.editions-schortgen.lu; art, literature, factual, cuisine, comics; Dir JEAN-PAUL SCHORTGEN.

Editpress Luxembourg SA: 44 rue du Canal, BP 147, 4050 Esch-sur-Alzette; tel. 54-71-31-1; fax 54-71-30; e-mail tageblatt@tageblatt .lu; internet www.tageblatt.lu; Dir ALVIN SOLD.

Edouard Kutter: BP 319, 2013 Luxembourg; tel. 22-35-71; fax 47-18-84; e-mail kuttered@pt.lu; internet www.kutter.lu; art, photography, facsimile edns on Luxembourg.

Imprimerie Beffort SA: 7A rue de Bitbourg, 1273 Luxembourg; tel. 25-44-55-1; fax 25-44-19; e-mail jmkerschen@beffort.lu; f. 1869; scientific, economic reviews; Dir JEAN-MARIE KERSCHEN.

Saint-Paul Luxembourg SA: 2 rue Christophe Plantin, 2988 Luxembourg; tel. 49-93-1; fax 49-93-386; e-mail direction@saint-paul.lu; internet www.saint-paul.lu; f. 1887; Man. Dir LÉON ZECHES.

PUBLISHERS' ASSOCIATION

Fédération Luxembourgeoise des Editeurs de Livres: 31 blvd Konrad Adenauer, BP 482, 2014 Luxembourg; tel. 43-94-44; fax 43-94-50; e-mail francoise.schlink@clc.lu; internet www.clc.lu; f. 1991; affiliated to Confédération Luxembourgeoise du Commerce (CLC).

Broadcasting and Communications

TELECOMMUNICATIONS

Regulatory Authority

Institut Luxembourgeois de Régulation (ILR): 45 allée Scheffer, 2922 Luxembourg; tel. 45-88-45-1; fax 45-88-45-88; e-mail info@ilr.lu; internet www.ilr.lu; Dir ODETTE WAGENER.

Major Service Providers

Cegecom SA: 3 rue Jean Piret, BP 2708, 1027 Luxembourg; tel. 26-49-91; fax 26-49-96-99; e-mail info@cegecom.net; internet www.cegecom.lu; Man. Dirs MICHAEL LEIDINGER, GEORGES MULLER, BERTHOLD WEGMANN.

Entreprise des Postes et Télécommunications (P&TLuxembourg): 8A ave Monterey, 2020 Luxembourg; tel. 47-65-1; fax 47-51-10; e-mail contact@pt.lu; internet www.pt.lu; f. 1992; post, telecommunications and internet service provider; Pres. GASTON REINESCH; CEO MARCEL GROSS.

LUXGSM SA: 90A rue de Strasbourg, 1171 Luxembourg; tel. 24-62-1; fax 24-62-60-00; e-mail communication@luxgsm.lu; internet www.luxgsm.lu; f. 1993; mobile cellular telephone operator; subsidiary of Entreprise des Postes et Télécommunications; Man. Dir MARC ROSENFELD.

Numericable: 283 route d'Arlon, 8011 Strassen; tel. 26-10-23-01; fax 34-93-98; internet www.numericable.lu; fmrly Coditel, name changed 2008; offers digital television, fixed-line telecommunications and broadband internet access; Dir-Gen. PASCAL DORMAL.

Tango: 177 route de Luxembourg, 8077 Bertrange; tel. 27-77-71-01; fax 27-77-78-88; e-mail info@tango.lu; internet www.tango.lu; fixed and mobile telephony, as well as broadband internet services; fmrly Tele2Tango; acquired by Belgacom SA (Belgium) in 2008; CEO DIDIER ROUMA.

VOXmobile SA: 8 Z.A.I. Bourmicht, 8070 Bertrange; e-mail ssidon@voxmobile.lu; internet www.vox.lu; mobile cellular and fixed-line telecommunications, broadband internet access; owned by Mobistar (Belgium); Group CEO BENOIT SCHEEN; 79,687 customers (2008).

BROADCASTING

Regulatory Authority

Commission Indépendante de la Radiodiffusion: 5 rue Large, 1917 Luxembourg; tel. 47-82-07-5; e-mail isabelle.marinov@smc.etat .lu; Pres. GEORGES SANTER.

Radio

Eldoradio: 47 Mühlenweg, BP 1344, 1013 Luxembourg; tel. 40-95-09-1; fax 40-95-09-509; e-mail eldoradio@eldoradio.lu; internet www.eldoradio.lu; popular music station; Dir CHRISTOPHE GOOSENS.

Radio 100,7: 45A ave Monterey, BP 1833, 2163 Luxembourg; tel. 44-00-44-1; fax 44-00-44-940; e-mail dweyler@100komma7.lu; internet www.100komma7.lu; f. 1993; non-commercial cultural broadcaster; Dir FERNAND WEIDES.

Radio Ara: 2 rue de la Boucherie, BP 266, 1247 Luxembourg; tel. 22-22-89; fax 22-22-66; e-mail radioara@pt.lu; internet www.ara.lu; music broadcaster.

Radio DNR: 12 rue Christophe Plantin, 2988 Luxembourg; tel. 40-70-60; fax 40-79-98; e-mail dnr@dnr.lu; internet www.dnr.lu; music broadcaster; Dir JEAN-MARC STURM.

Radio Latina: 3 rue du Fort Bourbon, 1249 Luxembourg; tel. 29-95-96-201; fax 40-24-76; internet www.radiolatina.lu; broadcasts programmes in Portuguese, French, Italian, Spanish and Cape-Verdean Créole; Dir LUIS BARREIRA.

Radio LRB: 4 rue Saint Benoît zu Peppeng, BP 8, 3201 Bettembourg; tel. 52-44-88-22; fax 52-44-88-33; e-mail info@lrb.lu; internet www.lrb.lu; popular music; Man. PATRICK CONSELMAN.

RTL Group: 45 blvd Pierre Frieden, 1543 Luxembourg; tel. 24-86-1; fax 24-86-51-39; e-mail oliver.herrgesell@rtlgroup.com; internet www.rtlgroup.com; f. 2000 by merger of CLT-UFA and Pearson TV; 90.3% owned by Bertelsmann AG (Germany), 9.7% by private shareholders; 32 radio stations and 43 television channels in 10 countries; CEO GERHARD ZEILER.

RTL Radio Lëtzebuerg: 45 blvd Pierre Frieden, 1543 Luxembourg; tel. 42-14-2; fax 42-14-22-737; e-mail news@rtl.lu; internet www.rtl.lu; f. 1959; broadcasts in Lëtzebuergesch; Station Man. FERNAND MATHES; Chief Editor MARC LINSTER.

Television

RTL Télé Lëtzebuerg: 45 blvd Pierre Frieden, 1543 Luxembourg; tel. 42-14-28-10; fax 42-14-27-43-1; e-mail online@rtl.lu; internet www.rtl.lu; f. 1969; 2 channels: RTL Télé Lëtzebuerg and Den 2. RTL; subsidiary of RTL Group; CEO ALAIN BERWICK; Station Man. LUCIEN LINSTER.

Finance

(cap. = capital; res = reserves; dep. = deposits; m. = million; brs = branches; amounts in euros unless otherwise indicated)

REGULATORY BODY

Commission de Surveillance du Secteur Financier (CSSF): 110 route d'Arlon, 2991 Luxembourg; tel. 26-25-11; fax 26-25-1-601; e-mail direction@cssf.lu; internet www.cssf.lu; f. 1998; supervision of financial sector; Dir-Gen. JEAN-NICOLAS SCHAUS; Dirs ARTHUR PHILIPPE, SIMONE DELCOURT.

BANKING

In January 2009 there were 152 banks in Luxembourg, most of which were subsidiaries or branches of foreign banks; a selection of the principal banks operating internationally is given below.

Central Bank

Banque centrale du Luxembourg: 2 blvd Royal, 2983 Luxembourg; tel. 47-74-1; fax 47-74-49-10; e-mail info@bcl.lu; internet www.bcl.lu; f. 1998; represents Luxembourg within the European System of Central Banks (ESCB); cap. 25m., res 143m., dep. 11,591m. (Dec. 2007); Pres. YVES MERSCH; Exec. Dirs ANDRÉE BILLON, SERGE KOLB.

Principal Banks

ABN AMRO Bank (Luxembourg) SA: 46 ave J. F. Kennedy, 185 Luxembourg; tel. 26-07-1; fax 26-07-29-99; internet www.abnamroprivatebanking.com/luxembourg; f. 1991 by merger; cap. 372m., res 63m., dep. 7,390m. (Dec. 2006); Chair. JAN KOOPMAN; Man. Dir TONIKA HERDMAN.

Banque et Caisse d'Epargne de l'Etat, Luxembourg: 1–2 pl. de Metz, 1930 Luxembourg; tel. 40-15-1; fax 40-15-20-99; e-mail info@bcee.lu; internet www.bcee.lu; f. 1856 as Caisse de l'Epargne de l'Etat du Grand-Duché de Luxembourg; present name adopted 1989; govt-owned; cap. 174m., res 1,059m., dep. 36,033m. (Dec. 2007); Chair. VICTOR ROD; Pres. and CEO JEAN-CLAUDE FINCK; 75 brs.

Banque Degroof Luxembourg SA: 12 rue Eugène Ruppert, 2453 Luxembourg; tel. 45-35-45-1; fax 25-07-21; e-mail investors .relation@degroof.lu; internet www.degroof.be; f. 1987; cap. 37m., res 75m., dep. 1,873m. (Sept. 2007); Chair., Supervisory Cttee ALAIN SIAENS; Chair., Management Cttee REGNIER HAEGELSTEEN.

Banque LBLux SA: 3 rue Jean Monnet, BP 602, 2180 Luxembourg; tel. 42-43-41; fax 42-43-45-09-9; e-mail bank@lblux.lu; internet www.lblux.lu; f. 1973; present name adopted 2002; 75% owned by BayernLB, 25% by Helaba (both Germany); cap. 300m., res 121m., dep. 11,755m. (Dec. 2007); Chair. RUDOLF HANISCH; Man. Dir HENRI STOFFEL.

Banque de Luxembourg SA: 14 blvd Royal, BP 2221, 1022 Luxembourg; tel. 26-20-26-60; fax 499-24-55-99; e-mail banque.de .luxembourg@bdl.lu; internet www.banquedeluxembourg.com; f. 1920; 71% owned by Crédit Industriel d'Alsace et de Lorraine (France); cap. 100m., res 316m., dep. 13,314m. (Dec. 2007); Pres. ROBERT RECKINGER; Man. Dir PIERRE AHLBORN; 4 brs.

LUXEMBOURG

Banque Raiffeisen SC: 46 rue Charles Martel, 2134 Luxembourg; tel. 24-50-1; fax 22-75-41; e-mail info@raiffeisen.lu; internet www.raiffeisen.lu; f. 1926 as Caisse Centrale Raiffeisen SC; present name adopted 2001; res 146m., dep. 3,746m., total assets 4,067m. (Dec. 2007); Chair. PAUL LAUTERBOUR; CEO and Gen. Man. ERNEST CRAVATTE.

Banque Safra Luxembourg SA: 10A blvd Joseph II, BP 887, 2018 Luxembourg; tel. 45-47-73-1; fax 45-47-86; internet www.safra.lu; cap. Swiss francs 14m., res Swiss francs 144m., dep. Swiss francs 1,748m. (Dec. 2006); Man. Dir JORGE ALBERTO KININSBERG.

BGL SA: 50 ave J. F. Kennedy, 2951 Luxembourg; tel. 42-42-20-00; fax 42-42-25-79; internet www.bgl.lu; f. 1919 as Banque Générale du Luxembourg SA; merged with Fortis Bank Luxembourg SA 2001, restyled Fortis Banque Luxembourg SA in 2005; present name adopted Dec. 2008; 50.1% stake owned by Fortis Bank SA/NV (Belgium), 49.9% owned by Luxembourg Govt; cap. 350m., res 2,983m., dep. 51,875m. (Dec. 2007); Chair. GASTON REINESCH; CEO CARLO THILL; 37 brs.

BHF-BANK International SA: 534 rue de Neudorf, 2220 Luxembourg; tel. 45-76-76-1; fax 45-83-24; e-mail direktion@bhf.lu; f. 1972; present name adopted 2005; subsidiary of BHF-Bank AG (Germany); cap. 26m., res 54m., dep. 5,221m. (Dec. 2007); Mans THOMAS KRUSE, THILO SCHIERING, ROLAND STEIES.

BNP Paribas Luxembourg: 10A blvd Royal, 2093 Luxembourg; tel. 46-46-1; fax 46-46-90-00; internet www.bnpparibas.lu; subsidiary of BNP Paribas SA (France); cap. 105m., res 986m., dep. 22,312m. (Dec. 2007); Chair. ALAIN PAPIASSE; Man. Dir ERIC MARTIN.

Clearstream Banking SA: 42 ave J. F. Kennedy, 1855 Luxembourg; tel. 243-0; fax 24-33-80-00; e-mail inquiries@clearstream.com; internet www.clearstream.com; f. 1970 as Cedelbank; present name adopted 2000; subsidiary of Deutsche Börse AG; private bank; acts as the central bank's securities depository; total assets 10,600,000m. (Dec. 2007); Chair. ANDRÉ ROELANTS; CEO JEFFREY TESSLER.

Commerzbank International SA (CISAL): 25 rue Edward Steichen, 2540 Luxembourg; tel. 47-79-11-1; fax 47-79-11-270; e-mail cisal@commerzbank.com; internet www.commerzbank.lu; f. 1969; cap. 580m., res 214m., dep. 8,953m. (Dec. 2007); Pres. and Chair. Dr ACHIM KASSOW; Man. Dir FALK FISCHER.

Crédit Agricole Luxembourg: 39 allée Scheffer, BP 1104, 1011 Luxembourg; tel. 47-67-1; fax 24-67–80-00; e-mail marketing@ca-luxembourg.com; internet www.e-private.com; f. 2005 by merger of Crédit Lyonnais Luxembourg and Crédit Agricole Indosuez Luxembourg; merged with Crédit Agricole Luxembourg Bank in 2008; cap. 84m., res 81m., dep. 584m. (Dec. 2007); Chair. JEAN-FRÉDÉRIC DE LEUSSE; Gen. Man. CHARLES HAMER.

Crédit Suisse (Luxembourg) SA: 56 Grand-Rue, BP 40, 2010 Luxembourg; tel. 46-00-11-1; fax 46-32-70; internet www.credit-suisse.com; f. 1974; cap. Swiss francs 43m., res Swiss francs 27m., dep. Swiss francs 5,104m. (Dec. 2006); Man. Dir HANS-ULRICH HÜGLI.

Danske Bank International SA: 13 rue Edward Steichen, BP 173, 2011 Luxembourg; tel. 46-12-75-1; fax 47-30-78; e-mail information@danskebank.lu; internet www.danskebank.lu; f. 1976; cap. 91m., res 35m., dep. 4,842m. (Dec. 2006); Chair. NIELS ERIK MOUSTEN; Man. Dir KLAUS MØNSTED PEDERSEN.

DekaBank Deutsche Girozentrale Luxembourg SA: 38 ave J. F. Kennedy, 1855 Luxembourg; tel. 34-09-35; fax 34-09-37; e-mail info@dekabank.lu; internet www.dekabank.lu; f. 1971 as Deutsche Girozentrale International SA; present name adopted 2002, after merger with DekaBank Luxembourg SA; cap. 50m., res 106m., dep. 6,380m. (Dec. 2007); Chair. OLIVER BEHRENS; Man. Dir RAINER MACH.

Deutsche Bank Luxembourg SA: 2 blvd Konrad Adenauer, 1115 Luxembourg; tel. 42-12-21; fax 42-12-24-49; internet www.db.com/luxembourg; f. 1970 as Deutsche Bank Compagnie Financière Luxembourg; present name adopted 1987; cap. 215m., res 1,437m., dep. 61,871m. (Dec. 2007); Chair. Dr HUGO BÄNZIGER; CEO ERNST WILHELM CONTZEN.

Deutsche Postbank International SA: PB Finance Centre, 18–20 Parc d'Activités Sydrall, 5365 Munsbach; tel. 34-95-31-1; fax 34-62-06; e-mail deutsche.postbank@postbank.lu; internet www.postbank.de; f. 1993; cap. 600m., res 71m., dep. 15,275m. (Dec. 2007); Chair. LOUKAS RIZOS; Gen. Mans CHRISTOPH SCHMITZ, JOCHEN BEGAS, TOBIAS GANZÄUER.

Dexia Banque Internationale à Luxembourg SA (Dexia BIL): 69 route d'Esch, 2953 Luxembourg; tel. 45-90-1; fax 45-90-20-10; e-mail contact.lu@dexia.com; internet www.dexia-bil.lu; f. 1856 as Banque Internationale à Luxembourg; present name adopted 2000; 99.9% owned by Dexia SA (Belgium); cap. 141m., res 1,104m., dep. 51,100m. (Dec. 2006); Chair. PIERRE RICHARD; 40 brs.

Dresdner Bank Luxembourg SA: 26 rue de Marché-aux-Herbes, 2097 Luxembourg; tel. 47-60-1; fax 47-60-33-1; e-mail info@dresdner-bank.lu; internet www.dresdner-bank.lu; f. 1967 as Cie Luxembourgeoise de Banque SA; present name adopted 1989; owned by Commerzbank Gruppe (Germany); cap. 125m., res 316m., dep. 11,442m. (Dec. 2007); Chair. HOLGER BOSCHKE; CEO FALK FISCHER; 1 br.

DZ Bank International SA: 4 rue Thomas Edison, 1445 Strassen; tel. 44-90-31; fax 44-90-32-00-1; e-mail info@dzi.lu; internet www.dzi.lu; f. 1978 as DG Bank Luxembourg SA; present name adopted 2001, after merger with GZ Bank International SA; 89.7% owned by DZ Bank AG Deutsche Zentral-Genossenschaftsbank; cap. 81m., res 230m., dep. 14,536m. (Dec. 2007); Chair. LARS HILLE; Man. Dir ANDREAS NEUGEBAUER.

EFG Bank (Luxembourg) SA: 14 allée Marconi, 2120 Luxembourg; tel. 26-45-41; fax 26-45-45-00; e-mail infolux@efgbank.com; internet www.efgbank.lu; f. 1986; owned by EFG Eurobank Ergasias (Greece); cap. 70m., res 37m., dep. 2,704m. (Dec. 2006); Chair. FRANÇOIS REIS; Man. Dir LENA LASCARI.

HSBC Private Bank (Luxembourg) SA: 32 blvd Royal, BP 733, 2017 Luxembourg; tel. 47-93-31-1; fax 47-93-31-33-7; e-mail hrlu@hsbcpb.com; internet www.hsbcpb.com; f. 1985; cap. 53m., res 57m., dep. 1,840m. (Dec. 2006); Chair. MICHEL S. ELIA; CEO PETER YEATES.

HSBC Trinkaus & Burkhardt (International) SA: 1–7 rue Nina et Julien Lefèvre, BP 579, 2015 Luxembourg; tel. 47-18-47-1; fax 47-18-47-61-3; e-mail privatebanking@hsbctrinkhaus.lu; internet www.hsbctrinkhaus.lu; f. 1977 as Trinkhaus & Burhardt (International) SA; present name adopted 1999; cap. 16m., res 67m., dep. 1,964m. (Dec. 2007); Pres. Dr OLAF HUTH; Man. Dirs HANS-JOACHIM ROSTECK, JÖRG MEIER.

HSH Nordbank Private Banking SA: 2 rue Jean Monnet, BP 612, 2016 Luxembourg; tel. 42-41-21-1; fax 42-41-21-50-9; e-mail info@hsh-nordbank-pb.com; internet www.hsh-nordbank-pb.com; f. 1983; cap. 13m., res 4m., dep. 1,120m. (Dec. 2007); Chair. BERNHARD VISKER; Man. Dirs ERNST-WILHELM MÜNSTER, JÜRGEN KÜHN, CARSTEN BÄCKER, BERNHARD STAHR.

HVB Banque Luxembourg SA (HVB Luxembourg): 4 rue Alphonse Weicker, 2721 Luxembourg; tel. 42-72-1; fax 42-72-45-00; e-mail contact@hvb.lu; internet www.hvb.lu; f. 1998 by merger of Hypobank International SA and Vereinsbank International SA Luxembourg; present name adopted 2001; owned by HVB Group (Germany); cap. 238m., res 738m., dep. 32,257m. (Dec. 2007); Pres. and Chair. ANDREAS WÖLFER; CEO ANGELO BRIZI.

IKB International SA: 12 rue Erasme, BP 771, 2017 Luxembourg; tel. 42-37-87-0; fax 42-37-87-59-9; e-mail ikb.luxemburg@ikb.de; internet www.ikb-international.de; f. 1979; cap. 273m., res 164m., dep. 8,056m. (March 2007); Dirs WOLFGANG GÜTH, LUTZ BREIDERT.

ING Luxembourg SA: 52 route d'Esch, 1470 Luxembourg; tel. 44-99-11; fax 44-99-12-31; internet www.ing.lu; f. 1960 as Crédit Européen SA; present name adopted 2003; owned by ING Belgium SA/NV; cap. 83m., res 1,260m., dep. 12,833m. (Dec. 2007); Man. Dir RICK VANDENBERGHE; 15 brs.

KBL European Private Bankers SA: 43 blvd Royal, 2955 Luxembourg; tel. 47-97-1; fax 47-97-73-91-2; internet www.kbl.lu; f. 1949; fmrly Kredietbank SA Luxembourgeoise; present name adopted 2008; 99% owned by KBC Bank NV (Belgium); cap. 187m., res 1,106m., dep. 17,693m. (Dec. 2007); Pres. and Gen. Man. ETIENNE VERWILGHEN; 3 brs.

LBBW Luxemburg SA: 10–12 blvd F.D. Roosevelt, BP 84, 2010 Luxembourg; tel. 47-59-21-1; fax 47-59-21-26-9; e-mail info@lbbw.lu; internet www.lbbw.lu; f. 2008, following acquisition of Landesbank Rheinland-Pfalz International by Landesbank Baden-Württemburg (Germany); cap. 315m., res 338m., dep. 13,752m. (Dec. 2007); Man. Dirs MARIE-ANNE VAN DEN BERG, ROBY HAAS.

Norddeutsche Landesbank Luxembourg SA: 26 route d'Arlon, BP 121, 2011 Luxembourg; tel. 45-22-11-1; fax 45-22-11-30-7; e-mail info@nordlb.lu; internet www.nordlb.lu; f. 1972; cap. 205m., res 421m., dep. 20,639m. (Dec. 2007); Man. Dir and CEO HARRY ROSENBAUM.

Nordea Bank SA: 672 rue de Neudorf-Findel, BP 562, 2015 Luxembourg; tel. 43-88-71; fax 43-93-76-11; e-mail nordea@nordea.lu; internet www.nordea.lu; f. 1976 as Privatbanken International (Denmark) SA, Luxembourg; changed name to Unibank SA in 1990, present name adopted 2001; cap. 25m., res 180m., dep. 3,044m. (Dec. 2007); Man. Dirs JHON MORTENSEN, CLAUS JØRGENSEN.

Sanpaolo Bank SA: 12 ave de la Liberté, BP 2062, 1020 Luxembourg; tel. 40-37-60-1; fax 40-37-60-35-0; e-mail sanpaolo@sanpaolo.lu; f. 1981 as Sanpaolo-Lariano Bank SA; present name adopted 1995; 99.99% stake owned by Intesa Sanpaolo SpA (Italy); cap. 140m., res 190m., dep. 3,325m. (Dec. 2006); Chair. STEFANO STANGONI.

Skandinaviska Enskilda Banken SA: 6A circuit de la Foire Internationale, BP 487, 2014 Luxembourg; tel. 26-23-1; fax 26-23-20-01; e-mail contact@sebprivatebank.com; internet www.sebgroup.lu; f. 1977; present name adopted 1999; cap. 118m., res 24m., dep. 2,035m. (Dec. 2006); Man. Dir LARS FRIBERG.

LUXEMBOURG

Société Européenne de Banque SA: 19–21 blvd du Prince Henri, BP 21, 2010 Luxembourg; tel. 46-14-11; fax 22-37-55; e-mail contact@seb.lu; internet www.seb.lu; f. 1976; cap. 45m., res 42m., dep. 3,898m. (Dec. 2006); subsidiary of Intesa Sanpaolo SpA (Italy); Chair. Prof. ANGELO CALOIA; Man. Dir and CEO MARCO BUS.

Société Générale Bank & Trust: 11 ave Emile Reuter, BP 1271, 2420 Luxembourg; tel. 47-93-11-1; fax 22-88-59; internet www.sgbt.lu; f. 1956 as International and General Finance Trust; present name adopted 1995; cap. 1,179m., res 630m., dep. 33,855m. (Dec. 2007); Chair. SYLVIE RUCAR; Pres. and Man. Dir VINCENT DECALF.

UBS (Luxembourg) SA: 33A ave J. F. Kennedy, 1855 Luxembourg; tel. 45-12-11; fax 45-12-12-70-0; internet www.ubs.lu; f. 1998 by merger of Swiss Bank Corporation (Luxembourg) SA and Union de Banques Suisses (Luxembourg) SA; cap. Swiss francs 150m., res Swiss francs 310m., dep. Swiss francs 19,350m. (Dec. 2006); Chair. ARTHUR DECURTINS; Man. Dir and CEO ROGER H. HARTMANN.

UniCredit International Bank (Luxembourg) SA: 8–10 rue Jean Monnet, 2180 Luxembourg; tel. 22-08-42-31-0; e-mail contact@unicreditgroup.lu; internet www.unicreditgroup.eu; merged with Capitalia Luxembourg SA in 2008; owned by Unicredito Italiano SpA; Group CEO ALESSANDRO PROFUMO.

WestLB International SA: 32–34 blvd Grande-Duchesse Charlotte, BP 420, 2014 Luxembourg; tel. 44-74-11; fax 44-74-12-10; e-mail info@westlb.lu; internet www.westlb.lu; f. 1972; owned by WestLB AG (Germany); cap. 65m., res 216m., dep. 7,651m. (Dec. 2007); Man. Dirs Dr JOHANNES SCHEEL, NORBERT LERSCH, UWE KRÖNERT.

Banking Association

Association des Banques et Banquiers Luxembourg (ABBL): 59 blvd Royal, BP 13, 2010 Luxembourg; tel. 46-36-60-1; fax 46-09-21; e-mail mail@abbl.lu; internet www.abbl.lu; f. 1939; Pres. JEAN MEYER.

STOCK EXCHANGE

Société de la Bourse de Luxembourg SA: 11 ave de la Porte-Neuve, BP 165, 2011 Luxembourg; tel. 47-79-36-1; fax 47-32-98; e-mail info@bourse.lu; internet www.bourse.lu; f. 1928; Chair. RAYMOND KIRSCH; CEO MICHEL MAQUIL.

INSURANCE

In 2007 there were 94 approved insurance companies and, in addition, 262 reinsurance companies. A selection of insurance companies is given below:

Aon Luxembourg: 19 rue de Bitbourg, BP 593, 2015 Luxembourg; tel. 31-72-35; fax 31-71-74; e-mail lambert_schroeder@aon.com; internet www.aon.com/luxembourg; f. 1994; insurance and reinsurance broker; subsidiary of Aon Corpn (USA); Man. Dir. LAMBERT SCHROEDER.

Assurances Mutuelles d'Europe SA (AME Lux): 7 blvd Joseph II, BP 787, 1840 Luxembourg; tel. 46-36-40; fax 46-36-44; e-mail ame@ame.lu; internet www.ame.lu; f. 1989; Man. Dir ALAIN HAUGLUSTAINE.

AXA Luxembourg: 7 rue de la Chapelle, 1325 Luxembourg; tel. 44-24-24-1; fax 44-24-24-45-90; e-mail info@axa.lu; internet www.axa.lu; f. 1977; all branches and life; Dir-Gen. PAUL DE COOMAN.

Fortis Assurances Luxembourg: 16 blvd Royal, 2449 Luxembourg; tel. 24-18-58-1; fax 24-18-58-90-00; e-mail info@fortisinsurance.lu; internet www.fortisinsurance.lu; f. 1996 by merger of AG Luxembourg and CGA Luxembourg; life and non-life insurance; CEO DIRK BILLEMON.

Groupe Foyer: 12 rue Léon Laval, 2986 Luxembourg; tel. 43-74-37; fax 43-74-32-49-9; e-mail contact@foyer.lu; internet www.foyer.lu; f. 1922; all branches and life; CEO PAUL FOHL.

La Luxembourgeoise SA d'Assurances: 10 rue Aldringen, 1118 Luxembourg; tel. 47-61-1; fax 47-61-30-0; e-mail groupell@lalux.lu; internet www.lalux.lu; f. 1989; all branches of non-life; Chair. ROBERT HENTGEN; Dir-Gen. PIT HENTGEN.

West of England Shipowners' Mutual Insurance Asscn (Luxembourg): 33 blvd du Prince Henri, BP 841, 1724 Luxembourg; tel. 47-00-67-1; fax 22-52-53; e-mail philip.aspden@westpandi.com; internet www.westpandi.com; f. 1970; marine mutual insurance; Gen. Man. PHILIP ASPDEN.

Insurance Association

Association des Compagnies d'Assurances (ACA): 75 rue de Mamer, BP 29, 8005 Bertrange; tel. 44-21-44-1; fax 44-02-89; e-mail aca@aca.lu; internet www.aca.lu; f. 1956; Pres. MARC LAUER; 71 mems.

Trade and Industry

GOVERNMENT AGENCY

Société Nationale de Crédit et d'Investissement (SNCI): 7 rue du Saint Esprit, BP 1207, 1475 Luxembourg; tel. 46-19-71-1; fax 46-19-79; e-mail snci@snci.lu; internet www.snci.lu; f. 1978; cap. €375m., res €185m., dep. €741m., assets €1,036m. (Dec. 2007); SNCI finances participations in certain cos, provides loans for investment and research and devt projects, provides export credit; Pres. GASTON REINESCH; Sec.-Gen. ÉVA KREMER.

CHAMBER OF COMMERCE

Chambre de Commerce du Grand-Duché de Luxembourg: 7 rue Alcide de Gasperi, 2981 Luxembourg-Kirchberg; tel. 42-39-39-1; fax 43-83-26; e-mail chamcom@cc.lu; internet www.cc.lu; f. 1841; Pres. MICHEL WURTH; 35,000 mems.

INDUSTRIAL AND TRADE ASSOCIATIONS

Centrale Paysanne Luxembourgeoise: BP 48, Agrocenter, 7501 Mersch, Luxembourg; tel. 64-64-48-0; fax 64-64-48-1; e-mail mfiedler@delpa.lu; f. 1945; Pres. MARC FISCH; Sec. LUCIEN HALLER; groups all agricultural organizations.

Chambre d'Agriculture (Landwirtschaftskammer): 261 route d'Arlon, BP 81, 8001 Strassen; tel. 31-38-76; fax 31-38-75; e-mail info@lwk.lu; internet www.lwk.lu; Pres. MARCO GAASCH; Sec.-Gen. ROBERT LEY.

Confédération Luxembourgeoise du Commerce (CLC): Bâtiment C, 2e étage, 7 rue Alcide de Gasperi, BP 482, 2014 Luxembourg; tel. 43-94-44; fax 43-94-50; e-mail info@clc.lu; internet www.clc.lu; f. 1909; Pres. MICHEL RODENBOURG; Dir THIERRY NOTHUM; 50,000 individual mems and 10,000 mem. cos.

Fédération des Artisans du Grand-Duché de Luxembourg: 2 circuit de la Foire Internationale, BP 1604, 1016 Luxembourg; tel. 42-45-11-1; fax 42-45-25; e-mail info@fda.lu; internet www.fda.lu; f. 1905; Pres. NORBERT GEISEN; Dir ROMAIN SCHMIT; 51 mem. feds.

FEDIL—Business Federation Luxembourg: 7 rue Alcide de Gasperi, BP 1304, 1013 Luxembourg; tel. 43-53-66-1; fax 43-23-28; e-mail fedil@fedil.lu; internet www.fedil.lu; f. 1918; Pres. ROBERT DENNEWALD; Dir NICOLAS SOISSON; c. 450 mems.

UTILITIES
Regulatory Authority

Institut Luxembourgeois de Régulation (ILR): see Broadcasting and Communications.

Electricity and Gas

Cegedel (Compagnie Grand-Ducale d'Electricité de Luxembourg): 2 rue Thomas Edison, 1445 Strassen; tel. 26-24-1; fax 26-24-61-00; e-mail mail@cegedel.lu; internet www.cegedel.lu; f. 1928; produces and distributes electricity; 82.8% owned by SOTEG SA; Chair. ROLAND MICHEL; Dir-Gen. ROMAIN BECKER.

Cegedel Net SA: 2 rue Thomas Edison, 1445 Strassen; tel. 26-24-1; fax 26-24-61-00; e-mail mail@cegedel.lu; internet www.cegedelnet.lu; f. 2004; operates the Cegedel distribution grid; Chair. ETIENNE SCHNEIDER; Dir-Gen. CARLO BARTOCCI.

Société Electrique de l'Our (SEO): 2 rue Pierre d'Aspelt, BP 37, 2010 Luxembourg; tel. 44-90-21; fax 44-90-28-00; e-mail seo@seo.lu; internet www.seo.lu; f. 1951; electricity production and supply; Pres. ETIENNE SCHNEIDER.

SOTEG SA: 19–21 bd Royal, 2449 Luxembourg; tel. 57-44-11-21-0; fax 26-55-20-05; internet www.soteg.lu; f. 1974 as Société de Transport de Gaz SA; 31% state-owned; transportation and supply of natural gas and electricity; Pres. MARCO HOFFMANN; Dir-Gen. JEAN LUCIUS.

SOTEL Réseau & Cie: 4 rue de Soleuvre, 4321 Esch-sur-Alzette; tel. 55-19-21; fax 57-22-13; f. 2001; distributor of electricity; Man. Dir NICO WIETOR.

SUDGAZ SA: 150 rue Jean-Pierre Michels, BP 383, 4004 Esch-sur-Alzette; tel. 55-66-551; fax 57-20-44; e-mail contact@sudgaz.lu; internet www.sudgaz.lu; f. 1899; gas distribution co; Pres. WILL HOFFMANN; Dir Jo SIMON.

Water

Responsibility for water supply lies with the municipalities. Many municipalities have formed syndicates to manage water supply, the largest of which is listed below.

Distribution d'Eau des Ardennes (DEA): BP 2, 8701 Useldange; tel. 23 64 24-1; fax 23 63 93 55; e-mail dea@dea.lu; internet www.dea.lu; f. 1929; distribution of drinking water in northern Luxembourg; comprises 36 municipalities; Dir PATRICK KOSTER.

LUXEMBOURG

TRADE UNIONS

FNCTTFEL—Landesverband der Eisenbahner, Transportarbeiter, Funktionäre und Beamten, Luxemburg (National Union of Luxembourg Railway and Transport Workers and Employees): 63 rue de Bonnevoie, 1260 Luxembourg; tel. 48-70-44-1; fax 48-85-25; e-mail info@landesverband.lu; internet www.landesverband.lu; f. 1909; affiliated to CGT and International Transport Workers' Federation; Pres. NICO WENNMACHER; Gen. Sec. GUY GREIVELDING; 8,000 mems.

Lëtzebuerger Chrëschtleche Gewerkschaftsbond (LCGB) (Confederation of Luxembourg Christian Trade Unions): 11 rue du Commerce, BP 1208, 1012 Luxembourg; tel. 49-94-24-1; fax 49-94-24-49; e-mail info@lcgb.lu; internet www.lcgb.lu; f. 1921; affiliated to ETUC and World Confederation of Labour; Pres. ROBERT WEBER; Gen. Sec. MARC SPAUTZ; 40,000 mems.

Onofhängege Gewerkschaftsbond-Lëtzebuerg/Confédération Syndicale Indépendente du Luxembourg (OGB-L) (Luxembourg Independent Confederation of Labour): 60 blvd J. F. Kennedy, BP 149, 4002 Esch-sur-Alzette; tel. 54-05-45-1; fax 54-16-20; e-mail ogbl@ogbl.lu; internet www.ogbl.lu; f. 1916; comprises 15 mem. unions; Pres. JEAN-CLAUDE REDING; c. 62,000 mems.

Transport

RAILWAYS

At 31 December 2007 there were 275 km of railway track, of which 262 km were electrified. A high-speed link from Luxembourg-Ville to Paris, France, opened in June 2007.

Société Nationale des Chemins de Fer Luxembourgeois: 9 place de la Gare, BP 1803, 1018 Luxembourg; tel. 49-90-0; fax 49-90-44-70; e-mail info@cfl.lu; internet www.cfl.lu; f. 1946; Pres. JEANNOT WARINGO; Dir-Gen. and CEO ALEX KREMER.

ROADS

At 1 January 2008 there were 2,894 km of roads, of which motorways comprised 147 km.

Ministry of Public Works: (see Ministries).

INLAND WATERWAYS AND SHIPPING

Rhine shipping has direct access to the Luxembourg inland port of Mertert as a result of the canalization of the Moselle river. An 'offshore' shipping register was established in 1991.

CIVIL AVIATION

There is an international airport situated at Findel, north-west of Luxembourg-Ville.

Luxair SA (Société Luxembourgeoise de Navigation Aérienne): Aéroport de Luxembourg, 2987 Luxembourg; tel. 456-42-55; fax 456-46-05; e-mail information@luxair.lu; internet www.luxair.lu; f. 1962; regular services to destinations in Europe and North Africa; Pres. and CEO ADRIEN NEY.

Cargolux Airlines International SA: Aéroport de Luxembourg, 2990 Luxembourg; tel. 42-11-1; fax 43-54-46; e-mail info@cargolux.com; internet www.cargolux.com; f. 1970; regular international all-freighter services; technological devt; owned by Luxair, a consortium of Luxembourg banks and SAir Logistics (Switzerland); Pres. and CEO ULRICH OGIERMANN.

Tourism

Many tourist resorts have developed around the ruins of medieval castles such as Clerf, Esch/Sauer, Vianden and Wiltz. The Benedictine Abbey at Echternach is also much visited. There is a thermal centre at Mondorf-les-Bains, supplied by three mineralized springs. In addition, there are numerous footpaths and hiking trails. Luxembourg-Ville, with its many cultural events and historical monuments, is an important centre for congresses. In 2007 there were 981,262 tourist arrivals at hotels and other accommodation establishments, of which there were 409. Receipts from tourism totalled US $3,889m. in 2004. In 2007 Luxembourg and Greater Region, which includes the German states of Saarland and Rhineland-Palatinate, the French region of Lorraine and the Belgian region of Wallonia, was a European Capital of Culture.

Office National du Tourisme (ONT): 68–70 blvd de la Pétrusse, BP 1001, 1010 Luxembourg; tel. 42-82-82-1; fax 42-82-82-38; e-mail info@ont.lu; internet www.ont.lu; f. 1931; 192 mems; Chair. M. SCHANK; Dir ROBERT L. PHILIPPART.

THE FORMER YUGOSLAV REPUBLIC OF MACEDONIA

Introductory Survey

Location, Climate, Language, Religion, Flag, Capital

The former Yugoslav republic of Macedonia (FYRM, or, according to its Constitution, the Republic of Macedonia), is situated in south-eastern Europe. The FYRM is a land-locked state and is bounded by Serbia to the north, Kosovo to the north-west, Albania to the west, Greece to the south and Bulgaria to the east. The republic is predominantly mountainous with a continental climate, although the Vardar (Axiós) river valley, which bisects the country from north-west to south-east, across the centre of the republic and into Greece, has a mild Mediterranean climate with an average summertime temperature of 27°C (80°F). The official language of the republic, under the Constitution of November 1991, was originally stipulated as Macedonian, and is most frequently written in the Cyrillic script. Constitutional amendments adopted in November 2001 accorded any minority language, such as Albanian, the status of official language in communities where its speakers constitute 20% of the population. Most of the population is nominally Christian and of the Eastern Orthodox faith. The ethnic Macedonians (who accounted for 64.2% of the total population at the 2002 census) are traditionally adherents of the Macedonian Orthodox Church, which claims autocephaly, although this is not recognized by other Orthodox churches. Most of the ethnic Albanians (officially recorded as 25.2% of the population) are Muslims, as are the majority of the remaining minority groups. The national flag (proportions 1 by 2) comprises, in the centre of a red field, a yellow disc, with eight yellow rays extending to the edges of the flag. The capital is Skopje.

Recent History

After the First World War, during which Macedonia was occupied by the Bulgarians and the Central Powers of Austria-Hungary and Germany, Vardar Macedonia, the area now known as the former Yugoslav republic of Macedonia (FYRM), became part of the new Kingdom of Serbs, Croats and Slovenes (formally named Yugoslavia in 1929), being widely referred to as 'South Serbia'. In the Second World War, however, the Bulgarian occupation of 1941–44 disillusioned many Yugoslav Macedonians. From 1943 the Partisans of Josip Broz (Tito), the General-Secretary of the Communist Party of Yugoslavia, began to increase their support in the region, and after the war the new Federal People's Republic of Yugoslavia and its communist rulers resolved to include a Macedonian nation as a federal partner (having rejected the idea of a united Macedonia under Bulgarian rule). A distinct Macedonian identity was promoted, and a linguistic policy that encouraged the establishment of a Macedonian literary language distinct from Bulgarian increased Macedonian self-awareness.

The presence of a large ethnic Albanian minority in western Macedonia added to Macedonian insecurities. The proximity of the neighbouring Serbian province of Kosovo, which had a majority ethnic Albanian population, and demands, from the late 1960s, for the creation of a Albanian republic, within Yugoslavia, alarmed the Macedonian authorities, which became particularly active against Albanian nationalism from 1981. In 1989 the communists amended the republican Constitution to allow for the introduction of a multi-party system; however, Macedonia was declared to be a 'nation-state' of the ethnic Macedonians, and mention of the 'Albanian and Turkish minorities' was excluded.

In November and December 1990 the first multi-party elections to a unicameral republican Sobranie (Assembly) were held in Macedonia. The Front for Macedonian National Unity, which principally comprised a nationalist party, the Internal Macedonian Revolutionary Organization—Democratic Party for Macedonian National Unity (IMRO—DPMNU), led by Ljubčo Georgievski, and which had previously declared its support for the return of territories within Serbia, alleged irregularities after failing to win any seats at the first round. Following two further rounds of voting, however, the IMRO—DPMNU unexpectedly emerged as the single party with the most seats (37) in the 120-member Sobranie. The League of Communists of Macedonia—Party for Democratic Reform (LCM—PDR, as the League of Communists of Macedonia had renamed itself), led by Petar Gosev, won 31 seats and the two predominantly Albanian parties (the Party for Democratic Prosperity—PDP—and the People's Democratic Party) a total of 25. The republican branch of the federal Alliance of Reform Forces (ARF, subsequently the Liberal Party of Macedonia—LPM) won 19 seats. Following lengthy coalition negotiations, in January 1991 Kiro Gligorov of the LCM—PDR was elected President of the Republic, with Georgievski as Vice-President; Stojan Andov of the ARF was elected President of the Sobranie. The three parties agreed to support a government largely comprising members without political affiliation. In March the Sobranie approved a new administration, headed by Nikola Kljušev. The LCM—PDR was renamed the Social Democratic Alliance of Macedonia (SDAM) in April.

On 25 January 1991 the Sobranie unanimously adopted a motion declaring the republic a sovereign territory. After June declarations of Croatian and Slovenian 'dissociation', Macedonia, wary of Serbian domination of the remaining federal institutions, declared its neutrality and emphasized its sovereign status. On 8 September a referendum (boycotted by the ethnic Albanian population) approved the sovereignty of Macedonia.

Georgievski resigned the vice-presidency in October 1991, and the IMRO—DPMNU announced that it had joined the opposition, stating that the party had been excluded from the decision-making process. The preparation of the new Constitution was delayed by the IMRO—DPMNU's proposal for an introductory nationalist statement, which was strongly opposed by the predominantly ethnic Albanian parties and was finally abandoned. On 17 November the Constitution, which declared the sovereignty of the Republic of Macedonia, was endorsed by 96 of the 120 Assembly members, with opposition from the majority of ethnic Albanian deputies. In January 1992 an unofficial referendum conducted among the ethnic Albanian population (declared illegal by the Macedonian authorities) reportedly resulted in 99.9% of votes being cast in favour of territorial and political autonomy for the ethnic Albanian population.

The complete withdrawal of federal troops from Macedonia in March 1992, in conjunction with the adoption in April of a new Constitution in the Federal Republic of Yugoslavia (FRY), referring only to Serbia and Montenegro, effectively signalled Yugoslav acceptance of Macedonian secession from the federation.

Macedonian affairs were subsequently dominated by the question of wider international recognition. The republic, although no longer part of Yugoslavia, was unable to act as an independent nation in the international community. Bulgaria recognized the state of Macedonia (although not the existence of a distinct Macedonian nationality or language) in January 1992, closely followed by Turkey in February, provoking mass protests in Thessaloníki, the capital of the Greek region of Macedonia. The Greek authorities insisted that 'Macedonia' was a geographical term delineating an area that included a large part of northern Greece, and expressed fears that the republic's independence under the name 'Macedonia' might foster a false claim to future territorial expansion. Greece was instrumental in the formulation of a European Community (EC, now European Union, EU, see p. 255) policy, adopted in early 1992, that the republic should be awarded no formal recognition of independence until stringent constitutional requirements had been fulfilled. In May Gligorov rejected a statement by the EC that it was 'willing to recognize Macedonia as a sovereign and independent state within its existing borders under a name that can be accepted by all concerned'. Negotiations with Greece ended in failure in June. In July, after a motion expressing no confidence in the Government received strong support in the Sobranie (and following large demonstrations at its failure to gain international recognition for an independent Macedonia), the Government resigned. The IMRO—DPMNU failed to form a new alliance and, eventually, in September Branko Crvenkovski, the Chairman of the SDAM, was installed as Prime Minister of a coalition Government.

The adoption of a new flag in August 1992 attracted particular opposition from Greece, which objected to the depiction outside Greece of the 'Vergina Star' (regarded as an ancient Greek symbol of Philip of Macedon and Alexander the Great). As a result of a blockade of petroleum deliveries imposed on Macedonia by Greece, reserves at the Skopje petroleum refinery were exhausted by September. In February 1993 Greece agreed to international arbitration over the issue of Macedonia's name, undertaking to abide by its final outcome. On 8 April the republic was admitted to the UN under the temporary name of 'the former Yugoslav republic of Macedonia', pending settlement of the issue of a permanent name by international mediators. However, Greece continued to assert, and the FYRM to deny, that the use of the 'Vergina Star' emblem and the name 'Macedonia' implied territorial claims on Greek territory, and in October Greece announced its withdrawal from UN-sponsored negotiations on the issue of a permanent name. In January 1994 Greece requested that the other nations of the EU prevail upon the FYRM (which was by this time recognized by all the other EU member states) to make concessions concerning its name, flag and Constitution, and threatened to ban trade with the FYRM. From February (shortly after Russia and the USA had formally recognized the FYRM) Greece blocked all non-humanitarian shipments to the FYRM through the port of Thessaloníki, and also road and rail transport links with the FYRM. In April the European Commission, which contested that the Greek embargo was in violation of EU trade legislation, initiated legal proceedings against Greece at the Court of Justice of the European Communities. In April 1995, however, the Court issued a preliminary opinion that the embargo was not in breach of Greece's obligations under the Treaty of Rome. Meanwhile, Greece agreed to resume negotiations in April with the FYRM, under the auspices of the UN; in May the Organization for Security and Co-operation in Europe (OSCE, see p. 366) announced that it was to join the mediation efforts. In September an interim accord was signed at the UN headquarters in New York, USA, by the FYRM Minister of Foreign Affairs and his Greek counterpart. The agreement provided for the mutual recognition of existing frontiers and respect for the sovereignty and political independence of each state, and for the free movement of goods and people between the two countries. Greece was to end its trade embargo and veto on the FYRM's entry into international organizations, while the FYRM undertook to abandon its use of the Vergina emblem in any form, and to amend parts of its Constitution that had been regarded by Greece as 'irredentist'. (The issue of a permanent name for the FYRM was to be the subject of further UN-mediated negotiations.) In early October the Sobranie approved a new state flag, depicting an eight-rayed sun in place of the Vergina emblem. The interim accord was ratified by the Sobranie on 9 October, and was formally signed in Skopje by representatives of the FYRM and Greece on 13 October. The border between the two countries was subsequently reopened.

The Albanian Government formally recognized the FYRM in April 1993. However, relations between the FYRM authorities and the minority Albanian population continued to deteriorate. In November several ethnic Albanians were arrested in the western towns of Gostivar and Tetovo and in Skopje. The Government announced that a conspiracy to form paramilitary groups, with the eventual aim of establishing an Albanian republic in the west of the FYRM, had been discovered. Further arrests followed, and in June 1994 Mithat Emini, the former General Secretary of the PDP, was sentenced to eight years' imprisonment, after being convicted of conspiring to engage in hostile activity; nine others received custodial sentences of between five and eight years. (In February 1995 all the sentences were reduced by two years.)

In February 1994, after months of disunity, the PDP split when a faction led by Xheladin Murati (the Deputy President of the Sobranie) and including the PDP's representatives in the Government and in the legislature, withdrew from the party's congress. The remaining grouping, led by Arben Xhaferi, made more radical demands regarding the status of ethnic Albanians in the FYRM. Organizations representing ethnic Albanians protested that inadequate preparations for a national census, conducted in mid-1994, effectively prevented the full enumeration of the ethnic Albanian community. The sentencing of Emini and his co-defendants prompted ethnic Albanian deputies to boycott the Sobranie in July (although they resumed their seats to defeat a motion, proposed by the IMRO—DPMNU, expressing no confidence in the Government). Murati resigned from the leadership of his PDP faction (and from his role at the Sobranie) later in July, reportedly in protest at the sentences; he was succeeded as party leader by Abdurahman Aliti.

Gligorov, representing the Alliance for Macedonia (a coalition of the SDAM, the LPM and the Socialist Party of Macedonia—SPM) was re-elected to the presidency on 16 October 1994, winning 78.4% of the valid votes cast; his only challenger was Georgievski of the IMRO—DPMNU. A first round of voting to the new Sobranie took place on the same day. The IMRO—DPMNU, which failed to secure any seats, alleged widespread electoral fraud in both elections, and boycotted the second round of legislative voting, which took place on 30 October (a third round was necessary in 10 constituencies on 13 November, owing to irregularities in earlier rounds). The final results confirmed that the Alliance for Macedonia had won the majority of seats in the Sobranie (with the SDAM taking 58 seats, the LPM 29 and the SPM eight). Aliti's 'moderate' PDP, which had been legally recognized as the successor to the original party, secured 10 seats; members of the 'radical' PDP had been obliged to stand as independent candidates (Xhaferi was among the independent candidates to be elected). Gligorov subsequently requested that Crvenkovski form a new government, and the SDAM-led administration, which also included members of the LPM, Aliti's PDP and the SPM, was approved by the Sobranie in December.

Tensions were exacerbated by efforts by the ethnic Albanian community to establish an Albanian-language university in Tetovo. Despite government objections that to establish such an institution would be unconstitutional, the university was formally founded in December 1994. In February 1995 the opening of the university provoked considerable unrest; an ethnic Albanian was killed in clashes with security forces. In July 1996 five of the university's founders, including its rector, received custodial sentences for inciting the riots, prompting protests by ethnic Albanians. (In May 2000 the Sobranie approved legislation granting the university at Tetovo legal status as a private foundation, and in January 2004 further legislation was passed, transforming it into a state university.)

In October 1995 Gligorov was injured in a car-bomb attack in Skopje; he resumed full presidential duties in January 1996. Meanwhile, divisions had emerged within the governing Alliance for Macedonia, which collapsed in February, prompting the LPM to be excluded from the Government. Andov resigned as President of the Sobranie in early March, stating that Crvenkovski had acted unconstitutionally in expelling the LPM from the Government.

In September 1996, prior to local elections scheduled for 17 November, the Sobranie approved legislation reorganizing the territorial division of the FYRM into 123 municipalities. In October three opposition parties, the IMRO—DPMNU, the PDP and the newly established Movement for All-Macedonian Action—Conservative Party, formed a coalition to contest the elections. Xhaferi's faction, which had been reconstituted as the Party of Democratic Prosperity of Albanians in Macedonia (PDPAM), and the (also ethnic Albanian) National Democratic Party (NDP) agreed to present joint candidates in some constituencies. The SDAM received the greatest number of votes, followed by the coalition led by the IMRO—DPMNU, and the PDP. Observers from the Council of Europe (see p. 236) declared that, overall, the elections had been conducted fairly.

In January 1997 legislation was adopted to permit Albanian to become the language of instruction at the teacher-training faculty of the university at Skopje, precipitating outrage among ethnic Macedonian students at the faculty. Ethnic tensions were further compounded by the civil conflict in Albania in early 1997. A financial scandal emerged in the FYRM in March, involving the embezzlement of funds invested in 'pyramid' savings schemes. Crvenkovski pledged an investigation to identify those responsible for the losses sustained by large numbers of investors, and several senior officials were subsequently arrested on suspicion of involvement. Although the Government won a vote of confidence in its management of the affair, the LPM deputies withdrew from the parliamentary chamber to register their disapproval of the measures undertaken. In April the Government announced plans to reimburse losses incurred by investors, following the failure of a major savings institution in the south-western town of Bitola; in May the Sobranie approved the replacement of the Governor of the central bank, who was believed to have been involved in the failure of the investment

gievski's Government was removed from power by a 10-party alliance (led by the SDAM and the LDP), known as Together for Macedonia, which secured 60 of the 120 seats in the Sobranie. The IMRO—DPMNU won 33 seats and the DUI 16 seats. The Together for Macedonia alliance and the DUI subsequently signed an agreement for the establishment of a coalition Government (which was, however, to exclude former NLA combatants). The new administration, comprising members of the SDAM, the LDP and the DUI, and headed by Crvenkovski, was officially approved by the Sobranie on 1 November.

In October 2002 NATO agreed to extend the mandate of Operation Amber Fox until December. On 14 December Operation Amber Fox was succeeded by a 450-member mission, Allied Harmony, with a mandate to protect international monitors and advise FYRM security forces. On 31 March 2003 this contingent was, in turn, replaced by an EU-led mission, Operation Concordia, comprising 350 military personnel; 13 EU member states and 14 non-EU nations were to participate in the force. The purpose of the operation, which was deployed at the official request of Trajkovski, was to maintain security in order to facilitate the implementation of the Ohrid peace agreement. Meanwhile, in early 2003 a newly emerged ethnic Albanian extremist group, the Albanian National Army (ANA), threatened to launch a military offensive against the Government. In September, after ethnic Albanian militants clashed with a security patrol at the border with Kosovo, the authorities dispatched security forces to the region in an operation to suppress dissident activity (a measure that was criticized by the DUI).

In May 2003 Nikola Gruevski became the new leader of the IMRO—DPMNU. In November Ljupco Jordanovski of the SDAM was elected as the new President of the Sobranie, replacing Nikola Popovski, who had been appointed as Deputy Prime Minister and Minister of Finance. In December Operation Concordia was replaced by a 200-member EU mission, Operation Proxima, which, in addition to maintaining security and combating organized crime in the country, was to advise the FYRM police forces (the mandate of Operation Proxima expired in December 2005). In early 2004 the Government announced plans to redemarcate municipal boundaries, as part of a process of administrative decentralization included in the provisions of the Ohrid agreement, although there was widespread popular opposition to the proposals.

On 26 February 2004 President Trajkovski, together with eight government officials, was killed, when an aircraft transporting him to a international investment conference in Bosnia and Herzegovina crashed in a southern, mountainous region of that country. Jordanovski, as speaker of the Sobranie, assumed the presidency in an acting capacity, pending an election, which, under the terms of the Constitution, was to take place within 40 days. At the presidential election, held on 14 April, Crvenkovski, representing the SDAM, won 42.5% of the votes cast; since he failed to secure the 50% of the votes necessary to be elected outright, he progressed to a second round with Saško Kedev, hitherto a parliamentary deputy and a member of the IMRO—DPMNU (who had won 34.1% of the votes). Two former NLA commanders, the DUI Secretary-General, Gzim Ostreni, and Zudi Xhelili of the DPA, also contested the election, obtaining 14.8% and 8.7% of the votes cast, respectively. On 28 April Crvenkovski was elected to the presidency with 62.7% of the votes. Kedev immediately claimed that widespread malpractice had been perpetrated and appealed against the election results, which were, however, described as legitimate by OSCE monitors. Crvenkovski was inaugurated on 12 May.

On 2 June 2004 the Sobranie approved the formation of a coalition administration, with Hari Kostov of the SDAM as Prime Minister, and comprising members of that party, the DUI and the LDP. The only new ministerial appointment was that of Siljan Avramovski as Minister of Internal Affairs, replacing Kostov. In July, after lengthy negotiations and under pressure from the international community, the parties of the governing coalition reached an agreement on the planned redemarcation of the country's municipal boundaries. The total number of administrative districts was to be reduced from 123 to 85, with the ethnic balance of 26 districts becoming predominantly Albanian, and the adoption of Albanian as a second official language in a number of these, including Skopje and Struga. The agreement prompted immediate strong public criticism. Protests in Struga escalated into violence; it was reported that 15 protesters and 24 members of the security forces had been injured. On 26 July a large demonstration was staged in Skopje, in protest at the draft agreement on decentralization, which been submitted for approval to the Sobranie.

On 7 November 2004, following a petition presented by Macedonian nationalist parties, a referendum on the proposed redemarcation of administrative districts was conducted. However, the governing coalition, together with representatives of the international community, urged a boycott and voter participation in the referendum was estimated at only 26%, thereby invalidating the results and allowing the local government reforms to proceed. In mid-November Kostov tendered his resignation as Prime Minister, claiming that the DUI had obstructed the parliamentary approval of reforms essential to attract foreign investment, and that the DUI Minister of Transport and Communications, in particular, had been involved in corrupt practices. Later that month Crvenkovski nominated Vlado Buckovski, hitherto the Minister of Defence, as Prime Minister, shortly after his election as Chairman of the SDAM. On 17 December the Sobranie approved a new Government, formed by Buckovski, who pledged his commitment to the implementation of economic reforms, and again comprising members of the SDAM, the LDP and the DUI. In mid-March 2005 the ICTY issued indictments against Boškovski and a former head of security, John Tarculovski, in connection with the August 2001 killings in Ljuboten. At the beginning of April Boškovski pleaded 'not guilty' to all charges before the Tribunal.

The first round of local government elections, which were to effect the significant devolution of powers to 85 municipal authorities (including the City of Skopje), took place, with some reported irregularities, on 13 March 2005. A second round of voting for 47 of the 85 municipalities was conducted on 27 March. After upholding claims of irregularities in the first round, the Supreme Court had ordered polls to be repeated in several constituencies, and an OSCE observer mission announced that the second round of the elections again failed to meet OSCE and Council of Europe standards in some municipalities. (Buckovski insisted, however, that irregularities had been recorded in only a small proportion of constituencies.) The DPA and the PDP, which had urged a boycott of the vote, refused to recognize the results. Supporters of the IMRO—DPMNU staged protests in Ohrid to demand that the second round be repeated in that municipality on grounds of malpractice. On 10 April further ballots were conducted in 19 municipalities and the City of Skopje, where electoral irregularities had occurred. According to official results, 36 of the mayoral contests were won by the Together for Macedonia governing coalition, and 15 by the DUI, with the IMRO—DPMNU securing 21 mayoralties. In mid-July, in accordance with the Ohrid Agreement, the Sobranie adopted legislation enabling any ethnic minority community to display its flag, together with the Macedonian flag, in regions where it constituted at least 50% of the population (in effect, in 19 municipalities, of which 16 were predominantly ethnic Albanian, two ethnic Turkish and one Roma).

In September 2005 the Government survived a motion of no confidence in the Sobranie, which had been proposed by opposition parties alleging economic mismanagement and demanding early elections. In December the Sobranie approved a series of constitutional amendments providing for extensive reform of the judicial system; the process of ensuring the complete independence of the judiciary, regarded as important to the country's application for EU membership (see below), was to be implemented over several years. In March 2006 the Sobranie adopted a series of amendments to electoral regulations, in preparation for legislative elections. In May the Sobranie abolished custodial sentences for those convicted of press offences.

In the legislative elections, held on 5 July 2006, the IMRO—DPMNU secured 32.5% of the votes cast, defeating Prime Minister Buckovski's SDAM, which obtained only 23.3% of the votes. A coalition of the DUI and the PDP secured the majority of ethnic Albanian votes, attracting 12.2% of the total ballot, while Xhaferi's DPA received 7.2% of the votes. Reported electoral irregularities caused the Supreme Court to demand that elections be repeated in eight constituencies, following which the IMRO—DPMNU's number of seats in the Sobranie was increased from 44 to 45. In August Gruevski, the Chairman of the IMRO—DPMNU, was formally appointed as Prime Minister and his Government was approved by the Sobranie a few days later. The new coalition administration comprised 10 members of the IMRO—DPMNU (including Trajko Slaveski as Minister of Finance and Antonio Milososki as Minister of Foreign Affairs) four of the DPA, three of the NSDP and one each of the LPM an of the SPM. Ljubiša Georgievski was appointed as President scheme. Following an IMRO—DPMNU demonstration in Skopje to demand the resignation of the Government, a reorganized administration was approved by the Sobranie at the end of May.

In May 1997 ethnic Albanians in Gostivar took part in protests against a ruling by the Constitutional Court that prohibited the use of the Albanian flag in the FYRM. In June the President of the Constitutional Court issued a statement demanding that the Government enforce the ruling. In early July the Sobranie adopted legislation stipulating that the use of the Albanian flag, and flags of other ethnic minorities, would only be permitted on national holidays, with the Macedonian flag being displayed at the same time. None the less, the mayors of Gostivar and Tetovo continued to refuse to comply with the order of the Constitutional Court, and government officials forcibly removed Albanian flags that had been displayed at municipal buildings. Ensuing protests in Gostivar resulted in violent clashes between security forces and demonstrators, as a result of which three ethnic Albanians were killed; some 500 protesters were arrested. In September the mayor of Gostivar, Rufi Osmani, received a custodial sentence of some 13 years (reduced to seven years in February 1998), after being convicted on charges of inciting ethnic tension and rebellion, while the Chairman of the municipal council was sentenced to three years' imprisonment for failing to adopt the ruling of the Constitutional Court. In April 1998 the Democratic Party of Albanians (DPA—which had been formed in July 1997 by the amalgamation of the PDPAM and the NDP) announced that it was to withdraw its representatives from all government bodies, in protest at Osmani's imprisonment.

In August 1998 the PDP and the DPA established an alliance to contest forthcoming legislative elections. In early September the IMRO—DPMNU and the newly formed Democratic Alternative (DA) formed an electoral coalition, For Changes. The legislative elections were conducted in two rounds on 18 October and 1 November 1998; the For Changes coalition secured an absolute majority in the Sobranie, with 58 seats, while the SDAM obtained 29 seats, and the alliance of the PDP and the DPA won 24. Owing to irregularities, a further round of voting took place in two electoral districts, at which one seat was won by the For Changes alliance, and the other by the PDP-DPA alliance. Later in November Georgievski was nominated as Prime Minister. The DPA was subsequently invited to join the governing coalition of the IMRO—DPMNU and the DA. In early December a new Government, comprising 14 representatives of the IMRO—DPMNU, eight of the DA and five of the DPA, was formed. At the end of December the Sobranie approved legislation (supported by the new Government) providing for the release of some 8,000 prisoners, among them Osmani. Although Gligorov refused to approve the amnesty in January 1999, in the following month the amnesty legislation was resubmitted to the Sobranie (in accordance with the Constitution) and subsequently adopted.

The first round of the presidential election on 31 October 1999 was contested by six candidates: Tito Petkovski, representing the SDAM, secured 33.2% of the votes cast, and Boris Trajkovski, the IMRO—DPMNU candidate, won 20.6%; Vasil Tupurkovski, the DA leader, took 16.0%, and Muharem Nexipi, the DPA candidate, 14.8%. Since no candidate had secured an outright majority of the votes, Petkovski and Trajkovski progressed to a second round, held on 14 November; Trajkovski secured the presidency with 52.8% of the votes cast (after DPA and DA voters transferred support to his candidacy). In late November the Supreme Court upheld a legal appeal by the SDAM against the results, and ruled that a further ballot take place in some western regions. A partial round, affecting about 10% of the total electorate, consequently took place on 5 December. However, the overall results were almost unchanged, with Trajkovski receiving 52.9% of the votes cast. Although the SDAM again claimed that irregularities had taken place, Petkovski finally accepted Trajkovski's election to the presidency. Trajkovski was formally inaugurated as President on 15 December. Following negotiations between the two leaders of the For Changes coalition, Georgievski and Tupurkovski, the IMRO—DPMNU, DA and DPA reached agreement on the formation of a new Government. The coalition administration, which contained seven new ministers (including Tupurkovski, as a Deputy Prime Minister), was formally approved by the Sobranie on 27 December.

In January 2000 the Government announced that amendments to the Constitution, which would allow higher education to be conducted in the language of ethnic minorities, would be submitted for approval by the Sobranie. In April legislation was adopted, obliging the authorities to return property expropriated under the communist regime. In the same month disaffected members of the IMRO—DPMNU, headed by a former Minister of Finance, Boris Zmejkovski, established a breakaway faction, which became known as the IMRO—True Macedonian Reform Option (IMRO—TMRO). In May the SDAM, the Liberal-Democratic Party (LDP) and the Democratic League—Liberal Party established an electoral alliance. In July Georgievski reorganized the Government, reducing the number of ministries from 21 to 14. Local government elections took place in two rounds on 10 and 24 September, amid reports of numerous violent incidents. After a further round of voting took place, owing to electoral irregularities, it was announced at the end of the month that the parties of the governing coalition had secured 75 of the 123 municipalities. Following prolonged dissent between Georgievski and Tupurkovski, the DA withdrew from the coalition Government and from the Sobranie at the end of November. Georgievski subsequently formed a new administration, which, for the first time, included members of the LDP.

In early 2001 ethnic Albanian militants, members of the self-styled National Liberation Army (NLA—which had emerged as the successor movement to the KLA), began to infiltrate northern parts of the FYRM from Kosovo, clashing with FYRM security forces. In early March NLA forces seized the border village of Tanusevci, north of Skopje, prompting counter-attacks from government troops. The border with Kosovo was officially closed after senior government officials visiting the border region were attacked and temporarily besieged by the NLA. Although the authorities succeeded in regaining control of Tanusevci, in mid-March some 200 NLA forces attempted to occupy Tetovo, precipitating the imposition of curfew regulations in the city. Following an appeal by the Government to the international community for military assistance, the North Atlantic Treaty Organization (NATO, see p. 351) reinforced its military presence at the border with Kosovo to prevent the NLA from receiving supplies from the province. On 21 March the UN Security Council adopted Resolution 1345, condemning the violence by ethnic Albanian nationalists in the FYRM as constituting a threat to the stability of the region. Despite reports that the ethnic Albanian rebels aimed to establish a 'greater Albania' (to include some northern and western regions of the FYRM), the NLA insisted that the conflict had been initiated to pressure the FYRM Government to institute constitutional changes guaranteeing equal rights for ethnic Albanians. The prolonged bombardment of rebel positions by government forces resulted in a withdrawal by the NLA from the Tetovo region, and hostilities temporarily subsided in early April. However, at the end of the month eight members of the state security forces were killed in an NLA attack near the border with Kosovo. Their funeral precipitated rioting and attacks by Macedonians on Albanian-owned property in the southern town of Bitola. Government troops subsequently launched an offensive against rebel ethnic Albanian positions near Kumanovo, after two further members of the armed forces were killed.

Meanwhile, in early April 2001, following the temporary suppression of the insurgency, inter-party discussions regarding the ethnic Albanian demands commenced. After signing a Stabilization and Association Agreement with the EU, the Government pledged to initiate political, social and economic reforms by mid-2001. Ethnic Albanian proposals included: the postponement of the ethnic census, due to take place in May, until October, to allow the return of refugees who had fled the conflict; state funding for the university at Tetovo; and the conversion of the state television's third service into an Albanian-language channel. However, the Government continued to oppose principal demands that the Constitution be amended to grant the ethnic Albanian population (hitherto officially categorized as a minority) equal rights with the Macedonian population, and Albanian the status of a second official language.

In early May 2001, following the resumption of intensive hostilities in the north of the country, the Government announced that the declaration of a state of war (which would allow the authorities to adopt emergency powers and Trajkovski to rule by decree) was under debate; the declaration, which required the approval of a two-thirds' majority in the Sobranie, was strongly opposed by ethnic Albanian deputies. Intensive discussions ensued between the principal political parties, with EU and NATO mediation, and it was agreed that the SDAM, the DPA and the PDP would join a government of national unity, and the parliamentary debate on the declaration of a state of war was suspended. The PDP subsequently demanded that the Government declare a cease-fire in the conflict in the north, as a precondition to the ethnic Albanian party's participation in the new administration. After the government offensive against the rebels was temporarily suspended, the Government of national unity (which was again headed by Georgievski) was approved by the Sobranie on 13 May. NLA leaders stated that the rebel movement (which still held several villages) would continue hostilities until the Government agreed to enter into negotiations.

On 8 June 2001 Trajkovski announced proposals for a comprehensive peace plan, which provided for the proportional representation of ethnic Albanians at all levels of government, the increased official use of the Albanian language, and a partial amnesty for NLA combatants. Despite EU support for the plan, the NLA demanded that the Government end hostilities and enter into negotiations on constitutional reforms, and rebel forces seized the town of Aracinovo, some 6 km east of Skopje. Later in June the Government announced the suspension of its offensive against the NLA, following pressure from international envoys. However, violent protests were staged by Macedonian nationalists at the parliament building in Skopje, in response to the NATO-mediated cease-fire arrangement at Aracinovo, which was perceived to be lenient towards the ethnic Albanian rebels. On 29 June NATO formally approved an operation to deploy a 3,500-member multinational force in the FYRM to assist in the disarmament of the NLA, which was, however, conditional on the imposition of a lasting cease-fire. On 5 July the Government announced that an official cease-fire agreement had been signed by both sides, and negotiations resumed between leaders of the principal Macedonian and ethnic Albanian parties regarding a permanent peace settlement. However, Georgievski and his nationalist cabinet supporters strongly opposed proposals, detailed by the EU and US special envoys, for the extension of the use of the Albanian language, and accused them of bias towards the rebels. The cease-fire collapsed after 17 days, when the NLA launched further attacks on government forces deployed near Tetovo. (By that time some 60,000 ethnic Albanians had fled to Kosovo, while a further 30,000 had become internally displaced.) International diplomatic efforts subsequently intensified, following renewed fears of widespread civil conflict. On 26 July it was announced that an accord had been reached to restore the cease-fire between government forces and the ethnic Albanian rebels, who had agreed to withdraw from newly captured territory near Tetovo. At the end of July further negotiations on the peace proposals, between government and ethnic Albanian representatives, commenced at the western town of Ohrid. Progress in the discussions was reported, following the resolution of the two main issues of contention (the extension of the official use of the Albanian language and the right to proportional representation of the ethnic Albanian community in the security forces). In response to increasing pressure from the EU and the USA, the Government announced a unilateral cease-fire, and on 13 August the Government and ethnic Albanian leaders at Ohrid signed a framework peace agreement, providing for the amendment of the Constitution to grant greater rights to the ethnic Albanian community. On the following day the NLA leader, Ali Ahmeti, agreed that the NLA, numbering an estimated 2,500–3,000, would relinquish its armaments to NATO troops. Following an assessment of the security situation, NATO announced that the cease-fire was generally being observed, and on 22 August the activation order for a NATO mission, Operation Essential Harvest, was released. The force, which had comprised 4,500 troops (of which the United Kingdom contributed about 1,900), had a mandate to disarm the ethnic Albanian combatants and destroy their weapons within 30 days of its deployment. The Ministry of Internal Affairs claimed the NLA to be in possession of some 85,000 armaments; however, NATO estimated the number of weapons to be collected at 3,000–4,000.

In early September 2001 parliamentary debate on constitutional reform was delayed by mass nationalist protests against the peace plan. Macedonian nationalist parties in the legislature continued to dispute the details of a number of the proposed amendments, while ethnic Albanian representatives insisted that attempts to limit the reforms would provoke renewed conflict. Meanwhile, investigators from the International Criminal Tribunal for the former Yugoslavia (ICTY, see p. 19) at the Hague, Netherlands, had been dispatched to the FYRM to conduct preliminary inquiries into the killing of six ethnic Albanian civilians in the village of Ljuboten in early August; the nationalist Minister of Internal Affairs, Ljube Boškovski, was suspected of responsibility for the operation. On 26 September NATO's 30-day disarmament programme was declared to have been successful, with the collection of some 3,875 armaments. On the same day the establishment of a further, reduced NATO mission, Operation Amber Fox, was authorized. In response to international pressure, the Government had insisted NATO to retain a military presence in the country, despite domestic opposition. The new mission, comprising 700 troops, together with 300 forces already stationed in the FYRM, was deployed under German leadership, with a three-month renewable mandate to protect EU and OSCE monitors supervising the implementation of the peace agreement. On 27 September Ahmeti announced that the NLA had been formally disbanded following the completion of the disarmament process. In early October the EU criticized delays in implementing constitutional reforms, after Macedonian parties announced that the legislative process would be suspended pending the release of Macedonian civilians allegedly seized by the NLA earlier in the year. Following pressure from Trajkovski, and the international community, which urged acceptance of the plan, discussion of the measures resumed in the Sobranie. Later that month Trajkovski approved plans for the deployment of ethnically mixed security units in regions formerly held by the NLA.

On 16 November 2001 the Sobranie finally adopted 15 amendments to the existing Constitution (although the extent of some provisions had been reduced at the insistence of Macedonian parties). The principal reforms were: the revision of the Constitution's preamble to include a reference to members of non-ethnic Macedonian communities as citizens of the country; the introduction in the Sobranie of a 'double majority' system, whereby certain legislation would require the approval of a minority group; the establishment of Albanian as the second official language in communities where ethnic Albanians comprised more than 20% of the population; and the right to proportional representation for ethnic Albanians on the Constitutional Court, all areas of government administration and the security forces. The adoption of the reforms was met with approval by the international community. Later in November the SDAM and the LDP withdrew from the coalition Government (which was subsequently reorganized), on the grounds that their participation was no longer necessary.

In early December 2001 NATO extended the mandate of Operation Amber Fox until 26 March 2002, and it was subsequently extended until 26 June. An EU-sponsored international donor conference on economic assistance for the FYRM, originally scheduled to take place in October 2001, was further postponed in December, pending the implementation of additional reforms. In January 2002 new legislation providing for the devolution of greater authority to local government (thereby granting a measure of self-rule to predominantly ethnic Albanian regions) was approved by the Sobranie, and the donor conference duly took place in March. Also in January a Deputy Prime Minister, Dosta Dimovska (who was considered a moderate), resigned from the Government, following disagreement with Georgievski over issues relating to the deployment of security units in previously NLA-controlled villages. In February the three principal ethnic Albanian political parties (the DPA, the PDP and the NDP) and the former NLA leaders officially established a co-ordinating council. In March the Sobranie adopted legislation granting immunity from prosecution to several thousand former NLA insurgents (excluding those indictable by the ICTY), in accordance with the peace settlement. In May the mandate of Operation Amber Fox was further extended, to 26 October. In accordance with the peace settlement, the Sobranie was dissolved on 18 July, prior to legislative elections, which were scheduled for 15 September and were to be monitored by the OSCE.

In May 2002 Ahmeti established a new political party, the Democratic Union for Integration (DUI), which was believed to comprise mainly former NLA combatants. Later that month three ministers belonging to the IMRO—TMRO resigned from the Government, on the grounds that former NLA members had become dominant within the principal ethnic Albanian regions. In the same month the Sobranie approved legislation whereby Albanian became an official language, in accordance with the Ohrid peace accord. At the end of August ethnic Albanians took hostage five Macedonian civilians at Gostivar; security forces surrounded an ethnic Albanian base and killed two of the kidnappers. None the less, the elections to the legislature took place peacefully on 15 September, attracting commendation from the international community, after OSCE observers declared them to have been conducted democratically the Sobranie. Gruevski identified his Government's main priorities as intensifying efforts to combat corruption, and improving living standards, the rate of employment and inter-ethnic relations.

In November 2006 the Sobranie adopted amendments to the FYRM's anti-corruption legislation, which included a widening of the range of activities that the Government was prohibited from engaging in during election campaigns. Meanwhile, in January 2007 the DUI and the PDP announced a boycott of parliamentary proceedings, in protest at their continued exclusion from Gruevski's Government. In February Ahmeti announced two preconditions to the resumption of political dialogue: a reconsideration by the Government of the composition of the Committee for Cross-Community Relations; and a constitutional amendment to ensure fairer representation for ethnic minorities within future governments. In mid-March representatives of the ruling coalition and of the DUI convened to discuss the political impasse; however, the DUI insisted that it would not commit to a return to the Sobranie until concessions had been made.

In February 2007 the Sobranie approved a government reorganization, which included the appointment of Imer Aliu (hitherto Minister of the Environment and Physical Planning) to the position of Deputy Prime Minister, responsible for the implementation of the Ohrid Framework Agreement. In April Boškovski and Tarculovski became the first of those accused of war crimes during the 2001 insurgency to stand trial at the ICTY; the trial concluded in May 2008.

At the end of May 2007 the PDP announced that its representatives were to resume participation in the Sobranie, after reaching an agreement with the IMRO—DPMNU permitting it to join the Government; members of the PDP received several state posts. The DUI also ended its boycott of the Sobranie, but criticized the PDP's admission to the Government. The return of the PDP and the DUI enabled the Sobranie to adopt, on 5 June, legislation providing for full co-operation with the ICTY by the Government. Two days later the Government survived a motion of no confidence proposed by the SDAM. In July DUI deputies withdrew from a parliamentary session, owing to their dissatisfaction that the regulation of use of minority languages was not under debate. In September the DUI again suspended participation in the Sobranie, following a violent disagreement between PDP and DUI deputies, prompted by criticism of the DUI by the PDP Chairman, Abduladi Vejseli. In December legislation amending the judicial system was approved, as part of the requirements for NATO accession.

In December 2007 Abduraman Memeti of the PDP announced his resignation as Minister of Local Self-Government. In January 2008 the Minister of the Economy, Vera Rafajlovska, also tendered her resignation, citing personal reasons. In March the DPA announced its withdrawal from the Government, in protest at the failure of the IMRO—DPMNU both to recognize the independence of Kosovo (see below), and to provide increased rights for the use of the Albanian language and flag. Later that month, however, it was reported that the DPA had retracted its decision (with only Aliu expected to resign from his post), after reaching an agreement with the IMRO—DPMNU on inter-party co-operation to adopt legislation on the use of language, in accordance with the Constitution and the Ohrid Framework Agreement. Following the failure of negotiations with Greece on the issue of the country's official name, and Greece's consequent decision to veto NATO membership for the FYRM at a summit meeting of the Alliance held on 2 April (see below), the DUI proposed a motion for the dissolution of the Sobranie. The motion received the support of the IMRO—DPMNU, on the grounds that the existing legislature had obstructed reforms and, was approved on 12 April by 70 deputies in the Sobranie, despite opposition from Crvenkovski (with SDAM representatives boycotting the vote). Early legislative elections were scheduled for 1 June.

At the elections on 1 June 2008 voting was disrupted in a number of constituencies by outbreaks of violence between rival ethnic Albanian groups, in which at least one person was killed and several injured. Elections were repeated on 15 June in those districts in which disorder had prevented voting from taking place, and in a small number of constituencies a further round of repeat voting was necessary on 29 June. According to provisional official results, a 19-party coalition led by IMRO—DPMNU, known as For a Better Macedonia, secured 48.8% of the votes cast and 63 of the 120 seats in the legislature, thereby becoming the first grouping to obtain an absolute majority in the Sobranie since its establishment. The Sun Coalition for Europe, an eighty-party coalition led by the SDAM, was placed second, with 23.7% and 27 seats. The DUI received 18 seats (with 12.8%) and the DPA 11 seats (8.5%). It was subsequently announced that the PDP, which failed to obtain legislative representation, was to merge with the DPA. On 12 July Gruevski announced a new Government, which was approved by the Sobranie on 26 July; the coalition administration principally comprised members of IMRO—DPMNU and the DUI, while the SPM, the Democratic Party of Turks in Macedonia and the United Party of Roma in Macedonia were also represented. In the same month Boškovski was acquitted of all charges at the ICTY, and returned to the FYRM shortly afterwards. (However, Tarculovski was sentenced to 12 years' imprisonment for the August 2001 killings in Ljuboten.)

In January 2009 the Speaker of the Sobranie scheduled the forthcoming presidential and municipal elections for 22 March; it was also announced that the major political parties had agreed that the minimum voter turnout required for a valid poll be reduced from 50% to 40%. Later in January a convention of the IMRO—DPMNU selected a university professor and non-party member, Gjorge Ivanov, as its presidential candidate, while a former minister, Ljubomir Frčkoski, was nominated by SDAM. Boškovski also declared his intention to contest the poll as an independent candidate. At the first round of the presidential election, which was contested by seven candidates on 22 March, Ivanov received about 35.1% of votes cast (according to official provisional results), while Frčkoski won 20.5%, Imer Selmani of New Democracy 15.0% and Boškovski 14.9% of votes. Consequently, a second round was scheduled for 5 April (when run-off ballots for the municipal elections were also conducted). According to official provisional results, Ivanov was elected to the presidency, with some 63.1% of votes cast. Voter turnout at the presidential poll was recorded at only 42.6% (owing, in part, to a boycott by ethnic Albanian voters), marginally exceeding the minimum rate of participation required for the poll to be valid. At the two rounds of municipal elections, held concurrently, the IMRO—DPMNU-led coalition secured 53 of the 85 mayoralties; the DUI won 12 and SDAM six mayoral posts. OSCE and Council of Europe observers declared that the organization of the elections met democratic commitments, but recommended further electoral reforms, including an end to the requirement of minimum 40% turnout. Ivanov was inaugurated as President on 12 May.

Both the September 1995 interim agreement with Greece and the November Dayton peace accord (for further details, see the chapter on Bosnia and Herzegovina) were of great significance for the FYRM, despite the unresolved issue of a permanent name for the country. The FYRM was admitted to the Council of Europe in late September, and to the OSCE in mid-October; in the following month the FYRM joined NATO's 'Partnership for Peace' programme (see p. 353). The agreement with Greece facilitated the establishment of full diplomatic relations with the EU from January 1996, and negotiations subsequently began for a co-operation accord; a declaration on co-operation was, furthermore, signed with the European Free Trade Association (see p. 426) in early April. By the end of 1996 more than 75 countries had recognized the FYRM, with about two-thirds using the country's constitutional name, the Republic of Macedonia. The FYRM Government signed a Stabilization and Association Agreement with the EU in April 2001, which came into effect on 1 April 2004. A formal application for membership of the EU was submitted on 22 March 2004 (having been postponed from February, following the death of President Trajkovski—see above). In November 2005 the European Commission recommended that the FYRM be granted the status of candidate country. The FYRM was officially declared to have candidate status at an EU summit meeting in Brussels, Belgium, in mid-December, prompting public celebrations in Skopje. However, this provided no guarantee of formal accession, although the holding of legislative elections in accordance with international standards in July 2006 did much to bolster Macedonian hopes of membership. The breakdown in political dialogue in early 2007 (see above) provoked considerable censure from, inter alia, the EU, NATO and the USA, which urged the FYRM Government more fully to implement reform measures announced in 2006. Prime Minister Gruevski assured the international community that his Government would accelerate the pace of reform. In October 2007 NATO member states adopted a resolution supporting the accession application of the FYRM (together with Albania and Croatia). The Government expressed confidence that an official invitation would be extended at a NATO summit meeting in Bucharest, Romania, on 2–4 April 2008; however, the unresolved dispute with Greece over the issue of the country's permanent name presented a continued obstacle, and, despite intensified diplomatic efforts by the UN special envoy (see below), Greece vetoed the FYRM's application. NATO confirmed that the country had fulfilled other membership pre-requisites, and that an invitation would be extended upon the settlement of the issue.

In July 1995 the FYRM and Turkey signed a 20-year co-operation agreement and a mutual security accord. Turkey, together with Albania, Bulgaria and Italy, was involved (between February 1994 and October 1995) in providing trading routes to permit the FYRM to bypass the Greek blockade. Nonetheless, the issue of ethnic Albanian rights in the FYRM was a frequent source of tension with Albania, and relations with Bulgaria continued to be impeded, specifically by the question of its recognition of a distinct Macedonian language and nationality.

Regular trade with Greece and the FRY resumed in late 1995, and, under the interim agreement of September (see above), UN-mediated discussions continued between FYRM and Greek officials regarding the issue of a permanent name for the FYRM. By 1999 the FYRM's relations with Greece had improved significantly, and the principal border crossing between the FYRM and Greece was reopened at the end of 2000. Meanwhile, work on the construction of a 214-km pipeline to transport petroleum from the FYRM's capital, Skopje, to Thessaloníki was officially completed in July 2002. Greece strongly opposed a decision by the USA, announced in November 2004, that it would henceforth recognize the FYRM by its constitutional name of 'Republic of Macedonia'. In April a UN proposal for the adoption of the name 'Republic of Macedonia-Skopje' was rejected by both countries, although Greece indicated that it might provide a basis for further dialogue. The announcement in December 2006 that the international airport near Skopje was to be renamed after Alexander 'the Great' (considered by Greece to be integral to its cultural heritage) provoked renewed tension. Discussions continued in Ohrid in January 2007, but again resulted in little progress; it was reported that the FYRM authorities were only prepared to accept a 'double formula', whereby 'Republic of Macedonia' would be used for international instances and a separate name adopted for bilateral communications with Greece. In October Prime Minister Kostas Karamanlis announced that Greece would veto the FYRM's NATO and EU applications if no resolution was reached on the issue. In March 2008 UN Special Envoy Matthew Nimetz increased pressure on both Governments to reach a compromise resolution prior to a NATO conference on 2–4 April. Demonstrations against changing the country's constitutional name were staged in Skopje, and at the end of March the Greek ambassador formally protested to the Macedonian Government at the public display of posters depicting the Greek flag overprinted with a Nazi swastika. Following the FYRM's failure to receive an invitation to join NATO in April, owing to the continued impasse, the Government pledged to intensify efforts to resolve the dispute, and early legislative elections were subsequently scheduled for June (see above), in the hope that the efficacy of governance would be improved. In November the FYRM Government submitted legal proceedings against Greece to the International Court of Justice (ICJ, see p. 22), claiming that it had violated the terms of the September 1995 interim accord regulating relations between the two countries, which stipulated that Greece would not veto the FYRM's accession to international institutions under that provisional name; a decision on the issue was expected within four years. In April 2009 the Greek Government reacted favourably to a proposal by Nimetz for the appellation 'Republic of Northern Macedonia'. However, President-elect Gjorge Ivanov (see above), who had declared that settlement of the issue would be a main priority for the Government, announced his intention to organize a national referendum on any name proposed as a compromise resolution to the dispute.

Although the FYRM formally supported the UN embargo on the FRY, there was frequent evidence that the FYRM Government permitted violations of the blockade. An agreement signed by the FYRM and the FRY in early April 1996, regulating bilateral relations and promoting mutual co-operation, was regarded as particularly significant in formalizing the FRY's recognition of the FYRM as a sovereign state, although it was criticized by most opposition groups within the FYRM. Meanwhile, the FYRM, Bosnia and Herzegovina, Croatia and Slovenia co-operated in efforts to secure international recognition for all the former republics as successor states to the SFRY, and thereby win access to a share of the assets of the former Yugoslavia. In September the FRY Prime Minister, Radoje Kontić, on his first official visit to the FYRM, signed several bilateral agreements. The Governments of the FYRM and Serbia and Montenegro (as the FRY was renamed in February 2003) increased bilateral co-operation in a number of areas, particularly measures to combat organized crime and promote regional stability.

In late 1992 the UN Security Council approved the deployment of members of the UN Protection Force (UNPROFOR) along the FYRM's border with the FRY and Albania, in an effort to protect the FYRM from any external threat to its security; in March 1995 the operation in the FYRM was renamed the UN Preventive Deployment Force (UNPREDEP). Following a reduction in UNPREDEP's authorized strength by the Security Council, the US contingent of military personnel was placed under direct US administration. In April 1997 the mandate of UNPREDEP was extended to the end of May, in view of the civil disorder in Albania (q.v.); it was further extended in June and December. Following the civil unrest in Albania, a number of border incursions by armed groups of Albanian rebels were reported. In October the Ministers of Defence of the FYRM and Albania signed an agreement providing for increased security along the joint border between the two countries.

In early 1998 increasing clashes were reported in Kosovo between members of the Serbian security forces and the ethnic Albanian KLA. In late July the UN Security Council extended the mandate of UNPREDEP until 28 February 1999 and agreed to increase the size of the contingent from 750 to about 1,100, with the aim of reinforcing border control. In early December 1998, following discussions between President Gligorov and NATO officials, it was announced that a NATO 'extraction force' was to be deployed in the FYRM to effect the evacuation of OSCE monitors in Kosovo in the event of large-scale conflict. In late February 1999 the People's Republic of China vetoed a UN Security Council resolution to extend the mandate of UNPREDEP for a further six months, following a decision by the FYRM Government to extend diplomatic recognition to Taiwan, which prompted the People's Republic of China to suspend diplomatic relations with the FYRM. Following the commencement by NATO forces of an intensive aerial bombardment of strategic targets in the FRY in late March (see the chapter on Serbia), by early April some 140,000 refugees had fled to the FYRM. By mid-April about 14,000 NATO troops were deployed near the FYRM border with Kosovo, and were involved in assisting the refugees. Owing to concern over internal destabilization, the FYRM authorities repeatedly closed the border with Kosovo to prevent the continued arrival of large numbers of ethnic Albanians, and demanded that the international community fulfil pledges to accept a proportion of the refugees. By late May some 60,000 refugees had been transported from the FYRM for provisional resettlement abroad, while an estimated 250,000 remained in the country. In early June the strength of NATO forces stationed in the FYRM was increased to 16,000. Shortly afterwards the Yugoslav Government accepted a peace plan, which provided for the withdrawal of Serbian forces from Kosovo, the return of ethnic Albanian refugees and the deployment of a NATO-led Kosovo Force (KFOR). NATO troops, which were to be deployed under the KFOR mandate, entered Kosovo from the FYRM. On 20 June NATO announced that the air campaign had officially ended, and large numbers of ethnic Albanian refugees subsequently began to return to the province from the FYRM.

In June 2001 the FYRM and the People's Republic of China agreed to restore diplomatic relations, thereby ensuring Chinese support in the UN Security Council for the deployment of a NATO peace-keeping operation from August (following an ethnic Albanian insurgency—see above); Taiwan subsequently severed relations with the FYRM. In March 2004, following an outbreak of violence in the province, the FYRM Minister of Foreign Affairs met the Head of the UN Interim Administration Mission in Kosovo (UNMIK) and NATO and US envoys for emergency discussions on Kosovo, amid concern that the clashes would result in further destabilization in the FYRM. In March 2005 Prime Minister Buckovski urged a resolution on demarcation of the border between the FYRM and Kosovo (contested since a 2001 agreement between the Governments of the FYRM and Serbia and Montenegro, owing to the continued unresolved status of Kosovo). Prolonged negotiations between Kosovan Albanian and Serbian delegations on the final status of Kosovo, which commenced in early 2006, and subsequent deliberations in the UN Security Council failed to result in a resolution. Kosovo's declaration of independence, with the support of many EU member states and the USA, on 17 February 2008 (see the chapter on Kosovo) was celebrated by ethnic Albanians in Skopje. The FYRM Government reacted with caution to the declaration and requested that the new Kosovo authorities rapidly proceed with demarcation of the border between the two countries in order to avert regional instability. In October the FYRM (together with Montenegro) announced the extension of diplomatic recognition to Kosovo, after a motion proposed by the DPA and the DUI was adopted by the Sobranie; the decision was welcomed by the USA and the EU but prompted an official protest from Serbia, which expelled the FYRM and Montenegrin ambassadors to Serbia in reprisal. Later in October the FYRM Government announced that an agreement had been reached on the demarcation of the border with Kosovo, after joint committees, meeting in Ohrid, completed operations.

Government

According to the 1991 Constitution, which was amended in November 2001, legislative power is vested in the Sobranie (Assembly), with 120 members, elected for a four-year term by universal adult suffrage (85 in single-seat constituencies and 35 members by proportional representation). The President is directly elected for a five-year term, and appoints a Prime Minister to head the Government. The Ministers are elected by the Sobranie. For the purposes of local government, the FYRM is divided into 85 municipalities (including the City of Skopje).

Defence

As assessed at November 2008, the armed forces of the FYRM totalled 10,890 in active service: army 9,760 and air force 1,130. Paramilitary forces comprised a police force of 7,600. There was also a reserve force of 21,000. Conscription was officially abolished from the beginning of 2007). On 31 March 2003 the North Atlantic Treaty Organization (NATO, see p. 351) contingent in the FYRM was replaced by a European Union (EU, see p. 255) mission, Operation Concordia, which was, in turn, replaced on 15 December by a 200-member EU police mission, Operation Proxima. The mandate of Operation Proxima, which had been renewed for one year, expired at the end of 2005. The EU subsequently provided support and assistance for the FYRM police force. The budget for 2008 allocated 7,480m. new denars to defence.

Economic Affairs

In 2007, according to World Bank estimates, the FYRM's gross national income (GNI), measured at average 2005–07 prices, was US $7,052m., equivalent to $3,460 per head (or $8,510 per head on an international purchasing-power parity basis). During 2000–07, it was estimated, the population increased by an average of 0.2% per year, while gross domestic product (GDP) per head increased, in real terms, at an average annual rate of 2.1%. Overall GDP increased, in real terms, at an average annual rate of 2.3% in 2000–07; real GDP increased by 5.1% in 2007.

Agriculture (including hunting, forestry and fishing) contributed 10.5% of GDP and engaged 18.2% of the employed labour force in 2007. Dairy farming is significant, and the principal agricultural exports are tobacco, vegetables and fruit. The wine industry is of considerable importance, and the FYRM is also a producer of wheat, maize and barley. During 2000–07, according to the World Bank, the GDP of the agricultural sector declined at an average annual rate of 0.1%; real agricultural GDP decreased by 2.9% in 2007.

Industry contributed 31.3% of GDP and engaged 31.3% of the employed labour force in 2007. During 2000–07, according to the World Bank, the GDP of the industrial sector increased, in real terms, at an average annual rate of 1.5%; real industrial GDP increased by 4.1% in 2007.

Mining contributed 0.8% of GDP and engaged 1.0% of the employed labour force in 2007. The only major mining activity is the production of lignite (brown coal), although there are also deposits of iron, zinc, lead, copper, chromium, manganese, antimony, silver, gold and nickel. Production in the mining and quarrying sector increased at an average annual rate of 5.9% in 1996–2000.

The manufacturing sector contributed an estimated 20.7% of GDP and engaged 24.8% of the employed labour force in 2007. The GDP of the manufacturing sector increased, in real terms, at an average annual rate of 0.9% in 2000–07; real manufacturing GDP increased by 5.1% in 2007.

Energy is derived principally from coal and lignite, which provided 78.3% of the electricity generated in 2005. Hydroelectric sources accounted for another 21.5% of production. The first stage of a pipeline from the Bulgarian border to carry natural gas to the FYRM from Russia became operational in 1995. A 214-km pipeline to transport petroleum from the Greek port of Thessaloníki to Skopje was inaugurated in July 2002. Mineral fuels accounted for 18.7% of the value of total imports in 2007, according to preliminary data.

Services accounted for 58.1% of GDP in 2007, when the sector engaged 50.4% of the employed labour force. During 2000–07, according to the World Bank, the GDP of the services sector increased, in real terms, at an average annual rate of 3.2%; services GDP increased by 7.3% in 2007.

In 2007 the FYRM recorded a visible trade deficit of US $1,626.9m., and there was a deficit of $246.7m. on the current account of the balance of payments. In 2007 the principal source of imports was Russia (accounting for an estimated 12.3% of total imports); other major sources were Germany, Serbia and Montenegro, Greece, Italy and Bulgaria. The principal markets for exports in that year were Serbia and Montenegro (taking a combined total of 19.1% of all exports, according to provisional data); other important purchasers were Germany, Greece, Italy, Bulgaria and Spain. The principal exports in 2007 were basic manufactures, miscellaneous manufactured articles, food and live animals, beverages and tobacco, and inedible crude materials. The main imports in that year were basic manufactures, machinery and transport equipment, mineral fuels and lubricants (notably petroleum and petroleum products), chemical products, food and live animals, miscellaneous manufactured articles, and inedible crude materials.

The FYRM recorded an overall budgetary deficit of 5,542m. new denars in 2008. At the end of 2006 the FYRM's external debt totalled US $2,661m., of which $1,498m. was long-term public debt. In that year the cost of debt-servicing was equivalent to 15.7% of the value of exports of goods and services. The annual rate of inflation averaged 2.0% in 2000–2007. Consumer prices increased by 2.2% in 2007. The rate of unemployment was 34.9% in 2007.

The FYRM is a member of the European Bank for Reconstruction and Development (EBRD, see p. 251). It became a member of the World Trade Organization (WTO, see p. 410) in 2003. The FYRM joined the Central European Free Trade Association (CEFTA) in February 2006.

Economic prospects in the FYRM advanced significantly following the removal, in late 1995, of a Greek embargo on trade (see Recent History), and UN sanctions against the Federal Republic of Yugoslavia (Montenegro and Serbia), which had severely disrupted trading links. A subsequent improvement in relations with Greece enabled substantial Greek investment, while in April 2001 a Stabilization and Association Agreement was signed with the European Union (EU, see p. 255). Although ethnic hostilities in the north of the FYRM in early 2001 caused a sizeable deterioration of the fiscal position, considerable pledges to support reconstruction ensued from a World Bank- and EU-sponsored donor aid conference in March 2002; a new stand-by credit agreement with the IMF was also signed in 2003. The new Government established in December 2003 made progress in attracting major investment projects, and in mid-2005 the IMF approved a further three-year stand-by arrangement. Notable measures adopted by the Government in 2008 included reducing the corporate tax rate (from 15% to 10%), removing the minimum capital requirement previously applied to new enterprises, increasing pensions (by 13% in January and by some 7% in July, despite the pension system being in deficit), and raising public sector wages by 10%. Critical areas of concern remained the widening current account deficit (estimated at 15% of GDP in 2008)— prompted by the growing trade deficit and driven by an increase in domestic demand—the need to diversify exports, and the high rate of unemployment (33.5% in late 2008). Inflation rose sharply in 2008 as a result of higher international prices for food and oil, and concerns were raised that the country would suffer some consequences of the global financial crisis, notably a decline in revenue from exports, remittances from workers abroad and foreign investment (the latter had, hitherto, accelerated, particularly in the export sector). The governing coalition planned a seven-year programme to invest €8,000m. in the country's infrastructure.

Education

Elementary education is free and compulsory for all children between the ages of seven and 15. Various types of secondary school, beginning at 15 and lasting for four years, are available to those who qualify. In 2005 some 91.8% of children in the relevant

THE FORMER YUGOSLAV REPUBLIC OF MACEDONIA

age-group were enrolled in primary education, while the comparable ratio for secondary education was 81.6%. According to the terms of the Constitution, nationals are granted the right to elementary and secondary education in their mother tongue. In 2001/02 Albanian was the language of education in 275 primary schools and 24 secondary schools, Turkish in 55 primary schools and five secondary schools, and Serbian in 13 primary schools. There are universities at Skopje and Bitola. New legislation on education was adopted in July 2000, permitting the use of Albanian and other languages in private tertiary institutions. In 2004, under further amendments to legislation on higher education, the Albanian-language Tetovo University became the third state-funded university. In 2006/07 some 45,624 students were enrolled in higher education. Expenditure on education by the central Government in 2002 was budgeted at 7,591m. new denars (11.4% of total expenditure).

Public Holidays

2009: 1 January (New Year), 6–7 January (Orthodox Christmas), 19–20 April (Orthodox Easter), 1 May (Labour Day), 24 May (Day of the Apostles SS Cyril and Methodius), 2 August (National Day), 8 September (Independence Day), 20 September* (Small Bayram, end of Ramadan), 11 October (Anti-Fascism Day), 23 October (Day of the Macedonian Revolution), 27 November* (Great Bayram, Feast of the Sacrifice), 8 December (St Clement of Ohrid Day).

2010: 1 January (New Year), 6–7 January (Orthodox Christmas), 4–5 April (Orthodox Easter), 1 May (Labour Day), 24 May (Day of the Apostles SS Methodius), 2 August (National Day), 8 September (Independence Day), 10 September* (Small Bayram, end of Ramadan), 11 October (Anti-Fascism Day), 23 October (Day of the Macedonian Revolution), 16 November* (Great Bayram, Feast of the Sacrifice), 8 December (St Clement of Ohrid Day).

* These holidays are dependent on the Islamic lunar calendar and may vary by one or two days from the dates given.

Weights and Measures

The metric system is in force.

Statistical Survey

Source (unless otherwise indicated): State Statistical Office of the Republic of Macedonia, 91000 Skopje, Dame Gruev 4, POB 506; tel. (2) 114904; fax (2) 111336; e-mail info@stat.gov.mk; internet www.stat.gov.mk.

Area and Population

AREA, POPULATION AND DENSITY

Area (sq km)	25,713*
Population (census results)†	
20 June 1994	1,945,932
31 October 2002	
Males	1,015,377
Females	1,007,170
Total	2,022,547
Population (UN estimates at mid-year)‡	
2006	2,038,000
2007	2,040,000
2008	2,041,000
Density (per sq km) at mid-2008	79.4

* 9,928 sq miles.
† Comprising persons with an official place of residence in the country (including those temporarily abroad for less than a year), persons from other countries who have been granted a residence permit in the FYRM and have been present there for at least a year and foreigners with refugee status; excluding foreign diplomatic and military personnel.
‡ Source: UN, *World Population Prospects: The 2008 Revision*.

PRINCIPAL ETHNIC GROUPS
(census of 31 October 2002)

	Number	%
Macedonian	1,297,981	64.2
Albanian	509,083	25.2
Turkish	77,959	3.9
Roma (Gypsy)	53,879	2.7
Serb	35,939	1.8
Muslim	17,018	0.8
Vlach	9,695	0.5
Others	21,193	1.0
Total	**2,022,547**	**100.0**

PRINCIPAL TOWNS
(official estimates, 2004)*

Skopje (capital)	515,419	Prilep		76,768
Kumanovo	105,484	Struga		63,376
Bitola	95,385	Ohrid		55,749
Tetovo	86,580	Velec		55,108
Gostivar	81,042	Strumica		54,676

* Population by municipality, except for Skopje, which comprises 10 municipalities.

Source: Ministry of Local Self-Government, Skopje.

Mid-2007 (incl. suburbs, UN estimate): Skopje 480,000 (Source: UN, *World Urbanization Prospects: The 2007 Revision*).

BIRTHS, MARRIAGES AND DEATHS

	Registered live births		Registered marriages		Registered deaths	
	Number	Rate (per 1,000)	Number	Rate (per 1,000)	Number	Rate (per 1,000)
2000	29,308	14.5	14,255	7.0	17,253	8.5
2001	27,010	13.3	13,267	6.5	16,919	8.3
2002	27,761	13.7	14,522	7.2	17,962	8.9
2003	27,011	13.3	14,402	7.1	18,006	8.9
2004	26,883	13.2	14,073	6.9	18,265	9.0
2005	22,697	11.1	14,500	7.1	18,406	9.0
2006	22,786	11.2	14,908	7.3	18,630	9.1
2007	22,688	11.1	15,490	7.6	19,594	9.6

Life expectancy (years at birth, World Bank estimates): 74.0 (males 71.7; females 76.4) in 2006 (Source: World Bank).

ECONOMICALLY ACTIVE POPULATION
(sample surveys, '000 persons aged 15 years and over)

	2005	2006	2007†
Agriculture, hunting and forestry	106.2	114.5	107.4
Fishing	0.4	0.3	0.3
Mining and quarrying	3.6	3.9	5.1
Manufacturing	120.0	123.1	126.2
Electricity, gas and water	17.0	16.0	15.6
Construction	35.2	43.2	38.0
Wholesale and retail trade, repair of motor vehicles, motorcycles and articles for personal use and for households	74.7	73.0	83.0
Hotels and restaurants	13.6	19.0	17.5

THE FORMER YUGOSLAV REPUBLIC OF MACEDONIA

—continued	2005	2006	2007+
Transport, storage and communications	32.7	30.0	35.5
Financial intermediation	6.3	7.1	9.0
Real estate, renting and business activities	14.8	15.4	15.9
Public administration and defence, compulsory social security	38.3	39.3	41.4
Education	31.7	33.4	34.4
Health and social work	31.3	32.6	32.9
Other community, social and personal services	18.2	18.3	24.7
Private households with employed persons	0.4	0.5	1.4
Extra-territorial organizations and bodies	0.9	1.0	1.9
Total employed	545.3	570.4	590.2
Unemployed	323.9	321.3	316.9
Total labour force	869.2	891.7	907.1
Males	523.3	543.8	548.1
Females	345.9	347.8	359.0

Source: ILO.

Health and Welfare

KEY INDICATORS

Total fertility rate (children per woman, 2006)	1.5
Under-5 mortality rate (per 1,000 live births, 2006)	17
HIV/AIDS (% of persons aged 15–49, 2007)	<0.1
Physicians (per 1,000 head, 2006)	2.6
Hospital beds (per 1,000 head, 2006)	4.6
Health expenditure (2006): US $ per head (PPP)	623
Health expenditure (2006): % of GDP	8.2
Health expenditure (2006): public (% of total)	71.6
Human Development Index (2006): ranking	68
Human Development Index (2006): value	0.808

For sources and definitions, see explanatory note on p. vi.

Agriculture

PRINCIPAL CROPS
('000 metric tons)

	2005	2006	2007
Wheat	333.9	293.3	157.4
Rice, paddy	12.6	13.9	12.9
Barley	136.9	135.2	83.2
Maize	148.2	147.5	99.7
Rye	9.5	8.6	7.4
Potatoes	186.7	188.1	192.5
Sugar beet	57.8	25.0*	5.9
Beans, dry	6.3	6.7	11.3*
Olives*	14.0	12.0	13.8
Cabbages and other brassicas	66.5	66.8	68.5*
Tomatoes	116.6	142.4	120.0*
Cucumbers and gherkins	36.2	39.3	32.4
Chillies and peppers, green*	100.0	100.0	108.0
Onions, dry	38.5	33.9	34.4*
Beans, green*	13.8	14.0	13.8
Watermelons	132.9	129.6	135.4
Apples	86.2	95.8	78.0*
Peaches and nectarines	11.0	10.5	9.4*
Plums and sloes	25.3	29.7	24.0*
Grapes	265.7	254.3	225.0
Tobacco, unmanufactured	27.7	25.0	20.6

* FAO estimate(s).

Aggregate production ('000 metric tons, may include official, semi-official or estimated data): Total cereals 644.6 in 2005, 602.3 in 2006, 364.2 in 2007; Total roots and tubers 186.7 in 2005, 188.1 in 2006, 192.5 in 2007; Total vegetables (incl. melons) 542.0 in 2005, 543.5 in 2006, 530.5 in 2007; Total fruits (excl. melons) 413.9 in 2005, 418.2 in 2006, 360.0 in 2007.

Source: FAO.

Statistical Survey

LIVESTOCK
('000 head, year ending September)

	2005	2006	2007
Horses*	57	58	57
Cattle	248	255	254
Pigs	156	167	255
Sheep	1,244	1,249	818
Chickens	2,617	2,585	2,264

* FAO estimates.

Source: FAO.

LIVESTOCK PRODUCTS
('000 metric tons)

	2005	2006	2007
Cattle meat	7.6	7.1	7.1
Sheep meat	6.9	7.2	6.5*
Pig meat	8.9	8.6	8.9
Chicken meat	3.8	3.7	3.5
Cows' milk	197.5	234.7	385.3
Sheep's milk	48.7	56.6	36.6
Hen eggs*	19.0	18.5	18.0
Honey	1.0	0.9	0.7
Wool, greasy	1.8	2.1	1.1

* FAO estimate(s).

Source: FAO.

Forestry

ROUNDWOOD REMOVALS
('000 cubic metres, excl. bark)

	2005	2006	2007
Sawlogs, veneer logs and logs for sleepers	144	138	142
Other industrial wood	14	24	27
Fuel wood	664	663	583
Total	822	825	752

Source: FAO.

SAWNWOOD PRODUCTION
('000 cubic metres, incl. railway sleepers)

	2005	2006	2007
Coniferous (softwood)	5	4	2
Broadleaved (hardwood)	13	13	12
Total	18	17	14

Source: FAO.

Fishing

(metric tons, live weight)

	2004	2005	2006
Capture	213	246	89
Trouts	125	142	1
Aquaculture	959	868	646
Common carp	248	187	167
Other freshwater fishes	n.a.	214	43
Trouts	711	442	378
Huchen	n.a.	n.a.	3
Total catch	1,172	1,114	735

Source: FAO.

THE FORMER YUGOSLAV REPUBLIC OF MACEDONIA   *Statistical Survey*

Mining

('000 metric tons, unless otherwise indicated)

	2004	2005	2006
Lignite	8,500	6,880	6,650
Copper concentrates*	—	22	34
Gold (kilograms)	—	750	700
Gypsum	150	190	268

* Figures refer to the metal content of concentrates.
Silver: 10,000 kg in 2003.
Source: US Geological Survey.

Industry

SELECTED PRODUCTS
('000 metric tons, unless otherwise indicated)

	2002	2003	2004
Flour	114	98	95
Refined sugar	37	33	n.a.
Wine ('000 hectolitres)	254	873	n.a.
Beer ('000 hectolitres)	657	680	716
Soft drinks ('000 hectolitres)	1,021	1,149	1,094
Cigars (million)	6,567	5,162	n.a.
Footwear, excl. rubber ('000 pairs)	1,654	1,586	n.a.
Sulphuric acid	95	45	n.a.
Motor spirit (petrol)	78	126	146
Naphthas	97	160	183
Gas-diesel (distillate fuel) oil	172	322	359
Residual fuel oils	254	343	282
Cement	777	832	812
Ferro-alloys*	77	65	70
Crude steel*	244.6	291.4	315.0
Lead: refined*	19.8	8.0	n.a.
Zinc: refined*	38.0	15.1	n.a.
Electric energy (million kWh)	6,090	6,737	6,665

* Data from US Geological Survey.
Source (unless otherwise indicated): UN, *Industrial Commodity Statistics Yearbook*.

Finance

CURRENCY AND EXCHANGE RATES

Monetary Units
100 deni = 1 new Macedonian denar.

Sterling, Dollar and Euro Equivalents (31 December 2008)
£1 sterling = 63.503 new denars;
US $1 = 43.561 new denars;
€1 = 60.624 new denars;
1,000 new denars = £15.75 = $22.96 = €16.50.

Average Exchange Rate (new denars per US $)
2006   48.802
2007   44.730
2008   41.868

BUDGET
(million new denars)*

Revenue	2006	2007	2008†
Tax revenue	58,688	66,734	73,669
Personal income tax	8,256	8,320	8,331
Profit tax	4,423	5,721	5,254
Value-added tax	27,374	31,841	36,305
Excises	11,652	13,200	14,185
Import duties	5,483	5,652	7,420
Special revenue accounts tax	240	211	401
Social contributions	30,579	31,325	33,217
Pension insurance	19,933	20,878	22,526
Unemployment contributions	1,370	1,390	1,457
Health insurance	9,276	9,057	9,234
Non-tax revenue	15,994	15,445	18,763
Capital revenue	700	564	695
Foreign donations	2,430	1,819	1,994
Repayment of loans	400	20	—
Total	**109,031**	**116,118**	**128,739**

Expenditure	2006	2007	2008†
Current expenditure	99,555	105,307	112,846
Wage, salaries and allowances	23,860	24,335	23,204
Other purchases of goods and services	14,392	17,166	18,696
Transfers	57,541	61,053	68,637
Pensions	26,884	28,532	30,798
Unemployment benefits	2,152	1,748	1,733
Social benefits	4,280	4,152	4,140
Health care	16,087	16,032	16,264
Interest payments	3,362	2,753	2,309
Guarantees	400	—	—
Capital expenditure	11,914	14,306	21,435
Total	**111,469**	**119,615**	**134,281**

* Figures refer to the consolidated accounts of the general Government, comprising the transactions of the central Government and the operations of extrabudgetary funds.
† Projections.
Source: Ministry of Finance, Skopje.

INTERNATIONAL RESERVES
(US $ million at 31 December)

	2006	2007	2008
Gold (national valuation)	138.8	182.6	188.8
IMF special drawing rights	3.0	1.5	1.4
Foreign exchange	1,747.6	2,080.8	1,919.0
Total	**1,889.4**	**2,264.9**	**2,109.2**

Source: IMF, *International Financial Statistics*.

MONEY SUPPLY
(million new denars at 31 December)

	2006	2007	2008
Currency outside banks	16,187	17,908	17,600
Demand deposits	18,084	27,342	33,728
Total (incl. others)	**36,788**	**48,858**	**56,945**

Source: IMF, *International Financial Statistics*.

COST OF LIVING
(Consumer Price Index; base: 2000 = 100)

	2005	2006	2007
Food	102.7	105.0	109.1
Fuel and light	114.0	118.2	125.0
Clothing (incl. footwear)	114.0	114.2	116.3
Housing	120.4	119.5	127.1
All items (incl. others)	**108.8**	**112.3**	**114.8**

Source: ILO.

THE FORMER YUGOSLAV REPUBLIC OF MACEDONIA

NATIONAL ACCOUNTS
(million new denars at current prices)

Expenditure on the Gross Domestic Product

	2005	2006	2007*
Government final consumption expenditure	53,990	57,583	61,902
Private final consumption expenditure	222,726	243,131	272,886
Changes in inventories	10,481	11,606	14,105
Gross fixed capital formation	48,868	56,485	71,557
Total domestic expenditure	336,065	368,805	420,450
Exports of goods and services	128,137	149,654	189,309
Less Imports of goods and services	177,582	207,544	255,971
GDP in purchasers' values	286,619	310,915	353,786
GDP at constant 1995 prices	210,486	n.a.	n.a.

* Preliminary figures.

Gross Domestic Product by Economic Activity

	2005	2006	2007*
Agriculture, hunting and forestry	31,018	33,550	33,100
Fishing	28	47	56
Mining and quarrying	1,415	1,594	2,637
Manufacturing	44,517	50,718	65,150
Electricity, gas and water supply	10,164	10,351	9,702
Construction	15,954	17,803	21,025
Wholesale and retail trade	39,022	43,707	51,579
Hotels and restaurants	4,280	4,753	5,596
Transport and communications	23,763	26,494	29,323
Financial services	8,299	10,027	12,117
Real estate and business services†	23,618	25,700	30,778
Public administration and defence	20,760	21,141	22,692
Education	10,253	10,820	12,069
Health care and social work	9,675	10,618	11,535
Other community, social and personal services	6,186	7,161	7,240
Sub-total	248,952	274,484	314,599
Less Imputed bank service charge	5,933	7,304	8,773
Gross value added at basic prices	243,019	267,180	305,826
Value-added tax	38,688	39,318	42,676
Import duties	5,398	5,423	6,198
Less Subsidies on products	486	1,006	915
GDP in purchasers' values	286,619	310,915	353,786

* Preliminary figures.
† Including imputed rents of owner-occupied dwellings.

BALANCE OF PAYMENTS
(US $ million)

	2005	2006	2007
Exports of goods f.o.b.	2,040.6	2,396.3	3,349.5
Imports of goods f.o.b.	−3,103.6	−3,681.2	−4,976.4
Trade balance	−1,063.0	−1,285.0	−1,626.9
Exports of services	515.4	601.2	818.0
Imports of services	−548.9	−573.0	−783.1
Balance on goods and services	−1,096.6	−1,256.7	−1,591.9
Other income received	97.5	134.9	213.1
Other income paid	−211.0	−171.6	−247.6
Balance on goods, services and income	−1,210.0	−1,293.4	−1,626.4
Current transfers received	1,094.9	1,279.1	1,479.5
Current transfers paid	−42.7	−42.1	−99.8
Current balance	−157.8	−56.4	−246.7
Capital account (net)	−2.0	−1.1	−1.6
Direct investment abroad	−2.8	−0.2	1.1
Direct investment from abroad	97.0	424.2	319.7
Portfolio investment assets	0.8	−0.5	−2.8
Portfolio investment liabilities	237.8	92.8	153.1
Other investment assets	−47.0	−149.4	−80.9
Other investment liabilities	291.9	68.2	83.9
Net errors and omissions	−7.3	7.7	−26.7
Overall balance	410.6	385.3	199.0

Source: IMF, *International Financial Statistics*.

External Trade

PRINCIPAL COMMODITIES
(distribution by SITC, US $ million)

Imports c.i.f.	2002	2003	2004
Food and live animals	246.5	270.6	337.1
Meat and meat preparations	70.9	70.2	86.5
Mineral fuels, lubricants, etc.	263.2	322.0	377.3
Petroleum, petroleum products, etc.	205.7	257.9	295.9
Crude petroleum and bituminous oils	96.2	192.0	220.3
Refined petroleum products	100.5	55.1	59.6
Chemicals and related products	211.7	254.7	303.7
Basic manufactures	264.8	332.8	696.1
Iron and steel	44.6	75.8	298.6
Machinery and transport equipment	408.0	433.4	545.7
Telecommunications, sound recording and reproducing equipment	50.6	89.4	73.7
Electrical machinery, apparatus, etc. (excl. telecommunications and sound equipment)	70.9	75.9	81.6
Road vehicles and parts*	130.9	101.9	184.1
Passenger motor vehicles (excl. buses)	91.3	59.2	129.8
Miscellaneous manufactured articles	113.3	128.5	171.3
Total (incl. others)	1,995.1	2,299.9	2,903.4

*Data on parts exclude tyres, engines and electrical parts.

Source: UN, *International Trade Statistics Yearbook*.

2005 (US $ million): Food and live animals 343.1; Crude materials (inedible) except fuels 106.7; Mineral fuels, lubricants, etc. 618.4; Chemicals and related products 333.9; Basic manufactures 947.6; Machinery and transport equipment 563.0; Miscellaneous manufactured articles 252.0; Total (incl. others) 3,228.0.

2006 (US $ million, preliminary): Food and live animals 369.0; Crude materials (inedible) except fuels 133.6; Mineral fuels, lubricants, etc. 760.1; Chemicals and related products 365.3; Basic manufactures 1,118.8; Machinery and transport equipment 688.6; Miscellaneous manufactured articles 260.9; Total (incl. others) 3,762.7.

2007 (US $ million, preliminary): Food and live animals 513.9; Crude materials (inedible) except fuels 293.5; Mineral fuels, lubricants, etc. 979.5; Chemicals and related products 482.8; Basic manufactures 1,483.1; Machinery and transport equipment 1,030.8; Miscellaneous manufactured articles 354.5; Total (incl. others) 5,227.6.

Exports f.o.b.	2002	2003	2004
Food and live animals	74.7	91.1	125.6
Vegetables and fruit	36.0	42.4	63.4
Beverages and tobacco	124.9	136.7	127.8
Beverages	48.7	55.4	54.9
Tobacco and tobacco manufactures	76.2	81.3	72.8
Crude materials (inedible) except fuels	35.4	39.9	47.7
Mineral fuels, lubricants, etc.	25.1	73.8	78.3
Refined petroleum products	22.5	68.6	70.4
Chemicals and related products	69.3	70.2	79.6
Basic manufactures	316.2	397.2	542.7
Textile yarn, fabrics, etc.	35.8	42.4	52.6
Iron and steel	156.1	250.5	401.8
Ferro-alloys	32.6	74.9	116.3
Sheets and plates	72.3	113.1	169.1
Non-ferrous metals	62.0	40.7	7.2
Zinc	40.1	20.4	0.7

THE FORMER YUGOSLAV REPUBLIC OF MACEDONIA

Statistical Survey

Exports f.o.b.—*continued*	2002	2003	2004
Machinery and transport equipment	74.5	80.6	98.8
Electrical machinery, apparatus, etc. (excl. telecommunications and sound equipment)	42.0	44.4	49.4
Miscellaneous manufactured articles	388.9	470.3	568.7
Clothing and accessories (excl. footwear)	334.1	409.3	488.3
Total (incl. others)	1,115.5	1,363.2	1,673.5

Source: UN, *International Trade Statistics Yearbook*.

2005 (US $ million): Food and live animals 167.2; Beverages and tobacco 163.1; Crude materials (inedible) except fuels 67.8; Mineral fuels, lubricants, etc. 163.6; Chemicals and related products 90.7; Basic manufactures 682.5; Machinery and transport equipment 109.9; Miscellaneous manufactured articles 589.9; Total (incl. others) 2,041.3.

2006 (US $ million, preliminary): Food and live animals 191.1; Beverages and tobacco 192.0; Crude materials (inedible) except fuels 111.8; Mineral fuels, lubricants, etc. 225.1; Chemicals and related products 100.5; Basic manufactures 852.6; Machinery and transport equipment 117.9; Miscellaneous manufactured articles 604.1; Total (incl. others) 2,400.7.

2007 (US $ million, preliminary): Food and live animals 248.1; Beverages and tobacco 207.3; Crude materials (inedible) except fuels 170.1; Mineral fuels, lubricants, etc. 165.1; Chemicals and related products 132.2; Basic manufactures 1,502.7; Machinery and transport equipment 149.8; Miscellaneous manufactured articles 776.5; Total (incl. others) 3,356.2.

PRINCIPAL TRADING PARTNERS
(US $ million)

Imports c.i.f.	2005	2006	2007*
Austria	69.2	80.6	101.4
Bulgaria	234.3	250.2	267.1
China, People's Republic	115.0	139.4	242.7
Croatia	75.2	79.0	109.7
France	61.0	66.3	n.a.
Germany	334.9	369.3	525.3
Greece	296.8	319.9	413.3
Italy	193.7	226.9	303.5
Netherlands	53.2	59.8	73.9
Poland	94.6	117.7	162.4
Romania	64.9	91.9	n.a.
Russia	424.5	569.6	643.3
Serbia and Montenegro	264.2	282.9	448.4
Slovenia	128.0	129.4	154.5
Spain	32.3	51.7	50.8
Switzerland-Liechtenstein	63.7	59.3	49.9
Turkey	113.6	123.9	194.8
Ukraine	72.0	105.6	n.a.
United Kingdom	44.0	37.2	49.9
USA	45.2	41.0	77.9
Total (incl. others)	3,228.0	3,762.7	5,227.6

Exports f.o.b.	2005	2006	2007*
Bosnia and Herzegovina	50.5	64.7	88.0
British Virgin Islands	83.6	n.a.	n.a.
Bulgaria	76.1	130.1	242.5
Croatia	81.1	124.2	163.9
France	19.9	10.3	n.a.
Germany	364.0	375.5	484.0
Greece	312.9	361.2	420.4
Italy	169.6	236.8	346.8
Netherlands	44.6	55.4	71.8
Russia	21.4	25.5	23.6
Serbia and Montenegro	459.5	55.8	639.4
Slovenia	31.8	41.2	68.7
Spain	50.4	50.4	173.0
Turkey	46.3	55.2	53.2
United Kingdom	42.9	36.5	75.1
USA	44.3	22.4	51.6
Total (incl. others)	2,041.3	2,400.7	3,356.2

* Preliminary.

Transport

RAILWAYS
(traffic)

	2005	2006	2007
Passenger journeys ('000)	903	962	1,102
Passenger-km (million)	94	101	109
Freight carried ('000 metric tons)	3,129	3,797	4,686
Freight ton-km (million)	531	614	778

ROAD TRAFFIC
(motor vehicles in use at 31 December)

	2000	2001	2002
Motorcycles	3,729	4,483	2,918
Passenger cars	299,588	309,562	307,581
Buses	2,498	2,620	2,497
Commercial vehicles	20,763	21,727	20,213
Special vehicles	8,552	9,554	10,292
Tractors and working vehicles	1,417	1,560	918

INLAND WATERS
(lake transport)

	2000	2001	2002
Passengers carried ('000)	10	3	6
Passenger-km ('000)	321	117	389

CIVIL AVIATION
(traffic on scheduled services)

	2002	2003	2004
Kilometres flown (million)	3	3	3
Passengers carried ('000)	166	201	211
Passenger-kilometres (million)	236	280	276
Total ton-kilometres (million)	21	25	25

Source: UN, *Statistical Yearbook*.

Tourism

TOURISTS BY COUNTRY OF ORIGIN*

	2004	2005	2006
Albania	12,470	15,392	14,402
Bosnia and Herzegovina	3,118	3,546	3,783
Bulgaria	11,110	15,894	15,548
Croatia	5,767	6,770	7,976
Germany	6,337	6,762	7,412
Greece	28,661	31,504	28,868
Italy	3,537	4,160	4,473
Netherlands	2,524	3,995	3,653
Serbia and Montenegro	27,141	33,212	33,032
Slovenia	4,848	6,754	8,156
Turkey	6,010	6,795	7,173
United Kingdom	3,988	4,976	5,219
USA	7,531	7,353	8,073
Total (incl. others)	153,644	181,484	185,185

* Figures refer to arrivals from abroad at all accommodation establishments.

Total tourist arrivals: 202,357 in 2006; 230,080 in 2007.

Tourism receipts (US $ million, incl. passenger transport): 77 in 2004; 92 in 2005; 156 in 2006.

Source: mainly World Tourism Organization.

Communications Media

	2000	2001	2002
Television receivers ('000 in use) .	570	n.a.	n.a.
Telephones ('000 main lines in use)	507.3	538.5	578.3
Mobile cellular telephones ('000 subscribers)	99.9	221.3	365.3
Internet users ('000) . . .	50	70	100
Book production: titles* . .	727	737	1,102
Book production: copies ('000)*	968	1,061	1,899
Daily newspapers: titles . .	6	8	9
Daily newspapers: average circulation ('000 copies) . .	32,640	43,689	45,536
Non-daily newspapers: titles .	33	29	30
Non-daily newspapers: average circulation ('000 copies) . .	2,619	2,961	2,618

* Including pamphlets.

Radio receivers ('000 in use): 410 in 1997.

Facsimile machines (number in use): 3,000 in 1997.

Telephones ('000 main lines in use): 533.2 in 2005; 490.9 in 2006; 463.6 in 2007.

Mobile cellular telephones ('000 subscribers): 1,261.3 in 2005; 1,417.0 in 2006; 1,946.7 in 2007.

Personal computers ('000 in use): 118 in 2003; 140 in 2004; 451 in 2005.

Internet users ('000): 159.9 in 2005; 268.0 in 2006; 416.4 in 2007.

Broadband subscribers ('000): 12.4 in 2005; 36.5 in 2006; 100.5 in 2007.

Sources: mainly International Telecommunication Union; UNESCO, *Statistical Yearbook*; and UN, *Statistical Yearbook*.

Education

(2006/07, unless otherwise indicated)

	Institutions	Teachers	Students
Primary and lower secondary .	1,000	15,106	228,207
Upper secondary	104	6,280	93,763
University level*	29	1,487	44,731
Other higher*	1	32	893

* 2002/03 figures.

Adult literacy rate (UNESCO estimates): 97.0% (males 98.6%; females 95.4%) in 2007 (Source: UNESCO Institute for Statistics).

Directory

The Constitution

The Constitution was promulgated on 17 November 1991. The following is a summary of the main provisions of the Constitution, as subsequently amended:

GENERAL PROVISIONS

The Republic of Macedonia is a sovereign, independent, democratic state, where sovereignty derives from democratically elected citizens, referendums and other forms of expression. The citizens of the Republic are the Macedonian people, as well as citizens living within its borders, including Albanians, Turks, Serbs and Vlach. State power is divided between legislative, executive and judicial bodies.

BASIC RIGHTS

The following rights and freedoms are guaranteed and protected in the Republic: the right to life, the inviolability of each person's physical and moral integrity, the right to freedom of speech, public appearance, public information, belief, conscience and religion, and the freedom to organize and belong to a trade union or a political party.

The Macedonian language is the official language in use throughout the Republic of Macedonia. Any other language spoken by at least 20% of the population in a locality is also an official language.

Any citizen who has reached the age of 18 years has the right to vote and to be elected to organs of government. The right to vote is equal, general and direct, and is realized in free elections by secret ballot. The proportional representation of each community must be assured in the public services and in all areas of public life. Citizens enjoy equal freedoms and rights without distinction. All religious creeds are separate from the State and are equal under the law.

GOVERNMENT

Legislature

Legislative power resides with the Sobranie (Assembly), which consists of between 120 and 140 deputies elected for four years. The Sobranie adopts and amends the Constitution, enacts laws and gives interpretations thereof, adopts the budget of the Republic, decides on war and peace, chooses the Government, elects judges and releases them from duty. The Sobranie may decide to call a referendum on issues within its competence. A decision is adopted at a referendum if the majority of voters taking part in the ballot votes in favour of it and if more than one-half of the electorate participates in the vote. The Sobranie forms a Council for Inter-Ethnic Relations, comprising seven representatives from each of the ethnic Macedonian and Albanian communities, and five representatives of other nationalities living in the Republic. Parliamentary legislation on issues of culture and identity, particularly in the areas of language and education, can only be adopted if a majority of the deputies representing these communities votes in favour, in addition to the overall majority. Three of the nine judges of the Constitutional Court and three of the seven members of the Republican Judicial Council must also be elected by a double majority vote.

President

The President of the Republic represents the country and is responsible for ensuring respect for the Constitution and laws. He appoints the Prime Minister and is Commander of the Armed Forces. He appoints three members of the Security Council of the Republic (over which he presides).

Ministers

Executive power in the Republic resides with the Prime Minister and Ministers, who may not concurrently serve as legislative deputies. Ministers are elected by the majority vote of all the deputies in the Sobranie. The Ministers implement laws and the state budget, and are responsible for foreign and diplomatic relations.

Judiciary

Judicial power is vested in the courts, and is autonomous and independent. The Supreme Court is the highest court. The election and dismissal of judges is proposed by the Republican Judicial Council.

Local Government

Legislation at local and municipal level is adopted by a two-thirds' majority vote of the total number of representatives. Legislation regulating such areas as local finance, elections and municipal boundaries must be adopted by a majority of the representatives representing the minority communities, as well as by an overall majority.

ON AMENDMENT

Revision of the Constitution must be approved by a two-thirds' majority in the Sobranie. Certain articles, such as the Preamble and those relating to local councils and minority rights, also require a majority of the vote by deputies from the minority communities.

The Government

HEAD OF STATE

President of the Republic: Dr GJORGE IVANOV (elected 5 April 2009; inaugurated 12 May).

GOVERNMENT
(April 2009)

Comprising representatives of the Internal Macedonian Revolutionary Organization—Democratic Party for Macedonian National Unity, the Democratic Union for Integration, the Socialist Party of Macedonia, the Democratic Party of Turks in Macedonia and the United Party of Roma in Macedonia.

Prime Minister: NIKOLA GRUEVSKI.
Deputy Prime Minister, responsible for Economic Affairs: ZORAN STAVRESKI.
Deputy Prime Minister, responsible for European Integration: IVICA BOCEVSKI.
Deputy Prime Minister, responsible for the implementation of the Ohrid Framework Agreement: ABDILAQIM ADEMI.
Minister of Foreign Affairs: ANTONIO MILOŠOSKI.
Minister of Defence: ZORAN KONJANOVSKI.
Minister of Internal Affairs: GORDANA JANKULOSKA.
Minister of Justice: MIHAJLO MANEVSKI.
Minister of Finance: TRAJKO SLAVESKI.
Minister of the Economy: FATMIR BESIMI.
Minister of Agriculture, Forestry and Water Resources: ACO SPASENOVSKI.
Minister of Health: BUJAR OSMANI.
Minister of Education and Science: PERO STOJANOVSKI.
Minister of the Information Society: IVO IVANOVSKI.
Minister of Local Self-Government: MUSA XHAFERI.
Minister of Culture: ELIZABETA KANČESKA MILEVSKA.
Minister of Transport and Communications: MILE JANAKIESKI.
Minister of the Environment and Physical Planning: NEXHATI JAKUPI.
Minister of Labour and Social Welfare: XHELAL BAJRAMI.
Minister without Portfolio: VELE SAMAK.
Minister without Portfolio: HADI NEZIRI.
Minister without Portfolio: NEŽDET MUSTAFA.

MINISTRIES

Office of the President: 1000 Skopje, 11 Oktomvri bb; tel. (2) 3113318; fax (2) 3112147; internet www.president.gov.mk.
Office of the Prime Minister: 1000 Skopje, Ilindenska bb; tel. (2) 3115455; fax (2) 3112561; internet www.vlada.mk.
Ministry of Agriculture, Forestry and Water Resources: 1000 Skopje, Leninova 2; tel. (2) 3134477; fax (2) 3239429; e-mail irena.ristoska@mzsv.gov.mk; internet www.mzsv.gov.mk.
Ministry of Culture: 1000 Skopje, ul. Gjuro Gjakovik 61; tel. (2) 3240600; fax (2) 3240561; e-mail info@kultura.gov.mk; internet www.kultura.gov.mk.
Ministry of Defence: 1000 Skopje, Orce Nikolov bb; tel. and fax (2) 3119577; fax (2) 3227835; e-mail info@morm.gov.mk; internet www.morm.gov.mk.
Ministry of the Economy: 1000 Skopje, Jurij Gagarin 15; tel. (2) 3093408; fax (2) 3084472; e-mail minister@economy.gov.mk; internet www.economy.gov.mk.
Ministry of Education and Science: 1000 Skopje, Dimitrija Čupovski 9; tel. (2) 3117288; fax (2) 3118414; e-mail contact@mon.gov.mk; internet www.mon.gov.mk.
Ministry of the Environment and Physical Planning: 1000 Skopje, ul. Drezdenska 52; tel. (2) 3066930; fax (2) 3066931; e-mail info@moepp.gov.mk; internet www.moepp.gov.mk.
Ministry of Finance: 1000 Skopje, Dame Gruev 14; tel. (2) 3117288; fax (2) 3117280; e-mail finance@finance.gov.mk; internet www.finance.gov.mk.
Ministry of Foreign Affairs: 1000 Skopje, Dame Gruev 6; tel. (2) 3110333; fax (2) 3115790; e-mail mailmnr@mfa.gov.mk; internet www.mfa.gov.mk.
Ministry of Health: 1000 Skopje, Vodnjanska bb; tel. (2) 3112500; fax (2) 3113014; internet www.zdravstvo.gov.mk.
Ministry of the Information Society: 1000 Skopje, bul. Ilinden 63A; tel. (2) 3200870; fax (2) 3221883; e-mail contact_mis@mis.gov.mk; internet www.mio.gov.mk.
Ministry of Internal Affairs: 1000 Skopje, ul. Dimče Mirčev bb; tel. (2) 3117222; fax (2) 3112468; e-mail kontakt@moi.gov.mk; internet www.mvr.gov.mk.
Ministry of Justice: 1000 Skopje, Dimitrija Čupovski 9; tel. (2) 3117277; fax (2) 3226975; internet www.pravda.gov.mk.
Ministry of Labour and Social Welfare: 1000 Skopje, Dame Gruev 14; tel. (2) 3106410; fax (2) 3110251; e-mail mtsp@mtsp.gov.mk; internet www.mtsp.gov.mk.
Ministry of Local Self-Government: 1000 Skopje, Dame Gruev 14; tel. (2) 3106302; fax (2) 3106303; internet www.mls.gov.mk.
Ministry of Transport and Communications: 1000 Skopje, pl. Crvena skopska opštinaopstina 4; tel. (2) 3145497; fax (2) 3126228; internet www.mtc.gov.mk.

President

Presidential Election, First Ballot, 22 March 2009

Candidate	Votes	% of votes
Gjorge Ivanov (IMRO—DPMNU)	343,374	35.05
Ljubomir Frčkoski (SDAM)	200,316	20.45
Imer Selmani (New Democracy)	146,795	14.98
Ljube Boškoski (Ind.)	145,638	14.87
Agron Buxhaku (DUI)	73,567	7.51
Nano Ružin (LDP)	39,645	4.05
Mirushe Hoxha (DPA)	30,281	3.09
Total	**979,616**	**100.00**

Second Ballot, 5 April 2009

Candidate	Votes	% of votes
Gjorge Ivanov (IMRO—DPMNU)	453,616	63.14
Ljubomir Frčkoski (SDAM)	264,828	36.86
Total	**718,444**	**100.00**

Legislature

Sobranie
(Assembly)

1000 Skopje, 11 Oktomvri bb; tel. (2) 3112255; fax (2) 3237947; e-mail sobranie@sobranie.mk; internet www.sobranie.mk.

President: TRAJKO VELJANOSKI.

General Election, 1 June 2008*

Party	Votes	%	Seats
For a Better Macedonia†	481,602	48.80	63
Sun Coalition for Europe‡	233,362	23.65	27
Democratic Union for Integration	125,997	12.77	18
Democratic Party of Albanians	83,678	8.48	11
Party for a European Future	14,473	1.47	1
Others	47,710	4.83	—
Total	**986,822**	**100.00**	**120**

* Provisional results, including the results of voting in six constituencies where voting was repeated on 15 June. A further repeated round of voting was held in a small number of polling stations on 29 June.
† An electoral coalition of 19 parties, led by Internal Macedonian Revolutionary Organization—Democratic Party for Macedonian National Unity.
‡ An electoral coalition of eight parties, led by the Social Democratic Alliance of Macedonia and the Liberal-Democratic Party.

Election Commission

State Election Commission (Drzhavna izborna komisija): 1000 Skopje, Makedonija 19; tel. (2) 3244744; fax (2) 3244745; e-mail izbori@sec.mk; internet www.dik.mk; Chair. ALEKSANDAR NOVAKOSKI.

THE FORMER YUGOSLAV REPUBLIC OF MACEDONIA

Political Organizations

Democratic Party of Albanians (DPA) (Partia Demokratike Shqiptare) (PDSh): Tetovo, Maršal Tito 2; tel. and fax (44) 7332572; e-mail m.thaci@gurra-pdsh.org; internet www.pdsh.info; f. 1997; officially registered 2002; absorbed the Party for Democratic Prosperity in 2008; Chair. MENDUH THAÇI.

Democratic Party of Serbs in Macedonia (DPSM): Skopje, 27 Mart 11; tel. (2) 3254274; f. 1996; contested 2008 legislative elections as mem. of For a Better Macedonia coalition; Pres. IVAN STOILKOVIĆ.

Democratic Party of Turks in Macedonia (DPTM) (Makedonya Türk Demokratik Partisi): 1000 Skopje, Üsküp, ul. Stiv Naumov bb; tel. and fax (2) 3214053; e-mail info@tdp.org.mk; internet www.tdp.org.mk; contested 2008 legislative elections as mem. of For a Better Macedonia coalition; Leader Dr KENAN HASIPI.

Democratic Renewal of Macedonia (Demokratska Obnova na Makedonija): 1000 Skopje, ul. Nikola Vapcarov 18/1; tel. (2) 3120901; fax (2) 3120902; e-mail dom@dom.org.mk; internet www.dom.org.mk; f. 2006; contested 2008 legislative elections as mem. of coalition led by IMRO—DPMNU (q.v.); Leader LILJANA POPOVSKA.

Democratic Union for Integration (DUI) (Bashkimi Demokratik për Integrim/Demokratska Unija za Integracija) (BDI): 1200 Tetovo, Rruga 170 Nr 2, Reçicë e Vogël; tel. (4) 4334398; fax (4) 4334397; e-mail bdi@bdi.org.mk; internet www.bdi.org.mk; f. 2002; ethnic Albanian, dominated by former mems of rebel National Liberation Army; Chair. ALI AHMETI; Sec.-Gen. GËZIM OSTRENI.

Internal Macedonian Revolutionary Organization—Democratic Party for Macedonian National Unity (IMRO—DPMNU) (Vnatrešno-Makedonska Revolucionerna Organizacija—Demokratska Partija za Makedonsko Nacionalno Edinstvo—VMRO—DPMNE): 1000 Skopje, Makedonija 17A; tel. (2) 3215550; fax (2) 3211586; e-mail info@vmro-dpmne.org.mk; internet www.vmro-dpmne.org.mk; nationalist; Pres. NIKOLA GRUEVSKI; Sec.-Gen. MARTIN PROTOGJER.

Internal Macedonian Revolutionary Organization—People's Party (IMRO—People's Party) (Vnatrešno Makedonska Revolucionerna Organizacija—Narodna Partija—VMRO—NP): 1000 Skopje, ul. Nikola Vapcarov br. 2; tel. and fax (2) 6131692; e-mail contact@vmro-np.org.mk; internet www.vmro-np.org.mk; f. 2004 by fmr mems of IMRO—DPMNU (q.v.); Leader LJUBČO GEORGIEVSKI; Chair. MARJAN DODOVSKI.

Liberal-Democratic Party (LDP) (Liberalno-Demokratska Partija): 1000 Skopje, Partizanski odredi 89; tel. (2) 3298261; fax (2) 3298268; e-mail contact@ldp.org.mk; internet www.ldp.org.mk; f. 1996; contested 2008 legislative elections as mem. of Sun Coalition for Europe; Chair. RISTO PENOV; Sec.-Gen. ROZA TOPUZOVA-KAREVSKA.

Liberal Party of Macedonia (LPM) (Liberalna Partija na Makedonija): 1000 Skopje, ul. Vasko Karangeleski bb; tel. (2) 2464955; fax (2) 2464956; e-mail info@lp.org.mk; internet www.lp.org.mk; contested 2008 legislative elections as mem. of Sun Coalition for Europe; Pres. BORČE STOJANOVSKI; Sec.-Gen. DUŠKO POPOVSKI.

New Democracy (Demokracia e Re): Rruga Hristijan Todorovski Karposh 94A; tel. (2) 2616220; fax (2) 2616217; e-mail info@demokraciaere.org; internet www.demokraciaere.org; f. 2008 by fmr mems of DPA (q.v.); Pres. IMER SELMANI.

New Social Democratic Party (NSDP) (Nova Socijaldemokratska Partija): 1000 Skopje, Dame Gruev 5; tel. and fax (2) 3238775; e-mail nsdp@nsdp.org.mk; internet www.nsdp.org.mk; f. 2005; contested 2008 legislative elections as mem. of Sun Coalition for Europe; Pres. TITO PETKOVSKI.

Social Democratic Alliance of Macedonia (SDAM) (Socijaldemokratski Sojuz na Makedonija—SDSM): 1000 Skopje, Bihakjka 8; tel. (2) 3293100; fax (2) 3293109; e-mail contact@sdsm.org.mk; internet www.sdsm.org.mk; f. 1943; fmrly League of Communists of Macedonia—Party of Democratic Reform; contested 2008 legislative elections as mem. of Sun Coalition for Europe; Chair. ZORAN ZAEV; Gen. Sec. IGOR IVANOVSKI.

Socialist Party of Macedonia (SPM) (Socijalistiska Partija na Makedonija): 1000 Skopje, 11 Oktomvri 17; tel. (2) 3228015; fax (2) 3220025; e-mail spm@mol.com.mk; f. 1990; left-wing; contested 2008 legislative elections as mem. of For a Better Macedonia coalition; Chair. LJUBISAV IVANOV.

United Party of Roma in Macedonia (Obedinita Partija na Romite na Makedonija): contested 2008 elections as mem. of For a Better Macedonia coalition; Leader NEZDET MUSTAFA.

Diplomatic Representation

EMBASSIES IN THE FORMER YUGOSLAV REPUBLIC OF MACEDONIA

Albania: 1000 Skopje, Majka Tereza 22; tel. (2) 3246726; fax (2) 3246727; e-mail ambshqip@mt.net.mk; Ambassador ARBEN ÇEJKU.

Austria: 1000 Skopje, Mile Popjordanov 8; tel. (2) 3083400; fax (2) 3083350; e-mail skopje-ob@bmeia.gv.at; Ambassador Dr ALOIS KRAUT.

Bosnia and Herzegovina: 1000 Skopje, Mile Pop-Jordanov 56; tel. (2) 3086216; fax (2) 3086221; e-mail emb.bih@neotel.net.mk; Ambassador MILAN BALABAN.

Bulgaria: 1000 Skopje, Zlatko Shnajder 3; tel. (2) 3229444; fax (2) 3246493; e-mail secretary@bgemb.org.mk; Ambassador MIHO MIHOV.

China, People's Republic: 1000 Skopje, 474 No 20; tel. (2) 3213163; fax (2) 3122500; e-mail chinaembmk@mfa.gov.cn; internet mk.china-embassy.org; Ambassador DONG CHUNFENG.

Croatia: 1000 Skopje, Mitropolit Teodosij Gologanov 44; tel. (2) 3248170; fax (2) 3246004; e-mail croemb.skopje@mvpei.hr; Ambassador IVAN KUJUNDŽIĆ.

Czech Republic: 1000 Skopje, Salvador Aljende 35; tel. (2) 3109805; fax (2) 3178380; e-mail skopje@embassy.mzv.cz; internet www.mzv.cz/skopje; Ambassador JOZEF BRAUN.

France: 1000 Skopje, Salvador Aljende 73; tel. (2) 3244300; fax (2) 3244313; e-mail franamba@mt.net.mk; internet www.ambafrance-mk.org; Ambassador BERNARD VALERO.

Germany: 1000 Skopje, Lerinska 59; tel. (2) 3093900; fax (2) 3093899; e-mail info@skop.auswaertiges-amt.de; internet www.skopje.diplo.de; Ambassador ULRIKE MARIA KNOTZ.

Hungary: 1000 Skopje, Mirka Ginova 27; tel. (2) 3063423; fax (2) 3063070; e-mail mission.skp@kum.hu; internet www.mfa.gov.hu/emb/skopje; Ambassador Dr FERENC KÉKESI.

Iran: 1000 Skopje, Vasil Stefanovski 25; tel. (2) 3217420; e-mail iriemb@t-home.mk; Ambassador MOHAMMED REZA SOKOUT (resident in Tehran, Iran).

Italy: 1000 Skopje, Osma Udarna brig. 22; tel. (2) 3236500; fax (2) 3236505; tel. segreteria@esteri.it; internet www.ambskopje.esteri.it; Ambassador DONATINO MARCON.

Montenegro: 1000 Skopje, Vasil Stefanovski 7; tel. (2) 3227277; fax (2) 3227254; e-mail mail@montenegroembassy.org.mk; internet www.montenegroembassy.org.mk; Ambassador DUŠKO LALIĆEVIĆ.

Netherlands: 1000 Skopje, Leninova 69–71; tel. (2) 3129319; fax (2) 3129309; e-mail sko@minbuza.nl; internet www.nlembassy.org.mk; Ambassador SIMONE FILIPPINI.

Norway: 1000 Skopje, Osma Udarna brig. 2; tel. (2) 3129165; fax (2) 3111138; e-mail embskp@mfa.no; internet www.norway.org.mk; Ambassador CARL SCHIØTZ WIBYE.

Poland: 1000 Skopje, Djuro Djakovic 50; tel. and fax (2) 3119744; e-mail ambasada@skopje.polemb.net; internet www.skopje.polemb.net; Ambassador DARIUSZ KAROL BACHURA.

Romania: 1000 Skopje, Rajko Zinzifov 42; tel. (2) 3245870; fax (2) 3245871; e-mail romanamb@cadis.net.mk; internet skopje.mae.ro; Ambassador ADRIAN STEFAN CONSTANTINESCU.

Russia: 1000 Skopje, Pirinska 44; tel. (2) 3117160; fax (2) 3117808; e-mail embassy@russia.org.mk; internet www.russia.org.mk; Ambassador VLADIMIR D. SOLOTSINSKII.

Serbia: 1000 Skopje, Pitu Guli 8; tel. (2) 3129298; fax (2) 3129427; e-mail srbamb@unet.com.mk; internet www.scgembassy.org.mk; Ambassador ZORAN POPOVIĆ.

Slovenia: 1000 Skopje, Vodnjanska 42; tel. (2) 3176663; fax (2) 3176631; e-mail vsk@gov.si; Ambassador ALAIN BRIAN BERGANT.

Spain: 1000 Skopje, 27 Mart 7; tel. (2) 3231002; fax (2) 3220612; e-mail ambspanija@mt.net.mk; Ambassador JOSÉ MANUEL PAZ Y AGÜERAS.

Sweden: 1000 Skopje, Osma Udarna Brigada 2; tel. (2) 3297880; fax (2) 3112065; e-mail ambassaden.skopje@foreign.ministry.se; internet www.swedenabroad.com/skopje; Ambassador LARS PETER FREDÉN.

Switzerland: 1000 Skopje, Maksim Gorki 19; tel. (2) 3103300; fax (2) 3103301; e-mail vertretung@sko.admin.ch; internet www.eda.admin.ch/skopje; Ambassador NICOLE WYRSCH.

Turkey: 1000 Skopje, Slavej Planina bb; tel. (2) 3113270; fax (2) 3117024; e-mail turkish@on.net.mk; Ambassador ARSLAN HAKAN OKÇAL.

Ukraine: 1000 Skopje, Pitu Guli 3; tel. and fax (2) 3178120; e-mail emb_mk@mfa.gov.ua; internet www.mfa.gov.ua/macedonia; Ambassador VITALIY A. MOSKALENKO.

United Kingdom: 1000 Skopje, Salvador Aljende 73; tel. (2) 3299299; fax (2) 3179726; e-mail britishembassyskopje@fco.gov.uk; internet ukinmacedonia.fco.gov.uk; Ambassador ANDREW KEY.

USA: 1000 Skopje, Ilindenska bb; tel. (2) 3116180; fax (2) 3117103; internet skopje.usembassy.gov; Ambassador PHILIP THOMAS REEKER.

Judicial System

The FYRM has 27 Courts of First Instance and three Courts of Appeal. The Republican Judicial Council, which comprises seven members elected by the Sobranie for a term of six years, proposes the election or dismissal of judges to the Sobranie. The Constitutional Court, comprising nine judges elected by the Sobranie with a mandate of nine years, is responsible for the protection of constitutional and legal rights, and ensures that there is no conflict in the exercise of legislative, executive and judicial powers. The Supreme Court is the highest court in the country, and guarantees the equal administration of legislation by all courts.

Constitutional Court (Ustaven Sud na Republika Makedonija): 1000 Skopje, 12 Udarna brig. 2; tel. and fax (2) 3119355; e-mail mail@ustavensud.mk; internet www.ustavensud.mk; Pres. TRENDAFIL IVANOVSKI.

Supreme Court: 1000 Skopje, Krste Misirkova bb; tel. (2) 3234064; fax (2) 3237538; Pres. SIMEON GELEVSKI.

Republican Judicial Council: 1000 Skopje, Veljko Vlahovikj bb; tel. (2) 3218130; fax (2) 3218131; Pres. LENČE SOFRONIEVSKA.

Office of the Public Prosecutor (Javno Obvinitelstvo na RM): 1000 Skopje, Krste Misirkova bb; tel. (2) 3219850; fax (2) 3219866; e-mail jorm@jorm.org.mk; internet www.jorm.org.mk; Public Prosecutor LJUPČO SVRGOVSKI.

Religion

Most ethnic Macedonians are adherents of the Eastern Orthodox Church, and since 1967 there has been an autocephalous Macedonian Orthodox Church. However, the Serbian Orthodox Church (of which the Macedonian Church formed a part) does not recognize the autocephalous church, and nor do other Orthodox Churches. There are some adherents of other Orthodox jurisdictions in the country. Those Macedonian (and Bulgarian) Slavs who converted to Islam during the Ottoman era are known as Pomaks or as ethnic Muslims. The substantial Albanian population is mostly Muslim (mainly Sunni, but there are some adherents of a Dervish sect); there are a few Roman Catholic Christians and a small Jewish community.

CHRISTIANITY

Macedonian Orthodox Church: 1000 Skopje, Partizanski Odredi 12, POB 69; tel. (2) 3230697; fax (2) 3230685; internet www.mpc.org.mk; Metropolitan See of Ohrid revived in 1958; autocephaly declared 1967; 1.5m. mems; comprises seven bishoprics in Macedonia and three abroad; Head of Church and Archbishop of Ohrid and Macedonia Metropolitan Archbishop of Skopje STEFAN VELJANOVSKI.

The Roman Catholic Church

The diocese of Skopje, suffragan to the archdiocese of Vrhbosna (based in Sarajevo, Bosnia and Herzegovina), covers most of the FYRM. The Bishop is also Apostolic Exarch for Catholics of the Byzantine Rite in the FYRM. At 31 December 2006 there were an estimated 3,762 adherents of the Latin Rite in the diocese, and the country had an estimated 15,175 adherents of the Byzantine Rite.

Bishop of Skopje: Rt Rev. KIRO STOJANOV, 1000 Skopje, Risto Šiškov 31; tel. and fax (2) 3164123; e-mail katbiskupija@mt.net.mk.

ISLAM

Islamic Community of Macedonia (Bashkësia Fetare Islame e Republikës së Maqedonisë): Skopje, Çairska 52; tel. (2) 3117410; fax (2) 3117883; e-mail bim@bim.org.mk; internet www.bim.org.mk; Leader Haji ARIF EMINI.

The Press

In 2002 a total of 39 newspapers and 178 magazines were published in the FYRM.

PRINCIPAL DAILY NEWSPAPERS

Denes (Today): 1000 Skopje, M. H. Jasmin 50; tel. (2) 3110239; fax (2) 3110150; e-mail denes@unet.com.mk; Editor NIK DENES.

Dnevnik (Daily): 1000 Skopje, Teodosij Gologanov 28; tel. (2) 3297555; fax (2) 3297554; e-mail dnevnik@dnevnik.com.mk; internet www.dnevnik.com.mk; independent; Editor-in-Chief CAŠO KOKALANOV.

Nova Makedonija (New Macedonia): 1000 Skopje, Atinska br. 12; tel. and fax (2) 5511711; e-mail nm@novamakedonija.com.mk; internet www.novamakedonija.com.mk; f. 1944; morning; in Macedonian; Dir RATKO LAZAREVSKI; Editor-in-Chief ALEKSANDAR DAMOVSKI; circ. 25,000.

Utrinski Vesnik (Morning Herald): 1000 Skopje, ul. Dimitrie Čuposki br. 11/5; tel. (2) 3236900; fax (2) 3236901; e-mail contact@utrinski.com.mk; internet www.utrinski.com.mk; Dir Dr SRGJAN KERIM; Editor-in-Chief LJUPČO POPOVSKI.

Večer (The Evening): 1000 Skopje, Nikola Vapcarov 2; tel. (2) 3219650; fax (2) 3219651; e-mail marketing@vecer.com.mk; internet www.vecer.com.mk; f. 1963; evening; Editor-in-Chief DRAGAN PAVLOVIKJ-LATAS; circ. 29,200.

Vest (News): Skopje; internet www.vest.com.mk; popular.

PERIODICALS

Delo: 1000 Skopje, Mihail Cokov bb; tel. (2) 3133306; e-mail delo@unet.com.mk; internet www.delo.com.mk; f. 1993; weekly; nationalist; Editor-in-Chief VLADO MOKROV.

Fokus: Skopje, Zheležniča 53; tel. (2) 3111327; fax (2) 3111685; weekly; independent; Editor-in-Chief NIKOLA MLADENOV.

Makedonsko Vreme/Macedonian Times: 1000 Skopje, Kliment Ohridski 52A; tel. and fax (2) 3121182; e-mail mian@mian.com.mk; internet www.mian.com.mk; f. 1994; monthly; politics and current affairs; in Macedonian and English; Editor-in-Chief JOVAN PAVLOVSKI.

Puls (Pulse): 1000 Skopje, Mito Hadživasilev bb; tel. (2) 3117124; fax (2) 3118024; internet www.puls.com.mk; weekly; business and technology; Editor-in-Chief MIRČE TOMOVSKI.

Roma Times: Skopje; e-mail mail@dostae.net.mk; internet www.dostae.net.mk/mk/press_mk_roma.htm; f. 2001; 3 a week; circ. 3,000.

Sport Magazine: 1000 Skopje, Mito Hadživasilev Jasmin bb; tel. and fax (2) 3116254; e-mail lav@unet.com.mk; f. 1991; weekly; circ. 6,000.

Trudbenik (Worker): 1000 Skopje, Udarna brigada 12; weekly; organ of Macedonian Trade Unions; Editor SIMO IVANOVSKI.

NEWS AGENCIES

Macedonian Information Agency (Makedonska Informativna Agencija—MIA): 1000 Skopje, Bojmija 2; tel. (2) 2461600; fax (2) 2464048; e-mail mia@mia.com.mk; internet www.mia.com.mk; f. 1992; news service in Macedonian, Albanian and English; Exec. Dir LJUPČO JAKIMOSKI.

Makfax: 1000 Skopje, Goce Delčev bb, POB 738; tel. (2) 3110125; fax (2) 3110181; e-mail makfax@makfax.com.mk; internet www.makfax.com.mk; f. 1992; independent; provides daily regional news service; in Macedonian, Albanian and English; Exec. Dir RISTO POPOVSKI.

PRESS ASSOCIATION

Journalists' Association of Macedonia: 1000 Skopje, Gradskizid 13, POB 498; tel. and fax (2) 3116447; e-mail znm@on.net.mk; internet www.znm.org.mk; Pres. IVAN ANDREEVSKI.

Publishers

Detska radost/Nova Makedonija (Children's Happiness/New Macedonia) Publishing House: 1000 Skopje, Mito Hadživasilev Jasmin bb; tel. (2) 3213059; fax (2) 3225830; f. 1944; children's books; Dir KIRIL DONEV.

Kultura: 1000 Skopje, Sv. Kliment Ohridski 68A; tel. (2) 3111332; fax (2) 3228608; e-mail ipkultura@kultura.com.mk; internet www.kultura.com.mk; f. 1945; history, philosophy, art, poetry, children's literature and fiction; in Macedonian; Dir DIMITAR BAŠEVSKI.

Kulturen Život (Cultural Life) Publishing House: 1000 Skopje, Ruzveltova 6; tel. (2) 3239134; f. 1971; Editor LJUBICA ARSOVSKA.

Makedonska kniga (Macedonian Book) Publishing House: 1000 Skopje, 11 Oktomvri; tel. (2) 3224055; fax (2) 3236951; f. 1947; arts, non-fiction, novels, children's books; Dir SANDE STOJČEVSKI.

Matica Makedonska: 1000 Skopje, ul. Kliment Ohridski 23; tel. (2) 3221138; fax (2) 3229244; f. 1991; Dir RADE SILJAN.

Metaforum: 1000 Skopje, Goce Delčev 6; tel. (2) 3114890; fax (2) 3115634; f. 1993; Dir RUŽICA BILKO.

Misla (Thought) Publishing House: 1000 Skopje, Partizanski odredi 1; tel. (2) 3221844; fax (2) 3118439; f. 1966; modern and classic Macedonian and translated literature; Pres. ZLATA BUNTESLEA.

Naša kniga (Our Book) Publishing House: 1000 Skopje, M. Gorki 21, POB 132; tel. (2) 3228066; fax (2) 3116872; f. 1948; Dir STOJAN LEKOVSKI.

Prosvetno delo (Educational) Publishing House: 1000 Skopje, Dimitrija Čupovski 15; tel. (2) 3117255; fax (2) 3225434; f. 1945; works of domestic writers and textbooks in Macedonian for elementary, professional and high schools; fiction and scientific works; Dir Dr KRSTE ANGELOVSKI.

Tabernakul: 1000 Skopje, POB 251, Mihail Cokov bb; tel. (2) 3127073; fax (2) 3115329; e-mail contact@tabernakul.com.mk; internet www.tabernakul.com.mk; f. 1989; religion, history, literature, philosophy, popular science; Dir CVETAN VRAŽIVIRSKI.

Broadcasting and Communications

TELECOMMUNICATIONS

Makedonski Telekom (MT): 1000 Skopje, Orce Nikolov bb; tel. (2) 3100200; fax (2) 3100300; e-mail kontakt@telekom.mk; internet www.telekom.mk; fmrly Makedonski telekomunikacii; present name adopted 2008; 51% owned by Stonebridge Communications AD Skopje (in liquidation in 2009), 34.8% state-owned; mem. of Deutsche Telekom group (Germany); CEO NIKOLAJ J. V. BEKERS.

Cosmofon: 1000 Skopje, Orce Nikolov bb; internet www.cosmofon.com.mk; f. 2003; majority share owned by Hellenic Telecommunications Organization (Greece); mobile cellular telecommunications; 140,000 subscribers (June 2004).

T-Mobile Macedonia: 1000 Skopje, Orce Nikolov bb; tel. (2) 3131131; fax (2) 3201269; e-mail kontakt@t-mobile.com.mk; internet www.t-mobile.com.mk; f. 1996 as Mobimak; present name adopted 2006; mobile cellular telecommunications; CEO RUBIN ZARESKI; 450,000 subscribers (Aug. 2003).

VIP operator DOOEL Skopje: 1000 Skopje, Dimitrie Čupovski 2; tel. (2) 3110077; e-mail kontakt@vipoperator.com.mk; internet www.vipoperator.com.mk; f. 2007; subsidiary of MobilKom (Austria); mobile cellular telecommunications services; Gen. Dir NIKOLA LJUŠEV.

BROADCASTING
Radio

Makedonska Radio-Televizija (MRT): 1000 Skopje, Goce Delčev bb; tel. (2) 3236839; fax (2) 3111821; e-mail mkrtvcor@mt.com.mk; internet www.mkrtv.com.mk; f. 1944; fmrly Radiotelevizija Skopje, name changed 1991; 3 radio channels; broadcasts in Macedonian, Albanian, Turkish, Serb, Roma and Vlach; Dirs JANEZ SAJOVIC, BORIS STAVROV; Dir of Radio GRIGORI POPOVSKI.

Antenna 5 Radio: 1000 Skopje, Tetovska 35; tel. (2) 3111911; fax (2) 3113281; e-mail mail@antenna5.com.mk; internet www.antenna5.com.mk; f. 1994; 12 transmitters broadcast to 90% of the country; Gen. Man. ZORAN PETROV.

Television

Makedonska Radio-Televizija (MRT): 1000 Skopje, Goce Delčev bb; tel. (2) 3112200; fax (2) 3111821; e-mail gstosic@unet.com.mk; internet www.mkrtv.com.mk; f. 1964; fmrly Radiotelevizija Skopje, name changed 1991; state broadcasting co; 3 television services; broadcasts in Macedonian, Albanian, Turkish, Serb, Roma and Vlach; Dirs JANEZ SAJOVIC, BORIS STAVROV; Dir of Television LJUBČO TOZIJA.

Al Television: 1000 Skopje, Pero Nakov bb; tel. (2) 2550350; fax (2) 2551970; e-mail altv@al.com.mk; internet www.al.com.mk; Gen. Man. DARKO PERUSEVSKI.

SITEL Television: 1000 Skopje, Gradski Stadion bb; tel. (2) 3116566; fax (2) 3229799; e-mail sitelvesti@on.net.mk; internet www.sitel.com.mk; Gen. Man. GOVAN IVANOVSKI.

Finance

(cap. = capital; res = reserves; dep. = deposits; m. = million; amounts in new Macedonian denars; brs = branches)

BANKS

A programme to privatize the banking sector of the FYRM was completed in early 2000. At September 2008 the banking system comprised 18 commercial banks and 11 savings houses; 14 of the banks were majority foreign-owned.

National Bank

National Bank of the Republic of Macedonia (Narodna Banka na Makedonija): 1000 Skopje, POB 401, Kompleks banki bb; tel. (2) 3108203; fax (2) 3124054; e-mail governorsoffice@nbrm.gov.mk; internet www.nbrm.gov.mk; f. 1992; central bank and bank of issue; cap. 1,289.8m., res 7,971.0m., dep. 65,042.9m. (Dec. 2007); Gov. PETAR GOŠEV.

Selected Banks

Alpha Banka a.d. Skopje: 1000 Skopje, Dame Gruev 1, POB 564; tel. (2) 3289400; fax (2) 3135206; e-mail contact@alphabank.com.mk; internet www.alphabank.com.mk; f. 1993; wholly owned by Alpha Bank AE Athens (Greece); present name adopted 2002; cap. 560.2m., res 1,021.0m., dep. 5,357.0m. (Dec. 2007); Chair. SPYROS FILARETOS; Gen. Man. IOANNIS PAPADOPOULOS; 24 brs.

InvestBanka a.d. Skopje: 1000 Skopje, Makedonija 9/11; tel. (2) 3200500; fax (2) 3200515; e-mail contact@investbanka.com.mk; internet www.investbanka.com.mk; f. 1992; 96% owned by Steiermärkische Bank und Sparkassen AG (Austria); cap. 677.5m., res 54.6m., dep. 5,266.8m. (Dec. 2007); Pres. JOSIF EFTIMOSKI.

Izvozna i Kreditna Banka a.d. (IK Banka—Export and Credit Bank): 1000 Skopje, bul. Partizanski odredi 3, POB 421; tel. (2) 3240800; fax (2) 3240833; e-mail ikbanka@ikbanka.com.mk; internet www.ikbanka.com.mk; f. 1993; 66.6% owned by Demir-Halk Bank (the Netherlands); cap. 414.2m., res 528.3m., dep. 3,915.9m. (Dec. 2007); Pres. PANČE MANČEVSKI; Chair. SVETLANA SHALJINSKA; 19 brs.

Komercijalna Banka a.d.—Skopje: 1000 Skopje, Kej Dimitar Vlahov 4; tel. (2) 3107107; fax (2) 3124064; e-mail contact@kbnet.com.mk; internet www.kb.com.mk; f. 1955 as Komunalna Banka; name changed as above in 1991; cap. 2,014.1m., res 2,105.4m., dep. 46,065.5m. (Dec. 2007); Pres. SAVA DIMITROVA; 33 brs.

Makedonska Banka za Poddrshka na Razvojot a.d. Skopje (Macedonian Bank for Development Promotion): Skopje, Veljko Vlahovikj 26; tel. (2) 3115844; fax (2) 3239688; e-mail info@mbdp.com.mk; internet www.mbdp.com.mk; f. 1998; cap. 932.4m., res 550.7m., total assets 3,080.7m. (Dec. 2007); Pres. MIHAIL PETKOVSKI.

NLB Tutunska Banka a.d. Skopje: 1000 Skopje, 12 Makedonska brigada 20; tel. (2) 3105600; fax (2) 3105681; e-mail tbanka1@tb.com.mk; internet www.tb.com.mk; f. 1985; fmrly Tutunska Banka; present name adopted 2006; cap. 785.6m., res 2,197.2m., dep. 29,531.8m. (Dec. 2007); Pres. MATEJ NARAT; 32 brs.

Ohridska Banka (Ohrid Bank): 6000 Ohrid, Makedonski Prosvetiteli 19; tel. (46) 206600; fax (46) 254130; e-mail obinfo@ob.com.mk; internet www.ob.com.mk; cap. 979.5m., res 48.1m., dep. 6,199.0m. (Dec. 2006); Pres. IVAN GOLABOSKI; 5 brs.

ProCredit Bank Macedonia: 1000 Skopje, Jane Sandanski 109A; tel. (2) 3219900; fax (2) 3219901; e-mail info@procreditbank.com.mk; internet www.procreditbank.com.mk; f. 2003; cap. 613.7m., res 33.7m., dep. 7,846.5m. (Dec. 2008); Chair. HELEN ALEXANDER.

Stopanska Banka a.d. Bitola: 7000 Bitola, Dobrivoe Radosavljević 21; tel. (47) 207500; fax (47) 207541; e-mail stbbt@stbbt.com.mk; internet www.stbbt.com.mk; f. 1948 as Komunalna Banka Bitola; present name adopted 1995; cap. 1,173.6m., res 254.0m., dep. 3,839.3m. (Dec. 2006); Pres. BLAGEJ DZALEV.

Stopanska Banka a.d. Skopje: 1000 Skopje, 11 Oktomvri 7; tel. (2) 3295295; fax (2) 3114503; e-mail sbank@stb.com.mk; internet www.stb.com.mk; f. 1944; cap. 3,602.2m., res 253.0m., dep. 47,046.0m. (Dec. 2007); 73.0% owned by National Bank of Greece, 10.8% by European Bank for Reconstruction and Development, 10.8% by International Finance Corpn (World Bank); Chair. IOANNIS PECHLIVANIDIS; 25 brs.

TTK Banka a.d. Skopje: 1000 Skopje, POB 198, ul. Naroden Front 19A; tel. (2) 3236401; fax (2) 3236444; e-mail ttk@ttk.com.mk; internet www.ttk.com.mk; f. 2001; present name adopted 2006; cap. 680.9m., res 196.3m., dep. 2,370.1m. (Dec. 2006); Pres. GLIGORIE GOGOVSKI.

UniBanka—Universalna Investiciona Banka a.d. Skopje (Universal Investment Bank): 1000 Skopje, M. Gorki 6; tel. (2) 3286100; fax (2) 3286000; e-mail info@unibank.com.mk; internet www.unibank.com.mk; f. 1993 as Balkanska Banka a.d. Skopje; present name adopted 2004; cap. 546.0m., res 183.9m., dep. 6,594.9m. (Dec. 2007); Pres. JORDAN SKORČEV.

STOCK EXCHANGE

Macedonian Stock Exchange (Makedonska Berza a.d. Skopje): 1000 Skopje, Orce Nikolov 75; tel. (2) 3122055; fax (2) 3122069; e-mail mse@mse.org.mk; internet www.mse.com.mk; f. 1995; Chair. LIDIJA TRAJKOVIKJ.

INSURANCE

In 2008 the insurance system in the FYRM comprised 12 insurance companies, seven insurance brokerage companies and three insurance agencies.

QBE Makedonija: 1000 Skopje, 11 Oktomvri 25; tel. (2) 3115188; fax (2) 3114020; internet www.qbeeurope.com/makedonija; subsid-

THE FORMER YUGOSLAV REPUBLIC OF MACEDONIA

iary of QBE Insurance Group (Australia); stock company for insurance and reinsurance; CEO FRANK O'HALLORAN.

Trade and Industry

CHAMBER OF COMMERCE

Economic Chamber of Macedonia (Stopanska Komora na Makedonija): 1000 Skopje, Dimitrija Čupovski 13; tel. (2) 3244000; fax (2) 3244088; e-mail ic@ic.mchamber.org.mk; internet www.mchamber.org.mk; f. 1962; Pres. BRANKO AZESKI.

UTILITIES

Electricity

EVN Macedonia: 1000 Skopje, 11 Oktombri 9; tel. (2) 3111077; fax (2) 3227827; e-mail lenche.karpuzovska@evn.com.mk; internet www.evn.com.mk; production and distribution of electric power; 90% owned by EVM AG (Austria); fmrly Electric Power Co of Macedonia (Elektrostopanstovo na Makedonija); Chair. GEORG VALDNER.

TRADE UNIONS

Federation of Trade Unions of Macedonia: 1000 Skopje; tel. (2) 3231374; fax (2) 3115787; 18 affiliated unions; Pres. VANCO MURATOVSKI.

Transport

RAILWAYS

In 2002 the rail network totalled 699 km, of which 233 km were electrified. Train services between Skopje and Prishtina, Kosovo, suspended since 1999, were resumed in 2006.

Makedonski Železnici (MZ) (Macedonian Railways): 1000 Skopje, Železnička 50; tel. (2) 3227903; fax (2) 3462330; e-mail muzunova@mz.com.mk; internet www.mz.com.mk; f. 1992; Chair. KOSANA MAZNEVA; Dir-Gen. NIKOLA DIMITROVSKI.

ROADS

The FYRM's road network totalled 12,974 km in 2002, of which about 6,806 km were paved.

CIVIL AVIATION

The FYRM has two international airports, at Ohrid, and the Aleksandar Veliki (Alexander the Great) Airport, near Skopje.

Macedonian Airlines (MAT): 1000 Skopje, Vasil Glavinov 3; tel. (2) 3292333; fax (2) 3229576; e-mail mathq@mat.com.mk; internet www.mat.com.mk; f. 1994; domestic services and flights within Europe; Man. Dir DUSKO GRUEVSKI.

Tourism

Tourist arrivals numbered 230,080 in 2007. In 2006 receipts from tourism amounted to US $156m.

Tourist Association of Macedonia: 1000 Skopje, Dame Gruev 28/5; tel. (2) 3290862; e-mail tarm@mt.net.mk.

MADAGASCAR

Introductory Survey

Location, Climate, Language, Religion, Flag, Capital

The Republic of Madagascar comprises the island of Madagascar, the fourth largest in the world, and several much smaller offshore islands, in the western Indian Ocean, about 500 km (300 miles) east of Mozambique, in southern Africa. The inland climate is temperate; in Antananarivo temperatures are generally between 8°C (48°F) and 27°C (81°F), with cooler, dryer weather between May and October. The coastal region is tropical, with an average daily maximum temperature of 32°C (90°F). The rainy season extends from November to April in the highlands (average annual rainfall is 1,000 mm–1,500 mm) but is more prolonged on the coast, where average annual rainfall can reach 3,500 mm. The official languages are Malagasy and French. Following a referendum held in April 2007, English was adopted as the third official language. Hova and other dialects are also widely spoken. More than 50% of the population follow animist beliefs, while about 41% are Christians and the remainder are Muslims. The national flag (proportions 2 by 3) has a vertical white stripe (one-third of the length) at the hoist and two equal horizontal stripes, of red and green, in the fly. The capital is Antananarivo.

Recent History

A French possession since 1896, Madagascar became an autonomous state within the French Community in October 1958, as the Malagasy Republic. In May 1959 Philibert Tsiranana, leader of the Parti social démocrate (PSD), was elected President. The country achieved full independence on 26 June 1960. Prior to independence France supported the PSD, which was identified with the majority coastal tribes (*côtiers*), as an alternative to the more nationalistic highland people, the Merina, who were the traditional ruling group in the island.

After 1967 the economy deteriorated, and there was growing opposition to the Government's alleged authoritarianism and subservience to French interests. In May 1972, following civil unrest, President Tsiranana transferred full powers to the Army Chief of Staff, Gen. Gabriel Ramanantsoa. In October 1973 pro-Government parties secured a decisive victory in legislative elections. A prolonged crisis followed an attempted military coup in December 1974, and in early February 1975 Ramanantsoa transferred power to Col Richard Ratsimandrava, hitherto Minister of the Interior; however, Ratsimandrava was assassinated shortly afterwards. On 12 February Brig.-Gen. Gilles Andriamahazo assumed power and imposed martial law. All political parties were suspended. In June Andriamahazo was succeeded as Head of State by Lt-Commdr (later Adm.) Didier Ratsiraka, a *côtier* and a former Minister of Foreign Affairs, who became Chairman of the Supreme Revolutionary Council (SRC).

In a referendum in December 1975 more than 94% of voters approved a new Constitution, which provided for radical administrative and agrarian reforms, and the appointment of Ratsiraka as President of the Republic for a term of seven years. The country's name was changed to the Democratic Republic of Madagascar, and a 'Second Republic' was proclaimed. In March the Avant-garde de la révolution malgache (AREMA—Antoky Ny Revolosiona Malagasy) was founded as the nucleus of the Front national pour la défense de la révolution socialiste malgache (FNDR), the only political organization permitted by the Constitution.

At local government elections in March–June 1977 AREMA secured the majority of votes, resulting in division within the FNDR. The left-wing Mouvement national pour l'indépendance de Madagascar (Monima Ka Miviombio, known as Monima), led by Monja Jaona, withdrew from the FNDR and was subsequently proscribed. At legislative elections in June AREMA secured 112 of the 137 seats in the National People's Assembly. A new Council of Ministers was formed in August, and the membership of the SRC was extended to include leaders of the former political parties and additional *côtiers*, in an effort to restore political equilibrium.

In November 1982 Ratsiraka was re-elected President, receiving 80.2% of the votes cast. At elections to the National People's Assembly in August 1983 AREMA won 117 of the 137 seats. Open dissatisfaction with the Government's policies persisted, however.

In February 1988 the Prime Minister, Col Désiré Rakotoarijaona, resigned, owing to poor health, and was replaced by Lt-Col Victor Ramahatra, formerly Minister of Public Works. Ratsiraka was re-elected to the presidency in March 1989 for a further seven-year term, with 62.7% of the total votes cast. At legislative elections in May AREMA won 120 seats. The Mouvement pour le pouvoir prolétarien (Mpitolona ho amin'ny Fonjakan'ny Madinika—MFM), which obtained only seven seats, rejected the official results, alleging electoral misconduct. The Elan populaire pour l'unité nationale (Vonjy Iray Tsy Mivaky, known as Vonjy) secured four seats, AKFM/Fanavaozana (a newly formed group, comprising former members of the Parti du congrès de l'indépendance de Madagascar—AKFM), won three seats, the original AKFM two seats, and Monima only one seat.

In August 1989 Ratsiraka assented to opposition demands for discussions about the future role and structure of the FNDR. In December the National People's Assembly adopted a constitutional amendment abolishing the requirement for political parties to be members of the FNDR (thereby effectively dissolving the FNDR), despite opposition from MFM deputies.

In March 1990 the Government formally permitted the resumption of multi-party politics. Numerous new organizations emerged, while other parties that had hitherto operated within the FNDR became official opposition movements. Several pro-Government political associations joined AREMA to form a new coalition, the Mouvement militant pour le socialisme malagasy (MMSM). The principal opposition movements included the Union nationale pour le développement et la démocratie (UNDD) and the MFM (restyled the Mouvement pour le progrès de Madagascar, or Mpitolona ho amin'ny Fandrosoan'ny Madagasikara). An informal alliance, the Comité des forces vives—subsequently known as Forces vives (FV, Hery Velona)—was formed by 16 opposition factions, and trade unions and other groups.

In May 1991 legislation providing for extensive constitutional amendments was submitted to the National People's Assembly. Opposition parties criticized the proposals, on the grounds that the revised Constitution would retain references to socialism. In June opposition leaders applied to the Haute Cour Constitutionnelle (High Constitutional Court—HCC) to effect Ratsiraka's removal from office, while the FV organized demonstrations in support of its demands for the resignation of the President and the convening of a national conference to draft a new constitution. Later in June the FV formed a 'parallel' administration, which it termed the 'Provisional Government'.

In July 1991 the FV organized a general strike, warning that it would continue until the Government acceded to its demands for constitutional reform. The FV appointed Jean Rakotoharison, a retired army general, as President of the 'Provisional Government', and Albert Zafy, the leader of the UNDD, as its Prime Minister. However, Manandafy Rakotonirina, the leader of the MFM, rejected the formation of the 'Provisional Government', favouring further negotiations, and withdrew his party from the FV. Members of the 'Provisional Government' subsequently occupied the premises of six official government ministries. Later in July Ratsiraka ordered the detention of several members of the 'Provisional Government' and imposed a state of emergency in Antananarivo. The FV withdrew from negotiations with the MMSM, in protest against the arrests, while the French Government appealed to Ratsiraka to release the opposition leaders. In response to increasing public pressure, Ratsiraka dissolved the Council of Ministers and pledged to organize a constitutional referendum before the end of 1991. Members of the 'Provisional Government' were released from custody, and Ratsiraka repealed legislation that authorized the detention of opponents of the Government.

In August 1991 Ratsiraka appointed Guy Razanamasy, the mayor of Antananarivo, as Prime Minister. Later that month Ratsiraka declared Madagascar to be a federation of six states, with himself as President, and claimed to command the support of five provinces where AREMA continued to hold the majority of seats in regional councils. At the end of August Razanamasy formed an interim Government, which did not include any members of the FV or the MFM.

On 31 October 1991 representatives of the Government, the FV, the MFM, church leaders and the armed forces signed an agreement providing for the suspension of the Constitution and the creation of a transitional Government, which was to remain in office for a maximum period of 18 months, pending presidential and legislative elections. The SRC and the National People's Assembly were to be replaced by interim bodies, respectively the High State Authority for Transition to the Third Republic and the National Committee for Economic and Social Regeneration. On an interim basis, Ratsiraka was to remain as President of the Republic and Razanamasy as Prime Minister. Zafy was designated President of the High State Authority, while Rakotonirina and Pastor Richard Andriamanjato, the leader of AKFM/Fanavaozana, were appointed as joint Presidents of the 131-member National Committee for Economic and Social Regeneration. The power to appoint or to dismiss government ministers, hitherto vested in the President, was granted to Razanamasy. A new constitution was to be submitted to a national referendum by the end of 1991. Zafy subsequently rejected the agreement, on the grounds that Ratsiraka was to retain the nominal post of Commander-in-Chief of the Armed Forces. In November Razanamasy formed a new interim Government, which included three representatives of the MFM and one MMSM member. Francisque Ravony, of the MFM, was appointed to the new post of Deputy Prime Minister. Owing to Zafy's refusal to participate in the Government, 10 portfolios that had been allocated to the FV remained vacant. Later in November, however, Zafy agreed to accept the presidency of the High State Authority.

In December 1991 Razanamasy announced that the formation of the coalition Government had proved unsuccessful, and 11 ministers, including Ravony, resigned. Razanamasy appointed a larger Government of national consensus, in which 14 (of 36) portfolios were allocated to the FV. In January 1992 it was announced that all political factions had now accepted the terms of the October 1991 agreement. The institutions that had been established by the accord were to prepare for the constitutional referendum, now scheduled for June 1992, and for local, presidential and legislative elections, which were to take place by the end of the year. In February the High State Authority for Transition to the Third Republic announced the dissolution of the SRC and the National People's Assembly, in accordance with the October 1991 agreement, and indicated that a new body was to be created to supervise local elections, replacing the existing system of government, based on village assemblies (*fokontany*). However, the MMSM claimed that the High State Authority was not empowered to dissolve the local government structure. The Government subsequently announced that control of local government was to be transferred from elected councils to special delegations, and that security commissions were to be established to organize the *fokontany*.

The draft Constitution of the Third Republic, as submitted to the Government in April 1992, envisaged a unitary state and provided for a bicameral legislature, comprising a Senate and a National Assembly. Two-thirds of the members of the Senate were to be selected by an electoral college, with the remaining one-third to be appointed by the President, while the 184-member National Assembly was to be elected by universal suffrage, under a system of proportional representation, for a four-year term. The authority of the President was reduced, and executive power was vested in the Prime Minister, who was to be appointed by the National Assembly. Ratsiraka reiterated his intention to contest the presidential election and demanded that a draft providing for a federal system of government also be submitted to the forthcoming referendum.

The new Constitution was approved by 72.2% of votes cast in a national referendum on 19 August 1992. Federalists forcibly prevented the electorate from voting in a number of regions, and several people were killed in clashes between supporters of the MMSM and members of the FV at Toamasina. In September MMSM supporters unilaterally declared Antsiranana, Toliary, Toamasina and Fianarantsoa to be federal states, and suspended infrastructural links between these provinces and Antananarivo. The following month federalists in Antsiranana, apparently supported by members of the presidential guard, took hostage members of the FV and seized control of the radio and television stations. Razanamasy declared the unilateral proclamation of independence of the four provinces to be illegal, but initiated negotiations with the federalists, in an effort to prevent disruption of the presidential election. Later that month there were further clashes in Toliary between supporters of the FV and federalists, led by Monja Jaona, who had declared himself to be Governor of the province. At the end of October, however, the federalists agreed to participate in the presidential election, although the MMSM continued officially to reject the new Constitution

The presidential election took place on 25 November 1992 at which Zafy secured 45.1% of votes cast, and Ratsiraka 29.2%. At a second round of voting, on 10 February 1993, Zafy secured 66.7% of the votes cast. Zafy's inauguration, on 27 March, was accompanied by violent clashes between security forces and federalists in the north. In accordance with the Constitution, Zafy resigned as President of the UNDD at a party congress in May; Emmanuel Rakotovahiny, the Minister of State for Agriculture and Rural Development, was elected as his successor.

Several constituent parties of the FV that had not supported Zafy in the first round of the presidential election subsequently presented independent lists of candidates for the forthcoming legislative elections; the remaining parties in the alliance became known as Forces vives Rasalama (Hery Velona Rasalama—HVR). The elections, to a reduced 138-member National Assembly, took place on 16 June 1993, and were contested by 121 political associations. The HVR secured 46 seats, the MFM 15, and a new alliance of pro-Ratsiraka parties 11 seats. The official results indicated that parties supporting Zafy had won 75 seats in the National Assembly. In August Francisque Ravony was elected Prime Minister and formed a new Council of Ministers. Richard Andriamanjato was elected President of the National Assembly.

In July 1995, apparently at Zafy's instigation, deputies belonging to the HVR, the UNDD and AKFM/Fanavaozana proposed a motion of censure against Ravony in the National Assembly (which was, however, rejected by a large majority). Zafy subsequently announced that he was unable to co-operate with Ravony and decreed that a constitutional amendment empowering the President, rather than the National Assembly, to select the Prime Minister, be submitted for approval in a national referendum. Ravony indicated that he would resign after the referendum, regardless of the outcome. In August Ravony formed a new Council of Ministers, comprising representatives of the parliamentary majority that had supported him in the previous month. The referendum proceeded in September, at which the constitutional amendment was approved by 63.6% of votes cast. Ravony duly resigned in October, and Zafy appointed Rakotovahiny as Prime Minister.

Dissension emerged between the parties that supported Zafy over the composition of the new Council of Ministers, and in December 1995 associates of Andriamanjato demanded that an alternative cabinet be appointed. In May 1996 a motion of censure against Rakotovahiny's Government was approved by a large majority in the National Assembly. Rakotovahiny submitted his administration's resignation, and Norbert Ratsirahonana, hitherto President of the HCC, was appointed Prime Minister.

Zafy refused to approve the new Government initially proposed by Ratsirahonana, insisting on the inclusion of five UNDD members who had served in the previous Council of Ministers. Ratsirahonana, however, won a vote of confidence in the legislature in July, by associating the vote with legislation providing for the implementation of economic reforms stipulated by the IMF and the World Bank. On 26 July a motion in the National Assembly to remove Zafy from office for numerous contraventions of the Constitution was supported by 99 of 131 votes cast. (Meanwhile, local elections, which had been scheduled for August, and were to replace the existing six provinces with 28 regions, were postponed as a result of the presidential crisis.) The HCC endorsed the President's impeachment in September, upholding the majority of the charges against him; Zafy maintained that his impeachment was illegal, but resigned the same day. Ratsirahonana was appointed interim President by the HCC, pending an election; he formed a new interim Government that represented the majority in the National Assembly and excluded members of the UNDD. Zafy announced his intention to contest the forthcoming election, as did Ratsiraka and Ratsirahonana.

In all, 15 candidates stood in the first round of the presidential election, which proceeded peacefully on 3 November 1996; Ratsiraka (with 36.6% of the votes cast) and Zafy (with 23.4%) qualified to contest the second round. The head of Libéralisme économique et action démocratique pour la reconstruction nationale (LEADER/Fanilo), Herizo Razafimahaleo, obtained 15.1%, and Ratsirahonana 10.1%, of the votes. Razafimahaleo urged his supporters to vote for Ratsiraka. None of the unsuccessful candidates chose to support Zafy, who declared his intention, if elected, to retain Ratsirahonana (who had successfully concluded an agreement with the IMF in August) as Prime Minister; Ratsirahonana, however, refused to endorse either candidate. At the second round, which took place on 29 December, Ratsiraka narrowly won, with 50.7% of the valid votes cast, although more than 50% of the registered electorate abstained from voting. Ratsiraka was inaugurated as President on 9 February. He appointed Pascal Rakotomavo (a former Minister of Finance) as Prime Minister. Rakotomavo's Government included Razafimahaleo as Deputy Prime Minister, responsible for Foreign Affairs.

In early 1998 Ratsiraka announced that a constitutional referendum would take place on 15 March 1998, to be followed by legislative elections. The draft amendments to the Constitution envisaged a 'federal-style' state, composed of six autonomous provinces, and also provided for increased presidential powers.

In February 1998 a motion of impeachment against Ratsiraka failed to gain the requisite two-thirds' majority in the National Assembly. Later that month the principal opposition parties urged voters to boycott the forthcoming referendum, claiming that the Government had ignored the views presented at the regional forums and the proposals of the National Consultative Commission, and had deliberately delayed discussion on legislation proposed by Rakotonirina (who had chaired the Commission) whereby any draft constitution would require the approval of more than 50% of all registered voters in order to become law. The referendum proceeded on 15 March 1998, when extensive revisions to the Constitution were narrowly endorsed by 50.96% of votes cast. Rakotonirina's proposed legislation was approved by the National Assembly later that month. However, Ratsiraka referred the legislation back to the National Assembly, and in April it was rejected after further deliberation.

Elections to an expanded National Assembly followed on 17 May 1998, under a new electoral law. Of the 150 seats, 82 were to be filled from single-member constituencies, with the remaining deputies to be elected by a system of proportional representation in 34 two-member constituencies. Ratsiraka's party, AREMA, performed well in the elections, winning 63 seats, while the pro-presidential LEADER/Fanilo and the Rassemblement pour le socialisme et la démocratie (RPSD) secured 16 and 11 seats, respectively. Ratsirahonana's party, Ny asa vita no ifampitsara (AVI), emerged as the strongest opposition party, with 14 seats, while Zafy's new party—Asa, Faharaminana, Fampandrasoana, Arinda (AFFA)—won six seats; independent candidates took 32 seats. The AVI and 24 independent deputies were subsequently reported to have joined the AREMA majority, leaving the AFFA and the remaining independents as the only significant parliamentary opposition. In July Tantely Andrianarivo, hitherto Deputy Prime Minister, was appointed as Prime Minister, retaining responsibility for finance and the economy. The 31-member Council of Ministers was dominated by AREMA, with the key portfolios largely unchanged; 12 new ministers were appointed.

The first local government elections—communal voting for 20,000 councillors and 1,392 mayors—since the reintroduction of the three-tier system of local government (provinces, regions and communes), under the amended Constitution of 1998, took place on 14 November 1999. The greatest successes were recorded by nominally independent candidates. Most notably, Marc Ravalomanana, the head of the country's largest agro-industrial processor, Tiko, was elected mayor of Antananarivo; Ravalomanana had been a principal donor of electoral funds to the AVI, but had stood as an independent. Roland Ratsiraka, a nephew of the President, was elected independent mayor of Toamasina. Provincial elections took place on 3 December 2000 to elect 336 councillors, as a preliminary step to the decentralization of certain powers to six autonomous provinces (legislation on the organization of which had been approved by the National Assembly in August). It was reported that AREMA had secured control of most of the major towns, although the AVI won a majority of seats in Antananarivo.

On 18 March 2001 a 1,727-member electoral college, which included mayors and local councillors, elected 60 members of the new Senate. AREMA won 49 of the 60 seats, while LEADER/Fanilo secured five seats and opposition parties a total of six, including two for the AVI. President Ratsiraka subsequently named the remaining 30 senators who would constitute the 90-seat upper house.

A presidential election took place on 16 December 2001, contested by six candidates, including Ratsiraka, Zafy, Razafimahaleo and Ravalomanana. According to the official results, Ravalomanana secured 46.2% of the votes cast and Didier Ratsiraka 40.9%, thereby necessitating a second round of voting. However, Ravalomanana's own electoral observers disputed this result, claiming that he had won an outright victory, with 52.2% of the votes, and demanded a public comparison of voting records. The opposition was supported in these demands by international electoral observers. A re-count was subsequently conducted, and on 25 January 2002 the HCC endorsed the official results and ruled that a second round of voting should take place within 30 days. Ravalomanana rejected this verdict and called for a national strike in protest. Some 500,000 people responded by gathering in Antananarivo; government offices, public utilities and banks ceased operations, and air traffic was suspended. Ravalomanana's supporters also closed the central bank in order to prevent Ratsiraka from withdrawing special funds from the treasury. Strike action continued, in varying forms, for eight weeks. Following a meeting between Ravalomanana and Ratsiraka in mid-February, negotiations were conducted between their representatives, with mediation by the Organization of African Unity (OAU); Ratsiraka's delegates rejected Ravalomanana's proposals for the formation of an interim government and new appointments to the HCC and electoral committee. Meanwhile, the Minister of the Armed Forces, Gen. Marcel Ranjeva, declared that the army would remain neutral in the electoral dispute.

On 22 February 2002 Ravalomanana accelerated events by unilaterally declaring himself President at a ceremony in Antananarivo attended by 100,000 supporters. The President of the Senate immediately declared Ravalomanana's proclamation to be illegal, and it was widely condemned by the international community. In response, President Ratsiraka declared a three-month 'state of national necessity', according himself broad powers, including the right to pass laws by decree. On 26 February Ravalomanana named Jacques Sylla, a former Minister of Foreign Affairs under Zafy's presidency, as his Prime Minister. On the following day Ratsiraka's Minister of Foreign Affairs and Minister of Post and Telecommunications both resigned. Violent clashes erupted between supporters of Ratsiraka and Ravalomanana in Antananarivo, prompting Ratsiraka to decree martial law and appoint a military governor, Gen. Léon-Claude Raveloarison, in the capital. None the less, Ravalomanana proceeded with the formation of his rival Government in early March, while opposition supporters erected barricades against the army and set fire to the military headquarters; 17 of those appointed to Ravalomanana's administration were successfully installed in government offices, accompanied by large crowds of supporters and unopposed by the military. On the same day the governors of the five remaining provinces of the country declared their allegiance to Ratsiraka, recognizing his hometown, Toamasina (where Ratsiraka and his ministers had relocated) as a temporary 'alternative capital'. A few days later Gen. Ranjeva resigned as Minister of the Armed Forces, shortly after Ravalomanana's rival Government had taken control of his offices in Antananarivo. Gen. Raveloarison resigned as military governor of Antananarivo some three weeks after his appointment, having failed to apply martial law and order troops to end protests, on the grounds that this would have incurred deaths. Later in March 58 of Madagascar's 150 deputies attended a parliamentary session called by Ravalomanana and elected an interim President of the National Assembly.

An OAU mission held talks with Ravalomanana and Ratsiraka in March 2002, in an attempt to resolve the ongoing political crisis, but its proposal for a 'government of national reconciliation' was rejected by both sides. At the beginning of April supporters of Ratsiraka, who had erected roadblocks to isolate Antananarivo in February, destroyed two of the bridges located on its supply routes to the rest of the island, in an effort to intensify the effective siege of the capital, which was already suffering from severe fuel shortages.

On 10 April 2002 the Supreme Court ruled that there had been irregularities in the appointment, shortly before the presidential election, of six of the nine judges of the HCC, which had endorsed the official results; one week later the Supreme Court annulled the disputed results and ordered a re-count of the votes. On the following day Ratsiraka and Ravalomanana signed a peace accord in Dakar, Senegal, where they had been holding talks under the auspices of the OAU and the UN, and with mediation by the Presidents of Senegal, Benin, Côte d'Ivoire and Mozambique. Following the completion of the re-count, in late April, the HCC ruled that Ravalomanana had secured the presidency, with 51.5% of the votes cast, while Ratsiraka had won 35.9%. Ratsiraka, who had failed to remove the blockade of Antananarivo (in contravention of the Dakar accord), refused to accept the Court's decision. Nevertheless, Ravalomanana was inaugurated as President on 6 May, largely without international recognition, and appointed a new Council of Ministers later that month. Four of the country's six provincial governors, who were loyal to Ratsiraka, subsequently threatened to secede. Heavy fighting ensued, as troops loyal to Ravalomanana conducted a military offensive against areas controlled by Ratsiraka, securing two provincial capitals, Mahajanga and Toliary, in mid-June.

In mid-June 2002 Ravalomanana dissolved the Government that he had formed in May, immediately reappointing Sylla as Prime Minister; however, despite nominating six new members of the Council of Ministers, he failed to appoint a government of national unity. At the end of June the USA recognized Ravalomanana as the legitimate leader of Madagascar; endorsement soon followed from France and, in contravention of the policy of the OAU, Senegal. Meanwhile, the OAU suspended Madagascar from its meetings, pending the staging of free and fair elections leading to the establishment of a legitimate government; this decision was upheld by the African Union (AU, see p. 172), which replaced the OAU in July. In early July Ravalomanana's government troops took control of Antsiranana and Toamasina, and Ratsiraka sought exile in France; this apparent admission of defeat allowed for an international conference to take place in Paris, France, on the donation of aid for the reconstruction of Madagascar. The new Government was in full control of the island by the middle of the month. Ravalomanana replaced the 30 presidentially appointed members of the Senate, with the approval of the HCC, despite the fact that those appointed by Ratsiraka had been appointed for a tenure of six years. In August six of the nine members of the HCC were also replaced.

In mid-October 2002 the National Assembly was dissolved in preparation for legislative elections, brought forward from May 2003, in response to pressure from aid donors, in order to finalize the legitimacy of Ravalomanana's mandate. At the elections, which took place on 15 December 2002, Ravalomanana's party, Tiako i Madagasikara (TIM—I Love Madagascar), won 104 of the 160 seats and the pro-Ravalomanana Firaisankinam-Pirenena, an alliance of the AVI and elements of the RPSD, secured a further 22 seats; notably, 23 independent deputies were elected, and the formerly incumbent AREMA party won only three seats. (Foreign observers were permitted to be present at the elections for the first time in Malagasy electoral history.) In mid-January 2003 a new Government was appointed, which included 10 new ministers and was reduced in overall size from 30 to 20 ministers; the former Minister of Public Works, Jean Lahiniriako, was elected President of the National Assembly. Madagascar's suspension from meetings of the AU—hitherto the only remaining significant authority not to have recognized the new Government—was formally revoked at the organization's General Assembly in July of that year; the legitimacy of the Ravalomanana administration was thus considered finally to have been established. In August former President Ratsiraka was sentenced, *in absentia*, to 10 years' hard labour for the embezzlement of public funds and declared unfit for public office.

In January 2004 Ravalomanana restructured and reshuffled the Council of Ministers, reducing its membership to 17 ministers and two secretaries of state. Several former supporters of Ratsiraka were appointed in order to diversify the ethnic composition of the Government, which had hitherto been dominated by the Merina. In March the President granted pardons to those sentenced to less than three years' imprisonment for involvement with the pro-Ratsiraka resistance; those with more serious sentences would have the right to apply individually for an amnesty.

In December 2004 the TIM held its first national congress, at which Sylla resigned as Secretary-General; a reshuffle of the Council of Ministers was effected early in the same month. President Ravalomanana increased the accountability of the Government with ministerial performances being graded, financial bonuses awarded for the attainment of performance targets and the introduction of possible dismissal from office as the result of failure to reach such targets.

In March 2005 Zaza Ramandimbiarisona resigned as Deputy Prime Minister in charge of Economic Programmes and the post was subsequently abolished, although a successor was appointed to his secondary role as Minister of Transport and Public Works. As part of that reorganization the office of Secretary of State for Decentralization and National and Regional Development was redesignated as a ministerial portfolio. In October a further minor reorganization was effected, with the appointment of Roger-Marie Rafanomezantsoa as Minister of Industry, Trade and the Development of the Private Sector and of Tombo Ramandimbisoa to the Ministry of Youth and Sports. Furthermore, the Minister of the Interior and Administrative Reform, Gen. Soja, was unexpectedly dismissed in November, following an alleged attempt on the President's life; he was replaced by Lt-Gen. Charles Rabemananjara. Meanwhile, in October the Government forcibly closed the Fiangonana Protestanta Vaovao eto Madagasikara (FPVM) protestant church, for illegally occupying churches of the Fiangonan' i Jesoa Kristy eto Madagasikara (FJKM), of which President Ravalomanana was a senior official, and posing a threat to public order. Some observers feared a threat to the secular status of the country, with the President declaring that he hoped for a Christian nation. The FPVM challenged the closure, but it was ruled by a civil court that only the President could overturn the decision.

In mid-November 2006 Gen. Randrianafidiosa, a senior member of the armed forces whose candidacy for the presidential election scheduled for the following month had been rejected by the HCC, attempted a military coup to overthrow what he termed an 'illegitimate' Government. An aircraft aboard which President Ravalomanana was returning from Europe was diverted as gunfire broke out near the airport at Antananarivo, and it was reported that a member of the security forces had been shot dead outside a military base. Randrianafidiosa initially evaded capture, but was arrested by the authorities in mid-December.

The presidential election was held on 3 December 2006. According to results released by the HCC on 23 December, Ravalomanana secured 54.79% of votes cast in the first-round ballot, thus obviating the requirement for a second round of voting. His closest rival was Jean Lahiniriko, who took 11.65% of the votes. The poll was generally accepted by independent observers as free and fair. President Ravalomanana was formally sworn in for a second term in office on 19 January 2007 and the following day he appointed Rabemananjara as Prime Minister. The majority of those appointed to the new Government announced later that month were members of the FJKM church, including, most notably, Harison Edmond Randriarimanana, who was appointed to head the newly created Ministry of the Economy, Planning, the Private Sector and Commerce.

At a national referendum conducted on 4 April 2007 75.3% of participants voted in favour of amendments to the Constitution, which included the abolition of autonomous powers for the six provinces. Voter turn-out was reported at just 44%. The new Constitution also adopted English as the country's third official language alongside Malagasy and French and granted extended powers to the President, including the right to legislate by decree in the event of the declaration of a state of emergency.

President Ravalomanana dissolved the National Assembly on 24 July 2007, claiming that its composition was no longer representative of the recently restructured regional and national administrative order. Elections to the 127-seat legislature (reduced from 160) were held on 23 September, in which the TIM secured 105 seats while independent candidates won 11. However, results in two constituencies were annulled owing to alleged voting irregularities. In October the President of the TIM, Razoharimihaja Solofonantenaina, resigned citing ill health; Yvan Randriasandratriniony, the Minister of Decentralization and Territorial Development, was selected as his successor. Later that month, in a governmental reorganization, Cécile Manorohanta was appointed Minister of National Defence, while Bakolalao Ramanandraibe Ranaivoharivony was named as Minister of Justice and Keeper of the Seals; Haja Nirina Razafinjatovo became Minister of Finance and the Budget. Further cabinet changes were effected in early January 2009 when Desiré Rasolofomanana was appointed Minister of Internal Security and Gervais Rakotonirina was named Minister of the Interior.

Meanwhile, relations between President Ravalomanana and the Mayor of Antananarivo and the leader of the Tanora Malagasy Vonona (TGV—Determined Malagasy Youth), Andry Rajoelina, had become strained in December 2008 when Ravalomanana closed Rajoelina's television station after it broadcast a number of anti-Government programmes and an interview with former President Ratsiraka. This prompted violent protests by several thousand of Rajoelina's supporters who attacked state-owned television and radio stations and began looting businesses. Tensions had also recently increased in the country as a result of the rising cost of fuel and foodstuffs, the perceived success of Ravalomanana's business interests, and the decision taken in November 2008 to lease some 1.3m. ha of agricultural land to the South Korean conglomerate Daewoo (on which it was to grow corn and palm oil) for a period of 99 years, and for which Madagascar would receive no direct financial benefit. A political impasse developed with Rajoelina, speaking at an opposition rally in late January 2009, accusing the President of failing in his duties and insisting that he resign. Violence continued to escalate and sizeable areas of the capital were destroyed by fire, resulting in at least 44 deaths. Ravalomanana appealed to Rajoelina to work with him to stabilize the situation; however, in early February Rajoelina, who had been gaining popular support, was dismissed from the mayoralty and replaced by Guy Randrianarisoa, resulting in days of further violent disturbances: some 28 people were killed and more than 200 injured when the security forces fired on demonstrators. Days later the Minister of Defence, Cécile Manorohanta, announced her resignation in protest at the actions of the security forces; she was replaced by Vice-Adm. Mamy Ranaivoniarivo. Meanwhile, Rajoelina declared himself President of a Haute autorité de la transition (HAT) and named, among others, Monja Roindefo as Prime Minister and Manantsoa Masimana as Minister of the Interior. The parallel administration was not recognized by the international community but received widespread internal popular support. Nevertheless, the security forces removed a number of Rajoelina's supporters who had attempted to seize four government buildings, including those of the interior and security ministries.

Ravalomanana and Rajoelina held a series of discussions with the aim of finding a resolution to the crisis and on 21 February 2009 agreed a five-point plan, which included steps to end the violence and the inflammatory statements emanating from both parties. However, several days later Rajoelina announced that talks between the two men had failed and urged his supporters to hold daily protests until Ravalomanana agreed to step down. Pressure continued to increase on the President—a number of military officers announced on 8 March that they would no longer take orders from Ravalomanana and two days later Ranaivoniarivo announced his resignation, although he subsequently claimed that it had been extracted under duress and that he remained in his post—and, following a military assault on the presidential residence and the central bank on 16 March and demands from Rajoelina that the President be arrested, Ravalomanana dissolved the Government and resigned, handing power over to a military executive committee led by the most senior figure in the armed forces, Vice-Adm. Hyppolite Ramaroson. Later that day the military transferred executive powers to Rajoelina despite the current terms of the Constitution stipulating that the President should be aged 40 years or above. Rajoelina, at just 34 years of age, was too young to fulfil this requirement. Although international organizations refused to acknowledge Rajoelina's authority, and what was perceived as a coup received widespread international condemnation, on 18 March the HCC endorsed Rajoelina's assumption of interim power (he was officially sworn in as President on 21 March), and on 19 March the new leader dissolved the National Assembly and the Senate. Rajoelina announced that elections would be held within two years and that a new constitution would be drafted. Both the AU and the Southern African Development Community subsequently suspended Madagascar's membership pending a return to constitutional order.

In late March 2009 Rajoelina appointed a 22-member Government, retaining those ministers named in February; other appointments included Col Noël Rakotonandrasana as Minister of the Armed Forces, Benja Joas Razafimahaleo as Minister of Finance and the Budget and Ny Hasina Andriamanjato as Minister of Foreign Affairs. In mid-April, Ravalomanana, who remained in exile in Swaziland, named Rakotonirina as his own 'legal' Prime Minister in an attempt to regain his authority and, despite the issuing of a warrant for his arrest, pledged to return to Madagascar. Later in April Rakotonirina was arrested in Antananarivo and charged with threatening the security of the state, illegitimately declaring himself Prime Minister, instigating the destruction of property and the illegal possession of firearms.

Madagascar's foreign policy is officially non-aligned: while it formerly maintained close links with communist countries (particularly the People's Republic of China, the Democratic People's Republic of Korea and the former USSR), the Zafy Government established relations with Israel, South Africa and the Republic of Korea. Relations with France have been affected by disputes over compensation for nationalized French assets and over the continuing French claim to the Iles Glorieuses, north of Madagascar, and three other islets in the Mozambique Channel. In 1980 the UN voted in favour of restoring all the disputed islets to Madagascar. In early 1986 the Government announced the extension of Madagascar's exclusive economic zone to include the Iles Glorieuses and the three islets. In 1997 government announcements regarding future privatization plans in Madagascar prompted renewed appeals from France for compensation for nationalized French assets. In response, the Government allocated some 50,000m. francs MG as initial compensation in the budget for 1998. In February 2000 it was agreed that the Iles Glorieuses would be co-administered by France, Madagascar and Mauritius, without prejudice to the question of sovereignty. In April 2004, during a state visit to Madagascar by Prime Minister Paul Bérenger of Mauritius, political and economic co-operation agreements between the two countries were signed.

Relations with China were strengthened in January 1999, during a visit by Vice-President Hu Jintao; agreements were signed on the expansion of bilateral economic relations and China's provision of preferential loans to Madagascar. In September 2000 the representative office for Taiwan in Madagascar was closed down, following an official visit by the Malagasy Minister of Foreign Affairs to China. (It was claimed that this was carried out by the Government in support of the 'one China' policy; however, the Taiwanese claimed that the office had never functioned effectively.) In 2005 Prime Minister Sylla denounced the Taiwanese authorities' decision to terminate the National Unification Council, which had been established in 1990 to oversee the island's eventual unification with China.

Government

The Constitution of the Third Republic was endorsed by national referendum on 19 August 1992, but was extensively revised by amendments that were endorsed by national referendum on 15 March 1998. The amended Constitution enshrined a 'federal-style' state, composed of six autonomous provinces (*faritany*), each with a provincial council (holding legislative power) elected by universal suffrage for a term of five years. Each provincial council elected a governor; however, these officials were replaced on an interim basis by presidentially appointed representatives following the governmental crisis in 2002 (see above). Legislation was passed subsequently whereby local administration was restructured into 22 regions and in September 2004 each region was nominated a regional chief responsible for decentralizing operations. A national referendum held on 4 April 2007 approved a number of further amendments to the Constitution, including the abolition of autonomy for the six provinces. The first local elections (for communal councillors and mayors) under the restored three-tier system of provinces, regions and communes, as envisaged in the Constitution, took place in November 1999. Provincial elections were held in December 2000 and in November 2003. The Constitution provides for a bicameral legislature, comprising a Senate (established in March 2001) and a National Assembly. Two-thirds of the members of the Senate are elected by the autonomous provinces, and the remaining one-third of the members are appointed by the President, while the National Assembly is elected by universal suffrage for a five-year term of office. The constitutional Head of State is the President, who is elected for a term of five years, and can be re-elected for two further terms. The President appoints the Prime Minister and, on the latter's recommendation, the other members of the Council of Ministers.

Defence

As assessed at November 2008, total armed forces numbered about 13,500 men: army 12,500, navy 500 and air force 500. There is a paramilitary gendarmerie of 8,100. The defence budget for 2008 was estimated at 176,000m. ariary.

Economic Affairs

In 2007, according to estimates by the World Bank, Madagascar's gross national income (GNI), measured at average 2005– prices, was US $6,331m., equivalent to about $320 per h (or $920 per head on an international purchasing-power p basis). During 2000–07, it was estimated, the popu increased at an average annual rate of 2.8%, while gross tic product (GDP) per head increased, in real term average of 0.4% per year. Overall GDP increased, in real terms, at an average annual rate of 3.2% in 2000–07; GDP increased by 6.5% in 2007.

In 2007 the agricultural sector (including forestry and fishing) accounted for an estimated 26.5% of GDP and employed an estimated 82.0% of the economically active population in 2005. Rice, the staple food crop, is produced on some 50% of cultivated land. Since 1972, however, imports of rice have been necessary to supplement domestic production. The most important cash crops are spices (which accounted for an estimated 7.6% of total export revenue in 2007). Following a long drought in 2003, vanilla production was estimated to have halved in that year, leading to a dramatic escalation in world prices and the development of the crop in other countries, as well as an increase in synthetic alternatives; however, prices had declined significantly at the beginning of 2005, having a negative impact on producers. Sugar, coconuts, tropical fruits, sweet potatoes and maize are also cultivated. Cattle-farming is important. Sea fishing by coastal fishermen (particularly for crustaceans) is being expanded, while vessels from the European Union fish for tuna and prawns in Madagascar's exclusive maritime zone, within 200 nautical miles (370 km) of the coast, in return for compensation. According to World Bank figures, agricultural GDP increased by an average of 2.1% per year in 2000–07; the sector's GDP increased by 2.4% in 2007.

Industry (including mining, manufacturing, construction and power) contributed an estimated 15.0% of Madagascar's GDP in 2007, and employed 3.4% of the employed labour force in 2005. According to the World Bank, industrial GDP increased at an average annual rate of 2.0% in 2000–07; the sector's GDP increased by 4.8% in 2007.

The mining sector contributed only 0.3% of GDP in 1991 and engaged 0.2% of the employed labour force in 2005. However, Madagascar has sizeable deposits of a wide range of minerals, principally chromite (chromium ore), which, with graphite and mica, is exported, together with small quantities of semi-precious stones. A major project to resume the mining of ilmenite (titanium ore) in south-eastern Madagascar, which would generate US $550m. over a 30-year period received approval from the Government in 2001. Construction of the mining facilities and rehabilitation of a deep-sea multi-purpose port at Ehoala, near Fort Dauphin (Tolagnaro) was nearing completion in early 2009. The facility began operations in January, with an initial capacity of 750,000 metric tons. Other potential mineral projects included the exploitation of an estimated 100m. tons of bauxite in the south-east of the country, and of nickel and cobalt deposits in Ambatovy, central Madagascar. The presence of significant grades of the platinum group of metals were confirmed, as well as copper and nickel, in 2004. Renewed interest was also shown in that year in reviving the country's long-inactive uranium mines. An agreement with the People's Republic of China in 2005 for the export of chrome ore held significant potential for the development of that sector. In late 2007 it was announced that a large nickel mining project was due to begin production by 2010, with annual output expected to reach 60,000 tons of nickel and 5,600 tons of cobalt. The project was expected to provide employment for some 5,000 workers. In early 2008 a pilot project in the north-west produced the first oil in the country for some 60 years, improving Madagascar's prospects for generating export revenue.

According to the World Bank, manufacturing contributed 14.1% of GDP in 2007 and engaged some 2.8% of the employed labour force in 2005. The petroleum refinery at Toamasina, using imported petroleum, provides a significant share of export revenue. Other important branches of manufacturing are textiles and clothing, food products, beverages and chemical products. The introduction of a new investment code in 1990 and the tion of a number of export-processing zones achieved some in attracting foreign private investment, particularly in facturing branches of textiles, cement, fertilizers and cals. According to the World Bank, manufacturing at an average annual rate of 2.0% in 2000–07; the increased by 4.8% in 2007.

depends on imports of petroleum (which ed 16.4% of the value of total imports in stallations, although hydroelectric loped, and accounted for an esti- duction in 2008. nted for an estimated 58.4% of GDP 14.6% of the employed labour force in nmunication technologies business park

was under development in Antananarivo as part of an effort to diversify Madagascar's economic growth. According to the World Bank, the GDP of the services sector increased by an average of 3.8% per year in 2000–07; services GDP increased by 9.5% in 2007.

In 2005 Madagascar recorded a visible trade deficit of US $592m., and there was a deficit of $626m. on the current account of the balance of payments. The principal source of imports in 2007 was the People's Republic of China (19.1%); other major suppliers were Bahrain, France and South Africa. France was the principal market for exports (accounting for 44.0% of exports in that year); the USA and Germany were also important purchasers. The principal exports in 2007 were spices and crustaceans; food and live animals constituted 28.1% of the value of total exports. The principal imports in that year were basic manufactures, machinery and transport equipment, mineral fuels and food and live animals.

Madagascar's overall budget deficit for 2007 (excluding grants) was estimated at 1,265,800m. ariary. Madagascar's external debt totalled US $1,453m. at the end of 2006, of which $1,236m. was long-term public debt. The cost of debt-servicing in 2005 was estimated to be equivalent to 5.7% of the value of exports of goods and services. The annual rate of inflation averaged 10.6% in 2000–07; consumer prices increased by 10.3% in 2007. About 2.8% of the labour force was unemployed in 2005.

Madagascar is a member of the Indian Ocean Commission (see p. 426) and of the Common Market for Eastern and Southern Africa (COMESA, see p. 215). In August 2005 Madagascar joined the Southern African Development Community (SADC, see p. 400).

Economic activity in Madagascar has been adversely affected by repeated instances of political instability during the 2000s. The economy was paralysed from the beginning of 2002—amid political uncertainty caused by the disputed presidential election (see Recent History)—by the strikes called by Marc Ravalomanana and the blockades ordered by Didier Ratsiraka. The closure of the central bank from the end of January resulted in the freezing of the nation's assets, rendering Madagascar unable to service its debts and at risk of default, while real GDP for the year declined by 11.9%. In July international donors pledged some US $2,300m. over a period of four years towards the reconstruction and development of the country and in October the IMF disbursed a structural adjustment credit of $100m. The economy recovered significantly in 2003, and in November 2004, following Madagascar's completion of its obligations under the IMF's initiative for heavily indebted poor countries, international creditors restructured the country's debt; many participants cancelled the entire amount owed to them, reaching a total reduction of some $836m. In July 2005 the World Bank announced $129.8m. of funding under an 'integrated growth poles' project, aimed at broadening the base of the country's growth and employment beyond the narrow sector of textiles in the export processing zone. In September 2008, following the fourth and fifth reviews under the three-year Poverty Reduction and Growth Facility, the IMF acknowledged continued progress in meeting the majority of its objectives and supported the Malagasy authorities' request for increasing the country's quota under the arrangement by 15% to guard against the impact of the global financial crisis and related increases in fuel and food prices. The World Bank, meanwhile, approved a loan of $40m. for poverty reduction as part of the Madagascar Action Plan, which aimed to reduce the poverty rate in the country to below 50% of the population and sustain economic growth of between 8%–10% from 2012. GDP growth for 2008 was estimated by the IMF at 2.1%, lower than previous estimates, although growth of 7.5% was projected for 2009, expected to be driven by a resurgent mining sector. However, following the removal of Ravalomanana in March 2009 (see Recent History), newly installed President Andry Rajoelina froze all mining contracts and announced a review of the sector in an attempt further to increase revenue therefrom.

Education

Six years' education, to be undertaken usually between six and 13 years of age, is officially compulsory. Madagascar has both public and private schools, although legislation that was enacted in 1978 envisaged the progressive elimination of private education. In 2002 primary school fees were abolished. Primary education generally begins at the age of six and lasts for five years. Secondary education, beginning at 11 years of age, lasts for a further seven years, comprising a first cycle of four years and a second of three years. According to UNESCO estimates, in 2006/07 primary enrolment included 98.5% of children in the relevant age-group (male 98.0%; females 98.9%), while in 2005/06 secondary enrolment included 17.4% of children in the relevant age-group (males 17.1%; females 17.7%). In 2006/07 58,300 students attended institutions providing tertiary education; there are six universities in Madagascar. In 2005 spending on education represented 25.3% of total budgetary expenditure.

Public Holidays

2009: 1 January (New Year), 29 March (Martyr's Day, Commemoration of 1947 Rebellion), 13 April (Easter Monday), 1 May (Labour Day), 21 May (Ascension Day), 25 May (Organization of African Unity Day), 31 May (Whitsun), 26 June (Independence Day), 15 August (Assumption), 1 November (All Saints' Day), 25 December (Christmas).

2010: 1 January (New Year), 29 March (Martyr's Day, Commemoration of 1947 Rebellion), 5 April (Easter Monday), 1 May (Labour Day), 13 May (Ascension Day), 23 May (Whitsun), 25 May (Organization of African Unity Day), 26 June (Independence Day), 15 August (Assumption), 1 November (All Saints' Day), 25 December (Christmas).

Weights and Measures

The metric system is in force.

Statistical Survey

Source (unless otherwise stated): Institut National de la Statistique Malagache, BP 485, Anosy Tana, 101 Antananarivo; tel. (20) 2227418; e-mail dridnstat@wanadoo.mg; internet www.instat.mg; Ministry of Economy, Finance and Budget, BP 61, 101 Antananarivo; internet www.mefb.gov.mg.

Area and Population

AREA, POPULATION AND DENSITY

Area (sq km)	587,041*
Population (census results)	
1974–75†	7,603,790
1–19 August 1993	
Males	5,991,171
Females	6,100,986
Total	12,092,157
Population (UN estimates at mid-year)‡	
2006	19,159,000
2007	19,683,000
2008	20,215,000
Density (per sq km) at mid-2008	34.4

* 226,658 sq miles.
† The census took place in three stages: in provincial capitals on 1 December 1974; in Antananarivo and remaining urban areas on 17 February 1975; and in rural areas on 1 June 1975.
‡ Source: UN, *World Population Prospects: The 2006 Revision*.

PRINCIPAL ETHNIC GROUPS
(estimated population, 1974)

Merina (Hova)	1,993,000	Sakalava	470,156*
Betsimisaraka	1,134,000	Antandroy	412,500
Betsileo	920,600	Antaisaka	406,468*
Tsimihety	558,100		

* 1972 figure.

PRINCIPAL TOWNS
(population at 1993 census)

Antananarivo (capital)	1,103,304	Mahajanga (Majunga)	106,780
Toamasina (Tamatave)	137,782	Toliary (Tuléar)	80,826
Antsirabé	126,062	Antsiranana (Diégo-Suarez)	59,040
Fianarantsoa	109,248		

2001 (estimated population, incl. Renivohitra and Avaradrano): Antananarivo 1,111,392.

Mid-2007 ('000, incl. suburbs, UN estimate): Antananarivo 1,697 (Source: UN, *World Urbanization prospects: The 2007 Revision*).

BIRTHS AND DEATHS

	2005	2006	2007
Birth rate (per 1,000)	37.5	36.9	36.4
Death rate (per 1,000)	10.2	10.0	9.7

Source: African Development Bank.

Life expectancy (years at birth, WHO estimates): 58.9 (males 57.1; females 60.8) in 2006 (Source: WHO, *World Health Statistics*).

ECONOMICALLY ACTIVE POPULATION
(labour force survey, '000 persons)

	2005
Agriculture, hunting and forestry	7,745.3
Fishing	99.0
Mining and quarrying	18.8
Manufacturing	267.5
Electricity, gas and water	27.5
Construction	13.0
Wholesale and retail trade; repair of motor vehicles, motor cycles and personal and household goods	470.5
Hotels and restaurants	63.9
Transport, storage and communications	86.3
Financial intermediation	4.1
Public administration and defence; compulsory social security	202.4
Education	44.5
Health and social work	9.9
Other community, social and personal service activities	517.7
Total employed	9,570.4
Unemployed	274.3
Total labour force	9,844.7
Males	4,942.2
Females	4,902.4

Source: ILO.

Health and Welfare

KEY INDICATORS

Total fertility rate (children per woman, 2006)	4.9
Under-5 mortality rate (per 1,000 live births, 2006)	115
HIV/AIDS (% of persons aged 15–49, 2007)	0.1
Physicians (per 1,000 head, 2004)	0.3
Hospital beds (per 1,000 head, 2005)	0.3
Health expenditure (2006): US $ per head (PPP)	34
Health expenditure (2006): % of GDP	3.2
Health expenditure (2006): public (% of total)	62.8
Access to water (% of persons, 2006)	47
Access to sanitation (% of persons, 2006)	12
Human Development Index (2006): ranking	143
Human Development Index (2006): value	0.533

For sources and definitions, see explanatory note on p. vi.

MADAGASCAR

Agriculture

PRINCIPAL CROPS
('000 metric tons)

	2005	2006	2007*
Rice, paddy	3,393	3,485	3,596
Maize	391	495	500
Potatoes	215	221	225
Sweet potatoes	879	869	870
Cassava (Manioc)	2,964	2,359	2,400
Taro (Cocoyam)*	200	200	200
Sugar cane	2,446	2,691	2,700
Beans, dry	78	88	88
Groundnuts, in shell	61	61	62
Coconuts*	85	85	85
Oil palm fruit*	21	21	21
Tomatoes*	22	22	22
Bananas*	290	290	290
Oranges*	87	83	83
Guavas, mangoes and mangosteens*	210	210	210
Avocados*	23	23	23
Pineapples*	51	51	51
Cashewapple*	68	68	68
Coffee, green	56	62	62
Vanilla	3	3	3
Cinnamon (Canella)*	2	2	2
Cloves*	10	10	10
Sisal	17*	n.a.	n.a.
Tobacco, unmanufactured	2	2*	2*

* FAO estimate(s).

Aggregate production ('000 metric tons, may include official, semi-official or estimated data): Total cereals 3,795 in 2005, 3,991 in 2006, 4,109 in 2007; Total roots and tubers 4,257 in 2005, 3,648 in 2006, 3,695 in 2007; Total vegetables (incl. melons) 344 in 2005, 344 in 2006, 344 in 2007; Total fruits (excl. melons) 965 in 2005, 769 in 2006, 769 in 2007.

Source: FAO.

LIVESTOCK
('000 head, year ending September)

	2005	2006	2007*
Cattle	9,500	9,573	9,600
Pigs	1,247	1,600*	1,610
Sheep	695	712	715
Goats	1,219*	1,249	1,250
Chickens*	24,214	24,727	25,000
Ducks*	3,775	3,873	3,900
Geese and guinea fowls*	3,000	3,000	3,000
Turkeys*	2,000	2,000	2,000

* FAO estimate(s).
Source: FAO.

LIVESTOCK PRODUCTS
('000 metric tons, FAO estimates)

	2004	2005	2006
Cattle meat	114.8	133.9	147.0
Sheep meat	3.1	2.6	2.5
Goat meat	6.9	6.2	6.2
Pig meat	28	51	70
Chicken meat	35.5	35.5	40.0
Duck meat	10.6	10.6	11.0
Goose meat	12.6	12.6	12.6
Turkey meat	8.4	8.4	8.4
Cows' milk	450	510	520
Hen eggs	14.9	14.9	14.9
Other eggs	4.5	4.5	4.6
Honey	3.9	3.9	4.0

2007: Production assumed to be unchanged from 2006 (FAO estimates).
Source: FAO.

Forestry

ROUNDWOOD REMOVALS
('000 cubic metres, excl. bark, FAO estimates)

	2005	2006	2007
Sawlogs, veneer logs and logs for sleepers	160	193	222
Pulpwood*	23	23	23
Fuel wood	11,055	13,100	13,100
Total	11,238	13,316	13,345

* Production assumed to be unchanged from 2000 (FAO estimates).
Source: FAO.

SAWNWOOD PRODUCTION
('000 cubic metres, incl. railway sleepers)

	2005	2006	2007
Coniferous (softwood)	8*	1	2
Broadleaved (hardwood)*	885	886	886
Total	893	887	888

* FAO estimate(s).
Source: FAO.

Fishing

('000 metric tons, live weight)

	2004	2005	2006
Capture	146.5	134.9	134.4
Cichlids	21.5	21.5	21.5
Other freshwater fishes	4.5	4.5	4.5
Narrow-barred Spanish mackerel	12.0	12.0	12.0
Other marine fishes	89.9	80.0	79.4
Shrimps and prawns	11.2	9.3	9.4
Aquaculture	8.8	9.4*	11.2
Giant tiger prawn	6.2	6.7*	8.5
Total catch	155.3	144.2*	145.6

* FAO estimate.

Note: Figures exclude aquatic plants ('000 metric tons, capture only): 5.2 in 2004; 5.2 in 2005; 5.3 in 2006. Also excluded are crocodiles, recorded by number rather than weight, and shells. The number of Nile crocodiles caught was: 4,760 in 2004; 4,850 in 2005; 6,660 in 2006.

Source: FAO.

Mining

(metric tons, estimates)

	2004	2005	2006
Chromite*	77,386	140,847	132,335
Salt (marine)	55,000	65,000	75,000
Graphite (natural)	15,000	15,000	15,000
Mica	90	90	90

* Figures refer to gross weight. The estimated chromium content is 27%.
Source: US Geological Survey.

MADAGASCAR

Industry

SELECTED PRODUCTS
(metric tons, unless otherwise indicated)

	1999	2000	2001
Raw sugar	61,370	62,487	67,917
Beer ('000 hectolitres)	610.1	645.5	691.7
Cigarettes	3,839	4,139	4,441
Woven cotton fabrics (million sq metres)	20.4	23.3	29.6
Leather footwear ('000 pairs)	460	570	568
Plastic footwear ('000 pairs)	375	303	291
Paints	1,918	1,487	1,554
Soap	15,884	15,385	15,915
Motor spirit—petrol ('000 cu metres)	98.0	122.6	128.3
Kerosene ('000 cu metres)	65.0	65.2	75.1
Gas-diesel (distillate fuel) oil ('000 cu metres)	119.0	150.4	150.2
Residual fuel oils ('000 cu metres)	198.8	225.7	247.2
Cement	45,701	50,938	51,882
Electric energy (million kWh)*	721.3	779.8	833.9

* Production by the state-owned utility only, excluding electricity generated by industries for their own use.

2002: Raw sugar 35,000 metric tons; Beer 439,000 hectolitres; Woven cotton fabrics 20m. sq metres; Soap 14,100 metric tons; Motor spirit—petrol 112,000 metric tons (estimate); Kerosene 66,000 metric tons (estimate); Gas-diesel (distillate fuel) oil 57,000 metric tons (estimate); Residual fuel oils 77,000 metric tons (estimate); Electric energy 790m. kWh (Source: mainly UN, *Industrial Commodity Statistics Yearbook*).

2003: Raw sugar 35,000 metric tons; Motor spirit—petrol 113,000 metric tons; Kerosene 67,000 metric tons; Gas-diesel (distillate fuel) oil 57,000 metric tons; Residual fuel oils 77,000 metric tons; Electric energy 900m. kWh (Source: mainly UN, *Industrial Commodity Statistics Yearbook*).

2004: Raw sugar 26,000 metric tons; Motor spirit—petrol 113,000 metric tons; Kerosene 67,000 metric tons; Gas-diesel (distillate fuel oil) 57,000 metric tons; Residual fuel oils 77,000 metric tons; Electric energy 990m. kWh (Source: UN, *Industrial Commodity Statistics Yearbook*).

2005: Raw sugar 27,000 metric tons; Motor spirit—petrol 114,000 metric tons; Kerosene 68,000 metric tons; Gas-diesel (distillate fuel oil) 58,000 metric tons; Residual fuel oils 78,000 metric tons; Electric energy 1,035m. kWh (Source: UN, *Industrial Commodity Statistics Yearbook*).

Cement ('000 metric tons, estimates): 170 in 2004; 150 in 2005; 150 in 2006 (Source: US Geological Survey).

Finance

CURRENCY AND EXCHANGE RATES

Monetary Units
5 iraimbilanja = 1 ariary.

Sterling, Dollar and Euro Equivalents (31 December 2008)
£1 sterling = 2,712.03 ariary;
US $1 = 1,860.36 ariary;
€1 = 2,589.06 ariary;
100,000 ariary = £3.69 = $5.38 = €3.86.

Average Exchange Rate (ariary per US $)
2006 2,142.3
2007 1,873.9
2008 1,708.4

Note: A new currency, the ariary, was introduced on 31 July 2003 to replace the franc malgache (franc MG). The old currency was to remain legal tender until 30 November. Some figures in this survey are still given in terms of francs MG.

BUDGET
('000 million ariary, central government operations)

Revenue and grants	2005	2006*	2007†
Tax revenue	1,020.0	1,259.2	1,523.8
Non-tax revenue	82.8	80.8	28.3
Grants	579.5	5,580.0	699.3
Total	1,682.3	6,920.0	2,251.4

Expenditure	2005	2006*	2007†
Current expenditure	1,107.2	1,240.6	1,411.1
Budgetary expenditure	1,021.5	1,226.2	1,397.5
Wages and salaries	456.4	596.9	721.0
Other non-interest expenditure	298.5	375.9	455.3
Interest payments	266.6	253.4	221.1
Treasury operations (net)	84.2	12.5	13.7
Counterpart funds-financed operations	1.5	1.9	—
Capital expenditure	1,038.3	1,290.3	1,406.8
Total	2,145.5	2,530.9	2,817.9

* Provisional.
† Forecasts.

INTERNATIONAL RESERVES
(US $ million at 31 December)

	2005	2006	2007
IMF special drawing rights	0.0	0.0	0.0
Foreign exchange	481.3	583.2	846.7
Total	481.3	583.2	846.7

Source: IMF, *International Financial Statistics*.

MONEY SUPPLY
('000 million ariary at 31 December)

	2005	2006	2007
Currency outside banks	599.12	715.05	840.64
Demand deposits at deposit money banks	815.57	1,035.75	1,234.18
Total money	1,414.69	1,750.81	2,074.83

Source: IMF, *International Financial Statistics*.

COST OF LIVING
(Consumer Price Index for Madagascans in Antananarivo; base: 2000 = 100)

	2005	2006	2007
Food	170.2	180.8	202.1
Electricity, gas and other fuels	156.5	207.3	214.9
Clothing*	122.0	149.6	144.4
Rent	233.7	268.7	289.2
All items (incl. others)	152.6	183.7	202.6

* Including household linen.
Source: ILO.

NATIONAL ACCOUNTS

Expenditure on the Gross Domestic Product
('000 million ariary at current prices)

	2004	2005	2006*
Government final consumption expenditure	778.0	849.1	993.4
Private final consumption expenditure	6,725.1	8,349.2	9,739.2
Increase in stocks	1,980.8	2,276.3	2,563.5
Gross fixed capital formation			
Total domestic expenditure	9,483.9	11,474.6	13,296.1
Exports of goods and services	2,650.7	2,674.8	3,230.6
Less Imports of goods and services	3,979.0	4,052.0	4,766.0
Statistical discrepancy†	—	461.7	33.0
GDP in purchasers' values	8,155.7	10,559.1	11,793.7
GDP at constant 1984 prices	498.8	521.7	546.4

* Provisional.
† Representing the difference between the expenditure and production approaches.

MADAGASCAR

Gross Domestic Product by Economic Activity
('000 million francs MG at current prices)

	2002	2003	2004
Agriculture, hunting, forestry and fishing	8,963	9,073	9,857
Mining and quarrying } Manufacturing } Electricity, gas and water	4,078	4,777	5,456
Construction	552	652	794
Trade, restaurants and hotels	3,555	3,909	4,316
Transport, storage and communications	4,817	5,154	5,796
Financial intermediation	246	293	324
Administration	1,641	2,140	2,281
Other services	4,610	5,289	5,644
Sub-total	28,462	31,287	34,468
Less imputed bank charges	196	226	251
GDP at factor cost	28,265	31,061	34,217
Indirect taxes, less subsidies	1,777	2,803	3,435
GDP in purchasers' values	30,042	33,863	37,651

Source: Ministry of the Economy, Finance and Budget.

2005 ('000 million ariary at current prices): Agriculture, hunting, forestry and fishing 2,668.8; Industry 1,476.6; Services 5,519.2; *Sub-total* 9,664.6; Imputed bank charges –70.2; *GDP at factor cost* 9,574.4; Indirect taxes, less subsidies 981.6; *GDP in purchasers' values* 10,559.1.

2006 ('000 million ariary at current prices, provisional): Agriculture, hunting, forestry and fishing 2,967.5; Industry 1,656.7; Services 6,143.1; *Sub-total* 10,767.3; Imputed bank charges –79.6; *GDP at factor cost* 10,688.0; Indirect taxes, less subsidies 1,105.6; *GDP in purchasers' values* 11,793.7.

2007 ('000 million ariary at current prices, estimates): Agriculture, hunting, forestry and fishing 3,363.6; Industry 1,906.1; Services 7,204.8; *Sub-total* 12,474.5; Imputed bank charges –94.7; *GDP at factor cost* 12,378.1; Indirect taxes, less subsidies 1,313.5; *GDP in purchasers' values* 13,691.6.

BALANCE OF PAYMENTS
(US $ million)

	2003	2004	2005
Exports of goods f.o.b.	854	990	834
Imports of goods f.o.b.	–1,111	–1,427	–1,427
Trade balance	–258	–437	–592
Exports of services	322	425	498
Imports of services	–619	–637	–615
Balance on goods and services	–555	–649	–710
Other income received	16	15	24
Other income paid	–94	–89	–104
Balance on goods, services and income	–632	–723	–790
Current transfers received	357	245	208
Current transfers paid	–183	–62	–45
Current balance	–458	–541	–626
Capital account (net)	143	182	192
Direct investment from abroad	13	53	85
Other investment assets	–29	295	11
Other investment liabilities	–110	–97	–102
Net errors and omissions	67	–35	91
Overall balance	–374	–143	–349

Source: IMF, *International Financial Statistics*.

External Trade

PRINCIPAL COMMODITIES
(US $ million)

Imports c.i.f.	2005	2006	2007
Food and live animals	214.6	200.2	286.3
Cereals and cereal preparations	124.6	75.3	118.2
Rice	92.9	40.2	61.4
Mineral fuels, lubricants and related materials	267.3	329.0	406.2
Petroleum, petroleum products and related materials	262.1	322.3	401.0
Petroleum and oils obtained from bituminous materials (not crude)	254.9	311.6	390.3
Residual petroleum products	7.2	10.7	10.7
Gas oils			
Chemicals and related products	122.6	150.8	179.7
Medicinal and pharmaceutical products	29.9	46.1	50.8
Basic manufactures	462.1	520.9	711.2
Textile yarn and related products	263.8	314.5	417.4
Woven cotton fabrics	68.7	70.0	97.9
Machinery and transport equipment	410.5	337.0	599.0
Electric machinery, apparatus and appliances	40.5	35.5	63.2
Road vehicles	126.4	87.6	141.2
Miscellaneous manufactures	109.5	133.9	153.7
Total (incl. others)	1,685.9	1,760.3	2,445.5

Exports f.o.b.	2005	2006	2007
Food and live animals	242.1	326.3	376.8
Fish, crustaceans and molluscs and preparations thereof	134.2	184.0	189.9
Crustaceans and molluscs	109.5	135.0	141.0
Vegetables and fruit	29.1	26.8	40.2
Coffee, tea, cocoa, spices	75.7	107.0	139.5
Spices	65.0	78.8	101.5
Vanilla	46.2	47.4	56.7
Cloves	16.6	27.0	38.1
Crude materials, inedible, except fuels	85.8	74.9	81.0
Basic manufactures	52.1	69.9	166.2
Miscellaneous manufactures	299.2	313.5	589.3
Articles of apparel and clothing accessories	256.6	251.8	496.5
Men's and boys' outerwear	59.3	52.5	74.3
Women's, girls' and infants' outerwear	73.6	73.0	111.0
Knitted or crocheted outerwear	13.9	17.7	29.0
Total (incl. others)	835.9	1,008.2	1,343.3

Source: UN, *International Trade Statistics Yearbook*.

MADAGASCAR

PRINCIPAL TRADING PARTNERS
(US $ million)

Imports	2005	2006	2007
Bahrain	220.1	288.4	372.6
Belgium	46.5	30.4	33.7
China, People's Repub.	235.1	312.5	467.1
France	249.4	232.8	261.5
Germany	43.2	43.1	59.3
Hong Kong	27.5	17.6	18.9
India	99.7	51.4	70.2
Indonesia	20.9	34.5	28.9
Italy	21.6	26.9	43.4
Japan	40.6	42.6	66.5
Korea, Republic	17.8	23.3	29.4
Malaysia	20.8	17.4	24.8
Mauritius	124.8	54.0	73.0
Pakistan	25.0	27.4	47.9
South Africa	98.8	100.7	129.7
Thailand	32.8	26.3	38.5
United Arab Emirates	20.3	13.3	18.6
United Kingdom	18.4	16.9	23.0
USA	40.6	62.5	86.6
Total (incl. others)	1,685.9	1,760.3	2,445.5

Exports	2005	2006	2007
Belgium	9.6	22.0	13.9
Canada	5.9	12.5	11.6
France	286.6	398.7	591.2
Germany	53.8	60.4	69.1
Hong Kong	11.7	10.6	9.8
Italy	23.1	42.0	47.6
Japan	17.5	13.7	8.9
Mauritius	16.0	14.5	38.5
Netherlands	13.9	16.4	26.5
Singapore	14.2	19.6	20.0
South Africa	4.8	10.1	8.1
Spain	12.0	24.2	29.2
Thailand	10.5	15.8	5.0
United Kingdom	16.0	30.7	42.9
USA	183.8	150.8	237.4
Total (incl. others)	835.9	1,008.2	1,343.3

Source: UN, *International Trade Statistics Yearbook*.

Transport

RAILWAYS
(traffic)

	1997	1998	1999
Passengers carried ('000)	359	293	273
Passenger-km (million)	37	35	31
Freight carried ('000 metric tons)	227	213	141
Ton-km (million)	81	71	46

Source: Réseau National des Chemins de Fer Malagasy.

2000: Passenger-km (million) 19; Ton-km (million) 26 (Source: UN, *Statistical Yearbook*).

ROAD TRAFFIC
(vehicles in use)

	1994	1995	1996*
Passenger cars	54,821	58,097	60,480
Buses and coaches	3,797	4,332	4,850
Lorries and vans	35,931	37,232	37,972
Road tractors	488	560	619

* Estimates.

Source: IRF, *World Road Statistics*.

1998 ('000): Passenger cars 64.0; Commercial vehicles 9.1 (Source: UN, *Statistical Yearbook*).

Statistical Survey

SHIPPING
Merchant Fleet
(registered at 31 December)

	2005	2006	2007
Number of vessels	103	103	106
Displacement ('000 gross registered tons)	33.2	33.6	35.4

Source: Lloyd's Register-Fairplay, *World Fleet Statistics*.

International Sea-borne Freight Traffic
('000 metric tons)

	1987	1988	1989
Goods loaded:			
Mahajanga	17	18	29
Toamasina	252	350	361
other ports	79	100	137
Total	348	468	527
Goods unloaded:			
Mahajanga	37	32	31
Toamasina	748	778	709
other ports	48	53	52
Total	833	863	792

1990 ('000 metric tons): Goods loaded 540; Goods unloaded 984 (Source: UN, *Monthly Bulletin of Statistics*).

CIVIL AVIATION
(traffic on scheduled services)

	2001	2002	2003
Kilometres flown (million)	7	2	4
Passengers carried ('000)	146	241	140
Passenger-km (million)	654	266	562
Total ton-km (million)	86	42	60

Source: UN, *Statistical Yearbook*.

Tourism

TOURIST ARRIVALS BY NATIONALITY

	2004	2005	2006
Canada and USA	9,151	13,808	15,587
France	129,263	145,192	163,180
Germany	9,609	12,025	13,526
Italy	17,159	22,657	25,556
Japan	3,432	5,952	6,697
Mauritius	9,609	9,825	11,253
Réunion	22,878	31,861	35,698
Switzerland	4,576	4,987	5,610
United Kingdom	6,864	6,732	7,594
Total (incl. others)	228,785	277,422	311,730

Tourism receipts (US $ million, incl. passenger transport): 239 in 2004; 290 in 2005; 386 in 2006.

Source: World Tourism Organization.

Communications Media

	2005	2006	2007
Telephones ('000 main lines in use)	66.9	129.8	133.9
Mobile cellular telephones ('000 subscribers)	510.3	1,045.9	2,217.6
Personal computers ('000 in use)	91	n.a.	n.a.
Internet users ('000)	100	110	n.a.

Source: International Telecommunication Union.

1995: Radio receivers ('000 in use) 2,850; Book production (incl. pamphlets): titles 131, copies ('000) 292; Daily newspapers: number 6, circulation ('000 copies) 59 (Source: UNESCO, *Statistical Yearbook*).

1996: Radio receivers ('000 in use) 2,950; Book production (incl. pamphlets): titles 119, copies ('000) 296; Daily newspapers: number 5, circulation ('000 copies) 66 (Source: UNESCO, *Statistical Yearbook*).

1997: Radio receivers ('000 in use) 3,050 (Source: UNESCO, *Statistical Yearbook*).

2000: Television receivers ('000 in use) 375.

2004: Daily newspapers (number) 9 (Source: UNESCO Institute for Statistics).

Education

(2006/07, unless otherwise indicated, UNESCO estimates, public and private schools)

	Teachers	Males	Females	Total
Pre-primary (all programmes)	4,949	75.2	77.4	152.6
Primary (all programmes)	78,743	1,950.8	1,886.6	3,837.3
Secondary	33,551	426.1	405.5	831.6
General	31,418	408.8	396.6	805.4
Vocational	2,133	17.3	8.9	26.2
Tertiary	3,032	30.9	27.4	58.3

Pupils ('000)

Source: UNESCO Institute for Statistics.

2005/06: 6 universities; 14 private institutes of higher education.

Adult literacy rate (UNESCO estimates): 70.7% (males 76.5%; females 65.3%) in 2000 (Source: UNESCO Institute for Statistics).

Directory

The Constitution

The Constitution of the Third Republic of Madagascar was endorsed by national referendum on 19 August 1992, but was substantially altered by amendments that were endorsed in a national referendum on 15 March 1998. The amended Constitution enshrines a 'federal-style' state, composed of six autonomous provinces—each with a governor and up to 12 general commissioners (holding executive power) and a provincial council (holding legislative power). It provides for a government delegate to each province, who is charged with supervising the division of functions between the state and the province. The bicameral legislature consists of the National Assembly (the lower house), which is elected by universal adult suffrage in single-seat constituencies for a five-year term of office. The Constitution also provides for a Senate (the upper house), of which one-third of the members are presidential nominees and two-thirds are elected by an electoral college of National Assembly members, regional councillors and mayors, for a term of six years. The constitutional Head of State is the President. If no candidate obtains an overall majority in the presidential election, a second round of voting is to take place a maximum of 30 days after the publication of the results of the first ballot. Any one candidate can be elected for a maximum of three five-year terms. The powers of the President were greatly increased by constitutional amendments of March 1998: the President has the power to determine general state policy in the Council of Ministers, to call referendums on all matters of national importance, and to dissolve the National Assembly not less than one year after a general election. Executive power is vested in a Prime Minister, who is appointed by the President. The President appoints the Council of Ministers, on the recommendation of the Prime Minister. In a national referendum held on 4 April 2007 a number of constitutional reforms were endorsed, including the abolition of autonomous powers for the six provinces. The amended Constitution conferred on the President new powers, including the right to legislate by decree in the event of a state of emergency. English was also adopted as the country's third official language.

Following the resignation of President Marc Ravalomanana on 17 March 2009, executive power was assumed by the Haute Autorité de la Transition (High Authority of Transition). That body's President, Andry Rajoelina, was appointed Head of State despite not fulfilling the constitutional requirement of being over 40 years of age. Rajoelina pledged to introduce a new constitution within two years.

The Government

HEAD OF STATE

President of the Haute Autorité de la Transition: ANDRY RAJOELINA (inaugurated 21 March 2009).

Following the resignation of President Marc Ravalomanana on 17 March 2009, executive power was assumed by the Haute Autorité de la Transition (HAT—High Authority of Transition), headed by Andry Rajoelina. The HAT was to oversee the activities of the 22-member Government, appointed in mid-April.

COUNCIL OF MINISTERS
(April 2009)

Prime Minister: MONJA ROINDEFO.
Minister of the Armed Forces: Col NOËL RAKOTONANDRASANA.
Minister of the Economy and Industry: FIENENA RICHARD.
Minister of Population and Social Affairs: NADINE RAMAROSON.
Minister of Transport: ROLLAND RANJATOELINA.
Minister of Energy: JEAN RODOLPHE RAMANANTSOA.
Minister of the Civil Service, Labour and Social Legislation: NOELSON WILLIAM.
Minister of Health and Family Planning: HENRI RANAIVOARISOA.
Minister of Higher Education and Scientific Research: ATHANASE TONGAVELO.
Minister of Tourism and Crafts: IRÈNE VICTOIRE ANDRÉAS.
Secretary of State responsible for the Gendarmerie: Col CLAUDE RAVELOMANANA.
Minister of Finance and the Budget: BENJA JOAS RAZAFIMAHALEO.
Minister of Justice: CHRISTINE RAZANAMAHASOA.
Minister of Foreign Affairs: NY HASINA ANDRIAMANJATO.
Minister of Internal Security: RÉMY SYLVAIN ORGANÈS RAKOTOMIHANTARIZAKA.
Minister of National Education: JULIEN RAZAFIMANAZATO.
Minister of Land Settlement and Decentralization: HAJO ANDRIANAINARIVELO.
Minister of the Interior: MANANTSOA MASIMANA.
Minister of the Environment and Forests: MARIOT JEAN FLORENT RAKOTOVAO.
Minister of Telecommunications, Post and New Technologies: AUGUSTIN RAZAFINARIVO ANDRIAMANANORO.
Minister of Communication and Culture: GILBERT HARISOA RAHARIZATOVO.
Minister of Water: NIRHY-LANTO ANDRIAMAHAZO.

MINISTRIES

Office of the President: Antananarivo; e-mail communication@presidency.gov.mg; internet www.madagascar-presidency.gov.mg.
Office of the Prime Minister: BP 248, Palais d'Etat Mahazoarivo, 101 Antananarivo; tel. (20) 2264498; fax (20) 2233116; e-mail dircom@primature.gov.mg; internet www.primature.gov.mg.
Ministry of Agriculture, Livestock and Fisheries: BP 301, Anosy, 101 Antananarivo; tel. (20) 2261002; fax (20) 2264308; e-mail info@maep.gov.mg; internet www.maep.gov.mg.

MADAGASCAR

Ministry of the Civil Service, Labour and Social Legislation: BP 207, Cité des 67 Hectares, 101 Antananarivo; tel. (20) 2224209; fax (20) 2233856; e-mail ministre@mfptls.gov.mg; internet www.mfptls.gov.mg.

Ministry of Decentralization: Antananarivo.

Ministry of the Economy, Commerce and Industry: Bâtiment Commerce, Ambohidahy, 101 Antananarivo; tel. (20) 2264681; fax (20) 2234530; e-mail sg@mepspc.gov.mg; internet www.mepspc.gov.mg.

Ministry of Energy and Mines: BP 527, Immeuble de l'Industrie, Antaninarenina, 101 Antananarivo; tel. (20) 2228928; fax (20) 2232554; internet www.mem.gov.mg.

Ministry of the Environment, Forests and Tourism: Fernand Kasanga, BP 610 Tsimbazaza, 101 Antananarivo; tel. (20) 2266805; fax (20) 2235410; e-mail sp@meeft.gov.mg; internet www.meeft.gov.mg.

Ministry of Finance and the Budget: BP 61, Antaninarenina, Antananarivo; tel. (20) 2230173; fax (20) 2264680; internet www.mefb.gov.mg.

Ministry of Foreign Affairs: BP 836, Anosy, 101 Antananarivo; tel. (20) 2221198; fax (20) 2234484; e-mail contact@madagascar-diplomatie.net; internet www.madagascar-diplomatie.net.

Ministry of Health and Family Planning: BP 88, Ambohidahy, 101 Antananarivo; tel. (20) 2263121; fax (20) 2264228; e-mail cabminsan@wanadoo.mg; internet www.sante.gov.mg.

Ministry of the Interior: BP 833, Anosy, 101 Antananarivo; tel. (20) 2223084; fax (20) 2235579; internet www.mira.gov.mg.

Ministry of Internal Security: BP 23 bis, 101 Antananarivo; tel. (20) 2221029; fax (20) 2231861; internet www.policenationale.gov.mg.

Ministry of Justice: rue Joel Rakotomalala, BP 231, Faravohitra, 101 Antananarivo; tel. (20) 2237684; fax (20) 2264458; e-mail presse.justice@justice.gov.mg; internet www.justice.gov.mg.

Ministry of National Defence: BP 08, Ampahibe, 101 Antananarivo; tel. (20) 2222211; fax (20) 2235420; e-mail mdn@wanadoo.fr; internet www.defense.gov.mg.

Ministry of National Education: BP 247, Anosy, 101 Antananarivo; tel. (20) 2224308; fax (20) 2223897; e-mail mlraharimalala@yahoo.fr; internet www.education.gov.mg.

Ministry of Public Works and Meteorology: BP 295, 101 Antananarivo; tel. (20) 2228715; fax (20) 2220890; e-mail secreab@mtpm.gov.mg; internet www.mtpm.gov.mg.

Ministry of Telecommunications, Post and Communications: pl. de l'Indépendance, Antaninarenina, 101 Antananarivo; tel. (20) 2222902; fax (20) 2234115; internet www.mtpc.gov.mg.

Ministry of Transport: BP 610, rue Fernand Kasanga Tsimbazaza, 101 Antananarivo; tel. (20) 2262816; fax (20) 2235410; internet www.mtt.gov.mg.

Ministry of Water: Antananarivo.

Ministry of Youth, Sports and Culture: Ambohijatovo, pl. Goulette, BP 681, 101 Antananarivo; tel. (20) 2227780; fax (20) 2234275; e-mail mjs_101@yahoo.fr; internet www.mscl.gov.mg.

President and Legislature

PRESIDENT

Presidential Election, 3 December 2006

Candidate	Votes	% of votes
Marc Ravalomanana	2,435,199	54.79
Jean Lahiniriko	517,994	11.65
Iarovana Roland Ratsiraka	450,717	10.14
Herizo J. Razafimahaleo	401,473	9.03
Norbert Lala Ratsirahonana	187,552	4.22
Ny Hasina Andriamanjato	185,624	4.18
Others	266,191	5.99
Total	4,444,750*	100.00

*Excluding 87,196 invalid votes.

LEGISLATURE

Senate

President: YVAN RANDRIASANDRATRINIONY.

Senatorial Election, 20 April 2008

Party	Seats
TIM	22
Total	22*

*Elected by an electoral college of National Assembly members, regional councillors and mayors. An additional 11 seats were appointed by the President.

National Assembly

President: JACQUES HUGUES SYLLA.

General Election, 23 September 2007, provisional results

Party	Seats
TIM	105
Independents	11
Others	9
Total	125*

*The total number of seats is 127; however, results in two constituencies were annulled, owing to alleged voting irregularities.

Election Commission

Conseil national électoral (CNE): Immeuble Microréalisation, 4 étage, 67 ha, 101 Antananarivo; tel. (20) 2225179; fax (20) 2225881; e-mail cne@wanadoo.mg; internet www.cne.mg; Pres. THÉODORE RANDREZASON.

Political Organizations

Following the restoration of multi-party politics in March 1990, more than 120 political associations emerged, of which six secured representation in the National Assembly in 2002. The following were among the more influential political organizations in 2008:

Association pour la renaissance de Madagascar (Andry sy riana enti-manavotra an'i Madigasikara) (AREMA): f. 1975 as Avant-garde de la révolution malgache; adopted present name 1997; party of fmr Pres. Adm. (retd) Ratsiraka (now in exile); control disputed between two factions, headed by Gen. Sec. PIERROT RAJAONARIVELO (in exile), and Asst. Gen. Sec. PIERRE RAHARIJAONA.

Comité pour la Réconciliation Nationale (CRN): Villa la Franchise, Lot II-I 160 A, Alarobia, Antananarivo; tel. (20) 2242022; f. 2002 by fmr President Zafy; radical opposition; formed part of the 3FN (Trois Forces Nationales) group of opposition parties, established in Sept. 2005; Leader ALBERT ZAFY.

Herim-Bahoaka Mitambatra (HBM) (Union of Popular Forces): formed part of the coalition supporting Marc Ravalomanana prior to the 2006 presidential election; Leader TOVONANAHARY RABETSITONTA.

Libéralisme économique et action démocratique pour la reconstruction nationale (LEADER/Fanilo) (Torch): f. 1993 by Herizo Razafimahaleo; Sec. Gen. MANASSÉ ESOAVELOMANDROSO.

Mouvement pour le progrès de Madagascar (Mpitolona ho amin'ny Fandrosoan'ny Madagasikara) (MFM): 42 & 44 Cité Ampefiloha Bldg, 101 Antananarivo; tel. (20) 2437560; e-mail contact@mfm-madagascar.com; internet www.mfm-madagascar.com; f. 1972 as Mouvement pour le pouvoir prolétarien (MFM); adopted present name in 1990; advocates liberal and market-orientated policies; Leader MANANDAFY RAKOTONIRINA; Sec.-Gen. OLIVIER RAKOTOVAZAHA.

Ny asa vita no ifampitsara (AVI) (People are judged by the work they do): f. 1997 to promote human rights, hard work and devt; Leader NORBERT RATSIRAHONANA.

Parti socialiste et démocratique pour l'union de Madagascar (PSDUM): f. 2006; Pres. JEAN LAHINIRIKO.

Rassemblement des forces nationales (RFN): f. 2005; a coalition of parties comprising the AKFM, LEADER/Fanilo and Fihavanantsika (led by Pasteur Daniel Rajakoba); formed part of the 3FN (Trois Forces Nationales) group of opposition parties, established in Sept. 2005; Leader Pasteur EDMOND RAZAFIMAHEFA.

Rassemblement pour le socialisme et la démocratie (RPSD): f. 1993 by fmr mems of PSD; also known as Renaissance du parti social-démocratique; Jean-Eugène Voninahitsy formed a breakaway party known as the RPSD Nouveau in 2003; Leader EVARISTE MARSON.

Tanora Malagasy Vonona (TGV) (Determined Malagasy Youth): Antananarivo; f. 2007; Leader ANDRY RAJOELINA.

MADAGASCAR

Tiako i Madagasikara (TIM) (I Love Madagascar): internet www.tim-madagascar.org; f. 2002; supports former Pres. Ravalomanana; Pres. YVAN RANDRIASANDRATRINIONY.

Diplomatic Representation

EMBASSIES IN MADAGASCAR

China, People's Republic: Ancien Hôtel Panorama, BP 1658, 101 Antananarivo; tel. (20) 2240129; fax (20) 2240215; e-mail chinaemb_mg@mfa.gov.cn; internet mg.china-embassy.org; Ambassador WO RUIDI.

Comoros: Antananarivo; tel. (20) 2265819; Ambassador MOURAD SAÏD IBRAHIM (designate).

Egypt: Lot MD 378 Ambalatokana Mandrosoa Ivato, BP 4082, 101 Antananarivo; tel. (20) 2245497; fax (20) 2245379; Ambassador MAGID FOAD SALEH FOAD.

France: 3 rue Jean Jaurès, BP 204, 101 Antananarivo; tel. (20) 2239898; fax (20) 2239927; e-mail ambatana@moov.mg; internet www.ambafrance-mada.org; Ambassador JEAN-MARC CHÂTAIGNER.

Germany: 101 rue du Pasteur Rabeony Hans, BP 516, Ambodirotra, 101 Antananarivo; tel. (20) 2223802; fax (20) 2226627; e-mail amballem@moov.de; internet www.antananarivo.diplo.de; Ambassador Dr WOLFGANG MOSER.

Holy See: Amboniloha Ivandry, BP 650, 101 Antananarivo; tel. (20) 2242376; fax (20) 2242384; e-mail nuntiusantana@wanadoo.mg; Apostolic Nuncio Most Rev. AUGUSTINE KASUJJA (Titular Archbishop of Caesarea de Numidia).

India: 4 Làlana Emile Rajaonson, Tsaralalana, BP 1787, 101 Antananarivo; tel. (20) 2223334; fax (20) 2233790; e-mail indembmd@blueline.mg; Ambassador AZAD SINGH TOOR.

Indonesia: 26–28 rue Patrice Lumumba, BP 3969, 101 Antananarivo; tel. (20) 2224915; fax (20) 2232857; Chargé d'affaires a.i. SLAMET SUYATA SASTRAMIHARDZA.

Iran: route Circulaire, Lot II L43 ter, Ankadivato, 101 Antananarivo; tel. (20) 2228639; fax (20) 2222298; Ambassador ABDOL RAHIM HOMATASH.

Japan: 8 rue du Dr Villette, BP 3863, Isoraka, 101 Antananarivo; tel. (20) 2226102; fax (20) 2221769; Ambassador TETSURO KAWAGUCHI.

Korea, Democratic People's Republic: 101 Antananarivo; tel. (20) 2244442; Ambassador RI YONG HAK.

Libya: Lot IIB, 37A route Circulaire Ampandrana-Ouest, 101 Antananarivo; tel. (20) 2221892; Chargé d'affaires a.i. Dr MOHAMED ALI SHARFEDIN AL-FITURI.

Mauritius: Villa David IV, Manakambahiny, 101 Antananarivo; tel. (20) 2221864; fax (20) 2221939; e-mail memad@moov.mg; Ambassador ERNEST GÉRARD LEMAIRE.

Morocco: Bâtiment D1, Rez-de-chaussée, Ankorondrano, BP 12, 104 Antananarivo; tel. (20) 2221347; fax (20) 2221124; e-mail amar_med@hotmail.com; Ambassador MUHAMMAD AMAR.

Norway: Explorer Business Park, Bâtiment 2D, Antananarivo; tel. (20) 2230507; fax (20) 2237799; e-mail emb.antananarivo@mfa.no; internet www.amb-norvege.mg; Ambassador DAG NISSEN.

Russia: BP 4006, Ivandry-Ambohijatovo, 101 Antananarivo; tel. (20) 2242827; fax (20) 2242642; e-mail ambrusmad@blueline.mg; Ambassador VLADIMIR B. GONCHARENKO.

Senegal: Lot II R, 179B Ambohirakely, Betongolo, Antananarivo; tel. (20) 2252186; fax (20) 2252186; Ambassador CÉSAR COLY.

South Africa: Lot IVO 68 bis, rue Ravoninahitriniarivo, Ankorondrano, BP 12101-05, 101 Antananarivo; tel. (20) 2243350; fax (20) 2249514; e-mail antananarivo@foreign.gov.za; Ambassador MOKGETHI SAMUEL MONAISA.

Switzerland: Immeuble ARO, Solombavambohaoka, Frantsay 77, BP 118, 101 Antananarivo; tel. (20) 2262997; fax (20) 2228940; e-mail ant.vertretung@eda.admin.ch; internet www.eda.admin.ch/antananarivo; Ambassador CARLOS ORGA.

USA: 14–16 rue Rainitovo, Antsahavola, BP 620, 101 Antananarivo; tel. (20) 2221257; fax (20) 2234539; internet www.antananarivo.usembassy.gov; Ambassador R. NIELS MARQUARDT.

Judicial System

HIGH CONSTITUTIONAL COURT

Haute Cour Constitutionnelle: POB 835, Ambohidahy, 101 Antananarivo; tel. (20) 2266061; e-mail hcc@hcc.gov.mg; internet www.hcc.gov.mg; interprets the Constitution and rules on constitutional issues; nine mems; Pres. JEAN-MICHEL RAJAONARIVONY.

HIGH COURT OF JUSTICE

Haute Cour de Justice: 101 Antananarivo; nine mems.

SUPREME COURT

Cour Suprême: Palais de Justice, Anosy, 101 Antananarivo; Pres. ALICE RAJAONAH (acting); Attorney-General COLOMBE RAMANANTSOA (acting); Chamber Pres YOLANDE RAMANGASOAVINA, FRANÇOIS RAMANANDRAIBE.

COURT OF APPEAL

Cour d'Appel: Palais de Justice, Anosy, 101 Antananarivo; Pres. AIMÉE RAKOTONIRINA; Pres of Chamber CHARLES RABETOKOTANY, PÉTRONILLE ANDRIAMIHAJA, BAKOLALAO RANAIVOHARIVONY, BERTHOLIER RAVELONTSALAMA, LUCIEN RABARIJHON, NELLY RAKOTOBE, ARLETTE RAMAROSON, CLÉMENTINE RAVANDISON, GISÈLE RABOTOVAO, JEAN-JACQUES RAJAONA.

OTHER COURTS

Tribunaux de Première Instance: at Antananarivo, Toamasina, Antsiranana, Mahajanga, Fianarantsoa, Toliary, Antsirabé, Ambatondrazaka, Antalaha, Farafangana and Maintirano; for civil, commercial and social matters, and for registration.

Cours Criminelles Ordinaires: tries crimes of common law; attached to the Cour d'Appel in Antananarivo but may sit in any other large town. There are also 31 Cours Criminelles Spéciales dealing with cases concerning cattle.

Tribunaux Spéciaux Economiques: at Antananarivo, Toamasina, Mahajanga, Fianarantsoa, Antsiranana and Toliary; tries crimes specifically relating to economic matters.

Tribunaux Criminels Spéciaux: judges cases of banditry and looting; 31 courts.

Religion

It is estimated that more than 50% of the population follow traditional animist beliefs, some 41% are Christians (about one-half of whom are Roman Catholics) and some 7% are Muslims.

CHRISTIANITY

Fiombonan'ny Fiangonana Kristiana eto Madagasikara (FFKM)/Conseil Chrétien des Eglises de Madagascar (Christian Council of Churches in Madagascar): Vohipiraisama, Ambohijatovo-Atsimo, BP 798, 101 Antananarivo; tel. (20) 2623433; e-mail ffkmfoibe@gmail.com; f. 1980; four mems and two assoc. mems; Pres. Pastor Dr MODESTE ENDOR RAKOTO; Gen. Sec. Rev. MAHERY RAKOTONANDRIANINA.

Fiombonan'ny Fiangonana Protestanta eto Madagasikara (FFPM)/Fédération des Eglises Protestantes à Madagascar (Federation of the Protestant Churches in Madagascar): VK 3 Vohipiraisana, Ambohijatovo-Atsimo, BP 4226, 101 Antananarivo; tel. (20) 2415888; e-mail edmrazafi@fuller.edu; f. 1958; two mem. churches; Pres Rev. Dr LALA RASENDRAHASINA; Gen. Sec. Rev. Dr EDMOND RAZAFIMANANTSOA.

The Anglican Communion

Anglicans are adherents of the Church of the Province of the Indian Ocean, comprising seven dioceses (five in Madagascar, one in Mauritius and one in Seychelles). The Archbishop of the Province is the Bishop of Antananarivo. The Church has about 160,000 adherents in Madagascar, including the membership of the Eklesia Episkopaly Malagasy (Malagasy Episcopal Church), founded in 1874.

Bishop of Antananarivo: Rt Revd. SAMOELA JAONA RANARIVELO, Evêché anglican, Lot VK57 ter, Ambohimanoro, 101 Antananarivo; tel. (20) 2220827; fax (20) 2261331; e-mail eemdanta@yahoo.com.

Bishop of Antsiranana: Rt Rev. ROGER CHUNG PO CHEN, Evêché anglican, 4 rue Grandidier, BP 278, 201 Antsiranana; tel. (20) 8222670; e-mail mgrchungpo@blueline.mg; internet www.antsirananadiocese.org.

Bishop of Fianarantsoa: Rt Rev. GILBERT RATELOSON RAKOTONDRAVELO, Evêché anglican, BP 1418, 531 Fianarantsoa.

Bishop of Mahajanga: Rt Rev. JEAN-CLAUDE ANDRIANJAFIMANANA, Evêché anglican, BP 169, 401 Mahajanga; e-mail eemdmaha@dts.mg.

Bishop of Toamasina: Rt Rev. JEAN PAUL SOLO, Evêché anglican, rue James Seth, BP 531, 501 Toamasina; tel. (20) 5332163; fax (20) 5331689.

MADAGASCAR

The Roman Catholic Church

Madagascar comprises four archdioceses and 17 dioceses. At 31 December 2006 the number of adherents in the country represented about 27.2% of the total population.

Bishops' Conference

Conférence episcopale de Madagascar, 102 bis, rue Cardinal Jerôme Rakotomalala, BP 667, 101 Antananarivo; tel. (20) 2220478; fax (20) 2224854; e-mail ecar@vitelcom.mg.

f. 1969; Pres. Most Rev. FULGENCE RABEMAHAFALY (Archbishop of Fianarantsoa).

Archbishop of Antananarivo: ODON ARSÈNE RAZANAKOLONA, Archevêché, Andohalo, BP 3030, 101 Antananarivo; tel. (20) 2220726; fax (20) 2264181; e-mail didih@simicro.org.

Archbishop of Antsiranana: Most Rev. MICHEL MALO, Archevêché, 5 blvd le Myre de Villers, BP 415, 201 Antsiranana; tel. (82) 21605; e-mail archevediego@blueline.mg.

Archbishop of Fianarantsoa: Most Rev. FULGENCE RABEMAHAFALY, Archevêché, pl. Mgr Givelet, BP 1440, Ecar Ambozontany, 301 Fianarantsoa; tel. (20) 7550027; fax (20) 7551436; e-mail ecarfianar@mel.wanadoo.mg.

Archbishop of Toliara: Most Rev. FULGENCE RABEONY, Archevêché, Maison Saint Jean, BP 30, 601 Toliary; tel. (20) 9442416; e-mail diocese_tulcar@wanadoo.mg.

Other Christian Churches

Fiangonan'i Jesoa Kristy eto Madagasikara/Eglise de Jésus-Christ à Madagascar (FJKM): Lot 11 B18, Tohatohabato Ranavalona 1, Trano 'Ifanomezantsoa', BP 623, 101 Antananarivo; tel. (20) 2228237; fax (20) 2227033; e-mail fjkm@wanadoo.mg; internet foibefjkm.mg; f. 1968; Pres. LALA HAJA RASENDRAHASINA; Gen. Sec. Rev. RÉMY RALIBERA; 2m. mems.

Fiangonana Loterana Malagasy (Malagasy Lutheran Church): BP 1741, 19, rue Jules Pochard, 101 Antananarivo; tel. (20) 2422703; fax (20) 2423856; e-mail drmodeste@yahoo.fr; internet www.flm-mada.org; f. 1867; Pres. Rev. Dr ENDOR MODESTE RAKOTO; 3m. mems (2009).

The Press

In December 1990 legislation was adopted guaranteeing the freedom of the press and the right of newspapers to be established without prior authorization.

PRINCIPAL DAILIES

Bulletin de l'Agence Nationale d'Information 'TARATRA' (ANTA): 8/10 Làlana Rainizanabololona, Antanimena, BP 194, 101 Antananarivo; tel. (20) 2234308; e-mail administration@taratramada.com; internet www.taratramada.com; f. 1977; Malagasy; Editor-in-Chief HANITRA RABETOKOTANY.

L'Express de Madagascar: BP 3893, 101 Antananarivo; tel. (20) 2221934; fax (20) 2262894; e-mail lexpress@malagasy.com; internet www.lexpressmada.com; f. 1995; French and Malagasy; Editor (vacant); circ. 10,000.

Gazetiko: rue Ravoninahitriniarivo, BP 1414 Ankorondrano, 101 Antananarivo; tel. (20) 2269779; fax (20) 2227351; e-mail gazetiko@midi-madagasikara.mg; internet www.gazetiko.mg; Malagasy; circ. 50,000.

La Gazette de la Grande Ile: Lot II, W 23 L Ankorahotra, route de l'Université, BP 8678, Antananarivo; tel. (20) 2261377; fax (20) 2265188; e-mail james@lagazette-dgi.com; internet www.lagazette-dgi.com; French; 24 pages; Pres. JAMES RAMAROSAONA; circ. 15,000–30,000.

Imongo Vaovao: 11K 4 bis Andravoahangy, BP 7014, 101 Antananarivo; tel. (20) 2233110; f. 1955; Malagasy; Dir ANDRÉ RATSIFEHERA; circ. 15,000.

Madagascar Tribune: Immeuble SME, rue Ravoninahitriniarivo, BP 659, Ankorondrano, 101 Antananarivo; tel. (20) 2222635; fax (20) 2222254; e-mail contact@madagascar-tribune.com; internet www.madagascar-tribune.com; f. 1988; independent; French and Malagasy; Editor RAHAGA RAMAHOLIMIHASO; circ. 12,000.

Maresaka: Cité Logt. 288, Analamahitsy, 101 Antananarivo; tel. (20) 2431665; f. 1953; independent; Malagasy; Editor R. RABEFANANINA; circ. 5,000.

Midi Madagasikara: Làlana Ravoninahitriniarivo, BP 1414, Ankorondrano, 101 Antananarivo; tel. (20) 2269779; fax (20) 2227351; e-mail contact@midi-madagasikara.mg; internet www.midi-madagasikara.mg; f. 1983; French and Malagasy; Dir MAMY RAKOTOARIVELO; circ. 21,000 (Mon.–Fri.), 35,000 (Sat.).

Les Nouvelles: BP 194, 101 Antananarivo; tel. (20) 2235433; fax (20) 2229993; e-mail administration@les-nouvelles.com; internet www.les-nouvelles.com; in French and Taratra; f. 2003; Dir-Gen. NAINA ANDRIANTSITOHAINA.

Ny Vaovaontsika: BP 11137, MBS Anosipatrana; tel. (20) 2227717; e-mail nyvaovaontsika@mbs.mg; f. 2004; re-estd as a daily; Malagasy; Malagasy Broadcasting System; Editor-in-Chief ROLAND ANDRIAMAHENINA; circ. 10,000.

Le Quotidien: BP 11 097, 101 Antananarivo; tel. (20) 2227717; fax (20) 2265447; e-mail lequotidien@mbs.mg; internet www.lequotidien.mg; f. 2003; owned by the Tiko Group plc; French.

PRINCIPAL PERIODICALS

Basy Vava: Lot III E 96, Mahamasina Atsimo, 101 Antananarivo; tel. (20) 2220448; f. 1959; daily; Malagasy; Dir GABRIEL RAMANANJATO; circ. 3,000.

Bulletin de la Société du Corps Médical Malgache: Imprimerie Volamahitsy, 101 Antananarivo; Malagasy; monthly; Dir Dr RAKOTOMALALA.

Dans les Médias Demain (DMD): 51 rue Tsiombikibo, BP 1734, Ambatovinaky, 101 Antananarivo; tel. (20) 2241664; fax (20) 2241665; e-mail admin@dmd.mg; internet www.dmd.mg; f. 1986; independent; economic information and analysis; weekly; Editorial Dir JEAN ERIC RAKOTOARISOA; circ. 4,000.

Feon'ny Mpiasa: Lot M8, Isotry, 101 Antananarivo; trade union affairs; Malagasy; monthly; Dir M. RAZAKANAIVO; circ. 2,000.

Gazetinao: Lot IPA 37, BP 1758, Anosimasina, 101 Antananarivo; tel. (33) 1198161; e-mail mitantanasymitarika@yahoo.fr; f. 1976; French and Malagasy; monthly; religion and culture; Editor-in-Chief DAVID ALDEN EINSTEN RAKOTOMAHANINA; circ. 3,000.

L'Hebdo: BP 3893, 101 Antananarivo; tel. (20) 2221934; e-mail courrier@hebdomada.com; internet www.hebdomada.net; f. 2005; French and Malagasy; weekly; Editor-in-Chief NASOLO VALIAVO ANDRIAMIHAJA.

Isika Mianakavy: Ambatomena, 301 Fianarantsoa; f. 1958; Roman Catholic; Malagasy; monthly; Dir J. RANAIVOMANANA; circ. 21,000.

Journal Officiel de la République de Madagascar/Gazetim-Panjakan' Ny Repoblika Malagasy: BP 248, 101 Antananarivo; tel. (20) 2265010; fax (20) 2225319; f. 1883; official announcements; Malagasy and French; weekly; Dir HONORÉE ELIANNE RALALAHARISON; circ. 1,545.

Journal Scientifique de Madagascar: BP 3855, Antananarivo; f. 1985; Dir Prof. MANAMBELONA; circ. 3,000.

Jureco: BP 6318, Lot IVD 48 bis, rue Razanamaniraka, Behoririka, 101 Antananarivo; tel. (20) 2255271; e-mail jureco@malagasy.com; internet www.jureco.com; law and economics; monthly; French; Dir MBOARA ANDRIANARIMANANA.

Lakroan'i Madagasikara/La Croix de Madagascar: BP 7524, CNPC Antanimena, 101 Antananarivo; tel. (20) 2266128; fax (20) 2224020; e-mail info@lakroa.org; internet www.geocities.com/lakroam; f. 1927; Roman Catholic; French and Malagasy; weekly; Dir Fr VINCENT RABEMAHAFALY; circ. 25,000.

La Lettre de Madagascar (LLM): Antananarivo; f. 2003; 2 a month; in French and English; economic; Editor-in-Chief DANIEL LAMY.

Mpanolotsaina: BP 623, 101 Antananarivo; tel. (20) 2226845; fax (20) 2226372; e-mail fjkm@wanadoo.mg; religious, educational; Malagasy; quarterly; Dir RAYMOND RAJOELISOL.

New Magazine: BP 7581, Newprint, Route des Hydrocarbures, 101 Antananarivo; tel. (20) 2233335; fax (20) 2236471; e-mail newmag@wanadoo.mg; internet www.newmagazine.mg; monthly; in French; Dir CLARA RAVOAVAHY.

Ny Mpamangy-FLM: 9 rue Grandidier Isoraka, BP 538, Antsahamanitra, 101 Antananarivo; tel. (20) 2232446; f. 1882; monthly; Dir Pastor JEAN RABENANDRASANA; circ. 3,000.

Ny Sakaizan'ny Tanora: BP 538, Antsahaminitra, 101 Antananarivo; tel. (20) 2228943; f. 1878; monthly; Editor-in-Chief ELISABETH RAHELINORO; circ. 5,000.

PME Madagascar: rue Hugues Rabesahala, BP 953, Antsakaviro, 101 Antananarivo; tel. (20) 2222536; fax (20) 2234534; f. 1989; French; monthly; economic review; Dir ROMAIN ANDRIANARISOA; circ. 3,500.

Recherche et Culture: BP 907, 101 Antananarivo; tel. (20) 2226600; f. 1985; publ. by French dept of the University of Antananarivo; 2 a year; Dir GINETTE RAMAROSON; circ. 1,000.

Revue de l'Océan Indien: Communication et Médias Océan Indien, rue H. Rabesahala, BP 46, Antsakaviro, 101 Antananarivo; tel. (20) 2222536; fax (20) 2234534; e-mail roi@dts.mg; internet www.madatours.com/roi; f. 1980; monthly; French; Man. Dir GEORGES RANAIVOSOA; Sec.-Gen. HERY M. A. RANAIVOSOA; circ. 5,000.

Sahy: Lot VD 42, Ambanidia, 101 Antananarivo; tel. (20) 2222715; f. 1957; political; Malagasy; weekly; Editor ALINE RAKOTO; circ. 9,000.

MADAGASCAR

Sosialisma Mpiasa: BP 1128, 101 Antananarivo; tel. (20) 2221989; f. 1979; trade union affairs; Malagasy; monthly; Dir PAUL RABEMANANJARA; circ. 5,000.

Vaovao: BP 271, 101 Antananarivo; tel. (20) 2221193; f. 1985; French and Malagasy; weekly; Dir MARC RAKOTONOELY; circ. 5,000.

NEWS AGENCIES

Agence Nationale d'Information 'TARATRA' (ANTA): 7 rue Jean Ralaimongo, Ambohiday, BP 386, 101 Antananarivo; tel. and fax (20) 2236047; e-mail taratra.mtpc@mtpc.gov.mg; f. 1977; Man. Dir JOÉ ANACLET RAKOTOARISON.

Mada: Villa Joëlle, Lot II J 161 R, Ivandry, 101 Antananarivo; tel. (20) 2242428; e-mail courrier@mada.mg; internet www.mada.mg; f. 2003; independent information agency; Dir RICHARD CLAUDE RATOVONARIVO.

Publishers

Edisiona Salohy: BP 4226, 101 Antananarivo; Dir MIRANA VOLOLOARISOA RANDRIANARISON.

Editions Ambozontany Analamalintsy: BP 7553, 101 Antananarivo; tel. and fax (20) 2243111; e-mail editionsj@moov.mg; f. 1962; religious, educational, historical, cultural and technical textbooks; Dir Fr GUILLAUME DE SAINT PIERRE RAKOTONANDRATONIARIVO.

Foibe Filankevitry Ny Mpampianatra (FOFIPA): BP 202, 101 Antananarivo; tel. (20) 2227500; f. 1971; textbooks; Dir Frère RAZAFINDRAKOTO.

Imprimerie Nouvelle: PK 2, Andranomahery, route de Majunga, BP 4330, 101 Antananarivo; tel. (20) 2221036; fax (20) 2269225; e-mail nouvelle@wanadoo.mg; Dir EUGÈNE RAHARIFIDY.

Imprimerie Takariva: 4 rue Radley, BP 1029, Antanimena, 101 Antananarivo; tel. (20) 2222128; f. 1933; fiction, languages, school textbooks; Man. Dir PAUL RAPATSALAHY.

Madagascar Print and Press Co (MADPRINT): rue Rabesahala, Antsakaviro, BP 953, 101 Antananarivo; tel. (20) 2222536; fax (20) 2234534; f. 1969; literary, technical and historical; Dir GEORGES RANAIVOSOA.

Maison d'Edition Protestante Antso: 19 rue Venance Manifatra, Imarivolanitra, BP 660, 101 Antananarivo; tel. (20) 2220886; fax (20) 2226372; e-mail fjkm@dts.mg; f. 1972; religious, school, social, political and general; Dir HANS ANDRIAMAMPIANINA.

Nouvelle Société de Presse et d'Edition (NSPE): Immeuble Jeune Afrique, 58 rue Tsiombikibo, BP 1734, Ambatorinaky, 101 Antananarivo; tel. (20) 2227788; fax (20) 2230629.

Office du Livre Malgache: Lot 111 H29, Andrefan' Ambohijanahary, BP 617, 101 Antananarivo; tel. (20) 2224449; f. 1970; children's and general; Sec.-Gen. JULIETTE RATSIMANDRAVA.

Société Malgache d'Edition (SME): BP 659, Ankorondrano, 101 Antananarivo; tel. (20) 2222635; fax (20) 2222254; e-mail tribune@wanadoo.mg; f. 1943; general fiction, university and secondary textbooks; Man. Dir RAHAGA RAMAHOLIMIHASO.

Société Nouvelle de l'Imprimerie Centrale (SNIC): Làlana Ravoninahitriniarivo, BP 1414, 101 Antananarivo; tel. (20) 2221118; e-mail mrakotoa@wanadoo.mg; f. 1959; science, school textbooks; Man. Dir MAMY RAKOTOARIVELO.

Société de Presse et d'Edition de Madagascar: Antananarivo; non-fiction, reference, science, university textbooks; Man. Dir RAJAOFERA ANDRIAMBELO.

Trano Printy Fiangonana Loterana Malagasy (TPFLM): BP 538, 9 ave Général Gabriel Ramanantsoa, 101 Antananarivo; tel. (20) 2223340; fax (20) 2262643; e-mail impluth@wanadoo.mg; f. 1877; religious, educational and fiction; Man. RAYMOND RANDRIANATOANDRO.

GOVERNMENT PUBLISHING HOUSE

Imprimerie Nationale: BP 38, 101 Antananarivo; tel. (20) 2223675; e-mail dinm@wanadoo.mg; all official publs; Dir JEAN DENIS RANDRIANIRINA.

Broadcasting and Communications

TELECOMMUNICATIONS

Office Malagasy d'Etudes et de Régulation des Télécommunications (OMERT): BP 99991, Route des Hydrocarbures-Alarobia, 101 Antananarivo; tel. (20) 2242119; fax (20) 2321516; e-mail omert@moov.mg; internet www.omert.mg; f. 1997; Gen. Man. GILBERT ANDRIANIRINA RAJAONASY.

Orange Madagascar: Antananarivo; internet www.orange.mg; f. 1998; fmrly Antaris, la Société Malgache de Mobiles; name changed as above 2003; mobile telecommunication GSM network provider; market leader; Dir-Gen. PATRICE PEZAT.

Télécom Malagasy SA (TELMA): BP 763, 101 Antananarivo; tel. (20) 2532705; fax (20) 2253871; e-mail telmacorporate@telma.mg; internet www.telma.mg; 68% owned by Distacom (Hong Kong); owns DTS Wanadoo internet service provider; Chair. DAVID WHITE; Dir-Gen. PATRICK PISAL-HAMIDA.

Zain Madagscar: Explorer Business Park, Ankorondrano, Antananarivo 101; tel. (33) 1100100; e-mail info.mg@zain.com; internet www.mg.zain.com; f. 1997 as Madacom; acquired by Celtel in 2006; name changed as above in 2008; Dir-Gen. IHAB EL FOULY.

BROADCASTING

Radio

In 2001 there were an estimated 127 radio stations.

Radio MBS (Malagasy Broadcasting System): BP 11137, Anosipatrana, Antananarivo; tel. (20) 2266702; fax (20) 2268941; e-mail marketing@mbs.mg; internet www.mbs.mg; broadcasts by satellite; Man. SARAH RAVALOMANANA.

Radio Nationale Malagasy: BP 442, Anosy, 101 Antananarivo; tel. (20) 2221745; fax (20) 2232715; e-mail rnmdir@dts.mg; internet www.takelaka.dts.mg/radmad; state-controlled; part of the Office de Radiodiffusion et de Télévision de Madagascar (ORTM); broadcasts in French and Malagasy; Dir ALAIN RAJAONA.

Le Messager Radio Evangélique: BP 1374, 101 Antananarivo; tel. (20) 2234495; broadcasts in French, English and Malagasy; Dir JOCELYN RANJARISON.

Radio Antsiva: BP 632, Enceinte STEDIC, Village des Jeux, Zone Industrielle Nord, Route des Hydrocarbures, 101 Antananarivo; tel. (20) 2254849; e-mail antsiva@freenet.mg; internet www.antsiva.mg; f. 1994; broadcasts in French and Malagasy; Dir LALATIONE RAKOTONDRAZAFY.

Radio Don Bosco: BP 60, 105 Ivato; tel. (20) 2244387; fax (20) 2244511; e-mail rdb@wanadoo.mg; internet www.radiodonbosco.mg; f. 1996; Catholic, educational and cultural; Chair. Fr GIUSEPPE MIELE.

Radio Feon'ny Vahoaka (RFV): 103 Immeuble Ramaroson, 8e étage, 101 Antananarivo; tel. (20) 2233820; broadcasts in French and Malagasy; Dir ALAIN RAMAROSON.

Radio Lazan'iarivo (RLI): Lot V A49, Andafiavaratra, 101 Antananarivo; tel. (20) 2229016; fax (20) 2267559; e-mail rli@simicro.mg; broadcasts in French, English and Malagasy; privately owned; specializes in jazz music; Dir IHOBY RABARLJOHN.

Radio Viva: Antananarivo; Owner ANDRY RAJOELINA.

Television

MA TV: BP 1414 Ankorondrano, 101 Antananarivo; tel. (20) 2220897; fax (20) 2234421.

MBS Television (Malagasy Broadcasting System): BP 11137, Anosipatrana, Antananarivo; tel. (20) 2266702; fax (20) 2268941; e-mail journaltv@mbs.mg; internet www.mbs.mg; broadcasts in French and Malagasy.

Radio Télévision Analamanga (RTA): Immeuble Fiaro, 101 Antananarivo; e-mail rta@rta.mg; internet www.rta.mg; incl. four provincial radio stations; Dir-Man. PATRICK COTTRELLE.

Télévision Nasionale Malagache: BP 1202, Anosy, 101 Antananarivo; tel. (20) 2222381; state-controlled; part of the Office de Radiodiffusion et de Télévision de Madagascar (ORTM); broadcasts in French and Malagasy; Gen. Man. JPHARY RAVAOJANAHARY.

Télévision Viva: Antananarivo; Owner ANDRY RAJOELINA.

Finance

(cap. = capital; res = reserves; dep. = deposits; m. = million; brs = branches; amounts in ariary)

BANKING

Central Bank

Banque Centrale de Madagascar: rue de la Révolution Socialiste Malgache, BP 550, 101 Antananarivo; tel. (20) 2221751; fax (20) 2234532; e-mail sbu@bfm.mg; internet www.banque-centrale.mg; f. 1973; bank of issue; cap. 200m., res 83,754.9m., dep. 921,164.2m. (Dec. 2006); Gov. FRÉDÉRIC RASAMOELY.

Other Banks

Bank of Africa (BOA)—Madagascar: 2 pl. de l'Indépendance, BP 183, 101 Antananarivo; tel. (20) 2239100; fax (20) 2266125; e-mail boa@boa.mg; internet www.boa.mg; f. 1976 as Bankin'ny Tantsaha

Mpamokatra; name changed as above 1999; 38.86% owned by Bank of Africa Group (Luxembourg), 10.00% state-owned; commercial bank, specializes in micro-finance; cap. 18,000.0m., res 19,023.4m., dep. 583,932.8m. (Dec. 2006); Chair. and Pres. PAUL DERREUMAUX; Gen. Man. RENÉ FORMEY DE SAINT-LOUVENT; 55 brs.

Banque Industrielle et Commerciale de Madagascar (BICM): 2 rue du Dr Raseta Andraharo, BP 889, 101 Antananarivo; tel. (20) 2356568; fax (20) 2356656; e-mail bicm@bicm.mg; internet www.bicm.mg; f. 2002; successor of the Banque Internationale Chine Madagascar, fmrly Compagnie Malgache de Banque; cap. 7,116.7m., res −1,804.6m., dep. 5,888.7m. (Dec. 2005); Chair. Dr HUANG WEI GUANG.

Banque Malgache de l'Océan Indien (BMOI) (Indian Ocean Malagasy Bank): pl. de l'Indépendance, BP 25 bis, Antaninarenina, 101 Antananarivo; tel. (20) 2238251; fax (20) 2238544; e-mail bmoi.st@simicro.mg; internet www.bmoi.mg; f. 1989; 75% owned by BNP Paribas SA (France); cap. and res 40,200.0m., dep. 377,700.0m. (Dec. 2006); Pres. GASTON RAMENASON; Dir JEAN LUC RAZAFISON; 8 brs.

Banque SBM Madagascar: rue Andrianary Ratianarivo Antsahavola 1, 101 Antananarivo; tel. (20) 2266607; fax (20) 2266608; e-mail bsbmmtana@sbm.intnet.mu; f. 1998; 79.99% owned by SBM Global Investments Ltd (Mauritius), 20.01% owned by Nedbank Africa Investments Ltd (South Africa); cap. 2,900.5m., res 2,348.5m., dep. 82,078.0m. (Dec. 2006); Chair. CHAITLALL GUNNESS; Gen. Man. KRISHNADUTT RAMBOJUN.

BFV—Société Générale: 14 rue Général Rabehevitra, BP 196, Antananarivo 101; tel. (20) 2220691; fax (20) 2237140; e-mail webmaster.mail@socgen.com; internet www.bfvsg.mg; f. 1977 as Banky Fampandrosoana ny Varotra; changed name in 1998; 70% owned by Société Générale (France), 28.5% state-owned; cap. 38,485.9m., res 15,320.6m., dep. 378,898.1m. (Dec. 2006); Pres. MARCEL LENGUIN; 40 brs.

BNI Madagascar: 74 rue du 26 Juin 1960, BP 174, 101 Antananarivo; tel. (20) 2222800; fax (20) 2233749; e-mail info@bni.mg; internet www.bni.mg; f. 1976 as Bankin 'ny Indostria; 51% owned by IUB Holding (France), 32.58% state-owned; cap. 2,700.0m., res 35,007.0m., dep. 543,236.7m. (Dec. 2005); Pres. and Chair. EVARISTE MARSON; Man. Dir PASCAL FALL; 25 brs.

Mauritius Commercial Bank (Madagascar) SA (MCB): 77 rue Solombavambahoaka Frantsay, Antsahavola, BP 197, 101 Antananarivo; tel. (20) 2227262; fax (20) 2228740; e-mail mcb.int@mcbmadagascar.com; internet www.mcbmadagascar.com; f. 1992 as Union Commercial Bank; name changed as above in 2007; 70% owned by Mauritius Commercial Bank Ltd; cap. and res 17,113.2m., dep. 105,991.2m. (Dec. 2007); Chair. JEAN FRANÇOIS DESVAUX DE MARIGNY; Gen. Man. MARC MARIE JOSEPH DE BOLLIVIER; 3 brs.

INSURANCE

ARO (Assurances Réassurances Omnibranches): Antsahavola, BP 42, 101 Antananarivo; tel. (20) 2220154; fax (20) 2234464; e-mail aro1@moov.mg; internet www.aro.mg; state-owned; Dir-Gen. GUY ROLLAND RASOANAIVO.

ASCOMA Madagascar: 13 rue Patrice Lumumba, BP 673, 101 Antananarivo; tel. (20) 2223162; fax (20) 2222785; e-mail madagascar@ascoma.com; f. 1952; Dir VIVIANE RAMANITRA.

Compagnie Malgache d'Assurances et de Réassurances 'Ny Havana': Immeuble 'Ny Havana', Zone des 67 Ha, BP 3881, 101 Antananarivo; tel. (20) 2226760; fax (20) 2224303; e-mail nyhavana@wanadoo.mg; f. 1968; state-owned; cap. 5,435.6m. (2006); Dir-Gen. BERA RAZANAKOLONA.

Mutuelle d'Assurances Malagasy (MAMA): Lot 1F, 12 bis Ambalavao-Isotry, BP 185, 101 Antananarivo; tel. (20) 2261882; fax (20) 2261883; e-mail assurancemama@moov.mg; f. 1968; Dir. SETH AIMÉ RANDRIANARIJAONA.

Trade and Industry

DEVELOPMENT ORGANIZATIONS

Bureau d'Information pour les Entreprises (BIPE): Nouvel Immeuble ARO, Ampefiloha, 101 Antananarivo; tel. (20) 2230512; internet www.bipe.mg; part of the Ministry of Industry, Trade and the Development of the Private Sector.

Economic Development Board of Madagascar (EDBM): ave Gabriel Ramanantsoa, Antaninarenina, Antananarivo 101; tel. (20) 2268121; fax (20) 2266105; e-mail edbm@edbm.mg; internet www.edbm.gov.mg; f. 2006; service for the facilitation and promotion of investment in Madagascar; advisory service for starting a business, obtaining visas and land acquisition; Interim CEO ERIC RAKOTO ANDRIANTSILAVO.

La maison de l'entreprise: rue Samuel Ramahefy Ambatonakanga, BP 74, 101 Antananarivo; tel. (20) 2225386; fax (20) 2233669; e-mail cite@cite.mg; internet www.cite.mg; f. 1967; supports and promotes Malagasy businesses; Dir-Gen. ISABELLE GACHIE.

Office des Mines Nationales et des Industries Stratégiques (OMNIS): 21 Làlana Razanakombana, BP 1 bis, 101 Antananarivo; tel. (20) 2224283; fax (20) 2222985; e-mail omnis@simicro.mg; internet www.omnis-madagascar.mg; f. 1976; promotes the exploration and exploitation of mining resources, in particular oil resources; Dir-Gen. JOELI VALÉRIEN LALAHARISAINA.

Société d'Etude et de Réalisation pour le Développement Industriel (SERDI): BP 3180, 101 Antananarivo; tel. (20) 2225204; fax (20) 2229669; f. 1966; Dir-Gen. RAOILISON RAJAONARY.

CHAMBER OF COMMERCE

Fédération des Chambres de Commerce, d'Industrie et d'Agriculture de Madagascar: BP 166, 20 rue Henri Razanatseheno, Antaninarenina, Antananarivo 101; tel. (20) 2220211; fax (20) 2220213; e-mail cciaa@tana-cciaa.org; internet www.tana-cciaa.org; 12 mem. chambers; Pres. SIMON RAKOTONDRAHOVA; Chair. HENRI RAZANATSEHENO; Sec.-Gen. HUBERT RATSIANDAVANA.

Chambre de Commerce, d'Industrie, d'Artisanat et d'Agriculture—Antananarivo (CCIAA): BP 166, 20 rue Henri Razanatseheno, Antaninarenina, 101 Antananarivo; tel. (20) 2220211; fax (20) 2220213; e-mail cciaa@tana-cciaa.org; internet cci-tana.org; f. 1993; Pres. BEZO ANDRIANARIVELO RAZAFY.

TRADE ASSOCIATION

Société d'Intérêt National des Produits Agricoles (SINPA): BP 754, rue Fernand-Kasanga, Tsimbazaza, Antananarivo; tel. (20) 2220558; fax (20) 2220665; f. 1973; monopoly purchaser and distributor of agricultural produce; Chair. GUALBERT RAZANAJATOVO; Gen. Man. JEAN CLOVIS RALIJESY.

EMPLOYERS' ORGANIZATIONS

Groupement des Entreprises de Madagascar (GEM): Kianja MDRM sy Tia Tanindrazana, Ambohijatovo, BP 1338, 101 Antananarivo; tel. (20) 2223841; fax (20) 2221965; e-mail gem@simicro.mg; internet www.gem-madagascar.com; f. 1975; 15 nat. syndicates and five regional syndicates comprising 1,000 cos and 49 directly affiliated cos; Pres. NAINA ANDRIANTSITOHAINA; Sec.-Gen. ZINAH RASAMUEL RAVALOSON.

Groupement National des Exportateurs de Vanille de Madagascar (GNEV): BP 21, Antalaha; tel. (13) 20714532; fax (13) 20816017; e-mail rama.anta@sat.blueline.mg; 18 mems; Pres. JEAN GEORGES RANDRIAMIHARISOA.

Malagasy Entrepreneurs' Association (FIV.MPA.MA): Lot II, 2e étage, Immeuble Santa Antaninarenina; tel. (20) 2229292; fax (20) 2229290; e-mail fivmpama@simicro.mg; comprises 10 trade assocs, representing 200 mems, and 250 direct business mems; Chair. HERINTSALAMA RAJAONARIVELO.

Syndicat des Industries de Madagascar (SIM): Immeuble Holcim, Lot 1 bis, Tsaralalàna; BP 1695, 101 Antananarivo; tel. (20) 2224007; fax (20) 2222518; e-mail syndusmad@wanadoo.mg; internet www.syndusmad.com; f. 1958; Chair. SAMUEL RAVELOSON; 82 mems (2006).

Syndicat des Planteurs de Café: 37 Làlana Razafimahandry, BP 173, 101 Antananarivo.

Syndicat Professionnel des Agents Généraux d'Assurances: Antananarivo; f. 1949; Pres. SOLO RATSIMBAZAFY; Sec. IHANTA RANDRIAMANDRANTO.

Syndicat Professionel des Producteurs d'Extraits Aromatiques, Alimentaires et Medicinaux de Madagascar (SYPEAM): 7 rue Rakotoson Toto Radona, Antsahavola, BP 5038, Antananarivo 101; tel. (20) 2235363; e-mail itd.madagascar@moov.mg.

UTILITIES

Electricity and Water

Office de Regulation de l'Electricité (ORE): Antananarivo; f. 2004; Dir MAMY RAKOTOMIZAO.

Jiro sy Rano Malagasy (JIRAMA): BP 200, 149 rue Rainandriamampandry, Faravohitra, 101 Antananarivo; tel. (20) 2220031; fax (20) 2233806; e-mail dgjirama@wanadoo.mg; internet www.jirama.mg; f. 1975; controls production and distribution of electricity and water; managed by Lahmeyer International (Germany) from April 2005; Pres. ANDRY RALIJAONA; Dir-Gen. Dr BERNARD P. ROMAHN.

TRADE UNIONS

Cartel National des Organisations Syndicales de Madagascar (CARNOSYMA): BP 1035, 101 Antananarivo.

Confédération des Travailleurs Malagasy Révolutionnaires (FISEMARE): Lot IV N 76-A, Ankadifotsy, BP 1128, Befelatanana-

MADAGASCAR

Antananarivo 101; tel. (20) 2221989; fax (20) 2267712; f. 1985; Pres. PAUL RABEMANANJARA.

Confédération des Travailleurs Malgaches (Fivomdronamben'ny Mpiasa Malagasy—FMM): Lot IVM 133 A Antetezanafovoany I, BP 846, 101 Antananarivo; tel. (20) 2224565; e-mail rjeannot2002@yahoo.fr; f. 1957; Sec.-Gen. JEANNOT RAMANARIVO; 30,000 mems.

Fédération des Syndicats des Travailleurs de Madagascar (Firaisan'ny Sendika eran'i Madagaskara—FISEMA): Lot III, rue Pasteur Isotry, BP 172, 101 Antananarivo; f. 1956; Pres. DESIRÉ RALAMBOTAHINA; Sec.-Gen. M. RAZAKANAIVO; 8 affiliated unions representing 60,000 mems.

Sendika Kristianina Malagasy (SEKRIMA) (Christian Confederation of Malagasy Trade Unions): Soarano, route de Mahajanga, BP 1035, 101 Antananarivo; tel. (20) 2223174; f. 1937; Pres. MARIE RAKOTOANOSY; Gen. Sec. RAYMOND RAKOTOARISAONA; 158 affiliated unions representing 40,000 mems.

Union des Syndicats Autonomes de Madagascar (USAM): Lot III M 33 BC, Andrefan'Ambohijanahary, BP 1038, 101 Antananarivo; tel. and fax (20) 2227485; e-mail usam@moov.mg; f. 1954; Pres. JEAN HENRI RANDRIAMBAOARISOA; Sec.-Gen. SAMUEL RABEMANANTSOA; 46 affiliated unions representing 30,000 mems.

Transport

RAILWAYS

In 2001 there were 893 km of railway, including four railway lines, all 1-m gauge track. The northern system, which comprised 720 km of track, links the east coast with Antsirabé, in the interior, via Moramanga and Antananarivo, with a branch line from Moramanga to Lake Alaotra and was privatized in 2001. The southern system, which comprised 163 km of track, links Manakara, on the east coast, with Fianarantsoa.

Réseau National des Chemins de Fer Malagasy (RNCFM): 1 ave de l'Indépendance, BP 259, Soarano, 101 Antananarivo; tel. (20) 2220521; fax (20) 2222288; f. 1909; in the process of transfer to private sector; Administrator DANIEL RAZAFINDRABE.

Fianarantsoa-Côte Est (FCE): FCE Gare, Fianarantsoa; tel. (20) 7551354; e-mail fce@blueline.mg; internet www.fce-madagascar.com; f. 1936; southern network, 163 km.

Madarail: Gare de Soarano, 1 ave de l'Indépendance, BP 1175, 101 Antananarivo; tel. (20) 2234599; fax (20) 2221883; e-mail madarail@wanadoo.mg; internet www.comazar.com/madarail.htm; f. 2001; jt venture, operated by Comazar, South Africa; 45% of Comazar is owned by Sheltam Locomotive and Rail Services, South Africa; 31.6% is owned by Transnet Freight Rail, South Africa; operates the northern network of the Madagascan railway (650 km); Chair. ERIC PEIFFER; Gen. Dir PATRICK CLAES; 878 employees.

ROADS

In 2001 there were an estimated 49,837 km of classified roads; about 11.6% of the road network was paved. In 1987 there were 39,500 km of unclassified roads, used only in favourable weather. A road and motorway redevelopment programme, funded by the World Bank (€300m.) and the European Union (EU—€61m.), began in June 2000. In August 2002 the EU undertook to disburse US $10m. for the reconstruction of 11 bridges destroyed during the political crisis in that year. In 2003 Japan pledged $28m. to build several bridges and a 15-km bypass. The Government planned to have restored and upgraded 14,000 km of highways and 8,000 km of rural roads to an operational status by 2015. In 2005, according to the IMF, 8,982 km of roads had been maintained or rehabilitated.

INLAND WATERWAYS

The Pangalanes canal runs for 600 km near the east coast from Toamasina to Farafangana. In 1990 432 km of the canal between Toamasina and Mananjary were navigable.

SHIPPING

There are 18 ports, the largest being at Toamasina, which handles about 70% of total traffic, and Mahajanga; several of the smaller ports are prone to silting problems. A new deep-sea port was to be constructed at Ehoala, near Fort Dauphin, in order to accommodate the activity of an ilmenite mining development by 2008.

CMA—CGM Madagascar: BP 12042, Village des jeux, Bat. C1 Ankorondrano, 101 Antananarivo; tel. (20) 2235949; fax (20) 2266120; e-mail tnr@cma-cgm.mg; internet www.cma-cgm.com; maritime transport; Gen. Man. JOËL LE JULIEN.

Compagnie Générale Maritime Sud (CGM): BP 1185, Lot II U 31 bis, Ampahibe, 101 Antananarivo; tel. (20) 2220113; fax (20) 2226530.

Compagnie Malgache de Navigation (CMN): rue Rabearivelo, BP 1621, 101 Antananarivo; tel. (20) 2225516; fax (20) 2230358; f. 1960; coasters; 13,784 grt; 97.5% state-owned; privatization pending; Pres. ELINAH BAKOLY RAJAONSON; Dir-Gen. ARISTIDE EMMANUEL.

SCAC-SDV Shipping Madagascar: rue Rabearivelo Antsahavola, BP 514, 102 Antananarivo; tel. (20) 2220631; fax (20) 2247862; operates the harbour in Antananarivo Port.

Société Malgache des Transports Maritimes (SMTM): 6 rue Indira Gandhi, BP 4077, 101 Antananarivo; tel. (20) 2227342; fax (20) 2233327; f. 1963; 59% state-owned; privatization pending; services to Europe; Chair. ALEXIS RAZAFINDRATSIRA; Dir-Gen. JEAN RANJEVA.

CIVIL AVIATION

The Ivato international airport is at Antananarivo, while the airports at Mahajanga, Toamasina and Nossi-Bé can also accommodate large jet aircraft. There are 211 airfields, two-thirds of which are privately owned. In 1996 the Government authorized private French airlines to operate scheduled and charter flights between Madagascar and Western Europe.

Air Madagascar (Société Nationale Malgache des Transports Aériens): 31 ave de l'Indépendance, Analakely, BP 437, 101 Antananarivo; tel. (20) 2222222; fax (20) 2233760; e-mail commercial@airmadagascar.com; internet www.airmadagascar.com; f. 1962; 90.60% state-owned; 3.17% owned by Air France (France); transfer to the private sector pending; restructured and managed by Lufthansa Consulting since 2002; extensive internal routes connecting all the principal towns; external services to France, Italy, the Comoros, Kenya, Mauritius, Réunion, South Africa and Thailand; Chair. HERINIAINA RAZAFIMAHEFA; Gen. Man. ROLAND RANJATOELINA.

Air Transport et Transit Régional (ATTR): tel. (32) 0518811; fax (32) 3205218; e-mail attr.reservation@blueline.mg; internet www.attrmada.com; f. 2006; private; regular local and regional services; Dir Gen. FRÉDÉRIC RABESAHALA.

Aviation Civile de Madagascar (ACM): BP 4414, 101 Tsimbazaza-Antananarivo; tel. (20) 2222438; fax (20) 2224726; e-mail acm@acm.mg; f. 2000; Chair. TOKIARITEFY RABESON; Dir-Gen. (vacant).

Transports et Travaux Aériens de Madagascar (TAM): 17 ave de l'Indépendance, Analakely, Antananarivo; tel. (20) 2222222; fax (20) 2224340; e-mail tamdg@wanadoo.mg; f. 1951; provides airline services; Administrators LALA RAZAFINDRAKOTO, FRANÇOIS DANE.

Tourism

Madagascar's attractions include unspoiled scenery, many unusual varieties of flora and fauna, and the rich cultural diversity of Malagasy life. In 2006 some 311,730 tourists visited Madagascar, the majority were from France (52.3%). Revenue from tourism in that year was estimated at US $386m.

Direction d'Appui aux Investissements Publiques: Ministry of Culture and Tourism, BP 610, rue Fernand Kasanga Tsimbazaza, 101 Antananarivo; tel. (20) 2262816; fax (20) 2235410; e-mail mintourdati@wandaoo.mg; internet www.tourisme.gov.mg.

Office National du Tourisme de Madagascar: 3 rue Elysée Ravelontsalama, Ambatomena, 101 Antananarivo; tel. (20) 2266115; fax (20) 2266098; e-mail ontm@moov.mg; internet www.madagascar-tourisme.com; Pres. JOEL RANDRIAMANDRANTO.

MALAWI

Introductory Survey

Location, Climate, Language, Religion, Flag, Capital

The Republic of Malawi is a land-locked country in southern central Africa, with Zambia to the west, Mozambique to the south and east, and Tanzania to the north. Lake Malawi forms most of the eastern boundary. The climate is tropical, but much of the country is sufficiently high above sea-level to modify the heat. Temperatures range from 14°C (57°F) to 18°C (64°F) in mountain areas, but can reach 38°C (100°F) in low-lying regions. There is a rainy season between November and April. The official language is English, although Chichewa is being promoted as the basis for a 'Malawi Language'. Chitumbuka, a national language, and Yao are also widely spoken. More than 70% of the population profess Christianity, while a further 20%, largely Asians, are Muslims. Most of the remaining Malawians follow traditional beliefs, although there is also a Hindu minority. The national flag (proportions 2 by 3) has three equal horizontal stripes, of black, red and green, with a rising sun, in red, in the centre of the black stripe. The capital is Lilongwe.

Recent History

Malawi was formerly the British protectorate of Nyasaland. In 1953 it was linked with two other British dependencies, Northern and Southern Rhodesia (now Zambia and Zimbabwe), to form the Federation of Rhodesia and Nyasaland. The Federation was dissolved in December 1963 and Nyasaland gained independence, as Malawi, on 6 July 1964. The country became a republic and a one-party state, with Dr Hastings Kamuzu Banda, the leader of the Malawi Congress Party (MCP), as its first President, on 6 July 1966. Malawi created a major controversy among African states in 1967 by officially recognizing the Republic of South Africa. In 1971 Banda, named Life President in that year, became the first African head of state to visit South Africa. In 1976, however, Malawi recognized the communist-backed Government in Angola in preference to the South African-supported forces. Malawi did not recognize the 'independence' granted by South Africa to four of its African 'homelands'.

Until 1993 all Malawian citizens were obliged to be members of the MCP; no political opposition was tolerated, and only candidates who had been approved by Banda were allowed to contest elections to the National Assembly. Frequent reorganizations of the Cabinet effectively prevented the emergence of any political rival to Banda. However, it was reported in 1983 that a conflict had developed between Dick Matenje, the Minister without Portfolio in the Cabinet and Secretary-General of the MCP, and John Tembo, the Governor of the Reserve Bank of Malawi, concerning the eventual succession to Banda. In May the authorities reported that Matenje and three other senior politicians had died in a road accident; Malawian exiles claimed that the four men had been shot while attempting to flee the country.

Opposition to the Government intensified during 1992: in March Malawi's Roman Catholic bishops criticized the Government's alleged abuses of human rights. In April Chakufwa Chihana, a prominent trade union leader who had demanded multi-party elections, was arrested. In July Chihana was charged with sedition, and in August the police detained 11 church leaders and prohibited a planned rally by pro-democracy supporters. In September opposition activists formed the Alliance for Democracy (AFORD), a pressure group operating within Malawi, under the chairmanship of Chihana, which aimed to campaign for democratic political reform. Another opposition grouping, the United Democratic Front (UDF), was formed in October. In that month Banda conceded that a referendum on the introduction of a multi-party system would take place. However, in November the Government banned AFORD. In the following month Chihana was found guilty of sedition and sentenced to two years' hard labour (reduced to nine months in March 1993).

At the referendum on the introduction of a multi-party system, held on 14 June 1993, 63.2% of those who participated (some 63.5% of the electorate) voted for an end to single-party rule. Banda rejected opposition demands for the immediate installation of an interim government of national unity. He agreed, however, to the establishment of a National Executive Council to oversee the transition to a multi-party system and the holding of free elections, and of a National Consultative Council to implement the necessary amendments to the Constitution. Both councils were to include members of the Government and the opposition. Banda announced an amnesty for thousands of political exiles, and stated that a general election would be held, on a multi-party basis, within a year. In late June the Constitution was amended to allow the registration of political parties other than the MCP: by mid-August five organizations, including AFORD and the UDF, had been accorded official status.

In September 1993 Banda carried out an extensive cabinet reshuffle, relinquishing the post of Minister of External Affairs, which he had held since 1964. In October 1993 Banda underwent neurological surgery in South Africa. Interim executive power was assumed by a three-member Presidential Council, chaired by the new Secretary-General of the MCP, Gwandaguluwe Chakuamba. In November a further cabinet reshuffle relieved Banda of all ministerial responsibilities. Later in November the National Assembly approved a Constitutional Amendment Bill, which, *inter alia*, abolished the institution of life presidency, ended the requirement that election candidates be members of the MCP and repealed the right of the President to nominate members of the legislature exclusively from the MCP.

Having made a rapid and unexpected recovery, Banda resumed full presidential powers in December 1993. Shortly afterwards, in response to increasing pressure from the opposition, the Government amended the Constitution to provide for the appointment of an acting President in the event of the incumbent being incapacitated. In February 1994 the MCP announced that Banda was to be the party's presidential candidate in the forthcoming general election (scheduled for May); Chakuamba was named as the MCP's candidate for the vice-presidency. Also in February the National Assembly approved an increase in the number of elective seats in the legislature from 141 to 177.

On 16 May 1994 the National Assembly adopted a provisional Constitution, which provided for the appointment of a Constitutional Committee and of a human rights commission, and abolished the system of 'traditional' courts. Malawi's first multi-party parliamentary and presidential elections took place on 17 May. In the presidential election the Secretary-General of the UDF, (Elson) Bakili Muluzi (a former government minister and MCP Secretary-General), took 47.3% of the votes cast, defeating Banda (who won 33.6% of the votes). Eight parties contested the legislative elections: of these, the UDF won 85 seats in the National Assembly, the MCP 56 and AFORD 36. The Constitution was introduced for a one-year period on 18 May; it was to be subject to further review prior to official ratification one year later.

President Muluzi and his Vice-President, Justin Malewezi, were inaugurated on 21 May 1994. The new UDF-dominated Government proclaimed an amnesty for the country's remaining political prisoners, and commuted all death sentences to terms of life imprisonment. In August it was announced that Banda, while remaining honorary Life President of the MCP, was to retire from active involvement in politics. Chakuamba, as Vice-President of the party, effectively became the leader of the MCP.

In September 1994 a number of AFORD members were appointed to the Government, including Chihana as Second Vice-President and Minister of Irrigation and Water Development. Meanwhile, the creation of the post of Second Vice-President had necessitated a constitutional amendment, and provoked severe criticism from the MCP. In March the National Assembly (in the absence of MCP deputies, who boycotted the vote) approved the retention of the second vice-presidency; the Assembly also endorsed recommendations for the establishment—although not before May 1999—of a second chamber of parliament. The Constitution took effect on 18 May 1995.

In June 1994 Muluzi established an independent commission of inquiry to investigate the deaths of Matenje and his associates in May 1983. In January 1995, in accordance with the findings of the commission, Banda was placed under house arrest and Tembo and two former police-officers were detained; the four were charged with murder and conspiracy to murder. A former inspector-general of police was charged later in the month. In

April Cecilia Kadzamira, Tembo's niece and the former President's 'Official Hostess', was also charged with conspiracy to murder. The trial opened later that month, but was immediately adjourned, owing to Banda's failure to appear in court (his defence counsel asserted that he was too ill to stand trial) and to the failure of the state prosecution to submit certain evidence to the defence. Hearings resumed, in Banda's absence, in July. In September Tembo and the two former police-officers were granted bail, and most restrictions on Banda's movements were ended. The case against Kadzamira was abandoned in December, owing to lack of evidence, and later that month Banda, Tembo and the other defendants were found not guilty of conspiracy to murder and conspiracy to defeat justice. In January 1996 an MCP-owned newspaper printed a statement by Banda in which he admitted that he might unknowingly have been responsible for brutalities perpetrated under his regime and apologized to Malawians for 'pain and suffering' inflicted during his presidency.

Meanwhile, there were further allegations that the Muluzi administration had been involved in dubious financial transactions. It emerged, in mid-1995, that the President had authorized the payment of some 6.2m. kwacha from the state poverty alleviation account to UDF deputies; there was also evidence of the involvement of government ministers in the smuggling of maize to neighbouring countries. In February 1996 Muluzi announced that an independent Anti-Corruption Bureau (ACB) was to be established to investigate allegations of corruption.

In November 1997 Banda died in South Africa, where he had been undergoing emergency medical treatment. He was accorded a state funeral, with full military honours.

In June 1998 the National Assembly approved legislation providing for the introduction of a single-ballot electoral system to replace the existing multiple-ballot system and for a strengthening of the authority and independence of the Malawi Electoral Commission (MEC). In November legislation was adopted to allow presidential and parliamentary elections to run concurrently (as Muluzi's term was due to end several weeks earlier than that of the National Assembly), and the elections were subsequently scheduled for 18 May 1999. An electoral alliance between the MCP and AFORD, which was officially announced in February 1999, created serious divisions within the MCP, when the party's leader and presidential candidate, Chakuamba, chose Chihana, who had resigned the post of Second Vice-President in May 1996, as the candidate for the vice-presidency, in preference to Tembo. Thousands of Tembo's supporters were reported to have mounted protests to demand Chakuamba's resignation. The Chakuamba-Chihana partnership also provoked a wider dispute with the UDF and the MEC, which claimed that the arrangement was unconstitutional. In February 1999 the National Assembly adopted a controversial report by the MEC that recommended the creation of a further 72 parliamentary seats, including an additional 42 in the Southern Region, a UDF stronghold. In response to widespread opposition to the proposals, however, only 16 of the 72 seats were approved.

Having been postponed twice, the presidential and legislative elections were held on 15 June 1999. Muluzi was re-elected to the presidency, securing 51.4% of the votes cast, while Chakuamba obtained 43.3%. Turn-out was high, with some 93.8% of registered voters reported to have participated. At the elections to the expanded National Assembly the ruling UDF won 94 seats, while the MCP secured 66 seats, AFORD 29 and independent candidates four. Despite declarations from international observers that the elections were largely free and fair, the MCP-AFORD alliance filed two petitions with the High Court, challenging Muluzi's victory and the results in 16 districts. The opposition alleged irregularities in the voter registration process and claimed that Muluzi's victory was unconstitutional, as he had failed to gain the support of 50% of all registered voters. Nonetheless, Muluzi was inaugurated later in June, and a new Cabinet was appointed. In mid-August the UDF regained a parliamentary majority when the four independent deputies decided to ally themselves with the UDF, of which they had previously been members.

Chakuamba, who had maintained a boycott of the new parliament pending the result of his party's challenge to the outcome of the elections, was suspended from the chamber in June 2000. Tembo assumed the leadership of the opposition and appointed his supporters to prominent posts within the MCP. Chakuamba was reinstated in September, and a dispute between the two factions ensued. In October the opposition's petitions against the election results were dismissed by the High Court.

In January 2001 deputies from the Tembo faction of the MCP ensured the approval by the National Assembly of a UDF proposal to abandon plans (ostensibly for financial reasons) for the creation of a second legislative chamber, the Senate, which would have had powers to impeach the President; AFORD boycotted the vote. In November seven deputies who had joined the opposition National Democratic Alliance (NDA) were excluded from the National Assembly for abandoning the political parties for which they had been elected, an action proscribed by law since May, when the UDF acted to prevent defections to the NDA; Sam Mpasu, the Speaker, defied an order of the High Court restraining him from expelling the deputies.

Proposed legislation to change the Constitution to allow Muluzi to seek a third presidential term failed to gain the requisite support of two-thirds of the members of the National Assembly in July 2002. A further attempt to introduce a constitutional amendment also failed in January 2003, when the bill was withdrawn. The UDF declared that it would hold a referendum on the issue later in the year. However, in late March Muluzi declared that he would not seek a third presidential term, and proposed Dr Bingu wa Mutharika, recently appointed Minister of Economic Planning and Development, as his successor, to contest the presidential election scheduled for May 2004. (Mutharika had represented the United Party at the 1999 presidential election, but subsequently defected to the UDF.) In early April 2003 Muluzi dismissed his entire Cabinet, apparently without explanation. However, several ministers reported that Muluzi had imposed the appointment of Mutharika on the party without sufficient consultation, and suggested that they had been dismissed for expressing opposition to the President's decision; Muluzi appointed a new administration later that month.

In May 2003, at a party convention in Blantyre that was disrupted by violent incidents, Tembo and Chakuamba were elected, respectively, as President and Vice-President of the MCP. Tembo was subsequently named as the MCP's candidate to contest the 2004 presidential election. Chakuamba resigned from the MCP and formed the Republican Party (RP). On 1 January 2004 Justin Malewezi, Malawi's First Vice-President and Minister responsible for Privatization, announced his resignation from the UDF for 'personal reasons'. He did not, however, relinquish his position in the Government, stating that he would remain in office, but on leave, until after the presidential election had taken place. One week after leaving the UDF Malewezi joined the People's Progressive Movement (PPM), an opposition party founded in April 2003. Later in January 2004 Aleke Banda, who had resigned from the UDF in May 2003, was elected as President of the PPM, while Malewezi was chosen as its Vice-President.

In February 2004 the Government initiated legal proceedings aimed at having Malewezi's position within the Cabinet declared vacant on the grounds that he had resigned as Vice-President 'by implication or by his own conduct'. Meanwhile, in late January several opposition parties, including the PPM and the RP, announced their formation of the Mgwirizano Coalition to contest the forthcoming presidential election; Chakuamba was elected as the coalition's presidential candidate in February. Malewezi subsequently announced that he would contest the election as an independent. A minor cabinet reorganization was effected in late February, and Muluzi appointed Hetherwick Ntaba, the leader of the New Congress for Democracy (NCD), as Minister of Energy and Mining at the end of March, following the NCD's decision to join the UDF-AFORD electoral alliance.

At the presidential election held on 20 May 2004 Mutharika, representing the ruling UDF, secured 35.89% of the valid votes cast, according to official results. Tembo, of the MCP, and Chakuamba, representing the Mgwirizano Coalition, took 27.13% and 25.72% of the vote, respectively. Cassim Chilumpha, of the UDF, was elected as Vice-President. At concurrent elections to the National Assembly, however, the MCP emerged as the largest party, winning 56 of the 193 seats in the legislature, while the UDF secured 49 seats and the Mgwirizano Coalition 25; 39 of the remaining seats were taken by independent candidates, while voting in six constituencies was not conducted owing to irregularities. International observers criticized the conduct of the polls and opposition parties disputed the results. Mutharika was sworn in as President on 24 May amid rioting by opposition supporters. The new Cabinet, appointed in mid-June 2004, comprised 21 ministers, compared with 32 under the previous administration. Mutharika, in defiance of critics who believed he would merely serve to act as Muluzi's 'puppet', pledged to take measures to combat corruption and to effect wide-ranging economic reforms. In late October the former Minister of Finance, Friday Jumbe, was arrested in connection with illegal sales of maize during 2001–02 when he held the position of General Manager of the Agriculture Development and Marketing Corporation; he was subsequently charged with four counts of corruption. The Director of Public Prosecutions, Ishmael Wadi, also announced in October 2004 that at least 10 former senior ministers were under investigation by the ACB following the disappearance of more than 10,000m. kwacha during the Muluzi presidency.

In early February 2005 Mutharika resigned from the leadership of the UDF—of which Muluzi was Chairman—claiming that the party was opposing his campaign against corruption. Prior to the announcement, Mutharika dismissed three members of the Government loyal to Muluzi, including the Minister of Labour, Lilian Patel, and Chihana, who was replaced as Minister of Agriculture, Irrigation and Food Security by Chakuamba. Later that month Mutharika announced his intention to form a new political party, the Democratic Progressive Party (DPP), which was formally registered in mid-March. In late May the Minister of Education and Human Resources, Yusuf Mwawa, was arrested on charges of corruption, fraud and misuse of public funds. He was replaced by the former Secretary-General of the MCP, Kate Kainja Kaluluma. (In February 2006 Mwawa was sentenced to five years' imprisonment.) Meanwhile, in late June 2005 the UDF introduced before the National Assembly a motion of impeachment against Mutharika, alleging statutory violations of the Constitution and misuse of public funds. The session was suspended following the collapse of the Speaker, Rodwell Munyenyembe, who died several days later. Louis Chimango of the MCP was elected as Speaker in early July and the impeachment debate resumed later that month.

In late July 2005 Mutharika faced criticism for increasing the size of the Cabinet from 27 members to 33. A new Ministry of Irrigation and Water Development was created, headed by Chakuamba, while the agriculture and food security portfolio was awarded to Uladi Mussa, who was replaced as Minister of Home Affairs and Internal Security by Anna Kachikho. In early September Sidik Mia replaced Chakuamba at the Ministry of Irrigation and Water Development. Chakuamba was dismissed in advance of an investigation by the ACB over misuse of World Bank funds; he was arrested later that month for allegedly slandering the President at a rally for the RP. Chakuamba subsequently formed the New Republican Party (NRP) and pledged his support to Muluzi.

In October 2005 Muluzi was summoned to appear before the ACB, which was investigating the misappropriation of 1,400m. kwacha in foreign aid during his presidency. It was alleged that much of this money had been diverted to personal bank accounts and had also been used to finance the 2004 presidential campaign. Muluzi was able to obtain an injunction from the High Court, which allowed him to refuse to answer the ACB's questions. However, later that month police and ACB officers raided three properties belonging to Muluzi, confiscating computer equipment and banking documents. In November Vice-President Chilumpha was arrested in connection with the alleged embezzlement of 187m. kwacha during his tenure as Minister of Education. Chilumpha obtained an injunction against criminal proceedings being initiated against him on the grounds that as the incumbent Vice-President he was immune from prosecution.

Following an agreement between the UDF and Tembo, in mid-October 2005 the National Assembly voted in favour of beginning proceedings to impeach Mutharika. Envoys from several donor countries (including the United Kingdom, the USA and South Africa) were signatories to a letter to the opposition requesting that they reconsider their decision in the interests of the country at large. Despite their appeal Mutharika was summoned to face indictment before the National Assembly later that month. However, the impeachment process was halted by the High Court after concern was expressed over the constitutionality of the process. At by-elections in December (following the deaths of five UDF members of the National Assembly and the conviction of a sixth) the DPP won all six seats, suggesting that there was general support for Mutharika among the populace. Later that month, in South Africa, former regional heads of state—Nelson Mandela of South Africa, Joachim Chissano of Mozambique and Sir Ketumile Masire of Botswana—brokered talks between Mutharika, Muluzi and Tembo in an attempt to halt the impeachment proceedings; however, they ended without success.

The impeachment motion was eventually withdrawn in late January 2006, prompting the resignation of seven UDF members, five of whom subsequently joined the DPP. The next session of Parliament, scheduled for February, was postponed owing to the continuing food crisis (see below) as it was believed that the allocated budget would be more beneficial to ongoing relief efforts. (Expenditure on the previous four-week session had amounted to 56m. kwacha and had been largely occupied with the failed impeachment proceedings.) In early February it was announced that Mutharika had accepted Chilumpha's 'constructive resignation'. In a letter to Chilumpha the President asserted that Chilumpha had abandoned his duties as Vice-President, leading the Cabinet to conclude that he had resigned. Chilumpha refuted the allegations made against him—*inter alia*, that he had only attended 16 out of 48 cabinet meetings and had left the country without informing Mutharika—and brought the matter before the High Court on the grounds that his dismissal was unconstitutional: as an elected minister he could only be dismissed by Parliament, not by the President. In March the High Court apparently ordered Chilumpha's full restitution; however, the Supreme Court ruled later that month that although Chilumpha was confirmed in his position as Vice-President the Government was permitted to strip him of all benefits and entitlements. In late April Chilumpha was arrested and charged with treason and conspiring to murder the President. In May he was granted bail but confined to house arrest; the restrictions on his movement were relaxed in November. Meanwhile in mid-May the Attorney-General, Ralph Kasambara, was dismissed, following allegations that he was implicated in events that led to Chilumpha's resignation; in July Jane Ansah was appointed to replace Kasambara.

In October 2006 Mutharika dismissed Mussa and the Minister of Economic Planning and Development, David Faiti. The President assumed responsibility for their respective portfolios. In February 2007 Mussa was questioned over his alleged involvement in the attempted assassination of the President the previous year, although this was not given as the reason for his dismissal from the Cabinet. Days later the President also accused Mussa of the misappropriation of fertilizer subsidies, which some small-scale farmers claimed not to have received. Mussa denied both allegations.

A High Court ruling in November 2006 stated that the section of the Constitution which stipulated that the Speaker must declare vacant the parliamentary seat of any member of the legislature wishing to move to a different political party did not breach any other principle of the Constitution. The decision was passed after it was noted that many deputies had realigned themselves with the ruling DPP without first consulting their constituency. It was alleged that only five of some 90 DPP parliamentarians had been elected while serving that party. The DPP challenged the decision; however, in June 2007 the Supreme Court of Appeal ruled that the Speaker had the authority to expel from the National Assembly any member of that body who switched party allegiances. Opposition deputies insisted upon the expulsions and in July members of the MCP and the UDF refused to participate in discussions regarding the budget for the 2007/08 financial year. The following month an injunction was granted allowing the opposition to continue their delay of the debate on the budget, although that order was overturned after an appeal by the Attorney-General. In mid-August the debate began without the participation of opposition deputies, and in mid-September the budget was finally approved. A similar dispute arose the following year, delaying the approval of the 2008/09 budget by one month.

In early February 2008 President Mutharika carried out a reorganization of the Cabinet, in which the Minister of Defence and the Minister of Health were replaced. Muluzi was nominated in April by the UDF as that party's candidate for the presidential election due to be held concurrently with legislative elections in May 2009; having previously served two terms in office, opponents objected to his candidacy. However, Muluzi's supporters maintained that the Constitution only stipulated that a President may not serve more than two 'consecutive' terms, permitting him to contest the election that could return him to the presidency. In mid-March 2009 the MEC ruled that Muluzi was ineligible to contest the election on the grounds that he had already served as President for the maximum period of two five-year terms. Muluzi appealed against the decision, but in mid-

May the Constitutional Court rejected his challenge. He subsequently declared his support for Tembo, who had been selected as the presidential candidate for the UDF-MCP-NRP alliance (see below).

Meanwhile, reports emerged in early May 2008 that eight high-ranking security officials, including former Commander-in-Chief of the Armed Forces Lt-Gen. Joseph Chimbayo, had been arrested following accusations by Mutharika that they had been acting under instruction from Muluzi in an attempt to remove him from office; seven were subsequently released on bail. Later that month Muluzi was questioned by police and placed under house arrest. Muluzi denied the allegations and was later released without charge. In December Chakuamba of the NRP was arrested for encouraging violence against Muthrika's Lhomwe tribe but was released on bail. In late February 2009 Muluzi was again detained on charges of corruption relating to the misappropriation donor funds during his presidency (see above). He appeared in court in April, but refused to enter a plea. Muluzi's legal representatives maintained that they were in possession of evidence which demonstrated that Mutharika had been responsible for instigating renewed investigation into the case by the country's Anti-Corruption Bureau.

Also in April 2009 Chakuamba announced that the NRP, together with the MCP and the UDF, had formed an alliance to contest the presidential and legislative elections scheduled for 19 May and to form the next administration. By late April several smaller parties had also indicated their willingness to join the new alliance.

Despite being the only African country to have maintained full diplomatic relations with South Africa during the apartheid era, Malawi joined the Southern African Development Co-ordination Conference (subsequently the Southern African Development Community, see p. 400—SADC), which originally aimed to reduce the dependence of southern African countries on South Africa.

Relations with Mozambique were frequently strained during the early and mid-1980s by the widely held belief that the Banda regime was supporting the Resistência Nacional Moçambicana (Renamo—see the chapter on Mozambique). Following the death of President Machel of Mozambique in an air crash in South Africa in October 1986, the South African Government claimed that documents discovered in the wreckage revealed a plot by Mozambique and Zimbabwe to overthrow the Banda Government. Angry protests from Malawi were answered by denials of the accusations from the Mozambican and Zimbabwean Governments. In December, however, Malawi and Mozambique signed an agreement on defence and security matters, which was believed to include co-operation in eliminating Renamo operations. In July 1988, during an official visit to Malawi, President Chissano of Mozambique stated that he did not believe Malawi to be supporting Renamo. In December of that year Malawi, Mozambique and the office of the UN High Commissioner for Refugees (UNHCR) signed an agreement to promote the voluntary repatriation of an estimated 650,000 Mozambican refugees who had fled into Malawi during the previous two years. However, by mid-1992 the number of Mozambican refugees in Malawi had reportedly reached 1m. Large numbers of refugees returned to Mozambique in 1993–94, but in May 1995 Malawi demanded the repatriation of the remainder—estimated to total some 39,000—stating that food aid and other assistance to those who failed to leave would be reduced. The programme of the Malawi-Mozambique-UNHCR commission officially ended in November: it was estimated that a total of 1m. refugees had been repatriated.

Until early 2008 Malawi was one of a small number of nations which accorded Taiwan recognition as an independent country. In January of that year, however, it was announced that Malawi had withdrawn its support for Taiwan and established diplomatic relations with the People's Republic of China.

Government

The Head of State is the President, who is elected by universal adult suffrage, in the context of a multi-party political system, for a term of five years. Executive power is vested in the President, and legislative power in the National Assembly, which has 193 elective seats. Members of the Assembly are elected for five years, by universal adult suffrage, in the context of a multi-party system. Cabinet ministers are appointed by the President. The country is divided into three administrative regions (Northern, Central and Southern), sub-divided into 24 districts.

Defence

Malawi's active defence forces, as assessed at November 2008, comprised a land army of 5,300, a marine force of 220 and an air force of 200; all form part of the army. There was also a paramilitary police force of 1,500. Budgetary expenditure on defence was 5,800m. kwacha in 2007.

Economic Affairs

In 2007, according to estimates by the World Bank, Malawi's gross national income (GNI), measured at average 2005–07 prices, was US $3,506m., equivalent to $250 per head (or $750 per head on an international purchasing-power parity basis). During 2000–07, it was estimated, the population increased at an average annual rate of 2.6%, while gross domestic product (GDP) per head increased, in real terms, by an average of 0.1% per year. Overall GDP increased, in real terms, at an average annual rate of 2.8% in 2000–07; real GDP increased by 7.4% in 2007.

Agriculture (including forestry and fishing) contributed an estimated 34.3% of GDP in 2007, and engaged an estimated 80.8% of the labour force in 2005. The principal cash crops are tobacco (which accounted for 48.7% of total export earnings in 2007), sugar cane and tea. The principal food crops are maize, cassava, potatoes, bananas and groundnuts. Periods of severe drought and flooding have necessitated imports of basic foods in recent years (see below). During 2000–07, according to the World Bank, agricultural GDP increased at an average annual rate of 0.3%; agricultural GDP declined by 8.5% in 2005; however, it increased by 11.9% in 2006 and by a further 5.9% in 2007.

Industry (including manufacturing, mining, construction and power) contributed an estimated 20.4% of GDP in 2007, and engaged 4.5% of the employed labour force in 1998. During 2000–07, according to the World Bank, industrial GDP increased by an average of 3.1% per year. Industrial GDP increased by 8.5% in 2007.

Mining and quarrying contributed an estimated 0.8% of GDP in 2006, and engaged less than 0.1% of the employed labour force in 1998. Limestone, coal and gemstones are mined, and there are plans to develop deposits of bauxite, high-calcium marble and graphite. There are also reserves of phosphates, uranium, glass sands, asbestos and vermiculite. Environmental and financial concerns have delayed plans to exploit an estimated 30m. metric tons of bauxite deposits at Mount Mulanje. Uranium mining, due to commence in 2009, was expected to increase the country's export revenue by some 25%. The GDP of the mining sector increased at an average annual rate of 15.1% in 1994–2003, according to official figures; mining GDP increased by 18.6% in 2003, but decreased by 12.1% in 2004.

Manufacturing contributed an estimated 19.7% of GDP in 2006, and engaged 2.7% of the employed labour force in 1998. During 2000–07, according to the World Bank, manufacturing GDP increased by an average of 1.4% per year. Manufacturing GDP increased by 9.1% in 2007.

Production of electrical energy is by hydroelectric (principally) and thermal installations. Some 95% of energy for domestic use is derived from hydroelectric power. In October 1997 an agreement was signed to link Malawi's electricity system to the Cahora Bassa hydroelectric dam in Mozambique. In October 2000 a hydroelectric power plant, with a generation capacity of 64 MW, was opened at Kapichira; in February 2009 the Government pledged funds amounting to some 2,500m. kwacha for the Kapichira Hydroelectric Power Phase II Project, aimed at addressing the country's power shortage. In 2009 full capacity of Malawi's hydroelectric power plants was 282.5 MW. In January 2001 the Government introduced a campaign to widen access to electricity, especially in rural areas; plans to open the power industry to foreign investors, increasing access to electricity by as much as 50%, were being considered in early 2009. By August 2008 some 14 coalfields had been identified in Malawi with speculated reserves of 800m. metric tons; at that time there was only one coal producer in Malawi, which mainly supplied domestic manufacturers. Imports of mineral fuels comprised 13.8% of the value of total imports in 2007.

The services sector contributed an estimated 45.3% of GDP in 2007, and engaged 11.0% of the employed labour force in 1998. The GDP of the services sector increased by an average of 3.7% per year in 2000–07, according to the World Bank. Services GDP increased by 4.0% in 2007.

Malawi recorded a visible trade deficit of 76,298.2m. kwacha in 2007, while there was a deficit of 100,592.5m. kwacha on the current account of the balance of payments. In 2007 the principal source of imports was South Africa (29.1%); Mozambique, the

United Arab Emirates and Tanzania were also notable suppliers. South Africa was also the principal market for exports (14.8%) in that year; other important markets were Zimbabwe, Belgium, the United Kingdom and Germany. The principal imports in 2007 were machinery and transport equipment (particularly road vehicles), chemicals and related products, and mineral fuels and lubricants. The principal exports in that year were tobacco and food and live animals.

Preliminary figures indicated that in the financial year ending 30 June 2008 Malawi's overall budget deficit was an estimated 14,843m. kwacha. The country's external debt totalled US $850m. at the end of 2006, of which $767m. was long-term public debt. In 2003 the cost of debt-servicing was equivalent to 9.0% of the value of exports of goods and services. The annual rate of inflation averaged 14.6% in 2000–06; consumer prices increased by an average of 13.9% in 2006. Some 1.4m. people were unemployed in 2007.

Malawi is a member of the Southern African Development Community (SADC, see p. 400) and the Common Market for Eastern and Southern Africa (COMESA, see p. 215). Nine members of COMESA, including Malawi, became inaugural members of the COMESA Free Trade Area in October 2000. The country belongs to the International Tea Promotion Association (see p. 423) and to the International Tobacco Growers' Association (see p. 423). Malawi was also a signatory to the Cotonou Agreement with the European Union (EU), which expired on 31 December 2007 and was to be superseded by an Economic Partnership Agreement (EPA). In January 2008 it emerged that the EU's EPA funding would be disbursed on the basis of membership of a single regional bloc. Malawi was therefore compelled to withdraw its membership from either SADC or COMESA; the terms of trade embodied in the new arrangement had not been finalized in early 2009.

Malawi's natural impediments to growth (including its landlocked position, the vulnerability of the dominant agricultural sector to drought, and a high rate of population growth) were compounded by the severe mismanagement of economic affairs during the early 2000s. The dispersal of funds under the IMF's Poverty Reduction and Growth Facility (PRGF) was delayed and it was not until August 2005 that approval was finally given for a three-year PRGF programme worth US $55m. In September 2006 the World Bank agreed that sufficient progress had been made under the initiative for heavily indebted poor countries and approved the disbursement of debt relief funds amounting to $646m. The report on the final review of Malawi's performance under the PRGF programme, published in July 2008, commended the Government for its efforts in meeting the majority of the programme's targets, while acknowledging that international pressure on monetary reserves needed to be addressed; the authorities requested that the PRGF arrangement be increased by 15%. The country remains vulnerable to the ongoing global financial crisis, in particular the rising cost of importing fuel and fertilisers, and in January 2009 Malawi became the first recipient country of the IMF's new Exogenous Shock Facility, under which a one-year loan of $77.1m. was approved. Meanwhile, a severe scarcity of food was experienced in 2005/06, with the 2005 harvest declared the worst in a decade by the UN World Food Programme; however, an improved harvest was recorded in 2006. Further improvements in this sector resulted in a 22% increase in maize production during 2007, thereby allowing Malawi to donate a portion of its surplus crop to less affluent countries in Southern Africa. However, despite a continued improvement in maize production, in May 2008 Malawi banned exports of that commodity to all countries except Zimbabwe to ensure sufficient stocks for domestic use following earlier flooding. In 2006 the Government had unveiled the Malawi Growth and Development Strategy, covering the period from 2006/07–2010/11, which sought to create wealth through sustainable economic growth and infrastructure development and promote manufacturing and exporting as a source of revenue. Real GDP increased by an estimated 7.1% in 2008 and the IMF forecast further growth of 7.8% for 2009.

Education

Primary education, which is officially compulsory, begins at six years of age and lasts for eight years. Secondary education, which begins at 14 years of age, lasts for four years, comprising two cycles of two years. According to UNESCO estimates, in 2006/07 primary enrolment included 87.0% of children in the relevant age-group (males 84.0%; females 90.1%), while secondary enrolment included 23.9% of children in the relevant age-group (males 25.0%; females 22.8%). A programme to expand education at all levels has been undertaken; however, the introduction of free primary education in September 1994 led to the influx of more than 1m. additional pupils, resulting in severe overcrowding in schools. In January 1996 the International Development Association granted US $22.5m. for the training of 20,000 new teachers, appointed in response to the influx. In 2004 there were some 45,300 primary school teachers, of whom 17,300 were female. In mid-1997 additional funding was provided by the African Development Bank for the construction of primary and secondary schools. The University of Malawi had 3,565 students in 1999. Some students attend institutions in the United Kingdom and the USA. Expenditure on education in 2003/04 was estimated at 8,714m. kwacha (equivalent to 19.6% of total expenditure).

Public Holidays

2009: 1 January (New Year's Day), 15 January (John Chilembwe Day), 3 March (Martyrs' Day), 10–13 April (Easter), 1 May (Labour Day), 14 June (Freedom Day), 6 July (Republic Day), 13 October (Mothers' Day), 25–26 December (Christmas).

2008: 1 January (New Year's Day), 15 January (John Chilembwe Day), 3 March (Martyrs' Day), 2–5 April (Easter), 1 May (Labour Day), 14 June (Freedom Day), 6 July (Republic Day), 13 October (Mothers' Day), 25–26 December (Christmas).

Weights and Measures

The metric system is in use.

Statistical Survey

Sources (unless otherwise indicated): National Statistical Office of Malawi, POB 333, Zomba; tel. 1524377; fax 1525130; e-mail enquiries@statistics.gov.mw; internet www.nso.malawi.net; Reserve Bank of Malawi, POB 30063, Capital City, Lilongwe 3; tel. 1770600; fax 1772752; e-mail webmaster@rbm.mw; internet www.rbm.mw.

Area and Population

AREA, POPULATION AND DENSITY

Area (sq km)	
Land	94,276
Inland water	24,208
Total	118,484*
Population (census results)	
1–21 September 1998	9,933,868
8–28 June 2008 (preliminary)	
Males	6,365,771
Females	6,700,549
Total	13,066,320
Density (per sq km) at 2008 census	138.6†

* 45,747 sq miles.
† Land area only, preliminary.

REGIONS
(population at census of June 2008, preliminary)

Region	Area (sq km)*	Population	Density (per sq km)	Regional capital
Southern	31,753	5,876,784	185.1	Blantyre
Central	35,592	5,491,034	154.3	Lilongwe
Northern	26,931	1,698,502	63.1	Mzuzu
Total	94,276	13,066,320	138.6	

* Excluding inland waters, totalling 24,208 sq km.

PRINCIPAL TOWNS
(population at census of June 2008, preliminary)

Lilongwe (capital)	669,021	Kasungu	42,351
Blantyre	661,444	Karonga	41,074
Mzuzu	128,432	Mangochi	39,369
Zomba	87,366	Salima	27,083

BIRTHS AND DEATHS
(annual averages, UN estimates)

	1990–95	1995–2000	2000–05
Birth rate (per 1,000)	49.1	47.0	43.8
Death rate (per 1,000)	17.1	17.2	17.5

Source: UN, *World Population Prospects: The 2006 Revision*.

Life expectancy (years at birth, WHO estimates): 50 (males 49; females 51) in 2006 (Source: WHO, *World Health Statistics*).

ECONOMICALLY ACTIVE POPULATION*
(persons aged 10 years and over, 1998 census)

	Males	Females	Total
Agriculture, hunting, forestry and fishing	1,683,006	2,082,821	3,765,827
Mining and quarrying	2,206	293	2,499
Manufacturing	94,545	23,938	118,483
Electricity, gas and water	6,656	663	7,319
Construction	70,196	3,206	73,402
Trade, restaurants and hotels	176,466	80,923	257,389
Transport, storage and communications	29,438	3,185	32,623
Financing, insurance, real estate and business services	10,473	3,484	13,957
Public administration	82,973	18,460	101,433
Community, social and personal services	52,980	33,016	85,996
Total employed	2,208,940	2,249,989	4,458,929
Unemployed	34,697	15,664	50,361
Total labour force	2,243,637	2,265,653	4,509,290

* Excluding armed forces.

Mid-2005 (estimates in '000): Agriculture, etc. 4,903; Total labour force 6,068 (Source: FAO).

Health and Welfare

KEY INDICATORS

Total fertility rate (children per woman, 2006)	5.7
Under-5 mortality rate (per 1,000 live births, 2006)	120
HIV/AIDS (% of persons aged 15–49, 2007)	11.9
Physicians (per 1,000 head, 2004)	0.02
Hospital beds (per 1,000 head, 2007)	1.1
Health expenditure (2006): US $ per head (PPP)	70
Health expenditure (2006): % of GDP	12.3
Health expenditure (2006): public (% of total)	72.1
Access to water (% of persons, 2006)	76
Access to sanitation (% of persons, 2006)	60
Human Development Index (2006): ranking	162
Human Development Index (2006): value	0.457

For sources and definitions, see explanatory note on p. vi.

Agriculture

PRINCIPAL CROPS
('000 metric tons)

	2005	2006	2007*
Rice, paddy	41.3	91.5*	91.5
Maize	1,225.2	2,576.7*	3,444.7
Millet	16.0	27.3*	32.3
Sorghum	18.2	54.3*	63.7
Potatoes*	1,800.0	1,850.0	1,900.0
Cassava (Manioc)	2,197.6	2,100.0*	2,150.0
Beans, dry	85.8	82.0*	85.0
Chick-peas*	37.0	35.0	35.0
Cow peas, dry*	54.0	54.0	54.0
Pigeon peas*	63.9	79.0*	79.0
Groundnuts, with shell	141.1	145.0†	150.0

MALAWI

—continued	2005	2006	2007*
Cabbages and other brassicas*	50.0	50.0	50.0
Tomatoes*	38.0	35.0	35.0
Onions, dry*	50.0	50.0	50.0
Guavas, mangoes and mangosteens*	65.0	33.0	33.0
Bananas*	380.0	385.0	385.0
Plantains*	300.0	300.0	300.0
Sugar cane*	2,400	2,450	2,500
Coffee, green	1.5†	1.5†	1.6
Tea	38.0	38.4	39.0
Tobacco, unmanufactured*	110.0	115.0	118.0

* FAO estimate(s).
† Unofficial figure.

Aggregate production ('000 metric tons, may include official, semi-official or estimated data): Total cereals 1,302 in 2005, 2,752 in 2006, 3,637 in 2007; Total roots and tubers 3,998 in 2005, 3,950 in 2006, 4,050 in 2007; Total vegetables (incl. melons) 313 in 2005, 310 in 2006, 310 in 2007; Total fruits (excl. melons) 946 in 2005, 720 in 2006, 720 in 2007.

Source: FAO.

LIVESTOCK
('000 head, year ending September, FAO estimates)

	2005	2006	2007
Cattle	750	750	752
Pigs	485.0	456.3	458.0
Sheep	130	115	116
Goats	1,920	1,900	1,900
Chickens	15,600	15,200	15,300

Source: FAO.

LIVESTOCK PRODUCTS
('000 metric tons, FAO estimates)

	2005	2006	2007
Cattle meat	16.0	16.0	16.0
Goat meat	6.9	6.7	6.7
Pig meat	22.0	21.0	21.0
Chicken meat	15.9	15.3	15.3
Cows' milk	35.0	35.0	35.5
Hen eggs	20.2	19.5	19.5

Source: FAO.

Forestry

ROUNDWOOD REMOVALS
('000 cubic metres, excluding bark, FAO estimates)

	2005	2006	2007
Sawlogs, veneer logs and logs for sleepers	130	130	130
Other industrial wood	390	390	390
Fuel wood	5,141	5,189	5,240
Total	5,661	5,709	5,760

Source: FAO.

SAWNWOOD PRODUCTION
('000 cubic metres, including railway sleepers)

	1991*	1992†	1993
Coniferous (softwood)	28	28	30
Broadleaved (hardwood)	15	15	15†
Total	43	43	45

* Unofficial figures.
† FAO estimate(s).

1994–2007: Annual production as in 1993 (FAO estimates).

Source: FAO.

Fishing

('000 metric tons, live weight)

	2004	2005	2006
Capture	56.5	58.8	71.3
Cyprinids	7.1	7.2	4.2
Tilapias	6.0	6.0	9.7
Cichlids	31.4	33.6	50.2
Torpedo-shaped catfishes	8.7	8.7	4.5
Other freshwater fishes	3.3	3.3	2.8
Aquaculture	0.7	0.8	1.5
Total catch	57.2	59.6	72.8

Note: Figures exclude aquatic mammals, recorded by number rather than weight. The number of Nile crocodiles caught was: 20 in 2004; 637 in 2005; 698 in 2006.

Source: FAO.

Mining

('000 metric tons, unless otherwise indicated)

	2005	2006	2007
Bituminous coal	51.9	60.4	58.6
Lime	22.7	21.1	19.0
Gemstones (kg)	1,994	2,171	3,710
Stone (crushed for aggregate)	171.3	192.0	226.4
Limestone	21.5	24.2	31.5

Source: US Geological Survey.

Industry

SELECTED PRODUCTS
('000 metric tons, unless otherwise indicated)

	2000	2001	2002
Raw sugar	96	107	260*
Beer ('000 hectolitres)	739	1,033	n.a.
Blankets ('000)	574	281	n.a.
Cement	198	111	174

* Natural sodium carbonate (Na_2Co_3).

2003 ('000 metric tons): Raw sugar (Na_2Co_3) 257; Cement 190 (Source: US Geological Survey).

Electric energy (million kWh): 1,129 in 2002; 1,177 in 2003; 1,270 in 2004.

Source (unless otherwise indicated): UN, *Industrial Commodity Statistics Yearbook*.

Cement ('000 metric tons, hydraulic): 166.0 in 2005; 187.6 in 2006; 185.3 in 2007 (Source: US Geological Survey).

Finance

CURRENCY AND EXCHANGE RATES

Monetary Units
100 tambala = 1 Malawi kwacha (K).

Sterling, Dollar and Euro Equivalents (31 October 2008)
£1 sterling = 227.408 kwacha;
US $1 = 140.601 kwacha;
€1 = 179.365 kwacha;
1,000 Malawi kwacha = £4.40 = $7.11 = €5.58.

Average Exchange Rate (kwacha per US $)
2005 118.420
2006 136.014
2007 139.957

MALAWI

Statistical Survey

BUDGET
(K million, year ending 30 June)

Revenue	2003/04	2004/05	2005/06*
Tax revenue	27,793.2	43,635.0	55,797.8
Taxes on income and profits	12,706.6	19,854.0	23,973.0
Companies	4,796.6	5,386.0	6,710.3
Individuals	7,910.0	14,468.0	17,263.5
Taxes on goods and services	12,160.4	18,830.0	25,909.8
Surtax	8,630.0	13,739.0	17,796.6
Excise duties	3,530.4	5,091.0	8,113.2
Taxes on international trade	3,766.1	5,952.0	7,374.4
Less Tax refunds	840.0	1,001.0	1,460.2
Non-tax revenue	4,874.0	4,461.0	8,127.0
Departmental receipts	1,173.2	2,447.0	4,595.3
Total	32,667.2	48,096.0	63,924.8

Expenditure	2003/04	2004/05	2005/06*
General public services	21,889.6	22,719.7	35,519.5
General administration	19,445.9	17,581.0	26,997.5
Defence	1,139.1	2,552.6	4,157.3
Public order and safety	1,304.6	2,586.1	4,364.7
Social and community services	12,606.7	17,509.0	24,363.2
Education	6,310.1	8,631.9	9,500.8
Health	3,692.4	5,247.6	11,057.9
Social security and welfare	2,105.7	2,706.4	2,221.3
Housing and community amenities	356.7	395.8	1,325.6
Recreational, cultural and other social services	75.4	76.8	106.2
Broadcasting and publishing	66.4	450.5	151.3
Economic affairs and services	4,799.0	8,721.1	6,927.3
Energy and mining	108.9	105.2	115.4
Agriculture and natural resources	2,482.4	4,345.5	2,837.2
Tourism	150.0	—	—
Physical planning and development	101.6	1,144.3	527.9
Transport and communications	1,496.3	2,048.5	2,299.1
Industry and commerce	210.7	390.0	599.6
Labour relations and employment	231.2	346.5	404.2
Environmental protection and conservation	—	—	—
Scientific and technological services	—	314.4	144.0
Other economic services	17.9	26.7	—
Unallocable expenditure	1,505.2	677.3	—
Total recurrent expenditure	40,800.5	49,627.0	66,810.0
Debt amortization	18,736.5	18,752.0	17,328.0
Total	59,537.0	68,379.0	84,138.0

*Estimates.

2006/07 (K million, year ending 30 June): *Revenue:* Tax revenue 77,321; Non-tax revenue 6,974; Total 84,295 (excl. grants 63,337). *Expenditure:* Current expenditure 99,464 (Wages and salaries 23,778, Interest payments 16,378, Other 59,307); Development expenditure 53,665; Total 153,128 (excl. net lending 452). (Source: IMF, *Malawi: Request for a One-Year Exogenous Shocks Facility Arrangement - Staff Report; Press Release on the Executive Board Discussion; and Statement by the Executive Director for Malawi*—January 2009).

2007/08 (K million, year ending 30 June, preliminary figures): *Revenue:* Tax revenue 96,387; Non-tax revenue 8,567; Total 104,954 (excl. grants 59,600). *Expenditure:* Current expenditure 115,622 (Wages and salaries 30,018, Interest payments 12,331, Other 73,272); Development expenditure 63,775; Total 179,397 (Source: IMF, *Malawi: Request for a One-Year Exogenous Shocks Facility Arrangement - Staff Report; Press Release on the Executive Board Discussion; and Statement by the Executive Director for Malawi*—January 2009).

2008/09 (K million, year ending 30 June, projected figures): *Revenue:* Tax revenue 112,299; Non-tax revenue 11,237; Total 123,536 (excl. grants 84,073). *Expenditure:* Current expenditure 175,827 (Wages and salaries 37,256, Interest payments 17,416, Other 121,155); Development expenditure 55,256; Total 231,084 (Source: IMF, *Malawi: Request for a One-Year Exogenous Shocks Facility Arrangement - Staff Report; Press Release on the Executive Board Discussion; and Statement by the Executive Director for Malawi*—January 2009).

INTERNATIONAL RESERVES
(US $ million at 31 December)

	2005	2006	2007
Gold (national valuation)	0.54	0.54	0.54
IMF special drawing rights	1.05	0.68	0.03
Reserve position in IMF	3.27	3.48	3.66
Foreign exchange	154.59	129.61	212.92
Total	159.45	134.31	217.15

Source: IMF, *International Financial Statistics*.

MONEY SUPPLY
(K million at 31 December)

	2005	2006	2007
Currency outside banks	11,947.0	15,470.9	20,587.5
Demand deposits at commercial banks	19,356.1	20,217.8	30,142.3
Total money (incl. others)	31,303.1	35,688.7	50,729.8

Source: IMF, *International Financial Statistics*.

COST OF LIVING
(Consumer Price Index; base: 2000 = 100)

	2004	2005	2006
Food (incl. beverages)	154.4	181.0	209.1
Clothing (incl. footwear)	179.5	192.8	208.8
Rent	211.7	236.9	266.9
All items (incl. others)	172.0	198.5	226.1

2007: Food (incl. beverages) 224.7; All items (incl. others) 244.1.
Source: ILO.

NATIONAL ACCOUNTS
Expenditure on the Gross Domestic Product
(K million at current prices)

	2004	2005	2006*
Government final consumption expenditure	34,990.1	41,344.5	49,124.8
Private final consumption expenditure	324,697.4	395,671.5	435,651.9
Gross capital formation	25,091.9	29,106.9	32,783.5
Total domestic expenditure	384,779.4	466,122.9	517,560.2
Exports of goods and services	58,914.3	61,785.8	84,188.8
Less Imports of goods and services	135,181.6	164,387.6	166,523.9
GDP in purchasers' values	308,512.1	363,521.1	435,225.0
GDP at 2002 factor cost	271,050.6	276,801.2	300,123.6

2007 (US $ million at current prices): General government final consumption expenditure 428.25; Household final consumption expenditure 2,440.17; Gross capital formation 349.85; *Total domestic expenditure* 3,218.27; Exports of goods and services 652.86; Imports of goods and services −1,291.41; *GDP at market prices* 2,579.73 (Source: African Development Bank).

MALAWI

Gross Domestic Product by Economic Activity
(K million at current prices)

	2004	2005	2006*
Agriculture, forestry and fishing	88,955.7	81,395.9	91,814.5
Mining and quarrying	1,450.5	2,177.2	2,386.2
Manufacturing	52,040.1	55,786.9	59,022.6
Electricity and water	3,434.4	3,740.0	4,016.8
Building and construction	3,904.4	4,189.5	4,759.2
Wholesale and retail trade services	53,418.1	58,118.9	62,826.6
Hotels and restaurants	10,804.3	11,470.0	12,341.3
Transport and communication	14,584.4	15,926.2	16,802.1
Financial intermediation and insurance	8,405.0	9,069.0	9,540.6
Business activities and real estate	9,815.1	10,050.6	10,362.2
Ownership of dwellings	2,407.2	2,457.8	2,583.1
Private social services	7,984.7	8,240.2	8,808.8
Government services	13,846.7	14,179.0	14,859.6
Sub-total	271,050.6	276,801.2	300,123.6
Net indirect taxes	25,706.2	31,813.3	40,000.0
Adjustment to current prices	11,755.2	54,906.6	95,101.4
GDP in market prices	308,512.0	363,521.1	435,225.0

* Projected figures.

BALANCE OF PAYMENTS
(K million)

	2005	2006	2007
Exports of goods f.o.b.	59,733.1	73,803.7	99,258.4
Imports of goods f.o.b.	−119,101.8	−141,302.4	−175,556.6
Trade balance	−59,368.7	−67,498.7	−76,298.2
Net services	−24,049.7	−28,659.0	−32,228.4
Balance on goods and services	−83,508.4	−96,157.7	−108,526.6
Net other income	−4,715.2	−4,847.3	−2,974.3
Balance on goods, services and income	−88,133.6	−101,005	−111,500.9
Net transfers	4,997.8	5,657.5	10,908.3
Current balance	−83,135.8	−95,347.5	−100,592.5
Government transfers (net)	23,361.7	20,634.5	38,346.6
Government drawings on loans	10,499.4	6,112.3	10,631.9
Public enterprises (net)	1,319.4	1,632.0	1,570.5
Private sector (net)	425.7	489.1	503.3
Short-term capital (net)	70.6	81.1	83.5
Errors and omissions	34,975.9	49,298.4	32,038.2
Statistical discrepancy	—	—	12,883.7
Overall balance*	−12,483.0	−17,100.1	−4,534.8

* Excluding debt relief (K million): 7,079.1 in 2005; 14,925.4 in 2006; 155.4 in 2007.

External Trade

PRINCIPAL COMMODITIES
(distribution by SITC, US $ million)

Imports c.i.f.	2005	2006	2007
Food and live animals	91.8	96.2	80.8
Cereals and cereal preparations	61.8	62.2	47.2
Beverages and tobacco	96.2	58.2	35.8
Tobacco and tobacco products	94.1	57.1	34.3
Mineral fuels, lubricants, etc.	122.7	138.1	190.3
Petroleum, petroleum products, etc.	120.4	136.2	188.6
Refined petroleum products	116.1	130.2	180.5
Chemicals and related products	249.8	223.9	383.4
Medicinal and pharmaceutical products	54.2	58.4	85.8
Manufactured fertilizers	116.5	73.3	188.2
Basic manufactures	179.3	175.3	199.2
Paper, paperboard, etc.	24.3	27.2	28.3
Textile yarn, fabrics, etc.	44.8	37.5	43.7

Imports c.i.f.—continued	2005	2006	2007
Iron and steel	32.3	35.0	42.5
Machinery and transport equipment	256.6	356.2	306.6
Machinery specialized for particular industries	49.5	36.0	43.5
General industrial machinery, equipment and parts	25.5	28.0	29.5
Office machinery and automatic data-processing equipment	17.0	15.1	21.3
Telecommunications, sound recording and reproducing equipment	30.9	31.6	25.8
Road vehicles	87.3	189.2	143.2
Goods vehicles (lorries and trucks)	25.2	127.0	31.7
Miscellaneous manufactured articles	125.0	112.1	133.2
Total (incl. others)	1,165.2	1,206.7	1,377.8

Exports f.o.b.	2005	2006	2007
Food and live animals	115.7	126.5	268.4
Sugar and honey	45.4	42.0	64.3
Raw cane sugars	45.3	38.0	60.5
Coffee, tea, cocoa and spices	54.5	56.7	61.4
Tea	49.6	49.5	55.4
Beverages and tobacco	264.6	409.5	423.8
Tobacco and tobacco products	264.6	409.3	422.7
Unstripped tobacco	237.9	340.2	336.6
Stripped or partly stripped tobacco	26.7	69.1	86.0
Crude materials (inedible) except fuels	33.2	36.3	83.8
Textile fibres	15.7	15.3	23.9
Basic manufactures	9.3	14.6	10.9
Machinery and transport equipment	16.3	16.9	11.8
Miscellaneous manufactured articles	53.9	57.7	50.2
Total (incl. others)	495.5	666.2	868.6

Source: UN, *International Trade Statistics Yearbook*.

PRINCIPAL TRADING PARTNERS
(US $ million)

Imports	2005	2006	2007
Belgium	17.6	9.8	9.2
China, People's Repub.	33.5	26.7	41.3
Denmark	13.8	20.7	32.9
France (incl. Monaco)	11.5	13.0	16.0
Germany	33.5	18.6	25.5
Hong Kong	5.9	13.5	8.0
India	54.5	49.9	69.2
Indonesia	5.4	9.1	9.1
Italy	9.1	10.6	7.1
Japan	14.7	10.7	16.2
Kenya	18.9	25.7	31.3
Korea, Repub.	9.9	5.2	8.7
Mozambique	147.6	151.1	167.8
Netherlands	13.4	17.7	26.4
South Africa	380.7	433.5	401.0
Tanzania	32.2	41.6	82.5
United Arab Emirates	27.0	72.6	96.6
United Kingdom	54.0	70.1	69.2
USA	30.3	38.6	49.5
Zambia	62.1	43.2	32.0
Zimbabwe	89.7	40.4	47.5
Total (incl. others)	1,165.2	1,206.7	1,377.8

MALAWI

Exports	2005	2006	2007
Belgium	7.1	31.9	69.9
Denmark	3.1	3.1	31.8
Egypt	15.4	34.0	20.4
France (incl. Monaco)	5.9	5.0	9.9
Germany	37.3	69.7	50.8
Japan	7.6	2.2	1.1
Kenya	6.9	6.5	7.1
Korea, Repub.	0.9	6.6	30.7
Mozambique	17.2	15.3	17.3
Netherlands	21.5	23.2	31.5
Poland	10.5	12.7	18.9
Portugal	5.5	2.8	28.9
Russia	18.0	23.3	29.8
South Africa	92.4	147.9	128.5
Spain	8.8	6.5	9.2
Switzerland (incl. Liechtenstein)	34.8	7.4	9.2
Turkey	2.5	8.9	17.1
United Kingdom	57.2	87.9	57.0
USA	55.3	54.3	36.3
Zambia	7.2	14.1	18.8
Zimbabwe	11.1	21.2	132.0
Total (incl. others)	495.5	666.2	868.6

Source: UN, *International Trade Statistics Yearbook*.

Transport

RAILWAYS
(traffic)

	2002	2003	2004
Passengers carried ('000)	402	488	394
Passenger-kilometres ('000)	23,845	30,311	29,523
Net freight ton-kilometres ('000)	86,018	26,009	26,055

ROAD TRAFFIC
(estimates, motor vehicles in use at 31 December)

	1994	1995	1996
Passenger cars	23,520	25,480	27,000
Lorries and vans	26,000	29,000	29,700

Source: International Road Federation, *World Road Statistics*.

SHIPPING

Inland Waterways
(lake transport)

	2002	2003	2004
Passengers carried ('000)	78	68	55
Passenger-km ('000)	6,955	5,659	4,299
Net freight-ton km	392	1,438	316

CIVIL AVIATION
(traffic on scheduled services)

	2002	2003	2004
Kilometres flown (million)	3	4	5
Passengers carried ('000)	105	109	122
Passenger-km (million)	140	147	167
Total ton-km (million)	14	16	18

Source: UN, *Statistical Yearbook*.

Tourism

FOREIGN TOURIST ARRIVALS BY COUNTRY OF RESIDENCE

	2003	2004	2005
Mozambique	92,200	104,698	95,019
North America	17,210	19,431	17,278
Southern Africa*	49,200	54,230	48,155
United Kingdom and Ireland	31,220	17,030	28,157
Zambia	50,540	45,817	43,855
Zimbabwe	63,910	57,518	60,807
Total (incl. others)	424,000	427,360	437,718

*Comprising South Africa, Botswana, Lesotho and Swaziland.

Tourism receipts (US $ million, incl. passenger transport): 36 in 2004; 43 in 2005; 43 in 2006.

Source: World Tourism Organization.

Communications Media

	2005	2006	2007
Telephones ('000 main lines in use)	102.7	130.0	175.2
Mobile cellular telephones ('000 subscribers)	421.2	620.2	1,050.9
Personal computers ('000 in use)	25	n.a.	n.a.
Internet users ('000)	52.5	59.7	139.5
Broadband subscribers ('000)	0.4	n.a.	1.6

Radio receivers ('000 in use): 4,929 in 1998.

Television receivers ('000 in use): 40 in 2001.

Facsimile machines (number in use): 1,250 in 1997.

Book production (first editions only): 120 titles in 1996.

Daily newspapers: 5 in 1998 (estimated average circulation 26,000 copies).

Non-daily newspapers: 4 in 1996 (estimated average circulation 120,000 copies).

Sources: UNESCO Institute for Statistics; UN, *Statistical Yearbook*; International Telecommunication Union.

Education

(2003 unless otherwise indicated)

	Institutions	Teachers	Students
Primary	3,160*	45,100	2,943,248†
Secondary	n.a.	7,076	574,003†
Tertiary	6	861†	6,458†

*1997 figure. Source: UNESCO Institute for Statistics.
†2006/07 figure.

Source: partly UNESCO Institute for Statistics.

Primary education (2004): Schools 5,103; Students 3,166,786; Teachers 43,952 (Source: partly Ministry of Education, Science and Technology).

Adult literacy rate (UNESCO estimates): 71.8% (males 79.2%; females 64.6%) in 2007 (Source: UNESCO Institute for Statistics).

Directory

The Constitution

A new Constitution, replacing the (amended) 1966 Constitution, was approved by the National Assembly on 16 May 1994, and took provisional effect for one year from 18 May. During this time the Constitution was to be subject to review, and the final document was promulgated on 18 May 1995. The main provisions (with subsequent amendments) are summarized below:

THE PRESIDENT

The President is both Head of State and Head of Government. The President is elected for five years, by universal adult suffrage, in the context of a multi-party political system. The Constitution provides for up to two Vice-Presidents.

PARLIAMENT

Parliament comprises the President, the Vice-President(s) and the National Assembly. The National Assembly has 193 elective seats, elections being by universal adult suffrage, in the context of a multi-party system. Cabinet ministers who are not elected members of parliament also sit in the National Assembly. The Speaker is appointed from among the ordinary members of the Assembly. The parliamentary term is normally five years. The President has power to prorogue or dissolve Parliament.

In 1995 the National Assembly approved proposals for the establishment of a second chamber, the Senate, to be implemented in 1999. The chamber was not established by that date, however, and in January 2001 the National Assembly approved a proposal to abandon plans for its creation.

EXECUTIVE POWER

Executive power is exercised by the President, who appoints members of the Cabinet.

The Government

HEAD OF STATE

President: Dr BINGU WA MUTHARIKA (took office 24 May 2004).
Vice-President: Dr CASSIM CHILUMPHA.

CABINET
(April 2009)

President and Commander-in-Chief of the Malawi Defence Force and Police Service, Minister of Agriculture and Food Security and Minister of Education, Science and Technology: Dr BINGU WA MUTHARIKA.
Minister for Presidential and Parliamentary Affairs: DAVIES KATSONGA.
Minister of Finance: Dr GOODALL E. GONDWE.
Minister of Foreign Affairs: JOYCE BANDA.
Minister of Industry and Trade: HENRY MUSSA.
Minister of Energy and Mines: TED KALEBE.
Minister of Local Government and Rural Development: Dr GEORGE CHAPONDA.
Minister of Transport, Public Works and Housing: HENRY CHIMUNTHU BANDA.
Minister of Economic Planning and Development: KEN LIPENGA.
Minister of Irrigation and Water Development: MOHAMMED SIDIK MIA.
Minister of National Defence: AARON SANGALA.
Minister of Information and Civic Education: PATRICIA KALIATI.
Minister of Lands and Natural Resources: JOHN B. KHUMBO CHIRWA.
Minister of Home Affairs and Internal Security: ERNEST MALENGA.
Minister of Justice: HENRY DAMA PHOYA.
Attorney-General: JANE ANSAH.
Minister of Labour: DAVIS KATSONGA.
Minister of Health: KUMBO KACHALI.
Minister of Women and Child Development: ANNA KACHIKO.
Minister of Youth Development and Sports: SYMON VUWA KAUNDA.
Minister of Persons with Disabilities and the Elderly: CLEMENT KHEMBO.
Minister of Tourism and Wildlife: CALLISTA CHAPOLA CHIMOMBO.
There were also 21 Deputy Ministers.

MINISTRIES

Office of the President and Cabinet: Private Bag 301, Capital City, Lilongwe 3; tel. 1789311; fax 1788456; internet www.malawi.gov.mw/opc/opc.htm.
Office of the Vice President: POB 30399, Capital City, Lilongwe; tel. 1788444; fax 1788218; e-mail vicepres@malawi.gov.mw.
Ministry of Agriculture and Food Security: POB 30134, Capital City, Lilongwe 3; tel. 1789033; fax 1789218; e-mail agriculture@agriculture.gov.mw; internet www.malawi.gov.mw/Agriculture/Home%20%20Agriculture.htm.
Ministry of Economic Planning and Development: POB 30136, Capital City, Lilongwe 3; tel. 1788390; fax 1788131; e-mail epd@malawi.net; internet www.malawi.gov.mw/Economic%20Planning/Home%20Economic%20Planning.htm.
Ministry of Education Science and Technology: Private Bag 328, Lilongwe 3; tel. 1789422; fax 1788064; e-mail education@malawi.gov.mw; internet www.malawi.gov.mw/Education/Home%20%20Education.htm.
Ministry of Energy and Mines: Private Bag 350, Lilongwe 3; tel. 1789488; fax 1773379; internet www.malawi.gov.mw/natres/natres.htm.
Ministry of Finance: Capital Hill, POB 30049, Lilongwe 3; tel. 1789355; fax 1789173; internet www.malawi.gov.mw/Finance/Home%20Finance.htm.
Ministry of Foreign Affairs: POB 30315, Lilongwe 3; tel. 1789323; fax 1788482; e-mail foreign@malawi.net; internet www.malawi.gov.mw/Foreign%20Affairs/Home%20ForeignAffairs.htm.
Ministry of Health: POB 30377, Capital City, Lilongwe 3; tel. 1789400; fax 1789431; e-mail doccentre@malawi.net; internet www.malawi.gov.mw/Health/Home%20Health.htm.
Ministry of Home Affairs and Internal Security: Private Bag 331, Lilongwe 3; tel. 1789177; fax 1789509; internet www.malawi.gov.mw/Home%20Affairs/Home%20HomeAffairs.htm; comprises the Immigration Dept, Prison and Police Services.
Ministry of Industry and Trade: POB 30366, Capital City, Lilongwe 3; tel. 1770244; fax 1770680; e-mail minci@malawi.net; internet www.malawi.gov.mw/Trade/Home%20%20Trade.htm.
Ministry of Information and Civic Education: Private Bag 326, Capital City, Lilongwe 3; tel. 1775499; fax 1770650; e-mail psinfo@sdnp.org.mw; internet www.malawi.gov.mw/Information/Home%20Information.htm.
Ministry of Irrigation and Water Development: Tikwere House, Private Bag 390, Capital City, Lilongwe 3; tel. 1770238; fax 1773737; internet www.malawi.gov.mw/water/Home%20%20Water.htm.
Ministry of Justice: Private Bag 333, Capital City, Lilongwe 3; tel. 1788411; fax 1788332; e-mail justice@malawi.gov.mw; internet www.malawi.gov.mw/Justice/Home%20%20Justice.htm; also comprises the Attorney-General's Chambers and the Directorate of Public Prosecutions.
Ministry of Labour: Private Bag 344, Capital City, Lilongwe 3; tel. 1773277; fax 1773803; e-mail labour@malawi.net; internet www.malawi.gov.mw/Labour/Home%20%20Labour.htm.
Ministry of Lands and Natural Resources: POB 30548, Lilongwe 3; tel. 1774766; fax 1773990.
Ministry of Local Government and Rural Development: POB 30312, Lilongwe 3; tel. 1789388; fax 1788083; internet www.malawi.gov.mw/LocalGovt/Home%20%20LocalGovt.htm.
Ministry of National Defence: Private Bag 339, Lilongwe 3; tel. 1789600; fax 1789176; internet www.malawi.gov.mw/Defence/Home%20Defence.htm.
Ministry of Persons with Disabilities and the Elderly: Lilongwe 3.
Ministry of Tourism and Wildlife: Lilongwe 3; tel. 1772702; fax 1770650; e-mail tourism@malawi.net.
Ministry of Transport, Public Works and Housing: Private Bag 322, Capital City, Lilongwe 3; tel. 1789377; fax 1789328; internet www.malawi.gov.mw/Transport/Home%20%20Transport.htm.
Ministry of Women and Child Development: Private Bag 330, Capital City, Lilongwe 3; tel. 1770411; fax 1770826.
Ministry of Youth Development and Sports: Lingadzi House, Private Bag 384, Lilongwe 3; tel. 1774999; fax 1771018; e-mail

MALAWI

sports@malawi.gov.mw; internet www.malawi.gov.mw/Youth/Home%20%20Youth.htm.

President and Legislature

PRESIDENT

Presidential Election, 20 May 2004

Candidate	Votes	% of votes
Bingu wa Mutharika (UDF)	1,119,738	35.89
John Tembo (MCP)	846,457	27.13
Gwandaguluwe Chakuamba (Mgwirizano Coalition*)	802,386	25.72
Brown Mpinganjira (NDA)	272,172	8.72
Justin Malewezi (Independent)	78,892	2.53
Total	3,119,645	100.00

* Comprising the Malawi Democratic Party, the Malawi Forum for Unity and Development, the Movement for Genuine Democratic Change (MGODE), the National Unity Party, the People's Progressive Movement, the People's Transformation Party and Chakuamba's Republican Party (RP); in early June 2004 MGODE and the RP signed a memorandum of understanding on co-operation with the UDF.

NATIONAL ASSEMBLY

National Assembly: Parliament Bldg, Private Bag B362, Lilongwe 3; tel. 1773566; fax 1774196; internet www.malawi.gov.mw/parliament/parliament.htm.

Speaker: LOUIS JOSEPH CHIMANGO.

General Election, 20 May 2004*

Party	Seats
Malawi Congress Party (MCP)	56
United Democratic Front (UDF)	49
Republican Party (RP)†	15
National Democratic Alliance (NDA)	8
Alliance for Democracy (AFORD)	6
People's Progressive Movement (PPM)†	6
Movement for Genuine Democratic Change (MGODE)†	3
Congress for National Unity (CONU)	1
People's Transformation Party (PETRA)†	1
Independents	39
Total	193‡

* Provisional results.
† Contested the election as part of the Mgwirizano Coalition, which also comprised the Malawi Democratic Party, the Malawi Forum for Unity and Development and the National Unity Party; in early June 2004 MGODE and the RP signed a memorandum of understanding on co-operation with the UDF.
‡ Disputed results in three constituencies remained under investigation in early June 2004, while voting in a further six constituencies was not conducted owing to irregularities.

Election Commission

Malawi Electoral Commission (MEC): Development House, Private Bag 113, Blantyre; tel. 1822033; fax 1823960; internet www.sdnp.org.mw/~solomon/mec/index.htm; f. 1998; Chair. ANASTASIA MSOSA; Chief Elections Officer DAVID KAMBAUWA (acting).

Political Organizations

Alliance for Democracy (AFORD): Private Bag 28, Lilongwe; f. 1992; in March 1993 absorbed membership of fmr Malawi Freedom Movement; Pres. CHAKUFWA CHIHANA; First Vice-Pres. KALUNDI CHIRWA; Sec.-Gen. WALLACE CHIUME.

Congress of Democrats (CODE): Mzuzu; Pres. RALPH KASAMBARA.

Congress for National Unity (CONU): Lilongwe; f. 1999; Pres. Bishop DANIEL KAMFOSI NKHUMBWA.

Democratic Progressive Party (DPP): Lilongwe 3; internet dppmw.org; f. 2005 following Bingu wa Mutharika's resignation from the UDF; Leader Dr BINGU WA MUTHARIKA; Sec.-Gen. HEATHERWICK NTABA.

Malawi Congress Party (MCP): Private Bag 388, Lilongwe 3; tel. 999223228; internet www.malawicongressparty.org; f. 1959; sole legal party 1966–93; Pres. JOHN TEMBO.

Malawi Democratic Party (MDP): Lilongwe; Pres. KAMLEPO KALUA.

Malawi Forum for Unity and Development (MAFUNDE): f. 2002; aims to combat corruption and food shortages; Pres. GEORGE MNESA.

Maravi People's Party (MPP): Lilongwe; Pres. ULADI MUSSA; Sec.-Gen. Dr YUSUF HAUDI (acting).

Movement for Genuine Democratic Change (MGODE): Plot No. 52, Kanjedza Drive, Mzuzu; f. 2003 by fmr mems of AFORD; Chair. SAM KANDODO BANDA (acting); Dir GREENE LULILO MWAMONDWE; Sec.-Gen. RODGER NKWAZI.

National Democratic Alliance (NDA): POB 994, Blantyre; tel. 1842593; f. 2001 by fmr mems of the UDF; officially merged with the UDF in June 2004 but maintained independent structure; Pres. BROWN JAMES MPINGANJIRA; Nat. Chair. JAMES MAKHUMULA NKHOMA.

National Solidarity Movement: Leader NGWAZI KAZUNI KUMWENDA.

National Unity Party (NUP): Blantyre; Pres. HARRY CHIUME; Sec.-Gen. HARRY MUYENZA.

New Dawn for Africa (NDA): Legends Compound, Blantyre, POB 76, Liwonde; f. 2003; associated with the UDF; Pres. THOM CHIUMIA; Sec.-Gen. CHIKUMBUTSO MTUMODZI.

New Republican Party (NRP): f. 2005; Pres. GWANDAGULUWE CHAKUAMBA; Vice-Pres. KEN ZIKHALE NG'OMA.

People's Progressive Movement (PPM): f. 2003 by fmr mems of the UDF; Pres. ALEKE KADONAPHANI BANDA; Sec.-Gen. KNOX VARELA.

People's Transformation Party (PETRA): POB 31964, Chichiri, Blantyre 3; tel. 1871577; fax 1871573; e-mail umunthu@sdnp.org.mw; internet www.petra.mw; f. 2002; Pres. KAMUZU CHIBAMBO; Sec.-Gen. DEREK LAKUDZALA.

United Democratic Front (UDF): POB 5446, Limbe; internet www.udf.malawi.net; f. 1992; officially merged with the NDA in June 2004 but maintained independent structure; Nat. Chair. Dr BAKILI MULUZI; Sec.-Gen. KENNEDY MAKWANGWALA.

United Front for Multi-party Democracy (UFMD): f. 1992 by three exiled political groups: the Socialist League of Malawi, the Malawi Freedom Party and the Malawi Dem. Union; Pres. EDMOND JIKA.

The Movement for the Restoration of Democracy in Malawi (f. 1996) is based in Mozambique and consists of fmr Malawi Young Pioneers; it conducts occasional acts of insurgency.

Diplomatic Representation

EMBASSIES AND HIGH COMMISSIONS IN MALAWI

China, People's Republic: No. 9, Area 11, Lilongwe; tel. 1794751; fax 1794752; e-mail chinaemb_mw@mfa.gov.cn; internet mw.chineseembassy.org/eng; LIN SONGTIAN.

Egypt: 10/247 Tsoka Rd, POB 30451, Lilongwe 3; tel. 1780668; fax 1794660; Ambassador AKRAM MOHSEN HAMDY.

Germany: Convention Dr., POB 30046, Lilongwe 3; tel. 1772555; fax 1770250; e-mail info@lilongwe.diplo.de; internet www.lilongwe.diplo.de; Ambassador ALBERT JOSEF GISY.

Ireland: Lilongwe; tel. 1706405; e-mail lilongweemdiplomats@dfa.ie; Ambassador LIAM MACGABHANN.

Mozambique: POB 30579, Lilongwe 3; tel. 1774100; fax 1771342; e-mail embamoc.malawi@minec.gov.mz; High Commissioner PEDRO JOÃO DE AZEVEDO DAVANE.

South Africa: Kang'ombe House, 3rd Floor, City Centre, POB 30043, Lilongwe 3; tel. 1773722; fax 1772571; e-mail sahc@malawi.net; High Commissioner N. M. TSHEOLE.

Tanzania: POB 922, Capital City, Lilongwe 3; tel. 1770150; fax 1770148; e-mail tanzanianhighcomm@tz.lilongwe.mw; High Commissioner Maj.-Gen. (retd) MAKAME RASHID.

United Kingdom: British High Commission Bldg, Capital Hill, POB 30042, Lilongwe 3; tel. 1772400; fax 1772657; e-mail bhclilongwe@fco.gov.uk; internet ukinmalawi.fco.gov.uk; High Commissioner RICHARD WILDASH.

USA: Area 40, Plot No. 18, 16 Jomo Kenyatta Rd, POB 30016, Lilongwe 3; tel. 1773166; fax 1770471; e-mail ConsularLilong@state.gov; internet lilongwe.usembassy.gov; Ambassador PETER W. BODDE.

Zambia: Area 40/2, City Centre, POB 30138, Lilongwe 3; tel. 1772100; fax 1774349; High Commissioner (vacant).

MALAWI

Zimbabwe: POB 30187, Lilongwe 3; tel. 1774988; fax 1772382; e-mail zimhighcomllw@malawi.net; High Commissioner THANDIWE S. DUMBUTSHENA.

Judicial System

The courts administering justice are the Supreme Court of Appeal, High Court and Magistrates' Courts.

The High Court, which has unlimited jurisdiction in civil and criminal matters, consists of the Chief Justice and five puisne judges. Traditional Courts were abolished under the 1994 Constitution. Appeals from the High Court are heard by the Supreme Court of Appeal in Blantyre.

High Court of Malawi

POB 30244, Chichiri, Blantyre 3; tel. 1670255; fax 1670213; e-mail highcourt@sdnp.org.mw; internet www.judiciary.mw; Registrar SYLVESTER KALEMBERA.

Chief Justice: LOVEMORE MUNLO.

Justices of Appeal: J. B. KALAILE, D. G. TAMBALA, H. M. MTEGHA, A. S. E. MSOSA, I. J. MTAMBO, A. K. TEMBO.

High Court Judges: D. F. MWAUNGULU, A. K. C. NYIRENDA, G. M. CHIMASULA PHIRI, B. S. CHIUDZA BANDA, E. B. TWEA, R. R. MZIKAMANDA, Dr J. M. ANSAH, R. R. CHINANGWA, A. C. CHIPETA, F. E. KAPANDA, L. P. CHIKOPA, H. S. B. POTANI, E. CHOMBO, J. N. KATSALA, J. S. MANYUNGWA, M. L. KAMWAMBE, M. C. C. MKANDAWIRE, I. C. KAMANGA.

Religion

More than 70% of the population profess Christianity. Islam, the fastest growing religion, is practised by about 20% of the population. Traditional beliefs are followed by about 10% of the population. The Asian community includes Hindus.

CHRISTIANITY

Malawi Council of Churches (MCC): POB 30068, Capital City, Lilongwe 3; tel. 1783499; fax 1783106; f. 1939; Chair. Rev. HOWARD MATIYA NKHOMA; Gen. Sec. Rev. Dr A. C. MUSOPOLE; 22 mem. churches.

The Anglican Communion

Anglicans are adherents of the Church of the Province of Central Africa, covering Botswana, Malawi, Zambia and Zimbabwe. The Church comprises 15 dioceses, including four in Malawi. There were about 230,000 adherents in Malawi at mid-2000.

Archbishop of the Province of Central Africa and Bishop of Upper Shire: (vacant), Private Bag 1, Chilema, Zomba; tel. and fax 1539203; e-mail dionorth@zamnet.zm.

Bishop of Lake Malawi: (vacant), POB 30349, Capital City, Lilongwe 3; tel. 1797858; fax 1797548; e-mail anglama@eomw.net.

Bishop of Northern Malawi: Rt Rev. CHRISTOPHER JOHN BOYLE, POB 120, Mzuzu; tel. 1331486; fax 1333805; e-mail angdioofnm@sdnp.org.mw.

Bishop of Southern Malawi: Rt Rev. JAMES TENGATENGA, POB 30220, Chichiri, Blantyre 3; tel. 1641218; fax 1641235; e-mail angsoma@sdnp.org.mw; internet www.angsoma.org.mw.

Protestant Churches

At mid-2001 there were an estimated 2.1m. Protestants in Malawi.

Assemblies of God in Malawi: POB 1220, Lilongwe; tel. 1761057; fax 1762056; Pres. LAZARUS CHAKWERA; 639,088 mems in 3,114 churches (2005).

Baptist Convention of Malawi (BACOMA): Lali Lubani Rd, POB 30212, Chichiri, Blantyre 3; tel. 1671170; e-mail bacoma@sdnp.org.mw; 175,000 adherents, 1,375 churches (2007); Gen. Sec. Rev. FLETCHER KAIYA.

Church of Central Africa Presbyterian (CCAP): Blantyre Synod, POB 413, Blantyre; tel. and fax 1633942; e-mail btsynod@malawi.net; internet www.blantyresynod.org; comprises three synods in Malawi (Blantyre, Livingstonia and Nkhoma); Co-ordinating Rev. J. J. MPHATSE; Gen. Sec. DANIEL GUNYA; Exec. Dir ROBSON CHITENGO; more than 1m. adherents in Malawi.

Evangelical Association of Malawi: POB 2120, Blantyre; tel. and fax 9936681; Chair. Rev. Dr LAZARUS CHAKWERA; Gen. Sec. FRANCIS MKANDAWIRE.

Evangelical Lutheran Church in Malawi: POB 650, Lutheran Church Centre, Plot 22, Chidzanja Rd, Lilongwe; tel. and fax 1724989; fax 1725910; e-mail elcmwi@elcmw.org; Bishop. Dr JOSEPH P. BVUMBWE; 60,000 mems (2009).

Seventh-day Adventist Church: Robins Rd, Kabula Hill, POB 951, Blantyre; tel. 1620264; fax 1620528; e-mail musda@malawi.net; Pres. SAUSTIN K. MFUNE; Exec. Sec. BAXTER D. CHILUNGA; 200,000 mems.

The African Methodist Episcopal Church, the Churches of Christ, the Free Methodist Church, the New Apostolic Church and the United Evangelical Church in Malawi are also active. At mid-2000 there were an estimated 2m. adherents professing other forms of Christianity.

The Roman Catholic Church

Malawi comprises one archdiocese and six dioceses. At 31 December 2006 there were some 3.6m. adherents of the Roman Catholic Church (equivalent to approximately 22.4% of the total population).

Episcopal Conference of Malawi

Catholic Secretariat of Malawi, Chimutu Rd, POB 30384, Capital City, Lilongwe 3; tel. 1782066; fax 1782019; e-mail ecm@malawi.net. f. 1969; Pres. Most Rev. TARCISIUS GERVAZIO ZIYAYE (Archbishop of Blantyre).

Archbishop of Blantyre: Most Rev. TARCISIUS GERVAZIO ZIYAYE, Archbishop House, POB 385, Blantyre; tel. and fax 1637905; e-mail archdblantyre@africa-online.net.

ISLAM

Muslim Association of Malawi (MAM): POB 497, Blantyre; tel. 1622060; fax 1623581; f. 1946 as the Nyasaland Muslim Asscn; umbrella body for Muslim orgs; provides secular and Islamic education; Sec.-Gen. MOHAMMED IMRAN SHAREEF.

BAHÁ'Í FAITH

National Spiritual Assembly: POB 30922, Lilongwe 3; tel. 1771177; fax 1771713; e-mail bahaimalawi@africa-online.net; f. 1970; mems resident in over 1,200 localities.

The Press

The Chronicle: Private Bag 77, Lilongwe; tel. 1756530; e-mail thechronicle@africa-online.net; f. 1993; publ. by Jamieson Publications; Mon. and Thur.; English; ceased publ. in Dec. 2006; Owner and Editor-in-Chief ROBERT JAMIESON; circ. c. 5,000 (2006).

The Daily Times: Scott Rd, Private Bag 39, Blantyre; tel. 1670115; fax 1671233; e-mail info@bnl.bppmw.com; internet www.dailytimes.bppmw.com; f. 1895; fmrly the *Nyasaland Times*; Mon.–Fri., Sun.; English; publ. by Blantyre Newspapers Ltd (Chayamba Trust); affiliated to the MCP; Editor JAMES MPHANDE; circ. Mon.–Fri. c. 20,000, Sun. c. 40,000 (2006).

The Democratus: Aquarius House, Convention Dr., City Centre, Box 1100, Lilongwe 3; tel. 1770033; internet democratusmalawi.blogspot.com; f. 2004; publ. by Democratus Ltd; Wed. and Sun.; Chair. ZIKHALE NG'OMA.

The Dispatch: The Dispatch Publications Ltd, POB 30353, Capital City, Lilongwe 3; tel. 1751639; fax 9510120; e-mail thedispatchmw@sdnp.org.mw; Thur. and Sun; Publr and Man. Editor MARTINES NAMINGAH; circ. Thur. 5,000, Sun. 7,000.

The Enquirer: POB 1745, Blantyre; tel. 1670022; e-mail pillycolette@yahoo.co.uk; English and Nyanja; affiliated to the UDF; Owner LUCIOUS CHIKUNI.

The Guardian: Captial Hill, Private Bag B341, Lilongwe; tel. 1761996; fax 1761996; internet guardian.ultinets.net; Man. Dir DUWA MUTHARIKA-KAFOTEKA; circ. c. 5,000 (2006).

The Lamp: Montfort Media, POB 280, Balaka, Zomba; tel. 1545267; e-mail montfortmedia@malawi.net; f. 1995; fortnightly; Roman Catholic and ecumenical; Editor Fr GAMBA PIERGIORGIO; circ. 5,500.

Malawi Government Gazette: Government Printer, POB 37, Zomba; tel. 1523155; fax 1522301; f. 1894; weekly.

Malawi News: Scott Rd, Private Bag 39, Blantyre; tel. 1871679; fax 1871233; internet www.malawinews.bppmw.com; f. 1959; weekly; English and Chichewa; publ. by Blantyre Newspapers Ltd (Chayamba Trust); Gen. Man. JIKA NKOLOKOSA; Man. Editor EDWARD CHISAMBO; Editor STEVEN NHLANE, Jr; circ. c. 40,000 (2006).

The Malawi Standard: POB 31781, Blantyre 3; tel. 1674013; e-mail bligomeka@yahoo.co.uk; fortnightly; Editor BRIAN LIGOMEKA.

The Mirror: POB 30721, Blantyre; tel. 1675043; f. 1994; weekly; English and Nyanja; affiliated to the UDF; Owner and Publr BROWN MPINGANJIRA; circ. 10,000.

The Nation: POB 30408, Chichiri, Blantyre 3; tel. 1673611; fax 1674343; e-mail nation@nationmalawi.com; internet www.nationmw.net; f. 1993; daily; publ. by Nation Publs Ltd; weekly edn

MALAWI

of *The Weekend Nation* (circ. 30,000); English and Nyanja; Owner ALEKE BANDA; Editor-in-Chief ALFRED NTONGA; circ. 15,000.

Odini: POB 133, Lilongwe; tel. 1721135; fax 1721141; f. 1949; fortnightly; Chichewa and English; Roman Catholic; Dir P. I. AKOMENJI; circ. 12,000.

UDF News: POB 3052, Blantyre; tel. 1645314; fax 1645725; e-mail echapusa@yahoo.co.uk; organ of the UDF; fortnightly; English and Nyanja.

Weekly Courier: Lilongwe 3; affiliated to the Democratic Progressive Party; Man. Editor DENIS MZEMBE; circ. c. 3,000 (2006).

The Weekly News: Dept of Information, POB 494, Blantyre; tel. 1642600; fax 1642364; f. 1996; English and Nyanja; publ. by the Ministry of Information; Editor-in-Chief GEORGE TUKHUWA.

PERIODICALS

Boma Lathu: POB 494, Blantyre; tel. 1620266; fax 1620039; internet www.maform.com/bomalathu.htm; f. 1973; quarterly; Chichewa; publ. by the Ministry of Information; circ. 100,000.

Business Monthly: POB 906646, Blantyre 9; tel. 16301114; fax 1620039; f. 1995; English; economic, financial and business news; Editor ANTHONY LIVUZA; circ. 10,000.

Fairlane Magazine: POB 1745, Blantyre; tel. 1880205; e-mail fairlane@sndp.org.mw; internet www.fairlane.emalawi.com; f. 2006; 6 a year; lifestyle magazine; English and Chichewa; Man. Dir MARIE FRANCE CHIKUNI; Editor AGNES DUMISANI MIZERE.

Kuunika (The Light): POB 17, Nkhoma, Lilongwe; tel. 1722807; e-mail nkhomasynod@globemw.net; f. 1909; monthly; Chichewa; publ. by the Church of Central Africa (Presbyterian) Nkhoma Synod; Presbyterian; Editor Rev. M. C. NKHALAMBAYAUSI; circ. 6,000.

Malawi Medical Journal: College of Medicine and Medical Asscn of Malawi, Private Bag 360, Blantyre 3; tel. and fax 1878254; e-mail mmj@medcol.mw; internet www.mmj.medcol.mw; f. 1980; replaced *Medical Quarterly*; quarterly; Chair. Prof. ERIC BORGSTEIN; Editor-in-Chief Prof. MALCOLM E. MOLYNEUX.

Moni Magazine: POB 5592, Limbe; tel. 1651833; fax 1651171; f. 1964; monthly; Chichewa and English; Editor PRINCE SHONGA; circ. 40,000.

Moyo Magazine: Health Education Unit, POB 30377, Lilongwe 3; 6 a year; English; publ. by the Ministry of Health; Editor-in-Chief JONATHAN NKHOMA.

Pride: POB 51668, Limbe; tel. 1640569; f. 1999; quarterly; Publr JOHN SAINI.

This is Malawi: POB 494, Blantyre; tel. 1620266; fax 1620807; f. 1964; monthly; English and Chichewa edns; publ. by the Dept of Information; Editor ANTHONY LIVUZA; circ. 12,000.

Together: Montfort Media, POB 280, Balaka, Zomba; tel. 1545267; e-mail together@sdnp.org.mw; f. 1995; quarterly; Roman Catholic and ecumenical, youth; Editor LUIGI GRITTI; circ. 6,000.

Other publications include *Dzukani*, *Inspiration* and *Msilikali*.

NEWS AGENCY

Malawi News Agency (MANA): POB 28, Blantyre; tel. 1622122; fax 1634867; f. 1966.

Publishers

Christian Literature Association in Malawi (CLAIM): POB 503, Blantyre; tel. 1620839; f. 1968; Chichewa and English; general and religious; Gen. Man. J. T. MATENJE.

Likuni Press and Publishing House: POB 133, Lilongwe; tel. 1721388; fax 1721141; f. 1949; English and Chichewa; general and religious.

Macmillan Malawi Ltd: Private Bag 140, Kenyatta Dr., Chitawira, Blantyre; tel. 1676449; fax 1675751; e-mail mayeso@macmillanmw.net; Gen. Man. HASTINGS MATEWERE.

Montfort Press and Popular Publications: POB 5592, Limbe; tel. 1651833; fax 1641126; f. 1961; general and religious; Gen. Man. VALES MACHILA.

GOVERNMENT PUBLISHING HOUSE

Government Press: Government Printer, POB 37, Zomba; tel. 1525515; fax 1525175.

Directory

Broadcasting and Communications

TELECOMMUNICATIONS

Regulatory Authority

Malawi Communications Regulatory Authority (MACRA): Salmon Amour Rd, Private Bag 261, Blantyre; tel. 1883611; fax 1883890; e-mail dg-macra@macra.org.mw; internet www.macra.org.mw; f. 1998; Chair. THENGO MALOYA; Dir-Gen. JAMES CHIMERA.

Service Providers

Malawi Telecommunications Ltd (MTL): Lamya House, Masauko Chipembere Highway, POB 537, Blantyre; tel. 1846977; fax 1846445; e-mail mtlceo@malawi.net; internet www.mtl.mw; f. 2000 following division of Malawi Posts and Telecommunications Corpn into two separate entities; privatized in 2006; 80% owned by Telecom Holdings Ltd, 20% state-owned; CEO PETER ZIMMER.

Telekom Networks Malawi (TNM): Livingstone Towers, Lower Ground Floor, POB 3039, Blantyre; tel. 1830888; fax 1830092; e-mail customercare@tnm.co.mw; internet www.tnm.co.mw; f. 1995; owned by Malawi Telecommunications Ltd; operates mobile cellular telephone network; CEO WERNER SCHRIJVER.

Zain Malawi: Mwai House, City Centre, POB 57, Lilongwe; tel. 1774800; fax 1774802; e-mail helpdesk.mw@zain.com; internet www.mw.zain.com; f. 1999; 80% owned by Mobile Systems Int. Cellular Investments Holding B.V., 10% owned each by Malawi Devt Corpn and Investment and Devt Bank of Malawi Ltd; Man. Dir FAYAZ KING.

BROADCASTING

Radio

Malawi Broadcasting Corpn: POB 30133, Chichiri, Blantyre 3; tel. 1671222; fax 1671257; e-mail dgmbc@malawi.net; internet www.mbcradios.com; f. 1964; statutory body; semi-commercial, partly state-financed; two channels: MBC 1 and Radio 2 (MBC 2); programmes in English, Chichewa, Chitonga, Chitumbuka, Kyangonde, Lomwe, Sena and Yao; Chair. LEONARD NAMWERA; Dir-Gen. OWEN MAUNDE.

Private commercial and religious radio stations include:

African Bible College Radio (Radio ABC): POB 1028, Lilongwe; tel. 1761965; e-mail radioabc@malawi.net; f. 1995; regional Christian religious programming; Asst Station Man. MCLEOD MUNTHALI.

Calvary Family Radio: POB 30239, Blantyre 3; tel. 1671627; fax 1671642; e-mail calvaryministries@hotmail.com; operated by the Calvary Family Church; religious community radio station.

Capital Radio 102.5 FM: 1st Floor, Kapeni House, cnr of Victoria Ave and Chilembwe Rd, Blantyre; Private Bag 437, Chichiri, Blantyre 3; tel. 1820858; fax 1823382; e-mail stationmanager@capitalradiomalawi.com; internet www.capitalradiomalawi.com; f. 1999; commercial radio station; music and entertainment; Man. Dir and Editor-in-Chief ALAUDIN OSMAN.

Channel for All Nations (CAN): POB 1220, Lilongwe; tel. 1761763; fax 1762056; e-mail kawembale@yahoo.com; f. 2004; operated by the Assemblies of God church; regional Christian religious programming.

Dzimwe Community Radio (DCR): POB 425, Chichiri, Blantyre; tel. 1672288; fax 1624330; e-mail mamwa@yahoo.com; f. 1997; operated by the Malawi Media Women's Asscn; focus on rural women's issues; Station Man. JANET KARIM.

Joy FM: Private Bag 17, Limbe, Blantyre; tel. 1638330; fax 1638329; e-mail joyradio@globemalawi.net; commercial radio station; Owner BAKILI MULUZI.

MIJ FM: POB 30165, Chichiri, Blantyre 3; tel. 1675087; fax 1675649; e-mail mij@clcom.net; f. 1996; operated by students of the Malawi Institute of Journalism; community radio station; closed by the Govt during May 2004.

Nkhota Kota Community Radio: Nkhota Kota; f. 2003 with assistance from UNESCO; focus on social and devt issues.

Power 101 FM: POB 761, Blantyre; tel. 1844101; fax 1841387; e-mail fm101@malawi.net; f. 1998; commercial radio station; music and entertainment; Dir and Station Man. OSCAR THOMSON.

Radio Alinafe: Maula Cathedral, POB 631, Lilongwe; tel. 1759971; fax 1752767; e-mail radioalinafe@sdnp.org.mw; f. 2002; Chichewa and English; operated by the Archdiocese of Lilongwe; regional Roman Catholic religious programming; Dir GABRIEL JANA; Editor MOSES KAUFA.

Radio Islam: PO Box 5400, Limbe; tel. 1641408; e-mail zakaat@globemw.net; f. 2001; operated by the Islamic Zakaat Fund; religious programming; Dir MAHMUD SARDAR ISSA.

Radio Maria Malawi: POB 408, Mangochi; tel. 1599626; fax 1599691; e-mail radiomaria@malawi.net; internet www.radiomaria.mw; f. 2003; operated by Asscn of Radio Maria Malawi as

MALAWI

part of the World Family of Radio Maria, Italy; Roman Catholic religious programming; Chichewa, Chiyao and English; Gen. Man. JOSEPH KIMU; Dir of Programmes HENRY SAINDI.

Radio Tigawane: Bishop's House, POB 252, Mzuzu; tel. 1332271; e-mail tigawane@sndp.org.mw; f. 2005; operated by the Diocese of Mzuzu; regional Roman Catholic religious programming; Tumbuka, Chichewa and English; Project Co-ordinator EUGENE NGOMA.

Star FM: Everest House, Lower Sclatter Rd, Blantyre; f. 2006; commercial radio station; Station Man. PATRICK KAMKWATIRA.

Trans World Radio Malawi (TWR): POB 52, Lilongwe; tel. and fax 1751763; e-mail twr@malawi.net; f. 2000; part of Trans World Radio-Africa, South Africa; Christian religious programming; Dir PATRICK SEMPHERE.

Zodiak Broadcasting Station (ZBS): Private Bag 312, Lilongwe 3; f. 2005; operated by Zodiak Broadcasting Services; programmes in Chichewa and English; Man. Dir GOSPEL KAZAKO.

Television

Television Malawi (TVM): Private Bag 268, Blantyre; tel. 1675033; fax 1762627; e-mail tvmalawi@sdnp.org.mw; internet www.tvmalawi.com; f. 1999; broadcasts 55 hours per week, of which 10 hours are produced locally; relays programmes from France, Germany, South Africa and the United Kingdom; Chair. INKOSI YA MAKOSI MBELWA IV; Dir-Gen. KENSON M'BWANA.

Finance

(cap. = capital; res = reserves; dep. = deposits; m. = million; br(s). = branch(es); amounts in kwacha)

BANKING

Central Bank

Reserve Bank of Malawi: Convention Dr., POB 30063, Capital City, Lilongwe 3; tel. 1770600; fax 1772752; e-mail webmaster@rbm.mw; internet www.rbm.mw; f. 1965; bank of issue; cap. 306m., res 348m., dep. 18,675m. (Dec. 2006); Gov. and Chair. VICTOR MBEWE; br. in Blantyre.

Commercial Banks

Finance Bank Malawi Ltd: Finance House, Victoria Ave, POB 421, Blantyre; tel. 1624232; fax 1622957; f. 1995; 93.6% owned by Finance Holdings Corpn Ltd (International), 6.4% owned by Finance Bank Zambia Ltd; cap. and res 439.2m., total assets 4,152m. (Dec. 2003); Chair. Dr RAJAN L. MAHTANI; CEO A. S. PILLAI; 5 brs, 1 agency.

INDEBank Ltd: INDEBank House, Kaohsiong Rd, Top Mandala, POB 358, Blantyre; tel. 1820055; fax 1823353; internet www.indebank.com; f. 1972 as Investment and Devt Bank of Malawi Ltd; total assets 2,162.6m. (Dec. 2003); 41.38% owned by Trans-Africa Holdings Ltd, 30% owned by Press Trust, 25.67% owned by ADMARC Investments Holding, 2.95% owned by Employee Ownership Scheme; commercial and devt banking; provides loans to statutory corpns and to private enterprises in the agricultural, industrial, tourism, transport and commercial sectors; Chair. FRANKLIN KENNEDY; Man. Dir and CEO WILLIAM CHATSALA; 6 brs.

Loita Bank Ltd: c/o Fintech (Malawi) Ltd, Peoples Bldg, 1st Floor, Victoria Ave, Private Bag 264, Blantyre; tel. 1822099; fax 1822683; e-mail lib@mw.loita.com; internet www.loita.com; total assets 3,100.3m. (Dec. 2003); 100% owned by Loita Capital Partners Int.; Chair. and CEO N. JUSTIN CHIMYANTA; 2 brs.

National Bank of Malawi: 19 Victoria Ave, POB 945, Blantyre; tel. 1820622; fax 1820321; e-mail chiefexec@natbankmw.com; internet www.natbank.co.mw; f. 1971; 51.7% owned by Press Corpn Ltd, 24.8% owned by Old Mutual Group; cap. 456m., res 895m., dep. 24,254m. (Dec. 2005); Chair. Dr M. A. P. CHIKAONDA; CEO GEORGE B. PARTRIDGE; 12 brs; 11 agencies.

NBS Bank Ltd: Ginnery Cnr, Chipembere Highway, off Masajico, POB 32251, Chichiri, Blantyre; tel. 1876222; fax 1875041; e-mail nbs@nbsmw.com; internet www.nbsmw.com; f. 2003; 60% owned by NICO, 30% state-owned, 10% owned by the Nat. Investment Trust; fmrly New Building Society; cap. 246.7m., res 574.7m., dep. 10,921m. (Dec. 2007); Chair. FELIX L. MLUSU; CEO JOHN S. BIZIWICK.

Nedbank (Malawi) Ltd: Development House, cnr Henderson St and Victoria Ave, POB 750, Blantyre; tel. 1620477; fax 1620102; e-mail office@mw.nedcor.com; f. 1999; fmrly Fincom Bank of Malawi Ltd; 68.8% owned by Nedbank Africa Investments Ltd, 28.4% owned by SBM Nedcor Holdings Ltd; total assets 1,426.9m. (Dec. 2003); Chair. C. DREW; Man. Dir PAUL TUBB.

Standard Bank Ltd: Kaomba Centre, cnr Glyn Jones Rd and Victoria Ave, POB 1111, Blantyre; tel. 1820144; fax 1820117; e-mail stanbicmw@standardbank.co.mw; internet www.standardbank.co.mw; f. 1970 as Commercial Bank of Malawi; present name adopted June 2003; 60.18% owned by Stanbic Africa Holdings Ltd, 12.50% owned by Nat. Insurance Co; cap. 200m., res 2,322m., dep. 15,605m. (Dec. 2006); Chair. ALEX CHITSIME; Man. Dir CHARLES MUDIWA; 8 brs.

Development Bank

Opportunity International Bank of Malawi Ltd (OIBM): Opportunity Bank Bldg, POB 1794, Lilongwe; tel. 1758403; fax 1758400; e-mail lilongwe@oibm.mw; internet www.oibm.mw; f. 2003; 63.7% owned by Opportunity Transformation Investments, USA, 25.3% owned by Opportunity Micro Investments (UK) Ltd, United Kingdom, 11% owned by Trust for Transformation; total assets 967.4m. (Dec. 2005); Chair. FRANCIS PELEKAMOYO; CEO RODGER VOORHIES.

Discount Houses

Continental Discount House: Unit House, 5th Floor, Victoria Ave, POB 1444, Blantyre; tel. 1821300; fax 1822826; e-mail info@cdh-malawi.com; internet www.cdh-malawi.com; f. 1998; 84% owned by Trans-Africa Holdings; total assets 6,728.8m. (Dec. 2005); Chair. ROBERT SEKOH ABBEY; Man. Dir and CEO MISHECK ESAU.

First Discount House Ltd: Umoyo House, Upper Ground Floor, 8 Victoria Ave North, POB 512, Blantyre; tel. 1820219; fax 1523044; e-mail fdh@fdh.co.mw; internet www.fdh.co.mw; f. 2000; 40.16% owned by Kingdom Financial Holdings Ltd, 39.84% owned by Thomson F. Mpinganjira Trust, 20% owned by Old Mutual Life Assurance Co (Malawi) Ltd; total assets 5,960.7m. (Dec. 2004); Man. Dir EDWARD CHILIMA; Chair. NIGEL CHAKANIRA.

Merchant Banks

First Merchant Bank Ltd: Livingstone Towers, Glyn Jones Rd, Private Bag 122, Blantyre; tel. 1821955; fax 1821978; e-mail fmb.headoffice@fmbmalawi.com; internet www.fmbmalawi.com; f. 1994; cap. 111.3m., res 1,416.7m., dep. 8,148m. (Dec. 2006); 44.9% owned by Zambezi Investments Ltd, 22.5% owned by Simsbury Holdings Ltd, 11.2% owned each by Prime Capital and Credit Ltd, Kenya, and Prime Bank Ltd, Kenya; Chair. RASIKBHAI C. KANTARIA; Man. Dir KASHINATH N. CHATURVEDI; 7 brs.

Leasing and Finance Co of Malawi Ltd: Livingstone Towers, Glyn Jones Rd, POB 1963, Blantyre; tel. 1820233; fax 1820275; f. 1986; subsidiary of First Merchant Bank Ltd since June 2002; total assets 2,087.4m. (Dec. 2006); Chair. HITESH ANADKAT; Gen. Man. MBACHAZWA LUNGU.

Savings Bank

Malawi Savings Bank: Umoyo House, Victoria Ave, POB 521, Blantyre; tel. 1625111; fax 1621929; internet www.msb.mw; f. 1994; 99.9% state-owned; total assets 1,191.7m. (Dec. 2003); Sec.-Treas. P. E. CHILAMBE; Gen. Man. IAN C. BONONGWE.

STOCK EXCHANGE

Malawi Stock Exchange: Old Reserve Bank Bldg, 17 Victoria Ave, Private Bag 270, Blantyre; tel. 1824233; fax 1823636; e-mail mse@mse-mw.com; internet www.mse.co.mw; f. 1996; Chair. KRISHNA SAVJANI; CEO SYMON W. MSEFULA; 11 cos listed in 2007.

INSURANCE

In 2005 the insurance sector comprised 10 local companies and one foreign company; there was also one reinsurance company. Of these, eight companies dealt in non-life insurance.

NICO Holdings Ltd: NICO House, 3 Stewart St, POB 501, Blantyre; tel. 1822699; fax 1822364; e-mail info@nicomw.com; internet www.nicomw.com; f. 1970; fmrly National Insurance Co Ltd; transferred to private sector in 1996; incorporates NICO Gen. Insurance Co Ltd, NICO Life Insurance Co Ltd and NICO Technologies Ltd; cap. and res 104.7m. (Sept. 1997); offices at Blantyre, Lilongwe, Mzuzu and Zomba; agencies country-wide; CEO and Man. Dir FELIX L. MLUSU.

Old Mutual Malawi: 30 Glyn Jones Rd, Old Mutual Building, POB 393, Blantyre; tel. 1820677; fax 1822649; e-mail info@oldmutual.co.mw; internet www.oldmutualmalawi.com; f. 1845; subsidiary of Old Mutual PLC, United Kingdom; Chair. MIKE LEVETT; Man. Dir JEAN DU PLESSIS.

REAL Insurance Co of Malawi Ltd: Hannover House, Independence Dr., POB 442, Blantyre; tel. 1824044; fax 1823862; e-mail blantyre@realinsurance.co.mw; internet www.realinsurance.co.mw; associate of Royal and SunAlliance PLC, United Kingdom; Man. Dir ROBERT G. NDUNGU; Gen. Man. DAMIANO K. PHIRI.

United General Insurance Co Ltd (UGI): Michiru House, Victoria Ave, POB 383, Blantyre; tel. 1621770; fax 1621980; e-mail ugiugimalawi.com; internet www.ugimalawi.com; f. 1986 as Pearl Assurance Co Ltd; latterly Property and Gen. Insurance Co Ltd;

present name adopted following merger with Fide Insurance Co Ltd in July 1998; 74% owned by ZimRE Holdings, Zimbabwe; Chair. ALBERT NDUNA; Man. Dir IAN K. KUMWENDA.

Vanguard Life Assurance Co (Pvt) Ltd: Centre House Arcade, Private Bag B389, Lilongwe; tel. 1775946; fax 1775960; e-mail vanguard@malawi.net; f. 1999; 90% owned by Fidelity Life Assurance Ltd, Zimbabwe; Man. Dir THEMBA MPALA.

Trade and Industry

GOVERNMENT AGENCIES

Agricultural Development and Marketing Corpn (ADMARC): POB 5052, Limbe; tel. 1840044; fax 1840486; e-mail admce@admarc.co.mw; internet www.admarc.co.mw; f. 1971; involved in cultivation, processing, marketing and export of grain and other crops; Chair. Prof. KANYAMA PHIRI; CEO Dr CHARLES J. MATABWA.

Malawi Export Promotion Council (MEPC): Kanabar House, 2nd Floor, Victoria Ave, POB 1299, Blantyre; tel. 1820499; fax 1820995; e-mail mepco@malawi.net; internet www.malawiepc.com; f. 1971; promotes and facilitates export and investment, and provides technical assistance and training to exporters; Gen. Man. LAWRENCE M. CHALULUKA.

Malawi Investment Promotion Agency (MIPA): Aquarius House, Private Bag 302, Lilongwe 3; tel. 1770800; fax 1771781; e-mail mipa@mipamw.org; internet www.malawi-invest.net; f. 1993; promotes and facilitates local and foreign investment; CEO JAMES R. KAPHWELEZA BANDA.

Petroleum Control Commission: POB 2827, Blantyre; e-mail sichioko@pccmalawi.com; state-owned; held monopoly on fuel imports until 2000; also serves regulatory role; Chair. Rev. Dr LAZARUS CHAKWERA; Gen. Man. ISHMAEL CHIOKO.

Privatisation Commission of Malawi: Livingstone Towers, 2nd Floor, Glyn Jones Rd, POB 937, Blantyre; tel. 1823655; fax 1821248; e-mail info@pcmalawi.org; internet www.pcmalawi.org; f. 1996; has sole authority to oversee divestiture of govt interests in public enterprises; Chair. EDWARD SAWERENGERA; CEO JIMMY LIPUNGA; 75 privatizations completed by January 2008.

Tobacco Control Commission: POB 40045, Kanengo, Lilongwe 4; tel. 1712777; fax 1712632; e-mail tcclib@tcc.mw.com; internet www.tccmw.com; f. 1993; regulates tobacco production and marketing; Chair. Dr ANDREW MZUMACHARO IV; Gen. Man. Dr GODFREY M. CHAPOLA; brs in Mzuzu and Limbe.

DEVELOPMENT ORGANIZATIONS

Council for Non-Governmental Organizations in Malawi (CONGOMA): Chitawira, Waya Bldg, POB 480, Blantyre; tel. 1676459; fax 1677908; internet www.congoma.org; f. 1992; promotes social and economic devt; Chair. TADEYO SHABA; Exec. Dir EMMANUEL TED NANDOLO; 86 mem. orgs (2004).

Small Enterprise Development Organization of Malawi (SEDOM): POB 525, Blantyre; tel. 1622555; fax 1622781; e-mail sedom@sdnp.org.mw; f. 1982; financial services and accommodation for indigenous small- and medium-scale businesses; Chair. STELLA NDAU.

CHAMBER OF COMMERCE

Malawi Confederation of Chambers of Commerce and Industry (MCCCI): Masauko Chipembere Highway, Chichiri Trade Fair Grounds, POB 258, Blantyre; tel. 1871988; fax 1871147; e-mail mccci@mccci.org; internet www.mccci.org; f. 1892; promotes trade and encourages competition in the economy; Chair. H. B. KALUA; CEO CHANCELLOR L. KAFERAPANJIRA; 400 mems.

INDUSTRIAL AND TRADE ASSOCIATIONS

Dwangwa Cane Growers Trust (DCGT): POB 156, Dwangwa; tel. 1295111; fax 1295164; e-mail dcgt@malawi.net; f. 1999; fmrly Smallholder Sugar Authority; CEO WILFRED CHAKANIKA.

National Hawkers and Informal Business Association (NAHIBA): Chichiri Trade Fair, POB 60544, Ndirande, Blantyre; tel. 1945315; fax 1624558; e-mail nazulug@yahoo.com; f. 1995; Exec. Dir EVA JOACHIM.

Smallholder Coffee Farmers Trust: POB 20133, Luwinga, Mzuzu 2; tel. 1332899; fax 1333902; e-mail mzuzucoffee@malawi.net; f. 1971; successor to the Smallholder Coffee Authority, disbanded in 1999; producers and exporters of arabica coffee; Gen. Man. HARRISON KALUA; 4,000 mems.

Smallholder Tea Co (STECO): POB 135, Mulanje; f. 2002 by the merger of the Smallholder Tea Authority and Malawi Tea Factory Co Ltd.

Tea Association of Malawi Ltd (TAML): Kidney Crescent Rd, POB 930, Blantyre; tel. 1671182; fax 1671427; e-mail taml@malawi.net; internet www.taml.co.mw; f. 1934; CEO CLEMENT C. THINDWA; 10 mems.

Tobacco Association of Malawi (TAMA): 13/64 Independence Dr., TAMA House, POB 31360, Lilongwe 3; tel. 1773099; fax 1773493; e-mail tama@tamalawi.com; internet www.tamalawi.com; f. 1929; Pres. RUEBEN JEFRED MAIGWA; Chief Exec. FELIX MKUMBA; brs in Mzuzu, Limbe and Chinkhoma; 75,000 mems.

Tobacco Exporters' Association of Malawi Ltd (TEAM): Private Bag 403, Kanengo, Lilongwe 4; tel. 1775839; fax 1774069; f. 1930; Chair. CHARLES A. M. GRAHAM; Gen. Man. H. M. MBALE; 9 mems.

EMPLOYERS' ORGANIZATIONS

Employers' Consultative Association of Malawi (ECAM): POB 2134, Blantyre; tel. and fax 1830151; e-mail ecam@malawi.net; internet www.ecam.co.mw; f. 1963; Pres. DAPTHER NAMANDWA; Exec. Dir BUXTON KAYUNI; 250 mem. asscns and six affiliates representing 80,000 employees.

Master Printers' Association of Malawi: POB 2460, Blantyre; tel. 1632948; fax 1632220; f. 1963; Chair. PAUL FREDERICK; 21 mems.

Motor Traders' Association: POB 311, Blantyre; tel. and fax 1624754; f. 1954; Chair. A. R. OSMAN; 24 mems (2003).

UTILITY

Electricity

Electricity Supply Corpn of Malawi (ESCOM): ESCOM House, Haile Selassie Rd, POB 2047, Blantyre; tel. and fax 1822000; fax 1822008; e-mail info@escommw.com; internet www.escommw.com; f. 1966; controls electricity generation and distribution; Chair. Prof. DONTON DONTON; CEO PETERSON ZEMBANI.

TRADE UNIONS

According to the Malawi Congress of Trade Unions, in 2005 some 18% of the workforce was unionized.

Congress of Malawi Trade Unions (COMATU): POB 1443, Lilongwe; tel. 1757255; fax 1770885; Pres. THOMAS L. BANDA; Gen. Sec. PHILLMON E. CHIMBALU.

Malawi Congress of Trade Unions (MCTU): POB 1271, Lilongwe; tel. 1752162; fax 1820716; e-mail mctusecretariat@mctumw.com; f. 1995 as successor to the Trade Union Congress of Malawi (f. 1964); affiliated to the Int. Trade Union Confed.; Pres. LUTHER MAMBALA; Sec.-Gen. ROBERT JAMES D. MKWEZALAMBA; 113,000 paid-up mems (2008).

Affiliated unions incl.:

Building Construction, Civil Engineering and Allied Workers' Union (BCCEAWU): c/o MCTU, POB 5094, Limbe; tel. 1620381; fax 1622304; e-mail johnmwafulirwa@yahoo.com; f. 1961; Pres. LAWRENCE KAFERE; Gen. Sec. JOHN O. MWAFULIRWA; 6,401 mems (2006).

Commercial Industrial and Allied Workers' Union (CIAWU): c/o MCTU, POB 5094, Limbe; tel. 1820716; fax 1622303; e-mail mareydzinyemba@yahoo.com; affiliated to the Int. Textile, Garment and Leather Workers' Fed. and Union Network Int.; Pres. TRYSON KALANDA; Gen. Sec. MARY DZINYEMBA; 3,075 mems (2006).

Communications Workers' Union of Malawi: Armarsi Odvarji Plaza, 1st Floor, Chipembere Highway, Private Bag 186, Blantyre; tel. 1820716; fax 1830830; e-mail cowuma@yahoo.co.uk; f. 1997; Pres. BATWELL KULEMERO; Gen. Sec. ROBERT JAMES DANIEL MKWEZALAMBA; 2,854 mems (2006).

Electronic Media Workers' Union: POB 30133, Chichiri, Blantyre 3; tel. 1871343; e-mail mmsowoya@hotmail.com; Pres. LASTEN KUNKEYANI; Gen. Sec. MALANI MSOWOYA; 243 mems (2006).

ESCOM Staff Union: POB 2047, Blantyre; tel. 1773447; Pres. OSCAR CHIMWEZI; affiliated to the Int. Fed. of Chemical, Energy, Mine and General Workers' Unions; Gen. Sec. RACHEL CHASWEKA; 1,899 mems (2006).

Hotels, Food and Catering Service Union: c/o MCTU 5094, Limbe; tel. 1820314; e-mail hfpcwu@sdnp.org.mw; affiliated to the Int. Union of Food, Agricultural, Hotel, Restaurant, Catering, Tobacco and Allied Workers' Asscns; Pres. AUSTIN KALIMANJIRA; Gen. Sec. DOROTHEA MAKHASU; 3,565 mems (2006).

Malawi Housing Co-operation Workers' Union: c/o MHC, POB 84, Mzuzu; tel. 1332655; Pres. GREY SADIKI; Gen. Sec. ROOSEVELT MSISKA; 236 mems (2006).

Plantation and Agriculture Workers' Union: POB 181, Lucheza; Pres. PATRICK KADYANJI; Gen. Sec. DENNIS BANDA; 2,086 mems (2006).

Private Schools Employees' Union of Malawi (PSEUM): c/o MCTU, Kepell Compton Cres., Area 3/089, POB 1271, Lilongwe; tel. 1755614; fax 1752162; e-mail hendrixbanda@yahoo.com; Pres. SAMUEL NJIWA; Gen. Sec. HENDRIX S. BANDA; 2,670 mems (2008).

Railway Workers' Union of Malawi (Central East African Railway Workers' Union—CEARWU): POB 5393, Limbe; tel. 1640844; e-mail cear@cearcdn.mw; f. 1954; affiliated to the Int. Transport Workers' Fed.; Pres. DINA M'MERA; Gen. Sec. LUTHER MAMBALA; 485 mems (2006).

Sugar Plantation and Allied Workers' Union (SPAWUM): c/o Illovo Sugar (Malawi) Ltd, Private Bag 50, Blantyre; tel. 1425200; e-mail spawum@illovo.co.za; Pres. KEEPER GUMBO; Gen. Sec. STEPHEN MKWAPATIRA; 8,598 mems (2006).

Teachers' Union of Malawi: Aphunzitsi Centre, Private Bag 11, Lilongwe; tel. 1727302; fax 1727302; e-mail tum@sdnp.org.mw; Pres. CHAULUKA MUWAKE; Gen. Sec. DENIS KALEKENI; 46,207 mems (2006).

Textile, Garment, Leather and Security Services Workers' Union: POB 5094, Limbe; tel. 8345576; e-mail textilegarmentunion@yahoo.com; f. 1995; affiliated to the Int. Textile, Garment and Leather Workers' Fed. and Malawi Congress of Trade Unions; Gen. Sec. GRACE NYIRENDA; 8,900 mems (2009).

Tobacco Tenants Workers' Union: POB 477, Nkhotakota; tel. 1292288; e-mail totawum@malawi.net; affiliated to the Int. Union of Food, Agricultural, Hotel, Restaurant, Catering, Tobacco and Allied Workers' Asscns; Pres. LUTHER MAMBALA; Gen. Sec. RAPHAEL SANDRAM; 5,579 mems (2006).

Transport and General Workers' Union: POB 2778, Blantyre; tel. 8877795; fax 1830219; e-mail ronaldmbewe2002@yahoo.com; f. 1945; affiliated to the Int. Transport Workers' Fed.; Pres. FRANCIS ANTONIO; Gen. Sec. RONALD MBEWE; 3,257 mems (2006).

Water Employees' Trade Union of Malawi (WETUM): c/o Lilongwe Water Board, Madzi House, off Likuni Rd, POB 96, Lilongwe; tel. 1750366; fax 1752294; affiliated to the Public Services Int.; Pres. ANTHONY A. CHIMPHEPO; Gen. Sec. OLIVIA KUNJE; 1,195 mems (2006).

Transport

RAILWAYS

The Central East African Railways Co (fmrly Malawi Railways) operates between Nsanje (near the southern border with Mozambique) and Mchinji (near the border with Zambia) via Blantyre, Salima and Lilongwe, and between Nkaya and Nayuchi on the eastern border with Mozambique, covering a total of 797 km. The Central East African Railways Co and Mozambique State Railways connect Malawi with the Mozambican ports of Beira and Nacala. These links, which traditionally form Malawi's principal trade routes, were effectively closed during 1983–85, owing to insurgent activity in Mozambique. The rail link to Nacala was reopened in October 1989; however, continued unrest and flooding in Mozambique prevented full use of the route until the completion of a programme of improvements in September 2000; the service was temporarily suspended in 2002 while safety was improved. There is a rail/lake interchange station at Chipoka on Lake Malawi, from where vessels operate services to other lake ports in Malawi.

Central East African Railways Co Ltd (CEAR): Station Rd, POB 5144, Limbe; tel. 1640844; fax 1643496; f. 1994 as Malawi Railways Ltd; sold to a consortium owned by Mozambique's Empresa Nacional dos Portos e Caminhos de Ferro de Moçambique and the USA's Railroad Corpn in mid-1999 and subsequently renamed as above; ceased passenger services in Oct. 2005; Dir RUSSELL NEELY.

ROADS

In 2004 Malawi had a total road network of some 15,500 km, of which 3,600 km was paved. In addition, unclassified community roads total an estimated 10,000 km. All main roads, and most secondary roads, are all-weather roads. Major routes link Lilongwe and Blantyre with Harare (Zimbabwe), Lusaka (Zambia) and Mbeya and Dar es Salaam (Tanzania). A 480-km highway along the western shore of Lake Malawi links the remote Northern Region with the Central and Southern Regions. A project to create a new trade route, or 'Northern Corridor', through Tanzania, involving road construction and improvements in Malawi, was completed in 1992.

Department of Road Traffic: c/o Ministry of Transport and Public Works, Private Bag 257, Capital City, Lilongwe 3; tel. 1756138; fax 1752592; comprises the Nat. Roads Authority.

National Roads Authority: Functional Bldg, off Chilambula Rd, Private Bag B346, Lilongwe 3; tel. 1753699; fax 1750307; e-mail nra@nramw.com; internet www.nra.malawi.net; f. 1997; CEO DAUPHIN MAKAKO.

Road Transport Operators' Association: Chitawira Light Industrial Site, POB 30740, Chichiri, Blantyre 3; tel. 1870422; fax 1871423; e-mail rtoa@sdnp.org.mw; f. 1956; Chair. P. CHAKHUMBIRA; Exec. Dir SHADRECK MATSIMBE; 200 mems (2004).

United Bus Co: POB 176, Blantyre; tel. 888863912; fax 1870038; e-mail ubc@ubcmw.com; internet www.ubcmw.com; f. 2008 by fmr employees of Shire Bus Lines Ltd following its liquidation in 2006; operates local and long-distance bus services between Makata, Blantyre, Malangalanga, Mzimba and Mzuzu and rural areas; services to Harare (Zimbabwe) and Johannesburg (South Africa); Chair. Al-haj Sheik ALIDI LIKONDE.

SHIPPING

There are 23 ports and landing points on Lake Malawi. The four main ports are at Chilumba, Nkhata Bay, Chipoka and Monkey Bay. Ferry services carry around 60,000 passengers annually; the principal cargoes transported are sugar, fertilizer, dried fish and maize. The amount of cargo transported was expected to increase from August 2005 with the inclusion of a new landing point at Ngala, near Dwangwa, to carry sugar to Chipoka. Smaller vessels are registered for other activities including fishing and tourism. Lake Malawi is at the centre of the Mtwara Development Corridor transport initiative agreed between Zambia, Malawi, Tanzania and Mozambique in mid-December 2004.

Department of Marine Services: c/o Department of Transport and Public Works, Private Bag A-81, Lilongwe; tel. 1751531; fax 1756290; e-mail marinedepartment@malawi.net; responsible for vessel safety and control, ports services, and maritime pollution control.

Malawi Lake Services Ltd (MLS): POB 15, Monkey Bay; tel. and fax 1587221; fax 1587309; e-mail ilala@malawi.net; f. 1994; state-owned; operates passenger and freight services to Mozambique, and freight services to Tanzania; Gen. Man. OWEN SINGINI; 9 vessels, incl. 3 passenger and 4 cargo vessels.

CIVIL AVIATION

Kamuzu (formerly Lilongwe) International Airport was opened in 1982. There are also international airports at Chileka, and at Mzuzu and Karonga in the Northern region. There is one domestic airport, Club Makokola, at Mangochi.

Department of Civil Aviation: c/o Ministry of Transport and Public Works, Private Bag B311, Lilongwe 3; tel. 1770577; fax 1774986; e-mail aviationhq@malawi.net; Dir L. Z. PHESELE.

Air Malawi Ltd: 4 Robins Rd, POB 84, Blantyre; tel. 1820811; fax 1820042; e-mail enquiries@airmalawi.com; internet www.airmalawi.com; f. 1967; privatization, begun in 1999, was postponed in 2003; scheduled domestic and regional services; owns five subsidiary cos incl. Air Cargo Ltd and Lilongwe Handling Co Ltd; Chair. JIMMY KOREIA-MPATSA; CEO Capt. A. B. W. MCHUNGULA.

Tourism

Fine scenery, beaches on Lake Malawi, big game and an excellent climate form the basis of the country's tourist potential. According to official figures, the number of foreign visitor arrivals was 437,718 in 2005. Receipts from tourism totalled US $43m. in 2006.

Department of Tourism: POB 402, Blantyre; tel. 1620300; fax 1620947; f. 1969; responsible for tourism policy; inspects and licenses tourist facilities, sponsors training of hotel staff and publishes tourist literature; Dir of Tourism Services ISAAC K. MSISKA.

Malawi Tourism Association (MTA): POB 1044, Lilongwe; tel. 1770010; fax 1770131; e-mail mta@malawi.net; internet www.malawi-tourism-association.org.mw; f. 1998; Exec. Dir SAM BOTOMANI.

MALAYSIA

Introductory Survey

Location, Climate, Language, Religion, Flag, Capital

The Federation of Malaysia, situated in South-East Asia, consists of 13 states. Eleven of these are in Peninsular Malaysia, in the southern part of the Kra peninsula (with Thailand to the north and the island of Singapore to the south), and two, Sabah and Sarawak, are on the north coast of the island of Borneo, two-thirds of which comprises the Indonesian territory of Kalimantan. Sarawak also borders Brunei, a coastal enclave in the north-east of the state. The climate is tropical, there is rain in all seasons and temperatures are generally between 22°C (72°F) and 33°C (92°F), with little variation throughout the year. The official language is Bahasa Malaysia, based on Malay, but English is also widely used. Chinese, Tamil and Iban are spoken by minorities. Islam is the established religion, practised by about 53% of the population (including virtually all Malays), while about 19%, including most of the Chinese community, follow Buddhism. The Indians are predominantly Hindus. There is a minority of Christians among all races, and traditional beliefs are practised, particularly in Sabah and Sarawak. Malaysia's national flag (proportions 1 by 2) has 14 horizontal stripes, alternating red and white, with a blue rectangular canton, containing a yellow crescent and a 14-pointed yellow star, in the upper hoist. The capital is Kuala Lumpur. A new administrative capital, Putrajaya, has been developed south of Kuala Lumpur.

Recent History

The 11 states of Malaya, under British protection, were united as the Malayan Union in April 1946 and became the Federation of Malaya in February 1948. An armed communist offensive began in 1948, and was not effectively suppressed until the mid-1950s. After 1960 the remainder of the banned Communist Party of Malaya (CPM) took refuge in southern Thailand. Meanwhile, Malaya was granted independence, within the Commonwealth, on 31 August 1957.

Malaysia was established on 16 September 1963, through the union of the independent Federation of Malaya (renamed the States of Malaya), the internally self-governing state of Singapore, and the former British colonies of Sarawak and Sabah (North Borneo). Singapore left the federation in August 1965, reducing the number of Malaysia's component states from 14 to 13. The States of Malaya were designated West Malaysia in 1966 and later styled Peninsular Malaysia.

In 1970 serious inter-communal rioting, engendered by Malay resentment of the Chinese community's economic dominance and of certain pro-Chinese electoral results, precipitated the resignation of Tunku Abdul Rahman, who had been Prime Minister of Malaya (and subsequently of Malaysia) since independence. The new Prime Minister, Tun Abdul Razak, widened the government coalition, dominated by the United Malays National Organization (UMNO), to create a national front, Barisan Nasional (BN). The BN originally comprised 10 parties, absorbing most of the former opposition parties. In January 1976 the Prime Minister died and was succeeded by the Deputy Prime Minister, Dato' Hussein bin Onn.

Political stability was subsequently threatened by the resurgence of the communist guerrilla movement, which conducted a series of terrorist attacks in Peninsular Malaysia during 1976–78. However, CPM activity subsequently declined, owing to co-operation between Malaysia and Thailand in military operations along their common border. In 1987, in a Thai-sponsored amnesty, about 700 Malaysian communists surrendered to the Thai authorities. In December 1989, following a year of negotiations with the Thai Government, the remaining 1,188 rebels (including recruits from Thailand and Singapore) agreed to terminate all armed activities. The peace agreements, signed by the leader of the CPM and representatives of the Malaysian and Thai Governments, made provision for the resettlement of the insurgents in either Malaysia or Thailand and their eventual participation in legitimate political activity in Malaysia.

In October 1977 the expulsion of the Chief Minister (Menteri Besar) of Kelantan from the dominant Parti Islam se Malaysia (PAS—Islamic Party of Malaysia) resulted in violent political disturbances in Kelantan and the declaration of a state of emergency by the federal Government. Direct rule was imposed in Kelantan, and the PAS was expelled from the BN coalition in December. In the federal and state elections of July 1978 Hussein consolidated the position of the BN, while the PAS, in opposition, suffered a serious reversal. In 1978, following the federal Government's rejection of proposals for a Chinese university, racial and religious tensions re-emerged.

In July 1981 Hussein was succeeded as Prime Minister by Dato' Seri Dr Mahathir Mohamad, Deputy Prime Minister since 1976. Mahathir called a general election in April 1982; the BN coalition won convincingly in all states and increased its overall strength in the House of Representatives.

A new political party, the Parti Bersatu Sabah (PBS—Sabah United Party), won control of the Sabah State Legislative Assembly at an election in April 1985. The legality of the new PBS Government was challenged by Muslim opponents, and in February 1986 the Chief Minister (Ketua Menteri) called a further election. In the May election the PBS won an increased majority of seats in the Assembly, and in June the BN agreed to admit the PBS into its ruling coalition, together with the United Sabah National Organization (USNO), which had been expelled in 1984.

In February 1986 Mahathir's leadership of the federal Government and of UMNO was challenged when Datuk Musa Hitam, the Deputy Prime Minister, resigned from the Government, owing to 'irreconcilable differences' with Mahathir. However, Musa retained his position as Deputy President of UMNO. During the following months Musa's supporters became increasingly critical of Mahathir. At an early general election in August, the BN coalition took 148 of the 177 seats in an enlarged House of Representatives: UMNO secured 83 seats, while the Malaysian Chinese Association (MCA) won 17. Of the opposition parties, the Democratic Action Party (DAP) won 24 seats, having gained support from ethnic Chinese voters who were disillusioned with the MCA. In state elections held simultaneously, the BN retained control of all the State Legislative Assemblies in Peninsular Malaysia. Several ministers who had supported Musa were subsequently demoted or removed from the Government.

In early 1987 there was a serious challenge for the presidency of UMNO from Tengku Razaleigh Hamzah, the Minister of Trade and Industry. At the UMNO General Assembly in April, none the less, Mahathir was elected UMNO President for the third time (and thus retained the position of Prime Minister at the head of the BN coalition), albeit with a greatly reduced majority. The General Assembly also narrowly elected Abdul Ghafar Baba (who had replaced Musa as Deputy Prime Minister in February 1986) as UMNO Deputy President. Mahathir subsequently announced the resignation of Razaleigh.

Criticism of Mahathir's leadership persisted during 1987, both from within UMNO and from other political parties. At the same time, racial tensions intensified in various parts of the country over Chinese-language education, religion and other issues. In October–November, allegedly to prevent violent racially-motivated riots between Chinese and Malays over politically sensitive issues, 106 people were detained under the provisions of the Internal Security Act (ISA), which allows detention without trial on grounds of national security. Those detained included politicians from all parties (most notably the leader of the DAP, Lim Kit Siang), lawyers, journalists and leaders of pressure groups. Three newspapers were closed by the Government, and political rallies were prohibited. In November the Government introduced legislation to impose stringent penalties on editors and publishers disseminating what the Government regarded as 'false' news. From December the Minister of Information was empowered to monitor all radio and television broadcasts, and to revoke the licence of any private broadcasting company not conforming with 'Malaysian values'. By April 1989 all the detainees under the ISA had been released (although often under restrictive conditions).

In February 1988 the High Court gave a ruling on a suit filed by dissatisfied members of UMNO, who claimed that, since some of the delegations taking part in the UMNO elections of April 1987 had not been legally registered, the elections should be declared null and void. On account of the irregularities, the Court ruled that UMNO was an 'unlawful society' and that there had been 'no election at all'. Mahathir maintained that the ruling did not affect the legal status of the Government, and the Head of State, Tunku Mahmood Iskandar, expressed support for Mahathir. Later in February 1988 Mahathir announced that UMNO Baru (New UMNO) had been formed and that members of the original party would have to re-register in order to join. In March it was stated that Razaleigh and his supporters were to be excluded from the new party. The assets of UMNO Baru (hereafter referred to as UMNO) were 'frozen' and placed under judicial control until the party's legal status had been resolved; they were finally returned in September 1994.

Tension between the executive and the judiciary was intensified by Parliament's approval in March 1988 of constitutional amendments limiting the power of the judiciary to interpret laws. The Lord President of the Supreme Court, Tun Mohammed Salleh bin Abas, wrote to the Head of State to complain about government attempts to reduce the independence of the judiciary, and was subsequently dismissed from office. In June 1989 the Government introduced a security law removing the right of persons being detained under provisions of the ISA to have recourse to the courts.

In September 1988 Razaleigh and 12 others followed two earlier dissidents and left the BN to join the opposition in the House of Representatives as independents. They were joined in October by Musa. In December Musa and his supporters drafted a six-point resolution (the Johore Declaration), specifying the terms under which they would consent to join UMNO. These terms were accepted by UMNO in January 1989 but were binding only in the state of Johor. Following the defeat at a by-election in that month of an opposition representative by an MCA candidate with UMNO support, Musa announced his membership of UMNO, prompting a further eight dissident representatives in Johor to join the party.

In March 1989 Razaleigh's movement established an alliance with the fundamentalist PAS. In May Razaleigh's party registered as Semangat '46 (Spirit of 1946, a reference to the year of foundation of the original UMNO). The DAP, whose followers were largely urban Chinese, agreed to co-operate with Semangat '46 and the PAS, but refused to join a formal alliance, owing to their opposition to the PAS's proclaimed policy of forming an Islamic state in Malaysia. In June a former breakaway faction from the PAS, Barisan Jama'ah Islamiah Sa-Malaysia, left the BN coalition to join Semangat '46, the PAS and the Parti Hisbul Muslimin Malaysia in an opposition coalition, Angkatan Perpaduan Ummah (APU—Muslim Unity Movement). APU subsequently won a by-election in Trengganu. In December Mahathir held a cordial but unproductive meeting with Razaleigh, in an attempt to heal the rift in the ethnic Malay community.

A general election took place in October 1990. The opposition parties formed an informal electoral alliance, Gagasan Rakyat (People's Might). (Gagasan Rakyat was formally registered in April 1992, and Razaleigh was elected as Chairman in July.) Prior to the election the PBS withdrew from the BN and aligned itself with the opposition. None the less, the BN controlled 127 of the 180 seats in the enlarged House of Representatives, thus retaining the two-thirds' majority necessary to amend the Constitution. Elections to 11 of the 13 State Legislative Assemblies (excluding Sabah and Sarawak) took place simultaneously. The BN obtained a majority of seats in every state except Kelantan, where APU won every seat in both the federal and state elections.

In November 1990, at a meeting of the UMNO General Assembly, Mahathir and Abdul Ghafar Baba were unanimously re-elected as President and Deputy President of the party. In February 1991 Mahathir appointed Anwar as Minister of Finance and Abdullah Badawi as Minister of Foreign Affairs.

In January 1991 the Chief Minister of Sabah and President of the PBS, Datuk Seri Joseph Pairin Kitingan, was arrested and charged with corruption. It was widely conjectured that his arrest and his press adviser's detention, under the ISA, were politically motivated. In May UMNO secured its first seat in Sabah, in a by-election necessitated by the defection to UMNO of USNO's founder and President, Tun Mustapha Harun. Shortly afterwards Jeffrey Kitingan (the brother of the Chief Minister) was detained under the ISA, accused of plotting Sabah's secession from Malaysia.

In 1992 Mahatir began drafting amendments to the constitution that reduced the nine hereditary rulers' privileges, an action which was widely suspected to be due, in part, to the Sultan of Kelantan's open support for Razaleigh (a prince of Kelantan) in the 1990 general election. By the end of the year, after initial resistance, the Sultans had agreed to the amendments with some slight modifications, and they were adopted in March 1993. The changes included ending the Sultans' legal immunity, curtailing their power to pardon the offences of family members, and allowing parliamentary criticism of their misdeeds.

In August 1993 Anwar announced his decision to contest the post of UMNO Deputy President in the party's divisional elections, which Mahathir had postponed until November. The post was particularly significant as the Deputy President of UMNO was traditionally also accorded the position of Deputy Prime Minister. In October Mahathir was returned unopposed as President of UMNO. By November Anwar, representing the *Malayu baru* (new Malays—younger, urban, mainly professional Malays who had prospered as a result of economic expansion), had secured overwhelming support for his candidacy, prompting the more traditional Ghafar to withdraw from the contest and also resign from UMNO. Anwar was duly elected Deputy President of UMNO, and all three vice-presidential posts were won by his self-styled 'Vision Team', which comprised Tan Sri Haji Muhyiddin Yassim (the Chief Minister of Johor), Dato' Seri Najib Razak (the Minister of Defence) and Tan Sri Dato' Mohammad Haji Mohammad Taib (the Chief Minister of Selangor). Anwar was appointed Deputy Prime Minister in December.

In April 1993 USNO, now led by Tun Mustapha Amirkahar (the son of Tun Mustapha Harun), left the opposition in the Sabah State Legislative Assembly to form a coalition with the ruling PBS. Prior to the announcement six of the 11 elected representatives of USNO joined UMNO. USNO's defection prompted the federal Government successfully to seek the party's deregistration in August, on the grounds that it had breached its own statutes. In the same month Tun Mustapha Harun was appointed to the federal post of Minister of Sabah Affairs.

In January 1994 Pairin Kitingan dissolved the Sabah State Legislative Assembly in preparation for early elections. Shortly afterwards Pairin Kitingan was convicted on charges of corruption by the High Court, but fined less than the minimum RM 2,000 required to disqualify him from office. Although Pairin Kitingan gained popular sympathy owing both to his perceived victimization in the corruption case and to his resistance to federal encroachment on Sabahan authority, a faction emerged in the PBS that favoured more harmonious relations with the federal Government. Former members of the deregistered USNO joined the PBS for the election, and the party also gained the support of Tun Mustapha Harun, who had resigned as Minister of Sabah Affairs and as a member of UMNO in January. (Tun Mustapha Harun died in January 1995.) At the election in February 1994 the PBS won a narrow majority, securing 25 of the 48 elective seats. Pairin Kitingan was sworn in as Chief Minister. In March, however, several PBS members defected to the opposition; among these was Jeffrey Kitingan, who had been released from detention under the ISA in December 1993. Although he was initially confined to Seremban town in Negeri Sembilan for two years, all restrictions on him were swiftly revoked, encouraging suspicions of an agreement with the federal authorities. In March 1994 Pairin Kitingan resigned as Chief Minister, and on the following day Tan Sri Sakaran Dandai, a leader of the Sabah wing of UMNO, was sworn in at the head of a new administration.

In June 1994 the BN coalition agreed to admit two breakaway parties from the PBS, the Parti Demokratik Sabah (Sabah Democratic Party), led by Datuk Bernard Dompok, and the Parti Bersatu Rakyat Sabah (PBRS—United Sabah People's Party), led by Joseph Kurup. In August Dompok was appointed as Minister in the Prime Minister's Department and Jeffrey Kitingan became Deputy Minister for Housing and Local Government. Also in June Jeffrey Kitingan was cleared of corruption in the High Court.

In May 1994 the House of Representatives approved the 1994 Constitution (Amendment) Act, which further restricted the powers of the monarchy and provided for the restructuring of the judiciary. Hitherto the Yang di-Pertuan Agong (Head of State) had been competent to withhold assent from and return legislation, within 30 days, to Parliament for further consideration. The amendment required the Yang di-Pertuan Agong to give his assent to a bill within 30 days; if he failed to do so, the bill would, none the less, become law. The changes to the judiciary in the amendment included the creation of a Court of Appeal, the restyling of the Supreme Court as the Federal Court and of the Lord President as the Chief Justice.

From June 1994 the Government took action to suppress the activities of Al-Arqam, an Islamic sect that had been founded by Ashaari Muhammad in 1968. Al-Arqam was believed to have about 10,000 members in Malaysia, many of whom were public servants, and was alleged to control considerable assets. Although Al-Arqam had traditionally eschewed politics, the Government asserted that the group was a threat to national security and denounced its Islamic teachings as 'deviationist'; moreover, the Malaysian authorities accused it of training a military force in Thailand, although this was denied by both Al-Arqam and the Thai Government. In July UMNO threatened to expel party members who refused to leave Al-Arqam, and in August the National Fatwa (Islamic Advisory) Council banned the sect on the grounds that its doctrine contravened Islamic principles.

In the April 1995 general election the BN won an overwhelming majority, taking 162 of the 192 seats in the House of Representatives (with some 64% of the total votes cast). The PBS won eight of Sabah's federal seats, including those held by Jeffrey Kitingan and Dompok. Although this constituted a loss of six seats, it was an indication that, despite the BN's assumption of power at state level through the defection of former PBS members of the legislature, the PBS remained a significant political force in Sabah. The BN also retained control of 10 of the 11 State Legislative Assemblies for which voting took place, in most cases securing a two-thirds' majority. In Kelantan, which remained the only state under opposition control, a coalition of the PAS and Semangat '46 took 35 of the 43 state seats.

Despite his overwhelming election victory, Mahathir's position appeared vulnerable during the divisional elections of UMNO in 1995. The defeat of several Mahathir supporters was widely attributed to the influence of Anwar's associates, and prompted speculation that Anwar might challenge Mahathir for the leadership. In November, however, UMNO's General Assembly adopted an unprecedented resolution to avoid any contest for the two senior party positions in 1996; Anwar finally declared that he would not challenge Mahathir, and Mahathir for the first time said that he would retire in the near future and again named Anwar as his successor.

Semangat '46 was formally dissolved in October 1996, and its members were admitted to UMNO. At that month's UMNO General Assembly Mahathir and Anwar were, as anticipated, returned unopposed to their posts. In contrast to the 1993 party elections, in which Anwar's supporters had been particularly successful, a large proportion of Mahathir loyalists were now elected. Notably, in the elections for the vice-presidencies, Muhyiddin Yassim, the only member of Anwar's 'Vision Team' who had remained loyal to the Deputy President, was defeated by Abdullah Badawi (the Minister of Foreign Affairs, who had been a vice-president prior to 1993); Najib Razak and Mohammad Taib were re-elected. However, the leadership of the women's wing and the youth wing, both previously held by Mahatir loyalists, were both taken by Anwar supporters. No former member of Semangat '46, including Razaleigh, secured a position on the UMNO Supreme Council.

In October 1996 the PAS announced that it was to abandon its attempt to replace secular criminal laws with *hudud*, the Islamic criminal code, in Kelantan: Mahathir was known to be strongly opposed to such a policy. The PAS won a by-election for the State Legislative Assembly in Kelantan in January 1997. Although the PAS took the seat from Semangat '46 by only a narrow margin, the results were nevertheless indicative of Razaleigh's weakened position in the state.

Mahathir's response to the currency crisis affecting the region in 1997, following Thailand's effective devaluation of the baht in early July, and his criticism of international investors, was widely perceived to have exacerbated Malaysia's economic position. Meanwhile, Anwar benefited politically from the situation, appearing to act responsibly in reassuring investors and rescinding the newly imposed financial restrictions. However, political opponents attempted to undermine Anwar through the circulation of a series of letters accusing him of sexual indiscretions. International criticism of Mahathir's outspokenness prompted popular demonstrations of support for the premier within Malaysia and near unanimous support for a vote of confidence in his leadership, which was held in the House of Representatives during November. In the same month Mahathir announced the formation of an executive authority to address the economic crisis, the National Economic Action Council, which was approved by the Cabinet in January 1998. At the UMNO annual convention in September 1997 Mahathir criticized the increasing tendency of Malaysian Muslims to attach excessive importance to external symbols of Islam (such as beards and headscarves) and warned of the dangers of extremism. Mahathir's speech, which was resented by many Muslims, followed the widely publicized arrest, in June, of three Muslim women for taking part in a beauty contest in Selangor. The arrests prompted debate concerning the position of women in Malaysian society and resulted in demands for the reform of the Islamic Syariah (Shariah) courts; a *fatwa* (religious edict) had the force of law in the state in which it was issued, which arguably violated the liberties of Malaysians as guaranteed under the federal Constitution. In November 10 men were detained under the ISA for disseminating Shia Muslim teachings (Malaysian Muslims belong predominantly to the Sunni sect) that were perceived as militant and a threat to national security. Many non-governmental organizations and political parties urged that the detainees be released or allowed to stand trial under the Sedition Act.

At internal elections for divisional committee members in UMNO, which took place in March 1998, most of Mahathir's supporters retained their positions. However, evidence of a growing division between Mahathir and Anwar became apparent at the UMNO annual party congress held in June, where Ahmad Zahid Hamidi, the head of the youth wing of UMNO and one of Anwar's supporters, made a speech criticizing what he termed the debilitating impact of corruption in the party. Zahid's speech, which was reminiscent of Anwar's recent condemnation of corruption and political restrictions, was perceived as an attack on the party's leadership; Mahathir responded by publishing a list of hundreds of people and companies who had received privatization contracts in recent years, which included close associates of Anwar and members of his family. During the following weeks Mahathir acted to counter the influence of Anwar, promoting allies and dismissing newspaper editors close to Anwar. The resignation in August of the Governor (a close ally of Anwar) and Deputy Governor of the central bank, reportedly owing to a disagreement over policy with Mahathir, served as an indication of the intensification of the rift within the Government. Supporters loyal to the Prime Minister responded to the perceived threat to Mahathir's leadership by circulating a brochure entitled *Fifty Reasons Why Anwar Cannot Become Prime Minister*, in which Anwar was accused of sexual offences and corruption.

Allegations of Anwar's supposed sexual misconduct increased throughout the months following the UMNO congress, and, following Anwar's refusal to resign, culminated in Mahathir's dismissal of Anwar as Deputy Prime Minister and Minister of Finance on 2 September 1998, on the grounds that he was morally unfit to hold office. On the following day Anwar was expelled from UMNO, and affidavits accusing him of sexual impropriety were filed with the High Court. The allegations were denied by Anwar, who asserted that they constituted part of a political conspiracy, at senior level, to discredit him. Anwar began a tour of the country, drawing extensive support for his calls for the wide-ranging reform of the political system from the many thousands who attended his public appearances. His supporters adopted the slogan *'reformasi'* (reform), which had united the popular forces that ousted President Suharto in Indonesia. In mid-September Anwar's adoptive brother, Sukma Darmawan Samitaat Madja, and a former speech-writer for Anwar, Munawar Ahmad Anees, were each sentenced to six months' imprisonment after they confessed to illegal homosexual activity with Anwar. The following day, at a meeting attended by at least 40,000 people in Kuala Lumpur, Anwar called directly for Mahathir's resignation; he was arrested shortly afterwards and detained under the ISA. A further 17 people, including a number of close associates of Anwar, were also detained under the same act. Anwar's arrest provoked demonstrations of protest, which erupted into violence when demonstrations involving up to 60,000 people were violently dispersed by the security forces; 132 people were arrested.

Following Anwar's arrest, his wife, Wan Azizah Wan Ismail, emerged as the de facto leader of the opposition movement. Despite a restriction order issued against Wan Azizah, barring her from holding rallies at her residence, demonstrations in protest at Anwar's detention were held throughout September 1998; these became the forum for demands for widespread political reform and for the removal of the restrictions on freedom of speech and assembly imposed under the ISA. At a court hearing in Petaling Jaya, Anwar pleaded not guilty to five charges of corruption and five charges of sexual impropriety. Allegations made by Anwar, who appeared in court with visible bruising to his face, that he had been severely beaten while in police custody and had subsequently been denied medical attention for a number of days, provoked expressions of extreme concern from foreign Governments—in particular from the Presidents of the Philippines and Indonesia—and the UN Secretary-General, Kofi Annan. In December the Inspector-General of the Malaysian police force, Tan Sri Abdul Rahim Noor, resigned after an initial inquiry blamed the police for the injuries Anwar had received. Malaysia's Attorney-General publicly admitted in January 1999 that Anwar had been assaulted by the police while in custody, and a Royal Commission of Inquiry into Anwar's injuries, which was completed in March, found Rahim Noor to be personally responsible for the beating. He was eventually sentenced to two months' imprisonment and fined RM 2,000 after pleading guilty to a charge of assault against Anwar.

Anwar's trial on four charges of corruption (which related to efforts allegedly made by him in 1997 to obtain through the police written denials that he was guilty of sexual misconduct and sodomy) began in November 1998, and in April 1999 Anwar was found guilty on each of the four charges of corruption and a sentence of six years' imprisonment was imposed (under Malaysian law, this would be followed by a five-year period of disqualification from political office). Following the delivery of the verdict, supporters of the former Deputy Prime Minister clashed with security forces outside the court. Violent protests continued for the next three days, resulting in the arrest of 18 demonstrators. Following the trial, three prosecution witnesses who had withdrawn their testimony against Anwar, including his adoptive brother and speech writer, who claimed their confessions had been obtained through police coercion, were charged with perjury. In late April Anwar was further charged with one count of illegal homosexual activity, to which he pleaded not guilty; it was announced that four other similar charges and one additional corruption charge against him had been suspended.

On the first day of Anwar's second trial in early June 1999 the prosecution amended the wording of its charge, changing the month and year (for the second time) in which the alleged crimes were supposedly committed. The trial was adjourned in September; Anwar was sent for medical examination following claims by the defence that he had proven high levels of arsenic in his blood and was possibly the victim of deliberate poisoning. In the same month some 10,000 supporters of Anwar gathered to demonstrate against the Government's treatment of him; following the protests, several of his prominent allies were reported to have been arrested. However, Anwar's trial resumed in late September after medical tests found that he showed no clinical signs of arsenic poisoning. In his testimony in court in October and November, Anwar made potentially damaging allegations of corruption against members of the Government who, he alleged, had conspired to remove him from office. In mid-November the trial of Anwar was adjourned indefinitely without explanation; supporters of Anwar claimed that the adjournment was a government attempt to silence him in the approach to the general election, which was to be held in late November. The trial resumed on 25 January 2000, but was adjourned again in late February at the request of the defence. Meanwhile, in April 2000 the Court of Appeal upheld Anwar's conviction on four charges of corruption.

Anwar suffered a further set-back in early June 2000, after the Court of Appeal rejected his plea for a stay of proceedings, ordering the trial on charges of sodomy to continue. In July the presiding judge ordered Anwar's defence lawyers to conclude their case, although they protested that they had intended to call further witnesses. The High Court found Anwar guilty of sodomy, sentencing him to a further nine years' imprisonment, thus bringing his term to a total of 15 years. His adopted brother, Sukma Darmawan, was sentenced to six years' imprisonment and four strokes of the cane for the same offence.

Although Anwar had been effectively removed from public office for 15 years, the affair continued to receive prominence in the media. Anwar was hospitalized in November, suffering from an acute back problem that required critical surgery. The Government refused a request for Anwar to travel abroad for surgery and in April 2001 issued an ultimatum to Anwar either to accept treatment in a state hospital or return to his cell. He returned to his cell in May. In the same month public prosecutors announced that the remaining charges of corruption and sodomy against him were to be abandoned and, in July, Anwar lodged an appeal against his sodomy conviction. Meanwhile, in June 2001 the contempt verdict against one of Anwar's lawyers was overruled when the High Court concluded that the lawyer had been acting only in the interests of his client. In July 2002 Anwar lost his final appeal against his corruption conviction. In October of the same year Mahathir launched bankruptcy proceedings against Anwar, following his refusal to pay the costs of a defamation lawsuit he had brought against the Prime Minister in 1999. In April 2003 Anwar's appeal against his final conviction for sodomy was rejected by the Court of Appeal. A few days previously he had completed his sentence for corruption, the last two years of his six-year sentence having been remitted for good behaviour.

In early September 2004 Anwar was released from prison after his appeal against his conviction for sodomy was upheld by the Federal Court, which found the evidence against Anwar unreliable. Shortly afterwards Anwar travelled to Germany for surgery on the back condition that he claimed had resulted from the severe beatings he had received in police custody in 1998, returning to Malaysia at the end of October 2004. Although he remained disqualified from holding political office until April 2008 owing to his corruption conviction, Anwar announced his intention to resume his campaign for political reform.

In January 1999, meanwhile, prior to the closure of the first trial of Anwar, Mahathir effected a major cabinet reorganization, in which Abdullah Badawi was appointed as Deputy Prime Minister and Minister for Home Affairs (a post relinquished by Mahathir) and Daim Zainuddin was allocated the finance portfolio. Also in January 1999 the UMNO Supreme Council announced its decision to postpone for 18 months elections for senior posts within the party, previously scheduled to be held in June, effectively preventing any potential challenge to Mahathir's leadership from within the party. The BN won a significant victory in the elections to the State Legislative Assembly in Sabah on 12–13 March, securing 31 of the 48 seats; however, Mahathir indicated that the result would not induce him to call an early general election. In early April a new opposition party, the Parti Keadilan Nasional (PKN—National Justice Party), was launched by Wan Azizah in anticipation of the general election; the new party reportedly aimed to establish itself as a multi-ethnic and multi-religious party and declared that its first act, should it come to power, would be to seek a royal pardon for Anwar. However, Anwar himself did not join the new party. Despite its stated aspirations to multi-ethnicity, the initial membership of the party appeared to be predominantly Muslim.

In November 1999 the Government unexpectedly announced that a general election was to be held later in the same month. The opposition expressed dissatisfaction at the limited period of time allowed for campaigning. At the election, which was held on 29 November, a decisive victory was won by the governing BN coalition, which gained 148 of a total of 193 seats in the House of Representatives, thereby retaining the two-thirds' majority required to allow the Government to amend the Constitution. The opposition coalition, the Barisan Alternatif (Alternative Front—which had been formed by the PAS, the PKN, the DAP and the Parti Rakyat Malaysia (PRM—Malaysian People's Party) in June 1999 and which subsequently selected Anwar as its prime ministerial candidate) won a total of 42 seats, while the opposition PBS (which remained outside the Barisan Alternatif) secured three seats. Despite the BN's victory, UMNO experienced a significant decline in support among Malay voters (mainly to the PAS, which secured 27 seats) and lost 23 seats, including those of four cabinet ministers. The party also performed poorly in the assembly elections held simultaneously in 11 Malaysian states: the PAS secured control of the state legislature in Trengganu, retained power in Kelantan and made significant gains in Mahathir's home state of Kedah. This erosion of confidence in UMNO was widely believed to be a result of the Government's treatment of Anwar and the concomitant decline of public confidence in the country's institutions, including the police and the judicial system. While there were a number of new appointments to the Cabinet, which was announced in early December, many of the important portfolios remained unchanged. However, in an unexpected development, Mahathir promoted the unelected academic, Musa Mohamad, neither an existing government minister nor a member of UMNO, to the influential post of Minister of Education; Musa replaced Najib Razak, who was transferred to the less powerful Ministry of Defence in what was perceived by many as an effective demotion. Also in December Mahathir announced that he intended this (his fifth) term of office to be his last, and for the first time formally identified the Deputy Prime Minister, Abdullah Badawi, as his preferred successor. In the same month the Barisan Alternatif nominated Fadzil Nor, President of the PAS, as the new parliamentary leader of the opposition. He replaced Lim Kit Siang, who had lost his seat in the general election and who in early December resigned as the Secretary-General of the DAP.

In May 2000, at the UMNO party elections, Mahathir and Abdullah Badawi were formally elected President and Deputy President of the party, respectively. In November the Prime Minister appointed Mohamed Dzaiddin Abdullah as the new Chief Justice, in a bid to enhance the credibility of the judiciary, tarnished by the Anwar trials. Later that month UMNO held a special general assembly, at which measures were approved to revitalize the image of the party and to attract more young professionals, including women. These developments failed to prevent the opposition PKN from taking a seat from the BN coalition at a by-election in the Lunas constituency of Kedah.

After taking leave in April 2001, the Minister of Finance, Daim Zainuddin, formally resigned from his post in June, following widespread allegations that he had taken advantage of public funds to help business associates, including the heavily indebted Malaysia Airlines and Time dotCom (the telecommunications unit of the Renong Group). Mahathir assumed the finance portfolio on an interim basis.

In a possible attempt to strengthen support from the Malay community, in August 2000 Mahathir criticized Suqiu, the Malaysian Chinese Organizations' Election Appeals Committee, describing some of its members as extremists and likening them to communists for urging the abolition of the New Vision Policy. The policy had for 30 years ensured favouritism for the Malay majority in education and commerce, in an attempt to reduce the inequality of wealth between Malays and Chinese. The effect of the criticism may have been merely to alienate Chinese supporters, integral to the BN's 1999 victory, although Suqiu did withdraw its demands after a series of meetings with UMNO in January 2001. In March Mahathir confirmed that the New Vision Policy, due to end in 2001, was to be extended for a further 10 years.

In January 2000, meanwhile, government suppression of dissent increased significantly. The deputy leader of the DAP and Anwar's legal representative, Karpal Singh, and the Vice-President of the PKN, Marina Yusoff, were charged under the Sedition Act. Mohamad Ezam Mohamad Noor was charged under the Official Secrets Act and subsequently placed on trial. In the same month the editor and the printer of the popular PAS newspaper, *Harakah*, were also charged with sedition in connection with an article concerning the trial of Anwar, and in early March 2000 the Government ordered that *Harakah* be published just twice a month instead of twice weekly and restricted sales of the publication to members of the PAS only. The group editor of the *New Straits Times*, Kadir Jasin, was forced to resign in January over an editorial that questioned the UMNO Supreme Council's rejection of demands that the party's two most senior positions be contested from within the party in the forthcoming UMNO internal elections. In January 2002 public prosecutors abandoned the sedition charges against Karpal Singh without explanation.

The Anwar issue continued to incite public unrest, and in April 2000 a protest to mark the anniversary of Anwar's conviction for corruption was broken up by riot police, 48 PKN activists being arrested. Public criticism of the Government, and subsequent detentions, became more frequent after Anwar's second conviction, as confidence in Mahathir's leadership continued to decline. Mohamad Ezam Mohamad Noor was arrested in March 2001 as a result of allegedly seditious comments, despite already being on trial for releasing a secret report on corruption. A month later he was detained again, along with six other opposition leaders, including the PKN Vice-President, Tian Chua, and the PKN youth Vice-Chairman, N. Gobala Krishnan, under the ISA (which allows for detention without trial for up to two years). The aim of these arrests seemed to be to dissuade protesters from gathering for the second anniversary of Anwar's conviction. The effect was significant as only 2,000 demonstrators defied the authorities' ban to attend the peaceful 'Black 14' rally, named after and coinciding with the date of Anwar's first conviction, 14 April. However, the seven detainees were not immediately released after the rally, and three more arrests were made under the ISA. During late April the PKN youth leaders, Dr Badrul Amin Baharom and Lokman Noor Adam, were arrested, as was the human rights activist, Badarudiin Ismail, thus bringing the total of recent detainees under the provisions of the ISA to 10. In August 2002 Mohamad Ezam Mohamad Noor was sentenced to a two-year prison term, having been convicted of 'leaking' state secrets. In June 2003 he was freed on bail, pending an appeal; his conviction was overruled by the High Court in April 2004.

In early August 2001 an extraordinary session of the Court of Final Appeal heard arguments against the detention of five people under the ISA. Significantly, the judges ruled that the onus was on the State to produce evidence that those arrested posed a real threat to national security. Meanwhile, Nik Adli Nik Abdul Aziz, son of PAS spiritual leader Datuk Haji Nik Abdul Aziz Nik Mat, was one of 10 men detained under the Act on suspicion of membership of the Kumpulan Mujahidin Malaysia (KMM), an Islamist fundamentalist group believed to be engaged in a long-term plot to overthrow the Government. Seven of those taken into custody were also members of the PAS. Soon afterwards 25 supporters of Anwar Ibrahim were freed from prison and promptly rearrested on new charges, before being granted bail. In September the Government announced that Nik Adli Nik Abdul Aziz was to be detained for two years without trial under the provisions of the ISA. Eight of the nine men arrested with him were also imprisoned. Human rights activists accused the Government of exploiting the aftermath of the terrorist attacks on the USA in the same month (see the chapter on the USA) to suppress national opposition groups. Further arrests continued to be made under the ISA, as the Government tightened its control of national security.

In September 2001 the opposition was destabilized by the withdrawal of the DAP from the Barisan Alternatif. The party accused the PAS of alienating Chinese voters through its support for an Islamic state. In the same month an election in Malaysia's largest state, Sarawak, confirmed the strength of the ruling coalition. The BN won 60 out of 62 available seats in the state legislature. The DAP secured one seat; an independent candidate the other. In January 2002 the PBS was formally readmitted to the BN following more than a decade of absence from power. Also in January, at a by-election in the Perlis district of Indera Kayangan, the PKN was heavily defeated by the BN. The PAS accused the Government of using devious methods to exploit popular fear of Islamist militancy in the aftermath of the September terrorist attacks.

On 21 November 2001 the Head of State, Sultan Salahuddin Abdul Aziz Shah Al-Haj ibni Al-Marhum Sultan Hisamuddin Alam Shah Al-Haj, died at the age of 75. On 13 December the Raja of Perlis, Tuanku Syed Sirajuddin Syed Putra Jamalullail, was sworn in as the new monarch, following his election by secret ballot from among the remaining eight Malay rulers. The Sultan of Terengganu continued as his deputy.

In December 2001 a court convicted 19 members of the Islamist cult al-Ma'unah of treason for plotting to overthrow the Government. The men had been arrested following the murder of two hostages during a confrontation with security forces after a weapons robbery in July 2000. Ten other cult members had pleaded guilty to lesser charges and received 10-year prison terms. Three of the sect's ringleaders were sentenced to death for their part in the armed rebellion. The remaining men were given life terms. (In November 2003 15 members of the cult, who had played only minor roles in the robbery and who later expressed remorse for their actions, were released, having been held under the ISA.) In January 2002 the Government announced that, with effect from May, students and staff at public universities would be required to sign a pledge declaring allegiance to their king, country and government. Students had played a leading role in the protests that had followed the dismissal of Anwar Ibrahim in 1998.

In June 2002, during a speech to the annual congress of UMNO, Prime Minister Mahathir made the dramatic announcement that he intended to resign from the Government, with immediate effect. However, he was persuaded to withdraw his resignation shortly afterwards and, following some discussion, it was decided that he would remain in power until October 2003, when he would be succeeded by the Deputy Prime Minister, Abdullah Badawi. During the transition period Abdullah Badawi would assume increased responsibility for the running of the Government. Fadzil Nor, President of the PAS, died following complications arising from heart surgery in June 2002; Abdul Hadi Awang assumed the party leadership on an interim basis.

In July 2002 Abdul Hadi Awang announced the imposition of Islamic law in Terengganu state, of which he was the Chief Minister. However, the Government continued to oppose efforts to enforce the new law code. In the same month, at a by-election to the Kedah seat of Pendang, which had become vacant upon the death of Fadzil Nor, the BN secured a narrow victory.

In October 2002 police arrested five men, believed to be members of the regional Islamist organization Jemaah Islamiah (JI), under the ISA. The arrests brought the total number of ISA detainees to approximately 70. Members of JI were believed to be responsible for the recent terrorist attack on the Indonesian island of Bali (see the chapter on Indonesia), which had resulted in the deaths of 202 people, including many tourists. In November the ISA attracted renewed criticism when a court ordered the release of Nasharuddin Nasir, who had been detained under its provisions since April of that year, on the grounds that no evidence had been provided to substantiate claims that he had engaged in terrorist activities. The Government, in contravention of the judicial order, rearrested him almost immediately after his release. It was announced subsequently that the ISA was to be strengthened in order to prevent further challenges by the courts. Meanwhile, Prime Minister Mahathir announced the appointment of Datuk Dr Jamaluddin Jarjis as Minister of Finance II; Mahathir himself continued to hold the other finance portfolio.

In May 2003 Minister of Transport Ling Liong Sik announced his resignation. In the following month it was announced that three members of the PKN who had been imprisoned under the ISA for more than two years were to be released. In August the PKN merged with the smaller PRM, forming the Parti Keadilan Rakyat (PKR—People's Justice Party), in advance of the general election scheduled to be held in 2004. It was hoped that the merger would strengthen opposition to the BN and promote Anwar's cause. The President of the PKN, Wan Azizah, continued as President of the new party. In September it was announced that nine suspected members of the KMM who had been detained under the ISA in August 2001, including Nik Adli Nik Abdul Aziz, would be imprisoned for a further two years.

On 31 October 2003 Prime Minister Mahathir Mohamad retired, having spent 22 years in power. His designated successor, Deputy Prime Minister Abdullah Badawi, was then sworn in as Prime Minister, retaining the home affairs portfolio and, in addition, assuming Mahathir's role as Minister of Finance. In November Abdullah Badawi was also endorsed as the new Chairman of the BN. Meanwhile, the PAS announced plans to transform Malaysia fully into an Islamic state should it come to power, attracting criticism not only from non-Muslim members of the BN but also from political allies of the PAS, including the PKR. In January 2004 the new Prime Minister effected his first cabinet reorganization, nominating Minister of Defence Najib Razak as Deputy Prime Minister.

In February 2004, as a result of an ongoing anti-corruption campaign initiated by the new Prime Minister, both the Minister of Land and Co-operative Development, Tan Sri Datuk Kasitah bin Gaddam, and the former head of the national steel company Perwaja Steel Bhd, Eric Chia Eng Hock, were arrested and charged with corruption. Kasitah announced his resignation shortly afterwards. (The charges against Chia were dismissed in June 2007; the judge in his trial criticized the prosecutors involved in the case, notably over their failure to call important witnesses. Kasitah's trial continued in early 2008.) Also in February 2004 a national service programme was introduced with the intention of promoting national unity; conscripts were to perform military service for three months. A Royal Commission into the police force released its final report in May 2005, in which it urged the swift establishment of an Independent Police Complaints and Misconduct Commission, in order to render the police more accountable to the public; the report noted that the incidence of corruption within the police force was higher than in other government agencies. Meanwhile, in early March 2004 it was announced that Parliament was to be dissolved and a general election held later in that month, several months before the constitutional deadline of November. Later in March it was reported that six suspected Indonesian members of JI had been captured in Malaysia and were being held under the ISA, bringing the total number of suspected militants detained under the ISA to 96.

On 21 March 2004, following a brief campaign period, elections took place to an enlarged 219-member House of Representatives and to 12 of the 13 State Legislative Assemblies (Sarawak was exempted, having held elections to its legislature in September 2001). The BN secured a commanding victory, winning 198 of the 219 seats in the House of Representatives and taking control of 11 of the 12 State Legislative Assemblies, including that of Terengganu, which had previously been governed by the PAS. The PAS retained control of Kelantan by a narrow margin. The DAP secured 12 seats in the House of Representatives, followed by the PAS, which won seven (compared with 27 at the election of 1999) and the PKR, which retained only one seat, that held by Wan Azizah. Having been sworn in again as head of government, Abdullah Badawi announced a major reorganization of his Cabinet, which was enlarged through the creation of two new ministries—the Ministry of Federal Territories and the Ministry of Natural Resources and the Environment—and the division of three existing ministries, those of Home Affairs, Education and Culture, Arts and Tourism. Najib Razak continued as Deputy Prime Minister and Minister of Defence.

The Prime Minister launched a National Integrity Plan in April 2004, aimed at reducing corruption and abuse of power. In late May the Government allowed journalists to visit a detention centre for those held under the ISA, in an attempt to dispel recent allegations, made by the US-based organization Human Rights Watch, that detainees had been tortured. In August the BN succeeded in retaining its seat at a state assembly by-election in Kuala Berang in Terengganu, increasing its majority in the constituency.

Abdullah Badawi's control over UMNO was questioned in September 2004, when three members of his Cabinet failed to secure re-election to the party's Supreme Council at its General Assembly; some observers attributed their defeat to a reaction by party members against the Prime Minister's anti-corruption campaign. None the less, Abdullah Badawi and Najib Razak were formally endorsed as the party's President and Deputy President. UMNO leaders ruled out a return to the party for Anwar Ibrahim, who had been freed from prison earlier in September (see above). Anwar's release was widely regarded as evidence that the Prime Minister was fulfilling a pledge to respect the independence of the judiciary. In December Anwar launched a nation-wide campaign against the ISA.

In January 2005 police responsible for religious matters conducted a raid on a night-club in Kuala Lumpur, arresting about 100 Muslims, including many women, on charges of public indecency and other 'anti-Islamic' crimes. Amid the ensuing public outcry, the legitimacy of these arrests was questioned, as the application of Islamic law in federal territories was restricted to marriage and related matters. In the following month the Government instructed the Federal Territories Islamic Department to abandon the charges. In July 21 members of the religious group Sky Kingdom, one of 22 organizations deemed by the Government earlier that month to be 'deviant sects of Islam', were arrested at the group's compound in Terengganu and charged with propagating teachings that 'humiliated' Islam. One of those arrested pleaded guilty and was sentenced to a one-year period of religious 'rehabilitation' under the supervision of local Islamic officials. Two of the detainees, who claimed to have previously renounced Islam, applied for a hearing at the Federal Court on the question of whether the right to profess a religion under Article 11 of the Constitution (which prescribes religious freedom for all) included the right of a Muslim to renounce Islam. In December the federal High Court in Kuala Lumpur rejected their application, ruling that the jurisdiction to decide whether or not a person had renounced Islam rested with the Syariah courts. (One of the two was sentenced to two years' imprisonment in March 2008 by the Syariah High Court, having been convicted of apostasy.) Meanwhile, the remaining 18 detainees pleaded not guilty and opted for trial before an Islamic Court. The forthcoming verdicts, regarded as being of considerable significance in the continuing debate about the issue of religious tolerance within Malaysia, were awaited with great interest by the international community. In August 2005 Anwar Ibrahim was awarded RM 4.5m. in damages by the High Court for the false allegations contained within the pamphlet *Fifty Reasons Why Anwar Ibrahim Cannot Become Prime Minister*, published in 1998.

In October 2005 Tan Sri Mohamed Isa Abdul Samad resigned from the position of Minister of Federal Territories, having been found guilty by the ruling party of vote-buying and political corruption pertaining to the UMNO party elections of September 2004. The UMNO Supreme Council subsequently rejected Isa's appeal against his three-year suspension from the party. In November 2005 a new Malaysian coastguard agency was launched, with operations initially focused on the Strait of Melaka, where piracy remained a serious problem. The Government was to disburse an estimated RM 578m. by the end of 2007 to finance the agency's operations, which were to be expanded gradually to cover Malaysia's other territorial waters. Malaysia, Indonesia and Singapore agreed to improve co-operation in their efforts to protect vessels traversing the busy maritime trade route. In the same month Azahari Husin, a notorious Malaysian bomb-maker thought to be responsible for many of JI's operations, was killed in Indonesia during a police raid on a property in Batu, near Malang, East Java. In January 2006 another prominent Malaysian Islamist militant, Noordin Mohammad Top, released a message in which he claimed responsibility for the bombings on the Indonesian island of Bali in 2005 (see the chapter on Indonesia) and declared himself to be the head of a new South-East Asian Islamist militant organization, namely Tanzam Qaedat al Jihad (Organization of the Basis of Jihad). The statement served to remind Malaysia of the threat posed by its own nationals to regional security. Later that month Anwar Ibrahim filed a lawsuit against former Prime Minister Mahathir Mohamad for falsely having depicted him as a homosexual and causing 'irreparable damage' to his reputation. (In September 2005 Mahathir had controversially admitted to reporters that he had dismissed Anwar in order to avert the prospect of the appointment of a homosexual prime minister.) However, in July 2007 the High Court dismissed the lawsuit, which Mahathir had claimed was a ploy by Anwar to 'rehabilitate himself for high office'.

In February 2006 the Prime Minister effected a reorganization of the Cabinet. Datuk Paduka Abdul Kadir Sheikh Fadzir had previously announced his resignation from the position of Minister of Information and was replaced by Datuk Zainuddin Maidin. Other notable changes included the appointment of Datuk Seri Radzi Sheikh as Minister of Home Affairs, in place of Datuk Azmi Khalid, and the appointment of Dato' Haji Zulhasnan Rafique as Minister of Federal Territories. In the same month the Malaysian Government suspended indefinitely the licence of the *Sarawak Tribune*, in response to the newspaper's decision to reprint controversial cartoons depicting the Prophet Muhammad, which had first been published in a Danish newspaper and had provoked outrage from the international Muslim community. This was the first time in almost two decades that a Malaysian publication had had its licence revoked, and the episode renewed concerns about the status of religious freedom and freedom of expression. Shortly afterwards the licences of *Guang Ming Daily* and *Berita Petang Sarawak* were also revoked, for a two-week period, after they too reprinted the cartoons. Also in February, the Government announced plans to slaughter all poultry in four villages, following official confirmation of the first outbreak of avian influenza ('bird flu') in the country for more than a year: 40 chickens on a farm near Kuala Lumpur had been diagnosed with the deadly H5N1 strain of the virus earlier that month, prompting the Singapore Government to ban all imports from the affected region. Further cases followed.

The Sarawak State Legislative Assembly was dissolved in April 2006 and an election held in May. The BN won 62 of the 71 seats in the expanded state legislature, while the DAP took six seats and the remaining three were divided among the PKR, the Sarawak National Party and an independent candidate.

In April 2006 relations with Singapore became a source of internal disharmony when the Malaysian Prime Minister suspended the construction of a bridge designed to replace the Johor Strait causeway to Singapore. It was hoped that the new bridge would reduce congestion on the route and allow the passage of ships through the waterway. Singapore had expressed uncertainty about the plan on financial and environmental grounds but, in the absence of a bilateral consensus, construction work on the Malaysian half of the bridge had nevertheless begun in January. Abdullah Badawi remarked that other related negotiations would also be suspended, in a statement that cast doubt over Singapore's request for the provision of Malaysian materials for the purposes of land reclamation work, as well as access to Malaysian airspace for military training. The incident provoked a harsh reaction from former Prime Minister Mahathir, who was outspoken in his criticism of what he regarded as a 'surrender (of) sovereignty' to Singapore. In June the rupture in relations deepened when the former leader, who remained powerful in many quarters, appeared to question his own choice of successor, and expressed disapproval at the Prime Minister's reluctance to complete certain projects started in the Mahathir era. The UMNO Supreme Council responded by voicing its support for Abdullah Badawi, both as Prime Minister and UMNO President. For some observers the episode signified the beginning of a power struggle that would reach its culmination at the forthcoming UMNO party election in 2008 (it was later announced that the party election would not take place until after the next legislative election). Mahathir continued his apparent campaign against Abdullah Badawi and his administration in the months that followed, warning in August 2006 that he had evidence to substantiate his accusations of government corruption. In September Mahathir was unable to secure election as a delegate to the annual UMNO assembly scheduled for November, amid speculation that he had intended to use the meeting to renew his offensive against the Government of Abdullah Badawi.

In October 2006 Nik Adli Nik Abdul Aziz was released from prison, having been incarcerated for more than five years without charge (see above). Sultan Tuanku Mizan Zainal Abidin ibni al-Marhum Sultan Mahmud, the Sultan of Terengganu, was sworn in as the country's Yang di-Pertuan Agong on 13 December and enthroned on 26 April 2007. Severe flooding in December 2006 and January 2007, particularly in the southern state of Johor, displaced more than 100,000 people.

Several corruption scandals, involving senior officials, emerged in early 2007. In March it was revealed that the Anti-Corruption Agency was investigating allegations that the Deputy Minister of Internal Security, Datuk Mohd Johari Baharum, had accepted more than RM 5m. in bribes in return for the release of three men suspected of being involved in organized crime. Meanwhile, the Director-General of the Anti-Corruption Agency, Datuk Seri Zulkipli Mat Noor, had himself been accused by a former colleague of illicit self-enrichment. The Prime Minister's Office announced at the end of March that Zulkipli's contract, which had just expired, would not be renewed. Moreover, the position of the Deputy Prime Minister and Minister of Defence, Najib Razak, was undermined by opposition attempts to link him to a murder that his political adviser, Abdul Razak Baginda, was charged with abetting. In late April Najib denied having any connection to the killing or the victim. The trial of Abdul Razak Baginda and the two members of a special police unit who were accused of perpetrating the murder commenced in June and continued in early 2008. In July 2007 the Attorney-General halted investigations into the activities of Johari and Zulkipli owing to lack of evidence.

A state assembly by-election held in Ijok, in Selangor, in late April 2007 marked the return to active politics of Anwar Ibrahim, who campaigned vigorously on behalf of the PKR candidate. None the less, the ruling BN retained the seat with an increased majority. Anwar declared his intention to contest the presidency of the PKR at its annual conference in late May, despite being barred from holding public office until April 2008, but at a very late stage withdrew his candidacy, amid some internal dissent over his decision to stand; Wan Azizah was consequently re-elected unopposed. Anwar's renewed prominence was not welcomed by all members of the PKR and prompted the resignation from the party of a number of senior members. Meanwhile, Abdullah Badawi's announcement that civil servants would receive pay rises of up to 35% (the first increase in 15 years) prompted speculation that the Prime Minister intended to call an early general election.

In late May 2007 the Federal Court rejected an appeal by a convert from Islam to Christianity to have the word 'Islam' removed from the religion section of her identity card, ruling that Syariah courts held jurisdiction in this area. Observers noted that the judgment effectively made it impossible to renounce Islam legally, given that apostasy was a criminal offence under Islamic law, and raised renewed questions about the right to religious freedom prescribed by Article 11 of the Constitution. This was perhaps the most high-profile of a number of similar cases that were provoking religious tension in Malaysia. In late August the Government suspended publication of the Tamil-language newspaper *Makkal Osai* for one month, after the newspaper published an image of Jesus Christ apparently smoking a cigarette and drinking alcohol. In December controversy arose over the use of the word 'Allah' by non-Muslims, when a Roman Catholic weekly newspaper, *The Herald*, encountered difficulties in renewing its publishing permit because its Malay-language section employed 'Allah' when referring to the Christian God. Dato' Abdullah bin Mohamad Zin, the Minister in the Prime Minister's Department responsible for Islamic affairs, reportedly stated that the Government had decided that the use of 'Allah' by non-Muslims might create confusion among Muslims.

In mid-November 2007 police used tear gas and water cannons to disperse up to 30,000 protesters who were marching in Kuala Lumpur to campaign for electoral reform. The demonstration, which had been declared illegal, was organized by the Gabungan Pilihanraya Bersih dan Adil (Bersih—the Coalition for Clean and Fair Elections), comprising a number of opposition parties, including the DAP, the PAS and the PKR, and civil society organizations. Bersih's main demands were equal access to the state-controlled media for all parties, a complete revision of the electoral register, the use of indelible ink to prevent multiple voting, and the abolition of postal voting except for diplomats and overseas voters. A second banned demonstration, involving at least 8,000 ethnic Indians, took place outside the British High Commission in Kuala Lumpur later that month, ending in violence, as police clashed with the protesters. The rally was organized by the Hindu Rights Action Force (Hindraf, a coalition of some 30 Hindu non-governmental organizations) to highlight perceived discrimination against Indians in Malaysia (who accounted for some 7% of the population) and, more specifically, in support of a lawsuit, filed in the British courts in August, demanding that the British Government pay reparations to the descendants of Indians transported to Malaysia as indentured labourers during the 19th century. In December five Hindraf members were detained under the ISA on the grounds that their actions had threatened national security.

The Minister of Health, Datuk Seri Chua Soi Lek, resigned in early January 2008 after admitting his involvement in a sexual scandal; he was replaced by Dato' Seri Ong Ka Ting. In mid-February Abdullah Badawi announced the dissolution of Parliament, and a general election was called for 8 March, more than one year earlier than the constitutional deadline. The Prime Minister gave no explanation for his decision, which observers attributed to a desire to secure a renewed mandate in advance of a widely anticipated deterioration in economic conditions. The timing of the election also ensured the exclusion of Anwar Ibrahim, whose disqualification from seeking public office was not due to expire until a month later. Also in mid-February, several hundred ethnic Indians participated in another banned demonstration organized by Hindraf in Kuala Lumpur to protest against the alleged marginalization of the Indian minority.

On 8 March 2008 the BN sustained heavy losses in elections to an enlarged House of Representatives and to 12 of the 13 State Legislative Assemblies (Sarawak having conducted elections to its legislature in May 2006). The ruling coalition failed to retain its two-thirds' majority in the House of Representatives, taking only 140 of the 222 seats, and lost control of the Legislative Assemblies of Kedah, Penang, Perak and Selangor. Of the opposition parties, which had pledged not to present candidates against each other, the PKR made the most significant gains in the House of Representatives, winning a total of 31 seats (compared with only one in 2004), while the DAP and the PAS both increased their representation by 16 seats, to 28 seats and 23 seats, respectively. The PAS also strengthened its majority in the Kelantan state legislature. The BN's poor performance was attributed to public discontent with renewed ethnic tensions and rising inflation, as well as concern about crime levels and corruption. Having dismissed demands for his resignation, including from within UMNO, Abdullah Badawi reorganized his Cabinet 10 days after the election. The Prime Minister retained the finance portfolio. Although Najib Razak remained Deputy Prime Minister and Minister of Defence, most other portfolios were affected by the reallocation. The most notable departure from the Government was perhaps that of Dato' Seri Paduka Rafidah binti Aziz, who had served as Minister of International Trade and Industry since 1987, but had been criticized in 2006 over procedures for the import of foreign vehicles; she was replaced by Tan Sri Dato' Haji Muhyiddin bin Mohd Yassin, hitherto Minister of Agriculture and Agro-Based Industry. Rais Yatim assumed responsibility for the foreign affairs portfolio. Other new appointees included Datuk Mohd Zaid bin Ibrahim, a former lawyer and member of UMNO, who had previously been critical of the Government, as a Minister in the Prime Minister's Department. Zaid was charged with reforming the judiciary, which had been damaged during the second half of 2007 by allegations of corruption in the appointment process for judges.

In May 2008 Anwar Ibrahim was accused of sodomy by a party aide, Mohd Saiful Bukhari Azlan; the allegations against him were similar to those made 10 years previously. At the end of June, fearing for his safety, Anwar sought temporary refuge at the Turkish embassy. He was arrested in mid-July and questioned by the police, before being released on the following day. The Kuala Lumpur Sessions Court formally charged Anwar with sodomy in early August, but released him on bail pending a further hearing. In November the Kuala Lumpur Sessions Court ruled against a decision by the Attorney-General to transfer the trial to the High Court. In July, meanwhile, Wan Azizah vacated the seat that she had occupied in the House of Representatives since her husband's conviction in 1999, thus enabling Anwar to stand as a candidate at the ensuing by-election for the seat that he had previously held. Polling took place in late August, when Anwar secured victory by a large majority. As the de facto leader of the opposition, he subsequently gained the support of the PAS.

In September 2008 the editor of an online newspaper, *Malaysia Today*, Raja Petra Kamaruddin, was arrested under the ISA on the grounds that he had published articles provoking racial tension. Later in that month Raja Petra received a two-year detention order on charges of insulting Islam, but this was overruled in early November when the High Court found that the Government had acted beyond its legal powers in issuing such an order. Raja Petra also implicated Najib Razak and his wife in the murder of a Mongolian translator (see below).

Datuk Mohd Zaid bin Ibrahim resigned from his position in the Prime Minister's Department in mid-September 2008. In a letter submitted to the Prime Minister, Zaid expressed frustration at the pace of legal reforms and criticized the use of the ISA to imprison three dissidents earlier in the month. Other cabinet ministers were also reported to have questioned the authorities' increasing recourse to the ISA. In December a Singapore newspaper reported that it had been informed of the unannounced release of more than a dozen Islamist militants closely linked to JI, who had been also been imprisoned under the ISA. The Malaysian Government appeared to defend the release of the prisoners on the grounds that they had been rehabilitated. A further 13 detainees, similarly held under the provisions of the ISA, were released in May 2009, without having been formally charged. Among those released were members of Hindraf who had been detained since organizing the anti-Government protests of 2007 (see above).

In March 2009 Gobind Singh Deo, a member of the DAP, was banned from Parliament for one year after accusing Prime Minister Najib Razak of involvement in the murder of a Mongolian translator, whose remains had been discovered in a jungle area of Shah Alam in 2006, a crime for which two Malaysian police officers were subsequently sentenced to death. Gobind's exclusion from the House of Representatives prompted opposition members to abandon the parliamentary session, protesting that Gobind had not been given an opportunity to defend his statement. Gobind's father, DAP Chairman Karpal Singh, who was also an eminent lawyer and was representing the murdered woman's family, was charged with sedition, allegedly having insulted the Sultan of Perak. Karpal accused the Government of using the Sedition Act as a 'political weapon against its political opponents'. Two leading opposition newspapers, *Harakah* and *Suara Keadilin*, were banned from publishing for three months by the Government in late March 2009, shortly before the anticipated appointment of Najib Razak as Prime Minister and the holding of three by-elections in April (only one of which was won by the BN). In early March riot police in Kuala Lumpur used tear gas to disperse thousands of demonstrators, who were protesting against the use of English as a medium of instruction in mathematics and science classes. More than 100 protesters were reported to have been detained.

Meanwhile, in October 2008 Abdullah Badawi had announced his intention to vacate the presidency of UMNO and to resign as Prime Minister in early 2009. In September 2008 Abdullah had transferred the finance portfolio to Najib Razak, in exchange for that of defence. Abdullah had been placed under increasing pressure to depart, owing to the recent electoral losses of the BN and to his perceived failure effectively to address the issue of corruption. Furthermore, the first ever parliamentary motion of no confidence against a Malaysian Prime Minister had been drafted in June 2008, only to be withdrawn on a technicality. In late March 2009 Abdullah Badawi officially resigned as UNMO President and was replaced by Najib Razak. In his farewell speech to party delegates, Abdullah stated that UMNO needed to reform if it were to remain in power. On 2 April 2009 Abdullah formally submitted his resignation as Prime Minister, and Najib Razak was inaugurated as Prime Minister on the following day. Najib, who retained the finance portfolio, had pledged to make use of the ISA in a more appropriate way and to address the problems encountered by minority communities, notably the grievances of Malaysia's ethnic Indians. The new Cabinet included Muhyiddin Yassin, hitherto the Minister of International Trade and Industry, who was promoted to the position of Deputy Prime Minister and Minister of Education. Mustapa Mohamed, Minister of Agriculture in the outgoing Government, replaced Muhyiddin Yassin. Ahmad Zahid Hamidi became the Minister of Defence, and Anifah Aman was appointed as Minister of Foreign Affairs.

In February 2009 the BN regained control of Perak state after four PKR members of the State Legislative Assembly defected to the BN. The Sultan of Perak confirmed the BN's majority in the state legislature and deposed the Chief Minister, Mohammad Nizar Jamaluddin, appointing a BN member, Datuk Zambry Abdul Kadir, in his place. The formation of a new Government was strongly contested by the PKR, which argued that the transition was unconstitutional; the opposition thus demanded the holding of state elections. Following a series of protests and parliamentary manoeuvres to obstruct the new Government, PKR legislators were prevented by the police from entering the assembly building. Nizar further challenged the leadership of Zambry by referring the matter to the High Court, which ruled in early March that the case could be heard only in the Federal Court. The Federal Court subsequently declared that the case could be heard only in the High Court, thereby prolonging the dispute. The High Court was due to announce its decision in late May; however, prior to the ruling, and amid protests and the arrests of dozens of protesters and opposition members, the BN Government forcibly removed the Assembly's Speaker and took control of the state legislature. The next session of the Assembly was then officially opened by the son of the Sultan of Perak. Four days later the High Court ruled that the opposition was the lawful Government of Perak and that Nizar Jamaluddin was the rightful Chief Minister. On the following day, however, the High Court reinstated Zambry, pending an appeal.

Malaysia's foreign policy was dominated by its membership of the regional grouping, the Association of South East Asian Nations (ASEAN, see p. 194), founded in 1967. In February 2008 Malaysia ratified the new ASEAN Charter, which codified the principles and purposes of the Association and had been signed in November 2007 at the 13th summit meeting in Singapore.

Mahathir was instrumental in bringing Myanmar into ASEAN in 1997 under the Policy of Constructive Engagement. Malaysia also played an integral role in bringing together the military junta and opposition leader Aung San Suu Kyi for negotiations in late 2000, although it was thought that financial considerations might have been significant, with a promise of direct investment in Myanmar by Malaysia's national petroleum corporation, PETRONAS, in return for a semblance of progress on the part of the junta. Mahathir's visit to Myanmar in January 2001 confirmed Malaysia's interest in Myanmar, a possible alternative source of natural gas. In September 2001 the Myanma leader, Gen. Than Shwe, paid an official visit to Malaysia during which a number of bilateral agreements were signed. In August 2002 Mahathir visited Myanmar again; during his visit he met with Aung San Suu Kyi and, it was thought, attempted to encourage the junta to engage in further dialogue with the opposition. In March 2006 the Malaysian Minister of Foreign Affairs, Syed Hamid Albar, was denied access to Aung San Suu Kyi on a visit to Myanmar as an ASEAN envoy to assess the country's progress towards political reform. Albar, who had held a meeting with Lt-Gen. Soe Win, the Myanma Prime Minister, was initially positive about the visit. However, ASEAN's forbearance with regard to the military regime of Myanmar seemed to be decreasing in July when Albar implied that the Association's development was being impeded by Myanmar, claiming that ASEAN could no longer defend the country as Myanmar was 'not making an attempt to co-operate or help itself'.

Relations with Singapore had always been characterized by mistrust, after the city-state left the Federation of Malaya in 1965. Resentment increased as Singapore advanced more swiftly than Malaysia economically, creating a certain acrimonious competition between the two countries. However, as Malaysia also developed, bilateral relations became more cordial, and co-operation increased. The visit in August 2000 by Singapore's Senior Minister and figurehead, Lee Kuan Yew, to Mahathir in Kuala Lumpur demonstrated the growing convergence of the two countries' viewpoints. In September 2001 Lee Kuan Yew travelled to Kuala Lumpur again, on a visit intended to further enhance links between the two countries. Relations were threatened from early 2002, however, as tensions arose over the renegotiation of a 1961 agreement by which Malaysia supplied Singapore with water. Negotiations took place in July and October 2002 in an attempt to resolve the problems arising from the water dispute, but without success. In February 2003 Prime Minister Mahathir stated that, while Malaysia would cease to supply Singapore with untreated water in 2011, it would continue to supply filtered water, at a reasonable price, for as long as necessary. Following the retirement of Mahathir in October 2003, bilateral relations showed signs of improvement under new Prime Minister Abdullah Badawi. In January 2004 the Malaysian Prime Minister and his Singaporean counterpart, Goh Chok Tong, exchanged visits and discussed the tensions in the relationship. In October, on his first official visit to Malaysia, the new Prime Minister of Singapore, Lee Hsien Loong, announced that his predecessor, Goh, now Senior Minister in the Prime Minister's Office, would lead his country's efforts to resolve outstanding bilateral issues. Abdullah Badawi and Goh held talks in Kuala Lumpur in December. Issues discussed included the dispute over the sale of water to Singapore; the use of Malaysian airspace by Singapore's air force; the joint development of unused railway land in Singapore; the release of pension funds owed to Malaysians who had worked in Singapore; and the proposed construction of a bridge between the two countries. In January 2005 Malaysia and Singapore appeared to have resolved a dispute over the latter's land reclamation project in the Straits of Johor, which separate the two countries. Malaysia accepted that the reclamation work could proceed, while Singapore agreed to co-operate with Malaysia to ensure navigational safety and environmental protection of the waterway. In 2006, however, relations became strained over the Johor Strait bridge dispute (see above), and deteriorated further in September, when Singapore's Minister Mentor and former Prime Minister, Lee Kuan Yew, remarked that Malaysia's Chinese minority was being systematically marginalized because of its success. Lee later apologized to Abdullah Badawi for causing him 'discomfort' and stated that he did not want to interfere in Malaysian politics. Prime Minister Lee Hsien Loong visited Malaysia in May 2007 for two days of informal talks with Abdullah Badawi. The main outcome of the discussions was a decision to form a joint ministerial committee to oversee collaboration on Malaysia's plan to establish a 2,217-sq-km economic development zone in southern Johor, to be known as the Iskandar Development Region, with both leaders agreeing that outstanding issues of dispute, such as water sales to Singapore and the suspended construction of the Johor Strait bridge, should not be allowed to impede bilateral co-operation in other areas.

In January 1993 Gen. Fidel Ramos visited Malaysia, the first Philippine President to do so since 1968, owing to strained relations over the Philippines' claim to Sabah. Mahathir and Ramos agreed to establish a joint commission to address bilateral problems. In February 1994 Mahathir made the first official visit by a Malaysian head of government to the Philippines. Relations with the Philippines were strained in April 2000, however, when Muslim separatists from the southern Philippines abducted a group of tourists from the Malaysian resort of Sipadan, off the coast of Sabah. Following a similar kidnapping incident in September, the Malaysian Government dispatched an additional 600 troops to the region. In August 2008 the Malaysia extended the deployment of its troops for a further three months. At the end of their mandate in late November all Malaysian troops were withdrawn, despite a request from the Philippine Government for them to remain.

Relations with Indonesia generally improved from the mid-1990s. In June 1996 the two countries agreed on joint measures to limit the flow of illegal workers into Malaysia. Wide-ranging amendments to the Immigration Act in Malaysia in October 1996 failed to halt the flow of illegal immigrants, which was blamed for rising social tensions. The regional economic crisis, which began in mid-1997, led to an increase in illegal immigrants arriving in Malaysia and prompted Malaysia to begin a repatriation programme to Indonesia and elsewhere. Violent protests against deportation took place in detention centres in March 1998. In addition, groups of illegal Indonesian immigrants entered the compounds of several foreign embassies and the office of the UN High Commissioner for Refugees in March and April and requested political asylum to prevent their repatriation to the Indonesian province of Aceh, where they claimed that, as members of secessionist groups, they would be subject to persecution. Some of the immigrants were subsequently granted asylum by Denmark and Norway. In November 2000 Malaysia and Indonesia agreed to intensify border patrols, after four Malaysians were detained by Indonesian police in June of that year for allegedly stealing logs.

Relations with both Indonesia and the Philippines, meanwhile, were strained in 1998 following the arrest in September of the former Malaysian Deputy Prime Minister and Minister of Finance, Anwar Ibrahim: both the President of Indonesia and the President of the Philippines made explicit criticisms of the Malaysian Government regarding its treatment of Anwar. Although the controversy surrounding Anwar's treatment receded as an international issue in 1999, bilateral relations with the Philippines were adversely affected by President Estrada's granting of an audience to Anwar's wife, Wan Azizah Wan Ismail, when she visited the Philippines in April. The new President of Indonesia, Abdurrahman Wahid, demonstrated the close relations between Indonesia and Malaysia by visiting Kuala Lumpur immediately after his election in October 1999.

In August 2001 President Wahid's successor, Megawati Sukarnoputri, visited Malaysia on the final stage of her tour of ASEAN nations. In the same month the new President of the Philippines, Gloria Macapagal Arroyo, also paid her first official visit to the country. However, relations with Indonesia soon threatened to deteriorate again. In 2001 the Government announced that it would deport 10,000 Indonesian illegal immigrants each month in an attempt to tighten controls on foreign labour in the country at a time of economic slowdown. In December 2001 and January 2002 a series of riots by Indonesian labourers led Prime Minister Mahathir to comment that Malaysia might give workers of different nationalities preference in the labour market owing to the problems caused by the illegal immigrants. In late January a temporary ban was imposed on new workers arriving from Indonesia. Soon afterwards the Indonesian Government issued a formal apology for the behaviour of its workers and stated that it hoped that the trouble caused would not affect an otherwise harmonious relationship. Relations with the Philippines were also threatened in November 2001 when the authorities arrested the fugitive Philippine rebel leader, Nur Misuari, on charges of attempting to enter Malaysia illegally. After much indecision, he was finally deported in January 2002 to stand trial in Manila (see the chapter on the Philippines).

In May 2002 Malaysia, Indonesia and the Philippines signed an anti-terrorism pact enabling them to exchange intelligence and to launch joint police operations, in an effort to combat regional terrorist organizations; Thailand and Cambodia also acceded to the pact later in the year. In August the implementation of new legislation requiring that all illegal immigrants leave the country, or risk penalties including fines, imprisonment and caning, strained relations with both the Philippines and Indonesia, as the majority of the workers affected were citizens of those countries. In September the Malaysian Government announced that, owing to diplomatic pressure, exacerbated by public protests being held in Indonesia and the Philippines over the apparently inhumane nature of the expulsions, deportations were being temporarily halted. In early 2004 relations with Indonesia were threatened again when the Indonesian Government urged a global boycott of Malaysian timber, following the release of a report alleging that protected trees from Indonesia were being smuggled across the joint border, 'laundered' and re-exported. The Government denied the claims. At the end of October a 17-day amnesty began for illegal migrant workers to leave Malaysia voluntarily without penalty. Thousands of Indonesians had fled to Malaysia since the Indonesian authorities had commenced military operations against separatists in the province of Aceh in May 2003. In November 2004 Malaysia agreed to extend the amnesty until the end of the year in response to disquiet expressed by the Indonesian Government. The amnesty was subsequently further extended following a written request from President Susilo Bambang Yudhoyono of Indonesia, who was concerned at the prospect of an influx of migrants, at a time when the country was still struggling to recover from the devastation caused by a series of tsunamis in late December (which had killed at least 111,000 people in Indonesia and some 68 in Malaysia). None the less, it was reported that around 380,000 of an estimated 1.2m. illegal foreign workers had left Malaysia by the end of January 2005. In mid-February, following talks with President Yudhoyono in Kuala Lumpur, the Malaysian Prime Minister announced that the amnesty would expire at the end of the month, and in March the forced repatriation of illegal immigrants recommenced. Human rights organizations, including Amnesty International, expressed serious misgivings about the standard of training and supervision given to officers of the Malaysian Immigration Department, amid allegations of widespread physical abuse of immigrants. In July 2006 it was estimated by the Minister of Home Affairs, Radzi Sheikh, that approximately 500,000 illegal immigrants were still living in Malaysia. According to the Minister, another major deportation campaign was to be undertaken by the Government. In October 2007 a temporary ban was imposed on Malaysian employers recruiting new workers from Bangladesh, following a series of cases of ill-treatment of migrants, including the abandonment of several thousand at Kuala Lumpur airport. In January 2008 it was reported that the Malaysian Government aimed to reduce the number of foreign workers in the country from some 2.3m. to 1.8m. in 2009, and to 1.5m. by 2015, by introducing stricter regulations on their employment. In early 2009 the Government announced the cancellation of work permits for nearly 100,000 Indonesian and 55,000 Bangladeshi migrant workers, who were to be sent home. In March 2009 the Philippine President, Gloria Arroyo, met with Prime Minister Abdullah Badawi to request further assistance in peace talks with the rebel Moro Islamic Liberation Front (MILF—see the chapter on the Philippines).

In August 2005 the Malaysian Government expressed frustration at the Indonesian authorities' apparent failure adequately to address the recurrent issue of the heavy smoke emanating from forest fires lit by farmers to clear land for crop plantations on the Indonesian island of Sumatra. Owing to the dangerously high levels of air pollution, the Government declared a state of emergency in western and central regions of the country, including Kuala Lumpur.

In 1994 Malaysian and Indonesian officials commenced discussions to resolve their conflicting claims to the sovereignty of Sipadan and Ligitan, two small islands off the coast of Borneo. In October 1996 an agreement was reached by both countries to refer the issue to the International Court of Justice (ICJ, see p. 22). In December 2002 the ICJ ruled that Malaysia would be awarded sovereignty of the islands, thus bringing an end to the dispute. Another territorial claim being pursued through negotiations was the dispute with Singapore over the island of Batu Putih (Pedra Branca). In February 2003 the two countries finally signed a formal agreement referring the dispute to the ICJ. The Court began deliberating its judgment in November 2007, following the conclusion of public hearings on the case. In May 2008 the ICJ ruled in favour of Singapore by 12 votes to four. Malaysia is also involved with Brunei, Viet Nam, the People's Republic of China, the Philippines and Taiwan in disputed sovereignty claims over the Spratly Islands in the South China Sea. In November 2002 the ASEAN member states approved a Code of Conduct for the islands; the agreement was also sanctioned by China.

Relations with Thailand were strained at the end of 1995 following the killing by the Malaysian navy of two Thai citizens fishing illegally in Malaysian waters. In December the two countries agreed to establish a committee to resolve a long-standing dispute over fishing rights. In February 1996 relations deteriorated, owing to Thailand's opposition to Malaysia's construction of a 27-km wall (completed in 1997) along its border with Thailand, intended to deter illegal immigration from that country. However, in January 1997 the two countries agreed to co-operate in preventing Bangladeshi migrant workers from entering Malaysia and in expediting the return of illegal Thai workers from Malaysia. The arrest in January 1998 of three Thai Muslim separatists by the Malaysian authorities and their deportation to Thailand demonstrated continued co-operation between the two countries since Malaysia was often regarded as a place of sanctuary for Muslim separatists in southern Thailand. Relations between Malaysia and Thailand were further enhanced in April, when the two countries signed an agreement to share equally the natural gas produced in an offshore area to which both countries had made territorial claims. However, the Thai Minister of Foreign Affairs, Surin Pitsuwan, was among a number of international political figures who expressed concern at the arrest and detention of the former Deputy Prime Minister and Minister of Finance, Anwar Ibrahim, in September. In April 2001 the Thai Prime Minister, Thaksin Shinawatra, made his first official visit to the country on a trip intended to enhance co-operation. Bilateral talks were also held in January 2002 in an attempt to resolve problems arising from a planned project to build a gas pipeline between the two countries. In January 2004 new Prime Minister Abdullah Badawi visited Thailand for security discussions, following several attacks believed to have been perpetrated by separatists along the Thai side of the joint border. The two countries agreed to co-operate in efforts to bring an end to the violence and began joint border patrols. The Thai Government subsequently announced that it intended to fence off parts of the border, owing to speculation that Muslim separatists thought to be responsible for the violence might be inside Malaysia. Malaysia rejected such suggestions by the Thai Prime Minister. Amid continuing unrest in southern Thailand, Thaksin Shinawatra visited Malaysia in mid-April for further talks with Abdullah Badawi on improving security along the border. In late April Malaysia increased its border security after militants launched a series of attacks on police posts in southern Thailand; the attacks were violently suppressed by the Thai security forces. Security at the border was heightened again in October following renewed clashes in southern Thailand between government troops and Muslim protesters in which 85 people died, many of whom suffocated after being forced into army trucks. Hundreds of Malaysians demonstrated outside the Thai embassy in Kuala Lumpur in protest at the deaths. Bilateral relations were further strained in December, when the Thai Government claimed to have photographic evidence that militants in southern Thailand had received training in the Malaysian state of Kelantan. In January 2005 the Malaysian authorities arrested Abdul Rahman Ahmad, whom Thailand held responsible for organizing the separatist violence in the south. A diplomatic dispute arose between the two countries in October, concerning the fate of 131 Muslim villagers who had fled from the violence-stricken province of Narathiwat, in southern Thailand, to neighbouring Malaysia. The Malaysian authorities insisted that they would not sanction the return of the asylum-seekers to Thailand unless they received a guarantee of their safety from the Thai authorities. One of the villagers, suspected of involvement in a raid on a Thai military camp in January 2004, was subsequently relinquished to the Thai authorities, while the other 130 refugees remained in a Malaysian detention centre in Terengganu. Discussions aimed at resolving the dispute were held in November 2005 between former Prime Minister Mahathir Mohamad and Thai Prime Minister Thaksin Shinawatra; negotiations were also held between Thaksin and Prime Minister Abdullah Badawi in the same month, during the course of the APEC summit meeting in Busan, the Republic of Korea. The ongoing dispute took relations between the two countries to their lowest point in recent years. In February 2006 the Thai Government indicated that it was prepared to cease its attempts to repatriate the villagers and was to allow them to remain in Malaysia. There was some improvement in bilateral relations from October, when Gen. Surayud Chulanont was appointed as Thai Prime Minister following a coup in which Thaksin was ousted from power. Surayud visited Malaysia later that month, holding talks with Abdullah Badawi on the ongoing insurgency in Thailand's southern provinces. An official visit to Thailand by Abdullah Badawi in February 2007 was reciprocated by Surayud in August. In December Abdullah Badawi and Surayud officially opened a new bridge across the Golok River, linking the Malaysian state of Kelantan to the Thai province of Narathiwat, as part of efforts to improve the economy of the border region and, as a consequence, reduce violence. In July 2008 the Malaysian Minister of Foreign Affairs, Rais Yatim, undertook a three-day visit to Thailand for discussions with the Thai Deputy Prime Minister, Somchai Wongsawat. Rais Yatim discussed the political situation in Thailand and pledged that Malaysia would continue to assist the Thai Government in resolving the ongoing violence in the country's Muslim-dominated southern provinces.

Malaysia's relations with the People's Republic of China remained extremely cordial, with Malaysia frequently offering public support to China, particularly in response to US criticism. Mahathir paid another of a long series of official visits to China in November 2000, and the Chinese Premier, Zhu Rongji, made an official visit to Malaysia in November 1999. In May 2001 the Yang di-Pertuan Agong paid an official state visit to China at the invitation of the Chinese President, Jiang Zemin.

Malaysia forged closer links with Japan in December 2005 with the signing of a bilateral free trade agreement, which entered into force in July 2006. Under the terms of the accord, the two countries were to eliminate tariffs on all industrial goods and on most agricultural, forestry and fishery products within a 10-year period. The agreement also covered intellectual property-rights protection, investment rules, competition policies, business facilitation and personnel training. In keeping with the spirit of invigorated relations, the Emperor and Empress of Japan paid a state visit to Malaysia in June 2006, their first official trip to the country since 1991, and Japanese Prime Minister Shinzo Abe visited Malaysia in August 2007, marking the 50th anniversary of the establishment of diplomatic relations between the two countries.

Mahathir's proposal to establish an East Asian Economic Caucus (EAEC), a trade group intended to exclude the USA, met with considerable resistance from the US Government (which continued to promote the US-dominated Asia-Pacific Economic Co-operation forum—APEC, see p. 185) and Australia. In July 1993 ASEAN agreed, despite the continuing reluctance of Japan to participate, that the EAEC should operate as an East Asian interest group within APEC. In November 1999 (although Mahathir was absent owing to the Malaysian general election) the third informal summit meeting of the 10 ASEAN countries and the People's Republic of China, Japan and the Republic of Korea (collectively known as 'ASEAN + 3') took place. At the meeting it was agreed to hold annual East Asian summits of all 13 nations and to strengthen present economic co-operation with the distant aim of forming an East Asian bloc with a common market and monetary union. This ambition was brought closer in April 2001 when, at a meeting of the ASEAN + 3 group, plans were agreed for a network of currency 'swap' arrangements to prevent a repetition of the regional financial crisis of 1997. At the annual ASEAN summit meeting held in Laos in November 2004 it was agreed to transform the ASEAN + 3 summit meeting, which was first held in 1997, into the East Asia summit, with the long-term objective of establishing an East Asian Community. In December 2005 Kuala Lumpur hosted the inaugural East Asia Summit, held during the course of the ASEAN summit meeting. At the first East Asia Summit, which was chaired by the Malaysian Prime Minister, representatives from the participating nations held discussions on a wide range of issues, including international terrorism, maritime security, the threat of avian influenza, trade and development and the promotion of human rights and democracy. It was agreed that the Summit should convene annually; the second meeting was held in Cebu, the Philippines, in January 2007.

In 1999 Mahathir objected to Australia's leadership of the UN-mandated peace-keeping mission in East Timor (now Timor-Leste, following the territory's accession to independence in May 2002), the UN Transitional Administration in East Timor (UNTAET), claiming that an ASEAN-led mission would be more appropriate. However, other ASEAN members were reluctant to assume responsibility for the peace-keeping body and Australia and East Timor both objected to the notion of Malaysia leading transitional arrangements, owing to its close relations with Indonesia. Only after the intervention of the UN Secretary-General did Malaysia finally contribute limited personnel to UNTAET. In February 2001 Malaysia announced that it would open a liaison office in Dili, East Timor, which became an embassy upon the declaration of East Timor as a fully independent state in May 2002.

Malaysia's relations with Australia, which were often strained under Mahathir, appeared to improve following the succession of Abdullah Badawi to the premiership in October 2003. In June 2004, during a visit to Malaysia by the Australian Minister for Foreign Affairs, Alexander Downer, agreement was reached to hold formal annual talks between the two countries' foreign ministers and separate regular consultations between senior security officials. At the same time Prime Minister Abdullah Badawi accepted an invitation to make a state visit to Australia. This took place in April 2005 and was the first by a Malaysian leader in more than 20 years. However, the Malaysian Government had dismissed a plan announced by the Australian Prime Minister, John Howard, in September 2004 to establish specialist counter-terrorist centres in South-East Asia and Australia, complaining that it had not been consulted about the proposal. None the less, formal negotiations on a free trade agreement between Malaysia and Australia commenced in mid-2005. In July 2008 Kevin Rudd embarked upon a one-day visit to Malaysia, where he had discussions with Abdullah Badawi. The two Prime Ministers agreed to implement an education programme to train teachers in Afghanistan, as part of a new initiative to enhance the regional forces' peace-keeping capacity in that country. The two leaders also agreed to strengthen diplomatic links through regular meetings.

In July 1997 Mahathir (who was often regarded as the international spokesperson for developing countries) indicated that he might submit a proposal to the UN to review its 1948 Universal Declaration of Human Rights, with regard to the specific priorities of less-developed countries. While this sentiment was supported by many Asian countries, the USA reacted angrily to any suggestion of compromise on the issue of human rights. Relations with the USA were also strained by the involvement of PETRONAS in a consortium that signed an agreement during September 1997 to invest in Iran, in contravention of US sanctions against Iran. In October Mahathir paid a formal visit to Cuba, the first such visit by a Malaysian leader, and urged Malaysian firms to invest in the country, in defiance of US legislation that threatened reprisals against firms conducting business with Cuba. Bilateral relations deteriorated further in the same month following Mahathir's suggestion that the economic crisis in the South-East Asian region was due to hostile Jewish currency speculation aimed at preventing progress among Muslim nations. A resolution tabled by 34 members of the US Congress calling for the withdrawal of the remarks or Mahathir's resignation was condemned by Mahathir and the Malaysian press. Relations with the USA were further strained in 1998 following US condemnation of the detention and treatment of the former Deputy Prime Minister and Minister of Finance, Anwar Ibrahim; the Malaysian Government was particularly angered by a speech delivered at the APEC summit meeting in Kuala Lumpur in November by the US Vice-President, Albert Gore, in which Gore expressed support for the movement for political reform in Malaysia. During a speech to UMNO members in June 1999, Mahathir criticized the influence on the country of non-Malaysians (and, in particular, ethnic Europeans), who Mahathir claimed were attempting to 're-colonize' Malaysia. Relations with the USA were improved following a visit by Adm. Dennis Blair, the Commander-in-Chief of the US Pacific Command, to Kuala Lumpur in January 2001. At his meeting with Mahathir, the first between the Prime Minister and a US Pacific commander, the two countries agreed to extend military co-operation. However, the new US President, George W. Bush, insisted that any further improvement in relations would depend on better treatment for Anwar Ibrahim and other detained members of the Malaysian opposition.

In September 2001 relations with the USA were greatly strengthened when Mahathir acted quickly to condemn attacks on the US mainland thought to have been carried out by the al-Qa'ida terrorist network. However, during a meeting with the US President at an APEC summit meeting in Shanghai in October, Mahathir refused to lend his Government's support to the US-led retaliatory attacks on Afghanistan that had begun earlier that month, voicing his concerns at the large numbers of civilian casualties resulting from the raids. At a meeting of ASEAN leaders in November, Malaysia agreed to co-operate with other member nations in the fight against terrorism. In January 2002 the USA congratulated the Malaysian Government on its demonstration of support for the international coalition against terrorism, following the detention of at least 15 suspected terrorists. However, it demanded assurances that the suspects would receive a fair trial under the ISA. In October it was reported that the US Government had requested that Malaysia be the host for a regional anti-terrorism training centre.

While Prime Minister Mahathir made clear his opposition to the US-led campaign to remove the regime of Saddam Hussain in Iraq in 2003, relations with the USA remained generally stable, owing largely to the Government's ongoing operation against suspected domestic terrorists, which was in line with the global anti-terrorism campaign being pursued by the Bush Administration. However, in October 2003, at a summit meeting of the Organization of the Islamic Conference (OIC, see p. 382) held in Putrajaya, Mahathir attracted criticism from the USA, Israel and several European countries when he attacked what he described as Jewish subjugation of Islamic countries during his opening address to the meeting. The Government later issued an apology for the comments. In early 2004 relations with the USA were threatened when new Prime Minister Abdullah Badawi accused the USA of using unreliable intelligence to implicate Malaysia in a global nuclear smuggling network. (The US Government had alleged that a company owned by the Prime Minister's son had supplied components to the network.) In May the USA welcomed the arrest, under the ISA, of Buhary Syed Abu Tahir, a Sri Lankan businessman resident in Malaysia, for his alleged involvement in the network. Meanwhile, in April the Deputy Prime Minister and Minister of Defence, Najib Razak, rejected a proposal by the Commander-in-Chief of the US Pacific Command, Adm. Thomas Fargo, that US warships should patrol the Strait of Melaka between Malaysia and Indonesia to deter terrorism. In July Malaysia, Indonesia and Singapore commenced co-ordinated patrols of the Strait, a critical maritime trade route through which 50% of the world's oil passes, in an attempt to curb piracy. On his first official visit to the USA as Prime Minister in the same month, Abdullah Badawi offered to consider dispatching a medical team to Iraq. In 2006 Malaysia and the USA began negotiations on the establishment of a free trade agreement, but discussions faltered in early 2007 over disagreements in a number of contentious areas, reported to include government procurement, labour, intellectual property rights and the labelling of genetically modified foodstuffs. Opposition to a free trade agreement came from several quarters in Malaysia, including farmers fearful of competition from US imports and trade unions concerned about the impact on local livelihoods, as well as from US politicians who disapproved of Malaysia's gas agreement with Iran. Negotiations resumed in January 2008, when the US chief negotiator expressed hope that an agreement could be concluded by the middle of the year, prior to the US presidential election in November, although significant differences remained to be resolved.

In December 2006 Prime Minister Abdullah Badawi visited Venezuela. Discussions with President Hugo Chávez resulted in initial agreements in the areas of trade and energy co-operation. Meanwhile, during a meeting in November, Abdullah Badawi and the Chilean President, Michelle Bachelet, agreed to initiate bilateral negotiations on the establishment of a free trade agreement; two sessions of talks were held in 2007.

A speech by the head of the European Commission delegation in Malaysia, Thierry Rommel, in June 2007, in which he criticized policies favouring ethnic Malays, prompted considerable anger among Malaysian leaders, who accused the diplomat of interfering in the internal administration of the country. He was summoned to the Ministry of Foreign Affairs to discuss his remarks.

In June 1997 the inauguration took place of a group that aimed to foster economic co-operation among Muslim developing countries, the Developing-Eight (D-8), comprising Malaysia, Bangladesh, Egypt, Indonesia, Iran, Nigeria, Pakistan and Turkey. Malaysia continued to express its close relationship with Arab countries after it denounced US and British air strikes against Iraq in February 2001, while demanding the removal of UN sanctions. It was hoped that a D-8 agreement on preferential tariffs signed in May 2006 would further strengthen economic relations between the group's members. In November 2007, furthermore, Malaysia and Pakistan signed a bilateral free trade agreement, which entered into force in January 2008.

In September 2008 the Malaysian Government dispatched three naval vessels and soldiers to the Gulf of Aden after the seizure by pirates of two Malaysian merchant ships in the previous month. At the end of September both commercial vessels and their crews were released by the pirates, reportedly in exchange for the payment of a large ransom by the Malaysian Government.

Government

Malaysia is a federation of 13 states. The capital, Kuala Lumpur, is a separate Federal Territory, as is the island of Labuan and the newly developed administrative capital of Putrajaya. The Head of State, or Supreme Head of Malaysia, is a monarch (Yang di-Pertuan Agong), elected for a five-year term (with a Deputy Head of State) by and from the hereditary rulers of nine of the states. The monarch acts on the advice of Parliament and the Cabinet. Parliament consists of the Dewan Negara (Senate) and the Dewan Rakyat (House of Representatives). The Senate has 70 members, including 44 appointed by the Head of State, four of which are from the Federal Territories, and 26 elected members, two chosen by each of the 13 State Legislative Assemblies. The House of Representatives consists of 222 members (increased from 219 at the March 2008 general election), elected for five years by universal adult suffrage: 165 from Peninsular Malaysia (including 11 from Kuala Lumpur and one from Putrajaya), 31 from Sarawak and 26 from Sabah (including one from Labuan). The Head of State appoints the Prime Minister and, on the latter's recommendation, other ministers. The Cabinet is responsible to Parliament. The country is divided into 137 administrative districts.

Defence

Malaysia participates in the Five-Power Defence Arrangements with Australia, New Zealand, Singapore and the United Kingdom. As assessed at November 2008, the active armed forces totalled 109,000 men: army 80,000 (although it was planned to reduce this to 60,000–70,000), navy 14,000 and air force 15,000. In February 2004 a programme of national service was introduced, initially on an experimental basis, requiring conscripts to perform three months of military service. Reserve forces numbered 51,600 (army 50,000, navy 1,000, air force 600). Paramilitary forces in 2006 included a General Operations Force (formerly the Police Field Force) of 18,000 men and a People's Volunteer Corps with about 240,000 members. Federal budget plans for 2008 allocated RM 13,920m. to defence.

Economic Affairs

In 2007, according to estimates by the World Bank, Malaysia's gross national income (GNI), measured at average 2005–07 prices, was US $173,705m., equivalent to $6,540 per head (or $13,570 per head on an international purchasing-power parity basis). During 2000–07, it was estimated, the population increased at an annual average of 1.9%, while gross domestic product (GDP) per head increased, in real terms, by an average of 2.8% per year. Overall GDP increased, in real terms, at an average annual rate of 4.8% in 2000–07. According to Bank Negara Malaysia (BNM) estimates, GDP increased by 6.3% in 2007 and by 4.6% in 2008.

Agriculture (including forestry and fishing) contributed 10.1% of GDP in 2008. The sector engaged 14.8% of the employed labour force in 2007. Malaysia is the world's leading producer of palm oil, exports of which contributed 6.9% of the value of total merchandise exports in 2008. Other important crops include rice, rubber, cocoa, coconuts, bananas, tea and pineapples. During 2000–07, according to World Bank figures, agricultural GDP increased, in real terms, at an average annual rate of 3.4%. According to figures from the BNM, agricultural GDP increased by 2.2% in 2007 and by 3.8% in 2008.

Industry (including mining, manufacturing, construction and utilities) contributed 47.7% of GDP in 2008. The sector engaged 28.5% of the employed labour force in 2007. During 2000–07, according to the World Bank, industrial GDP increased, in real terms, at an average annual rate of 4.6%. According to figures from the BNM, industrial GDP grew by 3.3% in 2007 and by 1.0% in 2008.

Mining contributed 16.9% of GDP in 2008. However, it engaged only 0.4% of the employed labour force in 2007. At the end of 2007 estimated proven gas reserves stood at 2,480,000m. cu m, and petroleum reserves at 5,400m. barrels. Petroleum production in 2007 averaged 755,000 barrels per day from Malaysia's oilfields. Exports of crude petroleum and condensates provided 4.7% of total export earnings in 2008. Malaysia is one of the world's leading producers of tin. Bauxite, copper, iron, gold and coal are also mined. The GDP of the mining sector increased at an average annual rate of 2.0% in 2000–07, according to figures from the BNM. Mining GDP increased by 3.3% in 2007, but contracted by 0.8% in 2008.

Manufacturing (the largest export sector) contributed 25.9% of GDP in 2008. The manufacturing sector engaged 18.8% of the employed labour force in 2007. The most important branches of manufacturing include electrical machinery and appliances, food products, metals and metal products, non-electrical machinery, transport equipment, rubber and plastic products, chemical products, wood products and furniture. According to figures from the World Bank, during 2000–07 manufacturing GDP increased, in real terms, at an average annual rate of 5.2%. Manufacturing GDP increased by 3.1% in 2007 and by 1.3% in 2008, according to the BNM.

Energy is derived principally from Malaysia's own reserves of hydrocarbons. The country's dependence on petroleum as a source of electric energy declined from 55.9% in 1990 to 2.9% in 2005. The share contributed by natural gas increased from 22.0% to 64.0% over the same period. In 2005 hydropower and coal accounted for 6.6% and 26.5%, respectively, of the country's electricity output. Production of electricity rose from 100,831m. kWh in 2006 to 104,950m. kWh in 2007. Plans for a controversial 2,400-MW hydroelectric dam at Bakun, in Sarawak, first received government approval in 1986, but construction work has been delayed by various issues; the project was not expected to be completed before 2008. Imports of mineral products comprised 9.1% of the value of merchandise imports in 2006.

The services sector contributed 42.2% of GDP in 2008. It engaged 56.7% of the employed labour force in 2007. Tourism makes a major contribution to the economy. Revenue from this source was reported to have reached RM 49m. in 2008. In that year tourist arrivals rose to a record 22.0m. In 2008 the financial sector contributed 7.7% of GDP. The GDP of the services sector increased by an average of 5.3% per year in 2000–07, according to the World Bank. According to the BNM, services GDP grew by 10.0% in 2007 and by 7.7% in 2008.

In 2007 Malaysia recorded a visible trade surplus of US $37,328m., with a surplus of $28,931m. on the current account of the balance of payments. In 2008 the principal sources of imports were the People's Republic of China, which provided 12.8% of the total, Japan (12.5%), Singapore (11.0%) and the USA (10.8%). Other important suppliers included Thailand, Taiwan and the Republic of Korea. The principal market for exports (purchasing 14.7%) was Singapore; other significant purchasers were the USA (12.5%), Japan (10.8%) and China (9.5%). The principal imports in 2008 were intermediate goods, mainly parts and accessories of capital goods and miscellaneous industrial supplies. The principal exports were electrical machinery and parts (particularly electronic components and semiconductors), chemicals, palm oil, crude petroleum and condensates, and liquefied natural gas.

The 2008 budget envisaged total spending of RM 196,020m. (including net development expenditure of RM 45,067m.). Revenue reached an estimated RM 161,558m., the preliminary budgetary deficit being equivalent to 4.7% of GDP. According to the ADB, at the end of 2008 Malaysia's external debt totalled US $70,479m.; the cost of debt-servicing in that year was equivalent to 3.1% of the value of exports of goods and services. The annual rate of inflation averaged 8.9% in 2000–07. Consumer prices increased by an average of 5.4% in 2008, according to the ADB. The rate of unemployment declined to 3.0% of the labour force in 2007, before rising to an estimated 5.5% in 2008.

Malaysia is a member of the World Trade Organization (WTO, see p. 410), the UN Economic and Social Commission for Asia and the Pacific (ESCAP, see p. 36), the Asian Development Bank (ADB, see p. 191), the Association of South East Asian Nations (ASEAN, see p. 194), the Colombo Plan (see p. 425) and Asia-Pacific Economic Co-operation (APEC, see p. 185), all of which aim to accelerate economic progress in the region. In January 1992 the member states of ASEAN agreed to establish a free trade zone, the ASEAN Free Trade Area (AFTA). The original target for the reduction of tariffs to between 0% and 5% was 2008, but this was subsequently advanced to 2003 and then 2002, when AFTA was formally established. However, Malaysia itself was granted a three-year delay in January 2001 for the opening of its politically sensitive automotive industry to the free trade agreements, fearing competition from Thailand; this was subsequently extended until 2008.

The Malaysian economy made a rapid recovery from the regional economic crisis of the late 1990s. The Ninth Malaysia Plan (2006–10) reiterated the aim of raising the country to the level of a developed nation by 2020. An important aim of the Ninth Plan was the eradication of poverty and the reduction of regional disparities. It was also planned to increase Malaysia's global competitiveness through the development of human resources and the improvement of business conditions. Foreign investment rose by 46.9% in 2007, reaching some RM 80,593m. However, adverse conditions resulting from the global recession precipitated a sharp decline in investment levels during 2008; foreign investment inflows to Malaysia declined by 27% in that year, to RM 58,861m. The substantial contraction in international economic activity also impeded the country's external sector, with exports of palm oil and petroleum beginning to decline in the latter part of 2008. Sales of these commodities had contributed to strong growth in 2007, owing to record international prices. Exports of manufactured goods also suffered the effects of the reduction in foreign demand, which was likely to increase the rate of unemployment. In January 2009 the authorities forbade employers from hiring additional foreign workers, owing to increased public concerns relating to the rate of unemployment. Furthermore, in an effort to reduce competition in the job market, the Government revoked the working visas of thousands of Indonesian and Bangladeshi nationals (see Recent History). In November 2008 a programme of economic stimulus, envisaging expenditure of RM 7,000m., was announced. In March 2009 a further allocation to economic stimulus measures was announced; this amounted to RM 60,000m. (equivalent to an estimated 9% of GDP) and aimed to create 163,000 jobs through investment in infrastructure projects and the provision of tax incentives for businesses. However, the increased expenditure required by the stimulus plan was likely to widen the fiscal deficit in 2009, which was projected to reach 5.4% of GDP. Forecasts of economic growth were subject to a number of downward revisions. Real GDP was expected to increase by 0.5% in 2009, although the authorities warned that the economy might contract by as much as 1.0%.

Education

Under the Malaysian education system, free schooling is provided at government-assisted schools for children between the ages of six and 18 years, although pupils are required to pay fees for public examinations. However, in September 2006 the Government announced that, with effect from the 2007/08 academic year, these charges were to be abolished for all candidates enrolled in government schools. There are also private schools, which receive no government financial aid. Bahasa Malaysia is the main medium of instruction, while English is taught as a second language; Chinese and Tamil are used for instruction only in primary institutions. In January 2003 new legislation came into effect, requiring that all mathematics and science classes in schools be taught in English. Only primary education, which begins at six years of age and lasts for six years, is compulsory. In 2002/03 enrolment in pre-primary education included 75% of the relevant age-group (males 72%; females 79%). In the same year enrolment in primary education included 93.2% of the relevant age-group (males 93%; females 93%). Secondary education, beginning at the age of 12, lasts for seven years, comprising a first cycle of three years and a second of four. Pupils may attend vocational and technical secondary schools instead of the final four years of academic education. In 2004/05 the total enrolment at secondary schools included 69% of the relevant age-group (males 66%; females 72%). At January 2004 Malaysia had 48 tertiary institutions, including nine universities and 31 teacher-training colleges; in 1995 total enrolment at tertiary level was equivalent to 12% of the relevant age-group. The Ninth Malaysia Plan for the period 2006–10 proposed the creation of two new universities, in the states of Kelantan and Terengganu.

The federal budget for 2007 allocated a combined sum of RM 25,938.8m. in operating expenditure (23.0% of the total) to the Ministries of Education and of Higher Education. The 2006–10 Plan allocated RM 40,300m. (about 21% of total development expenditure) to the improvement of education and training.

Public Holidays

Each state has its own public holidays, and the following federal holidays are also observed:

2009: 26–27 January* (Chinese New Year), 9 March† (Mouloud, Prophet Muhammad's Birthday), 1 May (Labour Day), 9 May (Vesak Day), 5 June (Official Birthday of HM the Yang di-Pertuan Agong), 31 August (National Day), 20 September† (Hari Raya Puasa, end of Ramadan), 17 October‡ (Deepavali), 27 November† (Hari Raya Haji, Feast of the Sacrifice), 18 December† (Muharram, Islamic New Year), 25 December (Christmas Day).

2010: 14–16 February* (Chinese New Year), 26 February† (Mouloud, Prophet Muhammad's Birthday), 1 May (Labour Day), 27 May (Vesak Day), 5 June (Official Birthday of HM the Yang di-Pertuan Agong), 31 August (National Day), 11 September† (Hari Raya Puasa, end of Ramadan), 5 November‡ (Deepavali), 17 November† (Hari Raya Haji, Feast of the Sacrifice), 7 December† (Muharram, Islamic New Year), 25 December (Christmas Day).

* The first two days of the first moon of the lunar calendar.

† These holidays are dependent on the Islamic lunar calendar and may vary by one or two days from the dates given.

‡ Except Labuan and Sarawak.

Weights and Measures

The metric system is in force. There is also a local system of weights and measures:

1 cupak = 1 quart (1.1365 litres)
1 gantang = 1 gallon (4.5461 litres)
1 tahil = 1 1/3 ounces (37.8 grams)
16 tahils = 1 kati = 1 1/3 lb (604.8 grams)
100 katis = 1 picul = 133 1/3 lb (60.48 kg)
40 piculs = 1 koyan = 5,333 1/3 lb (2,419.2 kg)

Statistical Survey

Sources (unless otherwise stated): Department of Statistics, Blok C6, Parcel C, Pusat Pentadbiran Kerajaan Persekutuan, 62514 Putrajaya; tel. (3) 88857000; fax (3) 88889248; e-mail jpbpo@stats.gov.my; internet www.statistics.gov.my; Bank Negara Malaysia (Central Bank of Malaysia), Jalan Dato' Onn, PO Box 10922, 50929 Kuala Lumpur; tel. (3) 26988044; fax (3) 26912990; e-mail info@bnm.gov.my; internet www.bnm.gov.my; Departments of Statistics, Kuching and Kota Kinabalu.

Note: Unless otherwise indicated, statistics refer to all states of Malaysia.

Area and Population

AREA, POPULATION AND DENSITY

Area (sq km)	
Peninsular Malaysia	131,686
Sabah (incl. Labuan)	73,711
Sarawak	124,450
Total	329,847*
Population (census results)	
14 August 1991	18,379,655
5–20 July 2000	
Males	11,853,432
Females	11,421,258
Total	23,274,690
Population (official estimate at mid-year)	
2006	26,640,200
2007	27,173,600
2008	27,728,700
Density (per sq km) at mid-2008	84.1

* 127,355 sq miles.

PRINCIPAL ETHNIC GROUPS
(at census of August 1991)*

	Peninsular Malaysia	Sabah†	Sarawak	Total
Malays and other indigenous groups	8,433,826	1,003,540	1,209,118	10,646,484
Chinese	4,250,969	218,233	475,752	4,944,954
Indians	1,380,048	9,310	4,608	1,393,966
Others	410,544	167,790	10,541	588,875
Non-Malaysians	322,229	464,786	18,361	805,376
Total	14,797,616	1,863,659	1,718,380	18,379,655

* Including adjustment for underenumeration.
† Including the Federal Territory of Labuan.

Mid-1997 ('000 persons, estimates): Malays 10,233.2; Other indigenous groups 2,290.9; Chinese 5,445.1; Indian 1,541.7; Others 685.7; Non-Malaysians 1,468.9; Total 21,665.5.

MALAYSIA

STATES
(census of 5–20 July 2000)

	Area (sq km)	Population*	Density (per sq km)	Capital
Johor (Johore)	18,987	2,740,625	144.3	Johor Bahru
Kedah	9,425	1,649,756	175.0	Alor Star
Kelantan	15,024	1,313,014	87.4	Kota Baharu
Melaka (Malacca)	1,652	635,791	384.9	Melaka
Negeri Sembilan (Negri Sembilan)	6,644	859,924	129.4	Seremban
Pahang	35,965	1,288,376	35.8	Kuantan
Perak	21,005	2,051,236	97.7	Ipoh
Perlis	795	204,450	257.2	Kangar
Pulau Pinang (Penang)	1,031	1,313,449	1,274.0	George Town
Sabah	73,619	2,603,485	35.4	Kota Kinabalu
Sarawak	124,450	2,071,506	16.6	Kuching
Selangor	7,960	4,188,876	526.2	Shah Alam
Terengganu (Trengganu)	12,955	898,825	69.4	Kuala Terengganu
Federal Territory of Kuala Lumpur	243	1,379,310	5,676.2	—
Federal Territory of Labuan	92	76,067	826.8	Victoria
Total	329,847	23,274,690	70.6	

* Including adjustment for underenumeration.

PRINCIPAL TOWNS
(population at 2000 census)

Kuala Lumpur (capital)*	1,297,526	Ampang	348,084
Kelang (Klang)	631,676	Shah Alam	319,612
Johor Baharu	630,603	Kota Kinabalu	305,382
Ipoh	574,041	Seremban	290,999
Petaling Jaya	438,084	Kuantan	289,395
Kuching	423,873	Sandakan	275,375
Sabang Jaya	423,338		

* The new town of Putrajaya is now the administrative capital.

Source: Thomas Brinkhoff, *City Population* (internet www.citypopulation.de).

Mid-2007 ('000, incl. suburbs, UN estimates): Kuala Lumpur 1,448; Kelang 956; Johor Baharu 875 (Source: UN, *World Urbanization Prospects: The 2007 Revision*).

BIRTHS AND DEATHS

	Registered live births		Registered deaths	
	Number	Rate (per 1,000)	Number	Rate (per 1,000)
2002	484,037	19.7	105,982	4.3
2003	480,083	19.2	113,644	4.5
2004	477,768	18.7	112,700	4.4
2005*	466,208	17.8	113,531	4.3
2006*	482,700	18.1	117,400	4.4

* Provisional figures.

Sources: UN, *Demographic Yearbook* and *Population and Vital Statistics Report*.

2007 (estimates): Birth rate 17.6 per 1,000; Death rate 4.4 per 1,000.

Life expectancy (years at birth, official estimates): 74 (males 72; females 76) in 2006.

ECONOMICALLY ACTIVE POPULATION*
(sample surveys, ISIC major divisions, '000 persons aged 15 to 64 years)

	2005	2006	2007
Agriculture, hunting and forestry	1,355.2	1,375.3	1,437.3
Fishing	115.2	128.2	120.9
Mining and quarrying	36.1	42.0	39.4
Manufacturing	1,989.3	2,082.8	1,977.3
Electricity, gas and water	56.6	75.4	60.8
Construction	904.4	908.9	922.5
Wholesale and retail trade; repair of motor vehicles, motorcycles and personal and household goods	1,620.3	1,650.5	1,712.1
Hotels and restaurants	671.8	721.3	760.7
Transport, storage and communications	544.7	539.7	538.2
Financial intermediation	247.4	242.3	282.2
Real estate, renting and business activities	459.0	508.4	558.1
Public administration and defence; compulsory social security	728.5	674.1	716.1
Education	607.1	600.1	632.7
Health and social work	212.6	223.2	238.9
Other community, social and personal service activities	234.9	247.1	266.5
Private households with employed persons	260.6	254.6	272.7
Extra-territorial organizations and bodies	1.7	1.2	1.7
Total employed	10,045.4	10,275.4	10,538.1
Unemployed	368.1	353.6	351.4
Total labour force	10,413.5	10,628.9	10,889.5

* Excluding members of the armed forces.

Source: ILO.

Health and Welfare

KEY INDICATORS

Total fertility rate (children per woman, 2006)	2.7
Under-5 mortality rate (per 1,000 live births, 2006)	12
HIV/AIDS (% of persons aged 15–49, 2007)	0.5
Physicians (per 1,000 head, 2002)	0.7
Hospital beds (per 1,000 head, 2006)	1.9
Health expenditure (2006): US $ per head (PPP)	500
Health expenditure (2006): % of GDP	4.3
Health expenditure (2006): public (% of total)	45.2
Access to water (% of persons, 2006)	99
Access to sanitation (% of persons, 2006)	94
Human Development Index (2006): ranking	63
Human Development Index (2006): value	0.823

For sources and definitions, see explanatory note on p. vi.

Agriculture

PRINCIPAL CROPS
('000 metric tons)

	2005	2006	2007
Rice, paddy	2,240	2,154*	2,231*
Maize	75*	80†	83*
Sweet potatoes†	27	27	27
Cassava (Manioc)	400†	430*	430*
Sugar cane	95*	80*	80*
Coconuts	584*	570†	568†
Oil palm fruit	75,650	75,400†	77,700†
Cabbages†	35	35	35
Tomatoes†	35	35	35
Cucumbers and gherkins†	45	45	45
Watermelons†	132	132	132
Bananas†	530	530	530
Pineapples	340†	350†	360†
Papayas†	72	72	72
Coffee, green	40*	40†	40†
Cocoa beans	28	32	30
Pepper	19	19†	19†
Natural rubber	1,126	1,284	1,270†

* Unofficial figure.
† FAO estimate(s).

Aggregate production ('000 metric tons, may include official, semi-official or estimated data): Total cereals 2,315 in 2005, 2,234 in 2006, 2,314 in 2007; Total oilcrops 16,907 in 2005, 17,854 in 2006, 18,423; Total vegetables (incl. melons) 511 in 2005, 511 in 2006, 511 in 2007; Total fruits (excl. melons) 1,317 in 2005, 1,003 in 2006, 1,019 in 2007.

Source: FAO.

LIVESTOCK
('000 head, year ending September)

	2005	2006*	2007*
Cattle	801	815	829
Buffaloes	137	137	138
Goats	271	278	285
Sheep	109	109	103
Pigs	2,168	2,230	2,290
Chickens*	185,000	187,000	190,000
Ducks*	16,000	16,000	16,000

* FAO estimates.
Source: FAO.

LIVESTOCK PRODUCTS
('000 metric tons, FAO estimates unless otherwise indicated)

	2005	2006	2007
Cattle meat	21.7	21.9	22.3
Buffalo meat	4.5	4.7	4.7
Pig meat	213.7	220.0	226.0
Chicken meat	860.0	922.0	931.0
Duck meat	107.0	108.0	111.0
Cows' milk	37.8	38.7	39.3
Buffaloes' milk	7.9	7.5	7.5
Hen eggs	442.0	453.0	465.0
Other poultry eggs	11.0	11.0	11.0

* Unofficial figures.
Source: FAO.

Forestry

ROUNDWOOD REMOVALS
('000 cubic metres, excl. bark)

	2005	2006	2007
Sawlogs, veneer logs and logs for sleepers	23,296	21,893	20,924
Pulpwood*	703	703	703
Other industrial roundwood	1,187	582	563
Fuel wood*	3,068	3,013	2,959
Total	28,254	26,191	25,149

* FAO estimates.
Source: FAO.

SAWNWOOD PRODUCTION
('000 cubic metres, incl. railway sleepers)

	2005	2006	2007
Total (all broadleaved)	5,173	5,129	5,122

Source: FAO.

Fishing

('000 metric tons, live weight)

	2004	2005	2006
Capture	1,335.8	1,214.2	1,296.3
Indian scad	67.3	81.0	99.1
Kawakawa	14.8	16.0	25.3
Indian mackerels	141.6	131.3	117.5
Squids	52.2	44.3	70.1
Aquaculture	171.3	175.8	168.3
Blood cockle	64.6	59.5	45.7
Total catch	1,507.0	1,390.0	1,464.7

Note: Figures exclude crocodiles, recorded by number rather than by weight. The number of estuarine crocodiles caught was: 1,450 in 2004; 1,058 in 2005; 1,790 in 2006. Also excluded are shells and corals. Catches of turban shells (metric tons, FAO estimates) were: 80 in 2004; 80 in 2005; 80 in 2006. Catches of hard corals (metric tons, FAO estimates) were: 4,000 in 2004; 4,000 in 2005; 4,000 in 2006.

Source: FAO.

Mining

PRODUCTION
(metric tons, unless otherwise indicated)

	2005	2006	2007
Tin-in-concentrates	2,857	2,398	2,263
Bauxite ('000 metric tons)	5	92	157
Iron ore ('000 metric tons)*	950	667	802
Kaolin	494,511	341,223	587,508
Gold (kg)	4,250	3,497	2,913
Hard coal	789,356	901,801	1,074,936
Crude petroleum ('000 barrels)	267,720	243,455	253,675
Natural gas (million cu m)†	70,471	70,191	71,170
Ilmenite*	38,196	45,649	59,310
Zirconium*	4,954	1,690	7,393

* Figures refer to the gross weight of ores and concentrates.
† Including amount reinjected, flared and lost.

Source: US Geological Survey.

Industry

SELECTED PRODUCTS
('000 metric tons, unless otherwise indicated)

	2006	2007	2008
Canned fish, frozen shrimps/prawns	41.6	45.5	45.6
Palm oil (crude)	15,881	15,823	17,734
Refined sugar	1,460.3	1,597.6	1,541.7
Soft drinks ('000 litres)	1,424.5	2,138.4	2,071.6
Cigarettes (metric tons)	22,799	23,723	23,004
Woven cotton fabrics (million metres)	156.2	159.7	200.8
Veneer sheets ('000 cu metres)	1,138.9	1,227.4	1,034.4
Plywood ('000 cu metres)	4,923.6	4,941.2	4,620.5
Kerosene and jet fuel	3,419.5	3,306.9	3,940.4
Liquefied petroleum gas	3,437.5	3,807.3	3,625.6
Inner tubes and tyres ('000)	31,530	34,378	35,533
Rubber gloves (million pairs)	20,527.6	20,513.2	21,733.9
Earthen brick and cement roofing tiles (million)	1,265.1	1,054.5	1,118.4
Cement	19,456	21,910	19,635
Iron and steel bars and rods	3,020.6	2,743.9	2,399.4
Television receivers ('000)	7,743.8	5,752.5	5,704.1
Radio receivers ('000)	24,876	46,471	65,880
Semiconductors (million)	17,440	21,274	21,975
Electronic transistors (million)	29,341	30,960	31,466
Integrated circuits (million)	33,209	32,733	31,077
Passenger motor cars ('000)*	365.6	333.7	419.6
Commercial vehicles ('000)*	95.7	79.6	85.2
Motorcycles and scooters ('000)	446.1	463.4	542.5
Electric energy (million kWh)†	100,831	104,950	n.a.

* Vehicles assembled from imported parts.
† Source: Asian Development Bank.

Tin (smelter production of primary metal, metric tons): 18,250 in 2003; 33,914 in 2004; 36,924 in 2005; 22,850 in 2006; 25,263 in 2007 (Source: US Geological Survey).

Finance

CURRENCY AND EXCHANGE RATES

Monetary Units
100 sen = 1 ringgit Malaysia (RM—also formerly Malaysian dollar).

Sterling, US Dollar and Euro Equivalents (31 December 2008)
£1 sterling = RM 5.050;
US $1 = RM 3.4640;
€1 = RM 4.8208;
RM 100 = £19.80 = US $28.87 = €20.74.

Exchange Rate
2006 3.668
2007 3.438
2008 3.336.

FEDERAL BUDGET
(RM million)

Revenue	2005	2006	2007*
Tax revenue	80,594	86,630	95,169
Taxes on income and profits	53,543	61,572	69,396
Companies (excl. petroleum)	26,381	26,477	32,149
Individuals	8,649	10,196	11,661
Petroleum	14,566	20,674	20,453
Export duties	2,085	2,362	2,322
Import duties	3,385	2,679	2,424
Excises on goods	8,641	8,577	8,990
Sales tax	7,709	6,532	6,642
Service tax	2,582	2,685	3,013
Others	2,648	2,225	2,380
Other revenue	25,709	36,915	44,716
Total	106,304	123,546	139,885

Expenditure	2005	2006	2007*
Emoluments	25,587	28,522	32,587
Pensions and gratuities	6,809	7,008	8,251
Debt service charges	11,604	12,495	12,911
Domestic	9,875	10,990	11,485
External	1,729	1,506	1,426
Supplies and services	17,984	20,923	23,622
Subsidies	13,387	10,112	10,481
Asset acquisition	1,603	1,949	2,532
Other grants and transfers	20,427	26,294	31,501
Other expenditure	343	391	1,197
Total	97,744	107,694	123,084

* Preliminary.

2008 (RM million, preliminary): Total revenue 161,558; Total expenditure 150,953 (Emoluments 36,214, Pensions and gratuities 8,412, Debt service charges 13,101, Supplies and services 25,900, Subsidies 34,103, Grants and transfers to state governments 4,402, Other expenditure 28,821).

FEDERAL DEVELOPMENT EXPENDITURE
(RM million)

	2005	2006	2007*
Defence and security	4,803	4,803	5,702
Social services	7,450	9,525	12,893
Education	3,736	5,349	6,271
Health	1,220	1,298	1,496
Housing	1,082	1,347	2,947
Economic services	14,957	17,404	20,116
Agriculture and rural development	2,482	3,999	3,842
Public utilities	1,481	2,244	2,358
Trade and industry	3,221	3,389	4,904
Transport	7,660	7,751	8,500
General administration	3,325	4,076	1,853
Sub-total	30,534	35,807	40,564
Less Loan recoveries	3,250	846	3,105
Total	27,284	34,961	37,460

* Preliminary.

2008 (RM million): Development expenditure (net) 45,067 (preliminary).

INTERNATIONAL RESERVES
(US $ million at 31 December)

	2006	2007	2008
Gold (national valuation)	62	65	63
IMF special drawing rights	214	229	226
Reserve position in IMF	195	155	317
Foreign exchange	81,724	100,635	90,511
Total	82,195	101,084	91,117

Source: IMF, *International Financial Statistics*.

MONEY SUPPLY
(RM million at 31 December)

	2005	2006	2007
Currency outside banks	30,166	33,500	36,246
Demand deposits at commercial banks	92,695	104,334	127,300
Total money (incl. others)	122,861	137,834	163,545

Source: IMF, *International Financial Statistics*.

MALAYSIA

COST OF LIVING
(Consumer Price Index; base 2000 = 100)

	2003	2004	2005
Food	102.8	105.0	108.8
Beverages and tobacco	111.0	119.7	132.3
Clothing and footwear	93.3	91.6	90.7
Rent and other housing costs, heating and lighting	103.1	104.0	105.3
Furniture, domestic appliances, tools and maintenance	99.2	99.5	101.5
Medical care	107.2	108.7	110.4
Transport and communications	112.3	113.0	118.1
Education and leisure	100.7	100.6	101.1
Other goods and services	103.1	105.0	107.5
All items	**104.4**	**105.9**	**109.1**

All items (Consumer Price Index; base: 2000 = 100): 112.9 in 2006; 115.2 in 2007; 121.7 in 2008 (Source: IMF, *International Financial Statistics*).

NATIONAL ACCOUNTS
(RM million at current prices)

Expenditure on the Gross Domestic Product

	2005	2007	2008
Government final consumption expenditure	68,526	78,297	93,067
Private final consumption expenditure	257,412	292,724	334,219
Change in stocks	577	1,654	−4,532
Gross fixed capital formation	119,596	139,142	146,127
Total domestic expenditure	**446,111**	**511,817**	**568,881**
Exports of goods and services	669,776	707,156	766,360
Less Imports of goods and services	542,150	577,110	594,520
GDP in purchasers' values	**573,737**	**641,864**	**740,721**
GDP at constant 1987 prices	n.a.	**505,353**	**528,804**

Gross Domestic Product by Economic Activity

	2006	2007	2008
Agriculture, forestry and fishing	50,512	65,701	76,219
Mining and quarrying	83,869	92,796	127,277
Manufacturing	169,761	179,522	195,027
Electricity, gas and water	15,388	16,373	17,345
Construction	15,941	17,584	19,519
Trade	60,373	69,209	81,386
Restaurants and hotels	12,428	14,368	16,399
Transport and storage	20,198	22,686	24,516
Communications	18,388	19,643	21,092
Finance and insurance	48,504	53,324	57,933
Real estate and business services	23,518	28,395	29,202
Government services	38,208	44,231	54,337
Other services	29,057	30,910	33,026
Sub-total	**586,145**	**654,742**	**753,278**
Import duties	5,659	5,969	7,387
Less Financial intermediation services indirectly measured	18,066	18,846	19,942
GDP in purchasers' values	**573,73**	**641,864**	**740,721**

BALANCE OF PAYMENTS
(US $ million)

	2005	2006	2007
Exports of goods f.o.b.	141,808	160,842	176,403
Imports of goods f.o.b.	−108,653	−124,144	−139,075
Trade balance	**33,156**	**36,698**	**37,328**
Exports of services	19,576	21,831	28,272
Imports of services	−21,956	−23,720	−27,986
Balance on goods and services	**30,776**	**34,809**	**37,613**
Other income received	5,373	8,463	11,302
Other income paid	−11,691	−13,192	−15,297
Balance on goods, services and income	**24,457**	**30,080**	**33,618**
Current transfers received	299	313	342
Current transfers paid	−4,776	−4,904	−5,029
Current balance	**19,980**	**25,488**	**28,931**
Capital account (net)	—	—	−28

—*continued*	2005	2006	2007
Direct investment abroad	−2,972	−6,043	−11,042
Direct investment from abroad	3,966	6,064	8,456
Portfolio investment assets	−715	−2,123	−3,940
Portfolio investment liabilities	−2,985	5,593	9,320
Financial derivatives assets	−59	8	198
Financial derivatives liabilities	1	21	−246
Other investment assets	−4,877	−8,531	−17,209
Other investment liabilities	−2,164	−6,883	3,614
Net errors and omissions	−6,555	−6,731	−4,910
Overall balance	**3,620**	**6,864**	**13,144**

Source: IMF, *International Financial Statistics*.

External Trade

PRINCIPAL COMMODITIES
(RM million)

Imports c.i.f.	2005	2006	2007*
Capital goods†	60,734	65,257	69,996
Intermediate goods	308,335	335,532	358,506
Miscellaneous industrial supplies, processed	87,704	96,471	110,718
Parts and accessories of capital goods (excl. transportation equipment)	163,660	172,047	172,667
Consumption goods	24,600	27,894	28,888
Total (incl. others)‡	**434,010**	**480,773**	**504,569**

Exports f.o.b.	2005	2006	2007*
Palm oil	19,036	21,643	31,983
Crude petroleum and condensates	28,508	30,814	31,880
Liquefied natural gas	20,790	23,285	26,157
Semi-conductors	89,967	93,505	96,471
Electronic components	118,265	127,751	116,978
Consumer electrical products	22,632	19,099	16,469
Industrial and commercial electrical products	28,608	34,489	29,690
Electrical industrial machinery and equipment	20,476	22,844	25,183
Chemicals and chemical products	29,718	32,893	37,421
Metal manufactures	17,157	22,817	26,410
Total (incl. others)	**533,788**	**588,965**	**605,193**

* Preliminary.
† Figures net of re-exports.
‡ Including re-exports.

2008 (RM million): *Imports:* Capital goods 69,957; Intermediate goods 378,997 (Miscellaneous industrial supplies, processed 120,204; Parts and accessories of capital goods, excl. transportation equipment 164,038); Consumption goods 32,273; Total (incl. others) 521,503. *Exports:* Palm oil 46,050; Crude petroleum and condensates 31,224; Liquefied natural gas 22,873; Semi-conductors 89,815; Electronic components 106,104; Consumer electrical products 21,525; Industrial and commercial electrical products 30,951; Electrical industrial machinery and equipment 25,391; Chemicals and chemical products 40,974; Metal manufactures 29,262; Total (incl. others) 663,514.

MALAYSIA

PRINCIPAL TRADING PARTNERS
(RM million)

Imports c.i.f.	2005	2006	2007
Australia	8,171	8,884	10,203
China, People's Republic	49,880	58,226	64,856
France	5,660	7,696	7,714
Germany	19,265	21,063	23,408
Hong Kong	10,797	12,650	14,676
India	4,164	4,884	7,064
Indonesia	16,566	18,166	21,370
Japan	62,982	63,568	65,495
Korea, Republic	21,604	25,911	24,917
Philippines	12,192	10,640	9,774
Singapore	50,828	56,188	57,920
Taiwan	23,974	26,220	28,706
Thailand	22,889	26,276	26,981
United Kingdom	6,522	6,809	7,264
USA	55,918	60,210	54,678
Total (incl. others)	434,010	480,773	504,569

Exports f.o.b.	2005	2006	2007
Australia	18,042	16,711	20,381
China, People's Republic	35,221	42,660	53,032
France	6,913	7,942	7,351
Germany	11,259	12,774	14,831
Hong Kong	31,205	29,144	27,966
India	14,972	18,783	20,204
Indonesia	12,580	14,916	17,739
Japan	49,918	52,215	55,239
Korea, Republic	17,945	21,291	23,026
Netherlands	17,452	21,429	23,586
Philippines	7,476	7,974	8,736
Singapore	83,333	90,751	88,509
Taiwan	14,813	16,044	16,461
Thailand	28,723	31,177	29,983
United Kingdom	9,470	10,714	9,899
USA	105,033	110,586	94,513
Total (incl. others)	533,788	588,965	605,099

2008 (RM million): *Imports:* Australia 11,764; China, People's Republic 66,854; France 7,554; Germany 22,489; Hong Kong 13,658; India 10,302; Indonesia 24,186; Japan 65,099; Korea, Republic 24,218; Philippines 9,640; Singapore 57,321; Taiwan 25,091; Thailand 29,269; United Kingdom 7,654; USA 56,454; Total (incl. others) 521,503. *Exports:* Australia 24,410; China, People's Republic 63,211; France 6,361; Germany 15,361; Hong Kong 28,326; India 24,733; Indonesia 20,719; Japan 71,793; Korea, Republic 25,880; Netherlands 22,443; Philippines 9,761; Singapore 97,765; Taiwan 16,230; Thailand 31,755; United Kingdom 9,467; USA 82,741; Total (incl. others) 663,514.

Transport

RAILWAYS
(traffic, Peninsular Malaysia only)

	2002	2003	2004
Passenger-km (million)	1,138	1,031	1,152
Freight ton-km (million)	1,073	887	1,017

Source: UN, *Statistical Yearbook*.

ROAD TRAFFIC
(registered motor vehicles at 31 December)

	2000	2001	2002
Passenger cars	4,212,567	4,624,557	5,069,412
Buses and coaches	48,662	49,771	51,158
Lorries and vans	665,284	689,668	713,148
Road tractors	315,687	329,198	345,604
Motorcycles and mopeds	5,356,604	5,609,351	5,842,617

Source: International Road Federation, *World Road Statistics*.

SHIPPING
Merchant Fleet
(registered at 31 December)

	2005	2006	2007
Number of vessels	1,052	1,101	1,151
Total displacement ('000 grt)	5,758.7	6,389.0	6,974.6

Source: Lloyd's Register-Fairplay, *World Fleet Statistics*.

Sea-borne Freight Traffic*
(Peninsular Malaysia, international and coastwise, '000 metric tons)

	2001	2002	2003
Goods loaded	70,092	81,648	87,960
Goods unloaded	68,184	74,460	73,416

* Including transshipments.

Source: UN, *Monthly Bulletin of Statistics*.

CIVIL AVIATION
(traffic on scheduled services)

	2002	2003	2004
Kilometres flown (million)	232	247	278
Passengers carried ('000)	16,275	16,710	19,227
Passenger-km (million)	36,923	38,415	44,642
Total ton-km (million)	5,345	5,689	6,672

Source: UN, *Statistical Yearbook*.

Tourism

TOURIST ARRIVALS BY COUNTRY OF RESIDENCE*

	2006	2007	2008
Brunei	784,446	1,172,154	1,085,115
China, People's Republic (incl. Hong Kong and Macao)	528,871	783,788	949,864
Indonesia	1,217,024	1,804,535	2,428,605
Japan	354,213	367,567	433,462
Singapore	9,634,506	10,492,692	11,003,492
Thailand	1,891,921	1,625,698	1,493,789
Total (incl. others)	17,546,863	20,972,822	22,052,488

* Including Singapore residents crossing the frontier by road through the Johore Causeway.

Source: Malaysia Tourism Promotion Board.

Tourism receipts (US $ million, including passenger transport): 9,181 in 2004; 10,389 in 2005; 12,355 in 2006 (Source: World Tourism Organization).

Communications Media

	2005	2006	2007
Telephones ('000 main lines in use)	4,365.6	4,342.1	4,350.0
Mobile cellular telephones ('000 subscribers)	19,545.0	19,463.7	23,347.0
Personal computers ('000 in use)	4,900	n.a.	n.a.
Internet users ('000)	12,537.3	13,989.0	15,867.7
Broadband subscribers ('000)	507.1	899.0	1,368.9

Radio receivers ('000 in use, 1997): 9,100.

Television receivers ('000 in use, 2001): 4,773.

Facsimile machines (estimate, '000 in use): 175.0 in 1998.

Book production (incl. pamphlets, 1999): 5,084 titles (29,040,000 copies in 1996).

Daily newspapers (2004): 35 (average circulation 2,753,000 copies).

Non-daily newspapers (1997): 3 (average circulation 312,000 copies).

Periodicals (1992): 25 titles (average circulation 996,000 copies).

Sources: International Telecommunication Union; UNESCO, *Statistical Yearbook*; UN, *Statistical Yearbook*.

Education

(January 2004, unless otherwise indicated)

	Institutions	Teachers	Students
Primary	7,557	179,622	3,044,797
Secondary	1,962	130,372	2,093,645
Regular	1,751	116,006	1,979,526
Fully residential	53	3,135	29,813
Technical	88	7,224	34,710
Religious	55	3,053	37,732
Special	3	140	884
Special Model	10	688	10,437
Sports*	2	142	912
Tertiary†	48	14,960	210,724
Universities	9	7,823	97,103
Teacher training	31	3,220	46,019
MARA Institute of Technology	1	2,574	42,174

* 2003 figures.
† 1995 figures.

Source: Ministry of Education.

Teachers (2004/05): Pre-primary 29,530; Primary 189,521; Secondary 146,503; Tertiary 45,246 (Source: UNESCO Institute for Statistics).

Students (2004/05): Pre-primary 668,291; Primary 3,202,008; Secondary 2,489,117; Tertiary 696,760 (Source: UNESCO Institute for Statistics).

Adult literacy rate (UNESCO estimates): 91.9% (males 94.2%; females 89.6%) in 2007 (Source: UNESCO Institute for Statistics).

Directory

The Constitution

The Constitution of the Federation of Malaya became effective at independence on 31 August 1957. As subsequently amended, it is now the Constitution of Malaysia. The main provisions are summarized below.

SUPREME HEAD OF STATE

The Yang di-Pertuan Agong (King or Supreme Sovereign) is the Supreme Head of Malaysia.

Every act of government is derived from his authority, although he acts on the advice of Parliament and the Cabinet. The appointment of a Prime Minister lies within his discretion, and he has the right to refuse to dissolve Parliament even against the advice of the Prime Minister. He appoints the Judges of the Federal Court and the High Courts on the advice of the Prime Minister. He is the Supreme Commander of the Armed Forces. The Yang di-Pertuan Agong is elected by the Conference of Rulers, and to qualify for election he must be one of the nine hereditary Rulers. He holds office for five years or until his earlier resignation or death. Election is by secret ballot on each Ruler in turn, starting with the Ruler next in precedence after the late or former Yang di-Pertuan Agong. The first Ruler to obtain not fewer than five votes is declared elected. The Deputy Supreme Head of State (the Timbalan Yang di-Pertuan Agong) is elected by a similar process. On election the Yang di-Pertuan Agong relinquishes, for his tenure of office, all his functions as Ruler of his own state and may appoint a Regent. The Timbalan Yang di-Pertuan Agong exercises no powers in the ordinary course, but is immediately available to fill the post of Yang di-Pertuan Agong and carry out his functions in the latter's absence or disability. In the event of the Yang di-Pertuan Agong's death or resignation he takes over the exercise of sovereignty until the Conference of Rulers has elected a successor.

CONFERENCE OF RULERS

The Conference of Rulers consists of the Rulers and the heads of the other states. Its prime duty is the election by the Rulers only of the Yang di-Pertuan Agong and his deputy. The Conference must be consulted in the appointment of judges, the Auditor-General, the Election Commission and the Services Commissions. It must also be consulted and concur in the alteration of state boundaries, the extension to the federation as a whole, of Islamic religious acts and observances, and in any bill to amend the Constitution. Consultation is mandatory in matters affecting public policy or the special position of the Malays and natives of Sabah and Sarawak. The Conference also considers matters affecting the rights, prerogatives and privileges of the Rulers themselves.

FEDERAL PARLIAMENT

Parliament has two Houses—the Dewan Negara (Senate) and the Dewan Rakyat (House of Representatives). The Senate has a membership of 70, comprising 26 elected and 44 appointed members. Each state legislature, acting as an electoral college, elects two Senators; these may be members of the State Legislative Assembly or otherwise. The Yang di-Pertuan Agong appoints the other 44 members of the Senate; these include four Senators representing the three Federal Territories—Kuala Lumpur, Labuan and Putrajaya. Members of the Senate must be at least 30 years old. The Senate elects its President and Deputy President from among its members. It may initiate legislation, but all proposed legislation for the granting of funds must be introduced in the first instance in the House of Representatives. All legislative measures require approval by both Houses of Parliament before being presented to the Yang di-Pertuan Agong for the Royal Assent in order to become law. A bill originating in the Senate cannot receive Royal Assent until it has been approved by the House of Representatives, but the Senate has delaying powers only over a bill originating from and approved by the House of Representatives. Senators serve for a period of three years, but the Senate is not subject to dissolution. Parliament can, by statute, increase the number of Senators elected from each state to three. The House of Representatives consists of 219 elected members (see Amendments). Of these, 165 are from Peninsular Malaysia (including 11 from Kuala Lumpur and one from Putrajaya), 28 from Sarawak and 26 from Sabah (including one from Labuan). Members are returned from single-member constituencies on the basis of universal adult franchise. The term of the House of Representatives is limited to five years, after which time a fresh general election must be held. The Yang di-Pertuan Agong may dissolve Parliament before then if the Prime Minister so advises.

THE CABINET

To advise him in the exercise of his functions, the Yang di-Pertuan Agong appoints the Cabinet, consisting of the Prime Minister and an unspecified number of Ministers (who must all be Members of Parliament). The Prime Minister must be a citizen born in Malaysia and a member of the House of Representatives who, in the opinion of the Yang di-Pertuan Agong, commands the confidence of that House. Ministers are appointed on the advice of the Prime Minister. A number of Deputy Ministers (who are not members of the Cabinet) are also appointed from among Members of Parliament. The Cabinet meets regularly under the chairmanship of the Prime Minister to formulate policy.

PUBLIC SERVICES

The Public Services, civilian and military, are non-political and owe their loyalty not to the party in power but to the Yang di-Pertuan Agong and the Rulers. They serve whichever government may be in power, irrespective of the latter's political affiliation. To ensure the impartiality of the service, and its protection from political interference, the Constitution provides for a number of Services Commissions to select and appoint officers, to place them on the pensionable establishment, to determine promotion and to maintain discipline.

THE STATES

The heads of nine of the 13 states are hereditary Rulers. The Ruler of Perlis has the title of Raja, and the Ruler of Negeri Sembilan that of Yang di-Pertuan Besar. The rest of the Rulers are Sultans. The heads of the States of Melaka (Malacca), Pulau Pinang (Penang), Sabah and Sarawak are each designated Yang di-Pertua Negeri and do not participate in the election of the Yang di-Pertuan Agong. Each of the 13 states has its own written Constitution and a single Legislative Assembly. Every state legislature has powers to legislate on matters not reserved for the Federal Parliament. Each State Legislative Assembly has the right to order its own procedure, and the members enjoy parliamentary privilege. All members of the Legislative Assemblies are directly elected from single-member constituencies. The head of the state acts on the advice of the State Government. This advice is tendered by the State Executive Council or Cabinet in precisely the same manner in which the Federal Cabinet tenders advice to the Yang di-Pertuan Agong.

The legislative authority of the state is vested in the head of the state in the State Legislative Assembly. The executive authority of the state is vested in the head of the state, but executive functions may be conferred on other persons by law. Every state has its own Executive Council or Cabinet to advise the head of the state, headed by its Chief Minister (Ketua Menteri in Melaka, Pulau Pinang, Sabah and Sarawak and Menteri Besar in other states), and collectively responsible to the state legislature. Each state in Peninsular Malaysia is divided into administrative districts, each with its District Officer. Sabah is divided into five divisions: West Coast, Interior, Sandakan, Tawau and Kudat. Sarawak is divided into 11 Divisions, each in the charge of a Resident: Betong, Bintulu, Kapit, Kota Samarahan, Kuching, Limbang, Miri, Mukah, Sarikei, Sibu and Sri Aman.

AMENDMENTS

From 1 February 1974, the city of Kuala Lumpur, formerly the seat of the Federal Government and capital of Selangor State, is designated the Federal Territory of Kuala Lumpur. It is administered directly by the Federal Government and returns five members to the House of Representatives.

In April 1981 the legislature approved an amendment empowering the Yang di-Pertuan Agong to declare a state of emergency on the grounds of imminent danger of a breakdown in law and order or a threat to national security.

In August 1983 the legislature approved an amendment empowering the Prime Minister, instead of the Yang di-Pertuan Agong, to declare a state of emergency.

The island of Labuan, formerly part of Sabah State, was designated a Federal Territory as from 16 April 1984.

The legislature approved an amendment increasing the number of parliamentary constituencies in Sarawak from 24 to 27. The amendment took effect at the general election of 20–21 October 1990. The total number of seats in the House of Representatives, which had increased to 177 following an amendment in August 1983, was thus expanded to 180.

In March 1988 the legislature approved two amendments relating to the judiciary (see Judicial System).

In October 1992 the legislature adopted an amendment increasing the number of parliamentary constituencies from 180 to 192. The Kuala Lumpur Federal Territory and Selangor each gained three seats, Johor two, and Perlis, Kedah, Kelantan and Pahang one. The amendment took effect at the next general election (in April 1995).

In March 1993 an amendment was approved that removed the immunity from prosecution of the hereditary Rulers.

In May 1994 the House of Representatives approved an amendment that ended the right of the Yang di-Pertuan Agong to delay legislation by withholding his assent from legislation and returning it to Parliament for further consideration. Under the amendment, the Yang di-Pertuan Agong was obliged to give his assent to a bill within 30 days; if he failed to do so, the bill would, none the less, become law. An amendment was simultaneously approved restructuring the judiciary and introducing a mandatory code of ethics for judges, to be drawn up by the Government.

In 1996 an amendment was approved, increasing the number of parliamentary constituencies from 192 to 193.

In July 2001 an amendment was approved banning all discrimination on grounds of gender.

From 1 February 2001 the city of Putrajaya, formerly part of Selangor State, was designated a Federal Territory.

In 2003 the legislature approved an amendment increasing the number of parliamentary constituencies from 193 to 219. The amendments took effect at the next general election, held in March 2004.

In 2005 an amendment was approved increasing the number of parliamentary constituencies from 219 to 222, following the delineation of additional constituencies in Sarawak. The changes were implemented at the general election of March 2008.

The Government

SUPREME HEAD OF STATE

HM Yang di-Pertuan Agong: HRH Sultan Tuanku MIZAN ZAINAL ABIDIN IBNI AL-MARHUM Sultan MAHMUD (Sultan of Terengganu) (took office 13 December 2006).

Deputy Supreme Head of State

Timbalan Yang di-Pertuan Agong: HRH Tuanku Haji ABDUL HALIM MU'ADZAM SHAH IBNI AL-MARHUM Sultan BADLISHAH (Sultan of Kedah).

CABINET
(April 2009)

Prime Minister and Minister of Finance: Dato' Seri NAJIB BIN Tun Haji ABDUL RAZAK.
Deputy Prime Minister and Minister of Education: Tan Sri Dato' Haji MUHYIDDIN BIN MOHD YASSIN.
Minister of Foreign Affairs: Datuk Seri ANIFAH AMAN.
Minister of Home Affairs: Datuk HISHAMMUDDIN Tun HUSSEIN.
Minister of Defence: Datuk Seri Dr AHMAD ZAHID HAMIDI.
Minister of International Trade and Industry: Datuk MUSTAPA MOHAMED.
Minister of Domestic Trade and Consumer Affairs: Datuk Seri ISMAIL SABRI.
Minister of Transport: Datuk ONG TEE KEAT.
Minister of Energy, Green Technology and Water: Datuk PETER CHIN FAH KUI.
Minister of Works: Datuk SHAZIMAN ABU MANSOR.
Minister of Education: Datuk HISHAMMUDDIN Tun HUSSEIN.
Minister of Higher Education: Dato' Seri MOHAMED KHALED BIN NORDIN.
Minister of Information, Communications and Culture: Datuk Seri Dr RAIS YATIM.
Minister of Human Resources: Datuk Dr S. SUBRAMANIAM.
Minister of Natural Resources and the Environment: Datuk DOUGLAS UGGAH EMBAS.
Minister of Plantation Industries and Commodities: Tan Sri BERNARD DOMPOK.
Minister of Tourism: Datuk Seri Dr NG YEN YEN.
Minister of Science, Technology and Innovation: Datuk Dr MAXIMUS JOHNITY ONGKILI.
Minister of Health: Dato' LIOW TIONG LAI.
Minister of Agriculture and Agro-Based Industry: Datuk NOH OMAR.
Minister of Rural and Regional Development: Datuk SHAFIE APDAL.
Minister of Federal Territories: Datuk Raja NONG CHIK ZAINAL ABIDIN.
Minister of Women, Family and Community Development: Datuk Seri SHAHRIZAT ABDUL JALIL.
Minister of Finance II: Datuk AHMAD HUSNI HANADZIAH.
Minister of Housing and Local Government: Datuk KONG CHO HA.
Minister of Youth and Sports: Datuk AHMAD SHABERY CHEEK.
Ministers in the Prime Minister's Department: Dr KOH TSU KOON, Dato' Seri MOHAMAD NAZRI BIN ABDUL AZIZ, Brig.-Gen. (retd) Datuk JAMIL KHIR BAHARUM, Tan Sri NOR MOHAMED YAKCOP.

MINISTRIES

Prime Minister's Office (Jabatan Perdana Menteri): Federal Government Administration Center, Bangunan Perdana Putra, 62502 Putrajaya; tel. (3) 88888000; fax (3) 88883444; e-mail ppm@pmo.gov.my; internet www.pmo.gov.my.

Ministry of Agriculture and Agro-Based Industry: Wisma Tani, Lot 4G1, Pusat Pentadbiran Kerajaan Persekutuan, 62624 Putrajaya; tel. (3) 88701000; fax (3) 88701845; e-mail pro@agri.moa.my; internet agrolink.moa.my.

Ministry of Defence (Kementerian Pertahanan): Wisma Pertahanan, Jalan Padang Tembak, 50634 Kuala Lumpur; tel. (3) 26921333; fax (3) 26914163; e-mail cpa@mod.gov.my; internet www.mod.gov.my.

Ministry of Arts, Culture and Heritage: 16th Floor, TH Perdana Tower, Maju Junction, 1001 Jalan Sultan Ismail, 50694 Kuala Lumpur; tel. (3) 26127600; fax (3) 26935114; e-mail info@heritage.gov.my; internet www.heritage.gov.my.

Ministry of Defence (Kementerian Pertahanan): Wisma Pertahanan, Jalan Padang Tembak, 50634 Kuala Lumpur; tel. (3) 26921333; fax (3) 26914163; e-mail cpa@mod.gov.my; internet www.mod.gov.my.

Ministry of Domestic Trade and Consumer Affairs (Kementerian Perdagangan Dalam Negeri Dan Hal Ehwal Pengguna): Lot 2G3, Presint 2, Pusat Pentadbiran Kerajaan Persekutuan, 62623 Putrajaya; tel. (3) 88825500; fax (3) 88825762; e-mail aduan@kpdnhep.gov.my; internet www.kpdnhep.gov.my.

Ministry of Education (Kementerian Pendidikan): Kompleks Kerajaan Persekutuan, Parcel E, Pusat Pentadbiran Kerajaan Persekutuan, 62604 Putrajaya; tel. (3) 88846000; fax (3) 88895235; e-mail webmaster@moe.gov.my; internet www.moe.gov.my.

Ministry of Energy, Water and Communications (Kementerian Tenaga, Air dan Komunikasi): Blok E4–5, Parcel E, Pusat Pentadbiran Kerajaan Persekutuan, 62668 Putrajaya; tel. (3) 88836000; fax (3) 88893712; e-mail webmaster@ktak.gov.my; internet www.ktak.gov.my.

Ministry of Federal Territories (Kementerian Wilayah Persekutuan): Aras 1–4, Blok 2, Menara PJH, Presint 2, 62100 Putrajaya; tel. (3) 88897888; fax (3) 88889140; e-mail pha@kwp.gov.my; internet www.kwp.gov.my.

Ministry of Finance (Kementerian Kewangan): Kompleks Kementerian Kewangan, Presint 2, Pusat Pentadbiran Kerajaan Persekutuan, 62592 Putrajaya; tel. (3) 88823000; fax (3) 88823893; e-mail pertanyaan@treasury.gov.my; internet www.treasury.gov.my.

Ministry of Foreign Affairs (Kementerian Luar Negeri): Wisma Putra, 1 Jalan Wisma Putra, Presint 2, 62602 Putrajaya; tel. (3) 88874000; fax (3) 88891717; e-mail webmaster@kln.gov.my; internet www.kln.gov.my.

Ministry of Health (Kementerian Kesihatan): Blok E1, Parcel E, Pusat Pentadbiran Kerajaan Persekutuan, 62590 Putrajaya; tel. (3) 88833888; fax (3) 26985964; e-mail csl@moh.gov.my; internet www.moh.gov.my.

Ministry of Higher Education (Kementerian Pengajian Tinggi): Blok E3, Parcel E, Pusat Perbadanan Kerajaan Persekutuan, 62505 Putrajaya; tel. (3) 88835000; fax (3) 88893921; e-mail menteri@mohe.gov.my; internet www.mohe.gov.my.

Ministry of Home Affairs (Kementerian Hal Ehwal Dalam Negeri): Blok D2, Parcel D, Pusat Pentadbiran Kerajaan Persekutuan, 62546 Putrajaya; tel. (3) 88863000; fax (3) 88891613; e-mail azmi@mofa.gov.my; internet www.moha.gov.my.

Ministry of Housing and Local Government (Kementerian Perumahan dan Kerajaan Tempatan): Paras 3–7, Blok K, Pusat Bandar Damansara, 50782 Kuala Lumpur; tel. (3) 20947033; fax (3) 20949720; e-mail menteri@kpkt.gov.my; internet www.kpkt.gov.my.

Ministry of Human Resources (Kementerian Sumber Manusia): Level 6–9, Blok D3, Parcel D, Pusat Pentadbiran Kerajaan Persekutuan, 62530 Putrajaya; tel. (3) 88865000; fax (3) 88892381; e-mail ksm1@mohr.gov.my; internet www.mohr.gov.my.

Ministry of Information (Kementerian Penerangan): 5th Floor, Wisma TV, Angkasapuri, Bukit Putra, 50610 Kuala Lumpur; tel. (3) 22825333; fax (3) 22821255; e-mail webmaster@kempen.gov.my; internet www.kempen.gov.my.

Ministry of International Trade and Industry (Kementerian Perdagangan Antarabangsa dan Industri): Blok 10, Kompleks Pejabat Kerajaan, Jalan Duta, 50622 Kuala Lumpur; tel. (3) 62033022; fax (3) 62012337; e-mail webmiti@miti.gov.my; internet www.miti.gov.my.

Ministry of Natural Resources and the Environment (Kementerian Sumber Asli dan Alam Sekitar): Aras 14, Blok Menara 4G3, Presint 4, Pusat Pentadbiran Kerajaan Persekutuan, 62574 Putrajaya; tel. (3) 88861111; fax (3) 88892672; e-mail adenan@nre.gov.my; internet www.nre.gov.my.

Ministry of Plantation Industries and Commodities (Kementerian Perusahaan Perladangan dan Komoditi): Aras 6–13, Lot 2G4, Presint 2, Pusat Pentadbiran Kerajaan Persekutuan, 62654 Putrajaya; tel. (3) 88803300; fax (3) 88803441; e-mail pybm@kppk.gov.my; internet www.kppk.gov.my.

Ministry of Rural and Regional Development (Kementerian Kemajuan Luar Bandar dan Wilayah): Aras 5–9, Blok D9, Parcel D, Pusat Pentadbiran Kerajaan Persekutuan, 62606 Putrajaya; tel. (3) 88863500; fax (3) 88892104; e-mail info@kplb.gov.my; internet www.rurallink.gov.my.

Ministry of Science, Technology and Innovation: Aras 1–7, Blok C5, Pusat Pentadbiran Kerajaan Persekutuan, 62662 Putrajaya; tel. (3) 88858000; fax (3) 88886070; e-mail pro@mosti.gov.my; internet www.mosti.gov.my.

Ministry of Tourism (Kementerian Pelancongan): Tingkat 17, Menara Dato' Onn, Pusat Dagangan Dunia Putra, 45 Jalan Tun Ismail, 50480 Kuala Lumpur; tel. (3) 26158188; fax (3) 26935884; e-mail enquiries@tourism.gov.my; internet www.tourism.gov.my.

Ministry of Transport (Kementerian Pengangkutan): Aras 4–7, Blok D5, Parcel D, Pusat Pentadbiran Kerajaan Persekutuan, 62616 Putrajaya; tel. (3) 88866000; fax (3) 88891569; e-mail saptuyah@mot.gov.my; internet www.mot.gov.my.

Ministry of Women, Family and Community Development (Kementerian Pembangunan Wanita, Keluarga dan Masyarakat): Aras 1–6, Blok E, Kompleks Petabat Kerajaan Bukit Perdana, Jalan Dato' Onn, 50515 Kuala Lumpur; tel. (3) 26930095; fax (3) 26934982; e-mail info@kpwkm.gov.my; internet www.kpwkm.gov.my.

Ministry of Works (Kementerian Kerja Raya): Tingkat 5, Blok B, Kompleks Kerja Raya, Jalan Sultan Salahuddin, 50580 Kuala Lumpur; tel. (3) 27111100; fax (3) 27112591; e-mail pro@kkr.gov.my; internet www.kkr.gov.my.

Ministry of Youth and Sports (Kementerian Belia dan Sukan): Lot 4G4, Presint 4, Pusat Pentadbiran Kerajaan Persekutuan, 62570 Putrajaya; tel. (3) 88713333; fax (3) 88888767; e-mail pa_menteri@kbs.gov.my; internet www.kbs.gov.my.

Legislature

PARLIAMENT

Dewan Negara
(Senate)

The Senate has 70 members, of whom 26 are elected. Each State Legislative Assembly elects two members. The Supreme Head of State appoints the remaining 44 members, including four from the three Federal Territories.

President: Dr ABDUL HAMID PAWANTEH.

Dewan Rakyat
(House of Representatives)

The House of Representatives has a total of 222 members: 165 from Peninsular Malaysia (including 11 from Kuala Lumpur and one from the Federal Territory of Putrajaya), 31 from Sarawak and 26 from Sabah (including one from the Federal Territory of Labuan).

Speaker: Tan Sri PANDIKAR AMIN MULIA.

Deputy Speakers: Datuk RONALD KIANDEE, Datuk Dr WAN JUNAIDI TUANKU JAAFAR.

General Election, 8 March 2008

Party	Seats
Barisan Nasional (National Front)	140
United Malays National Organization	79
Malaysian Chinese Association	15
Parti Pesaka Bumiputera Bersatu	14
Parti Rakyat Sarawak	6
Sarawak United People's Party	6
Sabah Progressive Democratic Party	4
United Kadazan People's Organization	3
Sabah Progressive Party	3
Malaysian Indian Congress	3
Parti Bersatu Sabah	3
Parti Gerakan Rakyat Malaysia	2
Parti Bersatu Rakyat Sabah	1
Liberal Democratic Party	1
Parti Keadilan Rakyat	31
Democratic Action Party	28
Parti Islam se Malaysia	23
Total	**222**

The States

JOHOR
(Capital: Johor Bahru)

Sultan: HRH Tuanku Mahmood Iskandar ibni Al-Marhum Sultan Ismail.

Menteri Besar: Datuk Haji Abdul Ghani Othman.

State Legislative Assembly: internet www.johor.gov.my; 56 seats: Barisan Nasional 50; Democratic Action Party 4; Parti Islam se Malaysia 2; elected March 2008.

KEDAH
(Capital: Alor Star)

Sultan: HRH Tuanku Haji Abdul Halim Mu'adzam Shah ibni Al-Marhum Sultan Badlishah.

Menteri Besar: Azizan Abdul Razak.

State Legislative Assembly: internet www.kedah.gov.my; 36 seats: Parti Islam se Malaysia 16; Barisan Nasional 14; Parti Keadilan Rakyat 4; Democratic Action Party 1; Independent 1; elected March 2008.

KELANTAN
(Capital: Kota Baharu)

Sultan: HRH Tuanku Ismail Petra ibni Al-Marhum Sultan Yahaya Petra.

Menteri Besar: Tuan Guru Haji Nik Abdul Aziz bin Nik Mat.

State Legislative Assembly: internet www.kelantan.gov.my; 45 seats: Parti Islam se Malaysia 38; Barisan Nasional 6; Parti Keadilan Rakyat 1; elected March 2008.

MELAKA (MALACCA)
(Capital: Melaka)

Yang di-Pertua Negeri: Tan Sri Khalil Yaakob.

Ketua Menteri: Datuk Wira Mohamed Ali Rustam.

State Legislative Assembly: internet www.melaka.gov.my; 28 seats: Barisan Nasional 23; Democratic Action Party 5; elected March 2008.

NEGERI SEMBILAN
(Capital: Seremban)

Yang di-Pertuan Besar: Tuanku Mukhriz ibni Al-Marhum Tuanku Munawir.

Menteri Besar: Datuk Mohamad Hasan.

State Legislative Assembly: 36 seats: Barisan Nasional 21; Democratic Action Party 10; Parti Keadilan Rakyat 4; Parti Islam se Malaysia 1; elected March 2008.

PAHANG
(Capital: Kuantan)

Sultan: HRH Haji Ahmad Shah Al-Musta'in Billah ibni Al-Marhum Sultan Abu Bakar Ri'ayatuddin Al-Mu'adzam Shah.

Menteri Besar: Dato' Adnan bin Yaakob.

State Legislative Assembly: Unit Pengurusan Teknologi Maklumat, Pejabat Setiausaha Kerajaan, Negeri Pahang, Tingkat 6, Wisma Sri Pahang, 25503 Kuantan, Pahang Darul Makmur; tel. (9) 5129425; fax (9) 5163490; internet www.pahang.gov.my; 42 seats: Barisan Nasional 37; Democratic Action Party 2; Parti Islam se Malaysia 2; Independent 1; elected March 2008.

PERAK
(Capital: Ipoh)

Note: the federal Government took direct control of the state legislature in May 2009. The ruling coalition installed its own Speaker in the Perak legislature.

Sultan: HRH Sultan Tuanku Azlan Muhibuddin Shah ibni Al-Marhum Sultan Yusuf Izuddin Ghafarullah Shah.

Menteri Besar: Datuk Zambry Abdul Kadir.

State Legislative Assembly: Pejabat Setiausaha Kerajaan Negeri Perak, Bangunan Perak Darul Ridzuan, Bahagian Majlis, Jalan Panglima Bukit Gantang Wahab, 30000 Ipoh; tel. (5) 2531957; fax (5) 2414869; e-mail prosuk@perak.gov.my; internet www.perak.gov.my; 59 seats: Barisan Nasional 28; Democratic Action Party 18; Parti Keadilan Rakyat 7; Parti Islam se Malaysia 6; elected March 2008.

PERLIS
(Capital: Kangar)

Raja: HM Tuanku Syed Sirajuddin ibni Al-Marhum Syed Putra Jamalullail.

Menteri Besar: Datuk Dr Mohammad Isa Sabu.

State Legislative Assembly: e-mail sukpls@perlis.gov.my; internet www.perlis.gov.my/webperlis/welcome.html; 15 seats: Barisan Nasional 14; Parti Islam se Malaysia 1; elected March 2008.

PULAU PINANG (PENANG)
(Capital: George Town)

Yang di-Pertua Negeri: HE Datuk Abdul Rahman Haji Abbas.

Ketua Menteri: Lim Guan Eng.

State Legislative Assembly: 40 seats: Democratic Action Party 19; Barisan Nasional 11; Parti Keadilan Rakyat 9; Parti Islam se Malaysia 1; elected March 2008.

SABAH
(Capital: Kota Kinabalu)

Yang di-Pertua Negeri: HE Datuk Ahmadshah Abdullah.

Ketua Menteri: Datuk Seri Musa Aman.

State Legislative Assembly: Dewan Undangan Negeri Sabah, Aras 4, Bangunan Dewan Undangan Negeri Sabah, Peti Surat 11247, 88813 Kota Kinabalu; tel. (88) 427533; fax (88) 427333; e-mail pejduns@sabah.gov.my; internet www.sabah.gov.my; 60 seats: Barisan Nasional 59; Democratic Action Party 1; elected March 2008.

SARAWAK
(Capital: Kuching)

Yang di-Pertua Negeri: HE Tun Datuk Patinggi Abang Haji Muhammed Salahuddin.

Ketua Menteri: Datuk Patinggi Tan Sri Haji Abdul Taib bin Mahmud.

State Legislative Assembly: Bangunan Dewan Undangan Negeri, Petra Jaya, 93502 Kuching, Sarawak; tel. (82) 441955; fax (82) 440628; e-mail abangof@sarawaknet.gov.my; internet www.dun.sarawak.gov.my; f. 1867; 71 seats: Barisan Nasional 62; Democratic Action Party 6; Parti Keadilan Rakyat 1; Sarawak National Party 1; Independent 1; elected May 2006.

SELANGOR
(Capital: Shah Alam)

Sultan: Tuanku Idris Salahuddin Abdul Aziz Shah.

Menteri Besar: Tan Sri Dato' Abdul Khalid bin Ibrahim.

State Legislative Assembly: internet www.selangor.gov.my; 56 seats: Barisan Nasional 20; Parti Keadilan Rakyat 15; Democratic Action Party 13; Parti Islam se Malaysia 8; elected March 2008.

TERENGGANU
(Capital: Kuala Terengganu)

Yang Di-Pertuan Muda (Regent): Tuanku Muhammad Ismail Sultan Mizan Zainal Abidin.

Menteri Besar: Datuk Ahmad Said.

State Legislative Assembly: internet www.terengganu.gov.my; 32 seats: Barisan Nasional 24; Parti Islam se Malaysia 8; elected March 2008.

Election Commission

Suruhanjaya Pilihan Raya (SPR): Aras 4–5, Blok C7, Parcel C, Pusat Pentadbiran Kerajaan Persekutuan, 62690 Putrajaya; tel. (3) 88856500; fax (3) 88889117; e-mail spr@spr.gov.my; internet www.spr.gov.my; f. 1957; Chair. Tan Sri Datuk Rashid bin Rahman.

Political Organizations

Barisan Nasional (BN) (National Front): Suites 1–2, 8th Floor, Menara Dato' Onn, Pusat Dagangan Dunia Putra, Jalan Tun Ismail, 50480 Kuala Lumpur; tel. (3) 26920384; fax (3) 26934743; e-mail info@bn.org.my; internet www.bn2008.org.my; f. 1973; the governing multiracial coalition of 14 parties; Chair. Dato' Seri Najib bin Tun Haji Abdul Razak; Sec.-Gen. Dato' Datuk Sri Mohammed Rahmat; comprises:

   Liberal Democratic Party: Tingkat 1, No. 33, Karamunsing Warehouse, POB 16033, 88868 Kota Kinabalu, Sabah; tel. (88) 218985; fax (88) 240598; e-mail ldpkk@tm.net.my; internet www.ldpsabah.com; f. 1989; Chinese-dominated; Pres. Datuk Liew Vui Keong; Sec.-Gen. Teo Chee Kang.

   Malaysian Chinese Association (MCA): Wisma MCA, 8th Floor, 163 Jalan Ampang, POB 10626, 50450 Kuala Lumpur;

tel. (3) 21618044; fax (3) 21619772; e-mail info@mca.org.my; internet www.mca.org.my; f. 1949; 1,121,403 mems; Pres. Dato' Seri ONG KA TING; Sec.-Gen. Dato' ONG KA CHUAN.

Malaysian Indian Congress (MIC): Menara Manickavasagam, 6th Floor, 1 Jalan Rahmat, 50350 Kuala Lumpur; tel. (3) 40424377; fax (3) 40427236; e-mail michq@mic.org.my; internet www.mic.org.my; f. 1946; 401,000 mems (1992); Pres. Dato' Seri S. SAMY VELLU; Sec.-Gen. Dr S. SUBRAMANIAM.

Parti Bersatu Rakyat Sabah (PBRS) (United Sabah People's Party): POB 20148, Luyang, Kota Kinabalu, 88761 Sabah; tel. and fax (88) 269282; f. 1994; breakaway faction of PBS; mostly Christian Kadazans; Leader Datuk JOSEPH KURUP.

Parti Bersatu Sabah (PBS) (Sabah United Party): Block M, Lot 4, 2nd and 3rd Floors, Donggongon New Township, 89500 Penampang, Sabah; tel. (88) 702111; fax (88) 718067; e-mail pbshq@pbs-sabah.org; internet www.pbs-sabah.org; f. 1985; multiracial party, left the BN in 1990 and rejoined in Jan. 2002; Pres. Datuk Seri JOSEPH PAIRIN KITINGAN; Sec.-Gen. Datuk RADIN MALLEH.

Parti Gerakan Rakyat Malaysia (GERAKAN) (Malaysian People's Movement): Tingkat 5, Menara PGRM, 8 Jalan Pudu Ulu, Cheras, 56100 Kuala Lumpur; tel. (3) 92876868; fax (3) 92878866; e-mail gerakan@gerakan.org.my; internet www.gerakan.org.my; f. 1968; 300,000 mems; Pres. Tan Sri KOH TSU KOON (acting); Sec.-Gen. CHIA KWANG CHYE.

Parti Pesaka Bumiputera Bersatu (PBB) (United Traditional Bumiputra Party): Lot 401, Jalan Bako, POB 1953, 93400 Kuching, Sarawak; tel. (82) 448299; fax (82) 448294; e-mail pbb1@bumiputerasarawak.org.my; internet www.bumiputerasarawak.org.my; f. 1983; Pres. Tan Sri Datuk Patinggi Amar Haji ABDUL TAIB MAHMUD; Dep. Pres. Datuk ALFRED JABU AK NUMPANG.

Parti Progresif Penduduk Malaysia (PPP) (People's Progressive Party): 27–29A Jalan Maharajalela, 50150 Kuala Lumpur; tel. (3) 2441922; fax (3) 2442041; e-mail info@ppp.com.my; internet www.ppp.com.my; f. 1953 as Perak Progressive Party; joined the BN in 1972; Pres. Datuk M. KAYVEAS.

Sabah Progressive Party (SAPP) (Parti Maju Sabah): Lot 23, 2nd Floor, Bornion Centre, 88300 Kota Kinabalu, Sabah; tel. (88) 242107; fax (88) 249188; e-mail sappkk@streamyx.com; internet www.sapp.org.my; f. 1994; non-racial; Pres. Datuk YONG TECK LEE; Sec.-Gen. Datuk RICHARD YONG WE KONG.

Sarawak Progressive Democratic Party (SPDP): Lot 4319–4320, Jalan Stapok, Sungai Maong, 93250 Kuching, Sarawak; tel. (82) 311180; fax (82) 311190; f. 2003 by breakaway faction of Sarawak National Party; Pres. Datuk WILLIAM MAWAN ANAK IKOM; Sec.-Gen. Agung Dr JUDSON SAKAI TAGAL.

Sarawak United People's Party (SUPP): 7 Jalan Tan Sri Ong Kee Hui, POB 454, 93710 Kuching, Sarawak; tel. (82) 246999; fax (82) 256510; e-mail supphq@yahoo.com; internet www.supp.org.my; f. 1959; Sarawak Chinese minority party; Pres. Datuk Dr GEORGE CHAN HONG NAM; Sec.-Gen. SIM KHENG HUI.

United Kadazan People's Organization (UPKO): Penampang Service Centre, Km 11, Jalan Tambunan, Peti Surat 420, 89507 Penampang, Sabah; tel. (88) 718182; fax (88) 718180; e-mail n4upko@yahoo.com; internet www.upko.org.my; f. 1994 as the Parti Demokratik Sabah (PDS—Sabah Democratic Party); formed after collapse of PBS Govt by fmr leaders of the party, represents mostly Kadazandusun, Rungus and Murut communities; Pres. Tan Sri BERNARD GILUK DOMPOK.

United Malays National Organization (Pertubuhan Kebangsaan Melayu Bersatu—UMNO Baru) (New UMNO): Menara Dato' Onn, 38th Floor, Jalan Tun Ismail, 50480 Kuala Lumpur; tel. (3) 40429511; fax (3) 40412358; e-mail email@umno.net.my; internet www.umno-online.com; f. 1988; replaced the original UMNO (f. 1946), which had been declared an illegal organization, owing to the participation of unregistered branches in party elections in April 1987; Supreme Council of 45 mems; 2.5m. mems; Pres. Dato' Seri NAJIB BIN TUN Haji ABDUL RAZAK; Sec.-Gen. Datuk Seri Tengku ADNAN; Tengku MANSOR.

Angkatan Keadilan Insan Malaysia (AKIM) (Malaysian Justice Movement): f. 1994 by fmr members of PAS and Semangat '46; Pres. HAMBALI YAZID.

Barisan Alternatif (Alternative Front): Kuala Lumpur; f. June 1999 to contest the general election; opposition electoral alliance originally comprising the PAS, the DAP, the PKN and the PRM; the DAP left in Sept. 2001; the PKN and the PRM merged in 2003 to form the PKR.

Barisan Jama'ah Islamiah Sa-Malaysia (Berjasa) (Pan-Malaysian Islamic Front): Kelantan; f. 1977; pro-Islamic; 50,000 mems; Pres. Dato' Haji WAN HASHIM BIN Haji WAN ACHMED; Sec.-Gen. MAHMUD ZUHDI BIN Haji ABDUL MAJID.

Bersatu Rakyat Jelata Sabah (Berjaya) (Sabah People's Union): Natikar Bldg, 1st Floor, POB 2130, Kota Kinabalu, Sabah; f. 1975; 400,000 mems; Pres. Haji MOHAMMED NOOR MANSOOR.

Democratic Action Party (DAP): 24 Jalan 20/9, 46300 Petaling Jaya, Selangor; tel. (3) 79578022; fax (3) 79575718; e-mail dap.Malaysia@pobox.com; internet www.dapmalaysia.org; f. 1966; main opposition party; advocates multiracial society based on democratic socialism; 12,000 mems; Chair. KARPAL SINGH; Sec.-Gen. LIM GUAN ENG.

Kongres Indian Muslim Malaysia (KIMMA): Kuala Lumpur; tel. (3) 2324759; f. 1977; aims to unite Malaysian Indian Muslims politically; 25,000 mems; Pres. SAMMY VELLU; Sec.-Gen. MOHAMMED ALI BIN Haji NAINA MOHAMMED.

Pakatan Rakyat (People's Alliance): f. 2008; est. following the legislative election; opposition alliance of the PKR, the DAP and PAS.

Parti Hisbul Muslimin Malaysia (Hamim) (Islamic Front of Malaysia): Kota Bahru, Kelantan; f. 1983 as an alternative party to PAS; Pres. Datuk ASRI MUDA.

Parti Ikatan Masyarakat Islam (Islamic Alliance Party): Terengganu.

Parti Islam se Malaysia (PAS) (Islamic Party of Malaysia): 318A Jalan Raja Laut, 50350 Kuala Lumpur; tel. (3) 26925000; fax (3) 26938399; e-mail editor@parti-pas.org; internet www.parti-pas.org; f. 1951; seeks to establish an Islamic state; 700,000 mems; Pres. ABDUL HADI AWANG; Sec.-Gen. KAMARUDDIN JAAFAR.

Parti Keadilan Rakyat (PKR) (People's Justice Party): 110–3 Jalan Tun Sambanthan, 50470 Kuala Lumpur; tel. (3) 22723220; fax (3) 22721220; e-mail contact@partikeadilanrakyat.org; internet www.keadilanrakyat.org; f. 2003 following merger of Parti Keadilan Nasional (PKN) and Parti Rakyat Malaysia (PRM); Pres. Datin Seri Dr WAN AZIZAH WAN ISMAIL; Sec.-Gen. Datuk KAMARUL BAHRIN ABAS.

Persatuan Rakyat Malaysia Sarawak (PERMAS) (Malaysian Sarawak Party): Kuching, Sarawak; f. March 1987 by fmr mems of PBB; Leader Haji BUJANG ULIS.

Sabah Chinese Consolidated Party (SCCP): POB 704, Kota Kinabalu, Sabah; f. 1964; 14,000 mems; Pres. JOHNNY SOON; Sec.-Gen. CHAN TET ON.

Sabah Chinese Party (PCS): Kota Kinabalu, Sabah; f. 1986; Pres. Encik FRANCIS LEONG.

Sarawak National Party (SNAP): 304–305 Bangunan Mei Jun, 1 Jalan Rubber, POB 2960, 93758 Kuching, Sarawak; tel. (82) 254244; fax (82) 253562; internet sarawak-national-party.blogspot.com; f. 1961; deregistered Nov. 2002, but deregistration deferred indefinitely in April 2003 following appeal; Pres. EDWIN DUNDANG BUGAK; Sec.-Gen. STANLEY JUGOL.

Setia (Sabah People's United Democratic Party): Sabah; f. 1994.

Diplomatic Representation

EMBASSIES AND HIGH COMMISSIONS IN MALAYSIA

Afghanistan: 2nd Floor, Wisma Chinese Chamber, 258 Jalan Ampang, 50450 Kuala Lumpur; tel. (3) 42569400; fax (3) 42566400; e-mail consular@afghanembassykl.org; internet www.afghanembassykl.org; Ambassador MOHAMMAD YUNOS FARMAN.

Albania: UBN Tower 10, 31st Floor, Jalan P. Pamlee, 50250 Kuala Lumpur; tel. (3) 20788690; fax (3) 20702285; e-mail albania@streamyx.com; Chargé d'affaires a.i. DILAVER QESJA.

Algeria: 5 Jalan Mesra, off Jalan Damai, 55000 Kuala Lumpur; tel. (3) 21488159; fax (3) 21488154; e-mail enquiries@algerianembassy.org.my; internet www.algerianembassy.org.my; Ambassador AMAR BELANI.

Argentina: Suite 16-03, 16th Floor, Menara Keck Seng, 203 Jalan Bukit Bintang, 55100 Kuala Lumpur; tel. (3) 21441451; fax (3) 21441428; e-mail emsia@pd.jaring.my; Ambassador (vacant).

Australia: 6 Jalan Yap Kwan Seng, 50450 Kuala Lumpur; tel. (3) 21465555; fax (3) 21415773; e-mail Public-Affairs-KLPR@dfat.gov.au; internet www.australia.org.my; High Commissioner PENNY WILLIAMS.

Austria: Suite 10.01–02, Level 10, Wisma Goldhill 67, Jalan Raja Chulan, 50200 Kuala Lumpur; tel. (3) 20570020; fax (3) 23817168; e-mail kuala-lumpur-ob@bmeia.gv.at; Ambassador Dr DONATUS KOECK.

Azerbaijan: 2nd Floor, Wisma Chinese Chamber, 258 Jalan Ampang, 50450 Kuala Lumpur; tel. (3) 42526800; fax (3) 42571800; e-mail azembkl@streamyx.com; Ambassador TAHIR KARIMOV.

Bangladesh: Block 1, Lorong Damai 7, Jalan Damai, 55000 Kuala Lumpur; tel. (3) 21487940; fax (3) 21413381; e-mail bddoot@streamyx.com; internet www.bangladesh-highcomkl.com; High Commissioner M. KHAIRUZZAMAN.

Belgium: Suite 10-02, 10th Floor, Menara Tan & Tan, 207 Jalan Tun Razak, 50400 Kuala Lumpur; tel. (3) 21620025; fax (3) 21620023;

MALAYSIA

e-mail kualalumpur@diplobel.org; internet www.diplomatie.be/kualalumpur; Ambassador FRANK VAN DE CRAEN.

Bosnia and Herzegovina: JKR 854, Jalan Bellamy, 50460 Kuala Lumpur; tel. (3) 21440353; fax (3) 21426025; e-mail hsomun@hotmail.com; Ambassador MUSTAFA MUJEZINOVIĆ.

Brazil: Suite 20-01, 20th Floor, Menara Tan & Tan, 207 Jalan Tun Razak, 50400 Kuala Lumpur; tel. (3) 21711420; fax (3) 21711427; e-mail embassy@brazilembassy.org.my; internet www.brazilembassy.org.my; Ambassador SÉRGIO DE SOUZA ARRUDA.

Brunei: Suite 19-01, 19th Floor, Menara Tan & Tan, 207 Jalan Tun Razak, 50400 Kuala Lumpur; tel. (3) 21612800; fax (3) 2631302; High Commissioner Dato' Paduka Haji ABDUL RAHMAN.

Cambodia: 46 Jalan U Thant, 55000 Kuala Lumpur; tel. (3) 42571150; fax (3) 42571157; e-mail reckl@tm.net.my; Ambassador HRH Samdech Preah ANOCH NORODOM ARUNRASMY.

Canada: 17th Floor, Menara Tan & Tan, 207 Jalan Tun Razak, 50400 Kuala Lumpur; tel. (3) 27183333; fax (3) 27183391; e-mail klmpr@dfait-maeci.gc.ca; internet www.dfait-maeci.gc.ca/kualalumpur; High Commissioner DAVID COLLINS.

Chile: 8th Floor, West Block, Wisma Selangor Dredging, 142-C Jalan Ampang, Peti Surat 27, 50450 Kuala Lumpur; tel. (3) 21616203; fax (3) 21622219; e-mail eochile@ppp.nasionet.net; Ambassador PATRICIO TORRES.

China, People's Republic: 229 Jalan Ampang, 50450 Kuala Lumpur; tel. (3) 21428495; fax (3) 21414552; e-mail cn@tm.net.my; internet my.china-embassy.org/eng; Ambassador LIU JIAN.

Colombia: Level 28, UOA Centre, 19 Jalan Pinang, 50450 Kuala Lumpur; tel. (3) 21645488; fax (3) 21645487; e-mail emcomal@streamyx.com; internet www.embcolombia.com.my; Ambassador SILVIA CASTAÑO DE GONZÁLEZ.

Croatia: 3 Jalan Menkuang, off Jalan Ru Ampang, 55000 Kuala Lumpur; tel. (3) 42535340; fax (3) 42535217; e-mail kuala-lumpur@mvpei.hr; Ambassador ZELJKO CIMBUR.

Cuba: 10 Lorong Gurney, 54100 Kuala Lumpur; tel. (3) 26911066; fax (3) 26911141; e-mail admin@cubemb.com.my; internet www.cubaemb.com.my; Ambassador CARLOS A. AMORES.

Czech Republic: 32 Jalan Mesra, off Jalan Damai, 55000 Kuala Lumpur; tel. (3) 21427185; fax (3) 21412727; e-mail kualalumpur@embassy.mzv.cz; internet www.mzv.cz/kualalumpur; Ambassador JAN FÜRY.

Denmark: Wisma Denmark, 22nd Floor, 86 Jalan Ampang, 50450 Kuala Lumpur; tel. (3) 20322001; fax (3) 20322012; e-mail kulamb@um.dk; internet www.ambkualalumpur.um.dk; Ambassador SVEND WAEVER.

Ecuador: 10th Floor, West Block, Wisma Selangor Dredging, 142C Jalan Ampang, 50450 Kuala Lumpur; tel. (3) 21635078; fax (3) 21635096; e-mail embecua@po.jaring.my; Ambassador MANUEL PESANTES.

Egypt: 12 Jalan Rhu, off Jalan Ampang, 55000 Kuala Lumpur; tel. (3) 42568154; fax (3) 42573515; e-mail egyembkl@tm.net.my; Ambassador HANI ABDEL KADER AHMED SHASH.

Fiji: Level 2, Menara Chan, 138 Jalan Ampang, 50450 Kuala Lumpur; tel. (3) 27323335; fax (3) 27327555; e-mail fhckl@pd.jaring.my; High Commissioner (vacant).

Finland: Wisma Chinese Chamber, 5th Floor, 258 Jalan Ampang, 50450 Kuala Lumpur; tel. (3) 42577746; fax (3) 42577793; e-mail sanomat.kul@formin.fi; Ambassador TAPIO SAARELA.

France: 192–196 Jalan Ampang, 50450 Kuala Lumpur; tel. (3) 20535500; fax (3) 20535501; e-mail ambassade.kuala-lumpur-amba@diplomatie.gouv.fr; internet www.ambafrance-my.org; Ambassador MARC BARÉTY.

Germany: 26th Floor, Menara Tan & Tan, 207 Jalan Tun Razak, 50400 Kuala Lumpur; tel. (3) 21709666; fax (3) 21619800; e-mail contact@german-embassy.org.my; internet www.kuala-lumpur.diplo.de; Ambassador GÜNTER GRUBER.

Ghana: 14 Ampang Hilir, off Jalan Ampang, 55000 Kuala Lumpur; tel. (3) 42526995; fax (3) 42578698; e-mail ghcomkl@tm.net.my; High Commissioner NANA KWADWO SEINTI.

Guinea: 5 Jalan Kedondong, off Jalan Ampang Hilir, 55000 Kuala Lumpur; tel. (3) 42576500; fax (3) 42511500; e-mail mwcnakry@sotelgui.net.gn; Ambassador MOHAMED SAMPIL.

Hungary: Menara Tan & Tan, 10th Floor, Suite 10-04, Jalan Tun Razak, 50400 Kuala Lumpur; tel. (3) 21637914; fax (3) 21637918; e-mail mission.kul@kum.hu; Ambassador TAMÁS TÓTH.

India: 2 Jalan Taman Duta, off Jalan Duta, 50480 Kuala Lumpur; tel. (3) 20933510; fax (3) 20933507; e-mail highcomm@po.jaring.my; internet www.indianhighcommission.com.my; High Commissioner ASHOK K. KANTHA.

Indonesia: 233 Jalan Tun Razak, POB 10889, 50400 Kuala Lumpur; tel. (3) 21452011; fax (3) 21417908; e-mail dubresi_kul@kbrikl.org.my; internet www.kbrikl.org.my; Ambassador DA'I BACHTIAR.

Iran: 1 Lorong U Thant Satu, off Jalan U Thant, 55000 Kuala Lumpur; tel. (3) 42514824; fax (3) 42562904; internet www.iranembassy.com.my; Ambassador MAHDI KHANDAGHABADI.

Iraq: 2 Jalan Langgak Golf, off Jalan Tun Razak, 55000 Kuala Lumpur; tel. (3) 21480555; fax (3) 21414331; Chargé d'affaires Dr HOSHIAR H. S. DAZAYI.

Ireland: Ireland House, The Amp Walk, 218 Jalan Ampang, POB 10372, 50450 Kuala Lumpur; tel. (3) 21612963; fax (3) 21613427; e-mail info@ireland-embassy.com.my; internet www.ireland-embassy.com.my; Ambassador EUGENE HUTCHINSON.

Italy: 99 Jalan U Thant, 55000 Kuala Lumpur; tel. (3) 42565122; fax (3) 42573199; e-mail ambasciata.kualalumpur@esteri.it; internet www.ambkualalumpur.esteri.it; Ambassador ALESSANDRO BUSACCA.

Japan: 11 Pesiaran Stonor, off Jalan Tun Razak, 50450 Kuala Lumpur; tel. (3) 21427044; fax (3) 21672314; internet www.my.emb-japan.go.jp; Ambassador MASAHIKO HORIE.

Jordan: 2 Jalan Kedondong, off Jalan Ampang Hilir, 55000 Kuala Lumpur; tel. (3) 42521268; fax (3) 42528610; e-mail general@jordanembassy.org.my; internet www.jordanembassy.org.my; Ambassador HASSAN MAHMOUD MOHAMMAD AL-JAWARNEH.

Kazakhstan: 115 Jalan Ampang Hilir, 55000 Kuala Lumpur; tel. (3) 42522999; fax (3) 42523999; e-mail kuala-lumpur@kazembassy.org.my; internet www.kazembassy.org.my; Ambassador MUKHTAR TILEUBERDI.

Kenya: 8 Jalan Taman U Thant, 55000 Kuala Lumpur; tel. (3) 21461163; fax (3) 21451087; e-mail kenya@po.jaring.my; High Commissioner DAVID GACHOKI NJOKA.

Korea, Democratic People's Republic: 4 Jalan Persiaran Madge, off Jalan U Thant, 55000 Kuala Lumpur; tel. (3) 42569913; fax (3) 42569933; Ambassador PAK RYONG YON.

Korea, Republic: Lot 9 and 11, Jalan Nipah, off Jalan Ampang, 55000 Kuala Lumpur; tel. (3) 42512336; fax (3) 42521425; e-mail korem-my@mofat.go.kr; internet mys.mofat.go.kr/eng/index.jsp; Ambassador BONG RYULL-YANG.

Kuwait: 229 Jalan Tun Razak, 50400 Kuala Lumpur; tel. (3) 21410033; fax (3) 21456121; e-mail kuwait@streamyx.com; Ambassador MONTHER BADER SULAIMAN AL-EISSA.

Kyrgyzstan: 10 Lorong Damai 9, 55000 Kuala Lumpur; tel. (3) 21649862; fax (3) 21632024; e-mail kyrgyz@tm.net.my; internet www.kyrgyz.net.my; Ambassador JEENBEK KULUBAEV (designate).

Laos: 12A Persiaran Madge, off Jalan Ampang Hilir, 55000 Kuala Lumpur; tel. (3) 42511118; e-mail embassylao-kualalumpur@hotmail.com; Ambassador Dr BOUNTHEUANG MOUNLASY.

Lebanon: 56 Jalan Ampang Hilir, 55000 Kuala Lumpur; tel. (3) 42516690; fax (3) 42603426; Ambassador KHALED AL KILANI.

Libya: 6 Jalan Madge, off Jalan U Thant, 55000 Kuala Lumpur; tel. (3) 21411293; fax (3) 21413549; Chargé d'affaires a.i. AHMAD MASAOUD B. ALGHALI.

Luxembourg: Menara Keck Seng Bldg, 16th Floor, 203 Jalan Bukit Bintang, 55100 Kuala Lumpur; tel. (3) 21433134; fax (3) 21433157; e-mail emluxem@po.jaring.my; Chargé d'affaires CHARLES SCHMIT.

Maldives: Suite 07-01, Menara See Hoy Chan, 374 Jalan Tun Razak, 50400 Kuala Lumpur; tel. (3) 21637244; fax (3) 21647244; e-mail mail@maldives.org.my; High Commissioner MOHAMED ZAKI.

Mauritius: 17th Floor, West Block, Wisma Selangor Dredging, Jalan Ampang, 50450 Kuala Lumpur; tel. (3) 21411870; e-mail maurhckl@streamyx.com; Chargé d'affaires a.i. D. P. GOKULSING.

Mexico: Suite 22-05, 22nd Floor, Menara Tan & Tan, 207 Jalan Tun Razak, 50400 Kuala Lumpur; tel. (3) 21646362; fax (3) 21640964; e-mail embamex@po.jaring.my; internet www.embamex.org.my; Ambassador JORGE ALBERTO LOZOYA LEGORRETA.

Morocco: Unit 9, 3rd Floor, East Block, Wisma Selangor Dredging, 142B Jalan Ampang, 50450 Kuala Lumpur; tel. (3) 21610701; fax (3) 21623081; e-mail sifmakl@po.jaring.my; Ambassador AHMED AMAZIANE.

Myanmar: 1 Lorong Ru Kedua, off Jalan Ampang Hilir, 55000 Kuala Lumpur; tel. (3) 42560280; fax (3) 42568320; e-mail mekl@tm.net.my; Ambassador U TIN LATT.

Namibia: Suite 15-01, Level 15, Menara HLA, 3 Jalan Kia Peng, 50450 Kuala Lumpur; tel. (3) 21433593; e-mail namhckl@streamyx.com; High Commissioner TJI-TJAI UANIVI.

Nepal: Suite 13A-01, 13th Floor, Wisma MCA, 163 Jalan Ampang, 50450 Kuala Lumpur; tel. (3) 21645934; fax (3) 21648659; e-mail mekl_88@streamyx.com; internet www.nepalembassy.com.my; Ambassador RISHIRAJ ADHIKARI.

Netherlands: The Amp Walk, 7th Floor, South Block, 218 Jalan Ampang, POB 10543, 50450 Kuala Lumpur; tel. (3) 21686200; fax (3) 21686240; e-mail kll@minbuza.nl; internet www.netherlands.org.my; Ambassador LODY EMBRECHTS.

MALAYSIA

New Zealand: Menara IMC, 21st Floor, 8 Jalan Sultan Ismail, 50250 Kuala Lumpur; tel. (3) 20782533; fax (3) 20780387; e-mail nzhckl@po.jaring.my; High Commissioner DAVID KERSEY.

Nigeria: 85 Jalan Ampang Hilir, 55000 Kuala Lumpur; tel. (3) 42517843; fax (3) 42524302; e-mail chancerykl@nigeria.org.my; internet www.nigeria.org.my; High Commissioner PETER ANEGBEH.

Norway: Suite CD, 53rd Floor, Empire Tower, Jalan Tun Razak, 50400 Kuala Lumpur; tel. (3) 21750300; fax (3) 21750308; e-mail emb.kualalumpur@mfa.no; internet www.norway.org.my; Ambassador ARILD BRAASTAD.

Oman: 6 Jalan Langgak Golf, off Jalan Tun Razak, 55000 Kuala Lumpur; tel. (3) 21452827; e-mail omanemb@po.jaring.my; Ambassador AFLAH BIN SULEIMAN ALTAEI.

Pakistan: 132 Jalan Ampang, 50450 Kuala Lumpur; tel. (3) 21618877; fax (3) 21645958; e-mail pahickl@gmail.com; internet www.pahickl.com; High Commissioner Maj.-Gen. (retd) TAHIR MAHMUD QAZI.

Papua New Guinea: 46 Jalan U Thant, 55000 Kuala Lumpur; tel. (3) 42575405; fax (3) 42576203; High Commissioner PETER P. MAGINDE.

Peru: Wisma Selangor Dredging, 6th Floor, South Block, 142A Jalan Ampang, 50450 Kuala Lumpur; tel. (3) 21633034; fax (3) 21633039; e-mail embperu@streamyx.com; Ambassador ALEJANDRO GORDILLO FERNÁNDEZ.

Philippines: 1 Changkat Kia Peng, 50450 Kuala Lumpur; tel. (3) 21484233; fax (3) 21483576; e-mail consular@philembassykl.org.my; internet www.philembassykl.org.my; Ambassador VICTORIANO M. LECAROS.

Poland: POB 10052, 50704 Kuala Lumpur; tel. (3) 42576733; fax (3) 42570123; e-mail info@ambasada.com.my; internet www.kualalumpur.polemb.net; Ambassador EUGENIOSZ SAWICKI.

Qatar: 113 Jalan Ampang Hilir, POB 13118, 55000 Kuala Lumpur; tel. (3) 42565552; fax (3) 42565553; e-mail qekl113@streamyx.com; Ambassador ABDULHAMEED MUBARAK AL-KUBAISI.

Romania: 114 Jalan Damai, off Jalan Ampang, 55000 Kuala Lumpur; tel. (3) 21423172; fax (3) 21448713; e-mail roemb@streamyx.com; Ambassador PETRU PETRA.

Russia: 263 Jalan Ampang, 50450 Kuala Lumpur; tel. (3) 42567252; fax (3) 42576091; e-mail ruemvvl@tm.net.my; internet www.malaysia.mid.ru; Ambassador ALEXANDER A. KARCHAVA.

Saudi Arabia: Level 4, Wisma Chinese Chamber, 258 Jalan Ampang, 50450 Kuala Lumpur; tel. (3) 42579433; fax (3) 42578751; e-mail saembssy@tm.net.my; Ambassador MOHAMMED REDA HUSSEIN ABU AL-HAMAYEL.

Senegal: 9 Lorong U Thant, off Jalan U Thant, 55000 Kuala Lumpur; tel. (3) 42567343; fax (3) 42563205; e-mail senamb_mal@yahoo.fr; Ambassador ABDEL KADER PIERRE FALL.

Singapore: 209 Jalan Tun Razak, 50400 Kuala Lumpur; tel. (3) 21616277; fax (3) 21616343; e-mail singhc_kul@sgmfa.gov.sg; internet www.mfa.gov.sg/kl; High Commissioner T. JASUDASEN.

Slovakia: 11 Jalan U Thant, 55000 Kuala Lumpur; tel. (3) 21150016; fax (3) 21150014; e-mail emb.kualalumpur@mzv.sk; Ambassador MILAN LAJČIAK.

South Africa: Menara HLA, Suite 22-01, 3 Jalan Kia Peng, 50450 Kuala Lumpur; tel. (3) 21688663; fax (3) 21643742; e-mail sahcadm@streamyx.com; High Commissioner S. NGOMBANE.

Spain: 200 Jalan Ampang, 50450 Kuala Lumpur; tel. (3) 21484868; fax (3) 21424582; e-mail embespmy@mail.mae.es; Ambassador JOSÉ RAMÓN BARAÑANO FERNÁNDEZ.

Sri Lanka: 12 Jalan Keranji Dua, off Jalan Kedondong, Ampang Hilir, 55000 Kuala Lumpur; tel. (3) 42568987; fax (3) 42532497; e-mail slhicom@streamyx.com; internet www.slhc.com.my; High Commissioner D. D. RANASINGHE.

Sudan: 2A Persiaran Ampang, off Jalan Ru, 55000 Kuala Lumpur; tel. (3) 42569104; fax (3) 42568107; e-mail assalamiz@hotmail.com; Ambassador ABDEL RAHMAN HAMZAH ELRAYA.

Swaziland: Suite 22-03 and 03 (A), Menara Citibank, 165 Jalan Ampang, 50450 Kuala Lumpur; tel. (3) 21632511; fax (3) 21633326; e-mail swazi@tm.net.my; High Commissioner MPUMELELO J. N. HLOPE.

Sweden: Wisma Angkasa Raya, 6th Floor, 123 Jalan Ampang, 50450 Kuala Lumpur; tel. (3) 20522550; fax (3) 21486325; e-mail ambassaden.kuala-lumpur@foreign.ministry.se; internet www.swedenabroad.se/kualalumpur; Ambassador HELENA SÅNGELAND.

Switzerland: 16 Persiaran Madge, 55000 Kuala Lumpur; tel. (3) 21480622; fax (3) 21480935; e-mail kua.vertretung@eda.admin.ch; internet www.eda.admin.ch/kualalumpur; Ambassador URS STEMMLER.

Syria: Suite 23-03, 23rd Floor, Menara Tan & Tan, 207 Jalan Tun Razak, 50400 Kuala Lumpur; tel. (3) 21634110; fax (3) 21634199; internet www.syrianembassy.com.my; Ambassador LAMIA MERIE AASI.

Thailand: 206 Jalan Ampang, 50450 Kuala Lumpur; tel. (3) 21488222; fax (3) 21486573; e-mail thaikl@pop1.jaring.my; internet www.mfa.go.th/web/1830.php?depcode=23000100; Ambassador PIYAWAT NIYOMRERKS.

Timor-Leste: 62 Jalan Ampang Hilir, 55000 Kuala Lumpur; tel. (3) 42562046; fax (3) 42562016; e-mail embaixada_tl_kl@yahoo.com; Ambassador JUVÊNCIO DE JESUS MARTINS.

Turkey: 118 Jalan U Thant, 55000 Kuala Lumpur; tel. (3) 42572225; fax (3) 42572227; e-mail turkbe@tm.net.my; Ambassador BARLAS OZENER.

Ukraine: Suite 22-02, 22nd Floor, Menara Tan & Tan, 207 Jalan Tun Razak, 50400 Kuala Lumpur; tel. (3) 21669552; fax (3) 21664371; e-mail emb_my@mfa.gov.ua; internet www.mfa.gov.ua/malaysia; Ambassador OLEKSANDR SHEVCHENKO.

United Arab Emirates: 1 Gerbang Ampang Hilir, off Persiaran Ampang Hilir, 55000 Kuala Lumpur; tel. (3) 42535221; fax (3) 42535220; e-mail uaemal@tm.net.my; Ambassador NASSER SALMAN ALABOODI.

United Kingdom: 185 Jalan Ampang, 50450 Kuala Lumpur; tel. (3) 21702200; fax (3) 21702303; e-mail political.kualalumpur@fco.gov.uk; internet ukinmalaysia.fco.gov.uk; High Commissioner BOYD MCCLEARY.

USA: 376 Jalan Tun Razak, POB 10035, 50400 Kuala Lumpur; tel. (3) 21685000; fax (3) 21422207; e-mail klconsular@state.gov; internet malaysia.usembassy.gov; Ambassador JAMES R. KEITH.

Uruguay: 6th Floor, UBN Tower, 10 Jalan P. Ramlee, 50250 Kuala Lumpur; tel. (3) 20313669; fax (3) 20315669; e-mail urukuala@streamyx.com; Ambassador PABLO SADER.

Uzbekistan: Suite 6-03, 6th Floor, North Block The Ampang Walk, 218 Jalan Ampang, 50450 Kuala Lumpur; tel. (3) 21618100; e-mail uzbekemb@streamyx.com; Ambassador AYBEK KHASANOV.

Venezuela: Suite 20-05, 20th Floor, Menara Tan & Tan, 207 Jalan Tun Razak, 50400 Kuala Lumpur; tel. (3) 21633444; fax (3) 21636819; e-mail venezuela@po.jaring.my; internet www.venezuela.org.my; Ambassador MANUEL ANTONIO GUZMÁN HERNÁNDEZ.

Viet Nam: 4 Jalan Persiaran Stonor, 50450 Kuala Lumpur; tel. (3) 21484036; fax (3) 21483270; e-mail daisevn@putra.net.my; internet www.mofa.gov.vn/vnemb.my; Ambassador HOANG TRONG LAP.

Yemen: 7 Jalan Kedondong, off Jalan Ampang Hilir, 55000 Kuala Lumpur; tel. (3) 42511793; fax (3) 42511794; e-mail yemenkl@tm.net.my; internet yemenembassykl.com; Ambassador Dr ABDULLA MOHAMED ALI AL-MONTSER.

Zimbabwe: 124 Jalan Sembilan, Taman Ampang Utama, 68000 Ampang, Selangor Darul Ehsan; tel. (3) 42516779; fax (3) 42517252; e-mail zhck@tm.net.my; Ambassador LUCAS PANDE TAVAYA.

Judicial System

The two High Courts, one in Peninsular Malaysia and the other in Sabah and Sarawak, have original, appellate and revisional jurisdiction as the federal law provides. Above these two High Courts is the Court of Appeal, which was established in 1994; it is an intermediary court between the Federal Court and the High Court. When appeals to the Privy Council in the United Kingdom were abolished in 1985 the former Supreme Court became the final court of appeal. Therefore, at that stage only one appeal was available to a party aggrieved by the decision of the High Court. Hence, the establishment of the Court of Appeal. The Federal Court (formerly the Supreme Court) has, to the exclusion of any other court, jurisdiction in any dispute between states or between the Federation and any state; and has special jurisdiction as to the interpretation of the Constitution. The Federal Court is headed by the Chief Justice (formerly the Lord President); the other members of the Federal Court are the President of the Court of Appeal, the two Chief Judges of the High Courts and the Federal Court Judges. Members of the Court of Appeal are the President and the Court of Appeal judges, and members of the High Courts are the two Chief Judges and their respective High Court judges. All judges are appointed by the Yang di-Pertuan Agong on the advice of the Prime Minister, after consulting the Conference of Rulers. In 1993 a Special Court was established to hear cases brought by or against the Yang di-Pertuan Agong or a Ruler of State (Sultans).

The Sessions Courts, which are situated in the principal urban and rural centres, are presided over by a Sessions Judge, who is a member of the Judicial and Legal Service of the Federation and is a qualified barrister or a Bachelor of Law from any of the recognized universities. Their criminal jurisdiction covers the less serious indictable offences, excluding those that carry the death penalty. Civil juris-

MALAYSIA

diction of a Sessions Court is up to RM 250,000. The Sessions Judges are appointed by the Yang di-Pertuan Agong.

The Magistrates' Courts are also found in the main urban and rural centres and have both civil and criminal jurisdiction, although of a more restricted nature than that of the Sessions Courts. The Magistrates consist of officers from the Judicial and Legal Service of the Federation. They are appointed by the State Authority in which they officiate on the recommendation of the Chief Judge.

There are also Syariah (Shariah) courts for rulings under Islamic law. In July 1996 the Cabinet announced that the Syariah courts were to be restructured with the appointment of a Syariah Chief Judge and four Court of Appeal justices, whose rulings would set precedents for the whole country.

Prior to February 1995 trials in the High Courts for murder and kidnapping were heard with jury and assessors, respectively. The amendment to the Criminal Procedure Code abolished both the jury and the assessors systems, and all criminal trials in the High Courts are heard by a judge sitting alone. In 1988 an amendment to the Constitution empowered any federal lawyer to confer with the Attorney-General to determine the courts in which any proceedings, excluding those before a Syariah court, a native court or a court martial, be instituted, or to which such proceedings be transferred.

Federal Court of Malaysia

Palace of Justice, Presint 3, 62506 Putrajaya; tel. (3) 88803500; internet www.kehakiman.gov.my.

Chief Justice of the Federal Court: Tan Sri Dato' ZAKI BIN TUN AZMI.

President of the Court of Appeal: Tan Sri Dato' ALAUDDIN BIN MOHD SHERIFF.

Chief Judge of the High Court in Peninsular Malaysia: Dato' ARIFIN ZAKARIA.

Chief Judge of the High Court in Sabah and Sarawak: Tan Sri Datuk Seri RICHARD MALANJUM.

Attorney-General: Tan Sri ABDUL GANI PATAIL.

Religion

Islam is the established religion. While freedom of religious practice is enshrined in the Constitution, Malaysia's parallel Islamic judicial system holds great sway over the Muslim majority on religious issues. In May 2005 21 members of the controversial sect known as 'Sky Kingdom' were arrested for propagating 'devious' teachings said to humiliate Islam. Almost all ethnic Malays are Muslims, representing 60.4% of the total population in 2000. In that year 19.2% of the population followed Buddhism, 9.1% followed Christianity and 6.3% followed Hinduism.

Malaysian Consultative Council of Buddhism, Christianity, Hinduism, Sikhism and Taoism (MCCBCHST): 8 Jalan Duku, off Jalan Kasipillai, 51200 Kuala Lumpur; tel. (3) 40414669; fax (3) 40444304; f. 1981; a non-Muslim group.

ISLAM

President of the Majlis Islam: Datuk Haji MOHD FAUZI BIN Haji ABDUL HAMID (Kuching, Sarawak).

Istitut Kefahaman Islam Malaysia (IKIM) (Institute of Islamic Understanding Malaysia): 2 Langgak Tunku, off Jalan Duta, 50480 Kuala Lumpur; tel. (3) 62010889; fax (3) 62014189; internet www.ikim.gov.my.

Jabatan Kemajuan Islam Malaysia (JAKIM) (Department of Islamic Development Malaysia): Aras 4–9, Blok D7, Pusat Pentadbiran Kerajaan Persekutuan, 62519 Putrajaya; tel. (3) 88864000; e-mail faizal@islam.gov.my; internet www.islam.gov.my.

BUDDHISM

Malaysian Buddhist Association (MBA): MBA Bldg, 182 Jalan Burmah, 10050 Pinang; tel. (4) 2262690; fax (4) 2263024; e-mail mbapg@po.jaring.my; internet www.mba.net.my; f. 1959; the national body for Chinese-speaking monks and nuns and temples from the Mahayana tradition; 9 state brs and 25 other brs nationwide; 27,950 mems; Pres. Ven. SECK JIT HENG.

Buddhist Missionary Society Malaysia (BMSM): 123 Jalan Berhala, off Jalan Tun Sambanthan, 50470 Kuala Lumpur; tel. (3) 22730150; fax (3) 22740245; e-mail president@bmsm.org.my; internet www.bmsm.org.my; f. 1962 as Buddhist Missionary Society; Pres. ANG CHOO HONG.

Buddhist Tzu-Chi Merit Society (Malaysia): 24 Jesselton Ave, 10450 Pinang; e-mail mtzuchi@po.jaring.my; internet www.tzuchi.org.my.

Malaysian Fo Kuang Buddhist Association: 2 Jalan SS3/33, Taman University, 47300 Petaling Jaya, Selangor; tel. (3) 78776512; fax (3) 78776511; e-mail myfoguang@yahoo.com.

Sasana Abhiwurdhi Wardhana Society: 123 Jalan Berhala, off Jalan Tun Sambanthan, 50490 Kuala Lumpur; f. 1894; the national body for Sri Lankan Buddhists belonging to the Theravada tradition.

Young Buddhist Association of Malaysia (YBAM): 9 Jalan SS25/24, 47301 Petaling Jaya, Selangor; tel. (3) 78049154; fax (3) 78049021; e-mail ybam@streamyx.com; internet www.ybam.org.my; f. 1970; Pres. ONG SEE YEW.

CHRISTIANITY

Majlis Gereja-Gereja Malaysia (Council of Churches of Malaysia): 10 Jalan 11/9, 46200 Petaling Jaya, Selangor; tel. (3) 75967092; fax (3) 79560353; e-mail ccchurchm@streamyx.org; internet www.ccmalaysia.org; f. 1947; 18 mem. churches; 10 associate mems; Pres. Rev. Dr THOMAS PHILIPS (Mar Thoma Syrian Church); Gen. Sec. Rev. Dr HERMEN SHASTRI.

The Anglican Communion

Malaysia comprises three Anglican dioceses, within the Church of the Province of South East Asia.

Primate: Most Rev. Dr JOHN CHEW (Bishop of Singapore).

Bishop of Kuching: Rt Rev. BOLLY ANAK LAPOK, The House of the Epiphany, POB 347, 93704 Kuching, Sarawak; tel. (82) 240187; fax (82) 426488; e-mail bishopk@streamyx.com; has jurisdiction over Sarawak, Brunei and part of Indonesian Kalimantan (Borneo).

Bishop of Sabah: Most Rev. ALBERT VUN CHEONG FUI, Rumah Bishop, Jalan Tangki, POB 10811, 88809 Kota Kinabalu, Sabah; tel. (88) 247008; fax (88) 245942; e-mail dosabah@streamyx.com.

Bishop of West Malaysia: Rt. Rev. NG MOON HING, Bishop's House, 16 Jalan Pudu Lama, 50200 Kuala Lumpur; tel. (3) 20312728; fax (3) 20313213; e-mail anglican@streamyx.com; internet www.anglicanwestmalaysia.org.my.

The Baptist Church

Malaysia Baptist Convention: 2 Jalan Dispensary 2/38, 46000 Petaling Jaya, Selangor; tel. (3) 77823564; fax (3) 77833603; e-mail mbcpj@tm.net.my; internet www.mbc.org.my; Chair. Rev. BERNARD ANG; Gen. Sec. Rev. RONNIE CHIU.

The Methodist Church

Methodist Church in Malaysia: 69 Jalan 5/31, 46000 Petaling Jaya, Selangor; tel. (3) 79541811; fax (3) 79541787; e-mail info@methodistchurch.org.my; internet www.methodistchurch.org.my; 164,400 mems; Bishop Dr HWA YUNG.

The Presbyterian Church

Presbyterian Church in Malaysia: Joyful Grace Church, Jalan Alsagoff, 82000 Pontian, Johor; tel. (7) 711390; fax (7) 324384; e-mail office@gpm.org.my; internet www.gpm.org.m; Moderator Rev. CHUA HUA PENG.

The Roman Catholic Church

Malaysia comprises two archdioceses and seven dioceses. At 31 December 2006 approximately 3.3% of the population were adherents.

Catholic Bishops' Conference of Malaysia, Singapore and Brunei
Xavier Hall, 133 Jalan Gasing, 46000 Petaling Jaya, Selangor Darul Ehsan; tel. and fax (3) 79581371; e-mail cbcmsb@pc.jaring.my; Pres. Most Rev. MURPHY NICHOLAS XAVIER PAKIAM (Archbishop of Kuala Lumpur).

Archbishop of Kuala Lumpur: Most Rev. MURPHY NICHOLAS XAVIER PAKIAM, Archbishop's House, 528 Jalan Bukit Nanas, 50250 Kuala Lumpur; tel. (3) 20788828; fax (3) 20313815; e-mail mpakiam@pd.jaring.my.

Archbishop of Kuching: Most Rev. JOHN HA TIONG HOCK, Archbishop's Office, 118 Jalan Tun Abang Haji Openg, POB 940, 93718 Kuching, Sarawak; tel. (82) 242634; fax (82) 425724; e-mail abcofku@pd.jaring.my.

BAHÁ'Í FAITH

Spiritual Assembly of the Bahá'ís of Malaysia: 4 Lorong Titiwangsa 5, off Jalan Pahang, 53200 Kuala Lumpur; tel. (3) 79819059; fax (3) 79819073; e-mail nsa-sec@bahai.org.my; internet www.bahai.org.my; f. 1964; mems resident in 800 localities.

MALAYSIA
Directory

The Press

PENINSULAR MALAYSIA DAILIES

English Language

Business Times: Balai Berita 31, Jalan Riong, 59100 Kuala Lumpur; tel. (3) 22822628; fax (3) 22825424; e-mail bt@nstp.com.my; internet www.btimes.com.my; f. 1976; morning; Editor MUSTAPHA KAMIL; circ. 15,000.

The Edge: G501–G801, Levels 5–8, Block G, Phileo Damansara I, Jalan 16/11, off Jalan Damansara, 46350 Petaling Jaya, Selangor; tel. (3) 77218000; fax (3) 77218018; e-mail eeditor@bizedge.com; internet www.theedgedaily.com; f. 1996; weekly, with daily internet edition; business and investment news; Editor-in-Chief HO KAY TAT.

Malay Mail: Balai Berita 31, Jalan Riong, 59100 Kuala Lumpur; tel. (3) 22822829; fax (3) 22849133; e-mail malaymail@nstp.com.my; internet www.mmail.com.my; f. 1896; afternoon; Editor AHIRUDIN ATTAN; circ. 75,000.

Malaysiakini: 48 Jalan Kemuja, Bangsar Utama, 59000 Kuala Lumpur; tel. (3) 22835567; fax (3) 22892579; e-mail enquiries@malaysiakini.com; internet www.malaysiakini.com; f. 1999; Malaysia's first online newspaper; English and Malay; Editor STEVEN GAN.

New Straits Times: Balai Berita 31, Jalan Riong, 59100 Kuala Lumpur; tel. (3) 22823322; fax (3) 22821434; e-mail mailed@nstp.com.my; internet www.nst.com.my; f. 1845; morning; Group Editor-in-Chief Datuk HISHAMUDDIN AUN; circ. 190,000.

The Star: 15 Jalan 16/11, 46350 Petaling Jaya, POB 12474, Selangor Darul Ehsan; tel. (3) 79671388; fax (3) 79550439; e-mail msd@thestar.com.my; internet www.thestar.com.my; f. 1971; morning; Group Chief Editor DATUK WONG CHUN WAI; circ. 302,658.

The Sun: Sun Media Corpn Sdn Bhd, Lot 6, Jalan 51/217, Section 51, 46050 Petaling Jaya, Selangor Darul Ehsan; tel. (3) 77846688; fax (3) 77835871; e-mail editor@thesundaily.com; internet www.thesundaily.com; f. 1993; free tabloid newspaper in print and online formats; Group Editor-in-Chief HO KAY TAT; Editor CHONG CHENG HAI; circ. 82,474.

Chinese Language

Chung Kuo Pao (China Press): 80 Jalan Riong, 59100 Kuala Lumpur; tel. (3) 2828208; fax (3) 2825327; f. 1946; Editor POON CHAU HUAY; Gen. Man. NG BENG LYE; circ. 210,000.

Guang Ming Daily: 19 Jalan Semangat, 46200 Petaling Jaya, Selangor; tel. (3) 7582888; fax (3) 7575135; licence suspended for two weeks in Feb. 2006 following the publication's reprinting of controversial cartoons depicting the Prophet Muhammad; Editor-in-Chief YE NING; circ. 87,144.

Kwong Wah Yit Poh: 19 Jalan Presgrave, 11300 Pinang; tel. (4) 2612312; fax (4) 2610510; e-mail editor@kwongwah.com.my; internet www.kwongwah.com.my; f. 1910; morning; Chief Editor WONG KWAN CHEUNG; circ. 100,000.

Nanyang Siang Pau (Malaysia): 1st Floor, 1 Jalan SS7/2, 47301 Petaling Jaya, Selangor; tel. (3) 78726888; fax (3) 78726800; e-mail info@nanyang.com; internet www.nanyang.com.my; f. 1923; morning and evening; Editor-in-Chief CHENG KHEE CHIEN; circ. 180,000 (daily), 220,000 (Sunday).

Shin Min Daily News: 31 Jalan Riong, Bangsar, 59100 Kuala Lumpur; tel. (3) 2826363; fax (3) 2821812; f. 1966; morning; Editor-in-Chief CHENG SONG HUAT; circ. 82,000.

Sin Chew Jit Poh (Malaysia): 19 Jalan Semangat, POB 367, Jalan Sultan, 46200 Petaling Jaya, Selangor; tel. (3) 7582888; fax (3) 7570527; internet www.sinchew-i.com; f. 1929; morning; Chief Editor LIEW CHEN CHUAN; circ. 227,067 (daily), 230,000 (Sunday).

Malay Language

Berita Harian: Balai Berita, 31 Jalan Riong, 59100 Kuala Lumpur; tel. (3) 22822323; fax (3) 22822425; e-mail bh@bharian.com.my; internet www.bharian.com.my; f. 1957; morning; Group Editor Datuk HISHAMUDDIN AUN; circ. 350,000.

Mingguan Perdana: 48 Jalan Siput Akek, Taman Billion, Kuala Lumpur; tel. (3) 619133; Group Chief Editor KHALID JAFRI.

Utusan Malaysia: 46M Jalan Lima, off Jalan Chan Sow Lin, 55200 Kuala Lumpur; tel. (3) 2217055; fax (3) 2220911; e-mail corpcomm@utusan.com.my; internet www.utusan.com.my; Editor ABDUL AZIZ ISHAK; circ. 239,385.

Watan: 23-1 Jalan 9A/55A, Taman Setiawangsa, 54200 Kuala Lumpur; tel. (3) 4523040; fax (3) 4523043; circ. 80,000.

Tamil Language

Malaysia Nanban: 1544-3 Batu Complex, off Jalan Ipoh, Batu 3 1/4, 51200 Kuala Lumpur; e-mail accounts@nanban.com.my; tel. (3) 62515981; fax (3) 62515986; circ. 45,000; Dir AHMAD MYDIN Dato' SIKANDAR BATCHA.

Tamil Nesan: 28 Jalan Yew, Pudu, 55100 Kuala Lumpur; tel. (3) 2216411; fax (3) 2210448; f. 1924; morning; Editor V. VIVEKA-NANTHAN; circ. 35,000 (daily), 60,000 (Sunday).

Tamil Thinamani: 9 Jalan Murai Dua, Batu Kompleks, off Jalan Ipoh, Kuala Lumpur; tel. (3) 66719; Editor S. NACHIAPPAN; circ. 18,000 (daily), 39,000 (Sunday).

SUNDAY NEWSPAPERS

English Language

New Sunday Times: Balai Berita 31, Jalan Riong, 59100 Kuala Lumpur; tel. (3) 2822328; fax (3) 2824482; e-mail news@nstp.com.my; f. 1931; morning; Group Editor Datuk HISHAMUDDIN AUN; circ. 191,562.

Sunday Mail: Balai Berita 31, Jalan Riong, 59100 Kuala Lumpur; tel. (3) 2822328; fax (3) 2824482; e-mail smail@nstp.com.my; f. 1896; morning; Editor JOACHIM S. P. NG; circ. 75,641.

Sunday Star: 13 Jalan 13/6, 46300 Petaling Jaya, POB 12474, Selangor Darul Ehsan; tel. (3) 7581188; fax (3) 7551280; f. 1971; Editor DAVID YEOH; circ. 232,790.

Malay Language

Berita Minggu: Balai Berita 31, Jalan Riong, 59100 Kuala Lumpur; tel. (3) 2822328; fax (3) 2824482; e-mail bharian@bharian.com.my; f. 1957; morning; Editor Dato' AHMAD NAZRI ABDULLAH; circ. 421,127.

Metro Ahad: Balai Berita 31, Jalan Riong, 59100 Kuala Lumpur; tel. (3) 22822328; fax (3) 22821482; e-mail metahad@nstp.com.my; internet www.nstp.com.my/Corporate/nstp/products/productMetroAhd.htm; f. 1995; morning; circ. 136,974.

Mingguan Malaysia: 11A The Right Angle, Jalan 14/22, 46100 Petaling Jaya; tel. (3) 7563355; fax (3) 7577755; f. 1964; Editor MOHD HASSAN MOHD NOOR; circ. 543,232.

Utusan Zaman: 11A The Right Angle, Jalan 14/22, 46100 Petaling Jaya; tel. (3) 7563355; fax (3) 7577755; f. 1939; Editor MUSTAFA FADULA SUHAIMI; circ. 11,782.

PENINSULAR MALAYSIA PERIODICALS

English Language

Her World: Berita Publishing Sdn Bhd, Balai Berita 31, Jalan Riong, 59100 Kuala Lumpur; tel. (3) 2824322; fax (3) 2828489; monthly; Editor ALICE CHEE LAN NEO; circ. 35,000.

Malaysia Warta Kerajaan Seri Paduka Baginda (HM Government Gazette): Percetakan Nasional Malaysia Berhad, Jalan Chan Sow Lin, 50554 Kuala Lumpur; tel. (3) 92212022; fax (3) 92220690; e-mail pnmb@po.jaring.my; fortnightly.

Malaysian Agricultural Journal: Ministry of Agriculture and Agro-based Industry, Publications Unit, Wisma Tani, Jalan Sultan Salahuddin, 50624 Kuala Lumpur; tel. (3) 2982011; fax (3) 2913758; f. 1901; 2 a year.

Malaysian Forester: Forestry Department Headquarters, Jalan Sultan Salahuddin, 50660 Kuala Lumpur; tel. (3) 26988244; fax (3) 26925657; e-mail skthai@forestry.gov.my; f. 1931; quarterly; Editor THAI SEE KIAM.

The Planter: Wisma ISP, 29–33 Jalan Taman U Thant, POB 10262, 50708 Kuala Lumpur; tel. (3) 21425561; fax (3) 21426898; e-mail isphq@tm.net.my; internet www.isp.org.my/index.php?id=4; f. 1919; publ. by Isp Management (M); monthly; Editor AZIZAN ABDULLAH; circ. 4,000.

Young Generation: 11A The Right Angle, Jalan 14/22, 46100 Petaling Jaya, Selangor; tel. (3) 7563355; fax (3) 7577755; monthly; circ. 50,000.

Chinese Language

Mister Weekly: 2A Jalan 19/1, 46300 Petaling Jaya, Selangor; tel. (3) 7562400; fax (3) 7553826; f. 1976; weekly; Editor WONG AH TAI; circ. 25,000.

Mun Sang Poh: 472 Jalan Pasir Puteh, 31650 Ipoh; tel. (5) 3212919; fax (5) 3214006; bi-weekly; circ. 77,958.

New Life Post: 80M Jalan SS21/39, Damansara Utama, 47400 Petaling Jaya, Selangor; tel. (3) 7571833; fax (3) 7181809; f. 1972; bi-weekly; Editor LOW BENG CHEE; circ. 231,000.

New Tide Magazine: Nanyang Siang Pau Bldg, 2nd Floor, Jalan 7/2, 47301 Petaling Jaya, Selangor; tel. (3) 76202118; fax (3) 76202131; e-mail newtidemag@hotmail.com; f. 1974; monthly; Editor NELLIE OOI; circ. 39,000.

MALAYSIA   *Directory*

Malay Language

Dewan Masyarakat: Dewan Bahasa dan Pustaka, Jalan Wisma Putra, POB 10803, 50926 Kuala Lumpur; tel. (3) 2481011; fax (3) 2484211; f. 1963; monthly; current affairs; Editor ZULKIFLI SALLEH; circ. 48,500.

Dewan Pelajar: Dewan Bahasa dan Pustaka, Jalan Wisma Putra, POB 10803, 50926 Kuala Lumpur; tel. (3) 2481011; fax (3) 2484211; f. 1967; monthly; children's; Editor ZALEHA HASHIM; circ. 100,000.

Dewan Siswa: POB 10803, 50926 Kuala Lumpur; tel. (3) 2481011; fax (3) 2484208; monthly; circ. 140,000.

Gila-Gila: 38-1, Jalan Bangsar Utama Satu, Bangsar Utama, 59000 Kuala Lumpur; tel. (3) 22824970; fax (3) 22824967; fortnightly; circ. 70,000.

Harakah: Jabatan Penerangan dan Penyelidikan PAS, 28A Jalan Pahang Barat, Off Jalan Pahang, 53000 Kuala Lumpur; tel. (3) 40213343; fax (3) 40212422; e-mail harakahenglish@yahoo.com; internet www.harakahdaily.net; two a month; organ of the Parti Islam se Malaysia; Editor ZULKIFLI SULONG.

Jelita: Berita Publishing Sdn Bhd, 16–20 Jalan 4/109E, Desa Business Park, Taman Desa, off Jalan Klang Lama, 58100 Kuala Lumpur; tel. (3) 76208111; fax (3) 76208114; e-mail jelita@beritapub.com.my; internet www.beritapublishing.com.my; monthly; fashion and beauty magazine; Editor SARIMAH HUSIN; circ. 80,000.

Mangga: 11A The Right Angle, Jalan 14/22, 46100 Petaling Jaya, Selangor; tel. (3) 7563355; fax (3) 7577755; monthly; circ. 205,000.

Mastika: 11A The Right Angle, Jalan 14/22, 46100 Petaling Jaya, Selangor; tel. (3) 7563355; fax (3) 7577755; monthly; illustrated magazine; Editor AZIZAH ALI; circ. 15,000.

Utusan Radio dan TV: 11A The Right Angle, Jalan 14/22, 46100 Petaling Jaya, Selangor; tel. (3) 7563355; fax (3) 7577755; fortnightly; Editor NORSHAH TAMBY; circ. 115,000.

Wanita: 11A The Right Angle, Jalan 14/22, 46100 Petaling Jaya, Selangor; tel. (3) 7563355; fax (3) 7577755; monthly; women; Editor NIK RAHIMAH HASSAN; circ. 85,000.

Punjabi Language

Navjiwan Punjabi News: 52 Jalan 8/18, Jalan Toman, 46050 Petaling Jaya, Selangor; tel. (3) 7565725; f. 1950; weekly; Assoc. Editor TARA SINGH; circ. 9,000.

SABAH DAILIES

Api Siang Pau (Kota Kinabalu Commercial Press): 24 Lorong Dewan, POB 170, Kota Kinabalu; f. 1954; morning; Chinese; Editor Datuk LO KWOCK CHUEN; circ. 3,000.

Borneo Mail (Nountan Press Sdn Bhd): 1 Jalan Bakau, 1st Floor, off Jalan Gaya, 88999 Kota Kinabulu; tel. (88) 238001; fax (88) 238002; English; circ. 14,610.

Daily Express: News House, 16 Jalan Pasar Baru, POB 10139, 88801 Kota Kinabalu; tel. (88) 256422; fax (88) 238611; e-mail sph@tm.net.my; internet www.dailyexpress.com.my; f. 1963; morning; English, Bahasa Malaysia and Kadazan; Editor-in-Chief SARDATHISA JAMES; circ. 30,000.

Hwa Chiaw Jit Pao (Overseas Chinese Daily News): News House, 16 Jalan Pasar Baru, POB 10139, 88801 Kota Kinabalu; tel. (88) 256422; e-mail sph@tm.net.my; internet www.dailyexpress.com.my; f. 1936; morning; Chinese; Editor HII YUK SENG; circ. 30,000.

Merdeka Daily News: Lot 56, BDC Estate, Mile 1½ North Road, POB 332, 90703 Sandakan; tel. (89) 214517; fax (89) 275537; e-mail merkk@tm.net.my; f. 1968; morning; Chinese; Editor-in-Chief FUNG KON SHING; circ. 8,000.

New Sabah Times: Jalan Pusat Pembangunan Masyarakat, off Jalan Mat Salleh, 88100 Kota Kinabalu; POB 20119, 88758 Kota Kinabalu; tel. (88) 230055; fax (88) 231155; internet www.newsabahtimes.com.my; English, Malay and Kadazan; Editor-in-Chief EDDY LOK; circ. 30,000.

Syarikat Sabah Times: Kota Kinabalu; tel. (88) 52217; f. 1952; English, Malay and Kadazan; circ. 25,000.

Tawau Jih Pao: POB 464, 1072 Jalan Kuhara, Tawau; tel. (89) 72576; Chinese; Editor-in-Chief STEPHEN LAI KIM YEAN.

SARAWAK DAILIES

Berita Petang Sarawak: Lot 8322, Lorong 7, Jalan Tun Abdul Razak, 93450 Kuching; POB 1315, 93726 Kuching; tel. (82) 480771; fax (82) 489006; f. 1972; evening; Chinese; Chief Editor HWANG YU CHAI; circ. 12,000.

Borneo Post: 40 Jalan Tuanku Osman, POB 20, 96000 Sibu; tel. (84) 332055; fax (84) 321255; internet www.borneopost.com.my; morning; English; Man. Dir LAU HUI SIONG; Editor NGUOI HOW YIENG; circ. 60,000.

International Times: Lot 2215, Jalan Bengkel, Pending Industrial Estate, POB 1158, 93724 Kuching; tel. (82) 482215; fax (82) 480996; e-mail news@intimes.com; internet www.intimes.com.my; f. 1968; morning; Chinese; Editor LEE FOOK ONN; circ. 37,000.

Malaysia Daily News: 7 Island Rd, POB 237, 96009 Sibu; tel. (84) 330211; tel. (84) 320540; f. 1968; morning; Chinese; Editor WONG SENG KWONG; circ. 22,735.

Sarawak Tribune and Sunday Tribune: Lot 231, Jalan Abell Utara, 93100 Kuching; tel. (82) 424411; fax (82) 415024; internet www.sarawaktribune.com.my; f. 1945; English; licence suspended indefinitely in Feb. 2006; Editor (vacant); circ. 29,598.

See Hua Daily News: 40 Jalan Tuanku Osman, POB 20, 96000 Sibu; tel. (84) 332055; fax (84) 321255; f. 1952; morning; Chinese; Man. Editor LAU HUI SIONG; circ. 80,000.

United Daily News: internet www.uniteddaily.com.my; f. 2004 following merger between Chinese Daily News and Miri Daily News; morning; Chinese; Dep. Publr WONG KEH HUONG; circ. 35,000.

SARAWAK PERIODICALS

Pedoman Rakyat: Malaysian Information Dept, Mosque Rd, 93612 Kuching; tel. (82) 240141; f. 1956; monthly; Malay; Editor SAIT BIN HAJI YAMAN; circ. 30,000.

Pemberita: Malaysian Information Services, Mosque Rd, 93612 Kuching; tel. (82) 247231; internet www.penerangan.gov.my; f. 1950; every 2 months; Iban; Editor PHILIP NYARU BUNDAK; circ. 20,000.

Sarawak Gazette: Sarawak Museum, Jalan Tun Abang Haji Openg, 93566 Kuching; tel. (82) 244232; fax (82) 246680; e-mail museum@po.jaring.my; f. 1870; 2 a year; English; Chief Editor Datu Haji SALLEH SULAIMAN.

Utusan Sarawak: Lot 231, Jalan Nipah, off Jalan Abell Utara, POB 138, 93100 Kuching; tel. (82) 424411; fax (82) 415024; internet www.utusansarawak.com.my; f. 1949; Malay; Editor Haji ABDUL AZIZ Haji MALIM; circ. 32,292.

NEWS AGENCY

Bernama (Malaysian National News Agency): Wisma Bernama, 28 Jalan 1/65A, off Jalan Tun Razak, POB 10024, 50400 Kuala Lumpur; tel. (3) 26919955; fax (3) 26919932; e-mail helpdesk@bernama.com; internet www.bernama.com; f. 1968; general and foreign news, economic features and photo services, public relations wire, screen information and data services, stock market on-line equities service, real-time commodity and monetary information services; daily output in Malay and English; in June 1990 Bernama was given the exclusive right to receive and distribute news in Malaysia; Editor-in-Chief Datuk YONG SOO HEONG.

PRESS ASSOCIATION

Persatuan Penerbit-Penerbit Akhbar Malaysia (Malaysian Newspaper Publishers' Asscn): Unit 706, Blok B, Phileo Damansara 1, 9 Jalan 16/11, off Jalan Damansara, 46350 Petaling Jaya; tel. (3) 76608535; fax (3) 76608532; e-mail mnpa@macomm.com.my; Chair. MOHD NASIR ALI.

Publishers

KUALA LUMPUR

Arus Intelek Sdn Bhd: Plaza Mont Kiara, Suite E-06-06, Mont Kiara, 50480 Kuala Lumpur; tel. (3) 62011558; fax (3) 62018698; e-mail afusint@streamyx.com; Man. Datin AZIZAH MOKHZANI.

Berita Publishing Sdn Bhd: 16–20 Jalan 4/109E, Desa Business Park, Taman Desa, off Jalan Klang Lama, 58100 Kuala Lumpur; tel. (3) 76208111; fax (3) 76208018; e-mail mbeditor@beritapub.com; internet www.beritapublishing.com.my; education, business, fiction, cookery; Chair. A. KADIR JASIN.

Dewan Bahasa dan Pustaka (DBP) (Institute of Language and Literature): Jalan Dewan Bahasa, 50460 Kuala Lumpur; tel. (3) 21481011; fax (3) 21447248; internet www.dbp.gov.my; f. 1956; textbooks, magazines and general; Chair. Dato' JOHAN JAAFFAR.

Jabatan Penerbitan Universiti Malaya (University of Malaya Press): University of Malaya, Lembah Pantai, 50603 Kuala Lumpur; tel. (3) 79574361; fax (3) 79574473; e-mail terbit@um.edu.my; internet umweb.um.edu.my/umpress; f. 1954; general fiction, literature, economics, history, medicine, politics, science, social science, law, Islam, engineering, dictionaries; Man. ABDUL MANAF SAAD.

Malaya Press Sdn Bhd: Kuala Lumpur; tel. (3) 5754650; fax (3) 5751464; f. 1958; education; Man. Dir LAI WING CHUN.

Pustaka Antara Sdn Bhd: Lot UG 07 and 09, Upper Ground Floor, Kompleks Wilayah, 2 Jalan Munshi Abdullah, 50100 Kuala Lumpur;

MALAYSIA   *Directory*

tel. (3) 26980044; fax (3) 26917997; e-mail pantara4@streamyx.com; textbooks, children's, languages, fiction; Man. Dir Datuk ABDUL AZIZ BIN AHMAD.

Utusan Publications and Distributors Sdn Bhd: 1 and 3 Jalan 3/91A, Taman Shamelin Perkasa, Cheras, 56100 Kuala Lumpur; tel. (3) 92856577; fax (3) 92856341; e-mail rose@utusan.com.my; f. 1976; school textbooks, children's, languages, fiction, general; Exec. Dir ROSELINA JOHARI.

JOHOR

Penerbitan Pelangi Sdn Bhd: 66 Jalan Pingai, Taman Pelangi, 80400 Johor Bahru; tel. (7) 89269553; fax (7) 3329201; e-mail info@pelangibooks.com; internet www.pelangibooks.com; f. 1979; children's books, guidebooks and reference; Man. Dir SAMUEL SUM KOWN CHEEK.

Textbooks Malaysia Sdn Bhd: 49 Jalan Tengku Ahmad, POB 30, 85000 Segamat, Johor; tel. (7) 9318323; fax (7) 9313323; school textbooks, children's fiction, guidebooks and reference; Man. Dir FREDDIE KHOO.

NEGERI SEMBILAN

Bharathi Press: 166 Taman AST, POB 74, 70700 Seremban, Negeri Sembilan Darul Khusus; tel. (6) 7622911; f. 1939; Mans M. SUBRAMANIA BHARATHI, BHARATHI THASAN.

PULAU PINANG

Syarikat United Book Sdn Bhd: 187–189 Lebuh Carnarvon, 10100 Pulau Pinang; tel. (4) 2626891; fax (4) 2626892; textbooks, children's, reference, fiction, guidebooks; Man. Dir CHEW SING GUAN.

SELANGOR

Federal Publications Sdn Bhd: Lot 46, Subang Hi-Tech Industrial Park, Batu Tiga, 40000 Shah Alam, Selangor; tel. (3) 56286888; fax (3) 56364620; e-mail fpsb@tpg.com.my; f. 1957; computer, children's magazines; Gen. Man. STEPHEN K. S. LIM.

FEP International Sdn Bhd: 6 Jalan SS 4C/5, POB 1091, 47301 Petaling Jaya, Selangor; tel. (3) 7036150; fax (3) 7036989; f. 1969; children's, languages, fiction, dictionaries, textbooks and reference; Man. Dir LIM MOK HAI.

International Law Book Services: 10 Jalan PJU 8/5 G, Perdana Business Centre, Bandar Damansara Perdana, 47820 Petaling Jaya, Selangor Darul Ehsan; tel. (3) 77273890; fax (3) 77273884; e-mail gbc@pc.jaring.my; internet www.malaysialawbooks.com; Man. Dr SYED IBRAHIM.

Mahir Publications Sdn Bhd: 39 Jalan Nilam 1/2, Subang Sq., Subang Hi-Tech Industrial Park, Batu Tiga, 40000 Shah Alam, Selangor; tel. (3) 7379044; fax (3) 7379043; e-mail mahirpub@tm.net.my; Gen. Man. ZAINORA BINTI MUHAMAD.

Minerva Publications (NS) Sdn Bhd: 51 Jalan SG 3/1, Tan Sri Gombak, Batu Caves, 68100 Selangor; tel. (3) 61882876; fax (3) 61883876; e-mail minerva@streamyx.com; internet www.minervaa.com; f. 1974; general, children's, reference, medical, law; Dir and Chief Editor SUJAUDEEN; Man. Dir THANJUDEEN.

Pearson Education Malaysia Sdn Bhd: Lot 2, Jalan 215, off Jalan Templer, 46050 Petaling Jaya, Selangor; tel. (3) 78012000; fax (3) 77818005; e-mail inquiry@pearsoned.com.my; internet www.pearsoned.com.my; textbooks, mathematics, physics, science, general, educational materials; Dir WONG WEE WOON; Man. WONG MEI MEI.

Pelanduk Publications (M) Sdn Bhd: 12 Jalan SS 13/3E, Subang Jaya Industrial Estate, 47500 Subang Jaya, Selangor; tel. (3) 56386885; fax (3) 56386575; e-mail pelpub@tm.net.my; internet www.pelanduk.com; f. 1984; politics, history, anthropology, religion, education, language, economics, business and management, culture, self-improvement, women's studies, law; Man. JACKSON TAN.

Penerbit Fajar Bakti Sdn Bhd: 4 Jalan U1/15, Seksyeen U1, Hicom-Glenmarie Industrial Park, 40150 Shah Alam, Selangor; tel. (3) 7047011; fax (3) 7047024; e-mail edes@pfb.po.my; school, college and university textbooks, children's, fiction, general; Man. Dir EDDA DE SILVA.

Penerbit Pan Earth Sdn Bhd: 11 Jalan SS 26/6, Taman Mayang Jaya, 47301 Petaling Jaya, Selangor; tel. (3) 7031258; fax (3) 7031262; Man. STEPHEN CHENG.

Penerbit Universiti Kebangsaan Malaysia: Universiti Kebangsaan Malaysia, 43600 UKM, Selangor; tel. (3) 8292840; fax (3) 8254375; Man. HASROM BIN HARON.

Pustaka Delta Pelajaran Sdn Bhd: Wisma Delta, Lot 18, Jalan 51A/22A, 46100 Petaling Jaya, Selangor; tel. (3) 7570000; fax (3) 7576688; economics, language, environment, geography, geology, history, religion, science; Man. Dir LIM KIM WAH.

Pustaka Sistem Pelajaran Sdn Bhd: Lot 17–22 and 17–23, Jalan Satu, Bersatu Industrial Park, Cheras Jaya, 43200 Cheras, Selangor; tel. (3) 9047558; fax (3) 9047573; Man. T. THIRU.

Sasbadi Sdn Bhd: Lot 12, Jalan Teknologi 3/4, Taman Sains Selangor 1, Kota Damansara, 47810 Petaling Jaya, Selangor; tel. (3) 61451188; fax (3) 61569080; e-mail enquiry@sasbadi.com; internet www.sasbadi.com; Man. Dir LAW KING HUI.

SNP Panpac (Malaysia) Sdn Bhd: Lot 3, Jalan Saham 23/3, Kawasan MIEL Phase 8, Section 23, 40300 Shah Alam, Selangor Darul Ehsan; tel. (3) 55481088; fax (3) 55481080; e-mail eastview@snpo.com.my; f. 1980; fmrly SNP Eastview Publications Sdn Bhd; school textbooks, children's, fiction, reference, general; Dir CHIA YAN HENG.

Times Educational Co Sdn Bhd: 22 Jalan 19/3, 46300 Petaling Jaya, Selangor; tel. (3) 79571766; fax (3) 79573607; e-mail presco@po.jaring.my; general and reference; Man. FOONG CHUI LIN.

GOVERNMENT PUBLISHING HOUSE

Percetakan Nasional Malaysia Bhd (Malaysia National Printing Ltd): Jalan Chan Sow Lin, 50554 Kuala Lumpur; tel. (3) 2212022; fax (3) 2220690; fmrly the National Printing Department, incorporated as a company under govt control in January 1993.

PUBLISHERS' ASSOCIATION

Malaysian Book Publishers Association: Lot 12, Jalan Teknologi, Taman Sains Selangor 1, 47810 Petaling Jaya, Selangor; tel. (3) 61451010; fax (3) 61451199; e-mail info@mabopa.com.my; internet www.mabopa.com.my; f. 1968; Pres. LAW KING HUI; 95 mems.

Broadcasting and Communications

TELECOMMUNICATIONS

Jabatan Telekomunikasi Malaysia (JTM) (Department of Telecommunications): c/o Ministry of Energy, Water and Communications, Blok E4–5, Parcel E, Pusat Pentadbiran Kerajaan Persekutuan, 62668 Putrajaya; tel. (3) 88836000; fax (3) 88893712; e-mail webmaster@ktak.gov.my; internet www.ktkm.gov.my; regulatory body for telecommunications industry.

Celcom (Malaysia) Sdn Bhd: Menara Celcom, 82 Jalan Raja Muda Abdul Aziz, 50300 Kuala Lumpur; tel. (3) 26883939; e-mail feedback@celcom.com.my; internet www.celcom.com.my; f. 1988; private co licensed to operate mobile cellular telephone service; merged with TM Cellular Sdn Bhd in 2003; Chair. Tan Sri Dato' Ir MUHAMMAD RADZI BIN Haji MANSOR; CEO Dato' MOHAMMED SHAZALLI RAMLY.

DiGi Telecommunications Sdn Bhd: Lot 30, Jalan Delima 1/3, Subang Hi-Tech Industrial Park, 40000 Shah Alam, Selangor; tel. (3) 57211800; fax (3) 57211857; internet www.digi.com.my; private co licensed to operate mobile telephone service; Chair. SIGVE BREKKE; CEO JOHAN DENNELIND.

Maxis Communications Bhd: Menara Maxis, Aras 18, Kuala Lumpur City Centre, off Jalan Ampang, 50088 Kuala Lumpur; tel. (3) 23307000; fax (3) 23300008; internet www.maxis.com.my; f. 1995; provides mobile, fixed-line and multimedia services; approx. 3.25m. subscribers in 2003; Chair. Datuk MEGAT ZAHARUDDIN BIN MEGAT MOHAMED NOR; CEO SANDIP DAS.

Technology Resources Industries Bhd (TRI): Menara TR, 23rd Floor, 161B Jalan Ampang, 50450 Kuala Lumpur; tel. (3) 2619555; fax (3) 2632018; operates mobile cellular telephone service; Chair. and Chief Exec. Tan Sri Dato' TAJUDIN RAMLI.

Telekom Malaysia Bhd: Level 51, North Wing, Menara Telekom, off Jalan Pantai Baru, 50672 Kuala Lumpur; tel. (3) 22401221; fax (3) 22832415; internet www.tm.com.my; f. 1984; public listed co responsible for operation of basic telecommunications services; 74% govt-owned; 4.22m. fixed lines (95% of total); Chair. Haji MUHAMMAD RADZI BIN Haji MANSOR; Chief Exec. Dato' MOHD ISA ZAMZAMZAIRANT.

Time dotCom Bhd: Wisma Time, 1st Floor, 249 Jalan Tun Razak, 50400 Kuala Lumpur; tel. (3) 27208000; fax (3) 27200199; internet www.time.com.my; f. 1996 as Time Telecommunications Holdings Bhd; name changed as above in Jan. 2000; state-controlled co licensed to operate trunk network and mobile cellular telephone service; Chair. Dato' WAN MUHAMAD WAN IBRAHIM; Man. Dir AFZAL ABDUL RAHIM.

BROADCASTING

Regulatory Authority

Under the Broadcasting Act (approved in December 1987), the Minister of Information is empowered to control and monitor all

MALAYSIA

radio and television broadcasting, and to revoke the licence of any private company violating the Act by broadcasting material 'conflicting with Malaysian values'.

Radio Televisyen Malaysia (RTM): Dept of Broadcasting, Angkasapuri, Bukit Putra, 50614 Kuala Lumpur; tel. (3) 22825333; fax (3) 22825103; internet www.rtm.gov.my; f. 1946; television introduced 1963; supervises radio and television broadcasting; Dir-Gen. ABDUL RAHMAN HAMID; Dep. Dir-Gen. ADILAH SHEK KUMAR.

Radio

Radio Malaysia: Radio Televisyen Malaysia (see Regulatory Authority), POB 11272, 50740 Kuala Lumpur; tel. (3) 2823991; fax (3) 2825859; f. 1946; domestic service; operates six networks; broadcasts in Bahasa Malaysia, English, Chinese (Mandarin and other dialects), Tamil and Aborigine (Temiar and Semai dialects); Dir of Radio MADZHI JOHARI.

Radio Televisyen Malaysia—Sabah: Jalan Tuaran, 88614 Kota Kinabalu; tel. (88) 213444; fax (88) 223493; f. 1955; television introduced 1971; a dept of RTM; broadcasts programmes over two networks for 280 hours a week in Bahasa Malaysia, English, Chinese (two dialects), Kadazan, Murut, Dusun and Bajau; Dir of Broadcasting JUMAT ENGSON.

Radio Televisyen Malaysia—Sarawak: Broadcasting House, Jalan P. Ramlee, 93614 Kuching; tel. (82) 248422; fax (82) 241914; e-mail pvgrtmsw@tm.net.my; f. 1954; a dept of RTM; broadcasts 441 hours per week in Bahasa Malaysia, English, Chinese, Iban, Bidayuh, Melanau, Kayan/Kenyah; Dir of Broadcasting NORHYATI ISMAIL.

Rediffusion Sdn Bhd: Rediffusion House, 17 Jalan Pahang, 53000 Kuala Lumpur; tel. (3) 4424544; fax (3) 4424614; f. 1949; two programmes; 44,720 subscribers in Kuala Lumpur; 11,405 subscribers in Pinang; 6,006 subscribers in Province Wellesley; 20,471 subscribers in Ipoh; Gen. Man. ROSNI B. RAHMAT.

Suara Islam (Voice of Islam): Islamic Affairs Division, Prime Minister's Department, Blok Utama, Tingkat 1–5, Pusat Pentadbiran Kerajaan Persekutuan, 62502 Putrajaya; f. 1995; Asia-Pacific region; broadcasts in Bahasa Malaysia on Islam.

Suara Malaysia (Voice of Malaysia): Wisma Radio, Angkasapuri, POB 11272, 50740 Kuala Lumpur; tel. (3) 22887824; fax (3) 22847954; f. 1963; overseas service in Bahasa Malaysia, Arabic, Myanmar (Burmese), English, Bahasa Indonesia, Chinese (Mandarin/Cantonese), Tagalog and Thai; Controller of Overseas Service STEPHEN SIPAUN.

Time Highway Radio: All Asia Broadcast Centre, Technology Park Malaysia, Bukit Jalil, 57000 Kuala Lumpur; tel. (3) 95438888; fax (3) 95439911; e-mail feedback@thr.fm; internet www.thr.fm; f. 1994; serves Kuala Lumpur region; broadcasts in English; CEO ABDUL AZIZ HAMDAN.

Television

Measat Broadcast Network Systems Sdn Bhd: All Asia Broadcast Centre, Technology Park Malaysia, Lebuhraya Puchong, Simpang Besi, Bukit Jalil, 57000 Kuala Lumpur; tel. (3) 74919888; fax (3) 95437333; e-mail custcare@astro.com.my; internet www.astro.com.my; nation-wide subscription service; Malaysia's first satellite, Measat 1, was launched in January 1996; a second satellite was launched in October of that year; Chair. T. ANANDA KRISHNAN.

Metropolitan Television Sdn Bhd (8TV): 3 Persiaran Bandar Utama, 47800 Petaling Jaya, Selangor; tel. (3) 77288282; fax (3) 77289593; e-mail izham@8tv.com.my; internet www.8tv.com.my; began broadcasting in July 1995; commercial station; operates only in Klang Valley; 100%-owned by Merit Idea Sdn Bhd; CEO AHMAD IZHAM OMAR.

Radio Televisyen Malaysia—Sabah: see Radio**Radio Televisyen Malaysia—Sarawak:** see Radio**Sistem Televisyen Malaysia Bhd (TV 3):** 3 Persiaran Bandar Utama, Bandar Utama, 47800 Petaling, Selangor Darul Ehsan; tel. (3) 77266333; fax (3) 77278455; e-mail enquiries@tv3.com.my; internet www.tv3.com.my; f. 1983; Malaysia's first private television network, began broadcasting in 1984; Chair. Dato' ABDUL MUTALIB BIN Datuk Seri MOHAMED RAZAK; Man. Dir Hisham Dato' ABDULLAH RAHMAN.

Televisyen Malaysia: Radio Televisyen Malaysia (see Regulatory Authority); f. 1963; operates two national networks, TV1 and TV2; Controller of Programmes ISMAIL MOHAMED JAH.

Under a regulatory framework devised by the Government, a ban on privately owned satellite dishes was ended in 1996.

Directory

Finance

(cap. = capital; auth. = authorized; res = reserves; dep. = deposits; m. = million; brs = branches; amounts in ringgit Malaysia)

BANKING

Following a series of mergers, 10 domestic banking groups and about 30 banks were operating in 2008. In February 2004 53 banks held 'offshore' licences in Labuan.

Central Bank

Bank Negara Malaysia: Jalan Dato' Onn, POB 10922, 50929 Kuala Lumpur; tel. (3) 26988044; fax (3) 26912990; e-mail info@bnm.gov.my; internet www.bnm.gov.my; f. 1959; bank of issue; financial regulatory authority; cap. 100.0m., res 29,647,119m., dep. 317,695,814m. (Dec. 2007); Gov. Tan Sri Dato' Sri Dr ZETI AKHTAR AZIZ; 6 brs.

Regulatory Authority

Labuan Offshore Financial Services Authority (LOFSA): Level 17, Main Office Tower, Financial Park Labuan, Jalan Merdeka, 87000 Labuan; tel. (87) 591200; fax (87) 413328; e-mail communication@lofsa.gov.my; internet www.lofsa.gov.my; regulatory body for the International Offshore Financial Centre of Labuan established in October 1990; Chair. Tan Sri Dato' Sri ZETI AKHTAR AZIZ (Gov. of Bank Negara Malaysia); Dir-Gen. Dato' AZIZAN ABDUL RAHMAN.

Commercial Banks

Peninsular Malaysia

ABN Amro Bank Bhd: Levels 25–27, MNI Twins, Tower II, 11 Jalan Pinang, POB 10094, 50704 Kuala Lumpur; tel. (3) 21627888; fax (3) 21625692; e-mail info@abnamro.com.my; internet www.abnamromalaysia.com; f. 1963.

Affin Bank Bhd: Menara AFFIN, 17th Floor, 80 Jalan Raja Chulan, 50200 Kuala Lumpur; tel. (3) 20559000; fax (3) 20261415; e-mail head.ccd@affinbank.com.my; internet www.affinbank.com.my; f. 1975 as Perwira Habib Bank Malaysia Bhd; name changed to Perwira Affin Bank Bhd 1994; merged with BSN Commercial Bank (Malaysia) Bhd Jan. 2001, and name changed as above; cap. 1,439.2m., res 500.0m., dep. 22,308.7m. (Dec. 2007); Chair. Gen. Tan Sri Dato' Seri ISMAIL Haji OMAR; Pres. and CEO Dato' ABDUL HAMIDY ABDUL HAFIZ; 106 brs.

Alliance Bank Malaysia Bhd: Menara Multi-Purpose, Ground Floor, Capital Sq., 8 Jalan Munshi Abdullah, 50100 Kuala Lumpur; POB 10069, 50704 Kuala Lumpur; tel. (3) 26948800; fax (3) 26946727; e-mail info@alliancebg.com.my; internet www.alliancebank.com.my; f. 1982 as Malaysian French Bank Bhd; name changed to Multi-Purpose Bank Bhd 1996; name changed as above Jan. 2001, following acquisition of six merger partners; cap. 598.5m., res 864.3m., dep. 20,478.5m. (March 2007); Chair. THOMAS LEE; CEO BRIDGET ANNE LAI HUNG YEE; 79 brs.

AmBank Bhd: 22nd Floor, Bangunan AmBank Group, 55 Jalan Raja Chulan, 50200 Kuala Lumpur; tel. (3) 20782633; fax (3) 20316453; e-mail customercare@ambg.com.my; internet www.ambg.com.my; f. 1994; fmrly Arab-Malaysian Bank Bhd; name changed as above 2002; cap. 505.5m., res −72.0m., dep. 9,036.3m. (March 2003); Chair. Tan Sri Dato' AZMAN HASHIM; Man. Dir KUNG BENG HONG.

Bangkok Bank Bhd (Thailand): 105 Jalan Tun H. S. Lee, 50000 Kuala Lumpur; tel. (3) 20724555; fax (3) 20788569; e-mail bbb@tm.net.my; internet www.bangkokbank.com; f. 1958; cap. 265.0m., res 98.6m., dep. 738.2m. (Dec. 2006); Chair. CHATRI SOPHONPANICH; Man. Dir SINGH TANGTATSWAS; 1 br.

Bank of America Malaysia Bhd: Wisma Goldhill, Jalan Raja Chulan, 50200 Kuala Lumpur; tel. (3) 20321133; fax (3) 20319087; internet www.bankofamerica.com.my; cap. 135.8m., res 244.0m., dep. 1,005.0m. (Dec. 2006); Chair. KRISTJAN DRAKE.

Bank of Nova Scotia Bhd: POB 11056, Menara Boustead, 69 Jalan Raja Chulan, 50200 Kuala Lumpur; tel. (3) 21410766; fax (3) 21412160; e-mail bns.kualalumpur@scotiabank.com; internet www.scotiabank.com.my; f. 1973; cap. 122.4m., res 352.4m., dep. 2,226.1m. (Oct. 2007); Man. Dir RASOOL KHAN.

Bank of Tokyo-Mitsubishi UFJ (Malaysia) Bhd (Japan): Levels 9–11, Menara IMC, 8 Jalan Sultan Ismail, 50250 Kuala Lumpur; tel. (3) 20788871; fax (3) 20788870; e-mail edpbtm@tm.net.my; f. 1996 following merger of the Bank of Tokyo and Mitsubishi Bank; fmrly known as Bank of Tokyo-Mitsubishi, name changed as above following merger with UFJ; cap. 200m., res 712.5m., dep. 4,414.5m. (Dec. 2006); Chair. TETSUO TANAKA; Pres. and CEO HAJIME WASHIZU.

Bumiputra Commerce Bank Bhd: 6 Jalan Tun Perak, 50050 Kuala Lumpur; tel. (3) 26931722; fax (3) 26986628; internet www.bcb

MALAYSIA

.com.my; f. 1999 following merger of Bank Bumiputra Malaysia Bhd with Bank of Commerce Bhd; cap. 2,064.0m., res 2,950.3m., dep. 59,632.6m. (Dec. 2005); Chair. Tan Sri HAIDAR MOHAMED NOOR; Group CEO Dato' MOHAMED NAZIR ABDUL RAZAK ALI; 230 brs.

Citibank Bhd (USA): 165 Jalan Ampang, POB 10112, 50450 Kuala Lumpur; tel. (3) 23830000; fax (3) 2328763; internet www.citibank.com.my; f. 1959; cap. 121.7m., res 1,816.6m., dep. 32,700.9m. (Dec. 2006); Country Officer AJAY BANGA; 3 brs.

Deutsche Bank (Malaysia) Bhd (Germany): 18–20 Menara IMC, 8 Jalan Sultan Ismail, 50250 Kuala Lumpur; tel. (3) 20536788; fax (3) 20319822; f. 1994; cap. 173.5m., res 670.1m., dep. 6,951.2m. (Dec. 2006); Man. Dir RAYMOND YEOH.

EON Bank Bhd: Menara EON Bank, 12th Floor, 288 Jalan Raja Laut, 50350 Kuala Lumpur; tel. (3) 26941188; fax (3) 26949588; e-mail caf@eonbank.com.my; internet www.eonbank.com.my; f. 1963; fmrly Kong Ming Bank Bhd; merged with Oriental Bank Bhd 2001; cap. 1,329.8m., res 1,845.2m., dep. 28,584.3m. (Dec. 2006); Chair. Datin Dr ASERI SYED JAMALULLAIL; CEO and Exec. Dir ALBERT LAU YIONG; 95 brs.

Hong Leong Bank Bhd: Wisma Hong Leong, Level 3, 18 Jalan Perak, 50450 Kuala Lumpur; tel. (3) 21642828; fax (3) 27156365; internet www.hlb.com.my; f. 1905; fmrly MUI Bank Bhd; merged with Wah Tat Bank Bhd 2001; cap. 1,580.1m., res 2,913.5m., dep. 59,113.7m. (June 2007); Chair. Tan Sri QUEK LENG CHAN; Man. Dir YVONNE CHIA; 187 local brs, 2 overseas brs.

HSBC Bank Malaysia Bhd (Hong Kong): 2 Leboh Ampang, POB 10244, 50912 Kuala Lumpur; tel. (3) 20700744; fax (3) 20702678; internet www.hsbc.com.my; f. 1860; fmrly Hongkong Bank Malaysia Bhd; adopted present name in 1999; cap. 114.5m., res 3,006.7m., dep. 40,756.7m. (Dec. 2006); Chair. SANDY FLOCKHART; CEO IRENE DORNER.

Malayan Banking Bhd (Maybank): Menara Maybank, 14th Floor, 100 Jalan Tun Perak, 50050 Kuala Lumpur; tel. (3) 20747037; fax (3) 20789761; e-mail publicaffairs@maybank.com.my; internet www.maybank2u.com; f. 1960; acquired Pacific Bank Bhd Jan. 2001; merged with PhileoAllied Bank (Malaysia) Bhd March 2001; cap. 3,889.2m., res 13,564.6m., dep. 192,748.9m. (June 2007); Chair. Tan Sri MOHAMED BASIR BIN AHMAD; Pres. and CEO Datuk ANDUL WAHID BIN OMAR; 327 domestic brs, 30 overseas brs.

OCBC Bank (Malaysia) Bhd: Menara OCBC, 18 Jalan Tun Perak, 50050 Kuala Lumpur; tel. (3) 83175000; fax (3) 26984363; internet www.ocbc.com.my; f. 1932; cap. 291.5m., res 1,925.8m., dep. 30,701.9m. (Dec. 2006); Group Chair. Tan Sri Dato' NASRUDDIN BIN BAHARI; CEO JEFFREY CHEW SUN TEONG; 25 brs.

Public Bank Bhd: Menara Public Bank, 146 Jalan Ampang, 50450 Kuala Lumpur; tel. (3) 21638888; fax (3) 21619307; e-mail customerservice@publicbank.com.my; internet www.publicbank.com.my; f. 1965; merged with Hock Hua Bank Bhd March 2001; cap. 3,527.8m., res 5,822.7m., dep. 145,185.5m. (Dec. 2007); Chair. Tan Sri Dato' Dr TEH HONG PIOW; 241 domestic brs, 3 overseas brs.

RHB Bank Bhd: Towers Two and Three, Menara AA, 426 Jalan Tun Razak, 50400 Kuala Lumpur; tel. (3) 92068118; fax (3) 92068088; e-mail md_ceo@rhbbank.com.my; internet www.rhbbank.com.my; f. 1997 as a result of merger between DCB Bank Bhd and Kwong Yik Bank Bhd; acquired Sime Bank Bhd 1999; merged with Bank Utama (Malaysia) Bhd 2003; cap. 3,318.1m., res 2,235.4m., dep. 71,447.9m. (Dec. 2007); Chair. (non-exec.) Datuk AZLAN ZAINOL; CEO MICHAEL JOSEPH BARRETT; 148 brs.

Standard Chartered Bank Malaysia Bhd: 1st Floor, 2 Jalan Ampang, 50450 Kuala Lumpur; tel. (3) 20726555; fax (3) 2010621; internet www.standardchartered.com.my; 31 brs.

United Overseas Bank (Malaysia) Bhd: Menara UOB, Level 2, Jalan Raja Laut, POB 11212, 50738 Kuala Lumpur; tel. (3) 26924511; fax (3) 26913110; e-mail uob121@uob.com.my; internet www.uob.com.my; f. 1920; merged with Chung Khiaw Bank (Malaysia) Bhd in 1997 and with Overseas Union Bank (Malaysia) Bhd in 2002; cap. 470m., res 1,902.2m., dep. 25,827.7m. (Dec. 2006); Chair. WEE CHO YAW; CEO CHAN KOK SEONG; 37 brs.

Merchant Banks

Affin Merchant Bank Bhd: Menara Boustead, 27th Floor, 69 Jalan Raja Chulan, POB 11424, 50744 Kuala Lumpur; tel. (3) 21423700; fax (3) 21423799; e-mail general@affinmerchantbank.com.my; internet www.affinmerchantbank.com.my; f. 1970 as Permata Chartered Merchant Bank Bhd; name changed as above March 2001; cap. 211.6m., res 293.9m., dep. 3,841.1m. (Dec. 2006); Chair. Tan Sri YAACOB MOHAMED ZAIN; CEO Datin ZURAIDAH ATAN-SHARARIMAN.

Alliance Investment Bank Bhd (AIB): Menara Multi-Purpose, 20th Floor, Capital Sq., 8 Jalan Munshi Abdullah, 50100 Kuala Lumpur; tel. (3) 26927788; fax (3) 26928787; e-mail ambb@allianceinvestment.com.my; internet www.allianceinvestmentbank.com.my; f. 1974 as Amanah-Chase Merchant Bank Bhd; name changed to Alliance Merchant Bank Bhd in 2001, following merger with Bumiputra Merchant Bankers Bhd; name changed as above in 2006, following merger with Kuala Lumpur City Securities (KLCS); cap. 365.0m., res 96.6m., dep. 1,904.7m. (March 2007); Chair. Dato' THOMAS MUN LUNG LEE; CEO BRIDGET LAI.

AmInvestment Bank Bhd: 22nd Floor, Bangunan AmBank Group, 55 Jalan Raja Chulan, 50200 Kuala Lumpur; tel. (3) 20782655; fax (3) 20782842; e-mail customercare@ambg.com.my; internet www.ambg.com.my; f. 1975; fmrly Arab-Malaysian Merchant Bank Bhd, later known as AmMerchant Bank Bhd; name changed as above 2006; cap. 340.0m., res 600.9m., dep. 17,757,6m. (March 2007); Chair. Tan Sri Dato' AZMAN HASHIM; Group Man. Dir CHEAH TEK KUANG; 5 brs.

Aseambankers Malaysia Bhd: Menara Maybank, 33rd Floor, 100 Jalan Tun Perak, 50050 Kuala Lumpur; tel. (3) 20591888; fax (3) 20784194; e-mail faudziah@maybank-ib.com; internet www.maybank-ib.com; f. 1973; cap. 50.1m., res 689.3m., dep. 7,903.6m. (June 2007); Chair. Dato' MOHAMED BASIR AHMAD; CEO Tan Sri MOHAMMED RASHDAN YUSOF; 2 brs.

CIMB Investment Bank Bhd: Bangunan CIMB, 10th Floor, Jalan Semantan, Damansara Heights, 50490 Kuala Lumpur; tel. (3) 2536688; fax (3) 2535522; e-mail info@cimb.com.my; internet www.cimbbank.com.my; f. 1974; fmrly known as Commerce International Merchant Bankers Bhd; name changed as above 2006; cap. 219.2m., res 623.5m., dep. 1,205.5m. (Dec. 2006); Chair. Dato' MD NOR YUSOF.

MIMB Investment Bank Bhd: Menara EON Bank, 21st Floor, 288 Jalan Raja Laut, 50350 Kuala Lumpur; tel. (3) 26910200; fax (3) 26985388; internet www.mimb.com.my; f. 1970; fmrly known as Malaysian International Merchant Bankers Bhd; wholly owned subsidiary of EON Bank Berhad; cap. 75m., res 122.1m., dep. 109.5m. (Dec. 2006); Chair. YEO KAR PENG; 2 brs.

Public Islamic Bank Bhd: 25th Floor, Menara Public Bank, 146 Jalan Ampang, 50450 Kuala Lumpur; tel. (3) 21669382; fax (3) 21669362; e-mail merchantbank@publicbank.com.my; f. 1973 as Asian International Merchant Bankers Bhd; became Sime Merchant Bankers Bhd 1996; name changed as above 2000; cap. 165.0m., res −28.9m., dep. 1,086.6m. (Dec. 2002); Chair. Tan Sri Dato' THONG YAW HONG.

RHB Investment Bank Bhd: Tower Three, 9th Floor, RHB Centre, 426 Jalan Tun Razak, 50400 Kuala Lumpur; tel. (3) 92805475; fax (3) 27118501; e-mail publicaffairs@rhb.com.my; internet www.rhb.com.my; f. 1974; fmrly known as RHB Sakura Merchant Bankers Bhd; name changed as above 2006; cap. 338.6m., res 359.5m., dep. 5,625.8m. (Dec. 2006); Chair. Encik ABDULLAH MAT NOH.

Southern Investment Bank Bhd: Menara Southern Bank, 83 Medan Setia 1, Plaza Damansara, Bukit Damansara, 50772 Kuala Lumpur; tel. (3) 62047788; fax (3) 23817198; e-mail sibb@sibb.com.my; f. 1988; fmrly Perdana Merchant Bankers Bhd; cap. 77.9m., res 0.5m., dep. 313.6m. (Dec. 2006); Chair. Dato' Nik IBRAHIM KAMIL; CEO Tan Sri Dato' TAN TEONG HEAN.

Utama Merchant Bank Bhd: Menara Maxis, Level 33, Suite A, 50088 Kuala Lumpur; tel. (3) 20789133; fax (3) 20725511; e-mail umbb@umbb.po.my; internet www.cmsb.com.my/ubg; f. 1975 as Utama Wardley Bhd; name changed as above 1996; cap. 156.5m., res 385.9m., dep. 8,746.2m. (Dec. 2006); Chair. Dato' MAHMUD ABU BAKIR TAIB; CEO DONNY KWA SOO CHUAN; 1 br.

Co-operative Bank

Bank Kerjasama Rakyat Malaysia Berhad: Bangunan Bank Rakyat, Jalan Tangsi, Peti Surat 11024, 50732 Kuala Lumpur; tel. (3) 2985011; fax (3) 2985981; f. 1954; 83,095 mems. of which 823 were co-operatives (Dec. 1996); Chair. Dr YUSUF YACOB; Man. Dir Dato' ANUAR JAAFAR; 67 brs.

Development Banks

Bank Pembangunan Malaysia Bhd: Menara Bank Pembangunan, POB 12352, Jalan Sultan Ismail, 50774 Kuala Lumpur; tel. (3) 26113888; fax (3) 26928520; e-mail enq_y@bpmb.com.my; internet www.bpmb.com.my; f. 1973; govt-owned; fmrly known as Bank Pembangunana & Infrastruktur Malaysia Bhd; name changed as above following merger with Bank Industri & Teknologi Malaysia Bhd in 2005; specializes in infrastructure, maritime and high-technology sectors; cap. 3,078.7m., res 2,444.3m., dep. 5,174.6m. (Dec. 2007); Pres. and Man. Dir Dato' TAJUDDIN ATAN; Chair. Datuk ABDUL SAMAD ALIAS; 15 brs.

Bank Perusahaan Kecil & Sederhana Malaysia Bhd (SME Bank): Menara SME Bank, Jalan Sultan Ismail, Peti Surat 12352, 50774 Kuala Lumpur; tel. (3) 26152020; fax (3) 26928520; e-mail enq_y@smebank.com.my; internet www.smebank.com.my; f. 2005; wholly owned subsidiary of Bank Pembangunan Malaysia Bhd; provides both financial and non-financial assistance to SMEs; cap. 1,350.0m., res −241.0m., dep 2,564.7m. (Dec. 2006); Chair. Dato' GUMURI HUSSAIN; Man. Dir Dato' AZMI ABDULLAH.

Sabah Development Bank Bhd: SDB Tower, Wisma Tun Fuad Stephens, POB 12172, 88824 Kota Kinabalu, Sabah; tel. (88) 232177; fax (88) 261852; e-mail info@sabahdevbank.com; internet www.sabahdevbank.com; f. 1977; wholly owned by State Government of Sabah; cap. 430.0m., res –84.8m., dep. 560.0m. (Dec. 2006); Chair. PETER SIAU WUI KEE; Man. Dir and CEO PETER LIM SIONG ENG.

Islamic Banks

Bank Islam Malaysia Bhd: Darul Takaful, 11th Floor, Jalan Sultan Ismail, 50250 Kuala Lumpur; tel. (3) 26168000; fax (3) 26980587; e-mail communications@bankislam.com.my; internet www.bankislam.com.my; f. 1983; cap. 1,725.4m., res –681.2m., dep. 17,650.8m. (June 2007); Chair. MOHD BAKKE SALEH; Man. Dir Dato' ZUKRI SAMAT; 90 brs.

Bank Muamalat Malaysia Bhd: Menara Bumiputra, 21 Jalan Melaka, 50100 Kuala Lumpur; tel. (3) 26988787; fax (3) 20325997; e-mail webmaster@muamalat.com.my; internet www.muamalat.com.my; f. 1999; CEO Tuan Haji MOHD SHUKRI HUSSIN; 40 brs.

'Offshore' Banks

ABN Amro Bank, Labuan Branch: Level 9 (A), Main Office Tower, Financial Park Labuan, Jalan Merdeka, 87000 Labuan; tel. (87) 423008; fax (87) 421078; Man. ANTHONY RAJAN.

Al-Hidayah Investment Bank (Labuan) Ltd: Level 7 (C), Main Office Tower, Financial Park Labuan, Jalan Merdeka, 87000 Labuan; tel. (87) 451660; fax (87) 583088.

AMInternational (L) Ltd: Level 12 (B), Block 4, Office Tower, Financial Park Labuan, Jalan Merdeka, 87000 Labuan; tel. (87) 413133; fax (87) 425211; e-mail felix-leong@ambg.com.my; internet www.ambg.com.my; f. 1995; Dir PAUL ONG.

AmMerchant Bank Bhd, Labuan Branch: Level 12 (B), Block 4, Main Office Tower, Financial Park Labuan, Jalan Merdeka, 87000 Labuan; tel. (87) 413133; fax (87) 425211; Gen. Man. PAUL ONG WHEE SEN.

Bank of America, National Trust and Savings Association, Labuan Branch: Level 13 (D), Main Office Tower, Financial Park Labuan, Jalan Merdeka, 87000 Labuan; tel. (87) 411778; fax (87) 424778; Gen. Man. Pengiran NUR FARHAH OOI ABDULLAH.

Bank of East Asia Ltd, Labuan Offshore Branch: Level 10 (C), Main Office Tower, Financial Park Labuan, Jalan Merdeka, 87000 Labuan; tel. (87) 451145; fax (87) 451148; e-mail arraisag@hkbea.com; Gen. Man. ALVIN ARRAIS.

Bank Islam (L) Ltd: Level 15 (A), Main Office Tower, Financial Park, Jalan Merdeka, 87000 Labuan; tel. (87) 451802; fax (87) 453077; e-mail engkuafandi@bankislam.com.my; Branch Man. ENGKU AFANDI TAIB.

Bank Muamalat Malaysia Bhd, Labuan Branch: Level 15 (A1), Main Office Tower, Financial Park Labuan, Jalan Merdeka, 87000 Labuan; tel. (87) 412898; fax (87) 451164; e-mail fuad@muamalat.com.my; Gen. Man. ZAINOL RASHID KHAIRUDDIN.

Bank of Nova Scotia, Labuan Branch: Level 10 (C2), Main Office Tower, Financial Park Labuan, Jalan Merdeka, 87000 Labuan; tel. (87) 451101; fax (87) 451099; Man. KWAN SING HUNG.

Bank of Tokyo-Mitsubishi UFJ Ltd, Labuan Branch: Level 12 (A & F), Main Office Tower, Financial Park Labuan, Jalan Merdeka, 87000 Labuan; tel. (87) 410487; fax (87) 410476; e-mail pulaubtm@tm.net.my; Gen. Man. WATURU TANAKA.

Barclays Bank PLC: Level 5 (A), Main Office Tower, Financial Park Labuan, Jalan Merdeka, 87000 Labuan; tel. (87) 425571; fax (87) 425575; e-mail barclay@tm.net.my; Man. MIAW SIAW LOONG.

Bayerische Landesbank Girozentrale, Labuan Branch: Level 14 (C), Block 4, Office Tower, Financial Park Labuan, Jalan Merdeka, 87000 Labuan; tel. (87) 422170; fax (87) 422175; e-mail blblab@tm.net.my; Exec. Vice-Pres., CEO and Gen. Man. LOUISE PAUL.

BNP Paribas, Labuan Branch: Level 9 (E), Main Office Tower, Financial Park Labuan, Jalan Merdeka, 87000 Labuan; tel. (87) 422328; fax (87) 419328; e-mail bnpkul@tm.net.my; Gen. Man. YAP SIEW YING.

Bumiputra Commerce Bank (L) Ltd: Level 14 (B), Main Office Tower, Financial Park Labuan, Jalan Merdeka, 87000 Labuan; tel. (87) 410302; fax (87) 410313; e-mail bumitrst@tm.net.my; Gen. Man. ASARAF ABU BAKAR.

Cathay United Bank, Labuan Branch: Level 3 (C), Main Office Tower, Financial Park Labuan, Jalan Merdeka, 87000 Labuan; tel. (87) 452168; fax (87) 453678; Gen. Man. YEH PIN HUNG.

CIMB (L) Ltd: Unit 11 (B1), Level 11, Main Office Tower, Financial Park Labuan, Jalan Merdeka, 87000 Labuan; tel. (87) 451608; fax (87) 451610; CEO ADHA AMIR ABDULLAH.

Citibank Malaysia (L) Ltd: Level 11 (F), Main Office Tower, Financial Park Labuan, Jalan Merdeka, 87000 Labuan; tel. (87) 421181; fax (87) 419671; Gen. Man. CLARA LIM AI CHENG.

City Credit Investment Bank Ltd: Level 11 (D1), Main Office Tower, Financial Park Labuan, Jalan Merdeka, 87000 Labuan; tel. (87) 582268; fax (87) 581268; Dir ABDUL RAHMAN ABDULLAH.

Commercial IBT Bank, Labuan Branch: 02-01, 2nd Floor, Wisma Lucas Kong Bldg, U0185 Jalan Merdeka, 87000 Labuan; tel. (87) 411868; fax (87) 416818; e-mail aong@cibtbank.com; Pres. Dir Dr ADRIAN ONG CHEE BENG.

Commerzbank AG, Labuan Branch: Level 6 (E), Main Office Tower, Financial Park Labuan, Jalan Merdeka, 87000 Labuan; tel. (87) 416953; fax (87) 413542; Prin. Officer HO KAH HENG.

Crédit Agricole Indosuez, Calyon Labuan Branch: Level 6 (B), Main Office Tower, Financial Park Labuan, Jalan Merdeka, 87000 Labuan; tel. (87) 408334; fax (87) 408335; Sr Country Officer TAN BOON EONG.

Crédit Industriel et Commercial: Level 11 (C2), Main Office Tower, Financial Park Labuan, Jalan Merdeka, 87000 Labuan; tel. (87) 452008; fax (87) 452009; Gen. Man. YEOW TIANG HUI.

Crédit Suisse First Boston, Labuan Branch: Level 10 (B), Main Office Tower, Financial Park Labuan, Jalan Merdeka, 87000 Labuan; tel. (87) 425381; fax (87) 425384; Gen. Man. RUDOLF ZAUGG.

Danaharta Managers (L) Ltd: Tingkat 10, Bangunan Setia 1, 15 Lorong Dungun, Bukit Damansara, 50490 Kuala Lumpur; tel. (3) 2531122; fax (3) 2534375; Gen. Man. (vacant).

Deutsche Bank AG, Labuan Branch: Level 9 (G2), Main Office Tower, Financial Park Labuan, Jalan Merdeka, 87000 Labuan; tel. (87) 439811; fax (87) 439866; Man. Dir KUAH HUN LIANG.

Development Bank of Singapore (DBS Bank) Ltd, Labuan Branch: Level 12 (E), Main Office Tower, Financial Park Labuan, Jalan Merdeka, 87000 Labuan; tel. (87) 423375; fax (87) 423376; Gen. Man. KEVIN WONG.

Dresdner Bank AG, Labuan Branch: Level 13 (C), Main Office Tower, Financial Park Labuan, Jalan Merdeka, 87000 Labuan; tel. (87) 419271; fax (87) 419272; Gen. Man. JAMALUDIN NASIR.

ECM Libra Investment Bank Ltd: Level 3 (I1), Main Office Tower, Financial Park Complex, Jalan Merdeka, 87000 Labuan; tel. (87) 408525; fax (87) 408527.

Hongkong & Shanghai Banking Corporation, Offshore Banking Unit: Level 11 (D), Main Office Tower, Financial Park Labuan, Jalan Merdeka, 87000 Labuan; tel. (87) 417168; fax (87) 417169; Man. PREM KUMAR.

ING Bank NV: Level 8 (B2), Main Office Tower, Financial Park Labuan, Jalan Merdeka, 87000 Labuan; tel. (87) 425733; fax (87) 425734; Gen. Man. MILLY TAN.

International Commercial Bank of China: Level 7 (E2), Main Office Tower, Financial Park Labuan, Jalan Merdeka, 87000 Labuan; tel. (87) 581688; fax (87) 581668; Gen. Man. TAI CHI-HSIEN.

J. P. Morgan Chase Bank, Labuan Branch: Level 5 (F), Main Office Tower, Financial Park Labuan, Jalan Merdeka, 87000 Labuan; tel. (87) 424384; fax (87) 424390; e-mail fauziah.hisham@chase.com; Gen. Man. LEONG KET TI.

J. P. Morgan Malaysia Ltd: Unit 5 (F), Level 5, Main Office Tower, Financial Park Labuan, Jalan Merdeka, 87000 Labuan; tel. (87) 459000; fax (87) 451328; Gen. Man. LEONG KET TI.

KBC Bank NV, Labuan Branch: Level 3 (B), Main Office Tower, Financial Park Labuan, Jalan Merdeka, 87000 Labuan; tel. (87) 581778; fax (87) 583787; Gen. Man. KONG KOK CHEE.

Lloyds TSB Bank PLC: Lot B, 11th Floor, Wisma Oceanic, Jalan OKK Awang Besar, 87007 Labuan; tel. (87) 418918; fax (87) 411928; e-mail labuan@lloydstsb.com.my; Dir and Gen. Man. BARRY FRANCIS LEA.

Macquarie Bank Ltd, Labuan Branch: Level 3 (A), Main Office Tower, Financial Park Labuan, Jalan Merdeka, 87000 Labuan; tel. (87) 583080; fax (87) 583088; Division Dir DARREN WOODWARD.

Maybank International (L) Ltd: Level 16 (B), Main Office Tower, Financial Park Labuan, Jalan Merdeka, 87000 Labuan; tel. (87) 414406; fax (87) 414806; e-mail millmit@tm.net.my; Gen. Man. LAM HEE.

Mizuho Corporate Bank Ltd, Labuan Branch: Level 9 (B and C), Main Office Tower, Financial Park Labuan, Jalan Merdeka, 87000 Labuan; tel. (87) 417766; fax (87) 419766; Gen. Man. ISAKU TANIMURA.

Natexis Banque Populaires: Level 9 (G), Main Office Tower, Financial Park Labuan, Jalan Merdeka, 87000 Labuan; tel. (87) 581009; fax (87) 583009; Gen. Man. RIZAL ABDULLAH.

National Australia Bank, Labuan Branch: Level 12 (C2), Main Office Tower, Financial Park Complex, Jalan Merdeka, 87008 Labuan; tel. (87) 426386; fax (87) 428387; e-mail natausm@po.jaring.my; Gen. Man. LIONEL LIM.

OSK Investment Bank (Labuan) Ltd: Lot 3B, Level 5, Wisma Lazenda, Jalan Kemajuan, Labuan; tel. (87) 581885; fax (87) 582885; Prin. Officer ONG LEONG HUAT.

MALAYSIA

Directory

Oversea-Chinese Banking Corporation Ltd, Labuan Branch: Level 8 (C), Main Office Tower, Financial Park Labuan, Jalan Merdeka, 87000 Labuan; tel. (87) 423381; fax (87) 423390; Gen. Man. BERNARD FERNANDO.

Public Bank (L) Ltd: Level 8 (A and B), Main Office Tower, Financial Park Labuan, Jalan Merdeka, 87000 Labuan; tel. (87) 411898; fax (87) 413220; Man. ALEXANDER WONG.

RHB Bank (L) Ltd: Level 15 (B), Main Office Tower, Financial Park Labuan, Jalan Merdeka, 87000 Labuan; tel. (87) 417480; fax (87) 417484; Gen. Man. TOH AY LENG.

RUSD Investment Bank, Inc.: Level 4 (A1), Main Office Tower, Financial Park Labuan, Jalan Merdeka, 87000 Labuan; tel. (87) 452100; fax (87) 543100; Man. Dir NASEERUDDIN A. KHAN.

Société Générale, Labuan Branch: Level 11 (B), Main Office Tower, Financial Park Labuan, Jalan Merdeka, 87000 Labuan; tel. (87) 421676; fax (87) 421669; Gen. Man. RAMZAN ABU TAHIR.

Standard Chartered Bank Offshore Labuan: Level 10 (F), Main Office Tower, Financial Park Labuan, Jalan Merdeka, 87000 Labuan; tel. (87) 417200; fax (87) 417202; Gen. Man. EDWARD NG.

Sumitomo Mitsui Banking Corpn, Labuan Branch: Level 12 (B and C), Main Office Tower, Financial Park Labuan, Jalan Merdeka, 87000 Labuan; tel. (87) 410955; fax (87) 410959; Gen. Man. JUNICHI IKENO.

UBS AG, Labuan Branch: Level 5 (E), Main Office Tower, Financial Park Labuan, Jalan Merdeka, 87000 Labuan; tel. (87) 421743; fax (87) 421746; Man. ZELIE HO SWEE LUM.

United Overseas Bank Ltd, Labuan Branch: Level 6 (A), Main Office Tower, Financial Park Labuan, Jalan Merdeka, 87000 Labuan; tel. (87) 424388; fax (87) 424389; Gen. Man. HO FONG KUN.

United World Chinese Commercial Bank: Level 3 (C), Main Office Tower, Financial Park Labuan, Jalan Merdeka, 87000 Labuan; tel. (87) 452168; fax (87) 453678; Gen. Man. PIN HUNG YEH.

Banking Associations

Association of Banks in Malaysia (ABM): UBN Tower, 34th Floor, 10 Jalan P. Ramlee, 50250 Kuala Lumpur; tel. (3) 20788041; fax (3) 20788004; e-mail banks@abm.org.my; internet www.abm.org.my; f. 1973; Chair. Dato' ABDUL HAMIDY ABDUL HAFIZ; Exec. Dir CHUAH MEI LIN.

Institute of Bankers Malaysia: Wisma IBI, 5 Jalan Semantan, Damansara Heights, 50490 Kuala Lumpur; tel. (3) 20956833; fax (3) 20952322; e-mail ibbm@ibbm.org.my; internet www.ibbm.org.my; f. 1977; professional and educational body for the banking and finance industry; Chair. Tan Sri Dato' Sri Dr ZETI AKHTAR AZIZ.

Malayan Commercial Banks' Association: POB 12001, 50764 Kuala Lumpur; tel. (3) 2983991.

Persatuan Institusi Perbankan Tanpa Faedah Malaysia (Association of Islamic Banking Institutions Malaysia—AIBIM): 23/F, Menara Tun Razak, Jalan Raja Laut, 50350 Kuala Lumpur; tel. (3) 2648002; fax (3) 2648012; e-mail admin@aibim.com; internet www.aibim.com; f. 1995; Exec. Dir MOHAMED SHAMSUDIN.

STOCK EXCHANGE

Bursa Malaysia: 15th Floor, Exchange Square, Bukit Kewangan, 50200 Kuala Lumpur; tel. (3) 20347000; fax (3) 27326437; e-mail enquiries@bursamalaysia.com; internet www.bursamalaysia.com; f. 1973; fmrly known as Kuala Lumpur Stock Exchange (KLSE); name changed as above in 2004; in 1988 KLSE authorized the ownership of up to 49% of Malaysian stockbroking companies by foreign interests; 988 listed cos (Jan. 2008); merged with Malaysian Exchange of Securities Dealing and Automated Quotation Bhd (MESDAQ) in March 2002; Chair. TUN MOHAMED DZAIDDIN Haji ABDULLAH; CEO Dato' YUSLI MOHAMED YUSOFF.

Regulatory Authority

Securities Commission (SC): 3 Persiaran Bukit Kiara, Bukit Kiara, 50490 Kuala Lumpur; tel. (3) 62048777; fax (3) 62015078; e-mail cau@seccom.com.my; internet www.sc.com.my; f. 1993; Chair. Dato' ZARINAH ANWAR.

INSURANCE

From 1988 onwards, all insurance companies were placed under the authority of the Central Bank, Bank Negara Malaysia. In 1997 there were 69 insurance companies operating in Malaysia, including nine reinsurance companies, 11 composite, 40 general and life and two takaful (compliant with Islamic law) insurance companies.

Principal Insurance Companies

Allianz General Insurance Malaysia Bhd: Wisma UOA II, Floors 23 and 23A, 21 Jalan Pinang, 50450 Kuala Lumpur; tel. (3) 21623388; fax (3) 21626387; e-mail partner@allianz.com.my; internet www.allianz.com.my/general; f. 2001; CEO WILLIAM MEI YORK LIANG; Chair. Tan Sri RAZALI ISMAIL.

Allianz Life Insurance Malaysia Bhd: Wisma UOA II, Floors 23 and 23A, 21 Jalan Pinang, 50450 Kuala Lumpur; tel. (3) 21616001; fax (3) 21626387; e-mail partner@allianz.com.my; internet life.allianz.com.my; fmrly MBA Life Assurance Sdn Bhd; CEO CHRIS JAMES.

Commerce Life Assurance Bhd: 338 Jalan Tunku Abdul Rahman, 50100 Kuala Lumpur; tel. (3) 26123600; fax (3) 26987035; f. 1992 as AMAL Assurance Bhd; name changed as above in 1999.

Great Eastern Life Assurance (Malaysia) Bhd: Menara Great Eastern, 303 Jalan Ampang, 50450 Kuala Lumpur; tel. (3) 42598888; fax (3) 42590500; e-mail wecare@lifeisgreat.com.my; internet www.lifeisgreat.com.my; CEO KOH YAW HUI.

Hong Leong Assurance Sdn Bhd: Menara HLA, 26th Floor, 3 Jalan Kia Peng, 50450 Kuala Lumpur; tel. (3) 27199228; fax (3) 27101735; internet www.hla.com.my; Chair. Tan Sri QUEK LENG CHAN; Man. Dir and CEO CHARLIE ESPINOLA OROPEZA.

ING Insurance Bhd: Menara ING, 84 Jalan Raja Chulan, POB 10846, 50927 Kuala Lumpur; tel. (3) 21617255; fax (3) 21610549; internet www.ing.com.my; f. 1987; fmrly Aetna Universal Insurance Bhd; Chair. Tengku ABDULLAH IBNI AL-MARHUM Sultan ABU BAKAR.

Jerneh Insurance Corpn Sdn Bhd: Wisma Jerneh, 12th Floor, 38 Jalan Sultan Ismail, POB 12420, 50788 Kuala Lumpur; tel. (3) 2427066; fax (3) 2426672; f. 1970; general; Gen. Man. GOH CHIN ENG.

Malaysia National Insurance Sdn Bhd: Tower 1, 26th Floor, MNI Twins, 11 Jalan Pinang, 50450 Kuala Lumpur; tel. (3) 21769000; fax (3) 21769090; e-mail askme@mni.com.my; internet www.mni.com.my; f. 1970; life and general; CEO MOHAMAD SALIHUDDIN AHMAD.

Malaysian Co-operative Insurance Society Ltd: Wisma MCIS, Jalan Barat, 46200 Petaling Jaya, Selangor; tel. (3) 7552577; fax (3) 7571563; e-mail info@mcis.po.my; internet www.mcis.com.my/mcis; f. 1954; CEO L. MEYYAPPAN.

Manulife Insurance (Malaysia) Bhd: Menara Manulife RB, 12th Floor, 6 Jalan Gelenggang, Damansara Heights, 50490 Kuala Lumpur; tel. (3) 20948055; fax (3) 20935487; internet www.manulife.com.my; f. 1963; life and non-life insurance; fmrly British American Life and General Insurance Bhd; name then changed to John Hancock Life Insurance (Malaysia) Bhd; name changed as above 2005, following 2004 merger between John Hancock Financial Services, Inc. and Manulife Financial Corpn; Chair. Tan Sri Dato' MOHAMED SHERIFF BIN MOHAMED KASSIM.

Mayban Assurance Bhd: Mayban Assurance Tower, Dataran Maybank, 1 Jalan Maarof, 50000 Kuala Lumpur; tel. (3) 22972888; fax (3) 22972828; e-mail mayassur@tm.net.my; internet www.maybank2u.com.my; Pres. and CEO Datuk AMIRSHAM A. AZIZ.

MBf Insurans Sdn Bhd: Plaza MBf, 5th Floor, Jalan Ampang, POB 10345, 50710 Kuala Lumpur; tel. and fax (3) 2613466; Man. MARC HOOI TUCK KOK.

MCIS Zürich Insurance Bhd: Wisma MCIS Zürich, Jalan Barat, 46200 Petaling Jaya, Selangor; tel. (3) 79552577; fax (3) 79574780; e-mail info@mciszurich.com.my; internet www.mciszurich.com.my; CEO MD ADNAN MD ZAIN; Chair. Dato' BALARAM ANAK LELAKI PETHA NAIDU.

Multi-Purpose Insurans Bhd: Menara Multi-Purpose, 9th Floor, Capital Square, 8 Jalan Munshi Abdullah, 50100 Kuala Lumpur; tel. (3) 26919888; fax (3) 26945758; e-mail info@mpib.com.my; fmrly Kompas Insurans Bhd; Senior Gen. Mans WONG FOOK WAH, VISWANATH A. L. KANDASAMY.

Oriental Capital Assurance Bhd: 36 Jalan Ampang, 50450 Kuala Lumpur; tel. (3) 20702828; fax (3) 20724150; e-mail oricap@oricap.net; internet www.oricap.net; f. 2002 as a result of the merger of Capital Insurance Bhd and United Oriental Assurance Sdn Bhd; Chair. Datuk Dr SHERIFF KASSIM; Exec. Dir MOHD YUSOF BIN IDRIS.

Overseas Assurance Corpn Ltd: Wisma Lee Rubber, 21st Floor, Jalan Melata, 50100 Kuala Lumpur; tel. (3) 2022939; fax (3) 2912288; Gen. Man. A. K. WONG.

Progressive Insurance Sdn Bhd: Plaza Berjaya, 9th, 10th and 15th Floors, 12 Jalan Imbi, POB 10028, 50700 Kuala Lumpur; tel. (3) 2410044; fax (3) 2418257; Man. JERRY PAUT.

RHB Insurance Bhd: Tower 1, 4th Floor, RHB Centre, Jalan Tun Razak, 50450 Kuala Lumpur; tel. (3) 9812731; fax (3) 9812729; Man. MOHAMMAD ABDULLAH.

Sime AXA Assurance Bhd: Wisma Sime Darby, 15th Floor, Jalan Raja Laut, 50350 Kuala Lumpur; tel. (3) 2937888; fax (3) 2914672; e-mail hkkang@simenet.com; Gen. Man. HAK KOON KANG.

South-East Asia Insurance Bhd: Tingkat 9, Menara SEA Insurance, 1008 Jalan Sultan Ismail, 50250 Kuala Lumpur; POB 6120 Pudu, 55916 Kuala Lumpur; tel. (3) 2938111; fax (3) 2930111; CEO HASHIM HARUN.

UMBC Insurans Sdn Bhd: Bangunan Sime Bank, 16th Floor, Jalan Sultan Sulaiman, 50000 Kuala Lumpur; tel. (3) 2328733; fax (3) 2322181; f. 1961; CEO ABDULLAH ABDUL SAMAD.

Trade and Industry

GOVERNMENT AGENCIES

Danamodal Nasional Bhd (Danamodal): 10th Floor, Bangunan Sime Bank, Jalan Sultan Sulaiman, 50000 Kuala Lumpur; tel. (3) 20312255; fax (3) 20310786; e-mail info@danamodal.com.my; f. 1998 to recapitalize banks and restructure financial institutions, incl. arranging mergers and consolidations; Chair. Raja Datuk ARSHAD Raja Tun UDA; Man. Dir MARIANUS VONG SHIN TZOI.

Federal Agricultural Marketing Authority (FAMA): Bangunan Fama Point, Lot 17304, Jalan Persiaran 1, Bandar Baru Selayang, 68100 Batu Caves, Selangor Darul Ehsan; tel. (3) 61262020; fax (3) 61365610; e-mail fama@fama.gov.my; internet www.famaxchange.org; f. 1965 to supervise, co-ordinate and improve marketing of agricultural produce, and to seek and promote new markets and outlets for agricultural produce; Chair. Datuk ABDUL RAHIM B. BAKRI; Dir-Gen. Dato' Haji MOHAMED SHARIFF ABDUL AZIZ.

Federal Land Development Authority (FELDA): Wisma FELDA, Jalan Perumahan Gurney, 54000 Kuala Lumpur; tel. (3) 2935066; fax (3) 2920087; e-mail upd@felda.net.my; internet www.felda.net.my; f. 1956; govt statutory body formed to develop land into agricultural smallholdings to eradicate rural poverty; 893,150 ha of land developed (1994); involved in rubber, oil palm and sugar-cane cultivation; Chair. Tan Sri Dr MOHD YUSOF NOOR; Dir-Gen. Dato' AHMAD TARMIZI ALIAS.

Khazanah Nasional: Level 33, Tower 2, Petronas Twin Towers, 50088 Kuala Lumpur; tel. (3) 20340000; fax (3) 20340300; e-mail info@khazanah.com.my; internet www.khazanah.com.my; f. 1994; state-controlled investment co; assumed responsibility for certain assets fmrly under control of the Ministry of Finance; holds 40% of Telekom Malaysia Bhd, 40% of Tenaga Nasional Bhd, 6.6% of HICOM Bhd and 17.8% of PROTON; Chair. Dato' Seri ABDULLAH BIN Haji AHMAD BADAWI; Man. Dir Dato' AZMAN BIN Haji MOKHTAR.

Malaysia External Trade Development Corpn (MATRADE): Menara MATRADE, Jalan Khidmat Usaha, off Jalan Duta, 50480 Kuala Lumpur; tel. (3) 62077077; fax (3) 62037037; e-mail info@matrade.gov.my; internet www.matrade.gov.my; f. 1993; responsible for external trade development and promotion; Chair. Tan Sri HALIM MOHAMMED.

Malaysian Institute of Economic Research: Menara Dayabumi, 9th Floor, Jalan Sultan Hishamuddin, POB 12160, 50768 Kuala Lumpur; tel. (3) 22725897; fax (3) 22730197; e-mail Admin@mier.po.my; internet www.mier.org.my; f. 1986; Exec. Dir Dr MOHAMED ARIFF; Chair. Tan Sri Dato' MOHAMED SHERIFF MOHAMED KASSIM.

Malaysian Palm Oil Board (MPOB): 6 Persiaran Institusi, Bandar Baru Bangi, 43000 Kajang, Selangor; tel. (3) 87694400; fax (3) 89259446; e-mail webmaster@mpob.gov.my; internet www.mpob.gov.my; f. 2000 by merger of Palm Oil Registration and Licensing Authority and Palm Oil Research Institute of Malaysia; Chair. Dato' SABRI AHMAD.

Malaysian Timber Industry Board (Lembaga Perindustrian Kayu Malaysia): 13–17 Menara PGRM, 8 Jalan Pudu Ulu, 56100 Cheras, Kuala Lumpur; tel. (3) 92822235; fax (3) 92851477; e-mail info@mtib.gov.my; internet www.mtib.gov.my; f. 1973 to promote and regulate the export of timber and timber products from Malaysia; Chair. Datuk WIRA ISMAEL SALEH; Dir-Gen. MOHD NAZURI BIN HASHIM SHAH.

Muda Agricultural Development Authority (MADA): MADA HQ, Ampang Jajar, 05990 Alor Setar, Kedah; tel. (4) 7728255; fax (4) 7722667; Chair. Dato' Seri MAHDZIR BIN KHALID.

National Economic Action Council: NEAC-MTEN, Prime Minister's Office, Blok Utama, Tingkat 1–5, Pusat Pentadbiran Kerajaan Persekutuan, 62502 Putrajaya; tel. (3) 88882903; fax (3) 88882902; e-mail effendi@epu.jpm.my; internet www.neac.gov.my; Exec. Dir Dato' Sri MOHAMED EFFENDI NORWAWI.

National Information Technology Council (NITC): Kuala Lumpur; Sec. Datuk Tengku Dr MOHD AZZMAN SHARIFFADEEN.

National Timber Certification Council: Kuala Lumpur; Chair. CHEW LYE TENG.

Perbadanan Nasional Bhd (PERNAS): Kuala Lumpur; tel. (3) 2935177; internet www.pns.com.my; f. 1969; govt-sponsored; promotes trade, banking, property and plantation development, construction, mineral exploration, steel manufacturing, inland container transportation, mining, insurance, industrial development, engineering services, telecommunication equipment, hotels and shipping; cap. p.u. RM 116.25m.; 10 wholly owned subsidiaries, over 60 jointly owned subsidiaries and 18 assoc. cos; Chair. Datuk AWANG ADEK BIN HUSSIN; Man. Dir Tuan SYED KAMARULZAMAN BIN SYED ZAINOL KHODKI SHAHABUDIN.

DEVELOPMENT ORGANIZATIONS

Fisheries Development Authority of Malaysia: 7th–11th Floors, Wisma PKNS, Jalan Raja Laut, 50784 Kuala Lumpur; tel. (3) 26177000; fax (3) 26911931; e-mail info@kim.moa.my; internet lkim.gov.my; Dir-Gen. Dato' MUSTAFA BIN Haji AHMAD.

Johor Corporation: 13th Floor, Menara Johor Corporation, Kotaraya, 80000 Johor Bahru; tel. (7) 2232692; fax (7) 2233175; e-mail pdnjohor@jcorp.com.my; internet www.jcorp.com.my; development agency of the Johor state govt; Chair. Dato' Haji ABDUL GHANI BIN OTHMAN; Chief Exec. Dato' MUHAMMAD ALI HASHIM.

Kumpulan FIMA Bhd (Food Industries of Malaysia): Suite 4-1, Level 4, Block C, Plaza Damansara, 45 Jalan Medan Setia 1, Bukit Damansara, 50490 Kuala Lumpur; tel. (3) 20921211; fax (3) 20925923; e-mail enquiry@fima.com.my; internet www.fima.com.my; f. 1972; fmrly govt corpn, transferred to private sector in 1991; promotes food and related industry through investment on its own or by co-ventures with local or foreign entrepreneurs; oil palm, cocoa and fruit plantation developments; manufacturing and packaging, trading, supermarkets and restaurants; Man. Dir Encik AHMAD RIZA BIN BASIR; 1,189 employees.

Majlis Amanah Rakyat (MARA) (Trust Council for the People): Bangunan Medan MARA, 13th Floor, 21 Jalan Raja Laut, 50609 Kuala Lumpur; tel. (3) 26915111; fax (3) 26913620; e-mail webmaster@mara.gov.my; internet www.mara.gov.my; f. 1966 to promote, stimulate, facilitate and undertake economic and social development; to participate in industrial and commercial undertakings and jt ventures; Dir-Gen. Datuk ZAMANI BIN MOHD NOOR.

Malaysian Agricultural Research and Development Institute (MARDI): POB 12301, General Post Office, 50774 Kuala Lumpur; tel. (3) 89437111; fax (3) 89483664; e-mail saharan@mardi.my; internet www.mardi.my; f. 1969; research and development in food and tropical agriculture; Dir-Gen. Datuk Dr ABD. SHUKOR BIN ABD. RAHMAN.

Malaysian Industrial Development Authority (MIDA): Plaza Sentral, Block 4, 5 Jalan Stesen Sentral, 50470 Kuala Lumpur; tel. (3) 22673633; fax (3) 22747970; e-mail promotion@mida.gov.my; internet www.mida.gov.my; f. 1967; Chair. Tan Sri Datuk ZAINAL ABIDIN BIN SULONG; Dir-Gen. Datuk JALILAH BABA.

Malaysian Industrial Development Finance Bhd: Level 21, Menara MIDF, 82 Jalan Raja Chulan, 50200 Kuala Lumpur; tel. (3) 21619011; fax (3) 21617580; e-mail inquiry@midf.com.my; internet www.midf.com.my; f. 1960 by the Govt; banks, insurance cos, industrial financing, advisory services, project development, merchant and commercial banking services; Chair. Tan Sri Dato' MAHMOOD TAIB; Man. Dir Dato' MOHAMED NAJIB ABDULLAH.

Malaysian Pepper Board: Lot 115, Jalan Utama, 93916 Kuching, Sarawak; tel. (82) 331811; fax (82) 336877; e-mail info@mpb.gov.my; internet www.mpb.gov.my; f. 2007; responsible for the statutory grading of all Sarawak pepper for export, licensing of pepper dealers and exporters, trading and the development and promotion of pepper grading, storage and processing facilities; Chair. Datuk RICHARD RIOT JAEM; Dir-Gen. GRUNSIN AYOM.

Pinang Development Corporation: 1 Pesiaran Mahsuri, Bandar Bayan Baru, 11909 Bayan Lepas, Pinang; tel. (4) 6340111; fax (4) 6424746; e-mail enquiry@pdc.gov.my; internet www.pdc.gov.my; f. 1969; development agency of the Pinang state government; Gen. Man. ROSLI JAAFAR.

Sarawak Economic Development Corpn: Menara SEDC, 6th–11th Floors, Sarawak Plaza, Jalan Tunku Abdul Rahman, POB 400, 93902 Kuching; tel. (82) 416777; fax (82) 424330; e-mail ssedc@pop1.jaring.my; internet www.sedc.com.my; f. 1972; statutory org. responsible for commercial and industrial development in Sarawak either solely or jtly with foreign and local entrepreneurs; responsible for the development of tourism infrastructure; Chair. Datuk Haji TALIB ZULPILIP.

Selangor State Development Corporation (PKNS): Persiaran Barat, off Jalan Barat, 46505 Petaling Jaya, Selangor; tel. (3) 79572955; fax (3) 79575250; e-mail general@pkns.gov.my; internet www.pkns.gov.my; f. 1964; partially govt-owned; Corporate Man. YUSOF OTHMAN.

CHAMBERS OF COMMERCE

Associated Chinese Chambers of Commerce and Industry of Malaysia: Lot 6.05, Menara Promet, 6th Floor, Jalan Sultan Ismail, 50250 Kuala Lumpur; tel. (3) 21452503; fax (3) 21452562; e-mail acccim@acccim.org.my; internet www.acccim.org.my; Pres. Tan Sri WILLIAM CHENG; Sec.-Gen. Tan Sri Dato' SOONG SIEW HOONG.

Malay Chamber of Commerce Malaysia: 33 & 35, Jalan Medan Setia 1, Bukit Damansara, 50490 Kuala Lumpur; tel. (3) 20962233; fax (3) 20962533; e-mail wmaster@dpmm.org.my; internet www

MALAYSIA   *Directory*

.dpmm.org.my; f. 1957 as Associated Malay Chambers of Commerce of Malaya; name changed as above 1992; Pres. SYED ALI MOHAMED ALATTAS; Sec.-Gen. ZAKI SAID.

Malaysian Associated Indian Chambers of Commerce and Industry: Megan AveDato 11, Block B, 9th Floor, Unit 1, 12 Jalan Yap Kwan Seng, 50450 Kuala Lumpur; tel. (3) 21712616; fax (3) 21711195; e-mail info@maicci.org.my; internet www.maicci.org.my; f. 1950; Pres. Datuk K. K ESWARAN; 8 brs.

Malaysian International Chamber of Commerce and Industry (MICCI) (Dewan Perniagaan dan Perindustrian Antarabangsa Malaysia): C-8-8, 8th Floor, Block C, Plaza Mont' Kiara, 50480 Kuala Lumpur; tel. (3) 62017708; fax (3) 62017705; e-mail micci@micci.com; internet www.micci.com; f. 1837; brs in Pinang, Perak, Johor, Melaka and Sabah; 1,000 corporate mems; Pres. RAJAH KUMAR; Exec. Dir STEWART J. FORBES.

National Chamber of Commerce and Industry of Malaysia: 6A, 6th Floor, Menara BGI, Plaza Berjaya, 12 Jalan Imbi, 55100 Kuala Lumpur; tel. (3) 2419600; fax (3) 2413775; e-mail enquiry@nccim.org.my; internet www.nccim.org.my; f. 1962; Pres. Tuan SYED ALI MOHAMED ALATTAS; Hon. Sec.-Gen. Dato' SYED HUSSEIN AL-HABSHEE.

Sabah Bumiputera Chamber of Commerce (SBCC): Lot 119, 4th Floor, S.B.C.C Bldg, Locked Bag 154, Jalan Gaya, 88999 Kota Kinabalu; tel. (88) 222442; fax (88) 223454; f. 1972; Pres. Datuk Haji AHMAD ALIP LOPE ABDUL AZIZ; Sec.-Gen. Encik JURIL Haji SUDIN.

Sabah United Chinese Chambers of Commerce (SUCCC): POB 12176, 88824 Kota Kinabalu; tel. (88) 225460; fax (88) 218185; e-mail succc01@tm.net.my; internet www.succc.org; f. 1955; Pres. Datuk Seri Panglima SARI NUAR.

Sarawak Chamber of Commerce and Industry (SCCI): POB A-841, Kenyalang Park Post Office, 93806 Kuching; tel. (82) 237148; fax (82) 237186; e-mail scci@su.cmsb.com.my; f. 1950; Chair. Datuk Haji MOHAMED AMIN Haji SATEM; Dep. Chair. Datuk Abang Haji ABDUL KARIM Tun Abang Haji OPENG.

INDUSTRIAL AND TRADE ASSOCIATIONS

Federation of Malaysian Manufacturers: Wisma FMM, 3 Persiaran Dagang, PJU 9 Bandar Sri Damansara, 52200 Kuala Lumpur; tel. (3) 62761211; fax (3) 62741266; e-mail webmaster@fmm.org.my; internet www.fmm.org.my; f. 1968; offers guidance and advice relating to trade and industry; presents problems and concerns to the Govt; 2,117 mems (Jan. 2005); Pres. Tan Sri Datuk MUSTAFA MANSUR; CEO LEE CHENG SUAN.

Federation of Rubber Trade Associations of Malaysia: 138 Jalan Bandar, 50000 Kuala Lumpur; tel. (3) 2384006.

Malayan Agricultural Producers' Association: Kuala Lumpur; tel. (3) 42573988; fax (3) 42573113; e-mail mapa@myjaring.net; f. 1997; 406 mem. estates and 108 factories/mills; Pres. Dato' Dr MOHD NOOR BIN ISMAIL; Dir MOHAMAD BIN AUDONG.

Malaysian Iron and Steel Industry Federation: 28E, 30E, 5th Floor, Block 2, Worldwide Business Park, Jalan Tinju 13/50, Section 13, 40675 Shah Alam, Selangor; tel. (3) 55133970; fax (3) 55133891; e-mail misif@po.jaring.my; internet www.misif.org.my; Pres. CHOW CHONG LONG; 150 mems.

Malaysian Palm Oil Association (MPOA): Bangunan Getah Asli I, 12th Floor, 148 Jalan Ampang, 50450 Kuala Lumpur; tel. (3) 27105680; fax (3) 27105679; e-mail kay@mpoa.org.my; internet www.mpoa.org.my; f. 1999 as result of rationalization of plantation industry; secretariat for producers of palm oil; Chief. Exec. Dato' MAMAT SALLEH.

Malaysian Pineapple Industry Board: Wisma Nanas, 5 Jalan Padi Mahsuri, Bandar Baru UDA, 81200 Johor Bahru; tel. (7) 2361211; fax (7) 2365694; e-mail mpib@tm.net.my; internet www.mpib.gov.my; Dir-Gen. Tuan Haji ISMAIL BIN ABD JAMAL.

Malaysian Rubber Board: Bangunan Getah Asli, Tingkat 17 and 18, 148 Jalan Ampang, 50450 Kuala Lumpur; tel. (3) 92062000; fax (3) 21634492; e-mail general@lgm.gov.my; internet www.lgm.gov.my; f. 1998; implements policies and development programmes to ensure the viability of the Malaysian rubber industry; regulates the industry (in particular, the packing, grading, shipping and export of rubber); Dir-Gen. Dr KAMARUL BAHARAIN BIN BASIR.

Malaysian Rubber Products Manufacturers' Association: 1 Jalan USJ 11/1J, Subang Jaya, 47620 Petaling Jaya, Selangor; tel. (3) 56316150; fax (3) 56316152; e-mail mrpma@po.jaring.my; f. 1952; Pres. Tan Sri Datuk ARSHAD AYUB; 144 mems.

Malaysian Timber Certification Council (MTCC): 19th Floor, Menara PGRM, 8 Jalan Pudu Ulu, Cheras, 56100 Kuala Lumpur; tel. (3) 92005008; fax (3) 92006008; e-mail info@mtcc.com.my; internet www.mtcc.com.my; f. 1999; operates a voluntary national timber certification scheme to encourage sustainable forest management; Chair. Dato' Dr FREEZAILAH CHE YEOM.

Malaysian Wood Industries Association: 19B, 19th Floor, Menara PGRM, 8 Jalan Pudu Ulu, Cheras, 56100 Kuala Lumpur; tel. (3) 92821789; fax (3) 92821779; e-mail mwia@tm.net.my; internet www.mtc.com.my; f. 1957; CEO CHEA KAM HUAN.

National Tobacco Board Malaysia (Ibu Pejabat Lembaga Tembakau Negara): Kubang Kerian, POB 198, 15720 Kota Bharu, Kelantan; tel. (9) 7652212; fax (9) 7655640; e-mail ltnm@ltn.gov.my; internet www.ltn.gov.my; Dir-Gen. TEO HUI BEK.

Northern Malaya Rubber Millers and Packers Association: 22 Pitt St, 3rd Floor, Suites 301–303, 10200 Pinang; tel. (4) 620037; f. 1919; 153 mems; Pres. HWANG SING LUE; Hon. Sec. LEE SENG KEOK.

Palm Oil Refiners' Association of Malaysia (PORAM): 801 C/802A Blok B, Executive Suites, Kelana Business Centre, 97 Jalan SS7/2, 47301 Kelana Jaya, Selangor; tel. (3) 74920006; fax (3) 74920128; e-mail poram@poram.org.my; internet www.poram.org.my; f. 1975 to promote the palm oil refining industry; Chair. Dato' YONG CHIN FATT (acting); CEO FRANKIE WEE; 90 mems.

Rubber Industry Smallholders' Development Authority (RISDA): Bangunan RISDA, Km 7, Jalan Ampang, Karung Berkunci 11067, 50990 Kuala Lumpur; tel. (3) 4564022; e-mail webmaster@risda.gov.my; internet www.risda.gov.my; Dir-Gen. ABDULLAH BIN ABDUL KADIR.

Tin Industry Research and Development Board: West Block, 8th Floor, Wisma Selangor Dredging, Jalan Ampang, POB 12560, 50782 Kuala Lumpur; tel. (3) 21616171; fax (3) 21616179; e-mail mcom@mcom.com.my; Chair. MOHAMED AJIB ANUAR; Sec. MUHAMAD NOR MUHAMAD.

EMPLOYERS' ORGANIZATIONS

Malaysian Employers' Federation: 3A06–3A07, Block A, Pusat Dagangan Phileo Damansara II, 15 Jalan 16/11, off Jalan Damansara, 46350 Petaling Jaya, Selangor; tel. (3) 79557778; fax (3) 79556808; e-mail mef-hq@mef.org.my; internet www.mef.org.my; f. 1959; Pres. Dato' AZMAN SHAH Dato' Seri HARUN; Exec. Dir Haji SHAMSUDDIN BARDAN; private-sector org. incorporating 13 employer organizations and 4,211 individual enterprises, including:

Association of Insurance Employers: c/o Royal Insurance (M) Sdn Bhd, Menara Boustead, 5th Floor, 69 Jalan Raja Chulan, 50200 Kuala Lumpur; tel. (3) 2410233; fax (3) 2442762; Pres. NG KIM HOONG.

Commercial Employers' Association of Peninsular Malaysia: c/o The East Asiatic Co (M) Bhd, 1 Jalan 205, 46050 Petaling Jaya, Selangor; tel. (3) 7913322; fax (3) 7913561; Pres. HAMZAH Haji GHULAM.

Malaysian Chamber of Mines: West Block, Wisma Selangor Dredging, 8th Floor, 142C Jalan Ampang, 50450 Kuala Lumpur; tel. (3) 21616171; fax (3) 21616179; e-mail mcom@mcom.com.my; internet www.mcom.com.my; f. 1914; promotes and protects interests of Malaysian mining industry; Pres. MOHAMED AJIB ANUAR; Exec. Dir MUHAMAD NOR MUHAMAD; 100 mems.

Malaysian Textile Manufacturers' Association: C-9-4, Megan Ave 1, 189 Jalan Tun Razak, 50400 Kuala Lumpur; tel. (3) 21621454; fax (3) 21625148; e-mail info@mtma.org.my; internet www.fashion-asia.com; Pres. YAP FUNG KONG; Exec. Dir ANDREW HONG; 150 mems.

Pan Malaysian Bus Operators' Association: 88 Jalan Sultan Idris Shah, 30300 Ipoh, Perak; tel. (5) 2549421; fax (5) 2550858; Sec. TEOH EWE HUN.

Sabah Employers' Consultative Association: Dewan SECA, No. 4, Block A, 1st Floor, Bandar Ramai-Ramai, 90000 Sandakan, Sabah; tel. and fax (89) 272846; Chair. LING AH HONG.

Stevedore Employers' Association: 5 Pengkalan Weld, POB 288, 10300 Pinang; tel. (4) 2615091; Pres. ABDUL RAHMAN MAIDIN.

UTILITIES

Electricity

Energy Commission of Malaysia: Levels 15, 19 and 20, Menara Dato' Onn, Putra World Centre, Jalan Tun Ismail, Kuala Lumpur; internet www.st.gov.my; f. 2002; regulatory body supervising electricity and gas supply.

Tenaga Nasional Bhd: 129 Jalan Bangsar, POB 11003, 50732 Kuala Lumpur; tel. (3) 2825566; fax (3) 22833686; e-mail webadmin@tnb.com.my; internet www.tnb.com.my; f. 1990 through the corporatization and privatization of the National Electricity Board; 53% govt-controlled; generation, transmission and distribution of electricity in Peninsular Malaysia; generating capacity of 7,621 MW (63% of total power generation); also purchases power from 12 licensed independent power producers; Chair. Tan Sri Dato' AMAR LEO MOGGIE; Pres. and CEO Dato' CHE KHALIB BIN MOHAMAD NOH.

Sabah Electricity Supply Board (SESB): Wisma SESB, Jalan Tunku Abdul Rahman, 88673 Kota Kinabalu; tel. (88) 211699; fax (88) 282314; e-mail webmaster@sesb.com.my; internet www.sesb.com.my; generation, transmission and distribution of electricity in Sabah; Man. Dir Ir BAHARIN BIN DIN.

MALAYSIA

Syarikat Sesco Bhd (SESCO): POB 149, 93700 Kuching, Sarawak; tel. (82) 441188; fax (82) 444433; e-mail public_enquiry@sesoc.com.my; internet www.sesco.com.my; fmrly known as Sarawak Electricity Supply Corpn; generation, transmission and distribution of electricity in Sarawak; Chair. Datuk ABDUL HAMED SEPAWI.

Gas

Energy Commission of Malaysia: see above **Gas Malaysia Sdn Bhd:** 5 Jalan Serendah 26/17, Seksyen 26, Peti Surat 7901, 40732 Shah Alam, Selangor Darul Ehsan; tel. (3) 51923000; e-mail ccu@gasmalaysia.com; internet www.gasmalaysia.com; f. 1992; Chair. Tan Sri Datuk Dr HAMZAH BAKAR; CEO MUHAMAD NOOR HAMID.

Water

Under the federal Constitution, water supply is the responsibility of the state Governments. In 1998, owing to water shortages, the National Water Resources Council was established to co-ordinate management of water resources at national level. Malaysia's sewerage system is operated by Indah Water Konsortium, owned by Prime Utilities.

National Water Resources Council: c/o Ministry of Works, Jalan Sultan Salahuddin, 50580 Kuala Lumpur; tel. (3) 2919011; fax (3) 2986612; f. 1998 to co-ordinate management of water resources at national level through co-operation with state water boards; Chair. Dato' Seri Dr MAHATHIR BIN MOHAMAD.

Regulatory Authorities

Johor State Regulatory Body: c/o Pejabat Setiausaha Kerajaan Negeri Johor, Aras 1, Bangunan Sultan Ibrahim, Jalan Bukit Timbalan, 80000 Johor Bahru; tel. (7) 223850; Dir Tuan Haji OMAR BIN AWAB.

Kelantan Water Department: Tingkat Bawah Blok 6, Kota Darul Naim, 15503 Kota Bahru, Kelantan; tel. (9) 7475240; e-mail hjabaziz@yahoo.com.my; Dir Tuan Haji ABDUL AZIZ BIN Haji ABDUL RAHMAN.

Water Supply Authorities

Kedah Public Works Department: Bangunan Sultan Abdul Halim, Jalan Sultan Badlishah, 05582 Alor Setar, Kedah; tel. (4) 7334041; fax (4) 7341616; internet kedah.jkr.gov.my; Dir BAHARANUDDIN BIN CHE ZAIN.

Kelantan Water Sdn Bhd: 14 Beg Berkunci, Jalan Kuala Krai, 15990 Kota Bahru, Kelantan; tel. (10) 9022222; fax (10) 9022236; Dir PETER NEW BERKLEY.

Kuching Water Board: Jalan Batu Lintang, 93200 Kuching, Sarawak; tel. (82) 240371; fax (82) 244546; internet www.kwb.gov.my; Gen. Man. Encik MOHAMMAD ARIS YUSOP.

Labuan Public Works Department: Jalan Kg. Jawa, POB 2, 87008 Labuan; tel. (87) 414040; fax (87) 412370; Dir Ir ZULKIFLY BIN MADON.

LAKU Management Sdn Bhd: Soon Hup Tower, 6th Floor, Lot 907, Jalan Merbau, 98000 Miri; tel. (85) 442000; fax (85) 442005; e-mail wtk@lakumyy.po.my; serves Miri, Limbang and Bintulu; CEO WONG TIONG KAI.

Melaka Water Corpn: Tingkat Bawah, 1 10–13, Graha Maju, Jalan Graha Maju, 75300 Melaka; tel. (6) 2825233; fax (6) 2827366; e-mail baharam@pamwtr.gov.my; Dir Ir Haji BAHARAM BIN Haji MOHAMAD.

Negeri Sembilan Water Department: Wisma Negeri, 70990 Seremban; tel. (6) 7610505; fax (6) 7617841; Dir Ir ZULKIFLI IBRAHIM.

Pahang Water Supply Department (Jabatan Bekalan Air Pahang): 9–10 Komplek Tun Razak, Bandar Indera Mahkota, 25582 Kuantan, Pahang; tel. (9) 5721222; fax (9) 5721221; e-mail p-jba@pahang.gov.my; Dir Ir Haji ISMAIL BIN Haji MAT NOOR.

Perak Water Board: Jalan St John, Peti Surat 589, 30760 Ipoh, Perak; tel. (5) 2551155; fax (5) 2556397; internet www.lap.com.my; Dir Ir SANI BIN SIDIK.

Pinang Water Supply Corpn: Level 32, KOMTAR, 10000 Pinang; tel. (4) 2633736; fax (4) 2633735; e-mail amiruddin@pba.com.my; internet www.pba.com.my; f. 1973; Gen. Man. Ir JASENI BIN MAIDINSA.

Sabah State Water Department: Wisma MUIS, Blok A, Tingkat 6, Beg Berkunci 210, 88825 Kota Kinabalu; tel. (88) 232364; fax (88) 232396; e-mail muis.air@sabah.gov.my; internet www.sabah.gov.my/air; Man. MOHAMAD TAHIR BIN MOHAMAD TALIB.

SAJ Holdings Sdn Bhd: Bangunan Ibu Pejabat SAJ Holdings, Jalan Garuda, Larkin, POB 262, 80350 Johor Bahru; tel. (7) 2244040; fax (7) 2240033; e-mail support@saj.com.my; internet www.saj.com.my; f. 1999; Exec. Chair. Tan Sri Dato' Paduka Dr SALEHUDDIN MOHAMED.

Sarawak Public Works Department: Wisma Seberkas, Jalan Tun Haji Openg, 93582 Kuching; tel. (82) 244041; fax (82) 429679; Dir MICHAEL TING KUOK NG.

Selangor Water Department: POB 5001, Jalan Pantai Baru, 59990 Kuala Lumpur; tel. (3) 2826244; fax (3) 2827535; f. 1972; Dir Ir LIEW WAI KIAT.

Sibu Water Board: Km 5, Jalan Salim, POB 405, 96007 Sibu, Sarawak; tel. (84) 211001; fax (84) 211543; e-mail swbs@swb.gov.my; internet www.swb.gov.my; Gen. Man. DANIEL WONG PARK ING.

Terengganu Water Department: Tkt 3, Wisma Negeri, Jalan Pejabat, 20200 Kuala Terengganu; tel. (9) 6222444; fax (9) 6221510; Dir Ir Haji WAN NGAH BIN WAN.

TRADE UNIONS

Congress of Unions of Employees in the Public Administrative and Civil Services (CUEPACS): tel. (3) 9285-6110; fax (3) 9285-9457; internet www.cuepacs.org.my; a nat. fed. with 53 affiliates, representing 120,000 govt workers (2005); Pres. Haji OMAR BIN Haji OSMAN.

Malaysian Trades Union Congress: Wisma MTUC, 10-5, Jalan USJ 9/5T, 47620 Subang Jaya, Selangor; POB 3073, 46000 Petaling Jaya, Selangor; tel. (3) 80242953; fax (3) 80243224; e-mail mtuc@tm.net.my; internet www.mtuc.org.my; f. 1949; 247 affiliated unions, representing approx. 500,000 workers; Pres. SYED SHAHIR BIN SYED MOHAMUD; Sec.-Gen. G. RAJASEKARAN.

Principal affiliated unions:

All Malayan Estates Staff Union: 29-3, Jalan USJ 1/1A, 47620 Subang Jaya; tel. (3) 80240375; fax (3) 80247822; e-mail mes@po.jaring.my; 2,654 mems; Pres. TITUS GLADWIN; Gen. Sec. D. P. S. THAMOTHARAM.

Amalgamated Union of Employees in Government Clerical and Allied Services: 32A Jalan Gajah, off Jalan Yew, Pudu, 55100 Kuala Lumpur; tel. (3) 9859613; fax (3) 9838632; 6,703 mems; Pres. IBRAHIM BIN ABDUL WAHAB; Gen. Sec. MOHAMED IBRAHIM BIN ABDUL WAHAB.

Chemical Workers' Union: 35B, Jalan SS 15/4B, Subang Jaya, 47500 Petaling Jaya, Selangor; 1,886 mems; Pres. RUSIAN HITAM; Gen. Sec. JOHN MATHEWS.

Electricity Industry Workers' Union: 55-2 Jalan SS 15/8A, Subang Jaya, 47500 Petaling Jaya, Selangor; tel. (3) 7335243; 22,000 mems; Pres. ABDUL RASHID; Gen. Sec. P. ARUNASALAM.

Federation of Unions in the Textile, Garment and Leather Industry: c/o Selangor Textile and Garment Manufacturing Employees Union, 9D Jalan Travers, 50470 Kuala Lumpur; tel. (3) 2742578; f. 1989; four affiliates; Pres. ABDUL RAZAK HAMID; Gen. Sec. ABU BAKAR IBRAHIM.

Harbour Workers' Union, Port Kelang: 106 Persiaran Raja Muda Musa, Port Kelang; 2,426 mems; Pres. MOHAMED SHARIFF BIN YAMIN; Gen. Sec. MOHAMED HAYAT BIN AWANG.

Kesatuan Pekerja-Pekerja FELDA: 2 Jalan Maktab Enam, Melalui Jalan Perumahan Gurney, 54000 Kuala Lumpur; tel. (3) 26929972; fax (3) 26913409; 2,900 mems; Pres. INDERA PUTRA Haji ISMAIL; Gen. Sec. MOHAMAD BIN ABDUL RAHMAN.

Kesatuan Pekerja-Pekerja Perusahaan Membuat Tekstil dan Pakaian Pulau Pinang dan Seberang Prai: 23 Lorong Talang Satu, Prai Gardens, 13600 Prai; tel. (4) 301397; 3,900 mems; Pres. ABDUL RAZAK HAMID; Gen. Sec. KENNETH STEPHEN PERKINS.

Kesatuan Pekerja Tenaga Nasional Bhd: 30 Jalan Liku Bangsar, POB 10400, 59100 Kuala Lumpur; tel. (3) 2745657; 10,456 mems; Pres. MOHAMED ABU BAKAR; Gen. Sec. IDRIS BIN ISMAIL.

Malayan Technical Services Union: 3A Jalan Menteri, off Jalan Cochrane, 55100 Kuala Lumpur; tel. (3) 92851778; fax (3) 92811875; e-mail mtsu@streamyx.com; 6,000 mems; Pres. SHUHAIMI OTHMAN; Gen. Sec. SAMUEL DEVADASAN.

Malaysian Rubber Board Staff Union: POB 10150, 50908 Kuala Lumpur; tel. (3) 42565102; 850 mems; Pres. HASNAH GANI; Gen. Sec. SUBRAMANIAM SINNASAMY.

Metal Industry Employees' Union: Metalworkers' House, 5 Lorong Utara Kecil, 46200 Petaling Jaya, Selangor; tel. (3) 79567214; fax (3) 79550854; e-mail mieum@tm.net.my; 15,491 mems; Pres. SAMUSUDDIN USOP; Gen. Sec. JACOB ENGKATESU.

National Union of Bank Employees (NUBE): 12 NUBE House, 3rd Floor, Jalan Tun Sambanthan 3, Brickfield, 50470 Kuala Lumpur; tel. (3) 20789800; fax (3) 20703800; e-mail nube_hq@streamyx.com; internet www.nube.org.my; 27,000 mems; Gen. Sec. JOSEPH SOLOMON.

National Union of Commercial Workers: Bangunan NUCW, 98A–D Jalan Masjid India, 50100 Kuala Lumpur; POB 12059, 50780 Kuala Lumpur; tel. (3) 26927385; fax (3) 26925930; f. 1959; 11,937 mems; Pres. TAIB SHARIF; Gen. Sec. C. KRISHNAN.

MALAYSIA

National Union of Plantation Workers: 428 A–B, Jalan 5/46, Gasing Indah, POB 73, 46700 Petaling Jaya, Selangor; tel. (3) 77827622; fax (3) 77815321; e-mail nupw@tm.net.my; f. 1946; 29,251 mems; Pres. NADARAJA A/L KUMARAN; Gen. Sec. Dato' G. SANKARAN.

National Union of PWD Employees: 32B Jalan Gajah, off Jalan Yew, 55100 Kuala Lumpur; tel. (3) 9850149; 5,869 mems; Pres. KULOP IBRAHIM; Gen. Sec. S. SANTHANASAMY.

National Union of Telecoms Employees: Wisma NUTE, 17A Jalan Bangsar, 59200 Kuala Lumpur; tel. (3) 2821599; fax (3) 2821015; 15,874 mems; Pres. MOHAMED SHAFIE B. P. MAMMAL; Gen. Sec. MOHD JAFAR BIN ABDUL MAJID.

Non-Metallic Mineral Products Manufacturing Employees' Union: 99A Jalan SS 14/1, Subang Jaya, 47500 Petaling Jaya, Selangor; tel. (3) 56339006; fax (3) 56333863; e-mail nonmet@tm.net.my; 10,000 mems; Pres. ABDULLAH ABU BAKAR; Sec. S. SOMAHSUNDRAM.

Railwaymen's Union of Malaya: Bangunan Tong Nam, 1st Floor, Jalan Tun Sambathan (Travers), 50470 Kuala Lumpur; tel. (3) 2741107; fax (3) 2731805; 5,500 mems; Pres. ABDUL GAFFOR BIN IBRAHIM; Gen. Sec. S. VEERASINGAM.

Technical Services Union—Tenaga Nasional Bhd: Bangunan Keselamatan, POB 11003, Bangsar, Kuala Lumpur; tel. (3) 2823581; 3,690 mems; Pres. RAMLY YATIM; Gen. Sec. CLIFFORD SEN.

Timber Employees' Union: 10 Jalan AU 5C/14, Ampang, Ulu Kelang, Selangor; 7,174 mems; Pres. ABDULLAH METON; Gen. Sec. MINHAT SULAIMAN.

Transport Workers' Union: 21 Jalan Barat, Petaling Jaya, 46200 Selangor; tel. (3) 7566567; 10,447 mems; Pres. NORASHIKIN; Gen. Sec. ZAINAL RAMPAK.

Independent Federations and Unions

Kongres Kesatuan Guru-Guru Dalam Perkhidmatan Pelajaran (Congress of Unions of Employees in the Teaching Services): Johor; seven affiliates; Pres. RAMLI BIN MOHD JOHAN; Sec.-Gen. KASSIM BIN Haji HARON.

Malaysian Medical Association: MMA House, 4th Floor, 124 Jalan Pahang, 53000 Kuala Lumpur; tel. (3) 40420617; fax (3) 40418187; e-mail info@mma.org.my; internet www.mma.org.my; 10 affiliates; Pres. Datuk Dr KHOO KAH LIN.

National Union of Journalists: 30B Jalan Padang Belia, 50470 Kuala Lumpur; tel. (3) 2742867; fax (3) 2744776; f. 1962; 1,700 mems; Gen. Sec. ONN EE SENG.

National Union of Newspaper Workers: 11B Jalan 20/14, Paramount Garden, 46300 Petaling Jaya, Selangor; tel. (3) 78768118; fax (3) 78751490; e-mail nunwl@tm.net.my; 3,000 mems; Pres. GAN HOE JIAN; Gen. Sec. R. CHANDRASEKARAN.

Sabah

Sabah Banking Employees' Union: POB 11649, 88818 Kota Kinabalu; e-mail sbeukk@tm.net.my; 729 mems; Gen. Sec. LEE CHI HONG.

Sabah Civil Service Union: Kota Kinabalu; f. 1952; 1,356 mems; Pres. J. K. K. VOON; Sec. STEPHEN WONG.

Sabah Commercial Employees' Union: Sinsuran Shopping Complex, Lot 3, Block N, 2nd Floor, POB 10357, 88803 Kota Kinabalu; tel. (88) 225971; fax (88) 213815; e-mail sceu-kk@tm.net.my; f. 1957; 980 mems; Gen. Sec. REBECCA CHIN.

Sabah Medical Services Union: POB 11257, 88813 Kota Kinabalu; tel. (88) 242126; fax (88) 242127; e-mail smsu65@hotmail.com; 4,000 mems; Pres. KATHY LO NYUK CHIN; Gen. Sec. LAURENCE VUN.

Sabah Petroleum Industry Workers' Union: POB 1087, Kota Kinabalu; tel. (88) 720737; e-mail victor.yb.sang@exxonmobil.com; internet www.sabah.org.my/spiwu; f. 1966; 168 mems; Pres. ABDULLAH JAMIL AHMAD.

Sabah Teachers' Union: POB 10912, 88810 Kota Kinabalu; tel. (88) 420034; fax (88) 431633; f. 1962; 3,001 mems; Pres. KWAN PING SIN; Sec.-Gen. PATRICK Y. C. CHOK.

Sarawak

Kepak Sarawak (Kesatuan Pegawai-Pegawai Bank, Sarawak): POB 62, Bukit Permata, 93100 Kuching, Sarawak; tel. (19) 8549372; e-mail kepaksar@tm.net.my; bank officers' union; 1,430 mems; Gen. Sec. DOMINIC CH'NG YUNG TED.

Sarawak Commercial Employees' Union: POB 807, Kuching; 1,636 mems; Gen. Sec. SONG SWEE LIAP.

Sarawak Teachers' Union: 139A Jalan Rock, 1st Floor, 93200 Kuching; tel. (82) 245727; fax (82) 245757; f. 1965; 12,832 mems; Pres. WILLIAM GHANI BINA; Sec.-Gen. THOMAS HUO KOK SEN.

Directory

Transport

RAILWAYS

Peninsular Malaysia

The state-owned Malayan Railways had a total length of 1,672 km in Peninsular Malaysia in 1996. The main railway line follows the west coast and extends 782 km from Singapore, south of Peninsular Malaysia, to Butterworth (opposite Pinang Island) in the north. From Bukit Mertajam, close to Butterworth, the Kedah line runs north to the Thai border at Padang Besar where connection is made with the State Railway of Thailand. The East Coast Line, 526 km long, runs from Gemas to Tumpat (in Kelantan). A 21-km branch line from Pasir Mas (27 km south of Tumpat) connects with the State Railway of Thailand at the border station of Sungei Golok. Branch lines serve railway-operated ports at Port Dickson and Telok Anson as well as Port Klang and Jurong (Singapore). Malaysia's first Light Rail Transit (LRT) system was opened the Kuala Lumpur area in 1996. A second line began operating within the same system in 1998; a second LRT system, comprising one line, also commenced operations in that year. An express rail link connecting central Kuala Lumpur and the new Kuala Lumpur International Airport (KLIA) opened in 2001.

Keretapi Tanah Melayu Bhd (KTMB) (Malayan Railways): KTMB Corporate Headquarters, Jalan Sultan Hishamuddin, 50621 Kuala Lumpur; tel. (3) 22631111; fax (3) 27105706; e-mail shahriza@ktmb.com.my; internet www.ktmb.com.my; f. 1885; inc as a co under govt control in 1992; privatized in 1997; managed by the consortium Marak Unggal (Renong, DRB and Bolton); Chair. MOHAMAD ISA BIN HUSSEIN.

Sabah

Sabah State Railway: Karung Berkunci 2047, 88999 Kota Kinabalu; tel. (88) 254611; fax (88) 236395; internet www.sabah.gov.my/railway; 134 track-km of 1-m gauge (2008); goods and passenger services from Tanjong Aru to Tenom, serving part of the west coast and the interior; diesel trains are used; Gen. Man. Ir BENNY WANG.

ROADS

Peninsular Malaysia

Peninsular Malaysia's road system is extensive, in contrast to those of Sabah and Sarawak. In 2004 the road network in Malaysia totalled an estimated 98,721 km, of which 1,821 km were motorways and 18,095 km were highways.

Sabah

Jabatan Kerja Raya Sabah (Sabah Public Works Department): Jalan Sembulan, Locked Bag 2032, 88582 Kota Kinabalu, Sabah; tel. (88) 244333; fax (88) 237234; e-mail pos@jkr.sabah.gov.my; internet www.jkr.sabah.gov.my; f. 1881; implements and maintains public infrastructures such as roads, bridges, buildings and sewerage systems throughout Sabah; maintains a road network totalling 15,756.6 km, of which 5,686.5 km were sealed roads; Dir JOHN ANTHONY.

Sarawak

Jabatan Kerja Raya Sarawak (Sarawak Public Works Department): Tingkat 11–18, Wisma Saberkas, Jalan Tun Abg. Haji Openg, 93582 Kuching, Sarawak; tel. (82) 203100; fax (82) 429679; e-mail limkh@sarawaknet.gov.my; internet www.jkr.sarawak.gov.my; implements and maintains public infrastructures in Sarawak; road network totalling 10,979 km, of which 3,986 km were sealed roads; Dir HUBERT THIAN CHONG HUI.

SHIPPING

The ports in Malaysia are classified as federal ports, under the jurisdiction of the federal Ministry of Transport, or state ports, responsible to the state ministries of Sabah and Sarawak.

Peninsular Malaysia

The federal ports in Peninsular Malaysia are Klang (the principal port), Pinang, Johor and Kuantan.

Johor Port Authority: 6A1–8A1 Pusat Perdagangan Pasir Gudang, Jalan Bandar, 81700 Pasir Gudang, Johor; tel. (7) 2534000; fax (7) 2517684; e-mail admin@lpj.gov.my; internet www.lpj.gov.my; f. 1976; Gen. Man. Encik NIK AZIZ BIN HUSSAIN.

Johor Port Bhd: POB 151, 81707 Pasir Gudang, Johor; tel. (7) 2535888; fax (7) 2510980; e-mail jpb@johorport.com.my; internet www.johorport.com.my; Exec. Chair. Dato' MOHD TAUFIK ABDULLAH.

Klang Port Authority: POB 202, Jalan Pelabuhan, 42005 Port Klang, Selangor; tel. (3) 31688211; fax (3) 31670211; e-mail onestopagency@pka.gov.my; internet www.pka.gov.my; f. 1963; Gen. Man. LIM THEAN SHIANG.

Kuantan Port Authority: Tanjung Gelang, POB 161, 25720 Kuantan, Pahang; tel. (9) 5858000; fax (9) 5833866; e-mail lpktn@lpktn.gov.my; internet www.lpktn.gov.my; f. 1974; Gen. Man. KHAIRUL ANUAR BIN ABDUL RAHMAN.

Penang Port Commission: 3A-6 Sri Weld Bldg, Weld Quay, Pinang; tel. (4) 2633211; fax (4) 2626211; e-mail sppp@po.jaring.my; internet www.penangport.gov.my; f. 1956; Gen. Man. NORLAILA BINTI IBRAHIM.

Sabah

The main ports, which are administered by the Sabah Ports Authority, are Kota Kinabalu, Sandakan, Tawau, Lahad Datu, Kudat, Semporna and Kunak. Many international shipping lines serve Sabah. Local services are operated by smaller vessels.

Sabah Ports Authority: Bangunan SPA, Jalan Tun Fuad, Tanjung Lipat, Locked Bag 2005, 88617 Kota Kinabalu, Sabah; tel. (88) 538400; fax (88) 223036; e-mail sabport@tm.net.my; internet www.lpps.sabah.gov.my; f. 1968; Gen. Man. Eng. MAYONG OMAR.

Sarawak

There are four port authorities in Sarawak: Kuching, Rajang, Miri and Bintulu. Kuching, Rajang and Miri are state ports, while Bintulu is a federal port. Kuching port serves the southern region of Sarawak, Rajang port the central region, and Miri port the northern region.

Kuching Port Authority: Jalan Pelabuhan, Pending, POB 530, 93450 Kuching, Sarawak; tel. (82) 482144; fax (82) 481696; e-mail hq@kuport.com.my; internet www.kpa.gov.my; f. 1961; Gen. Man. LIU MOI FONG.

Rajang Port Authority: Jalan Pulau, 96000 Sibu, Sarawak; tel. (84) 319004; fax (84) 318754; e-mail rpa@rajangport.gov.my; internet www.rajangport.gov.my; f. 1970; Gen. Man. HELEN LIM HUI SHYAN.

Principal Shipping Companies

Archipelago Shipping (Sarawak) Sdn Bhd: Lot 267/270, Jalan Chan Chin Ann, POB 2998, 93758 Kuching; tel. (82) 412581; fax (82) 416249; Gen. Man. MICHAEL M. AMAN.

Malaysia Shipping Corpn Sdn Bhd: Office Tower, Plaza Berjaya, Suite 14C, 14th Floor, 12 Jalan Imbi, 55100 Kuala Lumpur; tel. (3) 21418788; fax (3) 21429214; Chair. Y. C. CHANG.

Malaysian International Shipping Corpn Bhd (National Shipping Line of Malaysia): Menara Dayabumi, Level 25, Jalan Sultan Hishamuddin, 50050 Kuala Lumpur; tel. (3) 22738088; fax (3) 22736602; e-mail caffairs@miscbhd.com; internet www.misc.com.my; f. 1968; regular sailings between the Far East, South-East Asia, Australia, Japan and Europe; also operates chartering, tanker, haulage and warehousing and agency services; major shareholder, Petroliam Nasional Bhd (PETRONAS); Chair. Tan Sri Dato' MOHD HASSAN BIN MARICAN; Pres. and CEO Dato' AMIR HAMZA BIN AZIZAN.

Perbadanan Nasional Shipping Line Bhd (PNSL): Kuala Lumpur; tel. (3) 2932211; fax (3) 2930493; f. 1982; specializes in bulk cargoes; Chair. Tunku Dato' SHAHRIMAN BIN Tunku SULAIMAN; Exec. Dep. Chair. Dato' SULAIMAN ABDULLAH.

Persha Shipping Agencies Sdn Bhd: Bangunan Maybank Trust, Penthouse Suite, Jalan Pinang, 10200 Pinang; tel. (4) 2612400; fax (4) 2623122; Man. Dir MOHD NOOR MOHD KAMALUDIN.

Syarikat Perkapalan Kris Sdn Bhd (The Kris Shipping Co Ltd): 3AO7 Block A, Kelana Centre Point, 3 Jalan SS7/19, Kelana Jaya; POB 8428, 46700 Petaling Jaya, Selangor; tel. (3) 7046477; fax (3) 7048007; domestic services; Chair. Dato' Seri SYED NAHAR SHAHABUDIN; Gen. Man. ROHANY TALIB; Dep. Gen. Man. THO TEIT CHANG.

Trans-Asia Shipping Corpn Sdn Bhd: Unit 715–718, Block A, Kelana Business Centre, 97 Jalan SS7/2, Kelana Jaya, 47301 Petaling Jaya, Selangor; tel. (3) 51018800; fax (3) 78802200; e-mail bernard@tasco.com.my; internet www.tasco.com.my; f. 1974; Man. Dir LEE CHECK POH.

CIVIL AVIATION

The new Kuala Lumpur International Airport (KLIA), situated in Sepang, Selangor (50 km south of Kuala Lumpur) began operations in June 1998, with an initial capacity of 25m.–30m. passengers a year, which was projected to rise to 45m. by 2020. An express rail link between central Kuala Lumpur and KLIA opened in early 2001. There are regional airports at Kota Kinabalu, Pinang, Johor Bahru, Kuching and Pulau Langkawi. In addition, there are airports catering for domestic services at Alor Star, Ipoh, Kota Bahru, Kuala Terengganu, Kuantan and Melaka in Peninsular Malaysia, Sibu, Bintulu and Miri in Sarawak, and Sandakan, Tawau, Lahad Datu and Labuan in Sabah. There are also numerous smaller airstrips.

Department of Civil Aviation (Jabatan Penerbangan Awam Malaysia): Aras 1–4, Lot 4G4, Presint 4, Pusat Pentadbiran Kerajaan Persekutuan, 62570 Putrajaya; tel. (3) 88714000; fax (3) 88714331; e-mail webmaster@dca.gov.my; internet www.dca.gov.my; Dir-Gen. Dato' AZHARUDDIN ABDUL RAHMAN.

AirAsia Sdn Bhd: Asia Pacific Auction Center, 1st Floor, Sultan Abdul Aziz Shah Airport, 47200 Subang, Selangor; tel. (3) 78445555; fax (3) 78445400; e-mail tellus@airasia.com; internet www.airasia.com; f. 1993; a second national airline, budget carrier with a licence to operate domestic, regional and international flights; 85%-owned by HICOM; Chair. PAHAMIN A. RAJAB; Chief Exec. TONY FERNANDES.

Berjaya Air: Terminal 3, Lapangan Terbang Sultan Abdul Aziz Shah, Shah Alam, Selangor, 47200 Kuala Lumpur; tel. (3) 7476828; fax (3) 7476228; e-mail berjayaa@tm.net.my; internet www.berjaya-air.com; f. 1989; scheduled and charter domestic services; Pres. Tan Sri Dato' Seri VINCENT TAN CHEE YIOUN.

Firefly: Kuala Lumpur; internet www.fireflyz.com.my; f. 2007; low-cost domestic and regional flights; 100% owned by Malaysia Airlines; Man. Dir EDDY LEONG.

Malaysia Airlines: 31st Floor, Bangunan MAS, Jalan Sultan Ismail, 50250 Kuala Lumpur; tel. (3) 21655140; fax (3) 21633178; e-mail corpcomm@mas.com.my; internet www.malaysiaairlines.com.my; f. 1971 as the Malaysian successor to Malaysia Singapore Airlines (MSA); known as Malaysian Airline System (MAS) until Oct. 1987; 114 international routes and 118 domestic routes; Chair. Dato' Dr MOHAMED MUNIR BIN ABDUL MAJID; Man. Dir and CEO IDRIS JALA.

Transmile Air Sdn Bhd: Wisma Semantan, Mezzanine 2, Block B, 12 Jalan Gelenggang, Bukit Damansara, 50490 Kuala Lumpur; tel. (3) 2537718; fax (3) 2537719; internet www.transmile.com; f. 1992; scheduled and charter regional and domestic services for pasengers and cargo; Chair. Tun Dr LING LIONG SIK.

Tourism

Malaysia has a rapidly growing tourist industry, and tourism is an important source of foreign-exchange earnings. Receipts from tourism exceeded RM 36m. in 2006. In 2008 a record 22.1m. tourists, of whom 11.0m. were from Singapore, visited Malaysia.

Malaysia Tourism Promotion Board: Menara Dato' Onn, 15th–18th, 24th–27th, 29th–30th Floors, Putra World Trade Centre, 45 Jalan Tun Ismail, 50480 Kuala Lumpur; tel. (3) 26158188; fax (3) 26935884; e-mail enquiries@tourism.gov.my; internet www.tourismmalaysia.gov.my; f. 1972 to co-ordinate and promote activities relating to tourism in Malaysia; Chair. Dato' Sri AZALINA Dato' OTHMAN SAID.

Sabah Tourist Association: POB 12181, 88824 Kota Kinabalu; tel. (88) 221234; fax (88) 218909; f. 1963; 55 mems; parastatal promotional org.; Chair. THOMAS MORE WILLIE.

Sarawak Tourism Board: Levels 6 and 7, Bangunan Yayasan Sarawak, Jalan Masjid, 93400 Kuching; tel. (82) 423600; fax (82) 416700; e-mail stb@sarawaktourism.com; internet www.sarawaktourism.com; f. 1995; CEO GRACIE GEIKIE.

THE MALDIVES

Introductory Survey

Location, Climate, Language, Religion, Flag, Capital

The Republic of Maldives (commonly referred to as 'the Maldives') is in southern Asia. The country, lying about 675 km (420 miles) south-west of Sri Lanka, consists of 1,192 small coral islands (of which 197 are inhabited), grouped in 26 natural atolls (but divided, for administrative purposes, into 20 atolls), in the Indian Ocean. The climate is warm and humid. The annual average temperature is 27°C (80°F), with little daily or seasonal variation, while annual rainfall is generally between 2,540 mm and 3,800 mm (100 ins to 150 ins). The national language is Dhivehi (Maldivian), which is related to Sinhala. Islam is the state religion, and most Maldivians are Sunni Muslims. The national flag (proportions 2 by 3) is red, with a green rectangle, containing a white crescent, in the centre. The capital is Malé.

Recent History

The Maldives, called the Maldive Islands until April 1969, formerly had an elected Sultan as head of state. The islands were placed under British protection, with internal self-government, in 1887. They became a republic in January 1953, but the sultanate was restored in February 1954. The Maldives became fully independent, outside the Commonwealth, on 26 July 1965. Following a referendum, the country became a republic again in November 1968, with Amir Ibrahim Nasir, Prime Minister since 1957, as President.

In 1956 the Maldivian and British Governments agreed to the establishment of a Royal Air Force staging post on Gan, an island in the southernmost atoll, Addu. In 1975 the British Government's decision to close the base and to withdraw British forces created a large commercial and military vacuum. In October 1977 President Nasir rejected an offer of an annual payment of US $1m. from the USSR to lease the former base on Gan, announcing that he would not lease the island for military purposes, nor lease it to a superpower. In 1981 the President announced plans to establish an industrial zone on Gan. By 1990 there were two factories (producing ready-made garments) operating on Gan. The airport on Gan, which links the capital, Malé, with the south, is now fully operational and, following construction work carried out in the first half of the 2000s, had been upgraded to international standards by 2007 in preparation for international flights, with the opening of tourist resorts in the area.

A new Constitution, promulgated in 1968, vested considerable powers in the President, including the right to appoint and dismiss the Prime Minister and the Cabinet of Ministers.

In March 1975, following rumours of a coup conspiracy, President Nasir dismissed the Prime Minister, Ahmed Zaki, and the premiership was abolished. Unexpectedly, President Nasir announced that he would not seek re-election at the end of his second term in 1978. To succeed him, the Majlis (legislature) chose Maumoon Abdul Gayoom, Minister of Transport under Nasir, who was approved by referendum in July 1978 and took office in November. President Gayoom announced that his main priority would be the development of the poor rural regions, while in foreign affairs the existing policy of non-alignment would be continued.

Ex-President Nasir left the country after his resignation, but the authorities subsequently sought his return to the Maldives, where he was required to answer charges of misappropriating government funds. In 1980 President Gayoom confirmed an attempted coup against the Government and implicated Nasir in the alleged plot. Nasir was to stand trial, in his absence, on these and other charges. In April 1981 Ahmed Naseem, former Deputy Minister of Fisheries and brother-in-law of Nasir, was sentenced to life imprisonment for plotting to overthrow President Gayoom. Nasir himself denied any involvement in the coup, and attempts to extradite him from Singapore were unsuccessful. (In July 1990, however, President Gayoom officially pardoned Nasir *in absentia*, in recognition of the role that he had played in winning national independence.) In September 1983 Gayoom was re-elected as President, for a further five years, by a national referendum (with 95.6% of the popular vote).

In September 1988 he was again re-elected unopposed, for a third five-year term, obtaining a record 96.4% of the popular vote.

Another attempt to depose President Gayoom took place in November 1988, when a sea-borne mercenary force, which was composed of around 80 alleged Sri Lankan Tamil separatists (led by a disaffected Maldivian businessman, Abdullah Luthufi), landed in Malé and endeavoured to seize control of important government installations. At the request of President Gayoom, however, the Indian Government dispatched an emergency contingent of 1,600 troops, which rapidly and successfully suppressed the attempted coup. Nineteen people were reported to have been killed in the fighting. In September 1989 the President commuted to life imprisonment the death sentences imposed on 12 Sri Lankans and four Maldivians who had taken part in the aborted coup.

In February 1990, despite alleged opposition from powerful members of the privileged élite, President Gayoom announced that, as part of proposals for a broad new policy of liberalization and democratic reform, he was planning to introduce legislation enabling him to distribute powers, currently enjoyed by the President alone, amongst other official bodies. A further sign of growing democratization in the Maldives was the holding of discussions by the President's Consultative Council, in early 1990, concerning freedom of speech (particularly in the local press). In April, however, it became apparent that some Maldivians opposed political change when three pro-reform members of the Majlis received anonymous death threats. A few months later, following the emergence of several politically outspoken magazines, including *Sangu* (The Conchshell), there was an abrupt reversal of the Government's policy regarding the liberalization of the press. All publications not sanctioned by the Government were banned, and a number of leading writers and publishers were arrested.

As part of a major cabinet reshuffle in May 1990, President Gayoom dismissed the Minister of State for Defence and National Security, Ilyas Ibrahim (who also held the Trade and Industries portfolio and headed the State Trading Corporation), following the latter's abrupt and unannounced departure from the country. The Government later disclosed that Ibrahim (Gayoom's brother-in-law) was to have appeared before a presidential special commission investigating alleged embezzlement and misappropriation of government funds. On his return to the Maldives in August, Ibrahim was placed under house arrest. In March 1991, however, the special commission concluded that there was no evidence of involvement, either direct or indirect, by Ibrahim in the alleged financial misdeeds; in the same month the President appointed Ibrahim as Minister of Atolls Administration. In April the President established an anti-corruption board, which was to investigate allegations of corruption, bribery, fraud, misappropriation of government funds and property, and misuse of government office.

In early August 1993, a few weeks before the Majlis vote on the presidential candidate, Gayoom was informed that Ibrahim, whose position as Minister of Atolls Administration had afforded him the opportunity to build a political base outside Malé (where he already enjoyed considerable popularity), was seeking the presidency and attempting to influence members of the Majlis (at that time, the Majlis nominated and elected by secret ballot a single candidate, who was presented to the country in a referendum). In the Majlis vote held in late August, the incumbent President, who had previously been unanimously nominated for the presidency by the legislature, obtained 28 votes, against 18 for his brother-in-law. For his allegedly unconstitutional behaviour, however, Ibrahim was charged with attempting to 'influence the members of the Majlis' and he promptly left the country once again. Ibrahim was subsequently tried *in absentia* and sentenced to 15 years' imprisonment. In addition, his brother, Abbas Ibrahim, was removed from his post as Minister of Fisheries and Agriculture. (Ibrahim returned to the Maldives in 1996 when he was placed under house arrest; this restriction was lifted in 1997.) In October 1993 Gayoom's re-election as President for a further five years was endorsed by a national referendum, in which he obtained 92.8% of the popular vote.

In November 1994, at an official ceremony marking Republic Day, President Gayoom outlined various measures intended to strengthen the political system and to advance the process of democratization. These included the granting of greater autonomy and responsibilities to members of the Cabinet of Ministers, the introduction of regulations governing the conduct of civil servants (in order to increase their accountability), the introduction of democratic elections to island development committees and atoll committees, and the establishment of a Law Commission to carry out reforms to the judicial system.

In November 1996 President Gayoom effected an extensive cabinet reshuffle and a reorganization of government bodies, including the establishment of a Supreme Council for Islamic Affairs, which was to be under direct presidential control and was to advise the Government on matters relating to Islam. In early 1997 President Gayoom announced that the Citizens' Special Majlis (which was established in 1980 with the specific task of amending the Constitution) had resolved to complete the revision of the Constitution during that year and to implement the amended version by 1 January 1998. The Citizens' Special Majlis finished its 17-year-long task in early November 1997. The revised Constitution was ratified by the President on 27 November and came into effect, as planned, on 1 January 1998. Under the new 156-article Constitution, a formal, multi-candidate contest was permitted for the legislature's nomination for the presidency; no restriction was placed on the number of terms a president may serve; for administrative purposes, the number of atolls was increased from 19 to 20; the Majlis, which was henceforth known as the People's Majlis, was enlarged from 48 to 50 seats; the Citizens' Special Majlis was renamed the People's Special Majlis; the rights of the people were expanded; parliamentary immunity was introduced; the office of auditor-general was created; the post of commissioner of elections was constitutionalized; ministers were afforded greater power; public officers were made more accountable; parliamentary questions were allowed; and judges and magistrates were obliged to take special oaths of loyalty.

In September 1998 five individuals declared their candidacy for the presidency; the People's Majlis unanimously voted by secret ballot for the incumbent President Gayoom to go forward to the national referendum. In the referendum, which was held in mid-October, Gayoom was re-elected as President for a fifth term in office, obtaining 90.9% of the popular vote. Following his re-election, the President carried out a cabinet reorganization. In an unexpected move, Ilyas Ibrahim was appointed to hold the new portfolio of transport and civil aviation.

In November 1999 elections for 42 members of the 50-seat People's Majlis were conducted (on a non-partisan basis). In September 2000 the Comprehensive Nuclear Test Ban Treaty was ratified by the Maldives. As part of a government initiative to promote the advancement of women in public life, President Gayoom appointed a woman as the new Island Chief of Himmafushi in June 2001. In December a woman was appointed as Atoll Chief of Vaavu Atoll (the first woman to be assigned a senior executive position of responsibility for an atoll).

Meanwhile, in early 2001 an attempt by 42 prominent Maldivians, including members of the People's Majlis, former cabinet ministers and business executives, to register the newly formed Maldivian Democratic Party (MDP) was blocked by the People's Majlis on the grounds that the existence of political parties would encourage divisions among the public and, therefore, be counter-productive. It was believed by some, however, that President Gayoom had enforced the decision and, in doing so, had acted unconstitutionally.

In July 2002 three journalists were charged with defamation and inciting violence, and were sentenced to life imprisonment for writing articles criticizing the President and the Government. In early 2003 international activists demanded the release of the detainees, claiming that the journalists had not advocated violent opposition to President Gayoom or the Government, and that they had only been exercising their right to freedom of speech. In July a businessman was sentenced to life imprisonment for publishing an article via the internet urging that the Government be overthrown. Later that month the human rights group Amnesty International issued a report citing frequent cases of arbitrary detentions, unfair trials and long-term imprisonment and torture of political opponents in the Maldives. The organization urged the Government to release political prisoners, investigate allegations of torture and reform the criminal justice system. The Maldives authorities strongly rejected the allegations.

In September 2003 detainees at a prison in Malé held protests in response to the death of a fellow prisoner. Reports of the violent suppression of the rioting by the country's National Security Service (NSS), and the death of another two detainees, prompted major anti-Government protests in the capital, the first ever during President Gayoom's tenure. Large numbers of alleged demonstrators were arrested, and a curfew was imposed on the city. Gayoom appealed for calm and announced an investigation into the deaths of the prisoners (the subsequent demise of another detainee brought the number of deaths to four). Eleven members of the NSS were arrested for their alleged involvement in the over-zealous curbing of the riots, and the Deputy Chief of the NSS and Police Commissioner, Brig. Adam Zahir, was removed from office (he was appointed executive director of the Ministry of Information, Arts and Culture until his reinstatement as Police Commissioner in mid-February 2004, after the inquiry cleared him of any misconduct). Amnesty International reiterated demands for an end to widespread political repression and the violation of human rights and for reform of the judicial system.

On 25 September 2003 Gayoom was re-elected unanimously by secret ballot in the People's Majlis for a sixth presidential term, defeating three other candidates. His re-election was ratified at a public referendum on 17 October, where he secured 90.3% of the votes cast. One day after the beginning of his new term in office President Gayoom effected a cabinet reorganization, in which the Attorney-General, Dr Mohamed Munavvar, and the Minister of Planning and National Development, Ibrahim Hussain Zaki, were dismissed. Gayoom gave no reason for the dismissals, although it was alleged that the two had been removed for supporting reformers attempting to register a political party. Gayoom also announced that the judicial system, executive and legislature would be reformed over the next five years (without specifying what the changes would be) and that a human rights commission would be established in Malé. In the same month a group of political activists decided to establish the MDP (which had been prevented from registering as a political party in the Maldives in 2001—see above) in exile in Sri Lanka, in response to the rise in discontent with the Maldives Government. In mid-February 2004 members of the MDP claimed that more than 15 of the party's supporters had been arrested in Malé in an attempt to disrupt a planned protest march; however, the Government asserted that the raids were aimed at criminal offenders and that only eight people had been detained.

In December 2003 a Human Rights Commission was established in Malé. At the end of that month a report by the Presidential Commission investigating the deaths of the four prisoners in September was submitted to President Gayoom. In his speech on the findings of the Commission to the People's Majlis in January 2004, Gayoom stated that the security personnel implicated in the prisoners' deaths had acted illegally and would be prosecuted. The President also announced that a programme of penal reform was under way. However, the exiled leader of the MDP, Mohamed Latheef, criticized the report, claiming that the names of those responsible for the deaths had been omitted, and demanded the President's resignation.

In May 2004 the election, by universal suffrage, of a People's Special Majlis, which was empowered to amend the Constitution, took place. Voters chose 42 members from 121 independent candidates. The President appointed an additional eight people to serve on the council; the People's Special Majlis also included members of the People's Majlis and the Cabinet of Ministers. Gayoom invited members of the public to send him proposals for constitutional reform and in early June the President himself proposed a number of radical constitutional reforms. He suggested that a President's tenure should be limited to two five-year terms and that women should be allowed to stand for the presidency. According to the proposed reforms, the President would also lose the right to appoint eight members of the People's Majlis; the People's Majlis would become independent of the executive; the post of Prime Minister would be created; the judiciary would be restructured (a Supreme Court would be created as the highest court of appeal and would be appointed by the President, on the advice of the People's Majlis), and, perhaps most importantly, the formation and functioning of political parties would be permitted. The People's Special Majlis, which was sworn in on 15 June, convened in July to discuss the proposals.

In mid-August 2004 President Gayoom declared an indefinite state of emergency after a pro-democracy protest in the capital became violent. Four police officers were reportedly stabbed and about 185 people were arrested during the protests. The Government claimed that the demonstration had been a coup attempt, a charge denied by the opposition MDP. The exiled opposition leader Latheef accused the Government of 'ruthlessly suppressing dissent'. The Government invited a European Union (EU) fact-finding team to Malé. The EU envoys, however, were denied access to the detainees and expressed concern about the continuing detention without charge of the alleged protesters and the ongoing state of emergency. By early September 122 people had been released, while about 60 people remained in detention, including former Attorney-General Dr Mohamed Munavvar and members of the People's Special Majlis. On 1 September, meanwhile, Gayoom relinquished the defence and finance portfolios as part of a cabinet reorganization, in an apparent move towards government reform. Ismail Shafeeu and Mohamed Jaleel were appointed as the new Minister of Defence and National Security and Minister of Finance and Treasury respectively.

In October 2004 the state of emergency that had been declared in August was revoked. Although a curfew remained in place, the lifting of the state of emergency meant that the opposition members who had been indefinitely detained following the August pro-democracy protest would either have to be charged or released from prison. In December four of the detained opposition members were charged with treason; later in that month, however, President Gayoom announced that all charges of treason and public order offences against those taken into custody following the August protest were to be suspended.

On 26 December 2004 a tsunami generated by a massive earthquake in the Indian Ocean, off the coast of Indonesia, devastated many of the low-lying Maldive islands. While the resultant death toll was not as high as might have been expected, several of the islands were rendered uninhabitable and an estimated 15,000 people were left homeless by the disaster. The economic consequences of the catastrophe on the Maldives were extensive, owing in large part to the significant contribution made by the tourism industry to the economy.

On 22 January 2005 149 independent candidates contested elections to the People's Majlis. The elections had been postponed from the previous month owing to the tsunami. Candidates supported by the opposition MDP reportedly won 18 of the 42 elective legislative seats. However, the Government stated that only 12 opposition candidates had done so, claiming that the results were a sign of widespread popular support for its reform policies. Following the elections President Gayoom insisted that he intended to establish a multi-party democracy in the Maldives within one year.

In May 2005 the Maldivian dissident Fathimath Nisreen, who had been sentenced to 10 years' imprisonment in July 2002 for her alleged participation in subversive activities, was freed, having received a presidential pardon. In June 2005 the People's Majlis unanimously approved a constitutional amendment permitting the registration of political parties in the Maldives, reversing its 2001 decision opposing the establishment of a multi-party democracy. The MDP was subsequently officially registered in the Maldives as a political party, together with several others, including the Dhivehi Rayyithunge Party (DRP—Maldivian People's Party) established by President Gayoom. In mid-July 2005 Gayoom instigated a major reorganization of the Cabinet in which, most notably, the long-serving Minister of Foreign Affairs, Fathulla Jameel, was dismissed and replaced by Dr Ahmed Shaheed.

In August 2005 a protest took place in Malé demanding the release of all political prisoners. Shortly afterwards the Chairman of the MDP, Mohamed Nasheed, was arrested, provoking several days of unrest in the capital and on various other atolls. Nasheed was subsequently charged with terrorism and attempting to perpetrate anti-Government actions; his trial began in October. Also in October Jennifer Latheef, daughter of the exiled Mohamed Latheef, was convicted of having incited a riot in Malé in September 2003 (see above) and was sentenced to a 10-year prison term. Amnesty International condemned the trial, describing Jennifer Latheef as a 'prisoner of conscience'. In February 2006 two dissidents who had been sentenced to lengthy prison terms in 2002 were released, having received presidential pardons.

In a significant development towards the further democratization of the Maldives, from June 2006 representatives of the Government and the MDP conducted informal talks at the British High Commission in Colombo, Sri Lanka. These negotiations resulted in what subsequently became known as the Westminster House Agreement. The reported terms of the agreement included the release of a number of opposition detainees and the advancement of constitutional reform, on the part of the Government, in return for MDP assurances that the party would curb public demonstrations and renounce violent protest. In July charges against several detainees were dropped by the Government, and in the following month 11 prisoners were released. Jennifer Latheef was also freed and received a presidential pardon, which she rejected on the grounds of her alleged innocence and the continuing imprisonment of other activists. Mohamed Nasheed, whose trial had been resumed in May, was released in September, although the charges against him were not withdrawn.

In November 2006 more than 100 members of the MDP were arrested in the run-up to a planned demonstration to demand the swifter implementation of reforms; the rally was cancelled by the MDP amid fears for the welfare of protesters. Government officials alleged that the MDP had organized the rally as an attempt to overthrow the Government, and that, if held, it would have posed a threat to public safety. In a subsequent report Amnesty International expressed concern at reports of 'repressive measures' being used by government officials. These allegations were vehemently denied by the Government, but they prompted widespread calls for the urgent introduction of a reform programme to prevent the arbitrary detention, mistreatment and torture of dissidents. In December the trial of the acting President of the MDP, Ibrahim Hussain Zaki, recommenced; the initial charge of high treason, arising from a speech that Zaki had made on Dhidhoo island in defence of fishermen's right to protest, had been amended to a charge of 'enmity, contempt and disharmony'. However, no progress was made regarding the trial in 2007 and the charges were reportedly dropped. The issue of press freedom came to the fore again in January 2007, with the commencement of the trial of Nazim Sattar, the Deputy Editor of the independent daily newspaper *Minivan News*. Sattar was charged with 'disobedience to order' for an article published in August 2005 that had quoted criticism of the Star Force unit of the Maldivian police force, allegedly resulting in the persecution of the unit by the public. However, in May 2007 the Minister of Legal Reform, Information and Arts, Mohamed Nasheed, announced at the World Press Freedom Day conference in Medellin, Colombia, that charges against Sattar had been dropped.

Meanwhile, in early 2006 meetings of the People's Special Majlis, which had been established in mid-2004 to draw up and implement constitutional amendments, were obstructed by President Gayoom's refusal to permit the removal of presidential appointees from the body. The opposition MDP condemned the continued presence of representatives who had not been elected, stressing that they should be withdrawn in advance of the redrafting of the Constitution, and also proposed that the President's power to assent to the Constitution should be removed. Tensions were heightened in late February 2006 when the Speaker of the People's Special Majlis, Abbas Ibrahim, removed a scheduled debate on the matter from the legislative agenda. The MDP boycotted the opening of the People's Majlis in that month in protest at the President's alleged obstruction of the constitutional amendment process. In March, however, the Government published a 'Roadmap for the Reform Agenda', which projected the passing of a draft constitution by the People's Special Majlis by 31 May 2007 and its ratification within a month of that date; the document also forecast that multi-party elections would be held by 2008. Among the other stated aims of the agenda were judicial and electoral reforms, greater media freedom, the establishment of a Police Integrity Commission and greater autonomy for the atoll and island administrations.

A Police Integrity Commission was established in August 2006, and in November the Human Rights Commission was reconstituted as legally autonomous; however, the introduction of new regulations on press freedom and access to information was delayed indefinitely by the Government in January 2007. A referendum to determine whether to adopt a presidential or parliamentary system of government, which was originally scheduled to be held in September 2006, was postponed owing to disagreements between the Government and the opposition. In mid-February 2007 a meeting between the DRP and the MDP to address the faltering pace of constitutional reform was tentatively hailed as a positive development, although its conclusions and consequences remained unclear.

In mid-January 2007 the founder of the MDP, Mohamed Latheef, ended three years of voluntary exile in Sri Lanka with his return to the Maldives. In February the Deputy Chairman of the MDP's parliamentary group, Ibrahim Shareef, defected to the DRP, citing his disapproval of alleged militant elements within his former party. Later in the month a demonstration organized by the MDP in protest at police violence against civilians reportedly attracted an estimated 1,000 participants. In mid-April the discovery in Malé harbour of the corpse of a man who was alleged to have died in police custody prompted further demonstrations and numerous arrests; however, according to the subsequent autopsy, which was carried out in Sri Lanka, the man had not been tortured prior to his death. Meanwhile, in the same month the Minister of Higher Education, Employment and Social Security, Abdullah Yameen, resigned amid rumours of discord within the Cabinet of Ministers. Yameen also stood down as a member of the DRP, and was reported to be planning the creation of a new political party. In early May Qasim Ibrahim was elected Speaker of the People's Special Majlis, succeeding Abbas Ibrahim, who had resigned in the previous month.

The death of an inmate of Maafushi prison in the Kaafu atoll in unclear circumstances during a prison revolt in June 2007 precipitated a hunger strike by hundreds of the deceased's fellow prisoners and public outrage at the regulation and conditions of the prison. There was speculation that the subsequent cabinet reshuffle, in which Minister of Home Affairs Ahmed Thasmeen Ali was transferred to the position of Minister of Atolls Development and the home affairs portfolio was assigned to Abdullah Kamaaludheen, was related to the crisis. Further cabinet changes took place in August, when Minister of Justice Mohamed Jameel Ahmed and Attorney-General Hassan Saeed resigned, reportedly over their concerns regarding impediments and delays to the programme of democratic reforms. Minister of Foreign Affairs Dr Ahmed Shaheed resigned later in the month, and was replaced by Abdullah Shahid; Mohamed Muiz Adnan was appointed Minister of Justice. In October Azima Shakoor was sworn in as the new Attorney-General.

In August 2007 three dissident former government members—Mohamed Jameel Ahmed, Hassan Saeed and Dr Ahmed Shaheed—launched a new body entitled the New Maldives Movement (NMM) and encouraged the formation of a united front of pro-democracy groups as the National Unity Alliance. In early January 2008 the official newspaper of the governing DRP, *Hamaroalhi Daily News*, accused the NMM of fostering terrorism. Later in the month the Government declared that the movement had not sought official registration and was therefore illegal. Consequently the NMM was banned by the Government, which granted a licence to two members of the DRP to operate an NGO under the name of the New Maldives Movement. Meanwhile, a press freedom bill was approved by the People's Majlis in August 2007, despite criticisms by Article 19, an international campaign group for freedom of expression, that it fell short of international standards.

The potential threat of terrorism to the Maldives came to the fore when a bomb exploded in Malé on 29 September 2007, injuring 12 foreign tourists. The explosion—the first recorded terrorist attack to take place in the Maldives—was widely believed to have been perpetrated by Islamic extremists. In December three Maldivian men were each sentenced to 15 years in prison for their part in the incident, which they confessed to having planned as a deliberate attack on the country's vital tourism industry. In an attempt to combat the perceived threat of growing Islamic fundamentalism and to protect the lucrative tourism sector, the Government introduced a number of measures, including arresting suspected extremists, banning the wearing of the full veil in public, advocating the promotion of moderate Islamic views in schools and colleges, forbidding the convention of unlicensed Muslim prayer groups, and banning foreign Islamic clerics from visiting the islands unless they had been explicitly invited by the authorities. While visiting an atoll in the far north of the island chain in January 2008, President Gayoom himself escaped unhurt after an attempted knife attack by a 20-year-old Maldivian man. The Government claimed that the President's political rivals were the most likely organizers of the apparent assassination attempt, rather than Islamic extremists, as some early reports had suggested.

In June 2007 the People's Special Majlis announced a new deadline of 30 November 2007 for the drawing up of constitutional amendments and agreed that a referendum on the system of government should be held in August. The results of the ballot, which took place on 18 August, indicated popular support for retaining the presidential system, with a reported 62% of those who participated in favour. However, there were doubts among the opposition regarding the validity of the results and the alleged turn-out, and several complaints were lodged with the Election Commission. The November deadline for finalizing the draft constitutional amendments was not met by the People's Special Majlis and discussions on constitutional reform, including proposals with regard to new regulations on freedom of information, continued in 2008. In January the People's Special Majlis voted to amend the Constitution to limit the length of a President's tenure to two five-year terms (whether consecutive or not) and to remove the gender bar on the presidency. In late June 2008 the People's Special Majlis approved final amendments to the draft Constitution, which was then passed to the Cabinet of Ministers and the President in turn. The new Constitution was ratified by the President on 7 August; major points included the direct election of the President (and his declared Vice-President) and the restriction of presidential terms of office to two; the election, rather than presidential appointment, of the Speaker and Deputy Speaker of the People's Majlis; the establishment of a Supreme Court as the highest judicial authority; and the granting to citizens the right to hold peaceful demonstrations. The People's Special Majlis and Judicial Advisory Council were duly dissolved, while the Speaker of the People's Majlis, Ahmed Zahir, was replaced by the elected Mohamed Shihab. Meanwhile, the Cabinet of Ministers was in a state of flux as numerous ministers resigned for constitutional and other reasons. By early September a total of 12 political parties had registered in the Maldives. In that month the Election Commissioner, Ahmed Manik, who had been assigned the post by President Gayoom, was replaced by a new five-member Elections Commission, which was nominated and appointed by the People's Majlis.

The first multi-party presidential election in the Maldives was held on 8 October 2008. Despite opposition to Gayoom standing for a seventh presidential term, the DRP argued that the new two-term limit did not exclude him from contesting what would be the first election under the new Constitution. Five other candidates contested the presidency, including former political prisoner and leader of the MDP, Mohamed Nasheed. Gayoom secured 40.3% of the votes, Nasheed won 24.9%, Hassan Saeed, who was running as an independent candidate, secured 16.7%, and he was closely followed by Qasim Ibrahim of the Jumhooree Party (JP, Republican Party), with 15.2% of the votes. It was reported that 85.5% of the electorate participated in the poll. As no candidate secured more than 50% of the ballot in the first round of voting, the two leading candidates contested a second round on 28 October. In an historic victory, Nasheed secured the presidency with 54.2% of the votes, and was consequently inaugurated on 11 November 2008. On the same day the country's first elected Vice-President, Dr. Mohamed Waheed Hassan Manik of the National Unity Party (NUP, Gaumee Itthihaad), was also sworn in. The new President appointed a coalition Cabinet of Ministers, comprising members of the MDP, the NUP, the JP, the Social Liberal Party (SLP) and the Adhaalath Party. On appointing his new Government, Nasheed carried out a significant reorganization of the ministries, including the establishment of a Ministry of Islamic Affairs, which replaced the Supreme Council for Islamic Affairs that had operated under President Gayoom since 1996. In addition, President Nasheed appointed eight new members of the People's Majlis to replace the eight appointees of former President Gayoom to ensure that the Government had a working majority. One of Nasheed's first acts as new Head of State was to request the resignation of the National Police Commissioner, Adam Zahir, who had long been held personally accountable for various human rights abuses on the part of the police, including torture and custodial deaths. In December Nasheed's Cabinet suffered its first real set-back when the Minister of Home Affairs, Gasim Ibrahim, who was also the leader of the JP, resigned. Ibrahim claimed that his resignation had been prompted by the Government's unwillingness to allocate funds to prison reform, but several sources alleged that his departure came as a result of criticism of his heavy-handed response to a strike by employees at a tourist resort (the police reportedly used electric batons and pepper spray against the striking staff). The Minister of Defence, Ameen Faisal, assumed the home affairs portfolio in an acting capacity. In mid-February 2009 the President's Special Advisor, Dr. Hassan Saeed, resigned from his post; earlier that month he had formed a new political party entitled the Dhivehi Qaumee Party (DQP).

In early February 2009 the People's Majlis passed two electoral bills, paving the way for the holding of the Maldives' first multi-party legislative elections. One of the two bills was the Parliamentary Constituencies Bill, according to which the population of each administrative atoll would determine how many electoral constituencies would be created and two members of parliament would be elected for every 5,000 residents registered in each constituency. Although, according to the Constitution, the elections were due to be held by 1 March, the Elections Commission announced that a delay would be necessary to enable the required preparations to be carried out and that the poll would take place on 9 May.

A total of 77 seats were contested in the election and, according to preliminary results, the DRP won the highest number of seats (28), while the MDP gained 26 seats. Although independent candidates took 13 seats, the predominance of the leading parties in the voting illustrated the population's willing adoption of a party political system.

Environmental issues are becoming increasingly important in Maldivian politics, particularly given the fact that around 80% of the islands are just one metre above sea level or less and are thus extremely vulnerable to climate change. In November 1989 the Maldives hosted an international conference with delegates from other small island nations, to discuss the threat posed to low-lying island countries by the predicted rise in sea-level caused by heating of the earth's atmosphere as a result of pollution (the 'greenhouse effect'). In June 1990 an Environmental Research Unit, which was to operate under the Ministry of Planning and the Environment, was established in the Maldives. The Maldives reiterated its serious concern with regard to problems of world-wide environmental pollution when it hosted the 13th conference of the UN's Intergovernmental Panel on Climate Change (IPCC, see p. 167) in September 1997. In September 1999 a special session of the UN General Assembly was convened in New York to address the specific problems faced by the 43-member Alliance of Small Island States (see p. 437) (including the Maldives), notably climate change, rising sea levels and globalization. At the UN Millennium Summit meeting in September 2000 the President of the Maldives again took the opportunity to urge leaders to address environmental issues. The Government expressed its grave disappointment and concern at the USA's decision in April 2001 to reject the Kyoto Protocol to the UN's Framework Convention on Climate Change. A large part of the international community adopted the protocol in July after many of the emissions targets had been reduced. The USA proposed an alternative initiative in February 2002; however, most states dismissed it as potentially ineffective. In early March the Maldives, Kiribati and Tuvalu announced their decision to take legal action against the USA for refusing to sign the Kyoto Protocol and thus threatening the very survival of the low-lying island states. President Gayoom attended the South Asian Regional Conference on Ecotourism in India in January 2002. At the World Summit on Sustainable Development held in September in Johannesburg, South Africa, President Gayoom warned the international community that low-lying islands were at greater risk than ever before. He demanded urgent action, including the universal ratification and implementation of the Kyoto Protocol, to prevent a global environmental catastrophe. On his return to the Maldives, the President stated that some progress had been made in certain areas, although the decisions were not as far-reaching as desired by small island nations. The President again urged the international community to enforce the Kyoto Protocol during a television interview in August 2004, and in a speech at the Non-Aligned Movement Conference in Havana, Cuba, in September 2006, appealed for international action on climate change and environmental degradation. On assuming the presidency in November 2008, Mohamed Nasheed immediately announced government plans to use some of the revenue from the tourism sector to establish a sovereign wealth fund to finance a long-term plan to purchase land abroad should the relocation of the Maldivian population become necessary owing to rising sea levels. In March 2009 President Nasheed announced plans to make the Maldives 'carbon neutral' (i.e. a zero net contributor to greenhouse gas emissions) within 10 years by switching to using only renewable energy sources such as wind, wave and solar power. It was estimated that the ambitious plan would cost the country around US $110m. per year over the next decade and Nasheed expressed his hopes that it would serve as a blueprint to other nations considering adopting such measures.

The Maldives is a founder member of the South Asian Association for Regional Co-operation (SAARC, see p. 397), which was formally constituted in December 1985, and the country became a full member of the Commonwealth in June 1985. The Maldives' international standing was enhanced in November 1990, when it successfully hosted the fifth SAARC summit meeting, which was held in Malé. In November 2004 the Maldives opened its fourth resident diplomatic mission (in addition to those in Sri Lanka, at the UN headquarters in New York and in London, United Kingdom) in New Delhi, India. At the 12th SAARC Summit Conference, which was held in January 2004 in the Pakistani capital of Islamabad, the members agreed to form a South Asia Free Trade Area (SAFTA); this came into effect on 1 January 2006, but was not due to enter fully into force until 2016. In February 2009 the number of countries with which the Maldives had established diplomatic relations stood at 147.

Government

Legislative authority is vested in the People's Majlis. The People's Majlis shall consist of 77 members elected from Malé and the 20 administrative atolls for five years by universal adult suffrage. Executive power is vested in the President, who is elected directly by the people, with more than 50% of the vote, for a period of five years. The President (who is not permitted to serve for more than two terms) governs with the assistance of an appointed Cabinet of Ministers (including a Vice-President), which is responsible to the People's Majlis. The country has 21 administrative districts: the capital is under direct central administration while the 20 atolls are each under an atoll chief (verin) who is appointed by the President, under the general guidance of the Minister of Atolls Administration.

Defence

There is no army, navy or air force. The voluntary National Security Service was founded in 1892 and was renamed the Maldives National Defence Force (MNDF) in April 2006 when a separate police force was established to differentiate military duties from domestic law enforcement tasks. The MNDF, which has about 2,000 members and incorporates an expanded infantry unit, undertakes paramilitary security duties (including coast-guard duties). In 2008 budgetary expenditure on defence was estimated at 551.2m. rufiyaa (equivalent to 4.9% of total spending) and expenditure on public order and internal security was projected at 929.7m. rufiyaa (8.2% of total spending).

Economic Affairs

In 2007, according to estimates by the World Bank, the Maldives' gross national income (GNI), measured at average 2005–07 prices, was US $977.4m., equivalent to $3,200 per head (or $5,040 per head on an international purchasing-power parity basis). During 2000–07, it was estimated, the population increased at an average annual rate of 1.6%, while gross domestic product (GDP) per head grew, in real terms, by an average of 5.7% per year over the same period. Overall GDP increased, in real terms, at an average annual rate of 7.4% in 2000–07. According to the Asian Development Bank (ADB), GDP declined by 4.6% in 2005 following the devastating tsunami of December 2004; however, subsequent reconstruction efforts contributed to impressive growth, of 18.0%, in 2006, 7.2% in 2007 and 5.7% in 2008.

Agriculture and fishing contributed an estimated 6.7% of GDP (the primary fishing sector alone accounted for 4.9%) in 2008. About 11.5% of the total working population were employed in the sector (more than 7% in fishing) at the March 2006 census. In 2007 revenue from exports of marine products totalled 1,357.2m rufiyaas, thus accounting for 98% of total export earnings. The fisheries sector suffered significant damage as a result of the December 2004 tsunami disaster, with the destruction of boats and equipment contributing to the loss of many livelihoods. Small quantities of various fruits, vegetables and cereals are produced, but virtually all of the principal staple foods have to be imported. As a result of salt-water intrusion caused by the tsunami, a significant amount of cultivable land was ruined. The dominant agricultural activity (not including fishing) in the Maldives is coconut production. The GDP of the agriculture and fisheries sector increased, in real terms, at an average annual rate of 5.9% (3.6% for the fishing sector) in 2000–08. Real agricultural GDP grew by 12.2% in 2005, but declined by 0.7% in 2006. According to preliminary estimates, the sector's GDP declined by a massive 17.5% (23.7% for the fisheries sector alone) in 2007, but rose by 5.7% (8.4% for the fisheries sector) in 2008.

Industry (including mining, manufacturing, construction and utilities) contributed an estimated 17.6% of GDP in 2008, and employed 24.3% of the working population at the March 2006 census. Sectoral GDP increased, in real terms, at an average annual rate of 8.8% in 2000–08. Industrial GDP grew by 15.9% in 2006, by 11.2% in 2007 and by 8.1% in 2008.

Mining and quarrying (mostly for coral and sand) contributed 0.5% of GDP in 2008, and employed 0.3% of the working population at the March 2006 census. No reserves of petroleum or natural gas have, as yet, been discovered in Maldivian waters. Mining GDP increased, in real terms, at an average annual rate of 3.0% in 2000–08. The GDP of the mining sector grew by 2.3% in 2007 and by 1.7% in 2008.

The manufacturing sector contributed 6.4% of GDP in 2008, and employed 17.5% of the working population at the March 2006 census. There are only a small number of 'modern' manufacturing enterprises in the Maldives, including fish-canning, garment-making and soft-drink bottling. Although cottage industries (such as the weaving of coir yarn and boat-building) employ nearly one-quarter of the total labour force, there is little scope for expansion, owing to the limited size of the domestic market. Because of its lack of manufacturing industries, the Maldives has to import most essential consumer and capital goods. In the late 1980s and 1990s traditional handicrafts, such as lacquer work and shell craft, revived as a result of the expansion of the tourism sector. Manufacturing GDP increased, in real terms, at an average annual rate of 5.0% in 2000–08. Real manufacturing GDP rose by 7.3% in 2006, but declined by 7.0% in 2007 and by 6.7% in 2008.

Energy is derived principally from petroleum, and imports of mineral fuels and oils comprised 23.0% of the cost of imports in 2007. Owing to a surge in commercial activities and a significant increase in construction projects in Malé, demand for electricity in the capital grew rapidly in the late 1980s and early 1990s. Accordingly, plans were formulated in late 1991 to augment the generating capacity of the power station in Malé and to improve the distribution network. In 2004–07 the fourth phase of the Malé power project, further to increase the capital's power supply, was undertaken. Meanwhile, in December 2001 the ADB agreed to provide a loan to improve the supply of electricity to some 40 outer islands. By 2004 21 inhabited islands had been provided with electricity. In 2006 the ADB supplied another loan, of US $8m., to enable the electrification of those outer islands not included in the first project.

Following the decline of the shipping industry in the 1980s, tourism gained in importance as an economic sector, and by 1989 it had overtaken the fishing industry as the Maldives' largest source of foreign exchange. In 2003 the tourism sector provided 31.5% of GDP. In 2003 tourist arrivals increased by 16.3%, compared with the previous year, to reach 563,593. In that year receipts from tourism totalled an estimated 896.2m. rufiyaa. In 2004 tourist arrivals increased by a further 9.4%, to 616,716, and receipts from tourism reached 921.6m. rufiyaa. In March 2004 the Government announced that nine more atolls would be opened for tourism and that 11 further islands would be converted into resorts. The devastating impact upon the Maldives of the massive tsunami in the Indian Ocean in December 2004 significantly affected the performance of the tourism sector in 2005, with several tourist resorts damaged and adverse publicity surrounding the disaster further discouraging prospective tourists. Tourist arrivals amounted to just 395,320 in 2005, but receipts remained strong, at 909.3m. rufiyaa. However, the contribution of the tourism sector to GDP was only 21.8% in 2005, and the sector's GDP declined, in real terms, by 33.1% in that year. The reopening by the end of 2005 of all of the resorts affected by the tsunami provided the tourism industry with a considerable boost; arrivals increased by 52.3% in 2006 to reach 601,923 and the sector's GDP grew by 42.3% to an impressive total of 1,685.9m. rufiyaa. The tourism sector continued to recover in 2007, with arrivals rising by 12.3% to reach 675,889 and revenue increasing by 13.8%, from US $433.7m. in 2006 to $493.6m. The real GDP of the tourism sector increased, in real terms, at an average annual rate of 7.2% in 2000–08. The services sector as a whole contributed 79.4% of GDP in 2008. The GDP of the services sector increased, in real terms, by an average of 7.2% per year in 2000–08. Compared with the previous year, sectoral GDP declined by 8.2% in 2005, but expanded by a massive 21.3% in 2006. Growth in the services sector was sustained, at 8.6% in 2007 and 8.5% in 2008.

In 2007 the Maldives recorded a visible trade deficit of an estimated US $736.7m. and there was a deficit of approximately $422.9m. on the current account of the balance of payments. In 2007 the principal source of imports was Singapore (accounting for 22.5% of the total); other major sources were the United Arab Emirates, India and Malaysia. In 2007 the principal market for exports (traditionally the USA) was Thailand (accounting for 40.9% of the total); other major purchasers were Sri Lanka, France and the United Kingdom. The principal exports were marine products (tuna being the largest export commodity). The principal imports were machinery and mechanical appliances and electrical equipment, mineral products, and wood and metal manufactures.

Foreign grant aid in 2000 totalled an estimated US $17.7m. In the aftermath of the December 2004 tsunami, the Maldives received a significant amount of international aid, in the form of both grants and concessional loans, principally from the UN, the ADB, the World Bank and Japan (which has traditionally been the Maldives' largest aid donor). A total of $88m. had been pledged in assistance by the end of April 2005, of which $75m. was to be in the form of grants. In June 2006 the Japanese Government announced a $23m. loan to aid reconstruction. According to government figures, foreign financing rose by 119.7% in 2007, compared with the previous year, to reach an estimated 1,162.8m. rufiyaa. In 2008, in terms of central government finance, there was an estimated fiscal deficit of 1,564.6m. rufiyaa. The Maldives' total external debt was $574.8m. at the end of 2006, of which $362.2m. was long-term public debt. According to the ADB, total external debt had risen to $975m. by the end of 2008. In that year the cost of debt-servicing was equivalent to 5.0% of revenue from exports of goods and services. According to the IMF, during 2000–07 the average annual rate of inflation was 2.5%. According to the ADB, consumer prices increased by 3.5% in 2006 and, largely owing to a sharp rise in global commodity prices (notably petroleum and food), rose sharply, to 7.4%, in 2007 and to 12.3% in 2008. According to the March 2006 census, 14.4% of the total labour force was unemployed at that time (compared with around 2% in 2000).

The Maldives is a member of the UN Economic and Social Commission for Asia and the Pacific (ESCAP, see p. 36), the ADB (see p. 191), the Colombo Plan (see p. 425) and the South Asian Association for Regional Co-operation (SAARC, see p. 397).

In response to the rapid growth and increasing importance of the tourism sector in the Maldives from the late 1990s onwards, the Government made efforts to improve the infrastructure (including the development of communication systems, sanitation and the water supply). By 1999 the Maldivian telecommunications company, Dhivehi Raajjeyge Gulhun Ltd (Dhiraagu), had provided telephone facilities to all of the inhabited islands and by 2007 311,422 inhabitants had also subscribed to mobile cellular telephones. However, despite a recovery in fish exports and buoyant tourism receipts in the latter half of the 1990s, the current-account deficit persisted and the trade deficit continued to grow. In early 2001 the Government opened up the export of fresh and canned fish to the private sector, and in that year the Maldives Industrial Fisheries Company recorded a 13% increase in sales of fish, compared with the previous year. In 2002 the fisheries sector continued to expand and tourism gradually began to recover. The current-account deficit, however, remained high and the fiscal deficit continued to grow, largely owing to an increase in government expenditure. Furthermore, the islands continued to experience a shortage of domestic labour: in 2003 about 33,765 expatriate workers (mainly from India, Sri Lanka and Bangladesh) were employed in the Maldives, and it was estimated that in 1999 almost 20% of the country's GDP went to non-Maldivians. Development of an artificially constructed island—Hulhumalé—commenced from 1997 as a means to disperse the population, which was concentrated largely in the nearby overcrowded capital of Malé. A total of 1,500 people had been resettled in Hulhumalé by the end of December 2004 and the Government planned to move up to 45,000 people to the island by 2020. In December 2004 the tsunami generated by a massive earthquake in the Indian Ocean had a devastating effect on the Maldives, leading to widespread destruction of infrastructure and housing. An estimated 14 of the 200 inhabited islands were completely destroyed by the huge waves, which also damaged approximately 8% of the country's fishing fleet and several tourist resorts. The economic consequences of the disaster were profound; the cost of reconstruction was estimated at US $375m., the equivalent of approximately 50% of annual GDP. The Government was reckoned to have lost an estimated $40m. in revenue in 2005. In conjunction with a large increase in government expenditure, this contributed to a significant rise in both the fiscal and current-account deficits. As a direct result of the tsunami, the ADB estimated that GDP contracted by 4.6% in 2005. The increasing levels of capital expenditure that were required to proceed with reconstruction projects placed considerable pressure on the budget (despite high inflows of aid from international donors) and the budgetary deficit grew by 19.5% in 2005 and by 14.2% in 2006. In 2007, although the majority of public expenditure was unrelated to the tsunami, it nevertheless remained at a high level; the budget deficit in that year was estimated to have risen by 16.6%. The Government financed the deficit by leasing out islands and reducing the budget allocation of ministries by 20% in 2008. Public debt in 2007 was estimated at 38.9% of GDP. Tourism figures for 2007 indicated that the sector had recovered well and, moreover, that it remained the most dynamic subdivision of the economy. However, the tsunami disaster highlighted the vulnerability of the economy to external events, both economic and environmental, and as a result of the ongoing global financial crisis the ADB projected that real GDP growth would slow to 1.0% in 2009 from 5.7% in 2008.

Education

Education is not compulsory. There are three types of formal education: traditional Koranic schools (*Makthab*), Dhivehi-language primary schools (*Madhrasa*) and English-language primary and secondary schools. Schools of the third category are the only ones equipped to teach a standard curriculum. In 1984 a national curriculum was introduced in all schools. In 1989 the Government established a National Council on Education to oversee the development of education in the Maldives. Primary education begins at six years of age and lasts for five years. Secondary education, beginning at the age of 11, lasts for up to seven years, comprising a first cycle of five years and a second of two years. In 2005/06 enrolment at primary schools included 97.4% of children in the relevant age-group; the ratio for secondary enrolment of pupils in the relevant age-group was an estimated 67.1% in the same year. The construction of the first secondary school outside Malé was completed on Hithadoo Island, in Addu atoll, in 1992. By early 2005 there were 22 schools in Malé and 312 schools in the rest of the Maldives. There is a full-time vocational training centre, a teacher-training institute, an Institute of Hotel and Catering Services, an Institute of Management and Administration, a Science Education Centre, a Centre for Social Education, an Institute of Health Sciences, an Institute for Islamic Studies and a Centre for Continuing Education. The Maldives Institute of Technical Education, which was completed in late 1996, was expected to help to alleviate the problem of the lack of local skilled labour. The Maldives College of Higher Education, which was established to provide a uniform framework and policies for post-secondary education institutes, was opened in late 1998 and incorporates an Institute of Shari'a and Law. At least 116 of the country's schools were affected by the December 2004 tsunami. In the aftermath of the disaster eight schools required complete reconstruction. A large quantity of school equipment was also lost. Projected budgetary expenditure on education by the central Government in 2008 was 1,849.8m. rufiyaa, representing 16.3% of total spending.

Public Holidays

2009: 26 February* (National Day), 2 March† (Presidential Address), 9 March* (Birth of the Prophet Muhammad), 18 April (World Culture and Heritage Day), 10 May† (Day following General Election), 26–27 July (Independence Days), 22 August* (Ramadan begins), 20 September* (Id al-Fitr, end of Ramadan), 3 November (Victory Day), 11–12 November (Republic Days), 27 November* (Id al-Adha, feast of the Sacrifice), 10 December (Fishermen's Day), 18 December* (Islamic New Year).

2010: 15 February* (National Day), 26 February* (Birth of the Prophet Muhammad), 18 April (World Culture and Heritage Day), 26–27 July (Independence Days), 11 August* (Ramadan begins), 10 September* (Id al-Fitr, end of Ramadan), 3 November (Victory Day), 11–12 November (Republic Days), 16 November* (Id al-Adha, feast of the Sacrifice), 7 December* (Islamic New Year), 10 December (Fishermen's Day).

* These holidays are dependent on the Islamic lunar calendar and may vary by one or two days from the dates given.

† This is a 'one-off' holiday.

Weights and Measures

The metric system is in force, but imperial units are also used.

Statistical Survey

Source (unless otherwise stated): Ministry of Planning and National Development, Ghaazee Bldg, 4th Floor, Ameer Ahmed Magu, Malé 20-05; tel. 3322919; fax 3327351; internet www.planning.gov.mv.

AREA AND POPULATION

Area: 298 sq km (115 sq miles).

Population: 270,101 at census of 31 March–7 April 2000; 298,968 (males 151,459, females 147,509) at census of 21–28 March 2006. *Mid-2008* (official estimate): 309,575 (males 156,714, females 152,861).

Density (official estimate, mid-2008): 1,038.8 per sq km.

Administrative Divisions (population, 2006 census): *Capital City*: Malé 103,693. *Atolls*: North Thiladhunmathi 13,495; South Thiladhunmathi 16,237; North Miladhunmadulu 11,940; South Miladhunmadulu 10,015; North Maalhosmadulu 14,756; South Maalhosmadulu 9,578; Faadhippolhu 9,190; Malé 15,441; North Ari 5,776; South Ari 8,379; Felidhe 1,606; Mulakatholhu 4,710; North Nilandhe 3,765; South Nilandhe 4,967; Kolhumadulu 8,493; Hadhdhunmathi 11,990; North Huvadhu 8,262; South Huvadhu 11,013; Gnaviyani 7,636; Addu 18,026.

Births, Marriages and Deaths (2006 unless otherwise indicated): Registered live births 5,827 (birth rate 20 per 1,000); Marriages 5,556; Registered deaths 1,118 (death rate 3.7 per 1,000) (2007).

Life Expectancy (years at birth, WHO estimates): 72.3 (males 71.5; females 73.2) in 2006. Source: WHO, *World Health Statistics*.

Economically Active Population (persons aged 12 years and over, census of March 2006): Agriculture, hunting and forestry 4,236; Fishing 8,388; Mining and quarrying 339; Manufacturing 19,259; Electricity, gas and water 1,229; Construction 5,930; Wholesale and retail trade and repairs 11,711; Restaurants and hotels 12,090; Transport, storage and communications 7,098; Financing, insurance, real estate and business services 1,738; Public administration and defence 15,949; Education 9,872; Health and social work 4,182; Other community, social and personal service activities 3,248; Extra-territorial organizations and bodies 216; Activities not adequately defined 4,746; *Total employed* 110,231 (males 69,701, females 40,530); Unemployed 18,605; *Total labour force* 128,836.

HEALTH AND WELFARE

Key Indicators

Total Fertility Rate (children per woman, 2006): 2.6.

Under-5 Mortality Rate (per 1,000 live births, 2006): 30.0.

HIV/AIDS (% of persons aged 15–49, 2007): <0.1.

Physicians (per 1,000 head, 2004): 0.92.

Hospital Beds (per 1,000 head, 2003): 2.26.

Health Expenditure (2006): US $ per head (PPP): 882.

Health Expenditure (2006): % of GDP: 10.1.

Health Expenditure (2006): public (% of total): 84.1.

Access to Water (% of persons, 2006): 83.

Access to Sanitation (% of persons, 2006): 59.

Human Development Index (2006): ranking: 99.

Human Development Index (2006): value: 0.749.

For sources and definitions, see explanatory note on p. vi.

AGRICULTURE, ETC.

Principal Crops (production in long-term leased islands*, metric tons, 2007 unless otherwise indicated): Coconuts 94.4; Tender coconuts 116.2; Aubergines 31.7; Cucumbers 48.6; Pumpkins 48.4; Bitter gourds 4.4 (2006); Ridged peppers 63.6; Papayas 631.1; Watermelons 395.7; Bananas 499.

*Comprising the atolls of North Thiladhunmathi, South Thiladhunmathi, North Miladhunmadulu, South Ari, Mulakatholhu, North Nilandhe, Kolhumadulu and Hadhdhunmathi.

Coconuts (number): 40.6m. in 2004; 52.4m. in 2005; 64.1m. in 2006.

Sea Fishing ('000 metric tons, 2006): Total catch 184.2 (Skipjack tuna—Oceanic skipjack 138.5; Yellowfin tuna 21.8; Sharks, rays, skates, etc. 0.9). Source: FAO.

INDUSTRY

Selected Products (metric tons, 2003): Frozen tuna 47,546; Salted, dried or smoked fish 9.2; Canned fish 7,094. Source: FAO.

Electric Energy (million kWh): 204.1 in 2005; 233.3 in 2006; 269.8 in 2007.

FINANCE

Currency and Exchange Rates: 100 laari (larees) = 1 rufiyaa (Maldivian rupee). *Sterling, Dollar and Euro Equivalents* (31 December 2008): £1 sterling = 18.660 rufiyaa; US $1 = 12.800 rufiyaa; €1 = 17.814 rufiyaa; 1,000 rufiyaa = £53.59 = $78.13 = €56.14. *Exchange Rate* (rufiyaa per US dollar): since July 2001 the mid-point rate of exchange has been fixed at US $1 = 12.80 rufiyaa.

Budget (central government finance, million rufiyaa, 2008, estimates): *Revenue:* Tax revenue 3,291.5 (Import duty 2,409.3); Other current revenue 5,620.0 (Resort lease rents 1,403.6); Capital revenue 33.0; Grants 812.5; Total 9,757.0. *Expenditure:* General administration of public services 1,973.2; Defence 551.2; Public order and internal security 929.7; Environmental protection 152.5; Education 1,849.8; Health 1,286.8; Social security and welfare 626.0; Community programmes 1,968.8; Economic services 1,836.7 (Agriculture and fishing 249.1, Trade and industry 179.4, Electricity, gas and water 220.8, Transport and communications 1,016.8, Tourism 170.6); Interest on public debt 341.7; Net lending –194.8; Total 11,321.6 (Current 8,755.7, Capital and net lending 2,565.9).

International Reserves (US $ million at 31 December 2008): IMF special drawing rights 0.62; Reserve position in IMF 2.39; Foreign exchange 237.6; Total 240.6. Source: IMF, *International Financial Statistics.*

Money Supply (million rufiyaa at 31 December 2007): Currency outside banks 1,141.60; Demand deposits at commercial banks 3,221.37; Total money (incl. others) 4,404.73. Source: IMF, *International Financial Statistics.*

Cost of Living (Consumer Price Index; base: 2005 = 100): All items 103 in 2006; 111 in 2007. Source: IMF, *International Financial Statistics.*

Gross Value Added in Basic Prices (million rufiyaa at constant 1995 prices, 2008, estimates): Agriculture 206.6; Fishing and fisheries 553.3; Manufacturing 729.6; Electricity and water supply 485.9; Construction 699.2; Wholesale and retail trade 411.8; Transport and communications 1,993.2; Finance, real estate and business services 1,183.4; Tourism 2,991.2; Public administration 1,917.2; Other services 157.4; *Sub-total* 11,328.8; Financial intermediation services indirectly measured –427.1; *Gross value added in basic prices* 10,901.7.

Balance of Payments (US $ million, 2007): Exports of goods f.o.b. 228.0; Imports of goods f.o.b. –964.7; *Trade balance* –736.7; Exports of services 627.7; Imports of services –268.5; *Balance on goods and services* –377.5; Other income received 21.7; Other income paid –63.1; *Balance on goods, services and income* –418.9; Current transfers received –102.7; Current transfers paid 98.7; *Current balance* –422.9; Direct investment from abroad 15.0; Other investment assets 183.4; Other investment liabilities 246.7; Net errors and omissions 53.6; *Overall balance* 75.8. Source: IMF, *International Financial Statistics.*

EXTERNAL TRADE

Principal Commodities (million rufiyaa, 2007): *Imports c.i.f.:* Live animals and animal products 616.5; Vegetable products 803.8; Prepared foodstuffs; beverages, spirits and vinegar 862.6; Mineral products 3,233.1; Intermediate and capital goods 8,357.1 (Plastics and rubber and articles thereof 489.6; Wood, articles of wood, wood charcoal, cork and articles and pulp of wood 1,022.3; Construction materials 366.6; Base metal and articles of base metal 1,097.8; Machinery and mechanical appliances 2,997.2; Textiles 327.7; Chemicals and chemical products 650.3; Transport equipment and parts 653.3; Miscellaneous manufactured goods 752.1); Total (incl. others) 14,032.5. *Exports:* Marine products 1,357.2 (Fresh, chilled or frozen tuna 1,021.5, *of which* Skipjack 539.9; Yellowfin 272.7; Dried fish 98.5; Canned fish 137.9); Other products (mostly clothing and waste and scrap of alloy steel) 27.4; Total 1,384.6. *Re-exports:* (US $ million, 2007) 120.2.

Principal Trading Partners (million rufiyaa, 2007): *Imports:* Australia 326.5; China, People's Republic 313.1; France 150.6; Germany 304.6; India 1,611.4; Japan 264.6; Malaysia 1,195.5; Singapore 3,162.2; Sri Lanka 972.4; Thailand 678.6; United Arab Emirates 2,684.5; United Kingdom 205.8; USA 285.8; Total (incl. others) 14,032.5. *Exports:* France 102.1; Germany 21.9; Japan 63.1; Singapore 10.4; Sri Lanka 206.9; Thailand 566.5; United Kingdom 158.5; Total (incl. others) 1,384.6. *Re-exports:* (US $ million, 2007) 120.2.

TRANSPORT

Road Traffic (registered motor vehicles, 2007): Passenger cars 2,727; Buses, pick-ups and vans 2,172; Lorries and tractors 762; Motorcycles and mopeds 26,777; Total (incl. others) 33,803.

Merchant Shipping Fleet (displacement, '000 gross registered tons at 31 December): 87.4 in 2005; 99.9 in 2006; 125.5 in 2007. Source: Lloyd's Register-Fairplay, *World Fleet Statistics.*

International Shipping (freight traffic, '000 metric tons, 1990): Goods loaded 27; Goods unloaded 78. Source: UN, *Monthly Bulletin of Statistics.*

Civil Aviation (traffic at Malé International Airport, 2007): *International Flights:* Arrivals 833,436; Departures 824,592. *Domestic Flights:* Arrivals 398,430; Departures 411,112.

TOURISM

Tourist Arrivals: 395,320 in 2005; 601,923 in 2006; 675,889 in 2007.

Foreign Visitors by Country of Nationality (2007): Austria 13,673; China, People's Republic 35,976; France 45,301; Germany 72,269; India 17,327; Italy 117,246; Japan 41,121; Russia 31,845; Switzerland 26,183; United Kingdom 125,158; Total (incl. others) 675,889.

Tourism Receipts (US $ million): 286.6 in 2005; 433.7 in 2006; 493.6 in 2007.

COMMUNICATIONS MEDIA

Radio Receivers (July 2000): 29,724 registered.

Television Receivers (July 2000): 10,701 registered.

Telephones (main lines in use): 32,296 in 2005; 32,181 in 2006; 33,063 in 2007.

Mobile Cellular Telephones: 153,393 in 2005; 271,053 in 2006; 311,422 in 2007.

Personal Computers (2004): 36,000 in use.

Internet Users (registered): 1,288 in 2005; 1,323 in 2006; 1,311 in 2007.

Sources: Telecommunications Authority of Maldives, Malé; International Telecommunication Union.

EDUCATION

Schools (2007): 342 (government 219, community 45, private 78). Source: Ministry of Education.

Teachers (2007): Pre-primary 632 (males 27, females 605); Primary 3,463 (males 1,001, females 2,462); Lower secondary 2,569 (males 1,570, females 999); Upper secondary 322 (males 206, females 116). Source: Ministry of Education.

Pupils (2007): Pre-primary 14,851 (males 7,448, females 7,403); Primary 50,270 (males 26,221, females 24,049); Lower secondary 29,417 (males 14,407, females 15,010); Upper secondary 2,486 (males 1,300, females 1,186); Special needs 107 (males 59, females 48). Source: Ministry of Education.

Maldives College of Higher Education: Academic staff 138 (2003); Students 4,388 (2007). Source: Maldives College of Higher Education.

Adult Literacy Rate (UNESCO estimates): 97.0% (males 97.0%; females 97.1%) in 2007. Source: UNESCO Institute for Statistics.

Directory

The Constitution

On 7 August 2008 the President ratified a new 301-article Constitution. The main provisions are summarized below:

STATE, SOVEREIGNTY AND CITIZENS

The Maldives is a sovereign, independent, democratic republic based on the principles of Islam, and is a unitary State, to be known as the Republic of Maldives. In this Constitution, the Republic of Maldives shall hereinafter be referred to as 'the Maldives'.

The powers of the State of the Maldives shall be vested in the citizens. Legislative power is vested in the People's Majlis (People's Council), executive power is vested in the President and judicial power is vested in the courts of the Maldives.

The religion of the State of the Maldives is Islam. The national language of the Maldives shall be Dhivehi.

FUNDAMENTAL RIGHTS AND FREEDOMS

Maldivian citizens are equal before and under the law and are entitled to the equal protection and equal benefit of the law. The State has a duty to protect the natural environment, and undertakes to ensure citizens' rights to adequate nourishment, clothing, housing, healthcare and sewerage and electricity systems, and access to communications, transportation and natural resources.

The following are guaranteed: the right to privacy; the right to vote and run for public office; freedom of expression and the media; freedom of assembly and association; protection of the young, the elderly and the disadvantaged; the right to education, to work and to strike; the right to acquire and hold property; freedom of movement. No person shall be arrested or detained, except as provided by law.

Every citizen must respect the Constitution, the rule of law and the rights and freedoms of others.

THE PEOPLE'S MAJLIS

Legislative authority is vested in the People's Majlis. The People's Majlis shall consist of members elected from Malé and the 20 administrative atolls. The duration of the People's Majlis shall be five years from the first sitting. The Speaker and Deputy Speaker shall be elected from and by the members of the People's Majlis.

There shall be at least three regular sessions of the People's Majlis every year. Unless otherwise provided in the Constitution, matters proposed for passage in the People's Majlis shall be passed by a simple majority.

Prior to the commencement of each financial year, the Minister of Finance shall submit the proposed state budget for approval by the People's Majlis.

A bill passed by the People's Majlis shall become law and enter into force upon being assented to by the President.

Only under certain circumstances may the People's Majlis remove the President or Vice-President. A motion expressing want of confidence in a member of the Cabinet of Ministers may be moved in the People's Majlis.

THE PRESIDENT

Executive power is vested in the President. The President shall be the Head of State, Head of Government and the Commander-in-Chief of the Armed Forces. The term of office is five years, and no President shall serve for more than two terms.

The President shall be elected directly by the people, with more than 50% of the votes. Each presidential candidate must declare his or her proposed Vice-President.

In addition to the powers and functions expressly conferred on or assigned to the President by the Constitution and law, the President shall have the following powers and duties: to preside over the Cabinet of Ministers and to appoint, dismiss or accept the resignations of cabinet members; to appoint or remove members of diplomatic missions of the Maldives; to hold public referendums on major issues; to declare states of emergency, and war, and peace.

In the event that the presidency becomes vacant for any reason, the Vice-President shall become President.

THE CABINET OF MINISTERS

The Cabinet of Ministers is appointed by the President. The Cabinet of Ministers shall consist of the Vice-President, Ministers charged with responsibility for Ministries and the Attorney-General. All appointments to the Cabinet, except that of the Vice-President, must be approved by the People's Majlis.

The functions of the Cabinet of Ministers shall include the following: to advise and recommend draft bills and proposals to the President, to be prepared for submission to the People's Majlis; to assist the President in formulating government policy on important national and international matters and issues; and to direct, review and co-ordinate the political, economic and social development of the Maldives;

The Attorney-General shall advise the Government on all legal matters affecting the State.

The President may, at his discretion, remove any member of the Cabinet from office, but does not have the discretion to remove the Vice-President from office.

THE JUDICIARY

Judicial power is vested in the Supreme Court, the High Court and such Trial Courts as established by law. The Supreme Court shall be the highest authority for the administration of justice, and the Chief Justice shall be the highest authority on the Supreme Court.

The Supreme Court shall consist of the Chief Justice and such number of judges as provided by law. The Chief Justice and judges are appointed by the President following consultation with the Judicial Service Commission and approval by a majority in the People's Majlis.

INDEPENDENT COMMISSIONS AND OFFICES

The following independent and impartial institutions shall exist: the Judicial Service Commission, the Elections Commission, the Civil Service Commission, the Human Rights Commission and the Anti-Corruption Commission. There shall also be an independent and impartial Auditor-General and Prosecutor-General

PROCLAMATION OF EMERGENCY

In the event of natural disaster, dangerous epidemic disease, war, threat to national security or threatened foreign aggression, the President shall have the right to declare a state of emergency for a period not exceeding 30 days. The declaration must be submitted to the People's Majlis for approval; the People's Majlis has the right to approve, extend or revoke the declaration. Should the President wish to extend the declaration, the approval of the People's Majlis must be obtained.

GENERAL PROVISIONS

Other provisions made by the Constitution cover the areas of decentralized administration, security services, property, liabilities and legal actions of the State, amendment of the Constitution and transitional matters.

The Government

HEAD OF STATE

President: MOHAMED NASHEED (took office 11 November 2008).

THE CABINET OF MINISTERS
(May 2009)

A coalition of the Maldivian Democratic Party (MDP), the Jumhooree Party (JP, Republican Party), the Social Liberal Party (SLP), the National Unity Party (NUP, Gaumee Itthihaad), the Adhaalath Party (AP) and Independents (Ind.).

Vice-President: Dr MOHAMED WAHEED HASSAN MANIK (NUP).

Minister of Finance and Treasury and Acting Attorney-General: ALI HASHIM (MDP).

Minister of Foreign Affairs: Dr AHMED SHAHEED (Ind.).

Minister of Health and of Gender and Family: Dr AMINATH JAMEEL (MDP).

Minister of Defence and National Security and Acting Minister of Home Affairs: AMEEN FAISAL (MDP).

Minister of Education: Dr MUSTHAFA LUTHFY (NUP).

Minister of Economic Development: MOHAMED RASHEED (NUP).

Minister of Tourism, Arts and Culture: Dr AHMED ALI SAWAD (JP).

Minister of Human Resources, Youth and Sports: HASSAN LATHEEF (SLP).

THE MALDIVES

Minister of Housing, Transport and Environment: Mohamed Aslam (MDP).
Minister of Fisheries, Agriculture and Marine Resources: Dr Ibrahim Didi (MDP).
Minister of Civil Aviation and Communication: Dr Mohamed Jameel Ahmed (Ind.).
Minister of Islamic Affairs: Dr Abdul Majeed Abdul Bari (AP).

MINISTRIES

President's Office: Boduthakurufaanu Magu, Malé 20-05; tel. 3320701; fax 3325500; e-mail info@presidencymaldives.gov.mv; internet www.presidencymaldives.gov.mv.

Attorney-General's Office: Huravee Bldg, 3rd Floor, Ameer Ahmed Magu, Malé 20-05; tel. 3323809; fax 3314109; e-mail ashraf@agoffice.gov.mv.

Ministry of Atolls Development: Faashana Bldg, Boduthakurufaanu Magu, Malé 20-05; tel. 3323070; fax 3327750; e-mail info@atolls.gov.mv; internet www.atolls.gov.mv.

Ministry of Civil Aviation and Communication: 7th Floor, PA Complex, Hilaalee Magu, Malé 20–307; tel. 3324992; fax 3323039; e-mail civav@aviainfo.gov.mv; internet www.aviainfo.gov.mv.

Ministry of Construction and Public Infrastructure: Izzuddeenu Magu, Malé 20-01; tel. 3323234; fax 3328300; e-mail admin@construction.gov.mv; internet www.construction.gov.mv.

Ministry of Defence and National Security: Ameer Ahmed Magu, Malé 20-126; tel. 3322607; fax 3332689; e-mail admin@defence.gov.mv; internet www.defence.gov.mv.

Ministry of Economic Development: Ghaazee Bldg, Ameer Ahmed Magu, Malé 20-05; tel. 3323668; fax 3323840; e-mail contact@trademin.gov.mv; internet www.trade.gov.mv.

Ministry of Education: Ghaazee Bldg, 2nd Floor, Ameer Ahmed Magu, Malé 20-05; tel. 3323262; fax 3321201; e-mail foreign@moe.gov.mv; internet www.moe.gov.mv.

Ministry of Finance and Treasury: Block 379, Ameenee Magu, Malé 20-379; tel. 3349200; fax 3324432; e-mail admin@finance.gov.mv; internet www.finance.gov.mv.

Ministry of Fisheries, Agriculture and Marine Resources: Ghaazee Bldg, 1st Floor, Ameer Ahmed Magu, Malé 20-05; tel. 3322625; fax 3326558; e-mail it@fishagri.gov.mv; internet www.fishagri.gov.mv.

Ministry of Foreign Affairs: Boduthakurufaanu Magu, Malé 20-077; tel. 3323400; fax 3323841; e-mail admin@foreign.gov.mv; internet www.foreign.gov.mv.

Ministry of Gender and Family: FEN Bldg, 2nd Floor, Ameenee Magu, Malé 20-156; tel. 3328179; fax 3316237; e-mail admin@mgf.gov.mv; internet www.mgf.gov.mv.

Ministry of Health: Ameenee Magu, Malé 20-379; tel. 3328887; fax 3328889; e-mail moh@health.gov.mv; internet www.health.gov.mv.

Ministry of Higher Education, Employment and Social Security: Haveeree Hingun, Malé 20-125; tel. 3317172; fax 3331578; e-mail admin@employment.gov.mv; internet www.employment.gov.mv.

Ministry of Home Affairs: Huravee Bldg, 3rd Floor, Ameer Ahmed Magu, Malé 20-05; tel. 3323820; fax 3324739; e-mail minhah@dhivenhinet.net.mv; internet www.homeaffairs.gov.mv.

Ministry of Housing, Transport and Environment: 3rd Floor, Fen Bldg, Ameenee Magu, Malé 20-156; tel. 3324861; fax 3322286; e-mail secretariat@environment.gov.mv; internet www.environment.gov.mv.

Ministry of Human Resources, Youth and Sports: Haveeree Hingun, Malé 20-125; tel. 3347300; fax 3347490; e-mail admin@employment.gov.mv; internet www.employment.gov.mv.

Ministry of Islamic Affairs: POB 20103, Malé; tel. 3352671; fax 3323103.

Department of Justice: Justice Bldg, Orchid Magu, Malé 20-212; tel. 3322303; fax 3325447; e-mail admin@justice.gov.mv; internet www.justice.gov.mv.

Ministry of Planning and National Development: Ghaazee Bldg, 3rd Floor, Ameer Ahmed Magu, Malé 20-125; tel. 3348383; fax 3325371; e-mail info@planning.gov.mv; internet www.planning.gov.mv.

Ministry of Tourism, Arts and Culture: Ghazee Bldg, 1st Floor, Ameer Ahmed Magu, Malé 20-05; tel. 3323224; fax 3322512; e-mail info@maldivestourism.gov.mv; internet www.tourism.gov.mv.

President and Legislature

PRESIDENT

Presidential Election, First Ballot, 8 October 2008 (unofficial results)

Candidates	Votes	% of votes
Maumoon Abdul Gayoom (Dhivehi Rayyithunge Party)	71,731	40.34
Mohamed Nasheed (Maldivian Democratic Party)	44,293	24.91
Hassan Saeed (Independent)	29,633	16.67
Qasim Ibrahim (Jumhooree Party)	27,056	15.22
Umar Naseer (Islamic Democratic Party)	2,472	1.39
Ibrahim Ismail (Social Liberal Party)	1,382	0.77
Other (invalid)	1,235	0.69
Total	**177,802**	**100.0**

Presidential Election, Second Ballot, 28 October 2008 (unofficial results)

Candidates	Votes	% of votes
Mohamed Nasheed (Maldivian Democratic Party)	97,222	53.65
Maumoon Abdul Gayoom (Dhivehi Rayyithunge Party)	82,121	45.32
Other (invalid)	1,861	1.03
Total	**181,204**	**100.0**

LEGISLATURE
People's Majlis

The People's Majlis (People's Council) comprises members elected by the people of Malé and each of the 20 atolls (for a five-year term).

Speaker: Mohamed Shihab.
Deputy Speaker: Aneesa Ahmed.

Election, 9 May 2009 (preliminary results)

Party	Seats
Dhivehi Rayyithunge Party	28
Maldivian Democratic Party	26
Independents	13
People's Alliance	7
Dhivehi Qaumee Party	2
Jumhooree Party	1
Total	**77**

Elections Commission

Elections Commission of Maldives: PA Complex, 3rd Floor, Hilaalee Magu, Malé; tel. 3324426; fax 3323997; e-mail info@elections.gov.mv; internet www.elections.gov.mv; f. 1998; independent; five-mem. commission nominated and appointed by People's Majlis; Pres. Mohamed Ibrahim; Vice-Pres. Ahmed Shahid; Commrs Mohamed Mahir, Fuad Thaufeeq.

Political Organizations

In June 2005 legislation was approved permitting the establishment of political parties in the Maldives for the first time since 1952.

Adhaalath Party (Justice Party): Malé; internet www.adhaalath.org.mv; f. 2005; Leader Sheikh Hussain Rasheed Ahmed.

Dhivehi Qaumee Party (DQP): Malé; internet www.quamee.org.mv; f. 2009; Leader Dr Hassan Saeed; Gen. Sec. Abdulla Ameen.

Dhivehi Rayyithunge Party (DRP) (Maldivian People's Party): Sinamalé 3 Galolhu, Malé; tel. 3320456; fax 3344774; e-mail info@drp.org.mv; internet www.drp.org.mv; f. 2005; Leader Maumoon Abdul Gayoom; Sec.-Gen Dr Abdullah Mausoom.

Islamic Democratic Party: Malé; tel. 3326962; fax 3327385; e-mail info@idp.org.mv; internet www.idp.org.mv; f. 2005; Pres. Umar Naseer; Dep. Leader Mohamed Hassan Manik.

Jumhooree Party (JP) (Republican Party): M. Chan'beyleege, 4th floor, Malé; tel. 3309595; fax 3306699; Leader Gasim Ibrahim.

Maldivian Democratic Party (MDP): H. Sharaashaa, 1st Floor, Sosun Magu, Malé 20-059; tel. 3340044; fax 3322960; e-mail secretariat@mdp.org.mv; internet www.mdp.org.mv; f. 2001; fmrly based in Colombo, Sri Lanka; official registration in Maldives permitted June 2005; Chair. MARIYA AHMED DIDI; Vice-Pres. and Acting Pres. IBRAHIM HUSSAIN DIDI; Sec.-Gen. AISHATH ANIYA.

Maldivian National Congress (MNC): G. Blue Lagoon, 1st Floor, Faashanakilege Magu, Malé; tel. 3316944; fax 3348988; e-mail secretariat@mnc.org.mv; internet www.mnc.org.mv; f. 2007; Founder and Leader MOHAMED MONAZA NAEEM.

Maldivian Social Democratic Party: Malé; f. 2006; Leader IBRAHIM ('REEKO') MANIK.

National Unity Party (NUP, Gaumee Itthihaad): Malé; f. 2008; Chair. Dr MOHAMED WAHEED HASSAN MANIK.

People's Alliance: Malé; f. 2008; Founder and Leader ABDULLAH YAMEEN.

People's Party: Malé.

Poverty Alleviating Party (PAP): Malé; f. 2008; Vice-Pres. AHMED SALEEM (acting).

Social Liberal Party (SLP): Malé; f. 2008 as breakaway faction of the Maldivian Democratic Party; Leader MAZLAN RASHEED; Dep. Leader HASSAN LATHEEF.

Diplomatic Representation

HIGH COMMISSIONS IN THE MALDIVES

Bangladesh: M. Kurinbee Lodge, 5th Floor, Izzudheen Magu, Malé; tel. 3315541; fax 3315543; e-mail bdootmal@dhivehinet.net.mv; High Commissioner Prof. SELINA MOHSIN.

India: H. Athireege-Aage, Ameeru Ahmed Magu, Malé; tel. 3323015; fax 3324778; e-mail hcmale@hicomindia.com.mv; High Commissioner Dr D. M. MULAY.

Pakistan: G. Helengely, Lily Magu, Malé; tel. 3323005; fax 3321832; e-mail pahicmale@hotmail.com; High Commissioner Dr JAMALUDDIN.

Sri Lanka: H. Haifa Bldg, Bodufungadu Magu, Malé; tel. 3322845; fax 3321652; e-mail highcom@dhivehinet.net.mv; High Commissioner MOHAMED ALI FAROOK.

Judicial System

The administration of justice is undertaken in accordance with Islamic (*Shari'a*) law. In 1980 the Maldives High Court was established. There are four courts in Malé, and one island court in every inhabited island.

In January 1999 the Government declared that the island court of each atoll capital would thenceforth oversee the administration of justice in that atoll. At the same time it was announced that arrangements were being made to appoint a senior magistrate in each atoll capital.

According to the provisions of the new Constitution, which was enacted in August 2008, a Supreme Court—the highest authority for the administration of justice in the Maldives—was to be formed. In the following month the President appointed five judges to the interim Supreme Court after consultation with the newly established Judicial Service Commission and confirmation of the appointments by a two-thirds' majority of the People's Majlis. With the establishment of the Supreme Court, there was to be no further recourse of appeal from the High Court to the President. The interim Supreme Court was to function until a new Chief Justice and judges to the Supreme Court were appointed by the President after the election of a new People's Majlis in May 2009. The Maldives' first Prosecutor-General was appointed by the President in early September 2008, following approval by the People's Majlis.

Prosecutor-General: AHMED MUIZZU.

SUPREME COURT

Chief Justice: ABDULLA SAEED (acting).

Acting Judges: AHMED FAIZ HUSSAIN, ABDULLA ARIF, MUJTHAZ FAHUMY, YOOSUF HUSSAIN.

Religion

Islam is the state religion, and the majority of Maldivians are Sunni Muslims. In mid-1991 there were 724 mosques and 266 women's mosques throughout the country.

In November 2008 the new President, Mohamed Nasheed, established a new Ministry of Islamic Affairs to replace the Supreme Council for Islamic Affairs, which had been founded by former President Maumoon Abdul Gayoom in 1996 to authorize state policies with regard to Islam and to advise the Government on Islamic affairs.

The Press

In 1993 the Government established a National Press Council to review, monitor and further develop journalism in the Maldives.

DAILIES

Aafathis Daily News: Silver Cloud, Maafannu, Malé 20-02; tel. 3318609; fax 3312425; e-mail aafathis@dhivehinet.net.mv; internet www.aafathisnews.com.mv; f. 1979; Dhivehi and English; Editor ABDULLAH NAEEM IBRAHIM; circ. 3,000.

Dhives: Malé; f. 2009; organ of the Dhivehi Rayyithunge Party; Editor AHMED NIHAN.

Haama Daily: Ma. Night Rose, Dhilbahaaru Magu, POB 20232, Malé; tel. 3340077; fax 3343726; e-mail haama@haamadaily.com; internet www.haamadaily.com; Dhivehi and English; Chair. QASIM IBRAHIM.

Haveeru Daily: Ameenee Magu, POB 20103, Malé; tel. 3325671; fax 3323103; e-mail haveeru@haveeru.com.mv; internet www.haveeru.com.mv; f. 1979; Dhivehi and English; Chair. MOHAMED ZAHIR HUSSAIN; Editor ALI RAFEEQ; circ. 4,500.

Jazeera Daily: M. Zenthuram, Izzudheen Magu, Malé; tel. 3343738; fax 3343736; e-mail info@jazeera.com.mv; internet www.jazeera.com.mv.

Miadhu News: G. Mascot, Koimalaa Hingun, Malé 20-02; tel. 3320700; fax 3320500; e-mail miadhu@dhivehinet.net.mv; internet www.miadhu.com.mv; Chair. MOHAMED NABEEL; Editor JAUFAR RASHEED.

Minivan News: Malé; tel. 3334888; e-mail minivan.news@gmail.com; internet www.minivannews.com; f. 2005; independent; predominantly Dhivehi, with English section; Editor AMINATH NAJEEB.

Raajje Daily: Malé; f. 2008; independent; predominantly Dhivehi with English section; Editor HASSAN SAEED.

Sangu Daily: G. Aabin, Dhonadharaadhahigun, Malé; tel. 3300065; fax 3300064; e-mail sangu@sangudaily.com; internet www.sangudaily.com; Editor IKRAM ABDUL LATHEEF.

PERIODICALS

Adduvas: Malé; f. 2000; weekly; news, entertainment, health issues and social affairs; Editor AISHATH VELEZINEE.

Dhivehingetharika (Maldivian Heritage): National Centre for Linguistic and Historical Research, Soasun Magu, Malé 20-05; tel. 3323206; fax 3326796; e-mail nclhr@dhivehinet.net.mv; internet www.qaumiyyath.gov.mv; f. 1998; Dhivehi; Maldivian archaeology, history and language.

The Evening Weekly: Ameenee Magu, POB 20103, Malé; tel. 3325671; fax 3323103; e-mail info@eveningweekly.com.mv; internet www.haveeru.com.mv; weekly; English; owned by the Haveeru news group; Chair. MOHAMED ZAHIR HUSSAIN.

Faiythoora: National Centre for Linguistic and Historical Research, Soasun Magu, Malé 20-05; tel. 3323206; fax 3326796; e-mail nclhr@dhivehinet.net.mv; internet www.qaumiyyath.gov.mv; f. 1979; monthly magazine; Dhivehi; Maldivian history, culture and language; Editor UZ ABDULLA HAMEED; circ. 800.

Furadhaana: Dept of Information, Ministry of Tourism, Arts and Culture, Ghazee Bldg, 1st Floor, Ameer Ahmed Magu, Malé 20-05; tel. 3323224; fax 3322512; e-mail informat@dhivehinet.net.mv; internet www.maldivesinfo.gov.mv; f. 1990; monthly; Dhivehi; Editor IBRAHIM MANIK; circ. 1,000.

Hidhaayathuge Magu (The Road to Steadfastness): Malé; f. 2008; weekly; Dhivehi; religious; publ. by the Ministry of Islamic Affairs.

Huvaas Magazine: Ameenee Magu, POB 20103, Malé; tel. 3325671; fax 3323103; e-mail huvaas@haveeru.com.mv; internet www.haveeru.com.mv/huvaas; f. 2001; fortnightly; Chair. Dr MOHAMED ZAHIR HUSSAIN.

Jamaathuge Khabaru (Community News): Centre for Continuing Education, Salahudeen Bldg, Malé 20-04; tel. 3328772; fax 3322223; monthly; Dhivehi; Editor AHMED ZAHIR; circ. 1,500.

Maldives News Bulletin: Maldives News Bureau, Department of Information, Ministry of Tourism, Arts and Culture, Ghazee Bldg, 1st Floor, Ameer Ahmed Magu, Malé 20-05; tel. 3323224; fax 3322512; e-mail informat@dhivehinet.net.mv; internet www.maldivesinfo.gov.mv; f. 1980; weekly; English; Editor ALI SHAREEF; circ. 350.

Marine Research Centre Bulletin: Marine Research Centre, Ministry of Fisheries, Agriculture and Marine Resources, H. White Waves, Malé 20-06; tel. 3322242; fax 3322509; e-mail info@mrc.gov

.mv; f. 1984; biannual; fisheries and marine research; Exec. Dir Dr MOHAMED SHIHAM ADAM.

Monday Times: H. Neel Villa, Boduthakunufaanu Magu, Malé; tel. and fax 3315084; f. 2000; banned 2002; relaunched 2004; weekly.

Our Environment: Forum of Writers on the Environment, c/o Ministry of Planning and National Development, Ghaazee Bldg, Ameer Ahmed Magu, Malé 20-05; tel. 3324861; fax 3327351; f. 1990; monthly; Dhivehi; Editor FAROUQ AHMED.

Rasain: Ministry of Fisheries, Agriculture and Marine Resources, Ghaazee Bldg, Ameer Ahmed Magu, Malé 20-05; tel. 3322625; fax 3326558; e-mail fishagri@dhivehinet.net.mv; f. 1980; annual; fisheries devt.

Samugaa: Malé; f. 1995; publ. by the Government Employees' Club.

NEWS AGENCIES

Haveeru News Service (HNS): POB 20103, Malé; tel. 3313825; fax 3323103; e-mail haveeru@haveeru.com.mv; internet www.haveeru.com.mv; f. 1979; Chair. MOHAMED ZAHIR HUSSAIN; Man. Editor AHMED ZAHIR.

Maldives News Bureau (MNB): Department of Information, Ministry of Tourism, Arts and Culture, Ghazee Bldg, 1st Floor, Ameer Ahmed Magu, Malé 20-05; tel. 3323224; fax 3322512; e-mail informat@dhivehinet.net.mv; internet www.maldivesinfo.gov.mv.

Publishers

Corona Press: Feeroaz Magu, Maafannu, Malé; tel. 3310052; fax 3314741.

Cypea Printers: 25 Boduthakurufaanu Magu, Malé; tel. 3333883; fax 3323523; e-mail cyprea@dhivehinet.net.mv; f. 1984 as Cyprea Printers; Man. Dir ABDULLA SAEED.

Loamaafaanu Print: Alkariyya Bldg, Ground Floor, Ameenee Magu, Malé 20-354; tel. 3317209; fax 3313815; e-mail haveeru@netlink.net.mv.

Novelty Printers and Publishers: M. Vaarey Villa, Izzudhdheen Magu, Malé 20-317; tel. 3318844; fax 3327039; e-mail novelty@dhivehinet.net.mv; f. 1965; general and reference books; Man. Dir ASAD ALI.

Ummeedhee Press: M. Aasthaanaa Javaahirumagu, Malé 20-02; tel. 3325110; fax 3326412; e-mail ummpress@dhivehinet.net.mv; f. 1986; printing and publishing; Principal Officers ABDUL SHAKOOR ALI, MOHAMED SHAKOOR.

Broadcasting and Communications

TELECOMMUNICATIONS

In March 2007 a privately owned submarine fibre-optic cable link between the Maldives and India was inaugurated in an effort to provide more affordable, reliable telecommunications access to islanders and to enhance international connectivity.

Telecommunications Authority of Maldives: Telecom Bldg, Husnuheena Magu, Malé 20-04; tel. 3323344; fax 3320000; e-mail secretariat@tam.gov.mv; internet www.tam.gov.mv; f. 2003; regulatory authority; Chair. Dr HASSAN HAMEED; CEO MOHAMED AMIR.

Dhivehi Raajjeyge Gulhun Ltd (Dhiraagu): 19 Medhuziyaaraiy Magu, POB 2082, Malé 20-03; tel. 3322802; fax 3322800; e-mail 123@dhiraagu.com.mv; internet www.dhiraagu.com.mv; f. 1988; jtly owned by the Maldivian Govt (55%) and by Cable and Wireless PLC of the United Kingdom (45%); operates all nat. and int. telecommunications services in the Maldives (incl. internet service—Dhivehinet); CEO ISMAIL RASHEED.

Wataniya Telecom Maldives Pvt Ltd: 2nd Floor, Urban Development Bldg, Hulhumalé; tel. 9621111; fax 3350519; e-mail media@wataniya-maldives.com; internet www.wataniya.mv; f. 2005; provides advanced cellular mobile telephone services throughout the Maldives; Chair. SOLAH FAHUD SULTAN; CEO ABRAHAM SMITH.

> **WARF Telecom International (Pvt) Ltd:** Hulhumalé; f. 2005 by jt venture of Wataniya Telecom Maldives, Reliance Communications (India), and Focus Infocomm to lay fibre-optic cable between Hulhumalé and mainland India; owned by Wataniya Telecom Maldives (65%), Reliance Communications Ltd (20%) and Focus Infocomm (15%); awarded 15-year operating licence in March 2007; CEO AHMAD HALEEM.

RADIO

From May 2007 the Maldives Government permitted private broadcasting under its 'Roadmap for the Reform Agenda' programme. Five national radio stations and a number of small local operators secured terrestrial broadcasting rights. The first private radio station commenced broadcasting operations in July.

Capital Radio: 03 Marvel, Roashanee Magu, Malé 20-05; tel. 3310214; fax 3310213; e-mail info@capital956.fm; internet www.capital956live.com; f. 2007; operated by Asna Maldives Pte Ltd; broadcasts BBC news bulletins, music, current affairs and analysis programmes; Man. Dir MOHAMED NASHEED.

DhiFM 95.2: Malé; e-mail admin@dhifm.com; internet www.dhifm.fm; f. 2007; operated by Maldives Media Co Pvt; broadcasts news, music and general interest programmes in Dhivehi and English; operates 24-hour nationwide service; Chief Exec. Dir IBRAHIM KHALEEL; Editorial Dir MASOOD ALI.

HFM 92.6: Ma. Thimarafusheege, 8th Floor, Dhilbahaaru Magu, POB 20231, Malé; tel. 3301171; fax 3301170; e-mail info@hfm.com.mv; internet www.hfm.com.mv; f. 2008; operated by Haveeru Media Group; broadcasts 24 hrs daily.

Radio Atoll: Ma. Eastern Lagoon, POB 20193, Malé 20; tel. 3349696; fax 3319600; e-mail info@radioatoll.com; internet www.radioatoll.com; broadcasts current affairs, entertainment and general interest programmes.

Voice of Islam: Malé.

Voice of Maldives (VOM) (Dhivehi Raajjeyge Adu): Voice of Maldives Bldg, Maafaanu, Malé; tel. 3314515; fax 3317273; e-mail gs@vom.gov.mv; internet www.vom.gov.mv; radio broadcasting began in 1962 under name of Malé Radio; name changed as above in 1980; operates one channel for religious broadcasts and another for music and current affairs; home service in Dhivehi and English; began broadcasting 24 hrs daily from Jan. 2005; Dir-Gen. BADRU NASEER.

TELEVISION

Under the Maldivian Government's 'Roadmap for the Reform Agenda', licences for the establishment of national television stations were made available to bidders in May 2007. The development represented significant progress towards the liberalization of this previously state-dominated sector.

Atoll Television: Majeediyya Alimas Ufaa, Boduthakurufaanu Magu, Henveiru, Malé; tel. 326638; fax 327143; e-mail atoll@airatoll.com; f. 2007; operated by Atoll Investment Pvt Ltd.

DhiTV: Champa Bldg, Daisy Magu, Galolhu, Malé 20-02; tel. 3304555; fax 3307666; e-mail info@dhitv.com.mv; internet www.dhitv.com.mv; f. 2008; pvt cable television channel; Founder CHAMPA MOHAMED MOOSA.

Future Television: Malé; f. 2008; broadcasts for 12 hrs daily in Dhivehi; Man. Dir MOHAMED FAYAZ.

Television Maldives: Buruzu Magu, Malé 20-144; tel. 3342200; fax 3325083; e-mail comments@tvm.gov.mv; internet www.tvm.gov.mv; television broadcasting began in 1978; two channels: TVM broadcasts for an average of 18 hrs daily and TVM Plus (f. 1994) broadcasts for 10 hrs daily; covers a 40-km radius around Malé; Exec. Dir HUSSAIN MOHAMED.

Finance

(cap. = capital; res = reserves; dep. = deposits; m. = million; brs = branches; amounts in US dollars unless otherwise stated)

BANKING

Central Bank

Maldives Monetary Authority (MMA): Boduthakurufaanu Magu, Malé 20-182; tel. 3312343; fax 3323862; e-mail mail@mma.gov.mv; internet www.mma.gov.mv; f. 1981; bank of issue; supervises and regulates commercial bank and foreign-exchange dealings and advises the Govt on banking and monetary matters; authorized cap. 4m. rufiyaa, res 126.8m. rufiyaa, dep. 4,010.4m. rufiyaa (Dec. 2007); Gov. FAZEEL NAJEEB.

Commercial Bank

Bank of Maldives PLC: 11 Boduthakurufaanu Magu, Malé 20-094; tel. 3330100; fax 3328233; e-mail bmlho@dhivehinet.net.mv; internet www.bankofmaldives.com.mv; f. 1982; 75% state-owned; cap. 36.5m., res 597.0m., dep. 4,393.9m. (Dec. 2006); Chair. SALAH SHIHAB; Man. Dir and CEO SERENA HO OI KHUEN; 24 brs.

DEVELOPMENT FINANCE ORGANIZATION

Housing Development Finance Corpn: 4th Floor, H. Milani, Sosun Magu, Malé; tel. 3338810; fax 3315138; e-mail h@hdfc.com.mv; internet www.hdfc.com.mv; f. 2004 to provide public housing loans; 100% state-owned; Chair. IBRAHIM NAEEM.

THE MALDIVES

INSURANCE

Allied Insurance Co of the Maldives (Pte) Ltd: 04–06 STO Trade Centre, Orchid Magu, Malé 20-02; tel. 3324612; fax 3325035; e-mail info@alliedmaldives.net; internet www.alliedmaldives.com; f. 1985; all classes of non-life insurance; operated by State Trading Organization (see below); Chair. IBRAHIM SHAREEF MOHAMED; Man. Dir ABDUL WAHID THOWFEEQ.

Trade and Industry

GOVERNMENT AGENCY

Invest Maldives: Ministry of Economic Development, Ghazee Bldg, 1st Floor, Malé 20-05; tel. 3324767; fax 3322528; e-mail info@investmaldives.org; internet www.investmaldives.org; government agency established to promote, regulate and license foreign investment; under administration of Ministry of Economic Development; Dir-Gen. AHMED NASEEM.

CHAMBER OF COMMERCE AND INDUSTRY

Maldives National Chamber of Commerce and Industry (MNCCI): G. Viyafaari Hiya, Ameenee Magu, Malé 20-04; tel. 3326634; fax 3310233; e-mail mncci@dhivehinet.net.mv; internet www.mncci.com.mv; f. 1978; merged with the Maldivian Traders' Assen in 2000; Pres. IBRAHIM JIHAD.

INDUSTRIAL AND TRADE ASSOCIATIONS

Maldives Association of Construction Industry (MACI): PA Complex, Ground Floor, Hilaalee Magu, Malé; tel. 3318660; fax 3318796; e-mail maci@dhivehinet.net.mv; internet www.maci.org.mv; f. 2001; Pres. MOHAMED ALI JANAH; Treas. AHMED ABDULLA.

Sri Lanka Trade Centre: Girithereyege Bldg, 3rd Floor, Hithaffinivaa Magu, Malé; tel. 3315183; fax 3315184; e-mail dirsltc@avasmail.com.mv; f. 1993 to facilitate and promote trade, tourism, investment and services between Sri Lanka and the Maldives; Dir M. I. SUFIYAN.

State Trading Organization PLC (STO): STO Bldg, Boduthakurufaanu Magu, Maafanau, Malé 20-345; tel. 3344333; fax 3344334; e-mail info@stomaldives.net; internet www.stomaldives.com; f. 1964 as Athirimaafannuge Trading Account, renamed as above in 1976; became public limited company in 2001; state-controlled commercial org.; under administration of independent Board of Directors; imports and distributes staple foods, fuels, pharmaceuticals and general consumer items; acts as purchaser for govt requirements; undertakes long-term devt projects; Chair. FAROOQ UMAR; Man. Dir SHAHID ALI.

UTILITIES

Electricity

Maldives Energy Authority: 4th Floor, Fen Bldg, Ameeenee Magu, Malé 20-156; tel. 3331695; fax 3331043; e-mail mea@meew.gov.mv; f. 2006 to replace Maldives Electricity Bureau; under administration of Ministry of Housing, Transport and Environment; regulatory authority; Dir-Gen. ABDULLA WAHID.

State Electric Co (STELCO) Ltd: Ameenee Magu, Malé; tel. 3320982; fax 3327036; e-mail admin@stelco.com.mv; internet www.stelco.com.mv; f. 1997 to replace Maldives Electricity Board; under administration of Ministry of Economic Development; provides electricity, consultancy services, electrical spare parts service, etc.; operates 28 power stations; installed capacity 57,134.8 kW (2007); Chair. HASSAN ZAHIR; 650 employees (2006).

Gas

Maldive Gas Pvt Ltd: STO Trade Centre, 1st Floor, Orchid Magu, Malé; tel. 3335614; fax 3335615; e-mail info@maldivegas.com; internet www.maldivegas.com; f. 1999 as a jt venture between State Trading Organization and Champa Gas and Oil Co; Chair. MOHAMED MANIK.

Water

Maldives Water and Sanitation Authority (MWSA): Ameenee Magu, Malé; tel. 3317563; fax 3317569; e-mail shaheedha@mwsa.gov.mv; internet www.mwsa.gov.mv; f. 1973; Dir-Gen. Dr MOHAMED ALI.

Malé Water and Sewerage Co Pvt Ltd: Ameenee Magu, Machangolhi, POB 2148, Malé 20375; tel. 3323209; fax 3324306; e-mail mwsc@dhivehinet.net.mv; internet www.mwsc.com.mv; f. 1995; 76% govt-owned; produces approximately 8,500 metric tons of fresh, desalinated water daily, using seven plants; provides water and sewerage services to the islands of Malé, Hulhumalé and Villingili; provides water services to the islands of Maafushi and L. Gan; Chair. AHMED MANSOOR; Man. Dir MOHAMED AHMED DIDI.

Transport

Maldives Transport and Contracting Co Ltd (MTCC): MTCC Bldg, 5th Floor, Boduthakurufaanu Magu, POB 263, Malé 20-181; tel. 3326822; fax 3323221; e-mail info@mtcc.com.mv; internet www.mtcc.com.mv; f. 1980; 60% state-owned, 40% privately owned; marine transport, civil and technical contracting, harbour devt, shipping agents for general cargo, passenger liners and oil tankers; Chair. HUSSAIN HILMY; Man. Dir MOHAMED NASEEM IBRAHIM.

SHIPPING

Vessels operate from the Maldives to Sri Lanka and Singapore at frequent intervals, also calling at points in India, Pakistan, Myanmar (formerly Burma), Malaysia, Bangladesh, Thailand, Indonesia and the Middle East. In December 2005 the merchant shipping fleet of the Maldives numbered 70 vessels, with a combined aggregate displacement of 87,402 grt; by 31 December 2007 the displacement had increased to 125,500 grt. Smaller vessels provide services between the islands on an irregular basis. Malé is the only port handling international traffic. In 1986 a new commercial harbour was opened in Malé. The Malé Harbour Development Project was implemented during 1991–97, and improved and increased the capacity and efficiency of Malé Port. In July 2003 a new harbour was opened in Fuvah Mulah, on Gnaviyani atoll. Ambitious government-led plans for the construction of 60 new harbours and a transhipment port in the north of the country were under development in 2006–08.

Maldives Ports Authority (MPA): Boduthakurufaanu Magu, Maafaanu, Malé 20-250; tel. 3329339; fax 3325293; e-mail info@maldport.com.mv; internet www.maldport.com.mv; f. 1986; owned by govt-owned Maldives Ports Ltd; Chair. HUSSAIN NIZAR; Man. Dir MAHUDHY IMAD.

Island Enterprises Pvt Ltd: Maaram, 1st Floor, Ameeru Ahmed Magu, POB 2169, Malé 20-077; tel. 3323531; fax 3325645; e-mail info@ielmaldives.com; internet www.ielmaldives.com; f. 1978; fleet of eight vessels; exporters of frozen fish, owners of processing plant, shipping agents, chandlers, cruising agents, surveyors and repairs; Man. Dir MAIZAN OMAR MANIK.

   Precision Marine Pvt Ltd: H. Maaram, 1st Floor, Ameeru Ahmed Magu, Malé; tel. 3315663; fax 3315107; e-mail info@pmlboatyard.com.mv; internet www.pmlboatyard.com.mv; f. 1990; mfrs and repairers of fibreglass boats, launches, yachts, marine sports equipment, etc.; Man. Dir OMAR MANIKU.

Maldives National Shipping Ltd: Ship Plaza, 2nd Floor, 1/6 Orchid Magu, POB 2022, Malé 20-02; tel. 3323871; fax 3324323; e-mail male@maldiveshipping.com.mv; internet www.maldiveshipping.com; f. 1965; 100% state-owned; fleet of three container vessels; br. in Singapore; Chair. AIMON JAMEEL.

Matrana Enterprises (Pvt) Ltd: 79 Majeedhee Magu, Malé; tel. 3331166; fax 3322832; e-mail webmaster@matrana.org; Sr Exec. MOHAMED ABDULLA.

Villa Shipping and Trading Co (Pvt) Ltd: Villa Bldg, POB 2073, Malé 20-02; tel. 3325195; fax 3325177; e-mail info@villa.com.mv; internet www.villa.com.mv; operates five tourist resorts and owns a trading operation supported by a fleet of eight cargo vessels and tankers; Man. Dir QASIM IBRAHIM.

CIVIL AVIATION

The existing airport on Hululé Island near Malé, which was first opened in 1966, was expanded and improved to international standard with financial assistance from abroad and, as Malé International Airport, was officially opened in 1981. Charter flights from Europe subsequently began. Further expansion was completed in 2006, including the construction of the world's largest water aerodrome. Proposals have been put forward for the construction of a second runway.

In addition, there are four domestic airports covering different regions of the country. These are located on Gan Island, Addu atoll, on Kadhdhoo Island, Hadhdhummathi atoll, on Hanimaadhoo Island, South Thiladhummathi atoll, and on Kaadedhdhoo Island, South Huvadhu atoll; there are plans to build a further airport on Maamigili Island, Alif Dhaal atoll. The airport on Gan Island was expected to begin servicing international flights in 2009. In early 1995 there were 10 helipads in use in the Maldives.

Maldives Airport Co Ltd (MACL): Malé International Airport, Hululé 22-000; tel. 3338800; fax 3331515; e-mail info@maclnet.net; internet www.airports.com.mv; f. 2000; 100% govt-owned; under administration of Ministry of Civil Aviation and Communication; serviced by 13 charter airlines and 12 scheduled carriers; CEO MOHAMED AMIR.

Island Aviation Services Ltd: 26 Ameer Ahmed Magu, Malé; tel. 3335566; fax 3314806; e-mail info@island.com.mv; internet www.island.com.mv; f. 2000; 100% govt-owned; operates domestic flights;

THE MALDIVES

commenced flights to Sri Lanka in Jan. 2008; Chair. MOHAMED UMAR MANIK; Man. Dir BANDHU IBRAHIM SALEEM.

Maldivian Air Taxi: Kaafu Hulhulé, POB 2023, Malé; tel. 3315201; fax 3315203; e-mail fawzy@maldivianairtaxi.com; internet www.maldivianairtaxi.com; f. 1993; seaplane services between Malé and outer islands; operates 24 aircraft; Chair. LARS ERIK NIELSEN; Gen. Man. AUM FAWZY.

Trans Maldivian Airways (Pvt) Ltd: Malé International Airport, POB 2079, Malé; tel. 3348400; fax 3348409; e-mail mail@tma.com.mv; internet www.tma.com.mv; f. 1989 as Hummingbird Island Airways Pvt Ltd; name changed as above in 2000; operates 35 aircraft; Man. Dir EDWARD ALSFORD.

Tourism

The tourism industry brings considerable foreign exchange to the Maldives. The islands' attractions include white sandy beaches, excellent diving conditions and multi-coloured coral formations. At the end of 2004 there were 87 island resorts in operation, and some 16,858 hotel beds were available; a further 8,000 beds were to supplement capacity in 2007 when 35 new resorts were scheduled to commence operations. An additional 50 resorts were forecast to open between 2010 and 2012. The annual total of foreign visitors increased from only 29,325 in 1978 to 616,716 in 2004. Revenue from tourism amounted to 921.5m. rufiyaa in the latter year. It was feared that the devastating effect on the Maldives of the tsunami in the Indian Ocean in December 2004 would severely affect the country's tourism industry. By the end of 2005 all the resorts affected by the tsunami had reopened. However, tourist arrivals in that year totalled only 395,320, a decline of 35.9% compared with the previous year. The number of arrivals had almost completely recovered, to a reported 601,923, by the end of 2006 and estimated receipts from tourism in that year increased by an impressive 85.4%, compared with 2005, to reach 1,685.9m. rufiyaa. In 2007 a record number of visitor arrivals was achieved, at 675,889, and receipts from tourism (in US dollar terms) rose by 13.8%, compared with the previous year, to reach US $493.6m.

Maldives Association of Tourism Industry (MATI): Gadhamoo Bldg, 3rd Floor, Boduthakurufaanu Magu, POB 2056, Malé; tel. 3326640; fax 3326641; e-mail mati@dhivehinet.net.mv; internet www.mati.com.mv; f. 1984; promotes and develops tourism; Chair. MOHAMED UMAR MANIKU; Sec.-Gen. SIM I. MOHAMED.

Maldives Tourism Promotion Board: H. Aage, 3rd Floor, 12 Boduthakurufaanu Magu, Malé 20-05; tel. 3323228; fax 3323229; e-mail mtpb@visitmaldives.com; internet www.visitmaldives.com; f. 1998; Dir Dr ABDULLA MAUSOOM.

Air Maldives Travel Bureau/Tourist Information: Aifaan Bldg, Boduthakurufaanu Magu, Malé; tel. 3310917; fax 3318757; e-mail airmldvs@dhivehinet.net.mv; f. 1997.

MALI

Introductory Survey

Location, Climate, Language, Religion, Flag, Capital

The Republic of Mali is a land-locked country in West Africa, with Algeria to the north, Mauritania and Senegal to the west, Guinea and Côte d'Ivoire to the south, and Burkina Faso and Niger to the east. The climate is hot throughout the country. The northern region of Mali is part of the Sahara, an arid desert. It is wetter in the south, where the rainy season is from June to October. Temperatures in Bamako are generally between 16°C (61°F) and 39°C (103°F). The official language is French but a number of other languages, including Bambara, Fulfulde, Sonrai, Tamashek, Soninke and Dogon, are widely spoken. It is estimated that about 80% of the population are Muslims and 18% follow traditional animist beliefs; under 2% are Christians. The national flag (proportions 2 by 3) has three equal vertical stripes, of green, gold and red. The capital is Bamako.

Recent History

Mali, as the former French West African colony of Soudan, merged in April 1959 with Senegal to form the Federation of Mali, which became independent on 20 June 1960. Senegal seceded two months later, and the remnant of the Federation was proclaimed the Republic of Mali on 22 September. Its first President was Modibo Keita, the leader of the Union soudanaise—Rassemblement démocratique africain (US—RDA), who pursued authoritarian socialist policies. Mali withdrew from the Franc Zone (see p. 316) in 1962, and developed close relations with the communist bloc. Economic difficulties caused Mali to return to the Franc Zone in 1968, although the country was not fully reintegrated into the Zone's monetary union until 1984.

Following a series of purges of US—RDA and public officials, Keita was overthrown in November 1968 by a group of junior army officers, who assumed power as the Comité militaire pour la libération nationale (CMLN). The Constitution was abrogated, and all political activity was banned. Lt (later Gen.) Moussa Traoré became Head of State and President of the CMLN.

A draft Constitution, providing for the establishment of a one-party state at the end of a five-year transitional period of military rule, was approved by a national referendum in June 1974. Keita died in custody in 1977, prompting anti-Government demonstrations. The single political party, the Union démocratique du peuple malien (UDPM), was officially constituted in March 1979, and presidential and legislative elections took place in June. Traoré, the sole candidate for the presidency, was elected for a five-year term; a single list of UDPM candidates for the 82-member Assemblée nationale was elected for a four-year term.

A constitutional amendment in September 1981 increased the presidential term of office to six years and reduced that of the legislature to three years. Elections to the Assemblée nationale were thus held in June 1982 and June 1985, with UDPM candidates being elected unopposed on both occasions. In June 1985 Traoré was re-elected President, reportedly obtaining 99.9% of the votes cast. At legislative elections in June 1998 only about one-half of the incumbent deputies were returned to office, after provision was made for as many as three UDPM-nominated candidates to contest each seat.

Mali's first cohesive opposition movements began to emerge in 1990, among them the Comité national d'initiative démocratique (CNID) and the Alliance pour la démocratie au Mali (ADEMA), which together organized mass pro-democracy demonstrations in December. The security forces harshly repressed violent pro-democracy demonstrations in Bamako in March 1991: official figures later revealed that 106 people were killed, and 708 injured, in three days of unrest. On 26 March it was announced that Traoré had been arrested. A military Conseil national de réconciliation (CNR), led by Lt-Col (later Gen.) Amadou Toumani Touré, the commander of the army's parachute regiment, assumed power, and the Constitution and its institutions were abrogated. The CNR was succeeded by a 25-member Comité de transition pour le salut du peuple (CTSP), chaired by Touré. It was announced that a national conference would be convened, and that the armed forces would relinquish power to democratic institutions in January 1992. Soumana Sacko (who had briefly been Minister of Finance and Trade in 1987) returned to Mali from the Central African Republic to head a transitional, civilian-dominated government.

The transitional regime affirmed its commitment to the economic adjustment efforts of recent years, and undertook the reform of Malian political life. Among those arrested in subsequent months were Gen. Sékou Ly, Brig.-Gen. Mamadou Coulibaly (respectively, Minister of the Interior and Basic Development and Minister of Defence at the time of the violently repressed demonstrations in early 1991) and the former army Chief of Staff, Ousmane Coulibaly. In July 1991 an amnesty for most political prisoners detained under Traoré was proclaimed, and provision made for the legalization of political parties. The CNID was registered as the Congrès national d'initiative démocratique, and ADEMA adopted the additional title of Parti panafricain pour la liberté, la solidarité et la justice. Pre-independence parties, banned for many years, re-emerged, most notably the US—RDA.

The National Conference began in July 1991. Over a period of two weeks its 1,800 delegates adopted a draft Constitution, an electoral code and a charter governing the activities of political parties. In November the period of transition to democratic rule was extended until March 1992. The delay was attributed principally to the CTSP's desire to conclude a peace agreement with Tuareg rebels in the north of the country (see below). The draft Constitution was submitted to a national referendum on 12 January 1992, when it was endorsed by 99.8% of those who voted (about 43% of the registered electorate).

At municipal elections, held on 19 January 1992, ADEMA enjoyed the greatest success, winning 214 of 751 seats. At the elections to the Assemblée nationale, on 23 February and 8 March, ADEMA won 76 of the 129 seats, the CNID took nine seats, and the US—RDA eight. The date for the transition to civilian rule was again postponed, and the first round of the presidential election eventually proceeded on 12 April, contested by nine candidates. The leader of ADEMA, Alpha Oumar Konaré, won the largest share of the votes cast (some 45%). He and his nearest rival, Tiéoulé Mamadou Konaté (of the US—RDA), proceeded to a second round, on 26 April, at which Konaré secured 69% of the votes. Overall, only about 20% of the electorate were reported to have voted in the presidential election; a similar turn-out was reported in the legislative polls. Konaré was inaugurated as President on 8 June. He appointed Younoussi Touré (hitherto the national director of the Banque centrale des états de l'Afrique de l'ouest) as Prime Minister. Touré's first Council of Ministers was dominated by members of ADEMA, although a small number of portfolios were allocated to representatives of the US—RDA and of the Parti pour la démocratie et le progrès (PDP).

The trial of Traoré and his associates began in November 1992. In February 1993 Traoré, Ly, Mamadou Coulibaly and Ousmane Coulibaly were sentenced to death, having been convicted, *inter alia*, of premeditated murder at the time of the March 1991 unrest. The Supreme Court rejected appeal proceedings in May 1993; however, Konaré subsequently indicated that no death penalty would be exacted under his presidency. Charges remained against Traoré, his wife and several others in connection with the 'economic crimes' of the former administration.

Touré resigned in April 1993, following violent disturbances in Bamako, involving students and school pupils disaffected by the adverse effects of economic austerity measures. The new Prime Minister, Abdoulaye Sekou Sow (hitherto Minister of State, responsible for Defence, and who was not a member of any political party), implemented an extensive reorganization of the Government. The Council of Ministers remained dominated by ADEMA, but also included representatives of other parties, including the CNID. Following the resignation of ADEMA's Vice-President, Mohamed Lamine Traoré, from a senior government post, a major reorganization of the Council of Ministers was effected in November.

Meanwhile, a programme of austerity measures, announced in September 1993, provoked considerable political controversy and failed to prevent the suspension of assistance by the IMF and the World Bank. The 50% devaluation of the CFA franc, in January 1994, exacerbated differences regarding economic policy within the Government. Sow resigned in February, and was replaced by Ibrahim Boubacar Keïta, a member of ADEMA's 'radical' wing, which was opposed to Sow's economic policies. The withdrawal from the coalition of the CNID and the Rassemblement pour la démocratie et le progrès (RDP) prompted the appointment of a new Government, again dominated by ADEMA; the PDP in turn withdrew.

Following the election of Keïta as President of ADEMA in September 1994, Mohamed Lamine Traoré and other prominent figures resigned from the party and subsequently formed the Mouvement pour l'indépandance, la renaissance et l'intégration africaine (MIRIA). In January 1995 a party established by supporters of the UDPM, the Mouvement patriotique pour le renouveau (MPR), was granted official status. In October the Parti pour la renaissance nationale (PARENA), comprising several leading members of the CNID, who alleged excessive dominance by the party Chairman, Mountaga Tall, was registered. PARENA and ADEMA established a political alliance in February 1996, and PARENA's leaders, Yoro Diakité and Tiébilé Dramé, were appointed to the Government in July.

In early 1997 the first round of elections to the enlarged (147-seat) Assemblée nationale was postponed from 9 March until 13 April. As early results indicated that ADEMA was the only party to have won seats outright at this round, the main opposition parties denounced the results as fraudulent and announced their intention to withdraw from the second round. The opposition parties also withdrew their candidates from the forthcoming presidential and municipal elections. On 24 April the Constitutional Court invalidated the results of the first round of voting, citing irregularities in the conduct of the poll.

The presidential election was postponed, by one week, until 11 May 1997. Konaré stated that he did not wish to be the sole candidate and appealed to the opposition to participate. In early May the leader of the Parti pour l'unité, la démocratie et le progrès, Mamadou Maribatou Diaby, announced that he was prepared to contest the presidency. According to the final results, Konaré was re-elected to the presidency, securing 95.9% of the valid votes cast. Members of the radical opposition, which had campaigned for a boycott by voters, stated that the low rate of participation (28.4% of the registered electorate) effectively invalidated Konaré's victory. At the end of the month the municipal elections were postponed indefinitely. Violent protests occurred in Bamako in June, as Konaré was sworn in for a second term of office and the first round of the legislative elections (due on 6 July) was postponed by two weeks.

A small number of opposition parties announced their intention to present candidates for the Assemblée nationale, but the radical collective, known as the Collectif des partis politiques de l'opposition (COPPO), at this time numbering 18 parties of varying political tendencies, reiterated its refusal to re-enter the electoral process. Violent disturbances, in which two deaths were reported, preceded the first round of voting on 20 July 1997, which was contested by 17 parties (including five 'moderate' opposition parties) and a number of independent candidates. COPPO again asserted that its appeal for a boycott had been heeded, and that the low rate of participation by voters (at about 12% of the registered electorate in Bamako, and 22% outside the capital) would render the new parliament illegitimate. A second round of voting was necessary for eight seats on 3 August. The final results allocated 130 of the 147 seats to ADEMA, eight to PARENA, four to the Convention démocratique et sociale (CDS), three to the Union pour la démocratie et le développement (UDD) and two to the PDP.

In September 1997 Konaré held a meeting with some 20 opposition leaders, including representatives of COPPO, at which he presented proposals for a broadly based coalition government. A new Council of Ministers, under Keïta, was appointed in mid-September. The new administration included, in addition to members of ADEMA and its allies, a small number of representatives of the moderate opposition parties (among them the UDD and PDP). Further measures intended to promote national reconciliation were implemented, and in December Konaré commuted some 21 death sentences, including those imposed on ex-President Traoré and his associates, to terms of life imprisonment. Although several parties had withdrawn from COPPO, little progress was made towards a full political reconciliation.

In October 1998 the trial for 'economic crimes' began in Bamako of ex-President Traoré, his wife Mariam, her brother, Abraham Douah Cissoko (the former head of customs), a former Minister of Finance and Trade, Tiénan Coulibaly, and the former representative in France of the Banque de développement du Mali, Moussa Koné. In January 1999 Traoré, his wife and brother-in-law were sentenced to death, having been convicted of 'economic crimes' to the value of some US $350,000 (the original charges had cited embezzled funds amounting to $4m.). Coulibaly and Koné were acquitted. In September Konaré commuted the death sentences to terms of life imprisonment.

In February 2000 Keïta submitted his Government's resignation. An extensively reorganized Council of Ministers was subsequently appointed. The new Prime Minister, Mandé Sidibé, was widely regarded as a supporter of economic reform. In June Choguel Kokala Maïga, the leader of the MPR, was among opposition leaders who announced their intention to participate fully in the presidential and parliamentary elections to be held in 2002, stating that conditions for electoral fairness and transparency seemed likely to be achieved.

In July 2000 the Assemblée nationale approved legislation providing for state funding of political parties. The Assemblée also adopted a revision of the Constitution proposed by Konaré, according to which some 50 articles of the 1992 document would be amended, subject to approval by referendum. Notably, people of dual nationality were to be permitted to contest presidential elections, while the Supreme Court was to be abolished. Also in July COPPO, which now comprised 15 parties and was led by Almamy Sylla of the RDP, announced that it would henceforth participate in the electoral process.

Keïta resigned from the leadership of ADEMA in October 2000, following the announcement that his opponents within the party had succeeded in calling an extraordinary congress of the party, to be held in late November. At the congress, several new members were appointed to ADEMA's executive committee, and Dioncounda Traoré was elected as the new Chairman of the party. A minor ministerial reshuffle was effected in June 2001. In July a new party led by Keïta, the Rassemblement pour le Mali (RPM), was officially registered.

In November 2001 Konaré indefinitely postponed a referendum, which had been due to take place in December, on the constitutional amendments adopted by the legislature in July 2000, following pressure from opposition parties and the judiciary. In January 2002 Soumaïla Cissé was elected as ADEMA's candidate for the forthcoming presidential election. In March Modibo Keita, hitherto Secretary-General at the presidency, was appointed as Prime Minister, following Sidibé's resignation to contest the presidency as an independent candidate. In early April 16 opposition parties, including the CNID, the RPM and the MPR, formed an electoral alliance, Espoir 2002, agreeing to support a single opposition candidate (generally expected to be Ibrahim Boubacar Keïta, who was to contest the election on behalf of the RPM) in the event of a second round of voting. Meanwhile, an alliance of 23 political parties, including MIRIA, PARENA and the US—RDA declared their support for the candidacy of Gen. (retd) Amadou Toumani Touré.

At the first round of the presidential election, which was held on 28 April 2002, contested by 24 candidates, Touré secured the largest share of the votes cast, with 28.7%, followed by Cissé, with 21.3%, and Keïta, with 21.0%. As no candidate had secured an overall majority, Touré and Cissé progressed to a second round of voting, held on 12 May. Touré, was elected to the presidency, with 65.0% of the votes cast, having obtained the support of more than 40 parties, including those of Espoir 2002. The electoral process was marred by allegations of fraud and incompetence, which led the Constitutional Court to annul 25% of the votes cast in the first ballot. None the less, international observers described the elections as generally free, fair and open. Touré was inaugurated as President on 8 June, and subsequently formed an interim Government, comprising 21 ministers. The new Prime Minister and Minister of African Integration, Ahmed Mohamed Ag Hamani, was regarded as a technocrat; in addition to having previously held various ministerial posts under Traoré, he had, more recently, served as ambassador to Belgium and to Morocco and as High Commissioner of the Organisation pour la mise en valeur du fleuve Sénégal (see p. 426). President Touré emphasized that he was not affiliated to any particular political party, and would be prepared to govern with any future parliamentary majority.

The elections to the Assemblée nationale in July 2002 further demonstrated the lack of any one dominant political grouping in Mali, while the rate of participation, at 25.7% nation-wide, in the second round, was low. The first round of polls was largely inconclusive and, as a result of various irregularities in the conduct of the elections, several thousand votes were invalidated; following the publication, in early August, of the results by the Constitutional Court, the RPM emerged as the single largest party, with 46 of the 147 seats (although 20 of its seats had been won in local electoral alliances with other parties of the Espoir 2002 grouping), while other parties of Espoir 2002 obtained a further 21 seats, giving a total of 67 to allies of the RPM. ADEMA secured 45 seats, while the pro-ADEMA Alliance pour la République et la démocratie won an additional six seats, giving a total of 51. The CNID received 13 seats, while parties belonging to an informal alliance supportive of President Touré, the Convergence pour l'alternance et le changement (ACC), including PARENA and the US—RDA, won a total of 10 seats. The Constitutional Court declared void the results of voting in eight constituencies in Sikasso, in the south, and Tin-Essako, in the north, owing to administrative flaws; by-elections were held in October. In early September 19 deputies, comprising those of the ACC parties, several independent deputies and other declared supporters of Touré, formed a grouping within the legislature, with the declared intention of forming a stable presidential majority. Later in the month Ibrahim Boubakar Keïta was elected President of the Assemblée nationale.

In mid-October 2002 Touré announced the formation of a Government of National Unity. Although many of the principal posts remained unchanged from the interim administration appointed in June, one notable appointment was that of Bassari Touré, a former official of the World Bank, as Minister of the Economy and Finance, who was expected to institute an expedited process of reform. Meanwhile, ADEMA increased its representation in the Assemblée nationale to 53 deputies, becoming the largest party grouping, following its victory in by-elections in all eight constituencies where elections were rerun on 20 October. A minor government reorganization was announced in mid-November.

In late April 2004 Ag Hamani tendered his resignation as Prime Minister, apparently in response to a request by President Touré. A new administration, headed by Prime Minister Ousmane Issoufi Maïga, hitherto Minister of Equipment and Transport (and not affiliated to any political party), was formed in early May. Moktar Ouane was appointed Minister of Foreign Affairs and International Co-operation, and Aboubacar Traoré became Minister of the Economy and Finance. ADEMA was the most successful party at municipal elections held on 23 May (postponed from the previous month), winning 28% of the seats contested, followed by the URD, which secured 14%, and the RPM, with 13%; the rate of participation by the electorate was relatively high, at 43.6%. ADEMA and the RPM subsequently formed an alliance, which, with ADEMA holding 44 seats and the RPM 35, gave the new grouping a majority in the 147-seat Assemblée nationale (although still short of the two-thirds majority needed to enact a motion of 'no confidence' against the head of the Government).

From mid-2004 there was considerable speculation regarding potential realignments of political organizations ahead of the presidential and legislative elections due in 2007. In February and March 2005 the President held a series of consultations with the leaders of various political organizations. However, there were signs that the political consensus that had existed since Touré's election in 2002 was likely to come to an end before the elections, as parties began to distance themselves from the President. In November 2005 the RPM announced that it would henceforth oppose the Government, stating that it had been increasingly marginalized within the ruling coalition. The victory of an RPM candidate in a legislative by-election later that month was interpreted by some observers as reflecting a decline in support for the ruling coalition, and it was subsequently reported that the RMP and the URD were considering forming a common political programme. In February 2006 the executive committee of ADEMA announced that the party would support the candidacy of Touré at the presidential election due in April 2007 and that it would not, consequently, present its own candidate in the election.

The presidential election was duly held on 29 April 2007, at which 36.2% of the registered electorate participated. According to results released by the Constitutional Court in mid-May, Touré received 71.20% of the total votes cast, claiming an absolute majority and securing a second, and final, five-year term while avoiding a second round of voting. His closest rival was Keïta, who received 19.15% of the votes cast. Although a number of opposition candidates challenged the results, alleging that Touré had used public funds to finance his campaign and had manipulated the lists of voters, most independent observers believed the election to have been conducted fairly.

The first round of the legislative elections took place on 1 July 2007 and a second round followed on 22 July. According to official results, ADEMA secured 51 seats, while the URD took 34 seats and the RPM 11. Turn-out was, however, low at 12%, rising to 33% in rural areas. In total, parties supporting President Touré won 113 seats in the Assemblée nationale. In early September Dioncounda Traoré was elected President of that body

On 27 September 2007 Prime Minister Maïga tendered his resignation and that of his Government. The following day President Touré named Modibo Sidibé, hitherto Secretary-General of the Presidency, as Maïga's successor. Sidibé announced a new Council of Ministers in early October; the most notable appointments were Gen. Sadio Gassama as Minister of Internal Security and Civil Protection and a Tuareg, Mohammed El Moctar, as Minister of Culture. Ouane retained the foreign affairs portfolio and Gen. Kafougouna Koné was reappointed to head the Ministry of Territorial Administration and Local Communities. In April 2008 Ahmadou Abdoulaye Diallo replaced Bâ Fatoumata Nènè Sy as Minister of Economy, Industry and Commerce, while in October Mamadou Igor Diarra was appointed Minister of Energy and Water following the resignation of Ahmed Sow.

A predominant concern in the first half of the 1990s was the rebellion in the north of Mali, which began as large numbers of Tuareg nomads, who had migrated to Algeria and Libya at times of drought, began to return to West Africa (see also the chapter on Niger). A Tuareg attack in June 1990 on Menaka (near the border with Niger) precipitated a state of emergency in the Gao and Tombouctou regions, and the armed forces began a campaign against the nomads. A peace accord signed in January 1991 in Tamanrasset, Algeria, by representatives of the Traoré Government and delegates from two Tuareg groups, the Mouvement populaire de l'Azaouad (MPA) and the Front islamique-arabe de l'Azaouad (FIAA), failed to provide a lasting solution to the conflict. Following the overthrow of the Traoré regime, the transitional administration affirmed its commitment to the Tamanrasset accord, and Tuareg groups were represented in the CTSP. However, unrest continued. At the time of the National Conference it was reported that at least 150 members of the armed forces had been killed since 1990; meanwhile, thousands of Tuaregs, Moors and Bella (the descendants of the Tuaregs' black slaves, some of whom remained with the nomads) had fled to neighbouring countries.

In February 1992, following negotiations between representatives of the Malian Government and of the Mouvements et fronts unifiés de l'Azaouad (MFUA), comprising the MPA, the FIAA and the Armée révolutionnaire de l'Azaouad (ARLA), with Algerian mediation, a truce entered into force, and a commission of inquiry was inaugurated to examine acts of violence perpetrated and losses suffered during the conflict; the more militant Front populaire de libération de l'Azaouad (FPLA) was not reported to have attended the talks. Following further discussions, the Malian authorities and the MFUA signed a draft 'National Pact' in April: joint patrols were duly established, and in November President Konaré visited the north to inaugurate new administrative structures. In February 1993 the Malian Government and the MFUA signed an accord facilitating the integration of an initial 600 Tuaregs into the national army. In May it was announced that the office of the UN High Commissioner for Refugees (UNHCR) was to oversee a two-year voluntary repatriation programme, whereby 12,000 refugees would be resettled from southern Algeria to Mali by the end of 1993. However, the assassination, in February 1994, of the MPA's military leader—now, in accordance with the Pact, a senior officer in the Malian army—resulted in several weeks of clashes between the MPA and the ARLA, which was blamed for his death.

In May 1994 the Malian authorities and Tuareg leaders reached agreement regarding the integration of 1,500 former rebels into the Malian army and of a further 4,860 Tuaregs into civilian sectors. The success of the agreement was, however, undermined by an intensification of disorder in northern Mali. Meanwhile, a Songhaï-dominated black resistance movement, the Mouvement patriotique malien Ghanda Koy ('Masters of the Land'), emerged, amid rumours of official complicity in its offensives against the Tuaregs. In June one of the leaders of the FIAA died during clashes with members of the armed forces. Meeting in Tamanrasset shortly afterwards, the Malian authorities and the MFUA endorsed a reinforcement of the army presence in areas affected by the violence, and agreed procedures for the more effective integration of Tuareg fighters. Despite a serious escalation of violence in July, the ministers responsible for foreign affairs of Mali, Algeria, Burkina Faso, Libya, Mauritania and Niger met in Bamako in August to discuss the Tuareg issue, and a new agreement for the voluntary repatriation from Algeria of Malian refugees was reached. Although MFUA leaders welcomed the agreement, pledged the reconciliation of the Tuareg movements, and reiterated their commitment to the National Pact, sporadic hostilities continued.

In October 1994 both the Government and the MFUA appealed for an end to the violence, following an attack on Gao (for which the FIAA claimed responsibility) and retaliatory action, as a result of which 66 deaths were officially reported. A new Minister of the Armed Forces and Veterans was appointed shortly afterwards, and the authorities subsequently appeared to adopt a less conciliatory approach to the dissident rebel groups, with the FIAA becoming increasingly marginalized in the peace process. Further discussions involving Tuareg groups, Ghanda Koy and representatives of local communities resulted in the signing, in April 1995, of an agreement providing for co-operation in resolving hitherto contentious issues. In June the FIAA announced an end to its armed struggle, and expressed its willingness to join national reconciliation efforts. A programme for the encampment of former rebels, in preparation for their eventual integration into the national army or civilian structures, began in November and ended in February 1996, by which time some 3,000 MFUA fighters and Ghanda Koy militiamen had registered and surrendered their weapons. The MFUA and Ghanda Koy subsequently issued a joint statement affirming their adherence to Mali's Constitution, national unity and territorial integrity, urging the full implementation of the National Pact and associated accords and proclaiming the 'irreversible dissolution' of their respective movements.

In September 1997 the graduation of MFUA and Ghanda Koy contingents in the gendarmerie was reported as marking the accomplishment of the integration of all fighters within the national armed and security forces. In October the former FPLA leader, Rhissa Ag Sidi Mohamed, who had not previously been regarded as a party to the peace process, returned to Mali and expressed willingness to join efforts to consolidate peace and promote the development of the north. None the less, the Ministers of Justice and of the Armed Forces and Veterans expressed concern that the continued proliferation of weapons, as well as the inadequacy of military and administrative structures in the north, could result in renewed clashes. In November 2000 it was reported that Malian government forces had been dispatched to end widespread banditry by an armed group, led by Ibrahim Ag Bahanga, a former Tuareg rebel, in the Kidal area, near to the border with Algeria. In September 2001 Bahanga reportedly announced that his forces were to cease hostilities, following talks with a state official.

The presence of large numbers of refugees from the conflict in northern Mali dominated Mali's relations with its neighbours during the 1990s, and even after the completion of the process of repatriation in mid-1998 (and the conclusion of a UNHCR programme in June 1999) the north of the country remained vulnerable to cross-border banditry. In May 1998 the ministers responsible for the interior of Mali, Mauritania and Senegal met with a view to strengthening co-operation and border controls, and in December Mali and Senegal agreed to improve border security. In February 1999 Mali and Algeria agreed to revive their joint border committee to promote development and stability in the region. In March Konaré visited Mauritania to discuss border stability; however, in June a dispute over watering rights escalated into an armed conflict between neighbouring Malian and Mauritanian communities, in which 13 people were killed. The two Governments responded to the disturbances by increasing border controls and by sending a joint delegation to the villages involved. In August, at a meeting in Dakar, Senegal, the Malian, Mauritanian and Senegalese ministers responsible for the interior agreed to establish an operational unit drawn from the police forces of the three countries in order to ensure security in the area of their joint border. Bilateral relations between Mali and Mauritania were further strengthened by a military co-operation agreement regarding border security signed by the countries' respective Presidents in Nouakchott, Mauritania, in January 2005.

Concerns about insecurity in the region re-emerged in mid-2003, following reports, in late July, that some 15 German, Swiss and Dutch tourists, said to have been kidnapped in February by Islamist militants allegedly associated with the Groupe salafiste pour la prédication et le combat in southern Algeria, had been smuggled into Mali. Following negotiations with the kidnappers, conducted by a former rebel Tuareg leader, Iyad Ag Agaly, 14 hostages were released in mid-August (the remaining hostage had reportedly died earlier from heatstroke). In March 2004 Mali announced that it was to increase anti-terrorism co-operation with the authorities in Algeria, Chad and Niger. In November 2007 the Presidents of Mali and Algeria agreed to establish a joint border patrol.

Tensions arose again in May 2006 when Tuareg rebels launched an attack on the town of Kidal in the north-east of Mali. Two military bases were seized, as were two radio stations and a further military base south of Kidal, and it was reported that two government soldiers were shot and killed during army attempts to regain control of the installations. Military reinforcements were deployed to the region; however, the rebel group had taken much of the army's ammunition and weaponry and withdrawn to an area close to the Niger border, from where they demanded the commencement of negotiations with the Government over the conditions in which the Tuaregs had been forced to live since their integration into the armed forces. At a meeting between the Malian Government and the Tuareg group in June, mediated by Algerian officials, corruption and fraud were also cited among the reasons for the May attack. However, discussions were positive, including proposals for greater autonomy in the administration of the mountainous region of Kidal. In July a peace deal was signed in Algiers, Algeria, which included agreement on an investment programme for the region and the reintegration of rebels into the armed forces. There was some criticism of the Government for its relenting attitude towards the insurgents, but President Touré reiterated his determination to find a peaceful resolution to the conflict. A further reconciliation agreement was signed on 23 February 2007 between the Malian Government and the Tuareg rebels, stipulating guide-lines for the implementation of the agreement signed in July the previous year. The accord also outlined the establishment of special security units in the Kidal region, and measures for facilitating the reintegration of the Tuaregs into Malian society. In August several attacks on military personnel by Tuareg rebels were reported to have occurred near to the border with Niger. The main Tuareg group insisted that it was continuing to uphold the reconciliation agreement; however, a splinter group announced that it had formed an alliance with Tuareg militia in Niger, who had launched an offensive against the Niger Government. Following talks between the Tuareg rebels and the Malian Government in September, hostages taken in the attacks were released. Nevertheless, later that month a US aircraft carrying aid supplies into Mali came under fire from Tuareg troops, which prompted President Touré to demand the holding of an urgent conference on peace and security in the region.

In April 2008 a new agreement, brokered by Libyan authorities, was signed by the Malian Government and a Tuareg rebel group led by Bahanga, styled the Alliance tuareg Nord-Mali pour le changement (ATNMC); the accord committed both parties to reducing the number of troops stationed in the Kidal area. In addition, Libya pledged its support to the development of the region, which was believed to be one of the underlying causes of tension in the area. However, fighting subsequently intensified and in May it was reported that 27 soldiers and rebels had been killed in an attack on a military base in Abebara, north of Kidal. Despite President Touré reiterating his commitment to restoring peace to the region and to adhering to the terms of recent peace agreements, he maintained that he would not negotiate with individual Tuareg groups. Nevertheless, meeting in Algiers in July, the Government and the leaders of a group believed to be allied to the ATNMC, the Alliance démocratique du 23 mai pour le changement (ADC), reached an agreement on peace and security, and in September the rebels released 44 Government soldiers who had been held hostage in the north of the country (although a number remained in captivity). Despite the establishment in November of the first joint special unit comprising rebel fighters and Malian soldiers, raising hopes for continued progress towards peace, further unrest was reported the following month in which nine soldiers were killed. None the less, in January 2009 the ADC in Kidal released the last remaining Malian hostages following a period in which the Government used increased force to seize ammunition and weapons. It was later announced that three Tuareg factions, including the ADC, had united and agreed to rejoin peace negotiations. The Malian military then claimed in February that it had taken the last of the ATNMC positions (that organization was believed by this stage to number only some 165 members) and that Ag Bahanga and an unknown number of fighters had crossed the border into Algeria. Later that month it was reported that he had been granted refuge in Libya, while some 500 members of the ADC surrendered their weapons and agreed to join the peace process.

In February 1999 some 488 Malian troops joined the Economic Community of West African States (ECOWAS, see p. 246) Ceasefire Monitoring Group forces in Sierra Leone, although the Malian authorities emphasized that these troops would take on a purely peace-keeping role. However, following widespread demands in Mali for a withdrawal, during August the majority of the force departed Sierra Leone; it was later announced that seven Malian soldiers had been killed and 10 seriously injured while serving in Sierra Leone. As Chairman of ECOWAS, in March 2001 Konaré hosted a mini-summit, attended by the leaders of the three countries of the Mano River Union (see p. 427), Sierra Leone, Liberia and Guinea, in Bamako on the subject of the peace process in Sierra Leone. Konaré sought to emphasize the role of Mali in ECOWAS, and in November 2000 a 120-member ECOWAS parliament, which was to promote regional co-operation, was inaugurated in Bamako.

Mali has in recent years forged closer relations with Libya, and was a founder member of the Community of Sahel-Saharan States (see p. 425), established in Tripoli, Libya, in 1997.

Government

The Constitution of the Third Republic, which was approved in a national referendum on 12 January 1992, provides for the separation of the powers of the executive, legislative and judicial organs of state. Executive power is vested in the President of the Republic, who is elected for five years by universal suffrage. The President appoints a Prime Minister, who, in turn, appoints a Council of Ministers. Legislative power is vested in the 147-seat unicameral Assemblée nationale, elected for five years by universal suffrage. Elections take place in the context of a multiparty political system.

Mali has eight administrative regions, each presided over by a governor, and a district government in Bamako. Following a significant revision of local government structures in 1999, and a further minor revision in 2001, the number of elected mayors across Mali increased from 19 to 703. The Constitution makes provision for the establishment of a High Council of Local Communities.

Defence

As assessed at November 2008, the active Malian army numbered about 7,350 men, including a naval force of about 50 men (with patrol boats on the River Niger) and an air force of 400. Paramilitary forces comprised the gendarmerie (1,800), republican guard (2,000), militia (3,000) and national police (1,000). Military service is by selective conscription and lasts for two years. The defence budget for 2007 was estimated at 75,000m. francs CFA.

Economic Affairs

In 2007, according to estimates by the World Bank, Mali's gross national income (GNI), measured at average 2005–07 prices, was US $6,136m., equivalent to $500 per head (or $1,040 on an international purchasing-power parity basis). During 2000–07, it was estimated, the population increased at an average annual rate of 3.0%, while gross domestic product (GDP) per head increased, in real terms, by an average of 2.6% per year. Overall GDP increased, in real terms, at an average annual rate of 5.7% in 2000–07. According to the World Bank, real GDP increased by 2.8% in 2007.

Agriculture (including livestock-rearing, forestry and fishing) contributed 36.5% of GDP in 2007, according to the World Bank. An estimated 37.9% of the labour force were employed in the sector in 2004. Mali is among Africa's foremost producers and exporters of cotton (exports of which contributed an estimated 13.8% of the value of total exports in 2007). According to unofficial figures, having reached a peak of 635,000 metric tons in 2003, 250,400 tons of cotton were produced in 2005, with an estimated 160,000 tons produced the following year. Shea-nuts (karité nuts), groundnuts, vegetables and mangoes are also cultivated for export. The principal subsistence crops are millet, rice, sorghum and maize. Cereal imports remain necessary in most years and the agricultural sector was badly damaged by the large locust swarms that affected the countries of the Sahel region in mid-2004. The livestock-rearing and fishing sectors make an important contribution to the domestic food supply and (in the case of the former) to export revenue, providing an estimated 4.7% of total exports in 2004, although both are highly vulnerable to drought. According to the World Bank, agricultural GDP increased by an average of 4.9% per year in 2000–07; it increased by 2.4% in 2007.

Industry (including mining, manufacturing, construction and power) contributed 24.2% of GDP in 2007, according to the World Bank. It employed 15.1% of the labour force in 2004. Industrial GDP increased at an average annual rate of 6.0% in 2000–07. It increased by 3.7% in 2007.

Mining contributed 2.5% of GDP in 2007, according to the IMF. It employed 0.4% of the labour force in 2004. The importance of the sector has increased with the successful exploitation of the country's gold reserves: exports of gold contributed an estimated 70% of the value of total exports in 2008. Output of gold increased significantly in the second half of the 1990s, as new mining facilities commenced operations, and by 2001 Mali had become the third largest gold producer in Africa. Exports of gold were forecast at 46 metric tons for 2009, and would yield an estimated US $240m. despite a reduction in productivity as mines near the end of their reserves. Two new open-pit mines, at Yalea and Loulo, operated by Randgold Resources (of South Africa), commenced operations in late 2005; underground development at the same sites was expected, in due course, to produce 1.8m. oz of gold in total over a 10-year period. Salt, diamonds, marble and phosphate rock are also mined. The future exploitation of deposits of iron ore and uranium is envisaged. According to the IMF, the GDP of the mining sector increased at an average annual rate of 46.8% in 1996–2002; growth in mining GDP reached 181.3% in 1997, before slowing to an estimated 23.1% by 2002.

The manufacturing sector, including electricity and water, contributed 10.0% of GDP in 2006, according to the BCEAO. It employed 10.5% of the labour force in 2004. The main area of activity is agro-industrial (chiefly the processing of cotton, sugar and rice). Brewing and tobacco industries are represented, and some construction materials are produced for the domestic market. According to the World Bank, manufacturing GDP increased at an average annual rate of 3.6% in 2000–07. It grew by 4.5% in 2007.

Of total electric energy generated in 1995, about 80% was derived from hydroelectric installations. Mali began to receive power supplies from the Manantali hydroelectric project (constructed and operated under the auspices of the Organisation pour la mise en valeur du fleuve Sénégal—OMVS) from December 2001, and there were also plans to link the Malian network with those of Côte d'Ivoire, Burkina Faso and Ghana. An agreement on energy supply was also reached with Algeria in February 1998. In July 2000 Belgium provided a loan of 2,600m. francs CFA for the construction of two high-voltage power stations in Bamako. Imports of petroleum, petroleum products and related materials comprised an estimated 21.9% of the value of merchandise imports in 2007.

The services sector contributed 36.7% of GDP in 2006, according to the BCEAO. It employed 38.3% of the labour force in 2004. The GDP of the services sector increased at an average annual rate of 6.3% in 2000–07. Services GDP increased by 7.6% in 2007.

In 2006 Mali recorded a visible trade surplus of just US $75.0m., while there was a deficit of $230.5m. on the current account of the balance of payments. In 2007 the principal sources of imports were Senegal (which supplied 19.8% of total imports), France, the People's Republic of China and Côte d'Ivoire. The largest market for exports in that year was South Africa, which accounted for 67.1% of total exports. The principal export in 2007 was cotton, comprising 13.8% of total exports. The principal imports in that year were machinery and transport equipment (accounting for 24.5% of total imports), petroleum, petroleum products and related materials, manufactured goods, chemicals and related products, and food and live animals.

In 2007, according to the IMF, Mali recorded an overall budget deficit of 210,500m. francs CFA. Mali's total external debt was US $1,436m. at the end of 2006, of which $1,411m. was long-term public debt. In 2005 the cost of debt-servicing was equivalent to 5.6% of the value of exports of goods and services. The annual rate of inflation averaged 2.1% in 2000–07. Consumer prices increased by 1.6% in 2006 and by 1.4% in 2007.

Mali is a member of numerous international and regional organizations, including the Economic Community of West African States (ECOWAS, see p. 243), the West African organs of the Franc Zone (see p. 316), the African Groundnut Council (see

p. 421), the Liptako-Gourma Integrated Development Authority (see p. 427), the Niger Basin Authority (see p. 427) and the OMVS (see p. 426).

Mali's economic development is hindered by its vulnerability to drought, its dependence on imports and its narrow range of exports. The country also lacks facilities for the processing of its important cotton crop; it was reported in 2002 that only 1% of Mali's cotton crop was processed in the country. In the first half of the 2000s the cotton sector underwent restructuring and a partial transfer to private ownership, having been adversely affected by a decline in international prices during the late 1990s; the privatization of a majority share of the cotton ginning company, the Compagnie Malienne pour le Développement des Textiles (CMDT) was, however, postponed from 2006 until 2009, owing to technical delays and concerns regarding the transfer of the large debt accrued by the CMDT. It had also been reported that some 57,000 cotton farmers had turned to other crops since 2005, threatening Mali's export revenue. GDP growth slowed to 3.1% in 2007, according to the IMF, reflecting the impact of heavy rainfall on the agricultural sector and the continued difficulties within the cotton industry. Meanwhile, in March 2003 the Bretton Woods institutions announced that Mali had reached completion point under the terms of the initiative for heavily indebted poor countries, thus becoming eligible for additional debt-relief. Furthermore, in late 2006 the US Millennium Challenge Corpn pledged $461m. towards poverty alleviation and in early 2007 the World Bank awarded Mali a grant of $10m. to develop infrastructure, social services and reform programmes. In early 2008 the European Union pledged 366,000m. francs CFA in development aid to Mali in 2008–13, while in late 2008 the IMF completed its first review of Mali's performance under the Poverty Reduction and Growth Facility, which released a further $7.5m. in developmental assistance, bringing the total amount under the arrangement to some US $26.8m. The African Development Bank also approved further funding amounting to 23,000m. francs CFA to support the cotton sector. The IMF projected GDP growth of 4.8% in 2008 and of 5.2% in 2009. None the less, in the absence of a more diversified economic base, Mali's economy continued to remain vulnerable to the effects of the ongoing global financial crisis, particularly with regard to the global prices of gold and cotton.

Education
Education is provided free of charge and is officially compulsory for nine years between seven and 16 years of age. Primary education begins at the age of seven and lasts for six years. Secondary education, from 13 years of age, lasts for a further six years, generally comprising two cycles of three years. The rate of school enrolment in Mali is among the lowest in the world: in 1997 total enrolment at primary and secondary schools, excluding Medersas (Islamic schools), was equivalent to only 32% of the school-age population (males 39%; females 25%). According to UNESCO estimates, in 2006/07 primary enrolment included 63.0% of the appropriate age-group (males 69.8%; females 56.2%), while secondary enrolment in 2005/06 was equivalent to only 28.3% (males 35.2%; females 21.4%). Tertiary education facilities include the national university, developed in the mid-1990s; in 2004/05 there were some 32,600 students enrolled at that institution. Hitherto many students have received higher education abroad, mainly in France and Senegal. In 2005 spending on education represented 14.8% of total budgetary expenditure.

Public Holidays
2009: 1 January (New Year's Day), 20 January (Armed Forces Day), 9 March* (Mouloud, Birth of the Prophet), 16 March* (Baptism of the Prophet), 25 March (Commemoration of the overthrow of Moussa Traoré), 13 April (Easter Monday), 1 May (Labour Day), 25 May (Africa Day, anniversary of the OAU's foundation), 20 September* (Korité, end of Ramadan), 22 September (Independence Day), 27 November* (Tabaski, Feast of the Sacrifice), 25 December (Christmas Day).

2010: 1 January (New Year's Day), 20 January (Armed Forces Day), 26 February* (Mouloud, Birth of the Prophet), 5 March* (Baptism of the Prophet), 25 March (Commemoration of the overthrow of Moussa Traoré), 5 April (Easter Monday), 1 May (Labour Day), 25 May (Africa Day, anniversary of the OAU's foundation), 10 September* (Korité, end of Ramadan), 22 September (Independence Day), 16 November* (Tabaski, Feast of the Sacrifice), 25 December (Christmas Day).

* These holidays are determined by the Islamic lunar calendar and may vary by one or two days from the dates given.

Weights and Measures
The metric system is in force.

Statistical Survey

Source (unless otherwise stated): Direction Nationale de la Statistique et de l'Informatique, rue Archinard, porte 233, BP 12, Bamako; tel. 2022-2455; fax 2022-7145; e-mail cnpe.mali@afribonemali.net; internet www.dnsi.gov.ml.

Area and Population

AREA, POPULATION AND DENSITY

Area (sq km)	1,240,192*
Population (census results)†	
1–30 April 1987	7,696,348
17 April 1998	
Males	4,847,436
Females	4,943,056
Total	9,790,492
Population (UN estimates at mid-year)‡	
2006	12,118,000
2007	12,409,000
2008	12,706,000
Density (per sq km) at mid-2008	10.2

* 478,841 sq miles.
† Figures are provisional and refer to the *de jure* population.
‡ Source: UN, *World Population Prospects: The 2008 Revision.*

Ethnic Groups (percentage of total, 1995): Bambara 36.5; Peul 13.9; Sénoufo 9.0; Soninké 8.8; Dogon 8.0; Songhaï 7.2; Malinké 6.6; Diola 2.9; Bobo and Oulé 2.4; Tuareg 1.7; Moor 1.2; Others 1.8 (Source: La Francophonie).

ADMINISTRATIVE DIVISIONS
(*de jure* population at 1998 census, provisional figures)

District		Mopti	1,475,274
Bamako	1,016,167	Kayes	1,372,019
Regions		Tombouctou	461,956
Sikasso	1,780,042	Gao	397,516
Ségou	1,679,201	Kidal	42,479
Koulikoro	1,565,838		

PRINCIPAL TOWNS*
(*de jure* population at 1998 census, provisional figures)

Bamako (capital)	1,016,167	Koutiala	74,153
Sikasso	113,813	Kayes	67,262
Ségou	90,898	Gao	54,903
Mopti	79,840	Kati	49,756

* With the exception of Bamako, figures refer to the population of communes (municipalities).

Mid-2007 ('000, incl. suburbs, UN estimate): Bamako 1,494 (Source: UN, *World Urbanization Prospects: The 2007 revision*).

MALI

BIRTHS AND DEATHS
(annual averages, UN estimates)

	1990–95	1995–2000	2000–05
Birth rate (per 1,000)	46.0	44.1	43.3
Death rate (per 1,000)	20.6	19.1	17.4

Source: UN, *World Population Prospects: The 2008 Revision*.

Life expectancy (years at birth, WHO estimates): 46.4 (males 44.8; females 47.8) in 2006 (Source: WHO, *World Health Statistics*).

ECONOMICALLY ACTIVE POPULATION
('000 persons, 2004, estimates)

	Males	Females	Total
Agriculture, hunting and forestry	657.7	291.7	949.4
Fishing	33.3	2.0	35.2
Mining	8.4	3.0	11.4
Manufacturing	136.1	136.4	272.5
Electricity, gas and water	5.1	—	5.1
Construction	97.5	4.7	102.1
Wholesale and retail trade; repair of motor vehicles, motorcycles and personal household goods	266.1	402.1	668.1
Hotels and restaurants	1.4	6.3	7.6
Transport, storage and communications	51.8	3.5	55.3
Financial intermediation	4.4	—	4.4
Real estate	3.5	0.6	4.0
Public administration	33.3	6.6	39.9
Education	35.6	18.3	53.9
Health and social work	11.4	9.5	20.9
Other social services	42.6	97.5	140.1
Total employed	1,388.3	982.5	2,370.8
Unemployed	107.0	120.5	227.4
Total labour force	1,495.3	1,103.0	2,598.2

Source: ILO.

Mid-2005 (estimates in '000): Agriculture, etc. 4,978; Total labour force 6,378 (Source: FAO).

Health and Welfare

KEY INDICATORS

Total fertility rate (children per woman, 2006)	6.6
Under-5 mortality rate (per 1,000 live births, 2006)	217
HIV/AIDS (% of persons aged 15–49, 2007)	1.5
Physicians (per 1,000 head, 2004)	0.08
Hospital beds (per 1,000 head, 2005)	0.30
Health expenditure (2006): US $ per head (PPP)	65
Health expenditure (2006): % of GDP	6.0
Health expenditure (2006): public (% of total)	51.7
Access to water (% of persons, 2006)	60
Access to sanitation (% of persons, 2006)	45
Human Development Index (2006): ranking	168
Human Development Index (2006): value	0.391

For sources and definitions, see explanatory note on p. vi.

Agriculture

PRINCIPAL CROPS
('000 metric tons)

	2005	2006	2007*
Rice, paddy	945.8	1,053.2	955.3
Maize	634.5	706.7	542.1
Millet	1,157.8	1,128.8	1,074.4
Sorghum	629.1	769.7	908.0
Fonio	26.6	26.2	23.7
Sweet potatoes	133.1	185.4	185.0
Cassava (Manioc)	56.1	96.1	82.0
Yams	47.8	77.8	70.0
Sugar cane	348.0	319.5	350.0
Groundnuts, with shell	279.5	265.5	180.0
Karité nuts (Sheanuts)	85.0*	n.a.	n.a.
Cottonseed	311.0	300.0*	n.a.
Tomatoes	64.6	75.3	72.0
Onions, dry	34.9	34.8	35.0
Guavas, mangoes and mangosteens	61.4	65.4	70.0
Cotton (lint)	250.4†	160.0*	n.a.

* FAO estimate(s).
† Unofficial figure.

Aggregate production ('000 metric tons, may include official, semi-official or estimated data): Total cereals 3,398.7 in 2005, 3,693.3 in 2006, 3,509.6 in 2007; Total pulses 112.1 in 2005, 89.4 in 2006, 88.3 in 2007; Total roots and tubers 314.4 in 2005, 464.2 in 2006, 427.0 in 2007; Total vegetables (incl. melons) 646.2 in 2005, 495.1 in 2006, 531.4 in 2007; Total fruits (excl. melons) 325.8 in 2005, 362.1 in 2006, 369.5 in 2007.

Source: FAO.

LIVESTOCK
('000 head, year ending September)

	2005	2006*	2007*
Cattle	7,103	7,800	7,917
Sheep	8,403	8,500	8,595
Goats	12,000	12,500	13,010
Pigs	69	70	71
Horses*	172	173	174
Asses, mules or hinnies	720*	n.a.	n.a.
Camels*	472	474	476
Chickens*	31,00	32,000	33,000

* FAO estimate(s).

Source: FAO.

LIVESTOCK PRODUCTS
('000 metric tons, FAO estimates)

	2005	2006	2007
Cattle meat	97.8	101.4	134.0
Sheep meat	36.0	36.2	36.6
Goat meat	48.5	50.8	52.8
Chicken meat	36.0	37.1	38.3
Game meat	18.0	18.0	18.5
Pig meat	2.2	2.2	2.3
Cows' milk	188.7	191.1	194.1
Sheep's milk	126.0	127.5	36.6
Goats' milk	238.6	247.5	257.6
Camels' milk	55.2	55.5	55.7

Source: FAO.

MALI Statistical Survey

Forestry

ROUNDWOOD REMOVALS
('000 cubic metres, excl. bark, FAO estimates)

	2005	2006	2007
Sawlogs, veneer logs and logs for sleepers	4	4	4
Other industrial wood	409	409	409
Fuel wood	5,027	5,084	5,143
Total	5,440	5,497	5,556

Source: FAO.

SAWNWOOD PRODUCTION
('000 cubic metres, incl. railway sleepers)

	1987	1988	1989
Total (all broadleaved)	11	13	13*

* FAO estimate.

1990–2007: Production assumed to be unchanged from 1989 (FAO estimates).

Source: FAO.

Fishing

('000 metric tons, live weight)

	2000	2001*	2002*
Capture	109.9	100.0	100.0
Nile tilapia	33.0	30.0	30.0
Elephantsnout fishes	7.7	7.0	7.0
Characins	5.5	5.0	5.0
Black catfishes	4.4	4.0	4.0
North African catfish	27.5	25.0	25.0
Nile perch	6.6	6.0	6.0
Other freshwater fishes	25.3	23.0	23.0
Aquaculture	0.0	0.5	1.0
Total catch	109.9	100.5	101.0

* FAO estimates.

2003–06 (FAO estimates): Data assumed to be unchanged from 2002.

Source: FAO.

Mining

(metric tons, unless otherwise indicated, estimates)

	2004	2005	2006
Gold (kg)	37,911	44,230	51,957
Salt	6,000	6,000	6,000

Source: US Geological Survey.

Industry

SELECTED PRODUCTS
('000 metric tons, unless otherwise indicated)

	1999	2000	2001
Raw sugar*	31.2†	29.1	28.0
Salted, dried or smoked fish*	6.4	8.0	7.9
Cigarettes ('000 packets)	51.4	n.a.	n.a.
Cement‡	10	10	n.a.
Electric energy (million kWh)§	404	412	415

* Data from FAO.
† Unofficial figure.
‡ Data from the US Geological Survey.
§ Provisional or estimated figures.

2002: Raw sugar ('000 metric tons) 32.0 (data from FAO).

Electrical energy (million kWh): 417 in 2002; 449 in 2003; 455 in 2004.

Source: mainly UN, *Industrial Commodity Statistics Yearbook*.

Finance

CURRENCY AND EXCHANGE RATES

Monetary Units
100 centimes = 1 franc de la Communauté financière africaine (CFA).

Sterling, Dollar and Euro Equivalents (31 December 2008)
£1 sterling = 687.113 francs CFA;
US $1 = 471.335 francs CFA;
€1 = 655.957 francs CFA;
10,000 francs CFA = £14.55 = $21.21 = €15.24.

Average Exchange Rate (francs CFA per US $)
2006 522.89
2007 479.27
2008 447.81

Note: An exchange rate of 1 French franc = 50 francs CFA, established in 1948, remained in force until January 1994, when the CFA franc was devalued by 50%, with the exchange rate adjusted to 1 French franc = 100 francs CFA. This relationship to French currency remained in effect with the introduction of the euro on 1 January 1999. From that date, accordingly, a fixed exchange rate of €1 = 655.957 francs CFA has been in operation.

BUDGET
('000 million francs CFA)*

Revenue†	2006	2007	2008‡
Budgetary revenue	504.5	509.4	539.9
Tax revenue	478.6	487.2	504.7
Non-tax revenue	25.9	22.2	35.2
Special funds and annexed budgets	49.7	60.5	66.3
Total	554.2	569.9	606.2

Expenditure§	2006	2007	2008‡
Budgetary expenditure	752.6	832.7	856.3
Current expenditure	411.8	437.1	475.4
Wages and salaries	147.9	162.9	194.2
Interest payments (scheduled)	15.5	13.9	14.7
Other current expenditure	248.4	260.4	266.5
Capital expenditure	340.8	395.6	380.9
Externally financed	228.7	227.6	246.3
Special funds and annexed budgets	49.7	60.5	66.3
Total	802.3	893.2	922.6

* Figures represent a consolidation of the central government budget, special funds and annexed budgets.
† Excluding grants received ('000 million francs CFA): 1,244.5 in 2006; 160.4 in 2007; 162.8 in 2008 (projected).
‡ Projected.
§ Excluding net lending ('000 million francs CFA): –6.0 in 2006; –47.6 in 2007; 9.6 in 2008 (projected).

Source: IMF, *Mali-First Review Under the Three-Year Arrangement Under the Poverty Reduction and Growth Facility, and Requests for Waiver of Nonobservance of Performance Criteria, and Deletion and Modification of Performance Criteria-Staff Report; Staff Statement; Press Release; and Statement by the Executive Director for Mali* (December 2008).

INTERNATIONAL RESERVES
(excluding gold, US $ million at 31 December)

	2005	2006	2007
IMF special drawing rights	0.3	0.1	0.1
Reserve position in IMF	13.1	14.1	15.1
Foreign exchange	841.2	955.4	1,071.9
Total	854.6	969.5	1,087.1

Source: IMF, *International Financial Statistics*.

MONEY SUPPLY
('000 million francs CFA at 31 December)

	2005	2006	2007
Currency outside banks	344.9	344.4	327.5
Demand deposits	297.1	349.8	376.2
Total money (incl. others)	642.4	694.5	704.2

Source: IMF, *International Financial Statistics*.

MALI

Statistical Survey

COST OF LIVING
(Consumer Price Index for Bamako: base: 2000 = 100)

	2005	2006	2007
Food, beverages and tobacco	115.1	114.6	117.3
Clothing	96.3	98.2	97.3
Housing, water, electricity and gas	107.5	110.1	112.3
All items (incl. others)	112.3	114.1	115.7

Source: ILO.

NATIONAL ACCOUNTS
('000 million francs CFA at current prices)

Expenditure on the Gross Domestic Product

	2004	2005	2006
Final consumption expenditure	2,270.3	2,485.0	2,630.2
Households	1,797.7	1,994.6	2,122.5
General government	472.6	490.4	507.7
Gross capital formation	577.8	541.1	637.3
Gross fixed capital formation	446.6	446.7	467.3
Changes in inventories	131.2	94.4	170.0
Total domestic expenditure	2,848.1	3,026.1	3,267.5
Exports of goods and services	643.0	724.3	899.9
Less Imports of goods and services	859.1	952.5	1,071.3
Statistical discrepancy	—	13.6	—
GDP in market prices	2,632.1	2,811.5	3,096.1

Source: Banque centrale des états de l'Afrique de l'ouest.

2007 (US $ million): Final government consumption expenditure 1,262.49; Final household consumption expenditure 4,577.41; Gross capital formation 1,490.48; *Total domestic expenditure* 7,330.38; Exports of goods and services 2,080.72; *Less* Imports of goods and services 2,298.11; *GDP in market prices* 7,113.00 (Source: African Development Bank).

Gross Domestic Product by Economic Activity

	2004	2005	2006
Agriculture, livestock-rearing, forestry and fishing	900.7	991.5	1,037.5
Mining	162.3	202.6	250.1
Manufacturing	247.7	257.7	278.8
Electricity, gas and water	42.8	50.2	63.6
Construction and public works	116.5	115.1	128.8
Trade	323.5	363.8	359.0
Transport, storage and communications	115.4	125.3	152.7
Non-market services	289.2	286.6	318.3
Other services	173.6	209.2	191.1
Sub-total	2,371.7	2,601.9	2,779.9
Import duties	260.4	209.6	316.2
GDP in purchasers' values	2,632.1	2,811.5	3,096.1

Source: Banque centrale des états de l'Afrique de l'ouest.

BALANCE OF PAYMENTS
(US $ million)

	2004	2005	2006
Exports of goods f.o.b.	976.4	1,100.9	1,550.4
Imports of goods f.o.b.	−1,092.9	−1,245.5	−1,475.4
Trade balance	−116.4	−144.6	75.0
Exports of services	241.1	274.3	313.3
Imports of services	−531.8	−588.0	−674.5
Balance on goods and services	−407.1	−458.3	−286.2
Other income received	24.0	32.0	33.2
Other income paid	−218.8	−238.9	−302.6
Balance on goods, services and income	−601.9	−665.2	−555.6
Current transfers received	251.3	286.0	380.9
Current transfers paid	−58.3	−58.5	−55.8
Current balance	−409.0	−437.6	−230.5

—continued	2004	2005	2006
Capital account (net)	151.4	148.9	140.6
Direct investment abroad	−0.8	0.9	−1.2
Direct investment from abroad	101.0	223.8	83.4
Portfolio investment assets	−3.2	−18.0	−6.9
Portfolio investment liabilities	0.6	2.9	−4.2
Financial derivatives assets	−0.4	−0.1	—
Other investment assets	−130.9	−109.2	−209.3
Other investment liabilities	133.5	232.9	−1,771.9
Net errors and omissions	−26.3	−29.1	−34.9
Overall balance	−184.0	15.5	−2,035.0

Source: IMF, *International Financial Statistics*.

External Trade

PRINCIPAL COMMODITIES
(distribution by SITC, US $ million)

Imports c.i.f.	2005	2006	2007
Food and live animals	210.8	257.0	252.2
Cereals and cereal preparations	96.6	112.4	91.3
Mineral fuels, lubricants, etc.	372.8	435.7	484.9
Petroleum, petroleum products and related materials	368.9	430.8	478.4
Chemicals and related products	255.6	252.9	338.9
Medicinal and pharmaceutical products	55.7	67.3	140.2
Manufactured goods	291.8	312.2	399.7
Iron and steel	67.7	68.9	89.0
Machinery and transport equipment	295.4	407.9	534.5
Road vehicles	101.4	142.0	158.9
Miscellaneous manufactured articles	58.8	76.3	83.1
Total (incl. others)*	1,543.6	1,819.8	2,184.8

Exports f.o.b.	2005	2006	2007
Food and live animals	59.4	79.4	93.7
Crude materials, inedible, excluding fuels	265.4	260.5	207.4
Cotton	262.7	254.1	198.7
Machinery and transport equipment	28.3	19.4	27.3
Road vehicles	7.7	6.6	5.1
Total (incl. others)†	1,075.1	1,526.1	1,440.6

* Including commodities and transactions not classified elsewhere in SITC (US $ million): 3.2 in 2005; 9.2 in 2006; 3.6 in 2007.
† Including commodities and transactions not classified elsewhere in SITC (US $ million): 695.6 in 2005; 1,135.3 in 2006; 1,085.2 in 2007.

Source: UN, *International Trade Statistics Yearbook*.

SELECTED TRADING PARTNERS
(US $ million)

Imports	2005	2006	2007
Belgium	44.8	44.6	67.2
Benin	143.3	163.8	97.5
Brazil	40.7	37.8	36.4
Burkina Faso	7.7	17.1	35.8
China, People's Repub.	75.5	111.9	130.0
Côte d'Ivoire	158.2	197.6	277.0
France (incl. Monaco)	194.5	277.3	325.9
Germany	29.8	53.3	52.3
Ghana	51.1	46.1	65.3
India	37.8	39.7	78.3
Italy	12.6	21.8	21.4

MALI

Imports—continued	2005	2006	2007
Japan	35.3	48.2	41.1
Netherlands	13.3	15.4	15.8
Senegal	177.1	220.6	432.2
South Africa	63.2	67.8	79.5
Thailand	20.2	16.0	11.2
Togo	100.9	90.2	87.3
United Arab Emirates	17.3	17.6	14.6
Ukraine	27.2	34.5	12.1
USA	73.2	91.7	81.6
Total (incl. others)	1,543.6	1,819.8	2,184.8

Exports	2005	2006	2007
Bangladesh	21.4	12.4	11.8
Belgium	3.8	4.7	30.4
China, People's Repub.	62.4	94.5	32.1
Côte d'Ivoire	14.0	18.8	36.0
France (incl. Monaco)	24.0	16.6	12.6
Germany	18.4	4.2	2.9
Guinea	3.5	10.2	11.3
Indonesia	7.5	20.6	25.7
Italy	12.8	5.7	6.9
Malaysia	14.5	1.9	5.1
Pakistan	7.7	2.8	30.1
Senegal	73.7	40.6	61.1
South Africa	375.0	1,084.0	966.0
Switzerland-Liechtenstein	325.9	22.6	65.6
United Kingdom	0.5	19.6	26.5
Viet Nam	22.0	34.6	23.5
Total (incl. others)	1,075.1	1,526.1	1,440.6

Source: UN, *International Trade Statistics Yearbook*.

Transport

RAILWAYS
(traffic)

	1999	2000	2001
Passengers ('000)	778.7	682.3	649.0
Freight carried ('000 metric tons)	535	438	358

Passenger-km (million): 210 in 1999.
Freight ton-km (million): 241 in 1999.

ROAD TRAFFIC
(motor vehicles in use, estimates)

	1994	1995	1996
Passenger cars	24,250	24,750	26,190
Lorries and vans	16,000	17,100	18,240

1998 (motor vehicles in use): Passenger cars 29,374; Total road vehicles 47,374.

Source: IRF, *World Road Statistics*.

CIVIL AVIATION
(traffic on scheduled services)*

	1999	2000	2001
Kilometres flown (million)	3	3	1
Passengers carried ('000)	84	77	46
Passenger-km (million)	235	216	130
Total ton-km (million)	36	32	19

* Including an apportionment of the traffic of Air Afrique.

Source: UN, *Statistical Yearbook*.

Tourism

FOREIGN VISITORS BY NATIONALITY*

	2004	2005	2006
Austria	1,167	2,175	977
Belgium, Luxembourg and the Netherlands	6,591	9,002	9,258
Canada	3,543	3,646	4,285
France	37,971	37,851	42,661
Germany	3,676	5,885	6,623
Italy	6,087	7,066	8,615
Japan	3,117	2,090	1,636
Middle Eastern states	1,524	1,064	1,128
Scandinavian states	800	1,964	2,015
Spain	4,322	7,069	7,787
Switzerland	1,236	2,384	2,066
United Kingdom	560	5,180	5,006
USA	8,951	9,641	14,222
West African states	21,993	23,972	18,902
Total (incl. others)	112,654	142,814	152,660

* Arrivals at hotels and similar establishments.

Receipts from tourism (US $ million, excl. passenger transport): 140 in 2004; 148 in 2005; 167 in 2006.

Source: World Tourism Organization.

Communications Media

	2005	2006	2007
Telephones ('000 main lines in use)	75.0	82.5	80.0
Mobile cellular telephones ('000 subscribers)	869.6	1,512.9	2,530.9
Personal computers ('000 in use)	45	n.a.	n.a.
Internet users ('000)	60	88.4	100.0
Broadband subscribers ('000)	—	3.1	3.2

Source: International Telecommunication Union.

Television receivers ('000 in use): 160 in 2000 (Source: UNESCO, *Statistical Yearbook*).

Radio receivers ('000 in use): 570 in 1997 (Source: UNESCO, *Statistical Yearbook*).

Daily newspapers (national estimates): 3 (total circulation 12,350 copies) in 1997; 3 (total circulation 12,600) in 1998; 9 in 2004 (Source: UNESCO Institute for Statistics).

Book production: 14 titles (28,000 copies) in 1995 (first editions only, excluding pamphlets); 33 in 1998 (Sources: UNESCO, *Statistical Yearbook*, UNESCO Institute for Statistics).

Education

(2006/07, unless otherwise indicated)

	Institutions*	Teachers	Males	Females	Total
Pre-primary	212	1,510	n.a.	n.a.	54.6
Primary	2,871	33,230	954.4	762.5	1,717.0
Secondary	n.a.	15,013	308.8	225.1	533.9
Tertiary†	n.a.	1,112	22.3	10.3	32.6

* 1998/99.
† 2004/05.

Source: mainly UNESCO Institute for Statistics.

2005/06: *Pre-primary:* 412 institutions; 1,510 teachers; 51,071 students; *Primary and Secondary (lower):* 8,079 institutions; 39,109 teachers; 1,990,765 students (1,137,787 males, 852,978 females); *Secondary (higher):* 121 institutions; 1,904 teachers; 47,279 students (31,724 males, 15,555 females—estimates); *Secondary (technical and vocational):* 119 institutions; 41,137 students; *Secondary (teacher training):* 10,467 students (Source: Office of the Secretary-General of the Government, Bamako).

Adult literacy rate (UNESCO estimates): 23.3% (males 31.4%; females 16.0%) in 2007 (Source: UNESCO Institute for Statistics).

Directory

The Constitution

The Constitution of the Third Republic of Mali was approved in a national referendum on 12 January 1992. The document upholds the principles of national sovereignty and the rule of law in a secular, multi-party state, and provides for the separation of powers of the executive, legislative and judicial organs of state.

Executive power is vested in the President of the Republic, who is Head of State and is elected for five years by universal adult suffrage. The President appoints the Prime Minister, who, in turn, appoints other members of the Council of Ministers.

Legislative authority is exercised by the unicameral 147-member Assemblée nationale, which is elected for five years by universal adult suffrage.

The Constitution guarantees the independence of the judiciary. Final jurisdiction in constitutional matters is vested in a Constitutional Court.

The rights, freedoms and obligations of Malian citizens are enshrined in the Constitution. Freedom of the press and of association are guaranteed.

The Government

HEAD OF STATE

President: Gen. (retd) AMADOU TOUMANI TOURÉ (took office 8 June 2002; re-elected 29 April 2007).

COUNCIL OF MINISTERS
(April 2009)

Prime Minister: MODIBO SIDIBÉ.
Minister of Employment and Professional Training: IBRAHIMA N'DIAYE.
Minister of Health: OUMAR IBRAHIMA TOURÉ.
Minister of Crafts and Tourism: N'DIAYE BA.
Minister of Territorial Administration and Local Communities: Gen. KAFOUGOUNA KONÉ.
Minister of Stockbreeding and Fisheries: MADELEINE BA DIALLO.
Minister of Foreign Affairs and International Co-operation: MOCTAR OUANE.
Minister of Agriculture: AGATHANE AG ALASSANE.
Minister of Industry, Investment and Commerce: AHMADOU ABDOULAYE DIALLO.
Minister of Mining: ABOU-BACAR TRAORÉ.
Minister of Equipment and Transport: HAMED DIANE SEMEGA.
Minister of the Economy and Finance: SANOUSSI TOURÉ.
Minister of Internal Security and Civil Protection: Gen. SADIO GASSAMA.
Minister of Higher Education and Scientific Research: SIBY GINETTE BELLEGARDE.
Minister of Defence and Veterans: NATIÉ PLÉAH.
Minister of Education, Literacy and the National Languages: SALIKOU SANOGO.
Minister of Malians Abroad and African Integration: BADRA ALOU MACALOU.
Minister for the Promotion of Women, Children and the Family: SINA BAMBA MAIGA.
Minister of Communication and New Information Technologies: MARIAM FLANTIÉ DIALLO DIARRA.
Minister of the Environment and Sanitation: TIÉMOKO SANGARE.
Minister of Labour, Civil Service and State Reform: ABDOUL WAHAB BERTHE.
Minister of Social Development, Solidarity and the Elderly: SÉKOU DIAKITE.
Minister of Justice, Keeper of the Seals: MAHARAFA TRAORÉ.
Minister of Housing, Town Planning and Land Affairs: SALIMATA GAKOU FOFANA.
Minister of Culture: MOHAMMED EL MOCTAR.
Minister of Youth and Sports: HAMANE NIANG.
Minister in charge of Relations with the Institutions and Government Spokesperson: FATOUMATA DIABATE GUINDO.
Minister of Energy and Water: MAMADOU IGOR DIARRA.
Minister-delegate at the Ministry of the Economy, responsible for the Budget: LASSINE BOUARÉ.
Secretary of State at the Office of the Prime Minister, responsible for the Integrated Development of the Office du Niger Zone: ABOU SOW.

MINISTRIES

Office of the President: BP 1463, Koulouba, Bamako; tel. 2022-2572; fax 2023-0026; internet www.koulouba.pr.ml.

Office of the Prime Minister: Quartier du Fleuve, BP 790, Bamako; tel. 2022-4310; fax 2023-9595; internet www.primature.gov.ml.

Office of the Secretary-General of the Government: BP 14, Koulouba, Bamako; tel. 2022-2552; fax 2022-7050; e-mail sgg@sgg.gov.ml; internet www.sgg.gov.ml.

Ministry of Agriculture: BP 1676, Bamako; tel. 2022-2785; e-mail ministere@ma.gov.ml; internet www.maliagriculture.org.

Ministry of Communication and New Information Technologies: ave de l'Yser, Quartier du Fleuve, BP 116, Bamako; tel. and fax 2022-2054.

Ministry of Crafts and Tourism: Badalabougou, Semagesco, BP 2211, Bamako; tel. 2029-6450; fax 2029-3917; e-mail malitourisme@afribone.net.ml; internet www.malitourisme.com.

Ministry of Culture: rue 321, Porte 287, BP 4075, Bamako; tel. 2023-2640; fax 2023-2646; e-mail info@culture.gov.ml; internet www.maliculture.net.

Ministry of Defence and Veterans: route de Koulouba, BP 2083, Bamako; tel. 2022-5021; fax 2023-2318.

Ministry of the Economy and Finance: Bamako; internet www.finances.gov.ml.

Ministry of Education, Literacy and the National Languages: Bamako.

Ministry of Employment and Professional Training: Bamako; tel. 2022-3431.

Ministry of Energy and Water: Bamako.

Ministry of the Environment and Sanination: Bamako; tel. 2023-0539.

Ministry of Equipment and Transport: Bamako; tel. 2022-3937.

Ministry of Foreign Affairs and International Co-operation: Koulouba, Bamako; tel. 2022-8314; fax 2022-5226.

Ministry of Health: BP 232, Koulouba, Bamako; tel. 2022-5302; fax 2023-0203.

Ministry of Higher Education and Scientific Research: BP 71, Bamako; tel. 2022-5780; fax 2022-2126; e-mail info@education.gov.ml; internet www.education.gov.ml.

Ministry of Housing, Town Planning and Land Affairs: Bamako; tel. 2023-0539.

Ministry of Industry, Investment and Commerce: BP 234, Koulouba, Bamako; tel. 2022-5156; fax 2022-0192.

Ministry of Internal Security and Civil Protection: BP E 4771, Bamako; tel. 2022-0082.

Ministry of Justice: Quartier du Fleuve, BP 97, Bamako; tel. 2022-2642; fax 2023-0063; e-mail ucprodej@afribone.net.ml; internet www.justicemali.org.

Ministry of Labour, Civil Service and State Reform: Bamako; tel. 2022-3180.

Ministry of Malians Abroad and African Integration: Cité du Niger, route de l'Hotel Mandé, Bamako; tel. 2021-8148; fax 2021-2505; e-mail maliensdelexterieur@yahoo.fr; internet www.maliensdelexterieur.gov.ml.

Ministry of Mining: BP 238, Bamako; tel. 2022-4184; fax 2022-2160.

Ministry for the Promotion of Women, Children and the Family: porte G9, rue 109, Badalabougou, BP 2688, Bamako; tel. 2022-6659; fax 2023-6660; e-mail mpfef@cefib.com; internet www.mpfef.gov.ml.

Ministry of Social Development, Solidarity and the Elderly: Bamako; tel. 2023-2301.

Ministry of Stockbreeding and Fisheries: Bamako; tel. 2023-3696.

Ministry of Territorial Administration and Local Communities: face Direction de la RCFM, BP 78, Bamako; tel. 2022-4212; fax 2023-0247; internet www.matcl.gov.ml.

MALI

Ministry of Youth and Sports: route de Koulouba, BP 91, Bamako; tel. 2022-3153; fax 2023-9067; e-mail mjsports@mjsports.gov.ml; internet www.mjsports.gov.ml.

President and Legislature

PRESIDENT

Presidential Election, 29 April 2007

Candidate	Votes	% of votes
Gen. (retd) Amadou Toumani Touré (Independent)	1,612,912	71.20
Ibrahim Boubacar Keïta (RPM)	433,897	19.15
Tiébilé Dramé (PARENA)	68,956	3.04
Oumar Mariko (SADI)	61,670	2.72
Others	88,048	3.89
Total	**2,265,483**	**100.00**

LEGISLATURE

Assemblée nationale

BP 284, Bamako; tel. 2021-5724; fax 2021-0374; e-mail mamou@blonba.malinet.ml.

President: DIONCOUNDA TRAORÉ.

General Election, 1 and 22 July 2007

Party	Seats
Alliance pour la démocratie au Mali—Parti pan-africain pour la liberté, la solidarité et la justice (ADEMA)	51
Union pour la République et la démocratie (URD)	34
Rassemblement pour le Mali (RPM)	11
Mouvement patriotique pour le renouveau (MPR)	8
Congrès national d'initiative démocratique—Faso Yiriwa Ton (CNID)	7
Parti pour la renaissance nationale (PARENA)	4
Parti de la solidarité africaine pour la démocratie et l'indépendance (SADI)	4
Union pour la démocratie et le développement (UDD)	3
Bloc des alternances pour le renouveau, l'intégration et la coopération africaine (BARICA)	2
Mouvement pour l'indépendance, la renaissance et l'intégration africaine (MIRIA)	2
Parti de la solidarité et du progrès (PSP)	2
Bloc pour la démocratie et l'intégration africaine—Faso Jigi (BDIA)	1
Parti citoyen pour le renouveau (PCR)	1
Rassemblement national pour la démocratie (RND)	1
Union soudanaise—Rassemblement démocratique africaine (US—RDA)	1
Independents	15
Total	**147**

Election Commission

Commission électorale nationale indépendante (CENI): Bamako; Pres. FODIÉ TOURÉ.

Advisory Councils

Economic, Social and Cultural Council: BP E15, Koulouba, Bamako; tel. 2022-4368; fax 2022-8452; e-mail cesc@cefib.com; internet www.cesc.org.ml; f. 1987; Pres. MOUSSA BALLA COULIBALY.

High Council of Communities: Bamako; compulsorily advises the Govt on issues relating to local and regional devt; comprises national councillors, elected indirectly for a term of five years; Pres. OUMAROU AG MOHAMED IBRAHIM HAÏDARA.

Political Organizations

In 2007 there were 94 political parties officially registered in Mali, the most active of which included:

Alliance pour la démocratie au Mali—Parti pan-africain pour la liberté, la solidarité et la justice (ADEMA): rue Fankélé, porte 145, BP 1791, Bamako-Coura; tel. 2022-0368; internet www.adema-pasj.org; f. 1990 as Alliance pour la démocratie au Mali; Pres. DIONCOUNDA TRAORÉ; Sec.-Gen. MARIMATIA DIARRA.

Bloc des alternances pour le renouveau, l'intégration et la coopération africaine (BARICA): Bamako.

Bloc pour la démocratie et l'intégration africaine—Faso Jigi (BDIA): Bolibana, rue 376, porte 83, BP E 2833, Bamako-Coura; tel. 2023-8202; f. 1993; liberal, democratic; Leader SOULEYMANE MAKAMBA DOUMBIA.

Congrès national d'initiative démocratique—Faso Yiriwa Ton (CNID): rue 426, porte 58, Niarela, BP 2572, Bamako; tel. 2021-4275; fax 2022-8321; e-mail cnid@cefib.com; f. 1991; Chair. Me MOUNTAGA TALL; Sec.-Gen. N'DIAYE BA.

Convention démocratique et sociale (CDS): Ouolofobougou-Bolibana, rue 417, porte 46, Bamako; tel. 2029-2625; f. 1996; Chair. MAMADOU BAKARY SANGARÉ.

Convention parti du peuple (COPP): Korofina nord, BP 9012, Bamako; fax 2021-3591; e-mail lawyergakou@datatech.toolnet.org; f. 1996; Pres. Me MAMADOU GACKOU.

Mouvement patriotique pour le renouveau (MPR): Quinzambougou, BP E 1108, Bamako; tel. 2021-5546; fax 2021-5543; f. 1995; Pres. Dr CHOGUEL KOKALA MAÏGA.

Mouvement pour l'indépendance, la renaissance et l'intégration africaine (MIRIA): Dravéla, Bolibana, rue 417, porte 66, Bamako; tel. 2029-2981; fax 2029-2979; e-mail miria12002@yahoo.fr; f. 1994 following split in ADEMA; Pres. MOHAMED LAMINE TRAORÉ.

Parti citoyen pour le renouveau (PCR): Niaréla II, rue 428, porte 592, Bamako; tel. 6672-0988; internet pcrmali.net; f. 2005; supports administration of Pres. Touré; Pres. OUSMANE BEN FANA TRAORÉ.

Parti de la solidarité africaine pour la démocratie et l'indépendance (SADI): Djélibougou, rue 246, porte 559, BP 3140, Bamako; tel. 2024-1004; f. 2002; Leader CHEICK OUMAR SISSOKO.

Parti de la solidarité et du progrès (PSP): rue 552, porte 255, Quinzambougou, Bamako; tel. 2021-9960; f. 1945; Pres. OUMAR HAMMADOUN DICKO.

Parti malien pour le développement et le renouveau (PMDR): Sema I, rue 76, porte 62, BP 553, Badalabougou, Bamako; tel. 2022-2558; f. 1991; social democratic; Pres. Me ABDOUL WAHAB BERTHE.

Parti pour la démocratie et le progrès (PDP): Korofina sud, rue 96, porte 437, Bamako; tel. 2024-1675; fax 2020-2314; f. 1991; Leader MADY KONATÉ.

Parti pour la démocratie et le renouveau—Dounkafa Ton (PDR): Bamako; f. 1998; Pres. ADAMA KONÉ; Leader KALILOU SAMAKE.

Parti pour la renaissance nationale (PARENA): rue Soundiata, porte 1397, BP E 2235, Ouolofobougou, Bamako; tel. 2023-4954; fax 2022-2908; e-mail info@parena.org.ml; internet www.parena.org.ml; f. 1995 following split in CNID; Pres. TIÉBILÉ DRAMÉ; Sec.-Gen. AMIDOU DIABATÉ.

Parti pour l'indépendance, la démocratie et la solidarité (PIDS): Hippodrome, rue 250, porte 1183, BP E 1515, Bamako; tel. 2077-4575; f. 2001 by dissidents from US—RDA; Pres. DABA DIAWARA.

Rassemblement malien pour le travail (RAMAT): Marché, Hippodrome, rue 224, porte 1393, BP E 2281, Bamako; tel. 6674-4603; f. 1991; Leader ABDOULAYE MACKO.

Rassemblement national pour la démocratie (RND): Niaréla, route Sotuba, porte 1892, Hamdallaye, Bamako; tel. 2029-1849; fax 2029-0939; f. 1997 by 'moderate' breakaway group from RDP; Pres. ABDOULAYE GARBA TAPO.

Rassemblement pour la démocratie et le progrès (RDP): Niarela, rue 485, porte 11, BP 2110, Bamako; tel. 2021-3092; fax 2024-6795; f. 1991; Sec.-Gen. IBRAHIM DIAKITE (acting).

Rassemblement pour le Mali (RPM): Hippodrome, rue 232, porte 130, BP 9057, Bamako; tel. 2021-1433; fax 2021-1336; e-mail siegerpmbko@yahoo.fr; internet www.rpm.org.ml; f. 2001; Pres. IBRAHIM BOUBACAR KEÏTA; Sec.-Gen. Dr BOCARY TRETA.

Union des forces démocratiques pour le progrès—Sama-ton (UFDP): Quartier Mali, BP E 37, Bamako; tel. 2023-1766; f. 1991; mem. of informal alliance supportive of Pres. Touré, the Convergence pour l'alternance et le changement (ACC), during 2002 legislative elections; Sec.-Gen. Col YOUSSOUF TRAORÉ.

Union pour la démocratie et le développement (UDD): ave OUA, porte 3626, Sogoniko, BP 2969, Bamako; tel. 2020-3971; f. 1991 by supporters of ex-Pres. Traoré; Leader Me HASSANE BARRY.

Union pour la République et la démocratie (URD): Niaréla, rue 268, porte 41, Bamako; tel. 2021-8621; e-mail contact@urd-mali.net; internet www.urd-mali.net; f. 2003 by fmr mems of ADEMA (q.v.) allied to 2002 presidential candidate Soumaïla Cissé; Pres. YOUNOUSSI TOURÉ.

Union soudanaise—Rassemblement démocratique africain (US—RDA): Hippodrome, porte 41, BP E 1413, Bamako; tel. and fax 2021-4522; f. 1946; sole party 1960–68, banned 1968–1991; 'moderate' faction split from party in 1998; Leader Dr BADARA ALIOU MACALOU.

Diplomatic Representation

EMBASSIES IN MALI

Algeria: Daoudabougou, BP 02, Bamako; tel. 2020-5176; fax 2022-9374; Ambassador ABDELKREM GHRAIEB.

Burkina Faso: ACI-2000, Commune III, BP 9022, Bamako; tel. 2023-3171; fax 2021-9266; e-mail ambafaso@experco.net; Ambassador Prof. SANNÉ MOHAMED TOPAN.

Canada: route de Koulikoro, Immeuble Séméga, Hippodrome, BP 198, Bamako; tel. 2021-2236; fax 2021-4362; e-mail bmako@international.gc.ca; internet www.bamako.gc.ca; Ambassador ISABELLE ROY.

China, People's Republic: route de Koulikoro, Hippodrome, BP 112, Bamako; tel. 2021-3597; fax 2022-3443; e-mail chinaemb_ml@mfa.gov.cn; internet ml.china-embassy.org/fra; Ambassador ZHANG GUOQING.

Côte d'Ivoire: square Patrice Lumumba, Immeuble CNAR, BP E 3644, Bamako; tel. 2022-0389; fax 2022-1376; Ambassador ABOUBACAR SIRIKI DIABATÉ.

Cuba: porte 31, rue 328, Niarela, Bamako; tel. 2021-0289; fax 2021-0293; e-mail emcuba.mali@malinet.ml; Ambassador ALBERTO MIGUEL OTERO LÓPEZ.

Egypt: Badalabougou-est, BP 44, Bamako; tel. 2022-3565; fax 2022-0891; e-mail mostafa@datatech.net.ml; Ambassador MOSTAFA ABDEL HAMID GENDY.

France: square Patrice Lumumba, BP 17, Bamako; tel. 4497-5757; fax 2022-3136; e-mail ambassade@france-mali.org.ml; internet www.ambafrance-ml.org; Ambassador MICHEL REVEYRAND DE MENTHON.

Germany: Badalabougou-est, rue 14, porte 334, BP 100, Bamako; tel. 2022-3299; fax 2022-9650; e-mail allemagne.presse@afribonemali.net; internet www.bamako.diplo.de; Ambassador KARL FLITTNER.

Ghana: BP 3161, Bamako; Ambassador Maj.-Gen. C. B. YAACHIE.

Guinea: Immeuble Saybou Maïga, Quartier du Fleuve, BP 118, Bamako; tel. 2022-3007; fax 2021-0806; Ambassador (vacant).

Iran: ave al-Quds, Hippodrome, BP 2136, Bamako; tel. 2021-7638; fax 2021-0731; Ambassador (vacant).

Korea, Democratic People's Republic: Bamako; Ambassador KIM PONG HUI.

Libya: Badalabougou-ouest, face Palais de la Culture, BP 1670, Bamako; tel. 2022-3496; fax 2022-6697; Ambassador Dr SALAHEDDIN AHMED ZAREM.

Mauritania: route de Koulikoro, Hippodrome, BP 135, Bamako; tel. 2021-4815; fax 2022-4908; Ambassador SIDAMINE OULD AHMED CHALLA.

Morocco: Badalabougou-est, rue 25, porte 80, BP 2013, Bamako; tel. 2022-2123; fax 2022-7787; e-mail sifamali@afribone.net.ml; Ambassador MOULAY DRISS FADHILL.

Netherlands: rue 437, BP 2220, Hippodrome, Bamako; tel. 2021-5611; fax 2021-3617; e-mail bam@minbuza.nl; internet www.mfa.nl/bam; Ambassador ELLEN VAN DER LAAN.

Nigeria: Badalabougou-est, BP 57, Bamako; tel. 2021-5328; fax 2022-3974; e-mail ngrbko@malinet.ml; Ambassador MOHAMMED SANI KANGIWA.

Russia: BP 300, Niarela, Bamako; tel. 2021-5592; fax 2021-9926; Ambassador ANATOLII P. SMIRNOV.

Saudi Arabia: Villa Bal Harbour, 28 Cité du Niger, BP 81, Bamako; tel. 2021-2528; fax 2021-5064; e-mail mlemb@mofa.gov.sa; Ambassador FAUWAZ MISHIL AL TIMYAT.

Senegal: porte 341, rue 287, angle ave Nelson Mandela, BP 42, Bamako; tel. 2021-0859; fax 2016-9268; Ambassador SAOUDATOU NDIAYE SECK.

South Africa: bât. Diarra, Hamdallaye, ACI-2000, BP 2015, Bamako; tel. 2029-2925; fax 2029-2926; e-mail bamako@foreign.gov.za; Ambassador R. W. MOKOU.

Spain: porte 81, rue 13, Badalabougou-est, BP 3230, Bamako; tel. 2023-6527; fax 2023-6524; e-mail emb.bamako@maec.es; Ambassador Dr LOURDES MELÉNDEZ GARCÍA.

Tunisia: Quartier du Fleuve, Bamako; tel. 2023-2891; fax 2022-1755; Ambassador MOHAMED NACEUR QORT.

USA: ACI 2000, rue 243, porte 297, Bamako; tel. 2070-2300; fax 2070-2479; e-mail webmaster@usa.org.ml; internet mali.usembassy.gov; Ambassador GILLIAN ARLETTE MILOVANOVIC.

Judicial System

The 1992 Constitution guarantees the independence of the judiciary.

High Court of Justice: Bamako; competent to try the President of the Republic and ministers of the Government for high treason and for crimes committed in the course of their duties, and their accomplices in any case where state security is threatened; mems designated by the mems of the Assemblée nationale, and renewed annually.

Supreme Court: BP 7, Bamako; tel. 2022-2406; e-mail csupreme@afribone.net.ml; f. 1969; comprises judicial, administrative and auditing sections; judicial section comprises five chambers, administrative section comprises two chambers, auditing section comprises three chambers; Pres. DIALLO KAÏTA KAYENTAO; Sec.-Gen. ALKAÏDY SANIBIÉ TOURÉ.

President of the Bar: Me MAGATTÉ SÈYE.

Constitutional Court: BP E 213, Bamako; tel. 2022-5609; fax 2023-4241; e-mail tawatybouba@yahoo.fr; f. 1994; Pres. AMADI TAMBA CAMARA; Sec.-Gen. BOUBACAR TAWATY.

There are three Courts of Appeal, seven Tribunaux de première instance (Magistrates' Courts) and also courts for labour disputes.

Religion

According to the UN Development Programme's *Human Development Report*, around 80% of the population are Muslims, while 18% follow traditional animist beliefs and under 2% are Christians.

ISLAM

Association Malienne pour l'Unité et le Progrès de l'Islam (AMUPI): Bamako; state-endorsed Islamic governing body.

Chief Mosque: pl. de la République, Bagadadji, Bamako; tel. 2021-2190.

Haut Conseil Islamique: Bamako; f. 2002; responsible for management of relations between the Muslim communities and the State; Pres. MAHMOUD DICKO.

CHRISTIANITY

The Roman Catholic Church

Mali comprises one archdiocese and five dioceses. At 31 December 2006 there were an estimated 240,533 Roman Catholics, comprising about 1.7% of the total population.

Bishops' Conference

Conférence Episcopale du Mali, Archevêché, BP 298, Bamako; tel. 2022-5499; fax 2022-5214; e-mail cemali@afribone.net.ml. f. 1973; Pres. Most Rev. JEAN-GABRIEL DIARRA (Bishop of San).

Archbishop of Bamako: JEAN ZERBO, Archevêché, BP 298, Bamako; tel. 2022-5842; fax 2022-7850; e-mail mgrjeanzerbo@afribonemali.net.

Other Christian Churches

There are several Protestant mission centres, mainly administered by US societies.

BAHÁ'Í FAITH

National Spiritual Assembly: BP 1657, Bamako; e-mail ntirandaz@aol.com.

The Press

The 1992 Constitution guarantees the freedom of the press. In 2000 there were six daily newspapers, 18 weekly or twice-weekly publications and six-monthly or twice-monthly publications.

DAILY NEWSPAPERS

Les Echos: Hamdallaye, ave Cheick Zayed, porte 2694, BP 2043, Bamako; tel. 2029-6289; fax 2026-7639; e-mail lesechos@jamana.org; internet www.jamana.org/lesechos; f. 1989; daily; publ. by Jamana cultural co-operative; circ. 30,000; Dir ALEXIS KALAMBRY; Editor-in-Chief ABOUBACAR SALIPH DIARRA.

L'Essor: square Patrice Lumumba, BP 141, Bamako; tel. 2022-3683; fax 2022-4774; e-mail info@essor.gov.ml; internet www.essor.gov

MALI

.ml; f. 1949; daily; pro-Govt newspaper; Editor SOULEYMANE DRABO; circ. 3,500.

Info Matin: rue 56/350, Bamako Coura, BP E 4020, Bamako; tel. 2023-8209; fax 2023-8227; e-mail redaction@info-matin.com; internet www.info-matin.com; independent; Dir SAMBI TOURÉ; Editor-in-Chief MOHAMED SACKO.

Le Républicain: 116 rue 400, Dravéla-Bolibana, BP 1484, Bamako; tel. 2029-0900; fax 2029-0933; internet www.lerepublicain.net.ml; f. 1992; independent; Dir SALIF KONÉ.

PERIODICALS

26 Mars: Badalabougou-Sema Gesco, Lot S13, BP MA 174, Bamako; tel. 2029-0459; f. 1998; weekly; independent; Dir BOUBACAR SANGARÉ.

L'Aurore: Niarela 298, rue 438, BP 3150, Bamako; tel. and fax 2021-6922; e-mail aurore@timbagga.com.ml; f. 1990; 2 a week; independent; Dir KARAMOKO N'DIAYE.

Le Canard Déchaîné: Immeuble Koumara, bloc 104, Centre Commercial, Bamako; tel. 7621-2686; fax 2022-86-86; e-mail maison.presse@afribone.net.ml; weekly; satirical; Dir OUMAR BABI; circ. 3,000 (2006).

Le Carrefour: ave Cheick Zayed, Hamdallaye, Bamako; tel. 2023-9808; e-mail journalcarrefour@yahoo.fr; f. 1997; Dir MAHAMANE IMRANE COULIBALY.

Citoyen: Bamako; f. 1992; fortnightly; independent.

Le Continent: AA 16, Banankabougou, BP E 4338, Bamako; tel. and fax 2029-5739; e-mail le_continent@yahoo.fr; f. 2000; weekly; Dir IBRAHIMA TRAORÉ.

Le Courrier: 230 ave Cheick Zayed, Lafiabougou Marché, BP 1258, Bamako; tel. and fax 2029-1862; e-mail journalcourrier@webmails.com; f. 1996; weekly; Dir SADOU A. YATTARA; also *Le Courrier Magazine*, monthly.

L'Indépendant: Immeuble ABK, Hamdallaye ACI, BP E 1040, Bamako; tel. and fax 2023-2727; e-mail independant@cefib.com; 2 a week; Dir SAOUTI HAÏDARA.

L'Inspecteur: Immeuble Nimagala, bloc 262, BP E 4534, Bamako; tel. 6672-4711; e-mail inspecteurmali@yahoo.fr; f. 1992; weekly; Dir ALY DIARRA.

Jamana—Revue Culturelle Malienne: BP 2043, Bamako; BP E 1040; e-mail infos@jamana.org; f. 1983; quarterly; organ of Jamana cultural co-operative.

Journal Officiel de la République du Mali: Koulouba, BP 14, Bamako; tel. 2022-5986; fax 2022-7050; official gazette.

Kabaaru: Village Kibaru, Bozola, Bamako; f. 1983; state-owned; monthly; Fulbé (Peul) language; rural interest; Editor BADAMA DOUCOURÉ; circ. 5,000.

Kibaru: Village Kibaru, Bozola, BP 1463, Bamako; f. 1972; monthly; state-owned; Bambara and three other languages; rural interest; Editor NIANZÉ SAMAKÉ; circ. 5,000.

Liberté: Immeuble Sanago, Hamdallaye Marché, BP E 24, Bamako; tel. 2028-1898; e-mail ladji.guindo@cefib.com; f. 1999; weekly; Dir ABDOULAYE LADJI GUINDO.

Le Malien: rue 497, porte 277, Badialan III, BP E 1558, Bamako; tel. 2023-5729; fax 2029-1339; e-mail lemalien2000@yahoo.fr; f. 1993; weekly; Dir SIDI KEITA.

Match: 97 rue 498, Lafiabougou, BP E 3776, Bamako; tel. 2029-1882; e-mail bcissouma@yahoo.fr; f. 1997; 2 a month; sports; Dir BABA CISSOUMA.

Musow: BP E 449, Bamako; tel. 2028-0000; fax 2028-0001; e-mail musow@musow.com; internet www.musow.com; women's interest.

Nyéléni Magazine: Niarela 298, rue 348, BP 13150, Bamako; tel. 2029-2401; f. 1991; monthly; women's interest; Dir MAÏMOUNA TRAORÉ.

L'Observateur: Galérie Djigué, rue du 18 juin, BP E 1002, Bamako; tel. and fax 2023-0689; e-mail belcotamboura@hotmail.com; f. 1992; 2 a week; Dir BELCO TAMBOURA.

Le Reflet: Immeuble Kanadjigui, route de Koulikoro, Boulkassoumbougou, BP E 1688, Bamako; tel. 2024-3952; fax 2023-2308; e-mail lereflet@afribone.malinet.ml; weekly; fmrly Le Carcan; present name adopted Jan. 2001; Dir ABDOUL KARIM DRAMÉ.

Royal Sports: BP 98, Sikasso; tel. 6672-4988; weekly; also *Tatou Sports*, publ. monthly; Pres. and Dir-Gen. ALY TOURÉ.

Le Scorpion: 230 ave Cheick Zayed, Lafiabougou Marché, BP 1258, Bamako; tel. and fax 2029-1862; f. 1991; weekly; Dir MAHAMANE HAMÈYE CISSÉ.

Le Tambour: rue 497, porte 295, Badialan III, BP E 289, Bamako; tel. and fax 2022-7568; e-mail tambourj@yahoo.fr; f. 1994; 2 a week; Dir YÉRO DIALLO.

NEWS AGENCY

Agence Malienne de Presse et Publicité (AMAP): square Patrice Lumumba, BP 141, Bamako; tel. 2022-3683; fax 2022-4774; e-mail amap@afribone.net.ml; f. 1977; Dir SOULEYMANE DRABO.

PRESS ASSOCIATIONS

Association des Editeurs de la Presse Privée (ASSEP): BP E 1002, Bamako; tel. 6671-3133; e-mail belcotamboura@hotmail.com; Pres. BELCO TAMBOURA.

Association des Femmes de la Presse Privée: porte 474, rue 428, BP E 731, Bamako; tel. 2021-2912; Pres. FANTA DIALLO.

Association des Journalistes Professionels des Médias Privés du Mali (AJPM): BP E 2456, Bamako; tel. 2022-1915; fax 2023-5478; Pres. MOMADOU FOFANA.

Association des Professionnelles Africaines de la Communication (APAC MALI): porte 474, rue 428, BP E 731, Bamako; tel. 2021-2912; Pres. MASSIRÉ YATTASSAYE.

Maison de la Presse de Mali: 17 rue 619, Darsalam, BP E 2456, Bamako; tel. 2022-1915; fax 2023-5478; e-mail maison.presse@afribone.net.ml; internet www.mediamali.org; independent media asscn; Pres. SADOU A. YATTARA.

Union Interprofessionnelle des Journalistes et de la Presse de Langue Française (UIJPLF): rue 42, Hamdallaye Marché, BP 1258, Bamako; tel. 2029-9835; Pres. MAHAMANE HAMÉYE CISSÉ.

Union Nationale des Journalistes Maliens (UNAJOM): BP 1300, Bamako; tel. 2022-1915; fax 2023-5478; e-mail ibrafam@yahoo.fr; Pres. IBRAHIM FAMAKAN COULIBALY.

Publishers

EDIM SA: ave Kassé Keïta, BP 21, Bamako; tel. 2022-4041; fax 2029-3001; e-mail edim@afribone.net.ml; f. 1972 as Editions Imprimeries du Mali; general fiction and non-fiction, textbooks; Chair. and Man. Dir ALOU TOMOTA.

Editions Donniya: Cité du Niger, BP 1273, Bamako; tel. 2021-4646; fax 2021-9031; e-mail imprimcolor@cefib.com; internet www.imprimcolor.cefib.com; f. 1996; general fiction, history, reference and children's books in French and Bambara.

Le Figuier: 151 rue 56, Semal, BP 2605, Bamako; tel. and fax 2023-3211; e-mail lefiguier@afribone.net.ml; f. 1997; fiction and non-fiction.

Editions Jamana: BP 2043, Bamako; tel. 2029-6289; fax 2029-7639; e-mail jamana@timbagga.com.ml; internet www.jamana.org; f. 1988; literary fiction, poetry, reference; Dir BA MAÏRA SOW.

Editions Teriya: BP 1677, Bamako; tel. 2024-1142; theatre, literary fiction; Dir GAOUSSOU DIAWARA.

Broadcasting and Communications

TELECOMMUNICATIONS
Regulatory Authority

Comité de Régulation des Télécommunications (CRT): BP 2206, Bamako; tel. 2023-1490; fax 2023-1494; e-mail crtmali@crt.ml; internet www.crt-mali.org; f. 1999; Dir Dr CHOGUEL K. MAÏGA.

Service Providers

Orange Mali SA: Immeuble Orange Mali ACI-2000, BP E 3991, Bamako; tel. 4499-9000; fax 4499-9001; e-mail orange@orangemali.com; internet www.orangemali.com; f. 2003 as Ikatel; repackaged under brand name Orange in 2007; fixed-line and mobile cellular telecommunications; jtly owned by France Télécom and Société Nationale des Télécommunications du Sénégal; Dir-Gen. ALIOUME N'DIAYE; 100,000 subscribers (2003).

Société des Télécommunications du Mali—Malitel (SOTELMA): route de Koulikoro, Hippodrome, BP 740, Bamako; tel. 2021-5280; fax 2021-3022; e-mail segal@sotelma.ml; internet www.sotelma.ml; f. 1990; 51% owned by Itissalat al-Maghrib—Maroc Télécom (Morocco), 20% state-owned; operates fixed-line telephone services, also mobile and cellular telecommunications in Bamako, Kayes, Mopti, Ségou and Sikasso; 90,000 fixed lines and 480,000 subscribers to mobile cellular telecommunications services (2007); Pres. and Dir-Gen. LASSANA N'DIAYE.

BROADCASTING
Radio

Office de Radiodiffusion-Télévision Malienne (ORTM): 287 rue de la Marne, BP 171, Bamako; tel. 2021-2019; fax 2021-4205;

e-mail ortm@ortm.ml; internet www.ortm.ml; Dir-Gen. SIDIKI KONATÉ; Dir of Radio OUMAR TOURÉ.

Radio Mali–Chaîne Nationale: BP 171, Bamako; tel. 2021-2019; fax 2021-4205; e-mail ortm@spider.toolnet.org; f. 1957; state-owned; radio programmes in French, Bambara, Peulh, Sarakolé, Tamachek, Sonrai, Moorish, Wolof, English.

Chaîne 2: Bamako; f. 1993; radio broadcasts to Bamako.

In late 2003 there were an estimated 130 community, commercial and religious radio stations broadcasting in Mali.

Fréquence 3: Bamako; f. 1992; commercial.

Radio Balanzan: BP 419, Ségou; tel. 2132-0288; commercial.

Radio Bamakan: Marché de Médine, BP E 100, Bamako; tel. and fax 2021-2760; e-mail radio.bamakan@ifrance.com; internet bamakan.net; f. 1991; community station; 104 hours of FM broadcasts weekly; Man. MODIBO DIALLO.

Radio Espoir—La Voix du Salut: Sogoniko, rue 130, porte 71, BP E 1399, Bamako; tel. 2020-6708; e-mail accm@mali.maf.net; f. 1998; broadcasts 16 hours of radio programming daily on topics including Christianity, devt and culture; Dir DAOUDA COULIBALY.

Radio Foko de Ségou Jamana: BP 2043, Bamako; tel. 2132-0048; fax 2022-7639; e-mail radiofoko@cefib.com.

Radio Guintan: Magnambougou, BP 2546, Bamako; tel. 2020-0938; f. 1994; community radio station; Dir RAMATA DIA.

Radio Jamana: BP 2043, Bamako; tel. 2029-6289; fax 2029-7639; e-mail radio@jamana.org; internet www.jamana.org.

Radio Kayira: Djélibougou Doumanzana, BP 3140, Bamako; tel. 2024-8782; fax 2022-7568; internet www.kayira.org; f. 1992; community station; Dir OUMAR MARIKO.

Radio Klédu: Cité du Niger, BP 2322, Bamako; tel. 2021-0018; e-mail rkledudirect@cefib.com; internet www.kleducommunication.com; f. 1992; commercial; Dir-Gen. JACQUES DEZ.

Radio Liberté: BP 5015, Bamako; tel. 2023-0581; f. 1991; commercial station broadcasting 24 hours daily; Dir ALMANY TOURÉ.

Radio Patriote: Korofina-Sud, BP E 1406, Bamako; tel. 2024-2292; f. 1995; commercial station; Dir MOUSSA KEÏTA.

Radio Rurale: Plateau, BP 94, Kayes; tel. 2153-1476; e-mail rrk@afribone.net.ml; f. 1988; community stations established by the Agence de coopération culturelle et technique (ACTT); transmitters in Niono, Kadiolo, Bandiagara and Kidal; Dir FILY KEÏTA.

Radio Sahel: BP 394, Kayes; tel. 2152-2187; f. 1991; commercial; Dir ALMAMY S. TOURÉ.

Radio Tabalé: Bamako-Coura, BP 697, Bamako; tel. and fax 2022-7870; internet www.radiotabale.org; f. 1992; independent public-service station; broadcasting 57 hours weekly; Dir TIÉMOKO KONÉ.

La Voix du Coran et du Hadit: Grande Mosquée, BP 2531, Bamako; tel. 2021-6344; f. 1993; Islamic station broadcasting on FM in Bamako; Dir El Hadj MAHMOUD DICKO.

Radio Wassoulou: BP 24, Yanfolila; tel. 2165-1097; commercial.

Radio France International, the Voix de l'Islam and the Gabonese-based Africa No. 1 began FM broadcasts in Mali in 1993; broadcasts by Voice of America and the World Service of the British Broadcasting Corpn are also transmitted via private radio stations.

Television

Office de Radiodiffusion-Télévision Malienne (ORTM): see Radio; Dir of Television BALY IDRISSA SISSOKO.

Multicanal SA: Quinzambougou, BP E 1506, Bamako; tel. 2021-4964; e-mail sandrine@multi-canal.com; internet www.multi-canal.com; private subscription broadcaster; relays international broadcasts; Pres. ISMAÏLA SIDIBÉ.

TV Klédu: 600 ave Modibo Keïta, BP E 1172, Bamako; tel. 2023-9000; fax 2023-7050; e-mail info@tvkledu.com; private cable TV operator; relays international broadcasts; Pres. MAMADOU COULIBALY.

Finance

(cap. = capital; res = reserves; dep. = deposits; m. = million; br(s). = branch(es); amounts in francs CFA)

BANKING

Central Bank

Banque centrale des états de l'Afrique de l'ouest (BCEAO): BP 206, Bamako; tel. 2022-3756; fax 2022-4786; internet www.bceao.int; f. 1962; HQ in Dakar, Senegal; bank of issue for the mem. states of Union économique et monétaire ouest-africaine (UEMOA, comprising Benin, Burkina Faso, Côte d'Ivoire, Guinea-Bissau, Mali, Niger, Senegal and Togo); cap. and res 1,148,589m., total assets 5,099,908m. (Dec. 2005); Gov. PHILIPPE-HENRI DACOURY-TABLEY; Dir in Mali IDRISSA TRAORÉ; brs at Mopti and Sikasso.

Commercial Banks

Bank of Africa—Mali (BOA—MALI): 418 ave de la Marné, Bozola, BP 2249, Bamako; tel. 2070-0500; fax 2070-0560; e-mail information@boamali.net; internet www.bank-of-africa.net; f. 1983; cap. 4,100m., res 1,760m., dep. 91,841m. (Dec. 2008); Pres. BOUREIMA SYLLA; Dir-Gen. CHRISTOPHE LASSUS-LALANNE; 7 brs.

Banque Commerciale du Sahel (BCS–SA): ave Bozola 127, BP 2372, Bamako; tel. 2021-0535; fax 2021-1660; e-mail dg@bcss.mali.com; f. 1980; fmrly Banque Arabe Libyo-Malienne pour le Commerce Extérieur et le Développement; 96.61% owned by Libyan-Arab Foreign Bank; cap. 7,500m., res 1,046m., total assets 37,953m. (Dec. 2006); Pres. KABA DIAMINATOU DIALLO; Dir-Gen. IBRAHIM ABOUJAFAR SWEAI; 1 br.

Banque de l'Habitat du Mali (BHM): ACI 2000, ave Kwamé N'Krumah, BP 2614, Bamako; tel. 2022-9190; fax 2022-9350; e-mail bhm@bhm-sa.com; internet www.bhm-sa.com; f. 1990; present name adopted 1996; 37.1% owned by Institut National de Prévoyance Social, 25.9% by Agence Cession Immobilière; cap. and res 5,414.7m., total assets 98,237.5m. (Dec. 2003); Pres. and Dir-Gen. MODIBO CISSÉ; 1 br.

Banque Internationale pour le Commerce et l'Industrie au Mali (BICI–Mali): blvd du 22 octobre 1946, Quartier du Fleuve, BP 72, Bamako; tel. 2070-0700; fax 2023-3373; e-mail bicim-dg@africa.bnpparibas.com; f. 1998; 85% owned by BNP Paribas BDDI Participations (France); cap. and res 3,678m., total assets 40,076m. (Dec. 2003); Pres. and Dir-Gen. PIERRE BÉRÉGOVOY; 1 br.

Banque Internationale pour le Mali (BIM): ave de l'Indépendance, BP 15, Bamako; tel. 2022-5066; fax 2022-4566; e-mail bim@bim.com.ml; internet www.bim.com.ml; f. 1980; present name adopted 1995; 61.5% state-owned; privatization pending; cap. 4,254m., dep. 120,250m., total assets 131,159m. (Dec. 2006); Pres. and Dir-Gen. MAMADOU IGOR DIARRA; 14 brs.

Ecobank Mali: pl. de la Nation, Quartier du Fleuve, BP E 1272, Bamako; tel. 2023-3300; fax 2023-3305; e-mail ecobank@cefib.com; f. 1998; 49.5% owned by Ecobank Transnational Inc., 17.8% by Ecobank Bénin, 14.9% by Ecobank Togo, 9.9% by Ecobank Burkina; cap. and res 2,973.9m., total assets 46,222.7m. (Dec. 2003); Pres. SEYDOU DJIM SYLLA; Dir-Gen. KASSIM ABOU KABASSI; 2 brs.

Development Banks

Banque de Développement du Mali (BDM-SA): ave Modibo Keita, Quartier du Fleuve, BP 94, Bamako; tel. 2022-2050; fax 2022-5085; e-mail info@bdm-sa.com; internet www.bdm-sa.com; f. 1968; absorbed Banque Malienne de Crédit et de Dépôts in 2001; 22.1% state-owned, 20.7% owned by Banque Marocaine du Commerce Extérieur (Morocco), 16.0% by BCEAO, 16.0% by Banque ouest-africaine de développement; cap. and res 15,658m., total assets 276,148m. (Dec. 2002); Pres. and Dir-Gen. ABDOULAYE DAFFÉ; 14 brs.

Banque Malienne de Solidarité (BMS): ave du Fleuve, Immeuble Dette Publique, 2e étage, BP 1280, Bamako; tel. and fax 2023-5034; fax 2023-5413; e-mail bms-sa@bms-sa.com; f. 2002; cap. 2.4m.; Dir BABALI BAH; 1 br.

Banque Nationale de Développement Agricole—Mali (BNDA–Mali): Immeuble BNDA, blvd du Mali, ACI 2000, BP 2424, Bamako; tel. 2029-6464; fax 2029-2575; e-mail bnda@bndamali.com; internet www.bndamali.com; f. 1981; 36.5% state-owned, 22.8% owned by Agence française de développement (France), 21.4% owned by Deutsche Entwicklungsgesellschaft (Germany), 19.4% owned by BCEAO; cap. 10,988m., res 2,188m., dep. 107,896m. (Dec. 2004); Chair., Pres. and Gen. Man. MOUSSA ALASSAME DIALLO; Dir-Gen. ARNAUD BELLAMY BROWN; 22 brs.

Financial Institutions

Direction Générale de la Dette Publique: Immeuble ex-Caisse Autonome d'Amortissement, Quartier du Fleuve, BP 1617, Bamako; tel. 2022-2935; fax 2022-0793; management of the public debt; Dir NAMALA KONÉ.

Equibail Mali: rue 376, porte 1319, Niarela, BP E 566, Bamako; tel. 2021-3777; fax 2021-3778; e-mail equip.ma@bkofafrica.com; internet www.bkofafrica.net/jeux_de_cadres/equibail/equibail_mali/equibail_mali.htm; f. 1999; 50.2% owned by African Financial Holding, 17.5% by Bank of Africa—Benin; cap. 300m. (Dec. 2002); Mems of Administrative Council RAMATOULAYE TRAORÉ, PAUL DERREUMAUX, LÉON NAKA.

Société Malienne de Financement (SOMAFI): Immeuble Air Afrique, blvd du 22 octobre 1946, BP E 3643, Bamako; tel. 2022-1866; fax 2022-1869; e-mail somafi@malinet.ml; f. 1997; cap. and res 96.9m., total assets 3,844.9m. (Dec. 2002); Man. Dir ERIC LECLÈRE.

STOCK EXCHANGE

Bourse Régionale des Valeurs Mobilières (BRVM): Chambre de Commerce et de l'Industrie du Mali, pl. de la Liberté, BP E 1398, Bamako; tel. 2023-2354; fax 2023-2359; e-mail abocoum@brvm.org; f. 1998; nat. branch of BRVM (regional stock exchange based in Abidjan, Côte d'Ivoire, serving the mem. states of UEMOA); Man. AMADOU DJÉRI BOCOUM.

INSURANCE

Les Assurances Générales de France (AGF): ave de la Nation, BP E 4447, Bamako; tel. 2022-5818; e-mail agf.mali@agf-ml.com; internet www.agf-afrique.com/filiales/mali.htm; Dir-Gen. PATRICK PRADO.

Caisse Nationale d'Assurance et de Réassurance du Mali (CNAR): BP 568, square Patrice Lumumba, Bamako; tel. 2021-3117; fax 2021-2369; f. 1969; state-owned; cap. 50m.; Dir-Gen. F. KEITA; 10 brs.

Colina Mali SA: ave Modibo Keita, BP E 154, Bamako; tel. 2022-5775; fax 2023-2423; e-mail mali@groupecolina.com; internet www.colina-bd.accelance.net/fr/ml/; f. 1990; cap. 1,000m.; Dir-Gen. MARYVONNE SIDIBE.

Compagnie d'Assurance Privée—La Soutra: BP 52, Bamako; tel. 2022-3681; fax 2022-5523; f. 1979; cap. 150m.; Chair. AMADOU NIONO.

Compagnie d'Assurance et de Réassurance de Mali: BP 1822, Bamako; tel. 2022-6029.

Compagnie d'Assurance et de Réassurance Sabu Nyuman: rue 350, porte 129, Bamako-Coura, BP 1822, Bamako; tel. 2022-6029; fax 2022-5750; e-mail assur.sn@malinet.ml; f. 1984; cap. 250m.; Dir-Gen. MOMADOU SANOGO.

Gras Savoye Mali: Immeuble SOGEFIH, 3ème etage, Quartier du Fleuve, ave Moussa Travele, BP E 5691, Bamako; tel. 2022-6469; fax 2022-6470; e-mail grassavoyemali@ml.grassavoye.com; affiliated to Gras Savoye (France); Man. FAYEZ SAMB.

Lafía Assurances: ave de la Nation, BP 1542, Bamako; tel. 2022-3551; fax 2022-5224; e-mail assurlafia@yahoo.fr; f. 1983; cap. 50m.; Dir-Gen. ABDOULAYE TOURÉ.

Trade and Industry

GOVERNMENT AGENCIES

Agence Nationale pour l'Emploi (ANPE): BP 211, Bamako; tel. 2022-3187; fax 2023-2624; e-mail anpe@anpe-mali.org; internet www.anpe-mali.org; f. 2001; Dir-Gen. Prof. MAKAN MOUSSA SISSOKO.

Centre d'Etudes et de Promotion Industrielle (CEPI): BP 1980, Bamako; tel. 2022-2279; fax 2022-8085.

Direction Nationale des Affaires Economiques (DNAE): BP 210, Bamako; tel. 2022-2314; fax 2022-2256; involved in economic and social affairs.

Direction Nationale des Travaux Publics (DNTP): ave de la Liberté, BP 1758, Bamako; tel. and fax 2022-2902; administers public works.

Guichet Unique–Direction Nationale des Industries: rue Titi Niare, Quinzambougou, BP 96, Bamako; tel. and fax 2022-3166.

Office National des Produits Pétroliers (ONAP): Quartier du Fleuve, rue 315, porte 141, BP 2070, Bamako; tel. 2022-2827; fax 2022-4483; e-mail onapmali@afribone.net.ml; internet www.onapmali.com; Dir-Gen. TAPA NOUGA NADIO.

Office du Niger: BP 106, Ségou; tel. 2132-0292; fax 2132-0143; e-mail on@office-du-niger.org.ml; internet www.office-du-niger.org.ml; f. 1932; taken over from the French authorities in 1958; restructured in mid-1990s; cap. 7,139m. francs CFA; principally involved in cultivation of food crops, particularly rice; the Office du Niger zone is the western region of the Central Niger Delta; Pres. and Dir-Gen. SEYDOU IDRISSA TRAORÉ.

Office des Produits Agricoles du Mali (OPAM): BP 132, Bamako; tel. 2022-3755; fax 2021-0406; e-mail opam@cefib.com; f. 1965; state-owned; manages National (Cereals) Security Stock, administers food aid, responsible for sales of cereals and distribution to deficit areas; cap. 5,800m. francs CFA; Pres. and Dir-Gen. YOUSSOUF MAHAMANE TOURÉ.

DEVELOPMENT ORGANIZATIONS

Agence Française de Développement (AFD): Quinzambougou, route de Sotuba, BP 32, Bamako; tel. 2021-2842; fax 2021-8646; e-mail afdbamako@ml.groupe-afd.org; internet www.afd.fr; Country Dir JEAN-FRANÇOIS VAVASSEUR.

Agence pour le Développement du Nord-Mali (ADN): Gao; f. 2005 to replace l'Autorité pour le Développement Intégré du Nord-Mali (ADIN); govt agency with financial autonomy; promotes devt of regions of Tombouctou, Gao and Kidal; br. in Bamako.

Office de Développement Intégré du Mali-Ouest (ODIMO): square Patrice Lumumba, Bamako; tel. 2022-5759; f. 1991 to succeed Office de Développement Intégré des Productions Arachidières et Céréalières; devt of diversified forms of agricultural production; Man. Dir ZANA SANOGO.

Service de Coopération et d'Action Culturelle: square Patrice Lumumba, BP 84, Bamako; tel. 2021-8338; fax 2021-8339; administers bilateral aid from France; Dir BERTRAND COMMELIN.

CHAMBER OF COMMERCE

Chambre de Commerce et d'Industrie du Mali (CCIM): pl. de la Liberté, BP 46, Bamako; tel. 2022-5036; fax 2022-2120; e-mail ccim@cimali.org; f. 1906; Pres. JEAMILLE BITTAR; Sec.-Gen. DABA TRAORÉ.

EMPLOYERS' ASSOCIATIONS

Association Malienne des Exportateurs de Légumes (AMELEF): Bamako; tel. 7608-9048; fax 2029-2836; f. 1984; Pres. BAKARY YAFFA; Sec.-Gen. BIRAMA TRAORÉ.

Association Malienne des Exportateurs de Ressources Animales (AMERA): Bamako; tel. 2022-5683; f. 1985; Pres. AMBARKÉ YERMANGORE; Admin. Sec. ALI HACKO.

Fédération Nationale des Employeurs du Mali (FNEM): route de Sotuba, BP 2445, Bamako; tel. 2021-6311; fax 2021-9077; e-mail fnem@spider.toolnet; f. 1980; Pres. MOUSSA MARY BALLA COULIBALY; Permanent Sec. LASSINA TRAORÉ.

UTILITIES

Electricity

Energie du Mali (EdM): square Patrice Lumumba, BP 69, Bamako; tel. 2022-3020; fax 2022-8430; e-mail sekou.edm@cefib.com; f. 1960; 66% state-owned, 34% owned by Industrial Promotion Services (West-Africa); planning, construction and operation of power-sector facilities; cap. 7,880m. francs CFA.

Enertech GSA: marché de Lafiabougou, BP 1949, Bamako; tel. 2022-3763; fax 2022-5136; f. 1994; cap. 20m. francs CFA; solar energy producer; Dir MOCTAR DIAKITÉ.

Société de Gestion de l'Energie de Manantali (SOGEM): Parcelle 2501, ACI 2000, BP E 4015, Bamako; tel. 2023-3286; fax 2023-8350; to generate and distribute electricity from the Manantali HEP project, under the auspices of the Organisation pour la mise en valeur du fleuve Sénégal; Dir-Gen. SALOUM CISSÉ.

Gas

Maligaz: route de Sotuba, BP 5, Bamako; tel. 2022-2394; gas distribution.

TRADE UNION FEDERATION

Union nationale des travailleurs du Mali (UNTM): Bourse du Travail, blvd de l'Indépendance, BP 169, Bamako; tel. 2022-3699; fax 2023-5945; f. 1963; 13 nat. and 8 regional unions, and 52 local orgs; Sec.-Gen. SIAKA DIAKITÉ.

There are, in addition, several non-affiliated trade unions.

Transport

RAILWAYS

Mali's only railway runs from Koulikoro, via Bamako, to the Senegal border. The line continues to Dakar, a total distance of 1,286 km, of which 729 km is in Mali. The track is in very poor condition, and is frequently closed during the rainy season. In 1995 the Governments of Mali and Senegal agreed to establish a joint company to operate the Bamako–Dakar line, and the line passed fully into private ownership in 2003. Some 358,000 metric tons of freight were handled on the Malian railway in 2001. Plans exist for the construction of a new rail line linking Bamako with Kouroussa and Kankan, in Guinea.

Transrail SA: Immeuble la Roseraie, 310 ave de la liberté, BP 4150, Bamako; tel. 2022-5967; fax 2022-5433; e-mail ericpeiffer@transrailsa.com; f. 2003 on transfer to private management of fmr Régie du Chemin de Fer du Mali; jt venture of Canac (Canada) and Getma (France); Dir-Gen. ERIC PEIFFER.

ROADS

The Malian road network in 2004 comprised 18,709 km, of which about 3,370 km were paved. A bituminized road between Bamako and Abidjan (Côte d'Ivoire) provides Mali's main economic link to the coast; construction of a road linking Bamako and Dakar (Senegal) is to be financed by the European Development Fund. The African

MALI

Development Bank also awarded a US $31.66m. loan to fund the Kankan–Kouremale–Bamako road between Mali and Guinea. A road across the Sahara to link Mali with Algeria is also planned.

Compagnie Malienne de Transports Routiers (CMTR): BP 208, Bamako; tel. 2022-3364; f. 1970; state-owned; Man. Dir MAMADOU TOURÉ.

INLAND WATERWAYS

The River Niger is navigable in parts of its course through Mali (1,693 km) during the rainy season from July to late December. The River Senegal was, until the early 1990s, navigable from Kayes to Saint-Louis (Senegal) only between August and November, but its navigability was expected to improve following the inauguration, in 1992, of the Manantali dam, and the completion of works to deepen the river-bed.

Compagnie Malienne de Navigation (COMANAV): BP 10, Koulikoro; tel. 2026-2094; fax 2026-2009; f. 1968; 100% state-owned; river transport; Pres. and Dir-Gen. DEMBÉLÉ GOUNDO DIALLO.

Conseil Malien des Chargeurs (CMC): Dar-salam, BP E 4031, Bamako; tel. 2023-0486; fax 2023-0489; e-mail contact@cmchargeurs.com; internet www.cmchargeurs.com; f. 1999; Pres. OUSMANE BABALAYE DAOU.

Société Navale Malienne (SONAM): Bamako-Coura, BP 2581, Bamako; tel. 2021-6066; fax 2022-6066; f. 1981; transferred to private ownership in 1986; Chair. ALIOUNE KEÏTA.

Société Ouest-Africaine d'Entreprise Maritime (SOAEM): rue Mohamed V, BP 2428, Bamako; tel. 2022-5832; fax 2022-4024; maritime transport co.

CIVIL AVIATION

The principal airport is at Bamako-Senou. The other major airports are at Bourem, Gao, Goundam, Kayes, Kita, Mopti, Nioro, Ségou, Tessalit and Tombouctou. There are about 40 small airfields. Mali's airports are being modernized with external financial assistance. In early 2005 the Malian Government announced the creation of a new national airline, in partnership with the Aga Khan Fund for Economic Development and Industrial Promotion Services.

Agence Nationale de l'Aéronautique Civile (ANAC): Ministère de l'Equipement et des Transports, BP 227, Bamako; tel. 2029-5524; fax 2028-6177; e-mail anacmali@hotmail.com; f. 2005 to replace Direction Nationale de l'Aéronautique Civile (f. 1990); Dir-Gen. ADAMA KONE.

Air Affaires Mali: BP E 3759, Badalabougou, Bamako; tel. 2022-6136.

Compagnie Aérienne du Mali (CAM): Immeuble Tomota, ave Cheick Zayed, BP E 2286, Bamako; tel. 2022-2424; fax 2022-7111; e-mail dc.cam@cam-mali.org; internet www.camaero.com; f. 2005; 51% owned by Fonds Aga Khan pour le Développement Economique (AKAFED), 20% state-owned; domestic and international flights.

STA Trans African Airlines: Quartier du Fleuve, BP 775, Bamako; tel. 2022-4444; fax 2021-0981; internet www.sta-airlines.com; f. 1984 as Société des Transports Aériens; privately owned; local, regional and international services; Man. Dir MELHEM ELIE SABBAGUE.

Tourism

Mali's rich cultural heritage is promoted as a tourist attraction. In 1999 the Government launched a three-year cultural and tourism development programme centred on Tombouctou, Gao and Kidal. In 2006 152,660 tourists visited Mali, while receipts from tourism totalled some US $67m. in that year.

Ministry of Crafts and Tourism: see section on The Government.

MALTA

Introductory Survey

Location, Climate, Language, Religion, Flag, Capital

The Republic of Malta is in southern Europe. The country comprises an archipelago in the central Mediterranean Sea, consisting of the inhabited islands of Malta, Gozo and Comino, and the uninhabited islets of Cominotto, Filfla and St Paul's. The main island, Malta, lies 93 km (58 miles) south of the Italian island of Sicily and 288 km (179 miles) east of the Tunisian coast, the nearest point on the North African mainland. The climate is warm, with average temperatures of 22.6°C (72.7°F) in summer and 13.7°C (56.6°F) in winter. Average annual rainfall is 578 mm (22.8 ins). Maltese and English are the official languages, although Italian is widely spoken. About 94% of the inhabitants are Christians adhering to the Roman Catholic Church. The national flag (proportions 2 by 3) consists of two equal vertical stripes, white at the hoist and red at the fly, with a representation of the George Cross, edged with red, in the upper hoist. The capital is Valletta, on the island of Malta.

Recent History

Malta, which had been a Crown Colony of the United Kingdom since 1814, became an independent sovereign state, within the Commonwealth, on 21 September 1964. The Government, led by Dr Giorgio Borg-Olivier of the Nationalist Party (Partit Nazzjonalista—PN), negotiated defence and financial aid agreements, effective over a 10-year period, with the United Kingdom.

In June 1971 the Malta Labour Party (MLP—the official name of which was the Partit tal-Haddiema–Workers' Party), led by Dom Mintoff, assumed power after winning a general election. Pursuing a policy of non-alignment, the Government concluded agreements for cultural, economic and commercial co-operation with Italy, Libya, Tunisia, the USSR, several East European countries, the USA, the People's Republic of China and others. The MLP Government abrogated the 1964 Mutual Defence and Assistance Agreement with the United Kingdom. This agreement was replaced in 1972 by a new seven-year agreement, under which Malta was to receive substantially increased rental payments for the use of military facilities by the United Kingdom and other members of the North Atlantic Treaty Organization (NATO, see p. 351). British troops were finally withdrawn in March 1979.

Malta became a republic in December 1974. The MLP retained power at general elections held in September 1976 and in December 1981, when it secured a majority of three seats in the 65-seat House of Representatives, although obtaining only 49.1% of the votes cast. The PN, which had received 50.9% of the votes cast, contested the result, refused to take its seats in the legislature and organized a campaign of civil disobedience. In March 1983 the PN terminated its legislative boycott, but immediately withdrew again, in protest against a government resolution to loosen ties with the European Community (EC, now European Union—EU, see p. 255). Although Mintoff promised constitutional amendments and weekly consultations with the opposition, these arrangements collapsed in June, when the MLP blamed the PN for a bomb attack on government offices. In November a police raid on the PN headquarters was alleged to have discovered a cache of arms and ammunition.

In June 1983 the House of Representatives approved controversial legislation, under which about 75% of church property was to be expropriated to provide finance for a programme of universal free education and the abolition of fee-paying church schools. Opponents of the measure denounced it as both unconstitutional and a violation of religious liberty, and in September 1984 the courts disallowed the legislation. In April 1984 the House of Representatives approved legislation forbidding any school to accept fees (including voluntary gifts and donations). The Roman Catholic Archbishop of Malta rejected the government conditions and ordered the closure of all church schools, in response to growing tensions and public unrest. An agreement was finally reached in November, when the schools were reopened.

Mintoff retired in December 1984 and was replaced as Prime Minister by the new leader of the MLP, Dr Carmelo Mifsud Bonnici. In April 1985 the Government reached agreement with the Roman Catholic Church, providing for the phased introduction of free education in church secondary schools, and guaranteeing the autonomy of church schools. However, in July 1988 the enforced introduction of new licensing procedures for church schools led to demands by the Roman Catholic Church that the State should reduce its supervisory powers over church education.

At a general election held in May 1987 the PN obtained 50.9% of the votes cast, but won only 31 of the 65 seats in the House of Representatives, while the MLP, with 48.9% of the votes cast, won the remaining 34 seats. However, in accordance with a constitutional amendment that had been adopted in January (see Government, below), the PN was allocated four additional seats, giving it a majority of one in the legislature, thus ending the MLP's 16-year tenure in office. The leader of the PN, Dr Eddie Fenech Adami, became Prime Minister. The PN secured an increased majority of three seats over the MLP at a general election held in February 1992. This result was widely interpreted as an endorsement of the PN's pro-EC policies.

Malta has maintained a policy of non-alignment in its international relations, and has negotiated economic co-operation agreements with many countries. In 1984 the Governments of Malta and Libya signed a five-year treaty of co-operation. The treaty signified a return to the previously close relations between the two countries, which had deteriorated in 1980, owing to a dispute over a maritime boundary (eventually resolved in 1985). Malta also had an association agreement with the EU, which was originally signed in 1970 and periodically renewed until Malta's accession to the EU in 2004. On becoming Prime Minister in May 1987, Fenech Adami declared that the Government, while retaining Malta's non-aligned status and its links with Libya, would seek closer relations with the USA and other Western countries, and would apply for full membership of the EC.

A formal application for full membership of the EC was submitted by the Maltese Government in July 1990. In June 1993 the EC Commission recommended that, subject to the Government of Malta's satisfying EC requirements for regulatory reforms in financial services, competition and consumer protection, favourable consideration should be given to the future accession of Malta to the EU.

Domestic opposition to Maltese accession to the EU had been led by the MLP, on the grounds that EU agricultural policies would increase the cost of living, and that integration into the EU would conflict with the Republic's traditional neutrality in its foreign relations. In September 1996 the PN Government, seeking to confirm its mandate to pursue the goal of full membership of the EU, called a general election for the following month. Although the PN contested the election on its record of economic success, the Government's introduction of value-added tax (VAT), as a precondition of Malta's admission to the EU, had proved unpopular with the electorate, and its proposed abolition by the MLP (which would concurrently disqualify Malta from EU membership) was widely regarded as the decisive factor in the election. With a participation rate of 97.1% of eligible voters, the MLP won 50.7% of the votes cast, compared with 47.8% for the PN. The MLP obtained 31 seats in the House of Representatives, while the PN received 34. (As the MLP actually won three seats less than the PN in the election, four seats were added to its final total, giving it a one-seat majority in the legislature.) Dr Alfred Sant, the leader of the MLP, formed a new Government with the declared intention of replacing the 1970 association agreement (see above) with new arrangements providing for an eventual 'free-trade zone' between Malta and the EU.

In February 1997 the Government announced the initiation of a 'national discussion' of proposals to legalize divorce. However, the imposition of tax increases and levies on public utilities substantially diminished the Government's popularity. Sant called a general election for September, three years earlier than constitutionally required, at which the PN, led by Fenech Adami, obtained a five-seat majority (having obtained 51.8% of votes cast), while the MLP receiving 48.0%. Immediately following the election, Fenech Adami reactivated Malta's application for full membership of the EU. In December 1999 the European

Commission agreed that accession negotiations could recommence in February 2000, and in the following month the President of the Commission paid an official visit to the island. In November the Commission published a report which stated that Malta was among the best-equipped economically of those countries seeking to join the EU. Further action was required in Malta to reduce state aid (notably the politically sensitive LM 15m. annual subsidy to the island's dry docks), to implement privatization plans and to strengthen tax and customs administrations.

Talks over EU accession were formally concluded on 13 December 2002 in Copenhagen, Denmark. Malta had obtained 77 exemptions in the discussions, aimed largely at protecting its industrial and agricultural sectors, but also including cultural issues, such as the right to maintain the ban on divorce. A non-binding referendum was called for 8 March 2003 to determine whether the country would join the EU. Support for membership of the EU was led by the ruling PN and opposition to it by the MLP, which told voters to abstain, vote against the motion to join or spoil their ballots. Following an acrimonious campaign, 53.65% of the votes cast were in favour of EU membership, with 46.35% against. Sant refused to concede defeat, however, arguing that since the turn-out had been only 91% of the electorate the vote in support of membership of the EU did not represent an absolute majority. In accordance with the Constitution, Fenech Adami, whose mandate expired in 2004, called a general election for 12 April 2003 to confirm the referendum result, four days before the proposed signing of the EU accession treaty by 10 applicant countries, including Malta.

At the general election that took place on 12 April 2003 97.0% of the electorate participated; the PN won an absolute majority of 35 seats with 51.8% of the votes, while the MLP won 30 seats (47.5%). Fenech Adami was sworn in as Prime Minister on 14 April, announced the new Cabinet the following day (which included two new ministries with responsibility for rural affairs and the environment, and for youth and the arts) and signed the EU accession treaty in Athens, Greece, on 16 April. The House of Representatives eventually ratified the treaty on 14 July by 34 votes to 25 (with six members boycotting the vote), and the President signed it on 16 July. Malta thus became a full member of the EU on 1 May 2004.

Malta's accession to the EU marked the beginning of a change in the country's politics. Since independence Malta's politics had been deeply partisan and bitterly polarized over who could best govern the archipelago. Following the 2003 general election, however, the parties moved towards unity and consensus in order to obtain the maximum benefits for Malta from its EU membership. The MLP, which had previously been opposed outright to accession, accepted the result of the general election as a final arbiter of Maltese opinion on the question. Accordingly, following the MLP's defeat at the polls, the party leadership decided to embrace majority public opinion and work within the reality of EU membership. This decision proved divisive, and was resisted by a faction of the MLP led by Mifsud Bonnici. However, delegates at a subsequent party conference agreed that the MLP would not withdraw Malta from the EU if the party came to power. Moreover, it was agreed that the incumbent Government would henceforth be able to rely on the MLP's support in its efforts to defend Malta's influence within the EU, particularly with regard to negotiations relating to the draft EU constitutional treaty. In January 2004 the Minister of Foreign Affairs, Dr Joe Borg, was named as Malta's first member of the European Commission.

In early February 2004 Fenech Adami used the occasion of his 70th birthday to announce his intention to resign as leader of the PN. He had always maintained that he would relinquish this post, and that of Prime Minister, when he reached 70 years of age, and he indicated that he would step down as Prime Minister once the party had appointed his successor. At a party conference on 29 February the Deputy Prime Minister and Minister for Social Policy, Dr Lawrence Gonzi, was elected as the PN's new leader. Fenech Adami duly resigned from his seat in the House of Representatives and from his post as Prime Minister, and Gonzi was sworn in on 23 March. On his assumption of the premiership he stated that his main priorities in the post would be full participation in the EU, the creation of jobs and the improvement of the economy. When naming his Cabinet, Gonzi assumed responsibility for the finance portfolio and appointed his former rival for the party leadership, John Dalli, as Minister of Foreign Affairs.

On 29 March 2004 Fenech Adami was elected President by the House of Representatives, by 33 votes to 29, following his nomination by Gonzi. His appointment was controversial, as party leaders had not traditionally stood for the post, and it was bitterly opposed by the MLP. Fenech Adami was sworn in as Malta's seventh President on 4 April.

On 12 June 2004 Malta participated for the first time in elections to the European Parliament. The participation rate, at 82.4%, was the third highest among the member states, surpassed only by Belgium and Luxembourg (where voting is mandatory). The MLP won three seats and the PN two.

In July 2004 Dalli resigned his post as Minister of Foreign Affairs, claiming he was unable to continue amid attacks from 'different sides', which was thought to be a reference to criticism from within the PN. There were also allegations, which Dalli denied, of irregularities involving a large shipping deal and the handling of ministry travel expenses. He was replaced by his junior minister, Michael Frendo.

The Treaty establishing a Constitution for Europe was signed by the EU heads of state and of government on 29 October 2004, but adoption remained dependent on ratification by all 25 member states, either through a referendum or by parliamentary approval. Gonzi had confirmed in June, when the final text of the constitution was agreed, that there was no need for a referendum on the issue in Malta. On 6 July 2005 the House of Representatives unanimously ratified the constitutional treaty. However, the treaty was rejected at referendums in France and the Netherlands. At a meeting of the European Council in Brussels on 21–22 June 2007, a preliminary agreement was reached to replace the rejected constitutional treaty. On 13 December EU leaders signed the new Reform Treaty, which was to amend existing EU treaties, at a summit meeting in Lisbon, Portugal. The Treaty of Lisbon, as it was subsequently known, was approved by the House of Representatives in early February 2008. However, the treaty's future remained uncertain, following its rejection at a referendum held in Ireland in June.

Following its accession to the EU, illegal immigration became an increasing problem for Malta, partly owing to its proximity to North Africa. According to the Office of the UN High Commissioner for Refugees (UNHCR, see p. 69), of all EU states Malta received the second largest number of asylum seekers per 1,000 inhabitants in 2005 (after Cyprus). Given Malta's extremely high population density the European Commission supported the Government's request in July 2005 that a proportion of the migrants arriving there be transferred to other EU states. Malta received offers of assistance from the Czech Republic, Ireland, the Netherlands and the United Kingdom. The Commission also proposed that the detention period for illegal immigrants and asylum seekers be reduced from one year to six months. The detention centres reached capacity in September, with new arrivals housed in tents. An investigation was launched in that month to determine whether the recent influx of illegal immigrants was the result of human trafficking. In October the House of Representatives adopted amendments to refugee legislation aimed at facilitating the repatriation of failed asylum seekers. In December a first group of migrants granted refugee status was transferred to the Netherlands. The USA also pledged to accept a small group the following year. Malta also sought an agreement with Libya on the repatriation of illegal immigrants to that country. In February 2006 immigrants housed in detention centres across Malta protested, claiming that they were poorly fed and kept in unsanitary conditions. Malta had been criticized by UNHCR over its treatment of asylum seekers in January 2005.

In July 2006 Malta refused permission to a vessel transporting a group of 51 illegal migrants, originating mainly from sub-Saharan Africa, to enter the port of Valletta. The Government insisted that, as the vessel was Spanish-owned and had been rescued in Libyan waters, Malta would not accept responsibility for it, nor for its passengers. However, Spain also refused to accept responsibility for the migrants and the ship remained at sea for some eight days, during which discussions were held between Frendo, his Spanish counterpart, Miguel Ángel Moratinos, and the Vice-President of the European Commission, responsible for Justice, Freedom and Security, Franco Frattini. Under the resulting agreement, Malta allowed the passengers to disembark at Valletta and accepted eight migrants, while Spain accepted 18; the remainder were transferred to Libya, Italy and Andorra. Later that month the EU announced its intention to deploy a police force to patrol the borders of member countries experiencing problems with illegal immigration, which would include a maritime patrol in the Mediterranean Sea between Malta and North Africa. None the less, in May 2007 there were several incidents in which the Maltese authorities refused to take responsibility for migrants arriving by sea from Africa, usually setting off from Libya, including a case in which 27 African migrants were left in the water for several days by a Maltese vessel, until they were rescued by the Italian navy. In June Frattini accused the Maltese Government of failing to meet its international responsibilities to save lives at sea. The Deputy Prime Minister and Minister for Justice and Home Affairs, Dr Tonio Borg, subsequently defended Malta's record but insisted that Malta could not accept responsibility for all illegal immigrants rescued in the Mediterranean, particularly if they were in international and third country search and rescue areas. Borg proposed the creation of a system of shared responsibility for rescued migrants between EU member states on a quota basis. Although Frattini acknowledged Malta's predicament, immediate EU assistance was limited to the provision of an improved marine patrol force in the waters surrounding Malta, Sicily and Libya. In March 2009 Malta and Libya signed a memorandum of understanding on search and rescue, in order to enhance co-operation between the two countries. In the same month the Maltese Government offered to deploy Maltese military personnel to assist in planned joint patrols of Libyan waters by Italian and Libyan forces, which were intended to curtail the illegal transportation of migrants across the Mediterranean. Later that month the Italian Minister of the Interior, Roberto Maroni, announced that the patrols were to commence in mid-May.

On 8 March 2008 Malta held its first general election since joining the EU. The Prime Minister, Gonzi, emphasized the economic achievements of the PN, while the MLP leader, Sant, campaigned on an anti-corruption platform, with pledges for greater transparency in government. The ruling PN emerged victorious with 49.3% of the votes cast, while the MLP won 48.8%; voter turn-out was 93%. However, while the PN won the popular vote, the MLP won the majority of parliamentary seats (34 seats, compared with 31 for the PN). Consequently, the PN was assigned four additional seats to ensure that it had a parliamentary majority, as required by the Constitution. Following the results of the election, Sant immediately resigned as MLP leader. After his re-election as Prime Minister, Gonzi announced the composition of the new Cabinet, which comprised eight ministers (compared with the previous 12) and six parliamentary secretaries. The Minister for Gozo, Giovanna Debono, was the only member of the outgoing Cabinet to retain the same portfolio. Borg remained as Deputy Prime Minister but was allocated the foreign affairs portfolio in place of justice and home affairs, while the former parliamentary secretaries, Dr Tonio Fenech and Dr Carmelo Mifsud Bonnici, were appointed Minister for Finance, the Economy and Investment and Minister for Justice and Home Affairs, respectively. In early June five candidates contested the MLP leadership. As none won the requisite 51% in the first round, the leading candidates, Dr Joseph Muscat and Dr George Abela, took part in a second ballot the following day, when Muscat defeated Abela with 66.4% of the votes cast. However, as a member of the European Parliament, Muscat was unable officially to assume the role of Leader of the opposition until September, when he was co-opted to the House of Representatives. Following his election as MLP Leader, Muscat indicated his intention to rejuvenate the party's image and to reform its internal structures. At a special party conference held in late November, delegates approved a programme of reforms, most notably including changing the party's official title to Partit Laburista (PL) and dispensing with the historical emblem, the flaming torch.

On 1 April 2009 Abela was unanimously elected President by the House of Representatives, having been nominated by Gonzi, in accordance with an agreement reached by the two main parties earlier that year. It was the first time that a Maltese Prime Minister had proposed a member of an opposing party for the role of President. Abela was duly sworn in on 4 April.

Malta is a member of the Council of Europe (see p. 236) and the Organization for Security and Co-operation in Europe (see p. 366). Participation by Malta in the NATO 'Partnership for Peace' programme formally commenced in 1995, but was suspended by the MLP Government during 1996–98. In September 2005 Malta applied for full membership of the Organisation for Economic Co-operation and Development (OECD, see p. 358). On 1 January 2008 Malta adopted the single European currency, the euro, having submitted a formal application for membership of the euro area in February 2007 (see Economic Affairs, below).

In November 2005 Malta hosted the Commonwealth Heads of Government Meeting, at which leaders discussed improving co-operation in development, mass migration and combating terrorism. The British Prime Minister, Tony Blair, attended the meeting and later held talks with Gonzi on a number of issues, including illegal immigration. It was the first visit to Malta by a British Prime Minister in some 60 years.

In July 2005 Malta extended its maritime jurisdiction and established exclusive fisheries zones in response to similar measures adopted by Libya and Tunisia. Malta also requested permission from Libya for 15 vessels to operate within its unilaterally declared fisheries conservation zone at any one time during the year. In early 2006 Malta and Libya discussed reviving their 1984 co-operation agreement and agreed to consider a number of options with regard to petroleum, not limited to exploration. In February 2006 Malta and Tunisia signed an agreement on joint petroleum exploration and exploitation in zones of the continental shelf located between the two countries.

Government

Under the 1974 Constitution, legislative power is held by the unicameral House of Representatives, whose 65 members are elected by universal adult suffrage for five years (subject to dissolution) on the basis of proportional representation. The Constitution was amended in January 1987 to ensure that a party that received more than 50% of the total votes cast in a general election would obtain a majority of seats in the legislature (by the allocation—if necessary—of additional seats to that party). The President is the constitutional Head of State, elected for a five-year term by the House of Representatives, and executive power is exercised by the Cabinet. The President appoints the Prime Minister and, on the latter's recommendation, other Ministers. The Cabinet is responsible to the House of Representatives.

Defence

As assessed at November 2008, the armed forces of Malta comprised a regular army of 1,954. There was also a reserve of 167. Military service is voluntary. Budgetary expenditure on defence in 2007 was LM 13.6m.

Economic Affairs

In 2006, according to estimates by the World Bank, Malta's gross national income (GNI), measured at average 2004–2006 prices, was US $6,216m., equivalent to $15,310 per head (or $20,990 per head on an international purchasing-power parity basis). During 2000–07, it was estimated, the population increased at an average annual rate of 0.7%, while gross domestic product (GDP) per head increased, in real terms, at an average annual rate of 0.6% during 2000–06. Overall GDP increased, in real terms, at an average annual rate of 1.2% in 2000–06. According to official estimates, GDP increased by 3.8% in 2007.

Agriculture (including hunting, forestry and fishing) contributed an estimated 2.6% of GDP in 2007 and engaged 1.6% of the working population in 2008. The principal export crop is potatoes. Tomatoes and other vegetables, cereals (principally wheat and barley) and fruit are also cultivated. Livestock and livestock products are also important, and efforts are being made to develop the fishing industry. Food accounted for a provisional 6.2% of total exports in 2008 (excluding re-exports). According to FAO figures, Malta's agricultural production increased at an average rate of 0.7% per year in 1995–2004. Output increased by 4.4% in 2004.

Industry (including mining, manufacturing, construction and power) provided an estimated 21.5% of GDP in 2007 and engaged 26.6% of the employed labour force in 2008. According to the IMF, industrial production increased at an average rate of 3.4% per year in 1995–2004; it rose by 3.8% in 2003, but declined by 1.2% in 2004.

Mining and quarrying contributed an estimated 0.8% of GDP in 2007 and engaged 0.3% of the employed labour force in 2008. The principal activities are stone and sand quarrying. There are reserves of petroleum in Maltese offshore waters, and petroleum and gas exploration is proceeding.

Manufacturing contributed an estimated 17.0% of GDP in 2007 and engaged 15.3% of the working population in 2008. Based on the gross value of output, the principal branches of manufacturing, excluding ship-repairing, in 2007 were electrical and optical equipment (accounting for around 27.3% of the total), chemicals, chemical products and man-made fibres (15.3%) and food products and beverages (13.7%).

Energy is derived principally from imports of crude petroleum (the majority of which is purchased, at preferential rates, from Libya) and coal. Imports of mineral fuels comprised a provisional 17.0% of the value of total imports in 2008.

Services provided an estimated 75.9% of GDP in 2007 and engaged 71.8% of the employed labour force in 2008. Tourism is a major source of foreign exchange earnings. In 2008 Malta received 1,290,856 foreign visitors, and revenue from the sector reached US $970m. in 2006. In 2008 7.1% of the employed labour force were engaged in employment in the hotels and restaurants sub-sector.

In 2007 Malta recorded a visible trade deficit of US $1,387m., and there was a deficit of $489m. on the current account of the balance of payments. In 2008 the principal source of imports (accounting for a provisional 26.3% of the total value) was Italy (including San Marino); other major suppliers were the United Kingdom (12.7%) and France (7.8%). Singapore was the principal market for exports (taking 13.5% of the total value); other significant purchasers of exports were Germany (13.1%), France (11.5%), the USA (9.0%) and the United Kingdom (8.1%). According to provisional figures, the principal domestic exports in 2008 were machinery and transport equipment, accounting for 57.1% of the total, and miscellaneous manufactured articles (16.6%). The principal imports were machinery and transport equipment, accounting for 35.3% of the total, miscellaneous manufactured articles (11.8%) and basic manufactures (10.2%).

In 2007 Malta recorded a fiscal deficit equivalent to 1.8% of GDP. General government debt was equivalent to 61.9% of GDP in 2007. The annual rate of inflation averaged 2.2% in 2000–07, according to the ILO; consumer prices increased by 1.3% in 2007. In 2008 the average annual rate of unemployment was 5.9%.

Malta is a member of the World Trade Organization (WTO, see p. 410) and of the European Bank for Reconstruction and Development (EBRD, see p. 251). Malta joined the European Union (EU, see p. 255) on 1 May 2004 and adopted the single European currency, the euro, on 1 January 2008.

Following the closure, in 1979, of the British military base and naval docks, on which Malta's economy had been largely dependent, successive governments pursued a policy of restructuring and diversification. The domestic market is limited, owing to the small population. There are few natural resources, and almost all raw materials have to be imported. Malta's development has therefore been based on the promotion of the island as an international financial centre and on manufacturing for export (notably in non-traditional fields, such as electronics, information technology and pharmaceuticals), together with the continuing development of tourism. From 2004 Malta's EU membership entailed a commitment on the part of the Government to reduce Malta's budgetary deficit to below 3.0% of GDP in order to comply with the convergence criteria for participation in Economic and Monetary Union (EMU). Through the implementation of strict monetary policies, institutional reform and a privatization programme, Malta reduced its deficit from more than 10% of GDP in 2003 to 2.3% in 2006 and 1.8% in 2007. Malta joined the euro area on 1 January 2008, with the euro becoming the sole currency by the end of that month. Efforts to liberalize Malta's economy continued during 2007–08. In 2007 the Government completed the sale of a number of state assets, including stakes in Mid-Med Bank (now HSBC Bank Malta) and Malta Freeport. Labour market conditions continued to improve, following government measures intended to increase flexibility. In 2008 the rate of unemployment was 5.9%, although an increase of around 1.0% was forecast in 2009. Along with other European countries, Malta was affected by the global economic downturn of 2008. Income from both exports and tourism declined sharply in the second half of that year, owing to a decline in demand, particularly from France and the United Kingdom. However, in contrast to most other EU member states, Malta's economy was expected to continue to grow in 2009–10. Nevertheless, the projected rate of growth was significantly lower than in previous years. Real GDP growth was forecast to decrease to 0.7% in 2009, compared with 2.1% in 2008. The fiscal deficit was expected to decline slightly, from 3.5% in 2008, to 2.6% in the following year.

Education

Education is compulsory between the ages of five and 16 years, and is available free of charge in government schools and institutions, from kindergarten to university. Kindergarten education is provided for three- and four-year-old children. In 2003/04 enrolment at pre-primary level included 88% of children in the relevant age-group (males 87%; females 89%). Primary education begins at five years of age and lasts for six years. In 2004/05 enrolment at primary level included 86% of children in the relevant age-group (males 88%; females 84%). Secondary education, beginning at 11 years of age, lasts for a maximum of seven years, but this period is extended in the case of technology and vocational courses. Enrolment at secondary level in 2004/05 included 84% of children in the relevant age-group (males 86%; females 84%). After completing five years of secondary-level education, students having the necessary qualifications may opt to follow a higher academic or technical or vocational course. The junior college, administrated by the University of Malta, prepares students specifically for a university course. About 30% of the student population attend schools administered by the Roman Catholic Church, from kindergarten to higher secondary level. The Government subsidizes the provision of free education for students in church schools. Higher education is available at the University of Malta. There are also a number of technical institutes, specialist schools and an extended skills-training scheme for trade-school leavers. Enrolment at tertiary level was equivalent to 31% of those in the relevant age-group in 2004/05 (males 27%; females 36%). The Government also provides adult education courses. Of total recurrent budgetary expenditure in 2004 LM 50.2m. (6.9%) was allocated to education. In July 2005 the Government announced its intention to reform the education system. From September state primary schools, area secondary schools and junior colleges were to be grouped together into autonomous regional colleges. The Government also proposed establishing a national commission on higher education, and the inclusion of a scholarship fund in the 2006 budget.

Public Holidays

2009: 1 January (New Year's Day), 10 February (St Paul's Shipwreck), 19 March (St Joseph), 31 March (Freedom Day), 10 April (Good Friday), 1 May (St Joseph the Worker), 7 June (Memorial of the 1919 Riot), 29 June (St Peter and St Paul), 15 August (Assumption), 8 September (Our Lady of Victories), 21 September (Independence Day), 8 December (Immaculate Conception), 13 December (Republic Day), 25 December (Christmas Day).

2010: 1 January (New Year's Day), 10 February (St Paul's Shipwreck), 19 March (St Joseph), 31 March (Freedom Day), 2 April (Good Friday), 1 May (St Joseph the Worker), 7 June (Memorial of the 1919 Riot), 29 June (St Peter and St Paul), 15 August (Assumption), 8 September (Our Lady of Victories), 21 September (Independence Day), 8 December (Immaculate Conception), 13 December (Republic Day), 25 December (Christmas Day).

Weights and Measures

The metric system is in force.

Statistical Survey

Source (unless otherwise stated): National Statistics Office, Lascaris, Valletta VLT 1921; tel. 21223221; fax 21249841; e-mail nso@magnet.mt; internet www.nso.gov.mt.

AREA AND POPULATION

Area: 316 sq km (122 sq miles).

Population: 404,962 (males 200,819, females 204,143) at census of 27 November 2005 (figures refer to *de jure* population). *2007* (estimated population at 31 December): 410,290 (males 204,106, females 206,184).

Density (at 31 December 2007): 1,298.4 per sq km.

Principal Towns (total population at 31 December 2006): Birkirkara 21,658; Mosta 18,495; Qormi 16,459; Żabbar 14,671; San Ġwann 12,318; Sliema 11,890; San Pawl Il-Bahar 11,767; Valletta (capital) 6,166.

Births, Marriages and Deaths (2007): Registered live births 3,871 (birth rate 9.5 per 1,000); Marriages 2,479 (marriage rate 6.1 per 1,000); Registered deaths 3,111 (death rate 7.6 per 1,000).

Life Expectancy (years at birth, WHO estimates): 79.4 (males 77.2; females 81.4) in 2006. Source: WHO, *World Health Statistics*.

Migration (2004, unless otherwise indicated): Emigrants 70 (all to United Kingdom); Returning emigrants 459; Non-Maltese nationals settling in the islands 533 (in 2002). *2005:* Total emigrants 70.

Economically Active Population (persons in full-time employment, labour force survey, October 2008): Agriculture and hunting 1,803; Fishing 544; Mining and quarrying 480; Manufacturing 22,123; Electricity, gas and water supply 2,943; Construction 12,908; Wholesale and retail trade and repair of motor vehicles, motorcycles and personal and household goods 21,882; Hotels and restaurants 10,269; Transport, storage and communications 11,109; Financial intermediation 5,634; Real estate, renting and business activities 13,848; Public administration and defence and compulsory social security 10,918; Education 12,447; Health and social work 10,208; Other community, social and personal service activities 7,382; Private households with employed persons 0; Extra-territorial organizations and bodies 165; *Total employed* 144,663 (males 98,506, females 46,157); Registered unemployed 6,351; *Total labour force* 151,014. Note: figures exclude apprentices, trainees and students engaged in holiday work (715 in October 2008).

HEALTH AND WELFARE
Key Indicators

Total Fertility Rate (children per woman, 2006): 1.4.

Under-5 Mortality Rate (per 1,000 live births, 2006): 6.

HIV/AIDS (% of persons aged 15–49, 2007): 0.1.

Physicians (per 1,000 head, 2006): 3.9.

Hospital Beds (per 1,000 head, 2006): 8.

Health Expenditure (2006): US $ per head (PPP): 1,825.

Health Expenditure (2006): % of GDP: 8.3.

Health Expenditure (2006): public (% of total): 77.7.

Human Development Index (2006): ranking: 36.

Human Development Index (2006): value: 0.894.

For sources and definitions, see explanatory note on p. vi.

AGRICULTURE, ETC.

Principal Crops ('000 metric tons, 2007): Wheat 9.2*; Barley 1.6*; Potatoes 25.0†; Cabbages 3.3; Tomatoes 16.6; Cauliflowers and broccoli 6.9; Pumpkins, squash and gourds 1.6; Onions, dry 7.8; Garlic 0.5; Broad beans, dry 0.8*; Melons 9.4; Citrus fruit 1.9*; Grapes 5.0*.
* FAO estimate.
† Unofficial figure.

Livestock ('000 head, year ending September 2007): Cattle 19.2; Pigs 73.7; Sheep 12.2; Goats 5.8; Chickens 1,100*; Horses 1.1*.
* FAO estimate.

Livestock Products ('000 metric tons, 2007, FAO estimates): Cattle meat 1.4; Pig meat 8.5; Rabbit meat 1.6; Chicken meat 4.0; Cows' milk 41.0; Sheep's milk 1.8; Hen eggs 7.0.

Fishing (metric tons, live weight, 2006): Capture 2,411 (Atlantic bluefin tuna 263, Common dolphinfish 559, Swordfish 239; Antarctic krill 1,081); Aquaculture 1,126 (FAO estimate—European seabass 155, Gilthead seabream 912); *Total catch* 3,537 (FAO estimate).

Source: FAO.

INDUSTRY

Production ('000 metric tons, 2001, unless otherwise indicated): Limestone flux and calcareous stones 2,000 (Limestone only); Cigarettes (1992, million) 1,475; Washing powders and detergents 9.7; Quicklime (1992, incl. other types of lime) 5; Tankers, launched (1996, number, completions) 5; Other sea-going merchant vessels launched (number, 2002) 1 (5 grt); Electricity (2005, million kWh, by public utilities) 2,240 (Source: UN, *Industrial Commodity Statistics Yearbook*).

FINANCE

Currency and Exchange Rates: 100 cent = 1 euro (€). *Sterling and Dollar Equivalents* (31 December 2008): £1 sterling = 1.0475 euros; US $1 = 0.7185 euros; €10 = £9.55 = $13.92. *Average Exchange Rate* (euros per US dollar): 0.7971 in 2006; 0.7306 in 2007; 0.6827 in 2008. Note: The national currency was formerly the Maltese lira (LM; plural liri). Malta adopted the euro on 1 January 2008 at a fixed exchange rate of €1 = LM 0.429300. The euro and local currency circulated alongside each other until 31 January, after which the euro became the sole legal tender. Much of the relevant historical data in this survey continues to be presented in terms of Maltese liri.

Budget (€ million, consolidated fund, 2007): *Revenue:* Income tax 663.4; Customs and excise 185.0; Licences and fines 231.6; Value-added tax 421.8; Social security 480.2; Grants 56.3; Other recurrent revenue 186.1; Non-recurrent revenue 140.9; Total 2,365.4. *Expenditure:* Recurrent expenditure 1,896.6 (Personal emoluments 484.4; Programmes and initiatives 1,169.6); Public debt servicing 179.1; Capital expenditure 257.9; Total 2,333.6.

International Reserves (US $ million at 31 December 2007): Gold (national valuation) 13.0; IMF special drawing rights 59.8; Reserve position in IMF 63.6; Foreign exchange 3,662.0; Total 3,798.4. Source: IMF, *International Financial Statistics*.

Money Supply (LM million at 31 December 2007): Currency issued 291; Demand deposits 1,325; Other deposits 2,211. Source: IMF, *International Financial Statistics*.

Cost of Living (Consumer Price Index; base: 2000 = 100): All items 112.8 in 2005; 116.0 in 2006; 117.4 in 2007. Source: IMF, *International Financial Statistics*.

Gross Domestic Product (LM million at constant 2000 prices): 1,781.8 in 2005; 1,842.3 in 2006; 1,912.2 in 2007. Source: IMF, *International Financial Statistics*.

National Income and Product (€ million at current prices, 2007, provisional): Compensation of employees 2,328.4; Gross operating surplus and mixed income 2,402.4; *Gross domestic product at factor cost* 4,730.8; Taxes on production and imports 825.4; *Less* Subsidies 109.1; *GDP in purchasers' values* 5,447.2.

Expenditure on Gross Domestic Product (€ million at current prices, 2007, provisional): Final consumption expenditure 4,347.6 (General government 1,036.1, Households 3,225.5, Non-profit institutes serving households 86.0); Gross capital formation 1,237.5 (Gross fixed capital formation 1,076.1, Changes in stocks 167.2, Acquisitions, less disposals, of valuables –5.7); *Total domestic expenditure* 5,585.1; Exports of goods and services 4,891.7; *Less* Imports of goods and services 5,029.7; *GDP in purchasers' values* 5,447.2.

Gross Domestic Product by Economic Activity (€ million at current prices, 2007, provisional): Agriculture, hunting and forestry 79.1; Fishing 43.1; Mining and quarrying 13.3; Manufacturing 793.3; Electricity, gas and water supply 27.0; Construction 169.7; Wholesale and retail trade, repair of motor vehicles, motorcycles and household goods 559.6; Hotels and restaurants 252.3; Transport, storage and communications 449.5; Financial intermediation 204.2; Real estate, renting and business activities 773.4; Public administration and defence, compulsory social security 316.0; Education 274.7; Health and social work 274.0; Other community, social and personal services 437.1; Private households with employed persons 7.1; *Gross value added at basic prices* 4,673.4; Indirect taxes 799.3; *Less* Subsidies 25.6; *GDP in purchasers' values* 5,447.2.

Balance of Payments (US $ million, 2007): Exports of goods f.o.b. 3,228; Imports of goods f.o.b. –4,616; *Trade balance* –1,387; Exports of services 3,411; Imports of services –2,248; *Balance on goods and services* –224; Other income received 2,682; Other income paid –2,854; *Balance on goods, services and income* –396; Current transfers received 713; Current transfers paid –806; *Current balance* –489; Capital account (net) 72; Direct investment abroad –31; Direct investment from abroad 932; Portfolio investment assets 534; Portfolio investment liabilities 2; Financial derivatives assets –196; Financial derivatives liabilities 363; Other investment assets –10,282; Other investment liabilities 9,356; Net errors and omissions 234; *Overall balance* 495. Source: IMF, *International Financial Statistics*.

EXTERNAL TRADE

Principal Commodities (€ million, 2008, provisional): *Imports:* Food 408.1; Beverages and tobacco 65.7; Animal and vegetable oils and fats 9.0; Crude materials (inedible) except fuels 24.6; Mineral fuels, lubricants, etc. 574.6; Chemicals 333.3; Manufactured goods 400.2; Semi-manufactures 345.0; Machinery and transport equipment 1,193.8; Miscellaneous transactions 25.7; Total 3,379.9. *Exports:* Food 126.0; Beverages and tobacco 15.3; Crude materials (inedible) except fuels 12.5; Mineral fuels, lubricants, etc. 46.7; Chemicals 215.3; Manufactured goods 337.7; Semi-manufactures 111.9; Machinery and transport equipment 1,161.9; Miscellaneous transactions 7.0; Total 2,034.8.

Principal Trading Partners (€ million, 2008, provisional): *Imports:* European Union 2,354.5 (France—incl. Monaco 262.1; Germany 252.3; Italy—incl. San Marino 888.4; United Kingdom 429.0); Other Europe 221.2; Africa 72.8; Americas 121.0 (USA 75.0); Asia 596.4 (China, People's Republic 106.9; Singapore 200.8); Australasia 13.1; Total 3,379.9 (incl. ships' and aircraft stores and bunkers 0.9). *Exports:* European Union 916.8 (France—incl. Monaco 234.3; Germany 267.0; Italy—incl. San Marino 101.7; United Kingdom 165.1); Other Europe 38.6; Africa 132.4; Americas 222.8 (USA 182.9); Asia 678.8 (Japan 122.8; Singapore 275.0); Australasia 5.0; Total 2,034.8 (incl. ships' and aircraft stores and bunkers 40.4).

TRANSPORT

Road Traffic (motor vehicles in use, December 2008): Private cars 222,775; Commercial vehicles 48,210; Minibuses 433; Coaches and buses 743; Motorcycles 14,413; Total (incl. others) 294,658.

Shipping: *Merchant Fleet* (31 December 2007): Vessels 1,421; Total displacement 27,754,385 grt (Source: Lloyds Register-Fairplay, *World Fleet Statistics*). *International Freight Traffic* ('000 metric tons, 2007): Goods loaded 410.2; Goods unloaded 1,669.2.

Civil Aviation (traffic on scheduled services, 2003): Kilometres flown (million) 22; Passengers carried ('000) 1,309; Passenger-km (million) 2,174; Total ton-km (million) 209. Source: UN, *Statistical Yearbook*. 2007 Passenger movements on scheduled services 2,453,962.

TOURISM

Tourist Arrivals (based on departures by air and sea): 1,124,233 in 2006; 1,243,510 in 2007; 1,290,856 in 2008.

Arrivals by Country of Origin (based on departures by air and sea, 2008): France 81,152; Germany 150,793; Italy 144,456; Libya 9,403; Netherlands 36,920; United Kingdom 454,356; Total (incl. others) 1,290,856.

Tourism Receipts (US $ million, incl. passenger transport): 953 in 2004; 923 in 2005; 970 in 2006.

Source: partly World Tourism Organization.

COMMUNICATIONS MEDIA

Radio Receivers (1997): 255,000 in use*.

Television Receivers (1999): 212,000 in use*.

Telephones (main lines, 2007): 198,100 in use.

Facsimile Machines (1996): 6,000 in use (estimate)†.

Mobile Cellular Telephones (2007): 371,500 subscribers.

Personal Computers (2005): 126,000 in use‡.

Internet Users (2007): 158,000.

Broadband Subscribers (2007): 61,400.

Book Production (1998): 237 titles*.

Daily Newspapers (1999): 4 titles (combined average circulation 54,000 copies per issue).

Non-daily Newspapers (1999): 10 titles.

Other Periodicals (1992): 359 titles*.

* Source: UN, *Statistical Yearbook*.
† Source: UNESCO, *Statistical Yearbook*.
‡ Source: International Telecommunication Union.

EDUCATION

Pre-primary (2004/05, unless otherwise stated): 131 schools (1999/2000); 874 teachers; 8,551 students. Source: UNESCO.

Primary (2004/05, unless otherwise stated): 126 schools (1999/2000); 2,570 teachers; 29,596 students. Source: UNESCO.

Secondary (2004/05, unless otherwise stated): *General:* 75 schools (1999/2000); 3,610 teachers; 34,121 students. *Vocational:* 23 schools (1999/2000); 329 teachers; 4,358 students. *Junior College* (1995/96): 1 school; 1,800 students. Source: UNESCO, partly *Statistical Yearbook*.

Universities, etc. (2004/05): 825 teachers; 9,441 students. Source: UNESCO.

Adult Literacy Rate (UNESCO estimates): 87.9% (males 86.4%; females 89.2%) in 1995. Source: UNESCO Institute for Statistics.

Directory

The Constitution

On 13 December 1974 the Independence Constitution of 1964 was substantially amended to bring into effect a Republican Constitution, under the terms of which Malta became a democratic republic within the Commonwealth, founded on work and on respect for the fundamental rights and freedoms of the individual. The new Constitution provided for the creation of the office of President to replace that of Governor-General.

The religion of the Maltese people is recognized to be the Roman Catholic Apostolic Religion, and the Church Authorities have the constitutional right and duty to teach according to its principles. The religious teaching of the Roman Catholic Church is provided in all state schools as part of compulsory education.

The Constitution provides that the national language and the language of the Courts is Maltese, but that both Maltese and English are official languages.

An independent Public Services Commission, consisting of three to five members, is appointed by the President, on the advice of the Prime Minister, to make recommendations to the Prime Minister concerning appointments to public office and the dismissal and disciplinary control of persons holding public office.

The Constitution also provides for an Employment Commission, consisting of a chairman and four other members, the function of which is to ensure that, in respect of employment, no distinction, exclusion or preference that is not justifiable is made or given in favour of or against any person by reason of his or her political opinion.

The Judicature is independent.
Radio and television broadcasting is controlled by an independent authority.

DECLARATION OF PRINCIPLES

The Constitution upholds the right to work and to reasonable hours of work, the safeguarding of rights of women workers, the encouragement of private economic enterprise, the encouragement of cooperatives, the provision of free and compulsory primary education, and the provision of social assistance and insurance.

FUNDAMENTAL RIGHTS AND FREEDOMS OF THE INDIVIDUAL

The Constitution provides for the protection of the right to life, freedom from arbitrary arrest or detention, protection of freedom of conscience, protection from discrimination on the grounds of race, etc.

THE PRESIDENT

Under the Constitution, the office of President becomes vacant after five years from the date of appointment made by resolution of the House of Representatives. The President appoints the Prime Minister, choosing the member of the House of Representatives who is judged to be ablest to command the confidence of a majority of the members. On the advice of the Prime Minister, the President appoints the other ministers, the Chief Justice, the Judges and the Attorney-General.

MALTA

THE CABINET
The Cabinet consists of the Prime Minister and such number of other ministers as are recommended by the Prime Minister.

PARLIAMENT
The House of Representatives consists of such number of members, being an odd number and divisible by the number of divisions, as Parliament by law determines from time to time. In future the electoral divisions are not to be fewer than nine and not more than 15, as Parliament may from time to time determine. The normal life of the House of Representatives is five years, after which a general election is held. Election is by universal adult suffrage on the basis of proportional representation. The age of majority is 18 years. Under a constitutional amendment adopted in January 1987, it was ensured that a party receiving more than 50% of the total votes cast in a general election would obtain a majority of seats in the House of Representatives, by the allocation (if necessary) of additional seats to that party.

NEUTRALITY AND NON-ALIGNMENT
In January 1987 a constitutional amendment was adopted, aiming to entrench in the Constitution Malta's status of neutrality and adherence to a policy of non-alignment, and stipulating that no foreign military base was to be permitted on Maltese territory.

The Government

HEAD OF STATE
President: Dr GEORGE ABELA (took office 4 April 2009).

THE CABINET
(April 2009)

Prime Minister: Dr LAWRENCE GONZI.
Deputy Prime Minister and Minister of Foreign Affairs: Dr TONIO BORG.
Minister for Gozo: GIOVANNA DEBONO.
Minister for Infrastructure, Transport and Communications: Dr AUSTIN GATT.
Minister for Resources and Rural Affairs: GEORGE PULLICINO.
Minister for Education, Culture, Youth and Sport: DOLORES CRISTINA.
Minister for Social Policy: JOHN DALLI.
Minister of Finance, the Economy and Investment: Dr TONIO FENECH.
Minister for Justice and Home Affairs: Dr CARMELO MIFSUD BONNICI.

PARLIAMENTARY SECRETARIES (ATTACHED TO MINISTRIES)

Parliamentary Secretary for Public Dialogue and Information in the Office of the Prime Minister: Dr CHRIS SAID.
Parliamentary Secretary for Tourism in the Office of the Prime Minister: Dr MARIO DE MARCO.
Parliamentary Secretary for Youth and Sport in the Ministry of Education, Culture, Youth and Sport: CLYDE PULI.
Parliamentary Secretary for Health in the Ministry for Social Policy: Dr JOE CASSAR.
Parliamentary Secretary for the Elderly and Community Care in the Ministry for Social Policy: MARIO GALEA.
Parliamentary Secretary for Revenues and Land in the Ministry of Finance, the Economy and Investment: Dr JASON AZZOPARDI.

MINISTRIES

Office of the President: The Palace, Valletta VLT 1190; tel. 21221221; fax 21241241; e-mail president@gov.mt; internet www.president.gov.mt.
Office of the Prime Minister: Auberge de Castille, Valletta VLT 2000; tel. 22001400; fax 22001467; internet www.opm.gov.mt.
Ministry of Education, Culture, Youth and Sport: Great Siege Rd, Floriana CMR 02; tel. 21223622; fax 21242759; e-mail communications.moed@gov.mt; internet www.education.gov.mt.
Ministry of Finance, the Economy and Investment: Maison Demandols, 30 South St, Valletta VLT 2000; tel. 25998000; fax 25998311; e-mail info.mfin@gov.mt; internet www.mfin.gov.mt.
Ministry of Foreign Affairs: Palazzo Parisio, Merchants St, Valletta VLT 1171; tel. 21242191; fax 21235032; e-mail info.mfa@gov.mt; internet www.mfa.gov.mt.
Ministry for Gozo: St Francis Sq., Victoria VCT 2000, Gozo; tel. 21561482; fax 21559360; e-mail info.mog@gov.mt; internet www.gozo.gov.mt.
Ministry for Infrastructure, Transport and Communications: 168 Strait St, Valletta VLT 1433; tel. 21226808; fax 21250700; e-mail mitc@gov.mt; internet www.mitc.gov.mt.
Ministry for Justice and Home Affairs: Auberge d'Aragon, Independence Sq., Valletta VLT 2000; tel. 22957000; fax 22957348; e-mail mjha@gov.mt; internet www.mjha.gov.mt.
Ministry for Resources and Rural Affairs: Barriera Wharf, Valletta VLT 1970; tel. 22952000; fax 22952212; e-mail info.mrra@gov.mt; internet www.mrra.gov.mt.
Ministry for Social Policy: Palazzo Ferreria, 310 Republic St, Valletta VLT 2000; tel. 25903100; fax 25903216; e-mail info.msp@gov.mt; internet www.msp.gov.mt.

Legislature

House of Representatives
The Palace, Valletta VLT 1190; tel. 25596000; fax 25596314; e-mail parliament@gov.mt; internet www.parliament.gov.mt.

Speaker: LOUIS GALEA.

General Election, 8 March 2008

Party	Votes	% of votes	Seats
Partit Nazzjonalista (Nationalist Party)	143,468	49.34	35
Partit Laburista (Malta Labour Party)	141,888	48.79	34
Alternattiva Demokratika—The Green Party	3,810	1.31	—
Azzjoni Nazzjonali (National Action)	1,461	0.50	—
Others	172	0.06	—
Total	**290,799**	**100.00**	**69**

Election Commission

Electoral Commission: Electoral Office, Evans Bldg, St Elmo Pl., Valletta VLT 2000; tel. 21221994; fax 21248457; e-mail electoral.office@gov.mt; internet www.electoral.gov.mt; independent; Chair. and Chief Electoral Commr EDWARD R. GATT; Sec. JOE CALLEJA.

Political Organizations

Alternattiva Demokratika—The Green Party (AD): 10 Manwel Dimech St, Sliema SLM 1059; tel. 21314040; fax 21314046; e-mail info@alternattiva.org.mt; internet www.alternattiva.org.mt; f. 1989; emphasizes social and environmental issues; Chair. ARNOLD CASSOLA; Sec.-Gen. VICTOR GALEA.

Azzjoni Nazzjonali (AN) (National Action): 74 The Strand, Sliema; e-mail azzjoninazzjonali@gmail.com; internet www.azzjoninazzjonali.org; f. 2007; right-wing; Leader Dr JOSIE MUSCAT; Gen. Sec. WAYNE HEWITT (acting).

Partit Laburista (PL) (Labour Party): National Labour Centre, Mile End Rd, Hamrun HMR 1717; tel. 21249900; fax 21244204; e-mail mlp@mlp.org.mt; internet www.mlp.org.mt; f. 1921; fmrly known as the Malta Labour Party (official name Partit tal-Haddiema–Workers' Party); name changed as above in 2008; democratic socialist; Leader Dr JOSEPH MUSCAT; Pres. STEFAN ZRINZO AZZOPARDI; Gen. Sec. JASON MICALLEF.

Partit Nazzjonalista (PN) (Nationalist Party): Herbert Ganado St, Pietà PTA 1541; tel. 21243641; fax 21243640; e-mail admin@pn.org.mt; internet www.pn.org.mt; f. 1880; Christian democratic; Leader Dr LAWRENCE GONZI; Sec.-Gen. PAUL BORG OLIVIER.

Diplomatic Representation

EMBASSIES AND HIGH COMMISSIONS IN MALTA

Australia: Villa Fiorentina, Ta'Xbiex Terrace, Ta'Xbiex XBX 1034; tel. 21338201; fax 21344059; e-mail aushicom@onvol.net; internet www.malta.embassy.gov.au; High Commr JUREK JUSZCZYK.

MALTA — Directory

Austria: Whitehall Mansions, 3rd Floor, Ta'Xbiex Seafront, Ta'Xbiex XBX 1026; tel. 23279000; fax 21317430; e-mail valletta-ob@bmeia.gv.at; Ambassador Dr CAROLINE GUDENUS.

Belgium: Europa Centre, 8–9 John Lopez St, Floriana FLN 1400; tel. 21228214; fax 21243246; e-mail valletta@diplobel.fed.be; internet www.diplomatie.be/valletta; Ambassador JEAN-FRANÇOIS DELAHAUT.

China, People's Republic: Karmnu Court, Lapsi St, St Julian's STJ 1264; tel. 21384889; fax 21344730; e-mail chinaemb–mt@mfa.gov.cn; internet mt.chineseembassy.org; Ambassador CHAI XI.

Egypt: Villa Mon Rêve, 10 Sir Temi Zammit St, Ta'Xbiex XBX 1013; tel. 21314158; fax 21319230; e-mail embegmlt@onvol.net; Ambassador ABD AL-KARIM MAHMOUD SOLIMAN.

France: POB 408, Valletta VLT 1000; 130 Melita St, Valletta VLT 1000; tel. 22480600; fax 22480626; e-mail ambafrance@maltanet.net; internet www.ambafrance-mt.org; Ambassador DANIEL RONDEAU.

Germany: 'Il-Piazzetta', Entrance B, 1st Floor, Tower Rd, Sliema SLM 1605; tel. 21336531; fax 21341271; e-mail info@valletta.diplo.de; internet www.valletta.diplo.de; Ambassador KARL ANDREAS VON STENGLIN.

Greece: Villino Fondgalland, 6 Ir-Rampa, Ta'Xbiex XBX 1035; tel. 21320889; fax 21320788; e-mail embassy.malta@mfa.gr; internet malta.mfa.gr; Ambassador ALEXANDROS RALLIS.

Holy See: Apostolic Nunciature, V20/22 Pietru Caxaru St, Tal-Virtù, Rabat RBT 2604; tel. 21453422; fax 21453423; e-mail nuntius@onvol.net; Apostolic Nuncio Most Rev. TOMMASO CAPUTO (Titular Archbishop of Otricoli).

Ireland: Whitehall Mansions, Ta'Xbiex Seafront, Ta'Xbiex XBX 1026; tel. 21334744; fax 21334755; e-mail vallettaembassy@dfa.ie; internet www.embassyofireland.org.mt; Chargé d'affaires GERALD O'CONNOR.

Italy: 5 Vilhena St, Floriana FRN 1040; tel. 21233157; fax 21239217; e-mail ambasciata.lavalletta@esteri.it; internet www.amblavalletta.esteri.it; Ambassador PAOLO ANDREA TRABALZA.

Libya: Dar Jamahiriya, Notabile Rd, Balzan BZN 9033; tel. 21486347; fax 21483939; e-mail libyanpeople@waldonet.net.mt; Chargé d'affaires a.i. SALEM F. E. ASH-SHTEWI.

Netherlands: Whitehall Mansions, 3rd Floor, Ta'Xbiex Seafront, Ta'Xbiex XBX 1026; tel. 21313980; fax 21313990; e-mail val@minbuza.nl; internet www.mfa.nl/val; Ambassador JAN HEIDSMA.

Portugal: Whitehall Mansions, 3rd Floor, Ta'Xbiex Seafront, Ta'Xbiex XBX 1026; tel. 21322924; fax 21322927; e-mail info@embportmalta.com; internet www.embportmalta.com; Ambassador ANTÓNIO JOSÉ DA CÂMARA RAMALHO ORTIGÃO.

Russia: Ariel House, 25 Anthony Schembri St, Kappara, San Ġwann SGN 08; tel. 21371905; fax 21372131; e-mail rusemb@onvol.net; internet www.malta.mid.ru; Ambassador ANDREI E. GRANOVSKII.

Spain: Whitehall Mansions, Ta'Xbiex Seafront, Ta'Xbiex XBX 1026; tel. 21317365; fax 21317362; e-mail emb.valletta@mae.es; internet www.maec.es/embajadas/lavalletta; Ambassador MARÍA ISABEL VICANDI PLAZA.

Tunisia: Valletta Rd, Attard ATD 9052; tel. 21417070; fax 21413414; e-mail at.lavalette@maltanet.net; Ambassador MOHAMED ALI GHANZOUI.

United Kingdom: Whitehall Mansions, Ta'Xbiex Seafront, Ta'Xbiex XBX 1026; tel. 23230000; fax 23232216; e-mail bhcvalletta@fco.gov.uk; internet ukinmalta.fco.gov.uk; High Commr LOUISE STANTON.

USA: Development House, 3rd Floor, St Anne St, Floriana FRN 9010; tel. 25614000; fax 21243229; e-mail usembmalta@state.gov; internet malta.usembassy.gov; Chargé d'affaires a.i. JASON DAVIS.

Judicial System

The legal system consists of enactments of the Parliament of Malta, and those of the British Parliament not repealed or replaced by enactments of the Maltese legislature. Maltese Civil Law derives largely from Roman Law, while British Law has significantly influenced Maltese public law.

The Constitutional Court, composed of three judges, is appellate in cases involving alleged violations of human rights, the interpretation of the Constitution and the invalidity of laws. It has jurisdiction to decide questions as to membership of the House of Representatives and any reference made to it relating to voting for election of members of the House of Representatives.

The Court of Appeal is composed of three judges, when it hears appeals from the judgments of the Civil Court, and of one judge, when it hears appeals from the Court of Magistrates in its civil jurisdiction. An appeal also lies to the Court of Appeal from the decisions of a number of administrative tribunals, mostly on points of law.

The Court of Criminal Appeal consists of three judges and hears appeals from persons convicted by the Criminal Court. A person convicted on indictment may appeal against his conviction in all cases or against the sentence passed on his conviction, unless the sentence is one fixed by law. An appeal can never result in a sentence of greater severity. An accused person may also appeal against a verdict of not guilty on the grounds of insanity. In certain cases the Court may also order a retrial. The Attorney-General, who is the prosecutor before the Criminal Court, cannot appeal from a verdict of acquittal or, in certain cases, against the sentence passed. This Court, when formed of one judge, hears appeals from judgments delivered by the Court of Magistrates in its criminal jurisdiction.

The Criminal Court is formed by one judge, who sits with a jury of nine persons to try, on indictment, offences exceeding the competence of the Court of Magistrates. This court may, in certain exceptional cases, sit without a jury.

The Civil Court is divided into three sections. The First Hall takes cognisance of all causes of a civil and a commercial nature, exceeding the jurisdiction of the Courts of Magistrates. The Voluntary Jurisdiction Section (formerly the Second Hall) is assigned all matters of a civil nature, such as authority to proceed the tutorship of minors, adoption, the interdiction and incapacitation of persons, the opening of successions and the confirmation of testamentary executors. The Family Section is assigned matters of a civil nature regulated by titles I, II and IV of the First Book of the Civil Code; the Maintenance Orders (Facilities for Enforcement) Ordinance; the Maintenance Ordinance (Reciprocal Enforcement) Act; the Marriage Act and the Child Abduction and Child Custody Act. One Judge presides in all three sections.

The Magistrates' Court, which is composed of one Magistrate, exercises both a civil and a criminal jurisdiction. The Court of Magistrates, in civil matters, has an inferior jurisdiction of first instance, limited to claims exceeding LM 1,500 but not exceeding LM 5,000. In criminal matters, the Court has a two-fold jurisdiction, namely, as a court of criminal judicature for the trial of offences which fall within its jurisdiction, and as a court of inquiry in respect of offences which fall within the jurisdiction of a higher tribunal.

The Court of Magistrates for Gozo, in civil matters, has a two-fold jurisdiction—an inferior jurisdiction comparable to that exercised by its counterpart Court in Malta, and a superior jurisdiction, both civil and commercial, in respect of causes which in Malta are cognisable by the First Hall of the Civil Court. Within the limits of its territorial jurisdiction, this Court has also the powers of a Court of voluntary jurisdiction.

The Small Claims Tribunal is presided over by an adjudicator who decides cases on principles of equity, according to law. Adjudicators are appointed from amongst advocates for a term of five years, and decide cases brought before them without delay. The aim is to have claims not exceeding the sum of LM 1,500 decided summarily. Sittings of this Tribunal are held in Malta or Gozo. An appeal from the decision of the Tribunal lies to the Court of Appeal on specific cases listed in the Act establishing the Tribunal.

The Juvenile Court consists of a Magistrate, as Chairman, and two members. Sittings are held in Santa Venera. The Court hears charges against, and holds other proceedings relating to, minors under the age of 16 years, and may also issue Care Orders in their regard. Given the confidential nature of such sittings, attendance to hearings is restricted to persons mentioned in the law establishing the Court.

Chief Justice and President of the Court of Appeal and the Constitutional Court: Dr VINCENT A. DE GAETANO.

Judges: CARMEL A. AGIUS, JOSEPH D. CAMILLERI, JOSEPH A. FILLETTI, ALBERTO J. MAGRI, GEOFFREY VALENZIA, GIANNINO CARUANA DEMAJO, GINO CAMILLERI, CARMELO FARRUGIA SACCO, RAYMOND PACE, DAVID P. SCICLUNA, JOSEPH R. MICALLEF, JOSEPH GALEA DEBONO, TONIO MALLIA, PHILIP SCIBERRAS, NOEL CUSCHIERI, JOSEPH AZZOPARDI, ABIGAIL LOFARO, ANNA FELICE.

Attorney-General: Dr SILVIO CAMILLERI.

Religion

CHRISTIANITY

The Roman Catholic Church

Malta comprises one archdiocese and one diocese. At 31 December 2006 adherents of the Roman Catholic Church numbered an estimated 405,977 (representing some 93.9% of the total population).

Bishops' Conference

Conferenza Episcopale Maltese, Archbishop's Curia, St Calcedonius Sq., Floriana FRN 1535; tel. 25906403; fax 21226457; e-mail joe.magro@maltadiocese.org; internet www.maltadiocese.org.

f. 1971; Pres. Most Rev. PAUL CREMONA (Archbishop of Malta); Sec. Rev. JOE MAGRO.

MALTA

Archbishop of Malta: Most Rev. PAUL CREMONA, Archbishop's Curia, St Calcedonius Sq., Floriana FRN 1535; POB 29, Valletta; tel. 21235350; fax 21223307; e-mail info@maltadiocese.org.mt.

Bishop of Gozo: Rt Rev. MARIO GRECH, Chancery Office, POB 1, Republic St, Victoria VCT 1000, Gozo; tel. 21556661; fax 21551278; e-mail info@gozodiocese.org; internet gozodiocese.org.

The Anglican Communion

Malta forms part of the Diocese in Europe.

Church of England: Pro-Cathedral of St Paul, Independence Sq., Valletta VLT 1520; tel. 21225714; fax 21225867; e-mail anglican@onvol.net; internet www.anglicanmalta.org; Senior Chaplain and Chancellor of the Pro-Cathedral (vacant).

Other Christian Churches

In 2004 there were approximately 680 Jehovah's Witnesses and 148 members of the Church of Jesus Christ of Latter-day Saints (Mormons). The Bible Baptist Church had 30 members and the Fellowship of Evangelical Churches had about 100 affiliates.

OTHER RELIGIONS

There is one Muslim mosque and a Muslim primary school. There are an estimated 3,000 Muslims in the country. There is one Jewish congregation. Zen Buddhism and the Bahá'í Faith have about 30 members each.

The Press

DAILY NEWSPAPERS

The Malta Independent: Standard House, Birkirkara Hill, St Julian's STJ 1149; tel. 21345888; fax 21344860; e-mail scalleja@independent.com.mt; internet www.independent.com.mt; English; Editor STEPHEN CALLEJA.

In-Nazzjon (The Nation): Herbert Ganado St, POB 37, Pietà PTA 1450; tel. 21243641; fax 21243640; e-mail alex.attard@media.link.com.mt; internet www.mument.com.mt; f. 1970; Maltese; affiliated to Partit Nazzjonalista; Editor ALEX ATTARD.

L-Orizzont (The Horizon): Union Print Co, A-41 Industrial Estate, Valletta Rd, Marsa MRS 3000; tel. 21244557; fax 21238484; e-mail info@unionprint.com.mt; internet www.l-orizzont.com; f. 1962; Maltese; organ of the General Workers' Union; Editor FRANS GHIRXI; circ. 20,000 (2008).

The Times: Allied Newspapers Ltd, 341 St Paul St, Valletta VLT 1211; tel. 25594100; fax 25594116; e-mail daily@timesofmalta.com; internet www.timesofmalta.com; f. 1935; English; Editor RAY BUGEJA.

OTHER NEWSPAPERS

Business Today: Vjal ir-Ríhan, San Ġwann SGN 9020; tel. 21382741; fax 21385075; internet www.businesstoday.com.mt; Weds; Man. Editor SAVIOUR BALZAN.

Il-Gensillum (The People Today): Media Centre, National Rd, Blata il-Bajda HMR 1640; tel. 25699119; fax 25699151; e-mail gens@mediacentre.org.mt; internet www.mediacentre.org.mt; f. 2004 to succeed *Il-Gens* (The People); Maltese; Roman Catholic; Editor Fr JOHN AVELLINO; circ. 13,000 (2008).

Illum (Today): MediaToday Co Ltd, Vjal ir-Rihan, San Ġwann SGN 9016; tel. 21382741; fax 21385075; e-mail illum@mediatoday.com.mt; internet www.illum.com.mt; weekly; Maltese; Man. Editor SAVIOUR BALZAN.

KullHadd: Centru Nazzjonali Laburista, Mile End Rd, Hamrun HMR 1717; tel. 21235312; fax 21238252; e-mail felix@kullhadd.com; internet www.kullhadd.com; f. 1993; organ of Partit Laburista; Maltese; Editor FELIX AGIUS.

Lehen is-Sewwa: Catholic Institute, Floriana FRN 1441; tel. and fax 21225847; e-mail lehenissewwa@vol.net.mt; f. 1928; Roman Catholic; Editor Rev. Fr JOHN CIARLÓ; circ. 10,000 (2008).

The Malta Business Weekly: Standard House, Birkirkara Hill, St Julian's STJ 1149; tel. 21345888; fax 21344860; e-mail csultana@independent.com.mt; internet www.independent.com.mt; f. 1994; English; Editor CHRISTOPHER SULTANA.

The Malta Independent on Sunday: Standard House, Birkirkara Hill, St Julian's STJ 1149; tel. 21345888; fax 21344884; e-mail ngrima@independent.com.mt; internet www.independent.com.mt; English; Editor NOEL GRIMA.

MaltaToday: MediaToday Co Ltd, Vjal ir-Ríhan, San Ġwann SGN 9016; tel. 21382741; fax 21385075; e-mail maltatoday@mediatoday.com.mt; internet www.maltatoday.com.mt; f. 1998; Weds and Sun.; English; Editor SAVIOUR BALZAN.

Il-Mument (The Moment): Herbert Ganado St, POB 37, Pietà PTA 1450; tel. 21243641; fax 21243640; e-mail mument@media.link.com.mt; internet www.mument.com.mt; f. 1972; Maltese; affiliated to Partit Nazzjonalista; Editor VICTOR CAMILLERI.

The Sunday Times: Allied Newspapers Ltd, POB 328, Valletta VLT 1211; tel. 25594500; fax 25594510; e-mail sunday@timesofmalta.com; internet www.timesofmalta.com; f. 1922; English; Editor STEVE MALLIA; circ. 40,000 (2008).

It-Torċa (The Torch): Union Press, A 41, Marsa Industrial Estate, Marsa MRS 3000; tel. 21244557; fax 21238484; e-mail info@unionprint.com.mt; internet www.it-torca.com; f. 1944; Maltese; organ of the General Workers' Union; Editor ALEKS FARRUGIA.

SELECTED PERIODICALS

Commercial Courier: Malta Chamber of Commerce and Enterprise, Exchange Bldgs, Republic St, Valletta VLT 1117; tel. 21233873; fax 21245223; e-mail admin@chamber.org.mt; internet www.chamber.org.mt; bi-monthly; Editor KEVIN J. BORG.

The Employer: Malta Employers' Asscn, 35/1 South St, Valletta VLT 1100; tel. 21222992; fax 21230227; e-mail admin@maltaemployers.com; internet www.maltaemployers.com; quarterly; Editor JOSEPH FARRUGIA.

Malta Government Gazette: Department of Information, 3 Castille Pl., Valletta VLT 2000; tel. 22001770; fax 22001775; e-mail info.doi@gov.mt; internet www.doi.gov.mt; f. 1813; official notices; Maltese and English; 2 a week.

Malta In Figures: National Statistics Office, Lascaris, Valletta VLT 1921; tel. 25997000; fax 25997205; e-mail nso@gov.mt; internet www.nso.gov.mt; official statistics; annual.

Malta This Month: Advantage Advertising Ltd, 118 St John's St, Valletta VLT 1169; tel. 21249924; fax 21249927; e-mail advantage@onvol.net; publ. by Air Malta; monthly; Editor PETER DARMANIN.

The Retailer: Association of General Retailers and Traders, Exchange Bldgs, Republic St, Valletta VLT 1117; tel. 21230459; fax 21246925; internet www.grtu.eu; monthly; publ. by Malta Chamber of Small and Medium-sized Enterprises; Editor VINCENT FARRUGIA.

The Teacher: Teachers' Institute, 213 Republic St, Valletta VLT 1118; tel. 21237815; fax 21244074; e-mail info@mut.org.mt; internet www.mut.org.mt; f. 1919; journal of the Malta Union of Teachers; 2 a year; Editor FRANKLIN BARBARA.

Xpress: 149 Archbishop St, Valletta VLT 1442; tel. 21240334; fax 21224745; publ. of the Alternattiva Demokratika—The Green Party; Maltese; monthly; Editor NEIL SPITERI.

Publishers

Malta University Publishers Ltd: Old University Building, St. Paul's St, Valletta VLT 1216; tel. 21224067; fax 21248218; e-mail mupl@mus.com.mt; internet www.mus.com.mt; f. 1953; owned by University of Malta; Maltese folklore, history, law, bibliography and language; Admin. Officer TITA BONNICI.

Merlin Library Ltd: Mountbatten St, Blata l-Bajda HMR 08; tel. 21234438; fax 21221135; e-mail mail@merlinlibrary.com; internet www.merlinlibrary.com; dictionaries, educational, fiction and children's books; Dir CHRISTOPHER GRUPPETTA.

Mireva: Triq Mons Carmelo Zammit St, Msida MSD 06; tel. 21312616; fax 21319311; e-mail info@mireva.com; internet www.mireva.com; academic, fiction.

Publishers Enterprises Group (PEG) Ltd: PEG Bldg, UB7 Industrial Estate, San Ġwann SGN 3000; tel. 21440083; fax 21488908; e-mail contact@peg.com.mt; internet www.peg.com.mt; f. 1983; educational, children's, cookery, technical, tourism, leisure; Man. Dir EMANUEL DEBATTISTA.

Broadcasting and Communications

TELECOMMUNICATIONS

Regulatory Authority

Malta Communications Authority (MCA): Pinto Wharf, Valletta Waterfront, Floriana FRN 1913; tel. 21336840; fax 21336846; e-mail info@mca.org.mt; internet www.mca.org.mt; national agency responsible for regulating telecommunications; f. 2001; Exec. Chair. and Dir-Gen. PHILIP MICALLEF.

Service Providers

GO PLC: Spencer Hill, POB 40, Marsa MRS 1001; tel. 21210210; fax 25945895; e-mail info@go.com.mt; internet www.go.com.mt; f. 1975; fmrly Maltacom PLC; restyled 2007; mobile cellular and fixed-line

MALTA

telecommunications, broadband internet access, digital television services; 60% owned by TECOM Investments and the Dubai Investment Group, both mems of Dubai Holding; Chair. SONNY PORTELLI; CEO DAVID KAY.

GO Mobile: Fra Diego St, Marsa MRS 1501; tel. 21246200; fax 21234314; internet www.go.com.mt/gomobile.

Melita PLC: Gasan Centre, Mriehel Bypass, Mriehel BKR 3000; tel. 21490006; fax 22745050; e-mail info@melitaplc.com; internet www.melita.com; f. 1992; offers mobile and fixed-line telecommunications services, and broadband internet access; also digital television services; CEO JOSEPH R. AQUILINA.

BROADCASTING

Regulatory Authority

Broadcasting Authority, Malta: 7 Mile End Rd, Hamrun HMR 1719; tel. 21247908; fax 21240855; e-mail info@ba-malta.org; internet www.ba-malta.org; f. 1961; statutory body responsible for the supervision and regulation of radio and television broadcasting; Chair. JOSEPH SCICLUNA; CEO PIERRE CASSAR.

Radio and Television

Bay Radio: Eden Pl., St George's Bay, St Julian's STJ 3310; tel. 23710800; fax 23710845; e-mail 897@bay.com.mt; internet www.bay.com.mt; Station Man. TERRY FARRUGIA.

Campus FM: Old Humanities Bldg, University of Malta, Msida MSD 06; tel. 21333313; fax 21314485; e-mail campusfm@um.edu.mt; internet campusfm.um.edu.mt; Man. Fr JOSEPH BORG.

Education 22: Mile End St, Hamrun HMR 1716; tel. 21239274; fax 21240701; e-mail info@e22.com.mt; internet www.e22.com.mt; educational television channel.

Media.link Communications Co Ltd: Dar Centrali, Herbert Ganado St, Pietà PTA 1450; tel. 21243641; fax 21243640; e-mail antona@vol.net.mt; internet www.media.link.com.mt.

Net TV: Dar Centrali, Herbert Ganado St, Pietà PTA 1450; tel. 21243641; fax 21226645; CEO ANTON ATTARD.

Radio 101: Independence Point, Herbert Ganado St, Pietà PTA 1450; tel. 21241164; fax 21564111; e-mail news@media.link.com.mt; internet www.radio101.com.mt; Man. ANTON ATTARD.

One Productions Ltd: A28B, Industrial Estate, Marsa MRS 3000; tel. 25682568; fax 25688249; e-mail onenews@one.com.mt; internet www.one.com.mt; f. 1999; owned by Partit Laburista; Man. Dir Dr MICHAEL VELLA HABER.

Super One Radio: A28B, Industrial Estate, Marsa MRS 3000; tel. 2568 2600; fax 21231472; e-mail ray.azzopardi@one.com.mt; broadcasts 24 hours daily; Man. RAY AZZOPARDI.

One Television: A28B Industrial Estate, Marsa MRS 3000; tel. 25682568; fax 21231472; e-mail ruth.vella@one.com.mt; broadcasts 126 hours weekly; Dir of Television RUTH VELLA.

Public Broadcasting Services Ltd: 75 St Luke's Rd, Gwardamangia PTA 1025; tel. 21225051; fax 21244601; e-mail info@pbs.com.mt; internet www.pbs.com.mt; f. 1991; govt-owned; operates national radio and television services: Radju Malta, Radju Parlament, Magic 91.7 and Television Malta; Chair. CLARE THAKE VASSALLO; CEO ALBERT DEBONO.

Radio Calypso 101.8 FM: Calypso Media Communications, The Blues Complex, Gifen St, Bugibba; tel. 21578022; fax 21581224; e-mail charles.vella@calypsoradio.com; internet www.calypsoradio.com; Station Man. FRANK CAMILLERI.

Radju Marija: Kunvent Patrijiet Dumnikani, Misrah San Duminku, Rabat RBT 06; tel. 21453105; fax 21453103; e-mail info.mal@radiomaria.org; internet www.radjumarija.org.

RTK Radio: Media Centre, National Rd, Blata il-Bajda HMR 1640; tel. 25699150; fax 25699151; e-mail rtknews@rtk.org.mt; internet www.rtk.org.mt; f. 1992; radio station of the Catholic Church of Malta; Chair. FRANCO AZZOPARDI; Man. Dir MICHAEL FRANCALANZA.

Smash TV and Radio: Smash Communications, Thistle Lane, Paola PLA 19; tel. 21697829; fax 21697830; f. 1992; Man. Dir JOSEPH BALDACCHINO.

XFM 100.2 FM: 24 A. Cuschieri St, Fleur-de-Lys, Birkirkara BKR 4916; tel. 21378165; fax 21378167; e-mail donny@xfmmalta.com; internet www.xfmmalta.com; f. 2003; programmes in Maltese and English; music; Station Man. DONNY HUGHES.

Directory

Finance

(cap. = capital; res = reserves; dep. = deposits; m. = million; brs = branches; amounts in Maltese liri, unless otherwise stated)

REGULATORY AUTHORITY

Malta Financial Services Authority: Notabile Rd, Attard BKR 3000; tel. 21441155; fax 21441188; e-mail communications@mfsa.com.mt; internet www.mfsa.com.mt; f. 2002; supervises the financial services sector, incl. banking, insurance and investments; regulates activities of Malta Stock Exchange; houses Malta's Companies Registry; Chair. Prof. JOSEPH V. BANNISTER.

BANKING

Central Bank

Central Bank of Malta: Pjazza Kastilja, Valletta VLT 1060; tel. 25500000; fax 25502500; e-mail info@centralbankmalta.org; internet www.centralbankmalta.org; f. 1968; bank of issue; cap. 5m., res 73m., dep. 408m. (Dec. 2006); Gov. MICHAEL C. BONELLO.

Commercial Banks

APS Bank Ltd: APS House, 24 St Anne Sq., Floriana FRN 9020; tel. 21226644; fax 21226202; e-mail headoffice@apsbank.com.mt; internet www.apsbank.com.mt; f. 1910; cap. 7m., res 3m., dep. 249m. (Dec. 2007); Chair. Prof. EMMANUEL P. DELIA; CEO EDWARD CACHIA; 6 brs.

Banif Bank (Malta) PLC: Level 2, 203 Rue D'Argens, Gzira GZR 1368; tel. 22601000; fax 21312000; e-mail customercare@banif.com.mt; internet www.banif.com.mt; f. 2008; owned by Grupo Banif (Portugal); Chair. JOSEPH SAMMUT; CEO JOAQUIM SILVA PINTO; 5 brs.

Bank of Valletta PLC: BOV Centre, Cannon Rd. St Venera SVR 9030; tel. 21312020; fax 22753730; e-mail customercare@bov.com; internet www.bov.com; f. 1974; merged with Valletta Investment Bank Ltd in Oct. 2000; cap. 28m., res 9m., dep. 2,193m. (Sept. 2007); Chair. RODERICK CHALMERS; CEO TONIO DEPASQUALE; 41 brs.

HSBC Bank Malta PLC: 233 Republic St, Valletta VLT 1116; tel. 25970000; fax 23804923; e-mail infomalta@hsbc.com; internet www.hsbc.com.mt; f. 1975 as Mid-Med Bank; 70.03% owned by HSBC Europe BV; cap. 36m., res 11m., dep. 1,782m. (Dec. 2007); CEO ALAN RICHARDS; 43 brs.

Lombard Bank Malta PLC: Lombard House, 67 Republic St, Valletta VLT 1117; tel. 25581117; fax 25581151; e-mail mail@lombardmalta.com; internet www.lombardmalta.com; f. 1969; cap. 2m., res 7m., dep. 180m. (Dec. 2007); Chair. CHRISTIAN LEMMERICH; Dir and CEO JOSEPH SAID; 6 brs.

Volksbank Malta Ltd: 53 Dingli St, Sliema SLM 09; tel. 27777777; fax 21336090; e-mail info@volksbank.com.mt; f. 1995 as an 'offshore' bank; licensed to operate as a commercial bank in 2002; Chair. WINSTON V. ZAHRA; Man. Dir HERBERT SKOK.

Principal 'Offshore' Bank

FIMBank PLC: Plaza Commercial Centre, 7th Floor, Bisazza St, Sliema SLM 1640; tel. 21322100; fax 21322122; e-mail info@fimbank.com; internet www.fimbank.com; f. 1994 as First International Merchant Bank PLC; cap. US $43m., dep. US $369m., total assets US $438m. (Dec. 2006); Chair. NAJEEB H. M. AS-SALEH; Pres. MARGRITH LÜTSCHG-EMMENEGGER.

Bankers' Association

Malta Bankers' Association: 48/2 Birkirkara Rd, Attard ATD 1210; tel. 21412210; fax 21424580; e-mail info@maltabankers.org; internet www.maltabankers.org; f. 1962; Chair. TONIO DEPASQUALE; Sec.-Gen. JAMES BONELLO; 21 mems.

STOCK EXCHANGE

Malta Stock Exchange: Garrison Chapel, Castille Pl., Valletta VLT 1063; tel. 21244051; fax 25696316; e-mail borza@borzamalta.com.mt; internet www.borzamalta.com.mt; f. 1992; Chair. JOSEPH ZAMMIT TABONA; Chief Exec. MARK A. GUILLAUMIER.

INSURANCE

Aon Mediterranean Insurance Brokers (Malta) Ltd: 53 Mediterranean Bldg, Abate Rigord St, Ta'Xbiex XBX 1122; tel. 23433234; fax 21341597; e-mail info@mib.com.mt; internet www.aon.com/malta; f. 1976; Man. Dir JOSEPH CUTAJAR.

Middle Sea Insurance PLC: Middle Sea House, Floriana FRN 1442; tel. 21246262; fax 21248195; e-mail middlesea@middlesea.com; internet www.middlesea.com; f. 1981; Exec. Chair. MARIO C. GRECH.

Numerous foreign insurance companies, principally British, Canadian and Italian, are represented in Malta by local agents.

Insurance Association

Malta Insurance Association: 43A/2, St Paul's Bldgs, West St, Valletta VLT 1532; tel. 21232640; fax 21248388; e-mail mia@maltainsurance.org; internet www.maltainsurance.org; Dir-Gen. Dr ANTON FELICE; 19 mem. cos (2008).

Trade and Industry

GOVERNMENT AGENCIES

Malta Enterprise: Enterprise Centre, Industrial Estate, San Gwann SGN 3000; tel. 25420000; fax 25423401; e-mail info@maltaenterprise.com; internet www.maltaenterprise.com; f. 2003 by merger of Malta External Trade Corpn Ltd (METCO), Malta Development Corpn (MDC) and Institute for the Promotion of Small Enterprise (IPSE); national agency for the promotion of inward investment, external trade and the support of enterprises; Exec. Chair. ALAN CAMILLERI; CEO CHRIS FALZON.

Malta Investment Management Co Ltd (MIMCOL): Trade Centre, San Ġwann Industrial Estate, San Gwann SGN 3000; tel. 21497970; fax 21499568; e-mail info@mimcol.com; internet www.mimcol.com; f. 1988; manages govt investments in domestic commercial enterprises and encourages their transfer to private sector ownership; Chair. IVAN FALZON; CEO MARIO MIZZI.

CHAMBER OF COMMERCE

Malta Chamber of Commerce, Enterprise and Industry: Exchange Bldgs, Republic St, Valletta VLT 1117; tel. 21233873; fax 21245223; e-mail admin@chamber.org.mt; internet www.chamber.org.mt; f. 2008 by merger of Malta Chamber of Commerce and Industry and Malta Federation of Industry; Pres. HELGA ELLUL; 1,200 mems.

EMPLOYERS' ORGANIZATION

Malta Employers' Association: 35/1 South St, Valletta VLT 1100; tel. 21222992; fax 21230227; e-mail admin@maltaemployers.com; internet www.maltaemployers.com; f. 1965; Pres. PIERRE FAVA; Dir-Gen. JOSEPH FARRUGIA.

UTILITIES

Electricity and Gas

Enemalta Corporation: Church Wharf, Marsa HMR 01; POB 6, Ħamrun HMR 01; tel. 21223601; fax 21243055; e-mail info.emc@enemalta.com.mt; internet www.enemalta.com.mt; f. 1977; state energy corpn; purchases and distributes petroleum products and operates two petroleum-fired power stations for electricity generation; distributes electricity and petroleum products; Chair. ALEXANDER J. TRANTER; CEO (vacant).

Water

Water Services Corporation: Qormi Rd, Luqa LQA 9043; tel. 22445566; fax 22443900; e-mail customercare@wsc.com.mt; internet www.wsc.com.mt; f. 1992; govt corpn responsible for the production and distribution of drinking water and the local sewerage system; Chair. MICHAEL FALZON; CEO MARC MUSCAT.

TRADE UNIONS

Confederation of Malta Trade Unions (CMTU): 9C Mikiel Anton Vassalli St, Valletta VLT 1310; tel. 21237313; fax 21250146; e-mail info@cmtu.org.mt; internet www.cmtu.org.mt; f. 1958; affiliated to the World Confed. of Labour, to the Commonwealth Trade Union Council and to the ETUC; Pres. WILLIAM PORTELLI; Gen. Sec. CHARLES MAGRO.

The principal affiliated unions include:

General Retailers & Traders Union (GRTU) (Asscn of General Retailers and Traders): Exchange Bldgs, Republic St, Valletta VLT 1117; tel. 21230459; fax 21246925; e-mail info@grtu.org.mt; internet www.grtu.org.mt; f. 1948; Pres. PAUL ABELA; Dir-Gen. VINCE FARRUGIA; 7,000 mems.

Malta Union of Teachers: Teachers' Institute, 213 Republic St, Valletta VLT 1118; tel. 21237815; fax 21244074; e-mail info@mut.org.mt; internet www.mut.org.mt; f. 1919; Pres. JOHN BENCINI; Gen. Sec. FRANKLIN BARBARA.

Union Ħaddiema Magħqudin (UHM) (Malta Workers' Union): 'Dar Reggie Miller', 69 St Thomas St, Floriana FLN 1123; tel. 21220847; fax 21246091; e-mail info@uhm.org.mt; internet www.uhm.org.mt; f. 1966; Pres. GAETANO TANTI; Sec.-Gen. GETJU VELLA.

The General Workers' Union (GWU): Workers' Memorial Bldg, South St, Valletta VLT 1100; tel. 21244451; e-mail info@gwu.org.mt; internet www.gwu.org.mt; f. 1943; affiliated to the ITUC and to the ETUC; Pres. VICTOR CARACHI; Gen. Sec. TONY ZARB.

Transport

REGULATORY BODIES

Malta Transport Authority: Sa Maison Rd, Floriana FRN 1613; tel. 25608000; fax 21255740; e-mail info@maltatransport.com; internet www.maltatransport.com; regulatory body for all land transport in Malta; Chair. SIMON VELLA.

RAILWAYS

There are no railways in Malta.

ROADS

In 2004 there were 2,254 km of roads, of which 185 km were highways and 2,069 km were secondary roads. About 87.5% of roads are paved. Bus services serve all parts of the main island and most parts of Gozo.

Roads Department: Cannon Rd, St Venera SVR 9030; tel. 21483609; fax 21243753; e-mail carmel.zammit@magnet.mt; Chair. C. DEMICOLI; CEO M. FALZON.

SHIPPING

Malta's national shipping register is open to ships of all countries. At 31 December 2007 Malta's merchant fleet comprised 1,421 vessels, with a total displacement of 27,754,385 grt. The island's dry dock facilities are also an important source of revenue.

Malta Maritime Authority: Maritime Trade Centre, Xatt l-Ghassara ta' l-Gheneb, Marsa MRS 1912; tel. 21222203; fax 21250365; e-mail info@mma.gov.mt; internet www.mma.gov.mt; f. 1991; govt agency supervising the administration and operation of ports and yachting centres, and of vessel registrations under the Maltese flag; Chair. MARK PORTELLI; CEO Dr STANLEY PORTELLI.

Bianchi & Co (1916) Ltd: Palazzo Marina, 143 St Christopher St, Valletta VLT 1465; tel. 21232241; fax 21232991; e-mail info@bianchi.com.mt; Man. Dir R. BIANCHI.

Cassar & Cooper Ltd: Valletta Bldgs, 54 South St, POB 311, Valletta VLT 1103; tel. 25584000; fax 21237864; e-mail info@cassar-cooper.com; internet www.cassar-cooper.com; cargo shipping; also ship agency; Dir MICHAEL COOPER.

Gollcher Group: 19 Saint Zachary St, POB 268, Valletta VLT 1133; tel. 25691100; fax 21234195; e-mail contact@gollcher.com; internet www.gollcher.com; f. 1854; Dir MARK GOLLCHER.

Malta Freeport Terminals Ltd: Freeport Centre, Port of Marsaxlokk, Kalafrana BBG 3011; tel. 21650200; fax 22251900; e-mail marketing@maltafreeport.com.mt; internet www.maltafreeport.com.mt; f. 1988; two container terminals and a distribution centre; also operates petroleum products terminal and general warehousing facilities; Man. Dir JOHN PORTELLI.

Malta Motorways of the Sea Ltd: 21–22 St Barbara Bastion, Valletta VLT 1961; tel. 21251564; fax 21226876; e-mail info@mmos.com.mt; internet www.mmos.com.mt; f. 2005; owned by Grimaldi Group (Italy); operates ro-ro and passenger ferry services between Malta, Italy (including Sicily) and Libya; Man. Dir ERNEST SULLIVAN; Gen. Man. JOE BUGEJA.

Medserv PLC: Malta Freeport, Port of Marsaxlokk, Birzebbugia BBG 3011; tel. 22202302; fax 22202328; e-mail info@medservmalta.com; internet www.medservmalta.com; logistic and supply base for petroleum and gas extraction industry; Dirs ANTHONY S. DIACONO, ANTHONY J. DUNCAN; Gen. Man. GODWIN BORG.

Mifsud Brothers Ltd: 26 South St, Valletta VLT 1102; tel. 21232157; fax 21221331; e-mail info@mbl.com.mt; internet www.mbl.com.mt; f. 1860; shipping and travel agents; Man. Dir IVAN MIFSUD.

SMS Shipping: 131 East St, Valletta VLT 1252; tel. 21233127; fax 21234180; e-mail ship@sms.com.mt; internet www.sms.com.mt; ship and forwarding agency; also ship supplies and bunkering; subsidiary of SMS Group Ltd; Exec. Man. PAUL SAVONA.

Sullivan Shipping Agencies Ltd: Exchange Bldgs, Republic St, Valletta VLT 1117; tel. 21245127; fax 21233417; e-mail info@sullivanshipping.com.mt; internet www.sullivanshipping.com.mt; Man. Dir CHRISTIAN SULLIVAN.

Thomas Smith & Co Ltd: 12 St Christopher St, Valletta VLT 1468; tel. 22058000; fax 22058199; e-mail info@tcsmith.com; internet www.tcsmith.com; Man. Dir JOE GERADA.

Virtu Ferries Ltd: Ta' Xbiex Terrace, Ta'Xbiex XBX 1034; tel. 23491000; fax 21314533; e-mail info@virtuferries.com; internet www.virtuferries.com; f. 1945; Malta–Sicily (Italy) express passenger ferry service.

MALTA

CIVIL AVIATION

Malta International Airport is situated at Gudja (8 km from Valletta).

Air Malta PLC: Vjal l'Avjazzjoni, Luqa LQA 9023; tel. 21690890; fax 21692861; e-mail info@airmalta.com.mt; internet www.airmalta.com; f. 1973; national airline with a 96.4% state shareholding; scheduled passenger and cargo services to mainland Europe, the United Kingdom, North Africa and the Middle East; charter services to the United Kingdom and mainland Europe; Chair. LAWRENCE ZAMMIT; CEO JOE CAPPELLO.

Tourism

Malta offers climatic, scenic and historical attractions, including fine beaches. Tourism forms a major sector of Malta's economy, generating foreign-exchange earnings of US $970m. in 2006. In 2008 tourist arrivals totalled 1,290,856.

Malta Tourism Authority (MTA): Auberge d'Italie, Merchants St, Valletta VLT 2000; tel. 22915000; fax 22915893; e-mail info@visitmalta.com; internet www.visitmalta.com; Chair. SAM MIFSUD; CEO JOSEF FORMOSA GAUCI.

THE MARSHALL ISLANDS

Introductory Survey

Location, Climate, Language, Religion, Flag, Capital

The Republic of the Marshall Islands consists of two groups of islands, the Ratak ('sunrise') and Ralik ('sunset') chains, comprising 29 atolls (some 1,225 islets) and five islands, and covering about 180 sq km (70 sq miles) of land. The territory lies within the area of the Pacific Ocean known as Micronesia (which includes Kiribati, Tuvalu and other territories). The islands lie about 3,200 km (2,000 miles) south-west of Hawaii and about 2,100 km (1,300 miles) south-east of Guam. Rainfall decreases from south to north, with January, February and March being the driest months, although seasonal variations in rainfall and temperature are generally small. The native population comprises various ethno-linguistic groups, but English is widely understood. The principal religion is Christianity. The national flag (proportions 100 by 190) is dark blue, with a representation of a white star (with 20 short and four long rays) in the upper hoist; superimposed across the field are two progressively-wider stripes (orange above white), running from near the lower hoist corner to near the upper fly corner. The capital is the Dalap-Uliga-Darrit Municipality, on Majuro Atoll.

Recent History

The first European contact with the Marshall and Caroline Islands was by Spanish expeditions in the 16th century, including those led by Alvaro de Saavedra and Fernão de Magalhães (Ferdinand Magellan), the Portuguese navigator. The islands received their name from the British explorer, John Marshall, who visited them at the end of the 18th century. Spanish sovereignty over the Marshall Islands was recognized in 1886 by the Papal Bull of Pope Leo XIII, which also gave Germany trading rights there (German trading companies had been active in the islands from the 1850s). In 1899 Germany bought from Spain the Caroline Islands and the Northern Mariana Islands (except Guam, which had been ceded to the USA after the Spanish–American War of 1898). In 1914, at the beginning of the First World War, Japan occupied the islands, and received a mandate for its administration from the League of Nations in 1920. After the capture of the islands by US military forces in 1944 and 1945, most of the Japanese settlers were repatriated, and in 1947 the UN established the Trust Territory of the Pacific Islands (comprising the Caroline Islands, the Marshall Islands and the Northern Mariana Islands), to allow the USA to administer the region. The territory was governed by the US Navy from 1947 until 1951, when control passed to a civil administration—although the Northern Mariana Islands remained under military control until 1962.

From 1965 onwards there were increasing demands for local autonomy. In that year the Congress of Micronesia was formed; in 1967 a commission was established to examine the future political status of the islands. In 1970 it declared Micronesians' rights to sovereignty over their own lands, of self-determination, to their own constitution and to revoke any form of free association with the USA. In 1977, after eight years of negotiations, US President Jimmy Carter announced that his Administration intended to adopt measures to terminate the trusteeship agreement by 1981.

On 9 January 1978 the Marianas District achieved separate status as the Commonwealth of the Northern Mariana Islands (q.v.), but remained legally a part of the Trusteeship until 1986. The Marshall Islands District drafted its own Constitution, which came into effect on 1 May 1979, and the four districts of Yap, Truk (now Chuuk), Ponape (now Pohnpei) and Kosrae ratified a new Constitution, to become the Federated States of Micronesia (q.v.), on 10 May 1979. In the Palau District a referendum in July 1979 approved a proposed local constitution, which came into effect on 1 January 1981, when the district became the Republic of Palau (q.v.).

The USA signed a Compact of Free Association with the Republic of Palau in August 1982, and with the Marshall Islands and the Federated States of Micronesia in October of that year. The trusteeship of the islands was due to end after the principle and terms of the Compacts had been approved by the respective peoples and legislatures of the new countries, by the US Congress and by the UN Security Council. Under the Compacts, the four countries (including the Northern Mariana Islands) would be independent of each other and would manage their internal and foreign affairs separately, while the USA would be responsible for defence and security. Moreover, Marshallese citizens were granted the right to live and work in the USA. The Compacts with the Federated States of Micronesia and the Marshall Islands were approved in plebiscites in June and September 1983, respectively. The Congress of the Federated States of Micronesia ratified the country's decision in September. Under the Compact with the Marshall Islands, the USA was to retain its military bases in the Marshall Islands for at least 15 years and, over the same period, was to provide annual aid of US $30m.

The Compact between the Marshall Islands and the USA came into effect on 21 October 1986, following its approval by the islands' Government. In November President Ronald Reagan issued a proclamation formally ending US administration of Micronesia. The first President of the Republic of the Marshall Islands was Iroijlaplap (paramount chief) Amata Kabua, who was re-elected in 1984, 1988, 1992 and 1995. In December 1990 the UN Security Council finally ratified the termination of the trusteeship agreement; the Marshall Islands became a member of the UN in 1991. Prior to their scheduled expiry in 2001, the terms of Compact were extended for a further two-year period, pending negotiation of new arrangements (see below).

The Marshall Islands' atolls of Bikini and Enewetak were used by the USA for experiments with nuclear weapons: Bikini in 1946–58 and Enewetak in 1948–58. A total of 67 such tests were carried out during this period. The native inhabitants of Enewetak were evacuated before tests began, and were allowed to return to the atoll in 1980, after much of the contaminated area had supposedly been rendered safe. The inhabitants of Bikini Atoll campaigned for similar treatment, and in 1985 the US Administration agreed to decontaminate Bikini Atoll over a period of 10–15 years. In 1985 the entire population of Rongelap Atoll, which had been engulfed by radioactive fall-out from the tests at Bikini in 1954, was forced to resettle on Mejato Atoll, after surveys suggested that levels of radiation there remained dangerous. In April 2001, following the adoption by the USA of a new standard of radioactivity considered to be acceptable, some six times lower than the previous level, the Tribunal announced that Ailuk Atoll was to be evacuated and environmental studies conducted.

Under the terms of the Compact, the US Government consented to establish a US $150m. Nuclear Claims Fund to settle claims against the USA resulting from nuclear testing in the Marshall Islands during the 1940s and 1950s. Accordingly, the Marshall Islands Nuclear Claims Tribunal was established in 1988, with jurisdiction to 'render final determination upon all claims past, present and future, of the Government, citizens and nationals of the Marshall Islands' in respect of the nuclear testing programme. A compensation programme was implemented in 1991 for personal injuries deemed to have resulted from the testing programme. Following an approach defined in legislation adopted by the US Congress in 1990, which established a 'presumptive' programme of compensation for specified diseases contracted by US civilian and military personnel who had been physically present in what was termed the 'affected area' during periods of atmospheric testing in Nevada, the Marshall Islands Nuclear Claims Tribunal initially identified 25 diseases for which credible evidence demonstrated a significant statistical relationship between exposure to radiation and subsequent development of a disease; in response to the findings of later studies, the Tribunal's list had by 2003 been extended to include 11 further conditions. Compensation awards totalling $83m. had by the end of 2003 been made to, or on behalf of, 1,865 individuals who had contracted one or more of these conditions. Additionally, an award of some $578m. had been ordered in May 2000 in respect of a class action brought by the people of Enewetak for loss of and damage to property; and an award of $563m. had been made in March 2002 in settlement of a class action brought by the peoples of Bikini Atoll; settlements of similar class actions by the peoples of Rongelap and Utrik Atolls were being finalized, while a new class action had been submitted by the people of Ailuk Atoll. However, only $45.8m. had been made available for actual payment of awards decided by the Tribunal; furthermore, less than $6m. remained of the original value of the Fund. In view of the inadequacy of the Fund to meet the compensation awards made by the Tribunal, in September 2000 the Marshall Islands Government formally petitioned the US Congress for a renegotiation of the settlement agreed under the Compact; the basis of the petition, which sought additional compensation amounting to some $3,000m., was an article of the agreement providing for what were termed 'Changed Circumstances'. In early August 2004 the Tribunal declared a deadline for islanders' compensation claims of the end of that month (subsequently extended to 31 December). The reason given for the deadline was that the Tribunal's funds had diminished to some $5m., a level that not only jeopardized future compensation payments but also the very existence of the Tribunal itself.

In January 2005, following the publication of a report by the US State Department's Bureau of East Asian and Pacific Affairs, the Bush Administration recommended that Congress reject the Marshall Islands' request for additional compensation payments, citing a lack of a scientific or legal basis for the request. In late February delegates from Bikini, Rongelap, Enewetak and Utrik met in Seattle, Washington, with officials of the US Senate Committee on Energy and Natural Resources in preparation for a congressional hearing on the Marshall Islands' request for additional payments. At the hearing, held in May, the Bush Administration's rejection of the appeal was reiterated, although several committee members expressed support for further consideration of the matter. At a Small Islands Summit meeting held in October in the Papua New Guinean capital of Port Moresby, the Marshall Islands' delegation demanded a further $3,000m. in compensation from the US Government. In April 2006 it was announced that the people of Bikini were suing the US Government in the Court of Federal Claims for $561m. as compensation or damages: the original award of $563m. minus the actual payment of $2.3m. The Marshall Islands Government expressed its support for the action. In April 2007 the Marshall Islands Nuclear Claims Tribunal ruled that claimants of Rongelap should receive $1,000m. in compensation; at the same time, however, the funds available to the Tribunal had decreased to $1m. In August 2007 the Court of Federal Claims dismissed the lawsuit submitted against the US Government on the basis that it had been submitted after the expiry of a six-year statute of limitations for the filing of such claims. The lawyer representing the people of Bikini then took the case to the US Court of Appeals for the Federal Circuit, arguing that the Fifth Amendment forbade the acquisition of private property without compensation. In February 2009, however, the Court of Appeals upheld the judgment dismissing the claim. In September 2007 the US Senate was examining a request for additional compensation for inhabitants of Bikini, Rongelap, Enewetak and Utrik. In March 2009, following confirmation by France that further consideration was to be given to compensation claims by those affected by its nuclear tests, the Marshall Islands renewed its request for additional compensation from the US Government.

In January 1994, meanwhile, several senior members of the Marshall Islands' legislature, the Nitijela, demanded that the US authorities release detailed information on the effects of its nuclear-testing programme in the islands. In July documentation released by the US Department of Energy gave conclusive evidence that Marshall Islanders had been deliberately exposed to high levels of radiation in order that its effects on their health could be studied by US medical researchers. Further evidence emerged during 1995 that the USA had withheld the medical records of islanders involved in radiation experiments (which included tritium and chromium-51 injections and genetic and bone-marrow transplant experiments).

Despite the publication of a study conducted by US scientists (in 1992) into contamination levels on Bikini atoll, which suggested that radiation levels there remained dangerous, in February 1997 a group of Bikini Islanders returned for the first time since 1946 to assist in the rehabilitation of the atoll for resettlement. The operation was to involve the removal of radioactive topsoil (although the matter of its disposal presented a serious problem) and the saturation of the remaining soil with potassium, which was believed to inhibit the absorption of radioactive material by root crops. In early 1999 the Nuclear Claims Tribunal demanded the adoption of US Environmental Protection Agency standards in the rehabilitation of contaminated islands, claiming that Marshall Islanders deserved to receive the same treatment as US citizens would in similar circumstances. The US Department of Energy, however, expressed strong resistance to the suggestion. In February 2001 a report published by an eminent Japanese scientist stated that radiation levels on Rongelap Island, according to research conducted in 1999, had now declined to such a level that human habitation of the island was again possible. In early 2004 the Marshall Islands protested that a reduction, decided upon by the US Department of Energy without consultation with Island representatives, of some US $740,000 in congressional funding allocated to nuclear test-related studies would result in the closure of a centre on Bikini Atoll used to support scientific studies at the former test site.

Another atoll in the Marshall Islands, Kwajalein, has been used since 1947 as a target for the testing of missiles fired from California, USA. The Compact as ratified in 1986 committed the US Government to provide an estimated US $170m. in rent over a period of 30 years for land used as the site of a missile-tracking station, and a further $80m. for development projects. The inhabitants of Kwajalein Atoll were concentrated on the small island of Ebeye, adjacent to the US base on Kwajalein Island, before a new programme of weapons-testing began in 1961. Consequent overcrowding reportedly led to numerous social problems on Ebeye. In 1989 the Marshall Islands Government agreed that the USA could lease a further four islands in the atoll, for five years, for the purpose of military tests. A further lease agreement was signed in 1995 for the use of Biken Island (in Aur Atoll) and Wake Island in the missile-testing programme. The issue of the Kwajalein lease proved to be one of the most controversial aspects of the renegotiated terms of the Compact, as signed in 2003 (see below). In January 2003 it was announced that the Marshall Islands Government and the USA had reached agreement on new terms extending the lease of the Kwajalein site, previously scheduled to end in 2016, until 2066 (with the USA retaining the right to extend the lease by a further 20 years). The renegotiated terms envisaged that payments for use of the site would be increased from $13.5m. annually to $16.9m. (including continued provision of $1.9m. annually in social funding for the residents of Ebeye), with a further increase, to more than $19.9m. per year, to enter into effect from 2014. However, Kwajalein landowners, who deemed the new terms unacceptable, asserted that the new arrangement was invalid, since they had not consented, as constitutionally required, to its terms. The landowners refused to accept the terms of the agreement.

Following the legislative election of November 1995, at which eight incumbent members of the 33-seat Nitijela were defeated, President Kabua was re-elected for a fifth term. Upon his death in December 1996, Iroijlaplap Imata Kabua, a cousin of the late President, was elected to succeed him in January 1997.

In 1996 the Nitijela approved legislation allowing for the introduction of gambling in the islands, in order to provide an additional source of revenue. However, income earned from the venture did not fulfil expectations. Moreover, a vociferous campaign by local church leaders to revoke the legislation led to fierce debate in the Nitijela in early 1998. Divisions within the Cabinet ensued, with three members supporting the President's pro-gambling stance and four others opposing. In April the Nitijela voted to repeal the law legalizing gambling: several influential politicians (including Imata Kabua) known to have major gambling interests were disqualified from voting. A second bill containing further measures to ensure the prohibition of all gambling activity in the islands was narrowly approved. Three ministers who had supported the anti-gambling legislation were dismissed in a cabinet reorganization in August. In the following month one of the dismissed ministers proposed a motion of no confidence in Kabua. The President and his supporters boycotted subsequent sessions of the Nitijela, thereby rendering the legislature inquorate and effectively precluding the vote, as well as delaying the approval of the budget for the impending financial year. Despite opposition claims that Kabua's continued absence from the Nitijela violated the terms of the Constitution, the motion of no confidence in Kabua was eventually defeated by a margin of one vote in October.

At the legislative election of November 1999 the opposition United Democratic Party (UDP) secured a convincing victory over the incumbent administration, winning 18 of the 33 seats in the Nitijela. Five senior members of the outgoing Government were defeated, including the Ministers of Finance and of Foreign Affairs and Trade—both of whom had played a prominent role in the establishment of diplomatic relations with Taiwan in 1998 (see below). The former Nitijela Speaker, Kessai Note, was elected President on 3 January 2000 (the islands' first non-traditional leader to assume the post). The UDP Chairman, Litokwa Tomeing, became Speaker of the legislature. Note subsequently appointed a 10-member Cabinet, and reiterated his administration's intention to pursue anti-corruption policies. In May a task-force was established by the Government for the purposes of investigating misconduct and corruption; it was hoped that the task-force would help to render government more accountable.

In November 2000 it was reported that finance officials had discovered that Imata Kabua had used funds granted to the Marshall Islands under the terms of the Compact of Free Association to pay off a personal loan, although the former President denied any wrongdoing. In mid-January 2001 Imata Kabua and former ministers in his Government, including the former Minister of Education, Justin DeBrum, presented a no confidence motion against President Note to the Nitijela. Although it was suggested that the vote had been intended to delay the publication of a report into mismanagement and corruption on the part of the former Government, DeBrum stated that the motion resulted from a number of failings by the Note Government, including its unwillingness to renegotiate land rental payments with the USA for the use of the military base on Kwajalein Atoll and also the development of an economic relationship between the Note Government and Rev. Sun Myung Moon, the founder of the Unification Church (known as the 'Moonies'). However, the Government was successful in defeating the vote by a margin of 19 to 14.

In September 2000 the Nitijela approved legislation to ensure the closer regulation of the banking and financial sector. In May of that year the Group of Seven industrialized nations (G-7) had expressed its view that the Marshall Islands had become a significant centre for the 'laundering' of money generated by international criminal activity, and, in June the Marshall Islands was one of more than 30 countries and territories criticized by the Organisation for Economic Co-operation and Development (OECD, see p. 358) for the provision of inappropriate 'offshore' financial establishments. OECD threatened to implement sanctions against 'unco-operative tax havens' unless reforms were introduced before July 2001. The Marshall Islands remained on the OECD's list of unco-operative tax havens until 2007. In October 2002, meanwhile, following a commendation from the IMF on a series of new measures to combat fraud, including specific legislation and the establishment of a Domestic Financial Intelligence Unit, the Financial Action Task Force on Money Laundering (see p. 430) removed the Marshall Islands from its list of countries judged to be unhelpful in the combating of international financial crime.

Negotiations began between the US and Marshall Islands Governments in July 2001 to renew the provisions of the Compact of Free Association ratified in 1986, which was due to expire at the end of September 2001. A two-year extension was permitted while negotiations were under way, during which time annual assistance to the Marshall Islands was to increase by some US $5.5m. An agreement was originally scheduled for early 2002 in order to allow adequate time for the US Congress to review it and to approve the requisite legislation (by 1 October 2003), but the procedure was postponed until early May 2002 after the Marshall Islands Government submitted a proposal seeking financing of more than $1,000m. over 15 years. The Government had also objected to being allocated 25%–30% less in US grant assistance per caput than that apportioned to the Federated States of Micronesia since the year 2000. In a further attempt to increase the national income, the Government sought to raise significantly the level of taxes levied on the Kwajalein base (see above). In early November 2002 the USA and the Marshall Islands announced a programme of direct funding of $822m., to be disbursed over 20 years, in addition to the expansion of many US government services in the islands. It was envisaged that the Marshall Islands would receive some $30.5m. a year; furthermore, a trust fund would be established, to which the USA would contribute $7m. annually in order to provide a means of income after the termination of direct US assistance in 2023. The amended Compact of Free Association was signed by the Governments of the Marshall Islands and the USA in May 2003. Under the new Compact, Marshall Islanders would for the first time require passports in order to enter the USA. They would, however, retain the right to enter the USA to live, work and study, and would no longer be required to obtain work authorization documentation before taking up employment in the USA. Other than the issue of the Kwajalein lease, a principal obstacle to the negotiation of Compact amendments had been that of immigration: the USA, increasingly preoccupied by issues of homeland security, had been notably concerned to prevent future sales of Marshallese passports (a controversial programme of which had been implemented in the 1990s, although this had officially been suspended in 1997). Final terms, including the restoration of some rights of access to US health care and education programmes, were approved by the US Congress in November 2003, and ratified by President George W. Bush in December.

At a general election held on 17 November 2003 the UDP returned 20 Senators to the 33-member Nitijela. The opposition grouping Ailin Kein Ad (Our Islands), which had campaigned against the terms of the renewed Compact and which received particularly strong support from Marshall Islanders resident in the USA, secured 10 seats (the re-election of the incumbent Ailin Kein Ad Senator for Ailinglaplap Atoll was decided following a recount of votes conducted in late January 2004). Note was re-elected for a second presidential term in a vote held in the Nitijela on 4 January 2004, defeating Justin DeBrum, the candidate of Ailin Kein Ad, by 20 votes to nine. He and his new Cabinet were sworn in on 12 January.

In late March 2005 the Nitijela considered a bill providing for the establishment of a constitutional convention, to be made up of 43 representatives representing every district. Proposals for the direct election of the country's President and for the clear separation of the executive branch of government from the legislature were among the constitutional amendments to be considered. However, in February 2006 a spokesperson for Ailin Kein Ad argued that the establishment of the constitutional convention should be deferred at least until after the next legislative election, scheduled for November 2007. In April 2006, therefore, having failed to secure the requisite parliamentary majority enabling it to proceed with its programme, the ruling UDP announced that its proposals for a constitutional convention were to be submitted to the electorate in a national referendum. Voters were to be asked if they wished a constitutional convention to consider a total of 22 amendments to the country's Constitution. In January 2007 President Note confirmed that the date of the forthcoming referendum would be decided by the Speaker of the Nitijela and the Electoral Commission.

A legislative election was held on 19 November 2007. There were complaints in Majuro, where several polling stations failed to open at the appointed time; irregularities in the counting procedure were subsequently criticized. The level of participation was relatively low, at approximately 50%. According to unofficial results published in December, neither the incumbent UDP nor the opposition Ailin Kein Ad had succeeded in securing the requisite majority of 17 or more seats; both parties contested the results. While the UDP claimed that it should remain in power, Ailin Kein Ad—which had gained former Speaker and UDP leader Litokwa Tomeing as a member prior to the election—maintained that, with the support of independent candidates, its United People's Party coalition would be able to defeat the UDP. Recounts in two constituencies and negotiations between the parties and independent candidates followed. The United People's Party coalition prevailed in January 2008, when the Nitijela elected Tomeing as the country's President by 18 votes (to 15 for the incumbent President Kessai Note), and Jurelang Zedkaia as Speaker by the same margin. Tomeing's new Cabinet included Christopher Loeak in the position of Minister in Assistance to the President and Tony deBrum as Minister of Foreign Affairs.

In February 2008 President Tomeing established a commission of inquiry into the organizational failures of the 2007 election. The commission published its findings in August 2008; the election failures were attributed to the former Minister of Internal Affairs, Rien Morris, and to the Public Service Commission. It was concluded that Morris had unconstitutionally interfered in the election process by appointing Carl Alik as the Chief Electoral Officer against the wishes of the Public Service Commission. The commission of inquiry made numerous recommendations, which included the establishment of an election commission of five independent members, who would be responsible for the appointment of the Chief Electoral Officer.

In April 2008 the Attorney-General, Posesi Bloomfield, resigned in order to pursue studies overseas. He was replaced by Filimon Manoni, who had served as chairman of the commission of inquiry into the election of 2007. Manoni took up his position in May.

In mid-October 2008 the opposition UDP tabled a no-confidence motion against President Litokwa Tomeing, citing the Government's alleged failures in negotiations with the USA (notably with regard to the financing of health care for islanders affected by the nuclear tests—see above) and its refusal to proceed with an elementary school project in Majuro. However, the motion was withdrawn after the opposition conceded that it had been unable to secure the support of at least 17 of the 33 members of the Nitijela, needed for the motion to succeed.

Tony deBrum, the Minister of Foreign Affairs, was dismissed from the Cabinet in February 2009, following his public criticism of President Tomeing's administration; deBrum was particularly critical of the President's perceived failure to provide sufficient support to landowners in their attempts to secure an increase in the rents payable to them by the USA for the use of the military base at Kwajalein Atoll (see above); deBrum was subsequently replaced by John Silk.

In April 2009 the Ailin Kein Ad and the United People's Party coalition presented a motion of no confidence against President Tomeing, which was defeated by 18 ballots to 14, after UDP members of the Nitijela voted in Tomeing's favour. Following the defeat of the motion, President Tomeing announced the dismissal of several ministers in a cabinet reorganization. Ruben Zachras replaced Christopher Loak as Minister in Assistance to the President and Kenneth Kedi was appointed Minister of Transportation and Communication. Maynard Alfred became Minister of Public Works, and Matt Zackhras was appointed as Minister of Resources and Development. All of the new Ministers were members of the opposition UDP.

In 1989 a UN report on the 'greenhouse effect' (heating of the earth's atmosphere) predicted a possible resultant rise in sea-level of some 3.7 m by 2030, which would completely submerge the Marshall Islands. In early 2002 the Intergovernmental Panel on Climate Change (IPCC) projected that during the 21st century global sea-level rises would submerge over 80% of Majuro atoll. The islands appeared to be increasingly vulnerable to adverse weather conditions, as exemplified in December 2008 when a state of emergency was declared; hundreds of people were displaced by the widespread flooding that followed unusually high tides.

The Marshall Islands Government caused regional environmental concerns with regard to the possible establishment of large-scale facilities for the storage of nuclear waste. Criticism by the US Government of the plans, announced in 1994, was strongly denounced by the Marshall Islands authorities, which claimed that the project constituted the only opportunity for the country to generate sufficient income for the rehabilitation of contaminated islands and the provision of treatment for illnesses caused by the US nuclear-test programme. In mid-1997 President Imata Kabua announced the indefinite suspension of the project (despite the initiation of a feasibility study into the development of a nuclear waste storage facility). None the less, the Government approved plans for a new feasibility study on the subject in April 1998.

In November 1998 the Marshall Islands established full diplomatic relations with Taiwan. The action was immediately condemned by the People's Republic of China, which in December severed diplomatic ties with the islands, closing its embassy in Majuro and suspending all intergovernmental agreements. The Marshall Islands Government insisted that it wished to maintain cordial relations with both governments. The Note administration, which took office in January 2000, emphasized its commitment to the maintenance of diplomatic relations with Taiwan. In February 2001 a proposed visit by a flotilla of Taiwanese naval vessels to the Marshall Islands was vetoed by the USA, on the grounds that the defence protocol of the Compact of Free Association prohibited such a visit. In August 2004 the Chinese Vice-Minister of Foreign Affairs, Zhou Wenzhong, expressed his country's willingness to restore normal relations, on condition that the Marshall Islands withdraw its diplomatic recognition of Taiwan. In April 2005 it was alleged that members of the ruling UDP had accepted bribes from Chinese officials hoping to expedite a return to normal diplomatic relations and the end of Marshallese recognition of Taiwan; the Government denied the allegations. Meanwhile, in September 2004 it was announced that Taiwan was to contribute more than US $40m. over a 20-year period to the Marshall Islands trust fund established in May. In June 2006 a delegation of Marshall Islands parliamentary representatives paid a visit to the mainland Chinese capital of Beijing, at the invitation of the National People's Congress, causing consternation among some government officials over the effect on the Marshall Islands' relations with Taiwan, which in April had been bolstered by President Note's third trip to Taipei, where he met Taiwanese President Chen Shui-bian for discussions. The leader of the delegation, Vice-Speaker of the Nitijela Ruben Zackhras, insisted that the Marshall Islands was simply responding to an invitation, while the Ministry of Foreign Affairs reaffirmed the country's commitment to Taiwan. In January 2008 the newly elected President, Litokwa Tomeing, who had previously expressed support for alignment with China, nevertheless confirmed that strong links with Taiwan would continue, and reinforced this position during a visit by the Taiwanese Vice-President, Annette Lu, in late January. The Minister of Foreign Affairs, Tony deBrum, visited Taiwan in February; his visit was followed by that of President Tomeing in March. In July 2006 the Marshall Islands signed an extradition treaty with the Federated States of Micronesia and Palau, and an agreement on maritime boundaries with the Federated States of Micronesia.

In May 2008 the Government of the Marshall Islands signed five conventions of the International Maritime Organization (IMO). The IMO conventions included protocols on marine pollution, maritime navigation and security of fixed platforms.

The Marshall Islands Government has consistently supported Japan at the International Whaling Commission, voting in favour of commercial whaling, and also in the country's attempt to secure a permanent seat on the UN Security Council. By 2008 Japan was reported to be the third largest donor of aid to the Marshall Islands. In April of that year President Tomeing undertook an official visit to Japan, where he had discussions with Prime Minister Yasuo Fukuda. Climate change and rising sea levels were among the topics discussed. In December it was announced that Japan was to provide a grant of US $2.2m. to support the islands' energy sector (see Economic Affairs).

Government

The Constitution of the Republic of the Marshall Islands, which became effective on 1 May 1979, provides for a parliamentary form of government, with legislative authority vested in the 33-member Nitijela. The Nitijela (members of which are elected, by popular vote, for a four-year term) elects the President of the Marshall Islands (also a four-year mandate) from among its own members. Under the terms of the Compact of Free Association, the Republic of the Marshall Islands is a sovereign, self-governing state. The first Compact was signed by the Governments of the Marshall Islands and the USA on 25 June 1983, and was effectively ratified by the US Congress on 14 January 1986. A revised Compact was signed by the Governments of the two countries on 1 May 2003; it was ratified by the US Congress in November 2003, and signed by US President George W. Bush in December of that year. Amendments to the compact were signed in May 2004.

Local governmental units are the municipalities and villages. Elected Magistrates and Councils govern the municipalities. Village government is largely traditional.

Defence

Under the terms of the Compact of Free Association as ratified in 1986 and amended in 2003, the defence of the Marshall Islands is the responsibility of the USA, which maintains a military presence on Kwajalein Atoll.

Economic Affairs

In 2007, according to estimates by the World Bank, the Marshall Islands' gross national income (GNI), measured at average 2005–07 prices, was US $204m., equivalent to $3,070 per head. During 2000–07, it was estimated, the population increased at an average annual rate of 3.3%; gross domestic product (GDP) per head declined, in real terms, at an average rate of 0.2% per year over the same period. Overall GDP increased, in real terms, at an average annual rate of 3.1% in 2000–07. According to the Asian Development Bank (ADB), GDP increased by 1.3% in 2006/07 and by 1.5% in 2007/08.

Agriculture is mainly on a subsistence level. The sector (including fishing and livestock-rearing) contributed an estimated 10.0% of GDP in 2006, according to the ADB. According to FAO, the sector engaged 7,000 people (mainly in subsistence fishing) in mid-2005. Fishing engaged 5.1% of those employed in the private sector in 2006/07. The principal crops are coconuts, cassava and sweet potatoes. Copra production increased from 4,646 short tons in 2006 to an estimated 6,053 tons in 2007. Reports suggested that in 2007/08 the amount of copra processed exceeded 7,000 tons for only the third time since records began in

1951, assisted by improved shipping services and higher global prices for the commodity. In 2006/07 exports of coconut oil and copra cake accounted for 10.3% of the total value of exports. The fishing sector incorporates a commercial tuna-fishing industry, including a transshipment base on Majuro. A new tuna-processing plant, employing more than 600 local workers and built by a Chinese company, was scheduled to become fully operational by 2008. The sale of fishing licences is an important source of revenue and earned the islands an estimated US $1.4m. in 2006/07. The GDP of the agricultural sector increased by 0.2% in 2005 and by 10.2% in 2006, according to the ADB.

Industrial activities (including mining, manufacturing, construction and power) engaged 18.9% of the employed labour force in 1999, and contributed an estimated 21.4% of GDP in 2006. Construction and manufacturing employed 8.3% of private-sector wage-earners in 2006/07. Between 1990 and 1999 industrial GDP declined at an average annual rate of 1.5%. The islands have few mineral resources, although there are high-grade phosphate deposits on Ailinglaplap Atoll. The GDP of the industrial sector increased by 0.2% in 2005, before declining by 5.6% in 2006, according to the ADB.

Manufacturing activity, which provided 1.9% of GDP in 2002, consists mainly of the processing of coconuts (to produce copra and coconut oil) and other agricultural products, and of fish (see above). According to the IMF, manufacturing engaged 1.1% of those employed in the private sector in 2006/07.

The islands are heavily reliant on imported diesel fuel for energy supplies. Severe difficulties in financing purchases of fuel for the power plants at Majuro and Ebaye led to the declaration of a state of economic emergency in 2008 (see below). A rapid energy assessment, funded by the ADB, made numerous recommendations for greater energy efficiency in the islands. The wider use of alternative sources of energy, such as solar power, was under consideration.

The services sector (comprising trade, transport, storage, communications and other activities) engaged 59.8% of the employed labour force in 1999, and provided an estimated 68.6% of GDP in 2006. The international shipping registry experienced considerable expansion following political unrest in Panama in 1989, and subsequently continued to expand (largely as a result of US, Japanese and South Korean ships' reflagging in the islands). The number of vessels registered rose from 853 in December 2005 to 1,099 at the end of 2007. Tourist receipts reached US $6.6m. in 2006. However, in comparison with the previous year the number of tourist arrivals was reported to have declined by 17% in 2008, to 6,022 visitors. According to the ADB, the GDP of the services sector grew by 2.5% in 2005 and by 3.0% in 2006.

In 2006/07 the Marshall Islands recorded an estimated trade deficit of US $60.1m., while there was a deficit of $3.1m. on the current account of the balance of payments. According to the ADB, there was a current account deficit equivalent to 26.0% of GDP in 2007/08. The only significant domestic exports in 2006/07 were coconut products. Re-exports of diesel fuel totalled $13.3m. in 2005, their value greatly exceeding that of domestic exports. The principal imports in 2000 included mineral fuels and lubricants (which accounted for 37.3% of total expenditure on merchandise imports), food and live animals, and machinery and transport equipment. In 2006 the principal sources of imports were the USA (which provided 45.8% of total imports), Australia (8.4%) and Japan (8.1%). In 2000 the USA was also the principal export destination (providing 57.1% of total exports).

Financial assistance from the USA, in accordance with the terms stipulated in the Compact of Free Association, contributes a large part of the islands' revenue. Grants and military payments from the USA for use of the missile-testing site on Kwajalein, along with trust fund contributions, provide most government revenue. The 2007/08 budget provided for expenditure of US $96.5m., including grants of $59.1m., while revenue totalled $96.0m. A budget deficit equivalent to 0.3% of GDP was projected for 2007/08. The islands' external debt reached $100m. in 2007/08, when the cost of debt-servicing was estimated to be the equivalent of 17.3% of revenue from the export of goods and services. Annual inflation in Majuro averaged 2.0% in 2000–07. According to the ADB, consumer prices increased by 3.1% in 2007, and by 17.5% in 2008. The ADB estimated that 30.9% of the work-force were unemployed in 2007. The rate of youth unemployment was estimated at 60% in 2006.

The Marshall Islands is a member of the Pacific Community (see p. 391), the Pacific Islands Forum (see p. 393), the South Pacific Regional Trade and Economic Co-operation Agreement (SPARTECA, see p. 395), the UN Economic and Social Commission for Asia and the Pacific (ESCAP, see p. 36) and the Asian Development Bank (ADB, see p. 191). In 1996 the Marshall Islands and other countries and territories of Micronesia established the Council of Micronesian Government Executives. The new body aimed to facilitate discussion of economic developments in the region, and to examine possibilities for reducing the considerable cost of shipping essential goods between the islands.

The lack of internationally marketable natural resources and the high rate of unemployment have continued to present major challenges. The Marshall Islands' susceptibility to adverse climatic conditions was demonstrated by the declaration of a state of emergency in December 2008 after storm surges flooded parts of the capital of Majuro and elsewhere, damaging homes and roads. The amended Compact of Free Association, signed by the Governments of the Marshall Islands and the USA in 2003 (see Recent History), planned for the gradual decrease in grant assistance over a 20-year period. Retrenchment at the US military base of Kwajalein led to a reduction in income from this source in 2008. Taiwan has financed many development projects; it also planned to transfer a total of US $1m. to the Government's trust fund each year until 2009 and thereafter, until 2023, an annual sum of $2.4m. A reduction in the number of flights from Japan, combined with the failure of a major scuba diving operation on Bikini Atoll, had a negative impact on the country's tourism sector in 2008. Furthermore, the islands were badly affected by the sharp increases in the costs of imports of fuel and foodstuffs: in July 2008, unable to finance essential imports of fuel and with electricity supplies seriously jeopardized, the Government declared a state of economic emergency. About $4m. of Taiwanese funding was redirected to the purchase of fuel. In early 2009 Japan provided a grant of $2.2m. to help meet the costs of the islands' energy requirements. In the third quarter of 2008 the annual rate of inflation was reported to be approaching 30%. Import duties on staple foods such as rice, flour, poultry, fruit and vegetables were removed in August. The country's overseas investments, mainly in the USA, lost a significant portion of their value in the stock market volatility of 2008. Between January and November 2008 the value of the Government's trust fund was reported to have declined from $93.1m. to $72.1m. The ADB forecast that real GDP would grow by just 0.5% in the 12 months to September 2009, as weak global economic conditions continued to prevail.

Education

Education is compulsory between the ages of six and 14. In 2006/07 a total of 8,215 children attended primary schools in the Marshall Islands with 5,369 enrolled at secondary schools. In 2002/03 enrolment at pre-primary schools included 49% of pupils in the relevant age-group. In 2002/03 enrolment at primary schools included 89.6% of the relevant age-group, and enrolment at secondary schools included 74.4% of pupils. The College of the Marshall Islands (which became independent from the College of Micronesia in 1993) is based on Majuro and had 919 students enrolled in 2002/03. In 1995 the University of the South Pacific opened an extension centre on Majuro. The Fisheries and Nautical Center offers vocational courses for Marshall islanders seeking employment in the fishing industry or on passenger liners, cargo ships and tankers. Government expenditure on education in 2004/05 was US $7.4m., equivalent to 10.6% of total recurrent budgetary spending.

Public Holidays

2009: 1–2 January (New Year), 1 March (Nuclear Victims' Remembrance Day), 10 April (Good Friday), 1 May (Constitution Day), 3 July (Fishermen's Day), 4 September (Dri-Jerbal), 25 September (Manit—Culture Day), 17 November (Presidents' Day), 4 December (Kamolol—Gospel Day), 25 December (Christmas).

2010 (provisional): 1–2 January (New Year), 1 March (Nuclear Victims' Remembrance Day), 2 April (Good Friday), 1 May (Constitution Day), July (Fishermen's Day), September (Dri-Jerbal), September (Manit—Culture Day), 17 November (Presidents' Day), December (Kamolol—Gospel Day), 25 December (Christmas).

Weights and Measures

With certain exceptions, the imperial system is in force. One US cwt equals 100 lb; one long ton equals 2,240 lb; one short ton equals 2,000 lb. A policy of gradual voluntary conversion to the metric system is being undertaken.

Statistical Survey

Source (unless otherwise indicated): Economic Policy, Planning and Statistics Office (EPPSO), Office of the President, POB 7, Majuro, MH 96960; tel. (625) 3802; fax (625) 3805; e-mail planning@ntamar.net; internet www.spc.int/prism/country/mh/stats.

AREA AND POPULATION

Area: 181.4 sq km (70.0 sq miles) (land only); two island groups, the Ratak Chain (88.1 sq km) and the Ralik Chain (93.3 sq km).

Population: 43,380 at census of 13 November 1988; 50,840 (males 26,026, females 24,814) at census of 1 June 1999. *Mid-2007:* 52,300 (Asian Development Bank estimate). *By Island Group* (1999): Ratak Chain 30,925 (Majuro Atoll 23,676); Ralik Chain 19,915 (Kwajalein Atoll 10,902).

Density (mid-2007, land area only): 288.3 per sq km.

Principal Towns (population of urban places, 1999 census): Ebeye 9,345; Darrit (Djarrot) 7,103; Delap 6,339; Rairok 3,846; Laura 2,256; Uliga 2,044. Note: The country's capital is the combined municipality of Delap-Uliga-Darrit.

Births and Deaths (2006): Registered live births 1,576; Registered deaths 318. Note: Registered live births exclude US military personnel, their dependants and contract employees. Source: UN, *Population and Vital Statistics Report*.

Life Expectancy (years at birth, WHO estimates): 62.5 (males 60.8; females 64.3) in 2006. Source: WHO, *World Health Statistics*.

Economically Active Population (persons aged 15 years and over, 1999 census): Agriculture and fishery 2,114; Manufacturing 761; Electricity, gas and water 258; Construction 848; Wholesale and retail trade 788; Transport, storage and communication 763; Finance, insurance, real estate and business services 559; Community, social and personal services 3,803; Activities not reported 247; *Total employed* 10,141 (males 7,008, females 3,133); Unemployed 4,536 (males 2,671, females 1,865); *Total labour force* 14,677 (males 9,679, females 4,998). *2006/07* (private sector only): Fishing 281; Manufacturing 60; Construction 782; Wholesale and retail trade 1,791; Total employed (incl. others) 5,491 (Source: IMF, *Republic of the Marshall Islands: Selected Issues and Statistical Appendix*—June 2008).

HEALTH AND WELFARE

Key Indicators

Total Fertility Rate (children per woman, 2006): 3.9.

Under-5 Mortality Rate (per 1,000 live births, 2006): 56.

Physicians (per 1,000 head, 2000): 0.5.

Hospital Beds (per 1,000 head, 1999): 2.1.

Health Expenditure (2006): US $ per head (PPP): 607.

Health Expenditure (2006): % of GDP: 15.3.

Health Expenditure (2006): public (% of total): 97.1.

Access to Water (% of persons, 2004): 87.

Access to Sanitation (% of persons, 2004): 82.

For sources and definitions, see explanatory note on p. vi.

AGRICULTURE, ETC.

Principal Crop ('000 metric tons, 2007, FAO estimate): Coconuts 20.4.

Livestock ('000 head, year ending September 2003): Pigs 12.9; Poultry 86.0.

Fishing ('000 metric tons, live weight, 2006): Bigeye tuna 0.1; Skipjack tuna 37.7; Yellowfin tuna 3.2; Total catch (incl. others) 42.0.

Source: FAO.

INDUSTRY

Electric Energy (million kWh, Majuro only): 81.0 in 2004; 81.3 in 2005; 78.0 in 2006. Source: Asian Development Bank.

FINANCE

Currency and Exchange Rates: United States currency is used: 100 cents = 1 United States dollar (US $). *Sterling and Euro Equivalents* (31 December 2008): £1 sterling = US $1.4578; €1 = US $1.3917; US $100 = £68.60 = €71.85.

Budget (US $ million, year ending 30 September 2008, projections): *Revenue:* Recurrent 36.9 (Tax 26.4, Non-tax 10.5); Grants 59.1; Total 96.0. *Expenditure:* Recurrent 80.0; Capital (incl. net lending) 16.5; Total 96.5. Source: IMF, *Republic of the Marshall Islands: Selected Issues and Statistical Appendix* (June 2008).

Cost of Living (Consumer Price Index for Majuro, average of quarterly figures; base: Jan.–March 2003 = 100): All items 107.7 in 2005; 112.4 in 2006; 115.8 in 2007. Source: IMF, *Republic of the Marshall Islands: Selected Issues and Statistical Appendix* (June 2008).

Gross Domestic Product (US $ million at constant 2000 prices): 127.4 in 2005; 129.1 in 2006; 131.7 in 2007. Source: Asian Development Bank.

Gross Domestic Product by Economic Activity (US $ million at current prices, 2002): Agriculture 15; Mining, manufacturing, electricity, gas and water 5; Construction 10; Trade 19; Transport, storage and communications 7; Other activities 51; *Total* 106. Source: UN, *Statistical Yearbook for Asia and the Pacific*.

Balance of Payments (US $ million, year ending 30 September 2007, estimates): Merchandise exports f.o.b. 24.3; Merchandise imports c.i.f. −84.4; *Trade balance* −60.1; Services (net) −6.8; *Balance on goods and services* −66.9; Other income 36.8; *Balance on goods, services and income* −30.1; Private unrequited transfers (net) −12.9; Official unrequited transfers (net) 40.0; *Current balance* −3.1; Capital and financial account (net) 4.6; Net errors and omissions −1.5; Statistical discrepancy −1.4; *Overall balance* −1.4. Source: IMF, *Republic of the Marshall Islands: Selected Issues and Statistical Appendix* (June 2008).

EXTERNAL TRADE

Principal Commodities (US $ million): *Imports* (2000, estimates): Food and live animals 5.0; Beverages and tobacco 6.0; Crude materials, inedible, except fuels 2.6; Mineral fuels, lubricants and related materials 20.4; Animal and vegetable oils and fats 2.4; Chemicals 0.1; Basic manufactures 3.0; Machinery and transport equipment 8.2; Miscellaneous manufactured articles 1.4; Goods not classified by kind 5.8; Total 54.7. *Exports* (year ending September 2007): Coconut oil (crude) 2.0; Copra cake 0.1; Total (incl. others) 20.3. Sources: Asian Development Bank, *Key Indicators of Developing Asian and Pacific Countries* and IMF, *Republic of the Marshall Islands: Selected Issues and Statistical Appendix* (June 2008).

Principal Trading Partners (US $ million): *Imports* (2006): Australia 5.7; Hong Kong 1.2; Japan 5.5; New Zealand 2.2; USA 31.0; Total (incl. others) 67.7 (Source: Asian Development Bank). *Exports* (2000, estimates): USA 5.2; Total (incl. others) 9.1.

TRANSPORT

Road Traffic (vehicles registered, 1999): Trucks 64; Pick-ups 587; Sedans 1,404; Jeeps 79; Buses 75; Vans 66; Scooters 47; Other motor vehicles 253.

Shipping: *Merchant Fleet* (at 31 December 2007): Vessels 1,099; Displacement ('000 grt) 35,964.2 (Source: Lloyd's Register-Fairplay, *World Fleet Statistics*). *International Sea-borne Freight Traffic* (estimates, '000 metric tons, 1990):* Goods loaded 29; Goods unloaded 123 (Source: UN, *Monthly Bulletin of Statistics*).

* Including the Northern Mariana Islands, the Federated States of Micronesia and Palau.

Civil Aviation (traffic on scheduled services, 2004): Kilometres flown 1 million; Passengers carried 29,000; Passenger-km 38 million; Total ton-km 4 million. Source: UN, *Statistical Yearbook*.

TOURISM

Tourist Arrivals: 9,007 in 2004; 9,173 in 2005; 5,780 in 2006.

Arrivals by Country (2006): Japan 957; Other Asia 2,647; USA 1,768; Total (incl. others) 5,780.

Tourism Receipts (US $ million, incl. passenger transport): 5.0 in 2004; 5.7 in 2005; 6.6 in 2006.

Source: World Tourism Organization.

COMMUNICATIONS MEDIA

Telephones (main lines in use, estimate): 4,500 in 2006*.

Mobile Cellular Telephones (subscriptions, estimate): 700 in 2006*.

Facsimile Machines (number): 160 in 1996†.

Personal Computers: 5,000 in 2005*.

Internet Users: 2,200 in 2006*.

Non-daily Newspaper: 1 (average circulation 10,000 copies) in 1996‡.

* Source: International Telecommunication Union.
† Source: UN, *Statistical Yearbook*.
‡ Source: UNESCO, *Statistical Yearbook*.

EDUCATION

Primary (2006/07, unless otherwise indicated): 103 schools (1998); 526 teachers (2002/03, estimate); 8,215 pupils enrolled (estimate).

Secondary (2006/07, unless otherwise indicated): 16 schools (1998); 387 teachers (2002/03, estimate); 5,369 pupils enrolled (estimate).

Higher (2002/03, unless otherwise indicated): 1 college (1994); 49 teachers (estimate); 919 students enrolled (estimate).

Source: UNESCO Institute for Statistics.

Directory

The Constitution

On 1 May 1979 the locally drafted Constitution of the Republic of the Marshall Islands became effective. The Constitution provides for a parliamentary form of government, with legislative authority vested in the 33-member Nitijela. Members of the Nitijela are elected by a popular vote, from 25 districts, for a four-year term. There is an advisory council of 12 high chiefs, or Iroij. The Nitijela elects the President of the Marshall Islands (who also has a four-year mandate) from among its own members. The President then selects members of the Cabinet from among the members of the Nitijela. On 25 June 1983 the final draft of a Compact of Free Association was signed by the Governments of the Marshall Islands and the USA, and the Compact was effectively ratified by the US Congress on 14 January 1986. An amended Compact was signed by the Governments of the two countries on 1 May 2003; final terms were ratified by the US Congress in November, and signed by the US President in December of that year. By the terms of the Compact, free association recognizes the Republic of the Marshall Islands as an internally sovereign, self-governing state, whose policy concerning foreign affairs must be consistent with guide-lines laid down in the Compact. Full responsibility for defence lies with the USA, which undertakes to provide regular economic assistance. The economic and defence provisions of the Compact are renewable after 15 years, but the status of free association continues indefinitely.

The Government

HEAD OF STATE

President: LITOKWA TOMEING (took office 7 January 2008).

CABINET
(April 2009)

Minister in Assistance to the President: RUBEN ZACKHRAS.
Minister of Education: NIDEL LORAK.
Minister of Finance: JACK ADING.
Minister of Transportation and Communication: KENNETH KEDI.
Minister of Health: AMENTA MATTHEW.
Minister of Public Works: MAYNARD ALFRED.
Minister of Internal Affairs: NORMAN MATTHEW.
Minister of Justice: DAVID KRAMER.
Minister of Resources and Development: MATT ZACKHRAS.
Minister of Foreign Affairs: JOHN SILK.

MINISTRIES

Office of the President: Govt of the Republic of the Marshall Islands, POB 2, Majuro, MH 96960; tel. (625) 3445; fax (625) 4021; e-mail pressoff@ntamar.net; internet www.rmigovernment.org.

Ministry of Education: POB 3, Majuro, MH 96960; tel. (625) 5262; fax (625) 3861; e-mail rmimoe@rmimoe.net; internet www.rmimoe.net.

Ministry of Finance: POB P, Majuro, MH 96960; tel. (625) 3320; fax (625) 3607; e-mail secfin@ntamar.net.

Ministry of Foreign Affairs: POB 1349, Majuro, MH 96960; tel. (625) 3181; fax (623) 4979; e-mail mofasec@ntamar.net.

Ministry of Health: POB 16, Majuro, MH 96960; tel. (625) 3355; fax (625) 3432; e-mail jusmohe@ntamar.net.

Ministry of Internal Affairs: POB 18, Majuro, MH 96960; tel. (625) 8240; fax (625) 5353; e-mail rmihpo@ntamar.net.

Ministry of Justice: c/o Office of the Attorney General, Majuro, MH 96960; tel. (625) 3244; fax (625) 5218; e-mail agoffice@ntamar.net.

Ministry of Public Works: POB 1727, Majuro, MH 96960; tel. (625) 8911; fax (625) 3005; e-mail secpw@ntamar.net.

Ministry of Resources and Development: POB 1727, Majuro, MH 96960; tel. (625) 3206; fax (625) 7471; e-mail rndsec@ntamar.net; internet rmirnd.net.

Ministry of Transportation and Communication: POB 1079, Majuro, MH 96960; tel. (625) 8869; fax (625) 3486; e-mail rmimotc@ntamar.net.

STATE TRIBUNAL

Nuclear Claims Tribunal: POB 702, Majuro, MH 96960; tel. (625) 3396; fax (625) 3389; e-mail nctmaj@ntamar.net; internet www.nuclearclaimstribunal.com; f. 1988; authorized under Section 177 of the first Compact of Free Association between the Government of the Marshall Islands and the Government of the USA to decide all claims arising from the nuclear-testing programme conducted by the USA in the Marshall Islands in 1946–58; Chair. GREGORY DANZ (acting); Defender of the Fund PHILIP A. OKNEY; Public Advocate BILL GRAHAM.

Legislature

THE NITIJELA

The Nitijela (lower house) consists of 33 elected Senators. Following the national election held on 19 November 2007, the Ailin Kein Ad (Our Islands) party, supported by independent candidates, was able to secure a parliamentary majority.

Speaker: Sen. JURELANG ZEDKAIA.

THE COUNCIL OF IROIJ

The Council of Iroij is the upper house of the bicameral legislature, comprising 12 tribal chiefs who advise the Presidential Cabinet and review legislation affecting customary law, land tenure or any traditional practice.

Chairman: Iroij KOTAK LOEAK.

Election Commission

Electoral Commission: POB 18, Majuro, MH 96900; Chief Electoral Officer CARL ALIK.

Political Organizations

Ailin Kein Ad (Our Islands): Majuro; f. 2002; formed United People's Party coalition following 2007 elections; Chair. CHRISTOPHER LOEAK.

United Democratic Party: Majuro; Chair. RUBEN ZACKHRAS; Pres. KESSAI NOTE.

Diplomatic Representation

EMBASSIES IN THE MARSHALL ISLANDS

China (Taiwan): A5-6, Lojkar Village, Long Island, POB 1229, Majuro, MH 96960; tel. (247) 4141; fax (247) 4143; e-mail eoroc@ntamar.net; Ambassador BRUCE J. D. LINGHU.

Japan: A-1 Lojkar Village, POB 300, Majuro, MH 96960; tel. (247) 7463; fax (247) 7493; Ambassador SHOJI SATO.

USA: POB 1379, Majuro, MH 96960; tel. (247) 4011; fax (247) 4012; e-mail publicmajuro@state.gov; internet majuro.usembassy.gov; Ambassador CLYDE BISHOP.

THE MARSHALL ISLANDS

Judicial System

The judicial system consists of the Supreme Court and the High Court, which preside over District and Community Courts, and the Traditional Rights Court.

Supreme Court of the Republic of the Marshall Islands: POB 378, Majuro, MH 96960; tel. (625) 3201; fax (625) 3323; e-mail jutrep@ntamar.com; Chief Justice DANIEL CADRA.

High Court of the Republic of the Marshall Islands: Majuro; e-mail judrep@ntamar.net; Chief Justice CARL INGRAM.

District Court of the Republic of the Marshall Islands: Majuro, MH 96960; tel. (625) 3201; fax (625) 3323; Presiding Judge MILTON ZACKIOS.

Traditional Rights Court of the Marshall Islands: Majuro, MH 96960; customary law only; Chief Judge BERSON JOSEPH.

Religion

The population is predominantly Christian, mainly belonging to the Protestant United Church of Christ. The Roman Catholic Church, Assembly of God, Bukot Nan Jesus, Seventh-day Adventists, the Church of Jesus Christ of Latter-day Saints (Mormons), the Full Gospel and the Bahá'í Faith are also represented.

CHRISTIANITY

The Roman Catholic Church

The Apostolic Prefecture of the Marshall Islands included 4,872 adherents at 31 December 2006.

Prefect Apostolic of the Marshall Islands: Rev. Fr RAYMUNDO SABIO, POB 8, Majuro, MH 96960; tel. (625) 8307; fax (625) 6507; e-mail diocesemarshalls@yahoo.com.

Protestant Churches

The Marshall Islands come under the auspices of the United Church Board for World Ministries (475 Riverside Drive, New York, NY 10115, USA); Sec. for Latin America, Caribbean and Oceania Dr PATRICIA RUMER.

BAHÁ'Í FAITH

National Spiritual Assembly: POB 1017, Majuro, MH 96960; tel. (247) 3512; fax (247) 7180; e-mail nsamarshallislands@yahoo.com; internet www.mh.bahai.org; mems resident in 50 localities; Sec. Dr IRENE J. TAAFAKI.

The Press

Kwajalein Hourglass: POB 23, Kwajalein, MH 96555; tel. (355) 3539; e-mail jbennett@kls.usaka.smdc.army.mil; f. 1954; 2 a week; Editor JIM BENNETT; circ. 2,300.

Marshall Islands Gazette: monthly; government publ.

Marshall Islands Journal: POB 14, Majuro, MH 96960; tel. (625) 8143; fax (625) 3136; e-mail journal@ntamar.net; internet www.marshallislandsjournal.com; f. 1970; weekly; Editor GIFF JOHNSON; circ. 3,700.

Broadcasting and Communications

TELECOMMUNICATIONS

National Telecommunications Authority (NTA): POB 1169, Majuro, MH 96960; tel. (625) 3676; fax (625) 3952; e-mail info@ntamar.net; internet www.ntamar.net; privatized in 1991; sole provider of local and long-distance telephone services and internet communications in the Marshall Islands; Chair. ALEX BING; Pres. and CEO ANTHONY M. MULLER.

BROADCASTING

Radio

Marshall Islands Broadcasting Co: POB 19, Majuro, MH 96960; tel. (625) 3250; fax (625) 3505; Chief Information Officer PETER FUCHS.

Radio Marshalls V7AB: POB 3250, Majuro, MH 96960; tel. (625) 8411; fax (625) 5353; govt-owned; commercial; programmes in English and Marshallese; Station Man. ANTARI ELBON.

Other radio stations include Micronesia Heatwave and V7AA.

Television

Marshalls Broadcasting Co Television: POB 19, Majuro, MH 96960; tel. (625) 3413; Chief Information Officer PETER FUCHS.

The US Department of Defense operates the American Forces Radio and Television Service for the Bucholz Army Airfield on Kwajalein Atoll.

Finance

(cap. = capital; res = reserves; dep. = deposits; amounts in US dollars)

BANKING

Bank of Guam (USA): POB C, Majuro, MH 96960; tel. (625) 3322; fax (625) 3444; Man. ROMY A. ANGEL; brs in Ebeye, Kwajalein and Majuro.

Bank of the Marshall Islands: POB J, Majuro, MH 96960; tel. (625) 3636; fax (625) 3661; e-mail bankmar@ntamar.net; f. 1982; 40% govt-owned; dep. 47.5m., total assets 61.8m. (Dec. 2003); Chair. GRANT LABAUN; Pres. and Gen. Man. PATRICK CHEN; brs in Majuro, Kwajalein, Ebeye and Santo.

Marshall Islands Development Bank: POB 1048, Majuro, MH 96960; tel. (625) 3230; fax (625) 3309; e-mail rmimidb@ntamar.net; f. 1989; lending suspended in 2003; Man. Dir AMON TIBON.

INSURANCE

Majuro Insurance Company: POB 60, Majuro, MH 96960; tel. (625) 8885; fax (625) 8188; Man. LUCY RUBEN.

Marshalls Insurance Agency: POB 113, Majuro, MH 96960; tel. (625) 3366; fax (625) 3189; Man. TOM LIKOVICH.

Moylan's Insurance Underwriters (Marshall) Inc: POB 727, Majuro, MH 96960; tel. (625) 3220; fax (625) 3361; e-mail marshalls@moylans.net; internet www.moylansinsurance.com; Founder, Chair. and Pres. KURT S. MOYLAN; Br. Man. STEVE PHILLIP.

Trade and Industry

DEVELOPMENT ORGANIZATIONS AND STATE AUTHORITIES

Marshall Islands Development Authority: POB 1185, Majuro, MH 96960; tel. (625) 3417; fax (625) 3158; Gen. Man. DAVID KABUA.

Marshall Islands Environmental Protection Authority: POB 1322, Majuro, MH 96960; tel. (625) 3035; fax (625) 5202; e-mail eparmi@ntamar.net; Gen. Man. JOHN BUNGITAK.

Marshall Islands Marine Resources Authority (MIMRA): POB 860, Majuro, MH 96960; tel. (625) 8262; fax (625) 5447; e-mail kiko@mimra.com; internet www.mimra.com; specializes in farming techniques and research and devt; Exec. Dir GLEN JOSEPH.

Tobolar Copra Processing Authority: POB G, Majuro, MH 96960; tel. (625) 3116; fax (625) 7206; e-mail wpcandilas@ntamar.net; Plant Man. WILFREDO CANDILAS.

CHAMBER OF COMMERCE

Marshall Islands Chamber of Commerce: POB 1226, Majuro, MH 96960; tel. (625) 3177; fax (625) 2500; e-mail commerce@ntamar.net; internet marshallislandschamber.net; fmrly known as Majuro Chamber of Commerce; Pres. HIROBO OBEKETANG; Sec. JIM McLEAN.

UTILITIES

Electricity

Marshalls Energy Company: POB 1439, Majuro, MH 96960; tel. (625) 3827; fax (625) 3397; e-mail meccorp@ntamar.net; internet www.mecrmi.net; Gen. Man. WILLIAM F. ROBERTS; Man. STEVEN WAKEFIELD.

Kwajalein Atoll Joint Utility Resource (KAJUR): POB 5819, Ebeye Island, Kwajalein, MH 96970; tel. (329) 3799; fax (329) 3722; Man. WESLEY LEMARI.

Water

Majuro Water and Sewage Services: POB 1751, Majuro, MH 96960; tel. (625) 8934; fax (625) 3837; Man. TERRY MELLAN.

CO-OPERATIVES

These include the Ebeye Co-op, Farmers' Market Co-operative, Kwajalein Employees' Credit Union, Marshall Is Credit Union, Marshall Is Fishermen's Co-operative, and the Marshall Is Handicraft Co-operative.

Transport

ROADS

Macadam and concrete roads are found in the more important islands. In 1996 there were 152 km of paved roads in the Marshall Islands, mostly on Majuro and Ebeye. Other islands have stone and coral-surfaced roads and tracks. A road improvement programme was completed in 1999.

SHIPPING

The Marshall Islands operates an 'offshore' shipping register. At the end of 2007 the merchant fleet comprised 1,099 vessels, with a combined displacement of some 36.0m. grt.

Vessel Registry:

Marshall Islands Maritime and Corporate Administrators Inc: 11495 Commerce Park Drive, Reston, VA 20191-1507, USA; tel. (703) 620-4880; fax (703) 476-8522; e-mail info@register-iri.com; internet www.register-iri.com; Pres. WILLIAM R. GALLAGHER; Vice-Pres. MELISSA A. HURST.

The Trust Company of the Marshall Islands Inc: Trust Company Complex, Ajeltake Island, POB 1405, Majuro, MH 96960; tel. (247) 3018; fax (247) 3017; e-mail tcmi@ntamar.net; Pres. GUY EDISON CLAY MAITLAND.

Marshall Islands Ports Authority (MIPA): Majuro; tel. 625-8269; fax 625-4269; internet rmipa-aip.org; responsible for seaports and airports; Dir JACK CHONG GUM.

CIVIL AVIATION

Continental Micronesia operates three flights a week from Honolulu and Guam to Majuro. Air Marshall Islands provides a daily domestic service; Aloha Airlines provides a weekly service from Honolulu to Kwajalein and to Majuro; and Japan Airlines operates a charter service from Tokyo to Majuro.

Air Marshall Islands (AMI): POB 1319, Majuro, MH 96960; tel. (625) 3731; fax (625) 3730; e-mail amisales@ntamar.net; internet www.airmarshallislands.com; f. 1980; internal services for the Marshall Islands; also charter, air ambulance and maritime surveillance operations; agency for Aloha airlines; Chair. KUNIO LAMARI.

Continental Airlines Micronesia: POB 156, Majuro; tel. (625) 3209; fax (625) 3730; e-mail cmimaj@ntamar.net; international flights between Majuro, the Federated States of Micronesia, Guam and Honolulu; also internal services between Majuro and Kwajalein; based in Hagåtña, Guam; Man. LEO SION.

Tourism

The islands' attractions include excellent opportunities for diving, game-fishing and the exploration of sites and relics of Second World War battles. The Marshall Islands Visitor Authority has implemented a short-term tourism development programme focusing on special-interest tourism markets. In the longer term the Visitor Authority planned to promote the development of small-island resorts throughout the country. Tourism receipts totalled some US $6.6m. in 2006. In 2008 there were an estimated 6,022 tourist arrivals. The leading sources of visitors were the USA and Japan.

Marshall Islands Visitor Authority: POB 5, Majuro, MH 96960; tel. (625) 6482; fax (625) 6771; e-mail tourism@ntamar.net; internet www.visitmarshallislands.com; f. 1997; Gen. Man. DOLORES DE-BRUM-KATTIL.

MAURITANIA

Introductory Survey

Location, Climate, Language, Religion, Flag, Capital

The Islamic Republic of Mauritania lies in north-west Africa, with the Atlantic Ocean to the west, Algeria and the disputed territory of Western Sahara (occupied by Morocco) to the north, Mali to the east and south, and Senegal to the south. The climate is hot and dry, particularly in the north, which is mainly desert. Average annual rainfall in the capital in the 1990s was 131 mm (5.1 ins). The 1991 Constitution designates Arabic (which is spoken by the Moorish majority) as the official language, and Arabic, Poular, Wolof and Solinke as the national languages. The black population in the south is largely French-speaking, and French is widely used in commercial and business circles. Islam is the state religion, and the inhabitants are almost all Muslims. The national flag (proportions 2 by 3) comprises a green field, bearing, on the vertical median, a yellow five-pointed star between the upward-pointing horns of a yellow crescent. The capital is Nouakchott.

Recent History

Mauritania, formerly part of French West Africa, achieved full independence on 28 November 1960 (having become a self-governing member of the French Community two years earlier). Moktar Ould Daddah, leader of the Mauritanian Assembly Party (MAP) and Prime Minister since June 1959, became Head of State, and was elected President in August 1961. All parties subsequently merged with the MAP to form the Mauritanian People's Party (MPP), with Ould Daddah as Secretary-General, and Mauritania became a one-party state in 1964. In 1973 Mauritania joined the League of Arab States (see p. 344), and withdrew from the Franc Zone in the following year.

Under a tripartite agreement of November 1975, Spain ceded Spanish (now Western) Sahara to Mauritania and Morocco, to be apportioned between them. The agreement took effect in February 1976, when Mauritania occupied the southern portion of the territory. Fighting ensued between Moroccan and Mauritanian troops and the guerrilla forces of the Frente Popular para la Liberación de Saguia el-Hamra y Río de Oro (the Polisario Front), which sought independence for Western Sahara. Attacks within Mauritania by Polisario forces proved highly damaging to the economy. Diplomatic links with Algeria, which supported Polisario bases within its borders, were severed in March 1976. Meanwhile, relations with Morocco improved, following that country's renunciation of territorial claims that included Mauritania, and in mid-1977 a joint defence pact was formed.

By 1977 Mauritania was spending two-thirds of its budget on defending territory that promised no economic benefits. In July 1978 Ould Daddah was deposed in a bloodless coup, led by the armed forces Chief of Staff, Lt-Col (later Col) Moustapha Ould Mohamed Salek, who took power as Chairman of a Military Committee for National Recovery (MCNR). Polisario immediately declared a cease-fire with Mauritania, but the continuing presence of several thousand Moroccan troops in Mauritania impeded a full settlement. In April 1979 the MCNR was replaced by a Military Committee for National Salvation (MCNS). Salek resigned in June, and was replaced as Head of State by Lt-Col Mohamed Mahmoud Ould Ahmed Louly. In July Polisario announced a resumption of hostilities against Mauritania. Later that month the Organization of African Unity (OAU, now the African Union—AU, see p. 172) recommended that a referendum be held to determine the future of the disputed region. These events provided the impetus for Mauritania's withdrawal from the war: Lt-Col Mohamed Khouna Ould Haidalla, appointed premier in May, renounced Mauritania's territorial claims in Western Sahara, and a peace treaty was signed with Polisario in August. Morocco announced its annexation of the entire territory, and diplomatic relations between Mauritania and Algeria were re-established.

Ould Haidalla succeeded Louly as Head of State in January 1980; he retained the posts of Prime Minister and Minister of Defence until December, when Sid'Ahmed Ould Bneijara was appointed premier. Although a draft Constitution, envisaging a multi-party system, was prepared, an attempted coup in March 1981 prompted Ould Haidalla to end civilian participation in the Government. The new Prime Minister, Lt-Col (later Col) Maaouiya Ould Sid'Ahmed Taya (a prominent member of the MCNS and the army Chief of Staff) assumed the defence portfolio in April, and the draft Constitution was abandoned.

In December 1984, while Ould Haidalla was temporarily absent from the country, Taya assumed the presidency in a bloodless coup and also took the defence portfolio in the new Government. An amnesty was proclaimed for all political prisoners and exiles. Ould Haidalla was detained upon his return to Mauritania, but was released, with five of his associates, in December 1988.

At a national referendum on 12 July 1991, a draft Constitution, which accorded extensive powers to the presidency and provided for the introduction of a multi-party political system, was supported by 97.9% of those who voted (85.3% of the registered electorate), according to official reports. Meanwhile, legislation permitting the registration of political parties was promulgated: among the first organizations to be accorded official status was the Democratic and Social Republican Party (DSRP), which was closely linked with Taya.

Taya was elected President on 17 January 1992, with 62.7% of the votes cast, defeating three other candidates; his nearest rival was Ahmed Ould Daddah, with 32.8%. The rate of voter participation was 51.7%. In legislative elections, which were held on 6 and 13 March, Taya's party took 67 of the 79 seats in the National Assembly, and he was inaugurated as President on 18 April.

The DSRP secured control of 172 of Mauritania's 208 administrative districts at Mauritania's first multi-party municipal elections, held in January and February 1994. Ahmed Ould Daddah's Union of Democratic Forces—New Era (UDF—NE) won control of 17 districts, the remainder being taken by independent candidates.

In January 1996 Taya appointed Cheikh el Avia Ould Mohamed Khouna as Prime Minister, to head a new Council of Ministers. At legislative elections held on 11 and 18 October the DSRP won 71 of the 79 seats in the National Assembly. The Rally for Democracy and Unity (RDU), closely allied with the administration, also secured a seat. Action for Change (AC), which sought to represent the interests of Harratin (mainly dark-skinned Moors who had formerly been slaves), was the only opposition party to obtain representation in the Assembly; six independent candidates also secured election. Later in October the Prime Minister named a new Council of Ministers.

In January 1997 several opposition leaders, including Messaoud Ould Boulkheir, the AC Chairman, were arrested on charges of maintaining 'suspicious relations' with Libya. Although Ould Boulkheir and several others had been freed by February, five other opposition activists received prison sentences for conspiring to break the law; in April four of the five convicted were acquitted on appeal. In February five prominent opposition parties, including the AC and the UDF—NE, formed a coalition, the Forum of Opposition Parties (FOP).

At the presidential election, held on 12 December 1997, Taya was returned to office with 90.9% of the valid votes cast; his nearest rival, Mohamed Lemine Ch'Bih Ould Cheikh Melainine, won 7.0% of the vote. Opposition parties alleged that there had been widespread electoral fraud and disputed the official rate of voter participation, of 73.8%. Taya subsequently appointed Mohamed Lemine Ould Guig, a university academic, as Prime Minister, and a new Council of Ministers was installed. In November 1998 Khouna was again appointed Prime Minister.

Meanwhile, in March 1998 internal divisions in the UDF—NE resulted in a split in the party into two rival factions, led by Ahmed Ould Daddah and Moustapha Ould Bedreddine. In November the Government banned the pro-Iraqi Baathist National Vanguard Party (Taliaa), a constituent member of the FOP, following its criticism of the Mauritanian Government's decision to establish full diplomatic relations with Israel in the previous month.

From October 2000, following the onset of the second *intifada* (uprising) in the Palestinian Autonomous Areas, the Mauritanian Government experienced increasing pressure from opposition groups, including the UDF—NE, to break off diplomatic relations with Israel. In October several pro-Palestinian demonstrations in Nouakchott and Nouadhibou led to violent anti-Israeli protests. Arrests of members of clandestine Islamist groups and of UDF—NE activists were reported. In late October the Council of Ministers officially dissolved the UDF—NE, on the grounds that the party had incited violence and sought to damage Mauritanian national interests. Ould Daddah refused to recognize the dissolution of the party, and the UDF—NE's partners in the FOP condemned the Government's action as unconstitutional. Meanwhile, the faction of the UDF—NE led by Moustapha Ould Bedreddine, which remained authorized, restyled itself as the Union of Progressive Forces (UPF).

In December 2000 President Taya announced that an element of proportional representation would be introduced in subsequent elections to the National Assembly, and that the State would seek to facilitate funding and equal access to the media for all parties, although independent candidacies were to be prohibited. The National Assembly approved these measures in January 2001, although they were rejected as insufficient by the radical opposition, including the FOP.

Some 15 political parties contested legislative and municipal elections held on 19 and 26 October 2001, at which an electoral turn-out of some 55% was reported. The DSRP won 64 of the 81 seats in the enlarged National Assembly, and the RDU and the Union for Democratic Progress (UDP), which were now both allied with the ruling party, each secured three seats. The AC was the most successful of the opposition parties, winning four seats, while the UPF and the newly formed Rally of Democratic Forces (RDF), which replaced the banned UDF—NE, also each took three seats, and the Popular Front (PF) secured the remaining seat. In November President Taya reappointed Khouna as Prime Minister, and a reshuffled Council of Ministers was appointed.

In January 2002 Ould Daddah was elected President of the RDF; four former vice-presidents of the UDF—NE were also appointed to the 12-member executive committee of the RDF. In that month the Government officially dissolved the AC, on the grounds that the party promoted racism and extremism. At partial senatorial elections, held in April, the RDF won one seat, the first time that part of the radical opposition had secured representation in the Senate, in which the DSRP enjoyed a large majority. In August the Convention for Change (CC), an organization including many former members of the AC, and led by Ould Boulkheir, was denied the right to register as a political party.

In October 2002 the UFP announced that it was to organize a series of meetings intended to promote a 'national dialogue' between the authorities and the opposition parties. However, later that month seven other opposition parties, including the CC (which remained banned), the PF and the RDF, formed a new grouping, the United Opposition Framework (UOF), which also stated as its purpose the co-ordination of dialogue between the opposition and the Government pertaining to democratic reform; the UFP was, notably, excluded from the UOF. Consequently, the initial meeting was postponed indefinitely, and, expressing discontent at the situation, in mid-November the UFP announced its withdrawal from the National Assembly. As a result of the withdrawal of the three UFP deputies from the Assembly, the group of opposition deputies was dissolved, as it was now reduced to eight members, fewer than the 10 required for the formation of a parliamentary group. On 27 October a government reorganization was effected. Notably, Dah Ould Abdi was replaced as Minister of Foreign Affairs and Co-operation by Mohamed Ould Tobar.

In March 2003 US-led military action in Iraq, aimed at ousting the Baathist regime of Saddam Hussain, prompted protests in Mauritania, with widespread demonstrations held to demand that the Government break off diplomatic relations with the two principal nations involved in the conflict, the United Kingdom and the USA, and also with Israel. As opposition to the Government's broadly pro-US stance intensified in early May, police raided the headquarters of a tolerated—although not officially authorized—Baathist party, the National Renaissance Party (NRP—Nouhoudh). Three leaders of the NRP, including its Secretary-General, Mohamed Ould Abdellahi Ould Eyye, were arrested on unspecified charges; 13 other Baathists were also arrested over a period of four days, including the former Secretary-General of the Taliaa party. (Ten of those arrested were later charged with attempting to re-establish Taliaa.)

In early May 2003 Taya effected a minor government reorganization: the appointment of Lembrabott Ould Mohamed Lemine as Minister of Culture and Islamic Affairs was regarded as an attempt to reduce tensions between the Government and Islamic communities. However, at the end of May the publication of a pro-Islamist weekly journal, *Ar-Rayah*, was suspended, and nine Baathists were convicted by a Nouakchott court of engaging in illegal political activity. In early June four Islamic cultural associations were closed down, and, according to opposition reports, more than 100 alleged Islamists were detained, 36 of whom were charged with plotting against the constitutional order.

The tensions that had been escalating throughout the first half of 2003 culminated in an attempted *coup d'état*, which commenced on 8 June. Exchanges of fire were reported near the presidential palace and at other strategic locations in Nouakchott. According to official reports, 15 people (including six civilians) died in ensuing clashes between the insurgents and the security forces, including the Chief of Staff of the Armed Forces, Col Mohamed Lamine Ould Ndiayane, with a further 68 people injured. Government forces regained control of the city on 9 June. Although the exact identity and motives of the rebels were unclear, reports named the leaders of the coup as Saleh Ould Hnana, a former colonel and Baathist sympathizer, who had been expelled from the Mauritanian armed forces in 2002, and Mohammed Ould Sheikhna, a squadron leader in the national air force; Taya subsequently stated, however, that Islamists had been responsible for the rebellion. (Other sources claimed that the attempted coup had been prompted by tribal rivalries.)

In the days following the restoration of order at least 12 alleged rebel leaders were arrested, including Ould Sheikhna, although the whereabouts of Ould Hnana remained unknown. Ould Mansour fled to Senegal before later being granted political asylum in Belgium. Meanwhile, more than 30 detained Islamists, who had been freed during the disorder, were reported to have surrendered themselves to the authorities. In mid-June 2003 several senior officials, including the Chief of Staff of the National Gendarmerie, the President of the High Court of Justice and the Mayor of Nouakchott, were replaced by new appointees regarded as loyal to the President. In July another suspected coup leader, Lt Didi Ould M'Hamed, who had fled to Senegal, was extradited to Mauritania; it was subsequently announced that he would face a civil trial.

In early July 2003 Taya appointed a new Prime Minister: Sghaïr Ould M'Barek, a Harratin, was regarded as a close ally of the President. A new Government was subsequently formed. Although several of the high-ranking officials who had been arrested in mid-June had been released from custody by mid-July, it was reported that the former Prime Minister, Khouna, had been detained after having sought political asylum in Spain. Further arrests of Islamists were reported throughout the month. In early August more than 80 members of the military who had been arrested following the attempted coup were released, although many more remained in detention. At the end of the month Melainine was freed, having been granted a presidential pardon. Some 41 Islamists had also been released from detention by the end of the month, although others continued to face charges. In early September it was announced that some 30 members of the military, including 20 senior officers, were to be tried in connection with the coup attempt.

In October 2003 the Constitutional Council approved the nominations of six candidates, including Taya, Ould Daddah, Ould Boulkheir and former President Ould Haidalla, for the forthcoming presidential election. Ould Haidalla was widely regarded as the most credible challenger to Taya, but only secured 18.7% of the votes cast, and Taya was re-elected with 66.7%. Some 60.8% of the electorate participated in the election. Opposition candidates accused the Government of perpetrating fraud at the election, which international observers had not been permitted to monitor.

In mid-November 2003 the trial of Ould Haidalla (who had been arrested twice in November) and 14 of his supporters, on charges of seeking to obtain power by force and by threatening the strategic interests of Mauritania, commenced. The trial concluded at the end of December, when Ould Haidalla and four of his co-defendants, including one of his sons, were convicted of plotting to overthrow the Head of State; they received five-year suspended sentences, during which time they were forbidden to engage in political activity, and were fined the equivalent of US $1,600 each. Four others received lesser sentences and fines. Ould Haidalla's conviction and sentence were upheld on appeal in April 2004.

In August 2004 some 31 army officers were arrested after the security forces discovered a plot to overthrow Taya. The Mauritanian authorities accused the Governments of Libya and Burkina Faso of providing assistance to the alleged conspirators; however, both states strongly denied the allegations. In September the Government announced that it had averted another attempted *coup d'état*, seizing a large quantity of weapons and making a number of arrests; among those detained was Capt. Abderahmane Ould Mini, who, it was reported, had also participated in the failed *coup d'état* in June 2003, while Ould Hnana and Ould Sheikhna were also sought by the authorities in connection with the alleged conspiracy.

In October 2004 the Government announced that Ould Hnana had been arrested at the town of Rosso on the Senegalese border. The trial of more than 190 soldiers and civilians accused of participation in the attempted *coup d'état* in June 2003 and in subsequent conspiracies to overthrow the Head of State commenced in November. The defendants included the alleged leaders of the group, Ould Hnana, Ould Mini and Ould Sheikhna, the latter being one of 19 people tried *in absentia* (also among this number was Sidi Mohamed Mustapha Ould Limam Chavi, an adviser to Burkinabè President Blaise Compaoré); the civilians on trial, meanwhile, included opposition leaders Ould Haidalla, Ould Daddah and Cheikh Ould Horma. Ould Hnana pleaded guilty to the charge of conspiring to overthrow President Taya, while Ould Mini also admitted conspiring to overthrow the President; the remaining accused military personnel entered pleas of not guilty. In February 2005 Ould Hnana, Ould Mini, Ould Sheikhna and a fourth officer, Capt. Mohammed Ould Salek, were sentenced to life imprisonment with hard labour, while 79 others received lesser jail sentences; Ould Haidalla, Ould Daddah and Ould Horma were among the 111 acquitted. Following his release, Ould Daddah urged the Government to initiate dialogue with the opposition.

Some 15 soldiers were killed, and a further 17 injured, in an attack in June 2005 by some 150 assailants on a military post at Lemgheity, in north-eastern Mauritania, for which an Algerian radical Islamist militant group, the Groupe salafiste pour la prédication et le combat (GSPC), subsequently claimed responsibility. Later in June it was reported that the existence of a radical Islamist group based in Mauritania with links to the GSPC, the Mauritanian Group for Preaching and Jihad, had been uncovered, as had details of proposed targets of attack in the country. At the end of the month the Senate adopted legislation aimed at countering terrorism and money-laundering. In May 2007 the trial of 25 suspected Islamist militants commenced in Nouakchott; several of the accused were being tried *in absentia*. Some of the defendants were charged in connection with the attack in Lemgheity, while others were accused of having received training from the GSPC (which had reportedly restyled itself as the al-Qa'ida Organization in the Islamic Maghreb). In early June 24 of the defendants were acquitted owing to lack of evidence, and one defendant, who had escaped from prison in April 2006, was sentenced, *in absentia*, to two years' imprisonment for falsifying identity papers. The trial of a second group of 14 alleged militants began in late June 2007. Three were charged with participating in the attack at Lemgheity, while 11 were charged with having links to the GSPC.

Meanwhile, on 3 August 2005, while President Taya was absent from Mauritania, attending the funeral of the late King Fahd ibn Abd al-Aziz as-Sa'ud of Saudi Arabia, a group of army officers seized control of state broadcasting services and the presidential palace in a bloodless *coup d'état*. A 16-member Military Council for Justice and Democracy (MCJD) under the leadership of Col Ely Ould Mohamed Vall, hitherto the Director of National Security, who had been regarded as a close ally of Taya, announced that it had assumed power. The Council stated that it would preside over the country for a transitional period of up to two years, at the end of which democratic elections, in which members of the MCJD and the Government would be prohibited from participating, would be held; although the National Assembly elected in 2001 was dissolved, the 1991 Constitution and most of its institutions (including the Constitutional Council and judicial bodies) were to be retained, as supplemented and amended by the charter of the MCJD. Taya was prevented from re-entering the country and was flown initially to Niamey, Niger; he subsequently took up residence in The Gambia.

On 7 August 2005 Vall appointed Sidi Mohamed Ould Boubacar, hitherto Ambassador to France, as Prime Minister, a position that he had previously held in 1992–96; a new, civilian, government was named on 10 August, and Vall announced the intention of holding a constitutional referendum within the period of one year. None of the ministers in the outgoing Government were re-appointed, although, notably, Ahmed Ould Sid'Ahmed, who, in his former capacity as Minister of Foreign Affairs and Co-operation, had been largely responsible for Mauritania's rapprochement with Israel in 1999, was re-appointed to that position. In the immediate aftermath of the coup, which was initially widely condemned internationally, the AU announced the immediate suspension of Mauritania's membership. However, the overthrow of Taya's regime was reported to have widespread domestic support. In mid-August a delegation from the AU met members of the MCJD, subsequently announcing the willingness of the Union to co-operate with the new leadership of Mauritania, although the country was to remain suspended from the organization pending democratic elections, in accordance with the Constitutive Act of the AU.

In early September 2005 the new administration announced that it was to offer a general amnesty for political prisoners; 32 such detainees, principally from among those imprisoned in February 2005 for their role in attempted *coups d'état* in 2003 and 2004, were among the first to benefit from the amnesty. However, some Islamist detainees were not freed, prompting 19 such prisoners to commence a hunger strike demanding their release later in September. In mid-October, moreover, the authorities refused to recognize a recently formed Islamist political party, the Party for Democratic Convergence, on the grounds that its programme violated Mauritanian law. Indeed, Ould Vall announced that no Islamist party would be legalized.

In November 2005 the MCJD issued a timetable for the transition to democratic rule: a constitutional referendum was to be held in June 2006, followed by elections to municipal councils and to the National Assembly in November, elections to the Senate in January 2007 and, finally, a presidential election in March 2007. A 15-member National Independent Electoral Commission was inaugurated at the end of November 2005. Meanwhile, the former ruling DSRP, which had changed its name to the Republican Party for Democracy and Renewal (RPDR), elected Ethmane Ould Cheikh Ebi el Maali, hitherto ambassador to Kuwait, as its new President. In late December the MCJD replaced 12 of the country's regional governors, as well as most prefects and district administrators. A few days later Vall announced a 50% increase in civil servants' salaries, aimed at reducing corruption within the public sector.

An electoral census was conducted in February–April 2006. In late March the MCJD approved proposals presented by the transitional Government on constitutional amendments to be put to a national referendum on 25 June. The principal changes envisaged included: limiting the presidential term of office to five years, renewable only once; stipulating a maximum age of 75 years for presidential candidates; and prohibiting a President from holding any other official post, particularly the leadership of a political party. The proposed reforms were generally supported by most major political parties, including the RPDR. In early May the European Union (EU, see p. 255) announced the resumption of co-operation with Mauritania, which had been suspended following the coup in August 2005.

The constitutional referendum was held, as scheduled, on 25 June 2006. Several days earlier five associates of former President Taya had been arrested on suspicion of planning to sabotage the plebiscite, while a coalition of four parties critical of the Vall administration, the Bloc of Parties for Change, encouraged their supporters to boycott the referendum. None the less, observers from the AU and the Arab League declared their satisfaction with the conduct of the poll. According to official results proclaimed by the Constitutional Council at the end of the month, 96.9% of the valid votes cast were in favour of the amendments to the Constitution and a turn-out of 76.5% of the registered electorate was recorded. In late June 10 political parties, including the RDF, the PF, the Popular Progressive Alliance (PPA) and the RM—TEMAM, announced the formation of the Coalition of Forces for Democratic Change (CFDC) to contest the forthcoming legislative and local elections.

At the legislative elections, which were held as scheduled on 19 November and 3 December 2006, the RDF took 15 seats, the UPF eight, the RPDR seven and the PPA five, while the Centrist Reformists and the Mauritanian Party for Union and Change—Hatem both secured four seats; 41 seats were taken by independent candidates. Indirect elections to the Senate took place on 21 January and 4 February 2007 at which independent candidates secured 34 of the 56 seats, while representatives of the CFDC took 15.

The presidential election took place as scheduled over two rounds on 11 and 25 March 2007. At the first round, which was contested by 20 candidates, Sidi Mohamed Ould Cheikh Abdellahi took 24.79% of votes cast, while Ould Daddah won 20.68%, Zeine Ould Zeidane 15.27% and Ould Boulkheir 9.80%. The rate of voter participation was recorded at 70.1%. Abdellahi and Ould Daddah thus proceeded to the second round at which, according to results proclaimed by the Constitutional Council on 29 March, Abdellahi (a government minister under both Moktar Ould Daddah and Taya) was elected President, having secured 52.85% of the valid votes cast. Some 67.5% of the electorate participated in the second round. Ould Boubacar submitted the resignation of his Government on 31 March, although the administration was to remain in office in a 'caretaker' capacity pending the inauguration of the new President, scheduled for 19 April. Abdellahi was duly inaugurated on that date, assuming executive powers in place of the MCJD, which was disbanded, and on the following day he appointed Zeidane as Prime Minister. Later in April a new Government, mainly comprising technocrats with no previous ministerial experience, was installed. The elections were largely deemed to have been fair and democratic and on 10 April Mauritania was readmitted to the AU. In June President Abdellahi effected a minor cabinet reorganization.

In May 2008 Zeidane was dismissed as Prime Minister and replaced by Yahya Ould Ahmed el Waghef, leader of the National Party for Democracy and Development (NPDD). A 31-member Council of Ministers was named, and later approved by Abdellahi, which included members of the opposition UPF and the National Rally for Reform and Development. However, on 1 July a motion of no confidence was submitted by 39 legislators from the NPDD, and the Government resigned on 3 July. Abdellahi initially threatened to dissolve the legislature, but he subsequently accepted the cabinet's resignation and invited el Waghef to form a new Government, which was appointed on 10 July and included 14 new members. Most notably, Ahmedou Tidjane Bal was appointed as Minister of Justice and Abdellahi Ould Ben Hmeida was named as Minister of Foreign Affairs and Cooperation.

On 6 August 2008 President Abdellahi announced the dismissal of four senior military officials, including Gen. Mohamed Ould Abdel Aziz, the Presidential Chief of Staff. Later that day Ould Abdel Aziz led a bloodless military coup to overthrow Abdellahi and declared himself President of a new interim executive, the High Council of State (HCS), which included two other generals—Mohamed Ould Cheik Mohamed Ahmed and Felix Negre—and eight colonels. Prime Minister el Waghef was also removed from office and detained along with Abdellahi, although the former Prime Minister was released later in August, while Abdellahi remained under house arrest until December. There was little opposition to the coup: less than 100 demonstrators took to the streets of Nouakchott on 7 August and were quickly dispersed by the security forces, while 107 of the 146 members of the National Assembly declared their support for the new regime. Ould Abdel Aziz claimed that a presidential election would be held 'as soon as possible'. (A timetable was eventually announced which established the election date as 6 June 2009.) The HCS issued a constitutional ordinance, which stated that it would exercise the powers of the President as defined by the Constitution, and granted Ould Abdel Aziz the power to appoint a Prime Minister, military officials and civil servants. On 14 August 2008 Ould Abdel Aziz named Moulaye Ould Mohamed Laghdaf, hitherto Mauritania's Ambassador to Belgium and the EU, as the new Prime Minister, and in early September a new cabinet was formed which featured a number of ministers from the previous administration. Bal retained the justice portfolio and Mohamed Mahmoud Ould Mohamed Lemine was reappointed as Minister of National Defence. The coup received widespread international condemnation and on 9 August the AU announced Mauritania's suspension from the organization, pending the restoration of democratic government.

In April 2009 Ould Abdel Aziz resigned his position as head of the HCS, in order to contest the presidential election. He was elected as Chairman of a new political party, the Union for the Republic, which had been formed the previous month. A spokesman for the National Front for the Defence of Democracy (NFDD), a coalition of political parties opposed to the coup, denounced the planned election, claiming it was a means of legitimizing military rule; in May the NFDD and RDF held a joint demonstration in Nouakchott, in which several thousand people marched to protest against the proposed election.

The AU's Peace and Security Council imposed further sanctions, including travel restrictions and a freezing of funds, on some 60 Mauritanian nationals in early February 2009, among them five members of the HCS, seven government ministers and 10 parliamentary deputies, and called on AU member states to contribute to efforts to restore political order in Mauritania. However, the Chairman of the AU Assembly, Libyan Revolutionary Leader Col Muammar al-Qaddafi, endorsed the electoral timetable set by the HSC for presidential elections (which had been rejected by the opposition and numerous international bodies), while visiting Mauritania in March. Several members of the opposition walked out of the National Assembly during an address by al-Qaddafi, accusing him of supporting the military junta.

Meanwhile, in late December 2007 four French tourists were shot dead by a group of gunmen near the town of Aleg, in the south-west of Mauritania, in what was initially believed to be a robbery. However, the Government later attributed the killings to Islamist militants, and in January 2008 two Mauritanian men with previous convictions for training with the GSPC and having links to al-Qa'ida, were arrested in Guinea-Bissau in connection with the incident. According to the Guinea-Bissau police, both admitted to the killings and they were handed over to the Mauritanian authorities. In April one of the suspects, Sidi Ould Sidna, escaped from police custody in Nouakchott, although on 10 April the alleged leader of the group, Marouf Ould Hibba, was arrested; in the same month a police officer and an Islamist militant were killed in a shoot-out in the capital. In May Hibba was charged for his role in the murder of the French tourists, along with 28 other suspected Islamist militants who faced various charges. In September 12 Mauritanian soldiers who were abducted and later found dead, were believed to have been victims of an attack by al-Qa'ida militants.

A long-standing border dispute with Senegal was exacerbated by the deaths, in April 1989, of two Senegalese farmers, who had been involved in a dispute regarding grazing rights with Mauritanian livestock-breeders. Mauritanian nationals resident in Senegal were attacked, and their businesses (primarily those of the retail trade) looted, while Senegalese nationals in Mauritania and black Mauritanians suffered similar aggression. By early May it was believed that several hundred people, mostly Senegalese, had been killed. Operations to repatriate nationals of both countries commenced, with international assistance. Amid allegations that the Mauritanian authorities had begun to instigate expulsions of the indigenous black population to Senegal or to Mali, a prominent human rights organization, Amnesty International, expressed concern at the reported violation of black Mauritanians' rights. Mauritania and Senegal suspended diplomatic relations in August 1989, and sporadic outbreaks of violence were reported later that year. In late 1990 the Senegalese Government denied accusations made by the Mauritanian authorities that it was implicated in an alleged attempt to overthrow Taya. In December the arrests of large numbers of black Mauritanians were reported. In early 1991 Mauritanian naval vessels were reported to have opened fire on Senegalese fishing boats, apparently in Senegal's territorial waters; in March several deaths were reported to have resulted from a military engagement on Senegalese territory, following an incursion by Senegalese troops into Mauritania.

Following renewed diplomatic activity, diplomatic relations with Senegal were resumed in April 1992, and the process of reopening the border began in May. However, Mauritanian refugees in Senegal insisted that, as long as the Taya Government refused to recognize their national identity (*mauritanité*) and land and property rights, they would not return to Mauritania. In June 2000 relations between Mauritania and Senegal deteriorated after Mauritania accused the new Senegalese administration of relaunching an irrigation project, which involved the use of joint waters from the Senegal river, in contravention of the Organisation pour la mise en valeur du fleuve Sénégal project (see p. 428). The dispute escalated when the Mauritanian authorities requested that all of its citizens living in Senegal return home and issued the estimated 100,000 Senegalese nationals living in Mauritania with a 15-day deadline by which to leave the country. In mid-June, following mediation by King Muhammad VI of Morocco and the Presidents of The Gambia and Mali, the Mauritanian Minister of the Interior announced that the decision to expel Senegalese citizens had been withdrawn and that Mauritanians living in Senegal could remain there. President Abdoulaye Wade of Senegal visited Mauritania later that month and announced that the irrigation project had been abandoned. By late 2000 the number of Mauritanian refugees in Senegal had declined to 19,800 (compared with 65,500 in mid-1995). In April 2001 President Taya's presence as guest of honour at a ceremony in Dakar to commemorate the 41st anniversary of the independence of Senegal demonstrated an improvement in relations between the countries. At the end of 2007 some 19,503 Mauritanian refugees still remained in Senegal, according to provisional figures. In January 2008 about 100 Mauritanian refugees returned from Senegal, following the conclusion of a repatriation agreement between the Senegalese and the Mauritanian authorities, which envisaged the eventual resettlement of all remaining Mauritanian refugees in Senegal.

Diplomatic relations between Mauritania and Morocco were severed in 1981, following accusations, denied by both countries, of involvement in mutual destabilization attempts. In 1983 Mauritania sought to improve relations between the Maghreb countries (Algeria, Morocco, Mauritania, Tunisia and Libya) and was a signatory of the Maghreb Fraternity and Co-operation Treaty, drafted by Algeria and Tunisia. Relations with Morocco again deteriorated from February 1984, when Mauritania announced its recognition of the Sahrawi Arab Democratic Republic (the Western Saharan state proclaimed by Polisario in 1976), although Taya restored diplomatic relations with Morocco in April 1985. In February 1989 Mauritania was a founder member, with Algeria, Libya, Morocco and Tunisia, of the Union of the Arab Maghreb (UMA, see p. 429), although relations with Libya were reported to have deteriorated from the mid-1990s; Libya was a particularly vehement critic of Mauritania's decision to establish and maintain full diplomatic relations with Israel. Diplomatic relations with Libya, severed in 1995, were none the less restored in 1997. In September 2001 King Muhammad VI of Morocco paid a three-day official visit to Mauritania, aimed at improving bilateral relations between the two countries. In March 2004 President Taya led an official delegation to Morocco, and again met with King Muhammad. King Muhammad returned to Mauritania in March 2005 as part of a tour of West Africa. There was speculation that, during his visits to both Mauritania and Burkina Faso, the King had attempted to mediate informally between the two countries' Presidents (whose relations remained strained following Mauritania's accusation that Burkina Faso and Libya had supported an attempt to overthrow Taya), but without apparent success.

Relations with both Libya and Burkina Faso were severely strained in the wake of allegations by the Mauritanian Government that those two countries had provided support to rebel elements in the Mauritanian military, accused of participating in the failed *coup d'état* of June 2003 and of subsequently conspiring to overthrow President Taya (see above). It was alleged that Ould Hnana and Ould Sheikhna, who were held responsible by the Mauritanian authorities of leading the 2003 *coup d'état*, had been granted refuge in Burkina Faso and received weapons, money and training, while the Libyan Government was accused of supplying the rebels with weapons, vehicles and other equipment. Libya and Burkina Faso, meanwhile, strenuously denied the accusations. In March 2005 a ministerial commission appointed by the UMA to investigate the Mauritanian allegations against Libya concluded that the al-Qaddafi had 'no connection' to the events in Mauritania, which it described as a 'purely Mauritanian affair'.

In November 1995 Mauritania signed an agreement to recognize and establish relations with Israel. In October 1998 Mauritania's Minister of Foreign Affairs and Co-operation visited Israel, where he held talks with the Prime Minister, Binyamin Netanyahu. The Arab League strongly criticized the visit, claiming that it contravened the League's resolutions on the suspension of the normalization of relations with Israel, and threatened to impose sanctions on Mauritania. Widespread controversy was provoked both domestically, and in Arab countries, by the establishment of full diplomatic relations between Mauritania and Israel in October 1999. (Of Arab countries, only Egypt and Jordan had taken such a step, under the terms of their respective peace treaties with Israel.) Following the resumption of the Palestinian uprising in September 2000, the Mauritanian Government came under renewed pressure to suspend diplomatic relations with Israel. A visit by the Mauritanian Minister of Foreign Affairs and Co-operation, Dah Ould Abdi, to Israel in May 2001, when he met Israeli Prime Minister Ariel Sharon and President Moshe Katsav, and entered into negotiations with the Minister of Foreign Affairs, Shimon Peres, provoked further controversy, particularly as a result of an appeal by the Arab League, issued earlier that month, for all member countries to cease political contacts with Israel. A further meeting between Peres, Taya and Ould Abdi, in Nouakchott, in October 2002, provoked further controversy. A visit to Mauritania by the Israeli Deputy Prime Minister and Minister of Foreign Affairs, Silvan Shalom, in early May 2005 was preceded, and followed, by the detention of several Islamists (see above), although the Government denied that the arrests were linked to Shalom's presence. His visit was accompanied by a number of anti-Israeli protests in Nouakchott. Although some concern was initially expressed, following the *coup d'état* of August 2005, that diplomatic relations between the two countries might be terminated, the appointment, later in the month, of Ahmed Ould Sid'Ahmed as Minister of Foreign Affairs and Co-operation (who had held that position when Mauritania re-established full diplomatic relations with Israel in 1999) appeared to indicate that the new regime intended to maintain amicable relations with Israel. In April 2007 newly elected President Abdellahi appealed for a public debate on the future of Mauritania's diplomatic ties with Israel. In February 2008 the Israeli embassy in Nouakchott was attacked by gunmen who opened fire and injured three people. Nevertheless, relations did not seriously deteriorate until after the assumption of power in Mauritania by the HCS. In January 2009 Mauritania recalled its ambassador from Israel, and suspended diplomatic relations, in response to the Israeli invasion of the Gaza Strip in December 2008; in March 2009 it was reported that the Israeli embassy in Nouakchott had been closed down and the ambassador ordered to leave the country.

Mauritania withdrew from the Economic Community of West African States (see p. 243), with effect from 31 December 2000, owing to decisions adopted by the organization at its summit in December 1999, including the integration of the armed forces of member states and the removal of internal border controls and tariffs.

Government

Following the *coup d'état* of 3 August 2005, a 16-member Military Council for Justice and Democracy (MCJD) assumed power. The Council stated that it would preside over the country for a transitional period of up to two years, following which democratic elections would be held. The 1991 Constitution and most of its institutions, including judicial bodies, and the Constitutional Council, were to be retained, as supplemented and amended by the charter of the MCJD, although the existing legislative organs were dissolved. A referendum held on 25 June 2006 approved various amendments to the Constitution: notably, the presidential term of office was to be reduced to five years (from six), renewable only once, a maximum age of 75 years was to be stipulated for presidential candidates, and the President was to be prohibited from holding any other official post, including the leadership of a political party. Elections to the new bicameral legislature (a 95-member National Assembly, elected by universal suffrage for five years, and a 56-member Senate, elected by municipal leaders) took place during November 2006–February 2007. A presidential election took place in March 2007. Sidi Mohamed Ould Cheikh Abdellahi was inaugurated as President on 19 April, assuming executive powers in place of the MCJD, which was disbanded, and a new Government was unveiled on 28 April. Following the coup of 6 August 2008, the High Council of State (HCS) which deposed Ould Cheikh Abdellahi issued a constitutional ordinance, which stated that it would exercise the powers of the President as defined by the Constitution, and granted the President of the HCS, Gen. Mohamed Ould Abdel Aziz, the power to appoint a Prime Minister, military officials and civil servants. All elections are conducted in the context of a multi-party political system.

For the purpose of local administration, Mauritania is divided into 13 wilayat (regions), comprising a total of 53 moughataa (counties), which are subdivided into 216 communes (districts).

Defence

As assessed at November 2008, the total armed forces were estimated to number 15,870 men: army 15,000, navy 620, air force 250. Full-time membership of paramilitary forces totalled about 5,000. Military service is by authorized conscription, and lasts for two years. The defence budget for 2007 was estimated at UM 4,800m.

MAURITANIA

Economic Affairs

In 2007, according to estimates by the World Bank, Mauritania's gross national income (GNI), measured at average 2005–07 prices, was US $2,636m., equivalent to $840 per head (or $2,010 on an international purchasing-power parity basis). During 2000–07, it was estimated, the population increased at an average annual rate of 2.8%, while gross domestic product (GDP) per head increased, in real terms, by an average of 1.9% per year. According to the World Bank, overall GDP increased, in real terms, at an average annual rate of 4.8% in 2000–07; GDP increased by 1.9% in 2007.

According to World Bank figures, agriculture (including forestry and fishing) contributed 12.5% of GDP in 2007. In 2005, according to FAO estimates, about 51.6% of the labour force were employed in the sector. Owing to the unsuitability of much of the land for crop cultivation, output of staple foods (millet, sorghum, rice and pulses) is insufficient for the country's needs. Livestock-rearing is the principal occupation of the rural population. Fishing, which in 2005 provided 18.5% of export earnings, supplies 5%–10% of annual GDP and a sizeable proportion of budgetary revenue, and also makes a significant contribution to domestic food requirements. During 2000–07, according to the World Bank, agricultural GDP increased by an average of 0.5% per year; the sector's GDP increased by 1.9% in 2007.

Industry (including mining, manufacturing, construction and power) provided 46.7% of GDP in 2007, according to World Bank figures. An estimated 8% of the labour force were employed in the industrial sector in 2000. During 2000–07 industrial GDP increased at an average annual rate of 3.4%; it increased by 1.9% in 2006.

Mining contributed 31.6% of GDP in 2006, according to provisional figures. The principal activity in this sector is the extraction of iron ore, exports of which contributed an estimated 41.7% of total merchandise export earnings in 2006. Gypsum, salt, gold and copper are also mined. Other exploitable mineral resources include diamonds, phosphates, sulphur, peat, manganese and uranium. In October 1999 highly valuable blue granite deposits were discovered in the north of the country. Many international companies were involved in offshore petroleum exploration in Mauritania in the early 2000s, with reserves at the offshore Shafr el Khanjar and Chinguetti fields estimated at 450m.–1,000m. barrels; production commenced at Chinguetti in February 2006. In September 2000 a five-year programme intended to accelerate the growth of the mining sector commenced, with a US $16.5m. loan from the World Bank. According to the IMF, the GDP of the mining sector increased by an average of 8.9% per year in 1996–2005. The sector's GDP increased by an estimated 0.6% in 2005.

The manufacturing sector contributed 18.0% of GDP in 2007, according to World Bank figures. Fish processing (which contributed 3.9% of GDP in 2002) is the most important activity. The processing of minerals (including imported petroleum) is also of some significance. According to the World Bank, manufacturing GDP declined at an average annual rate of 2.7% in 2000–07; however, it increased by 11.6% in 2006 and by 1.9% in 2007.

Mauritania began to utilize electricity generated at hydroelectric installations constructed under the auspices of the Organisation pour la mise en valeur du fleuve Sénégal (OMVS) in late 2002, thus reducing the country's dependence on power generated at thermal stations. Imports of petroleum products comprised 30.7% of the value of merchandise imports in 2007.

According to World Bank figures, the services sector contributed 40.7% of GDP in 2007, and engaged an estimated 25.8% of the labour force in 1994. The combined GDP of the services sector increased by an average rate of 7.0% per year during 2000–07. Services GDP increased by 1.9% in 2007.

In 2007 Mauritania recorded a visible trade surplus of an estimated US $22.9m.; however, there was a deficit of an estimated $321.3m. on the current account of the balance of payments. In 2002 the principal source of imports (20.8%) was France; other major suppliers were the Belgo-Luxembourg Economic Union, Spain and Germany. The principal markets for exports in that year were Italy (14.8%), France (14.4%), Spain and the Belgo-Luxembourg Economic Union. The principal exports in 2005 were iron ore, petroleum and fish. The principal imports in that year were petroleum products, food products and construction materials.

Mauritania's overall budget deficit for 2007 was UM 33,500m. Mauritania's total external debt was US $1,630m. at the end of 2006, of which $1,401m. was long-term public debt. In 1998 the cost of debt-servicing was equivalent to 14.2% of the value of exports of goods and services. The annual rate of inflation averaged 6.0% in 1996–2006; consumer prices increased by an average of 6.8% in 2007. The overall rate of unemployment in 2000 was 28.9%.

Mauritania is a member of the Islamic Development Bank (see p. 340), of the OMVS (see p. 428) and of the Union of the Arab Maghreb (see p. 429).

The exploitation, from the mid-2000s, of previously untapped petroleum reserves, principally at offshore locations, was expected to have a significant impact on Mauritania's economy, and in particular on export revenues, which had hitherto been largely dependent on fishing and on the extraction of iron ore. The first major offshore field, at Chinguetti, began production, operated by Woodside Petroleum (of Australia), although initial estimates of output of 75,000 barrels per day (b/d) were drastically reduced owing to technical constraints and average output in 2008 was just 12,000 b/d. Nevertheless, the rise in international petroleum prices was expected to result in increased revenue from that sector and further potential for growth was represented by ongoing onshore petroleum and natural gas drilling operations. In recent years government revenue has also been bolstered by the sale of fishing licences to foreign fleets. In July 2006 the European Union (EU) revised its fishing partnership with the Mauritanian Government. The terms of this agreement span six years and, in exchange for financial aid of some €516m., Mauritania continued to allow EU vessels to fish in its waters. Despite these positive developments, serious concern has been raised by the political instability in the country as a result of the bloodless coups of August 2005 and August 2008. The latter resulted in widespread international condemnation and the suspension of all non-humanitarian aid from France and the USA. The rapid rise in the cost of foodstuffs—Mauritania is obliged to import more than 50% of its staple food requirements—had precipitated social unrest from late 2007 and exacerbated the already precarious food security situation in Mauritania, which was further adversely effected by poor local harvests and a reduction in the availability of imports from other countries in the region. Although the global financial crisis was predicted to have further negative consequences for the Mauritanian economy, GDP growth of 5.7% was projected for 2008.

Education

Primary education, which is officially compulsory, begins at six years of age and lasts for six years. In 2006/07 total enrolment at primary schools included 80.4% of children in the relevant age-group (78.1% of boys; 82.9% of girls), according to UNESCO estimates. Secondary education begins at 12 years of age and lasts for six years, comprising two cycles of three years each. Total enrolment at public secondary schools in 2005/06 included only 15.6% of children in the appropriate age-group (16.3% of boys; 14.7% of girls), according to UNESCO estimates. In 2005/06 a total of 10,157 students were enrolled at Mauritania's four higher education institutions (including the Université de Nouakchott, which was opened in 1983). In 2005 spending on education represented 8.3% of total budgetary expenditure.

Public Holidays

2009: 1 January (New Year's Day), 9 March* (Mouloud, Birth of Muhammad), 1 May (Labour Day), 25 May (African Liberation Day, anniversary of the OAU's foundation), 10 July (Armed Forces Day), 19 July* (Leilat al-Meiraj, Ascension of Muhammad), 20 September* (Korité—Id al-Fitr, end of Ramadan), 27 November* (Tabaski—Id al-Adha, Feast of the Sacrifice), 28 November (Independence Day), 18 December* (Islamic New Year).

2010: 1 January (New Year's Day), 26 February* (Mouloud, Birth of Muhammad), 1 May (Labour Day), 25 May (African Liberation Day, anniversary of the OAU's foundation), 8 July* (Leilat al-Meiraj, Ascension of Muhammad), 10 July (Armed Forces Day), 10 September* (Korité—Id al-Fitr, end of Ramadan), 16 November* (Tabaski—Id al-Adha, Feast of the Sacrifice), 28 November (Independence Day), 7 December* (Islamic New Year).

* These holidays are determined by the Islamic lunar calendar and may vary by one or two days from the dates given.

Weights and Measures

The metric system is in force.

MAURITANIA

Statistical Survey

Source (unless otherwise stated): Office National de la Statistique, BP 240, Nouakchott; tel. 525-28-80; fax 525-51-70; e-mail webmaster@ons.mr; internet www.ons.mr.

Area and Population

AREA, POPULATION AND DENSITY

Area (sq km)	1,030,700*
Population (census results)	
5–20 April 1988	1,864,236†
1–15 November 2000‡	
Males	1,241,712
Females	1,266,447
Total	2,508,159
Population (official estimates)	
2006	3,162,338
2007	3,075,267
2008	3,065,721
Density (per sq km) at mid-2008	3.0

* 397,950 sq miles.
† Including an estimate of 224,095 for the nomad population.
‡ Figures include nomads, totalling 128,163 (males 66,007, females 62,156), enumerated during 10 March–20 April 2001.

Ethnic Groups (percentage of total, 1995): Moor 81.5; Wolof 6.8; Toucouleur 5.3; Sarakholé 2.8; Peul 1.1; Others 2.5 (Source: La Francophonie).

REGIONS
(census of November 2000)

Region	Area ('000 sq km)	Population*	Chief town
Hodh Ech Chargui	183	281,600	Néma
Hodh el Gharbi	53	212,156	Aïoun el Atrous
Assaba	37	242,265	Kiffa
Gorgol	14	242,711	Kaédi
Brakna	33	247,006	Aleg
Trarza	68	268,220	Rosso
Adrar	215	69,542	Atâr
Dakhlet-Nouadhibou	22	79,516	Nouadhibou
Tagant	95	76,620	Tidjikja
Guidimagha	10	177,707	Sélibaby
Tiris Zemmour	253	41,121	Zouïrât
Inchiri	47	11,500	Akjoujt
Nouakchott (district)	1	558,195	Nouakchott
Total	**1,030**	**2,580,159**	

* Including nomad population, enumerated during 10 March–20 April 2001.

PRINCIPAL TOWNS
(population at census of 2000*)

Nouakchott (capital)	558,195	Kiffa	32,716
Nouadhibou	72,337	Bougadoum	29,045
Rosso	48,922	Atâr	24,021
Boghé	37,531	Boutilimit	22,257
Adel Bagrou	36,007	Theiekane	22,041
Kaédi	34,227	Ghabou	21,700
Zouïrât	33,929	Mal	20,488

*With the exception of Nouakchott, figures refer to the population of communes (municipalities), and include nomads.

Mid-2007 (incl. suburbs, UN estimate): Nouakchott 673,000 (Source: UN, *World Urbanization Prospects: The 2007 Revision*).

BIRTHS AND DEATHS
(annual averages, UN estimates)

	1990–95	1995–2000	2000–05
Birth rate (per 1,000)	39.1	37.4	35.8
Death rate (per 1,000)	11.2	10.8	10.6

Source: UN, *World Population Prospects: The 2008 Revision*.

Life expectancy (years at birth, WHO estimates): 57.5 (males 55.1; females 60.0) in 2006 (Source: WHO, *World Health Statistics*).

ECONOMICALLY ACTIVE POPULATION
(census of 2000, persons aged 10 years and over, including nomads)

	Males	Females	Total
Agriculture, hunting, forestry and fishing	219,771	94,535	314,306
Mining and quarrying	5,520	249	5,769
Manufacturing	18,301	11,855	30,156
Electricity, gas and water	2,655	182	2,837
Construction	15,251	311	15,562
Trade, restaurants and hotels	83,733	24,799	108,532
Transport, storage and communications	17,225	691	17,916
Financing, insurance, real estate and business services	1,557	454	2,011
Community, social and personal services	72,137	26,583	98,720
Other and unspecified	33,350	22,608	55,958
Total	**469,500**	**182,267**	**651,767**

Mid-2005 (estimates in '000): Agriculture, etc. 705; Total labour force 1,367 (Source FAO).

Health and Welfare

KEY INDICATORS

Total fertility rate (children per woman, 2006)	4.5
Under-5 mortality rate (per 1,000 live births, 2006)	125
HIV/AIDS (% of persons aged 15–49, 2007)	0.8
Physicians (per 1,000 head, 2004)	0.11
Hospital beds (per 1,000 head, 2006)	0.40
Health expenditure (2006): US $ per head (PPP)	45
Health expenditure (2006): % of GDP	2.2
Health expenditure (2006): public (% of total)	68.6
Access to water (% of persons, 2006)	60
Access to sanitation (% of persons, 2006)	24
Human Development Index (2006): ranking	140
Human Development Index (2006): value	0.557

For sources and definitions, see explanatory note on p. vi.

Agriculture

PRINCIPAL CROPS
('000 metric tons)

	2005	2006	2007*
Rice, paddy	72.0	70.5	77.0
Maize	12.2	17.3	17.0
Sorghum	88.0†	83.8	58.0
Millet	0.9†	1.8	1.8
Peas, dry*	10.0	10.0	10.0
Cow peas, dry	8.0	8.0*	7.2
Beans, dry*	10.0	10.0	10.0
Dates	22.0	22.0*	22.0

* FAO estimate(s).
† Unofficial figure.

Aggregate production ('000 metric tons, may include official, semi-official or estimated data): Total cereals 175 in 2005, 175 in 2006, 155 in 2007; Total pulses 44 in 2005, 35 in 2006, 34 in 2007; Total roots and tubers 7 in 2005, 7 in 2006, 7 in 2007; Total vegetables (incl. melons) 4 in 2005, 4 in 2006, 4 in 2007; Total fruits (excl. melons) 25 in 2005, 22 in 2006, 22 in 2007.

Source: FAO.

MAURITANIA

LIVESTOCK
('000 head, year ending September, FAO estimates)

	2005	2006	2007
Cattle	1,692	1,692	1,692
Goats	5,600	5,600	5,600
Sheep	8,850	8,850	8,850
Asses, mules or hinnies	158	n.a.	n.a.
Horses	20	20	20
Camels	1,603	1,603	1,600
Chickens	4,200	4,200	4,200

Source: FAO.

LIVESTOCK PRODUCTS
('000 metric tons, FAO estimates)

	2005	2006	2007
Goat meat	14.6	13.8	13.8
Camel meat	24.0	24.0	24.0
Chicken meat	4.4	4.3	4.4
Camel milk	28.0	28.0	28.0
Cows' milk	122.5	120.8	120.8
Sheep's milk	96.3	96.3	96.3
Goats' milk	109.8	109.8	110.0
Hen eggs	5.3	5.3	5.3

Source: FAO.

Forestry

ROUNDWOOD REMOVALS
('000 cubic metres, excl. bark, FAO estimates)

	2005	2006	2007
Sawlogs, veneer logs and logs for sleepers	1	1	1
Other industrial wood	2	2	2
Fuel wood	1,623	1,663	1,707
Total	1,626	1,666	1,710

Source: FAO.

Fishing

('000 metric tons, live weight)

	2004	2005	2006
Freshwater fishes*	12.0	13.0	15.0
Sardinellas	19.2	30.5	14.6
European pilchard (sardine)	8.1	14.8	9.1
European anchovy	33.4	37.4	16.3
Jack and horse mackerels	51.5	79.4	28.2
Chub mackerel	23.7	14.3	2.9
Octopuses	12.1	14.6	12.1
Total catch (incl. others)*	270.7	304.9	193.2

* FAO estimates.
Source: FAO.

Mining

('000 metric tons)

	2004	2005	2006
Gypsum	38.9	43.3	45.2
Iron ore: gross weight	10,674	10,752	11,155
Iron ore: metal content*	6,900	7,000	7,250

* Estimates.
Source: US Geological Survey.

Industry

SELECTED PRODUCTS
('000 metric tons, unless otherwise indicated)

	2004	2005	2006
Cement*	300	300	374
Crude steel*	5	1	1
Electric energy (million kWh)	336.0	375.5	394.1

* Data from US Geological Survey.
2007: Electric energy 415.3m. kWh.

Finance

CURRENCY AND EXCHANGE RATES

Monetary Units
5 khoums = 1 ouguiya (UM).

Sterling, Dollar and Euro Equivalents (30 June 2008)
£1 sterling = 467.431 ouguiyas;
US $1 = 234.740 ouguiyas;
€1 = 370.044 ouguiyas;
1,000 ouguiyas = £2.14 = $4.26 = €2.70.

Average Exchange Rate (ouguiyas per US $)
2005   265.528
2006   268.600
2007   258.587

BUDGET
('000 million ouguiyas)

Revenue*	2003	2004	2005†
Tax revenue	44.9	59.2	76.0
Taxes on income and profits	12.0	16.3	26.6
Tax on business profits	6.6	9.3	15.7
Tax on wages and salaries	4.8	6.3	9.9
Taxes on goods and services	24.7	30.8	36.2
Value-added tax	16.6	21.8	26.7
Turnover taxes	3.3	2.7	2.8
Tax on petroleum products	2.4	2.8	2.5
Other excises	1.6	2.7	3.3
Taxes on international trade	7.3	11.1	10.8
Other current revenue	42.9	47.4	38.8
Fishing royalties and penalties	32.6	36.6	35.3
Revenue from public enterprises	2.1	4.2	0.6
Capital revenue	16.1	11.3	6.2
Other revenue (incl. special accounts)	8.3	6.6	2.8
Total	103.9	117.9	121.0

MAURITANIA

Expenditure‡	2003	2004	2005†
Current expenditure	105.0	96.7	126.7
Wages and salaries	16.0	17.2	22.4
Goods and services	35.3	36.9	60.6
Transfers and subsidies	26.3	9.6	8.7
Military expenditure	16.4	18.6	17.7
Interest on public debt	9.3	11.9	16.1
Capital expenditure	44.0	43.1	36.7
Domestically financed	25.4	24.6	21.4
Financed from abroad	18.6	18.5	15.2
Unidentified	9.2	9.6	0.0
Total	158.1	149.3	163.4

* Excluding grants received ('000 million ouguiyas): 15.7 in 2003; 12.5 in 2004; 10.3 (preliminary) in 2005.
† Preliminary figures.
‡ Excluding restructuring and net lending ('000 million ouguiyas): 1.4 in 2003; 0.2 in 2004; 2.9 in 2005 (preliminary).

Source: IMF, *Islamic Republic of Mauritania: Statistical Appendix* (July 2006).

2005 ('000 million ouguiyas, revised estimates): Total revenue 131.3; Total expenditure 166.1.

2006 ('000 million ouguiyas, estimates): Total revenue 406.0; Total expenditure 206.4.

2007 ('000 million ouguiyas): Total revenue 184.4; Total expenditure 217.9.

INTERNATIONAL RESERVES
(US $ million at 31 December)

	2005	2006	2007
Gold*	5.6	5.9	9.5
IMF special drawing rights	0.1	—	0.1
Foreign exchange	64.3	187.1	197.8
Total	70.0	193.0	207.4

* Valued at market-related prices.

Source: IMF, *International Financial Statistics*.

MONEY SUPPLY
(million ouguiyas at 31 December)

	2001	2002	2003
Currency outside banks	6,688	6,282	6,412
Demand deposits at deposit money banks	21,033	22,628	25,790
Total money (incl. others)	27,721	28,910	32,202

Source: IMF, *International Financial Statistics*.

COST OF LIVING
(Consumer Price Index; base: 2000 = 100)

	2005	2006	2007
Food (incl. beverages)	149.3	157.3	173.9
Clothing (incl. footwear)	131.1	143.5	149.7
Rent	134.7	145.1	157.3
All items (incl. others)	139.3	147.9	158.7

Source: ILO.

NATIONAL ACCOUNTS
(million ouguiyas at current prices, provisional)

Expenditure on the Gross Domestic Product

	2004	2005	2006
Government final consumption expenditure	75,814	95,719	178,763
Private final consumption expenditure	291,296	332,156	361,369
Gross fixed capital formation	198,790	284,601	244,292
Changes in stocks	−23,602	33,795	−44,936
Total domestic expenditure	542,298	746,271	739,488
Exports of goods and services	152,411	210,463	419,365
Less Imports of goods and services	312,424	481,539	422,588
GDP in purchasers' values	382,285	475,194	736,265
GDP at constant 1998 prices	293,481	305,900	483,780

Gross Domestic Product by Economic Activity

	2004	2005	2006
Agriculture, hunting, forestry and fishing	85,433	101,714	112,140
Mining and quarrying	47,264	67,361	218,918
Manufacturing	6,933	14,237	22,971
Electricity, gas and water	3,192	4,251	5,894
Construction	35,528	47,363	40,999
Trade, restaurants and hotels	47,134	54,963	81,423
Transport and communications	23,129	28,139	39,947
Public administration	47,728	56,962	98,551
Other services	54,552	65,787	72,438
Sub-total	350,893	440,777	693,281
Less Imputed bank service charge	9,062	10,587	6,947
GDP at factor cost	341,831	430,189	686,333
Indirect taxes, less subsidies	40,454	45,005	49,932
GDP in purchasers' values	382,285	475,194	736,265

BALANCE OF PAYMENTS
(US $ million)

	2006*	2007†
Exports of goods f.o.b.	1,366.6	1,454.4
Imports of goods f.o.b.	−1,167.0	−1,431.5
Trade balance	199.6	22.9
Exports of services	86.7	84.2
Imports of services	−406.3	−511.8
Balance on goods and services	−120.0	−404.7
Other income received	119.0	140.9
Other income paid	−193.3	−201.7
Balance on goods, services and income	−194.3	−465.5
Private unrequited transfers (net)	66.5	70.2
Official transfers	92.1	74.0
Current balance	−35.6	−321.3
Capital account (net)	1,107.2	50.8
Direct investment (net)	154.6	138.3
Official medium- and long-term loans	−835.7	79.3
Other capital	−168.3	48.0
Net errors and omissions	60.2	20.8
Overall balance	282.3	15.8

* Preliminary figures.
† Estimated figures.

Source: IMF, *Islamic Republic of Mauritania: 2008 Article IV Consultation and Third Review Under the Three-Year Arrangement Under the Poverty Reduction and Growth Facility—Staff Report; Staff Supplement; Public Information Notice and Press Release on the Executive Board Discussion; and Statement by the Executive Director for the Islamic Republic of Mauritania* (July 2008).

External Trade

PRINCIPAL COMMODITIES
('000 million ouguiyas)

Imports	2006	2007
Food products	66.5	83.2
Cosmetic chemical products	6.5	6.3
Petroleum products	77.9	113.3
Construction materials	21.0	31.3
Road vehicles and parts	20.1	26.0
Various equipment and appliances	52.5	68.1
Total (incl. others)	294.0	368.9

Exports	2006	2007
Iron ore	123.4	144.4
Fish	53.9	64.0
Petroleum	170.5	87.5
Total (incl. others)	347.8	345.9

PRINCIPAL TRADING PARTNERS
(US $ million)*

Imports c.i.f.	2000	2001	2002
Belgium-Luxembourg	32.9	31.4	36.8
France	94.5	89.2	86.9
Germany	17.2	21.3	23.2
Italy	21.9	22.1	17.6
Japan	9.2	9.8	16.2
Netherlands	10.0	10.7	14.0
Spain	21.8	21.5	27.9
United Kingdom	8.5	7.2	14.0
USA	9.6	16.0	14.4
Total (incl. others)	336.2	372.3	418.0

Exports c.i.f.	2000	2001	2002
Belgium-Luxembourg	30.8	28.9	33.9
France	63.5	50.7	47.6
Germany	13.2	20.8	35.7
Italy	47.4	51.0	48.8
Japan	53.0	27.1	21.0
Portugal	7.6	7.0	7.8
Spain	38.1	42.2	39.9
United Kingdom	5.4	5.4	1.5
Total (incl. others)	344.7	338.6	330.3

* Data are compiled on the basis of reporting by Mauritania's trading partners. Data detailing imports and exports of trade with developing and emerging countries were not available.

Source: IMF, *Islamic Republic of Mauritania: Statistical Appendix* (October 2003).

Transport

RAILWAYS

1984: Passengers carried 19,353; Passenger-km 7m.; Freight carried 9.1m. metric tons; Freight ton-km 6,142m.

Freight ton-km (million): 6,365 in 1985; 6,411 in 1986; 6,473 in 1987; 6,535 in 1988; 6,610 in 1989; 6,690 in 1990; 6,720 in 1991; 6,810 in 1992; 6,890 in 1993 (figures for 1988–93 are estimates) (Source: UN Economic Commission for Africa, *African Statistical Yearbook*).

ROAD TRAFFIC
(motor vehicles registered)

	2004	2005	2006
Passenger cars	6,033	6,040	6,182
Government vehicles	251	317	369
Specialist vehicles	413	542	504

SHIPPING
Merchant Fleet
(registered at 31 December)

	2005	2006	2007
Number of vessels	152	153	152
Total displacement ('000 grt)	51.9	51.9	51.5

Source: Lloyd's Register-Fairplay, *World Fleet Statistics*.

International Sea-borne Freight Traffic
(Port of Nouakchott, '000 metric tons)

	2005	2006	2007
Goods loaded	113.2	80.4	250.8
Goods unloaded	1,712.9	1,696.6	2,045.1

Source: Port Autonome de Nouakchott.

CIVIL AVIATION
(traffic on scheduled services)*

	2002	2003	2004
Kilometres flown (million)	1	1	1
Passengers carried ('000)	106	116	128
Passenger-km (million)	45	49	56
Total ton-km (million)	4	5	5

* Including an apportionment of the traffic of Air Afrique.

Source: UN, *Statistical Yearbook*.

Tourism

Tourist arrivals (estimates, '000): 24 in 1999.

Receipts from tourism (US $ million, excl. passenger transport): 28 in 1999 (Source: World Tourism Organization).

MAURITANIA

Communications Media

	2004	2005	2006
Telephones ('000 main lines in use)	39.0	41.0	34.9
Mobile cellular telephones ('000 subscribers)	522.4	745.6	1,060.1
Personal computers ('000 in use)	42	42	n.a.
Internet users ('000)	14	20	30
Broadband subscribers	—	200	1,000

Mobile cellular telephones ('000 subscribers): 1,300.0 in 2007.

Television receivers ('000 in use): 247 in 1999.

Radio receivers ('000 in use): 570 in 1997.

Facsimile machines (number in use): 3,300 in 1999.

Daily newspapers: Number 2; Estimated average circulation ('000 copies) 12 in 1996; 3 in 2004.

Sources: UNESCO, *Statistical Yearbook*; UN, *Statistical Yearbook*; International Telecommunication Union.

Education

(2005/06, unless otherwise indicated)

	Institutions	Teachers	Males	Females	Total
Pre-primary	n.a.	251*	n.a.	n.a.	4,856*
Primary	2,676†	11,252	224,796	232,174	456,970
Secondary	n.a.	3,777	54,459	44,487	98,946
Tertiary	4‡	353	7,552	2,605	10,157

* 2004/05.
† 1998/99.
‡ 1995/96.

Adult literacy rate (UNESCO estimates): 55.8% (males 63.3%; females 48.3%) in 2007 (Source: UNESCO Institute for Statistics).

Sources: mainly UNESCO Institute for Statistics and Ministry of National Education, Nouakchott.

Directory

While no longer an official language under the terms of the 1991 Constitution (see below), French is still widely used in Mauritania, especially in the commercial sector. Many organizations are therefore listed under their French names, by which they are generally known.

The Constitution

The 1991 Constitution was supplemented and partially replaced by a Constitutional Charter introduced by the self-styled Military Council for Justice and Democracy (MCJD) which assumed power in August 2005. Those provisions of the Constitution pertaining to the role of Islam, individual and collective freedoms and the prerogatives of the State were to remain in force, while certain judicial organs (namely: the High Council of Magistrates; courts and tribunals; the High Council of Islam; the Audit Court; and the Constitutional Council) were to continue to function. A number of the legislative powers previously held by a bicameral legislature (which was abolished) were transferred to the MCJD, which was also to assume executive powers. A referendum held on 25 June 2006 approved various amendments to the Constitution: notably, the presidential term of office was to be reduced to five years, renewable only once, a maximum age of 75 years was to be stipulated for presidential candidates, and the President was to be prohibited from holding any other official post, including the leadership of a political party. Elections to a new bicameral legislature were held during November 2006–February 2007, while a presidential election was held over two rounds in March. Sidi Mohamed Ould Cheikh Abdellahi was inaugurated as President on 19 April, assuming executive powers in place of the MCJD, which was disbanded, and a new Government was unveiled on 28 April. Following the coup of 6 August 2008, the High Council of State (HCS) which deposed Ould Cheikh Abdellahi issued a constitutional ordinance, which stated that it would exercise the powers of the President as defined by the Constitution, and granted the President of the HCS, Gen. Mohamed Ould Abdel Aziz, the power to appoint a Prime Minister, military officials and civil servants.

The Constitution states that the official language is Arabic, and that the national languages are Arabic, Pular, Wolof and Solinké.

The Government

HEAD OF STATE

Acting President of the High Council of State: Bâ Mamadou dit M'Baré (appointed 15 April 2009).

COUNCIL OF MINISTERS
(April 2009)

Prime Minister: Moulaye Ould Mohamed Laghdaf.
Minister of Justice: Ahmedou Tidjane Bal.
Minister of Foreign Affairs and Co-operation: Mohamed Mahmoud Ould Mohamedou.
Minister of National Defence: Mohamed Mahmoud Ould Mohamed Lemine.
Minister of the Interior and Decentralization: Mohamed Ould Maaouya.
Minister of Economic Affairs and Development: Sidi Ould Tah.
Minister of Finance: Sid'Ahmed Ould Raiss.
Minister of National Education: Ahmed Ould Bah.
Minister of Islamic Affairs and Original Education: Othmane Ould Cheikh Ahmed Aboul Maali.
Minister of the Civil Service, Employment and Vocational Training: Hacen Ould Limam Ould Amar Jowda.
Minister of Health: Mohamed Abdellahi Ould Siyam.
Minister of Petroleum and Energy: Die Ould Zeine.
Minister of Fisheries and the Maritime Economy: Hacenna Ould Ely.
Minister of Trade, Handicrafts and Tourism: Bamba Ould Dermane.
Minister of Housing, Urban Development and Land Settlement: Sy Adama.
Minister of Rural Development: Messaouda Mint Baham.
Minister of Equipment and Transport: Camara Moussa Seydi Boubou.
Minister of Water Resources and Sanitation: Mohamed Lemine Ould Aboye.
Minister of Industry and Mines: Mohamed Abdellahi Ould Oudaa.
Minister of Culture, Youth and Sports: Sidi Ould Samba.
Minister of Communication and Relations with Parliament: Mohamed Ould Mohamed Abderrahmane Ould Moine.
Minister of Social Affairs, Childhood and Families: Selama Mint Cheikhna Ould Lemrabott.
Minister-delegate to the Prime Minister, in charge of the Environment and Sustainable Development: Mohamed Ould Ahmed Salem.
Secretary of State, responsible for Modernization, Administration and Information and Communications Technology: Sidi Ould Mayouf.
Secretary of State, responsible for Maghreb Affairs: Mohamed Abderrahmane Ould Mohamed Ahmed.
Minister-delegate to the Ministry of Foreign Affairs and Co-operation, in charge of the Union of the Arab Maghreb: Mekfoula Mint Agatt.
Secretary-General of the Government: Bâ Ousmane.
Commissioner for Human Rights, Humanitarian Action and Relations with Civil Society: Bâ Mohamed Lemine Ould Dadde.
Commissioner for Food Security: Mohamed Ould Mohamedou.
Commissioner for the Promotion of Investments: Bâ Houdou.

MAURITANIA

MINISTRIES

Office of the President: BP 184, Nouakchott; tel. and fax 525-26-36.

Office of the Prime Minister: BP 237, Nouakchott; tel. 525-33-37.

Ministry of Capital Works and Transport: BP 237, Nouakchott; tel. 525-33-37.

Ministry of the Civil Service and Employment: BP 193, Nouakchott; tel. and fax 525-84-10.

Ministry of Communication: Nouakchott.

Ministry of Culture, Youth and Sports: BP 223, Nouakchott; tel. 525-11-30.

Ministry of Economic Affairs and Development: 303 Ilot C, BP 5150, Nouakchott; tel. 525-16-12; fax 525-51-10; e-mail nfomaed@mauritania.mr; internet www.maed.gov.mr.

Ministry of Energy and Petroleum: Nouakchott; tel. 525-71-40.

Ministry of Finance: BP 181, Nouakchott; tel. 525-20-20.

Ministry of Fisheries and the Maritime Economy: BP 137, Nouakchott; tel. 525-46-07; fax 525-31-46; e-mail ministre@mpem.mr; internet www.mpem.mr.

Ministry of Foreign Affairs and Co-operation: BP 230, Nouakchott; tel. 525-26-82; fax 525-28-60.

Ministry of National Education: BP 387, Nouakchott; tel. 525-12-37; fax 525-12-22.

Ministry of Health and Social Affairs: BP 177, Nouakchott; tel. 525-20-52; fax 525-22-68.

Ministry of Higher Education and Scientific Research: Nouakchott.

Ministry of the Interior, Posts and Telecommunications: BP 195, Nouakchott; tel. 525-36-61; fax 525-36-40; e-mail paddec@mauritania.mr.

Ministry of Justice: BP 350, Nouakchott; tel. 525-10-83; fax 525-70-02.

Ministry of Mines and Industry: BP 199, Nouakchott; tel. 525-30-83; fax 525-69-37; e-mail mmi@mauritania.mr.

Ministry of Rural Development and the Environment: BP 366, Nouakchott; tel. 525-15-00; fax 525-74-75.

Ministry of Trade, Crafts and Tourism: BP 182, Nouakchott; tel. 525-35-72; fax 525-76-71.

Ministry of Water Resources: BP 4913, Nouakchott; tel. 525-71-44; fax 529-42-87; e-mail saadouebih@yahoo.fr.

Office of the Secretary-General of the Government: BP 184, Nouakchott.

President and Legislature

PRESIDENT

Presidential Election, First Round, 11 March 2007

Candidate	Votes	% of votes
Sidi Mohamed Ould Cheikh Abdellahi	183,743	24.79
Ahmed Ould Daddah	153,242	20.68
Zeine Ould Zeidane	113,194	15.27
Messaoud Ould Boulkheir	72,611	9.80
Ibrahim Moctar Sarr	58,818	7.94
Saleh Ould Mohamedou Ould Hanana	56,718	7.65
Mohamed Ould Maouloud	30,265	4.08
Dahane Ould Ahmed Mahmoud	15,316	2.07
Others	57,159	7.71
Total	**741,066**	**100.00**

Presidential Election, Second Round, 25 March 2007

Candidate	Votes	% of votes
Sidi Mohamed Ould Cheikh Abdellahi	373,519	52.85
Ahmed Ould Daddah	333,184	47.15
Total	**706,703**	**100.00**

Al-Jamiya al-Wataniyah
(National Assembly)

ave de l'Indépendance, BP 185, Nouakchott; tel. 525-11-30; fax 525-70-78; internet www.mauritania.mr/assemblee.

President: Messoud Ould Boulkheir.

General Election, 19 November and 3 December 2006

Party	Constituency seats	National list seats	Total seats
Rally of Democratic Forces	12	3	15
Union of Progressive Forces	7	1	8
Republican Party for Democracy and Renewal	5	2	7
Popular Progressive Alliance	4	1	5
Centrist Reformists	2	2	4
Mauritanian Party for Union and Change—Hatem	3	1	4
Union for Democracy and Progress	2	1	3
Rally for Democracy and Unity	2	1	3
Democratic Renewal	1	1	2
Alternative	1	—	1
Union of the Democratic Centre	1	—	1
Popular Front	—	1	1
Independents	41	—	41
Total	**81**	**14**	**95**

Majlis ash-Shuyukh
(Senate)

ave de l'Indépendance, BP 5838, Nouakchott; tel. 525-68-77; fax 525-73-73; internet www.senat.mr.

President: Bâ Mamadou dit M'Baré.

Election, 21 January and 4 February 2007

Party	Seats
Independents	34
Coalition of Forces for Democratic Change	15
Republican Party for Democracy and Renewal	3
Total*	**52**

*The total number of seats in the Senate is 56. The result from one constituency was annulled by the Constitutional Council and the remaining three seats, reserved for representatives of the Mauritanian diaspora, were yet to be allocated.

Election Commission

National Independent Electoral Commission: Nouakchott; 15 mems; Pres. Cheikh Saad Bouh Kamara.

Advisory Council

Economic and Social Council: Nouakchott.

Political Organizations

At the time of the legislative elections held in November–December 2006 some 35 political parties were legally recognized in Mauritania. Following the coup of August 2008 several new political parties and coalitions were established in preparation for the presidential election scheduled to be held in June 2009.

Alliance for Justice and Democracy (AJD): Nouakchott; Leader Cissé Amadou Chiekhou.

Alternative (Al-Badil): Nouakchott; f. 2006; Leader Mohamed Yehdhih Ould Moktar El Hassen.

Centrist Reformists: Nouakchott; f. 2006; mem. of Coalition of Forces for Democratic Change, formed in advance of legislative and local elections in 2006; moderate Islamist grouping; Co-ordinator Mohamed Jemil Ould Mansour.

Democratic Renewal: Nouakchott; f. 2005; mem. of Coalition of Forces for Democratic Change, formed in advance of legislative and local elections in 2006; Pres. Moustapha Ould Abeiderrahmane.

Mauritanian African Liberation Forces—Renovation (MALF—Renovation): Nouakchott; tel. 228-77-40; internet www.flam-renovation.org; f. 2006 in split from clandestine, exiled, Mauritanian African Liberation Forces; represents interests of Afro- (Black) Mauritanians; mem. of Coalition of Forces for Democratic Change, formed in advance of legislative and local elections in 2006; Leader Mamadou Bocar Bâ.

Mauritanian Labour Party: Nouakchott; f. 2001; Leader Mohamed El Hafedh Ould Denna.

MAURITANIA

Mauritanian Party for Renewal and Agreement: Nouakchott; f. 2001; Leader MOULAY EL-HASSEN OULD JIYID.

Mauritanian Party for the Defence of the Environment (MPDE—The Greens): Nouakchott; internet pmde.hautetfort.com; ecologist; mem. of Bloc of Parties for Change, formed in advance of legislative and local elections in 2006; Pres. MOHAMED OULD SIDI OULD DELLAHI.

Mauritanian Party for Union and Change—Hatem: Nouakchott; f. 2005 by leadership of the fmr prohibited Knights of Change militia and reformist elements of the fmr ruling Democratic and Social Republican Party; mem. of Coalition of Forces for Democratic Change, formed in advance of legislative and local elections in 2006; Pres. SALEH OULD HNANA; Sec.-Gen. ABDERAHMANE OULD MINI.

Mauritanian People's Rally Party (MPRP): Nouakchott; f. 2009 by parliamentary deputies in support of ruling military junta; Leader Dr LOULEID OULD WEDAD.

National Front for the Defence of Democracy (NFDD): f. 2008; coalition of parties opposed to the military coup in August 2008; Leader ABDEL KOUDOUSSE OULD ABDEIDNA.

National Party for Democracy and Development (NPDD): Nouakchott; Leader YAHYA OULD EL WAGHEF.

Popular Progressive Alliance (APP): Nouakchott; internet www.app-mauritanie.org; f. 1991; absorbed Convention for Change (the successor to the proscribed Action for Change, which sought to represent the interests of Harratin—black Moors who had frmly been slaves) in 2003; mem. of Coalition of Forces for Democratic Change, formed in advance of legislative and local elections in 2006; Pres. MESSAOUD OULD BOULKHAR.

Tawassoul Party: moderate Islamist party; Leader JEMIL OULD MANSOUR.

Union of Progressive Forces (UPF) (Ittihad Quwa al-Taqaddum): Nouakchott; e-mail ufpweb2@yahoo.fr; internet www.ufpweb.org; tel. 529-32-66; fax 524-35-86; e-mail infos@ufpweb.org; f. 2000, following the enforced dissolution of the fmr Union of Democratic Forces—New Era, which it had existed as a faction thereof since 1998; mem. of Coalition of Forces for Democratic Change, formed in advance of legislative and local elections in 2006; Pres. MOHAMED OULD MAOULOUD; Sec.-Gen. MOHAMED EL MOUSTAPHA OULD BEDREDDINE.

National Rally for Reform and Development (NRRD) (Tawassoul): f. 2007; Islamist; Leader MOHAMED JEMIL OULD MANSOUR.

Party for Liberty, Equality and Justice (PLEJ): Nouakchott; mem. of Bloc of Parties for Change, formed in advance of legislative and local elections in 2006; Pres. MAMADOU ALASSANE BÂ.

Popular Front (FP): Nouakchott; f. 1998; social-liberal; mem. of Coalition of Forces for Democratic Change, formed in advance of legislative and local elections in 2006; Leader MOHAMED LEMINE CH'BIH OULD CHEIKH MELAININE.

Rally for Democracy and Unity (RDU): Nouakchott; f. 1991; supported regime of fmr Pres. Taya; Chair. AHMED OULD SIDI BABA.

Rally of Democratic Forces (RDF): Ilot K, 120, BP 4986, Nouakchott; tel. 525-67-46; fax 525-65-70; e-mail info@rfd-mauritanie.org; internet www.rfd-mauritanie.org; f. 2001 by fmr mems of the officially dissolved Union of Democratic Forces—New Era (f. 1991); mem. of Coalition of Forces for Democratic Change, formed in advance of legislative and local elections in 2006; Pres. AHMED OULD DADDAH.

Republican Party for Democracy and Renewal (RPDR): ZRB, Tevragh Zeina, Nouakchott; tel. 529-18-36; fax 529-18-00; e-mail info@prdr.mr; internet www.prdr.mr; f. 2006 to replace Democratic and Social Republican Party, the fmr ruling party, prior to *coup d'état* of August 2005; Leader SIDI MOHAMED OULD MED VALL DIT GHRINY.

Reward (Sawab): Nouakchott; f. 2004; social democratic; Chair. of Central Council MOHAMED MAHMOUD OULD GHOULMA; Pres. Dr CHEIKH OULD SIDI OULD HANENA.

Social Democratic Union: Nouakchott; Pres. ISSELMOU OULD HANNEFI.

Union for Democracy and Progress (UDP): Ilot V, 70, Tevragh Zeina, BP 816, Nouakchott; tel. 525-52-89; fax 525-29-95; f. 1993; Pres. NAHA HAMDI MINT.

Union for the Republic: Nouakchott; f. 2009 ahead of presidential election scheduled for June; Chair. Gen. MOHAMED OULD ABDEL AZIZ.

Union of Democratic Youth (UDY): f. 2008; promotes patriotism and moderate Islamic values, opposes extremism; Pres. JEDDOU OULD AHMAD.

Union of the Democratic Centre (UDC): Nouakchott; f. 2005 by fmr mems of the Democratic and Social Republican Party, the fmr ruling party; Pres. CHEIKH SID'AHMED OULD BABA.

Unauthorized, but influential, is the Islamic **Ummah Party** (the Constitution prohibits the operation of religious political organizations), founded in 1991 and led by Imam SIDI YAHYA, and the Baathist **National Vanguard Party (Taliaa)**, which was officially dissolved by the Government in 1999 and is led by AHMEDOU OULD BABANA. The clandestine **Mauritanian African Liberation Forces (MALF)** was founded in 1983 in Senegal to represent Afro-Mauritanians (Point d'ébullition, BP 5811, Dakar-Fann, Senegal; tel. +221 822-80-77; e-mail ba_demba@yahoo.fr; internet members.lycos.co.uk/flamnet; Pres. SAMBA THIAM); a faction broke away from this organization and returned to Mauritania in early 2006, forming the Mauritanian African Liberation Forces—Renovation. A further group based in exile is the **Arab-African Salvation Front against Slavery, Racism and Tribalism—AASF** (e-mail faas@caramail.com; internet membres.lycos.fr/faas). In August 2007 a further 18 new parties were registered: included were an Islamist party, the **National Rally for Reform and Development**, and two parties led by women, the **National Party for Development**, led by SAHLA BINT AHMAD ZAYID, and the **Mauritanian Hope Party**, led by TAHI BINT LAHBIB.

Diplomatic Representation

EMBASSIES IN MAURITANIA

Algeria: Ilot A, Tevragh Zeina, BP 625, Nouakchott; tel. 525-35-69; fax 525-47-77; Ambassador CHEKIB RACHID EL-KAID.

China, People's Republic: rue 42-133, Tevragh Zeina, BP 257, Nouakchott; tel. 525-20-70; fax 525-24-62; e-mail chinaemb_mr@mfa.gov.cn; internet mr.china-embassy.org; Ambassador ZHANG XUN.

Congo, Democratic Republic: Tevragh Zeina, BP 5714, Nouakchott; tel. 525-46-12; fax 525-50-53; e-mail ambardc.rim@caramail.com; Chargé d'affaires a.i. TSHIBASU MFUAD.

Egypt: Villa no. 468, Tevragh Zeina, BP 176, Nouakchott; tel. 525-21-92; fax 525-33-84; Ambassador BAHAA EDDIN MOKHTAR MOWAFI.

France: rue Ahmed Ould Hamed, Tevragh Zeina, BP 231, Nouakchott; tel. 529-96-99; fax 529-69-38; e-mail ambafrance.nouakchott-amba@diplomatie.gouv.fr; internet www.france-mauritanie.mr; Ambassador MICHEL VENDEPOORTER.

Germany: Tevragh Zeina, BP 372, Nouakchott; tel. 525-17-29; fax 525-17-22; e-mail amb-allemagne@toptechnology.mr; Ambassador EBERHARD SCHANZE.

Korea, Democratic People's Republic: Nouakchott; Ambassador PAK HO IL.

Kuwait: Tevragh Zeina, BP 345, Nouakchott; tel. 525-33-05; fax 525-41-45; Ambassador TALAL MANSOUR AL-KOURAVI.

Libya: BP 673, Nouakchott; tel. 525-52-02; fax 525-50-53; Chargé d'affaires ISSA ALI EL-VENAS.

Mali: Tevragh Zeina, BP 5371, Nouakchott; tel. 525-40-81; fax 525-40-83; e-mail ambmali@hotmail.com; Chargé d'affaires SOULEIMANE KONÉ.

Morocco: 569 ave de Gaulle, Tevragh Zeina, BP 621, Nouakchott; tel. 525-14-11; fax 529-72-80; e-mail sifmanktt@mauritel.mr; Ambassador ABDERRAHMANE BENOMAR.

Nigeria: Ilot P9, BP 367, Nouakchott; tel. 525-23-04; fax 525-23-14; Ambassador Alhaji BALA MOHAMED SANI.

Qatar: BP 609, Nouakchott; tel. 525-23-99; fax 525-68-87; e-mail nouakchoti@mofa.gov.qa; Ambassador MOHAMMED KURDI TALEB AL-MERRI.

Russia: rue Abu Bakr, BP 221, Nouakchott; tel. 525-19-73; fax 525-52-96; e-mail ambruss@opt.mr; Ambassador LEONID V. ROGOV.

Saudi Arabia: Las Balmas, Zinat, BP 498, Nouakchott; tel. 525-26-33; fax 525-29-49; e-mail mremb@mofa.gov.sa; Ambassador SAOUD BEN ABDEL AZIZ EL-JABIRI.

Senegal: Villa 500, Tevragh Zeina, BP 2511, Nouakchott; tel. 525-72-90; fax 525-72-91; Ambassador MAHMOUDOU CHEIKH KANE.

South Africa: Hotel Tfeila, Mezzanine Floor, Salon el-Waha, ave Charles de Gaulle, BP 2006, Nouakchott; tel. 524-55-90; fax 524-55-91; e-mail nouakchott@foreign.gov.za; Ambassador SEGOGWANE KOTANE.

Spain: BP 232, Nouakchott; tel. 525-20-80; fax 525-40-88; e-mail emb.nouakchott@mae.es; Ambassador ALEJANDRO POLANCO MATA.

Syria: Tevragh Zeina, BP 288, Nouakchott; tel. 525-27-54; fax 525-45-00; Chargé d'affaires M. DABALLAH.

Tunisia: BP 631, Nouakchott; tel. 525-28-71; fax 525-18-27; Ambassador ABDEL WEHAB JEMAL.

United Arab Emirates: Tafarugh Zeena Quarter, ZRA 742 bis, Nouakchott; tel. 525-10-98; fax 525-09-92; e-mail embeau@mauritel.mr; Ambassador ABDULLAH MOHAMMED AT-TAKAWI.

USA: rue Abdallaye, BP 222, Nouakchott; tel. 525-26-60; fax 525-15-92; e-mail tayebho@state.gov; internet mauritania.usembassy.gov; Ambassador MARK M. BOULWARE.

MAURITANIA

Yemen: Tevragh Zeina, BP 4689, Nouakchott; tel. 525-55-91; fax 525-56-39.

Judicial System

The Code of Law was promulgated in 1961 and subsequently modified to incorporate Islamic institutions and practices. The main courts comprise three courts of appeal, 10 regional tribunals, two labour tribunals and 53 departmental civil courts. A revenue court has jurisdiction in financial matters. The members of the High Court of Justice are elected by the National Assembly and the Senate.

Shari'a (Islamic) law was introduced in February 1980. A special Islamic court was established in March of that year, presided over by a magistrate of Islamic law, assisted by two counsellors and two ulemas (Muslim jurists and interpreters of the Koran). A five-member High Council of Islam, appointed by the President, advises upon the conformity of national legislation to religious precepts, at the request of the President.

Audit Court (Cour des Comptes): Nouakchott; audits all govt institutions; Pres. SOW ADAMA SAMBA.

Constitutional Council: f. 1992; includes six mems, three nominated by the Head of State and three designated by the Presidents of the Senate and National Assembly; Pres. ABDOULLAH OULD ELY SALEM; Sec.-Gen. MOHAMED OULD M'REIZIG.

High Council of Islam (al-Majlis al-Islamiya al-A'la'): Nouakchott; f. 1992; Pres. AHMED OULD NEINI.

High Court of Justice: Nouakchott; f. 1961; comprises an equal number of appointees elected from their membership by the National Assembly and the Senate, following each partial or general renewal of those legislative bodies; competent to try the President of the Republic in case of high treason, and the Prime Minister and members of the Government in case of conspiracy against the state.

Supreme Court: BP 201, Palais de Justice, Nouakchott; tel. and fax 525-67-40; f. 1961; comprises an administrative chamber, two civil and social chambers, a commercial chamber and a criminal chamber; Pres. MOHAMED OULD HANNANI.

Religion

ISLAM

Islam is the official religion, and the population are almost entirely Muslims of the Malekite rite. The major religious groups are the Tijaniya and the Qadiriya. Chinguetti, in the region of Adrar, is the seventh Holy Place in Islam. A High Council of Islam supervises the conformity of legislation to Muslim orthodoxy.

CHRISTIANITY

Roman Catholic Church

Mauritania comprises the single diocese of Nouakchott, directly responsible to the Holy See. The Bishop participates in the Bishops' Conference of Senegal, Mauritania, Cape Verde and Guinea-Bissau, based in Dakar, Senegal. At 31 December 2006 there were an estimated 4,500 adherents, mainly non-nationals, in the country.

Bishop of Nouakchott: Most Rev. MARTIN ALBERT HAPPE, Evêché, BP 5377, Nouakchott; tel. 525-04-27; fax 525-37-51; e-mail mgr-martin-happe@mauritel.mr.

The Press

Of some 400 journals officially registered in Mauritania in mid-2004, some 30 were regular, widely available publications, of which the following were among the most important:

Al-Akhbar: BP 5346, Nouakchott; tel. 525-08-94; fax 525-37-57; e-mail fr.redaction@alakhbar.info; internet fr.alakhbar.info; f. 1995; weekly; Arabic.

Al-Qalam/Le Calame: BP 1059, Nouakchott; tel. 529-02-34; fax 525-75-55; e-mail calame@compunet.mr; internet www.calame.8k.com; f. 1994; weekly; Arabic and French; independent; Editors-in-Chief RIYAD OULD AHMED EL-HADI (Arabic edn), HINDOU MINT AININA (French edn).

Le Carrefour: Nouakchott; Dir MOUSSA OULD SAMBA SY.

Châab: BP 371, Nouakchott; tel. 525-29-40; fax 525-85-47; e-mail chaabrim@gmail.com; f. 1975; daily; Arabic; also publ. in French Horizons; publ. by Agence Mauritanienne de l'Information; Dir-Gen. MOHAMED EL-HAFED OULD MAHAM.

Challenge: BP 1346, Nouakchott; tel. and fax 529-06-26.

Ech-tary: BP 1059, Nouakchott; tel. 525-50-65; fortnightly; Arabic; satirical.

L'Essor: BP 5310, Nouakchott; tel. 630-21-68; fax 525-88-90; e-mail sidiel2000@yahoo.fr; monthly; the environment and the economy; Dir SIDI EL-MOCTAR CHEÏGUER; circ. 2,500.

El-Anba: BP 3901, Nouakchott; tel. and fax 525-99-27.

L'Eveil-Hebdo: BP 587, Nouakchott; tel. 525-67-14; fax 525-87-54; e-mail symoudou@yahoo.fr; f. 1991; weekly; independent; Dir of Publication SY MAMADOU.

Inimich al-Watan: Nouakchott; independent; Arabic; Dir of Publication MOHAMED OULD ELKORY.

Journal Officel: BP 188, Nouakchott; tel. 525-33-37; fax 525-34-74; fortnightly.

Maghreb Hebdo: BP 5266, Nouakchott; tel. 525-98-10; fax 525-98-11; f. 1994; weekly; Dir KHATTRI OULD DIÈ.

Nouakchott-Info: Immeuble Abbas, Tevragh Zeina, BP 1905, Nouakchott; tel. 525-02-71; fax 525-54-84; e-mail aboulmaaly@yahoo.com; internet www.ani.mr; f. 1995; daily; independent; Arabic and French; Dir of Publication and Editor-in-Chief MOHAMED MAHMOUD ABOUL MAALY.

L'Opinion Libre: Nouakchott; weekly; Editor ELY OULD NAFA.

Rajoul Echarée: Nouakchott; e-mail rajoul_echaree@toptechnology.mr; weekly; independent; Arabic; Dir SIDI MOHAMED OULD YOUNÈS.

Ar-Rayah (The Banner): Nouakchott; e-mail team@rayah.info; internet www.rayah.info; f. 1997; independent; weekly; pro-Islamist; publication prohibited in May 2003; Editor AHMED OULD WEDIAA.

Le Rénovateur: Nouakchott; every 2 months; f. 2001; Editor Chiekh TIDIANE DIA.

La Tribune: BP 6227, Nouakchott; tel. 525-44-92; fax 525-02-09; Editor-in-Chief MOHAMMED FALL OULD OUMÈRE.

NEWS AGENCY

Agence Mauritanienne de l'Information (AMI): BP 371, Nouakchott; tel. 525-29-40; fax 525-45-87; e-mail ami@mauritania.mr; internet www.ami.mr; fmrly Agence Mauritanienne de Presse; state-controlled; news and information services in Arabic and French; Dir MOHAMED CHEIKH OULD SIDI MOHAMED.

Publishers

Imprimerie Commerciale et Administrative de Mauritanie: BP 164, Nouakchott; textbooks, educational.

Imprimerie Nationale: BP 618, Nouakchott; tel. 525-44-38; fax 525-44-37; f. 1978; state-owned; Pres. RACHID OULD SALEH; Man. Dir ISSIMOU MAHJOUB.

GOVERNMENT PUBLISHING HOUSE

Société Nationale d'Impression: BP 618, Nouakchott; Pres. MOUSTAPHA SALECK OULD AHMED BRIHIM.

Broadcasting and Communications

TELECOMMUNICATIONS

Mauritel: BP 7000, Nouakchott; tel. 525-23-40; fax 525-17-00; e-mail webmaster@mauritel.mr; internet www.mauritel.mr; fmrly Société Mauritanienne des Télécommunications; 46% state-owned, 34% owned by Maroc Télécom (Morocco), 20% owned by Abdallahi Ould Noueigued group; Dir Col AHMEDOUL OULD MOHAMED EL KORY

El-Jawel Mauritel Mobiles: ave du Roi Fayçal, BP 5920, Nouakchott; tel. 529-80-80; fax 529-81-81; e-mail mminfos@mauritel.mr; internet www.mauritelmobiles.mr; f. 2000; operates a mobile cellular telephone network (El-Jawal) in Nouakchott and more than 27 other locations and three highways nation-wide; more than 350,000 subscribers (2005).

Société Mauritano-Tunisienne de Télécommunications (Mattel): BP 3668, Nouakchott; tel. 529-53-54; fax 529-81-03; e-mail mattel@mattel.mr; internet www.mattel.mr; f. 2000; privately owned Mauritanian-Tunisian co; operates mobile cellular communications network in Nouakchott and more than 10 other locations nation-wide.

BROADCASTING

Radio

Radio de Mauritanie (RM): ave Gamal Abdel Nasser, BP 200, Nouakchott; tel. and fax 525-21-64; e-mail rm@radiomauritanie.com; f. 1958; state-controlled; five transmitters; radio broadcasts in Arabic, French, Sarakolé, Toucouleur and Wolof; Dir SID BRAHIM OULD HAMDINOU.

Television

Télévision de Mauritanie (TVM): BP 5522, Nouakchott; tel. 525-40-67; fax 525-40-69; e-mail dg@tvmsat.mr; internet www.tvm.mr; f. 1982; Dir-Gen. HAMOUD OULD M'HAMED.

Finance

(cap. = capital; res = reserves; dep. = deposits; m. = million; br(s).= branch(es); amounts in ouguiyas)

BANKING

Central Bank

Banque Centrale de Mauritanie (BCM): ave de l'Indépendance, BP 623, Nouakchott; tel. 525-22-06; fax 525-27-59; e-mail info@bcm.mr; internet www.bcm.mr; f. 1973; bank of issue; cap. 200m., res 1,514m., dep. 108,233m. (2006); Gov. KANE OUSMANE; 4 brs.

Commercial Banks

Banque El Amana (BADH): BP 5559, Nouakchott; tel. 525-34-90; fax 525-34-95; e-mail info@bea.mr; internet www.bea.mr; f. 1997; 73% privately owned, 27% owned by Société Nationale Industrielle et Minière; cap. and res 1,297.4m., total assets 7,248.4m. (Dec. 2001); cap. 1,500m. (Dec. 2005); Pres. AHMED SALEM BOUNA MOKHTAR; Dir-Gen. AHMED SALEM EL KORY; 8 brs.

Banque Internationale d'Investissement (BII): Nouakchott; tel. 529-70-00; fax 524-53-00; internet www.bii.mr; f. 2005; cap. 4,000m. (Jan. 2006); Pres. and Dir-Gen. JEAN-PHILLIPE EQUILBECQ; 1 br.

Banque pour le Commerce et l'Industrie (BCI): ave Nasser, BP 5050, Nouakchott; tel. 529-28-76; fax 529-28-77; e-mail bci@bci-banque.com; internet www.bci-banque.com; f. 1999; privately owned; cap. 2,040m. (Dec. 2005); Pres. and Dir-Gen. ISSELMOU OULD DIDI OULD TAJEDINE; 9 brs.

Banque pour le Commerce et l'Investissement en Mauritanie (Bacim-Bank): BP 1268, Nouakchott; tel. 529-19-00; fax 529-13-60; e-mail bacim-bank@mauritel.mr; internet www.bacim.mr; f. 2002; privately owned; cap. 1,500m. (Dec. 2005); Pres. and Dir-Gen. AHMED OULD EL WAFI; 6 brs.

Banque Mauritanienne pour le Commerce International (BMCI): Immeuble Afarco, ave Nasser, BP 622, Nouakchott; tel. 525-28-26; fax 525-20-45; e-mail info@bmci.mr; internet www.bmci.mr; f. 1974; 95.82% owned by Group Abbas; cap. 4,000m. res 3,401m., dep. 31,004m. (Dec. 2006); Pres. and Dir-Gen. MOULAY SIDI OULD HACEN OULD ABASS; 18 brs.

Banque Nationale de Mauritanie (BNM): ave Gamal Abdel Nasser, BP 614, Nouakchott; tel. 525-26-02; fax 525-33-97; e-mail bnm10@bnm.mr; f. 1989; privately owned; res 977m., dep. 20,659m. (Dec. 2003); cap. 6,000m. (Dec. 2005); Pres. and Dir-Gen. MOHAMED OULD NOUEIGUED; 10 brs.

Chinguitty Bank: ave Gamal Abdel Nasser, BP 626, Nouakchott; tel. 525-21-73; fax 525-33-82; e-mail chinguittybank@mauritel.mr; f. 1972; 51% owned by Libyan Arab Foreign Bank, 49% state-owned; cap. and res 4,002.9m., total assets 11,428.7m. (Dec. 2007); cap. 3,500m. (Dec. 2007); Pres. MOHAMED OULD DIDI; Gen. Man. YOUNIS TAHER AS-SOUDI; 2 brs.

Générale de Banque de Mauritanie pour l'Investissement et le Commerce SA (GBM): ave de l'Indépendance, BP 5558, Nouakchott; tel. 525-36-36; fax 525-46-47; e-mail gbm@gbm.mr.com; f. 1995; 70% privately owned; cap. 7,200m., res 14,037.6m., dep. 15,142.5m. (Dec. 2006); Pres. and Dir-Gen. MOHAMED HMAYEN OULD BOUAMATOU; 1 br.

Islamic Bank

Banque al-Wava Mauritanienne Islamique (BAMIS): 758, rue 22–018, ave du Roi Fayçal, BP 650, Nouakchott; tel. 525-14-24; fax 525-16-21; e-mail bamis@bamis.mr; internet www.bamis.mr; f. 1985; fmrly Banque al-Baraka Mauritannienne Islamique; majority share privately owned; cap. 2,000m., res 2,821m., dep. 13,778m. (Dec. 2005); Pres. MOHAMED ABDELLAHI OULD ABDELLAHI; Dir-Gen. MOHAMED ABDELLAHI OULD SIDI; Exec. Dir MOHAMED OULD TAYA; 2 brs.

INSURANCE

Assurances Générales de Mauritanie: BP 2141, ave de Gaulle, TZA Ilot A 667, Nouakchott; tel. 529-29-00; fax 529-29-11; Man. MOULAYE ELY BOUAMATOU.

Compagnie Nationale d'Assurance et de Réassurance (NASR): 12 ave Nasser, BP 163, Nouakchott; tel. 525-26-50; fax 525-18-18; e-mail nasr@nasr.mr; internet www.nasr.mr; f. 1994; state-owned; Pres. MOHAMED ABDELLAHI OULD SIDI; Dir-Gen. AHMED OULD SIDI BABA.

Société Anonyme d'Assurance et de Réassurance (SAAR): ave J. F. Kennedy, Immeuble El-Mamy, BP 2841, Nouakchott; tel. 525-30-56; fax 525-25-36; e-mail saar@infotel.mr; f. 1999; Pres. and Dir-Gen. AHMED BEZEID OULD MED LEMINE.

TAAMIN: BP 5164, Nouakchott; tel. 529-40-00; fax 529-40-02; e-mail taamin@toptechnology.mr; Pres. and Dir-Gen. MOULAYE EL HASSEN OULD MOCTAR EL HASSEN.

Trade and Industry

DEVELOPMENT ORGANIZATIONS

Agence Française de Développement (AFD): rue Mamadou Kouaté prolongée, BP 5211, Nouakchott; tel. 525-25-25; fax 525-49-10; e-mail afdnouakchott@groupe-afd.org; internet www.afd.fr; Country Dir GILLES CHAUSSE.

Mission Française de Coopération et d'Action Culturelle: BP 203, Nouakchott; tel. 525-21-21; fax 525-20-50; e-mail mcap.coop.france@opt.mr; administers bilateral aid from France; Dir MAURICE DADOUCHE.

Société Nationale pour le Développement Rural (SONADER): BP 321, Nouakchott; tel. 521-18-00; fax 525-32-86; e-mail sonader@toptechnology.mr; f. 1975; Dir AHMED OULD BAH OULD CHEIKH SIDIA.

CHAMBER OF COMMERCE

Chambre de Commerce, d'Industrie et d'Agriculture de Mauritanie: BP 215, Nouakchott; tel. 525-22-14; fax 525-38-95; f. 1954; Pres. MAHMOUD OULD AHMEDOU; Dir HABIB OULD ELY.

EMPLOYERS' ORGANIZATION

National Confederation of Mauritanian Employers (CNPM): 824 ave de Roi Fayçal, Ksar, BP 383, Nouakchott; tel. 525-33-01; fax 525-91-08; e-mail germe@opt.mr; f. 1960; professional asscn for all employers active in Mauritania; Pres. MOHAMED OULD BOUAMATOU; Sec.-Gen. SEYID OULD ABDALLAHI.

UTILITIES

Electricity

Société Mauritanienne d'Electricité (SOMELEC): BP 355, Nouakchott; tel. 525-23-08; fax 525-39-95; e-mail dahane@somelec.mr; internet www.somelec.mr; f. 2001; state-owned; transfer to majority private sector ownership proposed; production and distribution of electricity; Dir-Gen. TALEB OULD ABDI VALL.

Gas

Société Mauritanienne des Gaz (SOMAGAZ): POB 5089, Nouakchott; tel. 525-18-71; fax 524-29-70; e-mail somagaz@somagaz.com; internet www.somagaz.com; production and distribution of butane gas; Dir-Gen. MOHAMED YAHYA OULD AHMEDOU.

Water

Société Nationale d'Eau (SNDE): ave 42-096, no. 106, Tevragh Zeina, BP 796, Nouakchott; tel. 525-52-73; fax 525-19-52; e-mail mfoudail@infotel.mr; f. 2001; Dir-Gen. THIAM SAMBA.

TRADE UNIONS

Confédération Générale des Travailleurs de Mauritanie: BP 6164, Nouakchott; tel. 525-60-24; fax 525-80-57; e-mail admin@cgtm.org; internet cgtm.org; f. 1992; obtained official recognition in 1994; Sec.-Gen. ABDALLAHI OULD MOHAMED.

Confédération Libre des Travailleurs de Mauritanie: BP 6902, Nouakchott; fax 525-23-16; f. 1995; Sec.-Gen. SAMORI OULD BEYI.

Union des Travailleurs de Mauritanie (UTM): Bourse du Travail, BP 630, Nouakchott; f. 1961; Sec.-Gen. ABDERAHMANE OULD BOUBOU; 45,000 mems.

Transport

RAILWAYS

A 670-km railway connects the iron-ore deposits at Zouérate with Nouadhibou; a 40-km extension services the reserves at El Rhein, and a 30-km extension those at M'Haoudat. Motive power is diesel-electric. The Société Nationale Industrielle et Minière (SNIM) operates one of the longest (2.4 km) and heaviest (22,000 metric tons) trains in the world.

SNIM—Direction du Chemin de Fer et du Port: BP 42, Nouadhibou; tel. 574-51-74; fax 574-53-96; e-mail m.khalifa.beyah@zrt

.snim.com; internet www.snim.com; f. 1963; Gen. Man. MOHAMED SALECK OULD HEYINE.

ROADS

In 2006 there were about 11,066 km of roads and tracks, of which only 2,966 km were paved. The 1,100-km Trans-Mauritania highway, completed in 1985, links Nouakchott with Néma in the east of the country. Plans exist for the construction of a 7,400-km highway, linking Nouakchott with the Libyan port of Tubruq (Tobruk). In August 1999 the Islamic Development Bank granted Mauritania a loan worth US $9.4m. to help finance the rebuilding of the Chouk–Kiffa road. The construction of a 470-km highway between Nouakchott and Nouadhibou was completed in 2004.

Société Mauritanienne des Transports (SOMATRA): Nouakchott; tel. 525-29-53; f. 1975; Pres. CHEIKH MALAININE ROBERT; Dir-Gen. MAMADOU SOULEYMANE KANE.

INLAND WATERWAYS

The River Senegal is navigable in the wet season by small coastal vessels as far as Kayes (Mali) and by river vessels as far as Kaédi; in the dry season as far as Rosso and Boghé, respectively. The major river ports are at Rosso, Kaédi and Gouraye.

SHIPPING

The principal port, at Point-Central, 10 km south of Nouadhibou, is almost wholly occupied with mineral exports. In 1998 the port handled 11.6m. metric tons of cargo and cleared 3,804 vessels. There is also a commercial and fishing port at Nouadhibou. The deep-water Port de l'Amitié at Nouakchott, built and maintained with assistance from the People's Republic of China, was inaugurated in 1986. The port, which has a total capacity of about 1.5m. tons annually, handled 843,000 tons in 1998 (compared with 479,791 tons in 1990); the port cleared 453 vessels in 1998 (compared with 244 in 1990). In 2007 Mauritania's merchant fleet consisted of 152 vessels and had a total displacement of 51,505 grt.

Port Autonome de Nouakchott (Port de l'Amitié): BP 5103, El Mina, Nouakchott; tel. 525-14-53; fax 525-17-94; e-mail ouldmohamedna@yahoo.fr; f. 1986; deep-water port; Dir-Gen. AHMEDOU OULD HAMED.

Port Autonome de Nouadhibou: BP 236, Nouadhibou; tel. 525-21-34; f. 1973; state-owned; Pres. BAL MOHAMED EL HABIB; Dir-Gen. BÉBAHA OULD AHMED YOURA.

Shipping Companies

Cie Mauritanienne de Navigation Maritime (COMAUNAM): 119 ave Nasser, BP 799, Nouakchott; tel. 525-36-34; fax 525-25-04; f. 1973; 51% state-owned, 49% owned by Govt of Algeria; nat. shipping co; forwarding agent, stevedoring; Chair. MOHAND TIGHILT; Dir-Gen. KAMIL ABDELKADER.

Société d'Acconage et de Manutention en Mauritanie (SAMMA): BP 258, Nouadhibou; tel. 574-52-63; fax 574-52-37; e-mail didi.samma@snim.com; internet www.samma.mr; f. 1960; freight and handling, shipping agent, forwarding agent, stevedoring; Man. Dir DIDI OULD BIHA.

Société Générale de Consignation et d'Entreprises Maritimes (SOGECO): 1765 rue 22-002, Commune du Ksar, BP 351, Nouakchott; tel. 525-22-02; fax 525-39-03; e-mail sogeco@sogeco.sa.mr; internet www.sogecosa.com; f. 1973; shipping agent, forwarding, stevedoring; Man. Dir SID'AHMED ABEIDNA.

Société Mauritanienne pour la Pêche et la Navigation (SMPN): BP 40254, Nouakchott; tel. 525-36-38; fax 525-37-87; e-mail smpn@toptechnology.mr; Dir-Gen. ABDALLAHI OULD ISMAIL.

VOTRA: Route de l'Aéroport, BP 454, Nouakchott; tel. 525-24-10; fax 525-31-41; e-mail votra@mauritel.mr; internet www.votra.net; Dir-Gen. MOHAMED MAHMOUD OULD MAYE.

CIVIL AVIATION

There are international airports at Nouakchott, Nouadhibou and Néma, and 23 smaller airstrips.

Mauritania Airways: Nouakchott; internet www.fly-mauritaniaairways.com; f. 2006; 10% state-owned, 51% owned by Tunisair (Tunisia); Gen. Man. MONCEF BADIS.

Tourism

Mauritania's principal tourist attractions are its historical sites, several of which have been listed by UNESCO under its World Heritage Programme, and its game reserves and national parks. Some 24,000 tourists visited Mauritania in 1999. Receipts from tourism in that year totalled an estimated US $28m.

Office National du Tourisme: BP 2884, Nouakchott; tel. 529-03-44; fax 529-05-28; e-mail ont@tourisme-mauritanie.com; f. 2002; Dir KHADIJÉTOU MINT BOUBOU.

SOMASERT: BP 42, Nouadhibou; tel. 574-29-91; fax 574-90-43; subsidiary of SNIM; responsible for promoting tourism, managing hotels and organizing tours; Dir-Gen. MOHAMED OULD BIYAH.

MAURITIUS

Introductory Survey

Location, Climate, Language, Religion, Flag, Capital

The Republic of Mauritius lies in the Indian Ocean. The principal island, from which the country takes its name, lies about 800 km (500 miles) east of Madagascar. The other main islands are Rodrigues, the Agalega Islands and the Cargados Carajos Shoals (St Brandon Islands). The climate is maritime sub-tropical and generally humid. The average annual temperature is 23°C (73°F) at sea-level, falling to 19°C (66°F) at an altitude of 600 m (about 2,000 ft). Average annual rainfall varies from 890 mm (35 ins) at sea-level to 5,080 mm (200 ins) on the highest parts. Tropical cyclones, which may be severe, occur between September and May. Most of the population are of Indian descent. The most widely spoken languages in 2000 were Creole (38.6%) and Bhojpuri (30.6%). English is the country's official language, and Creole (derived from French) the lingua franca. The principal religious group are Hindus, who comprise more than 50% of the population. About 30% are Christians and 17% are Muslims. The national flag (proportions 2 by 3) has four equal horizontal stripes, of red, blue, yellow and green. The capital is Port Louis.

Recent History

The islands of Mauritius and Rodrigues, formerly French possessions, passed into British control in 1810. Subsequent settlement came mainly from East Africa and India, and the European population has remained largely French-speaking.

A ministerial form of government was introduced in 1957. The first elections under universal adult suffrage, held in 1959, were won by the Mauritius Labour Party (MLP), led by Dr (later Sir) Seewoosagur Ramgoolam. Mauritius became independent, within the Commonwealth, on 12 March 1968, with Ramgoolam as Prime Minister.

In November 1965 the United Kingdom transferred the Chagos Archipelago (including the atoll of Diego Garcia), a Mauritian dependency about 2,000 km (1,250 miles) north-east of the main island, to the newly created British Indian Ocean Territory (BIOT, q.v.). Mauritius has subsequently campaigned for the return of the islands, which have been developed as a major US military base. Mauritius also claims sovereignty of the French-held island of Tromelin, about 550 km (340 miles) to the northwest.

During the 1970s political opposition to successive coalition governments formed by Ramgoolam was led by a radical left-wing group, the Mouvement Militant Mauricien (MMM), founded by Paul Bérenger. Although the MMM became the largest single party in the Legislative Assembly following a general election in December 1976, Ramgoolam was able to form a new coalition Government with the support of the Parti Mauricien Social Démocrate (PMSD). However, social unrest and rising unemployment undermined popular support for the Government, and at a general election in June 1982 the MMM, in alliance with the Parti Socialiste Mauricien (PSM), won all 60 contested seats on the main island. Anerood (later Sir Anerood) Jugnauth, the leader of the MMM, became Prime Minister, and Bérenger Minister of Finance.

The MMM/PSM coalition collapsed in March 1983, when Bérenger and his supporters resigned, following differences concerning economic policy. Jugnauth formed a new Government and a new party, the Mouvement Socialiste Militant (MSM), which subsequently merged with the PSM. A general election took place in August, at which an electoral alliance of the MSM, the MLP and the PMSD, led by Sir Gaëtan Duval, gained a legislative majority. Jugnauth formed a new coalition Government, in which Duval became Deputy Prime Minister. The MLP, however, withdrew from the coalition in February 1984.

Following a general election in August 1987, the MSM again formed an electoral alliance with the PMSD and the MLP; the three parties obtained 39 of the 62 elective seats. Bérenger, who failed to secure a seat, transferred his functions as leader of the opposition in the Legislative Assembly to Dr Paramhansa Nababsingh (while Bérenger himself replaced Nababsingh as Secretary-General of the MMM). A new coalition, led by Jugnauth, took office in September, and the Government subsequently announced plans to make Mauritius a republic within the Commonwealth. In August 1988, following a disagreement over employment policies, the PMSD withdrew from the coalition.

In July 1990 the MSM and the MMM agreed to form an alliance to contest the next general election, and to promote constitutional measures allowing Mauritius to become a republic within the Commonwealth. This proposal, however, was jointly opposed by the MLP and the PMSD, prompting Jugnauth to dismiss the MLP leader, Sir Satcam Boolell, from the Government, together with two dissident ministers from the MSM. A further three ministers representing the MLP resigned, leaving only one MLP member in the Government. Boolell subsequently relinquished the leadership of the MLP to Dr Navinchandra Ramgoolam (the son of the late Sir Seewoosagur Ramgoolam). In September Jugnauth formed a new coalition Government.

Jugnauth dissolved the Legislative Assembly in August 1991. At the subsequent general election, which took place on 15 September, an alliance of the MSM, the MMM and the small Mouvement des Travaillistes Démocrates (MTD), won 57 of the 62 directly elected seats, while the MLP/PMSD alliance obtained three seats. The two remaining seats were secured by the Organisation du Peuple Rodriguais (OPR). Four 'additional' seats were subsequently allocated to members of the MLP/PMSD alliance. Jugnauth formed a new government coalition, to which nine representatives of the MMM (including Bérenger, who became Minister of External Affairs) and one representative of the MTD were appointed.

In December 1991 the Legislative Assembly approved the constitutional framework for the country's transition to a republic within the Commonwealth. Following the proclamation of the Republic of Mauritius on 12 March 1992, the Legislative Assembly was redesignated as the National Assembly, and the incumbent Governor-General, Sir Veerasamy Ringadoo, became interim President. Later in March the Government announced its choice of Cassam Uteem, the Minister of Industry and Industrial Technology and a member of the MMM, to assume the presidency in June. Uteem was duly elected President by the National Assembly; Sir Rabindrah Ghurburrun, a member of the MMM, took office as Vice-President.

The government coalition came under increasing pressure during 1993, amid intensifying disputes between the MSM and the MMM. In August, following an unexpected success by the PMSD in municipal by-elections in a constituency that traditionally supported the MMM, a meeting between Bérenger and Ramgoolam prompted speculation that an MMM/MLP alliance was contemplated. Shortly afterwards Jugnauth dismissed Bérenger from the Council of Ministers, on the grounds that he had repeatedly criticized government policy.

The removal of Bérenger precipitated a serious crisis within the MMM, whose political bureau decided that the other nine members of the party who held ministerial portfolios should remain in the coalition Government. Led by Nababsingh, the Deputy Prime Minister, and Jean-Claude de l'Estrac, the Minister of Industry and Industrial Technology, supporters of the pro-coalition faction announced in October 1993 that Bérenger had been suspended as Secretary-General of the MMM. Bérenger and his supporters responded by expelling 11 MMM officials from the party, and seeking a legal ban on Nababsingh and de l'Estrac from using the party name. The split in the MMM led in November to a government reshuffle, in which the remaining two MMM ministers supporting Bérenger were replaced by members of the party's pro-coalition faction.

In April 1994 the MLP and the MMM announced that they had agreed terms for an alliance to contest the next general elections. Under its provisions, Ramgoolam was to be Prime Minister and Bérenger the Deputy Prime Minister, with ministerial portfolios allocated on the basis of 12 ministries to the MLP and nine to the MMM. In the same month, three deputies from the MSM, who had been close associates of a former Minister of Agriculture dismissed two months earlier, withdrew their support from the Government.

Nababsingh and the dissident faction of the MMM, having lost Bérenger's legal challenge for the use of the party name, formed a new party, the Renouveau Militant Mauricien (RMM), which formally commenced political activity in June 1994. In the same month Jugnauth declared that the Government, which retained a cohesive parliamentary majority, would remain in office to the conclusion of its mandate in September 1996.

During the course of a parliamentary debate in November 1994, Bérenger and de l'Estrac accepted a mutual challenge to resign their seats in the National Assembly and to contest by-elections. In the following month the MSM indicated that it would not oppose RMM candidates in the two polls. In January 1995, however, Jugnauth unsuccessfully sought to undermine the MLP/MMM alliance by offering electoral support to the MLP. The by-elections, held in February, were both won by MLP/MMM candidates, and Bérenger was returned to the National Assembly. Following these results, Jugnauth opened political negotiations with the PMSD, whose leader, Charles Gaëtan Xavier-Luc Duval (the son of Sir Gaëtan Duval), entered the coalition as Minister of Industry and Industrial Technology and Minister of Tourism. The post of Attorney-General and Minister of Justice was also allocated to the PMSD, and Sir Gaëtan Duval agreed to act as an economic adviser to the Prime Minister. As a result, however, of widespread opposition within the PMSD to participation in the coalition, Xavier-Luc Duval left the Government in October, and Sir Gaëtan Duval subsequently resumed the leadership of the party. The Minister for Rodrigues, representing the OPR, also left the Government.

In November 1995 the Government was defeated in a parliamentary vote, requiring a two-thirds' majority, to introduce a constitutional requirement for instruction in oriental languages to be provided in primary schools. Jugnauth dissolved the National Assembly, and at the subsequent general election in December the MLP/MMM alliance won a decisive victory: of the 62 elected seats, the MLP secured 35 seats, the MMM obtained 25 seats and the OPR two seats. Under constitutional arrangements providing representation for unsuccessful candidates attracting the largest number of votes, Sir Gaëtan Duval re-entered the National Assembly, together with two members of the Mouvement Rodriguais and one representative of Hizbullah, an Islamist fundamentalist group. Ramgoolam became Prime Minister of the new MLP/MMM coalition, with Bérenger as Deputy Prime Minister with responsibility for foreign and regional relations. Sir Gaëtan Duval died in May 1996 and was succeeded in the National Assembly and as leader of the PMSD by his brother, Hervé Duval, although Xavier-Luc Duval continued to command a significant following within the party.

Serious divisions began to emerge within the coalition Government in late 1996, when differences were reported between Ramgoolam and Bérenger over the allocation of ministerial responsibilities and the perception by the MMM of delays in the implementation of social and economic reforms. In January 1997 rumours had begun to circulate of a possible political alliance between the MMM and the MSM, and in March it was reported that Ramgoolam intended to seek support from certain members of the PMSD should the MMM decide to withdraw from the Government. Bérenger's criticism of the coalition's performance intensified in the following months, and culminated in June in his dismissal from the Government and the consequent withdrawal of the MMM from the coalition. Following unsuccessful efforts by Ramgoolam to draw the PMSD into a new administration, an MLP Council of Ministers was formed by Ramgoolam, who additionally assumed Bérenger's former responsibilities for foreign affairs. Ramgoolam emphasized his determination to remain in office for the full legislative term to December 2000. On 28 June 1997 the National Assembly re-elected Cassam Uteem to a second five-year term as President. A prominent supporter of the MLP, Angidi Verriah Chettiar, was elected Vice-President.

Following the dissolution of the MLP/MMM alliance, Bérenger sought to assume the leadership of a consolidated political opposition to the Government. In August 1997 two small parties, the Mouvement Militant Socialiste Mauricien (MMSM) and the Rassemblement pour la Réforme (RPR), agreed to support Bérenger in this aim. The alliance was extended to include a breakaway faction of the PMSD, known as the 'Vrais Bleus', under the leadership of Hervé Duval, who had been replaced as party leader by Xavier-Luc Duval, an opponent of co-operation with the MMM.

In April 1998 the MMM, the MMSM, the RPR and the 'Vrais Bleus' formed an electoral coalition, the Alliance Nationale, to contest a by-election for a vacant seat in the National Assembly. The seat, which was retained by the MLP, had also been sought by Jugnauth on behalf of the MSM, which remained unrepresented in the National Assembly. Jugnauth, seeking to revitalize his party's prospects in preparation for the next general election (which was constitutionally required to take place by December 2000), subsequently entered negotiations with Bérenger for an electoral alliance, and in December 1998 both parties agreed terms for a joint list of candidates.

The MLP announced in mid-1999 its endorsement of the candidature of Xavier-Luc Duval for a legislative by-election to be held in September. Xavier-Luc Duval, after obtaining the vacant seat, joined the Government as Minister of Industry, Commerce, Corporate Affairs and Financial Services, following an extensive government reshuffle completed at the end of the month. The selection in October of Pravind Jugnauth, the son of Sir Aneerod Jugnauth, as Deputy Leader of the MSM gave rise to speculation that Sir Aneerod was contemplating retirement from politics and intended his son to be his successor.

In August 2000 the MSM/MMM formed an alliance, in advance of the imminent general election, on the basis that Jugnauth would lead as Prime Minister for three years in the event of victory, before assuming the more honorary role of President, thus allowing Bérenger to become Prime Minister for the remaining two years.

A general election was held on 11 September 2000, with 81% of the 790,000 registered electors casting their ballots. The MSM/MMM alliance achieved an overwhelming victory, winning 54 of the 62 directly elected seats in the National Assembly, while the MLP/PMSD alliance gained only six seats and the OPR two seats. As agreed, Sir Aneerod Jugnauth became Prime Minister again, while Paul Bérenger was appointed Deputy Prime Minister and Minister of Finance. A new Council of Ministers was appointed one week later.

In November 2000 the British High Court of Justice ruled that the eviction of several thousand inhabitants of the Chagos Archipelago between 1967 and 1973, to allow the construction of a US military base on the atoll of Diego Garcia, had been unlawful, and overturned a 1971 ordinance preventing the islanders from returning to the Archipelago. (The majority of the displaced islanders had been resettled in Mauritius, which had administered the Chagos Archipelago until its transfer to BIOT in 1965.) Following the ruling, the Mauritian Government declared its right to sovereignty over the islands to be indisputable and sought international recognition as such. Jugnauth stated that he would be prepared to negotiate with the USA over the continued presence of the military base. The United Kingdom responded that it would return the islands if, as had been maintained for many years, the USA was prepared to move out of the base on Diego Garcia. India declared its support for the Mauritian Government's claim to sovereignty, as part of the close relationship being encouraged between the two countries.

In November 2001 exiled Chagos islanders demonstrated outside the British High Commission in Port Louis, in support of their demands for compensation from the British Government. In February 2002 legislation allowing the displaced islanders to apply for British citizenship received royal assent in the United Kingdom. At that time the British Government was also examining the feasibility of a return to the Chagos Archipelago for the islanders, who continued to seek compensation.

In January 2002 a commission on constitutional and electoral reform presented its proposals at a series of public forums, before submitting them to the Government for consideration. Recommendations included the introduction of a system of proportional representation in legislative elections and a reinforcement of presidential powers. In mid-February controversial legislation on the prevention of terrorism was finally promulgated by the Chief Justice of the Supreme Court, Arianga Pillay, acting as interim President, following the resignations of both President Uteem and his successor, Vice-President Chettiar, over the issue. The legislation had been rejected by opposition parties and proved unpopular with many sections of society for arrogating excessive powers to the authorities and infringing on citizens' rights. On 25 February Karl Offman was elected as President by an extraordinary session of the National Assembly, which was boycotted by opposition deputies. Although formally elected for five years, Offman was to relinquish the presidency to Jugnauth in October 2003; in preparation for this, in April 2003 Jugnauth announced his resignation from the leadership of the MSM, to be succeeded by his son, Pravind.

In August 2003, in preparation for the transfer of governing roles, a constitutional amendment was approved by the National Assembly to increase the powers of the President, giving the incumbent the right to refuse a request from the Prime Minister to dissolve the legislature following a vote of no confidence. As agreed, on 1 October Offman resigned as President and was replaced, in an acting capacity, by the Vice-President, Raouf Bundhun, pending the election by the National Assembly of Sir Anerood Jugnauth as his successor one week later. Jugnauth had resigned as Prime Minister on 30 September and was immediately replaced by Paul Bérenger, who appointed a new Council of Ministers. During his first months in office Bérenger conducted a premiership active in international diplomacy, visiting two of the country's principal trading partners, India and France, and signing co-operation agreements with Madagascar. In early 2004 he also renewed the campaign to reclaim sovereignty of the Chagos Archipelago from the United Kingdom, on the basis that international law does not allow the dismemberment of a country before independence, and of Tromelin from France. It was established in 2004 that Mauritius had the right to pursue the case of the Chagos islands at the International Court of Justice, in spite of British objections on the basis of restrictions imposed by membership of the Commonwealth.

In early February 2005 the Minister of Public Infrastructure, Land Transport and Shipping, Anil Bachoo, resigned, to be replaced by Govindranath Gunness; the Minister of Local Government and Solid Waste Management, Mookhesswur Choonee, also left office the following week and was succeeded by Prithvirajsing Roopun. The two erstwhile ministers formed a new opposition party the following month, the Mouvement Sociale Démocrate (MSD), having also resigned from the MSM alleging poor leadership of that party by Pravind Jugnauth. Bachoo and Choonee reportedly disapproved of an apparent pre-electoral agreement between the parties of the ruling coalition, whereby, should they successfully be re-elected to office, Bérenger would relinquish the premiership in mid-term in favour of Pravind Jugnauth, just as the incumbent President (Pravind Jugnauth's father) had in September 2003. The MSD announced the formation of an electoral alliance with the MLP, known as the Social Alliance, thus creating a credible rival political force to the governing parties for the forthcoming legislative elections.

At the elections, which were held on 3 July 2005, the Social Alliance bloc defeated the incumbent coalition, winning 38 of the 62 directly elected mandates. The MSM/MMM alliance took 22 seats while the OPR secured two. The rate of voter participation was 81.5%. Ramgoolam was appointed as Prime Minister and a new 19-member Council of Ministers was sworn into office later that month. At local elections held in early October the Social Alliance won 122 of the 126 seats contested, including many long-term MSM/MMM strongholds. Following the elections the PMSD withdrew from the opposition alliance in which it had participated with the MSM and MMM. Tensions between the politically opposed premier and President initially proved somewhat obstructive to the functioning of the Government, however, they subsequently eased.

The Social Alliance Government continued with efforts to regain sovereignty over the Chagos Archipelago. A group of 102 Chagossians was permitted to visit the Archipelago in late March 2006, accompanied by Deputy Prime Minister Duval and two other government ministers, principally in order to visit the graves of relatives. In May the British High Court of Justice overturned the Orders in Council issued by the British Government under the royal prerogative in June 2004, ruling them to be unlawful, and confirmed the right of the islanders to return to the Archipelago without any conditions. In February 2007 the British Government commenced proceedings in the Court of Appeal to overturn the May 2006 ruling. However, in May 2007 that court confirmed that the residents of the Chagos Archipelago had been unlawfully removed and upheld the displaced islanders' immediate right to return. In November the House of Lords granted the British Government the right to appeal against the Court of Appeal's decision, on the condition that the Chagossian's costs were met by the British Government. In November 2008 the House of Lords ruled in favour of the British Government, thus denying the Chagossians the right to return, citing as its main reason the fact that the United Kingdom would have been obliged to meet the costs of economic, social and educational advancement of the residents. It was estimated that only approximately 500 of the 2,000 deported during the 1960s and 1970s were still alive.

Meanwhile, in April 2006 the opposition was further weakened when the MSM/MMM alliance collapsed following weeks of increasing tension between Pravind Jugnauth and Bérenger, and the PMSD announced that it was joining the government coalition. The MSM withdrew its support from Bérenger as official leader of the opposition and he was succeeded by Nando Bodha, the Secretary-General of the MSM and a close ally of Pravind Jugnauth (who had failed to retain his seat in the legislature in July 2005), since the MSM held 11 seats in the National Assembly to the MMM's 10. Bodha's nomination was rejected by Ashock Jugnauth, a senior member of the MSM (and uncle of Pravind), who resigned from the party and established a new opposition party, the Union Nationale. In August 2007 Chettiar resumed the position of Vice-President, replacing Bundhun. In September Bodha resigned as leader of the opposition and in October Bérenger once again assumed the role. Prime Minister Ramgoolam dismissed Minister of Foreign Affairs, International Trade and Co-operation Madan Murlidhar Dulloo in March 2008, assuming responsibility for that portfolio himself in an acting capacity.

Ramgoolam carried out a further reorganization of the Government in mid-September 2008, appointing four new ministers, including Jean François Chaumiere as Minister of Labour, Industrial Relations and Employment. Anil Bachoo was reinstated as Minister of Public Infrastructure, Land Transport and Shipping, and Arvin Boolell, hitherto in charge of international trade, was awarded the newly created post of Minister of Foreign Affairs, Regional Integration and International Trade. On 19 September the National Assembly unanimously re-elected Jugnauth as President for a second five-year term, and on the following day legislation was approved which allowed for two ministers to hold the title of Vice-Prime Minister: these positions were taken up by Xavier-Luc Duval and Dr Rama Sithanen with the former also retaining the tourism, leisure and external communications portfolio, while Sithanen retained the finance and economic empowerment portfolio. (The position of Deputy Prime Minister remained the second most senior post in the Council of Ministers—Ahmed Rashid Beebeejaun was appointed to this office and also assumed responsibility for the renewable energy and public utilities portfolio.)

In February 2009 the Truth and Justice Commission Act came into force, providing for the establishment of a five-member commission, which would conduct inquiries into slavery and indenture labour in Mauritius during the colonial period; the commission was to be chaired by Professor Robert Shell, a South African national.

Government

Constitutional amendments, which were approved by the Legislative Assembly (henceforth known as the National Assembly) in December 1991 and came into effect on 12 March 1992, provided for the establishment of a republic. The constitutional Head of State is the President of the Republic, who is elected by a simple majority of the National Assembly for a five-year term of office. Legislative power is vested in the unicameral National Assembly, which comprises the Speaker, 62 members elected by universal adult suffrage for a term of five years, up to eight 'additional' members (unsuccessful candidates who receive the largest number of votes at a legislative election, to whom seats are allocated by the Electoral Supervisory Commission to ensure a balance in representation of the different ethnic groups), and the Attorney-General (if not an elected member). Executive power is vested in the Prime Minister, who is appointed by the President and is the member of the National Assembly best able to command a majority in the Assembly. The President appoints other ministers, on the recommendation of the Prime Minister.

Defence

The country has no standing defence forces, although as assessed at November 2008 paramilitary forces were estimated to number 2,000, comprising a special mobile force of 1,500, to ensure internal security, and a coastguard of 500. The defence budget for 2008 was estimated at Rs 1,013m.

Economic Affairs

In 2007, according to estimates by the World Bank, Mauritius' gross national income (GNI), measured at average 2005–07 prices, was US $6,878m., equivalent to $5,450 per head (or $11,390 per head on an international purchasing-power parity basis). During 2000–07, it was estimated, the population increased at an average annual rate of 0.9%, while gross domestic product (GDP) per head increased, in real terms, by an average of 3.2% per year. Overall GDP increased, in real terms, at an average annual rate of 4.1% in 2000–07; growth in 2007 was 4.7%.

Agriculture (including hunting, forestry and fishing) contributed an estimated 4.1% of GDP in 2008 and engaged 9.0% of the employed labour force in 2007. The principal cash crops are sugar cane (sugar accounted for 18.4% of domestic export earnings in 2007, according to provisional figures), tea and tobacco. Food crops include potatoes tomatoes and bananas. Chicken farming is also practised. During 2000–07, according to the World Bank, the GDP of the agricultural sector increased, in real terms, at an average rate of 2.0% per year; however, it declined by 3.9% in 2006 and by 4.6% in 2007.

Industry (including mining, manufacturing, construction and utilities) contributed an estimated 26.8% of GDP in 2008 and engaged 33.5% of the employed labour force in 2007. During 2000–07, according to the World Bank, industrial GDP increased, in real terms, at an average annual rate of 2.1%; it increased by 4.9% in 2007. Mining is negligible, accounting for less than 0.1% of employment in 2007 and less than 0.1% of GDP in 2008.

Manufacturing contributed an estimated 18.3% of GDP in 2008 and engaged 23.4% of the employed labour force in 2007. The principal branches of manufacturing are clothing and food products, mainly sugar. Clothing (excluding footwear) provided 31.9% of export earnings in 2006, according to official figures. Factories in the Export Processing Zone (EPZ) import raw materials to produce goods for the export market. Clothing and apparel firms accounted for 75.8% of total EPZ employment in September 2005. Other important products include fish preparations, textiles, and precious stones. Export receipts from EPZ products provisionally represented 46.1% of total export earnings (and 16.6% of import earnings) in 2005. During 2000–07, according to the World Bank, the GDP of the manufacturing sector increased, in real terms, at an average annual rate of 0.2%; however, manufacturing GDP decreased by 0.7% in 2006 and by 2.4% in 2007.

Electric energy is derived principally from thermal (oil-fired) and hydroelectric power stations. Bagasse (a by-product of sugar cane) is also used as fuel for generating electricity and in 2006 it accounted for 19.0% of electricity produced (93% of indigenous production; 20% of electricity was produced locally). Imports of mineral fuels comprised 18.3% of the value of merchandise imports in 2007. Thermal energy accounted for 96.7% of electricity generated in 2006.

The services sector contributed an estimated 69.1% of GDP in 2008 and engaged 57.5% of the employed labour force in 2007. Tourism is the third most important source of revenue, after manufacturing and agriculture. The number of foreign tourist arrivals increased to 930,456 in 2008 from 422,000 in 1995. Gross receipts from tourism were estimated to total Rs 41,213m. in 2008. An 'offshore' banking sector and a stock exchange have operated since 1989. According to the World Bank, the real GDP of the services sector increased at an average annual rate of 5.9% in 2000–07; growth in 2007 was 5.8%.

In 2007 Mauritius recorded a visible trade deficit of US $1,425.7m., and there was a deficit of $408.3m. on the current account of the balance of payments. In 2007 the principal source of imports (21.2%) was India; other major suppliers were the People's Republic of China, France and South Africa. The principal market for exports in that year (34.1%) was the United Kingdom; other significant purchasers were France, the USA, Madagascar and Italy. The principal exports (excluding re-exports) in 2007 were miscellaneous manufactured articles and food and live animals. The principal imports in that year were machinery and transport equipment, basic manufactures, mineral fuels and lubricants, and food and live animals.

In 2007/08 there was an estimated budgetary deficit of Rs 9,331.4m. (equivalent to 3.5% of GDP). Mauritius' external debt totalled US $1,997m. at the end of 2006, of which $634m. was long-term public debt. In that year the cost of debt-servicing was equivalent to 7.1% of the value of exports of goods and services. The annual rate of inflation averaged 5.9% in 1996–2006. Consumer prices increased by an average of 8.9% in 2006. About 8.2% of the labour force were unemployed in 2008.

Mauritius is a member of the Common Market for Eastern and Southern Africa (COMESA, see p. 215), the Southern African Development Community (SADC, see p. 400) and the Indian Ocean Commission (IOC, see p. 426), which aims to promote regional economic co-operation. Mauritius was among the founder members of the Indian Ocean Rim Association for Regional Co-operation (IOR—ARC, see p. 427) in 1997.

From the 1980s the Mauritius Government pursued a successful policy of economic diversification away from its traditional dependence on sugar production, encouraging labour-intensive manufacturing (particularly of clothing) in the EPZ, and implemented extensive reforms with IMF support. The geographical location of Mauritius, as well as a number of incentive measures implemented by the Government, has contributed to its successful establishment as an international financial centre. By the late 1990s the island had become a significant provider of 'offshore' banking and investment services for a number of south Asian countries (particularly India), as well as for members of SADC. Mauritius has also been promoted as a future hub of information and communications technology, with the aim of encouraging the next stage of economic development and transferring the emphasis towards services. Following the expiry of the preferential Multi-Fibre Arrangement (subsequently known as the Agreement on Textiles and Clothing) with the European Union (EU, see p. 255) in December 2004, which exposed the textiles industry to direct competition from countries with lower labour costs, particularly those in Asia, and the decision of the EU to reduce preferential trade terms for the African, Caribbean and Pacific Group of States (resulting in a reduction of 36% from 2005 in the price paid for sugar—European countries represent the biggest importers of Mauritian sugar), the authorities began to focus on the development of the high-end tourist sector and also sought to offer foreigners more opportunities to invest in Mauritius. Further to this aim, the Business Facilitation Act was introduced before the National Assembly in late 2006, as a result of which Mauritius saw foreign investment grow at a record 19.0% in 2006, followed by a more modest 8.6% in 2007. Although the banking sector in Mauritius remained relatively unaffected by the global financial crisis, with financial institutions reporting no serious capitalization or liquidity issues, there were nevertheless concerns that much weaker external demand for textiles and tourism would have serious repercussions for the country's economy, and GDP growth was projected to decline to just 2.0% in 2009, compared with 5.2% in 2008.

Education

Education is officially compulsory for seven years between the ages of five and 12. Primary education begins at five years of age and lasts for six years. Secondary education, beginning at the age of 11, lasts for up to seven years, comprising a first cycle of three years and a second of four years. Primary and secondary education are available free of charge and became compulsory in 2005. According to UNESCO estimates, in 2006/07 enrolment at primary schools included 95.4% of pupils in the relevant age-group (males 94.7%; females 96.1%), while the comparable ratio for secondary schools was 72.6% (males 68.0%; females 77.3%). The education system provides for instruction in seven Asian languages (71% of primary school children and 30% of secondary school children were studying at least one of these in 2005). The Government exercises indirect control of the large private sector in secondary education (in 2005 only 70 of 188 schools were state administered). The University of Mauritius had 7,531 students in 2006/07 (34.3% of whom were part-time students); in addition, many students receive further education abroad. Of total expenditure by the central Government in 2007/08, Rs 6,973.8m. (11.7%) was for education.

Public Holidays

2009: 1–3 January (New Year), 1 February (Abolition of Slavery Commemoration), 7 February (Chinese New Year), 23 February (Maha Shivaratree), 12 March (National Day), 25 March (Ougadi), 1 May (Labour Day), 15 August (Assumption), 23 August (Ganesh Chathurti), 20 September* (Id al-Fitr, end of Ramadan), 17 October (Diwali), 2 November (Arrival of Indentured Labourers), 25 December (Christmas Day).

2010: 1–2 January (New Year), 1 February (Abolition of Slavery Commemoration), 7 February (Chinese New Year), 12 February (Maha Shivaratree), 12 March (National Day), 14 March (Ougadi), 1 May (Labour Day), 15 August (Assumption), 10 September* (Id al-Fitr, end of Ramadan), 11 September (Ganesh Chathurti), 2 November (Arrival of Indentured Labourers), 5 November (Diwali), 25 December (Christmas Day).

Thaipoosam Cavadee is also celebrated in late January or early February. However, the exact date is dependent on the appearance of a full moon.

* This holiday is dependent on the Islamic lunar calendar and may vary by one or two days from the dates given.

Weights and Measures

The metric system is in standard use.

Statistical Survey

Source (unless otherwise stated): Central Statistics Office, LIC Bldg, President John F. Kennedy St, Port Louis; tel. 212-2316; fax 211-4150; e-mail cso@mail.gov.mu; internet statsmauritius.gov.mu.

Area and Population

AREA, POPULATION AND DENSITY

Area (sq km)	2,040*
Population (census results)	
1 July 1990	1,058,942†
2 July 2000‡	
Males	583,949
Females	595,188
Total	1,179,137
Population (official estimates at 31 December)	
2006	1,256,739
2007	1,264,863
2008	1,272,040
Density (per sq km) at 31 December 2008	623.4

* 788 sq miles.
† Including an adjustment of 2,115 for underenumeration.
‡ Excluding an adjustment for underenumeration.

ISLANDS

		Population	
	Area (sq km)	Official estimates 2000 census	31 December 2008
Mauritius	1,865	1,143,069	1,234,052
Rodrigues	104	35,779	37,699
Other islands	71	289	289

Ethnic Groups: Island of Mauritius, mid-1982: 664,480 Indo-Mauritians (507,985 Hindus, 156,495 Muslims), 264,537 general population (incl. Creole and Franco-Mauritian communities), 20,669 Chinese.

LANGUAGE GROUPS
(census of 2 July 2000)*

Arabic	806	Marathi	16,587
Bhojpuri	361,250	Tamil	44,731
Chinese	16,972	Telegu	18,802
Creole	454,763	Urdu	34,120
English	1,075	Other languages	169,619
French	21,171	Not stated	3,170
Hindi	35,782	**Total**	**1,178,848**

* Figures refer to the languages of cultural origin of the population of the islands of Mauritius and Rodrigues only. The data exclude an adjustment for underenumeration.

POPULATION BY DISTRICT
(estimates at mid-2007)

Plaine Wilhems	379,446	Riv du Rempart	106,782
Flacq	137,173	Moka	80,171
Pamplemousses	134,037	Black River	71,804
Port Louis	130,050	Savanne	69,870
Grand Port	113,756	Rodrigues	37,314

PRINCIPAL TOWNS
(mid-2007)

Port Louis (capital)	148,877	Curepipe	83,557
Beau Bassin/Rose Hill	109,411	Quatre Bornes	80,542
Vacoas/Phoenix	106,574		

BIRTHS, MARRIAGES AND DEATHS*

	Registered live births		Registered marriages		Registered deaths	
	Number	Rate (per 1,000)	Number	Rate (per 1,000)	Number	Rate (per 1,000)
2001	19,696	16.4	10,635	8.9	7,983	6.7
2002	19,983	16.5	10,484	8.6	8,310	6.9
2003	19,343	15.8	10,812	8.8	8,520	7.0
2004	19,230	15.5	11,385	9.2	8,475	6.8
2005	18,829	15.1	11,294	n.a.	8,648	7.0
2006	17,605	14.1	11,471	n.a.	9,162	7.3
2007	17,034	13.5	11,547	n.a.	8,498	6.7
2008	16,334	12.9	11,120	n.a.	8,957	7.1

* Figures refer to the islands of Mauritius and Rodrigues only. The data are tabulated by year of registration, rather than by year of occurrence.

Life expectancy (WHO estimates, years at birth, WHO estimates): 73 (males 69; females 76) in 2006 (Source: WHO, *World Health Statistics*).

ECONOMICALLY ACTIVE POPULATION
('000 persons aged 15 years and over, incl. foreign workers)

	2005	2006	2007
Agriculture, forestry and fishing	48.6	47.9	47.3
Sugar cane	18.6	18.2	17.8
Mining and quarrying	0.3	0.3	0.2
Manufacturing	120.1	120.9	122.5
EPZ	65.5	65.0	n.a.
Electricity and water	3.0	3.0	3.0
Construction	47.2	48.4	49.7
Wholesale and retail trade, repair of motor vehicles and household goods	76.6	78.8	78.4
Hotels and restaurants	30.9	31.6	32.1
Transport, storage and communications	36.5	36.9	37.4
Financial intermediation	8.8	9.4	10.6
Real estate, renting and business activities	20.0	21.1	24.7
Public administration and defence	39.4	39.6	39.1
Education	27.1	28.4	28.8
Health and social work	15.0	15.0	15.6
Other services	33.7	34.0	34.3
Total employed	**507.2**	**515.3**	**523.7**
Males	338.5	340.5	347.1
Females	168.7	174.8	176.6
Unemployed	51.9	49.8	46.8
Total labour force	**559.1**	**565.1**	**570.5**

Health and Welfare

KEY INDICATORS

Total fertility rate (children per woman, 2006)	1.9
Under-5 mortality rate (per 1,000 live births, 2006)	15
HIV/AIDS (% of persons aged 15–49, 2007)	1.7
Physicians (per 1,000 head, 2004)	1.1
Hospital beds (per 1,000 head, 2006)	3.0
Health expenditure (2006): US $ per head (PPP)	581
Health expenditure (2006): % of GDP	4.3
Health expenditure (2006): public (% of total)	50.4
Access to sanitation (% of persons, 2006)	94
Human Development Index (2006): ranking	74
Human Development Index (2006): value	0.802

For sources and definitions, see explanatory note on p. vi.

Agriculture

PRINCIPAL CROPS
('000 metric tons)

	2005	2006	2007
Potatoes	12.8	11.3	13.0
Sugar cane	4,984.1	4,748.9	4,400.0
Coconuts*	1.9	1.8	1.8
Cabbages and other brassicas	4.8	4.5	4.2
Lettuce and chicory	1.7	1.6	1.2
Tomatoes	12.8	15.1	13.0
Cauliflowers and broccoli	2.0	1.4	1.5
Pumpkins, squash and gourds	14.1	17.6	16.9
Cucumbers and gherkins	8.7	10.8	8.6
Aubergines (Eggplants)*	2.1	2.8	3.0
Onions, dry	5.6	4.5	4.8
Carrots and turnips	3.9	4.1	4.1
Bananas	11.6	10.8	10.5
Pineapples	4.9	5.6	6.5
Tea	1.4	1.6	1.7
Tobacco, unmanufactured	0.3	0.3	0.3

* FAO estimates.

Aggregate production ('000 metric tons, may include official, semi-official or estimated data): Total cereals 0.5 in 2005, 0.5 in 2006, 0.5 in 2007; Total roots and tubers 13.9 in 2005, 12.3 in 2006, 13.9 in 2007; Total vegetables (incl. melons) 79.1 in 2005, 86.3 in 2006, 80.7 in 2007; Total fruits (excl. melons) 17.6 in 2005, 16.7 in 2006, 17.4 in 2007.

Source: FAO.

LIVESTOCK
('000 head, year ending September, FAO estimates)

	2005	2006	2007
Cattle	28	29	29
Pigs	11	13	13
Sheep	11	12	12
Goats	88	92	92
Chickens	10,500	9,900	10,000

Source: FAO.

LIVESTOCK PRODUCTS
('000 metric tons)

	2005	2006	2007
Cattle meat	4*	2	2
Chicken meat	33	36	37
Cows' milk	4	4	4
Hen eggs*	5	5	5

* FAO estimate(s).
Source: FAO.

Forestry

ROUNDWOOD REMOVALS
('000 cubic metres, excl. bark)

	2005	2006	2007
Sawlogs, veneer logs and logs for sleepers	6*	7	6*
Other industrial wood	2	3	3
Fuel wood	5	7*	7*
Total	13	17	15

* FAO estimate.
Source: FAO.

SAWNWOOD PRODUCTION
('000 cubic metres, incl. railway sleepers)

	2005	2006	2007
Coniferous (softwood)	2	4	3
Broadleaved (hardwood)	1	1	—
Total	3	4	3

Source: FAO.

Fishing

(metric tons, live weight)

	2004	2005	2006
Capture	9,971	9,855	8,341*
Groupers and seabasses	794	633	44
Snappers and jobfishes	1,595	2,584	106
Emperors (Scavengers)	3,374	2,534	2,969
Goatfishes	425	456	204
Spinefeet (Rabbitfishes)	319	345	90
Swordfish	1,011	1,001	705
Tuna-like fishes	736	730	706
Octopuses	307	293	84
Aquaculture	350	400	443
Red drum	326	368	416
Total catch	10,321	10,255	8,784*

* Estimate.
Source: FAO.

Industry

SELECTED PRODUCTS
('000 metric tons, unless otherwise indicated)

	2003	2004	2005*
Fish	37.5	40.7	46.0
Frozen	6.3	5.7	5.9
Canned	30.5	34.2	38.9
Raw sugar	537.2	572.3	519.8
Molasses	160.0	155.8	145.4
Beer and stout (hectolitres)	400.8	363.7	339.0
Cigarettes (million)	938	918	900
Iron bars and steel tubes	58.7	59.9	60.5
Fertilizers	89.4	89.4	85.0
Electric energy (million kWh)	2,057	2,138	2,242

* Estimates.

Finance

CURRENCY AND EXCHANGE RATES

Monetary Units
100 cents = 1 Mauritian rupee.

Sterling, Dollar and Euro Equivalents (28 November 2008)
£1 sterling = 48.70 rupees;
US $1 = 31.76 rupees;
€1 = 40.42 rupees;
1,000 Mauritian rupees = £20.53 = $31.49 = €24.74.

Average Exchange Rate (Mauritian rupees per US $)
2005   29.496
2006   31.708
2007   31.314

MAURITIUS

Statistical Survey

BUDGET
(million rupees, year ending 30 June)

Revenue*

	2005/06	2006/07	2007/08†
Current revenue	38,508.7	41,818.2	47,566.0
Tax revenue	35,381.5	38,185.9	42,609.8
Taxes on income, profits and capital gains	7,468.9	7,607.6	8,865.0
Individual income tax	2,767.9	2,332.3	3,005.0
Corporate tax	4,701.0	5,275.3	5,495.0
Taxes on property	1,939.5	2,798.5	3,130.0
Domestic taxes on goods and services	18,762.0	21,403.6	23,764.6
Excise duties	2,467.8	2,998.9	3,220.6
Value-added tax	13,709.5	15,468.1	17,150.0
Taxes on international trade	7,195.4	6,299.2	6,697.4
Other tax revenue	15.7	77.0	152.8
Non-tax revenue	3,127.2	3,632.3	4,956.2
Property income	1,804.8	2,179.5	3,222.0
Other non-tax revenue	1,322.4	1,452.8	1,734.2
Capital revenue	221.7	28.7	—
Total	38,730.4	41,846.9	47,566.0

EXPENSE/OUTLAYS

Expense by economic type	2005/06	2006/07	2007/08†
Current expenditure	41,915.3	44,122.2	50,453.1
Wages and salaries	12,298.7	12,263.4	13,279.2
Other purchases of goods and services	4,593.6	4,111.8	4,253.8
Interest payments	7,354.7	8,882.5	12,048.0
Subsidies and other current transfers	17,668.3	18,864.5	20,872.1
Transfer to non-profit institutions and households	14,130.9	15,775.8	17,707.2
Capital expenditure	6,959.9	7,110.9	9,379.3
Acquisition of fixed capital assets	5,159.2	4,608.7	6,689.3
Capital transfers	1,653.0	2,348.5	2,555.6
Total	48,875.2	51,233.1	59,832.4

Outlays by function of government	2005/06	2006/07	2007/08†
General government services	7,419.0	7,499.6	8,101.8
General public services	3,439.3	3,438.3	3,801.8
Defence	345.4	334.5	—
Public order and safety	3,634.3	3,726.8	4,300.0
Community and Social Services	21,110.7	22,514.5	24,704.7
Education	6,127.7	6,387.4	6,973.8
Health	4,049.0	4,240.1	4,355.9
Social security and welfare	9,578.8	10,595.9	11,906.4
Housing and community amenities	869.6	821.0	989.0
Recreational, cultural and religious services	485.6	470.1	479.6
Economic services	3,884.8	3,067.1	3,365.0
Agriculture, forestry, fishing and hunting	1,187.6	1,193.0	1,281.5
Transportation and communications	822.3	982.2	1,136.9
Other current expenditure	9,500.8	11,041.0	14,281.6
Public debt interest	7,354.7	8,882.5	12,048.0
Capital expenditure	6,959.9	7,110.9	9,379.3
Total expenditure	48,875.2	51,233.1	59,832.4

* Excluding grants received (million rupees): 489.2 in 2005/06; 321.9 in 2006/07; 2,935.0 in 2007/08 (estimate).
† Budget estimates.

INTERNATIONAL RESERVES
(US $ million at 31 December)

	2005	2006	2007
Gold (market prices)	25.9	31.3	41.5
IMF special drawing rights	25.7	27.5	29.3
Reserve position in IMF	25.0	15.8	11.1
Foreign exchange	1,298.2	1,226.3	1,739.9
Total	1,374.8	1,300.9	1,821.8

Source: IMF, *International Financial Statistics*.

MONEY SUPPLY
(million rupees at 31 December)

	2005	2006	2007
Currency outside banks	11,664.1	13,028.3	14,260.2
Demand deposits at deposit money banks	24,711.2	26,780.5	32,560.0
Total money (incl. others)	36,702.8	40,206.6	47,225.9

Source: IMF, *International Financial Statistics*.

COST OF LIVING
(Consumer Price Index; base: July 2001–June 2002 = 100)

	2004	2005	2006
Food and non-alcoholic beverages	112.5	119.1	131.0
Alcoholic beverages and tobacco	119.8	127.0	143.6
Clothing and footwear	105.0	106.3	113.4
Housing, fuel and electricity	107.1	110.8	123.6
Household operations	107.6	112.8	120.3
All items (incl. others)	112.1	117.6	128.1

NATIONAL ACCOUNTS
(million rupees in current prices, revised estimates)

National Income and Product

	2006	2007	2008
Compensation of employees	74,575	83,659	94,954
Operating surplus / Consumption of fixed capital	105,692	121,146	134,392
Gross domestic product (GDP) at factor cost	180,267	204,805	229,346
Taxes on production and imports / Less Subsidies	26,061	30,656	34,543
GDP in purchasers' values	206,328	235,461	263,889
Primary incomes received from abroad / Less Primary incomes paid abroad	1,633	7,023	6,416
Gross national income	207,961	242,484	270,305
Current transfers from abroad / Less Current transfers paid abroad	2,269	3,882	5,878
Gross national disposable income	210,230	246,366	276,183

Expenditure on the Gross Domestic Product

	2006	2007	2008
Private final consumption expenditure	145,491	165,790	191,642
Government final consumption expenditure	29,355	30,743	34,657
Gross fixed capital formation	50,048	59,170	64,790
Increase in stocks	4,734	4,095	4,867
Total domestic expenditure	229,628	259,798	295,956
Exports of goods and services	127,128	138,530	144,329
Less Imports of goods and services	150,429	162,867	176,396
GDP in purchasers' values	206,328	235,461	263,889

MAURITIUS

Gross Domestic Product by Economic Activity

	2006	2007	2008
Agriculture, hunting, forestry, and fishing	10,130	9,834	9,987
Sugar cane	5,137	4,620	4,348
Mining and quarrying	101	96	97
Manufacturing	36,356	41,075	45,013
Electricity, gas and water	3,521	3,668	4,718
Construction	10,205	13,145	16,116
Wholesale and retail trade, repair of motor vehicles and personal goods	22,534	25,598	28,580
Hotels and restaurants	15,500	19,517	20,271
Transport, storage and communications	22,169	24,696	26,369
Financial intermediation	18,850	21,607	25,410
Real estate, renting and business activities	19,071	22,615	26,831
Public administration and defence; compulsory social security	12,199	12,674	14,747
Education	8,440	9,110	10,302
Health and social work	6,266	6,824	7,979
Other services	6,784	7,981	9,423
Sub-total	192,126	218,440	245,843
Less Financial intermediation services indirectly measured	10,117	11,528	14,000
Gross value added in basic prices	182,009	206,912	231,843
Taxes, less subsidies, on products	24,319	28,549	32,046
GDP in market prices	206,328	235,461	263,889

BALANCE OF PAYMENTS
(US $ million)

	2005	2006	2007
Exports of goods f.o.b.	2,138.4	2,328.8	2,230.7
Imports of goods f.o.b.	−2,935.2	−3,408.8	−3,656.4
Trade balance	−796.8	−1,080.0	−1,425.7
Exports of services	1,618.1	1,671.3	2,205.3
Imports of services	−1,197.7	−1,316.9	−1,545.4
Balance on goods and services	−376.5	−725.5	−765.8
Other income received	142.9	373.9	816.5
Other income paid	−151.3	−323.8	−577.6
Balance on goods, services and income	−385.0	−675.5	−526.9
Current transfers received	162.3	179.3	253.9
Current transfers paid	−101.3	−108.2	−135.3
Current balance	−324.0	−604.4	−408.3
Capital account (net)	−1.8	−2.7	−1.6
Direct investment abroad	−47.0	−9.6	−59.6
Direct investment from abroad	41.8	106.8	340.8
Portfolio investment assets	−41.6	−110.5	−138.5
Portfolio investment liabilities	25.4	80.6	153.7
Other investment assets	−230.9	−371.0	−671.5
Other investment liabilities	394.3	476.5	894.1
Net errors and omissions	18.7	294.2	327.1
Overall balance	−165.0	−140.1	436.0

Source: IMF, *International Financial Statistics*.

External Trade

PRINCIPAL COMMODITIES
(million rupees)

Imports c.i.f.	2005	2006	2007
Food and live animals	13,820	17,276	20,032
Fish and fish preparations	4,266	6,687	7,066
Mineral fuels, lubricants, etc.	15,394	19,321	22,180
Refined petroleum products	13,471	17,025	18,969
Chemicals	7,386	8,157	9,414
Basic manufactures	19,297	21,811	24,733
Textile yarn, fabrics, etc	3,167	4,097	3,867
Cotton fabrics	1,751	1,875	2,217
Machinery and transport equipment	26,110	35,931	28,529
Machinery specialized for particular industries	3,046	3,350	3,774
General industrial machinery, equipment and parts	2,795	3,049	4,278
Telecommunications and sound equipment	9,739	10,678	5,430
Other electrical machinery, apparatus, etc.	2,996	2,926	3,518
Road motor vehicles	4,216	4,505	5,228
Miscellaneous manufactured articles	7,257	8,208	9,583
Total (incl. others)	93,282	115,502	121,037

Exports f.o.b.*	2005	2006	2007
Food and live animals	17,248	20,185	19,666
Basic manufactures	5,002	5,532	5,675
Chemicals and related products	860	867	1,310
Machinery and transport equipment	9,335	12,077	4,078
Miscellaneous manufactured articles	25,757	28,973	31,972
Total (incl. others)	59,095	68,966	64,265

* Excluding stores and bunkers for ships and aircraft (million rupees): 4,124 in 2005; 5,071 in 2006; 5,443 in 2007.

PRINCIPAL TRADING PARTNERS
(million rupees)*

Imports c.i.f.	2005	2006	2007
Argentina	1,137	994	1,398
Australia	2,699	3,105	2,752
Bahrain	5,086	1,349	6
Belgium	1,488	1,758	1,607
China, People's Repub.	9,166	9,988	13,768
Denmark	1,010	240	421
Finland	4,485	2,784	1,187
France	6,958	16,440	12,813
Germany	3,794	4,613	3,268
Hong Kong	652	597	582
Hungary	2,141	4,007	955
India	6,461	15,687	25,633
Indonesia	2,112	2,346	2,799
Italy	2,402	2,950	3,321
Japan	3,333	3,254	4,334
Korea, Repub.	906	1,081	1,663
Madagascar	436	478	553
Malaysia	2,670	2,978	3,116
Pakistan	1,011	1,239	1,208
Saudi Arabia	3,409	4,000	1,346
Singapore	1,586	1,103	1,333
South Africa	8,066	8,433	8,910
Spain	2,091	2,325	3,136
Switzerland	1,121	1,296	2,011
Thailand	1,532	1,677	2,147
United Arab Emirates	3,588	3,309	1,482
United Kingdom	2,589	2,894	3,622
USA	1,972	2,328	2,777
Total (incl. others)	93,282	115,502	121,037

MAURITIUS

Statistical Survey

Exports f.o.b.	2005	2006	2007
Belgium	1,559	1,851	2,077
France	8,391	8,704	8,889
Germany	1,070	1,295	1,697
Italy	3,308	2,754	3,568
Madagascar	3,373	3,288	3,865
Netherlands	723	870	1,091
Portugal	558	187	732
Réunion	1,561	1,652	1,839
South Africa	788	1,488	1,981
Spain	1,589	2,447	2,048
Switzerland	644	662	833
United Arab Emirates	4,903	7,882	2,453
United Kingdom	19,215	22,362	21,924
USA	5,640	5,754	4,760
Total (incl. others)	59,095	68,966	64,265

* Imports by country of origin; exports by country of destination (including re-exports, excluding ships' stores and bunkers).

Transport

ROAD TRAFFIC
(motor vehicles registered at 31 December)

	2006	2007	2008
Private vehicles:			
Cars	120,046	137,520	155,528
Motorcycles and mopeds	138,174	142,606	147,988
Commercial vehicles:			
Buses	2,612	2,753	2,762
Taxis	6,860	6,885	6,941
Goods vehicles	36,794	37,470	38,060

SHIPPING
Merchant Fleet
(registered at 31 December)

	2005	2006	2007
Number of vessels	47	45	43
Total displacement ('000 grt)	70.6	68.6	39.7

Source: Lloyd's Register-Fairplay, *World Fleet Statistics*.

Sea-borne Freight Traffic
('000 metric tons)

	2005	2006	2007*
Goods unloaded	3,667	4,433	5,080
Goods loaded†	1,514	1,253	1,179

* Provisional.
† Excluding ships' bunkers.

CIVIL AVIATION
(traffic)

	2005	2006	2007*
Aircraft landings†	8,349	9,211	8,543
Freight unloaded (metric tons)‡	20,100	21,200	22,700
Freight loaded (metric tons)‡	21,200	24,400	24,900

* Provisional.
† Commercial aircraft only.
‡ Figures are rounded.

Tourism

FOREIGN TOURIST ARRIVALS

Country of residence	2006	2007	2008
France	182,295	240,028	260,054
Germany	57,251	65,165	61,484
India	37,498	42,974	43,911
Italy	69,407	69,510	66,432
Réunion	89,127	95,823	96,174
South Africa	70,796	81,733	84,448
Switzerland	16,161	17,546	16,037
United Kingdom	102,333	107,297	107,919
Total (incl. others)	788,276	906,971	930,456

Tourism earnings (gross, million rupees): 31,942 in 2006; 40,687 in 2007; 41,213 in 2008.

Communications Media

	2004	2005	2006
Telephones ('000 main lines in use)	353.8	357.5	357.3
Mobile cellular telephones ('000 subscribers)	547.7	656.8	772.4
Personal computers ('000 in use)	200	200	n.a.
Internet users ('000)	240	300	320
Broadband subscribers ('000)	2.6	3.1	21.9
Television sets licensed ('000)	260.3	275.8	277.4
Daily newspapers	7	9	8
Non-daily newspapers	35	37	38

1996: Book production: titles 80, copies ('000) 163.

1997: Facsimile machines (number in use) 28,000.

2007: Mobile cellular telephones ('000 subscribers) 936.0; Internet users ('000) 340.

Sources: partly UNESCO, *Statistical Yearbook*; UN, *Statistical Yearbook*; International Telecommunication Union.

Education

(March 2007)

	Institutions	Personnel	Students*
Pre-primary	1,076	3,386	36,421
Primary	289	6,679†	119,310
Secondary	186	7,423	116,706
Technical and vocational	153	701	9,573

* By enrolment.
† Excluding instruction in oriental language.

Adult literacy rate (official estimates): 87.4% (males 90.2%; females 84.7%) in 2007 (Source: UNESCO Institute for Statistics).

Directory

The Constitution

The Mauritius Independence Order, which established a self-governing state, came into force on 12 March 1968, and was subsequently amended. Constitutional amendments providing for the adoption of republican status were approved by the Legislative Assembly (henceforth known as the National Assembly) on 10 December 1991, and came into effect on 12 March 1992. The main provisions of the revised Constitution are listed below:

HEAD OF STATE

The Head of State is the President of the Republic, who is elected by a simple majority of the National Assembly for a five-year term of office. The President appoints the Prime Minister (in whom executive power is vested) and, on the latter's recommendation, other ministers.

COUNCIL OF MINISTERS

The Council of Ministers, which is headed by the Prime Minister, is appointed by the President and is responsible to the National Assembly.

THE NATIONAL ASSEMBLY

The National Assembly, which has a term of five years, comprises the Speaker, 62 members elected by universal adult suffrage, a maximum of eight additional members and the Attorney-General (if not an elected member). The island of Mauritius is divided into 20 three-member constituencies for legislative elections. Rodrigues returns two members to the National Assembly. The official language of the National Assembly is English, but any member may address the Speaker in French.

The Government

HEAD OF STATE

President: Sir ANEROOD JUGNAUTH (took office 7 October 2003; re-elected by vote of the National Assembly 19 September 2008).
Vice-President: ANGIDI VERRIAH CHETTIAR.

COUNCIL OF MINISTERS
(April 2009)

Prime Minister, Minister of Defence and Home Affairs: NAVINCHANDRA RAMGOOLAM.
Deputy Prime Minister and Minister of Renewable Energy and Public Utilities: AHMED RASHID BEEBEEJAUN.
Vice-Prime Minister and Minister of Tourism, Leisure and External Communications: CHARLES GAËTAN XAVIER-LUC DUVAL.
Vice-Prime Minister and Minister of Finance and Economic Development: Dr RAMA KRISHNA SITHANEN.
Minister of Public Infrastructure, Land Transport and Shipping: ANIL KUMAR BACHOO.
Minister of Foreign Affairs, Regional Integration and International Trade: ARVIN BOOLELL.
Minister of Industry, Science and Research: DHARAMBEER GOKHOOL.
Minister of Housing and Lands: ABU TWALIB KASENALLY.
Minister of Local Government, Rodrigues and Outer Islands: JAMES BURTY DAVID.
Minister of Social Security, National Solidarity and Senior Citizens' Welfare and Reform Institutions: SHEILABAI BAPPOO.
Minister of Women's Rights, Child Development and Family Welfare: INDRANEE SEEBUN.
Minister of Education, Culture and Human Resources: VASANT KUMAR BUNWAREE.
Attorney-General: JAYARAMA VALAYDEN.
Minister of Agro-industry, Food Production and Security: SATYA VEYASH FAUGOO.
Minister of Health and Quality of Life: RAJESHWAR JEETAH.
Minister of Business, Enterprise and Co-operatives: MAHENDRA GOWRESSOO.
Minister of Information and Communication Technology: MOHAMMED ASRAF ALLY DULULL.
Minister of Consumer Protection and the Citizens' Charter: SYLVIO HOCK SHEEN TANG WAH HING.
Minister of Labour, Industrial Relations and Employment: JEAN FRANÇOIS CHAUMIERE.
Minister of the Environment and the National Development Unit: LORMUS BUNDHOO.
Minister of Civil Service and Administrative Reforms: BALKISSOON HOOKOOM.
Minister of Youth and Sports: SATYAPRAKASH RITOO.

MINISTRIES

Office of the President: State House, Le Réduit, Port Louis; tel. 454-3021; fax 464-5370; e-mail president@mail.gov.mu; internet president.gov.mu.
Office of the Prime Minister: New Treasury Bldg, Port Louis; tel. 201-1003; fax 208-8619; e-mail primeminister@mail.gov.mu; internet pm.gov.mu.
Ministry of Agro-industry and Fisheries: Renganaden Seeneevassen Bldg, 8th and 9th Floor, cnr Jules Koenig and Maillard Sts, Port Louis; tel. 212-2335; fax 212-4427; e-mail moa-headoffice@mail.gov.mu; internet agriculture.gov.mu.
Ministry of Arts and Culture: Renganaden Seeneevassen Bldg, 7th Floor, cnr Pope Hennessy and Maillard Sts, Port Louis; tel. 212-9993; fax 212-9366; e-mail moac@mail.gov.mu; internet culture.gov.mu.
Ministry of Civil Service Affairs and Administrative Reform: New Government Centre, 7th Floor, Port Louis; tel. 201-2886; fax 212-9528; e-mail civser@mail.gov.mu; internet www.civilservice.gov.mu.
Ministry of Defence and Home Affairs: New Government Centre, 4th Floor, Port Louis; e-mail pmo@mail.gov.mu; internet pmo.gov.mu/dha.
Ministry of Education and Human Resources: IVTB House, Pont Fer, Phoenix; tel. 601-5200; fax 698-2550; e-mail moeps@mail.gov.mu; internet ministry-education.gov.mu.
Ministry of the Environment and the National Development Unit: Ken Lee Tower, Barracks St, Port Louis; tel. 212-3363; fax 212-8324; e-mail admenv@internet.mu; internet environment.gov.mu.
Ministry of Finance and Economic Development: Government House, Ground Floor, Port Louis; tel. 201-1146; fax 211-0096; e-mail mof@mail.gov.mu; internet mof.gov.mu.
Ministry of Foreign Affairs, International Trade and Co-operation: New Government Centre, 5th Floor, Port Louis; tel. 201-1648; fax 208-8087; e-mail mfa@mail.gov.mu; internet foreign.gov.mu.
Ministry of Health and Quality of Life: 5th Floor, Emmanuel Anquetil Bldg, Sir Seewoosagur Ramgoolam St, Port Louis; tel. 201-1912; fax 208-0376; e-mail moh@mail.gov.mu; internet health.gov.mu.
Ministry of Housing and Land: Moorgate House, Port Louis; tel. 212-6022; fax 212-7482; internet housing.gov.mu.
Ministry of Industry, Science and Research: Air Mauritius Centre, 7th Floor, John F. Kennedy St, Port Louis; tel. 210-7100; fax 212-8201; e-mail mind@mail.gov.mu; internet industry.gov.mu.
Ministry of Information Technology and Telecommunications: Air Mauritius Centre, Level 9, John F. Kennedy St, Port Louis; tel. 210-0201; fax 212-1673; e-mail mtel@mail.gov.mu; internet telecomit.gov.mu.
Ministry of Justice and Human Rights: Renganaden Seeneevassen Bldg, 2nd Floor, Port Louis; tel. 212-2139; fax 212-6742; e-mail ago@intnet.mu; internet attorneygeneral.gov.mu.
Ministry of Labour, Industrial Relations and Employment: Victoria House, cnr St Louis and Barracks Sts, Port Louis; tel. 207-2600; fax 212-3070; e-mail mol@mail.gov.mu; internet labour.gov.mu.
Ministry of Local Government: Emmanuel Anquetil Bldg, 3rd Floor, cnr Sir Seewoosagur Ramgoolam and Jules Koenig Sts, Port Louis; tel. 201-1216; fax 208-9729; e-mail mlg@mail.gov.mu; internet localgovernment.gov.mu.
Ministry of Public Infrastructure, Land Transport and Shipping: Moorgate House, 9th Floor, Sir William Newton St, Port Louis; tel. 210-7271; fax 210-6344; e-mail mpi@mail.gov.mu; internet publicinfrastructure.gov.mu.
Ministry of Public Utilities: Medcor Bldg, 10th Floor, John F. Kennedy St, Port Louis; tel. 210-3994; fax 208-6497; e-mail minpuuti@intnet.mu; internet publicutilities.gov.mu.
Ministry of Rodrigues and Outer Islands: Fon Sing Bldg, 1st floor, Edith Cavell St, Port Louis; tel. 208-8472; fax 212-6329; internet shipping.gov.mu.

MAURITIUS

Ministry of Social Security, National Solidarity and Senior Citizens' Welfare and Reform Institutions: Renganaden Seeneevassen Bldg, Jules Koenig St, Port Louis; tel. 207-0625; fax 212-8190; e-mail mss@mail.gov.mu; internet socialsecurity.gov.mu.

Ministry of Tourism, Leisure and External Communications: Air Mauritius Centre, Level 12, John F. Kennedy St, Port Louis; tel. 211-7930; fax 208-6776; e-mail mtou@mail.gov.mu; internet tourism.gov.mu.

Ministry of Women's Rights, Child Development, Family Welfare and Consumer Protection: CSK Bldg, cnr Remy Ollier and Emmanuel Anquetil Sts, Port Louis; tel. 206-3700; fax 240-7717; e-mail mwfwcd@mail.gov.mu; internet women.gov.mu.

Ministry of Youth and Sports: Emmanuel Anquetil Bldg, 3rd Floor, Sir Seewoosagur Ramgoolam St, Port Louis; tel. 201-2543; fax 210-7754; e-mail mys@mail.gov.mu; internet youthsport.gov.mu.

Legislature

National Assembly

Port Louis; tel. 201-1414; fax 212-8364; e-mail themace@intnet.mu; internet mauritiusassembly.gov.mu.

Speaker: KAILASH PURRYAG.

General Election, 3 July 2005

	Seats		
Party	Directly elected	Additional*	Total
Social Alliance†	38	4	42
Mouvement Socialiste Militant (MSM)/Mouvement Militant Mauricien (MMM)	22	2	24
Organisation du Peuple Rodriguais (OPR)	2	2	4
Total	62	8	70

* Awarded to those among the unsuccessful candidates who attracted the largest number of votes, in order to ensure that a balance of ethnic groups are represented in the Assembly.
† Alliance primarily comprising the Mauritius Labour Party, the Parti Mauricien Xavier-Luc Duval, the Mouvement Républicain and the Mouvement Militant Socialiste Mauricien.

Election Commission

Electoral Commissioner's Office (ECO): 4th Floor, Max City Bldg, cnr Louis Pasteur and Remy Ollier Sts, Port Louis; tel. 241-7000; fax 241-0967; e-mail elec@mail.gov.mu; internet www.gov.mu/portal/site/eco; under the aegis of the Prime Minister's Office; Commissioner appointed by the Judicial and Legal Service Commission; Electoral Commissioner M. I. ABDOOL RAHMAN.

Political Organizations

Mauritius Labour Party (MLP) (Parti Travailliste): 7 Guy Rozemont Sq., Port Louis; tel. 212-6691; fax 210-0189; e-mail labour@intnet.mu; internet labour.intnet.mu; f. 1936; formed part of the Social Alliance for the 2005 election and subsequently a govt; Leader Dr NAVINCHANDRA RAMGOOLAM; Chair. ETIENNE SINATAMBOU; Sec.-Gen. DEVENAND VIRAHSAWMY.

Mouvement Militant Mauricien (MMM): 21 Poudrière St, Port Louis; tel. 212-6553; fax 208-9939; internet mmm.mmmonline.org; f. 1969; socialist; formed an alliance with the Mouvement Socialiste Militant for both the 2000 and the 2005 elections; Pres. SAM LAUTHAN; Leader PAUL BÉRENGER; Sec.-Gen. STEVEN OBEEGADOO, RAJESH BHAGWAN.

Mouvement Militant Socialiste Mauricien (MMSM): Port Louis; forms part of the incumbent Social Alliance, elected in 2005; announced intention to merge with the MMM in July 2008; Leader MADUN DULLOO.

Mouvement Rodriguais (MR): Port Mathurin, Rodrigues; tel. 831-1876 (Port Mathurin); tel. and fax 831-2648 (Port Louis); e-mail numally@intnet.mu; f. 1992; represents the interests of Rodrigues; Leader LOUIS JOSEPH (NICHOLAS) VON-MALLY.

Mouvement Sociale Démocrate (MSD) (Social Democratic Movement): Port Louis; f. 2005; Leader ANIL BACHOO.

Mouvement Socialiste Militant (MSM): Sun Trust Bldg, 31 Edith Cavell St, Port Louis; tel. 212-8787; fax 212-9334; e-mail info@msmparty.org; internet www.msmparty.org; f. 1983 by fmr mems of the MMM; dominant party in subsequent coalition govts until Dec. 1995 and again from 2000–05; Leader PRAVIND JUGNAUTH; Pres. JOE LESJONGARD; Sec.-Gen. NANDO BODHA.

Organisation du Peuple Rodriguais (OPR): Mont Lubin, Rodrigues; represents the interests of Rodrigues; f. 1976; Leader LOUIS SERGE CLAIR.

Parti Mauricien Social Démocrate (PMSD): Melville, Grand Gaube; centre-right; participated in an alliance with the MSM and MMM for the 2005 legislative and municipal elections; Leader MAURICE ALLET; Sec.-Gen. JACQUES PANGLOSE.

Parti Mauricien Xavier-Luc Duval (PMXD): Port Louis; f. 1998; forms part of the Social Alliance; Leader CHARLES GAËTAN XAVIER-LUC DUVAL.

Union Nationale (Mauritian National Union): Port Louis; f. 2006; Chair. ASHOCK JUGNAUTH.

Some of the blocs and parties that participated in the 2005 election include the **Front Solidarité Mauricienne (FSM)**, **Les Verts Fraternels/The Greens** (Leader SYLVIO MICHEL), the **Mouvement Républicain** (Leader RAMA VALAYDEV), the **Parti du Peuple Mauricien (PPM)**, the **Mouvement Démocratique National Raj Dayal (MDN Raj Dayal)**, the **Rezistans ek Alternativ** (Secretary ASHOK SUBRON), **Lalit** (lalitmauritius.com) and the **Tamil Council**.

Diplomatic Representation

EMBASSIES AND HIGH COMMISSIONS IN MAURITIUS

Australia: Rogers House, 2nd Floor, John F. Kennedy St, POB 541, Port Louis; tel. 202-0160; fax 208-8878; e-mail ahc.portlouis@dfat.gov.au; internet www.mauritius.embassy.gov.au; High Commissioner CATHERINE JOHNSTONE.

China, People's Republic: Royal Rd, Belle Rose, Rose Hill; tel. 454-9111; fax 464-6012; e-mail chinaemb_mu@mfa.gov.cn; internet www.ambchine.mu; Ambassador GAO YUCHEN.

Egypt: Sun Trust Bldg, 2nd floor, Edith Cavell St, Port Louis; tel. 213-1765; fax 213-1768; Ambassador BAKRY ROSHDY EL-AMARY.

France: 14 St George St, Port Louis; tel. 202-0100; fax 202-0110; e-mail ambafr@intnet.mu; internet www.ambafrance-mu.org; Ambassador JACQUES MAILLARD.

India: Life Insurance Corpn of India Bldg, 6th Floor, John F. Kennedy St, POB 162, Port Louis; tel. 208-3775; fax 208-6859; e-mail hicom.ss@intnet.mu; internet indiahighcom.intnet.mu; High Commissioner BONDAL JAISHANKAR.

Madagascar: Guiot Pasceau St, Floreal, POB 3, Port Louis; tel. 686-5015; fax 686-7040; e-mail madmail@intnet.mu; Ambassador BRUNO RANARIVELO.

Pakistan: 9A Queen Mary Ave, Floreal, Port Louis; tel. 698-8501; fax 698-8405; e-mail pareportlouis@hotmail.com; High Commissioner SYED HASAN JAVED.

Russia: Queen Mary Ave, POB 10, Floreal, Port Louis; tel. 696-1545; fax 696-5027; e-mail rusemb.mu@intnet.mu; Ambassador OLGA IVANOVA.

South Africa: BAI Bldg, 4th Floor, 25 Pope Hennessy St, POB 908, Port Louis; tel. 212-6925; fax 212-6936; e-mail sahc@intnet.mu; High Commissioner MADUMANE M. MATABANE.

United Kingdom: Les Cascades Bldg, 7th Floor, Edith Cavell St, POB 1063, Port Louis; tel. 202-9400; fax 202-9408; e-mail bhc@intnet.mu; High Commissioner Dr JOHN MURTON.

USA: Rogers House, 4th Floor, John F. Kennedy St, POB 544, Port Louis; tel. 208-4400; fax 208-9534; e-mail usembass@intnet.mu; internet mauritius.usembassy.gov; Ambassador CESAR BENITO CABRERA.

Judicial System

The laws of Mauritius are derived both from the French Code Napoléon and from English Law. The Judicial Department consists of the Supreme Court, presided over by the Chief Justice and such number of Puisne Judges as may be prescribed by Parliament (currently nine), who are also Judges of the Court of Criminal Appeal and the Court of Civil Appeal. These courts hear appeals from the Intermediate Court, the Industrial Court and 10 District Courts (including that of Rodrigues). The Industrial Court has special jurisdiction to protect the constitutional rights of the citizen. There is a right of appeal in certain cases from the Supreme Court to the Judicial Committee of the Privy Council in the United Kingdom.

Supreme Court: Jules Koenig St, Port Louis; tel. 212-0275; tel. 212-9946; internet supremecourt.intnet.mu.

MAURITIUS — *Directory*

Chief Justice: ARIANGA PILLAY.
Senior Puisne Judge: B. YEUNG SIK YUEN.

Religion

Hindus are estimated to comprise more than 50% of the population, with Christians accounting for some 30% and Muslims 17%. There is also a small Buddhist community.

CHRISTIANITY

The Anglican Communion

Anglicans in Mauritius are within the Church of the Province of the Indian Ocean, comprising seven dioceses (five in Madagascar, one in Mauritius and one in Seychelles). The Archbishop of the Province is the Bishop of Antananarivo, Madagascar.

Bishop of Mauritius (also Archbishop of the Province of the Indian Ocean): Most Rev. GERALD JAMES (IAN) ERNEST, Bishop's House, Phoenix; tel. 686-5158; fax 697-1096; e-mail dioang@intnet.mu.

The Presbyterian Church of Mauritius

Minister: Pasteur ANDRÉ DE RÉLAND, cnr Farquhar and Royal Rds, Coignet, Rose Hill; tel. 464-5265; fax 395-2068; e-mail embrau@bow.intnet.mu; f. 1814.

The Roman Catholic Church

Mauritius comprises a single diocese, directly responsible to the Holy See, and an apostolic vicariate on Rodrigues. At 31 December 2006 there were an estimated 311,856 adherents in the country, representing about 26.4% of the total population.

Bishop of Port Louis: Rt Rev. MAURICE PIAT, Evêché, 13 Mgr Gonin St, Port Louis; tel. 208-3068; fax 208-6607; e-mail eveche@intnet.mu.

BAHÁ'Í FAITH

National Spiritual Assembly: Port Louis; tel. 212-2179; mems resident in 190 localities.

ISLAM

World Islamic Mission (Mauritius): Old Moka Rd, Bell Village, Port Louis; tel. 210-9445; fax 211-1092; e-mail wim@wimmauritius.org; internet www.wimmauritius.org; Gen. Sec. ABDUS SABOOR SALEH.

The Press

DAILIES

China Times: 24 Emmanuel Anquetil St, POB 325, Port Louis; tel. 240-3067; f. 1953; Chinese; Editor-in-Chief LONG SIONG AH KENG; circ. 3,000.

Chinese Daily News: 32 Rémy Ollier St, POB 316, Port Louis; tel. 240-0472; f. 1932; Chinese; Editor-in-Chief WONG YUEN MOY; circ. 5,000.

L'Express: 3 Brown Sequard St, POB 247, Port Louis; tel. 206-8200; fax 247-1010; internet www.lexpress-net.com; f. 1963; owned by La Sentinelle Ltd; English and French; Editor-in-Chief RAJ MEETARBHAN; circ. 35,000.

Le Matinal: AAPCA House, 6 La Poudrière St, Port Louis; tel. 207-0909; fax 213-4069; e-mail editorial@lematinal.com; internet www.lematinal.com; f. 2003; in French and English; AAPCA (Mauritius) Ltd; CEO S. P. SINGH.

Le Mauricien: 8 St George St, POB 7, Port Louis; tel. 208-3251; fax 208-7059; e-mail redaction@lemauricien.com; internet www.lemauricien.com; f. 1907; English and French; Editor-in-Chief GILBERT AHNEE; circ. 35,000.

Le Quotidien: Pearl House, 4th Floor, 16 Sir Virgile Naz St, Port Louis; tel. 208-2631; fax 211-7479; e-mail quotidien@bow.intnet.mu; f. 1996; English and French; Dirs JACQUES DAVID, PATRICK MICHEL; circ. 30,000.

Le Socialiste: Manilall Bldg, 3rd Floor, Brabant St, Port Louis; tel. 208-8003; fax 211-3890; English and French; Editor-in-Chief VEDI BALLAH; circ. 7,000.

The Tribune: Port Louis; f. 1999; Publr HARISH CHUNDUNSING.

WEEKLIES AND FORTNIGHTLIES

5-Plus Dimanche: 3 Brown Sequard St, Port Louis; tel. 213-5500; fax 213-5551; e-mail comments@5plusltd.com; internet www.5plusltd.com; f. 1994; English and French; Editor-in-Chief FINLAY SALESSE; circ. 30,000.

5-Plus Magazine: 3 Brown Sequard St, Port Louis; tel. 213-5500; fax 213-5551; e-mail comments@5plusltd.com; f. 1990; English and French; Editor-in-Chief PIERRE BENOÎT; circ. 10,000.

Bollywood Massala: Le Défi Bldg, Royal Rd, Port Louis; tel. 211-8131; fax 213-0959; e-mail ledefi.plus@intnet.mu; internet www.defimedia.info.

Business Magazine: TN Tower, 2nd Floor, 13 St George St, Port Louis; tel. 211-3048; fax 211-1926; e-mail businessmag@intnet.mu; internet www.businessmag.mu; f. 1992; owned by Business Publications Ltd; English and French; Editor-in-Chief LINDSAY RIVIÈRE; circ. 7,500.

Le Croissant: cnr Velore and Noor Essan Mosque Sts, Port Louis; tel. 240-7105; English and French; Editor-in-Chief RAYMOND RICHARD NAUVEL; circ. 25,000.

Le Défi-Plus: Le Défi Bldg, Royal Rd, Port Louis; tel. 211-8131; fax 213-0959; e-mail ledefi.plus@intnet.mu; internet www.defimedia.info; Saturdays.

Le Dimanche: 5 Jemmapes St, Port Louis; tel. 212-5887; fax 212-1177; e-mail ledmer@intnet.mu; f. 1961; English and French; Editor RAYMOND RICHARD NAUVEL; circ. 25,000.

L'Hèbdo: Le Défi Bldg, Royal Rd, Port Louis; tel. 211-8131; fax 213-0959; e-mail ledefi.plus@intnet.mu; internet www.defimedia.info.

Impact News: 10 Dr Yves Cantin St, Port Louis; tel. 211-5284; fax 211-7821; e-mail farhadr@wanadoo.mu; internet www.impactnews.info; English and French; Editor-in-Chief FARHAD RAMJAUN.

Lalit de Klas: 153B Royal Rd, G.R.N.W., Port Louis; tel. 208-2132; e-mail lalitmail@intnet.mu; internet www.lalitmauritius.org; English, French and Mauritian Creole; Editor RADA KISTNASAMY.

Mauritius Times: 23 Bourbon St, Port Louis; tel. and fax 212-1313; e-mail mtimes@intnet.mu; internet www.mauritiustimes.com; f. 1954; English and French; Editor-in-Chief MADHUKAR RAMLALLAH; circ. 15,000.

Mirror: 39 Emmanuel Anquetil St, Port Louis; tel. 240-3298; Chinese; Editor-in-Chief NG KEE SIONG; circ. 4,000.

News on Sunday: Dr Eugen Laurent St, POB 230, Port Louis; tel. 211-5902; fax 211-7302; e-mail newsonsunday@news.intnet.mu; internet newsonsunday.150m.com; f. 1996; owned by Le Défi Group; weekly; in English; Editor NAGUIB LALLMAHOMED; circ. 10,000.

Le Nouveau Militant: 21 Poudrière St, Port Louis; tel. 212-6553; fax 208-2291; f. 1979; publ. by the Mouvement Militant Mauricien; English and French; Editor-in-Chief J. RAUMIAH.

Le Rodriguais: Saint Gabriel, Rodrigues; tel. 831-1613; fax 831-1484; f. 1989; Creole, English and French; Editor JACQUES EDOUARD; circ. 2,000.

Star: 38 Labourdonnais St, Port Louis; tel. 212-2736; fax 211-7781; e-mail starpress@intnet.mu; internet www.mauriweb.com/star; English and French; Editor-in-Chief REZA ISSACK.

Sunday: Port Louis; tel. 208-9516; fax 208-7059; f. 1966; English and French; Editor-in-Chief SUBASH GOBIN.

Turf Magazine: 8 George St, POB 7, Port Louis; tel. 207-8200; fax 208-7059; e-mail bdlm@intnet.mu; internet www.lemauricien.com/turfmag; owned by Le Mauricien Ltd.

La Vie Catholique: 28 Nicolay Rd, Port Louis; tel. 242-0975; fax 242-3114; e-mail viecatho@intnet.mu; internet pages.intnet.mu/lavie; f. 1930; weekly; English, French and Creole; Editor-in-Chief (vacant); circ. 8,000.

Week-End: 8 St George St, POB 7, Port Louis; tel. 207-8200; fax 208-3248; e-mail redaction@lemauricien.com; internet www.lemauricien.com/weekend; f. 1966; owned by Le Mauricien Ltd; French and English; Editor-in-Chief GÉRARD CATEAUX; circ. 80,000.

Week-End Scope: 8 St George St, POB 7, Port Louis; tel. 207-8200; fax 208-7059; e-mail wes@lemauricien.com; internet www.lemauricien.com/wes; owned by Le Mauricien Ltd; English and French; Editor-in-Chief JACQUES ACHILLE.

OTHER SELECTED PERIODICALS

CCI–INFO: 3 Royal St, Port Louis; tel. 208-3301; fax 208-0076; e-mail mcci@intnet.mu; internet www.mcci.org; English and French; f. 1995; quarterly; publ. of the Mauritius Chamber of Commerce and Industry.

Ciné Star Magazine: 64 Sir Seewoosagur Ramgoolam St, Port Louis; tel. 240-1447; English and French; Editor-in-Chief ABDOOL RAWOOF SOOBRATTY.

Education News: Edith Cavell St, Port Louis; tel. 212-1303; English and French; monthly; Editor-in-Chief GIAN AUBEELUCK.

Le Message de L'Ahmadiyyat: c/o Ahmadiyya Muslim Asscn, POB 6, Rose Hill; tel. 464-1747; fax 454-2223; e-mail darussalaam@intnet

.mu; French; monthly; Editor-in-Chief MOHAMMAD AMEEN JOWAHIR; circ. 3,000.

Le Progrès Islamique: 51B Solferino St, Rose Hill; tel. 467-1697; fax 467-1696; f. 1948; English and French; monthly; Editor DEVINA SOOKIA.

La Voix d'Islam: Parisot Rd, Mesnil, Phoenix; f. 1951; English and French; monthly.

Publishers

Boukié Banané (The Flame Tree): 5 Edwin Ythier St, Rose Hill; tel. 454-2327; fax 465-4312; e-mail limem@intnet.mu; internet pages .intnet.mu/develop; f. 1979; Morisien literature, poetry and drama; Man. Dir DEV VIRAHSAWMY.

Business Publications Ltd: TN Tower, 2nd Floor, St George St, Port Louis; tel. 211-3048; fax 211-1926; internet www.businessmag .mu; f. 1993; English and French; Dir LYNDSAY RIVIÈRE.

Editions du Dattier: 82 Goyavier Ave, Quatre Bornes; tel. 466-4854; fax 446-3105; e-mail dattier@intnet.mu; English and French; Dir JEAN-PHILIPPE LAGESSE.

Editions de l'Océan Indien: Stanley, Rose Hill; tel. 464-6761; fax 464-3445; e-mail eoibooks@intnet.mu; internet www.eoi-info.com; f. 1977; general, textbooks, dictionaries, literature; English, French and Asian languages; Gen. Man. DEVANAND DEWKURUN.

Editions Le Printemps: 4 Club Rd, Vacoas; tel. 696-1017; fax 686-7302; e-mail elp@bow.intnet.mu; Man. Dir A. I. SULLIMAN.

Editions Vizavi: 9 St George St, Port Louis; tel. 211-3047; e-mail vizavi@intnet.mu; Dir PASCALE SIEW.

Broadcasting and Communications

TELECOMMUNICATIONS

Information and Communication Technologies Authority (ICTA): The Celicourt, 12th Floor, 6 Sir Celicourt Antelme St, Port Louis; tel. 211-5333; fax 211-9444; e-mail icta@intnet.mu; internet www.icta.mu; f. 1999; regulatory authority; Chair. TRILOK DWARKA.

Mauritius Telecom Ltd: Telecom Tower, Edith Cavell St, Port Louis; tel. 203-7000; fax 208-1070; e-mail ceo@mauritiustelecom.com .mu; internet www.mauritiustelecom.com; f. 1992; 60% owned by Govt of Mauritius, State Bank of Mauritius and National Pensions Fund, 40% owned by France Télécom through RIMCOM; privatized in 2000; provides all telecommunications services, including internet and digital mobile cellular services; Chair. APPALSAMY (DASS) THOMAS; CEO SARAT LALLAH.

Cellplus Mobile Communications Ltd: Telecom Tower, 9th Floor, Edith Cavell St, Port Louis; tel. 203-7500; fax 211-6996; e-mail cellplus@intnet.mu; internet www.cellplus.mu; f. 1996; introduced the first GSM cellular network in Mauritius and recently in Rodrigues (Cell-Oh); a wholly owned subsidiary of Mauritius Telecom.

Emtel: 1 Boundary Road, Rose Hill; tel. 454-5400; fax 454-1010; e-mail emtel@emtelnet.com; internet www.emtel-ltd.com; f. 1989; CEO SHYAM ROY.

Outremer Télécom Maurice: POB 113, Hassamal Bldg, Rémono St, Rose Hill; tel. 401-9400; fax 401-9422; e-mail info@outremer-telecom.mu; internet www.outremer-telecom.mu; Man. Dir MICHEL RIGOT.

BROADCASTING

In 1997 the Supreme Court invalidated the broadcasting monopoly held by the Mauritius Broadcasting Corporation.

Independent Broadcasting Authority: 5 de Courson St, Curepipe Rd, Curepipe; tel. 670-4621; fax 670-2335; e-mail iba@intnet .mu; internet iba.gov.mu; Dir PIERRE AH-FAT.

Radio

Mauritius Broadcasting Corpn: 1 Louis Pasteur St, Forest Side; tel. 602-1200; fax 674-0488; e-mail customercare@mbc.intnet.mu; internet www.mbcradio.tv; f. 1964; independent corpn operating eight national radio services and nine television channels; Chair. FAREED JANGEER-KHAN; Dir-Gen. BIJAYE COOMAR MADHOU.

Radio One: Port Louis; tel. 211-4555; fax 211-4142; e-mail sales@r1 .mu; internet www.r1.mu; f. 2002; owned by Sentinelle media group; news and entertainment; Dir-Gen. JEAN-MICHEL FONTAINE.

Radio Plus: 4B, Labourdonnais St, Port-Louis; tel. 208-6002; fax 212-0042; e-mail radioplus@intnet.mu; internet www.defimedia .info.

Top FM: The Peninsula, Caudan Bldg, 7th Floor, 2A Falcon ST, Caudan, Port Louis; tel. 213-2121; fax 213-2222; e-mail topfm@intnet .mu; internet www.topfmradio.com; f. 2003; part of the International Broadcasting Group, in partnership with the Sunrise Group; Chair. BALKRISHNA KAUNHYE.

Television

Independent television stations were to commence broadcasting from 2002, as part of the liberalization of the sector.

Mauritius Broadcasting Corpn: see Radio

Finance

(cap. = capital; res = reserves; dep. = deposits; m. = million; brs = branches; amounts in Mauritian rupees, unless otherwise stated)

BANKING

Central Bank

Bank of Mauritius: Sir William Newton St, POB 29, Port Louis; tel. 208-4164; fax 208-9204; e-mail governor.office@bom.intnet.mu; internet bom.intnet.mu; f. 1966; bank of issue; cap. 1,000.0m., res 19,212.2m., dep. 11,963.3m. (June 2006); Gov. RUNDHEERSING BHEENICK.

Principal Commercial Banks

Bank of Baroda: 32 Sir William Newton St, POB 553, Port Louis; tel. 208-1504; fax 208-3892; e-mail info@bankofbaroda-mu.com; internet www.bankofbaroda-mu.com; f. 1962; total assets 2,655,000m. (June 2007); Vice-Pres.(Mauritius Operations) PRABHAT AGARWAL; 7 brs.

Barclays Bank PLC, Mauritius: Harbour Front Bldg, 8th Floor, John F. Kennedy St, POB 284, Port Louis; tel. 208-9070; fax 208-2720; e-mail barclays.mauritius@barclays.com; f. 1919; absorbed Banque Nationale de Paris Intercontinentale in 2002; cap. 100.0m., res 616.1m., dep. 6,886.7m. (Dec. 2001); Man. Dir RAVIN DAJEE; 16 brs.

First City Bank Ltd: 16 Sir William Newton St, POB 485, Port Louis; tel. 202-9200; fax 208-5388; e-mail info@firstcitybank-mauritius.com; internet www.firstcitybank-mauritius .com; f. 1991 as the Delphis Bank Ltd; merged with Union International Bank in 1997; private bank; taken over by consortium in 2002; 50% owned by Investments & Mortgages Bank Ltd, Nairobi, 50% by Ciel Investments Ltd; cap. 450.0m., res 164.9m., dep. 4,130.1m. (June 2007); Chair. JEAN PIERRE DALAIS; Chief Exec. RAJ DUSSOYE.

Hongkong and Shanghai Banking Corpn Ltd (HSBC): pl. d'Armes, POB 50, Port Louis; tel. 208-1801; fax 210-0400; e-mail hsbcmauritius@hsbc.co.mu; internet www.hsbc.co.mu; f. 1916; CEO PHILLIP DAWE.

Indian Ocean International Bank Ltd (IOIB): 34 Sir William Newton St, POB 863, Port Louis; tel. 208-0121; fax 208-0127; e-mail ioibltd@intnet.mu; internet www.ioib.intnet.mu; f. 1978; 56% owned by the State Bank of India; cap. 168.8m., res 294.8m., dep. 4,069.1m. (March 2007); Chair. MADHUKARLAL BAGUANT; Man. Dir V. PATTABHIRAMAN; 10 brs.

Mauritius Commercial Bank Ltd: MCB Centre, 9–15 Sir William Newton St, POB 52, Port Louis; tel. 202-5000; fax 208-7054; e-mail mcb@mcb.co.mu; internet www.mcb.mu; f. 1838; cap. 2,503m., res 4,205.4m., dep. 85,157m. (June 2007); Pres. GERARD J. HARDY; CEO PIERRE-GUY NOEL; 42 brs.

Mauritius Post and Co-operative Bank Ltd: 1 Sir William Newton St, Port Louis; tel. 207-9999; fax 208-7270; e-mail mpcb@mpcb.mu; internet www.mpcb.mu; f. 2003; 44.3% owned by The Mauritius Post Ltd, 35.7% state owned, 10% owned by the Sugar Investment Trust; cap. 384.0m., res 72.0m., dep. 5,866.6m. (Dec. 2007); CEO RAJIV KUMAR BEEHARRY; Gen. Man. PAVADAY THONDRAYON.

South East Asian Bank Ltd (SEAB): 26 Bourbon St, Port Louis; tel. 208-8826; fax 241-7379; e-mail seab@intnet.mu; internet www .seab.mu; f. 1989; 60% owned by Bumiputra-Commerce Bank Berhad (Malaysia); cap. 200.0m., res 14.3m., dep. 3,359.7m. (Dec. 2006); Chair. TAN SRI HAIDAR BIN MOHAMED NOR; 6 brs.

Standard Chartered Bank (Mauritius) Ltd: Happy World House, Level 8, 37 Sir William Newton St, Port Louis; tel. 213-9000; fax 208-5992; e-mail scbmauritius@intnet.mu; internet www .standardchartered.com/mu; wholly owned subsidiary of Standard Chartered Bank Plc; offshore banking unit.

State Bank of Mauritius Ltd: State Bank Tower, 1 Queen Elizabeth II Ave, POB 152, Port Louis; tel. 202-1111; fax 202-1234; e-mail sbm@sbm.intnet.mu; internet www.sbmonline.com; f. 1973; cap. 303.7m., surplus and res 6,836.9m., dep. 46,103.2m.

MAURITIUS — Directory

(June 2007); Chair. GEERJA SHANKAR RAMDAURSINGH; Chief Exec. SOOPAYA PARIANEN (acting); 43 brs.

Development Bank

Development Bank of Mauritius Ltd: rue La Chaussée, POB 157, Port Louis; tel. 203-3600; fax 208-8498; e-mail dbm@intnet.mu; internet www.dbm.mu; f. 1964; name changed as above in 1991; 85% govt-owned; cap. 125m., res 2,114.1m., dep. 4,028.0m. (June 2007); Chair. CHANDAN KHESWAR JANKEE; Man. Dir B. CHOORAMUN; 6 brs.

Principal 'Offshore' Banks

Banque des Mascareignes Ltd: 1 Cathedral Square, Level 8, 16 Jules Koenig St, POB 43, Port Louis; tel. and fax 213-1675; e-mail serviceclient@bm.mu; internet www.banquedesmascareignes.mu; f. 2004; name changed as above 2005; 69.5% owned by Financière Océor (France), 27.7% owned by Banque de la Réunion; cap. 423.7m., res 43.3m., dep. 6,546.2m. (Dec. 2005); Chair. BERNARD BOBROWSKI; CEO CHRISTIAN MONTAGARD.

SBI International (Mauritius) Ltd: Harbour Front Bldg, 7th Floor, John F. Kennedy St, POB 376, Port Louis; tel. 212-2054; fax 212-2050; e-mail sbilmaur@intnet.mu; internet www.sbimauritius.com; f. 1989; 98% owned by the State Bank of India; cap. US $10.0m., res $13.3m., dep. $120.0m. (June 2007); Chair. S.K. HARIHARAN; Man. Dir V. SRINIVASAN.

Bank of Baroda, Barclays Bank PLC, African Asian Bank, PT Bank International Indonesia, Investec Bank (Mauritius) and HSBC Bank PLC also operate 'offshore' banking units.

STOCK EXCHANGE

Financial Services Commission: 4th Floor, Harbour Front Bldg, President John Kennedy St, Port Louis; tel. 210-7000; fax 208-7172; e-mail fscmauritius@intnet.mu; internet www.fscmauritius.org; f. 2001; regulatory authority for securities, insurance and global business activities; Chief Exec. MILAN J. N. MEETARBHAN.

Stock Exchange of Mauritius Ltd: 1 Cathedral Sq. Bldg, 4th Floor, 16 Jules Koenig St, Port Louis; tel. 212-9541; fax 208-8409; e-mail stockex@sem.intnet.mu; internet www.stockexchangeofmauritius.com; f. 1989; 11 mems; Chair. P. GOPALLEN MOOROOGEN; CEO SUNIL BENIMADHU.

INSURANCE

Albatross Insurance Co Ltd: 22 St George St, POB 116, Port Louis; tel. 207-9007; fax 208-4800; e-mail headoffice@albatross-insurance.com; internet www.albatross-insurance.com; f. 1975; Chair. VAUGHAN HEBERDEN.

Anglo-Mauritius Assurance Society Ltd: Swan Group Centre, 10 Intendance St, POB 837, Port Louis; tel. 202-8600; fax 208-8956; e-mail anglomtius@intnet.mu; internet www.groupswan.com; f. 1951; Chair. CYRIL MAYER; CEO LOUIS RIVALLAND.

British American Insurance Co (Mauritius) Ltd: BAI Bldg, 25 Pope Hennessy St, POB 331, Port Louis; tel. 202-3600; fax 208-3713; e-mail bai@intnet.mu; internet www.bai.mu; f. 1920; CEO SANSJIV C. NUCKCHADY.

Ceylinco Stella Insurance Co Ltd: 36 Sir William Newton St, POB 852, Port Louis; tel. 208-0056; fax 213-3882; e-mail tilakf@intnet.mu; f. 1977; CEO TILAK FERNANDO (acting).

Indian Ocean General Assurance Ltd: 35 Corderie St, POB 865, Port Louis; tel. 212-4125; fax 212-5850; e-mail info@iogaltd.com; internet iogaltd.com; f. 1971; total assets 221m. (June 2007); Gen. Man. R. L. MATHUR.

Island Insurance Co Ltd: Labourdonnais Court, 5th Floor, cnr Labourdonnais and St George Sts, Port Louis; tel. 212-4860; fax 208-8762; f. 1998; Chair. CARRIM A. CURRIMJEE; Man. Dir OLIVIER LAGESSE.

Jubilee Insurance (Mauritius) Ltd: PCL Bldg, 4th Floor, 43 Sir William Newton St, POB 301, Port Louis; tel. 210-3678; fax 212-7970; f. 1998; Chair. and CEO AUGUSTINE J. HATCH.

Lamco International Insurance Ltd: 12 Barracks St, Port Louis; tel. 212-4494; fax 208-0630; e-mail lamco@intnet.mu; internet www.lamcoinsurance.com; f. 1978; Chair. A. B. ATCHIA; Gen. Man. N. C. ADIA.

Life Insurance Corpn of India: LIC Centre, John F. Kennedy St, Port Louis; tel. 212-5316; fax 208-6392; e-mail liccmm@intnet.mu; f. 1956; Chief Man. NAVIN SINHA.

Mauritian Eagle Insurance Co Ltd: 1st Floor, IBL House, Caudan Waterfront, POB 854, Port Louis; tel. 203-2200; fax 203-2299; e-mail caudan@mauritianeagle.com; internet www.mauritianeagle.com; f. 1973; Chair. P. D'HOTMAN DE VILLIERS; Man. Dir ERIC A. VENPIN.

Mauritius Union Assurance Co Ltd: 4 Léoville L'Homme St, POB 233, Port Louis; tel. 207-5500; fax 212-2962; e-mail mua@mua.mu; internet www.mauritiusunion.com; f. 1948; Chair. BERNARD MARIE JOSEPH MAYER.

The New India Assurance Co Ltd: Bank of Baroda Bldg, 3rd Floor, 15 Sir William Newton St, POB 398, Port Louis; tel. 208-1442; fax 208-2160; e-mail niasurance@intnet.mu; internet www.niacl.com; f. 1935; general insurance; Chief Man. A. K. JAIN.

La Prudence Mauricienne Assurances Ltée: Le Caudan Waterfront, 2nd Floor, Barkly Wharf, POB 882, Port Louis; tel. 207-2500; fax 208-8936; e-mail prudence@intnet.mu; Chair. ROBERT DE FROBERVILLE; Man. Dir FÉLIX MAUREL.

Rainbow Insurance Co Ltd: 23 Edith Cavell St, POB 389, Port Louis; tel. 202-8800; fax 208-8750; e-mail raininsu@intnet.mu; internet www.rainbowinsurance.mu; f. 1976; Chair. B. GOKULSING; Gen. Man. PRAVIN RAMBURN.

State Insurance Co of Mauritius Ltd (SICOM): SICOM Bldg, Sir Célicourt Antelme St, Port Louis; tel. 203-8400; fax 208-7662; e-mail email@sicom.intnet.mu; internet www.sicom.mu; f. 1975; Chair. T. K. SERVANSINGH; Man. Dir K. BHOOJEDHUR-OBEEGADOO.

Sun Insurance Co Ltd: 2 St George St, Port Louis; tel. 208-0769; fax 208-2052; e-mail suninsco@intnet.mu; f. 1981; Chair. Sir KAILASH RAMDANEE; Man. Dir A. MUSBALLY.

Swan Insurance Co Ltd: Swan Group Centre, 10 Intendance St, POB 364, Port Louis; tel. 211-2001; fax 208-6898; e-mail swan@intnet.mu; f. 1955; Chair. J. M. ANTOINE HAREL; CEO LOUIS RIVALLAND.

L. and H. Vigier de Latour Ltd: Les Jamalacs Bldg, Old Council St, Port Louis; tel. 212-2034; fax 212-6056; Chair. and Man. Dir L. J. D. HENRI VIGIER DE LATOUR.

Trade and Industry

GOVERNMENT AGENCIES

Agricultural Marketing Board (AMB): Dr G. Leclézio Ave, Moka; tel. 433-4025; fax 433-4837; e-mail agbd@intnet.mu; internet amb.intnet.mu; f. 1964; operates under the aegis of the Ministry of Agro-industry and Fisheries; markets certain locally produced and imported food products (such as potatoes, onions, garlic, spices and seeds); provides storage facilities to importers and exporters; Gen. Man. PARMANAND RAMNAWAZ.

Mauritius Meat Authority: Abattoir Rd, Roche Bois, POB 612, Port Louis; tel. 242-5884; fax 217-1077; e-mail mauritiusmeat@intnet.mu; f. 1974; licensing authority; controls and regulates sale of meat and meat products; also purchases and imports livestock and markets meat products; Gen. Man. A. BALGOBIN.

Mauritius Sugar Authority: Ken Lee Bldg, 2nd Floor, Edith Cavell St, Port Louis; tel. 208-7466; fax 208-7470; e-mail msa@intnet.mu; regulatory body for the sugar industry; Chair. S. HANOOMANJEE; Exec. Dir Dr G. RAJPATI.

Mauritius Tea Board: Wooton St, Curepipe Rd, Curepipe; POB 28, Eau Coulée; tel. 675-3497; fax 676-1445; e-mail teaboard@intnet.mu; internet www.gov.mu/portal/site/teaboard; f. 1975; regulates and controls the activities of the tea industry; Gen. Man. A. SEEPERGAUTH.

Mauritius Tobacco Board: Plaine Lauzun, Port Louis; tel. 212-2323; fax 208-6426; e-mail tobaco@intnet.mu; internet tobaccoboard.intnet.mu; Chair. A. L. JADOO.

DEVELOPMENT ORGANIZATIONS

Board of Investment—Mauritius (BOI): Cathedral Square Bldg 1, 10th Floor, 16 Jules Koenig St, Port Louis; tel. 211-4190; fax 208-2924; e-mail invest@boi.intnet.mu; internet www.boimauritius.com; f. 2001 to promote international investment, business and services; Chair. of Bd MAURICE LAM; Gen. Man. RAJU JADDOO.

Enterprise Mauritius: 7th Floor, Saint James Court, Saint Denis St, Port-Louis; tel. 212-9760; fax 212-9767; e-mail info@em.intnet.mu; internet www.enterprisemauritius.biz; f. 2004 from parts of the Mauritius Industrial Development Authority, the Export Processing Zones Development Authority and the Sub-contracting and Partnership Exchange—Mauritius; comprises a Corporate Services Unit, a Strategic Direction Unit, a Business Development Unit, a Client-Services Unit and a Special Support Unit (estd from the former Clothing and Textile Centre); Chair. AMÉDÉE DARGA; CEO PRAKESH BEEHARRY.

Joint Economic Council (JEC): Plantation House, 3rd Floor, pl. d'Armes, Port Louis; tel. 211-2980; fax 211-3141; e-mail jec@intnet.mu; internet www.jec-mauritius.org; f. 1970; the co-ordinating body of the private sector of Mauritius, including the main business orgs of the country; Pres. ARIF CURRIMJEE; Dir RAJ MAKOOND.

Mauritius Freeport Authority (MFA): Level 10, One Cathedral Sq. Bldg 16, Jules Koeing St, Port Louis; tel. 203-3800; fax 208-2924;

MAURITIUS

e-mail contact@investmauritius.com; internet www.efreeport.com; f. 1990; Man. NANDA NARRAINEN.

National Productivity and Competitiveness Council (NPCC): 4th Floor, Alexander House, Cybercity, Reduit; tel. 467-7700; fax 467-3838; e-mail natpro@intnet.mu; internet www.npccmauritius.com; f. 2000; represents the Govt, the private sector and trade unions; Exec. Dir Dr KRISHNALALL COONJAN.

Small Enterprises and Handicraft Development Authority (SEHDA): Industrial Zone, Coromandel; tel. 233-0500; fax 233-5545; e-mail smido@intnet.mu; internet www.sehda.org; f. 2006 following the merger of the Small and Medium Industries Development Organization and the National Handicraft Promotion Agency; provides support to potential and existing small entrepreneurs.

State Investment Corpn Ltd (SIC): Air Mauritius Centre, 15th Floor, John F. Kennedy St, Port Louis; tel. 202-8900; fax 208-8948; e-mail contactsic@stateinvestment.com; internet www.stateinvestment.com; f. 1984; provides support for new investment and transfer of technology, in agriculture, industry and tourism; Man. Dir IQBAL MALLAM-HASHAM; Chair. RAJ RINGADOO.

CHAMBERS OF COMMERCE

Chinese Chamber of Commerce: Suite 206, Jade Court, Jummah Mosque St, Port Louis; tel. and fax 242-0156; e-mail admin@cccmauritius.org; f. 1908; Pres. ANNABELLE KOK SHUN.

Mauritius Chamber of Commerce and Industry: 3 Royal St, Port Louis; tel. 208-3301; fax 208-0076; e-mail mcci@intnet.mu; internet www.mcci.org; f. 1850; 400 mems; Pres. AHMED PARKAR; Sec.-Gen. MAHMOOD CHEEROO.

INDUSTRIAL ASSOCIATIONS

Association of Mauritian Manufacturers (AMM): c/o The Mauritius Chamber of Commerce and Industry, 3 Royal St, Port Louis; tel. 208-3301; fax 208-0076; e-mail mcci@intnet.mu; f. 1995; Pres. PATRICK RIVALLAND.

Mauritius Export Processing Zone Association (MEPZA): Unicorn House, 6th Floor, 5 Royal St, Port Louis; tel. 208-5216; fax 212-1853; internet www.mepza.org; f. 1976; consultative and advisory body; Chair. LOUIS LAI FAT FUR.

Mauritius Sugar Producers' Association (MSPA): Plantation House, 2nd Floor, Edinburgh Ave, Port Louis; tel. 212-0295; fax 212-5727; e-mail mspa@mspa.intnet.mu; f. 1947; Chair. JACQUES MARRIER D'UNIENVILLE; Dir JEAN LI YUEN FONG.

EMPLOYERS' ORGANIZATION

Mauritius Employers' Federation: MEF-MCCI Bldg, Ebène CyberCity, Ebène; tel. 466-3600; fax 465-8200; e-mail mef@intnet.mu; internet www.mef-online.org; f. 1962; Chair. ANWAR JOONAS; Dir Dr AZAD JEETUN.

UTILITIES

Electricity

Central Electricity Board: Royal Rd, POB 40, Curepipe; tel. 601-1100; fax 675-7958; e-mail ceb@intnet.mu; internet cebweb.intnet.mu; f. 1952; state-operated; Chair. PATRICK ASSIRVADEN; Gen. Man. C. DABEEDIN.

Water

Central Water Authority: Royal Rd, St Paul, Phoenix; tel. 601-5000; fax 686-6264; e-mail cwa@intnet.mu; corporate body; scheduled for privatization; f. 1973; Gen. Man. H. K. BOOLUCK; Chair. Prof. ANWAR HUSSEIN SUBRATTY.

Waste Water Management Authority: Sir Celicourt Antelme St, Port Louis; tel. 206-3000; fax 211-7007; e-mail wma@intnet.mu; internet wma.gov.mu; f. 2000; Chair. KHUSHAL LOBINE; Gen. Man. ROBIN SOONARANE.

TRADE UNIONS

Federations

Federation of Civil Service and Other Unions (FCSOU): Jade Court, Rm 308, 3rd Floor, 33 Jummah Mosque St, Port Louis; tel. 216-1977; fax 216-1475; e-mail f.c.s.u@intnet.mu; internet www.fcsu.org; f. 1957; 72 affiliated unions with 30,000 mems (2006); Pres. TOOLSYRAJ BENYDIN; Sec. AWADHKOOMARSINGH BALLUCK.

General Workers' Federation: 13 Brabant St, Port Louis; tel. 212-3338; Pres. FAROOK AUCHOYBUR; Sec.-Gen. DEVANAND RAMJUTTUN.

Mauritius Labour Congress (MLC): 8 Louis Victor de la Faye St, Port Louis; tel. 212-4343; fax 208-8945; e-mail mlcongress@intnet.mu; f. 1963; 55 affiliated unions with 70,000 mems (1992); Pres. NURDEO LUCHMUN ROY; Gen. Sec. JUGDISH LOLLBEEHARRY.

Mauritius Trade Union Congress (MTUC): Emmanuel Anquetil Labour Centre, James Smith St, Port Louis; tel. 210-8567; internet www.mtucmauritius.org; f. 1946.

Trade Union Trust Fund: Richard House, 2nd Floor, cnr Jummah Mosque and Remy Ollier Sts, Port Louis; tel. and fax 217-2073; internet www.gov.mu/portal/site/tradeuniontf; f. 1997 to receive and manage funds and other property obtained from the Govt and other sources; to promote workers' education and provide assistance to workers' orgs; Chair. RADHAKRISNA SADIEN.

Principal Unions

Government Servants' Association: 107A Royal Rd, Beau Bassin; tel. 464-4242; fax 465-3220; e-mail gsa@intnet.mu; internet www.gsa.mauritius.org; f. 1945; Pres. R. SADIEN; Sec.-Gen. P. RAMJUG.

Government Teachers' Union: 3 Mgr Gonin St, POB 1111, Port Louis; tel. 208-0047; fax 208-4943; f. 1945; Pres. JUGDUTH SEEGUM; Sec. MOHAMMAD SALEEM CHOOLUN; 4,550 mems (2005).

Nursing Association: 159 Royal Rd, Beau Bassin; tel. and fax 464-5850; e-mail nur.ass@intnet.mu; f. 1955; Pres. CASSAM KUREEMAN; Sec.-Gen. FRANCIS SUPPARAYEN.

Organization of Artisans' Unity: 42 Sir William Newton St, Port Louis; tel. and fax 212-4557; f. 1973; Pres. AUGUSTE FOLLET; Sec. ROY RAMCHURN; 2,874 mems (1994).

Plantation Workers' Union: 8 Louis Victor de la Faye St, Port Louis; tel. 212-1735; f. 1955; Pres. N. L. ROY; Sec. GOPAL BHUJAN; 13,726 mems (1990).

Port Louis Harbour and Docks Workers' Union: Port Louis; tel. 208-2276; Pres. JOSÉ FRANÇOIS; Sec.-Gen. GERARD BERTRAND.

Sugar Industry Staff Employees' Association: 1 Rémy Ollier St, Port Louis; tel. 212-1947; f. 1947; Chair. T. BELLEROSE; Sec.-Gen. G. CHUNG KWAN FANG; 1,450 mems (1997).

Textile, Clothes and Other Manufactures Workers' Union: Thomy d'Arifat St, Curepipe; tel. 676-5280; Pres. PADMATEE TEELUCK; Sec.-Gen. DÉSIRÉ GUILDAREE.

Union of Bus Industry Workers: Port Louis; tel. 212-3338; f. 1970; Pres. M. BABOOA; Sec.-Gen. F. AUCHOYBUR.

Union of Employees of the Ministry of Agriculture and other Ministries: 28 Hennessy Ave, Quatre-Bornes; tel. 465-1935; e-mail bruno5@intnet.mu; f. 1989; Sec. BRUNEAU DORASAMI; 2,500 mems (Dec. 2003).

Union of Labourers of the Sugar and Tea Industry: Royal Rd, Curepipe; f. 1969; Sec. P. RAMCHURN.

Transport

RAILWAYS

There are no operational railways in Mauritius.

ROADS

In 2006 there were 2,021 km of paved roads, of which 75 km were motorways, 955 km were other main roads, and 593 km were secondary roads. An urban highway links the motorways approaching Port Louis. A motorway connects Port Louis with Plaisance airport.

SHIPPING

Mauritius is served by numerous foreign shipping lines. In 1990 Port Louis was established as a free port to expedite the development of Mauritius as an entrepôt centre. At 31 December 2007 Mauritius had a merchant fleet of 43 vessels, with a combined displacement of 39,733 grt.

Mauritius Ports Authority: H. Ramnarain Bldg, Mer Rouge, Port Louis; tel. 206-5400; fax 240-0856; e-mail info@mauport.com; internet www.mauport.com; f. 1976; Chair. DAVID JOCELYN GRACIEUSE; Dir-Gen. SHEKUR SUNTAH.

Ireland Blyth Ltd: IBL House, Caudan, Port Louis; tel. 203-2000; fax 203-2001; e-mail iblinfo@iblgroup.com; internet www.iblgroup.com; Chair. THIERRY LAGESSE; CEO P. D'HOTMAN DE VILLIERS; 2 vessels.

Mauritius Freeport Development Co Ltd: Freeport Zone 5, Mer Rouge; tel. 206-2000; fax 206-2025; e-mail info@mfd.mu; internet www.mfd.mu; f. 1997; manages and operates Freeport Zone 5, more than 40,000 sq m of storage facility; facilities include dry warehouses, cold warehouses, processing and transformation units, open storage container parks and a container freight station; largest logistics centre in the Indian Ocean region; CEO DOMINIQUE DE FROBERVILLE.

Mauritius Shipping Corpn Ltd: St James Court, Suite 417/418, St Denis St, Port Louis; tel. 208-5900; fax 210-5176; internet www.mauritiusshipping.mu; f. 1985; state-owned; operates two passenger-cargo vessels between Mauritius, Rodrigues, Reunion and Madagascar; Man. Dir Capt. J. PATRICK RAULT.

Société Mauricienne de Navigation Ltée: 1 rue de la Reine, POB 53, Port Louis; tel. 208-3241; fax 208-8931; Man. Dir Capt. FRANÇOIS DE GERSIGNY.

CIVIL AVIATION

Sir Seewoosagur Ramgoolam International Airport is at Plaisance, 4 km from Mahébourg. From 2006 air routes with France and the United Kingdom were to be liberalized, allowing new carriers to operate on the routes.

Civil Aviation Department: Sir Seewoosagur Ramgoolam International Airport, Plaine Magnien; tel. 603-2000; fax 637-3164; e-mail civil-aviation@mail.gov.mu; internet civil-aviation.gov.mu; overseen by the Ministry of Tourism, Leisure and External Communications; Dir ANAND GUNGAH.

Air Mauritius: Air Mauritius Centre, John F. Kennedy St, POB 441, Port Louis; tel. 207-7070; fax 208-8331; e-mail contact@airmauritius.com; internet www.airmauritius.com; f. 1967; 51% state-owned; services to 28 destinations in Europe, Asia, Australia and Africa; Chair. SANJAY BUCKHORY; CEO MANOJ R. K. UJOODHA.

Tourism

Tourists are attracted to Mauritius by its scenery and beaches, the pleasant climate and the blend of cultures. Accommodation capacity totalled 21,072 beds in 2005. The number of visitors increased from 300,670 in 1990 to 930,456 in 2008, when the greatest numbers of visitors were from France (27.9%), the United Kingdom (11.6%) and Réunion (10.3%). Gross revenue from tourism in 2008 was estimated at MRs 41,213m. The Government sought to increase the volume of tourists visiting the country (to some 2m. people by 2015) by improving the jetty facilities in the port in order to welcome cruise ships and by liberalizing air transit routes.

Mauritius Tourism Promotion Authority: Victoria House, 4th and 5th Floor, St Louis St, Port Louis; tel. 210-1545; fax 212-5142; e-mail mtpa@intnet.mu; internet www.tourism-mauritius.mu; Chair. ROBERT DESVAUX.

Tourism Authority (TA): Victoria House, 1st and 2nd Floor, St Louis St, Port Louis; tel. 213-1740; fax 213-1745; e-mail tourism.authority@intnet.mu; f. 2003; parastatal; issues licences for and monitors compliance of the regulation of the tourism industry; Dir JOËL RAULT.

MEXICO
Introductory Survey

Location, Climate, Language, Religion, Flag, Capital

The United Mexican States is bordered to the north by the USA, and to the south by Guatemala and Belize. The Gulf of Mexico and the Caribbean Sea lie to the east, and the Pacific Ocean and Gulf of California to the west. The climate varies with altitude. The tropical southern region and the coastal lowlands are hot and wet, with an average annual temperature of 18°C (64°F), while the highlands of the central plateau are temperate. Much of the north and west is arid desert. In Mexico City, which lies at about 2,250 m (nearly 7,400 ft) above sea-level, temperatures are generally between 5°C (42°F) and 25°C (78°F). The country's highest recorded temperature is 58°C (136°F). The principal language is Spanish, spoken by more than 90% of the population, while about 8% speak indigenous languages, of which Náhuatl is the most widely spoken. Almost all of Mexico's inhabitants profess Christianity, and about 85% are adherents of the Roman Catholic Church. The national flag (proportions 4 by 7) has three equal vertical stripes from hoist to fly, of green, white and red, with the state emblem (a brown eagle, holding a snake in its beak, on a green cactus, with a wreath of oak and laurel beneath) in the centre of the white stripe. The capital is Mexico City.

Recent History

Conquered by Hernán Cortés in the 16th century, Mexico was ruled by Spain until the wars of independence of 1810–21. After the war of 1846, Mexico ceded about one-half of its territory to the USA. Attempts at political and social reform by the anti-clerical Benito Juárez precipitated civil war in 1857–60, and the repudiation of Mexico's external debts by Juárez in 1860 led to war with the United Kingdom, the USA and France. The Austrian Archduke Maximilian, whom France tried to install as Emperor of Mexico, was executed, on the orders of Juárez, in 1867. Order was restored during the dictatorship of Porfirio Díaz, which lasted from 1876 until the Revolution of 1910. The Constitution of 1917 embodied the aims of the Revolution by revising land ownership, drafting a labour code and curtailing the power of the Roman Catholic Church. From 1929–2000 the country was dominated by the Partido Revolucionario Institucional (PRI), for much of that time in an effective one-party system, although a democratic form of election was maintained. However, allegations of widespread electoral malpractice persistently arose in connection with PRI victories.

In a presidential election held in July 1976 the PRI candidate, José López Portillo, was elected with almost 95% of the votes cast. In 1977 López Portillo initiated reforms to increase minority party representation in the legislature and to widen democratic participation. The high level of political participation in the presidential election of July 1982 (held amid a financial crisis) was without precedent, with left-wing groups taking part for the first time; however, the PRI's candidate, Miguel de la Madrid Hurtado, was successful. The concurrent elections to the Cámara Federal de Diputados (Federal Chamber of Deputies) resulted in another overwhelming victory for the PRI. On taking office in December, the new President embarked on a programme of major economic reform, giving precedence to the repayment of Mexico's debts, a policy which imposed severe financial constraints upon the middle and lower classes and which led to growing disaffection among traditional PRI supporters. Notably, the Partido Acción Nacional (PAN), an opposition party, made important gains at municipal elections in two state capitals in mid-1983. The PRI's effective response ensured success at the remaining elections, but provoked opposition allegations of widespread electoral fraud. Contrary to expectations, at gubernatorial and congressional elections conducted in July 1985, the PRI secured all seven of the available state governorships and won 288 of the 300 directly elective seats in the Cámara Federal de Diputados.

The formation of a major left-wing alliance, the Partido Mexicano Socialista—PMS (comprising six parties), in 1987 and, in particular, the emergence of a dissident faction, the Corriente Democrática (CD), within the PRI in 1986 were disturbing political developments for the ruling party. In early 1988 the CD and four left-wing parties (including the PMS coalition) formed an electoral alliance, the Frente Democrático Nacional (FDN), headed by CD leader Cuauhtémoc Cárdenas Solórzano. The legitimacy of the PRI victory at the presidential and congressional elections, conducted in July, was fiercely challenged by the opposition groups, following a delay in the publication of official results, reports of widespread electoral fraud and the failure of the Federal Electoral Commission to release details of results from almost 50% of polling stations. Moreover, Cárdenas claimed victory on behalf of the broad-left coalition; for the first time ever, the opposition secured seats in the Senado (Senate), while the PRI suffered defeats in the Distrito Federal and at least three other states.

In August 1988 the new Congreso de la Unión (Congress) was installed and immediately assumed the function of an electoral college, in order to investigate the claims of both sides. In September the allocation of 200 seats in the Cámara Federal de Diputados by proportional representation afforded the PRI a congressional majority and effective control of the electoral college. Opposition members withdrew from the Cámara in protest at the PRI's obstruction of the investigation, enabling the ruling party to ratify Carlos Salinas de Gortari as the new President. The results, although widely regarded as having been manipulated by the PRI, revealed a considerable erosion in support for the party, particularly among the traditional bastions of the trade unions, peasant groups and bureaucracy.

Agreements on rescheduling Mexico's vast foreign debts were reached with the 'Paris Club' of official creditors in 1989, and with some 450 commercial banks in early 1990. Success for the Government in financial negotiations with creditors was largely dependent upon its ability to provide evidence of a stable and developing domestic economy. In January 1989 a Pact for Economic Stability and Growth was implemented, with the agreement of employers' organizations and trade unions, and was subsequently extended until the end of 1994. None the less, the country experienced severe labour unrest in 1989 in support of greater pay increases and in protest at the Government's divestment programme.

During 1989 political opposition to the PRI was strengthened by success in gubernatorial and municipal elections, and by further accusations against the PRI of electoral fraud. In October proposed constitutional amendments were approved with the unexpected support of the PAN. A 'governability clause', whereby an absolute majority of seats in the Cámara Federal de Diputados would be awarded to the leading party, should it receive at least 35% of the votes at a general election, was criticized by the Partido de la Revolución Democrática (PRD), the successor party to the FDN.

In July 1991 the Federal Electoral Code was approved by the Cámara Federal de Diputados with support from all represented parties, except the PRD. The legislation contained provisions for the compilation of a new electoral roll, the issue of more detailed identification cards for voters, the modification of the Instituto Federal Electoral (IFE—Federal Electoral Institute), and the creation of a Tribunal Federal Electoral (Federal Electoral Tribunal, which, in 1996, became the Tribunal Electoral del Poder Judicial de la Federación). The PRD was highly critical of many of the provisions, including alleged procedural obstacles to the formation of political alliances, and the power given to the President to appoint the head of the IFE (the Secretary of the Interior) and to nominate six 'independent' lawyers to its executive. Further constitutional reforms, with regard to agriculture, education and religion, were adopted in 1992.

Meanwhile, in June 1990, in response to continuing allegations of federal police complicity in abuses of human rights, President Salinas announced the creation of a national commission for human rights. In October the Government proposed legislation transferring responsibility for the interrogation of suspected criminals from the federal judicial police to the public magistrate's office. The proposed legislation also sought to undermine the validity of confession alone (often allegedly extracted under torture) as sufficient grounds for conviction.

The PRI continued to secure disputed electoral success at municipal and state level in 1991. At mid-term congressional elections in August, the party won almost all of the 300 directly elective seats in the Cámara Federal de Diputados (plus 30 of the 200 seats awarded by proportional representation) and 31 of the 32 contested seats in the Senado. The return to the level of support that the PRI had enjoyed prior to the 1988 elections was largely attributed to the success of the Government's programme of economic reform. The election results were less encouraging for the opposition; the PAN secured 10 directly elective seats in the Cámara and its first seat in the Senado, but the PRD failed to win a directly elective seat in either congressional house.

PRI victories at gubernatorial and legislative elections in several states during 1993 were denounced by the opposition as fraudulent. In September the Congreso approved electoral reforms that included provisions for greater access to the media for all parties, restrictions on party funding, and improved impartiality of supervision. Other measures sought to increase the representation of minority parties in the Senado, and to end over-representation of larger parties in the Cámara Federal de Diputados. The 'governability clause' introduced in 1989 was to be removed. Divisions within the PRI emerged in November, following the selection of Luis Donaldo Colosio, the Secretary of Social Development, as the party's candidate in the presidential elections. Additional electoral reforms, which claimed to end PRI control of the IFE, received congressional approval in March 1994, but failed to appease PRD leaders, who demanded that the incumbent head of the IFE should be replaced by an impartial president elected by the IFE's newly created six-member commission.

In March 1994 Colosio was assassinated at a campaign rally. Mario Aburto Martínez, arrested at the scene of the murder, was later identified as the apparently motiveless assassin. However, speculation that Colosio had been the victim of a conspiracy within the PRI establishment increased following the arrest, in connection with the incident, of a number of party members associated with police and intelligence agencies. The PRI subsequently named Ernesto Zedillo Ponce de León, a former cabinet minister who had most recently been acting as Colosio's campaign manager, as the party's presidential candidate. Zedillo was elected President on 21 August, with 49% of the votes, ahead of the PAN candidate, Diego Fernández de Cevallos (26%), and the PRD candidate, Cuauhtémoc Cárdenas (17%). The PRI also achieved considerable success at the concurrent congressional elections. Despite the participation of some 70,000 impartial monitors and the attendance of a UN advisory technical team, numerous incidents of electoral malpractice were reported. Zedillo identified the immediate aims of his administration as the promotion of the independence of the judiciary, the separation of party political activity from the functions of federal government and the further reform of the electoral system.

The report of a special investigation into Colosio's murder, published in July 1994, concluded that Aburto Martínez had acted alone in the assassination, reversing the findings of a preliminary investigation which had suggested the existence of a number of conspirators. Nevertheless, speculation that Colosio had been the first victim of a politically motivated campaign of violence, conducted by a cabal of senior PRI traditionalists in order to check the advance of the party's reformist wing, intensified following the murder, in September, of the PRI Secretary-General, José Francisco Ruiz Massieu. In February 1995, however, a report issued by the Attorney-General was highly critical of all previous investigations of the Colosio assassination, concluding that the assassination had involved at least two gunmen. Meanwhile, in November 1994 Ruiz Massieu's brother, Mario, resigned his post as Deputy Attorney-General, claiming that senior PRI officials, including the party's President and Secretary-General, had impeded his investigation into his brother's death, in an attempt to protect the identities of those responsible for the assassination. In February 1995 Raúl Salinas de Gortari, brother of former President Salinas, was arrested on charges of complicity in Ruiz Massieu's murder, and in April several new conspirators, including five state Governors, were implicated. In October two men were each sentenced to 18 years' imprisonment for perpetrating the murder of the PRI Secretary-General. In October 1996 the case against Raúl Salinas was prejudiced further by the discovery of a body buried in the grounds of his property in Mexico City.

In March 1995, following the arrest of his brother, former President Salinas began a public campaign to discredit the new administration and to defend himself from accusations of responsibility for the country's economic crisis and from allegations that he had obstructed attempts to bring to justice those responsible for Colosio's death. Salinas's efforts culminated in a highly publicized but brief hunger strike, which prompted the Attorney-General to issue a statement confirming that there was no evidence that Salinas had impeded the Colosio murder inquiry. Raúl Salinas was convicted of murder and, in January 1999, sentenced to 50 years' imprisonment (later reduced to almost 28 years); in August 2002 he was additionally charged with the embezzlement of up to 209m. new pesos from a secret presidential fund under his brother's control. In September 1999 Mario Ruiz Massieu committed suicide in the USA while awaiting trial on charges of 'laundering' money gained from drugs-trafficking; he left a note repeating his earlier accusations against the PRI and blaming Zedillo and other senior officials for his own death and the assassination of Colosio.

The Government's ongoing attempts to effect political reform were reactivated in January 1996 at a meeting of some 50 civil and political groups. In July the PRI, the PAN, the PRD and the Partido del Trabajo (PT, a labour party) reached consensus on reforms that would include introducing a directly elected governor of the Distrito Federal, increasing and regulating public financing for political parties, employing proportional representation in elections to the Senado, granting a right of vote to Mexican citizens resident abroad, and allowing the IFE greater independence. The reforms received congressional approval in August. However, in November, in apparent response to their diminishing share of the vote in recent municipal elections, PRI traditionalists secured the adoption by the Cámara Federal de Diputados of a series of amendments to the electoral reform bill, increasing public funding in 1997 for political parties by some 476%, pronouncing that to exceed campaign finance limits would no longer be a criminal or electoral offence, expanding the Government's access to the media, and restricting the right of opposition parties to form coalitions.

In May 1996 President Zedillo dismissed Mexico City's chief of police following public outcry at the violent tactics employed by his officers to disperse a group of striking teachers in the capital. In the following months hundreds of police employees throughout the country were dismissed for incompetence or corruption, while army officers were increasingly appointed to positions within the police force. In March 1997 some 2,500 members of Mexico City's police force were replaced by army personnel, and in October an élite police unit was disbanded after accusations that as many as 35 of its members were implicated in the torture and murder of three youths in September. Several officers at the anti-abduction unit in the state of Morelos were also accused of torture and murder in early 1998, precipitating the resignation of the state's PRI Governor in May.

At elections held in July 1997 for all 500 members of the Cámara Federal de Diputados the PRI lost its overall majority for the first time, while the PRD and the PAN made substantial gains. At concurrent elections held for one-quarter of the seats in the Senado the PRI retained its overall majority, albeit significantly reduced, while the PAN and the PRD increased their representation. An informal congressional alliance between the PAN, the PRD, the Partido Verde Ecologista de México (PVEM) and the PT meant that opposition parties were able to take control of important legislative committees. In addition to the poor legislative electoral performance, the PRI was defeated by the PAN in two of six gubernatorial elections conducted at the same time. Most significant, however, was the election of Cárdenas, the PRD candidate, as Head of Government of the Distrito Federal. The electoral defeats suffered by the PRI exacerbated tensions within the party and several party members defected to the PRD, some of whom were selected as candidates in gubernatorial elections.

In mid-1998 the PRI encountered strong opposition in the Congreso to its proposals to convert into public debt liabilities to the value of some US $65,000m. assumed by the bank rescue agency, the Fondo Bancario de Protección al Ahorro (FOBAPROA), after the financial crisis of late 1994. In December revised legislation establishing a successor to the FOBAPROA was approved by the Cámara Federal de Diputados, and the Government was forced to concede that FOBAPROA's liabilities would not automatically become public debt. FOBAPROA's successor, the Instituto de Protección al Ahorro Bancario, was created in May 1999.

A presidential election was held on 2 July 2000. The PRI's candidate was the former Secretary of the Interior, Francisco Labastida Ochoa, while the former Governor of Guanajuato state, Vicente Fox Quesada, represented a PAN-PVEM alliance known as the Alianza por el Cambio (AC), and Cárdenas was once again the PRD's nominee (officially he stood for the PRD-dominated Alianza por México—AM). Fox secured 43% of the votes cast, while Labastida attracted 37% and Cárdenas 17%. Fox was thus elected President, ending the PRI's 71-year hegemony in Mexican government. In the concurrent elections to the Congreso the AC secured 223 of the 500 seats, compared with 209 won by the PRI and 68 by the parties of the AM. The PRI remained the largest grouping in the Senado, however, with 60 seats. Fox took office as President on 1 December, stating that his priorities were a reduction in poverty, improved relations with the USA, and peace and reconciliation within Mexico.

In January 2002 the Government announced that an investigation was to be held into allegations that the state petroleum company, Petróleos Mexicanos (PEMEX), had covertly funded Labastida's presidential election campaign. The affair centred on the alleged diversion of PEMEX funds into PRI accounts by two leaders of the petroleum workers' union, the Sindicato de Trabajadores Petroleros de la República Mexicana. In May a former director of PEMEX, Manuel Gómez-Peralta, was detained in connection with the allegations; furthermore, a former PEMEX President, Rogelio Montemayor, was arrested in Houston, Texas, USA, in October. In that month opposition parties demanded that President Fox allow the reopening of investigations into allegations that the PAN organization Amigos de Fox, responsible for Fox's presidential campaign, had received substantial illegal foreign funding. (The investigation had been suspended on grounds of banking secrecy, but had been ordered to recommence by the electoral tribunal in May.) The PRI threatened to initiate a congressional investigation unless the Amigos de Fox accounts were made public. In October 2003 the IFE fined both the PAN and the PVEM for receiving illegal campaign funding from Amigos de Fox.

In May 2002 a total of 27 Zapotec Indians were killed in suspicious circumstances at Agua Fría, in Santiago Textitlán, Oaxaca; state authorities arrested 17 villagers, but local Indian organizations claimed that paramilitary groups had been involved in the attacks. Following the incident, an official from the human rights organization Amnesty International denounced the state Attorney-General's office for abuses.

In early November 2003 the Supreme Court ruled that prosecution for murder could proceed even in cases where no body had been found. The ruling enabled prosecutions to proceed for human rights abuses committed during the 'guerra sucia' ('dirty war') of the late 1970s; in February 2004 Miguel Nazar Haro, former director of the covert Dirección General de Seguridad, was arrested in connection with the disappearance of left-wing activist Jesús Piedra Ibarra in 1975. In mid-2004 the Supreme Court made a further ruling that cases concerning disappearance could be brought in connection with the suppression of dissent in the 1970s and 1980s. Meanwhile, a special prosecutor, Ignacio Carrillo, was appointed to investigate the role of, among others, the former President Luis Echeverría in the 'guerra sucia'; however, Carrillo's request that Echeverría be arrested was rejected. In February 2005 the Supreme Court ruled that the Vienna Convention on genocide, which came into force in 2002, could not be applied retrospectively, while in July 2005 the case against Echeverría was dismissed on the grounds that there was no evidence of genocide. This dismissal, however, was itself overruled on appeal in November 2006, thereby reopening the possibility of a prosecution.

In November 2003 the Government's budget proposals were rejected by the Cámara Federal de Diputados. The PRI, the largest congressional party, subsequently presented its own budget proposals to the legislature. However, divisions appeared within that party, ostensibly over the alternative proposals. In December 118 PRI deputies voted to replace Elba Esther Gordillo Morales, the party's Secretary-General, as leader of the PRI legislative bloc. Gordillo, who had originally supported the Government's proposed budget, initially refused to accept her dismissal and continued to rely on the support of 104 PRI deputies. It was widely believed that the underlying reason for the split was an ongoing feud between Gordillo and party President Roberto Madrazo Pintado over who would secure the PRI nomination for the presidential election due in 2006.

In March 2004 a scandal emerged surrounding the PRD Head of Government of the Distrito Federal, Andrés Manuel López Obrador, a popular political figure and a likely candidate in the 2006 presidential election. A videotape appeared to show López Obrador's finance chief, Gustavo Ponce Meléndez, gambling large amounts at a casino in the USA (Ponce was arrested in October). A further video recording came to light that apparently showed the Head of Government's former private secretary accepting money from a prominent Argentine businessman, Carlos Ahumada, who was accused of corruption. López Obrador denied any knowledge of either incident and claimed that a 'dirty tricks' campaign was being waged against him. In June 2004 the Attorney-General's office announced it was to prosecute López Obrador for allegedly ignoring an injunction against a compulsory purchase order and disregarding a federal ruling to re-employ numerous dismissed city officials; as a result, a formal request was made to the Congreso to rescind López Obrador's immunity from prosecution. In an indication of his popularity in Mexico City, however, in early August thousands of supporters attended a march in the capital against the move to impeach him. Following much deliberation, in April 2005 a four-member committee of the Cámara Federal de Diputados voted to recommend that López Obrador be stripped of his immunity; the lower house concurred with the committee's recommendation, in order that charges might be brought against López Obrador. Following the vote López Obrador took a leave of absence from office, although the Distrito Federal assembly approved a motion confirming him in office. Later in April as many as 1.2m. people participated in a demonstration in Mexico City in support of their mayor, who returned to his post the following day. The federal Attorney-General was subsequently dismissed; this was widely interpreted as an admission by the Government that its plan to prevent López Obrador from contesting the forthcoming presidential election had failed (people facing criminal charges were prohibited from running for office); indeed, in early May the new Attorney-General dismissed all charges against López Obrador and in July he secured the PRD's presidential nomination.

Discord continued within the PRI during 2005 between the supporters of Gordillo and Madrazo in their respective campaigns to secure the party's nomination for the presidential election. In January Gordillo and the powerful teachers' union, the Sindicato Nacional de Trabajadores de la Educación, of which she was President, launched the Nueva Alianza (NA) in order to consolidate support for her candidacy. Madrazo had been due to resign as President of the party in mid-2005 to contest the party's primary election; traditionally, he would have been succeeded by the Secretary-General, Gordillo, but the rivalry between the two meant that Madrazo delayed his departure until August. At the end of that month the party's national political council elected Mariano Palacios Alcocer, who had previously served as party President, as Madrazo's successor; Gordillo resigned as Secretary-General in September. In early August a third faction, Unidad Democrática, more commonly known as Todos Unidos Contra Madrazo (TUCOM—Everyone United against Madrazo), elected Arturo Montiel, the outgoing Governor of the Estado de México, as its nominee for the PRI's presidential candidate. However, in October, following allegations of corruption regarding his use of public money during his time as Governor, Montiel suddenly withdrew from the primary contest. It was widely assumed that Madrazo had been behind the allegations. A series of defections in late 2005 by prominent members of the PRI opposed to Madrazo further highlighted the divisions within the party. None the less, in November Madrazo won an overwhelming victory in the election for the PRI's presidential nomination.

Meanwhile, in October 2005 the former Secretary of Energy, Felipe Calderón Hinojosa, from the traditional, clericist wing of the PAN, unexpectedly won the election to decide that party's 2006 presidential nomination, defeating Santiago Creel Miranda, who had enjoyed the support of President Fox. In December the PRI and the PVEM announced an alliance, Alianza por México, in advance of the 2006 elections. The PRD also formed an alliance, named Por el Bien de Todos (For the Good of Everyone), with two smaller left-wing parties, Convergencia and the PT, to contest the ballots. This alliance later became the Frente Amplio Progresista (FAP).

At the presidential election, held on 2 July 2006, the PAN's Calderón secured an extremely narrow margin of victory, of just 0.6% (243,934 votes out of almost 42m. cast), over López Obrador. According to official results, Calderón polled 35.9% of the total votes cast, compared with López Obrador's 35.3%. Madrazo, the PRI nominee, trailed in third place with 22.2%, an historic low for the party. López Obrador did not accept the results, alleging that electoral irregularities, combined with the narrow margin of defeat, undermined their legitimacy. A rally was held in the capital by López Obrador's supporters on 8 July to demand a recount. The close election results were an important test of the autonomy of the IFE. Control of the IFE had been removed from the Secretariat of the Interior under President Zedillo, and the federal electoral body had secured an unprecedented degree of popular trust by overseeing the end to the PRI's monopoly on the presidency in 2000. However, there were fears that the official election result, with its echoes of Cuauhtémoc Cárdenas's defeat in 1988, would undermine the recent gains in legitimacy and lead to instability and institutional crisis. Calderón was inaugurated as President on 1 December in a ceremony notable for its lack of celebration and ostentation. A week earlier López Obrador had held a ceremony in Mexico City's main square, declaring himself to be Mexico's legitimate President in front of a large crowd.

Results of elections to the Congreso, also held on 2 July 2006, were evenly distributed among the three leading parties, ensuring that the new President would face a legislature dominated by the opposition. The PAN secured 206 of the 500 seats in the Cámara Federal de Diputados, with the PRD-led Por el Bien de Todos alliance winning 158 seats and the PRI's Alianza por México garnering 123 seats. In the 128-seat Senado, the PAN won 52 seats, the Alianza por México 39 seats and Por el Bien de Todos 36 seats. Political obstacles in the Congreso threatened to undermine the new Government's ability to introduce reforms to the state sector, just as they had during President Fox's administration.

One of the first major challenges that the new Government faced was the increasing unrest in Oaxaca. In June 2006 some 70,000 teachers had begun industrial action in support of salary increases. This had been accompanied by demonstrations, which became violent when police and protesters clashed, leaving around 100 people injured. Indigenous Indian rights activists and local farmers' co-operatives joined the protests, swelling their numbers to some 50,000. By September protesters had started to demand the resignation of the state Governor Ulises Ruiz Ortiz, accusing him of violently suppressing dissent and of winning the state election in April 2004 by fraudulent means; five of these people were shot dead by police. A further three protesters were shot dead in October, and by the end of that month President-elect Calderón had dispatched 5,000 security personnel supported by armoured trucks and helicopters to retake control of the centre of the city. More that 150 people were subsequently arrested for their part in the protests, and many more were injured during violent confrontations. In total, some 14 people were killed during the disturbances. A series of bomb explosions in Mexico City in early November, which caused severe damage to property but no loss of life, were reportedly in response to 'repression in Oaxaca'; although no particular group claimed responsibility for the attacks, the Ejército Popular Revolucionario (EPR), a left-wing guerrilla group hitherto active only in the southern states, was believed to have been linked to them. The EPR did claim responsibility for a series of bomb attacks affecting petroleum and gas pipelines belonging to PEMEX in central Mexico in early July, as well as another similar series of explosions in September, both of which caused severe disruption to major industries.

A series of substantial increases in the price of tortillas and other food staples, such as milk and eggs, prompted demonstrations by over 100,000 people in Mexico City in January 2007. The protests were led by the self-declared 'parallel President' López Obrador. Calderón responded by negotiating an agreement between producers and retailers to attempt to fix the price of tortillas for the remainder of 2007.

A law to reform the electoral system by reducing the influence of money in elections was approved with the votes of all three main parties in the Senado in September 2007 and entered into law in November. The provisions of the reform, *inter alia*, reduced from 270m. to 40m. new pesos the amount that a party could spend on an election campaign, granted each party a limited amount of publicity in the broadcast media and prohibited the diffusion of propaganda that denigrated parties or candidates; the latter provision was in response to the negative campaign conducted by opponents of López Obrador that had preceded the 2006 presidential election.

In January 2008 Calderón dismissed the Secretary of the Interior, Francisco Javier Ramírez Acuña, and the Secretary of Social Development, María Beatriz Zavala Peniche, appointing in their stead Juan Camilo Mouriño Terrazo and Ernesto Cordero Arroyo, respectively. The appointment of Mouriño, hitherto Chief of the Office of the President, caused controversy, with the PRD alleging that as the holder of dual Mexican and Spanish nationality he was constitutionally ineligible for ministerial office. In March the opposition further accused the minister of having taken advantage of his position as head of the congressional energy commission in the early 2000s and, later, adviser to the Secretary of Energy, to sign a series of contracts between his family's transportation company and PEMEX. Mouriño resisted demands for his resignation, and was cleared of any wrongdoing in May. In November, however, Mouriño and several other government officials were killed when their aeroplane crashed in central Mexico City.

Rapidly declining oil production, apparently owing to a lack of investment in exploration and refineries, led the PAN to propose energy reforms in early 2008. The proposed modernization was to liberalize the oil sector allowing PEMEX to form alliances with foreign companies. The reforms were strongly opposed by the PRD, and facilitated the political revival of López Obrador, who led the protests. López Obrador rejected the proposals as an unwelcome step towards privatization, and argued that any private investment in PEMEX would threaten national sovereignty. However, the Congreso approved the energy reforms in October.

Meanwhile, in late March 2008 an election to choose the President of the PRD highlighted the divisions in the party between a faction that supported López Obrador's continued claim to the presidency and refused to deal with what it considered to be an illegitimate Government, and those who favoured a more pragmatic approach. Preliminary indications suggested that Alejandro Encinas, representing the pro-López Obrador faction, had defeated the moderate candidate, Jesús Ortega; however, counting of ballots was suspended in several states following allegations of irregularities by both sides. After several months of deliberation, the PRD announced the annulment of its internal elections in July. In November the Tribunal Electoral del Poder Judicial de la Federación (TEPJF) ruled that Ortega was the rightful winner of the March election, provoking further tensions within the party. The defeat of Encinas led to López Obrador threatening to split away from the PRD in December. In November, the leader of the PRI, Beatriz Paredes Rangel, had offered the PRD an alliance for the mid-term legislative elections. Although Ortega did not accept the offer, the possibility of new alliances seemed likely to cause further divisions in the PRD.

An outbreak of the A(H1N1) strain of the influenza virus (commonly known as 'swine flu') in Mexico in April 2009 led to fears of a global pandemic. In an attempt to contain the spread of the virus, Calderón ordered the closure of schools, universities, government offices, factories, restaurants and markets across the country. The Government's decisive response to the crisis appeared to have had some success in controlling the spread of the disease within Mexico, although the international impact of the virus remained unclear in early May.

Mexico's poor human rights record was highlighted in late 2001 by the assassination in October of a leading civil liberties lawyer, Digna Ochoa, and by the publication, in December, of an Amnesty International report alleging that Mexican security forces were involved in widespread human rights violations. In response, President Fox, whose electoral campaign had made the elimination of corruption and an improvement in human rights a priority, announced an official inquiry into the 'disappearance' of 532 people detained by security forces in the 1970s and 1980s. In February 2002 Fox ordered the immediate release of Gen. José Francisco Gallardo, who had been sentenced to 28 years' imprisonment in 1993 after being convicted of misappropriating military property. Human rights groups and supporters of Gallardo had maintained that the charges were fabricated and that he had been incarcerated after demanding a reform of the military justice system. However, in August 2003 Amnesty International published a report that accused the Government of inefficiency and negligence in investigating the rape and murder of an estimated 307 women (and the disappearance of a further 500) in Ciudad Juárez over the previous 10 years. In 2004 some 130 government officials were investigated for negligence in the ongoing murder investigations. In mid-2004 a further Amnesty International report asserted that widespread abuse of human rights persisted. The report alleged that the police and military routinely abused peasants, and that torture was commonly used by police and in the justice system. According to official figures, 531 kidnappings occurred in Mexico in 2003; however, other sources estimated that the real figure was 3,000. In December 2004 President Fox announced a National Plan for Human Rights, aimed at eliminating torture and abuse. A report commissioned by Fox in 2002, which was published in November 2006, acknowledged government responsibility in the massacres, torture and 'disappearances' of the 1970s. In March 2007 the investigating magistrate ordered the murder case of

Digna Ochoa to be reopened. In December of the same year the Supreme Court concluded an investigation into allegations that the PRI Governor of Puebla, Mario Marín Torres, had violated the human rights of the investigative journalist Lydia Cacho. A recording of a telephone conversation implied that Marín had ordered Cacho's illegal arrest and torture in December 2005, in retaliation for a book published by the journalist that had implicated him in a child abuse scandal; however, after ruling the evidence inadmissible, the court absolved Marín of responsibility. The ruling was strongly condemned by left-wing critics.

An anti-narcotics effort by the Fox administration led to an increased number of arrests in 2002–04, including the leaders of the Tijuana and Golfo cocaine cartels. However, the anti-drugs programme was itself the subject of an anti-corruption drive in 2002, leading to a number of specialized army units being dismantled. Meanwhile, in November the investigation into the 'guerra sucia' of the late 1970s resulted in the convictions of Brig.-Gen. Mario Acosta and Gen. Francisco Quirós on charges of protecting the operations of the Juárez cartel; they also faced charges over the disappearance of 143 activists. Despite efforts by President Fox to address the crime problem, drugs-related crime continued to escalate as the amount of narcotics crossing the Mexican–US border increased. It appeared that an internecine war between the Tijuana, Golfo and Sinaloa cartels was taking place in the north of Mexico. During 2005 more than 180 people were killed in Nuevo Laredo, Tamaulipas, in what appeared to be an ongoing conflict between two drugs cartels. In November Ricardo García Urquiza, alleged to be the leader of the Juárez cartel, was arrested in Mexico City.

Upon his election in mid-2006 President Calderón announced that law enforcement would form one of his priorities in office. A major offensive was subsequently launched in December against the activities of the drugs cartels in Michoacán state with the deployment of 7,000 troops and federal police officers. A second major operation was launched in Tijuana, Baja California, in early January 2007, while later in the same month some 9,000 troops were sent into the states of Sinaloa, Durango and Chihuahua. Meanwhile, Calderón was highly commended by the US authorities for his decision in January to allow the extradition of 15 drugs-trafficking suspects to the USA. The extradition of the individuals (who included the head of the Golfo cartel and senior figures from the Sinaloa and Tijuana cartels) represented a significant change in policy from previous administrations, which had refused to allow extradition until suspects had faced a Mexican court. By mid-May the army and federal police had been deployed in a law-enforcement role in 10 states. Although these offensives against organized crime appeared to have little immediate impact (according to official figures, at least 2,500 people were killed by gangsters in 2007, compared with 2,350 in 2006), the Government emphasized that its strategy would take several years to accomplish. In January 2008 the arrest, in Culiacán, Sinaloa, of Alfredo Beltrán Leyva, a senior leader of the Sinaloa cartel, was one of a number of important successes in the offensive. The arrest, however, provoked further battles between rival factions of the Sinaloa-based Arellano Félix cartel, one loyal to Beltrán Levya and the other to the notorious drugs trafficker Joaquín Guzmán ('El Chapo'). Minor bomb explosions in Mexico City in February and March were also attributed to the Sinaloa cartel. Drugs-related violence escalated in 2008, with a reported 5,400 killings, more than twice the murder toll of the previous year. As previously, the violence was particularly, but not exclusively, concentrated in the states of Baja California, Chihuahua and Sinaloa, with 12 decapitated bodies also discovered in the Yucatán in August, and a further dozen found in Chilpancingo, Guerrero, in December. On 15 September 2008, the eve of Independence Day, a grenade exploded amid celebrations in the main square of Morelia, Michoacán, killing eight people and wounding many others. The violence continued unabated, and the start of October saw the murder of 50 people in Tijuana in a single week. Despite the deployment of some 40,000 troops in the war against drugs, army incursions into the problem areas had little impact and tended to exacerbate violence; one confrontation between the army and gang members in a border town of Chihuahua in February 2009 resulted in 21 deaths, including the six hostages taken by the gang. The armed forces launched a renewed campaign against drugs gangs in Ciudad Juárez in March 2009, sending 7,000 troops and police into the city.

Confronted by widespread insecurity about the increasing crime rate, Calderón held a summit in August 2008, during which state governors, congressmen and other representatives agreed on a three-year plan to introduce 75 anti-crime measures, including the construction of maximum-security gaols and a national database to track mobile telephone usage. The high-profile kidnap and murder of Fernando Martí, the 14-year-old son of a well-known businessman, incited Calderón to toughen sentences for kidnappers and to launch a new anti-kidnap squad. Nevertheless, the Government failed to inspire confidence about the security situation in many Mexicans. In late August more than 200,000 people filled the capital's main square in a night-time demonstration to denounce not only murders, kidnappings and drugs-trafficking, but also alleged police and government complicity and corruption. The arrest of one of the Arellano Félix brothers, Eduardo, in October, was followed by the revelation that two senior officials in the government unit for the investigation of organized crime, the Subprocuraduría de Investigación Especializada en Delincuencia Organizada (SIEDO), were in the pay of the Beltrán Leyva cartel. The SIEDO's reputation was damaged further in November when its former head, Noé Ramírez, was accused of having accepted US $450,000 from the Sinaloa cartel in exchange for supplying information about police investigations.

On 1 January 1994 armed Indian groups numbering 1,000–3,000 took control of four municipalities of the southern state of Chiapas. The rebels issued the Declaration of the Lacandona Jungle, identifying themselves as the Ejército Zapatista de Liberación Nacional—EZLN (after Emiliano Zapata, who championed the land rights of Mexican peasants during the 1910–17 Revolution), and detailed a series of demands for economic and social change in the region, culminating in a declaration of war against the Government and a statement of intent to depose the 'dictator', President Salinas. A charismatic rebel spokesman, identified as 'subcomandante Marcos' (later tentatively identified as Rafael Sebastián Guillén Vicente, a former professor at the Universidad Autónoma Metropolitana), stated that the insurgency had been timed to coincide with the implementation of the North American Free Trade Agreement (NAFTA—see below), which the rebels considered to be the latest in a series of segregative government initiatives adopted at the expense of indigenous groups. Negotiations between the Zapatistas and government representatives concluded with the publication of a document detailing 34 demands of the EZLN, and the Government's response to them. A preliminary accord was reached following the Government's broad acceptance of many of the rebels' stipulations, including an acceleration of the wide-ranging anti-poverty programme in the region, the incorporation of traditional Indian structures of justice and political organization, and a commitment from the Government to investigate the impact of NAFTA and recent land reform legislation on Indian communities. Official figures suggested that 100–150 guerrillas, soldiers and civilians had been killed during the conflict, while the Roman Catholic Church estimated that there had been as many as 400 casualties. In June the EZLN announced that the Government's peace proposal had been rejected by an overwhelming majority of the movement's supporters. However, a similar majority had rejected the resumption of hostilities with the security forces, and had endorsed the extension of the cease-fire pending renewed bilateral discussions. Tensions, however, continued over the following years, with attempts to reach an accord between the Zapatistas and the Government proving unsuccessful. In February 1996 the EZLN and the Government signed an agreement guaranteeing the cultural, linguistic and local government rights of indigenous groups. However, the EZLN withdrew from negotiations in September on the grounds that the agreement had not been implemented. In September 1997 several thousand Zapatistas and their sympathizers staged a peaceful demonstration in Mexico City, during which the EZLN inaugurated the Frente Zapatista de Liberación Nacional, a political movement that embodied the Zapatistas' ideology. In December there was widespread disquiet at the killing of 45 Indians in a church in the village of Acteal, in the municipality of Chenalhó, Chiapas. Emilio Chuayffet, the Secretary of the Interior, and Julio César Ruiz Ferro, the Governor of Chiapas, were forced to resign, following criticism of their roles in the events leading to the Acteal massacre. In April 1998 Gen. Julio César Santiago Díaz, who had been acting chief of staff of Chiapas state police at the time of the massacre, was arrested and charged with failing to intervene to prevent the bloodshed. In September 1999 Jacinto Arias, mayor of Chenalhó at the time of the massacre, was convicted on charges of supplying the weapons used in the massacre and sentenced to 35 years' imprisonment. In November 2002 some 18 people were each sentenced to 36 years' imprisonment for their involvement in the deaths as part of a paramilitary group with links to the PRI; they joined 70 others previously convicted.

In February 2001 subcomandante Marcos and other Zapatista leaders began a tour of Mexico which culminated in Mexico City in early March, where a rally in the capital's main square, attended by an estimated 150,000 people, was held in support of congressional approval of the proposed indigenous rights legislation. Following a congressional vote, four EZLN leaders were permitted to address both legislative chambers, and, in March, the EZLN announced that formal dialogue with the Government would recommence. Subcomandante Marcos successfully negotiated the dismantling of the remaining three garrisons in Chiapas, and in April the Congreso approved amendments to six articles of the Constitution, which recognized and guaranteed indigenous political, legal, social and economic rights, and prohibited discrimination against Indians based on race and tribal affiliation. However, the legislation fell short of granting indigenous peoples the right to autonomy over land and natural resources; in response, the EZLN suspended all contact with the Government. In August 2003 the EZLN declared that 30 municipalities in Chiapas, hitherto under Zapatista control, were to be granted autonomy. 'Councils of Good Government' (Juntas de Buen Gobierno) would oversee the transition from military to civilian control in these areas. The transformation of the EZLN into a political force was underlined in August 2005, when subcomandante Marcos announced his plans to create a left-wing alliance of peasants' organizations. In early 2006 the Zapatistas began an alternative presidential election campaign, although it failed to gather significant support.

Mexico's foreign policy has been determined largely by relations with the USA. The rapid expansion of petroleum production from the mid-1970s onwards gave Mexico a new independence, empowering it to favour the left-wing regimes in Cuba and Nicaragua, opposed by the USA, during the 1980s. In February 1985 relations between Mexico and the USA deteriorated following the murder of an agent of the US Drug Enforcement Administration (DEA) by Mexican drugs-traffickers. The situation worsened in April 1990, when a Mexican physician was abducted, in Mexico, by agents employed by the DEA, and transported to the USA to be arrested on charges relating to the murder. Meanwhile, relations between Mexico and the USA remained tense, largely because of disagreement over the problem of illegal immigration from Mexico into the USA and Mexico's failure to take effective action against the illegal drugs trade. This situation improved following the deportation to the USA in 1996 of Juan García Abrego, the alleged head of the Golfo drugs cartel, and in the following year the USA 'certified' Mexico as a country co-operating in its campaign against drugs-trafficking. Bilateral relations were strained in May 1998, when a major US counter-narcotics operation was conducted in Mexico, without Mexican authorization. None the less, additional co-operation agreements were signed by the two countries in early 1999, and Mexico continued to be 'certified' by the USA. Although President Fox advocated abolition of the certification practice, it was reaffirmed in 2001.

NAFTA, comprising Mexico, the USA and Canada, took effect from 1 January 1994. Among the Agreement's provisions are the gradual reduction of tariffs on 50% of products over a period of 10–15 years (some 57% of tariffs on agricultural trade between the USA and Mexico were removed immediately), and the establishment, by Mexico and the USA, of a North American Development Bank (NADBank) charged with the funding of initiatives for the rehabilitation of the two countries' common border. From January 2003 tariffs on a number of agricultural products were reduced or removed entirely, provoking widespread discontent among Mexico's 25m.-strong rural community. In particular, they pointed to the greater subsidies received by US farmers and to a poor transport infrastructure, which resulted in higher costs. A pledge by President Fox in May 2002 to repay Mexico's 'water debt' to the USA had also angered Mexican farmers. Following the collapse, in September 2003, of the fifth Ministerial Conference of the World Trade Organization (WTO) in Cancún, Mexico joined the group of developing countries led by Brazil that opposed US-European Union (EU, see p. 255) subsidies of agricultural products. At a summit meeting in March 2005 between President Fox, US President George W. Bush and Canadian Prime Minister Paul Martin, the three leaders announced an accord to increase regional co-operation on economic and security issues.

The Fox Government sought to persuade the US Administration of George W. Bush, which took office in 2001, to adopt a more liberal position on Mexican immigrants to the USA. However, progress on immigration policy was suspended following the terrorist attacks in the USA on 11 September 2001, and proposals to tighten security on the US–Mexican border were approved by the US Congress in 2002. In March of that year, nevertheless, following a summit meeting in Monterrey, the two Presidents announced a 'smart border' partnership agreement, intended to facilitate the legal entry of Mexican people and goods into the USA while, at the same time, securing the frontier against possible acts of terrorism. In September, however, Fox requested that the emphasis in US-Mexican relations be shifted back to bilateral issues, which had been neglected in favour of border security. In the same month Mexico unilaterally withdrew from the Inter-American Treaty of Reciprocal Assistance (the Rio Treaty), the defence pact linking Mexico to the USA, resulting in a downturn in relations with the USA.

In March 2003, with Mexican public opinion strongly against armed intervention to remove the regime of Saddam Hussain in Iraq, President Fox risked a deterioration of relations with both the USA and Spain by stating his opposition to war. His stance was all the more significant owing to Mexico's place as one of the 10 non-permanent members of the UN Security Council. In January 2004 the announcement of a revised US immigration initiative, which offered significantly less to Mexican immigrants in the USA than had been hoped, was met with disappointment by the Mexican Government, which had hoped to increase freedom of movement between the two countries. In the same month US officials began managing the security arrangements for US-bound flights leaving Mexico City's airport.

Throughout 2005 tensions remained high between Mexico and the USA over border security, specifically regarding illegal immigration from Mexico to the USA, and also escalating drugs-related violence in Mexico (see above). However, in October a Mexican-US joint effort to reduce lawlessness in the border area was announced: a bilateral agreement was signed in March 2006. None the less, the Mexican Government expressed strong opposition to a US plan, announced in late 2005, to build security fences along some 1,600 km of the most accessible sections of the border in order to deter illegal immigrants. By September 2006, despite the objections of the Mexican authorities, the proposal, involving the construction of a triple barrier, monitored by lookout towers, sensors and cameras, had been approved by the US Congress. The Mexican Government appealed direct to President Bush to veto the bill, claiming that it would harm bilateral relations and be contrary to the spirit of co-operation necessary in guaranteeing the security of the common border. Various indigenous groups whose territories straddled the border also expressed concern at the proposal. Other commentators speculated on the possibility that, by forcing Mexicans to take more dangerous routes into US territory, there would be an increase in the death rate of migrants.

US-Mexican relations deteriorated somewhat in 2007 following Calderón's accession to the presidency, as a result not only of the USA's continued uncompromising stance on border security but also of Mexico's improved relations with Cuba and Venezuela (see below). None the less, as a result of negotiations between Presidents Bush and Calderón in March in Mérida, Yucatán, in October Bush promised the Mexican Government some US $500m. per year in order to combat drugs-related crime. The Mérida Initiative, as it became known, was signed into law in July 2008. In March 2009, however, the US Senate voted to reduce the Mérida Initiative budget to $300m. None the less, the new US Administration of President Barack Obama pledged to increase border security and assist Mexico in fighting the drugs cartels, including increasing the presence of its own border officials and contributing $700m. for helicopters and law enforcement equipment. The move reflected concerns that drugs-related violence was increasingly affecting US border towns.

In April 2004 Mexico's relations with Cuba were strained after Mexico voted in favour of a UN motion to censure Cuba for human rights abuses. In early May the Cuban leader, Fidel Castro Ruz, criticized Mexico's stance and accused the Fox Government of interference in the island's affairs. In response, President Fox expelled the Cuban ambassador from the country and recalled the Mexican ambassador in Cuba; the ambassadors returned to their posts in July. Under President Calderón Mexico effected a rapprochement towards Cuba, and in June 2007 Mexico voted in favour of a UN Human Rights Council resolution to end UN scrutiny of human rights in Cuba. In late 2005 Mexico and Venezuela recalled their respective ambassadors, after left-wing President Lt-Col (retd) Hugo Chávez Frías of Venezuela criticized President Fox for being subservient to the USA. Full diplomatic relations between the two countries were restored in August 2007.

In January 1991 a preliminary free trade agreement was signed with Honduras, Guatemala, El Salvador, Nicaragua and Costa Rica, in order to facilitate the negotiation of bilateral agreements between Mexico and each of the five countries, leading to free trade in an increasing range of products over a six-year period. During the 1990s Mexico concluded agreements for greater economic co-operation and increased bilateral trade with Colombia and Venezuela (as the Group of Three, see p. 426), and with Bolivia, Costa Rica and the EU. A free trade accord with Nicaragua came into force in 1998; a similar accord with Chile was signed in 1998 and came into force in the following year. A further trade agreement with Guatemala, Honduras and El Salvador (the Northern Triangle) was concluded in 2000. In March 2000 Mexico and the EU signed a free trade agreement, the first to be signed between the EU and a Latin American country. The accord provided for the gradual elimination of tariffs on industrial and agricultural products, the progressive liberalization of trade in services, and preferential access to public procurement; it also obliged the signatories to respect democratic principles and human rights. In October 2003 Mexico signed an Organization of American States agreement on regional security, which was also aimed at increasing co-operation on social and environmental issues. In April 2004 the Secretary of Foreign Affairs, Luis Ernesto Derbez, announced Mexico's aim of becoming a full member of the Southern Common Market Mercado Común del Sur—Mercosur (see p. 405), and in late 2004 he declared Mexico's intention of seeking permanent representation on the UN Security Council.

Government

Mexico is a federal republic comprising 31 states and a Distrito Federal (Federal District, comprising the capital). Under the 1917 Constitution, legislative power is vested in the bicameral Congreso de la Unión, elected by universal adult suffrage. The Senado (Senate) has 128 members (four from each state and the Distrito Federal), serving a six-year term. The Cámara Federal de Diputados (Federal Chamber of Deputies), directly elected for three years, has 500 seats, of which 300 are filled from single-member constituencies. The remaining 200 seats, allocated so as to achieve proportional representation, are filled from parties' lists of candidates. Executive power is held by the President, directly elected for six years at the same time as the Senado. He governs with the assistance of an appointed Cabinet. Each state has its own constitution and is administered by a Governor (elected for six years) and an elected Chamber of Deputies. The Distrito Federal is administered by a Head of Government.

Defence

Military service, on a part-time basis (four hours per week), is compulsory for conscripts selected by lottery, for one year. As assessed in November 2008, the active armed forces totalled 255,506: 188,000 in the army, 55,961 in the navy (including naval air force—1,250—and marines—19,328) and 11,545 in the air force. Paramilitary forces numbered 30,700, comprising a federal preventive police force of 12,700 and a rural defence militia numbering 18,000. The reserve numbered 39,899. Defence expenditure for 2008 was budgeted at 48,200m. new pesos, an increase of some 11% on the previous year.

Economic Affairs

In 2007, according to estimates by the World Bank, Mexico's gross national income (GNI), measured at average 2005–07 prices, was US $878,020m., equivalent to $8,340 per head (or $12,580 per head on an international purchasing-power parity basis). During 2000–07, it was estimated, the population increased at an average annual rate of 1.0%, while gross domestic product (GDP) per head increased, in real terms, by an average of 1.4% per year. Overall GDP increased, in real terms, at an average annual rate of 2.4% in 2000–07; GDP increased by 3.3% in 2007.

Agriculture (including forestry and fishing) contributed 3.9% of GDP in 2007 and engaged 13.1% of the employed labour force in 2008. The staple food crops are maize, wheat, sorghum, barley, rice, beans and potatoes. The principal cash crops are coffee, cotton, sugar cane, and fruit and vegetables (particularly tomatoes). Livestock-raising and fisheries are also important. During 2000–07, according to World Bank estimates, agricultural GDP increased at an average annual rate of 2.1%; agricultural GDP increased by 2.2% in 2007. The reduction and eventual removal of import tariffs proposed under the North American Free Trade Agreement (NAFTA) was a significant blow to Mexico's agriculture sector, which had lower subsidies and higher overhead costs than in the USA. In late 2004 the Congreso approved a law regulating the use of genetically modified seeds.

Industry (including mining, manufacturing, construction and power) engaged 25.5% of the employed labour force in 2008 and provided an estimated 26.2% of GDP in 2007. According to the World Bank, during 2000–07 industrial GDP increased by an average of 1.5% per year; industrial GDP increased by 3.3% in 2007.

Mining contributed 1.6% of GDP in 2007, and, together with electricity production and distribution, engaged 0.9% of the employed labour force in 2008. During 2000–07 the GDP of the mining sector increased by an average of 1.9% per year; mining GDP increased by 0.2% in 2007. Mexico has large reserves of petroleum and natural gas (mineral products accounted for an estimated 17.9% of total export earnings in 2008). Zinc, salt, silver, copper, celestite and fluorite are also major mineral exports. In addition, mercury, bismuth, antimony, cadmium, manganese and phosphates are mined, and there are significant reserves of uranium.

Manufacturing provided 17.6% of GDP in 2007 and engaged 16.3% of the employed labour force in 2008. According to the World Bank, manufacturing GDP increased at an average annual rate of 1.0% in 2000–07; the sector's GDP increased by 3.0% in 2007. In the 1990s the *maquila* sector (where intermediate materials produced on US territory are processed or assembled on the Mexican side of the border) grew in importance. By December 2000 Mexico had 3,703 *maquila* export plants, providing an estimated 1.3m. jobs and making a significant contribution to the manufacturing sector; however, the sector suffered a downturn in the early 2000s, and the number of plants fell to an estimated 2,860 in 2005. *Maquila* exports were valued at an estimated 214,430.2m. new pesos in 2006, an increase of 4.5% from 2005 and equivalent to 45.3% of total revenue from manufacturing exports. In 2005 an estimated 1.2m. people were employed in the *maquila* sector.

Energy is derived principally from hydrocarbons, coal and hydroelectric power. In 2005, according to the World Bank, some 29.3% of total output of electricity production was derived from petroleum, 36.1% came from natural gas, and 14.0% came from coal-powered plants. The Fox Government's planned liberalization of the energy sector, including the troubled state-run Petróleos Mexicanos (PEMEX), ran into difficulties owing to congressional opposition. In late 2004 the IMF recommended that Mexico further open its energy sector to private investment. In 2007, according to PEMEX, oil production was an estimated 3.1m. barrels per day, representing a 5% decline on average output the previous year. However, production of natural gas was estimated to have increased by 13% in 2007, reaching 6,058m. cu ft per day. In 2008 mineral imports were estimated at 10.1% of total merchandise imports, while exports of petroleum accounted for an estimated 14.8% of the total export value in the same year. In January 2009 plans to construct a US $10m. oil refinery were announced, a move expected to lessen Mexico's reliance on imports of refined petroleum products. Meanwhile, the decision of the Government to purchase oil futures contracts at a price of $70 per barrel during 2008 was expected to provide some insurance against declining prices in the following year and enable much-needed investment in this sector's infrastructure. In late 2001 the Governments of Mexico and Guatemala reached agreement, under the regional 'Plan Puebla-Panamá' (a series of joint transport, industry and tourism projects intended to integrate the Central American region), to link their electricity grids.

The services sector contributed 69.8% of GDP in 2007 and engaged 61.4% of the employed labour force in 2008. According to World Bank figures, the GDP of the sector increased by an average of 2.9% per year in 2000–07; the sector experienced growth of 3.8% in 2007. Tourism is one of Mexico's principal sources of foreign exchange. In 2006 there were an estimated 21.4m. foreign visitors to Mexico (mostly from the USA and Canada), providing revenue of US $12,801m.

In 2007 Mexico recorded a visible trade deficit of an estimated US $10,074m., and there was a deficit of $5,539m. on the current account of the balance of payments. In 2008 the principal source of imports (49.0%) was the USA, which was also the principal market for exports (80.1%). The principal exports in 2008 (including data for the *maquila* sector) were mechanical and electrical appliances, mineral products and transport equipment; the same categories also represented the principal imports.

In 2008 there was an estimated budgetary deficit of 195,514m. new pesos, equivalent to 1.6% of GDP. Mexico's external debt totalled US $160,700m. at the end of 2006, of which $96,304m. was long-term public debt. In that year the cost of debt-servicing was equivalent to 18.9% of the value of exports of goods and services. The average annual rate of inflation was 4.6% in 2000–07. Consumer prices increased by an average of 4.0% in 2007. An estimated 3.5% of the total labour force were officially recorded as unemployed in 2008. In that year remittances from Mexicans living abroad totalled US $25,145m., a 3.6% decline on 2007. It was estimated that remittances were Mexico's second largest source of foreign income, after petroleum exports.

Mexico is a member of the Inter-American Development Bank (IDB, see p. 318), and of the Latin American Integration Association (see p. 342). Mexico was admitted to the Asia-Pacific Economic Co-operation group (APEC, see p. 185) in 1993, and joined the Organisation for Economic Co-operation and Development (OECD, see p. 358) in 1994. Mexico is also a signatory nation to NAFTA (see p. 350). In September 2004 Mexico concluded a free trade agreement with Japan.

Mexico's economic development, centred on the expansion of the petroleum industry, was impeded from the mid-1980s by the decrease in international petroleum prices, in addition to the persistent problems of the flight of capital, the depreciation of the peso, a shortage of foreign exchange and vast foreign debt. A programme of tax reform and economic liberalization was undertaken from the late 1980s, but in late 1994 and early 1995 a sharp devaluation of the peso provoked a financial crisis, necessitating a stringent policy of economic adjustment and the procurement of substantial international credit facilities. Strong export performance in the latter half of the decade, particularly in the *maquila* industries, prompted an economic recovery, and annual economic growth reached 6.6% in 2000. An economic slowdown occurred in the early 2000s, caused by the sluggish economy of Mexico's largest trading partner, the USA, particularly in the *maquila* sector. A deceleration in US economic growth, which began in 2007, led to a similar decline in Mexico's growth rate in that year (see above). Conditions continued to deteriorate in 2008, and, with the onset of the global banking crisis in September, the strength of Mexico's economic links with the USA were revealed. The recall of investment and the serious depreciation of the peso created problems in the financial and business sectors. The central bank attempted to counter depreciation through a large-scale purchase of Mexican pesos, a measure which drew on a significant portion of the country's international reserves. Elsewhere, inflows of remittances were observed to be in decline, owing to rising unemployment in the US construction sector, which had accounted for a large section of the migrant labour force. The official rate of unemployment increased for the first time in four years in September 2008. Foreign demand declined rapidly in late 2008 and early 2009, leading to further contraction in the manufacturing sector (particularly the *maquila* industries), which relied heavily on exports to the USA. The economy was forecast to contract by 0.3% in 2009, according to estimates released by the IMF in January of that year. However, uncertainty relating to the global economic climate meant that a more pronounced decline remained very possible. Moreover, the nation-wide closure of public buildings and commercial premises in April and May 2009, in response to widespread fears of a pandemic caused by the spread of a dangerous strain of the influenza virus ('swine flu', see Recent History), was expected to have an adverse impact on the Mexican economy. The services sector, particularly the tourist industry, was likely to be the worst affected. However, US President Barack Obama's decision not to close the US border with Mexico during the crisis was welcomed by the Mexican Government.

Education

Education in state schools is provided free of charge and is officially compulsory. It covers six years of primary education, beginning at six years of age, and three years of secondary education, either general or technical, from the age of 12. This can then be followed by another three-year cycle of higher or specialized secondary education. In 2005/06 enrolment at primary schools included 97.7% of pupils in the relevant age-group, while in the same year enrolment at secondary schools included 70.3% of pupils in the relevant age-group. In 2006 there were an estimated 5,466 institutes of higher education, attended by some 2,446,700 students. In 2002 there were 56 universities in Mexico. In 2001/02 nursery schools for the indigenous population numbered 8,487, while there were 9,065 primary schools for the indigenous population. However, in spite of the existence of more than 80 indigenous languages in Mexico, there were few bilingual secondary schools. Federal expenditure on education in 2003 was an estimated 265,238.1m. new pesos (equivalent to 21.4% of total central government expenditure).

Public Holidays

2009: 1 January (New Year's Day), 2 February (for Constitution Day), 16 March (for Birthday of Benito Juárez), 9 April (Maundy Thursday)*, 10 April (Good Friday)*, 1 May (Labour Day), 5 May (Anniversary of the Battle of Puebla)*, 16 September (Independence Day), 2 November (All Souls' Day)*, 16 November (for Anniversary of the Revolution), 12 December (Day of Our Lady of Guadalupe)*, 25 December (Christmas).

2010: 1 January (New Year's Day), 1 February (for Constitution Day), 15 March (for Birthday of Benito Juárez), 1 April (Maundy Thursday)*, 2 April (Good Friday)*, 1 May (Labour Day), 5 May (Anniversary of the Battle of Puebla)*, 16 September (Independence Day), 2 November (All Souls' Day)*, 15 November (for Anniversary of the Revolution), 12 December (Day of Our Lady of Guadalupe)*, 25 December (Christmas).

* Widely celebrated unofficial holidays.

Weights and Measures

The metric system is in force.

Statistical Survey

Sources (unless otherwise stated): Dirección General de Estadística, Instituto Nacional de Estadística, Geografía e Informática (INEGI), Edif. Sede, Avda Prolongación Héroe de Nacozari 2301 Sur, 20270 Aguascalientes, Ags; tel. (14) 918-1948; fax (14) 918-0739; e-mail webmaster@inegi.gob.mx; internet www.inegi.gob.mx; Banco de México, Avda 5 de Mayo 1, Col. Centro, Del. Cuauhtémoc, 06059 México, DF; tel. (55) 5237-2000; fax (55) 5237-2370; internet www.banxico.org.mx.

Area and Population

AREA, POPULATION AND DENSITY

Area (sq km)	
Continental	1,959,248
Islands	5,127
Total	1,964,375*
Population (census and by-census results)†	
14 February 2000	97,483,412
29 October 2005	
Males	50,249,955
Females	53,013,433
Total	103,263,388
Population (projected mid-year estimates)‡	
2006	104,874,282
2007	105,790,725
2008	106,682,518
Density (per sq km) at mid-2008	54.3

* 758,449 sq miles.
† Including adjustment for underenumeration (1,730,016 in 2000).
‡ Source: Consejo Nacional de Población, *Proyecciones de la Población de México 2005–2050*.

ADMINISTRATIVE DIVISIONS
(at by-census of October 2005)

States	Area (sq km)*	Population	Density (per sq km)	Capital
Aguascalientes (Ags)	5,623	1,065,416	189.5	Aguascalientes
Baja California (BC)	71,540	2,844,469	36.8	Mexicali
Baja California Sur (BCS)	73,937	512,170	6.9	La Paz
Campeche (Camp.)	57,718	754,730	13.1	Campeche
Chiapas (Chis)	73,680	4,293,459	58.3	Tuxtla Gutiérrez
Chihuahua (Chih.)	247,490	3,241,444	13.1	Chihuahua
Coahuila (de Zaragoza) (Coah.)	151,447	2,495,200	16.5	Saltillo
Colima (Col.)	5,629	567,996	100.9	Colima
Distrito Federal (DF)	1,485	8,720,916	5,87.7	Mexico City
Durango (Dgo)	123,364	1,509,117	12.2	Victoria de Durango
Guanajuato (Gto)	30,617	4,893,812	159.8	Guanajuato
Guerrero (Gro)	63,618	3,115,202	50.0	Chilpancingo de los Bravos
Hidalgo (Hgo)	20,855	2,345,514	112.5	Pachuca de Soto
Jalisco (Jal.)	78,624	6,752,113	85.9	Guadalajara
México (Méx.)	22,332	14,007,495	627.2	Toluca de Lerdo
Michoacán (de Ocampo) (Mich.)	58,672	3,966,073	67.6	Morelia
Morelos (Mor.)	4,894	1,612,899	329.6	Cuernavaca
Nayarit (Nay.)	27,861	949,684	34.1	Tepic
Nuevo León (NL)	64,206	4,199,292	65.4	Monterrey
Oaxaca (Oax.)	93,348	3,506,821	37.6	Oaxaca de Juárez
Puebla (Pue.)	34,246	5,383,133	157.2	Heroica Puebla de Zaragoza
Querétaro (de Arteaga) (Qro)	11,659	1,598,139	137.1	Querétaro
Quintana Roo (Q.Roo)	42,544	1,135,309	26.7	Ciudad Chetumal
San Luis Potosí (SLP)	61,165	2,410,414	39.4	San Luis Potosí
Sinaloa (Sin.)	57,334	2,608,442	45.5	Culiacán Rosales
Sonora (Son.)	179,527	2,394,861	13.3	Hermosillo
Tabasco (Tab.)	24,747	1,989,969	80.4	Villahermosa
Tamaulipas (Tam.)	80,155	3,024,238	37.7	Ciudad Victoria
Tlaxcala (Tlax.)	3,988	1,068,207	267.8	Tlaxcala de Xicohténcatl
Veracruz-Llave (Ver.)	71,856	7,110,214	99.0	Jalapa Enríquez
Yucatán (Yuc.)	39,675	1,818,948	45.8	Mérida
Zacatecas (Zac.)	75,412	1,367,692	18.1	Zacatecas
Total	1,959,248	103,263,388	52.7	—

* Excluding islands.

PRINCIPAL TOWNS
(population at census of 14 February 2000)

Ciudad de México (Mexico City, capital)	8,605,239
Guadalajara	1,646,183
Ecatepec de Morelos (Ecatepec)	1,621,827
Heroica Puebla de Zaragoza (Puebla)	1,271,673
Nezahualcóyotl	1,225,083
Ciudad Juárez	1,187,275
Tijuana	1,148,681
Monterrey	1,110,909
León	1,020,818
Zapopan	910,690
Naucalpan de Juárez (Naucalpan)	835,053
Tlalnepantla de Baz (Tlalnepantla)	714,735
Guadalupe	669,842
Mérida	662,530
Chihuahua	657,876
San Luis Potosí	629,208
Acapulco de Juárez (Acapulco)	620,656
Aguascalientes	594,092
Saltillo	562,587
Morelia	549,996
Mexicali	549,873
Hermosillo	545,928
Culiacán Rosales (Culiacán)	540,823
Querétaro	536,463
Torreón	502,964
San Nicolás de los Garzas	496,879
Santa María Chimalhuacán (Chimalhuacán)	482,530
Atizapán de Zaragoza	467,544
Tlaquepaque	458,674
Toluca de Lerdo (Toluca)	435,125
Cuautitlán Izcalli	433,830
Victoria de Durango (Durango)	427,135
Tuxtla Gutiérrez	424,579
Veracruz Llave (Veracruz)	411,582
Reynosa	403,718
Benito Juárez (Cancún)	397,191
Matamoros	376,279
Jalapa Enríquez (Xalapa)	373,076
Villahermosa	330,846
Mazatlán	327,989
Cuernavaca	327,162
Valle de Chalco (Xico)	322,784
Irapuato	319,148
Tonalá	315,278
Nuevo Laredo	308,828

Mid-2007 ('000, incl. suburbs, UN estimates): Ciudad de México 19,028; Guadalajara 4,198; Monterrey 3,712; Puebla 2,195; Tijuana 1,553; Toluca de Lerdo 1,531; León de los Aldamas 1,488; Ciudad Juárez 1,343; Torreón 1,144 (Source: UN, *World Urbanization Prospects: The 2007 Revision*).

MEXICO

BIRTHS, MARRIAGES AND DEATHS

	Registered live births Number	Rate (per 1,000)	Registered marriages Number	Rate (per 1,000)	Registered deaths Number	Rate (per 1,000)
2000	2,798,339	24.5	707,422	7.2	437,667	4.9
2001	2,767,610	22.9	665,434	6.7	443,127	4.8
2002	2,699,084	21.7	616,654	6.1	459,687	4.8
2003	2,655,894	20.6	584,142	5.7	472,140	4.8
2004	2,625,056	19.8	600,563	5.8	473,417	4.8
2005	2,567,906	19.3	595,713	5.7	495,240	4.8
2006	2,505,939	19.0	586,978	5.6	494,471	4.8
2007	2,655,083	18.6	595,209	5.6	514,420	4.9

Life expectancy (years at birth, UN estimates): 74.1 (males 71.6; females 76.6) in 2006 (Source: WHO, *World Health Statistics*).

ECONOMICALLY ACTIVE POPULATION
(sample surveys, '000 persons aged 14 years and over, April–June)

	2006	2007	2008
Agriculture, hunting, forestry and fishing	6,033.0	5,772.4	5,758.6
Mining, quarrying and electricity	350.3	406.3	389.4
Manufacturing	7,000.3	7,041.3	7,150.4
Construction	3,452.5	3,585.8	3,641.2
Trade	8,211.6	8,502.3	8,603.7
Hotels and restaurants	2,514.9	2,670.6	2,836.7
Transport and communications	2,222.7	2,133.1	2,184.7
Finance and business services	2,365.9	2,530.4	2,722.1
Social services	3,413.7	3,531.9	3,578.9
Other services	4,288.2	4,371.9	4,492.3
Public sector	2,034.9	2,048.5	2,175.8
Activities not adequately defined	309.7	312.2	333.0
Total employed	42,197.8	42,906.7	43,866.7
Unemployed	1,377.7	1,505.2	1,593.3
Total labour force	43,575.5	44,411.9	45,460.0
Males	27,409.4	27,726.2	n.a.
Females	16,166.1	16,685.6	n.a.

Health and Welfare

KEY INDICATORS

Total fertility rate (children per woman, 2006)	2.3
Under-5 mortality rate (per 1,000 live births, 2006)	35
HIV/AIDS (% of persons aged 15–49, 2007)	0.3
Physicians (per 1,000 head, 2002)	1.5
Hospital beds (per 1,000 head, 2004)	1.0
Health expenditure (2006): US $ per head (PPP)	756
Health expenditure (2006): % of GDP	6.2
Health expenditure (2006): public (% of total)	43.3
Access to water (% of persons, 2006)	95
Access to sanitation (% of persons, 2006)	81
Human Development Index (2006): ranking	51
Human Development Index (2006): value	0.842

For sources and definitions, see explanatory note on p. vi.

Agriculture

PRINCIPAL CROPS
('000 metric tons)

	2005	2006	2007*
Wheat	3,015	3,378	3,000
Rice, paddy	291	337	350
Barley	761	869	895
Maize	19,339	21,893	22,500
Oats	127	152	111
Sorghum	5,524	5,519	5,550
Potatoes	1,635	1,523	1,530
Sugar cane	51,646	50,676	50,680
Beans, dry	827	1,386	1,390
Chick peas	134	163	165
Soybeans (Soya beans)	187	81	82
Groundnuts, with shell	73	68	69
Coconuts	1,167	1,022	1,023
Safflower seed	94	27	27
Cabbages	221	204	205
Lettuce and chicory	275	274	275
Tomatoes	2,246	2,899	2,900
Cauliflower and broccoli	359	305	305
Pumpkins, squash and gourds	511	117	117
Cucumbers and gherkins	475	496	500
Chillies and peppers, green	1,617	1,681	1,690
Onions, dry	1,115	1,151	1,200
Carrots and turnips	376	382	385
Bananas	2,250	2,196	2,200
Oranges	4,113	4,157	4,160
Tangerines, mandarins, clementines and satsumas	403	350	355
Lemons and limes	1,807	1,867	1,880
Grapefruit and pomelos	350	387	390
Apples	584	602	605
Peaches and nectarines	208	222	225
Strawberries	163	155	160
Grapes	323	244	250
Watermelons	865	977	980
Cantaloupes and other melons	580	570	575
Guavas, mangoes and mangosteens	1,679	2,046	2,050
Avocados	1,022	1,134	1,140
Pineapples	552	634	635
Papayas	709	799	800
Coffee, green	294	310*	320
Cocoa beans	36	38	39
Tobacco, unmanufactured	16	19	20

* FAO estimate(s).

Aggregate production ('000 metric tons, may include official, semi-official or estimated data): Total cereals 29,059.9 in 2005, 32,154.7 in 2006, 32,361.8 in 2007; Total fruits (excl. melons) 15,243.3 in 2005, 14,978.7 in 2006, 15,041.3 in 2007; Total vegetables (incl. melons) 10,495.9 in 2005, 11,582.3 in 2006, 11,699.1 in 2007.

Source: FAO.

LIVESTOCK
('000 head, year ending September)

	2005	2006	2007*
Horses*	6,260	6,300	6,350
Asses	6,540*	n.a.	n.a.
Cattle	28,763	28,649	29,000
Pigs	15,342	15,370	15,500
Sheep	7,624	7,484	7,500
Goats	8,887	8,897	8,900
Chickens	287,612*	289,663	290,000
Ducks*	8,100	8,150	8,200
Turkeys	4,451	4,236	4,300

* FAO estimate(s).

Source: FAO.

MEXICO

LIVESTOCK PRODUCTS
('000 metric tons)

	2005	2006	2007*
Cattle meat	1,558	1,613	1,650
Sheep meat	46	48	50
Goat meat	42	43	45
Pig meat	1,103	1,109	1,200
Horse meat*	79	79	80
Chicken meat	2,437	2,464	2,500
Cows' milk	9,868	10,089	9,599
Goats' milk	164	164	165
Hen eggs	2,025	2,290	2,300
Honey	51	56	56

* FAO estimates.
Source: FAO.

Forestry

ROUNDWOOD REMOVALS
('000 cubic metres, excl. bark)

	2005	2006	2007
Sawlogs, veneer logs and logs for sleepers	5,022	4,878	5,210
Pulpwood	975	999	882
Other industrial wood	184	254	214
Fuel wood*	38,448	38,521	38,600
Total	44,629	44,652	44,906

* FAO estimates.
Source: FAO.

SAWNWOOD PRODUCTION
('000 cubic metres, incl. railway sleepers)

	2005	2006	2007
Coniferous (softwood)	2,222	2,324	2,366
Broadleaved (hardwood)	452	326	321
Total	2,674	2,650	2,687

Source: FAO.

Fishing

('000 metric tons, live weight)

	2004	2005	2006
Capture	1,287.2	1,304.8	1,300.0*
Tilapias	68.7	64.6	64.6*
California pilchard (sardine)	475.7	548.4	545.0*
Yellowfin tuna	132.1	143.2	138.7
Marine shrimps and prawns	58.1	—	—
American cupped oyster	45.0	43.7	44.0*
Jumbo flying squid	87.2	49.7	50.0*
Aquaculture	104.4	133.1	158.6*
Whiteleg shrimp	62.4	90.0	112.5
Total catch (incl. others)	1,391.5	1,437.9	1,458.6*

* FAO estimate.

Note: Figures exclude aquatic plants ('000 metric tons, capture only): 27.4 in 2004; 27.0 in 2005 (FAO estimate); 27.0 in 2006 (FAO estimate). Also excluded are aquatic mammals and crocodiles (recorded by number rather than by weight), shells and corals. The number of Morelet's crocodiles caught was: 609 in 2004; 855 in 2005; 102 in 2006. The catch of marine shells (metric tons) was: 183 in 2004; 190 in 2005; 183 in 2006.

Source: FAO.

Mining
(metric tons, unless otherwise indicated)

	2005	2006	2007
Antimony*	565	778	414
Arsenic*	1,664	1,595	513
Barytes	268,657	199,605	185,921
Bismuth*	970	1,186	1,170
Cadmium*	1,627	1,399	1,605
Celestite	110,833	128,321	96,902
Coal	9,940,326	10,882,685	11,886,757
Coke	1,491,847	1,569,561	1,536,325
Copper*	373,252	327,536	335,502
Crude petroleum ('000 barrels per day)	3,333	3,256	3,082
Diatomite	62,132	62,948	82,519
Dolomite	1,308,977	1,282,590	1,123,225
Feldspar	373,411	459,209	438,696
Flourite	875,450	936,433	933,361
Gas (million cu ft per day)	4,818	5,356	6,058
Gold (kg)*	26,762	35,899	39,259
Graphite	12,357	11,773	9,900
Gypsum	5,087,849	5,950,794	5,963,438
Kaolin	32,648	18,852	86,784
Iron*	7,012,306	6,589,586	7,323,121
Lead*	121,669	120,450	89,838
Manganese*	132,872	124,417	152,446
Molybdenum*	4,245	2,519	6,491
Salt	9,057,623	7,987,318	8,032,273
Silica	2,120,878	2,661,770	2,950,438
Silver*	2,565,586	2,413,147	2,351,396
Sulphur	1,016,822	1,073,567	1,026,300
Wollastonite	27,132	44,280	50,809
Zinc*	427,061	432,347	426,509

* Figures for metallic minerals refer to metal content of ores.

Industry

SELECTED PRODUCTS
('000 metric tons, unless otherwise indicated)

	2003	2004	2005
Wheat flour	2,647	2,609	2,646
Maize (corn) flour	1,588	1,592	1,617
Raw sugar	2,852	3,094	3,257
Beer ('000 hectolitres)	65,462	67,575	72,030
Soft drinks ('000 hectolitres)	132,642	138,289	141,451
Cigarettes (million units)	41,856	40,752	41,439
Cotton yarn (pure and mixed)	55	47	44
Tyres ('000 units)*	8,551	10,717	11,650
Cement	33,594	34,992	37,452
Non-electric, cooking or heating appliances—household ('000 units)	4,275	4,287	3,962
Refrigerators—household ('000 units)	2,162	2,291	2,844
Washing machines—household ('000 units)	1,091	1,074	988
Lorries, buses, tractors, etc. ('000 units)	517	530	501
Passenger cars ('000 units)	1,028	993	1,128
Electric energy (million kWh)	217,867	224,077	234,895

* Tyres for road motor vehicles.

Source: UN, *Industrial Commodity Statistics Yearbook*.

MEXICO

Finance

CURRENCY AND EXCHANGE RATES

Monetary Units
100 centavos = 1 Mexican nuevo peso.

Sterling, Dollar and Euro Equivalents (31 December 2008)
£1 sterling = 19.736 nuevos pesos;
US $1 = 13.538 nuevos pesos;
€1 = 18.841 nuevos pesos;
1,000 Mexican nuevos pesos = £50.67 = $73.86 = €53.08.

Average Exchange Rate (nuevos pesos per US $)
2006   10.8992
2007   10.9282
2008   11.1297

Note: Figures are given in terms of the nuevo (new) peso, introduced on 1 January 1993 and equivalent to 1,000 former pesos.

BUDGET*
(million new pesos)

Revenue	2006	2007	2008†
Taxation	890,078	1,002,670	995,106
Income taxes	448,100	527,184	607,610
Value-added tax	380,576	409,013	457,698
Excise tax	−5,242	−6,792	−168,310
Import duties	31,726	32,188	35,783
Other tax revenue	34,917	41,077	62,325
Other revenue	668,730	708,551	1,054,121
Total revenue	1,558,808	1,711,221	2,049,228

Expenditure	2006	2007	2008†
Programmable expenditure	1,198,813	1,392,394	1,607,041
Current expenditure	906,406	1,060,420	1,181,912
Personal services	438,707	468,934	508,911
Transfers, subsidies and aid	400,365	476,219	569,614
Other current expenditure	67,334	115,268	103,387
Capital expenditure	292,407	331,974	425,129
Non-programmable expenditure	540,653	587,266	637,701
Interest and fees	192,435	188,671	200,122
Revenue sharing	329,337	332,758	423,500
Other	18,881	15,837	14,080
Total expenditure	1,739,467	1,929,660	2,244,742

* Figures refer to the consolidated accounts of the central Government, including government agencies and the national social security system. The budgets of state and local governments are excluded.
† Preliminary.

INTERNATIONAL RESERVES*
(US $ million at 31 December)

	2005	2006	2007
IMF special drawing rights	445	482	466
Reserve position in the Fund	594	340	334
Foreign exchange	73,015	75,448	86,309
Total	74,054	76,270	87,109

* Excluding gold reserves.
Source: IMF, *International Financial Statistics*.

MONEY SUPPLY
(million new pesos at 31 December)

	2005	2006	2007
Currency outside banks	335,904	389,259	429,854
Demand deposits at deposit money banks	529,988	599,268	695,346
Total money	865,891	988,527	1,125,200

Source: IMF, *International Financial Statistics*.

COST OF LIVING
(Consumer Price Index; base: 2000 = 100)

	2005	2006	2007
Food, beverages and tobacco	129.4	134.1	142.6
Clothing and footwear	112.1	113.5	115.0
Electricity, gas and other fuel	160.6	173.1	n.a.
Rent	129.1	133.2	n.a.
All items (incl. others)	127.2	131.8	137.0

Source: ILO.

NATIONAL ACCOUNTS
(million new pesos at current prices)

National Income and Product

	2002	2003	2004
Compensation of employees*	2,039,094	2,184,544	2,341,996
Operating surplus*	3,660,762	4,022,863	4,580,602
Taxes on production and imports	583,552	712,221	819,276
Less Subsidies	20,271	27,636	32,778
GDP in purchasers' values	6,263,137	6,891,992	7,709,096
Net factor income received from abroad	−14,829	23,375	74,464
Gross national product (GNP)	6,248,308	6,915,367	7,783,560

* Including consumption of fixed capital.

Expenditure on the Gross Domestic Product

	2005	2006	2007
Government final consumption expenditure	965,931	1,074,923	1,144,781
Private final consumption expenditure	5,704,780	6,191,714	6,723,612
Increase in stocks	208,225	140,611	42,121
Gross fixed capital formation	1,616,445	1,867,356	2,030,503
Total domestic expenditure	8,495,381	9,274,604	9,941,017
Exports of goods and services	2,508,403	2,916,551	3,176,101
Less Imports of goods and services	2,637,578	3,033,590	3,354,255
GDP in purchasers' values	8,366,205	9,157,565	9,762,864
GDP at constant 1993 prices	1,753,595	1,837,926	1,898,398

Gross Domestic Product by Economic Activity

	2005	2006	2007
Agriculture, forestry and fishing	287,344	319,598	350,955
Mining and quarrying	112,312	129,083	143,781
Manufacturing	1,333,950	1,480,974	1,579,198
Electricity, gas and water	101,067	117,190	127,480
Construction	401,478	470,617	500,366
Trade, restaurants and hotels	1,585,987	1,739,110	1,888,211
Transport, storage and communications	788,525	865,075	944,649
Finance, insurance, real estate and business services	982,256	1,063,896	1,151,034
Community, social and personal services	1,994,288	2,136,693	2,274,628
Sub-total	7,587,207	8,322,236	8,960,302
Less Imputed bank service charge	90,419	101,621	113,824
GDP at factor cost	7,496,787	8,220,615	8,846,477
Indirect taxes, *less* subsidies	869,418	936,950	916,387
GDP in purchasers' values	8,366,205	9,157,565	9,762,864

MEXICO

BALANCE OF PAYMENTS
(US $ million)

	2005	2006	2007
Exports of goods f.o.b.	214,233	249,925	271,875
Imports of goods f.o.b.	−221,820	−256,059	−281,949
Trade balance	−7,587	−6,133	−10,074
Exports of services	16,137	16,392	17,736
Imports of services	−21,440	−22,833	−23,826
Balance on goods and services	−12,890	−12,574	−16,164
Other income received	5,359	6,406	7,876
Other income paid	−18,409	−20,186	−21,560
Balance on goods, services and income	−25,939	−26,353	−29,847
Current transfers received	20,774	24,197	24,409
Current transfers paid	−57	−88	−101
Current balance	−5,222	−2,244	−5,539
Direct investment abroad	−6,474	−5,759	−8,256
Direct investment from abroad	20,945	19,291	24,686
Portfolio investment liabilities	8,366	1,296	14,773
Other investment assets	−7,719	−12,156	−21,776
Other investment liabilities	−1,124	−4,652	8,880
Net errors and omissions	−1,808	2,921	−2,518
Overall balance	6,965	−1,303	10,250

Source: IMF, *International Financial Statistics*.

External Trade

PRINCIPAL COMMODITIES
(distribution by Harmonized System, US $ million)

Imports f.o.b.*	2006	2007	2008†
Live animals and products thereof	4,193.9	5,159.1	5,486.8
Vegetable products	6,155.5	7,580.6	10,079.0
Animal and vegetable oils and fats	755.2	1,064.5	1,518.3
Prepared food, beverages, spirits and tobacco	4,479.6	5,147.7	5,600.5
Mineral products	16,217.5	20,990.8	31,085.2
Chemicals and related industries	18,617.9	20,873.7	23,904.1
Plastics, rubber and articles thereof	19,547.1	20,136.2	20,240.6
Raw hides, skins, leather and furs	1,481.7	1,308.9	1,268.5
Wood, charcoal, cork, straw, etc.	1,436.1	1,517.2	1,509.1
Paper-making material; paper and paperboard and articles thereof	6,134.9	6,485.7	6,701.5
Textiles and textile articles	9,062.3	8,677.9	8,512.8
Footwear, headgear, umbrellas, etc.	586.9	643.3	729.4
Articles of stone, plaster, cement, asbestos, etc.; glass and glassware	2,219.6	2,425.6	2,153.6
Pearls, precious stones and metals and articles thereof; imitation jewellery and coins	1,032.4	1,226.6	1,127.7
Base metals and articles thereof	23,752.5	24,714.0	26,895.1
Machinery and mechanical appliances; electrical equipment, parts and accessories	96,375.4	102,372.1	110,258.2
Vehicles, aircraft, vessels and associated transport equipment	26,026.0	28,569.8	27,844.5
Optical, photographic, measuring, precision and medical apparatus; clocks and watches; musical instruments	10,258.5	13,060.1	12,786.9
Arms and ammunitions, parts and accessories	41.0	47.0	52.7
Miscellaneous manufactured articles	4,488.4	6,022.5	6,215.9
Works of art, collectors' pieces, antiques	13.0	19.7	13.8
Total (incl. others)	256,058.4	281,949.0	308,644.7

*Figures include data for the *maquila* sector (US $ million): 86,527.3 in 2006; n.a. in 2007; n.a. in 2008.
† Preliminary.

Exports f.o.b.*	2006	2007	2008†
Live animals and products thereof	1,729.6	1,751.8	1,733.2
Vegetable products	5,851.0	6,557.0	7,745.4
Animal and vegetable oils and fats	91.5	115.8	184.8
Prepared food, beverages, spirits and tobacco	5,982.7	6,303.2	7,101.0
Mineral products	40,042.4	44,419.1	52,194.9
Chemicals and related industries	6,894.3	7,819.7	8,752.1
Plastics, rubber and articles thereof	6,173.5	6,716.0	6,839.2
Raw hides, skins, leather and furs	549.1	565.9	514.4
Wood, charcoal, cork, straw, etc.	491.8	434.6	394.5
Paper-making material; paper and paperboard and articles thereof	1,862.8	1,920.8	1,944.8
Textiles and textile articles	8,451.1	7,318.2	7,862.7
Footwear, headgear, umbrellas, etc.	380.4	394.6	386.3
Articles of stone, plaster, cement, asbestos, etc.; glass and glassware	2,850.8	2,848.9	2,896.0
Pearls, precious stones and metals and articles thereof; imitation jewellery and coins	3,064.1	3,824.9	5,262.7
Base metals and articles thereof	13,267.1	15,073.5	16,163.0
Machinery and mechanical appliances; electrical equipment, parts and accessories	94,340.6	104,177.6	108,888.8
Vehicles, aircraft, vessels and associated transport equipment	40,889.0	43,933.2	45,022.9
Optical, photographic, measuring, precision and medical apparatus; clocks and watches; musical instruments	8,922.9	8,936.5	9,513.4
Arms and ammunitions, parts and accessories	17.5	17.6	20.8
Miscellaneous manufactured articles	7,393.1	8,060.7	8,078.4
Works of art, collectors' pieces, antiques	10.9	8.2	8.1
Total (incl. others)	249,925.1	271,875.3	291,807.0

*Figures include data for the *maquila* sector (US $ million): 111,823.8 in 2006; n.a. in 2007; n.a. in 2008.
† Preliminary.

PRINCIPAL TRADING PARTNERS*
(US $ million)

Imports c.i.f.	2006	2007	2008†
Argentina	1,798.5	1,609.7	1,436.4
Brazil	5,557.8	5,575.3	5,185.8
Canada	7,376.2	7,957.4	9,442.9
Chile	2,469.8	2,594.0	2,592.5
China, People's Republic	24,438.3	29,743.7	34,690.8
France	2,661.5	3,097.8	3,511.0
Germany	9,437.0	10,687.7	12,606.7
Italy	4,108.5	5,542.4	5,219.5
Japan	15,295.2	16,343.0	16,283.0
Korea, Republic	10,621.4	12,613.7	13,527.4
Malaysia	4,474.4	4,771.2	4,659.3
Philippines	1,232.3	1,198.3	1,238.4
Singapore	1,955.2	2,086.8	1,697.7
Spain	3,638.2	3,830.5	4,056.0
Switzerland	1,121.9	1,246.1	1,412.9
Taiwan	4,973.7	5,897.1	6,658.6
Thailand	1,783.9	2,105.8	2,207.9
United Kingdom	2,140.3	2,294.3	2,596.0
USA	130,854.2	139,472.8	151,351.9
Total (incl. others)	256,130.4	281,949.0	308,644.7

Exports f.o.b.	2006	2007	2008†
Aruba	1,469.4	1,517.8	1,494.6
Canada	5,176.2	6,491.0	7,113.4
China, People's Republic	1,688.1	1,895.3	2,045.4
Colombia	2,132.1	2,943.4	3,032.5
Germany	2,972.6	4,103.6	5,011.1
Japan	1,594.0	1,912.6	2,063.0
Spain	3,270.1	3,689.8	4,315.7
United Kingdom	924.9	1,562.7	1,751.4
USA	211,799.4	223,133.3	233,825.6
Venezuela	1,783.2	2,332.6	2,312.4
Total (incl. others)	249,925.2	271,875.3	291,807.0

*Imports by country of origin; exports by country of destination.
† Preliminary.

MEXICO

Transport

RAILWAYS
(traffic)

	2004	2005	2006
Passengers carried ('000)	253	253	260
Passenger-kilometres (million)	74	n.a.	n.a.
Freight carried ('000 tons)	88,097	89,814	94,751
Freight ton-kilometres (million)	69,926	72,185	73,726

Source: Dirección General de Planeación, Secretaría de Comunicaciones y Transportes.

ROAD TRAFFIC
('000 vehicles in use at 31 December, estimates)

	2003	2004	2005
Passenger cars	14,007	13,388	14,075
Lorries and vans	6,492	6,708	7,111
Buses	299	265	265
Motorcycles	442	518	n.a.

Source: IRF, *World Road Statistics*.

SHIPPING
Merchant Fleet
(registered at 31 December)

	2005	2006	2007
Number of vessels	718	753	780
Total displacement ('000 grt)	1,099.8	1,161.9	1,217.0

Source: Lloyd's Register-Fairplay, *World Fleet Statistics*.

Sea-borne Shipping
(domestic and international freight traffic, '000 metric tons)

	2002	2003	2004
Goods loaded	160,894	175,923	177,915
Goods unloaded	87,203	88,816	88,093

Source: Coordinación General de Puertos y Marina Mercante.

CIVIL AVIATION
(traffic on scheduled services)

	2002	2003	2004
Passengers carried ('000)	33,190	35,287	39,422
Freight carried ('000 tons)	389.0	410.0	466.7

Sources: Dirección General de Planeación, Secretaría de Comunicaciones y Transportes.

Tourism

VISITOR ARRIVALS BY COUNTRY OF ORIGIN

	2005	2006
Argentina	78,096	84,583
Brazil	78,026	31,890
Canada	675,216	785,428
Chile	35,543	41,230
Colombia	33,863	35,954
France	160,119	173,183
Germany	129,871	135,031
Guatemala	36,088	31,444
Italy	149,176	163,284
Japan	65,376	68,984
Korea, Republic	26,219	30,742
Netherlands	61,813	70,200
Spain	203,716	261,456
United Kingdom	231,421	260,121
USA	17,905,684	17,510,123
Venezuela	32,219	38,022
Total (incl. others)	21,914,917	21,352,605

Tourism receipts (US $ million, incl. passenger transport): 11,609 in 2005; 12,801 in 2006.

Source: World Tourism Organization.

Communications Media

	2005	2006	2007
Telephones ('000 main lines in use)	19,512.0	19,861.3	19,754.4
Mobile cellular telephones ('000 subscribers)	47,141.0	57,016.4	68,253.6
Personal computers ('000 in use)	14,000	n.a.	n.a.
Internet users ('000)	17,966.0	20,564.3	22,812.5
Broadband subscribers ('000)	1,922.4	3,087.1	4,548.8

Radio receivers ('000 in use): 31,000 in 1997.

Television receivers ('000 in use): 28,000 in 2000.

Facsimile machines ('000 in use): 285 in 1997.

Daily newspapers (2000): Number 311; Average circulation 9,251,000.

Non-daily newspapers (2000): Number 26; Average circulation 614,000.

Books published (titles): 15,542 in 2002.

Sources: partly International Telecommunication Union; UNESCO Institute for Statistics; UNESCO, *Statistical Yearbook*; UN, *Statistical Yearbook*.

Education

(2006/07, unless otherwise indicated)

	Institutions*	Teachers*	Students ('000)†
Pre-primary	91,954	218,497	4,452.2
Primary	97,775	562,777	14,548.2
Secondary (incl. technical)	33,415	360,871	5,979.3
Intermediate: professional/technical	1,501	29,498	357.2
Intermediate: Baccalaureate	12,020	236,506	3,301.6
Higher (incl. post-graduate)	5,466	284,147	2,446.7

* Estimates.
† 2005/06.

Adult literacy rate (UNESCO estimates): 92.4% (males 94.4%; females 90.6%) in 2007 (Source: UNESCO Institute for Statistics).

Directory

The Constitution

The present Mexican Constitution was proclaimed on 5 February 1917, at the end of the Revolution, which began in 1910, against the regime of Porfirio Díaz. Its provisions regarding religion, education, and the ownership and exploitation of mineral wealth reflect the long revolutionary struggle against the concentration of power in the hands of the Roman Catholic Church and the large landowners, and the struggle that culminated, in the 1930s, in the expropriation of the properties of the foreign petroleum companies. It has been amended from time to time.

GOVERNMENT

The President and Congress

The President of the Republic, in agreement with the Cabinet and with the approval of the Congreso de la Unión (Congress) or of the Permanent Committee when the Congreso is not in session, may suspend constitutional guarantees in case of foreign invasion, serious disturbance, or any other emergency endangering the people.

The exercise of supreme executive authority is vested in the President, who is elected for six years and enters office on 1 December of the year of election. The presidential powers include the right to appoint and remove members of the Cabinet and the Attorney-General and to appoint, with the approval of the Senado (Senate), diplomatic officials, the higher officers of the army, and ministers of the supreme and higher courts of justice. The President is also empowered to dispose of the Armed Forces for the internal and external security of the federation.

The Congreso is composed of the Cámara Federal de Diputados (Federal Chamber of Deputies), elected every three years, and the Senado, whose members hold office for six years. There is one deputy for every 250,000 people and for every fraction of over 125,000 people. The Senado is composed of two members for each state and two for the Distrito Federal (Federal District). Regular sessions of the Congreso begin on 1 September and may not continue beyond 31 December of the same year. Extraordinary sessions may be convened by the Permanent Committee.

The powers of the Congreso include the right to: pass laws and regulations; impose taxes; specify the criteria on which the Executive may negotiate loans; declare war; raise, maintain and regulate the organization of the Armed Forces; establish and maintain schools of various types throughout the country; approve or reject the budget; sanction appointments submitted by the President of the Supreme Court and magistrates of the superior court of the Distrito Federal; approve or reject treaties and conventions made with foreign powers; and ratify diplomatic appointments.

The Permanent Committee, consisting of 29 members of the Congreso (15 of whom are deputies and 14 senators), officiates when the Congreso is in recess, and is responsible for the convening of extraordinary sessions of the Congreso.

The States

Governors are elected by popular vote in a general election every six years. The local legislature is formed by deputies, who are changed every three years. The judicature is specially appointed under the Constitution by the competent authority (it is never subject to the popular vote).

Each state is a separate unit, with the right to levy taxes and to legislate in certain matters. The states are not allowed to levy inter-state customs duties.

The Federal District

The Distrito Federal (DF) consists of Mexico City and several neighbouring small towns and villages. The first direct elections for the Head of Government of the Distrito Federal were held in July 1997; hitherto, a Regent had been appointed by the President.

EDUCATION

According to the Constitution, the provision of educational facilities is the joint responsibility of the federation, the states and the municipalities. Education shall be democratic, and shall be directed to developing all the faculties of the individual students, while imbuing them with love of their country and a consciousness of international solidarity and justice. Religious bodies may not provide education, except training for the priesthood. Private educational institutions must conform to the requirements of the Constitution with regard to the nature of the teaching given. The education provided by the states shall be free of charge.

RELIGION

Religious bodies of whatever denomination shall not have the capacity to possess or administer real estate or capital invested therein. Churches are the property of the nation; the headquarters of bishops, seminaries, convents and other property used for the propagation of a religious creed shall pass into the hands of the state, to be dedicated to the public service of the federation or of the respective state. Institutions of charity, provided they are not connected with a religious body, may hold real property. The establishment of monastic orders is prohibited. Ministers of religion must be Mexican; they may not criticize the fundamental laws of the country in a public or private meeting; they may not vote or form associations for political purposes. Political meetings may not be held in places of worship.

A reform proposal, whereby constitutional restrictions on the Catholic Church were formally ended, received congressional approval in December 1991 and was promulgated as law in January 1992.

LAND AND MINERAL OWNERSHIP

Article 27 of the Constitution vests direct ownership of minerals and other products of the subsoil, including petroleum and water, in the nation, and reserves to the Federal Government alone the right to grant concessions in accordance with the laws to individuals and companies, on the condition that they establish regular work for the exploitation of the materials. At the same time, the right to acquire ownership of lands and waters belonging to the nation, or concessions for their exploitation, is limited to Mexican individuals and companies, although the State may concede similar rights to foreigners who agree not to invoke the protection of their governments to enforce such rights.

The same article declares null all alienations of lands, waters and forests belonging to towns or communities made by political chiefs or other local authorities in violation of the provisions of the law of 25 June 1856*, and all concessions or sales of communally held lands, waters and forests made by the federal authorities after 1 December 1876. The population settlements that lack *ejidos* (state-owned smallholdings), or cannot obtain restitution of lands previously held, shall be granted lands in proportion to the needs of the population. The area of land granted to the individual may not be less than 10 hectares of irrigated or watered land, or the equivalent in other kinds of land.

The owners affected by decisions to divide and redistribute land (with the exception of the owners of farming or cattle-rearing properties) shall not have any right of redress, nor may they invoke the right of *amparo*† in protection of their interests. They may, however, apply to the Government for indemnification. Small properties, the areas of which are defined in the Constitution, will not be subject to expropriation. The Constitution leaves to the Congreso the duty of determining the maximum size of rural properties.

In March 1992 an agrarian reform amendment, whereby the programme of land distribution established by the 1917 Constitution was abolished and the terms of the *ejido* system of tenant farmers were relaxed, was formally adopted.

Monopolies and measures to restrict competition in industry, commerce or public services are prohibited.

A section of the Constitution deals with work and social security.

POLITICAL ORGANIZATIONS AND ELECTORAL PROCEDURE

In December 1977 a Federal Law on Political Organizations and Electoral Procedure was promulgated. It includes the following provisions:

Legislative power is vested in the Congreso de la Unión, which comprises the Cámara Federal de Diputados and the Senado. The Cámara shall comprise 300 deputies elected by majority vote within single-member electoral districts and up to 100 deputies (increased to 200 from July 1988) elected by a system of proportional representation from regional lists within multi-member constituencies. The Senado comprises two members for each state and two for the Distrito Federal, elected by majority vote.

Executive power is exercised by the President of the Republic of the United Mexican States, elected by majority vote.

Ordinary elections will be held every three years for the federal deputies and every six years for the senators and the President of the Republic on the first Sunday of July of the year in question. When a vacancy occurs among members of the Congreso elected by majority vote, the house in question shall call extraordinary elections, and when a vacancy occurs among members of the Cámara elected by proportional representation it shall be filled by the candidate of the same party who received the next highest number of votes at the last ordinary election.

MEXICO

Voting is the right and duty of every citizen, male or female, over the age of 18 years.

A political party shall be registered if it has at least 3,000 members in each one of at least half the states in Mexico or at least 300 members in each one of at least half of the single-member constituencies. In either case, the total number of members must be no fewer than 65,000. A party can also obtain conditional registration if it has been active for at least four years. Registration is confirmed if the party obtains at least 1.5% of the popular vote. All political parties shall have free access to the media.

In September 1993 an amendment to the Law on Electoral Procedure provided for the expansion of the Senado to 128 seats, representing four members for each state and the Distrito Federal, three to be elected by majority vote, and one by proportional representation.

* The Lerdo Law against ecclesiastical privilege, which became the basis of the Liberal Constitution of 1857.
† The Constitution provides for the procedure known as *juicio de amparo*, a wider form of habeas corpus, which the individual may invoke in protection of his constitutional rights.

The Government

HEAD OF STATE

President: Felipe Calderón Hinojosa (took office 1 December 2006).

CABINET
(April 2009)

Secretary of the Interior: Fernando Francisco Gómez-Mont Urueta.
Secretary of Foreign Affairs: Patricia Espinosa Cantellano.
Secretary of Finance and Public Credit: Agustín Carstens Carstens.
Secretary of National Defence: Gen. Guillermo Galván Galván.
Secretary of the Navy: Adm. Mariano Francisco Saynez Mendoza.
Secretary of the Economy: Gerardo Ruiz Mateos.
Secretary of Social Development: Ernesto Cordero Arroyo.
Secretary of Public Security: Genaro García Luna.
Secretary of Public Function: Salvador Vega Casillas.
Secretary of Communications and Transport: Juan Molinar Horcasitas.
Secretary of Labour and Social Welfare: Javier Lozano Alarcón.
Secretary of the Environment and Natural Resources: Juan Rafael Elvira Quesada.
Secretary of Energy: Georgina Kessel Martínez.
Secretary of Agriculture, Livestock, Rural Development, Fisheries and Food: Alberto Cárdenas Jiménez.
Secretary of Public Education: Alonso Lujambio Irazábal.
Secretary of Health: José Angel Córdova Villalobos.
Secretary of Tourism: Rodolfo Elizondo Torres.
Secretary of Agrarian Reform: Abelardo Escobar Prieto.
Procurator-General: Eduardo Medina-Mora Icaza.

SECRETARIATS OF STATE

Office of the President: Los Pinos, Col. San Miguel Chapultepec, 11850 México, DF; tel. (55) 5091-1100; fax (55) 5277-2376; e-mail felipe.calderon@presidencia.gob.mx; internet www.presidencia.gob.mx.
Secretariat of State for Agrarian Reform: Edif. de Avda Heroica, 1°, Escuela Naval Militar 701, Col. Presidentes Ejidales, Del. Coyoacán, 04470 México, DF; tel. (55) 5695-6776; fax (55) 5695-6368; e-mail sra@sra.gob.mx; internet www.sra.gob.mx.
Secretariat of State for Agriculture, Livestock, Rural Development, Fisheries and Food: Avda Municipio Libre 377, Col. Santa Cruz Atoyac, Del. Benito Juárez, 03310 México, DF; tel. (55) 9183-1000; fax (55) 9183-1018; e-mail ofsec@sagarpa.gob.mx; internet www.sagarpa.gob.mx.
Secretariat of State for Communications and Transport: Avda Xola y Universidad, Col. Narvarte, Del. Benito Juárez, 03020 México, DF; tel. (55) 5723-9300; fax (55) 5530-0093; e-mail buzon_ucg@sct.gob.mx; internet www.sct.gob.mx.
Secretariat of State for the Economy: Alfonso Reyes 30, Col. Hipódromo Condesa, 06170 México, DF; tel. (55) 5729-9100; fax (55) 5729-9320; internet www.economia.gob.mx.

Secretariat of State for Energy: Insurgentes Sur 890, 17°, Col. del Valle, 03100 México, DF; tel. (55) 5000-6000; fax (55) 5000-6222; e-mail acastellanos@energia.gob.mx; internet www.energia.gob.mx.
Secretariat of State for the Environment and Natural Resources: Blvd Adolfo Ruíz Cortines 4209, Col. Jardines en la Montaña, Tlalpan, 14210 México, DF; tel. (55) 5628-0602; fax (55) 5628-0643; e-mail contactodgeia@semarnat.gob.mx; internet www.semarnat.gob.mx.
Secretariat of State for Finance and Public Credit: Palacio Nacional, Primer Patio Mariano, 3°, Of. 3045, Col. Centro, Del. Cuauhtémoc, 06000 México, DF; tel. (55) 9158-2000; fax (55) 9158-1142; e-mail secretario@hacienda.gob.mx; internet www.hacienda.gob.mx.
Secretariat of State for Foreign Affairs: Avda Ricardo Flores Magón 2, Col. Guerrero, Del. Cuauhtémoc, 06995 México, DF; tel. (55) 5063-3000; fax (55) 5063-3195; e-mail comentario@sre.gob.mx; internet www.sre.gob.mx.
Secretariat of State for Health: Lieja 7, 1°, Col. Juárez, Del. Cuauhtémoc, 06600 México, DF; tel. (55) 5286-2383; fax (55) 5553-7917; e-mail afrias@salud.gob.mx; internet www.salud.gob.mx.
Secretariat of State for the Interior: Bucareli 99, Col. Juárez, 06069 México, DF; tel. (55) 5592-1141; fax (55) 5546-5350; internet www.gobernacion.gob.mx.
Secretariat of State for Labour and Social Welfare: Edif. A, 4°, Anillo Periférico Sur 4271, Col. Fuentes del Pedregal, 14149 México, DF; tel. (55) 5645-3965; fax (55) 5645-5594; e-mail correo@stps.gob.mx; internet www.stps.gob.mx.
Secretariat of State for National Defence: Blvd Manuel Avila Camacho, esq. Avda Industria Militar, 3°, Col. Lomas de Sotelo, Del. Miguel Hidalgo, 11640 México, DF; tel. (55) 5557-5571; fax (55) 5395-2935; e-mail ggalvang@mail.sedena.gob.mx; internet www.sedena.gob.mx.
Secretariat of State for the Navy: Eje 2 oriente, Tramo Heroica, Escuela Naval Militar 861, Col. Los Cipreses, Del. Coyoacán, 04830 México, DF; tel. (55) 5624-6500; e-mail srio@semar.gob.mx; internet www.semar.gob.mx.
Secretariat of State for Public Education: Dinamarca 84, 5°, Col. Juárez, 06600 México, DF; tel. (55) 5510-2557; fax (55) 5329-6873; e-mail educa@sep.gob.mx; internet www.sep.gob.mx.
Secretariat of State for Public Function: Insurgentes Sur 1735, 10°, Col. Guadalupe Inn, Del. Alvaro Obregón, 01020 México, DF; tel. (55) 1454-3000; e-mail sactel@funcionpublica.gob.mx; internet www.funcionpublica.gob.mx.
Secretariat of State for Public Security: Londres 102, 7°, Col. Juaréz, 06600 México, DF; e-mail enlace@ssp.gob.mx; internet www.ssp.gob.mx.
Secretariat of State for Social Development: Avda Reforma 116, Col. Juárez, Del. Cuauhtémoc, 06600 México, DF; tel. (55) 5328-5000; e-mail secretariadelramo@sedesol.gob.mx; internet www.sedesol.gob.mx.
Secretariat of State for Tourism: Presidente Masaryk 172, Col. Chapultepec Morales, 11587 México, DF; tel. (55) 3002-6300; fax (55) 1036-0789; internet www.sectur.gob.mx.
Office of the Procurator-General: Avda Paseo de la Reforma 211–213, Col. Cuauhtémoc, Del. Cuauhtémoc, 06500 México, DF; tel. (55) 5346-0114; fax (55) 5346-0908; e-mail ofproc@pgr.gob.mx; internet www.pgr.gob.mx.

State Governors
(April 2009)

Aguascalientes: Luis Armando Reynoso (PAN).
Baja California: José Guadalupe Osuna Millán (PAN).
Baja California Sur: Narciso Agúndez (PRD).
Campeche: Jorge Carlos Hurtado Valdez (PRI).
Chiapas: Juan José Sabines Guerrero (PRD).
Chihuahua: José Reyes Baeza (PRI).
Coahuila (de Zaragoza): Humberto Moreira Valdes (PRI).
Colima: Jesús Silverio Cavazos Ceballos (PRI-PT-PVEM).
Durango: Ismael Hernández Deras (PRI).
Guanajuato: Juan Manuel Oliva Ramírez (PAN).
Guerrero: Carlos Zeferino Torreblanca Galindo (PRD).
Hidalgo: Miguel Angel Osorio Chong (PRI).
Jalisco: Emilio González Márquez (PAN).
México: Enrique Peña Nieto (PRI).
Michoacán (de Ocampo): Leonel Godoy Rangel (PRD).
Morelos: Marco Antonio Adame Castillo (PAN).

MEXICO

Nayarit: NEY GONZÁLEZ SÁNCHEZ (PRI).

Nuevo León: JOSÉ NATIVIDAD GONZÁLEZ PARÁS (PRI-PVEM-PLM-Fuerza Ciudadana).

Oaxaca: ULISES RUÍZ (PRI).

Puebla: MARIO MARÍN TORRES (PRI).

Querétaro (de Arteaga): FRANCISCO GARRIDO PATRÓN (PAN).

Quintana Roo: FÉLIX GONZÁLEZ CANTO (PRI).

San Luis Potosí: MARCELO DE LOS SANTOS FRAGA (PAN).

Sinaloa: JESÚS AGUILAR PADILLA (PRI).

Sonora: JOSÉ EDUARDO ROBINSON BOURS CASTELO (PRI-PVEM).

Tabasco: ANDRÉS RAFAEL GRANIER MELO (PRI).

Tamaulipas: EUGENIO HERNÁNDEZ FLORES (PRI).

Tlaxcala: HECTOR ISRAEL ORTIZ ORTIZ (PAN).

Veracruz-Llave: FIDEL HERRERA (PRI).

Yucatán: IVONNE ORTEGA PACHECO (PRI).

Zacatecas: AMALIA GARCÍA MEDINA (PRD).

Head of Government of the Distrito Federal: MARCELO LUIS EBRARD CASAUBON (PRD).

President and Legislature

PRESIDENT

Election, 2 July 2006

Candidate	Number of votes	% of votes
Felipe Calderón Hinojosa (PAN)	14,916,927	35.89
Andrés Manuel López Obrador (Por el Bien de Todos*)	14,683,096	35.33
Roberto Madrazo Pintado (Alianza por México†)	9,237,000	22.23
Patricia Mercado Castro (PASC‡)	1,124,280	2.71
Roberto Campa Cifrián (Nueva Alianza)	397,550	0.96
Total§	41,557,430	100.00

* An alliance of the PRD, the PT and Convergencia.
† An alliance of the PRI and the PVEM.
‡ The Partido Alternativa Socialdemócrata y Campesina, subsequently renamed the Partido Socialdemócrata.
§ Including 900,373 invalid votes and 298,204 votes for unregistered candidates.

CONGRESO DE LA UNIÓN

Senado

Senate: Xicoténcatl 9, Centro Histórico, 06010 México, DF; tel. (55) 5130-2200; internet www.senado.gob.mx.

President: SANTIAGO CREEL MIRANDA (PAN).

Elections, 2 July 2006

Party	Seats
Partido Acción Nacional (PAN)	52
Partido Revolucionario Institucional (PRI)*	33
Partido de la Revolución Democrática (PRD)†	29
Partido Verde Ecologista de México (PVEM)*	6
Convergencia†	5
Partido del Trabajo (PT)†	2
Nueva Alianza	1
Total	128

* Part of the Alianza por México.
† Part of the Por el Bien de Todos alliance.

Cámara Federal de Diputados

Federal Chamber of Deputies: Avda Congreso de la Unión 66, Col. El Parque, Del. Venustiano Carranza, 15969 México, DF; tel. (55) 5628-1300; internet www.diputados.gob.mx.

President: RUTH ZAVALETA SALGADO (PRD).

Elections, 2 July 2006

Party	Seats
Partido Acción Nacional (PAN)	206
Partido de la Revolución Democrática (PRD)*	126
Partido Revolucionario Institucional (PRI)†	104
Partido Verde Ecologista de México (PVEM)†	19
Convergencia*	16
Partido del Trabajo (PT)*	16
Nueva Alianza	9
Partido Alternativa Socialdemócrata y Campesina (PASC)‡	4
Total	500

* Part of the Por el Bien de Todos alliance.
† Part of the Alianza por México.
‡ Subsequently renamed the Partido Socialdemócrata.

Election Commission

Instituto Federal Electoral (IFE): Viaducto Tlalpan 100, Col. Arenal Tepepan, Del. Tlalpan, 14610 México, DF; e-mail info@ife.org.mx; internet www.ife.org.mx; f. 1990; independent; Pres. LEONARDO VALDÉS ZURITA.

Political Organizations

To retain legal political registration, parties must secure at least 1.5% of total votes at two consecutive federal elections. In 2006 eight national political parties were registered.

Convergencia: Louisiana 113, Col. Nápoles, Del. Benito Juárez, 03810 México, DF; tel. (55) 1167-6767; e-mail convergencia@prodigy.net.mx; internet www.convergencia.org.mx; f. 1995 as Convergencia por la Democracia; part of the Por el Bien de Todos alliance formed to contest 2006 presidential election, later renamed the Frente Amplio Progresista; Pres. LUIS VENEGAS MALDONADO; Sec.-Gen. PEDRO JIMÉNEZ LEÓN.

Partido Acción Nacional (PAN): Avda Coyoacán 1546, Col. del Valle, Del. Benito Juárez, 03100 México, DF; tel. (55) 5200-4000; e-mail correo@cen.pan.org.mx; internet www.pan.org.mx; f. 1939; democratic party; 150,000 mems; Pres. GERMÁN MARTÍNEZ CÁZARES; Sec.-Gen. ROGELIO CARBAJAL TRJADA.

Partido Popular Socialista de México (PPS): Avda Alvaro Obregón 185, Col. Roma, Del. Cuauhtémoc, 06797 México, DF; tel. (55) 5672-2057; fax (55) 5609-1896; e-mail ppsm@ppsm.org.mx; internet www.ppsm.org.mx; f. 1948; Marxist-Leninist; First Sec. CUAUHTÉMOC AMEZCUA DROMUNDO.

Partido de la Revolución Democrática (PRD): Avda Benjamín Franklin 84, Col. Escandón, 11800 México, DF; tel. (55) 1085-8000; fax (55) 1085-8144; e-mail comunicacion@prd.org.mx; internet www.prd.org.mx; f. 1989; centre-left; leading mem. of the Por el Bien de Todos alliance formed to contest 2006 presidential election, later renamed the Frente Amplio Progresista; factions include Izquierda Unida (radical faction supporting Andrés Manuel López Obrador's claim to the presidency) and Nueva Izquierda (moderate); Pres. JESÚS ORTEGA MARTÍNEZ; Sec.-Gen. HORTENSIA ARAGÓN CASTILLO.

Partido Revolucionario Institucional (PRI): Edif. 2, Insurgentes Norte 59, Col. Buenavista, Del. Cuauhtémoc, 06359 México, DF; tel. (55) 5729-9600; internet www.pri.org.mx; f. 1929 as the Partido Nacional Revolucionario; regarded as the natural successor to the victorious parties of the revolutionary period; broadly based and centrist; formed Alianza por México alliance with PVEM to contest 2006 presidential election; Pres. BEATRIZ ELENA PAREDES RANGEL; Sec.-Gen. JESÚS MURILLO KARAM; groups within the PRI include: the Corriente Crítica Progresista, the Corriente Crítica del Partido, the Corriente Constitucionalista Democratizadora, Corriente Nuevo PRI XIV Asamblea, Democracia 2000, México Nuevo and Galileo.

Partido Socialdemócrata (PSD): Avda Insurgentes Sur 1942, Col. Florida, Del. Alvaro Obregón, 01030 México, DF; tel. (55) 9150-5191; fax (55) 9150-5190; e-mail info@alternativa.org.mx; internet www.alternativa.org.mx; f. 2005 as Partido Alternativa Socialdemócrata y Campesina; adopted current name 2008; progressive and peasants' rights; Pres. JORGE CARLOS DÍAZ CUEVOS.

Partido del Trabajo (PT): Avda Cuauhtémoc 47, Col. Roma Norte, 06700 México, DF; tel. and fax (55) 5525-6287; internet www.partidodeltrabajo.org.mx; f. 1990; labour party; part of the Por el Bien de Todos alliance formed to contest 2006 presidential election, later renamed the Frente Amplio Progresista; Leader ALBERTO ANAYA GUTIÉRREZ.

MEXICO

Partido Verde Ecologista de México (PVEM): Loma Bonita 18, Col. Lomas Altas, 11950 México, DF; tel. and fax (55) 5257-0188; internet www.pvem.org.mx; f. 1987; ecologist party; formed Alianza por México alliance with PRI to contest 2006 presidential election; Pres. Jorge Emilio González Martínez; Sec.-Gen. Natalia Escudero Barrera.

The following parties are not officially registered but continue to be politically active:

Fuerza Ciudadana: Rochester 94, Col. Nápoles, 03810 México, DF; tel. (55) 5534-4628; e-mail info@fuerzaciudadana.org.mx; internet www.fuerzaciudadana.org.mx; f. 2002; citizens' asscn; Pres. Jorge Alcocer Villanueva; Dir-Gen. Karyna García Castillo Urdiales.

Nueva Alianza: Durango 199, Col. Roma, Del. Cuauhtémoc, 06700 México, DF; tel. (55) 3685-8485; e-mail oscar.desfassiaux@vinculacionnuevaalianza.org.mx; internet www.nueva-alianza.org.mx; f. 2005 by dissident faction of the PRI; includes mems of the Sindicato Nacional de Trabajadores de la Educación (SNTE, see Trade Unions) and supporters of Elba Esther Gordillo Morales; Pres. Jorge Kahwagi Macari; Sec.-Gen. Fermín Trujillo Fuentes.

Partido Democrático Popular Revolucionario: f. 1996; political grouping representing the causes of 14 armed peasant orgs, including the EPR and the PROCUP.

Partido Revolucionario Obrerista y Clandestino de Unión Popular (PROCUP): peasant org.

Illegal organizations active in Mexico include the following:

Ejército Popular Revolucionario (EPR): e-mail pdprepr@hotmail.com; f. 1994; left-wing guerrilla group active mainly in southern states, linked to the Partido Democrático Popular Revolucionario (q.v.).

Ejército Revolucionario Popular Insurgente (ERPI): f. 1996; left-wing guerrilla group active in Guerrero, Morelos and Oaxaca; Leader Jacobo Silva Nogales.

Ejército Zapatista de Liberación Nacional (EZLN): e-mail laotra@ezln.org.mx; internet www.ezln.org.mx; f. 1993; left-wing guerrilla group active in the Chiapas region; Leader 'Subcomandante Marcos'.

Frente Democrático Oriental de México Emiliano Zapata (FDOMEZ): peasant org.

Other armed groups include the Tendencia Democrática Revolucionaria-Ejército del Pueblo and the Comando Popular Revolucionario—La Patria es Primero.

Diplomatic Representation

EMBASSIES IN MEXICO

Algeria: Sierra Madre 540, Col. Lomas de Chapultepec, Del. Miguel Hidalgo, 11000 México, DF; tel. (55) 5520-6950; fax (55) 5540-7579; e-mail embajadadeargelia@yahoo.com.mx; Ambassador Merzak Belhimeur.

Angola: Gaspar de Zúñiga 226, Col. Lomas de Chapultepec, Sección Virreyes, Del. Miguel Hidalgo, 11000 México, DF; tel. (55) 5202-4421; fax (55) 5540-5928; e-mail info@embangolamex.org; Ambassador José Jaime Furtado Gonçalvez.

Argentina: Avda Palmas 910, Col. Lomas de Chapultepec, Del. Miguel Hidalgo, 11000 México, DF; tel. (55) 5520-9430; fax (55) 5540-5011; e-mail embajadaargentina@prodigy.net.mx; Ambassador Jorge Raúl Yoma.

Australia: Rubén Darío 55, Col. Polanco, Del. Miguel Hidalgo, 11580 México, DF; tel. (55) 1101-2200; fax (55) 1101-2201; e-mail embaustmex@yahoo.com.mx; internet www.mexico.embassy.gov.au; Ambassador Katrina Anne Cooper.

Austria: Sierra Tarahumara 420, Col. Lomas de Chapultepec, Del. Miguel Hidalgo, 11000 México, DF; tel. (55) 5251-0806; fax (55) 5245-0198; e-mail mexiko-ob@bmaa.gv.at; internet www.embajadadeaustria.com.mx; Ambassador Dr Werner Druml.

Belgium: Alfredo Musset 41, Col. Polanco, Del. Miguel Hidalgo, 11550 México, DF; tel. (55) 5280-0758; fax (55) 5280-0208; e-mail mexico@diplobel.org; internet www.diplomatie.be/mexico; Ambassador Gustavus J. M. Dierckx.

Belize: Bernardo de Gálvez 215, Col. Lomas de Chapultepec, Del. Miguel Hidalgo, 11000 México, DF; tel. (55) 5520-1274; fax (55) 5520-6089; e-mail embelize@prodigy.net.mx; Ambassador Rosendo Urbina.

Bolivia: Goethe 104, Col. Anzures, Del. Miguel Hidalgo, 11590 México, DF; tel. and fax (55) 5255-3620; e-mail embajada@embol.org.mx; internet www.embol.org.mx; Ambassador Jorge Mansilla Torres.

Brazil: Lope de Armendáriz 130, Col. Lomas Virreyes, Del. Miguel Hidalgo, 11000 México, DF; tel. (55) 5201-4531; fax (55) 5520-4929; e-mail embrasil@brasil.org.mx; internet www.brasil.org.mx; Ambassador Sergio Agosto de Abreu e Lima Florencio Sobrinho.

Bulgaria: Paseo de la Reforma 1990, Col. Lomas de Chapultepec, Del. Miguel Hidalgo, 11000 México, DF; tel. (55) 5596-3283; fax (55) 5596-1012; e-mail ebulgaria@yahoo.com; Ambassador Sergey Penchev Michev.

Canada: Schiller 529, Col. Polanco, Del. Miguel Hidalgo, 11560 México, DF; tel. (55) 5724-7900; fax (55) 5724-7980; e-mail embajada@canada.org.mx; internet www.canada.org.mx; Ambassador Guillermo E. Rishchynski.

Chile: Andrés Bello 10, 18°, Col. Polanco, Del. Miguel Hidalgo, 11560 México, DF; tel. (55) 5280-9681; fax (55) 5280-9703; e-mail echilmex@prodigy.net.mx; internet www.embajadadechile.com.mx; Ambassador Germán Guerrero Pavez.

China, People's Republic: Avda San Jerónimo 217B, Del. Alvaro Obregón, 01090 México, DF; tel. (55) 5616-0609; fax (55) 5616-0460; e-mail embchina@adetel.net.mx; internet www.embajadachina.org.mx; Ambassador Yin Hengmin.

Colombia: Paseo de la Reforma 379, 1°, 5° y 6°, Col. Cuauhtémoc, Del. Cuauhtémoc, 06500 México, DF; tel. (55) 5525-0277; fax (55) 5208-2876; e-mail emcolmex@prodigy.net.mx; internet www.colombiaenmexico.org; Ambassador Luis Camilo Osorio Isaza.

Costa Rica: Río Po 113, Col. Cuauhtémoc, Del. Cuauhtémoc, 06500 México, DF; tel. (55) 5525-7764; fax (55) 5511-9240; e-mail embcrica@ri.redint.com; Ambassador Gioconda Ubeda Rivera.

Côte d'Ivoire: Tennyson 67, Col. Polanco, Del. Miguel Hidalgo, 11560 México, DF; tel. 5280-8573; fax 5282-2954; Ambassador Anne Gnahouret Tatret.

Cuba: Presidente Masaryk 554, Col. Polanco, Del. Miguel Hidalgo, 11560 México, DF; tel. and fax (55) 5280-8039; e-mail canclleria@embacuba.com.mx; internet www.embacuba.com.mx; Ambassador Manuel Francisco Aguilera de la Páz.

Cyprus: Sierra Gorda 370, Col. Lomas de Chapultepec, Del. Miguel Hidalgo, 11000 México, DF; tel. (55) 5202-7600; fax (55) 5520-2693; e-mail chipre@att.net.mx; Ambassador Antonis Grivas.

Czech Republic: Cuvier 22, Col. Nueva Anzures, Del. Miguel Hidalgo, 11590 México, DF; tel. (55) 5531-2777; fax (55) 5531-1837; e-mail mexico@embassy.mzv.cz; internet www.mzv.cz/mexico; Ambassador Jiří Havlík.

Denmark: Tres Picos 43, Col. Chapultepec Morales, Del. Miguel Hidalgo, 11580 México, DF; tel. (55) 5255-3405; fax (55) 5545-5797; e-mail mexamb@um.dk; internet www.ambmexicocity.um.dk; Ambassador Johannes Dahl-Hansen.

Dominican Republic: Bahía Magdalena 148, Of. 307, (entre Bahía de Caracas y Bahía de las Palmas), Col. Verónica Anzures, Del. Miguel Hidalgo, 11300 México, DF; tel. and fax (55) 5260-7262; e-mail embajada@ambadom.org.mx; internet www.embadom.org.mx; Ambassador Pablo A. Mariñez Alvarez.

Ecuador: Tennyson 217, Col. Polanco, Del. Miguel Hidalgo, 11560 México, DF; tel. (55) 5545-3141; fax (55) 5254-2442; e-mail mecuamex@prodigy.net.mx; Ambassador Galo Galarza Dávila.

Egypt: Alejandro Dumas 131, Col. Polanco, Del. Miguel Hidalgo, 11560 México, DF; tel. (55) 5281-0823; fax (55) 5282-1294; e-mail embofegypt@prodigy.net.mx; Ambassador Aly Hosussam Eldin Elhefny Mahmoud.

El Salvador: Temístocles 88, Col. Polanco, Del. Miguel Hidalgo, 11560 México, DF; tel. (55) 5281-5725; fax (55) 5280-0657; e-mail embesmex@webtelmex.net.mx; Ambassador Hugo Roberto Carrillo Corleto.

Finland: Monte Pelvoux 111, 4°, Col. Lomas de Chapultepec, Del. Miguel Hidalgo, 11000 México, DF; tel. (55) 5540-6036; fax (55) 5540-0114; e-mail finmex@prodigy.net.mx; internet www.finlandia.org.mx; Ambassador Ulla Marianna Vaisto.

France: Campos Elíseos 339, Col. Polanco, Del. Miguel Hidalgo, 11560 México, DF; tel. (55) 9171-9893; fax (55) 9171-9703; e-mail prensa@ambafrance-mx.org; internet www.ambafrance-mx.org; Ambassador Daniel Parfait.

Germany: Horacio 1506, Col. Los Morales, Del. Miguel Hidalgo, 11530 México, DF; tel. (55) 5283-2200; fax (55) 5281-2588; e-mail info@mexi.diplo.de; internet www.mexiko.diplo.de; Ambassador Dr Roland Michael Wegener.

Greece: Sierra Gorda 505, Col. Lomas de Chapultepec, Del. Miguel Hidalgo, 11010 México, DF; tel. (55) 5520-2070; fax (55) 5202-4080; e-mail grecemb@prodigy.net.mx; Ambassador Vassilis Karantonis.

Guatemala: Explanada 1025, Col. Lomas de Chapultepec, Del. Miguel Hidalgo, 11000 México, DF; tel. (55) 5540-7520; fax (55) 5202-1142; e-mail embaguatemx@minex.gob.gt; Ambassador José Luis Chea Urruela.

Haiti: Presa Don Martín 53, Col. Irrigación, Del. Miguel Hidalgo, 11500 México, DF; tel. (55) 5557-2065; fax (55) 5395-1654; e-mail ambadh@mail.internet.com.mx; Ambassador Idalbert Pierre-Jean.

MEXICO

Holy See: Juan Pablo II 118, Col. Guadalupe Inn, Del. Alvaro Obregón, 01020 México, DF; tel. (55) 5663-3999; fax (55) 5663-5308; Apostolic Nuncio Most Rev. CHRISTOPHE PIERRE (Titular Archbishop of Gunela).

Honduras: Alfonso Reyes 220, Col. Condesa, Del. Cuauhtémoc, 06170 México, DF; tel. (55) 5211-5747; fax (55) 5211-5425; e-mail emhonmex@prodigy.net.mx; Ambassador ROSALINDA BUESO ASFURA.

Hungary: Paseo de las Palmas 2005, Col. Lomas de Chapultepec, Del. Miguel Hidalgo, 11000 México, DF; tel. (55) 5596-0523; fax (55) 5596-2378; internet www.mfa.gov.hu/kulkepviselet/MX/hu; Ambassador TEREZ DÖRÖMBÖZI DE DEHELAN.

India: Musset 325, Col. Polanco, Del. Miguel Hidalgo, 11550 México, DF; tel. (55) 5531-1050; fax (55) 5254-2349; e-mail indembmx@prodigy.net.mx; internet www.indembassy.org; Ambassador DINESH KUMAR JAIN.

Indonesia: Julio Verne 27, Col. Polanco, Del. Miguel Hidalgo, 11560 México, DF; tel. (55) 5280-6363; fax (55) 5280-7062; e-mail kbrimex@prodigy.net.mx; Ambassador ANDUNG ABDULLAH NITIMIHARDJA.

Iran: Paseo de la Reforma 2350, Col. Lomas Altas, Del. Miguel Hidalgo, 11950 México, DF; tel. (55) 9172-2691; fax (55) 9172-2694; e-mail iranembmex@hotmail.com; Ambassador MOHAMMAD HASSAN GHADIRI ABYANEH.

Iraq: Paseo de la Reforma 1875, Col. Lomas de Chapultepec, Del. Miguel Hidalgo, 11000 México, DF; tel. (55) 5596-0933; fax (55) 5596-0254; Chargé d'affaires a.i. SABIR MAHMOUD ABDULRAZZAK AL-ANI.

Ireland: Cerrada Blvd Manuel Avila Camacho 76, 3°, Col. Lomas de Chapultepec, Del. Miguel Hidalgo, 11000 México, DF; tel. (55) 5520-5803; fax (55) 5520-5892; e-mail emexicoembassy@dfa.ie; Ambassador DERMOT BRANGAN.

Israel: Sierra Madre 215, Col. Lomas de Chapultepec, Del. Miguel Hidalgo, 11000 México, DF; tel. (55) 5201-1500; fax (55) 5201-1555; e-mail embisrael@prodigy.net.mx; internet mexico-city.mfa.gov.il; Ambassador YOSEF LIVNE.

Italy: Paseo de las Palmas 1994, Col. Lomas de Chapultepec, Del. Miguel Hidalgo, 11000 México, DF; tel. (55) 5596-3655; fax (55) 5596-2472; e-mail segreteria.messico@esteri.it; internet www.ambcittadelmessico.esteri.it; Ambassador FELICE SCAUSO.

Jamaica: Schiller 326, 8°, Col. Chapultepec Morales, Del. Miguel Hidalgo, 11570 México, DF; tel. (55) 5250-6804; fax (55) 5250-6160; e-mail embajadadejamaica@prodigy.net.mx; Ambassador SHEILA IVOLINE SEALY-MONTEITH.

Japan: Paseo de la Reforma 395, Apdo 5-101, Col. Cuauhtémoc, Del. Cuauhtémoc, 06500 México, DF; tel. (55) 5211-0028; fax (55) 5207-7743; e-mail embjapmx@mail.internet.com.mx; internet www.mx.emb-japan.go.jp; Ambassador MASAAKI ONO.

Korea, Democratic People's Republic: Eugenio Sue 332, Col. Polanco, Del. Miguel Hidalgo, 11550 México, DF; tel. (55) 5545-1871; fax (55) 5203-0019; e-mail dpkoreaemb@prodigy.net.mx; Ambassador SO JAE MYONG.

Korea, Republic: Lope de Armendáriz 110, Col. Lomas Virreyes, Del. Miguel Hidalgo, 11000 México, DF; tel. (55) 5202-9866; fax (55) 5540-7446; e-mail coremex@prodigy.net.mx; internet mex.mofat.go.kr; Ambassador WON JONG-CHAN.

Lebanon: Julio Verne 8, Col. Polanco, Del. Miguel Hidalgo, 11560 México, DF; tel. (55) 5280-5614; fax (55) 5280-8870; e-mail embalib@prodigy.net.mx; Ambassador NOUHAD MAHMOUD.

Libya: Horacio 1003, Col. Polanco, Del. Miguel Hidalgo, 11550 México, DF; tel. (55) 5545-5725; fax (55) 5545-5677; e-mail libia.mexico@yahoo.com; Chargé d'affaires a.i. MUSTAFA M. E. ELHMALI.

Malaysia: Sierra Nevada 435, Col. Lomas de Chapultepec, Del. Miguel Hidalgo, 11000 México, DF; tel. (55) 5202-4923; fax (55) 5282-4910; e-mail mwmexico@prodigy.net.mx; Ambassador NAFISAH BINTI MOHAMED.

Morocco: Paseo de las Palmas 2020, Col. Lomas de Chapultepec, Del. Miguel Hidalgo, 11000 México, DF; tel. (55) 5245-1786; fax (55) 5245-1791; e-mail sifamex@infosel.net.mx; internet www.marruecos.org.mx; Ambassador MAHMOUD RMIKI.

Netherlands: Edif. Calakmul, 7°, Avda Vasco de Quiroga 3000, Col. Santa Fe, Del. Alvaro Obregón, 01210 México, DF; tel. (55) 5258-9921; fax (55) 5258-8138; e-mail nlgovmex@nlgovmex.com; internet www.paisesbajos.com.mx; Ambassador CORA MINDERHOUD.

New Zealand: Edif. Corporativo Polanco, 4°, Jaime Balmes 8, Col. Polanco, Del. Miguel Hidalgo, 11510 México, DF; tel. (55) 5283-9460; fax (55) 5283-9480; e-mail kiwimexico@prodigy.net.mx; Ambassador CECILE HILLYER.

Nicaragua: Prado Norte 470, Col. Lomas de Chapultepec, Del. Miguel Hidalgo, 11000 México, DF; tel. (55) 5540-5625; fax (55) 5520-6961; e-mail embanic@prodigy.net.mx; Ambassador HORACIO BRENES ICABALCETA.

Nigeria: Paseo de las Palmas 1880, Col. Lomas de Chapultepec, Del. Miguel Hidalgo, 11000 México, DF; tel. (55) 5245-1487; fax (55) 5245-0105; e-mail nigembmx@att.net.mx; Chargé d'affaires a.i. CHARLES AZUBUIKE ONONYE.

Norway: Avda de los Virreyes 1460, Col. Lomas Virreyes, Del. Miguel Hidalgo, 11000 México, DF; tel. (55) 5540-3486; fax (55) 5202-3019; e-mail emb.mexico@mfa.no; internet www.noruega.org.mx; Ambassador KNUT SOLEM.

Pakistan: Hegel 512, Col. Chapultepec Morales, Del. Miguel Hidalgo, 11570 México, DF; tel. (55) 5203-3636; fax (55) 5203-9907; Ambassador ZEHRA AKBARI.

Panama: Sócrates 339, Col. Polanco, Del. Miguel Hidalgo, 11560 México, DF; tel. (55) 5280-7857; fax (55) 5280-7586; e-mail informes@embpanamamexico.com; internet www.embpanamamexico.com; Ambassador RICARDO JOSÉ ALEMÁN ALFARO.

Paraguay: Homero 415, 1°, esq. Hegel, Col. Polanco, Del. Miguel Hidalgo, 11570 México, DF; tel. (55) 5545-0405; fax (55) 5531-9905; e-mail embapar@prodigy.net.mx; Ambassador JOSÉ FÉLIX FERNÁNDEZ ESTIGARRIBIA.

Peru: Paseo de la Reforma 2601, Col. Lomas Reforma, Del. Miguel Hidalgo, 11000 México, DF; tel. (55) 5570-2443; fax (55) 5259-0530; e-mail embaperu@prodigy.net.mx; Ambassador CARLOS BÉRNINZON DEVÉSCOVI.

Philippines: Sierra Gorda 175, Col. Lomas de Chapultepec, Del. Miguel Hidalgo, 11000 México, DF; tel. (55) 5202-8456; fax (55) 5202-8403; e-mail ambamexi@att.net.mx; Ambassador FRANCISCO ORTIGAS MIRANDA.

Poland: Cracovia 40, Col. San Angel, Del. Alvaro Obregón, 01000 México, DF; tel. (55) 5481-2050; fax (55) 5616-0822; e-mail meksyk.amb.sekretariat@msz.gov.pl; Chargé d'affaires a.i. JOANNA HALINA ADDEO-BRATKIEWICZ.

Portugal: Avda Alpes 1370, Col. Lomas de Chapultepec, Del. Miguel Hidalgo, 11000 México, DF; tel. (55) 5520-7897; fax (55) 5520-4688; e-mail embpomex@prodigy.net.mx; internet www.portugalenmexico.com.mx; Ambassador FRANCISCO DOMINGOS GARCÍA FALCÃO MACHADO.

Romania: Sófocles 311, Col. Polanco, Del. Miguel Hidalgo, 11560 México, DF; tel. (55) 5280-0197; fax (55) 5280-0343; e-mail secretariat@rumania.org.mx; internet www.rumania.org.mx; Ambassador MANUELA VULPE.

Russia: José Vasconcelos 204, Col. Hipódromo Condesa, Del. Cuauhtémoc, 06140 México, DF; tel. (55) 5273-1305; fax (55) 5273-1545; e-mail embrumex@mail.internet.com.mx; Ambassador VALERY I. MOROZOV.

Saudi Arabia: Paseo de las Palmas 2075, Col. Lomas de Chapultepec, Del. Miguel Hidalgo, 11000 México, DF; tel. (55) 5596-0173; fax (55) 5020-3160; e-mail saudiemb@prodigy.net.mx; Ambassador MUNEER IBRAHIM AL-BENJABI.

Serbia: Montañas Rocallosas Oeste 515, Col. Lomas de Chapultepec, Del. Miguel Hidalgo, 11000 México, DF; tel. (55) 5520-0524; fax (55) 5520-9927; e-mail embajadaserbia@att.net.mx; Ambassador MILISAV PAIC.

Slovakia: Julio Verne 35, Col. Polanco, Del. Miguel Hidalgo, 11560 México, DF; tel. (55) 5280-6669; fax (55) 5280-6294; e-mail eslovaquia@prodigy.net.mx; Ambassador JOZEF ADAMEC.

South Africa: Edif. Forum, 9°, Andrés Bello 10, Col. Polanco, Del. Miguel Hidalgo, 11560 México, DF; tel. and fax (55) 5282-9260; e-mail safrica@prodigy.net.mx; Ambassador MPHAKAMA NYANGWENI MBETE.

Spain: Galileo 114, esq. Horacio, Col. Polanco, Del. Miguel Hidalgo, 11550 México, DF; tel. (55) 5282-2271; fax (55) 5282-1520; e-mail embaes@prodigy.net.mx; internet www.mae.es/embajadas/mexico; Ambassador CARMELO ANGULO BARTUREN.

Sweden: Paseo de las Palmas 1375, Col. Lomas de Chapultepec, Del. Miguel Hidalgo, 11000 México, DF; tel. (55) 9178-5010; fax (55) 5540-3253; e-mail suecia@prodigy.net.mx; internet www.suecia.com.mx; Ambassador ANNA LINDSTEDT.

Switzerland: Paseo de las Palmas 405, 11°, Torre Óptima, Col. Lomas de Chapultepec, Del. Miguel Hidalgo, 11000 México, DF; tel. (55) 5520-3003; fax (55) 5520-8685; e-mail vertretung@mex.rep.admin.ch; internet www.eda.admin.ch/mexico_emb/s/home.html; Ambassador URS BREITER.

Thailand: Paseo de las Palmas 1610, Col. Lomas de Chapultepec, Del. Miguel Hidalgo, 11000 México, DF; tel. (55) 5540-4551; fax (55) 5540-4817; e-mail thaimex@prodigy.net.mx; internet www.thaiembmexico.co.nr; Chargé d'affaires a.i. SAROJ THANASUNTI.

Turkey: Monte Líbano 885, Col. Lomas de Chapultepec, Del. Miguel Hidalgo, 11000 México, DF; tel. (55) 5282-5446; fax (55) 5282-4894; e-mail turkem@mail.internet.com.mx; Chargé d'affaires a.i. YUNUS EMRE BAYRAK.

Ukraine: Paseo de la Reforma 730, Col. Lomas de Chapultepec, Del. Miguel Hidalgo, 11000 México, DF; tel. (55) 5282-4085; fax (55) 5282-4768; e-mail ukraniaemb@prodigy.net.mx; Ambassador OLEKSIY V. BRANASHKO.

United Kingdom: Río Lerma 71, Col. Cuauhtémoc, Del. Cuauhtémoc, 06500 México, DF; tel. (55) 5242-8500; fax (55) 5242-8517; e-mail ukinmex@att.net.mx; internet www.embajadabritanica.com.mx; Ambassador GILES PAXMAN.

USA: Paseo de la Reforma 305, Del. Cuauhtémoc, 06500 México, DF; tel. (55) 5080-2000; fax (55) 5080-2150; internet www.usembassy-mexico.gov; Chargé d'affaires a.i. LESLIE BASSETT.

Uruguay: Hegel 149, 1°, Col. Chapultepec Morales, Del. Miguel Hidalgo, 11560 México, DF; tel. (55) 5531-4029; fax (55) 5545-3342; e-mail uruazte@ort.org.mx; Ambassador JOSÉ IGNACIO KORZENIAK PASTORINO.

Venezuela: Schiller 326, Col. Chapultepec Morales, Del. Miguel Hidalgo, 11570 México, DF; tel. (55) 5203-4233; fax (55) 5203-5072; e-mail embemve.mxmdf@mre.gob.ve; Chargé d'affaires a.i. DALIA ELOISA LAGONELL CASTILLO.

Viet Nam: Sierra Ventana 255, Col. Lomas de Chapultepec, Del. Miguel Hidalgo, 11000 México, DF; tel. (55) 5540-1632; fax (55) 5540-1612; e-mail vietnam.mx@mofa.gov.vn; internet www.vietnamembassy-mexico.org/vi; Ambassador PHAM VAN QUE.

Judicial System

The principle of the separation of the judiciary from the legislative and executive powers is embodied in the 1917 Constitution. The judicial system is divided into two areas: the federal, dealing with federal law, and the local, dealing only with state law within each state.

The federal judicial system has both ordinary and constitutional jurisdiction, and judicial power is exercised by the Supreme Court of Justice, the Electoral Court, Collegiate and Unitary Circuit Courts and District Courts. The Supreme Court comprises two separate chambers: Civil and Criminal Affairs, and Administrative and Labour Affairs. The Federal Judicature Council is responsible for the administration, surveillance and discipline of the federal judiciary, except for the Supreme Court of Justice.

In 2006 there were 172 Collegiate Circuit Courts (Tribunales Colegiados), 62 Unitary Circuit Courts (Tribunales Unitarios) and 285 District Courts (Juzgados de Distrito). Mexico is divided into 29 judicial circuits. The Circuit Courts may be collegiate, when dealing with the *derecho de amparo* (protection of constitutional rights of an individual), or unitary, when dealing with appeal cases. The Collegiate Circuit Courts comprise three magistrates with residence in the cities of México, Toluca, Naucalpan, Guadalajara, Monterrey, Hermosillo, Puebla, Boca del Río, Xalapa, Torreón, Saltillo, San Luis Potosí, Villahermosa, Morelia, Mazatlán, Oaxaca, Mérida, Mexicali, Guanajuato, León, Chihuahua, Ciudad Juárez, Cuernavaca, Ciudad Victoria, Ciudad Reynosa, Tuxtla Gutiérrez, Tapachula, Acapulco, Chilpancingo, Querétaro, Zacatecas, Aguascalientes, Tepic, Durango, La Paz, Cancún, Tlaxcala and Pachuca. The Unitary Circuit Courts comprise one magistrate with residence mostly in the same cities as given above.

SUPREME COURT OF JUSTICE

Suprema Corte de Justicia de la Nación: Pino Suárez 2, Col. Centro, 06065 México, DF; tel. (55) 5522-0096; fax (55) 5522-0152; e-mail administrator@mail.scjn.gob.mx; internet www.scjn.gob.mx. **Chief Justice:** GUILLERMO I. ORTÍZ MAYAGOITIA.

First Chamber—Civil and Criminal Affairs
President: SERGIO ARMANDO VALLS HERNÁNDEZ.

Second Chamber—Administrative and Labour Affairs
President: JOSÉ FERNANDO FRANCO GONZÁLEZ SALAS.

ELECTORAL TRIBUNAL OF THE FEDERAL JUDICIARY

Tribunal Electoral del Poder Jucicial de la Federación (TEPJF): Carlota Amero 5000, Col. Culhuacán, Del. Coyoacán, 04480 México, DF; tel. (55) 5728-2300; fax (55) 5728-2400; internet www.trife.gob.mx; Pres. MARÍA DEL CARMEN ALANIS FIGUEROA.

Religion

CHRISTIANITY

The Roman Catholic Church

The prevailing religion is Roman Catholicism, but the Church, disestablished in 1857, was for many years, under the Constitution of 1917, subject to state control. A constitutional amendment, promulgated in January 1992, officially removed all restrictions on the Church. For ecclesiastical purposes, Mexico comprises 18 archdioceses, 65 dioceses, five territorial prelatures and two eparchies (both directly subject to the Holy See). An estimated 84.7% of the population are adherents.

Bishops' Conference

Conferencia del Episcopado Mexicano (CEM), Edif. S. S. Juan Pablo II, Prolongación Ministerios 26, Col. Tepeyac Insurgentes, Apdo 118-055, 07020 México, DF; tel. (55) 5781-8462; fax (55) 5577-5489; e-mail segcem@cem.org.mx; internet www.cem.org.mx; Pres. CARLOS AGUIAR RETES (Bishop of Texcoco); Sec.-Gen. JOSÉ LEOPOLDO GONZÁLEZ GONZÁLEZ.

Archbishop of Acapulco: FELIPE AGUIRRE FRANCO, Arzobispado, Quebrada 16, Apdo 201, Centro, 39300 Acapulco, Gro; tel. and fax (744) 482-0763; e-mail arzobispadoaca@aca.cableonline.com.mx; internet www.arquidiocesisacapulco.org.mx.

Archbishop of Antequera, Oaxaca: JOSÉ LUIS CHÁVEZ BOTELLO, García Virgil 600, Anexos de Catedral, Col. Centro, 68000 Oaxaca, Oax.; tel. (951) 516-4822; fax (951) 514-1348; e-mail arzobispadooaxaca@hotmail.com; internet arquidiocesisoaxaca.org.mx.

Archbishop of Chihuahua: JOSÉ FERNÁNDEZ ARTEAGA, Arzobispado, Avda Cuauhtémoc 1828, Apdo 7, Col. Cuauhtémoc, 31020 Chihuahua, Chih.; tel. (614) 410-3202; fax (614) 410-5621; e-mail ferar@megalink.com.mx; internet www.arquichi.org.mx.

Archbishop of Durango: HÉCTOR GONZÁLEZ MARTÍNEZ, Arzobispado, 20 de Noviembre 306, Poniente Centro, 34000 Durango, Dgo; tel. (618) 811-4242; fax (618) 812-8881; e-mail arqdgo@prodigy.net.mx.

Archbishop of Guadalajara: Cardinal JUAN SANDOVAL IÑIGUEZ, Arzobispado, Liceo 17, Apdo 1-331, Col. Centro, 44100 Guadalajara, Jal.; tel. (33) 3614-5504; fax (33) 3658-2300; e-mail arzgdl@arquinet.com.mx; internet www.arquidiocesisgdl.org.mx.

Archbishop of Hermosillo: JOSÉ ULISES MACÍAS SALCEDO, Arzobispado, Dr Paliza y Ocampo, Ala Sur de la Catedral, Col. Centenario, 83260 Hermosillo, Son.; tel. (662) 213-2138; fax (662) 213-1327; e-mail arzohmo@hotmail.com; internet www.iglesiahermosillo.com.mx.

Archbishop of Jalapa: HIPÓLITO REYES LARIOS, Arzobispado, Avda Manuel Avila Camacho 73, Apdo 359, Col. Centro, 91000 Jalapa, Ver.; tel. (228) 812-0579; fax (228) 817-5578; e-mail arzobispadoalxal@prodigy.net.mx.

Archbishop of León: JOSÉ GUADALUPE MARTÍN RÁBAGO, Arzobispado, Pedro Moreno 312, Apdo 108, 37000 León, Gto; tel. (477) 713-2747; fax (477) 713-1286; e-mail canciller@arquidiocesisleon.org.mx; internet www.arquidiocesisdeleon.org.mx.

Archbishop of Mexico City: Cardinal NORBERTO RIVERA CARRERA, Curia del Arzobispado de México, Durango 90, 5°, Col. Roma, Apdo 24433, 06700 México, DF; tel. (55) 5208-3200; fax (55) 5208-5350; e-mail arzobisp@arquidiocesismexico.org.mx; internet www.arzobispadomexico.org.mx.

Archbishop of Monterrey: Cardinal FRANCISCO ROBLES ORTEGA, Zuazua 1100 Sur con Ocampo Centro, Apdo 7, 64000 Monterrey, NL; tel. (81) 1158-2450; fax (81) 1158-2488; e-mail canclleria@arquidiocesismty.org; internet www.arquidiocesismty.org.mx.

Archbishop of Morelia: ALBERTO SUÁREZ INDA, Arzobispado, Costado Catedral, Frente Avda Madero, Apdo 17, 58000 Morelia, Mich.; tel. (443) 313-2493; fax (443) 312-0919; e-mail asuarexi@prodigy.net.mx; internet www.arquimorelia.org.mx.

Archbishop of Puebla de los Angeles: ROSENDO HUESCA PACHECO, Avda 2 Sur 305, Apdo 235, Col. Centro, 72000 Puebla, Pue.; tel. (222) 232-4591; fax (222) 246-2277; e-mail rhuesca@mail.cem.org.mx.

Archbishop of San Luis Potosí: LUIS MORALES REYES, Arzobispado, Francisco Madero 300, Apdo 1, Col. Centro, 78000 San Luis Potosí, SLP; tel. (444) 812-4555; fax (444) 812-7979; e-mail arqsanluis@iglesiapotosina.org; internet www.iglesiapotosina.org.

Archbishop of Tijuana: RAFAEL ROMO MUÑOZ, Arzobispado, Calle Décima y Avda Ocampo 8525, Apdo 226, 22000 Tijuana, BCN; tel. (664) 684-8411; fax (664) 684-7683; internet www.iglesiatijuana.org.

Archbishop of Tlalnepantla: RICARDO GUÍZAR DÍAZ, Arzobispado, Avda Juárez 42, Apdo 268, Col. Centro, 54000 Tlalnepantla, Méx.; tel. (55) 5565-3944; fax (55) 5565-2751; e-mail curia@arqtlalnepantla.org; internet www.arqtlalnepantla.org.

Archbishop of Tulancingo: DOMINGO DÍAZ MARTÍNEZ, Arzobispado, Plaza de la Constitución, Apdo 14, 43600 Tulancingo, Hgo; e-mail sgamitra@netpac.net.mx.

Archbishop of Tuxtla Gutiérrez: ROGELIO CABRERA LÓPEZ, Uruguay 500A, Col. El Retiro, Apdo 365, 29040 Tuxtla Gutiérrez, Chis; e-mail casaepiscopal@prodigy.net.mx.

Archbishop of Yucatán: EMILIO CARLOS BERLIE BELAUNZARÁN, Arzobispado, Calle 58 501, Col. Centro, 97000 Mérida, Yuc.; tel. (999) 924-7777; fax (999) 923-7983; e-mail aryu@prodigy.net.mx; internet www.arquidiocesisdeyucatan.org.

MEXICO
Directory

The Anglican Communion
Mexico is divided into five dioceses, which form the Province of the Anglican Church in Mexico, established in 1995.

Bishop of Cuernavaca: RAMIRO DELGADO VERA, Minerva 1, Col. Delicias, 62431 Cuernavaca, Mor.; tel. and fax (777) 315-2870; e-mail adoc@cableonline.com.mx; internet www.cuernavaca-anglican.org.

Bishop of Mexico City and Primate of the Anglican Church in Mexico: CARLOS TOUCHÉ PORTER, La Otra Banda 40, Avda San Jerónimo 117, Col. San Ángel, 01000 México, DF; tel. and fax (55) 5616-2205; e-mail contacto@iglesiaanglicanademexico.org; internet www.iglesiaanglicanademexico.org.

Bishop of Northern Mexico: MARCELINO RIVERA DELGADO, Simón Bolívar 2005 Nte, Col. Mitras Centro, 64460 Monterrey, NL; tel. (81) 8333-0922; fax (81) 8348-7362; e-mail diocesisdelnorte@att.net.mx.

Bishop of South-Eastern Mexico: BENITO JUÁREZ MARTÍNEZ, Avda de las Américas 73, Col. Aguacatl, 91130 Jalapa, Ver.; tel. and fax (228) 814-6951; e-mail dioste99@aol.com.

Bishop of Western Mexico: LINO RODRÍGUEZ-AMARO, Francisco Javier Gamboa 255, Col. Barrera, 45150 Guadalajara, Jal.; tel. (33) 3615-5070; fax (33) 3615-4413; e-mail iamoccidente@prodigy.net.mx; internet www.iamoccidente.org.mx.

Protestant Churches

Iglesia Luterana Mexicana: POB 1-1034, 44101 Guadalajara, Jal.; tel. (33) 3639-7253; e-mail dtrejocoria@hotmail.com; f. 1951; Pres. DANIEL TREJO CORIA; 1,500 mems.

Iglesia Metodista de México, Asociación Religiosa: Miravelle 209, Col. Albert, 03570 México, DF; tel. (55) 5539-3674; e-mail prenapro@iglesia-metodista.org.mx; internet www.iglesia-metodista.org.mx; f. 1930; 55,000 mems; Pres. Rev. MOISÉS VALDERRAMA GÓMEZ; 370 congregations; comprises six episcopal areas.

National Baptist Convention of Mexico: Tlalpan 1035-A, Col. Américas Unidas, 03610 México, DF; tel. (55) 5539-7720; fax (55) 5539-2302; e-mail comunicacion@cnbm.org.mx; internet www.cnbm.org.mx; f. 1903; Pres. Rev. JOSÉ TRINIDAD BONILLA MORALES.

BAHÁ'Í FAITH

National Spiritual Assembly of the Bahá'ís of Mexico: Emerson 421, Col. Chapultepec Morales, 11570 México, DF; tel. (55) 5545-2155; fax (55) 5255-5972; e-mail info@bahaimexico.org; internet www.bahaimexico.org; mems resident in 978 localities.

JUDAISM

The Jewish community numbered some 40,000 in 2004.

Comité Central de la Comunidad Judía de México: Cofre de Perote 115, Lomas Barrilaco, 11010 México, DF; tel. (55) 5520-9393; fax (55) 5540-3050; e-mail comitecentral@prodigy.net.mx; internet www.tribuna.org.mx; Pres. OSCAR GORODZINSKY.

The Press

DAILY NEWSPAPERS

México, DF

La Afición: Ignacio Mariscal 23, Apdo 64 bis, Col. Tabacalera, 06030 México, DF; tel. (55) 5546-4780; fax (55) 5546-5852; internet www.laaficion.com; f. 1930; sport; Pres. FRANCISCO A. GONZÁLEZ; circ. 85,000.

La Crónica de Hoy: Londres 36, Col. Juárez, 06600 México, DF; tel. and fax (52) 5512-3429; e-mail suscripciones@cronica.com.mx; internet www.cronica.com.mx; Pres. JORGE KAHWAGI GASTINE; Editorial Dir PABLO HIRIART LE BERT.

Cuestión: Laguna de Mayrán 410, Col. Anáhuac, 11320 México, DF; tel. (55) 5260-0499; fax (55) 5260-3645; internet www.cuestion.com.mx; f. 1980; midday; Dir-Gen. Lic. ALBERTO GONZÁLEZ PARRA; circ. 48,000.

Diario de México: Chimalpopoca 38, Col. Obrera, 06800 México, DF; tel. (55) 5442-6501; fax (55) 5588-4289; e-mail redaccion@diariodemexico.com.mx; internet www.diariodemexico.com.mx; f. 1949; morning; Dir-Gen. FEDERICO BRACAMONTES BAZ; Editorial Dir ABEL MAGAÑA CAMPUZANO; circ. 76,000.

El Economista: Avda Coyoacán 515, Col. del Valle, 03100 México, DF; tel. (55) 5326-5454; fax (55) 5687-3821; e-mail jppadilla@eleconomista.com.mx; internet www.economista.com.mx; f. 1988; financial; Pres. JOSÉ GÓMEZ CAÑIBE; Editor-in-Chief DAVID CUEN; circ. 37,448.

Esto: Guillermo Prieto 7, 1°, Col. San Rafael, Del. Cuauhtémoc, 06470 México, DF; tel. and fax (55) 5566-1511; e-mail esto@oem.com.mx; internet www.esto.com.mx; f. 1941; published by Organización Editorial Mexicana; morning; sport; Dir MARIO VÁZQUEX RAÑA; circ. 400,000, Mondays 450,000.

Excélsior: Paseo de la Reforma 18 y Bucareli 1, Apdo 120 bis, Col. Centro, 06600 México, DF; tel. (55) 5705-4444; fax (55) 5566-0223; e-mail foro@excelsior.com.mx; internet www.excelsior.com.mx; f. 1917; morning; independent; Pres. OLEGARIO VÁZQUEX RAÑA; Dir ERNESTO RIVERA AGUILAR; circ. 200,000.

El Financiero: Lago Bolsena 176, Col. Anáhuac entre Lago Peypus y Lago Onega, 11320 México, DF; tel. (55) 5227-7600; fax (55) 5254-6427; internet www.elfinanciero.com.mx; f. 1981; financial; Dir-Gen. PILAR ESTANDÍA DE CÁRDENAS; circ. 119,000.

El Heraldo de México: Dr Lucio, esq. Dr Velasco, Col. Doctores, 06720 México, DF; tel. (55) 5578-7022; fax (55) 5578-9824; e-mail heraldo@iwm.com.mx; internet www.heraldo.com.mx; f. 1965; morning; Dir-Gen. GABRIEL ALARCÓN VELÁZQUEZ; circ. 209,600.

La Jornada: Avda Cuauhtémoc 1236, Col. Santa Cruz Atoyac, Del. Benito Juárez, 03310 México, DF; tel. (55) 9183-0300; internet www.jornada.unam.mx; f. 1984; morning; Dir-Gen. CARMEN LIRA SAADE; Gen. Man. JORGE MARTÍNEZ JIMÉNEZ; circ. 86,275.

Milenio Diario: México, DF; internet www.milenio.com; publishes Mexico City and regional edns, and a weekly news magazine, *Milenio Semanal*; Pres. FRANCISCO A. GONZÁLEZ; Dir-Gen. FRANCISCO D. GONZÁLEZ A.

Novedades: Balderas 87, esq. Morelos, Col. Centro, 06040 México, DF; tel. (55) 5518-5481; fax (55) 5521-4505; internet www.novedades.com.mx; f. 1936; morning; independent; Pres. and Editor-in-Chief ROMULO O'FARRILL, Jr; Vice-Pres. JOSÉ ANTONIO O'FARRILL AVILA; circ. 42,990, Sundays 43,536.

Ovaciones: Lago Zirahuén 279, 20°, Col. Anáhuac, 11320 México, DF; tel. (55) 5328-0700; fax (55) 5260-2219; e-mail ovaciones@ova.com.mx; internet www.ovaciones.com; f. 1947; morning and evening editions; Pres. and Dir-Gen. MAURICIO VÁZQUEZ RAMOS; circ. 130,000; evening circ. 100,000.

La Prensa: Basilio Vadillo 40, Col. Tabacalera, 06030 México, DF; tel. (55) 5228-9977; fax (55) 5521-8209; e-mail bmedina@la-prensa.com.mx; internet www.la-prensa.com.mx; f. 1928; published by Organización Editorial Mexicana; morning; Pres. and Dir-Gen. MARIO VÁZQUEZ RAÑA; Dir MAURICIO ORTEGA CAMBEROS; circ. 270,000.

Reforma: Avda México Coyoacán 40, Col. Santa Cruz Atoyac, 03310 México, DF; tel. (55) 5628-7100; fax (55) 5628-7188; internet www.reforma.com; f. 1993; morning; Pres. and Dir-Gen. ALEJANDRO JUNCO DE LA VEGA ELIZONDO; circ. 94,000.

El Sol de México: Guillermo Prieto 7, 20°, Col. San Rafael, 06470 México, DF; tel. (55) 5566-1511; fax (55) 5535-5560; e-mail enlinea@elsoldemexico.com.mx; internet www.elsoldemexico.com.mx; f. 1965; published by Organización Editorial Mexicana; morning and midday; Pres. and Dir-Gen. MARIO VÁZQUEZ RAÑA; Man. EDGAR FIERRO GRANADOS; circ. 76,000.

El Universal: Bucareli 8, Apdo 909, Col. Centro, Del. Cuauhtémoc, 06040 México, DF; tel. (55) 5709-1313; fax (55) 5510-1269; e-mail rdirgral@eluniversal.com.mx; internet www.eluniversal.com.mx; f. 1916; morning; independent; centre-left; Pres. JUAN FRANCISCO EALY ORTIZ; Dir-Gen. JUAN FRANCISCO EALY, Jr; circ. 165,629, Sundays 181,615.

Unomásuno: Gabino Barreda 86, Col. San Rafael, México, DF; tel. (55) 1055-5500; fax (55) 5598-8821; e-mail cduran@servidor.unam.mx; internet www.unomasuno.com.mx; f. 1977; morning; left-wing; Pres. NAIM LIBIEN KAUI; Dir JOSÉ LUIS ROJAS RAMÍREZ; circ. 40,000.

PROVINCIAL DAILY NEWSPAPERS

Baja California

El Sol de Tijuana: Rufino Tamayo 4, Zona del Río, 22320 Tijuana, BC; tel. (664) 634-3232; fax (664) 634-2234; e-mail soltij@oem.com.mx; internet www.oem.com.mx/elsoldetijuana; f. 1989; published by Organización Editorial Mexicana; morning; Gen. Man. MARIO VALDÉS HERNÁNDEZ; Dir MIGUEL ANGEL TORRES PONCE; circ. 50,000.

La Voz de la Frontera: Avda Madero 1545, Col. Nueva, Apdo 946, 21100 Mexicali, BC; tel. (686) 562-4545; fax (686) 562-6912; e-mail ramondiaz@lavozdelafrontera.com.mx; internet www.oem.com.mx/lavozdelafrontera; f. 1964; morning; published by Organización Editorial Mexicana; Dir FELIPE DE JESÚS LÓPEZ RODRÍGUEZ; Gen. Man. Lic. MARIO VALDÉS HERNÁNDEZ; circ. 65,000.

Chihuahua

El Diario: Publicaciones Paso del Norte, Avda Paseo Triunfo de la República 2505, Zona Pronaf, 32310 Ciudad Juárez, Chih.; tel. (656) 629-6900; internet www.diario.com.mx; f. 1976; Pres. OSVALDO RODRÍGUEZ BORUNDA.

El Heraldo de Chihuahua: Avda Universidad 2507, Apdo 1515, 31240 Chihuahua, Chih.; tel. (614) 432-3800; fax (614) 413-5625; e-mail elheraldo@buzon.online.com.mx; internet www.oem.com.mx/elheraldodechihuahua; f. 1927; published by Organización Editorial

MEXICO

Mexicana; morning; Dir Lic. JAVIER H. CONTRERAS; circ. 27,520, Sundays 31,223.

El Mexicano de Ciudad Juárez: Ciudad Juárez, Chih.; e-mail director@pesquisasenlinea.org; f. 1959; published by Organización Editorial Mexicana; morning; Dir RAFAEL NAVARRO; Editor-in-Chief JAIME NÚÑEZ; circ. 80,000.

Coahuila

El Siglo de Torreón: Avda Matamoros 1056 Pte, Col. Centro, 27000 Torreón, Coah.; tel. (871) 759-1200; e-mail internet@elsiglodetorreon.com.mx; internet www.elsiglodetorreon.com.mx; f. 1922; morning; Pres. OLGA DE JUAMBELZ Y HORCASITAS; Dir-Gen. ANTONIO IRAZOQUI Y DE JUAMBELZ; circ. 38,611, Sundays 38,526.

Vanguardia: Blvd Venustiano Carranza 1918, esq. con Chiapas, República Oriente, 25280 Saltillo, Coah.; tel. (844) 450-1000; e-mail hola@vanguardia.com.mx; internet www.vanguardia.com.mx; Dir-Gen. DIANA MARÍA GALINDO DE CASTILLA.

Colima

Diario de Colima: Avda 20 de Noviembre 380, 28060 Colima, Col.; tel. (312) 312-5688; internet www.diariodecolima.com; f. 1953; Dir-Gen. HÉCTOR SÁNCHEZ DE LA MADRID; Man. Dir ENRIQUE ZÁRATE CANSECO.

Guanajuato

Correo de Guanajuato: Carreterra Guanajuato—Juventino Rosas Km 9.5, 36260 Guanajuato, Gto; tel. (477) 733-1253; fax (477) 733-0057; e-mail correo@correo-gto.com.mx; internet www.correo-gto.com.mx; Dir-Gen. ARNALDO CUÉLLAR.

El Sol de Salamanca: Faro de Oro 800, 36700 Salamanca, Gto; tel. (464) 647-0144; e-mail aherrera@elsoldeirapuato.com.mx; internet www.elsoldesalamanca.com.mx; published by Organización Editorial Mexicana; Dir-Gen. ALEJANDRO HERRERA SÁNCHEZ.

Jalisco

El Informador: Independencia 300, Apdo 3 bis, 44100 Guadalajara, Jal.; tel. (33) 3678-7700; e-mail webmanager@informador.com.mx; internet www.informador.com.mx; f. 1917; morning; Editor JORGE ÁLVAREZ DEL CASTILLO; circ. 50,000.

El Occidental: Calzada Independencia Sur 324, Apdo 1-699, 44100 Guadalajara, Jal.; tel. (33) 3613-0690; fax (33) 3613-6796; e-mail silvia@eloccidental.com.mx; internet www.eloccidental.com.mx; f. 1942; published by Organización Editorial Mexicana; morning; Pres. and Dir-Gen. Lic. MARIO VÁSQUEZ RAÑA; Dir JAVIER VALLE CHÁVEZ; circ. 49,400.

México

ABC: Avda Hidalgo Oriente 1339, Centro Comercial, Col. Ferrocarriles Nacionales, 50070 Toluca, Méx.; tel. (722) 217-9880; fax (722) 217-8402; e-mail miled1@mail.miled.com; internet www.miled.com; f. 1984; morning; Pres. and Editor MILED LIBIEN KAUI; circ. 65,000.

Diario de Toluca: Allende Sur 209, 50000 Toluca, Méx.; tel. (722) 215-9105; fax (722) 214-1523; f. 1980; also publishes *Siete Dias* and *El Noticiero*; morning; Pres. ANUAR MACCISE DIB; circ. 22,200.

El Heraldo de Toluca: Salvador Díaz Mirón 700, Col. Sánchez Colín, 50150 Toluca, Méx.; tel. (722) 217-3542; fax (722) 212-2535; e-mail editotol@prodigy.net.mx; internet www.heraldotoluca.com; f. 1955; morning; Editor ALBERTO BARRAZA SÁNCHEZ; circ. 90,000.

El Sol de Toluca: Santos Degollado 105, Apdo 54, Col. Centro, 50050 Toluca, Méx.; tel. (722) 214-7077; fax (722) 215-2564; internet www.oem.com.mx/elsoldetoluca; f. 1947; published by Organización Editorial Mexicana; morning; Dir RAFAEL VILCHIS GIL DE ARÉVALO; circ. 42,000.

Michoacán

La Voz de Michoacán: Blvd del Periodismo 1270, Col. Arriaga Rivera, Apdo 121, 58190 Morelia, Mich.; tel. (443) 327-3712; fax (443) 327-3728; e-mail jcgonzalez@voznet.com.mx; internet www.vozdemichoacan.com.mx; f. 1948; morning; Dir-Gen. MIGUEL MEDINA ROBLES; circ. 50,000.

Morelos

El Diario de Morelos: Morelos Sur 132, Col. Las Palmas, 62050 Cuernavaca, Mor.; tel. and fax (777) 362-0220; e-mail redaccion@diariodemorelos.com; internet www.diariodemorelos.com; f. 1978; morning; Propr Grupo BRACA de Comunicación; CEO and Editor-in-Chief MIGUEL BRACAMONTES; circ. 35,000.

Nayarit

Meridiano de Nayarit: Independencia 335, Fracc. Las Aves, Tepic, Nay.; tel. (311) 210-3211; e-mail ventas@meridiano.com.mx; internet meridiano.nayaritpuntocom.com; f. 1942; morning; Dir Dr DAVID ALFARO; circ. 60,000.

Nuevo León

ABC: Platón Sánchez Sur 411, 64000 Monterrey, NL; tel. (81) 8344-2510; fax (81) 8344-5990; f. 1985; morning; Dir-Gen. GONZALO ESTRADO TORRES; circ. 40,000, Sundays 45,000.

El Norte: Washington 629 Oeste, Apdo 186, 64000 Monterrey, NL; tel. (81) 8150-8100; fax (81) 8343-2476; internet www.elnorte.com.mx; f. 1938; morning; Man. Dir ALEJANDRO JUNCO DE LA VEGA; circ. 133,872, Sundays 154,951.

El Porvenir: Galeana Sur 344, Apdo 218, 64000 Monterrey, NL; tel. (81) 8345-4080; fax (81) 8345-7795; internet www.elporvenir.com.mx; f. 1919; morning; Dir-Gen. JOSÉ GERARDO CANTÚ ESCALANTE; circ. 75,000.

Oaxaca

El Imparcial: Armenta y López 312, Apdo 322, 68000 Oaxaca, Oax.; tel. (951) 516-2812; fax (951) 514-7020; e-mail subdireccion@imparcialenlinea.com; internet www.imparoax.com.mx; f. 1951; morning; Dir-Gen. BENJAMÍN FERNÁNDEZ PICHARDO; circ. 17,000, Sundays 20,000.

Puebla

La Opinión: 3 Oriente 1207, Barrio del Analco, 238 Puebla, Pue.; tel. (222) 246-4358; fax (222) 232-7772; internet www.opinion.com.mx; f. 1924; morning; Dir-Gen. OSCAR LÓPEZ MORALES; circ. 40,000.

El Sol de Puebla: Avda 3 Oriente 201, Col. Centro, 72000 Puebla, Pue.; tel. (222) 514-3300; fax (222) 246-0869; e-mail elsoldepuebla@elsoldepuebla.com.mx; internet www.oem.com.mx/elsoldepuebla; f. 1944; published by Organización Editorial Mexicana; morning; Dir SERAFÍN SALAZAR ARELLANO; circ. 67,000.

San Luis Potosí

El Heraldo: Villerías 305, 78000 San Luis Potosí, SLP; tel. (444) 812-3312; fax (444) 812-2081; e-mail redaccion@elheraldoslp.com.mx; internet www.elheraldoslp.com.mx; f. 1954; morning; Dir-Gen. ALEJANDRO VILLASANA MENA; circ. 60,620.

Pulso: Galeana 485, Centro, 78000 San Luis Potosí, SLP; tel. (444) 812-7575; fax (444) 812-3525; internet www.pulsoslp.com.mx; morning; Dir-Gen. PABLO VALLADARES GARCÍA; circ. 60,000.

El Sol de San Luis: Avda Universidad 565, Apdo 342, 78000 San Luis Potosí, SLP; tel. and fax (444) 812-4412; internet www.oem.com.mx/elsoldesanluis; f. 1952; published by Organización Editorial Mexicana; morning; Dir JOSÉ ANGEL MARTÍNEZ LIMÓN; circ. 60,000.

Sinaloa

El Debate de Culiacán: Madero 556 Pte, 80000 Culiacán, Sin.; tel. (667) 716-6353; fax (667) 715-7131; e-mail andrea.miranda@lai.com.mx; internet www.debate.com.mx; f. 1972; morning; Dir ROSARIO I. OROPEZA; circ. 23,603, Sundays 23,838.

Noroeste Culiacán: Grupo Periódicos Noroeste, Angel Flores 282 Oeste, Apdo 90, 80000 Culiacán, Sin.; tel. (667) 759-8100; fax (667) 712-8006; e-mail direccion@noroeste.com.mx; internet www.noroeste.com.mx; f. 1973; morning; Dir-Gen. BEATRIZ BECERRA GONZÁLEZ; Editor RODOLFO DIAZ; circ. 35,000.

El Sol de Sinaloa: Blvd G. Leyva Lozano y Corona 320, Apdo 412, 80000 Culiacán, Sin.; tel. (667) 713-1621; fax (667) 713-1800; internet www.elsoldesinaloa.com.mx; f. 1956; published by Organización Editorial Mexicana; morning; Dir JORGE LUIS TÉLLEZ SALAZAR; circ. 30,000.

Sonora

Expreso: Hermosillo, Son.; tel. (662) 108-3000; e-mail holguin@expreso.com.mx; internet www.expreso.com.mx; Dir-Gen. MARTÍN HOLGUÍN ALATORRE; circ. 17,000, Sundays 18,000.

El Imparcial: Sufragio Efectivo y Mina 71, Col. Centro, Apdo 66, 83000 Hermosillo, Son.; tel. (662) 259-4700; fax (662) 217-4483; e-mail lector@elimparcial.com; internet www.elimparcial.com; f. 1937; morning; Pres. and Dir-Gen. JUAN F. HEALY; circ. 32,083, Sundays 32,444.

Tabasco

Tabasco Hoy: Avda de los Ríos 206, Col. Tabasco 2000, 86035 Villahermosa, Tab.; tel. (993) 316-2135; internet www.tabascohoy.com.mx; f. 1987; morning; Dir-Gen. MIGUEL CANTÓN ZETINA; circ. 50,000.

Tamaulipas

El Bravo: Morelos y Primera 129, Apdo 483, 87300 Matamoros, Tamps; tel. (871) 816-0100; fax (871) 816-2007; e-mail comenta@

MEXICO

elbravo.com.mx; f. 1951; morning; Pres. and Dir-Gen. JOSÉ CARRETERO BALBOA; circ. 60,000.

El Diario de Nuevo Laredo: González 2409, Apdo 101, 88000 Nuevo Laredo, Tamps; tel. (867) 711-5500; fax (867) 712-8221; internet www.diario.net; f. 1948; morning; Editor RUPERTO VILLARREAL MONTEMAYOR; circ. 68,130, Sundays 73,495.

Expresión: Calle 3 y Novedades 3, Col. Periodistas, 87457 Matamoros, Tamps; tel. (868) 817-9555; fax (868) 817-3307; e-mail xpresion@prodigy.net.mx; morning; Dir-Gen. MIGUEL GARAY AVILA; circ. 50,000.

El Mañana: Juárez y Perú, Col. Juárez, Nuevo Laredo, Tamps; tel. (867) 711-9900; fax (867) 715-0405; e-mail elmanana@elmanana.com.mx; internet www.elmanana.com.mx; f. 1932; morning; Pres. NINFA DEÁNDAR MARTÍNEZ; Editor HERIBERTO CANTÚ DEÁNDAR; circ. 16,473, Sundays 20,957.

El Mañana de Reynosa: Calle Matías Canales 504, Apdo 14, Col. Ribereña, 88620 Ciudad Reynosa, Tamps; tel. (899) 921-9950; fax (899) 924-9348; internet www.elmananarey.com.mx; f. 1949; morning; Chief Editors HERIBERTO DEÁNDAR ROBINSON, HILDEBRANDO DEÁNDAR AYALA; circ. 52,000.

Prensa de Reynosa: Matamoros y González Ortega, Zona Centro, 88500 Reynosa, Tamps; tel. (899) 922-0299; fax (899) 922-2412; e-mail prensa_88500@yahoo.com; internet www.prensadereynosa.com; f. 1963; morning; Dir-Gen. FÉLIX GARZA ELIZONDO; circ. 60,000.

El Sol de Tampico: Altamira 311 Pte, Apdo 434, 89000 Tampico, Tamps; tel. (833) 212-1067; fax (833) 212-6821; internet www.oem.com.mx/elsoldetampico; f. 1950; published by Organización Editorial Mexicana; morning; Dir-Gen. RUBÉN DÍAZ DE LA GARZA; circ. 77,000.

Veracruz

Diario del Istmo: Avda Hidalgo 1115, Col. Centro, 96400 Coatzacoalcos, Ver.; tel. (921) 211-8000; e-mail info@istmo.com.mx; internet www.diariodelistmo.com; f. 1979; morning; Dir-Gen. HÉCTOR ROBLES BARAJAS; circ. 64,600.

El Dictamen: 16 de Septiembre y Arista, 91700 Veracruz, Ver.; tel. (229) 931-1745; fax (229) 931-5804; e-mail dovali@hotmail.com; internet www.eldictamen.com.mx; f. 1898; morning; Pres. BERTHA ROSALIA MALPICA DE AHUED; circ. 25,000, Sundays 28,000.

La Opinión: Poza Rica de Hidalgo, Ver.; e-mail publicidad@laopinion.com.mx; internet www.laopinion.com.mx; Dir ABEL ANDRADE LICONA.

Yucatán

Diario de Yucatán: Calle 60 521, 97000 Mérida, Yuc.; tel. (999) 942-2222; fax (999) 942-2204; internet www.yucatan.com.mx; f. 1925; morning; Dir-Gen. CARLOS R. MENÉNDEZ NAVARRETE; circ. 54,639, Sundays 65,399.

Por Esto!: Calle 60, No 576 entre 73 y 71, 97000 Mérida, Yuc.; tel. (999) 24-7613; fax (999) 28-6514; e-mail redaccion@poresto.net; internet www.poresto.net; f. 1991; morning; Dir-Gen. MARIO RENATO MENÉNDEZ RODRÍGUEZ; circ. 26,985, Sundays 28,727.

Zacatecas

Imagen: Calzada Revolución 24, Col. Tierra y Libertad, 98600 Guadalupe, Zac.; tel. and fax (492) 923-8898; e-mail buzon@imagenzac.com.mx; internet www.imagenzac.com.mx; Dir-Gen. EUGENIO MERCADO.

SELECTED WEEKLY NEWSPAPERS

El Heraldo Bajio: Hermanos Aldama 222, Apdo 299, Zona Centro, 37000 León, Gto; tel. (477) 719-8800; e-mail heraldo@el-heraldo-bajio.com.mx; internet www.el-heraldo-bajio.com.mx; f. 1957; Pres. and Dir-Gen. MAURICIO BERCÚN LÓPEZ; circ. 85,000.

Segundamano: Insurgentes Sur 619, Col. Nápoles, Del. Benito Juárez, 03810 México, DF; tel. (55) 5350-7070; e-mail soporte@segundamano.com.mx; internet www.segundamano.com.mx; f. 1986; Dir-Gen. LUIS MAGAÑA MAGAÑA; circ. 105,000.

Zeta: Avda las Américas 4633, Fraccionamiento El Paraíso, Tijuana, BC; e-mail zeta@zetatijuana.com; internet www.zetatijuana.com; f. 1980; news magazine; Dir JESÚS BLANCORNELOS.

SELECTED PERIODICALS

Boletín Industrial: Luis Khune 55-B, Col. Las Águilas, 01710 México, DF; tel. (55) 5337-2200; fax (55) 5337-2222; e-mail ventas@boletinindustrial.com; internet www.boletinindustrial.com; f. 1983; monthly; Dir-Gen. HUMBERTO VALADÉS DÍAZ; circ. 22,000.

Casas & Gente: Amsterdam 112, Col. Hipódromo Condesa, 06100 México, DF; tel. (55) 5286-7794; fax (55) 5211-7112; e-mail informac@casasgente.com; internet www.casasgente.com; 10 a year; interior design; Dir-Gen. IGNACIO DÍAZ SÁNCHEZ.

Contenido: Darwin 101, Col. Anzures, 11590 México, DF; tel. (55) 5531-3162; fax (55) 5545-7478; e-mail contenido@contenido.com.mx; internet www.contenido.com.mx; f. 1963; monthly; popular appeal; Editor-in-Chief MARIANA CHAVEZ RODRÍGUEZ; circ. 124,190.

Cosmopolitan México: Vasco de Quiroga 2000, Col. Santa Fe, Del. Alvaro Obregón, 01210 México, DF; tel. (55) 5261-2600; fax (55) 5261-2704; internet www2.esmas.com/cosmopolitan; f. 1973; fortnightly; women's magazine; Dir SARA MARÍA CASTANY; circ. 300,000.

Expansión: Avda Constituyentes 956, Col. Lomas Altas, 11950 México, DF; tel. and fax (55) 9177-4100; e-mail quien@expansion.com.mx; internet www.expansion.com.mx; fortnightly; business and financial; Editor ARMANDO TALAMANTES.

Fama: Avda Eugenio Garza Sada 2245 Sur, Col. Roma, Apdo 3128, 64700 Monterrey, NL; tel. (81) 8359-2525; internet www.revistafama.com; fortnightly; show business; Pres. JESÚS D. GONZÁLEZ; Dir RAÚL MARTÍNEZ; circ. 350,000.

Gaceta Médica de México: Academia Nacional de Medicina, Unidad de Congresos del Centro Médico Nacional Siglo XXI, Bloque B, Avda Cuauhtémoc 330, Col. Doctores, 06725 México, DF; tel. (55) 5578-2044; fax (55) 5578-4271; internet www.medigraphic.com; f. 1864; every 2 months; journal of the Academia Nacional de Medicina de México; Editor ALFREDO ULLOA AGUIRRE; circ. 20,000.

Kena Mensual: Río Balsas 101, Col. Cuauhtémoc, 06500 México, DF; tel. (55) 5442-9600; e-mail corporativo@grupoarmonia.com.mx; f. 1977; fortnightly; women's interest; Editor GINA URETA; circ. 100,000.

Letras Libres: Chilaque 9, Col. San Diego Churubusco, 04120 México, DF; tel. (55) 9183-7800; fax (55) 9183-7836; e-mail revista@letraslibres.infonegocio.com; internet www.letraslibres.com; monthly; culture; Dir ENRIQUE KRAUZE.

Manufactura: Avda Constituyentes 956, esq. Rosaleda, Col. Lomas Altas, 11950 México, DF; tel. (55) 9177-4369; e-mail valcantara@expansion.com.mx; internet www.manufacturaweb.com; f. 1994; monthly; industrial; Dir-Gen. DAVID LUNA ARELLANO; circ. 25,000.

Marie Claire: Editorial Televisa, SA de CV, Avda Vasco de Quiroga 2000, Edif. E, 3°, Col. Santa Fe, 01210 México, DF; tel. (55) 5261-2622; fax (55) 5261-2733; e-mail mmartinezgom@editorial.televisa.com.mx; internet www.esmas.com/editorialtelevisa; f. 1990; monthly; women's interest; Editor MÓNICA MARTÍNEZ GÓMEZ; circ. 145,000.

Mecánica Popular (Popular Mechanics en Español): Vasco de Quiroga 2000, Col. Santa Fe, Del. Alvaro Obregón, 01210 México, DF; tel. (55) 5447-4711; fax (55) 5261-2705; internet www.mimecanicapopular.com; f. 1947; monthly; crafts and home improvements; Dir ANDRÉS JORGE; circ. 55,000.

Men's Health: Vasco de Quiroga 2000, Col. Santa Fe, Del. Alvaro Obregón, 01210 México, DF; tel. (55) 5261-2645; fax (55) 5261-2733; internet www.menshealth.com.mx; f. 1994; monthly; health; Editor JUAN ANTONIO SEMPERE; circ. 130,000.

Muy Interesante: Vasco de Quiroga 2000, Col. Santa Fe, Del. Alvaro Obregón, 01210 México, DF; tel. (55) 5261-2600; fax (55) 5261-2704; internet www.esmas.com/editorialtelevisa; f. 1984; monthly; scientific devt; Dir PILAR S. HOYOS; circ. 250,000.

Negocios y Bancos: Bolívar 8-103, Apdo 1907, Col. Centro, 06000 México, DF; tel. (55) 5510-1884; fax (55) 5512-9411; e-mail nego_bancos@mexico.com; f. 1951; fortnightly; business, economics; Dir ALFREDO FARRUGIA REED; circ. 10,000.

Proceso: Fresas 7, Col. del Valle, 03100 México, DF; tel. (55) 5636-2028; e-mail buzon@proceso.com.mx; internet www.proceso.com.mx; f. 1976; weekly; news analysis; Dir RAFAEL RODRÍGUEZ CASTAÑEDA; circ. 98,784.

Quién: Avda Constituyentes 956, Col. Lomas Altas, CP 11950, México, DF; tel. (55) 9177-4100; e-mail quien@expansion.com.mx; internet www.quien.com; fortnightly; celebrity news, TV, radio, films; Editor BLANCA GÓMEZ MORERA.

La Revista Peninsular: Calle 35, 489 x 52 y 54, Zona Centro, Mérida, Yuc.; tel. and fax (999) 926-3014; e-mail direccion@larevista.com.mx; internet www.larevista.com.mx; f. 1988; weekly; news and politics; Dir-Gen. RODRIGO MENÉNDEZ CÁMARA.

Selecciones del Reader's Digest: Avda Prolongación Paseo de la Reforma 1236, 10°, Col. Santa Fe, Del. Alvaro Obregón, 05348 México, DF; tel. (55) 5351-2200; internet www.selecciones.com; f. 1940; monthly; Editor AUDÓN CORIA; circ. 611,660.

Siempre!: Vallarta 20, Col. Tabacalera, 06030 México, DF; tel. and fax (55) 5566-1804; e-mail suscripciones@siempre.com.mx; internet www.siempre.com.mx; f. 1953; weekly; left of centre; Dir Lic. BEATRIZ PAGÉS REBOLLAR DE NIETO; circ. 100,000.

Tele-Guía: Vasco de Quiroga 2000, Col. Santa Fe, Del. Alvaro Obregón, 01210 México, DF; tel. (55) 5261-2600; fax (55) 5261-2704; internet www.esmas.com/editorialtelevisa; f. 1952; weekly; television guide; Editor MARÍA EUGENIA HERNÁNDEZ; circ. 375,000.

MEXICO

Tiempo Libre: Holbein 75 bis, Col. Nochebuena Mixcoac, Del. Benito Juárez, 03720 México, DF; tel. (55) 5611-2884; fax (55) 5611-3982; e-mail buzon@tiempolibre.com.mx; internet www.tiempolibre.com.mx; f. 1980; weekly; entertainment guide; Dir JUAN ALBERTO BECERRA; Editor ALICIA LABRA GÓMEZ; circ. 95,000.

Tú: Vasco de Quiroga 2000, Col. Santa Fe, Del. Alvaro Obregón, 01210 México, DF; tel. (55) 5261-2600; fax (55) 5261-2730; internet www.esmas.com/editorialtelevisa; f. 1980; monthly; teenage; Editor MARÍA ANTONIETA SALAMANCA; circ. 250,000.

TV y Novelas: Vasco de Quiroga 2000, Col. Santa Fe, Del. Alvaro Obregón, 01210 México, DF; tel. (55) 5261-2600; fax (55) 5261-2704; f. 1982; weekly; television guide and short stories; Dir JESÚS GALLEGOS; circ. 460,000.

Ultima Moda: Morelos 16, 6°, Col. Centro, 06040 México, DF; tel. (55) 5518-5481; fax (55) 5512-8902; e-mail revista_ultimamoda@yahoo.com.mx; f. 1966; monthly; fashion; Pres. ROMULO O'FARRILL, Jr; Gen. Man. Lic. SAMUEL PODOLSKY RAPOPORT; circ. 110,548.

Vanidades: Vasco de Quiroga 2000, Col. Santa Fe, Del. Alvaro Obregón, 01210 México, DF; tel. (55) 5261-2600; fax (55) 5261-2704; e-mail vanidades@editorialtelevisa.com; internet www.esmas.com/vanidades; f. 1961; fortnightly; women's magazine; Dir JAQUELINE BLANCO; circ. 290,000.

Vogue (México): Condé Nast México, México, DF; tel. (55) 5095-8076; fax (55) 5245-7109; f. 1999; monthly; women's fashion; circ. 208,180.

ASSOCIATIONS

Asociación Nacional de Periodistas y Comunicadores, A.C.: Luis G. Obregón 17, Of. 209, Col. Centro, 06020 México, DF; tel. (55) 5341-1523; Pres. MOISÉS HUERTA.

Federación de Asociaciones de Periodistas Mexicanos (Fapermex): Humboldt 5, Col. Centro, 06030 México, DF; tel. (55) 5510-2679; e-mail fapermexmail@gmail.com; internet www.fapermex.com; Pres. ROBERTO PIÑÓN OLIVAS; 88 mem. asscns; c. 9,000 mems.

Federación Latinoamericana de Periodistas (FELAP): Nuevo Leon 144, 1°, Col. Hipódromo Condesa, 06170 México, DF; tel. (55) 5286-6055; fax (55) 5286-6085; internet www.ciap-felap.org; Pres. JUAN CARLOS CAMAÑO; Sec.-Gen. JOSÉ RAFAEL VARGAS.

Fraternidad de Reporteros de México (FREMAC): Avda Juárez 88, Col. Centro, Del. Cuauhtémoc, México, DF; e-mail info@fremac.org.mx; internet www.fremac.org.mx; f. 1995; Sec.-Gen. MARCELA YARCE VIVEROS.

NEWS AGENCIES

Agencia de Información Integral Periodística (AIIP): Tabasco 263, Col. Roma, Del. Cuauhtémoc, 06700 México, DF; tel. (55) 5514-7389; fax (55) 5514-7389; e-mail aiipmx@aiip.com.mx; internet www.aiip.com.mx; f. 1987; Dir-Gen. MIGUEL HERRERA LÓPEZ.

Agencia Mexicana de Información (AMI): Avda Cuauhtémoc 16, Col. Doctores, 06720 México, DF; tel. (55) 5761-9933; e-mail info@red-ami.com; internet www.ami.com.mx; f. 1971; Dir-Gen. JOSÉ LUIS BECERRA LÓPEZ; Gen. Man. EVA VÁZQUEZ LÓPEZ.

Notimex, SA de CV: Morena 110, 3°, Col. del Valle, 03100 México, DF; tel. (55) 5420-1163; fax (55) 5420-1188; e-mail ventas@notimex.com.mx; internet www.notimex.com.mx; f. 1968; services to press, radio and television in Mexico and throughout the world; Dir-Gen. SERGIO UZETA MURCIO.

Publishers

MÉXICO, DF

Aguilar, Altea, Taurus, Alfaguara, SA de CV: Avda Universidad 767, Col. del Valle, 03100 México, DF; tel. (55) 5688-8966; fax (55) 5604-2304; f. 1965; general literature; Dir SEALTIEL ALATRISTE.

Arbol Editorial, SA de CV: Avda Cuauhtémoc 1430, Col. Santa Cruz Atoyac, 03310 México, DF; tel. (55) 5688-4828; fax (55) 5605-7600; e-mail editorialpax@maxis.com; f. 1979; health, philosophy, theatre; Man. Dir GERARDO GALLY TEOMONFORD.

Artes de México y del Mundo, SA de CV: Cordoba 69, Col. Roma, 06700 México, DF; tel. (55) 5525-5905; fax (55) 5525-5925; e-mail artesdemexico@artesdemexico.com; internet www.artesdemexico.com; f. 1988; art, design, poetry; Dir-Gen. ALBERTO RUY SÁNCHEZ LACY.

Editorial Avante, SA de CV: Luis G. Obregón 9, 1°, Apdo 45-796, Col. Centro, 06020 México, DF; tel. (55) 5510-8804; fax (55) 5521-5245; e-mail didactips@editorialavante.com.mx; internet www.editorialavante.com.mx; f. 1948; educational, drama, linguistics; Man. Dir Lic. MARIO A. HINOJOSA SAENZ.

Directory

Editorial Azteca, SA: Calle de la Luna 225–227, Col. Guerrero, 06300 México, DF; tel. (55) 5526-1157; fax (55) 5526-2557; internet www.circuloeditorialazteca.com.mx; f. 1956; religion, literature and technical; Man. Dir ALFONSO ALEMÓN JALOMO.

Cía Editorial Continental, SA de CV (CECSA): Renacimiento 180, Col. San Juan Tlihuaca, Azcapotzalco, 02400 México, DF; tel. (55) 5561-8333; fax (55) 5561-5231; e-mail info@patriacultural.com.mx; f. 1954; business, technology, general textbooks; Pres. CARLOS FRIGOLET LERMA.

Ediciones de Cultura Popular, SA: Odontología 76, Copilco Universidad, México, DF; f. 1969; history, politics, social sciences; Man. Dir URIEL JARQUÍN GALVEZ.

Editorial Diana, SA de CV: Arenal 24, Edif. Norte, Ex-Hacienda Guadalupe, Chimalistac, Del. Alvaro Obregón, 01050 México, DF; tel. (55) 5089-1220; fax (55) 5089-1230; internet www.editorialdiana.com.mx; f. 1946; general trade and technical books; Pres. and CEO JOSÉ LUIS RAMÍREZ.

Ediciones Era, SA de CV: Calle del Trabajo 31, Col. La Fama, Tlalpan, 14269 México, DF; tel. (55) 5528-1221; fax (55) 5606-2904; e-mail edicionesera@laneta.apc.org; internet www.edicionesera.com.mx; f. 1960; general and social science, art and literature; Gen. Man. NIEVES ESPRESATE XIRAU.

Editorial Everest Mexicana, SA: Calzada Ermita Iztapalapa 1631, Col. Barrio San Miguel del Iztapalapa, 09360 México, DF; tel. (55) 5685-1966; fax (55) 5685-3433; f. 1980; general textbooks; Gen. Man. JOSÉ LUIS HUIDOBRO LEÓN.

Fernández Editores, SA de CV: Eje 1 Pte México-Coyoacán 321, Col. Xoco, 03330 México, DF; tel. (55) 5605-6557; fax (55) 5688-9173; f. 1943; children's literature, textbooks, educational toys; Man. Dir LUIS GERARDO FERNÁNDEZ PÉREZ.

Editorial Fondo de Cultura Económica, SA de CV: Carretera Picacho-Ajusco 227, Col. Bosques del Pedregal, 14200 México, DF; tel. (55) 5227-4672; fax (55) 5227-4640; e-mail juan.cortes@fondodeculturaeconomica.com; internet www.fondodeculturaeconomica.com; f. 1934; economics, history, philosophy, children's books, science, politics, psychology, sociology, literature; Dir JUAN FRANCISCO CORTÉS GONZÁLEZ.

Nueva Editorial Interamericana, SA de CV: Cedro 512, Col. Atlampa, Apdo 4-140, 06450 México, DF; tel. (55) 5541-6789; fax (55) 5541-1603; f. 1944; medical publishing; Man. Dir RAFAEL SÁINZ.

Distribuidora Intermex, SA de CV: Lucio Blanco 435, Azcapotzalco, 02400 México, DF; tel. (55) 5230-9500; fax (55) 5230-9516; f. 1969; romantic fiction; Gen. Dir Lic. ALEJANDRO PAILLÉS.

Editorial Jus, SA de CV: Avda Constituyentes 647, 3°, Col. 16 de Septiembre, 11810 México, DF; tel. (55) 5093-1925; fax (55) 5529-0951; internet www.jus.com.mx; f. 1938; history of Mexico, law, philosophy, economy, religion; Man. TOMÁS G. REYNOSO.

Ediciones Larousse, SA de CV: Londres 247, Col. Juárez, Del. Cuauhtémoc, 06600 México, DF; tel. (55) 1102-1300; fax (55) 5208-6225; e-mail psala@larousse.com.mx; internet www.larousse.com.mx; f. 1965; Dir-Gen. GERARDO GUERRERO (acting).

Libros para Todos (EDAMEX): Heriberto Frias 1104, Col. del Valle, 03100 México, DF; tel. (55) 5559-8588; fax (55) 5575-0555; e-mail octaviocolmenares@edamex.com; internet www.edamex.com; arts and literature, sport, journalism, education, philosophy, food, history, children's, health, sociology.

Editorial Limusa, SA de CV: Balderas 95, 1°, Col. Centro, 06040 México, DF; tel. (55) 5521-2105; fax (55) 5510-9415; internet www.noriega.com.mx; f. 1962; science, general, textbooks; Pres. CARLOS NORIEGA MILERA.

McGraw-Hill Interamericana de México, SA de CV: Torre A, 17°, Paseo de la Reforma 1015, Col. Santa Fé, 01376 México, DF; tel. (55) 1500-5000; internet www.mcgraw-hill.com.mx; education, business, science; Man. Dir CARLOS RIOS.

Medios Publicitarios Mexicanos, SA de CV: Eugenia 811, Eje 5 Sur, Col. del Valle, 03100 México, DF; tel. (55) 5523-3342; fax (55) 5523-3379; e-mail editorial@mpm.com.mx; internet www.mpm.com.mx; f. 1958; advertising media rates and data; Gen. Man. FERNANDO VILLAMIL.

Editorial Nuestro Tiempo, SA: Avda Universidad 771, Despachos 103–104, Col. del Valle, 03100 México, DF; tel. (55) 5688-8768; fax (55) 5688-6868; f. 1966; social sciences; Man. Dir ESPERANZA NACIF BARQUET.

Editorial Oasis, SA: Avda Oaxaca 28, 06700 México, DF; tel. (55) 5528-8293; f. 1954; literature, pedagogy, poetry; Man. MARÍA TERESA ESTRADA DE FERNÁNDEZ DEL BUSTO.

Editorial Orión: Sierra Mojada 325, 11000 México, DF; tel. (55) 5520-0224; f. 1942; archaeology, philosophy, psychology, literature, fiction; Man. Dir SILVIA HERNÁNDEZ BALTAZAR.

Editorial Patria, SA de CV: Renacimiento 180, Col. San Juan Tlihuaca, Del. Azcapotzalco, 02400 México, DF; tel. (55) 5354-9100; fax (55) 5354-9109; e-mail info@editorialpatria.com.mx; internet

MEXICO   Directory

www.patriacultural.com.mx; f. 1933; fiction, general trade, children's books; Pres. CARLOS FRIGOLET LERMA.

Editorial Planeta Mexicana, SA de CV: Clavijero 70, Col. Esperanza, México, DF; tel. (55) 5533-1250; internet www.editorialplaneta.com.mx; general literature, non-fiction; part of Grupo Planeta (Spain); Grupo Planeta incorporates Ariel, Crítica, Destino, Deusto, Ediciones del Bronce, Editorial Joaquín Mortiz, Emecé, Espasa, Martínez Roca, Seix Barral and Temas de Hoy; Man. Dir JOAQUIN DIEZ-CANEDO.

Editorial Porrúa Hnos, SA: Argentina 15, 5°, 06020 México, DF; tel. (55) 5704-7578; fax (55) 5702-6529; e-mail servicios@porrua.com; internet www.porrua.com; f. 1944; general literature; Dir JOSÉ ANTONIO PÉREZ PORRÚA.

Editorial Posada, SA de CV: Eugenia 13, Despacho 501, Col. Nápoles, 03510 México, DF; tel. (55) 5682-0660; f. 1968; general; Dir-Gen. CARLOS VIGIL ZUBIETA.

Editorial Quetzacoatl, SA: Medicina 37, Local 1 y 2, México, DF; tel. (55) 5548-6180; Man. Dir ALBERTO RODRÍGUEZ VALDÉS.

Random House Mondadori, SA de CV: Homero 544, Col. Chapultepec Morales, 11570, México, DF; tel. (55) 3067-8400; e-mail diredit@grijalbo.com.mx; internet www.randomhousemondadori.com.mx; f. 1954; owned by Mondadori (Italy); general fiction, history, sciences, philosophy, children's books; Man. Dir AGUSTÍN CENTENO RÍOS.

Reverté Ediciones, SA de CV: Río Pánuco 141A, Col. Cuauhtémoc, 06500 México, DF; tel. (55) 5533-5658; fax (55) 5514-6799; e-mail reverte@reverte.com.mx; internet www.reverte.com; f. 1955; science, technical, architecture; Man. RAMÓN REVERTÉ MASCÓ.

Salvat Mexicana de Ediciones, SA de CV: Presidente Masaryk 101, 5°, 11570 México, DF; tel. (55) 5250-6041; fax (55) 5250-6861; medicine, encyclopaedic works; Dir GUILLERMO HERNÁNDEZ PÉREZ.

Siglo XXI Editores, SA de CV: Avda Cerro del Agua 248, Col. Romero de Terreros, Del. Coyoacán, 04310 México, DF; tel. (55) 5658-7999; fax (55) 5658-7599; e-mail informes@sigloxxieditores.com.mx; internet www.sigloxxieditores.com.mx; f. 1966; art, economics, education, history, social sciences, literature, philology and linguistics, philosophy and political science; Dir-Gen. Dr JAIME LABASTIDA OCHOA; Gen. Man. JOSÉ MARÍA CASTRO MUSSOT.

Editorial Trillas, SA: Avda Río Churubusco 385 Pte, Col. Xoco, Apdo 10534, 03330 México, DF; tel. (55) 5688-4233; fax (55) 5601-1858; e-mail ftrillas@trillas.com.mx; internet www.trillas.com.mx; f. 1954; science, technical, textbooks, children's books; Man. Dir FRANCISCO TRILLAS MERCADER.

Universidad Nacional Autónoma de México: Dirección General de Fomento Editorial, Avda del Imán 5, Ciudad Universitaria, 04510 México, DF; tel. (55) 5622-6572; internet www.unam.mx; f. 1935; publications in all fields; Dir-Gen. ARTURO VELÁZQUEZ JIMÉNEZ.

ESTADO DE MÉXICO

Pearson Educación de México, SA de CV: Atlacomulco 500, 4°, Industrial Atoto, Naucalpan de Juárez, Méx.; tel. (55) 5387-0700; fax (55) 5358-6445; internet www.pearsoneducacion.net; f. 1984; educational books under the imprints Addison-Wesley, Prentice Hall, Allyn and Bacon, Longman and Scott Foresman; Pres. STEVE MARBAN.

ASSOCIATIONS

Cámara Nacional de la Industria Editorial Mexicana: Holanda 13, Col. San Diego Churubusco, 04120 México, DF; tel. (55) 5688-2011; fax (55) 5604-3147; e-mail consejodirectivo@caniem.com; internet www.caniem.com; f. 1964; Pres. JUAN LUIS ARZOZ ARBIDE; Sec. PATRICIA VAN RHIJN ARMIDA.

Instituto Mexicano del Libro, AC: México, DF; tel. (55) 5535-2061; Pres. KLAUS THIELE; Sec.-Gen. ISABEL RUIZ GONZÁLEZ.

Broadcasting and Communications

TELECOMMUNICATIONS

Regulatory Authorities

Comisión Federal de Telecomunicaciones (Cofetel): Bosque de Radiatas 44, 4°, Col. Bosques de las Lomas, Del. Cuajimalpa, 05120 México, DF; tel. and fax (55) 5015-4000; e-mail nuevaimagen@cft.gob.mx; internet www.cofetel.gob.mx; Pres. HÉCTOR OSUNA.

Dirección General de Política de Telecomunicaciones: Avda Xola y Universidad s/n, Col. Narvarte, Del. Benito Juárez, 03020 México, DF; tel. (55) 5723-9369; fax (55) 5723-9300; e-mail holavarr@sct.gob.mx; internet www.sct.gob.mx; part of Secretariat of State for Communications and Transport; Dir HECTOR OLAVARRÍA TAPIA.

Principal Operators

Alestra: Paseo de las Palmas 405, Col. Lomas de Chapultepec, 11000 México, DF; tel. (55) 8503-5000; internet www.alestra.com.mx; 49% owned by AT&T; Dir-Gen. ROLANDO ZUBIRÁN SHETLER.

América Móvil, SA de CV: Lago Alberto 366, Edif. Telcel 2, Col. Anáhuac, 11320 México, DF; tel. (55) 2581-3947; fax (55) 2581-3948; e-mail patricia.ramirez@americamovil.com; internet www.americamovil.com; f. 2000; subsidiaries operate mobile telephone services in 17 countries in the Americas; CEO DANIEL HAJJ ABOUMRAD.

   Telcel: internet www.telcel.com; subsidiary of above, providing mobile services in Mexico; COO PATRICIA RAQUEL HEVIA COTO.

AT&T México: Montes Urales 470, Col. Lomas de Chapultepec, 11000 México, DF; internet www.att.com.

Avantel: Liverpool 88, Col. Juárez, 06600 México, DF; e-mail servicioaclientes@avantel.com.mx; internet www.avantel.net.mx; f. 1994; Dir-Gen. OSCAR RODRÍGUEZ MARTÍNEZ.

Axtel: Blvd Díaz Ordáz Km 3.33, Zona Industrial, 66215 San Pedro Garza García, NL; tel. (81) 8114-0000; e-mail contacto@axtel.com.mx; internet www.axtel.com.mx; f. 1993; fixed-line operator.

Carso Global Telecom, SA de CV: Insurgentes Sur 3500, Col. Peña Pobre, 14060 México, DF; tel. (55) 5726-3686; fax (55) 5238-0601; internet www.cgtelecom.com.mx; f. 1996; subsidiaries include Telmex and Global Telecom; Pres. JAIME CHICO PARDO.

   Teléfonos de México, SA de CV (Telmex): Parque Vía 190, Col. Cuauhtémoc, 06599 México, DF; tel. (55) 5222-1212; fax (55) 5545-5500; e-mail ri@telmex.com; internet www.telmex.com.mx; Pres. CARLOS SLIM DOMIT; Dir-Gen. HÉCTOR SLIM SEADE.

Grupo Iusacell, SA de CV: Avda Prolongación Paseo de la Reforma 1236, Col. Santa Fe, 05438 México, DF; tel. (55) 5109-0611; e-mail webmaster@iusacell.com.mx; internet www.iusacell.com.mx; f. 1992; a merger with Unefon was announced in Sept. 2006; operates mobile cellular telephone network; 74% owned by Móvil Access; Dir-Gen. GUSTAVO GUZMÁN SEPÚLVEDA.

Maxcom Telecomunicaciones, SAB de CV: Guillermo González Camarena 2000, Col. Centro Ciudad Santa Fe, 01210 México, DF; tel. (55) 5147-1111; internet www.maxcom.com; f. 1996; fixed-line operator; Pres. ADRIÁN AGUIRRE GÓMEZ; Dir-Gen. RENÉ SAGASTUY FERRANDIZ.

Telecomunicaciones de México (TELECOMM): Torre Central de Telecomunicaciones, Eje Central Lázaro Cárdenas 567, 11°, Ala Norte, Col. Narvarte, Del. Benito Juárez, 03020 México, DF; tel. (55) 5090-1166; fax (55) 1035-2408; e-mail figueroa@telecomm.net.mx; internet www.telecomm.net.mx; govt-owned; Dir-Gen. ANDRÉS FIGUEROA COBIÁN.

Telefónica México: Prolongación Paseo de la Reforma 1200, Lote B-2, Col. Santa Fe, Cruz Manca, 05348 México, DF; tel. (55) 1616-5000; internet www.telefonicamoviles.com.mx; operates mobile telephone service Telefónica Móviles México (MoviStar), telecommunications co Telefónica Data; controls Pegaso, Cedetel, Norcel, Movitel and Baja Celular; owned by Telefónica, SA (Spain); Pres. FRANCISCO GIL DÍAZ; CEO MIGUEL MENCHEN.

Unefon: Periférico Sur 4119, Col. Fuentes del Pedregal, 14141 México, DF; tel. (55) 8582-5000; e-mail ainfante@unefon.com.mx; internet www.unefon.com.mx; mobile operator; a merger with Grupo Iusacell was announced in Sept. 2006.

BROADCASTING

Regulatory Authority

Dirección General de Sistemas de Radio y Televisión (DGSRT): Roma 41, Col. Juaréz, Del. Cuauhtémoc, 06600 México, DF; tel. (55) 5723-9300; fax (55) 5530-4315; e-mail jrodrigc@sct.gob.mx; internet www.rtc.gob.mx; Dir-Gen. JORGE ALBERTO RODRIGUEZ CASTAÑEDA.

Radio

There were 1,423 radio stations in Mexico in 2004. Among the most important commercial networks are:

ARTSA: Avda de Los Virreyes 1030, Col. Lomas de Chapultepec, 11000 México, DF; tel. (55) 5202-3344; fax (55) 5202-6940; Dir-Gen. Lic. GUSTAVO ECHEVARRÍA ARCE.

Corporación Mexicana de Radiodifusión: Tetitla 23, esq. Calle Coapa, Col. Toriello Guerra, 14050 México, DF; tel. (55) 5424-6380; fax (55) 5666-5422; e-mail comentarios@cmr.com.mx; internet www.cmr.com.mx; Pres. ENRIQUE BERNAL SERVÍN; Dir-Gen. OSCAR BELTRÁN.

Firme, SA: Gauss 10, Col. Nueva Anzures, 11590 México, DF; tel. and fax (55) 5250-7788; Dir-Gen. LUIS IGNACIO SANTIBÁÑEZ.

Grupo Acir, SA: Monte Pirineos 770, Col. Lomas de Chapultepec, 11000 México, DF; tel. (55) 5201-1700; fax (55) 5201-1771; e-mail chernandez@fundacionacir.org.mx; internet www.grupoacir.com

MEXICO   *Directory*

.mx; f. 1965; comprises 140 stations; Exec. Pres. Mari Carmen Ibarra Fariña; Dir Cecilia Hernández Avalos.

Grupo Radio Centro, SA de CV: Constituyentes 1154, Col. Lomas Atlas, Del. Miguel Hidalgo, 11950 México, DF; tel. (55) 5728-4947; fax (55) 5259-2915; e-mail rcentro@grc.com.mx; internet radiocentro .com.mx; f. 1965; comprises 100 radio stations; Pres. Adrián Aguirre Gómez; Dir-Gen. Ing. Gilberto Solis Silva.

Grupo Siete Comunicación: Montecito 38, 31°, Of. 33, México, DF; tel. (55) 9000-0787; fax (55) 9000-0747; e-mail jch@gruposiete.com .mx; internet www.gruposiete.com.mx; f. 1997; Pres. Lic. Francisco Javier Sánchez Campuzano.

Instituto Mexicano de la Radio (IMER): Mayorazgo 83, 2°, Col. Xoco, 03330 México, DF; tel. (55) 5628-1704; internet www.imer.com .mx; f. 1983; Dir-Gen. Ana Cecilia Terrazas Valdés.

MVS Radio Stereorey y FM Globo: Mariano Escobedo 532, Col. Anzures, 11590 México, DF; tel. (55) 5203-4574; fax (55) 5255-1425; e-mail vargas@data.net.mx; f. 1968; Pres. Lic. Joaquín Vargas G.; Vice-Pres. Lic. Adrián Vargas G.

Núcleo Radio Mil: Prolongación Paseo de la Reforma 115, Col. Paseo de las Lomas, Santa Fe, 01330 México, DF; tel. (55) 5258-1200; e-mail radiomil@rnm.com.mx; internet www.nrm.com.mx; f. 1942; comprises seven radio stations; Pres. and Dir-Gen. Lic. E. Guillermo Salas Peyró.

Organización Radio Centro: Artículo 123, No 90, Col. Centro, 06050 México, DF; tel. (55) 5709-2220; fax (55) 512-8588; nine stations in Mexico City; Pres. María Esther Gómez de Aguirre.

Organización Radiofónica de México, SA: Tuxpan 39, 8°, Col. Roma Sur, 06760 México, DF; tel. (55) 5264-2025; fax (55) 5264-5720; Pres. Jaime Fernández Armendáriz.

Radio Cadena Nacional, SA (RCN): Lago Victoria 78, Col. Granada, 11520 México, DF; tel. (55) 2624-0401; e-mail loregonzalez@rcn.com.mx; internet www.rcn.com.mx; f. 1948; Pres. Rafael C. Navarro Arronte; Dir-Gen. Sergio Fajardo Ortiz.

Radio Educación: Angel Urraza 622, Col. del Valle, 03100 México, DF; tel. (55) 4155-1050; e-mail direccion@radioeducacion.edu.mx; internet www.radioeducacion.edu.mx; f. 1968; Dir-Gen. Virginia Bello Méndez.

Radio Fórmula, SA: Privada de Horacio 10, Col. Polanco, 11560 México, DF; tel. (55) 5282-1016; e-mail www.radioformula.com.mx; Dir Rogerio Azcarraga.

Radiodifusoras Asociadas, SA de CV (RASA): Durango 341, 2°, Col. Roma, 06700 México, DF; tel. (55) 5286-1222; fax (55) 5211-6159; e-mail rasa@rasa.com.mx; internet www.rasa.com.mx; f. 1956; Exec. Pres. José Laris Rodríguez.

Radiodifusores Asociados de Innovación y Organización, SA: Emerson 408, Col. Chapultepec Morales, 11570 México, DF; tel. (55) 5203-5577; fax (55) 5545-2078; Dir-Gen. Lic. Carlos Quiñones Armendáriz.

Radiópolis, SA de CV: owned by Grupo Televisa and Grupo Prisa; owns 5 radio stations; affiliated to Radiorama, SA de CV (q.v.) in 2004; Dir-Gen. Raúl Rodríguez González.

Radiorama, SA de CV: Reforma 2620, 2°, Col. Lomas, 11950 México, DF; tel. (55) 1105-0000; fax (55) 1105-0002; e-mail grupo@ radiorama.com.mx; internet www.radiorama.com.mx; Dir José Luis C. Reséndiz.

Representaciones Comerciales Integrales: Avda Chapultepec 431, Col. Juárez, 06600 México, DF; tel. (55) 5533-6185; Dir-Gen. Alfonso Palma V.

Sistema Radio Juventud: Pablo Casals 567, Prados Providencia, 44670 Guadalajara, Jal.; tel. (33) 3641-6677; fax (33) 3641-3413; f. 1975; network of several stations including Estereo Soul 89.9 FM; Dirs Alberto Leal A., J. Jesús Orozco G., Gabriel Arregui V.

Sistema Radiofónico Nacional, SA: Baja California 163, Of. 602, 06760 México, DF; tel. (55) 5574-0298; f. 1971; represents commercial radio networks; Dir-Gen. René C. de la Rosa.

Sociedad Mexicana de Radio, SA de CV (SOMER): Paseo de la Reforma 115, 4°, Col. Lomas, Santa Fé, 01330 México, DF; tel. (55) 9177-6660; fax (55) 9177-6671; e-mail somer@somer.com.mx; internet www.somer.com.mx; Dir-Gen. Edilberto Huesca Perrotin.

Radio Insurgente, the underground radio station of the Ejército Zapatista de Liberación Nacional (EZLN—Zapatistas), is broadcast from south-eastern Mexico. Programmes can be found on www.radioinsurgente.org.

Television

There were 658 television stations in 2004. Among the most important are:

Asesoramiento y Servicios Técnicos Industriales, SA (ASTISA): México, DF; tel. (55) 5585-3333; commercial; Dir Roberto Chávez Tinajero.

MVS (Multivisión): Blvd Puerto Aéreo 486, Col. Moctezuma, 15500 México, DF; tel. (55) 5764-8100; e-mail orivas@mvs.com; internet www.mvs.com; subscriber-funded; Pres. Joaquín Vargas Guajardo; Vice-Pres. Ernesto Vargas.

Once TV: Carpio 475, Col. Casco de Santo Tomás, 11340 México, DF; tel. (55) 5166-4000; e-mail info@mail.oncetv.ipn.mx; internet www .oncetv.ipn.mx; f. 1959; Dir Fernando Sariñana Márquez.

Tele Cadena Mexicana, SA: Avda Chapultepec 18, 06724 México, DF; tel. (55) 5535-1679; commercial, comprises about 80 stations; Dir Jorge Armando Piña Medina.

Televisa, SA de CV: Edif. Televicentro, Avda Chapultepec 28, Col. Doctores, 06724 México, DF; tel. (55) 5709-3333; fax (55) 5709-3021; e-mail webmaster@televisa.com.mx; internet www.televisa.com; f. 1973; commercial; began broadcasts to Europe via satellite in Dec. 1988 through its subsidiary, Galavisión; 406 affiliated stations; Chair. and CEO Emilio Azcárraga Jean.

Televisión Azteca, SA de CV: Anillo Periférico Sur 4121, Col. Fuentes del Pedregal, 14141 México, DF; tel. (55) 5447-8844; fax (55) 5645-4258; e-mail webtva@tvazteca.com; internet www.tvazteca .com; f. 1992; assumed responsibility for fmr state-owned channels 7 and 13; Pres. Ricardo B. Salinas Pliego; CEO Pedro Padilla Longoria.

Televisión de la República Mexicana: Mina 24, Col. Guerrero, México, DF; tel. (55) 5510-8590; cultural; Dir Eduardo Lizalde.

Association

Cámara Nacional de la Industria de Radio y Televisión (CIRT): Avda Horacio 1013, Col. Polanco Reforma, Del. Miguel Hidalgo, 11550 México, DF; tel. (55) 5726-9909; fax (55) 5545-6767; e-mail cirt@cirt.com.mx; internet www.cirt.com.mx; f. 1942; Pres. Enrique Pereda Gómez; Dir-Gen. Andrés Massieu Fernández.

Finance

(cap. = capital; res = reserves; dep. = deposits; m. = million; brs = branches; amounts in new pesos unless otherwise stated)

BANKING

The Mexican banking system is comprised of the Banco de México (the central bank of issue), multiple or commercial banking institutions and development banking institutions. Banking activity is regulated by the Federal Government.

Commercial banking institutions are constituted as *Sociedades Anónimas*, with wholly private social capital. Development banking institutions exist as *Sociedades Nacionales de Crédito*; participation in their capital is exclusive to the Federal Government, notwithstanding the possibility of accepting limited amounts of private capital. In 2005 there were 34 commercial and development banks operating in Mexico, and 71 foreign banks maintained offices.

All private banks were nationalized in September 1982. By July 1992, however, the banking system had been completely returned to the private sector. Legislation removing all restrictions on foreign ownership of banks received congressional approval in 1999.

Supervisory Authority

Comisión Nacional Bancaria y de Valores (CNBV) (National Banking and Securities Commission): Avda Insurgentes Sur 1971, Torre Norte, Sur y III, Col. Guadalupe Inn, Del. Alvaro Obregón, 01020 México, DF; tel. and fax (55) 1454-6000; e-mail info@cnbv.gob .mx; internet www.cnbv.gob.mx; f. 1924; govt commission controlling all credit institutions in Mexico; Pres. Guillermo Enrique Babatz Torres.

Central Bank

Banco de México (BANXICO): Avda 5 de Mayo 2, Col. Centro, Del. Cuauhtémoc, 06059 México, DF; tel. (55) 5237-2000; fax (55) 5237-2070; e-mail comsoc@banxico.org.mx; internet www.banxico.org.mx; f. 1925; currency issuing authority; became autonomous on 1 April 1994; cap. 5,995m., res –96,843m., dep. 687,906m. (Dec. 2006); Gov. Dr Guillermo Ortiz Martínez; 6 brs.

Commercial Banks

Banco del Bajío, SA: Avda Manuel J. Clouthier 508, Col. Jardines del Campestre, 37128 León, Gto; tel. (477) 710-4600; fax (477) 710-4693; e-mail internacional@bancobajio.com.mx; internet www .bancobajio.com.mx; f. 1994; cap. 2,039.1m., res 4,364.6m., dep. 44,372.6m. (Dec. 2007); Pres. Salvador Oñate.

Banco Mercantil del Norte, SA (BANORTE): Avda Revolución 3000, Col. Primavera, 64830 Monterrey, NL; tel. (81) 3319-7200; fax (81) 3319-5216; internet www.banorte.com; f. 1899; merged with Banco Regional del Norte in 1985; cap. 11,811.0m., res 12,169.0m.,

MEXICO
Directory

dep. 220,561.0m. (Dec. 2007); Chair. ROBERTO GONZÁLEZ BARRERA; Dir-Gen. ALEJANDRO VALENZUELA; 457 brs.

Banco Nacional de México, SA (Banamex): Avda Isabel la Católica 44, 06089 México, DF; tel. (55) 5720-7091; fax (55) 5920-7323; internet www.banamex.com; f. 1884; transferred to private ownership in 1991; merged with Citibank México, SA in 2001; cap. 30,248.0m., res 53,010.0m., dep. 400,191.0m. (Dec. 2007); CEO MANUEL MEDINA MORA; 1,260 brs.

Banca Santander, SA: Mod 401, 4°, Prolongación Paseo de la Reforma 500, Col. Lomas de Santa Fe, Del. Alvaro Obregon, 01219 México, DF; tel. (55) 5261-1543; fax (55) 5261-5549; internet www.santander.com.mx; f. 1864 as Banco Serfin; acquired by Banco Santander Central Hispano (Spain) in Dec. 2000; adopted current name 2006; cap. 27,013.0m., res 3,309.0m., dep. 312,640m. (Dec. 2007); Chair. and Pres. CARLOS GÓMEZ; Dir-Gen. MARCOS MARTÍNEZ GAVICA; 554 brs.

BBVA Bancomer, SA: Centro Bancomer, Avda Universidad 1200, Col. Xoco, 03339 México, DF; tel. (55) 5621-3434; fax (55) 5621-3230; internet www.bancomer.com.mx; f. 2000 by merger of Bancomer (f. 1864) and Mexican operations of Banco Bilbao Vizcaya Argentaria (Spain); privatized in 2002; cap. 15,247.9m., res 31,795.5m., dep. 455,671.6m. (Dec. 2005); Pres. and Dir-Gen. IGNACIO DESCHAMPS GONZÁLEZ.

Dresdner Bank Mexico, SA: Blvd M. A. Camacho 164, 4°, Col. Lomas de Barrilaco, 11010 México, DF; tel. (55) 5258-3170; fax (55) 5258-3199; e-mail mexico@dbla.com; f. 1995; Man. Dir LUIS NIÑO DE RIVERA.

HSBC México: Paseo de la Reforma 156, Col. Juárez, Del. Cuauhtémoc, 06600 México, DF; tel. (55) 5721-2222; fax (55) 5721-2393; internet www.hsbc.com.mx; f. 1941; bought by HSBC (United Kingdom) in 2002; name changed from Banco Internacional, SA (BITAL) in 2004; cap. 3,929.6m., res 16,214.7m., dep. 239,916.6m. (Dec. 2006); CEO PAUL THURSTON; 1,400 brs.

Scotiabank Inverlat, SA: Blvd Miguel Avila Camacho 1, 18°, Col. Lomas de Chapultepec, Del. Miguel Hidalgo, 11009 México, DF; tel. (55) 5728-1000; fax (55) 5229-2019; internet www.scotiabankinverlat.com; f. 1977 as Multibanco Comermex, SA; changed name to Banco Inverlat, SA in 1995; 55% holding acquired by Scotiabank Group (Canada) and adopted current name 2001; cap. 7,451.0m., surplus and res 10,890.0m., dep. 106,756.0m. (Dec. 2007); Pres. PETER C. CARDINAL; 476 brs.

Development Banks

Banco Nacional de Comercio Exterior, SNC (BANCOMEXT): Periférico Sur 4333, Col. Jardines en la Montaña, Del. Tlalpan, 14210 México, DF; tel. (55) 5449-9100; fax (55) 5652-9342; internet www.bancomext.com; f. 1937; cap. 11,040.0m., res -2,504.0m., dep. 67,444.0m. (Dec. 2007); Dir-Gen. MARIO MARTÍN LABORÍN GÓMEZ.

Banco Nacional del Ejército, Fuerza Aérea y Armada, SNC (BANJERCITO): Avda Industria Militar 1055, Col. Lomas de Sotelo, 11200 México, DF; tel. and fax (55) 5626-0500; e-mail info@banjercito.com.mx; internet www.banjercito.com.mx; f. 1947; Dir-Gen. Maj.-Gen. FERNANDO MILLÁN VILLEGAS.

Banco Nacional de Obras y Servicios Públicos, SNC (BANOBRAS): Avda Javier Barros Sierra 515, Col. Lomas de Santa Fe, 01219 México, DF; tel. (55) 5270-1552; fax (55) 5270-1564; internet www.banobras.gob.mx; f. 1933; govt-owned; cap. 15,540.0m., res 327.0m., dep. 107,052.0m. (Dec. 2007); Dir-Gen. ALONSO GARCÍA TAMÉS.

Compartamos Banco: Insurgentes Sur 551, 1°, Col. Escandón, 11800 México, DF; tel. (55) 5276-7250; fax (55) 5276-7299; e-mail servicioalcliente@compartamos.com; internet www.compartamos.com; f. 1990; Dir-Gen. CARLOS LABARTHE COSTAS.

Financiera Rural: Agrarismo 227, Col. Escandón, Del. Miguel Hidalgo, CP 11800, México, DF; tel. (55) 5230-1600; internet www.financierarural.gob.mx; f. 2004; state-run devt bank, concerned with agricultural, forestry and fishing sectors; Dir-Gen. ENRIQUE DE LA MADRID CORDERO.

Nacional Financiera, SNC (NAFIN): Insurgentes Sur 1971, Torre IV, 13°, Col. Guadalupe Inn, 01020 México, DF; tel. (55) 5325-6700; fax (55) 5661-8418; e-mail info@nafin.gob.mx; internet www.nafin.com; f. 1934; cap. 7,661m., res 3,528m., dep. 178,860m. (Dec. 2006); Dir-Gen. MARIO MARTÍN LABORÍN GÓMEZ; 32 brs.

BANKERS' ASSOCIATION

Asociación de Bancos de México: 16 de Setiembre 27, Col. Centro Histórico, 06000 México, DF; tel. (55) 5722-4305; internet www.abm.org.mx; f. 1928; Pres. ENRIQUE CASTILLO; Dir-Gen. JUAN CARLOS JIMÉNEZ ROJAS; 52 mems.

STOCK EXCHANGE

Bolsa Mexicana de Valores, SA de CV: Paseo de la Reforma 255, Col. Cuauhtémoc, 06500 México, DF; tel. (55) 5726-6000; fax (55) 5726-6836; e-mail cinforma@bmv.com.mx; internet www.bmv.com.mx; f. 1894; Pres. GUILLERMO PRIETO DE CASTILLA; Dir-Gen. Ing. GERARDO FLORES DEUCHLER.

INSURANCE
México, DF

ACE Seguros: Bosques de Alisos, 47A, 1°, Col. Bosques de las Lomas, 5120 México, DF; tel. (5) 258-5800; fax (5) 258-5899; e-mail info@acelatinamerica.com; f. 1990; fmrly Seguros Cigna.

Aseguradora Cuauhtémoc, SA: Manuel Avila Camacho 164, 11570 México, DF; tel. (55) 5250-9800; fax (55) 5540-3204; f. 1944; general; Exec. Pres. JUAN B. RIVEROLL; Dir-Gen. JAVIER COMPEÁN AMEZCUA.

Aseguradora Hidalgo, SA: Presidente Masaryk 111, Col. Polanco, Del. Miguel Hidalgo, 11570 México, DF; f. 1931; life; Dir-Gen. JOSÉ GÓMEZ GORDOA; Man. Dir HUMBERTO ROQUE VILLANUEVA.

Grupo Nacional Provincial, SAB: Avda Cerro de las Torres 395, Col. Campestre Churubusco, Del. Coyoacán, 04200 México, DF; f. 1936; general; Chair. ALBERTO BAILLÈRES; CEO ALEJANDRO BAILLÈRES.

ING Mexico: Paseo de la Reforma 222, 4°, 5° y 6°, Col. Juárez 06600, México, DF; tel. (55) 5169-2500; internet www.ing.com.mx; f. 1936 as La Comercial; acquired by ING Group in 2000; life, etc.; CEO JAN HOMMEN.

La Nacional, Cía de Seguros, SA: México, DF; f. 1901; life, etc.; Pres. CLEMENTE CABELLO; Chair. Lic. ALBERTO BAILLERES.

Pan American de México, Cía de Seguros, SA: México, DF; f. 1940; Pres. Lic. JESS N. DALTON; Dir-Gen. GILBERTO ESCOBEDA PAZ.

Royal & SunAlliance Mexico: Blvd Adolfo López Mateos 2448, Col. Altavista, 01060 México, DF; tel. (55) 5723-7999; fax (55) 5723-7941; e-mail omar.antonio@mx.royalsun.com; internet www.royalsun.com.mx; f. 1941; acquired Seguros BBV-Probursa in 2001; general, except life.

Seguros Azteca, SA: Insurgentes 102, México, DF; internet www.segurosazteca.com.mx; f. 1933; general including life; Pres. JUAN CAMPO RODRÍGUEZ.

Seguros Banamex, SA: Isabel la Católica 44, Col. Centro Histórico, Del. Cuauhtémoc, 06000 México, DF; e-mail sbainternet@banamex.com; internet www.segurosbanamex.com; f. 1994; life, accident and health; Pres. AGUSTÍN F. LEGORRETA; Dir-Gen. JUAN OROZCO GÓMEZ PORTUGAL.

Seguros Constitución, SA: Avda Revolución 2042, Col. La Otra Banda, 01090 México, DF; tel. (55) 5550-7910; f. 1937; life, accident; Pres. ISIDORO RODRÍGUEZ RUIZ; Dir-Gen. ALFONSO DE ORDUÑA Y PÉREZ.

Seguros el Fénix, SA: México, DF; f. 1937; Pres. VICTORIANO OLAZÁBAL E.; Dir-Gen. JAIME MATUTE LABRADOR.

Seguros Internacional, SA: Abraham González 67, México, DF; f. 1945; general; Pres. Lic. GUSTAVO ROMERO KOLBECK.

Seguros La República, SA: Paseo de la Reforma 383, México, DF; f. 1966; general; 43% owned by Commercial Union (United Kingdom); Pres. LUCIANO ARECHEDERRA QUINTANA; Gen. Man. JUAN ANTONIO DE ARRIETA MENDIZÁBAL.

Seguros de México, SA: Insurgentes Sur 3496, Col. Peña Pobre, 14060 México, DF; tel. (55) 5679-3855; f. 1957; life, etc.; Dir-Gen. Lic. ANTONIO MIJARES RICCI.

Seguros Monterrey New York Life: Presidente Masaryk 8, Bosques de Chapultepec, Del. Miguel Hidalgo, México, DF; tel. (55) 5326-9000; fax (55) 5536-9610; e-mail clientes@monterrey-newyorklife.com.mx; internet www.monterrey-newyorklife.com.mx; f. 1940 as Monterrey Cía de Seguros, acquired by New York Life in 2000; casualty, life, etc.; Dir-Gen. MARIO VELA BERRONDO.

Monterrey, NL

Seguros Monterrey del Círculo Mercantil, SA, Sociedad General de Seguros: Padre Mier Pte 276, Monterrey, NL; f. 1941; life; Gen. Man. CARMEN G. MASSO DE NAVARRO.

Insurance Association

Asociación Mexicana de Instituciones de Seguros, AC (AMIS): Fco I Madero 21, Col. Tlacopac, San Angel, 01040 México, DF; tel. (55) 5662-6161; fax (55) 5662-8036; e-mail amis@mail.internet.com.mx; internet www.amis.com.mx; f. 1946; all insurance cos operating in Mexico are mems; Pres. ROLANDO VEGA SAÉNZ; Dir-Gen. RECAREDO ARIAS JIMÉNEZ.

MEXICO   *Directory*

Trade and Industry

GOVERNMENT AGENCIES

Comisión Federal de Protección Contra Riesgos Sanitarios (COFEPRIS): Monterrey 33, esq. Oaxaca, Col. Roma, Del. Cuauhtémoc, 06700 México, DF; tel. (55) 5080-5200; e-mail mdiosdado@salud.gob.mx; internet www.cofepris.gob.mx; f. 2003; pharmaceutical regulatory authority; Sec.-Gen. (vacant).

Comisión Nacional Forestal (CONAFOR): Carretera a Nogales s/n, esq. Periférico Poniente 5360, 5°, San Juan de Ocotán, 45019 Zapopan, Jal.; tel. (33) 3777-7047; fax (33) 3777-7028; e-mail cgonzalez@conafor.gob.mx; internet www.conafor.gob.mx; f. 2001; Dir-Gen. JOSÉ CIBRIÁN TOVAR.

Comisión Nacional de Inversiones Extranjeras (CNIE): Dirección General de Inversión Extranjera, Insurgentes Sur 1940, 8°, Col. Florida, 01030 México, DF; tel. (55) 5229-6100; fax (55) 5229-6507; e-mail gcanales@economia.gob.mx; f. 1973; govt commission to co-ordinate foreign investment; Exec. Sec. GREGORIO MANUEL CANALES RAMÍREZ.

Comisión Nacional de los Salarios Mínimos (CNSM): Avda Cuauhtémoc 14, 2°, Col. Doctores, 06720 México 7, DF; tel. (55) 5588-3800; fax (55) 5578-5775; e-mail cnsm1@conasami.gob.mx; internet www.conasami.gob.mx; f. 1962, in accordance with Section VI of Article 123 of the Constitution; national commission on minimum salaries; Pres. Lic. BASILIO GONZÁLEZ NÚÑEZ.

Instituto Nacional de Investigaciones Nucleares (ININ): Centro Nuclear de México, Carretera México–Toluca Km 36.5, La Marquesa, 52750 Ocoyoacac, Méx.; tel. (55) 5329-7200; e-mail maribel.rangel@inin.gob.mx; internet www.inin.mx; f. 1979 to plan research and devt of nuclear science and technology; also researches the peaceful uses of nuclear energy, for the social, scientific and technological devt of the country; administers the Secondary Standard Dosimetry Laboratory, the Nuclear Information and Documentation Centre, which serves Mexico's entire scientific community; operates a tissue culture laboratory for medical treatment; the 1-MW research reactor, which came into operation in 1967, supplies part of Mexico's requirements for radioactive isotopes; also operates a 12-MV Tandem van de Graaff; Mexico has two nuclear reactors, each with a generating capacity of 654 MW; the first, at Laguna Verde, became operational in 1989 and is administered by the Comisión Federal de Electricidad (CFE); Dir-Gen. RAÚL ORTÍZ MAGAÑA.

Instituto Nacional de Pesca (National Fishery Institute): Pitágoras 1320, Col. Santa Cruz Atoyac, Del. Benito Juárez, 03310 México, DF; tel. (55) 3871-9542; fax (55) 5604-9169; e-mail gerardo.garcia@inapesca.sagarpa.gob.mx; internet www.inp.sagarpa.gob.mx; f. 1962; Dir MIGUEL ANGEL CISNEROS MATA.

Procuraduría Federal del Consumidor (Profeco): Avda José Vasconcelos 208, Col. Condesa, Del. Cuauhtémoc, 06140 México, DF; tel. (55) 5625-6700; internet www.profeco.gob.mx; f. 1975; consumer protection; Procurator ANTONIO MORALES DE LA PEÑA.

Servicio Geológico Mexicano (SGM): Blvd Felipe Angeles, Carretera México–Pachuca, Km 93.5, Col. Venta Prieta, 42080 Pachuca, HI; tel. (771) 711-4266; fax (771) 711-4204; e-mail gintproc@sgm.gob.mx; internet www.coremisgm.gob.mx; f. 1957; govt agency for the devt of mineral resources; Dir-Gen. RAFAEL ALEXANDRI RIONDA.

DEVELOPMENT ORGANIZATIONS

Centro de Investigación para el Desarollo, AC (CIDAC) (Centre of Research for Development): Jaime Balmes 11, Edif. D, 2°, Col. Los Morales Polanco, 11510 México, DF; tel. (55) 5985-1010; fax (55) 5985-1030; e-mail info@cidac.org.mx; internet www.cidac.org; f. 1984; researches economic and political devt.

Comisión Nacional de las Zonas Aridas (CONAZA): Blvd Isidro Lopez Zertuche 2513, Col. Los Maestros, 25260 Saltillo, Coah.; tel. (844) 450-5200; e-mail contacto@conaza.gob.mx; internet www.conaza.gob.mx; f. 1970; commission to co-ordinate the devt and use of arid areas; Dir-Gen. FELIPE FLORES GUAJARDO.

Fideicomiso de Fomento Mineiro (FIFOMI): Puente de Tecamachalco 26, 2°, Col. Lomas de Chapultepec, Del. Miguel Hidalgo, 11000 México, DF; tel. (55) 5249-9500; e-mail pguerra@fifomi.gob.mx; internet www.fifomi.gob.mx; trust for the devt of the mineral industries; Dir-Gen. ALBERTO ORTIZ TRILLO.

Fideicomisos Instituídos en Relación con la Agricultura (FIRA): Km 8, Antigua Carretera Pátzucuaro, 58341 Morelia, Mich.; tel. (443) 322-2399; fax (443) 327-6338; e-mail webmaster@correo.fira.gob.mx; internet www.fira.gob.mx; a group of devt funds to aid agricultural financing, under the Banco de México, comprising Fondo de Garantía y Fomento para la Agricultura, Ganadería y Avicultura (FOGAGA); Fondo Especial para Financiamiento Agropecuarios (FEFA); Fondo Especial de Asistencia Técnica y Garantía para Créditos Agropecuarios (FEGA); Fondo de Garantía y Fomento para las Actividades Pesqueras (FOPESCA); Dir FRANCISCO MERÉ PALAFOX.

Fondo de Operación y Financiamiento Bancario a la Vivienda (FOVI): Ejército Nacional 180, Col. Anzures, 11590 México, DF; tel. (55) 5263-4500; fax (55) 5263-4541; e-mail jmartinez@fovi.gob.mx; internet www.fovi.gob.mx; f. 1963 to promote the construction of low-cost housing through savings and credit schemes; devt fund under the Banco de México; Dir-Gen. MANUEL ZEPEDA PAYERAS.

Instituto Mexicano del Petróleo (IMP): Eje Central Lázaro Cárdenas 152, Col. San Bartolo Atepehuacan, Del. Gustavo A. Madero, 07730 México, DF; tel. (55) 9175-6000; fax (55) 9175-8000; e-mail jalim@imp.mx; internet www.imp.mx; f. 1965 to foster devt of the petroleum, chemical and petrochemical industries; Dir JUAN ARTURO LIM MEDRANO.

CHAMBERS OF COMMERCE

Chambers of Commerce exist in the chief town of each state as well as in the larger centres of commercial activity. There are also other international Chambers of Commerce.

American Chamber of Commerce of Mexico (Amcham): Lucerna 78, Col. Juárez, 06600 México, DF; tel. (55) 5141-3800; fax (55) 5141-3833; e-mail amchammx@amcham.com.mx; internet www.amcham.com.mx; f. 1917; brs in Guadalajara and Monterrey; Pres. NEAL R. GOINS.

Cámara de Comercio, Servicios y Turismo Ciudad de México (CANACO) (Chamber of Commerce, Services and Tourism of Mexico City): Paseo de la Reforma 42, 3°, Col. Centro, Apdo 32005, 06048 México, DF; tel. (55) 3685-2269; fax (55) 5592-2279; e-mail lysasi@ccmexico.com.mx; internet www.ccmexico.com.mx; f. 1874; 50,000 mems; Pres. LORENZO YSASI MARTÍNEZ.

Cámara Nacional de la Industria de Transformación (CANACINTRA): Avda San Antonio 256, Col. Ampliación Nápoles, Del. Benito Juárez, 03849 México, DF; tel. (55) 5482-3000; fax 5598-8044; e-mail direcciongeneral@canacintra.org.mx; internet www.canacintra.org.mx; represents majority of smaller manufacturing businesses; Pres. MIGUEL MARON MANZUR.

Confederación de Cámaras Nacionales de Comercio, Servicios y Turismo (CONCANACO-SERVYTUR) (Confederation of National Chambers of Commerce, Services and Tourism): Balderas 144, 3°, Col. Centro, 06079 México, DF; tel. (55) 5722-9300; e-mail comentarios@concanacored.com; internet www.concanaco.com.mx; f. 1917; Pres. LUIS ANTONIO MAHBUB SARQUIS; Dir-Gen. EDUARDO GARCÍA VILLASEÑOR; comprises 283 regional Chambers.

CHAMBERS OF INDUSTRY

The 47 national chambers, 15 regional chambers, 3 general chambers and 42 associations, many of which are located in the Federal District, are representative of the major industries of the country.

Central Confederation

Confederación de Cámaras Industriales de los Estados Unidos Mexicanos (CONCAMIN) (Confed. of Industrial Chambers): Manuel María Contreras 133, 4°, Col. Cuauhtémoc, Del. Cuauhtémoc, 06500 México, DF; tel. (55) 5140-7800; fax 5140-7831; e-mail webmaster@concamin.org.mx; internet www.concamin.org.mx; f. 1918; represents and promotes the activities of the entire industrial sector; Pres. ISMAEL PLASCENCIA NÚÑEZ; Dir-Gen. FRANCISCO JAVIER JIMÉNEZ ROJAS; 108 mem. orgs.

INDUSTRIAL AND TRADE ASSOCIATIONS

Asociación Nacional de Importadores y Exportadores de la República Mexicana (ANIERM) (National Association of Importers and Exporters): Monterrey 130, Col. Roma, Del. Cuauhtémoc, 06700 México, DF; tel. (55) 5584-9522; fax (55) 5584-5317; e-mail anierm@anierm.org.mx; internet www.anierm.org.mx; f. 1944; Pres. JOSÉ OTHÓN RAMÍREZ GUTTIÉREZ; Exec. Vice-Pres. HUMBERTO SIMONEEN ARDILA.

Asociación Nacional de la Industria Química (ANIQ): Angel Urraza 505, Col. del Valle, 03100 México, DF; tel. (55) 5230-5100; internet www.aniq.org.mx; f. 1959; chemicals asscn; Dir-Gen. MIGUEL BENEDETTO; c. 200 mem. cos.

Comisión Nacional de Seguridad Nuclear y Salvaguardias (CNSNS): Dr José María Barragán 779, Col. Narvarte, Del. Benito Juárez, 03020 México, DF; tel. (55) 5095-3200; fax (55) 5095-3295; e-mail swaller@cnsns.gob.mx; internet www.cnsns.gob.mx; f. 1979; nuclear regulatory agency; Dir-Gen. JUAN EIBENSCHUTZ HARTMAN.

Comisión Petroquímica Mexicana: México, DF; promotes the devt of the petrochemical industry; Tech. Sec. Ing. JUAN ANTONIO BARGÉS MESTRES.

Consejo Mexicano de Asuntos Internacionales (COMEXI) Oficina 502, Torre Magnum, Sierra Mojada 620, Col. Lomas de Chapultepec, 11000 México, DF; tel. (55) 5202-3776; internet www.consejomexicano.org; Pres. FERNANDO SOLANA.

MEXICO

Consejo Mexicano del Café (CMCAFE): José María Ibarrarán 84, 1°, Col. San José Insurgentes, Del. Benito Juárez, 03900 México, DF; tel. and fax (55) 5611-9075; e-mail cmc@sagar.gob.mx; f. 1993; devt of coffee sector; Pres. JAVIER USABIAGA.

Consejo Mexicano de Comercio Exterior (COMCE): Lancaster 15, 2° y 3°, Col. Juárez, 06600 México, DF; tel. (52) 5231-7100; fax (55) 5321-7109; e-mail direccion@comce.org.mx; internet www.comce.org.mx; f. 1999 to promote international trade; Pres. VALENTÍN DIEZ MORODO.

Consejo Nacional de la Industria Maquiladora de Exportación (CNIME): Ejército Nacional 418, 12°, Of. 1204, Col. Chapultepec Morales, Del. Miguel Hidalgo, 11570 México, DF; tel. and fax (55) 5250-6093; e-mail dirgral@cnimme.org.mx; internet www.cnime.org.mx; f. 1975; Pres. CÉSAR CASTRO; Dir-Gen. CARLOS PALENCIA ESCALANTE.

Instituto Nacional de Investigaciones Forestales y Agropecuarios (INIFAP) (National Forestry and Agricultural Research Institute): Avda Progreso No 5, Col. Barrio de Santa Catarina, Del. Coyoacán, 04010 México, DF; tel. (55) 3871-8700; e-mail brajcich.pedro@inifap.gob.mx; internet www.inifap.gob.mx; f. 1985; conducts research into plant genetics, management of species and conservation; Dir-Gen. PEDRO BRAJCICH GALLEGOS.

EMPLOYERS' ORGANIZATIONS

Consejo Coordinador Empresarial (CCE): Lancaster 15, Col. Juárez, 06600 México, DF; tel. (55) 5229-1100; fax (55) 5592-3857; e-mail sistemas@cce.org.mx; internet www.cce.org.mx; f. 1976; coordinating body of private sector; Pres. ARMANDO PAREDES ARROYO; Dir-Gen. LUIS MIGUEL PANDO.

Consejo Mexicano de Hombres de Negocios (CMHN): México, DF; f. 1963; represents leading businesspeople; affiliated to CCE; Pres. CLAUDIO GONZÁLEZ LAPORTE.

STATE HYDROCARBONS COMPANY

Petróleos Mexicanos (PEMEX): Avda Marina Nacional 329, Col. Huasteca, 11311 México, DF; tel. (55) 1944-2500; fax (55) 5531-6354; internet www.pemex.com; f. 1938; govt agency for the exploitation of Mexico's petroleum and natural gas resources; Dir-Gen. JESÚS REYES HEROLES GONZÁLEZ GARZA; 106,900 employees.

UTILITIES

Regulatory Authorities

Comisión Nacional del Agua (CONAGUA): Avda Insurgentes Sur 2416, Col. Copilco el Bajo, Del. Coyoacán, 04340 México, DF; tel. (55) 5174-4000; fax (55) 5550-6721; e-mail direccion@cna.gob.mx; internet www.cna.gob.mx; commission to administer national water resources; Dir-Gen. JOSÉ LUIS LUEGE TAMARGO.

Comisión Reguladora de Energía (CRE): Horacio 1750, Col. Morales Polanco, Del. Miguel Hidalgo, 11510 México, DF; tel. (55) 5283-1500; e-mail calidad@cre.gob.mx; internet www.cre.gob.mx; f. 1994; commission to control energy policy and planning; Pres. FRANCISCO XAVIER SALAZAR DIEZ DE SOLLANO; Exec. Sec. CARLOS HANS VALADEZ MARTÍNEZ.

Secretariat of State for Energy: see section on The Government (Secretariats of State).

Electricity

Comisión Federal de Electricidad (CFE): 2 Sec. del Bosque de Chapultepec, Museo Tecnológico, Del. Miguel Hidalgo, México, DF; tel. (55) 5229-4400; fax (55) 5553-5321; e-mail alfredo.elias@cfe.gob.mx; internet www.cfe.gob.mx; state-owned power utility; Dir-Gen. ALFREDO ELÍAS AYUB.

Luz y Fuerza del Centro: Melchor Ocampo 171, Col. Tlaxpana, Del. Miguel Hidalgo, 11379 México, DF; tel. (55) 5140-0020; fax (55) 5140-0300; e-mail cis@lfc.gob.mx; internet www.lfc.gob.mx; state-owned; operates electricity network in the centre of the country; Dir-Gen. JORGE GUTIÉRREZ VERA.

Gas

Gas Natural México (GNM): Jaime Blames 8-703, Col. Los Morales Polanco, 11510 México, DF; e-mail sugerencias@gnm.com.mx; internet www.gasnaturalmexico.com.mx; f. 1994 in Mexico; distributes natural gas in the states of Tamaulipas, Aguascalientes, Coahuila, San Luis Potosí, Guanajuato, Nuevo León and México and in the Distrito Federal; subsidiary of Gas Natural (Spain); Pres. SALVADOR GABARRÓ SERRA.

Petróleos Mexicanos (PEMEX): see State Hydrocarbons Company; distributes natural gas.

TRADE UNIONS

Confederación Regional Obrera Mexicana (CROM) (Regional Confederation of Mexican Workers): República de Cuba 60, México, DF; f. 1918; Sec.-Gen. IGNACIO CUAUHTÉMOC PALETA; 120,000 mems, 900 affiliated syndicates.

Confederación Revolucionaria de Obreros y Campesinos de México (CROC) (Revolutionary Confederation of Workers and Farmers): Hamburgo 250, Col. Juárez, Del. Cuauhtémoc, 06600 México, DF; tel. (55) 5208-5449; e-mail crocmodel@hotmail.com; internet www.croc.org.mx; f. 1952; Sec.-Gen. ISIAS GONZÁLEZ CUEVAS; 4.5m. mems in 32 state federations and 17 national unions.

Confederación Revolucionaria de Trabajadores (CRT) (Revolutionary Confederation of Workers): Dr Jiménez 218, Col. Doctores, México, DF; f. 1954; Sec.-Gen. MARIO SUÁREZ GARCÍA; 10,000 mems; 10 federations and 192 syndicates.

Confederación de Trabajadores de México (CTM) (Confederation of Mexican Workers): Vallarta 8, Col. Tabacalera, Del. Cuauhtémoc, 06030 México, DF; tel. (55) 5141-1730; e-mail ctmorganizacion@prodigy.net.mx; internet ctmorganizacion.org.mx; f. 1936; admitted to ICFTU; Sec.-Gen. JOAQUÍN GAMBOA; 5.5m. mems.

Congreso del Trabajo (CT): Avda Ricardo Flores Magón 44, Col. Guerrero, 06300 México 37, DF; tel. (55) 5583-3817; internet www.congresodeltrabajo.org.mx; f. 1966; trade union congress comprising trade union federations, confederations, etc.; Pres. JOAQUÍN GAMBOA PASCOE.

Federación Nacional de Sindicatos Independientes (National Federation of Independent Trade Unions): Isaac Garza 311 Oeste, 64000 Monterrey, NL; tel. (81) 8375-6677; e-mail fnsi@prodigy.net.mx; internet www.fnsi.org.mx/esp; f. 1936; Sec.-Gen. JACINTO PADILLA VALDEZ; 230,000 mems.

Federación Obrera de Organizaciones Femeniles (FOOF) (Workers' Federation of Women's Organizations): Vallarta 8, México, DF; f. 1950; women workers' union within CTM; Sec.-Gen. HILDA ANDERSON NEVÁREZ; 400,000 mems.

Federación de Sindicatos de Trabajadores al Servicio del Estado (FSTSE) (Federation of Unions of Government Workers): Gómez Farías 40, Col. San Rafael, 06470 México, DF; internet www.fstse.com; f. 1938; Sec.-Gen. JOEL AYALA ALMEIDA; 2.5m. mems; 80 unions.

Frente Unida Sindical por la Defensa de los Trabajadores y la Constitución (United Union Front in Defence of the Workers and the Constitution): f. 1990 by more than 120 trade orgs to support the implementation of workers' constitutional rights.

Unión General de Obreros y Campesinos de México, Jacinto López (UGOCM-JL) (General Union of Workers and Farmers of Mexico, Jacinto López): José María Marroquí 8, 2°, 06050 México, DF; tel. (55) 5518-3015; f. 1949; admitted to WFTU/CSTAL; Sec.-Gen. JOSÉ LUIS GONZÁLEZ AGUILERA; 7,500 mems, over 2,500 syndicates.

Unión Nacional de Trabajadores (UNT) (National Union of Workers): Villalongen 50, Col. Cuauhtémoc, México, DF; tel. (55) 5140-1425; fax (55) 5703-2583; e-mail secretariageneral@strm.org.mx; internet www.unt.org.mx; f. 1998; Sec.-Gen. FRANCISCO HERNÁNDEZ JUÁREZ.

A number of major unions are non-affiliated, including:

Federación Democrática de Sindicatos de Servidores Públicos (Democratic Federation of Public Servants): México, DF; f. 2005.

Frente Auténtico de los Trabajadores (FAT): Godard 20, Col. Guadalupe Victoria, México, DF; tel. (55) 5556-9314; fax (55) 5556-9316; internet www.fatmexico.org.

Pacto de Unidad Sindical Solidaridad (PAUSS): comprises 10 independent trade unions.

Sindicato Nacional de Trabajadores de la Educación (SNTE) (Education Workers): Venezuela 44, Col. Centro, México, DF; tel. (55) 5702-0005; fax (55) 5702-6303; e-mail info@snte.org.mx; internet www.snte.org.mx; f. 1943; Pres. ELBA ESTHER GORDILLO MORALES; Sec.-Gen. RAFAEL OCHOA GUZMÁN; 1.4m. mems.

Coordinadora Nacional de Trabajadores de la Educación (CNTE): dissident faction; Leader TEODORO PALOMINO.

Sindicato Nacional de Trabajadores Mineros, Metalúrgicos y Similares de la República Mexicana (SNTMM) (Mine, Metallurgical and Related Workers): Avda Dr Vertiz 668, Col. Narvarte, 03020 México, DF; tel. (55) 5519-5690; f. 1933; Sec.-Gen. NAPOLEÓN GÓMEZ URRUTIA; 86,000 mems.

Sindicato de Trabajadores Ferrocarrileros de la República Mexicana (STFRM) (Railway Workers): Avda Ricardo Flores Magón 206, Col. Guerrero, México 3, DF; tel. (55) 5597-1133; e-mail secretarianacional@stfrm.org; internet www.stfrm.org; f. 1933; Sec.-Gen. VÍCTOR F. FLORES MORALES; 100,000 mems.

MEXICO

Sindicato de Trabajadores Petroleros de la República Mexicana (STPRM) (Union of Workers): Zaragoza 15, Col. Guerrero, 06300 México, DF; tel. (55) 5546-0912; close links with PEMEX; Sec.-Gen. CARLOS ROMERO DESCHAMPS; 110,000 mems; includes:

Movimiento Nacional Petrolero: reformist faction; Leader HEBRAÍCAZ VÁSQUEZ.

Sindicato Unico de Trabajadores Electricistas de la República Mexicana (SUTERM) (Electricity Workers): Río Guadalquivir 106, Col. Cuauhtémoc, 06500 México, DF; tel. (55) 5207-0578; internet www.suterm.org.mx; Sec.-Gen. VICTOR FUENTES DEL VILLAR.

Sindicato Unico de Trabajadores de la Industria Nuclear (SUTIN) (Nuclear Industry Workers): Viaducto Río Becerra 139, Col. Nápoles, 03810 México, DF; tel. (55) 5523-8048; fax (55) 5687-6353; e-mail exterior@sutin.org.mx; internet www.sutin.org.mx; Sec.-Gen. ARTURO DELFÍN LOYA.

Unión Obrera Independiente (UOI) (Independent Workers' Union): non-aligned.

The major agricultural unions are:

Confederación Nacional Campesina (CNC) (National Peasant Confederation): Mariano Azuela 121, Col. Santa María de la Ribera, México, DF; tel. (55) 5547-8042; internet www.cnc.org.mx; Sec.-Gen. CRUZ LOPEZ AGUILAR.

Confederación Nacional de Organizaciones Ganaderas (National Confederation of Stockbreeding Organizations): Calzada Mariano Escobedo 714, Col. Anzures, México, DF; tel. (55) 5203-3506; e-mail teresa.hernandez@cnog.com.mx; internet www.cnog.com.mx; Pres. OSWALDO CHÁZARO MONTALVO; 300,000 mems.

Consejo Agrarista Mexicano (Mexican Agrarian Council): 09760 Iztapalapa, México, DF; Sec.-Gen. HUMBERTO SERRANO.

Unión Nacional de Trabajadores Agriculturas (UNTA) (National Union of Agricultural Workers).

Transport

Road transport accounts for about 98% of all public passenger traffic and for about 80% of freight traffic. Mexico's terrain is difficult for overland travel. As a result, there has been an expansion of air transport, and there were 61 international and national airports in 2004. In 2002 plans to build a new airport in the capital were postponed after conflict over the proposed site. International flights are provided by a large number of national and foreign airlines. Mexico has 140 seaports, 29 river docks and a further 29 lake shelters. More than 85% of Mexico's foreign trade is conducted through maritime transport. In the 1980s the Government developed the main industrial ports of Tampico, Coatzacoalcos, Lázaro Cárdenas, Altamira, Laguna de Ostión and Salina Cruz in an attempt to redirect growth and to facilitate exports. The port at Dos Bocas, on the Gulf of Mexico, was one of the largest in Latin America when it opened in 1999. A 300-km railway link across the isthmus of Tehuantepec connects the Caribbean port of Coatzacoalcos with the Pacific port of Salina Cruz.

Secretariat of State for Communications and Transport: see section on The Government (Secretariats of State).

Caminos y Puentes Federales (CAPUFE): Calzada de los Reyes 24, Col. Tetela del Monte, 62130 Cuernavaca, Mor.; tel. (55) 5200-2000; e-mail contacto@capufe.gob.mx; internet www.capufe.gob.mx; Dir-Gen. MANUEL ZUBIRIA MAQUEO.

RAILWAYS

In 2004 there were 26,662 km of main line track. In 2006 the railway system carried an estimated 260,000 passengers and 73,726m. freight ton-km. Ferrocarriles Nacionales de México (FNM), government-owned since 1937, was liquidated in 2001 following a process of restructuring and privatization. A suburban train system for the Valle de México began operations in 2008. In that year plans were under way for the construction of a high-speed rail link between Mexico City and Guadalajara, and a new line from Manzanillo, Aguascalientes, to Mexico City.

Ferrocarril Mexicano, SA de CV (Ferromex): Bosque de Ciruelos 99, Col. Bosques de la Loma, 11700 México, DF; tel. (55) 5246-3700; e-mail webmaster@ferromex.com.mx; internet www.ferromex.com.mx; 50-year concession awarded to Grupo Ferroviario Mexicano, SA, (GFM) commencing in 1998; owned by Grupo México, SA de CV; 8,500 km of track and Mexico's largest rail fleet; links from Mexico City to Guadalajara, Hermosillo, Monterrey, Chihuahua and Pacific ports; Exec. Pres. ALFREDO CASAR PÉREZ; Dir-Gen. ROGELIO VÉLEZ LÓPEZ DE LA CERDA.

Ferrocarril del Sureste (Ferrosur): Bosque de Ciruelos 180, 1°, Col. Bosques de las Lomas, 11700 México, DF; tel. (55) 5387-6500; e-mail magarcia@ferrosur.com.mx; internet www.ferrosur.com.mx; 50-year concession awarded to Grupo Tribasa in 1998; 66.7% sold to Empresas Frisco, SA de CV, in 1999, owned by Grupos Carso, SA de CV; Dir MIGUEL ANGEL GARCÍA.

Kansas City Southern de México (KCSM): Avda Manuel L. Barragán 4850, Col. Hidalgo, 64420 Monterrey, NL; tel. (81) 8305-7800; fax (81) 8305-7766; e-mail werdman@kcsouthern.com; internet www.kcsouthern.com; formerly Ferrocarril del Noreste; 4,242 km of line, linking Mexico City with the ports of Lázaro Cárdenas, Veracruz, Tampico/Altamira and north-east Mexico; Pres. HENRY R. DAVIES; Chair. MICHAEL R. HAVERTY.

Servicio de Transportes Eléctricos del Distrito Federal (STE): Avda Municipio Libre 402, Col. San Andrés Tetepilco, México, DF; tel. (55) 2595-0000; fax (55) 5672-4758; e-mail sugiere@ste.df.gob.mx; internet www.ste.df.gob.mx; suburban tram route with 17 stops upgraded to light rail standard to act as a feeder to the metro; also operates bus and trolleybus networks; Pres. MARCELO LUIS EBRARD CASAUBÓN (Head of Govt of the Distrito Federal); Dir-Gen. RUFINO H. LEÓN TOVAR.

Sistema de Transporte Colectivo (Metro) (STC): Delicias 67, 06070 México, DF; tel. (55) 5709-1133; fax (55) 5512-3601; internet www.metro.df.gob.mx; f. 1967; the first stage of a combined underground and surface railway system in Mexico City was opened in 1969; 10 lines, covering 158 km, were operating, in 1998, and five new lines, bringing the total distance to 315 km, are to be completed by 2010; the system is wholly state-owned and the fares are partially subsidized; Dir-Gen. FRANCISCO BOJÓRQUEZ HERNÁNDEZ.

ROADS

In 2004 there were 352,072 km of roads, of which 34.5% were paved.

Long-distance buses form one of the principal methods of transport in Mexico, and there are some 600 lines operating services throughout the country.

Dirección General de Autotransporte Federal: Calzada de las Bombas 411, 11°, Col. Los Girasoles, Del. Goyoacán, 04920 México, DF; tel. (55) 5677-3561; internet dgaf.sct.gob.mx; co-ordinates long-distance bus services; Dir Dr LUIS TÉLLEZ KUENZLER.

SHIPPING

At the end of 2007 Mexico's registered merchant fleet numbered 780 vessels, with a total displacement of 1,217,000 grt. The Government operates the facilities of seaports. In 1994–95 management of several ports was transferred to the private sector.

Coordinación General de Puertos y Marina Mercante (CGPMM): Avda Nuevo León 210, Col. Hipódromo, 03310 México, DF; tel. (55) 5723-9300; fax (55) 5265-3108; e-mail egarciai@sct.gob.mx; internet cgpmm.sct.gob.mx; Co-ordinator ALEJANDRO CHACÓN DOMÍNGUEZ; Dir-Gen. de Puertos (vacant); Dir-Gen. de Marina Mercante ADOLFO XAVIER ZAGAL OLIVARES.

Port of Acapulco: Puertos Mexicanos, Malecón Fiscal s/n, Acapulco, Gro; Harbour Master Capt. RENÉ F. NOVALES BETANZOS.

Port of Coatzacoalcos: Administración Portuaria Integral de Coatzacoalcos, SA de CV, Interior Recinto Portuario s/n Coatzacoalcos, 96400 Ver.; tel. (921) 211-0270; fax (921) 211-0272; e-mail dirgral@puertocoatzacoalcos.com.mx; internet www.apicoatza.com; Dir-Gen. Ing. GILBERTO ANTÓNIO RIOS RUÍZ.

Port of Dos Bocas: Administración Portuaria Integral de Dos Bocas, SA de CV, Carretera Federal Puerto Ceiba–Paraíso 414, Col. Quintín Arzuz, 86600 Paraíso, Tab.; tel. (933) 353-2744; e-mail dosbocas@apidosbocas.com; internet www.apidosbocas.com; Dir-Gen. ROBERTO DE LA GARZA LICÓN.

Port of Manzanillo: Administración Portuaria Integral de Manzanillo, SA de CV, Avda Tte Azueta 9, Col. Burócrata, 28250 Manzanillo, Col.; tel. and fax (314) 331-1400; e-mail comercializacion@apimanzanillo.com.mx; internet www.puerto-de-manzanillo.com.mx; Dir-Gen. JOSÉ JULIÁN DIP LEOS.

Port of Tampico: Administración Portuaria Integral de Tampico, SA de CV, Edif. API de Tampico, 1°, Recinto Portuario, 89000 Tampico, Tamps; tel. (833) 241-1400; fax (833) 212-5744; e-mail contacto@puertodetampico.com.mx; internet www.port-of-tampico.com.mx; Gen. Dir MANUEL FLORES GUERRA.

Port of Veracruz: Administración Porturia Integral de Veracruz, SA de CV, Avda Marina Mercante 210, 7°, Col. Centro, 91700 Veracruz, Ver.; tel. (229) 932-2170; fax (229) 932-3040; e-mail mespinosa@puertodeveracruz.com; internet www.puertodeveracruz.com.mx; privatized in 1994; Dir-Gen. JUAN IGNACIO FERNÁNDEZ CARBAJAL.

Transportación Marítima Mexicana, SA de CV (TMM): Avda de la Cúspide 4755, Col. Parque del Pedregal, Del. Tlalpan, 14010 México, DF; tel. (55) 5629-8866; fax (55) 5629-8899; e-mail grupotmm@tmm.com.mx; internet www.tmm.com.mx; f. 1958; cargo services to Europe, the Mediterranean, Scandinavia, the USA, South and Central America, the Caribbean and the Far East; Pres. JOSÉ F. SERRANO SEGOVIA; Sec. IGNACIO RODRÍGUEZ PULLEN.

MEXICO

Directory

CIVIL AVIATION

There were 61 airports in Mexico in 2004, of which 47 were international. Of these, México, Cancún, Guadalajara, Monterrey and Tijuana registered the highest number of operations.

Aeropuertos y Servicios Auxiliares (ASA): Edif. B, Avda 602 161, Col. San Juan de Aragón, Del. Venustiano Carranza, 15620 México, DF; tel. (55) 5133-1000; fax (55) 5133-2985; e-mail glmeyer@asa.gob.mx; internet www.asa.gob.mx; oversees airport management and devt; Gen. Man. GILBERTO LÓPEZ MEYER.

Dirección General de Aeronáutica Civil (DGAC): Providencia No 807, Col. Del Valle, 03100 México, DF; tel. (55) 5523-6642; fax (55) 5523-7207; e-mail hgonzalw@sct.gob.m; internet dgac.sct.gob.mx; subdivision of Secretariat of State for Communications and Transport; regulates civil aviation; Dir-Gen. HECTOR GONZALEZ WEEKS.

Aerocalifornia: Aquiles Serdán 1955, 23000 La Paz, BCS; e-mail aeroll@aerocalifornia.uabcs.mx; f. 1960; services suspended in 2006 over safety concerns; regional carrier with scheduled passenger and cargo services in Mexico and the USA; Chair. PAUL A. ARECHIGA.

Aeromar, Transportes Aeromar: Hotel María Isabel Sheraton, Paseo de la Reforma 325, Local 10, México, DF; tel. (55) 5514-2248; e-mail web.aeromar@aeromar.com.mx; internet www.aeromar.com.mx; f. 1987; scheduled domestic passenger and cargo services; Dir-Gen. JUAN I. STETA.

Aeromexpress Cargo: Avda Texococo s/n esq., Avda Tahel, Col. Peñón de los Baños, 15620 México, DF; tel. (55) 5133-0203; internet www.aeromexpress.com.mx; owned by state holding co Consorcio Aeroméxico, SA; cargo airline.

Aerovías de México (Aeroméxico): Paseo de la Reforma 445, 3°, Torre B, Col. Cuauhtémoc, 06500 México, DF; tel. (55) 5133-4000; fax (55) 5133-4619; internet www.aeromexico.com; f. 1934 as Aeronaves de México, nationalized 1959; sold by state holding co Consorcio Aeroméxico, SA, to private investors in 2007; services between most principal cities of Mexico and the USA, Chile, Brazil, Peru, France and Spain; Pres. and Dir-Gen. ANDRÉS CONESA LABASTIDA.

Aviacsa: Aeropuerto Internacional, Zona C, Hangar 1, Col. Aviación General, 15520 México, DF; tel. (55) 5716-9005; fax (55) 5758-3823; internet www.aviacsa.com; f. 1990; operates internal flights, and flights to the USA; Pres. EDUARDO MEGA.

Click Mexicana: Avda Xola 3132, Col. del Valle, 03100 México, DF; tel. (55) 5284-3132; e-mail servicio.cliente@clickmx.com; internet www.clickmx.com; f. 2005; owned by Mexicana; fmrly known as Aerocaribe; budget airline operating internal flights; CEO ISAAC VOLIN BOLOK.

Interjet (ABC Aerolíneas, SA de CV): Aeropuerto Internacional de Toluca, Toluca, Méx.; tel. (55) 1102-5555; e-mail atencionaclientes@interjet.com.mx; internet www.interjet.com.mx; f. 2005; budget airline operating internal flights; Pres. MIGUEL ALEMÁN MAGNANI.

Mexicana (Compañía Mexicana de Aviación, SA de CV): Avda Xola 535, Col. del Valle, 03100 México, DF; tel. (55) 5448-3000; fax (55) 5448-3129; e-mail dirgenmx@mexicana.com.mx; internet www.mexicana.com; f. 1921; fmrly state-owned; sold to Grupo Posadas in 2005; international services between Mexico City and the USA, Central America and the Caribbean; domestic services; CEO MANUEL BORJA CHICO.

Volaris: Aeropuerto Internacional de la Ciudad de Toluca, 50500 Toluca, Méx.; tel. (55) 1102-8000; e-mail comentarios@volaris.com.mx; internet www.volaris.com.mx; f. 2006; operated by Vuela Compañía de Aviación; budget airline operating internal flights; Pres. PEDRO ASPE ARMELLA; Dir-Gen. ENRIQUE BELTRANENA.

Tourism

Tourism remains one of Mexico's principal sources of foreign exchange. Mexico received 21.4m. foreign visitors in 2006, as well as 78.6m. excursionists, and receipts from tourism in that year were US $12,801m. More than 90% of visitors come from the USA and Canada. The country is famous for volcanoes, coastal scenery and the great Sierra Nevada (Sierra Madre) mountain range. The relics of the Mayan and Aztec civilizations and of Spanish Colonial Mexico are of historic and artistic interest. Zihuatanejo, on the Pacific coast, and Cancún, on the Caribbean, were developed as tourist resorts by the Government. In 2004 an estimated 1.8m. people were employed in the tourism sector. In October 2005 'Hurricane Wilma' inflicted heavy damage on some tourist areas, notably Cancún. The government tourism agency, FONATUR, encourages the renovation and expansion of old hotels and provides attractive incentives for the industry. FONATUR is also the main developer of major resorts in Mexico.

Secretariat of State for Tourism: see section on The Government (Secretariats of State).

Asociación Mexicana de Agencias de Viajes (AMAV): Guanajuato 128, México, DF; tel. (55) 5584-9300; e-mail amavcun@prodigy.net.mx; internet www.amavnacional.com; f. 1945; asscn of travel agencies; Pres. JORGE HERNÁNDEZ DELGADO.

Fondo Nacional de Fomento al Turismo (FONATUR): Tecoyotitla 100, Col. Florida, 01030 México, DF; tel. (55) 5090-4200; fax (55) 5090-4469; e-mail jrbusquets@fonatur.gob.mx; internet www.fonatur.gob.mx; f. 1956 to finance and promote the devt of tourism; Dir-Gen. MIGUEL GÓMEZ-MONT URUETA.

THE FEDERATED STATES OF MICRONESIA

Introductory Survey

Location, Climate, Language, Religion, Flag, Capital

The Federated States of Micronesia forms (with Palau, q.v.) the archipelago of the Caroline Islands, about 800 km east of the Philippines. The Federated States of Micronesia comprises 607 islands and includes (from west to east) the states of Yap, Chuuk (formerly Truk), Pohnpei (formerly Ponape) and Kosrae. The islands are subject to heavy rainfall, although precipitation decreases from east to west. January, February and March are the driest months, although seasonal variations in rainfall and temperature are generally small. Average annual temperature is 27°C (81°F). The native population consists of various ethno-linguistic groups, but English is widely understood. The principal religion is Christianity, much of the population being Roman Catholic. The national flag (proportions 10 by 19) consists of four five-pointed white stars, arranged as a circle, situated centrally on a light blue field. The capital is Palikir, on Pohnpei.

Recent History

The Federated States of Micronesia was formerly part of the US-administered Trust Territory of the Pacific Islands (for history up to 1965, see the chapter on the Marshall Islands).

From 1965 there were increasing demands for local autonomy within the Trust Territory of the Pacific Islands. In that year the Congress of Micronesia was formed, and in 1967 a commission was established to examine the future political status of the islands. In 1970 it declared Micronesians' rights to sovereignty over their own lands, to self-determination, to devise their own constitution and to revoke any form of free association with the USA. In May 1977, after eight years of negotiations, US President Jimmy Carter announced that his administration intended to adopt measures to terminate the trusteeship agreement by 1981. Until 1979 the four districts of Yap, Truk (Chuuk since 1990), Ponape (Pohnpei since 1984) and Kosrae were governed by a local Administrator, appointed by the President of the USA. However, on 10 May 1979 the four districts ratified a new Constitution to become the Federated States of Micronesia. The Constitution was promulgated in 1980.

The USA signed the Compact of Free Association with the Republic of Palau in August 1982, and with the Marshall Islands and the Federated States of Micronesia in October. Under the Compacts, the four countries (including the Northern Mariana Islands) became independent of each other and took charge of both their internal and foreign affairs separately, while the USA remained responsible for defence and security. The Compact was approved by plebiscite in the Federated States of Micronesia in June 1983, and was ratified by the islands' Congress in September.

In May 1986 the UN Trusteeship Council endorsed the US Government's request for the termination of the existing trusteeship agreement with the islands. US administration of the Federated States of Micronesia was formally ended in November of that year. The UN Security Council ratified the termination of the trusteeship agreement in December 1990. Ponape was renamed Pohnpei in November 1984, when its Constitution came into effect. Truk was renamed Chuuk in January 1990, when its new Constitution was proposed (being later adopted). The Federated States of Micronesia was admitted to the UN in September 1991.

The incumbent President (since 1987), John Haglelgam, was replaced by Bailey Olter, a former Vice-President, in May 1991. At congressional elections in March 1995 Olter was re-elected to the Pohnpei Senator-at-Large seat, and in early May he was re-elected to the presidency unopposed. Similarly, Jacob Nena was re-elected as Vice-President. Allegations that financial mismanagement by the Governor of Chuuk, Sasao Gouland, had resulted in state debts of some US $20m. led to his resignation in June 1996, in order to avoid impeachment proceedings. In July Olter suffered a stroke. Jacob Nena served as acting President during Olter's absence from office, and in May 1997 was sworn in as President of the country. (Olter died in February 1999.)

Congressional elections took place in early March 1997 for the 10 Senators elected on a two-yearly basis, at which all of the incumbents were returned to office. A referendum held concurrently on a proposed amendment to the Constitution (which envisaged increasing the allocation of national revenue to the state legislatures from 50% to 80% of the total budget) was approved in Chuuk and Yap, but rejected in Pohnpei and Kosrae.

Allegations of government interference in the media became widespread when the editor of the country's principal newspaper, *FSM News*, was refused permission to re-enter the islands in June 1997. The Government had sought to deport the editor (who was a Canadian national) following publication in the periodical of reports on government spending, which the authorities claimed were false and malicious. It was also thought that by enforcing the exclusion order, the Government hoped to suppress the publication in the newspaper of information relating to alleged corruption among public officials. The newspaper ceased publication in late 1997.

In February 1998 Congress approved proposals to restructure and reorganize the Cabinet. Several ministerial portfolios were consequently merged or abolished, with the aim of reducing government expenditure. Congressional elections took place on 2 March 1999, at which President Nena was re-elected to the Kosrae Senator-at-Large seat and Vice-President Leo Falcam to the Pohnpei Senator-at-Large seat. On 11 May Congress elected Falcam as President and the Chuuk Senator-at-Large, Redley Killion, as Vice-President.

A first round of renegotiations of the Compact of Free Association (certain terms of which were due to expire in 2001) was completed in late 1999. The USA and the Federated States of Micronesia pledged to maintain defence and security relations. It was also agreed that the USA would continue to provide economic aid to the islands and assist in the development of the private sector, as well as in promoting greater economic self-sufficiency. In July 2001 the USA offered annual assistance of US $61m. and a trust fund of $13m., and expressed concern that the $2,600m. it had given to Micronesia and the Marshall Islands since 1986 had been mismanaged. The Compact's funding terms for Micronesia were originally due to expire on 3 November 2001, but negotiations regarding a new Compact were not completed by this time. Funding was, nevertheless, continued at the Compact's 15-year average level while negotiations remained in progress. Following a proposal by the USA in April 2002 to extend economic assistance for a period of 20 years, a new draft funding structure was agreed, and in March the US budget projections for 2004 granted Micronesian citizens access to private health care resources in the USA as part of the Federated States' continued entitlement to US federal programmes. On 1 May 2003 the amended Compact of Free Association was signed by representatives of the two countries in Pohnpei. The revised Compact envisaged direct annual grants of $76.2m. in 2004, in addition to a further $16m. annually, which was to be paid into a trust fund for Micronesia. From 2007, direct grants were to decrease by some $800,000, with this amount being transferred to the trust fund. (The total amount to be paid prior to the expected termination of US assistance in 2023 amounted, in 2004 terms, to some $1,760m.) Furthermore, the Micronesian Government also undertook to provide frequent, strictly monitored audit information on all US funding in order to ensure greater accountability. In October 2003 final agreement was reached on some outstanding security and immigration issues, and the US Congress approved the amended Compact in November. President George W. Bush signed the pact in December, and representatives of both Governments signed a document of implementation in June 2004. Nevertheless, there remained widespread concern in the Federated States of Micronesia that the new Compact represented a substantial overall reduction in annual income over the long term. Moreover, the formula for the distribution of Compact funds to each of Micronesia's states and the removal of certain US subsidies remained the subject of considerable controversy. In August representatives of Micronesia and the USA met to review the management of Compact funds in the first session of the Joint Economic Management Committee. In August 2008 these concerns were renewed when the US Department of the Interior partly suspended Compact funding for the state of Chuuk, citing financial management problems that needed to be resolved before the funds could be approved. In March 2008 the US Office of Insular Affairs had confirmed that in 2008/09 the sum of almost $20.3m. was to be allocated to the country's trust fund, in addition to the annual operating grants.

In September 2002 unrest occurred on the Faichuk islands, part of Chuuk, where the Faichuk Commission for Statehood continued its campaign to secede from Chuuk and gain equal status within the Federation. The secessionists believed that independence would bring more goods, services, medical treatment and capital improvement projects. Local dissatisfaction worsened in September following allegations of electoral manipulation against the village mayor of Udot island, with a large crowd appearing to support attempts by local security forces to prevent the mayor's arrest. In March 2005 Congressman Twiter Aritos introduced to the national Congress legislation to grant Faichuk the status of the Federation's fifth state.

Also in September 2002 a referendum was held on a number of proposed amendments to the Constitution. The prospective changes included a provision for the direct election of presidential candidates, the extension of the right of islanders to hold dual citizenship and changes to the distribution formula for Compact of Free Association funds. However, the measures did not receive the required three-quarters' majority of votes and were thus rejected.

At the congressional elections of 6 March 2003 President Leo Falcam unexpectedly failed to achieve re-election to a further four-year term as Senator-at-Large for Pohnpei. In mid-May Congress appointed the Senator-at-Large for Yap, Joseph J. Urusemal, to the presidency. The elections were the subject of some controversy, as it appeared that elected officials had disbursed a portion of the 2002 US funding for Micronesia in order to enhance their electoral prospects. The alleged misallocation of funds was reportedly a significant factor in the worsening fiscal positions of Chuuk, Pohnpei and Kosrae. Moreover, perceptions of official accountability continued to deteriorate in 2003; in November three serving Congressmen were indicted for their role in an alleged fraud involving some $1.2m. in public funds. In January 2004 the national Congress approved a resolution to dismiss the judge assigned to the case. President Urusemal lodged a petition against the dismissal on the grounds that it infringed the constitutionally guaranteed separation of powers. In August the Supreme Court ruled in favour of the petition and overturned the judge's dismissal. Also in January 2004, members of the national Congress attempted to introduce legislation effectively absolving public officials from corruption allegations relating to Compact of Free Association funds. The proposals aroused widespread public hostility, and several representatives of state legislatures threatened to secede from the federation unless the measure were withdrawn. In March the so-called 'amnesty bill' was returned to a congressional sub-committee for further discussion.

At congressional elections held on 7 March 2005 all but one of the four incumbent Senators-at-Large were re-elected, with results from Chuuk awaiting confirmation in early April. At congressional elections held on the following day eight of the 10 incumbent Senators with two-year mandates were re-elected. (Results from Chuuk were annulled, owing to alleged voting irregularities, and in late April a new round of voting was held in this state, at which, amid further allegations of electoral malpractice, Peter S. Sitan was elected.) Concurrent to the second round of congressional elections, a referendum was held over three proposed amendments to the Constitution, including the question of whether each state should recognize and uphold the laws and judicial rulings of other states, and whether to allow dual citizenship. Although a majority of voters favoured the proposed amendments, these could not be implemented because the majority of 75% or more of the votes, as required by the Constitution, had not been obtained.

In April 2006 the national Congress filed a lawsuit against President Urusemal in protest at his use of the presidential veto against certain items of proposed legislation. In June the Supreme Court approved the Department of Justice's decision, on behalf of the President, to dismiss the lawsuit, on the basis that the judicial system was not authorized to examine the reasons for a presidential veto. Urusemal had argued that these bills were unconstitutional because relevant first and second readings had been held on the same day; he later urged the Congress to resubmit them.

At congressional elections held on 6 March 2007 for all 14 seats of the chamber, the incumbent Senators-at-Large for Kosrae, Pohnpei and Yap were re-elected, while Immanuel Mori defeated Vice-President Redley Killion to become Senator-at-Large for Chuuk. On 11 May 2007, in a congressional vote, Mori was elected President of the Federated States of Micronesia, taking office on the same day; Alik L. Alik of Kosrae succeeded Redley Killion as Vice-President. 'Special' congressional elections were conducted in July to fill the seats vacated by Mori and Alik. In a protracted confirmation process, members of Mori's Government were individually nominated and sworn in during the latter half of 2007 and early 2008. A reorganization of ministries was also instigated, including the creation of a Department of Education.

In March 2008 Senator Roosevelt D. Kansou of Chuuk was found guilty of conspiracy and was consequently removed from his seat in Congress. In May a special congressional election was held to determine Kansou's successor. The election was won by Tesime Kofot, who took up the seat in September.

On 3 March 2009 elections were conducted for 10 of the 14 seats in the national Congress. Elections were also held to determine the Governor and Lieutenant-Governor of Chuuk. After initial results failed to provide a clear winner, a second round of polling was held in April when the incumbent Governor of Chuuk, Wesley Simina, and Lieutenant-Governor Johnson Elimo were both re-elected.

In foreign relations, in July 2006 the Chinese Minister of Foreign Affairs, Li Zhaoxing, became the most senior official of the People's Republic of China ever to visit the Federated States of Micronesia, meeting President Urusemal and Sebastian Anefal, the Secretary of the Department of Foreign Affairs. In September residences built by the Chinese for the President, Vice-President, Speaker of Congress and Chief Justice of the Federated States of Micronesia were presented to the Government at a ceremony that highlighted the strong links between the two countries. Relations between the Federated States of Micronesia and China were bolstered with the opening of a Micronesian embassy in Beijing in May 2007.

In December 2007 President Mori paid a visit to Japan, attending a meeting with the Japanese Prime Minister, Yasuo Fukuda. Fukuda reportedly acknowledged the challenge posed by global warming to island nations such as the Federated States of Micronesia, and he confirmed that the Japanese embassy in Kolonia would soon benefit from the presence of a resident ambassador.

Periodic extreme weather formations have caused loss of life and severe damage to crops, property and infrastructure in Micronesia. Following a severe typhoon in December 2002, President George W. Bush of the USA declared Micronesia a federal disaster area and ordered emergency US funding and resources to be allocated to the relief effort. A further typhoon which struck Yap in April 2004 left 1,200 people homeless; the US Government offered to assume 75% of the cost of the recovery effort.

In late 2000 marine biologists issued a warning regarding the erosion of the islands' coastlines, caused by the destruction of the coral reefs by pollution, overfishing and increasing sea temperatures. Furthermore, in late 2003 concerns over environmental pollution increased, owing to the environmental damage caused by former US and Japanese military equipment submerged in Micronesian waters. A former US Navy oil tanker submerged off the remote Ulithi Atoll was reported at this time to be leaking. Meanwhile, in September 2003 President Urusemal urged the UN General Assembly to work towards halting climate change and its consequent effects on sea-levels and weather systems. In March 2008 the Federated States of Micronesia's Permanent Representative to the UN, Masao Nakayama, attended a US congressional hearing on the subject of the environment. Nakayama argued that climate change was directly affecting Micronesia and urged the USA to take action to alleviate the problem.

In February 2003 Pohnpei hosted the first Summit of Micronesian Leaders. At the second summit, held in Koror, Palau, in March 2004, President Urusemal and the leaders of Palau, the Northern Mariana Islands and Guam undertook to increase co-operation among the Pacific island states in the areas of tourism and the environment. Further co-operation in the fields of

THE FEDERATED STATES OF MICRONESIA

health, the economy and labour were discussed at a summit meeting in late 2007.

Government

On 10 May 1979 the locally drafted Constitution of the Federated States of Micronesia, incorporating the four states of Kosrae, Yap, Ponape (later Pohnpei) and Truk (later Chuuk), became effective. The federal legislature, the Congress, comprises 14 members (Senators). The four states each elect one 'Senator-at-Large', for a four-year term. The remaining 10 Senators are elected for two-year terms: their seats are distributed in proportion to the population of each state. Each of the four states also has its own Constitution, Governor and legislature. The federal President and Vice-President are elected by the Congress from among the four Senators-at-Large; the offices rotate among the four states. (By-elections are then held for the seats to which the President and Vice-President had been elected.) In November 1986 the Compact of Free Association was signed by the Governments of the Federated States of Micronesia and the USA. Certain of its terms, due to expire in 2001, were renegotiated in late 1999, and an amended Compact was signed by the Governments of both countries on 1 May 2003. By the terms of the Compact, the Federated States of Micronesia is a sovereign, self-governing state.

Local government units are the municipalities and villages. Elected Magistrates and Councils govern the municipalities. Village government is largely traditional.

Defence

The USA is responsible for the defence of the Federated States of Micronesia.

Economic Affairs

In 2007, according to estimates by the World Bank, gross national income (GNI) in the Federated States of Micronesia, measured at average 2005–07 prices, was US $274m., equivalent to $2,470 per head (or $3,270 per head on an international purchasing-power parity basis). During 2000–07, it was estimated, the population increased at an average annual rate of 0.5%, while gross domestic product (GDP) per head decreased, in real terms, by an average of 0.1% per year. Overall GDP increased, in real terms, at an average annual rate of 0.4% in 2000–07. According to the Asian Development Bank (ADB), real GDP decreased by 3.1% in the fiscal year 2007 (ending in September) and by 1.0% in 2008.

Agriculture is mainly on a subsistence level, although its importance is diminishing. The principal crops are coconuts, bananas, betel nuts, cassava and sweet potatoes. White peppercorns are produced on Pohnpei. The sector (including forestry and fishing) contributed an estimated 18.8% of GDP in 2007. Agriculture engaged about 24% of the employed labour force in 2005. In the year to September 2005 fishing access fees, mainly from Japanese fleets, totalled US $13.3m. (some 25% of total government current revenue). Exports of fish are a major source of revenue. The GDP of the agricultural sector contracted by 2.3% in 2006 and by 2.0% in 2007, according to the ADB.

Industry (including mining, manufacturing, utilities and construction) provided an estimated 5.3% of GDP in 2007. There is little manufacturing, other than the production of buttons using trochus shells, and the mining sector is negligible. According to the ADB, industrial GDP contracted by 2.3% in 2006 and by 7.7% in 2007.

The islands are heavily dependent on imported fuels. Imports of mineral products accounted for 22.1% of the value of total imports in 2007. In April 2009 a new bio-gas project was initiated in Pohnpei, the first of four schemes financed by the Chinese province of Zhejiang.

The services sector provided an estimated 75.9% of GDP in 2007. A total of 6,524 people were employed by the national and state Governments in 2005/06. Tourism is an important industry, with receipts for 2005 totalling some US $17m. The number of tourist arrivals increased from 19,136 in 2006 to 21,146 in 2007. Remittances from overseas emigrants are a significant source of income support. The GDP of the services sector contracted by 2.3% in 2006 and by 1.3% in 2007, according to the ADB.

In the financial year ending September 2006 there was a visible trade deficit of an estimated US $128.9m., with a deficit of $38.4m. on the current account of the balance of payments. The principal sources of imports in 2007 were the USA (which supplied 41.2% of the total), Guam (14.4%) and Japan (8.5%). Guam was the principal market for exports in 2007, purchasing 22.5% of the total, while the USA accounted for 17.2%. The principal imports in 2007 were mineral products (22.1% of the total), prepared foodstuffs, beverages and tobacco (17.1%) and machinery, mechanical appliances and electrical equipment (14.4%). Fish is the major export commodity; marine products accounted for 76.0% of total exports in 2007. Other exports in that year included betel nuts and kava.

The budget deficit was estimated to be the equivalent of 3.0% of GDP in 2007/08, compared with a deficit of 16.0% of GDP in 2003/04. The proposed budget for 2009/10 projected a balancing of revenue and expenditure at $39.7m.; it was envisaged that expenditure would be 19% higher than in the previous year. The Federated States of Micronesia relies heavily on financial assistance, particularly from the USA, with funding made available under the Compact of Free Association (see Recent History). In 2008/09 the USA was to provide a total of $81.1m. of Compact funding to Micronesia. Of this sum, the national Government was to receive $7.9m. (of which $5.7m. was to be available for operational support), with the remainder being distributed among the four states. Bilateral grants have been provided by the People's Republic of China and Japan. Aid from Australia for 2008/09 was projected at $A6.6m. At the end of the 2007/08 financial year, according to the ADB, the islands' total external debt stood at $68m., and in 2006/07 the cost of debt-servicing was equivalent to 6.5% of the value of exports of goods and services. The annual rate of inflation averaged 2.0% in 2000–06. According to the ADB, the inflation rate increased from an annual average of 2.8% in 2007 to 5.0% in 2008. Some 22% of the labour force were unemployed at the 2000 census.

The Federated States of Micronesia is a member of the Pacific Community (see p. 391), the Pacific Islands Forum (see p. 393), the South Pacific Regional Trade and Economic Co-operation Agreement (SPARTECA, see p. 395), the UN Economic and Social Commission for Asia and the Pacific (ESCAP, see p. 36) and the Asian Development Bank (ADB, see p. 191). In November 2002 the Federated States of Micronesia was announced as the location of the headquarters for the Tuna Commission, a new multilateral agency to manage migratory fish stocks in the central and western Pacific region. The Council of Micronesian Government Executives, of which the Federated States of Micronesia was a founder member in 1996, aims to facilitate discussion of economic developments in the region and to examine possibilities for reducing the considerable cost of shipping essential goods between the islands.

Economic development has been constrained by the islands' remote position, the high rate of emigration, the lack of marketable commodities and vulnerability to adverse climatic conditions. It was hoped that Micronesia would be in a position to achieve financial self-sufficiency by 2023, but concerns continued with regard to the lack of progress in restructuring the economy in preparation for the impact of the withdrawal of direct US aid in that year (upon the expiry of the Compact of Free Association—see Recent History). Under the amended Compact, instead of general budgetary grants, US aid was to be directed more towards specific projects and government departments. Also, aid was to be conditional upon the efficiency of its management and use, and was to be reviewed annually. Of the total funding of US $81m. in 2008/09, at least 30% was required to be spent on infrastructure, with priority being accorded to education facilities and health services. Meanwhile, the trust fund established to support the Micronesian economy upon the expiry of the Compact remained vulnerable to the volatility of international financial markets; most of the fund's capital was invested in US stock markets. The value of the fund was reported to have decreased by 20% in 2008. In the longer term, an area identified as being in need of reform was that of public enterprises. Measures to encourage the development of the private sector were also required. The Government raised its fuel subsidies in 2008, in response to the rapid rise in international petroleum prices, thus reducing the funds available for other areas. The economy contracted for the fifth successive year in 2008, partly owing to the limitations placed on government expenditure by the reductions in US funding. The deterioration in global economic conditions, particularly in the USA and Japan (the leading sources of visitors to the islands), was expected to have a negative impact on the tourism sector. Remittances from overseas workers were also expected to decrease in 2009. The ADB forecast that the economic decline would continue in 2009, although GDP was expected to contract by only 0.1% in that year.

Education

Primary education, which begins at six years of age and lasts for eight years, is compulsory. Secondary education, beginning at 14

THE FEDERATED STATES OF MICRONESIA

years of age, comprises two cycles, each of two years. The Micronesia Maritime and Fisheries Academy, which was opened in Yap in 1990, provides education and training in fisheries technology at secondary and tertiary levels. The College of Micronesia offers two- and three-year programmes leading to a degree qualification. A summit meeting was held in September 2000 to discuss the improvement and reform of the education sector. In 2006/07 there were 18,512 pupils enrolled in primary education and 14,742 pupils enrolled in secondary education.

Public Holidays

2009: 1 January (New Year's Day), 10 April (Good Friday, Pohnpei only), 11 May (Constitution Day), 23 October (United Nations Day), 3 November (Independence Day), 25 December (Christmas Day).

2010: 1 January (New Year's Day), 2 April (Good Friday, Pohnpei only), 10 May (Constitution Day), 24 October (United Nations Day), 3 November (Independence Day), 25 December (Christmas Day).

Weights and Measures

With certain exceptions, the imperial system is in force. One US cwt equals 100 lb; one long ton equals 2,240 lb; one short ton equals 2,000 lb. A policy of gradual voluntary conversion to the metric system is being undertaken.

Statistical Survey

Source (unless otherwise indicated): Statistics Unit, Office of Statistics, Budget and Economic Management, Overseas Development Assistance and Compact Management (SBOC), POB PS-12, Palikir, Pohnpei, FM 96941; tel. (691) 320-2820; fax (691) 320-5854; e-mail fsmstat@sboc.fm; internet www.spc.int/prism/country/fm/stats.

AREA AND POPULATION

Area: 700.8 sq km (270.6 sq miles): Chuuk (Truk, 294 islands) 127.4 sq km; Kosrae (5 islands) 109.6 sq km; Pohnpei (Ponape, 163 islands) 345.2 sq km; Yap (145 islands) 118.6 sq km.

Population: 105,506 (males 53,923, females 51,583) at census of 18 September 1994; 107,008 (males 54,191, females 52,817) at census of 1 April 2000. *By State* (2000): Chuuk 53,595; Kosrae 7,686; Pohnpei 34,486; Yap 11,241. *2008* (official projections): 108,026 (males 54,350, females 53,676). *By State* (official projections, 2008): Chuuk 53,221; Kosrae 8,183; Pohnpei 34,886; Yap 11,736.

Density (2008): 154.1 per sq km.

Principal Towns (population of municipalities at 2000 census): Weno (Moen) 13,802; Palikir (capital) 6,444; Nett 6,158; Kitti 6,007. Source: Thomas Brinkhoff, *City Population* (internet: www.citypopulation.de).

Births and Deaths (1999/2000, official estimates): Birth rate 28.1 per 1,000; Death rate 6.7 per 1,000. *2003* (incomplete registration): Live births 2,483; Deaths 427 (Source: UN, *Population and Vital Statistics Report*). *2000–05* (annual averages, UN estimates): Birth rate 24.3 per 1,000; Death rate 5.3 per 1,000 (Source: UN, *World Population Prospects: The 2008 Revision*).

Life Expectancy (years at birth, WHO estimates): 68.5 (males 67.4; females 69.7) in 2006. Source: WHO, *World Health Statistics*.

Economically Active Population (persons aged 15 years and over, 2000 census): Agriculture, forestry and fishing 15,216; *Total employed* (incl. others) 29,175 (males 16,957, females 12,218); Unemployed 8,239 (males 4,419, females 3,820); *Total labour force* 37,414 (males 21,376, females 16,038). *Mid-2005* (estimates in '000): Agriculture, etc. 11; Total labour force 46 (Source: FAO).

HEALTH AND WELFARE
Key Indicators

Total Fertility Rate (children per woman, 2006): 3.9.

Under-5 Mortality Rate (per 1,000 live births, 2006): 41.

Physicians (per 1,000 head, 2003): 0.6.

Hospital Beds (per 1,000 head, 2006): 3.3.

Health Expenditure (2006): US $ per head (PPP): 491.

Health Expenditure (2006): % of GDP: 12.0.

Health Expenditure (2006): public (% of total): 90.5.

Access to Water (% of persons, 2006): 94.

Access to Sanitation (% of persons, 2006): 25.

For sources and definitions, see explanatory note on p. vi.

AGRICULTURE, ETC.

Principal Crops ('000 metric tons, 2007, FAO estimates): Coconuts 41; Cassava 12; Sweet potatoes 3; Vegetables 3; Bananas 2.

Livestock ('000 head, year ending September 2007, FAO estimates): Pigs 33; Cattle 14; Goats 4; Chickens 190.

Livestock Products (metric tons, 2007, FAO estimates): Cattle meat 260; Pig meat 880; Chicken meat 145; Hen eggs 175.

Fishing ('000 metric tons, live weight, 2006): Skipjack tuna 8.5; Yellowfin tuna 1.3; Bigeye tuna 0.2; Total catch (incl. others) 11.6.

Source: FAO.

FINANCE

Currency and Exchange Rates: United States currency is used: 100 cents = 1 United States dollar (US $). Sterling and Euro Equivalents (31 December 2008): £1 sterling = US $1.4578; €1 = US $1.3917; US $100 = £68.60 = €71.85.

Budget (US $ million, year ending 30 September 2006, estimates): *Revenue:* Current 54.7 (Tax 29.7, Non-tax 25.0); Grants 85.3; Total 140.0. *Expenditure:* Current 146.4; Capital 6.5; Total 153.0. Note: Figures represent a consolidation of the accounts of the national Government and the four state governments.

International Reserves (US $ '000 at 31 December 2007): IMF special drawing rights 2,127; Reserve position in IMF 0.0; Foreign exchange 46,352; *Total* 48,479. Source: IMF, *International Financial Statistics*.

Money Supply (US $ '000 at 31 December 2007): Demand deposits at banking institutions 22,449. Source: IMF, *International Financial Statistics*.

Cost of Living (Consumer Price Index, average of quarterly figures; base: 1999 = 100): All items 109.6 in 2005; 114.7 in 2006; 118.4 in 2007.

Gross Domestic Product (US $ million at constant 1998 prices, year ending 30 September): 208.7 in 2005; 203.9 in 2006; 187.5 in 2007 (projection).

Gross Domestic Product by Economic Activity (US $ million at current prices, 2002): Agriculture, hunting, forestry and fishing 34; Manufacturing 2; Mining, electricity, gas and water 3; Construction 21; Wholesale and retail trade, hotels and restaurants 34; Transport, storage and communications 29; Other activities 117; *GDP in purchasers' values* 240. Source: UN, *Statistical Yearbook for Asia and the Pacific*.

Balance of Payments (US $ million, year ending 30 September 2006, estimates): Merchandise exports f.o.b. 17.0; Merchandise imports f.o.b. −145.9; *Trade balance* −128.9; Exports of services 20.1; Imports of services −57.5; *Balance on goods and services* −166.2; Other income received 20.5; Other income paid −5.3; *Balance on goods, services and income* −151.0; Private unrequited transfers (net) 5.3; Official unrequited transfers (net) 107.3; *Current balance* −38.4; Capital account (net) 12.0; Other long-term capital (net) 1.9; Other short-term capital (net) 0.8; *Overall balance* (incl. errors and omissions) −23.6.

EXTERNAL TRADE

Principal Commodities (US $'000, 2007): *Imports c.i.f.*: Mineral products 31,476; Prepared foodstuffs, beverages and tobacco 24,390; Machinery, mechanical appliances and electrical equipment 20,553; Vegetable products 8,538; Animals and animal products 8,755; Transportation equipment 8,480; Chemicals 7,660; Base metals and articles thereof 6,216; Total (incl. others) 142,658. *Exports f.o.b.*: Marine products 12,301; Betel nuts 2,224; Citrus 416; Kava 2,224; Total (incl. others) 16,190.

Principal Trading Partners (US $'000, 2007): *Imports*: Australia 5,844; China, People's Republic 5,444; Guam 20,512; Hong Kong 8,955; Japan 12,067; Korea, Republic 5,820; Philippines 5,083;

THE FEDERATED STATES OF MICRONESIA

Singapore 12,413; USA 58,785; Total (incl. others) 142,658. *Exports*: Guam 3,641; Japan 660; USA (mainland only) 2,790; Total (incl. others) 16,190.

TRANSPORT

Shipping: *Merchant Fleet* (registered at 31 December 2007): Vessels 29; Total displacement ('000 grt) 12.9. Source: Lloyd's Register-Fairplay, *World Fleet Statistics*.

TOURISM

Foreign Tourist Arrivals: 18,958 in 2005; 19,136 in 2006; 21,146 in 2007.

Tourist Arrivals by Country or Region of Residence (2007): Europe 2,452; Japan 3,968; Philippines 1,566; Other Asia 1,965; USA 8,081; Total (incl. others) 21,146.

Tourism Receipts (US $ million, incl. passenger transport): 16.7 in 2003; 16.5 in 2004; 17.1 in 2005.

Source: World Tourism Organization.

COMMUNICATIONS MEDIA

Telephones ('000 main lines in use, 2007): 12.4*.

Facsimile Machines (number in use, 1998): 539*.
Mobile Cellular Telephones (2007): 27,400 subscribers.
Radio Receivers (1996): 22,000 in use.
Internet Users ('000, 2007): 15.0*.
Television Receivers (1996): 19,800 in use.

*Source: International Telecommunication Union.

EDUCATION

Primary (2006/07 unless otherwise indicated): 174 schools (1995); 1,051 teachers (1984); 18,512 pupils (Sources: UN, *Statistical Yearbook for Asia and the Pacific* and UNESCO Institute for Statistics).

Secondary (2006/07 unless otherwise indicated): 24 schools (1995); 314 teachers (1984); 14,742 pupils (Sources: UN, *Statistical Yearbook for Asia and the Pacific* and UNESCO Institute for Statistics).

Tertiary (1998/99): 1,510 students (Sources: UN, *Statistical Yearbook for Asia and the Pacific* and UNESCO Institute for Statistics).

Adult Literacy Rate (population aged 10 years and over, 2000 census): 92.4% (males 92.9%; females 91.9%).

Directory

The Constitution

On 10 May 1979 the locally drafted Constitution of the Federated States of Micronesia, incorporating the four states of Kosrae, Yap, Ponape (formally renamed Pohnpei in November 1984) and Truk (renamed Chuuk in January 1990), became effective. Each of the four states has its own Constitution, elected legislature and Governor. The Constitution guarantees fundamental human rights and establishes a separation of the judicial, executive and legislative powers. The federal legislature, the Congress of the Federated States of Micronesia, is a unicameral parliament with 14 members, popularly elected. The executive consists of the President, elected by the Congress, and a Cabinet. The Constitution provides for a review of the governmental and federal system every 10 years.

In November 1986 the Compact of Free Association was signed by the Governments of the Federated States of Micronesia and the USA. By the terms of the Compact, the Federated States of Micronesia is an internally sovereign, self-governing state, whose policy concerning foreign affairs must be consistent with guide-lines laid down in the Compact. Full responsibility for defence lies with the USA, and the security arrangements may be terminated only by mutual agreement. Furthermore, the Compact guaranteed exclusivity to US military forces in Micronesia's waters. The Governments of the Federated States of Micronesia and the USA signed an amended Compact on 1 May 2003, whereby its terms were renewed until 2023. The agreement was approved by the US Congress in November 2003 and ratified by President George W. Bush in December. The amended Compact came into force in June 2004 and was due to expire in 2023.

The Government

HEAD OF STATE

President: IMMANUEL (MANNY) MORI (took office 11 May 2007).
Vice-President: ALIK L. ALIK.

CABINET
(April 2009)

Secretary of the Department of Finance and Administration: FINLEY S. PERMAN.

Secretary of the Department of Foreign Affairs: LORIN S. ROBERT.

Secretary of the Department of Economic Affairs: (vacant).

Secretary of the Department of Resources and Development: PETER M. CHRISTIAN.

Secretary of the Department of Health and Social Affairs: Dr VITA AKAPITO SKILLING.

Secretary of the Department of Justice: MAKETO ROBERT.

Secretary of the Department of Transportation, Communications and Infrastructure: FRANCIS I. ITIMAI.

Secretary of the Department of Education: CASIANO SHONIBER.

Public Defender: JULIUS JOEY SAPELALUT.
Postmaster-General: Rev. MIDION G. NETH.

GOVERNMENT OFFICES

Office of the President: POB PS-53, Palikir, Pohnpei, FM 96941; tel. 320-2228; fax 320-2785; e-mail ppetrus@mail.fm; internet www.fsmpio.fm.

Department of Economic Affairs: POB PS-12, Palikir, Pohnpei, FM 96941; tel. 320-2646; fax 320-5854; e-mail fsmdea@mail.fm; internet www.fsminvest.fm.

Department of Education: POB PS-87, Palikir, Pohnpei, FM 96941; tel. 320-2643; fax 320-5500.

Department of Finance and Administration: POB PS-158, Palikir, Pohnpei, FM 96941; tel. 320-2640; fax 320-2380; e-mail fsmsofa@mail.fm.

Department of Foreign Affairs: POB PS-123, Palikir, Pohnpei, FM 96941; tel. 320-2641; fax 320-2933; e-mail foreignaffairs@mail.fm; internet www.fsmgov.org/ovmis.html.

Department of Health and Social Affairs: POB PS-70, Palikir, Pohnpei, FM 96941; tel. 320-2872; fax 320-5263; e-mail fsmhesa@mail.fm.

Department of Justice: POB PS-105, Palikir, Pohnpei, FM 96941; tel. 320-2644; fax 320-2234; e-mail doj@mail.fm.

Department of Resources and Development: POB PS-12, Palikir, Pohnpei, FM 96941; tel. 320-2646; fax 320-5854; e-mail fsmrd@dea.fm.

Department of Transportation, Communication and Infrastructure: POB PS-2, Palikir, Pohnpei, FM 96941; tel. 320-2865; fax 320-5853; e-mail transfsm@mail.fm; internet www.ict.fm.

Office of the Public Auditor: POB PS-05, Palikir, Pohnpei, FM 96941; tel. 320-2863; fax 320-5482; e-mail hhainrick@mail.fm; internet www.fsmopa.fm/index.htm.

Office of the Public Defender: POB PS-174, Palikir, Pohnpei, FM 96941; tel. 320-2648; fax 320-5775.

Public Information Office: POB PS-34, Palikir, Pohnpei, FM 96941; tel. 320-2548; fax 320-4356; e-mail fsmpio@mail.fm; internet www.fsmpio.fm/pio.htm.

The Legislature

CONGRESS OF THE FEDERATED STATES OF MICRONESIA

The Congress comprises 14 members (Senators), of whom four are elected for a four-year term and 10 for a two-year term. The most recent election was held on 3 March 2009.

Speaker: ISAAC V. FIGIR.

THE FEDERATED STATES OF MICRONESIA

STATE LEGISLATURES

Chuuk State Legislature: POB 189, Weno, Chuuk, FM 96942; tel. 330-2234; fax 330-2233; Senate of 10 mems and House of Representatives of 28 mems elected for four years; Gov. WESLEY W. SIMINA.

Kosrae State Legislature: POB 187, Tofol, Kosrae, FM 96944; tel. 370-3002; fax 370-3162; e-mail kosraelc@mail.fm; unicameral body of 14 mems serving for four years; Gov. ROBERT J. WEILBACHER.

Pohnpei State Legislature: POB 39, Kolonia, Pohnpei, FM 96941; tel. 320-2235; fax 320-2505; internet www.fm/pohnpeileg; 27 representatives elected for four years (terms staggered); Gov. JOHN EHSA.

Yap State Legislature: POB 39, Colonia, Yap, FM 96943; tel. 350-2108; fax 350-4113; 10 mems, six elected from the Yap Islands proper and four elected from the Outer Islands of Ulithi and Woleai, for a four-year term; Gov. SEBASTIAN L. ANEFAL.

Election Commission

National Election Commission: POB PS-355, Palikir, Pohnpei 96941; tel. 320-4283; fax 320-7534; e-mail ned@mail.fm; Dir Rev. KIMEUO KIMIUO.

Diplomatic Representation

EMBASSIES IN THE FEDERATED STATES OF MICRONESIA

Australia: POB S, Kolonia, Pohnpei, FM 96941; tel. 320-5448; fax 320-5449; e-mail australia@mail.fm; internet www.australianembassy.fm; Ambassador SUSAN COX.

China, People's Republic: POB 1530, Kolonia, Pohnpei, FM 96941; tel. 320-5575; fax 320-5578; e-mail chinaemb@mail.fm; internet fm.chineseembassy.org/eng; Ambassador LIU FEI.

Japan: Pami Bldg, 3rd Floor, POB 1847, Kolonia, Pohnpei, FM 96941; tel. 320-5465; fax 320-5470; Ambassador MASASHI NAMEKAWA.

USA: POB 1286, Kolonia, Pohnpei, FM 96941; tel. 320-2187; fax 320-2186; e-mail usembassy@mail.fm; internet www.fm/usembassy; Ambassador MIRIAM K. HUGHES.

Judicial System

Supreme Court of the Federated States of Micronesia: POB PS-J, Palikir Station, Pohnpei, FM 96941; tel. 320-2357; fax 320-2756; internet www.fsmlaw.org; Chief Justice ANDON L. AMARAICH.

State Courts and Appellate Courts have been established in Yap, Chuuk, Kosrae and Pohnpei.

Religion

The population is predominantly Christian, mainly Roman Catholic. The Assembly of God, Jehovah's Witnesses, Seventh-day Adventists, the Church of Jesus Christ of Latter-day Saints (Mormons), the United Church of Christ, Baptists and the Bahá'í Faith are also represented.

CHRISTIANITY

The Roman Catholic Church

The Federated States of Micronesia forms a part of the diocese of the Caroline Islands, suffragan to the archdiocese of Agaña (Guam). The Bishop participates in the Catholic Bishops' Conference of the Pacific, based in Fiji. At 31 December 2006 there were 68,500 adherents in the diocese.

Bishop of the Caroline Islands: Most Rev. AMANDO SAMO, Bishop's House, POB 939, Weno, Chuuk, FM 96942; tel. 330-2399; fax 330-4585; e-mail diocese@mail.fm; internet www.dioceseofthecarolines.org.

Other Churches

Calvary Baptist Church: Kolonia, Pohnpei, POB 2179, FM 96941; tel. 320-2830; fax 320-3887; e-mail cca_pohnpei@yahoo.com; Pastor ISAMO WELLES.

Liebenzell Mission: Rev. Seigbert Betz, POB 9, Weno, Chuuk, FM 96942; tel. 330-3869; e-mail missions@liebenzellusa.org; internet www.liebenzellusa.org.

Truth Independent Baptist Church: Kolonia, Pohnpei, POB 65, FM 969410065; tel. 320-3643; fax 320-6769; Pastor RICARDO P. VERACRUZ.

United Church of Christ in Pohnpei: Kolonia, Pohnpei, POB 864, FM 96941; tel. 320-2271; fax 320-4404; Pres. BERNELL EDWARD.

The Press

Da Rohng: Jano News Service, POB 510, Kolonia, Pohnpei FM 96941; tel. 320-6494; fax 320-4200; e-mail darohng2005@yahoo.com; Editor MARTIN JANO.

The Island Tribune: Pohnpei, FM 96941; f. 1997; fortnightly.

Kaselehlie Press: POB 2222, Pohnpei, FM 96941; tel. 320-6547; fax 320-6571; e-mail kpress@mail.fm; internet www.kpress.info; f. 2001; fortnightly; Man. Editor BILL JAYNES.

Micronesian Alliance: POB 543, Tofol, Kosrae, FM 96944; tel. 370-6131; e-mail equatormedia@yahoo.com.

Yap Networker: PB 1266, Yap, FM 96943; tel. 350-4949; fax 350-4525; e-mail microtech@mail.fm; internet www.yapnetworker.com; Editor BERNA GORONG.

Broadcasting and Communications

TELECOMMUNICATIONS

FSM Telecommunication Corporation: POB 1210, Kolonia, Pohnpei, FM 96941; tel. 320-2740; fax 320-2745; e-mail customerservice@telecom.fm; internet www.fm; provides domestic and international services; Gen. Man. TAKURO AKINAGA.

BROADCASTING

Radio

Federated States of Micronesia Public Information Office: POB PS-34, Palikir, Pohnpei, FM 96941; tel. 320-2548; fax 320-4356; e-mail fsmpio@mail.fm; internet www.fsmpio.fm/pio.htm; govt-operated; four regional stations, each broadcasting 18 hours daily; Information Officer PATRICK BLANK.

Station V6AH: POB 1086, Kolonia, Pohnpei, FM 96941; programmes in English and Pohnpeian; Man. WEIDEN MANUEL.

Station V6AI: POB 117, Colonia, Yap, FM 96943; tel. 350-2174; fax 350-4426; programmes in English, Yapese, Ulithian and Satawalese; Man. SEBASTIAN F. TAMAGKEN.

Station V6AJ: POB 147, Tofol, Kosrae, FM 96944; tel. 370-3040; fax 370-3880; e-mail kosraebroadcast@yahoo.com; programmes in English and Kosraean; Man. MCDONALD ITTU.

Station V6AK: Wenn, Chuuk, FM 96942; tel. 330-2596; programmes in Chuukese and English; Man. JOE COMMOR.

WSZA Yap: Dept of Youth and Civic Affairs, POB 30, Colonia, Yap 96943; tel. 350-2174; Media Dir PETER GARAMFEL.

WSZD Pohnpei: POB 1086, Kolonia, Pohnpei 96941; tel. 320-2296; programmes in English and Pohnpeian; Man. FRANCIS ZARRED.

Television

Island Cable TV—Pohnpei: POB 1628, Pohnpei, FM 96941; tel. 320-2671; fax 320-2444; e-mail ictv@mail.fm; f. 1991; Gen. Man. DAVID O. CLIFFE.

TV Station Chuuk (TTTK): Wenn, Chuuk, FM 96942; tel. 330-4475; commercial.

TV Station Pohnpei (KPON): Central Micronesia Communications, POB 460, Kolonia, Pohnpei, FM 96941; f. 1977; commercial; Tech. Dir DAVID CLIFFE.

TV Station Yap (WAAB): Colonia, Yap, FM 96943; tel. 350-2160; fax 350-4113; govt-owned; Man. LOU DEFNGIN.

Finance

BANKING

Regulatory Authority

Federated States of Micronesia Banking Board: POB 1887, Kolonia, Pohnpei, FM 96941; tel. 320-2015; fax 320-5433; e-mail fsmbb@mail.fm; e-mail wfwbb_gov@mail.fm; f. 1980; Chair. LARRY RAIGETAL; Commissioner WILSON F. WAGUK.

Banks are also supervised by the US Federal Deposit Insurance Corporation.

THE FEDERATED STATES OF MICRONESIA   *Directory*

Commercial Banks

Bank of the Federated States of Micronesia: POB BF, Tofol, Kosrae, FM 96944; tel. 370-3225; brs in Kosrae, Yap, Pohnpei and Chuuk.

Bank of Guam (USA): POB 367, Kolonia, Pohnpei, FM 96941; tel. 320-2550; fax 320-2562; e-mail bogpohn@mail.fm; internet www.bankofguam.com; Br. Mans JOANNE H. AKINAGA, VIDA B. RICAFRENTE; brs in Chuuk and Pohnpei.

Yap Credit Union: POB 610, Colonia, Yap; tel. 350-2142.

Development Bank

Federated States of Micronesia Development Bank: POB M, Kolonia, Pohnpei, FM 96941; tel. 320-2840; fax 320-2842; e-mail fsmdb@mail.fm; internet www.fsmdb.fm/index; f. 1979; total assets US $35.6m. (2007); Chair. IHLEN JOSEPH; Pres. ANNA MENDIOLA; 4 brs. Banking services for the rest of the islands are available in Guam, Hawaii and on the US mainland.

INSURANCE

Actouka Executive Insurance: POB 55, Kolonia, Pohnpei; tel. 320-5331; fax 320-2331.

Caroline Insurance Underwriters: POB 37, Chuuk; tel. 330-2705; fax 330-2207.

FSM Insurance Group: Kosrae; tel. 370-3788; fax 370-2120.

Islands Insurance: POB K, Kolonia, Pohnpei; tel. 320-3422; fax 320-3424.

Moylan's Insurance Underwriters: POB 96941, Kolonia, Pohnpei; tel. 320-2118; fax 320-2519; e-mail pohnpei@moylans.net; Pres. and Gen. Man. MELNER ISAAC.

Oceania Insurance Co: POB 1202, Weno, Chuuk, FM 96942; tel. 330-3036; fax 330-3764; e-mail oceanpac@mail.fm; also owns and manages Pacific Basin Insurance; Region Man. ERICSON MARAR.

Pacific Islands Insurance Underwriters: POB 386, Colonia, Yap; tel. 350-2340; fax 350-2341.

Transpacific Insurance: POB 510, Kolonia, Pohnpei; tel. 320-5525; fax 320-5524.

Yap Insurance Agency: POB 386, Colonia, Yap; tel. 350-2340; fax 350-2341.

Trade and Industry

GOVERNMENT AGENCIES

Coconut Development Authority: POB 297, Kolonia, Pohnpei, FM 96941; tel. 320-2892; fax 320-5383; e-mail fsmcda@mail.fm; responsible for all purchasing, processing and exporting of copra and copra by-products in the islands; Gen. Man. NAMIO NANPEI.

FSM National Fisheries Corporation: POB R, Kolonia, Pohnpei, FM 96941; tel. 320-2529; fax 320-2239; e-mail nfcairfreight@mail.fm; internet www.fsmgov.org/nfc; f. 1984; established in 1990, with the Economic Devt Authority and an Australian co, the Caroline Fishing Corpn (three vessels); promotes fisheries development; Pres. NICK SOLOMON.

Micronesian Fisheries Authority: PS122, Palikir, Pohnpei State, FM 96941; tel. 320-2700; fax 320-2383; e-mail fsmfish@mail.fm; name changed as above from Micronesian Maritime Authority in 2000.

National Oceanic Resource Management Authority (NORMA): POB PS-122, Palikir, Pohnpei, FM 96941; tel. 320-2700; fax 320-2383; e-mail info@norma.fm; internet norma.fm; fmrly Micronesian Fisheries Authority; name changed 2002; responsible for conservation, management and development of tuna resources and for issue of fishing licences; Exec. Dir BERNARD THOULAG; Deputy Dir EUGENE PANGELINAN.

Office of Compact Management: 253 Palikir Station, Pohnpei FM 96941; tel. 320-8375; fax 320-8377; Exec. Dir EHPEL ILON.

Pohnpei Economic Development Authority: POB 738, Kolonia, Pohnpei, FM 96941; tel. 320-2298; fax 320-2775; e-mail eda@mail.fm; chaired by the President of the Federated States of Micronesia; Exec. Dir SHELTEN NETH.

CHAMBERS OF COMMERCE

Chuuk Chamber of Commerce: POB 700, Weno, Chuuk, FM 96941; tel. 330-2318; fax 330-2314; e-mail larry.bruton@mail.fm; Pres. LARRY J. BRUTON.

Kosrae Chamber of Commerce: POB 1075, Tofol, Kosrae, FM 96944; tel. 370-2044; fax 370-2066; e-mail info@kosraechamberofcommerce.org; internet www.kosraechamberofcommerce.org; Chair. GEOFF RASCHOU.

Pohnpei Chamber of Commerce: POB 405, Kolonia, Pohnpei, FM 96941; tel. 320-2452; fax 320-5277; e-mail amc@mail.fm; Pres. AMBROS SENDA.

Yap Chamber of Commerce: Colonia, Yap, FM 96943; tel. 350-2298.

UTILITIES

Chuuk Public Works (CPW): POB 248, Weno, Chuuk, FM 96942; tel. 330-2242; fax 320-4815.

Kosrae Utility Authority: POB 277, Tofol, Kosrae, FM 96944; tel. 370-3799; fax 370-3798; e-mail kua@mail.fm; corporatized in 1994; Gen. Man. FRED SKILLING.

Pohnpei Utilities Corporation: POB C, Kolonia, Pohnpei, FM 96941; tel. 320-2374; fax 320-2422; e-mail info@puc.fm; internet www.puc.fm; f. 1992; provides electricity, water and sewerage services; Gen. Man. FELICIANO PERMAN.

Yap Public Services Corporation: POB 621, Colonia, Yap, FM 96943; tel. 350-2175; fax 350-2331; f. 1996; provides electricity, water and sewerage services.

CO-OPERATIVES

Chuuk: Chuuk Co-operative, Faichuk Cacao and Copra Co-operative Asscn, Pis Fishermen's Co-operative, Fefan Women's Co-operative.

Pohnpei: Pohnpei Federation of Co-operative Asscns (POB 100, Pohnpei, FM 96941), Kapingamarangi Copra Producers' Asscn, Kitti Minimum Co-operative Asscn, Kolonia Consumers' and Producers' Co-operative Asscn, Kosrae Island Co-operative Asscn, Metalanim Copra Co-operative Asscn, Mokil Island Co-operative Asscn, Ngatik Island Co-operative Asscn, Nukuoro Island Co-operative Asscn, PICS Co-operative Asscn, Pingelap Consumers' Co-operative Asscn, Pohnpei Fishermen's Co-operative, Pohnpei Handicraft Co-operative, Uh Soumwet Co-operative Asscn.

Yap: Yap Co-operative Asscn, POB 159, Colonia, Yap, FM 96943; tel. 350-2209; fax 350-4114; e-mail yca@mail.fm; f. 1952; Pres. FAUSTINO YANGMOG; Gen. Man. TONY GANNGIYAN; 1,832 mems.

Transport

ROADS

In 2000 the Federated States of Micronesia had a total road network of 240 km. Macadam and concrete roads are found in the more important islands. Other islands have stone and coral-surfaced roads and tracks.

SHIPPING

Pohnpei, Chuuk, Yap and Kosrae have deep-draught harbours for commercial shipping. The ports provide warehousing and transshipment facilities.

Caroline Fisheries Corporation (CFC): POB 7, Kolonia, Pohnpei, FM 96941; tel. 320-3926; fax 320-4733; e-mail cfc@mail.fm; Gen. Man. MILAN KAMBER.

Pacific Shipping Agency: POB 154, Lelu, Kosrae FM 96944; tel. 350-2475; Gen. Man. THEODORE SIGRAH.

Pohnpei Transfer & Storage, Inc: POB 340, Kolonia, Pohnpei FM 96941; tel. 320-2552; fax 320-2389; e-mail fsmlinejv@mail.fm; Gen. Man. JOE VITT.

Truk Transportation Company (TRANSCO): POB 99, Weno, Chuuk FM 96942; tel. 330-2143; fax 330-2726; e-mail transco@mail.fm; f. 1964; Pres. MYRON HASHIGUCHI; Gen. Man. GIDEON BISALEN.

Waab Transportation Company: POB 177, Colonia, Yap FM 96943; tel. 350-2301; fax 350-4110; e-mail waabtrans@mail.fm; agents for PM & O Lines (USA); Man. LOUIS GAW.

CIVIL AVIATION

The Federated States of Micronesia is served by Continental Micronesia, Our Airline (formerly Air Nauru) and Continental Airlines (USA). Pacific Missionary Aviation, based in Pohnpei and Yap, provides domestic air services. There are international airports on Pohnpei, Chuuk, Yap and Kosrae, and airstrips on the outer islands of Onoun and Ta in Chuuk.

Tourism

The tourist industry is a significant source of revenue, although it has been hampered by the lack of infrastructure. Visitor attractions include excellent conditions for scuba-diving (notably in Chuuk Lagoon), Second World War battle sites and relics (many underwater) and the ancient ruined city of Nan Madol on Pohnpei. The number of tourist arrivals was estimated to total 21,146 in 2007. Tourist receipts totalled an estimated US $17m. in 2005.

THE FEDERATED STATES OF MICRONESIA

Federated States of Micronesia Visitors Board: Dept of Economic Affairs, National Government, PO Box PS-12, Palikir, Pohnpei, FM 96941; tel. 320-5133; fax 320-3251; e-mail fsminfo@visit-fsm.org; internet www.visit-fsm.org.

Chuuk Visitors Bureau: POB FQ, Weno, Chuuk, FM 96942; tel. 330-4133; fax 330-4194; e-mail cvb@mail.fm.

Kosrae Visitors Bureau: POB 659, Tofol, Kosrae, FM 96944; tel. 370-2228; fax 370-3000; e-mail kosrae@mail.fm; internet www.kosrae.com.

Pohnpei Department of Tourism and Parks: POB 66, Kolonia, Pohnpei, FM 96941; tel. 320-2421; fax 320-6019; e-mail tourismparks@mail.fm; Deputy Chief BUMIO SILBANUZ.

Pohnpei Visitors Bureau: POB 1949, Kolonia, Pohnpei, FM 96941; tel. 320-4851; fax 320-4868; e-mail pohnpeiVB@mail.fm; internet www.visit-pohnpei.fm.

Yap Visitors Bureau: POB 988, Colonia, Yap, FM 96943; tel. 350-2298; fax 350-7015; e-mail yvb@mail.fm; internet www.visityap.com; Chair. ALPHONSO GANANG; Gen. Man. LAURENCE KENBAROY.

MOLDOVA

Introductory Survey

Location, Climate, Language, Religion, Flag, Capital

The Republic of Moldova is a small, land-locked country situated in south-eastern Europe. The republic is bounded to the north, east and south by Ukraine. To the west it borders Romania. The climate is favourable for agriculture, with long, warm summers and relatively mild winters. Average temperatures in Chişinău range from 21°C (70°F) in July to −4°C (24°F) in January. The 1994 Constitution describes the official language as Moldovan, a Romance language that is widely considered to be identical to Romanian. Most of the inhabitants of Moldova profess Eastern Orthodox Christianity. The national flag (proportions 1 by 2) consists of three equal vertical stripes, of light blue, yellow and red; the yellow stripe has at its centre the arms of Moldova (a shield bearing a stylized bull's head in yellow, set between an eight-pointed yellow star, a five-petalled yellow flower, and a yellow crescent, the shield being set on the breast of an eagle, in gold and red, which holds a green olive branch in its dexter talons, a yellow sceptre in its sinister talons, and a yellow cross in its beak). The capital is Chişinău.

Recent History

The area of the present-day Republic of Moldova corresponds to only part of the medieval principality of Moldova (Moldavia), which emerged as an important regional power in the 15th century. In the following century the principality came under Ottoman (Osmanlı) domination. Following a period of conflict between the Ottoman and Russian Empires, Moldova was divided into two parts in 1812: the eastern territory of Bessarabia, situated between the Prut and Dniester (Dnestr or Nistru) rivers (which roughly corresponds to the modern Republic of Moldova), was ceded to Russia, while the Ottomans retained control of western Moldova. A Romanian nationalist movement evolved in western Moldova and the neighbouring region of Wallachia during the 19th century, culminating in the proclamation of a Romanian state in 1877. In June 1918, after the collapse of the Russian Empire, Bessarabia was proclaimed an independent republic, although in November it voted to become part of Romania. This union was recognized in the Treaty of Paris (1920). However, the USSR (established in 1922) refused to recognize Romania's claims to the territory, and in October 1924 formed a Moldovan Autonomous Soviet Socialist Republic (ASSR) on the eastern side of the Dniester, within the Ukrainian Soviet Socialist Republic (SSR). In June 1940 Romania was forced to cede Bessarabia and northern Bucovina to the USSR, under the terms of the Treaty of Non-Aggression, concluded with Nazi Germany in August 1939. Northern Bucovina, southern Bessarabia and the Kotovsk-Balţa region of the Moldovan ASSR were incorporated into the Ukrainian SSR. The remaining parts of the Moldovan ASSR and of Bessarabia were merged to form the Moldovan SSR, which formally joined the USSR on 2 August 1940.

Between July 1941 and August 1944 the Moldovan SSR was reunited with Romania. However, the Soviet Army reannexed the region in 1944, and the Moldovan SSR was re-established. Soviet policy in Moldova concentrated on isolating the region from its historical links with Romania: cross-border traffic virtually ceased, the Cyrillic script was imposed on the Romanian language (which was referred to as Moldovan) and Russian and Ukrainian immigration was encouraged. In the 1950s thousands of ethnic Romanians were deported to Central Asia.

In May 1989 a number of independent cultural and political groups, which had recently emerged, but were denied legal status by the authorities, allied to form the Popular Front (PF). In June some 70,000 people attended a protest demonstration, organized by the PF, on the anniversary of the Soviet annexation of Bessarabia in 1940. In August 1989 mass demonstrations were convened in the capital, Chişinău, in support of proposals by the Moldovan Supreme Soviet (Supreme Council—legislature) to declare Romanian the official language of the republic. Following protests by non-ethnic Romanians, the proposals were amended: legislation was enacted providing for Russian to be retained as a language of inter-ethnic communication, but the official language was to be Romanian, written in the Latin script. Following disturbances in Chişinău, during the celebrations of the anniversary of the Bolshevik Revolution on 7 November, the First Secretary of the ruling Communist Party of Moldova (CPM), Semion Grossu, was dismissed. He was replaced by Petru Lucinschi.

The increasing influence of the Romanian-speaking population was strongly opposed by other inhabitants of the republic (who, at the 1989 census, comprised some 35% of the total population). In the areas east of the Dniester, Transnistria or Pridnestrovie, where Russians and Ukrainians predominated (and which had mostly constituted the Moldovan ASSR in 1924–40), the local authorities refused to implement the language law. Opposition to growing Moldovan nationalism was led by the Unity Movement (Yedinstvo), dominated by leading CPM members, and the Slav-dominated United Work Collectives. Both organizations had links with Gagauz Halky (Gagauz People), the most prominent of the political groups representing the 150,000-strong Gagauz minority (a Turkic, Orthodox Christian people, resident mostly in southern regions of Moldova). In January 1990 a referendum took place in the eastern town of Tiraspol, in which the predominantly Russian-speaking population voted to seek greater autonomy for Transnistria.

None of the independent political groups was officially allowed to endorse candidates in elections to the Moldovan Supreme Soviet in February 1990. About 80% of the 380 deputies elected were members of the CPM, but many were also sympathetic to the aims of the PF. The new Supreme Soviet convened in April, whereupon Mircea Snegur, a CPM member supported by the PF, was elected Chairman. In the following month the Government resigned after losing a vote of no confidence. A new Council of Ministers, chaired by an economist, Mircea Druc, implemented far-reaching political changes, revoking the CPM's constitutional right to power. On 23 June the Supreme Soviet adopted a declaration of sovereignty asserting the supremacy of Moldova's Constitution and law. The Supreme Soviet also declared the 1940 annexation of Bessarabia to have been illegal. In September Snegur was elected to the newly instituted post of President of the Republic.

The actions of the increasingly radical Romanian majority in the legislature provoked further anxiety among the country's minority ethnic groups during 1990. In August the Gagauz proclaimed a separate 'Gagauz SSR' in the southern region around Comrat (Komrat), and in September east-bank Slavs proclaimed their secession from Moldova and the establishment of the 'Transdnestrian SSR', with its self-styled capital at Tiraspol (this territory contained much of Moldova's industry, as well as three of the republic's five largest cities). Both declarations were immediately annulled by the Moldovan Supreme Soviet. In October Moldovan nationalists sought to thwart elections to a Gagauz Supreme Soviet by sending some 50,000 armed volunteers to the area. Violence was prevented only by the dispatch of Soviet troops to the region. The new Gagauz Supreme Soviet convened in Comrat and elected Stepan Topal as its President. Inter-ethnic violence occurred east of the Dniester in November, when elections were announced to a Transnistrian Supreme Soviet. Negotiations in Moscow, the Russian and Soviet capital, involving the Moldovan Government, the east-bank Slavs and the Gagauz, failed to resolve the crisis, but the elections proceeded without further violence.

In mid-December 1990 around 800,000 people, attending a 'Grand National Assembly', voted to reject any new union treaty (which was being negotiated by other Soviet republics), and in February 1991 the Moldovan Supreme Soviet resolved not to participate in the all-Union referendum on the future of the USSR. Despite the official boycott, in March some 650,000 people (mostly ethnic Russians, Ukrainians and Gagauz) did take part, voting almost unanimously for the preservation of the USSR. Nevertheless, the ethnic-Romanian-dominated Government and legislature continued the process of de facto secession. In May the designation 'Soviet Socialist' was removed from the republic's name and the Supreme Soviet was renamed Parlamentul (the Parliament). In the same month, following a vote of no confidence by the legislature, Druc was removed as Prime Minister.

Following the attempted coup by conservative communists in Moscow in August 1991, the commanders of the USSR's South-Western Military District sought to impose a state of emergency in Moldova. However, the republican leadership immediately announced its support for the Russian President, Boris Yeltsin, in his opposition to the coup. On 27 August, after the coup had collapsed, Moldova proclaimed its independence. In September President Snegur ordered the creation of national armed forces, and assumed control of the republican KGB (state security service), transforming it into a Ministry of National Security, while the CPM was proscribed.

At the election to the republican presidency on 8 December 1991, Snegur, the sole candidate, received 98.2% of the votes cast. On 21 December Moldova was among the 11 signatories to the Alma-Ata (Almaty) Declaration establishing the Commonwealth of Independent States (CIS, see p. 225). Moldovan affairs during the first half of 1992 were dominated by the armed conflict in Transnistria (see below) and by the question of possible unification with Romania, strongly advocated by the ruling PF (which in February was re-formed as the Christian Democratic Popular Front—CDPF). Moreover, a National Council for Reintegration had been established in December 1991, comprising legislators from both Moldova and Romania who were committed to the idea of a unified Romanian state. Within Moldova, however, popular support for unification remained insubstantial. In June 1992 the CDPF-dominated Government announced its resignation. Andrei Sangheli was appointed Prime Minister, and a new Government 'of national accord' was formed, led by the Agrarian Democratic Party (ADP), which largely comprised members of the former communist leadership. Several portfolios that had been reserved for representatives from Transnistria and Gagauz-Yeri (Gagauzia, the Gagauz-majority area) were refused. The CDPF became the main opposition party. The ADP declared its commitment to consolidating Moldovan statehood, rejecting any future union with Romania. These policies were strongly supported by President Snegur, who in January 1993 proposed that the issue be resolved in a referendum. This proposal was narrowly rejected by Parlamentul, but the ensuing political crisis led to several resignations, including that of the Chairman of Parlamentul, Alexandru Moşanu, who was replaced in February by Lucinschi.

During 1993 the ADP made substantial progress with the drafting of a new constitution, which was to be ratified following the election of a new parliament. The draft constitution provided, *inter alia*, for a reduced, 104-member legislature. Moldova's first multi-party elections were held on 27 February 1994, with the participation of more than 73% of the electorate. In Transnistria the local leadership did not open polling stations, although residents were able to vote on the west bank of the Dniester. In all, 13 parties and blocs contested the elections. The ADP obtained an overall majority in Parlamentul (56 seats). The successor party to the CPM, the Socialist Party (SP), in alliance with the Unity Movement, won 28 seats. Two pro-unification groups shared the remaining 20 seats: the Peasants' Party of Moldova/Congress of Intelligentsia alliance (11) and the CDPF (nine). In a referendum held on 6 March, more than 95% of the votes cast by 75% of the electorate were in favour of continued independence. A new Council of Ministers led by Sangheli, solely comprising members of the ADP, was appointed in April. In May the CPM was permitted to re-form, as the Party of Communists of the Republic of Moldova (PCRM).

The new Constitution, adopted by Parlamentul in July 1994, entered into force in August. As well as establishing the country's permanent neutrality, the Constitution provided for a 'special autonomous status' for Transnistria and Gagauz-Yeri within Moldova, the exact terms of which were to be determined at a later date. The state language was specified as Moldovan (rather than Romanian). In June, following the rejection by the ADP and its allies in Parlamentul of the proposal that the state language be constitutionally described as Romanian, Snegur resigned his membership of the ADP (which he had joined in 1994) and in August 1995 established the Party of Rebirth and Conciliation (PRC), with the support of several disaffected ADP deputies. In February 1996 Parlamentul again rejected the proposed redesignation of the state language as Romanian.

At the presidential election, held on 17 November 1996, Snegur received the largest share of the votes cast (39%) of any of the nine candidates; his failure to win an absolute majority necessitated a second round of voting, in which his opponent was Lucinschi, now supported by the ADP. In the second round of polling, held on 1 December, Lucinschi emerged as the winner, with 54% of the votes cast. The authorities in Transnistria again boycotted the poll, and there were reports that residents were prevented from leaving the region to vote. Lucinschi was inaugurated as President on 15 January 1997, and a new Government was announced later that month, headed by Ion Ciubuc, a non-party economist. In March the leader of the ADP, Dumitru Moţpan, was elected as Chairman of Parlamentul.

Parliamentary elections took place on 22 March 1998. In an apparent rejection of Lucinschi's economic reform programme, the elections were won by the PCRM, led by Vladimir Voronin, which took 30.1% of the votes cast (40 seats). The Democratic Convention of Moldova (CDM), an alliance led by Snegur, won 19.2% (26 seats), while the Movement for a Democratic and Prosperous Moldova (MDPM) received 18.2% (24 seats) and the Moldovan Party of Democratic Forces 8.8% (11 seats). The ADP failed to secure the 4% of the votes required for representation. The elections were again boycotted in Transnistria, but voters were permitted to cross the Dniester to vote.

At the first session of the new legislature, convened in April 1998, Dumitru Diacov was elected Chairman. The Government resigned shortly afterwards. Since none of the political parties had secured an overall parliamentary majority, the new Government, appointed in May (with Ciubuc retaining his post as Prime Minister), comprised members of the Alliance for Democracy and Reforms coalition led within Parlamentul by Snegur, including members of the MDPM, the CDM and the Moldovan Party of Democratic Forces.

Ciubuc resigned as Prime Minister in February 1999. Snegur resigned as parliamentary leader of the government coalition one day later, after his nominee for the premiership was rejected. Lucinschi then nominated the Mayor of Chişinău, Serafim Urechean, as Prime Minister. He was, however, unable to obtain the support of the parliamentary majority. Consequently, Lucinschi nominated Ion Sturza, the Deputy Prime Minister and Minister of the Economy and Reforms, as Prime Minister. Although Parlamentul twice failed to endorse his proposed government, Lucinschi nominated Sturza a third time. Confronted with a choice between acceptance or the constitutional requirement to hold an early general election, Parlamentul narrowly approved Sturza's Government in March.

Local elections were held on 23 May 1999, after which the country was reorganized into nine provinces and two autonomous entities (Gagauz-Yeri and Transnistria). A referendum held on the same day, approving increased presidential powers, was invalidated by the low rate of electoral participation, and was subsequently ruled to have been illegal, as it had not been announced and organized by Parlamentul.

In October 1999 the creation of a new, independent political bloc, principally comprising members of the MDPM, weakened the Government's support in Parlamentul. In November Sturza lost a vote of confidence in the legislature, after the defeat of legislation on the privatization of the wine and tobacco industries; the IMF and the World Bank subsequently suspended credits to Moldova (the bill was finally approved in October 2000). Following the failure of two candidates for the premiership (including Voronin) to secure the necessary support in the legislature, the President's nomination of Dumitru Braghiş, hitherto Deputy Minister of the Economy and Reform, as Prime Minister was approved in December.

In July 2000 Parlamentul voted in favour of amending the Constitution to permit the legislature to elect the Head of State. Parlamentul swiftly overturned President Lucinschi's decision to veto the proposed amendment, which duly took effect. In October Parlamentul announced that a presidential election would be contested within the legislature in December.

Neither of the two candidates in the presidential election—Voronin, for the PCRM, and Pavel Barbalat, the Chairman of the Constitutional Court, who had been proposed by a coalition of the Democratic Party of Moldova (PDM, as the MDPM had been renamed in April), the CDM, the Christian Democratic People's Party (PPCD, formerly the CDPF) and the Moldovan Party of Democratic Forces—obtained the requisite number of votes to secure an overall victory after three rounds of voting. The PDM, the CDM, the PPCD and the Moldovan Party of Democratic Forces boycotted a fourth round of voting on 21 December 2000, thereby permitting the President to dissolve the legislature and schedule early parliamentary elections.

At the legislative elections, held on 25 February 2001, the PCRM won an overall majority in Parlamentul, securing 49.9%

of the votes cast and 71 seats. The Braghiş Alliance, formed by the incumbent Prime Minister, obtained 19 seats, while the PPCD obtained 11 seats. The elections were described as free and fair by observers from the Organization for Security and Co-operation in Europe (OSCE, see p. 366). The rate of voter participation was some 70%. In the presidential election, which took place on 4 April, Voronin secured 71 votes, Braghiş obtained 15 and another communist candidate, Valerian Cristea, won three; the 11 PPCD deputies abstained from voting. Following his inauguration as President on 7 April, Voronin nominated Vasile Tarlev, a former businessman without party affiliation, as premier.

Proposals by the Minister of Education, Ilie Vancea, for the introduction of the compulsory teaching of Russian language and history to the national curriculum from 2002, were confirmed in December 2001. A demonstration, organized by the PPCD and involving an estimated 3,000 people, took place in Chişinău in early January 2002 to protest against these measures; protests continued throughout the month. In late January the Ministry of Justice suspended the PPCD from participation in political activities for a period of one month, thus preventing it from organizing further protests. However, in February, following intervention by the Council of Europe, the PPCD's suspension was annulled in order to allow the party to campaign for local elections, due to be held in April. In mid-February, however, the Constitutional Court ruled that the scheduling of early local elections for April was unconstitutional.

Meanwhile, in February 2002 the Deputy Prime Minister and Minister of the Economy, Andrei Cucu, and the reformist Minister of Finance, Mihai Manole, the only two non-PCRM members of the Council of Ministers, tendered their resignations. Following further protests against the proposed reform of the education system, Vancea announced that the proposed legislation would be retracted; he was consequently dismissed on 26 February. On the following day Vasile Draganel resigned as Minister of the Interior, amid reports that he had been unwilling to dispel protesters by force. Draganel was replaced by Gheorghe Papuc, a long-serving member of the security forces. Despite a ruling by the Supreme Court declaring the ongoing protests to be illegal and demanding that they be halted, in February 2002 demonstrators began to protest outside the headquarters of the national television company against state censorship and misinformation. In March the Deputy Chairman of the PPCD, Vlad Cubreacov, who had been involved in organizing the anti-Government protests, was declared missing; thousands of demonstrators subsequently gathered to protest against Cubreacov's disappearance. In May Cubreacov was discovered alive, although his kidnappers remained unidentified. In June judicial proceedings against members of the opposition involved in the organization of public protests (including Cubreacov) were suspended indefinitely.

Local elections took place on 25 May and 8 June 2003, in which the PCRM won the majority of seats, followed by the newly formed Our Moldova alliance, comprising the Alliance of Independents of Moldova, the National Liberal Party and the Social Democratic Alliance of Moldova. Following the elections, new legislation on administrative reform, approved by the Government in January, came into effect, according to which the nine provinces and two autonomous regions introduced in 1999 were replaced with a structure comprising 33 districts and two municipalities. In July 2003 the parties of the Our Moldova bloc formally merged, together with the Popular Democratic Party of Moldova, to form the Our Moldova Alliance (AMN), led by Braghiş, Urechean and Veaceslav Untilă.

Thousands of protesters took part in opposition demonstrations in November 2003, against the Government's initial support for a Russian proposal for the federalization of Moldova (see below). The proposals, rejected in late November, had envisaged the installation of a popularly elected president and new, bicameral legislature, with an upper house comprising nine representatives elected from Transnistria, four from Gagauz-Yeri and 13 from the remainder of Moldova; Transnistria and Gagauz-Yeri were to have been represented at federal level by deputy prime ministers. New legislation, which was approved on 19 December, which sought to promote the use of Russian as a language of inter-ethnic communication (as it had also been designated in the USSR), while retaining Moldovan as an official language, was a further source of demonstrations.

In February 2004 Andrei Strătan replaced Nicolae Dudău as Minister of Foreign Affairs. In the same month Parlamentul withdrew the immunity from prosecution of three members of the PPCD, including the party's Chairman, Iurie Roşca, to permit their prosecution on charges of organizing and participating in unauthorized protests. From April the PDM and the Social Liberal Party agreed to co-operate with the AMN, as the Democratic Moldova bloc, in preparation for parliamentary elections scheduled to be held in 2005. In October the Minister of Defence, Victor Gaicuc, was dismissed from office following the theft of substantial quantities of military ordnance from army depots. In December Strătan was appointed as Deputy Prime Minister, retaining the foreign affairs portfolio.

In the legislative elections, held on 6 March 2005, the PCRM won 46.0% of the votes cast and 56 seats, the Democratic Moldova bloc obtained 28.5% (34 seats) and the PPCD received 9.1% (11 seats). No other party or grouping obtained legislative representation. Although the PCRM held an absolute majority of seats in Parlamentul, it did not hold the quorum of 61 necessary for the election of a president. At the inaugural session of Parlamentul, the PDM withdrew from the Democratic Moldova bloc, forming its own eight-member faction, and three members of the Social Liberal Party subsequently also left the bloc, which was renamed the AMN faction in the legislature. Despite declarations that opposition deputies would boycott the presidential vote, in the event only the AMN did so. The election was held on 4 April, contested by the incumbent, Voronin, and another PCRM-nominated candidate, Gheorghe Duca, the President of the Moldovan Academy of Sciences. Voronin secured 75 of the 101 votes available (some 95 legislators were present); Duca received only one vote. Voronin was inaugurated as President on 7 April, and on 19 April Parlamentul approved a new Government, again led by Tarlev and retaining many members of the previous Council of Ministers.

In October 2005 members of the PCRM voted in Parlamentul to remove the parliamentary immunity of Urechean and two other deputies, following allegations of abuse of office. In the same month Mihai Pop was appointed Minister of Finance, in succession to Zinaida Grecianîi, who became First Deputy Prime Minister. In November Braghiş left the AMN, of which Urechean remained the sole leader, in order to form the Party of Social Democracy of Moldova. In January 2006 a former Minister of Defence, Valeriu Pasat, was sentenced to 10 years' imprisonment, after being convicted of defrauding the state when selling redundant fighter aircraft to the USA in 1997. In February 2006 Pasat was indicted on further, unrelated charges of having organized protests during the 2005 legislative elections in an attempt to overthrow Voronin and of conspiring to murder PPCD leader Iurie Roşca. (However, in July 2007 Pasat was released by the Court of Appeal.)

In September 2006 Voronin replaced the Minister of Justice, appointing the hitherto government representative to the European Court of Human Rights to the post. In June 2007 local elections were conducted throughout Moldova; voter turnout was recorded at 52.3% nation-wide and about 37.2% in Chişinău. Overall, the PCRM secured 334 mayoralties, 465 seats in district and municipal councils, and 4,040 seats in city and village councils; the AMN won 157 mayoralties, 220 seats in district and municipal councils, and 1,987 seats in city and village councils. The PCRM won 16 seats on Chişinău Municipal Council; however, Dorin Chrtoaca of the Liberal Party (PL), which had obtained 11 seats in the Council, was elected Mayor. In the same month Voronin dismissed the Minister of Defence, Valeriu Plesca, after a civilian was killed when journalists were permitted to participate in a military training exercise. In July he was replaced by Vitalie Vrabie, hitherto Deputy Prime Minister and Minister of Local Public Administration. In late 2007 a number of new political organizations were established in preparation for legislative elections due in early 2009.

In January 2008 Voronin appointed a prominent member of the PCRM, Victor Stepaniuc, as a Deputy Prime Minister. On 19 March Tarlev submitted his resignation and that of his Government. Voronin subsequently nominated Grecianîi to the premiership. On 31 March Parlamentul voted to approve a new Government by 56 votes, with opposition deputies abstaining from voting; Igor Dodon, the Minister of Economy and Trade, succeeded Grecianîi as First Deputy Prime Minister. In October the hitherto Minister of Internal Affairs, Valentin Mejinschi, became Deputy Prime Minister, while Gheorghe Papuc was reappointed to the internal affairs ministry. In the same month Tarlev was elected Chairman of the Centrist Union of Moldova.

Elections to Parlamentul on 5 April 2009 resulted in a decisive majority for the PCRM, which (according to preliminary results) secured about 49.5% of votes cast, while the PL won 13.1%, the

Liberal Democratic Party of Moldova (PLDM) obtained 12.4% and the AMN received 9.8% of the votes cast. Despite a positive assessment of the conduct of the elections by the OSCE and other international observers, protests at alleged electoral malpractice, involving some 20,000, began on 6 April, apparently having been organized spontaneously through social networking and micro-blogging websites. On the following day the anti-Government demonstrations degenerated into violent rioting, which included attacks on parliamentary and presidential buildings. The protests were suppressed by police, after clashes and the arrest of some 200 demonstrators; more than 270 people were reported to have been injured. Voronin accused the Romanian Government of organizing a coup attempt (since many of the protesters had exhibited pro-Romanian sentiments), and immediately expelled the Romanian ambassador and recalled the Moldovan envoy in Bucharest, the Romanian capital; a number of Romanian journalists were also refused entry into the country (as a result of the introduction of visa requirements). Romania denied the allegations of involvement and demanded that the European Union (EU, see p. 255) investigate alleged abuses by the Moldovan authorities. The Russian Government declared support for the Moldovan authorities and strongly condemned the protests. On 12 April the Constitutional Court officials ordered a recount of the preliminary results, following a request by Voronin. (However, the opposition parties dismissed the measure, claiming that malpractice had been perpetrated through the drafting of electoral lists.) Human rights groups corroborated claims that demonstrators in custody were subjected to assaults and other ill treatment by police, and it was reported that at least three protesters had died following the arrests. The EU Special Representative to Moldova, Kalman Mizsei, undertook the mediation of negotiations with opposition leaders; in mid-April, following a meeting with Mizsei, Voronin announced an amnesty for all suspects in detention or under investigation for involvement in the riots, excepting those with criminal records. (However, the Prosecutor-General's Office subsequently announced that 20 protesters had been officially charged in connection with the disturbances.) On 20 April the Electoral Commission announced that the recount had not resulted in a significant change to the official results of the poll: the PCRM had secured 60 seats in Parlamentul (one less than the number required to elect a President), while the PL and PLDM had each received 15 seats, and the AMN 11 seats. (None of the further eight parties, that, together with independent candidates, contested the elections, achieved the requisite 6% of votes cast to obtain representation.) On 23 April the Constitutional Court endorsed the election results, following an appeal against them, submitted by the PL, the PLDM and the AMN, based on alleged evidence of electoral malpractice. The PCRM subsequently nominated Voronin as its candidate for Chairman of Parlamentul; he was elected to the post on 12 May. On the following day the PCRM declared that it would present Grecianîi as its candidate to succeed Voronin as President. In mid-May it was announced that Grecianîi and a further candidate nominated by the PCRM, Stanislav Gropa, were to contest an election for the presidential office within Parlamentul on 20 May.

Following the proclamation of Transnistria's secession in September 1990, relations with the central Government in Chişinău remained tense. Armed conflict broke out in December 1991, as the leadership of the self-proclaimed republic, opposed to the Government's objective of reunification with Romania, launched a campaign to gain control of Transnistria (with the ultimate aim of unity with Russia). Over six months of military conflict ensued, as Moldovan government troops were dispatched to combat the local Slav militia. The situation was complicated by the presence (and alleged involvement in support of the east-bank Slavs) of the former Soviet 14th Army, which was still stationed in the region and jurisdiction over which had been transferred to Russia. Although peace negotiations were held at regular intervals, with the participation of Moldova, Russia, Ukraine and Romania, none of the agreed cease-fires was observed. By June 1992 some 700 people were believed to have been killed in the conflict, with an estimated 50,000 people forced to take refuge in Ukraine. On 21 July, however, a peace agreement was finally negotiated by President Snegur and his Russian counterpart, Boris Yeltsin, whereby Transnistria was to be accorded 'special status' within Moldova (the terms of which were to be formulated later). Later in July Russian, Moldovan and Transnistrian peace-keeping troops were deployed in the region to monitor the cease-fire.

Transnistria continued to demand full statehood, and in January 1994 the Moldovan Government accepted proposals by the Conference on Security and Co-operation in Europe (CSCE—later OSCE) for greater autonomy for Transnistria, within a Moldovan confederation. The Transnistrian leadership expressed approval of the proposals, and the result of the Moldovan parliamentary elections of the following month further enhanced the prospects for a settlement. In April President Snegur and the Transnistrian leader, Igor Smirnov, pledged their commitment to holding negotiations for a peaceful resolution of the conflict, based on the CSCE recommendations.

In July 1994, following the adoption of the new Moldovan Constitution, which provided for a 'special autonomous status' for Transnistria, negotiations commenced on the details of the region's future status within Moldova. Progress was obstructed, in particular, by disagreement over the future of the 15,000-strong 14th Army, the continued presence of which was demanded by the Transnistrian leadership as a guarantor of security. In October, however, the Moldovan and Russian Governments reached an agreement, under which Russia was gradually to withdraw the 14th Army, whereupon Transnistria's negotiated 'special autonomous status' would take effect. A referendum (declared illegal by President Snegur) was held in Transnistria in March 1995, in which some 91% of participants voted against the withdrawal of the 14th Army. In December two further referendums were held in Transnistria: 82.7% of the electorate endorsed a new constitution that proclaimed the region's independence, while 89.7% voted for Transnistria to join the CIS as a sovereign state. In February 1996, however, the CIS rejected admittance for Transnistria on such terms.

In July 1996 the executive and legislative authorities of Moldova and Transnistria initialled a memorandum, on normalizing relations. Smirnov was re-elected as 'President' of Transnistria in December. In May 1997 the memorandum was signed in Moscow by the new Moldovan President, Lucinschi, and Smirnov, with Russia and Ukraine acting as guarantors of the document. Representatives of the Moldovan and Transnistrian sides, meeting in Moscow in October, subsequently reached agreement on a number of 'confidence-building measures'. On 20 March 1998 a further agreement (the Odesa Accords) was signed by Lucinschi, Smirnov, Russian premier Viktor Chernomyrdin and President Leonid Kuchma of Ukraine, which envisaged a reduction in Moldovan and Transnistrian peace-keeping forces, while Russian troops were to remain in Transnistria until a final political settlement was reached.

In June 1998 Russian and Moldovan delegations to the joint commission monitoring the Odesa Accords agreed proposals for the composition of peace-keeping forces in the Transnistrian security zone, and Moldova's peace-keeping troops were gradually reduced in number. In late May 1999 Transnistria was formally designated an autonomous entity. In July a further joint declaration on the normalization of relations between Moldova and Transnistria was signed; however, Smirnov declared that differences remained.

In June 2000 the 'Transnistrian Supreme Soviet' was converted to a unicameral legislature, and in July Smirnov introduced a form of presidential rule. The Moldovan President elected in April 2001, Voronin, declared the pursuit of a final political settlement for Transnistria to be a priority. A deterioration in Transnistria's relations with the Moldovan Government took place in September, following the Government's introduction of new customs procedures, in accordance with World Trade Organization (WTO) specifications, leading to claims by Transnistria that the Moldovan Government was attempting to impose an 'economic blockade' on the region. Smirnov was re-elected as 'President' of the region in December, although the election was recognized by neither the Moldovan Government nor the international community. In December 2002 the OSCE amended a deadline agreed in 1999 for the removal of Russian forces from Moldova, extending it for a further year, until December 2003; however, Russia indicated that some troops might remain, with a possible mandate for maintaining peace and stability in the event of a final settlement.

In July 2002 mediators from Russia, Ukraine and the OSCE submitted a new draft agreement (the 'Kyiv agreement'), according to which Moldova would become a federal state, in which the autonomous territories would maintain their own legislature and constitution; however, Smirnov insisted that recognition of Transnistria's 'independence' was a fundamental prerequisite. On 27 February 2003 the EU and the USA, and subsequently other countries, imposed a travel ban on those Transnistrian officials considered to be 'primarily responsible for a lack of co-operation in promoting a political settlement'. In November the Russian President, Vladimir Putin, announced new proposals for a political settlement. Drafted by the deputy head of the Russian presidential administration, Dmitrii Kozak, the plan envisaged the establishment of an 'asymmetrical federation', comprising Moldova and Transnistria, with unified defence, customs and finance systems. The leaders of both Transnistria and Moldova initially responded positively to the proposals, but Voronin withdrew his support in late November, following opposition protests and reservations expressed by the OSCE. Although new proposals for Moldova's federalization were submitted to OSCE mediators in February 2004, the Transnistrian authorities argued that they offered the region insufficient autonomy, and representatives of Moldova also criticized the draft for its failure to clarify the issue of the presence of Russian troops. In mid-2004 controversy arose over the closure by the Transnistrian authorities of Moldovan-language schools teaching a Moldovan syllabus, in the Latin script. The Moldovan Government responded by withdrawing from the OSCE-mediated negotiation process and imposing economic sanctions on the separatist region, which retaliated in kind. The EU, the USA and other international parties condemned the closure of the schools as an infringement of human rights, adding a further 10 Transnistrian officials to the list of those prohibited from travelling to their countries, and a case was submitted to the European Court of Human Rights.

In December 2004, at an OSCE meeting held in Sofia, Bulgaria, the Russian delegation obstructed the adoption of a final statement containing a reference to the Russian commitment to withdraw troops and ammunition from Moldova. Russian representatives also refused to sign a Moldovan-drafted Declaration of Stability and Security, which proposed the inclusion of the EU and the USA in talks for the resolution of the Transnistrian conflict.

In April 2005 President Viktor Yushchenko of Ukraine presented a plan for the resolution of the Transnistrian conflict during a summit meeting in Chişinău. The plan envisaged that Transnistria would be awarded 'special status', as an autonomous entity within Moldova, and would be permitted to participate in foreign-policy decisions affecting its interests. In June Parlamentul endorsed the Yushchenko Plan, while noting that it made no mention of either the withdrawal of Russian troops or the establishment of border controls along the Transnistrian–Ukrainian border. In July Moldova removed the trade sanctions imposed against Transnistria in the previous year. In September all five parties to the negotiations on the status of Transnistria agreed to invite the EU and the USA (but not Romania) to participate in the process as observers; however, subsequent negotiations failed to record any substantive progress. Legislative elections (recognized by neither the Moldovan Government nor the international community) were held in Transnistria in December. Notably, the reformist Renewal bloc won the most seats in the region's Supreme Soviet.

At the end of November 2005 the EU launched a mission to help secure the Transnistrian–Ukrainian border, following appeals from Presidents Voronin and Yushchenko. As part of the same initiative, at the end of December the Prime Ministers of Moldova and Ukraine signed a joint declaration on external trade, whereby Ukraine agreed not to recognize Transnistria's customs regime and to deal only in goods processed through the Moldovan customs system, in an attempt to combat smuggling. The new measures came into force in March 2006. In response, the Transnistrian authorities withdrew from the internationally mediated negotiations. The Transnistrian authorities subsequently introduced legislation banning all foreign-financed non-governmental organizations, and Smirnov appealed to Russia to dispatch more troops to the region. (In February Russia had reportedly confirmed that it did not intend to complete the withdrawal of its troops from Transnistria before a final settlement on the region's status had been reached.) In late March Russia suspended the import of Moldovan wine and other agricultural products, ostensibly owing to hygiene concerns. At a CIS summit held in Minsk, Belarus, in November, President Putin declared an end to the trade ban against Moldova. In early 2007 the Russian authorities announced that the import of fruit and vegetables from Moldova had resumed. In October the Russian Government announced that those Moldovan wineries that had passed safety assessments were permitted to resume exports to Russia.

In March 2006, following the initiation in February of formal negotiations to determine the final status of the Serbian UN-administered province of Kosovo (see the chapter on Kosovo), Transnistrian officials declared their intention to schedule a referendum on future relations with Moldova, stating that the eventual secession of Kosovo from Serbia could set a precedent for the granting of statehood to other separatist territories. On 17 September the Transnistrian authorities conducted an internationally unrecognized referendum on the territory's independence and potential options for eventual integration, at which some 97% voted for a continuation of de facto independence from Moldova and an objective of eventual unification with Russia, while some 95% voted against the territory being ruled as part of Moldova. On 10 December a presidential election in Transnistria (again unrecognized by the international community) was won by Smirnov, with 82.4% of votes cast. Some 65.4% of registered voters participated in the election. Shortly after Kosovo's unilateral declaration of independence on 17 February 2008, Transnistria (together with Abkhazia and South Ossetia—see the chapter on Georgia) requested that the Russian legislature, the UN and other organizations recognize their independence. In March, following strong indications that Russia was not prepared to recognize Transnistria, Smirnov announced that he was willing to enter into discussions with the Moldovan Government. In April he and Voronin met for the first time since 2001 in Tighina (Bender), Transnistria; the discussions that followed between Moldovan and Transnistrian delegations in Odesa, Ukraine, were regarded as preparatory to the resumption of official negotiations on a political resolution of the status of Transnistria.

In February 2009 the Russian Minister of Foreign Affairs Sergei Lavrov made an official visit to Moldova, preparatory to a meeting between Voronin and Smirnov, to be conducted under the aegis of Russian President Dmitrii Medvedev in Moscow on 18 March. On that occasion the three leaders signed a Russian-drafted declaration providing for the conversion of the existing peace-keeping force in Transnistria into an OSCE-supervised operation (with the implication that the Moldovan Government would abandon demands for the withdrawal of Russian troops); the leaders expressed the intention to continue direct contacts but reiterated commitments to return to the '5 + 2' negotiating format (comprising Moldova, Transnistria, Russia, Ukraine and the OSCE, together with the USA and the EU).

During the Transnistrian conflict in 1991–92, the situation in Gagauz-Yeri (which, unlike Transnistria, constitutes several non-contiguous territories) remained peaceful, although the region continued to demand full statehood. The Moldovan Constitution adopted in 1994 provided for a 'special autonomous status' for Gagauz-Yeri, as for Transnistria, and negotiations duly commenced on the details of this status. Agreement was quickly reached between the Government and the Gagauz authorities, and in December Parlamentul adopted legislation on the status of Gagauz-Yeri. The regions of southern Moldova populated by the Gagauz were to enjoy broad self-administrative powers, and Gagauz was to be one of three official languages (with Moldovan and Russian). Legislative power was to be vested in a regional assembly, and a directly elected başkan (governor) was to hold a quasi-presidential position. The law entered into force in February 1995, and in March a referendum was held in the region to determine which settlements would form part of the region. Elections to the 35-seat Halk Toplusu (Popular Assembly) took place in May–June. Concurrent elections held to the post of Başkan were won by Gheorghe Tabunscic, the First Secretary of the Comrat branch of the PCRM. Under the new Constitution, Tabunscic, as Gagauz leader, became a member of the Council of Ministers of Moldova. In May 1999 Gagauz-Yeri, like Transnistria, was designated an autonomous entity within Moldova. Elections to the Halk Toplusu and to the post of Başkan were held in late August. Following a second round of voting in September, Dumitru Croitor was elected as Başkan, with 61.5% of the votes cast. In mid-February 2002 the Halk Toplusu adopted a vote of no confidence in Croitor, and scheduled a referendum in the hope of securing his dismissal. On 24 February, the date that the referendum was scheduled to take place, the regional security forces reportedly seized the offices of the regional electoral commission, declaring its mandate to have expired and the plebiscite to be illegal. President Voronin subsequently visited the region and demanded the resignations of both Croitor and the Chairman of the Halk Toplusu. Croitor finally resigned at the end of June. At a second round of voting in an election held on 11 October, Tabunscic regained the position of

Başkan. On 25 July 2003 Parlamentul officially recognized the autonomous status of Gagauz-Yeri through an amendment to the national Constitution, which awarded the Halk Toplusu the right to self-determination and to propose its own legislation. Legislative elections were held in the region in November and December, in which the PCRM and independent candidates each won almost one-half of the seats contested. On 17 December 2006 an independent candidate, Mihail Formuzal, was elected Başkan at a second round of voting. Further elections to the Halk Toplusu took place on 16 and 31 March 2008, with voter turnout estimated at 60.5%. A coalition formed by the PCRM with independent candidates commanded the greatest parliamentary representation, with 14 seats, while supporters of Formuzal won eight seats. Following prolonged disagreement between the factions in the Halk Toplusu over the election of a Chairman, at the end of July an independent deputy and prominent journalist, Ana Harlamenco, was elected unanimously to the post. On 22 September the Halk Toplusu narrowly approved a resolution formally recognizing the separatist regions of Abkhazia and South Ossetia as independent from Georgia, following Russian recognition of those territories as independent states, and declaring support for Russia's military action in Georgia in August (see the chapter on Georgia).

Owing to the changing domestic situation, Moldova's membership of the CIS was equivocal from its signature of the Alma-Ata Declaration in December 1991 until early 1994. In August 1993 Parlamentul failed by four votes to ratify the Alma-Ata Declaration, largely owing to the influence of deputies favouring unification with Romania, thus technically removing Moldova from the CIS. However, in September President Snegur signed a treaty to join the new CIS economic union. Following Moldova's parliamentary elections of February 1994 and the referendum in March, which strongly endorsed continued independence, Parlamentul reversed its earlier decision, and in April it finally ratified membership of the CIS.

The communist Government elected in 2001 initially undertook a policy of rapprochement with Russia, and in December Parlamentul ratified a treaty on friendship and co-operation, which had been signed by the two countries' respective Presidents in the previous month. The treaty was ratified by the Russian Gosudarstvennaya Duma (State Duma) in April 2002. However, in 2004 relations deteriorated, largely owing to developments associated with Transnistria (see above). From the beginning of 2006 Russia attempted to increase two-fold the price charged to Moldova for supplies of natural gas (from US $80 to $160 per 1,000 cu m). Gas supplies from Russia temporarily ceased in January, after Moldova refused to sign a new contract with the Russian state-controlled gas supplier, Gazprom. In mid-January a compromise agreement was reached, covering the first three months of the year; in return for agreeing to relinquish the Transnistrian assets of the joint-venture company MoldovaGaz to Gazprom (which already held a majority stake in the company), Moldova was be charged $110 per 1,000 cu m for its gas supplies from Russia. Leading officials of MoldovaGaz and Gazprom signed a five-year agreement, providing for staged increases in the price of gas supplied to Moldova, while the Moldovan Government was to transfer control of its gas distribution system to Gazprom.

Agreement on the delimitation of the Moldovan–Ukrainian border, apart from the Transnistrian section, was reached in November 1997, and the two countries finally defined their border in May 1999. In November 2004 Moldova condemned suspected electoral malpractice in Ukraine during the presidential election there and subsequently established cordial relations with the new administration of President Viktor Yushchenko in Ukraine. Moldova had also established good relations with the new, western-orientated Government in Georgia, under President Mikheil Saakashvili, who was inaugurated in early 2004. In December 2005 Moldova attended a meeting in Kyiv, Ukraine, to launch the new Community of Democratic Choice, originally conceived by Ukraine and Georgia. The nine-member alliance aimed to remove divisions and resolve conflicts in the Baltic, Black Sea and Caspian regions. In May 2006 the leaders of Georgia, Ukraine, Azerbaijan and Moldova met in Kyiv, Ukraine, to revive the regional GUAM organization, renaming it the Organization for Democracy and Economic Development—GUAM.

Relations with Romania were subject to tensions. A basic political treaty, in preparation for six years, was agreed in May 1999 and initialled in April 2000; however, it was not signed, and in late 2003 the Romanian Prime Minister, Adrian Năstase, indicated that the country no longer considered the treaty to be relevant to the political situation. In February 2000 many Moldovans applied to obtain Romanian citizenship as formal negotiations on Romania's accession to the EU commenced. The Romanian Government subsequently introduced measures to simplify the application process, angering the Moldovan authorities, since the Constitution did not permit dual citizenship. The situation was resolved when President Lucinschi drafted a new law, allowing Moldovans to hold dual citizenship with Israel, Romania and Russia, which was enacted in August. In March 2002 a Romanian diplomat was expelled from Moldova, after having reportedly met organizers of opposition protests (see above); Romania responded by expelling a Moldovan diplomat. From April 2003 ministerial co-operation between Moldova and Romania was resumed, together with discussions on the initiation of negotiations regarding a border agreement; it was confirmed that Romania would not require Moldovan citizens to possess entry visas until its accession to the EU. None the less, in October the Moldovan Government appealed to the Council of Europe for assistance with its deteriorating relations with Romania, after that country failed to sign a bilateral treaty confirming Moldova's borders. In January 2005 the new President of Romania, Traian Băsescu, visited Moldova and declared his support for the country's desire to achieve eventual membership of the EU, which had begun to formulate an official policy towards Moldova. In March 2007 the Moldovan Government strongly criticized Romania for granting Romanian citizenship to large numbers of Moldovans (with an estimated 800,000 applications pending), on the grounds that the policy undermined Moldova's statehood. Romania's accession to full EU membership, which took effect in January 2007, resulted in Moldovan citizens being required to possess entry visas to enter that country; in protest at this decision, the Moldovan authorities reversed a decision to allow Romania to open two new consulates in the country. In December Moldova expelled two Romanian diplomats, who had allegedly supplied funds to opposition newspapers, for activities 'incompatible with their status'.

The civil disturbances following legislative elections in early April 2009 (see above) prompted a number of retaliatory measures from the Moldovan Government, which accused Romania of organizing a coup attempt: the expulsion of the Romanian ambassador, the recall of the Moldovan envoy in Bucharest and the immediate introduction of visa requirements for Romanians entering the country. Băsescu subsequently pledged that the Romanian Government would expedite the process of granting Romanian citizenship to Moldovans, claiming that some 1m. applications had been received. In late April it was reported that the Moldovan authorities had refused to accredit a new Romanian ambassador. Following the European Commission's Eastern Partnership initiative for Moldova (together with Armenia, Azerbaijan, Georgia, Ukraine and Belarus), which had been approved at an EU summit meeting in March, the acting Prime Minister of the Czech Republic, Mirek Topolánek, in his capacity as President of the EU Council, visited Moldova in late April. During a meeting with Voronin, Topolánek extended officially an invitation to the Moldovan authorities for an Eastern Partnership summit meeting (which was scheduled to take place in early May). Topolánek also met principal opposition leaders, who presented alleged evidence to support their claims of electoral malpractice; he subsequently announced that he had recommended the establishment of a committee, comprising representatives of the European Commission and opposition parties, to investigate the violence.

Government

Under the Constitution of 1994, supreme legislative power is held by the unicameral Parlamentul (Parliament), which is directly elected every four years. Parlamentul comprises 101 members. The President is Head of State and holds executive power in conjunction with the Council of Ministers, led by the Prime Minister. According to constitutional amendments introduced in July 2000, the President is elected by the legislature for a four-year term. In 1999 the country was reorganized into nine provinces and two autonomous entities—Gagauz-Yeri and Transnistria. However, in January 2003 the Government approved new legislation on administrative reform, replacing the structure introduced in 1999 with one based upon 33 districts (rayons) and two municipalities, although the two autonomous entities retained that status.

Defence

Following independence from the USSR in 1991, the Moldovan Government initiated the creation of national armed forces. As assessed at November 2008, these numbered 6,000, with an army of 5,150 (including conscripts) and an air force of 850. In addition, reserves totalled 66,000. There were an estimated 2,379 paramilitary forces, attached to the Ministry of Internal Affairs. Military service is compulsory (with exemptions for students) and lasts for one year. Under an agreement concluded by the Moldovan and Russian Governments in late 1994, the former Soviet 14th Army (under Russian jurisdiction) was to have been withdrawn from Transnistria within three years, but in March 1998 it was announced that Russian forces would remain in Transnistria until a political settlement for the region was reached. Despite subsequent agreements providing for a withdrawal, some 1,500 Russian troops remained in Transnistria at November 2008. In early 1994 Moldova joined the North Atlantic Treaty Organization's (NATO) 'Partnership for Peace' (see p. 353) programme. The 2008 budget allocated 245m. Moldovan lei to defence.

Economic Affairs

In 2007, according to estimates by the World Bank, Moldova's gross national income (GNI), measured at average 2005–07 prices, was US $4,323m., equivalent to $1,260 per head (or $2,930 per head on an international purchasing-power parity basis). During 2000–07, it was estimated, the population decreased at an average annual rate of 1.3%, while gross domestic product (GDP) per head increased, in real terms, at an average annual rate of 7.5%. Overall GDP increased, in real terms, at an average annual rate of 6.2% in 2000–07; GDP increased by 3.0% in 2007.

As a result of its extremely fertile land and temperate climate, Moldova's economy is dominated by agriculture and related industries. Some 85% of the country's terrain is cultivated. In 2008 agriculture (including hunting, forestry and fishing) contributed 10.6% of GDP, according to preliminary figures. In 2007 the sector provided 32.8% of employment. Principal crops include wine grapes and other fruit, tobacco, vegetables and grain. The wine industry has traditionally occupied a central role in the economy. The private ownership of land was legalized in 1991, although the sale of agricultural land was not permitted until 2001. In 2004 some 73.1% of agricultural land was privately owned and the private sector accounted for some 99% of production. According to the World Bank, the GDP of the agricultural sector increased, in real terms, at an average rate of 1.6% per year during 2000–07. Agricultural GDP increased, in real terms, by 2.0% in 2007, according to World Bank estimates.

In 2008 industry (including mining, manufacturing, power and construction) contributed 23.0% of GDP, according to preliminary data. The sector provided 18.7% of employment in 2007. In 2000–07, according to the World Bank, industrial GDP increased at an average rate of 2.8% per year. Industrial GDP increased by 10.0% in 2007.

Mining and quarrying contributed 0.6% of GDP in 2008, according to preliminary figures, and employed just 0.3% of the working population in 2007. Moldova has extremely limited mineral resources. Activity is focused primarily on the extraction and processing of industrial minerals such as gypsum, limestone, sand and gravel. Deposits of petroleum and natural gas were discovered in southern Moldova in the early 1990s; total reserves of natural gas have been estimated at 22,000m. cu m.

The manufacturing sector contributed 13.7% of GDP in 2008, according to preliminary figures, and provided 10.3% of employment in 2007. The sector is dominated by food-processing, wine and tobacco production, machine-building and metal-working, and light industry. According to the World Bank, manufacturing GDP increased, in real terms, by an annual average of 5.8% in 2000–07. Manufacturing GDP increased by 10.0% in 2007.

Moldova relies heavily on imported energy—primarily natural gas and petroleum products—from Russia, Romania and Ukraine (such imports accounted for 76.7% of consumption in 2004). In the mid-2000s Moldova announced its intention to diversify its gas suppliers, and to increase domestic energy production substantially; domestic production represented 23.3% of consumption in 2004. A large proportion of natural gas imports supply the Moldoveneasca power station, located in Transnistria, which contributes much of the country's electricity-generating capacity. The growing importance of natural gas to the generation of electricity has been paralleled by the rapid decline, from the mid-1990s, in the importance of coal-fired power sources; whereas in 1995 some 31.5% of electricity generated in Moldova was of coal origin, by 2004 the contribution of coal to electricity generation was negligible. In February 2005 an Azerbaijani company purchased the unfinished Giurgiulesti petroleum terminal in southern Moldova; the terminal commenced operations in September 2007. Natural gas accounted for 98.1% of electricity production in 2005, when hydroelectric power accounted for 1.6% and petroleum for 0.2%. Mineral products comprised 24.2% of the value of total merchandise imports in 2006, according to the World Bank.

Services accounted for 66.4% of GDP in 2008, according to preliminary figures, and the sector provided 48.5% of total employment in 2007. The GDP of the services sector increased, in real terms, at an annual average rate of 8.0% in 2000–07. Services GDP increased by 2.4% in 2007.

In 2007 Moldova recorded a visible trade deficit of US $2,308.0m., while there was a deficit of $747.7m. on the current account of the balance of payments. In 2008 the principal source of imports was Ukraine (accounting for 17.1% of the value of total imports). Other major suppliers were Russia (13.6%), Romania (12.1%), Germany, the People's Republic of China and Italy. The main market for exports in that year was Romania (accounting for 21.0% of the value of total exports). Other important purchasers were Russia, Italy, Ukraine and Belarus. In 2008 the principal imports were mineral products, machinery and mechanical appliances, chemicals and related products, base metals, and foodstuffs, beverages and tobacco. The main exports in that year were textiles, foodstuffs, beverages and tobacco, and vegetable products.

In 2008 the consolidated state budget recorded a deficit of an estimated 1,802m. Moldovan lei (equivalent to 2.9% of GDP). At the end of 2006 Moldova's total external debt totalled US $2,416m., of which $735m. was long-term public debt. In that year the cost of debt-servicing was equivalent to 12.2% of the value of exports of goods and services. Consumer prices increased at an annual average rate of 10.9% during 2000–07. The average rate of inflation was 12.4% in 2007. The average rate of unemployment was 5.1% in 2007.

Moldova became a member of the IMF and the World Bank in 1992. It also joined the European Bank for Reconstruction and Development (EBRD, see p. 251) as a 'Country of Operations'. Moldova subsequently became a member of the Organization of the Black Sea Economic Co-operation (see p. 380), and it joined the World Trade Organization (see p. 410) in 2001.

After independence, economic performance was adversely affected by disruptions in inter-republican trade, as well as the armed conflict in Transnistria (the main industrial centre) in 1992 and the region's subsequent effective de facto secession from Moldova. After 1998 the reform process stalled, and from 1999 the IMF repeatedly suspended lending. Although the economy had recorded continued growth since 2000, by the mid-2000s the country was the poorest in Europe, and remittances from Moldovan workers abroad accounted for some 30% of GDP in 2005. The incidence of poverty remained notably high, although some progress was made in its reduction. The IMF suspended lending under its Poverty Reduction and Growth Facility (PRGF) in mid-2003, but agreement was reached on a new three-year PRGF in 2006. In 2006 economic growth was slower than forecast, not least because of an increase in prices for Russian gas, and Russia's prohibition on wine imports from Moldova, ostensibly on safety grounds. Wine exports to Russia resumed in late 2007, but in that year GDP expanded by only 3.0% (compared with 4.0% in 2006) as drought led to a contraction, of some 23%, in agricultural output. By the end of the year the current account deficit represented more than 15% of GDP, in part because of strong growth in imports. Legislation devised to rationalize budgetary operations was approved in 2007; it was hoped that the additional revenues thereby generated would offset increased expenditure on public sector salaries (which were scheduled to increase sharply in 2008, following concerns that low wages were precipitating emigration). The reorganization of the taxation system and a programme of privatization were undertaken in an effort to improve public finances and attract additional investment, but problems in the energy sector were expected in the absence of structural reform. Although there had been considerable success in fostering foreign direct investment (which represented 15% of GDP in 2008), investor confidence was seriously undermined by the violent protests that erupted in April 2009 after allegations of electoral fraud, and the ensuing political crisis (see Recent History). Meanwhile, the European Union's Eastern Partnership programme, due to be launched in May, envisaged the release of aid and the gradual creation of a free trade zone for Moldova and five other former Soviet states.

Education

Education is officially compulsory in Moldova between seven and 16 years of age. Primary education begins at seven years of age and lasts for four years. Secondary education, beginning at 11, lasts for a maximum of seven years, comprising a first cycle of five years and a second of two years. In 2005/06 total enrolment at primary schools included 87.8% (males 87.8%, females 87.7%) of children in the relevant age-group, while the comparable figure for secondary schools was 81.3% (males 79.7%, females 83.1%). In that year 74.9% of those enrolled in primary and secondary schools were taught in Moldovan and 20.4% in Russian. In the same year 544,032 students were enrolled at Moldova's 104 primary and 1,532 secondary (1,454 general; 78 vocational) schools, while 153,192 students were enrolled at one of the 86 higher education institutions. In 2004 general government expenditure on education amounted to 1,689m. lei (equivalent to 15.1% of GDP).

Public Holidays

2009: 1 January (New Year's Day), 7–8 January (Orthodox Christmas), 8 March (International Women's Day), 19–20 April (Orthodox Easter), 27 April (Parents' Day), 1 May (Labour Day), 9 May (Victory and Commemoration Day), 27 August (Independence Day), 31 August ('Limbă Noastră', National Language Day).

2010: 1 January (New Year's Day), 7–8 January (Orthodox Christmas), 8 March (International Women's Day), 4–5 April (Orthodox Easter), 12 April (Parents' Day), 1 May (Labour Day), 9 May (Victory and Commemoration Day), 27 August (Independence Day), 31 August ('Limbă Noastră', National Language Day).

Weights and Measures

The metric system is in force.

Statistical Survey

Principal sources (unless otherwise indicated): State Department for Statistics and Sociology, 2028 Chișinău, șos. Hîncești 53D; tel. (22) 73-37-74; fax (22) 22-61-46; e-mail dass@statistica.md; internet www.statistica.md.

Note: Most of the figures from 1993 onwards exclude the Transnistria (Pridnestrovie) region, which remained outside central government control.

Area and Population

AREA, POPULATION AND DENSITY

Area (sq km)	33,800*
Population (census results)†	
12 January 1989	4,335,360
5–12 October 2004	
Males	1,627,689
Females	1,755,643
Total	3,383,332
Population (official estimates at 1 January)‡	
2007	3,581,110
2008	3,572,703
2009§	3,567,500
Density (per sq km) at January 2009‡§	105.5

* 13,050 sq miles.
† Figures refer to the *de jure* population. The *de facto* total at the 1989 census was 4,337,592 (males 2,058,160, females 2,279,432).
‡ Excluding Transnistria.
§ Preliminary figure.

POPULATION BY ETHNIC GROUP*
(permanent inhabitants, 2004 census)

	Number	%
Moldovan	2,564,849	75.8
Ukrainian	282,406	8.4
Russian	201,218	5.9
Gagauz	147,500	4.4
Romanian	73,276	2.2
Bulgarian	65,662	1.9
Others and unknown	48,421	1.4
Total	**3,383,332**	**100.0**

* According to official declaration of nationality.

ADMINISTRATIVE DIVISIONS
('000, population estimates at 1 January 2009, preliminary figures)

Districts (raione)

Anenii Noi	83.1	Nisporeni	67.4
Basarabeasca	29.5	Ocnița	56.4
Briceni	76.2	Orhei	125.7
Cahul	123.9	Rezina	53.1
Cantemir	63.3	Rîșcani	70.9
Călărași	79.3	Sîngerei	93.8
Căușeni	92.7	Soroca	101.1
Cimișlia	62.6	Strășeni	91.4
Criuleni	72.8	Șoldănești	43.9
Dondușeni	46.0	Ștefan Vodă	72.5
Drochia	91.1	Taraclia	44.5
Dubăsari	35.2	Telenești	74.9
Edineț	83.4	Ungheni	117.2
Fălești	93.3	*Municipalities*	
Florești	91.0	Bălți	148.0
Glodeni	62.6	Chișinău	785.4
		Autonomous Territory	
Hîncești	123.3		
Ialoveni	98.2	Gagauz-Yeri	159.9
Leova	53.9	**Total**	**3,567.5**

Population of Transnistria (Pridnestrovie) (estimated figure obtained as residual from total country population estimates at 1 January 2003): 601,088.

PRINCIPAL TOWNS
(population at census of 5–12 October 2004)

Chișinău (capital)	589,455	Soroca	28,362
Bălți	122,669	Orhei	25,641
Cahul	35,488	Comrat	23,327
Ungheni	32,530	Ceadîr-Lunga	19,401

Principal Towns within Transnistria (estimated population at Moldovan census of 1 January 1996): Tiraspol 187,000; Tighina (Bender) 128,000; Rîbnița (Rybnitsa) 62,900.

IMMIGRATION AND EMIGRATION

	2005	2006	2007
Immigrants	2,056	1,968	2,070
Emigrants	6,827	6,685	7,172

MOLDOVA

BIRTHS, MARRIAGES AND DEATHS

	Registered live births Number	Rate (per 1,000)	Registered marriages Number	Rate (per 1,000)	Registered deaths Number	Rate (per 1,000)
2000	36,939	10.2	21,684	6.0	41,224	11.3
2001	36,448	10.0	21,065	5.8	40,075	11.0
2002	35,705	9.9	21,685	6.0	41,852	11.6
2003	36,471	10.1	24,961	6.9	43,079	11.9
2004	38,272	10.6	25,164	7.0	41,668	11.6
2005	37,695	10.5	27,187	7.6	44,689	12.4
2006	37,587	10.5	27,128	7.6	43,137	12.0
2007	37,973	10.6	29,213	8.2	43,050	12.0

Life expectancy (years at birth, WHO estimates): 68.0 (males 63.8; females 72.1) in 2006 (Source: WHO, *World Health Statistics*).

ECONOMICALLY ACTIVE POPULATION
(labour force survey, '000 persons aged 15 years and over)

	2005	2006	2007
Agriculture, hunting and forestry	534.0	421.6	407.8
Fishing	1.5	0.8	0.8
Mining and quarrying	1.8	3.4	3.7
Manufacturing	131.8	134.5	128.5
Electricity, gas and water supply	25.8	23.5	25.9
Construction	51.6	67.3	75.7
Wholesale and retail trade; repair of motor vehicles, motorcycles and personal and household goods	159.9	174.1	176.4
Hotels and restaurants	23.0	21.8	21.5
Transport, storage and communications	71.0	65.3	68.7
Financial intermediation	13.4	15.0	15.5
Real estate, renting and business activities	28.7	31.0	28.9
Public administration and defence; compulsory social security	61.5	71.9	66.3
Education	108.2	120.4	116.8
Health and social work	69.4	64.3	67.4
Other community, social and personal service activities	32.1	36.5	37.1
Private households with employed persons	3.3	4.7	5.3
Extra-territorial organizations and bodies	0.5	1.1	0.9
Total employed	1,318.7	1,257.3	1,247.2
Unemployed	103.7	99.9	66.7
Total labour force	1,422.3	1,357.2	1,313.9
Males	689.5	690.3	663.0
Females	732.9	666.9	650.8

Source: ILO.

Health and Welfare

KEY INDICATORS

Total fertility rate (children per woman, 2006)	1.4
Under-5 mortality rate (per 1,000 live births, 2006)	19
HIV/AIDS (% of persons aged 15–49, 2007)	0.4
Physicians (per 1,000 head, 2006)	2.7
Hospital beds (per 1,000 head, 2006)	6.3
Health expenditure (2006): US $ per head (PPP)	190
Health expenditure (2006): % of GDP	7.8
Health expenditure (2006): public (% of total)	56.4
Access to water (% of persons, 2006)	90
Access to sanitation (% of persons, 2006)	79
Human Development Index (2006): ranking	113
Human Development Index (2006): value	0.719

For sources and definitions, see explanatory note on p. vi.

Agriculture

PRINCIPAL CROPS
('000 metric tons)

	2005	2006	2007
Wheat	1,056.7	691.4	402.0*
Barley	212.0	200.1	115.0
Maize	1,492.0	1,322.2	363.0
Potatoes	378.2	377.0	199.0
Sugar beet	991.2	1,177.3	612.0
Beans, dry	27.4	26.6	14.5*
Peas, dry	33.9	33.8	18.7*
Sunflower seed	331.1	379.9	156.0
Cabbages and other brassicas	53.2	64.9	30.5*
Tomatoes	84.6	104.4	48.5*
Cucumbers and gherkins	28.0	38.1	17.8*
Chillies and peppers, green	32.1	46.0	21.5*
Aubergines (Eggplants)	7.2	8.6	4.0*
Onions, dry	52.3	54.4	25.5*
Carrots and turnips	19.3	25.4	12.0*
Watermelons	36.8	89.0	90.0*
Apples	278.4	202.8	172.0*
Plums and sloes	41.4	75.9	64.0*
Grapes	518.5	466.1	598.0
Tobacco, unmanufactured	6.7	4.9	4.0

* FAO estimate.

Aggregate production ('000 metric tons, may include official, semi-official or estimated data): Total cereals 2,771.7 in 2005, 2,222.4 in 2006, 884.6 in 2007; Total vegetables (incl. melons) 438.1 in 2005, 567.7 in 2006, 317.8 in 2007; Total fruits (excl. melons) 891.9 in 2005, 783.7 in 2006, 866.0 in 2007.

Source: FAO.

LIVESTOCK
('000 head at 1 January)

	2005	2006	2007
Horses	72.5	69.1	66.8
Cattle	330.6	310.5	299.1
Pigs	398.0	460.7	531.8
Sheep	822.8	818.3	835.1
Goats	119.4	119.4	111.9
Chickens	17,522*	22,100	22,390*

* FAO estimate.
Source: FAO.

LIVESTOCK PRODUCTS
('000 metric tons)

	2005	2006	2007
Cattle meat	15.6	15.0	16.8*
Sheep meat	2.4	2.3	2.6*
Pig meat	39.7	48.0	53.8*
Chicken meat	28.0	30.9	34.6*
Cows' milk	627.1	595.3	573.2*
Sheep's milk	21.1	19.9	18.8*
Goats' milk	10.4	12.3	11.5*
Hen eggs	42.5†	42.7*	39.3*
Honey	2.4	2.7	2.3*
Wool, greasy	2.1	2.2	2.1

* FAO estimate.
† Unofficial figure.
Source: FAO.

Forestry

ROUNDWOOD REMOVALS
('000 cubic metres, excl. bark)

	1999	2000	2001
Sawlogs, veneer logs and logs for sleepers	3	5	3
Other industrial wood	9	24	24*
Fuel wood	36	30	30*
Total	48	59	57

* FAO estimate.

2002–07: Annual production as in 2001 (FAO estimates).

Source: FAO.

SAWNWOOD PRODUCTION
('000 cubic metres, incl. railway sleepers)

	1998	1999	2000
Coniferous (softwood)	25	—	—
Broadleaved (hardwood)	5	6	5
Total	30	6	5

2001–07: Annual production as in 2000 (FAO estimates).

Source: FAO.

Fishing

(metric tons, live weight)

	2004	2005	2006
Capture	487	531	612
Common carp	128	160	239
Crucian carp	152	170	186
Aquaculture	4,470	4,470*	4,470*
Common carp	1,660	1,660*	1,660*
Grass carp (White amur)	21	21*	20*
Silver carp	2,780	2,780*	2,780*
Total catch	4,957	5,001*	5,082*

* FAO estimate.

Source: FAO.

Mining

('000 cu m)

	2005	2006	2007
Limestone	261.7	293.6	311.9
Gypsum	563	726	846
Sand and gravel	1,976.6	2,324.4	2,685.5

Peat ('000 metric tons, estimated production): 475 in 2005 (Source: US Geological Survey).

Industry

SELECTED PRODUCTS
('000 metric tons, unless otherwise indicated)

	2005	2006	2007
Fruit and vegetable preserves	81.3	91.4	94.0
Flour	144.0	133.5	113.3
Raw sugar	133.5	149.0	74.0
Wine ('000 hectolitres)†	3,630	1,930	1,230
Mineral water ('000 hectolitres)†	960	1,060	1,300
Soft drinks ('000 hectolitres)†	640	750	940
Cigars and cigarettes (million)	6,195	5,031	4,975
Carpets and rugs ('000 sq m)	4,430	5,224	5,246
Footwear ('000 pairs, excl. rubber)	3,650	3,673	3,796
Glasses and bottles (million)	354.6	321.4	302.7
Plaster	130,800	186,200	311,900
Electric energy (million kWh)	1,229	1,192	1,100

† Rounded figures.

Vegetable oil ('000 metric tons): 85.3 in 2004.

Cement ('000 metric tons): 439.7 in 2004.

Washing machines ('000 units): 53.8 in 2004.

Finance

CURRENCY AND EXCHANGE RATES

Monetary Units
100 bani (singular: ban) = 1 Moldovan leu (plural: lei).

Sterling, Dollar and Euro Equivalents (31 December 2008)
£1 sterling = 15.161 lei;
US $1 = 10.400 lei;
€1 = 14.474 lei;
1,000 Moldovan lei = £65.96 = $96.15 = €69.09.

Average Exchange Rate (Moldovan lei per US $)
2006   13.131
2007   12.140
2008   10.392

Note: The Moldovan leu was introduced (except in Transnistria) on 29 November 1993, replacing the Moldovan rouble at a rate of 1 leu = 1,000 roubles. The Moldovan rouble had been introduced in June 1992, as a temporary coupon currency, and was initially at par with the Russian (formerly Soviet) rouble.

STATE BUDGET
(million lei)*

Revenue†	2006	2007	2008‡
Tax revenue	14,889	18,154	20,020
Taxes on profits	1,079	1,388	418
Taxes on personal incomes	1,128	1,329	1,294
Value-added tax	6,194	7,587	8,885
Excises	1,071	1,392	1,501
Taxes on international trade	828	899	1,050
Social Fund contributions	3,691	4,350	5,257
Health Fund contributions	558	841	1,175
Other taxes	342	368	441
Non-tax revenue	1,154	1,627	1,450
Total	16,044	19,781	21,470

MOLDOVA

Expenditure§	2006	2007	2008‡
Current expenditure	14,312	18,448	20,126
Wages	4,123	4,875	5,517
Goods and services	3,703	4,779	5,357
Health insurance fund	1,485	1,895	2,646
Interest payments	455	635	692
Transfers	6,032	8,159	8,510
Other current expenditure	—	—	50
Capital expenditure	3,488	3,965	4,387
Total	17,800	22,413	24,513

* Figures refer to a consolidation of the operations of central (republican) and local governments, including the Social Fund.
† Excluding grants received (million lei): 315 in 2006; 919 in 2007; 1,175 in 2008 (preliminary).
‡ Preliminary.
§ Excluding net lending (million lei): –61 in 2006; –60 in 2007; –66 in 2008 (preliminary).

Source: IMF, *Republic of Moldova: 2007 Article IV Consultation and Third Review Under the Three-Year Arrangement Under the Poverty Reduction and Growth Facility—Staff Report; Staff Supplement; Public Information Notice and Press Release on the Executive Board Discussion; and Statement by the Executive Director for the Republic of Moldova* (April 2008).

INTERNATIONAL RESERVES
(US $ million at 31 December)

	2006	2007	2008
IMF special drawing rights	0.19	0.15	0.15
Reserve position in IMF	0.01	0.01	0.01
Foreign exchange	775.28	1,333.53	1,672.25
Total (excl. gold)	775.48	1,333.68	1,672.41

Source: IMF, *International Financial Statistics*.

MONEY SUPPLY
(million lei at 31 December)

	2006	2007	2008
Currency outside banks	5,145.81	6,664.94	7,578.66
Demand deposits at commercial banks	3,122.03	4,258.52	4,026.96
Total money (incl. others)	8,268.34	10,923.61	11,609.23

Source: IMF, *International Financial Statistics*.

COST OF LIVING
(Consumer Price Index; base: previous year = 100)

	2006	2007	2008
Food and beverages	108.7	109.5	106.5
Other consumer goods	115.7	111.6	102.1
Services	120.1	113.0	117.4
All items (incl. others)	114.1	113.1	107.3

NATIONAL ACCOUNTS
(million lei at current prices, excl. Transnistria)

Expenditure on the Gross Domestic Product

	2006	2007	2008*
Final consumption expenditure	50,972.5	60,618.1	71,534.4
Households			
Non-profit institutions serving households	42,027.7	49,178.3	57,944.4
General government	8,944.8	11,439.7	13,590.0
Gross capital formation	14,656.1	20,359.8	23,221.9
Gross fixed capital formation			
Acquisitions, less disposals, of valuables	12,691.5	18,221.7	21,413.3
Changes in inventories	1,964.6	2,138.1	1,808.6
Total domestic expenditure	65,628.6	80,977.9	94,756.3
Exports of goods and services	20,254.0	24,353.6	25,602.7
Less Imports of goods and services	41,128.2	51,901.9	57,518.8
GDP in market prices	44,754.4	53,429.6	62,840.3

Gross Domestic Product by Economic Activity

	2006	2007	2008*
Agriculture, hunting, forestry and fishing	6,488.8	5,333.9	5,617.0
Mining and quarrying	224.4	262.6	295.0
Manufacturing	5,599.2	6,300.2	7,298.7
Electricity, gas and water supply	757.2	1,053.1	1,485.3
Construction	1,776.5	2,585.9	3,162.0
Wholesale and retail trade; repair of motor vehicles, motorcycles and personal and household goods	5,144.8	6,713.8	8,223.5
Hotels and restaurants	468.9	612.0	886.4
Transport, storage and communications	5,288.7	6,582.0	7,652.3
Financial intermediation	2,224.8	3,223.3	3,958.1
Real estate, renting and business activities	3,003.5	3,712.3	4,509.9
Public administration and defence; compulsory social security	2,101.1	2,453.1	2,396.6
Education	2,632.0	3,058.0	3,478.0
Health and social work	1,582.1	2,033.3	2,415.4
Other community, social and personal services	1,163.3	1,705.1	1,834.8
Sub-total	38,455.2	45,628.7	53,212.9
Less Financial intermediation services indirectly measured	1,116.5	1,215.8	1,458.6
Gross value added in basic prices	37,338.7	44,412.9	51,754.3
Taxes, *less* subsidies, on products and imports	7,415.6	9,016.7	11,086.0
GDP in market prices	44,754.4	53,429.6	62,840.3

* Preliminary figures.

BALANCE OF PAYMENTS
(US $ million)

	2005	2006	2007
Exports of goods f.o.b.	1,104.6	1,058.7	1,368.4
Imports of goods f.o.b.	–2,296.1	–2,644.4	–3,676.4
Trade balance	–1,191.5	–1,585.7	–2,308.0
Exports of services	398.9	488.6	649.7
Imports of services	–419.7	–484.4	–630.0
Balance on goods and services	–1,212.2	–1,581.5	–2,288.3
Other income received	539.3	605.8	710.0
Other income paid	–128.4	–203.8	–295.7
Balance on goods, services and income	–801.4	–1,179.4	–1,874.0
Current transfers received	596.8	854.9	1,206.6
Current transfers paid	–43.2	–60.0	–80.3
Current balance	–247.7	–384.5	–747.7
Capital account (net)	–16.9	–22.8	–8.0
Direct investment abroad	0.2	0.7	–12.0
Direct investment from abroad	190.7	251.1	493.4
Portfolio investment assets	–1.2	–0.2	–0.1
Portfolio investment liabilities	–5.8	–4.6	–4.4
Financial derivatives assets	–1.7	–0.1	–0.5
Financial derivatives liabilities	0.1	0.3	0.1
Other investment assets	–78.2	–49.4	54.0
Other investment liabilities	96.3	161.6	458.6
Net errors and omissions	178.3	64.2	139.0
Overall balance	114.2	16.4	372.3

Source: IMF, *International Financial Statistics*.

MOLDOVA

External Trade

PRINCIPAL COMMODITIES
(distribution by Harmonized System, US $ million)

Imports c.i.f.	2006	2007	2008*
Vegetable products	72.8	150.4	167.0
Foodstuffs, beverages and tobacco	179.8	237.9	343.4
Mineral products	663.7	788.4	1,126.0
Mineral fuels, mineral oils and related materials	649.7	774.8	1,104.6
Chemicals and related products	223.3	317.7	416.8
Pharmaceutical products	84.9	114.2	151.4
Plastics, rubber and articles thereof	168.5	224.9	276.8
Plastics	137.1	178.3	213.5
Textiles and textile articles	206.5	249.6	285.4
Base metals and articles of base metals	219.4	336.7	372.6
Articles of iron or steel	83.6	112.7	147.0
Machinery and mechanical appliances	379.8	544.6	765.5
Apparatus such as nuclear reactors, boilers, machinery and mechanical appliances, and parts thereof	227.4	324.5	427.6
Electrical machinery and equipment and parts thereof; sound recorders and reproducers, television image and sound recorders and reproducers, and parts and accessories thereof	152.4	220.1	337.9
Vehicles and associated transport equipment	162.4	286.1	390.7
Vehicles other than railway or tramway rolling stock, and parts and accessories thereof	137.5	274.6	378.0
Total (incl. others)	2,693.2	3,689.5	4,898.9

Exports f.o.b.	2006	2007	2008*
Vegetable products	136.5	162.9	210.1
Edible fruit	64.6	92.9	85.4
Cereals	42.0	17.2	50.3
Oil seeds and oleaginous fruits, etc	22.6	47.2	68.2
Animal or vegetable fats	34.9	55.3	62.9
Foodstuffs, beverages and tobacco	276.4	276.0	312.2
Preparations of vegetables or fruits	42.7	79.5	51.4
Beverages, spirits and vinegar	186.8	135.5	196.0
Mineral products	27.4	57.1	63.5
Salt; sulphur; earths and stone; plastering materials, lime and cement	25.0	52.5	60.4
Articles of stone, plaster, cement, ceramic or glass	32.6	51.3	52.5

Exports f.o.b.—continued	2006	2007	2008*
Textiles and textile articles	228.3	276.3	314.0
Articles of apparel and clothing accessories, not knitted	78.5	96.2	108.2
Base metals and articles of base metals	75.8	110.5	119.1
Iron and steel	31.7	38.5	51.2
Machinery and mechanical appliances	53.1	90.7	171.1
Apparatus such as nuclear reactors, boilers, machinery and mechanical appliances, and parts thereof	31.0	51.7	51.2
Electrical machinery and equipment and parts thereof; sound recorders and reproducers, television image and sound recorders and reproducers, and parts and accessories thereof	22.1	39.0	119.8
Miscellaneous manufactured items	27.6	44.8	61.0
Furniture; bedding, mattresses, mattress supports, cushions and similar stuffed furnishings; lamps and lighting fittings, not elsewhere specified or included; illuminated signs, illuminated nameplates etc.; prefabricated buildings	21.3	35.4	48.8
Total (incl. others)	1,051.6	1,341.7	1,597.3

* Including provisional data for December.

PRINCIPAL TRADING PARTNERS
(US $ million)

Imports c.i.f.	2006	2007	2008
Austria	23.4	37.3	74.6
Belarus	74.6	118.7	199.1
Belgium	37.0	37.6	33.9
Bulgaria	35.1	50.4	45.1
China, People's Repub.	116.9	202.9	325.5
Czech Republic	32.6	43.6	57.5
France	62.7	94.8	103.4
Germany	214.1	319.3	364.5
Hungary	33.0	46.4	69.3
Italy	196.3	269.3	306.2
Japan	22.5	43.9	83.6
Korea, Republic	25.2	38.7	42.7
Netherlands	19.4	41.2	49.5
Poland	73.4	89.1	121.3
Romania	346.0	449.0	590.8
Russia	417.0	498.6	666.1
Turkey	113.8	166.8	231.9
Ukraine	516.5	687.0	839.0
United Kingdom	32.6	38.2	61.7
USA	35.9	46.8	93.3
Total (incl. others)	2,693.2	3,689.5	4,898.9

Exports f.o.b.	2006	2007	2008
Austria	13.1	30.8	12.5
Belarus	74.0	82.0	92.8
Belgium	14.1	11.2	9.7
Bulgaria	14.1	27.3	22.3
France	23.9	24.8	21.4
Germany	51.9	86.3	63.8
Hungary	14.6	5.1	18.5
Italy	116.9	140.2	167.1
Kazakhstan	24.2	45.5	44.5
Netherlands	9.3	14.4	13.2

MOLDOVA

Exports f.o.b.—continued	2006	2007	2008
Poland	39.2	48.3	56.1
Romania	155.6	211.2	335.8
Russia	182.0	232.7	318.4
Slovakia	22.7	8.9	7.6
Switzerland	14.2	22.6	39.7
Turkey	28.5	32.1	33.4
Ukraine	128.8	167.9	142.8
United Kingdom	27.3	34.1	52.3
USA	16.2	15.2	15.1
Total (incl. others)	1,051.6	1,341.7	1,597.3

Transport

RAILWAYS
(traffic)

	2006	2007	2008
Passenger journeys (million)	5.3	5.6	n.a.
Passenger-km (million)	471	468	n.a.
Freight transported (million metric tons)	11.1	11.8	11.0
Freight ton-km (million)	3,673	3,120	2,878

ROAD TRAFFIC
(motor vehicles in use)

	2005	2006	2007
Passenger cars	292,994	319,311	338,944
Buses and minibuses	19,825	21,056	21,095
Lorries and vans	81,798	84,087	94,828

INLAND WATERWAYS
(traffic)

	2006	2007	2008
Freight transported ('000 metric tons)	141.5	166.5	202.0
Freight ton-km (million)	0.6	0.6	0.8

CIVIL AVIATION
(traffic)

	2006	2007	2008
Passengers carried ('000)	396.6	415.2	473.9
Passenger-km (million)	481	550	638
Freight transported ('000 metric tons)	0.97	1.00	0.83
Freight ton-km (million)	1.3	1.3	1.2

Tourism

FOREIGN VISITOR ARRIVALS
(incl. excursionists)

Country of origin	2005	2006	2007
Belarus	1,161	580	290
Bulgaria	448	295	359
France	464	266	436
Germany	703	673	892
Italy	1,141	663	755
Netherlands	268	199	262
Romania	3,496	2,787	3,034
Russia	3,294	1,353	1,767
Turkey	3,038	1,687	1,400
Ukraine	3,406	1,472	1,335
United Kingdom	365	291	641
USA	3,088	1,066	515
Total (incl. others)	25,073	14,239	14,722

Receipts from tourism (US $ million, incl. passenger transport): 112 in 2004; 138 in 2005; 145 in 2006.

Source: World Tourism Organization.

Communications Media

	2005	2006	2007
Telephones ('000 main lines in use)	929.4	1,018.1	1,079.9
Mobile cellular telephones ('000 subscribers)	1,089.8	1,358.2	1,882.8
Internet users ('000)	550.0	727.7	700.0
Broadband subscribers ('000)	10.4	21.8	47.2

Television receivers ('000 in use): 1,300 in 2000.

Radio receivers ('000 in use): 3,220 in 1997.

Personal computers ('000 in use): 112 in 2005.

Book production (including pamphlets): 921 titles (2,779,000 copies) in 1996.

Facsimile machines ('000 in use): 716 in 1999.

Daily newspapers: 4 (average circulation 261,000) in 1996.

Non-daily newspapers: 206 (estimated average circulation 1,350,000) in 1996.

Other periodicals: 76 (average circulation 196,000) in 1994.

Sources: UNESCO, *Statistical Yearbook*; International Telecommunication Union.

Education

(2007/08)

	Institutions	Teachers	Students
Pre-primary	1,334	10,900*	120,100*
Primary and Secondary: general	1,541	38,700*	462,800*
Secondary: vocational	75	2,447	24,506
Higher: colleges	49	1,967	31,307
Higher: universities	31	6,447	122,939

* Rounded figures.

Adult literacy rate (UNESCO estimates): 99.2% (males 99.6%; females 98.9%) in 2007 (Source: UNESCO Institute for Statistics).

Directory

The Constitution

The Constitution of the Republic of Moldova, summarized below, was adopted by the Moldovan Parliament on 28 July 1994 and entered into force on 27 August. In 2000 amendments to the Constitution were enacted, which transformed Moldova into a parliamentary republic. The Constitution was further amended, to recognize the autonomous status of Gagauz-Yeri (Gagauzia) in July 2003.

GENERAL PRINCIPLES

The Republic of Moldova is a sovereign, independent, unitary and indivisible state. The rule of law, the dignity, rights and freedoms of the people, and the development of human personality, justice and political pluralism are guaranteed. The Constitution, the supreme law, upholds democracy and political pluralism, the separation and co-operation of the legislative, executive and judicial powers, respect for international law and treaties, and fundamental principles regarding property, free economic initiative and the right to national identity. The national language of the republic is Moldovan and its writing is based on the Latin alphabet, although the right to use other languages spoken within the country is acknowledged.

FUNDAMENTAL RIGHTS, FREEDOMS AND DUTIES

All citizens are equal before the law and are presumed innocent until proven guilty.

The State guarantees the right to life and to the freedoms of movement, conscience, expression, assembly and political association, and the enfranchisement of Moldovan citizens aged over 18 years. Moldovan citizens have the right of access to information and education, of health security, of establishing and joining a trade union, of working and of striking. Obligations of the citizenry include the payment of taxes and the defence of the motherland.

PARLAMENTUL

Parlamentul (The Parliament) is the sole legislative authority of Moldova, comprising 101 members, who are directly elected for a four-year term. The Chairman of Parlamentul is elected by members. Parlamentul's basic powers include: the enactment of laws, the calling of referendums, the approval of state policy, the approval or suspension of international treaties, the election of state officials and the declaration of the states of national emergency, martial law and war.

THE PRESIDENT OF THE REPUBLIC

The President of the Republic is the Head of State and is elected by the legislature for a four-year term. A candidate must be at least 40 years of age, a Moldovan citizen and a speaker of the official language. The candidate must be in good health and must submit the written support of a minimum of 15 parliamentarians. A decision on the holding of a presidential election is taken by parliamentary resolution, and the election must be held no fewer than 45 days before the expiry of the outgoing President's term of office. To be elected President, a candidate must obtain the support of three-fifths of the parliamentary quorum. If necessary, further ballots must then be conducted, contested by the two candidates who received the most votes. The candidate who receives more votes becomes President. The post of President may be held by the same person for not more than two consecutive terms.

The President's main responsibilities include the promulgation of laws, the issue of decrees, the scheduling of referendums, the conclusion of international treaties and the dissolution of Parlamentul. The President is allowed to participate in parliamentary proceedings. The President, after consultation with the parliamentary majority, is responsible for nominating a Prime Minister-designate and a Government. The President may preside over government meetings and may consult the Government on matters of special importance and urgency. On proposals submitted by the Prime Minister, the President may revoke or renominate members of the Government in cases of vacancies or the reallocation of portfolios. The President is Commander-in-Chief of the armed forces.

If the President has committed a criminal or constitutional offence, the votes of two-thirds of the members of Parlamentul are required to remove the President from office; the removal must be confirmed by the Supreme Court of Justice, for a criminal offence, or by a national referendum, for a constitutional offence.

THE COUNCIL OF MINISTERS

The principal organ of executive government is the Council of Ministers, which supervises state policy and public administration of the country. The Council of Ministers is headed by a Prime Minister, who co-ordinates the activities of the Government. The Council of Ministers must resign if Parlamentul votes in favour of a motion of 'no confidence' in the Council.

LOCAL ADMINISTRATION

For administrative purposes, the Republic of Moldova is divided into districts, towns and villages. At village and town level, elected local councils and mayors operate as autonomous administrative authorities. At district level, an elected council co-ordinates the activities of village and town councils.

The area on the left bank of the Dniester (Dnestr or Nistru) river, as well as certain other places in the south of the republic (i.e. Gagauz-Yeri) may be granted special autonomous status, according to special statutory provisions of organic law.

JUDICIAL AUTHORITY

Every citizen has the right to free access to justice. Justice shall be administered by the Supreme Court of Justice, the Court of Appeal, tribunals and courts of law. Judges sitting in the courts of law and the Supreme Court of Justice are appointed by the President following proposals by the Higher Magistrates' Council. They are elected for a five-year term, and subsequently for a 10-year term, after which their term of office expires on reaching the age limit. The Higher Magistrates' Council is composed of 11 magistrates, who are appointed for a five-year term. It is responsible for the appointment, transfer and promotion of judges, as well as disciplinary action against them.

The Prosecutor-General, who is appointed by Parlamentul, exercises control over the enactment of law, as well as defending the legal order and the rights and freedoms of citizens.

THE CONSTITUTIONAL COURT

The Constitutional Court is the sole authority of constitutional judicature in Moldova. It is composed of six judges, who are appointed for a six-year term. The Constitutional Court's powers include: the enforcement of constitutionality in laws, decrees and governmental decisions, as well as international treaties endorsed by the Republic; the confirmation of the results of elections and referendums; the explanation and clarification of the Constitution; and decisions over matters of the constitutionality of parties. The decisions of the Constitutional Court are final and are not subject to appeal.

CONSTITUTIONAL REVISIONS

A revision of the Constitution may be initiated by one of the following: a petition signed by at least 200,000 citizens from at least one-half of the country's districts and municipalities; no less than one-third of the members of Parlamentul; the President of the Republic; or the Government. Provisions regarding the sovereignty, independence, unity and neutrality of the State may be revised only by referendum.

The Government

HEAD OF STATE

President: VLADIMIR VORONIN (indirectly elected 4 April 2001; indirectly re-elected 4 April 2005).

Note: Following legislative elections on 5 April 2009, after which the outgoing President VLADIMIR VORONIN was elected as Chairman of Parlamentul (the Parliament), a presidential election was to be conducted within the new legislature on 20 May. The hitherto Prime Minister ZINAIDA GRECIANÎI and a further candidate, STANISLAV GROPA, also nominated by the Party of Communists of the Republic of Moldova, were to contest the election.

COUNCIL OF MINISTERS
(April 2009)

Prime Minister: ZINAIDA GRECIANÎI.

First Deputy Prime Minister and Minister of the Economy and Trade: IGOR DODON.

Deputy Prime Minister: VICTOR STEPANIUC.

Deputy Prime Minister and Minister of Foreign Affairs and European Integration: ANDREI STRĂTAN.

Deputy Prime Minister: VALENTIN MEJINSCHI.

Minister of Local Public Administration: VALENTIN GUZNAC.

Minister of Agriculture and the Food Industry: ANATOLIE GORODENCO.

Minister of Construction and Territorial Development: VLADIMIR BALDOVICI.

Minister of Finance: MARIANA DURLEŞTEANU.

Minister of Information Development: PAVEL BUCEAŢCHI.

Minister of Transport and Road Management: VASILE URSU.
Minister of Ecology and Natural Resources: VIOLETA IVANOV.
Minister of Education and Youth: LARISA ŠAVGA.
Minister of Health: LARISA CATRINICI.
Minister of Social Protection, the Family and Children: GALINA BALMOŠ.
Minister of Culture and Tourism: (vacant).
Minister of Justice: VITALIE PÎRLOG.
Minister of Internal Affairs: GHEORGHE PAPUC.
Minister of Defence: VITALIE VRABIE.
Minister of Reintegration: VASILE ȘOVA.

Note: the President of the Moldovan Academy of Sciences, GHEORGHE DUCA, and the Başkan (Governor) of the Autonomous Territory of Gagauz-Yeri (Gagauzia) are also members of the Government. MIHAIL FORMUZAL was elected to the latter position in December 2006.

MINISTRIES

Office of the President: 2073 Chișinău, bd. Ștefan cel Mare 154; tel. (22) 23-47-93; e-mail president@prm.md; internet www.president.md.

Office of the Council of Ministers: 2033 Chișinău, Piața Marii Adunări Naționale 1; tel. (22) 25-01-01; fax (22) 24-26-96; e-mail petitii@gov.md; internet www.gov.md.

Ministry of Agriculture and the Food Industry: 2012 Chișinău, bd. Ștefan cel Mare 162; tel. (22) 23-34-27; fax (22) 23-23-68; e-mail adm_maia@moldova.md; internet www.maia.gov.md.

Ministry of Construction and Territorial Development: Chișinău; internet www.mcdt.gov.md.

Ministry of Culture and Tourism: 2033 Chișinău, Piața Marii Adunări Naționale 1, Of. 326; tel. (22) 22-76-20; fax (22) 23-23-88; e-mail culture@turism.md; internet www.turism.md.

Ministry of Defence: 2021 Chișinău, șos. Hîncești 84; tel. (22) 25-22-22; fax (22) 23-26-31; e-mail ministru@army.md; internet www.army.md.

Ministry of Ecology and Natural Resources: 2005 Chișinău, str. Cosmonauților 9; tel. and fax (22) 21-45-33; e-mail cima@moldova.md; internet www.cim.moldova.md.

Ministry of the Economy and Trade: 2033 Chișinău, Piața Marii Adunări Naționale 1; tel. (22) 23-74-48; fax (22) 23-40-64; e-mail mineconcom@mec.gov.md; internet www.mec.gov.md.

Ministry of Education and Youth: 2033 Chișinău, Piața Marii Adunări Naționale 1; tel. (22) 23-33-48; fax (22) 23-35-15; e-mail consilier@edu.md; internet www.edu.md.

Ministry of Finance: 2005 Chișinău, str. Cosmonauților 7; tel. (22) 23-35-75; fax (22) 22-13-07; e-mail protocol@minfin.moldova.md; internet www.minfin.md.

Ministry of Foreign Affairs and European Integration: 2012 Chișinău, str. 31 August 80; tel. (22) 57-82-07; fax (22) 23-23-02; e-mail secdep@mfa.md; internet www.mfa.md.

Ministry of Health: 2009 Chișinău, str. Vasile Alecsandri 2; tel. (22) 72-99-07; fax (22) 73-87-81; e-mail cancelaria@mednet.md; internet www.ms.md.

Ministry of Information Development: Chișinău, str. Pușkin 42; tel. (22) 22-91-23; fax (22) 22-80-20; internet www.mdi.gov.md.

Ministry of Internal Affairs: 2012 Chișinău, bd. Ștefan cel Mare 75; tel. (22) 22-45-47; fax (22) 22-27-43; e-mail mai@mai.md; internet www.mai.md.

Ministry of Justice: 2012 Chișinău, str. 31 August 1989 82; tel. (22) 23-47-95; fax (22) 23-47-97; e-mail secretariat@justice.gov.md; internet www.justice.gov.md.

Ministry of Local Public Administration: 2033 Chișinău, Piața Marii Adunări Naționale 1; tel. (22) 20-01-70; fax (22) 23-89-22; e-mail info@mapl.gov.md; internet www.mapl.gov.md.

Ministry of Reintegration: Chișinău, str. A. Mateevici 109/1; tel. (22) 25-01-46; fax (22) 25-08-72; e-mail reintegrarea@moldova.md; internet www.reintegrarea.gov.md.

Ministry of Social Protection, the Family and Children: 2009 Chișinău, str. Vasile Alecsandri 1; tel. (22) 28-07-92; fax (22) 73-75-72; e-mail secretariat@mpsfc.gov.md; internet www.mpsfc.gov.md.

President

The President of the Republic is elected by parliamentary deputies, and is required to receive the support of at least 61 of the 101 members of Parlamentul. VLADIMIR VORONIN was re-elected President on 4 April 2005, receiving 75 votes. His sole opponent, GHEORGHE DUCA, obtained one vote. Following the expiry of Voronin's second term of office, elections for a new President were scheduled for 20 May 2009.

Legislature

Parlamentul
(Parliament)

2073 Chișinău, bd. Ștefan cel Mare 105; tel. (22) 23-33-52; fax (22) 23-30-12; e-mail info@parlament.md; internet www.parlament.md.

Chairman: VLADIMIR VORONIN.

General Election, 5 April 2009

Parties and alliances	Seats
Party of Communists of the Republic of Moldova	60
Liberal Party	15
Liberal Democratic Party of Moldova	15
Our Moldova Alliance	11
Total	**101**

Election Commission

Comisia Electorală Centrală a Republicii Moldova (Central Electoral Commission of the Republic of Moldova): Chișinău, str. Vasile Alecsandri 119; tel. (22) 25-14-51; fax (22) 25-14-50; e-mail cec@molddata.md; internet www.cec.md; Pres. EUGENIU ȘTIRBU.

Political Organizations

In January 2009 28 political parties were registered with the Ministry of Justice; the following were among the most important.

Centrist Union of Moldova (Uniunea Centristă din Moldova): Chișinău, str. A. Mateevici 47; tel. (22) 21-13-09; fax (22) 21-13-40; e-mail info@ucm.md; internet www.ucm.md; f. 2000; Chair. VASILE TARLEV.

Christian Democratic People's Party (PPCD) (Partidul Popular Creștin Democrat): 2009 Chișinău, str. N. Iorga 5; tel. (22) 23-33-56; fax (22) 23-86-66; e-mail echipa@ppcd.md; internet www.ppcd.md; f. 1989 as the People's Front of Moldova, renamed 1992, and as above 1999; advocates Moldova's entry into the EU and NATO; Chair. IURIE ROȘCA.

Democratic Party of Moldova (PDM) (Partidul Democrat din Moldova): 2001 Chișinău, str. Tighina 32; tel. (22) 27-82-29; fax (22) 27-82-30; e-mail secretariat@pdm.md; internet www.pdm.md; f. 1997; centrist; fmrly Movement for a Democratic and Prosperous Moldova, name changed in April 2000; contested 2005 legislative elections as mem. of the Democratic Moldova bloc; merged with Social Liberal Party in Feb. 2008; Chair. DUMITRU DIACOV.

Liberal Democratic Party of Moldova (PDLM) (Partidul Liberal Democrat din Moldova): 2012 Chișinău, str. București 88; tel. (22) 81-51-54; fax (22) 81-51-63; e-mail info@pldm.md; internet www.pldm.md; f. 2007; Pres. VLAD FILAT.

Liberal Party (PL) (Partidul Liberal): Chișinău, str. București 87; tel. (22) 23-26-89; fax (22) 22-80-97; e-mail liberal@pl.md; internet www.pl.md; f. 1993 as Party of Reform; renamed as above 2005; Chair. MIHAI GHIMPU; 12,000 mems.

Our Moldova Alliance (AMN) (Alianța 'Moldova Noastră'): 2012 Chișinău, str. M. Eminescu 68A; tel. (22) 26-00-07; fax (22) 21-13-94; e-mail alianta@amn.md; internet www.amn.md; f. 2003 by merger of the Alliance of Independents of Moldova, the Liberal Party (which left the Alliance in Dec. 2006), the Social Democratic Alliance of Moldova and the Popular Democratic Party of Moldova; supports Moldova's integration into Europe, a market economy and inter-ethnic harmony; contested 2005 legislative elections as mem. of the Democratic Moldova bloc; Chair. SERAFIM URECHEAN; c. 100,000 mems (2007).

Party of Communists of the Republic of Moldova (PCRM) (Partidul Comuniștilor din Republica Moldova): 2012 Chișinău, str. N. Iorga 11; tel. (22) 23-46-14; fax (22) 23-36-73; e-mail info@pcrm.md; internet www.pcrm.md; fmrly the Communist Party of Moldova (banned Aug. 1991); revived as above April 1994; Chair. VLADIMIR VORONIN.

Republican Party of Moldova (PRM) (Partidul Republican din Moldova): Chișinău, str. Cuza-Voda 35/2, ap. 21; tel. and fax (22) 76-94-22; e-mail acurteanma@yahoo.com; f. 1999; Chair. ION CURTEAN.

Social Democratic Party (PSD) (Partidul Social Democrat): 2005 Chișinău, str. Alexandru cel Bun 97; tel. and fax (22) 22-06-11; e-mail

MOLDOVA

info@psd.md; internet www.psd.md; f. 1990; merged with Party of Social Democracy in Dec. 2007; Leader DUMITRU BRAGHIȘ; Sec.-Gen. EDUARD ION MUȘUC.

Socialist Party of Moldova (Partidul Socialist din Moldova): Chișinău, str. V. Alecsandri 35A; tel. (22) 73-12-96; f. 1992 by mems of fmr Communist Party of Moldova; favours socialist economic and social policies, defends the rights of Russian and other minorities and advocates continued CIS membership; contested 2005 legislative election as mem. of the Fatherland-Motherland (Patria-Rodina) electoral bloc; Pres. VICTOR MOREV.

Parties and organizations in Transnistria include: **Renewal** (Obnovleniye), led by YEVGENII SHEVCHUK; **Transnistrian Communist Party (PKP)** (Pridnestrovskaya Kommunisticheskaya Partiya), led by OLEG KHORZHAN; **Patriotic Party of Transnistria (PPP)** (Patrioticheskaya Partiya Pridnestroviya), led by OLEG SMIRNOV; and **Republic** (Respublica), led by YURII SUKHOV.

Parties and organizations in Gagauz-Yeri include: **Fatherland** (Vatan), led by ANDREI CHESHMEJI; **Gagauz People** (Gagauz Halky), led by KONSTANTIN TAUSHANDJI; and **People's Republican Party** (Respublika Halk Partiyası), led by, among others, MIHAIL FORMUZAL.

Diplomatic Representation

EMBASSIES IN MOLDOVA

Azerbaijan: 2012 Chișinău, str. Kogelnichanu 64; tel. and fax (22) 21-42-09; e-mail chisinau@mission.mfa.gov.az; Ambassador ISFENDIYAR VAHABZADE.

Belarus: 2012 Chișinău, str. Mateevici 35; tel. (22) 23-82-73; fax (22) 23-83-00; e-mail moldova@belembassy.org; internet www.belembassy.org/moldova; Ambassador VASILIY A. SAKOVICH.

Bulgaria: 2012 Chișinău, str. București 92; tel. (22) 23-79-83; fax (22) 23-79-78; e-mail ambasada-bulgara@meganet.md; internet www.mfa.bg/kishinev; Ambassador NIKOLAI ILIYEV.

China, People's Republic: 2004 Chișinău, str. Mitropolit Dosoftei 124; tel. (22) 21-07-12; fax (22) 29-59-60; e-mail chnembassy@126.com; internet md.chineseembassy.org; Ambassador SHI LONGZHUANG.

Czech Republic: 2005 Chișinău, str. Moara Roșie 23; tel. (22) 29-64-19; fax (22) 29-64-37; e-mail chisinau@embassy.mzv.cz; internet www.mzv.cz/chisinau; Ambassador PETR KYPR.

France: 2012 Chișinău, str. V. Pîrcălab 6; tel. (22) 20-04-00; fax (22) 20-04-01; e-mail amb-fr@cni.md; internet www.ambafrance.md; Ambassador PIERRE ANDRIEU.

Germany: 2012 Chișinău, str. Maria Cibotari 35; tel. (22) 20-06-00; fax (22) 23-46-80; e-mail info@chisinau.diplo.de; internet www.chisinau.diplo.de; Ambassador NIKOLAUS VON DER WENGE GRAF LAMBSDORFF.

Hungary: 2004 Chișinău, bd. Ștefan cel Mare 131; tel. (22) 22-34-04; fax (22) 22-45-13; e-mail mission.kiv@kum.hu; internet www.mfa.gov.hu/emb/chisinau; Ambassador GYÖRGY VARNA.

Israel: 2001 Chișinău, str. Tighina 12; tel. (22) 54-42-84; Ambassador AVRAHAM SHARON (resident in Jerusalem, Israel).

Lithuania: 2001 Chișinău, str. I. Valilenco 24/1; tel. (22) 54-31-94; fax (22) 23-42-87; e-mail amb.md@urm.lt; internet md.mfa.lt; Ambassador VYTAUTAS ŽALYS.

Poland: 2019 Chișinău, str. Grenoble 126A; tel. (22) 28-59-50; fax (22) 28-90-00; e-mail polemb@mtc.md; internet www.kiszyniow.polemb.net; Ambassador KRZYSZTOF SUPROWICZ.

Romania: 2001 Chișinău, str. București 66/1; tel. (22) 21-30-37; fax (22) 22-81-29; e-mail ambrom@moldnet.md; internet chisinau.mae.ro; Ambassador (vacant).

Russia: 2004 Chișinău, bd. Ștefan cel Mare 153; tel. (22) 23-49-43; fax (22) 23-51-07; e-mail domino@mtc.md; internet www.moldova.mid.ru; Ambassador VALERII I. KUZMIN.

Turkey: Chișinău, str. Valeriau Cupcea 60; tel. (22) 50-91-00; fax (22) 22-55-28; e-mail tremb@moldova.md; Ambassador AHMET FERIT ÜLKER.

Ukraine: 2008 Chișinău, bd. Vasile Lupu 17; tel. (22) 58-21-51; fax (22) 58-51-08; e-mail emb_md@mfa.gov.ua; internet www.mfa.gov.ua/moldova; Ambassador SERHIY I. PYROZHKOV.

United Kingdom: 2012 Chișinău, str. N. Iorga 18; tel. (22) 22-59-02; fax (22) 25-18-59; e-mail enquiries.chisinau@fco.gov.uk; internet ukinmoldova.fco.gov.uk/en; Ambassador JOHN BEYER.

USA: 2009 Chișinău, str. Mateevici 103; tel. (22) 40-83-00; fax (22) 23-30-44; e-mail ircchisinau@state.gov; internet moldova.usembassy.gov; Ambassador ASIF J. CHAUDHRY.

Judicial System

Supreme Court of the Republic of Moldova (Curtea Supremă de Justiție a Republicii Moldova): 2009 Chișinău, str. M. Kogălniceanu 70; tel. and fax (22) 22-15-47; internet www.scjustice.md; Pres. ION MURUIANU.

Constitutional Court of the Republic of Moldova (Curtea Constitutionala a Republicii Moldova): 2004 Chișinău, str. A. Lapușneanu 28; tel. (22) 25-37-08; fax (22) 25-37-46; e-mail curtea@constcourt.md; internet www.constcourt.md; f. 1994; Chair. DUMITRU PULBERE.

Prosecutor-General: VALERIU GURBULEA, 2005 Chișinău, str. Mitropolit Bănulescu-Bodoni 26; tel. (22) 22-50-75; fax (22) 21-20-32; internet www.procuratura.md.

Religion

The majority of the inhabitants of Moldova profess Christianity, the largest denomination being the Eastern Orthodox Church. The Gagauz, of Turkic descent, are also adherents of Orthodox Christianity.

CHRISTIANITY

Eastern Orthodox Church

In December 1992 the Patriarch of Moscow and All Russia issued a decree altering the status of the Eparchy of Chișinău and Moldova to that of a Metropolitan See. In 2002 the Government permitted the registration of an Autonomous Metropolitate of Bessarabia. The recognition of the church, an exarchate of the Romanian Orthodox Church, was confirmed by the Supreme Court in late 2004. In late 2007 the Romanian Orthodox Church announced that three dioceses in Moldova, which had been abolished in 1944 following the Soviet occupation of the territory, were to be reactivated.

Metropolitanate of Bessarabia, Archbishop of Chișinău: 2004 Chișinău, str. 31 August 161; e-mail gbadea2006@yahoo.com; internet www.mitropoliabasarabiei.ro; Metropolitan of Bessarabia PETRU (PĂDURARU).

Orthodox Church in the Republic of Moldova (Moscow Patriarchate): 2004 Chișinău, str. București 119; tel. (22) 23-78-78; e-mail sec@mitropolia.md; internet www.mitropolia.md; 1,520 parishes (2004); Metropolitan of Chișinău and all-Moldova VLADIMIR (KANTARYAN).

Roman Catholic Church

In October 2001 the diocese of Chișinău, covering the whole country, was established. At 31 December 2006 there were an estimated 20,000 Roman Catholics in Moldova.

Bishop of Chișinău: Rt Rev. ANTON COȘA, 2012 Chișinău, str. Mitropolit Dosoftei 85; tel. (22) 22-34-70; fax (22) 22-52-10; e-mail episcopia@starnet.md.

The Press

The publications listed below are in Moldovan, except where otherwise indicated.

PRINCIPAL NEWSPAPERS

Analytique Moldpresa: 2200 Chișinău, str. 31 August 85; tel. (22) 22-12-83; fax (22) 22-67-04; f. 2006; weekly; in Russian; Chief Editor NATALIA UZUN; circ. 8,000 (2008).

Argumenty i Fakty v Moldove (Arguments and Facts in Moldova): 2000 Chișinău, str. Armenească 55/101; tel. (22) 27-89-28; fax (22) 54-65-80; e-mail aif@mld.net; internet www.aif.md; f. 1978; Moldovan version of *Argumenty i Fakty* (Russia); in Russian; weekly; Chief Editor YEVGENIYA ANOKHINA; circ. 25,000 (2008).

Curierul Agricol (The Agricultural Courier): 2012 Chișinău, str. Pușkin 22/311; e-mail curier06@mail.md; f. 2006; weekly; Chief Editor DUMITRU ȚIRA; circ. 4,000 (2008).

Curierul Economic (The Economic Courier): 2005 Chișinău, str. Bănulescu Bodoni 61/103; tel. (22) 40-28-33; fax (22) 24-52-57; e-mail curierul@ase.md; f. 1999; weekly; Dir TATIANA ROȘCA; circ. 4,000 (2008).

Ekonomicheskoye Obozreniye (Economic Review): 2000 Chișinău, str. S. Lazo 40, 5th floor; tel. (22) 88-77-77; fax (22) 88-77-89; e-mail red@logos.press.md; internet logos.press.md; f. 1990; weekly; in Russian; Chief Editor SERGEI MIȘIN; circ. 9,500 (2008).

Flux Continu: 2000 Chișinău, str. Corobceanu 17; tel. (22) 23-50-91; fax (22) 23-74-75; e-mail sergiu@flux.md; internet www.flux.md;

f. 1995; 5 a week; Chief Editor SERGIU PRAPORȘCIC; circ. 35,000 (Fri.), 3,000 (Mon.–Thur.) (2008).

Glasul Națiunii (The Voice of the Nation): 2000 Chișinău, str. 31 August 15; tel. and fax (22) 54-27-82; e-mail glasul_natiunii@yahoo.com; f. 1989; 4 a week; culture, arts, literature, sport, politics; Chief Editor VASILE NĂSTASE; circ. 10,000 (2008).

Jurnal de Chișinău (Chișinău Journal): 2012 Chișinău, str. Pușkin 22/444; tel. (22) 23-40-41; fax (22) 23-42-30; e-mail cotidian@jurnal.md; internet www.jurnal.md; f. 1999; 3 a week; Chief Editor RODICA MAHU; circ. 26,000 (2008).

Kishinevskii Obozrevatel (Chișinău Correspondent): Chișinău, str. B. Pirkalab 45/405; tel. and fax (22) 21-02-27; e-mail oboz@moldnet.md; internet www.ko.md; weekly; in Russian; Chief Editor IRINA ASTAKHOVA.

Kishinevskiye Novosti (Chișinău News): 2012 Chișinău, str. Pușkin 22; tel. and fax (22) 23-39-18; e-mail kn@kn.md; internet www.kn.md; f. 1991; weekly; in Russian; Chief Editor SERGHEI DROBOT; circ. 9,000 (2008).

Kommersant Plus (Businessman Plus): 2012 Chișinău, str. Pușkin 22/601; tel. (22) 23-36-94; fax (22) 23-33-31; e-mail inform@commert.press.md; internet www.km.press.md; weekly; in Russian; politics and economics, incl. coverage of Gagauz-Yeri and Transnistria; Chief Editor SVETLANA BURLAC; circ. 11,000 (2008).

Komsomolskaya Pravda v Moldove (Young Communist League Truth in Moldova): 2000 Chișinău, str. Vlaicu Pîrcălab 45; tel. (22) 22-07-13; fax (22) 22-12-74; e-mail kp@kp.md; internet www.kp.md; f. 1996; daily; in Russian; Moldovan edition of *Komsomolskaya Pravda* (Russia); Dir SERGEI CIURICOV; circ. 9,000 (2008).

Moldavskiye Vedomosti (Moldovan Gazette): 2012 Chișinău, str. Bănulescu-Bodoni 21; tel. and fax (22) 23-86-18; e-mail editor@mv.net.md; internet vedomosti.md; f. 1995; 2 a week; in Russian; Editor-in-Chief DMITRII A. CIUBAȘENCO; circ. 15,500 (2008).

Moldova Suverană (Sovereign Moldova): 2012 Chișinău, str. Pușkin 22, 3rd Floor; tel. and fax (22) 22-31-96; e-mail cotidian@moldova-suverana.md; internet www.moldova-suverana.md; f. 2005; daily; fmrly organ of the Govt; Editor ION BERLINSKI; circ. 20,000 (per week).

Nezavisimaya Moldova (Independent Moldova): 2012 Chișinău, str. Pușkin 22; tel. (22) 23-36-08; fax (22) 23-31-41; e-mail mail@nm.md; internet www.nm.md; f. 2005; daily; in Russian; Chief Editor IURII TIȘCENCO; circ. 92,700 (per month).

Vremya (Time): 2000 Chișinău, str. Ștefan cel Mare 13; tel. (22) 54-44-46; e-mail nata@vremea.md; f. 1998; daily; in Russian; Chief Editor EVGHENII PASCARI; circ. 8,800 (2008).

Gagauz-Yeri

Stolitsa Komrat (Capital City Comrat): 3800 Comrat, str. Tretiakov 36; tel. (298) 2-42-61; e-mail capitala@mail.ru; f. 2005; in Russian and Gagauz; Chief Editor ANA HARLAMENKO; circ. 8,000 (2008).

Vesti Gagauzii (Gagauz-Yeri News): 3800 Comrat, str. Lenin 200; tel. (298) 2-28-93; e-mail vesti@mtc-co.md; f. 1996; weekly; in Russian and Gagauz; politics, culture, language; Chief Editor DMITRII MARINOV; circ. 4,500 (2008).

Transnistria

Dnestrovskaya Pravda (Dnestr Truth): 3300 Tiraspol, str. 25 Octombrie 101/236–237; tel. and fax (533) 9-46-86; f. 1941; 3 a week; in Russian; Editor TATYANA M. RUDENKO; circ. 1,300 (2008).

Homin (The Echo): Rîbnița, str. Kirov, 130; tel. (555) 3-08-61; fax (555) 4-26-27; e-mail gomin130@mail.ru; f. 1996; weekly; in Ukrainian; Chief Editor DMITRII CERNEGA; circ. 2,460 (2008).

Pridnestrovye (Transnistria): 3300 Tiraspol, str. Lunacearski 13; tel. (533) 9-30-24; fax (533) 7-47-00; e-mail pridnestr@idknet.com; internet www.pridnestrovie-daily.net; f. 1994; 5 a week; in Russian; politics, economics, culture; Chief Editor VLADIMIR MASLENIKOV; circ. 4,241 (2008).

PRINCIPAL PERIODICALS

Alunelul (Little Hazelnut Tree): 2612 Chișinău, str. Pușkin 22; tel. (22) 22-26-41; f. 1982; for children aged 5–10 years; 10 a year; Chief Editor ȘTEFAN MELNIC; circ. 20,000 (2008).

Aquarelle: 2012 Chișinău, str. Pușkin 47/1A/3; tel. and fax (22) 22-07-73; e-mail aquarelle@aquarelle.md; internet www.aquarelle.md; f. 2003; in Russian; monthly; general women's interest; Chief Editor ANGELA SÎRBU; circ. 3,500 (2008).

Chipăruș Plus (Sharp Peppercorn): 2000 Chișinău, str. Ion Creangă 66/45; tel. and fax (22) 74-48-82; e-mail chiparusplus@yahoo.com; f. 2007; monthly; satirical; Dir MARGARETA CHIȚCATÎI; circ. 10,000 (2008).

Curierul Ortodox (The Orthodox Courier): 2060 Chișinău, bd. Traian 3, Biserica Sfîntul Dumitru; tel. (22) 77-25-33; e-mail fustei_nicolae@yahoo.com; internet www.geocities.com/cortodox; f. 1995; monthly; publ. of the Orthodox Church in the Republic of Moldova (Moscow Patriarchate); Chief Editor NICOLAE FUȘTEI; circ. 1,200 (2008).

Democrația (Democracy): 2012 Chișinău, str. Pușkin 22/518; tel. (22) 24-32-53; fax (22) 24-35-85; e-mail democratiasaptaminal@yahoo.com; f. 2001; monthly; economics, politics, sport; Editor-in-Chief CORNEL CIUREA; circ. 11,000 (2008).

Florile Dalbe (The White Flowers): 2012 Chișinău, str. Pușkin 22; tel. and fax (22) 23-37-78; e-mail florile_d@mtc.md; f. 1941; weekly; education; Dir ION ANTON; circ. 15,000 (2008).

Legea și Viața (The Law and Life): 2012 Chișinău, str. Pușkin 22/516; tel. (22) 23-37-90; e-mail legea@molddata.md; f. 1990; monthly; in Moldovan and Russian; Chief Editor LEONTIE ARSENIE; circ. 5,000 (2008).

Moldova (Moldova): 2012 Chișinău, str. Pușkin 22/539; tel. (22) 23-50-07; fax (22) 23-74-63; e-mail revistamoldova@list.ru; f. 2004; monthly; in Moldovan, Russian and English; the arts; Editor BORIS MARIAN; circ. 3,000 (2008).

Natura (Nature): 2000 Chișinău, str. S. Lazo 13; tel. and fax (22) 23-71-49; e-mail natura@natura.md; internet www.natura.md; f. 1990; monthly; nature and the environment; Chief Editor BORIS VIERU; circ. 7,800 (2008).

Noi (Us): 2012 Chișinău, str. Pușkin 22; tel. (22) 23-31-91; e-mail revistanoi@mail.md; f. 1935; for adolescents; Chief Editor VALERIU VOLONTIR; circ. 5,000 (2008).

Okhotnik i rybalov v Moldove (The Hunter and Fisherman in Moldova): 2000 Chișinău, str. Șipotelor 2; tel. (22) 24-20-27; fax (22) 24-26-42; e-mail ooorm_jurnal@mail.md; internet www.ohota.md; f. 2006; monthly; in Russian; hunting, shooting, fishing; Chief Editor SERGEI YAVTUSHENKO; circ. 3,000 (2008).

Omnibus: 2000 Chișinău, str. V. Alecsandri 35A; tel. (22) 73-39-72; e-mail omnibus@hotbox.ru; f. 1993; in Russian; agriculture; Chief Editor MIHAIL BEREZICOV; circ. 5,500 (2008).

Profit/ Banky i Finansy (Profit/ Banks and Finance): 2000 Chișinău, str. Kogălniceanu 76; tel. (22) 23-49-30; fax (22) 23-49-33; e-mail office@profit.md; internet www.profit.md; f. 1995; monthly; Romanian and Russian edns; economics and finance; Dir ALEXANDRU TARAS; total circ. 11,000 (2008).

Puls (Pulse): 2200 Chișinău, str. Dosoftei 118; tel. (22) 83-81-86; e-mail red@puls.md; internet www.puls.md; f. 2004; monthly; in Russian; politics and economics; Chief Editor DMITRII KAVRUK; circ. 5,000 (2008).

Săptămîna (The Week): 2012 Chișinău, str. 31 August 107; tel. (22) 22-43-42; fax (22) 22-44-61; e-mail saptamin@mdl.net; internet www.saptamina.md; f. 1992; weekly; politics, economics, social and cultural affairs; Chief Editor VIOREL MIHAIL; circ. 12,722 (2008).

Siesta: 2000 Chișinău, str. Kogălniceanu 88; tel. (22) 20-79-31; fax (22) 28-87-73; e-mail info@siesta.md; internet www.siesta.md; f. 2003; monthly; in Russian, Moldovan and English; coverage of cultural events in Chișinău; Chief Editor VLADIMIR GLADUN; circ. 6,000 (2008).

Timpul de Dimineața (The Morning Times): 2000 Chișinău, str. Mitropolitul Dosoftei 95; tel. (22) 29-40-45; e-mail timpul@mdl.net; internet www.timpul.md; f. 2003; daily; Chief Editor SORINA ȘTEFÎRȚĂ; circ. 46,750 (2008).

VIP Magazin (VIP Magazine): 2012 Chișinău, str. Pușkin 22/428–432; tel. (22) 23-31-64; fax (22) 23-40-01; e-mail vip_magazin@mld.net; internet www.vipmagazin.md; f. 2002; monthly; politics, business, entertainment; Chief Editor SERGIU GAVRILIȚĂ; circ. 3,500 (2008).

Transnistria

Obnovleniye (Renewal): 3300 Tiraspol, str. 25 Octombrie 118; f. 2000; monthly; in Russian; politics and economics; circ. 80,000 (2008).

Partner (Partner): 3300 Tiraspol, ul. Lenina 48, 4th floor; tel. (533) 9-42-03; e-mail makireeva@yandex.ru; internet www.tiraspol.ru/partner; f. 2004; monthly; in Russian; publ. by the Chamber of Trade and Industry of the 'Transnistrian Moldovan Republic'; Chief Editor MARINA KIREYEVA; circ. 999 (2008).

NEWS AGENCIES

Infotag News Agency: 2014 Chișinău, str. Kogâlniceanu 76; tel. (22) 23-49-30; fax (22) 23-49-33; e-mail office@infotag.md; internet www.infotag.md; f. 1993; Dir ALEXANDRU TANAS.

State Information Agency—Moldpres: 2012 Chișinău, str. Pușkin 22; tel. (22) 23-34-28; fax (22) 23-26-98; e-mail inform@moldpres.md; internet www.moldpres.md; f. 1940 as ATEM, reorganized 1990 and 1994; Dir VALERIU RENITA.

MOLDOVA

Directory

Transnistria

Olvia-Press: 3300 Tiraspol, str. Pravda 31; tel. (3022) 8-24-97; fax (3022) 8-20-04; e-mail olvia@idknet.com; internet www.olvia.idknet.com; f. 1992; sole press agency of the 'Transnistrian Moldovan Republic'; reports political, economic and cultural developments in the region; Editor-in-Chief OLEG A. YELKOV.

PRESS ASSOCIATIONS

Association of Independent Press (API): 2012 Chişinău, str. Bucureşti 77; tel. and fax (22) 22-09-96; e-mail api@api.md; internet www.api.md; f. 1997; Pres. ION MITITELU; Exec. Dir PETRU MACOVEI.

Independent Journalism Centre (IJC): 2012 Chişinău, str. Şciusev 53; tel. (22) 21-36-52; fax (22) 22-66-81; e-mail editor@ijc.md; internet www.ijc.md; f. 1994; non-governmental org.

Publishers

Editura Cartea Moldovei: 2004 Chişinău, bd. Ştefan cel Mare 180; tel. (22) 24-65-10; fax (22) 24-64-11; f. 1977; fiction, non-fiction, poetry, art books; Dir DUMITRU FURDUI; Editor-in-Chief RAISA SUVEICA.

Editura Hyperion: 2004 Chişinău, bd. Ştefan cel Mare 180; tel. (22) 24-40-22; f. 1976; fiction, literature, arts; Dir VALERIU MATEI.

Editura Lumina (Light): 2004 Chişinău, bd. Ştefan cel Mare 180; tel. (22) 24-63-95; f. 1966; educational textbooks; Dir VICTOR STRATAN; Editor-in-Chief ANATOL MALEV.

Editura Ştiinţa (Science): 2028 Chişinău, str. Academiei 3; tel. (22) 73-96-16; fax (22) 73-96-27; e-mail prini@stiinta.asm.md; f. 1959; textbooks, encyclopedias, dictionaries, children's books and fiction in various languages; Dir GHEORGHE PRINI.

Broadcasting and Communications

TELECOMMUNICATIONS

Regulatory Authority

National Regulatory Agency in Electronic Communications and Information Technology (ANRCETI) (Agenţia Naţională pentru Reglementare în Comunicaţii Electronice şi Tehnologia Informatiei): 2012 Chişinău, bd. Ştefan cel Mare 134; tel. (22) 25-13-17; fax (22) 22-28-85; e-mail office@anrceti.md; internet www.anrceti.md; f. 2000; Dir SERGIU SITNIC.

Service Providers

Eventis: Chişinău, str. Ghioceilor 1; tel. (22) 30-05-67; fax (22) 71-95-85; internet www.eventismobile.md; f. 2007; 51% owned by Eventis Telecom Holdings (Cyprus); mobile cellular telecommunications; Man. Dir IURIE CEBAN.

Moldcell: 2060 Chişinău, str. Belgrad 3; tel. (22) 20-62-06; fax (22) 20-62-07; e-mail moldcell@moldcell.md; internet www.moldcell.md; f. 1999; mobile telecommunications; owned by Fintur Holdings b.v. (Netherlands).

Moldtelecom: 2001 Chişinău, bd. Ştefan cel Mare 10; tel. (22) 57-01-01; fax (22) 57-01-11; e-mail office@moldtelecom.md; internet www.moldtelecom.md; f. 1993; telephone communication and internet service provider; scheduled for partial privatization; Gen. Dir STELA SCOLA.

Orange Moldova: 2071 Chişinău, str. Alba-Iulia 75; tel. (22) 57-50-10; e-mail orange@orange.md; internet www.orange.md; f. 1998 as Voxtel SA; present name adopted 2007; mobile cellular telecommunications; 56.7% owned by France Telecom Mobiles (France), 33.4% by MMT-BIS; Dir-Gen. BRUNO DUTOIT.

Unité: 2001 Chişinău, bd. Ştefan cel Mare 10; e-mail marketing@unite.md; internet www.unite.md; f. 2007; mobile cellular communications; 100% owned by Moldtelecom.

BROADCASTING

Regulatory Authorities

National Radio Frequencies Centre (Centrul National pentru Frecvente Radio): 2021 Chişinău, str. Drumul Viilor 28/2; tel. (22) 73-53-64; fax (22) 73-39-41; e-mail cnfr@cnfr.md; internet www.mdi.gov.md/main_gis_md; f. 1993; responsible for frequency allocations and monitoring, certification of post and communications equipment and services; Gen. Dir TEODOR CICLICCI.

Radio and Television Co-ordinating Council (Consiliul Coordonator al Audiovizualului): 2012 Chişinău, str. Mihai Eminescu 28; tel. (22) 27-74-70; fax (22) 27-74-71; e-mail office@cca.md; internet www.cca.md; f. 1995; state owned; regulatory and licensing body; Pres. GHEORGHE ION GORINCIOI.

Radio

State Radio and Television Company of Moldova (Teleradio) (Televiziunea de Stat a Republicii Moldova): 2028 Chişinău, str. Miorita 1; tel. (22) 72-10-77; fax (22) 72-33-52; e-mail info@trm.md; internet www.trm.md; f. 1994; Pres. VALENTIN TODERCAN; Exec. Dir (Radio) SERGIU PATOC.

Radio Moldova: 2028 Chişinău, str. Miorita 1; tel. and fax (22) 72-33-47; e-mail directorzodio@tzm.md; f. 1930; broadcasts in Romanian, Russian, Ukrainian, Gagauz and Yiddish; Exec. Dir GHEORGHIŞENCO VEACESLAV.

Television

State Radio and Television Company of Moldova (Teleradio) (Televiziunea de Stat a Republicii Moldova): 2028 Chişinău, str. Miorita 1; tel. (22) 72-10-77; fax (22) 72-33-52; e-mail info@trm.md; internet www.trm.md; f. 1994; Pres. VALENTIN TODERCAN; Exec. Dir (TV) ADELA RAILEANU.

Finance

(cap. = capital; res = reserves; dep. = deposits; m. = million; brs = branches; amounts in Moldovan lei, unless otherwise stated)

BANKING

The National Bank of Moldova, established in 1991, is independent of the Government (but responsible to Parlamentul) and has the power to regulate monetary policy and the financial system. At February 2009 there were 16 authorized commercial banks in operation (with total assets amounting to 38,092m. lei).

Central Bank

National Bank of Moldova (Banca Naţională a Moldovei): 2005 Chişinău, bd. Renaşterii 7; tel. (22) 40-90-06; fax (22) 22-05-91; e-mail official@bnm.org; internet www.bnm.org; f. 1991; cap. 288.9m., res 711.1m., dep. 3,639.4m. (Dec. 2006); Gov. LEONID TALMACI.

Commercial Banks

Banca de Economii a Moldovei: 2012 Chişinău, str. Columna 115; tel. (22) 21-80-05; fax (22) 21-80-06; e-mail bem@bem.md; internet www.bem.md; f. 1992; cap. 29.3m., res 18.8m., dep. 2,293.3m. (Dec. 2007); Pres. GRIGORE GACIKEVICI; 37 brs.

Banca de Finanţe şi Comerţ (FinComBank SA—Finance and Trade Bank JSC): 2012 Chişinău, str. Puşkin 26; tel. (22) 22-74-35; fax (22) 23-73-08; e-mail fincom@fincombank.com; internet www.fincombank.com; f. 1993; cap. 179.7m., dep. 854.7m., total assets 1,229.8m. (June 2007); Chair. VICTOR KHVOROSTOVSKY; 13 brs.

Banca Socială: 2005 Chişinău, str. Bănulescu-Bodoni 61; tel. (22) 22-14-94; fax (22) 22-42-30; e-mail office@socbank.md; internet www.socbank.md; f. 1991; jt-stock commercial bank; cap. 57.6m., res 27.5m., dep. 1,005.6m. (Dec. 2005); Pres. VLADIMIR SUETNOV; Chair. VALENTIN CUNEV; 20 brs.

Energbank: 2012 Chişinău, str. Vasile Alecsandri 78; tel. (22) 54-43-77; fax (22) 27-98-55; e-mail office@energbank.com; internet www.energbank.com; f. 1997; cap. 80m., dep. 681m., total assets 1,237m. (June 2008); Chair. IURII VASILACHI; 68 brs.

EuroCreditBank: 2001 Chişinău, str. Ismail 33; tel. (22) 50-01-01; fax (22) 54-88-27; e-mail info@ecb.md; internet www.telebank.md; f. 1992; jt-stock co; commercial investment bank; cap. 108.0m., res 8.4m. (March 2007), dep. 64.0m. (June 2008); Pres. AURELIU CINCILEI; 3 brs.

Eximbank: 2004 Chişinău, bd. Ştefan cel Mare şi Sfânt 171/1; tel. (22) 30-11-02; fax (22) 60-16-11; e-mail info@eximbank.com; internet www.eximbank.com; f. 1994; total assets 3,717.3m. (Dec. 2008); Gen. Dir MARCEL CHIRCĂ.

Investprivatbank: 2001 Chişinău, str. Şciusev 34; tel. (22) 26-78-03; fax (22) 54-05-10; e-mail ipb@ipb.md; internet www.ipb.md; f. 1994; cap. 123m., res 25m., dep. 1,294m. (Aug. 2008); Chair. IVAN CHIRPALOV; 20 brs.

Mobiasbanca: 2012 Chişinău, bd. Ştefan cel Mare şi Sfânt 81A; tel. and fax (22) 54-19-74; e-mail office@mobiasbanca.md; internet www.mobiasbanca.md; f. 1990; 67.9% owned by Société Générale (France); acquired Bancoop in 2001; commercial bank; cap. 100.0m., res 10.7m., dep. 1,948.1m. (Sept. 2008); Chair. of Bd JEAN-FRANÇOIS MYARD; 11 brs.

Moldova Agroindbank: 2006 Chişinău, str. Cosmonauţilor 9; tel. (22) 21-28-28; fax (22) 22-80-58; e-mail aib@maib.md; internet www.maib.md; f. 1991; joint-stock commercial bank; cap. 207.5m., res

31.0m., dep. 3,901.8m. (Dec. 2006); Chair. of Bd VICTOR MICULEȚ; Chair. NATALIA VRABIE; 45 brs.

Unibank: 2012 Chișinău, str. Mitropolit G. Bănulescu-Bodoni 45; tel. (22) 25-38-01; fax (22) 22-05-30; e-mail welcome@unibank.md; internet www.unibank.md; f. 1993; jt-stock commercial bank; cap. 186.1m., res 24.6m., dep. 232.2m. (Jan. 2008); Pres. DUMITRU TUGULSCHI; 5 brs.

Victoriabank: 2004 Chișinău, str. 31 August 1989 141; tel. (22) 57-61-00; fax (22) 23-45-33; e-mail office@vb.md; internet www.victoriabank.md; f. 1990; cap. 702.4m., res 170.8m., dep. 2,970.7m. (Aug. 2008); Pres. NATALIA POLITOV-CANGAS; 55 brs.

STOCK EXCHANGE

Moldovan Stock Exchange (Bursa de Valori a Moldovei SA): 2001 Chișinău, bd. Ștefan cel Mare 73; tel. (22) 27-75-94; fax (22) 27-73-56; e-mail dodu@moldse.md; internet www.moldse.md; f. 1994; Chair. Dr CORNELIU DODU.

INSURANCE

In April 2007 there were 32 insurance companies operating in Moldova.

State Inspectorate for the Supervision of Insurance and Non-state Pension Funds (Inspectoratul de Stat pentru Supravegherea Asigurarilor si Fondurilor Nestatale de Pensii—ISSA): 2001 Chișinău, bd. Ștefan cel Mare si Sfânt 124; tel. (22) 27-86-53; e-mail issa@tmg.md; internet www.issa.md; f. 1996; Dir ALEXANDRU MUNTEANU.

Asito: 2005 Chișinău, str. Bănulescu-Bodoni 57/1; tel. (22) 22-62-12; fax (22) 22-11-79; e-mail asito@qbe-asito.com; internet www.qbe-asito.com; f. 1991; 48.3% owned by Moldova Investment Group (United Kingdom); fmrly QBE Asito; Gen. Man. EUGEN SHLOPAK.

Donaris Group: 2012 Chișinău, str. Columna 72; tel. (22) 22-82-33; fax (22) 27-83-94; e-mail office@donaris.md; internet www.donaris.md; life and non-life, insurance and reinsurance.

Moldasig: 2009 Chișinău, str. M. Eminescu 2; tel. (22) 23-81-61; fax (22) 23-83-46; e-mail moldasig@dnt.md; internet www.moldasig.md; f. 2002; 51% owned by Banca de Economii SA, 25% owned by Calea Ferată din Moldova, 24% owned by Poșta Moldovei; 25% market share in Moldova in 2006; Gen. Dir VITALI I. BODYA.

Moldcargo: 2012 Chișinău, str. V. Alecsandri 97; tel. (22) 24-55-67; fax (22) 23-36-70; e-mail office@moldcargo.md; internet www.moldcargo.md; f. 1999; life and non-life; Pres. VLADIMIR FLOREA.

Trade and Industry

GOVERNMENT AGENCIES

State Department for Privatization (Departamentul Privatizarii al Republicii Moldova): 2012 Chișinău, str. Pușkin 26; tel. (22) 23-43-50; fax (22) 23-43-36; e-mail dep.priv@moldtelecom.md; Dir-Gen. ALEKSANDR BANNICOV.

Moldovan Investment and Export Promotion Organization (MEPO) (Organizația de Atragere a Investițiilor și Promovare a Exportului din Moldova): 2009 Chișinău, str. Mateevici 65; tel. (22) 27-36-54; fax (22) 22-43-10; e-mail office@miepo.md; internet www.miepo.md; f. 1999; assists enterprises in increasing exports and improving business environment; Dir.-Gen. ANDREI TIMUS.

CHAMBERS OF COMMERCE

Chamber of Commerce and Industry of the Republic of Moldova (Camera de Comerț și Industrie a Republicii Moldova): 2012 Chișinău, str. Ștefan cel Mare 151; tel. (22) 23-53-32; fax (22) 23-13-91; e-mail camera@chamber.md; internet www.chamber.md; f. 1991; brs in Bălți, Cahul, Ceadir-Lunga (Gagauz-Yeri), Edineț, Lapusna, Orhei, Soroca, Tighina (Bendery), Ungheni; 16 sub-brs; Pres. GHEORGHE CUCU.

Chamber of Commerce and Industry of the 'Transnistrian Moldovan Republic' (TPP PMR): 3300 Tiraspol, ul. Lenina 48; tel. (533) 9-42-03; e-mail tpp@tiraspol.ru; internet www.tiraspol.ru; f. 1996; brs in Bendery, Rybnitsa and Dubosarry; Pres. VASILII N. KOZHAN; Exec. Dir VIKTOR M. GUZIN.

UTILITIES

Regulatory Authority

National Energy Regulatory Agency (ANRE): 2012 Chișinău, str. Columna 90; tel. (22) 54-13-84; fax (22) 22-46-98; e-mail anre@anre.md; internet www.anre.md; f. 1997; autonomous public institution; Dir ANATOL BURLACOB; Gen. Dir NICOLAE TRIBOI.

Electricity

The sector comprises one transmission company, five distribution companies and four power generation plants.

MoldElectrica IS: 2012 Chișinău, str. V. Alecsandri 78; tel. (22) 22-22-70; fax (22) 25-31-42; e-mail disp@moldelectrica.md; internet www.moldelectrica.md; f. 2000 to assume the transmission and distribution functions of Moldtranselectro; Dir MARC RÎMIȘ.

Red Union Fenosa: 2024 Chișinău, str. A. Doga 4; tel. (22) 43-16-55; fax (22) 43-16-75; e-mail info@ufmoldova.com; internet www.ufmoldova.com; privatized in 2000; wholly owned by Unión Eléctrica Fenosa (Spain); distribution co supplying electricity to Chișinău; Pres. RADU SILVIA.

Gas

MoldovaGaz SA: 2005 Chișinău, str. Albișoara 38; tel. (22) 57-80-02; fax (22) 22-00-02; f. 1999; national gas pipeline and distribution networks; comprises 2 transmission companies and 18 distribution companies; 64% owned by Gazprom (Russia), 35% owned by Govt of Moldova; Gen. Dir GHENADIE ABAȘCHIN (acting).

TRADE UNIONS

Confederation of Trade Unions of the Republic of Moldova (Confederația Sindecatelor din Republica Moldova): 2012 Chișinău, str. 31 August 129; tel. (22) 23-76-74; fax (22) 23-76-98; e-mail cfsind@cni.md; f. 1990; Pres. PETRU CHIRIAC.

Transport

RAILWAYS

Calea Ferată din Moldova: 2012 Chișinău, str. Vlaicu Pîrcălab 48; tel. (22) 25-44-08; fax (22) 22-13-80; internet www.railway.md; f. 1992; total network 1,075 km; Dir-Gen. MIRON GAGAUZ.

ROADS

In 2000 Moldova's network of roads totalled 12,691 km (86.1% of which was hard-surfaced), including 3,328 km of main roads.

INLAND WATERWAYS

In 1997 the total length of navigable waterways in Moldova was 424 km. The main river ports are located within the separatist territory of Transnistria, at Tighina (Bendery) and at Râbnița.

CIVIL AVIATION

Moldova has four civilian airports, in Chișinău, Tiraspol, Bălți and Mărculești.

Civil Aviation Administration (Administrația de stat a Aviației Civile): 2026 Chișinău, Aeroportul Chișinău; tel. (22) 52-40-64; fax (22) 52-91-18; e-mail info@caa.md; internet www.caa.md; f. 1993; Dir-Gen. VALENTIN VIZANT.

Air Moldova (Compania Aeriana Moldova): 2026 Chișinău, bd. Dacia 80/2, Aeroportul Chișinău; tel. (22) 52-55-02; fax (22) 52-60-09; e-mail info@airmoldova.md; internet www.airmoldova.md; f. 1993; wholly state-owned; scheduled and charter passenger and cargo flights to destinations in Europe and the CIS; Dir-Gen. VASILE BOTNARI.

Moldavian Airlines: 2026 Chișinău, Aeroportul Chișinău; tel. (22) 52-93-56; fax (22) 52-50-64; e-mail sales@mdv.md; internet www.mdv.md; f. 1994; scheduled flights to Budapest (Hungary) and to Timisoara (Romania); also charter passenger and cargo flights; Pres. and Chief Exec. NICOLAE PETROV.

Tourism

There were 14,722 tourist arrivals in 2007; receipts from tourism (including passenger transport) totalled US $145m. in 2006.

Department of Tourism Development: 2004 Chișinău, bd. Ștefan cel Mare și Sfânt 180, bir. 901; tel. (22) 21-07-74; fax (22) 23-26-26; e-mail dept@turism.md; internet www.turism.md.

MONACO

Introductory Survey

Location, Climate, Language, Religion, Flag

The Principality of Monaco lies in western Europe. The country is a small enclave in south-eastern France, about 15 km east of Nice. It has a coastline on the Mediterranean Sea but is otherwise surrounded by French territory. The climate is Mediterranean, with warm summers and very mild winters. The official language is French, but Monégasque (a mixture of the French Provençal and Italian Ligurian dialects), Italian and English are also spoken. Most of the population profess Christianity, with about 91% belonging to the Roman Catholic Church. The national flag (proportions 4 by 5) has two equal horizontal stripes, of red and white. The state flag (proportions 4 by 5) displays the princely arms of Monaco (a white shield, held by two monks and superimposed on a pavilion of ermine) on a white background.

History

The Principality of Monaco is an hereditary monarchy, which has been ruled by the Grimaldi dynasty since 1297. It was abolished during the French Revolution but re-established in 1814. In 1861 Monaco became an independent state under the protection of France. The Constitution, promulgated in January 1911, vested legislative power jointly in the Prince and an 18-member Conseil national (National Council), selected for a term of five years by a panel comprising nine delegates of the municipality and 21 members elected by universal suffrage. Agreements in 1918 and 1919 between France and Monaco provided for Monaco's incorporation into France should the reigning prince die without leaving a male heir. Prince Louis II, the ruler of Monaco since 1922, died in May 1949, and was succeeded by his grandson, Prince Rainier III. A new Constitution, introduced in December 1962, abolished the principle of the divine right of the ruler, and stipulated that the Conseil national be elected by universal adult suffrage.

Supporters of Prince Rainier, grouped in the Union nationale et démocratique (UND), dominated at five-yearly elections in 1963–88, on all but two occasions taking all 18 seats on the Conseil national. In January 1993, however, two lists of candidates, the Liste Campora (led by Jean-Louis Campora, the President of the Principality's football team, AS Monaco) and the Liste Médecin, secured 15 and two seats, respectively, while an independent candidate won the remaining seat. At legislative elections in February 1998 UND candidates secured all 18 seats.

Controversy surrounding the use of Monaco's financial sector for the transfer of funds derived from criminal activities intensified in 1998 with the culmination of an investigation into the deposit of US $5.5m. in cash, suspected of originating from the illegal drugs trade, at a bank in Monaco in 1995. The affair led to a crisis in relations between France and the Principality, with the French Government overruling Prince Rainier by refusing to extend the mandate of Monaco's Chief Prosecutor, whom it suspected of not conducting a sufficiently thorough investigation of the scandal. Following further criticisms of Monégasque banking practice in a report by the Organisation for Economic Co-operation and Development (OECD, see p. 358) in 2000, the French Government recommended a rapid revision of the bilateral treaties between Monaco and France, proposing that Monégasque institutions be brought into greater conformity with French excise, fiscal and banking regulations. In a list published in April 2002, OECD defined Monaco as an 'unco-operative tax haven'; in early 2009 Monaco was removed from the list (see Economic Affairs). In December 2004 the EU signed an agreement with Monaco on the taxation of savings income. Under the agreement, savings income, in the form of interest payments made in Monaco to residents of the EU, was to be subject to a withholding tax from 1 July 2005. Monaco also agreed to exchange information on request with EU member states in criminal or civil cases of tax fraud or comparable offences.

In March 2002 the electoral law was amended, and in April the Conseil national approved a number of significant constitutional amendments. Both measures were in part intended to expedite Monaco's application for full membership of the Council of Europe (see p. 236), which had been submitted in October 1998. The age of majority was lowered from 21 years to 18 years, and several executive powers of the Prince were transferred to the Conseil national, the size of which was to be increased to 24 members following the elections in 2003. Additionally, the law of succession was modified, to permit succession through the female line.

In late 2002 discontent was reported at a proposal, supported by Campora, to sell AS Monaco to a Russian investment company based in the Principality, Fedcominvest, which was also the football club's principal sponsor. Following a report in *Le Monde*, in December 2002, which alleged that Fedcominvest was involved in money-laundering, Prince Rainier, who, on behalf of the Principality, retained ultimate control over the club, prohibited the sale. The ensuing scandal appeared to be a significant factor in appreciably reducing support for Campora's UND at the legislative elections, held on 9 February 2003, when the UND secured only three seats on the enlarged Conseil national; the remaining 21 seats were awarded to the Union pour Monaco (UpM) list, led by a former member of the UND, Stéphane Valéri.

In April 2004 the Parliamentary Assembly of the Council of Europe (PACE) ruled that Monaco was entitled to receive 'guest status' at PACE but that further reforms were required before the Principality could be considered for full membership; among the principal requirements were the extension of eligibility for several senior government positions, including the Minister of State (who, under the terms of a 1930 treaty, was required to be a French civil servant), to Monégasque citizens, and an enhancement of fiscal regulation. Following the decision of the Joint Committee of the Council of Europe (comprising representatives of the Parliamentary Assembly and the Committee of Ministers) that talks between France and Monaco had demonstrated significant progress towards the eventual reform of the 1930 convention, Monaco was admitted as the 46th member of the Council of Europe on 5 October.

In early 2005 a reorganization of the Council of Government took place. The number of Government Councillors was increased from three to five, with the creation of Government Councillors for Social Affairs and Health and for External Relations, and it was announced that Jean-Paul Proust was to replace Patrick Leclercq as Minister of State from the beginning of May.

On 6 April 2005, following a protracted period of ill health, Prince Rainier died at the age of 81. He was succeeded by his son, Prince Albert II, who had acted as Regent of the Principality since 31 March. In early July, several days before his formal inauguration as Head of State, it was confirmed that Prince Albert, who was unmarried and had no legal heir, had fathered a child in 2003. It was announced, however, that the Prince's son would neither bear the name Grimaldi nor be eligible to inherit the throne. (In June 2006 Prince Albert formally acknowledged paternity of a second child, who also would not take the family name or be eligible to inherit the throne.) Albert II was formally enthroned in mid-November 2005, marking the conclusion of the formal transfer of power.

A number of changes to the Council of Government were effected in 2006. In April Paul Masseron was appointed as Government Councillor for the Interior. In July the Government Councillor for Finance and the Economy, Franck Biancheri, assumed the newly created role of Head of Mission at the Ministry of State, responsible for International Financial Dossiers, and was replaced in his former post by Gilles Tonelli, hitherto Government Councillor for Facilities, the Environment and Urban Planning. In August Henri Fissore, hitherto ambassador to Italy, replaced Rainer Imperti as Government Councillor for External Relations. In May 2007 Jean-Jacques Campana was appointed as Government Councillor for Social Affairs and Health, following the death of Denis Ravera.

At legislative elections held on 3 February 2008, the UpM retained its 21 seats in the Conseil national. The remaining three seats were won by the Rassemblement et Enjeux pour Monaco list.

In December 2008 Prince Albert announced that a plan to extend the Principality (by some 5%) into the sea, by creating an artificial peninsula, had been abandoned due to funding constraints as a result of the international financial crisis and unresolved environmental concerns.

A minor reorganization of the Council of Government took place in March 2009. Sophie Thevenoux, who had hitherto held the post of Director General of the Department of Finance and the Economy, replaced Tonelli as Government Councillor for Finance and the Economy, while Tonelli returned to his previous portfolio of facilities, the environment and urban planning.

Monaco participates in the work of a number of international organizations, and in 1993 became a member of the UN. In February 2006 France upgraded the status of its diplomatic representation in Monaco from consular to ambassadorial level, becoming the first country to operate an embassy in the Principality. Italy also opened an embassy in Monaco later in the year.

Government

Legislative power is vested jointly in the Prince, an hereditary ruler, and the 24-member Conseil national (National Council), which is elected by universal adult suffrage, partly under a system of proportional representation, for a term of five years. The electorate comprises only Monégasque citizens aged 18 years or over. Executive power is exercised, under the authority of the Prince, by the five-member Council of Government, headed by the Minister of State (a French civil servant selected by the Prince from a list of three candidates presented by the French Government). The Prince represents the Principality in its relations with foreign powers, and signs and ratifies treaties. There is, additionally, a consultative Conseil communal (Communal Council), comprising 15 members elected for a term of four years, headed by a mayor.

Economic Affairs

In 2001, according to World Bank estimates, Monaco's gross national income (GNI), measured at average 1999–2001 prices, was equivalent to approximately US $24,700 per head. In 2000, according to World Bank estimates, GNI, measured at average 1998–2000 prices, was equivalent to approximately $25,200 per head, or approximately $25,700 on an international purchasing-power parity basis. According to UN estimates, Monaco's gross domestic product (GDP) was $847m. in 1995 (equivalent to $26,470 per head). During 1990–95 GDP increased, in real terms, at an average annual rate of 1.1%. GDP grew by 5.5% in 2006. The annual rate of population increase averaged 0.3% in 2003–07. Monaco has the highest population density of all the independent states in the world.

There is no agricultural land in Monaco. In 1990 a Belgian enterprise established an offshore fish farm for sea bass and sea bream. In 2005 there were just 28 private sector employees working in the primary sector.

Industry (including construction and public works) contributed 13.9% of the Principality's turnover in 2006. The sector engaged 16.3% of those employed in the private sector in 2007. Industry is mainly light in Monaco. The principal sectors, measured by gross value of output, are chemicals, pharmaceuticals and cosmetics (which together accounted for 43.4% of all industrial revenue in 2004), plastics (29.1%), electrical and electronic goods, paper and textile production.

Service industries represent the most significant sector of the economy in Monaco, contributing 86.1% of total turnover in 2006, and providing employment to 83.7% of those working in the private sector in 2007. Banking and finance accounted for more than 38% of the services sector and employed some 1,400 people in the late 1990s. At the end of 2006 the total value of deposits in Monaco's private banking sector was estimated at €23,450m. Trade accounted for 51.6% of national turnover in 2007, while banking and financial activities accounted for 21.6%.

Tourism is also an important source of income, providing an estimated 25% of total government revenue in 1991 and engaging some 20% of the employed labour force in the late 1990s, while the hotel business alone contributed 3.7% of the Principality's total turnover in 2007, and (together with restaurants and associated activities) engaged 16.5% of those employed in the private sector in the same year. In 2007 some 327,985 tourists (excluding excursionists) visited Monaco. The greatest number of visitors (excluding excursionists) in that year were from Italy (19.2%), France (17.7%), the United Kingdom (14.7%) and the USA (9.5%).

Monaco's external trade is included in the figures for France. Excluding trade within the association with France, in 2007 Monaco's principal merchandise imports were professional and business apparatus and road vehicles and machinery. The most significant exports were semi-finished non-metallic goods, consumer goods and processed agricultural manufactures. Excluding France, the most important source of imports in 2007 was the People's Republic of China (34.9% of the total value), followed by Italy and the United Kingdom. Germany was the most important market for exports (excluding France), contributing 10.7% of total export earnings. Italy, Spain and the United Kingdom were also important markets for exports.

In 2007 there was a budgetary surplus of €2.5m.; expenditure amounted to €843.1m. In 2000 value-added tax (VAT) contributed 52.8% of total government revenue. In the early 2000s it was estimated that less than 3% of the population were unemployed in the Principality.

Monaco is largely dependent on imports from France, owing to its lack of natural resources. There is a severe labour shortage in the Principality, and the economy is reliant on migrant workers (many of whom remain resident in France and Italy). Following the establishment of a casino in the 1860s, tourism became the dominant sector in the economy. In particular, the Principality has sought to establish itself as a major centre of the conference industry. From the 1980s the industry and real estate sectors expanded, as a series of land reclamation projects increased Monaco's area by 20%. A number of foreign companies and banks are registered in Monaco in order to take advantage of the low rates of taxation on company profits. Since the removal of French restrictions on foreign exchange in 1987, Monaco's banking industry (which includes an 'offshore' sector) has expanded. In February 2008 Monaco came under scrutiny when the German Federal Chancellor, Angela Merkel, called for more transparency in the Principality's banking sector. She criticized foreign nationals who avoid paying taxes in their own country by holding secret bank accounts in the Principality. Following an escalating German investigation into allegations of secret bank accounts held in Liechtenstein, it was reported in February 2008 that Monaco had pledged to improve co-operation with Germany on matters of tax evasion. At the EU summit in Brussels in July the European Commission was instructed by EU ministers responsible for finance to consider expanding the directive aimed at addressing the problem of tax evasion. Facing increasing international pressure, in mid-March 2009 Monaco became one of several states (including Andorra and Liechtenstein) to announce that it would adopt OECD standards on transparency and information exchange with regards to bank data, in an effort to combat tax evasion. Consequently, in the following month Monaco was removed from the OECD list of 'unco-operative tax havens'. A new state-owned company, the Société d'Exploitation des Ports de Monaco, was formed in 2003 to oversee the operations and future development of Monaco's two principal ports, at La Condamine (Port Hercule) and Fontvieille. The shipping sector is also significant, contributing some 4% of business revenue and providing employment for around 1,300 people. The telecommunications sector was also a focus of expansion in the Principality in the early 2000s.

Education

Education follows the French system, and is compulsory for 10 years for children aged six to 16 years. Primary education begins at six years of age and lasts for five years. Secondary education begins at 11 years of age and lasts for seven years. In 2004 expenditure on education was equivalent to 4.4% of GDP.

Public Holidays

2009: 1 January (New Year's Day), 27 January (Feast of St Dévote, Patron Saint of the Principality), 13 April (Easter Monday), 1 May (Labour Day), 21 May (Ascension Day), 1 June (Whit Monday), 15 August (Assumption), 1 November (All Saints' Day), 19 November (National Day/Fête du Prince), 8 December (Immaculate Conception), 25–26 December (Christmas).

2010: 1 January (New Year's Day), 27 January (Feast of St Dévote, Patron Saint of the Principality), 5 April (Easter Monday), 1 May (Labour Day), 13 May (Ascension Day), 24 May (Whit Monday), 15 August (Assumption), 1 November (All Saints' Day), 19 November (National Day/Fête du Prince), 8 December (Immaculate Conception), 25–26 December (Christmas).

Weights and Measures

The metric system is in force.

Statistical Survey

Source: (unless otherwise stated): Direction de l'expansion économique, division des statistiques et des études économiques, 9 rue du Gabian, MC 98000; tel. 93-15-41-59; fax 93-15-87-59.

AREA AND POPULATION

Area: 1.95 sq km.

Population: 29,972 at census of 23 July 1990; 32,020 (males 15,544, females 16,476) at census of July 2000. *2006* (estimate): 34,347.

Density (2006): 17,614 per sq km.

Population by Nationality (2000): French 10,229; Italian 6,410; Monégasque 6,089; Other 9,292. *2004* (official estimate at 31 December): Monégasque 7,716 (males 3,318, females 4,398).

Districts (population at 2000 census): Monte-Carlo 15,507; La Condamine 12,187; Fontvieille 3,292; Monaco-Ville (capital) 1,034.

Births, Marriages and Deaths (2006 unless otherwise indicated): Live births 880; Marriages 171 (2004); Deaths 535.

Life expectancy (years at birth, WHO estimates): 81.5 (males 77.9; females 84.9) in 2006. Source: WHO, *World Health Statistics*.

Employment (private sector only, December 2007): Agriculture, hunting, forestry and fishing 29; Mining and quarrying 2; Manufacturing 3,535; Construction 3,560; Electricity and gas 139; Services 37,217 (Hotels, restaurants and associated activities 7,323; Real estate, renting and business services 10,681); *Total* 44,482.

HEALTH AND WELFARE
Key Indicators

Total Fertility Rate (children per woman, 2006): 1.8.

Under-5 Mortality Rate (per 1,000 live births, 2006): 4.

Physicians (per 1,000 head, 1995): 5.80.

Hospital Beds (per 1,000 head, 1995): 19.6.

Health Expenditure (2006): US $ per head (PPP): 7,154.

Health Expenditure (2006): % of GDP: 4.6.

Health Expenditure (2006): public (% of total): 74.2.

For sources and definitions, see explanatory note on p. vi.

FINANCE

Currency and Exchange Rates: French currency: 100 cent = 1 euro (€). *Sterling and Dollar Equivalents* (31 December 2008): £1 sterling = 1.0475 euros; US $1 = 1.3917 euros; €10 = £9.55 = $13.92. *Average Exchange Rate* (euros per US dollar): 0.7971 in 2006; 0.7306 in 2007; 0.6827 in 2008. Note: The local currency was formerly the French franc, although some Monégasque currency, at par with the French franc, also circulated. From the introduction of the euro, with French participation, on 1 January 1999, a fixed exchange rate of €1 = 6.55957 French francs was in operation. Euro notes and coins were introduced on 1 January 2002. The euro and local currency circulated alongside each other until 17 February, after which the euro became the sole legal tender.

Budget (€ million, 2007): Revenue 845.6; Expenditure 843.1 (Current expenditure 548.5, Capital expenditure 294.6).

Turnover of the Principality (official figures, private sector only, € million, 2007): Industry 846.7; Public works and real estate 904.2; Hotel business 498.7; Banking and finance 2,894.7; Wholesale and retail trade 6,906.3; Transport 312.6; Other activities 3,022.2; *Total* 15,385.4.

Gross Domestic Product (€ million at constant 2000 prices): 3,131.7 in 2005; 3,306.2 in 2006.

National Income and Product (€ million at current prices, 2006): Compensation of employees 1,885; Gross operating surplus 1,538; Taxes, less subsidies, on production 295; *Gross domestic product* 3,717.

Gross Domestic Product by Economic Activity (€ million at current prices, 2006): Industry 519; Finance 495; Other services 2,704; *Total* 3,717.

EXTERNAL TRADE

Note: Monaco's imports and exports are included in the figures for France, and separate figures for Monaco's trade with France are not included here.

Principal Commodities (€ million, 2007): *Imports:* 850.2 (Professional and business apparatus 342.1; Road vehicles and machinery 16.5; Consumer goods 163.3; Semi-finished non-metallic goods 133.6). *Exports:* 834.1 (Semi-finished non-metallic goods 332.9; Consumer goods 101.8; Processed agricultural products 79.7).

Principal Trading Partners (€ million, 2007): *Imports:* Belgium 45.3; China, People's Republic 296.6; Germany 32.6; Italy 157.7; Japan 72.3; Madagascar 25.7; Spain 15.6; Switzerland 21.5; United Kingdom 60.1; USA 20.9; Total (incl. others) 850.2. *Exports:* Algeria 17.8; Canada 19.8; China, People's Republic 36.1; Estonia 22.9; Germany 89.0; Italy 69.9; Japan 41.5; Lithuania 43.6; Mauritania 8.8; Spain 65.6; Switzerland 17.6; United Kingdom 55.1; USA 41.9; Total (incl. others) 834.1.

TRANSPORT

Road Traffic (vehicles in use at 31 December 1996, estimates): Passenger cars 21,120; Buses and coaches 70; Lorries and vans 2,700; Road tractors 80; Motorcycles and mopeds 5,400. Source: IRF, *World Road Statistics*.

TOURISM

Tourist Arrivals (excluding excursionists): 285,675 in 2005; 313,070 in 2006; 327,985 in 2007. Figures refer to arrivals of foreign visitors at hotels and similar establishments.

Tourist Arrivals by Country (2007): France 57,976; Germany 12,807; Italy 62,975; Japan 6,444; Russia 10,523; Spain 7,455; Switzerland 8,818; United Kingdom 48,332; USA 31,007; Total (incl. others) 327,985.

COMMUNICATIONS MEDIA

Radio Receivers (1997): 34,000 in use.

Television Receivers (1997): 25,000 in use.

Daily Newspapers (1996): 1 title (estimated circulation 8,000 copies—1995). *2004:* 1 title.

Non-daily Newspapers (1996): 5 titles (estimated circulation 50,000 copies).

Telephones (2005): 34,000 main lines in use.

Facsimile Machines (1992): 1,880 in use.

Book production (1999): 72 titles.

Mobile Cellular Telephones (2005): 17,200 subscribers.

Internet Users (2006): 20,000.

Broadband Subscribers (2005): 9,400 (Sources: mostly International Telecommunication Union; UN, *Statistical Yearbook*; UNESCO Institute for Statistics).

EDUCATION

(2004/05)

Pre-primary: 40 teachers (33 public, 7 private); 903 pupils (736 public, 167 private).

Elementary: 133 teachers (108 public, 25 private); 1,827 pupils (1,365 public, 462 private).

Secondary: 330 teachers (277 public, 53 private); 3,095 pupils (2,399 public, 696 private).

Note: Educational establishments in Monaco in 2004/05 comprised the following: three public pre-primary schools; four primary schools (three public, one private), which integrate pre-primary and elementary age groups; one public elementary school; three public secondary schools, comprising one lower secondary school, one general upper secondary school, and one vocational secondary school; and one private school integrating primary and secondary age groups. There was also one private higher educational establishment, the International University of Monaco, a business school where instruction is conducted in English.

Source: Direction de l'éducation nationale, de la jeunesse et des sports.

Directory

The Constitution

The Constitution of 17 December 1962, as amended on 2 April 2002, vests legislative power jointly in the Ruling Prince and the 24-member Conseil national (National Council), which is elected by universal adult suffrage, partly under a system of proportional representation, for a term of five years. Executive power is exercised, under the authority of the Ruling Prince, by the Council of Government, headed by the Minister of State, who is appointed by the Ruling Prince and is assisted by five Government Councillors. The Constitution maintains the traditional hereditary monarchy, although the principle of the divine right of the ruler is renounced. The law of succession was modified to permit succession through the female line in April 2002. The right of association, trade union freedom and the right to strike are guaranteed. The Supreme Tribunal safeguards fundamental liberties. Constitutional amendments have to be submitted for approval by the Conseil national.

The Government

HEAD OF STATE

Ruling Prince: HSH Prince ALBERT II (succeeded 6 April 2005).

COUNCIL OF GOVERNMENT
(April 2009)

Minister of State: JEAN-PAUL PROUST.

Government Councillor for Finance and the Economy: SOPHIE THEVENOUX.

Government Councillor for the Interior: PAUL MASSERON.

Government Councillor for External Relations and International Economic and Financial Affairs: FRANCK BIANCHERI.

Government Councillor for Facilities, the Environment and Urban Planning: GILLES TONELLI.

Government Councillor for Social Affairs and Health: JEAN-JACQUES CAMPANA.

MINISTRY OF STATE AND DEPARTMENTS

Ministry of State: place de la Visitation, MC 98000; tel. 98-98-80-00; fax 98-98-82-17; e-mail sgme@gouv.mc; internet www.gouv.mc.

Department of Facilities, the Environment and Urban Planning: Ministère d'Etat, place de la Visitation, MC 98000; tel. 98-98-85-67.

Department of External Relations: Ministère d'Etat, place de la Visitation, BP 522, MC 98015 Cedex; tel. 98-98-89-04; fax 98-98-85-54; e-mail relext@gouv.mc; internet www.diplomatie.gouv.mc.

Department of Finance and the Economy: Ministère d'Etat, place de la Visitation, MC 98000; tel. 98-98-82-56; e-mail dfin@troisseptsept.mc.

Department of the Interior: Ministère d'Etat, place de la Visitation, MC 98000; tel. 98-98-84-56; fax 93-50-82-45.

Department of Social Affairs and Health: Ministère d'Etat, place de la Visitation, MC 98000; tel. 98-98-19-19; fax 98-98-19-99; e-mail afss@gouv.mc.

Legislature

Conseil national

12 rue Col Bellando de Castro, MC 98000; tel. 93-30-41-15; fax 93-25-31-90; e-mail vviora@conseil-national.mc; internet www.conseilnational.mc.

President: STÉPHANE VALÉRI.

Vice-President: BERNARD MARQUET.

Election, 3 February 2008

	% of votes	Seats
Union pour Monaco (Union for Monaco)	52.20	21
Rassemblement et Enjeux pour Monaco (Rally and Issues for Monaco)	40.49	3
Monaco Ensemble (Monaco Together)	7.31	—
Total	100.00	24

Advisory Councils

Conseil d'état: Palais de Justice, Monte-Carlo; advises on proposed laws or ordinances submitted for its approval by the Ruling Prince or by the Government, or on any other matter; 12 mems, appointed by the Ruling Prince, following the advice of the Minister of State and the Director of Judicial Services; Pres. PHILIPPE NARMINO; Sec. BRIGITTE GRINDA-GAMBARINI.

Conseil de la Couronne: Monte-Carlo; f. 1942; advises the Ruling Prince on matters of state, and must be consulted by the Ruling Prince prior to the implementation of certain constitutional matters, including the signature or ratification of treaties, the dissolution of the Conseil national, questions of naturalization or reintegration, the issuing of pardons or amnesties; 7 mems, appointed for renewable terms of 3 years; Pres. and 3 mems are appointed by free choice of the Ruling Prince, the remaining 3 mems are nominated by the Ruling Prince on the recommendation of the Conseil national; all mems must hold Monégasque nationality; Pres. CHARLES BALLERIO; Sec. RICHARD MILANESIO.

Conseil économique et social: Centre Administratif, 8 rue Louis-Notari, MC 98000; tel. 97-97-77-91; fax 93-50-05-96; f. 1945; advises on economic matters; 36 mems, appointed for a term of three years; 12 mems directly appointed by Govt, 12 appointed by Govt from list prepared by Union des Syndicats de Monaco, 12 appointed by Govt from list prepared by the Fédération Patronale Monégasque; the Ruling Prince appoints Pres. and 2 Vice-Pres from among the mems; Pres. ANDRÉ GARINO; Vice-Pres ANDRÉ THIBAULT, JACQUES WOLZOK.

Political Organizations

There are no political parties as such in Monaco; however, candidates are generally grouped into lists to contest elections to the Conseil national. Between 1963 and 1992, and 1998 and 2003 the Conseil national was dominated by representatives of the Union Nationale et Démocratique (UND). At the 1993 elections, however, the two main groupings were the Liste Campora, led by Jean-Louis Campora, and the Liste Médecin, led by Jean-Louis Médecin. The majority of seats at the 2003 elections were secured by the Union pour Monaco list, which comprised members of the Union pour la Principauté, the Union Nationale pour l'Avenir de Monaco (UNAM) and the Promotion de la Famille Monegasque. At the 2008 elections the Union pour Monaco list again secured the majority of seats, with the Rassemblement et Enjeux pour Monaco (comprising members of the Rassemblement pour Monaco and Valeurs et Enjeux) winning the remainder. Monaco Ensemble also contested the election, but failed to win representation.

Rassemblement et Enjeux pour Monaco (REM) (Rally and Issues for Monaco): 1 rue de Vedel, MC 98000; tel. 92-16-20-13; fax 93-25-20-09; e-mail info@rassemblement-enjeux.org; internet www.rassemblement-enjeux.org; coalition comprising members of the Rassemblement pour Monaco and Valeurs et Enjeux; Pres. LAURENT NOUVIAN.

Union Nationale pour l'Avenir de Monaco (UNAM) (National Union for the Future of Monaco): Monaco; e-mail unam@unam-monaco.com; internet www.unam-monaco.com; mem. of Union pour Monaco; Pres. ERIC GUAZZONE; Sec.-Gen. CHRISTIANE VATRICAN-SBARRATO.

Union pour Monaco (UpM) (Union for Monaco): Monaco; internet www.unionpourmonaco.com; coalition comprising members of the Union pour la Principauté and the Union Nationale pour l'Avenir de Monaco; Pres. STÉPHANE VALÉRI.

MONACO — *Directory*

Diplomatic Representation

In February 2006 France opened an embassy in Monaco, becoming the first country to institute ambassadorial-level diplomatic relations with the Principality. Italy opened an embassy in Monaco later in the year. By May 2008 ambassadors from 37 countries were accredited to Monaco.

France: Le Roc fleuri, 1 rue du Tenao, BP 345, MC 98006 Cedex; tel. 92-16-54-60; fax 92-16-54-64; e-mail courrier@ambafrance-mc.org; internet www.ambafrance-mc.org; Ambassador ODILE REMIK-ADIM.

Italy: L'Annonciade, 17 ave de l'Annonciade, MC 98000; tel. 93-50-22-71; fax 93-50-06-89; e-mail ambasciata.montecarlo@esteri.it; internet www.ambprincipatomonaco.esteri.it; Ambassador FRANCO MISTRETTA.

Judicial System

The organization of the legal system is similar to that of France. There is one Justice of the Peace, a Tribunal de Première Instance (Tribunal of First Instance), a Cour d'Appel (Court of Appeal), a Cour de Révision (High Court of Appeal), a Tribunal Criminel (Criminal Tribunal) and finally the Tribunal Suprême (Supreme Tribunal), which deals with infringements of the rights and liberties provided by the Constitution, and also with legal actions aiming at the annulment of administrative decisions for abusive exercise of power.

Palais de Justice

5 rue Col Bellando de Castro, MC 98000; tel. 98-98-88-11; fax 98-98-85-89.

Director of Judicial Services: PHILIPPE NARMINO.

President of the Supreme Tribunal: HUBERT CHARLES.

President of the Court of Revision: JEAN APOLLIS.

First President of the Court of Appeal: MONIQUE FRANÇOIS.

President of the Tribunal of First Instance: BRIGITTE GRINDA-GAMBARINI.

Attorney-General: ANNIE BRUNET-FUSTER.

Religion

CHRISTIANITY

The Roman Catholic Church

Monaco comprises a single archdiocese, directly responsible to the Holy See. At 31 December 2006 there were an estimated 29,000 adherents in the Principality, representing about 90.6% of the total population.

Archbishop of Monaco: Most Rev. BERNARD BARSI, Archevêché, 1 rue de l'Abbaye, BP 517, MC 98015 Cedex; tel. 93-30-88-10; fax 92-16-73-88; e-mail archeveche-mc@libello.com; internet www.eglise-catholique.mc.

The Anglican Communion

Within the Church of England, Monaco forms part of the diocese of Gibraltar in Europe.

Chaplain: Fr WALTER RAYMOND, St Paul's Church House, 22 ave de Grande Bretagne, Monte-Carlo, MC 98000; tel. 93-30-71-06; fax 93-30-50-39; e-mail chaplain@stpaulsmonaco.com; internet www.stpaulsmonaco.com.

The Principality also has two Protestant churches and a synagogue.

The Press

Gazette Monaco-Côte d'Azur: 1 ave Princesse Alice, MC 98000; tel. 97-97-61-20; fax 93-50-68-27; e-mail lagazette@aip.mc; f. 1976; monthly; regional information; Dir-Gen. MAX POGGI; Editor-in-Chief NOËLLE BINE-MULLER; circ. 10,000.

Journal de Monaco: Ministère d'Etat, place de la Visitation, BP 522, MC 98015; tel. 93-15-83-15; fax 93-15-82-17; e-mail journaldemonaco@gouv.mc; internet www.gouv.mc/DataWeb/jourmon.nsf; f. 1858; edited at the Ministry of State; official weekly; contains texts of laws and decrees; Editor ROBERT COLLE.

Monaco Actualité: 2 rue du Gabian, MC 98000; tel. 92-05-75-36; fax 92-05-75-34; e-mail actualite@monaco.mc; Dir-Gen. MAURICE RICCOBONO; circ. 15,000.

Monaco Hebdo: 27 blvd d'Italie, MC 98000; tel. 93-50-56-52; fax 93-50-19-22; e-mail monacohebdo@free.fr; internet monacohebdo.free.fr; Man. Editor ROBERTO TESTA.

Monte-Carlo Méditerranée: tel. 92-05-67-67; fax 92-05-37-01; Dir-Gen. GÉRARD COMMAN; Editor-in-Chief CAROLE CHABRIER.

French newspapers are widely read, and a special Monaco edition of the daily *Nice-Matin* is published in Nice, France.

NEWS AGENCY

Monte-Carlo Press: Le Beverly Palace, 13 blvd de Belgique, MC 98000; tel. 97-70-74-24; e-mail mcpress@mcpress.mc; internet www.mcpress.mc; f. 1987.

Publishers

EDIPROM: Monte-Carlo; tel. 92-05-67-67; fax 92-05-37-01; advertising material, official publications; Pres. GÉRARD COMMAN.

Editions Alphée: 28 rue Comte Félix Gastaldi, BP 524, MC 98015; tel. 93-30-40-06; fax 97-70-37-00; e-mail sophietatin@editions-alphee.com; internet www.editions-alphee.com; f. 1963; spirituality, personal devt; Dir JEAN-PAUL BERTRAND.

Editions EGC: 9 ave Albert II, BP 438, MC 98011 Cedex; e-mail multiprint@multiprintmc.com; economics, history, literature; Gen. Man. GÉRARD COMMAN.

Editions Victor Gadoury: 57 rue Grimaldi, MC 98000; tel. 93-25-12-96; fax 93-50-13-39; e-mail contact@gadoury.com; internet www.gadoury.com; f. 1967; numismatics.

Marsu Productions: 9 ave des Castelans, MC 98000; tel. 92-05-61-11; fax 92-05-76-60; e-mail marsuproductions@libello.com; internet www.marsupilami.com; comic strips, children's entertainment.

Editions de l'Oiseau-Lyre SAM: Les Remparts, BP 515, MC 98015 Cedex; tel. 93-30-09-44; fax 93-30-19-15; e-mail oiseaulyre@monaco.mc; internet www.oiseaulyre.com; f. 1932; owned by The Lyrebird Trust; classical music publishers; Pres. and Man. Dir KENNETH GILBERT.

Editions de Radio Monte Carlo: Monte-Carlo; tel. 93-15-17-57; general; Pres. JEAN PASTORELLI.

Editions Regain S.N.C. Boy et Cie: Monte-Carlo; tel. 93-50-62-04; f. 1946; fiction, essays, autobiography, travel, religion, philosophy, poetry; Dir-Gen. MICHÈLE G. BOY.

Editions du Rocher: 28 rue Comte Félix Gastaldi, BP 521, MC 98015; tel. 99-99-67-07; fax 99-99-67-18; internet www.editionsdurocher.fr; f. 1943; fiction, history, sciences; Pres. BÉATRICE GARETTE; Dir-Gen. PATRICK MAHÉ.

Editions André Sauret SAM: Monte-Carlo; tel. 93-50-67-94; fax 93-30-71-04; art, fiction; Dir RAYMOND LEVY.

Broadcasting and Communications

TELECOMMUNICATIONS

Direction du Controle des Concessions et des Télécommunications: 23 ave Albert II, MC 98000; tel. 98-98-88-00; fax 97-98-56-57; e-mail nic@nic.mc; internet www.nic.mc; Dir MARIE-PIERRE GRAMAGLIA.

Monaco Telecom: 25 blvd de Suisse, BP 14, MC 98000 Cedex; tel. 99-66-63-00; fax 99-66-63-01; e-mail communication@monaco-telecom.mc; internet www.monaco-telecom.mc; f. 1997; 49% owned by Cable & Wireless (United Kingdom), 45% by the Société Nationale de Financement (wholly owned by Govt of Monaco), 6% by the Compagnie Monégasque de Banque; incorporates the wholly owned subsidiaries Monaco Telecom International, Société Monégasque de Services de Telecoms (SMST), Société Monégasque de Télédistribution (SMT) and Divona; Pres. ETIENNE FRANZI; Dir-Gen. DENIS MARTIN.

BROADCASTING

Radio

Monte-Carlo Doualiya: 1 ave Henri Dunant, MC 98000; internet www.mc-doualiya.com; fmr subsidiary of RMC, transferred to Radio-France Internationale in 1996; in French and Arabic; Pres. ANTOINE SCHWARZ; Dir-Gen. PHILIPPE BEAUVILLARD.

Riviera Radio: 10 quai Antoine 1er, MC 98000; tel. 97-97-94-94; fax 97-97-94-95; e-mail info@rivieraradio.mc; internet www.rivieraradio.mc; owned by Morris Communications Co (USA); broadcasts in English; Man. Dir PAUL KAVANAGH.

Trans World Radio SC: c/o Courtin Global Assistance, BP 349, MC 98007; tel. 92-05-64-20; fax 92-16-56-01; e-mail testreete@twr.org; internet www.twr.org; f. 1955; evangelical Christian broadcaster; Pres. THOMAS J. LOWELL (acting).

MONACO

Television

TVI Monte-Carlo: 8 quai Antoine 1er, MC 98000; tel. 92-16-88-20; fax 93-25-46-39; e-mail tvimc@frateschi.mc; programmes in Italian; CEO LUIGI FRATESCHI.

Société Spéciale d'Entreprises Télé Monte-Carlo: 16 blvd Princesse Charlotte, BP 279, MC 98090; tel. 93-50-59-40; fax 93-25-01-09; f. 1954; Pres. JEAN-LOUIS MÉDECIN.

Finance

(cap. = capital, res = reserves, dep. = deposits, m. = million, br(s) = branch(es), amounts in euros)

BANKING

In 2008 a total of 41 banks, including major British, French, Italian and US banks, were represented in the Principality.

Banque de Gestion Edmond de Rothschild: BP 317, Les Terrasses, 2 ave de Monte-Carlo, MC 98000; tel. 93-10-47-47; fax 93-25-75-57; e-mail bger@lcf-rothschild.mc; internet www.lcf-rothschild.com; f. 1986; present name adopted 1993; cap. 12.0m., res 14.9m., dep. 696.4m. (Dec. 2006); Chair. LEONARDO P. A. POGGI; Gen. Man. GIAMPAOLO BERNINI.

Banque J. Safra (Monaco): La Belle Epoque, 15–17 bis ave d'Ostende, MC 98000; tel. 93-10-66-55; fax 93-50-60-71; internet www.safra.com; f. 1994 as Banque du Gothard (Monaco); present name adopted 2006; 100% owned by Banque Jacob Safra (Switzerland); cap. 40.0m., res 21.3m., dep. 849.9m. (Dec. 2004); Pres. JOSEPH SAFRA; Gen. Man. YVES BRACCALENTI.

BNP Paribas Private Bank Monaco: 15–17 ave d'Ostende, MC 98000; tel. 93-15-68-00; fax 93-15-68-01; e-mail privatebank.monaco@bnpparibas.com; internet www.privatebank.bnpparibas.mc; f. 2003 by merger of United European Bank—Monaco and BNP Paribas Private Bank Monaco; acquired Société Monégasque de Banque Privée and Bank Von Ernst (Monaco) 2005; private banking; cap. 13.0m. (April 2007); Dir-Gen. ERIC GEORGES.

Compagnie Monégasque de Banque: 23 ave de la Costa, BP 149, MC 98007; tel. 93-15-77-77; fax 93-25-08-69; e-mail cmb@cmb.mc; internet www.cmb.mc; f. 1976; 100% owned by Mediobanca—Banca di Credito Finanziario SpA (Italy); cap. 111.1m., res 142.2m., dep. 1,750.1m. (Dec. 2006); Chair. ETIENNE FRANZI; Deputy Chair. and Man. Dir EDOARDO LOEWENTHAL; 2 brs.

Crédit Foncier de Monaco (CFM Monaco): 11 blvd Albert 1er, BP 499, MC 98012 Cedex; tel. 93-10-20-00; fax 93-10-23-50; internet www.cfm.mc; f. 1922; 77.1% owned by Calyon (France); cap. 35.0m., res 113.5m., dep. 2,595.1m. (Dec. 2006); Chair. YVES BARSALOU; Gen. Man. GILLES MARTINENGO.

Crédit Suisse (Monaco): 27 ave de la Costa, BP 155, MC 98003; tel. 93-15-27-27; fax 93-25-27-99; e-mail alain.ucari@credit-suisse.com; f. 1987; cap. 12.0m., res 9.7m., dep. 1,042.8m. (Dec. 2006); Chair. FRANCO MULLER; Man ALAIN UCARI.

EFG Eurofinancière d'Investissements SAM: Villa Les Aigles, 15 ave d'Ostende, MC 98000; tel. 93-15-11-11; fax 93-15-11-12; e-mail enquiries_mco@efgbank.com; internet www.efggroup.com; f. 1990; merged with Banque Monegasque de Gestion SA in 2007; owned by EFG Bank (Switzerland); private banking; cap. 16.0m., res 3.3m., dep. 341.4m. (Dec. 2005); Dir-Gen. GEORGE CATSIAPIS.

HSBC Private Bank (Monaco): 17 ave d'Ostende, MC 98000; tel. 93-15-25-25; fax 93-15-25-00; internet www.hsbcprivatebank.com; f. 1997 as Republic National Bank of New York (Monaco) SA; present name adopted 2004; owned by HSBC Private Banking Holdings (Suisse) SA (Switzerland); private banking; cap. 131.0m., dep. 6,459.5m., total assets 6,740.2m. (Dec. 2007); Chief Exec. and Dir-Gen. GÉRARD COHEN.

KB Luxembourg (Monaco): 8 ave de Grande Bretagne, BP 262, MC 98005; tel. 92-16-55-55; fax 92-16-55-99; internet www.europeanprivatebankers.com; f. 1996; owned by KBL European Private Bankers S.A.; cap. 7.2m., res 1.8m., dep. 436.0m. (Dec. 2007); Chair. of Bd JEAN-PAUL LOOS; Man. Dir PAUL-MARIE JACQUES.

UBS (Monaco): 2 ave de Grande Bretagne, BP 189, MC 98007; tel. 93-15-58-15; fax 93-15-58-00; e-mail antonio.mancino@ubs.com; internet www.ubs.com/monaco; f. 1956; present name adopted 1998; owned by UBS AG (Switzerland); cap. 9.2m., res 28.7m., dep. 2,279.4m. (Dec. 2007); Chair. LUCA PEDROTTI; CEO PETER CONRAD; 1 br.

INSURANCE

Assurances J.P. et C. Sassi AXA: Le Suffren, 7 rue Suffren-Reymond, BP 25, MC 98001; tel. 93-30-45-88; fax 93-25-86-07; e-mail agence.sassi@axa.fr; f. 1968; Dir JEAN-PIERRE SASSI.

The Eric Blair Network: 33 blvd Princesse Charlotte, BP 265, MC 98005 Cedex; tel. 93-50-99-66; fax 97-70-72-00; e-mail eric@insure.monaco.mc; internet www.ericblairnet.com; Chief Exec. ERIC BLAIR.

Directory

Gramaglia Assurances: 14 blvd des Moulins, BP 153, MC 98003 Cedex; tel. 92-16-59-00; fax 92-16-59-16; e-mail assur@gramaglia.mc; internet www.gramaglia.mc; Dir ANTOINE GRAMAGLIA.

Monaco Insurance Services: 9 rue de Millo, MC 98000; tel. 97-97-39-39; fax 93-25-74-37; e-mail maoun@monaco377.com; Dir PIERRE AOUN.

Mourenon et Giannotti: 22 blvd Princesse Charlotte, MC 98000; tel. 97-97-08-88; fax 97-97-08-80; f. 1975; Dirs JEAN-PHILIPPE MOURENON, JOSÉ GIANNOTTI.

Silvain Assurances: 33 blvd Princesse Charlotte, BP 267, MC 98005; tel. 93-25-54-45; fax 93-50-39-05; Dir FRANÇOIS SILVAIN.

Société Française de Recours Cie d'Assurances: 28 blvd Princesse Charlotte, MC 98000; tel. 93-50-52-63; fax 93-50-54-49; Dir FLORIANO CONTE.

Trade and Industry

GOVERNMENT AGENCIES

Direction de l'Environnement: 3 ave de Fontvieille, MC 98013; tel. 98-98-80-00; fax 92-05-28-91; e-mail environnement@gouv.mc; Dir CYRIL GOMEZ.

Direction de l'Expansion Economique: 9 rue du Gabian, MC 98000; tel. 93-15-88-12; fax 92-05-75-20; e-mail expansion@gouv.mc; comprises 5 divisions: General Administration; Economic Development; Economic and Financial Enquiries; Intellectual Property; and Statistics and Economic Studies; Dir CATHERINE ORECCHIA-MATTHYSSENS.

Direction de la Prospective, de l'Urbanisme et de la Mobilité: 23 ave Albert II, MC 98000; tel. 98-98-22-99; fax 98-98-88-02; e-mail prospective@gouv.mc; Dir PATRICE CELLARIO.

Direction des Services Fiscaux: 'Le Panorama', 57 rue Grimaldi, BP 475, MC 98000; tel. 98-98-80-00; fax 93-15-81-55; Dir ANTOINE DINKEL.

CHAMBER OF COMMERCE

Jeune Chambre Economique de Monaco: 1 ave des Castelans, MC 98000; tel. 92-05-20-19; fax 92-05-31-29; e-mail jcemonaco@jcemonaco.mc; internet www.jcemonaco.mc; f. 1963; 102 mems; Pres. LUDOVIC MURE.

EMPLOYERS' ASSOCIATION

Fédération Patronale Monégasque (FPM) (Employers' Fed. of Monaco): 'Le Coronado', 20 ave de Fontvieille, MC 98000; tel. 92-05-38-92; fax 92-05-20-04; e-mail info@federation-patronale.mc; internet www.federation-patronale.mc; f. 1944; Pres. PHILIPPE ORTELLI; Sec.-Gen. CORINNE BERTANI; 25 mem. orgs, with 1,200 individual mems.

UTILITIES

Electricity and Gas

Société Monégasque de l'Electricité et du Gaz (SMEG): 10 ave de Fontvieille, BP 633, MC 98013 Cedex; tel. 92-05-05-00; fax 92-05-05-92; e-mail smeg@smeg.mc; internet www.smeg.mc; f. 1890; 64% owned by GDF SUEZ (France); 20% owned by the Govt of Monaco; Dir-Gen. GUY MAGNAN.

Water

Société Monégasque des Eaux (SME): 29 ave de Fontvieille, MC 98000; tel. 97-98-51-00; fax 92-05-23-83; e-mail sme@sme.mc; internet www.sme.mc; f. 1983; Pres. STÉPHANE GIACCARDI.

TRADE UNION FEDERATION

Union des Syndicats de Monaco (USM): 28 blvd Rainier III, MC 98000; tel. 93-30-19-30; fax 93-25-06-73; e-mail usm@usm.mc; internet www.usm.mc; f. 1944; Sec.-Gen. ANGÈLE BRAQUETTI; 41 mem. unions.

Transport

RAILWAYS

The 1.7 km of railway track in Monaco, running from France to Monte-Carlo, is operated by the French state railway, the Société Nationale des Chemins de fer Français (SNCF). As part of the Government's policy of land reclamation, an underground railway station was opened in 1999.

ROADS

In 2007 there were an estimated 50 km of major roads in the Principality.

SHIPPING

Direction des Affaires Maritimes: quai Jean-Charles Rey, BP 468, MC 98012 Cedex; tel. 98-98-86-78; fax 98-98-37-15; e-mail marine@gouv.mc; Dir JEAN-LOUIS BISSUEL.

Société d'Exploitation des Ports de Monaco (SEPM): 6 quai Antoine 1er, BP 453, MC 98011 Cedex; tel. 97-77-30-00; fax 97-77-30-01; e-mail info@ports-monaco.com; internet www.ports-monaco.com; f. 2002; state-owned; responsible for management and devt of the 2 principal ports in Monaco, at La Condamine (Port Hercule) and Fontvieille; Pres. ALECO KEUSSEOGLOU; Gen. Man. GIANBATTISTA BOREA D'OLMO.

Shipping Companies

D'Amico Dry Ltd: 20 blvd de Suisse, MC 98000 Cedex; tel. 93-10-57-20; fax 93-10-56-07; e-mail info@damicoship.com; internet www.cogema-sam.com; owned by d'Amico Società di Navigazione SpA (Italy); Group CEO CESARE D'AMICO.

MC Shipping Inc.: Gildo Pastor Center, 7 rue du Gabian, MC 98000; tel. 97-97-49-90; fax 97-97-49-99; e-mail operations@mcshipping.com; internet www.mcshipping.com; f. 1989; Chair. of Bd CHARLES LONGBOTTOM; Pres. and CEO ANTONY CRAWFORD.

Société Anonyme Monégasque d'Administration Maritime et Aérienne (SAMAMA): L'Estoril, Bloc B, 1er étage, 31 ave Princesse Grace, MC 98000; tel. 99-99-51-00; fax 99-99-51-09; e-mail general@samama-monaco.com; Pres. FRANK O. WALTERS; Dir-Gen. J. F. MEGGINSON.

CIVIL AVIATION

There is a helicopter shuttle service between the international airport at Nice, France, and Monaco's heliport at Fontvieille.

Héli Air Monaco SAM: Héliport de Monaco, MC 98000; tel. 92-05-00-56; fax 92-05-00-51; e-mail helico@heliairmonaco.com; internet www.heliairmonaco.com; Pres. JACQUES CROVETTO.

Tourism

Tourists are attracted to Monaco by the Mediterranean climate, dramatic scenery and numerous entertainment facilities, including a casino. In 2007 327,985 tourists (excluding excursionists) visited Monaco. There were 2,555 hotel rooms available in 2006.

Direction du Tourisme et des Congrès: 2A blvd des Moulins, MC 98030 Cedex; tel. 92-16-61-16; fax 92-16-60-00; e-mail dtc@gouv.mc; internet www.visitmonaco.com; Dir-Gen. of Tourism MICHEL BOUQUIER.

Monte-Carlo SBM: place du Casino, BP 139, MC 98000; tel. 92-16-25-25; fax 92-16-26-26; e-mail resort@sbm.mc; internet www.montecarloresort.com; f. 1863; corpn in which the Govt holds a 69.5% interest; controls the entertainment facilities of Monaco, including the casino and numerous hotels, clubs, restaurants and sporting facilities; Chair. JEAN-LUC BIAMONTI; Gen. Man. BERNARD LAMBERT.

MONGOLIA

Introductory Survey

Location, Climate, Language, Religion, Flag, Capital

Mongolia is a land-locked country in central Asia, with the Russian Federation to the north and the People's Republic of China to the south, east and west. The climate is dry, with generally mild summers but very cold winters. Temperatures in Ulan Bator (traditional spelling; Ulaanbaatar in transcription from Mongolian Cyrillic) range between −32°C (−26°F) and 22°C (71°F). The principal language is Khalkha Mongolian. Kazakh is spoken in the province of Bayan-Ölgii. There is no state religion, but Buddhist Lamaism is being encouraged once again. The national flag (proportions 1 by 2) has three equal vertical stripes, of red, blue and red, with the 'soyombo' symbol (a combination of abstract devices) in gold on the red stripe at the hoist. The capital is Ulan Bator.

Recent History

The country was formerly the Manchu province of Outer Mongolia. In 1911, following the republican revolution in China, Mongolian princes declared the province's independence. With support from Tsarist Russia, Outer Mongolia gained autonomy, as a feudal Buddhist monarchy, but Russia accepted Chinese suzerainty over the province in 1915. Following the Russian revolution of 1917, China began to re-establish control in Mongolia in 1919. In 1920 Mongol nationalists appealed to the new Soviet regime for assistance, and in March 1921 they met on Soviet territory to found the Mongolian People's Party (called the Mongolian People's Revolutionary Party—MPRP—from 1924) and established a Provisional People's Government. After nationalist forces, with Soviet help, drove anti-Bolshevik troops from the Mongolian capital, the People's Government was proclaimed on 11 July 1921. Soviet Russia recognized the People's Government in November of that year. In November 1924, after the death of Bogd Khan (King) Javzandamba Khutagt VIII, the Mongolian People's Republic was proclaimed.

The Mongolian People's Republic became increasingly dependent on the USSR's support. The Government conducted campaigns to collectivize the economy and to destroy the power of the nobility and Buddhist priests. In 1932 an armed uprising was suppressed with Soviet assistance. Following his reorganization of the MPRP and army leadership in 1936–39, power was held by Marshal Khorloogiin Choibalsan as Prime Minister and MPRP leader. The dictatorship of Choibalsan closely followed the model of the regime of Stalin (Iosif Dzhugashvili, 1924–53) in the USSR. Its thousands of victims included eminent politicians, military officers, religious leaders and intellectuals. In 1939 a Japanese invasion from Manchuria was repelled by Soviet and Mongolian forces at Khalkhyn Gol (Nomonhan). In accordance with the Yalta agreement to preserve the status quo in Mongolia, war was declared on Japan in August 1945, four days before the Japanese surrender, and northern China was invaded. In a Mongolian plebiscite in October, it was reported that 100% of the votes were cast in favour of independence, and this was recognized by China in January 1946.

Choibalsan died in January 1952 and was succeeded as Prime Minister by Yumjaagiin Tsedenbal, who had been the MPRP's First Secretary since 1940. Dashiin Damba became First Secretary of the MPRP in April 1954. In 1955 India became the first non-communist country to recognize Mongolia. Tsedenbal replaced Damba as First Secretary of the MPRP in November 1958, and a new Constitution was adopted in July 1960. Mongolia became a member of the UN in October 1961 and was subsequently accorded diplomatic recognition by the United Kingdom (1963), other Western European states and developing countries. By January 1987, when Mongolia was finally granted diplomatic recognition by the USA, it maintained diplomatic relations with more than 100 states.

Jamsrangiin Sambuu, Head of State since July 1954, died in May 1972. He was replaced in June 1974 by Tsedenbal, who remained First Secretary of the MPRP (restyled General Secretary in 1981) but relinquished the post of Chairman of the Council of Ministers to Jambyn Batmönkh. In August 1984 Tsedenbal was removed from the party leadership and state presidency, apparently owing to ill health, and Batmönkh replaced him as General Secretary of the MPRP. In December Batmönkh also became Head of State, while Dumaagiin Sodnom, hitherto a Deputy Chairman of the Council of Ministers and the Chairman of the State Planning Commission, was appointed Chairman of the Council of Ministers.

By the end of 1988 the MPRP Political Bureau was obliged to admit that economic renewal was not succeeding because of the need for social reforms. Batmönkh advocated greater openness and offered the prospect of multi-candidate elections. He criticized Tsedenbal for the country's 'stagnation', also stating that the former leader had belittled collective leadership.

Between December 1989 and March 1990 there was a great increase in public political activity, as several newly formed opposition movements organized a series of peaceful demonstrations in Ulan Bator, demanding political and economic reforms. The most prominent of the new opposition groups was the Mongolian Democratic Union (MDU), founded in December 1989. In January 1990 dialogue was initiated between MPRP officials and representatives of the MDU, including its chief co-ordinator, Sanjaasürengiin Zorig (a university lecturer). The emergence of further opposition groups, together with escalating public demonstrations (involving as many as 20,000 people), led to a crisis of confidence within the MPRP. At a party plenum in mid-March Batmönkh announced the resignation of the entire Political Bureau as well as of the Secretariat of the Central Committee. Gombojavyn Ochirbat, a former head of the Ideological Department of the Central Committee and a former Chairman of the Central Council of Mongolian Trade Unions, was elected the new General Secretary of the party, replacing Batmönkh. A new five-member Political Bureau was formed. The plenum voted to expel the former MPRP General Secretary, Yumjaagiin Tsedenbal, from the party and to rehabilitate several prominent officials who had been removed by Tsedenbal in the 1960s.

At a session of the People's Great Khural (legislature), held shortly after the MPRP plenum, Punsalmaagiin Ochirbat, hitherto the Minister of Foreign Economic Relations and Supply, was elected Chairman of the Presidium (Head of State), replacing Batmönkh, and other senior positions in the Presidium were reallocated. Dumaagiin Sodnom was dismissed from his post as Chairman of the Council of Ministers and was replaced by Sharavyn Gungaadorj, a Deputy Chairman and Minister of Agriculture and the Food Industry. The Khural also adopted amendments to the Constitution, including the deletion of references to the MPRP as the 'guiding force' in Mongolian society, and approved a new electoral law. It was decided that the next elections to the Khural would be held in mid-1990, and not in 1991 as originally planned. Meanwhile, all limits on personal livestock holdings were removed, and new regulations were introduced to encourage foreign investment in Mongolia. However, in late March 1990 an estimated 13,000 people, dissatisfied with the results of the Khural's session, demonstrated in Ulan Bator to demand the dissolution of the Khural. Opposition leaders declared that the changes introduced by the legislature were insufficient, and demanded the introduction of a multi-party electoral law.

In April 1990 the MPRP held an extraordinary congress, at which more than three-quarters of the membership of the Central Committee was renewed. General Secretary Gombojavyn Ochirbat was elected to the restyled post of Chairman of the party. The Political Bureau was renamed the Presidium, and a new, four-member Secretariat of the Central Committee was appointed. In May the People's Great Khural adopted a law on political parties, which legalized the new 'informal' parties through official registration, and also adopted further amendments to the Constitution, introducing a presidential system with a standing legislature called the State Little Khural, elected by proportional representation of parties.

At the July 1990 legislative election and consequent re-elections, 430 deputies were elected to serve a five-year term: 357 from the MPRP (in some instances unopposed), 16 from the Mongolian Democratic Party (MDP, the political wing of the MDU), 19 shared among the Mongolian Revolutionary Youth

League, the Mongolian National Progress Party (MNPP), and the Mongolian Social-Democratic Party (MSDP), and 39 without party affiliation. Under constitutional amendments adopted in May, the People's Great Khural was required to convene at least four times in the five years of its term.

In September 1990 the People's Great Khural elected Punsalmaagiin Ochirbat to be the country's first President, with a five-year term of office; the post of Chairman of the Presidium was abolished. Dashiin Byambasüren was appointed Prime Minister (equivalent to the former post of Chairman of the Council of Ministers) and began consultations on the formation of a multi-party government. The newly restyled Cabinet was elected by the State Little Khural in September and October. Under the amended Constitution, the President, Vice-President and Ministers were not permitted to remain concurrently deputies of the People's Great Khural; therefore, re-elections of deputies to the legislature were held in November.

The 20th Congress of the MPRP, held in February 1991, elected a new 99-member Central Committee, which, in turn, appointed a new Presidium. The Central Committee also elected a new Chairman, Büdragchaagiin Dash-Yondon, the Chairman of the Ulan Bator City Party Committee, who had become a Presidium member in November 1990.

A new Constitution was adopted by an almost unanimous vote of the Great Khural in January 1992, and entered into force in the following month. It provided for a unicameral Mongolian Great Khural, comprising 76 members, to replace the People's Great Khural, following elections to be held in June. (The State Little Khural was abolished.) The country's official name was changed from the Mongolian People's Republic to Mongolia, and the communist gold star was removed from the national flag.

At the elections to the Mongolian Great Khural in June 1992, contested by the MPRP, an alliance of the MDP, the MNPP and the United Party (UP), the MSDP, and six other parties and another alliance, a total of 293 candidates stood for 76 seats in 26 constituencies, comprising the 18 *aimag* (provinces), the towns of Darkhan and Erdenet, and Ulan Bator City (six). A total of 95.6% of the electorate participated in the elections. Candidates were elected by a simple majority, provided that they obtained the support of at least 50% of the electorate in their constituency. The MPRP candidates received some 57% of the total votes, while the candidates of the other parties (excluding independents) achieved a combined total of 40%. However, the outcome of the election was disproportionate, with the MPRP winning 70 seats (71 including a pro-MPRP independent). The remaining seats were taken by the MDP (two, including an independent), the MSDP, MNPP and UP (one each).

The first session of the Mongolian Great Khural opened in July 1992 with the election of officers, the nomination of Puntsagiin Jasrai (who had served as a Deputy Chairman of the Council of Ministers in the late 1980s) to the post of Prime Minister, and the approval of his Cabinet. Natsagiin Bagabandi, a Vice-Chairman of the MPRP Central Committee, was elected Chairman of the Great Khural. Jambyn Gombojav (Chairman of the People's Great Khural from late 1990 to late 1991) was elected Vice-Chairman of the new Khural. Meanwhile, a National Security Council was established, with the country's President as its Chairman, and the Prime Minister and Chairman of the Great Khural as its members.

In October 1992 the MDP, MNPP, UP and the Mongolian Renewal Party amalgamated to form the Mongolian National Democratic Party (MNDP), with a General Council headed by the MNPP leader, Davaadorjiin Ganbold, and including Sanjaasürengiin Zorig and other prominent opposition politicians. In the same month the MPRP Central Committee was renamed the MPRP Little Khural, and its membership was increased to 169 (and subsequently to 198). The Presidium was replaced by a nine-member Party Leadership Council, headed by Büdragchaagiin Dash-Yondon as its General Secretary.

The Great Khural adopted a Presidential Election Law in March 1993, and direct elections to the presidency were scheduled for June. Lodongiin Tüdev, a member of the Party Leadership Council and Editor-in-Chief of the MPRP organ, *Ünen*, was chosen as the MPRP's candidate, while President Ochirbat was nominated by a coalition of the MNDP and the MSDP. The result of the election was a convincing victory for Ochirbat, who received 57.8% of the votes cast, compared with 38.7% for Tüdev.

In early 1996 the MPRP forced through the Great Khural the passage of amendments that increased the number of constituencies from 26 to 76, making them all single-seat constituencies, while preserving the majority vote system. To be declared elected, a candidate was required to have received only 25% of the constituency votes. In response, opposition parties formed an election coalition, the Democratic Alliance, which received support from the Mongolian Green Party and the MDU.

At the legislative election, held at the end of June 1996, a resounding victory was achieved by the Democratic Alliance, which won 50 of the 76 seats in the Great Khural, receiving some 46.7% of the total votes cast. The MPRP took only 25 seats (40.6%), while one seat was won by a candidate of the United Heritage Party (UHP). Electoral turn-out was 92.2%. At the legislature's inaugural session, in mid-July, the leader of the MSDP, Radnaasümbereliin Gonchigdorj, was elected to the post of Chairman of the Great Khural. Mendsaikhany Enkhsaikhan, the leader of the Democratic Alliance and the group's choice for Prime Minister, was nominated by President Ochirbat and voted into office. Following the rejection of MPRP demands concerning the allocation of positions in the Great Khural, MPRP members organized a three-day boycott of the legislature, leaving it inquorate and unable to function. After the boycott ended, the MNDP leader, Tsakhiagiin Elbegdorj, was elected Vice-Chairman of the Great Khural; a new Government was formed at the end of July.

Following their election defeat, and amid growing evidence of a rift between supporters of tradition and advocates of the reform process, in July 1996 the MPRP Little Khural elected a new Leadership Council and General Secretary of the party, Nambaryn Enkhbayar. Indications of a division in the party increased in February 1997, when the leaders of the MPRP sought to enforce their uncompromising policies on the party congress. Several prominent dissenting members resigned from the party, and Natsagiin Bagabandi, who had been Chairman of the Great Khural in 1992–96, was elected Chairman of the party.

With a date in May 1997 set for the presidential election, the MNDP and the MSDP proposed a joint candidate for the post of President—the incumbent, Ochirbat. The MPRP nominated the party Chairman, Bagabandi, while the UHP adopted Jambyn Gombojav, a former Vice-Chairman of the Great Khural. The election was won convincingly by Bagabandi, with some 60.8% of the total votes cast. In a severe set-back to the democratic movement, Ochirbat received only 29.8%, a reflection of popular dissatisfaction at the rigorous economic reform policies implemented by the ruling Democratic Alliance. Gombojav obtained 6.6% of the votes. Following Bagabandi's success in the presidential election, Enkhbayar was elected Chairman of the MPRP in his place. In August he won a by-election for Bagabandi's former seat in the Great Khural.

In April 1998 the Democratic Alliance decided that, henceforth, the Cabinet was to comprise members of the Great Khural, headed by the leader of the Alliance. Tsakhiagiin Elbegdorj, leader of the MNDP, was thus appointed Prime Minister, and a new Cabinet was formed in May. The Government became embroiled in a dispute over the amalgamation of the state-owned Reconstruction Bank, declared bankrupt after over-extending its credit, with the private Golomt Bank. Amid accusations that Democratic Alliance leaders had obtained loans from the bank shortly before its failure, the MPRP effected a boycott of the Great Khural. The party rejected the Government's re-instatement of Reconstruction Bank and returned to the Great Khural in late July to pursue a motion of no confidence in the Government. The vote was carried by 42 votes to 33, with the support of 15 members of the Democratic Alliance.

In August 1998 the Democratic Alliance nominated as its candidate for Prime Minister Davaadorjiin Ganbold, Chairman of the Economic Standing Committee of the Great Khural (who had been chief Deputy Prime Minister in 1990–92 and President of the MNDP in 1992–96). President Bagabandi rejected Ganbold's nomination, on the grounds of his failure to act to resolve the bank merger crisis in his capacity as Chairman of the Committee. Ganbold was nominated a second time, and again rejected by Bagabandi, who proposed Great Khural member Dogsomyn Ganbold. The Democratic Alliance persisted, and by the end of the month Davaadorjiin Ganbold had been nominated and rejected five times. The Democratic Alliance then proposed Rinchinnyamyn Amarjargal, acting Minister of External Relations and a member of the MNDP General Council. President Bagabandi accepted the nomination, but it was rejected by one vote in the Great Khural in September. Two other candidates were subsequently rejected by Bagabandi.

In October 1998 Sanjaasürengiin Zorig, the Minister of Infrastructure Development and founder of the Mongolian Democratic Movement, was murdered. Although never nominated for the post, Zorig had been widely regarded as a potential prime ministerial candidate. Following Zorig's state funeral, Bagabandi named six more candidates of his own, including Dogsomyn Ganbold and the Mayor of Ulan Bator, Janlavyn Narantsatsralt. The Democratic Alliance disregarded the presidential list and for the sixth time nominated Davaadorjiin Ganbold. Although the nomination was supported by all 48 Democratic Alliance members of the Great Khural, Bagabandi once again rejected him. The political crisis was then deepened by a new Constitutional Court ruling that members of the Great Khural could not serve concurrently in the Government. Two months later the Democratic Alliance finally nominated Bagabandi's candidate, Narantsatsralt, who was appointed Prime Minister in December. The formation of his Government was completed in January 1999.

Narantsatsralt's Government remained in power for just over six months. In July 1999 the Prime Minister was challenged in the Great Khural over a letter that he had written in January to Yurii Maslyukov, First Deputy Chairman of the Russian Government, in which he seemingly acknowledged Russia's right to privatize its share in the Erdenet copper-mining joint venture without reference to Mongolia. Unable to offer a satisfactory explanation, in late July Narantsatsralt lost a vote of confidence, in which MSDP members of the Great Khural voted with the opposition MPRP. The Democratic Alliance nominated Rinchinnyamyn Amarjargal for the post of Prime Minister, but the proposal was immediately challenged by Bagabandi. The President insisted that, following the Constitutional Court ruling of late 1998, he could consider Amarjargal's suitability for nomination in the Great Khural only after the candidate had resigned from his seat. After several days of arguments, representatives of the Democratic Alliance and the President adopted a formula that allowed the Great Khural's approval of the prime ministerial nomination and the nominee's resignation of his Great Khural seat to take place simultaneously. Amarjargal was elected Prime Minister at the end of July. The ministers of Narantsatsralt's Government remained in office in an acting capacity until early September, when all but one (the Minister of Law) were reappointed. The formation of the Government was completed in late October with the appointment of Dashpuntsagiin Ganbold as Minister of Law. In November 1999 Amarjargal assumed the presidency of the MNDP, replacing Narantsatsralt.

The 1992 Constitution was amended for the first time in December 1999 by a Great Khural decree supported by all three parliamentary parties, which simplified the procedure for the appointment of the Prime Minister and allowed members of the Great Khural to serve as government ministers while retaining their seats in the legislature. An attempt by the President to veto the decree was defeated by the Great Khural in January 2000, but the Constitutional Court ruled in March that the decree had been illegal. When the Great Khural opened its spring session in April, members rejected the ruling and refused to discuss it. The Constitutional Court's demand for a statement on the issue was disregarded by the Great Khural.

As the legislative election approached, a breakaway grouping of the MNDP re-established the Mongolian Democratic Party, and a faction of the MSDP founded the Mongolian New Social Democratic Party. Sanjaasürengiin Oyuun, the sister of murdered minister Zorig, established the Civil Courage Party (CCP or Irgenii Zorig Nam, subsequently also known as Citizens' Will), drawing away from the MNDP several more members of the Great Khural, and formed an electoral alliance with the Mongolian Green Party. The MNDP, unable to reconstitute the previously successful Democratic Alliance with the MSDP, therefore formed a new Democratic Alliance with the Mongolian Believers' Democratic Party.

At the election, held in early July 2000, three coalitions and 13 parties were represented by a total of 603 candidates, including 27 independents. The MPRP won 72 of the 76 seats in the Great Khural. Prime Minister Rinchinnyamyn Amarjargal and his entire Cabinet lost their seats. The MPRP received 50.2% of the votes cast. The level of participation was 82.4% of the electorate. The MPRP's main support lay in rural constituencies, where it was widely seen as willing and able to halt the economic and social stagnation of the countryside. The Democratic Alliance won 13% of the votes cast, while the Mongolian Democratic New Socialist Party (MDNSP, which had amalgamated with the Mongolian Workers' Party in 1999) received 10.7% of the votes; each of them won one seat. The MSDP received 8.9% of the votes cast but won no seats.

When the Great Khural opened, Lkhamsürengiin Enebish, the MPRP General Secretary, was elected Chairman (Speaker) of the chamber. However, the nomination of the MPRP Chairman, Nambaryn Enkhbayar, for the post of Prime Minister was rejected by President Bagabandi, on the grounds that priority be given to the constitutional amendments. After a week of discussions a compromise was reached whereby Enkhbayar's nomination was presented to the Great Khural, while the amendments remained in force pending a Great Khural debate and a full nine-member session of the Constitutional Court. In July 2000 the Great Khural approved Enkhbayar's appointment as Prime Minister by 67 MPRP members' votes to three. Enkhbayar's Cabinet was approved in August.

At a conference in early December 2000 five parties—the MNDP, the MSDP, the Mongolian Democratic Party, the Believers' Democratic Party and the Democratic Renewal Party—decided to dissolve themselves and form a new Democratic Party (DP). Dambyn Dorligjav, a former Minister of Defence and director of the Erdenet copper enterprise, was elected Chairman, while Janlavyn Narantsatsralt and the former Minister of the Environment, Sonomtserengiin Mendsaikhan, were elected as Vice-Chairmen. The party's National Advisory Committee was formed in February 2001 and comprised two members from each of the Great Khural's 76 constituencies.

In mid-December 2000 the Great Khural readopted, unchanged and for immediate implementation, the decree of December 1999 amending the 1992 Constitution. The President's veto of the decree was rejected. However, the Constitutional Court was unable to meet in full session because the election of replacements for time-expired members was delayed in the Great Khural. President Bagabandi finally approved the amendments in May 2001.

In February 2001 the 23rd Congress of the ruling MPRP re-elected Prime Minister Nambaryn Enkhbayar as its Chairman, approved the establishment of a new Little Khural of 244 members and enlarged the Party Leadership Council from 11 to 15 members. At the end of September Lkhamsürengiin Enebish, Chairman of the Great Khural and recently re-elected as General Secretary of the MPRP, died; he was succeeded in the latter post by Doloonjingiin Idevkhten and as Chairman of the Great Khural by Sanjbegziin Tömör-Ochir, Secretary of the MPRP.

At the presidential election of May 2001, the incumbent Natsagiin Bagabandi, the MPRP candidate, was re-elected, having received 57.95% of the votes cast. Radnaasümbereliin Gonchigdorj of the DP won 36.58% of votes; Luvsandambyn Dashnyam, candidate of the CCP received 3.54%.

In March 2002 Sanjaasürengiin Oyuun's CCP merged with Bazarsadyn Jargalsaikhan's Mongolian Republican Party (MRP) to form the Civil Courage Republican Party, under Oyuun's leadership. However, in June 2003 the MRP leader Bazarsadyn Jargalsaikhan withdrew from the merger after disagreement about the formation of a coalition with the DP. Attempts in December to oust Oyuun from the party leadership failed, and in March 2004 she agreed to join the Motherland Democracy (MD) coalition comprising Erdenebat's MDNSP and the DP (see below).

In June 2002 the Great Khural approved the Law on Land and the Law on Land Privatization. Although less than 1% of the country's total territory was to be available for privatization, the laws generated much controversy. From November there were several demonstrations by farmers who were arrested for parking their tractors on Sükhbaatar Square in central Ulan Bator. The demonstrators, led by DP leader Erdeniin Bat-Üül, protested that the poor would be denied land by the 'oligarchy'. The privatization law duly entered into force in May 2003.

Meanwhile, an effective protest against the Government's silencing of the opposition was made by Lamjavyn Gündalai, a DP member of the Great Khural, who interrupted the Prime Minister's televised address and disrupted the opening ceremony of the autumn 2002 session of the Great Khural by displaying to television cameras a series of placards on which he demanded the right to speak, condemned the imprisonment of journalists and criticized the land privatization programme. When the 2003 spring session opened at the beginning of April Gündalai again displayed a range of slogans; the President and the Prime Minister were unable to deliver their speeches, and the televised session was suspended.

At the end of May 2003 Gündalai alleged that the Minister of Justice and Home Affairs, Tsendiin Nyamdorj, had links with the special services of a foreign country. In July Gündalai was removed from an aircraft at Ulan Bator airport, while on his way via the Republic of Korea (South Korea) to a conference in Singapore, and arrested for 'violation of the border'. This provoked an uproar regarding the breaching of Gündalai's parliamentary immunity, and the DP sought an investigation by the human rights committee of the Inter-Parliamentary Union (a non-governmental organization based in Geneva, Switzerland). In late July, on the same day as a newspaper published extracts from the material relating to the allegations against Nyamdorj, Gündalai was released. In August the charges against him were abandoned on the instructions of the Deputy Chief Prosecutor. In October Gündalai succeeded, for a third time, in disrupting the opening of the Great Khural's autumn session, with the result that the Prime Minister was once again unable to deliver his report to the cameras.

The National Human Rights Commission's 2003 annual report was highly critical of bureaucracy, corruption and cronyism, and the police were accused of numerous cases of brutality. The National Human Rights Programme was adopted in December. Also in 2003, Damirangiin Enkhbat, who had been suspected of the murder of Sanjaasürengiin Zorig in 1998 and had since been resident in France, was reported to have been abducted by Mongolian secret agents and subsequently imprisoned in Mongolia. In early 2004 reports from Amnesty International, the human rights organization, suggested that he had been tortured during interrogation. In June 2005 the UN's Special Rapporteur on torture, and other cruel, inhuman or degrading treatment or punishment, Manfred Nowak, carried out a prison inspection and met Enkhbat and his lawyer. Nowak's report, which was published in December but did not appear in the Mongolian press until a year later, condemned torture in Mongolian prisons and criticized the provisions of the Law on State Secrets for preventing dissemination of information about death sentences. (Enkhbat was released from prison in February 2006 on the grounds of ill health, and subsequently died.)

In the spring of 2004 political campaigning began for the election to the Mongolian Great Khural, which was held in late June. The new General Election Committee (GEC) incorporated many MPRP nominees. The opposition MD election pact, formed by Mendsaikhany Enkhsaikhan's DP and Badarchiin Erdenebat's 'Motherland' MDNSP, was joined by Sanjaasürengiin Oyuun's Civil Courage Republican Party, minus the followers of Bazarsadyn Jargalsaikhan, who left to re-establish the Republican Party.

After the registration of participating political parties and coalitions, the GEC examined the official lists, rejecting all Mongolian Youth Party candidates. Before polling day three candidates withdrew, leaving the final number at 241: 76 each for the MPRP and the MD coalition, 33 for the Republican Party, 23 for the National Solidarity Party, nine for the Mongolian Traditional United Party (also known as the United Heritage Party), five for the Mongolian Green Party, four for the Liberal Party and 15 Independents.

The initial results of the election of 27 June 2004 (compiled as percentages of the total ballot in each constituency) left the political scene in disarray: the MPRP and the MD coalition had each won about one-half of the seats, leaving neither with the necessary majority of 39 (one-half of the Great Khural seats plus one seat). The three Independents elected, although all DP members, were ruled as not counting in this process. The Republican Party won one seat. The rate of participation was 82.2% of registered voters. In 25 constituencies there was a straight contest between the MPRP and the MD coalition. Amid mutual accusations of bribery and electoral fraud in a number of constituencies, efforts to form a government soon became embroiled in disputes at the GEC and the recently established City Administrative Court.

The GEC submitted the results in 74 of the 76 constituencies to President Bagabandi in early July 2004, at the first session of the newly elected Great Khural, which was boycotted by the MPRP. The President stated that it was right to convene the first session, despite the fact that two results had yet to be confirmed, because of the need to address many important issues. However, the MD members were not allowed to take the oath. Meeting separately, 70 of the MPRP members elected in 2000 filed a lawsuit against the President on the grounds that he had contravened the Constitution and allowed the Great Khural to meet without a quorum (57 members being present) before the final session of the outgoing Great Khural had taken place. The closing session of the previous legislature was held in late July 2004. Among other decisions, it released the Great Khural's Deputy Chairman Jamsrangiin Byambadorj (who had lost his parliamentary seat in the recent election) to take up a vacant seat in the Constitutional Court and accused the President of acting unconstitutionally in convening the first session of the incoming legislature. All these decisions were vetoed by President Bagabandi in late July as unconstitutional. (Byambadorj was elected a member, then the Chairman, of the Constitutional Court in January 2005.)

Postponed after another MPRP boycott, the first plenary session of the new Great Khural was held in late July 2004, when 74 members were sworn in. The first business was the election of the new Chairman of the chamber. The MPRP group supported the candidacy of the MPRP leader and acting Prime Minister, Nambaryn Enkhbayar, but protracted discussion of this proposal with the MD members of the Khural continued for days without resolution. The MPRP members of the Great Khural proposed that the MD members should nominate the next Prime Minister, while the MD members proposed the formation of a joint working group to draw up a programme for a government of 'national accord'.

Eventually, at the end of August 2004, former Prime Minister Nambaryn Enkhbayar of the MPRP was appointed Chairman of the Great Khural, and Tsakhiagiin Elbegdorj of the MD coalition was appointed Prime Minister. Although the newly elected members of the Mongolian Great Khural agreed on the formation, chairmanship and membership of the Khural's standing committees and sub-committees, discussion of the basic principles for the establishment of a coalition government were protracted. In mid-September Prime Minister Elbegdorj forwarded to President Bagabandi proprosals for the composition of a new Cabinet, and in late September the new Government was appointed. The deputy ministers, one-half nominated by the MD coalition and one-half by the MPRP, were appointed in November and December respectively. The Government Action Programme 2004–2008, approved by the Great Khural in November 2004, included provision for a monthly grant of 3,000 tögrög from January 2005 to each child under the age of 18 in families with more than three children and a per caput income below the national minimum—a compromise of MPRP and MD election pledges.

The National Human Rights Commission's annual report for 2004 noted the need for the rights of vulnerable groups and the human rights activities of legal organizations to remain the 'centre of attention'. The report also noted that torture and severe punishment were still common activities and that many police officers equated punishment with physical torture. Provisions of the UN Convention against Torture and other Cruel, Inhumane or Degrading Treatment or Punishment, which Mongolia joined in 2000, were not widely known, and effective measures were not being taken to curb illegal acts, the report stated.

At the end of December 2004 Radnaasümbereliin Gonchigdorj took the chairmanship of the DP at a meeting of the executive of its National Consultative Committee (NCC) and installed his supporters in other senior posts. His predecessor, Mendsaikhany Enkhsaikhan, seemed to retain the support of the DP's National Assembly. Although a court ruled that the leadership change was contrary to the party's regulations, it declined to intervene. Badarchiin Erdenebat, the Minister of Defence and leader of the MDNSP, then withdrew from the MD coalition, which collapsed. The Civil Courage Republican Party leader, Sanjaasürengiin Oyuun, was obliged to relinquish her post of Deputy Chairwoman of the Great Khural in January 2005. Prime Minister Elbegdorj took over the defence portfolio from Erdenebat in February, and a new Minister of Defence, Tserenkhüügiin Sharavdorj, was appointed in March. The MD coalition's parliamentary group in the Great Khural disbanded, and many DP members, including Gonchigdorj (but not Enkhsaikhan), joined the Khural's MPRP group members to form a parliamentary 'combined group', of which Gonchigdorj was elected Deputy Chairman. Meanwhile, Doloonjingiin Idevkhten was replaced as General Secretary of the MPRP by Sanjaagiin (Sanjiin) Bayar, the Mongolian ambassador to Russia. In February Jügderdemidiin Gürragchaa (MPRP) and in September Zandaakhüügiin Enkhbold (MD) were declared the winners in the two constituencies where the results of the 2004 election to the Great Khural election had been contested. Gürragchaa was duly sworn in, but Enkhbold had already accepted the post of Chairman of the State Property Committee in the previous December.

In March 2005, in the fourth demonstration in Ulan Bator since January by the Healthy Society Citizens' Movement, protesters demanded the resignations of the Great Khural Chairman and MPRP leader, Nambaryn Enkhbayar, of Prime

Minister Elbegdorj and of the DP rebels in the Great Khural who had joined the MPRP's parliamentary group. Four of the five parliamentary political parties presented candidates for the forthcoming presidential election, scheduled for late May, and they were registered in early April. The candidates were Nambaryn Enkhbayar (of the MPRP), Bazarsadyn Jargalsaikhan (Republican Party), Badarchiin Erdenebat (Motherland Party, the recently renamed MDNSP) and Mendsaikhany Enkhsaikhan (DP). The election, held on 22 May, was won by Enkhbayar, who secured more than 53% of the votes cast, thereby receiving more votes than the other three candidates combined.

Enkhbayar's victory led to personnel changes in the MPRP and in the Great Khural. At the MPRP's congress in June 2005 the Mayor of Ulan Bator, Miyeegombyn Enkhbold, was chosen to replace Enkhbayar as the new party Chairman. The party's Leadership Council was enlarged to 21 members: nine re-elected (with four failing to secure re-election) and 10 new members, including Party Secretary Yondongiin Otgonbayar, the Ministers of Foreign Affairs, of Food and Agriculture, and of Health, and six MPRP Great Khural members. Two vacancies were held open, including one for a new head of the Presidential Secretariat. Enkhbayar was inaugurated as President of Mongolia on 24 June. At the beginning of July the Great Khural elected the Minister of Justice and Home Affairs, Tsendiin Nyamdorj (of the MPRP), to replace Enkhbayar as Chairman of the Great Khural.

After an attempt by the MPRP to force the Prime Minister to resign, including the expulsion of DP members from the 'combined' MPRP parliamentary group (the 'group of 62'), shortly before the closing of its spring 2005 session the Great Khural voted in favour of the formation of a DP parliamentary group, which 25 party members (headed by Gonchigdorj) joined. The by-election in Enkhbayar's former constituency was to be held at the end of August. The MPRP chose its Chairman, Miyeegombyn Enkhbold, as its candidate, and the DP nominated Prime Minister Tsakhiagiin Elbegdorj. However, Elbegdorj's nomination was withdrawn at the beginning of August, a coalition accord having been signed by the DP and the MPRP. The by-election was subsequently won by Miyeegombyn Enkhbold.

In January 2006 a Motherland Party deputy defected to the MPRP, thereby giving the latter its 38th seat in the Great Khural. Following demands by the MPRP for Prime Minister Elbegdorj's resignation, the 10 MPRP ministers in his Cabinet resigned and the 'grand coalition' Government was voted out of office. Miyeegombyn Enkhbold, MPRP Chairman and Mayor of Ulan Bator, was elected Prime Minister. He formed a new 'national solidarity' Government that included the Motherland and Republican Party leaders Erdenebat and Jargalsaikhan, ex-DP member Gündalai, who had recently established a new party, the Party of the People, and three DP members—Enkhsaikhan, Narantsatsralt and Sonompil—who were subsequently expelled from the rump DP, now excluded from the MPRP's new coalition. One newspaper described these politicians as 'unscrupulous'; another claimed that the MPRP's abandonment of its coalition with the DP was intended to halt the progress of a new anti-corruption bill that would focus on corruption within its ranks. The new Anti-Corruption Law was finally adopted in July, eight years after the first legislation.

Following his appointment in January 2006 to the post of Deputy Prime Minister, Mendsaikhany Enkhsaikhan and his supporters began forming a new party, which was named the National New Party at its first congress in May. After the death of Great Khural member Onomoogiin Enkhsaikhan in March, the resultant by-election was delayed (possibly unconstitutionally) until early September, when it was won by the Minister of Education, Culture and Science, Ölziisaikhany Enkhtüvshin (MPRP).

The political upheaval of early 2006 also delayed a decision on amendments to the 1997 Minerals Law, introduced at the end of December 2005, which caused disquiet among foreign investors in Mongolia's mining industry. Amid much public debate about the merits of state control of the country's resources and various protests, the Great Khural discussed the amendments, consolidated them in committee and finally adopted a new redaction of the 1997 law in July 2006. According to initial reports of the text prior to publication, mining licences were to be granted only to companies, not to individuals; foreign and domestic investors in mining were to be taxed at the same rate; stability agreements were to be replaced by investment contracts; and local people in proposed mining areas would be granted greater rights with regard to decisions on exploitation licences. Also, the Government would have the right to acquire up to 50% of the resources of deposits discovered with the help of state funds and to control up to 34% of resources obtained from privately funded deposits. Royalties were to be raised from 2.5% to 5.0%, severe penalties were envisaged for serious environmental damage and the size of foreign work-forces would be limited to 10%.

In October 2006 a parliamentary motion of no confidence was submitted against the Government: Enkhbold was accused of misconduct in relation to land sales during his tenure of the post of Mayor of Ulan Bator, while the Government was criticized for alleged incompetence and its failure to improve the living standards of the population. However, the motion failed to garner sufficient votes to succeed. In February 2007 Danzandarjaagiin Tuyaa of the MPRP was appointed Minister of Health, to replace Lamjavyn Gündalai of the Party of the People, who had been dismissed. (Gündalai subsequently abandoned the Party of the People and rejoined the DP.) The Minister of Social Welfare and Labour, Luvsangiin Odonchimed of the MPRP, resigned and was replaced by another MPRP member, Damdingiin Demberel. In April Tserengiin Davaadorj was appointed to succeed Bazaryn Jargalsaikhan as Minister of Industry and Trade.

Meanwhile, in preparation for the legislative election of mid-2008, the Great Khural approved amendments to the Law on Elections, restoring 26 large multi-candidate constituencies similar to those prevailing at the time of the 1992 legislative election and introducing a quota for female members.

In early 2007 it emerged that Tsendiin Nyamdorj, the Chairman of the Great Khural, had re-edited legislation, including the Election Law and the Minerals Law, after the final texts had been approved by the Great Khural. Nyamdorj's explanation was accepted by some of his MPRP colleagues, but, following a Constitutional Court ruling that his actions were unconstitutional, in June he was obliged to resign from his post. He was replaced by the Deputy Chairman, Danzangiin Lündeejantsan.

At the MPRP's 25th Congress in October 2007, delegates expressed their dissatisfaction with Miyeegombyn Enkhbold's performance by voting to remove him from the chairmanship of the party, in favour of General Secretary Sanjaagiin Bayar. The members of a new 255-member MPRP Little Khural and 23-member Leadership Council were later announced; in total, 13 of the 19 Leadership Council members elected in 2005 were replaced and three were re-elected. Former MPRP secretary Yondongiin Otgonbayar was elected General Secretary and six new secretaries were approved, including Enkhbold and Nyamdorj. For the first time intra-party political movements and factions were represented by three Leadership Council members; also of note was the inclusion of four women, one of them a Mongolian Kazakh. The reorganization of the Little Khural had been the subject of wide speculation and was regarded as an important stage in the preparation of the final list of MPRP candidates for the legislative election scheduled for June 2008.

An important consequence of these events was Enkhbold's resignation as Prime Minister in early November 2007, thus allowing Sanjaagiin Bayar's election to the position later in the month. Bayar's first acts included the appointment of Ravdangiin Bold, ambassador to the USA, to the post of head of the Main Directorate of Intelligence and the dismissal of the ministers for disaster reduction and professional inspection, their portfolios passing to the new Deputy Prime Minister, Enkhbold. After the signing of co-operation agreements with the CCP and the National New Party, Bayar formed a new Cabinet in December. Among the three female appointees was CCP leader Sanjaasürengiin Oyuun, who assumed the role of Minister of Foreign Affairs. Meanwhile, the Mayor and Governor of Ulan Bator, Tsogtyn Batbayar, was replaced in December by Tüdeviin Bilegt, head of the Presidential Secretariat.

Janlavyn Narantsatsralt, Minister of Construction and Urban Development and a former Prime Minister, was killed in a car accident in November 2007. He was replaced by Tserendashiin Tsolmon, who also became Chairman of the National New Party in February 2008. In the same month a new political organization was registered, the Mongolian Democratic Movement Party.

In preparation for the next election, in December 2007 the electoral law was amended to dispense with the requirement for a 30% quota of female members in the legislature. President Enkhbayar unsuccessfully attempted to veto the Great Khural's revision of the law. A total of 356 candidates were registered to contest the legislative election, which was held on 29 June 2008. The level of participation in the polls was reported to be 74.3%. Amid allegations of widespread irregularities, the Chairman of the DP, Tsakhiagiin Elbegdorj, demanded that the votes be recounted. The Citizens' Alliance (CA, a grouping that represented the Citizens' Movement Party, the Mongolian Green Party and the MSDP) accused both the MPRP and the DP of malpractice. Following the publication of provisional results awarding a narrow parliamentary majority to the MPRP, thousands of demonstrators took the streets of Ulan Bator to protest against the perceived electoral fraud. Several people were killed in the rioting that ensued, mostly from gunshot wounds, and hundreds were injured. About 700 demonstrators were reported to have been detained. The headquarters of the MPRP were damaged in an arson attack, and the GEC building was also attacked. On 1 July a state of emergency was declared by President Enkhbayar, which remained in place for four days.

It was reported in mid-July 2008 that the GEC had allocated 39 seats in the Great Khural to the MPRP, 25 to the DP, one to the CCP and one to an independent candidate. The winners of 10 of the 76 seats were yet to be declared. Nevertheless, the legislature was instructed by President Enkhbayar to convene its first session. The session duly opened but was swiftly abandoned by DP members, who refused to be inaugurated pending the announcement of the final election results. The withdrawal of the DP from the proceedings thus removed the quorum required for the registration of legislators. Futhermore, the DP demanded an investigation into the conduct of the election by the Chairman of the GEC, Bataagiin Battulga. After several unsuccessful attempts, the Great Khural finally convened at the end of August, with the participation of the DP and with 67 legislators in attendance. Damdingiin Demberel of the MPRP was chosen as the chamber's Chairman.

On 11 September 2008 the Great Khural re-elected Sanjaagiin Bayar as Prime Minister. Negotiations between the MPRP and the DP, which had encompassed the contentious issue of the development of the country's mineral resources, resulted in an agreement on the formation of a coalition Government, whereby 60% of the ministerial positions were to be allocated to the MPRP and 40% to the DP. Norovyn Altankhuyag, who in late August had replaced Elbegdorj as Chairman of the DP following the latter's resignation, became First Deputy Prime Minister. Miyeegombyn Enkhbold of the MPRP was appointed as Deputy Prime Minister. Sükhbaataryn Batbold (MPRP) was allocated responsibility for external relations, formerly the portfolio of foreign affairs, which had been modified to incorporate economic matters; the Ministry of Trade and Industry was abolished. A new Ministry of Mining and Energy was established.

As the GEC continued its investigations into the disputed results in six constituencies, the DP resumed its boycott of the Great Khural. In early 2009 the election results for four seats, in a constituency in Ulan Bator, remained outstanding. When these results were eventually declared, the MPRP held a total of 45 seats in the Great Khural and the DP 27; one seat was occupied by a representative of the CCP, one by a member of the Mongolian Green Party and another by an independent parliamentarian. Meanwhile, the winner of one seat had been imprisoned, pending an investigation into charges of fraud, allegedly committed during his tenure of a previous post.

With the presidential election scheduled for 24 May 2009, the MPRP confirmed in early April that the incumbent Nambaryn Enkhbayar was to stand for re-election. The other main contender for the presidency was Tsakhiagiin Elbegdorj, former Prime Minister and erstwhile Chairman of the DP, whose candidacy was supported by the Mongolian Green Party and the CCP, as well as by the DP.

For many years foreign affairs were dominated by Mongolia's relations with the Soviet Union. Following the dissolution of the USSR in 1991, co-operation with Russia, the largest of the successor states, continued. During an official visit to Russia in January 1993, President Ochirbat and the Russian President, Boris Yeltsin, issued a joint statement expressing regret at the execution and imprisonment of Mongolian citizens in the USSR during the Stalinist period. Ochirbat and Yeltsin also signed a new 20-year Mongolian-Russian Treaty of Friendship and Co-operation to replace the defunct Mongolian-Soviet treaty of 1986. A similar treaty had been signed with Ukraine in November 1992, during the official visit to Mongolia by Ukrainian President Leonid Kravchuk. In November 2000 the Russian President, Vladimir Putin, stayed overnight in Ulan Bator en route to an Asia-Pacific Economic Co-operation (APEC) conference in Brunei. He was the most senior Russian or Soviet visitor to Mongolia since 1974. Presidents Bagabandi and Putin issued a joint declaration on bilateral co-operation and the protection of each other's national interests. Russia affirmed its commitment to guaranteeing Mongolia's security in connection with its nuclear weapons-free status. Russian Prime Minister Mikhail Kasyanov officially visited Mongolia in late March 2002, to discuss economic and military co-operation, and also the issue of Mongolia's outstanding debt of 11,400m. transferable roubles that the Russian Government claimed it was owed for Soviet aid granted during 1947–91, which the Mongolian Government referred to as the 'big debt'. The two countries had been unable to agree terms for the previous 10 years. Mongolia disagreed with Russia's position that the debt should be paid in full at par value with the US dollar, and there was also Mongolian opposition pressure to offset the cost of damage done to the environment by Soviet military activity. The disagreement disrupted Mongolian-Russian discussions in early 2003 on a new contract for the Erdenet copper-mining joint venture.

However, when the two Prime Ministers did eventually meet in the Russian capital of Moscow in July 2003, a new five-year agreement on the operation of the Erdenet copper enterprise was reached, preserving Mongolia's 51% ownership of stock. Russia agreed that Mongolia had already repaid the cost of building the Erdenet plant. Otherwise, Mongolia's main concern was to reduce Russian taxes on imports of Mongolian goods. At the end of December Russia announced that it had received Mongolia's payment in settlement of the 'big debt'. Russia had waived 98% of the total debt and accepted US $250m. Prime Minister Nambaryn Enkhbayar celebrated a political and diplomatic victory for the MPRP Government, but the details of the settlement remained unclear. DP leader and ex-Prime Minister Enkhsaikhan pointed out that under the Constitution international agreements required approval by the Great Khural. Former Prime Minister Byambasüren revived charges of Soviet price-fixing, stating that from 1976 Mongolia had been paid only 0.39 roubles for every one rouble of the value of its exports to the USSR but had been charged 1.5 roubles for its imports of Soviet goods. In March 2005 the Great Khural established a parliamentary working group to investigate the circumstances of the repayment of the 'big debt'.

In July 2006 Russian Prime Minister Mikhail Fradkov visited Mongolia and participated in discussions with Mongolian Prime Minister Enkhbold concerning investment in the Mongolian mining sector. In December 2006 President Enkhbayar toured the Republics of Buryatiya and Kalmykiya, before flying to Moscow for the first state visit by a Mongolian president in 13 years. Following a meeting with President Putin, a treaty on the border regime and also trade and economic agreements were signed. In April 2008 Prime Minister Sanjaagiin Bayar visited Russia, for discussions with Vladimir Putin, now the country's Prime Minister, and in the following month President Enkhbayar also visited Moscow, where he had a meeting with President Dimitrii Medvedev.

Relations with the People's Rpublic of China were good until the onset of the Sino-Soviet dispute in the 1960s. In 1986, however, Sino-Mongolian relations improved significantly when the Chinese Vice-Minister of Foreign Affairs visited Ulan Bator, and the two countries signed agreements on consular relations and trade. In June 1987 a delegation from the Chinese National People's Congress visited Ulan Bator. A treaty concerning the resolution of border disputes was subsequently initialled by representatives of the two Governments.

A new Treaty of Friendship and Co-operation was concluded during a visit to Ulan Bator by Chinese Premier Li Peng in April 1994. An agreement on cultural, economic and technical co-operation was also signed. Mongolia continued to protest in 1995 at the ongoing series of nuclear tests being carried out in China (in the Xinjiang Uygur Autonomous Region). Mongolian human rights groups and the Ulan Bator press supported protests in Inner Mongolia against the arrest by the Chinese authorities of Inner Mongolian human rights activists in December. Prime Minister Jasrai's official visit to China in March 1996, focusing on trade and co-operation, appeared not to have been affected by these events. Relations with China were further consolidated in 1997 by the visits to Ulan Bator of Qiao Shi, the Chairman of the National People's Congress Standing Committee, in April, and of Qian Qichen, the Chinese Deputy Premier and Minister of Foreign Affairs, in August.

In July 1999 Chinese President Jiang Zemin undertook a state visit to Mongolia to promote bilateral relations. In November 1999 Prime Minister Amarjargal visited China. The Dalai Lama visited Ulan Bator in November 2002, travelling via Japan after Russia refused him a visa and Korean Air, the national carrier of South Korea, banned him on the grounds that he posed a security threat. Although his visit was at the invitation of Mongolia's

Buddhist leaders rather than of the Government, the Chinese authorities indicated their displeasure by halting rail traffic on their mutual border for 36 hours.

In June 2003 Chinese President Hu Jintao visited Ulan Bator, where he had discussions with President Bagabandi and Prime Minister Enkhbayar and addressed the Great Khural on the subject of 'neighbourly partnership of mutual trust' which, besides reiterating respect for each other's independence, sovereignty and territorial integrity, embodied in the handling of bilateral relations 'a spirit of consultation, co-operation and friendship'. China granted Mongolia 50m. yuan for the purposes of building a road across their border from Zamyn-Üüd to Erlian.

Natsagiin Bagabandi paid a state visit to China in July 2004, visiting Hainan and the Special Administrative Region of Macao, and discussing economic co-operation with President Hu Jintao. In August 2006 the Dalai Lama paid his seventh visit to Mongolia at the invitation of local Buddhists and presided over religious ceremonies in Ulan Bator. In November 2006 Enkhbold signed a trade and economic co-operation agreement with China, during his first official visit to Beijing since becoming Prime Minister in January. He also visited Urumqi, in the Xinjiang Uygur Autonomous Region, where Mongolia hoped to open a consulate. In April 2008 President Enkhbayar travelled to China to attend the Boao Forum for Asia where he had discussions with Chinese President Hu Jintao.

In July 1999 Prime Minister Keizo Obuchi of Japan made an official visit to Mongolia. In February 2001 Prime Minister Nambaryn Enkhbayar embarked upon his first visit to a foreign country, travelling to Japan, where he was by received by Emperor Akihito and participated in talks with Japanese Prime Minister Yoshio Mori. In August 2004 the Japanese Minister of Foreign Affairs, Yoriko Kawaguchi, visited Mongolia. Kawaguchi engaged in discussions with Prime Minister Tsakhiagiin Elbegdorj and President Natsagiin Bagabandi. The discussions focused on the strengthening of bilateral relations and the promotion of democratization in Mongolia. In July 2006 Mongolia received Japanese Prime Minister Junichiro Koizumi, who discussed joint efforts to develop energy resources in Mongolia, as well as issues relating to North Korea. In February 2007 President Enkhbayar visited Japan and signed a joint agreement with Japanese Prime Minister Shinzo Abe pledging to expand bilateral relations, including plans to utilize mineral resources in Mongolia. The two leaders agreed to co-operate in resolving tensions caused by the North Korean nuclear dispute and collaborate in Japan's quest to attain a permanent seat on the UN Security Council.

In May 1999 Mongolia received President Kim Dae-Jung of South Korea, marking the first such visit by a Korean head of state. Following talks with the Mongolian Minister of Defence, Sharavdorj Tuvdendorj, President Kim obtained the Mongolian Government's support for his policy of political engagement with North Korea. In November 1999 Mongolian Prime Minister Amarjargal made a reciprocal visit to South Korea and engaged in discussions to improve bilateral relations. In May 2006 the South Korean President Roh Moo-Hyun paid a state visit to Mongolia. During his visit President Roh discussed a range of issues with President Enkhbayar including trade and environmental co-operation. President Enkhbayar expressed support for South Korea's involvement in the six-party talks aimed at resolving the North Korean nuclear issue (see the chapter on the Democratic People's Republic of Korea).

In November 1999 Prime Minister Amarjargal visited North Korea and exchanged views with Premier Hong Song Nam on the development of bilateral relations. Prime Minister Amarjargal also met with the President of the Presidium of the Supreme People's Assembly, Kim Yong Nam. At the invitation of Kim Yong Nam, President Bagabandi visited North Korea in December 2005 to promote bilateral co-operation. In July 2007 Mongolia received Kim Yong Nam. At the conclusion of the visit the two countries signed an agreement to co-operate in the areas of public health, medical science and marine transport.

In March 2000 Prime Minister Amarjargal paid an official visit to the United Kingdom. In November 2004 Great Khural Chairman Nambaryn Enkhbayar was received by Queen Elizabeth during a visit to the United Kingdom. In April 2007 President Enkhbayar, as he had since become, revisited the United Kingdom, and had discussions with Prime Minister Tony Blair.

Nambaryn Enkhbayar's first overseas trip as Prime Minister was to the World Economic Forum in Davos, Switzerland, in January 2001. Enkhbayar's first official foreign travel after his inauguration as President of Mongolia was in July 2005 to Astana, the capital of Kazakhstan, where he attended a meeting of the Shanghai Co-operation Organization with Russian President Vladimir Putin, Chinese President Hu Jintao and other leaders (Mongolia had been granted observer status). In August 2007 President Enkhbayar returned to Astana for a further summit meeting of the Shanghai Co-operation Organization, where he had discussions with President Putin, President Nursultan Nazarbayev of Kazakhstan and other leaders.

During an official visit to the USA in November 2001, Prime Minister Enkhbayar addressed the UN General Assembly in New York and also had a meeting with President George W. Bush. Enkhbayar reaffirmed the strategic partnership with the USA and urged greater investment in Mongolia. Having condemned the terrorist attacks of 11 September against the USA, he informed President Bush of Mongolia's readiness to allow the use of its air space to help combat terrorism. The Secretary-General of the UN, Kofi Annan, paid a brief visit to Mongolia in October 2002. Following the US military intervention in Iraq in March 2003, soldiers of the Mongolian army's élite battalion were sent to Iraq for tours of duty with the Polish contingent stationed north of Baghdad. (The Mongolian deployment remained in Iraq until September 2008.)

In July 2004 President Bagabandi visited the USA, where he met President Bush and signed a Trade and Investment Framework Agreement. US Assistant Secretary of State James Kelly visited Ulan Bator in August 2004. The US Secretary of Defense, Donald Rumsfeld, visited Ulan Bator briefly in October 2005. Rumsfeld stated that the USA was willing to help Mongolia enhance its peace-keeping capabilities. In 2005 the USA provided Mongolia with US $18m. in military assistance, including regular training exchanges and bilateral peace-keeping exercises.

On the first visit to Mongolia by a sitting US President, in November 2005 George W. Bush spent four hours in Ulan Bator where he had discussions with President Enkhbayar. A joint statement noted that President Bush welcomed Mongolia's progress towards becoming a mature and stable democracy and the country's development of a free market economy, led by the private sector. The two Presidents also emphasized their commitment to combating terrorism.

In February 2006, following a closed meeting in Ulan Bator with foreign donors (the World Bank, the Asian Development Bank (ADB), the IMF, the UN, Japan, the USA and Germany), which urged greater accountability, the US Administration issued a statement noting that the US Agency for International Development had found that corruption in Mongolia was increasing at all levels. The Mongolian Government was to be required to draw up lists of specific actions to combat corruption and to detail all the changes needed within existing law in order that Mongolia might comply with the UN Convention Against Corruption (UNCAC). President George W. Bush sent a message in February to Mongolia's Kazakhs on the occasion of Kurban Ait (Id al-Adha), the first time a US President had done so.

In October 2007 President Enkhbayar visited the USA, meeting the UN Secretary-General and President George W. Bush; Enkhbayar and Bush signed a Millennium Challenge contract, which pledged US $285m. in funds for Mongolia.

In October 2004, President Bagabandi undertook a state visit to Canada for a meeting with Prime Minister Paul Martin. The two leaders agreed that regular meetings would be held to strengthen relations between the two countries. In January 2008 the Canadian Minister of International Trade, David Emerson, visited Mongolia to discuss the development of bilateral trade and investment, especially in Mongolia's mining sector.

In January 2005 President Bagabandi visited Laos and met with the President, Khamtay Siphandone. In September 2007 President Choummali Saignason of Laos embarked upon a three-day state visit to Mongolia. The Laotian President and President Enkhbayar signed a range of agreements relating to the areas of trade and international co-operation.

President Enkhbayar's travelled to France in 2007 where he was received by French President Jacques Chirac. Several trade agreements were signed between Mongolia and France at the conclusion of President Enkhbayar's visit.

Government

Supreme legislative power is vested in the 76-member Mongolian Great Khural (Assembly), elected by universal adult suffrage for four years. The Great Khural recognizes the President on his election and appoints the Prime Minister and members of the Cabinet, which is the highest executive body. The President, who is directly elected for a term of four years, is Head of State and Commander-in-Chief of the Armed Forces. A revision to the electoral law, adopted in December 2005, provided for the replacement of the 76 single-seat constituencies with 26 multi-seat constituencies, with effect from the 2008 election.

Mongolia is divided into 21 provinces (*aimag*) and one municipality (Ulan Bator), with appointed governors and elected local assemblies. However, plans to reduce the number of *aimag* to four (the original pre-revolutionary divisions) and to develop the town of Kharkhorin (the ancient Karakorum) as the future capital were under consideration in 2005.

Defence

Under the 1992 Constitution, the President of Mongolia is, ex officio, Commander-in-Chief of the Armed Forces. The defence roles of the President, the Mongolian Great Khural, the Government and local administrations are defined by the Mongolian Law on Defence (November 1993). Mongolia's *Military Doctrine*, a summary of which was issued by the Great Khural in July 1994, defines the armed forces as comprising general purpose troops, air defence troops, construction troops and civil defence troops. The border troops and internal troops, which are not part of the armed forces, are responsible for protection of the borders and of strategic installations, respectively. As assessed at November 2008 by the International Institute for Strategic Studies, Mongolia's defence forces numbered 10,000, comprising an army of 8,900 (of whom 3,300 were thought to be conscripts), 800 air defence personnel and 300 construction troops. There was a paramilitary force of about 7,200, comprising 1,200 internal security troops and 6,000 border guards. Military service is for 12 months (for males aged 18–25 years), but a system of alternative service is being introduced. Defence spending for 2009 was projected at 57,164.1m. tögrög, some 2.6% of total expenditure.

Economic Affairs

In 2007, according to estimates by the World Bank, Mongolia's gross national income (GNI), measured at average 2005–07 prices, was US $3,362m., equivalent to $1,290 per head (or $3,160 per head on an international purchasing-power parity basis). During 2000–07, it was estimated, the population increased at an average annual rate of 1.2%, while gross domestic product (GDP) per head increased, in real terms, at an average of 6.0% per year. Overall GDP increased, in real terms, at an average annual rate of 7.3% in 2000–07. According to revised Asian Development Bank (ADB) estimates published in early 2009, real GDP growth was 10.2% in 2007 and 8.9% in 2008.

Agriculture (including forestry) contributed 22.1% of GDP in 2007. The sector engaged 37.7% of the employed labour force in that year. Animal herding is the main economic activity and is practised throughout the country. Most livestock is privately owned. Following exceptionally severe weather, livestock numbers (sheep, goats, horses, cattle and camels) declined sharply in 2002, to fewer than 23.7m., before steadily recovering to reach almost 43.3m. by the end of 2008. The principal crops are wheat, potatoes and vegetables. Production of cereals rose from 114,800 metric tons in 2007 to 212,900 tons in 2008. During 2000–06, according to figures from the World Bank, the GDP of the agricultural sector increased, in real terms, at an average annual rate of 0.9%. According to the ADB, agricultural GDP increased by 15.8% in 2007 and by an estimated 15.2% in 2008.

Industry (comprising mining, manufacturing, construction and utilities) provided 38.4% of GDP in 2007 and the sector (excluding printing and publishing, but including fishing and logging) engaged 17.9% of the employed labour force in the same year. According to the World Bank, during 2000–06 industrial GDP increased, in real terms, at an average rate of 7.8% per year. According to the ADB, the industrial sector's GDP increased by 7.0% in 2007 and by 0.8% by 2008.

Mining contributed 29.4% of GDP in 2007, and some 13,700 workers were engaged in the sector in January of that year. Mongolia has significant, largely unexplored, mineral resources and is a leading producer and exporter of copper, gold, molybdenum and fluorspar concentrates. In 2006 the value of exports of copper concentrate increased by more than 90% to US $635.4m., reflecting the rise in world market prices for the commodity, and this trend continued in 2007, with a similar export volume valued at $811.5m. in that year. In 2008, however, the value of copper exports decreased sharply. The copper-molybdenum works at Erdenet, a Mongolian-Russian joint venture, is the most important mining operation in the country. The sites of other major deposits of copper and also of gold are being developed in collaboration with various foreign enterprises. However, gold production declined from 22.6 kg in 2006 to less than 17.5 kg in 2007. Other mineral resources include coal, tungsten, tin, uranium and lead. Output of coal rose from 8.1m. metric tons in 2006 to 9.2m. tons in 2007. Mongolia's production of crude petroleum rose from 366,800 barrels in 2006 to 850,200 barrels in 2007. According to the ADB, the GDP of the mining sector expanded at an average annual rate of 11.9% in 2003–07, but increased by only 1.7% in 2007.

The manufacturing sector accounted for 4.4% of GDP in 2007. Manufacturing industries are based largely on the products of the agricultural and animal husbandry sector. The principal branches of manufacturing include food products, beverages, textiles and garments. Mongolia is one of the world's foremost producers of cashmere, and the country also manufactures garments, leather goods and carpets. According to figures from the World Bank, manufacturing GDP increased by an annual average of 9.7% in 2000–06. The sector's GDP contracted by substantially in 2005, but a real growth rate of 13.3% was recorded in the sector in 2006. According to figures from the ADB, the manufacturing sector expanded by 32.4% in 2007.

Energy is derived principally from thermal power stations, fuelled by coal. Most provincial centres have thermal power stations or diesel generators, while minor rural centres generally rely on small diesel generators. In more isolated areas wood, roots, bushes and dried animal dung are used for domestic fuel. Mongolia imports electricity and petroleum products, including liquid petroleum gas. In 2007 the cost of Mongolia's imports of fuels and lubricants rose to US $634.8m., thus accounting for 29.3% of the total cost of merchandise imports.

The services sector contributed 39.5 of GDP in 2007 and engaged 35.1% of the employed labour force in the same year. During 2000–07, according to figures from the World Bank, the GDP of the sector increased, in real terms, by an average of 8.8% annually. According to the ADB, the GDP of the services sector increased by 10.7% in 2007 and by 15.9% in 2008. Receipts from tourism were estimated to have reached US $320m. in 2008. The number of visitor arrivals rose from 451,788 in 2007 (when about 47% of visitors came from the People's Republic of China) to 446,400 in 2008.

In 2006 Mongolia achieved its first ever visible trade surplus, but the trade balance reverted to deficit in the following year. The trade deficit rose to US $600m. in 2008, according to the ADB, and there was an estimated deficit of $677m. (equivalent to 12.9% of GDP in that year) on the current account of the balance of payments. In 2007 the principal source of imports was Russia, supplying 34.3% of the total, with the People's Republic of China providing 31.1%. Other significant suppliers were Japan, the Republic of Korea and the Germany. China was the principal market for exports, purchasing 72.5% of the total. Other important purchasers were Canada, the USA, Italy, Russia and the Republic of Korea. The principal imports in 2007 were fuels and lubricants (29.3%) and machinery and vehicles (28.3%). The leading export was copper concentrate (41.6%).

In 2008, following the revision of official figures, a budget deficit of 95,263.9m. tögrög was forecast. The ADB projected that the deficit would reach the equivalent of 5.0% of GDP in 2008. Mongolia's external debt totalled US $1,444m. at the end of 2006, of which $1,361m. was long-term public debt. In that year the cost of debt-servicing was equivalent to 2.2% of the value of exports of goods and services. According to figures from the IMF, the annual rate of inflation averaged 8.9% during 2000–08. Consumer prices rose by 25.0% in 2008. The number of registered unemployed persons decreased from 32,900 in 2006 to 29,900 in 2007. However, the number of unregistered unemployed persons was believed to be far greater. The ADB estimated the rate of unemployment at 3.0% of the (registered) labour force in 2008.

In 1989 Mongolia joined the Group of 77 (an organization of developing countries, founded under the auspices of UNCTAD, see p. 58, to promote economic co-operation). In February 1991 Mongolia became a member of the Asian Development Bank (ADB, see p. 191) as well as of the IMF and World Bank. In 1994 the European Union (EU, see p. 255) announced the inclusion of Mongolia in TACIS, the EU's programme of technical assistance to the Commonwealth of Independent States. In 1997 Mongolia became a member of the World Trade Organization (WTO, see p. 410). In July 1998 Mongolia was admitted to the ASEAN Regional Forum (ARF, see p. 197), and in May 2000 the country became a member of the European Bank for Reconstruction and Development (EBRD, see p. 251). Mongolia is also a member of the UN Economic and Social Commission for Asia and the Pacific (ESCAP, see p. 36). Mongolbank, the country's central bank, joined the Bank for International Settlements (see p. 204) in July 2008.

In January 2008 the Mongolian legislature approved a draft National Development Policy, encompassing the period to 2021. Strong international commodity prices sustained the performance of the mining sector in 2005–07, while relatively mild winters greatly benefited the agricultural sector. However, with the onset of the international financial crisis in the latter part of 2008, commodity prices decreased sharply. The erosion of the value of many of the country's mineral exports, notably copper, as well as a substantial decrease in cashmere prices in 2008, precipitated decline in many sectors, particularly that of construction. Although in comparison with the previous year the value of exports was reported to have increased by 29.7% in 2008 as a whole, the cost of merchandise imports rose by 56.3%. The deceleration in the economy of China, a major purchaser of Mongolian exports, was also expected to affect sales in 2009. Mongolia's financial services were also vulnerable to the global turmoil, and in December 2008 the authorities were required to take control of one of the country's largest banks, following the deterioration of its deposit base. In April 2009 the IMF approved an 18-month stand-by arrangement worth US $229.2m. An initial allocation of $76.4m. was provided, with the remainder to be disbursed quarterly, subject to review. The funds were to help finance Mongolia's economic stabilization programme, which was to address shortcomings in the banking sector and allow for greater exchange rate flexibility. The IMF advised that the Government reduce its high levels of capital spending. Another major objective of the Government's programme was the provision of greater support for poor families. In collaboration also with the World Bank and the ADB, a comprehensive restructuring of the system of social transfer programmes, in order to ensure that payments benefited the most impoverished of Mongolians, was to be undertaken. (In 2006 the incidence of poverty was estimated at 32.6%, while standards of health care and of education were reported to be deteriorating.) The ADB forecast a GDP growth rate of 3.0% in 2009.

Education

Ten-year general education is compulsory, beginning at six years of age, and 11-year schooling was being introduced as of early 2005. Pupils may attend vocational-technical schools from the ages of 16 to 18 years. In 2004/05 enrolment in primary schools included 93.3% of pupils in the relevant age-group, while enrolment in secondary schools included 91.8% of pupils. In 2007/08 754 general education schools, with a total enrolment of 537,500 pupils, employed 23,900 teachers. The 56 vocational training schools (some of them private) had a total enrolment of 29,900 in that year. In higher education, in 2007/08 there were 47 state-owned universities and colleges with 99,000 students, and 109 private universities and colleges with 50,800 students. Many Mongolian students continue their academic careers at universities and technical schools in Russia, Germany the United Kingdom and the USA. The state budget allocation to the Ministry of Education, Culture and Science for 2009 was 485,131.4m. tögrög (22% of planned budgetary expenditure).

Public Holidays

2009: 1 January (New Year), 25–26 February (Tsagaan Sar, lunar new year), 8 March (International Women's Day), 1 June (Children's Day), 11–13 July (Naadam, national sports festival), 26 November (Republic Day).

2010: 1 January (New Year), 14–16 February (Tsagaan Sar, lunar new year), 8 March (International Women's Day), 1 June (Children's Day), 11–13 July (Naadam, national sports festival), 26 November (Republic Day).

Weights and Measures

The metric system is in force.

Statistical Survey

Unless otherwise indicated, revised by Alan J. K. Sanders

Area and Population

AREA, POPULATION AND DENSITY

Area (sq km)	1,564,116*
Population (census results)	
5 January 1989	2,043,400
5 January 2000	
Males	1,177,981
Females	1,195,512
Total	2,373,493
Population (official estimates at 31 December)	
2006	2,594,800
2007	2,635,200
2008	2,683,400
Density (per sq km) at 31 December 2008	1.7

* 603,909 sq miles.

ADMINISTRATIVE DIVISIONS
(estimates at 31 December 2007)

Province (Aimag)	Area ('000 sq km)	Estimated population ('000)	Provincial centre
Arkhangai	55.3	92.8	Tsetserleg
Bayankhongor	116.0	84.2	Bayankhongor
Bayan-Ölgii	45.7	100.8	Ölgii
Bulgan	48.7	60.5	Bulgan
Darkhan-Uul	3.3	87.6	Darkhan
Dornod (Eastern)	123.6	72.9	Choibalsan
Dornogobi (East Gobi)	109.5	55.6	Sainshand
Dundgobi (Central Gobi)	74.7	48.8	Mandalgobi
Gobi-Altai	141.4	60.2	Altai
Gobi-Sümber	5.5	12.6	Choir

Province (Aimag)—continued	Area ('000 sq km)	Estimated population ('000)	Provincial centre
Khentii	80.3	71.3	Öndörkhaan
Khovd	76.1	88.6	Khovd
Khövsgöl	100.6	122.4	Mörön
Orkhon	0.8	80.1	Erdenet
Ömnögobi (South Gobi)	165.4	46.9	Dalanzadgad
Övörkhangai	62.9	115.7	Arvaikheer
Selenge	41.2	100.5	Sükhbaatar
Sükhbaatar	82.3	55.1	Baruun Urt
Töv (Central)	74.0	85.9	Zuun mod
Ulan Bator (Ulaanbaatar)*	4.7	1,031.2	(capital city)
Uvs	69.6	80.4	Ulaangom
Zavkhan	82.5	81.1	Uliastai
Total	**1,564.1**	**2,635.2**	

* Ulan Bator, including Nalaikh, and Bagakhangai and Baganuur districts beyond the urban boundary, has special status as the capital city.

MONGOLIA

ETHNIC GROUPS
(January 2000 census)

	Number	%
Khalh (Khalkha)	1,934,700	81.5
Kazakh (Khasag)	103,000	4.3
Dörvöd (Durbet)	66,700	2.8
Bayad (Bayat)	50,800	2.1
Buryat (Buriat)	40,600	1.7
Dariganga	31,900	1.3
Zakhchin	29,800	1.3
Uriankhai	25,200	1.1
Other ethnic groups	82,600	3.5
Foreign citizens	8,100	0.3
Total	**2,373,500**	**100.0**

PRINCIPAL TOWNS
(estimated population)

Ulan Bator (capital)	1,031,200*	Choibalsan	80,000‡
Darkhan	120,000†	Erdenet	74,300*

* December 2007.
† October 2006.
‡ June 2008.

BIRTHS, MARRIAGES AND DEATHS

	Registered live births Number	Rate (per 1,000)	Registered marriages* Number	Rate (per 1,000)	Registered deaths Number	Rate (per 1,000)
1999	49,461	21.0	13,722	10.1	16,105	6.8
2000	48,721	20.4	12,601	9.0	15,472	6.5
2001	49,658	20.5	12,393	8.6	15,999	6.6
2002	46,922	19.1	13,514	9.2	15,857	6.4
2003	45,723	18.4	14,572	9.6	16,006	6.4
2004	45,501	18.1	11,242	7.2	16,404	6.5
2005	45,326	17.8	14,993	9.3	16,480	6.5
2006	49,092	19.0	48,996	19.0	16,682	6.5
2007	56,636	21.7	40,965	15.7	16,259	6.2

* Persons aged 18 years and over.

2008: Registered live births 63,300 (birth rate 23.8 per 1,000); death rate 5.6 per 1,000.

Life expectancy (years at birth): 66.54 (males 63.13; females 70.23) in 2007 (Source: *Mongolian Statistical Yearbook*).

EMPLOYMENT
('000 employees at 31 December)

	2005	2006	2007
Agriculture and forestry	386.2	391.4	385.6
Industry*	113.9	118.9	123.1
Transport and communications	42.4	41.2	44.1
Construction	48.9	56.3	60.0
Trade	141.9	160.6	162.2
Public administration	46.7	46.9	48.5
Education			
Science, research and development	58.8	62.0	64.8
Health	39.5	39.3	40.2
Total (incl. others)	**968.3**	**1,009.9**	**1,024.1**

* Comprising manufacturing (except printing and publishing), mining and quarrying, electricity, water, logging and fishing.

Source: *Mongolian Statistical Yearbook*.

Unemployed ('000 registered at 31 December): 35.6 in 2004; 32.9 in 2005; 32.9 in 2006; 29.9 in 2007 (Sources: Asian Development Bank, *Key Indicators of Developing Asian and Pacific Countries*; Mongolian Statistical Directorate).

Health and Welfare

KEY INDICATORS

Total fertility rate (children per woman, 2006)	1.9
Under-5 mortality rate (per 1,000 live births, 2006)	42
HIV/AIDS (% of persons aged 15–49, 2007)	0.1
Physicians (per 1,000 head, 2002)	2.6
Hospital beds (per 1,000 head, 2006)	6.4
Health expenditure (2006): US $ per head (PPP)	149
Health expenditure (2006): % of GDP	5.1
Health expenditure (2006): public (% of total)	83.6
Access to water (% of persons, 2006)	72
Access to sanitation (% of persons, 2006)	50
Human Development Index (2006): ranking	112
Human Development Index (2006): value	0.720

For sources and definitions, see explanatory note on p. vi.

Agriculture

PRINCIPAL CROPS
(metric tons)

	2006	2007	2008
Cereals*	138,600	114,800	212,900
Potatoes	109,100	114,500	134,800
Other vegetables	70,400	76,400	78,900
Hay	983,300	933,100	1,009,800

* Mostly wheat, but also small quantities of barley and oats.

LIVESTOCK
(at December census)

	2006	2007	2008
Sheep	14,815,100	16,990,100	18,362,300
Goats	15,451,700	18,347,800	19,969,400
Horses	2,114,800	2,239,500	2,186,900
Cattle	2,167,900	2,425,800	2,503,400
Camels	253,500	260,600	266,400
Pigs	32,761	35,974	n.a.
Poultry	211,700	295,200	n.a.

LIVESTOCK PRODUCTS
('000 metric tons, unless otherwise indicated)

	2005	2006	2007
Meat	183.9	170.7	188.5
Beef	45.3	44.2	46.6
Mutton and goat meat	93.4	88.4	107.0
Sheep's wool	14.2	15.2	18.2
Cashmere	3.7	4.0	4.9
Hides and skins ('000)	6,927.1	6,374.0	7,219.3
Milk	425.9	450.1	465.6
Eggs (million)	21.3	19.0	46.2

Source: *Mongolian Statistical Yearbook*.

Forestry

ROUNDWOOD REMOVALS
('000 cubic metres)

	2001	2002	2003
Total	609.9	568.3	576.5

Source: *Mongolian Statistical Yearbook*.

MONGOLIA

SAWNWOOD PRODUCTION
('000 cubic metres, incl. railway sleepers)

	2005	2006	2007
Total	32.6	28.4	27.2

Source: *Mongolian Statistical Yearbook*.

Fishing

(metric tons, live weight)

	2004	2005	2006
Total catch (freshwater fishes)	305	366	289

Source: FAO.

Mining

(metric tons, unless otherwise indicated)

	2005	2006	2007
Salt	196	166	4
Coal	7,517,100	8,074,100	9,237,600
Fluorspar concentrate	134,100	137,600	131,800
Copper concentrate*	361,600	370,500	371,900
Molybdenum concentrate*	2,528	2,987	4,209
Zinc concentrate*	22,800	109,900	154,700
Iron ore	167,700	180,000	265,100
Gold (kilograms)	24,122	22,561	17,472
Crude petroleum (barrels)	200,700	366,800	850,200

* Figures refer to the gross weight of concentrates. Copper concentrate has an estimated copper content of 35%, while the metal content of molybdenum concentrate is 47% and that of zinc is 50%.

Source: *Mongolian Statistical Yearbook*.

Industry

SELECTED PRODUCTS

	2005	2006	2007
Flour ('000 metric tons)	58.3	63.6	70.8
Bread ('000 metric tons)	22.6	20.4	20.4
Confectionery ('000 metric tons)	8.3	10.2	13.0
Sheep's guts ('000 bunches)	612.3	700.4	644.3
Vodka and wine ('000 litres)	7,956.4	10,719.6	12,591.3
Beer ('000 litres)	7,996.9	7,393.0	18,377.7
Soft drinks ('000 litres)	42,260.6	38,813.2	69,732.1
Cashmere (combed) (metric tons)	581.9	1,388.2	1,554.7
Wool, scoured (metric tons)	900.0	1,100.0	1,700.0
Felt ('000 metres)	69.1	68.8	87.8
Camelhair blankets ('000 metres)	33.5	34.4	37.7
Spun thread (metric tons)	69.7	38.5	32.8
Knitwear ('000 garments)	3,448.5	4,529.3	4,220.1
Trousers ('000)	7,116.3	5,910.9	4,523.4
Shirts ('000)	10,366.0	7,208.9	4,375.4
Carpets ('000 sq metres)	586.9	606.3	658.1
Leather footwear ('000)	3.0	4.9	21.4
Felt footwear ('000 pairs)	10.5	7.8	9.3
Surgical syringes (million)	20.9	21.9	12.6
Bricks (million)	14.6	22.2	20.8
Lime ('000 metric tons)	81.2	60.4	43.3
Cement ('000 metric tons)	111.9	140.8	179.8
Ferroconcrete ('000 cu metres)	4.8	2.7	—
Copper (metric tons)	2,474.5	2,618.4	3,006.5
Electricity (million kWh)	3,418.9	3,544.2	3,700.7

Sources: *Mongolian Statistical Yearbook*; Ministry of Industry and Trade (Ulan Bator).

Finance

CURRENCY AND EXCHANGE RATES

Monetary Units
100 möngö = 1 tögrög (tughrik).

Sterling, Dollar and Euro Equivalents (31 December 2008)
£1 sterling = 1,847.78 tögrög;
US $1 = 1,267.51 tögrög;
€1 = 1,763.99 tögrög;
10,000 tögrög = £5.41 = $7.89 = €5.67.

Average Exchange Rate (tögrög per US $)
2006   1,165.37
2007   1,170.96
2008   1,165.74

BUDGET
(million tögrög)

Revenue	2005	2006	2007
Tax revenue	635,564.4	1,056,570.5	1,399,719.7
Income tax	168,078.0	462,911.3	636,138.2
Excise duty	78,959.2	100,131.8	133,757.8
Taxes on goods and services	254,017.5	331,315.2	389,912.4
Value-added tax	169,118.5	225,146.4	249,488.6
Other current revenue	128,797.8	213,703.0	324,332.1
Social insurance	98,343.2	115,498.6	163,720.7
Grants and transfers	28,147.6	29,159.3	29,378.9
Foreign aid	4,290.7	4,685.2	5,007.7
Total	792,509.8	1,299,432.7	1,753,430.7

Expenditure	2005	2006	2007
Current expenditure	566,169.9	938,053.3	1,361,462.7
Goods and services	350,310.1	646,160.6	663,525.7
Wages and salaries	132,476.2	182,819.4	292,458.8
Interest payments	20,682.8	18,081.7	18,320.2
Subsidies and transfers	195,176.9	273,811.1	679,616.8
Capital expenditure	77,145.0	159,618.7	286,980.0
Foreign financed	10,418.3	8,684.1	16,528.3
Lending (net)	74,490.3	78,986.9	100,725.7
Total	717,805.2	1,176,658.9	1,749,168.4

Source: *Mongolian Statistical Yearbook*.

2008 (million tögrög, revised forecasts): Total revenue 1,720,320.5; Total expenditure 1,815,584.4 (Source: *Töriin Medeelel*—State Information).

2009 (million tögrög, forecasts): Total revenue 1,847,794.5; Total expenditure 2,200,942.8 (Source: *Töriin Medeelel*—State Information).

INTERNATIONAL RESERVES
(US $ million at 31 December)

	2005	2006	2007
Gold (national valuation)	—	134.57	198.96
IMF special drawing rights	0.02	0.01	0.02
Reserve position in IMF	0.19	0.20	0.21
Foreign exchange	430.10	925.81	1,195.40
Total	430.31	1,060.59	1,394.59

Source: IMF, *International Financial Statistics*.

MONEY SUPPLY
(million tögrög at 31 December)

	2006	2007	2008
Currency outside banks	185,127	283,325	328,724
Demand deposits at deposit money banks	146,777	307,146	331,892
Total money	331,903	590,472	660,616

Source: IMF, *International Financial Statistics*.

MONGOLIA

COST OF LIVING
(Consumer Price Index at December; base: December 2005 = 100)

	2004	2006	2007
Foods	86.0	103.3	128.7
Clothing and footwear	100.4	107.5	110.7
Rent and utilities	95.9	108.7	121.0
All items (incl. others)	91.4	106.0	122.0

Source: *Mongolian Statistical Yearbook*.

All items (Consumer Price Index; base 2000 = 100): 144.6 in 2004; 157.7 in 2007; 197.2 in 2008 (Source: IMF, *International Financial Statistics*).

NATIONAL ACCOUNTS
Expenditure on the Gross Domestic Product
('000 million tögrög at current prices, unless otherwise indicated)

	2004	2005	2006
Government final consumption expenditure	312.8	344.5	425.3
Private final consumption expenditure	1,419.3	1,546.6	1,809.5
Increase in stocks	81.4	183.2	104.0
Gross fixed capital formation	661.0	844.5	1,199.9
Total domestic expenditure	2,474.5	2,918.8	3,538.7
Exports of goods and services Less Imports of goods and services	−230.3	−108.9	210.1
Sub-total	2,244.2	2,809.9	3,748.8
Statistical discrepancy*	−92.2	−30.3	−33.9
GDP in purchasers' values	2,152.1	2,779.6	3,715.0
GDP at constant 2005 prices	2,591.6	2,779.6	3,017.4

* Referring to the difference between the sum of the expenditure components and official estimates of GDP, compiled from the production approach.

2007 ('000 million tögrög): GDP at constant 2005 prices 3,316.5.

Source: Asian Development Bank, *Key Indicators of Developing Asian and Pacific Countries*.

Gross Domestic Product by Economic Activity
(million tögrög at current prices)

	2005	2006	2007
Agriculture	608,229.3	723,069.7	937,718.4
Fishing	105.8	111.3	113.5
Mining	608,208.9	1,112,604.7	1,248,592.9
Manufacturing	101,962.9	128,891.0	188,432.3
Electricity, heating and water supply	80,021.1	95,076.1	106,149.7
Construction	58,835.2	63,187.7	85,622.6
Trade	226,961.1	274,243.1	345,947.0
Hotels and restaurants	19,135.0	22,954.5	27,241.4
Transport and communications	309,100.0	334,975.2	415,281.4
Financial intermediation	99,966.8	106,265.7	129,921.2
Real estate, renting and other business activities	217,120.3	240,664.6	280,323.8
Public administration, defence and social security	66,847.2	117,960.8	175,525.7
Education, health and other services	151,205.2	210,444.7	301,692.9
Sub-total	2,547,698.8	3,430,449.1	4,242,562.8
Less Financial intermediation services indirectly measured	79,858.5	120,750.2	175,087.7
Gross value added in basic prices	2,467,840.3	3,309,698.9	4,067,475.1
Taxes, less subsidies, on products	311,738.0	405,253.9	490,037.0
GDP in market prices	2,779,578.3	3,714,952.8	4,557,512.1

Source: *Mongolian Statistical Yearbook*.

BALANCE OF PAYMENTS
(US $ million)

	2004	2005	2006
Exports of goods f.o.b.	872.1	1,068.6	1,545.2
Imports of goods f.o.b.	−901.0	−1,097.4	−1,356.7
Trade balance	−28.9	−28.8	188.5
Exports of services	338.4	414.5	485.8
Imports of services	−503.7	−476.0	−523.2
Balance on goods and services	−194.2	−90.8	151.0
Other income received	16.5	10.7	17.4
Other income paid	−27.7	−61.4	−161.9
Balance on goods, services and income	−205.3	−141.5	6.5
Current transfers received	230.9	177.6	179.8
Current transfers paid	−50.2	−41.2	−77.4
Current balance	−24.6	−5.1	108.9
Direct investment from abroad	92.9	184.6	344.0
Portfolio investment assets	−2.5	n.a.	n.a.
Portfolio investment liabilities	−50.0	n.a.	n.a.
Other investment assets	−132.2	−124.8	−223.4
Other investment liabilities	68.6	−14.2	60.8
Net errors and omissions	1.4	−74.9	−7.8
Overall balance	−46.3	−34.4	282.5

Source: IMF, *International Financial Statistics*.

External Trade

PRINCIPAL COMMODITIES
(US $ million, distribution by SITC)

Imports c.i.f.	2005	2006	2007
Food and live animals	121.5	142.6	208.3
Raw materials	8.7	9.8	14.3
Fuels and lubricants	314.7	434.6	634.8
Chemical products	59.7	81.0	118.3
Manufactured goods, classified chiefly by material	206.9	222.7	325.3
Machinery and vehicles	371.3	419.7	613.1
Miscellaneous manufactured articles	69.7	138.1	201.7
Total (incl. others)	1,184.3	1,485.6	2,170.1

Exports f.o.b.	2005	2006	2007
Food and live animals	12.7	26.6	33.6
Raw materials	515.9	997.4	1,366.9
Copper concentrate	326.2	635.4	811.5
Fuels and lubricants	40.2	70.4	88.9
Chemical products	1.1	1.6	2.0
Manufactured goods, classified chiefly by material	46.7	66.6	84.1
Machinery and vehicles	8.0	17.1	21.6
Miscellaneous manufactured articles	108.2	92.1	116.4
Gold, unwrought or in semi-manufactured forms	331.6	270.5	234.9
Total (incl. others)	1,064.9	1,542.8	1,949.2

Source: *Mongolian Statistical Yearbook*.

2008 (US $ million): Total imports 3,615.8; Total exports 2,539.3.

PRINCIPAL TRADING PARTNERS
(US $ million)

Imports c.i.f.	2005	2006	2007
China, People's Republic	307.3	415.0	674.3
Germany	37.6	43.0	76.5
Japan	75.5	97.6	140.2
Korea, Republic	63.7	82.5	119.6
Russia	417.9	547.8	745.0
USA	40.1	44.1	58.6
Total (incl. others)	1,184.3	1,485.6	2,170.1

MONGOLIA

Exports f.o.b.	2005	2006	2007
Canada	122.1	171.2	178.6
China, People's Republic	514.2	1,050.2	1,413.0
Italy	24.8	40.4	56.7
Russia	27.2	45.1	58.5
United Kingdom	87.1	38.6	22.1
USA	152.5	119.0	99.9
Total (incl. others)	1,064.9	1,542.8	1,949.2

Source: *Mongolian Statistical Yearbook*.

Transport

FREIGHT CARRIED
('000 metric tons)

	2006	2007	2008
Rail	14,779.8	14,076.2	14,600.0*
Road	9,189.4	9,207.1	9,300.0*
Air	2.1	1.9	1.8
Total (incl. other)	23,971.3	23,285.2	23,900.0*

* Rounded figure.

Source: Mongolian Statistical Directorate.

PASSENGERS CARRIED
(million)

	2006	2007	2008
Rail	4.3	4.5	4.4
Road	190.7	205.0	226.9
Air*	0.4	0.4	0.3
Total	195.4	209.9	231.6

* MIAT only.

Source: *Mongolian Statistical Yearbook*.

RAILWAYS
(traffic)

	2006	2007	2008
Passengers carried ('000)	4,322.8	4,473.9	4,400.0*
Freight carried ('000 metric tons)	14,779.8	14,076.2	14,600.0*
Freight ton-km (million)	9,225.6	8,372.5	n.a.

* Rounded figure.

Source: Mongolian Statistical Directorate.

ROAD TRAFFIC
(motor vehicles in use)

	2005	2006	2007
Passenger cars	87,792	94,442	100,150
Buses and coaches	11,067	11,726	13,038
Lorries, special vehicles and tankers	32,325	34,704	38,801

2008: Total vehicles 190,500.

Source: Mongolian Statistical Directorate.

CIVIL AVIATION
(traffic on scheduled services)

	2006	2007	2008
Passengers carried ('000)	364.8	388.3	365.5
International passengers ('000)	234.3	266.1	246.6
Freight carried (tons)	2,117.5	1,858.5	1,800.0

Source: Mongolian Statistical Directorate.

Tourism

FOREIGN ARRIVALS BY NATIONALITY

Country	2005	2006	2007
China, People's Republic	171,422	164,055	212,158
France	5,843	5,878	6,357
Germany	8,204	8,296	8,332
Japan	13,014	20,143	17,307
Korea, Republic	30,910	55,910	44,204
Russia	62,151	83,580	99,662
United Kingdom	5,224	5,633	6,743
USA	10,234	11,570	12,342
Total (incl. others)	338,715	385,989	451,788

Source: *Mongolian Statistical Yearbook*.

Tourism receipts (US $ million, incl. passenger transport): 205 in 2004; 203 in 2005; 261 in 2006 (Source: World Tourism Organization).

Communications Media

	2005	2006	2007
Television receivers ('000 in use)	320.0	362.5	400.1
Cable television subscribers ('000)	77.3	81.8	89.7
Telephones ('000 main lines in use)	160.5	156.6	149.6
Mobile cellular telephones ('000 subscribers)	570.9	770.1	1,175.1
Internet users ('000)	22.0	26.0	30.0
Personal computers ('000 in use)	85.0	99.6	119.5
Books (million printers' sheets)	24.3	23.6	27.7
Newspapers (million printers' sheets)	68.6	51.2	45.5

2008: 151,400 main telephone lines in use; 1,745,900 mobile cellular telephone subscribers; 101,300 cable television subscribers.

Book production (1994): 128 titles; 640,000 copies.

Newspapers (titles): 170 in 2004 (daily 6, non-daily 164).

Periodicals (titles): 60 in 2004.

Sources: mainly *Mongolian Statistical Yearbook*.

Education

(2007/08)

	Institutions	Teachers	Students ('000)
General education schools:			
Primary (grades 1–3)	71		239.7
Incomplete secondary (grades 4–8)	167	23,900	212.2
Complete secondary (grades 9–10)	516		85.6
Vocational schools			
State-owned	42	1,400	25.7
Private	14		4.2
Universities			
State-owned	11		70.0
Private	3	6,900	11.0
Other higher education			
State-owned	36		29.0
Private	106		39.8

Note: In addition, 700 students were studying abroad through inter-governmental agreements.

Pre-school institutions (2007/08): 768 kindergartens, with 3,900 teachers, attended by 105,500 infants.

Source: *Mongolian Statistical Yearbook*.

Adult literacy rate (UNESCO estimates): 97.3% (males 96.8%; females 97.7%) in 2007 (Source: UNESCO Institute for Statistics).

Directory

The Constitution

The Constitution was adopted on 13 January 1992 and came into force on 12 February of that year. It proclaims Mongolia (*Mongol Uls*), with its capital at Ulan Bator (Ulaanbaatar), to be an independent sovereign republic which ensures for its people democracy, justice, freedom, equality and national unity. It recognizes all forms of ownership of property, including land, and affirms that a 'multi-structured economy' will take account of 'universal trends of world economic development and national conditions'.

The 'citizen's right to life' is qualified by the death penalty for serious crimes, and the law provides for the imposition of forced labour. Freedom of residence and travel within the country and abroad may be limited for security reasons. The citizens' duties are to respect the Constitution and the rights and interests of others, pay taxes, and serve in the armed forces, as well as the 'sacred duty' to work, safeguard one's health, bring up one's children and protect the environment.

Supreme legislative power is vested in the Mongolian Great Khural (Assembly), a single chamber with 76 members elected by universal adult suffrage for a four-year term, with a Chairman and Vice-Chairman elected from among the members. The Great Khural recognizes the President on his election and appoints the Prime Minister and members of the Cabinet. A presidential veto of a decision of the Great Khural can be overruled by a two-thirds majority of the Khural. Decisions are taken by a simple majority.

The President is Head of State and Commander-in-Chief of the Armed Forces. He must be an indigenous citizen at least 45 years old who has resided continuously in Mongolia for the five years before election. Presidential candidates are nominated by parties with seats in the Great Khural; the winning candidate in general presidential elections is President for a four-year term.

The Cabinet is the highest executive body and drafts economic, social and financial policy, takes environmental protection measures, strengthens defence and security, protects human rights and implements foreign policy for a four-year term.

The Supreme Court, headed by the Chief Justice, is the highest judicial organ. Judicial independence is protected by the General Council of Courts. The Procurator General, nominated by the President, serves a six-year term.

Local administration in the 21 *aimag* (provinces) and Ulan Bator is effected on the basis of 'self-government and central guidance', comprising local khurals of representatives elected by citizens and governors (*zasag darga*), nominated by the Prime Minister to serve four-year terms.

The Constitutional Court, which guarantees 'strict observance' of the Constitution, consists of nine members nominated for a six-year term, three each by the Great Khural, the President and the Supreme Court. It accepts petitions from the public.

The first amendments to the Constitution, adopted by the Mongolian Great Khural in December 2000, despite opposition over procedure from the Constitutional Court, were finally approved by President Bagabandi in May 2001. The main effects of the amendments were to clarify the method of appointment of Prime Ministers, enable decision-making by a simple majority vote, and shorten the minimum length of sessions of the Khural from 75 days to 50.

The Government

PRESIDENCY

President and Commander-in-Chief of the Armed Forces: NAMBARYN ENKHBAYAR (elected 22 May 2005; inaugurated 24 June 2005).

Head of Presidential Secretariat: (vacant).

NATIONAL SECURITY COUNCIL

The President heads the National Security Council; the Prime Minister and the Chairman of the Mongolian Great Khural are its members. The Secretary is the President's national security adviser.

Chairman: NAMBARYN ENKHBAYAR.
Secretary: MANIBADRAKHYN GANBOLD.
Members: DANZANGIIN DEMBEREL, SANJAAGIIN BAYAR.

CABINET
(April 2009)

Prime Minister: SANJAAGIIN BAYAR (MPRP).
Chief Deputy Prime Minister: NOROVYN ALTANKHUYAG (DP).
Deputy Prime Minister: MIYEEGOMBYN ENKHBOLD (MPRP).

General Ministries

Minister of External Relations: SÜKHBAATARYN BATBOLD (MPRP).
Minister of Finance: SANGAJAVYN BAYARTSOGT (DP).
Minister of Justice and Home Affairs: TSENDIIN NYAMDORJ (MPRP).

Sectoral Ministries

Minister of Defence: LUVSANVANDANGIIN BOLD (DP).
Minister of Education, Culture and Science: YONDONGIIN OTGONBAYAR (MPRP).
Minister of Environment and Tourism: LÜIMEDIIN GANSÜKH (DP).
Minister of Food, Agriculture and Light Industry: TÜNJINGIIN BADAMJUNAI (MPRP).
Minister of Health: SAMBUUGIIN LAMBAA (DP).
Minister of Mineral Resources, Fuel and Power: DASHDORJIIN ZORIGT (MPRP).
Minister of Roads, Transport, Construction and Urban Development: KHALTMAAGIIN BATTULGA (DP).
Minister of Social Welfare and Labour: TÖGSJARGALYN GANDI (MPRP).
Head of Government Affairs Directorate: BADRAAGIIN DOLGOR (MPRP).

MINISTRIES AND GOVERNMENT DEPARTMENTS

All Ministries and Government Departments are in Ulan Bator.

Prime Minister's Office: State Palace, Sükhbaataryn Talbai 1, Ulan Bator; tel. (11) 322356; fax (11) 328329.

Ministry of Defence: Government Bldg 7, Dandaryn Gudamj 51, Bayanzürkh District, Ulan Bator; tel. (11) 458495; fax (11) 451727; e-mail mdef@mdef.pmis.gov.mn; internet www.mdef.pmis.gov.mn.

Ministry of Education, Culture and Science: Government Bldg 3, Baga Toiruu 44, Sükhbaatar District, Ulan Bator; tel. (11) 262480; fax (11) 323158; e-mail mecs@mecs.pmis.gov.mn; internet www.mecs.pmis.gov.mn.

Ministry of Environment and Tourism: Government Bldg 2, Negdesen Ündesnii Gudamj 5/2, Ulan Bator; tel. (11) 266171; fax (11) 321402; internet www.mne.mn.

Ministry of External Relations: Enkh Taivny Örgön Chölöö 7A, Sükhbaatar District, Ulan Bator; tel. (11) 262788; fax (11) 322127; e-mail mongmer@magicnet.mn.

Ministry of Finance: Government Bldg 2, Negdsen Ündestnii Gudamj 5/1, Chingeltei District, Ulan Bator; tel. and fax (11) 264891; internet www.mof.gov.mn.

Ministry of Food, Agriculture and Light Industry: Government Bldg 9, Enkh Taivny Örgön Chölöö 16A, Bayanzürkh District, Ulan Bator; tel. (11) 262376; fax (11) 453121; e-mail mofa@mofa.gov.mn; internet www.mofa.gov.mn.

Ministry of Health: Government Bldg 8, Olimpiin Gudamj 2, Sükhbaatar District, Ulan Bator; tel. (11) 261742; fax (11) 320916; e-mail moh@moh.mng.net; internet www.moh.mn.

Ministry of Justice and Home Affairs: Government Bldg 5, Khudaldaany Gudamj 6/1, Chingeltei District, Ulan Bator; tel. (11) 267014; fax (11) 325225; e-mail admin@mojha.gov.mn; internet www.mojha.gov.mn.

Ministry of Mineral Resources, Fuel and Power: Government Bldg 2, Negdsen Ündesnii Gudamj 5/2, Chingeltei District, Ulan Bator; tel. and fax (11) 330627; fax (11) 262626; internet www.mmre.energy.mn.

Ministry of Roads, Transport, Construction and Urban Development: Government Bldg 2, Negdsen Ündestnii Gudamj 5/2, Chingeltei District, Ulan Bator; tel. (11) 310597; fax (11) 310612; e-mail info@mrtt.pmis.gov.mn; internet www.mrtt.pmis.gov.mn.

Ministry of Social Welfare and Labour: Government Bldg 2, Negdsen Ündestnii Gudamj 5/1, Chingeltei District, Ulan Bator; tel. (11) 324918; fax (11) 328634; e-mail obaigalmaa@mswl.pmis.gov.mn; internet www.mswl.pmis.gov.mn.

Government Affairs Directorate (Cabinet Secretariat): State Palace, Sükhbaataryn Talbai 1, Ulan Bator; tel. and fax (11) 310011; internet www.pmis.gov.mn/cabinet.

President and Legislature

PRESIDENT

Office of the President: Government Palace, Sükhbaataryn Talbai, Ulan Bator; fax (11) 311121; internet www.president.mn.

Election, 22 May 2005

Candidate	Votes	%
Nambaryn Enkhbayar (MPRP)	495,975	53.46
Mendsaikhany Enkhsaikhan (Democratic Party)	182,990	19.73
Bazarsadyn Jargalsaikhan (Republican Party)	129,278	13.94
Badarchiin Erdenebat (Motherland Party)	106,762	11.51

Note: the next presidential election was scheduled for 24 May 2009.

MONGOLIAN GREAT KHURAL

Under the fourth Constitution, which came into force in February 1992, the single-chamber Mongolian Great Khural is the State's supreme legislative body. With 76 members elected for a four-year term, the Great Khural must meet for at least 50 working days in every six months. Its Chairman may act as President of Mongolia when the President is indisposed.

Chairman (Speaker): DAMDINGIIN DEMBEREL.
Vice-Chairmen: GAVAAGIIN BATKHÜÜ, NYAMAAGIIN ENKHBOLD.

General Election, 29 June 2008

Party	Seats
Mongolian People's Revolutionary Party (MPRP)	45
Democratic Party (DP)	27
Civil Courage Party (CCP)	1
Mongolian Green Party	1
Independent	1
Undeclared*	1
Total	**76**

* The winner of this seat was imprisoned on charges of fraud, relating to his conduct while in a previous post; in early 2009 the seat remained undeclared, pending the outcome of an investigation into the counting of the votes.

Election Commission

General Election Committee: Government Bldg 11, Sambuugiin Gudamj 11, Ulan Bator 38; tel. (11) 263383; e-mail gecm@mongol.net; internet www.gec.gov.mn; f. 1992; Chair. NAMSRAIJAVYN LUVSANJAV.

Political Organizations

Citizens' Movement Party: Rm 304, National Information and Technology Park, Baga Toiruu 49, Sükhbaatar District; tel. (11) 321900; f. 2007; 815 mems; Chair. NYAMAAGIIN DAVAA.

Civil Courage Party (CCP): Civil Courage Party Management Office, Baga Toiruu 24/2, Chingeltei District, Ulan Bator (POB 46/253); tel. 99098741; fax (11) 319009; e-mail oyun@mail.parl.gov.mn; f. 1994; merged with Mongolian National Solidarity Party in April 2008; also known as Citizens' Will; 35,000 mems (2008); Chair. SANJAASÜRENGIIN OYUUN; Sec.-Gen. MÖNKHCHULUUNY ZORIGT.

Democratic Party (DP): Democratic Party Central Bldg, Sükhbaataryn Talbai 8, Sükhbaatar District, Ulan Bator; tel. (11) 262055; fax (11) 312810; internet www.demparty.mn; f. 2000; est. by amalgamation of the Mongolian National Democratic Party, Mongolian Social-Democratic Party, Mongolian Democratic Party, Mongolian Democratic Renewal Party and the Mongolian Believers' Democratic Party; Mongolian Social-Democratic Party re-established as an independent party in Dec. 2004; c. 150,000 mems. (2008); Chair. NOROVYN ALTANKHUYAG; Sec.-Gen. DONDOGDORJIIN ERDENEBAT.

Development Programme Party: Rm 2, Poverty Reduction Programme Foundation Bldg, 14th Sub-District, Sükhbaatar District, Ulan Bator; tel. 96019222; f. 2007; 933 mems (2008); Chair. N. ZUUNAST.

Freedom Implementer Party: Varyeta Centre, 1st Sub-District, Bayangol District, Ulan Bator (POB 48/117); tel. 88113439; fax (11) 327899; e-mail freedom_ofmn@yahoo.com; 1,600 mems; f. 2006; Chair. SHOOVDORYN TÖMÖRSÜKH.

Mongolian Democratic Movement Party: Rm 306, Ikh Surguuliin Gudamj 3/2, 6th Sub-District, Sükhbaatar District, Ulan Bator (POB 20A/158); tel. 99009093; f. 2008; 850 mems (2008); Chair. S. BATBOLD.

Mongolian Green Party: Room 204, National Productivity Centre Bldg, Jamyangunii Gudamj, Sükhbaatar District, Ulan Bator; tel. 99114503; fax (11) 457146; f. 1990; political wing of the Alliance of Greens; 2,100 mems (2008); Chairs D. ENKHBAT, E. ZORIGT.

Mongolian Liberal Party: Ulan Bator Higher School of Intellect, 4th Sub-District, Chingeltei District, Ulan Bator (POB 23/320); tel. 99852957; fax (11) 328198; f. 1999 as Mongolian Civil Democratic New Liberal Party, renamed 2004; ruling body Little Khural of 90 mems with Leadership Council of nine; 1,300 mems (2008); Chair. B. BALDANGOMBO.

Mongolian People's Revolutionary Party (MPRP): Baga Toiruu 37/1, Ulan Bator (to be rebuilt following destruction in rioting of mid-2008); tel. and fax (6) 50067805; e-mail contact@mprp.mn; internet www.mprp.mn; f. 1921; est. as Mongolian People's Party, refounded in 1990; c. 166,000 mems (2008); ruling body Party Baga Khural (255 mems at Oct. 2007), which elects the Leadership (Steering) Council; Chair. SANJAAGIIN BAYAR; Gen. Sec. UKHNAAGIIN KHÜRELSÜKH.

Mongolian Social-Democratic Party (MSDP): Room 12, No 5 Bldg, 1st Sub-District, Sükhbaatar District, Ulan Bator (CPOB 680); tel. 99114273; fax (11) 323828; f. 1990; merged in Dec. 2000 to form part of Democratic Party; refounded Jan. 2005; c. 3,000 mems (2008); Chair. ARYAAGIIN GANBAATAR; Gen. Sec. LOSOLYN BYAMBAJARGAL.

Mongolian Traditional United Party (MTUP): Room 3, Mika Hotel, Elchingiin Gudamj, 1st Sub-District, Sükhbaatar District, Ulan Bator (POB 44/5240); tel. (11) 327690; fax (11) 310133; also known as the United Heritage (conservative) Party; f. 1994; est. as an amalgamation of the United Private Owners' Party and the Independence Party; 1,503 mems (2008); ruling body General Political Council; Gen. Sec. BATDELGERIIN BATBOLD.

Motherland Party: Motherland Party Central Bldg, Jukovyn Örgön Chölöö 7a, Ulan Bator (POB 49/404); tel. 90150268; fax (11) 453178; f. 1998; amalgamated with Mongolian Workers' Party 1999; fmrly Mongolian Democratic New Socialist Party, name changed as above Jan. 2005; c. 160,000 mems (2008); Chair. BADARCHIIN ERDENEBAT.

National New Party: No. 2 Bldg, Enkh Taivny Örgön Chölöö 12, 1st Sub-District, Sükhbaatar District, Ulan Bator; tel. (11) 260535; fax (11) 312596; f. 2006; est. after a split in the leadership of the Democratic Party upon the formation of the national solidarity government; 2,400 mems (2008); Chair. TSERENDASHIIN TSOLMON.

Party of the People: Room 301, Lucky Centre, 5th Sub-District, Sükhbaatar District, Ulan Bator; tel. 99114140; fax (11) 317982; e-mail info@ardtumen.mn; f. 2005; est. by fmr mem. of Democratic Party; 11,859 mems; Vice-Chair. B. ZORIGT.

Republican Party (RP): Rm 106, Buyan Holding Co Bldg, 3rd Sub-District, Bayangol District, Ulan Bator; tel. (11) 344844; fax (11) 344843; f. 2004; 50,000 mems (2008); Chair. BAZARSADYN JARGALSAIKHAN.

Diplomatic Representation

EMBASSIES IN MONGOLIA

Bulgaria: Olimpiin Gudamj 8, Ulan Bator (CPOB 702); tel. (11) 322841; fax (11) 324841; e-mail posolstvobg@magicnet.mn; Ambassador MIRCHO IVANOV.

China, People's Republic: Zaluuchuudyn Örgön Chölöö 5, Ulan Bator (CPOB 672); tel. (11) 320955; fax (11) 311943; internet mn.chineseembassy.org; Ambassador YU HONGYAO.

Cuba: Negdsen Ündestnii Gudamj 18, Ulan Bator (CPOB 710); tel. (11) 323778; fax (11) 327709; Ambassador MARÍA ORTENSIA FEBLES MIRABAL.

Czech Republic: Olimpiin Gudamj 12, Ulan Bator (CPOB 665); tel. (11) 321886; fax (11) 323791; e-mail czechemb@magicnet.mn; internet www.mzv.cz/ulaanbaatar; Ambassador VÁCLAV JÍLEK.

France: 3 Peace Ave, Ulan Bator (CPOB 687); tel. (11) 324519; fax (11) 319176; e-mail ambafrance@magicnet.mn; internet www.ambafrance-mn.org; Ambassador PATRICK CHRISMANT.

Germany: Negdsen Ündestnii Gudamj 7, Ulan Bator (CPOB 708); tel. (11) 323325; fax (11) 323905; internet www.ulan-bator.diplo.de; Ambassador PIUS A. FISCHER.

India: Zaluuchuudyn Örgön Chölöö 10, Ulan Bator (CPOB 691); tel. (11) 329522; fax (11) 329532; e-mail indembmongolia@magicnet.mn; Ambassador YOGESHWAR VARMA.

MONGOLIA

Japan: Olimpiin Gudamj 8, Ulan Bator (CPOB 1011); tel. (11) 320777; fax (11) 313332; e-mail eojmongol@magicnet.mn; internet www.eojmongolia.mn; Ambassador KIDOKORO TAKUO.

Kazakhstan: Diplomatic Corps Bldg 95, Apartment 2-11, Chingeltei District, Ulan Bator (CPOB 291); tel. (11) 312240; fax (11) 312204; e-mail kzemby@mbox.mn; Ambassador ORMAN NURBAYEV.

Korea, Democratic People's Republic: Khuvisgalchdyn Gudamj, Ulan Bator (CPOB 1015); tel. (11) 326153; fax (11) 330529; Ambassador PAK JONG DO.

Korea, Republic: Olimpiin Gudamj 10, Ulan Bator (CPOB 1039); tel. (11) 321548; fax (11) 311157; Ambassador CHEUNG IL.

Laos: Ikh Toiruu 59, Ulan Bator (CPOB 1030); tel. (11) 322834; fax (11) 321048; Ambassador PENG INTARAT.

Poland: Diplomatic Corps Bldg 95, Apartment 66, Ulan Bator (CPOB 1049); tel. (11) 320641; fax (11) 320576; e-mail polkonsulat@magicnet.mn; Ambassador ZBIGNIEW JERZY KULAK.

Russia: Enkh Taivny Gudamj 6-A, Ulan Bator (CPOB 661); tel. (11) 327191; fax (11) 327018; Ambassador BORIS ALEKSANDROVICH GOVORIN.

Turkey: Enkh Taivny Örgön Chölöö 5, Ulan Bator (CPOB 1009); tel. (11) 311200; fax (11) 313992; Ambassador AHMET ASIM ARAR.

United Kingdom: Enkh Taivny Gudamj 30, Ulan Bator 13 (CPOB 703); tel. (11) 458133; fax (11) 458036; Ambassador WILLIAM DICKSON (designate).

USA: Ikh Toiruu 59/1, Ulan Bator (CPOB 1021); tel. (11) 329095; fax (11) 320776; e-mail webmaster@us-mongolia.com; internet mongolia.usembassy.gov; Ambassador MARK C. MINTON.

Viet Nam: Enkh Taivny Örgön Chölöö 47, Ulan Bator (CPOB 670); tel. (11) 458917; fax (11) 458923; Ambassador UONG HUY THANH.

Judicial System

Under the fourth Constitution, judicial independence is protected by the General Council of Courts, consisting of the Chief Justice (Chairman of the Supreme Court), the Chairman of the Constitutional Court, the Procurator General, the Minister of Justice and Home Affairs and others. The Council nominates the members of the Supreme Court for approval by the Great Khural. The Chief Justice is chosen from among the members of the Supreme Court and approved by the President for a six-year term. Routine civil, criminal and administrative cases are handled by 30 rural district and inter-district courts and eight urban district courts. There are 22 appellate courts at provincial and capital city level. Some legal cases are required by law to be dealt with by the Supreme Court, appellate courts or special courts (military, railway etc.). The Procurator General and his deputies, who play an investigatory role, are nominated by the President and approved by the Great Khural for six-year terms.

Chief Justice: SODNOMDARJAAGIIN BATDELGER.

Procurator General: MONGOLYN ALTANKHUYAG.

Religion

The 1992 Constitution maintains the separation of Church and State. The Law on State-Church Relations (of November 1993) sought to make Buddhism the predominant religion and restricted the dissemination of beliefs other than Buddhism, Islam and shamanism. During the early years of communist rule Mongolia's traditional Mahayana Buddhism was virtually destroyed. In the early 1990s some 2,000 lamas established small communities at the sites of 120 former monasteries, temples and religious schools, some of which were being restored. The Kazakhs of western Mongolia are nominally Sunni Muslims. Mosques, also destroyed in the 1930s or closed subsequently, are only now being rebuilt or reopened. Traces of shamanism from the pre-Buddhist period still survive. In recent years there has been an increase in Christian missionary activity in Mongolia.

BUDDHISM

At the end of 2007 there were 138 Buddhist temples and monasteries in Mongolia, including 32 in Ulan Bator, with 1,333 lamas (monks), 2,836 employees and 1,076 students in religious schools. It is estimated that about 70% of the adult population (975,600) are Buddhists, that is, some 39% of the total population.

Living Buddha: The Ninth Javzandamba Khutagt (Ninth Bogd), Jambalnamdolchoijinjaltsan (resident in Dharamsala, India).

Asian Buddhists' Peace Assembly: Mongolian Office, Ulan Bator; Sec.-Gen. T. BULGAN.

Gandantegchinlen Monastery: Zanabazaryn Gudamj, Bayangol District, Ulan Bator; tel. (11) 360354; Centre of Mongolian Buddhists; Khamba Lama (Abbot) DEMBERELIIN CHOIJAMTS.

'Good Merit' Buddhist Society: Ulan Bator; Pres. Lama A. ERDENEBAT.

Karmapa Monastery: Khamba Lama (Abbot) DAVAASAMBUUGIIN TAIVANSAIKHAN.

Pethub Buddhist Institute: Ikh Toiruu, Chingeltei District, Ulan Bator (POB 38/105); tel. (11) 321867; fax (11) 320676; e-mail pethubmongolia@magicnet.mn; internet www.pethubmonastery.com; f. 2001 by Ven. Kushok Bakula Rinpoche (Indian Ambassador to Mongolia 1990–2000).

CHRISTIANITY

At the end of 2007 there were 89 Christian congregations in Mongolia, including 64 in Ulan Bator, with 116 priests and ministers, 668 employees and 189 students attending Christian studies.

Roman Catholic Church

The Church is represented in Mongolia by a single mission. At December 2006, according to Vatican sources, there were 340 Catholics in the country.

Catholic Mission: 18th Sub-District, Bayanzürkh District, Ulan Bator (CPOB 694); tel. (11) 458825; fax (11) 458027; e-mail info@ccmvatican.mn; internet www.ccmvatican.mn; f. 1992; Apostolic Prefect Bishop WENCESLAO PADILLA.

Protestant Church

Association of Mongolian Protestants: f. 1990; Pastor M. BOLDBAATAR.

Mongolian Evangelical Alliance: Kseni Bldg, Baga Toiruu, Chingeltei District, Ulan Bator; tel. (11) 312771; e-mail mea@magicnet.mn; internet www.mea.mn; f. 1998; a branch of the World Evangelical Alliance.

Other Christian Churches

Church of Jesus Christ of Latter-Day Saints (Mormon): Khudaldaany Gudamj, Chingeltei District, Ulan Bator; tel. (11) 312761.

Jesus Reigns Assembly: Ulan Bator; Pastor D. NARANMANDAKH.

Russian Orthodox Church: Holy Trinity Church, Jukovyn Gudamj 55, Ulan Bator; e-mail fatheraleksei@hotmail.com; internet www.pravoslavie.mn; opened in 1864, closed in 1927; services recommenced 1997 for Russian community; Head Father ALEKSEI TRUBACH.

Seventh-day Adventist Church: 5th Sub-District, Bayangol District, Ulan Bator; tel. (11) 688031; fax (11) 688032.

ISLAM

At the end of 2007 there were 20 Muslim congregations, all in western Mongolia, with 32 clergy, 90 employees and 986 students. A mosque was due to be built in Ulan Bator. It is assumed that the majority of Mongolia's ethnic Kazakh population (numbering 103,000 at the January 2000 census) are Muslim. It was stated in March 2005 that Mongolia had 32 mosques in Bayan-Ölgii and Khovd provinces and in the towns of Darkhan and Nalaikh.

Chief Imam (Ölgii): KH. BATYRBEK.

Imam of Gümyr shrine (Ölgii): DÖITENGIIN SHERKHAN.

Muslim Society: f. 1990; Hon. Pres. K. SAIRAAN; Chair. of Central Council M. AZATKHAN; Exec. Dir KH. BATYRBEK.

BAHÁ'Í FAITH

Bahá'í Society: Ulan Bator; tel. (11) 321867; f. 1989; Leader A. ARIUNAA.

SHAMANISM

Darkhad Shamanist Study Centre: Ulan Bator; Leader CH. TSERENBAAVAI.

Tengeriin Süld Shamanist Union: Ulan Bator; Pres. CH. CHINBAT.

The Press

PRINCIPAL NATIONAL NEWSPAPERS

State-owned publications in Mongolia were denationalized with effect from 1 January 1999, although full privatization could not proceed immediately. The number of newspapers published annually decreased from 134.1m. copies in 1990 to 18.5m. copies in 2003.

Ardchilal (Democracy): Democracy Palace, 11th Sub-District, Sükhbaatar District, Ulan Bator; tel. 70110187; 260 a year.

MONGOLIA

Ardyn Erkh (People's Power): Internom Shop Bldg, Amarsanaagiin Gudamj, Amaryn Gudamj 2, Ulan Bator; tel. and fax (11) 330116; e-mail ardiin_erkh@mongolnet.mn; f. 2004; original title ceased publication in 1999 (see *Ödriin Sonin*, below); subsequently assumed by new publr; 256 a year; Editor-in-Chief BAYARMAGNAIN TEMÜÜLEN; Sec. SOSORBARAMYN GANTOGOO.

Khödölmör (Labour): Sükhbaataryn Talbai 3, Ulan Bator; tel. (11) 323026; f. 1928; publ. by Confederation of Mongolian Trade Unions; 260 a year; Editor-in-Chief TSOODOLYN KHULAN; circ. 64,920.

Mongolyn Medee (Mongolian News): Jigjidjavyn Gudamj 6-1, Chingeltei District, Ulan Bator; tel. (11) 322005; fax (11) 311215; e-mail news-of-mon@mongolnet.mn; internet www.mongolmedia.com; 256 a year; Editor-in-Chief YO. GERELCHULUUN; circ. 2,900.

Montsame-giin Medee (Montsame News): Montsame News Agency, Jigjidjavyn Gudamj 8, Ulan Bator (CPOB 1514); tel. (11) 321324; e-mail localnews@montsame.mn; internet www.montsame.mn; daily news digest primarily for govt depts; 252 a year; Editor B. ZANDANKHÜÜ; Gen. Dir T. BAASANSÜREN.

Ödriin Sonin (Daily News): Mongol News Co Bldg, Ikh Toiruu, Ulan Bator; tel. 99030027; fax (11) 353897; internet www.dailynews.mn; f. 1924; restored 1990; fmrly Ardyn Erkh, Ardyn Ündesnii Erkh, Ündesnii Erkh and Ödriin Toli; 312 a year; Editor-in-Chief JAMBALYN MYAGMARSÜREN; circ. 14,200.

Öglöö Oroi (Morning and Evening): 1st Sub-District, Sükhbaatar District, Ulan Bator; tel. 99108810; e-mail ugluu_oroi2007@yahoo.com; 252 a year; Editor-in-Chief B. BOLOR-ERDENE.

Öglöönii Sonin (Morning News): No. 1 Bldg, 4th Sub-District, Chingeltei District, Ulan Bator (POB 46/411); tel. (11) 319386; fax (11) 315695; e-mail ugluuniisonin@yahoo.com; 260 a year; Editor-in-Chief O. MÖNKH-ERDENE.

Önöödör (Today): Mongol News Co Bldg, Juulchny Gudamj 40, Ulan Bator; tel. (11) 330797; fax (11) 330798; e-mail mntoday@mobinet.mn; internet www.mongolnews.mn; f. 1996; 300 a year; Editor-in-Chief B. NANDINTÜSHIG; circ. 5,500.

Önöödriin Mongol (Mongolia Today): Erkhüügiin Gudamj, Sükhbataar District, Ulan Bator (POB 20/374); tel. (11) 350345; fax (11) 354440; e-mail mongoliatoday@chinggis.com; 260 a year; Editor-in-Chief B. MÖNKHBAYAR.

Ulaanbaatar Taims (Ulan Bator Times): A. Amaryn Gudamj 1, Ulan Bator; tel. (11) 311187; fax (11) 322215; e-mail info@ubtimes.mn; internet www.ubtimes.mn; f. 1990; est. as Ulaanbaatar; publ. by Ulan Bator City Govt; 264 a year; Editor-in-Chief D. CHULUUNBAATAR; circ. 2,000.

Ünen (Truth): Baga Toiruu 11, Ulan Bator; tel. (11) 321287; fax (11) 323223; internet www.unen.mongolmedia.com; f. 1920; publ. by MPRP; 256 a year; Editor-in-Chief TSERENSODNOMYN GANBAT; circ. 8,330.

Zuuny Medee (Century's News): Amaryn Gudamj 1, Ulan Bator; tel. (11) 313499; fax (11) 321279; e-mail zuuniimedee@yahoo.com; internet www.zuuniimedee.mn; f. 1991; previously titled Zasgiin Gazryn Medee; 312 a year; Editor-in-Chief DAMDINSÜRENGIIN BOLDKHUYAG; circ 8,000.

Zuuny Shuudan (Century Post): Former Ardyn Erkh Bldg, Ikh Toiruu, Ulan Bator; tel. (11) 354632; fax (11) 354631; e-mail zuuniishuudan@yahoo.com; 312 a year; Editor-in-Chief BAASANJAVYN GANBOLD.

OTHER NEWSPAPERS AND PERIODICALS

4 dekh Zasaglal (Fourth Estate): Mongol Sonin Co, Gazar Holding Bldg, Variete Centre, Ulan Bator (POB 46A/81); tel. 99188125; e-mail dorovdekhzasaglal@yahoo.com; internet www.mongolmedia.com/4thEstate; 36 a year; Editor A. ENKHBAYAR.

81-r Suvag (Channel 81): Söüliin Gudamj, Bayangol District, Ulan Bator (POB 46A/81); tel. 96003992; fax (11) 460718; e-mail channel81@mongolmedia.com; internet www.channel81.mongolmedia.com; publishes views of the Mongolian Newspaper Asscn; 36 a year; Editor-in-Chief T. TSOGT-ERDENE.

Alag Shagai (Ankle-Bones): Bldg XVIII, Baga Toirog, Chingeltei District, Ulan Bator; tel. (11) 322005; fax (11) 311215; publ. by Mongolyn Medee; 300 a year; Editor-in-Chief YO. GERELCHULUUN.

Altangadas (Pole Star): AG Töv, Söüliin Gudamj, Bayanzürkh District, Ulan Bator (CPOB 430); tel. (11) 319411; fax (11) 319414; e-mail info@altangadas.mn; internet www.altangadas.mn; monthly political magazine; Editor NOROVYN ALTANKHUYAG.

Anagaakh Arga Bilig (The Healthy Way of Yin and Yang): Ulan Bator (CPOB 1053); tel. (11) 321367; e-mail arslny7144@magicnet.mn; twice monthly; Editor YA. ARSLAN.

Bagsh (Teacher): Rm 106, Teachers' College, Ulan Bator; tel. 99183398; f. 1989; by Ministry of Education; 24 a year.

Biznesiin Medee (Business News): Democratic Party Bldg, Sükhbaatar District, Ulan Bator (POB 20/335); tel. (11) 350541; fax (11) 350548; e-mail info@businessnews.mn; 48 a year; Editor-in-Chief S. KHÜREL.

Biznes, Uls Töriin Toim (Business and Political Review): Inforum Marketing and PR Centre, Ulan Bator; tel. (11) 319235; fax (11) 319236; e-mail toim@publicist.com; internet www.inforum.mn; monthly magazine; Editor-in-Chief A. BATPÜREV.

Bolson Yavdal (Events): Söüliin Gudamj, Sükhbaatar District, Ulan Bator (POB 36/346); e-mail bolsonyavdal@yahoo.com; 36 a year; Editor T. SANGAA.

Business Times: Chamber of Commerce and Industry, Government Bldg 11, Rm 712, Erkh Chölöönii Talbai, Ulan Bator; tel. and fax (11) 325374; e-mail marketing@mongolchamber.mn; internet www.businesstimes.mn; 36 a year; Editor BATSÜKHIIN SARANTUYAA.

Chansaa (Quality): Tergüün Chansaa Co, Jamyan Günii Gudamj, Ulan Bator; tel. (11) 335000; e-mail chansaa2005@yahoo.com; 36 a year; Editor-in-Chief DAVAADORJIIN AMARTÜVSHIN.

Deed Shüükhiin Medeelel (Supreme Court Information): Mongolian Supreme Court, Ulan Bator; quarterly journal.

Deedsiin Amidral (Elite's Life): Bldg 4, Rm 514, A. Amaryn Gudamj, Ulan Bator (CPOB 356); tel. 91189699; fax (11) 323847; e-mail deedsiinamidral@mongol.mn; internet www.elitslife.mongolmedia.com; 36 a year; Editor-in-Chief B. OTGONBAYAR.

Deedsiin Khüreelen (Elite's Forum): Ulan Bator (CPOB 1114); tel. and fax (11) 450602; e-mail deed_huree@yahoo.com; 36 a year; Publr M. SÜKHBAATAR; Editor KH. UYANGA; circ. 12,000.

Emiin Medeelel (Drug Newsletter): National Health Development Centre, Ministry of Health, Ulan Bator; tel. (11) 321485; fax (11) 320633; e-mail zorig@nchd.mn; bi-monthly magazine published by the National Health Development Centre; Editor T. ZORIG.

Erüül Mend (Health): Super Zuun Co, Ulan Bator (POB 20/412); tel. 99192239; fax (11) 321278; e-mail dr_jargal_d@yahoo.com; internet www.erul_mend.net; publ. by Ministry of Health; monthly; Editor D. JARGALSAIKHAN; circ. 5,600.

Il Tovchoo (Clear Summary): Chölööt Mongol Co Bldg, 8th Sub-District, Chingeltei District, Ulan Bator; tel. 91918674; Editor TSEND-AYUUSHIIN BUYANZAYAA.

Khani (Spouse): National Agricultural Co-operative Members' Association Bldg, Rm 201, Enkh Taivny Gudamj 18A, Bayanzürkh District, Ulan Bator (POB 49/600); tel. (11) 460698; fax (11) 458550; e-mail khani_sonin@yahoo.com; women and family issues; 36 a year; Editor-in-Chief DEMBERELIIN BATSÜKH; circ. 64,920.

Khiimori (Wind-Horse): Rm 305, Mongol News Co Bldg, Ikh Toiruu 20, Sükhbaatar District, Ulan Bator; tel. (11) 354565; 36 a year; Editor-in-Chief A. ERDENETUYAA.

Khökh Tolbo (Blue Spot): Mon-Azi Co Bldg, Ulan Bator (POB 24/306); tel. (11) 313405; fax (11) 312794; 36 a year; Publr BATYN ERDENEBAATAR; Editor-in-Chief E. ENKHTSOLMON; circ. 3,500.

Khöröngiin Zakh Zeel (Capital Market): Mongolian Stock Exchange, Sükhbaataryn Talbai 2, Ulan Bator; tel. (11) 313511; fax (11) 325170; e-mail info@mse.mn; monthly; Editor RENTSENGIIN SODKHÜÜ.

Khümüün Bichig (People and Script): Montsame News Agency, Jigjidjavyn Gudamj 8, Ulan Bator (CPOB 1514); tel. (11) 329486; fax (11) 327857; e-mail khumuun@montsame.mn; current affairs in Mongolian classical script; 48 a year; Editor T. GALDAN; circ. 15,000.

Khuuli Züin Medee (Legal News): Ministry of Justice and Home Affairs, Ulan Bator; f. 1990; 24 a year.

Khuviin Soyol (Personal Culture): Rm 2, Block 39, behind No. 5 School, Baga Toiruu, Ulan Bator (CPOB 1254); 24 a year; Editor BEKHBAZARYN BEKHSÜREN.

Leaders: Ulan Bator (POB 46A/455); tel. (11) 311322; magazine about political and business leaders; Editor AYUURBUMYAAGIIN LKHAGVA.

Mash Nuuts (Top Secret): Mongol Shaazan Bldg, Ulan Bator (POB 49/113); tel. (11) 328675; fax (11) 330690; e-mail tsecret@mongolnet.mn; 32 a year; Editor-in-Chief ONONGIIN CHINZORIG.

Mongolian Business Review: Green House, Baga Toiruu 29, Ulan Bator; tel. (11) 321312; Editor BADARALYN ZULBAYAR.

Mongoljin Goo (Mongolian Beauty): Mongolian Women's Federation, Ulan Bator (POB 44/717); tel. (11) 320790; fax (11) 367406; e-mail monwofed@magicnet.mn; f. 1990; monthly; Editor J. ERDENECHIMEG; circ. 3,000.

Mongolyn Anagaakh Ukhaan (Mongolian Medicine): Ulan Bator (CPOB 696); tel. (11) 112306; fax (11) 451807; e-mail nymadawa@hotmail.com; publ. by Scientific Society of Mongolian Physicians and Mongolian Academy of Sciences; quarterly; Editor-in-Chief Prof. PAGVAJAVYN NYAMDAVAA.

Mongolyn Khödöö (Mongolian Countryside): Agricultural University, Zaisan, Ulan Bator; tel. (11) 345211; e-mail haaint@magicnet.mn; publ. by Mongolian State University of Agriculture and

MONGOLIA

Academy of Agricultural Sciences; 24 a year; Editor-in-Chief Prof. BEGZIIN DORJ.

Mongolyn Neg Ödör (One Day of Mongolia): Bldg 31, Bayanzürkh District, Ulan Bator (POB 44/764); tel. (11) 450103; fax (11) 460718; e-mail onedai@mongolmedia.com; 48 a year; Editor-in-Chief SH. OTGONSETSEG.

Myangany Zuuch (Millennium Messenger): Mönkh Press Co, West side of Choijin Lama Temple, Sükbataar District, Ulan Bator (POB 46/390); tel. and fax (11) 319745; e-mail monkh@mobinet.mn; internet www.newspapers.mn; 36 a year; Deputy Editor G. ENKHJARGAL.

Notstoi Medee (Important News): Maximus Press Co, Ulan Bator (POB 20/359); tel. (11) 316953; 36 a year; Editor B. GALSANSÜKH.

Nyam Garig (Sunday): Mongol News Co Bldg, Juulchny Gudamj, Ulan Bator; tel. (11) 330797; fax (11) 330798; e-mail weekend@mongolnews.mn; supplement of *Önöödör*; Editor-in-Chief B. BOLDKHÜÜ.

Odoo Tsag (The Present): Baga Toiruu, Sükbataar District, Ulan Bator (POB 46A/161); tel. 88181260; 24 a year; Editor D. ÖRNÖKH.

Onigoo (Jokes): Konsulyn Gudamj 5-13, Bayanzürkh District, Ulan Bator (POB Sky Post 46/50); tel. 70150001; e-mail onigoosonin@yahoo.com; Editor S. SARANCHIMEG.

Önöögiin Törkh (Present Image): Rm 107, Mongolian Red Cross Society Bldg, Sükbataar District, Ulan Bator (POB 48/282); tel. and fax (11) 319007; 24 a year; Editor-in-Chief D. BADAMGARAV.

Sankhüügiin Medee (Financial News): Ulan Bator; 36 a year; Editor L. DONDOG.

Serüüleg (Alarm Clock): Business Plaza Bldg 2, Enkh Taivny Örgön Chölöö, Ulan Bator (CPOB 1094); tel. (11) 455570; fax (11) 459182; e-mail a.tsaschikher@yahoo.com; 48 a year; Editor-in-Chief BAYANMÖNKHIIN TSOOJCHULUUNTSETSEG; circ. 28,600.

Setgüülch (Journalist): Ulan Bator (POB 46/600); tel. (11) 325388; fax (11) 313912; f. 1982; publ. by Union of Journalists; journalism, politics, literature, art, economy; quarterly; Editor TSENDIIN ENKHBAT.

Shar Sonin (Yellow Newspaper): Ulan Bator (POB 46A/225); tel. (11) 313984; e-mail thesharsonin@yahoo.com; 36 a year; Editor B. NAMUUN.

Shine Erkh Chölöö (New Freedom): Ödriin Sonin Bldg, Ikh Toiruu, Ulan Bator (CPOB 2590); tel. and fax 70137010; e-mail erkhcholoo2007@yahoo.com; quarterly; social and political affairs; Editor-in-Chief TS. OYUUNCHIMEG.

Shine Yörtönts (New World): Empathy Centre, Baga Toiruu, 6th Sub-District, Ulan Bator; tel. (11) 313019; fax (11) 324657; quarterly; popular science magazine; Editor B. SARNAI.

Shinjlekh Ukhaany Akademiin Medee (Academy of Sciences News): Yörönkhii Said Amaryn Gudamj 1, Ulan Bator; tel. (11) 265163; fax (11) 261993; e-mail mas@mas.ac.mn; internet www.mas.ac.mn; f. 1961; publ. by Academy of Sciences; quarterly; Editor-in-Chief DUGER REGDEL.

Shuurkhai Zar (Quick Advertisement): Ulan Bator Bank Bldg, Rm 104, 1st Floor, Ulan Bator (POB 46A/151); tel. (11) 313778; e-mail shirevger@mobinet.mn; 100 a year; Editor E. TSEYENKHORLOO.

Solongo (Rainbow): Baruunselbe Service Centre, Ulan Bator (POB 23/628); tel. 99860276; f. 1992; monthly; Deputy Editor-in-Chief T. BAYANJARGAL.

Soyombo: Ministry of Defence, Ulan Bator; tel. 91177221; f. 1924; est. as *Ardyn Tsereg* (People's Soldier); renamed *Ekh Orny Tölöö* (For the Motherland), then *Ulaan Od* (Red Star); Dep. Editor-in-Chief Lt-Col G. NYAMDORJ.

Strategi Sudlal (Strategic Studies): Institute of Strategic Studies, Ulan Bator (CPOB 870); tel. (11) 260710; fax (11) 324055; f. 1991; 4 a year; owned by National Security Council; Editor DAVAADORJ BEGZ.

Tavan Tsagarig (Five Rings): National Olympic Committee, Ikh Toiruu 20, Ulan Bator; tel. (11) 70111095; fax (11) 343541; e-mail t_ts_sport@yahoo.com; noc@olympic.mn; internet www.mongolnews.mn/tavantsagarig; f. 1995; 100 a year; Editor-in-Chief BYAMBAA TSAGAANBAATAR.

Tengerleg Khümüüs (Heavenly People): Soyombo Press Co, Partizany Gudamj 17, Sükbataar District, Ulan Bator (POB 44/716); tel. (11) 325250; fax (11) 330383; internet www.soyomboprinting.com; 36 a year; Dir-Gen D. AMBARBAYASGALAN; Editor P. JARGALSAIKHAN.

Tonshuul (Woodpecker): Enkh Taivny Örgön Chölöö 4, Rm 148, Bayanzürkh District (CPOB 322), Ulan Bator; tel. 99118668; fax (11) 459265; e-mail ariun_tonshuul@yahoo.com; fortnightly magazine of cartoons, humour and satire; Editor TS. ARIUNAA.

Töriin Medeelel (State Information): Secretariat of the Mongolian Great Khural, Government Palace, Ulan Bator; tel. (11) 265958; fax (11) 322866; e-mail luvsanjav@mail.parl.gov.mn; internet www.parl.gov.mn; f. 1990; presidential and governmental decrees, state laws; 48 a year; circ. 5,000.

Tsenkher Delgets (Light Blue Screen): Ulan Bator; tel. (11) 312010; fax (11) 311850; e-mail bsnews@magicnet.mn; weekly guide to TV and radio programmes; Editor-in-Chief GALIGAAGIIN BAYARSAIKHAN.

Tsonkh (Window): Chingisiin Örgön Chölöö 1, Ulan Bator (CPOB 1085); tel. (11) 310717; publ. by the Democratic Party's Political Department; 24 a year.

Tsog (Ember): Mongolian Union of Writers, Ulan Bator; literary quarterly.

Üg (The Word): Bldg 86, Chingeltei District, Ulan Bator; tel. 55152675; fax (11) 329795; e-mail ugsonin@mol.mn; fmrly the journal of the Mongolian Social Democratic Party (until 2000); Editor-in-Chief A. GANBAATAR.

Uls Töriin Sonin (Political Newspaper): Delta Centre, Juulchny Gudamj, Chingeltei District, Ulan Bator (POB 46/796); tel. 99095040; fax (11) 312608; internet pnews.delhii.net; f. 2005 following closure of the *Mongol Times*; 48 a year; Editor GANTÖMÖRIIN UYANGA.

Utga Zokhiol Urlag (Literature and Art): Mongolian Union of Writers, Sükhbaataryn Gudamj 11, Ulan Bator (POB 46A/555); tel. (11) 318035; fax (11) 320817; e-mail info@utgazokhiol.mn; f. 1955; 36 a year; Editor J. BAYARAA; circ. 3,000.

Zar Medee (Advertisement News): Government Bldg 5, 1st Floor, Rm 130, Juulchny Gudamj, Chingeltei District, Ulan Bator; tel. and fax (11) 312379; e-mail advertisement-news@yahoo.com; personal and company advertisements; 100 a year; Editor D. BAYASGALAN.

Zindaa (Ranking): Room 305, former Ardyn Erkh Bldg, Sükhbaatar District, Ulan Bator; tel. (11) 354545; fax (11) 354555; internet www.zindaa.mongolmedia.com; wrestling news; 48 a year; Editor-in-Chief KH. MANDAKHBAYAR.

FOREIGN LANGUAGE PUBLICATIONS

Inspiring Mongolia: Mongolian National Chamber of Commerce and Industry, Sambuugiin Gudamj 11, Ulan Bator 38; tel. (11) 312501; fax (11) 324620; e-mail marketing@mongolchamber.mn; internet www.mongolchamber.mn; magazine in English, publ. twice a year; Editor-in-Chief SAMBUUGIIN DEMBEREL.

Menggu Xiaoxi Bao (News of Mongolia): Montsame News Agency, Ulan Bator (CPOB 1514); tel. (11) 320077; e-mail mgxxbao@chinggis.com; f. 1929; weekly; in Chinese; Sec. P. OYUUNTSETSEG.

Mongolian Magazine: Interpress Publishers, Ulan Bator; f. 2004; English-language monthly illustrated magazine about Mongolian history, culture, nature, life and customs.

Mongolia This Week: Ulan Bator; tel. and fax (11) 318339; e-mail mongoliathisweek@mobinet.mn; internet www.mongoliathisweek.mn; weekly in English, online daily; Editor-in-Chief D. NARANTUYAA; English Editor ERIC MUSTAFA.

Mongolia Today: Montsame News Agency, Jigjidjavyn Gudamj 8, Ulan Bator (CPOB 1514); quarterly; in English; Editor-in-Chief G. PÜREVSAMBUU.

Mongoliya Segodnya (Mongolia Today): Zoos Goyol Co Bldg, Chingeltei District, Ulan Bator (POB 46/609); tel. and fax (11) 324141; weekly; in Russian; Editor-in-Chief DÜNGER-YAICHILIIN SOLONGO.

The Mongol Messenger: Montsame News Agency, Jigjidjavyn Gudamj 8, Ulan Bator (CPOB 1514); tel. and fax (11) 325512; e-mail monmessenger@magicnet.mn; internet www.mongolmessenger.mn; f. 1991; weekly newspaper in English; owned by Montsame national news agency; Editor-in-Chief INDRA BORKHONDOIN; circ. 2,000.

Mongoru Tsushin (Mongolia News): Montsame News Agency, Jigjidjavyn Gudamj 8, Ulan Bator (CPOB 1514); weekly; in Japanese.

Montsame Daily News: Montsame News Agency, Jigjidjavyn Gudamj 8, Ulan Bator (CPOB 1514); tel. (11) 314574; fax (11) 327857; e-mail montsame@magicnet.mn; daily English news digest for embassies, etc.; Editor-in-Chief BAYANBATYN BAYASGALAN.

Novosti Mongolii (News of Mongolia): Montsame News Agency, Jigjidjavyn Gudamj 8, Ulan Bator (CPOB 1514); tel. (11) 310157; fax (11) 327857; e-mail novosty_mongolii@yahoo.co.uk; f. 1942; weekly; in Russian; Editor-in-Chief DÜGERSÜRENGIIN ARIUNBOLD.

The UB Post: Mongol News Co, Juulchny Gudamj, Ulan Bator; tel. (11) 70111095; fax (11) 330798; e-mail ubpost@mongolnews.mn; internet ubpost.mongolnews.mn; f. 1996; weekly; in English; Editor-in-Chief SUMIYABAZAR CHOIMBOROLJAV; circ. 4,000.

NEWS AGENCIES

Montsame (Mongol Tsakhilgaan Medeenii Agentlag) (Mongolian News Agency): Jigjidjavyn Gudamj 8, Ulan Bator (CPOB 1514); tel. (11) 266904; fax (11) 327857; e-mail montsame@magicnet.mn; internet www.montsame.mn; f. 1921; govt-controlled; Gen. Dir T. BAASANSÜREN; Editor-in-Chief B. NOMINCHIMED.

MONGOLIA

Mongolyn Medee (Mongolian News): Public Radio and Television, Khuvisgalyn Zam, Ulan Bator; Dir Ts. SÜKHBAATAR.

PRESS ASSOCIATIONS

Mongolian Newspaper Association: Ulan Bator; Pres. R. KHADBAATAR; Vice-Pres. D. BATSÜKH.

United Association of National Daily Newspapers: c/o Önöödör, Mongol News Co, Juulchny Gudamj, Ulan Bator; f. 2006; Pres. (vacant).

Publishers

The ending of the state monopoly has led to the establishment of several small commercial publishers, including Shuvuun Saaral (Ministry of Defence), Mongol Khevlel and Soyombo Co, Mongolpress (Montsame), Erdem (Academy of Sciences), Süülenkhüü children's publishers, Sudaryn Chuulgan, Interpress, Sükhbaatar Co, Öngöt Khevlel, Admon, Odsar, Khee Khas Co, etc.

Admon Co: Amaryn Gudamj 2, Sükhbaatar District, Ulan Bator (CPOB 92); tel. (11) 329253; fax (11) 327251; e-mail admon@magicnet.mn; Dir R. ENKHBAT.

Darkhan Sergelen Co: Naadamchdyn Gudamj, Darkhan; tel. (37) 23049; fax (37) 24741; internet www.munkhiin-useg.mn.

Chölööt Khevlel San (Free Press Foundation): Ikh Toiruu 11B, Ulan Bator (POB 20/357); tel. (11) 350016; e-mail mpfnph@magicnet.mn; f. 1996; the country's largest printer of newspapers and the biggest pre-press service provider; Man. Dir BAASTYN GALSANDORJ.

Khevleliin Khüreelen (Press Institute NGO): Ikh Toiruu 11, Sükhbaatar District, Ulan Bator; tel. and fax (11) 350012; e-mail ts_byambaa12@yahoo.com; internet www.owc.org.mn/pressinstitute; Chair. Ts. ENKHBAT.

Mongol News Group: Mongol News Group Bldg, Juulchny Gudamj, Ulan Bator; tel. (11) 330797; fax (11) 330798; e-mail mntoday@mobinet.mn; f. 1996; owns newspapers *MN-Önöödör*, *Tavan Tsagarig*, *Nyam Garig* and *The UB Post*, TV Channel 25 and ABM Co printers; Pres. B. NANDINTÜSHIG.

Mönkhiin Üseg Group: Teeverchdiin Gudamj, Songinokhairkhan District, Ulan Bator; tel. (11) 320807; fax (11) 321318; e-mail munuseg@mbox.mn; internet www.munkhiin-useg.mn; Chair. G. BATMÖNKH.

Novum Co: Migma Bldg, Ulan Bator; tel. (11) 319140; fax (11) 319319; e-mail print@mynovum.com; internet www.mynovum.com.

Öngöt Khevlel Co: Amaryn Gudamj 2, Sükhbaatar District, Ulan Bator; tel. (11) 323121; fax (11) 329519; e-mail ungut_khevlel@mongolnet.mn.

Soyombo Printing Co: Natsagdorjiin Gudamj, Sükhbaatar District, Ulan Bator; tel. (11) 325052.

Sükhbaatarprint Co: Amaryn Gudamj 2, Sükhbaatar District, Ulan Bator; tel. and fax (11) 320504; e-mail sukhprint@magicnet.mn.

Zurag Züi Co (Cartography): Ikh Toiruu 15, Ulan Bator; tel. (11) 322164; e-mail cart@magicnet.mn; publisher and retailer of maps and atlases.

PUBLISHERS' ASSOCIATIONS

Local Press and Information Association: Ulan Bator; f. 2006; Pres. S. SHARAVDORJ.

Mongolian Book Publishers' Association: Ulan Bator; Exec. Dir S. TSERENDORJ.

Mongolian Free Press Publishers' Association: POB 306, Ulan Bator 24; tel. and fax (11) 313405; Pres. BATYN ERDENEBAATAR.

Broadcasting and Communications

TELECOMMUNICATIONS

Digital exchanges have been installed in Ulan Bator, Darkhan, Erdenet, Sükhbaatar, Bulgan and Arvaikheer, while radio-relay lines have been digitalized between: Ulan Bator–Darkhan–Sükhbaatar; Ulan Bator–Darkhan–Erdenet; and Dashinchilen–Arvaikheer. Mobile telephone companies operate in Ulan Bator and other central towns, in addition to Arvaikheer, Sainshand and Zamyn-Üüd. By May 2005 a total of 1,776 km of fibre optic cable had been installed in Mongolia, with plans to lay another 1,400 km by the end of the year. The Ulan Bator–Bulgan cable was under construction.

Bodicom: Ulan Bator; tel. (11) 325144; fax (11) 318486; e-mail bodicom@mongolnet.mn; internet www.bodicom.mn.

Datacom: Rm 112, Mongolian Technology National Park, Baga Toiruu, Sükhbaatar District, Ulan Bator; tel. (11) 329688; fax (11) 320210; internet www.datacom.mn; service provider for Magicnet connection to internet; Dir DANGAASÜRENGIIN ENKHBAT.

G-Mobile: Gem International Co., 1st Sub-District, Chingeltei District, Ulan Bator; tel. (11) 333636; e-mail info@g-mobile.mn; internet www.g-mobile.mn; Dir-Gen. R. GANZORIG.

Incomnet: Enkh Taivny Örgön Chölöö, Bayanzürkh District, Ulan Bator (CPOB 582); tel. (11) 480606; fax (11) 480808; e-mail info@icn-mn.net; internet www.icn-mn.net; internet service provider, cable TV, satellite communications.

MagicNet Co: Rm 222, Ground Floor, Science and Technology Information Centre, Ulan Bator; tel. (11) 312061; fax (11) 311496; e-mail info@magicnet.mn; internet www.magicnet.mn; internet service provider.

MCSCom: MCS Plaza, 3rd Floor, Baga Toiruu 49, Ulan Bator; tel. (11) 327854; fax (11) 311323; e-mail mcscom@mcs.mn; internet www.mcscom.mn; internet service provider.

Medeelel Kholboony Süljee: Khasbaataryn Gudamj, Bayangol District, Ulan Bator; tel. and fax (11) 304824; internet www.icnc.mn; installation of digital radio relays and fibre optic cables for communications and internet, television and radio.

Micom: Mongol Tsakhilgaan Kholboo Co Bldg, Sükhbaataryn Talbai, Ulan Bator (CPOB 1124); tel. (11) 313229; fax (11) 322473; internet www.micom.mn; Dir CH. NARANTUNGALAG.

MobiCom: Mobicom Corp. Bldg, Enkh Taivny Örgön Chölöö 3/1, Ulan Bator; tel. (11) 318115; fax (11) 310411; e-mail feedback@mobicom.mn; internet www.mobicom.mn; mobile telephone service provider; Exec. Dir FUMIAKI SHIGA; Dir-Gen. R. ARVINTSOGT.

Moncom: Ulan Bator (POB 51/207); tel. (11) 329409; e-mail ch.enkhmend@hotmail.com; pager services.

Mongolia Telecom: Mongol Tsakhilgaan Kholboo Co Bldg, Sükhbaataryn Talbai, Ulan Bator (CPOB 1166); tel. (11) 320597; fax (11) 325412; e-mail mt@mtcone.net; internet www.mongol.net; 54.6% state-owned, 40.0% owned by Korea Telecom; Pres. and CEO OONOIGIIN SHAALUU.

Newcom LLC: Enkh Taivny Örgön Chölöö 3/1, Bayanzürkh District, Ulan Bator; tel. (11) 313183; fax (11) 318521; e-mail secretary@newcom.mn; internet www.newcom.mn.

Newtel Co: Sambuugiin Gudamj 36, Chingeltei District, Ulan Bator; tel. and fax (11) 311581; e-mail marketing@ntc.mn; internet www.ntc.mn; Exec. Dir D. BOLOR.

Orbitnet: New Horizon Bldg, Olimpiin Gudamj 6, Sükhbaatar District, Ulan Bator; tel. (11) 323705; fax (11) 312699; e-mail orbitnet@mcs.mn; internet www.orbitnet.mcs.mn.

Railcom: Mongolian Railways (MTZ), Zamchny Gudamj 1, Ulan Bator (CPOB 376); tel. (11) 252525; e-mail info@railcom.mn; internet www.railcom.mn; telephone, TV and internet service provider.

Skynetcom: 1st Sub-District, Chingeltei District, Ulan Bator; tel. 77007700; e-mail info@skynet.com; internet www.skynetcom.mn; mobile telephone service provider.

Skytel: Skytel Plaza Centre, Chingisiin Örgön Chölöö, Ulan Bator; tel. (11) 319191; fax (11) 318487; e-mail skytel@mongol.net; internet www.skytel.mn; mobile telephone and voice mail service provider; Mongolia-Republic of Korea jt venture; Dir-Gen. R. GANBOLD; Marketing Man. G. TÜVSHINTÖGS.

Unitel: Rokmon Bldg, Ündsen Khuuliin Gudamj 24, Ulan Bator; tel. (11) 328888; fax (11) 330708; e-mail info@unitel.mn; internet www.unitel.mn; f. 2005 by MBSB Telecom, Uangel Corpn (Republic of Korea) and Dream Choice Co (Canada); mobile telephone service provider; Dir-Gen. Ts. AMARAA.

Ulusnet: TEDY Centre, Sambuugiin Gudamj 18, Chingeltei District, Ulan Bator; tel. (11) 322686; e-mail service@ulusnet.mn; internet www.ulusnet.mn; Mongolia's first Wimax service provider.

BROADCASTING

A 1,900-km radio relay line from Ulan Bator to Altai and Ölgii provides direct-dialling telephone links as well as television services for western Mongolia. New radio relay lines have been built from Ulan Bator to Choibalsan, and from Ulan Bator to Sükhbaatar and Sainshand. Most of the population is in the zone of television reception, following the inauguration of relays via satellites operated by the International Telecommunications Satellite Organization (INTELSAT). In 2004 Mongolia had 30 radio stations and 35 television stations.

All provincial centres receive two channels of Mongolian national television; and all district centres can receive television, although only one-third can receive Mongolian television. At the beginning of 2005 the first legislative measures were taken to end state control, with the passing of the Law on Public Broadcasting, the provisions of which entered into force on 1 July 2005, creating an independent public service broadcaster to be known as Public Radio and Television. Also in 2005 it was planned to extend television coverage (UBS, TV-5, TV-9 and Channel 25) to outlying areas of Ulan Bator, includ-

MONGOLIA

Directory

ing Partizan, Songino and Gachuurt, by installing additional local transmitters.

Public Radio and Television (ONRT): Khuvisgalyn Zam 3, Bayangol District, Ulan Bator; f. 2006; replaced the govt-run Directorate of Radio and Television Affairs; Chair. of National Council KHAIDAVYN CHILAAJAV; Dir-Gen. MYANGANBUUGIIN NARANBAATAR; Editor-in-Chief DEMBERELIIN ERDENETSETSEG.

Radio

Mongolian National Public Radio: Khuvisgalyn Zam 3, Bayangol District, Ulan Bator; tel. (11) 323096; f. 1934; operates for 17 hours daily on three long-wave and one medium-wave frequency, and VHF; programmes in Mongolian (two) and Kazakh; part of Public Radio and Television; Dir B. PÜREVDASH; Dep. Dir B. KHANDDOLGOR.

Voice of Mongolia: Ulan Bator; e-mail radiomongolia@magicnet.mn; external service of Mongolradio; broadcasts in Russian, Chinese, English and Japanese on short wave; Dir B. NARANTUYAA.

AE and JAAG Co: Amryn Gudamj 2, Ulan Bator (POB 20/126); tel. (11) 352463; fax (11) 326545; e-mail aejaag@magicnet.mn; f. 1996; broadcasts for 4.5–5 hours daily; CEO Z. ALTAI.

FM 96.3 Avtoradio: Ulan Bator.

FM 98.9 Hi Fi (Hit First): Khair Tokhoi Co Bldg, Chingisiin Örgön Chölöö 10/1, Ulan Bator; tel. and fax (11) 330989; e-mail hifi@hi-fi.mn; internet www.hi-fi.mn.

FM 99.3 Ineemseglel (Smile): Central Palace of Culture, Sükhbaatar District, Ulan Bator; tel. 99147994; fax (11) 319789; Dir KH. IKHBAYAR.

FM 100.1 Kiss: Ulan Bator; tel. (11) 312234.

FM 100.5 Minii Mongol (My Mongolia): Central Palace of Culture, Sükhbaatar District, Ulan Bator; tel. (11) 323599.

FM 100.9 Khökh Tenger (Blue Sky Radio): Mongolian National Television Bldg, Chingeltei District, Ulan Bator; tel. (11) 320522; broadcasts for 12 hours Mon. to Sat. and shorter hours on Sun; short-wave transmitter on 4,850 kHz; Dir L. AMARZAYAA.

FM 101.7 Niisleliin Radio: Narny Titem, 5th Sub-District, Chingeltei District, Ulan Bator; tel. 70110981; fax (11) 322472; Dir U. BULGAN.

FM 102.1 Ekh Oron (Homeland): Central Palace of Culture, Sükhbaatar District, Ulan Bator; tel. (11) 327383; fax (11) 322472; operated by the Open Information Foundation.

FM 102.5 Radio Ulan Bator: Ulan Bator; tel. (11) 329269; Dir-Gen. U. BULGAN.

FM 103.1: Ulan Bator; BBC World Service Relay.

FM 103.6: Amaryn Gudamj, Sükhbaatar District, Ulan Bator; tel. 70110632; TV-9's radio station.

FM 104 Life: Alaska Centre, 13th Sub-District, Bayanzürkh District, Ulan Bator; tel. (11) 463782.

FM 104.5 Ger Büliin Radio (Family Radio): Mamba Datsan, Bayanzürkh District, Ulan Bator; tel. (11) 461045; fax (11) 452987.

FM 105 Tany Derged (Near You): Central Palace of Culture, Sükhbaatar District, Ulan Bator; tel. (11) 319789.

FM 105.5 Info Radio: Russian Foundation, Od Plaza, Sükhbaatar District, Ulan Bator; tel. (11) 319492; fax (11) 313687; internet www.inforadio.mn.

FM 106.6: Democratic Party Bldg, Chingisiin Örgön Chölöö, Ulan Bator; tel. (11) 329353; Voice of America news and information in Mongolian, English lessons and music.

FM 107.5 Shine Dolgion (New Wave): Namyanjügiin Gudamj 40, Bayanzürkh District, Ulan Bator; tel. and fax (11) 452444; e-mail info@fm1075.mn; internet www.fm1075.mn; relays of Voice of America broadcasts in English and Russian, entertainment programmes; Dir TS. ARIUNAA.

There are seven long- and short-wave radio transmitters and 49 FM stations in 23 towns.

Television

Bolovsrol (Education) TV Channel: Bayangol District, Behind Mongolian National Public TV Bldg, Ulan Bator; tel. (11) 300722; fax (11) 300710; e-mail develop@edutv.mn; internet www.edutv.mn; f. 2005; broadcasts 20–22 hours a day; Gen. Dir NATSAGDORJ SANJ.

C-1: Supermarket No. 1, Tömörchnii Gudamj, Chingeltei District, Ulan Bator; tel. (11) 312126; fax (11) 313651; f. 2006; daily 17-hour transmissions; news link with Reuters; Dir BEN MOYLE.

Channel 25: Mongol News Bldg, Juulchny Gudamj, Chingeltei District, Ulan Bator; tel. (11) 321989; daily 18-hour transmissions; Dir. ZORIGIIN ALTAI; Gen. Man. AYUUSHIIN AVIRMED.

Eagle Broadcasting Co: Erkhüüd Centre, Lkhagvasürengiin Gudamj, Ulan Bator; tel. (11) 463088; fax (11) 463087; internet www.eagle-tv.mn; f. 1994; several news bulletins a day; Christian message; commenced operations in 1996; broadcasts restarted 2005 after two years off air; Pres. THOMAS TERRY.

Khiimori Co: Bldg 3A, No. 2 Combined Clinical General Hospital, Ulan Bator; tel. (11) 458531; fax (11) 458569; f. 1995; cable TV service provider.

Mongolian National Public Television (MNTV): Mongolian National Television, Khuvisgalyn Zam 3, Bayangol District, Ulan Bator (CPOB 365); tel. (11) 327214; fax (11) 328939; e-mail mrtv@magicnet.mn; f. 1967; daily 16-hour transmissions, except Mon; short news bulletins in English Mon., Wed. and Fri; part of Public Radio and Television; Dir A. GANBAATAR.

New TV (NTV): Media Group Co Bldg, Chingisiin Örgön Chölöö, Khan-Uul District, Ulan Bator; tel. (11) 326047; internet www.ntv.mn.

Sansar KATV: Sansar Bldg, Enkh Taivny Örgön Chölöö, 3rd Sub-District, Chingeltei District, Ulan Bator; tel. (11) 313752; fax (11) 313770; e-mail sansarll@magicnet.mn.

Supervision KATV: No. 3 Bldg, Enkh Taivny Örgön Chölöö, 3rd Sub-District, Bayanzürkh District, Ulan Bator; tel. (11) 455082; fax (11) 320396; internet www.supervision.mn.

TV-5: Sapporo Centre, 1st Sub-District, Songinokhairkhan District; tel. (11) 680327; fax (11) 680326; e-mail feedback@tv5.mn; internet www.tv5.mn; daily 18-hour transmissions.

TV-8: Amaryn Gudamj, 8th Sub-District, Sükhbataar District, Ulan Bator; tel. (11) 315680; fax (11) 318006; Dep. Dir A. TSASCHIKHER.

TV-9: Media Holding Co, TV9 Television Bldg, Ulan Bator; tel. 70110628; fax (11) 70110631; e-mail programm@tv9.mn; internet www.tv9.mn; f. 2003; 24-hour broadcaster; Dir TS. ENKHBAT.

UBS (Ulan Bator Broadcasting System): Khuvisgalchdyn Gudamj 3, Bayangol District, Ulan Bator (POB 24/983); tel. (11) 301973; fax (11) 368108; e-mail ext_affairs@ubs.mn; internet www.ubs.mn; f. 1992; fmrly state-owned; privatized in 2005; two channels; 17 hours a day; Dir-Gen. LKHAGVADORJ BALKHJAV.

Cable television companies (29 in total) operate in 19 towns. There are local television stations in Ulan Bator (three), Darkhan, Sükhbaatar and Baganuur. Chinese, Kazakh, Russian, German and French television services are among those that can also be received.

Finance

(cap. = capital; res = reserves; dep. = deposits; m. = million; brs = branches; amounts in tögrög, unless otherwise stated)

BANKING

Before 1990 the State Bank was the only bank in Mongolia, responsible for issuing currency, controlling foreign exchange and allocating credit. With the inauguration of market reforms in Mongolia in the early 1990s, the central and commercial functions of the State Bank were transferred to the newly created specialized commercial banks: the Bank of Capital Investment and Technological Innovation and the State Bank International. In May 1991 the State Bank became an independent central bank, and the operation of private, commercial banks was permitted. In November 1996 amendments were made to banking legislation to improve the regulation and supervision of commercial banks, and two major insolvent banks were liquidated. Restructuring of the banking sector subsequently continued.

Central Bank

Bank of Mongolia (Mongolbank): Baga Toiruu 9, Ulan Bator; tel. (11) 310413; fax (11) 311471; e-mail ad@mongolbank.mn; internet www.mongolbank.mn; f. 1924; est. as the State Bank of the Mongolian People's Republic; cap. 5,000m., res 23,555m., dep. 775,149m. (Dec. 2006); Pres. LKHNAASÜRENGIIN PÜREVDORJ; Chief Vice-Pres. BATSÜKHIIN ENKHKHUYAG.

Other Banks

Anod Bank: Juulchny Gudamj 18, Chingeltei District, Ulan Bator (CPOB 361); tel. (11) 315315; fax (11) 315431; e-mail anod@anodbank.com; internet www.anod.com; cap. 11,504.2m., res 60.8m., dep. 178,512.3m. (Dec. 2006); Chair. ERDENEIIN GÜR-ARANZ; Exec. Dir L. ULAMBAYAR; Pres. NYAMAAGIIN DAVAA.

Capital Bank: Sambuugiin Gudamj 48, Ulan Bator; tel. (11) 315500; fax (11) 310833; e-mail info@capitalbank.mn; internet www.capitalbank.mn; cap. 8,000m., res 806m., dep. 14,397m. (June 2007); f. 1990; Bishrelt Holding; CEO AGVAANJAMBYN ARIUNBOLD; Dep. CEO DAMDINGIIN DÜGER; 24 brs.

Capitron Bank: Capitron Bank Bldg, Usny Gudamj 4, Enkhtaivny Örgön Chölöö, Sükhbaatar District, Ulan Bator; tel. (11) 328373; fax (11) 328372; e-mail info@capitronbank.mn; internet www.capitronbank.mn; f. 2001; cap. 8,000.5m., res 3.4m., dep. 74,746.7m. (Dec. 2006); CEO BALBARYN MEDREE.

MONGOLIA

Chinggis Khaan Bank: New Century Plaza, Chingisiin Örgön Chölöö 15, Sükhbaatar District, Ulan Bator; tel. (11) 317178; fax (11) 318367; e-mail bank@ckbank.mn; internet www.ckbank.mn; f. 2001; est. by Millennium Securities Management Ltd and Coral Sea Holdings Ltd (British Virgin Islands); cap. 39,373.2m., dep. 49,529.1m. (Dec. 2007); Chair. S. B. GROMOV; CEO CHIMIDIIN SAINTSOGT.

Credit Bank: Government Palace Bldg (east side), Sükhbaataryn Talbai, Sükhbaatar District, Ulan Bator; tel. (11) 326053; fax (11) 321897; e-mail creditbk@creditbank.mn; internet www.creditbank.mn; f. 1997; owned by Russian interests; cap. 8,090m., res 20,594m., dep. 12,363m. (July 2006); Exec. Dir B. TSENGEL.

Erel Bank: Erel Co No. 2 Bldg, Chingisiin Örgön Chölöö, Khan-Uul District, Ulan Bator (POB 36/500); tel. (11) 344550; fax (11) 343387; e-mail info@erelbank.mn; internet www.erelbank.mn; f. 1997; cap. 4,000m., res 45.9m., dep. 3,163.4m. (Dec. 2005); Owner BADARCHIIN ERDENEBAT; CEO GOMBOJAVYN DORJ.

Golomt Bank of Mongolia: Bodi Tower, Sükhbaataryn Talbai 3, 4th Floor, Ulan Bator; tel. (11) 311530; fax (11) 311958; e-mail mail@golomtbank.com; internet www.golomtbank.com; f. 1995; est. by Mongolian-Portuguese IBH Bodi International Co Ltd; cap. 21,934.1m., dep. 303,944.3m. (Dec. 2006); Chair. DANZANDORJIIN BAYASGALAN; Exec. Dir JOHN FINIGAN; 14 brs.

Khadgalamjiin Bank (Savings Bank): Peace Ave 13, Ulan Bator; tel. (11) 312043; fax (11) 327467; e-mail bank@savingsbank.mn; internet www.savingsbank.mn; f. 1996; est. as Ardyn Bank; owned by MD Securities Co, a consortium of Chinggis Khaan Bank, Mongol Daatgal and Bratsk People's Bank (Russian Federation); cap. 8,031.0m., res 2,544.5m., dep. 65,986.0m. (Dec. 2007); CEO POLUEKTOV O. E.; 60 brs.

Khan Bank (KhAAN or Agricultural Bank): Söuliin Gudamj 25, Sükhbaatar District, Ulan Bator (POB 44/192); tel. (11) 332333; fax (11) 70117023; e-mail info@khanbank.com; internet www.khanbank.com; f. 1991; purchased by H and S Securities (Japan) in Feb. 2003; cap. 14,307m., dep. 179,098m. (June 2005); Chair. HIDEO SAWADA; CEO J. PETER MORROW; Dep. Exec. Dir R. MÖNKHTUYAA; 380 brs.

Mongol Shuudan Bank (Post Bank): Kholboochdyn Gudamj 4, Ulan Bator (CPOB 874); tel. (11) 310103; fax (11) 328501; e-mail info@postbank.mn; internet www.postbank.mn; f. 1993; cap. 8,017.9m., res 1,732.0m., dep. 128,964.6m. (Dec. 2006); 100% in private ownership; Exec. Dir D. OYUUNJARGAL; Chair. D. ZORIGT.

Trade and Development Bank of Mongolia (Khudaldaa Khögjliin Bank): Cnr of Juulchny Gudamj 7 and Baga Toiruu 12, Ulan Bator; tel. (11) 312362; fax (11) 327028; e-mail tdbank@tdbm.mn; internet www.tdbm.mn; f. 1991; carries out Mongolbank's foreign operations; cap. 6,610.1m., res. 6,338.7m., dep. 482,329.6m. (Dec. 2007); 76% equity bought by Banca Commerciale (Lugano) and Gerald Metals (Stanford, CT), May 2002; Pres. RANDOLPH KOPPA; CEO B. MEDREE.

Transport and Development Bank (Trans Bank): Juulchny Gudamj, 1st Sub-District, Chingeltei District, Ulan Bator; tel. (11) 319590; fax (11) 319591; internet www.transbank.mn; owned by Russian interests; CEO A. E. NOVOZHILOV; Chair. DANZANBALJIRYN ENKHTAIVAN.

Ulaanbaatar City Bank: Sükhbaataryn Gudamj 16, Ulan Bator (POB 46/370); tel. (11) 319041; fax (11) 330508; e-mail info@ubcbank.mn; internet www.ubcbank.mn; f. 1998; est. by Capital City with assistance from the Bank of Taipei (Taiwan); cap. 5,349m., dep. 50,064m. (June 2005); CEO DASHDORJIN BADRAA.

XacBank: Yörönkhii Said Amaryn Gudamj, Sükhbaatar District, Ulan Bator (POB 46/721); tel. (11) 318185; fax (11) 328701; e-mail bank@xacbank.mn; internet www.xacbank.org; f. 2001; cap. 10,947.8m., res 7,780.7m., dep. 76,982.1m. (Dec. 2008); CEO BOLD MAVGAN.

Zoos Bank: Baga Toiruu 7/1, Ulan Bator (POB 44/304); tel. (11) 312107; fax (11) 329537; e-mail secretary@zoosbank.mn; internet www.zoosbank.mn; f. 1999; cap. 10,000m., res 1,789.6m., dep. 112,284.1m. (Dec. 2006); Exec. Dir SHARAVYN CHUDANJII.

Banking Associations

Mongolian Banks Association: Ulan Bator; e-mail monba@mongolnet.mn; Pres. SHARAVYN CHUDANJII; Exec. Dir GOTOVYN TSERENPÜREV.

STOCK EXCHANGE

At the end of 2007 there were 383 listed companies, of which 56 were wholly or partly state-owned. Over the course of the 253 trading days of 2007 business to the value of 62,100m. tögrög was conducted, including 40,500m. tögrög in bonds. Government bonds were traded on 10 occasions, reaching a total value of 39,600m. tögrög.

Stock Exchange: Sükhbaataryn Talbai 2, Ulan Bator; tel. (11) 310501; fax (11) 325170; internet www.mse.mn; f. 1991; Dir RENTSENGIIN SODKHÜÜ.

INSURANCE

Ard Daatgal: Tavan Bogd Plaza, Amaryn Gudamj 8, Ulan Bator; tel. (11) 331185; fax (11) 330083; est. with Omni Whittington Guernsey.

Bodi Daatgal Co: Bodi Tower, Sükhbaataryn Talbai, Ulan Bator; tel. 70110280; fax (11) 326535; e-mail bodi@bodiinsurance.mn; internet www.bodiinsurance.mn; Dir L. BOLDKHUYAG.

Ganzam Insurance: Mongolian Railways (MTZ), Zamchdyn Gudamj, Ulan Bator; tel. and fax (11) 242643.

MIG Daatgal: 1st Sub-District, Chingeltei District, Ulan Bator; tel. (11) 330130; fax (11) 330132; e-mail mig@magicnet.mn; internet www.mig.mn; f. 1997; Exec. Dir J. BAT-ORSHIKH.

Mongol Daatgal: Enkh Taivny Örgön Chölöö 13, Ulan Bator; tel. (11) 313615; fax (11) 310347; e-mail insurance@mongoldaatgal.mn; internet www.mongoldaatgal.mn; f. 1934; sold Dec. 2003 to consortium formed by Angara-SKB and Chinggis Khan Bank; Chair. and CEO BADARCHIIN ENKHBAT; Sr Vice-Pres. CHIMIDYN BATTSOGT.

National Life Daatgal: Financial Service Corpn, Ambassador Bldg, Enkh Taivny Örgön Chölöö 15A/5, 1st Sub-District, Sükhbaatar District, Ulan Bator; tel. 70110784; fax 70110781; e-mail national.life@fscomongolia.mn; internet www.fscomongolia.mn; Exec. Dir B. BATBAYAR.

Nomin Daatgal: State Department Store, Enkh Taivny Örgön Chölöö, Ulan Bator; tel. (11) 330023; fax (11) 325528; e-mail insurance@nomin.net; internet www.insurance.nomin.net.

Ochir Undraa Daatgal: Söuliin Gudamj 15/2, 4th Sub-District, Sükhbaatar District, Ulan Bator (POB 44/398); tel. (11) 324248; fax (11) 326466; e-mail insurance@ochir-undraa.com; internet www.ochir-undraa.com.

UB Daatgal Co: Baga Toiruu 37B, Sükbataar District, Ulan Bator (POB 46/385); tel. (11) 324828; fax (11) 322362; e-mail sanal_huselt@ubdaatgal.mn; internet www.ubdaatgal.mn.

Trade and Industry

GOVERNMENT AGENCIES

Energy Directorate: Ulan Bator; f. 2008; subordinate to Minister of Mineral Resources and Energy; Head TSENDSÜRENGIIN BAYARBAATAR.

Foreign Capital Investment Directorate: Ulan Bator; f. 2008; subordinate to Minister of External Relations; Head BAASANKHÜÜGIIN GANZORIG.

Minerals Directorate: Ulan Bator; f. 2008; subordinate to Minister of Mineral Resources and Energy; Head DORJPÜREVIIN BATKHUYAG.

Nuclear Energy Directorate: Ulan Bator; f. 2008; subordinate to Prime Minister; Head SODNOMYN ENKHBAT.

Petroleum Directorate: Ulan Bator; f. 2008; subordinate to Minister of Mineral Resources and Energy; Head DASHZEVEGIIN AMARSAIKHAN.

Small and Medium Enterprise Directorate: Ulan Bator; f. 2008; subordinate to Minister of Food, Agriculture and Light Industry; Head T. NYAM-OSOR.

DEVELOPMENT ORGANIZATIONS

Economics and Market Research Center: Government Bldg 1, J. Sambuugiin Gudamj 11, Ulan Bator; tel. (11) 324258; fax (11) 324620; e-mail emrc@mongolchamber.mn; internet www.mongolchamber.mn; Dir J. BOZKHÜÜKHEN.

Mongolian Business Development Agency: Yörönkhii Said Amaryn Gudamj, Ulan Bator (CPOB 458); tel. (11) 311094; fax (11) 311092; internet www.mbda-mongolia.org; f. 1994; Gen. Man. D. BAYARBAT.

Mongolian Development Research Centre: Rm 50, Baga Toiruu 13, Chingeltei District, Ulan Bator (POB 20A/63); tel. and fax (11) 315686; internet www.mdrc.mn; f. 1998; Chair. TSEDENDAMBYN BATBAYAR.

CHAMBERS OF COMMERCE

Junior Chamber of Commerce: Youth Union Bldg, Ulan Bator; tel. (11) 328694; Chair NATSAGDORJ.

Mongolian National Chamber of Commerce and Industry: Sambuugiin Gudamj 11, Ulan Bator 38; tel. (11) 312501; fax (11) 324620; e-mail chamber@mongolchamber.mn; internet www.mongolchamber.mn; f. 1960; responsible for establishing economic and trading relations, contacts between trade and industrial organizations, both at home and abroad, and for generating foreign trade; organizes commodity inspection, press information, and international exhbns and fairs at home and abroad; registration of trademarks and patents; issues certificates of origin and of quality; Chair. and CEO SAMBUUGIIN DEMBEREL.

MONGOLIA

INDUSTRIAL AND TRADE ASSOCIATIONS

Association of Exporters of Livestock, Raw Materials and Semi-Processed Products: Ulan Bator; Exec. Dir B. TÖRMÖNKH.

Association of Mongolian Sewn Goods and Knitwear Products Manufacturers: Ulan Bator; Pres. N. DASH-ÖLZII.

Building Materials Industry Association: Ulan Bator; Exec. Dir O. LKHAGVADORJ.

Financial Market Association: Ulan Bator; Pres. Ö. GANZORIG.

Grain Producers' Association: Ulan Bator; Pres. TSEVEENJAVYN ÖÖLD.

Mongolian Air Traffic Controllers' Association: National Air Traffic Services, Chinggis Khaan International Airport, Buyant-Ukhaa 210634, Ulan Bator; tel. (11) 282008; fax (11) 282108; e-mail monatca@mcaa.gov.mn.

Mongolian Association of Container and Packaging Makers and Users: Ulan Bator; Pres. DEMBERELIIN OTGONBAATAR.

Mongolian Builders' Association: Block 3, Urt Tsagaan, Chingeltei District, Ulan Bator; tel. 99112636; fax (11) 318685; Pres. MÖNKHBAYARYN BATBAATAR.

Mongolian Coal Association: Ulan Bator; Exec. Dir T. NARAN.

Mongolian Export Association: Ulan Bator; Exec. Dir D. GALSANDORJ.

Mongolian Farmers and Flour Producers' Association: Agro-Pro Business Centre, 19th Sub-District, Bayangol District, Ulan Bator; tel. (11) 300114; fax (11) 362875; e-mail agropro@magicnet.mn; f. 1997; research and quality inspection services in domestic farming and flour industry; Pres. SHARAVYN GUNGAADORJ.

Mongolian Foodstuffs Traders' Association: Ulan Bator; Exec. Dir KH. GIIMAA.

Mongolian Franchising Council of the Mongolian National Chamber of Commerce and Industry: Ulan Bator; tel. (11) 327178; fax (11) 324620; e-mail tecd@mongolchamber.mn; Head J. BATZANDAN.

Mongolian Institute of Internal Auditors: Ulan Bator; tel. (11) 312773; e-mail miia@bizcon.mn; internet www.bizcon.mn/miia; Pres. L. OTGONBAYAR.

Mongolian Marketing Association: Ulan Bator; Pres. D. DAGVADORJ.

Mongolian Metallurgists' Association: School of Technology, Darkhan-Uul Province; tel. (37) 24723; Pres. DO. GANBOLD; Exec. Dir TS. MÖNKHJARGAL.

Mongolian National Industrialists' Association: Ulan Bator; Pres. NAMJAAGIIN DASHZEVEG.

Mongolian National Mining Association: 501 Geosan Company Bldg, Ikh Surguuliin Gudamj 8, Ulan Bator; tel. (11) 314877; fax (11) 330032; e-mail info@miningmongolia.mn; internet www.miningmongolia.mn; f. 1994; provides members of the mining sector with legal protection, and reflects their views in Government mining policy and mineral sector development; Pres. DOGSOMYN GANBOLD; Exec. Dir NAMGARYN ALGAA.

Mongolian PR Association: Ulan Bator; Chair. D. BOLDKHUYAG.

Mongolian Printing Works Association: Ulan Bator; Pres. E. MYAGMARPÜREV.

Mongolian Timber Industry Association: Mon-Frukt Co, 1st Sub-District, Bayangol District, Ulan Bator (POB 36/51); tel. 91111191; fax (11) 343145.

Mongolian Wool and Cashmere Federation: Khan-Uul District, Ulan Bator; tel. (11) 341871; fax (11) 342814; Pres. D. GANKKHUYAG.

Petroleum Gas Association: Ulan Bator; f. 2005; Pres. SH. GUNGAADORJ.

EMPLOYERS' ORGANIZATIONS

Employers' and Owners' United Association: Rm 401, 4th Floor, Mongolian Youth Association 'B' Bldg, Ulan Bator; tel. (11) 326513; Exec. Dir. B. SEMBEEJAV.

Federation of Professional Business Women of Mongolia: Ulan Bator; tel. and fax (11) 315638; e-mail mbpw@mongolnet.mn; f. 1992; provides education, training, and opportunities for women to achieve economic independence, and the running of businesses; Pres. OCHIRBATYN ZAYAA; 7,000 mems, 14 brs.

Immovable Property (Real Estate) Business Managers' Association: Ulan Bator; Pres. J. BYAMBADORJ.

Mongolian Employers' Federation: Baga Toiruu 44A, Ulan Bator 48; tel. and fax (11) 325635; e-mail monef@magicnet.mn; internet www.monef.mn; f. 1990; fmrly Private Industry Owners' Association; 7,900 mems; Pres. LUVSANBALDANGIIN NYAMSAMBUU.

Mongolian Management Association: Ulan Bator; Chair. Exec. Council DAGVADORJIIN TSERENDORJ.

Private Business Owners' Association: Tsatsral Mon Bldg, 1st Sub-District, Songinokhairkhan District, Ulan Bator; tel. (11) 682905; Pres. T. NYAMDORJ.

Private Employers' Association: Ulan Bator; Pres. O. NATSAGDORJ.

Refuse Disposal Business Managers' Association: Ulan Bator; Chair. SH. BAASANJAV.

Scrap Business Managers' Association: Ulan Bator; Dir S. ALTANTSETSEG.

UTILITIES

Electricity

Darkhan-Selenge TsTS Co: Darkhan; management of electric power network in northern Mongolia; Exec. Dir CH. ENKHBOLD.

Dulaan Tsakhilgaan Stants-IV Co: 20th Sub-District, Bayangol District, Ulan Bator; tel. (11) 631768; Mongolia's biggest power station; Exec. Dir TS. BAYARBAATAR.

TsTS Co: Ulan Bator; tel. (11) 41294; management of electric power network in Ulan Bator; Exec. Dir DASHJAMTSYN BATTULGA.

Ulaanbaatar Power Distribution Network: Chingisiin Örgön Chölöö 45, Ulan Bator; tel. (11) 341674; fax (11) 343061; e-mail info@ubedn.mn; internet www.ubedn.mn; Exec. Dir BATTULGA DASHJAMTS.

Water

Dulaany Süljee Co: Ulan Bator; tel. (11) 343047; e-mail engineer@dhc.mn; internet www.dhc.mn; supervision of hot water district heating network in Ulan Bator; Exec. Dir D. BYAMBA-OCHIR.

USAG: Khökh Tengeriin Gudamj 5, Ulan Bator; tel. (11) 455055; fax (11) 450120; e-mail usag@magicnet.mn; supervision of water supply network in Ulan Bator; Chair. OSORYN ERDENEBAATAR.

IMPORT AND EXPORT ORGANIZATIONS

Agrotekhimpeks: Ulan Bator; imports agricultural machinery and implements, seed, fertilizer, veterinary medicines and irrigation equipment.

Altjin: Ulan Bator; company importing and distributing oil and oil products and also running distilleries, a spin-off from APU; Dir G. ALTAN.

Arisimpex: Ulan Bator; tel. (11) 343007; fax (11) 343008; exports hides and skins, fur and leather goods; imports machinery, chemicals and accessories for leather, fur and shoe industries; Pres. A. TSERENBALJID.

Avtoimpeks: Ulan Bator; f. 1934; state-owned; international trader in motor vehicles; Exec. Dir S. CHULUUNBAT.

Barter and Border: Khuvisgalchdyn Gudamj, Ulan Bator; tel. (11) 324848; barter and border trade operations.

Khorshoololimpeks: Tolgoit, Ulan Bator (CPOB 262); tel. (11) 332926; fax (11) 331128; f. 1964; exports sub-standard skins, hides, wool and furs, handicrafts and finished products; imports equipment and materials for housing, and for clothing and leather goods; Dir L. ÖLZIIBUYAN.

Kompleksimport: Enkh Taivny Gudamj 7, Ulan Bator; tel. and fax (11) 688948; f. 1963; imports consumer goods, foodstuffs, sets of equipment and turnkey projects; training of Mongolians abroad; state-owned pending planned privatization; cap. 3,500m. tögrög.

Makhimpeks: 4th Sub-District, Songinokhairkhan District, Ulan Bator; tel. (11) 632471; fax (11) 632517; f. 1946; abattoir, meat processing, canning, meat imports and exports; 51% share privatized in 1999; cap. 7,800m. tögrög; Exec. Dir B. BÜDRAGCHAA.

Materialimpex: Teeverchdiin Gudamj, Ulan Bator; tel. (11) 365143; fax (11) 367904; e-mail matimpex@magicnet.mn; internet www.materialimpex.com; f. 1957; exports cashmere, wool products, animal skins; imports glass, roofing material, dyes, sanitary ware, metals and metalware, wallpaper, bitumen, wall and floor tiles; partially privatized Feb. 1999, but most shares still state-owned; Gen. Dir B. ZORIG; 126 employees.

Medimpex International: Khan Holdings Bldg, Olimpiin Gudamj, 1st Sub-District, Sukhbaatar District, Ulan Bator; tel. (11) 310429; fax (11) 318254; e-mail medimpex@mcs.mn; internet www.medimpex.mcs.mn.

Metallimpeks (Metalimpex): Ulan Bator; tel. (11) 331154; Dir D. GANBAT.

Monfa Trade: Monfarma Trade Co, Bldg 69, First 40,000, 4th Sub-District, Sükhbaatar District, Ulan Bator; tel. and fax (11) 324420; e-mail monfatrade@mongol.net; procurement and distribution of pharmaceuticals.

Mongoleksport Co Ltd: Government Bldg 7, 8th Fl., Erkh Chölöönii Talbai, Ulan Bator; tel. (11) 329234; fax (11) 327884; exports wool, hair, cashmere, mining products, antler, skins and hides; Dir-Gen. D. CHIMEDDAMBAA.

Mongolemimpex: Teeverchdiin Gudamj 39, Ulan Bator; tel. (11) 322695; fax (11) 323877; e-mail moemim@magicnet.mn; internet www.mongolemimpex.mn; f. 1923; procurement and distribution to hospitals and pharmacies of drugs and surgical appliances; Dir-Gen. BATBAYARYN BOLORMAA.

Mongolimpeks: Khuvisgalchdyn Örgön Chölöö, Ulan Bator; tel. (11) 326081; exports cashmere, camels' wool, hair, fur, casings, powdered blood and horn, antler, wheat gluten, alcoholic drinks, cashmere and camels' wool knitwear, blankets, copper concentrate, souvenirs, stamps and coins; imports light and mining industry machinery, scientific instruments, chemicals, pharmaceuticals and consumer goods; state-owned; Dir-Gen. DORJPALAMYN DÖKHÖMBAYAR.

Mongol Safari Co Ltd: Baigal Ordon 38, Ulan Bator; tel. (11) 360267; fax (11) 360067; e-mail monsafari@magicnet.mn; internet www.monsafari.com; f. 1990; exports hunting products; imports hunting equipment and technology; organizes hunting and trekking tours; Dir-Gen. U. BUYANDELGER.

Monnis International: Chingisiin Gudamj 25, Sükhbaatar District, Ulan Bator; tel. (11) 311687; fax (11) 323248; e-mail monnis@monnis.com; Nissan distributor.

Monnoos: Ulan Bator (POB 36/450); tel. (11) 343201; fax (11) 342591; e-mail monnoos@mongolnet.mn; wool trade enterprise; Dir SANJIIN BAT-OYUUN.

Monos Cosmetics: Monos Group, Bldg 25, II-40,000, 2nd Sub-District, Chingeltei District, Ulan Bator; tel. and fax (11) 315908; fax (11) 320967; e-mail info@monoscosmetics.mn; internet www.monoscosmetics.mn; f. 1990; production, export and import of cosmetics; Chair. and CEO BALDANDORJIIN ERDENEKHISHIG; Exec. Dir KH. SOLONGO; 90 employees.

Monos Pharm Trade: Monos Group, Namyaanjugiin Gudamj 23, 18th Sub-District, Bayanzürkh District, Ulan Bator; tel. and fax (11) 450054; fax (11) 463158; internet www.monos.mn; f. 1990; production, export and import of medicine, medical equipment and health food; Dir-Gen. LUVSANGIIN ERDENECHIMEG; 280 employees.

Noosimpeks: Ulan Bator; tel. (11) 341577; exports scoured sheep's wool, yarn, carpets, fabrics, blankets, mohair and felt boots; imports machinery and chemicals for wool industry.

Nüürs: Ulan Bator; tel. (11) 327428; exports and imports in coal-mining field; Man. D. DÜGERJAV.

Packaging: Tolgoit, Ulan Bator; tel. (11) 31053; exports raw materials of agricultural origin, sawn timber, consumer goods, unused spare parts and equipment, and non-ferrous scrap; imports machinery and materials for packaging industry, and consumer goods.

Petrovis: Petrovis Co Bldg, Yörönkhii Said Amaryn Gudamj 8, Sükhbaatar District, Ulan Bator; tel. (11) 327051; fax (11) 327288; e-mail info@petrovis.mn; internet www.petrovis.mn; oil products importer and distributor; in Feb. 2004 acquired the 80% state-owned shares in the country's biggest distributor NIK (Neft Import Kontsern) for US $8.5m; CEO and Pres. J. OYUUNGEREL.

Raznoimpeks: 3rd Sub-District, Bayangol District, Ulan Bator; tel. (11) 329465; fax (11) 329901; f. 1933; exports wool, cashmere, hides, canned meat, powdered bone, alcoholic drinks, macaroni and confectionery; imports cotton and woollen fabrics, silk, knitwear, shoes, fresh and canned fruit, vegetables, tea, milk powder, acids, paints, safety equipment, protective clothing, printing and packaging paper; state-owned pending planned privatization; cap. 6,100m. tögrög; Exec. Dir TS. BAT-ENKH.

Tekhnikimport: Ulan Bator; tel. (11) 685149; imports machinery, instruments and spare parts for light, food, wood, building, power and mining industries, road-building and communications; state-owned; Dir-Gen. DASHDONDOGIIN GANBAT.

Tüshig Trade Co Ltd: Enkh Taivny Örgön Chölöö, Ulan Bator (POB 44/481); tel. (11) 314062; fax (11) 314052; exports sheep and camel wool, and cashmere goods; imports machinery for small enterprises, foodstuffs and consumer goods; Dir-Gen. D. GANBAATAR.

Whole Sale: Songinokhairkhan District, Ulan Bator; tel. 99112100; fax (11) 632119; e-mail boch30@mobinet.mn; f. 1952; wholesale trader; privately owned; Dir-Gen. OCHBADRAK BALJINNYAM.

YuniGaz: Petrovis Co Bldg, Yörönkhii Said Amaryn Gudamj 8, Sükhbaatar District, Ulan Bator; tel. (11) 314018; fax (11) 327253; e-mail info@unigas.mn; internet www.unigas.mn; petrol, diesel and LPG distributor; Dir-Gen. B. TÜMENTSOGT.

CO-OPERATIVES

Association of Private Herders' Co-operatives: Ulan Bator (POB 21/787); tel. (11) 633601; fax (11) 325935; e-mail mongolherder@magicnet.mn; f. 1991; Pres. R. ERDENE; Exec. Dir TS. MYAGMAR-OCHIR.

Central Association of Consumer Co-operatives: Ulan Bator; tel. and fax (11) 329025; f. 1990; wholesale and retail trade; exports animal raw materials; imports foodstuffs and consumer goods; Chair. G. MYANGANBAYAR.

Mongolian Association of Production Co-operatives: Urt Tsagaan, Khudaldaany Gudamj 12, Chingeltei District, Ulan Bator; tel. (11) 310956; e-mail cumic@mol.mn.

Mongolian Association of Savings and Credit Co-operatives: Bldg 2, State Property Committee, Chingeltei District, Ulan Bator; tel. (11) 313665; Pres. SH. GOOKHÜÜ.

Mongolian Co-operatives Development Centre: Ulan Bator; Dir DANZANGIIN RADNAARAGCHAA.

National Association of Mongolian Agricultural Co-operative Members: Enkhtayvny Örgön Chölöö, 18 A/1, Ulan Bator; tel. (11) 453535; fax (11) 458899; e-mail namac63@mongolnet.mn; internet www.namac.mn; f. 1992; Pres. NADMIDYN BAYARTSAIKHAN.

Union of Mongolian Production and Services Co-operatives: Bldg 16, II-40,000, 3rd Sub-District, Chingeltei District, Ulan Bator (POB 46/470); tel. (11) 327583; fax (11) 328446; e-mail umpscoop@hotmail.com; f. 1990; Pres. SAMDANY ENKHTUYAA.

TRADE UNIONS

Confederation of Mongolian Trade Unions: Sükhbaataryn Talbai 3, Ulan Bator; tel. (11) 327253; fax (11) 322128; e-mail mpcd@cmtu.mn; internet www.cmtu.mn; brs throughout the country; Chair. S. GANBAATAR; Sec.-Gen. M. GANAA.

Mongolian United Confederation of Trade Unions: Ulan Bator; Chair. D. TSEYEN-OIDOV.

Transport

MTT (Mongol Transport Team): MTT Bldg, 5th Sub-District, Bayangol District, Ulan Bator; tel. (11) 689000; fax (11) 684953; e-mail mtt@mtteam.mn; internet www.mtteam.mn; international freight forwarding by air, sea, rail and road; offices in Beijing, Berlin, Moscow and Prague.

Tuushin Co Ltd: Tuushin Bldg, Yörönkhii Said Amaryn Gudamj, Sükhbaatar District, Ulan Bator; tel. (11) 312092; fax (11) 325570; e-mail tuushin@magicnet.mn; internet www.tuushin.mn; f. 1990; international freight forwarders; transport and forwarding policy and services, warehousing, customs agent; tourism; offices in Beijing, Moscow and Prague; Dir-Gen. N. ZORIGT.

RAILWAYS

In 2008 the total single-track length was 2,083 km, of which 1,815 km was the main-line track, including passing loops and sidings.

Mongolian Railway Affairs Directorate: Zamchdyn Gudamj, Ulan Bator; internet www.gate1.pmis.gov.mn/tzheg; Dir T. BATBOLD.

Ulan Bator Railway: Zamchdyn Gudamj, Ulan Bator (CPOB 376); tel. (21) 944409; fax (11) 328360; internet www.mtz.mn; f. 1949; jt-stock co with Russian Federation; Dir VANCHIGDORJIIN OTGONDEMBEREL; Chair. I. V. ROMASHOV.

External Lines: from the Russian frontier at Naushki/Sükhbaatar (connecting with the Trans-Siberian Railway) to Ulan Bator and on to the Chinese frontier at Zamyn-Üüd/Erenhot, connecting with Beijing (total length 1,110 km).

Branches: from Darkhan to Sharyn Gol coalfield (length 63 km); branch from Salkhit near Darkhan, westwards to Erdenet (Erdenetiin-ovoo open-cast copper mine) in Bulgan Province (164 km); from Bagakhangai to Baganuur coal-mine, south-east of Ulan Bator (96 km); from Khar Airag to Bor-Öndör fluorspar mines (60 km); from Sainshand to Züünbayan oilfield (63 km).

Eastern Railway, linking Mongolia with the Trans-Siberian and Chita via Borzya; from the Russian frontier at Solovyevsk to Choibalsan (238 km), with branch from Chingis Dalan to Mardai uranium mine near Dashbalbar (110 km), possibly inactive.

IFFC (International Freight-forwarding Centre of Mongolian Railways): Mongolian Railway Headquarters, Zamchdyn Gudamj 1, Bayangol District, Ulan Bator (CPOB 376); tel. (11) 312509; fax (11) 313165; e-mail iffc@railcom.mn; internet www.iffc.mn; international freight forwarding.

ROADS

Main roads link Ulan Bator with the Chinese frontier at Zamyn Üüd/Erenhot and with the Russian frontier at Altanbulag/Kyakhta. A road from Chita in Russia crosses the frontier in the east at Mangut/Onon (Ölzii) and branches for Choibalsan and Öndörkhaan. In the west and north-west, roads from Biisk and Irkutsk in Russia go to Tsagaannuur, Bayan-Ölgii aimag, and Khankh, on Lake Khövsgöl, respectively. The total length of the road network was 45,000 km in 2005, of which asphalted roads comprised 1,500 km (incl. 400 km in Ulan Bator), gravel roads comprised 1,400 km, and improved earth roads comprised 1,300 km. The first section of a hard-surfaced road between Ulan Bator and Bayankhongor was completed in 1975. The road from Darkhan to Erdenet was also surfaced. Construction has been focused on the routes from Ulan Bator southwards to Choir and Sainshand and eastward to Öndörkhaan. In 2005 a further 389 km of hard-surfaced road was built, and 747 km of gravel road. The length of 'improved' roads reached 6,461.2 km in 2007, of which hard-surfaced roads accounted for 2,597.2 km (an increase of 204.4 km in comparison with the previous year). Mongolia divides its road system into state-grade and country-grade roads. State-grade roads (of which there were 11,000 km in 2005) run from Ulan Bator to provincial centres and from provincial centres to the border. Country-grade roads account for the remaining roads, but they are mostly rough cross-country tracks.

To mark the millennium, the Government announced its decision to construct a new east–west road, linking the Chinese and Russian border regions via Ölgii, Lake Khar Us, Zavkhan and Arkhangai provinces, Dashinchilen, Lün, Ulan Bator, Nalaikh, Baganuur, Öndörkhaan and Sümber (Khalkh Gol). Construction was expected to take about 10 years, but because of the cost, the road was not expected to be surfaced for the whole length.

There are bus services in Ulan Bator and other large towns, and road haulage services throughout the country on the basis of motor transport depots, mostly situated in provincial centres.

CIVIL AVIATION

Civil aviation in Mongolia, including the provision of air traffic control and airport management, is the responsibility of the Main Directorate of Civil Aviation, which provides air traffic and airport management services. It also supervises the Mongolian national airline (MIAT) and smaller operators such as Khangarid and Tengeriin Ulaach, which operate local flights. Aeroflot (Russia) and Air China operate flights to Ulan Bator (Chinggis Khaan International Airport).

Main Directorate of Civil Aviation: Chinggis Khaan International Airport, Buyant-Ukhaa, Ulan Bator; tel. (11) 282004; fax (11) 282102; e-mail webmaster@mcaa.gov.mn; internet internet www.mcaa.gov.mn; Dir-Gen. (vacant).

A-Jet Aviation: Olimpiin Gudamj, 1st Sub-District, Sükhbaatar District, Ulan Bator (POB 46/202); tel. (11) 318480; fax (11) 319780; e-mail flt_ops@jetmongol.com; internet www.jetmongol.com; f. 2000; fmrly Central Mongolia Airways; 3 Mi-8 helicopters for tourist travel; Exec. Dir LKHAMJAV NYAMBARYN.

Aero Mongolia Co Ltd: Chinggis Khaan International Airport, Buyant-Ukhaa, Ulan Bator (POB 34/105); tel. (11) 283212; fax (11) 379616; e-mail management@aeromongolia.mn; internet www.aeromongolia.mn; f. 2001; began operations June 2003; scheduled international flights to Irkutsk and Hohhot and scheduled internal flights to five provincial centres and Juulchin's South Gobi tourist camp by Fokker-50 aircraft; twice-weekly flights by Fokker-100 to the Republic of Korea inaugurated in Feb. 2006; Dir B. CHULUUN-BAATAR, D. DORJ.

Blue Sky Aviation: Door 2, Apt S-61, 1st Sub-District, Sükhbaatar District, Ulan Bator; tel. (11) 312085; fax (11) 322857; e-mail bsa@maf-europe.org; internet www.blueskyaviation.mn; jt venture of Mission Aviation Fellowship and Exodus International; operates charter flights and medical emergency services; f. 1999; Dir PAUL BROOKS; Operations Man. BATSURIN BAYARJIN.

Eznis (Easiness) Airways: Naiman Zokhis Bldg, Söüliin Gudamj, Sükhbaatar District, Ulan Bator; tel. (11) 313689; fax (11) 314258; internet www.eznis.com; f. 2006; operates two SAAB 340B aircraft on internal routes; Exec. Dir L. OYUUNBAT.

Khangarid: Room 210, MPRP Bldg, Baga Toiruu 37/1, Ulan Bator; tel. (11) 320138; fax (11) 311333; e-mail hangard_air_co@magicnet.mn; domestic and international passenger and freight services; Dir L. SERGELEN.

Mongolian Civil Air Transport (MIAT): MIAT Bldg, Chinggis Khaan International Airport, Buyant-Ukhaa, Khan-Uul District, Ulan Bator; tel. (11) 379935; fax (11) 379919; e-mail contact@miat.com; internet www.miat.com; f. 1956; scheduled services to Moscow, Irkutsk, Beijing, Seoul, Osaka, Berlin and Hohhot; carried 303,500 passengers in 2004; Dir R. BAT-ERDENE.

Tengeriin Ulaach (Sky Horse Aviation): Chinggis Khaan International Airport, Buyant-Ukhaa, Khan-Uul District, Ulan Bator (POB 34/17); tel. (11) 282023; fax (11) 379765; e-mail skyhorsenew@mbox.mn; internal helicopter transport for tourists and businesspeople; Dir L. TÖMÖR.

Trans-Ölgii: Ölgii, Bayan-Ölgii Province; f. 2006; operates one leased An-24 on Ölgii–Ulan Bator route twice a week.

Tourism

The country's main attractions are its scenery, wildlife and historical relics. A foreign tourist service bureau was established in 1954, but the tourism sector remained undeveloped. At March 2008 there were 248 tour operators, 326 hotels (with 8,000 beds) and 30 tourist camps (with 6,400 beds). Of the 30 or more hotels in Ulan Bator, all but four are relatively small, and in the peak summer season there is a shortage of rooms. The outlying tourist centres (Terelj, South Gobi, Öndör-Dov and Khujirt) have basic facilities. Total tourist arrivals increased from 451,788 in 2007 to 446,400 in 2008. Tourism revenue in 2008 reportedly reached US $320m.

Juulchin World Tours Corporation: Jamyan Gunii Gudamj 5/3, Ulan Bator; tel. (11) 312091; fax (11) 320246; e-mail info@juulchinworld.com; internet www.juulchinworld.com; f. 1954; offices in Berlin, Washington, DC, Beijing and Tokyo; tours, trekking, safaris, jeep tours, expeditions; Exec. Dir SH. NERGÜI.

Mongolian Adventure Tourism Association: Ulan Bator; Sec.-Gen. B. JIYAANDORJ.

Mongolian Tourism Association: 3/F, Rm 318, Building of the Mongolian Trade Unions Confederation, Sükhbaataryn Talbai, Ulan Bator; tel. (11) 327820; fax (11) 323026; e-mail info@travelmongolia.org; internet www.travelmongolia.org; Pres. BAYARSAIKHANY TSEVELMAA.

MONTENEGRO

Introductory Survey

Location, Climate, Language, Religion, Flag, Capital

Montenegro is situated in the central Balkan peninsula, in south-eastern Europe. Montenegro has frontiers with Bosnia and Herzegovina to the west and north-west, Serbia to the north, Kosovo to the east, and Albania to the south-east, as well as a short frontier with Croatia in the south-west. There is a western coastline along the Adriatic Sea (part of the Mediterranean). Montenegro has a rugged mountainous terrain, being dominated by the Black Mountains (Crna Gora), from which the country takes its name. The climate is Mediterranean near the coast, and continental inland. Mountainous areas have a colder climate with heavy snowfall in winter. Average temperatures range from between −7°C (19.4°F) and 23°C (73.4°F) inland, and between 11°C (51.8°F) and 28°C (84.2°F) on the coast. Montenegro's mountainous regions receive some of the highest amounts of rainfall in Europe. The 2007 Constitution defines the principal language as Montenegrin, with the Cyrillic and Latin alphabets in equal use. Serbian, Bosnian, and Croatian (all of which, in common with Montenegrin, were formerly described as variants of Serbo-Croat) and Albanian are also in official use. The principal religion is Orthodox Christianity, and there are significant Roman Catholic and Muslim communities. The national flag (proportions 1 by 2) is red, with a golden coat of arms depicting a double-headed eagle. Podgorica is the capital of Montenegro. The historical capital is Cetinje.

Recent History

After the Second World War, Montenegro became one of the six constituent republics of the federal Yugoslavia established by the Communist Party of Yugoslavia (later the League of Communists of Yugoslavia—LCY) under Josip Broz (Tito). Montenegrins were strongly represented among the ranks of the LCY and of the Yugoslav People's Army. Montenegro generally supported the Serbian reassertion of dominance within Yugoslavia after the death of Tito in the 1980s. Institutionally, this was helped by the installation of a new party leadership in the republic, following demonstrations during 1988 in favour of the Serbian leader, Slobodan Milošević. Subsequent reforms transformed the Skupština Crne Gore (Assembly of Montenegro) into a unicameral body of 125 members and replaced Montenegro's collective Presidency with a directly elected state President. The elections, in December 1990, represented a victory for the ruling League of Communists of Montenegro (subsequently renamed the Democratic Party of Socialists of Montenegro—DPS), which secured 83 seats in the new legislature, while its presidential candidate, Momir Bulatović, became President, after a second round of voting. In February 1991 Bulatović invited one of his party colleagues, Milo Đukanović, to head the republican Government. The third member of the new Montenegrin leadership was Svetozar Marović, the chairman of the Skupština.

The onset of armed conflict in Yugoslavia prompted Montenegro to adopt a pragmatic response to the disintegration of the federation. Although Montenegro adopted a declaration of state sovereignty on 18 October 1991 and a new Constitution in November, it remained committed to the federation with Serbia, confirming this conclusively in a referendum in March 1992. As a result, the two republics announced a new federal Constitution, which was a continuation of the old state, but effectively acknowledged the secession of the other four federal units. The Federal Republic of Yugoslavia (FRY) came into effect on 27 April. On 12 October a new Montenegrin Constitution declared the republic to be part of the FRY and, early in 1993, the disposition of power was confirmed by the re-election of Bulatović as State President and the continuation of Đukanović as premier. Meanwhile, another Montenegrin, Radoje Kontić, became the federal Prime Minister.

Relations between Montenegro and Serbia deteriorated from the mid-1990s. Montenegro was generally committed to the federal union, but resisted encroachments on its autonomy, in particular the attempts of Serbian leader Milošević to disassemble separate republican defence and foreign policy structures. Montenegro also wished to obtain international aid, which entailed its pursuit of a distinct foreign policy, often at variance with that of the federal authorities. The divergence in economic interests had mainly stemmed from Serbia's introduction, in mid-1993, of an export-import licensing system, which had prompted Montenegro to enact similar inter-republican trade controls. The federal authorities also tried to assert control over some state assets in Montenegro, which was a contentious issue, as privatization and the structures of a free market were further advanced in Montenegro than Serbia. Increasingly, however, the principal division in Montenegrin politics was not so much that between Serbia and Montenegro, as that between the republican presidency and premiership. Bulatović became more and more identified by his support for Milošević, who was attempting to control all opposition within the FRY, thereby threatening Montenegrin autonomy. Đukanović was more reform-minded than the federal authorities, and resistant to Milošević's dominance of Montenegro as well as Yugoslav politics, but in May 1996, none the less, maintained that most Montenegrins favoured the union with Serbia. Đukanović and Bulatović appeared united in their pursuit of separate negotiation of Montenegro's status in the international economic community, but relations between the two were strained by the premier's expressed support for Serbian anti-Government protesters later that year. In February 1997 Đukanović publicly declared Milošević unfit to hold public office, and in the following month he resisted the demands of Bulatović that he dismiss all anti-Milošević ministers in the republican Government. The ruling DPS (the parliamentary dominance of which had been conclusively confirmed in legislative elections in November 1996) split into two factions during 1997, as a result of Bulatović's support for the Serbian leader (who became the federal President in July). In July supporters of Đukanović within the DPS voted to remove Bulatović from the leadership of the party. Bulatović and Đukanović became the leading candidates in the Montenegrin presidential election of October. Đukanović won the second round of voting, with 50.8% of votes cast, although his opponent refused to accept the result as legitimate.

Đukanović was inaugurated as the President of Montenegro in January 1998, amid violent protests from supporters of Bulatović. A compromise agreement on early legislative elections in May was reached, pending which a transitional Government, led by the Đukanović faction of the DPS, was formed in February. Bulatović's faction refused to participate and renamed itself the Socialist People's Party of Montenegro (SPPM). However, support for the anti-Milošević stance of Đukanović and his party was confirmed in the elections of May, when the DPS won an outright majority (it formed a coalition Government, led by Filip Vujanović, in July). Montenegro had become increasingly suspicious of Serbia's intentions, particularly with the appointment of Bulatović as federal Prime Minister in May (in succession to Kontić). He proceeded to purge many Montenegrin officials from federal institutions, in response to the DPS appointing its own nominees to the federal chamber of the Yugoslav parliament in June; the republican authorities were anxious to resist institutional reforms that would enhance the powers of the federal presidency. Montenegro refused to acknowledge the administration of Bulatović, suspending all links with the federal Government in August.

Relations between the federal partners of the FRY continued to deteriorate during 1999. Escalating civil conflict in the Serbian province of Kosovo, a majority of the population of which comprised ethnic Albanians, led to aerial bombardment of the FRY by forces of the North Atlantic Treaty Organization (NATO, see p. 351) in March–June. Despite Montenegro's appeals to be spared such damage, the republic suffered during the military action. None the less, Montenegro continued to distance itself from Serbian military actions; in March refused to recognize the state of war declared by the federal Government at the commencement of the NATO bombardment, and in April Đukanović refused to place Montenegrin security forces under federal military command, as ordered by President Milošević.

In the aftermath of the open conflict in Kosovo, the Yugoslav federation became increasingly unstable, as internal wrangling and external forces combined to drive the two constituent republics apart. In mid-1999 the Government of Montenegro proposed the replacement of the federal system with an association of two states, threatening a referendum on full independence if Milošević did not agree; in October the Skupština enacted a citizenship law, which was viewed as progress towards such an arrangement. Economically, Montenegro attempted to insulate itself from the isolated Serbian economy; in November Montenegro replaced the depreciating Yugoslav dinar with the German Deutsche Mark as its official currency (the federal Constitutional Court declared the measure illegal in January 2000, to little effect). Serbia confirmed the economic rupture by imposing a partial blockade and then, in January 2000, a ban on the export of foodstuffs to Montenegro followed by a full economic embargo in March. While most of the Montenegrin Government preferred a looser confederation with Serbia, fears of Milošević increasing his political influence or of Serbian military action (such as the federal army's seizure of control over Montenegro's main airport in December 1999) escalated tensions.

Partial municipal elections in Montenegro in mid-2000 indicated the divided state of public opinion. In Podgorica, the DPS-led ruling coalition commanded an overall majority, but the Bulatović-led alliance remained robust, while the pro-independence Liberal Alliance of Montenegro (LAM) did not perform strongly. Attempts to reform federal institutions so as to weaken the influence of Montenegro in the federation were viewed with alarm, and the Skupština voted against the proposals in July. However, the anti-Milošević stance of Đukanović was to prove less useful following the change of regime in Serbia in October (the ruling Montenegrin coalition had boycotted the federal polls of the previous month), which included Bulatović resigning as federal Prime Minister. Đukanović began to advocate full independence for Montenegro, urging a referendum on the issue. This prompted the pro-federation People's Party of Montenegro to withdraw from the ruling republican coalition, precipitating legislative elections in April 2001. The DPS-led pro-independence coalition won 36 of the 77 seats, the SPPM-led alliance 33 and the LAM six. Vujanović was reappointed as premier. Meanwhile, negotiations about a new form of federal association were ongoing, and, from November, were mediated by the European Union (EU, see p. 255). The federal and republican leaderships signed a framework agreement on confederation on 14 March 2002, providing for the maintenance of separate economies and state structures by each of Serbia and Montenegro, which would be united by a shared presidency and legislature in charge of foreign and defence policies. Crucially, Montenegro had the right to refer the issue of independence to a referendum after three years. However, despite the appeals of other pro-independence groups, later in March the LAM resigned from the Government in protest at the agreement. The Skupština approved the accord on 9 April, although further resignations from the Government forced Vujanović to seek a new coalition, which he was unable to achieve by July.

On 20 October 2002 the DPS-led, pro-independence ruling coalition, now known as the Democratic List for a European Montenegro, won 39 of the 75 seats in the republican legislature. Together for Changes, which had opposed looser union with Serbia and was led by the SPPM (under a new leadership), retained 30 seats. Vujanović, who continued to act as premier until a new coalition was formed, was elected Speaker of the Skupština on 5 November. Vujanović became acting President of the Republic of Montenegro 20 days later, when Đukanović resigned, so that he could be nominated to form a government. A dispute over the allocation of ministerial portfolios with the DPS's ally, the Social Democratic Party of Montenegro (SDP), delayed the formalization of the coalition, but the new Government headed by Đukanović was finally approved by the legislature on 8 January 2003. Meanwhile, the pro-federation SPPM and the pro-independence LAM had organized a boycott of the presidential election, held on 22 December 2002, which was consequently won by Vujanović, with 83.7% of the votes cast, but with those votes amounting to less than the one-half of the total electorate legally required. Vujanović was the Democratic List candidate, but, owing to the boycott, the election was not contested by the main opposition group, Together for Change. He won 82.0% of votes in the repeated poll held on 9 February 2003, but with only 47% of the electorate participating, prompting the Skupština to abolish the regulation on participation in advance of a further attempt to elect a President. Vujanović was duly elected President on 11 May, with 62.9% of the votes cast (about 48% of the electorate participated). His nearest rival was Miodrag Živković of the LAM, who received 30.7%. Upon his election, Vujanović pledged to schedule a referendum on independence for Montenegro after a period of three years.

Meanwhile, on 29 January 2003 the Skupština approved the new arrangements for confederation with Serbia. On 4 February the federal parliament formally adopted a Constitutional Charter, thereby transforming the FRY into a new State Union of Serbia and Montenegro. A Skupština, President (former Montenegrin parliamentary Speaker and DPS leader, Marović) and Prime Minister of the State Union were elected in late February and March. In July, when the Skupština adopted a new Montenegrin flag and anthem, and declared 13 July (the anniversary of the 1878 recognition of Montenegrin independence by the Congress of Berlin and of the 1941 start of a popular revolt against the occupying Axis powers) a national holiday.

Politicians in Serbia and Montenegro agreed that the EU should set the conditions for and supervise the conduct of any referendum on Montenegrin independence. In February 2006, amid much controversy, the EU announced that any proposal of Montenegrin independence would require the approval of 55% of those voting (with a minimum rate of participation of 50% of the registered electorate), in order to secure international recognition. The Government, which favoured a simple majority, reluctantly agreed to the conditions. Legislation providing for a referendum to be held on 21 May was duly enacted on 1 March. In April the Government formally presented to the Serbian Government a guarantee of equal status for Serbian citizens within Montenegro in the event of independence.

Two days after the referendum of 21 May 2006 the electoral authorities declared Montenegro to have voted in favour of independence. With a participation rate of over 86%, some 55.5% of votes cast at the referendum were in favour of independence and 44.5% against, thereby narrowly fulfilling the EU criteria. The EU and other international organizations declared the vote to have been free and fair. The Skupština duly declared Montenegro independent on 3 June, and international recognition followed. Some two weeks later, Serbia acknowledged the dissolution of the Union and adopted its own independence. A new Ministry of Defence formally assumed responsibility for all military units of the Union on Montenegrin territory, while in July the respective finance ministers and central bank governors agreed the division of the financial rights and obligations of the former State Union (Montenegro was to receive 5.9% of the convertible currency and gold reserves of Serbia and Montenegro). On 11 July President Vujanović announced that legislative and local elections had been scheduled for September.

The general election of 10 September 2006 was won outright by the ruling coalition of the DPS and the SDP, which secured 41 of the 81 seats in an expanded Skupština. The SPPM-led alliance only obtained 11 seats (eight for the SPPM itself), being displaced as the largest opposition grouping by the Serbian List, led by Andrija Mandić of the Serb People's Party of Montenegro, which won 12 seats. A new party, the Movement for Changes, which was pro-European and anti-corruption, also obtained 11 seats. The Liberal Party of Montenegro (the only surviving successor to the LAM, which split in 2004), in alliance with the Bosniak Party of Montenegro, secured two seats. In October 2006 Đukanović announced that he would not seek to continue his premiership, as he wished to develop his business interests (although he would remain leader of the DPS). (Đukanović had been accused of involvement with organized crime, and was under investigation by the Italian authorities, mainly in connection with large-scale illicit tobacco trade in the Balkans.) He reportedly favoured Minister of Finance Igor Lukšić as his nominated successor, but a compromise was agreed with another senior party leader, Marović, and the Minister of Justice, Željko Šturanović, became the DPS candidate. Once the new Skupština met, Šturanović and his Government were duly installed, despite the delaying tactics of the pro-Serbian bloc, on 10 November. The legislature was subsequently also to act as a constituent assembly and to debate a new constitution.

Montenegro was admitted to the Organization for Security and Co-operation in Europe (see p. 366) on 22 June 2006 and to the UN on 28 June. The country then proceeded to seek membership of other international organizations. Montenegro has ambitions to join NATO and the EU (which, in July 2006, agreed to adapt negotiations for a Stabilization and Association Agreement—SAA—with the former Union to the new situation). Serbia, which had declared its own independence from the defunct Union with Montenegro on 5 June, extended recognition on 15 June, establishing diplomatic relations one week later. Montenegro acceded to the Geneva Conventions on 2 August. On

14 December Montenegro (together with Serbia, and Bosnia and Herzegovina) was admitted to NATO's 'Partnership for Peace' (see p. 353) programme. On 18 January 2007 Montenegro officially became a member of the World Bank, also joining the IMF and the other associated institutions. Montenegro initialled the SAA with the EU on 15 March. (The adoption of a new constitution in accordance with EU standards was required for the official signing of the SAA and its ratification by EU member states.) On 2 April the Skupština approved a new draft Constitution, which, however, included several alternative amendments regarding the regulation of state symbols, official languages and religious communities, owing to the failure of the ruling coalition and the opposition to reach agreement in these areas. On 11 May Montenegro was admitted to the Council of Europe (see p. 236).

After prolonged acrimonious debate, a new Constitution was finally approved by 55 of the 76 deputies present in the Skupština on 19 October 2007, narrowly achieving the requisite two-thirds' majority of votes; the Constitution was officially promulgated on 22 October. Serbian parties denounced the new Constitution (which described the main official language as Montenegrin, in place of Serbian), and the Serbian List issued a declaration repudiating its ratification. The adoption of the Constitution allowed the official signature of the SAA at a meeting of EU foreign ministers in the same month.

In mid-January 2008 the parliamentary Speaker announced that the forthcoming presidential election would take place on 6 April. On 31 January Šturanović resigned as Prime Minister, on grounds of ill health. On 29 February the appointment of Đukanović as premier and of his Government (which remained unchanged from the previous administration) was narrowly approved, with 41 votes cast in the Skupština. (Although the Italian investigation into organized crime allegations continued, Đukanović's immunity from prosecution was restored by his return to office.) In March Đukanović and his Croatian counterpart, meeting in Zagreb, agreed to refer the issue of demarcation of the maritime boundary between the two countries to the International Court of Justice at The Hague, the Netherlands. At a NATO summit meeting, which took place in Bucharest, Romania, in early April, Montenegro (together with Bosnia and Herzegovina) was invited to enter into an intensified dialogue towards membership.

Vujanović's re-election to the presidency on 6 April 2008, with 52.3% of the votes cast, further consolidated the strength of the DPS. Mandić won 19.3% of the votes; the reformist leader of the Movement for Changes, Nebojša Medojević, won 17.3%; and Srđan Milić of the SPPM won 11.1%. The rate of voter participation was estimated at about 69% (considerably higher than in 2003). Vujanović, who was inaugurated on 21 May, pledged to work towards EU accession. In October Montenegro (together with the former Yugoslav republic of Macedonia—FYRM) announced official recognition of Kosovo as a sovereign state, following its declaration of independence on 17 February; the decision was welcomed by the USA and the EU, while Serbia expressed outrage and expelled the Montenegrin ambassador in reprisal (but declared that discussions on dual citizenship between the two countries would, nevertheless, continue). Pro-Serbian opposition parties demanded that a referendum be conducted on the issue and organized a protest in Podgorica at which demonstrators clashed with security personnel. On 4 December Montenegro, together with Bosnia and Herzegovina, joined the Adriatic Charter, a US-supported initiative that had been established by Albania, Croatia and the FYRM in 2003 for accelerated military reform and regional security co-operation during the process of integration into NATO. On 15 December 2008 Montenegro submitted an official application for EU membership.

In January 2009 the governing coalition (which had already agreed that legislative elections, due in 2010, be brought forward to September 2009) submitted a proposal to the Skupština that the elections take place that March in order to allow the administration a stronger mandate to fulfil Montenegro's commitments in the EU integration process. On 26 January the Skupština voted in favour of ending its mandate to allow an early poll; on the following day Vujanović announced that the legislative elections would be conducted on 29 March. Later in January Mandić merged his Serb People's Party of Montenegro with the People's Socialist Party to form a new party, New Serbian Democracy, and initiated discussions with the SPPM in an effort to form a broad alliance against Đukanović's ruling coalition. (However, in the event, the SPPM contested the elections separately.)

In early March 2009 Mirek Topolánek, Prime Minister of the Czech Republic (which held the six-month rotational Presidency of the EU Council), expressed support for Montenegro's EU application following discussions with Đukanović in Podgorica, but emphasized that further reforms of the state administration and judiciary, and the instigation of further sustained measures against corruption and organized crime, were necessary before the opening of accession negotiations could be agreed. However, it was reported that several EU member states, notably the Netherlands, opposed a rapid decision to grant Montenegro EU candidate status. The elections to the Skupština on 29 March were contested by a total of 16 parties and alliances; Đukanović's For a European Montenegro coalition secured a decisive victory, with 51.9% of votes cast and 48 seats in the chamber, while the SPPM won 16.8% of votes and 16 seats, and New Serbian Democracy 9.2% of votes and eight seats. Four other groups each obtained one seat. A participation rate of about 66.2% of the electorate was recorded. The EU Commissioner for Enlargement, Olli Rehn, praised the democratic organization of the poll, but urged the Government to reform electoral legislation.

Government

In accordance with the provisions of the Constitutional Charter of February 2003, Montenegro became independent of the former State Union of Serbia and Montenegro on 3 June 2006, following a national referendum held on 21 May. The Constitution of Montenegro was adopted by the legislature on 19 October 2007 and was officially promulgated on 22 October. Legislative power is vested in the 81-member Skupština Crne Gore (Assembly of Montenegro), which is directly elected for a period of four years. Executive power is vested in the Government and judicial power in the courts of law. The President is directly elected for a term of five years, and is restricted to two terms in office. Constitutionality and legality are protected by the Constitutional Court. The President nominates the Prime Minister for approval by the Skupština. The Prime Minister proposes the composition of the Government to the Skupština.

Defence

Following Montenegro's independence in June 2006, the Montenegrin Government established a Ministry of Defence and revoked compulsory military service. In December Montenegro was admitted to the 'Partnership for Peace' (see p. 353) programme of the North Atlantic Treaty Organization (NATO). In May 2007 Montenegro and the USA signed a Status of Forces Agreement, providing for increased military co-operation and allowing US military personnel to operate in Montenegro. As assessed at November 2008, Montenegro's total armed forces numbered 4,500, comprising an army of 2,500 and a navy of 2,000. There was, in addition, a paramilitary force of 10,100, which included 6,000 personnel of the Ministry of Internal Affairs and Public Administration. The Government planned to reduce the size of the army to about 2,400. The budget for 2007 allocated an estimated €43m. to defence.

Economic Affairs

In 2007, according to estimates by the World Bank, Montenegro's gross national income (GNI), measured at average 2005–07 prices, was US $3,109.5m., equivalent to $5,180 per head (or $10,290 per head on an international purchasing-power parity basis). During 2000–07, it was estimated, the population decreased at an average annual rate of 1.6%, while gross domestic product (GDP) per head increased, in real terms, by an average of 5.6% per year during 2000–07. Overall GDP increased, in real terms, at an average annual rate of 4.0% in 2000–07. According to official figures, real GDP increased by 7.5% in 2007.

Agriculture (including hunting, forestry and fishing) contributed 8.5% of GDP and engaged 1.7% of the employed labour force in 2007. The principal crops are potatoes, maize and wheat. The cultivation of fruit (particularly grapes, plums, oranges and tangerines) and vegetables is also important. Agricultural output increased by an annual average of 2.2% during 2002–06; output decreased by 5.3% in 2007.

Industry (including mining, manufacturing, construction and power) contributed 17.8% of GDP and engaged 26.7% of the employed labour force in 2007. Industrial production declined by an annual average of 1.0% during 1996–2001, and increased by an annual average of 3.7% during 2002–06. Industrial output increased by 8.0% in 2007.

MONTENEGRO

Statistical Survey

The mining and quarrying sector contributed an estimated 1.4% of GDP and engaged 2.4% of the employed labour force in 2007. The principal minerals extracted are lignite, red bauxite and sea salt. Production in the sector declined by an annual average rate of 2.0% during 2002–06. Output increased by 8.3% in 2007.

The manufacturing sector contributed an estimated 8.5% of GDP and engaged 16.4% of the employed labour force in 2007. In 2005 the principal branches of manufacturing were metals, building materials, chemicals, woodworking, and food and tobacco products. Production in the sector remained constant during 2002–06; output increased by 15.9% in 2007.

Energy in Montenegro is derived principally from hydroelectric power (which provided about 65.2% of total electricity generated in 2005) and thermoelectric power (34.8%). Imports of mineral fuels accounted for 45.9% of the value of total imports in 2007.

Services contributed an estimated 73.7% of GDP and engaged 71.6% of the employed labour force in 2007. Total foreign tourist arrivals increased from 377,798 in 2006 to 594,710 in 2007.

In 2007 Montenegro recorded a trade deficit of €1,341.6m., and there was a deficit of €1,007.6m. on the current account of the balance of payments. In 2007 the principal source of imports was Serbia (30.2%); other major sources were Germany, Italy and Greece. The principal market for exports in that year was Italy (32.1%); other important purchasers were Serbia, Greece and Slovenia. The main exports in 2007 were basic manufactures and miscellaneous manufactured articles. The principal imports in that year were machinery and transport equipment, mineral fuels and lubricants, and basic manufactures.

In 2007, according to preliminary figures, the overall budgetary surplus was €29m., which was equivalent to 1.0% of GDP. The rate of unemployment was estimated at 30.3% in 2005.

Following the official declaration of independence from the Union with Serbia on 3 June 2006, Montenegro was recognized as an independent state by the European Union (EU, see p. 255) on 12 June, admitted to the Organization for Security and Co-operation in Europe (OSCE, see p. 366) on 22 June, and became the 192nd member state of the UN on 28 June. Montenegro joined the IMF and World Bank on 18 January 2007.

While the Republic formed part of the Federal Republic of Yugoslavia, the Government of Montenegro adopted the German currency, the Deutsche Mark (DM), as the official currency in November 1999, in place of the Yugoslav dinar; this was replaced in turn by the European common currency, the euro, in January 2002. In November 2006 the EU issued a progress report on Montenegro's first months of independence, which emphasized the need for economic reform to combat a continuing over-reliance on certain sectors of the economy, high unemployment and regulatory obstacles. Agreements on bilateral economic relations were signed with neighbouring and other European countries. High levels of growth followed, with GDP growth of 8.6% recorded in 2006, rising again to 10.7% in 2007, based largely on capital growth and massive inflows of foreign direct investment (FDI), particularly in the tourism, banking and construction sectors. Furthermore, unemployment was nearly halved, from 19.7% in 2005 to 10.7% in 2008. Montenegro initialled a Stabilization and Association Agreement with the EU in March 2007; it was officially signed on 15 October (shortly before a new Constitution entered into effect). The restructuring of public enterprises prior to privatization and improvement of state administration to meet EU requirements were priorities for the administration of Prime Minister Milo Đukanović, installed in February 2008; the country submitted its application for EU membership in December. FDI and tourism were expected to decline markedly in 2009 as a result of the global economic slowdown. The country's competitiveness was also being eroded as a result of high wage increases. The IMF therefore forecast a sharp decrease in the rate of annual GDP growth to 2.0% in 2009–10. In March 2009 Đukanović's governing coalition was returned to power in early legislative elections; he had pledged major investments in infrastructural projects to counteract the effects of the international economic crisis and rapid EU integration (notably requiring measures to combat endemic corruption and organized crime).

Education

Elementary education is free and compulsory for all children between the ages of seven and 15, when children attend the 'eight-year school'. Various types of secondary education are available to all who qualify, but the vocational and technical schools are the most popular. Alternatively, children may attend a general secondary school (gymnasium), where they follow a four-year course. At the secondary level there are also a number of art schools, apprentice schools and teacher-training schools. Higher education is offered at the University of Montenegro, which was established in 1974, and at post-secondary schools. Some 12,903 students were enrolled in higher education in 2005/06.

Public Holidays

2009: 1–2 January (New Year), 7–8 January (Christmas), 17–20 April (Orthodox Easter), 1–2 May (Labour Day), 21 May (Independence Day), 13 July (National Day).

2010: 1–2 January (New Year), 7–8 January (Christmas), 2–5 April (Orthodox Easter), 1–2 May (Labour Day), 21 May (Independence Day), 13 July (National Day).

Weights and Measures

The metric system is in force.

Statistical Survey

Sources: Statistical Office of Montenegro, 81000 Podgorica, IV Proleterske 2; tel. (20) 241206; fax (20) 241270; e-mail statistika@cg.yu; internet www.monstat.cg.yu.

AREA AND POPULATION

Area: 13,812 sq km (5,333 sq miles). *By Municipality* (sq km): Andrijevica 283; Bar 598; Berane 717; Bijelo Polje 924; Budva 122; Cetinje 910; Danilovgrad 501; Herceg Novi 235; Kolašin 897; Kotor 335; Mojkovac 367; Nikšić 2,065; Plav 486; Pljevlja 1,346; Plužine 854; Podgorica 1,441; Rožaje 432; Šavnik 553; Tivat 46; Ulcinj 255; Žabljak 445.

Population: 620,145 (males 305,225, females 314,920) at census of 31 October 2003. *Mid-2007* (official estimate) 626,188.

Density (mid-2007, official estimate): 45.3 per sq km.

Population by Municipality (census of 31 October 2003): Andrijevica 5,785; Bar 40,037; Berane 35,068; Bijelo Polje 50,284; Budva 15,909; Cetinje 18,482; Danilovgrad 16,523; Herceg Novi 33,034; Kolašin 9,949; Kotor 22,947; Mojkovac 10,066; Nikšić 75,282; Plav 13,805; Pljevlja 35,806; Plužine 4,272; Podgorica 169,132; Rožaje 22,693; Šavnik 2,947; Tivat 13,630; Ulcinj 20,290; Žabljak 4,204; Total 620,145.

Ethnicity (population as declared at 2003 census): Montenegrin 267,669; Serb 198,414; Bosniak 48,184; Albanian 31,163; Muslim 24,625; Croat 6,811.

Principal Towns (population in '000, official estimates on 1 January 2007): Podgorica 174; Nikšić 75; Bijelo Polje 50; Bar 41; Berane 35; Rožaje 23.

Births, Marriages and Deaths (2007): Live births 7,834 (birth rate 12.5 per 1,000); Marriages 4,005 (marriage rate 6.4 per 1,000); Deaths 5,979 (death rate 9.5 per 1,000).

Life Expectancy (WHO estimates, years at birth): 74.0 (males 71.5; females 76.4) in 2006 (Source: WHO, *World Health Statistics*).

Employment (persons aged 15 years and over, annual averages, 2007): Agriculture, hunting, forestry and fishing 2,698; Mining and quarrying 3,753; Manufacturing 25,697; Electricity, gas and water supply 5,594; Construction 6,647; Wholesale and retail trade, repair of motor vehicles, motorcycles, and personal and household goods 30,750; Hotels and restaurants 11,307; Transport, storage and communications 11,358; Financial intermediation 3,143; Real estate, renting and business activities 5,354; Public administration and defence, and compulsory social security 17,575; Education 12,687; Health and social work 12,004; Other community, social and personal service activities 7,841; *Total employed* 156,408 (males 86,190, females 70,218). *Unemployed* (persons aged 15 years and over, labour force survey at October 2007): 52,100 (males 27,200, females 24,900).

HEALTH AND WELFARE
Key Indicators

Total Fertility Rate (children per woman, 2006): 1.8.

Under-5 Mortality Rate (per 1,000 live births, 2006): 10.

Physicians (per 1,000 head, 2006): 2.0.

Hospital Beds (per 1,000 head, 2006): 4.1.

Health Expenditure (2006): US $ per head (PPP): 243.

Health Expenditure (2006): % of GDP: 6.8.

Health Expenditure (2006): public (% of total): 79.5.

Access to Water (% of persons, 2006): 98.

Access to Sanitation (% of persons, 2006): 91.

Human Development Index (2006): ranking: 64.

Human Development Index (2006): value: 0.822.

AGRICULTURE, ETC.

Principal Crops (metric tons, 2007, FAO estimates): Wheat 2,500; Maize 9,000; Barley 2,000; Potatoes 130,000; Tobacco 400; Plums 5,500; Olives 1,900; Oranges and tangerines 7,200; Grapes 41,000. Source: FAO.

Livestock ('000 head, 2007): Cattle 114.9; Horses 6.3; Pigs 13.3; Sheep 249.3; Poultry 449.0. Source: FAO.

Livestock Products (metric tons unless otherwise indicated, 2007): Cattle meat 11,056; Pigmeat 2,969; Sheep meat 4,729; Chicken meat 310; Milk 172.7m. litres; Eggs 71.3m. units; Honey 485.

Forestry ('000 cubic metres, 2007): *Timber Removals:* 548.2 (Broadleaved 236.3, Coniferous 311.8); *Assortments:* 446.7 (Broadleaved 195.8, Coniferous 250.9).

Fishing (metric tons, 2007): Total catch 1,130 (marine 689, freshwater 441).

MINING

Selected Products ('000 metric tons, 2007): Lignite 1,195.5; Red bauxite 667.1; Sea salt 20.0.

INDUSTRY

Selected Products ('000 metric tons unless otherwise indicated, 2007): Wheat flour 21.3; Wines ('000 hl) 110.2; Beer ('000 hl) 534.4; Spruce and fir lumber ('000 cu metres) 74.5; Oxygen, nitrogen and acetylene 12.9; Cut marble panels ('000 sq metres) 51.2; Steel ingots 38.2; Steel castings 135.6; Aluminium oxide 240.2; Aluminium ingots 124.1; Electric energy (kWh) 2,144.0m.

FINANCE

Currency and Exchange Rates: 100 cent = 1 euro (€). *Sterling and Dollar Equivalents* (31 December 2008): £1 sterling = 1.047 euros; US $1 = 0.719 euros; €10 = £9.55 = $13.92. *Average Exchange Rate* (euros per US dollar): 0.7971 in 2006; 0.7306 in 2007; 0.6827 in 2008.

Budget (€ million, 2007, preliminary): Total current revenues 785.4 (Taxes 708.0, Duties 18.4, Reimbursements 22.9, Other current revenues 36.1); Property disbursements 5.4; Loan repayment revenues and assets from the previous year 5.5; Grants and loans 2.5; *Total revenue* 798.8; Total expenses 605.6 (Gross wages and salaries 192.9, Other personal income and fringe benefits 17.2, Expenditure for materials and services 75.4, Maintenance 20.6, Interest rates 25.1, Leasing 4.9, Subventions 13.1, Transfers to individuals and institutions 128.6, Social protection transfers 44.7, Other current expenses 5.7, Capital expenses 77.4); Total loans and loan repayments 153.4; Total reserves 10.8; *Total expenditure* 769.8. Source: Central Bank of Montenegro.

International Reserves (US $ million at 31 December 2007; excl. gold): IMF special drawing rights 0.20; Reserve position in IMF 10.43; Foreign exchange 721.97; Total 732.60. Source: IMF, *International Financial Statistics.*

Money Supply (€ million at 31 December 2007): Demand deposits 791.2. Source: IMF, *International Financial Statistics.*

Cost of Living (Consumer Price Index for 2007; base: 2006 = 100): Food 104.4; Tobacco and beverages 100.6; Clothing and footwear 101.9; Housing 104.0; Fuel and light 114.4; All items (incl. others) 104.2.

Expenditure on the Gross Domestic Product (€ million at current prices, 2007): Government final consumption expenditure 776.2; Private final consumption expenditure 2,157.6; Gross fixed capital formation 683.6; Changes in inventories 103.2; *Total domestic expenditure* 3,720.6; Exports of goods and services 1,305.1; *Less* Imports of goods and services 2,217.8; *GDP in purchasers' values* 2,807.9.

Gross Domestic Product by Economic Activity (€ million at current prices, 2007): Agriculture, hunting, forestry and fishing 194.0; Mining and quarrying 31.5; Manufacturing 193.1; Electricity, gas and water supply 83.8; Construction 95.7; Wholesale and retail trade, repair of motor vehicles, motorcycles, and personal and household goods 337.0; Hotels and restaurants 91.5; Transport, storage and communications 282.6; Financial intermediation 106.7; Real estate, renting and business activities 360.1; Public administration and defence, and compulsory social security 247.3; Education 102.3; Health and social work 86.8; Other community, social and personal service activities 59.6; *Sub-total* 2,271.9; Financial intermediation services indirectly measured −10.2; *Gross value added in basic prices* 2,261.7; Taxes, less subsidies, on products 546.3; *GDP in purchasers' values* 2,807.9.

Balance of Payments (€ million, 2007): Exports of goods 627.7; Imports of goods −2,151.9; *Trade balance* −1,524.2; Exports of services 674.1; Imports of services −233.9; *Balance on goods and services* −1,084.0; Other income received 89.4; Other income paid −72.4; *Balance on goods, services and income* −1,067.0; Current transfers received 100.8; Current transfers paid −41.4; *Current balance* −1,007.6; Capital and financial account (net) 1,164.8; *Overall balance* 157.2. Source: Central Bank of Montenegro.

EXTERNAL TRADE

Principal Commodities (excluding trade with Serbia, € million, 2007): *Imports:* Food and live animals 216.6; Mineral fuels, lubricants, etc. 275.9; Chemicals products 146.0; Basic manufactures 317.2; Machinery and transport equipment 485.3; Total (incl. others) 2,317.7. *Exports:* Crude materials (except fuels) 38.1; Basic manufactures 431.1; Machinery and transport equipment 19.4; Miscellaneous manufactured articles 12.3; Total (incl. others) 600.8.

Principal Trading Partners (€ million, 2007): *Imports:* Austria 73.9; China, People's Republic 27.4; Germany 93.8; Greece 93.3; Italy 159.6; Serbia 699.1; Switzerland 108.0; Total (incl. others) 2,317.8. *Exports:* Bosnia and Herzegovina 26.6; Greece 85.7; Italy 193.1; Serbia 109.2; Slovenia 35.6; Total (incl. others) 600.8.

TRANSPORT

Road Transport (2006): 152,581 passenger cars in use.

Railways (traffic, 2006): Passengers carried ('000) 1,067; Passenger-km ('000) 131,500; Freight carried ('000 metric tons) 2,494; Total ton-km ('000) 182,163.

Shipping (freight handled, '000 metric tons, 2005): Goods loaded 1,167; Goods unloaded 851.2.

Civil Aviation (2006): Passenger movements 833,715; Freight carried 1,067 metric tons.

TOURISM

Foreign Tourist Arrivals: 272,005 in 2005; 377,798 in 2006; 594,710 in 2007.

Arrivals by Nationality (2007): Albania 37,801; Bosnia and Herzegovina 101,394; Croatia 12,809; Czech Republic 33,100; Germany 17,891; Italy 37,211; Russia 102,350; Slovakia 10,258; Slovenia 20,663; USA 7,426; Total (incl. others) 594,710.

COMMUNICATIONS MEDIA

Telephones (main lines in use, 2006): 175,794.

Mobile Cellular Telephones (subscribers, 2006): 703,053.

EDUCATION

Pre-primary (2006/07): Schools 88; Pupils 10,511; Teaching staff 693.

Primary (2007/08): Schools 444; Pupils 75,038; Teaching staff 4,889.

Secondary (2007/08): Schools 47; Students 31,557; Teaching staff 2,254.

Higher (incl. faculties, art academies and private institutions, 2005/06): Schools 21; Students 12,903.

Adult Literacy Rate: 97.65% (males 99.63; females 95.70) at 2003 census.

Directory

Constitution

Following a national referendum on 21 May 2006, Montenegro became independent from the State Union of Serbia and Montenegro on 3 June. The Constitution of Montenegro was adopted by the Constitutional Assembly on 19 October 2007 and was officially proclaimed, replacing the Constitution of 1992, on 22 October. The Constitution's main provisions are summarized below.

BASIC PROVISIONS

Montenegro is an independent and sovereign state, with a republican form of government. Sovereignty is vested in Montenegrin citizens, who exercise it directly and through the freely elected representatives. The territory of Montenegro is unified and inalienable. Human rights and liberties are guaranteed and protected. Ratified international agreements and generally accepted rules of international law have supremacy over national legislation and are directly applicable when they regulate relations differently from internal legislation. The official language in Montenegro is Montenegrin. The Cyrillic and Latin alphabets are equal. The Serbian, Bosnian, Albanian and Croatian languages are also in official use. Religious communities, which are equal and free in the exercise of religious affairs, are separated from the state. Montenegro will co-operate and develop friendly relations with other states, and regional and international organizations, based on the principles and rules of international law. The Skupština Crne Gore (Assembly of Montenegro) shall decide on the manner of accession to the European Union. Montenegro shall not enter into a union with another state by which it loses its independence and full international personality.

HUMAN RIGHTS AND LIBERTIES

Rights and liberties are exercised on the basis of the Constitution and confirmed international agreements. The right to local self-government is guaranteed. The death penalty is prohibited. Elections, which are free and direct, are conducted by secret ballot. The freedom of the press and other forms of public information are guaranteed. The freedom to operate political, trade union and other associations is guaranteed. The rights and liberties of persons belonging to minority national communities are guaranteed.

LEGISLATURE

The Skupština comprises 81 members, who are elected for a term of four years. The first session of a new Skupština will be held within 15 days of the date of publication of the final results of the legislative elections. The Skupština adopts decisions by majority vote of members at a session attended by more than one-half of the total number of members, unless otherwise regulated by the Constitution. The Skupština decides by a two-thirds' majority of the total number of members on the laws regulating the electoral system and property rights of foreign nationals. The Skupština decides by a two-thirds' majority of the total number of members in the first round of voting and by a majority of the total number of members in the second round of voting, on the laws regulating the manner of exercising obtained minority rights and the use of military units in international forces. The Skupština will be dissolved if it fails to elect a Government within 90 days of the President having nominated a candidate for Prime Minister.

PRESIDENT

The President of Montenegro is directly elected for a term of five years. The same person may be elected President for a maximum of two terms. A Montenegrin citizen who has resided in Montenegro for a minimum of 10 years in the previous 15 years may be elected President. The President proposes to the Skupština the President and judges of the Constitutional Court and, after consultations with the representatives of the political parties represented in the Skupština, the candidate for the office of Prime Minister.

THE GOVERNMENT

The Government comprises the Prime Minister, one or more Deputy Prime Ministers, and ministers. The President nominates a Prime Minister within 30 days of the Skupština being convened. The nominated candidate presents a programme to the Skupština and proposes the composition of the Government. The resignation of the Prime Minister is regarded as marking the resignation of the Government. The right to local self-government includes the right of citizens and local bodies of self-government to regulate and manage certain public and other affairs. The basic form of local self-government is the municipality.

JUDICIARY

The judiciary is independent. The Supreme Court is the highest court in Montenegro. The President of the Supreme Court is elected and dismissed by the Skupština, at the joint proposal of the President of Montenegro, the Speaker of the Skupština and the Prime Minister. The Judicial Council comprises a President and nine members, and the President of the Judicial Council is the President of the Supreme Court. Judges and Presidents of lower courts are elected and dismissed by the Judicial Council.

ECONOMIC SYSTEM

The economic system of Montenegro is based on a free and open market and the protection and equality of all forms of property. The Central Bank Council governs the Central Bank of Montenegro. The National Audit Institution of Montenegro is an independent and supreme authority of the national audit.

THE CONSTITUTIONAL COURT

The Constitutional Court monitors the enforcement of constitutionality and legality. The Constitutional Court comprises seven judges, who are elected by the Skupština for a period of nine years, and adopts decisions by a majority vote of judges. The President of the Constitutional Court is elected from amongst the judges for three years. A proposal to change the Constitution may be submitted by the President, the Government, or a minimum of 25 members of the Skupština. A proposal to change the Constitution may be adopted in the Skupština by a vote of two-thirds of the members of the Skupština. Constitutional legislation providing for the enforcement of the Constitution may be adopted by the Skupština with a majority vote of all members.

The Government

HEAD OF STATE

President: FILIP VUJANOVIĆ (elected 11 May 2003; took office 13 June 2003; re-elected 6 April 2008).

COUNCIL OF MINISTERS
(April 2009)

The Government comprises members of the Democratic Party of Socialists of Montenegro (DPS), the Social Democratic Party of Montenegro (SDP) and the Democratic Union of Albanians (DUA).

Prime Minister: MILO ĐUKANOVIĆ (DPS).

Deputy Prime Minister, responsible for European Integration: GORDANA ĐUROVIĆ (DPS).

Deputy Prime Minister, responsible for Economic Policy and the Information Society: VUJICA LAZOVIĆ (SDP).

Deputy Prime Minister and Minister of Finance: Dr IGOR LUKŠIĆ (DPS).

General Secretary of the Government: ŽARKO ŠTURANOVIĆ.

Minister of Justice: MIRAŠ RADOVIĆ (DPS).

Minister of Foreign Affairs: MILAN ROĆEN (DPS).

Minister of Education and Science: Prof. SRETEN ŠKULETIĆ (DPS).

Minister of Culture, Sports and Media: BRANISLAV MIĆUNOVIĆ (DPS).

Minister of Defence: BORO VUČINIĆ (DPS).

Minister of Economic Development: BRANIMIR GVOZDENOVIĆ (DPS).

Minister of Maritime Affairs, Transportation and Telecommunications: Dr ANDRIJA LOMPAR (SDP).

Minister of Agriculture, Forestry and Water Management: MILUTIN SIMOVIĆ (DPS).

Minister of Internal Affairs and Public Administration: JUSUF KALAMPEROVIĆ (SDP).

Minister of Tourism and Environmental Protection: PREDRAG NENEZIĆ (DPS).

Minister of Health, Labour and Social Welfare: Dr MIODRAG RADUNOVIĆ (DPS).

Minister for the Protection of Human and Minority Rights: FUAD NIMANI (DUA).

Minister without Portfolio: SUAD NUMANOVIĆ (DPS).

MONTENEGRO

MINISTRIES

Office of the President: 81000 Podgorica, Sveti Petar Cetinjski 3; tel. (20) 242388; fax (20) 246608; e-mail predsjednik@cg.yu; internet www.predsjednik.cg.yu.

Office of the Prime Minister: 81000 Podgorica, Jovana Tomaševića bb; tel. (20) 242530; fax (20) 242329; e-mail kabinet.premijera@mn.yu; internet www.gov.me.

Ministry of Agriculture, Forestry and Water Management: 81000 Podgorica, Poslovni centar Vektra, Cetinjski put bb; tel. (20) 482109; fax (20) 234306; e-mail milutins@mn.yu; internet www.minpolj.vlada.cg.yu.

Ministry of Culture, Sports and Media: 81000 Podgorica, Vuka Karadžića 3; tel. (20) 231561; fax (20) 231540; e-mail min.kulture.rcg@cg.yu; internet www.ministarstvokulture.vlada.cg.yu.

Ministry of Defence: 81000 Podgorica, Jovana Tomaševića 29; tel. (20) 224042; fax (20) 224702; e-mail kabinet@mod.co.me; internet www.gov.me/odbrana.

Ministry of Economic Development: 81000 Podgorica, Rimski trg 46; tel. (20) 234156; fax (20) 234131; internet www.minekon.vlada.cg.yu.

Ministry of Education and Science: 81000 Podgorica, Rimski trg bb; tel. (20) 405301; fax (20) 405343; e-mail mpin@cg.yu; internet www.mpin.vlada.cg.yu.

Ministry of Finance: 81000 Podgorica, Stanka Dragojevića 2; tel. (20) 242835; fax (20) 224450; e-mail mf@mn.yu; internet www.vlada.cg.yu/minfin.

Ministry of Foreign Affairs: 81000 Podgorica, Stanka Dragojevića 2; tel. (20) 224609; fax (20) 224670; e-mail mip@mn.yu; internet www.mip.vlada.cg.yu.

Ministry of Health, Labour and Social Welfare: 81000 Podgorica, Rimski trg 46; tel. (20) 242276; fax (20) 242762; e-mail mzdravlja@mn.yu; internet www.mzdravlja.vlada.cg.yu.

Ministry of Internal Affairs and Public Administration: 81000 Podgorica, bul. Svetog Petra Cetinjskog 22; tel. (20) 241590; fax (20) 246779; e-mail mup.kabinet@cg.yu; internet www.mup.vlada.cg.yu.

Ministry of Justice: 81000 Podgorica, Vuka Karadžića 3; tel. (20) 407501; fax (20) 407515; e-mail zeljkos@cg.yu; internet www.pravda.vlada.cg.yu.

Ministry of Maritime Affairs, Transportation and Telecommunications: 81000 Podgorica, Rimski trg 46; tel. (20) 234179; fax (20) 234331; e-mail angelinaz@mn.yu; internet www.minsaob.vlada.cg.yu.

Ministry for the Protection of Human and Minority Rights: 81000 Podgorica, Cetinjski put bb; tel. (20) 482126; fax (20) 234198; e-mail min.manj@cg.yu; internet www.minmanj.vlada.cg.yu.

Ministry of Tourism and Environmental Protection: 81000 Podgorica, Rimski trg 46; tel. (20) 482145; fax (20) 234168; e-mail ministarstvo.turizma@mn.yu; internet www.mturizma.vlada.cg.yu.

President

Presidential Election, 6 April 2008

Candidate	% of votes
Filip Vujanović (Democratic Party of Socialists of Montenegro)	52.3
Andrija Mandić (Serb People's Party of Montenegro)	19.3
Nebojša Medojević (Movement for Changes)	17.3
Srđan Milić (Socialist People's Party of Montenegro)	11.1
Total	**100.0**

Legislature

Skupština Crne Gore
(Assembly of Montenegro)

81000 Podgorica, bul. Svetog Petra Cetinjskog 10; tel. (20) 241083; fax (20) 242192; e-mail ranko.krivokapic@skupstina.cg.yu; internet www.skupstina.cg.yu.

Speaker: Ranko Krivokapić.

Election, 29 March 2009

Party	Votes	%	Seats
Coalition for A European Montenegro*	168,290	51.94	48
Socialist People's Party of Montenegro	54,545	16.84	16
New Serbian Democracy	29,885	9.22	8
Movement for Changes	19,546	6.03	5
People's Party/Democratic Serbian Party of Montenegro	9,448	2.92	—
Liberal Party of Montenegro/Democratic Centre of Montenegro	8,777	2.71	—
Democratic Union of Albanians	4,747	1.47	1
New Democratic Power	2,939	0.91	1
Democratic League of Montenegro/Albanian Alternative	2,898	0.89	1
Albanian Coalition—Perspective	2,619	0.81	1
Others	20,296	6.26	—
Total	**323,990**	**100.00**	**81**

*Comprising the Democratic Party of Socialists of Montenegro, the Social Democratic Party of Montenegro, the Croatian Civic Initiative and the Bosniak Party.

Political Organizations

Albanian Alternative: Leader Vaselj Sinistaj.

Albanian Coalition—Perspective (Albanska Koalicija—Perspektiva): Podgorica; Leader Amir Holaj.

Bosniak Party (Bošnjačka Stranka): 84310 Rožaje; tel. (51) 270164; fax (51) 270165; e-mail info@bosnjackastranka.org; internet www.bosnjackastranka.org; f. 2006; Leader Rafet Husović.

Croatian Civic Initiative (Hrvatska građanska inicijativa—HGI): 85320 Tivat; tel. (32) 660345; fax (32) 660348; e-mail hgicg@t-com.me; internet www.hgi.co.me; f. 2003; joined Democratic Party of Socialists of Montenegro coalition 2006; Pres. Marija Vučinović.

Democratic Centre of Montenegro (Demokratski Centar Crne Gore): Podgorica, Hercegovačka 13; tel. (78) 101011; e-mail dcinfo@dccg.me; internet www.dccg.me; f. 2009; Pres. Dr Goran Batrićević.

Democratic League of Montenegro (Demokratski Savez Crne Gore): Podgorica; ethnic Albanian party; Leader Mehmet Barhdi.

Democratic Party of Socialists of Montenegro (DPS) (Demokratska Partija Socijalista Crne Gore): 81000 Podgorica, Jovana Tomaševića bb; tel. (20) 243952; fax (20) 243347; e-mail office@dps.me; internet www.dpscg.org; fmrly League of Communists of Montenegro in 1991; Chair. Milo Đukanović.

Democratic Serbian Party of Montenegro (DSP) (Demokratska Srpska Stranka Crne Gore—DSS): Podgorica; f. 2003; centre-right; Leader Ranko Kadić.

Democratic Union of Albanians (DUA) (Demokratska Unija Albanaca): 85360 Ulcinj; tel. (20) 242261; e-mail dscg@skupstina.mn.yu; Leader Ferhat Dinoša.

Liberal Party of Montenegro (LPM) (Liberalna Partija Crne Gore—LPCG): 81000 Podgorica, Slobode 78; tel. (20) 232364; e-mail info@lpcg.org; internet www.lpcg.org; f. 2004; Leader Miodrag Živković.

Movement for Changes (MFC) (Pokret za Promjene—PZP): 81000 Podgorica, Dalmatinska 130 D; tel. and fax (20) 269336; e-mail gzp@cg.yu; internet www.promjene.org; f. 2002 as non-governmental org.; became political party in 2006; supports European integration; Leader Nebojša Medojević.

New Democratic Power (Nova Demokratska Snaga—FORCA): Tuzi; tel. (30) 409084; fax (30) 409085; internet www.forca.me; f. 2005; Chair. Nazif Cungu.

New Serbian Democracy (Nova Srpska Demokratija—NOVA): 81000 Podgorica, Vojislava Grujića 4; tel. and fax (20) 652147; e-mail centar@nova.org.me; internet www.nova.org.me; f. 2009 by merger of Serbian People's Party with People's Socialist Party and other small groups; Pres. Andrija Mandić.

People's Party (PP) (Narodna Stranka): 81000 Podgorica, Vasa Raickovića bb; tel. (20) 238715; fax (20) 238717; e-mail narodna@cg.yu; internet www.narodnastranka.com; conservative; supports close relations with Serbia; Chair. Predrag Popović.

Social Democratic Party of Montenegro (SDP) (Socijaldemokratska Partija Crne Gore): 81000 Podgorica, Jovana Tomasévića bb; tel. (20) 248648; fax (20) 612133; e-mail sdp@sdp.cg.yu; internet www.sdp.co.me; Pres. Ranko Krivokapić.

Socialist People's Party of Montenegro (SPPM) (Socijalistička Narodna Partija Crne Gore—SNP): 81000 Podgorica, Vaka Đurovića 5; tel. and fax (20) 272421; e-mail kabinet@snp.cg.yu; internet www.snp.co.me; Leader Srđan Milić.

MONTENEGRO

Diplomatic Representation

Albania: 81000 Podgorica, Zmaj Jovina 30, Stari Aerodrom; tel. (20) 652796; fax (20) 652798; e-mail embassy.potgorica@mfa.gov.al; Ambassador TONIN BECI.

Austria: 81000 Podgorica, Kralja Nikole 104; tel. (20) 601580; fax (20) 624344; e-mail podgorica-ob@bmeia.gv.at; Ambassador FLORIAN RAUNIG.

Bosnia and Herzegovina: 81000 Podgorica, Atinska 58; tel. (20) 618105; fax (20) 618016; Ambassador BRANIMIR JUKIĆ.

Bulgaria: 81000 Podgorica, Vukice Mitrovića 10; tel. (20) 655009; fax (20) 655008; e-mail bg.embassy.me@abv.bg; internet www.mfa.bg/podgorica; Ambassador MAYA N. DOBREVA.

China, People's Republic: 81000 Podgorica, Radosava Burića 4A; tel. and fax (20) 609275; Ambassador LI MANCHANG.

Croatia: 81000 Podgorica, Vladimira Ćetkovića 2; tel. (20) 269760; fax (20) 269810; e-mail croemb.podgorica@mvpei.hr; Ambassador PETAR TURČINOVIĆ.

France: 81000 Podgorica, Atinska 35; tel. and fax (20) 665348; e-mail france@cg.yu; internet www.ambafrance-me.org; Ambassador BERNARD GARANCHER.

Germany: 81000 Podgorica, Hercegovačka 10; tel. and fax (20) 667285; e-mail deutsche.botschaft@cg.yu; internet www.podgorica.diplo.de; Ambassador PETER PLATTE.

Greece: 81000 Podgorica, Atinska 4C; tel. (20) 655544; fax (20) 655543; e-mail hellas@cg.yu; Ambassador GEORGIOS AVGOUSTIS.

Hungary: 81000 Podgorica, Kralja Nikole 104; tel. (20) 602910; fax (20) 625243; e-mail mission.pdg@kum.hu; Ambassador Dr ZOLTÁN SOMOGYI.

Italy: 81000 Podgorica, Džordža Vašingtona 83; tel. (20) 234661; fax (20) 234663; e-mail segreteria.podgorica@esteri.it; internet www.ambpodgorica.esteri.it; Ambassador SERGIO BARBANTI.

Macedonia, former Yugoslav republic: 81000 Podgorica, Hercegovačka 49; tel. (20) 667415; fax (20) 667205; e-mail mkgkpodgorica@cg.yu; Ambassador STEFAN NIKOLOVSKI.

Poland: 81000 Podgorica, 8 Marta 72; tel. and fax (20) 658593; e-mail ambaspol@cg.yu; Chargé d'affaires a.i. JAROSŁAW LINDENBERG.

Romania: 81000 Podgorica, Vukice Mitrovića 40; tel. (20) 618040; fax (20) 655081; e-mail ambs.romania.mne@cg.yu; Ambassador MIHAIL FLOROVICI.

Russia: 81000 Podgorica, Veliše Mugoše 1; tel. and fax (20) 272460; e-mail gencons.ru@cg.yu; Chargé d'affaires YAKOV F. GERASIMOV.

Serbia: 81000 Podgorica, Hercegovačka 18; tel. (20) 667305; fax (20) 664301; e-mail embassy.podgorica@mfa.rs; Ambassador ZORAN LUTOVAC.

Slovenia: 81000 Podgorica, 13 Jula bb, PC 'Čelebić'; tel. (20) 208020; fax (20) 237095; e-mail kpg@gov.si; Ambassador JERNEJ VIDETIČ.

Turkey: 81000 Podgorica, Svetog Petra Cetinjskog 145, Hotel Best Western Premier; tel. (20) 406500; fax (20) 406558; Ambassador MEHMET MURAT OUZ.

United Kingdom: 81000 Podgorica, Ulcinjska 8, Gorica C; tel. (20) 618010; fax (20) 618020; e-mail podgorica@britishembassy.co.me; internet ukinmontenegro.fco.gov.uk; Ambassador KEVIN LYNE.

USA: 81000 Podgorica, Ljubljanska bb; tel. (20) 225417; fax (20) 241358; e-mail podgorica@state.gov; internet podgorica.usembassy.gov; Ambassador RODERICK V. MOORE.

Judicial System

Constitutional Court: 81000 Podgorica, Lenjina 3; tel. (20) 41846; 5 judges; Pres. MLADEN VUKČEVIĆ.

Supreme Court: 81000 Podgorica, Njegoševa 6; tel. (20) 43070; 13 judges; Pres. VESNA MEDENICA.

Office of the Public Prosecutor: 81000 Podgorica, Njegoševa 6; tel. (20) 43053; Public Prosecutor VESNA MEDENICA.

Religion

CHRISTIANITY

The Eastern Orthodox Church

Montenegrin Orthodox Church (Crnogorska Pravoslavna Crkva): 81250 Cetinje, Gruda bb; tel. and fax (41) 31310; e-mail crkva@moc-cpc.org; internet www.moc-cpc.org; autocephalous until 1920, when it was dissolved and annexed to the Serbian Orthodox Church; restored 1993; Archbishop of Cetinje and Metropolitan of Montenegro MIHAILO (DEDEIĆ).

Orthodox Metropolitanate of Montenegro and the Littoral—Serbian Orthodox Church (Pravoslavna Mitropolitija Crnogorsko Primorska—Srpska Pravoslavna Crkva): 81250 Cetinje; e-mail euo@mitropolija.me; internet www.mitropolija.me; Metropolitan of Montenegro and the Littoral AMFILOHIJE (RADOVIĆ).

The Roman Catholic Church

At 31 December 2006 there were an estimated 12,165 adherents in the archdiocese of Bar (which is directly answerable to the Holy See) and an estimated 11,000 adherents in the Diocese of Kotor (which is suffragan to the archdiocese of Split-Makarska, based in Croatia).

Archbishop of Bar: Most Rev. ZEF GASHI, 85000 Bar, Popovići 98; tel. (30) 344236; fax (30) 344233; e-mail zega_bar@cg.yu.

Bishop of Kotor: Most Rev ILIJA JANJIĆ, 85330 Kotor, Stari grad 336; tel. (32) 322315; fax (32) 322175; e-mail carbicot@cg.yu.

ISLAM

Almost 20% of the Montenegrin population profess Islam as their faith, many being ethnic Slav Muslims (Bosniaks) of the Sandžak region (which was partitioned between Montenegro and Serbia in 1913).

The Press

PRINCIPAL DAILIES

Dan (The Day): 81000 Podgorica, 13 Jula 10; tel. (20) 239106; fax (20) 239102; e-mail dan@cg.yu; internet www.dan.cg.yu; f. 1999; Chief Editor MLADEN MILUTINOVIĆ.

Pobjeda (Victory): 81000 Podgorica, bul. Revolucije 11, POB 101; tel. (20) 245955; fax (20) 224901; e-mail direktor@pobjeda.cg.yu; internet www.pobjeda.co.yu; f. 1944; morning; Editor-in-Chief ANDRIJA RACKOVIĆ; circ. 18,000 (2003).

Republika (The Republic): 81000 Podgorica, trg Republike bb; tel. (20) 215260; fax (20) 215270; e-mail direktor@republika.cg.yu; internet www.republika.cg.yu; Editor-in-Chief VELIZAR BRAJOVIĆ.

Vijesti (The News): 81000 Podgorica, bul. Revolucije 9; tel. (20) 406901; fax (20) 242306; e-mail vijesti@cg.yu; internet www.vijesti.cg.yu; f. 1997; Editor-in-Chief SLAVOLJUB SĆEKIČ.

PERIODICALS

Crnogorski Književni List (Montenegrin Literary Paper): 81000 Podgorica, Bożane Vucinić 1; tel. (20) 623552; fax (20) 623285; e-mail ckl@cg.yu; internet www.ckl.cg.yu; f. 2000; literature, culture, science, politics; Editor-in-Chief JEVREM BRKOVIĆ.

Monitor: 81000 Podgorica, ul. 19 Decembra 19; tel. (20) 242479; fax (20) 243739; e-mail monitor@cg.yu; internet www.monitor.cg.yu; f. 1990; weekly; independent; politics, general; Editor-in-Chief ESAD KOČAN.

PRESS ASSOCIATION

Asscn of Professional Journalists of Montenegro: 81000 Podgorica, 13 Jula 25; tel. and fax (20) 243169; e-mail publika@cg.yu; Pres DANILO BURZAN, RADOVAN MILJANIĆ.

Publishers

Obod: 81250 Cetinje, Njegoševa 3; tel. (41) 21331; fax (41) 21953; general literature; Dir VASKO JANKOVIĆ.

Pobjeda (Victory) Publishing House: 81000 Podgorica, Južni bul. bb; tel. (20) 44433; f. 1974; poetry, fiction, lexicography and scientific works.

Broadcasting and Communications

TELECOMMUNICATIONS

Regulatory Agency

Agency for Telecommunications: 81000 Podgorica, bul. Revolucije 1; tel. (20) 246786; fax (20) 241805; e-mail agentel@cg.yu; internet www.agentel.cg.yu; f. 2001; independent regulatory body; Dir ZORAN SEKULIĆ.

Service Providers

Crnogorski Telekom: 81000 Podgorica, Moskovska 29; tel. (20) 433433; fax (20) 432400; e-mail office@telekom-cg.com; internet www.telekom-cg.com; 76.53% owned by Magyar Telekom (Hungary); Chair. of Bd of Dirs BENCE MAKAI.

m:tel: 81000 Podgorica, Kralja Nikole 27A; internet www.mtel-cg.com; f. 2007; owned by Telekom Srbija (Serbia) and Ogalar (Netherlands); mobile cellular telecommunications services; Chair. of Bd of Dirs Branko Radujko.

Promonte: 81000 Podgorica, bul. Džordža Vašingtona 83; tel. (20) 235000; fax (20) 235035; e-mail info@promonte.com; internet www.promonte.com; f. 1996; 100% owned by Telenor (Norway); mobile cellular telecommunications services; Gen. Dir Kare Gustad.

T-Mobile Crna Gora: 81000 Podgorica, bul. Svetog Petra Cetinjskog bb; tel. (20) 400801; fax (20) 225752; e-mail office@monetcg.com; internet www.t-mobile-cg.com; f. 2000; fmrly Monet; present name adopted 2006; subsidiary of Crnogorski Telekom; mobile cellular telecommunications services.

BROADCASTING
Regulatory Agency

Montenegro Broadcasting Agency (Agencija za radio-diffuziu Crne Gore): 81000 Podgorica, bul. Svetog Petra Cetinjskog 9; fax (20) 201440; e-mail sard@ard.mn.yu; internet www.ard.cg.yu; Dir Abaz Beli Džafić.

Television and Radio

Radiotelevizija Crne Gore (Radio and Television of Montenegro): 81000 Podgorica, Cetinjski put bb; tel. (20) 225602; fax (20) 225108; internet www.rtcg.org; f. 1944 (radio) and 1971 (television); 2 terrestrial television channels and 1 satellite channel; 2 radio channels—Prvi program (Channel 1) and Radio 98; Dir-Gen. Radovan Miljanić; Dir of Television Veljo Jauković; Dir of Radio Budimir Raičević.

Radio D: 81000 Podgorica, 13 Jula bb; tel. (20) 238909; e-mail mladenm@cg.yu; f. 2000; independent; Dir Svetlana Vučeljić.

Finance
(cap. = capital; res = reserves; dep. = deposits; m. = million; amounts in euros; br. = branch)

BANKING
Central Bank

The Central Bank of Montenegro was established in 2001.

Central Bank of Montenegro (Centralna Banka Crne Gore—CBCG): 81000 Podgorica, bul. Petra Cetinjskog 7; tel. (20) 403191; fax (20) 664140; e-mail info@cb-cg.org; internet www.cb-mn.org; f. 2001; cap. 2.6m., res 41.9m., dep. 438.9m. (Dec. 2007); Gov. Ljubiša Krgović.

Selected Banks

In 2008 some 11 banks were operating in Montenegro, seven of which were foreign-owned.

Crnogorska komercijalna banka a.d. Podgorica (CKB): 81000 Podgorica, Moskovska bb; tel. (20) 404211; fax (20) 404358; e-mail info@ckb.cg.yu; internet www.ckb.cg.yu; f. 1997; 100% owned by National Savings and Commercial Bank—OTP Bank (Hungary); cap. 18.0m., res 0.9m., dep. 457.2m. (Dec. 2006); Pres. Jozsef Windheim; 40 brs.

NLB Montenegrobanka a.d. Podgorica: 81000 Podgorica, Dragojevića 46; tel. (20) 402000; fax (20) 402133; e-mail info@montenegro-banka.com; internet www.montenegrobanka.com; f. 1905; frmly MNB Crnogorska banka—Banque de Montenegro; present name adopted Jan. 2006; 86.97% owned by Nova Ljubljanska Banka d.d. (Slovenia); cap. 4.1m., dep. 60.9m. (Dec. 2005); Pres. Andrej Hazabent; Gen. Man. Crtomir Mesarić.

Opportunity Bank a.d. Podgorica: 81000 Podgorica, Marka Miljanova 46; tel. (20) 625615; fax (20) 625997; e-mail info@opportunitybank.cg.yu; internet www.opportunitybank.cg.yu; f. 2002; cap. 5.3m., res 2.1m., dep. 133.8m. (Dec. 2007); Pres. Keith Flintham.

STOCK EXCHANGE

Montenegro Stock Exchange (Montenegroberza): 81000 Podgorica, Moskovska 77; tel. and fax (20) 244422; e-mail mberza@cg.yu; internet www.montenegroberza.com; f. 1993; CEO Dejana Suškavčević.

INSURANCE

Lovćen Osiguranje a.d. Podgorica (Lovćen Insurance Co Podgorica): 81000 Podgorica, ul. Slobode 13 A; tel. (20) 404400; fax (20) 245482; e-mail lovosig@cg.yu; internet www.lovcenosiguranje.cg.yu; insurance and reinsurance; Sec. Purić Radenko.

Trade and Industry
CHAMBER OF COMMERCE

Chamber of Commerce of Montenegro (Privredna Komora Crne Gore): 81000 Podgorica, Novaka Miloševa 29; tel. (20) 31071; fax (20) 34926; e-mail pkcg@cg.yu; internet www.pkcg.org; Pres. Vojin Đukanović.

UTILITIES
Electricity

Elektroprivreda Crne Gore a.d. Nikšić (EPCG) (Montenegro Electricity Co): 81400 Nikšić, Vuka Karadžića 2; tel. and fax (40) 214252; e-mail Listepcg@cg.yu; internet www.epcg.cg.yu; production, transmission and distribution of electric power.

Transport
RAILWAYS

Željeznica Crne Gore: 81000 Podgorica, trg Golootočkih žrtava 13; tel. (20) 441302; fax (20) 633957; e-mail zcg-uprava@cg.yu; internet www.zeljeznica.cg.yu; 60.1% state-owned; Chair. of Bd of Dirs Ranko Medenića; Gen. Man. Rešad Nuhodžić.

SHIPPING

The principal coastal outlet is the port of Bar, which is linked to the Italian ports of Ancona and Bari by a regular ferry service.

CIVIL AVIATION

Montenegro Airlines: 81000 Podgorica, Beogradska 10; tel. (20) 405501; fax (20) 405548; e-mail contact@mgx.cg.yu; internet www.montenegroairlines.com; f. 1994; operations commenced 1997; direct flights between Podgorica and Tivat (Montenegro), Belgrade and Niš (Serbia), Frankfurt (Germany), Ljubljana (Slovenia), Paris (France), Rome (Italy), Vienna (Austria), and Zurich (Switzerland); Pres. Zoran Durišić.

Tourism

There were 594,710 tourist arrivals in 2007, compared with 272,005 in 2005.

National Tourism Organization of Montenegro: 81000 Podgorica, Omladinskih brigada 7; tel. (20) 230959; fax (20) 230979; e-mail tourism@cg.yu; internet www.visit-montenegro.com; Man. Dir Predrag Jelušić.

MOROCCO

Introductory Survey

Location, Climate, Language, Religion, Flag, Capital

The Kingdom of Morocco is situated in the extreme north-west of Africa. It has a long coastline on the shores of the Atlantic Ocean and, east of the Strait of Gibraltar, on the Mediterranean Sea, facing southern Spain. Morocco's eastern frontier is with Algeria, while to the south lies the disputed territory of Western Sahara (under Moroccan occupation), which has a lengthy Atlantic coastline and borders Mauritania to the east and south. Morocco's climate is semi-tropical. It is warm and sunny on the coast, while the plains of the interior are intensely hot in summer. Average temperatures are 27°C (81°F) in summer and 7°C (45°F) in winter for Rabat, and 38°C (101°F) and 4°C (40°F), respectively, for Marrakesh. The rainy season in the north is from November to April. The official language is Arabic, but a large minority speak Berber. Spanish is widely spoken in the northern regions, and French in the rest of Morocco. The established religion is Islam, and most of the country's inhabitants are Muslims. There are small minorities of Christians and Jews. The national flag (proportions 2 by 3) is red, with a green pentagram (intersecting lines in the form of a five-pointed star), known as 'Solomon's Seal', in the centre. The capital is Rabat.

Recent History

In 1912, under the terms of the Treaty of Fez, most of Morocco became a French protectorate, while a smaller Spanish protectorate was instituted in the north and far south of the country. Spain also retained control of Spanish Sahara (now Western Sahara), and Tangier became an international zone in 1923. A nationalist movement developed in Morocco during the 1930s and 1940s, led by the Istiqlal (Independence) grouping, and on 2 March 1956 the French protectorate achieved independence as the Sultanate of Morocco. Sultan Muhammad V, who had reigned since 1927 (although he had been temporarily removed from office by the French authorities between 1953 and 1955), became the first Head of State. The northern zone of the Spanish protectorate joined the new state in April 1956, and Tangier's international status was abolished in October. The southern zone of the Spanish protectorate was ceded to Morocco in 1958, but no agreement was reached on the enclaves of Ceuta and Melilla, in the north, the Ifni region in the south, or the Saharan territories to the south of Morocco, which all remained under Spanish control. The Sultan was restyled King of Morocco in August 1957, and became Prime Minister in May 1960. He died in February 1961, and was succeeded by his son, Moulay Hassan, who took the title of Hassan II.

Elections to Morocco's first House of Representatives took place in May 1963, and six months later King Hassan relinquished the post of Prime Minister. In June 1965, however, increasing political fragmentation prompted Hassan to declare a 'state of exception', and to resume full legislative and executive powers. The emergency provisions remained in force until July 1970, when a new Constitution was approved. Elections in the following month resulted in a pro-Government majority in the new Majlis an-Nuab (Chamber of Representatives).

In July 1971 an attempted *coup d'état* was suppressed by forces loyal to the King. Among those subsequently arrested were numerous members of the left-wing Union nationale des forces populaires (UNFP), five of whom were sentenced to death. Although a revised Constitution was approved in March 1972 by popular referendum, a general election did not take place until June 1977. Two-thirds of the deputies in the Chamber of Representatives were directly elected, the remainder being elected by local government councils, professional associations and labour organizations. Supporters of the King's policies won a majority of seats in the new legislature. A Government of national unity was formed, including opposition representatives from Istiqlal and the Mouvement populaire (MP) in addition to the pro-monarchist independents.

In October 1981, when it was announced that the term of office of the Chamber of Representatives was to be extended from four to six years, all 14 deputies belonging to the Union socialiste des forces populaires (USFP) withdrew from the assembly. Elections to the legislature were postponed and an interim Government of national unity was appointed, headed by Muhammad Karim Lamrani (Prime Minister in 1971–72). The new Government included members of the six main political parties: Istiqlal, the MP, the Parti national démocrate (PND), the Rassemblement national des indépendants (RNI), the Union constitutionnelle (UC) and the USFP. The postponed legislative elections took place in September and October 1984. Despite significant gains by the USFP, the Chamber of Representatives was again dominated by the centre-right parties. A new Cabinet, appointed in April 1985, included members of the MP, the PND, the RNI and the UC. Lamrani resigned in September 1986, on the grounds of ill health, and was replaced by Az ad-Dine Laraki (hitherto Deputy Prime Minister and Minister of National Education).

In March 1992 King Hassan announced that the Constitution was to be revised and submitted for approval in a national referendum, in preparation for legislative elections (which had been postponed since 1990, pending settlement of the Western Sahara dispute). The King indicated in July that the elections would take place in November, and that voting would be extended to include Western Sahara—irrespective of the UN's progress in organizing a referendum on the territory's status (see below). In August the King dissolved the Government, and named Lamrani as Prime Minister in an interim, non-partisan Government. According to official results, the revised Constitution was overwhelmingly endorsed by 99.96% of voters in the national referendum, which was held in September; approval was officially reported to be unanimous in the major cities and in three of the four provinces of Western Sahara. Under the terms of the new Constitution, the King would retain strong executive powers, including the right to appoint the Prime Minister, although government members would henceforth be nominated by the premier. The Government would be required to reflect the composition of the Chamber of Representatives, and was obliged to submit its legislative programme for the Chamber's approval; new legislation would automatically be promulgated one month after having been endorsed by parliament, regardless of whether royal assent had been received. Provision was also made for the establishment of a Constitutional Council and of an Economic and Social Council, and guarantees of human rights were enshrined in the document.

Legislative elections eventually took place on 25 June 1993. Parties of the Bloc démocratique (also known as the Koutla démocratique)—grouping Istiqlal, the USFP, the Parti du progrès et du socialisme (PPS), the Organisation de l'action démocratique et populaire (OADP) and the UNFP—won a combined total of 99 of the 222 directly elective seats in the enlarged chamber. (Within the Bloc, the USFP won 48 seats and Istiqlal 43.) The MP won 33 seats, the RNI 28 and the UC 27. The indirect election (by an electoral college) of the remaining 111 members of the Chamber, which followed on 17 September, was less favourable to the Bloc démocratique, which won only 21 further seats. Of the 333 seats in the Chamber, the USFP now controlled 56, the UC 54, Istiqlal 52, the MP 51 and the RNI 41. In November the King reappointed Lamrani as premier. The new Government comprised technocrats and independents, and did not include any representatives of the parties that had contested the legislative elections. (By-elections took place in April 1994 in 14 constituencies—in all but one of which the Constitutional Council had annulled results of the previous year's elections.)

In May 1994 Hassan replaced Lamrani with Abd al-Latif Filali, hitherto Minister of State for Foreign Affairs and Co-operation. Although the new Prime Minister held consultations with the political groupings represented in parliament, the composition of the new Government (in which he retained the foreign affairs portfolio) was effectively unchanged. In July the King appealed to all political parties to participate in a government of national unity, and in October he announced his intention to select a premier from the ranks of the opposition. However, negotiations on the formation of a coalition government failed, apparently owing to the Bloc démocratique's refusal to join an administration in which Driss Basri (a long-serving government member and close associate of the King) remained as Minister of the Interior and Information, and in January 1995

Hassan instructed Filali to form a new cabinet. The interior and information portfolios were, notably, separated in the new Government: Basri remained Minister of the Interior, while Driss Alaoui M'Daghri assumed responsibility for the restyled Ministry of Communication.

Muhammad Basri, a prominent opposition figure (sentenced to death in absentia in 1974) and founder member of both the UNFP and the USFP, returned to Morocco from France in June 1995, after 28 years in exile. It was widely believed that his rehabilitation had been precipitated by the royal amnesty of July 1994 and by the return to Morocco (also from France) in May 1995 of the First Secretary of the USFP, Abd ar-Rahman el-Youssoufi, both of which seemed to indicate a greater level of political tolerance on the part of the Moroccan authorities. In December Abdessalam Yassine, the leader of the unauthorized Islamist movement Al-Adl wal-Ihsan (Justice and Charity), was briefly released after six years of house arrest, but restrictions on his movement were reinstated after Yassine criticized the Government. Despite the King's assertion that there were no longer any political detainees in Morocco, a report published by the Association marocaine des droits humains (AMDH) in February 1996 claimed that 58 political prisoners (primarily radical Islamists, supporters of independence for Western Sahara and left-wing activists) remained in detention.

In August 1996 the King presented further constitutional amendments, including the creation of an indirectly elected second parliamentary assembly, the Majlis al-Mustasharin (Chamber of Advisers), and the introduction of direct elections for all members of the Chamber of Representatives. Most political parties supported the reforms; however, an appeal by the OADP leadership for a boycott of a planned referendum on the amendments led to a split in the party and the subsequent creation of the Parti socialiste démocratique (PSD). According to official results of the referendum, held in September, the reforms were approved by 99.6% of voters. Legislation regarding the new bicameral parliament was promulgated in August 1997: the Chamber of Representatives was to comprise 325 members, directly elected for a five-year term; the 270 members of the Chamber of Advisers would be indirectly elected, for a nine-year term, by local councils (which would chose 162 members), chambers of commerce (81) and trade unions (27).

At elections to the Chamber of Representatives held on 14 November 1997, the Bloc démocratique won a combined total of 102 seats (of which the USFP took 57 and Istiqlal 32); the centre-right Entente nationale took 100 (50 secured by the UC, 40 by the MP), and centrist parties 97 (including 46 obtained by the RNI). The Mouvement populaire constitutionnel et démocratique (MPCD), which earlier in the year had formally absorbed members of the Islamist Al Islah wa Attajdid, won nine seats, securing parliamentary representation for the first time. (In October 1998 the MPCD changed its name to the Parti de la justice et du développement—PJD.) At indirect elections to the Chamber of Advisers, which followed on 5 December, centrist parties won 90 of the seats (42 secured by the RNI, 33 by the Mouvement démocratique et social), the Entente nationale 76 (28 obtained by the UC, 27 by the MP) and the Bloc démocratique 44 (21 won by Istiqlal). In February 1998 the King appointed el-Youssoufi as the new Prime Minister, in an apparent attempt to appease opposition parties dissatisfied with the outcome of the legislative elections. This was the first time since independence that a socialist had been appointed to the Moroccan premiership. In March a new Cabinet was formed, including members of the USFP, the RNI, Istiqlal, the PPS, the Mouvement national populaire (MNP), the Front des forces démocratiques and the PSD.

King Hassan died on 23 July 1999, after several years of ill health. His eldest son, Crown Prince Sidi Muhammad, succeeded as King Muhammad VI. At the end of July the new King decreed an amnesty whereby some 8,000 prisoners were freed and more than 38,000 had their sentences reduced. In August the King ordered the creation within the Conseil Consultatif des Droits de l'Homme (CCDH)—established by King Hassan in April 1990—of an independent commission to determine levels of compensation for families of missing political activists and for those subjected to arbitrary detention. In April 1999 the CCDH had announced that it had been agreed to compensate the families of 112 people who were now officially acknowledged as having 'disappeared' between 1960 and 1990. However, independent Moroccan human rights organizations asserted that the number of missing people amounted to almost 600. In November 1999 King Muhammad approved the return to Morocco of the family of former opposition activist and UNFP leader Mehdi Ben Barka, who had been abducted and apparently murdered in Paris, France, in 1965.

Meanwhile, in November 1999 King Muhammad dismissed the long-serving Minister of State for the Interior, Driss Basri, apparently in response to the violent suppression of protests in Western Sahara in September (see below). The new Minister of the Interior, Ahmed Midaoui (a former Director of National Security), immediately pledged to work towards the strengthening of democracy and the reconciliation of the administration and the people of Morocco. Victims of repression and their families, together with left-wing political parties and non-governmental organizations, subsequently formed a 'Justice and Trust' organization, which aimed to investigate human rights abuses in Morocco since independence. In April 2000 the Government commenced payments, reportedly totalling 40m. dirhams, in respect of the cases of an initial 40 victims of arbitrary detention, from the fund established in the previous year. Abdessalam Yassine of Al-Adl wal-Ihsan was again released from house arrest in May.

In March 2001 King Muhammad announced the establishment of a royal commission to revise the country's laws on personal rights and responsibilities; the commission was to be chaired by the First President of the Supreme Court and included leading Islamic scholars and jurists. Meanwhile, the King demonstrated a commitment to greater rights for Moroccan women by appointing women as royal advisers, ambassadors and to other senior public offices. In September King Muhammad appointed Driss Jettou, a former Minister of Finance and Industry, as Minister of the Interior. (Ahmed Midaoui became an adviser to the King.) In October Muhammad established a royal institute charged with preserving the language and culture of the country's Berber population; the institute would also work towards integrating the Berber language into the education system.

In June 2001 the Moroccan authorities granted Jean-Baptiste Parlos, the French judge leading the inquiry into the disappearance of Mehdi Ben Barka (see above), permission to visit Morocco as part of his investigation. Later that month Ahmed Boukhari, a former member of the Moroccan special services, alleged in a newspaper article that Ben Barka had been kidnapped in Paris by French police officers in the employ of the Moroccan secret service and had been tortured to death by Morocco's then Minister of the Interior, Gen. Muhammad Oufkir. In July Boukhari received a summons to appear before the French investigation into Ben Barka's disappearance; however, the Moroccan authorities refused to grant Boukhari a passport, and in the following month he was arrested on charges of financial irregularity. Boukhari's detention was condemned by human rights organizations, which claimed that the Moroccan Government was attempting to prevent Boukhari from testifying at the Parlos inquiry. In December 2002 the Moroccan authorities announced that they would co-operate fully with the French investigation into the Ben Barka affair, and in January 2003 a French judge travelled to Rabat where he interviewed Boukhari about the disappearance of Ben Barka. In October 2007 a French magistrate issued arrest warrants for five Moroccan officials suspected of involvement in Ben Barka's disappearance.

Meanwhile, in January 2002 el-Youssoufi stated that he would stand down as Prime Minister after the legislative elections scheduled for September, but would remain as First Secretary of the USFP. In March the Government agreed a number of changes to the electoral system, including the abandonment of the simple majority system in favour of proportional representation. The Government insisted that the new system would reduce fraudulent practices and increase public confidence in the electoral process; at least 10% of the 325 seats in the lower house were to be reserved for women. The general election took place on 27 September 2002. According to official figures, the USFP won the largest number of seats, although its representation in the Chamber of Representatives was reduced from 57 to 50 seats. Istiqlal increased its parliamentary representation to 48 members, while the PJD took 42 seats, the RNI 41, the MP 27, the MNP 18 and the UC 16. The rate of voter participation was recorded at just 51.6% of the electorate. In October King Muhammad appointed Jettou as the new Prime Minister, and a new Government was announced in the following month. Despite securing the third highest number of seats in the Chamber of Representatives, the PJD was not allocated any ministerial portfolios. The new Cabinet comprised members of the USFD, Istiqlal, the RNI, the MNP, the MP and the PPS, as well as a number of non-affiliated technocrats—one of whom, Al Mustapha Sahel, replaced Jettou as Minister of the Interior. Three women were appointed to the Government. In early May 2003 King Muhammad marked the occasion of the birth of a son and heir to the throne, Prince Moulay Hassan, by ordering the release of an estimated 9,000 prisoners and reducing the gaol terms of a further 38,000.

In mid-May 2003 45 people died and more than 100 others were injured in a series of suicide bomb attacks in central Casablanca, which targeted the Belgian consulate, a Spanish restaurant and a Jewish cultural centre. Among those killed were reported to be 12 suicide bombers, and two other suspected attackers were detained by the security forces along with some 30 others thought to have been involved in the bombings. The Moroccan authorities believed that the bombers were linked to a small Moroccan-based militant Islamist group, al-Assirat al-Moustaquim (Righteous Path), but that the attacks had been orchestrated by an international terrorist network operating in Europe, possibly the al-Qa'ida (Base) organization of the fugitive Saudi Arabian-born Islamist Osama bin Laden. In late May the suspected co-ordinator of the attacks, who had been arrested in Fez, died in police custody as a result of ill health. Later in May stricter anti-terrorism measures were approved by the legislature, including an increase in the number of offences punishable by the death sentence.

In mid-July 2003 10 of the alleged 31 members of the radical Islamist group Salafia Jihadia, who had been arrested during police operations against Islamist networks in mid-2002, were sentenced to death by a court in Casablanca, having been convicted of murder and attempted murder. The remainder of the accused received lengthy prison terms. Later in July 2003 it was announced that more than 700 people would be tried in connection with the bomb attacks; 52 defendants subsequently appeared before Casablanca's criminal court. In August four men, including the two suspected surviving suicide bombers, received death sentences for their roles in the violence; 39 others were sentenced to life imprisonment for plotting further attacks in Essaouira, Agadir and Marrakesh. In February 2005 10 men were imprisoned for eight years for membership of Salafia Jihadia, and in July two members of Salafia Jihadia were sentenced to death, having been convicted of the murders in Casablanca of five people, including an official of the Ministry of the Interior. In April 2008 nine of the men convicted for their links to the suicide bombings in Casablanca escaped from prison in Kénitra, north of Rabat. Seven of the fugitives were reportedly serving life sentences, while the other two were serving terms of 20 years. One of the escaped prisoners was apprehended by Moroccan police a few weeks later, but the others remained at large.

Despite the clampdown on Islamist activity following the Casablanca bombings, King Muhammad continued to pursue his policies of reform and modernization of Moroccan society, including provision for the teaching of the Berber language in schools. In October 2003 King Muhammad announced major revisions to the *mudawana* (family code), which he claimed would promote female equality and protect children's rights. The reforms (originally outlined in 2000) would raise the legal age of marriage for women from 15 to 18 and simplify the procedure for women seeking a divorce from their husband. Although polygamy was not to be outlawed under the new legislation, women would be able to prevent their husbands from taking a second wife and would also be provided with equal authority and property rights within the marriage. In January 2004 the changes to the *mudawana* were approved by the legislature.

In February 2004 an earthquake measuring 6.4 on the Richter scale hit the province of Al-Hoceima in the north of the country, killing more than 600 people and leaving thousands more homeless. While international aid organizations were quick to respond to the disaster, relief efforts were hampered by a reported lack of organization on the part of the Moroccan authorities, leading to angry demonstrations by hundreds of people demanding food, medical assistance and tents.

In June 2005 Nadia Yassine, the daughter of Abdessalam Yassine and spokesperson for Al-Adl wal-Ihsan, was charged with attacking the monarchy following the publication of an interview in which she stated that the monarchy was no longer relevant for Morocco. Along with Abdelaziz Koukas, the editor of the magazine in which the interview appeared, Yassine was liable to up to five years' imprisonment if found guilty. However, the trial was immediately postponed, and was still pending, following several further adjournments, in May 2009.

A series of attempts by large organized groups of African migrants to scale fences along the border between Morocco and the Spanish enclaves of Ceuta and Melilla resulted in the deaths of at least 11 people in late September and early October 2005. Moroccan troops later admitted to shooting dead four of the victims and seven others were reported to have been crushed. In mid-October the Government denied allegations that groups of migrants sent back to Morocco from Spain had been transported to the country's southern desert region and abandoned without food or water. Later the same month the Moroccan authorities repatriated more than 1,000 migrants by air to various sub-Saharan African countries. Illegal immigration from Morocco in 2006 was reported to have fallen sharply compared with 2005, owing in part to tighter border controls by Morocco and Spain. However, in July 2006 another attempt by some 70 migrants to scale the six-metre-high fence surrounding Melilla resulted in two deaths, at least one of which, according to the Spanish authorities, was likely to have been the result of a gunshot.

In February 2006 King Muhammad appointed Chakib Benmoussa, a non-affiliate, as Minister of the Interior to replace Sahel, who became Morocco's ambassador to the UN. In May–June the police arrested more than 500 members of Al-Adl wal-Ihsan, most of whom were quickly released, after unconfirmed reports that the Islamist movement was planning an uprising. Al-Adl wal-Ihsan, which is unauthorized but generally tolerated by the Moroccan authorities, had launched an 'open doors' campaign earlier in 2006 to disseminate information among the general public and recruit new members outside its traditional areas of support such as mosques and universities. Indications of a possible threat from militant Islamism surfaced in August, when 56 members of a group called Ansar al-Mahdi were arrested on suspicion of planning a campaign of violence against the monarchy. Among those detained were several members of the police and armed forces as well as three women, two of whom were married to pilots of the national airline, Royal Air Maroc. In January 2008 the leader of Ansar al-Mahdi, Hassan Khattab, was sentenced to 25 years in prison, while 49 other members of the group were given prison terms of between two and 20 years, having been convicted of various crimes including plotting to attack government buildings and stealing funds to enable them to pursue militant activities.

In March 2007 a suicide bomb attack at an internet café in Casablanca resulted in three people being injured. In April, during a police operation in Casablanca in connection with the previous month's suicide attack, three suspected Islamist militants detonated explosive belts and a fourth was shot dead by police as he attempted to do so. Four days later two suicide bombers targeted the US consulate and a US cultural centre in the city. The series of attacks coincided with two large explosions in Algiers that were claimed by al-Qa'ida in the Islamic Maghreb (formerly the Groupe salafiste pour la prédication et le combat—see the chapter on Algeria). Although a statement on the internet purporting to be from al-Qa'ida claimed responsibility for the explosions in Casablanca, Moroccan police insisted that they were the work of a group with no links to external organizations. In October 2008 more than 40 people received prison sentences, ranging from two to 30 years, for their involvement in the Casablanca bombings; in April 2009 a further 51 suspects were awaiting trial for their alleged connection to the same incidents. Meanwhile, in February 2008 32 members of the small Islamist party al-Badil al-Hadari (Alternative Civilization) were arrested in Morocco on suspicion of being involved in plans to carry out politically motivated attacks. The Secretary-General of the party, Mustapha Moatassim, was among those detained. The party was subsequently banned by the Moroccan authorities following the discovery of weapons at the houses of suspects and allegations of links with international terrorist networks, including having maintained contacts with al-Qa'ida in Afghanistan in 2001. Moroccan police claimed to have dismantled at least 50 terrorist cells and to have made nearly 3,000 arrests since the Casablanca suicide bombings in 2003. Extensive anti-terrorism operations continued throughout 2008 and early 2009, with 32 people imprisoned in October 2008, charged with recruiting militants to fight in Iraq. In April 2009 43 people were convicted on charges of belonging to terrorist organizations, including al-Qa'ida in the Islamic Maghreb; 29 received prison sentences of between two and 20 years; the remainder were fined.

Meanwhile, in April 2006 one of Morocco's principal weekly newspapers, *Le Journal Hebdomadaire*, was ordered by the

Court of Appeal to pay damages of 3m. dirhams for defamation to the Belgium-based European Strategic Intelligence and Security Centre (ESISC); additionally, the publication's editor and one of its journalists were each fined 50,000 dirhams. The newspaper had questioned the impartiality of a report published by ESISC that had been highly critical of the separatist Polisario Front (see below), claiming that it had been guided by the Moroccan authorities. The damages were the highest ever awarded in a defamation case in the country. Mustapha Hormatallah, a journalist for the *Al Watan Al An* weekly, was sentenced to eight months' imprisonment in August 2007 for publishing 'confidential documents' pertaining to anti-terrorism operations in Morocco. An appeals court in Casablanca subsequently reduced Hormatallah's sentence to a term of seven months, but granted him a provisional release. The editor of the newspaper, Abderrahim Ariri, was given a five-month suspended sentence, and both men were fined 1,000 dirhams.

At the general election held on 7 September 2007, Istiqlal won a majority of seats (52) in the Chamber of Representatives. The PJD came in second place with 46 seats, followed by the MP (which had merged with the MNP and the Union démocratique in 2006) with 41, and the RNI with 39. The USFP, which previously held the majority of seats in the legislature, only managed to secure 38. Voter turn-out for the election was at a record low of 37% of eligible participants. On 19 September Abbas el-Fassi, the leader of Istiqlal and Minister of State in the outgoing Government, was appointed as the new Prime Minister by King Muhammad. In October a new Government made up of a coalition of four parties (Istiqlal, the RNI, the USFP and the PPS), along with several independent ministers, was sworn into office. Former Minister of Industry Salaheddine Mezouar was named as Minister of the Economy and Finance and the Deputy Minister of Foreign Affairs and Co-operation, Taieb Fassi Fihri, was promoted to head the foreign affairs portfolio. The new Cabinet included seven women (two of these becoming deputy ministers).

A new political organization, the Parti de l'authenticité et de la modernité, was founded in August 2008 by Fouad Ali el-Himma, a former Deputy Minister of the Interior and a close ally of King Muhammad. A number of existing parties, including the Parti Al Ahd, the Parti de l'environnement et du développement and the PND, entered into an alliance with the new grouping. In January 2009, following the announcement that municipal elections would be held in June, a new quota reserving 2,822 seats (some 12% of the total) for female candidates was introduced. The initiative followed a year-long campaign, supported by female members of parliament and various NGOs, demanding a quota of one-third of seats for women candidates. In the previous municipal elections in 2003 women candidates had won just 127 seats.

Following the cession of the Spanish enclave of Ifni to Morocco in 1969, political opinion in Morocco was united in opposing the continued occupation by Spain of areas considered to be historically parts of Moroccan territory: namely Spanish Sahara and Spanish North Africa (q.v.)—a number of small enclaves on Morocco's Mediterranean coast. A campaign to annex Spanish Sahara, initiated in 1974, received active support from all Moroccan political parties. In October 1975 King Hassan ordered a 'Green March' by more than 300,000 unarmed Moroccans to occupy the territory. The marchers were stopped by the Spanish authorities when they had barely crossed the border, but in November Spain agreed to cede the territory to Morocco and Mauritania, to be apportioned equally between them. Spain formally relinquished sovereignty of Spanish Sahara in February 1976. Moroccan troops moved into the territory to confront a guerrilla uprising led by the Frente Popular para la Liberación de Saguia el-Hamra y Río de Oro (the Polisario Front), a national liberation movement supported by Algeria and (later) Libya which aimed to achieve an independent Western Saharan state. On 27 February the Polisario Front declared the 'Sahrawi Arab Democratic Republic' (SADR), and shortly afterwards established a 'Government-in-exile' in Algeria. In protest, Morocco severed diplomatic relations with Algeria.

Moroccan troops inflicted heavy casualties on the insurgents, and ensured the security of Western Sahara's main population centres, but they failed to prevent constant infiltration, harassment and sabotage by Polisario forces. Moreover, Polisario had considerable success against Mauritanian troops, and in August 1979 Mauritania renounced its claim to Saharan territory and signed a peace treaty with the Polisario Front. Morocco immediately asserted its claim to the whole of Western Sahara and annexed the region.

In July 1980 the SADR applied to join the Organization of African Unity (OAU—now African Union, see p. 172) as a sovereign state. Although 26 of the 50 members then recognized the Polisario Front as the rightful government of Western Sahara, Morocco insisted that a two-thirds' majority was needed to confer membership. Morocco rejected an OAU proposal for a cease-fire and a referendum on the territory, and in 1981 heavy fighting resumed in the region. The SADR was accepted as the OAU's 51st member in early 1982, but a threat by 18 members to leave the organization in protest necessitated a compromise whereby the SADR, while remaining a member, agreed not to attend OAU meetings. In late 1984 a SADR delegation did attend a summit meeting of the OAU with little opposition from other states, causing Morocco to resign from the organization. Meanwhile, fighting continued in Western Sahara; decisive victories for Polisario proved impossible, however, as Morocco constructed a 2,500-km defensive wall of sand, equipped with electronic detectors, to surround Western Sahara.

In October 1985 Morocco announced a unilateral cease-fire in Western Sahara, and invited the UN to supervise a referendum to be held there the following January. A series of indirect talks between the two sides, arranged by the UN and the OAU in 1986–87, failed to achieve a solution, and in January 1988 Polisario forces renewed their offensive against Moroccan positions in Western Sahara. In August, however, it was announced that the Polisario Front and Morocco had provisionally accepted a peace plan proposed by the UN Secretary-General, Javier Pérez de Cuéllar, which envisaged the conclusion of a formal cease-fire, a reduction in Moroccan military forces in Western Sahara and the withdrawal of Polisario forces to their bases, to be followed by a referendum on self-determination in Western Sahara. A list of eligible voters was to be based on the Spanish census of 1974. A meeting in Marrakesh in January 1989 between King Hassan and officials of the Polisario Front and the SADR—the first direct contact for 13 years—was apparently limited to exchanges of goodwill, but was followed, in February, by the announcement of a unilateral cease-fire by Polisario. In September, however, Hassan rejected the possibility of official negotiations with the SADR and, later that month, Polisario renewed its military attacks on Moroccan positions.

UN Security Council Resolution No. 690 of April 1991 established a peace-keeping force, the UN Mission for the Referendum in Western Sahara (MINURSO, see p. 85), which was to implement the 1988 plan for a referendum on self-determination. In June 1991 Polisario agreed to a formal cease-fire, with effect from 6 September, from which date the 2,000-strong MINURSO delegation would undertake its duties in the region. Reports in September suggested that some 30,000 people had entered Western Sahara from Morocco, prompting claims that the Moroccan authorities were attempting to alter the region's demography in advance of the referendum. It was also reported that more than 170,000 Sahrawis who had fled the region since 1976 were being repatriated in order that they might participate in the referendum. By November 1991 some 200 MINURSO personnel had been deployed in Western Sahara, and the peace process was undermined further by Morocco's failure to withdraw any of its forces from the region (under the terms of the cease-fire agreement, Morocco was to have withdrawn one-half of its 130,000 troops from Western Sahara by mid-September). In May 1992 Pérez de Cuéllar's successor as UN Secretary-General, Dr Boutros Boutros-Ghali, announced that Morocco and Polisario representatives were to begin indirect talks under his auspices. In the same month, however, Morocco appeared to prejudge the result of the proposed referendum by including the population of Western Sahara in the voting lists for its own regional and local elections. In June the SADR Government, which by this time was recognized by 75 countries, appealed to the international community and the UN to condemn alleged Moroccan violations of the cease-fire and to exert pressure for the implementation of the UN peace plan. UN-sponsored negotiations in the USA in September failed to formulate acceptable criteria for the drafting of lists of eligible voters at an eventual referendum.

In March 1993 the UN Security Council approved plans for the holding of the referendum on Western Sahara by the end of the year. In July the first direct negotiations took place between the Moroccan Government and Polisario, although little progress was achieved. In March 1994 Boutros-Ghali submitted a report to the UN Security Council detailing possible procedures for overcoming the impasse on the Western Saharan issue, including the effective withdrawal of the UN from the peace process. The Security Council subsequently agreed to a continuation of negotiations for a further three months, and undertook to review the future of MINURSO if a referendum was not organized before the end of the year. In April Polisario accepted the UN programme for the registration of voters. However, the work of a UN voter identification commission, which had been due to commence in June, was delayed by the Moroccan Government's objection to the inclusion of OAU observers in the process.

In mid-1995 Polisario withdrew from the voter identification process, in protest at the severity of sentences placed upon pro-independence Sahrawi protesters by the Moroccan authorities and at alleged Moroccan violations of the cease-fire. In September the SADR announced the formation of a new 14-member Government, headed by Mahfoud Ali Beïba, and in October the first elected Sahrawi National Assembly was inaugurated at a refugee camp in Tindouf, Algeria.

The UN Security Council voted periodically to extend MINURSO's mandate on a short-term basis, noting in January 1996 that it was improbable that the referendum would take place during that year. In May the Security Council voted to suspend the registration of voters in Western Sahara until 'convincing proof' was offered by the Moroccan Government and the Sahrawi leadership that they would not further obstruct preparations for the referendum. The mandate of MINURSO was extended, but its personnel was to be reduced by 20%.

In March 1997 the new UN Secretary-General, Kofi Annan, appointed James Baker (a former US Secretary of State) as his Personal Envoy to Western Sahara. In June Baker mediated in talks in Portugal between representatives of Morocco and the SADR. The process of voter identification resumed in December for a referendum scheduled to be held one year later. However, disagreement between Morocco and Polisario regarding the eligibility of voters delayed the identification process and led the UN to revise the proposed date for the referendum on several occasions. By September 1998 a total of 147,350 voters had been identified since the commencement of the process in August 1994, but the issue of the disputed tribes remained unresolved. In June 1998, meanwhile, as Morocco intensified its efforts to rejoin the OAU, several OAU member states debated the expulsion from the organization of the SADR; only a minority of member countries continued to recognize its independent status.

During talks with Moroccan and SADR officials in November 1998, the UN Secretary-General warned that the UN would withdraw from Western Sahara if the two parties failed to show political will towards resolving the conflict. Annan presented proposals regarding the disputed tribes, the publication of a list of voters not contested by either party, and the repatriation of refugees under the auspices of the UN High Commissioner for Refugees. Although the proposals were accepted by Polisario, the Moroccan authorities expressed reservations. Morocco delayed the signing of a technical agreement with the UN until February 1999: Algeria and Mauritania had signed similar accords with the UN in November 1998. In July 1999 MINURSO published a list of 84,251 people provisionally entitled to vote in the referendum, which was scheduled to be held on 31 July 2000.

In February 1999, meanwhile, the SADR announced the formation of a new Government, led by Beïba's predecessor, Bouchraya Hammoudi Bayoune. In September the Polisario Front congress re-elected the President of the SADR, Muhammad Abd al-Aziz, as Secretary-General of the organization. In October a delegation comprising several ministers of the Moroccan Government was dispatched to el-Aaiún (the principal city in Western Sahara, also known as Laâyoune) for consultations with the Sahrawi population at the behest of King Muhammad—who had in September established a royal commission to monitor affairs in Western Sahara.

In response to indications by UN officials in November 1999 that the referendum was likely to be subject to a further postponement, Polisario stated that it could not rule out a return to an armed struggle. Nevertheless, in late November Polisario released 191 Moroccan prisoners. In December the mandate of MINURSO was once again extended to enable it to complete its work on the identification of possible voters in the referendum. In January 2000 it was announced that 86,381 out of a total of 198,481 people identified in Western Sahara would be eligible to vote in the referendum. In February, however, Annan postponed the referendum indefinitely, and warned, furthermore, of the possibility that it might never take place, owing to the persistent differences regarding criteria for eligibility to vote. By March the number of appeals lodged by those deemed ineligible to vote exceeded 130,000, and Abd al-Aziz reiterated the threat of the resumption of armed hostilities if Morocco continued to obstruct the UN peace plan.

In May 2000 in London, United Kingdom, Baker chaired the first direct talks between representatives of Morocco and Polisario for three years; however, the meeting failed to make any substantive progress. In October Annan urged Morocco partially to devolve authority in Western Sahara, stating that if no such concessions were granted, the UN would reactivate plans to hold a referendum in the territory. In February 2001 Annan announced that if Morocco failed to offer or support some devolution of governmental authority, MINURSO would be directed to begin the process of hearing appeals regarding eligibility to vote in the referendum.

In June 2001 the UN Security Council unanimously approved a compromise resolution (No. 1359), formulated by Baker, which encouraged Polisario and Morocco to discuss an autonomy plan for Western Sahara without abandoning the delayed referendum. Under the terms of the autonomy proposal the inhabitants of Western Sahara would have the right to elect their own legislative and executive bodies and have control over most areas of local government for a period of at least five years, during which Morocco would retain control over defence and foreign affairs. A referendum on the final status of the territory would take place within this five-year period. In August Baker hosted talks in Wyoming, USA, attended by representatives from Polisario, Mauritania and Algeria; however, Polisario subsequently accused the UN of ceding to Moroccan pressure and in September Polisario announced its formal rejection of Baker's proposal. In the following month King Muhammad visited Western Sahara for the first time since his accession to the throne, and in November he granted an amnesty to 56 prisoners in Western Sahara.

In February 2002 Annan outlined four possible measures to be considered by the UN Security Council in order to attempt to resolve the continuing impasse over Western Sahara: to resume attempts to implement the 1988 settlement plan, with or without the agreement of Polisario and the Moroccan Government; to charge Baker with revising his earlier draft framework agreement; to commence discussions regarding the division of the territory; or to terminate MINURSO's mandate, which had continued to be extended by Security Council resolutions for periods of between two and six months. In July 2002 the UN Security Council admitted that it had been unable to agree on the resolution of the Western Sahara issue, since none of the four proposals had secured the required support, but had voted unanimously to allow Baker to pursue efforts to find a political solution which would provide for self-determination.

Following exploratory negotiations held between Baker and government officials in Mauritania and Algeria, as well as with Abd al-Aziz and King Muhammad, in May 2003 Annan formally released details of a new peace plan aimed at ending the Western Sahara dispute and urged Morocco, Polisario and Algeria to accept the proposals. The new plan, known as 'Baker Plan II', proposed immediate self-government for Western Sahara for a period of four to five years, after which time a referendum would be held in order to give all bona fide residents the opportunity to decide the long-term future of the territory. The Security Council approved Annan's proposals in June. At the end of that month Polisario, under strong pressure from Algeria, accepted the Baker plan as a basis for negotiation. Morocco, however, refused to accept any 'imposed decision' on Western Sahara.

On 31 July 2003 the UN Security Council unanimously adopted Resolution 1495, which supported Baker Plan II and called on parties and states of the region to co-operate fully with the Secretary-General and his Personal Envoy in working towards the implementation of the peace plan. (However, following strong opposition from France, the resolution did not demand that Morocco and Polisario comply with the plan.) It also called on Polisario to release without further delay all remaining Moroccan prisoners of war, and for Morocco and Polisario to co-operate with the International Committee of the Red Cross (ICRC) to resolve the fate of persons unaccounted for since the beginning of the conflict. Polisario released 243 Moroccan prisoners of war in September, 300 in November, and a further 100 in February 2004. In April, having urged Morocco to accept and implement Baker Plan II on several occasions, Annan stated that he required a 'final response' from Morocco with regard to the plan.

In late April 2004 the UN Security Council unanimously adopted Resolution 1541, which urged the two sides to accept the UN plan to grant Western Sahara immediate self-government and which extended MINURSO's mandate until October. (The Security Council continued thereafter to extend MINURSO's mandate at regular intervals.) Morocco, however, continued to reject this proposal, maintaining that it could not accept a plan for a referendum that included independence as an option, and remained insistent on granting the territory 'autonomy within the framework of Moroccan sovereignty'. In June 2004 James Baker resigned as Annan's Personal Envoy for Western Sahara; at the request of Annan, he was replaced by Alvaro de Soto, a former Peruvian diplomat who had hitherto been the Secretary-General's Special Representative for the region. In September de Soto commenced talks with the Moroccan authorities and Polisario to attempt to resolve the impasse, and a resolution (No. 1570) adopted by the Security Council in October calling for an end to the deadlock and an advancement towards a political solution was welcomed by the Moroccan authorities. Protests against Moroccan policy towards the region took place in several cities in Western Sahara towards the end of 2004, and in December King Muhammad expressed his country's readiness to find a suitable political solution, while emphasizing that he was not prepared to jeopardize Morocco's sovereignty. In early 2005 de Soto left his role of Special Representative and immediately assumed the position of UN Special Co-ordinator for the Middle East Peace Process. In July Annan appointed Peter van Walsum of the Netherlands as his new Personal Envoy for Western Sahara, and in August it was announced that Francesco Bastagli of Italy would replace de Soto as Special Representative of the Secretary-General and MINURSO Chief of Mission. Later that month Polisario released the remaining 408 Moroccan prisoners of war, some of whom had been held in Tindouf for more than 20 years, one month after Abd al-Aziz had urged Morocco to release 150 Sahrawis he claimed were still in detention. In November one person was killed during violent confrontations in el-Aaiún, which preceded celebrations to mark the 30th anniversary of the Green March, between protesters demanding independence and Moroccan security forces. In a televised address on the anniversary, King Muhammad announced his intention to consult with Morocco's political parties on the issue of autonomy for Western Sahara 'within the sovereignty of the kingdom'. However, Polisario immediately rejected the plan and stated that a referendum was the only viable solution.

In March 2006 King Muhammad visited Western Sahara for the third time since his accession to the throne in 1999, and royal pardons were granted to 216 Sahrawi prisoners. (In April the King ordered the release of all the remaining 48 Sahrawi prisoners held by Morocco.) During the visit Muhammad also announced the appointment of a revised Royal Advisory Council for Saharan Affairs (CORCAS), a body that had been originally established in 1981 by King Hassan II. The 140 newly appointed members were to assist with the formulation of draft proposals for Sahrawi autonomy. In mid-April 2006 Annan submitted a report to the UN Security Council in which he noted the demise of Baker Plan II, which had not been mentioned in any of the relevant Security Council resolutions since Morocco rejected the proposal in 2004, and called on all parties in the dispute, including Algeria, to engage in direct negotiations with no preconditions in order to reach a consensual solution to the impasse. In February 2007 the new UN Secretary-General, Ban Ki-Moon, appointed Julian Harston of the United Kingdom as his Special Representative.

The 'Moroccan initiative for negotiating an autonomy statute for the Sahara region' was finally presented to the UN Security Council in April 2007. It proposed the granting of extensive legislative, executive and judicial autonomy to the region, with Morocco retaining sovereignty and control of borders, national security, foreign and religious affairs, among other areas. The plan was rejected by Polisario, which described it as 'null and void' and on the same day offered the UN a rival plan for a referendum with three options—full independence, autonomy within Morocco or full integration—including proposals for a special political and economic relationship with Morocco in the event of a vote for independence. On 30 April the Security Council unanimously adopted Resolution 1754, which described Morocco's plan as 'serious and credible', while also noting the Polisario proposal, and again called on both sides to enter into direct negotiations without preconditions under the aegis of the Secretary-General. Following the adoption of the resolution, both Morocco and Polisario agreed to begin negotiations, and UN-mediated talks between the two sides (attended by representatives of Algeria and Mauritania) took place in June and again in August in the New York suburb of Manhasset, USA. Two further rounds of negotiations between Moroccan officials and Polisario were held in January and March 2008. While the talks failed to achieve any significant progress, the two sides agreed to consider relaxing restrictions on people travelling by road to visit families in the disputed territory. A further resolution (No. 1813), adopted by the Security Council on 30 April, emphasized the legitimacy of the Moroccan autonomy proposal.

A renewed UN effort to facilitate another round of peace talks began in January 2009 with the appointment of Christopher Ross, a former US diplomat, as Personal Envoy to the Secretary-General for Western Sahara. Ross visited the region in February for consultations with all parties in the dispute. In late April the UN Security Council unanimously adopted Resolution 1871, which reiterated the principles of the preceding resolution and extended MINURSO's mandate for a further year.

Relations with other North African states, which had been strained due to the situation in Western Sahara, improved significantly in the late 1980s. In May 1988 Algeria and Morocco agreed to re-establish diplomatic relations. (Relations with Mauritania had been suspended in 1981 and resumed in April 1985.) In February 1989 North African heads of state, meeting in Marrakesh, signed a treaty establishing the Union du Maghreb arabe (UMA—Union of the Arab Maghreb, see p. 429). The new body, grouping Morocco, Algeria, Libya, Mauritania and Tunisia, aimed to promote trade by allowing the free movement of goods, services and workers. During 1990 bilateral agreements on economic co-operation were concluded by Morocco with Algeria and Libya, and there were further discussions within the UMA on the formation of a North African free trade area. However, there were political disagreements particularly concerning Algeria's continued support for the Polisario Front, and over Moroccan condemnation of Iraq's invasion of Kuwait in August 1990. In early 1993 it was announced that the five UMA members had decided there should be a 'pause' in the development of a closer union; of 15 conventions signed since the inauguration of the UMA, none had as yet been fully applied. However, the organization continued to hold meetings on an annual basis. In December 1995 King Hassan expressed disapproval at Algeria's continued support for the independence of Western Sahara, and demanded that UMA activities be suspended. An impending UMA summit was subsequently postponed.

In March 1999 President Zine al-Abidine Ben Ali of Tunisia made his first official visit to Morocco, during which he pledged to improve bilateral relations and to reactivate the UMA. At bilateral meetings during 2000 with other Maghreb heads of state King Muhammad also pledged to take measures to revive the UMA. A summit meeting of ministers responsible for foreign affairs of the five UMA states proceeded in the Algerian capital in March 2001. However, the meeting, which was to have made preparations for the first summit meeting of UMA heads of state since 1995, quickly broke down following disagreements between Moroccan and Algerian representatives. Libya assumed the chairmanship of the UMA in December 2003, and Libyan leader Col Muammar al-Qaddafi subsequently pledged to host a summit meeting of the UMA heads of state in Tripoli, Libya, in May 2005. However, a statement of renewed support for the Polisario Front by the Algerian President, Abdelaziz Bouteflika, provoked a fresh dispute between Morocco and Algeria days before the summit meeting was due to begin and King Muhammad declined to attend. Despite the ongoing failure to convene an official UMA summit, a meeting was held in Tangiers in late April 2008 to celebrate the 50th anniversary of the first proposal of a union of Arab states in the Maghreb. This was attended by both Prime Minister Abbas el-Fassi and the Prime Minister of Algeria, Abdelaziz Belkhadem, along with delegates from the three other UMA member states. In spite of a dispute between Belkhadem and the Minister of State and leader of the Moroccan USFP, Muhammad el-Yazghi, over the situation in Western Sahara, the meeting ended amicably, with renewed calls for regional co-operation. A year later ministers responsible for foreign affairs from the UMA member states met again in Tripoli, where they reiterated their commitment to improving regional political and economic co-operation.

Relations with Algeria had been further undermined in mid-1994 by the murder, apparently by radical Islamists, of two Spanish tourists in Marrakesh, which the Moroccan authorities attributed in part to Algerian nationals. The imposition by Morocco of entry restrictions on Algerian citizens prompted the Algerian Government to introduce reciprocal visa restrictions and to close its border with Morocco. Tensions eased somewhat in September, however, when Algeria announced the appointment of a new ambassador to Morocco. In January 1995 three people, including one Algerian, were sentenced to death for their part in acts of terrorism, including the murders in Marrakesh; three others were sentenced to life imprisonment. The French security forces made further arrests in connection with the murder of the two Spaniards during 1995–96, and in early 1997 a French court sentenced another 29 alleged conspirators (two Moroccans, the remainder French citizens of Maghreb origin) to terms of imprisonment ranging from one to eight years. The Western Sahara issue remained a source of tension between Morocco and Algeria, but in mid-1998 the Moroccan authorities indicated their desire to normalize relations with Algeria and to reopen the common border. In September 1999, however, Algeria's new President, Abdelaziz Bouteflika, claimed that radical Islamist rebels were launching attacks on Algeria from Morocco, and accused Morocco of ignoring the increasing trade in illicit drugs between the two countries. Bouteflika also criticized Morocco for negotiating a separate trade agreement with the European Union (EU, see p. 255), claiming that this was not in the interests of the UMA. None the less, both Morocco and Algeria subsequently reiterated their commitment to reviving the activities of the UMA.

Although relations remained generally co-operative, Bouteflika was vocal in opposing the UN proposals for Western Sahara in mid-2001, which he claimed favoured Morocco. In February 2002, furthermore, Morocco asserted that Algerian support for the partition of Western Sahara risked destabilizing the region; for its part, Algeria accused Morocco of blocking a UN-sponsored solution to the Western Sahara issue. During a visit to Algiers by the Moroccan Minister of Foreign Affairs and Co-operation in June 2003, it was agreed to establish three bilateral commissions to consider political, economic and social matters. Following talks in July 2004 between the Moroccan Minister of the Interior, Al Mustapha Sahel, and his Algerian counterpart, Noureddine Yazid Zerhouni, the two countries signalled their desire to improve diplomatic relations. In May 2005, however, Bouteflika issued a statement renewing Algeria's support for the Polisario Front, and in October allegations by Polisario that Morocco had abandoned African migrants in the Western Saharan desert further increased tensions between the two countries. Prime Minister Jettou accused Algeria of instigating the allegations, and claimed that Algeria had exacerbated the problem by allowing some illegal immigrants to establish camps close to their joint border. In April 2009, at the Tripoli meeting of UMA ministers of foreign affairs, the Moroccan Minister of Foreign Affairs, Taieb Fassi Fihri, declared his country's readiness to renew bilateral relations with Algeria.

From the late 1990s Morocco was actively involved in wider regional integration efforts, as a member of the Community of Sahel-Saharan States (CEN-SAD, see p. 425), and also through bilateral and multilateral free trade arrangements; in May 2001, notably, the Governments of Morocco, Iraq, Jordan and Tunisia agreed, at a meeting in Agadir, to establish a free trade zone.

A visit to Rabat by the Israeli Prime Minister, Itzhak Rabin, in September 1993 was regarded as an indication of improved relations between Morocco and Israel, and of the role played by King Hassan in the Middle East peace process. In September 1994 Morocco became only the second Arab country (after Egypt) to establish direct links with Israel; liaison offices were subsequently opened in Rabat and Tel-Aviv. In March 1997, however, in condemnation of recent Israeli settlement policy, ministers of foreign affairs of the League of Arab States (the Arab League, see p. 344) recommended a number of sanctions against Israel, including the closure of representative missions. In January 2000 Morocco and Israel agreed in principle to upgrade diplomatic relations to ambassadorial level, although no indication was given as to when embassies would be established. In October, however, as the crisis in Israeli–Palestinian relations deepened, Morocco announced that it had closed down Israel's liaison office in Rabat and its own representative office in Tel-Aviv. There was widespread outrage in Morocco in response to the Israeli military offensive in Palestinian-controlled areas of the West Bank from March 2002. A national march in solidarity with the Palestinian people took place in Rabat in April, attracting more than 1m. people—the biggest demonstration in the Arab world. Public demonstrations also took place throughout Morocco in January 2009 in response to the military offensive launched by Israel against Islamic Resistance Movement (Hamas) targets in the Gaza Strip in late December 2008 (see the chapters on Israel and the Palestinian Autonomous Areas).

Morocco has generally maintained close relations with France. However, the French Government expressed considerable concern following the imposition of death sentences on three defendants in January 1995 (see above), all of whom had been resident in France prior to their arrest. As the development of a Maghreb union slowed, Morocco attempted to improve relations with the EU, which had been critical of Morocco's human rights record. In February 1996, after two years of negotiations, Morocco signed an association agreement with the EU, which provided for greater political and economic co-operation, financial aid and the eventual establishment of a free trade zone. In March 2000 King Muhammad attended talks with President Jacques Chirac in France, during which he expressed his hope that Morocco would be accorded partnership status with the EU and, ultimately, full membership of the union. A fisheries agreement between Morocco and the EU entered into force in July 2006, despite opposition from Sweden, which claimed that Morocco had no right to include the territorial waters of Western Sahara in the agreement.

In 2007 Nicolas Sarkozy proposed the idea of a Mediterranean Union as part of his election campaign for the French presidency. Envisaged as an international body capable of fostering economic, political and cultural links between Mediterranean states, the initiative was described by Sarkozy as building upon the Barcelona Process launched by Euro-Mediterranean foreign ministers in November 1995. By the beginning of 2008 the project had been modified to encompass not just those nations bordering the Mediterranean Sea, but all EU member states, and had been renamed the Union for the Mediterranean. However, King Muhammad was not among the many heads of state of the 43 EU and Mediterranean member nations in attendance at the official inauguration of the union in Paris in July 2008; his absence was officially attributed to scheduling problems, rather than to any political or diplomatic concerns. (Morocco was represented by the King's brother, Prince Moulay Rachid.) Meanwhile, in April 2008 Morocco and France signed a number of agreements aimed at consolidating their economic and social co-operation. The agreements were a result of decisions reached during the ninth Franco-Moroccan intergovernmental seminar in October 2007, during a visit by President Sarkozy to Morocco.

Morocco was accorded 'advanced status' relations with the EU in October 2008. The new status, which was the culmination of more than eight years of negotiations, was expected to enable Morocco to attract more European investment and financial aid, as well as allowing for Moroccan participation in some EU agencies and committees. Morocco was the first Maghreb country to attain such a relationship with the EU, and the development was widely regarded as signifying European recognition of Morocco's programme of social and political reforms.

In February 1995, following the approval by the Spanish parliament of statutes of autonomy for the enclaves of Ceuta and Melilla, Morocco intensified its diplomatic campaign to obtain sovereignty over the territories. Relations between Morocco and Spain deteriorated in April, when responsibility for two bomb explosions in Ceuta was claimed by a guerrilla group suspected by the Spanish authorities of receiving clandestine support from Morocco. In January 1998 the two countries established a joint commission to examine security issues including illegal immigration (to Spain) and drugs-trafficking. In August 1999 Prime Minister el-Youssoufi urged a review of the statutes of Ceuta and Melilla; however, Spain asserted that no Moroccan sovereignty claims with regard to this issue would be considered. The Spanish premier, José María Aznar, visited Morocco in May 2000, and in September, during King Muhammad's first visit to Spain since his accession, two economic co-operation agreements were signed. Nevertheless, relations remained strained owing to lack of progress in negotiations with the EU regarding a new fisheries accord and attacks by Spanish fishermen on lorries carrying Moroccan products through Spanish ports.

In July 2001, in an attempt to limit the increasing number of Moroccans entering Spain illegally, the two countries signed an agreement that would allow as many as 20,000 Moroccans to enter Spain each year in search of employment. In September, however, Spain refuted allegations made by King Muhammad that Spanish criminal associations were responsible for the large increase in numbers of Moroccan economic migrants attempting illegally to cross the Straits of Gibraltar, asserting that collusion between Moroccan police and the smugglers was ongoing. Later that month Morocco recalled its ambassador from Spain. The Moroccan Government was critical of border controls introduced by the Spanish authorities for Moroccans entering the Spanish enclaves of Ceuta and Melilla, and the breakdown, in April 2002, of talks on renewing the EU fisheries accord also contributed to strained bilateral relations. Moroccan-Spanish relations were further strained in mid-July, when a small detachment of Moroccan troops occupied the uninhabited rocky islet of Perejil (known as Leila to Morocco), west of the Spanish enclave of Ceuta and close to the Moroccan coastline. Morocco claimed that it was establishing a surveillance post on the island as part of its campaign against illegal emigration and drugs-smuggling. However, Spain insisted that there had been since 1990 an agreement that neither Morocco nor Spain would occupy Perejil, and, with the support of the EU and NATO, demanded the immediate evacuation of Moroccan troops from the island. A few days later Spain's ambassador to Morocco was recalled, and Spanish special forces intervened and forcibly removed Moroccan troops from Perejil. Spanish officials insisted that their troops would be withdrawn if King Muhammad gave assurances that Moroccan forces would not reoccupy the island, and the Spanish Minister of Foreign Affairs, Ana Palacio, stated that Spain had no interest in maintaining a permanent military presence on the island. Following mediation by the US Secretary of State, Colin Powell, Spanish forces withdrew from the island. Talks held later in July 2002 in Rabat between Palacio and her Moroccan counterpart Muhammad Benaïssa resulted in an accord whereby both states agreed to return to the *status quo ante*. In January 2003 Muhammad temporarily allowed Spanish boats to fish in Moroccan waters, and in the following month the two countries agreed to the return of their respective ambassadors. In December Morocco and Spain announced plans to construct a 39-km underwater rail tunnel between the two countries.

In March 2004 a series of bomb attacks on commuter trains in the Spanish capital, Madrid, killed 191 people. A number of Moroccans from the Groupe islamique combattant marocain (GICM), who had also been linked with the Casablanca bombings of 2003, were among a group of suspected militant Islamists detained by the Spanish authorities in connection with the attacks, and in December 2004 a Moroccan man, Hassan al-Haski, was charged with having planned the bombings. (Al-Haski was sentenced to 14 years' imprisonment in Spain for his involvement in the Madrid bombings, and, following his extradition to Morocco in 2008, was also convicted of involvement in the Casablanca bombings and sentenced to 10 years' imprisonment.) The Moroccan authorities were quick to show their commitment to fighting terrorism, and in April 2004, following an official visit to Morocco by the new Spanish Prime Minister, José Luis Rodríguez Zapatero, the two countries announced renewed diplomatic ties. In May the two Governments revealed plans to establish a joint task force to tackle terrorism and organized crime. However, during June–July 2005 six delegations of Spanish politicians and journalists, seeking to conduct investigations following demonstrations in Western Sahara, were accused by Morocco of supporting Sahrawi independence and were refused permission to enter the disputed territory (see above).

In September–October 2005 at least 11 African migrants were reported to have died while attempting to enter Ceuta and Melilla illegally. Four were shot dead by Moroccan troops as the migrants scaled fences constructed to protect the borders between Morocco and the Spanish enclaves. The Spanish Government urged its Moroccan counterpart to increase its efforts to prevent illegal border crossings but later ended the practice of returning unsuccessful migrants to Morocco, amid claims by human rights organizations that migrants had been taken to the southern Moroccan desert and abandoned by the authorities. In January 2006 Zapatero visited Ceuta and Melilla, the first visit by an incumbent Spanish premier for 25 years. At a summit meeting held between Spain and Morocco in March 2007 and attended by Zapatero, the two countries reached an agreement on the prevention of unaccompanied child migrants. Zapatero also welcomed Morocco's plan for autonomy in Western Sahara (see above) as a means to the opening of dialogue within the framework of the UN, while maintaining that Spain was committed to a consensual solution to the issue that respected the principles laid down by the UN. However, diplomatic relations between Morocco and Spain deteriorated in November, when it was announced that King Juan Carlos of Spain would pay his first royal visit to Ceuta and Melilla. The trip provoked criticism from the Moroccan Government and the country recalled its ambassador to Spain, Omar Azziman, in protest. Azziman returned to his post in January 2008. Relations between Morocco and Spain improved markedly in late 2008, and Prime Ministers Zapatero and el-Fassi attended a bilateral summit in Madrid in December. Talks at the summit, which was also attended by high-ranking ministerial delegations from both countries, encompassed bilateral relations, immigration, the issue of Western Sahara, and economic and security co-operation. Following the summit a Spanish investment fund of more than €520m. for infrastructure projects in Morocco was announced. In January 2009 agreements between the two countries on increased co-operation in security and law-enforcement were finalized. In March it was announced that the first EU-Morocco summit (a product of Morocco's 'advanced status' relations with the EU—see above) was to be hosted by Spain during its presidency of the EU in 2010.

The Moroccan Government was swift to condemn the September 2001 attacks on New York and Washington, DC, USA, for which the al-Qa'ida network was believed to be responsible. In June 2002 the Moroccan authorities announced that they had arrested three Saudi nationals who were alleged to be members of an Islamist cell linked to al-Qa'ida that was preparing terrorist attacks on US and British warships in the Strait of Gibraltar. Seven Moroccans, including two of the suspects' wives, had also been arrested for allegedly acting as couriers between the Saudis in Morocco and al-Qa'ida, which had provided them with funds and logistical support. In February 2003 the three Saudis were sentenced to 10 years' imprisonment by a court in Casablanca; six of the Moroccans received sentences ranging from four months to one year for their roles in the plot. Also in February a Moroccan student, Mounir al-Motassadek, who was alleged to have been a member of the cell that had planned and executed the September 2001 attacks, was convicted by a court in Hamburg, Germany, of belonging to a terrorist group and of aiding and abetting the murder of 3,066 people. He was sentenced to 15 years' imprisonment. In March 2004 al-Motassadek's conviction was quashed by the German Federal Criminal Court and he was released from detention in April. A retrial began in August, and al-Motassadek was acquitted in August 2005 of involvement in the September 2001 attacks; he was nevertheless convicted of belonging to a terrorist organization and sentenced to seven years' imprisonment. In November 2006 the German Federal Court of Justice overturned al-Motassadek's acquittal on charges of accessory to murder, and he was again sentenced to 15 years' imprisonment in January 2007. A final appeal was rejected by the Federal Court of Justice in May 2007.

In June 2004 Morocco became only the second Arab country (after Jordan in 2001) to sign a free trade agreement with the USA. Both the Moroccan Chamber of Representatives and Chamber of Advisers ratified the accord in January 2005.

Morocco's relations with Iran deteriorated in February 2009 following a speech by Ali Akbar Nateq Nouri, a senior political figure in Iran, in which he described Bahrain as a former province of Iran. The remark, which was interpreted by many as an attack on Bahrain's sovereignty, provoked vociferous condemnation from numerous regional and international leaders, including King Muhammad. According to the Moroccan Government, its chargé d'affaires in Tehran was the only diplomatic representative to be summoned by the Iranian authorities to explain their country's response to the incident. The Moroccan representative was recalled from Iran in late February and, in early March the Ministry of Foreign Affairs announced the suspension of diplomatic relations with Iran. The Ministry also accused Iran of interfering in the religious unity of Morocco through its promotion of Shi'a Islam in the mainly Sunni country.

Government

The 1992 Constitution (amended by referendum in 1996) provides for a modified constitutional monarchy, with an hereditary King as Head of State. Legislative power is vested in the Majlis an-Nuab (Chamber of Representatives), with 325 members directly elected, on the basis of universal adult suffrage, for five years, and in the Majlis al-Mustasharin (Chamber of Advisers), with 270 members chosen by electoral colleges (representing mainly local councils, with the remainder selected from professional associations and trade unions) for a nine-year term. Executive power is vested in the King, who appoints (and may dismiss) the Prime Minister and (on the latter's recommendation) other members of the Cabinet. The King may also dissolve the legislature.

Defence

As assessed at November 2008, Morocco's active armed forces numbered 195,800, consisting of an army of an estimated 175,000 (including some 100,000 conscripts), a navy of 7,800 and an air force of 13,000. In addition, there was a paramilitary 'gendarmerie royale' of 20,000, and a paramilitary 'force auxiliaire' of 30,000 men (including a mobile intervention corps of 5,000). Army reserve forces totalled 150,000. Military service of 18 months is by authorized conscription. The defence budget for 2008 was 23,100m. dirhams.

Economic Affairs

In 2007, according to estimates by the World Bank, Morocco's gross national income (GNI), measured at average 2005–07 prices, was US $69,352m., equivalent to $2,250 per head (or $3,990 per head on an international purchasing-power parity basis). During 2000–07, it was estimated, the population increased at an average annual rate of 1.2%, while gross domestic product (GDP) per head increased, in real terms, by an average of 3.8% per year. Overall GDP increased, in real terms, at an average annual rate of 5.0% in 2000–07; it increased by 2.3% in 2007.

Agriculture (including forestry and fishing) contributed 13.7% of GDP in 2007, according to provisional figures, and engaged 42.1% of the employed labour force in that year. The principal crops are cereals (mainly wheat and barley), potatoes, sugar beet and sugar cane, tomatoes, melons and citrus fruit. Almost all of Morocco's meat requirements are produced within the country. The sale of licences to foreign fishing fleets is an important source of revenue. In 2007 seafoods and seafood products accounted for 7.3% of total exports. According to the World Bank, during 2000–07 agricultural GDP increased at an average annual rate of 5.0%; sectoral GDP grew by 23% in 2006, but declined by 20% in 2007, owing to a prolonged period of drought.

Industry (including mining, manufacturing, construction and power) provided 27.3% of GDP in 2007, according to provisional figures, and engaged 21.1% of the employed labour force in the same year. According to the World Bank, during 2000–07 industrial GDP increased by an average of 4.3% per year; it grew by 4.8% in 2007.

Mining and quarrying contributed 2.4% of GDP in 2007, according to provisional figures; the sector engaged 0.5% of the employed labour force in 2000. The major mineral exports are phosphate rock and phosphoric acid, which together earned 12.3% of export revenues in 2007. Morocco is the world's largest exporter of phosphate rock. Petroleum exploration activity was revived at the end of the 1990s, and the discovery of major oil and natural gas reserves in the Talsinnt region of eastern Morocco was announced in August 2000. Coal, salt, iron ore, barytes, lead, copper, zinc, silver, gold and manganese are mined. Deposits of nickel, cobalt and bauxite have been discovered. During 1990–2002 mining GDP increased at an average annual rate of 1.3%. According to official estimates, mining GDP increased by 1.8% in 2006.

Manufacturing, together with oil refining, contributed 15.2% of GDP in 2007, according to provisional figures. The manufacturing sector engaged 11.8% of the employed labour force in the same year. The most important branches, measured by gross value of output, are oil refining and energy products, food-processing, textiles, and chemicals. In 2007 manufactured garments accounted for 16.6% of export revenues. During 2000–07 manufacturing GDP increased at an average annual rate of 3.7%; the sector's GDP expanded by 4% in 2007.

In 2005 electric energy was derived principally from coal (69.2%), petroleum (23.6%) and hydroelectric power stations (6.3%). Facilities for generating wind power have also been developed. Imports of energy and lubricants comprised an estimated 20.2% of the value of total merchandise imports in 2007.

The services sector contributed an estimated 59.0% of GDP and engaged 36.8% of the employed labour force in 2007. The tourism industry is generally a major source of revenue, and tourist arrivals totalled some 4.3m. in 2007. The GDP of the services sector increased by an average of 5.1% per year during 2000–07, and by 7.4% in 2007.

In 2007 Morocco recorded a visible trade deficit of US $14,170m., but there was a surplus of $224m. on the current account of the balance of payments. In 2007 the principal source of imports was France (which provided 16.0% of merchandise imports); other major suppliers in that year included Spain, Italy and the People's Republic of China. France was also the principal market for exports (27.4%) in 2007; Spain and Italy were also important purchasers of Moroccan exports. The principal exports in 2007 were finished consumer products (notably manufactured garments and hosiery), semi-finished products (including phosphoric acid and electronic components) and foodstuffs, beverages and tobacco (particularly seafoods and seafood products). The principal imports in that year were semi-finished and finished products products, and fuel and energy products (notably crude petroleum).

In 2007 Morocco recorded an overall budget surplus of 5,600m. dirhams, equivalent to 0.9% of GDP. Morocco's total external debt in 2006 was US $18,493m., of which $14,108m. was long-term public debt. The cost of debt-servicing in that year was equivalent to 12.2% of exports of goods and services. The annual rate of inflation averaged 1.8% in 2000–07; consumer prices increased by an average of 2.0% in 2007, and by 3.9% in 2008. According to official figures, some 9.8% of the labour force were unemployed in 2007.

Morocco is a member of the African Development Bank (ADB, see p. 170), the Islamic Development Bank (see p. 340) and of the Arab Fund for Economic and Social Development (see p. 183). It is a founder member of the Union du Maghreb arabe (Union of the Arab Maghreb, see p. 429).

Following generally strong and sustained growth in the mid-2000s, Morocco's overall rate of GDP growth slowed in 2007, reflecting low levels of agricultural production as a result of drought, although non-agricultural GDP increased by 6.6%. A recovery in the agricultural sector in 2008, in conjunction with the strong performance of the construction and services industries, and high levels of private sector activity, was expected to result in a stronger rate of overall growth (of a projected 6.5%). The inflationary impact of high international prices for food and fuel was, meanwhile, partially tempered by government subsidies. Higher international prices, together with increased imports of cereals and strong domestic demand for consumer and capital investment goods, were reflected in a widening in the trade deficit in 2007, to the equivalent of some 19.2% of GDP, from 14.8% in the previous year, despite strong exports. Meanwhile, an increase of 19.4% in tax revenue in 2007 resulted in a narrowing in the budget deficit, excluding grants, to just 0.2% of GDP (from 1.9% in 2006); including grants and other disbursements, a surplus was achieved. Assessing Morocco's economic performance in mid-2008, the IMF considered that Morocco's diversified economy, improved public finances and resilient financial sector allowed a favourable outlook. Notwithstanding the potential impact on the economy of continued high international prices for commodities, the assessment urged a better targeting of subsidies over the medium term. The issue of unemployment, particularly among the young, was emphasized as an area of particular concern. The global economic downturn was expected to have a negative impact on sectors such as tourism: under its 'Vision 2010' strategy, the Government had aimed to raise the number of tourist visitors to Morocco to 10m., and to increase tourism revenues to approach 20%, by 2010; the strategy also envisaged the creation of around 600,000 new jobs in the tourism industry. Furthermore, as labour markets diminished in European Union countries, it was anticipated that there would be an increase in the number of migrant workers returning to Morocco, putting further pressure on the domestic labour force. In April 2009 the Government announced that some US $7,300m. would be invested in export-orientated industries (such as automotives, aeronautics, electronics, textiles and agri-business), as well as in the promotion of 'outsource' facilities, with the aim of further reducing dependence on the agricultural sector in the long term.

Education

Morocco has state-controlled primary, secondary and technical schools, and there are also private schools. Education (at the primary level) is compulsory for seven years, to be undertaken between the ages of six and 13 years. Secondary education, beginning at the age of 13, lasts for up to six years (comprising two cycles of three years). Primary enrolment in 2006/07 included 88.8% of children in the relevant age-group, while in 2002/03, according to UNESCO estimates, secondary enrolment included 34.5% of the relevant age-group. The Government has recently taken steps to expand the teaching of the Berber language in primary schools (see Recent History). There were 277,442 students enrolled at state universities and equivalent-level institutions in 2003/04. Under the 2004 budget, expend-

MOROCCO

Statistical Survey

iture on education by the central Government was 28,485m. dirhams (20.8% of total spending).

Public Holidays

2009: 1 January (New Year), 7 January*† (Ashoura), 11 January (Independence Manifesto), 9 March* (Mouloud, Birth of the Prophet), 1 May (Labour Day), 23 May (National Day), 30 July (Festival of the Throne, anniversary of King Muhammad's accession), 14 August (Oued ed-Dahab Day, anniversary of the 1979 annexation), 22 August* (Ramadan begins), 20 September* (Eid es-Seghir—Id al-Fitr, end of Ramadan), 6 November (Anniversary of the Green March), 18 November (Independence Day), 27 November* (Eid el-Kebir—Id al-Adha, Feast of the Sacrifice), 18 December* (Muharram, Islamic New Year), 27 December*† (Ashoura).

2010: 1 January (New Year), 11 January (Independence Manifesto), 26 February* (Mouloud, Birth of the Prophet), 1 May (Labour Day), 23 May (National Day), 30 July (Festival of the Throne, anniversary of King Muhammad's accession), 11 August* (Ramadan begins), 14 August (Oued ed-Dahab Day, anniversary of the 1979 annexation), 10 September* (Eid es-Seghir—Id al-Fitr, end of Ramadan), 6 November (Anniversary of the Green March), 18 November (Independence Day), 7 December* (Muharram, Islamic New Year), 9 December* (Eid el-Kebir—Id al-Adha, Feast of the Sacrifice), 16 December* (Ashoura).

* These holidays are dependent on the Islamic lunar calendar and may vary by one or two days from the dates given.

† This festival occurs twice (in the Islamic years AH 1430 and 1431) within the same Gregorian year.

Weights and Measures

The metric system is in force.

Statistical Survey

Sources (unless otherwise stated): Haut Commissariat au Plan, Direction de la Statistique, rue Muhammad Belhassan el-Ouazzani, BP 178, Rabat 10001; tel. (3) 7773606; fax (3) 7773217; e-mail statguichet@statistic.gov.ma; internet www.hcp.ma; Bank Al-Maghrib, 277 ave Muhammad V, BP 445, Rabat; tel. (3) 7702626; fax (3) 7706677; e-mail dai@bkam.gov.ma; internet www.bkam.ma.

Note: Unless otherwise indicated, the data exclude Western (formerly Spanish) Sahara, a disputed territory under Moroccan occupation.

Area and Population

AREA, POPULATION AND DENSITY

Area (sq km)	710,850*
Population (census results)†	
2 September 1994	
Males	12,944,517
Females	13,074,763
Total	26,019,280
2 September 2004	29,891,708
Population (UN estimate at mid-year)‡	
2006	30,853,000
2007	31,224,000
2008	31,606,000
Density (per sq km) at mid-2008	44.5

* 274,461 sq miles. This area includes the disputed territory of Western Sahara, which covers 252,120 sq km (97,344 sq miles).

† Including Western Sahara, with an estimated population of 417,000 at the 2004 census.

‡ Source: UN, *World Population Prospects: The 2008 Revision*.

REGIONS
(population at 2004 census)

	Population
Oued ed-Dahab Lagouira*	99,367
El-Aaiún Boujdour*	256,152
Guelmim es-Semara†	462,410
Souss Massa-Draa	3,113,653
Gharb Chrarda Beni-Hsen	1,859,540
Chaouia Ouardigha	1,655,660
Marrakech Tensift al-Haou	3,102,652
Oriental	1,918,094
Grand Casablanca	3,631,061
Rabat Salé Zemmour Zaer	2,366,494
Doukkala Abda	1,984,039
Tadla Azilal	1,450,519
Meknès Tafilalet	2,141,527
Fès Boulemane	1,573,055
Taza al-Hoceima Taounate	1,807,113
Tanger Tétouan	2,470,372
Total	**29,891,708**

* Regions situated in Western Sahara.
† Region partly situated in Western Sahara.

PRINCIPAL TOWNS
(population at 2004 census)

Casablanca	2,933,684	Tétouan	320,539
Rabat (capital)*	1,622,860	Safi	284,750
Fès (Fez)	946,815	Mohammedia	188,619
Marrakech (Marrakesh)	823,154	El-Aaiún†	183,691
Agadir	678,596	Khouribga	166,397
Tanger (Tangier)	669,685	Beni-Mellal	163,286
Meknès	536,232	El-Jadida	144,440
Oujda	400,738	Taza	139,686
Kénitra	359,142		

* Including Salé and Temara.
† Town situated in Western Sahara.

Source: Thomas Brinkhoff, *City Population* (internet www.citypopulation.de).

Mid-2007 ('000, incl. suburbs, UN estimates): Casablanca 3,181; Rabat 1,705; Fès 1,002; Marrakech 872 (Source: UN, *World Urbanization Prospects: The 2007 Revision*).

BIRTHS AND DEATHS
(annual averages, UN estimates)

	1990–95	1995–2000	2000–05
Birth rate (per 1,000)	27.3	23.4	20.9
Death rate (per 1,000)	7.2	6.4	6.0

Source: UN, *World Population Prospects: The 2008 Revision*.

Life expectancy (years at birth, WHO estimates): 72.0 (males 70.0; females 74.0) in 2006 (Source: WHO, *World Health Statistics*).

MOROCCO

ECONOMICALLY ACTIVE POPULATION
(sample surveys, '000 persons aged 15 years and over)

	2005	2006	2007
Agriculture, hunting, forestry and fishing	4,505.2	4,303.3	4,235.1
Mining and quarrying	41.8	39.9	48.4
Manufacturing	1,153.9	1,142.0	1,191.3
Electricity, gas and water	31.7	42.8	39.4
Construction	705.4	789.6	838.9
Wholesale and retail trade; repairs; hotels and restaurants	1,656.9	1,602.3	1,637.0
Transport, storage and communications	380.3	394.7	401.9
General administration and community services	1,301.4	1,449.5	1,478.7
Financial intermediation, real estate and business services	130.2	152.4	171.9
Activities not adequately defined	6.5	11.1	13.7
Total employed	9,913.3	9,927.7	10,056.2
Unemployed	1,226.4	1,062.5	1,088.9
Total labour force	11,139.7	10,990.2	11,145.1

Source: ILO.

Health and Welfare

KEY INDICATORS

Total fertility rate (children per woman, 2006)	2.4
Under-5 mortality rate (per 1,000 live births, 2006)	37
HIV/AIDS (% of persons aged 15–49, 2007)	0.1
Physicians (per 1,000 head, 2004)	0.51
Hospital beds (per 1,000 head, 2004)	0.90
Health expenditure (2006): US $ per head (PPP)	273
Health expenditure (2006): % of GDP	5.1
Health expenditure (2006): public (% of total)	35.9
Access to water (% of persons, 2006)	83
Access to sanitation (% of persons, 2006)	72
Human Development Index (2006): ranking	127
Human Development Index (2006): value	0.646

For sources and definitions, see explanatory note on p. vi.

Agriculture

PRINCIPAL CROPS
('000 metric tons)

	2005	2006	2007
Wheat	3,043	6,327	1,583
Rice, paddy	43	34	30*
Barley	1,102	2,535	763
Maize	50	297	120*
Potatoes	1,479	1,569	1,450*
Sugar cane	782	997	900*
Sugar beet	3,302	2,252	3,000*
Broad beans, dry	73	181	110*
Peas, dry	14	24	22*
Chick peas	33	66	47*
Lentils	15	34	32*
Almonds, with shell	71	83	73*
Groundnuts, with shell	47	38	30†
Olives	750	631	657*
Sunflower seed	18	28	8†
Cabbages and other brassicas	46	44	43*
Artichokes	53	55	52*
Tomatoes	1,206	1,245	1,140*
Cauliflowers and broccoli	37	73	73*
Pumpkins, squash and gourds	150	169	155*
Cucumbers and gherkins	54	70	50*
Aubergines (Eggplants)	50	57	43*
Chillies and peppers, green	190	236	192*
Onions, dry	716	882	755*
Peas, green	65	147	110*
String beans	142	163	115*
Carrots and turnips	373	290*	310*
Carobs*	26	25	25

Statistical Survey

—continued	2005	2006	2007
Watermelons	402	712	530*
Cantaloupes and other melons	649	648	615*
Figs	83	77	77*
Grapes	334	356	325*
Dates	48	45	52*
Apples	309	374	350*
Pears	42	35	40*
Quinces	30	28	30*
Peaches and nectarines	55	55*	55*
Plums and sloes	61	54*	52*
Strawberries	119	112	100*
Oranges	835	788	740*
Tangerines, mandarins, clementines and satsumas	463	454	480*
Apricots	104	129	100*
Bananas	190	203	180*
Anise, badian, fennel and coriander*	23	23	23

* FAO estimate(s).
† Unofficial figure.

Aggregate production ('000 metric tons, may include official, semi-official or estimated data): Total cereals 4,283 in 2005, 9,239 in 2006, 2,541 in 2007; Total pulses 182 in 2005, 361 in 2006, 270 in 2007; Total roots and tubers 1,486 in 2005, 1,579 in 2006, 1,459 in 2007; Total vegetables (incl. melons) 4,863 in 2005, 5,569 in 2006, 4,867 in 2007; Total fruits (excl. melons) 2,793 in 2005, 2,797 in 2006, 2,653 in 2007.

Source: FAO.

LIVESTOCK
('000 head, year ending September)

	2005	2006	2007*
Cattle	2,722	2,755	2,700
Sheep	16,872	17,260	17,250
Goats	5,332	5,355	5,300
Camels*	40	36	36
Horses	159	161	160
Asses and mules or hinnies	1,522	n.a.	n.a.
Chickens*	137	140	140

* FAO estimates.

Source: FAO.

LIVESTOCK PRODUCTS
('000 metric tons)

	2005	2006	2007*
Cattle meat	157	160	160
Sheep meat	115	120	120
Goat meat	21	22	17
Chicken meat	350	340	380
Cows' milk	1,400	1,500	1,500
Sheep's milk*	27	27	27
Goats' milk*	34	34	34
Hen eggs*	195	168	168
Honey	3	4	4
Wool, greasy*	40	40	40

* FAO estimates.

Source: FAO.

Forestry

ROUNDWOOD REMOVALS
('000 cubic metres, excl. bark)

	2005	2006	2007
Sawlogs, veneer logs and logs for sleepers	259	215	238
Pulpwood	315	384	377
Fuel wood	383	345	425
Total	957	944	1,040

Source: FAO.

MOROCCO

SAWNWOOD PRODUCTION
('000 cubic metres, incl. railway sleepers)

	1987*	1988	1989
Coniferous (softwood)	40	26*	43*
Broadleaved (hardwood)	40	27	40
Total	80	53	83

* FAO estimate(s).

1990–2007: Production assumed to be unchanged from 1989 (FAO estimates).

Source: FAO.

Fishing

('000 metric tons, live weight)

	2004	2005	2006
Capture	940.9	1,024.5	864.9
European pilchard (sardine)	644.7	629.5	452.2
Chub mackerel	68.1	67.9	62.5
Marine fishes	83.5	133.7	147.4
Octopuses	19.2	44.9	43.7
Aquaculture	1.7	2.3	1.2
Total catch (incl. others)	942.7	1,026.7	866.1

Source: FAO.

Mining

('000 metric tons)

	2004	2005	2006
Crude petroleum	32.3	32.3	11.2
Iron ore*	9.9	8.1	4.6
Copper concentrates*	14.2	12.7	17.8
Lead concentrates*	44.7	59.9	59.1
Manganese ore*	9.0	11.3	4.8
Zinc concentrates*	146.2	151.3	148.7
Phosphate rock†	25,369.0	27,254.0	27,386.0
Fluorspar (acid grade)	112.1	114.7	98.1
Barytes	355.8	475.7	612.8
Salt (unrefined)	253.8	319.9	319.9
Bentonite	85.4	54.4	34.0

* Figures refer to the gross weight of ores and concentrates.
† Including production in Western Sahara.

Industry

SELECTED PRODUCTS
('000 metric tons, unless otherwise indicated)

	2003	2004	2005
Wine*	34	35	38
Olive oil (crude)	45	100	50
Motor spirit—petrol	132	257	372
Naphthas	553	625	650
Kerosene	52	12	2
Distillate fuel oils	1,535	2,254	2,295
Residual fuel oils	1,747	2,264	2,545
Jet fuel	108	174	264
Petroleum bitumen—asphalt	58	141	198
Liquefied petroleum gas ('000 barrels)†	1,000	3,000‡	3,000
Cement	9,277	9,796	10,289
Phosphate fertilizers*§	1,118	1,057	1,042
Carpets and rugs ('000 sq m)	384	301	313
Electric energy (million kWh)	15,385	16,459	19,243

* Source: FAO.
† Source: US Geological Survey.
‡ Provisional figure.
§ Estimated production in terms of phosphoric acid.

Source: partly UN, *Industrial Commodity Statistics Yearbook*.

Finance

CURRENCY AND EXCHANGE RATES

Monetary Units
100 centimes (santimat) = 1 Moroccan dirham.

Sterling, Dollar and Euro Equivalents (31 December 2008)
£1 sterling = 12.11 dirhams;
US $1 = 8.31 dirhams;
€1 = 11.56 dirhams;
100 Moroccan dirhams = £8.26 = $12.04 = €8.65.

Average Exchange Rate (dirhams per US $)
2006   8.796
2007   8.192
2008   7.754

GENERAL BUDGET
('000 million dirhams)*

Revenue†	2006	2007	2008‡
Tax revenue	128.2	153.1	149.2
Direct taxes	50.6	60.5	59.0
Indirect taxes	55.1	67.1	67.1
Import taxes	13.4	14.4	12.2
Other tax revenues	9.1	11.1	11.1
Non-tax revenue	16.5	14.8	11.9
Total	144.7	167.9	161.1

Expenditure§	2006	2007	2008‡
Current	123.9	132.6	138.9
Wages	63.2	65.2	67.0
Food and petroleum subsidies	13.1	16.2	15.4
Food subsidies	5.5	5.8	6.7
Petroleum subsidies	7.6	10.4	8.7
Other	29.0	32.0	37.3
Interest	18.7	19.2	19.2
Capital	22.2	25.7	30.2
Road fund	1.7	1.8	2.0
Transfers to local government‖	11.7	14.9	15.0
Total	159.5	175.1	186.0

* Excluding grants ('000 million dirhams): 2.5 in 2006; 2.4 in 2007; 2.5 in 2008 (budget forecast), GSM revenues and receipts from privatization ('000 million dirhams): 4.8 in 2006; 6.1 in 2007; 3.0 in 2008 (budget forecast) and net transactions associated with the Hassan II Fund ('000 million dirhams): –2.2 in 2006; –2.1 in 2007; –1.5 in 2008 (budget forecast).
† Includes tariffs destined for food subsidies and road fund revenues.
‡ Budget forecasts.
§ Excluding net lending ('000 million dirhams): –0.5 in 2006; 0.0 in 2007; 0.0 in 2008 (budget forecast).
‖ Equivalent to 30% of value-added tax revenue.

Source: IMF, *Morocco: 2008 Article IV Consultation-Staff Report; Staff Statement; Public Information Notice; and Statement by the Executive Director for Morocco* (September 2008).

INTERNATIONAL RESERVES
(US $ million at 31 December)

	2006	2007	2008
Gold (national valuation)	450	593	613
IMF special drawing rights	53	32	19
Reserve position in IMF	106	111	109
Foreign exchange	20,182	23,980	21,976
Total	20,791	24,716	22,717

Source: IMF, *International Financial Statistics*.

MOROCCO

Statistical Survey

MONEY SUPPLY
(million dirhams at 31 December)

	2005	2006	2007
Currency outside banks	89,304	108,601	119,844
Demand deposits at deposit money banks	283,997	325,677	398,196
Total money (incl. others)	375,663	436,364	519,829

Source: IMF, *International Financial Statistics*.

COST OF LIVING
(Consumer Price Index for urban areas; base: 1989 = 100)

	2006	2007	2008
Food	176.1	181.8	194.2
Clothing	172.3	174.5	177.3
Shelter	175.7	180.6	181.8
Household equipment	144.9	147.7	151.5
All items (incl. others)	174.3	177.8	184.7

NATIONAL ACCOUNTS
(million dirhams at current prices)

Expenditure on the Gross Domestic Product

	2005	2006	2007*
Government final consumption expenditure	102,110	107,071	112,230
Private final consumption expenditure	303,172	331,996	359,134
Change in inventories	6,699	7,446	7,611
Gross fixed capital formation	145,256	162,456	192,573
Total domestic expenditure	557,237	608,969	671,548
Exports of goods and services	170,513	197,459	220,302
Less Imports of goods and services	200,071	229,084	276,477
GDP in purchasers' values	527,679	577,344	615,373
GDP at chained 1998 prices	500,525	539,365	554,009

* Provisional figures.

Gross Domestic Product by Economic Activity

	2005	2006	2007*
Agriculture, hunting and forestry	62,932	81,147	68,716
Fishing and aquaculture	6,633	6,335	6,212
Mining and quarrying	8,994	10,534	13,155
Manufacturing	77,166	81,202	82,074
Oil refining and energy products	1,484	1,296	841
Electricity and water	14,583	14,687	15,749
Construction	31,522	32,912	37,233
Commerce	56,454	60,956	65,058
Hotels and restaurants	12,963	13,265	16,294
Transport	17,961	18,357	23,264
Post and communications	16,561	18,134	19,887
Public administration and social security	47,917	50,664	51,906
Other services	118,786	128,459	145,300
Sub-total	473,956	517,948	545,689
Taxes, less subsidies, on imports	53,723	59,396	69,684
GDP in purchasers' values	527,679	577,344	615,373

* Provisional figures.

BALANCE OF PAYMENTS
(US $ million)

	2005	2006	2007
Exports of goods f.o.b.	10,690	11,926	15,146
Imports of goods f.o.b.	−18,894	−21,683	−29,316
Trade balance	−8,204	−9,756	−14,170
Exports of services	8,098	9,789	12,165
Imports of services	−3,845	−4,473	−5,416
Balance on goods and services	−3,951	−4,441	−7,421
Other income received	689	750	961
Other income paid	−1,072	−1,227	−1,365
Balance on goods, services and income	−4,335	−4,918	−7,825
Current transfers received	5,441	6,410	7,786
Current transfers paid	−158	−177	−185
Current balance	949	1,315	−224
Capital account (net)	−5	−3	−3
Direct investment abroad	−74	−451	−632
Direct investment from abroad	1,620	2,366	2,807
Portfolio investment assets	−4	3	−16
Portfolio investment liabilities	64	−298	−64
Other investment assets	−891	−762	−1,617
Other investment liabilities	−803	−1,043	−1,195
Net errors and omissions	−407	−499	105
Overall balance	449	628	−840

Source: IMF, *International Financial Statistics*.

External Trade

PRINCIPAL COMMODITIES
(million dirhams)

Imports c.i.f.	2005	2006	2007
Foodstuffs, beverages and tobacco	15,617	15,417	26,726
Wheat	4,155	3,090	9,407
Energy and lubricants	39,510	44,911	52,448
Crude petroleum	23,947	25,172	26,250
Crude products	12,017	12,691	15,847
Semi-finished products	40,880	49,393	59,782
Chemical products	7,579	8,694	10,010
Finished capital goods	38,514	46,933	55,819
Finished consumer products	37,560	41,026	48,906
Pharmaceutical products	2,382	2,526	2,936
Textile and cotton fabrics	7,223	7,245	7,614
Total (incl. others)	184,098	210,372	259,527

Exports f.o.b.	2005	2006	2007
Foodstuffs, beverages and tobacco	19,431	21,176	24,162
Crustaceans and molluscs	3,945	4,266	5,165
Prepared and preserved fish	3,626	4,213	3,899
Energy and lubricants	2,359	2,107	2,803
Crude mineral products	7,122	8,842	10,240
Phosphates	4,593	5,081	6,086
Semi-finished products	27,875	29,489	33,937
Phosphoric acid	7,641	7,891	9,069
Natural and chemical fertilizers	3,939	4,694	7,182
Finished industrial capital goods	8,442	11,962	14,038
Electric wire and cable	5,155	6,606	8,206
Finished consumer products	31,489	35,030	35,844
Manufactured garments	17,899	20,699	20,474
Hosiery	6,847	7,192	7,882
Total (incl. others)	99,099	111,799	123,614

MOROCCO

PRINCIPAL TRADING PARTNERS
(million dirhams)*

Imports c.i.f.	2005	2006	2007
Algeria	3,169	4,087	6,793
Belgium-Luxembourg	3,350	4,410	4,683
Brazil	4,014	4,034	4,534
Canada	1,881	1,546	2,097
China, People's Republic	9,399	11,069	15,146
France	33,483	37,141	41,607
Germany	8,866	9,794	12,900
India	1,341	1,616	2,566
Italy	11,103	13,299	16,695
Japan	3,219	3,575	4,281
Netherlands	3,510	4,683	8,252
Spain	21,448	24,128	27,544
United Kingdom	4,127	4,365	7,109
USA	6,104	9,492	15,442
Total (incl. others)	184,380	210,554	259,747

Exports f.o.b.	2005	2006	2007
Belgium-Luxembourg	2,755	3,281	3,030
Brazil	2,198	2,609	4,247
France	29,829	32,518	34,010
Germany	3,177	3,423	3,580
India	3,939	4,456	4,853
Italy	4,962	5,587	6,480
Japan	1,012	894	1,313
Netherlands	2,511	2,640	2,587
Spain	19,844	22,620	25,069
United Kingdom	6,289	6,867	6,388
USA	2,535	2,254	2,994
Total (incl. others)	99,265	111,979	123,941

* Imports by country of production; exports by country of last consignment.

Transport

RAILWAYS
(traffic)*

	2002	2003	2004
Passengers carried ('000)	14,685	16,516	18,543
Passenger-km (million)	2,145	2,374	2,645
Freight ('000 metric tons)	29,945	30,552	32,901
Freight ton-km (million)	4,974	5,146	5,563

* Figures refer to principal railways only.

ROAD TRAFFIC
('000 motor vehicles in use at 31 December)

	1999	2000	2001
Passenger cars	1,161.9	1,211.1	1,253.0
Commercial vehicles	400.3	415.7	431.0

Motorcycles and scooters: 20,388 in 2000; 20,569 in 2001.

Passenger cars: 1,326,108 passenger cars in 2003.

Sources: IRF, *World Road Statistics*; UN, *Statistical Yearbook*.

SHIPPING
Merchant Fleet
(registered at 31 December)

	2005	2006	2007
Number of vessels	514	513	517
Total displacement ('000 grt)	544.0	526.8	489.6

Source: Lloyd's Register-Fairplay, *World Fleet Statistics*.

International Sea-borne Freight Traffic
('000 metric tons)

	2002	2003	2004*
Goods loaded	24,891	24,355	27,355
Goods unloaded	32,097	31,785	34,149

* Provisional figures.

CIVIL AVIATION
(traffic on scheduled services)

	2002	2003	2004
Kilometres flown (million)	58	59	70
Passengers carried ('000)	3,146	2,638	3,004
Passenger-km (million)	6,045	4,905	5,551
Total ton-km (million)	626	528	642

Source: UN, *Statistical Yearbook*.

Tourism

FOREIGN TOURIST ARRIVALS*

Country of nationality	2005	2006	2007
France	1,337,204	1,481,610	1,605,503
Germany	144,200	151,396	159,844
Italy	120,955	140,923	160,047
Spain	367,811	467,956	540,186
United Kingdom	193,552	265,536	338,304
Other European countries	117,383	143,438	188,727
Maghreb countries	93,549	107,164	122,750
USA	82,980	93,646	109,079
Total (incl. others)	3,289,010	3,790,256	4,320,898

* Excluding Moroccans resident abroad (2,787,825 in 2005; 2,986,372 in 2006; 3,376,719 in 2007).

Cruise-ship passengers: 233,458 in 2005; 218,295 in 2006; 290,000 in 2007.

Receipts from tourism (US $ million, incl. passenger transport): 4,540 in 2004; 5,426 in 2005; 6,899 in 2006 (Source: World Tourism Organization).

Communications Media

	2005	2006	2007
Telephones ('000 main lines in use)	1,341.2	1,266.1	2,393.8
Mobile cellular telephones ('000 subscribers)	12,392.8	16,004.7	20,029.3
Personal computers ('000 in use)	740	n.a.	n.a.
Internet users ('000)	4,600	6,100	6,600
Broadband subscribers ('000)	249.1	391.9	477.4

1997: Radio receivers ('000 in use) 6,640; Facsimile machines (number in use) 18,000 (estimate).

1999: Book production (titles) 386.

2000: Television receivers ('000 in use) 4,700; Daily newspapers 23 (average circulation 846,000 copies); Other newspapers 507 (average circulation 4,108,000 copies); Periodicals 364 (average circulation 4,956,000 copies).

Sources: UNESCO, *Statistical Yearbook*; UN, *Statistical Yearbook*; and International Telecommunication Union.

Education

(2006/07, unless otherwise indicated)

	Institutions	Teachers	Males	Females	Total
Pre-primary	33,577*	40,379	416,991	288,762	705,753
Primary	6,565†	143,846	2,108,849	1,830,328	3,939,177
public	5,940†	n.a.	1,934,545	1,674,758	3,609,303
private	625†	n.a.	174,304	155,570	329,874
Secondary (public and private)	1,664†	100,367‡	n.a.	n.a.	2,173,454
Tertiary	68*	18,464	193,549	175,593	369,142

* 1997/98 figure.
† 1999/2000 figure.
‡ 2003/04 figure.

Source: Ministry of National Education, Higher Education, Training and Scientific Research; UNESCO Institute for Statistics.

Adult literacy rate (UNESCO estimates): 55.6% (males 68.7%; females 43.2%) in 2007 (Source: UNESCO Institute for Statistics).

Directory

The Constitution

The following is a summary of the main provisions of the Constitution, as approved in a national referendum on 4 September 1992, and as amended by referendum on 13 September 1996.

PREAMBLE

The Kingdom of Morocco, a sovereign Islamic State whose official language is Arabic, constitutes a part of the Great Arab Maghreb. As an African State, one of its aims is the realization of African unity. It adheres to the principles, rights and obligations of those international organizations of which it is a member and works for the preservation of peace and security in the world.

GENERAL PRINCIPLES

Morocco is a constitutional, democratic and social monarchy. Sovereignty pertains to the nation and is exercised directly by means of the referendum and indirectly by the constitutional institutions. All Moroccans are equal before the law, and all adults enjoy equal political rights including the franchise. Freedoms of movement, opinion and speech and the right of assembly are guaranteed. Islam is the state religion. All Moroccans have equal rights in seeking education and employment. The right to strike, and to private property, is guaranteed. All Moroccans contribute to the defence of the Kingdom and to public costs. There shall be no one-party system.

THE MONARCHY

The Crown of Morocco and its attendant constitutional rights shall be hereditary in the line of HM King Hassan II, and shall be transmitted to the oldest son, unless during his lifetime the King has appointed as his successor another of his sons. The King is the symbol of unity, guarantees the continuity of the state, and safeguards respect for Islam and the Constitution. The King appoints, and may dismiss, the Prime Minister and other Cabinet Ministers (appointed upon the Prime Minister's recommendation), and presides over the Cabinet. He shall promulgate adopted legislation within a 30-day period, and has the power to dissolve the Chamber of Representatives and/or the Chamber of Advisers. The Sovereign is the Commander-in-Chief of the Armed Forces; makes appointments to civil and military posts; appoints Ambassadors; signs and ratifies treaties; presides over the Supreme Council of the Magistracy, the Supreme Council of Education and the Supreme Council for National Reconstruction and Planning; and exercises the right of pardon. In cases of threat to the national territory or to the action of constitutional institutions, the King, having consulted the President of the Chamber of Representatives, the President of the Chamber of Advisers and the Chairman of the Constitutional Council, and after addressing the nation, has the right to declare a State of Emergency by royal decree. The State of Emergency shall not entail the dissolution of Parliament and shall be terminated by the same procedure followed in its proclamation.

LEGISLATURE

This consists of a bicameral parliament: the Chamber of Representatives and the Chamber of Advisers. Members of the Chamber of Representatives are elected by direct universal suffrage for a five-year term. Three-fifths of the members of the Chamber of Advisers are elected by electoral colleges of local councils; the remainder are elected by electoral colleges representing chambers of commerce and trade unions. Members of the Chamber of Advisers are elected for a nine-year term, with one-third renewable every three years. Deputies in both chambers enjoy parliamentary immunity. Parliament shall adopt legislation, which may be initiated by members of either chamber or by the Prime Minister. Draft legislation shall be examined consecutively by both parliamentary chambers. If the two chambers fail to agree on the draft legislation the Government may request that a bilateral commission propose a final draft for approval by the chambers. If the chambers do not then adopt the draft, the Government may submit the draft (modified, if need be) to the Chamber of Representatives. Henceforth the draft submitted can be definitively adopted only by absolute majority of the members of the Chamber of Representatives. Parliament holds its meetings during two sessions each year, commencing on the second Friday in October and the second Friday in April.

GOVERNMENT

The Government, composed of the Prime Minister and his Ministers, is responsible to the King and Parliament and ensures the execution of laws. The Prime Minister is empowered to initiate legislation and to exercise statutory powers except where these are reserved to the King. He presents to both parliamentary chambers the Government's intended programme and is responsible for co-ordinating ministerial work.

RELATIONS BETWEEN THE AUTHORITIES

The King may request a second reading, by both Chambers of Parliament, of any draft bill or proposed law. In addition, he may submit proposed legislation to a referendum by decree; and dissolve either Chamber or both if a proposal that has been rejected is approved by referendum. He may also dissolve either Chamber by decree after consulting the Chairman of the Constitutional Council, and addressing the nation, but the succeeding Chamber may not be dissolved within a year of its election. The Chamber of Representatives may force the collective resignation of the Government either by refusing a vote of confidence or by adopting a censure motion. The election of the new Parliament or Chamber shall take place within three months of its dissolution. In the interim period the King shall exercise the legislative powers of Parliament, in addition to those conferred upon him by the Constitution. A censure motion must be signed by at least one-quarter of the Chamber's members, and shall be approved by the Chamber only by an absolute majority vote of its members. The Chamber of Advisers is competent to issue 'warning' motions to the Government and, by a two-thirds' majority, force its resignation.

MOROCCO

THE CONSTITUTIONAL COUNCIL

The Constitutional Council consists of six members appointed by the King (including the Chairman) for a period of nine years, and six members appointed for the same period—three selected by the President of the Chamber of Representatives and three by the President of the Chamber of Advisers. One-third of each category of the Council are renewed every three years. The Council is empowered to judge the validity of legislative elections and referendums, as well as that of organic laws and the rules of procedure of both parliamentary chambers, submitted to it.

JUDICIARY

The Judiciary is independent. Judges are appointed on the recommendation of the Supreme Council of the Magistracy presided over by the King.

THE ECONOMIC AND SOCIAL COUNCIL

An Economic and Social Council shall be established to give its opinion on all matters of an economic or social nature. Its constitution, organization, prerogatives and rules of procedure shall be determined by an organic law.

THE HIGH AUDIT COUNCIL

The High Audit Council exercises the general supervision of the implementation of fiscal laws. It ensures the regularity of revenues and expenditure operations of the departments legally under its jurisdiction, as it assesses the management of the affairs thereof. It is competent to penalize any breach of the rules governing such operations. Regional audit councils exercise the supervision of the accounts of local assemblies and bodies, and the management of the affairs thereof.

LOCAL GOVERNMENT

Local government in the Kingdom consists of establishing regions, governorships, provinces and communes.

REVISING THE CONSTITUTION

The King, the Chamber of Representatives and the Chamber of Advisers are competent to initiate a revision of the Constitution. The King has the right to submit the revision project he initiates to a national referendum. A proposal for a revision by either parliamentary chamber shall be adopted only if it receives a two-thirds' majority vote by the chamber's members. Revision projects and proposals shall be submitted to the nation for referendum by royal decree; a revision of the Constitution shall be definitive after approval by referendum. Neither the state, system of monarchy nor the prescriptions related to the religion of Islam may be subject to a constitutional revision.

The Government

HEAD OF STATE

Monarch: HM King MUHAMMAD VI (acceded 23 July 1999).

CABINET
(April 2009)

A coalition of Istiqlal, the Union socialiste des forces populaires (USFP), the Rassemblement national des indépendants (RNI), the Parti du progrès et du socialisme (PPS) and independents (Ind.).

Prime Minister: ABBAS EL-FASSI (Istiqlal).
Minister of State: MUHAMMAD EL-YAZGHI (USFP).
Minister of Justice: ABDELWAHAD RADI (USFP).
Minister of the Interior: CHAKIB BENMOUSSA (Ind.).
Minister of Foreign Affairs and Co-operation: TAIEB FASSI FIHRI (Ind.).
Minister of Habous (Religious Endowments) and Islamic Affairs: AHMED TOUFIQ (Ind.).
Secretary-General of the Government: DRISS DAHAK (Ind.).
Minister in charge of Relations with Parliament: MUHAMMAD SAÂD EL-ALAMI (Istiqlal).
Minister of the Economy and Finance: SALAHEDDINE MEZOUAR (RNI).
Minister of Agriculture and Fisheries: AZIZ AKHENOUCH (RNI).
Minister of Employment and Vocational Training: JAMAL AGHMANI (USFP).
Minister of National Education, Higher Education, Staff Training and Scientific Research: AHMED AKHCHICHINE (Ind.).
Minister of Culture: TOURIYA JABRANE KRYATIF (Ind.).
Minister of Tourism and Handicrafts: MUHAMMAD BOUSSAID (RNI).
Minister of Equipment and Transport: KARIM GHELLAB (Istiqlal).
Minister of Housing, Town Planning and Development: AHMED TAOUFIQ HEJIRA (Istiqlal).
Minister of Industry, Trade and New Technologies: AHMED REDA CHAMI (USFP).
Minister of Health: YASMINA BADDOU (Istiqlal).
Minister of Youth and Sports: NAWAL EL-MOUTAWAKIL (RNI).
Minister of Energy, Mining, Water and the Environment: AMINA BENKHADRA (RNI).
Minister of Communication and Government Spokesperson: KHALID NACIRI (PPS).
Minister of Foreign Trade: ABDELLATIF MAÂZOUZ (Istiqlal).
Minister of Social Development, the Family and Solidarity: NOUZHA SKALLI (PPS).
Minister-delegate to the Prime Minister, in charge of Economic and General Affairs: NIZAR BARAKA (Istiqlal).
Minister-delegate to the Prime Minister, in charge of National Defence: ABDERRAHMANE SBAÏ (Ind.).
Minister-delegate to the Prime Minister, in charge of the Modernization of the Public Sector: MUHAMMAD ABBOU (RNI).
Minister-delegate to the Prime Minister, in charge of Moroccans Resident Abroad: MUHAMMAD AMEUR (USFP).

There are also six Secretaries of State.

MINISTRIES

Office of the Prime Minister: Palais Royal, Touarga, Rabat; tel. (3) 7219400; fax (3) 7768656; e-mail courrier@pm.gov.ma; internet www.pm.gov.ma.

Ministry of Agriculture, Rural Development and Fisheries: Quartier Administratif, pl. Abdellah Chefchaouni, BP 607, Rabat; tel. (3) 7760933; fax (3) 7776411; e-mail info@mardrpm.gov.ma; internet www.madrpm.gov.ma.

Ministry of Communication: ave Allal al-Fassi, Madinat al-Irfane Souissi, 10000 Rabat; tel. (3) 7772412; fax (3) 7767815; e-mail webmaster@mincom.gov.ma; internet www.mincom.gov.ma.

Ministry of Culture: 1 rue Ghandi, Rabat; tel. (3) 7209494; fax (3) 7209400; e-mail webmaster@minculture.gov.ma; internet www.minculture.gov.ma.

Ministry of the Economy and Finance: blvd Muhammad V, Quartier Administratif, Chellah, Rabat; tel. (3) 7677501; fax (3) 7677527; e-mail internet@finances.gov.ma; internet www.finances.gov.ma.

Ministry of Employment and Vocational Training: ave Muhammad V, Hassan, BP 5015, Rabat; tel. (3) 7760521; fax (3) 7765312; e-mail communication@emploi.gov.ma; internet www.emploi.gov.ma.

Ministry of Energy, Mining, Water and the Environment: rue Abou Marouane Essaadi, BP 6208, Agdal, Rabat; tel. (3) 7688857; fax (3) 7688863; e-mail dsi@mem.gov.ma; internet www.mem.gov.ma.

Ministry of Equipment and Transport: Quartier Administratif, Chellah, Rabat; tel. (3) 7684151; fax (3) 7764825; internet www.mtpnet.gov.ma.

Ministry of Foreign Affairs and Co-operation: ave Franklin Roosevelt, Rabat; tel. (3) 7761583; fax (3) 7765508; e-mail mail@maec.gov.ma; internet www.maec.gov.ma.

Ministry of Foreign Trade: 63 ave Moulay Youssef, Rabat; tel. (3) 7707320; fax (3) 7703231; e-mail ministere@mce.gov.ma; internet www.mce.gov.ma.

Ministry of Habous (Religious Endowments) and Islamic Affairs: Al-Mechouar Essaid, Rabat; tel. (3) 7766801; fax (3) 7765282; e-mail infos@habous.gov.ma; internet www.habous.gov.ma.

MOROCCO   Directory

Ministry of Health: 335 blvd Muhammad V, Rabat; tel. (3) 7761025; fax (3) 7768401; e-mail inas@sante.gov.ma; internet www.sante.gov.ma.

Ministry of Housing, Town Planning and Development: rues al-Jouaze and al-Joumaize, Hay Ryad, Secteur 16, 10000 Rabat; tel. (3) 7577000; fax (3) 7577373; e-mail zerrad@mhuae.gov.ma; internet www.mhuae.gov.ma.

Ministry of Industry, Trade and New Technologies: Quartier Administratif, Chellah, Rabat; tel. (3) 7761868; fax (3) 7766265; e-mail leministre@mcinet.gov.ma; internet www.technologies.gov.ma.

Ministry of the Interior: Quartier Administratif, Chellah, Rabat; tel. (3) 7761868; fax (3) 7762056.

Ministry of Justice: pl. Mamounia, Rabat; tel. (3) 7732941; fax (3) 7730772; e-mail kourout@justice.gov.ma; internet www.justice.gov.ma.

Ministry of the Modernization of the Public Sector: Quartier Administratif, rue Ahmed Cherkaoui, Agdal, BP 1076, Rabat; tel. (3) 7773106; fax (3) 7778438; e-mail info@mmsp.gov.ma; internet www.mmsp.gov.ma.

Ministry of National Education, Higher Education, Staff Training and Scientific Research: Bab Rouah, Rabat; tel. (3) 7771822; fax (3) 7201385; e-mail divcom@men.gov.ma; internet www.men.gov.ma.

Ministry in charge of Relations with Parliament: Nouveau Quartier Administratif, Agdal, Rabat; tel. (3) 7775159; fax (3) 7777719; e-mail mirepa@mcrp.gov.ma; internet www.mcrp.gov.ma.

Ministry of Social Development, the Family and Solidarity: 47 ave Ibn Sina, Agdal, Rabat; tel. (3) 7684060; fax (3) 7671967; e-mail mdsfs@mdsfs.ma; internet www.social.gov.ma.

Ministry of Youth and Sports: blvd ibn Sina, Rabat; tel. (3) 7680028; fax (3) 7680145; e-mail masterweb@mjs.gov.ma; internet www.secj.gov.ma.

Legislature

MAJLIS AN-NUAB
(Chamber of Representatives)

President: MUSTAPHA MANSOURI.
General Election, 7 September 2007

Party	Votes	% of votes	Seats
Istiqlal	494,256	10.7	52
Parti de la justice et du développement (PJD)	503,396	10.9	46
Mouvement populaire (MP)	426,849	9.3	41
Rassemblement national des indépendants (RNI)	447,244	9.7	39
Union socialiste des forces populaires (USFP)	408,945	8.9	38
Union constitutionnelle (UC)	335,116	7.3	27
Parti du progrès et du socialisme (PPS)	248,103	5.4	17
Parti national démocrate (PND)/ Parti Al Ahd	253,816	5.5	14
Front des forces démocratiques (FFD)	207,982	4.5	9
Mouvement démocratique et social (MDS)	168,960	3.7	9
Parti de l'avant-garde démocratique socialiste (PADS)/ Congrès national ittihadi (CNI)/ Parti socialiste unifié (PSU)	123,897	2.7	6
Parti travailliste (PT)	140,224	3.0	5
Parti de l'environnement et du développement (PED)	131,524	2.9	5
Parti du renouveau et de l'équité (PRE)	83,516	1.8	4
Other parties	552,301	12.0	8
Independents	81,364	1.8	5
Total	**4,607,493***	**100.0***	**325†**

* Excluding votes for the seats reserved for women (see below).
† 30 of the 325 seats were reserved for women. Of these, the PJD and Istiqlal each won six seats; the RNI, the MP and the USFP all secured five; and the PPS received three.

MAJLIS AL-MUSTASHARIN
(Chamber of Advisers)

President: MAATI BENKADDOUR.
Election, 5 December 1997*

	Seats
Rassemblement national des indépendants (RNI)	42
Mouvement démocratique et social (MDS)	33
Union constitutionnelle (UC)	28
Mouvement populaire (MP)	27
Parti national démocrate (PND)	21
Istiqlal	21
Union socialiste des forces populaires (USFP)	16
Mouvement national populaire (MNP)	15
Parti de l'action (PA)	13
Front des forces démocratiques (FFD)	12
Parti du progrès et du socialisme (PPS)	7
Parti social et démocratique (PSD)	4
Parti démocratique pour l'indépendance (PDI)	4
Trade unions	
Confédération Démocratique du Travail (CDT)	11
Union Marocaine du Travail (UMT)	8
Union Générale des Travailleurs Marocains (UGMT)	3
Others	5
Total	**270**

* Of the Chamber of Advisers' 270 members, 162 were elected by local councils, 81 by chambers of commerce and 27 by trade unions.

Note: Elections were conducted in September 2000, October 2003 and September 2006, with one-third of the membership of the Chamber of Advisers being renewed at each. At the 2006 elections the seats were allocated as follows: Istiqlal 17, MP 14, RNI 13, USFP 11, UC 6, PPS 4, Parti Al Ahd 4, PND 4, Parti de l'environnement et du développement (PED) 2, FFD 2, Parti de la Choura et de l'Istiqlal 1, MDS 1, Parti des forces citoyennes (PFC) 1, Parti du renouveau et de l'équité 1.

Political Organizations

Congrès national ittihadi (CNI): 209 blvd Strasbourg, Résidence C, 2ème étage, Casablanca; tel. and fax (2) 2447664; e-mail onittihadi@caramail.com; f. 2001 by dissident mems of USFP; Sec.-Gen. ABDELMAJID BOUZOUBÂA.

Front des forces démocratiques (FFD): 13 ave Tariq ibn Ziad, Hassan, Rabat; tel. (3) 7661625; fax (3) 7660621; e-mail forces@menara.ma; internet www.ffd.ma; f. 1997 after split from PPS; Sec.-Gen. THAMI EL-KHYARI.

Istiqlal (Independence): 4 ave Ibnou Toumert, Bab el-Had, 50020 Rabat; tel. (3) 7730951; fax (3) 7729107; e-mail istiqlal@istiqlal.ma; internet www.istiqlal.ma; f. 1944; aims to raise living standards and to confer equal rights on all; emphasizes the Moroccan claim to Western Sahara; Sec.-Gen. ABBAS EL-FASSI.

Mouvement démocratique et social (MDS): 4 ave Imam Malik, route des Zaërs, Rabat; tel. (7) 3834771; fax (3) 7764767; f. 1996 as Mouvement national démocratique et social after split from Mouvement national populaire (MNP); adopted current name in Nov. 1996; Leader MAHMOUD ARCHANE.

Mouvement populaire (MP): 66 rue Patrice Lumumba, Rabat; tel. (3) 7766431; fax (3) 7767537; e-mail parti_mp@hotmail.fr; internet www.harakamp.org; f. 1958; merged with the MNP and Union démocratique in 2006; liberal; Sec.-Gen. MOHAND LAENSER.

Parti de l'action (PA): 113 ave Allal ben Abdallah, Rabat; tel. (3) 7206661; f. 1974; advocates democracy and progress; Sec.-Gen. MUHAMMAD EL-IDRISSI.

Parti Al Ahd: 14 rue Idriss al-Akbar, rue Tafraout, Hassan, Rabat; tel. (3) 7204816; fax (3) 7204786; e-mail alhakika@iam.net.ma; f. 2002; Chair. NAJIB EL-OUAZZANI.

Parti de l'authenticité et de la modernité (PAM): f. 2008; Founder FOUAD ALI EL-HIMMA; Sec.-Gen. MUHAMMAD CHEIKH BIADILLAH.

Parti de l'avant-garde démocratique socialiste (PADS): BP 2091, 54 ave de la Résistance Océan, Rabat; tel. (3) 7200559; fax (3) 7708491; an offshoot of USFP; legalized in April 1992; Sec.-Gen. AHMAD BENJELLOUNE.

Parti démocratique et de l'indépendance (PDI): 9 Lalla Yakout, rue Araar, Apt 11, 2ème étage, blvd d'Anfa, Casablanca; tel. (2) 2200949; fax (2) 2200928; f. 1946; Sec.-Gen. ABD AL-WAHID MAÂCH.

Parti de l'environnement et du développement (PED): 3 rue Azilal, Hassan, Rabat; tel. and fax (3) 7702174; e-mail alamiahmed@

MOROCCO

hotmail.com; internet www.geocities.com/ped_maroc; f. 2002; Sec.-Gen. AHMAD AL-ALAMI.

Parti des forces citoyennes (PFC): 353 blvd Muhammad V, 9ème étage, Casablanca; tel. (2) 2400608; fax (2) 2400613; e-mail citoyennes@menara.ma; f. 2001; Sec.-Gen. ABDERRAHIM LAHJOUJI.

Parti de la justice et du développement (PJD): ave Abdelwahed Elmorakechi, rue Elyafrani, 4 les Orangers, Rabat; tel. (3) 7208862; fax (3) 7208854; e-mail info@pjd.ma; internet www.pjd.ma; f. 1967 as Mouvement populaire constitutionnel et démocratique; breakaway party from MP; formally absorbed mems of the Islamic asscn Al Islah wa Attajdid in June 1996; adopted current name in Oct. 1998; Sec.-Gen. ABDELILLAH BENKIRANE.

Parti marocain libéral (PML): 114 ave Allal ben Abdellah, 2ème étage, Rabat; tel. (3) 7733670; fax (3) 7733611; e-mail pml@menara.ma; f. 2002; Nat. Co-ordinator MUHAMMAD ZIANE.

Parti national démocrate (PND): 18 rue de Tunis, Hassan, Rabat; tel. (3) 7732127; fax (3) 7720170; e-mail annidal@menara.ma; internet www.pnd.ma; f. 1981 from split within RNI; Sec.-Gen. ABDULLAH KADIRI.

Parti du progrès et du socialisme (PPS): 29 ave John Kennedy, Youssoufia, Rabat; tel. (3) 7759464; fax (3) 7759476; e-mail sg@pps.maroc.org; internet www.pps-maroc.com; f. 1974; successor to Parti communiste marocain (banned in 1952) and Parti de la libération et du socialisme (banned in 1969); left-wing; advocates modernization, social progress, nationalization and democracy; 35,000 mems; Sec.-Gen. ISMAÏL ALAOUI.

Parti de la réforme et du développement (PRD): 34 ave Pasteur, Rabat; tel. and fax (3) 7703801; f. 2001 by fmr mems of RNI; Leader ABD AR-RAHMANE EL-KOUHEN.

Parti de la renaissance et de la vertu (Renaissance and Virtue Party): Bouznika; f. 2005; national democratic party based on the principles of Islam; Sec.-Gen. MUHAMMAD KHALIDI.

Parti du renouveau et de l'équité (PRE): 16 rue Sebou, Apt 5, Agdal, Rabat; tel. (3) 7777266; fax (3) 7777452; f. 2002; Pres. CHAKIR ACHAHBAR.

Parti socialiste unifié (PSU): Casablanca; f. 2005 by merger of Parti de la gauche socialiste unifieé and Fidélité à la démocratie; Sec.-Gen. MUHAMMAD MOUJAHID.

Parti travailliste (PT): 9 rue Ksar Essouk, Hassan, Rabat; f. 2005; centre-left; Sec.-Gen. ABDELKRIM BENATIQ.

Rassemblement national des indépendants (RNI): 6 rue Laos, ave Hassan II, Rabat; tel. (3) 7721420; fax (3) 7733824; internet rni.leguide.ma; f. 1978 from the pro-Govt independents' group that then formed the majority in the Chamber of Representatives; Leader MUSTAPHA MANSOURI.

Union constitutionnelle (UC): 158 ave des Forces Armées Royales, Casablanca; tel. (2) 2441144; fax (2) 2441141; e-mail union_constit@menara.ma; internet www.unionconstitutionnelle.org; f. 1983; 51-mem. Political Bureau; Sec.-Gen. MUHAMMAD ABIED.

Union Marocaine pour la démocratie (UMD): Rabat; f. 2006; Sec.-Gen. ABDELLAH AZMANI.

Union socialiste des forces populaires (USFP): 9 ave al-Araâr, Hay Riad, Rabat; tel. (3) 7565511; fax (3) 7565510; e-mail usfp@usfp.ma; internet www.usfp.ma; f. 1959 as Union nationale des forces populaires (UNFP); became USFP in 1974 after UNFP split into two separate entities; merged with Parti socialiste démocratique in 2005; democratic socialist and progressive party; 160,000 mems; First Sec. ABDELWAHAD RADI.

The following movement is not authorized as a political party by the Government, but is generally tolerated:

Al-Adl wal-Ihsan (Justice and Charity): internet www.aljamaa.net; advocates an Islamic state based on *Shari'a* law; rejects violence; Leader ABDESSALAM YASSINE.

The following group is active in the disputed territory of Western Sahara:

Frente Popular para la Liberación de Saguia el-Hamra y Río de Oro (Frente Polisario) (Polisario Front): BP 10, el-Mouradia, Algiers; tel. (2) 747907; fax (2) 747206; e-mail dgmae@mail.wissal.dz; f. 1973 to gain independence for Western Sahara, first from Spain and then from Morocco and Mauritania; signed peace treaty with Mauritanian Govt in 1979; supported by Algerian Govt; in February 1976 proclaimed the Sahrawi Arab Democratic Republic (SADR); admitted as the 51st mem. of the OAU in Feb. 1982 and currently recognized by more than 75 countries worldwide; its main organs are a 33-mem. National Secretariat, a 101-mem. Sahrawi National Assembly (Parliament) and a 13-mem. Govt; Sec.-Gen. of the Polisario Front and Pres. of the SADR MUHAMMAD ABD AL-AZIZ; Prime Minister of the SADR ABDELKADER TALEB OUMAR.

Diplomatic Representation

EMBASSIES IN MOROCCO

Algeria: 46–48 blvd Tariq ibn Ziad, BP 448, 10001 Rabat; tel. (3) 7661574; fax (3) 7762237; e-mail algerabat@iam.net.ma; Ambassador LARBI BELKHEIR.

Angola: km 5, 53 Ahmed Rifaï, BP 1318, Souissi, Rabat; tel. (3) 7659239; fax (3) 7659238; e-mail amb.angola@menara.ma; Ambassador Dr LUIS JOSÉ DE ALMEIDA.

Argentina: 4 ave Mehdi Ben Barka, Souissi, 10000 Rabat; tel. (3) 7755120; fax (3) 7755410; e-mail emarr@mrecic.gov.ar; Ambassador ALBERTO DE NÚÑEZ.

Austria: 2 rue Tiddas, BP 135, 10000 Rabat; tel. (3) 7761698; fax (3) 7765425; e-mail rabat-ob@bmeia.gv.at; Ambassador Dr GEORG MAUTNER-MARKHOF.

Azerbaijan: rue 3 Abu Hanifa, Aqdal, Rabat; tel. (3) 7671915; fax (3) 7671918; e-mail azembma@menara.ma; Ambassador SABIR AGHA-BAYOV.

Bahrain: rue beni Hassan, km 6.5, route des Zaêrs, Souissi, Rabat; tel. (3) 7633500; fax (3) 7630732; e-mail rabat.mission@mofa.gov.bh; Ambassador KHALID BIN SALMAN AL-KHALIFA.

Bangladesh: 25 ave Tarek ibn Ziad, BP 1468, Rabat; tel. (3) 7766731; fax (3) 7766729; e-mail bdoot@mtds.com; Ambassador MOSUD MANNAN (designate).

Belgium: 6 ave de Muhammad el-Fassi, Tour Hassan, Rabat; tel. (3) 7268060; fax (3) 7767003; e-mail rabat@diplobel.org; internet www.diplomatie.be/rabat; Ambassador PATRICK VERCAUTEREN DRUBBEL.

Benin: 30 ave Mehdi ben Barka, BP 5187, Souissi, 10105 Rabat; tel. (3) 7754158; fax (3) 7754156; e-mail benin@menara.ma; Ambassador ISSIRADJOU IBRAHIM GOMINA.

Brazil: 10 ave el-Jacaranda, Secteur 2, Hay Riad, 10000 Rabat; tel. (3) 7714663; fax (3) 7714808; e-mail brabat@menara.ma; internet www.ambassadedubresil.org; Ambassador CARLOS ALBERTO SIMAS MAGALHÃES.

Bulgaria: 4 ave Ahmed el-Yazidi, BP 1301, 10000 Rabat; tel. (3) 7765477; fax (3) 7763201; e-mail bulemrab@yahoo.com; internet www.mfa.bg/rabat; Ambassador KATIA PETROVA TODOROVA.

Burkina Faso: 7 rue al-Bouziri, BP 6484, Agdal, 10101 Rabat; tel. (3) 7675512; fax (3) 7675517; e-mail ambfrba@smirt.net.ma; Ambassador Brig.-Gen. IBRAHIM TRAORÉ.

Cameroon: 20 rue du Rif, BP 1790, Souissi, Rabat; tel. (3) 7754194; fax (3) 7750540; e-mail ambacam@iam.net.com; Ambassador MAHAMAT PABA SALÉ.

Canada: 13 bis rue Jaâfar as-Sadik, BP 709, Agdal, Rabat; tel. (3) 7687400; fax (3) 7687430; e-mail rabat@dfait-maeci.gc.ca; internet www.dfait-maeci.gc.ca/morocco; Ambassador MICHÈLE LÉVESQUE.

Central African Republic: Villa No 4, ave Souss, Cité Saâda, Quartier Administratif, BP 770, Agdal, 10000 Rabat; tel. (3) 7631654; fax (3) 7631655; e-mail centrafricaine@iam.net.ma; Ambassador ISMAÏLA NIMAGA.

Chile: 35 ave Ahmed Balafrej, Souissi, Rabat; tel. (3) 7636065; fax (3) 7636067; e-mail echilema@menara.net.ma; Ambassador MARCIA COVARRUBIAS.

China, People's Republic: 16 ave Ahmed Balafrej, 10000 Rabat; tel. (3) 7754056; fax (3) 7757519; e-mail chinaemb_ma@mfa.gov.cn; internet ma.china-embassy.org; Ambassador GONG YUANXING.

Congo, Democratic Republic: 34 ave de la Victoire, BP 553, 10000 Rabat; tel. and fax (3) 7262280; Chargé d'affaires a.i. WAWA BAMIALY.

Congo, Republic: 197 ave Général Abdendi Britel, Souissi II, Rabat; tel. (3) 7659966; fax (3) 7659959; Ambassador JEAN-MARIE EWENGUE.

Côte d'Ivoire: 21 rue de Tiddas, BP 192, 10001 Rabat; tel. (3) 7763151; fax (3) 7762792; e-mail ambcim@clam.net.ma.

Croatia: 73 rue Marnissa, Souissi, Rabat; tel. (3) 7638824; fax (3) 7638827; e-mail croemb.rabat@mvpei.hr; Ambassador DARKO BEKIĆ.

Czech Republic: Villa Merzaa, km 4.5, route des Zaêrs, BP 410, Zankat Aït Melloul, Souissi, 10200 Rabat; tel. (3) 7755421; fax (3) 7754393; e-mail rabat@embassy.mzv.cz; internet www.mzv.cz/rabat; Ambassador TOMÁŠ BURIL.

Egypt: 31 rue al-Jazair, 10000 Rabat; tel. (3) 7731833; fax (3) 7706821; e-mail embegypt@mtds.com; Ambassador KADRY FATHI ABD EL-MOTTELEB.

Equatorial Guinea: ave President Roosevelt, angle rue d'Agadir 9, Rabat; tel. and fax (3) 7769454; Ambassador JUAN NDONG NGUEMA MBENGONO.

Finland: 145 rue Soufiane Ben Wahb, BP 590, 10002 Rabat; tel. (3) 7658775; fax (3) 7658904; e-mail sanomat.rab@formin.fi; internet www.finlande.ma; Ambassador ANTTI RYTÖVUORI (resident in Lisbon, Portugal).

MOROCCO

France: 3 rue Sahnoun, BP 602, Rabat; tel. (3) 7689700; fax (3) 7689701; internet www.ambafrance-ma.org; Ambassador JEAN-FRANÇOIS THIBAULT.

Gabon: km 3.5, route des Zaêrs, BP 1239, 10100 Rabat; tel. (3) 7751950; fax (3) 7757550; Ambassador FRANÇOIS BANGA EBOUMI.

Gambia: 11 rue Cadi ben Hammadi Senhaji, Souissi, Rabat; tel. (3) 7638045; fax (3) 7638189; Ambassador OUSMANE BADJIE.

Germany: 7 Zankat Madnine, BP 235, 10001 Rabat; tel. (3) 7709662; fax (3) 7706851; e-mail amballma@mtds.com; internet www.rabat.diplo.de; Ambassador ULF-DIETER KLEMM.

Ghana: 27 rue Ghomara, La Pinede, Souissi, Rabat; tel. (3) 7757620; fax (3) 7757630; Ambassador KOBINA ANNAN.

Greece: km 5, route des Zaêrs, Villa Chems, Souissi, 10000 Rabat; tel. (3) 7638964; fax (3) 7638990; e-mail gremb.rab@mfa.gr; Ambassador GIORGIOS GEORGOUNTZOS.

Guinea: 15 rue Hamzah, Agdal, 10000 Rabat; tel. and fax (3) 7674148; Ambassador MAHMADOUBA DIABATE.

Holy See: rue Béni M'tir, BP 1303, Souissi, Rabat (Apostolic Nunciature); tel. (3) 7772277; fax (3) 7756213; e-mail nuntius@iam.net.ma; Apostolic Nuncio Most Rev. ANTONIO SOZZO (Titular Archbishop of Concordia).

Hungary: route des Zaêrs, 17 Zankat Aït Melloul, BP 5026, Souissi, Rabat; tel. (3) 7750757; fax (3) 7754123; e-mail ambhongrie@menara.ma; internet www.mfa.gov.hu/emb/rabat; Ambassador LÁSZLÓ VÁRADI.

India: 13 ave de Michlifen, Agdal, 10000 Rabat; tel. (3) 7671339; fax (3) 7671269; e-mail india@maghrebnet.net.ma; internet www.indianembassymorocco.ma; Ambassador PRABHU DAYAL.

Indonesia: 63 rue Béni Boufrah, km 5.9, route des Zaêrs, BP 576, 10105 Rabat; tel. (3) 7757860; fax (3) 7757859; e-mail kbrirabat@iam.net.ma; internet www.indonesie.ma; Ambassador SJACHWIEN ADENAN.

Iran: ave Imam Malik, BP 490, 10001 Rabat; tel. (3) 7752167; fax (3) 7659118; e-mail iranembassy@iam.net.ma; Ambassador WAHID AHMADI.

Iraq: 39 blvd Mehdi ben Barka, 10100 Rabat; tel. (3) 7754466; fax (3) 7759749; e-mail rbtemb@iraqmofamail.net; Ambassador ABD AL-MUHSIN MUHAMMAD SAID.

Italy: 2 rue Idriss al-Azhar, BP 111, 10001 Rabat; tel. (3) 7219730; fax (3) 7706882; e-mail ambassade.rabat@esteri.it; internet www.ambrabat.esteri.it; Ambassador UMBERTO LUCCHESI PALLI.

Japan: 39 ave Ahmed Balafrej, Souissi, 10100 Rabat; tel. (3) 7631782; fax (3) 7750078; e-mail amb-japon@fusion.net.ma; internet www.ma.emb-japan.go.jp; Ambassador HARUKO HIROSE.

Jordan: 65 Villa al-Wafaa, Souissi, 10000 Rabat; tel. (3) 7759270; fax (3) 7758722; Ambassador FAISAL ASH-SHOUBAKI.

Korea, Republic: 41 ave Mehdi ben Barka, Souissi, 10100 Rabat; tel. (3) 7756791; fax (3) 7750189; e-mail morocco@mofat.go.kr; internet mar.mofat.go.kr; Ambassador YOO JUNG-HEE.

Kuwait: km 4.3, route des Zaêrs, BP 11, 10001 Rabat; tel. (3) 7631111; fax (3) 7753591; e-mail alrabat@mofa.gov.kw; Ambassador SALAH MUHAMMAD AL-BIJAN.

Lebanon: 19 ave Abd al-Karim ben Jalloun, 10000 Rabat; tel. (3) 7760728; fax (3) 7766667; Ambassador AHMAD OTHMANE ABDELLAH.

Liberia: Lot no 7, Napabia, rue Ouled Frej, Souissi, Rabat; tel. (3) 7638426.

Libya: 1 rue Chouaïb Doukkali, BP 225, 10000 Rabat; tel. (3) 7769566; fax (3) 7705200; Ambassador MUHAMMAD BELKACEM EZZAOUI.

Malaysia: 17 ave Bir Kacem, Souissi, Rabat; tel. (3) 7658324; fax (3) 7658363; e-mail malrabat@kln.gov.my; internet www.kln.gov.my/perwakilan/rabat; Ambassador OTHMAN SAMIN.

Mali: 58 cité Olm, Souissi, Rabat; tel. (3) 7759125; fax (3) 7754742.

Mauritania: 6 rue Thami Lamdour, BP 207, Souissi, 10000 Rabat; tel. (3) 7656678; fax (3) 7656680; e-mail ambassadeur@mauritanie.org.ma; Ambassador CHAIKH OULD AÂL.

Mexico: 6 rue Cadi Mohamed Brebi, BP 1789, Rabat; tel. (3) 7631969; fax (3) 7631971; e-mail embamexmar@smirt.net.ma; Ambassador PORFIRIO THIERRY MUÑOZ-LEDO CHEVANNIER.

Netherlands: 40 rue de Tunis, BP 329, Hassan, 10001 Rabat; tel. (3) 7219600; fax (3) 7219665; e-mail rab@minbuza.nl; internet www.mfa.nl/rab; Ambassador A. H. F. VAN AGGELEN.

Niger: 14 bis, rue Jabal al-Ayachi, Agdal, Rabat; tel. (3) 7674615; fax (3) 7674629; Ambassador DIORI HAMANI RAMATOU.

Nigeria: 70 ave Omar ibn al-Khattab, BP 347, Agdal, Rabat; tel. (3) 7671857; fax (3) 7672739; e-mail nigerianrabat@menara.ma; Ambassador ALHAJI ABUBAKAR SHEHU WURNO.

Norway: 9 rue Khénifra, BP 757, Agdal, 10006 Rabat; tel. (3) 7764084; fax (3) 7764088; e-mail emb.rabat@mfa.no; internet www.norvege.ma; Ambassador ARNE AASHEIM.

Oman: 21 rue Hamza, Agdal, 10000 Rabat; tel. (3) 7673788; fax (3) 7674567; Ambassador ABDULLAH BIN MUHAMMAD BIN ABDULLAH AL-FARISSI.

Pakistan: 37 ave Ahmed Balafrej, Souissi, Rabat; tel. (3) 7631367; fax (3) 7631243; e-mail pareprabat@menara.ma; Ambassador QAZI RIZWAN-UL-HAQ MAHMOOD.

Peru: 16 rue d'Ifrane, 10000 Rabat; tel. (3) 7723236; fax (3) 7702803; e-mail leprurabat@menara.ma; Ambassador LUIS MANUEL MÁRCOVICH MONASI.

Poland: 23 rue Oqbah, Agdal, BP 425, 10000 Rabat; tel. (3) 7771173; fax (3) 7775320; e-mail apologne@menara.ma; internet www.rabat.polemb.net; Ambassador JOANNA WRONECKA.

Portugal: 5 rue Thami Lamdouar, Souissi, 10100 Rabat; tel. (3) 7756446; fax (3) 7756445; e-mail embport-rabat@hotmail.com; Ambassador JOÃO ROSA LA.

Qatar: 4 ave Tarik ibn Ziad, BP 1220, 10001 Rabat; tel. (3) 7765681; fax (3) 7765774; e-mail rabat@mofa.gov.qa; Ambassador SAQR MUBARAK AL-MANSOURI.

Romania: 10 rue d'Ouezzane, Hassan, 10000 Rabat; tel. (3) 7724694; fax (3) 7700196; e-mail bazilpopovici@yahoo.fr; internet rabat.mae.ro; Ambassador VASILE POPOVICI.

Russia: km 4 route des Zaêrs, 10100 Rabat; tel. (3) 7753509; fax (3) 7753590; e-mail ambrus@iam.net.ma; internet www.morocco.mid.ru; Ambassador BORIS BOLOTIN.

Saudi Arabia: 322 ave Imam Malik, km 6, route des Zaêrs, Rabat; tel. (3) 657789; fax (3) 7768587; e-mail ambassd@goodinfo.net.ma; Ambassador Dr MUHAMMAD ABD AR-RAHMAN BIN ABD AL-AZIZ BACHAR.

Senegal: 17 rue Cadi ben Hamadi Senhaji, Souissi, BP 365, 10000 Rabat; tel. (3) 7754171; fax (3) 7754149; e-mail ambassene@iam.net.ma; Ambassador IBOU NDIAYE.

Serbia: BP 5014, 23 ave Mehdi ben Barka, Souissi, 10105 Rabat; tel. (3) 7752201; fax (3) 753258; e-mail sermont@menara.ma; Ambassador MEHMED BECOVIĆ.

South Africa: 34 rue Saâdiens, Rabat; tel. (3) 7706760; fax (3) 7724550; e-mail sudaf@menara.ma; Chargé d'affaires N. K. M. SELEKA.

Spain: 3 rue Aïn Khalouiya, km 5.3, route des Zaêrs, Souissi, 10000 Rabat; tel. (3) 7633900; fax (3) 7630600; e-mail emb.rabat@maec.es; internet www.mae.es/Embajadas/Rabat; Ambassador D. LUIS PLANAS PUCHADES.

Sudan: 5 ave Ghomara, Souissi, 10000 Rabat; tel. (3) 7752863; fax (3) 7752865; e-mail soudanirab@maghrebnet.net.ma; Ambassador YAHIA ABDELJALIL MAHMOUD.

Sweden: 159 ave John Kennedy, BP 428, Souissi, 10001 Rabat; tel. (3) 7633210; fax (3) 7758048; e-mail ambassaden.rabat@foreign.ministry.se; internet www.swedenabroad.com/rabat; Ambassador KLAS GIEROW.

Switzerland: square de Berkane, BP 169, 10001 Rabat; tel. (3) 7268030; fax (3) 7268040; e-mail rab.vertretung@eda.admin.ch; internet www.eda.admin.ch/rabat; Ambassador LOUIS BERTRAND.

Syria: km 5.2, route des Zaêrs, BP 5158, Souissi, Rabat; tel. (3) 7755551; fax (3) 7757522; Ambassador NABIH ISMAIL.

Thailand: 11 rue de Tiddes, BP 4436, Rabat; tel. (3) 7634603; fax (3) 7634607; e-mail thaima@menara.ma; Ambassador SUWIT SAICHEUA.

Tunisia: 6 ave de Fès et 1 rue d'Ifrane, 10000 Rabat; tel. (3) 7730636; fax (3) 7730637; Ambassador SALAH BACCARI.

Turkey: 7 ave Abdelkrim Benjelloun, 10000 Rabat; tel. (3) 7661522; fax (3) 7660476; e-mail amb-tur-rabat@menara.ma; internet rabat.emb.mfa.gov.tr; Ambassador HALUK ILICAK.

Ukraine: rue Mouaouya ben Houdaig, Villa 212, Cité OLM, Souissi II, Rabat; tel. (3) 7657840; fax (3) 7754679; e-mail emb_ma@mfa.gov.ua; internet www.mfa.gov.ua/morocco; Ambassador VITALIY YOHNA.

United Arab Emirates: 11 ave des Alaouines, 10000 Rabat; tel. (3) 7702085; fax (3) 7724145; e-mail eua@menara.ma; Ambassador SAID HAMAD AL-KITBI.

United Kingdom: 28 ave S.A.R. Sidi Muhammad, Souissi, Rabat; tel. (3) 7633333; fax (3) 7758709; e-mail generalenquiries.rabat@fco.gov.uk; internet ukinmorocco.fco.gov.uk; Ambassador TIMOTHY MORRIS.

USA: 2 ave de Muhammad el-Fassi, Rabat; tel. (3) 7762265; fax (3) 7765661; e-mail ircrabat@usembassy.ma; internet rabat.usembassy.gov; Chargé d'affaires a.i. ROBERT P. JACKSON.

Venezuela: 58 Lot OLM, Villa Yasmine, rue Capitaine Abdeslam el-Moudden el-Alami, Souissi, Rabat; tel. (3) 7650315; fax (3) 7650372; e-mail emvenez@menara.ma; internet ambassadevenezuela-maroc.com; Ambassador LUISA REBECA SÁNCHEZ BELLO.

Yemen: ave Imam Malek, Rabat; tel. (3) 7631220; fax (3) 7674769; e-mail info@yemenembassyrabat.com; internet www.yemenembassyrabat.com; Ambassador AHMAD A. AL-BASHA.

Judicial System

SUPREME COURT

Al-Majlis al-Aala

Hay Ryad, Ave an-Nakhil, Rabat; tel. (3) 7714931; fax (3) 7715106; e-mail coursupreme@coursupreme.ma; internet www.coursupreme.ma.

Responsible for the interpretation of the law and regulates the jurisprudence of the courts and tribunals of the Kingdom. The Supreme Court sits at Rabat and is divided into six Chambers.

First President: TAÏEB CHARKAOUI.
Attorney-General: MUSTAPHA MEDDAH.

The 21 Courts of Appeal hear appeals from lower courts and also comprise a criminal division.

The 65 Courts of First Instance pass judgment on offences punishable by up to five years' imprisonment. These courts also pass judgment, without possibility of appeal, in personal and civil cases involving up to 3,000 dirhams.

The Communal and District Courts are composed of one judge, who is assisted by a clerk or secretary, and hear only civil and criminal cases.

The seven Administrative Courts pass judgment, subject to appeal before the Supreme Court pending the establishment of administrative appeal courts, on litigation with Government departments.

The nine Commercial Courts pass judgment, without the possibility of appeal, on all commercial litigations involving up to 9,000 dirhams. They also pass judgment on claims involving more than 9,000 dirhams, which can be appealed against in the commercial appeal courts.

The Permanent Royal Armed Forces' Court tries offences committed by the armed forces and military officers.

Religion

ISLAM

About 99% of Moroccans are Muslims (of whom about 90% are of the Sunni sect), and Islam is the state religion.

CHRISTIANITY

There are about 69,000 Christians, mostly Roman Catholics.

The Roman Catholic Church

Morocco (excluding the disputed territory of Western Sahara) comprises two archdioceses, directly responsible to the Holy See. At 31 December 2006 there were an estimated 23,300 adherents in the country, representing less than 0.1% of the population. The Moroccan archbishops participate in the Conférence Episcopale Régionale du Nord de l'Afrique (f. 1985).

Bishops' Conference: Conférence Episcopale Régionale du Nord the l'Afrique, 1 rue Hadj Muhammad Riffaï, BP 258, 10001 Rabat; tel. (37) 709239; fax (37) 706282; e-mail archev.rabat@wanadoo.net.ma; f. 1985; Pres. Most Rev. VINCENT LANDEL (Archbishop of Rabat).

Archbishop of Rabat: Most Rev. VINCENT LANDEL, Archevêché, 1 rue Hadj Muhammad Riffaï, BP 258, 10001 Rabat; tel. (3) 7709239; fax (3) 7706282; e-mail landel@wanadoo.net.ma.

Archbishop of Tangier: Most Rev. JOSÉ ANTONIO PETEIRO FREIRE, Archevêché, 55 rue Sidi Bouabid, BP 2116, 9000 Tangier; tel. (3) 9932762; fax (3) 9949117; e-mail igletanger@wanadoo.net.ma.

Western Sahara comprises a single Apostolic Prefecture, with an estimated 80 Catholics (2006).

Prefect Apostolic of Western Sahara: Fr ACACIO VALBUENA RODRÍGUEZ, Misión Católica, BP 31, 70001 el-Aaiún; tel. 893270; e-mail omisahara@menara.ma.

The Anglican Communion

Within the Church of England, Morocco forms part of the diocese of Gibraltar in Europe. There are Anglican churches in Casablanca and Tangier.

Protestant Church

Evangelical Church: 33 rue d'Azilal, 20000 Casablanca; tel. (2) 2302151; fax (2) 2444768; e-mail eeam@lesblancs.com; f. 1920; established in eight towns; Pres. Pastor JEAN-LUC BLANC; 1,000 mems.

JUDAISM

It is estimated that there are fewer than 7,000 Jews in Morocco, of whom approximately 5,000 reside in Casablanca, with smaller communities in Rabat and other cities.

Conseil des Communautés Israélites du Maroc: 52 Bne-Snassen, Souissi, Rabat; tel. (2) 222861; fax (2) 266953; Pres. SERGE BERDUGO.

The Press

DAILIES

Casablanca

Al-Ahdath al-Maghribia (Moroccan Events): 5 rue Saint-Emilion, Casablanca; tel. (2) 2443038; fax (2) 2442976; e-mail y.benjelloun@alahdath.info; internet www.ahdath.info; f. 1998; Arabic; Dir MUHAMMAD AL-BRINI; circ. 38,559 (2006).

Assabah (The Morning): Groupe Ecomedia, 70 blvd al-Massira al-Khadra, Casablanca; tel. (2) 2953660; fax (2) 2364358; e-mail assabah@assabah.press.ma; internet www.assabah.press.ma; Arabic; sister publication of l'Economiste; Dir-Gen. KHALID BELYAZID; circ. 61,737 (2006).

Assahra al-Maghribia: 17 rue Othman ben Affan, Casablanca; tel. (2) 2489120; fax (2) 2203935; e-mail web.master@almaghribia.ma; internet www.almaghribia.ma; f. 1989; Arabic; Dir HASSAN EL-ATTAFI.

Aujourd'hui le Maroc: 213 Rond-Point d'Europe, Casablanca; tel. (2) 2262674; fax (2) 2262443; e-mail alm@aujourdhui.ma; internet www.aujourdhui.ma; French; Dir KHALIL HACHIMI IDRISSI; Editor-in-Chief OMAR DAHBI; circ. 12,262 (2006).

Al-Bayane (The Manifesto): blvd Emile Zola, 8ème étage, BP 13152, Casablanca; tel. (2) 2307882; fax (2) 2308080; internet www.albayane.ma; Arabic and French; organ of the Parti du progrès et du socialisme; Dir ISMAÏL ALAOUI; Editor AHMED ZAKI; circ. 3,239 (2006).

L'Economiste: Groupe Ecomedia, 70 blvd al-Massira al-Khadra, Casablanca; tel. (2) 2953600; fax (2) 2365926; e-mail info@leconomiste.com; internet www.leconomiste.com; f. 1991; French; Pres. ABDELMOUNAÏM DILAMI; Dir-Gen. KHALID BELYAZID; Editor-in-Chief NADIA SALAH; circ. 17,254 (2006).

Al-Ittihad al-Ichtiraki (Socialist Unity): 33 rue Amir Abdelkader, BP 2165, Casablanca; tel. (2) 2407385; fax (2) 2619405; e-mail ail@menara.ma; internet www.alittihad.press.ma; Arabic; f. 1983; organ of the Union socialiste des forces populaires; Dir ABD AL-HADI DATE; Editor MUSTAPHA LAÂRAKI; circ. 14,669 (2006).

Libération: 33 rue Amir Abdelkader, BP 2165, Casablanca; tel. (2) 2619400; fax (2) 2620972; e-mail liberation@usfp.ma; internet www.liberation.press.ma; f. 1964; French; organ of the Union socialiste des forces populaires; Dir ABDELHADI KHAÏRAT; circ. 3,735 (2006).

Al-Massae (The Evening): 10 ave des Forces Armées Royales, 2ème étage, Casablanca; tel. (2) 2275918; fax (2) 2275597; e-mail chaouki.samir@gmail.com; internet www.almassae.press.ma; f. 2006; Arabic; independent; Dir RACHID NINI; circ. 41,085 (2006).

Le Matin du Sahara et du Maghreb: 17 rue Othman ben Affane, Casablanca; tel. (2) 2489100; fax (2) 2203048; e-mail m.jouahri@lematin.ma; internet www.lematin.ma; f. 1971; French; Dir-Gen. MUHAMMAD JOUAHRI; circ. 22,762 (2006).

Rissalat al-Oumma (The Message of the Nation): 152 ave des Forces Armées Royales, BP 20005, Casablanca; tel. (2) 2901925; fax (2) 2901926; Arabic; weekly edn in French; organ of the Union constitutionnelle; Dir MUHAMMAD TAMALDOU.

Rabat

Al-Alam (The Flag): ave Hassan II, rue Casablanca, Lot Vita, BP 141, Rabat; tel. (3) 7293002; fax (3) 7292639; e-mail alalam@alalam.ma; internet www.alalam.ma; f. 1946; Arabic; literary supplement on Saturdays; organ of the Istiqlal party; Dir ABD AL-JABBAR SUHEIMAT; Editor in Chief HASSAN ABDELKHALEK; circ. 11,943.

Attajdid (Reform): 3 blvd al-Moukawama, BP 9173, Rabat; tel. (3) 7705854; fax (3) 7705852; e-mail attajdid@attajdid.ma; internet www.attajdid.ma; f. 1999; Arabic; associated with the Parti de la justice et du développement; Dir ABDELILLAH BENKIRAN; circ. 4,581 (2006).

Al-Haraka (Progress): 66 rue Patrice Lumumba, BP 1317, Rabat; tel. (3) 7768667; fax (3) 7767537; e-mail harakamp@menara.ma; internet www.harakamp.ma; Arabic; organ of the Mouvement populaire; Dir ALI ALAOUI; circ. 1,034 (2006).

An-Nahar al-Maghribia (The Moroccan Day): 12 pl. des Alaouites, 2ème étage, Rabat; tel. (3) 7737568; fax (3) 7737547; e-mail annaharalmaghribia@menara.fr; internet www.annahar.ma; Arabic; Dir and Editor-in-Chief BADI ABD AL-HAKIM; circ. 11,221 (2006).

L'Opinion: ave Hassan II, Lot Vita, Rabat; tel. (3) 7293002; fax (3) 7292639; e-mail lopinion@lopinion.ma; internet www.lopinion.ma; f. 1965; French; organ of Istiqlal; Dir MUHAMMAD IDRISSI KAÏTOUNI; Editor-in-Chief JAMAL HAJJAM; circ. 20,662 (2006).

MOROCCO   *Directory*

SELECTED PERIODICALS

Casablanca

Al-Ayam (The Days): Espace Paquet, 508 rue Muhammad Smiha, Casablanca; tel. (2) 2442694; fax (2) 2441173; e-mail alayams75@yahoo.fr; f. 2001; Arabic; weekly; Editor NOUREDDINE MIFTAH; circ. 24,399 (2006).

CGEM Infos: 23 blvd Muhammad Abdou, Palmiers, Casablanca; tel. (2) 2997000; fax (2) 2983971; e-mail cgem@cgem.ma; internet www.cgem.ma; weekly; French; organ of the Confédération Générale des Entreprises du Maroc; Dir MOULAY HAFID ELALAMY.

Challenge Hebdo: Tour des Habous, 13ème étage, 58 ave des Forces Armées Royales, Casablanca; tel. (2) 2548150; fax (2) 2318094; e-mail redaction@challengehebdo.com; internet www.challengehebdo.com; weekly; French; business; Dir ADIL LAHLOU; Editor-in-Chief KHALID TRITKI; circ. 5,151 (2006).

Construire: 744 rue Boukraâ, Résidence Hanane Jassim I, Bourgogne, Casablanca; tel. (2) 2220271; fax (2) 2273627; e-mail nlleconstruire@yahoo.fr; internet www.nouvelleconstruire.com; f. 1940; weekly; French; Dir ABDELKRIM TALAL.

Femmes du Maroc: Immeuble Zénith I, Lot Attaoufik, route de Nouaceur, Sidi Maârouf, Casablanca; tel. (2) 2973949; fax (2) 2973929; internet www.femmesdumaroc.com; monthly; French; lifestyle magazine for women; Dir AÏCHA ZAÏMI SAKHRI; Editor-in-Chief GÉRALDINE DULAT; circ. 15,368 (2006).

La Gazette du Maroc: ave des Forces Armées Royales, Tour des Habous, 13ème étage, Casablanca; tel. (2) 2548150; fax (2) 2318094; e-mail info@lagazettedumaroc.com; internet www.lagazettedumaroc.com; weekly; French; Dir KAMAL LAHLOU; Editor-in-Chief ABD AL-LATIF EL-AZIZI; circ. 9,291 (2006).

Le Journal Hebdomadaire: 61 ave des Forces Armées Royales, BP 20000, Casablanca; tel. (2) 2546670; fax (2) 2446185; e-mail courrier@lejournal-hebdo.com; internet www.lejournal-hebdo.com; weekly; French; news, politics, economics; Dir ALI AMAR; circ. 14,832 (2006).

Maroc Fruits: 283 blvd Zerktouni, Casablanca; tel. (2) 2363946; fax (2) 2363996; f. 1958; fortnightly; Arabic and French; organ of the Association des Producteurs d'Agrumes du Maroc; Pres. LYOUSSI HASSAN; circ. 6,000.

Maroc Hebdo International: 4 rue des Flamants, Casablanca; tel. (2) 2238176; fax (2) 2981346; e-mail mhi@maroc-hebdo.press.ma; internet www.maroc-hebdo.com; f. 1991; weekly; French; Editor-in-Chief MUHAMMAD SELHAMI; 11,848 (2006).

Al-Mountakhab (The Team): 42 bis rue de Madagascar, Rabat; tel. (2) 2261951; fax (2) 2264638; e-mail almocom.j@menara.ma; internet www.almountakhab.com; f. 1986; fortnightly; Arabic; sport; Dir BADREDDINE IDRISSI; circ. 21,876 (2006).

Nissae min al-Maghrib (Women of Morocco): Immeuble Zénith I, Lot Attaoufik, route de Nouaceur, Sidi Maârouf, Casablanca; tel. (2) 2973949; fax (2) 2973929; e-mail y.guennoun@akwagroup.com; monthly; Arabic edn of *Femmes du Maroc*; circ. 32,564 (2006).

La Nouvelle Tribune: 320 blvd Zerktouni, angle rue Bouardel, Casablanca; tel. (2) 2424670; fax (2) 2200031; e-mail courrier@lanouvelletribune.com; internet www.lanouvelletribune.com; f. 1996; weekly (Thurs.); French; Dir FAHD YATA.

Parade: Immeuble Zénith I, Lot Attaoufik, route de Nouaceur, Sidi Maârouf, Casablanca; tel. (2) 2973949; fax (2) 2973929; e-mail y.guennoun@akwagroup.com; monthly; French; circ. 4,716 (2006).

Perspectives du Maghreb: 8 blvd Yacoub el Mansour, Maârif, Casablanca; tel. (2) 2257617; fax (2) 2257738; e-mail popmedia@menara.ma; f. 2005; monthly; French; circ. 4,973 (2006).

La Quinzaine du Maroc: 53 rue Dumont d'Urville, Casablanca; tel. (2) 2440033; fax (2) 2440426; e-mail mauro@wanadoopro.ma; internet quinzainedumaroc.com; f. 1951; fortnightly; English and French; visitors' guide; Dir HUBERT MAURO.

Le Reporter: 1 Sahat al-Istiqlal, 2ème étage, Casablanca; tel. (2) 2541103; fax (2) 2541105; e-mail redaction@lereporter.ma; internet www.lereporter.ma; f. 1998; weekly; French; Dir BAHIA AMRANI.

Assahifa al Maghribiya (The Moroccan Newspaper): 61 ave des Forces Armées Royales, Casablanca; e-mail ibargach2@yahoo.fr; tel. (2) 2546671; fax (2) 2446185; weekly; Arabic; Dir ISSAM BARGACH.

TelQuel: 28 ave des Forces Armées Royales, Casablanca; fax (2) 220563; e-mail courrier@telquel.info; internet www.telquel-online.com; weekly; French; Dir AHMAD BENCHEMSI; Editor-in-Chief KARIM BOUKHARI; circ. 21,747 (2006).

La Vérité: 174 blvd Zerktouni, 6ème étage, Casablanca; tel. (2) 2206411; fax (2) 2206423; e-mail elamrani321@yahoo.fr; internet www.laverite.ma; weekly (Fri.); French; Dir ABDALLAH EL-AMRANI.

Version Homme: ave des Forces Armées Royales, Tour des Habous, 13ème étage, Casablanca; tel. (2) 2450089; fax (2) 2442213; e-mail redaction@versionhomme.com; internet www.versionhomme.com; monthly; lifestyle magazine for men; Dir ADIL LAHLOU; circ. 5,745 (2006).

La Vie éco: 5 blvd Abdallah ben Yassine, 20300 Casablanca; tel. (2) 2450555; fax (2) 2304542; e-mail vieeco@marocnet.net.ma; internet www.lavieeco.com; f. 1921; weekly; French; economics; Dir FADEL AGOUMI; Editor-in-Chief SAÂD BEN MANSOUR; circ. 14,671 (2006).

La Vie Touristique Africaine: 17 rue El Houcine Ben Ali, Casablanca; tel. (2) 2227643; fax (2) 2275319; e-mail vietouristique@wanadoo.net.ma; internet www.vietouristique.ma; fortnightly; French; tourist information; Dir AHMED ZEGHARI.

Al-Watan al-An (The Nation Now): 33 rue Muhammad Bahi, Casablanca; tel. (2) 2251295; fax (2) 2251325; e-mail alwatanpress@menara.ma; internet www.alwatan.press.ma; weekly; Arabic; news; Editor ABDERRAHIM ARIRI; circ. 12,195 (2006).

Rabat

Al-Alam al-Amazighi: Éditions Amazigh, 5 rue Dakar, BP 477, Rabat; tel. (6) 1767073; fax (3) 7727283; e-mail lemondeamazigh@hotmail.com; weekly; Berber.

Asdae (Echoes): 30 ave Okba, Rabat; tel. (3) 7773706; e-mail asdae@menara.ma; internet www.asdae.com; weekly; Arabic; Dir EL-HASSAN ARBAI.

Ach-Chorta (The Police): BP 437, Rabat; tel. (3) 7652087; monthly; Arabic; Dir MUHAMMAD AD-DRIF.

Da'ouat al-Haqq (Call of the Truth): al-Michwar as-Said, Rabat; tel. (3) 7766851; e-mail direction_haq@habous.gov.ma; internet www.daouatalhaq.ma; publ. by Ministry of Habous (Religious Endowments) and Islamic Affairs; f. 1957; monthly; Arabic.

An-Nidal ad-Dimokrati (The Democratic Struggle): 18 rue de Tunis, Hassan, Rabat; tel. (3) 7732127; fax (3) 7720170; e-mail annidal@menara.ma; internet www.pnd.ma; f. 1984; weekly; Arabic; organ of the Parti national démocrate; Dir ABDELHAMID KHATIR.

At-Tadamoun (Solidarity): 6 rue Aguensous, BP 1740, Rabat; tel. (3) 7730961; fax (3) 7738851; e-mail amdh1@mtds.com; internet www.amdh.org.ma; monthly; Arabic; organ of the Association marocaine des droits humains; Dir ABD AL-MAJID SEMLALI EL-HASANI.

La Voix du Centre: 4 ave Imam Malik, route des Zaërs, Rabat; tel. (7) 3834771; fax (3) 7764767; weekly; French; organ of the Mouvement démocratique et social; Editor-in-Chief MUSTAPHA SHIMI.

Tangier

Achamal 2000: 137 ave Prince Héritier, Tangier; tel. (3) 9373927; fax (3) 9944216; e-mail ashamal@menara.ma; weekly; Arabic; Editor-in-Chief KHALID MECHBAL.

Le Journal de Tanger: 7 bis rue Omar Ben Abdelaziz, Tangier; tel. (3) 9943008; fax (3) 9945709; e-mail direct@lejournaldetanger.com; internet www.lejournaldetanger.com; f. 1904; weekly; French, English, Spanish and Arabic; Dir ABDELHAK BAKHAT; Editor-in-Chief MUHAMMAD ABOUABDILLAH; circ. 10,000.

NEWS AGENCY

Maghreb Arabe Presse (MAP): 122 ave Allal ben Abdallah, BP 1049, 10000 Rabat; tel. (3) 7279464; fax (3) 7279465; e-mail mapweb@map.co.ma; internet www.map.ma; f. 1959; Arabic, French, English and Spanish; state-owned; Dir-Gen. ALI BOUZERDA.

PRESS ASSOCIATIONS

Fédération Marocaine des Editeurs de Journaux (FMEJ): Groupe Ecomedia, 70 blvd al-Massira al-Khadra, Casablanca; tel. (2) 2953600; fax (2) 2365926; f. 2005; Pres. ABDELMOUNAIM DILAMI.

Organisme de Justification de la Diffusion (OJD Maroc): 4 rue des Flamants, Casablanca; tel. (2) 2238176; fax (2) 2981346; e-mail asmae@maroc-hebdo.press.ma; internet www.ojd.ma; f. 2004; compiles cir. statistics; Pres. MUHAMMAD SELHAMI; Dir ASMAE HASSANI.

Publishers

Afrique Orient: 159 bis blvd Yacoub el-Mansour, Casablanca; tel. (2) 2259813; fax (2) 2440080; f. 1983; sociology, philosophy and translations; Dir MUSTAPHA CHAJII.

Belvisi: 17 rue Abbas Ibnou Farnass, BP 8044, Casablanca; tel. (2) 2250973; fax (2) 2986258; f. 1986.

Dar el-Kitab: place de la Mosquée, Quartier des Habous, BP 4018, Casablanca; tel. (2) 2305419; fax (2) 3026630; f. 1948; Arabic and French; philosophy, history, Africana, general and social science; state-controlled; Dir BOUTALEB ABDOU ABD AL-HAY; Gen. Man. KHADIJA EL-KASSIMI.

Editions Le Fennec: 89B blvd d'Anfa, 14ème étage, Casablanca; tel. (2) 2209314; fax (2) 2277702; e-mail info@lefennec.com; internet www.lefennec.com; f. 1987; fiction, social sciences; Dir LAYLA B. CHAOUNI.

Editions La Porte: 281 blvd Muhammad V, BP 331, Rabat; tel. (3) 7709958; fax (3) 7706476; e-mail la_porte@meganet.net.ma; law, guides, economics, educational books.

Les Editions Maghrébines: Quartier Industriel, blvd E, N 15, Sin Sebaâ, Casablanca; tel. (2) 2351797; fax (2) 2357892; f. 1962; general non-fiction.

Les Editions Toubkal: Immeuble I.G.A, pl. de la Gare Voyageurs, Bélvèdere, 20300 Casablanca; tel. and fax (2) 22342323; e-mail contact@toubkal.ma; internet www.toubkal.ma; f. 1985; economy, history, social sciences, literature, educational books; Dir ABDELJALIL NADEM.

Malika Editions: 60 blvd Yacoub el-Mansour, 20100 Casablanca; tel. (2) 2235688; fax (2) 2251651; e-mail edmalika@connectcom.net.ma; internet www.malikaedition.com; art publications.

Tarik Editions: 321 route el-Jadida, 20000 Casablanca; tel. (2) 2259007; fax (2) 2232550; e-mail tarik.editions@wanadoo.net.ma; f. 2000; history and social sciences; Dir BICHR BENNANI.

Yomad: rue Boronia, secteur 17, Hay Riad, Rabat; tel. (3) 7717590; fax (3) 7717589; e-mail yomadeditions@yahoo.com; f. 1998; children's literature; Dir NADIA ES-SALMI.

GOVERNMENT PUBLISHING HOUSE

Imprimerie Officielle: ave Yacoub el-Mansour, Rabat-Chellah; tel. (3) 7765024; fax (3) 7765179.

Broadcasting and Communications

TELECOMMUNICATIONS

Regulatory Authority

Agence Nationale de Réglementation des Télécommunications (ANRT): Centre d'Affaires, blvd ar-Ryad, BP 2939, Hay Ryad, 10100 Rabat; tel. (3) 7718400; fax (3) 7203862; e-mail com@anrt.ma; internet www.anrt.ma; f. 1998; Dir-Gen. AZDIR EL MOUNTASSIR BILLAH.

Principal Operators

Itissalat al-Maghrib—Maroc Télécom: ave Annakhil Hay Riad, Rabat; tel. (3) 7719000; fax (3) 7714860; e-mail webmaster@iam.ma; internet www.iam.ma; f. 1998 to take over telephone services from the ONPT; privatized in 2004; Vivendi Universal (France) holds a 51% stake; Chair. ABDESLAM AHIZOUNE.

Méditel: Twin Centre, angle blvd Zerktouni et blvd Massira al-Khadra, Casablanca; internet www.meditel.ma; f. 1999; subsidiary of Telefónica SA and Portugal Telecom; provides national mobile telecommunications services; CEO MUHAMMAD EL-MANDJRA; Chair. OTHMAN BENJELLOUN.

BROADCASTING

Morocco can receive broadcasts from Spanish radio stations, and the main Spanish television channels can also be received in northern Morocco.

Radio

Radio Casablanca: c/o Loukt s.a.r.l, BP 16011, Casa Principal, 20001 Casablanca; tel. (2) 311914; e-mail i-RC@maroc.net; internet www.maroc.net/rc; f. 1996; Gen. Man. AMINE ZARY.

Radio Méditerranée Internationale: 3 rue Emsallah, BP 2055, 9000 Tangier; tel. (3) 9936363; fax (3) 9935755; e-mail medi1@medi1.com; internet www.medi1.com; Arabic and French; Man. Dir PIERRE CASALTA.

Voice of America Radio Station in Tangier: c/o US Consulate-General, chemin des Amoureux, Tangier.

Television

Société Nationale de Radiodiffusion et de Télévision: 1 rue el-Brihi, BP 1042, 1000 Rabat; tel. (3) 7766885; fax (3) 7766888; internet www.snrt.ma; govt station; transmission commenced 1962; 45 hours weekly; French and Arabic; carries commercial advertising; Dir-Gen. and Dir Television FAIÇAL LARAICHI.

SOREAD 2M: Société d'études et de réalisations audiovisuelles, km 7.3 route de Rabat, Aïn-Sebaâ, Casablanca; tel. (2) 2667373; fax (2) 2677856; e-mail portail@tv2m.co.ma; internet www.2m.tv; f. 1988; transmission commenced 1989; public television channel, owned by Moroccan Govt (72%) and by private national foreign concerns; broadcasting in French and Arabic; Man. Dir SAMI EL-JAI.

Finance

(cap. = capital; res = reserves; dep. = deposits; m. = million; brs = branches; amounts in dirhams)

BANKING

Central Bank

Bank Al-Maghrib: 277 ave Muhammad V, BP 445, Rabat; tel. (3) 7702626; fax (3) 7706667; e-mail webmaster@bkam.ma; internet www.bkam.gov.ma; f. 1959 as Banque du Maroc; name changed as above in 1987; bank of issue; cap. 500.0m., res 5,001.3m., dep. 59,630.0m. (Dec. 2008); Gov. ABDELLATIF JOUAHRI; Gen. Man. ABDELLATIF FAOUZI.

Other Banks

Attijariwafa Bank: 2 blvd Moulay Youssef, BP 11141, 20000 Casablanca; tel. (2) 2298888; fax (2) 2294125; e-mail contact@attijariwafa.com; internet www.attijariwafabank.com; f. 2005 by merger between Banque Commerciale du Maroc SA and Wafabank; 33.2% owned by Groupe ONA, 14.6% by Grupo Santander (Spain); cap. 1,929.9m., res 10,690.8m., dep. 146,188.4m. (Dec. 2007); Chair. and CEO MUHAMMAD EL-KETTANI.

Banque Centrale Populaire (Crédit Populaire du Maroc): 101 blvd Muhammad Zerktouni, BP 10622, 21100 Casablanca; tel. (2) 2202533; fax (2) 2229699; e-mail bcp@banquepopulairemorocco.ma; internet www.cpm.co.ma; f. 1961; 51% state-owned, 49% privately owned; merged with Société Marocaine de Dépot et Crédit in 2003; cap. 2,264.0m., res 9,256.2m., dep. 136,776.8m. (Dec. 2007); Pres. and Gen. Man. NOUREDDINE OMARY; 530 brs.

Banque Marocaine du Commerce Extérieur SA (BMCE): 140 ave Hassan II, BP 13425, 20000 Casablanca; tel. (2) 2200496; fax (2) 2200512; e-mail communicationfinanciere@bmcebank.co.ma; internet www.bmcebank.ma; f. 1959; transferred to majority private ownership in 1995; cap. 1,587.5m., res 4,281.6m., dep. 68,387.0m. (Dec. 2006); Chair. and CEO OTHMAN BENJELLOUN; 412 brs.

Banque Marocaine pour le Commerce et l'Industrie SA (BMCI): 26 pl. des Nations Unies, BP 15573, Casablanca; tel. (2) 22461000; fax (2) 22299406; e-mail adiba.lahbabi@africa.bnpparibas.com; internet www.bmcinet.com; f. 1964; 65.05% owned by BNP Paribas (France); cap. 1,000.3m., res 1,818.1m., dep. 38,350.8m. (Dec. 2006); Chair. MOURAD CHERIF; CEO JOËL SIBRAC; Gen. Man. RACHID MARRAKCHI; 221 brs.

Citibank-Maghreb: Zénith Millenium, Immeuble 1, Lot Attaoufik, Sidi Maârouf, BP 13362, Casablanca; tel. (2) 2489600; fax (2) 2974197; f. 1967; total assets 1,211.0m.; cap. and res 194.0m. (Dec. 2003); Pres. NUHAD SALIBA; 2 brs.

Crédit Agricole du Maroc SA: 29 rue Abou Faris al-Marini, BP 49, 10000 Rabat; tel. (3) 7208219; fax (3) 7445063; e-mail m_kettani@creditagricole.ma; internet www.creditagricole.ma; f. 1961 as Caisse Nationale de Crédit Agricole; became a limited co and adopted present name in 2003; 78% owned by Ministry of the Economy and Finance; cap. 1,820.5m., res 840.7m., dep. 33,055.0m. (Dec. 2005); Man. Dir KARIM BELMAACHI.

Crédit Immobilier et Hôtelier: 187 ave Hassan II, Casablanca; tel. (2) 2479000; fax (2) 2479363; e-mail info-client@cih.co.ma; internet www.cih.co.ma; f. 1920; transferred to majority private ownership in 1995; cap. 3,323.4m., res −4,443.9m., dep. 19,502.7m. (Dec. 2005); Pres. KHALID ALIOUA; Gen. Mans GILLES THERRY, SAID LAFTIT; 91 brs.

Crédit du Maroc SA: 48–58 blvd Muhammad V, BP 13579, 20000 Casablanca; tel. (2) 2477477; fax (2) 2477127; e-mail mohammadine.menjra@ca-cdm.ma; internet www.cdm.co.ma; f. 1963 as Crédit Lyonnais Maroc; name changed as above in 1966; 52.6% owned by Crédit Agricole (France); cap. 833.8m., res 933.3m., dep. 21,453.7m. (Dec. 2005); Chair. and CEO SAÏDA LAMRANI KARIM; 163 brs.

Société Générale Marocaine de Banques SA: 55 blvd Abdelmoumen, BP 13090, 21100 Casablanca; tel. (2) 2438888; fax (2) 2234931; e-mail contact@sgmaroc.com; internet www.sgmaroc.com; f. 1962; cap. 1,170.0m., res 1,496.9m., dep. 36,206.3m. (Dec. 2006); Pres. ABDELAZIZ TAZI; 132 brs.

Bank Organizations

Association Professionnelle des Sociétés de Bourse du Maroc: angle rue Muhammad Errachid et ave des Forces Armées Royales, 20000 Casablanca; tel. (2) 2542333; fax (2) 2542336; e-mail apsb@apsb.org.ma; internet www.apsb.org.ma; f. 1995; groups all brokers in the stock exchange of Casablanca for studies, inquiries of general interest and contacts with official authorities; 16 mems; Pres. YOUSUF BENKIRANE; Vice-Pres. OMAR AMINE.

Groupement Professionnel des Banques du Maroc: 71 ave des Forces Armées Royales, Casablanca; tel. (2) 2314824; fax (2) 2314903; f. 1967; groups all commercial banks for studies, inquiries of general interest, and contacts with official authorities; 18 mems; Pres. OTHMAN BENJELLOUN.

STOCK EXCHANGE

Bourse de Casablanca: angle ave des Forces Armées Royales et rue Muhammad Errachid, Casablanca; tel. (2) 2452626; fax (2) 2452625; e-mail contact@casablanca-bourse.com; internet www.casablanca-bourse.com; f. 1929; Chair. AOMAR YIDAR; CEO HICHAM ELAMY (acting).

INSURANCE

Assurances Al-Amane: 122 ave Hassan II, 20000 Casablanca; tel. (2) 2267272; fax (2) 2265664; f. 1975; cap. 120m.; Pres. and Dir-Gen. MUHAMMAD BOUGHALEB.

Atlanta Assurances: 181 blvd d'Anfa, BP 13685, 20001 Casablanca; tel. (2) 2957676; fax (2) 2369812; e-mail info@atlanta.ma; internet www.atlanta.ma; f. 1947; cap. 591.6m.; Dir-Gen. MUHAMMAD HASSAN BENSALAH.

AXA Assurance Maroc: 120–122 ave Hassan II, 21000 Casablanca; tel. (2) 2224185; fax (2) 2260150; internet www.axa.ma; cap. 900m.; Dir-Gen. DANIEL ANTUNÈS.

Compagnie d'Assurances et de Réassurances SANAD: 181 blvd d'Anfa, Tours Balzac, Casablanca; tel. (2) 2957878; fax (2) 2360712; e-mail atahiri@sanad.ma; internet www.sanad.ma; f. 1946; cap. 125m.; Chair. MUHAMMAD HASSAN BENSALAH; Dir-Gen. ABDELTIF TAHIRI.

CNIA Assurance: 216 blvd Muhammad Zerktouni, 20000 Casablanca; tel. (2) 2474040; fax (2) 2206081; internet www.cnia.ma; f. 1949; cap. 30m.; Pres. and Dir-Gen. MOULAY HAFID ELALAMY.

La Marocaine Vie: 37 blvd Moulay Youssef, Casablanca; tel. (2) 2206320; fax (2) 2297307; f. 1978; 83% owned by Société Générale Marocaine de Banques SA; Pres. MARC DUVAL; Gen. Man. KARIM MOULTAKI.

Mutuelle Centrale Marocaine d'Assurances (MCMA): 16 rue Abou Inane, BP 27, Rabat; tel. (3) 7767800; fax (3) 7766440; part of the MAMDA-MCMA group; Pres. ABED YACOUBI SOUSSANE; Man. Dir ANNIE GUERRAWI.

Mutuelle d'Assurances des Transporteurs Unis (MATU): 215 blvd Muhammad Zerktouni, Casablanca; tel. (2) 2367097; Pres. HADJ MUHAMMAD HAKAM; Dir-Gen. BENYAMNA MUHAMMAD.

RMA Watanya: 83 ave des Forces Armées Royales, 20000 Casablanca; tel. (2) 2312163; fax (2) 2313137; e-mail contact@rmawatanya.com; internet www.rmawatanya.com; f. 2005 by merger of Al-Wataniya and La Royale Marocaine d'Assurances; cap. 1,774m.; Pres. SÉBASTIEN CASTRO.

Es-Saâda, Compagnie d'Assurances et de Réassurances: 123 ave Hassan II, BP 13860, 20000 Casablanca; tel. (2) 2497100; fax (2) 2262655; e-mail es-saada@techno.net.ma; internet www.essaada.com; f. 1961; cap. 107.6m.; Pres. MEHDI OUAZZANI; Man. Dir ABDELFETTAH ALAMI.

Société Centrale de Réassurance (SCR): Tour Atlas, pl. Zallaqa, BP 13183, Casablanca; tel. (2) 2460400; fax (2) 2460460; e-mail scr@scrmaroc.com; internet www.scrmaroc.com; f. 1960; cap. 30m.; Chair. MUSTAPHA BAKKOURY; Man. Dir AHMAD ZINOUN.

Société Marocaine d'Assurance à l'Exportation (SMAEX): 24 rue Ali Abderrazak, BP 15953, Casablanca; tel. (2) 2982000; fax (2) 2252070; e-mail smaex@smaex.com; internet www.smaex.com; f. 1988; insurance for exporters in the public and private sectors; assistance for export promotion; Pres. and Dir-Gen. NEZHA LAHRICHI; Asst Dir-Gen. ABDERRAZZAK M'HAIMDAT.

WAFA Assurance: 1–3 blvd Abd al-Moumen, BP 13420, 20001 Casablanca; tel. (2) 2224575; fax (2) 2209103; e-mail webmaster@wafaassurance.com; internet www.attijariwafabank.com; subsidiary of Attijariwafa Bank; Pres. SAÂD KETTANI; Dir-Gen. JAOUAD KETTANI.

Zurich Assurances Maroc: Residence City Park Centre, 106 rue Abderrahmane Sahraoui, 20000 Casablanca; tel. (2) 2279015; fax (2) 2276718; e-mail customerservice@zurich.com; f. 1954; cap. 90m.; all kinds of insurance; Pres. and Dir-Gen. BERTO FISLER.

INSURANCE ASSOCIATION

Fédération Marocaine des Sociétés d'Assurances et de Réassurances: 154 blvd d'Anfa, Casablanca; tel. (2) 2391850; fax (2) 2391854; e-mail a.boughaleb@fmsar.ma; internet www.fmsar.org.ma; f. 1958; 15 mem. cos; Pres. MUSTAPHA BAKHOURY.

Trade and Industry

GOVERNMENT AGENCIES

Agence National pour la Promotion de Petite et Moyenne Entreprise (ANPME): 10 rue Gandhi, BP 211, 10001 Rabat; tel. (3) 7708460; fax (3) 7707695; e-mail anpme@anpme.ma; internet www.anpme.ma; f. 1973 as the Office pour le Développement Industriel; name changed as above in 2002; state agency to develop industry; Dir-Gen. LATIFA ECHIHABI.

Centre Marocain de Promotion des Exportations (CMPE): 23 blvd Bnou Majid el-Bahar, BP 10937, 20000 Casablanca; tel. (2) 2302210; fax (2) 2301793; e-mail cmpe@cmpe.org.ma; internet www.cmpe.org.ma; f. 1980; state org. for promotion of exports; Man. Dir ALI EL-ALAOUI (acting).

Direction des Entreprises Publiques et de la Privatisation (DEPP): rue Haj Ahmed Cherkaoui, Quartier Administratif, Agdal, Rabat; tel. (3) 7689303; fax (3) 7689347; e-mail talbi@depp.finances.gov.ma; part of the Ministry of the Economy and Finance; in charge of regulation, restructuring and privatization of state enterprises; Dir ABDELAZIZ TALBI.

Office National des Hydrocarbures et des Mines (ONHYM): 5 ave Moulay Hassan, BP 99, 10050 Rabat; tel. (3) 7239898; fax (3) 7709411; e-mail benkhadra@onhym.com; internet www.onhym.com; f. 2003 to succeed Bureau de Recherches et de Participations Minières and Office National de Recherches et d'Exploitations Pétrolières; state agency conducting exploration, valorization and exploitation of hydrocarbons and mineral resources; Dir-Gen. AMINA BENKHADRA.

Société de Gestion des Terres Agricoles (SOGETA): 35 rue Daïet-Erroumi, BP 731, Agdal, Rabat; tel. (3) 7772778; fax (3) 7772765; f. 1973; oversees use of agricultural land; Man. Dir BACHIR SAOUD.

DEVELOPMENT ORGANIZATIONS

Caisse de Dépôt et de Gestion: pl. Moulay el-Hassan, BP 408, 10001 Rabat; tel. (3) 7765520; fax (3) 7763849; internet www.cdg.ma; f. 1959; finances small-scale projects; Dir-Gen. MUSTAPHA BAKKOURI; Sec.-Gen. HASSAN BOUBRIK.

Caisse Marocaine des Marchés (Marketing Fund): Résidence el-Manar, 52 blvd Abd al-Moumen, 20100 Casablanca; tel. (2) 2259118; fax (2) 2252316; e-mail y.chraibi@cmm.ma; internet www.cmm.ma; f. 1950; cap. 10m. dirhams; Man. HASSAN KISSI.

Société de Développement Agricole (SODEA): ave Hadj Ahmed Cherkaoui, BP 6280, Rabat; tel. (3) 7770825; fax (3) 7774798; internet www.sodea.com; f. 1972; state agricultural devt org.; Man. Dir AHMED HAJJAJI.

Société Nationale d'Investissement (SNI): 60 rue d'Alger, BP 38, 20000 Casablanca; tel. (2) 2224102; fax (2) 2484303; f. 1966; transferred to majority private ownership in 1994; cap. 10,900m. dirhams; Pres. HASSAN BOUHEMOU; Sec.-Gen. SAÂD BENDIDI.

CHAMBERS OF COMMERCE

Fédération des Chambres de Commerce et d'Industrie du Maroc (FCCIM): 6 rue d'Erfoud, BP 218, Hassan, Rabat; tel. (3) 7767078; fax (3) 7767076; f. 1962; groups the 28 Chambers of Commerce and Industry; Pres. DRISS HOUAT; Dir-Gen. MUHAMMAD LARBI EL-HARRAS.

Chambre de Commerce, d'Industrie et de Services de la Wilaya de Rabat-Salé: 1 rue Gandhi, BP 131, Rabat; tel. (3) 7706442; fax (3) 7706768; e-mail ccisrs@ccisrs.org.ma; Pres. OMAR DERRAJI; Dir MOUNJI ZNIBER.

Chambre de Commerce, d'Industrie et de Services de la Wilaya du Grand Casablanca: 98 blvd Muhammad V, BP 423, Casablanca; tel. (2) 2264327; fax (2) 2268436; Pres. LAHCEN EL-WAFI.

INDUSTRIAL AND TRADE ASSOCIATIONS

Office National Interprofessionnel des Céréales et des Légumineuses (ONICL): 3 ave Moulay Hassan, BP 154, Rabat; tel. (3) 7217300; fax (3) 7709626; e-mail directeur@onicl.org.ma; internet www.onicl.org.ma; f. 1937; Dir-Gen. ABDELLATIF GUEDIRA.

Office National des Pêches: 15 rue Lieutenant Mahroud, BP 16243, 20300 Casablanca; tel. (2) 2242084; fax (2) 2242305; e-mail onp@onp.co.ma; internet www.onp.co.ma; f. 1969; state fishing org.; Man. Dir MAJID KAISSAR EL-GHAIB.

EMPLOYERS' ORGANIZATIONS

Association Marocaine des Exporteurs (ASMEX): 36B blvd Anfa, Casablanca; tel. (2) 2261033; fax (2) 2484191; e-mail asmex@asmex.org; internet www.asmex.org; f. 1982; Pres. ABDELLATIF BEN MADANI.

MOROCCO

Association Marocaine des Industries Textiles et de l'Habillement (AMITH): 92 blvd Moulay Rachid, Casablanca; tel. (2) 2942085; fax (2) 2940587; e-mail amith@amith.ma; internet www.amith.org.ma; f. 1958; 700 mems; textile, knitwear and ready-made garment manufacturers; Pres. MUHAMMAD TAMER; Dir-Gen. MUHAMMAD TAZI.

Association des Producteurs d'Agrumes du Maroc (ASPAM): 283 blvd Zerktouni, Casablanca; tel. (2) 2363946; fax (2) 2364041; f. 1958; links Moroccan citrus growers; has its own processing plants; Pres. LYOUSSI HASSAN.

Association Professionnelle des Agents Maritimes, Consignataires de Navires, et Courtiers d'Affrètement du Maroc (APRAM): 219 blvd des Forces Armées Royales, 5ème étage, 20000 Casablanca; tel. (2) 2541112; fax (2) 2541415; e-mail apram@wanadoopro.ma; internet www.apram.ma; f. 1999; 37 mems; Pres. ABDELAZIZ MANTRANCH.

Association Professionnelle des Cimentiers (APC): 239 blvd Moulay Ismaïl, Casablanca; tel. (2) 2401342; fax (2) 2248208; internet www.apc.ma; 4 mems; cement manufacturers; Pres. MUHAMMAD CHAIBI.

Confédération Générale des Entreprises du Maroc (CGEM): angle ave des Forces Armées Royales et rue Muhammad Errachid, 20100 Casablanca; tel. (2) 2997000; fax (2) 2983971; e-mail cgem@cgem.ma; internet www.cgem.ma; 25 affiliated feds; Pres. MOULAY HAFID ELALAMY.

UTILITIES

Electricity and Water

Office National de l'Eau Potable (ONEP): Station de Traitement ONEP, ave Muhammad Belhassan El Ouazzani, BP 10002 Rabat-Chellah, Rabat; tel. (3) 7759600; fax (3) 7759106; e-mail onepbo@onep.ma; internet www.onep.org.ma; f. 1972; responsible for drinking-water supply; Dir-Gen. ALI FASSI-FIHRI.

Office National de l'Electricité (ONE): 65 rue Othman ben Affan, BP 13498, 20001 Casablanca; tel. (2) 2668080; fax (2) 2220038; e-mail offelec@one.org.ma; internet www.one.org.ma; f. 1963; state electricity authority; Dir-Gen. ALI FASSI FIHRI.

Gas

Afriquia Gaz: 139 blvd Moulay Ismail, Aïn Sebaâ, Casablanca; tel. (2) 22639600; fax (2) 22639666; e-mail r.idrissi@akwagroup.com; internet www.afriquiagaz.com; f. 1992; Morocco's leading gas distributor; Pres. ALI WAKRIM; Dir-Gen. TAWFIK HAMOUMI.

TRADE UNIONS

Confédération Démocratique du Travail (CDT): 64 rue al-Mourtada, Quartier Palmier, BP 13576, Casablanca; tel. (2) 2994470; fax (2) 2994473; e-mail cdtmaroc@cdt.ma; internet www.cdt.ma; f. 1978; Sec.-Gen. NOUBIR EL-AMAOUI.

Fédération Démocratique du Travail (FDT): 12 rue Muhammad Diouri, Sidi Belyoute, Casablanca; tel. (2) 2446362; fax (2) 2444764; internet www.fdt.ma; f. 2003 by fmr mems of CDT associated with USFP; Sec.-Gen. TAYEB MOUNCHID.

Union Générale des Travailleurs du Maroc (UGTM): 9 rue du Rif, blvd Muhammad VI, Casablanca; tel. (2) 2281788; fax (2) 2282144; e-mail info@ugtm.ma; internet www.ugtm.ma; f. 1960; associated with Istiqlal; supported by unions not affiliated to UMT; Sec.-Gen. HAMID CHABAT.

Union Marocaine du Travail (UMT): Bourse du Travail, 232 ave des Forces Armées Royales, Casablanca; tel. (2) 2302292; fax (2) 2307854; f. 1955; left-wing; most unions are affiliated; Sec. MAHJOUB BENSEDDIQ.

Union Nationale du Travail du Maroc (UNTM): 352 ave Muhammad V, immeuble Saâda, Rabat; tel. (3) 7793196; fax (3) 7263546; f. 1976; Islamist, associated with the PJD; Sec.-Gen. MUHAMMAD YATIM.

Transport

Société Nationale des Transports et de la Logistique (SNTL): rue al-Fadila, Quartier Industriel, BP 114, Chellah, Rabat; tel. (3) 7289300; fax (3) 7797850; e-mail ahachemi@sntl.ma; internet www.sntl.ma; f. 1958; Dir-Gen. OUSSAMA LOUDGHIRI.

RAILWAYS

In 2005 there were 1,907 km of railways, of which 418 km were double track; 1,022 km of lines were electrified and diesel locomotives were used on the rest. In that year the network carried some 18.5m. passengers and 32.7m. metric tons of freight. All services are nationalized. A feasibility study took place in 1998 into the construction of a 28-km tram system in Casablanca; the project was finally approved in late 2008. In 2007 another feasibility study was begun into plans for a 40-km railway tunnel under the Strait of Gibraltar linking Morocco and Spain.

Office National des Chemins de Fer (ONCF): 8 bis rue Abderrahmane el-Ghafiki, Rabat-Agdal; tel. (3) 7774747; fax (3) 7774480; e-mail ketary@oncf.ma; internet www.oncf.ma; f. 1963; administers all Morocco's railways; Dir-Gen. MUHAMMAD RABIE KHLIE.

ROADS

In 2004 there were 57,493 km of classified roads, of which 56.9% were paved. The motorway network covered 640 km in 2007, and was due to be extended to 1,420 km by 2010.

Autoroutes du Maroc (ADM): Hay Riad, Rabat; tel. (3) 7711056; fax (3) 7711059; e-mail naitbrahim.ismail@adm.co.ma; internet www.adm.co.ma; responsible for the construction and upkeep of Morocco's motorway network.

Compagnie de Transports au Maroc (CTM—SA): km 13.5, autoroute Casablanca–Rabat, Casablanca; tel. (2) 2762100; fax (2) 2765428; e-mail webmaster@ctm.co.ma; internet www.ctm.co.ma; f. 1919; agencies in Tangier, Rabat, Meknès, Oujda, Marrakesh, Agadir, El Jadida, Safi, Casablanca, Essaouira, Fez and Ouarzazate; privatized in 1993, with 40% of shares reserved for Moroccan citizens; Pres. and Dir-Gen. MUHAMMAD BOUDA.

SHIPPING

According to official figures, Morocco's 21 ports handled 61.5m. metric tons of goods in 2004. The most important ports, in terms of the volume of goods handled, are Casablanca, Jorf Lasfar, Safi and Mohammadia. Tangier is the principal port for passenger services. Construction work on new ports at Tangier (to handle merchandise traffic) and Agadir commenced in 2000.

Office d'Exploitation des Ports (ODEP): 175 blvd Muhammad Zerktouni, 20100 Casablanca; tel. (2) 2232324; fax (2) 2232325; e-mail administrateur@odep.org.ma; f. 1985; port management and handling of port equipment; Gen. Man. MUSTAPHA BARROUG.

Principal Shipping Companies

Agence Med SARL: 3 rue ibn Rochd, 90000 Tangier; tel. (3) 9935875; fax (3) 9933239; e-mail agencemed@menara.ma; f. 1904; owned by the Bland Group; also at Agadir, Casablanca, Jorf Lasfar, Nador and Safi; Operations Man. MUHAMMAD CHATT.

Compagnie Chérifienne d'Armement: 5 blvd Abdallah ben Yacine, 21700 Casablanca; tel. (2) 2309455; fax (2) 2301186; f. 1929; regular services to Europe; Man. Dir MAX KADOCH.

Compagnie Marocaine d'Agences Maritimes (COMARINE): 45 ave des Forces Armées Royales, BP 60, 20000 Casablanca; tel. (2) 2548510; fax (2) 2548570; e-mail comarine@comarine.co.ma.

Compagnie Marocaine de Navigation (COMANAV): 7 blvd de la Résistance, BP 628, Casablanca 20300; tel. (2) 2303012; fax (2) 2302006; e-mail comanav@comanav.co.ma; internet www.comanav.ma; f. 1946 as Cie Franco-Chérifienne de Navigation; name changed as above in 1959; privatization pending; regular services to Mediterranean, North-west European, Middle Eastern and West African ports; tramping; Pres. and Dir-Gen. TOUFIQ IBRAHIMI; Sec.-Gen. MEHDI BELGHITI; 12 agencies.

Intercona SA: 7 rue Hariri, 4ème étage, Tangier; tel. (3) 9945907; fax (3) 9945909; e-mail intercona-sa@menara.ma; f. 1943; daily services from Algeciras (Spain) to Tangier and Ceuta (Spanish North Africa); Pres. VICENTE JORRO.

Limadet-ferry: 3 rue ibn Rochd, Tangier; tel. (3) 933639; fax (3) 937173; e-mail headoffice@limadet.com; f. 1966; daily services between Algeciras (Spain) and Tangier; Dir-Gen. RACHID BEN MANSOUR.

Société Marocaine de Navigation Atlas: 81 ave Houmane el-Fatouaki, 21000 Casablanca; tel. (2) 2224190; fax (2) 2200164; e-mail atlas@marbar.co.ma; f. 1976; Chair. HASSAN CHAMI; Man. Dir MUHAMMAD SLAOUI.

Union Maritime Maroc-Scandinave (UNIMAR): 12 rue de Foucauld, BP 746, Casablanca; tel. (2) 2279590; fax (2) 2223883; f. 1974; chemicals; Dir-Gen. ABD AL-WAHAB BEN KIRANE.

Voyages Paquet: 65 ave des Forces Armées Royales, 20000 Casablanca; tel. (2) 2761941; fax (2) 2442108; f. 1970; Pres. MUHAMMAD ELOUALI ELALAMI; Dir-Gen. NAÏMA BAKALI ELOUALI ELALAMI.

CIVIL AVIATION

The main international airports are at Casablanca (King Muhammad V), Rabat, Tangier, Marrakesh, Agadir Inezgane, Fez, Oujda, Al-Hocima, el-Aaiún, Ouarzazate, Agadir al-Massira and Nador. The completion of a second runway at King Muhammad V airport was followed by the inauguration, in September 2007, of a second terminal, which increased the airport's annual passenger capacity from 5m. to 11m.

Atlas Blue: Aéroport Marrakesh Ménara, BP 440, Medina, Marrakesh; fax (2) 44424222; e-mail contact@atlas-blue.com; internet www.atlas-blue.com; f. 2004; wholly owned by Royal Air Maroc (RAM); low-cost airline; domestic flights and services to six European countries; Chair ZOUHAIR MUHAMMAD EL-AOUFIR.

Office Nationale des Aéroports: Siège Social Nouasseur, BP 8101, Casablanca; tel. (2) 2539040; fax (2) 2539901; e-mail onda@onda.ma; internet www.onda.ma; f. 1990; Dir-Gen. MUHAMMAD NOURI.

Regional Air Lines: Aéroport de Muhammad V, BP 83, 20240 Casablanca; tel. (2) 2538020; fax (2) 2538411; e-mail customer-service@regionalmaroc.com; internet www.regionalmaroc.com; f. 1997; privately owned; domestic flights and services to southern Spain, Portugal and the Canary Islands; Pres. MUHAMMAD HASSAN BENSALAH; CEO HICHAM NECHAD.

Royal Air Maroc (RAM): Aéroport de Casablanca-Anfa; tel. (2) 2912000; fax (2) 2912087; e-mail callcenter@royalairmaroc.com; internet www.royalairmaroc.com; f. 1953; 94.4% state-owned; scheduled for partial privatization; domestic flights and services to countries in Western Europe, Scandinavia, the Americas, North and West Africa, the Canary Islands and the Middle East; Chair. and CEO DRISS BENHIMA.

Tourism

Tourism is Morocco's second main source of convertible currency. The country's tourist attractions include its sunny climate, ancient sites (notably the cities of Fez, Marrakesh, Meknès and Rabat) and spectacular scenery. There are popular holiday resorts on the Atlantic and Mediterranean coasts. In 2007 foreign tourist arrivals totalled 4.32m., compared with 1.63m. in 1996. Tourism receipts, including passenger transport, amounted to US $6,899m. in 2006.

Office National Marocain du Tourisme: 31 angle ave al-Abtal et rue Oued Fès, Agdal, Rabat; tel. (3) 7674013; fax (3) 7674015; e-mail website@onmt.org.ma; internet www.tourisme-marocain.com/onmt; f. 1918; Dir-Gen. FATHIA BENNIS.

MOZAMBIQUE

Introductory Survey

Location, Climate, Language, Religion, Flag, Capital

The Republic of Mozambique lies on the east coast of Africa, bordered to the north by Tanzania, to the west by Malawi, Zambia and Zimbabwe, and to the south by South Africa and Swaziland. The country has a coastline of about 2,470 km (1,535 miles) on the shores of the Indian Ocean, and is separated from Madagascar, to the east, by the Mozambique Channel. Except in a few upland areas, the climate varies from tropical to sub-tropical. Rainfall is irregular, but the rainy season is usually from November to March, when average temperatures in Maputo are between 26°C (79°F) and 30°C (86°F). In the cooler dry season, in June and July, the average temperatures are 18°C (64°F) to 20°C (68°F). Portuguese is the official language, while there are 39 indigenous languages, the most widely spoken being Makhuwa, Tsonga, Sema and Lomwe. Many of the inhabitants follow traditional beliefs. There are about 5m. Christians, the majority of whom are Roman Catholics, and 4m. Muslims. The national flag (proportions 2 by 3) has three equal horizontal stripes, of green, black and yellow, separated by narrow white stripes. At the hoist is a red triangle containing a five-pointed yellow star, on which are superimposed an open book, a hoe and a rifle. The capital is Maputo (formerly Lourenço Marques).

Recent History

Mozambique became a Portuguese colony in the 19th century and an overseas province in 1951. Nationalist groups began to form in the 1960s. The Frente de Libertação de Moçambique (Frelimo—Mozambique Liberation Front) was formed in 1962 and launched a military campaign for independence in 1964. After the coup in Portugal (q.v.) in April 1974, negotiations between Frelimo and the new Portuguese Government resulted in a period of rule in Mozambique by a transitional Government, followed by full independence on 25 June 1975. The leader of Frelimo, Samora Machel, became the first President of Mozambique. Between September and December 1977 elections took place to local, district and provincial assemblies and, at national level, to the Assembléia Popular (People's Assembly).

In March 1976 Mozambique closed its border with Rhodesia (now Zimbabwe) and applied economic sanctions against that country. Mozambique was the principal base for Rhodesian nationalist guerrillas, and consequently suffered considerable devastation as a result of offensives launched by Rhodesian government forces against guerrilla camps. The border was reopened in January 1980.

After Zimbabwean independence in April 1980, South Africa adopted Rhodesia's role as supporter of the Mozambican opposition guerrilla group, Resistência Nacional Moçambicana (Renamo), also known as the Movimento Nacional da Resistência de Moçambique. The activities of Renamo subsequently increased, causing persistent disruption to road, rail and petroleum pipeline links from Mozambican ports, which were vital to the economic independence of southern African nations from South Africa. In March 1984 Mozambique and South Africa signed a formal joint non-aggression pact, known as the Nkomati accord, whereby each Government undertook to prevent opposition forces on its territory from launching attacks against the other, and a Joint Security Commission was established. The accord effectively implied that South Africa would withdraw its covert support for Renamo in return for a guarantee by Mozambique that it would prevent any further use of its territory by the then banned African National Congress of South Africa (ANC). However, following an intensification of Renamo activity, in 1985 the Frelimo Government appealed to foreign powers for increased military assistance, and in June it was agreed that Zimbabwe would augment its military presence in Mozambique. A major military offensive against Renamo in July resulted in the capture, in August, of the rebels' national operational command centre. Mozambique subsequently alleged that South Africa had repeatedly violated the Nkomati accord by providing material support for the rebels. The Joint Security Commission ceased to meet in 1985.

General elections were scheduled to take place in 1982, but were postponed several times because of the security situation. Legislative elections eventually began in August 1986, but were delayed, owing to the internal conflict. The post of Prime Minister was created in July and allocated to Mário Machungo. President Machel died in an air crash in South Africa in October. The causes of the incident were unclear, and the Mozambican Ministry of Information declared that it did not exclude the possibility of South African sabotage. (In May 1998 it was announced that South Africa's Truth and Reconciliation Commission—TRC—was to examine evidence relating to the crash. The TRC's final report stated that the evidence was inconclusive, but a number of questions merited further investigation. In early 2006 the South African Government announced that it was to reopen the inquiry into Machel's death.) In November 1986 the Central Committee of Frelimo appointed Joaquim Alberto Chissano, hitherto Minister for Foreign Affairs, as President. The elections were then resumed. In contrast to the 1977 elections, the voters were given a choice of candidates; nevertheless, all government and party leaders had been re-elected when the poll was completed in December 1986.

In June 1988, following six months of negotiations, Mozambique, South Africa and Portugal signed an agreement to rehabilitate the Cahora Bassa hydroelectric plant in Mozambique (potentially one of the greatest sources of electricity in southern Africa). In May Mozambican and South African officials had agreed to reactivate the Nkomati accord and to re-establish the Joint Security Commission; subsequently a joint commission for co-operation and development was established.

At Frelimo's fifth congress, held in July 1989, the party's exclusively Marxist-Leninist orientation was renounced, and party membership was opened to Mozambicans from all sectors of society. In January 1990 Chissano announced the drafting of a new constitution.

In mid-1989 Presidents Daniel arap Moi of Kenya and Robert Mugabe of Zimbabwe agreed to mediate between the Mozambique Government and Renamo. In August Renamo rejected the Government's peace proposals, and demanded recognition as a political entity, the introduction of multi-party elections and the withdrawal of Zimbabwean troops from Mozambique as preconditions for peace. However, further talks between the Government and the rebels resulted in an agreement, in December 1990, for a partial cease-fire. Under the terms of the agreement, all Zimbabwean troops present in Mozambique were required to retire to the Beira and Limpopo transport 'corridors' linking Zimbabwe to the Mozambican ports of Beira and Maputo. The cease-fire was confined to these areas.

The agreement followed the introduction, on 30 November 1990, of a new Mozambican Constitution, formally ending Frelimo's single-party rule and committing the State to political pluralism and a free-market economy, while also enshrining private property rights and guarantees of press freedom. The official name of the country was changed from the People's Republic of Mozambique to the Republic of Mozambique. Renamo refused to recognize the new Constitution, declaring that it had been drafted without democratic consultation. The President was henceforth to be elected by direct universal suffrage, and the legislature was renamed the Assembléia da República (Assembly of the Republic). A new law concerning the formation, structure and function of political parties came into effect in February 1991. In accordance with the Constitution, Renamo would not be recognized as a legitimate political party until it had renounced violence completely.

In December 1990 negotiations between the Government and Renamo resumed in Rome, Italy, and a Joint Verification Commission, comprising independent representatives from 10 nations, in addition to those of the Mozambican Government and Renamo, was established to monitor the partial cease-fire. Further talks took place in Rome in January 1991, but collapsed following the presentation of a report by the Joint Verification Commission containing accusations that Renamo had violated the cease-fire agreement, and did not resume until May.

In October 1991 Renamo and the Government signed a protocol agreeing fundamental principles and containing a set of mutual guarantees as a basis for a peace accord. Throughout the discussions Renamo continued guerrilla attacks, many of which were launched (despite the Nkomati accord) from South Africa. Under the terms of the protocol, Renamo effectively recognized the legitimacy of the Government and agreed to enter the multi-party political framework. In return, the Government pledged not to legislate on any of the points under negotiation in Rome until a general peace accord had been signed. In November a second protocol was signed by both parties, enabling Renamo to begin functioning as a political party immediately after the signing of a general peace accord.

In March 1992, following discussions conducted in Rome, a third protocol was signed establishing the principles for the country's future electoral system. Under its terms, the elections, to be held under a system of proportional representation, were to be supervised by international observers. An electoral commission was to be established, with one-third of its members to be appointed by Renamo. On 7 August, following three days of discussions in Rome, Chissano and the Renamo leader, Afonso Macacho Marceta Dhlakama, signed a joint declaration committing the two sides to a total cease-fire by 1 October, as part of an Acordo Geral de Paz (AGP—General Peace Agreement). In September Chissano and Dhlakama met in Gaborone, Botswana, to attempt to resolve the deadlocked military and security issues. Chissano offered to establish an independent commission to monitor and guarantee the impartiality of the Serviço de Informação e Segurança do Estado (SISE—State Information and Security Service). In addition, the figure of 30,000 was agreed upon as the number of troops to comprise the joint national defence force.

The AGP was finally signed on 4 October 1992. Under the terms of the agreement, a general cease-fire was to come into force immediately after ratification of the treaty by the legislature. Both the Renamo troops and the government forces were to withdraw to assembly points within seven days of ratification. The new national defence force, the Forças Armadas de Defesa de Moçambique (FADM), would then be created, drawing on equal numbers from each side, with the remaining troops surrendering their weapons to a UN peace-keeping force within six months. A Cease-fire Commission, incorporating representatives from the Government, Renamo and the UN, was to be established to assume responsibility for supervising the implementation of the truce regulations. Overall political control of the peace process was to be vested in a Comissão de Supervisão e Controle (CSC—Supervision and Control Commission), comprising representatives of the Government, Renamo and the UN. In addition, Chissano was to appoint a Comissão Nacional de Informação (COMINFO—National Information Commission), with responsibilities including supervision of the SISE. Presidential and legislative elections were to take place, under UN supervision, one year after the signing of the AGP, provided that it had been fully implemented and the demobilization process completed. The AGP was duly ratified by the Assembléia da República and came into force on 15 October. On that day UN observers arrived in Maputo to supervise the first phase of the cease-fire. However, shortly afterwards the Government accused Renamo of systematically violating the accord. Dhlakama subsequently claimed that Renamo's actions had been defensive manoeuvres and, in turn, accused government forces of violating the accord by advancing into Renamo territory.

In November 1992, owing to considerable delays in the formation of the various peace commissions envisaged in the AGP, the timetable for the cease-fire operations was redrafted. In December the UN Security Council finally approved a plan for the establishment of the UN Operation in Mozambique (ONUMOZ), providing for the deployment of some 7,500 troops, police and civilian observers to oversee the process of demobilization and formation of the FADM, and to supervise the forthcoming elections. However, there were continued delays in the deployment of ONUMOZ. In March the peace process was effectively halted when Renamo withdrew from the CSC and the Cease-fire Commission, protesting that proper provisions had not been made to accommodate its officials, and in April Dhlakama announced that his forces would begin to report to assembly points only when Renamo received US $15m. to finance its transition into a political party. Meanwhile, the first UN troops became operational on 1 April.

In June 1993 Renamo rejoined the CSC. The commission subsequently agreed to a formal postponement of the election date to October 1994. A meeting in Maputo of international aid donors, also in June 1993, produced promises of additional support for the peace process, bringing the total pledged by donors to US $520m., including support for the repatriation of 1.5m. refugees from neighbouring countries, the resettlement of 4m.–5m. displaced people and the reintegration of some 80,000 former combatants into civilian life. The UN also agreed to establish a trust fund of $10m. to finance Renamo's transformation into a political party, with the disbursement of funds dependent on UN approval.

Renamo announced new preconditions to the advancement of the peace process in July 1993, insisting initially on the recognition of its own administration, to operate parallel to that of the Government, and later on the appointment of its members to five of the country's 11 provincial governorships. Under the terms of an agreement signed in September, Renamo was to appoint three advisers to each of the incumbent provincial governors to make recommendations relating to the reintegration of areas under Renamo control into a single state administration. In October 1993 the CSC approved a new timetable covering all aspects of the peace process, including the elections in October 1994. In November 1993 the UN Security Council renewed the mandate of ONUMOZ for a further six months. In addition, it acceded to the joint request by the Government and Renamo for a UN police corps. In the same month consensus was finally reached on the text of the electoral law, which was promulgated at the end of December. At a meeting of the CSC in mid-November an agreement was signed providing for the confinement of troops, to be concluded by the end of the year.

In February 1994 the UN Security Council announced that, in response to demands made by Renamo, it would be increasing the membership of the UN police corps monitoring the confinement areas from 128 to 1,144. By the end of February only 50% of troops had entered designated assembly points, and none had officially been demobilized. In March, in an effort to expedite the confinement process, the Government announced that it was to commence the unilateral demobilization of its troops. Renamo began the demobilization of its troops shortly afterwards. In April Lt-Gen. Lagos Lidimo, the nominee of the Government, and the former Renamo guerrilla commander, Lt-Gen. Mateus Ngonhamo, were inaugurated as the high command of the FADM. In the same month Chissano issued a decree scheduling the presidential and legislative elections for 27–28 October, and in May the UN Security Council renewed the mandate of ONUMOZ for the final period, ending on 15 November.

On 16 August 1994, in accordance with the provisions of the AGP, the government Forças Armadas de Moçambique were formally dissolved and their assets transferred to the FADM, which was inaugurated as the country's official armed forces on the same day. In December the Cease-fire Commission issued its final report, according to which ONUMOZ had registered a combined total of 91,691 government and Renamo troops during the confinement process, of whom 11,579 had enlisted in the FADM (compared with the 30,000 envisaged in the AGP).

In August 1994 Renamo formally registered as a political party. In the same month the Partido Liberal e Democrático de Moçambique, the Partido Nacional Democrático and the Partido Nacional de Moçambique formed an electoral coalition, the União Democrática (UD). The presidential and legislative elections took place on 27–29 October. The extension of voting to a third day had become necessary following the withdrawal of Renamo from the elections only hours before the beginning of the poll, claiming that conditions were not in place to ensure free and fair elections. However, following concerted international pressure, Renamo abandoned its boycott after the first day. In the presidential election Chissano secured an outright majority (53.3%) of the votes. His closest rival was Dhlakama, who received 33.7% of the votes. In the legislative elections Frelimo also secured an overall majority, winning 129 of the 250 seats in the Assembléia da República; Renamo obtained 112 seats, and the UD the remaining nine. Later in November the UN Security Council extended the mandate of ONUMOZ until the end of January 1995.

Chissano was inaugurated as President on 9 December 1994, and the new Government, in which all portfolios were assigned to members of Frelimo, was sworn in on 23 December. Demands by Renamo that it be awarded governorships in the five provinces where it won a majority of the votes in the legislative elections were rejected by Chissano. At the first session of the new legislature, which began on 8 December, a dispute resulted in the withdrawal of the Renamo and UD deputies, although both groups abandoned their boycott by the end of December.

By the end of March 1995 only a small unit of ONUMOZ officials remained in the country. In February 1996 the Government proposed that municipal elections, which the Constitution stipulated must be conducted no later than October 1996, be held in 1997. Delays in the election process had resulted from a dispute between the parliamentary opposition, which demanded simultaneous local elections throughout Mozambique, and the Government, which sought to hold elections only in those areas that had attained municipal status. In October 1996 the Assembléia da República approved a constitutional amendment differentiating between municipalities and administrative posts. In August 1997 the Government postponed the elections until 1998, owing to delays in the disbursement by international donors of funding for the voter registration process. In January 1998 Renamo alleged that the voter registration process had been fraudulent, and threatened to boycott the elections unless a further registration of voters was conducted. In April Renamo was among 16 opposition parties that officially withdrew from the elections. Renamo subsequently campaigned vigorously to dissuade the electorate from participating in the ballot. At the elections, which took place on 30 June, Frelimo secured all the mayoral posts and won control of all the municipal authorities contested. Very few opposition parties contested the election, and Frelimo's main competition came from independent candidates. Moreover, the voter turn-out was only 14.6%, prompting Renamo to demand the annulment of the elections.

Under the Constitution, presidential and legislative elections were to take place by November 1999. However, political disputes and administrative delays threatened to force a postponement of the elections. A principal cause of the delay was Renamo's insistence on the need to re-register the entire electorate. In June Frelimo announced that Chissano would stand as its presidential candidate. In the following month 11 opposition parties, led by Renamo, signed an agreement to contest the forthcoming elections as a coalition, styled Renamo—União Eleitoral (Renamo—UE). The coalition was to present a single list of legislative candidates, with Dhlakama as its presidential candidate.

Presidential and legislative elections took place on 3–5 December 1999. In the presidential contest, Chissano defeated Dhlakama (his sole challenger), taking 52.3% of the valid votes cast. Frelimo secured 133 of the 250 seats in the Assembléia da República; Renamo—UE obtained the remaining seats, although Renamo rejected the outcome, claiming that the vote had been fraudulent. On 15 January 2000 Chissano was sworn in for a further five-year presidential term.

In November 2000 one of the country's most influential journalists, Carlos Cardoso, was killed in Maputo. It was alleged by Dhlakama that Cardoso had been murdered as a result of an article, published in his newspaper *Metical*, in which he had criticized the Government's involvement in protests over the 1999 election earlier in November 2000; however, it was announced in March 2001 that three people, including the former manager of a branch of the Banco Comercial de Moçambique—BCM, had been arrested in connection with Cardoso's murder; shortly before his death Cardoso had apparently uncovered details relating to the theft of some 144,000m. meticais from a branch of the BCM in 1996. In 2002 six men were tried for the murder, three of whom accused President Chissano's eldest son, Nyimpine Chissano, of having ordered or paid for the assassination; Nyimpine Chissano denied any involvement in the murder. In January 2003 the six men were convicted of the murder and imprisoned. In June 2004 seven people, including three who were serving prison sentences for Cardoso's murder, were convicted of charges relating to the disappearance of funds from the BCM and were sentenced to terms of imprisonment. In December 2008 it was reported that one of the killers, Aníbal António dos Santos, had escaped from custody in Maputo for the third time since he was initially arrested for the murder.

Meanwhile, in late December 2000 Dhlakama and President Chissano held talks (the first since the disputed election of December 1999) in an attempt to resolve the growing tension between their two parties. The two leaders agreed to hold further talks in 2001, and to establish inquiries into the violence of November 2000. Moreover, Dhlakama stated that he was prepared to accept the results of the 1999 elections, and Chissano pledged to consult Renamo about future state appointments. However, comments by Dhlakama, accusing Frelimo of violence and intimidation towards Renamo, subsequently jeopardized the future of talks between the two parties. In a second meeting between the two leaders in January 2001 it was agreed that a number of working groups (including groups on defence and security, constitutional and parliamentary affairs, and the media) would be established in February. At a further meeting, in March, Chissano referred Dhlakama's demand for the appointment of Renamo state governors to the Assembléia da República, whose Frelimo representatives were strongly opposed to accommodating Renamo demands. In protest, Dhlakama ceased negotiations in April.

President Chissano announced in May 2001 that he would not stand for re-election on the expiry of his term in 2004. At the long-postponed Renamo congress, held in October 2001, Dhlakama was re-elected party President, obtaining over 95% of votes cast; Joaquim Vaz was elected Secretary-General. The holding of a party congress by Renamo for the first time since the end of the civil war, as well as the establishment of a 10-member Political Committee, were regarded as confirmation of the movement's decision to establish itself as a full political party, and to decentralize the party leadership and structure.

In June 2002, at the party's eighth congress, Frelimo elected Armando Guebuza as its Secretary-General, and thus also its candidate for the 2004 presidential election. During July Renamo's attempt to establish itself as a legitimate opposition party was threatened after Dhlakama dismissed Vaz as Secretary-General, assuming the position himself, and dissolved the party's Political Committee. In October Renamo announced its intention to contest municipal elections (due in 2003) alone, rather than in coalition, while in November 2002 the party regained some stability with the appointment of Viana Magalhaes as Secretary-General. In December, however, further controversy arose when Renamo demanded the exclusion from the Assembléia da República of five deputies who had resigned or been expelled from the party, including Raul Domingos, formerly a senior member of Renamo, who had been expelled from the party in 2000. Renamo protesters caused an estimated US $11,000 of damage to the Assembléia. The former Renamo deputies retained their right to participate in the Assembléia.

In February 2003, in response to Renamo's decision to run alone in the municipal elections, 10 opposition parties announced the formation of a new coalition, the União Eleitoral, led by Domingos, who had previously announced his intention of standing as an independent in the presidential election. In October Domingos founded his own party, the Partido para a Paz, Democracia e Desenvolvimento (PPDD). From mid-2003 divisions became apparent within Frelimo between supporters of its presidential candidate, Guebuza, and Chissano loyalists. The Conselho Constitucional (Constitutional Council), which was to supervise elections and determine the constitutionality of new legislation, was inaugurated in early November, with Rui Baltazar dos Santos Alves as its first Chairman. Municipal elections were held on 19 November. Despite allegations by Renamo of irregularities, the elections proceeded smoothly, and their conduct was later commended by an observer mission from the European Union (EU, see p. 255), although voter turn-out, at 24.2%, was low. Frelimo won a majority in 29 municipalities, while Renamo won a majority in four, including Beira. The results were verified by the Conselho Constitucional in January 2004.

In mid-February 2004 Luísa Dias Diogo was appointed as Prime Minister, to replace Mocumbi, who resigned the premiership to take up an executive post in an EU-sponsored initiative specializing in clinical research. Diogo retained the responsibilities of Minister of Planning and Finance, the post she had held under Mocumbi.

By the deadline for submissions in October 2004, eight candidates, five of whom were subsequently approved by the Conselho Constitucional, had registered their intention to contest the presidential election. Three candidates were rejected on the grounds that they had not gathered the requisite 10,000 signatures to support their nominations. The five candidates were Guebuza, Dhlakama, Domingos, Yaqub Sabindy of the Partido Independente de Moçambique, reportedly an Islamist party (although the Constitution prohibited religious affiliations in political organizations), and Carlos Alexandre dos Reis, the leader of the União Nacional Moçambicana. A total of 25 political organizations and coalitions registered to contest the legislative elections, although there were serious misgivings regarding the credibility of a number of the parties. In mid-November the Assembléia da República approved changes to the Constitution, which were to take effect on the day following the declaration of the results of the elections. Notably, the President would no longer be afforded immunity from prosecution and a Conselho de Estado (Council of State) was to be created, which would act as an advisory body to the President. It was also envisaged that elections to provincial assemblies, which were to mirror in structure those to the Assembléia, would take place in 2008. In March 2007 the Assembléia approved the first reading of legislation that was to govern the provincial elections. The first phase of voter registration for the provincial elections began in September, followed by a second that commenced in December; however, the process was hampered by severe flooding that affected the country in January 2008. Nevertheless, the registration of the electorate was scheduled to be completed by March, although the Assembléia enforced its right to extraordinary powers of amendment to the Constitution and altered the date for the holding of provincial elections to 2009; having been amended in 2004, under normal circumstances the Constitution should not have undergone further review for at least five years.

Meanwhile, the presidential and legislative elections took place as scheduled on 1–2 December 2004, and proceeded without notable incident, although 37 voting stations did not open, reportedly owing to bad weather. For the first time Mozambicans living abroad were able to vote. Although national and international observers stated that the elections had been generally free and fair, they did express concern at the lack of access that they had been granted to the counting process and about the low rate of voter participation, which was recorded at just 36.3%. Renamo, later joined by other opposition parties, announced that it would not recognize the results, due to alleged irregularities produced by the computer system used to tabulate the votes and demanded that the elections be rerun. Official results, which were released on 21 December, revealed that Guebuza had won 63.7% of the votes cast at the presidential election, while Dhlakama took 31.7% and Domingos 2.7%. In the legislative elections, Frelimo won 62.0% of the votes, securing 160 of the available 250 seats, while Renamo took 29.7% and 90 seats (a significant decline compared with the 117 seats it had won in the 1999 elections). No other party achieved the minimum of 5% of total votes cast required to secure parliamentary representation. Protests lodged by Renamo with the Comissão Nacional de Eleições (CNE—National Elections Commission) and the Conselho Constitucional were rejected in January 2005, and Renamo announced that it would accept the election results and participate in the new legislature.

In mid-January 2005 the election results were approved by the Conselho Constitucional. The new Assembléia da República was inaugurated on 31 January, and Eduardo Mulémbue was re-elected to the post of Chairman. Guebuza was sworn in as President on 2 February and in his inauguration speech pledged to promote rural development and to take measures to combat corruption and poverty. The new Government, featuring a number of new appointees, was announced the following day. Diogo retained her position as Prime Minister; however, in a reorganization of ministerial functions, Manuel Chang became Minister of Finance, while Aiuba Cuereneia headed the newly created Ministry of Planning and Development. Alcinda Abreu was appointed Minister of Foreign Affairs and Co-operation, and José Pacheco became Minister of the Interior. In mid-February a further three ministers were appointed to the justice, science and technology and veterans' affairs portfolios. In March Chissano resigned as President of Frelimo and was replaced by Guebuza.

Meanwhile, in February 2005 it was reported that members of Dhlakama's guard, protesting against the non-payment of wages and poor living conditions, had taken five Renamo officials hostage. The following month the Government announced plans to integrate the guards (estimated to number 100–150), who had been maintained by Dhlakama as his personal defence force following the end of the civil war in 1992, into the state security forces, however such attempts were consistently stalled by Dhlakama. In September 2005 conflict between Frelimo and Renamo supporters led to the deaths of 12 people in Mocímboa da Praia, in Cabo Delgado province, following a disputed by-election earlier in the year.

In November 2005 the Assembléia da República passed legislation providing for the formation of the Conselho de Estado, as envisaged in changes to the Constitution approved in late 2004. Members of the Conselho, including Dhlakama, were subsequently appointed by Guebuza and the Assembléia da República, and took office in late December 2005.

In December 2006 the Assembléia da República passed the final reading of amendments to the electoral legislation. Among the amendments were provisions for the restructuring of the CNE, which had been reduced in size to 13 members. Five members were henceforth to be nominated by the Assembléia in proportion to the number of seats held by each political party, while the remaining eight members were to be nominated by legally constituted civil society bodies. A 14th member was to be appointed by the Government, but would not have the right to vote. The procedure for voter registration was also amended with the electorate required to re-register every five years. Further changes to the election procedure included the abolition of the 5% 'barrier clause', whereby parties must secure at least 5% of votes cast in order to win seats in the Assembléia.

In March 2007 an explosion at a munitions storage facility in a residential area of Maputo resulted in the deaths of more than 100 people and left over 500 others injured. A commission of inquiry was established in April to investigate the incident. The Government admitted that it had been storing equipment since the end of the civil war and weapons experts were later deployed to dispose of obsolete military equipment. In June a munitions expert from South Africa was killed in an explosion whilst assisting with the destruction of unexploded missiles. A further explosion was reported in October, after which the Government agreed to relocate weapons stores away from residential areas.

In early 2008 severe flooding devastated parts of Mozambique, causing 25 deaths, destroying an estimated 117,000 ha of crops, and displacing 95,000 people. A further 200,000 were displaced, and 10 people were killed, by Cyclone Jokwe in March: subsequently, in July, the Government established a new relief agency, the Gabinete de Coordenação da Reconstrução, with responsibility for the resettlement of those displaced by natural disasters.

In late March 2008 Minister of National Defence Gen. (retd) Tobias Joaquim Dai was dismissed and replaced by Filipe Nhussi, hitherto a senior official at the Empresa Nacional dos Portos e Caminhos de Ferro de Moçambique; no official reason was given for the change, although Dai had been severely criticized for the military's negligence with regard to the 2007 armaments explosions. Earlier that month President Guebuza effected a reorganization of the Council of Ministers in which Oldemiro Baloi replaced Alcinda Abreu as Minister of Foreign Affairs and Co-operation, the latter having been demoted to the role of Minister of Environmental Co-ordination. Maria Benvida Levy became Minister of Justice, while Paulo Zucula assumed responsibility for the transport and communications portfolio.

In September 2008 the Central Committee of Frelimo selected Guebuza as the party's candidate for the 2009 presidential election: 155 of the 167 members present voted for Guebuza, who faced no challengers for the candidacy. In mid-November municipal elections were held, which resulted in a resounding victory for Frelimo. That party secured a majority in 42 of the 43 municipal assemblies, while Renamo lost four of the five municipalities it had gained in the elections in 2003. International observers stated that despite some minor problems, the elections had been conducted in a transparent and fair manner.

Meanwhile, in early February 2008 riots broke out in Maputo, as people took to the streets in protest against rising fuel prices and government plans to increase fares on public transport. Some 12 people were killed and hundreds more injured when the police opened fire on the demonstration. The Government subsequently reduced fuel costs for privately operated taxis and minibuses, and cancelled the increase in transport fares. The shootings were detailed in a report by the human rights organization, Amnesty International, which was published in April: the report accused the police force of acting with impunity and excessive violence in response to rising crime rates. In March 2009 it was reported that three senior police officers had been arrested after 13 prisoners died of asphyxiation while in police detention. According to a local human rights agency, more than 40 detainees were held in a cell with a capacity for just 10 people. The dead were among those arrested in connection with the murders of two Red Cross workers, who had been killed in the village of Quinga, in Nampula province. (Locals believed that they had deliberately contaminated a well with cholera when they had, in fact, been administering chlorine with which to decontaminate it.) According to the Red Cross, there were over 12,000 cases of cholera recorded between January and March 2009, resulting in 157 deaths.

During 1995 the activities, principally in the border province of Manica, of a group of mainly Zimbabwean dissidents, known as Chimwenje, came under increasing scrutiny. The group, which was alleged to have links with Renamo, was believed to be preparing for military incursions into Zimbabwe, where it sought the overthrow of President Mugabe. In early 1996 the Chissano Government announced its intention to expel the dissidents from Mozambique. In June, following a series of armed attacks on both sides of the Mozambique–Zimbabwe border, which were believed to have been perpetrated by Chimwenje, the Governments of Mozambique and Zimbabwe agreed to combine and intensify efforts to combat the activities of the dissidents. The group was suppressed in late 1996. During late 2002 and early 2003 Mozambique resettled a number of white Zimbabwean farmers whose land had been appropriated by the Mugabe regime.

After stepping down as President following the election of December 2004, Chissano increasingly took on an international role. In mid-2005, as the UN Secretary-General's special envoy, he monitored the presidential election in Guinea-Bissau, while in August he was appointed mediator for the African Union (see p. 172) in Zimbabwe.

After independence, Mozambique developed strong international links with the USSR and other countries of the communist bloc, and with neighbouring African states: it is a member of the Southern African Development Community (SADC, see p. 400), founded in 1979, as the Southern African Development Co-ordination Conference, then with the aim of reducing the region's economic dependence on South Africa, principally by developing trade routes through Mozambique. In December 1996 Mozambique, Malawi, Zambia and Zimbabwe (also SADC members) formally agreed to establish the Beira Development Corridor as a trading route avoiding South Africa's ports. In 1993 full diplomatic relations were established with South Africa. In July 1994 Mozambique and South Africa established a new Joint Defence and Security Commission, replacing the Joint Security Commission originally established in 1984. In November 1995 Mozambique was admitted, by special dispensation, as a full member of the Commonwealth (see p. 217). In 2006 Mozambique was admitted as an observer member of the Organisation Internationale de la Francophonie (see p. 440).

Following widespread xenophobic violence in South African townships in May 2008, at least 23 Mozambicans were believed to have been killed and around 40,000 were forced to return home. Refugee camps were set up on the common border and near Maputo to deal with the influx of refugees.

Government

The Constitution of 30 November 1990 (amended in 1996 and 2004) provides for a multi-party political system. Legislative power is vested in the Assembléia da República, with 250 members, who are elected for a five-year term. Members are elected by universal, direct adult suffrage in a secret ballot, according to a system of proportional representation. The President of the Republic, who is Head of State, is directly elected for a five-year term; the President holds executive power and governs with the assistance of an appointed Council of Ministers. A Council of State advises the President, who, however, has no obligation to follow its advice. Provincial governors, appointed by the President, have overall responsibility for the functions of government within each of the 11 provinces. For the purposes of local government, Mozambique is divided into 33 municipalities. The 2004 amendments to the Constitution provided for the creation of provincial assemblies, scheduled to be elected in 2009.

Defence

As assessed at November 2008, total active armed forces were estimated at 11,200 (army 10,000, navy 200, air force 1,000). At that time Mozambican forces were deployed in two overseas peace-keeping missions. Military service is compulsory and lasts for two years. Expenditure on defence was budgeted at an estimated 1,480,000m. meticais in 2007.

Economic Affairs

In 2007, according to estimates by the World Bank, Mozambique's gross national income (GNI), measured at average 2005–07 prices, was US $6,878m., equivalent to $320 per head (or $690 per head on an international purchasing-power parity basis). During 2000–07, it was estimated, the population increased at an average annual rate of 2.3%, while gross domestic product (GDP) per head increased, in real terms, by an average of 5.8% per year. Overall GDP increased, in real terms, at an average annual rate of 8.3% in 2000–07; growth in 2007 was 7.0%.

Agriculture (including forestry and fishing) contributed 28.4% of GDP in 2007. In mid-2005 an estimated 79.9% of the economically active population were employed in the sector. Fishing is a significant export activity: fish, crustaceans and molluscs accounted for 2.9% of total export earnings in 2007. The principal cash crops are fruit and nuts, cotton, sugar cane and copra. After production fell sharply in the 1990s, the Government attempted to increase revenue from the cashew crop by promoting production and improving processing facilities. The main subsistence crop is cassava. During 2000–07, according to the World Bank, agricultural GDP increased by an average of 7.9% per year. Growth in 2007 was 7.5%.

Industry (including mining, manufacturing, construction and power) employed 5.6% of the economically active population in 1997, and provided 24.7% of GDP in 2007. According to the World Bank, during 2000–07 industrial GDP increased at an average annual rate of 10.2%; growth in 2007 was 8.6%.

Mining contributed 1.6% of GDP in 2006, and employed 0.5% of the economically active population in 1997. Only coal, bauxite, marble, gold and salt are exploited in significant quantities, although gravel and crushed rocks are also mined. In November 2004 the Companhia Vale do Rio Doce (Brazil) was granted a coal mining concession in Moatize; production was expected to begin in 2010, with forecast annual production of 11m. metric tons. There are reserves of other minerals, including high-grade iron ore, precious and semi-precious stones, and natural gas. Plans began in 1994 to exploit natural gas reserves at Pande, in the province of Inhambane, which were estimated at 55,000m. cu m. A South African company, SASOL Ltd, was granted a 25-year concession to develop gasfields at Pande and Temane (also in Inhambane province); it was anticipated that the Government would receive revenues of some US $900m. from the project, and the construction of a pipeline to transport the gas to South Africa was completed in early 2004. A gas-processing centre opened in Temane in early 2004. In 1999 the largest reserve of titanium in the world (estimated at 100m. tons) was discovered in the district of Chibuto, in the province of Gaza; production from the Limpopo Corridor Sands Project in Chibuto was, however, put on hold in early 2009 after studies concluded that the potential value that could be obtained from the deposit was inadequate to justify its development. In mid-2007 the British company Pan African Resources plc was investigating the viability of developing a new gold mine in Manica province. Preliminary estimates suggested that production could amount to 2,600 kg per year. According to official figures, mining GDP increased at an average annual rate of 20.6% in 1996–2006; growth in 2006 was 4.5%.

Manufacturing contributed 14.5% of GDP in 2007, and employed 3.0% of the economically active population in 1997. A large aluminium smelter, Mozal, was opened in 2000 and expanded in 2003, with the completion of Mozal 2, which was expected to double capacity, to some 506,000 metric tons of aluminium ingots per year. Aluminium production was valued at 19,067,000m. meticais in 2003, equivalent to 16.8% of GDP. In 2004 unwrought aluminium and alloys accounted for 60.8% of total export earnings. During 2000–07, according to the World Bank, manufacturing GDP increased at an average annual rate of 12.2%; growth in 2007 was 7.0%.

Electrical energy is derived principally from hydroelectric power, which provided some 99.8% of total electricity production in 2005. Mozambique's important Cahora Bassa hydroelectric plant on the Zambezi River supplies electricity to South Africa and Zimbabwe. By 2004 an extended power supply from Cahora Bassa to Zambézia, Manica and Sofala was in operation. From 1999 a consortium involving Mozambican, French and German companies financed a feasibility study for the construction of a hydroelectric power plant at Mepanda Uncua, some 70 km downstream of Cahora Bassa, which would help to support the 900-MW energy requirement of the Mozal smelter. Construction of the plant, which would have a generating capacity of 2,500 MW, was projected to cost some US $1,500m. It was envisaged that power from the plant, which would not be in production before 2010, would also be exported to South Africa. Mozambique currently imports all of its petroleum requirements. Imports of mineral fuels and lubricants comprised 16.2% of the value of total imports in 2007.

The services sector engaged 12.3% of the economically active population in 1997, and contributed 46.9% of GDP in 2007. By the end of the 1990s tourism was the fastest growing sector of the economy, and in 2006 receipts from tourism totalled US $145m. It was hoped that the formal opening, in April 2002, of the Great Limpopo Transfrontier Park, comprising South Africa's Kruger National Park, Zimbabwe's Gonarezhou National Park and Mozambique's Limpopo National Park, would attract additional tourists; in 2006 some 1.1m. tourists visited Mozambique, compared with about 711,000 in 2004. The GDP of the services sector increased by an average of 7.4% per year in 2000–07, according to the World Bank; services GDP increased by 4.0% in 2007.

In 2007 Mozambique recorded a trade deficit of US $399.0m., and there was a deficit of $795.1m. on the current account of the balance of payments. In 2007 the principal source of imports was South Africa (31.8%). In 2006 the Netherlands was the principal market for exports (receiving 59.7%); South Africa was the other significant purchaser. The principal exports in 2007 were aluminium, mineral fuels and lubricants, and food, live animals and tobacco. The principal imports in 2003 were machinery and transport equipment, mineral fuels and lubricants, food and live animals, and chemicals. Production from the Mozal aluminium smelter provided around 60% the value of total exports in 2007.

In 2005 there was an overall budgetary deficit of 4,060,000m. meticais. Mozambique's total external debt was US $3,265m. at the end of 2006, of which $2,511m. was long-term public debt. In that year the cost of debt-servicing was equivalent to 1.9% of the total value of exports of goods and services. The average annual rate of inflation was 11.5% in 2000–07; consumer prices increased by an average of 8.2% in 2007. The number of unemployed was 118,000 at the end of 1996.

Mozambique is a member of the Southern African Development Community (SADC, see p. 400). In November 2000 Mozambique was invited by the Common Market for Eastern and Southern Africa (COMESA, see p. 215) to rejoin the organization (Mozambique left COMESA in 1993, when it joined SADC).

During the 1990s Mozambique's economy was one of the fastest growing in the world and in the early 2000s significant amounts of the country's foreign debt that had been accrued during the civil war was deferred and subsequently cancelled; most notably, as a result of the successful implementation of economic reforms, in December 2005 the IMF cancelled Mozambique's outstanding debt to the Fund, worth an estimated US $153m. The country possesses considerable mineral wealth and the Government signalled its intention to join the Extractive Industrial Transparency Initiative in anticipation of increased revenues from the mining sector (particularly petroleum, of which large scale exploration was expected to ensue following the allocation of concessions to foreign companies, and coal, reserves of which were estimated at 10,000m. metric tons). Mozambique is, however, prone to natural disasters, and floods in early 2008, which destroyed more than 117,000 ha of crops, exacerbated the increasingly precarious food security situation. The Government was obliged to import some 470,000 tons of wheat and more than 300,000 tons of rice in that year and local shortages, coupled with rising food prices on international markets, left thousands of Mozambicans unable to provide sufficiently for themselves. In order to alleviate these conditions in mid-2008 the authorities announced the introduction of a three-year agricultural campaign as part of a national 'green revolution' strategy, which aimed to guarantee food security. Although Mozambique has recorded strong macroeconomic performance in recent years, growth was expected to slow as a result of the ongoing global financial crisis and while the Government took steps to mitigate the social impact of higher fuel and food prices, inflation was projected to have risen to more than 10.0% in 2008. The Government targeted GDP growth of 7.0% in 2009 (compared with the 6.5% recorded in the previous year) and an inflation rate of no greater than 8.0%. However, price declines for commodities have had a substantial impact on Mozambique's external trade and a deeper slowdown in global demand would also adversely affect export volumes, thus jeopardizing further economic expansion.

Education

Education is officially compulsory for seven years from the age of six. Primary schooling begins at six years of age and lasts for seven years. It is divided into two cycles, of five and two years. Secondary schooling, from 13 years of age, lasts for six years and comprises two cycles, each lasting three years. According to UNESCO estimates, in 2005/06 76.0% of children in the relevant age-group were enrolled at primary schools (males 79.0%; females 73.1%), while secondary enrolment included only 4.2% of children in the relevant age-group (males 4.4%; females 4.0%). There were 11,619 students in higher education in 1999. Two privately owned higher education institutions, the Catholic University and the Higher Polytechnic Institute, were inaugurated in 1996. In late 2003 it was announced that education would no longer take place solely in Portuguese, but also in some Mozambican dialects. In 2005 an estimated 5,000 new teachers were to be recruited. In 2006 some US $39m. was granted by international donors to develop educational resources. Education was allocated 20.2% of total current expenditure in that year.

Public Holidays

2009: 1 January (New Year's Day), 3 February (Heroes' Day, anniversary of the assassination of Eduardo Mondlane), 7 April (Day of the Mozambican Woman), 1 May (Workers' Day), 25 June (Independence Day), 7 September (Victory Day—anniversary of the end of the Armed Struggle), 25 September (Anniversary of the launching of the Armed Struggle for National Liberation, and Day of the Armed Forces of Mozambique), 4 October (Peace and National Reconciliation Day), 25 December (National Family Day).

2010: 1 January (New Year's Day), 3 February (Heroes' Day, anniversary of the assassination of Eduardo Mondlane), 7 April (Day of the Mozambican Woman), 1 May (Workers' Day), 25 June (Independence Day), 7 September (Victory Day—anniversary of the end of the Armed Struggle), 25 September (Anniversary of the launching of the Armed Struggle for National Liberation, and Day of the Armed Forces of Mozambique), 4 October (Peace and National Reconciliation Day), 25 December (National Family Day).

Weights and Measures

The metric system is in force.

Statistical Survey

Source (unless otherwise stated): Instituto Nacional de Estatística, Comissão Nacional do Plano, Av. Ahmed Sekou Touré 21, CP 493, Maputo; tel. 21491054; fax 21490384; e-mail webmaster@ine.gov.mz; internet www.ine.gov.mz.

Area and Population

AREA, POPULATION AND DENSITY

Area (sq km)	799,380*
Population (census results)	
1 August 1997	16,099,246
1 August 2007 (preliminary)	
Males	9,787,135
Females	10,743,579
Total	20,530,714
Density (per sq km) at August 2007	25.7

* 308,641 sq miles. The area includes 13,000 sq km (5,019 sq miles) of inland water.

MOZAMBIQUE

PROVINCES
(at census of 1 August 2007)

Province	Area (sq km)	Population (preliminary)	Density (per sq km)
Cabo Delgado	82,625	1,632,809	19.8
Gaza	75,709	1,219,013	16.1
Inhambane	68,615	1,267,035	18.5
Manica	61,661	1,418,927	23.0
City of Maputo	300	1,099,102	3,663.7
Maputo Province	26,058	1,259,713	48.3
Nampula	81,606	4,076,642	50.0
Niassa	129,056	1,178,117	9.1
Sofala	68,018	1,654,163	24.3
Tete	100,724	1,832,339	18.2
Zambézia	105,008	3,892,854	37.1
Total	**799,380**	**20,530,714**	**25.7**

PRINCIPAL TOWNS
(at 2007 census, preliminary)

Maputo (capital)	1,099,102	Nacala-Porto	207,894
Matola	675,422	Quelimane	192,876
Nampula	477,900	Tete	152,909
Beira	436,240	Xai-Xai	116,343
Chimoio	238,976		

BIRTHS AND DEATHS

	2005	2006	2007
Crude birth rate (per 1,000)	41.1	40.3	39.5
Crude death rate (per 1,000)	19.6	19.7	19.8

Source: African Development Bank.

Life expectancy (years at birth, WHO estimates): 50.3 (males 49.5; females 51.0) in 2006 (Source: WHO, *World Health Statistics*).

ECONOMICALLY ACTIVE POPULATION
(persons aged 12 years and over, 1980 census)

	Males	Females	Total
Agriculture, forestry, hunting and fishing	1,887,779	2,867,052	4,754,831
Mining and quarrying	} 323,730	23,064	346,794
Manufacturing			
Construction	41,611	510	42,121
Commerce	90,654	21,590	112,244
Transport, storage and communications	74,817	2,208	77,025
Other services*	203,629	39,820	243,449
Total employed	**2,622,220**	**2,954,244**	**5,576,464**
Unemployed	75,505	19,321	94,826
Total labour force	**2,697,725**	**2,973,565**	**5,671,290**

* Including electricity, gas and water.

Source: ILO, *Yearbook of Labour Statistics*.

1997 (percentage distribution of economically active population at census of 1 August): Agriculture, forestry and hunting: 91.3% of females, 69.6% of males; Mining: 0.0% of females, 1.0% of males; Manufacturing: 0.8% of females, 5.5% of males; Energy: 0.0% of females, 0.3% of males; Construction: 0.3% of females, 3.9% of males; Transport and communications: 0.1% of females, 2.3% of males; Commerce and finance: 4.3% of females, 9.7% of males; Services: 2.2% of females, 3.4% of males; Unknown: 0.9% of females, 1.4% of males.

Mid-2005 (estimates in '000): Agriculture, etc. 8,250; Total labour force 10,321 (Source: FAO).

Health and Welfare

KEY INDICATORS

Total fertility rate (children per woman, 2006)	5.2
Under-5 mortality rate (per 1,000 live births, 2006)	138
HIV/AIDS (% of persons aged 15–49, 2007)	12.5
Physicians (per 1,000 head, 2004)	0.03
Hospital beds (per 1,000 head, 2006)	0.8
Health expenditure (2006): US $ per head (PPP)	56
Health expenditure (2006): % of GDP	4.7
Health expenditure (2006): public (% of total)	69.4
Access to water (% of persons, 2006)	42
Access to sanitation (% of persons, 2006)	31
Human Development Index (2006): ranking	175
Human Development Index (2006): value	0.366

For sources and definitions, see explanatory note on p. vi.

Agriculture

PRINCIPAL CROPS
('000 metric tons)

	2005	2006	2007
Rice, paddy	174*	183†	196†
Maize	1,403*	1,534†	1,579†
Millet	36*	49†	45†
Sorghum	307*	340†	350†
Potatoes†	80	80	80
Sweet potatoes†	66	66	66
Cassava (Manioc)†	6,500	7,500	7,350
Cashew nuts, with shell†	58	58	58
Groundnuts, with shell	100*	104*	105†
Coconuts†	285	265	265
Sunflower seed†	11	11	11
Tomatoes†	9	9	9
Bananas†	90	90	90
Oranges†	14	14	14
Grapefruits and pomelos†	13	13	13
Guavas, mangoes and mangosteens†	24	24	24
Pineapples†	13	13	13
Papayas†	43	41	41
Tobacco, unmanufactured†	12	11	11

* Unofficial figure.
† FAO estimate(s).

Aggregate production ('000 metric tons, may include official, semi-official or estimated data): Total cereals 1,922 in 2005, 2,107 in 2006, 2,173 in 2007; Total roots and tubers 6,652 in 2005, 7,652 in 2006, 7,502 in 2007; Total vegetables (incl. melons) 117 in 2005, 117 in 2006, 117 in 2007; Total fruits (excl. melons) 335 in 2005, 199 in 2006, 199 in 2007.

Source: FAO.

LIVESTOCK
('000 head, year ending September, FAO estimates)

	2005	2006	2007
Asses, mules or hinnies	23	n.a.	n.a.
Cattle	1,500	1,320	1,330
Pigs	200	180	182
Sheep	182	125	126
Goats	415	392	393
Chickens	30,000	28,000	28,500

Source: FAO.

MOZAMBIQUE

LIVESTOCK PRODUCTS
('000 metric tons, FAO estimates)

	2005	2006	2007
Cattle meat	42	38	38
Goat meat	2	2	2
Pig meat	14	13	13
Chicken meat	38	40	40
Cows' milk	69	61	61
Goats' milk	9	9	9
Hen eggs	15	14	14

Source: FAO.

Forestry

ROUNDWOOD REMOVALS
('000 cubic metres, excl. bark)

	2003	2004	2005
Sawlogs, veneer logs and logs for sleepers	128	123	113
Other industrial wood	1,191	1,191	1,191
Fuel wood	16,724	16,724	16,724
Total	18,043	18,038	18,028

2006–07: Figures assumed to be unchanged from 2005 (FAO estimates).
Source: FAO.

SAWNWOOD PRODUCTION
('000 cubic metres, incl. railway sleepers)

	2005	2006	2007
Total	38	43	57

Source: FAO.

Fishing

(metric tons, live weight)

	2004	2005	2006
Dagaas	18,759	13,007	16,220
Penaeus shrimps	12,403	13,005	10,855
Knife shrimp	992	1,774	1,968
Total catch (incl. others)	45,129*	43,736	43,710

* FAO estimate.

Note: Figures exclude crocodiles, recorded by number rather than by weight. The number of Nile crocodiles caught was: 0 in 2004; 1,323 in 2005; 2,179 in 2006.
Source: FAO.

Mining

('000 metric tons, unless otherwise indicated)

	2005	2006	2007*
Bauxite	9.5	11.1	12.0
Coal	3.4	41.0	72.0
Gold (kilograms)†	63	85	450
Quartz (metric tons)	294.7	195.1	200.0
Gravel and crushed rock ('000 cubic metres)	850.9	1,179.0	1,200.0
Marble (slab) ('000 square metres)	12.3	12.8	15.0
Salt (marine)*	80	80	80
Natural gas (million cu m)	2,393	2,330	2,800

* Estimates.
† Figures exclude artisanal gold production; total gold output is estimated at 360 kg–480 kg per year.
Source: US Geological Survey.

Industry

SELECTED PRODUCTS
('000 metric tons, unless otherwise indicated)

	2003	2004	2005
Flour (cereals other than wheat)	1	n.a.	n.a.
Wheat flour	163	160	204
Raw sugar	26	199	164
Groundnut oil ('000 metric tons)*	15.8	20.2	15.8
Beer ('000 hl)	1,044	1,025	1,412
Soft drinks ('000 hl)	30	n.a.	n.a.
Cigarettes (metric tons)	n.a.	1,332	1,735
Footwear (excl. rubber, '000 pairs)	12	24	37
Cement	582	552	564
Electric energy (million kWh)	10,602	11,713	13,289

* FAO estimates.
Sources: FAO; UN, *Industrial Commodity Statistics Yearbook*.
2006 ('000 metric tons): Groundnut oil 16.5 (FAO estimate) (Source: FAO).

Finance

CURRENCY AND EXCHANGE RATES

Monetary Units
100 centavos = 1 metical (plural: meticais).

Sterling, Dollar and Euro Equivalents (30 September 2008)
£1 sterling = 43.48 meticais;
US $1 = 24.16 meticais;
€1 = 34.56 meticais;
1,000 meticais = £2.30 = $4.14 = €2.89.

Average Exchange Rate (meticais per US $)
2005   23.06
2006   25.40
2007   22.84

Note: Between April 1992 and October 2000 the market exchange rate was the rate at which commercial banks purchased from and sold to the public. Since October 2000 it has been the weighted average of buying and selling rates of all transactions of commercial banks and stock exchanges with the public. A devaluation of the metical, with 1 new currency unit becoming equivalent to 1,000 of the former currency, was implemented on 1 July 2006.

MOZAMBIQUE

BUDGET
('000 million meticais)

Revenue*	2007	2008	2009†
Taxation	29,080	32,570	39,060
Taxes on income	9,280	11,100	12,110
Domestic taxes on goods and services	15,510	17,280	22,630
Taxes on petroleum products	2,260	2,540	3,590
Customs duties	3,780	3,530	3,510
Other taxes	520	660	810
Non-tax revenue	3,980	4,640	5,930
Total	33,060	37,200	44,980

Expenditure‡	2007	2008	2009†
Current expenditure	31,840	37,720	43,590
Compensation of employees	16,090	18,860	22,460
Goods and services	8,340	9,930	11,560
Interest on public debt	1,280	1,310	1,390
Transfer payments	6,130	7,620	8,180
Capital expenditure	24,310	35,010	43,320
Total	56,150	72,730	86,910

* Excluding grants received ('000 million meticais): 19,270 in 2007; 28,160 in 2008; 32,210 in 2009 (provisional).
† Provisional.
‡ Excluding net lending ('000 million meticais): 2,300 in 2007; 3,310 in 2008; 4,700 in 2009 (provisional).

Note: Totals may not be equal to the sum of components, owing to rounding.

Source: IMF, *Republic of Mozambique: Third Review Under the Policy Support Instrument—Staff Report; Staff Supplement; and Press Release* (February 2009).

INTERNATIONAL RESERVES
(US $ million at 31 December)

	2005	2006	2007
IMF special drawing rights	0.23	0.23	0.18
Reserve position in IMF	0.01	0.01	0.01
Foreign exchange	1,053.58	1,155.49	1,444.50
Total	1,053.82	1,155.73	1,444.69

Source: IMF, *International Financial Statistics*.

MONEY SUPPLY
('000 million meticais at 31 December)

	2005	2006	2007
Currency outside banks	6,417.9	7,152.0	8,950.4
Demand deposits at commercial banks	12,809.4	17,095.4	21,078.7
Total money (incl. others)	19,227.4	24,247.5	30,029.0

Source: IMF, *International Financial Statistics*.

COST OF LIVING
(Consumer Price Index; base: 1998 = 100)

	2002	2003	2004
Food, beverages and tobacco	151	175	187
Clothing and footwear	126	122	125
Firewood and furniture	190	215	263
Health	119	133	134
Transportation and communications	205	232	234
Education, recreation and culture	145	150	151
Other goods and services	136	154	159
All items	157	179	195

Source: IMF, *Republic of Mozambique: Selected Issues and Statistical Appendix* (August 2005).

All items (Consumer Price Index; base: 2000 = 100): 174.4 in 2005; 197.5 in 2006; 213.6 in 2007 (Source: IMF, *International Financial Statistics*).

NATIONAL ACCOUNTS
('000 million meticais at current prices)

Expenditure on the Gross Domestic Product

	2005	2006	2007
Government final consumption expenditure	19,662.9	22,228.5	24,738.1
Private final consumption expenditure	126,354.4	143,381.6	166,653.8
Change in stocks	−1,543.6	1,187.2	−1,724.7
Gross capital formation	28,360.7	31,818.6	36,009.9
Total domestic expenditure	172,834.4	198,615.9	225,677.1
Exports of goods and services	46,212.6	54,861.3	61,624.0
Less Imports of goods and services	67,340.0	70,861.1	77,639.9
GDP in purchasers' values	151,706.9	180,241.7	209,661.3
GDP at constant 2003 prices	129,763.5	141,030.4	151,453.0

Gross Domestic Product by Economic Activity

	2005	2006	2007
Agriculture, livestock and forestry	34,837.8	43,042.4	52,637.0
Fishing	2,284.0	2,810.4	3,056.3
Mining	1,476.4	2,337.1	3,193.7
Manufacturing	21,304.1	26,355.2	28,530.5
Electricity and water	7,605.6	9,578.9	11,089.0
Construction	4,506.8	5,213.3	5,739.3
Wholesale and retail trade	17,656.6	22,440.8	27,056.4
Repairs	556.7	630.5	740.6
Restaurants and hotels	2,141.7	2,508.1	3,080.8
Transport and communications	14,559.6	16,458.0	18,418.4
Financial services	6,748.8	7,657.9	9,030.9
Real estate and business services	11,307.1	11,659.9	12,225.2
Public administration and defence	5,658.9	6,639.6	7,350.2
Education	5,613.7	6,521.1	7,788.8
Health	1,846.0	2,396.4	3,024.8
Other services	2,725.1	3,066.1	3,302.9
Sub-total	140,828.9	169,315.7	196,264.8
Less Financial services indirectly measured	3,137.3	4,731.8	5,334.6
Gross value added in basic prices	137,691.6	164,583.9	190,930.2
Taxes on products / *Less* Subsidies on products	14,015.3	15,657.6	18,731.0
GDP in market prices	151,706.9	180,241.7	209,661.3

BALANCE OF PAYMENTS
(US $ million)

	2005	2006	2007
Exports of goods f.o.b.	1,745.3	2,381.1	2,412.1
Imports of goods f.o.b.	−2,242.3	−2,648.8	−2,811.1
Trade balance	−497.1	−267.7	−399.0
Exports of services	341.9	386.4	458.7
Imports of services	−648.6	−758.1	−855.6
Balance on goods and services	−803.8	−639.5	−795.9
Other income received	98.9	159.8	193.6
Other income paid	−458.8	−794.3	−785.2
Balance on goods, services and income	−1,163.6	−1,273.9	−1,387.5
Current transfers received	479.0	574.5	657.8
Current transfers paid	−76.0	−73.8	−65.4
Current balance	−760.7	−773.2	−795.1
Capital account (net)	187.9	488.5	415.1
Direct investment (net)	107.9	153.7	427.7
Portfolio investment (net)	−88.8	−124.2	−117.8
Financial derivatives (net)	—	—	−16.0
Other investment assets	−78.5	−13.8	−359.3
Other investment liabilities	154.3	−1,517.5	417.5
Errors and omissions (net)	281.0	143.8	83.9
Overall balance	−196.6	−1,642.6	56.7

Source: IMF, *International Financial Statistics*.

MOZAMBIQUE

External Trade

PRINCIPAL COMMODITIES
(US $ million)

Imports c.i.f.	2005	2006	2007
Food and live animals	290.2	325.8	473.7
Cereals	185.2	192.9	204.0
Mineral fuels, lubricants etc.	38.4	485.0	494.5
Chemicals and related products	148.8	188.3	197.8
Basic manufactures	265.3	337.5	338.3
Iron and steel	51.6	78.2	90.0
Machinery and transport equipment	622.1	711.3	745.6
General industrial machinery, equipment and parts	83.2	80.2	107.3
Electrical machinery, apparatus, etc.	77.7	78.6	112.3
Road vehicles and parts	226.3	270.2	282.9
Miscellaneous manufactured articles	163.0	148.8	148.3
Commodities and transactions not classified elsewhere	794.8	564.2	550.3
Total (incl. others)	2,408.2	2,869.3	3,049.7

Exports f.o.b.	2005	2006	2007
Food, live animals and tobacco	147.8	244.0	181.6
Fish, crustaceans, molluscs and preparations thereof	84.8	96.6	70.1
Crude materials	1,116.8	121.2	119.4
Cotton	36.2	45.7	31.5
Mineral fuels, lubricants, etc.	267.6	349.1	373.4
Electric current	141.8	177.8	225.3
Basic manufactures	27.1	1,416.7	1,541.3
Aluminium	0.0	1,401.6	1,516.1
Machinery and transport equipment	60.3	79.9	85.2
Total (incl. others)	1,783.0	2,381.1	2,412.1

Source: UN, *International Trade Statistics Yearbook*.

PRINCIPAL TRADING PARTNERS
(US $ million)

Imports c.i.f.	2005	2006	2007
Australia	7.5	211.3	2.7
France-Monaco	22.3	23.5	26.0
Germany	28.8	53.7	34.1
India	68.0	132.5	131.8
Japan	20.4	18.6	94.0
Malawi	29.4	17.7	9.3
Pakistan	25.8	34.9	41.6
Portugal	88.9	95.2	103.6
Saudi Arabia	2.5	36.8	23.8
South Africa	701.9	1,074.1	970.8
Spain	30.4	25.3	13.0
United Kingdom	20.1	19.1	16.7
USA	63.8	100.1	80.8
Total (incl. others)	2,408.2	2,869.3	3,049.7

Exports f.o.b.	2004	2006*
Belgium	7.9	3.3
Germany	0.8	25.9
Malawi	49.5	24.7
Netherlands	916.5	1,422.2
Portugal	47.0	29.7
South Africa	211.4	335.8
Spain	37.9	43.5
Swaziland	5.6	8.2
United Kingdom	2.6	16.3
USA	10.7	6.5
Zimbabwe	33.4	76.1
Total (incl. others)	1,503.8	2,381.1

* Total exports 1,783.0 in 2005 and 2,412.1 in 2007; complete data were not available for these years.

Source: UN, *International Trade Statistics Yearbook*.

Transport

RAILWAYS
(traffic)

	2002	2003	2004
Freight ton-km (million)	808	778	794
Passenger-km (million)	138	82	106

Source: UN, *Statistical Yearbook*.

ROAD TRAFFIC
(motor vehicles in use at 31 December)

	1999	2000	2001
Passenger cars	78,600	81,600	81,600
Lorries and vans	46,900	76,000	76,000

Source: UN, *Statistical Yearbook*.

SHIPPING

Merchant Fleet
(registered at 31 December)

	2005	2006	2007
Number of vessels	126	129	129
Total displacement ('000 grt)	35.4	36.5	37.9

Source: Lloyd's Register-Fairplay, *World Fleet Statistics*.

Freight Handled
('000 metric tons)

	2001	2002	2003
Goods loaded and unloaded	7,423	8,201	8,421

International Sea-borne Freight Traffic
('000 metric tons)

	2001	2002	2003
Goods loaded	2,962	2,780	2,982
Goods unloaded	3,144	4,062	3,837

CIVIL AVIATION
(traffic on scheduled services)

	2004	2005	2006
Kilometres flown (million)	7.5	8.4	9.7
Passengers carried ('000)	299.7	353.3	379.9
Passenger-km (million)	386.6	428.6	404.7

Tourism

TOURIST ARRIVALS BY COUNTRY OF RESIDENCE

Country	2004	2005	2006
Malawi	74,933	100,580	115,405
Portugal	11,898	15,970	18,324
South Africa	288,104	306,177	351,307
Swaziland	17,773	23,856	27,372
United Kingdom	6,700	8,993	10,319
USA	5,647	7,878	9,039
Zimbabwe	65,896	88,450	101,487
Total (incl. others)	711,060	954,433	1,095,000

Tourism receipts (US $ million, incl. passenger transport): 96 in 2004; 138 in 2005; 145 in 2006.

Source: World Tourism Organization.

Communications Media

	2004	2005	2006
Telephones ('000 main lines in use)	69.7	69.7	67.0
Mobile cellular telephones ('000 subscribers)	708.0	1,503.9	2,339.3
Personal computers ('000 in use)	138	138	n.a.
Internet users ('000)	112	178	180

1998: Daily newspapers 12 (average circulation 43,099); Non-daily newspapers 40 (estimated average circulation 205,800); Periodicals 32 (average circulation 83,000).

2007: Mobile cellular telephones ('000 subscribers) 3,300.0; Internet users ('000) 200.

Television receivers ('000 in use): 230 in 2001.

Radio receivers ('000 in use): 730 in 1997.

Facsimile machines ('000 in use): 7.2 in 1996.

Sources: International Telecommunication Union; UN, *Statistical Yearbook*; UNESCO Institute for Statistics.

Education

(2005, unless otherwise indicated)

	Institutions	Teachers	Students
Pre-primary*†	5,689	28,705	1,745,049
Primary‡			
First level	8,696	45,887	3,393,677
Second level	1,320	11,011	452,888
Secondary§			
First level	156	210,128	5,004
Second level	35	25,737	861
Technical	41	1,028	21,752
Teacher training‖	18	n.a.	9,314

* Public education only.
† 1997 figures.
‡ Primary education is divided into two cycles of five years followed by two years.
§ Secondary education is divided into two cycles of three years.
‖ 2002 figures.

Source: mainly Ministry of Education.

Adult literacy rate (UNESCO estimates): 44.4% (males 57.2%; females 33.0%) in 2007 (Source: UNESCO Institute for Statistics).

Directory

The Constitution

The Constitution came into force on 30 November 1990, replacing the previous version, introduced at independence on 25 June 1975 and revised in 1978. Its main provisions, as amended in 1996 and 2004, are summarized below. There are 306 articles in the Constitution.

GENERAL PRINCIPLES

The Republic of Mozambique is an independent, sovereign, unitary and democratic state of social justice. Sovereignty resides in the people, who exercise it according to the forms laid down in the Constitution. The fundamental objectives of the Republic include:

the defence of independence and sovereignty;

the defence and promotion of human rights and of the equality of citizens before the law; and

the strengthening of democracy, of freedom and of social and individual stability.

POLITICAL PARTICIPATION

The people exercise power through universal, direct, equal, secret, personal and periodic suffrage to elect their representatives, by referendums and through permanent democratic participation. Political parties are prohibited from advocating or resorting to violence.

FUNDAMENTAL RIGHTS AND DUTIES OF CITIZENS

All citizens enjoy the same rights and are subject to the same duties, irrespective of colour, race, sex, ethnic origin, place of birth, religion, level of education, social position or occupation. In realizing the objectives of the Constitution, all citizens enjoy freedom of opinion, assembly and association. All citizens over 18 years of age are entitled to vote and be elected. Active participation in the defence of the country is the duty of every citizen. Individual freedoms are guaranteed by the State, including freedom of expression, of the press, of assembly, of association and of religion. The State guarantees accused persons the right to a legal defence. No Court or Tribunal has the power to impose a sentence of death upon any person.

STATE ORGANS

Public elective officers are chosen by elections through universal, direct, secret, personal and periodic vote. Legally recognized political parties may participate in elections.

THE PRESIDENT

The President is the Head of State and of the Government, and Commander-in-Chief of the armed forces. The President is elected by direct, equal, secret and personal universal suffrage on a majority vote, and must be proposed by at least 10,000 voters, of whom at least 200 must reside in each province. The term of office is five years. A candidate may be re-elected on only two consecutive occasions, or again after an interval of five years between terms. The President is advised by a Conselho de Estado (Council of State), but is not obliged to follow its advice.

COUNCIL OF STATE

The Conselho de Estado is an advisory body presided over by the President of the Republic. It comprises the President of the Assembléia da República (Assembly of the Republic), the Prime Minister, the President of the Conselho Constitucional (Constitutional Council), the President of the Supreme Court, those former Presidents of the Republic not deposed, the former Presidents of the Assembléia and the second placed candidate in the most recent presidential election. In addition, seven representatives are nominated by the

MOZAMBIQUE

President of the Assembléia for the term of the legislature and four representatives are nominated by the President of the Republic for the duration of the presidential mandate. The Conselho de Estado rules on the dissolution of the Assembléia and the declaration of war and oversees general elections and public referenda.

THE ASSEMBLY OF THE REPUBLIC

Legislative power is vested in the Assembléia da República. The Assembléia is elected by universal direct adult suffrage on a secret ballot, and is composed of 250 Deputies. The Assembléia is elected for a maximum term of five years, but may be dissolved by the President before the expiry of its term. The Assembléia holds two ordinary sessions each year. The Assembléia, with a two-thirds majority, may impeach the President.

THE COUNCIL OF MINISTERS

The Council of Ministers is the Government of the Republic. The Prime Minister assists and advises the President in the leadership of the Government and presents the Government's programme, budget and policies to the Assembléia da República, assisted by other ministers.

THE JUDICIARY

Judicial functions shall be exercised through the Supreme Court and other courts provided for in the law on the judiciary, which also subordinates them to the Assembléia da República. Courts must safeguard the principles of the Constitution and defend the rights and legitimate interests of citizens. Judges are independent, subject only to the law.

LOCAL STATE ORGANS

The Republic is administered in provinces, municipalities and administrative posts. The highest state organ in a province is the provincial government, presided over by a governor, who is answerable to the central Government. There shall be assemblies at each administrative level.

CONSTITUTIONAL COUNCIL

The Conselho Constitucional rules, *inter alia*, on the constitutionality of legislation, the eligibility of presidential candidates and the legitimacy of electoral results. The Conselho Constitucional also formally declares the death or deposition of the Head of State and rules on the incapacity of the President of the Republic to remain in office. It comprises seven judges: one nominated by the President of the Republic, five elected by the Assembléia da República according to proportional representation and one nominated by the Supreme Court, each to serve a term of five years, which is renewable. Councillors must be aged 35 or over.

The Government

HEAD OF STATE

President of the Republic and Commander-in-Chief of the Armed Forces: ARMANDO EMÍLIO GUEBUZA (took office 2 February 2005).

COUNCIL OF MINISTERS
(April 2009)

Prime Minister: LUÍSA DIAS DIOGO.
Minister of Foreign Affairs and Co-operation: OLDEMIRO BALOI.
Minister of National Defence: FILIPE NHUSSI.
Minister of Finance: MANUEL CHANG.
Minister of Justice: MARIA BENVIDA LEVY.
Minister of the Interior: JOSÉ PACHECO.
Minister of Development and Planning: AIUBA CUERENEIA.
Minister of State Administration: LUCAS CHOMERA.
Minister of Agriculture: SOARES NHACA.
Minister of Fisheries: CADMIEL FILIANE MUTHEMBA.
Minister of Industry and Trade: ANTÓNIO FERNANDO.
Minister of Energy: SALVADOR NAMBURETE.
Minister of Mineral Resources: ESPERANÇA BIAS.
Minister of Transport and Communications: PAULO ZUCULA.
Minister of Education and Culture: AIRES BONIFÁCIO ALI.
Minister of Health: PAULO IVO GARRIDO.
Minister of Environmental Co-ordination: ALCINDA ABREU.
Minister of Labour: MARIA HELENA TAIPO.
Minister of Public Works and Housing: FELÍCIO ZACARIAS.
Minister of Women's Affairs and Social Welfare Co-ordination: VIRGÍLIA BERNARDA NETO ALEXANDRE SANTOS MATABELE.
Minister of Tourism and of Youth and Sport: FERNANDO SUMBANA, Jr.
Minister of Veterans' Affairs: FELICIANO SALOMÃO GUNDANA.
Minister of Science and Technology: VENÂNCIO MASSINGUE.
Minister in the Presidency with responsibility for Parliamentary Affairs: ISABEL MANUEL NKAVANDEKA.
Minister in the Presidency with responsibility for Diplomatic Affairs: FRANCISCO CAETANO MADEIRA.

MINISTRIES

Office of the President: Av. Julius Nyerere 1780, Maputo; tel. 21491121; fax 21492065; e-mail gabimprensa@teldata.mz; internet www.presidencia.gov.mz.

Office of the Prime Minster: Praça da Marinha Popular, Maputo; tel. 21426861; fax 21426881; internet www.govmoz.gov.mz.

Ministry of Agriculture: Praça dos Heróis Moçambicanos, CP 1406, Maputo; tel. 21460011; fax 21460055; internet www.minag.gov.mz.

Ministry of Development and Planning: Av. Ahmed Sekou Touré 21, CP 4087, Maputo; tel. 21490006; fax 21495477; internet www.mpd.gov.mz.

Ministry of Education and Culture: Av. 24 de Julho 167, CP 34, Maputo; tel. 21492006; fax 21492196; internet www.mec.gov.mz.

Ministry of Energy: Av. 25 de Setembro, 1218 3° andar, CP 1831, Maputo; tel. 21303265; fax 21313971; e-mail asi@me.gov.mz; internet www.me.gov.mz.

Ministry of Environmental Co-ordination: Rua Kassoende 167, Maputo; tel. 21492403; e-mail jwkacha@virconn.com; internet www.micoa.gov.mz.

Ministry of Finance: Praça da Marinha Popular, CP 272, Maputo; tel. 21315000; fax 21306261.

Ministry of Fisheries: Rua Consiglieri Pedroso 347, CP 1723, Maputo; tel. 21431266; fax 21425087; internet www.mozpesca.gov.mz.

Ministry of Foreign Affairs and Co-operation: Av. 10 de Novembro, 620–640, Maputo; tel. 21327000; fax 21327020; e-mail minec@minec.gov.mz; internet www.minec.gov.mz.

Ministry of Health: Avs Eduardo Mondlane e Salvador Allende 1008, CP 264, Maputo; tel. 21427131; fax 21427133; e-mail mdgedge@dnsdee.misau.gov.mz; internet www.misau.gov.mz.

Ministry of Industry and Trade: Praça 25 de Junho 300, CP 1831, Maputo; tel. 21352600; fax 214262301; e-mail infomic@mic.gov.mz; internet www.mic.gov.mz.

Ministry of the Interior: Av. Olof Palme 46/48, CP 290, Maputo; tel. 21303510; fax 21420084.

Ministry of Justice: Av. Julius Nyerere 33, Maputo; tel. 21491613; fax 21494264.

Ministry of Labour: Av. 24 de Julho 2351, CP 281, Maputo; tel. 21428301; fax 21421881; internet www.mitrab.gov.mz.

Ministry of Mineral Resources: Av. Fernão de Magalhães 34, CP 294, Maputo; tel. 21314843; fax 21427103; internet www.mireme.gov.mz.

Ministry of National Defence: Av. Mártires de Mueda 280, CP 3216, Maputo; tel. 21492081; fax 21491619.

Ministry of Public Works and Housing: Av. Karl Marx 606, CP 268, Maputo; tel. 21430028; fax 21421369.

Ministry of Science and Technology: Av. Patrice Lumumba 770, Maputo; tel. 21352800; fax 21352860; e-mail secretariado@mct.gov.mz; internet www.mct.gov.mz.

Ministry of State Administration: Rua da Rádio Moçambique 112, CP 4116, Maputo; tel. 21426666; fax 21428565.

Ministry of Tourism: Av. 25 de Setembro 1018, CP 4101, Maputo; tel. 21306210; fax 21306212; internet www.moztourism.gov.mz.

Ministry of Transport and Communications: Av. Mártires de Inhaminga 336, CP 276, Maputo; tel. 21430152; fax 21431028.

Ministry of Veterans' Affairs: Rua General Pereira d'Eça 35, CP 3697, Maputo; tel. 21490601.

Ministry of Women's Affairs and Social Welfare Co-ordination: Rua de Tchamba 86, CP 516, Maputo; tel. 21490921; fax 21492757; internet www.mmas.gov.mz.

Ministry of Youth and Sport: Av. 25 de Setembro 529, CP 2080, Maputo; tel. 21312172; fax 21300040; e-mail mjd@tvcabo.co.mz; internet www.mjd.gov.mz.

MOZAMBIQUE

PROVINCIAL GOVERNORS
(March 2009)

Cabo Delgado Province: Eliseu Joaquim Machava.
Gaza Province: Raimundo Maico Diomba.
Inhambane Province: Francisco Meque.
Manica Province: Maurício Vieira Jocob.
Maputo Province: Telmina Pereira.
Nampula Province: Felismino Ernesto Tocoli.
Niassa Province: Arnaldo Vicente Bimbe.
Sofala Province: Alberto Clementino Vaquina.
Tete Province: Ildefonso Muanantapha.
Zambézia Province: Carvalho Muária.
City of Maputo: Rosa Manuel Andrande da Silva.

President and Legislature

PRESIDENT

Presidential Election, 1–2 December 2004

Candidate	Votes	% of votes
Armando Guebuza (Frelimo)	2,004,226	63.74
Afonso Macacho Marceta Dhlakama (Renamo—União Eleitoral)	998,059	31.74
Raul Domingos (PPDD)	85,815	2.73
Yaqub Sabindy (PIMO)	28,656	0.91
Carlos Alexandre dos Reis (FMBG)	27,412	0.87
Total*	3,144,168	100.00

*Excluding 96,684 blank votes and 81,315 spoilt votes.

LEGISLATURE

Assembléia da República: CP 1516, Maputo; tel. 21400826; fax 21400711; e-mail cdi@sortmoz.com.
Chair.: Eduardo Mulémbue.

General Election, 1–2 December 2004

Party	Votes	% of votes	Seats*
Frente de Libertação de Moçambique (Frelimo)	1,889,054	62.03	160
Resistência Nacional Moçambicana—União Eleitoral (Renamo—UE)	905,289	29.73	90
Partido para a Paz, Democracia e Desenvolvimento (PPDD)	60,758	2.00	—
Partido para a Liberdade e Solidariedade (PAZS)	20,686	0.68	—
Partido de Reconciliação Nacional (PARENA)	18,220	0.60	—
Partido Independente de Moçambique (PIMO)	17,960	0.59	—
Partido Social de Moçambique (PASOMO)	15,740	0.52	—
Others	117,722	3.87	—
Total (incl. others)†	3,045,429	100.00	250

*Parties must obtain a minimum of 5% of the vote in order to gain representation in the Assembléia da República.
†Excluding 166,540 blank votes and 109,957 spoilt votes.

Election Commission

Comissão Nacional de Eleições (CNE): Maputo; f. 1997; 13 mems; Dir-Gen. António Carrasco.

Political Organizations

In mid-2004 there were five coalitions and 42 parties registered with the Comissão Nacional de Eleiçoes. The parties listed below secured votes in the December 2004 legislative elections.

Congresso dos Democratas Unidos (CDU): Maputo; f. 2001; Leader António Palange.

Frente de Libertação de Moçambique (Frelimo): Rua Pereira do Lago 10, Bairro de Sommerschield, Maputo; tel. 21490181; fax 21490008; e-mail info@frelimo.org.mz; internet www.frelimo.org.mz; f. 1962 by merger of three nationalist parties; reorg. 1977 as a 'Marxist-Leninist vanguard movement'; in 1989 abandoned its exclusive Marxist-Leninist orientation; Pres. Armando Guebuza.

Frente de Mudança e Boa Governa (FMBG): f. 2004; comprises:

Partido de Todos os Nativos Moçambicanos (Partonamo): f. 1996; Pres. Mussagy Abdul Remane.

União Nacional Moçambicana (Unamo): f. 1987; breakaway faction of Renamo; social democratic; obtained legal status 1992; fmr mem. of União Eleitoral; Pres. Carlos Alexandre dos Reis; Sec.-Gen. Florencia João da Silva.

Partido Democrático de Libertação de Moçambique (Padelimo): based in Kenya; Pres. Joaquim José Nhota.

Partido Independente de Moçambique (PIMO): f. 1993; Islamist; Leader Yaqub Sabindy; Sec.-Gen. Magalhães Bramugy.

Partido Liberal e Democrático de Moçambique (Palmo): f. 1991; obtained legal status 1993; Pres. António Muedo.

Partido para a Paz, Democracia e Desenvolvimento (PPDD): Quelimane; f. 2003; liberal; Leader Raul Domingos.

Partido Popular Democrático (PPD): f. 2004; Leader Marciano Fijama.

Partido de Reconciliação Nacional (PARENA): Maputo; f. August 2004; Leader André Balate.

Partido Social, Liberal e Democrático (Sol): breakaway faction of Palmo; Leader Casimiro Miguel Nhamithambo.

Partido Social de Moçambique (Pasomo): Maputo; Leader Francisco Campira.

Partido do Trabalho (PT): f. 1993; breakaway faction of PPPM; Pres. Miguel Mabote; Sec.-Gen. Luís Muchanga.

Partido Verde de Moçambique (PVM): Leader Bruno Sapemba.

Resistência Nacional Moçambicana-União Eleitoral (Renamo-UE): f. 1999; coalition comprising Renamo and the União Eleitoral which, in late 2004, consisted of 10 minor parties.

Constituent members include:

Resistência Nacional Moçambicana (Renamo): Av. Julius Nyerere 2541, Maputo; tel. 21493107; internet www.renamo.org.mz; also known as Movimento Nacional da Resistência de Moçambique (MNR); f. 1976; fmr guerrilla group, in conflict with the Govt between 1976 and Oct. 1992; obtained legal status in 1994; Pres. Afonso Macacho Marceta Dhlakama; Sec.-Gen. Ossufo Momade.

Aliança Independente de Moçambique (Alimo): Maputo; f. 1998; Sec.-Gen. Ernesto Sergio.

Frente de Ação Patriótica (FAP): Maputo; f. 1991; Pres. José Carlos Palaço.

Frente Democrática Unida—United Democratic Front (UDF): Maputo; Pres. Janeiro Mariano.

Frente Unida de Moçambique (Fumo): Av. Mao Tse Tung 230, 1° andar, Maputo; tel. 21494044; in early 2005 the party was reported to have split, with the faction led by Simeão Cuamba and Pedro Loforte supporting a withdrawal from the UE; Sec.-Gen. José Samo Gudo.

Partido de Convenção Nacional (PCN): Av. de 25 Setembro 1123, 3° andar, Maputo; tel. 21426891; obtained legal status in 1992; Chair. Lutero Chimbirimbiri Simango; Sec.-Gen. Dr Gabriel Mabunda.

Partido Ecologista de Moçambique (PEMO): Maputo.

Partido do Progresso do Povo de Moçambique (PPPM): Av. de 25 Setembro, 1123, 4° andar, Maputo; tel. 21426925; f. 1991; obtained legal status 1992; Pres. Dr Padimbe Mahose Kamati; Sec.-Gen. Che Abdala.

Partido Renovador Democrático (PRD): obtained legal status 1994; Pres. Maneca Daniel.

Partido de Unidade Nacional (PUN): TV Sado 9, Maputo; tel. 21419204; Pres. Hipolito Couto.

União para a Salvação de Moçambique (Usamo): f. 2004; coalition comprising the União para a Mudança (UM), PADRES, PSDM, and the PSM; Chair. Julio Nimuire.

Partido Socialista de Moçambique (PSM): Leader João Nkalamba.

In 2005 a coalition comprising 18 small parties, including the **Partido Popular Democrático (PPD)**, the **Partido Nacional de Moçambique (Panamo)** and the **Partido Progressivo e Liberal de Moçambique (PPLM)**, was formed.

MOZAMBIQUE   *Directory*

Diplomatic Representation

EMBASSIES AND HIGH COMMISSIONS IN MOZAMBIQUE

Algeria: Rua de Mukumbura 121–125, CP 1709, Maputo; tel. 21492070; fax 21490582; e-mail ab220261@virconn.com; Ambassador FOUAD BOUTTOURA.

Angola: Av. Kenneth Kaunda 783, CP 2954, Maputo; tel. 21493139; fax 21493930; Ambassador JOÃO GARCIA BIRES.

Brazil: Av. Kenneth Kaunda 296, CP 1167, Maputo; tel. 21484800; fax 21484806; e-mail ebrasil@teledata.mz; internet www.ebrasil.co.mz; Ambassador ANTONIO DE SOUZA E SILVA.

China, People's Republic: Av. Julius Nyerere 3142, CP 4668, Maputo; tel. 21491560; fax 21491196; e-mail emb.chi@tvcabo.co.mz; Ambassador TIAN GUANGFENG.

Congo, Democratic Republic: Av. Kenneth Kaunda 127, CP 2407, Maputo; tel. 21497154; fax 21494929; Chargé d'affaires a.i. MULUMBA TSHIDIMBA MARCEL.

Congo, Republic: Av. Kenneth Kaunda 783, CP 4743, Maputo; tel. 21490142; Chargé d'affaires a.i. MONSEGNO BASHA OSHEFWA.

Cuba: Av. Kenneth Kaunda 492, CP 387, Maputo; tel. 21492444; fax 21491905; e-mail residcuba.mozambique@tvcabo.co.mz; Ambassador MARCELINA EVANGELINA SEOANE DOMÍNGUEZ.

Denmark: Av. Julius Nyerere 1162, CP 4588, Maputo; tel. 21480000; fax 21480010; e-mail mpmamb@um.dk; internet www.ambmaputo.um.dk; Ambassador JOHNNY FLENTØ.

Egypt: Av. Mao Tse Tung 851, CP 4662, Maputo; tel. 21491118; fax 21491489; e-mail egypt2@tropical.co.mz; Ambassador ABDEL KADER TANTAWY ES-SAYED.

Finland: Av. Julius Nyerere 1128, CP 1663, Maputo; tel. 21482400; fax 21491662; e-mail sanomat.map@formin.fi; internet www.finland.org.mz; Ambassador KARI ALANKO.

France: Av. Julius Nyerere 2361, CP 4781, Maputo; tel. 21484600; fax 21484680; e-mail ambafrancemz@tvcabo.co.mz; internet www.ambafrance-mz.org; Ambassador (vacant).

Germany: Rua Damião de Góis 506, CP 1595, Maputo; tel. 21492700; fax 21492888; e-mail germaemb@tvcabo.co.mz; internet www.maputo.diplo.de; Ambassador KLAUS-CHRISTIAN KRAEMER.

Holy See: Av. Kwame Nkrumah 224, CP 2738, Maputo; tel. 21491144; fax 21492217; Apostolic Nuncio Most Rev. GEORGE PANIKULAM (Titular Archbishop of Caudium).

Iceland: Av. Zimbabwe 1694, Maputo; tel. 21483509; fax 21483511; e-mail mozambique@iceida.is; internet www.iceland.org/mo; Chargé d'affaires a.i. JÓHANN PÁLSSON.

India: Av. Kenneth Kaunda 167, CP 4751, Maputo; tel. 21492437; fax 21492364; e-mail hicomind@tvcabo.co.mz; internet www.hicomind-maputo.org; High Commissioner RAJINDER BHAGAT.

Ireland: Av. Julius Nyerere 3332, Maputo; tel. 21491440; fax 21493023; e-mail maputoembassy@dfa.ie; Ambassador FRANK SHERIDAN.

Italy: Av. Kenneth Kaunda 387, CP 976, Maputo; tel. 21492229; fax 21492046; e-mail ambasciata.maputo@esteri.it; internet www.ambmaputo.esteri.it; Ambassador CARLO LO CASCIO.

Japan: Av. Julius Nyerere 2832, CP 2494, Maputo; tel. 21499819; fax 21498957; Ambassador TATSUYA MIKI.

Korea, Democratic People's Republic: Rua da Kaswende 167, Maputo; tel. 21491482; Ambassador PAK KUN GWANG.

Malawi: Av. Kenneth Kaunda 75, CP 4148, Maputo; tel. 21492676; fax 21490224; High Commissioner MARTIN O. KANSICHI.

Mauritius: Rua Dom Carlos 42, Av. de Zimbabwe, Sommerscheid, Maputo; tel. 21494624; fax 21494729; e-mail maputo@mail.gov.mu; High Commissioner ALAIN LARIDON.

Netherlands: Av. Kwame Nkrumah 324, CP 1163, Maputo; tel. 21484200; fax 21484248; e-mail map@minbuza.nl; internet www.hollandinmozambique.org; Ambassador FRANS BIJVOET.

Nigeria: Av. Kenneth Kaunda 821, CP 4693, Maputo; tel. and fax 21490991; High Commissioner ALBERT G. PIUS OMOTAIO.

Norway: Av. Julius Nyerere 1162, CP 828, Maputo; tel. 21480100; fax 21480107; e-mail emb.maputo@mfa.no; internet www.norway.org.mz; Ambassador THORBJØRN GAUSTADSÆTHER.

Portugal: Av. Julius Nyerere 720, CP 4696, Maputo; tel. 21490316; fax 21491172; e-mail embaixada@embpormaputo.org.mz; Ambassador JOSÉ JOAQUIM ESTEVES DOS SANTOS DE FREITAS FERRAZ.

Russia: Av. Vladimir I. Lénine 2445, CP 4666, Maputo; tel. 21417372; fax 21417515; e-mail embrus@tvcabo.co.mz; internet www.mozambique.mid.ru; Ambassador IGOR V. POPOV.

South Africa: Av. Eduardo Mondlane 41, CP 1120, Maputo; tel. 21493030; fax 21493029; e-mail sahc@tropical.co.mz; High Commissioner THANDI LUJABE-RANKOE.

Spain: Rua Damião de Góis 347, CP 1331, Maputo; tel. 21492048; fax 21494769; e-mail emb.maputo@mae.es; Ambassador JUAN MANUEL MOLINA LAMOTHE.

Swaziland: Av. Kwame Nkrumah, CP 4711, Maputo; tel. 21491601; fax 21492117; High Commissioner Prince TSHEKEDI.

Sweden: Av. Julius Nyerere 1128, CP 338, Maputo; tel. 21480300; fax 21480390; e-mail ambasseden.maputo@foreign.ministry.se; internet www.swedenabroad.se/maputo; Ambassador TORVALD ÅKESSON.

Switzerland: Av. Ahmed Sekou Touré 637, CP 135, Maputo; tel. 21315275; fax 21315276; e-mail map.vertretung@eda.admin.ch; internet www.eda.admin.ch/maputo; Ambassador THOMAS LITSCHER.

Tanzania: Ujamaa House, Av. dos Mártires da Machava 852, CP 4515, Maputo; tel. 21490110; fax 21494782; e-mail ujamaa@zebra.eum.mz; High Commissioner ISSA MOHAMED ISSA.

Timor-Leste: Maputo; Chargé d'affaires a.i. MARINA ALKATIRI.

United Kingdom: Av. Vladimir I. Lénine 310, CP 55, Maputo; tel. 21356000; fax 21356060; e-mail bhc.consular@tvcabo.co.mz; internet www.britishhighcommission.gov.uk/mozambique; High Commissioner ANDREW SOPER.

USA: Av. Kenneth Kaunda 193, CP 783, Maputo; tel. 21492797; fax 21490114; e-mail consularmaputo@state.gov; internet www.usembassy-maputo.gov.mz; Ambassador WILLIAM R. STEIGER (designate).

Zambia: Av. Kenneth Kaunda 1286, CP 4655, Maputo; tel. 21492452; fax 21491893; e-mail zhcmmap@zebra.uem.mz; High Commissioner SIMON GABRIEL MWILA.

Zimbabwe: Av. Kenneth Kaunda 816, CP 743, Maputo; tel. 21490404; fax 21492237; e-mail maro@isl.co.mz; Ambassador AGRIPA MUTAMBARA.

Judicial System

The Constitution of November 1990 provides for a Supreme Court and other judicial courts, an Administrative Court, courts-martial, customs courts, maritime courts and labour courts. The Supreme Court consists of professional judges, appointed by the President of the Republic, and judges elected by the Assembléia da República. It acts in sections, as a trial court of primary and appellate jurisdiction, and in plenary session, as a court of final appeal. The Administrative Court controls the legality of administrative acts and supervises public expenditure.

President of the Supreme Court: MÁRIO MANGAZE.
Attorney-General: AUGUSTO PAULINO.

Religion

There are an estimated 5m. Christians and 4m. Muslims, as well as small Hindu, Jewish and Baháʼí communities. In 2004 over 100 religious groups were officially registered.

CHRISTIANITY

There are many Christian organizations registered in Mozambique.

Conselho Cristão de Moçambique (CCM) (Christian Council of Mozambique): Av. Agostino Neto 1584, CP 108, Maputo; tel. 21322836; fax 21321968; f. 1948; 22 mems; Pres. Rt Rev. ARÃO MATSOLO; Gen. Sec. Rev. DINIS MATSOLO.

The Roman Catholic Church

Mozambique comprises three archdioceses and nine dioceses. At 31 December 2006 it was estimated that there were some 4,466,472 adherents, representing some 21.5% of the total population.

Bishops' Conference

Conferência Episcopal de Moçambique (CEM), Secretariado Geral da CEM, Av. Paulo Samuel Kankhomba 188/RC, CP 286, Maputo; tel. 21490766; fax 21492174.
f. 1982; Pres. Most Rev. TOMÉ MAKHWELIHA (Archbishop of Nampula).

Archbishop of Beira: Most Rev. JAIME PEDRO GONÇALVES, Cúria Arquiepiscopal, Rua Correia de Brito 613, CP 544, Beira; tel. 23322313; fax 23327639; e-mail arquidbeira@teledata.mz.

Archbishop of Maputo: Most Rev. FRANCISCO CHIMOIO, Paço Arquiepiscopal, Avda Eduardo Mondlane 1448, CP 258, Maputo; tel. 21326240; fax 21321873.

Archbishop of Nampula: Most Rev. TOMÉ MAKHWELIHA, Paço Arquiepiscopal, CP 84, 70100 Nampula; tel. 26213024; fax 26214194; e-mail arquidiocesenpl@teledata.mz.

MOZAMBIQUE

The Anglican Communion

Anglicans in Mozambique are adherents of the Anglican Church of Southern Africa (formerly the Church of the Province of Southern Africa). There are two dioceses in Mozambique. The Metropolitan of the Province is the Archbishop of Cape Town, South Africa.

Bishop of Lebombo: Rt Rev. DINIS SALOMÃO SENGULANE, CP 120, Maputo; tel. 21734364; fax 21401093; e-mail bispo_sengulane@virconn.com.

Bishop of Niassa: Rev. MARK VAN KOEVERING, CP 264, Lichinga, Niassa; tel. 27112735; fax 27112336; e-mail bishop.niassa@gmail.com.

Other Churches

Baptist Convention of Mozambique: Av. Maguiguane 386, CP 852, Maputo; tel. 2126852; Pres. Rev. BENTO BARTOLOMEU MATUSSE; 78 churches, 25,000 adherents.

The Church of Jesus Christ of the Latter-Day Saints: Maputo; 9 congregations, 1,975 mems.

Free Methodist Church: Pres. Rev. FRANISSE SANDO MUVILE; 214 churches, 21,231 mems.

Igreja Congregational Unida de Moçambique: Rua 4 Bairro 25 de Junho, CP 930, Maputo; tel. 21475820; Pres., Sec. of the Synod A. A. LITSURE.

Igreja Maná: Rua Francisco Orlando Magumbwe 528, Maputo; tel. 21491760; fax 21490896; e-mail adm_mocambique@igrejamana.com; Bishop DOMINGOS COSTA.

Igreja Reformada em Moçambique (IRM) (Reformed Church in Mozambique): CP 3, Vila Ulongue, Anogonia-Tete; f. 1908; Gen. Sec. Rev. SAMUEL M. BESSITALA; 60,000 mems.

Presbyterian Church of Mozambique: Av. Ahmed Sekou Touré 1822, CP 21, Maputo; tel. 21421790; fax 21428623; e-mail ipmoc@zebra.uem.mz; f. 1887; 100,000 adherents; Pres. of Synodal Council Rev. ORIENTE SIBANE.

Seventh-Day Adventist Church: Av. Maguiguana 300, CP 1468, Maputo; tel. and fax 21427200; e-mail victormiconde@teledata.co.mz; 937 churches, 186,724 mems (2004).

Other denominations active in Mozambique include the Church of Christ, the Church of the Nazarene, the Greek Orthodox Church, the United Methodist Church of Mozambique, the Wesleyan Methodist Church, the Zion Christian Church, and Jehovah's Witnesses.

ISLAM

Comunidade Mahometana: Av. Albert Luthuli 291, Maputo; tel. 21425181; fax 21300880; internet www.paginaislamica.8m.com/pg1.htm; Pres. MOMAD BACHIR SULEMAN.

Congresso Islâmico de Moçambique (Islamic Congress of Mozambique): represents Sunni Muslims; Chair. ASSANE ISMAEL MAQBUL.

Conselho Islâmico de Moçambique (Islamic Council of Mozambique): Leader Sheikh AMINUDDIN MOHAMAD.

The Press

DAILIES

Correio da Manha: Av. Filipe Samuel Magaia 528, CP 1756, Maputo; tel. 21305322; fax 21305321; e-mail refi@virconn.com; f. 1997; published by Sojornal, Lda; also publishes weekly Correio Semanal; Dir REFINALDO CHILENGUE.

Diário de Moçambique: Av. 25 de Setembro 1509, 2° andar, CP 2491, Beira; tel. and fax 23427312; f. 1981; under state management since 1991; Dir EZEQUIEL AMBRÓSIO; Editor FARUCO SADIQUE; circ. 5,000 (2003).

Expresso da Tarde: Av. Patrice Lumumba 511, 1° andar, Maputo; tel. 21314912; subscription only; distribution by fax; Dir SALVADOR RAIMUNDO HONWANA.

Mediafax: Av. Amílcar Cabral 1049, CP 73, Maputo; tel. 21301737; fax 21302402; e-mail mediafax@tvcabo.co.mz; f. 1992 by co-operative of independent journalists Mediacoop; news-sheet by subscription only, distribution by fax and internet; Editor BENEDITO NGOMANE.

Notícias de Moçambique: Rua Joaquim Lapa 55, CP 327, Maputo; tel. 21420119; fax 21420575; f. 1926; morning; f. 1906; under state management since 1991; Dir BERNARDO MAVANGA; Editor HILÁRIO COSSA; circ. 12,793 (2003).

Further newspapers available solely in e-mail or fax format include Diário de Notícias and Matinal.

WEEKLIES

Campeão: Av. 24 de Julho 3706, CP 2610, Maputo; tel. and fax 21401810; sports newspaper; Dir RENATO CALDÉIRA; Editor ALEXANDRE ZANDAMELA.

Correio Semanal: Av. Filipe Samuel Magaia 528, CP 1756, Maputo; tel. 21305322; fax 21305312; Dir REFINALDO CHILENGUE.

Desafio: Rua Joaquim Lapa 55, Maputo; tel. 21305437; fax 21305431; Dir ALMIRO SANTOS; Editor BOAVIDA FUNJUA; circ. 3,890 (2003).

Domingo: Rua Joaquim Lapa 55, CP 327, Maputo; tel. 21431026; fax 21431027; f. 1981; Sun.; Dir JORGE MATINE; circ. 15,000 (2007).

Fim de Semana: Rua da Resistência 1642, 1° andar, Maputo; tel. and fax 21417012; e-mail fimdomes@tvcabo.co.mz; internet www.fimdesemana.co.mz; f. 1997; independent.

Savana: Av. Amílcar Cabral 1049, CP 73, Maputo; tel. 21301737; fax 21302402; e-mail savana@mediacoop.co.mz; internet www.savana.co.mz; f. 1994; owned by mediacoop, SA; CEO FERNANDO LIMA; Publr KOK NAM; Editor FERNANDO GONÇALVES; circ. 15,000 (2009).

Tempo: Av. Ahmed Sekou Touré 1078, CP 2917, Maputo; tel. 21426191; f. 1970; magazine; under state management since 1991; Dir ROBERTO UAENE; Editor ARLINDO LANGA; circ. 40,000.

Zambeze: Rua José Sidumo, Maputo; tel. 21302019; Dir SALOMÃO MOYANE; circ. 2,000 (2003).

PERIODICALS

Agora: Afrisurvey, Lda, Rua General Pereira d'Eça 200, 1° andar, CP 1335, Maputo; tel. 21494147; fax 21494204; internet www.agora.co.mz; f. 2000; monthly; economics, politics, society; Pres. MARIA DE LOURDES TORCATO; Dir JOVITO NUNES; Editor-in-Chief ERCÍLIA SANTOS; circ. 5,000.

Agricultura: Instituto Nacional de Investigação Agronómica, CP 3658, Maputo; tel. 2130091; f. 1982; quarterly; publ. by Centro de Documentação de Agricultura, Silvicultura, Pecuária e Pescas.

Aro: Av. 24 de Julho 1420, CP 4187, Maputo; f. 1995; monthly; Dir POLICARTO TAMELE; Editor BRUNO MACAME, Jr.

Arquivo Histórico: Av. Filipe Samuel Magaia 715, CP 2033, Maputo; tel. 21421177; fax 21423428; f. 1934; Editor JOEL DAS NEVES TEMBE.

Boletim da República: Av. Vladimir I. Lénine, CP 275, Maputo; govt and official notices; publ. by Imprensa Nacional da Moçambique.

Moçambique–Novos Tempos: Av. Ahmed Sekou Touré 657, Maputo; tel. 21493564; fax 21493590; f. 1992; Dir J. MASCARENHAS.

Mozambiquefile: c/o AIM, Rua da Radio Moçambique, CP 896, Maputo; tel. 21313225; fax 21313196; e-mail aim@aim.org.mz; internet www.sortmoz.com/aimnews; monthly; Dir GUSTAVO MAVIZ; Editor PAUL FAUVET.

Mozambique Inview: c/o Mediacoop, Av. Amílcar Cabral 1049, CP 73, Maputo; tel. 21430722; fax 21302402; e-mail inview@mediacoop.co.mz; internet www.mediacoop.odline.com; f. 1994; 2 a month; economic bulletin in English; Editor FRANCES CHRISTIE.

Portos e Caminhos de Ferro: CP 276, Maputo; English and Portuguese; ports and railways; quarterly.

Revista Maderazinco: CP 477, Maputo; tel. 823004770; e-mail maderazinco@yahoo.com; internet www.tropical.maderazinco.co.mz; f. 2002; quarterly; literature; Editor ROGÉRIO MANJATE.

Revista Médica de Moçambique: Instituto Nacional de Saúde, Ministério da Saúde e Faculdade de Medicina, Universidade Eduardo Mondlane, CP 264, Maputo; tel. 21420368; fax 21431103; e-mail mdgedge@malarins.uem.mz; f. 1982; 4 a year; medical journal; Editor MARTINHO DGEDGE.

NEWS AGENCY

Agência de Informação de Moçambique (AIM): Rua da Rádio Moçambique, CP 896, Maputo; tel. 21313225; fax 21313196; e-mail aim@aim.org.mz; internet www.sortmoz.com/aimnews; f. 1975; daily reports in Portuguese and English; Dir GUSTAVO LISSETIANE MAVIE.

Publishers

There are an estimated 30 printing and publishing companies in Mozambique.

Arquivo Histórico de Moçambique (AHM): Av. Filipe Samuel Magaia 715, CP 2033, Maputo; tel. 21421177; fax 21423428; internet www.ahm.uem.mz; Dir JOEL DAS NEVES TEMBE.

Central Impressora: c/o Ministério da Saúde, Avs Eduardo Mondlane e Salvador Allende 1008, CP 264, Maputo; tel. 21427131; fax 21427133; owned by the Ministry of Health.

MOZAMBIQUE   *Directory*

Centro de Estudos Africanos: Universidade Eduardo Mondlane, CP 1993, Maputo; tel. 21490828; fax 21491896; f. 1976; social and political science, regional history, economics; Dir Col SERGIO VIEIRA.

Editora Minerva Central: Rua Consiglieri Pedroso 84, CP 212, Maputo; tel. 2122092; f. 1908; stationers and printers, educational, technical and medical textbooks; Man. Dir J. F. CARVALHO.

Editorial Ndjira, Lda: Av. Ho Chi Minh 85, Maputo; tel. 21300180; fax 21308745; f. 1996.

Empresa Moderna, Lda: Av. 25 de Setembro, CP 473, Maputo; tel. 21424594; f. 1937; fiction, history, textbooks; Man. Dir LOUIS GALLOTI.

Fundo Bibliográfico de Língua Portuguesa: Av. 25 de Setembro 1230, 7° andar, Maputo; tel. 21429531; fax 21429530; e-mail palop@zebra.uem.mz; f. 1990; state owned; Pres. LOURENÇO ROSÁRIO.

Imprensa Universitária: Universidade Eduardo Mondlane, Praça 19 de Maio, Maputo; internet www.uem.mz/imprensa_universitaris; university press.

Instituto Nacional do Livro e do Disco: Av. 24 de Julho 1921, CP 4030, Maputo; tel. 21434870; govt publishing and purchasing agency; Dir ARMÉNIO CORREIA.

Moçambique Editora: Rua Armando Tivane 1430, Bairro de Polana, Maputo; tel. 21495017; fax 21499071; e-mail info@me.co.mz; internet www.me.co.mz; f. 1996; educational textbooks, dictionaries.

Plural Editores: Av. 24 de Julho 414, Maputo; tel. 21486828; fax 21486829; e-mail plural@pluraleditores.co.mz; internet www.pluraleditores.co.mz; f. 2003; educational textbooks; part of the Porto Editora Group.

GOVERNMENT PUBLISHING HOUSE

Imprensa Nacional de Moçambique: Rua da Imprensa, CP 275, Maputo; tel. 21427021; fax 21424858; internet www.imprensanac.gov.mz; part of Ministry of State Administration; Dir VENÂNCIO T. MANJATE.

Broadcasting and Communications

TELECOMMUNICATIONS

Regulatory Authority

Instituto Nacional das Comunicações de Moçambique (INCM): Av. Eduardo Mondlane 123–127, CP 848, Maputo; tel. 21490131; fax 21494435; e-mail info@incm.gov.mz; internet www.incm.gov.mz; regulates post and telecommunications systems.

Major Telecommunications Companies

TDM currently has a monopoly on fixed lines; however, plans were announced in 2004 to open this sector to competition in the late 2000s.

Telecomunicações de Moçambique, SARL (TDM): Rua da Sé 2, CP 25, Maputo; tel. 21431921; fax 21431944; e-mail scatdm@tdm.mz; internet www.tdm.mz; f. 1993; Chair. JOAQUIM RIBEIRO PEREIRA DE CARVALHO; Man. Dir MAMUDO IBRAIMO.

Moçambique Celular (mCel): Edif. Mcel, Esquina Av. 25 de Setembro e Rua Belmiro Obede Muianga, CP 1463, Maputo; tel. 21351111; fax 21351119; internet www.mcel.co.mz; f. 1997 as a subsidiary of TDM; separated from TDM in 2003; mobile cellular telephone provider.

Vodacom Moçambique: Time Square Complex, Bloco 3, Av. 25 de Setembro, Maputo; tel. 840900000; fax 840901775; e-mail yumna.bhikha@vm.co.mz; internet www.vm.co.mz; f. 2002; owned by Vodacom Group (South Africa) and local shareholders; Chair. SALIMO ABDULA; Man. Dir JOSÉ DOS SANTOS.

BROADCASTING

Radio

Rádio Encontro: Av. Francisco Manyanga, CP 366, Nampula; tel. 26215588.

Rádio Feba Moçambique: Av. Julius Nyerere 441, Maputo; tel. 21440002.

Rádio Maria: Rua Igreja 156A, Machava Sede, Matola, Maputo; tel. 21750505; fax 21752124; e-mail ramamo@virconn.com; f. 1995; evangelical radio broadcasts; Dir Fr JOÃO CARLOS H. NUNES.

Rádio Miramar: Rede de Comunicação, Av. Julius Nyerere 1555, Maputo; tel. and fax 21488613; e-mail jose.guerra@tvcabo.co.mz; owned by Brazilian religious sect, the Universal Church of the Kingdom of God.

Rádio Moçambique: Rua da Rádio 2, CP 2000, Maputo; tel. 21431687; fax 21321816; e-mail sepca_mz@yahoo.com.br; internet www.rm.co.mz; f. 1975; programmes in Portuguese, English and vernacular languages; Chair. RICARDO MADAUANE MALATE.

Rádio Terra Verde: fmrly Voz da Renamo; owned by former rebel movement Renamo; transmitters in Maputo and Gorongosa, Sofala province.

Rádio Trans Mundial Moçambique: Av. Eduardo Mondlane 2998, Maputo; tel. 21407358; fax 21407357.

Television

The Portuguese station RTP-Africa also broadcasts in Mozambique.

Rádio Televisão Klint (RTK): Av. Agostinho Neto 946, Maputo; tel. 21422956; fax 21493306; Dir CARLOS KLINT.

Televisão Miramar: Rua Pereira Lago 221, Maputo; owned by Brazilian religious sect, the Igrega Universal do Reino de Deus (Universal Church of the Kingdom of God).

Televisão de Moçambique, EP (TVM): Av. 25 de Setembro 154, CP 2675, Maputo; tel. 21308117; fax 21308122; e-mail tvm@tvm.co.mz; internet www.tvm.co.mz; f. 1981; Chair. and CEO SIMÃO JORDÃO ANGUILAZE.

TV Cabo Moçambique: Av. dos Presidentes 68, CP 1750, Maputo; tel. 21480500; fax 21480501; e-mail tvcabo@tvcabo.co.mz; internet www.tvcabo.co.mz; cable television and internet services in Maputo.

Finance

(cap. = capital; res = reserves; dep. = deposits; m. = million; brs = branches; amounts in meticais, unless otherwise stated)

BANKING

Central Bank

Banco de Moçambique: Av. 25 de Setembro 1679, CP 423, Maputo; tel. 21318000; fax 21429029; e-mail cdi@bancomoc.mz; internet www.bancomoc.mz; f. 1975; bank of issue; cap. 249.0m., res 2,268.2m., dep. 26,835.5m. (Dec. 2006); Gov. ERNESTO GOUVEIA GOVE; 4 brs.

National Banks

Barclays Bank Mozambique SA: Av. 25 de Setembro 1184, CP 757, Maputo; tel. 21351739; fax 21301094; internet www.bancoaustral.co.mz; f. 1995 as Banco Popular de Desenvolvimento (BPD); name changed to Banco Austral SARL in 1998; name changed as above in 2007; 80% owned by Amalgamated Banks of South Africa, 20% owned by União, Sociedade e Participacões, SARL, which represents employees of the bank; cap. 315m., res 46.4m., dep. 4,395.8m. (Dec. 2006); Chair. CASIMIRO FRANCISCO; Man. Dir PAUL NICE; 52 brs and agencies.

BCI Fomento (BCI) (Banco Comercial e de Investimentos, SARL): Edif. John Orr's, Av. 25 de Setembro 1465, CP 4745, Maputo; tel. 21307777; fax 21307762; e-mail bci@bci.co.mz; internet www.bci.co.mz; f. 1996; renamed as above following 2003 merger between Banco Comercial e de Investimentos and Banco de Fomento; 42% owned by Caixa Geral de Depósitos (Portugal), 30% Banco Português de Investimento; dep. US $360.0m. (Dec. 2004); Chair. ABDUL MAGID OSMAN; 34 brs.

Banco de Desenvolvimento e de Comércio de Moçambique, SARL (BDCM): Av. 25 de Setembro 420, 1° andar, sala 8, Maputo; tel. 21313040; fax 21313047; f. 2000; 42% owned by Montepio Geral (Portugal).

BIM—Investimento (Banco Internacional de Moçambique—Investimento): Av. Kim Il Sung 961, Maputo; tel. 21354896; fax 21354897; e-mail mpinto@bim.co.mz; internet www.bimnet.co.mz; f. 1998; 50% owned by Millennium bim, 25% by BCP Investimento and 15% by International Finance Corpn; total assets US $2.7m. (Dec. 2003); Chair. Dr MÁRIO FERNANDES DA GRAÇA MACHUNGO; Gen. Dir Dr JOSÉ A. FERREIRA GOMES.

Banco Mercantil e de Investimento, SARL (BMI): Av. 24 de Julho 3549, Maputo; tel. 21407979; fax 21408887.

Banco Terra: Av. Samora Machel 47 R/C, CP 69, Maputo; tel. 21359300; fax 21316120; internet www.bancoterra.co.mz; f. 2008; provides access to a full range of financial services to the rural and peri urban population in Mozambique; cap. 185m.; 30.7% owned by Rabobank (Netherlands); Chair. A. J.A. M. KUIJPERS; CEO MAARTEN SUSAN.

ICB-Banco Internacional de Comércio, SARL: Av. 25 de Setembro 1915, Maputo; tel. 21311111; fax 21314797; e-mail icbm@icbank-mz.com; internet www.icbank-mz.com; f. 1998; cap. and res 44,923,748m., total assets 164,773,569m. (Dec. 2003); Chair. JOSEPHINE SIVARETNAM; CEO LEE SANG HUAT; 4 brs.

Millennium bim: Av. 25 de Setembro 1800, CP 865, Maputo; tel. 21351500; fax 21354808; e-mail fxavier@millenniumbim.co.mz; internet www.millenniumbim.co.mz; f. 1995; name changed from Banco Internacional de Moçambique in 2005; 66.7% owned by Banco

MOZAMBIQUE

Comercial Português, 17.8% by the state; cap. 741,000m. (Dec. 2007); Pres. MÁRIO FERNANDES DA GRAÇA MACHUNGO; CEO JOÃO FILIPE DE FIGUEIREDO JÚNIOR; 86 brs.

Moza Banco: Av. Kwame Nrumah 97, CP 1012, Maputo; tel. 21480800; fax 21480801; e-mail info@mozabanco.co.mz; internet www.mozabanco.co.mz; f. 2008; cap. US $15m.; Chair. PRAKASH RATILAL.

Novo Banco, SARL: Av. do Trabalho 750, Maputo; tel. and fax 21407705; f. 2000; cap. and res 51,995m., total assets 108,847m. (Dec. 2003).

Standard Bank, SARL (Moçambique): Praça 25 de Junho 1, CP 2086, Maputo; tel. 21352500; fax 21426967; e-mail camal.daude@standardbank.co.mz; internet www.standardbank.co.mz; f. 1966 as Banco Standard Totta de Moçambique; 96.0% owned by Stanbic Africa Holdings, UK; cap. 174,000m., res 173,295m., dep. 6,080,437m. (Dec. 2003); Man. Dir ANTONIO COUTINHO; 24 brs.

Foreign Banks

African Banking Corporation (Moçambique), SA: ABC House, Av. Julius Nyerere 999, Polana, CP 1445, Maputo; tel. 21482100; fax 21487474; e-mail abcmoz@africanbankingcorp.com; internet www.africanbankingcorp.com; f. 1999; 100% owned by African Banking Corpn Holdings Ltd (Botswana); fmrly BNP Nedbank (Moçambique), SARL; changed name as above after acquisition in 2002; cap. 148m., res 173m., dep. 1,094m. (Dec. 2007); Chair. BENJAMIM ALFREDO; Man. Dir JOSEPH SIBANDA; 2 brs.

African Banking Corporation Leasing, SARL: Rua da Imprensa 256, 7° andar, CP 4447, Maputo; tel. 21300451; fax 21431290; e-mail ulcmoz@mail.tropical.co.mz; 66% owned by African Banking Corpn Holdings Ltd (Botswana); fmrly ULC (Moçambique); changed name as above in 2002; total assets US $1.8m. (Dec. 1998); Chair. ANTÓNIO BRANCO; Gen. Man. VICTOR VISEU.

União Comercial de Bancos (Moçambique), SARL: Av. Friedrich Engels 400, Maputo; tel. 21481900; fax 21498675; e-mail contact@mcbmozambique.com; f. 1999; 81.24% owned by Mauritius Commercial Bank Group; total assets US $46,777m. (Dec. 2006); Chair. PIERRE GUY NOEL; Gen. Man. ROBERT CANTIN.

DEVELOPMENT FUND

Fundo de Desenvolvimento Agrário: Rua Joaquim Lapa 192, 2° Andar, Maputo; tel. 21302814; fax 21430044; e-mail antonio.andre@ffa.org.mz; f. 2006 to provide credit for small farmers and rural co-operatives; promotes agricultural and rural devt; Sec. ANTÓNIO ANDRÉ.

STOCK EXCHANGE

Bolsa de Valores de Moçambique: Av. 25 de Setembro 1230, Prédio 33, 5° andar, Maputo; tel. 21308826; fax 21310559; internet www.bvm.co.mz; Chair. Dr JUSSUB NURMAMAD.

INSURANCE

In December 1991 the Assembléia da República approved legislation terminating the state monopoly of insurance and reinsurance activities. In 2005 five insurance companies were operating in Mozambique.

Companhia de Seguros de Moçambique, IMPAR: Rua da Imprensa 625, Prédio 33, Maputo; tel. 21429695; fax 21430640; f. 1992; Pres. INOCÊNCIO A. MATAVEL; Gen. Man. MANUEL BALANCHO.

Empresa Moçambicana de Seguros, EE (EMOSE): Av. 25 de Setembro 1383, CP 1165, Maputo; tel. 21356300; fax 21424526; f. 1977 as state insurance monopoly; took over business of 24 fmr cos; 80% govt-owned, 20% private; cap. 150m.; Chair. VENÂNCIO MONDLANE.

Seguradora Internacional de Moçambique: Av. 25 Setembro 1800, Maputo; tel. 21430959; fax 21430241; e-mail simseg@zebra.uem.mz; Pres. MÁRIO FERNANDES DA GRAÇA MACHUNGO.

Trade and Industry

GOVERNMENT AGENCIES

Centro de Promoção de Investimentos (CPI) (Investment Promotion Centre): Rua da Imprensa 332, CP 4635, Maputo; tel. 21313295; fax 21313325; e-mail cpi@cpi.co.mz; internet www.cpi.co.mz; f. 1987; encourages domestic and foreign investment and IT ventures with foreign firms; evaluates and negotiates investment proposals; Dir MAHOMED RAFIQUE JUSOB MAHOMED.

Instituto de Algodão de Moçambique (IAM): Av. Eduardo Mondlane 2221, 1° andar, CP 806, Maputo; tel. 21424264; fax 21430679; e-mail iampab@zebra.uem.mz; responsible for promotion and devt of the cotton industry; Dir (vacant).

Instituto do Fomento do Cajú (INCAJU): Maputo; national cashew institute; Dir CLEMENTINA MACHUNGO.

Instituto Nacional de Açúcar (INA): Rua da Gávea 33, CP 1772, Maputo; tel. 21326550; fax 21427436; e-mail gpsca.ina@tvcabo.co.mz; Chair. ARNALDO RIBEIRO.

Instituto Nacional de Petróleo (INP): Av. Fernão de Magalhães 34, CP 4724, Maputo; tel. 21320935; fax 21430850; e-mail info@inp.gov.mz; internet www.inp.gov.mz; f. 2005; regulates energy sector; Dir ARSÉNIO MABOTE.

Instituto para a Promoção de Exportações (IPEX): Av. 25 de Setembro 1008, 2° andar, CP 4487, Maputo; tel. 21307257; fax 21307256; e-mail ipex@tvcabo.co.mz; internet www.ipex.gov.mz; f. 1990 to promote and co-ordinate national exports abroad; Pres. Dr JOÃO MACARINGUE.

Unidade Técnica para a Reestruturação de Empresas (UTRE): Rua da Imprensa 256, 7° andar, CP 4350, Maputo; tel. 21426514; fax 21421541; implements restructuring of state enterprises; Dir MOMADE JUMAS.

CHAMBERS OF COMMERCE

Câmara de Comércio de Moçambique (CCM): Rua Mateus Sansão Muthemba 452, CP 1836, Maputo; tel. 21491970; fax 21490428; e-mail ccm@tvcabo.co.mz; internet www.ccmoz.org.mz; f. 1980; Pres. JACINTO VELOSO; Sec.-Gen. MANUEL NOTIÇO.

Mozambique-USA Chamber of Commerce: Rua Matheus Sansão Muthemba 452, CP 1836, Maputo; tel. 21492904; fax 21492739; e-mail ccmusa@tvcabo.co.mz; internet www.ccmusa.co.mz; f. 1993; Sec. PETER MUCHIRI.

South Africa-Mozambique Chamber of Commerce (SAMOZACC): e-mail info@samozacc.co.za; internet www.samozacc.co.za; f. 2005; Chair. (Mozambique) ANTÓNIO MATOS.

TRADE ASSOCIATIONS

Associação das Indústrias do Cajú (AICAJU): Maputo; cashew processing industry asscn; Chair. CARLOS COSTA; 12 mem. cos.

Confederação das Associações Económicas de Moçambique (CTA): Rua de Castanheda, CP 2975, Maputo; tel. 21491914; fax 21493094; internet www.cta.org.mz; Pres. SALIMO ABDULA; Exec. Dir SÉRGIO CHITARÁ; 58 mem. cos.

STATE INDUSTRIAL ENTERPRISES

Empresa Nacional de Carvão de Moçambique (CARBOMOC): Rua Joaquim Lapa 108, CP 1773, Maputo; tel. 21427625; fax 21424714; f. 1948; mineral extraction and export; transfer to private ownership pending; Dir JAIME RIBEIRO.

Empresa Nacional de Hidrocarbonetos de Moçambique (ENH): Av. Fernão de Magalhães 34, CP 4787, Maputo; tel. 21429456; fax 21421608; controls concessions for petroleum exploration and production; Dir MÁRIO MARQUES.

Petróleos de Moçambique (PETROMOC): Praça dos Trabalhadores 9, CP 417, Maputo; tel. 21427191; fax 21430181; internet www.petromoc.co.mz; f. 1977 to take over the Sonarep oil refinery and its associated distribution co; formerly Empresa Nacional de Petróleos de Moçambique; state directorate for liquid fuels within Mozambique, incl. petroleum products passing through Mozambique to inland countries; CEO MATEUS KATHUPA.

UTILITIES

Electricity

Electricidade de Moçambique (EDM): Av. Agostinho Neto 70, CP 2447, Maputo; tel. 21490636; fax 21491048; e-mail ligacaoexpresso@edm.co.mz; internet www.edm.co.mz; f. 1977; 100% state-owned; production and distribution of electric energy; in 2004 plans were announced to extend EDM grid to entire country by 2020, at an estimated cost of US $700m; Pres. MANUEL JOÃO CUAMBE; Dir PASCOAL BACELA; 2,700 employees.

Companhia de Transmissão de Moçambique, SARL (MOTRACO) (Mozambique Transmission Co): Prédio JAT, 4° andar, Av. 25 de Setembro 420, Maputo; tel. 21313427; fax 21313447; e-mail asimao@motraco.co.mz; internet www.motraco.co.mz; f. 1998; jt venture between power utilities of Mozambique, South Africa and Swaziland; electricity distribution; Gen. Man. FRANCIS MASAWI.

Water

Direcção Nacional de Águas: Av. 25 de Setembro 942, 9° andar, CP 1611, Maputo; tel. 21420469; fax 21421403; e-mail watco@zebra.uem.mz; internet www.dnaguas.gov.mz; Dir AMÉRICO MUIANGA.

TRADE UNIONS

Freedom to form trade unions, and the right to strike, are guaranteed under the 1990 Constitution.

Confederação de Sindicatos Livres e Independentes de Moçambique (CONSILMO): Sec.-Gen. JEREMIAS TIMANE.

Organização dos Trabalhadores de Moçambique—Central Sindical (OTM—CS) (Mozambique Workers' Organization—Trade Union Headquarters): Rua Manuel António de Sousa 36, Maputo; tel. 21426786; fax 21421671; internet www.otm.org.mz; f. 1983; Pres. AMÓS JÚNIOR MATSIUHE; Sec.-Gen. (vacant); 15 affiliated unions with over 94,000 mems including:

Sindicato Nacional dos Empregadores Bancários (SNEB): Av. Fernão de Magalhães 785, 1° andar, CP 1230, Maputo; tel. 21428627; fax 21303274; e-mail snebmoz@tvcabo.co.mz; internet www.snebmoz.co.mz; f. 1992; Sec.-Gen. CARLOS MELO.

Sindicato Nacional da Função Pública (SNAPF): Av. Ho Chi Min 365, Maputo; Sec.-Gen. MANUEL ABUDO MOMAD.

Sindicato Nacional dos Profissionais da Estiva e Ofícios Correlativos (SINPEOC): Av. Paulo Samuel Kakhomba 1568, Maputo; tel. and fax 21309535; Sec.-Gen. BENTO MADALA MAUNGUE.

Sindicato Nacional dos Trabalhadores Agro-Pecuários e Florestais (SINTAF): Av. 25 de Setembro 1676, 1° andar, CP 4202, Maputo; tel. 21306284; f. 1987; Sec.-Gen. EUSÉBIO LUÍS CHIVULELE.

Sindicato Nacional dos Trabalhadores da Aviação Civil, Correios e Comunicações (SINTAC): Av. 25 de Setembro 1509, 2° andar, Porta 5, Maputo; tel. 21309574; e-mail sintacnacional@tdm.co.mz; Sec.-Gen. ARMANDO MAZOIO.

Sindicato Nacional dos Trabalhadores do Comércio, Seguros e Serviços (SINECOSSE): Av. Ho Chi Minh 365, 1° andar, CP 2142, Maputo; tel. 21428561; Sec.-Gen. AMÓS JÚNIOR MATSINHE.

Sindicato Nacional dos Trabalhadores da Indústria do Açúcar (SINTIA): Av. das FPLM 1912, Maputo; tel. 21461772; fax 21461975; f. 1989; Sec.-Gen. ALEXANDRE CÂNDIDO MUNGUAMBE.

Sindicato Nacional dos Trabalhadores da Indústria Alimentar e Bebidas (SINTIAB): Av. Eduardo Mondlane 1267, CP 394, Maputo; tel. 21324709; fax 21324123; f. 1986; Gen. Sec. SAMUEL FENIAS MATSINHE.

Sindicato Nacional dos Trabalhadores da Indústria de Cajú (SINTIC): Rua do Jardim 574, 4° andar, Maputo; tel. 21477732; Sec.-Gen. BOAVENTURA MONDLANE.

Sindicato Nacional dos Trabalhadores da Indústria Metalúrgica, Metalomecânica e Energia (SINTIME): Av. Samora Machel 30, 6°, Maputo; Sec.-Gen. SIMIÃO NHATUMBO.

Sindicato Nacional dos Trabalhadores da Indústria Química, Borracha, Papel e Gráfica (SINTIQUIGRA): Av. Olof Palme 255, CP 4439, Maputo; tel. 21320288; fax 21321096; f. 1987; chemical, rubber, paper and print workers' union; due to merge with SINTEVEC in 2007; Co-ordinator JESSICA GUNE; 4,970 mems.

Sindicato Nacional dos Trabalhadores da Indústria Têxtil Vestuário, Couro e Calçado (SINTEVEC): Av. do Trabalho 1276, 1° andar, CP 2613, Maputo; tel. 21404669; fax 21409295; clothing, leather and footwear workers' union; due to merge with SINTIQUIGRA in 2007; Sec.-Gen. MARIO RAIMUNDO SITOE; 1,700 mems.

Sindicato Nacional dos Trabalhadores da Marinha Mercante e Pesca (SINTMAP): Rua Joaquim Lapa 22, 5° andar, No. 6, Maputo; tel. 21305593; Sec.-Gen. DANIEL MANUEL NGOQUE.

Sindicato Nacional dos Trabalhadores dos Portos e Caminhos de Ferro (SINPOCAF): Av. Guerra Popular, esquina 24 de Setembro, CP 2158, Maputo; tel. 21403912; fax 21303839; Sec.-Gen. SAMUEL ALFREDO CHEUANE.

Sindicato Nacional de Jornalistas (SNJ): Av. 24 de Julho 231, Maputo; tel. 21492031; fax 823015912; f. 1978; Sec.-Gen. EDUARDO CONSTANTINO.

Transport

Improvements to the transport infrastructure since the signing of the Acordo Geral de Paz (General Peace Agreement) in 1992 have focused on the development of 'transport corridors', which include both rail and road links and promote industrial development in their environs. The Beira Corridor, with rail and road links and a petroleum pipeline, runs from Manica, on the Zimbabwean border, to the Mozambican port of Beira, while the Limpopo Corridor joins southern Zimbabwe and Maputo. Both corridors form a vital outlet for the land-locked southern African countries, particularly Zimbabwe. The Maputo Corridor links Ressano Garcia in South Africa to the port at Maputo, and the Nacala Corridor runs from Malawi to the port of Nacala. Two further corridors were planned: the Mtwara Development Corridor was to link Mozambique, Malawi, Tanzania and Zambia, while the Zambezi Corridor was to link Zambézia province with Malawi. In February 2000 much of the country's infrastructure in the southern and central provinces was devastated as the result of massive flooding. Railway lines, roads and bridges suffered considerable damage.

RAILWAYS

In 2003 the total length of track was 3,114 km, of which 2,072 km was operational. There are both internal routes and rail links between Mozambican ports and South Africa, Swaziland, Zimbabwe and Malawi. During the hostilities many lines and services were disrupted. Improvement work on most of the principal railway lines began in the early 1980s. In the early 2000s work began on upgrading the railway system and private companies were granted non-permanent concessions to upgrade and run the railways.

Beira Railway Co: Dondo; f. 2004; 51% owned by Rites & Ircon (India), 49% owned by CFM; rehabilitating and managing Sena and Zimbabwe railway lines.

Empresa Nacional dos Portos e Caminhos de Ferro de Moçambique (CFM): Praça dos Trabalhadores, CP 2158, Maputo; tel. 21327173; fax 21427746; e-mail cfmnet@cfmnet.co.mz; internet www.cfmnet.co.mz; fmrly Empresa Nacional dos Portos e Caminhos de Ferro de Moçambique; privatized and restructured in 2002; Chair. RUI FONSECA; comprises four separate systems linking Mozambican ports with the country's hinterland, and with other southern African countries, including South Africa, Swaziland, Zimbabwe and Malawi:

CFM—Centro (CFM—C): Largo dos CFM, CP 236, Beira; tel. 23321000; fax 23329290; lines totalling 994 km linking Beira with Zimbabwe and Malawi, as well as link to Moatize (undergoing rehabilitation); Exec. Dir JOAQUIM VERÍSSIMO.

CFM—Norte: Av. do Trabalho, CP 16, Nampula; tel. 26214320; fax 26212034; lines totalling 872 km, including link between port of Nacala with Malawi; management concession awarded to Nacala Corridor Development Co (a consortium 67% owned by South African, Portuguese and US cos) in January 2000; Dir of Railways MANUEL MANICA.

CFM—Sul: Praça dos Trabalhadores, CP 2158, Maputo; tel. and fax 21430894; lines totalling 1,070 km linking Maputo with South Africa, Swaziland and Zimbabwe, as well as Inhambane-Inharrime and Xai-Xai systems; Exec. Dir JOAQUIM ZUCULE.

CFM—Zambézia: CP 73, Quelimane; tel. 24212502; fax 24213123; 145-km line linking Quelimane and Mocuba; Dir ORLANDO J. JAIME.

ROADS

In 2006 there were an estimated 17,805 km of roads in Mozambique, of which 5,083 km were paved. In 2003 827 km of roads were built or upgraded. Under its Road Sector Strategic Plan for 2007–11, the Administraçao Nacional de Estradas pledged to improve or redevelop 5,590 km of roads in 40 separate projects at a cost of some US $786m.

Administraçao Nacional de Estradas (ANE): Av. de Moçambique 1225, CP 1294, Maputo; tel. 21475157; fax 21475290; internet www.ane.gov.mz; f. 1999 to replace the Direcção Nacional de Estradas e Pontes; implements government road policy through the Direcção de Estradas Nacionais (DEN) and the Direcção de Estradas Regionais (DER); Pres. Eng. CARLOS FRAGOSO; Dir-Gen. IBRAIMO REMANE.

SHIPPING

Mozambique has three main sea ports, at Nacala, Beira and Maputo, while inland shipping on Lake Niassa and the river system was underdeveloped. At December 2007 Mozambique's registered merchant fleet consisted of 129 vessels, totalling 37,914 grt.

Empresa Portos e Caminhos de Ferro de Moçambique (CFM-EP): Praça dos Trabalhadores, CP 2158, Maputo; tel. 21427173; fax 21427746; e-mail cfmnet@cfmnet.co.mz; internet www.cfmnet.co.mz; fmrly Empresa Nacional dos Portos e Caminhos de Ferro de Moçambique; privatized and restructured in 2002; Port Dir CFM-Sul BOAVENTURA CHAMBAL; Port Dir CFM-Norte AGOSTINHO LANGA, Jr; Port Dir CFM-Centro CHINGUANE MABOTE.

Agência Nacional de Frete e Navegação (ANFRENA): Rua Consiglieri Pedroso 396, CP 492, Maputo; tel. 21427064; fax 21427822; Dir FERDINAND WILSON.

Empresa Moçambicana de Cargas, SARL (MOCARGO): Rua Consiglieri Pedroso 430, 1°–4° andares, CP 888, Maputo; tel. 21428318; fax 21302067; e-mail msamaral@teledata.mz; internet www.mocargo.co.mz; f. 1982; shipping, chartering and road transport; Man. Dir MANUEL DE SOUSA AMARAL.

MOZAMBIQUE

Manica Freight Services, SARL: Praça dos Trabalhadores 51, CP 557, Maputo; tel. 21356500; fax 21431084; e-mail fdimande@manica.co.mz; internet www.manica.co.mz; international shipping agents; Man. Dir A. Y. CHOTHIA.

Maputo Port Development Co, SARL (MPDC): Port Director's Building, Porto de Maputo, CP 2841, Maputo; tel. 21313920; fax 21313921; e-mail info@portmaputo.com; internet www.portmaputo.com; f. 2002; private-sector international consortium with concession (awarded 2003) to develop and run port of Maputo until 2018; CEO RON HERMAN.

Mozline, SARL: Av. Karl Marx 478, 2° andar, Maputo; tel. 21303078; fax 21303073; e-mail mozline1@virconn.com; shipping and road freight services.

Navique, SARL: Av. Mártires de Inhaminga 125, CP 145, Maputo; tel. 21312705; fax 21426310; e-mail smazoi@navique.co.mz; internet www.navique.com; f. 1985; Chair. J. A. CARVALHO; Man. Dir PEDRO VIRTUOSO.

CIVIL AVIATION

In 2006 there were five international airports.

Instituto de Aviação Civil de Moçambique (IACM): Maputo; civil aviation institute; Dir ANÍBAL SAMUEL.

Air Corridor, SARL: Av. Eduardo Mondlane 945, Nampula; tel. 26213333; fax 26213355; e-mail fagadit@aircorridor.com.mz; internet www.aircorridor.co.mz; f. 2004; domestic carrier and cargo transport; Chair. MOMADE AQUI RAJAHUSSEN; Commercial Dir FARUK ALY GADIT.

Linhas Aéreas de Moçambique, SARL (LAM): Aeroporto Internacional de Maputo, CP 2060, Maputo; tel. 21465137; fax 21422936; e-mail jrviegas@lam.co.mz; internet www.lam.co.mz; f. 1980; 80% state-owned; operates domestic services and international services to South Africa, Tanzania, Mayotte, Zimbabwe and Portugal; Pres. JOSÉ RICARDO ZUZARTE VIEGAS.

Sociedade de Transportes Aéreos/Sociedade de Transporte e Trabalho Aéreo, SARL (STA/TTA): Rua da Tchamba 405, CP 665, Maputo; tel. 21491765; fax 21491763; e-mail sta.tta@sta.co.mz; internet www.sta.co.mz; f. 1991; domestic airline and aircraft charter transport services; acquired Empresa Nacional de Transporte e Trabalho Aéreo in 1997; Chair. ROGÉRIO WALTER CARREIRA; Man. Dir JOSÉ CARVALHEIRA.

Other airlines operating in Mozambique include Serviço Aéreo Regional, South African Airlines, Moçambique Expresso, SA—Airlink International, Transairways (owned by LAM) and TAP Air Portugal.

Tourism

Tourism, formerly a significant source of foreign exchange, ceased completely following independence, and was resumed on a limited scale in 1980. There were 1,000 visitors in 1981 (compared with 292,000 in 1972 and 69,000 in 1974). With the successful conduct of multi-party elections in 1994 and the prospect of continued peace, there was considerable scope for development of this sector. By the late 1990s tourism was the fastest growing sector of the Mozambique economy, and in 2000 it was announced that a comprehensive tourism development plan was to be devised, assisted by funding from the European Union. In 2005 there were 5,030 hotels in Mozambique. The opening of the Great Limpopo Transfrontier Park, linking territories in Mozambique with South Africa and Zimbabwe, was expected to attract additional tourists. Further national parks were planned. Foreign tourist arrivals in 2006 were 1,095,000; tourism receipts totalled US $145m. in 2006.

Fundo Nacional do Turismo: Av. 25 de Setembro 1203, CP 4758, Maputo; tel. 21307320; fax 21307324; internet www.futur.org.mz; f. 1993; hotels and tourism; CEO Dr ZACARIAS SUMBANA.

MYANMAR

Introductory Survey

Location, Climate, Language, Religion, Flag, Capital

The Republic of the Union of Myanmar (Myanma Naing-ngan—formerly Burma) lies in the north-west region of South-East Asia, between the Tibetan plateau and the Malay peninsula. The country is bordered by Bangladesh and India to the north-west, by the People's Republic of China and Laos to the north-east and by Thailand to the south-east. The climate is tropical, with an average temperature of 27°C (80°F) and monsoon rains from May to October. Average annual rainfall is between 2,500 mm and 5,000 mm in the coastal and mountainous regions of the north and east, but reaches a maximum of only 1,000 mm in the lowlands of the interior. Temperatures in Yangon (Rangoon) are generally between 18°C (65°F) and 36°C (97°F). The official language is Myanmar (Burmese), and there are also a number of tribal languages. About 87% of the population are Buddhists. There are animist, Muslim, Hindu and Christian minorities. The national flag (proportions 5 by 9) is red, with a blue canton in the upper hoist, bearing two ears of rice within a cog-wheel and a ring of 14 five-pointed stars (one for each state), all in white. In 2006 the functions of the capital city were transferred from Yangon to the new administrative centre of Nay Pyi Taw.

Recent History

Burma (now Myanmar) was annexed to British India during the 19th century, and became a separate British dependency, with a limited measure of self-government, in 1937. Japanese forces invaded and occupied the country in 1942, and Japan granted nominal independence under a Government of anti-British nationalists. The Burmese nationalists later turned against Japan and aided Allied forces to reoccupy the country in 1945. They formed a resistance movement, the Anti-Fascist People's Freedom League (AFPFL), led by Gen. Aung San, which became the main political force after the defeat of Japan. Aung San was assassinated in July 1947 and was succeeded by U Nu. On 4 January 1948 the Union of Burma became independent, outside the Commonwealth, with U Nu as the first Prime Minister.

During the first decade of independence Burma was a parliamentary democracy, and the Government successfully resisted revolts by communists and other insurgent groups. In 1958 the ruling AFPFL split into two wings, the 'Clean' AFPFL and the 'Stable' AFPFL, and U Nu invited the Army Chief of Staff, Gen. Ne Win, to head a caretaker Government. Elections to the Chamber of Deputies in February 1960 gave an overwhelming majority to U Nu, leading the 'Clean' AFPFL (which was renamed the Union Party in March), and he resumed office in April. Despite its popularity, the U Nu administration proved ineffective, and in March 1962 Gen. Ne Win staged a coup to depose U Nu (who was subsequently detained until 1966). The new Revolutionary Council suspended the Constitution and instituted authoritarian control through the government-sponsored Burma Socialist Programme Party (BSPP). All other political parties were outlawed in March 1964.

During the next decade a more centralized system of government was created, in an attempt to win popular support and to nationalize important sectors of the economy. A new Constitution, aiming to transform Burma into a democratic socialist state, was approved in a national referendum in December 1973. The Constitution of the renamed Socialist Republic of the Union of Burma, which came into force in January 1974, confirmed the BSPP as the sole authorized political party, and provided for the establishment of new organs of state. Elections to a legislative People's Assembly took place in January 1974, and in March the Revolutionary Council was dissolved. U Ne Win (who, together with other senior army officers, had become a civilian in 1972) was elected President by the newly created State Council. However, Burma's economic problems increased, and in 1974 there were riots over food shortages and social injustices. Student demonstrations took place in 1976, as social problems increased. Following an attempted coup by members of the armed forces in July, the BSPP reviewed its economic policies, and in 1977 a new economic programme was adopted in an attempt to quell unrest.

An election in January 1978 gave U Ne Win a mandate to rule for a further four years, and in March he was re-elected Chairman of the State Council. In May 1980 a general amnesty was declared for political dissidents, including exiles (as a result of which U Nu, who had been living abroad since 1969, returned to Burma). Gen. San Yu, formerly the Army Chief of Staff, was elected Chairman of the State Council in November 1981. In August 1985 U Ne Win was re-elected Chairman of the BSPP. Elections for a new People's Assembly were held in November.

In August 1987, owing to the country's increasing economic problems, an unprecedented extraordinary meeting, comprising the BSPP Central Committee, the organs of the State Council and other state bodies, was convened. U Ne Win proposed a review of the policies of the past 25 years. In September the announcement of the withdrawal from circulation of high-denomination banknotes, coupled with rice shortages, provoked student riots (the first civil disturbances since 1976). Owing to continued economic deprivation, further student unrest in Rangoon (now Yangon) in March 1988 culminated in major protests, which were violently suppressed by riot police under the direct command of U Sein Lwin, the BSPP Joint General Secretary. Further demonstrations started in June. The Government's response was again extremely brutal, and many demonstrators were killed. In July vain attempts were made to counter the growing unpopularity of the Government, including the removal from office of the Minister of Home and Religious Affairs and the head of the People's Police Force in Rangoon. (The Prime Minister, also, was subsequently dismissed.) Finally, at an extraordinary meeting of the BSPP Congress, U Ne Win resigned as party Chairman and asked the Congress to approve the holding of a national referendum on the issue of a multi-party political system. The Congress rejected the referendum proposal and the resignation of four other senior members of the BSPP, including that of U Sein Lwin, but accepted the resignation of U San Yu, the BSPP Vice-Chairman.

The subsequent election of U Sein Lwin to the chairmanship of the BSPP, and his appointment as Chairman of the State Council and as state President, provoked further student-led riots. Martial law was imposed on Rangoon, and thousands of unarmed demonstrators were reportedly massacred by the armed forces throughout the country. In August 1988 U Sein Lwin was forced to resign after only 17 days in office. He was replaced by the more moderate Dr Maung Maung, hitherto the Attorney-General, whose response to the continued rioting was conciliatory. Martial law was revoked; Brig.-Gen. Aung Gyi (formerly a close colleague of U Ne Win, now an outspoken critic of the regime), who had been detained under U Sein Lwin, was released; and permission was given for the formation of the All Burma Students' Union. However, demonstrations continued, and by September students and Buddhist monks had assumed control of the municipal government of many towns. In that month U Nu requested foreign support for his formation of an 'alternative government'. The emerging opposition leaders, Aung Gyi, Aung San Suu Kyi (daughter of Gen. Aung San) and Gen. (retd) Tin Oo (a former Chief of Staff and Minister of Defence), then formed the National United Front for Democracy, which was subsequently renamed the League for Democracy and later the National League for Democracy (NLD).

At an emergency meeting of the BSPP Congress in September 1988 it was decided that free elections would be held within three months and that members of the armed forces, police and civil service could no longer be affiliated to a political party. Now distanced from the BSPP, the armed forces, led by Gen. (later Senior Gen.) Saw Maung, seized power on 18 September, ostensibly to maintain order until multi-party elections could be arranged. A State Law and Order Restoration Council (SLORC) was formed, all state organs (including the People's Assembly, the State Council and the Council of Ministers) were abolished, demonstrations were banned and a night-time curfew was imposed nation-wide. Despite these measures, opposition movements demonstrated in favour of an interim civilian government, and it was estimated that more than 1,000 demonstrators were killed in the first few days following the coup. The SLORC announced the formation of a nine-member Government, with Saw Maung as Minister of Defence and of Foreign Affairs and subsequently also Prime Minister. Although ostensibly in retirement, it was widely believed that U Ne Win retained a controlling influence over the new leaders. The new Government changed the official name of the country to the Union of Burma (as it had been before 1973). The law maintaining the BSPP as the sole party was abrogated, and new parties were encouraged to register for the forthcoming elections. The BSPP registered as the National Unity Party (NUP). In December 1988, owing to disagreements with Suu Kyi, Aung Gyi was expelled from the NLD after he had founded the Union National Democracy Party. Tin Oo was elected as the new NLD Chairman. U Nu returned to prominence as the leader of a new party, the League for Democracy and Peace (LDP), and also commanded the support of the new Democracy Party.

From October 1988 to January 1989 Suu Kyi campaigned in townships and rural areas across the nation, and elicited much popular support, despite martial law regulations banning public gatherings of five or more people. In March 1989 there were anti-Government demonstrations in many cities, in protest at the increasing harassment of Suu Kyi and the arrest of many NLD supporters and activists. In July Suu Kyi cancelled a rally to commemorate the anniversary of the assassination of her father, owing to the threat of government violence; two days later, both she and Tin Oo were placed under house arrest, accused of 'endangering the State'.

In May 1989 electoral legislation was ratified, providing for multi-party elections to be held on 27 May 1990. In June 1989 the SLORC changed the official name of the country to the Union of Myanmar (Myanma Naing-ngan), on the grounds that the previous title conveyed the impression that the population consisted solely of ethnic Burmans. The transliteration to the Roman alphabet of many other place names was changed, to correspond more closely with pronunciation.

In December 1989 Tin Oo of the NLD was sentenced by a military tribunal to three years' imprisonment, with hard labour, for his part in the anti-Government uprising in 1988. U Nu was disqualified from contesting the forthcoming general election, owing to his refusal to dissolve the 'alternative government' that he had proclaimed in September 1988. In January 1990 U Nu and 13 members of the 'alternative government' were placed under house arrest. Five members subsequently resigned and were released. Later in January, Suu Kyi was barred from contesting the election, owing to her 'entitlement to the privileges of a foreigner' (a reference to her marriage to a British citizen) and her alleged involvement with insurgents.

Martial law was revoked in eight townships in November 1989, and in a further 10 in February 1990. It was reported that during 1989 tens of thousands of residents had been forcibly evicted from densely populated areas in major cities, where anti-Government demonstrations had received much support, and resettled in rural areas. In January and April 1989 Amnesty International, the human rights organization, published information regarding violations of human rights in Myanmar, including the torture and summary execution of dissident students. This was followed by criticism from the UN later in the year.

In May 1990 93 parties presented a total of 2,296 candidates to contest 492 seats at the general election for the new assembly; there were also 87 independent candidates. The voting was reported to be free and orderly. The NLD received 59.9% of the total votes and won 396 of the 485 seats that were, in the event, contested; the NUP obtained 21.2% of the votes, but won only 10 seats. The NLD demanded the immediate opening of negotiations with the SLORC, and progress towards popular rule. However, the SLORC announced that the election had been intended to provide not a legislature but a Constituent Assembly, which was to draft a constitution establishing a 'strong government', to come under the direction of a national convention to be established by the SLORC. The resulting draft constitution would have to be endorsed by referendum, and subsequently approved by the SLORC. In July the SLORC announced Order 1/90, stating that the SLORC would continue as the de facto Government until a new constitution was drafted. Elected members of the NLD responded (independently of their leadership) with the 'Gandhi Hall Declaration', urging that an assembly of all elected representatives be convened by September.

In August 1990, at an anti-Government protest held in Mandalay to commemorate the killing of thousands of demonstrators in 1988, troops killed four protesters, including two Buddhist monks. In September the SLORC arrested six members of the NLD, including the acting Chairman, Kyi Maung, and acting Secretary-General, Chit Hlaing, on charges of passing state secrets to unauthorized persons. Kyi Maung was replaced as acting NLD Chairman by U Aung Shwe. Also in September NLD representatives discussed plans to declare a provisional government in Mandalay, without the support of the party's Central Executive Committee. Influential monks agreed to support the declaration, but the plan was abandoned after government troops surrounded monasteries. The SLORC subsequently ordered the dissolution of all Buddhist organizations involved in anti-Government activities (all except nine sects) and empowered military commanders to impose death sentences on rebellious monks. More than 50 senior members of the NLD were arrested, and members of all political parties were required to endorse Order 1/90: in acquiescing, the NLD effectively nullified its demand for an immediate transfer of power.

In December 1990 a group of candidates who had been elected to the Constituent Assembly fled to Manerplaw, on the Thai border, and announced a 'parallel government', the National Coalition Government of the Union of Burma (NCGUB), with the support of the Democratic Alliance of Burma (DAB), a broadly based organization uniting ethnic rebel forces with student dissidents and monks. The self-styled Prime Minister of the NCGUB was Sein Win, the leader of the Party for National Democracy (PND) and a cousin of Suu Kyi. The NLD leadership expelled members who had taken part in the formation of the 'parallel government', despite broad support for the move in the NLD. The SLORC subsequently annulled the registration as a political party of the PND, the LDP and two other parties and the elected status of the eight members of the NCGUB. In April 1991 Gen. (later Senior Gen. and Field Marshal) Than Shwe, the Vice-Chairman of the SLORC and the Deputy Chief of Staff of the armed forces, officially announced that the SLORC would not transfer power to the Constituent Assembly, as the political parties involved were 'subversive' and 'unfit to rule'. In response to continued pressure from the SLORC, the NLD carried out a complete reorganization of the party's Central Executive Committee, replacing Suu Kyi as General Secretary with the previously unknown U Lwin, and Tin Oo (as distinct from Tin Oo of the SLORC) with the former acting Chairman, U Aung Shwe.

In July 1991 the SLORC retroactively amended electoral legislation adopted in May 1989, extending the grounds on which representatives of the Assembly could be disqualified or debarred from contesting future elections to include convictions for breaches of law and order. More than 80 elected representatives had already died, been imprisoned or been forced into exile since the election in May 1990. In September 1991 the SLORC declared its intention to remain in charge of state administration for a further five to 10 years. In that month U Ohn Gyaw was appointed Minister for Foreign Affairs in place of Saw Maung, becoming the first civilian in the Cabinet.

In October 1991 Suu Kyi was awarded the Nobel Peace Prize. Sein Win attended the presentation of the award to Suu Kyi's family in Oslo, Norway, in December, gaining the Norwegian Government's de facto recognition of the NCGUB. In Myanmar students who staged demonstrations (the first since 1989) to coincide with the ceremony were dispersed by security forces. It was subsequently announced that Suu Kyi had been expelled from the NLD. In January 1992 Tin Oo's expulsion from the NLD was announced in a broadcast.

Three additional members were appointed to the SLORC in January 1992, and the Cabinet was expanded to include seven new ministers, four of whom were civilians. The changes, together with a reorganization of senior ministers in February, were widely perceived to benefit the Chief of Military Intelligence, Maj.-Gen. (later Lt-Gen.) Khin Nyunt (First Secretary of the SLORC). Khin Nyunt was widely regarded as the most powerful member of the SLORC, owing to U Ne Win's continued patronage. Divisions within the ruling junta between Khin Nyunt and the more senior officers were becoming increasingly evident. In March Than Shwe replaced Saw Maung as Minister of Defence, and in April Saw Maung retired as Chairman of the SLORC and Prime Minister for reasons of ill health. Than Shwe was subsequently appointed to both these posts. The SLORC promptly ordered the release of several political prisoners, including U Nu, and announced that Suu Kyi could receive a visit from her family. Than Shwe indicated that he was prepared to meet Suu Kyi personally to discuss her future. In June the first meeting took place between members of the SLORC and opposition representatives from the remaining 10 legal parties, in preparation for the holding of a national convention to draft a new constitution.

In January 1993 the National Convention finally assembled, but was adjourned several times during the year, owing to the objections of the opposition members to SLORC demands for a leading role in government for the armed forces. The SLORC reacted to what it regarded as opposition intransigence by suspending any conciliatory gestures (which had included the revocation of two martial law decrees and amnesties for a total of 534 political prisoners), and many arrests were reported. Towards the end of the year the Chairman of the National Convention's Convening Committee, U Aung Toe (the Chief Justice), announced (seemingly without grounds) that a consensus existed in favour of the SLORC's demands, which comprised: the inclusion, in both the lower and upper chambers of a proposed parliament, of military personnel (to be appointed by the Commander-in-Chief of the Armed Forces); the election of the President by an electoral college; the independent self-administration of the armed forces; and the right of the Commander-in-Chief to exercise state power in an emergency (effectively granting legitimate status to a future coup).

In September 1993 an alternative mass movement to the NUP (which had lost credibility through its election defeat) was formed to establish a civilian front through which the armed forces could exercise control. The Union Solidarity and Development Association (USDA), the aims of which were indistinguishable from those of the SLORC, was not officially registered as a political party, thus enabling civil servants to join the organization, with the incentive of considerable privileges.

In January 1994 the National Convention reconvened, and in April it was adjourned, having adopted guidelines for three significant chapters of the future Constitution. Accordingly, Myanmar was to be renamed the Republic of the Union of Myanmar, comprising seven states (associated with some of the country's minority ethnic groups) and seven divisions in central and southern Myanmar (largely representing the areas populated by the ethnic Bamars—Burmans). The Republic would be headed by an executive President, elected by the legislature for five years; proposals for the disqualification of any candidate with a foreign spouse or children would prevent Suu Kyi from entering any future presidential election. Reconvening in September, the Convention again stressed that the central role of the military (as 'permanent representatives of the people') be enshrined in the new Constitution. It was proposed that legislative power be shared between a bicameral Pyidaungsu Hluttaw (Union Parliament) and divisional and state assemblies, all of which were to include representatives of the military. The Pyidaungsu Hluttaw was to comprise the Pyithu Hluttaw (House of Representatives) and the Amyotha Hluttaw (House of Nationalities): the former would comprise 330 elected deputies and 110 members of the armed forces, and would be elected for five years. The latter would be constituted with equal numbers of representatives from the proposed seven regions and seven states of the Republic, as well as members of the military, and was to comprise a maximum of 224 deputies. A general election was scheduled for September 1997 (but never held). The session was adjourned in April 1995.

In September 1994, following mediation by a senior Buddhist monk between Suu Kyi and leading members of the SLORC, Suu Kyi was permitted to leave her home to meet Than Shwe and Khin Nyunt. In October Suu Kyi held a second meeting with senior SLORC members. In November it was reported that Suu Kyi had met other detained members of the NLD, including Tin Oo. In January 1995 the SLORC announced that Suu Kyi would be freed only when the new Constitution had been completed; Suu Kyi simultaneously rejected suggestions that she might reach a compromise with the SLORC on the terms for her release. In February leading members of the SLORC held talks in Yangon with an envoy of the UN Secretary-General. In March the Government released 31 political prisoners, including Tin Oo and Kyi Maung.

In July 1995 Suu Kyi was unexpectedly granted an unconditional release from house arrest. The SLORC, which thus hoped to attract greater foreign investment, was in a powerful position: the armed forces were united; political dissent had been effectively suppressed; and cease-fire accords had been reached with nearly all the ethnic insurgent groups. On her release Suu Kyi made a conciliatory speech, urging negotiations with the SLORC and a spirit of compromise. Suu Kyi swiftly reconciled the early leaders of the NLD with the new leadership, which had compromised with the SLORC. Hundreds of supporters gathered daily to hear Suu Kyi speak outside her house in Yangon. Suu Kyi was reinstated as General Secretary of the NLD in October, in a reorganization of the party's executive committee; Tin Oo and Kyi Maung were named Vice-Chairmen. Aung Shwe, who had led the 'legal' NLD and represented the party at the National Convention, was retained as party Chairman.

In November 1995 the National Convention reconvened. The NLD attended the opening session of the Convention, but later withdrew when the SLORC ignored its requests to expand the Convention to make it truly representative. (Suu Kyi was, of course, not a member of the National Convention.) Denouncing the Convention as illegitimate and undemocratic, the NLD for the first time appealed for international support for its cause. The SLORC, which had already begun to imprison NLD supporters for petty crimes, reacted strongly to the NLD boycott, officially expelling the party from the Convention and threatening to 'annihilate' anyone who placed national interests at risk.

In May 1996 more than 260 members of the NLD (mostly delegates elected to the Constituent Assembly in 1990) were arrested prior to the opening of the party's first congress. The majority were detained for the duration of the congress, which only 18 NLD members were able to attend. The congress resolved to draft an alternative constitution. In June the SLORC intensified its action against the NLD with an order banning any organization that held illegal gatherings or obstructed the drafting of the new Constitution by the National Convention; members of a proscribed party could be liable to between five and 20 years' imprisonment. In September police erected road-blocks around Suu Kyi's house, and again detained NLD activists, in order to prevent the holding of a further congress. Suu Kyi's telephone line was disconnected, and she was unable to deliver her regular weekend speech for the first time since her release from house arrest. From October the road-block was resumed each week with the purpose of preventing access to Suu Kyi's speech. The SLORC recommenced talks with NLD officials later that month. However, relations quickly deteriorated following an attack on vehicles in which Suu Kyi and other NLD leaders were travelling.

In October 1996 student action in Yangon, in protest against the detention and brutal treatment of fellow students, prompted further repression and numerous arrests (among those detained was Kyi Maung). This was followed in early December by the largest pro-democracy demonstration since 1988, involving more than 2,000 students. The gathering was dispersed peacefully, although some 600 demonstrators were temporarily detained. Smaller student demonstrations continued sporadically until mid-December, when Suu Kyi was briefly confined to her home, and tanks were deployed in Yangon; university establishments were closed indefinitely. At the end of December some 50 members of the Communist Party of Burma (CPB) and of the NLD were arrested in connection with the protests. In January 1997 14 people, including at least five NLD members, were convicted of involvement in the unrest and sentenced to seven years' imprisonment.

In January 1997 Suu Kyi was allowed to deliver her weekly speech for the first time in three months. However, the SLORC imposed new restrictions on media access to Suu Kyi, and barricades remained outside her home. In March there were further arrests of NLD members, together with an increased army presence in several towns. Also in March a series of attacks on Muslim targets by Buddhist monks took place across the country. These attacks were rumoured to have been organized by opponents within the regime of Myanmar's application to join the Association of South East Asian Nations (ASEAN, see p. 194), in an attempt to alienate Muslim-dominated members of the grouping.

In April 1997 a bomb attack at the home of the Second Secretary of the SLORC, Tin Oo, resulted in the death of his daughter. The Government attributed the bombing to anti-Government groups based in Japan; however, major opposition groups in exile denied involvement in the attack. The attack was rumoured to be related to a power struggle between Khin Nyunt, who was increasingly regarded as a moderate, and the more conservative Commander-in-Chief of the Army and Vice-Chairman of the SLORC, Gen. Maung Aye, who commanded the support of Tin Oo. The detention of NLD members increased during 1997, while government propaganda vilifying the opposition grew more frequent and Suu Kyi's freedom of movement and association remained restricted. In July, however, Khin Nyunt invited the NLD Chairman, Aung Shwe, to a meeting, which constituted the first senior-level contact between the

SLORC and the NLD since the release of Suu Kyi from house arrest in July 1995. The SLORC granted permission for an NLD congress to be held in September 1997.

On 15 November 1997 the ruling junta unexpectedly announced the dissolution of the SLORC and its replacement with the State Peace and Development Council (SPDC). The 19-member SPDC comprised exclusively military personnel; younger regional military commanders were included (largely, it appeared, to prevent them from developing local power bases), while the four most senior members of the SLORC retained their positions at the head of the new junta: Than Shwe was appointed Chairman, Maung Aye Vice-Chairman, Khin Nyunt First Secretary and Tin Oo Second Secretary. A number of former members of the SLORC were ostensibly promoted to an 'Advisory Group', which was subsequently abolished; five members of this group, who had also held positions in the Cabinet, were placed under house arrest in December, pending investigations into allegations of corruption. The SPDC immediately implemented a reorganization of the Cabinet. The new 40-member Cabinet included 25 former ministers, but, in contrast to the SLORC (the members of which had virtually all held cabinet portfolios), only one member of the SPDC, Than Shwe, was appointed to serve concurrently as a cabinet minister. Several supporters of Maung Aye were removed from power. In December the SPDC announced a further cabinet reorganization and the appointment of a new Chairman (the Minister of Hotels and Tourism, Maj.-Gen. Saw Lwin) and Vice-Chairmen of the National Convention Convening Commission; however, the Convention, which had adjourned in March 1996, remained in recess.

Harassment and persecution of members of the NLD and other opposition movements continued throughout 1998. In March 40 people were arrested on charges of complicity in a conspiracy allegedly led by the exiled All-Burma Students Democratic Front (ABSDF, an armed movement formed in 1988 by students within the DAB, which had officially renounced its armed struggle in 1997) to assassinate leaders of the military junta and initiate terrorist attacks on government offices and foreign embassies. The ABSDF, which rejected the allegations, was accused of complicity with the NLD. Six of the accused were sentenced to death at the end of April 1998. However, the SPDC unexpectedly authorized an NLD party congress, attended by 400 delegates, at the end of May to celebrate the eighth anniversary of the general election. In June the NLD demanded that the SPDC reconvene the Pyithu Hluttaw, in accordance with the results of the 1990 election, by 21 August. Some 40 elected NLD representatives were detained at the end of June, and others were forced to sign pledges restricting their freedom of movement. In July the SPDC ordered NLD elected representatives to report to their local police station twice a day and confined them to their townships. During July and August Suu Kyi attempted to visit NLD members outside the city, in an effort to exert pressure on the SPDC to comply with the NLD's demands. On four separate occasions the opposition leader was prevented from continuing her journey by road-blocks set up by the ruling junta. On one such occasion in July Suu Kyi was forcibly returned to her home by security forces after a six-day protest in her car, following government refusals to comply with her demands for the release of detained opposition members and the commencement of substantive dialogue with the NLD. In a further incident, in August, she was returned to her home by ambulance after spending 13 days in her car, prompting considerable international criticism of the SPDC.

Shortly before the NLD's prescribed deadline of 21 August 1998 for convening the Pyithu Hluttaw, the SPDC published an official rejection of the NLD's demands. The NLD responded by declaring its intention unilaterally to convene a 'People's Parliament', which would include elected representatives of all the ethnic minority groups. On the day that Suu Kyi abandoned her protest at the road-block, student demonstrations took place in Yangon (for the first time since December 1996), in support of the NLD's demands. In September 1998 thousands of students staged anti-Government demonstrations, which were dispersed by security forces. Arrests of opposition activists increased dramatically, and by early September 193 elected NLD members of the Pyithu Hluttaw and hundreds of party supporters had been detained. In the same month a 10-member Representative Committee, led by Suu Kyi and Aung Shwe, was established by the NLD to act on behalf of the 'People's Parliament' until a legislature could be convened under the 1990 election law. The Committee asserted that no laws passed by the military junta over the previous 10 years had legal authority, and also demanded the immediate and unconditional release of all political prisoners. Four parties representing Shan, Mon, Arakanese and Zomi ethnic groups expressed their support for the 'People's Parliament', together with the ABSDF. In the same month 15 senior military officers were reportedly arrested for allegedly planning to meet with Suu Kyi, and a number of large pro-Government rallies were held in Yangon. The NLD condemned the alleged use of coercion, intimidation and threats by government military intelligence units to secure the involuntary resignations of vast numbers of NLD members and the closure of a number of regional party headquarters. Following the death in custody in October of a member of the NLD, detained by the SPDC since early in the previous month, the NLD also formally condemned the junta's treatment of detained opposition party members in a letter to Than Shwe. (In August of the same year an elected representative of the NLD, Saw Win, had died in prison while serving an 11-year term of imprisonment, the third NLD member of the Pyithu Hluttaw to die in custody.) In October UN Assistant Secretary-General Alvaro de Soto met with SPDC leaders and also with Suu Kyi during a visit to Myanmar. He reportedly offered large-scale financial and humanitarian aid to the junta in exchange for the initiation of substantive dialogue with the NLD. During October and November about 300 opposition members were released by the Government; however, a further 500 were believed to remain in detention.

In March 1999, despite requests from several foreign Governments, the ruling junta refused to grant a visa to Suu Kyi's terminally ill husband, Michael Aris. The junta instead encouraged Suu Kyi to visit Aris in the United Kingdom; however, Suu Kyi declined to leave the country for fear that she would not be permitted to return. Following Aris's death that month, more than 1,000 supporters of Suu Kyi were permitted to attend a Buddhist ceremony at Suu Kyi's home marking her husband's demise.

In April 1999 the UN adopted a unanimous resolution deploring the escalation in the persecution of the democratic opposition in Myanmar. Nevertheless, the harassment and intimidation of NLD members continued, with the resignations from the party of nearly 300 members reported in July; further resignations were reported in November and in January 2000. In December 1999 it was reported that an elected representative of the People's Assembly, U Maung Maung Myint, had been forced to resign by the ruling SPDC. The lack of political progress by the NLD in 1999 led to the formation of a breakaway faction of the party by a prominent party member, Than Tun, who was subsequently expelled from the NLD.

In August 1999 a series of protests was staged by opposition supporters to mark the anniversary of the massacre of thousands of pro-democracy demonstrators by the military Government in 1988. In October the Supreme Court rejected a claim by the NLD that its activities had been 'continuously disrupted, prevented and destroyed' and that hundreds of its members had been illegally detained. In April 2000 Suu Kyi alleged that more than 40 youth members of the NLD had been arrested by the SPDC for their involvement in party activities.

Opposition radio sources continued to give details of small-scale protests throughout 2000 and 2001. A rare bomb explosion in May 2001 reportedly killed 12 people and injured eight others in a market in Mandalay. In the same month it was reported that religious riots in Toungoo, Bago Division, had led to the deaths of 24 Buddhist monks. The disturbances spread to other towns, prompting allegations that the SPDC had instigated the riots in an attempt to divert public attention from political and economic problems.

In August 2000 Suu Kyi and 14 NLD colleagues attempted to visit members of the party in Kunyangon, a town just outside Yangon. The group was stopped by a military road-block, but refused to return home. A nine-day confrontation finally ended with Suu Kyi and the NLD members being forcibly returned to Yangon. Suu Kyi and eight others were kept under house arrest for the next two weeks. In early September the SPDC ordered a raid on the NLD headquarters, and detained a number of other party leaders in their homes. Undeterred, the NLD announced that it was to draft a new constitution for the country, an act declared illegal in 1996 and punishable by 20 years' imprisonment. Later in the month Suu Kyi attempted to leave Yangon again, this time by train to Mandalay, only to be told that all trains were full. The NLD leader was once again returned home and placed under house arrest, while NLD Vice-Chairman Tin Oo and eight other party workers were taken to a government 'guest house'. Pressure on the NLD increased in October 2000, when a deadline for an eviction order for the party to vacate its premises expired. The landladies responsible for the eviction order had been incarcerated by the SPDC for allowing the NLD to use loudspeakers.

Despite the sustained suppression of the opposition party and the prevention of protest, the SPDC's treatment of its political rivals became markedly more liberal from mid-2000. In July the SPDC reportedly allowed 60,000 university students to resume their education. However, the undergraduate universities were relocated in the suburbs, in order to avoid demonstrations in the city centres that might draw in other civilians. Razali Ismail, a Malaysian diplomat newly appointed as the UN Secretary-General's Special Envoy to Myanmar, was allowed access to Suu Kyi during a four-day visit in October 2000, and in the same month James Mawdsley, a British human rights activist sentenced to 17 years' imprisonment in Myanmar in September 1999, was released (see below).

Conciliation between the SPDC and the NLD was confirmed in January 2001, when it was announced that the two parties had been holding secret talks since the previous October, the first senior-level discussions between the opponents since 1994. Lt-Gen. Khin Nyunt met with Suu Kyi several times. Some analysts feared that the resumption of discussions was merely a ploy by the Government to attract foreign investment, a view supported by the initial lack of progress.

Also in January 2001, in a further placatory gesture, the SPDC ordered the media to stop the regular acrimonious attacks on Suu Kyi and the NLD. The government-controlled Yangon division court dismissed a lawsuit brought by Suu Kyi's US-based brother, Aung San Oo, who claimed ownership of half of Suu Kyi's house. Although foreigners could not buy or transfer property in Myanmar, San Oo had been granted an exemption by the Government in July 2000, and thus requested half the family property according to Myanma inheritance law. In October 2001, however, the court rejected Suu Kyi's application to have her brother's claim dismissed. The hearing was subsequently adjourned on several occasions and in December 2003 was postponed until February 2004. At the end of January 2001 the SPDC released NLD Vice-Chairman Tin Oo and 84 other party supporters, who had been detained since Suu Kyi's attempted train journey in September 2000. A few days later a delegation of the European Union (EU, see p. 255) was permitted to meet with Suu Kyi, as was Dr Paulo Sérgio Pinheiro, UN human rights envoy to Myanmar, in April 2001.

In February 2001 Lt-Gen. Tin Oo, the army chief of staff and, as the Council's Second Secretary, the SPDC's fourth most powerful member, was killed in a helicopter crash, amid rumours of assassination; Lt-Gen. Tin Oo had survived two previous attempts on his life.

In mid-2001, as discussions continued, the Government ordered the release of a number of NLD members from prison and permitted the reopening of the NLD headquarters and several branch offices in Yangon. In August the release of Aung Shwe, Chairman of the NLD, and of Vice-Chairman Tin Oo, was hailed as an indication of progress. Shortly afterwards Ismail held further discussions with Suu Kyi during a visit to Yangon.

In November 2001 two senior army generals—Lt-Gen. Win Myint (widely regarded as the fourth most powerful individual in the country) and Deputy Prime Minister Tin Hla—were dismissed. While no official explanation was given, the two men were under investigation for corruption. As both had expressed only muted support for the ongoing talks with Suu Kyi, there was also speculation that their replacement would be more conducive to the attainment of a political settlement. Two days later the SPDC announced that five government ministers were to retire. While two Deputy Prime Ministers, Rear Adm. Maung Maung Khin and Lt-Gen. Tin Tun, had been expected to relinquish their positions, the other departures had not been foreseen. In the same month Razali Ismail visited the country again. Upon his departure, Ismail expressed satisfaction with the progress that had been made.

In January 2002 it was reported that Suu Kyi had met privately with Gen. Than Shwe for the first time since 1994, raising hopes that the two sides might be close to reaching a breakthrough. However, in February 2002 international pressure on the SPDC to release all remaining political prisoners (an estimated 1,500, according to Amnesty International) and begin a more substantive dialogue with the NLD increased, prompted by the release of a critical report by the US Government (see below). The Myanma Government responded by releasing five further detainees and expressing its confidence that a successful conclusion to the negotiation process was imminent.

In March 2002 the son-in-law and three grandsons of U Ne Win were arrested on charges of plotting to overthrow the Government. It was alleged that they had intended to abduct three government leaders and force them to form a figurehead government under U Ne Win's influence. Four senior military officials—the Commander-in-Chief of the Air Force, Maj.-Gen. Myint Swe, the Chief of Police, Maj.-Gen. Soe Win, and two regional commanders—were dismissed and questioned in connection with the attempted coup. Ne Win and his daughter, Sandar Win, were placed under house arrest. Despite suspicions that the coup allegations were linked to internal conflicts within the military, owing to the insubstantial nature of the evidence gathered to support the charges, in September U Ne Win's four relatives were convicted of high treason and sentenced to death. They entered appeals against the sentences. In December U Ne Win himself died while under house arrest.

In May 2002 Aung San Suu Kyi was finally released from house arrest. The SPDC stated that her release was unconditional and that it would not attempt to impose any restrictions upon her travel. Suu Kyi travelled to Mandalay without incident in June. In August Razali Ismail returned to the country with the intention of promoting further political dialogue between the NLD and the SPDC, but made little progress. Meanwhile, Suu Kyi challenged the SPDC to prove its commitment to the achievement of democracy by ordering the release of all political prisoners. In the following month a delegation from the EU visited Myanmar and met with Suu Kyi, but failed to secure a meeting with any members of the SPDC. In November the junta announced the release of 115 prisoners, the largest number to have been freed since negotiations began.

In early 2003 representatives from Amnesty International were permitted to enter Myanmar for the first time and to hold talks with Suu Kyi. Following the visit, the human rights organization condemned Myanmar's judicial system. Meanwhile, 12 political activists in the country were arrested on suspicion of planning anti-Government activities. In February it was reported that Suu Kyi wanted economic sanctions to be maintained against the Myanma Government until it began a meaningful dialogue with the opposition. In the same month it was announced that Lt-Gen. Soe Win would assume the previously vacant post of Second Secretary of the SPDC. Meanwhile, the Minister of Health, Maj.-Gen. Ket Sein, and the Minister of Finance and Revenue, U Khin Maung Thein, were permitted to retire. They were replaced, respectively, by Dr Kyaw Myint and Maj.-Gen. Hla Tun. In the following month UN envoy Paulo Sérgio Pinheiro restated a UN demand that the junta release all remaining political prisoners, estimated to number 1,200, and enter into serious dialogue with the opposition. Later in that month a bomb exploded in Yangon, killing one person, during celebrations being held to commemorate Armed Forces Day. An unexploded bomb was also discovered near the US embassy on the same day.

In April 2003 Suu Kyi issued a rare criticism of the SPDC for refusing to enter into any substantive dialogue with the opposition. In May 10 members of the NLD were imprisoned on charges that they had organized public protests and participated in clandestine activities. Later in the same month the political situation in Myanmar deteriorated further when violent confrontations occurred in the town of Ye-u, in the north of the country, between government supporters and opposition members travelling with an entourage conveying Suu Kyi. While the SPDC insisted that the violence had been provoked by the opposition, it was subsequently reported that the clashes had occurred when Suu Kyi and her supporters were ambushed and attacked by pro-Government forces. It was estimated that around 80 members of the entourage had died as a result. On the following day it was reported that Suu Kyi had been taken into 'protective custody' by the SPDC; meanwhile, the headquarters of the NLD, together with NLD offices across the country, were closed down, 17 other members of the NLD were also detained, and all universities under the control of the Ministry of Education were shut indefinitely. UN envoy Razali Ismail proceeded with a planned visit to Myanmar in June, when he was permitted to meet with Suu Kyi. The junta's detention of Suu Kyi prompted widespread international criticism. At a meeting of ASEAN ministers of foreign affairs held later in that month the organization departed from its traditional policy of non-interference in the affairs of other member states, urging Suu Kyi's release and a peaceful transition to democratic practices. Later in June, following the failure of its appeal to the SPDC for the release of Suu Kyi, the country's largest aid donor, Japan, announced that it had suspended all economic aid. In July the Government announced that it had freed 91 of the NLD activists detained after the violence of May and permitted a delegation from the International Committee of the Red Cross (ICRC) to visit Suu Kyi; the delegates subsequently confirmed that she was in good health, contradicting reports from the US Department of State, which claimed that she had gone on a hunger strike.

In July 2003 it was reported that three cabinet ministers—Minister of Industry (No. 1) U Aung Thaung, Minister of Forestry Aung Phone and Minister of Agriculture and Irrigation Maj.-Gen. Nyunt Tin—had all been dismissed. In late August a major reorganization of the Government was announced, during which the former First Secretary of the SPDC, Lt.-Gen. Khin Nyunt, replaced Field Marshal Than Shwe as Prime Minister. However, Than Shwe remained as Chairman of the SPCD and retained the defence portfolio. Lt.-Gen. Soe Win became First Secretary and was replaced as Second Secretary by Lt-Gen. Thein Sein. Khin Nyunt subsequently announced that the Government intended to reconvene the National Convention, which had been in recess since 1996, in order to draw up a new constitution.

In September 2003 it was announced that Aung San Suu Kyi had returned to her home and was being held under house arrest, having undergone major surgery in hospital. A visit to Myanmar by Razali Ismail in the following month failed to secure her release or to end the political deadlock. Paulo Sérgio Pinheiro returned to the country in late October. In November five members of the NLD's Central Executive Committee, who had been held in connection with the violence in May, were released. In December nine people were sentenced to death, having been convicted of high treason; they were among 12 people arrested in July for allegedly plotting to overthrow the ruling junta. (Four of the nine people subsequently had their sentences commuted to two years' imprisonment on appeal, and that of another was reduced to five years' imprisonment, while the remaining four were to serve sentences of life imprisonment.) In January 2004 the release of a further 26 members of the NLD was announced and, in the following month, Vice-Chairman of the NLD Tin Oo was placed under house arrest, having been imprisoned since May 2003. Also in January 2004, following a meeting with government officials, representatives from 25 ethnic groups and alliances rejected the proposed 'road map' to democracy outlined by Prime Minister Gen. Khin Nyunt in August 2003 and reiterated demands for the Government to begin talks with the opposition. However, following a visit to the country in March 2004, Razali Ismail expressed confidence that the SPDC would adhere to the 'road map'. In April the SPDC released the NLD's Chairman, Aung Shwe, and its Secretary, U Lwin, who had both been under house arrest since May 2003, and allowed the party's headquarters to reopen.

The National Convention was reconvened in mid-May 2004, despite a boycott by some ethnic minority groups and the NLD, which demanded that the SPDC release Suu Kyi and Tin Oo from house arrest and reopen the party's branch offices. More than 1,000 delegates attended the opening session, which was chaired by Lt-Gen. Thein Sein, the SPDC Second Secretary. It was emphasized that the Convention was to be a continuation of the discussions held between 1993 and 1996, at which a number of constitutional provisions had already been drafted (see above). Strict regulations governing the conduct of the delegates were imposed by the SPDC. The National Convention was adjourned in July 2004. In August courts in Yangon and Mandalay refused to accept petitions from the NLD for the release of Suu Kyi and Tin Oo, and for the reopening of the party's branch offices. Shortly afterwards the UN Secretary-General, Kofi Annan, released a statement urging the Myanma Government to free Suu Kyi and to hold substantive talks with the NLD and other political parties, noting that the National Convention would otherwise lack credibility. Meanwhile, Razali Ismail had been unable to return to Myanmar since his visit in March, as the authorities had rejected his requests for a visa. In September four members of the NLD were reportedly convicted of threatening national security and sentenced to seven years' imprisonment.

In mid-September 2004 a cabinet reorganization took place. The civilian Minister of Foreign Affairs, U Win Aung, and his deputy, Khin Maung Win, were replaced by senior military officers, Maj.-Gen. Nyan Win and Col Maung Myint, respectively. Amid reports of a power struggle within the SPDC, Khin Nyunt was removed from the premiership and from his position as Chief of Military Intelligence in October, and was placed under house arrest, apparently owing to his alleged involvement in corruption related to smuggling by military intelligence staff. Lt-Gen. Soe Win was appointed as Prime Minister, while Lt-Gen. Thein Sein replaced Soe Win as First Secretary of the SPDC. The National Intelligence Bureau was abolished, and associates of Khin Nyunt, including several members of his family and many military intelligence officers, were subsequently arrested. In November it was reported that three senior military intelligence officers had been convicted of corruption charges and sentenced to 22 years' imprisonment, and that 12 senior judicial officials, who were either linked to Khin Nyunt or had resisted the removal of those loyal to the former Prime Minister, had been dismissed. Meanwhile, in early November the SPDC announced that the Minister of Home Affairs, Col Tin Hlaing, the Minister of Science and Technology and of Labour, Tin Win, and four deputy ministers had been permitted to retire. It was reported that Tin Hlaing, an ally of Khin Nyunt, had also been placed under house arrest.

In late November 2004 the SPDC ordered the release of 9,248 prisoners who, it claimed, had been wrongly imprisoned owing to improper conduct by the dissolved National Intelligence Bureau. However, according to the opposition, the mass amnesty included only 43 of an estimated 1,300 political prisoners held by the authorities. Moreover, the NLD announced that Aung San Suu Kyi's detention under house arrest had been extended for at least a further year. In mid-December the SPDC freed a further 5,070 prisoners, 11 of whom were reported to be political prisoners, including the Chairman of the Democracy Party, U Thu Wai. However, a number of NLD members were arrested in the same month for allegedly inciting public unrest. In January 2005 widespread rumours of a gun battle involving Maung Aye, Than Shwe, Soe Win and their aides, which were prompted by the unexplained death of Maung Aye's personal assistant, Lt-Col Bo Win Tun, appeared to be unfounded, although speculation about tension within the leadership continued. In the same month it was reported that four associates of Khin Nyunt who had been arrested in October 2004 had died in detention, while the closed trials of some 300 others on corruption charges had commenced in a prison in Yangon. The National Convention resumed in mid-February 2005, again without the participation of the NLD and several ethnic minority groups and amid criticism from the EU, the UN and the USA. A few days earlier Tin Oo's detention under house arrest had been extended for a further year.

Following months of speculation, in July 2005 it was announced at the ASEAN Ministerial Meeting held in the Laotian capital of Vientiane that Myanmar was to relinquish the chair of ASEAN, which it had been due to assume in 2006. Myanmar had recently come under increasing pressure from the international community, and in particular from the other member states of ASEAN (a notable departure from the organization's usual policy of non-interference in the internal affairs of members), to forgo its turn to assume the rotating chair in order to enable the Myanma Government instead to focus its attention on addressing the country's human rights situation. Also in July 2005 former Prime Minister Khin Nyunt was convicted on eight charges, including corruption and bribery, and was given a suspended prison sentence of 44 years; his two sons were also convicted and sentenced to prison terms. In the same month the Government authorized the release of dozens of political prisoners; however, in September the UN Special Rapporteur for human rights in Myanmar, Paulo Sérgio Pinheiro, stated in an address to the UN General Assembly that approximately 1,100 dissidents remained in detention in Myanmar. Pinheiro's report was based on information derived from various independent sources, as Pinheiro himself had been repeatedly refused entry to Myanmar since November 2003. In August 2005 UN Special Envoy to Myanmar Ali Alatas had been allowed to visit the country, the first special envoy to be granted entry since Razali Ismail in March 2004.

Meanwhile, in August 2005 the World Food Programme (WFP) published a report stating that one-third of young children in Myanmar were malnourished; in some border areas afflicted by fighting between rival ethnic rebel groups, the figure was believed to be as high as 60%. The report also noted with concern the high number of Myanma children who received little or no formal education. In September Amnesty International released a report detailing the 'unacceptable' use by the military of tens of thousands of ethnic minority citizens to carry out forced labour;

MYANMAR

Introductory Survey

the report also drew attention to the military's use of physical abuse against such labourers.

In November 2005 the Government announced that it had initiated the first phase of a relocation of the country's administrative capital from Yangon to Pyinmana, a sparsely populated mountainous region approximately 400 km (nearly 250 miles) to the north of Yangon. Minister of Information Brig.-Gen. Kyaw Hsan announced that the decision to move to Pyinmana had been made owing to its central location and resultant ease of access to and from other parts of the country. The new administrative centre was officially named Nay Pyi Taw in March 2006. Also in November 2005 the NLD announced that Aung San Suu Kyi's detention under house arrest had again been extended by an additional 12 months.

In January 2006, after having being refused access to the country for almost two years, Razali Ismail, the UN Secretary-General's Special Envoy to Myanmar, relinquished his post. In a statement announcing his decision to resign, Ismail urged ASEAN to adopt a more forceful role in exerting pressure for democratic reform in Myanmar. Earlier in that month the US-based organization Human Rights Watch had dismissed the junta's pledges of democratic reform as 'empty rhetoric'. In late January the SPDC adjourned a session of the National Convention, with a view to reconvening towards the end of 2006. In February the former Minister of Foreign Affairs, U Win Aung, went on trial in Yangon, charged with corruption and bribery; in April he was convicted and sentenced to seven years' imprisonment. Meanwhile, in February the detention under house arrest of Tin Oo was again extended by a further year. In May UN envoy Ibrahim Gambari was permitted to enter the country, holding discussions with Than Shwe and attending a brief meeting with Suu Kyi. The visit was regarded by many as a positive development, partly because Gambari had been allowed access to Suu Kyi but also owing to Gambari's conclusion that SPDC leaders seemed willing to strengthen links with the international community. Later in the month UN Secretary-General Kofi Annan urged Than Shwe to free Suu Kyi; on the following day, however, her term of house arrest was extended for a further year. At the end of September the UN Security Council reviewed the human rights situation in Myanmar for the first time. Gambari paid a second visit to Myanmar in November and was again allowed to hold a brief meeting with Suu Kyi, who, according to Gambari, welcomed discourse between the UN and the Government of Myanmar. In January 2007 a draft resolution urging the Myanma Government to release all political prisoners and end its violation of human rights was submitted to the UN Security Council, sponsored by the USA and the United Kingdom. However, the resolution was defeated when, in an unusual development, both the People's Republic of China and Russia, two of the five permanent members of the Security Council, exercised their right of veto.

Meanwhile, in April 2006 the ABSDF, the Federation of Trade Unions—Burma (FTUB), the NCGUB and the National League for Democracy—Liberated Area (NLD—LA) were denounced as terrorist organizations by the Government, in relation to bomb attacks and attempted bombings in 2000–06. Several cabinet changes were implemented in May 2006: the Minister of Culture, Maj.-Gen. Kyi Aung, retired and was replaced by Khin Aung Myint, while the Minister of Immigration and Population and of Social Welfare, Relief and Resettlement, Maj.-Gen. Sein Htwa, was replaced by Maj.-Gen. Maung Maung Swe. Col Zaw Min, hitherto Minister of Co-operatives, became Minister of Electric Power (No. 1), succeeding Maj.-Gen. Tin Htut, who assumed responsibility for the co-operatives portfolio; the hotels and tourism portfolio was allocated to Maj.-Gen. Soe Naing, a new appointee to the Cabinet. In June a Supreme Court judge and several deputy ministers were said to have retired, prompting speculation that they had been dismissed. The National Convention reconvened in October. The admission of the foreign press to the proceedings represented progress to some observers, but the absence of the NLD and the relatively small number of delegates from other political parties did not bode well for democratic reform. In early January 2007 it was reported that the SPDC had released 2,831 prisoners, including some 30 political prisoners, in an amnesty to mark Independence Day. However, the detention under house arrest of Tin Oo was extended for a further year in the following month, as was that of Suu Kyi in late May, despite ongoing international pressure for their release. More than 50 people were arrested in mid-May while attending prayer vigils in support of Suu Kyi; most of the detainees had been freed by late June.

In May 2007 Lt-Gen. Thein Sein, the First Secretary of the SPDC, assumed the role of Prime Minister in an acting capacity, amid conjecture about Lt-Gen. Soe Win's health. The final session of the National Convention commenced in July and was formally closed in September. Thein Sein announced that the Convention had adopted detailed principles for a new constitution. As proposed in the 1994 sessions (see above), legislative power was to be vested in a bicameral Pyidaungsu Hluttaw, comprising the Pyithu Hluttaw and the Amyotha Hluttaw, with 25% of the seats to be allocated to representatives of the military nominated by the Commander-in-Chief of the Armed Forces. The principles approved by the Convention provided for the election of the President by members of the Pyidaungsu Hluttaw, from among three Vice-Presidents selected by an electoral college. The Commander-in-Chief of the Armed Forces was also to designate the government ministers responsible for defence, security, home affairs and border affairs, and was to assume executive, legislative and judicial power in the event of a state of emergency being declared. A 54-member commission, chaired by Chief Justice U Aung Toe, was appointed by the SPDC in October to draft the new Constitution and commenced work in December without the participation of the opposition.

Meanwhile, substantial unexpected increases in fuel prices in mid-August 2007 provoked a series of anti-Government protests in Yangon and other towns. More than 60 demonstrators had been arrested by the end of the month; those detained included leaders of the '88 Generation' students' group who had participated in the 1988 pro-democracy uprising. The protests escalated in September 2007 with the involvement of Buddhist monks. In early September, during two days of demonstrations in Pakokku, in central Myanmar, monks held some 20 government officials captive for several hours after the security forces had forcibly dispersed some 300–400 monks, detaining around 10 and injuring several. On 9 September the Alliance of All Burmese Buddhist Monks, a previously unknown group, made a series of demands to the SPDC—an apology for the force used in Pakokku, a reduction in commodity and fuel prices, the release of all political prisoners and those detained for participating in the recent protests, and the initiation of a dialogue with pro-democracy forces—threatening to withdraw all religious services from the authorities if they did not comply by 17 September. The SPDC accused the NLD and 'external groups' of instigating the unrest. Some of the marches were allowed to proceed peacefully, but on 18 September tear gas was used to disperse a rally of some 1,000 monks and other citizens in the western town of Sittwe. Meanwhile, with the monks' demands unfulfilled, daily marches commenced in Yangon. The Alliance of All Burmese Buddhist Monks issued a statement describing the military Government as 'the enemy of the people' and pledging to continue protesting until the Government was removed from office. On 22 September, the sixth consecutive day of demonstrations in Yangon, Suu Kyi made a brief public appearance when the monks were permitted to pass the house in which she was confined. On the same day up to 10,000 monks were reported to have marched in Mandalay. Around 150 Buddhist nuns joined some 5,000 monks on 23 September in Yangon, and on the following day the largest protest yet was held in the city, attended by an estimated 50,000–100,000 monks and civilians, including NLD leaders, while demonstrations also took place in more than 20 other towns.

Having thus far exercised relative restraint in response to the protests, on 25 September 2007 the SPDC imposed a night-time curfew in Yangon and Mandalay, banned gatherings of more than five people and deployed armed troops on the streets. On the following day, as up to 10,000 monks and other protesters defied government warnings to halt the marches, troops fired live ammunition, reportedly killing up to five people. Some 200 monks were later reportedly detained in overnight raids on several monasteries, during which many were allegedly beaten. Two NLD members were also arrested. The UN Security Council expressed concern at the situation in an emergency meeting, but China, Myanmar's closest ally, rejected a US proposal to consider the imposition of sanctions against the Myanma authorities. Despite the rising tension, anti-Government protests continued on 27–28 September, but were violently suppressed. The Government claimed that 10 people had died as a result of the violence (later increasing this figure to 15), but diplomats and witnesses reported that the death toll was much higher, with some estimating that up to 200 had been killed. As international condemnation of the military action mounted, the Myanma authorities sought to block telecommunications networks. By the end of the month the uprising had been largely quashed, with many monks in detention, while others were reportedly being prevented from leaving their monasteries. During October the security forces continued to arrest those suspected of involvement in the street protests, and reports emerged of ill-treatment in detention centres, including claims that an NLD member had died as a result of being tortured in custody. In mid-October the authorities announced that 2,927 protesters (including 596 monks) had been arrested since 26 September, 2,459 of whom had been released after pledging not to participate in further demonstrations. However, other estimates suggested that some 6,000 people had been detained, including 2,400 monks. (In December the UN human rights envoy to Myanmar, Paulo Sérgio Pinheiro, reported that at least 31 people had died and that 3,000–4,000 people had been arrested in September and October, 500–1,000 of whom were still in detention; according to the security forces, only 80 people, including 21 monks, remained in custody at this time.) Meanwhile, the curfew in Yangon and Mandalay was removed on 20 October. At the end of the month more than 100 monks marched through Pakokku, their progress reportedly unimpeded by the security forces.

UN envoy Ibrahim Gambari visited Myanmar in late September 2007, initially holding discussions with acting Prime Minister Thein Sein and other government ministers, as well as with Suu Kyi, and in early October he was finally permitted to meet Than Shwe and Maung Aye. The SPDC agreed to Gambari's recommendation that a government official be appointed to enter into dialogue with Suu Kyi, assigning this role (Minister of Relations) to the Deputy Minister of Labour, U Aung Kyi. Than Shwe had reportedly told Gambari that he would be willing to meet Suu Kyi personally, but only if she withdrew her support for international sanctions against his regime and abandoned her 'confrontational attitude'. In mid-October the UN Security Council unanimously adopted a statement deploring the use of violence against peaceful demonstrators, calling for the early release of all political prisoners and remaining detainees, and urging the Government to create the necessary conditions for a 'genuine dialogue' with Suu Kyi. WFP reported that it was able to assist only 500,000 of some 5m. people who were suffering food shortages in Myanmar, and urged the Myanma Government to pursue reforms aimed at reducing poverty.

Thein Sein was formally appointed Prime Minister in late October 2007, following Soe Win's death earlier in that month, and was replaced as First Secretary of the SPDC by Lt-Gen. Thiha Thura Tin Aung Myint Oo. At the same time U Aung Kyi was promoted to the position of Minister of Labour, while retaining responsibility for liaising with Suu Kyi. On the following day Aung Kyi and Suu Kyi held their first talks.

In early November 2007 the Myanma Government announced the expulsion of Charles Petrie, the most senior UN official resident in the country. Petrie had recently publicly linked the pro-democracy protests to economic hardship and a 'deteriorating humanitarian situation'. Shortly afterwards Gambari arrived for a further visit, during which he held discussions with the Prime Minister and Suu Kyi, although not with Than Shwe. It was reported by the Myanma state media that the SPDC had rejected an offer by Gambari to mediate in the dialogue between Suu Kyi and Aung Kyi. However, following the visit, Gambari issued a statement on behalf of Suu Kyi, in which she declared her willingness to co-operate with the SPDC 'in the interest of the nation'. A second meeting subsequently took place between Aung Kyi and Suu Kyi, who was also permitted to meet other members of the NLD for the first time in more than three years. In mid-November the UN Secretary-General, Ban Ki-Moon, urged the SPDC to conduct a 'meaningful and substantive dialogue' with the opposition, amid some scepticism among diplomats and other observers regarding the junta's commitment to genuine dialogue aimed at democratic reform. In early December the Government announced that it had granted amnesty to 8,585 prisoners since mid-November to mark the conclusion of the National Convention, although it was reported that only 10 were political detainees. Suu Kyi held two rounds of talks with Aung Kyi in January 2008, and was also permitted to meet NLD colleagues again at the end of the month, after which the party announced that its General Secretary was not satisfied with the progress of the dialogues. Meanwhile, in mid-January the UN Security Council expressed regret at the slow rate of progress towards meeting the objectives outlined in its October statement (i.e. the release of political prisoners and dialogue with Suu Kyi), and urged Myanmar to allow another visit by Gambari. In late January Amnesty International claimed that 96 pro-democracy activists had been arrested since November 2007, increasing the total number in detention to 1,850, of whom 700 were accused of participating in the August and September protests. A few days later 10 activists, including Min Ko Naing and Ko Ko Gyi of the '88 Generation' students' group, were reportedly charged with making illegal statements.

In February 2008 the SPDC unexpectedly announced that a constitutional referendum would be held in May, followed by multi-party elections in 2010. Chief Justice Aung Toe subsequently confirmed that his commission had completed the draft constitution. The NLD expressed surprise that elections had been planned before the results of the constitutional referendum were known. A few days later the detention under house arrest of Tin Oo was again extended by a further year; Suu Kyi's house arrest was similarly extended in May. Ibrahim Gambari returned to Myanmar in March, meeting Suu Kyi and several government officials, the most senior of whom was the Minister of Information, Brig.-Gen. Kyaw Hsan. However, no apparent progress was made during the visit, with the Government rejecting Gambari's proposal that independent observers be allowed to monitor the forthcoming referendum and refusing to consider amending the draft constitution to allow Suu Kyi to contest elections. Suu Kyi reportedly refused to meet with Gambari during the envoy's visit to Myanmar in August, arousing speculation about her dissatisfaction with the pace of developments. The newly appointed UN Special Rapporteur, Tomás Ojea Quintana, also paid a visit in that month. In his subsequent report, Ojea Quintana recommended the implementation of four major elements of reform prior to the holding of an election: the revision of domestic legislation governing fundamental rights; the release of all political prisoners (who were estimated to total more than 2,000); reform of the military; and the transition to a fully independent judiciary.

In early May 2008 the devastating Cyclone Nargis struck southern Myanmar. Yangon and four other regions, including the Ayeyarwady (Irrawaddy) Delta were declared disaster areas. The Government was criticized for its weak response to the developing crisis and for the restrictions it imposed on international aid efforts, which exacerbated the difficulties of the survivors, many of whom had no access to clean drinking water, food or shelter. Although some provisions supplied by the UN and foreign donors were eventually allowed into the country, the Government refused entry to foreign aid workers. In mid-May the UN Secretary-General, Ban Ki-Moon, stated that the Government's reaction to the disaster had been 'unacceptably slow'. By late June the official death toll had risen to more than 84,500. However, the ICRC had suggested that the number of fatalities might be as high as 128,000, while the UN estimated that 2.5m. people had been affected by Cyclone Nargis. In July ASEAN estimated the cost of disaster relief and longer-term reconstruction to be close to US $1,000m.

Meanwhile, the text of the draft constitution went on sale at government bookshops in early April 2008. The draft included the changing of the country's official name to the 'Republic of the Union of Myanmar'. Also reportedly enshrined in the draft was the ultimate establishment of a multi-party democracy. Nevertheless, a significant role for the military in future governments was envisaged, with military appointees to be allocated some 25% of seats in both chambers of the proposed legislature. Under another constitutional requirement, Suu Kyi's marriage to a foreign citizen would disqualify her from contesting elections. Despite the widespread destruction caused by Cyclone Nargis, which prompted the Government to postpone the constitutional referendum in the affected regions, the poll proceeded as scheduled in other areas on 10 May. Reporters without Borders, an international group campaigning for press freedom, claimed that debate on the referendum had been subject to severe restrictions. According to official reports, turn-out was high, at 99%, with 92.4% of voters endorsing the new Constitution, thereby completing the ratification process. Observers were sceptical about the validity of the results. In late 2008 Than Shwe confirmed that his regime's so-called 'road map' to democracy was progressing, with an election scheduled for 2010.

In June 2008 reorganizations took place within the cabinet and the military. Vice-Admiral Soe Thein, hitherto the Commander-in-Chief of the Navy, was appointed Minister of Industry (No. 2), while the Minister of Immigration and Population and of Social Welfare, Relief and Resettlement, Maj.-Gen. Maung Maung Swe, was transferred to a new post-cyclone management and resettlement portfolio. Five senior-level generals also reportedly retired. Media sources suggested that further changes would be implemented in anticipation of the

2010 election, with reports of the resignation of the Minister of Immigration and Population, Maj.-Gen. Saw Lwin, and the Minister of Construction, Maj.-Gen. Saw Tun, in early 2009. The Minister of Home Affairs, Maj.-Gen. Maung Oo, was said to have assumed responsibility for the former portfolio, while the latter was transferred to the Minister of Electric Power (No. 2), Maj.-Gen. Khin Maung Myint, although official confirmation of the reorganization was not forthcoming.

On the 20th anniversary of the 1988 pro-democracy uprising, several protesters were arrested in Taunggok in August 2008. Tensions rose in Yangon and surrounding areas as the anniversary of the September 2007 protests approached, with bomb explosions resulting in several fatalities in September 2008; large numbers of dissidents were thought to remain in custody. Also in September, the junta announced a large-scale amnesty involving as many as 9,000 detainees. Among those released was Win Tin, a senior political activist and founding member of the NLD who had been imprisoned for 19 years; however, in early October Ohn Kyaing, another veteran NLD member, was detained. This was followed by the culmination of dozens of trials that had begun in July, with the sentencing of more than a hundred activists and dissidents in November. Many defendants received substantial prison terms, some as long as 65 years, which were criticized as being unduly harsh. Those convicted included senior members of the '88 Generation', the NLD and monks' groups who were accused of having organized and participated in the September 2007 uprising. A well-known comedian, Zarganar (Maung Thura), who had organized relief efforts in the aftermath of the cyclone disaster, was convicted of the violation of electronic communications laws and sentenced to 59 years' imprisonment. In discussions with Ibrahim Gambari in Yangon in early February 2009, Suu Kyi reportedly criticized the trial process and suggested that the UN Secretary-General's visit should be conditional upon the freeing of political prisoners. Tomás Ojea Quintana also returned to Myanmar in February, and during his six-day mission he was granted access to a number of political detainees, including some held in the notorious Insein Prison in Yangon. His itinerary also incorporated the Karen (renamed Kayin in 1989), Rakhine and northern Kachin regions (see below).

In May 2009, shortly before her term of house arrest was due to expire, Suu Kyi was removed from her home and taken to Insein Prison, following an unauthorized visit to her residence by an uninvited US citizen who had gained access by swimming across the adjacent lake. It was then announced that Suu Kyi was to be tried on charges of violating the conditions of her house arrest. Despite appeals from the UN Secretary-General and numerous world leaders for Suu Kyi's immediate release, her trial opened soon afterwards.

After Burma gained independence in 1948, various groups conducted armed insurgency campaigns against government forces. The most effective of the ethnic-based insurgency groups was the Karen (Kayin) National Union (KNU), founded in 1948, which led a protracted campaign for the establishment of an independent state for the Karen ethnic group (restyled Kayin in the transliteration changes of 1989), partly through the activities of its military wing, the Karen (Kayin) National Liberation Army (KNLA). The KNU was a member of the National Democratic Front (NDF), an organization which at one time comprised 11 ethnic minority groups—including Kachin, Karenni (Kayinni), Mon, Shan, Pa-O, Palaung, Wa, Arakanese (Rakhine) and Lahu parties—formed in 1975 (by five groups, originally) with the aim of making Burma a federal union and opposing both the Government and, initially, the CPB. The CPB was one of the most well-organized insurgent movements, in military terms, and gained control of significant areas in northern Burma. By May 1986 the various minority groups in the NDF had agreed to relinquish their individual demands for autonomy, in favour of a unified demand for a federal system of government. At the same time, the CPB withdrew its demand for a 'one-party' government and entered into an alliance with the NDF. At the second NDF Congress, in June 1987, Maj.-Gen. Bo Mya, the President of the KNU and Chief of Staff of the KNLA, was replaced as NDF President by Saw Maw Reh, a former Chairman of the Karenni (Kayinni) National Progressive Party (KNPP), and further leadership changes removed all KNU representatives from senior NDF positions. The new NDF leaders advocated the establishment of autonomous, ethnic-based states within a Burmese union.

The insurgent groups were sympathetic to anti-Government movements in the major cities. Continued attacks throughout 1988 engaged the government forces in the border areas, leaving fewer of them to impose order in the towns. In September the Karen announced plans to co-operate with protesting students and Buddhist monks to work towards the achievement of democracy. After the armed forces seized power, insurgents intensified operations, aided by at least 3,000 students whom the Karen rebels agreed to train and arm. In November 22 anti-Government groups, led by members of the NDF, formed the DAB. Bo Mya was elected President.

In April 1989 dissatisfaction with the leadership of the CPB led to a mutiny by Wa tribesmen, who constituted an estimated 80%–90% of the CPB's membership. Rebellious Wa soldiers captured the CPB headquarters, and the party's leaders were forced into exile in China. The leaders of the mutiny subsequently accepted SLORC proposals for the former forces of the CPB army to become government-controlled militia forces in exchange for supplies of rice, financial support and development aid. The former CPB troops agreed to use their main forces against the 25,000-strong rebel separatist Mong Tai (Shan State) Army (formerly the Shan United Army), whose leader, Khun Sa, controlled much of the drug trade in the 'Golden Triangle', the world's major opium-producing area, where the borders of Myanmar, Laos and Thailand meet. The SLORC also approached members of the NDF, and was successful in securing agreements with the Shan State Progressive Party in September 1989, the Pa-O National Organization in March 1991 and the Palaung State Liberation Organization in May of that year. In July, at the third NDF Congress, these three movements were expelled, reducing the NDF's membership to eight organizations, and Nai Shwe Kyin was elected as the NDF's new President.

In December 1988, following a visit by the Prime Minister of Thailand, the SLORC granted licences to Thai business interests to exploit raw materials in Burma, in return for much-needed foreign exchange. Although there was no announcement of any official Thai-Burmese agreement, subsequent offensives by government forces against rebel groups achieved unprecedented success, with troops frequently attacking insurgent bases from Thai territory. By December 1989 six KNU bases along the Thai border had been captured, and in January 1990 two more camps, harbouring a large number of student dissidents, were seized. In January 1990 the armed forces launched an offensive against Mon separatists. In February they succeeded in capturing Three Pagodas Pass, a principal 'black market' trade route between Thailand and Myanmar, and the headquarters of the New Mon State Party.

Intense fighting between government and rebel forces continued as the KNLA advanced into the lower central Ayeyarwady Delta in late 1991. This potentially diversionary tactic failed to prevent a concerted attempt by government troops to seize control of the KNU and DAB headquarters, which was also the seat of the NCGUB. However, despite the use of sophisticated weaponry purchased from China, government troops failed to capture the camp at Manerplaw. In March 1992 the Thai Government fulfilled prior threats of strong retaliation, forcing hundreds of Myanma troops out of entrenched positions taken up in order to attack the KNU headquarters from the rear. In April the SLORC officially suspended its offensive against the KNU, 'in the interests of national unity'. In October, however, government troops resumed hostilities, making several incursions into Thai territory. In December the Thai and Myanma Governments agreed to 'relocate' the Myanma armed forces, and in February 1993 they resolved to demarcate their common border.

In February and March 1993 the Kachin Independence Organization (KIO) attended peace talks with the Government in the Kachin state capital of Myitkyina. The Kachins were in a vulnerable position, since they were no longer able to obtain arms from the practically defunct CPB or through Thailand (as the Mong Tai Army controlled the territory between Kachin encampments and the Thai border). The SLORC was anxious to reach an accommodation with the Kachins, as the NCGUB would be severely weakened by the loss of their support (although a de facto national cease-fire had been in effect since October 1992). The KIO appeared to have signed a peace agreement in April but, owing to attempts by the Kachins to persuade other members of the DAB to enter discussions with the SLORC, the cease-fire was not announced until October. The agreement was ratified in Yangon in February 1994. The KIO was suspended from the DAB in October 1993 for negotiating separately with the SLORC, and the DAB reiterated its conditions for discussions with the

SLORC in a series of open letters. Its stipulations included: the recognition of the DAB as a single negotiating body (the SLORC insisted on meeting each ethnic group separately); the location of the negotiating process in a neutral country; an immediate end to the forcible mass relocation of villagers; a new body to draft a constitution; and the release of all political detainees, beginning with Suu Kyi. However, under Thai pressure, the DAB policy of negotiating as a front was unofficially abandoned. In February 2001, ostensibly owing to ill health, Chairman Lt-Gen. Zau Mai was replaced by his deputy, Maj.-Gen. Tu Jai.

In May 1994 the Karenni (Kayinni) National People's Liberation Front concluded a cease-fire agreement with the SLORC, reportedly the 11th insurgent group to do so. This was followed in July by the declaration of a cease-fire by the Kayan New Land Party, and in October by the declaration of a cease-fire by the Shan State Nationalities Liberation Organization. In December government forces launched a new offensive against the KNU, recapturing its headquarters at Manerplaw in January 1995 (and forcing many hundreds of KNU fighters across the border into Thailand). The virtual defeat of the KNU forces was attributed to their reportedly severe lack of ammunition and funds and also to the recent defection from the Christian-led KNU of a mainly Buddhist faction, which established itself as the Democratic Karen (Kayin) Buddhist Army (DKBA). The DKBA, which had comprised about 10% of the strength of the KNLA, allegedly supported the government forces in their offensive. In February 1995 the Myanma army captured the KNU's last stronghold, and in the following month Bo Mya resigned as the Commander-in-Chief of the KNLA (although he remained the leader of the KNU). In March the KNU declared a unilateral cease-fire, with the aim of initiating negotiations with the SLORC. Earlier in the month the KNPP reportedly became the 14th ethnic insurgent group to abandon its armed struggle against the SLORC. This agreement collapsed in June, however, as government troops entered areas designated in the accord to be under KNPP control. In August 5,000 troops were dispatched to suppress the KNPP rebellion. Clashes continued throughout the year, and in January 1996 government forces captured a major Kayinni stronghold. However, the KNPP continued fighting, with support from the ABSDF. In February 1996 talks between the KNU and the SLORC in Mawlamyine (Moulmein), calling for tripartite negotiations between the NLD, the NCGUB (which had re-elected Sein Win as its head in Sweden in July 1995) and the SLORC, were inconclusive.

Further talks between the SLORC and the KNU began in November 1996, but had collapsed by December. In January 1997 the DKBA, allegedly supported by government forces, attacked Kayin refugee camps in Thailand. The KNU claimed that requests in late January for further peace negotiations were rejected by the SLORC, which then initiated a new offensive against the KNU. Fighting between the KNU and government forces continued in March, forcing several thousand Kayin across the border into Thailand. As a result of the forcible relocation of tens of thousands of Kayin away from KNU bases in Myanmar during 1997, further refugees fled to Thailand. The Thai armed forces denied collusion with the Myanma troops in the process of forced repatriations of Kayin refugees, who were believed to number more than 100,000 in mid-1997. In March 1998 the DKBA, supported by government troops, launched two further attacks on Kayin refugee camps in Thailand, prompting a retaliatory attack by the KNU on DKBA forces. In April 1999 the KNU issued a statement confirming the deaths of seven members of a group of 13 government officials whom they had abducted in February; the remaining six were said to have been released unharmed.

In January 2000 it was reported that 800–1,000 Kayin had fled across the border into Thailand, following clashes between government forces and the KNU. In the same month Gen. Bo Mya was succeeded as the Chairman of the KNU by the former General Secretary of the organization, Saw Ba Thin. Following his appointment as leader, Ba Thin announced that, while the KNU intended to continue its struggle against the ruling SPDC, the movement was prepared to negotiate a political settlement with the military regime. It was subsequently reported by both government and independent sources that an initial but inconclusive round of talks between the KNU and the SPDC was held in February, followed by further discussions in March. However, in late 2000 the Government began to use 'scorched-earth' tactics to deprive the KNU of its support base, displacing up to 30,000 people in eastern Myanmar.

In January 2001 Johnny and Luther Htoo, teenage leaders of the Kayin rebel group, God's Army, surrendered with 12 of their followers to the Thai authorities. While much smaller than the KNU or the KNLA, God's Army had gained international notoriety owing to the leadership of the twin boys, thought to be aged 13 or 14. Two of the 12 members who surrendered were believed to have been involved in a raid on a Thai village that had left six civilians dead in December 2000.

In April 2003 the KNU claimed responsibility for a series of explosions that had destroyed sections of a gas pipeline in Kayin State over the previous two months, declaring that they had intended to draw the attention of the international community to the human rights abuses being perpetrated by government troops in the area. Several bombings along the border with Thailand in the following month were also attributed to the KNU. In December, however, Vice-Chairman of the KNU Bo Mya led a personal delegation to Yangon to explore the possibility of a potential cease-fire arrangement with the Government. In January 2004, having unified the KNU behind his initiative, Bo Mya and other KNU officials held talks with government representatives in Yangon, which resulted in the conclusion of an informal cease-fire arrangement between the two sides. Bo Mya had previously made any peace agreement conditional both on the release of Aung San Suu Kyi and other NLD detainees and on the Government's adherence to UN resolutions delineating a return to democracy for the country. At further talks, held in Mawlamyine in February, the KNU and the Government discussed the demarcation of KNU territory, the relocation of the armed forces and the resettlement of some 200,000 internally displaced civilians in Kayin State. However, despite the informal cease-fire, sporadic fighting continued between government troops and the KNLA. Further negotiations in Yangon in October were curtailed at the Government's request following the dismissal of Prime Minister Khin Nyunt. Bo Mya retired as Vice-Chairman of the KNU in December because of ill health; he was replaced by Gen. Tamalabaw. In January 2005 10 government troops were reportedly killed in clashes with the KNU after attacking one of the group's bases near the border with Thailand. Later in that month the KNU demanded a resumption of the peace talks, which remained stalled. In the mean time, government forces were reported to have launched an offensive against a KNPP stronghold in Yamu, again close to the Thai border. In March 2006 it was reported that an army offensive was being conducted against the KNU in Kayin state, resulting in the displacement of several hundred people. In May reports emerged of a military campaign against the KNU in another part of the state, following which an estimated 15,000 Kayin people were reported to have fled from the violence. Bo Mya died in a Thai hospital in December 2006. In February 2007 a relatively small breakaway faction of the KNU led by Htain Maung negotiated a peace agreement with the Government, but the goals of the KNU itself were said to be unaffected. In April it was reported that DKBA and government forces had captured four KNU bases near the Thai border. In June 27 people were killed in two separate ambushes on buses in Kayah and Kayin states; the KNU and the KNPP claimed responsibility for the attacks, but insisted that the victims were armed troops and not civilians. Three people were killed in four minor bomb explosions in January 2008, which the authorities attributed to the KNU and other ethnic insurgent groups. The KNU suffered a reverse in February, when its General Secretary, Pado Mahn Sha, was killed by two unknown gunmen at his home in the Thai border town of Mae Sot; it was speculated that the DKBA was responsible for the assassination. The Chairman of the KNU, Saw Ba Thin, died in May 2008; in October Vice-Chairman Gen. Tamalabaw was appointed as his replacement, while Tamalabaw's daughter, Zipporah Sein, succeeded Mahn Sha as General Secretary.

Meanwhile, in December 1993 the SLORC initiated a major offensive against Khun Sa's Mong Tai Army encampments on the Thai border. During that month Khun Sa convened a Shan 'parliament' in his base of Homong, which was attended by hundreds of delegates. This was followed, in May 1994, by Khun Sa's declaration of an independent Shan State, of which he declared himself 'President'. In the same month fighting intensified between government forces and the Mong Tai Army near the Thai border, with heavy losses reported on both sides. However, Khun Sa claimed that his army retained control of two-thirds of the Shan State. In July he was reported to have offered to end opium cultivation and to surrender to the government forces, in exchange for their withdrawal from the

Shan State and a guarantee of Shan independence. In March 1995 government forces launched an intensive campaign, lasting several months, against the Mong Tai Army. In August a faction calling itself the Shan State National Army broke away from the Mong Tai Army, accusing Khun Sa of using Shan nationalism as a 'front' for drugs-trafficking. Khun Sa subsequently offered to relinquish areas under his control to an international force that could ensure the safety of the Shan while eradicating illicit drugs. Khun Sa's position was considerably weakened in September, as improving relations between Thailand and Myanmar led to a Thai pledge to close the common border, thus obstructing his supply routes, and cease-fires with neighbouring ethnic groups allowed the Government to deploy troops in hitherto inaccessible areas. Certain ethnic groups, notably the Wa, were also actively engaged in fighting the Mong Tai Army to gain control of the opium trade. In November Khun Sa announced his retirement from all political and military positions, citing his betrayal by the breakaway group. In January 1996 government troops entered Homong without resistance, and thousands of his former supporters surrendered. Although no formal agreement with the SLORC was announced, it was widely believed that Khun Sa had previously negotiated a settlement with the authorities since he was not detained and it was officially announced that he would not be extradited to the USA on drugs-trafficking charges. (Khun Sa was, moreover, later accorded the status of an honoured elder. He died in Yangon in October 2007.) The Mong Tai Army was subsequently transformed into a militia volunteer unit under the command of the armed forces.

Between November 1996 and February 1997 there were reports of clashes between the Shan United Revolutionary Party (a faction of the Mong Tai Army that had not surrendered in January 1996) and government forces. In September 1997 the alliance between three of the major Shan groups who continued their resistance—including the Shan State National Army (SSNA), remnants of the Mong Tai Army, and the Shan State Peace-keeping Council (SSPC) and its military wing, the Shan State Army (SSA)—was formalized, and the groups joined together in an enlarged SSA. In November it was reported that Shan separatist groups had launched a further offensive against government troops. In May 1999 it was reported that at least 300,000 Shan had been forced from their villages into resettlement camps by government troops. Clashes between SSA units and government forces were reported in December. In March 2000, following the group's announcement that it wished to seek a peaceful settlement with the ruling junta, the SSA issued a statement outlining cease-fire terms. It was later claimed by the SSA that these terms had been misinterpreted by the Government. In May several senior army officers died in an SSA ambush. In the following month more than 60 Shan and hill tribespeople, who had been forcibly relocated and had then attempted to return to their village, were reportedly killed by the Myanma military in a retaliatory attack. In similar incidents in the region in June, as many as 50 other villagers were believed to have been murdered. In 2001 the Government launched several offensives against SSA border camps, causing hundreds more Shan to flee the area. In September the leader of the SSA, Col Yodsuek, stated that the group would be willing to enter into peace talks with the SPDC.

In late 1996 Gen. Maung Aye ordered that the forces of the United Wa State Army (UWSA—who reached an accommodation with the SLORC in 1989) should withdraw from its principal base or surrender to the Government by the end of 1997. As the deadline approached, tension between the two sides increased until the UWSA was given permission to remain at the base for a further year. In January 2000 it was reported that the SPDC was to launch an operation to relocate 50,000 people from UWSA-controlled opium-growing areas, with the alleged intention of eradicating the production of drugs in the areas by 2005. The relocation programme began to cause ethnic tension early in 2001, as the Shan complained that the Wa tribespeople were occupying land that they had previously owned. It was also claimed that the Wa were still growing opium, in spite of the fact that the scheme had been introduced supposedly to prevent heroin production. In February 2001 the office of the UN High Commissioner for Refugees (UNHCR) investigated reports that 300,000 Shan had fled over the border to Thailand as a result of the Wa influx.

In late 1989 the SLORC began resettling Bamar (Burman) Buddhists in the predominantly Muslim areas of Arakan (renamed Rakhine), displacing the local Rohingya Muslims. In April 1991 Rohingya refugees were forced over the border into Bangladesh, as a result of the brutal operations of the Myanma armed forces, including the destruction of villages, widespread killings and pillaging. The Rohingyas had been similarly persecuted in 1976–78, when more than 200,000 of them had sought refuge in Bangladesh. The Rohingyas had finally been repatriated, only to lose their citizenship following the introduction of new nationality legislation in 1982. In November 1991 the SLORC pledged to repatriate genuine Myanma citizens, but claimed that many of the refugees were illegal Bengali immigrants. In April 1992 the Myanma and Bangladeshi Governments signed an agreement providing for the repatriation of those Rohingya refugees in possession of official documentation. However, the repatriation programme was delayed, owing to the continuing flow of refugees to Bangladesh (reaching an estimated 270,000 by the end of June). The first Rohingya refugees were returned to Myanmar in September, without the supervision of UNHCR. Despite demonstrations by Rohingyas in Bangladesh against forced repatriation, refugees continued to be returned to Myanmar. The SLORC's agreement, in November 1993, to allow UNHCR access to repatriated Rohingyas was expected to accelerate the programme. In April 1994 guerrillas of the Rohingya Solidarity Organization carried out attacks in the Maungdaw area of Rakhine. By May 1995 more than 216,000 refugees had been repatriated. In July 1999, however, about 20,000 Rohingya refugees remained in camps in Bangladesh, despite the expiry of the official deadline for their repatriation in August 1997. In April 2000 the International Federation of Human Rights Leagues (FIDH) issued a report condemning the treatment of Rohingya Muslims by the Myanma Government, including forced labour, punitive taxes and extrajudicial killings. The FIDH claimed that the regime was attempting to force the exodus of Rohingyas from their native Rakhine and criticized UNHCR for its effective complicity with the Myanma regime in designating the more recent refugees as economic migrants. In February 2001 violence between Buddhist and Muslim communities in the state capital, Sittwe, was reported to have resulted in at least 12 deaths, prompting the Government to regulate further the movement of Rohingya and other Muslims in and out of Rakhine. In 2003 UNHCR assisted more than 3,000 refugees to return to Myanmar from Bangladesh, following the removal of technical restrictions on their repatriation. Nevertheless, more than 28,800 remained in two camps in Bangladesh in early 2009, many of whom were reportedly unwilling to return to Myanmar. In addition, it was estimated that some 200,000 Rohingyas were residing in Bangladesh without refugee status. In early February 2009, during a visit to Bangladesh, the US Assistant Secretary of State urged Myanmar to halt the mistreatment of the Rohingyas. Relations between Myanmar and Bangladesh deteriorated in November 2008 with the escalation of a territorial dispute in the Bay of Bengal, the location of substantial reserves of natural gas; both countries deployed naval vessels to the area. In bilateral talks the two countries were unable to resolve the disagreement.

In other foreign relations, the People's Republic of China restored diplomatic relations with Burma in 1978. From 1988, as Burma's international isolation deepened, China assumed an increasingly important role. It became Myanmar's principal aid donor, supplier of weapons and source of consumer goods. In May 1997 an agreement was reached to establish a trade route through Myanmar to provide the Chinese province of Yunnan with access to the Indian Ocean. In the same year the Chinese Government signed a 30-year agreement with Myanmar that allowed for more than 200 Chinese fishing boats to operate in Myanma waters; the agreement was widely perceived as an indication of increasing Chinese influence in Myanmar. Furthermore, China announced the construction in Myanmar of two liquefied petroleum gas plants in October 2000 and also of a dry dock in February 2001. In December 2001 the Chinese President, Jiang Zemin, travelled to Myanmar, becoming the first Chinese Head of State to visit the country since 1985. Before his arrival the Government announced that it had ordered the release of more than 200 Chinese prisoners as a gesture of goodwill. Following successful discussions, the two Governments signed a series of bilateral agreements intended to enhance co-operative ties. It was reported that China had offered Myanmar US $100m. in aid and investment, although this was thought to be linked to Chinese demands that the ruling junta increase its efforts to eradicate the drug trade between the two countries. Relations between the two countries were further strengthened in March 2004, during a visit to Yangon by Chinese Vice-Premier Wu Yi, by the signing of 24 agreements on economic and technical co-operation and, in February 2006, by a visit to Beijing by the Prime Minister of Myanmar, Lt-Gen. Soe Win, during which the two heads of government agreed further to promote cordial bilateral relations.

In April 2007 Myanmar and the Democratic People's Republic of Korea (North Korea) agreed to restore diplomatic relations, which had been severed in 1983 after the latter was held responsible for a bomb attack in Yangon during a visit by the President of the Republic of Korea (South Korea). It was speculated that North Korea hoped to gain access to Myanmar's energy resources, while Myanmar would benefit from North Korean military co-operation.

During the 1990s Japan and the member states of ASEAN were anxious to halt Myanmar's excessive dependence on China for aid and trade. Myanmar, in its turn, applied to join ASEAN (which maintained a policy of 'constructive engagement' in relation to Myanmar) in an attempt to end its isolation, accelerate economic growth and gain protection from Western criticism of its internal affairs. In July 1994 Myanmar was invited to attend the annual meeting of ASEAN ministers responsible for foreign affairs, and in July 1995 it signed the organization's founding Treaty of Amity and Co-operation, a precursor to full membership. In July 1996 Myanmar was granted observer status, and in July 1997 the country was admitted as a full member of the organization. In May 1996 Myanmar joined the ASEAN Regional Forum (ARF, see p. 197) and in May 2000 the country hosted a senior-level meeting of the economic ministers of the ASEAN member countries; the meeting, which was also attended by ministers from China, Japan and the Republic of Korea, attracted strong criticism from the NLD. Myanmar enjoyed particularly cordial relations with Indonesia, and the military regime aspired to Indonesia's internationally accepted political system, in which the dominant role of the armed forces was enshrined in the Constitution. ASEAN links were strengthened by official visits from the Prime Minister of Cambodia, Hun Sen, in February 2000, and the Vietnamese Minister of Foreign Affairs, Nguyen Dy Nien, in October of the same year. In January 2001 Dr Mahathir Mohamad, Prime Minister of Malaysia and an influential figure in gaining entry for Myanmar into ASEAN, visited Yangon. Gen. Than Shwe and Gen. Khin Nyunt paid a reciprocal visit in September. Mahathir visited the country again in August 2002. In March 2006 the Malaysian Minister of Foreign Affairs, Syed Hamid Albar, was denied a meeting with Aung San Suu Kyi by the military junta. Albar, acting as an ASEAN envoy to assess the progress of political reform, had held a meeting with Lt-Gen. Soe Win, the Myanma Prime Minister, and was initially positive about the visit. However, he claimed in July that ASEAN's development was being impeded by Myanmar, and that ASEAN could no longer defend Myanmar as it was 'not making an attempt to co-operate or help itself'. In late September 2007, in a rare departure from the Association's policy of non-interference in member states' internal affairs, ASEAN ministers responsible for foreign affairs, meeting in New York, USA, issued a statement in which they declared that they had expressed their 'revulsion' to their Myanma counterpart over reports that anti-Government protests (see above) were being suppressed violently, and had urged the Myanma Government to resume efforts at national reconciliation and release all political detainees. ASEAN came under pressure to take action against Myanmar in advance of its summit meeting in November, at which member states signed a new charter committing themselves *inter alia* to strengthening democracy and promoting and protecting human rights, with the US Senate notably approving a resolution urging the Association to suspend Myanmar. However, ASEAN's Secretary-General rejected this suggestion, deeming it confrontational, and the Myanma Government also succeeded in forcing the cancellation of a planned address by UN envoy Ibrahim Gambari. None the less, the President of the Philippines warned that her country's legislature was unlikely to ratify the new ASEAN charter unless Myanmar agreed to release Suu Kyi.

In the late 1990s bilateral relations between Myanmar and Thailand were rather less cordial than previously, with the Thai Government advocating a more limited 'flexible engagement' with Myanmar, in place of the ASEAN policy of 'constructive engagement' formerly endorsed by the country. Relations between the two countries were placed under some strain in late 1999 when a group of armed Myanma student activists, styled the Vigorous Burmese Student Warriors, seized control of the Myanma embassy in Bangkok in early October, demanding the release of all political prisoners in Myanmar and the opening of a dialogue between the military Goverment and the opposition. All 89 hostages were released by the activists within 24 hours, in exchange for the Thai Government's provision of helicopter transport to the Thai–Myanma border. The Thai Government's release of the perpetrators angered the ruling junta in Myanmar, and Myanmar closed its border with Thailand immediately after the incident. The border was re-opened to commerce in late November, although relations between the two countries remained strained. In January 2000 Thai troops shot dead 10 armed Myanma rebels who had taken control of a hospital in Ratchaburi, holding hundreds of people hostage. The rebels, who were reported by some sources to be linked to the Kayin insurgent group, God's Army, had issued several demands, including that the shelling of their base on the Thai–Myanma border by the Thai military be halted, that co-operation between the Thai and Myanma armies against the Kayin should cease, and that Kayin tribespeople be allowed to seek refuge in Thailand. While the Thai Government denied reports that the perpetrators had been summarily executed after handing over their weapons, the brutal resolution of the incident was praised by the military Government in Myanmar.

There was renewed tension on the Thai–Myanma border in October 2000 when a Thai soldier was killed and two others were injured. It was unclear whether the clash was with Myanma troops or a faction allied to the Government. Tension was further heightened in November as 2,000 Myanma troops were deployed along the border, in preparation for an offensive against the KNU. In January 2001 it was reported that a Thai F-16 fighter aircraft had intruded into Myanma airspace, prompting the Government to announce the building of air defence systems along the border. Another border transgression occurred in February, when five Myanma soldiers were arrested by the Thai Border Patrol Police (BPP). The soldiers claimed that they were searching for food, whereas the BPP believed them to be gathering intelligence on Thai positions. On the previous day an offensive had been launched against the KNU, involving 300 Myanma troops, of whom five were killed. In mid-February there was a major incursion into Thai territory by some 200 Myanma troops, in pursuit of 100 SSA rebels. The troops clashed with Thai soldiers and occupied a hill that was within Thai territory for two days. At least two Thai villagers were killed, and officially 14 Myanma soldiers and two civilians also died. A cease-fire was signed, but this did not prevent Myanmar from ordering all SPDC troops on the border to be placed on full combat-ready status. By the end of February Thailand had detained 40 Myanma nationals for spying, according to Myanma figures, while the SPDC accused Thailand of providing support to the SSA.

In May 2001 Thai-Myanma relations deteriorated further when the Thai Government lodged a formal protest over an incident in which members of the DKBA had allegedly attacked a military unit situated in a Thai border village, causing the deaths of three civilians. A further protest was made several days later when the UWSA captured a hill believed to lie within Thai territory; the hill was later recaptured by Thai troops. In response, the Myanma Government demanded the withdrawal of Thai troops from 35 border outposts and claimed that the Thai army had launched air strikes into its territory, an accusation denied by the Thai authorities. The situation was further exacerbated by the publication of an article in a Myanma newspaper that Thailand claimed was insulting to its monarchy. In June Thai Prime Minister Thaksin Shinawatra arrived in Yangon for discussions, which defused the tensions, although the two sides failed to reach any firm agreement as to how they would overcome the problems affecting their relations. In the following month the Thai Minister of Defence, Chavalit Yongchaiyudh, visited Myanmar and agreed to work with the SPDC to aid the forced repatriation of refugees on the Thai–Myanma border. In September Gen. Khin Nyunt made a three-day trip to Thailand, which was seen by many to constitute a starting point for a new era of improved bilateral relations. In January 2002 a joint Thai-Myanma commission (meeting for the first time since 1999) agreed to establish a task force to assist in the repatriation of illegal workers. In February 2002 the Thai Minister of Foreign Affairs, Surakiart Sathirathai, visited Yangon. During his stay both countries agreed to co-operate in controlling the cross-border drugs trade.

In mid-2002 relations with Thailand deteriorated sharply when fighting broke out on the border between government troops, allied with the UWSA, and the SSA. It was alleged that

Thai troops had fired shells into the country, in the belief that the fighting had encroached upon Thai territory. In response, the Myanma Government again accused Thailand of lending its support to the SSA. The joint border was closed shortly afterwards as tensions escalated. Border incursions continued as the bilateral relationship worsened. In August Surakiart Sathirathai met with leaders of the SPDC in an attempt to defuse the tensions; the border subsequently reopened in October. Relations continued to improve, owing in large part to the adoption of a policy of 'soft engagement' by the Thai Government and, in early 2003, the two countries signed an unprecedented agreement pledging that future military exercises would be conducted at a suitable distance from the border.

In December 2003 Thailand hosted an international forum, called the 'Bangkok Process', at which the Myanma Minister for Foreign Affairs, U Win Aung, presented the 'road map' on democratic reform (see above) to government representatives from 10 other Asian and European countries. In early 2004, in a reflection of the improved relationship between Myanmar and Thailand, Myanmar announced that it was to award Thailand fishing concessions in its waters for one year. Fishing rights had been terminated in May 2001 following tensions on the joint border. (A second 'Friendship Bridge' linking the two countries opened in January 2006.) However, a second round of talks in the 'Bangkok Process', scheduled for late April 2004, was postponed indefinitely at Myanmar's request. Prime Minister Khin Nyunt visited Thailand in June, and discussed various economic, development and border issues with Prime Minister Thaksin Shinawatra. In December the Thai Prime Minister paid a visit to Myanmar, his first since the ousting of Khin Nyunt, and held talks with the new Prime Minister, Lt-Gen. Soe Win. In January 2005 Thailand increased security along the border with Myanmar, amid renewed concerns that fighting between Myanma troops and KNPP rebels might encroach upon Thai territory. In April Thailand again intensified security along its border with Myanmar in response to renewed fighting between the UWSA and the SSA close to Thai territory. In December the Thai Government announced that it was not prepared to host the delayed second meeting of the 'Bangkok Process' since Myanmar had not kept it sufficiently informed of its progress towards democracy; it was unclear whether any future efforts would be made to revive the initiative. In December 2007 UNHCR reported that 124,300 Myanma refugees remained resident in nine camps in Thailand, while a total of 20,878 had been resettled in third countries since January 2005, more than one-half having been accepted by the USA. In early 2009 it was alleged that groups of Myanma and Bangladeshi asylum-seekers, attempting to reach Thailand, had been picked up by Thai security forces and left at sea in boats without engines. The claims, which were made by survivors, prompted the Thai Prime Minister, Abhisit Vejjajiva, to order an investigation into the matter.

In October 2002 the Australian Minister of Foreign Affairs, Alexander Downer, arrived in Myanmar; he was the most senior Australian politician to have visited the country for 20 years. During his stay he met with senior members of the SPDC and with Aung San Suu Kyi. However, following his departure Suu Kyi reportedly claimed that she would prefer Australia to lend its support to the international sanctions against the country rather than attempt to engage with its leaders. In October 2007 the Australian Government imposed financial sanctions on more than 400 Myanma leaders and associates.

Despite the killing of three Indian soldiers in a clash with Myanma troops in October 2000, relations between the two countries subsequently improved. Gen. Maung Aye paid a seven-day visit to India in November 2000, meeting both the country's President and the Prime Minister. In mid-February 2001 India's Minister of External Affairs, Jaswant Singh, visited Myanmar, the first Indian cabinet minister to do so since the SLORC's assumption of power in 1988. While there, Singh officially opened the Tamu–Kalewa highway, a road built by India at a cost of US $22m. in order to increase bilateral trade with Myanmar. In January 2003 Minister of Foreign Affairs U Win Aung paid a visit to India, during which he met with the Prime Minister and several cabinet ministers. The two Governments agreed to hold regular consultations and to co-operate in counter-terrorism activities. In October 2004 the Chairman of the SPDC, Than Shwe, paid the first visit to India by a Myanma Head of State in 24 years, agreeing to further bilateral co-operation at meetings with the Indian President and Prime Minister. Following discussions between the two countries' respective Ministers of Home Affairs in October 2005, Myanmar and India agreed to a policy of joint interrogation of persons arrested for militant activities and on charges of smuggling drugs or weapons. In March 2006 President Aavul Pakkiri Jainulabidin Abdul Kalam visited Yangon, the first ever state visit to Myanmar by an Indian President. In September senior officials of the Myanma and Indian Ministries of Home Affairs signed an agreement to increase security co-operation. A claim by Amnesty International that India intended to sell a military helicopter to Myanmar provoked controversy in July 2007 because many of the components of the helicopter had been developed or manufactured in EU member states, meaning that such a sale would infringe the Union's arms embargo against Myanmar. However, the Indian Government rejected Amnesty's allegations.

Following the release of Suu Kyi from house arrest in July 1995, Japan resumed substantial economic aid to Myanmar, which had been halted in 1988. In November 1999 the Japanese Prime Minister met with Than Shwe during an ASEAN summit meeting in Manila; the meeting was the first between the leader of a major world power and a senior member of the military Government since the junta's suppression of the democratic opposition in 1988. In April 2001 Japan accelerated its policy of engagement, promising a US $28m. aid programme intended to facilitate the upgrading of a hydroelectric power plant in Kayah. The renewal of aid to the country was widely perceived to be a political gesture intended to reward the SPDC for its efforts to reach a settlement with the NLD. The international community criticized Japan's decision to resume aid as being premature in the light of Myanmar's failure to end forced labour and other human rights abuses in the country. In June 2003, following the junta's reimprisonment of Suu Kyi in May of that year, the Japanese Government suspended all economic aid to Myanmar. However, in early 2004 it was announced that Japan was to resume aid once again, having been satisfied that the release of some political prisoners by the SPDC constituted adequate progress towards democracy in the country. Tension arose between Japan and Myanmar in late September 2007, when a Japanese journalist was killed during the violent suppression of anti-Government protests in Yangon (see above). After evidence emerged that suggested that the journalist might have been deliberately targeted by the security forces, the Japanese Deputy Minister of Foreign Affairs visited Myanmar to investigate the incident. In the following month Japan cancelled some $4.7m. in funding for an educational centre at Yangon University, as Myanmar continued to maintain that the journalist had been accidentally shot.

In July 1996, as repression increased, Suu Kyi for the first time urged the imposition of international economic sanctions against Myanmar. From March 1997 the EU withdrew Myanmar's special trading status, in response to concerns over Myanmar's human rights record; later in that year a meeting scheduled to take place in November between the EU and ASEAN was cancelled by the EU, owing to its objection to the representation of Myanmar at the talks. In early 1999 a further meeting between the EU and ASEAN, scheduled to be held in February, was postponed indefinitely as a result of continued disagreement between the two organizations regarding the proposed representation of Myanmar. However, an agreement was subsequently reached by the two sides to allow Myanmar to take a 'passive role' in the Joint Co-operation Committee meeting between the EU and ASEAN scheduled to take place in May. The SPDC became more open to the development of external relations when it allowed an EU delegation to visit Myanmar and hold talks with Suu Kyi in January 2001. Despite this, the EU extended its sanctions against Myanmar for a further six months in April 2001, owing to the human rights situation. However, in October the EU announced that it had decided to ease its sanctions. After Razali Ismail's fourth visit to Myanmar in November 2001, plans for a US $16m. HIV/AIDS prevention programme were mooted. Several countries, particularly Japan and the EU, indicated that they would be willing to support a carefully monitored international aid programme, and it was hoped that the prospect of the resumption of limited aid would encourage the Government to release more political prisoners. In January 2003 the Myanma Deputy Minister of Foreign Affairs, Khin Maung Win, was permitted to attend an EU-ASEAN summit meeting for the first time since Myanmar's suspension from the meetings in 1997. However, in April the EU elected to extend its sanctions against the country and to increase the list of SPDC officials subject to visa sanctions and 'freezing' of their assets. These sanctions were subsequently renewed annually.

Relations between the EU and ASEAN were strained by pressure from some EU member states to exclude ASEAN's three newest members (Cambodia, Laos and Myanmar) from an Asia-Europe Meeting of heads of government (ASEM) in Viet Nam in October 2004. The EU initially insisted that the SPDC should release Aung San Suu Kyi from house arrest and commit to a number of other reforms before Myanmar be allowed to attend. However, ASEAN responded that if its new members were not allowed to participate, then the EU's 10 new members should also be excluded. The result was that Myanmar was represented at the summit meeting by a more junior-level delegation, led by the newly appointed Minister of Foreign Affairs, Maj.-Gen. Nyan Win. Two days after the ASEM summit EU ministers responsible for foreign affairs implemented an earlier threat to broaden sanctions against Myanmar if the country did not make progress towards democratization in time for the meeting. The ministers agreed to widen the list of Myanma officials subject to visa sanctions and to co-ordinate international bans on investment in the country (although France secured an exclusion from such a ban for European countries that had already invested in Myanmar). In November 2007, in response to the use of force to quell anti-Government protests in Myanmar in September, the EU formally increased the number of officials subject to visa sanctions and asset 'freezing', expanded the scope of an investment ban on state-owned enterprises and imposed a new ban on some Myanma exports, including timber, metals and gemstones.

In September 1999, meanwhile, a diplomatic dispute began between Myanmar and the United Kingdom after British consular staff were refused permission to visit two Britons in detention in Myanmar for their separate involvement in pro-democracy protest action. The British Government expressed its grave concern over their treatment. One of the two Britons was released in November. The second detainee, James Mawdsley, who had received a prison sentence of 17 years for entering the country illegally and carrying pro-democracy leaflets, was released in October 2000, following international pressure; he confirmed that he had been beaten heavily while in captivity.

In May 1997 the USA imposed trade sanctions in protest at persistent and large-scale repression by the SLORC. The sanctions prohibited further investment in Myanmar, but did not affect existing US interests in the country. In July, at a ministerial meeting that followed the ASEAN conference, the US Secretary of State, Madeleine Albright, denounced Myanmar publicly for its poor human rights record and the country's lack of progress towards democracy. During 1998 the USA criticized the military junta in Myanmar for its treatment of Suu Kyi and also demanded the release of hundreds of political prisoners. In March 1999 Albright publicly criticized the regime for taking insufficient action to combat the production of and trade in narcotics within Myanmar. The USA showed its support for the SPDC-NLD talks with a visit by a senior Department of State official to Suu Kyi in February 2001. However, while welcoming the discussions, the US Government renewed its sanctions later in the year. In December pro-democracy activists in Myanmar accused the USA of neglecting their cause after a reappraisal of its foreign policy in the wake of the terrorist attacks on the country in September (see the chapter on the USA). They claimed that the US Government had moderated its criticism of the ruling military junta because it suspected that the international terrorist network, al-Qa'ida, had a presence in the country. In February 2002 a report issued by the US Government offered the prospect of an easing of sanctions, but only if the military junta released all remaining political prisoners and made further tangible progress towards democracy. However, following the detention of Aung San Suu Kyi in May 2003, in July the US President, George W. Bush, approved the Burmese Freedom and Democracy Act, already passed by Congress, banning all imports from Myanmar for three years and extending visa sanctions already imposed on SPDC officials. The USA extended economic sanctions against Myanmar for another year in May 2004 and again in subsequent years. In August 2006 President Bush renewed the Burmese Freedom and Democracy Act of 2003 for a further three years. In September 2007 the US Department of State expanded its visa ban to more than 35 additional government and military officials; a further 14 senior officials were also designated subject to 'freezing' of their assets. In October Bush announced the imposition of stricter controls on imports from Myanmar, as well as sanctions affecting the property interests of senior Myanma leaders. At the beginning of May 2008, furthermore, the US Treasury was ordered to 'freeze' the assets of state-owned companies in Myanmar. Meanwhile, in April the US Senate approved legislation to award the Congressional Gold Medal to Suu Kyi.

In November 1998 the SPDC strongly denied claims made by the UN that the Myanma Government was responsible for the widespread abuse of human rights within the country. However, a report published in August by the International Labour Organization (ILO, see p. 113), following an investigation into the alleged use of forced labour and the suppression of trade unions in Myanmar, found the use of forced labour to be 'pervasive' throughout the whole country, and accused the military regime of using beatings, torture, rape and murder in the exaction of its forced labour policy, constituting a 'gross denial of human rights'. In June 1999 a resolution condemning Myanmar for its widespread use of forced labour was adopted by the member countries of the ILO, and the country was barred from participating in any ILO activities. (In the same month the ruling junta was accused by the human rights organization Amnesty International of perpetrating widespread abuses against ethnic minority groups.) Following the failure of the military Government to carry out the recommendations made by the ILO Commission of Inquiry in 1998 after the organization's initial investigation, in March 2000 the governing body of the ILO recommended that at its meeting in June the International Labour Conference take action to secure compliance by the ruling junta with the ILO's recommendations. In a statement issued in late March, the SPDC categorically rejected the governing body's decision and recommendations. Despite the Government's assurance in November 2000 that it would accept ILO monitors to verify the cessation of forced labour practices, the UN labour body voted to proceed with sanctions against Myanmar. This was the first time such action, the strongest available to the ILO, had been undertaken in the organization's 81-year history. The ILO subsequently requested its members to review their relations with Myanmar and to adopt sanctions. China, India, Malaysia and Russia voted against the action.

In September 2001 an ILO contingent arrived in Myanmar for a three-week visit intended to ascertain whether the military junta had honoured its promise to bring about the abolition of forced labour. In November the ILO issued a report concluding that, while some progress had been made, the practice was still endemic in many parts of the country. It recommended that a permanent ILO presence be established in Myanmar to monitor continued efforts to end forced labour in the region; discussions as to how this could be implemented headed the agenda during a further visit by the ILO in February 2002. However, the ILO delegation was not permitted to see the NLD leader, Suu Kyi, during its visit and, upon departure, the head of the delegation expressed disappointment at the lack of co-operation it had received from the Myanma authorities. Despite this, in March the ILO agreed to establish a liaison office in the country and, in October, an ILO mission visited the country to assist further in the development of good labour practices. In early 2004, following a visit by an ILO envoy, the SPDC agreed to allow ILO representatives to work freely towards the elimination of forced labour practices in the country. At the ILO's annual International Labour Conference in June, it was reported that the use of forced labour remained widespread in Myanmar, particularly on local infrastructure projects and by the army, although there had been some improvement since the 1990s, with forced labour no longer routinely used on national infrastructure projects. In February 2007 the ILO announced that the Myanma authorities had tentatively agreed to allow investigations into submitted forced labour cases without negative repercussions for alleged victims.

In October 1999 the UN Secretary-General's Special Envoy for Myanmar, Alvaro de Soto, arrived in the country to attempt, for the fifth time, to promote a dialogue between the military Government and the NLD; however, de Soto's efforts were fruitless. In April 2000 de Soto was replaced as Special Envoy for Myanmar by Razali Ismail, a Malaysian diplomat, who subsequently arranged the secret dialogue between Suu Kyi and Lt-Gen. Khin Nyunt in October (see above). In November the UN human rights envoy to Myanmar, Rajsoomer Lallah, resigned from his position, citing lack of financial and administrative assistance. Lallah had previously produced a damning report of Myanmar's human rights situation, but had not been granted a visa throughout his four-year term. His successor, Dr Paulo Sérgio Pinheiro, was able to visit Myanmar in April 2001, within six months of taking office. He returned for a further visit in October, but was criticized by the NLD for his failure to spend enough time consulting with local communities. His visit had to be curtailed for reasons of ill health. In February 2002 Pinheiro visited the country for a third time and held further discussions with senior members of the SPDC and with Suu Kyi and other political prisoners. The Government released 11 political prisoners during his stay and, upon leaving, he declared his visit to have been a success. In October Pinheiro travelled to the country again; during his time there he investigated allegations, made by several human rights groups, that members of the Myanma armed forces routinely raped ethnic women along the border with Thailand. He also met with Suu Kyi. In March 2003 he paid a further visit to the country but curtailed his stay, having discovered a hidden microphone in a room where he was interviewing NLD prisoners. He later urged the SPDC to release all remaining political prisoners and enter into a serious dialogue with the opposition. In the first half of 2004 Pinheiro was twice denied entry to Myanmar, and in June he described the ongoing National Convention as a 'meaningless and undemocratic exercise' owing to the restrictions imposed on free discussion and to the absence of the NLD. In early October 2007 the UN Human Rights Council adopted a resolution deploring the violent repression of peaceful demonstrations in the previous month and calling for the release of peaceful protesters and all other political detainees. In November, during his first visit to Myanmar since 2003, Pinheiro held talks with government ministers and several prominent political prisoners, although he was not permitted to meet Suu Kyi. Following his visit, Pinheiro stated that the Myanma authorities had admitted that 15 people had been killed during the suppression of the anti-Government protests in September (five more than previously acknowledged), and in the following month he reported that his investigations indicated that at least a further 16 people had died, that 500–1,000 people were still being detained by the authorities (far more than claimed by the Government) and that 74 people were missing. Pinheiro also reported that the ill-treatment of detainees and the poor conditions in which they were being held had resulted in several deaths in custody.

In May 1999 the ICRC, which had withdrawn from Myanmar in 1995 but reopened its office there in October 1998, regained permission from the ruling junta to visit a limited number of prisons in the country. Despite having been initially critical of the ICRC for reaching an agreement with the SPDC, Suu Kyi was reported subsequently to have expressed her support for the Committee's work with political prisoners. The ICRC sent a delegation to the country in July 2003, in order to ascertain that Suu Kyi was in good health following her recent imprisonment by the SPDC. In June 2007, in an unusual departure from its policy of neutrality, the ICRC issued a statement severely criticizing the Myanma authorities, claiming that human rights violations in Myanmar were causing 'immense suffering' for thousands of people. The Committee explained that the continued refusal of Myanma officials to discuss the alleged abuses had prompted it to make its concerns public.

In May 2007 it was announced that Russia was to assist with the construction of a 10-MW nuclear research reactor in Myanmar. An earlier agreement (concluded in 2002) had reportedly not been implemented because of Russian concerns that payment would not be made.

Government

Following the military coup of September 1988, all state organs, including the People's Assembly, the State Council and the Council of Ministers, were abolished by the State Law and Order Restoration Council (SLORC), and the country was placed under martial law. Legislative elections took place in May 1990, but the SLORC subsequently announced that the opposition-dominated elected body was a Constituent Assembly, which was accorded no legislative power. During September 1992 a night curfew, imposed in 1988, and two martial law decrees, in force for three years, were revoked. However, a ban remained on gatherings of more than five people. In early 1993 a National Convention, comprising members of the SLORC and representatives of the opposition parties, met to draft a new constitution; discussions continued until March 1996, when the National Convention was adjourned. In November 1997 the ruling military junta announced the dissolution of the SLORC and its replacement by the newly created State Peace and Development Council (SPDC). In August 2003 the SPDC announced its intention to reconvene the National Convention, which had remained in recess since 1996, in order that proceedings for the drafting of a new constitution could begin. The Convention entered its final session in mid-2007, and in October a 54-member constitution-drafting committee was established. The resultant document was officially published in April 2008, and the new Constitution was approved in a national referendum in May. The SPDC envisaged that the promulgation of the new Constitution would be followed by multi-party elections in 2010.

Defence

Myanmar maintains a policy of neutrality and has no external defence treaties. The armed forces are largely engaged in internal security duties. As assessed at November 2008, the armed services totalled some 406,000 men, of whom a reported 375,000 were in the army, an estimated 16,000 in the navy and 15,000 in the air force. Paramilitary forces included the People's Police Force of 72,000 men and the People's Militia of 35,000 men. In 2007 the defence budget was an estimated US $7,000m.

Economic Affairs

In 1986, according to estimates by the World Bank, Myanmar's gross national income (GNI), measured at average 1984–86 prices, was US $7,450m., equivalent to $200 per head. In 2000–07, it was estimated, the population increased at an annual average rate of 0.9%, while gross domestic product (GDP) per head increased, in real terms, by an average of 8.7% per year. Overall GDP increased, in real terms, by an annual average of 11.3% between 1996 and 2006. According to the Asian Development Bank (ADB), real GDP expanded by 11.9% in 2007.

According to figures from the ADB, agriculture (including forestry and fishing) contributed an estimated 43.7% of GDP in 2006/07. The sector engaged an estimated 68.6% of the employed labour force in mid-2005, according to FAO. Rice is the staple crop, and production reached an estimated 32.6m. metric tons in 2007. In 2007/08 pulses and beans accounted for an estimated 9.8% of total exports. Other crops include sugar cane, maize, groundnuts, sesame seed, plantains and rubber. The fishing sector is also important. The total catch reached an estimated 2.6m. metric tons in 2006. Sales of teak and other hardwood provided an estimated 8.4% of total export revenue in 2007/08. In 2007 Myanmar remained one of the world's largest sources of illicit opium. According to a survey conducted by the UN Office on Drugs and Crime (see p. 49) (formerly the UN Office of Drug Control and Crime Prevention), the area under opium poppy cultivation expanded by 29% in 2007 to reach an estimated 27,700 ha, increasing further, to 28,500 ha, in the following year. However, production of dry opium was believed to have decreased from an estimated 460 metric tons in 2007 to 410 tons in 2008. According to figures from the ADB, the real GDP of the agricultural sector increased by an annual average of 9.6% in 2001–04. Having reportedly expanded by 13.6% in 2005, agricultural GDP increased by a further 9.7% in 2006 and by 8.0% in 2007, according to revised estimates by the ADB. However, crop damage resulting from a strong cyclone in May 2008 was likely to have resulted in a substantial contraction in this sector in that year.

Industry (including mining, manufacturing, construction and utilities) provided an estimated 19.8% of GDP in 2006/07, according to the ADB. The industrial sector engaged 22.0% of the employed labour force (excluding activities not adequately defined) in 2005. Between 2000 and 2004, according to figures from the ADB, industrial GDP increased by an annual average of 25.6%. The GDP of the industrial sector was reported to have continued to expand strongly, rising by 19.9% in 2005. The sector's GDP was estimated by the ADB to have grown by 20.0% in 2006 and by 19.6% in 2007.

Mining and quarrying contributed an estimated 0.6% of GDP in 2004/05 and engaged 0.7% of the employed labour force in 1997/98. Significant new onshore and offshore discoveries of natural gas and petroleum resulted from exploration and production-sharing agreements with foreign companies, the first of which was signed in 1989. In March 2005, however, the Government announced that henceforth all onshore oil and gas blocks would be exclusively operated by the Myanma Oil and Gas Enterprise under the Ministry of Energy. Other important minerals that are commercially exploited include tin, copper, coal, lead, jade, gemstones, silver and gold; some of Myanmar's potentially lucrative mineral resources remain largely unexploited. According to figures from the ADB, the GDP of the mining sector increased by an annual average of 7.0% between 2000 and 2004, rising by 13.4% in the latter year.

Manufacturing contributed an estimated 11.6% of GDP in 2004/05 and engaged 9.1% of the employed labour force in 1998. The most important branches are food and beverage processing, the production of industrial raw materials (cement, plywood and fertilizers), petroleum refining and textiles. The sector is adversely affected by shortages of electricity and the high price of machinery and spare parts. From mid-2003 a US ban on imports from Myanmar had a serious impact upon the textile sector, and revenue from garment exports subsequently declined. However, alternative external markets for these products were rapidly established, and the revenue from garment exports rose from 1,586.0m. kyats in 2005/06 to 1,601.8m. kyats in 2006/07. The garment sector provided an estimated 1,554.6m. kyats in export revenue in 2007/08, equivalent to 4.4% of total exports in that year. The real GDP of the manufacturing sector expanded, according to figures from the ADB, at an average annual rate of 25.2% between 2000 and 2004, increasing by 24.8% in 2004.

Energy is derived principally from natural gas, which accounted for 39.8% of electricity production in 2005; hydroelectric power contributed 49.8% and petroleum 10.3%. In 2005 a 280-MW hydropower plant, financed by a Chinese company, was opened at Paung Laung. The same Chinese company was also involved in the ongoing construction of the 790-MW Yeywa hydropower station in Mandalay, and the Shweli Hydel hydroelectric power project in northern Shan State, which was expected to generate 3,042m. kWh annually. Imports of mineral oils accounted for around 11.1% of total imports in 2007/08.

The services sector contributed 36.5% of GDP in 2006/07, according to the ADB, and engaged 25.1% of the employed labour force in 1997/98. Tourism revenue is an important source of foreign exchange. The number of tourist arrivals increased from 232,218 in 2005 to 263,514 in 2006. However, revenue from this sector declined from US $85m. in 2005 to $59m. in 2006. According to figures from the ADB, the GDP growth rate of the services sector ranged between 12.9% and 14.8% annually in 2000–04. GDP growth in the sector was reported to have reached 13.1% in 2005 and 14.2% in 2006, decelerating slightly to an estimated 12.9% in 2007.

In 2006 Myanmar recorded a visible trade surplus of US $2,211.3m., and there was a surplus of $802.0m. on the current account of the balance of payments. In 2007/08 the principal sources of imports were the People's Republic of China (which supplied 29.7% of the total), Singapore (24.4%) and Thailand (11.4%); other major suppliers were Japan and Indonesia. The principal market for exports (44.0%) was Thailand; other significant purchasers were India (11.4%), China (10.9%), Hong Kong and Singapore. According to preliminary figures, the principal imports in 2007/08 were machinery and transport equipment, refined mineral oils and base metals and manufactures. The principal exports in that year included gas, dried pulses, teak and other hardwoods and also garments.

In the financial year ending 31 March 2006 there was an estimated budgetary deficit of 189,251m. kyats (excluding the capital account). The budget deficit was estimated by the ADB to have decreased from the equivalent of 6.0% of GDP in 2004 to 4.0% in 2005. Myanmar's external debt at the end of 2006 totalled US $6,828m., of which $5,234m. was long-term public debt; in that year the cost of servicing external debt was equivalent to 1.7% of exports of goods and services. The annual rate of inflation averaged 25.2% in 2000–07. According to the ADB, consumer prices increased by 26.4% in 2008. The ADB estimated the rate of unemployment in 2003 at 4.0% of the labour force.

Myanmar is a member of the World Trade Organization (WTO, see p. 410), the UN Economic and Social Commission for Asia and the Pacific (ESCAP, see p. 36), the Asian Development Bank (ADB, see p. 191) and the Colombo Plan (see p. 425), which promote economic development in the region. In July 1997 Myanmar acceded to the Association of South East Asian Nations (ASEAN, see p. 194). Myanmar was granted a 10-year period from 1 January 1998 to comply with the tariff reductions (to between 0% and 5%) required under the ASEAN Free Trade Area (AFTA), which was formally established on 1 January 2002.

Weaknesses in data, compounded by the vast disparity between the official and market values of the country's currency, have impeded accurate assessments of Myanmar's economy. Although official statistics continued to indicate strong growth in most sectors of the economy in the early 21st century, other sources suggested that progress was more modest. The Government's ambitious development plan for 2006–10 projected annual GDP growth of 10%, and while growth was officially estimated to have exceeded this level in 2007, some sources placed the figure closer to 5.9%. While the official exchange rate remained at an average of less than six kyats to the US dollar in 2004–07, the unofficial rate was believed to have reached 1,140 kyats to the dollar in May 2008. The unofficial exchange rate remained stable throughout the 2008/09 fiscal year and had reportedly declined slightly, to 1,030 kyats per US dollar, in April 2009. The hydrocarbons sector benefited from high levels of investment during 2007, and stronger international prices during the first half of 2008 boosted export revenues. However, the sudden decline in commodity prices that followed the global financial crisis in the latter part of 2008 was likely to erode the balance of payments situation in 2009. Furthermore, the continued imposition of trade sanctions on Myanmar by both the European Union and the USA (see Recent History) was likely to constrain the performance of other merchandise exports, despite the expansion of trade relations with India, China and Thailand. A sharp decline in world rice prices was expected to aid Myanmar, which had struggled to meet consumption requirements in 2008, following the imposition of export bans by leading suppliers in the early part of the year and the severe damage inflicted upon the domestic crop by a devastating cyclone in May. The authorities estimated that Cyclone Nargis had cost the economy 2.7% of projected growth in 2008. Rice exports were suspended for five months to allow for a revival in domestic supply chains. An economic recovery plan was drafted for the period 2009–11; the projected budget of US $690m. was to be largely financed by international donors. However, the contraction in the global economy was expected to delay the impact of these measures. More positively, there were hopes that the relative freedom with which international aid was dispensed in the aftermath of the cyclone might augur well for greater levels of co-operation between Myanmar and international organizations in the future.

Education

Education is provided free of charge, where available, and is compulsory at primary level. Primary education begins at five years of age and lasts for five years. Primary enrolment was equivalent to 100% of children in the relevant age-group in 2005/06 (males 99%; females 101%). Secondary education, beginning at 10 years of age, lasts for a further six years, comprising a first cycle of four years and a second of two years. In 2005/06 enrolment at secondary schools was equivalent to 54% of children in the relevant age-group (males 49%; females 59%). In 1994 total enrolment at tertiary level was equivalent to 5.4% of the relevant age-group (males 4.2%; females 6.7%). In 2001/02 an estimated 587,300 students were enrolled at a total of 958 tertiary level institutions. Emphasis is placed on vocational and technical training. Current expenditure on education by the central Government in 2005/06 was 68,676m. kyats, representing 6.8% of total expenditure.

Public Holidays

2009: 4 January (Independence Day), 12 February (Union Day), 2 March (Peasants' Day, anniversary of the 1962 coup), 10 March* (Full Moon of Tabaung), 27 March (Armed Forces' Day), 13–16 April* (Maha Thingyan—Water Festival), 17 April* (Myanma New Year), 1 May (Workers' Day), 8 May* (Full Moon of Kason), 6 July* (Full Moon of Waso and beginning of Buddhist Lent), 19 July (Martyrs' Day), 3 October* (Full Moon of Thadingyut and end of Buddhist Lent), 18 October* (Deepavali), 1 November* (Tazaungdaing Festival), 11 November* (National Day), 16 December* (Kayin New Year), 25 December (Christmas Day).

2010: 4 January (Independence Day), 12 February (Union Day), 2 March (Peasants' Day, anniversary of the 1962 coup), March* (Full Moon of Tabaung), 27 March (Armed Forces' Day), 13–16 April* (Maha Thingyan—Water Festival), April* (Myanma New Year), May* (Full Moon of Kason), 1 May* (Workers' Day), 19 July (Martyrs' Day), July* (Full Moon of Waso and beginning of Buddhist Lent), October* (Full Moon of Thadingyut and end of Buddhist Lent), October* (Deepavali), November* (Tazaungdaing Festival), November/December* (National Day), December* (Kayin New Year), 25 December (Christmas Day).

* A number of holidays depend on lunar sightings.

Weights and Measures

The imperial system is in force.

MYANMAR

Statistical Survey

Source (unless otherwise stated): Central Statistical Organization, Ministry of National Planning and Economic Development, Building 32, Nay Pyi Taw; tel. (67) 406325; fax (67) 407265; e-mail cso.stat@mptmail.net.mm; internet www.csostat.gov.mm.

Area and Population

AREA, POPULATION AND DENSITY

Area (sq km)	676,552*
Population (census results)	
31 March 1973	28,885,867
31 March 1983†	
Males	17,507,837
Females	17,798,352
Total	35,306,189
Population (UN estimates at mid-year)‡	
2006	48,723,000
2007	48,129,000
2008	49,563,000
Density (per sq km) at mid-2008	73.3

* 261,218 sq miles.
† Figures exclude adjustment for underenumeration. Also excluded are 7,716 Myanma citizens (males 5,704, females 2,012) abroad.
‡ Source: UN, *World Population Prospects: The 2008 Revision*.

PRINCIPAL TOWNS
(population at census of 31 March 1983)

Yangon (Rangoon)	2,513,023		Pathein (Bassein)	144,096
Mandalay	532,949		Taunggyi	108,231
Mawlamyine (Moulmein)	219,961		Sittwe (Akyab)	107,621
Bago (Pegu)	150,528		Manywa	106,843

Source: UN, *Demographic Yearbook*.

Mid-2007 ('000, incl. suburbs, UN estimates): Yangon 4,088; Mandalay 961 (Source: UN, *World Urbanization Prospects: The 2007 Revision*).

BIRTHS AND DEATHS
(annual averages, UN estimates)

	1990–95	1995–2000	2000–05
Birth rate (per 1,000)	25.2	22.2	21.5
Death rate (per 1,000)	10.3	10.1	10.0

Source: UN, *World Population Prospects: The 2008 Revision*.

Life expectancy (years at birth, WHO estimates): 59.6 (males 56.8; females 62.7) in 2006 (Source: WHO, *World Health Statistics*).

ECONOMICALLY ACTIVE POPULATION*
('000 persons, official estimates)

	1997	1998
Agriculture, hunting, forestry and fishing	11,381	11,507
Mining and quarrying	132	121
Manufacturing	1,573	1,666
Electricity, gas and water	21	48
Construction	378	400
Trade, restaurants and hotels	1,746	1,781
Transport, storage and communications	470	495
Financing, insurance, real estate and business services	577	597
Community, social and personal services†	1,686	1,744
Total employed	17,964	18,359
Unemployed‡	535	452
Total labour force	18,499	18,811

* Excludes members of the armed forces.
† Includes activities not adequately defined.
‡ Persons aged 18 years and over.

Unemployed ('000 persons aged 18 years and over): 291.3 in 2004; 189.7 in 2005; n.a. in 2006; 118.7 in 2007 (Source: ILO).

Mid-2005 (estimates in '000): Agriculture, etc. 19,479; Total labour force 28,390 (Source: FAO).

Health and Welfare

KEY INDICATORS

Total fertility rate (children per woman, 2006)	2.1
Under-5 mortality rate (per 1,000 live births, 2005)	104
HIV/AIDS (% of persons aged 15–49, 2007)	0.7
Physicians (per 1,000 head, 2004)	0.4
Hospital beds (per 1,000 head, 2000)	0.7
Health expenditure (2006): US $ per head (PPP)	43
Health expenditure (2006): % of GDP	2.3
Health expenditure (2006): public (% of total)	16.8
Access to water (% of persons, 2006)	80
Access to sanitation (% of persons, 2006)	82
Human Development Index (2006): ranking	135
Human Development Index (2006): value	0.585

For sources and definitions, see explanatory note on p. vi.

Agriculture

PRINCIPAL CROPS
('000 metric tons)

	2005	2006	2007
Wheat*	145	148	143
Rice, paddy	25,364	30,600*	32,610*
Maize	918	950*	789*
Millet	205†	163*	166*
Potatoes	478	500†	510†
Sweet potatoes	52	56†	57†
Cassava	202	207†	211†
Sugar cane	6,937	7,300†	7,450†
Beans, dry†	1,700	1,750	1,765
Peas, dry†	36	38	40
Chick peas†	230	220	225
Cow peas, dry†	130	132	133
Pigeon peas	556	535†	540†
Arecanuts†	58	59	60
Soybeans (Soya beans)	189	120*	124†
Groundnuts, with shell	910*	910*	1,000†
Coconuts†	350	365	370
Sunflower seed	353*	350*	365†
Sesame seed	570*	580*	600†
Onions, dry†	780	735	740
Garlic†	126	125	128
Plantains†	650	625	630
Tea†	25	27	27
Jute†	28	30	30
Tobacco, unmanufactured†	33	35	36
Natural rubber	40*	43†	45†

* Unofficial figure.
† FAO estimate(s).

Aggregate production ('000 metric tons, may include official, semi-official or estimated data): Total cereals 26,644 in 2005, 31,874 in 2006, 33,720 in 2007; Total roots and tubers 732 in 2005, 763 in 2006, 778 in 2007; Total vegetables (incl. melons) 3,906 in 2005, 4,010 in 2006, 4,068 in 2007; Total fruits (excl. melons) 1,800 in 2005, 625 in 2006, 630 in 2007.

Source: FAO.

MYANMAR

LIVESTOCK
('000 head, year ending September)

	2005	2006	2007*
Horses*	130	130	130
Cattle	12,123	12,364	12,500
Buffaloes	2,705	2,770	2,820
Pigs	5,677	6,293	6,300
Sheep	517	567	570
Goats	1,846	2,024	205
Chickens	81,518	93,737	94,500
Ducks	9,112	10,098	10,500
Geese*	660	680	685

* FAO estimates.
Source: FAO.

LIVESTOCK PRODUCTS
('000 metric tons)

	2005	2006	2007*
Cattle meat	105.7	119.8	122.0
Buffalo meat	23.6	26.8	27.0
Goat meat	16.5	18.8	19.0
Pig meat	327.8	369.9	380.0
Chicken meat	560.7	649.6	653.0
Cows' milk	807.8	883.5	900.0
Buffaloes' milk	170.6	198.0	205.0
Goats' milk*	9.2	10.5	12.0
Hen eggs	186.6	209.9	212.0
Other poultry eggs*	14.2	16.8	17.5

* FAO estimates.
Source: FAO.

Forestry

ROUNDWOOD REMOVALS
('000 cubic metres, excl. bark)

	2003	2004	2005
Sawlogs, veneer logs and logs for sleepers	2,885	2,816	2,849
Other industrial wood	1,353	1,380	1,413
Fuel wood	37,954	37,560	38,286
Total	42,192	41,756	42,548

2006–07: Figures assumed to be unchanged from 2005 (FAO estimates).
Source: FAO.

SAWNWOOD PRODUCTION
('000 cubic metres, incl. railway sleepers)

	2003	2004	2005
Total (all broadleaved)	1,001	1,056	1,530

2006–07: Production assumed to be unchanged from 2005 (FAO estimate).
Source: FAO.

Fishing
('000 metric tons, live weight)

	2004	2005	2006
Capture	1,586.6*	1,732.3	2,006.8*
Freshwater fishes	454.3	503.5	631.1
Marine fishes	1,109.6	1,206.3	1,351.7
Aquaculture*	400.4	485.2	575.0
Common carp*	50.0	50.0	50.0
Roho labeo*	100.0	100.0	100.0
Total catch*	1,987.0	2,217.5	2,581.8

* FAO estimate(s).
Source: FAO.

Mining
(metric tons, unless otherwise indicated)

	2004	2005	2006
Coal and lignite	237,949	229,647	331,445
Crude petroleum ('000 barrels)	7,160	8,133	7,675
Natural gas (million cu m)*	10,277	11,648	12,501
Copper ore†	31,756	34,500	20,400
Lead ore†	2,000	2,000	2,000
Zinc ore†	196	78	46
Tin concentrates†	330	402	566
Chromium ore (gross weight)	364	409	400‡
Silver ore (kilograms)†	1,120	2,302	684
Gold ore (kilograms)†§‡	90	90	100
Feldspar‡§	10,000	10,000	10,000
Barite (Barytes)	2,224	2,058	2,930
Salt (unrefined, excl. brine)‡	35,000	35,000	35,000
Gypsum (crude)	71,155	67,522	68,651
Rubies, sapphires and spinel ('000 metric carats)§	6,199	5,220	3,017
Jade	12,408	19,446	20,647

* Marketed production.
† Figures refer to the metal content of ores and concentrates (including mixed concentrates).
‡ Estimated production.
§ Twelve months beginning 1 April of year stated.
Source: US Geological Survey.

Industry

SELECTED PRODUCTS OF STATE-OWNED ENTERPRISES
('000 metric tons unless otherwise indicated)

	2005/06	2006/07	2007/08
Sugar	38.1	34.8	25.5
Beer ('000 gallons)	2,727.9	1,978.1	1,653.5
Cigarettes (million)	2,818.9	2,754.9	3,037.6
Cotton fabrics ('000 yards)	17.7	20.5	15.5
Cotton yarn ('000 lbs)	9.1	16.4	16.6
Plywood ('000 sq ft)	116.2	444.4	525.0
Fertilizers	100.1	115.1	110.0
Diesel oil ('000 gallons)	54,079	72,698	55,802
Furnace oil ('000 gallons)	13,442	11,068	15,962
Liquefied petroleum gas ('000 gallons)	3,960	3,842	3,573
Motor spirit (petrol, '000 gallons)	106,683	109,327	109,940
Cement	543.1	576.6	611.4
Paper	19.0	18.6	14.9
Soap	69.7	73.4	76.8
Electric energy (million kWh)	6,064.2	6,172.3*	6,603.9*

* Provisional.

MYANMAR

Finance

CURRENCY AND EXCHANGE RATES

Monetary Units
100 pyas = 1 kyat.

Sterling, Dollar and Euro Equivalents (31 December 2008)
£1 sterling = 8.094 kyats;
US $1 = 5.552 kyats;
€1 = 7.727 kyats;
100 kyats = £12.36 = $18.01 = €12.94.

Average Exchange Rate (kyats per US $)
2006 5.784
2007 5.560
2007 5.397

Note: Since January 1975 the value of the kyat has been linked to the IMF's special drawing right (SDR). Since May 1977 the official exchange rate has been fixed at a mid-point of SDR 1 = 8.5085 kyats. On 1 June 1996 a new customs valuation exchange rate of US $1 = 100 kyats was introduced. In September 2001 the free market exchange rate was $1 = 450 kyats.

CENTRAL GOVERNMENT BUDGET
(million kyats, year ending 31 March, excl. capital account)

Current revenue and grants	2003/04	2004/05	2005/06
Tax revenue	170,569	297,104	476,945
Taxes on income, profits and capital gains	91,860	138,866	206,676
Domestic taxes on goods and services	74,107	136,626	251,821
General sales, turnover or value-added tax	58,214	112,543	225,121
Taxes on international trade and transactions	4,602	21,613	18,448
Other revenue	213,542	290,190	342,273
Grants	111	171	316
Total	384,222	587,465	819,534

Current expenditure	2003/04	2004/05	2005/06
General public services, incl. public order	114,195	206,848	354,848
Defence	172,633	173,558	197,792
Education	71,665	101,936	68,676
Health	18,808	26,545	21,963
Social security and welfare	7,865	9,933	8,406
Recreational, cultural and religious affairs	4,112	5,863	4,511
Economic affairs and services	194,354	234,513	346,361
Agriculture, forestry, fishing and hunting	61,056	71,028	93,300
Transportation	119,190	131,839	198,261
Housing and community amenities	7,397	8,622	6,228
Total	591,029	767,818	1,008,785

Source: IMF, *Government Finance Statistics Yearbook*.

INTERNATIONAL RESERVES
(US $ million at 31 December)

	2004	2005	2006
Gold (national valuation)	12.6	11.6	12.2
IMF special drawing rights	0.0	0.2	0.2
Foreign exchange	672.1	770.5	1,235.4
Total	684.7	782.3	1,247.8

Source: IMF, *International Financial Statistics*.

MONEY SUPPLY
(million kyats at 31 December)

	2005	2006	2007
Currency outside banks	1,743,654	2,152,917	2,696,621
Demand deposits at deposit money banks	209,324	318,897	520,490
Total money (incl. others)	1,953,337	2,471,900	3,217,307

Source: IMF, *International Financial Statistics*.

COST OF LIVING
(Consumer Price Index; base: 2000 = 100)

	2005	2006	2007
Food (incl. beverages)	303.2	365.7	493.9
Fuel and light	281.6	370.0	491.7
Clothing (incl. footwear)	299.6	337.6	462.9
Rent	333.0	388.8	518.7
All items (incl. others)	297.1	356.5	481.3

Source: ILO.

NATIONAL ACCOUNTS
(million kyats at current prices, year ending 31 March)

National Income and Product
Expenditure on the Gross Domestic Product

	2002/03	2003/04	2004/05
Final consumption expenditure	5,049,366	6,865,352	7,979,598
Increase in stocks	19,095	418	33,934
Gross fixed capital formation	551,749	850,124	1,060,038
Total domestic expenditure	5,620,210	7,715,894	9,073,570
Exports of goods and services	19,955	14,119	16,697
Less Imports of goods and services	14,910	13,398	11,339
GDP in purchasers' values	5,625,255	7,716,616	9,078,929
GDP at constant 2000/01 prices	3,184,117	3,624,926	4,119,435

Gross Domestic Product by Economic Activity

	2002/03	2003/04	2004/05
Agriculture, hunting, forestry and fishing	3,067,357	3,906,194	4,389,837
Mining and quarrying	25,163	34,583	56,636
Manufacturing	516,243	756,183	1,050,447
Electricity, gas and water	4,654	5,992	7,470
Construction	185,611	303,496	356,770
Wholesale and retail trade	1,326,615	1,743,643	2,022,045
Transport, storage and communications	358,124	776,704	933,588
Finance	4,799	5,297	6,602
Government services	50,724	64,742	103,890
Other services	85,965	119,782	151,644
GDP in purchasers' values	5,625,255	7,716,616	9,078,929

Source: Asian Development Bank, *Key Indicators of Developing Asian and Pacific Countries*.

BALANCE OF PAYMENTS
(US $ million)

	2004	2005	2006
Exports of goods f.o.b.	2,926.6	3,787.8	4,554.7
Imports of goods f.o.b.	−1,998.7	−1,759.4	−2,343.4
Trade balance	927.9	2,028.4	2,211.3
Exports of services	254.7	259.1	279.5
Imports of services	−459.6	−502.0	−562.9
Balance on goods and services	723.0	1,785.5	1,928.0
Other income received	40.4	55.5	97.8
Other income paid	−785.8	−1,427.3	−1,346.2
Balance on goods, services and income	−22.4	413.8	679.6
Current transfers received	160.6	197.8	161.4
Current transfers paid	−26.7	−23.8	−39.0
Current balance	111.5	587.7	802.0
Direct investment from abroad	213.5	237.2	278.6
Other investment liabilities	−88.3	−71.1	−25.6
Net errors and omissions	−142.7	−610.3	−632.1
Overall balance	94.0	143.6	422.9

Source: IMF, *International Financial Statistics*.

MYANMAR

External Trade

PRINCIPAL COMMODITIES
(distribution by SITC, million kyats, year ending 31 March)

Imports c.i.f.	2005/06	2006/07	2007/08*
Edible vegetable oil and other hydrogenated oils	571.1	478.2	1,057.7
Pharmaceutical products	362.1	554.9	635.6
Base metals and manufactures	1,164.0	1,183.6	1,206.2
Machinery and transport equipment	1,786.2	2,718.2	4,161.7
Electrical machinery and apparatus	645.8	707.6	861.1
Paper, paperboard and manufactures	295.8	302.8	292.3
Refined mineral oils	1,560.9	3,966.6	2,034.0
Fabric of artificial materials and synthetics	917.2	1,059.7	1,168.5
Plastic	574.3	719.7	857.0
Total (incl. others)	11,514.2	16,835.0	18,405.5

Exports f.o.b.	2005/06	2006/07	2007/08*
Dried beans, peas, etc. (shelled)	1,875.8	3,497.9	3,462.5
Fresh and dried prawns	576.1	608.0	556.3
Fish and fish products	544.4	725.4	1,059.4
Teak	1,723.1	1,750.1	1,540.0
Other hardwood	1,027.2	1,189.0	1,423.8
Base metals and ores	646.2	637.8	474.7
Gas	6,234.7	11,676.2	13,937.9
Garments	1,586.0	1,601.8	1,554.6
Total (incl. others)	20,646.6	30,026.1	35,294.0

* Preliminary.

PRINCIPAL TRADING PARTNERS
(million kyats, year ending 31 March)

Imports	2005/06	2006/07	2007/08*
China, People's Republic	2,716.0	4,185.8	5,468.8
Hong Kong	119.0	135.0	115.6
India	465.2	916.5	954.7
Indonesia	336.1	539.8	1,139.9
Japan	610.7	896.3	1,335.0
Korea, Republic	498.6	486.9	590.8
Malaysia	810.8	634.5	635.8
Singapore	3,240.2	5,928.0	4,489.8
Thailand	1,376.2	1,749.4	2,101.1
Total (incl. others)	11,514.2	16,835.0	18,405.5

Exports	2005/06	2006/07	2007/08*
China, People's Republic	2,125.2	3,530.4	3,832.7
Hong Kong	1,488.1	2,316.6	3,573.0
India	2,841.6	4,217.2	4,005.9
Indonesia	380.5	506.4	477.0
Japan	790.4	952.4	1,021.3
Malaysia	540.4	507.6	652.6
Singapore	1,532.7	1,047.9	2,210.1
Thailand	7,868.6	13,533.8	15,527.7
United Kingdom	356.1	290.7	316.5
Total (incl. others)	20,646.6	30,026.1	35,294.0

* Preliminary.

Transport

RAILWAYS
(traffic, million)

	2005/06	2006/07	2007/08*
Passenger-miles	2,969	3,298	3,323
Freight ton-miles	570	551	538

* Provisional.

ROAD TRAFFIC
(registered motor vehicles at 31 March)

	2005/06	2006/07	2007/08
Passenger cars	196,314	206,020	222,661
Trucks	54,801	55,382	57,211
Buses	18,038	18,857	19,291
Motorcycles	641,777	646,872	658,997
Others	68,358	69,625	74,682
Total	979,288	996,756	1,032,842

INLAND WATERWAYS
(traffic by state-owned vessels)

	2005/06	2006/07	2007/08
Passenger-miles (million)	589	655	721
Freight ton-miles (million)	455	520	582

SHIPPING

Merchant Fleet
(registered at 31 December)

	2005	2006	2007
Number of vessels	125	126	118
Displacement ('000 grt)	435.5	397.3	203.2

Source: Lloyd's Register-Fairplay, *World Fleet Statistics*.

International Sea-Borne Traffic
('000 metric tons)

	2005/06	2006/07	2007/08
Goods loaded	1,173	1,479	1,951
Goods unloaded	3,252	3,582	4,252

CIVIL AVIATION
(traffic on scheduled services)

	2002	2003	2004
Kilometres flown (million)	15	16	19
Passengers carried ('000)	1,186	1,117	1,392
Passenger-km (million)	1,154	1,083	1,339
Total ton-km (million)	106	100	122

Source: UN, *Statistical Yearbook*.

2005/06 (million): Passenger-miles 73.1.
2006/07 (million): Passenger-miles 75.3.
2007/08 (million): Passenger-miles 77.6.

Tourism

TOURIST ARRIVALS BY COUNTRY OF NATIONALITY

	2004	2005	2006
Australia	6,069	6,342	6,583
China, People's Republic	17,890	19,596	24,893
France	13,372	15,295	15,498
Germany	14,112	13,689	18,003
India	8,357	7,679	7,540
Italy	7,924	7,083	10,774
Japan	20,296	19,584	18,945
Korea, Republic	10,405	10,934	18,265
Malaysia	12,478	9,858	9,588
Singapore	11,292	9,674	10,952
Taiwan	20,424	17,600	15,827
Thailand	32,735	27,199	30,400
United Kingdom	7,720	8,126	7,465
USA	16,432	16,598	18,052
Total (incl. others)	241,938	232,218	263,514

Tourism receipts (US $ million, incl. passenger transport): 97 in 2004; 85 in 2005; 59 in 2006.

Source: World Tourism Organization.

MYANMAR

Communications Media

	2004	2005	2006
Telephones ('000 main lines in use)	424.9	503.9	n.a.
Mobile cellular telephones ('000 subscribers)	92.5	128.7	214.2
Personal computers ('000 in use)	325	400	n.a.
Internet users ('000)	12	32	35
Broadband subscribers ('000)	n.a.	0.2	0.8

2007: Internet users 40,000; Broadband subscribers 1,500.

Book production (1999): 227 titles.

Newspapers (1998): 4 dailies (average circulation 400,000).

Facsimile machines (number in use): 2,540 in 1999.

Radio receivers ('000 in use): 3,157 in 1999.

Television receivers ('000 in use): 344.3 in 2000.

Sources: International Telecommunication Union; UNESCO, *Statistical Yearbook*; UN, *Statistical Yearbook*.

Education

(1994/95, provisional)

	Institutions	Teachers	Students
Primary schools*	35,856	169,748	5,711,202
Middle schools	2,058	53,859	1,390,065
High schools	858	18,045	389,438
Vocational schools	86	1,847	21,343
Teacher training	17	615	4,031
Higher education	45	6,246	247,348
Universities	6	2,901	62,098

* Excluding 1,152 monastic primary schools with an enrolment of 45,360.

2001/02 (provisional): *Primary:* Institutions 36,010, Teachers 143,490, Students ('000) 4,793.5; *General Secondary:* Institutions 2,110, Teachers 53,896, Students ('000) 1,600.9; *Tertiary:* Institutions 958, Teachers 15,947, Students ('000) 587.3 (Source: UN, *Statistical Yearbook for Asia and the Pacific*).

Adult literacy rate (UNESCO estimates): 89.9% (males 93.9%; females 86.4%) in 2000 (Source: UNESCO Institute for Statistics).

Directory

The Constitution

In August 2003 the ruling State Peace and Development Council (SPDC) announced that it planned to reconvene the National Convention in 2004 in order to commence the drafting of a new constitution. The National Convention met in May 2004 and several times thereafter. The resultant draft Constitution was officially published in April 2008. It was submitted to a national referendum on 10 May (postponed until 24 May in regions affected by a major cyclone earlier in the month). The new Constitution, which according to the SPDC was approved by 92.48% of voters, was enacted on 29 May.

The official name of the country is the Republic of the Union of Myanmar. The capital is Nay Pyi Taw, which stands as a region directly under the administration of the Chairman. The nation is divided into seven regions and seven states of national races, with six self-administered zones of six ethnic minorities.

The Chairman is the Head of State. Of the three candidates for the position of Chairman, at least one must be a member of the military, and a member of the military must be at least one of the two Vice-Chairmen. The Chairman is not answerable to court or to parliament in exercising his or her duties. The Chairman can declare a state of emergency, during which time the Commander-in-Chief of the defence forces, with the aid of the National Defence and Security Council (six of the 11 members of which are military personnel) assumes legislative, executive and judicial powers.

The Pyidaungsu Hluttaw (Union Parliament) consists of a Pyithu Hluttaw (House of Representatives, the lower chamber) and Amyotha Hluttaw (House of Nationalities, the upper chamber). Legislative power is shared by the Union Parliament, regional parliaments and state parliaments, as well as self-administered zones and divisions.

The Pyithu Hluttaw consists of 224 seats, of which 56 are reserved for the military. The Amyotha Hluttaw consists of 440 seats, of which 110 are reserved for the military. Military representatives must comprise one-third of the members of the state and regional assemblies.

Multi-party democratic elections will be held in 2010. Candidates are barred from standing for election if they or their parties accept support from foreign governments or religious organizations. Persons married to a foreign national are barred from holding political office. Members of religious orders and destitute persons are not permitted to vote.

The military has a leading role in the country's national politics. Ministers for defence, home affairs, security and border affairs must be members of the military. The Commander-in-Chief of the defence forces is authorized to exercise all state power should an emergency arise that threatens the disintegration of the union, the disintegration of sovereignty or the loss of national sovereignty. A state of emergency may be extended to a period of at least a year. The military is immune from prosecution for any actions undertaken during emergency rule.

Citizens may not be detained for more than 24 hours without trial, except on security or similar grounds.

The Constitution can be amended only with the approval of 75% of parliamentarians and one-half of the eligible voters.

The Government

HEAD OF STATE

Chairman of the State Peace and Development Council: Field Marshal THAN SHWE (took office as Head of State 23 April 1992).

STATE PEACE AND DEVELOPMENT COUNCIL
(April 2009)

Chairman: Field Marshal THAN SHWE.

Vice-Chairman: Dep. Senior Gen. MAUNG AYE.

First Secretary: Lt-Gen. Thiha Thura TIN AUNG MYINT OO.

Other members: Rear-Adm. KYI MIN, Lt-Gen. KYAW THAN, Lt-Gen. AUNG HTWE, Lt-Gen. YE MYINT, Lt-Gen. KHIN MAUNG THAN, Maj.-Gen. KYAW WIN, Maj.-Gen. Thura SHWE MANN, Maj.-Gen. MYINT AUNG, Lt-Gen. MAUNG BO, Lt-Gen. TIN AYE.

CABINET
(April 2009)

Prime Minister: Gen. THEIN SEIN.

Minister of Defence: Field Marshal THAN SHWE.

Minister of Military Affairs: Lt-Gen. Thiha Thura TIN AUNG MYINT OO.

Minister of Agriculture and Irrigation: Maj.-Gen. HTAY OO.

Minister of Industry (No. 1): AUNG THAUNG.

Minister of Industry (No. 2): Vice-Adm. SOE THEIN.

Minister of Foreign Affairs: Maj.-Gen. NYAN WIN.

Minister of National Planning and Economic Development: SOE THA.

Minister of Transport: Maj.-Gen. THEIN SHWE.

Minister of Culture: Maj.-Gen. KHIN AUNG MYINT.

Minister of Co-operatives: Maj.-Gen. TIN HTUT.

Minister of Post-Cyclone Management and Resettlement: Maj.-Gen. MAUNG MAUNG SWE.

Minister of Rail Transportation: Maj.-Gen. AUNG MIN.

Minister of Energy: Brig.-Gen. LUN THI.

Minister of Education: CHAN NYEIN.

Minister of Health: Dr KYAW MYINT.

Minister of Commerce: Brig.-Gen. TIN NAING THEIN.

Minister of Communications, Posts and Telegraphs: Brig.-Gen. THEIN ZAW.

Minister of Finance and Revenue: Maj.-Gen. HLA TUN.

Minister of Religious Affairs: Brig.-Gen. THURA MYINT MAUNG.

Minister of Construction and Electric Power (2): Maj.-Gen. KHIN MAUNG MYINT.

Minister of Science and Technology: U THAUNG.

Minister of Labour and of Relations with Aung San Suu Kyi: AUNG KYI.

MYANMAR

Minister of Immigration and Population and Home Affairs: Maj.-Gen. MAUNG OO.
Minister of Information: Brig.-Gen. KYAW HSAN.
Minister of Progress of Border Areas, National Races and Development Affairs: Col THEIN NYUNT.
Minister of Electric Power (No. 1): Col ZAW MIN.
Minister of Sports: Brig.-Gen. THURA AYE MYINT.
Minister of Forestry: Brig.-Gen. THEIN AUNG.
Minister of Mines: Brig.-Gen. OHN MYINT.
Minister of Livestock and Fisheries: Brig.-Gen. MAUNG MAUNG THEIN.
Minister of Hotels and Tourism: Maj.-Gen. SOE NAING.
Minister at the Office of the Prime Minister: U KO LAY.

MINISTRIES

Office of the Chairman of the State Peace and Development Council: 15–16 Windermere Park, Yangon; tel. (1) 282445.
Prime Minister's Office: Minister's Office, Theinbyu St, Botahtaung Township, Yangon; tel. (1) 283742.
Ministry of Agriculture and Irrigation: Bldg 15, Nay Pyi Taw; tel. (67) 410004; fax (67) 140130; e-mail dap.moai@mptmail.net.mm; internet www.moai.gov.mm.
Ministry of Commerce: Bldg 3, Nay Pyi Taw; tel. (67) 408002; fax (67) 408007; e-mail moc@commerce.gov.mm; internet www.commerce.gov.mm.
Ministry of Communications, Posts and Telegraphs: Bldg 2, Nay Pyi Taw; tel. (67) 407037; internet www.mcpt.gov.mm.
Ministry of Construction: Office No 11, Nay Pyi Taw; tel. (67) 407073; fax (67) 407181; e-mail pwscon@constuction.gov.mm; internet www.construction.gov.mm.
Ministry of Co-operatives: Bldg 16, Nay Pyi Taw; tel. (67) 410032; fax (67) 410036; e-mail mcop@mptmail.net.mm; internet www.myancoop.gov.mm.
Ministry of Culture: Bldg 35, Nay Pyi Taw; tel. (67) 408023; fax (1) 283794; internet www.myanmar.com/Ministry/culture.
Ministry of Defence: Ahlanpya Phaya St, Yangon; tel. (1) 281611.
Ministry of Education: Bldg 13, Nay Pyi Taw; tel. (67) 407131; internet www.myanmar-education.edu.mm.
Ministry of Electric Power: Bldg 38, Nay Pyi Taw; tel. (67) 411083; internet www.energy.gov.mm/MEP_1.htm.
Ministry of Energy: Bldg 6, Nay Pyi Taw; tel. (67) 411060; e-mail myanmoe@mptmail.net.mm; internet www.energy.gov.mm.
Ministry of Finance and Revenue: Bldg 26, Nay Pyi Taw; tel. (67) 410046; internet www.myanmar.com/Ministry/finance.
Ministry of Foreign Affairs: Bldg 19, Nay Pyi Taw; tel. (67) 412009; e-mail mofa.aung@mptmail.net.mm; internet www.mofa.gov.mm.
Ministry of Forestry: Bldg 28, Nay Pyi Taw; tel. (67) 405004; internet www.energy.gov.mm/MOF_1.htm.
Ministry of Health: Bldg 4, Nay Pyi Taw; tel. (67) 411358; internet www.moh.gov.mm.
Ministry of Home Affairs: Bldg 10, Nay Pyi Taw; tel. (67) 412079; internet www.moha.gov.mm.
Ministry of Hotels and Tourism: Bldg 33, Nay Pyi Taw; tel. (67) 406056; fax (67) 406057; e-mail dg.dht@mptmail.net.mm; internet www.hotel-tourism.gov.mm.
Ministry of Immigration and Population: Bldg 23, Nay Pyi Taw; tel. (67) 404026; internet www.myanmar.com/Ministry/imm&popu.
Ministry of Industry (No. 1): Bldg 37, Nay Pyi Taw; tel. (67) 408080; e-mail moi1@myanmar.com.mm; internet www.myanmar.com/Ministry/MOI-1.
Ministry of Industry (No. 2): Bldg 30, Nay Pyi Taw; tel. (67) 405042; e-mail dmip@mptmail.net.mm; internet www.industry2.gov.mm.
Ministry of Information: Bldg 7, Nay Pyi Taw; tel. (67) 412321.
Ministry of Labour: Bldg 21, Nay Pyi Taw; tel. (67) 404339.
Ministry of Livestock and Fisheries: Bldg 36, Nay Pyi Taw; tel. (67) 408045; e-mail dolf@mptmail.net.mm; internet www.livestock-fisheries.gov.mm.
Ministry of Military Affairs: Nay Pyi Taw.
Ministry of Mines: Bldg 19, Nay Pyi Taw; tel. (67) 409001; internet www.energy.gov.mm/MOM_1.htm.
Ministry of National Planning and Economic Development: Bldg 1, Nay Pyi Taw; tel. (67) 407023; e-mail ministry.nped@mptmail.net.mm; internet www.mnped.gov.mm.
Ministry of Progress of Border Areas, National Races and Development Affairs: Bldg 14, Nay Pyi Taw; tel. (67) 409022.
Ministry of Rail Transportation: Bldg 29, Nay Pyi Taw; tel. (67) 405034.
Ministry of Religious Affairs: Bldg 31, Nay Pyi Taw; tel. (67) 406008; internet www.mora.gov.mm.
Ministry of Science and Technology: Bldg 21, Nay Pyi Taw; tel. (67) 404451.
Ministry of Social Welfare, Relief and Resettlement: Bldg 23, Nay Pyi Taw; tel. (67) 404021; e-mail social-wel-myan@mptmail.net.mm; internet www.myanmar.gov.mm/ministry/MSWRR/index.htm.
Ministry of Sports: Bldg 31, Nay Pyi Taw; tel. (67) 406028; e-mail MOCYGN.MYA@mptmail.net.mm.
Ministry of Transport: Bldg 5, Nay Pyi Taw; tel. (67) 411039; fax (67) 411038; e-mail minotran@mptmail.net.mm; internet www.mot.gov.mm.

Legislature

CONSTITUENT ASSEMBLY

Following the military coup of 18 September 1988, the 489-member Pyithu Hluttaw (People's Assembly), together with all other state organs, was abolished. A general election was held on 27 May 1990. It was subsequently announced, however, that the new body was to serve as a constituent assembly, responsible for the drafting of a new constitution, and that it was to have no legislative power. The next legislative election was provisionally scheduled for September 1997, but did not take place.

General Election, 27 May 1990

Party	% of Votes	Seats
National League for Democracy	59.9	392
Shan Nationalities League for Democracy	1.7	23
Arakan (Rakhine) League for Democracy	1.2	11
National Unity Party	21.2	10
Mon National Democratic Front	1.0	5
National Democratic Party for Human Rights	0.9	4
Chin National League for Democracy	0.4	3
Kachin State National Congress for Democracy	0.1	3
Party for National Democracy	0.5	3
Union Pa-O National Organization	0.3	3
Zomi National Congress		2
Naga Hill Regional Progressive Party		2
Kayah State Nationalities League for Democracy		2
Ta-ang (Palaung) National League for Democracy		2
Democratic Organization for Kayan National Unity		2
Democracy Party		1
Graduates' and Old Students' Democratic Association		1
Patriotic Old Comrades' League	12.8	1
Shan State Kokang Democratic Party		1
Union Danu League for Democracy Party		1
Kamans National League for Democracy		1
Mara People's Party		1
Union Nationals Democracy Party		1
Mro (or) Khami National Solidarity Organization		1
Lahu National Development Party		1
United League of Democratic Parties		1
Karen (Kayin) State National Organization		1
Independents		6
Total	**100.0**	**485**

Political Organizations

A total of 93 parties contested the general election of May 1990. By October 1995 the ruling military junta had deregistered all except nine political parties:

Kokang Democracy and Unity Party: Yangon.

MYANMAR

Directory

Mro (or) Khami National Solidarity Organization: Kyauktaw; f. 1988; Leader SAN THA AUNG.

National League for Democracy (NLD): 97B West Shwegondine Rd, Bahan Township, Yangon; f. 1988; initially known as the National United Front for Democracy, and subsequently as the League for Democracy; present name adopted in Sept. 1988; central exec. cttee of 10 mems; Gen. Sec. AUNG SAN SUU KYI; Chair. AUNG SHWE; Vice-Chair. TIN OO.

National Unity Party (NUP): 93C Windermere Rd, Kamayut, Yangon; tel. (1) 278180; f. 1962; est. as the Burma Socialist Programme Party; sole legal political party until Sept. 1988, when present name was adopted; 15-mem. Cen. Exec. Cttee and 280-mem. Cen. Cttee; Chair. THA KYAW; Gen. Secs TUN YI, THAN TIN.

Shan Nationalities League for Democracy (SNLD): f. 1988; Chair. KHUN HTUN OO; Sec.-Gen. SAI NYUNT LWIN.

Shan State Kokang Democratic Party: 140 40 St, Kyauktada; f. 1988; Leader YANKYIN MAW.

Union Karen (Kayin) League: Saw Toe Lane, Yangon.

Union Pa-O National Organization: f. 1988; Leader KHUN SEIN WIN HLA.

Wa National Development Party: Byuhar St, Yangon.

The following parties contested the general election of March 1990 but subsequently had their legal status annulled:

Anti-Fascist People's Freedom League: Bo Aung Kyaw St, Bahan Township, Yangon; f. 1988; assumed name of wartime resistance movement that became Myanmar's major political force after independence; Chair. BO KYAW NYUNT; Gen. Sec. CHO CHO KYAW NYEIN.

Democracy Party: f. 1988; comprises supporters of fmr Prime Minister U NU; Chair. THU WAI; Vice-Chair. KHUN YE NAUNG.

Democratic Front for National Reconstruction: Yangon; f. 1988; left-wing.

Lahu National Development Party: f. 1988; deregistered 1994; Leader DANIEL AUNG.

League for Democracy and Peace: 10 Wingaba Rd, Bahan Township, Yangon; f. 1988; Gen. Sec. THEIN SEIN.

Party for National Democracy: Yangon; f. 1988; Chair. Dr SEIN WIN.

Union National Democracy Party (UNDP): 2–4 Shin Saw Pu Rd, Sanchaung Township, Yangon; f. 1988; est. by Brig.-Gen. AUNG GYI (fmr Chair. of the National League for Democracy); Chair. KYAW MYINT LAY.

United League of Democratic Parties: 875 Compound 21, Ledauntkan St, Sa-Hsa Ward, Thingangyun Township, Yangon; f. 1989.

United Nationalities League for Democracy: Yangon; an alliance of parties representing non-Bamar nationalities; won a combined total of 65 seats at the 1990 election.

Other deregistered parties included the Arakan (Rakhine) League for Democracy, the Mon National Democratic Front, the National Democratic Party for Human Rights, the Chin National League for Democracy, the Kachin State National Congress for Democracy, the Zomi National Congress, the Naga Hill Regional Progressive Party, the Kayah State Nationalities League for Democracy, the Ta-ang (Palaung) National League for Democracy, the Democratic Organization for Kayan National Unity, the Graduates' and Old Students' Democratic Association, the Patriotic Old Comrades' League, the Union Danu League for Democracy, the Kamans National League for Democracy, the Mara People's Party and the Karen (Kayin) State National Organization.

The following groups are, or have been, in armed conflict with the Government:

Burma Democratic Alliance (BDA): f. 2004; opposition alliance composed of several dissident organizations; Leader Dr NAING AUNG.

Chin National Army: Chin State.

Chin National Front: f. 1988; forces trained by Kachin Independence Army 1989–91; first party congress 1993; conference in March 1996; carried out an active bombing campaign in 1996–97, mainly in the Chin State; Pres. THOMAS TANG NO.

Communist Party of Burma (CPB): f. 1939; reorg. 1946; operated clandestinely after 1948; participated after 1986 in jt military operations with sections of the NDF; in 1989 internal dissent resulted in the rebellion of about 80% of CPB members, mostly Wa hill tribesmen and Kokang Chinese; the CPB's military efficacy was thus completely destroyed; Chair. of Cen. Cttee Thakin BA THEIN TIN (exiled).

Democratic Alliance of Burma (DAB): Manerplaw; f. 1988; formed by members of the NDF to incorporate dissident students, monks and expatriates; Pres. Maj.-Gen. BO MYA; Gen. Sec. TIN MAUNG WIN; remaining organizations include:

All-Burma Student Democratic Front (ABSDF): Dagwin; f. 1988; in 1990 split into two factions, under MOE THI ZUN and NAING AUNG; the two factions reunited in 1993; Chair. THAN KHE; Sec.-Gen. MYO WIN.

Karen (Kayin) National Union (KNU): f. 1948; Chair. Gen. TAMALABAW; Vice-Chair. DAVID TAKAPAW; Gen. Sec. ZIPPORAH SEIN; military wing: Karen (Kayin) National Liberation Army (KNLA); c. 6,000 troops; Chief of Staff MU TU.

Karenni (Kayinni) National Progressive Party: agreement with the SLORC signed in March 1995 but subsequently collapsed; resumed fighting in June 1996; Chair. Gen. AUNG THAN LAY; military wing: Karenni (Kayinni) Revolutionary Army.

God's Army: breakaway faction of the KNU; Leaders JOHNNY HTOO, LUTHER HTOO (surrendered to the Thai authorities in Jan. 2001).

National Democratic Front (NDF): f. 1975; aims to establish a federal union based on national self-determination; largely defunct.

National Socialist Council of Nagaland: Sagaing Division; comprises various factions.

Shan State Army (SSA): enlarged in Sept. 1997 through formal alliance between the following:

Shan State National Army (SSNA): Shan State; f. 1995; breakaway group from Mong Tai Army (MTA); Shan separatists; 5,000–6,000 troops; Leader KARN YORD.

Shan State Peace Council (SSPC): fmrly Shan State Progressive Party; Pres. HSO HTEN; Gen. Sec. KARN YORD; cease-fire agreement signed in Sept. 1989, but broken by SSA elements following establishment of above alliance in Sept. 1997; military wing: original **Shan State Army** (5,000 men); Leaders SAI NONG, KAI HPA, PANG HPA.

Other MTA remnants also participated in the alliance.

Vigorous Burmese Student Warriors (VBSW): f. 1999.

Most of the following groups have signed cease-fire agreements, or reached other means of accommodation, with the ruling military junta (the date given in parentheses indicates the month in which agreement with the junta was concluded):

Democratic Karen (Kayin) Buddhist Organization: Manerplaw; breakaway group from the KNU; military wing: Democratic Karen (Kayin) Buddhist Army.

Kachin Democratic Army: (Jan. 1991); fmrly the 4th Brigade of the Kachin Independence Army; Leader ZAW MAING.

Kachin Independence Organization (KIO): (Oct. 1993); Chair. U LAMON TU JAI; military wing: Kachin Independence Army.

Karen (Kayin) Solidarity Organization (KSO): f. 1997; fmrly All Karen Solidarity and Regeneration Front; breakaway group from the KNU; 21-mem. exec. cttee; advocates nation-wide cease-fire and the settlement of all national problems through negotiations; Pres. SAW W. P. NI; Sec.-Gen. MAHN AUNG HTAY.

Karenni (Kayinni) National People's Liberation Front: (May 1994); Leader TUN KYAW.

Kayan National Guard: (Feb. 1992).

Kayan New Land Party: (July 1994); Leader THAN SOE NAING.

Myanmar National Democracy Alliance: (March 1989).

National Democracy Alliance Army: (June 1989).

New Democratic Army: Kachin; (Dec. 1989).

New Mon State Party: (June 1995); Chair. (vacant); military wing: Mon National Liberation Army.

Palaung State Liberation Organization: (April 1991); military wing: Palaung State Liberation Army; 7,000–8,000 men.

Pa-O National Organization: (Feb. 1991); Chair. AUNG KHAM HTI; military wing: Pa-O National Army.

Shan State Nationalities People's Liberation Organization: (Oct. 1994); Chair. THA KALEI.

United Wa State Party: (May 1989); fmrly part of the Communist Party of Burma; military wing: **United Wa State Army** (10,000–15,000 men); Leaders CHAO NGI LAI, PAO YU CHANG.

Since 1991 the National Coalition Government of the Union of Burma, constituted by representatives elected in the general election of 1990, has served as a government-in-exile:

National Coalition Government of the Union of Burma (NCGUB): 77 South Washington Street, Suite 308, Rockville, Maryland 20850, USA; tel. (301) 424-4810; fax (301) 424-4812; e-mail ncgub@ncgub.net; internet www.ncgub.net; Prime Minister Dr SEIN WIN.

MYANMAR   *Directory*

Diplomatic Representation

EMBASSIES IN MYANMAR

Australia: 88 Strand Rd, Yangon; tel. (1) 251810; fax (1) 246159; internet www.burma.embassy.gov.au; Ambassador MICHELLE CHAN.

Bangladesh: 11B Than Lwin Rd, Yangon; tel. (1) 515275; fax (1) 515273; e-mail bdootygn@mptmail.net.mm; Ambassador Maj.-Gen. ABU ROSHDE ROKONUDDAWLA.

Brunei: 317/319 U Wisara Rd, Sanchaung Township, Yangon; tel. (1) 524285; fax (1) 512854; Ambassador Brig.-Gen. Dato' Paduka Haji MOHAMAD YUSOF BIN ABU BAKAR.

Cambodia: 34 Kaba Aye Pagoda Rd, Yangon; tel. (1) 549609; fax (1) 546156; e-mail recyangon@mptmail.net.mm; Ambassador HUL PHANY.

China, People's Republic: 1 Pyidaungsu Yeiktha Rd, Yangon; tel. (1) 221281; fax (1) 227019; e-mail chinaemb_mm@mfa.gov.cn; internet mm.china-embassy.org; Ambassador YE DABO.

Egypt: 81 Pyidaungsu Yeiktha Rd, Yangon; tel. (1) 222886; fax (1) 222865; Ambassador YOUSSEF KAMAL BOUTROS HANNA.

France: 102 Pyidaungsu Yeiktha Rd, POB 858, Yangon; tel. (1) 212523; fax (1) 212527; e-mail ambafrance-rangoun@diplomatie .gouv.fr; internet www.ambafrance-mm.org; Ambassador JEAN-PIERRE LAFOSSE.

Germany: 9 Bogyoke Aung San Museum Rd, POB 12, Yangon; tel. (1) 548951; fax (1) 548899; e-mail info@rangun.diplo.de; internet www.rangun.diplo.de; Ambassador JULIUS GEORG LUY.

India: 545–547 Merchant St, POB 751, Yangon; tel. (1) 282552; fax (1) 254086; e-mail amb.indembygn@mptmail.net.mm; internet www .indiaembassy.net.mm; Ambassador ALOKE SEN.

Indonesia: 100 Pyidaungsu Yeiktha Rd, POB 1401, Yangon; tel. (1) 254465; fax (1) 254468; e-mail kbriygn@indosat.net.id; internet www .indonesia.com.mm; Ambassador WYOSO PROJOWARSITO.

Israel: 15 Khabaung Road, Hlaing Township, Yangon; tel. (1) 515115; fax (1) 515116; e-mail info@yangon.mfa.gov.il; internet yangon.mfa.gov.il; Ambassador YARON MAYER.

Italy: 3 Inya Myaing Rd, POB 866, Golden Valley, Bahan Township, Yangon 11201; tel. (1) 527100; fax (1) 514565; e-mail ambitaly@ ambitaly.net.mm; internet www.italian-embassy.org.ae/ ambasciata_yangon; Ambassador GIUSEPPE CINTI.

Japan: 100 Natmauk Rd, POB 841, Bahan Township, Yangon 11021; tel. (1) 549644; fax (1) 549643; e-mail jembassy@baganmail .net.mm; internet www.mm.emb-japan.go.jp; Ambassador YASUAKI NOGAWA.

Korea, Republic: 97 University Ave, Yangon; tel. (1) 515190; fax (1) 513286; e-mail myanmar@mofat.go.kr; internet mmr.mofat.go.kr; Ambassador PARK GI-JONG.

Laos: A1 Diplomatic Quarters, Franser Rd, Yangon; tel. (1) 222482; fax (1) 227446; Ambassador KOUILY SOUPHAKET.

Malaysia: 82 Pyidaungsu Yeiktha Rd, Dagon Township, Yangon; tel. (1) 220249; fax (1) 221840; e-mail malyangon@kln.gov.my; internet www.kln.gov.my/perwakilan/yangon; Ambassador Datuk MAZLAN MUHAMMAD.

Nepal: 16 Natmauk Yeiktha Rd, POB 84, Tamwe, Yangon; tel. (1) 545880; fax (1) 549803; e-mail nepemb@mptmail.net.mm; Ambassador GUNA LAXMI SHARMA BISWAKARMA.

Pakistan: A4 Diplomatic Quarters, Pyay Rd, Dagon Township, Yangon; tel. (1) 222881; fax (1) 221147; e-mail parepygn@ myanmar.com.mm; Ambassador QAZI M. KHALILULLAH.

Philippines: 50 Saya San Rd, Bahan Township, Yangon; tel. (1) 558149; fax (1) 558154; e-mail phyangon@mptmail.net.mm; Ambassador PHOEBE ABAYA GOMEZ.

Russia: 38 Sagawa Rd, Yangon; tel. (1) 241955; fax (1) 241953; e-mail rusinmyan@mptmail.net.mm; internet www.rusembmyanmar.org; Ambassador MIKHAIL M. MGELADZE.

Serbia: 114A Inya Rd, POB 943, Yangon; tel. (1) 515282; fax (1) 504274; e-mail serbemb@yangon.net.mn; Chargé d'affaires a.i. DRAGAN JANEKOVIĆ.

Singapore: 238 Dhamazedi Rd, Bahan Township, Yangon; tel. (1) 559001; fax (1) 559002; e-mail singemb_ygn@sgmfa.gov.sg; internet www.mfa.gov.sg/yangon; Ambassador ROBERT CHUA.

Sri Lanka: 34 Taw Win Rd, POB 1150, Yangon; tel. (1) 222812; fax (1) 221509; e-mail srilankaemb@mpt.net.mm; Ambassador P. A. D. SAMARASEKERA.

Thailand: 73 Manawhari St, Dagon Township, Yangon; tel. (1) 224647; fax (1) 225929; e-mail thaiygn@mfa.go.th; Ambassador BANSARN BUNNAG.

United Kingdom: 80 Strand Rd, Kyauktada Township, Yangon; tel. (1) 370863; fax (1) 370866; e-mail chancery.Rangoon@fco.gov.uk; Ambassador ANDREW HEYN (designate).

USA: 581 Merchant St, POB 521, Yangon; tel. (1) 379880; fax (1) 256018; e-mail info.rangoon@state.gov; internet rangoon.usembassy .gov; Chargé d'affaires LARRY DINGER.

Viet Nam: 317–319 U Wisara Rd, Sanchaung Township, Yangon; tel. (1) 524656; fax (1) 524285; e-mail vnembmyr@bertech.net.mm; internet www.vietnamembassy-myanmar.org; Ambassador TRAN VAN TUNG.

Judicial System

A new judicial structure was established in March 1974. Its highest organ, composed of members of the People's Assembly, was the Council of People's Justices, which functioned as the central Court of Justice. Below this Council were the state, divisional, township, ward and village tract courts formed with members of local People's Councils. These arrangements ceased to operate following the imposition of military rule in September 1988, when a Supreme Court with five members was appointed. A chief justice, an attorney-general and a deputy attorney-general were also appointed. In March 2003 a deputy chief justice, four more justices and two further deputy attorney-generals were appointed.

Office of the Supreme Court

Bldg 24, Nay Pyi Taw; tel. (67) 404140.

Chief Justice: AUNG TOE.

Attorney-General: AYE MAUNG.

Religion

Freedom of religious belief and practice is guaranteed. In 1992 an estimated 87.2% of the population were Buddhists, 5.6% Christians, 3.6% Muslims, 1.0% Hindus and 2.6% animists or adherents of other religions.

BUDDHISM

State Sangha Maha Nayaka Committee: c/o Dept of Promotion and Propagation of the Sasana, Kaba Aye Pagoda Precinct, Mayangone Township, Yangon; tel. (1) 660759.

CHRISTIANITY

Myanmar Naing-ngan Khrityan Athin-dawmyar Kaung-si (Myanmar Council of Churches): 601 Pyay Rd, University PO, Kamayut, Yangon 11041; tel. (1) 537957; fax (1) 296848; e-mail oikoumedia@gmail.com; internet mcc-mm.org; f. 1914 as Burma Representative Council of Mission; reconstituted as Burma Council of Churches in 1974; 13 mem. nat. churches, 9 mem. nat. Christian orgs; Pres. Rev. SAW MAR GAY GYI; Gen. Sec. Rt Rev. SMITH N. ZA THAWNG.

The Roman Catholic Church

Myanmar comprises three archdioceses and 11 dioceses. At 31 December 2006 an estimated 1.2% of the total population were adherents.

Catholic Bishops' Conference of Myanmar

292 Pyay Rd, POB 1080, Sanchaung PO, Yangon 11111; tel. (1) 525868; fax (1) 527198; e-mail clspcbcm@mptmail.net.mm.

f. 1982; Pres. Most Rev. PAUL ZINGTUNG GRAWNG (Archbishop of Mandalay).

Archbishop of Mandalay: Most Rev. PAUL ZINGTUNG GRAWNG, Archbishop's House, 81st and 25th St, Mandalay 06011; tel. (2) 33916; e-mail paulgrawng@mandalay.net.mm.

Archbishop of Taunggyi: Most Rev. MATTHIAS U SHWE, Archbishop's Office, Bayint Naung Rd, Taunggyi 06011; tel. (81) 21689; fax (81) 22164; e-mail matthias@myanmar.com.mm.

Archbishop of Yangon: Most Rev. CHARLES MAUNG BO, Archbishop's House, 289 Theinbyu St, Botataung, 11161 Yangon; tel. (1) 246710; fax (1) 379059.

The Anglican Communion

Anglicans are adherents of the Church of the Province of Myanmar, comprising six dioceses. The Province was formed in February 1970, and contained an estimated 45,000 adherents in 1985.

Archbishop of Myanmar and Bishop of Yangon: Most Rev. STEPHEN THAN MYINT OO, Bishopscourt, 140 Pyidaungsu Yeiktha Rd, Dagon PO (11191), Yangon; tel. (1) 285379; fax (1) 251405.

MYANMAR   *Directory*

Protestant Churches

Lutheran Bethlehem Church: 181–183 Theinbyu St, Mingala Taung Nyunt PO 11221, POB 773, Yangon; tel. (1) 246585; Pres. Rev. JENSON RAJAN ANDREWS.

Myanmar Baptist Convention: 143 Minye Kyawswa Rd, POB 506, Yangon; tel. (1) 223231; fax (1) 221465; e-mail mbc@mptmail.net.mm; f. 1865; est. as Burma Baptist Missionary Convention; present name adopted 1954; 650,293 mems (2003); Pres. Rev. Dr HONOR NYO; Gen. Sec. Rev. K. D. TU LOM.

Myanmar Methodist Church: 47 Baho Rd, Thazin Lane, Ah Lone Township 65, Alanpya Pagoda Rd, Dagon, Yangon; Pres. Bishop ZOTHAN MAWIA.

Presbyterian Church of Myanmar: Synod Office, Falam, Chin State; 22,000 mems; Pres. Rev. SUN KANGLO.

Other denominations active in Myanmar include the Lisu Christian Church and the Salvation Army.

The Press

DAILIES

Botahtaung (The Vanguard): 22–30 Strand Rd, Botahtaung PO, POB 539, Yangon; tel. (1) 274310; Myanmar.

Guardian: 392–396 Merchant St, Botahtaung PO, POB 1522, Yangon; tel. (1) 270150; English.

Kyahmon (The Mirror): 77 52nd St, Dazundaung PO, POB 819, Yangon; tel. (1) 282777; internet www.myanmar.com/newspaper/kyaymon/index.html; Myanmar.

Myanmar Alin (New Light of Myanmar): 58 Komin Kochin Rd, Bahan PO, POB 21, Yangon; tel. (1) 544309; internet www.myanmar.com/newspaper/myanmarahlin/index.html; f. 1963; fmrly Loktha Pyithu Nezin (Working People's Daily); organ of the SPDC; morning; Myanmar; Chief Editor WIN TIN; circ. 400,000.

New Light of Myanmar: 22–30 Strand Rd, Yangon; tel. (1) 297028; e-mail webmaster@myanmar.com; internet www.myanmar.com/newspaper/nlm/index.html; f. 1963; fmrly Working People's Daily; organ of the SPDC; morning; English; Chief Editor KYAW MIN; circ. 14,000.

PERIODICALS

A Hla Thit (New Beauty): 46 90th St, Yangon; tel. (1) 287106; international news.

Dana Business Magazine: 72 8th St, Lanmadaw Township, Yangon; tel. and fax (1) 224010; e-mail dana@mptmail.net.mm; economic; Editor-in-Chief WILLIAM CHEN.

Do Kyaung Tha: Myawaddy Press, 184 32nd St, Yangon; tel. (1) 274655; f. 1965; monthly; Myanmar and English; circ. 17,000.

Gita Padetha: Yangon; journal of Myanma Music Council; circ. 10,000.

Guardian Magazine: 392–396 Merchant St, Botahtaung PO, POB 1522, Yangon; tel. (1) 296510; f. 1953; nationalized 1964; monthly; English; literary; circ. 11,600.

Kyee Pwar Yay (Prosperity): 296 Bo Sun Pat St, Yangon; tel. (1) 278100; economic; Editor-in-Chief MYAT KHINE.

Moethaukpan (Aurora): Myawaddy Press, 184 32nd St, Yangon; tel. (1) 274655; f. 1980; monthly; Myanmar and English; circ. 27,500.

Myanma Dana (Myanmar's Economy): 210A 36th St, Kyauktada PO, Yangon; tel. (1) 284660; economic; Editor-in-Chief THIHA SAW.

Myanmar Morning Post: Yangon; f. 1998; weekly; Chinese; news; circ. 5,000.

Myanmar Times & Business Review: 379–383 Bo Aung Kyaw St, Kyauktada Township, Yangon; tel. (1) 392928; fax (1) 254158; e-mail management@myanmartimes.com.mm; internet www.mmtimes.com; f. 2000; Editor-in-Chief ROSS DUNKLEY.

Myawaddy Journal: Myawaddy Press, 184 32nd St, Yangon; tel. (1) 274655; f. 1989; fortnightly; news; circ. 8,700.

Myawaddy Magazine: Myawaddy Press, 184 32nd St, Yangon; tel. (1) 274655; f. 1952; monthly; literary magazine; circ. 4,200.

Ngwetaryi Magazine: Myawaddy Press, 184 32nd St, Yangon; tel. (1) 274655; f. 1961; monthly; cultural; circ. 3,400.

Pyinnya Lawka Journal: 529 Merchant St, Yangon; tel. (1) 283611; publ. by Sarpay Beikman Management Board; quarterly; circ. 18,000.

Shwe Thwe: 529 Merchant St, Yangon; tel. (1) 283611; weekly; bilingual children's journal; publ. by Sarpay Beikman Management Board; circ. 100,000.

Taw Win Journal (Royal Journal): 149 37th St, Yangon; news; Editor-in-Chief SOE THEIN.

Teza: Myawaddy Press, 184 32nd St, Yangon; tel. (1) 274655; f. 1965; monthly; English and Myanmar; pictorial publication for children; circ. 29,500.

Thwe Thauk Magazine: Myawaddy Press, 184 32nd St, Yangon; f. 1946; monthly; literary.

Ya Nant Thit (New Fragrance): 186 39th St, Yangon; tel. (1) 276799; international news; Editor-in-Chief CHIT WIN MG.

NEWS AGENCY

Myanmar News Agency (MNA): 212 Theinbyu Rd, Botahtaung, Yangon; tel. (1) 270893; f. 1963; govt-controlled; Chief Editors ZAW MIN THEIN (domestic section), KYAW MIN (external section).

Publishers

Hanthawaddy Press: 157 Bo Aung Kyaw St, Yangon; f. 1889; textbooks, multilingual dictionaries; Man. Editor ZAW WIN.

Knowledge Publishing House: 130 Bo Gyoke Aung San St, Yegyaw, Yangon; art, education, religion, politics and social sciences.

Kyipwaye Press: 84th St, Letsaigan, Mandalay; tel. (2) 21003; arts, travel, religion, fiction and children's.

Myawaddy Press: 184 32nd St, Yangon; tel. (1) 276889; journals and magazines; CEO THEIN SEIN.

Sarpay Beikman Management Board: 529 Merchant St, Yangon; tel. (1) 283611; f. 1947; encyclopaedias, literature, fine arts and general; also magazines and translations; Chair. AUNG HTAY.

Shumawa Press: 146 West Wing, Bogyoke Aung San Market, Yangon; mechanical engineering.

Shwepyidan: 12A Haiaban, Yegwaw Quarter, Yangon; politics, religion, law.

Smart and Mookerdum: 221 Sule Pagoda Rd, Yangon; arts, cookery, popular science.

Thu Dhama Wadi Press: 55–56 Maung Khine St, POB 419, Yangon; f. 1903; religious; Propr TIN HTOO; Man. PAN MAUNG.

GOVERNMENT PUBLISHING HOUSE

Printing and Publishing Enterprise: 365–367 Bo Aung Kyaw St, Kyauktada Township, Yangon; tel. (1) 294645; f. 1880 as the Government Printing Office; Man. Dir AUNG NYEIN.

PUBLISHERS' ASSOCIATION

Myanma Publishers' Union: 146 Bogyoke Market, Yangon.

Broadcasting and Communications

TELECOMMUNICATIONS

Posts and Telecommunications Department: Block 68, Ayeyar Wun Rd, South Dagon Township, Yangon; tel. (1) 591388; fax (1) 591383; e-mail dg.ptd@mptmail.net.mm; internet www.mcpt.gov.mm/ptd/index.htm; regulatory authority responsible for supervising radio communication, telephone, telegraph and post operations; Dir-Gen. U TIN HTWE.

Myanma Posts and Telecommunications (MPT): No. 2 Office Bldg, Special Development Zone, Nay Pwi Taw; tel. (1) 407333; fax (1) 407008; internet www.mpt.net.mm; fmrly the Posts and Telecommunications Corpn; Man. Dir THAR OO.

BROADCASTING

Radio

Myanma TV and Radio Department (MTRD): 426 Pyay Rd, Kamayut 11041, Yangon; POB 1432, Yangon 11181; tel. (1) 531850; fax (1) 530211; f. 1946; broadcasts in Bamar, Arakanese (Rakhine), Shan, Karen (Kayin), Kachin, Kayah, Chin, Mon and English; Dir-Gen. KHIN MAUNG HTAY; Dir of Radio Broadcasting KO KO HTWAY.

Television

Myanma TV and Radio Department (MTRD): 426 Pyay Rd, Kamayut 11041, Yangon; tel. (1) 535553; fax (1) 525428; f. 1946; colour television transmissions began in 1980; Dir-Gen. KHIN MAUNG HTAY; Dir of Television Broadcasting MYINT OO.

TV Myawaddy: Hmawbi, Hmawbi Township, Yangon; tel. (1) 620270; f. 1995; military broadcasting station transmitting public information, education and entertainment programmes via satellite.

MYANMAR

Directory

In 2005 the Democratic Voice of Burma (DVB) began broadcasting Myanmar-language news and educational programmes via satellite from Norway. At the start of operations, the DVB broadcast two hours of transmissions per week, but planned to expand operations over the latter half of 2005. Despite the existence of strict regulations concerning ownership of satellite receiver equipment in Myanmar, it was believed that a considerable number of Myanma households owned an unlicensed satellite dish.

Finance

(cap. = capital; res = reserves; dep. = deposits; m. = million; brs = branches; amounts in kyats)

BANKING

Central Bank

Central Bank of Myanmar: 26A Settmu Rd, POB 184, Yankin Township, Yangon; tel. (1) 285300; fax (1) 543621; e-mail cbm.ygn@mptmail.net.mm; f. 1947 as People's Bank of the Union of Burma; name changed as above in 1990; bank of issue; cap. 350m., dep. 13,545m.; Gov. THAN NYEIN; 37 brs.

State Banks

Myanma Economic Bank (MEB): 564 Merchant St, Yangon; tel. (1) 289345; fax (1) 283679; f. 1975; provides domestic banking network throughout the country; Man. Dir MYAT MAW.

Myanma Foreign Trade Bank: 80–86 Maha Bandoola Garden St, POB 203, Kyauktada Township, Yangon; tel. (1) 284911; fax (1) 289585; e-mail mftb-hoygn@mptmail-net.mm; f. 1976; handles all foreign exchange and international banking transactions; Chair. and Man. Dir THAN YE; Man. and Sec. HTIN KYAW THEIN.

Development Banks

Myanma Agricultural Development Bank (MADB): 1–7 cnr of Latha St and Kanna Rd, Yangon; tel. (1) 226734; f. 1953; est. as State Agricultural Bank, reconstituted as Myanma Agricultural and Rural Development Bank 1990 and as above 1996; state-owned; Man. Dir CHIT SWE.

Myanma Investment and Commercial Bank (MICB): 170/176 Bo Aung Kyaw St, Botahtaung Township, Yangon; tel. (1) 256871; fax (1) 250518; e-mail micb.hoygn@mptmail.net.mm; f. 1989; state-owned; cap. 400m., res 786m., dep. 7,035m. (March 2000); Chair. and Man. Dir MYA THAN; 1 br.

Private Banks

Asian Yangon Bank Ltd: 319–321 Maha Bandoola St, Botahtaung Township, Yangon; tel. (1) 245825; fax (1) 245865; f. 1994 as Asian Yangon International Bank Ltd; name changed as above in 2000; Gen. Man. MYO MYINT.

Co-operative Bank Ltd: 334–336 Kanna Rd, Yangon; tel. (1) 272641; fax (1) 283063; e-mail cbbank@mptmail.net.mm; f. 1992; Gen. Man. NYUNT HLAING.

First Private Bank Ltd (FPB): 619–621 Merchant St, Pabedan Township, Yangon; tel. (1) 251750; fax (1) 242320; e-mail myintzaw@fpbank-myanmar.com; internet www.fpb-myanmar.com; f. 1992; est. as the first publicly subscribed bank; fmrly the Commercial and Development Bank Ltd; provides loans to private business and small-scale industrial sectors; cap. 5,000m. (March 2008); Chair. Dr SEIN MAUNG; 15 brs.

Innwa Bank Ltd: 554–556 Merchant St, Cnr of 35th and 36th Streets, Kyauktada Township, Yangon; tel. (1) 254642; fax (1) 254431; f. 1997.

Kanbawza Bank Ltd: 615/1 Pyay Rd, Kamayut Township, Yangon; tel. (1) 538075; fax (1) 538069; e-mail kbz@mptmail.net.mm; internet www.kbzbank.com; f. 1994; Chair. U AUNG KO WIN; 22 brs.

Myanma Citizens Bank Ltd (MCB): 383 Maha Bandoola St, Kyauktada Township, Yangon; tel. (1) 379176; fax (1) 245932; e-mail mcbankygn@mptmail.net.mm; f. 1991; Chair. HLA TIN; Man. Dir AUNG THIN WIN.

Myanma Oriental Bank Ltd (MOB): 166–168 Pansodan St, Kyauktada Township, Yangon; tel. (1) 246594; fax (1) 253217; e-mail mobl.ygn@mptmail.net.mm; f. 1993; Chair. MYAT KYAW; Man. Dir and CEO WIN MYINT.

Myanma Universal Bank (MUB): 81 Theinbyu Rd, Yangon; tel. (1) 297339; fax (1) 201428; f. 1995.

Myanmar Industrial Development Bank Ltd: 26–42 Pansodan St, Kyauktada Township, Yangon; tel. (1) 249536; fax (1) 249529; f. 1996; cap. US $335m.

Myawaddy Bank Ltd: 24–26 Sule Pagoda Rd, Kyauktada Township, Yangon; tel. (1) 283665; fax (1) 250093; e-mail mwdbankygn@mtpt400.stems.com; f. 1993; Gen. Mans TUN KYI, MYA MIN.

Tun Foundation Bank Ltd: 165–167 Bo Aung Kyaw St, Yangon; tel. (1) 240710; e-mail tfbbank@mptmail.net.mm; f. 1997; Chair. THEIN TUN.

Yadanabon Bank Ltd: 58A 26th St, cnr of 84th and 85th Sts, Aung Myay Thar Zan Township, Mandalay; tel. (2) 23577; f. 1992.

Yangon City Bank Ltd: 12–18 Sepin St, Kyauktada Township, Yangon; tel. (1) 289256; fax (1) 289231; f. 1993; auth. cap. 500m.; 100% owned by the Yangon City Development Committee; Chair. Col MYINT AUNG.

Yoma Bank Ltd: 1 Kungyan St, Mingala Taung Nyunt Township, Yangon; tel. (1) 242138; fax (1) 246548; f. 1993; Chair. SERGE PUN.

Foreign Banks

By November 2003 18 foreign banks had opened representative offices in Yangon.

STOCK EXCHANGE

Myanmar Securities Exchange Centre: 1st Floor, 21–25 Sule Pagoda Rd, Yangon; tel. (1) 283984; f. 1996; jt venture between Japan's Daiwa Institute of Research and Myanma Economic Bank; Man. Dir EIJI SUZUKI.

INSURANCE

At the end of November 2003 there were three representative offices of foreign insurance companies in Myanmar.

Myanma Insurance: 627–635 Merchant St, Yangon; tel. (1) 252373; fax (1) 250275; e-mail myansure@mptmail.net.com; internet www.soft-comm.com/myanma_insurance/index.html; f. 1976; govt-controlled; Man. Dir Col THEIN LWIN.

Trade and Industry

GOVERNMENT AGENCIES

Inspection and Agency Services: 383 Maha Bandoola St, Yangon; tel. (1) 284821; fax (1) 284823; works on behalf of state-owned enterprises to promote business with foreign companies; Man. Dir OHN KHIN.

Myanmar Economic Corpn (MEC): 74/76 Shwedagon Pagoda Rd, Dagon Township, Yangon; tel. (1) 254738.

Myanmar Investment Commission: Ministry of National Planning and Economic Development, 653–691 Merchant St, Pabedan Township, Yangon; tel. (1) 241918; fax (1) 282101; Chair. U THAUNG; Vice-Chair. Maj.-Gen. TIN HTUT.

Union of Myanmar Economic Holdings: 72–74 Shwedagon Pagoda Rd, Yangon; tel. (1) 78905; f. 1990; public holding co; auth. cap. 10,000m. kyats; 40% of share capital subscribed by the Ministry of Defence and 60% by members of the armed forces.

CHAMBER OF COMMERCE

Union of Myanmar Federation of Chambers of Commerce and Industry (UMFCCI): 29 Min Ye Kyawswa Rd, Lanmadaw Township, Yangon; tel. (1) 214344; fax (1) 214484; e-mail umcci@mptmail.net.mm; internet www.umfcci.com.mm; f. 1919 as Burmese Chamber of Commerce; name changed as above in 1999; Pres. WIN MYINT; Gen. Sec. SEIN WIN HLAING.

INDUSTRIAL AND TRADE ASSOCIATIONS

Myanmar Aquaculture and Fisheries Association: 74/86, Bo Sun Pat St, Pabedan Township, Yangon; tel. (1) 243150; fax (1) 248177.

Myanmar Construction Entrepreneurs' Association: Thanthumar Rd, cnr Thuwunna Rd, Thingankyun Township, Yangon; tel. (1) 579547; fax (1) 575947.

Myanmar Edible Oil Dealers' Association: 81/82 Kantgaw St, Bayint Naung Warehouse, Mayangon Township, Yangon; tel. (1) 680910.

Myanmar Engineers' Association: Bldg 6, Rm 5, MICT Park, Hlaing Township, Yangon; tel. (1) 652294.

Myanmar Fisheries Federation (MFF): cnr Bayint Naung Rd and Say War Sat Yone St, West Gyo Gone, Insein Township, Yangon; tel. (1) 683652; fax (1) 683662; e-mail fish-fed@mff.com.mm; internet www.mff.com.mm; six mem. asscns; Pres. HTAY MYINT.

Myanmar Forest Products and Timber Merchants' Association: 29 Min Ye Kyaw Swa St, Lanmadaw Township, Yangon; tel. (1) 214838; e-mail mfptma@mptmail.net.mm; internet www.myanmartimberassociation.org; f. 1993; Chair. SEIN LWIN.

Myanmar Garment Manufacturers' Association (MGMA): J V-2 Bldg, between Lanthit St and Wardan St, Seikkan Township, Yangon; tel. (1) 220879; fax (1) 222706; Chair. MYINT SOE.

MYANMAR

Myanmar Industries Association: 504/506 Merchant St, Kyauktada Township, Yangon; tel. (1) 241919; fax (1) 241919; internet www.mia.com.mm; f. 1993.

Myanmar Livestock Federation: Livestock Breeding and Veterinary Department Compound, Insein Rd, Insein Township, Yangon; tel. (1) 640820; fax (1) 225955.

Myanmar Rice and Paddy Wholesalers' Association: 504/506 Merchant St, Kyauktada Township, Yangon; tel. (1) 241920.

Myanmar Rice Millers' Association: 69 Theinbyu St, Botahtaung Township, Yangon; tel. (1) 296284.

Myanmar Women Entrepreneurs' Association: 288/290 Shwedagon Pagoda Rd, Dagon Township, Yangon; tel. (1) 253765; fax (1) 248177; f. 1995.

UTILITIES

Electricity

Myanma Electric Power Enterprise (MEPE): 197–199 Lower Kyimyindine Rd, Yangon; tel. (1) 220918; fax (1) 221006; e-mail mepe@mptmail.net.mm; Man. Dir ZAW WIN.

Water

Mandalay City Development Committee (Water and Sanitation Dept): cnr of 26th and 72nd Sts, Mandalay; tel. (2) 36173; f. 1992; Head of Water and Sanitation Dept TUN KYI.

Water Resources Utilization Department (WRUD): Ministry of Agriculture and Irrigation, Thiri Mingala Lane, off Kaba Aye Pagoda Rd, Yangon; tel. (1) 666359; fax (1) 667456; f. 1995.

Yangon City Development Committee (Water and Sanitation Dept): City Hall, cnr of Maha Bandoola Rd and Sule Pagoda Rd, Kyauktada Township, Yangon; tel. (1) 248112; fax (1) 246016; e-mail priycdc@mptmail.net.mm; internet www.yangoncity.com.mm/ycdc/index.asp; f. 1992; Head of Water and Sanitation Dept ZAW WIN.

CO-OPERATIVES

In 2003, according to official reports, there were 18,041 co-operative societies.

Central Co-operative Society Ltd: Saya San Plaza, Cnr Saya Rd and New University Ave, Bahan Township, Yangon; tel. (1) 557640; fax (1) 555745; e-mail ccscencoop@mptmail.net.mm; internet www.ccsmyanmar.com; Chair. KHIN MAUNG AYE.

Co-operative Department: Bldg 16, Nay Pyi Taw, Yangon; tel. (1) 410339; fax (1) 410024; e-mail myancoop@mptmail.net.mm; internet www.myancoop.gov.mm/co-department.htm; Dir-Gen. MAUNG HTI.

WORKERS' AND PEASANTS' COUNCILS

Peasants' Asiayone (Organization): Yangon; tel. (1) 82819; f. 1977; peasants' representative org.; Chair. Brig.-Gen. THAN NYUNT; Sec. SAN TUN.

Workers' Unity Organization: Central Organizing Committee, 61 Thein Byu St, Yangon; tel. (1) 284043; f. 1968; workers' representative org.; Chair. OHN KYAW; Sec. NYUNT THEIN.

Transport

All railways, domestic air services, passenger and freight road transport services and inland water facilities are owned and operated by state-controlled enterprises.

RAILWAYS

The railway network comprised 3,955 km of track in 1996/97, most of which was single track.

Myanma Railways: 361 Theinbyu Rd, Botataung Township, Yangon; tel. (1) 298585; fax (1) 284220; f. 1877; govt-operated; Man. Dir MIN SWE; Gen. Man. HLA YI.

ROADS

In 2005 the total length of the road network in Myanmar was an estimated 27,000 km.

Road Transportation Department: 375 Bogyoke Aung San St, Yangon; tel. (1) 284426; fax (1) 289716; f. 1963; controls passenger and freight road transport; Man. Dir OHN MYINT.

INLAND WATERWAYS

The principal artery of traffic is the River Ayeyarwady (Irrawaddy), which is navigable as far as Bhamo, about 1,450 km inland, while parts of the Thanlwin and Chindwinn rivers are also navigable.

Inland Water Transport: 50 Pansodan St, Yangon; tel. (1) 222399; fax (1) 286500; govt-owned; operates cargo and passenger services throughout Myanmar; Man. Dir KHIN MAUNG.

SHIPPING

Yangon is the chief port. Vessels with a displacement of up to 15,000 grt can be accommodated. In December 2007 the Myanma merchant fleet totalled 118 vessels, with a combined displacement of 203,200 grt.

Myanma Port Authority: 10 Pansodan St, POB 1, Yangon; tel. (1) 382722; fax (1) 295134; internet www.mot.gov.mm/mpa/index.html; f. 1880; general port and harbour duties; Man. Dir HTIEN HTAY; Gen. Man. HLAING SOON.

Myanma Five Star Line: 132–136 Theinbyu Rd, POB 1221, Yangon; tel. (1) 295279; fax (1) 297669; e-mail mfslhq@mptmail.net.mm; internet www.mfsl-shipping.com; f. 1959; cargo services to the Far East and Australia; Man. Dir MAUNG MAUNG NYEIN; Gen. Man. WIN PE; fleet of 26 coastal and ocean-going vessels.

CIVIL AVIATION

Mingaladon Airport, near Yangon, is equipped to international standards. Mandalay International Airport was inaugurated in September 2000. In 2002 plans for the construction of the country's third international airport, Hanthawaddy International Airport in Bago (Pegu), were finally approved.

Department of Civil Aviation: Mingaladon Airport, Yangon; tel. (1) 665144; fax (1) 665124; e-mail dca.myanmar@mpt.mail.net.mm; internet www.mot.gov.mm/dca/index.html; Dir-Gen. WIN MAUNG.

Air Bagan Ltd: 56 Shwe Taung Gyar St, Bahan Township, Yangon; tel. (1) 514861; fax (1) 515102; e-mail info@airbagan.com.mm; internet www.airbagan.com; f. 2004; domestic services to 14 destinations; Chair. TAY ZA; Man. Dir SOE WIN.

Air Mandalay: 146 Dhammazedi Rd, Bahan Township, Yangon; tel. (1) 501520; fax (1) 525937; e-mail info@airmandalay.com; internet www.airmandalay.com; f. 1994; Myanmar's first airline; jt venture between Air Mandalay Holding and Myanma Airways; operates domestic services and regional services to Chiang Mai and Phuket, Thailand, and Siem Reap, Cambodia; Chair. Dr TUN CHIN; Man. Dir ERIC KANG TIAN LYE; 242 employees.

Myanmar Airways (MA): 104 Kanna Rd, Yangon; tel. (1) 284566; fax (1) 89583; e-mail 8mpr@maiair.com.mm; internet www.mot.gov.mm/ma/index.html; f. 1993; govt-controlled; internal network operates services to 21 airports; Man. Dir TIN MAUNG TUN.

Myanmar Airways International (MAI): 08–02 Sakura Tower, 339 Bogyoke Aung San Rd, Yangon; tel. (1) 255260; fax (1) 255305; e-mail management@maiair.com; internet www.maiair.com; f. 1993; govt-owned; established by Myanmar Airways in jt venture with Highsonic Enterprises of Singapore to provide international services; operates services to Bangkok, Dhaka, Hong Kong, Kuala Lumpur and Singapore; Man. Dir AUNG GYI.

United Myanmar Air: Summit Parkview Hotel, Yangon; internet www.unitedmyanmar.com; f. 2003; jt venture between Myanmar Airways and Sunshine Strategic Investments Holdings of Hong Kong; international services to Bangkok, Hong Kong, Kuala Lumpur and Singapore; CEO EDWARD TAN.

Yangon Airways: MMB Tower, Level 5, 166 Upper Pansodan Rd, Mingalar Taungnyunt Township, Yangon; tel. (1) 383100; fax (1) 383109; e-mail info@yangonair.com; internet www.yangonair.com; f. 1996; domestic services to 13 destinations; Man. Dir TIN SOE.

Tourism

Yangon, Mandalay, Taunggyi and Pagan possess outstanding palaces, Buddhist temples and shrines. In 2006 there were 263,514 foreign tourist arrivals. Revenue from tourism (including passenger transport) totalled an estimated US $59m. in 2006.

Myanmar Hotels and Tourism Services: 77–91 Sule Pagoda Rd, Yangon 11141; tel. (1) 282013; fax (1) 254417; e-mail mtt.mht@mptmail.net.mm; govt-controlled; manages all hotels, tourist offices, tourist department stores and duty-free shops; Gen. Man. TIN HTAY.

Myanmar Tourism Promotion Board: Level 3, Business Centre, 223 Signal Pagoda Rd, Yangon; tel. (1) 242828; fax (1) 242800; e-mail mtpb@mptmail.net.mm; internet www.myanmar-tourism.com; Chair. AUNG MYAT KYAW.

Myanmar Travels and Tours: 118–120, Mahabandoola St, Kyauktada Township, Yangon; tel. (1) 371286; fax (1) 254417; e-mail mtt.mht@mptmail.net.mm; internet www.myanmartravelsandtours.com; f. 1964; govt tour operator and travel agent; handles all travel arrangements for groups and individuals; Gen. Man. HTAY AUNG.

Union of Myanmar Travel Association (UMTA): Bldg 69, No 609B, 6th Floor, Yuzana Condo Tower, cnr Shwegonedaing Rd and Kabaraye Pagoda Rd, Bahan Township, Yangon; tel. (1) 559673; fax (1) 545707; e-mail UMTA@mptmail.net.mm; internet www.umtanet.org; f. 2002; organizes private travel agencies and tour operators; promotes Myanmar as a tourist destination; Chair. KHIN ZAW.

NAMIBIA

Introductory Survey

Location, Climate, Language, Religion, Flag, Capital

The Republic of Namibia (formerly known as South West Africa) lies in south-western Africa, with South Africa to the south and south-east, Botswana to the east and Angola to the north. The country has a long coastline on the Atlantic Ocean. The narrow Caprivi Strip, between Angola and Botswana in the north-east, extends Namibia to the Zambezi river, giving it a border with Zambia. The climate is generally hot, although coastal areas have relatively mild temperatures. Most of the country is subject to drought and unreliable rainfall. The average annual rainfall varies from about 50 mm (2 ins) on the coast to 550 mm (22 ins) in the north. The arid Namib Desert stretches along the west coast, while the easternmost area is part of the Kalahari Desert. The official language is English; however, most of the African ethnic groups have their own languages. At the 2001 census the most widely spoken African languages were Oshiwambo (used in 48% of households), Nama/Damara (11%), Rukavango (10%) and Otjiherero (8%). In addition, Afrikaans is spoken (11%) and German is also used. About 90% of the population are Christians. The national flag (proportions 2 by 3) comprises a blue triangle in the upper hoist corner, bearing a yellow sun (a blue-bordered disc, surrounded by 12 triangular rays), separated from a green triangle in the lower fly corner by a white-bordered, broad red stripe. The capital is Windhoek.

Recent History

South West Africa became a German possession in 1884. The territory excluded the port of Walvis Bay and 12 small offshore islands, previously annexed by the United Kingdom and subsequently incorporated into South Africa. During the First World War South African forces occupied South West Africa in 1914, and in 1915 Germany surrendered the territory. In 1920 the League of Nations entrusted South Africa with a mandate to administer South West Africa. In 1925 South Africa granted a Constitution giving limited self-government to European (white) inhabitants only. No trusteeship agreement was concluded with the UN after the Second World War, and in 1946 the UN refused South Africa's request for permission to annex South West Africa. In 1949 the territory's European voters were granted representation in the South African Parliament. The following year the International Court of Justice (ICJ, see p. 22) issued a ruling that the area should remain under international mandate and that South Africa should submit it to UN control. South Africa refused to comply with this judgment. In October 1966 South Africa's security and apartheid laws were extended to South West Africa, retrospective to 1950.

Opposition within South West Africa to South African rule led to the establishment of two African nationalist organizations, the South West Africa People's Organisation (SWAPO—founded in 1957 as the Ovamboland People's Congress) and the South West African National Union (SWANU—formed in 1959). During 1966 SWAPO's military wing, the People's Liberation Army of Namibia (PLAN), launched an armed struggle for the liberation of the territory. PLAN operated from bases in Angola and Zambia, and was controlled by the external wing of SWAPO (led by Sam Nujoma—the organization's President from 1959). SWAPO also had a legal wing, which was tolerated in South West Africa.

South Africa was consistently criticized at the UN over its extension of apartheid to the territory. The UN General Assembly voted to terminate South Africa's mandate in October 1966, established a UN Council for South West Africa in May 1967, and changed the name of the territory to Namibia in June 1968. In 1971 the ICJ ruled that South Africa's presence was illegal. In 1973 the UN General Assembly recognized SWAPO as 'the authentic representative of the Namibian people', and appointed a UN Commissioner for Namibia to undertake 'executive and administrative tasks'.

A multiracial constitutional conference on the territory's future, organized by the all-white South West Africa Legislative Assembly, was convened in Windhoek in September 1975, attended by representatives of the territory's 11 main ethnic groups. However, neither the UN nor the Organization of African Unity (OAU, now the African Union, see p. 172) recognized this so-called Turnhalle Conference, owing to its ethnic and non-democratic basis. In 1976 and 1977 proposals for procedures whereby Namibia was to achieve independence and formulate a constitution were made by the Turnhalle Conference, but rejected by SWAPO, the UN and the OAU. In September 1977 South Africa appointed an Administrator-General to govern the territory. In November the Turnhalle Conference was dissolved, and the Democratic Turnhalle Alliance (DTA), a coalition of conservative political groups representing the ethnic groups involved in the Turnhalle Conference, was formed.

In early 1978 talks were held between South Africa, SWAPO and a 'contact group' comprising Canada, France, the Federal Republic of Germany, the United Kingdom and the USA. In September the contact group's proposals for a Namibian settlement, including the holding of UN-supervised elections, were conditionally accepted by both South Africa and SWAPO and were incorporated in UN Security Council Resolution 435. However, South Africa continued to implement its own internal solution for Namibia with an election for a Constituent Assembly in December. The election was contested by five parties, but boycotted notably by SWAPO. Of the 50 seats in the Assembly, 41 were won by the DTA. In May 1979 South Africa unilaterally established a legislative National Assembly, without executive powers, from the existing Constituent Assembly.

All-party negotiations, held under UN auspices in Geneva, Switzerland, in January 1981, failed in their aim of arranging a cease-fire and eventual UN-supervised elections. Later in 1981 the contact group attempted to secure support for a three-phase independence plan. However, South Africa's insistence (supported by the USA) that any withdrawal of South African forces must be linked to the withdrawal of Cuban troops from Angola was rejected by Angola and the UN. Meanwhile, the Ministerial Council, formed in 1980 and chaired by Dirk Mudge (also Chairman of the DTA), assumed much of the Administrator-General's executive power in September 1981. However, the Ministerial Council was dissolved in January 1983, when, after several months of disagreement with the South African Government regarding the future role of the DTA in the territory, Mudge resigned as Council Chairman. South Africa disbanded the National Assembly and resumed direct rule of Namibia, with Willem van Niekerk as Administrator-General.

The Multi-Party Conference (MPC) was established in November 1983, grouping, initially, seven internal political parties. Boycotted by SWAPO, it appeared to be promoted by South Africa as a means of settling the independence issue outside the framework of Resolution 435, and of reducing SWAPO's dominance in any future post-independence government for Namibia. None the less, South Africa continued to negotiate on the independence issue with SWAPO and Angola. In February 1984 South Africa and Angola agreed to a cease-fire on the Angola-Namibia border, and set up a joint commission to monitor the withdrawal of all South African troops from Angola. Angola undertook to ensure that neither Cuban nor SWAPO forces would move into the areas vacated by the South African troops. Discussions on the independence issue in mid-1984, involving van Niekerk, SWAPO and the MPC, ended inconclusively, as did negotiations in 1984–86 between the South African Government and the US Assistant Secretary of State for African Affairs.

In April 1985 the South African Government accepted a proposal by the MPC for a 'Transitional Government of National Unity' (TGNU) in Namibia. This was formally established in Windhoek in June, although the arrangement was condemned in advance by the contact group and was declared 'null and void' by the UN Secretary-General. The TGNU consisted of an executive Cabinet, drawn from a National Assembly of 62 members who were appointed from among the parties constituting the MPC. Its establishment was accompanied by the proclamation of a 'bill of rights', drafted by the MPC, which prohibited racial discrimination. A Constitutional Council was also established to prepare a constitution for an independent Namibia. The South African Government retained responsibility for foreign affairs, defence and internal security, and all legislation was to be subject to approval by the Administrator-General. Louis Pienaar replaced van Niekerk in this post in July.

During 1987, following the liberalization of labour laws and the legalization of trade unions for black workers in 1986, the trade union movement became increasingly active. In mid-1987 the Constitutional Council published a draft document; however, South Africa indicated that it could not accept the lack of a guarantee of minority rights in the proposal. In March 1988 the Namibian Supreme Court declared the 'AG8' law of 1980 (providing for the election of 'second-tier' legislative assemblies and for the administration of education and health facilities on an ethnic, rather than a geographical, basis) to be in conflict with the 1985 'bill of rights'.

Both Angola and Cuba were reported in January 1988 to have accepted, in principle, the US demand for a complete withdrawal of Cuban troops from Angola, but they reiterated that this would be conditional on the cessation of South African support for the insurgent União Nacional para a Independência Total de Angola (UNITA). In July Angola, Cuba and South Africa reached agreement on 14 'essential principles' for a peaceful settlement, and in August it was agreed that the implementation of Resolution 435 would begin on 1 November. Also in August the Governments of South Africa, Cuba and Angola announced a cease-fire, to which SWAPO agreed, and South Africa undertook to withdraw all its forces from Angola. The November deadline was not met, owing to failure to agree on an exact schedule for the evacuation of Cuban troops from Angola. In December Angola, Cuba and South Africa signed a formal treaty designating 1 April 1989 as the implementation date for Resolution 435 and establishing a joint commission to monitor the treaty's implementation. (A further agreement was signed by Angola and Cuba, requiring the evacuation of all Cuban troops from Angola by July 1991.) A Constituent Assembly was to be elected in Namibia on 1 November 1989. South African forces in Namibia were to be confined to their bases, and their numbers reduced to 1,500 by July 1989; all South African troops were to have been withdrawn from Namibia one week after the November election. SWAPO forces were to be confined to bases in Angola in April, before being disarmed and repatriated. A multinational military observer force, the UN Transition Assistance Group (UNTAG), was to monitor the South African withdrawal, and civilian administrators and an international police force were to supervise the election. At the end of February the TGNU was formally disbanded, and on 1 March the National Assembly voted to dissolve itself: until independence the territory was governed by the Administrator-General, in consultation with a Special Representative of the UN Secretary-General, Martti Ahtisaari. Pienaar and Ahtisaari were to be jointly responsible for arranging the November election.

Implementation of Resolution 435 was disrupted by large-scale movements, from April 1989, of SWAPO guerrillas into Namibia from Angola, as a result of which the South African security forces, with the consent of the UN, suspended the ceasefire. About 280 SWAPO troops were reported to have been killed in the subsequent conflict. Following negotiations by the joint monitoring commission, conditions were arranged for an evacuation of the SWAPO forces to Angola, and in May the commission certified the cease-fire to be once more in force. In June most racially discriminatory legislation was repealed, and an amnesty was granted to Namibian refugees and exiles: by late September nearly 42,000 people, including Nujoma, had returned to Namibia. Meanwhile, South Africa completed its troop reduction ahead of schedule.

Voting proceeded peacefully on 7–11 November 1989, with the participation of more than 95% of the electorate. SWAPO received 57.3% of all votes cast and won 41 of the Constituent Assembly's 72 seats, while the DTA, with 28.6% of the votes, secured 21 seats. (In 1991 the South African Government admitted that it had contributed funds to the electoral campaigns of the DTA and several other political parties opposed to SWAPO.) Following the election, South Africa's remaining troops were evacuated from Namibia, while SWAPO's bases in Angola were decommissioned. The SWAPO Government subsequently reached an agreement with South Africa that no legal action would be taken for atrocities committed by either side. The agreement also precluded the establishment of a truth and reconciliation commission.

In February 1990 the Constituent Assembly adopted a draft Constitution, providing for a multi-party democracy based on universal adult suffrage. Later in the month the Constituent Assembly elected Nujoma as Namibia's first President. On 21 March Namibia finally achieved independence; the Constituent Assembly was redesignated the National Assembly, and Nujoma assumed executive power. A Cabinet, headed by the Constituent Assembly Chairman, Hage Geingob (a long-serving SWAPO activist), was also sworn in.

Following Namibia's independence, the port of Walvis Bay, its surrounding territory of 1,124 sq km and the 12 offshore Penguin Islands remained under South African jurisdiction. In September 1991 the Namibian and South African Governments agreed to administer the disputed territories jointly, pending a final settlement on sovereignty, and in August 1992 the two countries announced the forthcoming establishment of a joint administration authority. In August 1993, however, South Africa's multi-party constitutional negotiating committee instructed the Government to prepare legislation for the transfer of sovereignty over Walvis Bay to Namibia. Accordingly, negotiations between Namibia and South Africa resulted in bilateral agreements regarding the future of South African interests in the Walvis Bay area. Namibia formally took control of Walvis Bay and its islands from 1 March 1994. In August SWAPO won eight seats, and the DTA two, in Walvis Bay's first non-racial local elections.

Namibia's first post-independence presidential and legislative elections in December 1994 resulted in overwhelming victories for Nujoma and SWAPO. Nujoma was elected for a second term as President, securing 76.3% of the votes cast, while SWAPO secured 53 of the elective seats in the National Assembly, with 73.9% of the valid votes cast. The DTA won 15 seats (with 20.8% of the votes), and the United Democratic Front (UDF) two. The remaining two seats were won by the Democratic Coalition of Namibia (an alliance of the National Patriotic Front and the German Union) and the Monitor Action Group (MAG).

At the SWAPO Congress in May 1997 Nujoma was re-elected unopposed as party President. Among the resolutions endorsed by the Congress was a proposal that Nujoma should seek re-election for a third term as national President. It was agreed that the Constitution, which stipulates that a President may serve no more than two consecutive terms, could be exceptionally amended to allow Nujoma to seek a further mandate, since the incumbent had initially been appointed by the Constituent Assembly, and had only once been elected President on a popular mandate. In August 1998 a senior SWAPO official, Ben Ulenga, resigned as Namibia's High Commissioner to the United Kingdom, in protest at the proposed arrangement to allow Nujoma to seek a renewed mandate. In October the exceptional constitutional amendment was approved by the requisite two-thirds' majority in the National Assembly, having received the support of SWAPO's members; the amendment was similarly endorsed by the National Council in November. In March 1999 it was reported that Ulenga was to establish a new political party, the Congress of Democrats (CoD), with a view to contesting the presidential and legislative elections due later in the year.

In August 1998 the DTA's executive announced the suspension of Mishake Muyongo as party President, and dissociated the party from Muyongo's overt support for the secession of the Caprivi Strip—a narrow area of land extending in the north-east, between Angola and Botswana, as far as the Zambezi river (Namibia's border with Zambia). In November it emerged that Muyongo, leading the so-called Caprivi Liberation Movement (CLM), was among more than 100 people who, apparently armed, had crossed into Botswana in October, and who were now seeking asylum in that country. The Namibian Government stated that it had discovered plans for a secessionist rebellion, led by Muyongo and a chief of the Mafwe tribe, Boniface Mamili, in Caprivi. Representatives of the office of the UN High Commissioner for Refugees (UNHCR) subsequently advised the Botswana authorities that the secessionists' fears of persecution, should they be returned to Namibia, were 'plausible'. In subsequent weeks many more people crossed into Botswana, claiming to be fleeing harassment and persecution by the Namibian security forces: among those who left the country were many San, who were not believed to be associated with the secessionist movement. (In mid-2001 it was reported that many more San were considering leaving Namibia, again alleging harassment by the security forces.) During a visit to Botswana in March 1999 Nujoma reached an agreement with President Festus Mogae of that country, whereby the separatist leaders (whose extradition had hitherto been sought by Namibia in order that they could be tried on terrorist charges) would be accorded refugee status, on condition that they be resettled in a third country. Muyongo and Mamili were subsequently granted asylum in Denmark. The agreement also provided for the return to Namibia, under the auspices of UNHCR and without fear of prosecution or persecution, of the estimated 2,500 refugees who had crossed into Botswana since late 1998.

A period of apparent calm in the Caprivi region ended abruptly in early August 1999 with an armed attack by members of an organization styling itself the Caprivi Liberation Army (CLA), who targeted a military base at Mpacha airport and the police headquarters and offices of the Namibian Broadcasting Corpn in the regional capital, Katima Mulilo. At least eight members of the Namibian security forces and five CLA fighters were killed during the attack and its suppression. Nujoma responded by declaring a state of emergency in the region. While there was support within Namibia for the declaration, the CoD, as well as church leaders and human rights organizations, expressed concern at evidence of the ill-treatment of detainees. Several members of the Government were subsequently reported to have admitted that 'mistakes' were made in the aftermath of the attack; however, the army Chief of Staff maintained that the decisive response of the forces under his command had been justified. Visiting Katima Mulilo in late August, Nujoma announced an end to the state of emergency, although army and police reinforcements were to remain in Caprivi. Initially, 12 alleged rebels were remanded on charges of high treason, murder, public violence and illegal possession of firearms; the prosecution asserted that 17 known leaders of the CLA remained at large. Meanwhile, a further 47 suspects were charged with aiding and abetting the rebels. Repatriations of refugees from Botswana were halted following the attack on Katima Mulilo, although UNHCR expressed the hope that voluntary repatriations would resume as soon as the security situation in Caprivi was adequate to guarantee the safe return of refugees. In early 2000, however, following an escalation of instability in the region of the Namibia–Angola border, a further 400 Namibian nationals were reported to have fled to Botswana. In late 2001 officials from Botswana and Namibia held talks regarding the repatriation of about 500 Namibian refugees. In September of that year, in response to a request from the Namibian Government, the Gaborone Magistrates' Court in Botswana ordered the extradition of a group of suspected Caprivi separatists who were wanted to stand trial for high treason in connection with the attack on Katima Mulilo. The Namibian Government was also seeking to extradite Muyongo from Denmark to answer similar charges; the Danish Government stated that it was awaiting advice from UNHCR before making a decision. In October 2003, after numerous delays, the trial commenced of 121 Namibians charged with offences related to the attack on Katima Mulilo. In February 2004 the trial judge ruled that 13 of the defendants were 'irregularly before the court', as a result of a process of 'disguised extradition' whereby they had been removed from Zambia and Botswana, and ordered their release. The Government indicated that it would seek permission to appeal to the Supreme Court against this ruling. It was reported that the 13 defendants thus acquitted had been immediately rearrested on their release. In August 2007 10 individuals were convicted in relation to the rebellion and given sentences of up to 32 years' imprisonment. The trial of the remaining defendants was ongoing in early 2008.

Meanwhile, presidential and legislative elections, which were held on 30 November and 1 December 1999, resulted in an overwhelming victory for Nujoma and SWAPO, with Ulenga and the CoD apparently winning support at the expense of the DTA. In the presidential election Nujoma was returned for a third (and final) term of office with 76.8% of the votes cast, while Ulenga took 10.5% and Katuutire Kaura (Muyongo's successor as President of the DTA) 9.6%. SWAPO won 55 of the elective seats in the National Assembly, with 76.1% of the votes cast (thus ensuring that it retained the two-thirds' majority required to amend the Constitution); the CoD and the DTA each won seven seats (taking, respectively, 9.9% and 9.5% of the total votes cast).

In August 2002 Nujoma reorganized his Cabinet; Theo-Ben Gurirab was appointed Prime Minister, replacing Geingob, who Nujoma reportedly considered to be a threat to his authority. Hidipo Hamutenya became Minister of Foreign Affairs, Information and Broadcasting, but was dismissed without explanation in late May 2004: many observers regarded the decision as part of a plan by the President to manoeuvre his own choice of successor, the Minister of Lands, Resettlement and Rehabilitation, Hifikepunye Pohamba, into a stronger position. Pohamba was duly selected as the presidential candidate of the SWAPO party later that month.

At national elections held on 15–16 November 2004 Pohamba was elected President with, according to official results, 76.44% of the votes cast; his nearest rival, Ulenga, secured 7.28%. SWAPO also recorded a decisive victory in the elections to the National Assembly, retaining 55 of the 72 seats with 76.1% of the national vote. The CoD increased its share of the vote but won only five seats, compared with seven in the 1999 elections. The DTA took four seats, the UDF three and the MAG one seat, while two newly reactivated parties, the National Unity Democratic Organization and the Republican Party, won three seats and one seat, respectively. The Electoral Commission of Namibia recorded voter turn-out at 85%. (Following claims of electoral irregularities by members of the opposition a recount was held in March 2005: with the exception of the CoD all parties received a smaller number of votes; however, the overall allocation of seats remained the same.) Pohamba was due to take office in March 2005, upon the expiry of Samuel Nujoma's third term as President.

Nujoma stood down as President on 21 March 2005, but was expected to remain as leader of SWAPO until 2007. Following his swearing in as President that day, Pohamba unveiled his Cabinet, which included six new appointees. The former Minister of Higher Education, Training and Employment Creation, Nahas Angula, and the former Minister of Health and Social Services, Dr Libertina Amathila, were appointed as Prime Minister and Deputy Prime Minister, respectively. The overall structure of the ministries was reorganized and several were renamed to reflect their changed remits. Responsibility for prisons and correctional services was transferred to the newly created Ministry of Safety and Security under Peter Tshirumbu-Tsheehama, who was also appointed acting Minister of Defence. (Maj.-Gen. (retd) Charles Namoloh was appointed Minister of Defence in April 2005.) Albert Kawana was awarded the newly created post of Minister of Presidential Affairs, while the new Ministry of Education, headed by Nangolo Mbumba, assumed the functions of the former ministries of Higher and Basic Education. The incumbent Attorney-General, Pendukeni Ivula-Ithana, assumed the justice portfolio. Despite the structural changes, the composition of the new Government was interpreted as an indication that it would continue with the policies set down under the previous administration. The National Assembly subsequently unanimously elected Gurirab as Speaker.

Meanwhile, in April 2001 the Government announced that it had allocated N $100m. to acquire land for redistribution on a voluntary basis over a five-year period. At that time approximately 4,000 (mainly white-owned) farms occupied 52% of the total land area, while the Government had acquired only some 6% of the land required for resettlement. In October 2002 the Government announced that it was considering the seizure of white-owned farms for redistribution to the landless black population, and criticized white farmers for taking advantage of the voluntary basis for land redistribution by charging excessively high prices for their land. In March 2004 the Government estimated that it would cost more than US $150m. over a five-year period to redistribute some 9m. ha of land among an estimated 243,000 applicants. (It was reported that land prices had increased three-fold between 1990 and 2005.) By September the Government had bought just over 140 farms at a cost of N $131m.—under the 'willing buyer, willing seller' scheme—and resettled 9,156 people. The expropriation of the first white-owned commercial farm was carried out in November 2005; a further 19 farms were listed for expropriation under compulsory purchase orders. However, an independent report, issued by the Legal Assistance Centre, criticized the Government programme, concluding that the resettlement targets were 'logistically impossible' and 'economically unrealistic'. In early December 2005 the National Assembly approved legislation granting former President Nujoma the title of 'Founding Father'.

In November 2007 a new political party, the Rally for Democracy and Progress (RDP), was registered under the leadership of two former cabinet ministers and members of SWAPO. Jesaya Nyamu, who was named as acting Chairman of the party, had been Minister of Trade and Industry until 2004 and Hidipo Hamutenya, acting President of the RDP, was formerly Minister of Foreign Affairs. Both had resigned from SWAPO a week prior to the RDP's registration. The resignations appeared to have instigated a crisis of legitimacy for the party, which subsequently proposed to abolish the role of the Prime Minister and introduce the position of Vice-President. The constitutional amendment required to implement the proposal was to be discussed at the party's congress in late 2007. A second new opposition party—the All People's Party of Namibia, founded by Herbert and Ignatius Shixwameni—was registered in January 2008 following a split within the CoD. In July another new party, the Democratic Party of Namibia (DPN), was established. According to the party's interim President, Salomon Dawid Isaacks, the DPN had been founded in order to represent minority groups in the country which, he maintained, had been neglected by the main political parties.

A state of emergency was declared by President Pohamba in March 2008, after widespread flooding in central and northern regions of the country killed 42 people and displaced thousands more. In March 2009 Pohamba again declared a state of emergency, when severe flooding affected northern Namibia, killing at least 92 people and displacing hundreds of thousands.

Meanwhile, in April 2008 President Pohamba announced a major reorganization of the Cabinet. The most notable appointment was that of former Prime Minister Geingob to the post of Minister of Trade and Industry, while the Minister of Security, Peter Tshirumbu-Tsheehama, was replaced by Dr Nickey Iyambo, hitherto the Minister of Agriculture, Water and Forestry.

In May 2008 workers at the Skorpion Zinc Mine in southern Namibia commenced industrial action following a wage dispute. The strike lasted for 19 days before a compromise was reached between Skorpion Zinc and the Mineworkers Union of Namibia, which agreed to a 12% pay increase. There was further industrial action in September when over 1,900 workers at TransNamib Holdings, a transport services company, went on strike, paralysing the country's rail network. The strike lasted for seven days and was strongly condemned by the Government due to the severe disruption caused: according to the Minister of Works, Transport and Communications, Helmut Angula, the cost to the Namibian economy was estimated at N $180m.

In March 1993 UNITA alleged that members of the Namibia Defence Force (NDF) had crossed the border into southern Angola to assist Angolan government forces in offensives against UNITA, and subsequently claimed that some 2,000 Cuban troops had landed at Namibia's southern port of Lüderitz, from where they had been transferred to Angola to assist government forces. The Namibian authorities denied any involvement in the Angolan conflict, however. A 550-km stretch of the Okavango river border was closed from September 1994, following the deaths of three Namibians in an attack attributed by the Namibian authorities to UNITA. In September 1995 the Namibian Government announced the formation of a border control unit to assist police and NDF troops deployed along the Okavango. In November the two countries' defence and security commission agreed new measures aimed at facilitating the work of border patrols. Namibia subsequently announced that the Government was to contribute 200 NDF troops to the UN peace-keeping mission in Angola.

Following the attack on Katima Mulilo by Caprivi separatists in August 1999, the Namibian Government alleged that UNITA was lending military and logistical support to the CLA. (Links were also reported with the separatist Barotse Patriotic Front in Zambia, and the Namibian authorities alleged that the CLA had received training on Zambian territory.) There was considerable speculation that not only was Caprivi an important supply route for UNITA, but also that the Angolan rebel movement was attempting to divert resources of the Namibian armed forces away from the conflict in the Democratic Republic of the Congo (DRC, q.v.).

Tensions in the region of the Namibia–Angola border escalated from late 1999, after the two countries began joint patrols targeting UNITA, and the Namibian Government authorized the Angolan armed forces to launch attacks against UNITA from Namibian territory. In February 2000 it was announced that Nujoma and President José Eduardo dos Santos of Angola had agreed to implement measures to restore security in the border region; by June, when a curfew was imposed on the north-eastern border with Angola, more than 50 Namibians had been killed in cross-border raids by the Angolan rebels. Continuing conflict in southern Angola resulted in a large number of refugees entering Namibia (some 6,000 arrived from Angola between November 1999 and August 2000, although increased border security subsequently reduced the flow). In March 2001 President Nujoma ordered a further reinforcement of the Namibian military presence in Caprivi. In October UNITA rebels were reported to have destroyed an electricity substation in the Kavango region, and in November a group of unidentified gunmen killed four people in western Caprivi before escaping to Angola.

In April 2002 the Namibian Government welcomed the signing of a formal cease-fire agreement by the Angolan Government and UNITA, some six weeks after the death of Jonas Savimbi, the UNITA leader. Some stability was restored in the Kavango and Caprivi regions in mid-2002, and in August a number of Angolan refugees were repatriated; the majority of them, estimated at around 20,000, were due to return home in mid-2003, under the auspices of UNHCR. In February 2005 Namibia and Angola reached agreement on a maritime border; negotiations had begun in 1993 but were not formalized until 2003 when a joint commission for delimitation and demarcation was established. In September 2008 Namibia's National Society for Human Rights (NSHR) reported that it had discovered what were believed to be unmarked mass graves near the border with Angola. The organization claimed that it had 'reasonable cause' to believe the remains it had discovered belonged to victims of the Namibian security forces, who were killed between 1994 and 2003. According to the NSHR, in 1994 the Namibian authorities ordered that all illegal immigrants be cleared from the northern border area, some of whom were accused of being members of UNITA. This allegedly resulted in systematic attacks on local people, who were subject to summary executions and 'forced disappearances': the Namibian Government, however, strongly denied these claims.

Following independence, Namibia became a member of the UN, the Commonwealth, the OAU and the Southern African Development Co-ordination Conference—now the Southern African Development Community (SADC, see p. 400). Despite expressed concerns at South African dominance of the regional economy, the Nujoma regime has forged close links with post-apartheid South Africa, and in 1994 SWAPO contributed funds to the electoral campaigns of the African National Congress of South Africa and the Pan-Africanist Congress. In February 1997 legislation providing for the cancellation of the debt (now amounting to N $1,200m.) was formally approved by the South African Parliament. In August 2001 the foreign ministers of Namibia and South Africa held talks regarding their 400 km border; Namibia claimed its southern border extended to the middle of the Orange river, while South Africa claimed that its territory stretched to the northern bank. (When South Africa's borders were reassessed in 1994, following its first democratic elections, the Surveyors-General of both Namibia and South Africa had agreed to place the border in the middle of the river, but the agreement was never signed.) The confusion over the location of the border has led to differences over mineral and fishing rights in the river, as well as grazing rights on its islands.

In February 1995 it was announced that Namibia and Botswana were to refer a dispute regarding the demarcation of their joint border on the Chobe river (specifically, the issue of the sovereignty of the small, uninhabited island of Kasikili-Sedudu) for adjudication by the ICJ. The dispute was formally submitted to the Court in mid-1996. The ICJ ruled in December 1999 that the island formed part of the territory of Botswana; the judgment further ruled that nationals of (and vessels flying the flags of) Botswana and Namibia should enjoy equal treatment in the two channels around the island. In January 1998 the two countries' Joint Commission on Defence and Security held an emergency meeting, following allegations by Namibia that troops from Botswana had taken control of a further island in disputed border territory—Situngu Island in the Caprivi Strip. The Joint Commission agreed to expedite the establishment of a Joint Technical Commission for the demarcation of the border. Relations were complicated by the issue of Caprivi secessionism (see above). Situngu is claimed as Mafwe land; furthermore, Namibia's representative in discussions regarding the island, said to be a member of the secessionist movement, was reported to have fled to Angola. In 2003 Botswana and Namibia accepted the demarcation by a joint commission of their joint border along the Kwando, Linyanti and Chobe rivers.

From August 1998 Namibia, which was participating in regional efforts to resolve the conflict in the DRC, supported a Zimbabwean-led initiative by members of SADC (notably excluding South Africa) for military intervention in support of the regime of President Laurent-Désiré Kabila; as many as 2,000 Namibian troops were subsequently dispatched to the DRC, provoking vociferous criticism by opponents of Nujoma. Namibia's continuing military commitments in the DRC following the failure of the 1999 Lusaka accord (to which Namibia was a signatory), together with the need for additional army resources in north-east Namibia as a result of the Caprivi rebellion and the intensification of operations against UNITA (see above), necessitated the allocation of an additional N $173m. to defence in the supplementary budget for 1999/2000, announced in early 2000.

President Laurent-Désiré Kabila was assassinated in January 2001, and was succeeded by his son, Maj.-Gen. Joseph Kabila. Efforts to resolve the conflict in the DRC were accelerated, and in February proposals for the withdrawal of troops involved in the regional military intervention, including the estimated 2,000 Namibians, were approved by the participating countries, under the aegis of the UN Security Council. In March it was announced that Namibian forces would remain in the DRC until the specified date for withdrawal in May. All but an estimated 150 Namibian troops eventually withdrew from the DRC in September, although other foreign forces were still deployed in large numbers; at least 30 Namibian troops were reported to have been killed in three years of service. All Namibian troops had been withdrawn by the end of 2002.

Germany has been a major aid donor to Namibia since independence, and relations are generally close. In September 1995, none the less, during a visit by the German Chancellor, Helmut Kohl, some 300 members of the Herero ethnic group staged a demonstration outside the German embassy in Windhoek to demand compensation for suffering inflicted on the Herero under German rule. In June 2001 the Herero filed a lawsuit in Washington, DC, USA, against three German companies (Deutsche Bank AG, Woermann Line and Terex Corporation), claiming US $2,000m. in reparation for the alleged exploitation and eventual extermination of some 65,000 Herero in 1904–07; a second lawsuit, for a further US $2,000m., was filed against the German Government in September 2001. The case against Terex Corpn was subsequently withdrawn, after the company claimed that it was under different management at the time of the atrocities. In October 2003 it was reported that the Federal Court in Washington, DC, had ruled that it did not have jurisdiction over the Herero case, and that the Herero were consequently considering filing a lawsuit in New York. In January 2004, at a commemoration of the Herero uprising against German rule in 1904, the Government of Germany expressed its regret for the extermination of Herero, but declared itself unwilling to pay compensation to descendants of the victims. During a visit to Namibia in August 2004 the German Minister of Economic Co-operation and Development, Heidemarie Wieczorek-Zeul, apologized to the Herero Community for the atrocities carried out during 1904–07. During a visit to Germany in early December 2005 President Pohamba rejected an offer of reparations valued at N $160m. Bilateral consultations took place in May 2006 and included a German proposal to invest N $150m., over a 10-year period, in regions inhabited by descendants of populations that suffered during the colonial occupation. The money would be made available in addition to existing aid commitments, which were reported to amount to some €11m. per year. However, the German Government denied that the additional money was intended as war reparations. Germany has also provided military assistance in the from of training and equipment donation. In September 2008 it was reported that the German Advisory Group in Namibia had supplied the Namibian Defence Force with an Integrated Logistics System, completing a N $16.5m. project to establish a communications network linking together all military bases in the country.

Government

On 21 March 1990 Namibia became independent, and the Constitution took effect. Executive authority is held by the President, who is the Head of State. According to the Constitution, the President shall be directly elected by universal adult suffrage for a term of five years, and permitted to hold office for a maximum of two terms. (In late 1998 legislation was approved whereby the Constitution was to be exceptionally amended to allow the incumbent President to seek a third term of office.) Legislative power is vested in the National Assembly, comprising 72 members directly elected by universal adult suffrage and as many as six non-voting members nominated by the President. The National Assembly has a maximum term of five years. An advisory National Council, comprising two representatives from each of the country's 13 regional councils, elected for a six-year period, operates as the second chamber of parliament. Each region has its own Governor.

Defence

As assessed at November 2008, the Namibian Defence Force numbered an estimated 9,000 men; there was also a 200-strong navy, operating as part of the Ministry of Fisheries and Marine Resources, and a paramilitary force of 6,000. Projected budgetary expenditure on defence for 2008 was N $2,370m.

Economic Affairs

In 2007, according to estimates by the World Bank, Namibia's gross national income (GNI), measured at average 2005–07 prices, was US $6,970m., equivalent to US $3,360 per head (or US $5,120 per head on an international purchasing-power parity basis). During 2000–07, it was estimated, the population increased at an average annual rate of 1.4% per year, while gross domestic product (GDP) per head increased, in real terms, by an average of 3.2% per year. Overall GDP increased, in real terms, at an average annual rate of 4.7% in 2000–07. Real GDP increased by 5.9% in 2007.

Agriculture (including hunting, forestry and fishing) contributed 10.1% of GDP in 2007, according to the Bank of Namibia. About 37.4% of the labour force were employed in the sector in 2005. Government revenue from sales of fishing concessions was projected at N $70m. in the financial year ending 31 March 1999, and exports of fish and fish products provided 11.4% of total export earnings in 2007. The principal agricultural activity is beef production; the production of karakul sheepskins is also important. In addition, sealing and ostrich farming are practised on a commercial basis. The main subsistence crops are root crops, millet and maize, although Namibia remains highly dependent on imports of basic foods, especially in drought years. Plantations of seedless grapes were developed on the banks of the Orange river in the late 1990s, and projected growth in production was expected to increase significantly their contribution to export revenue. In recent years Namibia's traditionally rich fisheries have suffered a reverse and in February 2006 fishing quotas were further lowered and a five-year moratorium was declared on new fishing rights. Legislation aimed at developing aquaculture was adopted in 2003 and a number of fish farms were established. Agricultural GDP increased at an average annual rate of 0.7% in 2000–07; it declined by 0.7% in 2006, but increased by 1.1% in 2007.

Industry (including mining, manufacturing, construction and power) contributed 35.5% of GDP in 2007, and engaged 14.8% of the employed labour force in 2004. During 2000–07 industrial GDP increased by an average of 5.8% per year. Industrial GDP increased by 8.3% in 2007.

Mining and quarrying contributed 13.2% of GDP in 2007 and engaged 2.0% of the employed labour force in 2004. Namibia has rich deposits of many minerals, and is among the world's leading producers of gem diamonds (some 98% of diamonds mined in Namibia are of gem quality). Diamond-mining contributed 46.9% of the sector's GDP in 2007, and diamonds are the principal mineral export, accounting for 17.4% of export earnings in that year. Total production was 2.4m. carats in 2006. In July 2004 the Israeli company Lev Leviev Diamonds established a diamond-cutting and -polishing factory in Windhoek, the first in Namibia and the largest of its kind in Africa. Copper production, which ceased in 1998, following the liquidation of the Tsumeb Corpn, resumed at the former Tsumeb sites in September 2000. In 2005 the smelter at Tsumeb, operated by Ongopolo, remained the only one in the country; imports of foreign ore accounted for around 40% of its production. The Skorpion zinc mine and refinery near Rosh Pinah, opened in mid-2003 by Anglo American plc, was expected to contribute some 4% of GDP on reaching full production in the second half of 2004. Production of an estimated 150,000 metric tons of zinc per year was anticipated over a period of 15 years. Despite health and environmental concerns, a new uranium mine was expected to begin production at Langer Heinrich in 2007, making Namibia the third largest producer in the world of that commodity; the mine was expected to contribute some N $1,400m. to the economy. In addition, zinc, lead, gold, salt, fluorspar, marble and semi-precious stones are extracted, and there are also considerable deposits of hydrocarbons, lithium, manganese, tungsten, cadmium and vanadium. Namibia is also believed to have substantial reserves of coal, iron ore and platinum. Mining GDP increased at an average annual rate of 13.2% in 2000–07; the sector's GDP grew by 27.6% in 2006, but declined by 0.4% in 2007.

Manufacturing contributed 16.8% of GDP in 2007 and engaged 6.2% of the employed labour force in 2004. The sector has hitherto remained underdeveloped, largely owing to Namibia's economic dependence on South Africa. The principal manufacturing activities are the processing of fish and minerals for export; brewing, meat processing and the production of chemicals are also significant. Manufacturing GDP increased by an average of 4.2% per year in 2000–07; the sector declined by 8.6% in 2006, but expanded by 14.0% in 2007.

In 2005 97.0% of Namibia's electricity production was derived from hydroelectric power. There is a hydroelectric station at Ruacana, on the Cunene river at the border with Angola, and a second hydroelectric power station was planned at Divundu on the Okavango river. Final agreement was reached on developing the Kudu offshore gasfield in early 2006. An 800-MW 'gas-to-power' plant would supply the domestic market and the surplus would be exported to South Africa under an agreement with that country's Electricity Supply Commission. Construction of the plant was scheduled to begin in 2007, for completion by 2009. The construction of a further 400-MW gas fired plant at Walvis Bay was proposed in late 2006, and it was envisaged that Namibia would become a significant exporter of electric power. Imports of mineral fuels and lubricants accounted for 10.3% of the value of total merchandise imports in 2007. South Africa supplies all of Namibia's petroleum requirements.

The services sector contributed 54.4% of GDP in 2007. Tourism is expanding rapidly, and has been the focus of a major privatization initiative. The acquisition of Walvis Bay in March 1994, and subsequent establishment there of a free-trade zone, was expected to enhance Namibia's status as an entrepôt for regional trade. By March 2004 it was estimated that the free-trade zone had attracted some N $80m. of direct foreign investment. In 2006 the Government remained the largest employer, accounting for some 70,000 jobs. The GDP of the services sector increased at an average annual rate of 5.3% in 2000–07. Services GDP increased by 5.8% in 2007.

In 2007 Namibia recorded a visible trade deficit of US $180.0m., but there was a surplus of US $693.1m. on the current account of the balance of payments. South Africa was the dominant source of imports in 2007, providing 78.1% of the total. In that year South Africa was also the principal market for Namibian exports (29.0%), followed by the United Kingdom, Italy, Angola and Spain. The principal exports were food and live animals (notably fish and meat), diamonds, and metal ores and scrap. The principal import groups in that year included machinery and transport equipment, manufactured goods, food and live animals and mineral fuels and lubricants.

In the financial year ending 31 March 2008 Namibia recorded an estimated overall budget deficit of N $747.6m. In 1997 South Africa officially cancelled the external public debt inherited by Namibia at independence. Namibia's external debt was estimated at US $716m. in 2003. The annual rate of inflation averaged 4.7% in 2001–07; consumer prices increased by 6.7% in 2007. According to the 2001 census some 31% of the labour force were unemployed.

Namibia is a member of the Common Market for Eastern and Southern Africa (see p. 215), of the Southern African Development Community (see p. 400), and of the Southern African Customs Union (with Botswana, Lesotho, South Africa and Swaziland); and is also a signatory to the Cotonou Agreement with the European Union.

Namibia's potential for economic prosperity remains high, given its abundant mineral reserves and well-developed infrastructure, both of which were enhanced in 1994 by the acquisition of sovereignty over Walvis Bay and of important diamond-mining rights. The mining of offshore diamond deposits is of increasing importance: the leading diamond producer in the country, Namdeb (a joint venture between the Government and De Beers), accounts for some 10% of national GDP and 30% of export earnings. However, Namibia's economic progress continues to be largely influenced by its dependence on South Africa.

(The Namibian dollar, introduced in 1993, is at par with the rand.) The 1995 Export Processing Zones (EPZ) Act aimed to industrialize the economy, which was dominated by primary sector industries, and by mid-2005 companies in the EPZ were reported to have attracted more than N $5,200m. in foreign direct investment and contributed N $11,600m. to the economy. Some 7,000 workers were directly employed within the EPZ, principally in the manufacturing industry, which included automotive parts and rebuilding and reconditioning motor vehicles; zinc and copper refinery; and the production of textiles, garments and leatherwear. The Government hoped that the Namibia Diamond Trading Company (established in January 2007) would stimulate production in the country's diamond-cutting industry. However, the threat of prolonged recession in most developed economies during 2009 was likely to curb external demand and diamond output was subsequently forecast to slow. Adverse market conditions which ensued as a consequence of the international banking crisis impeded other areas of Namibia's minerals sector, as rapidly declining prices diminished profit margins. Copper production was suspended in the final quarter of 2008, a decision that eventually led to significant job losses. Meanwhile, fewer exploration licences were granted in 2008, owing to the deteriorating investment climate. High rates of poverty and unemployment (the latter estimated at 36.7% in 2008) and that fact that more than 20% of the population was infected with HIV/AIDS, also remained causes for serious concern.

Education

Under the Constitution, education is compulsory between the ages of six and 16 years, or until primary education has been completed (whichever is the sooner). Primary education consists of seven grades, and secondary education of five. According to UNESCO estimates, in 2006/07 enrolment at primary schools included 86.5% of children in the relevant age-group (males 84.1%; females 89.0%), while the comparable ratio for secondary enrolment in 2005/06 was 48.9% (males 44.3%; females 53.5%). In that year there were some 442,244 children enrolled in pre-primary and primary education, and 158,162 in secondary education. Higher education is provided by the University of Namibia, the Technicon of Namibia, a vocational college and four teacher-training colleges. In 2005/06 13,185 students were enrolled in tertiary education. Various schemes for informal adult education are also in operation in an effort to combat illiteracy. Under the 2004/05 budget N $2,613.2m. was allocated to education (20.6% of total government expenditure).

Public Holidays

2009: 1 January (New Year's Day), 21 March (Independence Day), 10–13 April (Easter), 1 May (Workers' Day), 4 May (Cassinga Day), 21 May (Ascension Day), 25 May (Africa Day, anniversary of the OAU's foundation), 26 August (Heroes' Day), 10 December (Human Rights Day), 25–26 December (Christmas), 26 December (Family Day),

2010: 1 January (New Year's Day), 21 March (Independence Day), 2–5 April (Easter), 1 May (Workers' Day), 4 May (Cassinga Day), 13 May (Ascension Day), 25 May (Africa Day, anniversary of the OAU's foundation), 26 August (Heroes' Day), 10 December (Human Rights Day), 25–26 December (Christmas), 26 December (Family Day).

Weights and Measures

The metric system is in use.

NAMIBIA

Statistical Survey

Source (unless otherwise indicated): Central Bureau of Statistics, National Planning Commission, Government Office Park, Block D2, Luther St, Windhoek; Private Bag 13356, Windhoek; tel. (61) 2834056; fax (61) 237620; e-mail info@npc.gov.na; internet www.npc.gov.na.

Area and Population

AREA, POPULATION AND DENSITY*

Area (sq km)	824,292†
Population (census results)	
21 October 1991	1,409,920
28 August 2001	
Males	936,718
Females	890,136
Total	1,826,854
Population (UN estimates at mid-year)‡	
2006	2,048,000
2007	2,089,000
2008	2,130,000
Density (per sq km) at mid-2008	2.6

* Including data for Walvis Bay, sovereignty over which was transferred from South Africa to Namibia with effect from March 1994. Walvis Bay has an area of 1,124 sq km (434 sq miles) and had a population of 22,999 in 1991.
† 318,261 sq miles.
‡ Source: UN, *World Population Prospects: The 2008 Revision*.

ETHNIC GROUPS
(population, 1988 estimates)

Ovambo	623,000	Caprivian	47,000	
Kavango	117,000	Bushmen	36,000	
Damara	94,000	Baster	31,000	
Herero	94,000	Tswana	7,000	
White	80,000	Others	12,000	
Nama	60,000	**Total**	1,252,000	
Coloured	51,000			

PRINCIPAL TOWNS
(population at 2001 census)

Windhoek	233,529	Rehoboth	21,300
Rundu	44,413	Otjiwarongo	19,614
Walvis Bay	42,015	Keetmanshoop	15,543
Oshakati	28,255	Gobabis	13,856
Katima Mulilo	22,694	Tsumeb	13,108

Mid-2007 (including suburbs, UN estimate): Windhoek (capital) 313,000 (Source: UN, *World Urbanization Prospects: The 2007 Revision*).

BIRTHS AND DEATHS
(annual averages, UN estimates)

	1990–95	1995–2000	2000–05
Birth rate (per 1,000)	39.6	32.7	30.0
Death rate (per 1,000)	8.0	8.3	10.5

Source: UN, *World Population Prospects: The 2008 Revision*.

Life expectancy (WHO estimates, years at birth): 61.0 (males 59.2; females 62.7) in 2006 (Source: WHO, *World Health Statistics*).

EMPLOYMENT
(persons aged 15 to 69 years, 2004 labour force survey)

	Males	Females	Total
Agriculture, hunting and forestry	64,991	37,645	102,636
Fishing	7,933	4,787	12,720
Mining and quarrying	5,909	1,653	7,562
Manufacturing	12,082	11,673	23,755
Electricity, gas and water	5,031	1,120	6,151
Construction	18,296	1,309	19,605
Wholesale and retail trade, repair of motor vehicles, motorcycles and personal and household goods	27,004	26,891	53,895
Restaurants and hotels	5,889	7,243	13,132
Transport, storage and communications	12,744	3,117	15,861
Financial intermediation	3,506	4,076	7,582
Real estate, renting and business activities	5,280	4,095	9,375
Public administration and defence; compulsory social security	20,216	10,469	30,685
Education	12,313	18,855	31,168
Health and social work	3,533	10,477	14,010
Other community, social and personal services	7,480	5,152	12,632
Private households with employed persons	4,067	20,014	24,081
Extra-territorial organizations and bodies	72	—	72
Not classifiable by economic activity	305	102	407
Total employed	216,651	168,678	385,329

Source: ILO.

Mid-2005 ('000 persons, FAO estimates): Agriculture, etc. 311; Total labour force 832 (Source: FAO).

Health and Welfare

KEY INDICATORS

Total fertility rate (children per woman, 2006)	3.3
Under-5 mortality rate (per 1,000 live births, 2006)	61
HIV/AIDS (% of persons aged 15–49, 2007)	15.3
Physicians (per 1,000 head, 2004)	0.3
Hospital beds (per 1,000 head, 2006)	3.3
Health expenditure (2006): US $ per head (PPP)	338
Health expenditure (2006): % of GDP	4.9
Health expenditure (2006): public (% of total)	64.4
Access to water (% of persons, 2006)	80
Access to sanitation (% of persons, 2006)	35
Human Development Index (2006): ranking	129
Human Development Index (2006): value	0.634

For sources and definitions, see explanatory note on p. vi.

Agriculture

PRINCIPAL CROPS
('000 metric tons)

	2005	2006	2007*
Wheat	11.0	12.9	10.0
Maize	40.7	60.9	40.0
Millet	47.9	49.0	58.0
Sorghum*	6.5	6.0	6.0
Grapes*	15.5	8.5	8.5

* FAO estimates.

Aggregate production ('000 metric tons, may include official, semi-official or estimated data): Total cereals 106.1 in 2005, 138.7 in 2006, 114.0 in 2007; Total roots and tubers 315.0 in 2005, 295.0 in 2006, 290.0 in 2007; Total vegetables (incl. melons) 15.4 in 2005, 14.7 in 2006, 14.9 in 2007; Total fruits (excl. melons) 30.0 in 2005, 9.0 in 2006, 9.0 in 2007.

Source: FAO.

LIVESTOCK
('000 head, year ending September)

	2005	2006	2007*
Horses	47.4	46.2	50.0
Asses, mules or hinnies*	147.0	n.a.	n.a.
Cattle	3,133.9	2,384.0	2,500.0
Sheep	2,663.8	2,660.3	2,700.0
Goats	2,043.5	2,061.4	2,000.0
Chickens*	3,500	3,500	3,500

* FAO estimates.

Source: FAO.

LIVESTOCK PRODUCTS
('000 metric tons)

	2005	2006	2007
Cattle meat	39.2*	36.2	42.0*
Sheep meat*	7.2	6.7	6.7
Chicken meat*	9.6	5.2	5.2
Cows' milk*	150	110	110
Hen eggs*	3.0	1.9	1.9
Wool, greasy*	2.2	2.1	2.1

* FAO estimate(s).

Source: FAO.

Forestry

Separate figures are not yet available. Data for Namibia are included in those for South Africa.

Fishing

('000 metric tons, live weight)*

	2004	2005	2006
Capture†	571.7	554.0	509.4
Cape hakes (Stokvisse)	173.9	158.1	135.9
Kingklip	7.5	5.6	4.7
Devil anglerfish	9.0	11.1	9.8
Southern African pilchard	28.6	27.3	2.3
Cape horse mackerel (Maasbanker)	314.5	324.5	307.9
Aquaculture†	0.1	0.1	0.1
Total catch†	571.8	554.0	509.4

* Figures include quantities caught by licensed foreign vessels in Namibian waters and processed in Lüderitz and Walvis Bay. The data exclude aquatic mammals (whales, seals, etc.). The number of South African fur seals caught was: 31,971 in 2004; 64,167 in 2005; 40,000 (FAO estimate) in 2006. The number of Nile crocodiles caught was: 400 in 2005.
† FAO estimates.

Source: FAO.

Mining

(metric tons, unless otherwise indicated)

	2004	2005	2006*
Copper ore†	11,174	10,157	6,262
Lead concentrates†	14,338	14,320	11,830
Zinc concentrates†	66,028	69,368	55,455‡
Silver ore (kilograms)†	27,153	30,003	31,307
Uranium oxide	3,583	3,711	3,617
Gold ore (kilograms)†	2,205	2,703	2,790
Fluorspar (Fluorite)§	104,785	114,886	132,249
Salt (unrefined)	754,351	573,248	603,501
Diamonds ('000 metric carats)	2,004	1,902	2,356

* Provisional.
† Figures refer to the metal content of ores and concentrates.
‡ Estimate.
§ Figures (on a wet-weight basis) refer to acid-grade material.

Source: US Geological Survey.

Industry

SELECTED PRODUCTS
(metric tons)

	2004	2005	2006
Unrefined (blister) copper (unwrought)	24,704	23,551	21,918

Source: US Geological Survey.

Finance

CURRENCY AND EXCHANGE RATES

Monetary Units
100 cents = 1 Namibian dollar (N $).

Sterling, US Dollar and Euro Equivalents (31 December 2008)
£1 sterling = N $13.565;
US $1 = N $9.305;
€1 = N $12.950;
N $100 = £7.37 = US $10.75 = €7.72.

Average Exchange Rate (N $ per US $)
2006   6.7716
2007   7.0454
2008   8.2612

Note: The Namibian dollar was introduced in September 1993, replacing (at par) the South African rand. The rand remained legal tender in Namibia.

CENTRAL GOVERNMENT BUDGET
(N $ million, year ending 31 March)

Revenue*	2005/06	2006/07	2007/08†
Taxation	11,963.5	14,591.5	12,982.0
Taxes on income and profits	4,575.7	4,689.0	4,872.0
Taxes on property	110.1	122.0	140.0
Domestic taxes on goods and services	3,272.4	3,186.1	3,296.0
Taxes on international trade and transactions	3,891.9	6,471.4	4,538.0
Other taxes	113.4	123.0	136.0
Non-tax revenue	1,105.3	1,545.5	953.0
Entrepreneurial and property income	542.9	1,048.9	531.4
Fines and forfeitures	17.6	23.5	23.5
Administrative fees and charges	512.4	407.1	364.1
Return on capital from lending and equity	32.4	66.0	34.0
Total	13,068.8	16,137.0	13,935.0

NAMIBIA

Expenditure	2005/06	2006/07	2007/08†
Current expenditure	11,541.7	12,538.8	12,587.1
Personnel expenditure	5,888.3	6,139.4	6,183.2
Expenditure on goods and other services	1,922.4	2,198.5	2,208.0
Interest payments	1,186.3	1,478.1	1,477.7
Subsidies and other current transfers	2,544.7	2,722.8	2,718.2
Capital expenditure	1,650.9	2,749.0	2,143.5
Capital investment	1,337.4	1,848.2	1,462.5
Capital transfers	106.0	248.8	247.1
Total lending and equity participation	207.5	652.4	433.9
Total	13,192.6	15,287.8	14,730.6

* Excluding grants received from abroad (N $ million): 153.2 in 2005/06; 72.0 in 2006/07; 48.0 in 2007/08 (estimate).
† Estimates.

Source: Bank of Namibia, *Quarterly Bulletin* (December 2007).

INTERNATIONAL RESERVES
(US $ million at 31 December, excl. gold)

	2005	2006	2007
IMF special drawing rights	0.03	0.03	0.03
Reserve position in IMF	0.10	0.11	0.12
Foreign exchange	311.98	449.44	895.87
Total	312.10	449.58	896.02

Source: IMF, *International Financial Statistics*.

MONEY SUPPLY
(N $ million at 31 December)

	2005	2006	2007
Currency outside banks	680.0	763.4	820.3
Demand deposits at deposit money banks	8,728.8	12,915.6	13,815.7
Total money	9,408.8	13,678.9	14,636.1

Source: IMF, *International Financial Statistics*.

COST OF LIVING
(Consumer Price Index; base: December 2001 = 100)

	2005	2006	2007
Food and non-alcoholic beverages	124.4	132.5	148.7
Alcoholic beverages and tobacco	130.1	139.7	149.9
Clothing and footwear	108.2	105.0	108.5
Housing, fuel and power	124.3	128.3	132.7
Health	112.6	110.1	115.2
Transport	132.3	143.0	151.5
Communications	108.5	109.2	110.8
Recreation and culture	111.1	113.9	119.1
Education	140.6	149.9	158.8
All items (incl. others)	122.9	129.1	137.7

NATIONAL ACCOUNTS
(N $ million at current prices)

National Income and Product

	2005	2006	2007
Compensation of employees	19,630	21,317	23,635
Operating surplus	17,423	22,670	26,248
Domestic factor incomes	37,053	43,987	49,883
Consumption of fixed capital	5,261	5,896	6,920
Gross domestic product (GDP) at factor cost	42,314	49,883	56,804
Taxes, less subsidies, on production and imports	3,864	4,133	4,653
GDP in purchasers' values	46,177	54,017	61,457
Primary income received from abroad	955	1,304	1,911
Less Primary income paid abroad	−1,670	−1,661	−2,635
Gross national income	45,463	53,659	60,733
Less Consumption of fixed capital	5,261	5,896	6,920
National income in market prices	40,202	47,763	53,813
Other current transfers from abroad	4,547	6,733	7,421
Less Other current transfers paid abroad	−286	−306	−369
National disposable income	44,463	54,190	60,865

Expenditure on the Gross Domestic Product

	2005	2006	2007
Government final consumption expenditure	8,905	9,964	11,781
Private final consumption expenditure	26,735	30,223	37,610
Change in stocks	498	342	166
Gross fixed capital formation	8,594	11,962	12,705
Total domestic expenditure	44,732	52,491	62,262
Exports of goods and services	18,678	24,559	29,419
Less Imports of goods and services	18,615	22,454	30,573
Statistical discrepancy	1,382	−578	349
GDP in purchasers' values	46,177	54,017	61,457
GDP in constant 2004 prices	43,758	46,886	48,789

Gross Domestic Product by Economic Activity

	2005	2006	2007
Agriculture and forestry	2,861	3,275	3,626
Fishing	1,932	1,948	2,218
Mining and quarrying	4,257	6,654	7,591
Diamond mining	3,182	4,591	3,561
Manufacturing	5,738	7,792	9,661
Electricity and water	1,091	1,020	1,128
Construction	1,259	1,901	2,047
Wholesale and retail trade, repairs, etc.	5,202	5,879	6,769
Hotels and restaurants	829	940	1,090
Transport, storage and communications	2,662	2,544	2,922
Financial intermediation	1,823	2,190	2,508
Real estate and business services	4,218	4,479	4,924
Public administration and defence	4,115	4,434	5,101
Education	3,208	3,705	3,940
Health	1,579	1,535	1,683
Community, social and personal services	1,699	1,840	1,984
Private household with employed person	358	384	419
Sub-total	42,829	50,518	57,611
Less Financial services indirectly measured	517	637	807
GDP at basic prices	42,314	49,883	56,804
Taxes, less subsidies, on products	3,864	4,133	4,653
GDP in purchasers' values	46,177	54,017	61,457

Source: Bank of Namibia, *Quarterly Bulletin* (December 2008).

NAMIBIA

BALANCE OF PAYMENTS
(US $ million)

	2005	2006	2007
Exports of goods f.o.b.	2,069.9	2,646.6	2,921.6
Imports of goods f.o.b.	−2,326.2	−2,544.2	−3,101.6
Trade balance	−256.3	102.4	−180.0
Exports of services	412.6	525.7	599.1
Imports of services	−368.8	−429.7	−513.6
Balance on goods and services	−212.4	198.4	−94.5
Other income received	225.4	256.0	273.2
Other income paid	−352.6	−318.9	−431.5
Balance on goods, services and income	−339.6	135.6	−252.9
Current transfers received	651.1	925.6	998.3
Current transfers paid	−44.7	−45.4	−52.3
Current balance	266.8	1,051.8	693.1
Capital account (net)	79.6	83.3	83.4
Direct investment abroad	12.3	12.6	−2.7
Direct investment from abroad	166.1	−30.9	169.9
Portfolio investment assets	−1,052.8	−1,133.0	−1,482.9
Portfolio investment liabilities	5.1	4.7	4.5
Other investment assets	43.2	−353.7	136.2
Other investment liabilities	−48.6	−25.0	−292.0
Net errors and omissions	127.9	121.6	490.0
Overall balance	−400.5	−304.5	−200.5

Source: IMF, *International Financial Statistics*.

External Trade

PRINCIPAL COMMODITIES
(US $ million)

Imports c.i.f.	2005	2006	2007
Food and live animals	319.5	335.7	502.8
Mineral fuels and lubricants	51.3	86.7	416.4
Petroleum and petroleum products	48.4	83.1	399.4
Chemicals and related products	270.4	294.4	368.4
Basic manufactures	434.4	471.8	671.1
Non-metallic mineral manufactures	90.1	80.7	133.2
Metal products	123.2	152.6	247.5
Machinery and transport equipment	943.5	1,082.0	1,383.5
Machinery specialized for particular industries	78.4	134.9	167.2
General industrial machinery, equipment and parts	98.8	106.2	119.6
Telecommunications and sound equipment	69.1	104.4	111.2
Telecommunications equipment, parts and accessories	48.1	80.4	80.3
Electrical machinery, apparatus, etc.	101.4	124.7	143.1
Road vehicles	379.8	413.3	485.2
Passenger motor vehicles (excl. buses)	217.3	243.8	287.0
Other transport equipment	88.1	92.4	169.0
Miscellaneous manufactured articles	327.1	366.7	513.4
Clothing and accessories	86.8	86.8	130.6
Total (incl. others)	2,515.7	2,797.0	4,026.0

Exports f.o.b.	2005	2006	2007
Food and live animals	674.9	745.6	807.9
Fish, shellfish and preparations thereof	359.4	434.5	458.9
Fresh or frozen fish	323.4	415.2	431.7
Beverages and tobacco	106.6	111.9	137.7
Beverages	103.1	107.1	135.6
Alcoholic beverages	93.4	100.7	126.4
Beer made from malt	77.1	85.4	110.5
Crude materials (inedible) except fuels	118.9	335.9	647.9
Metal ores and scrap	10.2	188.6	474.5
Ores and concentrates of uranium and thorium	0.0	163.0	350.3
Basic manufactures	957.5	1,516.6	1,556.5
Non-metallic mineral manufactures	720.3	911.7	723.0
Pearl, precious and semi-precious stones	709.5	900.8	705.0
Diamonds	709.1	900.4	704.6
Machinery and transport equipment	135.9	121.0	280.3
Miscellaneous manufactured articles	284.4	362.0	422.1
Printed matter	215.5	292.7	357.0
Total (incl. others)	2,503.6	3,374.6	4,040.3

Source: UN, *International Trade Statistics Yearbook*.

PRINCIPAL TRADING PARTNERS
(US $ million)

Imports c.i.f.	2005	2006	2007
China, People's Repub.	40.0	96.8	101.5
Germany	48.2	62.4	83.9
South Africa	2,093.1	2,304.5	3,143.0
Spain	35.6	19.8	91.4
United Kingdom	26.9	23.6	45.2
USA	19.6	41.5	54.8
Total (incl. others)	2,515.7	2,797.0	4,026.0

Exports f.o.b.	2005	2006	2007
Angola	179.8	192.8	260.9
Belgium	9.0	12.2	12.9
Canada	80.3	127.6	199.3
Congo, Democratic Republic of	11.6	45.4	43.1
France	15.6	53.7	106.4
Germany	93.2	109.0	99.8
Italy	62.1	243.5	570.9
Netherlands	34.4	36.7	74.8
South Africa	763.4	829.2	1,172.3
Spain	180.6	202.0	242.8
United Kingdom	514.1	865.2	682.9
USA	229.2	81.7	102.1
Total (incl. others)	2,503.6	3,374.6	4,040.3

Source: UN, *International Trade Statistics Yearbook*.

Transport

RAILWAYS

	2002/03	2003/04
Freight (million net ton-km)	1,244.6	1,247.4
Passengers carried	125,656	112,033

Source: TransNamib Holdings Ltd, *2004 Annual Report*.

NAMIBIA

ROAD TRAFFIC
(motor vehicles in use at 31 December)

	1994*	1995*	1996
Passenger cars	61,269	62,500	74,875
Buses and coaches	5,098	5,200	10,175
Lorries and vans	60,041	61,300	59,352
Motorcycles and mopeds	1,450	1,480	1,520

* Estimates.

Total vehicles in use (excl. motorcycles and mopeds): 146,999 in 2000; 152,794 in 2001; 166,998 in 2002.

2002: Passenger cars 82,580; Buses and coaches 4,922; Lorries and vans 79,496; Motorcycles and mopeds 3,416.

Source: International Road Federation, *World Road Statistics*.

SHIPPING
Merchant Fleet
(at 31 December)

	2005	2006	2007
Number of vessels	178	173	173
Displacement (gross registered tons)	106,350	102,901	126,062

Source: Lloyd's Register-Fairplay, *World Fleet Statistics*.

Sea-borne Freight Traffic
('000 freight tons*, year ending 30 August, unless otherwise indicated)

	1999/2000†	2000/01	2001/02
Port of Lüderitz:			
Goods loaded	93.6	143.3	171.2
Goods unloaded	39.5	105.1	101.7
Goods transshipped	14.1	10.0	4.6
Containers handled (total TEUs)	2,311	2,320	2,480
Port of Walvis Bay:			
Goods loaded	723.4	720.7	915.8
Goods unloaded	1,460.3	1,452.1	1,443.1
Goods transshipped	40.0	56.6	60.3
Containers handled (total TEUs)	24,859	25,768	31,569

* One freight ton = 40 cu ft (1.133 cu m) of cargo capacity.
† Year ending 30 September 2000.
Source: Namibian Ports Authority.

CIVIL AVIATION
(traffic on scheduled services)

	2001	2002	2003
Kilometres flown (million)	9	9	11
Passengers carried ('000)	215	222	266
Passenger-km (million)	754	760	930
Total ton-km (million)	151	98	139

Source: UN, *Statistical Yearbook*.

Tourism

FOREIGN TOURIST ARRIVALS*

Country of origin	2003	2005†	2006
Angola	222,752	281,365	278,058
Botswana	22,679	22,333	24,719
Germany	58,036	61,222	68,214
South Africa	222,009	230,949	239,885
United Kingdom	19,291	20,978	24,736
Zimbabwe	17,795	22,765	30,622
Total (incl. others)	695,221	777,890	833,345

* Excluding same-day visitors: 917,000 in 2003; 973,168 in 2005; 1,031,677 in 2006.
† Figures for 2004 were not available.

Tourism receipts (US $ million, incl. passenger transport): 426 in 2004; 363 in 2005; 473 in 2006.

Source: World Tourism Organization.

Communications Media

	2005	2006	2007
Telephones ('000 main lines in use)	139.0	136.2	138.1
Mobile cellular telephones ('000 subscribers)	448.9	608.8	800.3
Internet users ('000)	80.6	90.1	101.0
Broadband subscribers ('000)	0.1	0.2	0.3

Personal computers ('000 in use): 220 in 2004.
Television receivers ('000 in use): 67 in 2000.
Source: International Telecommunication Union.
Radio receivers ('000 in use): 232 in 1997 (Source: UNESCO, *Statistical Yearbook*).
Daily newspapers (2004): 4 (average circulation 55,800) (Source: UNESCO, *Statistical Yearbook*).
Non-daily newspapers (2004): 3 (average circulation 240,000) (Source: UNESCO, *Statistical Yearbook*).

Education

(2005/06, unless otherwise indicated)

	Teachers	Males	Females	Total
Pre-primary	1,314*	16,414	16,322	32,736
Primary	13,675†	206,398	203,110	409,508
Secondary	6,423†	72,983	85,179	158,162
Tertiary	763	7,023	6,162	13,185

* Estimate for 1999/2000.
† 2006/07.

Institutions (1998/99): Primary 1,362.
Source: UNESCO, Institute for Statistics.

Adult literacy rate (UNESCO estimates): 88.0% (males 88.6%; females 87.4%) in 2007 (Source: UNESCO Institute for Statistics).

Directory

The Constitution

The Constitution of the Republic of Namibia took effect at independence on 21 March 1990. Its principal provisions are summarized below:

THE REPUBLIC

The Republic of Namibia is a sovereign, secular, democratic and unitary State and the Constitution is the supreme law.

FUNDAMENTAL HUMAN RIGHTS AND FREEDOMS

The fundamental rights and freedoms of the individual are guaranteed regardless of sex, race, colour, ethnic origin, religion, creed or social or economic status. All citizens shall have the right to form and join political parties. The practice of racial discrimination shall be prohibited.

THE PRESIDENT

Executive power shall be vested in the President and the Cabinet. The President shall be the Head of State and of the Government and

NAMIBIA

the Commander-in-Chief of the Defence Force. The President shall be directly elected by universal and equal adult suffrage, and must receive more than 50% of the votes cast. The term of office shall be five years; one person may not hold the office of President for more than two terms.*

THE CABINET
The Cabinet shall consist of the President, the Prime Minister and such other ministers as the President may appoint from members of the National Assembly. The President may also appoint a Deputy Prime Minister. The functions of the members of the Cabinet shall include directing the activities of ministries and government departments, initiating bills for submission to the National Assembly, formulating, explaining and assessing for the National Assembly the budget of the State and its economic development plans, formulating, explaining and analysing for the National Assembly Namibia's foreign policy and foreign trade policy and advising the President on the state of national defence.

THE NATIONAL ASSEMBLY
Legislative power shall be vested in the National Assembly, which shall be composed of 72 members elected by general, direct and secret ballots and not more than six non-voting members appointed by the President by virtue of their special expertise, status, skill or experience. Every National Assembly shall continue for a maximum period of five years, but it may be dissolved by the President before the expiry of its term.

THE NATIONAL COUNCIL
The National Council shall consist of two members from each region (elected by regional councils from among their members) and shall have a life of six years. The functions of the National Council shall include considering all bills passed by the National Assembly, investigating any subordinate legislation referred to it by the National Assembly for advice, and recommending legislation to the National Assembly on matters of regional concern.

OTHER PROVISIONS
Other provisions relate to the administration of justice (see under Judicial System), regional and local government, the public service commission, the security commission, the police, defence forces and prison service, finance, and the central bank and national planning commission. The repeal of, or amendments to, the Constitution require the approval of two-thirds of the members of the National Assembly and two-thirds of the members of the National Council; if the proposed repeal or amendment secures a majority of two-thirds of the members of the National Assembly, but not a majority of two-thirds of the members of the National Council, the President may make the proposals the subject of a national referendum, in which a two-thirds' majority is needed for approval of the legislation.

* In late 1998 the National Assembly and National Council approved legislation whereby the Constitution was to be exceptionally amended to allow the incumbent President to seek a third term of office.

The Government

HEAD OF STATE
President and Commander-in-Chief of the Defence Force: HIFIKEPUNYE POHAMBA (elected by direct suffrage 15–16 November 2004; took office 21 March 2005).

THE CABINET
(April 2009)

President: HIFIKEPUNYE POHAMBA.
Prime Minister: NAHAS ANGULA.
Deputy Prime Minister: Dr LIBERTINA AMATHILA.
Minister of Presidential Affairs: ALBERT KAWANA.
Minister of Home Affairs and Immigration: ROSALIA NGHIDINWA.
Minister of Safety and Security: Dr NICKEY IYAMBO.
Minister of Defence: Maj.-Gen. (retd) CHARLES NAMOLOH.
Minister of Foreign Affairs: MARCO HAUSIKO.
Minister of Information and Communication Technology: JOEL KAAPANDA.
Minister of Education: NANGOLO MBUMBA.
Minister of Mines and Energy: ERRKI NGHIMTINA.
Minister of Justice and Attorney-General: PENDUKENI IVULA-ITHANA.
Minister of Trade and Industry: Dr HAGE GEINGOB.
Minister of Agriculture, Water and Forestry: JOHN MUTORWA.
Minister of Finance: SAARA KUUGONGELWA-AMADHILA.
Minister of Health and Social Services: RICHARD KAMWI.
Minister of Labour and Social Welfare: IMMANUEL NGATJIZEKO.
Minister of Regional and Local Government and Housing and Rural Development: JERRY EKANDJO.
Minister of Environment and Tourism: NETUMBO NANDI-NDAITWAH.
Minister of Works, Transport and Communications: HELMUT ANGULA.
Minister of Lands, Resettlement and Rehabilitation: ALPHEUS NARUSEB.
Minister of Fisheries and Marine Resources: Dr ABRAHAM IYAMBO.
Minister of Gender Equality and Child Welfare: MARLENE MUNGUNDA.
Minister of Youth, National Service, Sport and Culture: WILLEM KONJORE.
Minister of War Veterans: Dr NGARIKUTUKE TJIRIANGE.

Also attending Cabinet
Dir-Gen. of the Namibia Central Intelligence Agency: Lt-Gen. LUCAS HANGULA.
Dir-Gen. of the National Planning Commission: PETER KATJAVIVI.

MINISTRIES
Office of the President: State House, Robert Mugabe Ave, PMB 13339, Windhoek; tel. (61) 2707111; fax (61) 221780; e-mail angolo@op.gov.na; internet www.op.gov.na.

Office of the Prime Minister: Robert Mugabe Ave, PMB 13338, Windhoek; tel. (61) 2879111; fax (61) 230648; internet www.opm.gov.na.

Ministry of Agriculture, Water and Forestry: Government Office Park, PMB 13184, Windhoek; tel. (61) 2087111; fax (61) 221733; internet www.mawf.gov.na.

Ministry of Defence: PMB 13307, Windhoek; tel. (61) 2042055; fax (61) 232518; e-mail psecretary@mod.gov.na; internet www.mod.gov.na.

Ministry of Education: Government Office Park, PMB 13186, Windhoek; internet www.mec.gov.na; tel. (61) 2933358; fax (61) 2933368.

Ministry of Environment and Tourism: Swabou Bldg, Post St Mall, PMB 13346, Windhoek; tel. (61) 2842111; fax (61) 221930; e-mail kshangula@met.gov.na; internet www.met.gov.na.

Ministry of Finance: Fiscus Bldg, John Meinert St, PMB 13185, Windhoek; tel. (61) 2092931; fax (61) 227702; internet www.mof.gov.na.

Ministry of Fisheries and Marine Resources: Uhland and Goethe Sts, Private Bag 13355, Windhoek; tel. (61) 2059111; fax (61) 233286; e-mail mfmr@mfmr.gov.na; internet www.mfmr.gov.na.

Ministry of Foreign Affairs: Govt Bldgs, Robert Mugabe Ave, PMB 13347, Windhoek; tel. (61) 2829111; fax (61) 223937; e-mail headquarters@mfa.gov.na; internet www.mfa.gov.na.

Ministry of Gender Equality and Child Welfare: Private Bag 13359, Windhoek; tel. (61) 2833111; fax (61) 238941; e-mail genderequality@mgecw.gov.na; internet www.mgecw.gov.na.

Ministry of Health and Social Services: Old State Hospital, Harvey St, PMB 13198, Windhoek; tel. (61) 2039111; fax (61) 227607; internet www.mhss.gov.na.

Ministry of Home Affairs and Immigration: Cohen Bldg, Kasino St, PMB 13200, Windhoek; tel. (61) 2922111; fax (61) 2922185; internet www.mha.gov.na.

Ministry of Information and Communication Technology: Windhoek.

Ministry of Justice: Justitia Bldg, Independence Ave, PMB 13248, Windhoek; tel. (61) 2805111; fax (61) 221615; includes the office of the Attorney-General.

Ministry of Labour and Social Welfare: 32 Mercedes St, Khomasdal, PMB 19005, Windhoek; tel. (61) 2066111; fax (61) 212323; internet www.mol.gov.na.

Ministry of Lands, Resettlement and Rehabilitation: Brendan Simbwaye Bldg, Goethe St, PMB 13343, Windhoek; tel. (61) 2852111; fax (61) 254240.

Ministry of Mines and Energy: 1st Aviation Rd, PMB 13297, Windhoek; tel. (61) 2848111; fax (61) 238643; e-mail info@mme.gov.na; internet www.mme.gov.na.

Ministry of Presidential Affairs: Windhoek.

NAMIBIA

Ministry of Regional and Local Government and Housing and Rural Development: PMB 13289, Windhoek; tel. (61) 2975111; fax (61) 226049; internet www.mrlgh.gov.na.

Ministry of Safety and Security: Brendan Simbwaye Bldg, Goethe St, PMB 13323, Windhoek; tel. (61) 2846111; fax (61) 233879.

Ministry of Trade and Industry: Uhland St, cnr Goethe St, Private Bag 13340, Windhoek; tel. (61) 2837111; fax (61) 220227; internet www.mti.gov.na.

Ministry of War Veterans: Windhoek.

Ministry of Works, Transport and Communications: PMB 13341, Windhoek; tel. (61) 2088111; fax (61) 228560.

Ministry of Youth, National Service, Sport and Culture: Windhoek.

President and Legislature

PRESIDENT

Presidential Election, 15–16 November 2004

Candidate	Votes	% of votes
Hifikepunye Pohamba (SWAPO)	625,605	76.44
Ben Ulenga (CoD)	59,547	7.28
Katuutire Kaura (DTA)	41,905	5.12
Kuaima Riruako (NUDO)	34,616	4.23
Justus Garoeb (UDF)	31,354	3.83
Henk Mudge (RP)	15,955	1.95
Kosie Pretorius (MAG)	9,738	1.15
Total	**818,360**	**100.00**

NATIONAL ASSEMBLY*

Speaker: THEO-BEN GURIRAB.

General Election, 15–16 November 2004

Party	Votes	% of votes	Seats
South West Africa People's Organisation of Namibia (SWAPO)	620,787	76.11	55
Congress of Democrats (CoD)	59,465	7.29	5
Democratic Turnhalle Alliance of Namibia (DTA)	41,714	5.11	4
National Unity Democratic Organisation (NUDO)	33,874	4.15	3
United Democratic Front (UDF)	29,336	3.60	3
Republican Party	15,965	1.96	1
Monitor Action Group (MAG)	6,920	0.85	1
Namibia Movement for Democratic Change (NMDC)	4,138	0.51	—
South West African National Union (SWANU)	3,438	0.42	—
Total	**815,637**	**100.00**	**72**

* In addition to the 72 directly elected members, the President of the Republic is empowered to nominate as many as six non-voting members.

NATIONAL COUNCIL

Chairman: ASSER KUVERI KAPERE.

The second chamber of parliament is the advisory National Council, comprising two representatives from each of the country's 13 Regional Councils, elected for a period of six years.

Election Commission

Electoral Commission of Namibia (ECN): 11 Goethe St, POB 13352, Windhoek; tel. (61) 376200; fax (61) 237618; e-mail mndjarakana@opm.gov.na; internet www.ecn.gov.na; f. 1992; independent; Chair. VICTOR L. TONCHI; Dir of Elections and CEO MOSES K. NDJARAKANA.

Political Organizations

All People's Party of Namibia (APP): f. 2008 in Kavango region; splinter group of the CoD, which split in late 2007; Chair. IGNATIUS SHIXWAMENI.

Congress of Democrats (CoD): 8 Storch St, POB 40905, Windhoek; tel. (61) 256954; fax (61) 256980; internet www.cod.org.na; f. 1999 after split from SWAPO; Leader BEN ULENGA; Nat. Chair. TSUDAO GURIRAB; Sec.-Gen. KALA GERTZE.

Democratic Party of Namibia (DPN): Windhoek; f. 2008; Interim Pres. SALOMON DAWID ISAACKS.

Democratic Turnhalle Alliance of Namibia (DTA): POB 173, Windhoek 9000; tel. 238530; fax 226494; e-mail m.venaani@parliament.gov.na; f. 1977 as a coalition of 11 ethnically based political groupings; reorg. in 1991 to allow dual membership of coalition groupings and the main party; Pres. KATUUTIRE KAURA; Chair. JOHAN DE WAAL; Sec.-Gen. ALOIS GENDE.

Monitor Action Group (MAG): POB 80808, Olympia, Windhoek; tel. (61) 252008; fax (61) 229242; e-mail mag@iway.na; f. 1991 by mems of the National Party of South West Africa alliance; Leader and Chair. J. W. F. (KOSIE) PRETORIUS.

Namibia Democratic Movement for Change (NDMC): POB 60043, Katutura; tel. and fax (61) 297795; f. 2004; Pres. FRANS GOAGOSEB; Sec.-Gen. JOSEPH KAUANDENGE.

National Unity Democratic Organisation (NUDO): POB 60043, Katutura; tel. and fax (61) 297795; f. 1964 by the Herero Chiefs' Council; joined the DTA in 1977; broke away from the DTA in 2003; Pres. Chief KUAIMA RIRUAKO; Sec.-Gen. JOSEPH KAUANDENGE.

Rally for Democracy and Progress (RDP): f. 2007 by fmr mems of ruling SWAPO party; Chair. JESAYA NYAMU (acting); Pres. HIDIPO HAMUTENYA (acting).

Republican Party: 6 Hügel St, POB 20020, Windhoek; tel. (61) 225632; fax (61) 225636; f. 1977 after breaking away from the National Party; joined the DTA later in 1977; dissolved in 1991; reactivated in 2003 after breaking away from the DTA; Pres. HENK MUDGE; Sec.-Gen. CAROLA ENGELBRECHT.

SWAPO Party of Namibia (SWAPO): POB 1071, Windhoek; tel. (61) 238364; fax (61) 232368; f. 1957 as the Ovamboland People's Congress; renamed South West Africa People's Organisation in 1960; adopted present name in 1997; Pres. Dr SAMUEL DANIEL NUJOMA; Vice-Pres. HIFIKEPUNYE POHAMBA; Sec.-Gen. NGARIKUTUKE TJIRIANGE.

South West African National Union (SWANU): Windhoek; f. 1959 by mems of the Herero Chiefs' Council; formed alliance with the Workers' Revolutionary Party in 1999; Pres. RIHUPISA KANDANDO.

United Democratic Front (UDF): POB 20037, Windhoek; tel. (61) 230683; fax (61) 237175; f. 1989 as a centrist coalition of eight parties; reorg. as a single party in 1999; Nat. Chair. ERIC BIWA; Pres. JUSTUS GAROEB.

Workers' Revolutionary Party: Windhoek; f. 1989; Trotskyist; Leaders WERNER MAMUGWE, HEWAT BEUKES.

The **Caprivi Liberation Army (CLA)**, f. 1998 as the Caprivi Liberation Movement, seeks secession of the Caprivi Strip; conducts military operations from bases in Zambia and Angola; political wing operates from Denmark as the **Caprivi National Union**, led by MISHAKE MUYONGO and BONIFACE MAMILI.

Diplomatic Representation

EMBASSIES AND HIGH COMMISSIONS IN NAMIBIA

Algeria: 111A Gloudina St, Ludwigsdorf, POB 3079, Windhoek; tel. (61) 221507; fax (61) 236376; Chargé d'affaires a.i. YOUCEF DELILECHE.

Angola: Angola House, 3 Dr Agostinho Neto St, Ausspannplatz, PMB 12020, Windhoek; tel. (61) 227535; fax (61) 221498; Ambassador MANUEL A. D. RODRIGUEZ.

Botswana: 101 Nelson Mandela Ave, POB 20359, Windhoek; tel. (61) 221942; fax (61) 221948; High Commissioner NORMAN MOLEBOGE.

Brazil: 52 Bismarck St, POB 24166, Windhoek; tel. (61) 237368; fax (61) 233389; e-mail brasemb@mweb.com.na; Ambassador CHRISTIANO WINDHOEK.

China, People's Republic: 13 Wecka St, POB 22777, Windhoek; tel. (61) 222089; fax (61) 225544; e-mail chinaemb@iafrica.com.na; internet na.chineseembassy.org; Ambassador REN XIAOPING.

Congo, Republic: 9 Korner St, POB 22970, Windhoek; tel. (61) 257517; fax (61) 240796; Ambassador PATRICE NDOUNGA.

Cuba: 31 Omuramba Rd, Eros, POB 23866, Windhoek; tel. (61) 227072; fax (61) 231584; Ambassador ANA VILMA VALLEJERA RODRÍGUEZ.

Egypt: 10 Berg St, POB 11853, Windhoek; tel. (61) 221501; fax (61) 228856; Ambassador MOHAMED HADI MOSTAFA EL-TONSI.

NAMIBIA

Directory

Finland: 2 Crohn St (cnr Bahnhof St), POB 3649, Windhoek; tel. (61) 221355; fax (61) 221349; e-mail sanomat.win@formin.fi; internet www.finland.org.na; Chargé d'affaires a.i. SEIJA KINNI-HUTTUNEN.

France: 1 Goethe St, POB 20484, Windhoek; tel. (61) 2276700; fax (61) 231436; e-mail frambwdk@iafrica.com.na; internet www.ambafrance-na.org; Ambassador JEAN-LOUIS ZOËL.

Germany: Sanlam Centre, 6th Floor, 154 Independence Ave, POB 231, Windhoek; tel. (61) 273100; fax (61) 222981; e-mail germany@iway.na; internet www.windhuk.diplo.de; Ambassador EGON KOCHANKE.

Ghana: 5 Nelson Mandela Ave, POB 24165, Windhoek; tel. (61) 221341; fax (61) 221343; High Commissioner MAUREEN A. AMEMA-TEKPOR.

India: 97 Nelson Mandela Ave, POB 1209, Windhoek; tel. (61) 226037; fax (61) 237320; e-mail hicomind@mweb.com.na; internet www.highcommissionofindia.web.na; High Commissioner TSEWANG TOPDEN.

Indonesia: 103 Nelson Mandela Ave, POB 20691, Windhoek; tel. (61) 2851000; fax (61) 2851231; e-mail kbri@iafrica.com.na; internet www.indonesiawindhoek.org; Ambassador LEONARDUS WIDAYATMO.

Kenya: Kenya House, 5th Floor, 134 Robert Mugabe Ave, POB 2889, Windhoek; tel. (61) 226836; fax (61) 221409; e-mail rjeboit@yahoo.co.uk; High Commissioner ROSE BOIT.

Libya: 69 Burg St, Luxury Hill, POB 124, Windhoek; tel. (61) 234454; fax (61) 234471; Ambassador SALAM MOHAMMED KRAYEM (designate).

Malawi: 56 Bismarck St, POB 13254, Windhoek 9000; tel. (61) 221391; fax (61) 227056; e-mail mhc@mweb.co.na; High Commissioner F. CHIKUTA.

Malaysia: 12 Babs Street, Ludwigsdorf, POB 312, Windhoek; tel. (61) 259344; fax (61) 259343; e-mail malwdhoek@kln.gov.my; High Commissioner HAYATI BT ISMAIL.

Mexico: Southern Life Tower, 3rd Floor, 39 Post St Mall, POB 13220, Windhoek; tel. (61) 229082; fax (61) 229180; Ambassador MAURICIO DE MARÍA Y CAMPOS.

Nigeria: 4 Omuramba Rd, Eros Park, POB 23547, Windhoek; tel. (61) 232103; fax (61) 221639; High Commissioner OKUN AYODEJI.

Russia: 4 Christian St, POB 3826, Windhoek; tel. (61) 228671; fax (61) 229061; Ambassador NIKOLAI M. GRIBKOV.

South Africa: RSA House, cnr Jan Jonker St and Nelson Mandela Ave, POB 23100, Windhoek; tel. (61) 2057111; fax (61) 224140; e-mail sahcwin@iafrica.com.na; Chargé d'affaires a.i. P. J. COETZEE.

Spain: 58 Bismarck St, POB 21811, Windhoek-West; tel. (61) 223066; fax (61) 223046; e-mail emb.windhoek@mae.es; Ambassador MARÍA VICTORIA SCOLA PLIEGO.

Sweden: Sanlam Centre, 9th Floor, POB 23087, Windhoek; tel. (61) 2859111; fax (61) 2859222; e-mail ambassaden.windhoek@sida.se; Chargé d'affaires a.i. LENA JOHANSSON BLOMSTRAND.

United Kingdom: 116 Robert Mugabe Ave, POB 22202, Windhoek; tel. (61) 274800; fax (61) 228895; e-mail general.windhoek@fco.gov.uk; internet www.ukinnamibia.fco.gov.uk; High Commissioner MARK BENSBERG.

USA: 14 Lossen St, Ausspannplatz, PMB 12029, Windhoek 9000; tel. (61) 221601; fax (61) 229792; internet windhoek.usembassy.gov; Ambassador GAIL DENNISE MATHIEU.

Venezuela: Southern Life Tower, 3rd Floor, 39 Post St Mall, PMB 13353, Windhoek; tel. (61) 227905; fax (61) 227804; Chargé d'affaires a.i. JORGE JIMÉNEZ.

Zambia: 22 Sam Nujoma Dr., cnr Mandume Ndemufayo Rd, POB 22882, Windhoek; tel. (61) 237610; fax (61) 228162; e-mail zahico@iway.na; internet www.zahico.iway.na; High Commissioner GRIFFIN NYIRONGO.

Zimbabwe: cnr Independence Ave and Grimm St, POB 23056, Windhoek; tel. (61) 228134; fax (61) 226859; Ambassador CHIPO ZINDOGA.

Judicial System

Judicial power is exercised by the Supreme Court, the High Court, and a number of Magistrate and Lower Courts. The Constitution provides for the appointment of an Ombudsman.

Chief Justice: PETER SHIVUTE.

Religion

It is estimated that about 90% of the population are Christians.

CHRISTIANITY

Council of Churches in Namibia: 8 Mont Blanc St, POB 41, Windhoek; tel. (61) 374054; fax (61) 62786; e-mail ccn.gensec@mweb.com.na; f. 1978; eight mem. churches; Pres. Bishop JOHANNES SINDANO; Gen. Sec. Rev. PHILLIP STRYDOM.

The Anglican Communion

Namibia comprises a single diocese in the Anglican Church of Southern Africa (formerly the Church of the Province of Southern Africa). The Metropolitan of the Province is the Archbishop of Cape Town, South Africa. In 2006 there were an estimated 110,000 Anglicans in the country.

Bishop of Namibia: Rt Rev. NATHANIEL NDAXUMA NAKWATUMBAH, POB 57, Windhoek; tel. (61) 238920; fax (61) 225903; e-mail shirley@mweb.com.na.

Dutch Reformed Church

Dutch Reformed Church in Namibia (Nederduitse Gereformeerde Kerk): 34 Feldstreet, POB 389, Windhoek; tel. (61) 374350; fax (61) 227287; e-mail clem@ngkn.com.na; internet www.ngkerk.org.za/namibie; f. 1898; Sec. Rev. CLEM MARAIS; 21,712 mems in 44 congregations (2008).

Evangelical Lutheran

Evangelical Lutheran Church in Namibia (ELCIN): PMB 2018, Ondangwa; tel. (65) 240241; fax (65) 240472; e-mail gen.sec@elcin.org.na; internet www.elcin.org.na; f. 1870; became autonomous in 1954; Presiding Bishop Dr THOMAS SHIVUTE; Gen. Sec. Rev. ELIKAIM N. K. SHAANIKA; 637,229 mems (2009).

Evangelical Lutheran Church in the Republic of Namibia (ELCRN) (Rhenish Mission Church): POB 5069, 6 Church St, Ausspanplatz, 9000 Windhoek; tel. (61) 224531; fax (61) 226775; e-mail bishoppa@elcrnam.org; f. 1957; became autonomous in 1972; Pres. Bishop Dr ZEPHANIA KAMEETA; 350,000 mems (2009).

German Evangelical-Lutheran Church in Namibia (ELCIN—GELC): POB 233, Windhoek; tel. (61) 224294; fax (61) 221470; e-mail bishop-office@elcin-gelc.org; internet www.elcin-gelc.org; Pres. Bishop ERICH HERTEL; 5,200 mems.

Methodist

African Methodist Episcopal Church: POB 798, Keetmanshoop; tel. (63) 222347; fax (63) 223026; e-mail erikke5@hotmail.com; bishop resident in Cape Town, South Africa; Rep. Rev. Dr ANDREAS BIWA; c. 8,000 mems in 33 churches.

Methodist Church of Southern Africa: POB 143, Windhoek; tel. (61) 228921; fax (61) 229202; e-mail central@iway.na; internet www.methodist.org.za; Rep. Rev. EDGAR LUKEN.

The Roman Catholic Church

Namibia comprises one archdiocese, one diocese and one apostolic vicariate. At 31 December 2006 there were 404,924 adherents of the Roman Catholic Church, representing some 17.7% of the total population.

Bishops' Conference

Namibian Catholic Bishops' Conference, POB 11525, Windhoek 9000; tel. (61) 224798; fax (61) 228126; e-mail ncbc@windhoek.org.na.

f. 1996; Pres. LIBORIUS NDUMBUKUTI NASHENDA (Archbishop of Windhoek).

Archbishop of Windhoek: LIBORIUS NDUMBUKUTI NASHENDA, POB 272, Windhoek 9000; tel. (61) 227595; fax (61) 229836; e-mail rcarch@iafrica.com.na; internet www.rcchurch.na.

Other Christian Churches

Among other denominations active in Namibia are the Evangelical Reformed Church in Africa, the Presbyterian Church of Southern Africa, Seventh Day Adventists and the United Congregational Church of Southern Africa. At mid-2000 there were an estimated 820,000 Protestants and 192,000 adherents professing other forms of Christianity.

JUDAISM

Windhoek Hebrew Congregation: POB 563, Windhoek; tel. (61) 221990; fax (61) 226444.

BAHÁ'Í FAITH

National Spiritual Assembly: POB 20372, Windhoek; tel. (61) 302663; fax (61) 230729; e-mail bahainamibia@iway.na; Sec. ROSI STEVENSON; mems resident in 215 localities.

NAMIBIA

The Press

The African Magazine: NCCI, 2 Jenner St, POB 1770, Windhoek; tel. and fax (61) 255018; e-mail info@theafricanmagazin.org; internet www.theafricanmagazin.org.

AgriForum: 114 Robert Mugabe Ave, POB 86641, Eros, Windhoek; tel. (61) 256023; fax (61) 256035; e-mail agriforum@agrinamibia.com.na; internet www.agrinamibia.com.na; f. 1978; monthly; Afrikaans and English; publ. by the Namibia Agricultural Union; Editor MARIETJIE VAN STADEN; circ. 5,000.

Allgemeine Zeitung: Omurambaweg 11, POB 86695, Eros, Windhoek; tel. (61) 225822; fax (61) 220225; e-mail azinfo@az.com.na; internet www.az.com.na; f. 1916; publ. by Newsprint Namibia; daily; German; Editor-in-Chief STEFAN FISCHER; circ. 5,300 (Mon.–Thur.), 6,500 (Fri.).

The Big Issue Namibia: 37 Bahnhof St, POB 97140, Maerua Park, Windhoek; tel. (61) 242216; fax (61) 242232; e-mail jo@bigissue.com.na; internet www.bigissuenamibia.org; f. 2002; monthly; Man. Dir JO ROGGE; Editor CATHERINE SASMAN.

Insight Namibia: 34 Sam Nujoma Dr., POB 86058, Windhoek; tel. (61) 301437; fax (61) 240385; e-mail editor@insight.com.na; internet www.insight.com.na; f. 2004; monthly; business and current affairs; Editor ROBIN SHERBOURNE.

Namib Times: Sam Nujoma Ave, POB 706, Walvis Bay; tel. (64) 205854; fax (64) 204813; e-mail ntimes@iway.na; internet www.namibtimes.net; 2 a week; Afrikaans, English, German and Portuguese; Editor FLORIS STEENKAMP; circ. 4,300.

Namibia Brief: Independence Ave, POB 2123, Windhoek; tel. and fax (61) 251044; fax (61) 237251; e-mail cblatt@iafrica.com.na; quarterly; English; Editor CATHY BLATT; circ. 7,500.

Namibia Economist: 7 Schuster St, POB 49, Windhoek 9000; tel. (61) 221925; fax (61) 220615; e-mail daniel@economist.com.na; internet www.economist.com.na; f. 1986; weekly; English; business, finance and economics; Editor DANIEL STEINMANN; circ. 7,000.

Namibia Magazin: POB 6870, Windhoek; tel. and fax (61) 224929; e-mail evonwiet@iafrica.com.na; publ. by Klaus Hess Verlag; German; politics, tourism and culture; Rep. ERIKA VON WIETERSHEIM.

Namibia Review: Directorate Print Media and Regional Offices, Regular Publications, Turnhalle Bldg, Bahnhof St, PMB 13344, Windhoek; tel. (61) 222246; fax (61) 224937; e-mail bupe@webmail.co.za; f. 1992; publ. by the Ministry of Information and Broadcasting; monthly; information on govt policy and developmental issues; Editor ELIZABETH KALAMBO-M'ULE; circ. 5,000.

Namibia Sport: POB 1246, Windhoek; tel. (61) 224132; fax (61) 224613; e-mail editor@namibiasport.com.na; internet www.namibiasport.com.na; f. 2002; monthly; Editor HELGE SCHUTZ; circ. 2,500.

Namibia Today: 21 Johan Albrecht St, POB 24669, Windhoek; tel. (61) 276730; fax (61) 276381; 2 a week; Afrikaans, English, Oshiherero and Oshiwambo; publ. by SWAPO; Editor KAOMO-VIJINDA TJOMBE; circ. 5,000.

The Namibian: 42 John Meinert St, POB 20783, Windhoek; tel. (61) 279600; fax (61) 279602; e-mail editor@namibian.com.na; internet www.namibian.com.na; daily; English; Editor GWEN LISTER; circ. 23,000 (Mon.–Thur.), 32,000 (Fri.).

The Namibian Worker: POB 50034, Bachbrecht, Windhoek; tel. (61) 215037; fax (61) 215589; e-mail nunw@mweb.com.na; newsletter publ. by National Union of Namibian Workers; revived in 2003; Afrikaans, English and Oshiwambo; Editor-in-Chief C. RANGA HAIKALI; circ. 1,000.

NCCI Namibia Business Journal: NCCI Head Office, 2 Jenner St, POB 9355, Windhoek; tel. (61) 228809; fax (61) 228009; publ. by the Namibia Chamber of Commerce and Industry; 6 a year; English; CEO TARAH SHAANIKA; Editor CHARITY MWIYA; circ. 4,000.

New Era: Daniel Tjongarero House, cnr Kerby and W. Kulz Sts, Private Mail Bag 13364, Windhoek; tel. (61) 273300; fax (61) 220583; internet www.newera.com.na; e-mail editor@newera.com.na; f. 1991; daily; publ. by the Ministry of Information and Broadcasting; English; Chair. VILBARD USIKU; CEO SYLVESTER BLACK; Editor RAJAH MUNAMAVA; circ. 10,000.

Plus Weekly: POB 21506, Windhoek; tel. (61) 233635; fax (61) 230478; e-mail info@namibiaplus.com; internet www.namibiaplus.com; publ. by Federsen Publications; Afrikaans, English and German.

Republikein: 11 Omuramba Rd, POB 3436, Eros, Windhoek; tel. (61) 2972000; fax (61) 223721; e-mail republkn@republikein.com.na; internet www.republikein.com.na; f. 1977; daily; Afrikaans and English; publ. by Newsprint Namibia; Group Gen. Man. CHRIS JACOBIE; circ. 17,500 (Mon.–Wed.), 21,000 (Thur.–Fri.).

Sister Namibia: POB 87753, Windhoek; tel. (61) 230618; fax (61) 236371; e-mail sister@iafrica.com.na; f. 1989; 6 a year; publ. by Sister Namibia human rights org.; women's issues; Editor LIZ FRANK; circ. 9,000.

The Southern Times: cnr Dr W. Külz and Kerby Sts, POB 32235, Windhoek; tel. (61) 301094; fax (61) 301095; e-mail tstnews@newera.com.na; internet www.southerntimesafrica.com; f. 2004; weekly (Sun.); owned by New Era and Zimpapers, Zimbabwe; printed in Namibia and Zimbabwe; regional; CEO PETER MIETZNER; Editor INNOCENT GORE.

Space Magazine: Sanlam Centre, 3rd Floor, POB 3717, Windhoek; tel. (61) 225155; e-mail space@mweb.com.na; monthly; English; family life; Publr ESTER SMITH; Editor YANNA SMITH.

Windhoek Observer: 6 Schuster St, POB 2255, Windhoek; tel. (61) 221737; fax (61) 226098; e-mail whkob@africaonline.com.na; f. 1978; weekly; English; Editor HANNES SMITH; circ. 14,000.

NEWS AGENCY

Namibia Press Agency (Nampa): cnr Keller and Eugene Marais Sts, POB 61354, Windhoek 9000; tel. (61) 374000; fax (61) 221713; e-mail admin@nampa.org; internet www.nampa.org; f. 1990; Chair. MAUREEN HINDA; CEO NGHIDINUA HAMUNIME; Editor TOMMY KATAMILA.

PRESS ASSOCIATION

Press Club Windhoek: POB 2032, Windhoek; tel. (61) 2796000; fax (61) 279602; e-mail carmen@namibian.com.na; Chair. CARMEN HONEY.

Publishers

ELOC Printing Press: PMB 2013, Oniipa, Ondangwa; tel. and fax (65) 240211; fax (65) 240536; e-mail elocbook@iway.na; internet www.elocbook.iway.na; f. 1901; Exec. Dir JOEL AKUDHENGA.

Gamsberg Macmillan Publishers (Pty) Ltd: 19 Faraday St, POB 22830, Windhoek; tel. (61) 232165; fax (61) 233538; e-mail gmp@iafrica.com.na; internet www.macmillan-africa.com; imprints incl. New Namibia Books and Out of Africa; Man. Dir HERMAN VAN WYK.

Longman Namibia: POB 9251, Eros, Windhoek; tel. (61) 231124; fax (61) 224019; Publr LINDA BREDENKAMP.

National Archives of Namibia: 1–9 Eugène Marais St, PMB 13250, Windhoek; tel. (61) 2935213; fax (61) 2935217; e-mail natarch@mec.gov.na; f. 1939; Chief Archivist WERNER HILLEBRECHT.

PUBLISHERS' ASSOCIATION

Association of Namibian Publishers: POB 40219, Windhoek; tel. (61) 228284; fax (61) 231496; f. 1991; Chair. Dr H. MELBER.

Broadcasting and Communications

TELECOMMUNICATIONS

Africa Online Namibia: Ground Floor, NAU Bldg, 114 John Meinert St (cnr of Robert Mugabe Ave), Windhoek; tel. (61) 2058111; fax (61) 2058244; e-mail info@africaonline.com.na; internet www.africaonline.com.na; f. 2000; subsidiary of Africa Online Holdings Ltd (Kenya); Gen. Man. GIDEON NHUNDU.

Telecom Namibia Ltd (Telecom): POB 297, Windhoek; tel. (61) 2019211; fax (61) 248723; internet www.telecom.na; f. 1992; state-owned; Chair. T. HAIMBILI; Man. Dir FRANS NDOROMA.

Mobile Telecommunications Ltd (MTC): cnr Mosé Tjitendero and Hamutenya Wanahepo Ndadi Sts, Olympia, Windhoek; POB 23051, Windhoek; tel. (61) 2802000; fax (61) 2802124; e-mail feedback@mtc.com.na; internet www.mtc.com.na; f. 1995 as jt venture between Namibia Post and Telecommunications Holdings (NPTH), Telia and Swedfund; 34% owned by Portugal Telecom, 64% by NPTH; Chair. STEVE MOTINGA; Man. Dir MIGUEL GERALDES.

BROADCASTING

Radio

In 2004 there were a total of 19 radio stations broadcasting from Windhoek including:

Namibian Broadcasting Corpn (NBC): POB 321, Windhoek; tel. (61) 2913133; fax (61) 215767; e-mail tnandjaa@nbc.com.na; internet www.nbc.com.na; f. 1990; runs 10 radio stations, broadcasting daily to 90% of the population in English (24 hours), Afrikaans, German and eight indigenous languages (10 hours); Chair. PONHELE YA FRANCE; Dir-Gen. VEZERA BOB KANDETU.

Channel 7/Kanaal 7: POB 20500, Windhoek; tel. (61) 235815; fax (61) 240190; e-mail channel7@k7.com.na; internet www.k7.com.na;

Christian community radio station; English and Afrikaans; Man. NEAL VAN DEN BERGH.

Katutura Community Radio: POB 22355, Windhoek; tel. (61) 263768; fax (61) 262786; f. 1995 by non-governmental orgs; Dir FREDERICK GOWASEB.

Kudu FM: 158 Jan Jonker St, POB 5369, Windhoek; tel. (61) 247262; fax (61) 247259; e-mail radiokudu@radiokudu.com.na; internet www.radiokudu.com.na; f. 1998; commercial station affiliated to Omulunga Radio; English, Afrikaans and German.

Omulunga Radio: POB 40789, Windhoek; tel. (61) 239706; fax (61) 247259; e-mail omulunga@omulunga.com.na; internet www.omulunga.com.na; f. 2002; Ovambo interest station affiliated to Kudu FM; Oshiwambo and English.

Radio Antenna Namibia (Pty) Ltd (Namibia FM 99): 6 Teinert St, POB 11849, Windhoek; tel. (61) 223634; fax (61) 230964; e-mail radio99@namfm99.com; f. 1994; Man. Dir GERT JACOBIE.

Radio Energy (Radio 100): 17 Bismarck St, Windhoek West; POB 676, Windhoek; tel. (61) 256380; fax (61) 256379; internet www.energy100fm.com; commercial radio station; Man. Dir MARIO AITA.

Other radio stations included: Kosmos Radio, Radio France International (via relay), Radio 99, and Radio Wave. There were six community radio stations including: Radio Ecclesia (Catholic), Live FM (in Rehoboth), Ohangwenga Community Radio, and UNAM Radio (University of Namibia). A further four community stations were planned in 2005 at Oshakti, Gobabis, Keetmanshoop and Swakopmund.

Television

Namibian Broadcasting Corpn (NBC): POB 321, Windhoek; tel. (61) 2913111; fax (61) 216209; internet www.nbc.com.na; f. 1990; broadcasts television programmes in English to 45% of the population, 18 hours daily; Chair. UAZUVA KAUMBI; Dir-Gen. GERRY MUNYAMA.

Multi-Choice Namibia: POB 1752, Windhoek; tel. (61) 222222; fax (61) 227605; commercial television channels; Gen. Man. KOBUS BEZUIDENHOUT.

Finance

(cap. = capital; res = reserves; dep. = deposits; m. = million; brs = branches; amounts in Namibian dollars)

BANKING

Central Bank

Bank of Namibia: 71 Robert Mugabe Ave, POB 2882, Windhoek; tel. (61) 2835111; fax (61) 2835228; e-mail jerome.mutumba@bon.com.na; internet www.bon.com.na; f. 1990; cap. 40.0m., res 1,149.5m., dep. 5,334.5m. (Dec. 2007); Gov. TOM K. ALWEENDO; Dep. Gov. P. HARTMAN.

Commercial Banks

Bank Windhoek Ltd: Bank Windhoek Bldg, 262 Independence Ave, POB 15, Windhoek; tel. (61) 2991223; fax (61) 223188; e-mail info@bankwindhoek.com.na; internet www.bankwindhoek.com.na; f. 1982; cap. 4.7m., res 531.7m., dep. 6,589.7m. (June 2006); Chair. J. C. 'KOOS' BRANDT; Man. Dir JAMES HILL; 32 brs.

First National Bank of Namibia Ltd: 209–211 Independence Ave, POB 195, Windhoek; tel. (61) 2992111; fax (61) 2220979; e-mail info@fnbnamibia.com.na; internet www.fnbnamibia.com.na; f. 1987 as First Nat. Bank of Southern Africa Ltd; present name adopted 1990; total assets 4,731.9m. (June 2003); Chair. H. DIETER VOIGTS; CEO L. J. HAYNES; 28 brs and 12 agencies.

Namibian Banking Corpn: Carl List Haus, Independence Ave, POB 370, Windhoek; tel. (61) 225946; fax (61) 223741; Chair. J. C. WESTRAAT; Man. Dir P. P. NIEHAUS; 3 brs.

Nedbank Namibia Ltd: 12–20 Dr Frans Indongo St, POB 1, Windhoek; tel. (61) 2959111; fax (61) 2952046; e-mail service@nedbank.com; internet www.nedbanknamibia.com; f. 1973; fmrly Commercial Bank of Namibia Ltd; subsidiary of Nedbank Ltd, South Africa; cap. 16m., res. 75m., dep. 3,747m. (Dec. 2006); Chair. T. J. FRANK; Man. Dir BILL TURTON; 16 brs and 3 agencies.

Standard Bank Namibia Ltd: Standard Bank Centre, cnr Werner List St and Post St Mall, POB 3327, Windhoek; tel. (61) 2949111; fax (61) 2942323; e-mail info@standardbank.com.na; internet www.standardbank.com.na; f. 1915; controlled by Standard Bank Africa; cap. 2m., res. 149.5m., dep. 496.1m. (Dec. 2006); Chair. LEAKE S. HANGALA; Man. Dir T. MBERIRUA; 23 brs.

Agricultural Bank

Agricultural Bank of Namibia (AgriBank): 10 Post St Mall, POB 13208, Windhoek; tel. (61) 2074111; fax (61) 2074289; e-mail agribank@iafrica.com.na; f. 1922; state-owned; total assets 739.1m. (March 2001); Chair. HANS-GUENTHER STIER; Acting CEO S. E. NDJABA.

Development Bank

Development Bank of Namibia (DBN): POB 235, Windhoek; tel. (61) 2908000; fax (61) 2908071; e-mail info@dbn.com.na; internet www.dbn.com.na; f. 2004; Chair. SVEN THIEME; CEO DAVID NUYOMA.

STOCK EXCHANGE

Namibian Stock Exchange (NSX): Kaiser Krone Centre, Shop 8, Post St Mall, POB 2401, Windhoek; tel. (61) 227647; fax (61) 248531; e-mail loiden@nsx.com.na; internet www.nsx.com.na; f. 1992; Chair. Exec. Cttee P. HANGO; Gen. Man. HEIKO NIEDERMEIER.

INSURANCE

Corporate Guarantee and Insurance Co of Namibia Ltd (CGI): Corporate House, Ground Floor, 17 Lüderitz St, POB 416, Windhoek; tel. (61) 259525; fax (61) 255213; e-mail info@corporateguarantee.com; internet www.corporateguarantee.com; f. 1996; wholly owned subsidiary of Nictus Group Ltd since 2001; Chair. J. L. OLIVER; Man. Dir and Principal Officer F. R. VAN STADEN.

Insurance Co of Namibia (INSCON): POB 2877, Windhoek; tel. (61) 275900; fax (61) 233808; f. 1990; short-term insurance; Chair. CHARLES KAURAISA; Man. Dir FERDINAND OTTO.

Legal Shield: 140–142 Robert Mugabe Ave, POB 11363, Windhoek; tel. (61) 2754200; fax (61) 2754090; internet www.legalshield.com.na; f. 2000; legal, funeral and medical insurance; Man. Dir QUINTON VAN ROOYEN.

Metropolitan Namibia: Metropolitan Pl., 1st Floor, cnr Bülow and Stubel Sts, POB 3785, Windhoek; tel. (61) 2973000; fax (61) 248191; internet www.metropolitan.com.na; f. 1996; subsidiary of Metropolitan Group, South Africa; acquired Channel Life in 2004; Chair. M. L. SMITH; Man. Dir LEEBA FOUCHÉ.

Mutual and Federal Insurance Co Ltd: Mutual and Federal Centre, 5th–7th Floors, 227 Independence Ave, POB 151, Windhoek; tel. (61) 2077111; fax (61) 2077205; f. 1990; subsidiary of Mutual and Federal, South Africa; acquired CGU Holdings Ltd in 2000 and FGI Namibia Ltd in 2001; Man. Dir G. KATJIMUNE; Gen. Man. J. W. B. LE ROUX.

Namibia National Reinsurance Corpn Ltd (NamibRE): Capital Centre, 2nd Floor, Levinson Arcade, POB 716, Windhoek; tel. (61) 256905; fax (61) 256904; e-mail administrator@namibre.com; f. 2001; 100% state-owned; Man. Dir ANNA NAKALE-KAWANA.

Old Mutual Life Assurance Co (Namibia) Ltd: Mutual Platz, 5th Floor, Post St Mall, POB 165, Windhoek; tel. (61) 2993999; fax (61) 2993520; e-mail nambusdev@oldmutual.com; internet www.oldmutual.com.na; Chair. G. S. VAN NIEKERK; Chief Exec. BERTIE VAN DER WALT.

Sanlam Namibia: 154 Independence Ave, POB 317, Windhoek; tel. (61) 2947418; fax (61) 2947416; e-mail marketing@sanlam.com.na; internet www.sanlam.com.na; f. 1928; subsidiary of Sanlam Ltd, South Africa; merged with Regent Life Namibia, Capricorn Investments and Nam-Mic Financial Services in Dec. 2004; Chair. ROY ANDERSEN; CEO Dr JOHAN VAN ZYL.

Santam Namibia Ltd: Ausspannplaza Complex, Ausspannplatz, POB 204, Windhoek; tel. (61) 2928000; fax (61) 235225; 60% owned by Santam, South Africa; 33.3% owned by Bank Windhoek Holdings Ltd; acquired Allianz Insurance of Namibia Ltd in 2001; Chief Exec. NAMA SIMON GOABAB.

Swabou Insurance Co Ltd: Swabou Bldg, Post St Mall, POB 79, Windhoek; tel. (61) 2997528; fax (61) 2997551; internet www.swabouinsurance.com.na; f. 1990; acquired by FNB Namibia Holdings Ltd in 2004; short-term insurance; Man. Dir RENIER TALJAARD.

Swabou Life Assurance Co Ltd: 209–211 Independence Ave, POB 79, Windhoek; tel. (61) 2997502; fax (61) 2997550; e-mail tgurirab@fnbnamibia.com.na; internet www.swaboulife.com.na; f. 1990; acquired by FNB Namibia Holdings Ltd in 2004; life assurance; CEO GERHARD MANS.

Trade and Industry

GOVERNMENT AGENCIES

Karakul Board of Namibia—Swakara Fur Producers and Exporters: Private Bag 13300, Windhoek; tel. (61) 235168; fax (61) 2909300; e-mail swakara@agra.com.na; internet www.swakara.net; Chair. H. J. VAN WYK; Man. W. H. VISSER.

Meat Board of Namibia: POB 38, Windhoek; tel. (61) 275830; fax (61) 228310; f. 1935; Chair. JOHN LE ROUX; Gen. Man. PAUL STRYDOM.

NAMIBIA

Meat Corpn of Namibia (Meatco Namibia): POB 3881, Windhoek; tel. (61) 3216400; fax (61) 3216401; e-mail hoffice@meatco.com.na; internet www.meatco.com.na; f. 1986; processors of meat and meat products at four abattoirs and one tannery; CEO KOBUS DU PLESSIS.

Namibian Agronomic Board: 30 Hochland Rd, POB 5096, Ausspannplatz, Windhoek; tel. (61) 379500; fax (61) 225371; internet www.nab.com.na; e-mail nabdesk@nammic.com.na; f. 1985; CEO CHRISTOF BROCK.

National Petroleum Corpn of Namibia (NAMCOR): Petroleum House, 1 Aviation Rd, Private Bag 13196, Windhoek; tel. (61) 2045000; fax (61) 221785; internet www.namcor.com.na; f. 1965 as Southern Oil Exploration Corpn (South-West Africa) (Pty) Ltd—SWAKOR; present name adopted 1990; state petroleum co; responsible for importing 50% of national oil requirements; Chair. F. KISTING; Man. Dir SAM BEUKES (acting).

DEVELOPMENT ORGANIZATIONS

Namibia Investment Centre (NIC): Ministry of Trade and Industry, Brendan Simbwaye Sq., Block B, 6th Floor, Goethe St, Private Bag 13340, Windhoek; tel. (61) 2837335; fax (61) 220278; e-mail nic@mti.gov.na; f. 1990; promotes foreign and domestic investment; Exec. Dir BERNADETTE ARTIVOR.

Namibia Non-Governmental Organisation Forum (NANGOF): 18 Axalie Doeseb St, POB 70433, Khomasdal, Windhoek; tel. (61) 239469; fax (61) 239471; e-mail nangof@iafrica.com.na; f. 1991; umbrella body representing 95 community-based orgs; Chair. SANDY TJARONDA.

National Housing Enterprise: 7 Omuramba Rd, Eros, POB 20192, Windhoek; tel. (61) 2927111; fax (61) 2927271; internet www.nhe.com.na; f. 1983; replaced Nat. Building and Investment Corpn; provides low-cost housing; manages Housing Trust Fund; 100% state-owned; total assets N $496.4m. (Dec. 2001); Chair. V. R. RUKORO; CEO VINCENT HAILULU.

CHAMBERS OF COMMERCE

Chamber of Mines of Namibia (CoM): Channel Life Tower, 4th Floor, Post St Mall, POB 2895, Windhoek; tel. (61) 237925; fax (61) 222638; e-mail dmeyer@chamberofmines.org.na; internet www.chamberofmines.org.na; f. 1979; Pres. OTTO SHIKONGO; Gen. Man. VESTON MALANGO; 60 mems (2009).

Namibia Chamber of Commerce and Industry (NCCI): 2 Jenner St, cnr Simpson and Jenner Sts, POB 9355, Windhoek; tel. (61) 228809; fax (61) 228009; e-mail ncciinfo@ncci.org.na; internet www.ncci.org.na; f. 1990; Chair. JOHN ENDJALA; CEO TARAH SHAANIKA; c. 3,000 mems (2008).

Windhoek Chamber of Commerce and Industries: SWA Building Society Bldg, 3rd Floor, POB 191, Windhoek; tel. (61) 222000; fax (61) 233690; f. 1920; Pres. H. SCHMIDT; Gen. Man. T. D. PARKHOUSE; 230 mems.

EMPLOYERS' ORGANIZATIONS

Construction Industries Federation of Namibia: cnr Stein and Schwabe Sts, POB 1479, Klein Windhoek; tel. (61) 230028; fax (61) 224534; e-mail info@cif.namibia.na; internet www.cifnamibia.com; Pres. RENATE SCHMIDT; Sec. RICKI WILSON; 60 contracting mems, 12 trade mems, 5 affiliated mems.

Namibia Agricultural Union (NAU): PMB 13255, Windhoek; tel. (61) 237838; fax (61) 220193; e-mail nau@agrinamibia.com.na; internet www.agrinamibia.com.na; f. 1947; represents commercial farmers; Pres. RAIMAR VON HASE; Exec. Man. SAKKIE COETZEE.

Namibia National Farmers' Union (NNFU): 4 Axalie Doeseb St, Windhoek West; POB 3117, Windhoek; tel. (61) 271117; fax (61) 271115; e-mail info@nnfu.org.na; internet www.nnfu.org.na; represents communal farmers; Pres. PINTILE DAVIDS.

Namibia Professional Hunting Association (NAPHA): 318 Sam Nujoma Dr., Klein Windhoek; POB 11291, Windhoek; tel. (61) 234455; fax (61) 222567; e-mail napha@mweb.com.na; internet www.napha.com.na; f. 1974; represents hunting guides and professional hunters; Pres. DIETHELM METZGER; c. 460 mems.

Retail Motor Industry of Namibia (RMI Namibia): POB 2110, Windhoek; tel. (61) 240280; fax (61) 240276; fmrly Motor Industries Federation of Namibia; present name adopted 2002; affiliated to RMI South Africa; Chair. HAROLD PUPKEWITZ; Pres. NEELS SWIEGERS; 40 mems (2003).

UTILITIES

ELECTRICITY

Electricity Control Board: 8 Bismarck St, ECB House, POB 2923, Windhoek; tel. (61) 374300; fax (61) 374304; e-mail info@ecb.org.na; internet www.ecb.org.na; f. 2000; CEO SISEHO C. SIMASIKU.

Namibia Power Corpn (Pty) Ltd (NamPower): NamPower Centre, 15 Luther St, POB 2864, Windhoek; tel. (61) 2054111; fax (61) 232805; e-mail paulinus.shilamba@nampower.com.na; internet www.nampower.com.na; f. 1964; state-owned; Chair. ANDRIES LEEVI HUNGAMO; Man. Dir PAULINUS SHILAMBA.

Northern Electricity: POB 891, Tsumeb; tel. (67) 222243; fax (67) 222245; private electricity supply co; first regional electricity distributor in Namibia, operating in the north of the country; Man. Dir C. G. N. HUYSEN.

WATER

Namibia Water Corporation Ltd (NamWater): 176 Iscor St, Northern Industrial Area, POB 13389, Windhoek; tel. (61) 710000; fax (61) 713000; e-mail shigwedhaj@namwater.com.na; internet www.namwater.com.na; f. 1997; state-owned; CEO Dr VAINO SHIVUTE.

TRADE UNIONS

In 2004 there were 27 unions representing more than 100,000 workers.

Trade Union Federations

National Union of Namibian Workers (NUNW): Mungunda St, Katutura; POB 50034, Windhoek; tel. (61) 215037; fax (61) 215589; f. 1972; affiliated to the SWAPO party; Pres. RISTO KAPENDA; Sec.-Gen. EVILASTUS KAARONDA; c. 70,000 mems.

The NUNW has 10 affiliates, which include:

Metal and Allied Namibian Workers' Union (MANWU): Mingunda St, POB 22771, Windhoek 9000; tel. (61) 263100; fax (61) 264300; e-mail manwu@mweb.com.na; f. 1987; affiliated to the Building and Wood Workers Int. and Int. Metalworkers' Fed.; Pres. J. NAOBEB; Gen. Sec. MOSES SHIIKWA (acting); 5,500 mems.

Mineworkers' Union of Namibia (MUN): POB 1566, Windhoek; tel. (61) 261723; fax (61) 217684; f. 1986; Pres. ANDRIES EISEB; 12,500 mems.

Namibia Farm Workers' Union (NAFWU): NUNW Centre, Mungunda Street, Katutura, POB 21007, Windhoek; tel. (61) 218653; fax (61) 263714; e-mail nafwu@iafrica.com.na; internet www.nunw.org.na/nafwu.htm; f. 1994; Pres. ASSER HENDRICKS; Sec.-Gen. ALFRED ANGULA.

Namibia Financial Institutions Union (NAFINU): POB 61791, Windhoek; tel. (61) 239917; fax (61) 215589; f. 2000; Pres. ALEX KAMAUNDJU; Gen. Sec. ASNATH ZAMUEE.

Namibia Food and Allied Workers' Union (NAFAU): Mungunda St, Katutura; POB 1553, Windhoek; tel. (61) 218213; fax (61) 263714; e-mail nafau@mweb.com.na; f. 1986; affiliated to the Int. Textile, Garment and Leather Workers' Fed. and Int. Union of Food, Agricultural, Hotel, Restaurant, Catering, Tobacco and Allied Workers' Asscns; Pres. DAVID NAMALENGA; Gen. Sec. KIROS SACARIAS; 12,000 mems.

Namibia National Teachers' Union (NANTU): POB 61009, Windhoek; tel. (61) 262247; fax (61) 261926; e-mail nantu@nantu.org.na; internet www.nantu.org.na; f. 1989; affiliated to Education Int.; Pres. SIMEON KAVILA; Gen. Sec. BASILIUS HAINGURA; 13,000 mems (2002).

Namibia Public Workers' Union (NAPWU): POB 50035, Bachbrecht, Windhoek; tel. (61) 261961; fax (61) 263100; e-mail napwu@namibnet.com; f. 1987; affiliated to the Public Services Int.; Pres. ELIPHAS NDINGARA; Sec.-Gen. PETRUS NEVONGA; 11,000 mems.

Namibia Transport and Allied Workers' Union (NATAU): POB 7516, Katutura, Windhoek; tel. (61) 218514; fax (61) 263767; f. 1988; affiliated to the Int. Transport Workers' Fed.; Pres. DAWID TJOMBE; Gen. Sec. JOHN KWEDHI; 7,500 mems.

Trade Union Congress of Namibia (TUCNA): POB 2111, Windhoek; tel. (61) 246143; fax (61) 212828; f. 2002 following the merger of the Namibia People's Social Movement (f. 1992 as the Namibia Christian Social Trade Unions) and the Namibia Fed. of Trade Unions (f. 1998); Pres. PAULUS HANGO; c. 45,000 mems (2005).

TUCNA has 14 affiliates including:

Local Authorities Union of Namibia (LAUN): Frans Indongo St, Windhoek; POB 22060, Windhoek; tel. (61) 234625; fax (61) 230035; Pres. FRANCOIS ADONIS.

Namibia Building Workers' Union (NABWU): 3930 Verbena St, Khomasdal; POB 22679, Windhoek; tel. (61) 212828.

Namibia Seamen and Allied Workers' Union (NASAWU): Nataniel Maxuilli St, Walvis Bay; POB 1341, Walvis Bay; tel. (64) 204237; fax (64) 205957; Pres. PAULUS HANGO.

Namibia Wholesale and Retail Workers' Union (NWRWU): 19 Verbena St, Khomasdal; POB 22769, Windhoek; tel. (61) 212378; fax (61) 212828; Sec.-Gen. JOSHUA MABUKU.

Public Service Union of Namibia (PSUN): 45–51 Kroon Rd, Khomasdal, Windhoek; POB 21662, Windhoek; tel. (61) 213083; fax (61) 213047; e-mail psun@iway.na; internet www.psun.com.na; f. 1991; successor to the Govt Service Staff Asscn; Pres. JOHANES HOESEB; Sec.-Gen. VICTOR KAZONJATI.

Teachers' Union of Namibia (TUN): PSUN Bldg, Dollar St 4551, Khomasdal, POB 30800, Windhoek; tel. (61) 229115; fax (61) 246360; e-mail tun@mweb.com.na; Pres. CHANVILLE GREGORY MACKRILL.

Transport

RAILWAYS

The main line runs from Nakop, at the border with South Africa, via Keetmanshoop to Windhoek, Kranzberg, Tsumeb, Swakopmund and Walvis Bay. There are three branch lines, from Windhoek to Gobabis, Otavi to Grootfontein and Keetmanshoop to Lüderitz. The total rail network covers 2,382 route-km. There are plans for a railway line connecting Namibia with Zambia, as part of a programme to improve transport links among the members of the Common Market for Eastern and Southern Africa; plans to extend the northern railway line by 248 km, from Tsumeb to Ondangwa, were announced in 2001. In 2006 the Namibian and Botswana Governments commenced discussions regarding a proposed railway linking the two countries.

TransNamib Holdings Ltd: TransNamib Bldg, cnr Independence Ave and Bahnhof St, PMB 13204, Windhoek; tel. (61) 2982437; fax (61) 2982386; e-mail pubrelation@transnamib.com.na; internet www.transnamib.com.na; f. 1998; state-owned; Chair. FOIBE JACOBS; CEO TITUS HAIMBILI.

ROADS

Between 2000 and 2002 the total road network decreased from 66,467 km to 42,237 km of roads, of which 12.8% was paved in 2002. A major road link from Walvis Bay to Jwaneng, northern Botswana, the Trans-Kalahari Highway, was completed in 1998, along with the Trans-Caprivi Highway, linking Namibia with northern Botswana, Zambia and Zimbabwe. The Government is also upgrading and expanding the road network in northern Namibia. In 2001 total spending on the road network was equivalent to US $17.7m.

SHIPPING

The ports of Walvis Bay and Lüderitz are linked to the main overseas shipping routes and handle almost one-half of Namibia's external trade. Walvis Bay has a container terminal, built in 1999, and eight berths; it is a hub port for the region, serving landlocked countries such as Botswana, Zambia and Zimbabwe. In 2005 NAMPORT added a N $30m. floating dock to the Walvis Bay facilities with a view to servicing vessels used in the region's expanding petroleum industry. Traditionally a fishing port, a new quay was completed at Lüderitz in 2000, with two berths, in response to growing demand from the offshore diamond industry. At the end of 2007 Namibia's merchant fleet comprised 173 vessels, with a combined displacement of 126,062 gross registered tons.

African Portland Industrial Holdings (APIH): Huvest Bldg, 1st Floor, AE/Gams Centre, Sam Nujoma Dr., POB 40047, Windhoek; tel. (61) 248744; fax (61) 239485; e-mail jacques@apiholdings.com; f. 1994; 80% owned by Grindrod (South Africa); bulk port terminal operator; Man. Dir ATHOL EMERTON; Sec. JACQUES CONRADIE.

Namibian Ports Authority (NAMPORT): 17 Rikumbi Kandanga Rd, POB 361, Walvis Bay; tel. (64) 2082207; fax (64) 2082320; e-mail jerome@namport.com.na; internet www.namport.com; f. 1994; Chair. SHAKESPEARE MASIZA; Man. Dir (vacant).

Pan-Ocean Shipping Services Ltd: POB 2613, Walvis Bay; tel. (64) 203959; fax (64) 204199; f. 1995; Man. Dir JÜRGEN HEYNEMANN; Gen. Man. GEORGE KIROV.

CIVIL AVIATION

There are international airports at Windhoek (Hosea Kutako) and Walvis Bay (Rooikop), as well as a number of other airports throughout Namibia, and numerous landing strips.

Air Namibia: TransNamib Bldg, cnr Independence Ave and Bahnhof St, POB 731, Windhoek; tel. (61) 2996000; fax (61) 2996101; e-mail aarickerts@airnamibia.com.na; internet www.airnamibia.com.na; f. 1946 as South West Air Transport; present name adopted in 1991; state-owned; part-privatization postponed indefinitely in 2003; services to Angola, Botswana, South Africa, Zimbabwe, Germany and the United Kingdom; Chair. H. PIUS ASHEEKE; Man. Dir KOSMOS EGUMBO.

Kalahari Express Airlines (KEA): POB 40179, Windhoek; tel. (61) 245665; fax (61) 245612; f. 1995; domestic and regional flights; Exec. Dir PEINGONDJABI SHIPOH.

Namibia Airports Company Limited: GIPF House, cnr Uhland and Goethe Sts, POB 23061, Windhoek; tel. (61) 2955000; fax (61) 2955022; e-mail pr@airports.com.na; internet www.airports.com.na; f. 1998; Chair. E. HAIHAMBO; CEO VEMUNJENGUA KAVARI.

Tourism

Namibia's principal tourist attractions are its game parks and nature reserves, and the development of 'eco-tourism' is being promoted. Tourist arrivals in Namibia in 2006 totalled 833,345. In that year tourism receipts amounted to US $473m.

Namibia Tourism Board: 1st Floor, Channel Life Towers, 39 Post Street Mall, Private Bag 13244, Windhoek; tel. (61) 2906000; fax (61) 254848; e-mail info@namibiatourism.com.na; internet www.namibiatourism.com.na; Chair. ERICKA AKUENJE; CEO DIGU NAOBEB.

NAURU

Introductory Survey

Location, Climate, Language, Religion, Flag, Capital

The Republic of Nauru is a small island in the central Pacific Ocean, lying about 40 km (25 miles) south of the Equator and about 4,000 km (2,500 miles) north-east of Sydney, Australia. Its nearest neighbour is Banaba (Ocean Island), in Kiribati, about 300 km (186 miles) to the east. The climate is tropical, with a westerly monsoon season from November to February. The average annual rainfall is about 2,060 mm (80 ins), but actual rainfall is extremely variable. Day temperatures vary between 24°C and 34°C (75°–93°F). Of the total resident population in 2002, 77% were Nauruans. Their language is Nauruan, but English is also widely understood. The majority of Nauruans are Christians, mostly adherents of the Nauruan Protestant Church. The national flag (proportions 1 by 2) is royal blue, divided by a narrow horizontal yellow stripe, with a 12-pointed white star at the lower hoist. The island state has no official capital, but the seat of the legislature and most government offices are in Yaren district.

Recent History

Nauru, inhabited by a predominantly Polynesian people, organized in 12 clans, was annexed by Germany in 1888. In 1914, shortly after the outbreak of the First World War, the island was captured by Australian forces. It continued to be administered by Australia under a League of Nations mandate (granted in 1920), which also named the United Kingdom and New Zealand as cotrustees. Between 1942 and 1945 Nauru was occupied by the Japanese, who deported 1,200 islanders to Truk (now Chuuk), Micronesia, where many died in bombing raids or from starvation. In 1947 the island was placed under UN Trusteeship, with Australia as the administering power on behalf of the Governments of Australia, New Zealand and the United Kingdom. The UN Trusteeship Council proposed in 1964 that the indigenous people of Nauru be resettled on Curtis Island, off the Queensland coast. This offer was made in anticipation of the progressive exhaustion of the island's phosphate deposits, and because of the environmental devastation resulting from the mining operations. However, the Nauruans elected to remain on the island. Between 1906 and 1968 41m. metric tons of phosphate were mined. Nauru was accorded a considerable measure of self-government in January 1966, with the establishment of Legislative and Executive Councils, and proceeded to independence on 31 January 1968 (exactly 22 years after the surviving Nauruans returned to the island from exile in Micronesia). In early 1998 Nauru announced its intention to seek UN membership and full Commonwealth membership (Nauru had hitherto been a 'special member' of the Commonwealth, not represented at meetings of Heads of Government). The decision was largely based on the islanders' desire to play a more prominent role in international policies relating to issues that affect them, most notably climate change (see below). Nauru became a full member of the Commonwealth in May 1999, and a member of the UN in September of that year.

The Head Chief of Nauru, Hammer DeRoburt, was elected President in May 1968 and re-elected in 1971 and 1973. Dissatisfaction with his increasingly personal rule led to the election of Bernard Dowiyogo (leader of the recently established, informal Nauru Party) to the presidency in 1976. Dowiyogo was re-elected President after a general election in late 1977. However, DeRoburt's supporters adopted tactics of obstruction in Parliament, and in December 1977 Dowiyogo resigned, in response to Parliament's refusal to approve budgetary legislation; he was re-elected shortly afterwards, but was again forced to resign in April 1978, following the defeat of a legislative proposal concerning phosphate royalties. Lagumot Harris, another member of the Nauru Party, succeeded him, but resigned three weeks later when Parliament rejected a finance measure, and DeRoburt was again elected President. He was re-elected in December of that year, in December 1980 and in May and December 1983.

In September 1986 DeRoburt resigned, following the defeat of a government budget proposal; he was replaced as President by Kennan Adeang, who was elected in Parliament by nine votes to DeRoburt's eight. However, after holding office for only 14 days, Adeang was defeated in a parliamentary vote of no confidence, and DeRoburt subsequently resumed the presidency. Following a general election in December, Adeang was again narrowly elected President, but he was subsequently ousted by another vote of no confidence; DeRoburt was reinstated as President. The atmosphere of political uncertainty generated by the absence of a clear majority in Parliament led DeRoburt to dissolve Parliament in preparation for another general election in January 1987, following which which the incumbent was re-elected to the presidency by 11 votes to six. In February Adeang announced the establishment of the Democratic Party of Nauru, essentially a revival of the Nauru Party. Eight members of Parliament subsequently joined the new party, which declared that its aim was to curtail the extension of presidential powers and to promote democracy. In August 1989 a parliamentary motion of no confidence in DeRoburt (proposed by Adeang) was approved by 10 votes to five, and Kenas Aroi, a former Minister for Finance, was subsequently elected President. Aroi resigned in December, owing to ill health, and after a general election in the same month Bernard Dowiyogo was re-elected President, defeating DeRoburt by 10 votes to six. The next presidential election, held shortly after a general election in November 1992, resulted in victory for Dowiyogo, by 10 parliamentary votes to seven, over Buraro Detudamo.

At a general election held in November 1995, when a total of 67 candidates contested the 18 parliamentary seats, all cabinet members were re-elected. A subsequent presidential election resulted in Lagumot Harris's defeat of the incumbent Dowiyogo by nine votes to eight. The resignation of the Chairman of Air Nauru, following allegations of misconduct, prompted Parliament to vote on a motion of no confidence in the Government in November 1996. The motion was narrowly approved and Harris was replaced by Dowiyogo as President. Later that month, however, Dowiyogo's new Government was itself defeated in a parliamentary vote of no confidence, and Kennan Adeang was elected to the presidency. A widespread perception that the new Government lacked experience was thought to be a major factor prompting a further motion of 'no confidence' in December, at which Adeang was similarly removed from office. At a subsequent presidential contest Reuben Kun, a former Minister for Finance, defeated Adeang by 12 votes to five, on the understanding that his administration would organize a general election. An election duly took place in February 1997, at which four new members were elected to Parliament, following an apparent agreement between the supporters of Harris and those of Dowiyogo to end the political manoeuvring that had resulted in several months of instability in Nauru. At the subsequent election to the presidency Kinza Clodumar (nominated by Dowiyogo) defeated Harris by nine parliamentary votes to eight.

In early 1998 five members of Parliament (including former President Lagumot Harris) were dismissed by Adeang, the Speaker, for refusing to apologize for personal remarks about him that had been published in an opposition newsletter. At the resultant by-elections, held in late February 1998, three of the five members were re-elected. A motion expressing no confidence in the President was approved in June, and Dowiyogo was consequently elected to replace Clodumar. In a further vote of no confidence, in late April 1999 Dowiyogo was defeated by 10 votes to seven; his replacement was Rene Harris, previously Chairman of the Nauru Phosphate Corporation. Former President Lagumot Harris died in September 1999.

Following the legislative election held on 8 April 2000, Rene Harris was re-elected President, narrowly defeating Dowiyogo by nine parliamentary votes to eight. Ludwig Scotty was elected Speaker of Parliament. However, Scotty and his deputy, Ross Cairn, subsequently resigned, stating only that they were unable to continue under the 'current political circumstances'. Harris therefore tendered his resignation and was replaced by Dowiyogo, whereupon Scotty and Cairn were re-elected to their posts in the legislature. Observers attributed the manoeuvring to shifting political allegiances within the legislature.

In early 2001, in another reversal to Dowiyogo's leadership, Anthony Audoa, the Minister for Home Affairs, Culture, Health and Women's Affairs, resigned and requested that Parliament be recalled. He claimed that Dowiyogo had squandered Nauru's wealth during his various tenures as President and that in promoting the island as a tax haven he had allowed Nauru to be used by Russian criminal gangs to 'launder' their illegal funds, prompting speculation that he intended to mount a challenge for the presidency.

In late March 2001 Dowiyogo was ousted from the presidency in a parliamentary vote of no confidence while he was undergoing hospital treatment in Australia. The motion, which was adopted by two votes, led to Rene Harris regaining the presidency. In October, however, Harris was flown to Australia for emergency medical treatment for a diabetes-related illness, during which time Remy Namaduk performed the role of acting President. Allegations that Nauru's 'offshore' financial centre was being used extensively by Russian criminal organizations for 'laundering' the proceeds of their illegal activities had led Dowiyogo to order a full review of the industry in March 1999. In early 2000 President Rene Harris announced that Nauru was to suspend its 'offshore' banking services and improve the accountability of existing banks on the island, as part of the Government's efforts to bring Nauru's financial services regulations into conformity with international standards. Dowiyogo similarly reaffirmed his commitment to reform the 'offshore' sector, following his election in April 2000. However, in February 2001 11 members of Nauru's 18-member legislature signed a petition requesting that Dowiyogo attend a special session of Parliament to answer questions relating to the island's alleged role in 'laundering' significant funds from Russian criminal organizations. The allegations originated in claims by Russia's central bank that some US $70,000m. of illegal funds had been processed in 'offshore' banks in Nauru. It was estimated that 400 such banks existed on the island in early 2001. The Government subsequently drew up an Anti-Money Laundering Act in August 2001, but the Paris-based Financial Action Task Force (FATF, see p. 430) found that the new laws contained several deficiencies and imposed sanctions in December. (The FATF had been established in 1989 on the recommendation of the Group of Seven (G-7) industrialized nations.) The Government announced revised anti-money-laundering legislation in the same month, and was considering legal action against the FATF in early 2002. Meanwhile, following Islamist attacks on New York and Washington, DC, on 11 September 2001, Nauru's financial system was subject to international scrutiny, amid suspicion that it might have been used as a conduit for the terrorists' funds.

As a result of continued US pressure, Nauru's Parliament approved a new law in February 2004 to address the problem of 'money-laundering', along with legislation to close down the country's 'offshore' banks. In October 2004 the FATF withdrew counter-measures against the country, and in October 2005, following the implementation of the requisite legislation, Nauru became the last of the Pacific islands to be removed from the FATF list of non-co-operative countries and territories. Nauru's removal from the list coincided with the final preparations for the presentation of the National Sustainable Development Strategy, announced at the international donor meeting held in Nauru at the end of November (see below). In December 2003 following the island's commitment to improve transparency and to exchange information on tax matters with other countries, Nauru had been removed from a list of unco-operative tax havens, issued in April 2002 by the Organisation for Economic Co-operation and Development (OECD, see p. 358).

In January 2003 meanwhile, President Rene Harris was defeated in a motion of no confidence by eight votes to three and was replaced by Bernard Dowiyogo. The vote followed a political crisis resulting from the defeat of the Government's budget proposals at the end of December 2002, as well as reports of increasing dissatisfaction with Harris's alleged economic mismanagement of the country. Nauru's deteriorating financial situation, in addition to the Government's decision to accept more than 1,000 asylum-seekers in return for aid from Australia, were believed to be major factors in the loss of confidence in Harris, which had led to the defection to the opposition of two cabinet ministers, two backbenchers and the Speaker in late 2002. However, Harris applied to the Supreme Court, and on 10 January 2003 an injunction was issued against Dowiyogo accepting the presidency. This decision had been based on the fact that only 11 of the 18 members of Parliament had attended the session when the vote took place, thus rendering it invalid; Harris and his Cabinet had staged a boycott of Parliament when the motion was to be proposed. Despite the injunction, Dowiyogo maintained his position and appointed a new Cabinet. Several days of confusion and political instability ensued. Finally, Harris was reinstated as President, after the intervention of Nauru's Melbourne-based Chief Justice, but he resigned from the presidency on the following day. In the resultant contest Dowiyogo defeated Kinza Clodumar by nine votes to eight to become the new President on 20 January. However, a lack of support for Dowiyogo within Parliament continued to create problems, amid appeals for an early election to resolve the impasse.

Meanwhile, a complete collapse of Nauru's telecommunications system in early January 2003 increased the problems experienced by the island. Nauru thus effectively became cut off from the rest of the world, with external contact possible only when ships equipped with satellite telephones were calling. A speech by Dowiyogo claiming that Nauru was on the verge of bankruptcy, unable to pay its public servants or to send its sick citizens to Australia for treatment, and appealing to donor countries for emergency assistance, could not be transmitted for almost a month. Telecommunications services were restored in early March following a visit from a technician supplied by Australia's government aid agency, AusAID.

In early March 2003 Dowiyogo travelled to Washington, DC, at the request of the US Government, which had threatened to impose harsh economic sanctions on the island and to repossess Air Nauru's only aircraft, if Nauru did not discontinue its 'offshore' banking services. The administration of George W. Bush was reported to have been angered by the possibility that individuals with links to terrorist organizations might have used the island's financial services to 'launder' their funds; some 400 'offshore' banks were registered on the island in the early 2000s. Consequently, Dowiyogo agreed to sign executive orders not to renew any banking licences or to issue any further so-called 'investor passports'. However, shortly after the meeting, Dowiyogo collapsed and, following emergency heart surgery, died on 9 March. Derog Gioura was appointed acting Head of State and on 20 March was elected President by nine parliamentary votes to seven. Legislation providing for the expiry of most 'offshore' banking licences within 30 days (and for the remainder within six months) was approved by Parliament in late March, in accordance with the agreement that Dowiyogo had signed in the USA. At the end of March acting President Derog Gioura himself suffered a heart attack and was flown to Australia for treatment.

A general election took place on 3 May 2003, at which six new members were elected to the legislature. However, the new Speaker resigned one day after his election, and with no further nominations for the position, Parliament was unable to proceed to a presidential election. The impasse was resolved when a Speaker was finally elected in late May and Ludwig Scotty won the subsequent presidential election, defeating Kinza Clodumar with 10 parliamentary votes to seven. Scotty, who named a new six-member Cabinet in June, stated his Government's intention to focus on 'prudent management and financial stability'. However, on 8 August Scotty was ousted from office by a no confidence motion and replaced by Rene Harris, who became the fourth President of 2003. The reasons for Scotty's removal were not clear, although concerns had been expressed about his plans to close the recently opened embassies in Washington, DC, and Beijing, and there had been speculation that he intended to switch Nauru's diplomatic allegiance from the People's Republic of China back to Taiwan (see below).

In August 2003 workers at the Nauru Phosphate Corporation began a strike in support of demands for almost six months of unpaid salaries. Opposition politicians claimed that the dispute was an indication of more widespread dissatisfaction with corruption and mismanagement in the industry and within the Government.

In January 2004 President Rene Harris was flown to Australia amid rumours that he had suffered a physical collapse and was in a poor state of health. Officials declined to respond to queries surrounding the President, merely stating that Derog Gioura would be acting President in his absence. In the following month the Minister for Justice resigned, precipitating a vote of no confidence in the President. A further political crisis arose when the motion received an equal number of votes in favour and against. Moreover, when Parliament was unable to agree on the election of a new Speaker, following the resignation of the incumbent in early April, the resulting impasse meant that Parliament could not be formally convened. As the country's financial crisis deepened, President Harris travelled to Australia in mid-April to request assistance in averting imminent bankruptcy for the island. On his return to Nauru Harris confronted angry demonstrations by hundreds of government employees protesting at the hardship imposed on them as a result of their salaries having been unpaid for 12 months. Reports indicated that government employees (who constituted the majority of paid employees on the island) were surviving on subsistence diets of fish and coconuts. In the same month receivers were appointed to manage the assets of the Nauru Phosphate Royalties Trust (including Nauru's extensive property portfolio in Australia) which was unable to pay off debts of some $A230m. to US interests. Nauruans working in government-owned buildings in Melbourne and Sydney were served with eviction notices. Meanwhile, with neither the Government nor the opposition willing to nominate a Speaker from among its members (thereby giving the other side a majority in Parliament), the legislature was unable to produce a budget. In May, however, during another of Harris's overseas trips, the opposition elected one of its members as Speaker and immediately approved legislation making it illegal for a government to operate without a budget. In the following month, and before the Supreme Court had ruled on the matter, Kinza Clodumar, the Minister of Finance, crossed the floor, thereby allowing the opposition to approve a motion of no confidence in Harris. Ludwig Scotty was subsequently elected to the presidency. In late July Australian Treasury official Peter Depta arrived in Nauru to take up the post of Financial Secretary, effectively assuming control of the country's finances.

Nauru's precarious political situation deteriorated during September 2004, and by the end of the month President Ludwig Scotty had dissolved Parliament and declared a state of emergency. His action had been prompted by the Speaker Russell Kun's suspension of the Minister of Health, Kieren Keke, on the grounds that he held dual Nauruan and Australian nationality. Keke's suspension had resulted in the loss of the Government's one-seat majority and a consequent stalemate in Parliament, during which budget legislation had been unable to be approved. Scotty assumed sole responsibility over the government of the country until a general election took place on 23 October. At the election all nine members of Scotty's Government retained their seats in the legislature, while seven of the nine opposition members of parliament were not re-elected. The result thus gave President Scotty an ample majority in Parliament. Within days of its election the new Government approved a budget that included a reduction in public-sector salaries and increased import duties. In the following month legislation aimed at discouraging criminals, particularly terrorists, from using the country's financial sector was approved, in addition to the establishment of a procedure for conducting possible future referendums and of reviewing the Constitution. The sudden death of the Speaker, Vassal Gadoengin, from a heart attack in December 2004 led to the election of Valdon Dowiyogo, a new member of Parliament and son of the former President, to the position in the following month.

In January 2005 a committee of members of Parliament began a review of Nauru's Constitution, motivated partly by a desire to achieve greater political stability in the country. In 2006 the committee formed the Independent Commission on Constitutional Review, and in mid-2007 a Constitutional Convention, comprising 18 directly elected members and 18 appointees, met to discuss the Commission's conclusions.

At the legislative election held on 25 August 2007 several members and supporters of the Scotty Government were re-elected to Parliament. Later in that month Scotty was re-elected as the island's President, defeating Marcus Stephen by a considerable margin of parliamentary votes. Scotty's new Cabinet retained all the ministers of the previous Government. In December, however, Scotty was removed from office in a vote of no confidence, amid allegations of corruption against the Minister of Foreign Affairs and of Finance, David Adeang, and the withdrawal of support of several members of the Government. Marcus Stephen was subsequently elected to replace Scotty, appointing a Cabinet that included Kieren Keke (who had served as a minister under Scotty) as Minister of Foreign Affairs, Trade, Telecommunications and Transport.

The new Government's progress was hampered by increasing discord and its lack of a majority in the legislature, and in April 2008 Speaker David Adeang, a member of the opposition, announced the suspension of all nine government members of Parliament. Stephen subsequently declared a state of emergency and dissolved Parliament, setting in motion the procedure for the holding of an early election. At the election, held on 26 April, the incumbent Government was able to increase its representation in Parliament to 12 of the 18 legislators, at the expense of three members of the opposition who lost their seats. Riddell Akua was elected Speaker. On 29 April Parliament re-elected Stephen as the country's President and confirmed the membership of the Cabinet, which remained largely unchanged. Former President Rene Harris lost his seat at the parliamentary election and died in July.

In September 2001 Nauru agreed to accept 310 of 460 predominantly Afghan asylum-seekers who were on board a Norwegian freighter, the *MV Tampa*, unable to disembark on Christmas Island as Australia refused to grant them entry into its territory (see the chapter on Christmas Island). The Australian Government agreed to fund the processing of the asylum-seekers and to pay an undisclosed sum to Nauru, which was to accommodate the asylum-seekers for three months while their claims for asylum were assessed. Following the interception of several other boats carrying asylum-seekers in Australian waters later the same month, Nauru received a pledge of $A20m. from the Australian Government for agreeing to host 800 asylum-seekers. In December 2001 Nauru signed an agreement with Australia's Minister for Foreign Affairs to accommodate a total of 1,200 at any one time, in return for a further $A10m. of aid, to be allocated to education, health and infrastructure programmes. Local residents and owners of the land upon which the camps were located expressed concern over the delays in processing the asylum-seekers' claims, which were due to be completed by July 2002. In May Australia offered monetary assistance to Afghan asylum-seekers as an incentive to return to their homeland, and in the following month the President announced that he anticipated that all the asylum-seekers would have left Nauru by the end of the year. However, in December some 700 people remained in the camps, despite the deportation of more than 100 Afghan asylum-seekers to Kabul. In the same month the President signed a new agreement with Australia's Minister for Foreign Affairs to extend the duration of the camps' operations and to accommodate up to 1,500 asylum-seekers.

In mid-2003 the Australian Government was accused of cruelty for detaining some 100 children in the camps on Nauru and for failing to reunite families held in separate camps for extended periods. The Nauruan Government was subject to further criticism when the visa of a Catholic priest and prominent human rights activist was withdrawn hours before he was due to visit detainees on the island. It was believed that Nauruan officials had been instructed to cancel the visa by the Australian Government. Concerns about the conditions at the camps and the welfare of the detainees increased during 2003, and in December some of those held began a hunger strike in order to attract attention to their situation. A reported 40 asylum-seekers participated in the strike, some of whom stitched their lips together. The Nauruan Government's subsequent appeals for medical assistance from Australia to care for the hunger strikers, many of whom required hospital treatment during the following weeks, were refused. The emerging rift between the two countries intensified when Nauru's Minister of Finance, Kinza Clodumar, condemned remarks made by Australia's Minister for Immigration, Amanda Vanstone, who had said that the health of the hunger strikers was of no concern to Australia. Clodumar, who stated that his country's limited medical resources could not cope with a problem of this scale, accused Australia of failing to recognize its obligations in continuing to ignore the plight of the asylum-seekers on Nauru. The strike ended about one month after it had begun, and in mid-January 2004 the Australian Government sent a delegation to inspect medical facilities available to asylum-seekers on the island. However, the resultant report, which found services for those held in detention to be adequate, was widely regarded as flawed, as it had failed to examine any of the detainees and had been compiled solely by Australian government officials. In late June 2004 the first of 146 Afghan asylum-seekers, approved for entry to Australia, left the detention centre. In November 2005, after four years of detention on the island, a total of 25 asylum-seekers were transferred to Melbourne. It was reported that only two detainees, who had failed to meet security requirements, remained on Nauru; their departure from the centre was finally arranged in late 2006. In early 2007 the claims of 82 Sri Lankan asylum-seekers, who had been intercepted by the Australian navy in February, were being processed on Nauru, along with those of seven detainees from Myanmar. In February 2008 the 21 remaining detainees left Nauru, marking the end of Australia's policy of accommodating asylum-seekers on the island. The

Australian Government's decision was not welcomed by all Nauruans, in view of its likely impact on the island's economy.

In July 2008, following the closure of the island's processing centre, the Nauruan Minister of Foreign Affairs, Kieren Keke, signed a memorandum of understanding with the Australian Minister for Foreign Affairs, Stephen Smith, confirming that in 2008/09 Australia would provide $A29m. in official development assistance to Nauru. Australia reiterated its commitment to assisting Nauru in the improvement of its financial management, the upgrading of its infrastructure and the improvement of services such as health and education.

In February 1987 representatives of the British, Australian and New Zealand Governments signed documents effecting the official demise of the British Phosphate Commissioners, who from 1919 until 1970 had overseen the mining of Nauru's phosphate deposits. President DeRoburt subsequently expressed concern about the distribution of the Commissioners' accumulated assets, which were estimated to be worth $A55m. His proposal that part of this sum be spent on the rehabilitation of areas of the island that had been mined before independence was rejected by the three Governments involved. DeRoburt subsequently established a commission of inquiry to investigate proposals for rehabilitation. The commission proposed that the three Governments provide one-third ($A72m.) of the estimated rehabilitation costs. In 1989 Australia's refusal to contribute to the rehabilitation of former phosphate-mining areas prompted Nauru to institute proceedings, claiming compensation from Australia for damage to its environment, at the International Court of Justice. However, in 1993, following negotiations between President Dowiyogo and the Australian Prime Minister, Paul Keating, a Compact of Settlement was signed, under which the Australian Government was to pay some $A107m. to Nauru. New Zealand and the United Kingdom subsequently agreed to contribute $A12m. each towards the settlement. An investigation into methods for the rehabilitation of the damaged areas of the island included plans to use landfill to encourage the restoration of vegetation to the mined areas, and the re-establishment of many of the species of flora and fauna that had previously been abundant on the island. In mid-1995 a report commissioned by the Government published details of a rehabilitation programme extending over the next 20–25 years and costing $A230m. However, the success of the rehabilitation scheme was dependent on the co-operation of landowners, some of whom were expected to continue to allow areas to be mined for residual ore once phosphate reserves had been exhausted. In mid-1997 Parliament approved the Nauru Rehabilitation Corporation (NRC) Act, providing for the establishment of a corporate body to manage the rehabilitation programme. The NRC held its inaugural meeting in May 1999. The rehabilitation programme (which was to be partly financed from the Compact of Settlement with Australia) was expected to transform the mined areas into sites suitable for agriculture, new housing and industrial units, but the project was hampered considerably by delays. In early 2004 the chair of the NRC resigned, reportedly in frustration at problems regarding the implementation of a feasibility study into the mining of residual phosphate. Results published in September 2004 from a series of test sites on the island indicated that the potential for residual phosphate mining might be greater than had been previously thought. A major refurbishment of the island's mining plant was subsequently undertaken, and exports of phosphates resumed in 2006 (see Economic Affairs). In March 2008 protests reportedly related to the export of phosphates escalated into violence, with a group of approximately 100 demonstrators setting fire to a police station. A team of volunteers was appointed by local Australian police officers to maintain stability on the island.

In February 2001, following the revelation of various safety concerns in recent years, Air Nauru suspended all its operations. In December 2005 the carrier risked closure following a court order for the seizure of the carrier's only aircraft, on account of the airline's non-payment of loan instalments to the Export-Import Bank of the United States. Discussions with Taiwan began in the hope that Air Nauru, which had consistently operated at a loss, might be revived, and in January 2006 Nauru's Minister of Civil Aviation announced that Taiwan had agreed to offer support. Meanwhile, Air Pacific (of Fiji), Air Vanuatu and Air Marshall Islands (which had hitherto provided only domestic services) were operating on sectors of the routes formerly serviced by Air Nauru. In September Air Nauru was relaunched under the new name of Our Airline after Taiwan provided sufficient funding for the Government's acquisition of an aircraft with which it could resume services. The future of the airline was discussed at a meeting held in the Marshall Islands later in the year, and it was resolved that a task force be established to analyse the possibility of Our Airline becoming a sub-regional carrier, jointly owned by Nauru, the Federated States of Micronesia, Kiribati, Solomon Islands, the Marshall Islands and Tuvalu.

Nauru was persistently critical of France's use of the South Pacific region for nuclear-weapons testing, and was one of the most vociferous opponents of the French Government's decision in mid-1995 to resume its nuclear-testing programme. Diplomatic relations, suspended between the two countries in 1995, were formally resumed in early 1998.

In early 2001 Nauru voiced strong opposition to the US Government's plans to develop a missile defence system, in which missiles are deployed to shoot down other missiles in flight. Government officials in Nauru expressed fears that testing of the system in the region could result in missile debris landing on the Pacific islands.

The President of Nauru met the Cuban Minister of Foreign Affairs in November 2001 at a UN meeting, where they agreed to establish diplomatic relations between their two countries and discussed a proposed technical and economic co-operation agreement whereby Nauru would be provided with health experts from Cuba.

In 1989 a UN report on the 'greenhouse effect' (the heating of the earth's atmosphere and a resultant rise in sea-level) listed Nauru as one of the countries that might disappear beneath the sea in the 21st century, unless drastic action were taken. The Government of Nauru strongly criticized Australia's refusal, at the December 1997 Conference of the Parties to the Framework Convention on Climate Change (see UN Environment Programme, see p. 65), in Kyoto, Japan, to reduce its emission of pollutant gases known to contribute to the 'greenhouse effect'.

In August 2001 Nauru hosted the Pacific Islands Forum (see p. 393) summit meeting, despite a problematic shortage of accommodation, caused by the presence of contingents of officials from Australia, refugee agencies, the UN and Eurest (the company subcontracted to operate Nauru's refugee camp). Fiji had been expected to perform this role, but its participation had been opposed owing to its failure to reinstate democratic rule following the coup of the previous year.

In July 2004 President Ludwig Scotty held emergency discussions with the Presidents of Kiribati and Tuvalu regarding at least US $2m. in outstanding salary payments owed to their nationals employed in Nauru by the Nauru Phosphate Corporation. Nauru's financial crisis (see above) led it to appeal for assistance from the Pacific region and the international community. Consequently, in September 2004 the Pacific Islands Forum offered to help pay the salaries of Nauruan government employees (which had been unpaid for many months, resulting in considerable hardship), while the Cuban Government responded to an appeal for health care workers (as discussed in a co-operation agreement in late 2001—see above) by sending 11 doctors to Nauru to alleviate an increasingly serious situation, in which only three doctors were available to sick Nauruans. In May 2006 the Government embarked upon a programme to improve the health of the population, having developed a draft national strategy for addressing the high prevalence of obesity and lifestyle diseases such as diabetes.

In July 2002 a political crisis had emerged after President Rene Harris decided unilaterally to recognize the People's Republic of China, thus ending 22 years of diplomatic relations with Taiwan. Several cabinet ministers opposed the shift in policy, and the controversy increased after Harris immediately accepted US $60m. in aid and $77m. in debt annulment from the People's Republic of China. Following the switch in allegiance, Taiwan announced that it would take legal action to recover a loan of $12.5m., which it had arranged to make available to Nauru.

In March 2005 President Ludwig Scotty made an official visit to mainland China where he took part in discussions on bilateral aid and economic and technical co-operation. However, in May the Chinese Government announced that Nauru had severed its diplomatic relations with the People's Republic by switching its allegiance back to Taiwan. In July it was reported that Taiwan was to pay the outstanding salaries of some 1,000 workers from Kiribati and Tuvalu, who had remained stranded on Nauru since the island's financial crisis had resulted in the Government's inability to pay their wages. In March 2006 it was announced that Taiwan was providing US $3m. in overdue salary payments to the former phosphate miners from Kiribati and Tuvalu.

In February 2003 two diplomatic missions were opened, in Washington, DC, and in Beijing, primarily to address US concerns over 'money-laundering' and international terrorism (fears regarding the latter increased when, in the same month, two members of al-Qa'ida were found to be travelling on Nauruan passports). However, in July President Scotty announced plans to close the missions, citing economic constraints and his belief that they were not serving their intended purpose. Representatives in China and the USA expressed surprise at the announcement and queried the President's motives, in particular his commitment to ending the lucrative sale of Nauruan passports.

Nauru attracted considerable controversy in June 2005 when, at a meeting of the International Whaling Commission (IWC) in the Republic of Korea, it voted with Japan to remove the moratorium on commercial whaling introduced in 1986. Japan was accused by some observers of encouraging small, developing countries to join the IWC and then of attempting to influence their voting with financial incentives. However, Nauru denied that it had been subjected to any form of manipulation by the Japanese Government, stating that it had voted to remove the ban on whaling in order to preserve its tuna stocks.

Government

Legislative power is vested in the unicameral Parliament, with 18 members elected by universal adult suffrage for up to three years. Executive authority is vested in a Cabinet, which consists of the President of the Republic, elected by the Parliament, and ministers appointed by him. The Cabinet is collectively responsible to Parliament. Responsibilities for administration are divided between the Nauru Local Government Council and the Government. The Council, an elected body of nine members from the country's 14 districts, elects one of its members to be Head Chief.

Defence

Nauru has no defence forces: under an informal arrangement, Australia is responsible for the country's defence.

Economic Affairs

In 2007, according to official sources, Nauru's gross domestic product (GDP), measured at current prices, was $A27m., equivalent to $A3,064 per head. In 1995–2004, it was estimated, GDP decreased, in real terms, at an average annual rate of 1.5%. The population decreased by an annual average of 1.8% per year in 2000–07. Real GDP expanded by 6.4% in the fiscal year 2006 (ending in June), according to the Asian Development Bank (ADB). However, GDP contracted by 27.5% in the fiscal year 2007 (ending in June), before expanding by an estimated 1.0% in 2008.

Agricultural activity comprises mainly the small-scale production of tropical fruit, vegetables and livestock, although the production of coffee and copra for export is increasingly significant. According to FAO, agriculture and fishing engaged some 33% of the economically active population in mid-2005. The sector provided an estimated 13.8% of GDP in 2006/07. Following a period of decline, agricultural GDP increased, in real terms, by 25.5% in 2003. Coconuts are the principal crop. Bananas, pineapples and the screw-pine (*Pandanus*) are also cultivated as food crops, while the islanders keep pigs and chickens. Almost all Nauru's requirements are imported. Increased exploitation of the island's marine resources was envisaged following the approval by Parliament of new fisheries legislation in the late 1990s. However, the sector failed to develop as hoped, and in early 2009 it was reported that a fisheries adviser, funded by Australia, had been engaged. Meanwhile, revenue from fishing licence fees totalled an estimated $A7m. in 2005/06.

Industrial activity (mining, manufacturing, construction and utilities) accounted for 8.5% of GDP in 2006/07. In real terms, industrial GDP declined by 7.5% in 2002 and by 9.8% in 2003. Nauru's economy was traditionally based on the mining of phosphate rock, which constituted four-fifths of the island's surface area. Phosphate extraction was conducted largely by indentured labour, notably by I-Kiribati and Tuvaluan workers. Revenue from phosphate sales was invested in a long-term trust fund, the Nauru Phosphate Royalties Trust (NPRT—see below) and the Nauru Local Government Council. As the depletion of primary (surface) deposits continued, in 2004 an Australian company undertook a detailed survey of the island's potential for secondary phosphate mining (see Recent History). The discovery of substantial new reserves of high-grade phosphate was announced in 2005. It was hoped that secondary deposits might yield sufficient phosphate to sustain exports for 20–30 years, thereby providing revenue of as much $A1,000m. for the island. Meanwhile, an agreement with an Australian fertilizer company was signed in late 2005, and in early 2006 it was announced that a Thai company was also to become involved in phosphate-mining operations on Nauru. In September 2006, following the upgrading of processing facilities, the first major shipment of phosphate for nearly 10 years was exported to India. However, in 2007 operations were disrupted after the island's port facilities were damaged in severe weather conditions. Australia's imports of crude fertilizer from Nauru totalled almost $A5.0m. in 2007/08.

Energy is derived principally from imported petroleum. Output of electrical energy totalled 32m. kWh in 2005, the same production level as in the previous year.

The services sector, accounting for 77.7% of Nauru's GDP in 2006/07, comprises mainly those employed in public service. The real GDP of services rose by 3.4% in 2002, but decreased by 0.4% in 2003. The sector recorded no growth in 2004, with many salaries remaining in arrears (see Recent History). According to official estimates, public administration accounted for 30.3% of GDP in 2006/07. There is no tourism sector. Commercial banking services are not widely available.

The country's trade balance improved in the year to June 2007, when a surplus of US $35.0m. was recorded. The deficit on the current account of the balance of payments was estimated at 10.3% of GDP in 2006/07. According to the ADB, a substantial decline in exports in 2004/05 was followed by an increase of 85.6% in the following year, and in 2006/07 the value of Nauru's exports was estimated to have risen by 618.6% (owing to the resumption of phosphate sales). The cost of imports increased by 11.1% in 2006/07. The principal imports are manufactured goods, machinery and transport equipment, food and live animals, and chemical products. Phosphates have traditionally been the most important export. The main exports in 2005 included manufactured goods and crude materials. The principal export markets in 2005 were the Republic of Korea (which purchased about 23% of the total) and Canada (20%). Australia's imports from Nauru totalled almost $A5.4m. in 2007/08. The principal sources of Nauru's imports in 2005 were the Republic of Korea (supplying 43%) and Australia (36%). Australia's exports to Nauru, largely comprising refined petroleum and goods vehicles, reached $A24.4m. in 2007/08.

The 2006/07 budget envisaged revenue of $A22,288m. and expenditure of $A22,226m., a modest surplus of $A62,000 thus being forecast. The ADB estimated the budget surplus at the equivalent of 0.6% of GDP in 2007/08, compared with a deficit of 36.3% in 2005/06. Development assistance from Australia was projected at $A26.6m. for 2008/09. Nauru's external debt was estimated by the ADB at US $A310m. in 2007. In that year the level of international and domestic debt was reported to be the equivalent of 30 times the country's GDP. Consumer prices increased by 17.9% in 2000, but inflation subsequently moderated. The annual rate of inflation was estimated by the ADB at 3.5% in 2006, 2.3% in 2007 and 4.5% in 2008. The rate of unemployment in 2002 was estimated at 22.7% of the labour force.

Nauru is a member of the Pacific Community (see p. 391), of the Pacific Islands Forum (see p. 393) and of the UN Economic and Social Commission for Asia and the Pacific (ESCAP, see p. 36), all of which aim to promote regional development. Nauru is also a member of the Asian Development Bank (ADB, see p. 191).

After gaining independence in 1968, Nauru benefited from sole control of earnings from phosphate mining, and as a result its income per head was among the highest in the world. However, this had serious repercussions for the country, which became excessively dependent on expatriate labour and on imports of consumer goods and convenience foods, causing environmental, health and social problems. The assets of the NPRT, meanwhile, became seriously depleted; these were estimated to have decreased from $A1,300m. in 1991 to only $A300m. in 2003, following which the portfolio was placed into receivership. In November 2005 Nauru hosted an international donor meeting, attended by representatives of about 20 donor nations and agencies, at which it requested support for its National Sustainable Development Strategy. The aims of this programme included an increase in revenue from phosphate production, better use of fish resources and the encouragement of agricultural activities, with particular emphasis on local food production. The substantial contraction in the economy during 2006/07 was primarily due to a decline in the public sector and to the

NAURU

suspension of phosphate exports (see above). Although GDP growth resumed in 2007/08, this was curtailed by the closure of a processing centre for asylum-seekers (see Recent History), which had been an important source of government revenue, as well as employment for islanders. However, strong expansion was recorded in the phosphate sector, which further benefited from the high international price for the commodity. The continued strength of global phosphate prices was expected to maintain modest economic growth in 2008/09, when GDP was forecast by the ADB to increase by 1.5%. Inflationary pressures were expected to ease during 2009, partly owing to the anticipated moderation of the level of inflation in Australia. (Nauru imports a large percentage of its supplies from Australia and uses the Australian dollar as its official currency.) The high level of public debt remained a major concern: the Government assessed its total debt at $A1,005m., equivalent to 20 times Nauru's GDP, in 2006/07. In August 2008 the Pacific Islands Forum agreed to extend its Pacific Regional Assistance to Nauru initiative.

Education

Education is compulsory for Nauruan children between six and 16 years of age. Primary education begins at the age of six and lasts for seven years. Secondary education, beginning at 13 years of age, lasts for up to four years. In 2002/03 enrolment at pre-primary schools was equivalent to 71% of the relevant age-group. In 2003/04 enrolment at primary level was equivalent to 83.7% and enrolment at secondary level was equivalent to 47.8%. In 2007 there were four pre-primary schools, two primary schools and four secondary schools with a total of 134 teachers. In 2003 there were four vocational level teachers with 38 students. In 2001 Nauruans studying overseas at secondary and tertiary levels numbered 85. There is a university extension centre, linked with the University of the South Pacific in Suva, Fiji. The education sector was particularly badly affected by the country's economic crisis during 2004. With payment of their salaries in arrears, many expatriate teachers left the country. The sector also continued to be constrained by the lack of adequate teaching materials.

Public Holidays

2009: 1 January (New Year's Day), 31 January (Independence Day), 10–13 April (Easter), 17 May (Constitution Day), 26 October (Angam Day), 25–26 December (Christmas).

2010: 1 January (New Year's Day), 31 January (Independence Day), 2–5 April (Easter), 17 May (Constitution Day), 26 October (Angam Day), 25–26 December (Christmas).

Weights and Measures

The imperial system is in force.

Statistical Survey

Source (unless otherwise indicated): Bureau of Statistics, Ministry of Finance, Government Offices, Yaren District; tel. (674) 444-3142; fax (674) 444-3125; e-mail bos@cenpac.net.nr; fax www.spc.int/prism/country/nr/stats.

AREA AND POPULATION

Area: 21.3 sq km (8.2 sq miles).

Population: 8,042 (Nauruan 4,964, Other Pacific Islanders 2,134, Asians 682, Caucasians—mainly Australians and New Zealanders—262) at census of 13 May 1983; 9,919 (males 5,079, females 4,840) at census of 17 April 1992; 10,065 (males 5,136, females 4,929) at census of 23 September 2002. *2008* (mid-year estimate): 10,163.

Density (mid-2008): 477.1 per sq km.

Principal Districts (population, 2002 census): Denigomudu 2,381; Meneng 1,323; Aiwo 1,051; Boe 731; Yaren (capital) 632; Buada 673.

Births, Marriages and Deaths (1995): Registered live births 203 (birth rate 18.8 per 1,000); Registered marriages 57 (marriage rate 5.3 per 1,000); Registered deaths 49 (death rate 4.5 per 1,000). *2002:* Registered live births 219; Registered deaths 75.

Life Expectancy (years at birth, WHO estimates): 61.3 (males 58.7; females 64.3) in 2006. Source: WHO, *World Health Statistics*.

Economically Active Population (census of 17 April 1992): 2,007 (Elementary occupations 401, Clerks and office workers 355, Craft and related workers 299, Service, shop and market sales workers 250, Professionals 208, Plant, machine operators and assemblers 136, Technicians and associate professionals 115, Legislators, senior officials and managers 18, Agriculture and related workers 2, Not classified 223). *2002* (census of 23 September): Total employed 2,534; Unemployed 746; Total labour force 3,280. *Mid-2005* (estimates): Agriculture, etc. 2,000; Total labour force 6,000 (Source: FAO).

HEALTH AND WELFARE
Key Indicators

Total Fertility Rate (children per woman, 2006): 3.1.

Under-5 Mortality Rate (per 1,000 live births, 2006): 30.

Physicians (per 1,000 head, 2004): 0.8.

Hospital Beds (per 1,000 head, 2004): 5.9.

Health Expenditure (2006): US $ per head (PPP): 803.

Health Expenditure (2006): % of GDP: 10.8.

Health Expenditure (2006): public (% of total): 55.3.

For sources and definitions, see explanatory note on p. vi.

AGRICULTURE, ETC.

Principal Crop and Livestock (2007, FAO estimates): Coconuts 1,800 metric tons; Pigs 2,900 head; Chickens 5,000 head.

Livestock Products (metric tons, 2007, FAO estimates): Pig meat 75; Chicken meat 4; Hen eggs 16.

Fishing (metric tons, live weight of capture, 2006): Yellowfin tuna 12; Bigeye tuna 3; Skipjack tuna 13; Total catch (incl. other marine fishes) 39.

Source: FAO.

MINING

Phosphate Rock ('000 metric tons, estimates): 84 in 2003; 22 in 2004; 11 in 2005. The phosphoric acid content ('000 metric tons, estimates) was: 26 in 2003; 7 in 2004; 3 in 2005. Source: US Geological Survey.

INDUSTRY

Electric Energy (million kWh): 32 in 2003; 32 in 2004; 32 in 2005. Source: UN, *Industrial Commodity Statistics Yearbook*.

FINANCE

Currency and Exchange Rates: Australian currency: 100 cents = 1 Australian dollar ($A). *Sterling, US Dollar and Euro Equivalents* (31 December 2008): £1 sterling = $A2.1042; US $1 = $A1.4434; €1 = $A2.0088; $A100 = £47.53 = US $69.28 = €49.78. *Average Exchange Rate* (Australian dollars per US $): 1.3280 in 2006; 1.1951 in 2007; 1.1922 in 2008.

Budget ($A '000, year ending 30 June 2007, provisional figures): *Total Revenue:* 22,288 (Tax revenue 8,646, Non-tax revenue 13,643); *Total Expenditure:* 22,226 (Employee expenses 5,890, Operating expenses 8,543, Property expenses 505, Current transfers 2,150, Gross fixed capital formation 4,682, Other 457).

Gross Domestic Product ($A '000, year ending 30 June at current prices): 34,009 in 2005; 36,881 in 2006; 26,897 in 2007 (preliminary).

Gross Domestic Product by Economic Activity ($A million, year ending 30 June at current prices, preliminary): Agriculture, hunting and fishing 3.7; Mining 4.6; Manufacturing 0.6; Electricity, gas and water −3.5; Construction 0.6; Trade 8.0; Transport and communications 0.3; Finance 0.7; Public administration 8.1; Other services 3.8; *GDP in market prices* 26.9. Source: Asian Development Bank, *Key Indicators of Developing Asian and Pacific Countries*.

EXTERNAL TRADE

Principal Commodities (US $ '000, year ending 30 June 2005): *Imports:* Food and live animals 4,548; Beverages and tobacco 1,891; Crude materials (except food and fuel) 1,741; Mineral fuels and lubricants 1,528; Animal fats and vegetable oils 1,698; Chemical products 3,300; Manufactured goods 11,898; Machinery and transport equipment 5,375; Miscellaneous manufacture articles 1,705; Total (incl. others) 33,683. *Exports:* Food and live animals 293; Crude materials (except food and fuel) 1,489; Chemical products 408; Manufactured goods 2,039; Machinery and transport equipment 616; Miscellaneous manufacture articles 113; Total (incl. others) 4,959.

Principal Trading Partners (US $ million, year ending 31 December 2005): *Imports:* Australia 10.7; Fiji 0.7; Germany 1.3; Korea, Republic 13.0; USA 1.8; Total (incl. others) 29.9. *Exports:* Canada 0.9; Germany 0.4; India 0.5; Korea, Republic 1.0; Total (incl. others) 4.4. Source: Asian Development Bank, *Key Indicators of Developing Asian and Pacific Countries*.

Trade Totals (US $ '000, year ending 30 June): *Imports c.i.f.:* 37,196 in 2003; 24,292 in 2004; 33,683 in 2005. *Exports f.o.b.:* 43,221 in 2003; 19,656 in 2004; 4,959 in 2005.

TRANSPORT

Road Traffic (1989): 1,448 registered motor vehicles.

Shipping: *Merchant Fleet* (displacement, '000 grt at 31 December): 15 in 1991 (at 30 June); 5 in 1992; 1 in 1993. Source: Lloyd's Register of Shipping. *International Freight Traffic* (estimates, '000 metric tons, 1990): Goods loaded 1,650; Goods unloaded 59. Source: UN, *Monthly Bulletin of Statistics*.

Civil Aviation (traffic on scheduled services, 2004): Kilometres flown (million) 3; Passengers carried ('000) 195; Passenger-km (million) 338; Total ton-km (million) 34. Source: UN, *Statistical Yearbook*.

COMMUNICATIONS MEDIA

Radio Receivers (1997): 7,000 in use*.

Television Receivers (1997): 500 in use*.

Telephones (main lines, 2001): 2,000 in use†.

Mobile Cellular Telephones (2001): 1,500 subscribers†.

Internet Users (2001): 300†.

* Source: UNESCO, *Statistical Yearbook*.
† Source: International Telecommunication Union.

EDUCATION

Pre-primary (2007): 4 schools; 38 teachers; 669 pupils.

Primary (2007): 2 schools; 53 teachers; 1,235 pupils.

Secondary (2007): 4 schools; 43 teachers; 689 pupils.

Vocational (2003, unless otherwise indicated): 2 schools (2004); 4 teachers; 38 students.

Note: Nauruans studying at secondary and tertiary levels overseas in 2001 numbered 85.

Source: Department of Education, Yaren, Nauru.

Directory

The Constitution

The Constitution of the Republic of Nauru came into force at independence on 31 January 1968, having been adopted two days previously. It protects fundamental rights and freedoms, and vests executive authority in the Cabinet, which is responsible to a popularly elected Parliament. The President of the Republic is elected by Parliament from among its members. The Cabinet is composed of five or six members, including the President, who presides. There are 18 members of Parliament, including the Cabinet. Voting is compulsory for all Nauruans who are more than 20 years of age, except in certain specified instances.

The highest judicial organ is the Supreme Court and there is provision for the creation of subordinate courts with designated jurisdiction.

There is a Treasury Fund from which monies may be taken by Appropriation Acts.

A Public Service is provided for, with the person designated as the Chief Secretary being the Commissioner of the Public Service.

Special mention is given to the allocation of profits and royalties from the sale of phosphates.

The Government

HEAD OF STATE

President: MARCUS STEPHEN (elected by Parliament 19 December 2007; re-elected 29 April 2009).

CABINET
(April 2009)

President and Minister of Public Service, Home Affairs, Police, Prisons and Emergency Services, and the Nauru Phosphate Royalties Trust: MARCUS STEPHEN.

Minister of Finance, Economic Planning, Foreign Affairs and Trade, responsible for assisting the President: Dr KIEREN KEKE.

Minister of Commerce, Industry and Resources: FREDERICK PITCHER.

Minister of Education and Fisheries: ROLAND KUN.

Minister of Health, Sports and Justice: MATTHEW BATSIUA.

Minister of Telecommunications and Transport: SPRENT DABWIDO.

MINISTRIES

Office of the President: Yaren; tel. 444-3772; fax 444-3776; e-mail the.president@naurugov.nr.

Ministry of Commerce, Industry and Resources: Yaren; e-mail minister.cir@naurugov.nr.

Ministry of Education: Yaren; tel. 444-3130; fax 444-3718; e-mail minister.education@naurugov.nr.

Ministry of Finance: Government Treasury Bldg, Aiwo; tel. 444-3140; fax 555-4477; e-mail minister.finance@naurugov.nr.

Ministry of Fisheries: e-mail minister.fisheries@naurugov.nr.

Ministry of Foreign Affairs: fax 444-3105; e-mail minister.foreignaffairs@naurugov.nr.

Ministry of Health: tel. 444-3133; fax 444-3188; e-mail minister.health@naurugov.nr.

Ministry of Home Affairs: fax 444-3891; e-mail minister.homeaffairs@naurugov.nr.

Ministry of Justice: Yaren; tel. 444-3160; fax 444-3108; e-mail minister.justice@naurugov.nr.

Ministry for Nauru Phosphate Royalties Trust: e-mail minister.nprt@naurugov.nr.

Ministry of Police: e-mail minister.police@naurugov.nr.

Ministry of Public Service: e-mail minister.publicservice@naurugov.nr.

Ministry of Sport: e-mail minister.sport@naurugov.nr.

Ministry of Telecommunications: e-mail minister.telecommunications@naurugov.nr.

Ministry of Transport: e-mail minister.transport@naurugov.nr.

Ministry of Utilities: e-mail minister.utilities@naurugov.nr.

Ministry of Youth Affairs: e-mail minister.youthaffairs@naurugov.nr.

Legislature

PARLIAMENT

Parliament comprises 18 members. The most recent general election took place on 26 April 2008.

Speaker: RIDDELL AKUA.

Political Organizations

Democratic Party of Nauru: c/o Parliament House, Yaren; f. 1987; revival of Nauru Party (f. 1975); Leader KENNAN ADEANG.

Naoero Amo (Nauru First): c/o Parliament House, Yaren; e-mail visionary@naoeroamo.com; f. 2001; Co-Leaders DAVID ADEANG, KIEREN KEKE.

NAURU

Diplomatic Representation

EMBASSY IN NAURU

China (Taiwan): Civic Center, 1st Floor, Aiwo; tel. 444-3239; fax 444-3846; e-mail nru@mofa.gov.tw.

Judicial System

The Chief Justice presides over the Supreme Court, which exercises original, appellate and advisory jurisdiction. The Resident Magistrate presides over the District Court, and he also acts as Coroner under the Inquests Act 1977. The Supreme Court is a court of record. The Family Court consists of three members, one being the Resident Magistrate as Chairman, and two other members drawn from a panel of Nauruans. The Chief Justice is Chairman of the Public Services Appeals Board and of the Police Appeals Board.

Supreme Court

Yaren; tel. 444-3163; fax 444-3104.

Chief Justice: BARRY CONNELL (non-resident).

DISTRICT COURT

Resident Magistrate: G. N. SAKSENA.

FAMILY COURT

Chairman: G. N. SAKSENA.

Religion

Nauruans are predominantly Christians, adhering either to the Nauruan Protestant Church or to the Roman Catholic Church.

Nauruan Protestant Church: Head Office, Nauru; Moderator (vacant).

Roman Catholic Church: POB 16, Nauru; tel. and fax 444-3708; Nauru forms part of the diocese of Tarawa and Nauru, comprising Kiribati and Nauru. The Bishop resides on Tarawa Atoll, Kiribati.

The Press

Central Star News: Nauru; f. 1991; fortnightly.

Nasero Bulletin: Nauru; tel. 444-3847; fax 444-3153; e-mail bulletin@cenpac.net.nr; fortnightly; English; local and overseas news; Editor SEPE BATSIUA; circ. 500.

The Nauru Chronicle: Nauru; Editor RUBY DEDIYA.

Broadcasting and Communications

TELECOMMUNICATIONS

Nauru Telecommunications Service: Nauru; tel. 444-3324; fax 444-3111; Dir EDWARD W. R. H. DEYOUNG.

BROADCASTING

Radio

Nauru Broadcasting Service: Information and Broadcasting Services, Chief Secretary's Department, POB 77, Nauru; tel. 444-3133; fax 444-3153; f. 1968; state-owned and non-commercial; broadcasts in the mornings in English and Nauruan; operates Radio Nauru; Station Man. RIN TSITSI; Man. Dir GARY TURNER.

Television

Nauru Television (NTV): Nauru; tel. 444-3133; fax 444-3153; began operations in June 1991; govt-owned; broadcasts 24 hrs per day on 3 channels; most of the programmes are supplied by foreign television companies via satellite or on videotape; a weekly current affairs programme is produced locally; Man. MICHAEL DEKARUBE; Dir of Media GARY TURNER.

Finance

(cap. = capital; res = reserves; dep. = deposits; m. = million; amounts in Australian dollars unless otherwise stated)

BANKING

State Bank

Bank of Nauru: Civic Centre, POB 289, Nauru; tel. 444-3238; fax 444-3203; e-mail bonauru@yahoo.com; f. 1976; state-owned; Chair. NAGENDRA GOSWAMI.

INSURANCE

Nauru Insurance Corporation: POB 82, Nauru; tel. 444-3346; fax 444-3731; f. 1974; sole licensed insurer and reinsurer in Nauru; Chair. NIMES EKWONA.

Trade and Industry

GOVERNMENT AGENCIES

Nauru Agency Corporation: POB 300, Aiwo; tel. 444-3782; fax 444-3730; e-mail info@nauruoffshore.com; internet nauruoffshore.com; f. 1972; management service to assist entrepreneurs in the incorporation of holding and trading corpns and the procurement of trust and insurance licences; CEO R. MOSES.

Nauru Corporation: Civic Centre, Yaren; f. 1925; operated by the Nauru Council; the major retailer in Nauru; Gen. Man. A. EPHRAIM.

Nauru Fisheries and Marine Resources Authority: POB 449, Aiwo; tel. 444-3733; fax 444-3812; e-mail nfmra@cenpac.net.nr; f. 1997; Man. KARLICK AGIR.

Nauru Phosphate Corporation: Aiwo; tel. 444-3839; fax 444-2752; f. 1970; has operated the phosphate industry and several public services of the Republic of Nauru (including provision of electricity and fresh water) on behalf of the Nauruan people; responsibility for phosphate-mining operations assumed by Republic of Nauru Phosphate Company (Ronphos), overseen from 2005 by Astro Pacific Group (New Zealand); Chair. RIDDELL AKUA; Gen. Man. LESI OLSSON.

Nauru Phosphate Royalties Trust (NPRT): Nauru; statutory corpn; invests phosphate royalties to provide govt revenue; extensive international interests, incl. hotels and real estate; assets put into receivership in 2004; Sec. NIRAL FERNANDO.

Nauru Rehabilitation Corporation (NRC): Civic Centre, Aiwo; tel. 444-3200; fax 444-3272; e-mail nrcadm@cenpac.net.nr; f. 1999; manages and devises programmes for the rehabilitation of those parts of the island damaged by the over-mining of phosphate; Chair. ALI AMWANO.

UTILITIES

Nauru Phosphate Corporation: Aiwo; tel. 444-3839; fax 444-2752; operates generators for the provision of electricity and water supplies; Chair. RIDDELL AKUA; Gen. Man. LESI OLSSON.

Transport

RAILWAYS

There are 5.2 km of 0.9-m gauge railway serving the phosphate workings.

ROADS

A sealed road, 16 km long, circles the island, and another serves Buada District.

SHIPPING

In 1998 finance was secured from the Japanese Government for the construction of a harbour in Anibare district, which was opened in 2000.

Nauru Pacific: Government Bldg, Yaren; tel. 444-3133; f. 1969; operates cargo charter services to ports in Australia, New Zealand, Asia, the Pacific and the west coast of the USA; Man. Dir (vacant).

CIVIL AVIATION

Our Airline: Directorate of Civil Aviation, Government of Nauru Offices, POB 40, Yaren; tel. 444-3746; fax 444-3705; e-mail info@ourairline.com.au; internet www.ourairline.com.au; f. 1970; corporatized in 1996 and moved to Australian aviation register in mid-1997; operates passenger and cargo services to Kiribati, Solomon Islands and Australia; fmrly Air Nauru; name changed as above in 2006; Chair. Capt. KEVIN POWER; CEO KARAM CHAND.

NEPAL

Introductory Survey

Location, Climate, Language, Religion, Flag, Capital

Nepal is a land-locked Asian country in the Himalaya mountain range, with India to the east, south and west, and Tibet (the Xizang Autonomous Region), in the People's Republic of China, to the north. The climate varies sharply with altitude, from arctic on the higher peaks of the Himalaya mountains (where the air temperature is permanently below freezing point) to humid subtropical in the central valley of Kathmandu, which is warm and sunny in summer. Temperatures in Kathmandu, which is 1,337 m (4,386 ft) above sea-level, are generally between 2°C (35°F) and 30°C (86°F), with an annual average of 11°C (52°F). The rainy season is between June and October. Average annual rainfall varies from about 1,000 mm (40 ins) in western Nepal to about 2,500 mm (100 ins) in the east. The official language is Nepali, which was spoken by 48.6% of the population in 2001. Other languages include Maithir (12.3% in 2001) and Bhojpuri (7.5%). Some 80.6% of the population were Hindus in 2001, with 10.7% Buddhists and 4.2% Muslims. The national flag (proportions 4 by 3) is composed of two crimson pennants, each with a blue border. The upper section contains a white crescent moon (horns upwards and surmounted by a disc with eight rays) and the lower section a white sun in splendour. The capital is Kathmandu.

Recent History

Although Nepal was an hereditary monarchy, for more than 100 years, until 1951, effective power was held by the Rana family, who created the post of hereditary Prime Minister. A popular revolution, led by the Nepali Congress Party (NCP), ousted the Ranas and restored King Tribhuvan to power. A limited constitutional monarchy was established in 1951. During most of the 1950s government was controlled by the monarchy, first under Tribhuvan and then, after his death in 1955, under his son, Mahendra. In February 1959 King Mahendra promulgated Nepal's first Constitution, providing for a bicameral parliament, including a popularly elected lower house. Elections held later that month resulted in victory for the NCP, led by Bisweswor Prasad (B. P.) Koirala, who became Prime Minister. However, the King retained a certain degree of power, and persistent differences between the King and the Prime Minister led to a royal coup in December 1960: Nepal's first brief period of democracy was thus brought to an abrupt end. The King dismissed the Council of Ministers and dissolved Parliament. A royal decree of January 1961 banned political parties. King Mahendra accused the Koirala administration of corruption, and in December 1962 he introduced a new Constitution, reasserting absolute royal power and providing for a 'partyless' system of government, based on the Panchayat (village council), with a Prime Minister appointed by the King. This office was filled successively by Dr Tulsi Giri (1962–65), Surya Bahadur Thapa (1965–69) and Kirti Nidhi Bista (1969–70, 1971–73). King Mahendra himself was Prime Minister from April 1970 to April 1971. In January 1972 King Mahendra died and was succeeded by his son, Birendra. Nagendra Prasad Rijal became Prime Minister in July 1973, and held office until December 1975, when Dr Giri was reappointed. The new Government made major changes to the Constitution, which allowed for a widening of the franchise and more frequent elections to the Rashtriya Panchayat (National Assembly), but in no way were the King's powers eroded. In September 1977 Dr Giri resigned and was succeeded by Bista.

B. P. Koirala, the former Prime Minister and an advocate of parliamentary democracy, was acquitted of treason in February 1978. Returning from abroad a year later, he was placed under house arrest in April 1979, but then released, partly to appease students who had been demonstrating for reforms. National unrest grew and, after King Birendra announced in May that there would be a national referendum on whether to restore multi-party democracy, Bista resigned and was succeeded as Prime Minister by Thapa. In the referendum, held in May 1980, 54.8% of the voters supported the Panchayat system with reforms. As a result, the King formed a Constitutional Reforms Commission, and in December he issued a decree under which amendments to the Constitution were made, including the proviso that the appointment of the Prime Minister by the King would henceforth be on the recommendation of the Rashtriya Panchayat. In accordance with the new provisions, direct legislative elections were held in May 1981, the first of their kind since 1959, although still on a non-party basis. Thapa was re-elected by the Rashtriya Panchayat as Prime Minister in June 1981, and the King installed a new Council of Ministers (on the recommendation of the Prime Minister). An extensive ministerial reorganization took place in October 1982, but this failed to stem increasing official corruption and economic mismanagement. In July 1983, for the first time in the 23-year history of the Panchayat system, the incumbent Prime Minister, Surya Bahadur Thapa, was ousted, and a new Council of Ministers was formed by a former Chairman of the Rashtriya Panchayat, Lokendra Bahadur Chand, who had successfully introduced a motion expressing no confidence in Thapa.

In March 1985 the NCP held a convention in Kathmandu, and in May it embarked upon a campaign of civil disobedience, aimed at restoring a multi-party political system and parliamentary rule under a constitutional monarchy. In June there was a series of bomb explosions, resulting in loss of life. The explosions were apparently co-ordinated by two newly formed anti-monarchist and anti-Government groups, the Janawadi Morcha (Democratic Front) and the Samyukta Mukti Bahini (United Liberation Torch-bearers). These bombings united an otherwise seriously divided legislature against the terrorists, and forced the predominantly moderate opposition to abandon the campaign of civil disobedience and to disclaim any responsibility for the explosions. In August the Rashtriya Panchayat approved a stringent anti-terrorist law, and more than 1,000 people were arrested in connection with the unrest.

In May 1986 a general election was held. About 64% of the electorate voted, in spite of appeals by the NCP and the pro-China faction of the Communist Party of Nepal (CPN) (neither of which presented candidates) for a boycott of the polls. All the candidates in the election were nominally independents, but it was reported that among the 72 new entrants to the Rashtriya Panchayat (40 members retained their seats) were at least 16 members of the Marxist-Leninist faction of the CPN. In June the King nominated 25 additional members of the new Rashtriya Panchayat, and Marich Man Singh Shrestha (previously Chairman of the Rashtriya Panchayat) was elected unopposed by the Assembly as the new Prime Minister. In late 1986, to counter the growing influence of the communist faction in the Rashtriya Panchayat, several senior figures (including Jog Meher Shrestha, a former government minister, and Chand) established a 'Democratic Panchayat Forum', which expressed full support for the non-party system.

In June 1987, in an apparent attempt to improve the image of the Panchayat system, the Government initiated an anti-corruption campaign, during the course of which several senior officials were arrested for drugs-trafficking and other offences. In early 1988 the Government continued its policy of suppressing opposition. In January the President of the NCP was arrested, and in February more than 100 people, who were planning to demonstrate in support of the NCP mayor of Kathmandu (who had been suspended from office for his anti-Panchayat stance), were also detained.

In September 1989 the Government arrested more than 900 NCP supporters, in an apparent effort to prevent them from celebrating the anniversary of the birth of Nepal's first elected Prime Minister, B. P. Koirala (who died in 1982). During these celebrations the NCP demonstrated in protest against the failings of the country's non-party political system. In November the leaders of the NCP held a meeting in Kathmandu with members of several other left-wing and communist political groups, to discuss the proposed formation of a country-wide peaceful 'movement for the restoration of democracy'; the movement's aims would be the alleviation of Nepal's severe economic problems (including the trade dispute with India, see below), the restoration of full democracy, the transfer from absolute to constitutional monarchy, the immediate replacement of the Panchayat Government by an interim national government, the removal of the ban on political activities, and the introduction of a multi-party system. In January 1990 a co-ordination committee to conduct the Jana Andolan (People's Movement) was formed by the NCP and the newly formed United Left Front (ULF, which was led by Sahana Pradhan and comprised six factions of the CPN and a labour group), despite the Government's efforts to pre-empt its inauguration by arresting hundreds of activists (including many students) and by banning, or heavily censoring, more newspapers. During the consequent violent confrontations between protesters and police that took place in February, it was officially estimated that 12 people were killed and hundreds more arrested. Violent demonstrations, strikes and mass arrests continued throughout March. At the end of the month the Minister of Foreign Affairs, Shailendra Kumar Upadhayaya, resigned from his post, following differences with the Prime Minister regarding the Government's management of the crisis. A few days later there was an extensive government reshuffle, including the dismissal of nine ministers who allegedly opposed the Government's acts of repression against the pro-democracy movement. In an effort to end the political unrest, the King dismissed Shrestha's Government on 6 April and nominated a restricted four-member Council of Ministers, under the leadership of the more moderate Chand. King Birendra also offered to establish a body that would examine the possibility of altering the Constitution and to hold discussions with the opposition, and he promised to initiate an official inquiry into the 20 deaths that had occurred during demonstrations since February. Despite these concessions, the situation worsened later the same day. A temporary curfew was imposed on the capital, and many political agitators were arrested. The Government immediately initiated talks with the opposition, and on 8 April the King announced that the 30-year ban on political parties was to be ended, thus enabling the future holding of multi-party elections, and that a commission to study constitutional reform was to be established. At the same time, the Jana Andolan suspended its campaign of demonstrations. However, many political activists continued to agitate, demanding the removal of the formal structure of the Panchayat system. A week later, the King accepted the resignation of Chand from his post as Prime Minister, dismissed the Council of Ministers and announced the dissolution of the Rashtriya Panchayat. King Birendra then invited the opposition alliance of the NCP and the ULF to form an interim government. On 19 April a new 11-member coalition Council of Ministers (including two ministers nominated by the King and two independents), under the premiership of the President of the NCP, Krishna Prasad (K. P.) Bhattarai, was sworn in. The new Prime Minister announced that a general election would be held, on a multi-party basis, within a year. The principal task of the interim Government was to prepare a new constitution in accordance with the spirit of multi-party democracy and constitutional monarchy. King Birendra stated that he was committed to transforming his role into that of a constitutional monarch, and, following further violent clashes in Kathmandu between anti-royalists and police, he ordered the army and the police to comply with the orders of the interim Government in order to facilitate a smooth transition to democracy.

In mid-May 1990 King Birendra announced a general amnesty for all religious and political prisoners. On 21 May he delegated the legislative powers of the dissolved Rashtriya Panchayat to the new Council of Ministers, empowering it to enact, amend and repeal legislation in order to bring about the introduction of a multi-party democracy. At the end of the month the King formed a nine-member Constitutional Recommendation Commission (based on the suggestions of the Prime Minister), which, after consulting the various parties, was to prepare a draft constitution and present it to the King within three months. In July the death sentence was abolished and the laws restricting freedom of the press and freedom of association were repealed. In addition, the King suspended almost one-half of the articles in the Constitution to enable the interim Government to function smoothly. The draft of the new Constitution, which was published at the end of August, recommended the introduction of a constitutional monarchy; a democratic multi-party system and a bicameral legislature, composed of a 205-member House of Representatives (Pratinidhi Sabha) and a 60-member National Assembly (Rashtriya Sabha); the official guarantee of fundamental rights (including freedom of expression); an independent judiciary; and the placing of the army under the control of a three-member National Defence Council, headed by the Prime Minister. The draft Constitution recognized Hinduism as the country's dominant religion. However, it also guaranteed freedom for religious minorities to practise their beliefs (although restrictions on proselytizing were to remain in force). Under the draft Constitution, the King would be allowed to declare a state of emergency on the advice of the Council of Ministers, but such declarations would have to be approved by the House of Representatives within three months. A crucial clause in the new Constitution required the King 'to obey and protect' the Constitution: under the old regime, the King was considered to be above the Constitution. The draft Constitution was approved by the Council of Ministers on 15 October and sent to the King for his endorsement. However, King Birendra amended the draft in a final effort to retain sovereign authority and full emergency powers. This retrograde action provoked violent protests. The Council of Ministers rejected most of the proposed amendments in the royal counter-draft, but agreed to the King's proposal to establish a Council of State (Raj Parishad), with a standing committee headed by a royal appointee. The 15-member committee was to be composed of eight royal appointees and seven other members, including the Prime Minister, the Ministers of Defence and Foreign Affairs, the Chief Justice of the Supreme Court and the Chief of Army Staff. However, Bhattarai stressed that the formation of this committee would not alter the democratic nature of the new Constitution, since it would not function as a parallel body to the Council of Ministers. He also emphasized that the King would only be permitted to act on judicial, executive and legislative matters on the advice of the Council of Ministers. The new Constitution was officially promulgated by the King on 9 November.

The communist movement in Nepal suffered a set-back in December 1990, when four of the seven constituent members of the ULF broke away from the front, citing their lack of representation in the interim coalition Council of Ministers. However, Sahana Pradhan stated that the three remaining factions would continue to operate as the ULF. In January 1991 two major factions of the CPN (the Marxist and Marxist-Leninist factions) merged to form the CPN (Unified Marxist-Leninist—UML).

The general election was held on 12 May 1991. However, of the 44 political parties that had been registered by the Election Commission, only 20 actually participated. The NCP decided to contest the election alone and not on the basis of an electoral alignment with any of its former Jana Andolan partners. The communists interpreted the NCP's move as the result of an increased understanding between the palace and the NCP on the basis that both wanted to forestall the rise of communism in the country. Consequently, relations between the NCP and the UML became strained and competitive. The general election was not only peaceful, but was also characterized by a high turn-out (65.2% of the electorate). The NCP won a comfortable majority, but it was soundly defeated by the UML in the eastern hill districts and in some parts of the Terai. In Kathmandu, supposedly an NCP stronghold, the party lost all of the seats but one. The UML established itself as the second largest party in the House of Representatives, followed by the United People's Front (UPF), an amalgam of radical, Maoist groups. The Rashtriya Prajatantra Party (Chand) and the Rashtriya Prajatantra Party (Thapa), led by the former Prime Ministers of those names, fared badly in the election, winning only four seats between them. Acting Prime Minister Bhattarai lost his seat in the capital, and was replaced in the premiership by Girija Prasad (G. P.) Koirala, the General Secretary of the NCP and brother of the late B. P. Koirala.

By the end of 1991 unity within the ruling NCP was threatened by growing internal dissent among its leadership, particularly between the senior leader, Ganesh Man Singh, and G. P. Koirala. The Government suffered a further set-back in April 1992 when a *bandh* (general strike), organized by the communist and other opposition parties in Kathmandu in protest against price rises, water shortages and alleged government corruption, resulted in the deaths of at least seven demonstrators following violent clashes with the police. Despite the consequent imposition of curfews in the capital and in the neighbouring town of Lalitpur, the opposition staged a number of anti-Government protest marches and demonstrations during the following week. The success of a second general strike, which was held in early May, demonstrated the continuing strength of the radical left. It brought Kathmandu to a standstill and, unlike the earlier general strike, passed off without violent incidents. Despite the strikes and the rising cost of living, the NCP performed well in the local elections held throughout the country in May and June. However, there were widespread reports of corruption and electoral malpractice.

Under the leadership of G. P. Koirala, the centrist NCP Government shifted to the right. The public image of the monarchy and leading members of the former Panchayat regime were rehabilitated with government support. No charges were brought against senior officials of the former administration for corruption or human rights violations. Replicating the patronage system of the Panchayat regime, the NCP rapidly began to dominate the public administration structure. The ruling party's persistent failure to democratize its internal bodies and the absence of open election to posts in the party leadership met with criticism both within and outside the NCP.

In addition to opposition from the leadership of his own party, G. P. Koirala faced increasing criticism from the opposition parties themselves, which focused on an agreement drawn up by the Prime Minister in December 1991 granting India access to water from the Tanakpur barrage on the Mahakali River, the terms of which were only subsequently revealed to the Nepalese House of Representatives. Alleging that the agreement constituted a treaty affecting national sovereignty, and therefore requiring a two-thirds' majority in the House of Representatives, the opposition launched a campaign calling for the resignation of Koirala on the grounds of unconstitutional behaviour. An indeterminate Supreme Court ruling in December 1992 on Koirala's action only intensified the protest.

In January–February 1993 the national UML congress abandoned much of the party's Marxist dogma and tacitly acknowledged its commitment to working within a democratic multiparty system. However, the untimely deaths of the party's General Secretary, Madan Bhandari, and Politburo member Jiv Raj Ashrit, following a road accident in mid-May, threw the UML into disarray. The rejection by the UML of the findings of a government inquiry, which concluded that the deaths had been accidental, provoked nation-wide protests in support of demands for an independent inquiry into the so-called 'Dhasdunga Incident'. In late May Madhav Kumar Nepal was appointed as the new General Secretary of the UML.

In the mean time, the rehabilitation of officials of the former Panchayat regime continued. In January 1993 the King appointed senior figures of the old administration, including former Prime Ministers Chand and Shrestha, to the 121-member Council of State (Raj Parishad), in a move designed both to rehabilitate former Panchayat officials and to reassert his leadership role over them. In June the right-wing Rashtriya Prajatantra Party (RPP, formed in February 1992, following a merger of the Chand and Thapa factions) held its first national conference in Kathmandu, an event that would have been inconceivable three years previously, when its leaders were forced into hiding by the democracy movement.

In August 1993 the UML signed an agreement with the NCP, providing for the permanent withdrawal of the UML from anti-Government agitation in return for the ruling party's pledge to establish an independent commission to investigate the 'Dhasdunga Incident'. However, the UPF and other left-wing groups continued their campaign of nation-wide general strikes and demonstrations. Further serious rifts became apparent within the ruling NCP when the party's President, K. P. Bhattarai, lost a legislative by-election to the UML candidate in Kathmandu in February 1994; his defeat was widely attributed to G. P. Koirala's public opposition to his candidature. In March the Government survived a vote of no confidence (by 113 votes to 81) presented to the House of Representatives by the UML. The opposition itself suffered from internal dissension in mid-1994 when both the UPF and the CPN (Unity Centre) split into competing factions, while the UML continued to be divided between radical and conservative camps. The crisis within the NCP culminated on 10 July when followers of Ganesh Man Singh withdrew their support for Koirala, who thereby lost his parliamentary majority. Consequently, the Prime Minister offered his resignation, and on the following day the King dissolved the House of Representatives. Koirala was appointed as interim Prime Minister pending the holding of a general election, which was brought forward from mid-1996 to 15 November 1994. At the general election, which attracted a turn-out of 58%, the UML unexpectedly emerged as the single largest party, winning 88 of the 205 seats in the House of Representatives, while the NCP won 85 seats. At the end of the month the UML formed a minority Government under the premiership of its moderate Chairman, Man Mohan Adhikari. In late December the communist Government won a vote of confidence in the House of Representatives (as required by the Constitution for a new administration to continue in power).

On 11 June 1995 the NCP registered a parliamentary motion of no confidence against the communist Government and, in conjunction with the RPP and the Nepali Sadbhavana Party (NSP), submitted a memorandum to King Birendra, staking their claim to form an alternative government. On the recommendation of the Prime Minister, who wished to avert the passage of the motion, the King dissolved the legislature on 13 June and announced that fresh elections were to be held on 23 November. Adhikari and his Council of Ministers were to function as a caretaker Government, pending the general election. In an apparent attempt to win popular support in the run-up to the election, Adhikari's interim administration substantially increased budgetary expenditure and implemented a number of welfare programmes. The opposition, angered by the communists' mode of electioneering, challenged the dissolution of the House of Representatives in the Supreme Court. In a controversial ruling, declared on 28 August, the Supreme Court decided that the dissolution of the lower house on the advice of a minority administration (when a majority coalition was ready to assume power) had, indeed, been unconstitutional. The House of Representatives was consequently reconvened and the election abandoned. The UML Government was defeated in a vote of no confidence on 10 September, by 107 votes to 88. On 12 September a coalition Government, composed of members of the NCP, the RPP and the NSP, and headed by the NCP's parliamentary leader, Sher Bahadur Deuba, was formed.

In early March 1996 the Government introduced a number of security measures following a series of violent clashes between a group of Maoist activists and the police in western Nepal, which resulted in the deaths of at least 11 people (by the end of the year more than 100 people had been killed as a result of the insurgency). The left-wing extremists (many of whom were members of the underground Communist Party of Nepal—Maoist and the UPF) had launched a 'people's revolutionary war' in the hills of Nepal in February, demanding the abolition of the constitutional monarchy and the establishment of a republic. In May G. P. Koirala was elected to replace Bhattarai as President of the NCP; for the first time since its foundation, the party elected its leader by ballot. In early December seven RPP members of the Council of Ministers resigned from their posts and the faction of the party led by Chand withdrew from the ruling coalition; however, the Government, which continued to enjoy the support of the RPP faction led by Thapa, narrowly survived a legislative vote of no confidence (presented by the UML) later that month. In early January 1997 five of the former RPP ministers who had resigned from the Government in the previous month reversed their position and pledged their support for Deuba's administration; a few days later four of these politicians were reinstated in the Government as part of a ministerial reorganization. The Government suffered a set-back at the end of the month when the UML, already the largest party in the House of Representatives, increased its strength from 87 to 90 deputies, following its success in three by-elections. Deuba's administration finally collapsed in early March when it lost a vote of confidence in the House of Representatives. Chand was appointed as the new Prime Minister (for the fourth time) at the head of a coalition Government composed of members of the RPP, the UML, the NSP and the Nepal Workers' and Peasants' Party. However, the new Government seemed unstable from the outset, since the members of the Thapa faction of the RPP refused to support Prime Minister Chand and the ideological differences between the communists and the former pro-monarchists appeared insuperable. Although Chand held the premiership, the UML, as the largest component of the coalition, was responsible for more ministerial posts than the RPP. In May and June the communists replaced the NCP as the country's dominant force in local government, following resounding successes in local elections. However, these elections were marred by violent clashes between supporters of the main political parties in which about 30 people were killed. In mid-June more than 10,000 NCP supporters demonstrated in Kathmandu in protest over alleged electoral irregularities on the part of the UML during the recent polls. During 1997 the UML suffered from factional infighting, with a major rift developing between Deputy Prime Minister Bam Dev Gautam and the General Secretary of the party, Madhav Kumar Nepal. This factionalism served to destabilize the coalition Government further. In August a strike organized by an alliance of left-wing groups (known as the National Democratic Front) in protest at the rise in the price of fuel and a proposed anti-terrorist law brought Kathmandu and surrounding towns to a standstill. In the following month an anti-defection bill, the aim of which was to prevent politicians from deserting their own party and thus to bring stability to Nepal's politics, was unanimously approved by the House of Representatives.

On 4 October 1997 the Government lost a parliamentary vote of no confidence tabled by the NCP. A few days later King Birendra appointed Thapa, the President of the RPP, to replace Chand as Prime Minister. A new coalition Government, comprising members of the RPP and the NSP, took office on the following day. In December Prime Minister Thapa expanded the Council of Ministers in a reshuffle that introduced members of the NCP and a number of independents into the coalition. In January 1998 Nepal was once again faced with political upheaval when Thapa recommended to the King that he dissolve the House of Representatives and set a date for mid-term elections. The Prime Minister presented the petition for fresh polls following a decision by the UML and dissident members of the RPP (including Chand) to introduce a parliamentary vote of no confidence against the Government. Uncertain as to how to act in this political impasse, the King referred the matter to the Supreme Court (the first time a Nepalese monarch had ever done so). In early February the Court advised King Birendra to convene a special session of the House of Representatives to discuss a no confidence motion against Thapa's Government. Although the Supreme Court's advice was not binding, the King called the parliamentary session. However, the no confidence motion, which was presented on 20 February, was narrowly defeated. Meanwhile, in mid-January Chand and nine other rebel deputies were expelled from the RPP; they immediately re-established a breakaway faction known as the RPP (Chand). In March the UML suffered a serious reverse when about one-half of the party's parliamentary deputies formed a breakaway faction entitled the Communist Party of Nepal (Marxist-Leninist) (ML). Bam Dev Gautam was unanimously elected as the new party's leader. The creation of the new party left the UML with 49 deputies, while the ML claimed the support of 40 deputies.

Under an agreement reached in October 1997 when Thapa assumed power, the Prime Minister was to transfer the leadership of the coalition Government to the NCP within an agreed time frame. By early April 1998, however, Thapa appeared reluctant to relinquish his post, and the NCP threatened to withdraw support for the Government unless the Prime Minister resigned immediately. Thapa tendered his resignation, and the President of the NCP, G. P. Koirala, was appointed Prime Minister in mid-April, taking office with only two other ministers. After obtaining a parliamentary vote of confidence, by 144 votes to four, the Prime Minister substantially expanded his Council of Ministers. Koirala stated that among the top priorities of the one-party minority Government would be the tackling of the Maoist insurgency (which had escalated in recent months). In August, in a seeming attempt to strengthen his own precarious administration and to encourage the UML's communist rivals, the Prime Minister invited the ML to join in alliance with the NCP and to form a coalition government. A new coalition administration was consequently established on 26 August (with the NCP retaining the most important ministries), giving Prime Minister Koirala an adequate parliamentary majority. Meanwhile, the 'people's war' waged by the Maoist activists in the hills of west Nepal gathered momentum. In May the Government launched a large-scale police operation in an effort to curb the guerrilla violence.

In December 1998 the ML withdrew from the coalition Government, alleging that its ruling partner, the NCP, had failed to implement a number of agreements drawn up between the two parties and other political groups in August. Prime Minister G. P. Koirala tendered his resignation, but was asked to head a new coalition Council of Ministers, which was to hold power in an acting capacity pending the holding of a general election. On the recommendation of the Prime Minister, the King appointed a new coalition administration, comprising members of the NCP, the UML and the NSP, and, for the first time in eight years, a nominee of the King, on 25 December. In mid-January 1999 the acting Government won a convincing vote of confidence in the House of Representatives, and on the following day the King dissolved the legislature in preparation for the forthcoming general election.

In late April 1999 the UML suffered a set-back when its veteran leader and former Prime Minister, Man Mohan Adhikari, died during the electoral campaign. In May the NCP won an outright majority in the general election (held over two rounds), securing 110 of the 205 seats in the lower house; the UML obtained 68 seats and the RPP (Thapa) took 11 seats, while the ML and the RPP (Chand) both failed to win a single seat. Voting was conducted relatively peacefully, according to government sources, despite threats by the Maoist insurgents to disrupt the electoral process. A new Council of Ministers, headed by the veteran NCP leader, K. P. Bhattarai, and composed solely of NCP members, was appointed at the end of the month. In late June the UML won all six seats in elections to the National Assembly, and in August Dr Mohammad Mohasin of the RPP was elected Chairman of the upper house.

In late November 1999, in an effort to resolve the Maoist insurgency, which, according to government sources, now affected (moderately to severely) 31 of Nepal's 75 districts and had led to the deaths of more than 1,000 people, the Prime Minister offered to grant the guerrillas an amnesty and various rehabilitation measures if they surrendered their arms and entered into negotiations with the Government. In response, the insurgents (who were estimated to number 5,000–6,000 and to have the support of about 8,000 sympathizers) stated that they were not prepared to enter into peace talks until arrest warrants issued against their leaders were withdrawn, official investigations were carried out into alleged extrajudicial killings of suspected militants by the police, and imprisoned activists were released. In an attempt to facilitate the peace process, the Government established a six-member high-level negotiation commission under the convenorship of former Prime Minister Sher Bahadur Deuba, which was charged with finding a solution to the Maoist situation that met with the approval of all political parties and the insurgents themselves.

In mid-December 1999 the ruling NCP, despite a number of by-election victories, was once again beset by internecine strife when about 80 pro-Koirala legislators initiated an attempt to oust (by means of a petition) the Prime Minister from his position as the NCP's parliamentary party leader (which would automatically lead to his removal from the premiership). Koirala had initially been supportive of Bhattarai's premiership, but had since become a vociferous critic of his rival's administration, particularly with regard to the Government's perceived mismanagement of the Maoist crisis. In February 2000 a minor reorganization of the Council of Ministers took place, which included the appointment of Ram Chandra Poudel, a former Speaker of the lower house, as Deputy Prime Minister; the ministerial reshuffle was prompted by the earlier resignation of the Minister of Finance, Mahesh Acharya, following a disagreement with the Prime Minister over the appointment of the new Governor of the Central Bank. A few days after the government reorganization, the Minister of Education, Yog Prasad Upadhyaya, resigned in protest at the appointment of Poudel as Deputy Prime Minister. The political unrest culminated in the registration of a vote of no confidence by 58 dissident NCP legislators against Prime Minister Bhattarai; this move led to the immediate resignation of 11 government ministers. The NCP's parliamentary party was scheduled to vote on the no-confidence motion in late February; however, following the reaching of a secret agreement between the Prime Minister and the NCP President, G. P. Koirala, including Bhattarai's reported assurance that he would stand down voluntarily within two weeks, the proposal was withdrawn. A second motion of no confidence in Bhattarai was registered by 69 predominantly pro-Koirala legislators in the NCP secretariat in mid-March. Under such pressure, Bhattarai tendered his resignation to the King. It was announced that G. P. Koirala was to be the new Prime Minister (for the fourth time), following his election as parliamentary party leader of the NCP; this election process replaced the party's traditional method of choosing a parliamentary leader through consensus. Koirala and a new Council of Ministers were sworn in by the King on 22 March, and vowed to continue the basic programmes and policies that the previous NCP Government had adopted. In May a Human Rights Commission was formed following accusations by various bodies that both the security forces and the Maoist guerrillas had committed human rights violations, including murder and torture.

In early April 2000 Prime Minister Koirala activated the National Defence Council, which, according to the Constitution, comprised the Prime Minister, the Minister of Defence and the Commander-in-Chief of the Royal Nepal Army, to resolve the Maoist crisis. In comparison to the inadequately trained and poorly armed police force, which had suffered numerous casualties, the army was much better equipped to deal with the insurgency, and Koirala expressed his wish to mobilize the armed forces in the ongoing fight against militant activity. The possibility of the deployment of the armed forces met with immediate criticism from various Nepalese human rights groups, which claimed that mobilization of the army would lead to an escalation in corruption.

At the end of August 2000 the Maoist crisis worsened. During two Maoist attacks in Dolpa and Lamjung, 24 police officers were killed and 44 were injured. The Royal Nepal Army was criticized for failing to intervene to protect the police from insurgents. The Minister of Home Affairs, Govinda Raj Joshi, resigned after admitting his failure to 'maintain law and order in the country'. The Prime Minister responded to the confusion over the command and control structure of the army by giving Mahesh Acharya, the Minister of Finance, the additional portfolio of defence. G. P. Koirala had hitherto held charge of this portfolio, but it had become clear that the Government and army needed an independent defence minister, clarification of the army's ambiguous role and the development of a procedure for mobilizing the army (such matters not being incorporated in the 1991 Constitution). It was later decided that the Government would employ a dual approach: using the army, as well as encouraging negotiations, in order to resolve the Maoist crisis. In the mean time, the RPP (Chand) again merged with the RPP (Thapa); the former was officially closed down in late 2000.

At the end of October 2000 the first direct unofficial negotiations began between the Government and the Communist Party of Nepal (Maoist)—CPN (M); however, they were short-lived, and the violence resumed in early November. In the same month the high-level commission charged with finding a solution to the Maoist crisis produced a report advising the Government and Maoist insurgents to cease violence and participate in negotiations. The report also recommended that the Government improve and modernize its security forces. The UML leader, who had earlier held negotiations with the insurgents, ruled out any alliance with the CPN (M) until it abandoned the use of force.

In January 2001 the Minister for Tourism and Civil Aviation, Tarani Datta Chataut, resigned following a controversial agreement to lease an Austrian aircraft to the Royal Nepal Airlines Corporation. In early February leading opposition parties issued a memorandum to the Prime Minister, demanding his resignation over the aircraft deal and also the worsening security situation. Koirala strongly denied his involvement in the leasing of the Austrian aircraft. The King then approved a reorganization of the Council of Ministers, on the recommendation of Prime Minister Koirala. However, shortly after the new administration was announced, two ministers withdrew their names, criticizing Koirala for making decisions without consulting other senior leaders. Palten Gurung later reneged on his decision, but Khum Bahadur Khadka refused to join the Council of Ministers. In March the Prime Minister faced increasing opposition from within and outside his party. Further ministerial resignations followed. The opposition continued to disrupt parliamentary proceedings, and, as a result, the King prorogued the National Assembly and House of Representatives in early April. At the end of the month the anti-corruption commission cleared the Prime Minister of involvement in the controversial aircraft agreement, but filed cases against 10 other people, including the former minister, Chataut. At the same time, Koirala was accused of accepting bribes in another aircraft deal. The opposition continued to demand his resignation and organized a nation-wide strike in protest against the Government's alleged misuse of power.

On 1 June 2001 King Birendra, Queen Aishwarya and six other members of the royal family were shot dead; the heir to the throne, Crown Prince Dipendra, was gravely wounded. Another family member, Dhirendra Shah, died later in hospital. Initial reports suggested that Prince Dipendra had shot members of his family before shooting himself, following a dispute between himself and his mother regarding his intentions to marry Devyani Rani (the daughter of a prominent Nepalese politician), of whom the Queen disapproved. However, Prince Gyanendra, the deceased King Birendra's brother, issued a statement claiming that the deaths were the result of an accidental discharge of an automatic weapon. Immediately after the incident Prince Dipendra was pronounced King, and Prince Gyanendra was appointed regent. On 4 June King Dipendra died and was succeeded by Prince Gyanendra. These events caused considerable unrest in Kathmandu, and a curfew was imposed. In the mean time, rumours about the killings began to spread. Few believed the statement given by Gyanendra. Some suggested that Maoist insurgents were to blame, while others claimed that India was responsible. Following his accession, King Gyanendra established a commission to investigate the deaths. The commission, comprising the Chief Justice, K. P. Upadhyaya, and the Speaker of the House of Representatives, T. Ranabhat, duly concluded that Dipendra had been responsible for the shootings and that at the time had been under the influence of drugs and alcohol. King Gyanendra bestowed the title of Queen on his wife, Princess Komal, but did not declare his son the Crown Prince until the end of October, owing to the latter's unpopularity among the public, caused by his profligate behaviour.

In late June 2001 elections to 16 seats in the National Assembly took place. The UML won eight seats, bringing its total to 23 and rendering it the largest bloc in the chamber. In June–July Maoist leaders, taking advantage of the discontent in Nepal, intensified their activities. On 13 July the Deputy Prime Minister, Ram Chandra Poudel, resigned, owing to disagreements with the Prime Minister over government policy towards the insurgency. Several days later a senior Maoist leader declared that he would enter negotiations with the Government on the condition that the Prime Minister resigned. On 19 July Prime Minister Koirala stood down, citing his failure to curb the Maoist insurgency and long-standing corruption allegations. A few days later the NCP elected former premier Sher Bahadur Deuba as its new leader; King Gyanendra appointed Deuba as Prime Minister on the same day and a new Council of Ministers was sworn in on 26 July. Prime Minister Deuba retained a number of Koirala's former ministers in an effort to ensure stability and initially took personal charge of many of the more important portfolios.

Immediately after his appointment Prime Minister Deuba persuaded the Maoist leaders to reciprocate his offer of a cease-fire and agree to enter into dialogue. Prior to the negotiations, both sides took part in a series of confidence-building measures: the Maoist activists released 31 kidnapped police officers, and the Government set free more than 30 Maoist leaders and published the names of 273 guerrillas who remained in prison. At the same time Parliament passed legislation to establish an armed police force and to develop the co-ordination of regional development and security. The Government released a further 68 insurgents after the first two rounds of negotiations in August and September 2001. However, despite the cease-fire, Maoist insurgents continued to carry out violent acts. During the peace talks tens of thousands of people held demonstrations against the fighting. The third round of negotiations, which took place in November, ended in failure, owing to the Maoists' continued demand for the dissolution of the Constitution, the establishment of an interim government, the election of a constituent assembly and, ultimately, a republic. The Government, in contrast, was prepared to offer a much less radical set of changes. Two days later the leader of the CPN (M), Pushpa Kamal Dahal (better known under his pseudonym, 'Prachanda'—'The Fierce One'), announced the end of the cease-fire. The Maoists established a parallel central government, the 'United People's Revolutionary Government', and resumed their violent campaign. The Maoists set up parallel governments in 40 of the country's 75 districts, and established direct rule in 22 districts in western Nepal. The violence escalated; on 26 November the King declared a state of emergency and authorized, for the first time, the deployment of the army to curb the insurgency. The King termed the Maoists as 'terrorists' and promulgated the Terrorist and Disruptive Activities Ordinance 2001, which sanctioned a number of counter-terrorist measures, including the suspension of civil liberties and the imposition of media restrictions. In mid-December Prime Minister Deuba declared that he would not resume negotiations with the Maoists until they had surrendered their arms.

Meanwhile, in early September 2001 the Government implemented a radical land reform programme, which was designed to help poor, landless farmers. The programme was supported by the UML, but opposed by smaller parties. Major landowners who risked losing part of their land because of the programme opposed the limit to the size of individual landholdings. In mid-August Deuba announced that discrimination against Dalits (or 'untouchables') would henceforth be illegal and pledged to pass legislation ending the caste system. A national commission for Dalit welfare and a National Women's Commission were also to be established.

In January 2002 the Nepal Rastra Bank 'froze' the bank accounts of individuals and organizations associated with Maoist militants. In mid-February Maoist insurgents launched their heaviest-ever offensive against government outposts. More than 150 people, mainly soldiers and police officers, were killed in the fighting. In response to the attacks, the army was instructed to use offensive as well as defensive measures to combat the insurgency. On 21 February the legislature voted to extend the state of emergency for three months. Although the opposition criticized the Government for its handling of the insurgency and for failing to react to warnings that major attacks were imminent, it voted for the extension after the Prime Minister agreed to establish social and economic development programmes in poor rural areas where Maoists were active, and ensured the fair use of the emergency powers.

In the mean time, in mid-February 2002 the UML and its breakaway faction, the ML, merged. The merger of the more moderate communist parties was regarded largely as a move to counter the influence of the Maoist insurgents. Strikes occurred in March, severely affecting businesses and schools. In its first annual report, the Human Rights Commission of Nepal accused the Maoist insurgents of committing serious human rights abuses. The commission also criticized the Government for allegedly violating human rights. In early April the Government reduced the controversial restrictions it had imposed on the media and political parties as part of the state of emergency. The violent campaign escalated in mid-April, leading to hundreds of fatalities. In May Deuba tabled a parliamentary motion proposing an extension of the six-month state of emergency (which was due to expire on 25 May), prompting strong opposition from within and outside his party. Members of the governing NCP, led by former premier G. P. Koirala, accused Deuba of not consulting them before recommending an extension and urged the Government to withdraw its parliamentary motion. The rift in the party led King Gyanendra to dissolve unexpectedly the House of Representatives on 22 May, on the recommendation of the Prime Minister. A general election was scheduled to take place on 13 November, and the incumbent Government was instructed to rule the country in the interim. Political leaders strongly condemned this decision. On 23 May Deuba was suspended from his party and three days later was expelled from the NCP for three years. In the mean time, three ministers, including the Minister of Finance, resigned in protest at the calling of early elections. In late May King Gyanendra extended the state of emergency by three months. Meanwhile, in early May the army launched a heavy attack against Maoist insurgents in Rolpa district, resulting in the deaths of more than 500 guerrillas, according to government sources. A series of counter-attacks and attacks ensued, leading to further hundreds of fatalities; by the end of May some reports estimated that more than 4,000 people had been killed since the beginning of the insurgency. On 9 May the Maoist leader made an offer of a one-month cease-fire by e-mail to newspapers in Kathmandu; Deuba promptly rejected the proposal, repeating his request for the insurgents to renounce violence.

In mid-June 2002 the NCP officially split during a 'general convention' held by the Deuba faction. Eventually, in mid-September the Election Commission recognized the faction led by G. P. Koirala as the official NCP. Several days later Deuba's minority breakaway faction registered as a new political party, the Nepali Congress Party—Democratic (NCP—D). Meanwhile, in April the Nepal Sadbhavana Party split into two factions and in July two communist parties, the National People's Front and the UPF, merged to form the People's Front Nepal (Janamorcha Nepal).

In the mean time, the state of emergency expired in late August 2002 and the Maoists consequently intensified their violent campaign. In mid-September the Government rejected Prachanda's offer of a cease-fire, on the grounds that it lacked credibility. In early October Deuba requested King Gyanendra to postpone the general election by one year, citing the deteriorating law and order situation. However, King Gyanendra dismissed the Prime Minister and the interim Council of Ministers for reportedly failing to organize the election. The King assumed executive power and postponed indefinitely parliamentary elections scheduled for November. In October King Gyanendra appointed a nine-member interim Government, headed by the former premier and monarchist Lok Bahadur Chand. The NCP, UML and legal experts condemned the dismissal of Deuba and his Government and the establishment of a new Council of Ministers as unconstitutional. In mid-November the King disregarded demands by political parties to create a new government composed of their members, instead reorganizing and expanding the interim Council of Ministers to include a former UML member, businessmen and independents. At the same time, amid continuing violence and disruption, the Deputy Prime Minister stated that the interim Government was prepared to enter negotiations with the CPN (M) and would consider the latter's demand for an elected constituent assembly. In December the human rights organization Amnesty International issued a damning report on the human rights situation in Nepal since the collapse of peace talks in November 2001. The army and Armed Police Force were severely criticized for the reported 'unprecedented levels' of human rights abuses, including torture, arbitrary detention and deaths in custody. In addition, the report accused Maoist insurgents of torturing and killing captives, taking hostages and recruiting children. The report claimed that nearly one-half of the 4,366 people who had died in the conflict since late 2001 were civilians, killed by both security forces and Maoists.

In January 2003 suspected Maoist militants shot dead the chief of the Armed Police Force, Inspector-General Krishna Mohan Shrestha, in Kathmandu; his wife and bodyguard were also killed. Three days later the CPN (M) and the Government announced an immediate cease-fire and agreed to resume peace negotiations after the Government agreed to declassify Maoist activists as terrorists, to withdraw rewards offered for the arrest of Maoist leaders and to cancel international police warrants issued for the guerrilla leaders. In February a series of informal talks took place; at the end of the month the Maoists presented two conditions for the resumption of formal negotiations: the release of Maoist prisoners and the return of the army to barracks. A 22-point code of conduct was signed by the chief government negotiator and Minister of Physical Planning and Construction, Narayan Singh Pun, and the Maoist leader, Baburam Bhattarai, in mid-March. According to the code, the Government would release prisoners gradually and give Maoists equal access to the state-controlled media; however, there was no mention of the army moving back to barracks. Both sides also agreed formally to cease hostilities. The following day a Maoist negotiator declared that, while a communist republic continued to be the CPN (M)'s goal, the militant group would comply with the public's decision on the future of the monarchy. In the mean time, Chand continued to prove unsuccessful in his attempts to involve political parties in the peace process and therefore to form a broad-based negotiating team. The country's political parties and the Maoists questioned the interim Government's authority to negotiate with the Maoists.

The interim Government and Maoist representatives commenced formal negotiations at the end of April 2003; it was reported that the CPN (M) demanded the release of Maoist prisoners, participation in an interim government and the creation of a constituent assembly, but did not include the abolition of the monarchy in its agenda. At the second round of peace talks, which took place in May, the Government agreed to release several Maoist detainees and to restrict army troops to within 5 km of their barracks. Both sides also achieved consensus on the composition of a committee to monitor the code of conduct guiding the cease-fire. The third round of negotiations, which eventually took place on 17–19 August, ended in impasse over the Maoists' demand for an elected assembly to draft a new constitution. Although the two sides agreed to meet again the following week, on 27 August Prachanda ended the seven-month cease-fire and withdrew from the peace process. On the following day the Government reclassified the insurgents as 'terrorists' after violent activity resumed. Thousands of people marched in Kathmandu at the end of August to urge the Government and the CPN (M) to resume peace talks.

In the mean time, at the end of May 2003 Prime Minister Chand resigned in response to pressure from leaders of the major political parties. The parties (the NCP, UML, Nepal Workers' and Peasants' Party, Nepali Sadbhavan Party—Anandi Devi, and People's Front Nepal), with the support of students, had held frequent demonstrations against the Chand Government and the King. On 4 June the King appointed the monarchist and former premier Surya Bahadur Thapa as Prime Minister, rejecting the nomination by the five opposition parties of Madhav Kumar Nepal, the General Secretary of the UML. One week later the King appointed a new interim Council of Ministers, which was composed entirely of members of the monarchist RPP. Thapa had invited M. K. Nepal and Deuba to join the Government, but the leading politicians refused, maintaining that Thapa's appointment had been unconstitutional. Opposition parties held a large demonstration in Kathmandu, demanding Thapa's resignation, the reinstatement of the legislature and the establishment of an all-party government. In late August Nepal's major political parties refused Thapa's appeal for co-operation, instead pledging to launch a new series of nation-wide protests demanding the return of parliamentary democracy. On 1 September, however, the Government banned all demonstrations or public gatherings of five or more people in the Kathmandu valley, citing fears of infiltration by Maoist guerrillas. None the less, about a week later more than 1,000 pro-democracy protesters, including former premier G. P. Koirala, were arrested for defying the ban and taking part in a demonstration.

The CPN (M) fully resumed its violent campaign in September 2003. In the same month it organized a three-day general strike, which severely affected businesses, transport services and schools throughout most of the country. In mid-September the police filed charges against 21 members of the CPN (M), including Prachanda and Baburam Bhattarai, for the murder in January of the Inspector-General of the Armed Police Force and two others (see above). According to a report published at the end of October by the Nepal human rights group the Informal Sector Service Centre (INSEC), more than 1,000 people had died in the violence since the collapse of the cease-fire. Meanwhile, Prachanda had issued a statement declaring that the CPN (M) would, henceforth, target US-supported organizations instead of infrastructure targets. In response, the US Administration announced at the end of the month that it had proscribed the CPN (M), listing the group as a threat to national security (the USA was already providing the Nepalese army with military assistance for its campaign against the Maoist insurgents).

In mid-November 2003 it was reported that a high-ranking Nepalese army officer had died in the violence. At the end of the month the international police agency Interpol issued arrest warrants for 11 senior CPN (M) officials, including Prachanda and Baburam Bhattarai. In mid-December the Government announced that it would grant an amnesty to anyone who surrendered by mid-February 2004; this message was dismissed by Maoist leaders. In January the Maoists announced the formation of autonomous people's governments in 10 districts under their control. At the end of the month the CPN (M) stated that it would give priority to development in these areas, and that representatives of the King and the USA were banned from operating in districts under Maoist influence. At the same time, the Nepalese army announced that 15 soldiers had been convicted of human rights violations and other criminal activities, and had been sentenced to up to six years' imprisonment; six other soldiers had been dismissed from the army for illegal activity committed during military operations against Maoist guerrillas. It was reported in mid-February that more than 500 Maoist militants had surrendered to security forces since the launch of the amnesty in December 2003; the deadline of the amnesty was extended to mid-April 2004. The violence increased, meanwhile, and the Maoists organized a further number of disruptive nation-wide general strikes. The number of people killed in the eight-year 'people's war' had risen sharply to more than 9,130 by mid-March, of whom more than 1,500 had died since the collapse of the cease-fire in August 2003. It was also reported that more than 250 people had 'disappeared' since August.

Meanwhile, it was reported in mid-November 2003 that the central committee of the RPP had requested Prime Minister Thapa to resign for failing to form an all-party government following his appointment. However, Thapa maintained the support of the King and was thus able to remain in his position. In January 2004 there were almost daily student-led pro-republic protests held in Kathmandu. At the end of the month the five main opposition parties issued a joint statement offering formal support to the student movement. This action provided evidence that the NCP, a committed supporter of the constitutional monarchy, and the UML were reconsidering their views towards the monarchy. In early February, as part of a two-week tour around the troubled mid-western region, King Gyanendra gave a public address in the city of Nepalganj. During the speech, the King appealed for an end to the insurgency and appeared to seek an active role in governing democracy. Opposition parties criticized the King, claiming that he was not committed to multi-party democracy and the constitutional monarchy, and pledged to intensify their protests against 'regression'. Prime Minister Thapa, meanwhile, announced that the interim Government was preparing to hold a general election in the near future. However, the opposition maintained that the Thapa Government was illegitimate and should be replaced by an all-party government, which would, in turn, hold elections and enter a peace process with the Maoist militants. In March the leaders of the five main opposition parties announced that a constitutional monarchy had not been successful and that, henceforth, their movement would be directed at achieving the establishment of a republic. Meanwhile, in the same month King Gyanendra reorganized and expanded the Council of Ministers. In early May the Prime Minister tendered his resignation as a result of the continuing political impasse. The resignation prompted the collapse of the entire Government; King Gyanendra authorized Thapa to remain in office in an acting capacity pending the formation of a new administration. Later in the same month the CPN (M) called a three-day general strike, which disrupted communications throughout the country and brought Kathmandu to a standstill. Violence during the strike resulted in the deaths of at least 45 people.

In June 2004 King Gyanendra appointed Sher Bahadur Deuba as Prime Minister for the third time. Several days later the King appointed two members of the NCP—D to the new Council of Ministers, in which Deuba held the majority of portfolios. The Council was expanded to 31 members in the following month and incorporated ministers from the four-party coalition (comprising the NCP—D, the UML, the RPP and the NSP) that had been formed following the resignation of Prime Minister Thapa.

In August 2004, for the first time since it had launched its campaign in 1996, the CPN (M) instigated a blockade of Kathmandu, stating that it would be of indefinite duration and would last until the Government released all remaining Maoist prisoners and initiated an investigation into the fates of Maoist activists who had reportedly died while in custody. The blockade was lifted after a week, reportedly in response to pleas from ordinary people, who were suffering significant hardship as the prices of food and other essential items had risen steeply. In response, at the end of the month the Government announced the formation of a peace committee, headed by Prime Minister Deuba, which, it was hoped, would commence peace talks with the Maoists in an attempt to end the ongoing insurgency. However, the rebels rejected a subsequent offer of peace negotiations. In September a riot in Kathmandu resulted in the deaths of two protesters, who were shot dead by police attempting to control the demonstrations (an estimated 3,000 demonstrators had gathered to protest against the murder of 12 Nepalese hostages by Iraqi insurgents during the US-led campaign in Iraq).

In October 2004 the Government agreed to observe a cease-fire that had been proposed by the CPN (M) for the duration of the Hindu religious festival of Dasain. Both sides were reported to have adhered, for the most part, to the halt in military operations during the nine-day festival. In the following month Prime Minister Deuba set the rebels a deadline of 13 January 2005 to commence peace talks with the Government. Deuba stated that if the Maoists did not agree to begin discussions, he would ensure that legislative elections were held by mid-April 2005, using the mandate that had been granted to him by King Gyanendra. However, Prachanda later rejected the proposed deadline. The rejection reportedly led to disagreement within the Government over the feasibility of holding elections amidst the ongoing insurgency. The violence had intensified following the expiry of the short-lived cease-fire in late October 2004. The Government was destabilized further in November when the founding President of the RPP, former Prime Minister Thapa, announced that he intended to launch a new political party, effectively creating a split within the RPP.

In February 2005 the political situation in Nepal seriously deteriorated when King Gyanendra abruptly dismissed Prime Minister Deuba and his Government, declared an indefinite state of emergency in the kingdom and announced that, henceforth, he would rule Nepal directly. All communications links into and out of Nepal were severed temporarily, censorship was imposed on the media and former ministers were placed under house arrest. The King claimed that his actions were a result of the Prime Minister's failure to halt the Maoist insurgency and to hold legislative elections in the country. In an attempt to prevent protests, the King ordered the detention of large numbers of political activists. Maoist rebels subsequently instigated a two-week blockade of national highways in protest at the King's actions. Shortly after he had assumed supreme power, the King appointed a new, 10-member Council of Ministers, under his chairmanship. Former Prime Ministers Dr Tulsi Giri and Kirti Nidhi Bista were appointed to serve as Vice-Chairmen. King Gyanendra's assumption of power met with an unfavourable international response, with Nepal's key allies, India and the United Kingdom, suspending military aid to the country and several nations recalling their ambassadors from Nepal in protest.

In March 2005 Thapa announced the foundation of his new political party, the Rashtriya Janashakti Party (RJP—National People's Power Party). In the same month several political leaders who had been detained following the royal coup were released from house arrest, including former Prime Minister Deuba. Meanwhile, protests against the King's actions, orchestrated by an opposition alliance comprising five of the country's main political parties, gathered momentum. At the same time, the Maoist insurgency intensified, with several clashes taking place between rebels and government troops. The state of emergency was lifted at the end of April, although there were few indications that normal political activity would be able to resume. Public meetings and demonstrations continued to be prohibited, and police powers of arrest and detention were extended. Meanwhile, former Prime Minister Deuba was re-arrested and charged with corruption offences by the newly established Royal Commission for Corruption Control (RCCC). Deuba refused to acknowledge the legitimacy of the body.

In May 2005 seven political parties, including the NCP, announced a joint agenda for the restoration of democracy in Nepal, calling for King Gyanendra to end his period of direct rule and for the House of Representatives, which had been dissolved in 2002, to be recalled. Later that month the alliance organized a demonstration in Kathmandu in protest against the King. In June Maoist rebels were responsible for the detonation of a land-mine under a bus in the southern district of Chitwan, which resulted in the deaths of 39 civilians. The Maoists subsequently apologized for the attack, claiming that the bomb had been intended to target security forces, and announced that, henceforth, all attacks on unarmed civilians would be suspended.

In June 2005 Deuba and six of his former government colleagues were cleared by the RCCC of charges relating to the misappropriation of money from the Prime Minister's Relief Fund. However, Deuba remained in custody pending a further judgment against him. In the following month Deuba, along with four other defendants, was convicted of charges of embezzlement relating to the issuing of a water contract and sentenced to a two-year prison term. Meanwhile, a reorganization and expansion of the Council of Ministers was carried out.

In August 2005, as opposition to King Gyanendra's ongoing direct rule intensified, it was announced that the seven-party alliance had decided to begin talks with the CPN (M) and to plan joint protests against the King. It cited positive gestures by the Maoist group, such as its suspension of attacks on unarmed civilians, as the reason for co-operation, having consistently maintained that it would be willing to hold discussions with the rebels only if they renounced violence. In September the Maoists announced a three-month unilateral cease-fire, an offer welcomed by the international community but one to which the Government responded cautiously. By the middle of that month, according to the INSEC, 12,809 people had been killed since the beginning of the 'people's war' in 1996. In October 2005 the Government declared that elections would take place to Nepal's 58 municipal councils in February 2006. The seven-party alliance announced that it intended to boycott the polls, although two of its members, the RPP and the RJP, later claimed that they had not yet decided whether to participate. Shortly afterwards King Gyanendra stated that elections to the House of Representatives would take place in April 2007. In November 2005, following talks with the CPN (M), the opposition alliance announced that it had reached a 12-point agreement with the rebels intended to restore democracy to Nepal. The agreement included a boycott of the February 2006 municipal elections and the election of a constituent assembly, the latter being a long-standing Maoist demand.

In December 2005 an extensive reorganization of the Council of Ministers took place, in which eight ministers were dismissed and several ministers from the RPP and RJP were appointed. In the same month the CPN (M) announced that it would extend its cease-fire by one month. However, in January 2006 the Maoists stated that the cease-fire had come to an end, owing to the lack of response from the Government, which had continued to authorize offensive operations against them. The insurgency subsequently intensified. In the following month the municipal elections were held, taking place in only 36 of the 58 municipal councils owing to an insufficient number of candidates and against the background of a four-day general strike, which was co-ordinated by the Maoists and was intended to disrupt the polls. Turn-out reached an estimated 20% of registered voters, according to official figures, although the major opposition parties, which boycotted the polls, claimed that the figure was significantly lower. Later that month the RCCC was outlawed after the Supreme Court ruled that its orders were not valid. Former Prime Minister Deuba was subsequently freed from prison, having been convicted of corruption offences by the body in the previous year. In March the Maoists instigated an indefinite blockade of Kathmandu in another attempt to force King Gyanendra to end his period of direct rule. Meanwhile, the Government offered an amnesty to any Maoist rebels who surrendered before a mid-June 2006 deadline.

In April 2006 the opposition alliance called a nation-wide general strike. Mass demonstrations followed, in response to which the Government announced the imposition of a 'shoot on sight' curfew. As thousands of protesters defied the curfew and violent clashes ensued, King Gyanendra's position appeared increasingly untenable. Following almost three weeks of popular demonstrations, the King offered to permit the opposition alliance to name a new Prime Minister. However, this offer was rejected and the protests continued to escalate. Several days later, in accordance with opposition demands, the King announced that he would reinstate Parliament, thus quelling the unrest. The CPN (M) rejected the royal offer and vowed to continue its insurgency, accusing the political parties of betraying the 12-point agreement. It did, none the less, agree to observe a three-month cease-fire. The opposition alliance subsequently nominated former Prime Minister G. P. Koirala to lead a new Government. The House of Representatives formally convened later in that month and approved legislation enabling the establishment of a constituent assembly to redraft the country's Constitution. The formation of a complete Council of Ministers, announced by Koirala at the beginning of May, was delayed for three weeks owing to disagreement over the distribution of ministerial portfolios among the political parties. Appointments included K. P. Sharma Oli of the UML as Deputy Prime Minister and Minister of Foreign Affairs, and the NCP's Krishna Sitaula and Dr Ram Sharan Mahat as Minister of Home Affairs and Minister of Finance respectively; Koirala himself assumed responsibility for the portfolios of defence, health and population, and industry, commerce and supplies. In June Koirala expanded the Council of Ministers to include representatives of a further two members of the seven-party alliance—namely the People's Front Nepal and the NSP. At this stage all of the seven-party alliance members were represented in the Government, with the exception of the Nepal Workers' and Peasants' Party.

On 3 May 2006 the Council of Ministers had announced a cease-fire with the CPN (M), offering to declassify the group as a terrorist organization and to abandon terrorism charges in exchange for the holding of peace talks. According to government figures, 467 of an estimated 1,000 Maoist prisoners had been freed by 25 May. Despite the Maoists' assertions that they would not enter into negotiations until all their prisoners had been released, and their insistence that the formation of a constituent assembly was subject to the abolition of the existing Constitution, legislature and monarchy, the Government and the CPN (M) engaged in a preliminary round of discussions on 26 May, establishing a code of conduct for the duration of peace talks. Meanwhile, on 12 May four former ministers, including Kamal Thapa, the former Minister of Home Affairs, and Ramesh Nath Pandey, the former Minister of Finance, were arrested and charged with use of excessive force in containing the April pro-democracy protests (three of the four detainees were later released on the orders of the Supreme Court). On 18 May the House of Representatives passed a resolution divesting the King of his role as Commander-in-Chief of the Army, his authority to make military appointments and nominate an heir, and his legal immunity and exemption from taxes. Nepal was pronounced a secular state in an attempt to extricate the concept of a divinely instituted monarchy from the national ideology. The transfer of power away from the monarchy continued in June: the King was no longer able to veto legislation, he was not required to open and close parliamentary sessions, and he lost the authority to announce government policy.

In mid-June 2006 talks between Koirala and Prachanda in Kathmandu led to the announcement that the CPN (M) would be included in a new interim government, which was to oversee elections for a constituent assembly. At Koirala's request, a UN team arrived in Nepal at the end of July to determine weapons management strategies for the Nepalese army and the People's Liberation Army (PLA) of the Maoists; Koirala reportedly deemed the decommissioning of weapons as a prerequisite of the entry of the CPN (M) into government. Also at the end of July, Prachanda extended the cease-fire by three months. On 9 August

Koirala and Prachanda agreed to a system of management for the Nepalese army and the PLA, which stipulated that the former would remain in barracks, while the latter would reside in holding camps. Two days later Lt-Gen. Rukmangad Katuwal assumed the post of Chief of Army Staff in an acting capacity, replacing Gen. Pyar Jung Thapa, who had been among those accused of using excessive force to quell the April uprising. In October further talks between the negotiating teams of the Government and the Maoists produced a tentative schedule for elections to the constituent assembly, which was to draw up a new constitution, with a deadline of the end of June 2007 for the assembly's first session. Prachanda reiterated his demand for the declaration of a republic, stating that an agreement to this effect would ensure the disarmament of Maoist forces. He announced a further three-month extension of the cease-fire in October 2006. The Comprehensive Peace Agreement (CPA), which was signed by Koirala and Prachanda on 21 November, provided for the establishment of an interim constitution, assembly and council of ministers by 1 December, and was hailed as the end of a civil war that had claimed the lives of more than 13,000 people. A disarmament agreement soon followed, the terms of which included the complete cessation of hostilities by both sides. The Maoist military forces were to be contained in cantonments and their weapons registered and impounded under UN supervision, while the Nepalese army, which was to remain in barracks, would also have its arms locked away. With the signing of an Interim Constitution in December 2006, constitutional powers of governance were reassigned from the monarchy to the Prime Minister. The National Assembly and House of Representatives were dissolved with the promulgation of the Interim Constitution in mid-January 2007. In their place an Interim Parliament, or 'Legislature-Parliament' was established; this body included members of the original 1999 Parliament as well as appointees selected by the seven-party alliance and the CPN (M) (which itself controlled 83 seats in its first parliamentary participation). A few days later the Maoists announced the closure of their 'People's Governments' and 'People's Courts'.

However, tensions among the Madhesi people in southern Nepal threatened to hinder the peace process in 2007. Madhesi groups, who were demanding increased independence for their region and greater representation in government, organized demonstrations and called strikes to draw attention to their campaign. The protests were at times violent and clashes with police resulted in several fatalities. At the end of January Koirala, reportedly in response to Madhesi demands, asserted that, under the terms of the forthcoming permanent constitution, Nepal would become a federal state. However, the ethnic unrest continued into the following month amid claims that the Government had not adequately addressed Madhesi needs. A government committee was subsequently established to negotiate with Madhesi groups. Constitutional amendments approved by the Interim Parliament in March provided for proportional representation and a federal style of government, and the revision of constituency boundaries to grant one-half of parliamentary seats to the southern plains, where an estimated 50% of the population resided. Despite these concessions, an element of dissatisfaction remained, with the Madhesi People's Rights Forum calling for total autonomy.

Progress in other areas of reform was halting. Conditions in the PLA holding camps were reported to be poor, with hundreds of troops departing, in contravention of the peace agreement. As late as March 2007, Prachanda commented that the arms decommissioning process had not been completed, and large numbers of Maoist troops had yet to move into the camps. Meanwhile, in February the King's image was removed from bank notes as part of a general move to eradicate symbols of the monarchy from public life; nationalization of the monarchy's assets was also proposed. In the following month Koirala suggested that the voluntary abdication of the King and the Crown Prince would be a positive outcome. According to the Interim Constitution, the future of the monarchy was to be decided at the inaugural session of the constituent assembly.

At the beginning of April 2007 an Interim Council of Ministers was approved by the Interim Parliament. G. P. Koirala was reappointed interim Prime Minister, heading an administration that included five members of the CPN (M), who assumed responsibility for information and communications, among other portfolios. Sahana Pradhan and Ram Chandra Poudel, both of the UML, were assigned the key portfolios of foreign affairs and peace and reconstruction respectively; the latter post was a newly created position that reflected the stated primary objective of the interim Government to promote domestic concord and tolerance. Later in April the Chief Election Commissioner expressed doubt that preparations for the constituent assembly elections, scheduled for 20 June, would be completed on time; at the end of May the Government decided to postpone the elections until November. In July the CPN (M) registered itself as a political party with the Election Commission of Nepal.

Although it had been agreed that the fate of the monarchy lay with the constituent assembly, demands for the declaration of a republic continued to be made. In June 2007 the Interim Parliament approved a constitutional amendment giving the legislature power to vote on the issue should the King attempt to influence the constituent assembly election process. Seven royal palaces were nationalized by the Government in August. In September the NCP and the NCP—D announced their merger. In the same month the CPN (M) withdrew from the Government, citing the continuing existence of the monarchy and disagreement over the composition of the constituent assembly—contrary to the dictates of the Interim Constitution, the CPN (M) demanded that constituent assembly members be determined solely through proportional representation—as major obstacles to co-operation with its coalition partners. As a result, the CPN (M) members of the Interim Council of Ministers tendered their resignations. A period of intense negotiations ensued, during which the CPN (M)'s numerous demands were considered by the remaining parties of the governing alliance, amid fears for the future of the peace process. In early October the elections were postponed indefinitely. In November the Interim Parliament approved a motion that reiterated the CPN (M)'s key stipulations: the declaration of a republic and the utilization of the proportional representation system for all constituent assembly seats. The Maoists had gained the support of the UML but not the NCP, and the motion, although approved, was consequently unable to garner the two-thirds' majority required for a constitutional amendment. However, at the end of December an amended version of the motion secured the requisite two-thirds of the vote, specifying that, although the monarchy was to be abolished, this change would only come into effect upon the approval of the constituent assembly. More than one-half of the assembly was to be determined by a system of proportional representation, with the bulk of the remainder directly elected and several appointees; elections were scheduled for April 2008. A few days later, the CPN (M) returned to government, with five of its members resuming their positions in the Interim Council of Ministers.

Meanwhile, in the latter half of 2007 tensions remained and the security situation deteriorated in the Terai region, where the Madhesi People's Rights Forum (MPRF) and numerous other groups continued to campaign for autonomy. In December the Minister of Environment, Science and Technology, Mahantha Thakur, resigned, together with several Madhesi members of the Interim Parliament, citing the Government's unwillingness to address the ongoing unrest in the Terai. Shortly after these resignations, the United Democratic Madhesi Front (UDMF), an alliance of three political organizations—the MPRF, the NSP and the Terai-Madhes Democratic Party—was established. In February blockades orchestrated by the UDMF caused widespread disruption in the south of the country and led to fuel shortages in Kathmandu and elsewhere. Later in the month, the Government and the UDMF signed an agreement ending the blockade and allowing for increased autonomy and representation of Madhesis on party lists and institutions such as the Nepal Army. However, concerns remained regarding the campaigns of more hardline Madhesi groups operating outside the negotiations.

At the constituent assembly elections, which were held on 10 April 2008, the CPN (M) won 220 out of a total of 575 elected seats under the mixed electoral system, twice as many as the NCP, which came second. The UML expressed disappointment at its election to only 103 seats, putting it in third place and prompting the resignation of the party's General Secretary, Madhav Kumar Nepal, while the MPRF won 52. Although the period leading up to the polls had been marked by bombings and violent clashes, the day of the election was largely peaceful, with a relatively large proportion of the electorate participating (around 60%). Prachanda declared victory on behalf of the CPN (M) and indicated that he would lead a coalition government. The CPN (M) also urged the King to abdicate voluntarily in advance of the inevitable declaration of a republic. This declaration was duly made following overwhelming approval at the inaugural session of the Constituent Assembly on 28 May, when the monarchy was abolished; King Gyanendra voluntarily vacated the royal palace in Kathmandu in June, opting to move to his summer residence outside the city. Meanwhile, the CPN (M)'s lack of a parliamentary majority proved to be an obstacle in the formation of a new government, with a lack of consensus between the three major parties over the mandate of the new post of president, a position Prachanda was keen to assume. Although by early June the CPN (M) had accepted the notion of a civilian president, the impasse continued, with the CPN (M) ministers of the interim Government tendering their resignations over a dispute with Prime Minister Koirala and his NCP. In late June Koirala stated that his resignation would come into effect upon the election of somebody to the presidency, which, it was decided, would be a largely ceremonial role. In a separate development, the seven-party alliance had reportedly been dissolved. A presidential election finally took place in the Constituent Assembly on 19 July, but the leading candidate, Ram Baran Yadav, who was supported by the NCP, was unable to secure a majority. Paramananda Jha, who had been nominated by the Madhesi Jana Adhikar Forum Party, was elected Vice-President. At a second round of voting two days later, Yadav defeated the CPN (M) candidate, Ramraja Prasad Singh, securing the support of the UML as well as the MPRF. Notably, Yadav, Singh and Jha were all Madhesis. Yadav took office on 23 July, and on the following day Subas Chandra Nembang was elected Chairman of the Constituent Assembly. The CPN (M), disgruntled with the alliance between the NCP, the UML and the MPRF and the resulting failure of its presidential candidate, initially warned that it would decline to form a government. However, with the support of the UML and MPRF, in mid-August Prachanda was able to defeat NCP candidate and former Prime Minister Sher Bahadur Deuba in a vote held in the Constituent Assembly for the post of prime minister. Prachanda assumed the premiership on 18 August, and shortly after appointed a new Council of Ministers, comprising members of the CPN (M), the MPRF, the Sadbhavana Party, the People's Front Nepal (Janamorcha Nepal) and the Communist Party of Nepal (United) (CPN—U). The NCP remained outside the Government, forming the opposition. The UML was absent from the coalition until it was given the deputy prime ministership: Bamdev Gautam was later appointed as both Deputy Prime Minister and Minister of Home Affairs. The CPN (M) retained the key portfolios of finance and defence, which were allocated to Baburam Bhattarai and Ram Bahadur Thapa Badal, respectively, while MPRF member Upendra Yadav assumed responsibility for the foreign affairs portfolio. In the following month the Minister of Land Reforms and Management, Matrika Yadav of the CPN (M), resigned; his portfolio was subsequently transferred to Prachanda. In mid-November the Constituent Assembly approved a timetable for the new constitution, with a deadline of May 2010 for its promulgation. The first draft of the constitution was expected to be made public in September 2009. A constitutional committee appointed by the Constituent Assembly began drafting the document in mid-December 2008. However, ongoing disputes between the Government and the opposition, and the unresolved issue of the integration of former Maoist fighters into the army—which strained relations between the Government and the military in early 2009—continued to hamper progress in other areas. In January 2009 the CPN (M) was restyled the CPN (Unified Maoist)—CPN (UM)—following merger with the CPN (Unity Centre-Masal).

On 4 May 2009 Nepal was faced with a serious political crisis and the peace process appeared increasingly fragile following the resignation of Prime Minister Prachanda and the withdrawal of the CPN (UM) from the ruling coalition. This dramatic development resulted from the President's refusal to accept Prachanda's earlier dismissal of the Chief of Army Staff, Lt-Gen. Rukmangad Katuwal, who was allegedly defying government orders to integrate former rebel fighters into the national army (claiming that they were politically indoctrinated). A series of protests by Maoist activists demanding the removal of the reinstated army chief subsequently took place in the capital and a number of clashes occurred between the protestors and the riot police. President Yadav set a deadline of 9 May for the formation of a new coalition government, but this date passed without any resolution to the political impasse. The CPN (UM) refused to participate in negotiations unless the President reversed his decision on the reinstatement of Lt-Gen. Katuwal. On 10 May President Yadav directed the Constituent Assembly to elect a new Prime Minister by a majority vote in an attempt to end the political crisis. On 17 May an alliance of 22 political parties, including the NCP and the UML, filed a claim to form a new coalition government and called for a parliamentary vote to elect their candidate, the veteran communist leader Madhav Kumar Nepal, as the new prime minister. In response, Prachanda stated that the move to form a new administration that excluded that Maoists was a conspiracy to derail the peace process.

In 1978 the old Trade and Transit Treaty between Nepal and India was replaced by two treaties (renewed in the mid-1980s), one concerning bilateral trade between the two countries, the other allowing Nepal to develop trade with other countries via India. Relations with India deteriorated considerably in March 1989, however, when India decided not to renew the treaties, insisting that a common treaty covering both issues be negotiated. Nepal refused, stressing the importance of keeping the treaties separate, on the grounds that trade issues are negotiable, whereas the right of transit is a recognized basic right of land-locked countries. In response, India closed 13 of the 15 transit points through which most of Nepal's trade was conducted. Severe shortages of food and fuel ensued. It was widely believed that a major issue aggravating the dispute was Nepal's purchase of weapons (including anti-aircraft guns) from the People's Republic of China in 1988, which, according to India, violated the Treaty of Peace and Friendship concluded by India and Nepal in 1950. Diplomatic relations between Nepal and India remained strained throughout 1989, with trade at a virtual standstill. Following several rounds of senior-level talks, a joint communiqué was signed by the two countries in June 1990, restoring trade relations and reopening the transit points, and assuring mutual consultations on matters of security. A few days earlier, as an apparent gesture of goodwill to India, the Nepalese Government had told the Chinese Government to defer indefinitely the delivery of the final consignment of weapons destined for Nepal. The visit to Kathmandu by the Indian Prime Minister in February 1991 (the first official visit to Nepal by an Indian head of government since 1977) helped to reaffirm the traditionally amicable ties between the two countries. Separate trade and transit treaties (valid for five and seven years respectively) were signed during a visit by Prime Minister Koirala to India in December 1991; these treaties were both subsequently renewed. A major breakthrough in Indo-Nepalese relations was achieved in February 1996, when the Prime Ministers of the two countries formally signed a treaty in New Delhi regarding the shared utilization of the waters of the Mahakali River basin (for irrigation, general consumption and the production of hydroelectric power). The costs and benefits of the project, which involved the construction of a massive hydroelectric power plant, were to be divided between Nepal and India, although not, some critics claimed, to Nepal's benefit. During a visit to Nepal by the Indian Prime Minister in June 1997, the Mahakali Treaty was formally endorsed, and India granted Nepal access to Bangladeshi ports through a new transit facility across Indian territory via the Karkavita-Phulbari road (this facility was extended and improved in 1998). Some tension in Indo-Nepalese relations, nevertheless, remained; this centred on border demarcation disputes and, in particular, on the Indian border police's use of territory that Nepal claimed as its own in the far west of the country (namely the strategically-situated Kalapani junction between India, Nepal and China, which covers an area of about 35 sq km). In late 2001 India supplied Nepal with two helicopters and arms to assist its neighbour in its struggle against the Maoist insurgency. In early 2002 the Nepalese and Indian Governments held talks on the civil disorder problem in Nepal and India repeated its offer of financial assistance. From early 2003, however, the Indian Government became increasingly concerned about King Gyanendra's perceived disregard for democracy. In February 2005 its concerns were realized when the King dismissed the Government and assumed executive power. India condemned the King's actions and suspended military aid to Nepal. It also intensified security along the shared border, owing to increased fears of infiltration by Maoist insurgents and their possible co-operation with rebels operating in India's fractious north-eastern states. In July India resumed non-lethal military aid to Nepal. In June 2007 Prime Minister Koirala paid an official visit to India, during which the Indian Prime Minister, Manmohan Singh, pledged Rs 10,000m. in developmental and infrastructural aid to Nepal. Following the Maoists' accession to power in Nepal in mid-2008 there was increasing concern expressed among certain sectors of the Indian authorities regarding the Nepalese Maoists' links with China and with India's own troublesome Maoist insurgencies. However, relations between India and the new ruling power in Kathmandu appeared amicable when the new Nepalese Prime Minister, Prachanda, met with Singh on a visit to India in mid-September.

The People's Republic of China has contributed a considerable amount to the Nepalese economy. The first meeting of a joint committee on economic co-operation took place in 1984. This committee met for a second time (and thenceforth annually) in Kathmandu in 1986, when China agreed to increase its imports from Nepal in order to minimize trade imbalances. Relations between Nepal and China improved further during the late 1980s and 1990s, as indicated by reciprocal visits made by high-ranking Nepalese and Chinese officials (notably, a state visit to Nepal was conducted by the Chinese President, Jiang Zemin, in 1996). In May 2001 the leaders of Nepal and China signed a six-point co-operation agreement to improve cross-border trade, increase road and aviation links and promote tourism.

In 1985 it was agreed that Nepal's border with Tibet (the Xizang Autonomous Region) should be opened. Following the outbreak of ethnic violence in Tibet in 1989, however, the border between Nepal and Tibet was closed indefinitely. The Nepalese authorities have been consistent in their commitment to the 'One China' policy and in their efforts to repatriate refugees fleeing from Tibet. In 1993 G. P. Koirala paid an informal visit to Tibet—the first visit to the region by a Nepalese Premier since the 1950s. In 1995, however, the Nepalese authorities banned a proposed peace march by Tibetans through Nepalese territory. During a visit to China by the Nepalese Minister of Foreign Affairs in August 2000, an agreement was reached to allow Nepal increased use of a new road in Tibet. Greater technological and economic co-operation was also achieved, therefore noticeably increasing bilateral trade. Nepal provoked strong criticism from the UN and Western governments in late May 2003, after it helped Chinese officials to deport 18 Tibetan refugees from Kathmandu to Tibet (Nepal's usual policy was to transfer Tibetan refugees to officials of the UN High Commissioner for Refugees—UNHCR). It was reported in late June that a further 19 Tibetans had been arrested in the western Nepalese district of Accham. In 2008 a series of demonstrations were held by Tibetan refugees in Kathmandu, as the approach of the Beijing Olympic Games drew international attention to the Tibet issue. The Nepalese police force was widely criticized for its reportedly violent suppression of the protests and the arrests of hundreds of activists; at the same time, China urged the Nepalese Government to control the demonstrations more stringently.

Ties with Bangladesh are also significant, particularly regarding the utilization of joint water resources. Large-scale migration from Bangladesh has resulted in a notable demographic transformation in Nepal, with the Muslim population increasing from around 4% of the total in the early 1990s to, unofficially, about 10% by the end of the decade. In January 2001 the Nepalese Minister of Foreign Affairs visited Bangladesh, where agreements on greater economic and transport co-operation were reached. In December 1982 Nepal and Pakistan strengthened their trade links by renewing a 1962 agreement, and in 1983 they established a joint economic commission and a regular air link. In March 2005 the joint economic commission met for the first time in 10 years, when a delegation of Pakistani economic officials visited Nepal.

In late 1991 thousands of Bhutanese of Nepalese origin began to arrive at refugee camps in eastern Nepal, following the outbreak of political and ethnic unrest in Bhutan. By early 1996 nearly 100,000 refugees were living in eight camps in the districts of Jhapa and Morang. In the first half of 1993 talks were held between Bhutanese and Nepalese government officials regarding proposals to resolve the issues at stake. The Nepalese Government steadfastly refused to consider any solution that did not include the resettlement in Bhutan of all ethnic Nepalese refugees living in the camps. This proposal was rejected by the Bhutanese Government, which claimed that the majority of the camp population were not actually Bhutanese. The deadlock was broken, however, when a joint statement was signed by the Ministers of Home Affairs of Bhutan and Nepal in July, which committed each side to establishing a 'high-level joint committee' to work towards a settlement (including the categorization of the refugees). In a notable shift in strategy, in January 1996 the Nepalese Government transferred the responsibility of handling the Bhutanese refugee problem from the Ministry of Home Affairs to the Ministry of Foreign Affairs. In April 1997 more than 10,000 Bhutanese refugees gathered at a mass demonstration in the eastern Nepalese town of Damak to call for UN intervention in the crisis. They also demanded that the Nepal Government either resolve the refugee problem or, failing that, 'internationalize' it. Nepal and Bhutan finally achieved a breakthrough at the 10th round of negotiations in December 2000. Both countries agreed that nationality would be verified on the basis of the head of the refugee family for those under 25 years of age; refugees over 25 years of age would be verified on an individual basis. By the end of January 2001 a Joint Verification Team (JVT) had concluded the inspection of refugee camps, and by late 2001 the verification of individuals in the Khudanabari camp had been completed. However, despite two further rounds of negotiations, the process reached a standstill in early 2002, with Bhutan reluctant to accept the individuals already verified, and both Governments undecided over the most suitable way to continue the verification process. In January 2003 Nepal and Bhutan finally harmonized their positions on the categorization of the refugees into four different groups and arrangements were commenced to conduct the repatriation to Bhutan of about 70 families (comprising around 300 people who were in the category of being Bhutanese nationals who had been forcefully evicted—Category I) by the end of the year. The majority of residents of the Khudanabari camp were categorized as either Bhutanese nationals who had left Bhutan voluntarily (Category II) or as non-Bhutanese (Category III); the remainder were classified as Bhutanese who had committed criminal acts (Category IV). It was agreed that the JVT would review the remaining appeals from people in the Khudunabari camp in November and then begin verification of the Sanischare camp. The two countries also decided that Bhutan would be fully responsible for any Category I persons, while Category II people could apply for either Bhutanese or Nepalese citizenship, in accordance with the respective laws. However, in December the Bhutanese members of the JVT were attacked in the Khudanabari camp by several thousand refugees protesting against the terms and conditions of the agreement. The JVT members were subsequently withdrawn to Thimphu and talks between Bhutan and Nepal were suspended. In October 2006 the US Government offered to resettle as many as 60,000 of the refugees (who by now totalled around 106,000). This met with a mixed response: some argued that third-country resettlement would amount to an exoneration of Bhutan's actions, while others welcomed the proposal. In the following month Australia, Canada and New Zealand also offered asylum to the refugees, although proposed intake numbers were not supplied. Following a visit to the refugee camps in November 2007, the US Assistant Secretary of State for Population, Refugees and Migration, Ellen Sauerbrey, stated that the refugees were facing 'severe intimidation' from political leaders who were opposed to the offers of resettlement abroad on the grounds that this would undermine their political struggle to settle all the 'camp people' in Bhutan. Nevertheless, in February 2008 Nepal began issuing exit permits to those who had opted for resettlement, and in March the resettlement of refugees in the USA and New Zealand began. According to the International Organization for Migration, which had become involved in resettlement efforts following the signing of a memorandum of understanding with the Nepalese Government in September 2007, between January 2008 and February 2009 more than 10,000 people claiming to be from Bhutan were resettled overseas (more than 9,000 in the USA), with many more expected to follow. At the 15th summit meeting of the South Asian Association for Regional Co-operation (SAARC, see p. 397), which was held in Colombo, Sri Lanka, in early August 2008, Bhutan's Prime Minister, Jigmi Yozer Thinley, met with his Nepalese counterpart, G. P. Koirala; the two leaders agreed that their respective Governments would resume the stalled talks regarding the refugee problem.

Nepal pursues a non-aligned foreign policy, and had diplomatic relations with 128 countries in early 2008. Nepal (with seven other countries) is a member of SAARC, which was formally established in 1985; the Association's permanent secretariat was established in Kathmandu in 1987. Kathmandu hosted a SAARC summit meeting in January 2002, despite rising tension in the region. Nepal is a signatory to the organization's agreement on the South Asian Free Trade Area (SAFTA), which came into force in January 2006 (SAFTA, however, was not due to enter fully into force until 2016).

Government

On 15 January 2007 the bicameral legislature instituted by the 1990 Constitution was dissolved upon the promulgation of a new Interim Constitution, and a 330-member Interim Parliament, or 'Legislature-Parliament', was convened by agreement of the seven-party alliance and the Maoists. In accordance with articles stipulated in the Interim Constitution, constitutional powers of governance were reassigned from the monarchy to the acting Prime Minister and the temporary legislature was to facilitate preparations for the democratic election of a constituent assembly by the end of June of that year. The constituent assembly, with a term of two years, would be responsible for drawing up a new permanent constitution. According to the Interim Constitution, the future of the monarchy was to be decided at the first official sitting of the constituent assembly. In December 2007 a parliamentary resolution declaring Nepal a republic received the requisite two-thirds' majority for a constitutional amendment, but this decision did not come into effect until the inaugural session of the Constituent Assembly, held in May 2008. At this stage the Interim Parliament was dissolved. In mid-2008 the Constituent Assembly elected a new President, Vice-President and Prime Minister; the presidency was a largely ceremonial position.

For the purposes of local administration, Nepal is divided into five development regions, 14 zones, 75 districts, 3,913 village development committees and 58 municipalities.

Defence

As assessed at November 2008, Nepal's total armed forces numbered 69,000 men. Paramilitary forces numbered 62,000 men. Military service is voluntary. An Armed Police Force was formed in 2001 and numbered 15,000 in November 2008. The defence budget for 2008 was projected at NRs 12,300m.

Economic Affairs

In 2007, according to estimates by the World Bank, Nepal's gross national income (GNI), measured at average 2005–07 prices, was US $9,660m., equivalent to $340 per head (or $1,040 per head on an international purchasing-power parity basis). During 2000–07, it was estimated, the population increased at an average annual rate of 2.0%, while gross domestic product (GDP) per head increased, in real terms, by an average of 1.1% per year. Overall GDP increased, in real terms, at an average annual rate of 3.1% in 2000–07. According to the Asian Development Bank (ADB), real GDP grew by 3.7% in 2005/06, by 2.7% in 2006/07 and by 5.3% in 2007/08.

Agriculture (including forestry and fishing) contributed an estimated 33.1% of GDP in the fiscal year ending 15 July 2007. The sector engaged an estimated 92.9% of the economically active population in mid-2005, according to FAO figures. The principal crops are rice, maize, millet, wheat, sugar cane, potatoes and vegetables, and melons. According to the World Bank, during 2000–07 agricultural GDP increased by an average of 3.1% per year. According to the ADB, the agricultural sector grew by 1.8% in 2005/06, by 1.0% in 2006/07 and by 4.7% in 2007/08.

Industry (comprising mining, manufacturing, construction and utilities) employed only 9.8% of the labour force in 1999, but provided an estimated 16.9% of GDP in 2006/07, according to the ADB. About 60% of Nepal's industrial output comes from traditional cottage industries, and the remainder from modern industries. During 2000–07 industrial GDP increased at an average annual rate of 2.9%. According to the ADB, industrial production rose by 4.5% in 2005/06, by 3.9% in 2006/07 and by 1.9% in 2007/08.

Mining employed only 0.08% of the labour force in 1999, and contributed an estimated 0.5% of GDP in 2006/07. Mining GDP increased by 11.4% in 2005/06 and by 8.0% in 2006/07. Mica is mined east of Kathmandu, and there are also small deposits of lignite, copper, talc, limestone, cobalt and iron ore. Geophysical investigations have indicated that the Siwalik range and the Terai belt are potential prospective areas for petroleum.

Manufacturing contributed an estimated 7.5% of GDP in 2006/07, and employed about 5.8% of the labour force in 1999. Manufacturing GDP increased by an average annual rate of 1.0% in 2000–07. Manufacturing production rose by 6.6% in 2005/06 and by 8.5% in 2006/07. The principal branches of the sector include textiles, particularly carpets and rugs, food products, wearing apparel and tobacco products. Traditional cottage industries include basket-making and the production of cotton fabrics and edible oils.

Energy is derived principally from traditional sources (particularly fuelwood). However, imports of mineral fuel and lubricants (mainly for the transport sector) comprised an estimated 20.8% of the cost of total imports in 2005/06. In addition, Nepal's rivers are exploited for hydroelectric power (HEP) production, but in July 2002 it was estimated that only about 1% of the country's huge potential generating capacity (83m. kW) was being utilized. In January 2004 the 144,000-kW Kali Gandaki A HEP plant was officially inaugurated. The project, the country's largest, began generating electricity in 2002. Nepal was hoping to export excess electricity to India. Several other HEP projects were under construction in the early 2000s. In August 2004 Cairn Energy Co of the United Kingdom signed an agreement with the Nepalese Government to explore for petroleum and gas in a 22,000-sq km area in the Terai plain, near the border with India.

The services sector employed 14.0% of the labour force in 1999. The sector contributed an estimated 49.1% of GDP in 2007. The GDP of the services sector increased at an average annual rate of 3.3% in 2000–07. According to the ADB, sectoral GDP grew by 5.6% in 2005/06, by 4.5% in 2006/07 and by 7.0% in 2007/08. By 1996 tourism had emerged as Nepal's major source of foreign exchange; in 1999/2000 revenue from tourism amounted to 12.9% of total foreign-exchange earnings. The Maoist insurgency affected visitor levels in the first half of the 2000s. In 2003 tourist arrivals showed some improvement, with 338,132 tourists visiting Nepal in that year. Arrivals increased further in 2004, reaching 385,297. However, in 2005 arrivals declined by 2.6% to 375,398, owing to the King's assumption of power in February and a concomitant deterioration in the domestic security situation, reflected in a particularly significant decrease in arrivals in the first five months of that year. The cessation of Maoist hostilities in 2006 and the subsequent peace agreement between the former insurgents and the political parties' alliance—combined with the introduction of additional airline services between Nepal and other Asian countries—led to a significant recovery in the tourism sector. Tourism arrivals witnessed massive growth, from 383,926 in 2006 to 526,000 in 2007, and over the same period revenue from tourism increased by more than 40%, from US $157.0m. to $230.6m. The industry continued to be buoyant in 2008, when a record 547,040 tourists were estimated to have visited Nepal.

In 2007 Nepal recorded a visible trade deficit of US $2,007.6m. and there was a deficit of $130.0m. on the current account of the balance of payments. In 2006/07 India was the principal source of imports (supplying 61.4% of the total) and the principal market for exports (68.9%). Other major trading partners were the People's Republic of China, the USA, Indonesia and Singapore. The principal exports were basic manufactures, manufactured goods and articles and garments. The principal imports were basic manufactures, machinery and transport equipment, and mineral fuels and lubricants.

In 2006/07 there was an estimated overall budget deficit of NRs 14,629.5m. (equivalent to 2.1% of GDP). Foreign aid plays a vital role in the Nepalese economy. According to the ADB, Nepal's total external debt was US $3,269m. at the end of 2008. In that year the cost of debt-servicing was equivalent to 9.9% of receipts from exports of goods and services. The annual rate of inflation averaged 5.0% in 2000–07. Inflation increased by 7.7% in 2007/08, but by mid-October 2008 the rate of inflation had soared to an estimated 14.1%, largely owing to rapidly escalating food and non-food prices. During the first decade of the 2000s it was estimated that more than 40% of Nepali workers were underemployed, while urban unemployment, a major problem, particularly among educated youths, stood at around 7%. According to the ADB, the unemployment rate in rural areas in 2004 was 2%.

Nepal is a member of the UN Economic and Social Commission for Asia and the Pacific (ESCAP, see p. 36), the ADB (see p. 191), the Colombo Plan (see p. 425) and the South Asian Association for Regional Co-operation (SAARC, see p. 397), all of which seek to encourage regional economic development. Nepal became the 147th member of the World Trade Organization (WTO, see p. 410) in April 2004.

With an inhospitable terrain comprising isolated valleys and very high mountains, Nepal is among the least developed countries in the world. Successive administrations since 1991 have followed a policy of economic liberalization: many state enterprises have been privatized (although there have been numerous delays in the process), and there have been attempts to reduce the fiscal deficit, to increase revenue mobilization, to restructure and improve the financial sector, and to institute and operate open trade and investment policies. In 2001/02, for the first time in 19 years, Nepal's GDP registered a negative growth rate: the economy contracted by 0.6%. Tourism and foreign trade fared particularly poorly, owing to a worsening internal security situation, regional tension and the terrorist attacks on the USA. In November 2003 the IMF approved a three-year

US $72m. Poverty Reduction and Growth Facility for Nepal, in support of the country's poverty reduction strategies. By 2003/04 the level of poverty had declined from more than 40% to 31%, owing in part to an increase in remittances from Nepalese workers overseas. The country's accession to the WTO in April 2004 would, it was hoped, lead to the further integration of Nepal into the global economy. Meanwhile, foreign investment in Nepal remained negligible, with significant reforms needed if the country's attractiveness as an investment destination was to increase. Following the Maoists' unexpected accession to power in 2008 (see Recent History) and the country's political transition from a monarchy to a republic, the new Government attempted to allay the fears of worried investors by insisting that Nepal's economy would be safe in their hands and that they were committed to capitalism. The Maoists' election manifesto for the 2008 Constituent Assembly elections referred to a 'transitional economic policy' that would focus on public–private partnership and thus create a favourable environment for private-sector investment (both domestic and foreign), for increased productivity and employment generation, and for an improvement in labour relations. Furthermore, they promised that the general thrust of the Three-Year Interim Development Plan devised in mid-2007, particularly its emphasis on agriculture and infrastructure investment, would continue to guide the developmental trajectory of the country. These assurances notwithstanding, structural reforms had to be tackled and the new Maoist-led Government had to demonstrate its capacity to handle immediate challenges such as rising food and fuel prices and serious power shortages, without endangering fiscal austerity or the environment conducive to investment and higher rates of growth. However, the collapse of the Government in early May 2009 and the ensuing political confusion did not bode well for the country's short-term economic future.

Education
Primary education, beginning at six years of age and lasting for five years, is officially compulsory and is provided free of charge in government schools. Secondary education, beginning at the age of 11, lasts for a further seven years, comprising a first cycle of three years (lower secondary), a second of two years (secondary) and a third of two years (higher secondary). In 2006/07 enrolment at primary schools included 76.1% of children in the relevant age-group (boys 77.9%, girls 74.2%). In 2005/06 secondary enrolment was equivalent to 43.2% of pupils in the relevant age-group (boys 45.7%, girls 40.5%). There are four state universities: the Tribhuvan University in Kathmandu, the Mahendra Sanskrit Viswavidyalaya in Beljhundi, Dang, the Purbanchal University and the Pokhara University. In addition, there is one private university in Banepa. Altogether, the universities had more than 120,000 students in 1999/2000. Proposed expenditure on education by the central Government in the 2007/08 budget was NRs 28,072m. (16.6% of total spending).

Public Holidays
The public holidays observed in Nepal vary locally. The dates given below apply to Kathmandu.
2009: 14 January (Maghi Sankranti), 16 January (Day of Reconciliation), 27 January (Lhosar, Tibetan New Year), 29 January (Martyrs' Day), 31 January (Vasant Panchami—Advent of Spring Day), 18 February (Rashtriya Prajatantra Divas—National Democracy Day), 23 February (Maha Shivaratri—in honour of Lord Shiva), March (Ghode Jatra—Horse Festival), 11 March (Phagu Purnima—Holi Festival Day), 3 April (Ram Nawami—Lord Ram's Birthday), 14 April (Navabarsha—New Year's Day), 1 May (Labour Day), 9 May (Lord Gautam Buddha's Birthday), 5 August (Janai Purnima—Sacred Thread Ceremony), 14 August (Janmashtami—Lord Krishna's Birthday), 20 August (Children's Day), September (Haritalika Teej—Women's Festival), 3 September (Indra Jatra—Festival of Rain God), 19 September (Ghatasthapana and, over nine days, Dasain), October (Durga Puja Festival), 17 October (Diwali—Festival of Lights, over three days), 20 October (Bhai Tika—Brothers' Day), November (Laxmi Puja), 9 November (Constitution Day).
2010: January (Day of Reconciliation), 15 January (Maghi Sankranti), 16 January (Lhosar, Tibetan New Year), 20 January (Vasant Panchami—Advent of Spring Day), 30 January (Martyrs' Day), 12 February (Maha Shivaratri—in honour of Lord Shiva), 19 February (Rashtriya Prajatantra Divas—National Democracy Day), 28 February (Phagu Purnima—Holi Festival Day), 15 March (Ghode Jatra—Horse Festival), 24 March (Ram Nawami—Lord Ram's Birthday), April (Navabarsha—New Year's Day), 1 May (Labour Day), 21 May (Lord Gautam Buddha's Birthday), August (Janai Purnima—Sacred Thread Ceremony), 20 August (Children's Day), September (Haritalika Teej—Women's Festival), September/October/November (Indra Jatra—Festival of Rain God), 2 September (Janmashtami—Lord Krishna's Birthday), October (Ghatasthapana and, over nine days, Dasain), October (Durga Puja Festival), October/November (Bhai Tika—Brothers' Day), November (Laxmi Puja), 5 November (Diwali—Festival of Lights, over three days), 9 November (Constitution Day).

Weights and Measures
The metric system has been officially adopted but traditional local and Indian systems of weights and measures are widely used.

Statistical Survey

Sources (unless otherwise stated): National Planning Commission Secretariat, Singha Durbar, POB 1284, Kathmandu; tel. (1) 4225879; fax (1) 4226500; e-mail npcs@wlink.com.np; internet www.npc.gov.np; Federation of Nepalese Chambers of Commerce and Industry (FNCCI), Pachali Shahid Shukra FNCCI Milan Marg, Teku, POB 269, Kathmandu; tel. (1) 4262061; fax (1) 4261022; e-mail fncci@mos.com.np; internet www.fncci.org.

Area and Population

AREA, POPULATION AND DENSITY

Area (sq km)	147,181*
Population (census results)	
22 June 1991	18,491,097
22 June 2001†‡	
Males	11,563,921
Females	11,587,502
Total	23,151,423
Population (estimates at mid-year)§	
2006	27,641,000
2007	28,196,000
2008	28,757,000
Density (per sq km) at mid-2008	195.4

* 56,827 sq miles.
† Population is *de jure*.
‡ Includes estimates for certain areas in 12 districts where the census could not be conducted, owing to violence and disruption.
§ Source: UN, *World Population Prospects: The 2006 Revision*.

PRINCIPAL TOWNS
(population at 2001 census)

Kathmandu*	671,846		Mahendranagar	80,839
Biratnagar	166,674		Butawal	75,384
Lalitpur	162,991		Janakpur	74,192
Pokhara	156,312		Bhaktapur	72,543
Birgunj	112,484		Hetaunda	68,482
Dharan	95,332		Dhangadhi	67,447
Bharatpur	89,323			

* Total for urban agglomeration 1,081,845.

Mid-2007 (incl. suburbs, UN estimate): Kathmandu 895,000 (Source: UN, *World Urbanization Prospects: The 2007 Revision*).

BIRTHS AND DEATHS
(annual averages, UN estimates)

	1990–95	1995–2000	2000–05
Birth rate (per 1,000)	38.1	34.5	30.2
Death rate (per 1,000)	12.0	9.8	8.7

Source: UN, *World Population Prospects: The 2006 Revision*.

2001 (estimates): Birth rate 33.1 per 1,000; Death rate 9.6 per 1,000.

Life expectancy (years at birth, WHO estimates): 62.4 (males 61.8; females 62.8) in 2006 (Source: WHO, *World Health Statistics*).

ECONOMICALLY ACTIVE POPULATION
(1999 labour force survey, '000 persons aged 15 years and over)

Agriculture, hunting and forestry	7,190
Fishing	13
Mining and quarrying	8
Manufacturing	553
Electricity, gas and water	26
Construction	344
Wholesale and retail trade	408
Hotels and restaurants	114
Transport, storage and communications	135
Financial intermediation	19
Real estate, renting and business activities	32
Public administration and defence	70
Education	164
Health and social work	34
Other community, social and personal services	57
Private households with employed persons	289
Extra-territorial organizations and bodies	8
Total employed	**9,463**

Source: Central Bureau of Statistics, Kathmandu.

Mid-2005 (official estimates in '000): Agriculture, etc. 12,078; Total labour force 12,998 (Source: FAO).

Health and Welfare

KEY INDICATORS

Total fertility rate (children per woman, 2006)	3.4
Under-5 mortality rate (per 1,000 live births, 2006)	59
HIV/AIDS (% of persons aged 15–49, 2007)	0.5
Physicians (per 1,000 head, 2004)	0.21
Hospital beds (per 1,000 head, 2001)	0.2
Health expenditure (2006): US $ per head (PPP)	78
Health expenditure (2006): % of GDP	5.7
Health expenditure (2006): public (% of total)	30.5
Access to water (% of persons, 2006)	89
Access to sanitation (% of persons, 2006)	27
Human Development Index (2006): ranking	145
Human Development Index (2006): value	0.530

For sources and definitions, see explanatory note on p. vi.

Agriculture

PRINCIPAL CROPS
('000 metric tons)

	2005	2006	2007
Wheat	1,442	1,394	1,515
Rice, paddy	4,290	4,209	3,681
Barley	29	28	28
Maize	1,716	1,734	1,820
Millet	290	291	285
Potatoes	1,739	1,975	1,943
Sugar cane	2,376	2,463	2,600
Beans, dry*	30	29	29
Pigeon peas	18	19	19
Lentils	161	158	165
Mustard seed	142	139	141
Garlic	29	29	30
Oranges	35	36	36
Apples	35	33	34
Ginger	154	154	159
Jute	18	17	17
Tobacco, unmanufactured	3	3	3

* FAO estimate(s).

Aggregate production ('000 metric tons, may include official, semi-official or estimated data): Total cereals 7,767 in 2005, 7,657 in 2006, 7,329 in 2007; Total roots and tubers 1,864 in 2005, 2,085 in 2006, 2,053 in 2007; Total vegetables (incl. melons) 1,891 in 2005, 2,233 in 2006, 2,374 in 2007; Total fruits (excl. melons) 995 in 2005, 491 in 2006, 494 in 2007.

Source: FAO.

LIVESTOCK
('000 head, year ending September)

	2005	2006	2007
Cattle	6,994	7,003	7,044
Buffaloes	4,081	4,203	4,367
Pigs	948	961	989
Sheep	817	812	814
Goats	7,154	7,422	7,848
Chickens	22,790	23,221	23,925

Source: FAO.

NEPAL

LIVESTOCK PRODUCTS
('000 metric tons)

	2005	2006	2007*
Cattle meat*	48.9	49.0	50.0
Buffalo meat	139.0	142.0	142.5
Sheep meat	2.7	2.7	2.8
Goat meat	41.7	42.8	43.0
Pig meat	15.7	15.8	15.8
Chicken meat	15.5	15.6	15.2
Cows' milk	380.0	385.3	386.0
Buffaloes' milk	894.6	926.9	930.0
Goats' milk*	65.0	65.0	67.0
Hen eggs*	28.8	26.5	26.6

* FAO estimates.
Source: FAO.

Forestry

ROUNDWOOD REMOVALS
('000 cubic metres, excl. bark, FAO estimates)

	2005	2006	2007
Sawlogs, veneer logs and logs for sleepers	1,260	1,260	1,260
Fuel wood	12,692	12,654	12,619
Total	13,952	13,914	13,879

Source: FAO.

SAWNWOOD PRODUCTION
('000 cubic metres, incl. railway sleepers)

	1999	2000	2001
Coniferous (softwood)*	20	20	20
Broadleaved (hardwood)	610	610	610
Total	630	630	630

* FAO estimates.
2002–07: Production as in 2001 (FAO estimates).
Source: FAO.

Fishing

('000 metric tons, live weight)

	2004	2005	2006
Capture	19.9	20.0	20.0
Aquaculture	20.0	22.5	25.4
Common carp	4.1	4.6	5.2
Bighead carp	3.0	3.4	3.9
Silver carp	6.0	6.8	7.7
Total catch	39.9	42.5	45.4

Source: FAO.

Industry

SELECTED PRODUCTS
('000 metric tons unless otherwise indicated, year ending 15 July)

	2004/05	2005/06	2006/07
Cement	610.0	613.6	644.3
Iron rods	166.5	n.a.	n.a.
Jute goods	32.8	n.a.	n.a.
Raw sugar	97.7	98.5	103.4
Tea	11.5	11.6	12.2
Vegetable ghee	199.6	179.2	188.2
Beer and liquor (million litres)	39.6	n.a.	n.a.
Soft drinks (million litres)	46.3	n.a.	n.a.
Paper	29.0	29.9	31.4
Cigarettes ('000 million)	9.4	9.5	10.0
Cotton clothing (million metres)	1.5	n.a.	n.a.
Synthetic clothing (million metres)	11.8	n.a.	n.a.
Soap	44.3	44.8	47.1

Finance

CURRENCY AND EXCHANGE RATES

Monetary Units
100 paisa (pice) = 1 Nepalese rupee (NR).

Sterling, Dollar and Euro Equivalents (31 December 2008)
£1 sterling = NRs 113.20;
US $1 = NRs 77.65;
€1 = NRs 108.07;
1,000 Nepalese rupees = £8.83 = $12.88 = €9.25.

Average Exchange Rate (rupees per US $)
2006   72.756
2007   66.415
2008   69.762

BUDGET
(NRs million, year ending 15 July)*

Revenue†	2004/05	2005/06	2006/07‡
Taxation	54,104.8	57,427.0	69,931.5
Taxes on external trade	15,701.6	15,343.7	18,328.0
Value-added tax	18,885.4	21,613.0	26,423.0
Excise duties	6,445.9	6,508.8	8,587.5
Income and property transfer tax	13,071.9	13,961.5	16,593.0
Other revenue	14,770.3	13,341.5	14,534.3
Interest	1,466.6	1,734.6	925.0
Civil administration	3,943.2	4,705.5	4,719.3
Dividend	4,589.9	3,394.8	3,960.0
Miscellaneous	3,504.0	2,356.0	3,550.0
Total	68,875.1	70,768.5	84,465.8

Expenditure	2004/05	2005/06	2006/07‡
Recurrent expenditure§	61,686.4	67,017.6	83,767.9
General administration	4,359.4	4,891.2	6,260.3
Defence	15,429.4	17,415.7	17,142.9
Social services	23,208.8	25,382.6	33,558.7
Education	15,960.2	17,729.8	20,942.9
Health	4,273.0	4,851.3	7,890.6
Economic services	7,167.8	7,529.8	9,950.9
Agriculture-related	2,117.2	2,437.5	3,045.9
Forestry	1,582.1	1,675.2	1,797.2
Interest payments	6,218.0	6,158.7	7,859.9
Other purposes	5,303.0	5,639.6	8,995.1
Capital expenditure	27,340.7	28,109.4	44,385.5

NEPAL

Statistical Survey

Expenditure—*continued*	2004/05	2005/06	2006/07‡
Administration and defence	3,570.1	3,151.7	1,929.8
Social services	7,940.7	10,151.8	18,314.3
Education	1,260.4	1,609.6	1,825.3
Health	409.3	948.2	1,413.3
Provision of drinking water	1,440.0	1,949.8	5,575.6
Economic services	15,394.9	14,797.1	23,585.3
Irrigation	1,921.5	2,462.7	3,457.1
Transport	4,149.6	4,178.1	7,337.7
Electricity	7,219.1	6,256.4	8,285.7
Total	89,027.1	95,127.0	128,153.4

* Figures refer to the recurrent and capital budgets of the central Government.

† Excluding grants received (NRs million): 14,391.2 in 2004/05; 13,827.5 in 2005/06; 23,728.6 in 2006/07 (budget estimate).

‡ Budget estimates.

§ Excluding net lending (NRs million): –1,247.7 in 2004/05; –16.4 in 2005/06; –319.1 in 2006/07 (budget estimate).

2006/07 (revised estimate): Total revenue (incl. grants) 100,836.2; Total expenditure (incl. net lending) 115,465.7.

Source: Nepal Rastra Bank, Kathmandu.

INTERNATIONAL RESERVES
(US $ million at mid-December)

	2003	2004	2005
Gold*	6.5	6.5	5.4
IMF special drawing rights	0.8	9.7	8.8
Reserve position in IMF	8.6	—	—
Foreign exchange	1,213.1	1,452.5	1,490.2
Total	1,229.0	1,468.7	1,504.4

* Valued at US $42.5 per troy ounce in 2003 and 2004, and at $41.9 in 2005.

2006 (US $ million at mid-December): IMF special drawing rights 9.0.

2007 (US $ million at mid-December): IMF special drawing rights 9.1.

Source: IMF, *International Financial Statistics*.

MONEY SUPPLY
(NRs million at mid-December)*

	2005	2006	2007
Currency outside banks	70,684	78,314	85,987
Demand deposits at commercial banks	37,522	45,515	51,254
Total money (incl. others)	109,755	125,804	138,793

* Excluding Indian currency in circulation.

Source: IMF, *International Financial Statistics*.

COST OF LIVING
(Consumer Price Index; base: 2000 = 100)

	2005	2006	2007
Food (incl. beverages)	120.3	129.1	139.6
Fuel and light	157.4	185.4	191.4
Clothing (excl. footwear)	111.5	114.1	116.6
Rent	126.2	131.9	179.0
All items (incl. others)	123.2	132.6	140.5

Source: ILO.

NATIONAL ACCOUNTS
(NRs million at current prices, year ending 15 July)

Expenditure on the Gross Domestic Product

	2004/05	2005/06*	2006/07†
Government final consumption expenditure	52,453	56,822	62,793
Private final consumption expenditure	468,849	538,533	589,377
Increase in stocks	38,368	32,616	36,186
Gross fixed capital formation	117,539	135,375	146,198
Total domestic expenditure	677,209	763,346	834,554
Exports of goods and services	85,958	87,952	89,825
Less Imports of goods and services	173,754	204,828	204,903
GDP in purchasers' values	589,412	646,471	719,477
GDP at constant 2000/01 prices	496,026	509,911	522,666

* Revised estimates.
† Preliminary estimates.

Gross Domestic Product by Economic Activity

	2004/05	2005/06*	2006/07†
Agriculture, forestry and fishing	199,368	211,010	228,677
Mining and quarrying	2,748	3,060	3,306
Manufacturing	44,885	47,840	51,887
Electricity, gas and water	12,782	13,130	13,530
Construction	36,644	40,811	44,186
Wholesale and retail trade	79,839	90,214	96,284
Restaurants and hotels	8,895	9,257	9,802
Transport, storage and communications	51,336	64,711	81,341
Financial intermediation	17,342	20,633	22,686
Real estate, renting and business	49,242	51,387	58,546
Public administration and defence	9,548	10,967	12,500
Education	31,671	34,623	39,661
Health and social work	7,017	7,925	8,890
Other community and social services	15,262	17,515	20,263
Sub-total	566,579	623,083	691,559
Less Imputed bank service charges	18,094	19,412	20,971
Gross value added in basic prices	548,485	603,671	670,588
Indirect taxes, *less* subsidies	40,927	42,798	48,888
GDP in market prices	589,412	646,471	719,477

* Revised estimates.
† Preliminary estimates.

BALANCE OF PAYMENTS
(US $ million)

	2005	2006	2007
Exports of goods f.o.b.	902.9	848.8	924.9
Imports of goods f.o.b.	–2,276.5	–2,441.0	–2,932.6
Trade balance	–1,373.6	–1,592.2	–2,007.6
Exports of services	380.3	385.7	511.3
Imports of services	–434.7	–492.8	–722.6
Balance on goods and services	–1,428.0	–1,699.4	–2,218.9
Other income received	139.9	158.2	224.3
Other income paid	–91.6	–96.1	–87.6
Balance on goods, services and income	–1,379.7	–1,637.3	–2,082.2
Current transfers received	1,441.3	1,695.7	1,993.7
Current transfers paid	–60.5	–68.9	–41.5
Current balance	1.1	–10.4	–130.0
Capital account (net)	40.3	46.3	75.4
Direct investment from abroad	2.5	–6.6	5.7
Other investment assets	–242.4	–250.9	–161.0
Investment liabilities	–36.5	260.3	23.1
Net errors and omissions	139.0	108.5	19.1
Overall balance	–96.1	147.2	–167.7

Source: IMF, *International Financial Statistics*.

External Trade

PRINCIPAL COMMODITIES
(NRs million, year ending 15 July)

Imports from India

Imports	2004/05	2005/06	2006/07*
Rice	437.1	2,309.8	1,505.0
Cotton textiles	1,607.5	1,273.0	902.1
Synthetic thread	404.2	1,536.4	2,190.9
Medicines	3,691.6	4,389.0	4,442.4
Chemicals	3,401.9	3,281.4	2,567.5
Coal	803.1	1,193.5	940.8
Cement	1,410.2	1,933.6	2,327.9
Diesel	10,243.3	12,843.3	12,635.0
Kerosene	7,677.2	11,995.8	10,275.5
Transport vehicles and parts	5,133.1	5,213.7	9,794.5
Other machine equipment and parts	3,010.8	3,509.4	3,530.5
Motor spirit (petrol)	4,723.7	5,813.6	6,675.8
Liquefied petroleum gas	3,557.7	2,351.1	2,989.2
Electrical equipment and goods	1,129.5	1,570.9	2,360.1
Agricultural equipment and parts	527.4	671.6	1,073.1
Total (incl. others)	88,675.5	107,143.1	117,740.4

IMPORTS FROM OTHER COUNTRIES

Imports	2004/05	2005/06	2006/07*
Crude palm oil	2,085.5	4,051.1	7,121.5
Betel nut	638.7	806.7	1,418.3
Crude soybean oil	834.6	1,572.9	1,924.2
Textile dyes	380.9	2,095.9	2,344.6
Medicines	701.2	1,108.1	1,536.9
Gold	4.9	2.9	3,519.9
Zinc ingot	1,266.3	2,327.1	2,372.5
Copper wire rod, scrapes and sheet	1,387.2	2,089.1	1,878.6
Polyethylene granules	1,972.7	3,696.7	2,959.7
Electrical equipment and goods	1,326.4	2,872.7	2,693.7
Computers and parts	1,227.0	1,353.8	2,662.5
Transport vehicles and parts	1,751.5	2,155.7	2,660.7
Other machine equipment and parts	2,695.9	2,830.7	2,007.4
Telecommunications equipment and parts	1,860.7	1,720.5	2,531.0
Aircraft and parts	980.5	1,071.3	1,462.8
Total (incl. others)	149,473.6	173,780.3	191,708.8

EXPORTS TO INDIA

Exports	2004/05	2005/06	2006/07*
Banaspati ghee	4,635.9	3,861.7	4,136.5
Juice	1,091.3	1,139.6	1,591.3
Cardamom	607.0	608.1	848.1
Polyester yarn	1,896.3	3,476.3	2,240.4
Twines	1,051.2	906.9	973.1
Other threads	2,213.7	1,898.3	4,055.9
Textiles (cotton, synthetic and others)	2,996.6	2,154.6	3,056.9
Ready-made garments	365.9	1,137.3	765.0
Sacks	1,456.2	1,265.4	1,408.6
Chemicals	1,407.5	1,057.5	911.5
Toothpaste	256.6	346.5	577.4
Galvanized iron sheet	3,070.3	2,345.2	1,967.3
Copper wire and rods	530.1	305.8	206.0
Other wire	1,221.4	1,504.1	1,610.7
Steel pipes	316.6	105.7	761.9
Total (incl. others)	38,916.9	40,714.7	41,874.8

EXPORTS TO OTHER COUNTRIES

	2004/05	2005/06	2006/07*
Pulses	106.5	191.7	488.1
Cardamom	205.3	109.2	129.6
Tea	106.7	107.6	114.7
Herbs	54.7	19.0	39.5
Perfume oil	48.3	8.2	21.4
Niger seeds	—	7.0	8.8
Hide and skins	235.8	310.4	275.5
Ready-made leather goods	30.2	14.4	111.1
Woollen carpet	5,868.7	5,838.7	5,600.2
Ready-made garments	6,124.6	6,204.1	5,205.5
Pashmina goods	1,049.8	1,577.8	931.0
Nepalese paper and paper products	239.8	257.0	190.6
Wooden handicraft goods	124.1	173.1	65.3
Metal handicraft goods	520.1	257.8	130.8
Gold and silver ornaments	363.2	282.4	325.4
Total (incl. others)	19,788.8	19,519.4	18,921.0

* Provisional figures.

PRINCIPAL TRADING PARTNERS
(NRs million, year ending 15 July)

Imports	2004/05	2005/06	2006/07
Australia	1,521.1	1,415.3	1,854.7
China, People's Republic	12,859.2	12,083.5	16,678.6
Germany	1,570.9	2,761.8	2,432.7
Hong Kong	1,286.4	930.9	1,029.5
India	88,675.5	107,143.1	117,740.4
Indonesia	5,222.7	5,647.8	11,172.1
Japan	2,565.2	1,935.1	3,229.0
Korea, Republic	2,784.6	1,788.9	2,380.5
Malaysia	2,820.9	2,474.7	2,794.6
New Zealand	1,229.7	1,018.8	841.1
Saudi Arabia	3,138.5	2,329.7	2,592.7
Singapore	7,746.8	3,375.3	5,496.9
Taiwan	825.7	567.9	796.0
Thailand	3,117.5	2,602.1	3,459.5
United Kingdom	1,452.2	961.4	1,727.1
USA	1,763.8	1,677.5	4,260.0
Total (incl. others)	149,473.6	173,780.3	191,708.8

Exports	2004/05	2005/06	2006/07
China, People's Republic	1,888.5	892.6	378.0
France	617.8	1,297.5	904.0
Germany	3,121.7	2,843.8	2,573.7
India	38,916.9	40,714.7	41,874.8
Italy	582.8	712.3	684.3
United Kingdom	1,050.0	1,184.1	998.7
USA	7,570.7	6,993.4	5,571.3
Total (incl. others)	58,705.7	60,234.1	60,795.8

Transport

ROAD TRAFFIC
(vehicles registered)

	2000/01	2001/02	2002/03
Cars, jeeps and vans	5,152	4,374	2,906
Buses and minibuses	1,453	1,343	730
Tractors	3,519	3,189	2,485
Other agro-industrial vehicles	1,271	1,798	1,212
Motorcycles	29,291	38,522	29,404
Total (incl. others)	40,995	49,560	37,610

Source: Department of Transport Management, Kathmandu.

CIVIL AVIATION

Royal Nepal Airlines Corporation
(traffic on scheduled services)

	2002	2003	2004
Kilometres flown (million)	10	8	9
Passengers carried ('000)	681	356	445
Passenger-km (million)	1,211	663	816
Total ton-km (million)	127	64	77

Source: UN, *Statistical Yearbook*.

Tourism

FOREIGN TOURIST ARRIVALS

Country of residence	2004	2005	2006
Australia	9,839	7,093	8,204
Bangladesh	14,640	19,206	16,623
China, People's Republic	12,733	21,092	15,777
France	18,992	14,108	14,293
Germany	16,031	14,345	13,686
India	89,861	95,685	88,857
Italy	12,121	8,785	7,472
Japan	24,196	18,239	21,664
Korea, Republic	10,654	10,121	12,413
Netherlands	11,064	8,890	6,848
Sri Lanka	16,045	18,686	27,382
Thailand	14,680	13,614	14,332
United Kingdom	24,644	24,950	21,180
USA	20,584	18,476	19,039
Total (incl. others)	385,297	375,398	383,926

Tourism receipts (US $ million, estimates): 157.0 in 2006; 230.6 in 2007.

Tourist arrivals (estimates): 526,000 in 2007; 547,040 in 2008.

Communications Media

	2005	2006	2007
Telephones ('000 main lines in use)	484.6	611.5	766.4
Mobile cellular telephones ('000 subscribers)	227.3	1,157.1	n.a.
Personal computers ('000 in use)	116	n.a.	n.a.
Internet users ('000)	225.0	316.8	337.1

2003: Daily newspapers 251 titles; Non-daily newspapers 3,490 titles.

Facsimile machines ('000 in use, year ending 15 July): 8 in 1999.

Radio receivers ('000 in use): 840 in 1997.

Television receivers ('000 in use): 170 in 2000; 193 in 2001.

Sources: UNESCO, *Statistical Yearbook*; International Telecommunication Union.

Education

(2006/07 unless otherwise indicated)

	Teachers	Males	Females	Total
Pre-primary	12,190*	289.1	264.9	554.0
Primary	112,827	2,333.8	2,181.2	4,515.1
Secondary	52,528*	1,081.7†	901.8†	1,983.6†
Tertiary	n.a.	106.5‡	40.6‡	147.1‡

Students ('000)

* 2002/03.
† 2005/06.
‡ 2003/04.

Source: UNESCO Institute for Statistics.

Institutions (2004): Primary 24,746; Lower secondary 7,436; Secondary 4,547. Note: Many schools offer education at more than one level. The total number of primary, lower secondary and secondary institutions was 26,277 (Source: Ministry of Education and Sports, Kathmandu).

Adult literacy rate (UNESCO estimates): 56.5% (males 70.3%; females 43.6%) in 2007 (Source: UNESCO Institute for Statistics).

Directory

Interim Constitution

In May 2006, prior to the convening of a Constituent Assembly, the House of Representatives approved a provisional proclamation significantly curtailing the powers of the King. All existing constitutional provisions that contradicted the proclamation were to be nullified. The most significant declarations of the proclamation were: that Nepal would henceforth be designated a secular state; that all legislative powers in the country would be exercised by the House of Representatives; that all executive authority in Nepal would reside with the Council of Ministers; that the Council of State (Raj Parishad) would be abolished; that the 'Royal Nepal Army' would be renamed the 'Nepal Army'; that the monarch would no longer hold the position of Supreme Commander-in-Chief of the Royal Nepal Army; that the monarch would no longer possess the authority to enact laws concerning the royal succession; that the monarch's acts could henceforth be challenged by both the House of Representatives and the courts; and that henceforth sessions of the House of Representatives would no longer be convened by the monarch, but by the Speaker, on the advice of the Prime Minister. In addition, in June, following a unanimous parliamentary vote, King Gyanendra was stripped of his right to veto laws, and in July his mandate to appoint judges was also taken away. The proclamation of May 2006 effectively overrode the Constitution promulgated by the King on 9 November 1990.

Following extensive negotiations between members of the seven-party alliance (a political coalition demanding an end to autocratic governance in Nepal), the Communist Party of Nepal (Maoist) and a UN peace delegation to Nepal, an Interim Constitution was presented in December 2006 and subsequently endorsed on 15 January 2007. (Maoist inclusion in the interim legislature was agreed according to the conditions of a Comprehensive Peace Agreement, which was signed on 21 November 2006 and which promised the disarmament of the Maoist militant groups and the containment of insurgent military personnel in government-supervised camps.) The enactment of the Interim Constitution effected the dissolution of the National Assembly and the House of Representatives and instituted a 330-member Interim Parliament, or 'Legislature-Parliament', which was mandated to formulate a model for the election of a Constituent Assembly, which would draft a permanent Constitution. All constitutional powers of governance formerly commanded by King Gyanendra were transferred to Prime Minister Girija Prasad Koirala, who was nominated Head of State. Executive power was conferred upon the Council of Ministers.

Further requested amendments to the Interim Constitution were confirmed in February 2007, particularly with respect to proportional and comprehensive representation of the Madhesi people and federal governance structure; following the submission of concerns from international observers in the USA, the process of judicial appointments and the administration of justice were also highlighted as issues for revision. A two-thirds' majority parliamentary vote was required to initiate all constitutional amendments. In December the Interim Parliament endorsed a constitutional amendment providing for the abolition of the monarchy; however, the change was to come into effect only upon the approval of the Constituent Assembly. At the same time, the membership of the Constituent Assembly was increased, with a significant number to be elected under the system of proportional representation. Following a legislative election on 10 April 2008, the Constituent Assembly voted to abolish the monarchy and declare Nepal a republic at its first session in May. As earlier agreed, the Interim Parliament was dissolved following the inaugural meeting of the Constituent Assembly.

NEPAL

The preamble to the Interim Constitution of Nepal, 2063 (2007), envisages the guarantee of the fundamental and human rights of every citizen and the protection of his civil liberty; the rights of the Nepalese people to structure their own Constitution and to engage in the unrestricted, impartial election of a Constituent Assembly; the resolution of class, caste, gender and regional tensions through systematic state restructure; universal adult suffrage and the multi-party system; complete freedom of press; and the provision of an independent judicial system. Democracy, peace, prosperity, economic and social progress, integrity and independence are national priorities. Sovereignty and state governance reside in the Nepalese people. The Constitution is the fundamental law of the land and nullifies any other extraneous laws that it may be attempted to introduce.

Nepal is a multi-ethnic, multi-lingual, religiously multi-denominational, independent, indivisible, sovereign, secular and inclusive democratic state. Nepali is recognized as the national language; Nepali in the Devnagari representation is the official language.

CITIZENSHIP AND FUNDAMENTAL RIGHTS

At the effective implementation of the Constitution, persons domiciled in Nepal who are eligible to apply for or have acquired citizenship are regarded as Nepali citizens. Honorary or naturalized citizenship may be endowed by the Government in accordance with legal provisions, and shall not be acquired or revoked unless dictated by law. Part Three of the Constitution provides for the fundamental rights of the citizen: all citizens are equal before the law and shall be awarded equal protection from the law; no discrimination is to be practised on the basis of religion, race, sex, caste, tribe, origin, language or ideology; acts of racial discrimination or untouchability shall be punishable by law and the victim eligible for compensation; no person can be deprived of his liberty except in accordance with the law; capital punishment remains abolished; freedom of expression and opinion, freedom to assemble peaceably and without arms, freedom to form political parties or organizations, freedom to form trade unions and associations, freedom of profession, and freedom of movement are also guaranteed. Similarly, pre-censorship of publications and impediment to communication media is prohibited and, thus, the right to press and publications is ensured. In the sphere of criminal justice, the following rights are specified in the Constitution: no person is to be regarded as an offender unless proven so by law, nor punished unless made punishable by law; any indicted person is entitled to confidential legal counsel at the time of arrest and may be represented by their chosen legal practitioner; those persons with insufficient financial means are to be entitled to free legal aid; no person may be tried more than once for the same offence; no one is compelled to testify against himself; no one is to be given punishment greater than that which the law at the time of the offence has prescribed; torture of detainees is prohibited; no person is to be detained without having first been informed about the grounds for such an action; and the detainee must appear before the judicial authorities within 24 hours of his arrest. In addition, provision has also been made to compensate any person who is wrongfully detained. Every citizen is entitled to a clean living environment and state-funded basic health care. A person's right to property and compensation for land reclaimed by the State under national programmes is ensured, and the right to protect and promote one's own language, script and culture have been safeguarded. The right to state-funded education up to secondary level (provided in the child's mother tongue up to primary level) is similarly ensured, while all persons are guaranteed the right to employment, and social security is to benefit all social groups. Exploitation and exile are guarded against. The rights of women to inheritance, protection from violence and sexual discrimination are assured, as are those of children to protection, nurture and state privileges in the case of disadvantaged birth. Additionally, social justice is guaranteed for women and tribal, oppressed and deprived social groups, and all citizens are to be permitted access to information pertaining to themselves or matters of national importance. The right to practise religion and to manage and protect religious places and trusts has been granted to the country's various religious groups. The right to secrecy and inviolability of the person, residence, property, documents, letters and other information is also guaranteed. The right to constitutional resolution secures the enforcement of all other rights designated by the Constitution.

GOVERNMENT AND LEGISLATURE

The executive powers of the country are vested in the Council of Ministers. The direction, supervision and conduct of the general administration of Nepal are the responsibility of the Council of Ministers. The Prime Minister and Council of Ministers are appointed according to political consensus. The Constituent Assembly comprises 601 members, of whom 575 are elected under the mixed electoral system and 26 are nominated. The Constituent Assembly is responsible for drafting a new Constitution; the tenure of office of its members is two years.

GOVERNANCE

Part Four of the Constitution details the responsibilities, policies and regulatory tenets of the State, particularly citing the objectives of electoral reform to provide for free and impartial election of the Constituent Assembly, the institution of a multi-party democratic and inclusive political system adherent to citizens' fundamental and human rights, the restructuring of the State to eliminate discrimination against or marginalization of any social group and actively promote full social and economic integration, the promotion of a national socio-economic development programme and prohibition of assets procurement by corrupt means, provision for the relief and rehabilitation of victims of the conflict, including the institution of an investigatory Truth and Reconciliation Commission, and prevention of further violence and conflict through institutionalized peace. In addition, the promotion of national economic independence and growth, enhancement of the people's basic quality of life and state infrastructure, and the adoption of a co-operative and equality driven foreign policy are ensured. No legal challenge may be submitted as to the implementation or otherwise of any such policies.

Part 17 of the Constitution makes provision for local self governance through the institution of district, municipal and village interim organizations. The State, through national and local government, is empowered to marshal revenue and resources in the interests of fulfilling such state policies.

THE JUDICIARY

The judicial system has three tiers: the Supreme Court, the Appellate Courts and the District Courts. The Supreme Court is the principal court and is also a Court of Record. The Supreme Court consists of a Chief Justice and a maximum of 14 other judges. The Chief Justice is appointed by the Prime Minister on the recommendation of the Constitutional Council; other Supreme Court, Appellate Court and District Court judges are nominated by the Chief Justice on the recommendation of the Judicial Council. A Constituent Assembly Court was established in February 2008 to address election issues.

OTHER INSTITUTIONS

The Interim Constitution also makes provisions for the establishment of a Constitutional Council, Public Service Commission, Election Commission, National Human Rights Commission, Commission for the Investigation of Abuse of Authority, Auditor-General and Attorney-General.

POLITICAL PARTIES

Political parties are required to register with the Election Commission, and must be non-discriminatory, have democratic aims, and produce the signatures of at least 10,000 voters in support of their application. It has been specifically provided that no law that bans, or imposes restrictions on, political parties may be enacted. Parties whose aims run 'contrary' to the Preamble of the Interim Constitution will be disqualified from registering.

DEFENCE

The Commander-in-Chief of the Nepal Army is appointed by the Council of Ministers. The Council of Ministers shall work towards the democratization and human rights awareness of the Nepal Army. The Nepal Army is administered and deployed by the Council of Ministers on the recommendation of the National Defence Council, which consists of the Prime Minister, the Minister of Defence, three other ministerial nominees and the Commander-in-Chief. The Council of Ministers shall establish a committee to oversee the assimilation and rehabilitation of Maoist combatants. Certain other procedures are governed by agreements between the (former) Government of Nepal and the Communist Party of Nepal (Maoist).

The Government

HEAD OF STATE

President: Dr RAM BARAN YADAV (assumed office 23 July 2008).
Vice-President: PARAMANANDA JHA.

COUNCIL OF MINISTERS
(May 2009)

Following the constituent assembly elections on 10 April 2008, a coalition Government was formed, comprising members of the Communist Party of Nepal (Maoist) (CPN—M) (restyled the CPN (Unified Maoist)—CPN—UM—following merger with CPN—Unity Centre-Masal in January 2009), the Communist Party of Nepal (Unified Marxist-Leninist—UML), the Madhesi Jana Adhikar Forum Nepal (Madhesi People's Rights Forum Nepal—MPRF), the Sadbhavana Party, the People's Front Nepal (Janamorcha Nepal) and the Communist Party of Nepal (United) (CPN—U).

NEPAL

On 4 May 2009 Nepal faced another period of political uncertainty following the unexpected resignation of Prime Minister Pushpa Kamal Dahal ('Prachanda') and the withdrawal of the CPN (UM) from the coalition Government.

Prime Minister and Minister of Women, Children and Social Welfare, and of Land Reform and Management: (vacant).

Deputy Prime Minister and Minister of Home Affairs: BAMDEV GAUTAM (UML).

Minister of Finance: (vacant).

Minister of Defence: (vacant).

Minister of Foreign Affairs: UPENDRA YADAV (MPRF).

Minister of Peace and Reconstruction: (vacant).

Minister of Law, Justice and the Constituent Assembly: (vacant).

Minister of Environment, Science and Technology: GANESH SAH (CPN—U).

Minister of Culture and State Restructuring: (vacant).

Minister of Commerce and Supplies: RAJENDRA MAHATO (Sadbhavana Party).

Minister of Agriculture and Co-operatives: JAY PRAKASH PRASAD GUPTA (MPRF).

Minister of Forests and Soil Conservation: KIRAN GURUNG (UML).

Minister of Physical Planning and Works: BIJAY KUMAR GACHHADAR (MPRF).

Minister of Local Development: RAM CHANDRA JHA (UML).

Minister of Tourism and Civil Aviation: (vacant).

Minister of Education: RENU KUMARI YADAV (MPRF).

Minister of Industry: ASTHA LAXMI SHAKYA (UML).

Minister of Information and Communications: (vacant).

Minister of Health and Population: GIRI RAJ MANI POKHAREL (People's Front Nepal).

Minister of Labour and Transportation: (vacant).

Minister of Water Resources: BISHNU POUDEL (UML).

Minister of Youth and Sports: GOPAL SHAKYA (UML).

Minister of General Administration: (vacant).

MINISTRIES

Prime Minister's Office: Singha Durbar, POB 43312, Kathmandu; tel. (1) 421000; e-mail info@opmcm.gov.np; internet www.opmcm.gov.np.

Ministry of Agriculture and Co-operatives: Singha Durbar, Kathmandu; tel. (1) 4228371; fax (1) 4229139; e-mail memoac@moac.gov.np; internet www.moac.gov.np.

Ministry of Culture, Tourism and Civil Aviation: Bhrikutimandap, Kathmandu; tel. (1) 4256217; fax (1) 4227281; e-mail info@tourism.gov.np; internet www.tourism.gov.np.

Ministry of Defence: Singha Durbar, Kathmandu; tel. (1) 4211290; fax (1) 4211294.

Ministry of Education and Sports: Keshar Mahal, Kantipath, Kathmandu; tel. (1) 4418784; fax (1) 412199; e-mail infomoe@most.gov.np; internet www.moe.gov.np.

Ministry of Environment, Science and Technology: Singha Durbar, Kathmandu; tel. (1) 4244609; fax (1) 4225474; e-mail info@most.gov.np; internet www.most.gov.np.

Ministry of Finance: Singha Durbar, Kathmandu; tel. (1) 4211809; fax (1) 4211831; e-mail admindivision@mof.gov.np; internet www.mof.gov.np.

Ministry of Foreign Affairs: Shital Niwas, Maharajganj, Kathmandu; tel. (1) 4416011; fax (1) 4416016; e-mail adm@mofa.gov.np; internet www.mofa.gov.np.

Ministry of Forests and Soil Conservation: Singha Durbar, Kathmandu; tel. (1) 4220067; fax (1) 4223868; e-mail info@mosc.gov.np; internet www.mofsc.gov.np.

Ministry of General Administration: Singha Durbar, Kathmandu; tel. (1) 4245367; fax (1) 4242138; e-mail moga@most.gov.np; internet www.moga.gov.np.

Ministry of Health and Population: Singha Durbar Plaza, Ramshah Path, Kathmandu; tel. (1) 4262862; fax (1) 4262896; e-mail info@moh.gov.np; internet www.moh.gov.np.

Ministry of Home Affairs: Singha Durbar, Kathmandu; tel. (1) 4211224; e-mail moha@wlink.com.np; internet www.moha.gov.np.

Ministry of Industry, Commerce and Supplies: Singha Durbar, Kathmandu; tel. (1) 4211967; fax (1) 4211619; e-mail info@moics.gov.np; internet www.moics.gov.np.

Ministry of Information and Communications: Singha Durbar, Kathmandu; tel. (1) 4211556; fax (1) 4221729; e-mail moicppme@ntc.net.np; internet www.moic.gov.np.

Ministry of Labour and Transport Management: Singha Durbar, Kathmandu; tel. (1) 4247842; fax (1) 4256877; e-mail info@moltm.gov.np; internet www.moltm.gov.np.

Ministry of Land Reform and Management: Singha Durbar, Kathmandu; tel. (1) 4225366; fax (1) 4220108; e-mail lrm@most.gov.np; internet www.molrm.gov.np.

Ministry of Law, Justice and Parliamentary Affairs: Singha Durbar, Kathmandu; tel. (1) 4223727; fax (1) 4220684; e-mail info@moljpa.gov.np; internet www.moljpa.gov.np.

Ministry of Local Development: Sri Mahal, Pulchowk, Lalitpur; tel. (1) 5521727; fax (1) 5522045; e-mail info@mld.gov.np; internet www.mld.gov.np.

Ministry of Physical Planning and Works: Singha Durbar, Kathmandu; tel. (1) 4228285; fax (1) 4228420; e-mail info@moppw.gov.np; internet www.moppw.gov.np.

Ministry of Water Resources: Singha Durbar, Kathmandu; tel. (1) 4211511; e-mail mowr@most.gov.np; internet www.mowr.gov.np.

Ministry of Women, Children and Social Welfare: Singha Durbar, Kathmandu; tel. (1) 4241728; fax (1) 4241516; internet www.mowcsw.gov.np.

Legislature

CONSTITUENT ASSEMBLY

The Constituent Assembly, which is responsible for drafting a new Constitution, comprises 601 members, of whom 575 were elected (using the mixed electoral system) and 26 nominated by the incumbent Interim Parliament. The term of office of its members is two years.

Chairman: SUBAS CHANDRA NEMBANG.

Election, 10 April 2008

Party	Seats*
Communist Party of Nepal (Maoist—M)†	220
Nepali Congress Party (NCP)	110
Communist Party of Nepal (Unified Marxist–Leninist—UML)	103
Madhesi People's Rights Forum Nepal	52
Terai Madhes Loktantrik Party	20
Sadbhavana Party	9
Communist Party of Nepal (Marxist–Leninist)	8
Rashtriya Prajatantra Party (RPP)	8
Janamorcha Nepal	7
Communist Party of Nepal (United)	5
Nepal Workers' and Peasants' Party	4
Rashtriya Prajatantra Party Nepal	4
Rastriya Janamorcha	4
Rashtriya Janashakti Party	3
Communist Party of Nepal (Unified)	2
Nepali Janata Dal	2
Nepali Sadbhavana Party (Anandi Devi)	2
Rastriya Janamukti Party	2
Sanghiya Loktantrik Rastriya Manch	2
Churevawar Rastriya Ekata Party Nepal	1
Dalit Janajati Party	1
Nepal Loktantrik Samajbadi Dal	1
Nepal Pariwar Dal	1
Nepal Rastriya Party	1
Samajwadi Prajatantrik Janata Party Nepal	1
Independents	2
Nominated	26
Total	**601**

* Includes seats determined by proportional representation and 'first past the post' systems.

† Name changed to Communist Party of Nepal (Unified Maoist—UM) following merger in January 2009.

Election Commission

Election Commission of Nepal: Bahadur Bhawan, Kantipath, Kathmandu; tel. (1) 4228663; fax (1) 4229227; e-mail info@election.gov.np; internet www.election.gov.np; independent; appointed by the Prime Minister, on recommendation of a Constitutional Council, for a six-year term; Chief Election Commr BHOJ RAJ POKHAREL.

NEPAL

Political Organizations

According to the Interim Constitution (which was formally endorsed in January 2007), political parties are required to register with the Election Commission, and must be non-discriminatory, have democratic aims, and produce the signatures of at least 10,000 voters supporting them. No law that bans or imposes restrictions on political parties may be enacted. Parties whose aims run 'contrary' to the Preamble of the Interim Constitution will not be permitted to register. By mid-2007 11 major political parties of the interim Parliament had been registered as official national parties with the Election Commission and confirmed as eligible to contest the constituent assembly elections, which were held in April 2008.

Communist Party of Nepal (Unified): Kathmandu; f. 2007; Gen. Sec. RAJ SINGH SHRIS.

Communist Party of Nepal (Unified Maoist) (CPN—UM): internet www.cpnm.org; f. 1990 as Communist Party of Nepal (Unity Centre), renamed as CPN (Maoist) in 1995; fmr underground political movement, represented in Interim Parliament in 2007; orchestrated 'people's war' in hills of west Nepal (1996–2006); merged with CPN (Unified Marxist-Leninist-Maoist) in Sept. 2007; merged with CPN (Marxist) in Feb. 2008; merged with CPN (Unity Centre-Masal) in Jan. 2009 and name changed as above; 175-mem. central committee; Chair. PUSHPA KAMAL DAHAL ('Prachanda').

Communist Party of Nepal (Unified Marxist–Leninist) (UML): Madan Nagar, Balkhu, POB 5471, Kathmandu; tel. (1) 4278081; fax (1) 4278084; e-mail uml@ntc.net.np; internet www.cpnuml.org; f. 1991 when two major factions of the Communist Party of Nepal (CPN; f. 1949; banned 1960; legalized 1990)—the Marxist and Marxist–Leninist factions—merged; the Communist Party of Nepal (Marxist–Leninist—ML) seceded in 1998 and rejoined the UML in 2002; the Communist Party of Nepal (Verma) merged with the UML in 2001; Gen. Sec. JHALA NATH KHANAL.

Communist Party of Nepal (United): Kathmandu; f. 2007 following a split in the Communist Party of Nepal (United Marxist); Gen. Sec. GANESH SHAH.

Green Nepal Party: Kalikasthan, POB 890, Kathmandu; tel. and fax (1) 4438402; fax (1) 4416547; e-mail greennepal96@wlink.com.np; internet web.greens.org/nepalm; f. 1996; Chair. KUBER SHARMA; Pres. M. K. RIMAL.

Madhesi Jana Adhikar Forum Nepal (Madhesi People's Rights Forum Nepal): f. 2006; Chair. UPENDRA YADAV.

Nepal Workers' and Peasants' Party: Golmadhi Tole-7, Bhaktapur, Kathmandu; tel. (1) 6610974; fax (1) 6613207; e-mail nwpp@ntc.net.np; Chair. NARAYAN MAN BIJUKCHHEN (Comrade Rohit).

Nepali Congress Party (NCP): B. P. Smriti Bhavan, B. P. Nagar, Sanepa, Lalitpur; tel. (1) 5555263; fax (1) 5555188; e-mail ncparty@wlink.com.np; internet www.nepalicongress.org; f. 1947; banned 1960; legalized 1990; Nepali Congress Party—Democratic formed as breakaway faction in 2002, rejoined Sept. 2007; Pres. GIRIJA PRASAD KOIRALA; Gen. Secs K. B. GURUNG, BIMALENDRA NIDHI, Dr RAM BARAN YADAV; 101,000 active members, 500,000 ordinary members.

Nepali Janata Dal: Tripureshwor, Kathmandu; tel. (1) 4212389; f. 1990; advocates the consolidation of the multi-party democratic system and supports the campaign against corruption; Leader KESHAR JUNG RAYAMAJHI.

Nepali Sadbhavana Party (NSP) (Nepal Goodwill Party): Shantinagar, New Baneshwor, Kathmandu; tel. (1) 4488068; fax (1) 4470797; f. 1990; promotes the rights of the Madhesiya community, who are of Indian origin and reside in the Terai; demands that the Government recognize Hindi as an official language, that constituencies in the Terai be allocated on the basis of population, and that the Government grant citizenship to those who settled in Nepal before April 1990; in 2003 the party split into two factions, one led by Badri Prasad Mandal, known as the Mandal Group, and the other led by Anandi Devi Singh, known as the Anandi Devi group.

People's Front Nepal (Janamorcha Nepal): Kathmandu; f. 2002 following merger of Rashtriya Jana Morcha (National People's Front) and United People's Front; split into three factions in Dec. 2006; Pres. AMIK SHERCHAN; Vice-Chair. LILAMANI POKHAREL.

Rashtriya Janashakti Party (National People's Power Party): Ramalphokhari, Kathmandu; tel. (1) 4437063; fax (1) 4437064; e-mail rjpnepal@info.com.np; f. 2005; Leader SURYA BAHADUR THAPA.

Rashtriya Prajatantra Party (RPP) (National Democratic Party—NDP): Charumati Bahal, Chabahil, Kathmandu; tel. (1) 4471071; fax (1) 4423384; e-mail info@rppnepal.com; internet www.rppnepal.org; liberal democratic party; Pres. PASHUPATI SHUMSHERE J. B. RANA; Sec.-Gen. DEEPAK BOHARA.

Rashtriya Prajatantra Party Nepal: Kathmandu; tel. (1) 4375455; f. 2008; Pres. RABINDRA NATH SHARMA; Chair. KAMAL THAPA.

Rastriya Janamorcha: Kathmandu; tel. (1) 4420226; Pres. CHITRA BAHADUR K. C.

Directory

Rastriya Janamukti Party: Maha Laxmisthan, Lagan Khel, POB 5569, Kathmandu; tel. (1) 5542212; fax (1) 5525531; e-mail zhedi43@yahoo.com; internet www.janamuktiparty.com; f. 1990; Pres. MALBAR SINGH THAPA.

Sadbhavana Party: Kathmandu; Chair. RAJENDRA MAHATO.

Sanghiya Loktantrik Rastriya Manch: Kathmandu; Pres. KAMAL CHARAHANG.

Terai Janatantrik Party (TJP): Kathmandu; f. 2009 by merger; Chair. JAYA KRISHNA GOIT; Vice-Chair. PAWAN GIRI; Gen. Sec. JWALA SINGH.

Terai Madhes Loktantrik Party (Terai Madhes Democratic Party): Kathmandu; tel. (1) 4462398; Pres. MAHANTHA THAKUR.

United Left Front: coalition of Nepali communist parties; f. 2002.

Other parties elected to the Constituent Assembly in April 2008 were Churevawar Rastriya Ekata Party Nepal, Dalit Janajati Party, Nepal Loktantrik Samajbadi Dal, Nepal Pariwar Dal, Nepal Rastriya Party, and Samajwadi Prajatantrik Janata Party Nepal.

Diplomatic Representation

EMBASSIES IN NEPAL

Australia: Suraj Niwas, Bansbari, POB 879, Kathmandu; tel. (1) 4371678; fax (1) 4371533; internet www.nepal.embassy.gov.au; Ambassador SUSAN GRACE.

Bangladesh: Maharajgunj Ring Rd, POB 789, Kathmandu; tel. (1) 4372843; fax (1) 4373265; e-mail bdootktm@wlink.com.np; Ambassador IMTIAZ AHMED.

China, People's Republic: Baluwatar, POB 4234, Kathmandu; tel. (1) 4419053; fax (1) 4414045; e-mail chinaemb_np@mfa.gov.cn; internet www.fmprc.gov.cn/ce/cenp; Ambassador QIU GUOHONG.

Denmark: 761 Neel Saraswati Marg, Lazimpat, POB 6332, Kathmandu; tel. (1) 4413010; fax (1) 4411409; e-mail ktmamb@um.dk; internet www.ambkathmandu.um.dk; Ambassador FINN THILSTED.

Egypt: Pulchowk, Lalitpur, POB 792, Kathmandu; tel. (1) 5524812; fax (1) 5522975; Ambassador ABDUL HAMEED MAHMOUD SOLIMAN.

Finland: Bishalnagar, POB 2126, Kathmandu; tel. (1) 4416636; fax (1) 4416703; e-mail sanomat.kat@formin.fi; internet www.finland.org.np; Chargé d'affaires a.i. PIRKKO-LIISA KYÖSTILÄ.

France: Lazimpat, POB 452, Kathmandu; tel. (1) 4412332; fax (1) 4419968; e-mail consulat@ambafrance-np.org; internet www.ambafrance-np.org; Ambassador GILLES-HENRY GARAULT.

Germany: Gyaneshwar, POB 226, Kathmandu; tel. (1) 4412786; fax (1) 4416899; e-mail info@kathmandu.diplo.de; internet www.kathmandu.diplo.de; Ambassador VERENA GRÄFIN VON ROEDERN.

India: 336 Kapurdhara Marg, POB 292, Kathmandu; tel. (1) 4410900; fax (1) 4428279; e-mail pic@eoiktm.org; internet www.south-asia.com/embassy-India; Ambassador RAKESH SOOD.

Israel: Bishramalaya House, Lazimpat, POB 371, Kathmandu; tel. (1) 4411811; fax (1) 4413920; e-mail info@kathmandu.mfa.gov.il; internet kathmandu.mfa.gov.il; Ambassador DAN STAV.

Japan: Panipokhari, POB 264, Kathmandu; tel. (1) 4426680; fax (1) 4414101; e-mail comjpn@mos.com.np; internet www.np.emb-japan.go.jp; Ambassador TATSUO MIZUNO.

Korea, Democratic People's Republic: Jhamsikhel, Lalitpur, Kathmandu; tel. (1) 5521855; fax (1) 5525394; Ambassador JANG YONG CHOL.

Korea, Republic: Red Cross Marg, Tahachal, POB 1058, Kathmandu; tel. (1) 4270172; fax (1) 4272041; e-mail koreaemb@mos.com.np; Ambassador HONG SUNG-MOG.

Malaysia: Block B, 2nd Floor, Karmachari Sanchaya Kosh Bldg, Pulchowk, POB 24372, Lalitpur, Kathmandu; tel. (1) 5010004; fax (1) 5010492; e-mail malkatmandu@kln.gov.my; internet www.kln.gov.my/perwakilan/kathmandu; Ambassador DATO' ILANKOVAN KOLANDAVELU.

Myanmar: Chakupath, Patan Gate, Lalitpur, POB 2437, Kathmandu; tel. (1) 5521788; fax (1) 5523402; Ambassador U AUNG KHIN SOE.

Norway: Surya Court, Pulchowk, Lalitpur, POB 20765, Kathmandu; tel. (1) 5545307; fax (1) 5545226; e-mail emb.kathmandu@mfa.no; internet www.norway.org.np; Ambassador THOR GISLESEN.

Pakistan: Pushpanjali, Maharajgunj, Chakrapath, POB 202, Kathmandu; tel. (1) 4374024; fax (1) 4374012; e-mail parepktm@wlink.com.np; Ambassador SYED ABRAR HUSSAIN.

Russia: Baluwatar, POB 123, Kathmandu; tel. (1) 4412155; fax (1) 4416571; e-mail ruspos@info.com.np; internet www.nepal.mid.ru; Ambassador ANDREI LEONIDOVICH TROFIMOV.

NEPAL   Directory

Sri Lanka: 'Shah Villa', Chundevi Rd, Maharajgunj, POB 8802, Kathmandu; tel. (1) 4720623; fax (1) 4720128; e-mail embassy@srilanka.info.com.np; Ambassador SUMITH NAKANDALA.

Thailand: 167/4 Ward No. 3, Maharajgunj-Bansbari Rd, POB 3333, Kathmandu; tel. (1) 4371410; fax (1) 4371409; e-mail thaiemb@wlink.com.np; internet www.thaiembassy.org/kathmandu; Ambassador VANVISA THAMRONGNAVASAWAT.

United Kingdom: Lainchaur, POB 106, Kathmandu; tel. (1) 4410583; fax (1) 4411789; e-mail bekathmandu@fco.gov.uk; internet ukinnepal.gov.uk; Ambassador Dr ANDREW HALL.

USA: Panipokhari, POB 295, Kathmandu; tel. (1) 4411179; fax (1) 4419963; e-mail usembktm@state.gov; internet nepal.usembassy.gov; Ambassador NANCY J. POWELL.

Judicial System

According to the Interim Constitution (which was officially endorsed in January 2007), the judicial system has three tiers: the Supreme Court (which is also a Court of Record), the Appellate Courts and the District Courts. The Supreme Court consists of a Chief Justice and a maximum of 14 other judges. The Chief Justice is appointed by the Prime Minister on the recommendation of the Constitutional Council; other Supreme Court, Appellate Court and District Court judges are nominated by the Chief Justice on the recommendation of the Judicial Council. A Constituent Assembly Court was established in February 2008 to deal with election matters.

Supreme Court: Ramashah Path, Kathmandu; e-mail info@supremecourt.gov.np; internet www.supremecourt.gov.np.

Chief Justice: KEDAR PRASAD GIRI.

Judges of the Supreme Court: MIN BAHADUR RAYAMAJHEE, ANUP RAJ SHARMA, RAM PRASAD SHRESTHA, KHIL RAJ REGMI, SHARDA SHRESTHA, BALA RAM K. C., TAP BAHADUR MAGAR, DAMODAR PRASAD SHARMA, RAM KUMAR PRASAD SHAH, KALYAN SHRESTHA, GAURI DHAKAL, TAHIR ALI ANSARI, RAJENDRA KOIRALA, KRISHNA PRASAD UPADHYAYA, PREM SHARMA, RANA BAHADUR BAM, MOHAN PRAKASH SITAULA, ABADESH KUMAR YADAV, GIRISH CHANDRA LAL, SHUSHILA KARKI, PRAKASH CHANDRA SHARMA WASTI, BHARAT RAJ UPRETI.

Registrar: Dr RAM KRISHNA TIMALSENA.

Attorney-General: YAGYAMURTI BANJADE.

Religion

At the 2001 census, an estimated 80.6% of the population professed Hinduism (the religion of the royal family), while 10.7% were Buddhists and 4.2% Muslims. The actual number of Muslims in the country was considered to be much higher, owing to immigration from Bangladesh. There were an estimated 101,976 Christians in Nepal in 2001.

BUDDHISM

All Nepal Bhikkhu Association: Vishwa Shanti Vihara (World Peace Temple), 465 Ekadantamarga, Minbhavan, New Baneshwor, POB 8973 NPC-327, Kathmandu; tel. (1) 4482984; fax (1) 4482250; e-mail vishwa@ntc.net.np; Treas. BHIKSHU BODHIJNANA.

Nepal Buddhist Council: Nahtole, Lalitpur 20; tel. (1) 5534277; Contact MAHISWOR RAJ BAJRACHARYA.

United Trungram Buddhist Foundation: Hattigauda, Bansbari, POB 3157, Kathmandu; tel. (1) 4370089; fax (1) 4370292; e-mail info@utbf.org; internet www.utbf.org; Spiritual Dir GYALTRUL RINPOCHE.

CHRISTIANITY

Protestant Church

Presbyterian Church of the Kingdom of Nepal: POB 3237, Kathmandu; tel. and fax (1) 4524450.

The Roman Catholic Church

The Church is represented in Nepal by a single apostolic prefecture. In March 2009 there were an estimated 6,515 adherents in the country.

Apostolic Vicariate: Church of the Assumption, Everest Postal Care P. Ltd, POB 8975 EPC-343, Kathmandu; tel. (1) 5542802; fax (1) 5521710; e-mail anath@wlink.com.np; f. 1983 as Catholic Mission; Vicar Apostolic Bishop ANTHONY FRANCIS SHARMA.

The Press

PRINCIPAL DAILIES

The Commoner: Naradevi, POB 203, Kathmandu; tel. (1) 4228236; f. 1956; English; Publr and Chief Editor GOPAL DASS SHRESTHA; circ. 7,000.

Daily News: Bhimsensthan, POB 171, Kathmandu; tel. (1) 4279147; fax (1) 4279544; e-mail manju_sakya@hotmail.com; f. 1983; Nepali and English; Chief Editor MANJU RATNA SAKYA; Publr SUBHA LAXMI SAKYA; circ. 20,000.

Dainik Nirnaya: Bhairawa; tel. (71) 520117; Nepali; Editor P. K. BHATTACHAN.

Gorkhapatra: Dharma Path, POB 23, Kathmandu; tel. (1) 4244438; fax (1) 4222921; e-mail gopa@gorkhapatra.org.np; internet www.gorkhapatra.org.np; f. 1901; Nepali; govt-owned; Exec. Chair. MASTRIKA PRASAD TIMSINA; Editor-in-Chief KRISHNA SHRESTHA; circ. 75,000.

The Himalayan Times: International Media Network Nepal (Pvt) Ltd, APCA House, Baidya Khana Rd, Anam Nagar, POB 11651, Kathmandu; tel. (1) 4771489; fax (1) 4770701; e-mail editorial@thehimalayantimes.com; internet www.thehimalayantimes.com; f. 2001; English; Editor AJAYA BHADRA KHANAL.

Janadoot: Ga 2-549, Kamal Pokhari (in front of the Police Station), Kathmandu; tel. (1) 4412501; f. 1970; Nepali; Editor GOVINDA BIYOGI; circ. 6,500.

Kantipur: Kantipur Complex, Subhidhanagar, POB 8559, Kathmandu; tel. (1) 4480100; fax (1) 4470178; e-mail sudheer@kantipur.com.np; internet www.kantipuronline.com; f. 1993; Nepali; Chair. and Man. Dir KAILASH SIROHIYA; Editor SUDHIR SHARMA; circ. 210,000.

Kathmandu Post: Kantipur Complex, Subhidhanagar, POB 8559, Kathmandu; tel. (1) 4480100; fax (1) 4466320; e-mail au@kantipur.com.np; internet www.kantipuronline.com; f. 1993; English; Editor AKHILESH UPADHYAY; circ. 40,000.

Motherland: POB 1184, Kathmandu; English; Editor MANINDRA RAJ SHRESTHA; circ. 5,000.

Nepal Samacharpatra: Sagarmatha Press, Ramshah Path, Kathmandu; tel. (1) 4287777; e-mail pushkarlal@newsofnepal.com; internet newsofnepal.com; f. 1945; Nepali; Editor-in-Chief PUSHKAR LAL SHRESTHA; circ. 1,000.

Nepali Hindi Daily: 72 Kalinchok Marg, Maitidevi, POB 49, Kathmandu; tel. (1) 4436374; fax (1) 4435931; e-mail das@ntc.net.np; f. 1954; evening; Hindi; Publr UMA KANT DAS; Chief Editor VIJOY KUMAR DAS; circ. 100,000.

Rajdhani: Kathmandu; internet www.rajdhani.com.np; Editor KAPIL KAFLE; circ. 50,000.

Rising Nepal: Dharma Path, POB 1623, Kathmandu; tel. (1) 4224435; fax (1) 4224381; e-mail trn@gorkhapatra.org.np; internet www.gorkhapatra.org.np; f. 1965; English; Editor-in-Chief AJAY SHUMSHER RANA; circ. 20,000.

Samaj: National Printing Press, Dillibazar, Kathmandu; f. 1954; Nepali; Editor MANI RAJ UPADHYAYA; circ. 5,000.

Samaya: Kamal Press, Ramshah Path, Kathmandu; f. 1954; Nepali; Editor MANIK LALL SHRESTHA; circ. 18,000.

Space Time Dainik: Iceberg Bldg, 3rd Floor, Putali Sadak, Kathmandu; tel. (1) 4419133; fax (1) 4419504; e-mail info@spacetimenetwork.com; f. 2000; Nepali; Man. Dir JAMIM SHAH; circ. 60,000.

Swatantra Samachar: Kathmandu; tel. (1) 4419285; f. 1957; Editor MADAN DEV SHARMA; circ. 2,000.

SELECTED PERIODICALS

Agricultural Credit: Agricultural Training and Research Institute, Agricultural Development Bank, Head Office, Ramshah Path, Panchayat Plaza, Kathmandu; tel. (1) 4220756; fax (1) 4225329; 2 a year; publ. by the Agricultural Development Bank; Chair. Dr NARAYAN N. KHATRI; Editor RUDRA PD DAHAL.

Arpan: Bhimsensthan, POB 285, Kathmandu; tel. (1) 4244450; fax (1) 4279544; e-mail manju_sakya@hotmail.com; internet www.nepalnews.com.arpan.php; f. 1964; weekly; Nepali; Publr and Chief Editor MANJU RATNA SAKYA; circ. 18,000.

Awake Weekly Chronicle: Kathmandu; English.

Commerce: Bhimsensthan, POB 171, Kathmandu; tel. (1) 4279636; fax (1) 4279544; e-mail manju_sakya@hotmail.com; f. 1971; monthly; English; Publr and Chief Editor MANJU RATNA SAKYA; Editor SUBHA LAXMI SAKYA; circ. 12,000.

Current: Gautam Marg, Kamalpokhari, Kathmandu; tel. (1) 4419484; fax (1) 4445406; f. 1982; weekly; Nepali; publ. by private limited co; Man. Editor KIRAN GAUTAM; Chief Editor DEVENDRA GAUTAM; circ. 10,000.

NEPAL

Cyber Post: Kathmandu; fortnightly; computers, electronics.

Foreign Affairs Journal: 5/287 Lagon, Kathmandu; f. 1976; 3 a year; articles on Nepalese foreign relations and diary of main news events; Publr and Editor BHOLA BIKRUM RANA; circ. 5,000.

Himal Southasian: Patan Dhoka, Lalitpur, POB 24393; tel. (1) 5547279; fax (1) 5552141; e-mail info@himalmag.com; internet www.himalmag.com; f. 1987; monthly; political, business, social and environmental issues throughout South Asia; Editor-in-Chief KANAK MANI DIXIT; Marketing Man. KOMAL MORE.

The Independent: Shankher Deep Bldg, Khichhapokhari, POB 3543, Kathmandu; tel. (1) 4249256; fax (1) 4226293; e-mail independ@mos.com.np; internet www.nepalnews.com/independent .htm; f. 1991; weekly; English; Editor SUBARNA B. CHHETRI.

Janadharana (People's Opinion): Kathmandu; e-mail janadharana@gmail.com; internet www.nepalnews.com.np/janadharana; weekly; independent; Editor NIMKANT PANDEY.

Janmabhumi: Janmabhumi Press, Tahachal, Kathmandu; tel. (1) 4280979; fax (1) 4274795; e-mail sirishnp@hotmail.com; f. 1970; weekly; Nepali; Publr and Editor SHIRISH BALLABH PRADHAN.

Koseli: Kathmandu; weekly; Nepali.

Madhuparka: Dharmapath, POB 23, Kathmandu; tel. (1) 4222278; f. 1986; monthly; Nepali; literary; Editor-in-Chief KRISHNA BHAKTA SHRESTHA; circ. 20,000.

Matribhoomi (Nepali Weekly): Ga-2-549, Kamal Pokhari (in front of the Police Station), Kathmandu; tel. (1) 4412501; weekly; Nepali; Editor GOVINDA BIYOGI.

Mulyankan: Kathmandu; monthly, left-wing; Editor SHYAM SHRESTHA.

Nepal Chronicle: Maruhiti; weekly; English; Publr and Editor CHANDRA LAL JHA.

Nepal National Weekly: Kantipur Publications Pvt Ltd, Kantipur Complex, Subhidhanagar, POB 8559, Kathmandu; tel. (1) 4480100; fax (1) 4496548; e-mail prashanta@kantipur.com.np; internet www.ekantipur.com/nepal; f. 2000; fortnightly; Nepali; Editor PRASHANT ARYAL; circ. 40,000.

Nepal Overseas Trade Statistics: Trade and Export Promotion Centre, Pulchowk, Lalitpur, POB 825, Kathmandu; tel. (1) 5525348; fax (1) 5525464; e-mail info@tepc.gov.np; internet www.tepc.gov.np; f. 2006; annual; English; Dir BADRI BAHADUR KARKI.

Nepal Post: 10/31 Gautam Marg, Kamalpokhari, Kathmandu, POB 191; tel. (1) 4419484; fax (1) 4445406; e-mail info@nayanepalpost.com; internet www.nayanepalpost.com; f. 1973; monthly; Chief Editor DEVENDRA GAUTAM.

Nepal Trade and Export Bulletin: Trade and Export Promotion Centre, Pulchowk, Lalitpur, POB 825, Kathmandu; tel. (1) 5532642; fax (1) 5525464; e-mail info@tepc.gov.np; internet www.tepc.gov.np; f. 2006; 3 a year; English; Dir BADRI BAHADUR KARKI (acting).

Nepali Times: Himalmedia Pvt Ltd, POB 7251, Kathmandu; tel. (1) 5250333; fax (1) 5251013; e-mail editors@nepalitimes.com; internet www.nepalitimes.com; f. 2000; weekly; English; publ. by Himalmedia Pvt Ltd; Publr and Chief Editor KUNDA DIXIT; circ. 15,000.

People's Review: Pipalbot, Dillibazar, POB 3052, Kathmandu; tel. (1) 4438797; fax (1) 4438797; e-mail preview@ntc.net.np; internet www.peoplesreview.com.np; weekly; English; Editor-in-Chief PUSHPA RAJ PRADHAN; circ. 15,000.

Rastrabani: Kathmandu; tel. (1) 4410339; weekly; Nepali; Chief Editor HARI LAMSAL.

Sanghu Weekly: Kathmandu; weekly; Editor GOPAL BUDHATHOKI.

Sanibariya: Kathmandu; weekly.

Saptahik Weekly: Kantipur Complex, Subhidhanagar, POB 8559, Kathmandu; tel. (1) 4480100; fax (1) 4470178; internet www.kantipuronline.com/saptahik_html/saptahik; f. 1997; weekly; Nepali; news and entertainment; Editor SUBASH DHAKAL.

Spotlight: POB 7256, Kathmandu; tel. (1) 4410772; e-mail spotlight@mos.com.np; f. 1991; weekly; English; Editor MADHAV KUMAR RIMAL.

Swatantra Manch Weekly: POB 49, Kathmandu; tel. (1) 4436374; fax (1) 4435931; e-mail das@ntc.net.np; f. 1985; independent; weekly; Nepali; Publr and Chief Editor VIJOY KUMAR DAS; circ. 30,000.

The Telegraph: Ghattekulo, Dillibazar, POB 4063, Kathmandu; tel. (1) 4419370; e-mail tgw@ntc.net.np; weekly; English; Chief Editor NARENDRA P. UPADHYAYA.

Vashudha: Makhan, Kathmandu; monthly; English; social, political and economic affairs; Publr and Editor T. L. SHRESTHA.

NEWS AGENCY

Rastriya Samachar Samiti (RSS): Bhadrakali Plaza, Kathmandu; tel. (1) 4262912; fax (1) 4262744; e-mail info@rss.com.np; internet www.rss.com.np; f. 1962; state-operated; Gen. Man. JAYA SHANKAR MAHATO; Chair. KOMAL NATH BARAL.

PRESS ASSOCIATIONS

Federation of Nepalese Journalists (FNJ): Media Village, Sinamangal, Kathmandu; tel. (1) 4490063; fax (1) 4490085; e-mail fnjnepal@mail.com.np; internet www.fnjnepal.org; f. 1956; Pres. DHARMENDRA JHA; Gen. Sec. K. C. POSHAN.

Nepal Journalists' Association (NJA): Maitighar, POB 285, Kathmandu; tel. (1) 4262426; fax (1) 4279544; e-mail manju_sakya@hotmail.com; internet www.nja.org.np; 5,400 mems; Pres. MANJU RATNA SAKYA; Gen. Sec. NIRMAL KUMAR ARYAL.

Press Council: Sanchargram, Tilganga, POB 3077, Kathmandu; tel. (1) 4469799; fax (1) 4469894; e-mail prescoun_mdf@wlink.com.np; internet www.presscouncilnepal.org; f. 1970; Chair. NARAYAN PRASAD SHARMA; Sec. SHREE DAR GAUTAM.

Publishers

Educational Publishing House: POB 5178, Kathmandu; tel. (1) 4241255; e-mail ishwarbshrestha@yahoo.com; f. 1962; educational and technical; Dir JYOTSNA SHRESTHA.

Himal Books: Himal Association, Patan Dhoka, POB 166, Lalitpur, Kathmandu; tel. (1) 5542544; fax (1) 5541196; e-mail books@himalassociation.org; internet www.himalassociation.org/himalbooks; f. 1992; subsidiary operation of Himal Association; general interest and academic publications in English and Nepali; Exec. Dir BASANTA THAPA.

International Standards Books and Periodicals (Pvt) Ltd: Bhotahity Bazaar, Chowk Bhitra, POB 3000, Kathmandu 44601; tel. (1) 4262815; fax (1) 4264179; e-mail u2@ccsl.com.np; f. 1991; Chief Man. Dir YOGYNDRA LALL CHHIPA; Chief Exec. and Man. Dir GANESH LALL SINGH CHHIPA.

Lakoul Press: Palpa-Tansen, Kathmandu; educational and physical sciences.

Mahabir Singh Chiniya Main: Makhan Tola, Kathmandu.

Mandass Memorials Publications: Kathmandu; Man. BASANT RAJ TULADHAR.

Pilgrims Book House: Thamel, POB 3872, Kathmandu; tel. (1) 4700942; fax (1) 4700943; e-mail pilgrims@wlink.com.np; internet www.pilgrimsbooks.com; f. 1986; Asian studies, religion and travel; Propr PUSHPA TIWARI.

Pilgrims Publishing Nepal (Pvt) Ltd: Goldhunga 4, POB 21646, Kathmandu; tel. (1) 4356764; fax (1) 4700544; internet www.pilgrimsbooks.com; f. 2000; Exec. Dir JOHN SNYDER; Man. Dir BISHOW BHATTA.

Ratna Pustak Bhandar: 71 Ga Bank Marg, POB 98, Kathmandu; tel. (1) 4223026; fax (1) 4248421; e-mail rpb@wlink.com.np; f. 1945; textbooks, general, non-fiction and fiction; Propr GOVINDA PRASAD SHRESTHA.

Royal Nepal Academy: Kamaladi, Kathmandu; tel. (1) 4221241; fax (1) 4221175; f. 1957; languages, literature, social sciences, art and philosophy; Dep. Admin. Chief T. D. BHANDARI.

Sajha Prakashan: Pulchowk, Lalitpur, POB 20259, Kathmandu; tel. (1) 5521118; fax (1) 5544236; e-mail sajhap@wlink.com.np; internet www.sajha.org.np; f. 1964; educational, literary and general; Chair. RAM VAROS KAPADI VRAMAR; Gen. Man. VICTOR PRADHAN.

Trans Asian Media Pvt Ltd: Thapathali Crossing, POB 5320, Kathmandu; tel. (1) 4242895; fax (1) 4223889; Man. Editor SHYAM GOENKA.

GOVERNMENT PUBLISHING HOUSE

Department of Information: Ministry of Information and Communications, Singha Durbar, Kathmandu; tel. (1) 483254; fax (1) 483252; e-mail info@doinepal.gov.np; internet www.doinepal.gov.np.

Broadcasting and Communications

TELECOMMUNICATIONS

Nepal Telecommunications Authority: Bluestar Office Complex, Tripureswor, POB 9754, Kathmandu; tel. (1) 4101030; fax (1)4101034; e-mail info@nta.gov.np; internet www.nta.gov.np; telecommunications regulatory body; f. 1998; Chair. DINESH KUMAR SHARMA.

Nepal Telecom (Nepal Doorsanchar Co Ltd): Bhadrakali Plaza, POB 11803, Kathmandu; tel. (1) 4210202; fax (1) 4222424; e-mail rkt@ntc.net.np; internet www.ntc.net.np; f. 1975; operates landline and mobile services; 85% state-owned, 10% owned by Nepalese public, 5% owned by Nepal Telecom employees; Man. Dir AMAR NATH SINGH.

NEPAL   *Directory*

Spice Nepal (Pvt) Ltd (SNPL): Krishna Tower, Buddhanagar, New Baneshwor, Kathmandu; tel. (1) 5554444; fax (1) 5554538; e-mail info@spicenepal.com; internet www.spicenepal.com; f. 2002; jt venture between Kazakhstan-based VISOR Group (75%), Raj Group (20%) and India-based Spice Cell (5%); operates GSM mobile network; Chair. RAJ BAHADUR SINGH; CEO DMITRY ZAIKA.

STM Telecom Sanchar: 768/47 Thirbam Sadak, Baluwatar, Kathmandu; tel. (1) 4445981; fax (1) 44419366; e-mail marketing@stmnetworks.com; internet www.stmi.com; f. 2003 as jt venture between the USA, Thailand and Nepal; awarded World Bank-funded project to provide rural telecommunication services to eastern region of Nepal; CEO ABHINAV PURI.

United Telecom: Ground Floor, Triveni Complex, Putali Sadak, Kathmandu; tel. (1) 2000050; fax (1) 2499999; e-mail info@utlnepal.com; internet www.utlnepal.com; f. 2003; jt venture between Indian-owned Mahanagar Telephone Nigam Ltd, Videsh Sanchar Nigam Ltd, Telecom Consultants India, and Nepal Venture (Pvt) Ltd; Chair. Shri S. K. GUPTA.

BROADCASTING

Radio

In July 2005 there were 47 commercial and community radio stations in Nepal. A media ordinance adopted by the King in October of that year banned private radio stations in the country from broadcasting news or information-related programmes. Following the April 2006 uprising and revocation of the King's direct rule, the seven-party alliance Government resumed issuing licences to independent broadcasters; by February 2008 licences had been granted to 254 FM operators.

Radio Nepal: Radio Broadcasting Service, Government of Nepal, Singha Durbar, POB 634, Kathmandu; tel. (1) 4211910; fax (1) 4211952; e-mail radio@rne.wlink.com.np; internet www.radionepal.org; f. 1951; broadcasts on short wave, medium wave and FM frequencies in 20 regional languages, incl. Nepali and English, for 18 hours daily (incl. two hours of regional broadcasting in the morning and evening); short-wave station at Khumaltar and medium-wave stations at Bhainsepati, Pokhara, Surkhet, Dipayal, Bardibas and Dharan; FM stations at Kathmandu, Kanchanpur, Rupandhi, Chitwan, Makawanpur, Bara, Jumla, Mustang, Ilam, Simikot and Humla; Exec. Dir R. S. KARKI.

Himalaya Broadcasting Co (Radio HBC 94 FM): POB 8974, CPC 94, Kathmandu; tel. (1) 4489618; fax (1) 4499788; e-mail hbc94fm@hbc.com.np; internet www.hbc.com.np; f. 1999.

Hits FM: POB 21912, Baneshwor, Kathmandu; tel. (1) 4780534; fax (1) 4780543; e-mail info@hitsfm.com.np; internet www.hitsfm.com.np; f. 1996; broadcasts 24 hrs daily; Exec. Dir JEEVAN SHRESTHA.

Image FM (Kath FM): POB 5566, Kathmandu; tel. (1) 4230368; fax (1) 4241260; e-mail kath979@wlink.com.np; internet www.imagechannels.com; f. 1999; Station Man. BHARAT SHAKYA.

Kantipur FM: Kantipur Complex, Subhidhanagar, POB 8559, Kathmandu; tel. (1) 4480100; fax (1) 4470178; e-mail kfm@kanti.mos.com.np; f. 1998; broadcasts 24 hrs daily; Man. Dir BINOD RAJ GYAWALI; Station Man. PRABHAT RIMAL.

Radio Lumbini: Aanandabane VDC, Ward No. 3, Manigram, Rupandehi, Lumbini; tel. (71) 561003; fax (71) 561545; e-mail lumbinifm@mos.com.np; internet www.radiolumbini.org; f. 2000; Station Man. MOHAN CHAPAGAIN.

Radio Sagarmatha: Bakhundol, Lalitpur, GPOB 6958, Kathmandu; tel. (1) 5528091; fax (1) 5530227; e-mail stationmanager@radiosagarmatha.org; internet www.radiosagarmatha.org; f. 1997; independent; Chair. LAXMAN UPRETI; Station Man. GHAMA RAJ LUITEL.

Times FM: GPOB 8975, EPC 906, Jawalakhel, Lalitpur, Kathmandu; tel. and fax (1) 5539171; e-mail timesfm@hotnepal.com; Man. Dir R. K. SHRESTHA.

Television

In 1986 Nepal's first television station began broadcasting within the Kathmandu valley.

Nepal Television Corpn: Singha Durbar, POB 3826, Kathmandu; tel. (1) 4220348; fax (1) 4228312; internet neptv.com.np; f. 1985; operates NTV and NTV2; programmes in Nepali (50%), English (25%) and Hindi/Urdu (25%); regional station at Kohalpur; Chair. PURNA BAHADUR GHARTI MAGUR.

Avenues TV: 11 Avenues Plaza, Teku Rd, Ganeshman Marga, Kathmandu; tel. (1) 4227222; fax (1) 4248811; e-mail atv@avenues.tv; f. 2003; news service.

Image Channel: 369 Narayan Gopal Sadak, POB 9581, Lazimpat, Kathmandu; tel. (1) 4433141; fax (1) 4432707; e-mail ichannel@wlink.com.np; internet www.imagechannels.com; f. 2003; privately owned; Chair. R. K. MANANDHAR.

Kantipur Television Network (KTV): Kantipur Complex, Subhidhanagar, POB 8559, Kathmandu; tel. (1) 4480100; fax (1) 4470178; internet www.kantipurtv.com; f. 2003; Chair. HEM RAJ GYAWALI; Man. Dir JEEWA LAMICHHANE.

Finance

(auth. = authorized; cap. = capital; m. = million; dep. = deposits; res = reserves; brs = branches; amounts in Nepalese rupees)

BANKING

Central Bank

Nepal Rastra Bank: Central Office, Baluwatar, POB 73, Kathmandu; tel. (1) 4411250; fax (1) 4410159; e-mail gsd@nrb.org.np; internet www.nrb.org.np; f. 1956; bank of issue; 100% state-owned; cap. 3,000.0m., res 32,374.1m., dep. 36,914.9m. (July 2006); Gov. DEEPENDRA BAHADUR KSHETRY (acting); 9 brs.

Domestic Commercial Banks

Kumari Bank Ltd: Putalisadak, POB 21128, Kathmandu; tel. (1) 4232112; fax (1) 4231960; e-mail info@kbl.com.np; internet www.kumaribank.com; f. 2001; auth. cap. 750.0m., res 240.6m., dep. 10,770.4m. (July 2007); Chair. SHIVA RATAN SHARADA.

Nepal Bank Ltd: Nepal Bank Bldg, Dharmapath, New Rd, POB 36, Kathmandu; tel. (1) 4222397; fax (1) 4220414; e-mail info@nepalbank.com.np; internet www.nepalbank.com.np; f. 1937; 40% state-owned, 60% owned by Nepalese public; cap. 380.4m., res 1,523.6m., dep. 30,014.2m. (July 2007); CEO BINOD ATREYA; 96 brs.

Nepal Industrial and Commercial Bank Ltd (NIC Bank): Kamaladi, Ganeshthan, POB 7367, Kathmandu; tel. (1) 4222336; fax (1) 4241865; e-mail kamaladi@nicbank.com.np; internet www.nicbank.com; f. 1998; privately owned; cap. 660.0m., res 246.1m., dep. 10,299.9m. (July 2007); Chair. JAGDISH PRASAD AGRAWAL; CEO SASHIN JOSHI; 10 brs.

Rastriya Banijya Bank (National Commercial Bank): POB 8368, Singha Durbar Plaza, Kathmandu; tel. (1) 4252595; fax (1) 4252931; e-mail rbb.info@rbb.com.np; internet www.rbb.com.np; f. 1966; 100% state-owned; cap. 1,172.3m., dep. 46,195.5m. (July 2006); Chair. KHRISNA HARI BASKOTA; CEO JANARDAN ACHARYA; 114 brs, 4 regional offices.

Joint-venture Banks

Bank of Kathmandu Ltd: Kamal Pokhari, POB 9044, Kathmandu; tel. (1) 4414541; fax (1) 4418990; e-mail info@bok.com.np; internet www.bok.com.np; f. 1993; 58% owned by Nepalese public, 42% by local promoters; cap. 603.1m., res 372.1m., dep. 12,614.7m. (July 2007); Chair. SANJAY B. SHAH; Man. Dir RADHESH PANT.

Everest Bank Ltd: POB 13384, EBL House, Lazimpat, Kathmandu; tel. (1) 4443377; fax (1) 4443160; e-mail ebl@mos.com.np; internet www.everestbankltd.com; f. 1994; 50% owned by directors, 20% by Punjab National Bank (India) and 30% by the Nepalese public; cap. 518.0m., res 553.0m., dep. 18,513.0m. (July 2007); Chair. BISHNU KRISHNA SHRESTHA; 22 brs.

Global Bank Ltd: Adarshanagar, Birgunj 13, POB 45, Parsa; tel. (1) 530337; fax (1) 530339; internet www.globalbanknepal.com; f. 2006; Chair. CHANDRA PRASAD DHAKAL; CEO ANIL GYAWALI.

Himalayan Bank Ltd: Karmachari Sanchaya Kosh Bldg, Tridevi Marg, Thamel, POB 20590, Kathmandu; tel. (1) 4227749; fax (1) 4222800; e-mail hbl@hbl.com.np; internet www.himalayanbank.com; f. 1993; 20% owned by Habib Bank Ltd (Pakistan); cap. 810.8m., res 1,151.3m., dep. 30,499.7m. (July 2007); Chair. MANOJ BAHADUR SHRESTHA; CEO ASOKE S. J. B. RANA; 8 brs.

Laxmi Bank Ltd: Hattisar, POB 19593, Kathmandu; tel. (51) 530394; fax (51) 530393; e-mail info@laxmibank.com; internet www.laxmibank.com; f. 2001; cap. 609.9m., res 15.7m., dep. 4,449.1m. (July 2006); Chair. RAJENDRA K. KHETAN; CEO SUMAN JOSHI.

Nabil Bank Ltd (Nabil): Nabil House, Kamaladi, POB 3729, Kathmandu; tel. (1) 4429546; fax (1) 4429548; e-mail nabil@nabilbank.com; internet www.nabilbank.com; f. 1984 as Nepal Arab Bank Ltd, name changed as above Jan. 2000; 50% owned by National Bank of Bangladesh, 30% by the Nepalese public and 20% by Nepalese govt financial institutions; cap. 491.7m., res 2,068.7m., dep. 23,342.3m. (July 2007); Chair. SATYENDRA PYARA SHRESTHA; Chief. Exec. ANIL SHAH; 27 brs.

Nepal Bangladesh Bank Ltd: Bijuli Bazar, New Baneshwor, POB 9062, Kathmandu; tel. (1) 4783976; fax (1) 4780316; e-mail nbblho@nbbl.com.np; internet www.nbbl.com.np; f. 1994; 50% owned by International Finance Investment and Commerce Bank Ltd (Bangladesh), 20% by Nepalese promoters and 30% public issue; cap. 359.9m., res 324.0m., dep. 10,580.7m. (July 2003); CEO SHOVAN DEV PANT; Chair. JEET BAHADUR SHRESTHA; 15 brs.

NEPAL

Directory

Nepal Credit and Commerce Bank Ltd: NB Bldg, Bagh Bazar, Kathmandu; tel. (1) 4246991; fax (1) 4244610; e-mail nccb@nccbank.com.np; internet www.nccbank.com.np; f. as Nepal Bank of Ceylon, reconstituted as above in Sept. 2002 after Bank of Ceylon (Sri Lanka) sold its shares to NB Group (Nepal); Chair. PRITHIVI RAJ LIGAL; CEO RATNA RAJ BAJRACHARYA; 17 brs.

Nepal Investment Bank Ltd: Durbar Marg, POB 3412, Kathmandu; tel. (1) 4228229; fax (1) 4226349; e-mail info@nibl.com.np; internet www.nibl.com.np; f. 1986 as Nepal Indosuez Bank Ltd, name changed as above in June 2002; 50% owned by a consortium of Nepalese investors, 20% by general public, 15% by Rastriya Banijya Bank and 15% by Rastriya Beema Sansthan; cap. 801.4m., res 955.4m., dep. 25,321.3m. (July 2007); Chair. and Chief Exec. PRITHIVI BAHADUR PANDE; 12 brs.

Nepal SBI Bank Ltd: Corporate Office, Hattisar, POB 6049, Kathmandu; tel. (1) 4435516; fax (1) 4435612; e-mail nsblco@nsbl.com.np; internet www.nepalsbi.com.np; f. 1993; 50% owned by State Bank of India, 30% by Nepalese public, 15% by Employees' Provident Fund (Nepal) and 5% by Agricultural Development Bank (Nepal); Chair. B. K. SHRESTHA; Man. Dir N. K. CHARI.

Nepal Sri Lanka Merchant Bank Ltd: NSLMB Bldg, Kalamadi, POB 12248, Kathmandu; tel. (1) 4440300; fax (1) 4441034; e-mail nslmb@info.com.np; Exec. Dir VED MAN SINGH MALLA.

Standard Chartered Bank Nepal Ltd: Grindlays Bhavan, Naya Baneshwor, POB 3990, Kathmandu; tel. (1) 4246753; fax (1) 4226762; internet www.standardchartered.com/np; f. 1986 as Nepal Grindlays Bank; name changed in July 2001; 75% owned by Standard Chartered Bank (United Kingdom) and 25% by the Nepalese public; cap. 413.3m., res 1,198.4m., dep. 25,047.0m. (July 2007); Chair. CHRISTOPHER LOW; CEO SUJIT MUNDUL; 7 brs.

Banking Organization

Nepal Bankers' Association (NBA): Heritage Plaza, C and D Block, 2nd Floor, Kamaladi, Kathmandu; e-mail info@nepalbankers.com; internet www.nepalbankers.com; Pres. RADHESH PANT.

Development Finance Organizations

Agricultural Development Bank: Ramshah Path, Kathmandu; tel. (1) 4262885; fax (1) 4262616; e-mail info@adbn.gov.np; internet www.adbn.gov.np; f. 1968; 93.6% state-owned, 2.1% owned by the Nepal Rastra Bank, and 4.3% by co-operatives and private individuals; specialized agricultural credit institution providing credit for agricultural development to co-operatives, individuals and asscns; receives deposits from individuals, co-operatives and other asscns to generate savings in the agricultural sector; acts as Government's implementing agency for small farmers' group development project, assisted by the Asian Development Bank and financed by the UN Development Programme; operational networks include 14 zonal offices, 37 brs, 92 sub-brs, 52 depots and 160 small farmers' development projects, three Zonal Training Centres, two Appropriate Technology Units; Chair. BAMDEV CHHETRI; CEO JANAK RAJ SHAH.

Nepal Development Bank: Heritage Plaza, POB 11017, Kamaladi, Kathmandu; tel. (1) 4254639; fax (1) 4245753; e-mail ndevbank@ndbl.com.np; internet www.ndevbank.com; f. 1998; Chair. AMAR GURUNG; CEO SUNANDA B. SHRESTHA.

Nepal Housing Development Finance Co Ltd: New Baneshwor, POB 5624, Kathmandu; tel. (1) 4780259; fax (1) 4792753; e-mail info@nepalhousing.com; internet www.nepalhousing.com; Chair. BINOD KUMAR GURAGAI; Gen. Man. ACHUT RAJ SAPKOTA.

STOCK EXCHANGE

Nepal Stock Exchange Ltd (NEPSE): Singha Durbar Plaza, POB 1550, Kathmandu; tel. (1) 4250735; fax (1) 4262538; e-mail info@nepalstock.com; internet www.nepalstock.com; f. 1976; reorg. 1984; converted in 1993 from Securities Exchange Centre Ltd to Nepal Stock Exchange Ltd; 147 listed cos, 139 scripts; Chair. NARAYAN PRASAD POUDEL; Gen. Man. SHANKER MAN SINGH.

INSURANCE

Alliance Insurance Co Ltd: Durbar Marg, POB 10811, Kathmandu; tel. (1) 4222836; fax (1) 4241411; e-mail sk@aic.wlink.com.np.

Everest Insurance Co Ltd: Hattisar, POB 10675, Kathmandu; tel. (1) 4444717; fax (1) 4444366; e-mail evensco@mos.com.np; internet www.everestinsurance.com; Chair. RAJENDRA K. KHETAN.

Himalayan General Insurance Co Ltd: Babar Mahal, POB 148, Kathmandu; tel. (1) 4231788; fax (1) 4241517; e-mail ktm@hgi.com.np; internet www.hgi.com.np; f. 1993; CEO MAHENDRA KRISHNA SHRESTHA.

National Insurance Co Ltd: Tripureswor, POB 376, Kathmandu; tel. (1) 4250710; fax (1) 4261289; e-mail natinsur@ccsl.com.np; Man. A. S. KOHLI.

National Life and General Insurance Co Ltd: Lazimpat, POB 4332, Kathmandu; tel. (1) 4412625; fax (1) 4416427; e-mail nlgi@mail.com.np; Chief Exec. S. K. SINGH; Pres. OM SINGH.

Neco Insurance Ltd: Hattisar, POB 12271, Lal Durbar, Kathmandu; tel. (1) 4427354; fax (1) 4418761; e-mail info@necoins.com.np; f. 1994; Chair. JANARDAN AACHARYA; CEO ANIL SHARMA.

Nepal Insurance Co Ltd: NIC Bldg, Kamaladi, POB 3623, Kathmandu; tel. (1) 4221353; fax (1) 4225446; e-mail info@nepalinsurance.com; internet www.nepalinsurance.com; Chair. BHARAT KARKI; Man. Dir NIRMAL KUMAR BARAL.

The Oriental Insurance Co Ltd: Jyoti Bhavan, POB 165, Kathmandu; tel. (1) 4221448; fax (1) 4223419; e-mail oriental@wlink.com.np; CEO Dr MADHUSUDAN KUMAR.

Premier Insurance Co (Nepal) Ltd: Tripureswor Plaza, Tripureswor, POB 9183, Kathmandu; tel. (1) 4259567; fax (1) 4249708; e-mail premier@picl.com.np; internet www.premier-insurance.com.np; f. 1994; Pres. RADHE SHYAM GORKHALI; Chair. RAM LAL SHRESHTHA.

Rastriya Beema Sansthan (National Insurance Corpn): RBS Bldg, Ramshah Path, POB 527, Kathmandu; tel. (1) 4213882; fax (1) 4262610; e-mail beema@wlink.com.np; internet www.beema.com.np; f. 1967; Gen. Man. BIR BIKRAM RAXAMAJHI.

Sagarmatha Insurance Co Ltd: Kathmandu Plaza, Block Y, 4th Floor, Kamaladi, POB 12211, Kathmandu; tel. (1) 4240896; fax (1) 4247947; e-mail sagarmatha@insurance.wlink.com.np; Exec. Dir K. B. BASNYAT.

United Insurance Co (Nepal) Ltd: I. J. Plaza, Durbar Marg, POB 9075, Kathmandu; tel. (1) 4246686; fax (1) 4246687; e-mail uic@mail.com.np; internet www.unitedinsurance.com.np; Chair. RAVI BHAKTA SHRESTHA; Gen. Man. RABI MAN JOSHI.

Trade and Industry

GOVERNMENT AGENCY

National Planning Commission (NPC): Singha Durbar, POB 1284, Kathmandu; tel. (1) 4225879; fax (1) 4226500; e-mail npcs@npcnepal.gov.np; Vice-Chair. JAGADISH CHANDRA POKHAREL.

DEVELOPMENT ORGANIZATIONS

National Productivity and Economic Development Centre: Balaju Industrial District, POB 1318, Kathmandu; tel. (1) 4350566; fax (1) 4350530; e-mail npedc@wlink.com.np; internet www.npedc-nepal.org; functions as secretariat of National Productivity Council; provides services for industrial promotion and productivity improvement through planning research, consultancy, training, seminars and information services; Gen. Man. SHAMBHU NATH PANT (acting).

National Tea and Coffee Development Board (NTCDB): New Baneshwor, POB 9683, Kathmandu; tel. (1) 4495792; fax (1) 4497941; e-mail ntcdb@hons.com.np; internet teacoffee.gov.np; f. 1992 to promote and expand the Nepalese tea industry; Vice-Chair. SURAJ VAIDYA.

National Trading Ltd: Teku, POB 128, Kathmandu; tel. (1) 4225799; fax (1) 4225151; e-mail info@nationaltrading.com.np; internet www.nationaltrading.com.np; f. 1962; govt-owned; imports and distributes construction materials and raw materials for industry; also machinery, vehicles and consumer goods; operates bonded warehouse, duty-free shop and related activities; brs in all major towns; Chair. L. P. AGRAWAL.

Nepal Foreign Trade Association: Bagmati Chamber, 1st Floor, Milan Marg, Teku, POB 541, Kathmandu; tel. (1) 4223784; fax (1) 4247159; e-mail nfta@mos.com.np; f. 1972; Pres. AKHIL KUMAR CHAPAGAIN; Vice-Pres. SATISH KUMAR MORE; 431 mems.

Nepal Tea Development Corpn Ltd: Triveni Complex, Putali Sadak, Kathmandu; tel. (1) 4224074; fax (1) 4266133; e-mail ntdc@trivenionline.com; internet www.ntdcltd.com; f. 1966; privatized in early 2000s; commercial production of tea; Contact SUBHASH C. SHANGHAI.

Trade and Export Promotion Centre (TEPC): Na Tole, Pulchowk, Lalitpur, POB 825, Kathmandu; tel. (1) 5525898; fax (1) 5525464; e-mail info@tepc.gov.np; internet www.tepc.gov.np; f. 1971; govt-owned; Exec. Dir DILPI ARYAL (acting).

CHAMBERS OF COMMERCE

Federation of Nepalese Chambers of Commerce and Industry (FNCCI): Pachali Shahid Shukra FNCCI Milan Marg, Teku, POB 269, Kathmandu; tel. (1) 4262061; fax (1) 4261022; e-mail fncci@mos

.com.np; internet www.fncci.org; f. 1965; comprises 91 District Municipality Chambers (DCCIs), 66 Commodity Associations, 376 leading industrial and commercial undertakings in both the public and private sector, and 10 Bi-national Chambers; publishes annual *Nepal and the World: A Statistical Profile* and directory of members every three years; Pres. KUSH KUMAR JOSHI; Dir-Gen. NEGH NATH NEUPANE.

Birganj Chamber of Commerce and Industries: Hospital Rd, Birganj; tel. (51) 522290; fax (51) 526049; e-mail bicci@atcnet.com.np; 605 mems; Pres. VIJAY KUMAR SARAWAGI.

Lalitpur Chamber of Commerce and Industry: Mangal Bazar, Patan Durbar Sq., POB 26, Lalitpur; tel. (1) 5530663; fax (1) 5530661; e-mail lcci@mos.com.np; internet www.lcci.org.np; f. 1967; Pres. UMESH LAL AMATYA; Sec.-Gen. NARESH KUMAR SHRESTHA.

Nepal Chamber of Commerce: Chamber Bhavan, Kantipath, POB 198, Kathmandu; tel. (1) 4230947; fax (1) 4229998; e-mail chamber@wlink.com.np; internet www.nepalchamber.org; f. 1952; non-profit org. promoting industrial and commercial development; 8,000 regd cos and 1,600 ordinary mems; Pres. SURENDRA BIR MALAKAR; Sec.-Gen. BHAKTA BAHADUR MALLA.

INDUSTRIAL AND TRADE ASSOCIATIONS

Association of Craft Producers: Ravi Bhavan Mode, POB 3701, Kathmandu; tel. (1) 4275108; fax (1) 4272676; e-mail craftacp@mos.com.np; internet acp.org.np; f. 1984; local non-profit org. providing technical, marketing and management services for craft producers; manufacturer, exporter and retailer of handicraft goods; Exec. Dir MEERA BHATTARAI; Programme Dir REVITA SHRESTHA.

Association of Forest-based Industries and Trade: Thapathali, POB 2798, Kathmandu; tel. (1) 4216020.

Association of Nepalese Rice, Oil and Pulses Industries: POB 20782, Radha Bhavan, Tripureshwor, Kathmandu; tel. (1) 4215676; e-mail nfma@mcmail.com.np; Pres. TOLA RAM DUGAR; Gen. Sec. CHANDRA KRISHNA KARMACHARYA.

Association of Pharmaceutical Producers of Nepal: Babar Mahal, POB 21721, Maitighar, Kathmandu; tel. and fax (1) 4231871; e-mail appon@wlink.com.np; Pres. PRADEEP MAN VAIDYA; Sec.-Gen. UMESH LAL SHRESTHA.

Cargo Agents' Association of Nepal: Thamel, POB 5355, Kathmandu; tel. (1) 4419019; fax (1) 4419858.

Central Carpet Industries Association of Nepal: Maitighar, Babar Mahal, POB 2419, Kathmandu; tel. (1) 4259400; fax (1) 4262458; e-mail ccia@enet.com.np; internet www.nepalcarpet.org; Pres. A. G. SHERPA; Gen. Sec. KAPIL PRASAD BAZGAIN.

Computer Association of Nepal: 235/39 Maitidevi Marga, Kathmandu; tel. (1) 4432700; fax (1) 4441998; e-mail info@can.org.np; internet www.can.org.np; f. 1992; asscn of the IT Businessmen's Organization; Pres. SURESH K. KARNA.

Federation of Handicrafts Associations of Nepal: Upma Marg, Thapathali, POB 784, Kathmandu; tel. (1) 4244231; fax (1) 4222940; e-mail han@wlink.com.np; internet www.nepalhandicraft.org.np; f. 1972; Pres. PUSKAR MAN SHAKYA.

Federation of Nepal Cottage and Small Industries (FNCSI): Chabahil, POB 6530, Kathmandu; tel. (1) 4491528; fax (1) 4468337; e-mail fncsi@ntc.net.np; internet www.fncsi.org.np; business networks in 70 districts; represents interests and promotes development of nation's micro, cottage and small industries; 30,000 general mems (2007); Pres. ANG DENDI SHERPA.

Garment Association of Nepal: Shankhamul Rd, New Baneshwor, POB 21332, Kathmandu; tel. (1) 4780691; fax (1) 4780173; e-mail gan@ntc.net.np; internet www.ganasso.org; Pres. KIRAN P. SAAKHA.

Himalayan Orthodox Tea Producers' Association of Nepal: Bakhundole, Lalitpur; internet www.nepaltea.com.np; f. 1998; non-profit making org.; represents and promotes the Himalayan tea sector; Chair. DEEPAK PRAKASH BASKOTA.

Leather Footwear and Goods Manufacturers' Association of Nepal: Bag Bazar, POB 19732, Kathmandu; tel. (1) 4219349; e-mail lfgman@ntc.net.np; Pres. RAM KRISHNA PRASAI.

Nepal Forest Industries Association: Naxal, Nag Pokhari, POB 5623, Kathmandu; tel. (1) 4411865; fax (1) 4413838; e-mail padmasri@ccsl.com.np; Pres. HARI PRASAD GIRI; Sec.-Gen. ROHINI THAPALIYA.

Nepal Leather Industries Association: POB 9944, Anamnagar, Kathmandu; tel. (1) 4265248; fax (1) 4228978; e-mail giris@atcnet.com.np; Pres. SANJAY GIRI; Sec.-Gen. RAMESH RAJ POKHAREL.

Nepal Plastic Manufacturers' Association: Kandevsthan, Kupandol, POB 2350, Lalitpur; tel. and fax (1) 5528185; Pres. SHAILENDRA LAL PRADHAN; Sec.-Gen. RAJESWOR LAL JOSHI.

Nepal Tea Planters' Association: Bhadrapur-4, Jhapa; tel. (23) 520059; fax (23) 420679; Pres. CHANDI PRASAD PARAJULI; Sec.-Gen. MAL CHAND GOYAL.

Nepal Textile Industries Association: Krishna Galli, Lalitpur; tel. (1) 5529290; fax (1) 5520291; Pres. GOPAL P. KSHATRIYA; Sec.-Gen. RAM K. MAHARJAN.

Nepal Trans-Himalayan Trade Association: Jyoti Bhavan, Kantipath, POB 133, Kathmandu; tel. (1) 4225490; fax (1) 4254048; e-mail syamukapu@unilever.wlink.com.np; Pres. TRIBHUWAN D. TULADHAR; Gen. Sec. MAHESH TULADHAR.

UTILITIES

Electricity

Butwal Power Co Ltd: 313 Ganga Devi Marga, Buddha Nagar, POB 11728, Kathmandu; tel. (1) 4781776; fax (1) 4780994; e-mail service@bpc.com.np; internet www.bpc.com.np; f. 1966; partially privatized in 2003; principal shareholders: 68.95% owned by Shangri-La Energy Ltd, 9.09% by Ministry of Water Resources and 6.05% by Interkraft Norway; 5.91% divided between Nepalese energy orgs and employees; public sector retains 10% ownership; owns and operates Jhimruk and Andhi Khola Hydropower Plants; supplies electricity to the national grid; 326 employees; Chair. PADMA JYOTI.

Chilime Hydropower Co Ltd: Kalikasthan, POB 25210, Kathmandu; tel. (1) 44439163; fax (1) 4443077; e-mail chpcl@wlink.com.np; internet www.chilime.com.np; 51% owned by Nepal Electricity Authority; Dir UTTAR KUMAR SHRESTHA.

Department of Electricity Development: 576 Bhakti Thapa Sadak-4, POB 2507, Anamnagar, Kathmandu; tel. (1) 4496800; fax (1) 4480257; e-mail info@doed.gov.np; internet www.doed.gov.np; f. 1993; fmrly Electricity Development Centre; name changed as above 1999; under Ministry of Water Resources; Dir-Gen. SRIRANJAN LACOUL.

Nepal Electricity Authority: Durbar Marga, Kathmandu; tel. (1) 4252835; fax (1) 4256091; e-mail sapkota.pawan@gmail.com; internet www.nea.org.np; f. 1985 following merger; govt-owned; Chair. BISHNU POUDEL; Man. Dir and CEO UTTAR KUMAR SHRESTHA.

Water

Nepal Water Supply Corpn: Tripureshwor Marg, POB 5349, Kathmandu; tel. (1) 4262202; fax (1) 4262229; e-mail info@nwsc.com.np; internet www.nwsc.gov.np; f. 1990; govt-owned; Gen. Man. GAUTAM BAHADUR AMATYA.

TRADE UNIONS

Trade unions were banned in Nepal in 1961, but were legalized again in 1990, following the success of the pro-democracy movement and the collapse of the Panchayat system.

Nepal Trade Union Congress—I (NTUC—I): POB 5507, Kathmandu; tel. (1) 5527443; fax (1) 5527469; e-mail ntuc@mos.com.np; internet www.ntuc.org.np; f. 1947 as the Nepal Trade Union Congress; 28 affiliated unions; affiliated to ICFTU; operates in association with Nepali Congress Party; merged with Democratic Confederation of Nepalese Trade Unions in March 2008 and name changed to the above; Co-Pres LAXMAN BASNET, KHILA NATH DAHAL; 192,000 mems.

General Federation of Nepalese Trade Unions (GEFONT): Man Mohan Labour Bldg, GEFONT Plaza, Putali Sadak, POB 10652, Kathmandu; tel. (1) 4248072; fax (1) 4248073; e-mail dfa@gefont.org; internet www.gefont.org; f. 1989; 19 affiliated unions; Chair. MUKUNDA NEUPANE.

Transport

Ministry of Labour and Transport Management: Singha Durbar, Kathmandu; tel. (1) 4247842; fax (1) 4256877; e-mail info@moltm.gov.np; internet www.moltm.gov.np; Sec. YUBA RAJ PANDEY.

Interstate Multi-Modal Transport (Pvt) Ltd: Shiva Sabitri Sadan, 240 Red Cross Marg, Kalimati, Kathmandu; tel. (1) 4271473; fax (1) 4271570; e-mail rauniar@mos.com.np; f. 1975; provides freight forwarding, transport contracting, customs clearance, warehousing and shipping services, transport consultancy, terminal operations, logistics solutions; Gen. Man. ANAND S. RAUNIAR.

RAILWAYS

Nepal Railways Corpn Ltd (NRC): Khajuri, Janakpur; tel. (41) 52082; HQ Jayanagar, India; f. 1937 as Janakpur-Jayanagar Railways; name changed as above June 2004; 53 km open, linking Jayanagar with Janakpur and Bijalpura; narrow gauge; 11 steam engines, 25 coaches and vans, and 20 wagons; Gen. Man. MADAN SINGH MAHAT.

Nepal Government Railway: Birganj; f. 1927; 7 steam engines, 12 coaches and 82 wagons; Man. D. SINGH (acting).

NEPAL

ROADS

In 2007 there were 17,609 km of roads, of which 5,222 km were black-topped and 4,738 km gravel-covered. Around Kathmandu there are short sections of roads suitable for motor vehicles, and there is a 28-km ring road round the valley. A 190-km mountain road, Tribhuwana Rajpath, links the capital with the Indian railhead at Raxaul. The Siddhartha Highway, constructed with Indian assistance, connects the Pokhara valley, in mid-west Nepal, with Sonauli, on the Indian border in Uttar Pradesh. The 114-km Arniko Highway, constructed with Chinese help, connects Kathmandu with Kodari, on the Chinese border. In the early 1990s the final section of the 1,030-km East–West Highway (Mahendra Highway) was constructed. A number of north–south roads were also constructed to connect the district headquarters with the East–West Highway.

A fleet of container trucks operates between Kolkata and Raxaul in India and other points in Nepal for transporting exports to, and imports from, third countries. Trolley buses provide a passenger service over the 13 km between Kathmandu and Bhaktapur.

ROPEWAY

A 42-km ropeway links Hetauda and Kathmandu and can carry 22 metric tons of freight per hour throughout the year. Food grains, construction goods and heavy goods on this route are transported by the ropeway.

CIVIL AVIATION

Tribhuvan International Airport is situated about 6 km from Kathmandu. In 2007 Nepal had 47 airports, of various standards; in mid-2007, however, only 33 of these airports were in operation.

Civil Aviation Authority of Nepal (CAAN): Babar Mahal, Kathmandu; tel. (1) 262518; fax (1) 262516; e-mail cnsatm@mos.com.np; internet www.caanepal.org.np; f. 1998; Dir-Gen. YAJNA PRASAD GAUTAM.

Nepal Airlines Corpn (NAC): RNAC Bldg, Kantipath, POB 401, Kathmandu 711000; tel. (1) 4220757; fax (1) 4225348; e-mail info@nac.com.np; internet www.royalnepal-airlines.com; f. 1958; fmrly Royal Nepal Airlines Corpn (RNAC); 100% state-owned (scheduled for transfer to private ownership); scheduled services to 30 domestic airfields, international scheduled flights to 10 destinations in Europe, the Middle East and the Far East, charter flights; Man. Dir S. R. KANSAKAR.

The monopoly of the RNAC in domestic air services came to an end in 1992. By 2007 there were about 16 private airlines in Nepal providing domestic cargo and passenger services. The Government of Nepal announced in August 2007 that foreign airlines operating services to Nepal would be permitted to increase flight frequencies during the height of the tourist season that year—between September and December—in order to ease pressure on existing services and those provided by the national NAC.

Buddha Air: Jawalakhal, Lalitpur, POB 2167, Kathmandu; tel. (1) 5521015; fax (1) 5537726; e-mail buddhaair@buddhaair.com; internet www.buddhaair.com; f. 1997; domestic passenger services; Man. Dir BIRENDRA B. BASNET; Chair. SURENDRA B. BASNET.

Cosmic Air: Kalimatidole, Sinamangal, POB 3488, Kathmandu; tel. (1) 4490146; fax (1) 4497569; e-mail soi@wlink.com.np; internet www.cosmicair.com; f. 1997; operates domestic cargo, passenger and mountain flights; began operating flights to a limited no. of Indian destinations in 2004; Exec. Chair. SANJAYA PRADHAM; Man. Dir M. B. MATHEMA.

Gorkha Airlines: Maharajgunj, POB 9451, Kathmandu; tel. (1) 4435122; fax (1) 4444525; e-mail gorkha@mos.com.np; internet www.gorkhaairlines.com; f. 1996; scheduled and charter passenger and cargo flights to domestic destinations; Gen. Man. RABINDRA SILWAL.

Yeti Airlines: Tilganga, POB 20011, Kathmandu; tel. (1) 4465888; fax (1) 4464977; e-mail yetiair@wlink.com.np; internet www.yetiairlines.com; f. 1998; operates scheduled and chartered domestic flights; Chair. LHAKPA SONAM SHERPA; Man. Dir ANG TSHERING SHERPA.

Tourism

Tourism is being developed through the construction of new tourist centres in the Kathmandu valley, Pokhara valley and Chitwan. Regular air services link Kathmandu with Pokhara and Chitwan. Major tourist attractions include Lumbini, the birthplace of Buddha, the lake city of Pokhara and the Himalaya mountain range, including Mt Everest, the world's highest peak. In 1989, in an effort to increase tourism, the Government abolished travel restrictions in 18 areas of north-western Nepal that had previously been inaccessible to foreigners. Following the restoration of parliamentary democracy in 1990, tourist arrivals in Nepal rose considerably. Further travel restrictions in the remote areas of the country were abolished in 1991, and efforts were made to attract foreign investment in the Nepalese tourism industry, but the insurgency in the west hindered development in the early and mid-2000s. The cessation of Maoist hostilities in 2006 and the subsequent peace agreement between the former insurgents and the political parties' alliance—combined with the introduction of additional airline services between Nepal and other Asian countries—led to a significant recovery in the tourism sector. Tourism arrivals witnessed massive growth, from 383,926 in 2006 to 526,000 in 2007, and over the same period revenue from tourism increased by more than 40%, from US $157.0m. to $230.6m. The industry continued to be buoyant in 2008, when a record 547,040 tourists were estimated to have visited Nepal. Since 2005, in an effort further to promote tourism, access has been granted to an additional 175 mountains, raising the total number of mountains open to climbers to 326.

Nepal Tourism Board: Tourist Service Centre, Bhrikuti Mandap, POB 11018, Kathmandu; tel. (1) 4256909; fax (1) 4256910; e-mail info@ntb.org.np; internet www.welcomenepal.com; f. 1998; Chair. LEELA MANI POUDEL; CEO PRACHANDA MAN SHRESTHA.

Hotel Association Nepal (HAN): Subarna Shamsher Marg, Gairidhara, POB 2151, Kathmandu; tel. (1) 4412705; fax (1) 4424914; e-mail info@hotelassociation.org.np; internet www.hotelassociation.org.np; f. 1966; Pres. NARENDRA BAJRACHARYA.

Nepal Association of Tour and Travel Agents (NATTA): Gairidhara Rd, Goma Ganesh, Naxal, POB 362, Kathmandu; tel. (1) 4419409; fax (1) 4418684; e-mail natta@mail.com.np; internet www.natta.org.np; f. 1966 to promote and regulate development in the tourism industry; non-governmental org.; 360 mems; Pres. RAM KAJI KONEY.

Tourist Guide Association of Nepal (TURGAN): POB 5344, Kamaladi, Kathmandu; tel. (1) 4225102; fax (1) 4423939.

Trekking Agents Association of Nepal: Maligaun Ganesthan, POB 3612, Kathmandu; tel. (1) 4427473; fax (1) 4419245; e-mail info@taan.org.np; internet www.taan.org.np; Pres. JYOTI ADHIKARI; Sec.-Gen. NAVA RAJ DAHAL.

THE NETHERLANDS

Introductory Survey

Location, Climate, Language, Religion, Flag, Capital

The Kingdom of the Netherlands is situated in western Europe, bordered to the east by Germany and to the south by Belgium. Its northern and western shores face the North Sea. The climate is temperate: the average temperature in January is 0°C (32°F), and the summer average is 21°C (70°F). The national language is Dutch. There is a Frisian-speaking minority (numbering about 400,000). About one-third of the inhabitants are Roman Catholics and about one-quarter are Protestants, while most of the remainder do not profess any religion. The national flag (proportions 2 by 3) has three equal horizontal stripes, of red, white and blue. The capital is Amsterdam, but the seat of government is The Hague (Den Haag or 's-Gravenhage).

Recent History

The Netherlands was occupied by Germany during the Second World War. Following its liberation in 1945, the country chose to abandon its traditional policy of neutrality, subsequently becoming a member of Western European Union (WEU, see p. 442) and the North Atlantic Treaty Organization (NATO, see p. 351). The Treaty establishing the Benelux Economic Union (see p. 425) between the Netherlands, Belgium and Luxembourg was signed in 1958 and came into force in 1960. The Netherlands was a founder member of the European Community (EC, now European Union—EU, see p. 255). Indonesia, formerly the Netherlands East Indies, was granted independence in 1949, except for West New Guinea, which was transferred to Indonesia in 1963. In 1975 Suriname became independent, leaving the Netherlands Antilles as the only remaining Dutch dependency. Aruba, formerly part of the Netherlands Antilles, was granted separate status within the Kingdom of the Netherlands in 1986. A commission, established jointly by the Governments of the Netherlands and the Netherlands Antilles, recommended in October 2004 that the islands of Curaçao and St Maarten (in the Netherlands Antilles) should be given autonomous status within the Kingdom of the Netherlands (i.e. have *status aparte*, like that of Aruba), while the three other islands of the dependency, Saba, Bonaire and St Eustatius, should be placed under direct rule. In a series of non-binding referendums between 2000 and 2005 a majority of voters in St Maarten and Curaçao favoured obtaining *status aparte*, while the electorates of both Bonaire and Saba strongly favoured direct rule. St Eustatius was the only island to favour remaining part of the Netherlands Antilles. None the less, in late October 2005 the Dutch Minister of Government Reform and Kingdom Relations, Alexander Pechtold, concluded an outline agreement on constitutional reform with all five islands. Curaçao and St Maarten were to be granted *status aparte*, while Bonaire, Saba and St Eustatius would become *koninkrijkseilanden* (kingdom islands) with direct ties to the Netherlands. The future status of Bonaire, Saba and St Eustatius was subsequently refined to that of *bijzondere gemeente* (special municipalities), similar in most ways to other metropolitan Netherlands municipalities, although with separate social security and currency arrangements, for example. However, the populations of the Antillean municipalities would be able to vote in Dutch and European elections (the province of Noord-Holland offered to include the three territories). Following the negotiation of further details, the Dutch Prime Minister, Jan Peter Balkenende, and the Antillean premier, Emily de Jongh-Elhage, signed an agreement confirming the new status of the five islands at a meeting in Curaçao on 15 December 2008; the reforms were expected to take effect by 2010.

Queen Juliana, who had reigned since 1948, abdicated in favour of her eldest daughter, Beatrix, in April 1980, following the adoption in February of a constitutional amendment that allowed for the accession of the reigning monarch's eldest child, regardless of sex.

All post-war administrations have been formed by various coalitions between the several 'confessional' Roman Catholic and Protestant and 'progressive' Socialist and Liberal parties. At a general election held in 1971 left-wing parties made substantial gains. In July 1972 the Government was forced to resign after losing its working majority in the Second Chamber of the States-General (see Government, below). Another general election took place in November, at which the 'confessional' parties suffered a major reverse, and in May 1973 a new Government was formed by a left-of-centre coalition under the leadership of Dr Joop den Uyl of the Partij van de Arbeid (PvdA—Labour Party).

The coalition collapsed in March 1977; a general election followed in May. Attempts to form a left-of-centre coalition between the PvdA, the Christen Democratisch Appèl (CDA—Christian Democratic Appeal)—an alliance of 'confessional' groupings, which united in 1980 to form a single party—and Democraten '66 were unsuccessful, and in December 1977 Andries van Agt, of the CDA, formed a centre-right coalition Government of the CDA and the right-wing Volkspartij voor Vrijheid en Democratie (VVD—People's Party for Freedom and Democracy). Despite retaining only a narrow majority in the Second Chamber and several ministerial disagreements, the Government survived its full term in office. A general election was held in May 1981, and a centre-left coalition Government was formed in September, led by van Agt and comprising the CDA, the PvdA and Democraten '66. The Council of Ministers resigned after only five weeks in office, owing to its failure to agree on economic strategy. In November the coalition partners accepted a compromise economic programme, but deep divisions within the Government continued. The coalition collapsed again in May 1982, when all six PvdA ministers resigned, after which van Agt led a minority interim Government of the CDA and Democraten '66.

Although at a general election held in September 1982 the PvdA became the largest party in the Second Chamber (with 47 of 150 deputies), the election produced a significant swing to the right. In November a centre-right CDA-VVD coalition was established under the leadership of Ruud Lubbers, who had recently succeeded van Agt as Chairman of the CDA. The CDA-VVD coalition was returned to power at a general election in May 1986, having retained its majority in the Second Chamber. A loss of nine seats by the VVD was offset by a corresponding gain by the CDA, which, with 54 seats, became the party with the largest representation in the Second Chamber. The election did, none the less, produce a shift towards the centrist parties, with the PvdA and Democraten '66 (D66, as the party was restyled) both gaining seats at the expense of smaller radical groups. Following the election, Wim Kok replaced den Uyl as parliamentary leader of the PvdA. A new CDA-VVD coalition was formed in July.

In May 1989 the VVD caused the collapse of the Government by refusing to support Lubbers' proposals for the financing of a 20-year National Environment Policy (NEP), which was to involve a reduction in government spending in sectors such as defence and housing, an increase in taxes on motor fuels and the abolition of tax concessions for commuters using private transport. A general election was called for September, at which the CDA again secured 54 seats in the Second Chamber, while the PvdA took 49 seats. The VVD lost five seats. An alliance of left-wing organizations, GroenLinks, won six. In October negotiations between the CDA and the PvdA culminated in the formation of a centre-left coalition, again led by Lubbers. The coalition accord envisaged increased welfare provision, to be funded by a reduction in defence expenditure, as well as a programme of job creation and reductions in certain categories of taxation. Kok was appointed Deputy Prime Minister and Minister of Finance. In August 1990 the Government introduced an amended version of the NEP, designated the National Environment Policy Plus (NEPP), which placed strong emphasis on energy conservation and improvements in waste disposal and recycling, and was to be financed by both the Government and the industrial sector.

In November 1992 the Second Chamber ratified the Treaty on European Union, which had been signed by EC Heads of Government at Maastricht in December 1991; the First Chamber similarly approved the Treaty in December 1992.

The CDA performed poorly at the May 1994 general election, winning only 34 seats in the Second Chamber. The PvdA, which had focused its election manifesto on unemployment and reductions in social welfare, became the party with the largest representation in the Chamber, with 37 seats. Both the VVD and D66 improved upon their performances at the previous general election, securing 31 and 24 seats respectively. The remaining 24 seats were distributed among eight smaller parties and special issue groups. Negotiations on a three-party coalition agreement between the PvdA, the VVD and D66 were initially retarded by deeply entrenched disagreement between the VVD and PvdA over the latter's reluctance to sanction severe reductions in social welfare spending. Following several concessions by the PvdA, a tripartite coalition, with Kok as Prime Minister, was eventually agreed in August.

The PvdA won increased representation at the general election to the Second Chamber held on 6 May 1998, taking 45 seats. The VVD secured 38 seats, while the CDA's representation was further reduced, to 29 seats. D66 won only 14 seats, having lost votes to GroenLinks and the Socialistische Partij (SP—Socialist Party). None the less, the PvdA, VVD and D66 agreed to renew their coalition (it was considered that D66 would be useful as an intermediary in conflicts of policy between the two leading partners), and a new Government, led by Kok, was inaugurated in August.

A parliamentary committee was established in October 1998 to investigate the Government's response to the crash, six years earlier, of a cargo aircraft belonging to El Al, the Israeli national carrier, into a densely populated suburb of Amsterdam, in which 43 people had died. The inquiry was ordered after the Israeli Government had confirmed reports published in a Dutch newspaper that the cargo on the flight had included depleted uranium and chemical components of sarin nerve gas. The inquiry investigated claims that residents and workers who had been in contact with the wreckage had suffered ill health since the disaster, as well as allegations that Dutch ministers had been aware of the nature of the cargo. The committee's report, published in April 1999, found that there was a direct link between the accident and the high incidence of ill health around the site of the crash, and was severely critical of the failure of the Prime Minister to coordinate government action with respect to the disaster. The report, none the less, concluded that there was no evidence of attempts by the Netherlands Government to conceal details of the flight's cargo.

In May 1999 the First Chamber rejected the Government's proposal to allow the use of referendums on policy issues, a key demand of D66, after the refusal of a prominent member of the VVD to support the measure. D66 subsequently announced that it could no longer work with the VVD, and withdrew from the ruling coalition, prompting the resignation of the Council of Ministers. However, following a series of talks between the three parties, in June the Government formally withdrew its resignation. In January 2001 the three coalition parties reached a new agreement on the introduction of the use of referendums. The new proposals were for a judicially non-binding referendum and would not require a change to the Constitution. The temporary referendum law entered into force on 1 January 2002 and expired three years later. Legislation was subsequently adopted to allow a national referendum to be held exceptionally on the proposed EU constitutional treaty in June 2005 (see below).

In September 2000 the First Chamber approved laws giving same-sex couples the same legal status as heterosexuals, including the right to marriage and adoption (the legislation took effect in April 2001). Legal recognition of homosexual partnerships had been granted in 1998.

During 1992–93 parliament debated and approved legislation codifying a procedure for the practice of euthanasia in circumstances where it was repeatedly requested by an incurably ill patient. In April 2001 the First Chamber passed a bill legalizing euthanasia by 46 votes to 28. (In November 2000 the Second Chamber had passed the bill by 104 votes to 40.) The practice was to be subject to strict criteria. The key conditions according to which life could lawfully be ended were that the patient was terminally ill and in unbearable pain with no prospect of improvement. Euthanasia became legal in April 2002. In October 2005 the practice was extended to include terminally ill infants in acute suffering, with the express consent of the parents.

In August 2001 Kok announced that he would not seek re-election for a further term in office at the general election, scheduled for May 2002. He also announced that he would step down as Party Leader of the PvdA and subsequently endorsed the appointment of Ad Melkert, the Parliamentary Leader of the party, as his successor. Jaap de Hoop Scheffer, the Parliamentary Leader of the CDA, resigned in September 2001.

He was replaced by Jan Peter Balkenende in the following month.

In April 2002 the entire Council of Ministers resigned following the publication of a report by the Netherlands Institute for War Documentation into the massacre of some 7,000 Bosnian Muslims by Bosnian Serb troops in Srebrenica, Bosnia and Herzegovina, in 1995. The report blamed the Dutch Government, the Dutch military and the UN for their respective roles in failing to prevent the atrocity and claimed that the 100 lightly armed Dutch peace-keeping troops who had been stationed in the town at the time had been ill-trained and had no clear mandate. At the request of Queen Beatrix, the Government agreed to remain in office in a caretaker capacity pending the forthcoming general election, which was scheduled to be held on 15 May 2002.

Further investigations by a parliamentary commission, in November 2002, into the failure of the Dutch authorities to prevent the massacre at Srebrenica in 1995 revealed that the former Government had been aware of the likelihood of atrocities occurring in the UN camp, and that the possibility of such killings had, in fact, been discussed during a meeting of the Council of Ministers on 11 July 1995, the very day the mass murders had occurred. In January 2003 the commission concluded that the Netherlands bore responsibility for the massacre, that the Government had failed adequately to plan the mission and that the Netherlands army had suppressed details of its failures. In September 2004 about 50 women who had survived the massacre held a demonstration outside the States-General to demand compensation from the Government for the failure of Dutch peace-keepers to protect Srebrenica. In November 2007 a court in The Hague ruled that a case against both the UN and the Netherlands Government brought by a group of relatives of those killed at Srebrenica in 1995 was admissible under Dutch law and in June 2008 civil proceedings began in The Hague. However, the following month the court ruled that the UN enjoyed immunity from prosecution with regard to its peace-keeping operations. In September the court dismissed a case against the Netherlands Government brought by the relatives of two Bosnian Muslims killed in the 1995 massacre, stating that the Government could not be held liable for the actions of Dutch peace-keepers in Srebrenica, as they had been operating under a UN mandate.

On 6 May 2002 the controversial politician Pim Fortuyn was shot dead in Hilversum, in the central Netherlands, just days before the general election, in which his newly established party, the populist and anti-immigration Lijst Pim Fortuyn (LPF—Pim Fortuyn List), was expected to secure a substantial proportion of votes. Fortuyn had formed the movement following his dismissal in January as leader of the Leefbaar Nederland (LN—Livable Netherlands) party for his anti-immigration rhetoric. In November Volkert van der Graaf, an animal-rights activist who had been arrested shortly after Pim Fortuyn's murder, confessed to the murder. At his trial, which began in March 2003, van der Graaf claimed that he believed Fortuyn had presented a threat to vulnerable members of society. He was convicted in April and received a prison sentence of 18 years.

At the general election of 15 May 2002 the CDA won 43 of the 150 seats in the Second Chamber, with 27.9% of the valid votes cast. The LPF took 26 seats (with 17.0% of the votes), the VVD 24 (15.4%) and the PvdA 23 (15.1%). In the light of their electoral defeats, both the PvdA and the VVD changed their Parliamentary Leaders, to Jeltje van Nieuwenhoven and Gerrit Zalm, respectively.

Balkenende was inaugurated as Prime Minister on 21 July 2002, leading a coalition Government comprising the CDA, the LPF and the VVD. However, the same day, a Suriname-born LPF minister in the Ministry of Emancipation and Family Affairs, Philomena Bijhout, resigned when it was confirmed that she had been linked to a Surinamese militia group involved in political killings in the former Dutch colony in December 1982. The LPF suffered a further reverse when allegations were made by a newspaper that their new leader, Mat Herben, had tried unfairly to influence the selection procedure for the LN's electoral candidates when Fortuyn was still leader and Herben a party member. Herben resigned at the end of July 2002 and was subsequently replaced by Harry Wijnschenk.

The new Government detailed policies to reform the health insurance and social security system and reduce the number of illegal immigrants to the Netherlands. In October 2002 the Minister of Immigration and Integration opened a new college for the instruction of Muslim religious leaders (*imams*) in Dutch values and social conventions. The course was compulsory for new *imams*, who faced deportation if they practised without passing an examination.

Meanwhile, the LPF was riven by factionalism and personal acrimony. In addition to the expulsion of two party members who objected to Wijnschenk's leadership style, in early October 2002 a feud developed between two ministers. Herman Heinsbroek, the Minister of Economic Affairs, articulated his ambition to assume the deputy premiership, which resulted in a dispute with the incumbent Deputy Prime Minister and Minister of Public Health, Welfare and Sport, Dr Eduard Bomhoff. Despite the subsequent resignations of Heinsbroek and Bomhoff from the Council of Ministers, the LPF's coalition partners refused to co-operate further with the party and the Government resigned on 16 October, after just 87 days in power. Balkenende presided over a minority Government, comprising the CDA and the VVD, pending a general election, which was scheduled for January 2003.

In the general election of 22 January 2003, in which 79.9% of the electorate participated, the CDA won 44 seats in the Second Chamber (securing 28.6% of total votes cast), while the PvdA increased its number of seats from 23 to 42 (27.3%), under its new leader, Wouter Bos. The LPF, again led by Herben, following the resignation of Wijnschenk in late 2002, secured only eight seats, while the D66 obtained six. Although the popularity of the right-wing LPF had declined sharply, the electoral manifestos of the mainstream parties addressed the issues raised by the movement. Of these, immigration became a prominent subject of debate, the VVD echoing Fortuyn's statement that the Netherlands was already 'full'. In late January 2003 negotiations began regarding the formation of a coalition administration under Balkenende. Disagreements between the CDA and the PvdA over Dutch support for an impending US-led military campaign to remove the regime of Saddam Hussein in Iraq hindered progress. In March, in his capacity as Prime Minister of the interim administration, Balkenende announced that, while Dutch troops would not assist in the campaign, some units of the armed forces and weapons would be supplied to help defend Turkey, should the conflict escalate. Negotiations resumed in late March and, as the US-led coalition entered Iraq, both parties expressed their support for the military operation. In early April, however, talks collapsed following the failure of the two sides to agree on reductions in budgetary expenditure necessary to revive a stagnant economy. The following month the CDA negotiated the formation of a centre-right coalition with the VVD and the D66, thereby gaining a slender majority of six in the 150-seat Second Chamber. The coalition Government, under the renewed premiership of Balkenende, was formally sworn in on 27 May.

In late May 2003 the provincial councils elected a new First Chamber in which the CDA-VVD-D66 coalition also obtained a majority, securing 41 of the 75 seats. The new Council of Ministers largely resembled the caretaker administration formed in October 2002. The CDA held eight portfolios, the VVD six and the D66 two. Two new Deputy Prime Ministers were appointed: Zalm of the VVD, who was also assigned the post of Minister of Finance, and Thom de Graaf of the D66, who was also named as Minister of Government Reform and Kingdom Relations. In accordance with its pledge to tackle the problems of illegal drugs and crime, the new administration proposed the extension of police powers to stop and search people and the introduction of compulsory identity cards for citizens from the age of 14 years.

In September 2003 the Government announced its intention to reform the Netherlands' generous social security system, which had been rendered increasingly expensive by the combination of an ageing population and a decline in the work-force. The proposed reforms included the reduction of hospital budgets by 5% and the introduction of charges for non-prescription drugs. The Government planned to increase the involvement of the private sector in health care, thereby transferring certain costs from the State to the individual. Under the proposed reforms, in 2006 the public and private health care systems would merge and a standard insurance scheme would be offered by the various private health insurance companies. In an effort to encourage more people to work (the rate of unemployment had risen from only 3% in 2001 to 6.5% in 2004), the Government planned to make the eligibility criteria for disability and unemployment benefits more stringent; in addition, incentives for early retirement were to be abolished.

In December 2003 Rotterdam City Council adopted a highly controversial policy paper that aimed to restore the city's socio-economic balance by building expensive rather than affordable housing and by restricting the issue of residence permits to those who earned at least 20% more than the minimum wage and who spoke a good level of Dutch. A parliamentary report published the following month highlighted a perceived unwillingness to integrate on the part of some immigrants and judged that the tolerant and multiculturalist policies practised over the previous 30 years had generally failed.

The Government also introduced a number of stringent new policies regarding immigrants and asylum seekers. In late January 2004 the Government announced that, in order to prevent the destabilization of the employment market, a maximum of 22,000 immigrants from the 10 new EU member states (which were scheduled to join the EU on 1 May) would be permitted to settle in the Netherlands. In February parliament approved a bill that would permit the deportation of 26,000 failed asylum seekers over the following three years. The legislation applied to asylum seekers who had arrived in the Netherlands before 1 April 2001 and who had exhausted their appeals. It authorized the removal of their welfare benefits, and the provision of a repatriation payment and a free flight to their country of origin. The law was condemned by human rights groups and considered too severe by left-wing groups, but was welcomed by certain sectors of society that felt threatened by the rising level of unemployment. The 'voluntary returns' policy came into effect in June 2004. By early 2005 some 8,636 cases had been processed, of which an estimated 41% were granted residence permits. Of the remainder, the majority had returned to their country of origin of their own volition, while 519 people were compulsorily repatriated. Moreover, emigration from the Netherlands rose by 8.9% in 2004, while the number of immigrants entering the country declined by 10.0% overall and by 33.7% among those from outside Europe.

At elections on 10 June 2004 to the enlarged European Parliament, in which 39.1% of the electorate participated, the CDA and the opposition PvdA each won seven of the 27 Dutch seats, while the VVD obtained four. A new party called Europa Transparant (Transparent Europe) won two seats by campaigning against corruption within the EU. The decline in support for the CDA and the VVD (which had previously held nine and six seats, respectively) was interpreted as a protest against the stagnant economy and the deployment of troops to Iraq. Nonetheless, Balkenende subsequently extended the mandate of the troops by eight months to March 2005.

In September 2004 the Government announced proposals for an austerity budget for 2005, in an attempt to reduce the budget deficit and prepare for the economic effects of an ageing population. The proposed measures included reforms to unemployment and disability benefits, reductions in health care expenditure and the elimination of tax benefits for those saving for early retirement. The proposals provoked widespread industrial action in September and October, culminating in a demonstration in Amsterdam in early October attended by some 200,000 protesters. However, as a result of negotiations with representatives of the Government, a compromise was reached in November whereby the trade union leaders accepted the proposed disincentive to early retirement and the restriction of eligibility for disability benefits, and agreed to demand only minimal wage increases over the forthcoming year.

The murder in November 2004 of Theo van Gogh, who had made a controversial film about Islamic culture, raised concerns regarding the threat to the Netherlands' liberalism presented by the country's failure to assimilate ethnic minorities. Mohammed Bouyeri, who was convicted of van Gogh's murder and sentenced to life imprisonment in late July 2005, was suspected of membership of a militant Islamist organization, known as the Hofstad group. Other members of this group were arrested in connection with threats to kill prominent politicians who were openly critical of Islam, including the writer of van Gogh's screenplay and VVD deputy in the Second Chamber, Ayaan Hirsi Ali. Following van Gogh's murder, a number of arson attacks and acts of vandalism took place, damaging Islamic schools, mosques and other Muslim community buildings. Arson attacks, presumed to be have been committed by Islamists, also took place at five churches. The trial of another alleged member of the Hofstad group, Samir Azzouz, began in February 2005 on charges of planning bomb attacks on Schiphol airport (Amsterdam), the parliament building and a nuclear power station. Azzouz was acquitted of these charges in April on the grounds of a lack of direct evidence, although he was sentenced to three months' imprisonment for the illegal possession of weapons; his acquittal was confirmed on appeal in December. Also in December the trial began of Bouyeri and 13 other alleged members of the Hofstad group on charges of membership of a terrorist organization. In

March 2006 nine of the defendants were convicted and sentenced to terms of imprisonment ranging from one year to 15 years; Bouyeri was found guilty of leading the organization. In an attempt to improve security, parliament adopted legislation in January 2005 requiring all citizens and foreigners to carry official identification.

In March 2005 de Graaf tendered his resignation as Deputy Prime Minister and Minister of Government Reform. His resignation followed the rejection by parliament of an electoral reform bill that would have introduced direct election of mayors. The governing coalition was further destabilized when the two remaining D66 cabinet members announced that they were also reconsidering their positions. However, following negotiations between representatives of the coalition partners, an agreement was reached that ensured the continuance of the incumbent Government. Pechtold, the Chairman of the D66 and the Mayor of Wageningen, was appointed Minister of Government Reform and Kingdom Relations, while the D66 Minister of Economic Affairs, Laurens Jans Brinkhorst, assumed the additional role of Deputy Prime Minister.

In October 2005 the Minister of Immigration and Integration, Rita Verdonk, announced proposals that would prohibit the wearing of traditional Islamic dress, such as the burka and other face veils, in certain public places. Despite criticism by Muslim and human rights organizations, a motion in support of such measures was narrowly approved by the Second Chamber in December. In March 2006, however, following an investigation into the implications of human rights law on such a ban, the Government failed to reach agreement on the issue, and the proposals were to be reconsidered. In the same month further measures to control immigration were introduced, requiring potential immigrants from the majority of non-EU countries to pass an examination in their country of origin on their knowledge of Dutch culture and language.

In May 2006 the Secretary of State for Education, Culture and Science, Mark Rutte, defeated Verdonk in a contest for the VVD leadership, which had emphasized deep divisions within the party, particularly regarding immigration and the integration of ethnic minorities into Dutch society. (Rutte was widely regarded as holding moderate views on such issues, in contrast to Verdonk.) During the leadership election campaign, Verdonk had publicly questioned the right to Dutch citizenship of her Somali-born parliamentary colleague, Hirsi Ali, and threatened to revoke Hirsi Ali's passport after irregularities were discovered in her original application. Verdonk's intervention was unfavourably received, not only by opposing political parties and the electorate, but within the VVD itself. None the less, later that month Hirsi Ali admitted to falsifying elements of her application for citizenship and announced that she would resign as a member of the Second Chamber. On 27 June, however, Verdonk announced that an inquiry into Hirsi Ali's original application for citizenship had found that her claim was legitimate. Two days later Verdonk survived a motion of censure in the Second Chamber urging her departure from office. The motion had been supported by the D66, the three Government members of which subsequently resigned. On 30 June the remaining members of the Government followed suit. Owing to the timing of the resignations, just prior to the parliamentary summer recess, an early election in September was considered undesirable. Consequently, following discussions between party leaders, a minority interim administration comprising the CDA and the VVD was sworn in on 7 July, with a general election scheduled for November.

In September 2006 the Minister of Justice, Piet Hein Donner, and the Minister of Housing, Spatial Planning and the Environment, Sybilla Dekker, resigned, following the conclusion of an inquiry into a fire at a detention centre for illegal immigrants near Schiphol airport in October 2005, in which 11 people had died. The inquiry found that state bodies under the jurisdiction of the two ministers had failed to ensure that safety procedures at the detention centre were followed adequately.

A general election was held on 22 November 2006. The three largest parties all suffered a reduction in support among the electorate (80.1% of whom voted). The CDA emerged as the largest party in the Second Chamber, with 26.5% of the valid votes cast (41 seats, a decrease of three on 2003). The PvdA won 21.2% of the valid votes cast (33 seats, from 42 in 2003) and the VVD 14.7%, (22 seats, from 28). The SP achieved the largest electoral gain, winning some 16.6% of the votes (25 seats, from eight) and the 'confessional' ChristenUnie (CU—Christian Union) party also increased its representation, achieving 4.0% of the vote (six seats, from three in the previous parliament). The nationalist Partij voor de Vrijheid (PVV—Freedom Party), which was formed in February 2006 by former VVD parliamentarian Geert Wilders, won 5.9% of the valid votes cast (nine seats).

Following protracted negotiations between the main parties, in late February 2007 a centre-left coalition of the CDA, the PvdA and the CU was formed under the renewed premiership of Balkenende. The PvdA leader, Bos, became Deputy Prime Minister and Minister of Finance, and the CU leader, André Rouvoet, Deputy Prime Minister and Minister of Youth and the Family. In total, the CDA held eight portfolios, the PvdA six and the CU two. The appointment of two foreign-born Muslim Secretaries of State, Ahmed Aboutaleb and Nebahat Albayrak, both of the PvdA, provoked some controversy. Wilders strongly criticized Aboutaleb and Albayrak after it was revealed that they, respectively, retained Moroccan and Turkish nationality in addition to their Dutch citizenship. The PVV and some VVD representatives, including Verdonk, demanded that the two ministers renounce their foreign nationality—despite the fact that this was not legally possible—and proposed legislation to prevent government members from holding dual nationality. The proposal was later withdrawn. The new coalition agreement signalled the Government's intention to reverse some of the policies of the previous administration, including a slowing in the reduction of disability payments and a relaxation of restrictions on immigration. However, its programme was criticized by some observers as lacking substantial measures for economic reform. In June the Second Chamber approved a government-proposed amnesty for asylum seekers whose applications had been rejected. Under the legislation, around 30,000 asylum seekers who had arrived in the Netherlands before April 2001 would be eligible for the scheme, reversing legislation approved in February 2004 that allowed for their voluntary repatriation (see above). However, later in June 2007 negotiations between the Government, trade union federations and employers' organizations ended with only a minor agreement over plans to create 200,000 new jobs, while more contentious proposals for the deregulation of dismissal procedures remained unresolved. In 2008 the Government considered alternative measures to expand the size of the labour force, including raising the age of retirement to 67 years or higher.

The limited progress of the Government in implementing its reform programme allowed nationalist groups to dominate the political agenda in late 2007. In October Verdonk resigned her membership of the VVD, following her expulsion from the party's parliamentary group in September for criticizing the leadership. None the less, Verdonk retained her seat in the Second Chamber and a week later she announced the formation of a new political movement, Trots op Nederland (Proud of the Netherlands), under her leadership; Trots op Nederland was formally inaugurated in April 2008. Meanwhile, in March 2008 Wilders provoked controversy when a film he had produced, entitled *Fitna* (an Arabic word commonly translated as strife), which was critical of the Islamic religion, was broadcast on an internet site. Following the broadcast, the Government accused Wilders of attempting deliberately to cause offence, having previously expressed its fears that the film's release would provoke acts of violence and economic boycotts of Dutch interests, citing the reaction to the publication in 2005 of cartoons depicting the Islamic Prophet Muhammad, initially in a Danish newspaper (and their circulation, by a group of *imams*, alongside several more inflammatory images, in various countries of the Middle East), which were deemed to be offensive towards Islam (see the Recent History of Denmark). However, despite limited criticism from politicians in some Islamic countries, initial reaction to Wilders' film was calm.

None the less, in January 2009 the Amsterdam Court of Appeal ordered that Wilders should be prosecuted for 'initiating hatred and discrimination'. The ruling, which took into account not only Wilders' controversial film, but also a letter that had been published by the Dutch daily *De Volkskrant* in August 2007, in which Wilders described the Koran as 'fascist', reversed an earlier decision by the Dutch prosecution service. The subsequent ruling was described by Wilders as a 'black day' for himself and for freedom of speech. Wilders expressed further indignation in February 2009, following the decision by the British Government to prevent him from entering the United Kingdom, on the grounds that he was a potential 'threat to public security'. (Wilders had been invited to attend a screening of *Fitna* in the British Parliament building later that month.) The decision was strongly criticized by Dutch politicians of all parties, including the Minister for Foreign Affairs, Maxime Verhagen, who insisted that the PVV leader should not have been prohibited from entering another EU country.

Meanwhile, in mid-November 2008 Ella Vogelaar, of the PvdA, resigned as Minister for Housing, Communities and Integration, having been the subject of increasing criticism from party colleagues since assuming the post in February 2007; she was replaced the following day by Eberhard van der Laan.

By late 2008 the Netherlands began to suffer the effects of the global financial crisis. In early October the Government was forced to nationalize the Dutch operations of the Belgian-Dutch financial services group, Fortis, after partial nationalization in conjunction with the Belgian and Luxembourg Governments in the previous month had proved insufficient to stabilize the bank. It was also announced later in October that the Dutch Government was to acquire a minority stake in the country's largest bank, ING. By February 2009 the Prime Minister acknowledged that the Netherlands had entered a 'deep recession'. Following strained negotiations between the coalition parties, along with business representatives and trade unions, in March the Government announced a package of fiscal stimulus measures valued at some €6,000m., most notably including a reduction in expenditure on health care; increased spending on public infrastructure projects and an extension of the retirement age to 67 years. Nevertheless, the opposition parties criticized the measures, claiming that they were insufficiently radical to address the country's economic decline. Moreover, the opposition parties expressed consternation that members of the Second Chamber would have little opportunity to amend the stimulus package, and pointed out that the proposal to raise the retirement age was uncertain, as the Government had allowed trade unions until October that year to formulate an alternative scheme that would generate comparable savings.

Relations within the governing coalition were strained further in April 2009 when representatives of the PvdA withdrew their support for plans to purchase two prototype Joint Strike Fighter (JSF) aircraft, stating that their acquisition was inappropriate in light of the difficult economic circumstances. It had been stipulated in the 2007 coalition agreement that a decision regarding the purchase of both the prototype JSFs and a further order of 85 aircraft must be made by the end of 2010. However, without support from the PvdA, the plan was unlikely to be approved; thus, seeking to avert potential discord, the three coalition parties agreed, in principle, to purchase just one of the prototype aircraft and to delay any decision regarding a larger order until at least 2012.

Government plans to commit troops to a NATO peace-keeping mission to southern Afghanistan prompted fierce opposition in late 2005. (Some 350 soldiers from the Netherlands were already stationed in the provinces of Baghlan and Kabul, in the north and east of Afghanistan, while a further 250 were engaged in counter-terrorism operations.) Opponents of further participation in the International Security Assistance Force referred to events in Srebrenica (see above), and claimed that Afghanistan's southern provinces were not sufficiently stable for peace-keeping exercises. However, following a debate in the Second Chamber, in February 2006 the Minister of Defence, Henk Kamp, announced that 1,200 military personnel were to join the mission in the province of Uruzgan, in central Afghanistan, from August. (Dutch troops had been withdrawn from Iraq in March 2005.) In December 2007 the Second Chamber voted to extend the mandate of Dutch troops in Uruzgan province until December 2010.

The EU Treaty establishing a Constitution for Europe was signed by the EU heads of state and of government in October 2004. It required ratification by all 25 EU member countries, either through a referendum or by a vote in the national legislature, before it could come into force. In February 2005 the Council of Ministers confirmed that a non-binding referendum on the treaty would take place on 1 June. As the referendum was consultative, the States-General would still be competent to ratify the constitutional treaty even if it were rejected in the popular vote. However, the Government pledged to abide by a clear result. At the referendum, which was held, as scheduled, on 1 June, 61.6% of those who voted (63% of the electorate) were opposed to the treaty's ratification. On the following day the Government formally withdrew the proposed legislation. This decisive rejection of the treaty by Dutch voters, and by French voters a few days earlier, prompted several other member countries to postpone indefinitely their own referendums. In March 2007 Balkenende expressed his new coalition Government's opposition to proposals by Germany and some other EU member countries to introduce a new treaty that would contain some of the main elements of the constitutional treaty. The following month Balkenende reiterated his opposition to a new EU constitutional treaty, instead favouring a new treaty similar to those signed in Maastricht in 1992 and Amsterdam in 1997. In late June 2007, at a meeting of the European Council in Brussels, Belgium, EU heads of state and of government reached a preliminary agreement for a comprehensive reform treaty. In September Balkenende announced that the new treaty would be approved by parliamentary vote, thus avoiding the prospect of a further defeat at a national referendum. The Treaty of Lisbon was formally signed by EU leaders on 13 December at a summit meeting in Lisbon, Portugal. The treaty was ratified by parliamentary vote in July 2008. Nevertheless, the future of the treaty was uncertain, following its rejection by the Irish electorate at a referendum held in June.

At a summit meeting held in The Hague on 17 June 2008 Balkenende, along with the Prime Ministers of Belgium and Luxembourg, signed a new Benelux Treaty on political and economic co-operation. The document expanded the scope of the previous treaty, signed in 1958, to provide for greater co-operation between the three Governments on justice and home affairs, as well as customs and cross-border trade. In recognition of this, the official title of the organization was to change from the Benelux Economic Union to the Benelux Union. The treaty was expected to be ratified by all three countries during 2009, to enter into effect on 1 January 2010.

Government

The Netherlands is a constitutional and hereditary monarchy. Legislative power is held by the bicameral States-General (Staten-Generaal). The First Chamber (Eerste Kamer) or Senate (Senaat) has 75 members and is indirectly elected for four years by members of the 12 Provincial Councils. The Second Chamber (Tweede Kamer) comprises 150 members and is directly elected by universal adult suffrage for four years (subject to dissolution), on the basis of proportional representation. The Head of State has mainly formal prerogatives, and executive power is exercised by the Council of Ministers, which is led by the Prime Minister and is responsible to the States-General. The monarch appoints the Prime Minister and, on the latter's recommendation, other ministers. Each of the 12 provinces is administered by a directly elected Provincial Council, a Provincial Executive and a Sovereign Commissioner, who is appointed by Royal Decree.

Defence

The Netherlands is a member of the North Atlantic Treaty Organization (NATO, see p. 351). Conscription to the armed forces was ended in August 1996, and a gradual reduction in the number of military personnel is ongoing. The total strength of the armed forces, as assessed at November 2008, was 40,537: army 21,483; navy 9,468; and air force 9,586. There were also some 5,953 military police. Total reserves stood at 3,339 (army 3,005; air force 296; military police 38). In August 1995 a joint Dutch-German army corps, numbering 28,000 men, was inaugurated, and in January 1996 the operational units of the Royal Netherlands Navy merged with the Belgian navy under the command of the Admiral of the Benelux. In November 2000 the Netherlands committed 5,000 troops to a proposed joint European Union (EU) rapid reaction force, which was to be ready to be deployed by 2003. The logistics of assembling this force proved problematic, however, and in November 2004 the EU defence ministers agreed to create a number of 'battlegroups' (each comprising about 1,500 men), which could be deployed at short notice (within 10 days) to carry out peace-keeping activities at crisis points around the world. The battlegroups, two of which were to be ready for deployment at any one time, following a rotational schedule, reached full operational capacity from 1 January 2007. The Netherlands was committed to contributing troops to two of the battlegroups; one with the participation of Germany and Finland, and one with the United Kingdom. Budgeted defence expenditure in 2008 totalled €8,090m.

Economic Affairs

In 2007, according to estimates by the World Bank, the Netherlands' gross national income (GNI), measured at average 2005–07 prices, was US $750,526m., equivalent to $45,820 per head (or $39,310 per head on an international purchasing-power parity basis). During 2000–07, it was estimated, the population grew at an average annual rate of 0.4%, while gross domestic product (GDP) per head increased, in real terms, at an average annual rate of 1.3% over the same period. Overall GDP increased, in real terms, at an average annual rate of 2.0% in 2000–07; real GDP increased by 3.5% in 2007.

Agriculture (including hunting, forestry and fishing) contributed 2.0% of GDP in 2007, although only 3.3% of the employed labour force were engaged in the sector in that year. According to provisional figures, the Netherlands is a net exporter of agricultural products: in 2007 exports of food and live animals provided 11.0% of total export earnings. The principal crops are potatoes, sugar beet, wheat and onions. The main agricultural activity is horticulture; market gardening is highly developed, and the production of cut flowers and bulbs has traditionally been a significant industry, although its contribution to export earnings showed some decline in the early years of the 21st century (partly compensated for by re-exports from other growers to European markets). Livestock farming is also an important activity. According to the Central Bureau of Statistics, during 2000–07 agricultural GDP increased, in real terms, at an average annual rate of 0.4%; the sector's GDP rose by 1.7% in 2007.

Industry (including mining, manufacturing, construction and power) contributed 24.4% of GDP and engaged 20.1% of the employed labour force in 2007. The Central Bureau of Statistics put the increase in industrial GDP, in real terms, at an average annual rate of 1.1% in 2000–07; real industrial GDP rose by 3.2% in 2007.

Mining and quarrying provided 3.0% of GDP and engaged 0.1% of the employed labour force in 2007. The principal mineral resource is natural gas. Total extraction in 2007 was an estimated 64,500m. cu m. Reserves of petroleum and salts are also exploited. The GDP of the mining sector declined, in real terms, at an average annual rate of 1.3% in 2000–07; it declined by 0.2% in 2007.

Manufacturing contributed 13.7% of GDP and accounted for 13.0% of the employed labour force in 2007. Several multinational companies are domiciled in the Netherlands, including the electrical firm Philips, the brewer Heineken, and two British-Dutch firms, the food industry company Unilever and the petroleum firm Royal Dutch Shell. According to the Central Bureau of Statistics, manufacturing GDP increased at an average annual rate of 1.4% in 2000–07; it rose by 3.2% in 2007.

In 2005 natural gas provided 57.7% of total electricity production and coal 26.9%. Imports of mineral fuels and lubricants comprised 10.4% of the value of total imports in 2003; by 2007 this figure had increased to 15.8%. In recent years the gradual depletion of the Groningen natural gas field has prompted the exploration of investment possibilities in smaller fields, while successive Governments have sought to promote the utilization of renewable energy resources.

The services sector contributed 73.6% of GDP and engaged 76.6% of the employed labour force in 2007. Within the sector, financial services, tourism and transport are of considerable importance. The GDP of the services sector increased, in real terms, at an average annual rate of 2.4% in 2000–07; it grew by 3.8% in 2007.

In 2007 the Netherlands recorded a visible trade surplus of €54,909m. and there was a surplus of €59,506m. on the current account of the balance of payments. The principal source of imports in 2007 was Germany (contributing 20.1% of the total); other major suppliers were Belgium (10.8%), the People's Republic of China (8.6%), the USA (7.9%), the United Kingdom (6.4%) and France (4.9%). Germany was also the principal market for exports in that year (accounting for 23.6% of the total); other major purchasers in 2007 were Belgium (11.9%), the United Kingdom (9.1%), France (8.2%) and the USA (5.0%). The principal exports in 2007 were machinery and transport equipment, chemicals and related products, food and live animals, and petroleum. The principal imports in that year were also machinery and transport equipment, followed by mineral fuels and lubricants, chemicals and related products, and basic manufactures.

In 2007 the Netherlands recorded an overall budgetary surplus of €3,272m., equivalent to 0.6% of GDP. In 2007 government debt, according to IMF figures, was estimated to be equivalent to 46.0% of GDP. In 2000–07 the annual rate of inflation averaged 2.2%. Consumer prices increased by 1.6% in 2007. The annual average rate of registered unemployment was 3.5% in 2007.

The Netherlands is a founder member of the European Union (EU, see p. 255), of the Benelux Economic Union (see p. 425), of the Organisation for Economic Co-operation and Development (OECD, see p. 358) and of the European Bank for Reconstruction and Development (EBRD, see p. 251).

The Netherlands was particularly vulnerable to external economic shocks in the first decade of the twenty-first century, as a result of the country's small size, its dependence on external trade (exports and imports of goods and services were equivalent to around 74% and 66% of GDP, respectively, in 2007), decreasing industrial production and increasing labour costs. Moreover, an ageing population and rising levels of unemployment resulted in increased demands for state-funded pensions, health care and welfare benefits. In an attempt to reduce the budget deficit to comply with the limit of 3% of GDP imposed by the EU's Stability and Growth Pact, the Government introduced measures to encourage participation in the labour market, including a comprehensive reform of the health system, in addition to restricting access to unemployment and disability payments, and the abolition of tax benefits for early retirement. The measures enabled the Government to reduce the budget deficit to the equivalent of 0.2% of GDP in 2005; small surpluses, of 0.8% in 2006 and 0.6%, were recorded in 2007, respectively. The economy was observed to have performed well overall: in 2007 real GDP increased by 3.5% (the highest rate of GDP growth recorded in the Netherlands since 2000), owing partly to an increase in revenue from exports and higher levels of investment. However, the economy's reliance on external trade that worsening global economic conditions had a significant effect. The rate of GDP growth decreased, to 2.1%, in 2008, while exports declined sharply in the fourth quarter of that year. It was expected that government finances would deteriorate substantially in 2009, following the announcement of a fiscal stimulus package, valued at €6,000m., in March of that year. The package included greater investment in construction and infrastructure projects, as well as investment in part-time unemployment benefits and retraining schemes, as well as a plan to ensure continued liquidity for companies connected with Schiphol airport. The Netherlands Bureau for Economic Policy Analysis projected that GDP would contract by 3.5% in 2009, while the rate of unemployment was forecast to increase significantly, to 5.5%, in that year.

Education

There are two types of school in the Netherlands: public schools, which are maintained by municipalities, and attended by about 35% of all school children; and private schools, which are, for the most part, denominational and are attended by almost 65% of the school-going population. Both types of school are fully subsidized by the State. Schools are administered by school boards, responsible to the local authorities or to the private organizations that operate them, thus providing teachers with considerable freedom. The Minister of Education, Culture and Science, advised by an education council, is responsible for educational legislation and its enforcement.

Full-time education is compulsory in the Netherlands from five to 16 years of age, and part-time education is compulsory for a further two years. Some 98% of four-year-old children also attend primary schools. Primary education lasts for eight years and is followed by various types of secondary education. In 2005/06 enrolment in primary education included 98.1% of children in the relevant age-group, while enrolment in secondary education included 88.3% of children in the relevant age-group. Pre-university schools provide various six-year courses that prepare pupils for university education. General secondary education comprises senior and junior secondary schools, providing five- and four-year courses that prepare pupils for higher vocational institutes and senior secondary vocational education respectively. In all types there is latitude in the choice of subjects taken. In 2004/05 199,350 students were enrolled at the Netherlands' 13 universities, while some 346,210 students were enrolled at the 54 institutes of higher vocational education. In addition, 21,004 students were registered with the Open University at 31 December 2003. Education, culture and science were allocated €32,500m. (equivalent to some 19.3% of total expenditure) by the central Government in the 2008 budget.

Public Holidays

2009: 1 January (New Year's Day), 10 April (Good Friday), 13 April (Easter Monday), 30 April (Queen's Day), 21 May (Ascension Day), 1 June (Whit Monday), 25–26 December (Christmas).

2010: 1 January (New Year's Day), 2 April (Good Friday), 5 April (Easter Monday), 30 April (Queen's Day), 13 May (Ascension Day), 24 May (Whit Monday), 25–26 December (Christmas).

Weights and Measures

The metric system is in force.

Statistical Survey

Source: Netherlands Central Bureau of Statistics, Prinses Beatrixlaan 428, POB 959, 2270 AZ Voorburg; tel. (70) 3373800; fax (70) 3877429; e-mail infoservice@cbs.nl; internet www.cbs.nl.

Area and Population

AREA, POPULATION AND DENSITY

Area (sq km)	
Land	33,873
Inland waters	3,479
Coastal water	4,175
Total	41,528*
Population (census results)†	
1 January 1991‡	15,010,445
1 January 2001‡	
Males	7,909,855
Females	8,077,220
Total	15,987,075
Population (official estimate at 1 January)†	
2007	16,357,992
2008	16,405,399
2009	16,486,587
Density (per sq km of land) at 1 January 2009	486.7§

* 16,034 sq miles.
† Population is *de jure*.
‡ Based on a compilation of continuous accounting and sample surveys.
§ Land area only.

PROVINCES

	Land area (sq km)*	Population (1 January 2008)†	Density (per sq km)
Groningen	2,340	573,459	245
Friesland	3,356	643,189	192
Drenthe	2,649	488,135	184
Overijssel	3,337	1,119,994	336
Flevoland	1,421	378,688	266
Gelderland	4,983	1,983,869	398
Utrecht	1,363	1,201,350	881
Noord-Holland	2,657	2,626,163	988
Zuid-Holland	2,867	3,461,435	1,207
Zeeland	1,805	380,585	211
Noord-Brabant	4,929	2,424,827	492
Limburg	2,164	1,123,705	519
Total	33,871	16,405,399	484

* Figures refer to area at 1 January 2000.
† Provisional.

PRINCIPAL TOWNS
(population of municipalities at 1 January 2008)*

Amsterdam (capital)†	747,093	Haarlem	147,640
Rotterdam	582,951	Arnhem	143,582
's-Gravenhage/Den Haag (The Hague)†	475,681	Zaanstad	142,863
Utrecht	294,737	Amersfoort	141,211
Eindhoven	210,333	Haarlemmermeer	140,648
		's-Hertogenbosch/Den Bosch	136,481
Tilburg	202,091		
Almere	183,270	Zoetermeer	119,504
Groningen	182,484	Dordrecht	118,182
Breda	170,960	Maastricht	118,004
Nijmegen	161,251	Leiden	116,878
Apeldoorn	155,108	Zwolle	116,365
Enschede	154,753		

* Provisional figures.
† Amsterdam is the capital, while The Hague is the seat of government.

BIRTHS, MARRIAGES AND DEATHS

	Live births* Number	Rate (per 1,000)	Marriages Number	Rate (per 1,000)	Deaths* Number	Rate (per 1,000)
2000	206,619	13.0	88,074	5.5	140,527	8.8
2001	202,603	12.6	82,091	5.0	140,270	8.7
2002	202,083	12.5	85,808	5.3	142,355	8.8
2003	200,297	12.3	80,427	5.0	141,936	8.7
2004	194,007	11.9	72,231	4.5	136,553	8.4
2005	187,910	11.5	72,263	4.4	136,402	8.4
2006	185,057	11.3	72,369	4.4	135,372	8.3
2007	181,336	11.1	72,485	4.4	133,022	8.1

* Including residents outside the country if listed in a Netherlands population register.

Life expectancy (years at birth, WHO estimates): 79.9 (males 77.7; females 82.0) in 2006 (Source: WHO, *World Health Report*).

IMMIGRATION AND EMIGRATION

	2005	2006	2007
Immigrants	92,297	101,150	116,819
Emigrants	83,399	91,028	91,287

ECONOMICALLY ACTIVE POPULATION
('000 persons aged 15–64, labour force survey)

	2005	2006	2007
Agriculture, hunting, forestry and fishing	273	262	260
Mining and quarrying	7	7	9
Manufacturing	1,033	1,020	1,033
Electricity, gas and water supply	43	43	42
Construction	488	499	505
Wholesale and retail trade and repair	1,153	1,193	1,196
Hotels and restaurants	319	332	357
Transport, storage and communications	489	497	508
Financial intermediation	258	264	260
Real estate, renting and business activities	945	964	1,001
Public administration, social security and defence	529	528	543
Education	508	519	531
Health and social work	1,204	1,245	1,314
Other community, social and personal service activities	316	330	356
Private households with employed persons	4	5	5
Activities not adequately defined	390	354	389
Total employed	7,959	8,061	8,310
Unemployed	425	354	300
Total labour force	8,384	8,415	8,610
Males	4,642	4,617	4,690
Females	3,742	3,798	3,919

Source: ILO.

THE NETHERLANDS
Statistical Survey

Health and Welfare

KEY INDICATORS

Total fertility rate (children per woman, 2006)	1.7
Under-5 mortality rate (per 1,000 live births, 2006)	5
HIV/AIDS (% of persons aged 15–49, 2007)	0.2
Physicians (per 1,000 head, 2005)	3.7
Hospital beds (per 1,000 head, 2003)	5
Health expenditure (2006): US $ per head (PPP)	3,383
Health expenditure (2006): % of GDP	9.3
Health expenditure (2006): public (% of total)	81.8
Human Development Index (2006): ranking	6
Human Development Index (2006): value	0.958

For sources and definitions, see explanatory note on p. vi.

Agriculture

PRINCIPAL CROPS
('000 metric tons)

	2005	2006	2007
Wheat	1,175	1,184	990
Barley	307	269	260
Maize	253	237*	217*
Rye	11	11	11
Triticale (wheat-rye hybrid)	20	21	20
Potatoes	6,777	6,240	7,200
Sugar beet	5,931	5,414	5,400*
Cabbages and other brassicas	209	210	216*
Lettuce and chicory	74	72	73*
Spinach	43	41	43*
Tomatoes	660	675	690*
Cauliflowers and broccoli	56	53	54*
Cucumbers and gherkins	440	440	445*
Aubergines (Eggplants)	42	40	42*
Chillies and green peppers	345	318	340*
Onions and shallots, green*	36	20	22
Onions, dry	1,060	920	925*
Leeks and other alliaceous vegetables	82	82*	n.a.
Beans, green	71	68	70*
Peas, green	30	28	30*
Carrots and turnips	487	541	545*
Mushrooms and truffles	245	225	245*
Apples	359	365	370*
Pears	195	222	224*
Strawberries	39	39	39*

* FAO estimate(s).

Aggregate production ('000 metric tons, may include official, semi-official or estimated data): Total cereals 1,775 in 2005, 1,730 in 2006, 1,506 in 2007; Total roots and tubers 6,777 in 2005, 6,240 in 2006, 7,200 in 2007; Total vegetables (incl. melons) 4,117 in 2005, 4,049 in 2006, 4,157 in 2007; Total fruits (excl. melons) 608 in 2005, 634 in 2006, 642 in 2007.

Source: FAO.

LIVESTOCK
('000 head, year ending September)

	2005	2006	2007*
Horses*	129	129	130
Cattle	3,799	3,749	3,730
Chickens	92,914	91,789	91,000
Sheep	1,363	1,376	1,388
Goats	310	340	373
Pigs	11,312	11,356	11,600

* FAO estimates.
Source: FAO.

LIVESTOCK PRODUCTS
('000 metric tons)

	2005	2006	2007*
Cattle meat	396	384	382
Sheep meat	13	15*	15
Pig meat	1,297	1,270	1,296
Chicken meat	628	621	610
Turkey meat*	40	40	42
Cows' milk	10,847	10,500*	10,750
Hen eggs	607	611	610

* FAO estimate(s).
Source: FAO.

Forestry

ROUNDWOOD REMOVALS
('000 cubic metres, excl. bark)

	2005	2006	2007
Sawlogs, veneer logs and logs for sleepers	448	443	396
Pulpwood	328	343	316
Other industrial wood	44	32	20
Fuel wood	290	290	290
Total	1,110	1,108	1,022

Source: FAO.

SAWNWOOD PRODUCTION
('000 cubic metres, incl. railway sleepers)

	2005	2006	2007
Coniferous (softwood)	176	179	184
Broadleaved (hardwood)	103	86	87
Total	279	265	271

Source: FAO.

Fishing

('000 metric tons, live weight)

	2004	2005	2006
Capture*	521.6	549.2	435.3
European plaice	25.1	23.1	23.9
Blue whiting	77.2	128.4	96.6
Atlantic herring	129.6	128.0	95.9
Round sardinella	55.6	70.9	45.4
European pilchard	46.8	31.8	20.3
Atlantic horse mackerel	66.7	67.8	63.6
Chub mackerel	7.5	3.5	1.2
Atlantic mackerel	28.0	23.5	22.1
Aquaculture	78.6	71.4	43.9*
Blue mussel	67.2	59.5	31.3
Total catch*	600.2	620.6	479.3

* FAO estimate(s).

Note: Figures exclude aquatic plants and aquatic mammals. Aquatic mammals are recorded by number rather than by weight. The number of porpoises caught was: 100 in 2004; 150 in 2005; 250 in 2006.

Source: FAO.

THE NETHERLANDS

Mining

(estimates)

	2004	2005	2006
Crude petroleum ('000 barrels)	15,564	11,858	11,426
Salt ('000 metric tons)	5,000	5,000	5,000

Source: US Geological Survey.

Natural gas (million cu m, excl. gas flared or recycled): 68,800 in 2004; 62,900 in 2005; 65,300 in 2006; 64,500 in 2007 (Source: BP, *Statistical Review of World Energy 2008*).

Industry

SELECTED PRODUCTS
('000 metric tons unless otherwise indicated)

	2003	2004	2005
Gravel and crushed stone	5,412	5,538*	5,223*
Margarine	307	296*	284*
Cocoa powder (metric tons)	179,241	182,386*	108,050*
Cocoa butter (metric tons)	192,932	198,115*	182,512*
Prepared animal feeds	12,482	13,553*	12,479*
Beer ('000 hectolitres)	25,699	24,546*	23,851*
Mineral waters ('000 hectolitres)	1,732	2,444*	3,016*
Soft drinks ('000 hectolitres)	15,823	15,529*	15,713*
Mechanical wood pulp†	124	119	107
Newsprint†	427	422	421
Printing and writing paper†	910	962	931
Wrapping and packaging paper and paperboard†	1,875	1,941	1,976
Packing containers of paper or paperboard	1,190	1,812*	1,736*
Synthetic dyestuffs*	11,546	10,844	10,690
Synthetic rubber*	283	287	273
Washing powders and detergents	441	405*	422*
Jet fuels	6,669	6,935	6,990
Kerosene	498	379	469
Motor spirit (petrol)	15,730	15,539	14,234
Naphthas	10,222	11,084	13,906
Gas-diesel (distillate fuel) oil	20,787	20,234	21,346
White spirit	294	314	300
Residual fuel (Mazout) oils	12,333	13,073	12,394
Lubricating oils	625	638	589
Petroleum bitumen (asphalt)	297	521	408
Liquefied petroleum gas	4,780	5,070	4,579
Coke	2,249	2,314	2,343
Coke-oven gas (TJ)	19,054	19,379	19,141
Cement‡§	2,450	2,380	2,400
Pig-iron‖	5,846	6,011	6,031
Crude steel‖	6,571	6,848	6,919
Aluminium (unwrought):‡			
primary	278	326	341
secondary§	5	50	50
Refined lead: secondary‡	22§	20§	17
Zinc (unwrought): primary‡	223	228	232
Passenger vessels launched ('000 grt)	38.0	n.a.	42.7
Tankers launched ('000 grt)	17.3	11.2	8.6
Bicycles ('000)	1,058	887*	903*
Electricity (million kWh)	96,763	100,770	100,219

* Refers to amounts sold by establishments employing 20 persons or more.
† Source: FAO.
‡ Data from US Geological Survey.
§ Estimate(s).
‖ Source: International Iron and Steel Institute (Brussels).

Source: unless otherwise indicated, UN, *Industrial Commodity Statistics Yearbook*.

2006 ('000 metric tons unless otherwise indicated): Mechanical wood pulp 109 (Source: FAO); Newsprint 422 (Source: FAO); Printing and writing paper 1,008 (Source: FAO); Wrapping and packaging paper and paperboard 1,828 (Source: FAO); Cement 2,400 (estimate); Aluminium (unwrought, primary) 312; Aluminium (unwrought, secondary) 30 (estimate); Pig-iron 5,417 (estimate); Crude steel 6,372; Refined lead (secondary) 17 (estimate); Zinc (unwrought, primary) 236 (estimate); (Source: unless otherwise indicated, US Geological Survey).

2007 ('000 metric tons): Mechanical wood pulp 113; Newsprint 421; Printing and writing paper 924; Wrapping and packaging paper and paperboard 1,764 (Source: FAO).

Finance

CURRENCY AND EXCHANGE RATES

Monetary Units
100 cent = 1 euro (€).

Sterling and Dollar Equivalents (31 December 2008)
£1 sterling = 1.0475 euros;
US $1 = 0.7185 euros;
€10 = £9.55 = $13.92.

Average Exchange Rate (euros per US $)
2006   0.7971
2007   0.7306
2008   0.6827

Note: The national currency was formerly the guilder. From the introduction of the euro, with the Netherlands' participation, on 1 January 1999, a fixed exchange rate of €1 = 2.20371 guilders was in operation. Euro notes and coins were introduced on 1 January 2002. The euro and local currency circulated alongside each other until 28 January, after which the euro became the sole legal tender.

BUDGET
(€ million)

Revenue	2002	2003	2004
Taxation	110,900	111,700	106,300
Wage and income taxes	28,300	27,500	26,100
Company tax	19,100	18,100	15,900
Dividend tax	3,700	3,800	3,300
Inheritance tax	1,700	1,600	1,400
Gambling tax	200	200	200
Value-added tax	35,000	36,200	35,500
Motor vehicle taxes	9,300	10,100	9,800
Excise duties	8,000	8,500	9,200
Environmental taxes	3,600	4,000	3,200
Import duties	1,800	1,500	1,500
Consumer tax	200	200	200
Other revenue	18,700	17,600	17,400
Total	**129,600**	**129,300**	**123,700**

Expenditure	2002	2003	2004
Education, culture and science	23,100	24,800	25,700
Social security and employment	19,500	20,600	22,700
General public services	13,300	14,200	13,300
Housing and community amenities	11,900	12,600	11,900
Public health, welfare and sport	8,300	9,500	11,100
Foreign affairs and development co-operation	10,400	9,900	9,400
Transport and public works	8,000	8,700	8,200
Defence	7,000	7,300	7,700
Home affairs	4,500	4,900	5,000
Justice	4,800	4,600	5,000
Finance	3,400	3,700	3,800
Housing, planning regulation and environmental management	3,400	3,500	3,500
Agriculture, nature and food quality	2,100	2,100	1,900
Economic affairs	1,800	1,700	1,600
Other	4,200	4,700	3,600
Total	**125,700**	**132,800**	**134,400**

2005 (€ million): *Revenue:* Current 127,790 (Taxes on income and wealth 54,693, Taxes on production and imports 59,582, Other revenue 13,516); Capital revenue 5,474; Total 133,263. *Expenditure:* Current 122,451 (Personnel 33,400, Subsidies on products 2,412, Taxes paid on production and imports 44, Social transfers 86,595); Capital 10,310; Total 132,760.

2006 (€ million): *Revenue:* Current 139,631 (Taxes on income and wealth 59,488, Taxes on production and imports 63,801, Other revenue 16,342); Capital revenue 5,628; Total 145,259. *Expenditure:* Current 130,641 (Personnel 34,418, Subsidies on products 2,517, Social transfers 93,661); Capital 10,533; Total 141,174.

2007 (€ million, provisional): *Revenue:* Current 147,550 (Taxes on income and wealth 64,844, Taxes on production and imports 66,735, Other revenue 15,971); Capital revenue 5,760; Total 153,310. *Expenditure:* Current 138,456 (Personnel 36,279, Taxes paid on production and imports 45, Subsidies on products 3,434, Social transfers 98,698); Capital 11,583; Total 150,038.

THE NETHERLANDS

INTERNATIONAL RESERVES
(US $ million at 31 December)

	2006	2007	2008
Gold (market prices)	13,100	16,713	17,033
IMF special drawing rights	785	981	1,021
Reserve position in IMF	691	540	1,087
Foreign exchange	9,327	8,749	9,369
Total	23,903	26,983	28,510

Source: IMF, *International Financial Statistics*.

MONEY SUPPLY
(€ '000 million at 31 December)

	2006	2007	2008
Currency issued*	32.93	35.46	39.82
Demand deposits at banking institutions	204.52	201.20	199.56

*Currency put into circulation by De Nederlandsche Bank: €24,420m. in 2006; €24,190m. in 2007; €24,500m. in 2008.

Source: IMF, *International Financial Statistics*.

COST OF LIVING
(Consumer Price Index; base: 2000 = 100)

	2005	2006	2007
Food	106.5	108.3	109.4
Electricity, gas and other fuels	153.5	168.2	175.1
Clothing (incl. footwear)	97.3	97.8	99.0
Rent	115.1	117.8	120.1
All items (incl. others)	113.1	114.4	116.2

Source: ILO.

2008 (Consumer Price Index; base: 2000 = 100): 119.1 (Source: IMF, *International Financial Statistics*).

NATIONAL ACCOUNTS
(€ million at current prices)

National Income and Product

	2005	2006	2007
Compensation of employees	254,563	264,745	279,714
Net operating surplus/mixed income	124,334	133,415	139,762
Domestic primary incomes	378,897	398,160	419,476
Consumption of fixed capital	75,709	78,538	81,547
Gross domestic product (GDP) at factor cost	454,606	476,698	501,023
Taxes, less subsidies, on production and imports	58,801	63,231	66,043
GDP in market prices	513,407	539,929	567,066

Expenditure on the Gross Domestic Product

	2005	2006	2007
Government final consumption expenditure	121,685	135,469	142,481
Private final consumption expenditure	250,343	255,038	264,345
Increase in stocks	598	−339	−1,649
Gross fixed capital formation	97,016	106,379	113,173
Total domestic expenditure	469,642	496,547	518,350
Exports of goods and services	357,453	394,396	424,827
Less Imports of goods and services	313,688	351,014	376,111
GDP in purchasers' values	513,407	539,929	567,066
GDP at constant 2000 prices	446,282	461,349	477,315

Gross Domestic Product by Economic Activity

	2005	2006	2007
Agriculture, hunting, forestry and fishing	9,535	10,353	10,169
Mining and quarrying	12,587	15,736	15,289
Manufacturing	65,163	65,804	68,917
Electricity, gas and water supply	7,910	8,808	10,198
Construction	24,587	26,466	28,339
Wholesale and retail trade; repair of motor vehicles, motorcycles and personal household goods	59,198	62,660	65,868
Hotels and restaurants	8,470	8,765	9,332
Transport and storage	20,770	21,615	22,834
Post and telecommunications	12,419	12,346	12,297
Financial activities	35,093	32,299	30,381
Real estate activities	33,897	37,820	41,992
Activities of employment agencies	10,681	12,640	15,031
Other business activities	46,071	50,283	54,773
General government	52,520	53,593	55,619
Care and other service activities	57,281	59,546	62,049
GDP at basic prices	456,182	478,734	503,088
Taxes, less subsidies, on imports	56,587	61,084	64,712
Value-added tax, less imputed bank service charge*	638	111	−734
GDP in purchasers' values	513,407	539,929	567,066

*Figure obtained as a residual.

BALANCE OF PAYMENTS
(€ million)

	2005	2006	2007
Exports of goods f.o.b.	344,734	390,785	462,226
Imports of goods f.o.b.	−297,088	−342,317	−407,317
Trade balance	47,647	48,469	54,909
Exports of services	80,085	84,809	96,727
Imports of services	−73,307	−75,481	−84,536
Balance on goods and services	54,425	57,796	67,099
Other income received	98,776	131,137	159,667
Other income paid	−94,839	−112,858	−154,853
Balance on goods, services and income	58,362	76,076	71,912
Current transfers received	11,177	12,521	13,983
Current transfers paid	−22,921	−25,555	−26,309
Current balance	46,618	63,042	59,586
Capital account (net)	−1,764	−2,617	−3,450
Direct investment abroad	−129,925	−64,230	−26,764
Direct investment from abroad	47,328	6,666	123,609
Portfolio investment assets	−83,831	−45,311	−39,759
Portfolio investment liabilities	160,315	70,200	−71,282
Financial derivatives assets	150,955	131,817	159,511
Financial derivatives liabilities	−155,136	−138,561	−155,723
Other investment assets	−65,310	−194,263	−278,208
Other investment liabilities	36,189	173,306	259,804
Net errors and omissions	−7,229	752	−28,733
Overall balance	−1,790	780	−1,409

Source: IMF, *International Financial Statistics*.

THE NETHERLANDS

External Trade

PRINCIPAL COMMODITIES
(distribution by SITC, € '000)

Imports c.i.f.	2005	2006	2007*
Food and live animals	19,195	20,886	23,835
Crude materials (inedible) except fuels	9,768	11,134	12,896
Mineral fuels, lubricants, etc.	36,956	47,553	48,386
Petroleum, petroleum products, etc.	30,670	38,564	39,533
Crude petroleum	18,971	22,893	22,461
Chemicals and related products	32,502	36,030	41,469
Organic chemicals	8,399	9,750	11,172
Basic manufactures	28,323	34,365	39,141
Machinery and transport equipment	89,066	97,608	102,560
Office machines and automatic data-processing equipment	29,045	33,547	25,738
Telecommunications and sound equipment	13,518	13,893	22,260
Other electrical machinery, apparatus, etc.	16,044	14,939	14,964
Road vehicles (incl. air-cushion vehicles) and parts (excl. tyres, engines, and electrical parts)	14,319	15,776	17,458
Passenger motor vehicles (excl. buses)	7,142	7,490	7,796
Miscellaneous manufactured articles	29,162	32,487	33,149
Total (incl. others)	249,845	285,370	307,012

Exports f.o.b.	2005	2006	2007*
Food and live animals	32,430	34,568	38,171
Vegetables and fruit	8,647	9,755	10,950
Crude materials (inedible) except fuels	15,414	17,602	18,667
Mineral fuels, lubricants, etc.	30,813	41,430	41,733
Petroleum, petroleum products, etc.	20,905	28,067	28,652
Chemicals and related products	47,678	53,072	60,001
Organic chemicals	12,509	14,166	16,556
Plastics in primary form	9,764	10,770	11,421
Basic manufactures	27,063	32,310	36,878
Machinery and transport equipment	90,731	97,936	113,126
Office machines and automatic data-processing equipment	30,557	32,974	29,063
Automatic data-processing machines	17,245	17,646	12,206
Telecommunications and sound equipment	11,841	13,193	21,026
Other electrical machinery, apparatus, etc.	17,688	17,028	17,688
Thermionic tubes, transistors, etc.	7,944	6,423	6,748
Road vehicles (incl. air-cushion vehicles) and parts (excl. tyres, engines, and electrical parts)	11,044	12,070	13,323
Miscellaneous manufactured articles	28,875	32,384	28,916
Total (incl. others)†	281,300	318,953	347,958

* Preliminary figures.
† Including victuals and stores supplied to foreign ships and aircraft.

Statistical Survey

PRINCIPAL TRADING PARTNERS
(€ million)

Imports c.i.f.	2005	2006	2007*
Belgium	26,960	31,036	33,090
Brazil	3,978	2,972	2,801
China, People's Republic	19,056	23,007	26,363
Denmark	2,724	3,308	3,140
France	12,808	14,266	15,009
Germany	47,563	55,504	61,624
Hong Kong	1,776	1,928	1,613
Ireland	3,569	3,524	3,688
Italy	6,592	7,121	7,655
Japan	6,109	6,479	7,184
Korea, Republic	2,315	2,620	2,270
Malaysia	4,146	4,571	4,965
Norway	4,133	3,839	4,310
Russia	8,342	10,969	10,404
Saudi Arabia	4,092	4,389	3,295
Singapore	2,977	3,209	3,093
Spain	4,843	5,380	5,985
Sweden	4,187	4,975	5,507
Switzerland	2,175	2,209	2,217
Taiwan	3,325	2,962	2,571
United Kingdom	15,571	18,136	19,566
USA	19,674	23,757	24,110
Total (incl. others)	249,845	285,370	307,012

Exports f.o.b.	2005	2006	2007*
Austria	3,780	4,359	4,913
Belgium	32,899	39,613	41,393
Denmark	4,276	4,338	4,773
France	25,734	26,285	28,551
Germany	66,957	78,917	81,949
Italy	16,087	16,007	17,226
Japan	2,217	2,206	2,541
Poland	3,998	4,826	6,259
Spain	10,900	11,371	12,559
Sweden	5,812	6,059	6,324
Switzerland	4,070	4,825	4,738
United Kingdom	25,907	28,427	31,694
USA	13,596	16,166	17,397
Total (incl. others)	281,300	318,953	347,958

* Figures are provisional.

Transport

RAILWAYS
(traffic)

	1996	1997	1998
Passenger-km (million)	14,131	14,485	14,879
Freight ton-km (million)	3,123	3,406	3,778

Passenger-km (million): 14,730 in 2005; 15,414 in 2006; 15,546 in 2007 (Source: Nederlandse Spoorwegen NV, *Annual Report 2007*).

ROAD TRAFFIC
('000 motor vehicles)

	2001	2002	2003
Passenger vehicles	6,539	6,711	6,855
Commercial passenger vehicles	753	788	780
Buses and coaches	11	11	11
Vans	756	798	856
Lorries	143	145	144
Motorcycles	438	461	494

SHIPPING

Inland Waterways
(transport fleet at 1 January)

	1997	1998	1999
Number of vessels	5,067	5,003	4,577
Carrying capacity ('000 metric tons)	5,859	5,589	5,212

Inland Waterways
(freight traffic, million metric tons)

	1996	1997	1998
Internal transport: Commercial	61.2	75.7	79.3
Internal transport: Private	28.2	20.9	19.3
International transport	201.1	224.5	219.7

Merchant Fleet
(at 31 December)

	2005	2006	2007
Number of vessels	1,257	1,258	1,258
Displacement ('000 grt)	5,669.0	5,818.4	6,139.4

Source: Lloyd's Register-Fairplay, *World Fleet Statistics*.

Sea-borne Freight Traffic
('000 metric tons)

	1997	1998	1999
Goods loaded	88,667	85,137	92,000
Goods unloaded	312,864	319,684	305,000

CIVIL AVIATION*
(Netherlands scheduled air services)

	2002	2003	2004
Kilometres flown (million)	424	429	460
Passengers carried ('000)	22,119	22,590	24,627
Passenger-km (million)	68,979	68,688	75,706
Total ton-km (million)	11,244	11,331	12,487

* Figures include data for airlines based in the territories and dependencies of the Netherlands.

Source: UN, *Statistical Yearbook*.

Tourism

FOREIGN TOURIST ARRIVALS
('000)*

Country of origin	2004	2005	2006
Belgium	811	917	991
France	510	527	608
Germany	2,649	2,570	2,812
Italy	369	374	398
Spain	298	322	392
United Kingdom	1,760	1,853	1,913
Total (incl. others)	9,647	10,012	10,739

* Arrivals at all accommodation establishments.

Tourism receipts (US $ million, excl. passenger transport): 10,308 in 2004; 10,446 in 2005; 11,381 in 2006 (Source: World Tourism Organization).

Communications Media

	2005	2006	2007
Telephones ('000 main lines in use)	7,600	7,450	7,334
Mobile cellular telephones ('000 subscribers)	15,834	17,300	n.a.
Internet users ('000)	12,060	14,000	15,000
Broadband subscribers ('000)	4,100	5,192	5,507

Personal computers ('000 in use): 11,110 in 2004.

Daily newspapers: 35 in 2000 (circulation 4,443,000).

Non-daily newspapers (regional or local): 49 in 2000 (circulation 317,000).

Book production (1993): 34,067 titles, excluding pamphlets.

Radio receivers ('000 in use): 15,300 in 1997.

Television receivers ('000 in use): 8,600 in 1997.

Facsimile machines ('000 in use): 600 in 1997.

Sources: UNESCO, *Statistical Yearbook*; UN, *Statistical Yearbook*; International Telecommunication Union.

Education

(2007/08)

	Institutions	Students ('000)
Primary	7,229	1,597.5
Secondary	658	941.5
Higher vocational	51	374.4
University	13	212.7

Directory

The Constitution

The Netherlands' first Constitution was adopted in 1814–15. The present Constitution, the first new one since 1848, came into force on 17 February 1983. Its main provisions are summarized below:

THE KINGDOM OF THE NETHERLANDS

The Kingdom of the Netherlands consists of territories in Europe (the Netherlands) and in the Caribbean (the Netherlands Antilles and Aruba). Under the Charter for the Kingdom of the Netherlands, signed by Queen Juliana in 1954, these territories constitute a single realm, ruled by the House of Orange-Nassau.

THE MONARCHY

The Netherlands is a constitutional monarchy with a parliamentary system of government. The Constitution regulates the royal succession and the regency in great detail. A successor to the Throne may be appointed by Act of Parliament if it appears that there will otherwise be no successor. The Bill for this purpose shall be discussed and decided upon in a joint session of the two Chambers of the States-General (Staten-Generaal). The Sovereign is succeeded by his or her eldest child. The age of majority of the Sovereign is 18 years. Until the Sovereign has attained that age, the royal prerogative shall be exercised by a Regent.

ELECTORAL SYSTEM

The parliament of the Netherlands is the Staten-Generaal and is composed of two Chambers, a First and a Second Chamber. The Second Chamber (Tweede Kamer), which is the more important politically, consists of 150 members, and is directly elected for four years on the basis of proportional representation. The First Chamber (Eerste Kamer), or Senate (Senaat), comprises 75 members and is elected by the (directly elected) members of the Provincial Councils.

THE NETHERLANDS

Nearly all Dutch nationals who have attained the age of 18 years are entitled to take part in the election for the Second Chamber. Those not entitled to vote are certain groups of non-resident nationals, mentally disordered and legally incompetent persons.

To be eligible for membership of the Staten-Generaal, a person must be a Dutch national, must have attained the age of 18 years and must not have been disqualified from voting.

MINISTERIAL RESPONSIBILITY

The Ministers, led by the Prime Minister, are responsible to the Staten-Generaal for all acts of government. This means, for example, that the power of the Government (Sovereign and Ministers) to dissolve one or both Chambers of the Staten-Generaal is ultimately subject to the judgment of the Staten-Generaal. The right to declare war and conclude treaties can, in principle, only be exercised subject to prior parliamentary approval. The Constitution contains provisions concerning the transferral of legislative, executive and judicial power to international institutions and on the legal supremacy of self-executing provisions of treaties.

The Prime Minister and the other Ministers are appointed and dismissed by Royal Decree. Ministries are established by Royal Decree.

A Council of Ministers is formed by a so-called 'formateur' (usually the future Prime Minister), who will have been assured of the support of a majority in the Second Chamber of the Staten-Generaal.

A Minister may not be a member of the Staten-Generaal. However, Ministers have the right to attend sittings of the Chambers and may take part in the deliberations. They must supply the Chambers, either orally or in writing, with any information requested, provided that this cannot be deemed to conflict with the interests of the State.

A statement of the policy that is to be pursued by the Government is given by the Sovereign every year on the third Tuesday in September before a joint session of the two Chambers of the Staten-Generaal.

Acts of Parliament are passed jointly by the Government and the Staten-Generaal. Bills, including the draft budget, must be introduced into the Second Chamber. The Second Chamber has the right to amend bills; the First Chamber can only accept or reject a bill. Revision of the Constitution requires two parliamentary readings of the bills that contain the proposed changes. In between the two readings, the Staten-Generaal must be dissolved and elections held.

THE COUNCIL OF STATE

The Council of State is the Government's oldest and most important advisory body. It must be consulted on all bills and draft general administrative orders. The Council is also an important court for administrative disputes.

The Sovereign is President of the Council of State, but the day-to-day running of the Council is the responsibility of its Vice-President. Its other members—usually former politicians, scholars, judges and business executives—are appointed for life.

LOCAL GOVERNMENT

The Netherlands is divided into 12 provinces. Provinces may be dissolved and established by Act of Parliament. The provincial administrative organs are the Provincial Council, the Provincial Executive and the Sovereign's Commissioner. The Provincial Council—directly elected on the basis of proportional representation—forms the provincial equivalent of the parliament. Each Provincial Council elects, from among its members, a Provincial Executive.

The Sovereign's Commissioner is appointed and dismissed by Royal Decree. Each Commissioner presides over both the Provincial Council and the Provincial Executive. The provincial administrative organs have the constitutionally guaranteed power to regulate and administer their own internal affairs. They may also be required by, or pursuant to, Act of Parliament to provide regulation and administration. In January 2009 there were 441 municipalities in the Netherlands. The municipal administrative organs are the Municipal Council (directly elected by the local inhabitants), the Municipal Executive (chosen by the Council from among its members) and the Burgemeester (appointed and dismissed by Royal Decree). The Burgemeester (mayor) presides over both the Municipal Council and the Municipal Executive. The Municipal Council has the power to make local regulations.

The Government

HEAD OF STATE

Queen of the Netherlands: HM Queen BEATRIX WILHELMINA ARMGARD (succeeded to the throne 30 April 1980).

COUNCIL OF MINISTERS
(April 2009)

A coalition comprising the Christen Democratisch Appèl (CDA—Christian Democratic Appeal), the Partij van de Arbeid (PvdA—Labour Party) and the ChristenUnie (CU—Christian Union).

Prime Minister, Minister of General Affairs: Dr JAN PIETER (JAN PETER) BALKENENDE (CDA).

Deputy Prime Minister, Minister of Finance: WOUTER JACOB BOS (PvdA).

Deputy Prime Minister, Minister of Youth and the Family: ANDRÉ ROUVOET (CU).

Minister of Economic Affairs: MARIA JOSEPHINA ARNOLDINA VAN DER HOEVEN (CDA).

Minister of Foreign Affairs: MAXIME JACQUES MARCEL VERHAGEN (CDA).

Minister of the Interior and Kingdom Relations: Dr GUUS (GUUSJE) TER HORST (PvdA).

Minister of Defence: EIMERT VAN MIDDELKOOP (CU).

Minister of Housing, Communities and Integration: EBERHARD VAN DER LAAN (PvdA).

Minister of Justice: Dr ERNST MAURITS HENRICUS HIRSCH BALLIN (CDA).

Minister of Agriculture, Nature and Food Quality: GERRITJE (GERDA) VERBERG (CDA).

Minister of Education, Culture and Science: Dr RONALD HANS ANTON PLASTERK (PvdA).

Minister of Social Affairs and Employment: JAN PIET HEIN (PIET HEIN) DONNER (CDA).

Minister of Health, Welfare and Sport: Dr ABRAHAM (AB) KLINK (CDA).

Minister of the Environment and Spatial Planning: Dr JACQUELINE MARIAN CRAMER (PvdA).

Minister of Development Co-operation: ALBERT GERARD (BERT) KOENDERS (PvdA).

Minister of Transport, Public Works and Water Management: CAMIEL MARTINUS PETRUS STEPHANUS EURLINGS (CDA).

Minister Plenipotentiary for the Netherlands Antilles: PAUL RALSTON JOSEPH COMENENCIA.

Minister Plenipotentiary for Aruba: Dr FRANCISCO WALFRIDO (FRIDO) CROES.

There are, in addition, nine Secretaries of State.

MINISTRIES

Office of the Prime Minister, Ministry of General Affairs: Binnenhof 20, POB 20001, 2500 EA The Hague; tel. (70) 3564100; fax (70) 3564683; internet www.minaz.nl.

Ministry of Agriculture, Nature and Food Quality: Bezuidenhoutseweg 73, POB 20401, 2500 EK The Hague; tel. (70) 3786868; fax (70) 3786100; e-mail webredactie@minlnv.nl; internet www.minlnv.nl.

Ministry of Defence: Plein 4, POB 20701, 2500 ES The Hague; tel. (70) 3188188; fax (70) 3187888; e-mail defensievoorlichting@mindef.nl; internet www.mindef.nl.

Ministry of Economic Affairs: Bezuidenhoutseweg 30, POB 20101, 2500 EC The Hague; tel. (800) 6463951; internet www.ez.nl.

Ministry of Education, Culture and Science: Rijnstraat 50, POB 16375, 2500 BJ The Hague; tel. (70) 4123456; fax (70) 4123450; e-mail ocwinfo@postbus51.nl; internet www.minocw.nl.

Ministry of the Environment and Spatial Planning: Rijnstraat 8, POB 20951, 2500 EZ The Hague; tel. (70) 3393939; e-mail vrominfo@postbus51.nl; internet www.vrom.nl.

Ministry of Finance: Prinses Beatrixlaan 512, POB 20201, 2500 EE The Hague; tel. (70) 3428000; fax (70) 3427900; e-mail webmaster@minfin.nl; internet www.minfin.nl.

Ministry of Foreign Affairs: Bezuidenhoutseweg 67, POB 20061, 2500 EB The Hague; tel. (70) 3486486; fax (70) 3484848; e-mail minbuza@buza.minbuza.nl; internet www.minbuza.nl; incorporates Development Co-operation.

Ministry of Housing, Communities and Integration: operates under the Ministry of the Environment and Spatial Planning (see above).

Ministry of the Interior and Kingdom Relations: Schedeldoekshaven 200, POB 20011, 2500 EA The Hague; tel. (70) 4266426; fax (70) 3639153; e-mail info@minbzk.nl; internet www.minbzk.nl.

Ministry of Justice: Schedeldoekshaven 100, POB 20301, 2500 EH The Hague; tel. (70) 3707911; fax (70) 3707900; e-mail voorlichting@minjus.nl; internet www.justitie.nl.

THE NETHERLANDS

Ministry of Public Health, Welfare and Sport: Parnassusplein 5, POB 20350, 2500 EJ The Hague; tel. (70) 3407911; fax (70) 3407834; internet www.minvws.nl.

Ministry of Social Affairs and Employment: Anna van Hannoverstraat 4, POB 90801, 2509 LV The Hague; tel. (70) 3334444; fax (70) 3334033; internet www.szw.nl.

Ministry of Transport, Public Works and Water Management: Plesmanweg 1–6, POB 20901, 2500 EX The Hague; tel. (70) 3516171; fax (70) 3517895; e-mail venwinfo@postbus51.nl; internet www.minvenw.nl.

Ministry of Youth and the Family: operates under the Ministry of Public Health, Welfare and Sport (see above).

Office of the Minister Plenipotentiary for Aruba: R. J. Schimmelpennincklaan 1, 2517 JN The Hague; tel. (70) 3566200; fax (70) 3451446; e-mail info@arubahuis.nl; internet www.arubahuis.nl.

Office of the Minister Plenipotentiary for the Netherlands Antilles: Badhuisweg 175, POB 90706, 2509 LS The Hague; tel. (70) 3066111; fax (70) 3066110; e-mail info@antillenhuis.nl; internet www.antillenhuis.nl.

Legislature

STATEN-GENERAAL
(States-General)

Eerste Kamer
(First Chamber)

Binnenhof 22, POB 20017, 2513 AA The Hague; tel. (70) 3129200; fax (70) 3129390; e-mail postbus@eerstekamer.nl; internet www.eerstekamer.nl.

President: YVONNE TIMMERMAN-BUCK (CDA).

Election, 29 May 2007

	Seats
Christen Democratisch Appèl	21
Volkspartij voor Vrijheid en Democratie	14
Partij van de Arbeid	14
Socialistische Partij	12
GroenLinks	4
ChristenUnie	4
Democraten 66	2
Staatkundig Gereformeerde Partij	2
Partij voor de Dieren	1
Independent	1
Total	**75**

Tweede Kamer
(Second Chamber)

Binnenhof 4, 2513 AA The Hague; tel. (70) 3183040; internet www.tweedekamer.nl.

President: GERDI A. VERBEET (PvdA).

General Election, 22 November 2006

	Votes	%	Seats
Christen Democratisch Appèl	2,608,573	26.51	41
Partij van de Arbeid	2,085,077	21.19	33
Socialistische Partij	1,630,803	16.58	25
Volkspartij voor Vrijheid en Democratie	1,443,312	14.67	22
Partij voor de Vrijheid	579,490	5.89	9
GroenLinks	453,054	4.60	7
ChristenUnie	390,969	3.97	6
Democraten 66	193,232	1.96	3
Partij voor de Dieren	179,988	1.83	2
Staatkundig Gereformeerde Partij	153,266	1.56	2
Others	120,919	1.23	—
Total	**9,838,683**	**100.00**	**150**

Election Commission

Kiesraad (Dutch Electoral Council): Herengracht 21, POB 20011, 2500 EA The Hague; tel. (70) 4266266; fax (70) 4266489; e-mail kiesraad@kiesraad.nl; internet www.kiesraad.nl; f. 1917; independent; Chair. Prof. HENK KUMMELING.

Advisory Councils

Raad van State (Council of State): Paleisstraat 3, POB 20019, 2500 EA The Hague; tel. (70) 4264426; fax (70) 3651380; e-mail voorlichting@raadvanstate.nl; internet www.raadvanstate.nl; comprises a Vice-Pres. and up to 28 mems nominated by the Sovereign, who formally presides over the Council; advises on legislation, constitutional issues, international treaties and all matters of national importance; Vice-Pres. H. D. TJEENK WILLINK; Sec. R. VAN DER BRUG.

Sociaal-Economische Raad (Social and Economic Council): Bezuidenhoutseweg 60, POB 90405, 2509 LK The Hague; tel. (70) 3499499; fax (70) 3832535; e-mail m.vander.burg@ser.nl; internet www.ser.nl; f. 1950; tripartite advisory body; to advise Govt on social and economic policy; monitors commodity and industrial boards; 33 mems, of which 11 belong to the Netherlands trade union federations, 11 belong to the employers' organizations, and 11 are independent experts in social and economic affairs appointed by the Crown; Chair. Dr ALEXANDER RINNOOY KAN; Sec.-Gen. Dr VÉRONIQUE TIMMERHUIS.

Political Organizations

Christen Democratisch Appèl (CDA) (Christian Democratic Appeal): Buitenom 18, POB 30453, 2500 GL The Hague; tel. (70) 3424888; fax (70) 3643417; e-mail cda@cda.nl; internet www.cda.nl; f. 1980; by merger of three 'confessional' parties; Chair. PETER VAN HEESWIJK; Party Leader JAN PIETER (JAN PETER) BALKENENDE; Parliamentary Leader PETRUS LEONARDUS BASTIAAN ANTONIUS (PIETER) VAN GEEL; 69,000 mems.

ChristenUnie (CU) (Christian Union): Puntenburgerlaan 91, POB 439, 3800 AK Amersfoort; tel. (33) 4226969; fax (33) 4226968; e-mail bureau@christenunie.nl; internet www.christenunie.nl; f. 2000 by merger of two 'evangelical' parties, the Gereformeerd Politiek Verbond and the Reformatorische Politieke Federatie; interdenominational, based on biblical precepts; mem. of European Christian Political Movement; Chair. PETER BLOKHUIS; Party Leader ANDRÉ ROUVOET; Parliamentary Leader ARIE SLOB; c. 27,500 mems (2008).

Democraten 66 (D66) (Democrats 66): Laan van Meerdervoort 50, POB 660, 2501 CR The Hague; tel. (70) 3566066; fax (70) 3641917; e-mail info@d66.nl; internet www.d66.nl; f. 1966; Chair. INGRID VAN ENGELSHOVEN; Parliamentary Leader ALEXANDER PECHTOLD; 12,500 mems.

EénNL (One NL): Rotterdam; tel. (10) 2085971; e-mail info@eennl.nl; internet www.eennl.nl; f. 2006 by fmr mems of Leefbaar Rotterdam and List Pim Fortuyn; right-wing, nationalist; agenda broadly similar to that of Pim Fortuyn; Leaders MARCO PASTORS, JOOST EERDMANS.

Europa Transparant (Transparent Europe): POB 3196, 4800 DD Breda; tel. (76) 5317946; fax (76) 5397701; e-mail paul.vanbuitenen-assistant@europarl.europa.eu; internet www.europatransparant.nl; f. 2004; aims to encourage openness within the European Union; Pres. PAUL VAN BUITENEN.

Fryske Nasjonale Partij (FNP) (Frisian National Party): FNP-hûs, Obrechtstrjitte 32, 8916 EN Ljouwert; tel. (58) 2131422; fax (58) 2131420; e-mail fnphus@globalxs.nl; internet www.fnp.nl; f. 1962; promotes federalism and greater regional autonomy; Leader JOHANNES KRAMER; c. 1,300 mems.

De Groenen (The Greens): POB 1251, 3500 BG Utrecht; tel. (30) 2341545; e-mail info@degroenen.nl; internet www.degroenen.nl; f. 1983; founding mem. of the European Green Party; Pres. PAUL FRERIKS, OTTO TER HAAR.

GroenLinks (GL) (Green Left): Oudegracht 312, POB 8008, 3503 RA Utrecht; tel. (30) 2399900; fax (30) 2300342; e-mail info@groenlinks.nl; internet www.groenlinks.nl; f. 1990 by merger of Communistische Partij van Nederland, Evangelische Volkspartij, Pacifistisch-Socialistische Partij and Politieke Partij Radicalen; Chair. HENK NIJHOF; Parliamentary Leader FEMKE HALSEMA; c. 20,000 mems.

Nieuwe Communistische Partij Nederland (NCPN) (New Communist Party of the Netherlands): Haarlemmerweg 177, 1051 LB Amsterdam; tel. (20) 6825019; fax (20) 6828276; e-mail manifest@wanadoo.nl; internet www.ncpn.nl; f. 1992; Chair. JOB PRUIJSER.

Nieuwe Midden Partij (NMP) (New Centre Party): POB 2087, 8203 AB Lelijstad; tel. and fax (320) 281412; e-mail info@nmp.nl; internet www.sdnl.nl/nmp.htm; f. 1970; campaigns on economic issues; Leader MARTIN DESSING.

Partij van de Arbeid (PvdA) (Labour Party): Herengracht 54, POB 1310, 1000 BH Amsterdam; tel. (20) 5512155; fax (20) 5512250; e-mail voorzitter@pvda.nl; internet www.pvda.nl; f. 1946 by merger of progressive and liberal organizations; social democratic; Chair.

THE NETHERLANDS

LILIANE PLOUMEN; Party Leader WOUTER BOS; Parliamentary Leader MARIËTTE HAMER; c. 60,000 mems.

Partij voor de Vrijheid (PVV) (Freedom Party): POB 20018, 2500 EA The Hague; internet www.pvv.nl; f. 2004 as Groep Wilders; present name adopted 2006; populist, anti-immigration; Leader GEERT WILDERS.

Socialistische Alternatieve Politiek (SAP) (Socialist Political Alternative): Postbus 2096, 3000 CB Rotterdam; tel. (20) 6259272; e-mail redactie@grenzeloos.nl; internet www.grenzeloos.org; f. 1974; Trotskyist.

Socialistische Partij (SP) (Socialist Party): Vijverhofstraat 65, 3032 SC Rotterdam; tel. (10) 2435555; fax (10) 2435566; e-mail sp@sp.nl; internet www.sp.nl; f. 1972; Chair. JAN MARIJNISSEN; Parliamentary Leader AGNES KANT; Gen. Sec. HANS VAN HEIJNINGEN; 50,238 mems (2008).

Staatkundig Gereformeerde Partij (SGP) (Reformed Political Party): Burgemeester van Reenensingel 101, 2803 Gouda; tel. (82) 696900; fax (82) 573222; e-mail info@sgp.nl; internet www.sgp.nl; f. 1918; Calvinist; female membership banned in 1996; Chair. Rev. A. VAN HETEREN; Parliamentary Leader B. J. (BAS) VAN DER VLIES; Gen. Sec. V. A. SMIT; 25,900 mems (2005).

Trots op Nederland (TON) (Proud of the Netherlands): POB 60, 2501 CB The Hague; tel. (47) 7638384; e-mail pers@trotsopnederland.com; internet www.trotsopnederland.com; f. 2007; right-wing, nationalist; Leader RITA VERDONK.

Verenigde Senioren Partij (VSP) (United Senior Citizens' Party): Israëlslaan 37, 3431 AS Nieuwegein; tel. (30) 6300208; fax (30) 6300209; e-mail secretariaat@verenigdeseniorenpartij.nl; internet www.verenigdeseniorenpartij.nl; Chair. H. J. (HERMAN) TROOST; Sec. JACK KOEHORST.

Volkspartij voor Vrijheid en Democratie (VVD) (People's Party for Freedom and Democracy—Netherlands Liberal Party): Laan Copes van Cattenburch 52, POB 30836, 2500 GV The Hague; tel. (70) 3613061; fax (70) 3608276; e-mail info@vvd.nl; internet www.vvd.nl; f. 1948; advocates free enterprise, individual freedom and responsibility, but its programme also supports social security and recommends the participation of workers in profits and management; Chair. IVO OPSTELTEN; Parliamentary Leader MARK RUTTE; 38,000 mems.

Diplomatic Representation

EMBASSIES IN THE NETHERLANDS

Albania: Anna Paulownastraat 109B, 2518 BD The Hague; tel. (70) 4272101; fax (70) 4272083; e-mail embalba@xs4all.nl; Ambassador ROLAND BIMO.

Algeria: Van Stolklaan 1–3, 2585 JS The Hague; tel. (70) 3522954; fax (70) 3061961; e-mail ambalg1@wanadoo.nl; internet www.embalgeria.nl; Ambassador BENCHAÄ DANI.

Argentina: Javastraat 20, 2585 AN The Hague; tel. (70) 3118411; fax (70) 3118410; e-mail argentina@xs4all.nl; internet www.embassyargentina.nl; Ambassador SANTOS GOÑI MARENCO.

Australia: Carnegielaan 4, 2517 KH The Hague; tel. (70) 3108200; fax (70) 3107863; e-mail austemb_thehague@dfat.gov.au; internet www.netherlands.embassy.gov.au; Ambassador LYDIA MORTON.

Austria: Van Alkemadelaan 342, 2597 AS The Hague; tel. (70) 3245470; fax (70) 3282066; e-mail den-haag-ob@bmeia.gv.at; internet www.bmeia.gv.at/denhaag; Ambassador WOLFGANG PAUL.

Azerbaijan: Laan Copes van Cattenburch 127, 2585 EZ The Hague; tel. (70) 3538205; fax (70) 3469604; e-mail info@azembassy.nl; Ambassador FUAD ISKANDAROV.

Bangladesh: Wassenaarseweg 39, 2596 CG The Hague; tel. (70) 3283722; fax (70) 3283524; e-mail amb.vanbangladesh@wanadoo.nl; internet www.bangladeshembassy.nl; Ambassador MIZANUR RAHMAN.

Belarus: Anna Paulownastraat 34, 2518 BE The Hague; tel. (70) 3631566; fax (70) 3640555; e-mail netherlands@belembassy.org; internet www.netherlands.belembassy.org; Ambassador ELENA GRITSENKO.

Belgium: Alexanderveld 97, 2585 DB The Hague; tel. (70) 3123456; fax (70) 3645579; e-mail thehague@diplobel.fed.be; internet www.diplomatie.be/thehague; Ambassador LUC CARBONEZ.

Bolivia: Nassaulaan 5, 2514 JS The Hague; tel. (70) 3616707; fax (70) 3620039; e-mail embolned@xs4all.nl; Ambassador ROBERTO CALZADILLA SARMIENTO.

Bosnia and Herzegovina: Bezuidenhoutseweg 223, 2495 AL The Hague; tel. (70) 3588505; fax (70) 3584367; e-mail fuad.sabeta@mfa.gov.ba; internet www.xs4all.nl/~bih; Ambassador ŽELJKO JERKIC.

Brazil: Mauritskade 19, 2514 HD The Hague; tel. (70) 3023959; fax (70) 3023950; e-mail brasil@brazilianembassy.nl; internet www.brazilianembassy.nl; Ambassador JOSÉ ARTUR DENOT MEDEIROS.

Bulgaria: Duinroosweg 9, 2597 KJ The Hague; tel. (70) 3503051; fax (70) 3584688; e-mail info@embassy-bulgaria.nl; internet www.embassy-bulgaria.nl; Ambassador ZLATIN V. TRAPKOV.

Cameroon: Amaliastraat 14, 2514 JC The Hague; tel. (70) 3469715; fax (70) 3652979; e-mail ambacam-la-haye@planet.nl; internet www.cameroon-embassy.nl; Chargé d'affaires a.i. MATHIEU BLAISE BANOUM.

Canada: Sophialaan 7, POB 30820, 2500 GV The Hague; tel. (70) 3111600; fax (70) 3111620; e-mail info@canada.nl; internet www.canada.nl; Ambassador JAMES CORNELIUS WALL.

Chile: Mauritskade 51, 2514 HG The Hague; tel. (70) 3123640; fax (70) 3616227; e-mail echilenl@echile.nl; internet www.echile.nl; Ambassador CECILIA MACKENNA ECHAURREN.

China, People's Republic: William Lodewijklaan 10, 2517 JT The Hague; tel. (70) 3065091; fax (70) 3551651; e-mail chinaemb_nl@mfa.gov.cn; internet www.chinaembassy.nl; Ambassador ZHANG JUN.

Colombia: Groot Hertoginnelaan 14, 2517 EG The Hague; tel. (70) 3614545; fax (70) 3614636; e-mail info@colombiaemb.nl; internet www.colombiaemb.nl; Chargé d'affaires a.i. FRANCISCO JOSÉ LLOREDA MERA.

Congo, Democratic Republic: Violenweg 2, 2597 KL The Hague; tel. (70) 3547904; fax (70) 3541373; Ambassador JACQUES MASANGU-A-MWANZA.

Costa Rica: Laan Copes van Cattenburch 46, 2585 GB The Hague; tel. (70) 3540780; fax (70) 3584754; e-mail embajada@embacrica.demon.nl; Ambassador FRANCISCO JOSÉ AGUILAR URBINA.

Croatia: Amaliastraat 16, 2514 JC The Hague; tel. (70) 3623638; fax (70) 3623195; e-mail croemb.haag@mvpei.hr; internet nl.mfa.hr; Chargé d'affaires a.i. ALEKSANDAR SUNKO.

Cuba: Scheveningseweg 9, 2517 KS The Hague; tel. (70) 3606061; fax (70) 3647586; e-mail embacuba@cistron.nl; internet www.embacuba.nl; Ambassador OSCAR DE LOS REYES RAMOS.

Cyprus: Surinamestraat 15, 2585 GG The Hague; tel. (70) 3466499; fax (70) 3924024; e-mail cyprus@xs4all.nl; internet www.mfa.gov.cy/embassythehague; Ambassador JAMES DROUSHIOTIS.

Czech Republic: Paleisstraat 4, 2514 JA The Hague; tel. (70) 3130031; fax (70) 3563349; e-mail hague@embassy.mzv.cz; internet www.mfa.cz/hague; Ambassador PETR MAREŠ.

Denmark: Koninginnegracht 30, 2514 AB The Hague; tel. (70) 3025959; fax (70) 3025950; e-mail haaamb@um.dk; internet www.ambhaag.um.dk; Ambassador KIRSTEN BIERING.

Dominican Republic: Raamweg 21–22, 2596 HL The Hague; tel. (70) 3317553; fax (70) 4049890; e-mail embajada@embajadadominicana.nl; Ambassador GUIDO D'ALESSANDRO.

Ecuador: Koninginnegracht 84, 2514 AJ The Hague; tel. (70) 3463763; fax (70) 3658910; e-mail ambassade@ambassadevanecuador.nl; internet www.embajadaecuador.nl; Ambassador Dr RODRIGO GUILLERMO RIOFRÍO MACHUCA.

Egypt: Badhuisweg 92, 2587 CL The Hague; tel. (70) 3542000; fax (70) 3543304; e-mail ambegnl@wanadoo.nl; Ambassador AHMED AMIN FATHALLAH.

El Salvador: Riouwstraat 137, 2585 HP The Hague; tel. (70) 3249855; fax (70) 3247842; Ambassador EDGAR HERNÁN VARELA ALAS.

Eritrea: Nassauplein 13, 2585 EB The Hague; tel. (70) 4276812; fax (70) 4277236; e-mail eritrea@xs4all.nl; Ambassador MOHAMMED SULEIMAN AHMED.

Estonia: Zeestraat 92, 2518 AD The Hague; tel. (70) 3029050; fax (70) 3029051; e-mail embassy.haag@mfa.ee; internet www.estemb.nl; Ambassador GITA KALMET.

Finland: Groot Hertoginnelaan 16, 2517 EG The Hague; tel. (70) 3469754; fax (70) 3107174; e-mail info.haa@formin.fi; internet www.finlande.nl; Ambassador MIKKO JOKELA.

France: Smidsplein 1, 2514 BT The Hague; tel. (70) 3125800; fax (70) 3125824; e-mail info@ambafrance-nl.org; internet www.ambafrance-nl.org; Ambassador JEAN-FRANÇOIS BLAREL.

Georgia: Groot Hertoginnelaan 28, 2517 EG The Hague; tel. (70) 3029080; fax (70) 3029081; e-mail thehague.emb@mfa.gov.ge; internet www.netherlands.mfa.gov.ge; Ambassador Dr MAIA PANJIKIDZE.

Germany: Groot Hertoginnelaan 18–20, 2517 EG The Hague; tel. (70) 3420600; fax (70) 3651957; e-mail ambduits@euronet.nl; internet www.den-haag.diplo.de; Ambassador Dr THOMAS LÄUFER.

Ghana: Laan Copes van Cattenburch 70, 2585 GD The Hague; tel. (70) 3384380; fax (70) 3062800; e-mail gaababio@ghanaembassy.nl; internet www.ghanaembassy.nl; Ambassador Dr GRACE AMPONSAH-ABABIO.

THE NETHERLANDS

Greece: Amaliastraat 1, 2514 JC The Hague; tel. (70) 3638700; fax (70) 3563040; e-mail grembhag@planet.nl; internet www.greekembassy.nl; Ambassador CONSTANTINOS IOANNIS RALLIS.

Guatemala: Javastraat 44, 2585 AP The Hague; tel. (70) 3020253; fax (70) 3602270; e-mail embpaisesbajos@minex.gob.gt; Ambassador ROBERTO PALOMO SILVA.

Honduras: Burgemeester Patijnlaan 1932, 2585 CB The Hague; tel. (70) 3641684; fax (70) 3649134; e-mail eholan@honduras.demon.nl; Ambassador JULIO ANTONIO RENDÓN BARNICA.

Holy See: Carnegielaan 5 (Apostolic Nunciature), 2517 KH The Hague; tel. (70) 3503363; fax (70) 3521461; e-mail apost.nuntiatuur@inter.nl.net; Apostolic Nuncio Most Rev. FRANÇOIS BACQUÉ (Titular Archbishop of Gradisca).

Hungary: Hogeweg 14, 2585 JD The Hague; tel. (70) 3500404; fax (70) 3521749; e-mail mission.hga@kum.hu; internet www.hungarianembassy.nl; Ambassador IVÁN UDVARDI.

India: Buitenrustweg 2, 2517 KD The Hague; tel. (70) 3469771; fax (70) 3617072; e-mail ambassador@indianembassy.nl; internet www.indianembassy.nl; Ambassador MANBIR SINGH.

Indonesia: Tobias Asserlaan 8, 2517 KC The Hague; tel. (70) 3108100; fax (70) 3643331; e-mail bidpen@indonesia.nl; internet www.indonesia.nl; Ambassador JUNUS EFFENDI HABIBIE.

Iran: Duinweg 20–22, 2585 JX The Hague; tel. (70) 3548483; fax (70) 3503224; e-mail info@iranembassy.nl; internet www.iranianembassy.nl; Ambassador BOZORGMEHR ZIARAN.

Iraq: Johan de Wittlaan 16, 2517 JR The Hague; tel. (70) 3101260; fax (70) 3924958; e-mail info@embassyofiraq.nl; internet www.embassyofiraq.nl; Ambassador SIAMAND BANAA.

Ireland: Dr Kuyperstraat 9, 2514 BA The Hague; tel. (70) 3630993; fax (70) 3617604; internet www.embassyofireland.nl; Ambassador RICHARD RYAN.

Israel: Buitenhof 47, 2513 AH The Hague; tel. (70) 3760500; fax (70) 3760555; e-mail info@hague.mfa.gov.il; internet thehague.mfa.gov.il; Ambassador HARRY KNEY-TAL.

Italy: Alexanderstraat 12, 2514 JL The Hague; tel. (70) 3021030; fax (70) 3614932; e-mail embitaly.denhaag@esteri.it; internet www.amblaja.esteri.it; Ambassador FRANCO GIORDANO.

Japan: Tobias Asserlaan 2, 2517 KC The Hague; tel. (70) 3469544; fax (70) 3106341; e-mail japan.cultural@planet.nl; internet www.nl.emb-japan.go.jp; Ambassador MINORU SHIBUYA.

Jordan: Badhuisweg 79, 2587 CD The Hague; tel. (70) 4167200; fax (70) 4167209; e-mail info@jordanembassy.nl; internet www.jordanembassy.nl; Ambassador AHMAD S. AL-HASSAN.

Kazakhstan: Nieuwe Parklaan 69, 2597 LB The Hague; tel. (70) 3634757; fax (70) 3657600; e-mail info@kazakhembassy.nl; internet www.kazakhembassy.nl; Ambassador MAINURA S. MURZAMADIYEVA.

Kenya: Nieuwe Parklaan 21, 2597 LA The Hague; tel. (70) 3504215; fax (70) 3553594; e-mail info@kenya-embassy.nl; Ambassador Prof. RUTHIE CHEPKOECH RONO.

Korea, Republic: Verlengde Tolweg 8, 2517 JV The Hague; tel. (70) 3586076; fax (70) 3504712; e-mail koremb@euronet.nl; internet www.mofat.go.kr/netherlands; Ambassador JONG-MOO CHOI.

Kuwait: Carnegielaan 9, 2517 KH The Hague; tel. (70) 3123400; fax (70) 3924588; e-mail info@kuwaitembassy.nl; Ambassador YOUSEF ABDULLAH AL-ONAIZI.

Latvia: Balistraat 88, 2585 XX The Hague; tel. (70) 3063934; fax (70) 3062858; e-mail embassy.netherlands@mfa.gov.lv; Ambassador SANITA PAVLUTA-DESLANDES.

Lebanon: Frederikstraat 2, 2514 LK The Hague; tel. (70) 3658906; fax (70) 3620779; e-mail amb.lib@wanadoo.nl; Ambassador ZEIDAN AS-SAGHIR.

Libya: 15 Parkweg, 2585 JH The Hague; tel. (70) 355886; fax (70) 3559075; e-mail libyanembassy@wanadoo.nl; Sec. of the People's Bureau ZAKIA ABDUSSALAM M. SAHLI.

Lithuania: Laan van Meerdervoort 20, 2517 AK The Hague; tel. (70) 3855418; fax (70) 3853940; e-mail amb.nl@urm.lt; internet nl.mfa.lt; Ambassador VAIDOTAS VERBA.

Luxembourg: Nassaulaan 8, 2514 JS The Hague; tel. (70) 3647589; fax (70) 3462000; e-mail lahaye.amb@mae.etat.lu; Ambassador JEAN-MARC HOSCHEIT.

Macedonia, former Yugoslav republic: Laan van Meerdervoort 50C, 2517 AM The Hague; tel. (70) 4274464; fax (70) 4274469; e-mail repmak@wanadoo.nl; Ambassador Dr DOBRINKA TASKOVSKA.

Malaysia: Rustenburgweg 2, 2517 KE The Hague; tel. (70) 3506506; fax (70) 3506536; e-mail malaysia@euronet.nl; internet www.kln.gov.my/perwakilan/thehague; Ambassador Dr FAUZIAH MOHD TAIB.

Malta: Carnegielaan 4–14, 2517 KH The Hague; tel. (70) 3561252; fax (70) 3464796; e-mail maltaembassy.thehague@gov.mt; Ambassador Dr IVAN FSADNI.

Mexico: Nassauplein 28, 2585 EC The Hague; tel. (70) 3602900; fax (70) 3560543; e-mail embamex@embamex-nl.com; internet www.embamex-nl.com; Ambassador JORGE LOMÓNACO TONDA.

Morocco: Oranjestraat 9, 2514 JB The Hague; tel. (70) 3469617; fax (70) 3562829; e-mail ambamar.lahaye@wanadoo.nl; Ambassador JAWAD EL-HIMDI.

New Zealand: Eisenhowerlaan 77N, 2517 KK The Hague; tel. (70) 3469324; fax (70) 3632983; e-mail nzemb@xs4all.nl; internet www.nzembassy.com/netherlands; Ambassador RACHEL FRY.

Nicaragua: Statenlaan 81, 2582 GE, The Hague; tel. (70) 3225063; fax (70) 3508331; e-mail embajador@embanic.nl; Ambassador CARLOS ARGÜELLO GÓMEZ.

Nigeria: Wagenaarweg 5, 2597 LL The Hague; tel. (70) 3501703; fax (70) 3551110; e-mail nigembassy@nigerianembassy.nl; internet www.nigerianembassy.nl; Ambassador Dr NIMOTA NIHINLOLA AKANBI.

Norway: Lange Vijverberg 11, 2513 AC The Hague; tel. (70) 3117611; fax (70) 3659630; e-mail emb.hague@mfa.no; internet www.noorwegen.nl; Ambassador EVA BUGGE.

Oman: Nieuwe Parklaan 9, LA The Hague; tel. (70) 3615800; fax (70) 3605364; e-mail info@embassyofoman.nl; Ambassador KHADIJA HASSAN SALMAN AL-LAWATI.

Pakistan: Amaliastraat 8, 2514 JC The Hague; tel. (70) 3648948; fax (70) 3106047; Ambassador SIBTE YAHYA NAQVI.

Peru: Nassauplein 4, 2585 EA The Hague; tel. (70) 3653500; fax (70) 3651929; e-mail info@embassyofperu.nl; Chargé d'affaires a.i. PEDRO ROBERTO REATEGUI GAMARRA.

Philippines: Laan Copes van Cattenburch 125, 2585 EZ The Hague; tel. (70) 3604820; fax (70) 3560030; e-mail ph@bart.nl; internet www.philembassy.nl; Ambassador ROMEO A. ARGUELLES.

Poland: Alexanderstraat 25, 2514 JM The Hague; tel. (70) 7990100; fax (70) 7990137; e-mail ambhaga@polamb.nl; internet www.haga.polamb.net; Ambassador Dr JANUSZ STAŃCZYK.

Portugal: Bazarstraat 21, 2518 AG The Hague; tel. (70) 3630217; fax (70) 3615589; e-mail info@portembassy.nl; Ambassador MANUEL NUNO TAVARES SOUSA.

Qatar: Borweg 7, 2597 LR The Hague; tel. (70) 4166666; fax (70) 4166660; e-mail info@embassyofqatar.nl; internet www.embassyofqatar.nl; Ambassador SALEH ABDULLAH AL-BOUANIN.

Romania: Catsheuvel 55, 2517 KA The Hague; tel. (70) 3543796; fax (70) 3541587; e-mail sicrned@tip.nl; internet haga.mae.ro; Ambassador CĂLIN FABIAN.

Russia: Andries Bickerweg 2, 2517 JP The Hague; tel. (70) 3451300; fax (70) 3617960; e-mail ambrusnl@euronet.nl; internet www.netherlands.mid.ru; Ambassador KIRILL G. GEVORGIYAN.

Saudi Arabia: Alexanderstraat 19, 2514 JM The Hague; tel. (70) 3614391; fax (70) 4276183; e-mail saudiembassy@casema.nl; Ambassador WALID A. AL-KHEREIJI.

Serbia: Groot Hertoginnelaan 30, 2517 EG The Hague; tel. (70) 3632397; fax (70) 3602421; e-mail embassy.hague@mfa.gov.yu; internet users.bart.nl/~yuambanl; Ambassador CEDOMIR RAJKOVIĆ (designate).

Slovakia: Parkweg 1, 2585 JG The Hague; tel. (70) 4167777; fax (70) 4167783; e-mail emb.hague@mzv.sk; internet www.haag.mfa.sk; Ambassador OKSANA TOMOVÁ.

Slovenia: Anna Paulownastraat 11, 2518 BA The Hague; tel. (70) 3108690; fax (70) 3626608; e-mail vhg@gov.si; internet www.haagvelepeslanistvo.si; Ambassador LEON MARC.

South Africa: Wassenaarseweg 40, 2596 CJ The Hague; tel. (70) 3924501; fax (70) 3460669; e-mail info@zuidafrika.nl; internet www.zuidafrika.nl; Ambassador HLENGIWE BUHLE MKHIZE.

Spain: Lange Voorhout 50, 2514 EG The Hague; tel. (70) 3024999; fax (70) 3617959; e-mail ambassade.spanje@worldonline.nl; internet www.mae.es/embajadas/lahaya; Ambassador JUAN PRAT Y COLL.

Sri Lanka: Jacob de Graeffaan 2, 2517 JM The Hague; tel. (70) 3655910; fax (70) 3465596; e-mail mission@infolanka.nl; Ambassador PAMELA JAYASEKERA DEEN.

Sudan: Laan Copes van Cattenburch 81, 2585 EW The Hague; tel. (70) 3620939; fax (70) 3617975; e-mail sudan@tiscali.nl; Ambassador ABUELGASIM ABDELWAHID SHEIKH IDRIS.

Suriname: Alexander Gogelweg 2, 2517 JH The Hague; tel. (70) 3650844; fax (70) 3617445; e-mail ambassade.suriname@wxs.nl; Ambassador URMILA JOELLA.

Sweden: Jan Willem Frisolaan 3, 2517, JS The Hague; tel. (70) 4120200; fax (70) 4120211; e-mail ambassaden.haag@foreign.ministry.se; internet www.swedenabroad.com/thehague; Ambassador HANS OSCAR MAGNUSSON.

Switzerland: Lange Voorhout 42, 2514 EE The Hague; tel. (70) 3642831; fax (70) 3561238; e-mail hay.vertretung@eda.admin.ch;

THE NETHERLANDS

internet www.eda.admin.ch/denhaag; Ambassador Dominik Matthias Alder.

Thailand: Laan Copes van Cattenburch 123, 2585 EZ The Hague; tel. (70) 3450766; fax (70) 3451929; e-mail thaihag@thaihag.demon.nl; internet www.thaiembassy.org/hague; Ambassador Suchitra Hiranprueck.

Tunisia: Gentsestraat 98, 2587 HX The Hague; tel. (70) 3512251; fax (70) 3514323; e-mail ambassadetunisie@wanadoo.nl; Ambassador Muhammad Salah Tekaya.

Turkey: Jan Evertstraat 15, 2514 BS The Hague; tel. (70) 3604912; fax (70) 3617969; e-mail turkishembassy@euronet.nl; Ambassador Selahattin Alpar.

Ukraine: Zeestraat 78, 2518 AD The Hague; tel. (70) 3626095; fax (70) 3615565; e-mail embukr@wxs.nl; internet www.oekraine.com; Ambassador Vasyl H. Korzachenko.

United Arab Emirates: Eisenhowerlaan 130, 2517 KN The Hague; tel. (70) 3384370; fax (70) 3384373; e-mail info@uae-embassy.nl; internet www.uae-embassy.nl; Ambassador Ali Thani as-Suwaidi.

United Kingdom: Lange Voorhout 10, 2514 ED The Hague; tel. (70) 4270427; fax (70) 4270345; internet www.britain.nl; Ambassador Lyn Parker.

USA: Lange Voorhout 102, 2514 EJ The Hague; tel. (70) 3102209; fax (70) 3102307; e-mail ircthehague@state.gov; internet thehague.usembassy.gov; Chargé d'affaires a.i. Michael Gallagher.

Uruguay: Mauritskade 33, 2514 HD The Hague; tel. (70) 3609815; fax (70) 3562826; e-mail uruholan@wxs.nl; Ambassador Dr Carlos Antonio Mora Medero.

Venezuela: Nassaulaan 2, 2514 JS The Hague; tel. (70) 3651256; fax (70) 3656954; e-mail embvene@xs4all.nl; internet www.embven.nl; Ambassador Augustín Pérez Celis.

Viet Nam: Nassauplein 12, 2585 EB The Hague; tel. (70) 3648917; fax (70) 3648656; e-mail emviet@wanadoo.nl; Ambassador Hà Huy Thông.

Yemen: Nassaulaan 2a, 2514 JS The Hague; tel. (70) 3653936; fax (70) 3563312; e-mail yemenembassy@planet.nl; internet www.yemenembassy.nl; Ambassador Naguib Ahmed Obeid Obeid.

Judicial System

Justices and judges must have graduated in law at a Dutch university, and are nominated for life by the Crown. The justices of the Supreme Court are nominated from a list of three compiled by the Second Chamber of the States-General.

SUPREME COURT

De Hoge Raad der Nederlanden

Kazernestraat 52, POB 20303, 2500 EH The Hague; tel. (70) 3611311; fax (70) 3658700; internet www.rechtspraak.nl/Gerechten/HogeRaad.

For appeals in cassation against decisions of courts of lower jurisdiction. As a court of first instance, the Supreme Court tries offences committed in their official capacity by members of the States-General and Ministers. When dealing with appeals in cassation, the court is composed of five or, in more straightforward cases, of three justices (Raadsheren).

President of the Supreme Court: G. J. M. Corstens.

Procurator-General: J. W. Fokkens.

Secretary of the Court: E. Hartogs.

COURTS OF APPEAL

Gerechtshoven: Five courts: Amsterdam, Arnhem, 's-Hertogenbosch, Leeuwarden, The Hague. A court is composed of three judges (Raadsheren); appeal is from decisions of the District Courts of Justice. Fiscal Divisions (Belastingkamers) of the Courts of Appeal deal with appeals against decisions relating to the enforcement of the fiscal laws (administrative jurisdiction). The court of Arnhem has a Tenancy Division (Pachtkamer), composed of three judges and two assessors (a tenant and a landlord), and a Penitentiary Division (Penitentiaire Kamer), composed of three judges and two experts. The Tenancy Division hears appeals from decisions of all Canton Tenancy Divisions. The Penitentiary Division hears appeals against refusals of release on license, which is usually granted after two-thirds of a prison sentence longer than one year, unless there are special objections from the Minister of Justice. A Companies Division (Ondernemingskamer) is attached to the court at Amsterdam, consisting of three judges and two experts as assessors

Directory

DISTRICT COURTS OF JUSTICE

Arrondissementsrechtbanken: There are 19 courts for important civil and penal cases and for appeals from decisions of the Canton Judges. A court is composed of three judges (Rechter); no jury; summary jurisdiction in civil cases by the President of the Court; simple penal cases, including economic offences, generally by a single judge (Politierechter). Offences committed by juveniles are (with certain exceptions) tried by a specialized judge (Kinderrechter), who is also competent to take certain legal steps when the upbringing of a juvenile is endangered. Economic offences, and in particular environmental offences, are also dealt with by a specialized judge sitting alone.

CANTON COURTS

Kantongerechten: There are 62 courts for civil and penal cases of minor importance. A court consists of a single judge, the Canton Judge (Kantonrechter). Each Canton Court has a Tenancy Division (Pachtkamer), presided over by the Canton Judge who is assisted by two assessors (a landlord and a tenant).

ADMINISTRATIVE COURTS

The administrative courts regulate relations between the authorities and citizens according to the provisions of the General Administrative Law Act. The majority of cases are heard by the Administrative Law Sections of the District Courts, while appeals are heard by the Administrative Law Division of the Council of State (Afdeling Bestuursrechtspraak van de Raad van State), which also acts as the court of sole and last instance in the majority of cases concerning education, the environment and spatial planning. In addition, cases relating to certain areas of administrative law are heard by the following bodies:

Centrale Raad van Beroep (Central Appeals Council): Graadt van Roggenweg 200–250, POB 16002, 3500 DA Utrecht; tel. (30) 8502100; fax (30) 8502198; e-mail crvb@rechtspraak.nl; internet www.rechtspraak.nl/gerechten/crvb; hears appeals against decisions of the District Courts in matters concerning the public service and social security; Pres. T. G. M. Simons.

College van Beroep voor het Bedrijfsleven (Trade and Industry Appeals Tribunal): Prins Clauslaan 60, POB 20021, 2500 EA The Hague; tel. (70) 3813910; fax (70) 3813999; internet www.rechtspraak.nl/gerechten/cbb; hears in first and last instance appeals against decisions enforcing socio-economic and agricultural legislation made by certain bodies, such as regulatory bodies and Chambers of Commerce, and by certain ministers; Pres. R. R. Winter.

Administration Law Section, Aliens Division, District Court of The Hague: court of sole and last instance in cases involving immigration; brs in Zwolle, 's-Hertogenbosch, Amsterdam and Haarlem. The introduction of a limited right of further appeal is pending.

Tariefcommissie (Tariff Commission): court of sole and last instance for all customs and excise disputes.

Religion

CHRISTIANITY

Raad van Kerken in Nederland (Council of Churches in the Netherlands): Koningin Wilhelminalaan 5, 3818 HN Amersfoort; tel. (33) 4633844; e-mail rvk@raadvankerken.nl; internet www.raadvankerken.nl; f. 1968; 12 mem. churches; Pres. Drs H. J. van Hout; Gen. Sec. Drs K. van der Kamp.

The Roman Catholic Church

The Netherlands comprises one archdiocese and six dioceses. At 31 December 2006 there were an estimated 4,647,300 adherents in the country (28.6% of the population).

Bishops' Conference

Nederlandse Bisschoppenconferentie, Biltstraat 121, POB 13049, 3507 LA Utrecht; tel. (30) 2334244; fax (30) 2332103; e-mail secrbk@rkk.nl; internet www.katholieknederland.nl/rkkerk.

f. 1986; Pres. Mgr Rev. Adrianus Herman van Luyn.

Archbishop of Utrecht: Most Rev. Willem Jacobus (Wim) Eijk, Aartsbisdom, Maliebaan 40, POB 14019, 3508 SB Utrecht; tel. (30) 2338030; fax (30) 2311962; e-mail secretariaat@aartsbisdom.nl; internet www.aartsbisdom.nl.

Protestant Churches

Christelijke Gereformeerde Kerken in Nederland (Christian Reformed Churches in the Netherlands): Vijftien Morgen, POB 334, 3900 AH Veenendaal; tel. (318) 582350; e-mail lkb@cgk.nl; internet

THE NETHERLANDS

www.cgk.nl; f. 1834; Relations Dir Rev. J. G. H. VAN DER VINNE; c. 73,400 mems; 180 churches.

First Church of Christ, Scientist: Andries Bickerweg 1B, 2517 JP The Hague; tel. (70) 3636652; e-mail peter.faas@hccnet.nl; churches in Amsterdam, Haarlem and The Hague.

Deutsche Evangelische Gemeinde (German Evangelical Church): Bleijenburg 3B, 2511 VC, The Hague; tel. (70) 3465727; e-mail deg.haag@tiscali.nl; internet www.evangelischekirche-denhaag.nl; Leaders Pastor E. BENZ-WENZLAFF, Pastor B. WENZLAFF.

Dutch Mennonites: Algemene Doopsgezinde Sociëteit, Singel 454, 1017 AW Amsterdam; tel. (20) 6230914; fax (20) 6278919; e-mail info@doopsgezind.nl; internet www.doopsgezind.nl; f. 1811; Pres. OTTO BLEKER; Sec.-Gen. H. W. STENVERS; 9,000 mems; 118 parishes.

Evangelische Broedergemeente (Hernhutters): Zusterpl. 20, 3703 CB Zeist; tel. (30) 6924833; fax (30) 6922677; e-mail provinciaalbestuur@ebg.nl; internet www.ebg.nl; f. 1746; Pres. RITA HARRY; 10,000 mems in Holland; seven parishes.

Hersteld Apostolische Zendingkerk (Restored Apostolic Missionary Church): Hogerbeetsstraat 32, 2242 TR Wassenaar; tel. and fax (70) 5113995; e-mail s.de.jong.hazk@hazknederland.org; internet www.hazknederland.org; f. 1863; Pres. Apostle for the Netherlands H. F. RIJNDERS; Sec. J. L. M. STRAETEMANS; 500 mems; 10 parishes.

Protestante Kerk in Nederland (Protestant Church in the Netherlands): Joseph Haydnlaan 2A, POB 8504, 3503 RM Utrecht; tel. (30) 8801880; fax (30) 8801300; e-mail info@pkn.nl; internet www.pkn.nl; f. 2004; unification of the Nederlandse Hervormde Kerk with the Gereformeerde Kerken in Nederland and the Evangelisch-Lutherse Kerk; 2.5m. mems, 3,000 parishes in 77 districts; Pres. Rev. G. DE FIJTER; Sec.-Gen. Rev. Dr B. PLAISIER; 1.9m. mems.

Remonstrantse Broederschap (Remonstrant Brotherhood): Nieuwe Gracht 27A, 3512 LC Utrecht; tel. (30) 2316970; fax (30) 2311055; e-mail info@remonstranten.org; internet www.remonstranten.org; f. 1619; Pres. J. W. VAN DER KAMP; Gen. Sec. A.A.I.M. MIKKERS; 6,000 mems; 46 parishes.

Unie van Baptistengemeenten in Nederland (Union of Baptist Churches in The Netherlands): Biltseweg 10, 3735 MC Bosch en Duin; tel. (30) 2255660; fax (30) 2251798; e-mail administratie@baptisten.nl; internet www.baptisten.nl; f. 1881; Pres. JANS HOFMAN; 11,500 mems.

Other Christian Churches

Anglikaans Kerkgenootschap (Anglican Church): Ary van der Spuyweg 1, 2585 HA The Hague; tel. (70) 3555359; e-mail churchoffice@stjohn-stphilip.org; internet www.stjohn-stphilip.org; f. 1698; Chaplain Rev. TONY ROAKE.

Katholiek Apostolische Gemeenten (Catholic Apostolic Church): 1E De Riemerstraat 3, 2513 CT The Hague; tel. (70) 3555018; f. 1867; seven parishes in the Netherlands and three in Belgium.

Oud-Katholieke Kerk van Nederland (Old Catholic Church): Koningin Wilhelminalaan 3, 3818 HN Amersfoort; tel. (33) 4620875; e-mail info@okkn.nl; internet www.okkn.nl; f. 1723 in the Netherlands with Jansenist influence; refuses to accept papal infallibility and other 'new' dogmas of the Roman Catholic Church; full communion with the Anglican Churches since 1931; Leader Archbishop of Utrecht Mgr JORIS A. O. L. VERCAMMEN (18 parishes), Bishop of Haarlem Mgr JAN LAMBERT WIRIX-SPEETJENS (10 parishes); 10,000 mems.

ISLAM

At 1 January 2004 there were around 944,000 Muslims in the Netherlands, representing some 5.8% of the total population.

Contactorgaan Moslims en Overheid (CMO) (Contact Group for Muslims and the Government): POB 85518, 2506 CE The Hague; tel. (70) 3028224; internet www.islamenburgerschap.nl; f. 2004; promotes dialogue between Muslim community and the Government; includes eight Muslim groups.

JUDAISM

Nederlands Israëlitisch Kerkgenootschap (Organization of Jewish Communities in the Netherlands): Postbus 7967, 1008 AD Amsterdam; tel. (20) 3018484; fax (20) 3018485; e-mail info@nik.nl; internet www.nik.nl; f. 1814; 36 communities with around 5,000 mems; Rabbi RAPHAEL EVERS.

Portugees-Israëlietische Gemeente (Portuguese-Israelite Community): Mr. Visserplein 3, 1011 RD Amsterdam; tel. (20) 6245351; fax (20) 6254680; e-mail info@esnoga.com; internet www.esnoga.com; Gen. Sec. NATHAN MOKED.

BAHÁ'Í FAITH

National Spiritual Assembly (Bahá'í Community of the Netherlands): Riouwstraat 27, 2585 GR The Hague; tel. (70) 3554017; fax (70) 3506161; e-mail nsa@bahai.nl; internet www.bahai.nl; f. 1962; mems resident in 179 locations (2008).

The Press

PRINCIPAL DAILIES

Alkmaar

Noordhollands Dagblad: Edisonweg 10, POB 2, 1800 AA Alkmaar; tel. (72) 5196196; fax (72) 5124152; e-mail redactie@nhd.nl; internet www.nhd.nl; morning; eight regional editions; Editors GEERT TEN DAM, JAN-GEERT MAJOOR; circ. 147,064 (2006).

Amersfoort

AD Amersfoortse Courant: POB 1262, 3800 BG Amersfoortse; tel. (33) 4647911; fax (33) 4647334; e-mail ac.redactie@ad.nl; internet www.ad.nl/amersfoort; f. 1887; publ. by AD NieuwsMedia; evening; Editor-in-Chief ARJEH KALMANN.

Amsterdam

Het Financieele Dagblad (Dutch Financial Daily): Prins Bernhardplein 173, POB 216, 1000 AE Amsterdam; tel. (20) 5928888; fax (20) 5928700; e-mail rsc@fd.nl; internet www.fd.nl; f. 1796; morning; Mon.–Sat.; Editor ULKO JONKER; circ. 58,350 (2006).

Metro: Metro Holland BV, Delflandlaan 4, POB 90009, 1006 BA Amsterdam; tel. (20) 5114000; fax (20) 5114090; e-mail info@metronieuws.nl; internet www.metronieuws.nl; f. 2004 in Rotterdam; separate Amsterdam edition since 2005; morning; owned by Metro International SA; Editor ROBERT VAN BRANDWIJK; circ. 560,000 (2008).

Het Parool: Jacob Bontiusplaats 9, POB 433, 1000 AK Amsterdam; tel. (20) 5584444; fax (20) 5584351; e-mail redactie@parool.nl; internet www.parool.nl; f. 1940; evening; Editor BARBARA VAN BEUKERING; circ. 86,656 (2006).

Sp!ts: POB 2620, 1000 CP Amsterdam; tel. (20) 5853045; fax (20) 5853065; e-mail redactie@spitsnieuws.nl; internet www.spitsnieuws.nl; f. 1998; morning; distributed free of charge; publ. by BasisMedia BV; Editor B. BROUWERS; circ. 450,000 (2008).

De Telegraaf: POB 376, 1000 EB Amsterdam; tel. (20) 5859111; fax (20) 5858017; e-mail redactie@telegraaf.nl; internet www.telegraaf.nl; f. 1893; morning; Editor EEF BOS; circ. 714,563 (2006).

Trouw (Loyalty): Jacob Bontiusplaats 9, POB 859, 1000 AW Amsterdam; tel. (20) 5629444; e-mail redactie@trouw.nl; internet www.trouw.nl; f. 1943; morning; Editor WILLEM SCHOONEN; circ. 108,435 (2006).

De Volkskrant (The People's Journal): Jacob Bontiusplaats 9, POB 1002, 1000 BA Amsterdam; tel. (20) 5626222; fax (20) 5626289; e-mail redactie@volkskrant.nl; internet www.volkskrant.nl; f. 1919; morning; Editor PIETER I. BROERTJES; circ. 284,801 (2006).

Apeldoorn

Reformatorisch Dagblad: Laan van Westenenk 12, POB 670, 7300 AR Apeldoorn; tel. (55) 5390222; fax (55) 5412288; e-mail redactie@refdag.nl; internet www.refdag.nl; f. 1971; evening; publ. by Erdee Media Groep; Editor-in-Chief WIM B. KRANENDONK; circ. 58,000 (2008).

De Stentor: Laan van Westenenk 6, POB 99, 7336 AZ Apeldoorn; tel. (55) 5388388; fax (55) 5388200; e-mail redactiesecretariaat@destentor.wegener.nl; internet www.destentor.nl/apeldoorn; f. 2003; evening; publishes nine regional versions; Editor ALEX ENGBERS; circ. 140,757 (2006).

Barneveld

Nederlands Dagblad: Hermesweg 20, POB 111, 3770 AC Barneveld; tel. (342) 411711; fax (342) 411611; e-mail redactie@nd.nl; internet www.nd.nl; f. 1944; morning; Editor-in-Chief P. A. BERGWERFF; circ. 33,200 (2006).

Breda

BN/De Stem (The Voice): Spinveld 55, POB 3229, 4800 MB Breda; tel. (76) 5312311; fax (76) 5312355; e-mail redactie@bndestem.nl; internet www.bndestem.nl; f. 1998 by merger of Brabants Nieuwsblad and De Stem; owned by Koninklijke Wegener NV; morning; Editor JOHAN VAN UFFELEN; circ. 124,213 (2006).

THE NETHERLANDS

Dordrecht

AD De Dordtenaar: POB 54, 3300 AB Dordrecht; tel. (78) 6324705; fax (78) 6324729; e-mail dd.redactie@ad.nl; internet www.ad.nl; f. 1946; morning; Editor BART VERKADE.

Eindhoven

Eindhovens Dagblad (ED): Wal 2, POB 534, 5600 AM Eindhoven; tel. (40) 2336336; fax (40) 2436244; e-mail redactie@eindhovensdagblad.nl; internet www.ed.nl; owned by Wegener; Editor HENK VAN WEERT; circ. 116,901 (2006).

Enschede

De Twentsche Courant Tubantia: Getfertsingel 41, POB 28, 7500 AA Enschede; tel. (53) 4842842; fax (53) 4842200; e-mail lezers@tubantia.wegener.nl; internet www.tctubantia.nl; f. 1844; publ. by Koninklijke Wegener NV; Editor ANDRÉ VIS; circ. 124,070 (2006).

's-Gravenhage/Den Haag
(The Hague)

AD Haagsche Courant: POB 16050, 2500 AA The Hague; tel. (70) 3190911; fax (70) 3954783; e-mail hc.lezers@ad.nl; internet www.ad.nl/denhaag; evening; Editor DENNIS MULKENS.

Nederlandse Staatscourant: Prinses Margrietplantsoen 88, POB 20020, 2500 EA The Hague; tel. (70) 3789639; fax (70) 3855505; e-mail staatscourant@sdu.nl; internet www.staatscourant.nl; f. 1814; morning; Editor W. M. C. DE JONG; circ. 5,913 (2006).

Groningen

Dagblad van het Noorden: Lübeckweg 2, POB 60, 9700 MC Groningen; tel. (50) 5844444; fax (50) 5844209; e-mail redactie@dvhn.nl; internet www.dvhn.nl; f. 1888; morning; Editor PIETER SIJPERSMA; circ. 156,247 (2006).

Haarlem

Haarlems Dagblad: Stationsplein 86, POB 507, 2003 PA Haarlem; tel. (88) 8241200; fax (88) 8241212; e-mail stadsredactie@haarlemsdagblad.nl; internet www.haarlemsdagblad.nl; f. 1656; evening; Editors GEERT TEN DAM, JAN GEERT MAJOOR; circ. 44,123 (2006).

IJmuider Courant: Marktplein 1, 1972 GA IJmuiden; tel. (255) 561800; fax (255) 561888; e-mail redactie@ijmuidercourant.nl; internet www.ijmuidercourant.nl; evening; Editors GEERT TEN DAM, JAN GEERT MAJOOR.

's-Hertogenbosch/Den Bosch

Brabants Dagblad: Emmaplein 25, POB 235, 5201 HB 's-Hertogenbosch; tel. (73) 6157157; fax (73) 6157105; e-mail stadsredactie@brabantsdagblad.nl; internet www.brabantsdagblad.nl; f. 1771; morning; publ. by Koninklijke Wegener NV; Editor ANNEMIEKE BESSELING; circ. 136,068 (2006).

Hilversum

De Gooi- en Eemlander: Seinstraat 14, 1223 DA Hilversum; tel. (35) 6477000; fax (35) 6477108; e-mail redactie@gooieneemlander.nl; internet www.gooieneemlander.nl; f. 1871; evening; Editors GEERT TEN DAM, JAN-GEERT MAJOOR; circ. 29,752 (2006).

Leeuwarden

Leeuwarder Courant: Sixmastraat 15, POB 394, 8901 BD Leeuwarden; tel. (58) 2845655; fax (58) 2845419; e-mail redactie@leeuwardercourant.nl; internet www.leeuwardercourant.nl; f. 1752; evening; Editor RIMMER MULDER; circ. 103,489 (2006).

Leiden

Leidsch Dagblad: 3e Binnenvestgracht 23, POB 54, 2300 AB Leiden; tel. (71) 5356356; fax (71) 5356415; e-mail stadsredactie@leidschdagblad.nl; internet www.leidschdagblad.nl; f. 1860; publ. by HDC Media; evening; Editors GEERT TEN DAM, JAN-GEERT MAJOOR; circ. 34,781 (2006).

Nijmegen

De Gelderlander: Voorstadslaan 2, POB 36, 6500 DA Nijmegen; tel. (24) 3650611; fax (24) 3650479; e-mail redactie@gelderlander.nl; internet www.gelderlander.nl; f. 1848; owned by Koninklijke Wegener NV; morning; Editor K. PIJNAPPELS; circ. 163,780 (2006).

Rotterdam

AD: Marten Meesweg 35, POB 8983, 3009 TC Rotterdam; tel. (10) 4067211; e-mail ad@ad.nl; internet www.ad.nl; f. 1946; fmrly Algemeen Dagblad; morning; Editor JAN BONJER; circ. 524,974 (2006, incl. regional editions).

AD Rotterdams Dagblad: Westblaak 180, POB 2999, 3000 CZ Rotterdam; tel. (10) 4004400; fax (10) 4128509; e-mail rd.redactie@ad.nl; internet www.ad.nl/rotterdam; f. 1991; evening; Editor BART VERKADE.

NRC Handelsblad: Marten Meesweg 35, POB 8987, 3009 TH Rotterdam; tel. (10) 4066111; fax (10) 4066967; e-mail nrc@nrc.nl; internet www.nrc.nl; f. 1970; evening; Editor BIRGIT DONKER; circ. 239,211 (2006).

Sittard

Dagblad De Limburger: POB 1056, 6201 MK Maastricht; tel. (43) 3502000; fax (43) 3501879; e-mail redactievenlo@mgl.nl; internet www.limburger.nl; f. 1845; morning; Editor-in-Chief KITTY BORGHOUTS; circ. 180,000.

Limburgs Dagblad: Mercator 3, 6135 KW Sittard; tel. (46) 4116000; fax (46) 4116471; e-mail marketing@mgl.nl; internet www.limburger.nl; f. 1918; morning; Editor JOS ADRIAENS; circ. 53,904 (2006).

Utrecht

AD Utrechts Nieuwsblad: Essenkade 2, POB 500, 3990 DM Houten; tel. (30) 6399911; fax (30) 6399937; e-mail un.lezers@ad.nl; internet www.ad.nl; f. 1993; evening; Editor-in-Chief ARJEH KALMANN.

Vlissingen

Provinciale Zeeuwse Courant: POB 31, 4460 AA Goes; tel. (113) 315600; fax (113) 315669; e-mail redactie@pzc.nl; internet www.pzc.nl; f. 1758; morning; Editor PETER JANSEN; circ. 56,868 (2006).

SELECTED WEEKLIES

Adformatie: POB 75462, 1070 AL Amsterdam; tel. (20) 5733644; fax (20) 6793581; e-mail redactie@adformatie.nl; internet www.adformatie.nl; advertising, marketing and media; Editor-in-Chief LÉON BOUWMAN; circ. 40,000.

Avrobode: 's-Gravelandseweg 52, 1217 ET Hilversum; tel. (35) 6717911; fax (35) 717443; e-mail redactie@avrobode.nl; internet www.avrobode.nl; publ. by Algemene Omroepvereniging; radio and TV guide; circ. 791,986.

Boerderij: Hanzestraat 1, POB 4, 7000 BA Doetinchem; tel. (314) 349446; fax (314) 344397; e-mail boerderij@reedbusiness.nl; internet www.boerderij.nl; f. 1915; farming; Editor-in-Chief MARCEL HENST; circ. 65,000.

Donald Duck: Haaksbergseweg 75, 1101 BR Amsterdam; tel. (20) 4300300; fax (20) 4300315; internet www.donaldduck.nl; f. 1952; children's interest; weekly; Publr SUZAN SCHOUTEN HAAGMANS; Editor JESSICA HAAGMANS; circ. 62,784.

Elsevier: POB 152, 1000 AD Amsterdam; tel. (20) 5159944; fax (20) 5159900; e-mail redactie.elsevier@elsevier.nl; internet www.elsevier.nl; f. 1945; current affairs; Chief Editor ARENDO JOUSTRA; circ. 160,000.

Fancy: POB 1610, 2130 JA Hoofddorp; tel. (23) 5565117; fax (23) 5565116; e-mail fancy@sanoma-uitgevers.nl; internet www.fancy.nl; teenage girls' interest; Editor ANNET NITERINK; circ. 120,000.

HP/De Tijd (The Times): Amsterdam; tel. (20) 5734811; fax (20) 5734406; f. 1845 as daily; changed to weekly in 1974; Christian progressive; current affairs; Dir A. VISSER; circ. 37,580.

Libelle: POB 1742, 2130 JC Hoofddorp; tel. (23) 5564002; fax (23) 5564003; e-mail libelle@libelle.nl; internet www.libelle.nl; f. 1934; women's interest; Editor-in-Chief FRANSKA STUY; circ. 587,754.

Margriet: POB 1640, 2130 JA Hoofddorp; tel. (23) 5564123; e-mail redactie@margriet.nl; internet www.margriet.nl; f. 1938; women's interest; Editor-in-Chief LEONTINE VAN DEN BOS; circ. 499,868.

Mikro-Gids: Zeverijnstraat 6, 1216 GK Hilversum; tel. (35) 6726751; fax (35) 6726752; internet www.mikrogids.nl; f. 1974; radio and TV guide; Dir H. SCHEENSTRA; circ. 468,280.

NCRV-Gids: POB 25900, 1202 HW Hilversum; tel. (35) 6726801; fax (35) 6726863; internet www.ncrvgids.nl; f. 1966; publ. by Nederlandse Christelijke Radio Vereniging; radio and TV guide; Dir C. ABBENHUIS; circ. 419,363.

Nederlands Tijdschrift voor Geneeskunde (Dutch Journal of Medicine): POB 75971, 1070 AZ Amsterdam; tel. (20) 6620150; fax (20) 6735481; e-mail redactie@ntvg.nl; internet www.ntvg.nl; f. 1856; Editors Prof. Dr P. W. DE LEEUW, Prof. Dr F. W. A. VERHEUG, Prof. Dr J. O. M. ZAAT; circ. 30,000.

Nieuwe Revu: Haaksbergseweg 75, POB 23059, 1100 DN Amsterdam; tel. (20) 7518380; fax (20) 7518381; e-mail redactie@revu.nl; internet www.revu.nl; f. 1968; general interest; Editor-in-Chief ALTAN ERDOGAN; circ. 127,802.

THE NETHERLANDS

Panorama: Ceylonpoort 5–25, 2037 AA Haarlem; tel. (23) 5304304; fax (23) 5361624; e-mail panorama@smm.nl; internet www.panorama.nl; f. 1913; general interest; Editor FRANS LOMANS; circ. 194,466.

Privé: POB 1980, 1000 BZ Amsterdam; tel. (20) 5853375; fax (20) 5854225; e-mail redactie@prive.nl; internet www.prive.nl; f. 1977; women's interest; Editor EVERT SANTEGOEDS; circ. 490,000.

Story: POB 1760, 2130 JD Hoofddorp; tel. (23) 5564894; fax (23) 5564911; internet www.story.nl; f. 1974; women's interest; Editor PETRA BAKKER-SCHUT; circ. 272,700.

TeleVizier: Zeverijnstraat 6, POB 20002, 1202 AB Hilversum; tel. (35) 6726834; fax (35) 6726712; e-mail redactie@televizier.nl; internet www.televizier.nl; publ. by Algemene Omroepvereniging; radio and TV guide; circ. 258,487.

Tina: Ceylonpoort 5–25, 2037 AA Haarlem; tel. (23) 5304304; fax (23) 5352554; f. 1967; teenage interest; circ. 112,191.

TrosKompas: POB 28600, 1202 LR Hilversum; tel. (35) 6728798; fax (35) 6728631; internet www.troskompas.nl; f. 1966; radio and TV guide; Editor EDGER HAMER.

TV Krant: POB 28600, 1202 LR Hilversum; tel. (35) 6728798; fax (35) 6728631; f. 1990; radio and TV guide; Editor EDGER HAMER.

Vara TV Magazine: POB 175, 1200 AD Hilversum; tel. (35) 6711445; fax (35) 6711429; e-mail tv.magazine@vara.nl; internet vara.nl; radio and TV guide; circ. 500,000.

Veronica: POB 22000, 1202 CA Hilversum; tel. (35) 6463333; fax (35) 6463300; e-mail bladredactie@veronicapublishing.nl; internet www.veronica.nl; f. 1971; radio and TV guide; Editor PETER CONTANT; circ. 1,250,000.

Viva: POB 1630, 2130 JA Hoofddorp; tel. (23) 5565165; fax (23) 5565200; e-mail redactie@viva.nl; internet www.viva.nl; women's interest; Editor KARIN VAN GILST; circ. 149,461.

VNU: Ceylonpoort 5–25, 2037 AA Haarlem; POB 1, 2000 MA Haarlem; tel. (23) 5463463; fax (23) 5463912; e-mail vnupr@hq.vnu.com; circ. 174,250.

VPRO-Gids: POB 11, 1200 JC Hilversum; tel. (35) 6712665; fax (35) 6712285; e-mail gids@vpro.nl; internet www.vpro.nl/gids; radio and TV guide; Dir H. VAN DALFSEN; circ. 254,000.

Vrij Nederland: Raamgracht 4, POB 1254, 1000 BG Amsterdam; tel. (20) 5518711; fax (20) 6247476; e-mail redactie@vn.nl; f. 1940; current affairs; Editor EMILE FALLAUX; circ. 80,000.

SELECTED PERIODICALS

Art, History and Literature

De Architect: POB 34, 2501 AG The Hague; tel. (70) 3045833; fax (70) 3045806; e-mail architect@wkths.nl; internet www.deArchitect.nl; Dir HARM TILMAN; circ. 8,000.

Kunstbeeld: POB 256, 1110 AG Diemen; tel. (20) 5310900; fax (20) 5310971; e-mail redactie@kunstbeeld.nl; internet www.kunstbeeld.nl; monthly; art, sculpture; Editor ROBBERT ROOS; circ. 11,000 (2007).

Spiegel Historiael: Molukkenstraat 200, E5, 1098 TW Amsterdam; tel. (20) 6652759; fax (20) 6657831; e-mail s.h@inter.nl.net; f. 1966; monthly; history and archaeology; circ. 8,000.

Tableau Fine Arts Magazine: Capellalaan 65, 2132 JL Hoofddorp; tel. (23) 5565377; fax (23) 5565376; e-mail tableau@sanoma-uitgevers.nl; internet www.tableaufineartsmagazine.nl; f. 1978; every 2 months; Editor RONALD KRAAYEVELD; circ. 14,000.

Tijdschrift voor Geschiedenis (Historical Review): Instituut Geschiedenis UU, Kromme Drift 10, 3512 BS Utrecht; tel. (30) 2537868; e-mail tvg@let.uu.nl; f. 1886; quarterly; Chair. M. GREVER.

Economics and Business

Computable: POB 1905, 2003 BA Haarlem; tel. (23) 5463413; e-mail computable@vnumedia.nl; internet www.computable.nl; Editor ALEX BESHUIZEN; circ. 96,636.

Elektronica + Embedded Systems: POB 23, 7400 AB Deventer; tel. (570) 504381; fax (570) 504399; e-mail h.vries@mybusinessmedia.nl; internet www.engineersonline.nl; f. 1953; 11 a year; electronics design; Editor HENK DE VRIES; circ. 5,000.

Intermediair: POB 1900, 2003 BA Haarlem; tel. (23) 5463455; fax (23) 5465530; e-mail redactie@intermediair.nl; internet www.intermediair.nl; f. 1965; weekly; business recruitment; Editor PETER TER HORST; circ. 240,678.

Management Team: VNU Business Publications, POB 1907, 2003 BA Haarlem; tel. (318) 521422; fax (318) 523136; e-mail redactie@mt.nl; internet www.mt.nl; f. 1980; monthly; management; Editor JAN DIJKGRAAF; circ. 142,000 (2001).

PCM (Personal Computer Magazine): Ceylonpoort 5–25, 2037 AA Haarlem; tel. (23) 5463704; fax (23) 5465524; internet www.pcmweb.nl; f. 1982; monthly; computing; Editor-in-Chief EDWIN AMMERLAAN; circ. 94,997.

Trade Channel: Holland Business Press BV, Sophiastraat 1, 2011 VT Haarlem; tel. (23) 5319022; fax (23) 5317974; e-mail pvroom@tradechannel.com; internet www.tradechannel.com; f. 1945; monthly, 2 edns: Trade Channel Consumer Goods and Trade Channel Industrial & Technical Products; promote imports and exports; Editor HENK VAN CAPELLE; circ. 13,286 (consumer edn), 55,000 (technical edn).

Home, Fashion and General

Ariadne at Home: Capellalaan 65, POB 1919, 2130 YM Hoofddorp; tel. (23) 5566770; fax (23) 5361624; e-mail redactie@ariadneathome.nl; internet www.ariadneathome.nl; f. 1946; monthly; home decoration; Editor BRIGITTE SPEEKMAN; circ. 169,198.

Het Beste uit Reader's Digest: POB 23330, 1100 DV Amsterdam; tel. (20) 56789111; fax (20) 6976422; e-mail hetbeste@readersdigest.nl; internet www.readersdigest.nl; f. 1957; monthly; general interest; Man. Dir OELE STEENKS; circ. 304,453.

Cosmopolitan: Capellalaan 65, POB 1730, 2132 JL Hoofddorp; fax (23) 5565259; e-mail c.straatmans@sanoma-uitgevers.nl; internet www.cosmopolitan.nl; f. 1982; monthly; women's interest; Editor CLAUDIA STRAATMANS; circ. 108,406.

Delicious: POB 1632, 2130 JA Hoofddorp; tel. (23) 5565466; fax (23) 5565488; e-mail deliciousmagazine@sanoma-uitgevers.nl; internet www.deliciousmagazine.nl; f. 1977; monthly; cookery; Editor-in-Chief MAKKIE MULDER; circ. 70,000.

Kijk: Ceylonpoort 5–25, 2037 AA Haarlem; tel. (20) 4300455; fax (20) 4300450; sports, science, technology and adventure; circ. 92,993.

Knipmode: Capellalaan 65, POB 1900, 2130 JL Hoofddorp; tel. (23) 5565006; fax (23) 5566771; internet www.knipmode.nl; monthly; DIY fashion; Editor-in-Chief MARGREET HAGDORN; Publr GERT JAAP SCHOPPINK; circ. 124,000.

Nouveau: Ceylonpoort 5–25, 2037 AA Haarlem; tel. (23) 304304; fax (23) 350621; f. 1986; women's interest; Dir K. P. M. VAN DE PAS; circ. 134,669.

Opzij: POB 2748, 1000 CS Amsterdam; tel. (20) 5518525; fax (20) 6227265; e-mail redactie@opzij.nl; internet www.opzij.nl; f. 1972; monthly; feminist themes; Editor MARGRIET VAN DER LINDEN; circ. 80,000.

Ouders van Nu: POB 740, 2400 AS Alphen Aan Den Ryn; tel. (23) 5565066; fax (23) 5565095; e-mail ouders@jongezinnen.nl; internet www.oudersvannu.nl; f. 1967; monthly; childcare; Editor K. KROON-STUIVER; circ. 156,720.

SEN: Mathenesserlaan 179, 3014 HA Rotterdam; fax (102) 092629; e-mail info@senmagazine.com; internet www.senmagazine.com; f. 2004; monthly; women's interest; Publr SENAY OZDEMIR; circ. 20,000.

VT-Wonen: Ceylonpoort 5-25, 2037 AA Haarlem; tel. (30) 822511; fax (30) 898388; e-mail vtwonen@sanoma-utigevers.nl; internet www.vtwonen.nl; f. 1964; monthly; home-owning and decorating, circ. 210,374; Editors MONIQUE WIEMEYER, FRANCIEN DE VET.

101 Woonideeën: POB 1702, 2130 JC Hoofddorp; tel. (23) 5564590; fax (23) 5564505; e-mail 101woonideeen@sanoma-uitgevers.nl; internet www.101woonideeen.nl; f. 1957; monthly; home ideas; Editor ANNET NITERINK; circ. 95,000.

Leisure Interests and Sport

Autokampioen: POB 93200, 2509 BA The Hague; tel. (88) 2696688; fax (88) 2696279; e-mail autokampioen@anwb.nl; internet www.anwb.nl/auto; f. 1908; publ. by Royal Dutch Touring Club (ANWB); motoring; fortnightly; Chief Editor JOS VROOMANS; circ. 70,000.

Grasduinen (Browsing): POB 23209, 1100 DT Amsterdam; tel. (20) 7510110; fax (20) 7510111; e-mail grasduinen@smm.nl; internet www.grasduinen.nl; monthly; leisure, healthy living, art; Editor KEES LOOGMAN; circ. 51,000.

Kampeer en Caravankampioen: POB 93200, 2509 BA The Hague; tel. (70) 3146691; fax (70) 3146692; e-mail kck@anwb.nl; internet www.kck-online.nl; f. 1941; monthly; camping and caravanning; publ. by Royal Dutch Touring Club (ANWB); Editor-in-Chief F. VOORBERGEN; circ. 139,601.

Kampioen: POB 93200, 2509 BA The Hague; tel. (70) 3146285; fax (70) 3146983; e-mail kampioen@anwb.nl; internet www.kampioen.nl; f. 1885; monthly; recreation and tourism; publ. by Royal Dutch Touring Club (ANWB); Editor E. LODEWYKS; circ. 3,700,000.

Reizen Magazine: POB 93200, 2509 BA The Hague; tel. (88) 2696670; fax (88) 2697610; e-mail reizen@anwb.nl; internet www.reizen.nl; monthly; tourism, travel; publ. by Royal Dutch Touring Club (ANWB); Editor-in-Chief HARRI THEIRLYNCK; circ. 48,000.

Sport International: POB 225, 2800 AE Gouda; tel. (182) 599366; fax (182) 516650; f. 1981; five a year; Editor J. LINSE; circ. 47,350.

THE NETHERLANDS

Voetbal International: WP Sport Media BV, POB 764, 1000 AT Amsterdam; tel. (20) 5518510; e-mail webmaster@vi.nl; internet www.vi.nl; weekly; football; Editor-in-Chief JOHAN DERKSEN.

Waterkampioen: POB 93200, 2509 BA The Hague; tel. (70) 3145796; fax (70) 3147356; e-mail waterkampioen@anwb.nl; internet www.waterkampioen.nl; f. 1927; fortnightly; water sports and yachting; publ. by Royal Dutch Touring Club (ANWB); Editor INGEBORG BERGHUIJS; circ. 54,000.

Scientific and Medical

Huisarts en Wetenschap: POB 3231, 3502 GE Utrecht; tel. (30) 2881700; fax (30) 2870668; e-mail redactie@nhg-nl.org; monthly; medical; Editor Dr JOOST VAAT; circ. 8,500.

Natuur & Techniek: Segment Special Interest Media, POB 75, 6190 AB Beek (L); tel. (46) 4389444; fax (46) 4370161; e-mail natutech@xs4all.nl; internet www.natutech.nl; f. 1932; monthly; Editor R. DOBBELAER; circ. 47,360.

Technische Revue: POB 4, 7000 BA Doetinchem; tel. (314) 349911; fax (314) 361522; internet www.ebi.nl; monthly; review of new products; Chief Editor M. L. MATSER; circ. 28,000.

NEWS AGENCY

Algemeen Nederlands Persbureau (ANP) (Netherlands News Agency): POB 1, 2501 AA The Hague; tel. (70) 4141414; fax (70) 4140560; e-mail redactie@anp.nl; internet www.anp.nl; f. 1934; official agency of the Netherlands Daily Press Asscn; Man. Dir LUC VAN GOMPEL; Editor-in-Chief ERIK VAN GRUIJTHUIJSEN.

PRESS ORGANIZATIONS

Buitenlandse Persvereniging in Nederland (Foreign Press Asscn in the Netherlands): Oudezijds Voorburgwal 129, 1012 EP Amsterdam; tel. (20) 4221209; e-mail ccorder@ap.org; internet www.bpv-fpa.nl; f. 1925; Pres. KERSTIN SCHWEIGHÖFER; 120 mems.

Nederlandse Dagbladpers (NDP) (Dutch Asscn of Daily Newspaper Publrs): Hogehilweg 6, POB 12040, 1100 AA Amsterdam-Zuidoost; tel. (20) 4309171; fax (20) 4309199; e-mail ndp@nuv.nl; internet www.nuv.nl; f. 1908; affiliated to Nederlands Uitgeversverbond; Chair. C. G. G. SPAAN; Gen. Sec. T. NAUTA; 31 mems.

De Nederlandse Nieuwsbladpers (NNP) (Organization of Local News Media in the Netherlands): Hogebrinkerweg 23C, 3871 KM Hoevelaken; tel. (33) 4481650; fax (33) 4481652; e-mail nnpnl@nnp.nl; internet www.nnp.nl; f. 1945; asscn of publrs of non-daily local newspapers and other local news media; Pres. P. V. J. H. (PAUL) JANSSEN; Dir J. P. (PAUL) BOS; 131 mems.

Nederlandse Vereniging van Journalisten (Netherlands Union of Journalists): Johannes Vermeerstraat 22, POB 75997, 1070 AZ Amsterdam; tel. (20) 6766771; fax (20) 6624901; e-mail vereniging@nvj.nl; internet www.villamedia.nl/n/nvj; f. 1884; publ. *De Journalist* (fortnightly); Chair. (vacant); Sec. T. BRUNING; 9,000 mems.

Publishers

Uitgeverij Altamira BV: Blekersvaartweg 19A, Heemstede; tel. (23) 5286882; e-mail altamira@tip.nl; internet www.altamira-becht.nl; f. 1985; philosophy, psychology, New Age, health and spirituality.

Uitgeverij Ankh-Hermes BV: Smyrnastraat 5, POB 125, 7400 AC Deventer; tel. (57) 0678900; fax (57) 0624632; e-mail info@ankh-hermes.nl; internet www.ankh-hermes.nl; health, eastern and western religions, astrology, alternative medicine, psychology, esoterics; Dir A. STEENBERGEN; Publrs E. TEN SELDAM, W. DE VEER.

Ambo Anthos: Herengracht 435–437, 1017 BR Amsterdam; tel. (20) 5245411; fax (20) 4200422; e-mail info@amboanthos.nl; internet www.amboanthos.nl; literature, cultural history, biographies, history, politics; Dir R. AMMERLAAN.

APA (Academic Publishers Associated): POB 806, 1000 AV Amsterdam; tel. (20) 6265544; fax (20) 5285298; e-mail apa@apa-publishers.com; internet www.apa-publishers.com; f. 1966; subsidiaries: Apantiqua, Holland University Press, Fontes Pers, Oriental Press, Philo Press, van Heusden, Hissink & Co; new and reprint edns in the arts, humanities and science; Man. Dir G. VAN HEUSDEN.

BV Uitgeverij De Arbeiderspers: Herengracht 370–372, POB 2877, 1000 CW Amsterdam; tel. (20) 5247500; fax (20) 6224937; e-mail info@arbeiderspers.nl; internet www.ap-archipel.nl; participant in Weekbladpers holdings group; general, fiction and non-fiction; Dir R. C. HAANS.

A. Asher & Co BV: Zeeweg 264, POB 258, 1971 AG IJmuiden; tel. (25) 5523839; fax (25) 5510352; e-mail info@asherbooks.com; internet www.asherbooks.com; f. 1830; natural history; Dirs M. J. ROOS, J. W. STEINER.

Bert Bakker BV: Herengracht 540, POB 1662, 1000 BR Amsterdam; tel. (20) 6241934; fax (20) 6225461; e-mail info@pbo.nl; internet www.uitgeverijprometheus.nl/bb; f. 1893; Dutch and international literature, sociology, history, politics, science; Editor JOB LISMAN.

John Benjamins BV: Klaprozenweg 105, POB 36224, 1020 ME Amsterdam; tel. (20) 6304747; fax (20) 6739773; e-mail customer.services@benjamins.nl; internet www.benjamins.com; f. 1964; linguistics, philology, psychology and art history; antiquarian scholarly periodicals; Man. Dirs J. L. BENJAMINS, C. L. BENJAMINS-SCHALEKAMP, SELINE BENJAMINS.

Uitgeverij De Bezige Bij BV: Van Miereveldstraat 1, POB 75184, 1070 AD Amsterdam; tel. (20) 3059810; fax (20) 3059824; e-mail info@debezigebij.nl; internet www.debezigebij.nl; f. 1945; Publr MICHIEL GAAF.

Erven J. Bijleveld: Janskerkhof 7, 3512 BK Utrecht, POB 1238, 3500 BE Utrecht; tel. (30) 2317008; fax (30) 2368675; e-mail bijleveld.publishers@wxs.nl; internet www.bijleveldbooks.nl; f. 1865; psychology, sociology, philosophy, religion and history; computer books (as Bijleveld Press); Mans J. B. BOMMELJÉ, L. S. BOMMELJÉ.

Boekencentrum Uitgevers: Goudstraat 50, POB 29, 2700 AA Zoetermeer; tel. (79) 3615481; fax (79) 3615489; e-mail info@boekencentrum.nl; internet www.boekencentrum.nl; bibles, books and magazines; Dir N. A. DE WAAL.

Bohn Stafleu Van Hoghum BV: Het Spoor 2, POB 246, 3990 GA Houten; tel. (30) 6385838; fax (30) 6383839; e-mail klantenservice@bsl.nl; internet www.bsl.nl; mem. of Wolters Kluwer NV holdings group; social sciences, humanities, medical, dental and nursing; Dir P. J. A. SNAKKERS.

Boom Uitgevers Amsterdam BV: Prinsengracht 747–751, 1017 JX Amsterdam; tel. (20) 6226107; fax (20) 6253327; e-mail info@boomamsterdam.nl; internet www.boomamsterdam.nl; f. 1842; fmrly Boom Pers BV, Meppel; philosophy, educational and social sciences, environment, history; Man. Dir DRIES VAN INGEN.

Brill Academic Publishers: Plantijnstraat 2, POB 9000, 2300 PA Leiden; tel. (71) 5353500; fax (71) 5317532; e-mail cs@brill.nl; internet www.brill.nl; f. 1683; academic books and periodicals (mainly in English); classics, medieval, renaissance and oriental studies, comparative religion, biology; CEO HERMAN PABBRUWE.

A. W. Bruna Uitgevers BV: Kobaltweg 23–25, POB 40203, 3504 AA Utrecht; tel. (30) 2470411; fax (30) 2410018; e-mail info@awbruna.nl; internet www.awbruna.nl; f. 1868; general fiction and non-fiction; Dir J. A. A. BOEZEMAN.

Uitgeverij Cantecleer BV: Julianalaan 11, POB 309, 3740 AM Baarn; tel. (35) 5486600; fax (35) 5486645; e-mail cantecleer@worldonline.nl; internet www.cantecleer.nl; f. 1948; mem. of Bosch & Keuning Uitgevers group; Man. Dir H. SCHWURMANS.

Uitgeverij De Fontein BV: Prinses Marielaan 8, POB 1, 3740 AA Baarn; tel. (35) 5486311; fax (35) 5423855; f. 1981; mem. of NDC/VBK; commercial fiction, non-fiction and children's books; Dir T. AKVELD.

Uitgeverij van Gennep BV: Keizersgracht 524, 1017 EK Amsterdam; tel. (20) 6247033; fax (20) 6247035; e-mail vangennep@wxs.nl; history, social theory, political science, biographies, literature.

Uitgeverij J. H. Gottmer/H. J. W. Becht BV: Wilhelminapark 6, POB 317, 2000 AH Haarlem; tel. (23) 5411190; fax (23) 5274404; e-mail info@gottmer.nl; internet www.gottmer.nl; f. 1937; fiction, non-fiction, children's books, religion, spirituality, travel guides; imprints incl. Aramith, Becht, Dominicus and Hollandia; Dir C. G. A. VAN WIJK.

> **Uitgeverij Hollandia BV:** e-mail info@hollandia-boeken.nl; internet www.hollandia-boeken.nl; f. 1899; travel, yachting and nautical books; Dir TONNIS MUNTINGA.

Uitgeverij Holland BV: Spaarne 110, 2011 CM Haarlem; tel. (23) 5323061; fax (23) 5342908; e-mail info@uitgeverijholland.nl; internet www.uitgeverijholland.nl; f. 1922; literature, reference, science, children's books; Publr J. B. VAN ULZEN.

Uitgeefmaatschappij J. H. Kok: IJsseldijk 31, POB 5019, 8260 GA Kampen; tel. (38) 3392555; fax (38) 3327331; e-mail algemeen@kok.nl; internet www.kok.nl; f. 1894; theology, belles-lettres, science, periodicals; mem. of Veen Bosch & Keuning Uitgevers; nine subsidiaries; Dir B. A. ENDEDIJK.

> **Ten Have BV:** IJsseldijk 31, POB 5018, 8266 DA Kampen; tel. (38) 3328912; fax (38) 3392500; e-mail info@uitgeverijtenhave.nl; internet www.uitgeverijtenhave.nl; f. 1831; imprint of Uitgeefmaatschappij J. H. Kok; religious; Dir B. A. ENDEDIJK; Editor P. DE BOER.

> **Uitgeverij Voorhoeve:** Stationsplein 62, POB 133, 3740 AC Baarn; tel. (35) 5418855; fax (35) 5413174; f. 1876; imprint of Uitgeversmaatschappij J. H. Kok; general non-fiction, children's books; Dir B. A. ENDEDIJK.

Kosmos Uitgevers: Maliebaan 74, POB 13288, 3507 LG Utrecht; tel. (30) 2349211; fax (30) 2349247; e-mail info@kosmosutigevers.nl;

internet www.kosmosutigevers.nl; f. 1992; mem. of Veen Bosch & Keuning Uitgevers; Dir ROBBERT SCHUURMANS.

Lemniscaat BV: Vijverlaan 48, POB 4066, 3006 AB Rotterdam; tel. (10) 2062929; fax (10) 4141560; e-mail info@lemniscaat.nl; internet www.lemniscaat.nl; f. 1963; philosophy, psychology, care of the disabled and mentally handicapped, books for juveniles and young adults, picture books; Dir J. C. BOELE VAN HENSBROEK.

Uitgeverij Leopold BV: Singel 262, POB 3879, 1001 AR Amsterdam; tel. (20) 5511250; fax (20) 4204699; e-mail info@leopold.nl; internet www.leopold.nl; f. 1923; mem. Weekbladpers BV; children's books; Dir MARTINE SCHAAP.

Uitgeverij Luitingh-Sijthoff BV: Leidsegracht 105A, 1017 ND Amsterdam; tel. (20) 5307340; fax (20) 626251; e-mail info@luitingh-sijthoff.nl; Luitingh; f. 1946; Sijthoff; f. 1851; merged in 1989; mem. of Veen Bosch en Keuning Uitgevers publishing group; fiction and popular non-fiction; Man. Dir J. A. B. LEPPINK.

Malmberg BV: Leeghwaterlaan 16, POB 233, 5201 AE Den Bosch; tel. (73) 6288811; fax (73) 6210512; e-mail malmberg@malmberg.nl; internet www.malmberg.nl; f. 1885; part of SanomaWSOY Group (Finland); educational; Dir J. DRIESSEN.

J. M. Meulenhoff BV: Nieuwe Spiegelstraat 26, POB 100, 1000 AC Amsterdam; tel. (20) 5533500; fax (20) 6251135; e-mail info@meulenhoff.nl; internet www.meulenhoff.nl; f. 1895; literature, historical, political, social/cultural, art, paperbacks and pocket books; Dir ROB HOGENES.

NDC/VBK de Uitgevers B.V.: Sixmastraat 15, POB 394, 8932 PA Leeuwarden; tel. (30) 2845245; e-mail communicatie@ndcvbk.nl; internet www.ndcvbk.nl; f. 2005; merger between NDC Holding BV and Veen Bosch en Keuning Uitgevers NV; Chair. JAN K. W. DE ROOS.

Nienhuis Montessori International BV: Industriepark 14, POB 16, 7020 AA Zelhem; tel. (314) 627127; fax (314) 627128; e-mail info@nienhuis.nl; internet www.nienhuis.nl; f. 1800; holdings group; publrs and printers specializing in scientific books and periodicals; Dir A. J. NIENHUIS.

Uitgeverij Ploegsma BV: Keizersgracht 616, POB 19857, 1000 GW Amsterdam; tel. (20) 6262907; fax (20) 6242994; internet www.ploegsma.nl; subsidiary: Uitgeverij De Brink; Dir M. BRINKMAN.

Em. Querido's Uitgeverij BV: Singel 262, POB 3879, 1001 AR Amsterdam; tel. (20) 5511262; fax (20) 6391968; internet www.querido.nl; f. 1915; subsidiary: Uitgeverij Nijgh & van Ditmar; participant in 'Singel 262' holdings group; general fiction, history, children's books, translations from Latin and Greek texts; Dir ARY T. LANGBROEK.

Reed Elsevier NV: VRadarweg 29, 1043 NX Amsterdam; POB 152, 1000 AD Amsterdam; tel. (20) 5159944; fax (20) 5159900; internet www.elsevier.nl; f. 1979 by merger; subholdings include some 60 subsidiaries in the Netherlands and abroad specializing in reference works, handbooks, weekly magazines, newspapers, trade and technical pubs, (postgraduate) scientific books and journals, audiovisual materials, further education study courses, databases; CEO IAN SMITH.

 Elsevier B.V. Excerpta Medica: Radarweg 29, 1043 NX Amsterdam; tel. (20) 4853975; fax (20) 4853188; e-mail excerptamedica@elsevier.com; internet www.excerptamedica.com; Man. Dir EDWARD ROOS.

Editions Rodopi BV: Tijnmuiden 7, 1046 AK Amsterdam; tel. (20) 6114821; fax (20) 4472979; e-mail info@rodopi.nl; internet www.rodopi.nl; f. 1966; Dir Y. L. SCHIPPERS.

SDU: Prinses Beatrixlaan 116, POB 20025, 2500 EA The Hague; tel. (70) 3789911; fax (70) 3854321; e-mail sdu@sdu.nl; internet www.sdu.nl; Chair. Dr L. JONGSMA.

Springer: Van Godewijckstraat 30, POB 989, 3311 GX Dordrecht; tel. (78) 6576050; fax (78) 6576467; internet www.springeronline.com; merged with Kluwer Academic Publrs in 2004; publrs of books and journals in the fields of science, technology and medicine, incl., *inter alia*, natural sciences, mathematics, engineering, computer science and psychology; CEO DERK HAANK.

Uitgeverij Strengholt: Hofstede Oud-Bussem, Flevolaan 41, POB 338, 1400 AH Bussum; tel. (35) 6958411; fax (35) 6946173; e-mail info@utigeverijstrengholt.nl; internet www.uitgeverijstrengholt.nl; f. 1928; health, biography, music, current affairs, psychology, parapsychology, sports, cookery; Dir T. M. JANSEN.

Taylor & Francis The Netherlands (T&F NL): Schipholweg 107C, POB 447, 2300 AK Leiden; tel. (71) 5243080; fax (71) 5234571; e-mail pub.nl@tandf.co.uk; internet www.taylorandfrancis.com; f. 1901 as Swets & Zeitlinger Publishers; acquired by Taylor & Francis (United Kingdom) in 2003; publr of books in civil engineering, water, geosciences and earth sciences; Sr Publr JANJAAP BLOM.

Uitgeverij De Tijdstroom BV: Janskerkhof 26, POB 775, 3500 AT Utrecht; tel. (30) 2364450; fax (30) 23699354; e-mail info@tijdstroom.nl; internet www.tijdstroom.nl; f. 1921; educational and professional publications on health and welfare, periodicals in these fields; Dir N. F. VAN 'T ZET.

Unieboek BV: Papiermolen 14–24, POB 97, 3990 DB Houten; tel. (30) 7998300; fax (30) 7998398; e-mail info@unieboek.nl; internet www.unieboek.nl; f. 1890; holding group incorporating 10 publishing houses; general and juvenile literature, fiction, popular science, history, art, social, economics, religion, textbooks, etc.; Dir W. VAN GILS.

VNU Business Publications BV: Ceylonpoort 5–25, POB 4020, 2031 EA Haarlem; tel. (23) 5463463; fax (23) 5463931; e-mail info@bp.vnu.com; internet www.vnubp.nl; trade and fashion, careers, IT, personal computer, management, training.

West Friesland BV: Slijksteeg 4, POB 2308, 1620 EH Hoorn; tel. (22) 9248820; fax (22) 9218944; f. 1943; novels, biographies, children's books, paperbacks, young adults; Man. Dir B. E. ENDEDIJK; Editor-in-Chief F. H. JONKERS.

Wolters Kluwer NV: Apollolaan 153, POB 75248; 1070 AE Amsterdam; tel. (20) 6070400; fax (20) 6070490; e-mail info@wolterskluwer.com; internet www.wolterskluwer.com; health, accounting, finance, legal; Chair. ADRI BAAN; CEO NANCY MCKINSTRY.

Wolters-Noordhoff BV: Damsport 157, POB 58, 9700 MB Groningen; tel. (50) 5226922; fax (50) 5277599; e-mail info@wolters.nl; internet www.wolters-noordhoff.nl; f. 1836; educational and scientific books, educational software, geographical and historical atlases and maps; Man. Dir Dr A. M. W. HOLL.

PUBLISHERS' ASSOCIATIONS

Koninklijke Vereniging van het Boekenvak (KVB) (Royal Asscn for the Book Trade): Frederiksplein 1, POB 15007, 1001 MA Amsterdam; tel. (20) 6240212; fax (20) 6208871; e-mail info@kvb.nl; internet www.kvb.nl; f. 1815; Chair. E. BRINKMAN; Exec. Dir CONNIE VERBERNE; 1,500 mems.

Nederlands Uitgeversverbond (NUV) (Dutch Publrs' Asscn): Hogehilweg 6, POB 12040, 1100 AA Amsterdam Zuidoost; tel. (20) 4309150; fax (20) 4309179; e-mail info@nuv.nl; internet www.nuv.nl; Chair. L. M. L. H. A. HERMANS; Dir J. BOMMER; 142 mems.

Broadcasting and Communications

TELECOMMUNICATIONS

Regulatory Authority

Onafhankelijke Post en Telecommunicatie Autoriteit (OPTA): Babylon Bldg, Tower B, Koningin Julianaplein 30, POB 90420, 2509 LK The Hague; tel. (70) 3153500; fax (70) 3153501; e-mail mail@opta.nl; internet www.opta.nl; f. 1997; supervises compliance with legislation, settles disputes, manages the telephone number database; Chair. CHRIS A. FONTEIJN.

Service Providers

debitel Nederland BV: POB 6700, 2130 LT Hoofddorp; internet www.debitel.nl; f. 1993; mobile cellular telecommunications; subsidiary of debitel AG (Germany); CEO HUIB KLOOSTERHUIS.

Enertel NV: Toren op Zuid, Wilhelminakade 123, POB 70024, 3000 LE Rotterdam; tel. (10) 8803800; fax (10) 8803700; e-mail info@enertel.nl; internet www.enertel.nl; f. 1994; fixed-line telecommunications and internet access; acquired by Koninklijke KPN NV in 2006.

Koninklijke KPN NV: Maanplein 55, POB 30000, 2500 GA The Hague; tel. (70) 3434343; fax (70) 3436568; e-mail webmaster@kpn.com; internet www.kpn.com; privatized 1989; fmrly Koninklijke PTT NV, present name adopted 1998; operates KPN Mobile; fixed-line operator and internet access provider; CEO ADRIANUS (AD) SCHEEPBOUWER.

Orange Nederland NV: Groenhovenstr. 2, POB 95313, 2509 CH The Hague; tel. (06) 48999000; e-mail info@dutchtone.nl; internet www.orange.nl; mobile cellular telecommunications and internet access; owned by Deutsche Telekom; Man. Dir NIEK JAN VAN DAMME.

Telfort BV: POB 23079, 1100 DN Amsterdam Zuid-Oost; tel. 0800-1771; internet www.telfort.com; f. 1996; mobile cellular telecommunications and internet access; owned by Koninklijke KPN NV; Man. Dir MARCO VISSER.

T-Mobile: Rijswijkseweg 60, POB 16272, 2500 BG The Hague; tel. (61) 4095000; internet www.t-mobile.nl; owned by Deutsche Telekom; mobile telephone operator.

UPC Nederland NV: POB 80900, 1005 DA Amsterdam; tel. (20) 7755731; fax (20) 7756724; e-mail mediarelations@upc.nl; internet www.upc.nl; subsidiary of UPC Broadband; broadband internet, telephone, digital television and radio service provider; Man. Dir DIEDERIK KARSTEN.

THE NETHERLANDS

Vodafone: POB 1500, 6201 BM Maastricht; e-mail press.nl@vodafone.com; internet www.vodafone.nl; f. 1999; owned by Vodafone Group PLC (United Kingdom); CEO JENS SCHULTE-BOCKUM.

BROADCASTING

Under the Netherlands public broadcasting system the two co-ordinating bodies work with the seven licensed broadcasters to provide a complete range of programmes.

Co-ordinating Bodies

Nederlandse Programma Stichting (NPS) (Dutch National Broadcasting Service): Sumatralaan 49, POB 29000, 1202 MA Hilversum; tel. (35) 6779333; fax (35) 6774959; e-mail publiek@nps.nl; internet www.nps.nl; Dir JOOP DAALMEŸER.

Nederlandse Publieke Omroep (NPO) (Netherlands Public Broadcasting): POB 26444, 1202 JJ Hilversum; tel. (35) 6779222; fax (35) 6772649; e-mail npo.communicatie@omroep.nl; internet www.omroep.nl; f. 1969; co-ordination of Dutch national public broadcasting and news, sports and teletext programmes on six national public radio and three television channels; fmrly Nederlandse Omroep Stichting; Chair. HENK N. HAGOORT.

Broadcasting Associations

Algemene Omroepvereniging AVRO: 's-Gravelandseweg 80, POB 2, 1200 JA Hilversum; tel. (35) 6717911; fax (35) 6717439; e-mail info@avro.nl; internet www.avro.nl; f. 1923; independent; general broadcaster; 800,000 mems; Pres. PAUL SMITS.

Evangelische Omroep (EO): Oude Amersfoortseweg 79, POB 21000, 1202 BA Hilversum; tel. (35) 6474747; fax (35) 6474727; e-mail eo@eo.nl; internet www.eo.nl; f. 1967; Protestant; Chair. ARIE VAN DER VEER; Man. Dir HENK HAGOORT.

Katholieke Radio Omroep (KRO): 's-Gravelandseweg 80, POB 23000, 1202 EA Hilversum; tel. (35) 6713911; fax (35) 6713666; internet www.kro.nl; f. 1925; Catholic; 615,000 mems; Pres. Dr F. C. H. SLANGEN; Sec.-Gen. Dr H. A. M. HOOFT.

Nederlandse Christelijke Radio Vereniging (NCRV): 's-Gravelandseweg 80, POB 25000, 1202 HB Hilversum; tel. (35) 6719911; fax (35) 6719285; e-mail info@ncrv.nl; internet www.ncrv.nl; f. 1924; Protestant; more than 550,000 mems; Chair. LEO BORN; Dir COEN ABBENHUIS.

Omroepvereniging VARA: Sumatralaan 49, POB 175, 1200 AD Hilversum; tel. (35) 6711911; fax (35) 6711333; e-mail vara@vara.nl; internet vara.nl; f. 1925; social-democratic and progressive; 515,000 mems; Pres. VERA M. M. KEUR.

Omroepvereniging VPRO: Villa VPRO, Mediapark, Sumatralaan 49, POB 11, 1200 JC Hilversum; tel. (35) 6712911; fax (35) 6712220; e-mail info@vpro.nl; internet www.vpro.nl; f. 1926; progressive; 380,000 mems; Pres. PETER VAN LIESHOUT; Dir of Radio KEES SCHAEPMAN; Dirs of Television KAREN DE BOK, FRANK WIERING.

TROS: Lage Naarderweg 45–47, POB 28450, 1202 LL Hilversum; tel. (35) 6715715; fax (35) 6715236; e-mail publiekservice@tros.nl; internet www.tros.nl; f. 1964; independent; general broadcaster; 573,664 mems; Chair. K. VAN DOODEWAERD.

Radio

There are six privately owned national radio stations that are operated on a public-service basis, as well as 13 regional stations and about 330 local stations.

Radio 1: internet www.radio1.nl; 24-hour news and sports programming.

Radio 2: internet www.radio2.nl; broadcasts popular music.

3FM: internet www.3fm.nl; broadcasts contemporary music.

Radio 4: internet www.radio4.nl; broadcasts popular classical music.

Radio 5: internet www.radio5.nl; broadcasts popular music, current affairs and cultural programmes; aimed at people aged over 55.

Radio 6: internet www.radio6.nl; broadcasts Americana, electronica, folk, jazz and 'world' music.

Television

Television programmes are transmitted on three public channels, each of which is allocated to a different combination of broadcasting associations and other organizations, and on the commercially funded channels operated by RTL Nederland.

RTL Nederland: Sumatralaan 47, Postbus 15016, 1200 TV Hilversum; tel. (35) 6718718; fax (35) 6236892; e-mail info@rtl.nl; internet www.rtl.nl; f. 1996 as Holland Media Groep; present name adopted 2004; operates four television channels: RTL 4, RTL 5, RTL 7 and RTL 8; subsidiary of RTL Group (Luxembourg); CEO FONS VAN WESTERLOO.

SBS 6/NET5: Plantage Middenlaan 14, POB 18179, 1001 ZB Amsterdam; e-mail sbs6@publieksservice.sbs.nl; internet www.sbs6.nl; private broadcaster; Man. JORIS BOUMAN.

United Pan-Europe Communications NV: POB 80900, 1005 DA Amsterdam; tel. (20) 7729729; fax (20) 7729988; e-mail service@upc.nl; internet www.upc.nl; cable broadcaster; Chair. MICHAEL T. FRIES.

Overseas Broadcasting

BVN TV: Witte Kruislaan 55, POB 222, 1200 JG Hilversum; tel. (35) 6724333; fax (35) 6724343; e-mail bvn@rnw.nl; internet www.bvn.nl; f. 1998; by Radio Nederland Wereldomroep, VRT and Nederlandse Publieke Omroep(NPO); daily international transmissions of news and cultural programmes from public-service broadcasters in Flanders and the Netherlands; Dir of Programmes R. VAN BAAREN.

Radio Nederland Wereldomroep (Radio Netherlands International): Witte Kruislaan 55, POB 222, 1200 JG Hilversum; tel. (35) 6724211; fax (35) 6724352; e-mail wereldomroep@rnw.nl; internet www.rnw.nl; f. 1947; public-service broadcaster; daily transmissions in Arabic, Dutch, English, Indonesian, Papiamento, Portuguese, Sarnami Hindi and Spanish; programme and transcription services for foreign radio and TV stations; Radio Nederland Training Centre (for students from developing countries); Dir-Gen. JAN HOEK.

Finance

(cap. = capital; res = reserves; dep. = deposits; m. = million; br(s). = branch(es); amounts in euros)

BANKING

Central Bank

De Nederlandsche Bank NV: Westeinde 1, POB 98, 1000 AB Amsterdam; tel. (20) 5249111; fax (20) 5242500; e-mail info@dnb.nl; internet www.dnb.nl; f. 1815; nationalized 1948; merged with Pensioen- en Verzekeringskamer (Chamber of Insurance and Pensions) in 2004; cap. 500m., res 17,253m., dep. 26,290m. (Dec. 2007); Pres. A. H. E. M. (NOUT) WELLINK; Exec. Dirs HENK BROUWER, ARNOLD SCHILDER, JOANNE KELLERMANN, FLIP KLOPPER.

Principal Commercial Banks

ABN AMRO Bank NV: Gustav Mahlerlaan 10, POB 283, 1082 PP Amsterdam; tel. (20) 6289393; fax (20) 6287740; e-mail postbox@abnamro.com; internet www.abnamro.com; f. 1991 by merger of Algemene Bank Nederland NV and Amsterdam-Rotterdam Bank NV; acquisition by consortium comprising Royal Bank of Scotland PLC (United Kingdom), Grupo Santander (Spain) and Fortis agreed in Oct. 2007; Dutch Govt replaced Fortis as stakeholder in Oct. 2008; cap. 1,085m., res 2,840m., dep. 900,157m. (Dec. 2007); Chair., Management Bd MARK FISHER; 915 brs nationally.

Amsterdam Trade Bank NV: Herengracht 475, 1017 BS Amsterdam; tel. (20) 5209209; fax (20) 5209219; e-mail info@atbank.nl; internet www.atbank.nl; f. 1994 as Stolichny Bank International NV; present name adopted 1999; 100% owned by Alfa-Bank (Russia); cap. 117.3m., res 40.21m., dep. 2,578.7m. (Dec. 2007); Chair., Supervisory Bd P. SMIDA; Man. Dirs ALEXEI V. DROVOSSEKOV, J. P. J. KONIJN, ANTON H. DEN HELD.

Bank Nederlandse Gemeenten NV (BNG): Koninginnegracht 2, POB 30305, 2500 GH The Hague; tel. (70) 3750750; fax (70) 3454743; e-mail info@bng.nl; internet www.bng.nl; f. 1914 as NV Gemeentelijke Credietbank; present name adopted 1992; 50% Govt-owned, 50% by provincial and municipal authorities; cap. 139m., res 1,748m., dep. 82,707m. (Dec. 2007); Pres. P. O. VERMEULEN.

Banque Artesia Nederland NV (GE Artesia Bank): Herengracht 539–543, POB 274, 1000 AG Amsterdam; tel. (20) 5204911; fax (20) 6247502; e-mail info@artesia.nl; internet www.artesia.nl; f. 1863 as the Nederlandsche Credit & Depositobank; became Banque Paribas Nederland in 1984; present name adopted 1998; acquired by GE Commercial Finance (USA) in 2006; cap. 73.7m., res 131.4m., dep. 3,935.1m. (Dec. 2006); Chair. S. W. PRINS; Man. Dirs V. SNEYDERS, D. E. A. WAEBENS, J. H. M. EVERY; 9 brs.

Dexia Bank Nederland NV: Piet Heinkade 55, POB 808, 1000 AV Amsterdam; tel. (20) 3485000; fax (20) 5571414; e-mail klantenservie@dexiabank.nl; internet www.dexiabank.nl; f. 2001 by merger of Bank Labouchere NV (f. 1990) and Kempen and Co NV; owned by Dexia banking group; Chair. B. F. M. KNÜPPE; 1 br.

Fortis Bank (Nederland) NV: Blaak 555, POB 1045, 3000 BA Rotterdam; tel. (10) 2701010; fax (10) 4148391; e-mail info@fortis.com; internet www.fortisbank.nl; f. 1999 by merger of VSB Bank and Generale Bank Nederland; nationalized in Oct. 2008; cap. 566m., res 3,333m., dep. 3,314m. (Dec. 2004); Chair. JAN VAN RUTTE.

Friesland Bank NV: Beursplein 1, POB 1, 8900 AA Leeuwarden; tel. (58) 2994499; fax (58) 2994591; e-mail service@frieslandbank.nl; internet www.frieslandbank.nl; f. 1913 as Coöperatieve Zuivel-Bank; present name adopted 1995; dep. 8,557.7m., total assets

10,188.8m. (Dec. 2007); Chair. Dr W. F. C. CRAMER; Dirs T. BRANBERGEN, A. VLASKAMP; 33 brs.

ING Bank NV: Amstelveenseweg 500, 1081 KL Amsterdam; tel. (20) 5415411; fax (20) 5415444; e-mail ing@ing.com; internet www.ing.com; f. 1990 by merger of Nationale-Nederlanden and NMB Postbank Groep; Govt acquired an 8.5% stake in Oct. 2008; cap. 525m., res 24,986m., dep. 919,497m. (Dec. 2007); Chair., Supervisory Bd PETER A. F. W. ELVERDING; more than 400 brs.

KAS BANK NV: Spuistraat 172, POB 24001, 1000 DB Amsterdam; tel. (20) 5575911; fax (20) 5576100; e-mail info@kasbank.com; internet www.kasbank.com; f. 1806 by merger; present name adopted 2002; cap. 15.7m., res 1952.4m., dep. 7,966.7m. (Dec. 2007); Chair., Managmement Bd ALBERT A. RÖELL.

F. van Lanschot Bankiers NV: Hooge Steenweg 29, POB 1021, 5200 HC 's-Hertogenbosch; tel. (73) 5483548; fax (73) 5483648; e-mail vanlanschot@vanlanschot.nl; internet www.vanlanschot.nl; f. 1737; merger with CenE Bankiers NV completed 2005; cap. 32.4m., res 837.7m., dep. 16,436.2m. (Dec. 2006); Chair. F. G. H. DECKERS; 32 brs.

Mizuho Corporate Bank Nederland NV: Apollolaan 171, POB 7075, 1007 JB Amsterdam; tel. (20) 5734343; fax (20) 5734372; f. 2000 by merger of Dai Ichi Kangyo Bank Europe NV and Fuji Bank Nederland NV; cap. 141.8m., res 18.5m., dep. 1,447.8m. (Dec. 2006); Man. Dir A. UJITA.

NIBC Bank NV: Carnegieplein 4, POB 380, 2501 BH The Hague; tel. (70) 3425425; fax (70) 3651071; e-mail info@nibc.com; internet www.nibc.com; f. 1945 as Herstelbank; present name adopted 2005; cap. 1,363m., res 448m., dep. 28,272m. (Dec. 2006); Chair., Management Bd and CEO JEROEN DROST; 1 br.

Postbank NV: Haarlemmerweg 506, POB 21009, 1000 EX Amsterdam; tel. (20) 5846133; fax (20) 5846132; internet www.postbank.nl; f. 1985; retail bank operating through post offices; 100% owned by ING Group NV; Chair. MICHEL TILMANT.

Rabobank Nederland (Coöperatieve Centrale Raiffeisen-Boerenleenbank BA): Croeselaan 18, POB 17100, 3500 HG Utrecht; tel. (30) 2160000; fax (30) 2162672; e-mail rabocomm@rn.rabobank.nl; internet www.rabobank.nl; f. 1972 by merger of Coöperatieve Centrale Raiffeisenbank of Utrecht and Coöperatieve Centrale Boerenleenbank of Eindhoven; dep. 533,673m., total assets 570,503m. (Dec. 2007); Chair. H. HEEMSKERK; 1,727 brs.

SNS Bank NV: Croeselaan 1, 3503 BJ Utrecht; tel. (30) 2915100; fax (30) 2915300; e-mail info@snsbank.nl; internet www.sns.nl; f. 1971 as Bank der Bondsspaarbanken NV; present name adopted 2002; cap. 426m., res 2,791m., dep. 69,484m. (Dec. 2007); Group Chair. and CEO S. VAN KEULEN; 256 brs.

Staalbankiers NV: Lange Houtstraat 8, POB 327, 2501 CH The Hague; tel. (70) 3101510; fax (70) 3650819; e-mail info@staalbankiers.nl; internet www.staalbankiers.nl; f. 1916 as Bankierskantoor Staal & Co NV; present name adopted 2005; mem. of Achmea Groep; dep. 2,136.6m., total assets 2,518.4m. (Dec. 2006); Chair. and CEO P. A. DE RUIJTER; Man. Dirs P. J. HUURMAN, D. BECK.

Bankers' Association

Nederlandse Vereniging van Banken (NVB) (Netherlands Bankers' Asscn): Singel 236, POB 3543, 1001 AH Amsterdam; tel. (20) 5502888; fax (20) 6239748; e-mail info@nvb.nl; internet www.nvb.nl; f. 1989; Chair. B. STAAL; Dir HEIN G. M. BLOCKS; 91 mems.

STOCK EXCHANGES

A supervisory authority, the Netherlands Securities Board, commenced activities in 1989.

Euronext Amsterdam: Beursplein 5, POB 19163, 1000 GD Amsterdam; tel. (20) 5505555; fax (20) 5504899; e-mail info@euronext.nl; internet www.euronext.com; subsidiary of NYSE Euronext; Euronext NV was formed by merger of Amsterdam, Paris and Brussels exchanges and joined in 2002 by the London futures exchange LIFFE and the Lisbon stock exchange; merged with New York Stock Exchange in 2007 to form NYSE Euronext; unitary stock and options exchange; Chair. JOOST VAN DER DOES DE WILLEBOIS.

There are also financial futures, grain, citrus fruits and insurance bourses in the Netherlands; a 'spot' market for petroleum operates from Rotterdam.

INSURANCE

Principal Companies

AEGON Nederland: AEGONplein 50, POB 202, 2501 CE The Hague; tel. (70) 3443210; fax (70) 3475238; internet www.aegon.nl; f. 1983 by merger; life, accident, health, general and linked activities; Chair. MARCO B. A. KEIM.

Delta Lloyd Verzekeringen NV: Spaklerweg 4, POB 1000, 1000 BA Amsterdam; tel. (20) 5949111; fax (20) 937968; internet www.deltalloyd.nl; f. 1807; Chair. NIEK HOEK.

De Eerste Nederlandsche/Enfas: POB 325, 1170 AH Badhoevedorp; tel. (562) 445090; fax (562) 445150; e-mail info@eerste.nl; internet www.eerste.nl; Chair. G. VAN PLATERINGEN.

Fiducia Assurantiën: Park Hoornwijck 6B, 2289 CZ Rijswijk; tel. (70) 4150506; fax (70) 4150507; e-mail info@fiducia.nl; internet www.fiducia.nl; f. 1990; home, vehicle, non-life; Dir BJORN DE HAAN.

Fortis ASR Verzekeringsgroep NV: Archimedeslaan 10, POB 2072, 3500 HB Utrecht; tel. (30) 2579111; internet www.fortisasr.nl; f. 2000 by merger of ASR Verzekeringsgroep NV (f. 1720) and AMEV Nederland NV (f. 1883); owned by the Fortis group; Group CEO JEAN-PAUL VOTRON.

Generali Verzekeringsgroep: Diemerhof 42, 1112 XN Diemen; tel. (20) 6604444; fax (20) 3983000; e-mail info@generali.nl; internet www.generali.nl; f. 1870; life and non-life; Gen. Dir FREEK WANSINK.

ING Groep NV: Amstelveenseweg 500, 1081 KL Amsterdam; tel. (20) 5415411; fax (20) 5415497; e-mail nanne.bos@ing.com; internet www.ing.com; f. 1963; Dir, Insurance Europe JACQUES DE VAUCLEROY.

Nationale-Nederlanden NV: Kantoor Delftse Poort, Weena 505, 3013 AL Rotterdam; tel. (10) 5130303; internet www.nn.nl; f. 1863; Chair. LUDO WIJNGAARDEN.

RVS: Loevestein 33, POB 225, 6710 DA Ede; tel. (318) 662054; e-mail rvs@rvs.nl; internet www.rvs.nl; f. 1838; subsidiary of ING Groep NV; mem. of Internationale-Nederlanden group; life and non-life; Chair. MARC VAN DER PLOEG.

Insurance Association

Verbond van Verzekeraars (Asscn of Insurers): Bordewijklaan 2, POB 93450, 2509 AL The Hague; tel. (70) 3338500; fax (70) 338510; e-mail info@verzekeraars.nl; internet www.verzekeraars.nl; f. 1978; Chair. LUDO WIJNGAARDEN; Gen. Man. R. WEURDING.

Trade and Industry

GOVERNMENT AGENCY

Netherlands Foreign Investment Agency: Bezuidenhoutseweg 16A, POB 20101, 2594 AV The Hague; tel. (70) 3798818; fax (70) 3796322; e-mail info@nfia.nl; internet www.nfia.nl; govt agency; facilitates foreign direct investment.

CHAMBERS OF COMMERCE

There are 12 autonomous Chambers of Commerce and Industry in the Netherlands. The most important are:

Kamer van Koophandel Amsterdam (Chamber of Commerce and Industry for Amsterdam): De Ruyterkade 5, 1013 AA Amsterdam; POB 2852, 1000 CW Amsterdam; tel. (20) 5314000; fax (20) 5314799; e-mail info@amsterdam.kvk.nl; internet www.amsterdam.kvk.nl; f. 1811; Dir-Gen. H. E. VAN BAARSBANK.

Kamer van Koophandel Rotterdam (Chamber of Commerce for Rotterdam): Blaak 40, 3011 TA Rotterdam; POB 450, 3000 AL Rotterdam; tel. (10) 4027777; fax (10) 4145754; e-mail post@rotterdam.kvk.nl; internet www.rotterdam.kvk.nl; f. 1803; Pres. (vacant).

EMPLOYERS' ORGANIZATIONS

LTO-Nederland (Netherlands Agricultural Organization): Bezuidenhoutseweg 225, 2594 AL The Hague; POB 29773, 2502 LT The Hague; tel. (70) 3382700; fax (70) 3382810; e-mail info@lto.nl; internet www.lto.nl; f. 1995; Chair. A. J. MAAT; 50,000 mems.

Nederlands Centrum voor Handelsbevordering (NCH) (Netherlands Council for Trade Promotion): Juliana van Stolberglaan 148, POB 10, 2501 CA The Hague; tel. (70) 3441544; fax (70) 3853531; e-mail info@nchnl.nl; internet www.handelsbevordering.nl; Man. Dir JOCHUM HAAKMA; 800 mem. cos.

Nederlandsche Maatschappij voor Nijverheid en Handel (NMNH) (Netherlands Society for Industry and Trade): Jan van Nassaustraat 75, 2596 BP The Hague; tel. (70) 3141940; fax (70) 3247515; e-mail info@nmnh.nl; internet www.nmnh.nl; f. 1777; Pres. R. J. A. DE LANGE; Dir-Gen. GEERT VAN DER TANG; more than 5,500 mems.

De Nederlandse Tuinbouwraad (NTR) (Netherlands Horticultural Council): Schipholweg 1, 2316 XB Leiden; tel. (71) 5659596; fax (71) 5659610; e-mail informatie@tuinbouwraad.nl; internet www.tuinbouwraad.nl; f. 1908; Chair. Dr N. C. A. (NICO) KOOMEN; Sec. GEORGE FRANKE.

NERG (Nederlands Elektronica- en Radiogenootschap): POB 39, 2260 AK Leidschendam; tel. (70) 3325112; fax (70) 3326477; internet www.nerg.nl; f. 1921; Chair. Prof. Dr N. H. G. BAKEN; Sec. E. BOTTELIER; c. 500 mems.

Vereniging VNO-NCW (Confederation of Netherlands Industry and Employers): Bezuidenhoutseweg 12, POB 93002, 2509 AA The Hague; tel. (70) 3490349; fax (70) 3490300; e-mail informatie@

THE NETHERLANDS

vno-ncw.nl; internet www.vno-ncw.nl; f. 1997 as merger of Verbond van Nederlandse Ondernemingen (VNO) and Nederlands Christelijk Werkgeversverbond (NCW); represents almost all sectors of the Dutch economy; Pres. B. E. M. (BERNARD) WIENTJES; mems: 160 asscns representing more than 115,000 enterprises.

UTILITIES

Electricity

ENECO: POB 96, 2900 AB Capelle a/d IJssel; tel. (10) 4576979; fax (10) 4577784; internet www.eneco.nl; Chair. J. F. (JEROEN) DE HAAS; 5,300 employees.

E.ON Benelux BV: POB 909, 2270 AX Voorburg; tel. (70) 3820028; fax (70) 3383901; e-mail info@eon-benelux.com; internet www.eon-benelux.com; f. 2000; replaced Electriciteitsbedrijf Zuid Holland (f. 1941); supplies energy to large-volume customers and distributors; CEO JOOST VAN DIJK.

Essent: Nieuwe Stationsstraat 20, 6811 KS Arnhem; internet www.essent.nl; f. 1999 by merger of Edon Group and Pnem Mega Group; electricity generation and supply, also supplier of gas; Chair., Management Bd MICHIEL BOERSMA.

Nuon NV: Spaklerweg 20, POB 41920, 1009 DC Amsterdam; tel. (20) 5972729; e-mail nuon@nuon.com; internet www.nuon.com; f. 1999; energy and water; Chair. and CEO ØYSTEIN LØSETH.

Tennet BV: Utrechtseweg 310, POB 718, 6812 AS Arnhem; tel. (26) 3731111; fax (26) 3731112; e-mail servicedesk@tennet.org; internet www.tennet.org; f. 1999; independent; Dutch Transmission System operator; manages 220/380–kW national grid and supplies electricity to direct suppliers; Dir J. M. KROON.

Gas

Full liberalization of the gas market in the Netherlands took effect from the beginning of July 2004. Although retaining ownership of the main transport network, NV Nederlandse Gasunie passed the legal tasks of the national transmission system operator to a new, state-owned organization, Gas Transport Services BV, founded on 2 July 2004.

ENECO: see above.

Essent: see above.

Gas Transport Services BV: POB 181, 9700 AD Groningen; tel. (50) 3626000; fax (50) 3626100; e-mail info@gastransport.nl; internet www.gastransportservices.nl; f. 2004; independent; transmission system operator; CEO GEERT H. GRAAF.

NV Nederlandse Gasunie: Concourslaan 17, POB 19, 9700 MA Groningen; tel. (50) 5219111; fax (50) 5211999; e-mail communicatie@gasunie.nl; internet www.gasunie.nl; f. 2005; Chair. and CEO MARCEL P. KRAMER.

RWE Obragas NV: POB 300, 5700 AH Helmond; tel. (49) 2594888; fax (49) 2594990; internet www.rwe.nl.

Water

Nuon: see above.

Vewin: POB 1019, 2280 CA Rijswijk; tel. (70) 4144750; fax (70) 4144420; e-mail info@vewin.nl; internet www.vewin.nl; Chair J. A. M. HENDRIKX.

TRADE UNIONS

Central federations and affiliated unions are mainly organized on a religious, political or economic basis. The most important unions are those of the transport, metal, building and textile industries, the civil service and agriculture.

Central Federations

Christelijk Nationaal Vakverbond in Nederland (CNV) (Christian National Federation of Trade Unions): Tiberdreef 4, POB 2475, 3500 GL Utrecht; tel. (30) 7511100; fax (30) 7511109; e-mail cnvinfo@cnv.nl; internet www.cnv.nl; f. 1909; affiliated to ITUC and European Trade Union Confederation; Pres. RENÉ PAAS; Gen. Sec. BERT VAN BOGGELEN; 330,000 mems.

Eleven affiliated unions, of which the principal unions are:

CNV Bedrijvenbond (Industry, Food and Transport): Tiberdreef 4, POB 2525, 3500 GM Utrecht; tel. (30) 7511007; e-mail info@cnv.net; internet www.cnvbedrijvenbond.nl; Chair. JAAP JONGEJAN; 85,000 mems.

CNV Dienstenbond (Service Industries, Media and Printing): Polarisave 175, POB 3135, 2130 KC Hoofddorp; tel. (23) 5651052; fax (23) 5650150; e-mail cnvdienstenbond@cnvdibo.nl; internet www.cnvdienstenbond.nl; f. 1894; Pres. D. SWAGERMAN; Sec. R. J. ROTSHUIZEN; 36,500 mems.

CNV Hout en Bouw (Wood and Building): Oude Haven 1, 3984 KT Odijk; tel. (30) 6597711; fax (30) 6571101; e-mail info@cnvhb.nl; internet www.cnvhb.nl; f. 1900; Chair. A. A. VAN WIJNGAARDEN; Gen. Sec. J. T. SLOK; 48,000 mems.

CNV Onderwijs (Education): Tiberdreef 4, POB 2510, 3500 ZC Utrecht; tel. (30) 75117000; fax (30) 7511709; e-mail info@cnvo.nl; internet www.cnvo.nl; f. 2000; Pres. (vacant).

CNV Publieke Zaak (Public Sector Union): Carnegielaan 1, POB 84500, 2508 AM The Hague; tel. (70) 4160600; fax (70) 4160690; e-mail denhaag@cnvpubliekezaak.nl; internet www.cnvpubliekezaak.nl; Pres. P. J. KOESLAG; Sec. K. KRUITHOF; 79,000 mems.

Federatie Nederlandse Vakbeweging (FNV) (Netherlands Trade Union Confederation): Naritaweg 10, POB 8456, 1005 AL Amsterdam; tel. (20) 5816300; fax (20) 6844541; e-mail persvoorlichting@vc.fnv.nl; internet www.fnv.nl; f. 1975 as confederation of the Netherlands Federation of Trade Unions (f. 1906) and the Netherlands Catholic Trade Union Federation (f. 1909); Pres. AGNES JONGERIUS; Vice-Pres. PETER GORTZAK; Gen. Sec. WILNA WIND; 1,234,361 mems.

Seventeen affiliated unions, of which the principal are:

ABVAKABO FNV (Government Personnel, Civil Servants, Private Health Workers, Social Workers, Post and Telecom Workers, Public Utility Workers): Boerhaavelaan 1, POB 3010, 2700 KT Zoetermeer; tel. (79) 3536161; fax (79) 3521226; e-mail post@abvakabo.nl; internet www.abvakabofnv.nl; f. 1982; Pres. EDITH SNOEY; Gen. Sec. XANDER DEN UYL; 365,000 mems.

Algemene Onderwijsbond (AOb) (Education): Jaarbeursplein 22, POB 2875, 3500 GW Utrecht; tel. (30) 2989898; fax (30) 2989862; e-mail info@aob.nl; internet www.aob.nl; f. 1997 as merger between Algemene Bond van Onderwijspersoneel and NGL—Dordrecht; Pres. WALTER DRESSCHER; Gen. Sec. MARTIN KNOOP; 76,000 mems.

FNV Bondgenoten (Transport, Metal and Steel, Information Technology, Electrotechnical, Textiles, Financial Services, Retail, Wholesale, Foods, Agriculture): Varrolaan 100, POB 9208, 3506 GE Utrecht; tel. (30) 2738222; fax (30) 2738225; e-mail info@bg.fnv.nl; internet www.fnvbondgenoten.nl; f. 1998 by merger; Pres. HENK VAN DER KOLK; Sec. ELLEN DEKKERS; 460,000 mems.

FNV Bouw (Building): Houttuinlaan 3, POB 520, 3440 AM Woerden; tel. (348) 575575; fax (348) 423610; e-mail info@fnvbouw.nl; internet www.fnvbouw.nl; f. 1917; Pres. DICK VAN HAASTER; 150,000 mems.

FNV KIEM (Printing and Allied Trades): J. Tooropstraat, POB 9354, 1006 AJ Amsterdam; tel. (20) 3553636; fax (20) 3553737; e-mail algemeen@fnv-kiem.nl; internet www.fnv-kiem.nl; Chair. HERMAN LEISINK; Gen. Sec. BEA VAN DEN BOSCH; 40,000 mems.

Nederlandse Politiebond (NPB) (Police): Steinhagenseweg 2D, POB 68, 3440 AB Woerden; tel. (34) 8707444; fax (34) 8707411; e-mail info@politiebond.nl; internet www.politiebond.nl; f. 1946; Pres. HANS VAN DUIJN; Gen. Sec. FRANS VAN DER HEIDEN; 22,500 mems.

Vakcentrale voor Middengroepen en Hoger Personeel (MHP) (Federation for Professional and Managerial Staff): Multatulilaan 12, POB 575, 4100 AN Culemborg; tel. (345) 851900; fax (345) 851915; e-mail info@vc-mhp.nl; internet www.vakcentralemhp.nl; f. 1974; mem. of the European Trade Union Confederation; Pres. RICHARD STEENBORG; 160,000 mems.

Four affiliated unions, of which the following is the largest:

Unie van Onafhankelijke Vakorganisaties (UoV) (United Independent Trade Unions): Multatulilaan 12, POB 400, 4100 AK Culemborg; tel. (345) 851851; fax (345) 851500; e-mail info@unie.nl; internet www.uov.nl; 16 affiliated independent trade unions, including De Unie; 93,900 mems.

Consultative Organization

Stichting van de Arbeid (Labour Foundation): Bezuidenhoutseweg 60, 2594 AW The Hague; tel. (70) 3499577; fax (70) 3499796; internet www.stvda.nl; f. 1945; central organ of co-operation and consultation between employers and employees; 16 bd mems; Jt Pres B. E. M. WIENTJES, Dr A. M. JONGERIUS.

Land Reclamation and Development

Without intensive land-protection schemes, nearly the whole of the north and west of the Netherlands (about one-half of the total area of the country) would be inundated by sea water twice a day. A large part of the country (including a section of the former Zuiderzee, now the IJsselmeer) has already been drained.

The Delta Plan, which was adopted in 1958 and provided for the construction of eight dams, a major canal, several locks and a system of dykes, aimed to shorten the southern coastline by 700 km and to protect the estuaries of Zeeland and Southern Holland. The final cost of the delta works project, which had originally been projected at 2,500m. guilders, totalled around 14,000m. guilders, as the result of a

THE NETHERLANDS

complex adaptation to ensure the preservation of the delta's ecological balance.

The Ministry of Transport, Public Works and Water Management is responsible for land reclamation and waterways.

Transport

RAILWAYS

About 70% of the Dutch railway network is electrified; the remaining track carries diesel electric and diesel stock. There were approximately 6,500 km of railways in 2007, providing mainly passenger services. The infrastructure of the Dutch railway network remains wholly under public ownership. Until early 2002 the main railway operator, Nederlandse Spoorwegen (NS), was partially privatized, but, following a sharp deterioration in the quality of service, it was taken back under government control. NS retains a majority of the passenger and freight rolling stock, and station premises, while there is a small number of additional, privately owned network service providers.

Nederlandse Spoorwegen NV (NS): Laan van Puntenberg 100, POB 2025, 3500 HA Utrecht; tel. (30) 2359111; fax (30) 2332458; internet www.ns.nl; f. 1937; partially privatized until early 2002, when the Govt reasserted management control; operates most railway lines in the Netherlands; Pres. and Man. Dir BERT MEERSTADT.

Arriva Nederland: Trambaan 3, POB 626, 8440 AP Heerenveen; tel. (51) 3655855; fax (51) 3655808; internet www.arriva.nl; f. 1999; operates 50 trains and 920 buses, including cross-border rail services into Germany; Man. Dir ANNE HETTINGA.

ProRail: POB 2038, 3500 GA Utrecht; tel. (30) 2357104; fax (30) 2359056; internet www.prorail.nl; f. 2003; manages and maintains railway infrastructure, and controls passenger and freight traffic; independent; Chair. B. J. (BERT) KLERK.

Railion Nederland: Moreelspark 1, 3511 Utrecht; tel. (3) 2354127; fax (30) 2359310; e-mail info@railion.nl; internet www.railion.nl; frmly Railon Benelux NV; international goods transport by rail; Man. Dir DETLEF HEYDT.

ROADS

In 2003 there were 2,500 km of motorway, 6,700 km of main roads, 57,500 km of secondary roads and 59,400 km of other roads in the Netherlands.

INLAND WATERWAYS

An extensive network of rivers and canals navigable for ships of 50 metric tons and over, totalling 5,046 km, has led to the outstanding development of Dutch inland shipping. About one-third of goods transported inside the Netherlands are carried on the canals and waterways. Dutch inland shipping has access to Germany and France along the Rhine and its branch rivers, and to France and Belgium along the Meuse and Scheldt (including the Rhine-Scheldt link). Ocean traffic reaches Rotterdam via the New Waterway, and the 21-km long North Sea Canal connects Amsterdam to the North Sea.

SHIPPING

The Netherlands is one of the world's leading shipping countries. At the end of 2007 the merchant fleet comprised 1,258 vessels, with a combined displacement of 6.1m. grt. The Port of Rotterdam complex, incorporating Europoort (for large oil tankers and bulk carriers), is the main European Union port and the busiest in the world, handling over 350m. metric tons of cargo per year.

Principal Companies

Amasus Chartering BV: Zijlvest 26, Farmsum, POB 250, 9930 Delfzijl; tel. (596) 610744; fax (596) 616551; e-mail info@amasus.nl; internet www.amasus.nl; shipowners, managers and operators.

Hudig Freight Services: Debussystraat 2, POB 1030, 3160 AE Rhoon; tel. (10) 5066550; fax (10) 5012827; e-mail info@hudig.nl; internet www.hudig.com; f. 1795; international freight services; Man. Dir A. D. FONTEIN.

Koninklijke Vopak NV: Westerlaan 10, POB 863, 3000 AW Rotterdam; tel. (10) 4002911; fax (10) 4139829; internet www.vopak.com; f. 1999; Chair. JOHN PAUL BROEDERS.

Koninklijke Wagenborg BV: Marktstraat 10, POB 14, 9930 AA Delfzyl; tel. (596) 636911; fax (596) 636250; e-mail info@wagenborg.com; internet www.wagenborg.com; shipowners, managers and operators; Man. Dirs Dr E. VUURSTEEN, Dr G. R. WAGENBORG.

Seatrade Groningen BV: Laan Corpus den Hoorn 200, POB 858, 9700 AW Groningen; tel. (50) 5215300; fax (50) 5215399; e-mail info@seatrade.nl; internet www.seatrade.nl; shipowners, managers and operators; Man. Dir Capt. MARK JANSEN.

Spliethoff's Bevrachtingskantoor BV: Radarweg 36, POB 409, 1000 AK Amsterdam; tel. (20) 4488400; fax (20) 4488500; e-mail gogracht@spliethoff.com; internet www.spliethoff.nl; shipowners, managers and operators; Man. ROLF G. W. ERIKSSON.

Stena Line: Stationsweg 10, POB 2, 3150 AA Hoek van Holland; tel. (17) 4389333; fax (17) 4389309; e-mail info.nl@stenaline.nl; internet www.stenaline.nl; operates daily (day and night) ferry services for accompanied private cars, commercial freight vehicles and trailers between Hoek van Holland and Harwich (UK); Man. Dir GUNNAR BLOMDAHL.

Van Uden Maritime BV: POB 1123, 3000 BC, Rotterdam; tel. (10) 2973100; fax (10) 4851044; e-mail group@van-uden.nl; internet www.van-uden.nl; f. 1848; agencies in Rotterdam, Amsterdam; liner operators and representatives; international chartering; Man. D. P. F. DUTILH.

Vroon BV: Haven Westzijde 21, POB 28, 4510 AA Breskens; tel. (117) 384910; fax (117) 384218; e-mail info@vroon.nl; internet www.vroon.nl; shipowners, managers and operators; Man. Dir F. D. VROON.

Wijnne & Barends' Cargadoors- en Agentuurkantonen BV: Handelskade Oost 5, POB 123, 9930 AC Delfzijl; tel. (596) 637777; fax (596) 637790; e-mail info@wijnne-barends.nl; internet www.wijnne-barends.nl; f. 1855; became part of Spliethoff Group in 2003; shipowners, managers and operators; cargo services and agents; Man. Dir D. P. MAKKINJE.

Shipping Associations

Federatie van Werknemers in de Zeevaart (Dutch Seafarers' Federation): Heemraadssingel 323, POB 25131, 3001 HC Rotterdam; tel. (10) 4771188; fax (10) 4773846; e-mail fwz.nl@wxs.nl; internet www.fnv.nl/zeevaart.

Koninklijke Vereniging van Nederlandse Reders (KVNR) (Royal Asscn of Netherlands' Shipowners): Wijnhaven 65B, POB 2442, 3000 CK Rotterdam; tel. (10) 4146001; fax (10) 2330081; e-mail kvnr@kvnr.nl; internet www.kvnr.nl; f. 1905; Chair. T. NETELENBOS; Man. Dir G. X. HOLLAAR; 300 mems.

Vereniging Nederlandse Scheepsbouw Industrie (VNSI) (Netherlands Shipbuilding Industry Asscn): Boerhaavelaan 40, POB 138, 2700 AC Zoetermeer; tel. (79) 3531165; fax (79) 3531155; e-mail info@vnsi.nl; internet www.vnsi.nl; promotes Dutch shipbuilding on a national basis; Chair M. J. VAN DER WAL; 95 mems.

CIVIL AVIATION

The main Dutch airport is at Schiphol, near Amsterdam. There are also international airports at Zestienhoven for Rotterdam, Beek for Maastricht and at Eelde for Groningen. Schiphol has expanded rapidly since the late 1990s, from 25.3m. passengers in 1995 to 47.7m. in 2007. A fifth runway was opened in early 2003, while the planned privatization of Schiphol was abandoned in February 2007.

KLM (Koninklijke Luchtvaart Maatschappij) NV (Royal Dutch Airlines): Amsterdamseweg 55, 1182 GP Amstelveen; tel. (20) 6499123; fax (20) 6488069; internet www.klm.com; f. 1919; world's oldest commercial airline; regular international air services; merged with Air France in 2004 to create Europe's largest airline; subsidiaries: KLM cityhopper, transavia.com; Pres. and CEO PETER F. HARTMAN; Dir JAN ERNST DE GROOT.

Martinair Holland NV: Havenmeesterweg 201, POB 7507, 1118 ZG Schiphol Airport; tel. (20) 6011767; fax (20) 6011303; internet www.martinair.nl; f. 1958; world-wide passenger and cargo services; Pres. and CEO ARIE VERBERK.

transavia.com: Westelijke Randweg 3, POB 7777, 1118 ZM Schiphol Airport; tel. (20) 6046555; fax (20) 6015093; internet transavia.com; f. 1965 as Transavia Limburg N.V.; scheduled and charter services to leisure destinations; subsidiary of KLM; Pres. and CEO ONNO P. M. VAN DEN BRINK.

Tourism

The principal tourist attractions in the Netherlands are the cosmopolitan city of Amsterdam (which receives nearly one-half of all tourist visits), the historic towns, the canals, the cultivated fields of spring flowers, the outlying islands, the art galleries and modern architecture. Some 10.7m. foreign tourists stayed in hotels and boarding houses in the Netherlands in 2006. Receipts from tourism totalled an estimated US $11,381m. in that year.

Royal Dutch Touring Club ANWB: POB 93200, 2596 EC The Hague; tel. (70) 3147147; fax (70) 3146969; e-mail info@anwb.nl; internet www.anwb.nl; f. 1883; CEO GUIDO H. N. L. VAN WOERKOM; 55 brs in Europe; 3.9m. mems.

Toerisme Recreatie Nederlands (Netherlands Board of Tourism): Vlietweg 15, POB 458, 2260 MG Leidschendam; tel. (70) 3705705; fax (70) 3201654; e-mail info@holland.com; internet www.holland.com; f. 1968; Man. Dir HANS VAN DRIEM.

NETHERLANDS DEPENDENCIES

ARUBA

Introductory Survey

Location, Climate, Language, Religion, Flag, Capital

Aruba is one of the group of Benedenwindse Eilands or 'Leeward Islands', which it forms with part of the Netherlands Antilles (q.v.), and lies in the southern Caribbean Sea, 25 km north of Venezuela and 68 km west of the island of Curaçao (Netherlands Antilles). The climate is tropical, with an average annual temperature of 28°C (82°F), but is tempered by north-easterly winds. Rainfall is very low, averaging only about 426 mm (16.8 ins) annually. The official language is Dutch, but the dominant language is Papiamento (a mixture of Dutch, Spanish, English, Arawak Indian and several West African dialects). Spanish and English are also spoken. Most of the inhabitants profess Christianity and belong to the Roman Catholic Church, although a wide variety of other denominations are represented. The national flag (proportions 2 by 3) is blue, with two narrow yellow horizontal stripes in the lower section and a white-bordered four-pointed red star in the upper hoist. The capital is Oranjestad.

Recent History

The Caribbean island of Aruba was claimed for Spain in 1499, but was first colonized by the Dutch in 1636 and subsequently formed part of the Dutch possessions in the West Indies. Administered from Curaçao after 1845, in 1954 Aruba became a member of the autonomous federation of the Netherlands Antilles. The establishment in 1929 of a large petroleum refinery on the island, at Sint Nicolaas, led to the rapid expansion of the economy and a high standard of living for the islanders. However, many Arubans resented the administrative dominance of Curaçao, and what they regarded as the excessive demands made upon Aruban wealth and resources by the other five islands within the Netherlands Antilles. The island's principal political party, the Movimentu Electoral di Pueblo (MEP), campaigned, from its foundation in 1971 onwards, for Aruban independence and separation from the other islands. In a referendum held in Aruba in March 1977 82% of voters supported independence and withdrawal from the Antillean federation. The MEP used its position in the coalition Government of the Netherlands Antilles, formed in 1979, to press for concessions from the other islands towards early independence for Aruba. In 1981 (after the MEP had withdrawn from the Government of the Netherlands Antilles) a provisional agreement regarding Aruba's future was reached between the Dutch and Antillean Governments. Following further discussions, it was agreed in March 1983 that Aruba should receive separate status (*status aparte*), within the Kingdom of the Netherlands, from 1 January 1986, achieving full independence in 1996. The Dutch Government would remain responsible for defence and external relations until independence, while Aruba was to form a co-operative union with the Netherlands Antilles (the Antilles of the Five) in economic and monetary affairs.

At local elections in April 1983 the MEP increased its representation to 13 of the 21 seats in the Staten (parliament), and the leader of the MEP, Gilberto F. (Betico) Croes, remained as leader of the island Government. Austerity measures, introduced in an attempt to alleviate the adverse effects of the closure (announced in October 1984) of the Sint Nicolaas petroleum refinery, provoked a series of strikes and demonstrations by civil servants in protest at wage reductions and price rises. The MEP consequently lost popular support and, following elections to the Staten in November 1985, was succeeded in government by a coalition of four opposition parties led by the Arubaanse Volkspartij (AVP). Aruba achieved separate status, as planned, on 1 January 1986, and Jan Hendrik Albert (Henny) Eman, leader of the AVP, became its first Prime Minister. Croes died in November 1986; he was succeeded as leader of the MEP by Nelson O. Oduber.

From 1988 Aruba began to enjoy an economic recovery, based on tourism. However, the MEP claimed that the benefits to the whole community were limited, and also criticized Eman's stated reservations about independence in 1996 and his refusal to negotiate with the Netherlands about transitional arrangements. At a general election in January 1989 the MEP came within 28 votes of securing an absolute majority in the Staten. The number of seats held by the MEP increased from eight to 10, and in February Oduber formed a Government in coalition with the Partido Patriótico Arubano (PPA) and the Acción Democrático Nacional (ADN). (Both these parties had been in the previous Government, and retained one seat each at the election.)

The MEP and the AVP each secured nine seats in the Staten at the January 1993 general election, while the three remaining seats were won by the ADN, the PPA and the Organisacion Liberal Arubano (OLA). Despite gaining fewer votes than the AVP, the MEP administration remained in office, renewing the coalition with the ADN and the PPA. In April 1994, however, Oduber announced the Government's resignation, following the withdrawal of the ADN and the PPA from the coalition. In May, following lengthy inter-party negotiations, it was agreed that a fresh general election would be held. Government functions were to be undertaken in the interim by the MEP. The general election was held on 29 July: the AVP secured 10 seats, while the MEP won nine seats and the OLA the remaining two. In late August Eman formed a Government in coalition with the OLA.

In March 1994 the Governments of Aruba, the Netherlands and the Netherlands Antilles convened in The Hague, Netherlands, and decided to cancel plans for Aruba's transition to full independence, due to take place in 1996. The possibility of a transition to full independence at a later date was not excluded, but was not considered a priority, and would, moreover, require the approval of the Aruban people, by referendum, as well as the support of a two-thirds' majority in the Staten.

In September 1997 the Staten was dissolved after the OLA withdrew from the coalition. A general election was thus held on 12 December; this resulted in a political composition identical to that of the 1993 polls. Following protracted negotiations, the AVP and the OLA renewed their coalition in mid-1998, and a new Council of Ministers, headed by Eman, was appointed.

In June 2001 the governing coalition collapsed, following the withdrawal of the OLA's support for the AVP's plan to privatize the Aruba Tourism Authority. As a result, the legislative elections that had been scheduled to be held in December were brought forward to 28 September. The MEP comfortably defeated the incumbent AVP in the elections, securing 52% of the votes cast and 12 seats in the Staten. The AVP legislative representation was reduced to six seats. The three remaining seats were shared between the PPA (two) and the OLA (one). Oduber was once again appointed Prime Minister and a new single-party Government, with an unprecedented opportunity to pass legislation through the Staten, took office in November.

In early 2004, after several months of discussion, the Aruban and Dutch Governments agreed to appoint Fredis Refunjol, hitherto Minister of Education, as Governor. The Dutch Government objected to the fact that there was only one candidate for the position and argued that the appointment was overtly political. Nevertheless, since Refunjol's candidature had strong cross-party support in the Staten, he was duly sworn in on 7 May. The erstwhile President of the Staten, Francisco Walfrido Croes, assumed the vacant education portfolio. Meanwhile, in January the Staten voted against becoming an Ultra Periphery Area of the European Union (EU, see p. 255). The island thus remained an Overseas Territory of the EU.

At a general election on 23 September 2005 the MEP again won a majority of seats (11, from 43% of the popular vote) in the 21-seat Staten. The victory came in spite of broad public criticism of the Government's unwillingness to defend wage levels from the downward pressure caused by large-scale immigration from South America. Notably, the minimum wage had not been adjusted for five years. The AVP won eight seats, an improvement on its result in the 2001 election, and the Movimento Patriotico Arubano and RED Democratico each won one legislative seat. The electoral turn-out among those eligible to vote was 85%. Oduber, who continued as Prime Minister, defended his economic policies and pledged to continue to develop the tourism sector and to balance the budget, which is heavily dependent on external creditors, by 2009.

Aruba's relations with the Antilles of the Five improved after 1986. In 1987 Aruba agreed to undertake economic co-operation, and in 1988 the three Dutch 'Leeward Islands' initiated a joint project for the development of tourism. Aruba's relations with the 'metropolitan' Netherlands were dominated at this time by the latter's pressure for more control to be exercised over the large amount of aid that it gave to Aruba, and by the issue of independence, in particular the future arrangements for the island's security: Aruba's strategic position, close to the South American mainland, and the possibility of it being used as a base for drugs-trafficking, were matters of particular concern. In September 1990 Aruba announced that it was to adopt the 1988 UN Convention on measures to combat trade in illegal drugs; a joint Dutch and Aruban team was formed to conduct investigations. In December 1996, however, the USA included Aruba on its list of major drugs-producing or transit countries. New legislation to facilitate the extradition of suspected drugs-traffickers and money-launderers took effect in October 1997. US naval and air force patrols began operating from a base in Aruba in May 1999 in an effort to counter the transport of illicit drugs. In 2001 the Caribbean Financial Action Task Force commended the Government on its efforts in combating money-laundering. In the same year the territory was removed from the list of so-called 'un-co-operative tax havens' drawn up by the Organisation for Economic Co-operation and Development (OECD, based in Paris, France), after the Government pledged to reform the territory's financial sector in order to conform to OECD's guidelines by 2005; however, in April 2009 Aruba was included in OECD's so-called 'grey list' of territories that had committed to improving financial transparency, but had yet substantially to implement reform. In October 2005 the Minister of Justice, Rudy Croes, visited The Hague to discuss the issue of independence with the Dutch Government. Relations between Aruba and the Netherlands deteriorated, however, when the Dutch Government forced Aruba to introduce a more stringent policy on visa conditions. In November 2003 Aruba signed an agreement with the USA to exchange tax information in order to combat illegal financial activities, such as money-laundering, that are associated with international terrorism and drugs-trafficking. The issue of immigration arose again in late 2004: in the first 10 months of the year Aruba deported 864 Colombians, most of whom arrived on the island from Venezuela. In late 2006 Aruba was collaborating with the Netherlands towards drafting its first anti-corruption legislation, which would equip the Caribbean state with the legislative means to ratify international anti-corruption treaties. By early 2009 any such legislation was still in the planning stages.

In May 2005 the disappearance of a US teenager, Natalee Holloway, on the island and the attendant negative publicity in her home country led to tension in the relationship between Aruba and the USA and placed severe strain on the island's crucial tourism industry, which is heavily dependent upon US custom. Later in the year the Governor of Alabama, the missing girl's home state, blamed the Aruban Government for the failure to discover her whereabouts and, backed by overwhelming US public support (and, in January 2006, by the Alabama Senate), unsuccessfully requested that the US Government impose sanctions on Aruba. Several arrests were made during 2006, but suspects were subsequently released, exacerbating criticism of the investigation's perceived mismanagement. In early 2007 legal representatives for two of the original suspects (resident in Aruba) applied to the Superior Court in Los Angeles, California, USA, for the dismissal of a 'wrongful death' action filed by Holloway's parents against the defendants in December 2006.

Amendments to the Western Hemisphere Travel Initiative, ratified by the US Congress on 4 October 2006, requiring all US citizens and foreign nationals travelling to and from the Caribbean to hold a valid passport, were implemented from 8 January 2007. The initiative precipitated myriad travel incentives within Aruba and other Caribbean states in an attempt to offset the anticipated decline in tourism. Unified by the perceived threat, several of the Caribbean states' tourism officials lobbied for the deadline to be extended to June 2009, when the legislation would also become applicable to cruise-ship passengers. The new visa requirements were, however, enacted as scheduled, but in June delays experienced in the processing of applications prompted the US Department of State to issue a limited extension of existing regulations until September 2007.

After acquiring separate status, Aruba fostered relations with some of its Caribbean neighbours and with countries in Latin America. This included the development of ties with Venezuela, which had traditionally laid claim to the Dutch 'Leeward Islands', including Aruba, and the signing of a memorandum of understanding with Brazil in September 2006, which sought to promote more extensive air transport links.

Government

Aruba has separate status within the Kingdom of the Netherlands. Legislative power is held by the unicameral Staten (parliament) of 21 members, elected by universal adult suffrage for four years (subject to dissolution). Executive power in all domestic affairs is vested in the Council of Ministers (led by the Prime Minister), responsible to the Staten. The Governor, appointed by the Dutch Crown for a term of six years, represents the monarch of the Netherlands on Aruba and holds responsibility for external affairs and defence. The Governor is assisted by an advisory council.

Defence

The Netherlands is responsible for Aruba's defence, and military service is compulsory. The Governor is Commander-in-Chief of the armed forces on the island. A Dutch naval contingent is stationed in Aruba, primarily to combat drugs-trafficking and organized crime. In May 1999 the USA began air force and navy patrols from a base on Aruba as part of efforts to prevent the transport of illegal drugs.

Economic Affairs

In 2000, according to the UN, Aruba's gross national income (GNI) was US $1,756m. During 2000–07 the population increased at an average annual rate of 4.0% per year. According to the central bank, gross domestic product (GDP) per head increased, in real terms, by an average of 2.5% per year in 2000–07. Overall GDP increased, in real terms, at an average annual rate of 0.7% in 2000–07. Real GDP increased by 2.1% in 2007.

Owing to the poor quality of the soil and the prohibitive cost of desalinated water, the only significant agricultural activity is the cultivation of aloes (used in the manufacture of cosmetics and pharmaceuticals); aloe-based products are exported. Some livestock is raised, and there is a small fishing industry (although in the mid-1990s fishing production contributed only some 12.5% of Aruba's annual consumption of fish and fish products). In 2000 the agricultural sector engaged 0.6% of the employed labour force, although FAO estimated that it employed 20.8% of the employed labour force in mid-2005. The sector contributed 0.4% of total GDP in 2003, according to UN estimates.

The industrial sector, and the island's economy, was formerly based on the refining and transshipment of imported petroleum and petroleum products. In the early 1980s this sector accounted for one-quarter of GDP and provided almost all Aruba's exports. The Sint Nicolaas petroleum refinery ceased operations in 1985; however, in 1990 the plant partially reopened, following renovation; after more construction and revision works, production reached an estimated 202,000 barrels per day (b/d) in 1999, an increase of 26% on the previous year's total. Following a further US $250m. renovation in 2000, production increased to 280,000 b/d. In March 2004 the refinery was purchased by the US-based Valero Energy Corporation, which, in 2005, announced that it was considering a US $6,000m. expansion of the plant in order to increase production to as much as 800,000 b/d by about 2012. In 2005 Aruba refined 78.2m. barrels of crude petroleum; imports of crude petroleum were valued at A Fl. 5,910m. and exports at A Fl. 7,602m. (total exports excluding mineral fuels and free trade zone transactions amounted to just A Fl. 36.1m. in the same year). There is a large petroleum transshipment terminal on Aruba, and a small petrochemicals industry. An advanced-technology coker plant opened in 1995 to supply liquefied petroleum gas, largely for export to the USA. There are believed to be exploitable reserves of hydrocarbons within Aruban territory, and Aruba also has reserves of salt. The industrial sector contributed an estimated 16.6% of GDP in 2003, and engaged 16.4% of the employed labour force in 2000.

Light industry is engaged in the production of beverages, building materials, paints and solvents, paper and plastic products, candles, detergents, disinfectants, soaps and aloe-based cosmetics. There is a 'free zone', and the ports of Oranjestad and Barcadera provide bunkering and repair facilities for ships. In 1996 a ports development initiative was announced, proposing the relocation (over a 20-year period) of all cargo operations to Barcadera, leaving Oranjestad's port to accommodate commercial, recreation and resort activities. The construction sector, which grew steadily in the 1980s, declined in importance following a moratorium on the construction of new hotels in 1992. In 2005–07, however, some US $150m. was invested in the renovation and expansion of existing hotels and resorts in an attempt to reinvigorate the construction sector. Manufacturing, meanwhile, contributed an estimated 2.8% of GDP in 2003 and, along with electricity, gas and water, engaged 7.0% of the employed labour force in 2000.

The service industries are Aruba's principal economic activity, employing 83.1% of the active labour force in 2000, and contributing an estimated 82.9% of the island's GDP in 2003. Financial services are well established in Aruba, particularly the data-processing sector, an important service to US companies in particular. Aruba's principal source of income is tourism; the hotels and restaurants sector alone was estimated to provide 10.5% of Aruba's GDP in 2002. In 2001 there was a slight decrease in the number of visitor arrivals, attributed mainly to the global economic slowdown and to the effects on tourism of the terrorist attacks on the USA in September of that year. The sector finally recorded positive growth again in 2004, when the number of stop-over arrivals increased by 13.4%, to 728,157. The number of cruise-ship passengers also increased significantly in that year (by 6.3% to 567,320), and receipts from tourism increased by 23.3% to a total of A Fl. 1,875.8m. Thereafter, however, visitor numbers remained more or less static, at around 1.3m., and in 2007 there was a 2.5% decrease in total visitor numbers, to 1,253,848 (772,073 stop-over visitors and 481,775 cruise-ship passengers). Total tourist expenditure reached A Fl. 2,244.3m. in 2007.

Aruba is obliged to import most of its requirements, particularly machinery and electrical equipment, chemical products and foodstuffs; in 2007 the island recorded a visible trade deficit of US $159.4m., but there was also a surplus on the current account of the balance of payments of US $214.9m. In 2007 the principal source of imports, excluding the petroleum sector and the 'free zone', was the USA (58.1% of the total value); other major sources were the

NETHERLANDS DEPENDENCIES

Netherlands, Venezuela and the Netherlands Antilles. The principal export commodity is refined petroleum (see above). Excluding the petroleum sector and the 'free zone', the principal market for exports in 2007 was also the USA (accounting for 34.9% of the total value of exports), followed by the Netherlands, the Netherlands Antilles and Venezuela.

In 2008 the budget deficit was A Fl.11.0m., equivalent to 0.2% of GDP in that year. At the end of 2007 total government debt was A Fl. 2,112m. (equivalent to 44.9% of GDP), much of which was owed to the Government of the Netherlands. The average annual rate of inflation was 4.0% in 2000–07; consumer prices increased by 5.8% in 2007. Some 7.1% of the labour force were unemployed in 2007.

As part of the Kingdom of the Netherlands, Aruba is classed as an Overseas Territory in association with the European Union (see p. 255). It forms a co-operative union with the Antilles of the Five in monetary and economic affairs. Aruba also has observer status with the Caribbean Community and Common Market (CARICOM, see p. 206).

The closure of the Sint Nicolaas petroleum refinery in 1985 and Aruba's separation from the rest of the Netherlands Antilles in 1986 prompted the Aruban administration to institute a policy of retrenchment and austerity, except for investment in tourism development. In 1992, following six consecutive years of rapid economic growth, a moratorium was imposed on construction in the tourism industry, partly in recognition of the adverse environmental impact on the island and also to preserve the island's reputation as an exclusive holiday destination for the wealthy. Economic growth subsequently slowed to a more sustainable level during the remainder of the decade. Aruba also maintained reasonably low levels of inflation and of unemployment, and was considered to be one of the most prosperous islands in the Caribbean. Concern, however, has been expressed that Aruba's high public sector wage bill and the generous nature of the island's social welfare system, combined with its ageing population, would threaten the future stability of public finance, already hindered by a narrow taxation base and poor revenue collection. The budgetary deficit increased markedly during the early 2000s, and in May 2005 the IMF re-emphasized the need for the Government to gain control of the worsening ratio of public debt to GDP. Government efforts to address the current account deficit in 2006 included a review of the Civil Servants Pension Fund and its universal health scheme. It was hoped that an increase of the import duty tariffs on a more comprehensive range of goods would help to redress the fiscal deficit. Increased efficiency in tax administration and greater discipline over fiscal expenditure were also pursued during 2006. Overall tourist arrivals decreased in 2007, although this was mainly owing to a fall in cruise-ship passengers, and tourism receipts continued to rise. It was hoped that investments of over US $350m. to be implemented during 2007 (including the renovation and upgrade of the island's cruise-ship terminals, facility improvements at Queen Beatrix International Airport, the inauguration of a new private jet terminal, and extensive hotel and resort renovation and expansion) would reinvigorate the tourism industry and further advance its economic performance. From January to September 2008 arrivals of cruise-ship passengers rose by 21.4%, compared with the same period in 2007. However, there was a sharp decrease in the number of ships docking in September, which coincided with the onset of the global financial crisis. In late 2007 the Government announced measures to balance Aruba's budget and reduce debt to under 40% of GDP by 2009, although the realization of this objective was dependent on a growing tourism sector, which presented a challenge during a global economic downturn.

Education

A Compulsory Education Act was introduced in 1999, to cover the 4–16 age-group. Kindergarten begins at four years of age. Primary education begins at six years of age and lasts for six years. Secondary education, beginning at the age of 12, lasts for up to six years. In 2006/07 enrolment at primary schools included 99.6% of pupils in the relevant age-group, while the comparable enrolment ratio at secondary schools was 82.5%. The main language of instruction is Dutch, but Papiamento (using a different spelling system from that of the Antilles of the Five) is used in kindergarten and primary education and in the lower levels of technical and vocational education. Papiamento is also being introduced onto the curriculum in all schools. In Aruba there are two institutes of higher education: the University of Aruba, comprising the School of Law and the School of Business Administration, which had 208 students in 1999/2000; and the Teachers' College, which had 180 students in 2000/01. There is also a community college. The majority of students, however, continue their studies abroad, generally in the Netherlands. Public expenditure on education was put at 15.4% of total government expenditure in 2005, according to UNESCO.

Public Holidays

2009: 1 January (New Year's Day), 25 January (Gilberto F. Croes's Birthday), 23 February (Lenten Carnival), 18 March (National Anthem and Flag Day), 10–13 April (Easter), 30 April (Queen's Day), 1 May (Labour Day), 21 May (Ascension Day), 25–26 December (Christmas).

2010: 1 January (New Year's Day), 25 January (Gilberto F. Croes's Birthday), 15 February (Lenten Carnival), 18 March (National Anthem and Flag Day), 2–5 April (Easter), 30 April (Queen's Day), 1 May (Labour Day), 13 May (Ascension Day), 25–26 December (Christmas).

Weights and Measures

The metric system is in force.

Statistical Survey

Sources (unless otherwise stated): Department of Economic Affairs, Commerce and Industry (Direktie Economische Zaken, Handel en Industrie), Sun Plaza Bldg, L. G. Smith Blvd 160, Oranjestad; tel. 5821181; fax 5834494; e-mail deaci@setarnet.aw; internet www.arubaeconomicaffairs.aw; Centrale Bank van Aruba, J. E. Irausquin Blvd 8, POB 18, Oranjestad; tel. 5252100; fax 5252101; e-mail cbaua@setarnet.aw; internet www.cbaruba.org.

AREA AND POPULATION

Area: 193 sq km (74.5 sq miles).

Population: 66,687 (males 32,821, females 33,866) at census of 6 October 1991; 105,859 at 31 December 2008 (official estimate).

Density (31 December 2008): 548.4 per sq km.

Principal Towns (population estimates, 2002): Oranjestad (capital) 20,700; Sint Nicolaas 17,400. Source: Stefan Helders, *World Gazetteer* (internet www.world-gazetteer.com). *Mid-2007* (UN estimate, incl. suburbs): Oranjestad 32,000 (Source: UN, *World Urbanization Prospects: The 2007 Revision*).

Births and Deaths (2006): Live births 1,227 (birth rate 11.9 per 1,000); Deaths 537 (death rate 5.2 per 1,000). *2008:* Birth rate 13.6 per 1,000; Death rate 7.2 per 1,000. Sources: UN, *Population and Vital Statistics Report*; Pan American Health Organization.

Life Expectancy (years at birth, 2008): 74.4 (males 71.4; females 77.2). Source: Pan American Health Organization.

Economically Active Population (persons aged 15 years and over, 2000): Agriculture, hunting and forestry 251; Manufacturing, electricity, gas and water 2,940; Construction 3,892; Wholesale and retail trade, repairs 7,112; Hotels and restaurants 7,651; Transport, storage and communications 2,905; Financial intermediation 1,485; Real estate, renting and business activities 3,722; Public administration, defence and social security 3,573; Education 1,431; Health and social work 1,986; Other community, social and personal services 2,776; Private households with employed persons 1,870; Other 324; Total employed 41,918; Unemployed 3,118; Total labour force 45,036. *September 2005* (estimate): Total employed 47,350; Unemployed 3,114; Total labour force 50,464.

HEALTH AND WELFARE

Total Fertility Rate (children per woman, 2008): 2.0.

Under-5 Mortality Rate (per 1,000 live births, 2006): 20.0.

Physicians (per 1,000 head, 1999): 1.28.

Hospital Beds (per 1,000 head, 2003): 3.2.

Health Expenditure (% of GDP, 2005): 8.5.

Source: partly Pan American Health Organization.

For definitions, see explanatory note on p. vi.

FISHING

Total catch (metric tons, live weight, 2006): 145 (Groupers 15, Snappers and jobfishes 40, Wahoo 50, Other marine fishes 40). Source: FAO.

INDUSTRY

Electric Energy (million kWh, 2007): 781.1.

FINANCE

Currency and Exchange Rates: 100 cents = 1 Aruban gulden (guilder) or florin (A Fl.). *Sterling, Dollar and Euro Equivalents* (31 December 2008): £1 sterling = A Fl. 2.609; US $1 = A Fl. 1.790; €1 = A Fl. 2.491; A Fl. 100 = £38.32 = $55.87 = €40.14. Note: The Aruban florin was introduced in January 1986, replacing (at par) the Netherlands Antilles guilder or florin (NA Fl.). Since its introduction, the currency has had a fixed exchange rate of US $1 = A Fl. 1.79.

NETHERLANDS DEPENDENCIES

Budget (A Fl. million, 2008, preliminary): *Revenue:* Tax revenue 1,001; Non-tax revenue 133 (incl. grants 15); Total 1,134. *Expenditure:* Wages 314; Goods and services 215; Interest payments 112; Investments 36; Transfer to the General Health Insurance (AZV) 98; Other 370; Total (incl. others) 1,145.

International Reserves (US $ million at 31 December 2007): Gold 92.9; Foreign exchange 372.1; Total 465.0. Source: IMF, *International Financial Statistics*.

Money Supply (A Fl. million at 31 December 2007): Currency outside banks 174.79; Demand deposits at commercial banks 972.47; Total money (incl. others) 1,148.05. Source: IMF, *International Financial Statistics*.

Cost of Living (Consumer Price Index; base: 2000 = 100): All items 116.9 in 2005; 121.3 in 2006; 128.3 in 2007. Source: IMF, *International Financial Statistics*.

Gross Domestic Product (A Fl. million at constant 1995 prices): 3,092 in 2005; 3,110 in 2006; 3,176 in 2007.

Expenditure on the Gross Domestic Product (A Fl. million at current prices, 2007): Final consumption expenditure 3,509; Gross capital formation 1,534; *Total domestic expenditure* 5,043; Exports of goods and services 3,063; *Less* Imports of goods and services 3,518; *GDP in purchasers' values* 4,588.

Gross Domestic Product by Economic Activity (A Fl. million at current prices, 2000): Agriculture, hunting, forestry and fishing, and mining and quarrying 14; Manufacturing 91; Electricity, gas and water (incl. petroleum-refining) 212; Construction 202; Trade 440; Restaurants and hotels 355; Transport, storage and communications 287; Finance, insurance, real estate and business services 877; Government services 390; Other community, social and personal services 365; *Sub-total* 3,234; *Less* Imputed bank service charges 163; Indirect taxes, *less* subsidies 255; *GDP in purchasers' values* 3,326. *2003* (A Fl. million at current prices): Agriculture, hunting, forestry and fishing 15; Mining, manufacturing and utilities 331 (Manufacturing 99); Construction 248; Wholesale and retail trade, restaurants and hotels 851; Transport, storage and communications 298; Activities not adequately defined 1,735; *Total value added* 3,478. Source: UN, mostly *National Accounts Statistics*.

Balance of Payments (US $ million, 2007): Exports of goods f.o.b. 2,690.8; Imports of goods f.o.b. −2,850.3; *Trade balance* −159.4; Exports of services 1,492.1; Imports of services −941.4; *Balance on goods and services* 391.3; Other income received 79.3; Other income paid −157.0; *Balance on goods, services and income* 313.7; Current transfers received 57.8; Current transfers paid −156.6; *Current balance* 214.9; Capital account (net) 18.2; Direct investment abroad −29.3; Direct investment from abroad −116.2; Portfolio investment assets −320.7; Portfolio investment liabilities 85.5; Financial derivatives assets −1.0; Other investment assets 198.9; Other investment liabilities −14.2; Net errors and omissions 7.0; *Overall balance* 43.2. Source: IMF, *International Financial Statistics*.

EXTERNAL TRADE

Principal Commodities (A Fl. million, 2007): *Imports c.i.f.:* Live animals and animal products 109.7; Food products 199.2; Chemical products 184.1; Base metals and articles thereof 156.1; Machinery and electrical equipment 320.3; Transport equipment 125.9; Total (incl. others) 1,875.5. *Exports f.o.b.:* Live animals and animal products 1.1; Machinery and electrical equipment 7.9; Transport equipment 5.1; Art objects and collectors' items 9.4; Total (incl. others) 55.8. Note: Figures exclude transactions involving mineral fuels and those of the Free Trade Zone of Aruba.

Principal Trading Partners (A Fl. million, 2007): *Imports c.i.f.:* Japan 34.2; Netherlands 238.8; Netherlands Antilles 56.1; USA 1,089.3; Venezuela 42.4; Total (incl. others) 1,875.5. *Exports f.o.b.:* Colombia 0.9; Netherlands 13.7; Netherlands Antilles 8.9; USA 19.5; Venezuela 3.2; Total (incl. others) 55.8. Note: Figures exclude transactions of the petroleum sector and those of the Free Trade Zone of Aruba.

TRANSPORT

Road Traffic (motor vehicles registered, December 2005): Passenger cars 49,521; Lorries 907; Buses 300; Taxis 398; Rental cars 3,514; Other cars 578; Motorcycles 1,499; Total 56,717.

Shipping: *Arrivals* (2006): 1,971 vessels. *Merchant Fleet* (vessels registered at 31 December 2006): Number of vessels 2; Total displacement 400 grt (Source: Lloyd's Register-Fairplay, *World Fleet Statistics*).

Civil Aviation: *Aircraft Landings:* 17,866 in 2004; 16,270 in 2005; 16,842 in 2006. *Passenger Arrivals:* 875,021 in 2004; 860,212 in 2005; 810,322 in 2006.

TOURISM

Tourist Arrivals: 1,285,333 (732,514 stop-over visitors, 552,819 cruise-ship passengers) in 2005; 1,285,846 (694,372 stop-over visitors, 591,474 cruise-ship passengers) in 2006; 1,253,848 (772,073 stop-over visitors, 481,775 cruise-ship passengers) in 2007.

Tourism Receipts: A Fl. 1,953.0m. in 2005; A Fl. 1,917.0m. in 2006; A Fl. 2,244.3m. in 2007.

COMMUNICATIONS MEDIA

Radio Receivers (1997): 50,000 in use.

Television Receivers (1997): 20,000 in use.

Telephones (2007): 38,600 main lines in use.

Facsimile Machines (1996): 3,600 in use.

Mobile Cellular Telephones (2007): 145,800 subscribers.

Internet Users (2007): 24,000.

Broadband Subscribers (2007): 15,100.

Daily Newspapers (1996): 13 titles (estimated circulation 73,000 copies per issue).

Sources: mainly UNESCO, *Statistical Yearbook*; International Telecommunication Union; UN, *Statistical Yearbook*.

EDUCATION

Pre-primary (2000/01): 23 schools; 2,737 pupils; 105 teachers.

Primary (2000/01): 33 schools; 8,849 pupils; 415 teachers.

General Secondary (2000/01): 10 schools; 4,251 pupils; 242 teachers.

Technical-Vocational (2000/01): 2 schools; 3,237 pupils; 263 teachers.

Community College (1999/2000): 1 school; 1,187 pupils; 106 teachers.

University (1999/2000): 1 university; 208 students; 24 tutors.

Teacher Training (2000/01): 1 institution; 180 students; 25 teachers.

Special Education (2000/01): 4 schools; 272 pupils; 56 teachers.

Private, Non-aided (1999/2000): 4 schools; 553 pupils; 58 teachers.

International School (2000/01): 1 school; 154 pupils; 25 teachers.

2007/08 (unless otherwise indicated): *Pre-primary:* 2,914 pupils (males 1,464, females 1,450), 141 teachers (males 1, females 140); *Primary:* 10,346 pupils (males 5,319, females 5,027), 594 teachers (males 102, females 492); *Lower Secondary:* 3,423 pupils (males 1,774, females 1,649), 243 teachers (males 117, females 126) (2004/05); *Upper Secondary:* 4,430 pupils (males 2,083, females 2,347), 259 teachers (males 125, females 134) (2004/05); *Tertiary:* 2,232 students (males 928, females 1,304), 222 teachers (males 111, females 111) (Source: UNESCO Institute for Statistics).

Adult Literacy Rate (UNESCO estimates, 2007): 98.1% (males 98.2%; females 98.1%) (Source: UNESCO Institute for Statistics).

Directory

The Constitution

On 1 January 1986 Aruba acquired separate status (*status aparte*) within the Kingdom of the Netherlands. The form of government is similar to that for the Netherlands Antilles, and is embodied in the Charter of the Kingdom of the Netherlands (operational from 20 December 1954. The Netherlands, the Netherlands Antilles (Antilles of the Five) and Aruba each enjoy full autonomy in domestic and internal affairs, and are united on a basis of equality for the protection of their common interests and the granting of mutual assistance. In economic and monetary affairs there is a co-operative union between Aruba and the Antilles of the Five, known as the 'Union of the Netherlands Antilles and Aruba'.

The Governor, who is appointed by the Dutch Crown for a term of six years, represents the monarch of the Netherlands in Aruba. The Government of Aruba appoints a minister plenipotentiary to represent it in the Government of the Kingdom. Whenever the Netherlands Council of Ministers is dealing with matters coming under the heading of joint affairs of the realm (in practice mainly foreign affairs and defence), the Council assumes the status of Council of Ministers of the Kingdom. In that event, Aruba's Minister Plenipotentiary takes part, with full voting powers, in the deliberations.

A legislative proposal regarding affairs of the realm and applying to Aruba as well as to the metropolitan Netherlands is sent, simultaneously with its submission, to the Staten Generaal (the Netherlands parliament) and to the Staten (parliament) of Aruba. The latter body can report in writing to the Staten Generaal on the draft Kingdom Statute and designate one or more special delegates to attend the debates and furnish information in the meetings of the Chambers of the Staten Generaal. Before the final vote on a draft the Minister Plenipotentiary has the right to express an opinion on it. If he disapproves of the draft, and if in the Second Chamber a three-fifths' majority of the votes cast is not obtained, the discussions on the draft are suspended and further deliberations take place in the Council of Ministers of the Kingdom. When special delegates attend the meetings of the Chambers, this right devolves upon the delegates of the parliamentary body designated for this purpose.

The Governor has executive power in external affairs, which he exercises in co-operation with the Council of Ministers. He is assisted by an advisory council, which consists of at least five members appointed by him.

Executive power in internal affairs is vested in a nominated Council of Ministers, responsible to the Staten. The Aruban Staten consists of 21 members, who are elected by universal adult suffrage for four years (subject to dissolution), on the basis of proportional representation. Inhabitants have the right to vote if they have Dutch nationality and have reached 18 years of age.

The Government

HEAD OF STATE

Queen of the Netherlands: HM Queen BEATRIX.

Governor: FREDIS J. REFUNJOL (took office 7 May 2004).

COUNCIL OF MINISTERS
(April 2009)

Prime Minister and Minister of General Affairs and Utilities: NELSON ORLANDO ODUBER.

Deputy Prime Minister and Minister of Education, Social Affairs and Infrastructure: MARISOL J. LOPEZ-TROMP.

Minister of Finance and Economic Affairs: NILO J. J. SWAEN.

Minister of Justice: HYACINTHO RUDOLFO CROES.

Minister of Labour, Culture and Sports: TAI FOO RAMON LEE.

Minister of Public Health, the Environment, Administrative Affairs and Immigration Affairs: CANDELARIO A. S. D. (BOOSHI) WEVER.

Minister of Tourism and Transportation: EDISON BRIESEN.

Minister Plenipotentiary and Member of the Council of Ministers of the Realm for Aruba in the Netherlands: FRANCISCO WALFRIDO CROES.

Minister Plenipotentiary of the Realm for Aruba in Washington, DC (USA): JOCELYNE CROES.

MINISTRIES

Office of the Governor: Plaza Henny Eman 3, Oranjestad; tel. 834445; fax 834930.

Office of the Prime Minister: Government Offices, L. G. Smith Blvd 76, Oranjestad; tel. 5880300; fax 5880024.

Ministry of Education, Social Affairs and Infrastructure: Caya Betico Croes 38, Oranjestad; tel. 5226700; fax 5880032; e-mail minszi@setarnet.aw; internet www.minszi.aw.

Ministry of Finance and Economic Affairs: Cumana 69, Oranjestad; tel. 5880269; fax 5880347.

Ministry of General Affairs and Utilities: L. G. Smith Blvd 76, Oranjestad; tel. 5839022; fax 5838958.

Ministry of Justice: Macuarima 65, Santa Cruz; tel. 5221100; fax 5851155.

Ministry of Labour, Culture and Sports: Wilhelminastraat 6, Oranjestad; tel. 5880900; fax 5880331; e-mail macs@setarnet.aw.

Ministry of Public Health, the Environment, Administrative Affairs and Immigration Affairs: Bernardstraat 75, Sint Nicolaas; tel. 5841199; fax 5849744.

Ministry of Tourism and Transportation: L. G. Smith Blvd 78, Oranjestad; tel. 5880114; fax 5880121.

Office of the Minister Plenipotentiary for Aruba: R. J. Schimmelpennincklaan 1, 2517 JN The Hague, Netherlands; tel. (70) 3566200; fax (70) 3451446; e-mail info@arubahuis.nl; internet www.arubahuis.nl.

Legislature

STATEN

President: MERVIN WYATT-RAS, Staten, L. G. Smith Blvd 72, Oranjestad.

General Election, 23 September 2005

Party	Seats
Movimentu Electoral di Pueblo	11
Arubaanse Volkspartij	8
Movimento Patriotico Arubano	1
RED Democratico	1
Total	**21**

Political Organizations

Arubaanse Volkspartij (AVP) (Aruba People's Party): Avda Alo Tromp 56, Oranjestad; tel. 5830911; fax 5837963; e-mail info@avparuba.net; internet www.avparuba.net; f. 1942; advocates Aruba's separate status; Leader MICHIEL GODFRIED EMAN.

Movimentu Electoral di Pueblo (MEP) (People's Electoral Movement): Santa Cruz 74D, Oranjestad; tel. 5854495; fax 5850768; e-mail mep@setarnet.aw; f. 1971; socialist; 1,200 mems; Pres. and Leader NELSON ORLANDO ODUBER.

Movimento Patriotico Arubano (MPA) (Aruban Patriotic Movement): Oranjestad; Leader MONICA KOCK ARENDS.

Organisacion Liberal Arubano (OLA) (Aruban Liberal Organization): Oranjestad; f. 1991; Leader GLENBERT FRANCOIS CROES.

Partido Patriotico di Aruba (PPA) (Patriotic Party of Aruba): Oranjestad; internet www.ppa-aruba.org; f. 1949; social democratic; opposed to complete independence for Aruba; Leader BENEDICT (BENNY) JOCELYN MONTGOMERY NISBET.

RED Democratico (RED Democratic Network): Oranjestad; internet www.red.aw; f. 2003; Leader Fr RUDY LAMPE.

Judicial System

Legal authority is exercised by the Court of First Instance. Appeals are heard by the Joint High Court of Justice of the Netherlands Antilles and Aruba.

Attorney-General of Aruba: ROBERT PIETERSZ.

Solicitor-General of Aruba: NICO JÖRG.

Courts of Justice: J. G. Emanstraat 51, Oranjestad; tel. 5822294; fax 5821241; e-mail griffiekopie@setarnet.aw.

Religion

Roman Catholics form the largest religious community, numbering more than 80% of the population. The Anglicans and the Methodist, Dutch Protestant and other Protestant churches have a total membership of about 6,500. There are approximately 130 Jews.

CHRISTIANITY

The Roman Catholic Church

Aruba forms part of the diocese of Willemstad, comprising the Netherlands Antilles and Aruba. At 31 December 2006 there were an estimated 224,809 adherents in the diocese. The Bishop resides in Willemstad (Curaçao, Netherlands Antilles).

Roman Catholic Church: J. Yrausquin Plein 3, POB 702, Oranjestad; tel. 5821434; fax 5821409.

The Anglican Communion

Within the Church in the Province of the West Indies, Aruba forms part of the diocese of the North Eastern Caribbean and Aruba. The Bishop is resident in The Valley, Anguilla.

Anglican Church: Holy Cross, Weg Seroe Pretoe 31, Sint Nicolaas; tel. 5845142; fax 5843394; e-mail holycross@setarnet.aw.

Protestant Churches

Baptist Church: Aruba Baptist Mission, SBC, Paradera 98-C; tel. 5883893.

Church of Christ: Pastoor Hendrikstraat 107, Sint Nicolaas; tel. 5848172.

Church of Jesus Christ of Latter Day Saints: Dadelstraat 16, Oranjestad; tel. 5823507.

Dutch Protestant Church: Wilhelminastraat 1, Oranjestad; tel. 5821435.

Evangelical Church: Jasmijnstraat 7, Sint Nicolaas; tel. 5848973.
Faith Revival Center: Rooi Afo 10, Paradera; tel. 5831010; fax 5833070.
Iglesia Evangelica Pentecostal: Asamblea di Dios, Reamurstraat 2, Oranjestad; tel. 5831940.
Jehovah's Witnesses: Guyabastraat 3, Oranjestad; tel. 5828963.
Methodist Church: Longfellowstraat, Oranjestad; tel. 5845243.
New Apostolic Church: Goletstraat 5A, Oranjestad; tel. 5833762.
Pentacostal Apostolic Assembly: Bernhardstraat 185; tel. 5848710; fax 5845699.
Seventh-day Adventist: Weststraat, Oranjestad; tel. 5845896.

JUDAISM

Beth Israel Synagogue: Adriaan Laclé Blvd, Oranjestad; tel. 5823272; fax 5823534; e-mail jcommaruba@gmail.com; internet bethisrael-aruba.blogspot.com; Rabbi MARIO GUREVICH.

BAHÁ'Í FAITH

Spiritual Assembly: Bucutiweg 19, Oranjestad; tel. 5823104; Contact M. CHRISTIAN.

The Press

DAILIES

Amigoe di Aruba: Patriastraat 13, POB 323, Oranjestad; tel. 5824333; fax 5822368; e-mail amigoearuba@setarnet.aw; internet www.amigoe.com; f. 1884; Dutch; Man. BRENDA BOUWMAN; circ. 12,000 (in Aruba and Netherlands Antilles).
Aruba Today: Weststraat 22, Oranjestad; tel. 5827800; fax 5827093; e-mail info@arubatoday.com; internet www.arubatoday.com; Editor-in-Chief JULIA C. RENFRO.
Bon Dia Aruba: Weststraat 22, Oranjestad; tel. 5827800; fax 5827044; e-mail bondia.aruba@gmail.com; internet www.bondia.com; Dirs JOHN CHEMALY, JOHN CHEMALY, Jr.
Diario: Engelandstraat 29, POB 577, Oranjestad; tel. 5826747; fax 5828551; e-mail diario@setanet.aw; internet www.diarioaruba.com; f. 1980; Papiamento; morning; Editor and Man. JOSSY M. MANSUR; circ. 15,000.
Extra: Dominicanessenstraat 17, Oranjestad; tel. 58834034; fax 5821639; Papiamento; Dir C. FRANKEN.
The News: Italiestraat 5, POB 300, Oranjestad; tel. 5824725; fax 5889430; e-mail thenewsaruba@setarnet.aw; f. 1951; English; Dir SONIA WEVER-SCHOUTEN; Editor-in-Chief MARGARET BONARRIVA-WEVER; circ. 6,900.
La Prensa: Bachstraat 6, POB 566, Oranjestad; tel. 5821199; fax 5828634; e-mail laprensa@laprensacur.com; internet www.laprensacur.com; f. 1929; Papiamento; Editor THOMAS C. PIETERSZ.

NEWS AGENCIES

Algemeen Nederlands Persbureau (ANP) (The Netherlands): Caya G. F. (Betico) Croes 110, POB 323, Oranjestad; tel. 5824333; fax 5822368; internet www.anp.nl.
Aruba News Agencies: Bachstraat 6, Oranjestad; tel. 5821243.

Publishers

Aruba Experience Publications NV: Verbindingsweg 2, POB 634, Oranjestad; tel. 5834467; fax 5384520; e-mail info@arubaexperience.com; internet www.arubaexperience.com; f. 1985; Gen. Man. MICHEL J. M. JANSSEN.
Caribbean Publishing Co Ltd (CPC): L. G. Smith Blvd 116, Oranjestad; tel. 5820485; fax 5820484.
De Wit Stores NV: L. G. Smith Blvd 110, POB 386, Oranjestad; tel. 5823500; fax 5821575; e-mail info@dewitvandorp.com; f. 1948; Gen. Man. LYANNE BEAUJON.
Editorial Charuba: Lagoenweg 31, Oranjestad; tel. 7301512; fax 5884574; e-mail alivaro@hotmail.com; f. 1982; Pres. ALICE VAN ROMONDT.
Gold Book Publishing: L. G. Smith Blvd 116, Oranjestad; tel. 5820485; fax 5820484; e-mail drosario@caribbeanhotels.org; internet www.caribbeanhotels.org; a division of the Caribbean Hotel Asscn, based in the Cayman Islands.
Oranjestad Printing NV: Italiestraat 5, POB 300, Oranjestad; Man. Dir GERARDUS J. SCHOUTEN.
ProGraphics Inc: Italiestraat 5, POB 201, Oranjestad; tel. 5824550; fax 5833072; e-mail prographics@setarnet.aw; f. 2001; fmrly VAD Printers Inc; Publr WILBERT WEVER.

Publicidad Exito Aruba SA: Domenicanessenstraat 17, POB 142, Oranjestad; tel. 5822020; fax 5824242; f. 1958.
Van Dorp Aruba NV: Caya G. F. (Betico) Croes 77, POB 596, Oranjestad; tel. 5823076; fax 5823573.

Broadcasting and Communications

TELECOMMUNICATIONS

Digicel Aruba: Marisol Bldg, L. G. Smith Blvd 60, POB 662, Oranjestad; tel. 5222200; fax 5222231; e-mail customercare@digicelcuracao.com; internet www.digicelaruba.com; f. 2003; owned by an Irish consortium; established a mobile cellular telephone network connecting Aruba with Bonaire and Curaçao in July 2006; Chair. DENIS O'BRIEN; CEO (Dutch Caribbean) HANS LUTE.
Servicio di Telecomunicacion di Aruba NV (SETAR): Seroe Blanco z/n, POB 13, Oranjestad; tel. 5251000; fax 5251515; e-mail sysop@setarnet.aw; internet www.setar.aw; f. 1986; Man. Dir ROLAND CROES.

BROADCASTING

Radio

Canal 90 FM Stereo: Van Leeuwenhoekstraat 26, Oranjestad; tel. 5828952; fax 837340; e-mail info@canal90fm.aw.
Cristal Sound 101.7 FM: J. G. Emanstraat 124A, Oranjestad; tel. 5827726; fax 5820144.
Hit 94 FM: Oranjestad; e-mail hit94fm@hotmail.com; internet www.hit94fm.com; f. 1993; Dir JOHNNY HABIBE.
Magic 96.5 FM: Oranjestad; internet www.magic965.com.
Radio 1270: Bernardstraat 138, POB 28, Sint Nicolaas; tel. 5845602; fax 5827753; commercial station; programmes in Dutch, English, Spanish and Papiamento; Dir F. A. LEAUER; Station Man. J. A. C. ALDERS.
Radio Carina FM: Datustraat 10A, Oranjestad; tel. 5821450; fax 5831955; commercial station; programmes in Dutch, English, Spanish and Papiamento; Dir-Gen. ALBERT R. DIEFFENTHALER.
Radio Caruso Booy FM: G. M. de Bruynewijk 49, Savaneta; tel. 5847752; fax 5843351; e-mail sira@setarnet.aw; internet www.geocities.com/carusobooy; commercial station; broadcasts for 24 hrs a day; programmes in Dutch, English, Spanish and Papiamento; Pres. HUBERT ERQUILLES ANTONIO BOOY; Gen. Man. SIRA BOOY.
Radio Kelkboom: Bloemond 14, POB 146, Oranjestad; tel. 5821899; fax 5834825; e-mail radiokelkboom@setarnet.aw; internet www.watapana-aruba.com; f. 1954; commercial radio station; programmes in Papiamento, Dutch, English, Spanish and Creole; Owners CARLOS A. KELKBOOM, E. A. M. KELKBOOM.
Radio Victoria: Washington 23A, POB 5291, Oranjestad; tel. 5873444; fax 5873444; e-mail radiovictoria@setarnet.aw; internet www.radiovictoriaaruba.org; f. 1958; religious and cultural FM radio station owned by the Radio Victoria Foundation; programmes in Dutch, English, Spanish and Papiamento; Pres. N. J. F. ARTS.
Voz di Aruba (Voice of Aruba): Van Leeuwenhoekstraat 26, POB 219, Oranjestad; tel. 5823355; fax 5837340; commercial radio station; programmes in Dutch, English, Spanish and Papiamento; also operates Canal 90 on FM; Dir A. M. ARENDS, Jr.

Television

ABC Aruba Broadcasting Co NV (ATV): Royal Plaza Suite 223, POB 5040, Oranjestad; tel. 5838150; fax 5838110; e-mail 15atv@setarnet.aw.
Telearuba NV: Pos Chiquito 1A, POB 392, Oranjestad; tel. 5851000; fax 5851111; e-mail info@telearuba.aw; internet www.telearuba.aw; f. 1963; fmrly operated by Netherlands Antilles Television Co; commercial; acquired by SETAR in March 2005; Gen. Man. M. MARCHENA.

Finance

(cap. = capital; res = reserves; dep. = deposits; m. = million; brs = branches; amounts in Aruban florin, unless otherwise stated)

BANKING

Central Bank

Centrale Bank van Aruba: J. E. Irausquin Blvd 8, POB 18, Oranjestad; tel. 5252100; fax 5252101; e-mail cbaua@setarnet.aw; internet www.cbaruba.org; f. 1986; cap. 10.0m., res 210.8m., dep. 418.4m. (Dec. 2007); Chair. A. J. SWAEN; Pres. JANE R. FIGAROA-SEMELEER.

NETHERLANDS DEPENDENCIES
Aruba

Commercial Banks

Aruba Bank NV: Camacuri 12, POB 192, Oranjestad; tel. 5277777; fax 5277715; e-mail info@arubabank.com; internet www.arubabank.com; f. 1925; acquired Interbank Aruba NV in Dec. 2003; total assets US $260m. (Dec. 2004); Man. Dir and CEO EDWIN TROMP; 5 brs.

Banco di Caribe NV: Vondellaan 31, POB 493, Oranjestad; tel. 5232000; fax 5832422; e-mail bdcaua@setarnet.aw; internet www.bancodicaribe.com; f. 1987; Gen. Man. and CEO IDEFONS D. SIMON; 1 br.

Caribbean Mercantile Bank Aruba: Caya G. F. (Betico) Croes 53, POB 28, Oranjestad; tel. 5823118; fax 5830919; e-mail executive_office@cmbnv.com; internet www.cmbnv.com; f. 1963; cap. 4.0m., res 100.6m., dep. 951.1m. (Dec. 2007); Pres. LIONEL CAPRILES, II; Gen. Man. Dir J. E. WOLTER; 6 brs.

RBTT Bank Aruba NV: Italiestraat 36, Sasakiweg, Oranjestad; tel. 5233100; fax 58821576; e-mail info@tt.rbtt.com; internet www.rbtt.com; f. 2001; fmrly First National Bank of Aruba NV (f. 1985 and acquired by Royal Bank of Trinidad and Tobago Ltd in 1998); total assets US $111.5m. (Dec. 2003); Chair. PETER J. JULY; 6 brs.

Investment Bank

AIB NV: Wilhelminastraat 34–36, POB 1011, Oranjestad; tel. 5827327; fax 5827461; e-mail info@aib-bank.com; internet www.aib-bank.com; f. 1987 as Aruban Investment Bank; name changed as above in April 2004; total assets 149.0m. (Dec. 2005); Man. Dir FRENDSEL W. GIEL; Asst Man. Dir HERRY M. KOOLMAN.

Mortgage Bank

Fundacion Cas pa Comunidad Arubano (FCCA): Sabana Blanco 66, Oranjestad; tel. 5238800; fax 5836272; e-mail info@fcca.com; internet www.fcca.com; f. 1979; Man. Dir PETER VAN POPPEL.

'Offshore' Bank

Citibank Aruba NA: Arulex Bldg, Punta Bravo z/n, Oranjestad; tel. 5822138; fax 5832363; e-mail fred.aarons@citicorp.com.

INSURANCE

There were eight life insurance companies and 14 non-life insurance companies active in Aruba in December 2005.

Association

Insurance Association of Aruba (IAA): L. G. Smith Blvd 160, Oranjestad; tel. 5821111; fax 5826138; 10 mems.

Trade and Industry

DEVELOPMENT ORGANIZATIONS

Department of Agriculture, Husbandry, and Fisheries: Piedra Plat 114A, Oranjestad; tel. 5858102; fax 5855639; e-mail dlvv@aruba.gov.aw; internet www.overheid.aw; f. 1976; Dir T. G. DAMIAN.

Department of Economic Affairs, Commerce and Industry (Directie Economische Zaken, Handel en Industrie): Sun Plaza Bldg, L. G. Smith Blvd 160, Oranjestad; tel. 5821181; fax 5834494; e-mail deaci@setarnet.aw; internet www.arubaeconomicaffairs.aw; f. 1986; Dir MARIA DIJKHOFF-PITA.

CHAMBER OF COMMERCE AND INDUSTRY

Chamber of Commerce and Industry Aruba: J. E. Irausquin Blvd 10, POB 140, Oranjestad; tel. 5821120; fax 5883200; e-mail secretariat@arubachamber.com; internet www.arubachamber.com; f. 1930; Pres. EDWIN A. ROOS; Exec. Dir LORRAINE C. DE SOUZA.

TRADE ASSOCIATION

Aruba Trade and Industry Association (ATIA): ATIA Bldg, Pedro Gallegostraat 6, POB 562, Oranjestad; tel. 5827593; fax 5833068; e-mail atiaruba@setarnet.aw; internet www.atiaruba.org; f. 1945; Pres. JUAN YRAUSQUIN; 230 mems.

UTILITIES

Electricity and Water

Utilities Aruba NV: Arulex Center, Punta Brabo z/n; tel. 5828277; fax 5828682; e-mail utilities@setarnet.aw; govt-owned holding co; Man. Dir HAROLD HENRIQUEZ.

Electriciteit-Maatschappij Aruba (ELMAR) NV: Wilhelminastraat 110, POB 202, Oranjestad; tel. 5237100; fax 5828991; e-mail info@elmar.aw; internet www.elmar.aw; independently managed co, residing under Utilities Aruba NV; electricity distribution; Man. Dir ING. A. O. RAFINÉ; 167 employees.

Water en Energiebedrijf Aruba (WEB) NV: Balashi 76, POB 575, Oranjestad; tel. 5254600; fax 5857681; e-mail web@webaruba.com; internet www.webaruba.com; f. 1991; independently managed co, residing under Utilities Aruba NV; production and distribution of industrial and potable water, and electricity generation; Man. Dir JOSSY M. LACLÉ.

Gas

Aruba Gas Supply Company Ltd (ARUGAS): Barcadera z/n, POB 190, Oranjestad; tel. 5851198; fax 5852187; e-mail webmaster@arugas.com; internet www.arugas.com.

BOC Gases Aruba NV: Balashi z/n, POB 387, Oranjestad; tel. 5852624; fax 5852823; e-mail bocaruba@setarnet.aw; internet www.boc-gases.com; acquired by the Linde Group global industrial gases and engineering org. in Sept. 2006.

TRADE UNIONS

Federacion di Trahadornan di Aruba (FTA) (Aruban Workers' Federation): Bernhardstraat 23, Sint Nicolaas; tel. 5845448; fax 5845504; e-mail fetraua@setarnet.aw; f. 1964; independent; affiliated with the International Trade Union Confederation; Pres. JOSÉ RUDOLF (RUDY) GEERMAN; Vice-Pres. JANE ANASTACIA BRAAFHART.

There are also several unions for government and semi-government workers and employees.

Transport

There are no railways, but Aruba has a network of all-weather roads.

Arubus NV: Sabana Blanco 67, Oranjestad; tel. 5882300; fax 5828633; e-mail info@arubus.com; internet www.arubus.com; f. 1979; state-owned company providing public transport services; runs a fleet of 48 buses; Dir FRANKLIN KUIPERI.

SHIPPING

The island's principal seaport is Oranjestad, whose harbour can accommodate ocean-going vessels. There are also ports at Barcadera and Sint Nicolaas, the latter administered by the Valero Aruba Refining Company.

Aruba Ports Authority NV: Port Administration Bldg, L. G. Smith Blvd 23, Oranjestad; tel. 5826633; fax 5832896; e-mail info@arubaports.com; internet www.arubaports.com; f. 1981; responsible for the administration of the ports of Oranjestad and Barcadera; Man. Dir JUAN ALFONSO BOEKHOUDT.

Principal Shipping Companies

Beng Lian Shipping S. de R. L. A. V. V.: Dominicanessenstraat 22, Oranjestad.

Rodoca Shipping and Trading SA: Parkietenbos 30, Barcadera Harbour; tel. 5850096; fax 5850097; fmrly Aruba Shipping and Chartering Co NV.

Valero Aruba Marine Services: Lagoweg, POB 2150, Sint Nicolaas; tel. 5894742; fax 5894554.

VR Shipping NV: Anthony Veder Bldg, POB 3677, Willemstad; tel. 4615700; fax 4612576; e-mail info@vrshipping.com; internet www.vrshipping.com; f. 1975 as Anthony Veder & Co; name changed as above 2000.

Windward Island Agencies: Heyligerweg, POB 66, Oranjestad.

CIVIL AVIATION

The Queen Beatrix International Airport (Aeropuerto Internacional Reina Beatrix), about 2.5 km from Oranjestad, is served by numerous airlines (including Dutch Antilles Express, based in Curaçao, Netherlands Antilles), linking the island with destinations in the Caribbean, Europe, the USA, and Central and South America. After renovation and expansion, the airport was expected to be able to handle 2.6m. passengers per year by 2010. In November 2000 the national carrier, Air Aruba, was declared bankrupt.

Aruba Airport Authority NV: Queen Beatrix International Airport, Wayaca z/n, Oranjestad; tel. 5242424; fax 5834229; internet www.airportaruba.com; Man. Dir PETER STEINMETZ.

Tourism

Aruba's white sandy beaches, particularly along the southern coast, are an attraction for foreign visitors, and tourism is a major industry. The number of hotel rooms totalled 7,226 in 2004. Most stop-over visitors came from the USA (71.0% in 2006), Venezuela (8.2%) and the Netherlands (5.3%). In 2007 some 1,253,848 tourists visited Aruba, of which 772,073 were stop-over visitors and 481,775 were cruise ship passengers. Receipts from tourism totalled A Fl. 2,244.3m. in that year.

Aruba Cruise Tourism: Suite 230, Royal Plaza Mall, L. G. Smith Blvd 94, POB 5254, Oranjestad; tel. 5833648; fax 5835088; e-mail info@arubabycruise.com; internet www.arubabycruise.com; f. 1995 as the Cruise Tourism Authority—Aruba; name changed as above in 2005; non-profit government organization; Exec. Dir KATHLEEN ROJER.

Aruba Hotel and Tourism Association (AHATA): L. G. Smith Blvd 174, POB 542, Oranjestad; tel. 5822607; fax 5824202; e-mail info@ahata.com; internet www.ahata.com; f. 1965; 101 mems; Pres. and CEO ROB SMITH; Chair. EWALD BIEMANS.

Aruba Tourism Authority (ATA): L. G. Smith Blvd 172, Eagle, Oranjestad; tel. 5823777; fax 5834702; e-mail ata.aruba@aruba.com; internet www.aruba.com; f. 1953; Man. Dir MYRNA JANSEN-FELICIANO.

THE NETHERLANDS ANTILLES

Introductory Survey

Location, Climate, Language, Religion, Flag, Capital

The Netherlands Antilles (Antilles of the Five) consists of two groups of islands in the Caribbean Sea, about 800 km (500 miles) apart. The main group, lying off the coast of Venezuela, consists of Bonaire and Curaçao, which (together with Aruba, 68 km to the east of Curaçao) are known as the Benedenwindse Eilands or 'Leeward Islands'; to the north-east lie the small volcanic islands of St (Sint) Eustatius (also known as Statia), Saba and St (Sint) Maarten (the northern half of the last island being a dependency of the French overseas department of Guadeloupe), known as the Bovenwindse Eilands or 'Windward Islands' (although actually in the Leeward group of the Lesser Antilles). The climate is tropical, moderated by the sea, with an average annual temperature of 27.5°C (81°F) and little rainfall. The official languages are Dutch and Papiamento (a mixture of Dutch, Spanish, Portuguese, English, Arawak Indian and several West African dialects), which is the dominant language of the 'Leeward Islands'. English is the official and principal language of the 'Windward Islands'. Spanish is also widely spoken. Almost all of the inhabitants profess Christianity: the people of the 'Leeward Islands' and Saba are predominantly Roman Catholics, while those of St Eustatius and St Maarten are predominantly Protestants. The state flag (proportions 2 by 3) is white, with a red vertical stripe in the centre, crossed by a horizontal blue stripe on which there are five white five-pointed stars (one for each of the main islands) arranged in an oval. The capital is Willemstad, on the island of Curaçao.

Recent History

The 'Leeward Islands', already settled by communities of Arawak Indians, were discovered by the Spanish in 1499 and were seized by the Dutch in the 1630s. Curaçao became prosperous in the late 17th and 18th centuries as an entrepôt for trade in the Caribbean. The Dutch settled the 'Windward Islands', once settled by Carib Indians, in the mid-17th century. After frequent changes in possession, the islands (including Aruba) were finally confirmed as Dutch territory in 1816. The two groups were administered as Curaçao and Dependencies between 1845 and 1948. Slavery was abolished in 1863, and the islands suffered from an economic decline until the establishment of petroleum refineries on Curaçao and Aruba, in 1918 and 1929, respectively. During the Second World War Queen Wilhelmina of the Netherlands promised independence, and in 1954 a Charter gave the federation of six islands full autonomy in domestic affairs, and declared it to be an integral part of the Kingdom of the Netherlands.

Divisions of political allegiance within the territory have been along island, rather than policy, lines, and a series of coalition Governments has frequently paralysed decision-making. In 1969 serious rioting and looting broke out in Willemstad after a demonstration by workers in the petroleum industry. Troops had to be sent from the Netherlands to quell the disturbances and to restore order. In February 1970 the socialist Government of Ciro Kroon resigned over the nomination of a new Governor, and in 1971 the Government of E. Petronia resigned over the rejection by the Staten (parliament) of new financial measures.

Following elections to the Staten in June 1977, a coalition Government was formed, with the leader of the Democratische Partij (DP), Silvio Rozendal, as Prime Minister. After a boycott of the session by the Movimentu Electoral di Pueblo (MEP) of Aruba and the Frente Obrero i Liberashon 30 di mei (FOL), the Staten was eventually convened by a Governor's decree in October. Rozendal resigned in April 1979, and elections were held in July. A coalition administration was formed by the Movimentu Antiyas Nobo (MAN), the MEP and the Unión Patriótico Bonairiano (UPB), with Dominico (Don) Martina, the leader of the MAN, as Prime Minister. The DP joined the coalition Government in December 1980.

In Aruba resentment of the administrative dominance of Curaçao resulted, in 1971, in the establishment of the pro-independence MEP. In 1981 a series of talks regarding Aruba's future began with the Netherlands Government. However, in September the MEP representatives in the Staten withdrew their support for the Government on the question of Aruba's rights to possible discoveries of petroleum off its coast. The Government's majority was restored by the inclusion of the DP—St Maarten (DP—StM) member for the 'Windward Islands' in the coalition, but a DP resignation in January 1982 precipitated a further crisis. A general election in June failed to resolve the situation, and it was not until October that agreement was reached on the formation by Martina of a new coalition, which excluded the MEP.

In March 1983 agreement was finally reached whereby Aruba would be given separate status (*status aparte*) within the Kingdom of the Netherlands from January 1986, with the prospect of full independence in 1996 (for further details, see Aruba, q.v.). Arguments persisted regarding the division of the Antilles' financial reserves, and over rights to explore for petroleum and other minerals. In June 1984 Martina's coalition Government resigned. A five-party coalition was eventually formed in September, with Maria Liberia-Peters of the conservative Partido Nashonal di Pueblo (PNP) as Prime Minister.

At a general election in November 1985 the PNP gained the largest number of seats in the Staten for the Antilles of the Five (six out of 22), but was unable to secure enough support from other parties to form a government. Martina once again became Prime Minister and formed a coalition Government. During 1986–87 the Government was forced to introduce a series of economic austerity measures, following Aruba's separation from the Netherlands Antilles and the decline of both the petroleum-refining industry and 'offshore' financial services. The Government resigned in March 1988, after losing the support of the DP—StM and the FOL. In May Liberia-Peters formed a coalition with all the parties represented in the Staten except for the MAN and the DP—Curaçao (DP—C).

In January 1989 Martina revealed that successive Curaçao administrations had diverted revenues from the 'offshore' financial sector into a fund that had not been declared to The Hague, Netherlands, during negotiations for budgetary support. The Netherlands had recently exerted pressure for more control to be exercised over the large amount of aid that it provided for the Netherlands Antilles. By the early 1990s it appeared that, while the 'metropolitan' Government was unwilling to allow the complete disintegration of the federation, it was prepared to consider a less centralized system or the creation of two federations in the separate island groups.

At a general election in March 1990 the PNP increased the number of its seats (all on Curaçao) to seven, again making it the largest single party in the Staten, and, after some weeks of negotiations, Liberia-Peters assumed the leadership of a broadly based coalition. In March 1992 the FOL and its partner at the 1990 election, the Social Independiente, withdrew from the Government. Liberia-Peters formed a new coalition with the DP—StM, the UPB and the DP—C. In September 1993 the DP—StM withdrew, although the Government maintained its majority in the Staten with the support of an independent deputy and subsequently that of the Windward Islands People's Movement (WIPM).

A referendum was conducted on Curaçao in November 1993 regarding its constitutional status; 74% of the electorate voted for a continuance of the island's status as a member of the Antillean federation. The option of *status aparte* within the Kingdom of the Netherlands, favoured by the Government, received only 18% of the votes cast. As a result of this defeat, the WIPM and the UPB withdrew their support, leaving the Government without a majority in the Staten. Liberia-Peters resigned, and Alejandro Felippe Paula, a professor at the University of the Netherlands Antilles, subsequently agreed to head an interim Government. A general election took place in February 1994, at which a new, Curaçao-based party, the Partido Antía Restrukturá (PAR), led by Miguel A. Pourier, became the largest single party in the Staten. Pourier assumed the leadership of a broadly based coalition Government, which was inaugurated in March.

Referendums on status were conducted on St Maarten, St Eustatius, Saba and Bonaire in October 1994. On St Maarten 60% of the electorate voted to remain within the Antillean federation, while the option of *status aparte* received 32% of the vote. On St Eustatius 86% of voters opted for continued membership of the Antillean federation, while the equivalent vote on Saba was 91%. On Bonaire (where voting took place one week later) some 88% of voters favoured continued federation.

A general election was held on 30 January 1998, at which the PAR lost four of its eight seats in the Staten. The PNP retained its three seats, while a new party, the Partido Laboral Krusada Popular (PLKP), also took three seats. The loss of support for the PAR was attributed to the unpopularity of austerity measures imposed by the outgoing Government. Pourier failed in his attempts to form a new coalition, largely owing to opposition to the PAR's economic policies. A new coalition Government, with Susanne F. C. Camelia-Römer of the PNP as Prime Minister, was finally agreed in early May, only to collapse later in the month, when it was revealed that a designated cabinet member was under criminal investigation. A new Government was sworn in on 1 June. The coalition comprised six parties, with the support of 13 of the 22 members of the Staten.

In late 1998 the Government adopted a National Recovery Plan, which aimed both to reduce the fiscal deficit and also to generate growth in the economy through the introduction of measures intended to stimulate investment. However, the Government's subsequent attempts to reduce state expenditure proved to be highly controversial, and proposals to reduce the public sector work-force by some 2,400—principally through cuts in the civil service of the central Government and of the island Government of Curaçao—caused great tension between Camelia-Römer's PNP and its fellow Curaçao-based coalition partners, the PLKP and the FOL, which led, in October 1999, to the collapse of both the central Government and the island Government of Curaçao. In the following month former Prime Minister Pourier formed a new broad-based coalition Government, which had the support of 18 of the 22 members of the Staten. Concerns were, however, expressed that Pourier's Government would confront the same problems as the previous administration in its attempt fully to implement the National Recovery Plan, and this was, to some extent, anticipated by the appointment of Camelia-Römer as Minister for the National Recovery Plan and Economic Affairs.

A referendum on the constitutional future of St Maarten took place on 23 June 2000. Only 4% of participants in St Maarten favoured maintaining the status quo. Some 69% favoured obtaining *status aparte* within the Kingdom of the Netherlands, 14% favoured complete independence and 12% preferred a restructuring of the Antilles of the Five. Although the Dutch Government indicated that it would not support a request by St Maarten to receive *status aparte*, it supported the establishment of a commission to explore the possibilities of St Maarten adopting *status aparte*. In February 2003 Johan Remkes, the Dutch Minister of Interior and Kingdom Relations, confirmed that the Netherlands would not permit St Maarten to leave the federation. Despite this set-back, St Maarten had signed an agreement with the central Government in August 2002, which would permit the island's executive council to take out loans on its own initiative, without seeking permission from the central bank. Furthermore, in late 2002 the executive council proposed to the central bank that discussions should begin on a separate monetary system for St Maarten.

The elections of 18 January 2002 were won by the FOL, led by Anthony Godett, which had campaigned against the stringent measures imposed by the IMF. Despite the party's victory, attempts by the FOL to form a coalition government failed because of allegations of corruption and mismanagement of funds by party leaders. Eventually, in June 2002 a coalition Government that included representatives of the PAR, the PNP, the PLKP, the DP—StM, the UPB and the Democratische Partij—Statia (DP—StE) took office, under the leadership of the new PAR leader, Etienne Ys, replacing Pourier's caretaker Government.

Local elections in Curaçao in May 2003 were won by the FOL under the leadership of Anthony Godett, who had been detained by the police in April for alleged corrupt activities. The victory of Godett's party, known for its independent and assertive attitude towards the Netherlands and the IMF, was expected to impact negatively on the implementation of IMF measures and the island's political relationship with the Netherlands, which had improved under the PAR leadership. Later in the same month Prime Minister Ys' cabinet resigned to allow the FOL to form a fresh governing coalition (comprised of the FOL, the PNP, the PLKP, the UPB, the DP—StE and the WIPM), based on new local political alliances. In late July Ben Komproe of the FOL was sworn in as Prime Minister on a temporary basis, as Godett could not be approved for the post while he faced corruption charges. In August Mirna Luisa Godett, the sister of the FOL leader, was elected by the party to the post of Prime Minister, despite not being a member of the Staten. Komproe, meanwhile, was appointed Minister of Justice. Following the conviction in December of Anthony Godett (and 16 other party members, business leaders and officials) for fraud, embezzlement and corruption, in January 2004 the governing coalition almost lost control of the legislature when the WIPM and the UPB withdrew their support. The Government managed to retain its majority, however, when the Democratische Partij—Bonaire (DP—B) agreed to join the coalition later in the same month. In February the Staten rejected a motion proposed by the opposition (and directed at Anthony Godett) that legislators found guilty of corruption be prevented from retaining their parliamentary seats.

Meanwhile, as anticipated, relations between the Netherlands Antilles and the Dutch Government worsened following the advent of the FOL-dominated Government. In August 2003 Mirna Luisa Godett announced that a delegation of Dutch MPs would not be officially received when they visited the territory. Godett's administration further alienated the Dutch Government by its support of a proposal to remove a body scanner at Curaçao's international airport, which had been installed in an attempt to combat the increasing drugs trade between the Netherlands and the Caribbean. Relations continued to worsen during the remainder of 2003, and in January 2004 Godett accused Dutch officials of spying on her Government after it emerged that local justice officials had met two visiting Dutch ministers without her knowledge. Tension was further exacerbated by Godett's rejection of a Dutch proposal to ban known drugs-traffickers from Antillean airlines.

The Government lost its parliamentary majority in early April 2004 after four parties (the PNP, the PLKP, the DP—B and the DP—StE) withdrew from the FOL-led coalition, having failed to effect the resignation of the Minister of Justice, Ben Komproe. The coalition partners accused Komproe of allowing the FOL's main political donor, Nelson Monte, who was serving a custodial sentence for corruption, to stay in a luxury hospital rather than be gaoled. After the Staten voted in favour of a 'no confidence' motion against the Government, the Prime Minister submitted her resignation on 6 April; Komproe, along with two ministers, also resigned. Komproe's position had already been weakened by his failure to reverse the rising crime rate on Curaçao and by his brother's alleged involvement in fraud. In the wake of the resignations, the Governor, Fritz Goedgedrag, assumed the task of forming a new government; a seven-party coalition (consisting of the PAR, the PNP, the PLKP, the UPB, the DP—StM, the DP—StE and the WIPM) led by Etienne Ys was duly appointed in June and charged with the responsibility of repairing the territory's relationship with the Netherlands and reducing the huge national debt. Meanwhile, in July Anthony Godett was sentenced to 15 months' imprisonment on corruption-related charges; the sentence was confirmed by the High Court in The Hague. However, five of the original 15 months were suspended, and the FOL leader—who had retained his parliamentary and Island Council membership owing to anomalies in existing legislation—was released in March 2007.

In November 2005 Ys announced that the PAR-led Government had lost its slim majority following the withdrawal from the coalition of the UPB. (The UPB was reportedly dissatisfied with the central Government's financial support for Bonaire's San Francisco Hospital and Flamingo Field Airport.) A general election, intended to be the final election to the Netherlands Antilles Staten, was consequently held on 27 January 2006. The PAR, led by Ys, secured the largest number of seats (five) in the 22-seat legislature. In addition, the MAN won three seats, the PNP, the National Alliance (NA—comprising the National Progressive Party and the St Maarten Patriotic Alliance), the UPB, the FOL and Fòrsa Kòrsou each won two seats, and the DP—StM, the WIPM, the DP—StE and the DP—B each secured one legislative seat. In total, 27 parties contested the election. Negotiations to form a new coalition government were, as usual, protracted. Eventually, on 26 March, a coalition Government comprising representatives of the PAR, the MAN, the PNP, the NA, the UPB, the DP—StE and the WIPM, and headed by the PAR leader, Emily de Jongh-Elhage, was sworn into office. (The DP—StE and the WIPM had representatives at the rank of State Secretary rather than at full ministerial level.) De Jongh-Elhage pledged to ensure that the best interests of all the constituent parts of the federation would be considered during the transition period, and that education and the eradication of poverty would be her Government's main concerns.

On 8 October 2004 the Jesurun Commission, established by the Dutch and Antillean Governments and headed by Edsel Jesurun—a former Governor of the territory—recommended the dissolution of the Netherlands Antilles; support for the federation had, it was argued, virtually disintegrated on most of the islands. In particular, changes were needed to combat the rise in unemployment, poverty, violent crime and drugs-smuggling in the territory. The Commission proposed that Curaçao and St Maarten should become autonomous states within the Netherlands (i.e., have *status aparte*), while Saba, Bonaire and St Eustatius should be directly administered by the Dutch Government. In September and November, respectively, in official referendums, a majority of voters on both Bonaire (59%) and Saba (86%) strongly favoured becoming part of the Netherlands. Further referendums on the constitutional futures of Curaçao and St Eustatius took place on 8 April 2005: 68% of participants in Curaçao favoured *status aparte*, in line with the recommendations of the Commission, 23% voted for closer ties with the Netherlands and 5%

voted for complete independence—there was a 54% voter turn-out. In St Eustatius, from a voter turn-out of 55%, 76% of the electorate favoured remaining part of the Netherlands Antilles, while 20% voted for closer ties with the Netherlands and 1% preferred to seek complete independence for the tiny island. Taking into account the results of the referendum on St Maarten in 2000 (see above), since St Eustatius was the only island of the dependency to favour the status quo, the future of the Antillean federation appeared to be limited. On 3 December 2005 a preliminary agreement with the Dutch Government that the extant federation be dissolved by 1 July 2007 was duly signed in Curaçao. Under the new structure, Curaçao and St Maarten were, as expected, to become autonomous members of the Kingdom of the Netherlands, while Saba, Bonaire and St Eustatius were to become 'Kingdom Islands', a status that was likely to be equivalent to that of a Dutch province.

Arrangements towards effecting the proposed dissolution of the Netherlands Antilles federation advanced considerably in 2006. An agreement confirming the three smaller islands' impending accession to 'special municipality' status was signed in The Hague on 12 October, and included provisions for citizens of Saba, Bonaire and St Eustatius to participate in Dutch national and local elections and in the election of candidates to the European Parliament. On 2 November the Dutch Government granted St Maarten and Curaçao independent governance within the Kingdom of the Netherlands; endorsement of this latter agreement was contingent upon the two larger islands ceding authority for the administration of defence, foreign policy and law enforcement matters to the Dutch Government. Responsibility for the Netherlands Antilles' substantial collective debt, estimated at NA Fl. 5,000m., was to be assumed by the Dutch administration, assuming comprehensive ratification of the 2 November accord by the respective heads of Island Councils. The Common Court of Justice of the Netherlands Antilles and Aruba was to be retained as the islands' principal judicial authority.

However, while St Maarten acceded to the agreement on 28 November 2006, Curaçao's Island Council voted by a decisive 13–6 majority against the accord, averring that further negotiations were required in order to safeguard the interests of the island's citizens, specifically over the administration of justice (over which they regarded the Dutch Government as having too great an influence). Particular concern had been expressed by the detractors with regard to stipulations for the management of the islands' respective budgets—entailing submission to a joint central bank—and the supervision of their judicial and police departments by the Dutch Government; furthermore, potential deficiencies had been identified within the Dutch system regarding the regulation of political practices, freedom of expression, the synthesis of European Union (see p. 255) directives with national democratic tenets, and the integration of foreign nationals into Dutch society. Representatives of the PAR and PNP, who had voted in favour of the final agreement, left the Island Council in protest at the decision. Their departure left Curaçao without a legitimate government. Furthermore, in January 2007 the Netherlands Government rejected the island's request for a renegotiation of the 2 November accord. Curaçao's abstention was regarded as having jeopardized certain provisions of the agreement that were dependent upon all five islands becoming signatories and provoked polarized responses from the island's people. The urgency of addressing Curaçao's already burdensome public debt, estimated as constituting approximately one-half of the entire federation's total obligation, was rendered more acute in light of the fact that the island would no longer benefit from the debt relief awarded by the Netherlands to signatories of the 2 November agreement.

A further 'transition accord' was signed by the Netherlands Antilles central Government, the Island Councils of Saba, Bonaire, St Eustatius and St Maarten, and the Netherlands on 12 February 2007, envisaging the islands' complete secession from the federation. Curaçao was conspicuously absent from the provisions of the agreement and consequently attended the signing ceremony in an observer capacity only. Under the terms of this covenant, the Netherlands was to pledge over NA Fl. 1,000m. (in addition to existing financial assistance) to facilitate the process of disintegration; of this sum, NA Fl. 224m. was designated specifically for debt relief, while the remaining funds were to be disseminated through social and economic development programmes and budgetary aid, with each of the four participating islands receiving individual allocations. Curaçao's exclusion from the restructured Netherlands Antilles precipitated serious concerns for the island's pursuit of autonomy and its future status and relations with the Dutch Government, and, consequently, on 9 July the Curaçao Island Council signed the November accord's 'closing statement', although its late accession to the arrangement precluded the island from the Netherlands Government's debt-restructuring provisions.

In early 2007 the Curaçao Island Council—now comprised of the FOL, the Liste Ni'un Paso Atras (LNPA), the MAN and the Movimentu Sosial Laboral (MSL)—was reportedly exploring the possibility of greater involvement in the Caribbean Community and Common Market (CARICOM, see p. 206), while St Maarten, Saba and St Eustatius had expressed an interest in acceding to the Organization of Eastern Caribbean States (OECS). State Secretary of Finance Alex Rosaria reaffirmed the islands' commitment to further regional integration after an official visit by the Secretary-General of the OECS, Edwin Carrington, in September.

Local government elections were staged on all five islands of the federation on 20 April 2007, representing the final elections prior to dissolution of the Netherlands Antilles, anticipated before the end of the following year. The PAR received the greatest number of votes and obtained seven seats in the Curaçao Island Council. The MAN won five seats and the FOL's representation was reduced to two seats, along with the PNP and the LNPA.

Opposition-led protests took place in late 2007 in Curaçao in response to the continuing constitutional negotiations with the Dutch Government. On 12 November riot police were deployed to disperse a crowd of around 300 protesters when violence broke out. The demonstrators objected to the Dutch Government having the power to intervene in the island's future financial and legal affairs. One week later the Island Council formally ratified the results of the 2005 referendum: at a second peaceful demonstration held in early December and attended by several thousand people, opposition parties demanded an end to the negotiations and for the Government to seek to achieve the autonomous status of Curaçao, in accordance with the results of the ballot.

A round table conference was held in Willemstad on 14–16 December 2008, at which representatives of all five islands of the federation and the Dutch Prime Minister, Jan Pieter Balkenende, agreed on the new political structure of the Netherlands Antilles. As previously established, Bonaire, St Eustatius and Saba would become Dutch municipalities, while Curaçao and St Maarten (and Aruba) would gain autonomy. Agreement was reached on the extent of the administrative powers of the Netherlands Government within the two seceding territories. In return for retaining some legal and financial controls over Curaçao and St Maarten, the Netherlands agreed to write off almost three-quarters of the Antilles' debt, beginning in 2009. The agreement was subject to a referendum in Curaçao, held on 15 May 2009; according to preliminary results, the agreement was narrowly endorsed by those participating in the plebiscite. Further negotiations to agree the details of the reform were to be held throughout 2009, and, although no definite target date for secession was fixed, it was widely hoped that the dissolution of the Netherlands Antilles would take place in 2010.

In December 2000 an agreement was reached with the Dutch Government on the compulsory acculturation of Antillean migrants to the Netherlands. The high level of unemployment, particularly among the younger members of the Antillean community in the Netherlands, and the steady influx of new migrants in recent years had led the Dutch Government to propose that the Netherlands Antilles adopt legislation whereby those under 25 years of age would be granted permission to emigrate to the Netherlands only after attending acculturation classes designed to facilitate their integration into Dutch society. In May 2005 the Netherlands announced plans to introduce legislation to require citizens of the Netherlands Antilles aged between 16 and 24 years to find work or begin studies within three months of arriving in the Netherlands, or face deportation; it was estimated by the Dutch Government that immigrants from the Netherlands Antilles aged under 25 years were four times more likely to turn to crime than the general Dutch population. Prime Minister Ys described the policy as discriminatory and threatened to take the Dutch Government to court.

In December 2004 the Dutch Government pledged to send 60 police officers to the Netherlands Antilles, primarily Curaçao, to combat the increase in crime on the islands. In addition, 25 Dutch customs and military officials were sent to Curaçao and Bonaire airports in January 2005 to improve security against drugs-transshipment between the Netherlands and its dependent territory. Proposals announced by the Dutch Ministry of Immigration and Integration in September 2006 for the forcible return of Antillean juvenile offenders to the Caribbean, even if they held Dutch citizenship, were condemned as being in violation of European Human Rights legislation (by discriminating in favour of Netherlands-born nationals). In January 2007 draft legislation was submitted to the Island Council of St Maarten for the proposed repatriation of persons who had assumed illegal residence on the island since 2005. It was estimated that over 25,000 people were living in the territory at that time, although the proportion of this number to which compulsory expulsion would apply was unclear. The measure appeared to coincide with requirements for immigration and security reforms ahead of the proposed redesignation of St Maarten within the Kingdom of the Netherlands (see above).

Efforts by the Netherlands Antilles Government to improve its regulation of financial transactions and tax administration—and to attain recognition as an international financial centre—were bolstered by the formation of a 'double taxation task force' in October 2006. One of the new organization's stated principal objectives was to extend its network of Double Taxation Agreements (DTA); to this end, the Government announced plans to negotiate such agreements with Mexico, Spain, Suriname, the United Arab Emirates and

Colombia in 2008. The Staten approved a series of amendments to the national tax legislation in November 2006 that would render the Netherlands Antilles compliant with requirements for the establishment of a Tax Information and Exchange Agreement with the USA and facilitate future discussions towards a bilateral DTA; a similar agreement for the exchange of tax information was reached with New Zealand in March 2007.

Government

The Governor of the Netherlands Antilles, appointed by the Dutch Crown for a term of six years, represents the monarch of the Netherlands in the territory, and has executive power over external affairs. The Governor is assisted by an advisory council. Executive power in internal affairs is vested in the Council of Ministers. The Council is responsible to the Staten (parliament), which has 22 members elected by universal adult suffrage for four years (subject to dissolution). The administration of each island is conducted by its own Island Council, Executive Council and Lieutenant-Governor.

Defence

Although defence is the responsibility of the Netherlands, compulsory military service is laid down in an Antilles Ordinance. The Governor is the Commander-in-Chief of the armed forces in the islands, and a Dutch contingent is stationed in Willemstad, Curaçao. The Netherlands also operates a Coast Guard Force (to combat organized crime and drugs-smuggling), based at St Maarten and Aruba. In May 1999 the US air force and navy began patrols from a base on Curaçao to combat the transport of illegal drugs.

Economic Affairs

In 2007 the gross national income (GNI) of the Netherlands Antilles, measured at current prices, was an estimated US $3,452m., equivalent to some $18,017 per head. Gross domestic product (GDP) was some $3,463m. in 2007 (equivalent to $17,894 per head), according to UN estimates. In 2000–07 the population increased at an average annual rate of 0.8%, while GDP per head increased, in real terms, by an average of 1.9% per year during 2000–07. According to UN estimates, GDP increased, in real terms, at an average annual rate of 1.0% in 2000–07; real GDP increased by 0.9% in 2007.

Agriculture, together with forestry, fishing and mining, contributed only 0.7% of GDP in 2004. The sector employed an average of 1.4% of the working population on Curaçao in 2005–07. Some 8% of the total land area is cultivated. The chief products are aloes (Bonaire is a major exporter), sorghum, divi-divi, groundnuts, beans, fresh vegetables and tropical fruit. A bitter variety of orange is used in the production of Curaçao liqueur. There is also some fishing.

Industry (comprising manufacturing, construction, power and water, but excluding mining) contributed 16.5% of GDP in 2004, and employed an average of 15.9% of the working population on Curaçao in 2005–07.

The mining and quarrying sector employed only 0.3% of the working population on Curaçao in 2000. Apart from some phosphates on Curaçao (exploited until the mid-1980s), and some limestone and salt on Bonaire, the islands have no other significant mineral reserves. Aggregate is quarried on St Maarten and consumed primarily by the local construction industry.

Manufacturing contributed 5.9% of GDP in 2004, and employed an average of 6.6% of the working population on Curaçao in 2005–07; activities include food-processing, production of Curaçao liqueur, and the manufacture of paint, paper, soap and cigarettes. Bonaire has a textile factory, and Curaçao's 'free zone' is of considerable importance in the economy, but the 'Windward Islands' have very few manufacturing activities. Petroleum-refining (using petroleum imported from Venezuela) is the islands' principal industrial activity, with the Curaçao refinery leased to the Venezuelan state petroleum company. Production capacity at the refinery was 116.8m. barrels per year in 2001, according to the US Geological Survey; however, industrial action in Venezuela led to the closure of the refinery during December 2002–March 2003, impacting heavily upon the islands' economy. Petroleum transshipment is also important, and ship repairs at the Curaçao dry dock make a significant contribution to the economy. In 2002 petroleum imports comprised 68.4% of total merchandise imports.

The services sector contributed 82.9% of GDP in 2004, and engaged an average of 82.7% of the employed labour force on Curaçao in 2005–07. The Netherlands Antilles is a major 'offshore' financial centre. In June 2000 the Netherlands Antilles was urged by the Organisation for Economic Co-operation and Development (OECD, based in Paris, France) to improve the accountability and transparency of its financial services; in response, the Government announced that it was to review its taxation legislation to comply more closely with OECD's standards. In April 2002 the Netherlands Antilles was removed from the list of those countries deemed to be 'un-co-operative tax havens' after OECD favourably assessed the Government's legislative amendments. In the same month an agreement was signed with the USA, pledging to share information on tax matters, with the aim of combating money-laundering and associated criminal activities. Nevertheless, in 2009 the Netherlands Antilles was included on OECD's so-called 'grey list' of territories that had committed to improving financial transparency, but had yet substantially to implement reform. The financial and business services sector contributed 31.6% of GDP in 2004, and employed an average of 17.6% of the Curaçao working population in 2005–07. Operational income from the 'offshore' sector increased significantly from the 1990s. A major industry for all the islands (particularly St Maarten) is tourism, which is the largest employer after the public sector. Significant improvements in the number of stop-over tourists, the number of cruise-ship passengers and the level of tourism revenue were recorded in 2003 and 2004. Figures for the whole of the latter year were the best since 1994. Tourism continued to improve in 2004–07. The number of cruise-ship passengers visiting Bonaire, Curaçao and St Maarten alone increased further, to 1,860,448, in 2007. In addition to tourism, Curaçao, in particular, has sought to establish itself as a centre for regional trade, exploiting its excellent harbours. In 1998 a free trade zone was established at the island's airport, which further enhanced Curaçao's entrepôt status.

In 2007 the Netherlands Antilles recorded a visible trade deficit of US $1,866.7m., and there was a deficit of $589.7m. on the current account of the balance of payments. The petroleum industry dominates the trade figures of the Netherlands Antilles, particularly of the 'Leeward Islands'. In 2002 the principal source of imports (60.4%) was Venezuela (which provides crude petroleum), and the principal market for exports (22.1%) was the USA. The USA is an important trading partner for all the islands of the Netherlands Antilles, as are the Netherlands and other Caribbean countries. Petroleum is the principal commodity for both import and export, and accounted for 68.4% of imports and 94.7% of exports in 2002. The Netherlands Antilles also imports machinery and transport equipment, manufactured goods, and chemicals and related products, while it exports aloes, Curaçao liqueur and some light manufactures.

In 2006 the general Government (including island governments) recorded a budgetary deficit of NA Fl. 153.7m., which was equivalent to 2.7% of GDP in 2004. In 2007 the central Government recorded a deficit of NA Fl. 94.6m. on its budget. The administrations of the islands tend to operate with deficits. At the end 2006 the combined public domestic debts of the central Government and the island Government of Curaçao were NA Fl. 4,698.6m. (72.0% of GDP). Total foreign debt stood at NA Fl. 820.8m. (12.6% of GDP). The average annual rate of inflation was 2.2% in 2000–07; consumer prices increased by an average of 3.3% in 2006 and by 3.0% in 2007. The rate of unemployment in the labour force was an estimated 15.1% for the Netherlands Antilles as a whole in June 2005. According to a sample survey of the labour force, 12.0% of the Curaçao work-force were unemployed in 2005–07. Figures from the 2001 census showed that the rate of unemployment in St Maarten stood at 12.2%, with the rate of youth unemployment at 24.1%.

The Netherlands Antilles, as part of the Kingdom of the Netherlands, has the status of an Overseas Territory in association with the European Union (see p. 255). The Netherlands Antilles enjoys observer status in the Caribbean Community and Common Market (CARICOM, see p. 206).

The relative isolation of the individual islands has led to the development of semi-independent economies, and economic conditions vary considerably between them. Notwithstanding, the Netherlands Antilles experienced relatively strong economic growth in the early 1990s, but, owing mainly to a decline in both the financial services and the petroleum-refining sectors, the next decade witnessed a progressive weakening of the economy, leading to a prolonged recession, high unemployment and increasing rates of emigration. Following stringent measures announced by the Pourier Government in 2001, the Dutch Government released NA Fl. 153m. (to be spent in 2002–06) to encourage sustained economic development and to support the Netherlands Antilles Government in improving the quality of its administration and education systems. The Netherlands approved the release of €125m. in additional funds in 2003, and the Dutch and Netherlands Antillean Governments agreed on a more prominent role for the central bank in the monitoring and implementation of the IMF targets. Some optimism was engendered by the improving tourism industry: the addition of a new US $87m. terminal at the Princess Juliana International Airport on St Maarten in October 2006, expanding the airport's passenger-handling capabilities by 2.5m., was expected to result in increased visitor numbers. Growth in activity in Curaçao's free trade zone and a consequent increase in arrivals from Venezuela and the Dominican Republic was reportedly an important boost for the tourism and retail sectors. The tourism industry continued to expand in 2008, particularly in Curaçao, where six new resorts were being constructed and five existing ones were expanded. In the second quarter of 2008 tourism visitors from Venezuela increased year-on-year by 143%. However, because of the favourable fixed exchange rate in the Netherlands Antilles and a limit to how much US currency Venezuelans can buy, many Venezuelan visitors travel to Curaçao in order to purchase dollars, which they then sell on the 'black market' at an inflated exchange rate. The lowering of Venezuelans' travel allowances was expected negatively to affect the Netherlands Antilles tourism sector—Venezuelans represent typically one-third of all arrivals to the islands. The recession in the USA in 2009 was also expected to hurt tourism numbers. Under the agreement to dissolve the Netherlands Antilles (see Recent History), the Dutch Government was to restructure some 70% of the islands' public debt, a large proportion of which was owed to the Netherlands. The three islands to gain municipal status (Bonaire, St Eustatius and Saba) following secession were expected to start to benefit from an enhanced association with the Netherlands from 2009. Dutch financial relief for Curaçao was dependent on the outcome of the 15 May referendum on proposed secession: only a 'yes' vote would release funds and debt relief from the Netherlands. Real GDP growth was estimated at 2.0% in 2008, while in 2009 the economy was forecast to remain at 2008 levels as the global economic downturn took effect.

Education

Education was made compulsory in 1992. The islands' educational facilities are generally of a high standard. The education system is the same as that of the Netherlands. Dutch is used as the principal language of instruction in schools on the 'Leeward Islands', while English is used in schools on the 'Windward Islands'. Instruction in Papiamento (using a different spelling system from that adopted by Aruba) has been introduced in primary schools. Primary education begins at six years of age and lasts for six years. Secondary education lasts for a further five years. In 2003/04 enrolment in all levels of education, with the exception of primary schools, was equivalent to 88% of students in the relevant age categories. The University of the Netherlands Antilles, sited on Curaçao, had 2,032 students in 2006/07. In April 2002 the Netherlands Government made more than €12.7m. available for improvements to education provision in the Netherlands Antilles. In 1995 local government expenditure on education in the Antilles of the Five was NA Fl. 178.9m. (19.3% of total spending by the island governments).

Public Holidays

2009: 1 January (New Year's Day), 19 January (Bonaire only: Carnival Rest Day), 23 February (Curaçao and Bonaire only: Lenten Carnival), 10–13 April (Easter), 30 April (Queen's Day), 1 May (Labour Day), 8 May (St Maarten, Saba and St Eustatius only: Celebration of World War II Victory), 21 May (Ascension Day), 1 June (St Maarten, Saba and St Eustatius only: Whit Monday), 1 July (Emancipation Day), 2 July (Curaçao Day), 21 July (St Maarten, Saba and St Eustatius only: Schoelcher Day), 31 July (Carnival), 6 September (Bonaire Day), 21 October (Antillian Day), 1 November (St Maarten, Saba and St Eustatius only: All Saints' Day), 11 November (St Maarten Day), 16 November (St Eustatius Day), 6 December (Saba Day), 15 December (St Maarten, Saba and St Eustatius only: Kingdom Day), 25–26 December (Christmas).

2010: 1 January (New Year's Day), 19 January (Bonaire only: Carnival Rest Day), 4 February (Curaçao and Bonaire only: Lenten Carnival), 2–5 April (Easter), 30 April (Queen's Day), 1 May (Labour Day), 8 May (St Maarten, Saba and St Eustatius only: Celebration of World War II Victory), 13 May (Ascension Day), 24 May (St Maarten, Saba and St Eustatius only: Whit Monday), 1 July (Emancipation Day), 2 July (Curaçao Day), 21 July (St Maarten, Saba and St Eustatius only: Schoelcher Day), 31 July (Carnival), 6 September (Bonaire Day), 21 October (Antillian Day), 1 November (St Maarten, Saba and St Eustatius only: All Saints' Day), 11 November (St Maarten Day), 16 November (St Eustatius Day), 6 December (Saba Day), 15 December (St Maarten, Saba and St Eustatius only: Kingdom Day), 25–26 December (Christmas).

Weights and Measures

The metric system is in force.

Statistical Survey

Sources (unless otherwise stated): Centraal Bureau voor de Statistiek, Fort Amsterdam, Willemstad, Curaçao; tel. (9) 461-1031; fax (9) 461-1696; internet www.central-bureau-of-statistics.an; Bank van de Nederlandse Antillen, Simon Bolivar Plein 1, Willemstad, Curaçao; tel. (9) 434-5500; fax (9) 461-5004; e-mail info@centralbank.an; internet www.centralbank.an.

AREA AND POPULATION

Area (sq km): Curaçao 444; Bonaire 288; St Maarten (Dutch sector) 34; St Eustatius 21; Saba 13; Total 800 (309 sq miles).

Population: 189,474 at census of 27 January 1992 (excluding adjustment for underenumeration, estimated at 3.2%); 175,653 (males 82,521, females 93,132) at census of 29 January 2001; 197,184 at 1 January 2008 (estimate). *By Island* (at 1 January 2008, estimates): Curaçao 140,796; Bonaire 12,103; St Maarten (Dutch sector) 40,007; St Eustatius 2,754; Saba 1,524.

Density (per sq km, 1 January 2008, estimates): Curaçao 317.1; Bonaire 42.0; St Maarten (Dutch sector) 1,176.7; St Eustatius 131.1; Saba 117.2; Total 246.5.

Principal Town: Willemstad (capital), population (incl. suburbs, UN estimate) 120,000 at mid-2007. Source: UN, *World Urbanization Prospects: The 2007 Revision*.

Births, Marriages and Deaths (2007 unless otherwise indicated): Registered live births 2,554; Registered marriages 1,104 (marriage rate 5.8 per 1,000) in 2006; Registered deaths 1,337 (death rate 6.8 per 1,000). *2008:* Birth rate 12.3 per 1,000; death rate 7.9 per 1,000. Source: Pan American Health Organization.

Life Expectancy (years at birth): 75.3 (males 71.5; females 78.9) in 2008. Source: Pan American Health Organization.

Economically Active Population (sample survey, Curaçao only, persons aged 15 years and over, average 2005–07): Agriculture, forestry, fishing and mining 747; Manufacturing 3,563; Electricity, gas and water 822; Construction 4,157; Wholesale and retail trade, repairs 9,559; Hotels and restaurants 4,358; Transport, storage and communications 3,226; Financial intermediation 3,976; Real estate, renting and business activities 5,504; Public administration, defence and social security 5,156; Education 2,690; Health and social work 4,561; Other community, social and personal services 3,389; Private households with employed persons 1,998; Extra-territorial organizations and bodies 73; *Total employed* 53,779; Unemployed 7,346; *Total labour force* 61,125.

HEALTH AND WELFARE

Total Fertility Rate (children per woman, 2008): 1.9.

Under-5 Mortality Rate (per 1,000 live births, 2006): 16.8.

Physicians (per 1,000 head, 1999): 1.4.

Hospital Beds (per 1,000 head, 2002): 7.24.

Health Expenditure (% of GDP, 2005): 4.8.

Source: mostly Pan American Health Organization.

For other sources and definitions, see explanatory note on p. vi.

AGRICULTURE, ETC.

Livestock ('000 head, year ending September 2007, FAO estimates): Cattle 0.7; Pigs 2.6; Goats 13.6; Sheep 9.1; Chickens 140.

Livestock Products (metric tons, 2007, FAO estimates): Pig meat 200; Chicken meat 300; Cows' milk 450; Hen eggs 530.

Fishing (metric tons, live weight, 2006): Skipjack tuna 3,042; Yellowfin tuna 1,939; Bigeye tuna 416; *Total catch* (incl. others) 6,247 (FAO estimate).

Source: FAO.

MINING

Production ('000 metric tons, 2003, estimate): Salt 500. *2004–06:* Production assumed to be unchanged from 2003 (estimates). Source: US Geological Survey.

INDUSTRY

Production ('000 metric tons, 2004, unless otherwise indicated): Jet fuel 790; Kerosene 46; Residual fuel oils 4,188; Lubricating oils 384; Petroleum bitumen (asphalt) 994; Liquefied petroleum gas 118; Motor spirit (petrol) 1,716; Aviation gasoline 21; Distillate fuel oils (gas-diesel oil) 2,202; Sulphur (recovered) 30 (2002); Electric energy (million kWh) 1,248 (2005).

Sources: mainly UN, *Industrial Commodity Statistics Yearbook*, and US Geological Survey.

FINANCE

Currency and Exchange Rates: 100 cents = 1 Netherlands Antilles gulden (guilder) or florin (NA Fl.). *Sterling, Dollar and Euro Equivalents* (31 December 2008): £1 sterling = NA Fl. 2.609; US $1 = NA Fl. 1.790; €1 = NA Fl. 2.491; NA Fl. 100 = £38.32 = $55.87 = €40.14. *Exchange Rate:* In December 1971 the central bank's mid-point rate was fixed at US $1 = NA Fl. 1.80. In 1989 this was adjusted to $1 = NA Fl. 1.79. The US dollar also circulates on St Maarten.

Central Government Budget (NA Fl. million, 2007): *Revenue:* Tax revenue 710.7 (Taxes on property 44.6, Taxes on goods and services 492.3, Taxes on international trade and transactions 166.1, Other taxes 7.7); Non-tax revenue 95.6 (Entrepreneurial and property income 77.8, Administrative fees and charges, non-industrial and incidental sales 16.5, Other 1.3); Grants (from other levels of government, excluding overseas development aid) 30.8; Total 837.2. *Expenditure:* Wages and salaries 312.2; Other goods and services 105.7; Interest payments 175.3; Subsidies 0.0; Current transfers 324.2; Capital expenditure (incl. transfers and net lending) 14.4; Total 931.8.

International Reserves (US $ million at 31 December 2007): Gold (national valuation) 244; Foreign exchange 661; Total 905. Source: IMF, *International Financial Statistics.*

Money Supply (NA Fl. million at 31 December 2007): Currency outside banks 304.4; Demand deposits at commercial banks 1,433.8; Total (incl. others) 1,786.0. Source: IMF, *International Financial Statistics.*

Cost of Living (Consumer Price Index; base: 2000 = 100): All items 109.6 in 2005; 113.1 in 2006; 116.5 in 2007. Source: IMF, *International Financial Statistics.*

Gross Domestic Product (US $ million at constant 1990 prices): 2,334 in 2005; 2,355 in 2006; 2,377 in 2007. Source: UN Statistics Division, National Accounts Main Aggregates Database.

Expenditure on the Gross Domestic Product (million NA Fl. at current prices, 2007): Final consumption expenditure 4,790 (Government 1,364, Households and non-profit institutions serving households 3,426); Gross fixed capital formation 1,573; Change in inventories 53; *Total domestic expenditure* 6,416; Exports of goods and services 5,473; *Less* Imports of goods and services 5,687; Statistical discrepancy (relating to the disparity between the expenditure and production approaches to GDP) –3; *GDP in market prices* 6,199. Source: UN Statistics Division, National Accounts Main Aggregates Database.

Gross Domestic Product (million NA Fl. at current prices, 2004): Agriculture, fishing, mining, etc. 35.7; Manufacturing 311.7; Electricity, gas and water 263.7; Construction 286.8; Wholesale and retail trade 678.8; Hotels and restaurants 219.5; Transport, storage and communications 553.7; Financial intermediation 808.0; Real estate, renting and business activities 848.1; Public administration, defence, etc. 444.9; Education 194.0; Health care and social services 266.4; Other community, social and personal services 305.8; Private households with employed persons 21.8; *Sub-total* 5,238.9; *Less* Financial intermediation services indirectly measured 123.1; *Gross value added at basic prices* 5,115.8; Taxes, less subsidies, on products 549.0; *Gross domestic product in market prices* 5,665.0.

Balance of Payments (US $ million, 2007): Exports of goods f.o.b. 676.5; Imports of goods f.o.b. –2,543.2; *Trade balance* –1,866.7; Exports of services 2,099.7; Imports of services –802.6; *Balance on goods and services* –569.6; Other income received 175.8; Other income paid –165.6; *Balance on goods, services and income* –559.4; Current transfers received 296.4; Current transfers paid –326.8; *Current balance* –589.7; Capital account (net) 121.6; Direct investment abroad 3.2; Direct investment from abroad 231.8; Portfolio investment assets –67.9; Portfolio investment liabilities –9.6; Financial derivatives assets –4.2; Other investment assets 427.7; Other investment liabilities –66.2; Net errors and omissions 82.4; *Overall balance* 129.2. Source: IMF, *International Financial Statistics.*

EXTERNAL TRADE

Principal Commodities (US $ million, 2002): *Imports c.i.f.:* Food and live animals 145.5; Petroleum, petroleum products, etc. 1,552.1 (Crude petroleum 1,354.4); Basic manufactures 110.4; Machinery and transport equipment 126.3 (Road vehicles 72.9); Total (incl. others) 2,268.5. *Exports f.o.b.:* Refined petroleum products 1,609.0; Total (incl. others) 1,699.2. Source: UN, *International Trade Statistics Yearbook.*

Principal Trading Partners (US $ million, 2002): *Imports c.i.f.:* Colombia 30.3; Germany 39.0; Iraq 151.1; Japan 36.7; Netherlands 187.4; USA 305.1; Venezuela 1,370.9; Total (incl. others) 2,268.5. *Exports f.o.b.:* Antigua and Barbuda 22.0; Aruba 22.7; Bahamas 129.9; Belize 26.1; Canada 68.6; Colombia 18.2; Cuba 61.5; El Salvador 80.0; Guatemala 66.5; Guyana 69.7; Haiti 34.2; Honduras 74.2; Netherlands 73.7; Nicaragua 36.3; Panama 68.0; Suriname 24.1; United Arab Emirates 40.6; USA 375.0; Venezuela 169.9; Total (incl. others) 1,699.2. Source: UN, *International Trade Statistics Yearbook.*

TRANSPORT

Road Traffic (Curaçao and Bonaire, motor vehicles registered, excl. government-owned vehicles, 2004): Passenger cars 64,729; Lorries 14,873; Buses 462; Taxis 218; Other cars 207; Motorcycles 1,498.

Shipping: *International Sea-borne Freight Traffic* (Curaçao, TEUs moved, 2004): 82,087. *Merchant Fleet* (registered at 31 December 2007): Number of vessels 172; Total displacement 1,264,043 grt (Source: Lloyd's Register-Fairplay, *World Fleet Statistics*).

Civil Aviation (aircraft landings): *Bonaire* (2005): 15,900 (Commercial 13,577). *Curaçao* (2003): 20,902 (Commercial 18,066).

TOURISM

Tourist Arrivals: *Stop-overs:* 770,187 in 2005; 782,161 in 2006; 862,116 in 2007. *Cruise-ship Passengers* (Bonaire, Curaçao and St Maarten only): 1,804,495 in 2005; 1,805,040 in 2006; 1,860,448 in 2007.

Tourism Receipts (NA Fl. million, incl. passenger transport): 1,683.5 in 2002; 1,761.0 in 2003; 1,906.5 in 2004.

COMMUNICATIONS MEDIA

Radio Receivers (1997): 217,000 in use.

Television Receivers (1999): 71,000 in use.

Telephones (2004): 81,000 main lines in use.

Mobile Cellular Telephones (2005): 200,000 subscribers.

Internet Users (1999, UN estimate): 2,000.

Daily Newspapers: 6 titles (estimated circulation 70,000 copies per issue) in 1996; 5 in 2004.

Sources: UNESCO, *Statistical Yearbook*; UNESCO Institute for Statistics; UN, *Statistical Yearbook*; International Telecommunication Union.

EDUCATION

Pre-primary (2002/03): 5,972 pupils; 309 teachers.

Primary (2002/03): 22,667 pupils; 1,145 teachers.

General Secondary (2002/03): 9,180 pupils; 639 teachers.

Vocational (2002/03): 6,088 pupils; 542 teachers.

Tertiary (2001/02): 2,285 students; 340 teachers.

English Language Secondary (2000/01): 377 pupils.

Special Education (2000/01): 2,337 pupils; 178 teachers.

Teacher Training (2000/01): 133 students; 22 teachers.

Adult Literacy Rate (2007, UNESCO estimates): 96.4% (males 96.3%; females 96.4%).

Source: partly UNESCO Institute for Statistics.

Directory

The Constitution

The form of government for the Netherlands Antilles is embodied in the Charter of the Kingdom of the Netherlands, which came into force on 20 December 1954. The Netherlands, the Netherlands Antilles and, since 1986, Aruba each enjoy full autonomy in domestic and internal affairs and are united on a basis of equality for the protection of their common interests and the granting of mutual assistance.

The monarch of the Netherlands is represented in the Netherlands Antilles by the Governor, who is appointed by the Dutch Crown for a term of six years. The central Government of the Netherlands Antilles appoints a Minister Plenipotentiary to represent the Antilles in the Government of the Kingdom. Whenever the Netherlands Council of Ministers is dealing with matters coming under the heading of joint affairs of the realm (in practice mainly foreign affairs and defence), the Council assumes the status of Council of Ministers of the Kingdom. In that event, the Minister Plenipotentiary appointed by the Government of the Netherlands Antilles takes part, with full voting powers, in the deliberations.

A legislative proposal regarding affairs of the realm and applying to the Netherlands Antilles as well as to the 'metropolitan' Netherlands is sent, simultaneously with its submission, to the Staten Generaal (the Netherlands parliament) and to the Staten (parliament) of the Netherlands Antilles. The latter body can report in writing to the Staten Generaal on the draft Kingdom Statute and designate one or more special delegates to attend the debates and furnish information in the meetings of the Chambers of the Staten Generaal. Before the final vote on a draft the Minister Plenipotentiary has the right to express an opinion on it. If he disapproves of the draft, and if in the Second Chamber a three-fifths' majority of the votes cast is not obtained, the discussions on the draft are suspended and further deliberations take place in the Council of Ministers of the Kingdom. When special delegates attend the meetings of the Chambers this right devolves upon the delegates of the parliamentary body designated for this purpose.

The Governor has executive power in external affairs, which he exercises in co-operation with the Council of Ministers. He is assisted

NETHERLANDS DEPENDENCIES

by an advisory council, which consists of at least five members appointed by him.

Executive power in internal affairs is vested in the nominated Council of Ministers, responsible to the Staten. The Netherlands Antilles Staten consists of 22 members, who are elected by universal adult suffrage for four years (subject to dissolution). Each island forms an electoral district. Curaçao elects 14 members, Bonaire three members, St Maarten three members and Saba and St Eustatius one member each. In the islands where more than one member is elected, the election is by proportional representation. Inhabitants have the right to vote if they have Dutch nationality and have reached 18 years of age. Voting is not compulsory. Each island territory also elects its Island Council (Curaçao 21 members, Bonaire 9, St Maarten 7, St Eustatius and Saba 5), and its internal affairs are managed by an executive council, consisting of the Gezaghebber (Lieutenant-Governor), and a number of commissioners. The central Government of the Netherlands Antilles has the right to annul any local island decision which is in conflict with the public interest or the Constitution. Control of the police, communications, monetary affairs, health and education remain under the jurisdiction of the central Government.

On 1 January 1986 Aruba acquired separate status (*status aparte*) within the Kingdom of the Netherlands. However, in economic and monetary affairs there is a co-operative union between Aruba and the Antilles of the Five, known as the 'Union of the Netherlands Antilles and Aruba'.

The islands of Saba, Bonaire and St Eustatius ratified an agreement with the Government of the Netherlands on 12 October 2006 under which they would be redesignated as 'special municipalities' of the Kingdom of the Netherlands. A further accord was signed by St Maarten and Curaçao on 28 November 2006 and 9 July 2007, respectively, confirming these islands' secession from the federation to achieve a degree of independent governance and status similar to that enjoyed by Aruba. While the transition process was well advanced by mid-2009, final dissolution of the Netherlands Antilles was not expected until 2010.

The Government

HEAD OF STATE

Queen of the Netherlands: HM Queen BEATRIX.
Governor: Dr FRITZ M. DE LOS SANTOS GOEDGEDRAG.

COUNCIL OF MINISTERS
(April 2009)

A coalition of the Partido Antía Restrukturá (PAR), the Movimentu Antiyas Nobo (MAN), the Frente Obrero i Liberashon 30 di mei (FOL), the Partido Nashonal di Pueblo (PNP), the National Alliance (NA), the Unión Patriótico Bonairiano (UPB), the Democratic Partij—Statia (DP—StE) and the Windward Islands People's Movement (WIPM).

Prime Minister and Minister of General Affairs and Foreign Relations: EMILY DE JONGH-ELHAGE (PAR).
Deputy Prime Minister and Minister of Finance: ERSILIA T. M. DE LANNOOY (PNP).
Minister of Economic Affairs and Labour: ELVIS E. J. TJIN ASJOE (UPB).
Minister of Constitutional Affairs and the Interior: ROLAND E. DUNCAN (NA).
Minister of Justice: DAVID A. DICK (PAR).
Minister of Education and Culture and of Public Health and Social Development: OMAYRA VICTORIA ELISABETH LEEFLANG (PAR).
Minister of Transport and Telecommunications: MAURICE H. P. P. ADRIAENS (FOL).
State Secretary of Constitutional Affairs and the Interior, with responsibility for the Transfer of Tasks and Authority: HUBERT MARTIS.
State Secretary of Finance, with responsibility for Tax Affairs: ALEX ROSARIA.
State Secretary of Finance, with responsibility for the Solidarity Fund: ALEX ROSARIA.
State Secretary of Justice, with responsibility for Police Affairs and the Penal Institution of the Windward Isles: E. C. SIMMONS.
State Secretary of Health, with responsibility for Medical Care in the Windward Isles and Bonaire: JOAN A. BERKEL (NA).
Minister Plenipotentiary and Member of the Council of Ministers for the Realm of the Netherlands Antilles in the Netherlands: PAUL R. J. COMENENCIA (PAR).
Minister Plenipotentiary for the Realm of the Netherlands Antilles in Washington, DC (USA): NORBERTO V. RIBEIRO.

The Netherlands Antilles

Attorney-General of the Netherlands Antilles: DICK A. PIAR.

MINISTRIES

Office of the Governor: Fort Amsterdam 2, Willemstad, Curaçao; tel. (9) 461-1289; fax (9) 461-1412; e-mail rojer@kgna.an; internet www.gouverneur.an.
Ministry of Constitutional Affairs and the Interior: Willemstad, Curaçao.
Ministry for Economic Affairs and Labour: Directorate of Labour, Schouwburgweg 22, Willemstad, Curaçao; tel. (9) 461-9999; fax (9) 461-5553; e-mail info@diraz.an; internet www.diraz.an.
Ministry of Education and Culture: Schouwburgweg 24–26 (APNA Bldg), Willemstad, Curaçao; tel. (9) 434-3711; fax (9) 462-4471; e-mail minoc@gov.an; internet www.minoc.an; Dep. Dir FLORENTINA NG.
Ministry of Finance: Pietermaai 17, Willemstad, Curaçao; tel. (9) 432-8000; fax (9) 461-3339; e-mail g.d.dirfin@curinfo.an.
Ministry of Foreign Affairs: Plasa Horacio Hoyer 9, Willemstad, Curaçao; tel. (9) 461-1866; fax (9) 461-1268.
Ministry of Justice: Willhelminaplein, Willemstad, Curaçao; tel. (9) 463-0650; fax (9) 465-8083.
Ministry of Public Health and Social Development: Santa Rosaweg 122, Willemstad, Curaçao; tel. (9) 736-3530; fax (9) 736-3531; e-mail vornil@cura.net.
Ministry of Transport: Fort Amsterdam 17, Willemstad, Curaçao; tel. (9) 461-3988.
Office of the Minister Plenipotentiary for the Netherlands Antilles: Kabinet van de Gevolmachtigde Minister van de Nederlanse Antillen, Badhuisweg 175, POB 90706, 2509 LS The Hague, Netherlands; tel. (70) 3066111; fax (70) 3066110; e-mail info@antillenhuis.nl; internet www.antillenhuis.nl.

GEZAGHEBBERS
(Lieutenant-Governors)

Bonaire: HERBERT F. DOMACASSE, Wilhelminaplein 1, Kralendijk, Bonaire; tel. 717-5330; fax 717-5100; e-mail gezag@bonairelive.com.
Curaçao: LIZANNE M. RICHARDS-DINDIAL, Voorlichtingscentrum 'Bentana di informashon', Johan van Walbeeckplein 11, Willemstad, Curaçao; tel. (9) 433-3131; fax (9) 433-3130; e-mail info@curacao-gov.an; internet www.curacao-gov.an.
Saba: SYDNEY A. E. SORTON, The Bottom, Saba; tel. 416-3215; fax 416-3274.
St Eustatius: HYDEN C. I. GITTENS, Oranjestad, St Eustatius; tel. 318-2552; fax 318-2324; e-mail lt.governor@statiagovernment.com; internet www.statiagovernment.com.
St Maarten: FRANKLYN E. RICHARDS, Government Administration Bldg, Clem Labega Sq., POB 943, Philipsburg, St Maarten; tel. 542-6085; fax 542-4172; e-mail hodge@governorsxm.com; internet www.governorsxm.com.

Legislature

STATEN

Speaker: DWIGNO PURIEL.
General Election, 27 January 2006

Party	Seats
Partido Antía Restrukturá	5
Movimentu Antiyas Nobo	3
Frente Obrero i Liberashon 30 di mei	2
Partido Nashonal di Pueblo	2
Forsa Kòrsou	2
National Alliance	2
Unión Patriótico Bonairiano	2
Democratische Partij—St Maarten	1
Democratische Partij—Bonaire	1
Democratische Partijy—Statia	1
Windward Islands People's Movement	1
Total	**22**

Political Organizations

Democratische Partij—Bonaire (DP—B) (Democratic Party—Bonaire): Kaya America 13A, POB 294, Kralendijk, Bonaire; tel. 717-8903; fax 717-5923; f. 1954; also known as Partido Democratico Boneriano; liberal; Leader JOPIE ABRAHAM.

Democratische Partij—Curaçao (DP—C) (Democratic Party—Curaçao): Neptunusweg 28, Willemstad, Curaçao; f. 1944; Leader NORBERT GEORGE.

Democratische Partij—Sint Maarten (DP—StM): Tamarind Tree Dr. 4, Union Rd, Cole Bay, St Maarten; tel. 543-1166; fax 542-4296; Leader SARAH WESCOTT-WILLIAMS.

Democratische Partij—Statia (DP—StE): Oranjestad, St Eustatius; Leader JULIAN WOODLEY.

Forsa Kòrsou: F. D. Rooseveltweg 347, Willemstad, Curaçao; tel. (9) 888-3041; fax (9) 888-3504; e-mail direktiva@forsakorsou.info; internet www.forsakorsou.info; Leader NELSON NAVARRO.

Frente Obrero i Liberashon 30 di mei (FOL) (Workers' Liberation Front of 30 May): Mayaguanaweg 16, Willemstad, Curaçao; tel. (9) 461-8105; f. 1969; socialist; Leaders ANTHONY GODETT, RIGNALD LAK, EDITHA WRIGHT.

Liste Ni'un Paso Atras (LNPA): Willemstad, Curaçao; Leader NELSON PIERRE.

Movimentu Antiyas Nobo (MAN) (Movement for a New Antilles): Landhuis Morgenster, Willemstad, Curaçao; tel. (9) 468-4781; f. 1971; socialist; Leader DOMINICO (DON) F. MARTINA.

Movimentu Sosial Laboral (MSL): Willemstad, Curaçao; Leader CÉSAR PRINCE.

National Alliance (NA): Philipsburg, St Maarten; internet www.sxmnationalalliance.org; Leader WILLIAM MARLIN.

Partido Antía Restrukturá (PAR) (Restructured Antilles Party): Fokkerweg 26, Unit 3, Willemstad, Curaçao; tel. (9) 465-2566; fax (9) 465-2622; e-mail omi7@ibm.net; internet www.cura.net/archives/par/frame.html; f. 1993; social-Christian ideology; Leader MIGUEL ARCHANGEL POURIER.

Partido Laboral Krusado Popular (PLKP): Winston Churchillweg 57, Willemstad, Curaçao; tel. (9) 868-1924; internet www.plkp.an; f. 1997; progressive; Leader ERROL A. COVA.

Partido Nashonal di Pueblo (PNP) (National People's Party): Winston Churchillweg 133, Willemstad, Curaçao; tel. (9) 869-6777; fax (9) 869-6688; f. 1948; also known as Nationale Volkspartij; social-Christian party; Pres. FAROE METRY; Leader ERSILIA DE LANNOOY.

People's Democratic Party (PDP): Philipsburg, St Maarten; tel. 542-2696; Leader MILLICENT DE WEEVER.

People's Progressive Alliance: Philipsburg, St Maarten; Leader GRACITA ARRINDELL.

Pueblo Soberano: Willemstad, Curaçao; Leader HERMAN WIELS.

Saba United Democratic Party (SUDP): Saba; tel. 416-3311; fax 416-3434; Leader STEVE HASSELL.

Saint Eustatius Alliance (SEA): Oranjestad, St Eustatius; Leader INGRID WHITFIELD-HOUTMAN.

Unión Patriótico Bonairiano (UPB) (Patriotic Union of Bonaire): Kaya Sabana 22, Kralendijk, Bonaire; tel. 717-8906; fax 717-5552; 2,134 mems; Christian democratic; Leader RAMONSITO T. BOOI; Sec.-Gen. C. V. WINKLAAR.

Windward Islands People's Movement (WIPM): Windwardside, POB 525, Saba; tel. 416-2244; Chair. and Leader RAY HASSELL; Sec.-Gen. DAVE LEVENSTONE.

Judicial System

Legal authority is exercised by the Court of First Instance (which sits in all the islands) and in appeal by the Joint High Court of Justice of the Netherlands Antilles and Aruba. The members of the Joint High Court of Justice sit singly as judges in the Courts of First Instance. The Chief Justice of the Joint High Court of Justice, its members (a maximum of 30) and the Attorneys-General of the Netherlands Antilles and of Aruba are appointed for life by the Dutch monarch, after consultation with the Governments of the Netherlands Antilles and Aruba. The Supreme Court of the Netherlands (based in The Hague) is the court of Final Instance for any appeal. Under a provision of the agreement for the dissolution of the five-island federation by December 2008 (subsequently revised to January 2010), reforms to the judicial system were to be implemented from 2007.

Joint High Court of Justice

Wilhelminaplein 4, Willemstad, Curaçao; tel. (9) 463-4111; fax (9) 461-8341; e-mail hofcur@cura.net.

Chief Justice of the Joint High Court: LISBETH HOEFDRAAD.

Secretary-Executive of the Joint High Court: M. E. N. ROJER-DE FREITAS (acting).

Religion

CHRISTIANITY

Most of the population are Christian, the predominant denomination being Roman Catholicism. According to the 1992 census, Roman Catholics formed the largest single group on four of the five islands: 82% of the population of Bonaire, 81% on Curaçao, 65% on Saba and 41% on St Maarten. On St Eustatius the Methodists formed the largest single denomination (31%). Of the other denominations, the main ones were the Anglicans and the Dutch Reformed Church. There were also small communities of Jews, Muslims and Bahá'ís.

Curaçaose Raad van Kerken (Curaçao Council of Churches): Periclesstraat 6, Willemstad, Curaçao; tel. (9) 465-3207; fax (9) 461-0733; e-mail ddtic@yahoo.com; f. 1958; six mem. churches; Chair. IDA VISSER; Exec. Sec. PAUL VAN DER WAAL.

The Roman Catholic Church

The Netherlands Antilles and Aruba together form the diocese of Willemstad, suffragan to the archdiocese of Port of Spain (Trinidad and Tobago). At 31 December 2006 the diocese numbered an estimated 224,809 adherents (about 78% of the total population). The Bishop participates in the Antilles Episcopal Conference, currently based in Trinidad and Tobago.

Bishop of Willemstad: Rt Rev. LUIGI ANTONIO SECCO, Bisdom, Breedestraat 31, Otrobanda, Willemstad, Curaçao; tel. (9) 462-5857; fax (9) 462-7437; e-mail bisdomwstad@curinfo.an.

The Anglican Communion

Saba, St Eustatius and St Maarten form part of the diocese of the North Eastern Caribbean and Aruba, within the Church in the Province of the West Indies. The Bishop is resident in The Valley, Anguilla.

Other Churches

Iglesia Protestant Uni (United Protestant Church): Fortkerk, Fort Amsterdam, Willemstad, Curaçao; tel. (9) 461-1139; fax (9) 465-7481; e-mail vpg-cur@curlink.com; internet www.vpg-curacao.com; f. 1825 by union of Dutch Reformed and Evangelical Lutheran Churches; associated with the World Council of Churches; Pres. MARITZA BEAUJON-BAKHUIS; 3 congregations; 11,280 adherents; 3,200 mems.

Methodist Church: Oranjestad, St Eustatius.

Other denominations active in the islands include the Moravian, Apostolic Faith, Wesleyan Holiness and Norwegian Seamen's Churches, the Baptists, Calvinists, Jehovah's Witnesses, Evangelists, Seventh-day Adventists, the Church of Christ and the New Testament Church of God.

JUDAISM

Congregation 'Shaarei Tsedek' Ashkenazi Orthodox Jewish Community: 37 Magdalenaweg, Willemstad, Curaçao; tel. and fax (9) 738-5949; e-mail rel_yes@yahoo.com; 140 mems; Rabbi ARIEL YESHURUN.

Reconstructionist Shephardi Congregation Mikvé Israel-Emanuel: Hanchi di Snoa 29, POB 322, Willemstad, Curaçao; tel. (9) 461-1067; fax (9) 465-4141; e-mail information@snoa.com; internet www.snoa.com; f. 1732 on present site; about 350 mems.

The Press

Algemeen Dagblad: ABCourant NV, Prof. Kernkampweg z/n, POB 725, Willemstad, Curaçao; tel. (9) 747-2200; fax (9) 747-2257; e-mail algemeen@antilliaansdagblad.com; internet www.antilliaansdagblad.com; daily; Dutch; Editor NOUD KÖPER.

Amigoe: Kaya Fraternan di Skèrpenè z/n, POB 577, Curaçao; tel. (9) 767-2000; fax (9) 767-4084; e-mail management@amigoe.com; internet www.amigoe.com; f. 1884; Christian; daily; evening; Dutch; Dir ERNEST VOGES; Editor-in-Chief WILLEM DA COSTA GOMEZ; circ. 12,000.

Bala: Noord Zapateer nst 13, Willemstad, Curaçao; tel. (9) 467-1646; fax (9) 467-1041; e-mail bala@cura.net; daily; Papiamento.

Beurs en Nieuwsberichten: A. M. Chumaceiro Blvd 5, POB 741, Willemstad, Curaçao; tel. (9) 465-4544; fax (9) 465-3411; f. 1935; daily; evening; Dutch; Editor L. SCHENK; circ. 8,000.

Bonaire Holiday: POB 569, Curaçao; tel. (9) 767-1403; fax (9) 767-2003; f. 1971; tourist guide; English; 3 a year; circ. 95,000.

Bonaire Reporter: Kaya Gob. Debrot 200-6, POB 407, Bonaire; tel. and fax 717-8988; e-mail info@bonairereporter.com; internet bonairereporter.com; English; weekly.

The Business Journal: Indjuweg 30A, Willemstad, Curaçao; tel. (9) 461-1367; fax (9) 461-1955; monthly; English.

NETHERLANDS DEPENDENCIES

Curaçao Holiday: POB 569, Curaçao; tel. (9) 767-1403; fax (9) 767-2003; f. 1960; tourist guide; English; 3 a year; circ. 300,000.

De Curaçaosche Courant: Frederikstraat 123, POB 15, Willemstad, Curaçao; tel. (9) 461-2766; fax (9) 462-6535; f. 1812; weekly; Dutch; Editor J. KORIDON.

Daily Herald: Bush Rd 22, POB 828, Philipsburg, St Maarten; tel. 542-5253; fax 542-5913; e-mail editorial@thedailyherald.com; internet www.thedailyherald.com; daily; English.

Extra: W. I. Compagniestraat 41, Willemstad, Curaçao; tel. (9) 462-4595; fax (9) 462-7575; e-mail redactie@extra.an; daily; morning; Papiamento; Man. R. YRAUSQUIN; Editor MIKE OEHLERS; circ. 20,000.

Newsletter of Curaçao Trade and Industry Association: Kaya Junior Salas 1, POB 49, Willemstad, Curaçao; tel. (9) 461-1210; fax (9) 461-5422; f. 1972; monthly; English and Dutch; economic and industrial paper.

Nobo: Scherpenheuvel w/n, POB 323, Willemstad, Curaçao; tel. (9) 467-3500; fax (9) 467-2783; daily; evening; Papiamento; Editor CARLOS DAANTJE; circ. 15,000.

Nos Isla: Refineria Isla (Curazao) SA, Emmastad, Curaçao; 2 a month; Papiamento; circ. 1,200.

La Prensa: W. I. Compagniestraat 41, Willemstad, Curaçao; tel. (9) 462-3850; fax (9) 462-5983; e-mail webmaster@laprensacur.com; internet news.laprensacur.com; f. 1929; daily; evening; Papiamento; Man. R. YRAUSQUIN; Editor SIGFRIED RIGAUD; circ. 10,750.

Saba Herald: The Level, Saba; tel. 416-2244; f. 1968; monthly; news, local history; Editor WILL JOHNSON; circ. 500.

St Maarten Guardian: Vlaun Bldg, Pondfill, POB 1046, Philipsburg, St Maarten; tel. 542-6022; fax 542-6043; e-mail guardian@sintmaarten.net; f. 1989; daily; English; Man. Dir RICHARD F. GIBSON; Man. Editor JOSEPH DOMINIQUE; circ. 4,000.

St Maarten Holiday: POB 569, Curaçao; tel. (9) 767-1403; fax (9) 767-2003; f. 1968; tourism guide; English; 3 a year; circ. 175,000.

Teen Times: c/o The Daily Herald, Bush Rd 22, POB 828, Philipsburg, St Maarten; tel. 542-5597; e-mail info@teentimes.com; for teenagers by teenagers; sponsored by The Daily Herald; English; Editor-in-Chief MICHAEL GRANGER.

Ultimo Noticia: Frederikstraat 123, Willemstad, Curaçao; tel. (9) 462-3444; fax (9) 462-6535; daily; morning; Papiamento; Editor A. A. JONCKHEER.

La Unión: Rotaprint NV, Willemstad, Curaçao; weekly; Papiamento.

NEWS AGENCY

Algemeen Nederlands Persbureau (ANP) (Netherlands): Panoramaweg 5, POB 439, Willemstad, Curaçao; tel. (9) 461-2233; fax (9) 461-7431; Representative RONNIE RENS.

Publishers

Curaçao Drukkerij en Uitgevers Maatschappij: Willemstad, Curaçao.

Drukkerij Scherpenheuvel NV: Scherpenheuvel, POB 60, Willemstad, Curaçao; tel. (9) 467-1134.

Drukkerij de Stad NV: W. I. Compagniestraat 41, POB 3011, Willemstad, Curaçao; tel. (9) 462-3566; fax (9) 462-2175; e-mail management@destad.an; internet www.destad.an; f. 1929; Dir KENRICK A. YRAUSQUIN.

Ediciones Populares: W. I. Compagniestraat 41, Willemstad, Curaçao; f. 1929; Dir RONALD YRAUSQUIN.

Holiday Publications: POB 569, Curaçao; tel. (9) 767-1403; fax (9) 767-2003.

Offsetdrukkerij Intergrafia NV: Esseweg 54, Willemstad, Curaçao; tel. (9) 464-3180.

Broadcasting and Communications

TELECOMMUNICATIONS

Digicel Curaçao: Schottegatweg Oost 19, Willemstad, Curaçao; tel. (9) 736-1056; fax (9) 736-1057; e-mail customercare@digicelcuracao.com; internet www.digicelcuracao.com; f. 1999; bought by Digicel (Ireland) in 2005; bought into Bonaire market through majority shareholding of Antilliano Por NV in April 2006; known as Curaçao Telecom until 2006; telephone and internet services; Digicel acquired mobile business of TELBO (Bonaire) in Dec. 2006; also operates in Aruba; Chair. DENIS O'BRIEN; CEO (Dutch Caribbean) HANS LUTE.

East Caribbean Cellular NV (ECC): 13 Richardson St, Philipsburg, St Maarten; tel. 542-4100; fax 542-5678; e-mail info@eastcaribbeancellular.com; internet www.eastcaribbeancellular.com; f. 1989.

Scarlet: Fokkerweg 26, Suite 106, Willemstad, Curaçao; tel. (9) 461-6063; fax (9) 461-8301; internet www.scarlet.an; telecommunications provider in Curaçao and St Maarten.

SMITCOMS NV (St Maarten International Telecommunications Services): Falcon Dr. No. 3, Harbor View, Philipsburg, St Maarten; tel. 542-9140; fax 542-9141; e-mail Sales@smitcoms.com; internet www.smitcoms.com; f. 2000; international telephone network provider; affiliated with TelEm group in Jan. 2006; Man. Dir ELDERT LOUISA (acting).

St Maarten Telephone Co (TelEm): C. A. Cannegieter St 17, POB 160, Philipsburg, St Maarten; tel. 542-2278; fax 543-0101; e-mail webmaster@sintmaarten.net; internet www.telemgroup.an; f. 1975; local fixed line services; also operates TelCell digital cellular service and TelNet internet service provider; sister company Smitcoms; 15,000 subscribers; Man. Dir CURTIS K. HAYNES.

Telefonia Bonairiano NV (TELBO NV): Kaya Libertador Simon Bolivar 8, POB 94, Bonaire; tel. 717-7000; fax 717-5007; e-mail telbo@telbo.an; internet www.telbo.net; f. 1983; fixed line telecommunications and internet service provider; TELBO's mobile operations on Bonaire were purchased by Digicel in December 2006; Gen. Man. EDSEL WINKLAAR.

United Telecom Services (UTS): UTS Headquarters, Rigelweg 2, Willemstad, Curaçao; tel. (9) 777-0101; fax (9) 777-1284; e-mail info@uts.an; internet www.uts.an; f. 1999 following merger of Antelecom NV (f. 1908) and SETEL (f. 1979); Antelecom and SETEL still operate under own names; Chair. DAVID DICK; Man. Dir HENDRIK J. EIKELENBOOM.

Servicio de Telekomunikashon (UTS Wireless Curaçao) (SETEL): UTS Headquarters, Rigelweg 2, Willemstad, Curaçao; tel. (9) 777-0101; fax (9) 777-1284; e-mail info@uts.an; internet www.uts.an; f. 1979; telecommunications equipment and network provider; forms part of UTS; state-owned, but privatization pending; Pres. ANGEL R. KOOK; Man. Dir JULIO CONSTANCIA; 400 employees.

BROADCASTING

Radio

Curom Broadcasting Inc: Roodeweg 64, POB 2169, Willemstad, Curaçao; tel. (9) 462-2020; fax (9) 462-5796; internet www.curom.com; f. 1933; broadcasts in English, Papiamento, Dutch and Spanish; Dir ORLANDO CUALES.

Mi 95: f. 1988; FM; music station, aimed at adults.

Z-86: news station.

88 Ròckòrsou: rock music station, aimed at young people.

Easy 97.9 FM: Arikokweg 19A, Willemstad, Curaçao; tel. (9) 462-3162; fax (9) 462-8712; e-mail radio@easyfm.com; internet www.easyfm.com; f. 1995; Dir KEVIN CARTHY.

Laser 101 (101.1 FM): Suite 2, 106 A. T. Illidge Rd, Philipsburg, St Maarten; tel. 543-2200; fax 543-2229; e-mail master@laser101.com; internet www.laser101.fm; 24 hours a day; music; English and Papiamento.

Radio Caribe: Ledaweg 35, Brievengat, Willemstad, Curaçao; tel. (9) 736-9555; fax (9) 736-9569; f. 1955; commercial station; programmes in Dutch, English, Spanish and Papiamento; Dir-Gen. C. R. HEILLEGGER.

Radiodifusión Boneriana NV: Kaya Gobernador Debrot 2, Kralendijk, Bonaire; tel. 717-8273; fax 717-8220; e-mail vdb@vozdibonaire.com; internet www.vozdibonaire.com; f. 1980; Owner FELICIANO DA SILVA PILOTO.

Alpha FM: broadcasts in Spanish.

Mega FM: broadcasts in Dutch.

Voz di Bonaire (PJB2) (Voice of Bonaire): broadcasts in Papiamento.

Radio Exito: Julianaplein 39, Curaçao; tel. (9) 462-5577; fax (9) 462-5580.

Radio Hoyer NV: Plasa Horacio Hoyer 21, Willemstad, Curaçao; tel. (9) 461-1678; fax (9) 461-6528; e-mail hoyer1@radiohoyer.com; internet www.radiohoyer.com; f. 1954; commercial; two stations: Radio Hoyer I (mainly Papiamento, also Spanish) and II (mainly Dutch, also English) in Curaçao; Man. Dir HELEN HOYER.

Radio Korsou FM: Bataljonweg 7, POB 3250, Willemstad, Curaçao; tel. (9) 737-3012; fax (9) 737-2888; e-mail master@korsou.com; internet www.korsou.com; f. 1976; 24 hrs a day; programmes in Papiamento and Dutch; Gen. Man. ALAN H. EVERTSZ.

Radio Tropical: Kaya W. F. G. Mensing, Willemstad, Curaçao; tel. (9) 465-0190; fax (9) 465-2470; e-mail tropi@cura.net; Dir DWIGHT RUDOLPHINA.

Trans World Radio (TWR): Kaya Gobernador N. Debrot 64, Kralendijk, Bonaire; tel. 717-8800; fax 717-8808; e-mail 800am@twr.org; internet www.twr.org; f. 1964; religious, educational and cultural station; programmes to South, Central and North America,

NETHERLANDS DEPENDENCIES

and Caribbean in five languages; Pres. LAUREN LIBBY; Station Dir JOSEPH BARKER.

Voice of St Maarten (PJD2 Radio): Plaza 21, Backstreet, POB 366, Philipsburg, St Maarten; tel. 542-2580; fax 542-4905; also operates PJD3 on FM (24 hrs); commercial; programmes in English; Gen. Man. DON R. HUGHES.

Voice of Saba (PJF1): The Bottom, POB 1, Saba; studio in St Maarten; tel. 546-3213; also operates The Voice of Saba FM; Man. MAX W. NICHOLSON.

There is a relay station for Radio Nederland on Bonaire.

Television

Antilliaanse Televisie Maatschappij NV (TeleCuraçao): Berg Ararat z/n, POB 415, Willemstad, Curaçao; tel. (9) 461-1288; fax (9) 461-4138; e-mail web@telecuracao.com; internet www.telecuracao.com; f. 1960; fmrly operated Tele-Aruba; commercial; owned by United Telecommunication Services; also operates cable service, offering programmes from US satellite television and two Venezuelan channels; Dir PAUL DE GEUS; Gen. Man. HUGO LEW JEN TAI.

Leeward Broadcasting Corporation—Television: Postbus 375, Philipsburg, St Maarten; tel. (5) 23491; transmissions for approx. 10 hours daily.

Five television channels can be received on Curaçao in total. Relay stations provide Bonaire with programmes from Curaçao, St Maarten with programmes from Puerto Rico, and Saba and St Eustatius with programmes from St Maarten and neighbouring islands. Curaçao has a publicly owned cable television service, TDS.

Finance

(cap. = capital; res = reserves; dep. = deposits; m. = million; br.(s) = branch(es); amounts in Netherlands Antilles guilders unless otherwise stated)

BANKING

Central Bank

Bank van de Nederlandse Antillen (Bank of the Netherlands Antilles): Simon Bolivar Plein 1, Willemstad, Curaçao; tel. (9) 434-5500; fax (9) 461-5004; e-mail info@centralbank.an; internet centralbank.an; f. 1828 as Curaçaosche Bank, name changed as above Jan. 1962; cap. 30.0m., res 339.8m., dep. 1,320.7m. (Dec. 2006); Chair. RALPH PALM; Pres. Dr EMSLEY D. TROMP; 2 brs in St Maarten and Bonaire.

Commercial Banks

Banco di Caribe NV: Schottegatweg Oost 205, POB 3785, Willemstad, Curaçao; tel. (9) 432-3000; fax (9) 461-5220; e-mail info@bancodicaribe.com; internet www.bancodicaribe.com; f. 1973; cap. 4.7m., res 121.1m., dep. 951.5m. (Dec. 2006); Chair. WILFRED J. CURIEL; CEO and Gen. Man. Dir EDUARDO DE KORT; Man. Dirs KENNETH ABRAHAM, PERCIVAL VIRGINIA; 5 brs.

CITCO Banking Corporation NV: Kaya Schottengatweg Oost 44, POB 707, Willemstad, Curaçao; tel. (9) 732-2322; fax (9) 732-2330; e-mail curacao-bank@citco.com; f. 1980 as Curaçao Banking Corpn NV; Man. Dir and Gen. Man. RONALD F. IRAUSQUIN; Man. Dirs CHARLES RUND, GLENDA E. C. SOON-TRAPENBERG, RUPERT E. WALLÉ.

FirstCaribbean International Bank (Curaçao) NV: De Ruyterkade 61, POB 3144, Willemstad, Curaçao; tel. (9) 433-8000; fax (9) 433-8198; e-mail bank.curacao@firstcaribbeanbank.com; internet www.firstcaribbeanbank.an; f. 1964 as ABN AMRO Bank NV; part of FirstCaribbean Group, based in Barbados; 91.5% owned by CIBC, Canada; Man. Dir W. M. (PIM) VAN DER BERG; 6 brs.

Fortis Bank (Curaçao) NV: Berg Ararrat 1, POB 3889, Willemstad, Curaçao; tel. (9) 463-9200; fax (9) 461-3769; internet www.fortisbank.com; f. 1952 as Pierson, Heldring and Pierson (Curaçao) NV; became Meespierson (Curaçao) NV in 1993, name changed as above in 2000; international banking/trust co; Man. Dir GREGORY ELIAS.

Girobank NV: Scharlooweg 35, Willemstad, Curaçao; tel. (9) 433-9999; fax (9) 461-7861; e-mail info@gironet.com; internet www.girobank.net; Man. Dir ERIC GARCIA.

Maduro & Curiel's Bank NV: Plaza Jojo Correa 2–4, POB 305, Willemstad, Curaçao; tel. (9) 466-1100; fax (9) 466-1122; e-mail info@mcb-bank.com; internet www.mcb-bank.com; f. 1916 as NV Maduro's Bank; merged with Curiel's Bank in 1931; affiliated with Bank of Nova Scotia NV, Toronto, Canada; br. in Bonaire; cap. 50.6m., res 137.7m., dep. 4,386.8m. (Dec. 2007); Chair. LIONEL CAPRILES; Man. Dirs WILLIAM H. L. FABRO, RON GOMES CASSERES; 31 brs.

Orco Bank NV: Dr Henry Fergusonweg 10, POB 4928, Willemstad, Curaçao; tel. (9) 737-2000; fax (9) 737-6741; internet www.orcobank.com; f. 1986; cap. 30.7m., res 27.5m., dep. 523.9m. (Dec. 1999); Chair. E. L. GARCIA; Man. Dirs R. KOELEWIJN, K. R. CANWORD; 1 br.

Rabobank Curaçao NV: Zeelandia Office Park, Kaya W. F. G. (Jombi), Mensing 14, POB 3876, Willemstad, Curaçao; tel. (9) 465-2011; fax (9) 465-2066; e-mail l.an.curacao.ops@rabobank.com; internet www.rabobank.com; f. 1978; cap. US $53.0m., res $17.8m., dep. $4,535.2m. (Dec. 2003); Chair. BERT HEEMSKERK; Gen. Man. J. S. KLEP.

RBTT Bank NV: Kaya Flamboyan 1, Willemstad; tel. (9) 763-8000; fax (9) 763-8449; e-mail info@tt.rbtt.com; internet www.rbtt.com; f. 1997 as Antilles Banking Corpn; name changed to RBTT Bank Antilles in 2001; name changed as above in 2002; cap. 114.5m., res 125.4m., dep. 2,770.1m. (Dec. 2006); Pres. RODNEY S. PRASAD; Chair. PETER J. JULY; 4 brs.

Windward Islands Bank Ltd: Clem Labega Sq. 7, POB 220, Philipsburg, St Maarten; tel. 542-2313; fax 542-4761; e-mail info@wib-bank.net; internet www.wib-bank.net; affiliated to Maduro & Curiel's Bank NV; f. 1960; cap. and res 53.2m., dep. 662.2m. (Dec. 2006); Man. Dir JAN J. BEAUJON.

'Offshore' Banks

Abu Dhabi International Bank NV: Kaya W. F. G. (Jombi), Mensing 36, POB 3141, Willemstad, Curaçao; tel. (9) 461-1299; fax (9) 461-5392; internet www.nbad.com; f. 1981; cap. US $20.0m., res $30.0m., dep. $112.2m. (Dec. 2006); Pres. QAMBAR AL MULLA; Man. Dir NAGY S. KOLTA.

FirstCaribbean International Wealth Management (Curaçao) NV: De Ruyterkade 61, Curaçao; tel. (9) 433-8000; fax (9) 433-8198; f. 1976 as ABN AMRO Bank Asset Management (Curaçao) NV; acquired by FirstCaribbean Bank in Dec. 2005; Man. Dir E. J. W. HERMENS.

F. Van Lanschot Bankiers (Curaçao) NV: Schottegatweg Oost 32, POB 4799, Willemstad, Curaçao; tel. (9) 737-1011; fax (9) 737-1086; e-mail info@vanlanschot.an; f. 1962; wholly owned by F. Van Lanschot Bankiers NV (Netherlands); Man. A. VAN GEEST.

Development Banks

Ontwikkelingsbank van de Nederlandse Antillen NV: Schottegatweg Oost 3C, POB 267, Willemstad, Curaçao; tel. (9) 747-3000; fax (9) 747-3320; e-mail obna@obna-bank.com; f. 1981; Man. Dir DENNIS CIJNTJE.

Stichting Korporashon pa Desaroyo di Korsou (Curaçao Development Corporation—KORPODEKO): Schottegatweg Oost 36, Willemstad, Curaçao; tel. (9) 738-1799; fax (9) 738-1766; e-mail info@korpodeko.an; internet www.korpodeko.an.

Savings Banks

Postspaarbank van de Nederlandse Antillen: Waaigatplein 1, Willemstad, Curaçao; tel. (9) 433-1100; fax (9) 461-7561; e-mail info@postpaarbank.com; f. 1905; post office savings bank; Chair. H. J. J. VICTORIA; cap. 21m.; 20 brs.

Spaar- en Beleenbank van Curaçao NV: MCB Salinja Bldg, Schottegatweg Oost 130, Willemstad, Curaçao; tel. (9) 466-1585; fax (9) 466-1590; e-mail chbsbb@mcb-bank.com.

There are also several mortgage banks and credit unions.

Banking Associations

Association of International Bankers in the Netherlands Antilles (IBNA): Chumaceiro Blvd 3, POB 220, Curaçao; tel. (9) 461-5367; fax (9) 461-5369; e-mail info@ibna.an; internet www.ibna.an; f. 1980; 32 mems; Pres. FRANKLIN GIRIGORI.

Bonaire Bankers' Association: Maduro & Curiel's Bank (Bonaire) NV, Kaya L. D. Gerharts 1, POB 366, Kralendijk, Bonaire; tel. 717-5520; fax 717-5884; Pres. R. GOMEZ.

Curaçao Bankers' Association (CBA): Banco di Caribe NV, Schottegatweg Oost 205, POB 3785, Willemstad, Curaçao; tel. (9) 432-3000; fax (9) 432-3343; e-mail florisela.bentoera@an.rbtt.com; f. 1972; Pres. E. A. DE KORT; Sec. FLORISELA BENTOERA.

Federashon di Kooperativanan di Spar i Kredito Antiyano (Fekoskan): Curaçaostraat 50, Willemstad, Curaçao; tel. (9) 462-3676; fax (9) 462-4995; e-mail fekoskan@attglobal.net; Vice-Pres. R. FRANS.

International Bankers' Association in the Netherlands Antilles: A. M. Chumaceiro Blvd 3, Willemstad, Curaçao; tel. (9) 461-5367; fax (9) 461-5369; Pres. F. GIRIGORI.

The Windward Islands Bankers' Association: Clem Labega Sq., Philipsburg, St Maarten; tel. 542-2313; fax 542-6355; Pres. J. BEAUJON.

INSURANCE

Amersfoortse Antillen NV: Kaya W. F. G. Mensing 19, Willemstad, Curaçao; tel. (9) 461-6399; fax (9) 461-6709.

Aseguro di Kooperativa Antiyano (ASKA) NV: Scharlooweg 15, Willemstad, Curaçao; tel. (9) 461-7765; fax (9) 461-5991; accident and health, motor vehicle, property.

Ennia Caribe Schaden NV: J. B. Gorsiraweg 6, POB 581, Willemstad, Curaçao; tel. (9) 434-3800; fax (9) 434-3873; e-mail mail@ennia.com; f. 1948; general; life insurance as Ennia Caribe Leven NV; Pres. DONALD BAKHUIS; Man. Dir ALBARTUS WILLEMSEN.

ING Fatum: Cas Coraweg 2, Willemstad, Curaçao; tel. (9) 777-7777; fax (9) 461-2023; f. 1904; property insurance.

MCB Group Insurance NV: MCB Bldg Scharloo, Scharloo, Willemstad, Curaçao; tel. (9) 466-1370; fax (9) 466-1327.

Netherlands Antilles and Aruba Assurance Company (NA&A) NV: Pietermaai 135, Willemstad, Curaçao; tel. (9) 465-7146; fax (9) 461-6269; accident and health, motor vehicle, property.

Seguros Antilliano NV: S. b. N. Doormanweg/Reigerweg 5, Willemstad, Curaçao; tel. (9) 736-6877; fax (9) 736-5794; general.

A number of foreign companies also have offices in Curaçao, mainly British, Canadian, Dutch and US firms.

Insurance Association

Insurance Association of the Netherlands Antilles (NAVV): c/o ING Fatum, Cas Coraweg 2, POB 3002, Willemstad, Curaçao; tel. (9) 777-7777; fax (9) 736-9658; Pres. R. C. MARTINA-JOE.

Trade and Industry

DEVELOPMENT ORGANIZATIONS

Curaçao Industrial and International Trade Development Company NV (CURINDE): Emancipatie Blvd 7, Landhuis Koningsplein, Curaçao; tel. (9) 737-6000; fax (9) 737-1336; e-mail info@curinde.com; internet www.curinde.com; f. 1980; state-owned; manages the harbour free zone, the airport free zone and the industrial zone; Man. Dir ERIC R. SMEULDERS.

Foreign Investment Agency Curaçao (FIAC): Luchthavenweg 55, 5657 EA Eindhoven, Netherlands; tel. (40) 2518674; fax (40) 2572098.

World Trade Center Curaçao: POB 6005, Piscadera Bay, Curaçao; tel. (9) 463-6271; fax (9) 462-4408; e-mail info@wtccuracao.com; internet www.wtccuracao.com; Man. Dir JOSÉ VICENTE SANCHES PIÑA.

CHAMBERS OF COMMERCE

Bonaire Chamber of Commerce and Industry: Princess Mariestraat, POB 52, Kralendijk, Bonaire; tel. 717-5595; fax 717-8995.

Curaçao Chamber of Commerce and Industry: Kaya Junior Salas 1, POB 10, Willemstad, Curaçao; tel. (9) 461-1451; fax (9) 461-5652; e-mail management@curacao-chamber.an; internet www.curacao-chamber.an; f. 1884; Chair. RUUD THUIS; Exec. Dir JOHN H. JACOBS.

St Maarten Chamber of Commerce and Industry: Cannegieterstraat 11, POB 454, Philipsburg, St Maarten; tel. 542-3590; fax 542-3512; e-mail info@sintmaartenchamber.org; internet www.sintmaartenchamber.org; f. 1979; Pres. GLEN CARTY; Exec. Dir (vacant).

INDUSTRIAL AND TRADE ASSOCIATIONS

Curaçao Exporters' Association (CEA): c/o Seawings NV, Maduro Plaza z/n CEA, POB 6049, Curaçao; tel. (9) 733-1591; fax (9) 733-1599; e-mail albert.elens@seawings-curacao.com; f. 1993; Dir ALBERT ELENS.

Curaçao International Financial Services Association (CIFA): Chumaceiro Blvd 3, POB 220, Curaçao; tel. (9) 461-5371; fax (9) 461-5378; e-mail info@cifa.an; internet www.cifa.an; Chair. HERMAN J. BEHR.

Curaçao Trade and Industry Association (Vereniging Bedrijfsleven Curaçao—VBC): Kaya Junior Salas 1, POB 49, Willemstad, Curaçao; tel. (9) 461-1210; fax (9) 461-5422; e-mail vbc1@cura.net; f. 1944; Pres. BASTIAN KOOYMAN; Exec. Dir R. P. J. LIEUW.

St Maarten Hospitality and Trade Association (SHTA): 33A WJA Nisbeth Rd, POB 486, Philipsburg, St Maarten; tel. 542-0108; fax 542-0107; e-mail info@shta.com; internet www.shta.com; Pres. EMIL LEE.

UTILITIES

Electricity and Water

Aqualectra Production NV (KAE): Rector Zwijsenstraat 1, POB 2097, Curaçao; tel. (9) 433-2200; fax (9) 462-6685; e-mail mgmt@aqualectra.com; internet www.aqualectra.com; present name adopted in 2001 following the restructuring of Curaçao's energy sector; Dir S. MARTINA.

EcoPower Bonaire BV: Bonaire; f. 2007; consortium of Econcern (Germany), MAN (Germany) and Enercon (Netherlands); sustainable energy producer.

GEBE NV: Pond Fill, W. J. A. Nisbeth Rd 35, POB 123, St Maarten; tel. 542-2213; fax 542-4810; e-mail gebesxm@sintmaarten.net; f. 1961; generates and distributes electricity via island network; operates island water supply system; Man. Dir WILLIAM GODFREY BROOKS.

Water & Energiebedrijf Bonaire (WEB) NV: Carlos Nicolaas 3, Kralendijk, Bonaire; tel. 717-8244.

TRADE UNIONS

Algemene Bond van Overheidspersoneel (ABVO) (General Union of Civil Servants): POB 3604, Willemstad, Curaçao; tel. (9) 737-6097; fax (9) 737-3145; e-mail abvo_na@cura.net; internet www.abvo-informa.org; f. 1936; Pres. ROLAND H. IGNACIO; Sec. R. C. SAEZ; 4,000 mems.

Central General di Trahado di Corsow (CGTC) (General Headquarters for Workers of Curaçao): POB 2078, Willemstad, Curaçao; tel. (9) 737-6097; fax (9) 737-3145; e-mail abvo_na@cura.net; f. 1949; Sec.-Gen. ROLAND H. IGNACIO.

Curaçaosche Federatie van Werknemers (Curaçao Federation of Workers): Schouwburgweg 44, Willemstad, Curaçao; tel. (9) 737-6300; fax (9) 737-1426; f. 1964; Pres. WILFRED SPENCER; Sec.-Gen. GILBERT POULINA; 204 affiliated unions; about 2,000 mems.

Federashon Bonaireana di Trabou (FEDEBON): Kaya Krabè 6, Nikiboko, POB 324, Bonaire; tel. and fax 717-8845; Pres. GEROLD BERNABELA.

Petroleum Workers' Federation of Curaçao: Willemstad, Curaçao; tel. (9) 737-0255; fax (9) 737-5250; affiliated to Int. Petroleum and Chemical Workers' Federation; f. 1955; Pres. R. G. GIJSBERTHA; approx. 1,500 mems.

Sentral di Sindikatonan di Korsou (SSK) (Central Trade Unions of Curaçao): Schouwburgweg 44, POB 3036, Willemstad, Curaçao; tel. (9) 737-0255; fax (9) 737-5250; Pres. PABLO COVA; 6,000 mems.

Sindikato di Trahado den Edukashon na Korsou (SITEK) (Curaçao Schoolteachers' Trade Union): Landhuis Stenen Koraal, POB 3545, Willemstad, Curaçao; tel. (9) 468-2902; fax (9) 469-0552; 1,234 mems.

Windward Islands' Federation of Labour (WIFOL): Pond Fill, Long Wall Rd, POB 1097, St Maarten; tel. 542-2797; fax 542-6631; e-mail wifol@sintmaarten.net; Pres. THEOPHILUS THOMPSON.

Transport

RAILWAYS

There are no railways.

ROADS

All the islands have a good system of all-weather roads. There were 845 km of roads in 2004, of which 31% were paved.

SHIPPING

Curaçao is an important centre for the refining and transshipment of Venezuelan and Middle Eastern petroleum. Willemstad is served by the Schottegat harbour, set in a wide bay with a long channel and deep water. Facilities for handling containerized traffic at Willemstad were inaugurated in 1984. A Mega Cruise Facility, with capacity for the largest cruise ships, has been constructed on the Otrobanda side of St Anna Bay. Ports at Bullen Bay and Caracas Bay also serve Curaçao. St Maarten is one of the Caribbean's leading ports for visits by cruise ships, and in January 2001 new pier facilities were opened that could accommodate up to four cruise ships and add more cargo space. Each of the other islands has a good harbour, except for Saba, which has one inlet, equipped with a large pier. In May 2002 the Netherlands provided NA Fl. 9.6m. for the repair of Saba's port, which sustained severe hurricane damage in 1999. Many foreign shipping lines call at ports in the Netherlands Antilles.

Curaçao Ports Authority: Werf de Wilde z/n, POB 689, Willemstad, Curaçao; tel. (9) 434-5999; fax (9) 461-3907; e-mail info@curports.com; internet curports.com; Man. Dir RICHARD LÓPEZ-RAMÍREZ.

Curaçao Shipping Association (SVC): c/o Dammers & van der Heide (Antilles) Inc, Kaya Flamboyan 11, Willemstad, Curaçao; tel. (9) 737-0600; fax (9) 737-3875; Pres. K. Ponsen.

St Maarten Ports Authority: J. Yrausquin Blvd, POB 146, Philipsburg, St Maarten; tel. 542-2307; fax 542-5048; e-mail kfranca@smpanv.com; internet www.portofstmaarten.com; Man. Dir Keith Franca.

Principal Shipping Companies

Anthony Veder & Co NV: Zeelandia z/n, POB 3677, Curaçao; tel. (9) 461-4700; fax (9) 461-2576; e-mail anveder@vrshipping.com; Man. Dir Joop van Vliet.

Caribbean Moving Services NV: Caracasbaaiweg 328, POB 442, Willemstad, Curaçao; tel. (9) 767-2588; fax 747-1155; internet www.ccs.an; fmrly Caribbean Cargo Services NV; Man. Dir Loes van der Woude.

Curaçao Dry-dock Co Inc: POB 3012, Curaçao; tel. (9) 733-0000; fax (9) 736-5580; e-mail info@cdmnv.com; f. 1958; Man. Dir Mario Raymond Evertsz.

Curaçao Ports Services Inc NV (CPS): Curaçao Container Terminal, POB 170, Curaçao; tel. (9) 461-5177; fax (9) 461-6536; e-mail cps@cps.an; Man. Dir Karel Jan O. Aster.

Dammers & van der Heide, Shipping and Trading (Antilles) Inc: Dammers Bldg, Kaya Flamboyan 11, POB 3018, Willemstad, Curaçao; tel. (9) 737-0600; fax (9) 737-3875; e-mail general@dammers-curacao.com; internet www.dammers-curacao.com; f. 1964; Man. Dir (Finance) Peter Govers; Man. Dir (Marketing and Sales) Robert van Heulen.

Gomez Transport NV: Zeelandia z/n, Willemstad, Curaçao; tel. (9) 461-5900; fax (9) 461-3358; e-mail info@gomezshipping.an; Man. Fernando da Costa Gómez.

Hal Antillen NV: De Ruyterkade 63, POB 812, Curaçao.

Intermodal Container Services NV: Salinja Galleries, 1st Floor Unit 201, POB 3747, Curaçao; tel. (9) 461-3330; fax (9) 461-3432; Mans A. R. Beaujon, N. N. Harms.

Lagendijk Maritime Services: POB 3481, Curaçao; tel. (9) 465-5766; fax (9) 465-5998; e-mail ims@ibm.net.

S. E. L. Maduro Shipping: Dokweg 19, Maduro Plaza, Curaçao; tel. (9) 733-1510; fax (9) 733-1538; e-mail maduroship@madurosons.com; internet www.madurosons.com; f. 1837; Vice-Pres. Ronald Corsen.

St Maarten Port Services: POB 270, Philipsburg, St Maarten; tel. 542-2304.

CIVIL AVIATION

There are international airports at Curaçao (Dr Albert Plesman, or Hato, 12 km from Willemstad), Bonaire (Flamingo Field) and St Maarten (Princess Juliana, 16 km from Philipsburg), and airfields for inter-island flights at St Eustatius and Saba. In 1998 a free trade zone was inaugurated at the international airport on Curaçao. The second phase of a US $118m. project to expand Princess Juliana Airport, which commenced in June 2004, was completed in November 2006. The development comprised a new terminal, enhancing the airport's passenger-handling capacity by 2.5m. Financing was secured for the construction of a new passenger terminal building at Dr Albert Plesman Airport in September 2003. The national carrier of the Netherlands Antilles, known as Dutch Caribbean Airlines (DCA) from 2002, was declared bankrupt in late 2004.

Dutch Antilles Express: Pietermaai 33–35, POB 4101, Willemstad, Curaçao; tel. 461-2502; fax 461-2508; e-mail curacao@flydae.com; internet www.flydae.com; f. 2005; scheduled passenger flights within the Netherlands Antilles and to other Caribbean and South American destinations.

Windward Express Airways: Princess Juliana International Airport, St Maarten; tel. 545-2001; fax 545-2224; e-mail windwardexpressreservations@hotmail.com; internet www.windwardexpress.com; domestic and limited Caribbean island charter flights, incl. destinations with restricted access; passenger and cargo flights; Man. Dir Curletta Halley.

Windward Islands Airways International (WIA—Winair) NV: Princess Juliana Airport, POB 2088, Philipsburg, St Maarten; tel. 545-4237; fax 545-2002; e-mail info@fly-winair.com; internet www.fly-winair.com; f. 1961; govt-owned since 1974; scheduled and charter flights throughout north-eastern Caribbean; Man. Dir Edwin Hodge.

Tourism

Tourism is a major industry on all the islands. The principal attractions for tourists are the white, sandy beaches, marine wildlife and diving facilities. There are marine parks in the waters around Curaçao, Bonaire and Saba. The numerous historic sites are of interest to visitors. The largest number of tourists visit St Maarten, Curaçao and Bonaire. In 2007 stop-over visitors totalled some 862,116. In the same year 1,860,448 cruise-ship passengers visited St Maarten, Curaçao and Bonaire. Tourism generated earnings of NA Fl. 1,906.5m. in 2004.

Curaçao Tourist Board: Pietermaai 19, POB 3266, Willemstad, Curaçao; tel. (9) 434-8200; fax (9) 461-5017; e-mail ctdbcur@ctdb.net; internet www.ctb.an; f. 1989; supervised by the Curaçao Tourism Development Bureau; Marketing Dir E. Nita.

Saba Tourist Office: Windwardside, POB 527, Saba; tel. 416-2231; fax 416-2350; e-mail tourism@sabagov.com; internet www.sabatourism.com; Dir Glenn C. Holm.

St Eustatius Tourist Office: St Eustatius Tourism Development Foundation, Fort Oranje, Oranjestad, St Eustatius; tel. and fax 318-2433; e-mail euxtour@goldenrocknet.com; internet www.statiatourism.com; Dir Alida Francis.

St Maarten Tourist Bureau: Vineyard Office Park, W. G. Buncamper Rd 33, Philipsburg, St Maarten; tel. 542-2337; fax 542-2734; e-mail info@travelsxm.com; internet www.st-maarten.com; Commr Roy Marlin; Dir Regina La Bega.

Tourism Corporation Bonaire (TCB): Kaya Grandi 2, Kralendijk, Bonaire; tel. 717-8322; fax 717-8408; e-mail info@tourismbonaire.com; internet www.infobonaire.com; Commr Jeffrey Levenstone.

HOTEL ASSOCIATIONS

Bonaire Hotel and Tourism Association (BONHATA): Kaya Soeur Bartola 15B, Kralendijk, Bonaire; tel. 717-5134; fax 717-8534; e-mail info@bonhata.org; internet www.ilovebonaire.com; f. 1980; Pres. Sara Matera; Vice-Pres. Martin Van Bekkum.

Curaçao Hospitality and Tourism Association (CHATA): Kaya Junior Salas 01, Curaçao; tel. (9) 465-1005; fax (9) 465-1052; e-mail info@chata.org; internet www.chata.org; f. 1967 as Curaçao Hotel Asscn; Pres. Jeanette Bonet.

St Maarten Hospitality and Trade Association: W. J. A. Nisbeth Rd 33A, POB 486, Philipsburg, St Maarten; tel. 542-0108; fax 542-0107; e-mail info@shta.com; internet www.shta.com; Pres. Emil Lee.

NEW ZEALAND

Introductory Survey

Location, Climate, Language, Religion, Flag, Capital

The Dominion of New Zealand lies in the South Pacific Ocean, about 1,750 km (1,100 miles) south-east of Australia. It consists of North Island and South Island, separated by the narrow Cook Strait, and several smaller islands, including Stewart Island (or Rakiura) in the south. The climate is temperate and moist, with an average temperature of 12°C (52°F), except in the far north, where higher temperatures are reached. The official languages are English and Maori. At the 2001 census, 15.7% of respondents professed adherence to the Anglican Church, 13.0% being Roman Catholics and 11.5% Presbyterians. At the 2006 census, 55.6% of respondents professed adherence to the Christian religion. The national flag (proportions 1 by 2) is dark blue, with a representation of the United Kingdom flag as a canton in the upper hoist. In the fly are four five-pointed red stars, edged in white, in the form of the Southern Cross constellation. The capital is Wellington, on North Island.

Recent History

New Zealand is a former British colony. It became a dominion, under the British Crown, in 1907 and achieved full independence by the Statute of Westminster, adopted by the British Parliament in 1931 and accepted by New Zealand in 1947.

In 1962 Western Samoa (now Samoa, q.v.), formerly administered by New Zealand, achieved independence, and in 1965 the Cook Islands attained full internal self-government, but retained many links, including common citizenship, with New Zealand. In October 1974 Niue, one of New Zealand's island territories, obtained similar status 'in free association with New Zealand'. New Zealand retains two Dependent Territories, Ross Dependency and Tokelau (see the chapter on New Zealand's Dependent Territories).

In December 1972 the first Labour Government for more than 12 years came to power, under the leadership of Norman Kirk, after a succession of New Zealand National Party administrations, most recently led by John Marshall, who had replaced Sir Keith Holyoake upon Marshall's retirement in February of that year. The New Zealand Labour Party took office at a time when the economy was thriving, mainly as a result of a sharp increase in international prices for agricultural commodities. However, this prosperity was accompanied by inflation, and the international energy crisis of 1973–74 led to a rapid deterioration in the country's economy.

Norman Kirk died in August 1974, and Wallace Rowling, hitherto Minister of Finance, became Prime Minister in September. The economic recession worsened, and in November 1975 a general election resulted in victory for the National Party, which won 55 of the 87 seats in the House of Representatives, while the Labour Party took the remaining 32 seats. The new Government, under Robert (later Sir Robert) Muldoon, who had led the National Party since July 1974, introduced austere economic policies, and in 1976 reduced the annual intake of migrants from 30,000 to 5,000, while conducting a campaign against illegal immigrants.

Popular dissatisfaction with Muldoon's sometimes controversial leadership was reflected at the general election in November 1978. The National Party retained power, with 50 of the 92 seats in the enlarged House of Representatives, but its share of the total vote decreased markedly. Labour won 41 seats. The Social Credit Party substantially increased its share of the votes cast but obtained only one seat. In the November 1981 election Muldoon's majority was further reduced. The National Party won 47 of the 92 seats in the House, while Labour, which again received more votes, won 43 seats and Social Credit (despite obtaining 20.6% of votes cast) only two.

In February 1984 Muldoon's Government antagonized New Zealand's trade unions by effecting legislation to ban 'closed shop' agreements with employers, thus giving employees the right to choose whether or not to join a trade union. Further legislation was used in June to compel striking construction workers to return to work. In the same month, owing to dissent within his own party, Muldoon called an early general election for July. The Labour Party secured 56 of the 95 seats in an enlarged House of Representatives, while the National Party took 37 seats: it was thought that the National Party had lost considerable support to the newly formed New Zealand Party, a right-wing party which won more than 12% of the votes cast but no seats, after campaigning for a minimum of government intervention in the economy. David Lange (the leader of the Labour Party since February 1983) became Prime Minister. James McLay, who had been deputy leader of the National Party since March 1984, defeated Muldoon in an election for the leadership of the party in November 1984, but he was replaced as party leader by his deputy, James (Jim) Bolger, in March 1986.

The Labour Government introduced controversial deregulatory measures to improve the country's economic situation. The initial success of these measures, together with widespread popular support for the Government's anti-nuclear policy (see below), contributed to a second victory for the Labour Party in a general election in August 1987. Of the 97 seats in the expanded House of Representatives, the Labour Party secured 58, and the National Party 39. (The Democratic Party lost both the seats that its predecessor, the Social Credit Party, had won at the 1984 election.)

In 1987 Lange's Government initiated a controversial policy of 'privatization' of state-owned enterprises. In November 1988 policy disagreements prompted Lange to dismiss the minister responsible for the privatization programme, Richard Prebble. Lange was accused by cabinet colleagues of acting without consultation, and in December Roger (later Sir Roger) Douglas, the Minister of Finance, declared that he would not serve another term under Lange. Douglas was promptly dismissed from office, and later that month unsuccessfully challenged Lange for the leadership of the Labour Party. In May 1989 the formation of the NewLabour Party (led by a former president of the Labour Party, Jim Anderton) was announced: the party aimed to appeal to disillusioned Labour supporters. In early August Douglas was elected by Labour MPs to a vacant cabinet post, thus prompting Lange to resign. Shortly afterwards, Geoffrey Palmer, hitherto the deputy leader of the Labour Party, was elected the Labour Party's parliamentary leader and Prime Minister.

In January 1990 Palmer effected an extensive government reorganization. The return of Richard Prebble to the Cabinet, in his former post as Minister for State-Owned Enterprises, provoked considerable anger within the Labour Party. The Government aroused further hostility by its introduction of a substantial fee for tertiary-level students. The continued sale of state assets, especially that of the telecommunications company, Telecom, was also unpopular. In September 1990, less than eight weeks before the next general election, Palmer resigned as Prime Minister. Public opinion polls had indicated that Labour, under his leadership, had lost support to the National Party, and members of the Cabinet had consequently urged him to resign. Michael Moore, the Minister of External Relations and Trade (who had also contested the August 1989 leadership election), replaced Palmer as Prime Minister and Labour Party leader. Moore promised to act promptly to avert the enormous budget deficit forecast for 1991/92 and, two weeks later, he secured an agreement with the country's trade union leaders regarding restricted pay settlements. At the general election of October 1990, none the less, the National Party took 67 of the 97 seats in the House of Representatives. The Labour Party won 29 seats, while the NewLabour Party retained its sole seat. Jim Bolger, as leader of the National Party, thus became Prime Minister at the head of a Government that promised to continue Labour's strict budgetary and monetary controls. The sale of state assets would also continue.

In November 1990 the new Government's first economic proposals were outlined. They included the repeal of legislation on equal pay for women, and envisaged reductions in public spending, particularly in the field of social welfare. In December the Government announced measures that entailed proposed reductions in unemployment benefit, family benefits, and in medical and sickness payments, in preparation for the introduction of a system whereby users of medical and educational services (hitherto provided free of charge) would be required to pay, according to a means test. These measures were received with anger by social and church groups. Protest marches took place in April 1991, and plans for a 'freeze' in the levels of old-age pensions prompted groups representing the elderly unsuccessfully to petition the British monarch (through the Governor-General) to dismiss the Government. Two National Party members of the House of Representatives resigned from the party in August, in protest against the proposals, and the Minister of Maori Affairs, Winston Peters (who had openly criticized the Government's economic strategy), was dismissed in October. In November Sir Robert Muldoon announced that he would resign from the legislature in early 1992, in protest against the Government's economic policies. Earlier in the month criticism had prompted the Government to withdraw its stringent means-testing measures for the allocation of state pensions, but the overall level of payments remained lower than previously.

In December 1991 a coalition was formed by minor parties as a challenge to the two main parties. The grouping, known as the Alliance, consisted of the NewLabour Party, the New Zealand Democratic Party, the Green Party of Aotearoa—New Zealand and Mana Motuhake. In its first electoral test (the by-election in February 1992 that had been necessitated by Muldoon's resignation) the Alliance campaigned for the provision of education and health care free of charge and the return to the public sector of 'privatized' state assets. The National Party retained the seat in the by-election, but with a greatly reduced majority.

In September 1992 a preliminary referendum on proposed electoral reform was held. The electorate voted overwhelmingly in favour of the abolition of the 'first-past-the-post' system and for its replacement by a form of proportional representation; of the four alternatives offered, the mixed member proportional (MMP) system (similar to that used in Germany) received the greatest support. The new rules were to be implemented at the 1996 election, following a second, binding referendum.

In March 1993 the outspoken Winston Peters resigned from his parliamentary seat in order to stand for re-election as an independent candidate. The by-election in April resulted in an overwhelming victory for Peters, the major political parties having declined to present candidates. In July Peters established New Zealand First, and announced that the party would contest all 99 seats at the forthcoming general election.

At the election, held in November 1993, the National Party, which had campaigned mainly on the Government's record of economic recovery, was narrowly returned to office, securing 50 seats in the House of Representatives. The Labour Party won 45 seats, the Alliance two and New Zealand First two. At a concurrent, second referendum on electoral reform, 54% of voters favoured the adoption of the MMP system. A new Government was appointed in late November.

In October 1994 Peter Dunne, a former cabinet minister, resigned from the Labour Party, following differences over the party's policy on taxation, and declared his intention to remain in the House of Representatives as an independent member. He subsequently established a new party, Future New Zealand. The traditional two-party system was further challenged in early 1995, when support for ACT New Zealand, co-founded by Sir Roger Douglas (reformist Minister of Finance in 1984–88), who had recently announced his return to politics, began to increase rapidly. In June 1995, however, the position of the ruling party was strengthened by the formation of United Future New Zealand (UFNZ) by seven members of the House of Representatives (four National, two Labour and the leader of Future New Zealand, Peter Dunne). The new grouping pledged its support for the Government on issues of confidence. In February, for the first time since the early 1930s, a formal coalition Government was established when the National Party formed an official alliance with United New Zealand. In the ensuing government reorganization, Peter Dunne joined the Cabinet as Minister of Revenue and Internal Affairs. As a result of a number of parliamentary defections and realignments, by April 1996 the number of parliamentary seats held by the National Party had been reduced to 41. In March, meanwhile, Sir Michael Hardie Boys replaced Dame Catherine Tizard as Governor-General.

The first general election under the MMP system was held in October 1996. No party achieved an outright majority. The National Party received 34.1% of the votes cast and took 44 of the 120 seats in the expanded House of Representatives, the Labour Party (28.3%) secured 37 seats and New Zealand First (13.1%) garnered 17 seats, while the Alliance won 13 seats, ACT New Zealand eight and United New Zealand one. A notable development was the increase in the number of Maori MPs from six to 15, a figure almost equivalent to the proportion of Maori (the country's aboriginal inhabitants) in the population as a whole. Although the election result initially appeared to favour the formation of a centre-left coalition under the leadership of Helen Clark, complex negotiations finally led to the establishment in December of an alliance between the National Party and New Zealand First, led by Winston Peters.

Jim Bolger thus continued as Prime Minister, while Winston Peters was appointed Deputy Prime Minister and Treasurer, the latter newly created post carrying responsibility for the drafting of the country's budget. Although Peters had previously discounted the possibility of a reconciliation and of entering into a coalition with the National Party, he had unexpectedly altered his stance in exchange for concessions on economic policy. The incoming Cabinet incorporated a total of five members of New Zealand First. Don McKinnon of the National Party retained the foreign affairs portfolio, and Bill Birch continued to hold nominal responsibility for finance.

In September 1997 proposals for the introduction of a compulsory retirement savings scheme were overwhelmingly rejected by the electorate in a referendum. The holding of the referendum had been a condition of New Zealand First's participation in the ruling coalition, but the Prime Minister had also actively supported the proposed pension reforms. In the following month thousands of protesters took to the streets to demand the resignation of the Government, its policies on health and education having drawn particular criticism.

In November 1997, following a leadership challenge from Jenny Shipley, a cabinet minister whose portfolios now included transport and women's affairs, the Prime Minister announced his intention to resign. Shipley was thus sworn in as New Zealand's first woman Prime Minister in December, reiterating the National Party's commitment to a continuation of the partnership with New Zealand First. In the ensuing government reorganization, most supporters of Jim Bolger retained their portfolios but were downgraded. Winston Peters continued as Deputy Prime Minister, while other members of New Zealand First also remained in the Cabinet.

In November 1997, meanwhile, following the Alliance's rejection of a Greens' proposal to establish a coalition arrangement, the Green Party of Aotearoa decided that at the next general election it would stand as a separate political party but would remain a member of the Alliance until that time. In January 1998 the Liberal Party announced that it was to be dissolved and would merge with the Alliance.

In May 1998 the outcome of a parliamentary by-election to fill the seat vacated by Jim Bolger confirmed the electorate's growing disillusionment with the coalition Government. Although the seat was retained by the National Party, its majority was greatly reduced. In August, following an acrimonious dispute regarding the sale of the Government's stake in Wellington airport, Winston Peters was dismissed from the post of Deputy Prime Minister and Treasurer; the dissolution of the coalition Government was announced. Rejecting demands for an early general election, Jenny Shipley reallocated many cabinet portfolios. Although Tau Henare (who in late 1998 founded a new party, Mauri Pacific, having been removed as deputy leader of New Zealand First in July), the Minister of Maori Affairs, was the only former New Zealand First minister to retain his post within the Cabinet, three other erstwhile members of the National Party's former coalition partner remained as ministers outside the Cabinet. Despite the defection of Winston Peters to the opposition, the Prime Minister was able to secure the support of eight of the 16 New Zealand First representatives in the legislature, and in September she survived a vote of confidence in the House. In the same month, in an attempt to raise public concern over the social effects of government policy, in particular the plight of low-income families, the Anglican Church initiated an ecumenical 'Hikoi of Hope', in which protesters from both ends of the country marched to Wellington and converged upon the House of Representatives.

In December 1998 the minority Government's position was further weakened by the unexpected resignation of a supporting independent (and former New Zealand First) MP, following the administration's decision to proceed with its acquisition of 28 F-16 fighter aircraft from the USA. (However, the contract to lease the aircraft was cancelled in March 2000 by the new Labour Government.) The Prime Minister was placed under further pressure in early 1999, when it was alleged that the Minister of

Tourism, Murray McCully, had acted inappropriately with regard to the handling of a major contract for the advertising business of the New Zealand Tourism Board. In February, as the Prime Minister became personally implicated in the affair and as opposition MPs accused her of deliberately misleading the legislature over her association with the head of the advertising agency in question, the Government won a motion of no confidence by 61 votes to 59. Claiming that the ruling party had intended to exploit its links with the agency during the next general election campaign, the Labour Party demanded an inquiry into the Government's alleged payments to departing members of the New Zealand Tourism Board and into the Board's expenditure on overseas promotions. In March the $NZ53m. marketing contract with the agency was terminated. McCully relinquished the tourism portfolio in April.

At the general election, conducted in late November 1999, the opposition Labour Party won the largest share of votes cast. A recount of votes in one constituency, where the Green Party candidate then unexpectedly took the seat from the incumbent National MP, combined with the incorporation of 'special votes' (which included those cast by New Zealanders overseas), led to a substantial modification of the initial results. Having secured 38.7% of the votes cast, the Labour Party was finally allocated 49 of the 120 seats in the House of Representatives, while the National Party, which had won 30.5% of the votes, received 39 seats. The Alliance was allocated 10 seats and ACT New Zealand nine seats. Under the recently introduced system of proportional representation, the Green Party's victory in the one constituency automatically entitled the movement to a further six seats in the legislature. New Zealand First's representation declined to five seats; the party's leader, Winston Peters, only narrowly retained his seat. United New Zealand took the one remaining seat. Having previously discounted any co-operation with the Green Party, the Labour Party was thus obliged to seek the support not only of the Alliance but also of the seven Green MPs.

The leader of the Labour Party, Helen Clark (who had served as Deputy Prime Minister in 1989–90), thus became Prime Minister. The minority Government, which incorporated several members of the Alliance, took office in December 1999. Jim Anderton, the leader of the Alliance, was appointed Deputy Prime Minister, Minister for Economic Development and Minister for Industry and Regional Development. The treasury and finance portfolios were assigned to Dr Michael Cullen, while Phil Goff became Minister of Foreign Affairs and Trade and also assumed responsibility for the justice portfolio.

In a non-binding, citizen-initiated referendum held on the same day as the general election, a majority of voters favoured a reduction in the number of members of the House of Representatives from 120 to 99; voters also favoured a reform of the criminal justice system.

One of the new Government's stated priorities was the 'Closing the Gaps' initiative, which aimed to address the socio-economic disparities between the Maori and non-Maori communities, particularly in health, housing, education, income and the incidence of crime. Among its first actions were the repeal of the Employment Contracts Act, the restoration of the state monopoly in the provision of accident compensation and the cancellation of the contract to lease 28 F-16 fighter aircraft from the USA. The new Government was strongly criticized by opposition politicians and accused of racism, following its decision in mid-2000 to sell a 25% share of a lucrative radiowaves company (which auctioned high frequency radio positions to telecommunications companies) to a Maori trust under its 'Closing the Gaps' policy.

In June 2000 the Prime Minister was obliged to dismiss the Minister of Maori Affairs, Dover Samuels, following allegations of sexual misconduct. On 4 April 2001 Dame Silvia Cartwright (New Zealand's first female High Court Judge) took office as Governor-General. Her appointment represented a significant achievement for women in New Zealand public life, and created an unprecedented situation in which the five most important public roles in the country (those of Prime Minister, Leader of the Opposition, Attorney-General, Chief Justice and Governor-General) were all occupied by women.

In October 2001 Jenny Shipley resigned as leader of the National Party and was replaced by Bill English, a former Minister of Health. The incoming leader renamed the party the New National Party. In December Jim Anderton was placed under considerable pressure from left-wing members of the Alliance to withdraw his support for the Government's military involvement in Afghanistan, following the Prime Minister's confirmation that New Zealand transport aircraft had landed in Afghanistan, to assist in the US-led military campaign there (see the chapter on Afghanistan). In early April 2002, after months of discord, the Alliance split. Anderton and six other members of the party agreed to form a breakaway party, later named the Progressive Coalition, but continued to support the ruling coalition. The seven members of the legislature were expelled from the Alliance in late April. At the same time Laila Harré, Minister of Women's Affairs, Youth Affairs and Statistics, succeeded Anderton as leader of the Alliance and confirmed her support for the Government until the next legislative election. In June the Prime Minister announced that the next election was to be held earlier than planned, in late July, largely owing to the disintegration of the Alliance, and a dispute between the Labour Party and the Greens over the Government's decision not to renew a moratorium banning the commercial release of genetically modified organisms (which expired in October 2003).

In April 2002, following extensive consultations, the Government announced the proposed replacement of the monarch's Privy Council (based in London, United Kingdom) as New Zealand's court of final appeal by an independent Supreme Court, consisting of five judges headed by the Chief Justice. The requisite legislation was approved in October 2003; the new court began functioning in July 2004.

Some 77% of registered voters participated in the general election, which took place on 27 July 2002. The Labour Party won 41% of the party votes cast, thereby gaining a second term in office. However, the party failed to secure an overall majority in the House of Representatives, winning 52 of the 120 seats. New Zealand First received 10% of the votes (13 seats); ACT New Zealand 7% (nine seats); the Greens 7% (nine seats) and UFNZ 7% (eight seats). The Progressive Coalition won 1.7% of the party votes and secured two seats, while the Alliance failed to secure any parliamentary representation. The National Party performed badly at the election, winning only 21% of the party votes; its representation declined by 12 seats to 27. Unable to reach an agreement with the Greens on the issue of genetically modified organisms, Clark formed a minority coalition Government with the Progressive Coalition. The Labour Party leader secured the support of UFNZ. In May 2003 the Prime Minister carried out a government reorganization.

In June 2003 Clark announced that the Government intended to draw up new legislation to ensure that the country's coastline and seabed were owned by the Crown, following a ruling by the Court of Appeal that Maori tribes could pursue their own claims to ownership of the Marlborough Sands foreshore and seabed in South Island. Maori condemned the Government's 'draconian' and 'colonialist' actions. In October the legislature voted overwhelmingly in favour of the Anti-Terrorism Act, which widened the powers of the police force. The act, an extension of the 2002 Terrorism Suppression Act, created various new offences. The Green Party opposed the legislation, claiming that the law would infringe upon civil liberties.

In February 2004 the Minister of Commerce and of Immigration, Lianne Dalziel, was forced to resign after it transpired that she had lied over the disclosure to the media of a document relating to the deportation of a Sri Lankan youth. The Prime Minister ordered an inquiry into the acquisition by Dalziel of a confidential legal document and into officials' involvement in its subsequent circulation. A cabinet reorganization was subsequently effected. Meanwhile, in the same month the new leader of the opposition National Party, Don Brash, a former governor of the central bank, announced that if he won power he would discontinue all forms of positive discrimination for Maori, considering 'special privileges' to be unnecessary and divisive. Brash also pledged to abolish the parliamentary seats reserved for Maori and to repeal 'divisive, race-based' legislation. Clark accused Brash of creating disharmony by breaking the national consensus on dealing with Maori affairs; nevertheless, two days later she promised a review of state assistance for Maori, agreeing that policies should be based on need and not on any perceived privilege. In the February government reorganization, Clark also created the post of Co-ordinating Minister for Race Relations after opinion polls showed a decline in support for her administration over its policies towards the Maori. The portfolio was assigned to the Minister of Education, of State Services, and for Sport and Recreation, Trevor Mallard; he was given the immediate responsibility of conducting a full review of government policy.

In April 2004 the Progressive Coalition was renamed the Progressive Party. In the same month Clark dismissed the Associate Minister of Maori Affairs, Tariana Turia, after Turia stated that she intended to vote against the Government's Seabed and Foreshore Bill, which ensured that coastal areas were owned by the Crown, on the grounds that the new legislation was in contravention of the rights of indigenous Maori. Following her dismissal, in the following month Turia resigned from the Labour Party and the House of Representatives. In May the Prime Minister secured a narrow victory in a vote of no confidence precipitated by Turia's resignation. Meanwhile, a two-week hikoi (protest march) against the planned legislation, which had commenced in mid-April, arrived outside the Parliament building in Wellington.

In July 2004 Tariana Turia secured victory in a by-election to the seat of Te Tai Hauauru on North Island, necessitated by her resignation from the House of Representatives in the previous month. Turia was the candidate of the newly formed Maori Party. In November the controversial Seabed and Foreshore Bill was narrowly approved by the House of Representatives, after the Government secured the support of New Zealand First. In the same month the Minister of Youth Affairs, for Land Information and of Statistics, John Tamihere, resigned following the revelation that a report on his activities had been sent to the Serious Fraud Office for investigation. In December a major government reorganization was announced, in which Tamihere's portfolios were reassigned. The appointments took effect in February 2005, when Attorney-General Margaret Wilson left the Cabinet in order to succeed Jonathan Hunt as Speaker of the House of Representatives. Deputy Prime Minister Michael Cullen became the new Attorney-General, while retaining his existing portfolios. In March the Serious Fraud Office announced that, following its investigation, it did not intend to charge Tamihere with any offence.

In May 2005 Minister of Fisheries David Benson-Pope resigned from his cabinet post, following the commencement of a police inquiry into allegations that he had abused children during his former career as a teacher. However, he was reinstated to the Cabinet in the following month. In July Prime Minister Helen Clark announced that a general election would take place in September. At the election, which was held on 17 September, Clark's Labour Party secured victory by a narrow margin, winning 41.1% of the votes cast and 50 seats. The National Party won 39.1% of the votes and 48 seats for the National Party, a significant improvement in comparison with its performance at the 2002 election. The newly formed Maori Party secured 2.1% of the vote, winning four of the seven seats reserved for Maoris. As the Labour Party had failed to gain an overall majority, it subsequently entered into a coalition with the Progressive Party, which had won only one seat. With the support of New Zealand First and UFNZ, secured on a more informal basis, this brought the total number of seats controlled by the Government in the new legislature to 61.

In October 2005 the new Government was sworn in. Controversial New Zealand First leader Winston Peters was appointed Minister of Foreign Affairs. Peter Dunne of UFNZ was allocated the revenue portfolio, but with the unusual provision that both would remain outside the Cabinet. The appointment of Peters met with widespread criticism, owing largely to his anti-immigration views. In March 2006 David Parker, who had been appointed as Attorney-General in the new Government, resigned from the position, having admitted that he had made an error while filing an annual return for a company with which he was involved. However, he retained the cabinet portfolios of energy and transport. Deputy Prime Minister Michael Cullen subsequently became Attorney-General for the second time, holding the post concurrently with the finance and tertiary education portfolios. In the same month Maj.-Gen. Jerry Mateparae, hitherto Chief of the Army, became the first Maori to be appointed Chief of the New Zealand Defence Force; he took up the position in May. In mid-August 2006 Te Arikinui (Dame Te Atairangikaahu, the Maori Queen) died, bringing to an end her 40-year reign. Te Arikinui's son, Tuheitia Paki, took the throne, shortly before a traditional Maori funeral ceremony for Dame Te Ata, which was attended by thousands of mourners, including Prime Minister Clark. Also in August Anand (later Sir Anand) Satyanand, a retired judge of Indo-Fijian descent, replaced Dame Silvia Cartwright as Governor-General upon the expiry of her term of office. While Dame Silvia used her farewell speech to highlight the pressing issue of domestic and other violence in New Zealand society, Satyanand, who was sworn in on 23 August, emphasized the country's diversity and the importance of greater cohesion among the various communities.

In October 2006 the Auditor-General, Kevin Brady, published a report on an investigation into campaign funding during the 2005 legislative election, a controversy that had led to a dispute between the Government and the opposition. Brady found that the Labour Party had improperly spent $NZ768,000 of taxpayers' money on its election campaign; several other parties, including New Zealand First and the Green Party, were similarly implicated in breaches of regulations, albeit for smaller sums. Labour promptly announced that it was to reimburse the funds. Legislation retrospectively validating the relevant election campaign expenditure was swiftly enacted by the House of Representatives, but controversy continued. In November 2006 Don Brash resigned as leader of the National Party, citing concerns that increased speculation about his position was having a negative effect on the party. Brash had applied for an injunction against the publication of his e-mails in a book that attempted to prove a link between himself and the Exclusive Brethren, a business-orientated Christian group that had allegedly been involved in improperly influencing the outcome of the 2005 election; he denied allegations of irregular campaign practices and maintained that his resignation was not related to the impending publication of the book. John Key, hitherto the National Party's finance spokesman and a former investment banker, was subsequently elected unopposed to the National Party leadership.

In July 2007 David Benson-Pope, the Minister for Social Development and Employment and for the Environment, resigned in connection with the allegedly unfair dismissal of an employee of the Ministry for the Environment. Amid opinion poll results suggesting an increase in support for the National Party, Prime Minister Clark announced a ministerial reorganization in October 2007, referring to the changes as part of the Government's preparations for the general election due to be held in the latter part of 2008. Steve Chadwick was appointed Minister of Conservation and of Women's Affairs, Maryan Street Minister for the Accident Compensation Corporation and of Housing, and Shane Jones Minister for Building and Construction. Another notable change was the allocation of the justice portfolio to Annette King, in addition to her existing responsibilities for transport and police.

In October 2007 a nation-wide police operation, carried out in various cities as well as in a remote part of North Island, resulted in the arrest of 17 people under the Terrorism Suppression Act. Some of the detainees were reported to be activists for causes including Maori independence and the environment, and were alleged to have been involved in illegal training camps where firearms and other weapons were found. Tame Iti, a well-known Maori campaigner, was among those arrested. Hundreds of people took part in demonstrations to protest against the police action, while the development prompted a wide debate about the possibility of an insurgency within the country. In early November the Solicitor-General concluded that the detainees could not be charged under the Terrorism Suppression Act, but charges such as the illegal possession of weapons were not ruled out.

In August 2008 the Minister of Foreign Affairs and for Racing, Winston Peters, relinquished his portfolios, following the commencement of an investigation by the Serious Fraud Office into allegations of irregularities with regard to donations intended for his New Zealand First party. Prime Minister Helen Clark assumed responsibility for the portfolios, pending the outcome of the inquiry. In October the investigation concluded that Peters had not committed any fraud. However, he did not resume his ministerial role, owing to the imminence of the general election, which was scheduled for early November.

At the election held on 8 November 2008, the National Party won 58 of the 122 seats in the House of Representatives, having received 44.9% of the party votes cast. The Labour Party took 43 seats, with 34.0% of the votes. The rate of participation in the polls was almost 79.5% of the registered electorate. In the absence of an overall majority of parliamentary seats for the National Party, John Key announced his intention to establish an informal coalition administration, and he proceeded to secure the support of members of ACT New Zealand, UFNZ and the Maori Party. Following the defeat of the Labour Party, Helen Clark resigned as leader; she was replaced by Phil Goff, whose portfolios in the outgoing Government had included that of defence.

On 19 November 2008 John Key was sworn in as Prime Minister, at the head of a coalition Government. Key also assumed the tourism portfolio. Bill English was appointed as Deputy Prime Minister and Minister of Finance. Other notable appointments to the new Cabinet included Murray McCully as Minister of Foreign Affairs, who in addition was allocated responsibility for sport and recreation. The new Government also included New Zealand's first minister of Asian origin, Pansy Wong, who was appointed as Minister of Ethnic and Women's Affairs. Five 'support party ministers' included Dr Pita Sharples as Minister of Maori Affairs; Tariana Turia, also a member of the Maori Party, as Minister for the Community and Voluntary Sector; and Peter Dunne of UFNZ as Minister of Revenue. As global financial conditions rapidly deteriorated and as New Zealand entered recession, the incoming Government's immediate priority was to address the country's economic difficulties (see Economic Affairs).

During 1987, meanwhile, there were protests by the Maori concerning their cultural and economic rights and, in particular, their claims to land in accordance with the Treaty of Waitangi, concluded in 1840 by the British Government and Maori leaders, whereby sovereignty had been ceded to the United Kingdom in return for the Maori people's retention of hunting and fishing grounds. In November 1987 a ruling by the Waitangi Tribunal, reconvened in 1975 to consider retrospectively the claims of Maori land rights activists, recommended the restoration of an Auckland harbour headland to the Maori people. By 1994 about 75% of the country was subject to land claims by Maori groups. In December of that year the Government offered the sum of $NZ1,000m., payable over a 10-year period from September 1992, in full and final settlement of outstanding claims for compensation. However, the condition that all future land claims be renounced was rejected by most Maori groups. In the same month an historic agreement between the Government and the Tainui people of Waikato provided for the return of land confiscated in 1863 and for the deposit over a period of five years of $NZ65m. in a land acquisition trust.

In May 1995 the Prime Minister and the Queen of the Tainui people signed an agreement relating to a full and final settlement, valued at $NZ170m., of land grievances dating back to 1863. However, increasing ethnic tension was demonstrated by the destruction in September 1995 of an old school building by Maori protesters involved in a land dispute and by the burning down in October of an historic church, known as the 'Maori Cathedral', at Otaki, in an apparent retaliatory arson attack by white extremists. In November, in a highly significant ceremony in Wellington, Queen Elizabeth II gave her personal assent to the legislation ending the Tainui grievances when she signed the Waikato Raupatu Claims Settlement Act: this implemented the $NZ170m. agreement, including the return of 15,780 ha of land, and incorporated an apology from the Crown for the loss of lives and for the confiscation of property. A final settlement payment of $NZ13m. was made to the Tainui tribe in late 2000. In October 1996, as more modest agreements continued to be reached, the Government announced a $NZ170m. provisional settlement with the South Island's Ngai Tahu (one of New Zealand's smallest Maori tribes) regarding the group's long-standing claim for compensation. In early 1997 Maori leaders, pursuing a claim first lodged by tribal advocates in 1991, embarked upon a lawsuit aimed at the official alteration of New Zealand's name to Aotearoa ('Land of the Long White Cloud').

In July 1997 a Maori tribe that had been driven off its land in the 1840s lodged a claim to the site of the Parliament building in Wellington. The Ngati Tama also presented claims to other areas of the capital, while declaring their willingness to negotiate. At a ceremony in Wellington in September 1997, following six years of negotiations, the Government and the Ngai Tahu reached a formal agreement, subject to approval by the tribe's members, regarding the compensation of $NZ170m. The Government's offer also included the right to name mountains and rivers, often in combination with the English equivalents, and incorporated a full apology from the Crown. In November, the tribal beneficiaries having voted overwhelmingly in favour of the arrangements, the historic deed of full and final settlement was signed by the Prime Minister and representatives of the Ngai Tahu. In March 1998 the Ngai Tahu Claims Settlement Bill was duly submitted to the House of Representatives, where it received approval six months later. In July, exercising for the first time its power of compulsory recommendation, the Waitangi Tribunal ordered the Government to return to the Ngati Turangitukua land (now valued at $NZ6.1m.) which had been confiscated from its Maori owners more than 30 years previously to permit the construction of housing for workers engaged on an electric power project in the central North Island. In early 2000 a joint land claim was lodged by five Maori tribes of the central North Island. With the forestry claim alone worth an estimated $NZ588m., the application was potentially the largest ever submitted to the Waitangi Tribunal. In March 2001 the Ngati Ruanui became the first Taranaki tribe to conclude a deed of settlement with the Government, amounting to $NZ41m. In early 2003 the Ngati Awa voted in favour of a treaty settlement with the Government, which included an apology from the Crown, the return of 64 ha of land and $NZ42m. In August 2005 Prime Minister Helen Clark announced that all Maori land claims under the Treaty of Waitangi would have to be filed by 1 September 2008, in order that they could be settled by 2020. The announcement constituted one of the Labour Party's pledges in advance of the general election. According to reports, by 2007 the Waitangi Tribunal had been able to settle only about 20 claims. On the closing date for registration the Waitangi Tribunal received more than 1,000 new historical grievance claims from Maori communities. In October 2007 the Government instigated a campaign to persuade Maoris living in Australia to return to New Zealand.

In June 2008, in a settlement valued at $NZ418m., the New Zealand Government signed an agreement with seven Maori tribes to transfer ownership of 176,000 ha of Crown forestry land in the central North Island, originally ceded under the Treaty of Waitangi. The Maori tribes, who represented approximately 100,000 people, also stood to receive backdated forest rental payments of $NZ223m., in addition to future annual rental income and carbon credits.

At a Waitangi Day ceremony in February 2009, the Prime Minister was accosted by two Maori activists but was unharmed in the incident. In the same month the Government awarded $NZ300m. in compensation to eight Maori tribes, comprising more than 12,000 members, in recognition of historic injustices arising from violations of the Treaty of Waitangi and illegal seizures of land. Furthermore, in the first such decision relating to an issue of intellectual property, the Government recognized that the Ka Mate haka, the 'war dance' traditionally performed by the New Zealand rugby team at international games but increasingly being used for commercial exploitation, had been written in the 1820s by Maori chief Te Rauparaha, an ancestor of the Ngati Toa tribe.

In response to Maori grievances over fishing rights, in 1988 the Government introduced a Maori Fisheries Bill, under the provisions of which 2.5% of current fishing quotas were to be restored to the Maori people annually for the following 19 years. However, Maori activists alleged that the proposed legislation was racially discriminatory, since it stipulated that no other Maori fishing claim would be considered by the Waitangi Tribunal until the 19 years had elapsed. The bill was also condemned by some white New Zealanders, as, if implemented as proposed, it would guarantee the Maori people about 50% of the country's entire fishing rights by the year 2008. In August 1992, finding that the Government had failed to honour its obligations under the Treaty of 1840, the Waitangi Tribunal recommended that ownership of most of the fisheries of South Island be transferred to the Ngai Tahu. In November 1992, in the hope of reaching a permanent settlement, the Government advanced the sum of $NZ150m. to a Maori consortium to enable the latter's purchase of a 50% stake in the country's biggest inshore fishing company. In early 1996 the Treaty of Waitangi Fisheries Commission, established to resolve the issue of the allocation among Maori of resources valued at $NZ200m., had yet to deliver its recommendations. In April the Court of Appeal declared that, despite having no coastline, urban Maori constituted an *iwi* (tribe) and were therefore directly entitled to a share of these fishery assets. The case was subsequently referred to the Privy Council in London. Its decision, announced in January 1997, overruled the Court of Appeal's definition of an *iwi*. In mid-1998 the Waitangi Tribunal ruled that urban Maori without blood ties should be accorded similar negotiating rights to those of traditional *iwi*. The historic decision thus acknowledged urban Maori trusts as modern tribes. In August, however, a High Court judge ruled in favour of traditional Maori tribes, effectively declaring that urban Maori groups had no claim to fishery assets. In October 1999, furthermore, the urban Maori claim was rejected by the Court of Appeal. In June 2004 it was reported that Maori tribes had been offered 20% of all new aquaculture or marine farming areas and 20% of aquaculture areas that had been allocated since 1992 in an attempt to resolve the 1992 fisheries settlement. The offer was believed to be, in part, an inducement to Maori to accept the controversial Seabed and Foreshore Bill (see above).

In April 1997 urban Maori were outraged at a proposal by the Treaty of Waitangi Fisheries Commission to allocate up to $NZ300m. of fishery assets on a tribal basis, rather than according to *iwi* size as the populous northern tribes demanded. The Ngai Tahu and other *iwi*, meanwhile, argued that the length of coastline and traditional fishing grounds should determine the allocation of assets. In early 1998, following an incident in late 1997 when a fishing boat reportedly landed several metric tons of snapper without commercial quota rights, it was announced that new regulations were to govern the management of 'customary' fishing by *tangata whenua* (people of the land), whereby Maori were permitted to take an unlimited amount of seafood provided that it was not for pecuniary gain.

In foreign affairs, between 1964 and 1971 about 3,500 New Zealand soldiers served in Viet Nam. However, New Zealand's decision to contribute troops in support of the US war effort was not popular, and it was only in May 2008 that the New Zealand Prime Minister issued a public apology to the veterans for their lack of recognition. The Labour Government that took office at the end of 1972 adopted a more independent policy than that of its predecessors. It phased out New Zealand's military commitments under the South-East Asia Treaty Organization and established diplomatic relations with the People's Republic of China. From 1984, however, the Lange Government's pledge to ban from New Zealand's ports all vessels believed to be carrying nuclear weapons, or powered by nuclear energy, caused considerable strain in the country's relations with Australia and the USA, its partners in the ANZUS military pact (see p. 437). The ban was duly imposed in February 1985. In July 1986 the US Government announced its intention to devise new, bilateral defence arrangements with Australia, and in August the USA's military obligations to New Zealand under the ANZUS Treaty were formally suspended. In February 1987 the US Government announced its decision not to renew a 1982 memorandum of understanding (due to be renegotiated in June of that year), whereby New Zealand was able to purchase military equipment from the USA at favourable prices. The Lange Government subsequently defined a new defence strategy, based on increased self-reliance for the country's military forces. In June 1987 legislation banning nuclear-armed ships was formally enacted by the House of Representatives, despite strong opposition from the National Party. In September 1989 New Zealand agreed the terms for a joint venture with Australia to build as many as 12 naval frigates to patrol the South Pacific. The decision proved to be very contentious because of the high costs and because of allegations that the Government was succumbing to political pressure from Australia to return to the ANZUS alliance and abandon its independent anti-nuclear stance. In March 1990 the opposition National Party announced its support for the anti-nuclear policy, a position that it retained after its election to office in October.

Following the US Government's decision, in September 1991, to remove nuclear weapons from surface naval vessels, Bolger announced that his administration would reconsider the law banning visits from nuclear-armed and nuclear-propelled warships. The review would focus on the nuclear propulsion ban, which was seen as the obstacle to a renegotiated alliance with Australia and the USA. In July 1992 the USA announced that its warships no longer carried tactical nuclear weapons. In December the report commissioned by the Prime Minister was released. The committee of scientists concluded that the dangers of permitting nuclear-powered vessels to enter New Zealand waters were minimal. Despite these findings, no immediate change to the anti-nuclear legislation was envisaged. In February 1994 the Prime Minister welcomed the US decision to resume senior-level contacts with New Zealand, suspended since 1985. As relations continued to improve, in December 1994 the USA announced that nuclear-armed warships would not be dispatched to New Zealand, thus acknowledging the latter's ban. In August 1998, during a visit by Madeleine Albright, the US Secretary of State, the Prime Minister of New Zealand strongly reiterated her country's long-standing ban on visits by nuclear-armed or nuclear-powered vessels. In July 2005 a private member's bill proposing the removal of the ban was rejected by a large majority by the House of Representatives. Following his attendance at the summit meeting of the Asia-Pacific Economic Co-operation (APEC) forum held in Auckland in September 1999, US President Bill Clinton announced the end of the 14-year ban on New Zealand's participation in military exercises with the USA, in preparation for the dispatch of a multinational peacekeeping force to East Timor (now Timor-Leste—q.v.), of which New Zealand troops were to form part.

Meanwhile, New Zealand's trading relations with the USA were strained during 1999 by the latter's imposition of tariffs on imports of New Zealand lamb. However, in December 2000 the World Trade Organization (WTO, see p. 410) ruled in favour of New Zealand's case against the tariffs, and upheld the decision when the USA appealed against the ruling. The Prime Minister visited the USA in March 2002 for a series of meetings with the US President, Secretary of State and other senior officials, raising hopes within New Zealand's business community that a free trade agreement between the two nations might ultimately be achieved, despite New Zealand's adherence to its anti-nuclear policy.

The Government quickly expressed support for the USA following the suicide attacks of 11 September 2001 and offered to share intelligence in the effort to combat terrorism. In October the administration provided troops from the Special Air Service (SAS) for the US-led military campaign against the al-Qa'ida (Base) organization, held principally responsible for the attacks, and its Taliban hosts in Afghanistan. However, US policy in the 'war on terror' was a source of concern in New Zealand. In 2003, during preparations for the US-led military campaign to remove the regime of Saddam Hussain in Iraq, the Government stated that it would favour action in Iraq only through the UN, a stance that was popularly supported in New Zealand. Relations with the US Administration were affected as a result. In May Prime Minister Clark warned the USA and the United Kingdom that they had set a dangerous precedent by invading Iraq without the endorsement of a UN resolution. None the less, New Zealand decided to provide humanitarian support for Iraq and sent a team of army engineers and defence force staff to assist in the rehabilitation of the country once the UN had authorized reconstruction efforts following the ousting of Saddam Hussain. The Government had already sent forces to Afghanistan to assist in the reconstruction there, and in March 2004 it agreed to send SAS troops back to the South Asian country to take part in the search for senior al-Qa'ida leaders. In February 2005 the Prime Minister announced an extension to the New Zealand Defence Force's deployment in Afghanistan, and in March 2007 it was stated that an expanded force would remain in Afghanistan until at least September 2008 (subsequently extended to September 2009). Meanwhile, in June 2006 New Zealand deported Rayed Mohammed Abdullah Ali, a Saudi-born Yemeni citizen who was alleged to have links with one of the perpetrators of the attacks on the USA in 2001. In August 2007 it emerged that earlier in the year Air New Zealand, the national carrier, had flown Australian soldiers to Kuwait and the United Arab Emirates, en route to military service in Iraq; the revelation was reported to have appalled Prime Minister Clark.

A subsequent improvement in relations with the USA was exemplified in July 2008 by the visit to New Zealand of Condoleezza Rice, the US Secretary of State and thus the most senior representative of the US Government to visit the country since the late 1990s. Rice's discussions with Prime Minister Clark and with the Minister of Foreign Affairs focused on trade issues, renewing hopes that a free trade agreement between the two countries might be negotiated. Matters such as the reconstruction programme in Afghanistan and the situation in Fiji were also discussed.

In July 1985 the *Rainbow Warrior*, the flagship of the anti-nuclear environmentalist group, Greenpeace (which was to have led a flotilla to Mururoa Atoll, in French Polynesia, to protest against France's testing of nuclear weapons in the South Pacific), was blown up and sunk in Auckland Harbour. One member of the crew was killed as a result of the explosion. Two agents of the French secret service were tried for manslaughter in November and sentenced to 10 years' imprisonment, initially in Auckland. The French Government made repeated requests for the release or repatriation of the agents, and in July 1986 the two Governments eventually reached an agreement, whereby the agents were to be transferred to detention on Hao Atoll, in French Polynesia, for three years. The French Government made a formal apology for its part in the sabotage operation, and paid the New Zealand Government $NZ7m. in compensation. By May 1988, however, both the agents had been taken back to France, ostensibly for medical reasons. When neither agent was returned to the atoll, Lange referred the matter to the UN: in May 1990 an arbitration panel ruled that France's repatriation of the agents constituted a substantial violation of the 1986 agreement, but it announced that the agents would not be required to return to

Hao Atoll. France agreed to pay an initial US $2m. into a joint fund intended to foster close and friendly relations between the two countries. In April 1991 the French Prime Minister, Michel Rocard, visited New Zealand and again apologized for the sinking of the *Rainbow Warrior*, while reiterating that French testing of nuclear weapons in the Pacific was to continue. Relations between the two countries deteriorated in July, following the French Government's announcement that it had conferred an honour for distinguished service on one of the two agents responsible for the sabotage of the *Rainbow Warrior*. The issue re-emerged in November, when a third French agent, also suspected of involvement in the 1985 incident, was arrested, at New Zealand's instigation, in Switzerland. In December 1991, however, the New Zealand Government decided against seeking the man's extradition, on the grounds that the case was now considered to be closed. In October 2006 the New Zealand Government responded in a similar manner to the naming of another French agent allegedly involved in the incident. In July 2005 an article in a French newspaper confirmed that the sinking of the *Rainbow Warrior* had been authorized by the then French President, François Mitterrand. France announced the suspension of its nuclear testing in the South Pacific in April 1992. In May 1993 the first French warship to visit New Zealand since 1985 entered Auckland Harbour. (Similarly, in June 1995 the first British warship to visit New Zealand for 12 years arrived in Wellington.)

In June 1995 President Jacques Chirac's announcement that France was to resume its nuclear-testing programme in the South Pacific aroused international condemnation. New Zealand suspended military relations with France, and the New Zealand ambassador to Paris was recalled. In August, in response to public pressure, the New Zealand Government dispatched a naval research vessel to the test area. The first in the new series of tests was carried out in early September. Later in the month the International Court of Justice ruled that it could not reopen New Zealand's case against France, brought in 1973. France's continuation of its testing programme, in defiance of world opinion, was a major issue at the Commonwealth heads of government meeting held in Auckland in November 1995. New Zealand's relations with the United Kingdom were strained by the British Prime Minister's apparent support for France's position; upon his arrival in Auckland, thousands of anti-nuclear demonstrators took to the streets to express their outrage. In March 1996 (the French tests having been concluded) France, the United Kingdom and the USA finally acceded to the South Pacific Nuclear-Free Zone Treaty (Treaty of Rarotonga—Pacific Islands Forum, see p. 393), thus opening the way to improved relations with New Zealand and other Pacific nations. In October 1997, following a two-day official visit to Paris by the New Zealand Prime Minister, the resumption of normal relations with France was declared.

Although New Zealand's trade with the People's Republic of China assumed increasing significance from the 1990s, relations were strained by the issue of China's nuclear-testing programme. Relations were further strained in September 1996 when the Dalai Lama, the exiled spiritual leader of Tibet, paid a four-day visit to New Zealand, where he was welcomed by the Prime Minister. In September 1997, however, the New Zealand Deputy Prime Minister expressed support for China's application to join the WTO. In November 1998 New Zealand's decision to accord Taiwanese government officials similar privileges to those granted to representatives of the People's Republic provoked serious concern in China. During a visit to China in July 1999, however, the Prime Minister of New Zealand reaffirmed her country's support for the 'one China' policy. An official visit to China by the Prime Minister in April 2001 was intended to improve New Zealand's trading position with the country, prior to its accession to the WTO. A senior Chinese official, on a diplomatic tour of the Asia-Pacific region, met with New Zealand's Deputy Prime Minister in April 2002, when New Zealand reconfirmed its 'one China' policy. The Chinese Prime Minister, Wen Jiabao, paid an official visit to New Zealand in April 2006. In March 2008 it was reported that China had agreed to grant 'most favoured nation' status to New Zealand as part of a free trade agreement between the two countries, which was signed in the following month. During his first official visit to China in April 2009, Prime Minister John Key expressed his firm commitment to the consolidation of the bilateral trading relationship. In addition to wider economic co-operation, Key also urged an expansion in cultural exchanges with China, which had become the largest source of New Zealand's students from overseas.

New Zealand remained committed to its aim of the global elimination of all nuclear weapons, and in November 1996 was a co-sponsor of a UN resolution, overwhelmingly adopted by the General Assembly, to promote the establishment of a nuclear-weapons-free southern hemisphere. In December the Deputy Prime Minister of New Zealand announced that the Government was to finance a lawsuit against the United Kingdom that was being prepared by former servicemen (and veterans' widows) who had long campaigned for compensation for their exposure to the effects of British hydrogen bomb tests conducted in the South Pacific region in the late 1950s. In January 1997 New Zealand lodged a strong protest with the Japanese Government regarding the proposed route of a ship transporting nuclear waste to Japan from France. In March 1998 the New Zealand Prime Minister travelled to Japan, the first official visit by the country's head of government for 22 years. Relations with Japan, however, continued to be strained by a fishing dispute relating to Japan's perceived failure to conserve stocks of southern bluefin tuna, as agreed in a treaty of 1993, of which Australia was also a signatory. In July 1998, following a protest to Japan's ambassador in Wellington, New Zealand closed its ports to all Japanese tuna-fishing vessels. In August 1999 an international tribunal ruled in favour of New Zealand and Australia. In early 2000, the Labour Party's commitment to the protection of the environment having been reaffirmed, the new Government of New Zealand became embroiled in a further dispute with Japan, this time relating to the latter's controversial whaling programme. The Prime Minister, Helen Clark, announced her intention to raise the issue with Japan on an official visit to that country in April 2001, and she expressed her Government's desire to pursue proposals for a southern seas whale sanctuary through the International Whaling Commission (see p. 418). In December 2000 New Zealand reiterated its opposition to nuclear waste shipments in response to the news that a shipment of high-level waste had left the United Kingdom for Japan, warning that the vessel must not enter New Zealand's exclusive economic zone. In October of that year New Zealand had ratified the Waigani Convention (signed by all South Pacific Forum members in 1995, except Marshall Islands and Tuvalu), which banned the export of hazardous and radioactive waste to the Pacific islands.

Meanwhile, New Zealand continued to play an active role in Pacific island affairs. In 1997, in the quest for peace in Papua New Guinea, it participated in a peace-keeping force on the secessionist island of Bougainville. New Zealand hosted discussions between the Papua New Guinea Government and representatives of the secessionist movement, and in January 1998 a permanent ceasefire agreement was signed in Christchurch. The agreement was successfully implemented at the end of April. New Zealand strongly condemned the coup in Fiji in May 2000, which led to the overthrow of the Indian-led, elected Government of the country and prompted outbreaks of racially motivated violence throughout the islands. New Zealand's Minister of Foreign Affairs and Trade, Phil Goff, led a Commonwealth delegation, together with his Australian counterpart, to negotiate with the ethnic militias involved in a coup in Solomon Islands in June 2000. The New Zealand naval frigate, *Te Kaha*, was dispatched to the islands to serve as a venue for peace talks, and the country pledged to contribute to a group of international peace-keepers following the signing of a ceasefire agreement in October. In mid-2003 New Zealand troops joined forces from Australia and several Pacific islands to provide a peace-keeping force in Solomon Islands. New Zealand, together with Australia, deployed security forces to Tonga in November 2006 to restore stability following violent pro-reform demonstrations. In December Prime Minister Clark condemned the military coup in Fiji as an 'outrage'; the Government subsequently imposed defence, travel and development sanctions. Further sanctions were announced in June 2007 after New Zealand's high commissioner to Fiji was expelled because of his alleged interference in the country's internal affairs. In December 2008, as the restoration of democracy in Fiji appeared increasingly unlikely, the acting high commissioner of New Zealand in Fiji was expelled, in response to which her Fijian counterpart was asked to leave New Zealand. Nevertheless, New Zealand was one of several nations to offer, via non-governmental agencies, immediate aid to the emergency flood relief effort in Fiji in January 2009. In April New Zealand was particularly critical of the abrogation of the Fijian Constitution and subsequent developments in the country (see the chapter on Fiji).

In June 2008 the New Zealand Government released details of its Pacific Development Strategy Plan, which envisaged expenditure of $NZ2,000m. in official development assistance to the Pacific region over an eight-year period. This new initiative aimed to improve health services and education facilities, to strengthen governance, to reduce poverty and to promote economic growth in the Pacific islands.

In September 2001 relations with Australia were strained by the failure of Ansett, the Melbourne-based airline. Ansett's owner, Air New Zealand, had been unable to find a purchaser for the loss-making company, which was therefore placed in receivership. In Melbourne irate Ansett staff blockaded an aircraft upon which the New Zealand Prime Minister was due to travel, and the Australian media demanded a boycott of New Zealand products. Nevertheless, in the same month the New Zealand Government helped Australia to resolve an international crisis, when it agreed to accept up to 150 of the refugees stranded aboard the Norwegian vessel, the *MV Tampa* (see the chapter on Christmas Island). Despite international pressure, neither Australia nor Indonesia (where they had embarked) were willing to accept the asylum-seekers for the duration of the processing of their claims.

In July 2004 New Zealand's relations with Israel were strained when two alleged agents from the Israeli secret service, Mossad, were fined and sentenced to six-month prison terms by the Auckland High Court, having been convicted of fraudulently attempting to obtain New Zealand passports. Prime Minister Helen Clark stated that the available evidence strongly suggested that the men were acting as Israeli agents, but that no explanation had been forthcoming from the Israeli Government. New Zealand subsequently suspended senior-level diplomatic contact with Israel, demanding an apology for the incident. In connection with the deterioration in bilateral relations, in July several graves in a Jewish cemetery in Wellington were desecrated, in what was believed to have been the first anti-Semitic attack to take place in the country. In September, having been released from prison early, the Israelis were deported from the country. Relations remained strained into 2005. However, in June of that year the Israeli Government issued a formal apology for the incident, following which cordial diplomatic relations were restored.

As part of her golden jubilee tour of the Commonwealth, Queen Elizabeth II visited New Zealand in February 2002. Having previously stated that New Zealand's eventual transition to a republic was inevitable, the Prime Minister attracted some criticism for her absence from the country on the day of the Queen's arrival. In response to the international condemnation of the conduct of Zimbabwe's presidential election of March 2002, which subsequently led to that country's suspension from the Commonwealth, New Zealand followed the European Union, Canada and the USA in imposing a travel ban on senior members of the Zimbabwe Government in April. New Zealand also announced a ban on sales of armaments to Zimbabwe and declared that any New Zealand-based assets and investments found to belong to the Zimbabwean President or his associates would be 'frozen'.

Relations with the countries of South-East Asia continued to assume greater significance. In June 2001 President Abdurrahman Wahid undertook an official visit to New Zealand, the first by an Indonesian head of state for 26 years. In July 2005 New Zealand signed the Treaty of Amity and Co-operation of the Association of South East Asian Nations (ASEAN, see p. 194). In December 2005 New Zealand was represented at the inaugural East Asia Summit meeting, convened in Malaysia and attended by leaders of ASEAN members and various other countries of the Asia-Pacific region. In February 2009, along with Australia, New Zealand signed a free trade agreement with ASEAN.

Government

Executive power is vested in the British monarch, as Head of State, and is exercisable by an appointed representative, the Governor-General, who must be guided by the advice of the Executive Council (Cabinet), led by the Prime Minister. Legislative power is vested in the unicameral House of Representatives, elected for three years by universal adult suffrage. A system of mixed member proportional representation was introduced in 1996. At the 2008 election the legislature was expanded to 122 seats: 70 electorate members, including seven seats reserved for Maori, and 52 being chosen from party lists. The Governor-General appoints the Prime Minister and, on the latter's recommendation, other Ministers. The Cabinet is responsible to the House.

Defence

The ANZUS Security Treaty (see p. 437) was signed by New Zealand in 1951. New Zealand also participates in the Five-Power Defence Arrangements with Australia, Malaysia, Singapore and the United Kingdom. The total strength of active forces as assessed at November 2008 was 9,278: army 4,754, navy 2,020, air force 2,504. Reserves totalled 2,197. The defence budget for 2007/08 was estimated at $NZ1,980m.

Economic Affairs

In 2007, according to estimates by the World Bank, New Zealand's gross national income (GNI), measured at average 2005–07 prices, was US $121,708m., equivalent to US $28,780 per head (or US $26,340 per head on an international purchasing-power parity basis). During 2000–07, it was estimated, the population increased at an average annual rate of 1.3%, while gross domestic product (GDP) per head increased, in real terms, by an average of 1.9% per year. Overall GDP increased, in real terms, at an average annual rate of 3.2% in 2000–07. According to official figures, GDP growth reached 1.8% in the year to March 2007 and 3.1% in 2007/08.

Agriculture (including fishing, forestry and logging) contributed, along with mining, 6.2% of GDP in the year ending March 2005. About 7.2% of the employed labour force were engaged in the sector in 2007. The principal crops are barley, maize and wheat. Fruit (particularly kiwi fruit, apples and pears) and vegetables are also cultivated. New Zealand is a major producer of wool, although its significance as a source of export earnings has declined in recent years. Meat and dairy products are important, contributing 12.0% and 21.5% of provisional export earnings, respectively, in 2008. The forestry industry showed strong expansion in the early 1990s. In 2008 exports of logs, wood and wood articles totalled a provisional $NZ2,195m. (equivalent to 5.1% of total export earnings). The fisheries sector is of increasing significance, with exports worth a provisional $NZ1,217m. (equivalent to 2.8% of total export earnings) in 2008. Between 2000/01 and 2007/08 agricultural GDP (including fishing and forestry), together with mining, increased by an average of 1.8% per year. Compared with the previous year, the combined GDP of these sectors declined by 0.1% in 2006/07 but grew by 4.7% in 2007/08.

Industry (including mining, manufacturing, construction and utilities) engaged 22.0% of the employed labour force in 2007. The industrial sector provided 24.6% of GDP in the year ending March 2005. Between 2000/01 and 2007/08 industrial GDP (excluding mining) increased at an average annual rate of 2.6%. Compared with the previous year, industrial GDP decreased by 1.4% in 2006/07, but grew by 1.2% in 2007/08.

Mining contributed only 1.1% of GDP in the year ending March 2005 and engaged just 0.2% of the employed labour force in 2007. New Zealand has substantial coal reserves; petroleum, natural gas, iron, gold and silica are also exploited. A considerable amount of natural gas is used to produce synthetic petrol.

Manufacturing contributed an estimated 15.3% of GDP in the year ending March 2005. The sector engaged 12.8% of the employed labour force in 2007. The principal branches of manufacturing are food products, printing and publishing, wood and paper products, chemicals, metals and metal products, machinery and transport equipment. Between 2000/01 and 2007/08 manufacturing GDP increased by an average of 1.9% per year. Manufacturing GDP contracted by 2.0% in 2006/07, but grew by 1.0% in 2007/08.

Energy is derived mainly from domestic supplies of natural gas, coal and petroleum. Hydroelectric power supplied about 54.6% of total electricity output in 2005, gas 22.0% and coal 13.5%. Imports of petroleum and its products comprised a provisional 17.5% of the total value of merchandise imports in 2008.

The services sector provided 69.1% of GDP in 2004/05. This sector engaged 70.8% of the employed labour force in 2007. Tourism became the single largest source of foreign exchange in 1987/88. Receipts rose to $NZ6,147m. in 2007, but decreased to $NZ5,947 in 2008, when international visitor arrivals reached almost 2.5m. Between 2000/01 and 2007/08 the GDP of the services sector increased at an average annual rate of 4.0%. Compared with the previous year, the sector's GDP expanded by 3.8% in 2007/08.

In 2007 New Zealand recorded a visible trade deficit of US $1,761m., and there was a deficit of US $10,635m. on the current account of the balance of payments. In 2008 the principal sources of imports were Australia (18.0%), the People's Republic of China (13.3%) and the USA (9.5%). Australia was also the principal market for exports in that year (23.3%), followed by the USA (10.2%) and Japan (8.4%). The principal exports in 2008 were dairy products, meat, logs, wood and wood articles, machinery and equipment and fruit. The principal imports were petroleum and petroleum products, boilers and mechanical appliances, vehicles, parts and accessories and electrical machinery and equipment.

In the year ending June 2008 a budgetary surplus of $NZ1,318m. was projected. Overseas debt was officially estimated to have reached a total of $NZ219,463m. by March 2008, when it represented 123% of GDP. The average rate of unemployment decreased to 3.6% of the labour force in 2007. Annual inflation averaged 2.6% in 2000–07. Consumer prices increased by 3.4% in 2008.

New Zealand is a member of the World Trade Organization (WTO, see p. 410), the Organisation for Economic Co-operation and Development (see p. 358), Asia-Pacific Economic Co-operation (APEC, see p. 185), the Pacific Community (see p. 391), the Pacific Islands Forum (see p. 393) and the Cairns Group (see p. 479). New Zealand is also a member of the Colombo Plan (see p. 425) and the UN Economic and Social Commission for Asia and the Pacific (ESCAP, see p. 36). In 1982 New Zealand signed an agreement for a 'closer economic relationship' (CER) with Australia; trade barriers between the two countries were eliminated in July 1990.

The Government of John Key took office in November 2008, having pledged to reduce taxes, to increase expenditure on the country's infrastructure and to implement a programme of regulatory reform in the hope of raising investment. The immediate challenge for the incoming Prime Minister was to address the recent deterioration in New Zealand's economy. In mid-2008, for the first time in nine years, the economy had entered recession following two consecutive quarters of contraction. The downturn was attributed largely to the sharp decline in the availability of credit, which preceded the subsequent global financial crisis. Although continuing to rise in terms of value, the volume of New Zealand's exports declined by 1.8% in 2008. Nevertheless, in the longer term, New Zealand's trade prospects were greatly enhanced by the signing of a free trade agreement with the People's Republic of China in April 2008. Free trade negotiations with both the Republic of Korea and India were reported to have commenced in early 2009. However, the short-term outlook remained poor, and a large current account deficit was expected to impede an early economic recovery. Although the relatively high rate of inflation began to ease in the first quarter of 2009, serious concerns remained with regard to the low rates of household saving, declining consumption and rising levels of personal debt. Business confidence continued to weaken, and investment decreased. In December 2008 the new Government announced a financial stimulus programme focusing on reductions in the rates of personal taxation, valued at about $NZ9,000m. In July 2008, after remaining at 8.25% for a protracted period, the interest rate set by the Reserve Bank of New Zealand was reduced by 0.25%. Following a succession of further decreases, at the end of April 2009 the rate stood at a record low level of 2.5%. In real terms, despite four consecutive quarters of declining activity in 2008, in the year as a whole GDP expanded by 0.2% (the rate of growth in 2007 having been greater than the rate of contraction in the following year). Real GDP was forecast to contract by 0.4% in 2009.

Education

State education is free and, for children between six and 16 years of age, compulsory. Primary education lasts from five to 11 years of age, after which children transfer to secondary schools until a maximum age of 18. As a proportion of children in the relevant age-groups, the enrolment ratios in 2005 were equivalent to 93% in pre-primary schools and 99% in primary schools. In 2002 enrolment at secondary level included 92% of the relevant age-group. In July 2007 a total of 439,287 students were enrolled in primary schools and 270,085 in secondary schools. In addition, 47,735 pupils attended composite schools, providing both primary and secondary education. There are eight universities, as well as 20 polytechnics, offering education at the post-secondary level. Changes introduced in 1991 obliged most students to pay part of their fees: parental income is tested to determine the level of allowances. Projected budgetary expenditure on education by the central Government in the financial year ending 30 June 2009 was $NZ11,017m., representing 14.0% of total spending.

Public Holidays

2009: 1–2 January (New Year), 6 February (Waitangi Day, anniversary of 1840 treaty), 10–13 April (Easter), 25 April (ANZAC Day, anniversary of 1915 landing at Gallipoli), 1 June (Queen's Official Birthday), 26 October (Labour Day), 25 December (Christmas Day), 26 December (Boxing Day).

2010: 1–2 January (New Year), 6 February (Waitangi Day, anniversary of 1840 treaty), 2–5 April (Easter), 25 April (ANZAC Day, anniversary of 1915 landing at Gallipoli), 7 June (Queen's Official Birthday), 27 October (Labour Day), 25 December (Christmas Day), 26 December (Boxing Day).

In addition to these national holidays, each region celebrates an anniversary day.

Weights and Measures

The metric system is in force.

Statistical Survey

Source (unless otherwise stated): Statistics New Zealand, Aorangi House, 85 Molesworth St, POB 2922, Wellington 1; tel. (4) 495-4600; fax (4) 472-9135; e-mail info@stats.govt.nz; internet www.stats.govt.nz.

Area and Population

AREA, POPULATION AND DENSITY

Area (sq km)	270,534*
Population (census results)†	
6 March 2001	3,737,277
7 March 2006	
Males	1,965,618
Females	2,062,329
Total	4,027,947
Population (official estimate at 31 December)	
2007	4,252,600
2008‡	4,291,900
Density (per sq km) at 31 December 2008	15.9

* 104,454 sq miles.
† Figures refer to the population usually resident. The total population (including foreign visitors) was: 3,820,749 in 2001; 4,143,282 in 2006.
‡ Provisional.

ADMINISTRATIVE REGIONS
(census of March 2006)

	Area (sq km)	Population	Density (per sq km)
North Island			
Northland	13,296	148,470	11.2
Auckland	5,048	1,303,068	258.1
Waikato	26,170	382,713	14.6
Bay of Plenty	11,428	257,379	22.5
Gisborne	8,355	44,499	5.3
Hawke's Bay Region	13,764	147,783	10.7
Taranaki	7,227	104,124	14.4
Manawatu-Wanganui	22,687	222,423	9.8
Wellington	8,056	448,959	55.7
Total North Island	116,031	3,059,418	26.4

NEW ZEALAND

—continued

	Area (sq km)	Population	Density (per sq km)
South Island			
Tasman	14,538	44,625	3.1
Nelson	444	42,891	96.6
Marlborough	12,493	42,558	3.4
West Coast	23,351	31,326	1.3
Canterbury	45,845	521,832	11.4
Otago	31,476	193,800	6.2
Southland	25,392	90,876	3.6
Total South Island	153,540	967,908	38.1
Area outside regions	963	618	0.6
Total	270,534	4,027,947	14.9

Note: Totals may not be equal to the sum of components, owing to rounding.

PRINCIPAL CENTRES OF POPULATION
(census of March 2006, enumerated totals, incl. visitors)

Auckland city	404,658	Palmerston North	75,543
Christchurch	348,435	Hastings district	70,842
Wellington (capital)	179,466	Rotorua district	65,901
Hamilton	129,249	Napier	55,359
Dunedin	118,683	Nelson	42,888
Tauranga	103,635		

BIRTHS, MARRIAGES AND DEATHS

	Live births* Number	Rate (per '000)	Marriages† Number	Rate (per '000)	Deaths* Number	Rate (per '000)
2001	55,799	14.4	19,972	5.1	27,825	7.2
2002	54,021	13.7	20,690	5.2	28,065	7.1
2003	56,134	13.9	21,419	5.3	28,010	7.0
2004	58,073	14.2	21,006	5.1	28,419	7.0
2005	57,745	14.0	20,470	5.0	27,034	6.5
2006	59,193	14.1	21,423	5.1	28,245	6.8
2007	64,044	15.1	21,494	5.1	28,522	6.7
2008	64,343	15.1‡	n.a.	n.a.	29,188	6.8‡

* Data for births and deaths are tabulated by year of registration rather than by year of occurrence.
† Based on the resident population concept, replacing the previous de facto concept.
‡ Provisional.

Life expectancy (years at birth, WHO estimates): 80.3 (males 78.3; females 82.1) in 2006 (Source: WHO, *World Health Statistics*).

IMMIGRATION AND EMIGRATION

	2006	2007	2008
Long-term immigrants*	82,732	82,572	87,463
Long-term emigrants†	68,123	77,081	83,649

* Figures refer to persons intending to remain in New Zealand for 12 months or more, and New Zealand citizens returning after an absence of 12 months or more.
† Figures refer to New Zealand citizens intending to remain abroad for 12 months or more, and overseas migrants departing after a stay of 12 months or more.

ECONOMICALLY ACTIVE POPULATION
('000 persons aged 15 years and over, excl. armed forces)

	2005	2006	2007
Agriculture, hunting and forestry	145.3	149.2	152.2
Fishing	2.7	1.7	2.2
Mining and quarrying	4.0	4.8	5.1
Manufacturing	282.5	275.8	274.4
Electricity, gas and water	8.1	8.2	8.8
Construction	161.6	184.1	183.1
Wholesale and retail trade; repair of motor vehicles, motorcycles and personal and household goods	363.2	368.4	377.9
Restaurants and hotels	99.6	96.6	107.8
Transport, storage and communications	118.8	116.7	115.4
Financial intermediation	65.8	70.7	71.4
Real estate, renting and business activities	234.8	246.9	249.0
Public administration and defence; compulsory social security	126.8	134.5	136.1
Education	163.1	163.0	167.2
Health and social work	187.1	193.4	200.1
Other community, social and personal service activities	101.7	92.0	90.7
Private households with employed persons	2.5	3.2	3.7
Activities not adequately defined	5.4	8.1	10.5
Total employed	2,072.9	2,117.2	2,155.5
Unemployed	79.3	82.6	79.8
Total labour force	2,152.2	2,199.8	2,235.4
Males	1,157.9	1,184.0	1,201.0
Females	994.3	1,015.8	1,034.4

Source: ILO.

Health and Welfare

KEY INDICATORS

Total fertility rate (children per woman, 2006)	2.0
Under-5 mortality rate (per 1,000 live births, 2006)	6
HIV/AIDS (% of persons aged 15–49, 2007)	0.1
Physicians (per 1,000 head, 2002)	2.1
Hospital beds (per 1,000 head, 2002)	6.0
Health expenditure (2006): US $ per head (PPP)	2,447
Health expenditure (2006): % of GDP	9.4
Health expenditure (2006): public (% of total)	77.8
Human Development Index (2006): ranking	20
Human Development Index (2006): value	0.944

For sources and definitions, see explanatory note on p. vi.

NEW ZEALAND

Statistical Survey

Agriculture

PRINCIPAL CROPS
('000 metric tons)

	2005	2006	2007
Wheat	319	262	275*
Barley	302	277	400†
Maize	210	227	230*
Oats	25	28	30*
Potatoes	500	501	505*
Peas, dry*	38	32	35
Cabbages and other brassicas	40	43*	44*
Lettuce and chicory*	31	31	32
Tomatoes	90	92	93*
Cauliflowers and broccoli*	56	56	60
Pumpkins, squash and gourds	124	154	155*
Onions and shallots, green	165	170*	175*
Peas, green	63	63*	63*
Carrots and turnips	65	65	65*
Maize, green	97	100*	102*
Grapes	142	185	190*
Apples	524	354	380*
Pears*	32	33	35
Kiwi fruit	318	318	315

* FAO estimate(s).
† Unofficial figure.

Aggregate production ('000 metric tons, may include official, semi-official or estimated data): Total cereals 866 in 2005, 805 in 2006, 945 in 2007; Total roots and tubers 518 in 2005, 519 in 2006, 524 in 2007; Total vegetables (incl. melons) 908 in 2005, 1,160 in 2006, 1,176 in 2007; Total fruits (excl. melons) 1,131 in 2005, 969 in 2006, 1,002 in 2007.

Source: FAO.

LIVESTOCK
('000 head at 30 June)

	2005	2006	2007*
Cattle	9,511	9,609	9,650
Sheep	39,880	40,098	40,000
Goats*	155	155	160
Pigs	341	356	360
Horses*	77	78	80
Chickens	20,939	17,596	18,000
Ducks*	180	180	190
Geese and guinea fowls*	70	75	80
Turkeys*	75	75	76

* FAO estimates.

Source: FAO.

LIVESTOCK PRODUCTS
('000 metric tons)

	2005	2006	2007
Cattle meat	651.8	642.9	632.4
Sheep meat	542.8	542.2	573.2
Pig meat	50.5	50.6	50.5
Chicken meat	157.0	149.0	149.0*
Game meat	41.8	38.6	39.0*
Cows' milk	14,638	15,332	15,842
Hen eggs	50.9†	51.0*	51.5*
Other poultry eggs*	2.5	2.5	2.5
Honey	9.7	10.4	9.7
Wool, greasy	215.5	224.7	217.9

* FAO estimate(s).
† Unofficial figure.

Source: FAO.

Forestry

ROUNDWOOD REMOVALS
('000 cubic metres)

	2005	2006	2007
Sawlogs, veneer logs and logs for sleepers	8,801	8,835	9,336
Pulpwood	3,317	3,208	3,271
Other industrial roundwood	6,887	7,257	7,651
Total	19,005	19,300	20,258

Source: FAO.

SAWNWOOD PRODUCTION
('000 cubic metres, year ending 31 March)

Species	2005/06	2006/07	2007/08
Radiata pine	4,038	4,102	4,122
Other introduced pines	5	6	4
Douglas fir	156	157	175
Rimu and miro	n.a.	3	3
Total (incl. others)	4,234	4,301	4,341

Source: Forestry Statistics Section, Ministry of Agriculture and Forestry, Wellington.

Fishing

('000 metric tons, live weight)

	2004	2005	2006
Capture*	546.0	545.1	470.7
Southern blue whiting	21.6	30.3	23.4
Blue grenadier (Hoki)	134.4	127.6	105.0
Pink cusk-eel	18.7	16.0	14.8
Oreo dories	19.6	17.4	16.9
Jack and horse mackerels	43.2	45.7	36.3
Snoek (Barracouta)	22.5	31.1	25.9
Wellington flying squid	84.4	87.8	69.2
Aquaculture	92.2	105.3	107.5
New Zealand mussel	85.0	95.0	97.0
Total catch	638.2	650.4	578.2

* Excluding catches made by chartered vessels and landed outside New Zealand.

Note: Figures exclude aquatic mammals (recorded by number rather than by weight) and sponges. The number of whales and dolphins caught was: 31 in 2004; 12 in 2005; 11 in 2006.

Source: FAO.

Mining

('000 metric tons, unless otherwise indicated)

	2005	2006	2007
Coal (incl. lignite)	5,267	5,768	4,835
Gold (kg)	10,583	10,618	10,762
Crude petroleum ('000 barrels)	7,032	6,808	14,873
Gross natural gas (million cu m)	4,223	4,100	4,712
Liquid petroleum gas ('000 barrels)	1,946	1,786	654
Iron sands	2,207	2,146	1,723
Silica sand	65.4	58.7	86.5
Limestone	5,226	5,032	5,092

Source: US Geological Survey.

Industry

SELECTED PRODUCTS
(metric tons, unless otherwise indicated)

	2002	2003	2004
Wine (million litres)	89.0	55.0	119.2
Beer (sales, '000 hectolitres)	3,093	3,127	2,902
Chemical wood pulp*	711,361	623,437	743,671
Mechanical wood pulp*	838,963	795,394	852,787
Newsprint*	351,585	362,130	379,913
Other paper and paperboard*	518,155	447,512	537,350
Fibre board (cu m)*	880,301	868,539	873,408
Particle board (cu m)*	204,650	221,855	243,798
Veneer (cu m)*	552,738	637,556	680,687
Plywood (cu m)*	299,056	343,715	402,147
Jet fuels ('000 metric tons)	869	832	930
Motor spirit—petrol ('000 metric tons)	1,530	1,520	1,627
Gas-diesel (Distillate fuel) oils ('000 metric tons)	2,049	2,018	1,763
Residual fuel oils ('000 metric tons)	427	359	350
Cement ('000 metric tons)	1,090	1,100	1,110
Aluminium—unwrought ('000 metric tons):			
primary	335.0	342.0	351.4
secondary†	21.5	21.5	21.5
Electric energy (million kWh)	40,346	40,441	41,813

* Source: Ministry of Agriculture and Forestry, Wellington.
† Estimates.

Sources (unless otherwise stated): UN, *Industrial Commodity Statistics Yearbook* and *Monthly Bulletin of Statistics*; US Geological Survey; New Zealand Wine Online.

2005: Wine (million litres) 102.0; Chemical wood pulp (metric tons, provisional) 747,768; Mechanical wood pulp (metric tons, provisional) 852,961; Newsprint (metric tons) 379,628; Other paper and paperboard (metric tons) 541,711; Fibre board (cu m) 845,663; Particle board (cu m) 229,971; Veneer (cu m) 694,301; Plywood (cu m) 408,635 (Sources: New Zealand Wine Online; Ministry of Agriculture and Forestry, Wellington).

2006: Wine (million litres) 133.2; Chemical wood pulp (metric tons, provisional) 751,349; Mechanical wood pulp (metric tons, provisional) 749,679; Newsprint (metric tons) 367,064; Other paper and paperboard (metric tons) 573,396; Fibre board (cu m) 906,938; Particle board (cu m) 238,205; Veneer (cu m) 665,206; Plywood (cu m) 403,808 (Sources: New Zealand Wine Online; Ministry of Agriculture and Forestry, Wellington).

2007: Wine (million litres) 147.6; Newsprint (metric tons) 292,015; Other paper and paperboard (metric tons) 579,931; Fibre board (cu m) 836,755; Particle board (cu m) 256,239; Veneer (cu m) 688,312; Plywood (cu m) 421,794 (Sources: New Zealand Wine Online; Ministry of Agriculture and Forestry, Wellington).

2008: Wine (million litres) 205.2; Newsprint (metric tons) 285,654; Other paper and paperboard (metric tons) 585,429; Fibre board (cu m) 765,044; Particle board (cu m) 245,309; Veneer (cu m) 512,575; Plywood (cu m) 416,383 (Sources: New Zealand Wine Online; Ministry of Agriculture and Forestry, Wellington).

Finance

CURRENCY AND EXCHANGE RATES

Monetary Units
100 cents = 1 New Zealand dollar ($NZ).

Sterling, US Dollar and Euro Equivalents (31 December 2008)
£1 sterling = $NZ2.520;
US $1 = $NZ1.729;
€1 = $NZ2.406;
$NZ100 = £39.68 = US $57.85 = €41.57.

Average Exchange Rate (New Zealand dollars per US $)
2006 1.5421
2007 1.3601
2008 1.4227

BUDGET
($NZ million, year ending 30 June)

Revenue	2006/07	2007/08*	2008/09*
Taxation	53,064	56,186	55,911
Compulsory fees, fines, penalties and levies	3,496	3,851	4,037
Sales of goods and services	12,613	13,682	14,222
Interest revenue and dividends	2,995	3,203	3,358
Other	2,421	2,891	2,591
Total	74,589	79,813	80,119

Expenditure	2006/07	2007/08*	2008/09*
Social security and welfare	19,829	22,274	22,843
GSF pension expenses	645	714	652
Health	10,661	10,765	12,024
Education	9,853	10,803	11,017
Core government services	4,628	3,163	3,412
Law and order	2,822	3,192	3,341
Defence	1,478	1,524	1,697
Transport and communications	6,990	7,185	8,027
Economic and industrial services	4,723	7,433	7,918
Primary services	1,233	1,404	1,364
Heritage, culture and recreation	2,043	2,366	3,130
Housing and community development	865	965	1,036
Other	74	84	83
Finance costs	2,885	2,954	2,503
Future spending forecast	—	—	249
Adjustment	—	–240	–495
Total (incl. others)	68,729	74,586	78,801

* Forecasts.
Source: New Zealand Treasury, Wellington.

INTERNATIONAL RESERVES
(US $ million at 31 December)

	2006	2007	2008
IMF special drawing rights	33	28	22
Reserve position in IMF	119	95	175
Foreign exchange	13,916	17,124	10,955
Total	14,068	17,247	11,152

Source: IMF, *International Financial Statistics*.

MONEY SUPPLY
($NZ million at 31 December)

	2006	2007	2008
Currency outside banks	3,016	3,191	3,526
Demand deposits at banking institutions	19,610	19,834	20,180
Total money (incl. others)	22,672	23,025	23,707

Source: IMF, *International Financial Statistics*.

COST OF LIVING
(Consumer Price Index; base: 2000 = 100)

	2005	2006	2007
Food (incl. beverages)	113.1	116.2	120.6
Fuel and light	131.8	140.2	149.5
Clothing (incl. footwear)	101.6	101.6	101.6
Rent	100.0	102.3	105.2
All items (incl. others)	113.0	116.8	119.6

Source: ILO.

NEW ZEALAND

Statistical Survey

NATIONAL ACCOUNTS
($NZ million at current prices, year ending 31 March)

Expenditure on the Gross Domestic Product

	2005/06	2006/07	2007/08
Government final consumption expenditure	28,542	30,890	33,125
Private final consumption expenditure	93,394	98,656	103,730
Change in inventories	848	–459	1,340
Gross fixed capital formation	38,084	38,568	40,872
Total domestic expenditure	160,869	167,655	179,067
Exports of goods and services	43,786	48,199	51,421
Less Imports of goods and services	47,444	50,528	52,876
GDP in market prices	157,210	165,325	177,613
GDP at constant 1995/96 prices	128,510	130,533	134,391

Gross Domestic Product by Economic Activity

	2002/03	2003/04	2004/05
Agriculture	6,924	7,539	7,656
Fishing	274	268	261
Forestry and logging	1,217	1,021	1,016
Mining and quarrying	1,489	1,339	1,581
Manufacturing	20,048	20,374	22,044
Electricity, gas and water	3,318	3,812	4,032
Construction	5,809	6,623	7,803
Wholesale and retail trade	17,292	18,560	19,271
Hotels and restaurants	2,418	2,585	2,844
Transport, storage and communications	9,445	10,011	10,615
Financial intermediation (incl. insurance)	8,033	8,651	9,041
Property and business activities	18,645	20,161	21,728
Ownership of dwellings	8,780	9,280	9,669
Public administration and defence	5,487	5,842	6,344
Education	5,170	5,624	6,087
Health and community services	6,761	7,371	8,108
Cultural and recreational services	3,105	3,407	3,545
Personal and other services	1,911	2,042	2,248
Sub-total	126,128	134,512	143,892
Less Financial intermediation services indirectly measured	4,725	4,875	5,108
Gross value added at basic prices	121,403	129,637	138,784
Goods and services tax on production	8,851	9,571	10,282
Import duties	742	719	870
GDP in market prices	130,996	139,928	149,936

BALANCE OF PAYMENTS
(US $ million)

	2005	2006	2007
Exports of goods f.o.b.	22,006	22,576	27,291
Imports of goods f.o.b.	–24,583	–24,573	–29,052
Trade balance	–2,577	–1,997	–1,761
Exports of services	8,602	8,108	9,282
Imports of services	–8,253	–7,887	–9,114
Balance on goods and services	–2,228	–1,776	–1,593
Other income received	1,554	1,554	2,765
Other income paid	–8,844	–9,456	–12,224
Balance on goods, services and income	–9,517	–9,677	–11,052
Current transfers received	1,242	1,292	1,425
Current transfers paid	–1,006	–880	–1,008
Current balance	–9,281	–9,265	–10,635
Capital account (net)	–195	–214	–559
Direct investment abroad	1,504	–490	–3,198
Direct investment from abroad	1,489	7,762	2,469
Portfolio investment assets	–587	–945	–1,188
Portfolio investment liabilities	581	–313	12,081
Other investment assets	4,090	–1,434	–1,999
Other investment liabilities	3,926	8,184	6,333
Net errors and omissions	914	969	–216
Overall balance	2,441	4,255	3,087

Source: IMF, *International Financial Statistics*.

External Trade

PRINCIPAL COMMODITIES
($NZ million)

Imports (c.i.f.)	2006	2007	2008*
Vehicles, parts and accessories	4,771	5,136	5,062
Boilers, machinery and mechanical appliances	5,157	5,360	6,218
Petroleum, petroleum products, etc.	6,029	5,985	8,515
Electrical machinery and equipment	3,555	3,719	4,000
Paper and paperboard	995	991	1,045
Plastic and plastic articles	1,543	1,557	1,724
Iron and steel and articles	1,379	1,487	1,736
Optical, medical and measuring equipment	1,216	1,136	1,299
Total (incl. others)	40,716	41,869	48,530

Exports f.o.b.	2006	2007	2008*
Dairy produce; birds' eggs; natural honey; edible products or animal origin, not elsewhere specified or included	6,255	7,495	9,213
Meat and edible offal	4,668	4,346	5,147
Logs, wood and wood articles	2,136	2,089	2,195
Boilers, machinery and mechanical appliances; parts thereof	1,886	1,893	1,881
Fruit and nuts; peel of citrus fruit or melons	1,202	1,285	1,445
Fish, crustaceans and molluscs	1,195	1,103	1,217
Aluminium and aluminium articles	1,484	1,517	1,428
Electrical machinery and equipment	1,099	1,051	1,075
Total (incl. others)†	34,634	36,557	42,915

* Provisional figures.
† Including re-exports.

NEW ZEALAND

Statistical Survey

PRINCIPAL TRADING PARTNERS
($NZ million)

Imports (c.i.f.)*	2006	2007	2008*
Australia	8,194	8,622	8,740
Belgium	295	288	340
Canada	681	584	728
China, People's Republic	4,964	5,587	6,445
France	778	667	805
Germany	1,801	1,958	2,077
Indonesia	674	731	1,155
Italy	832	960	979
Japan	3,709	3,945	3,952
Korea, Republic	1,191	1,189	1,318
Malaysia	1,196	1,126	2,009
Netherlands	296	517	389
Qatar	n.a.	410	1,522
Saudi Arabia	n.a.	590	550
Singapore	1,850	2,149	2,211
Sweden	343	339	378
Taiwan	729	918	974
Thailand	1,030	1,125	1,318
United Arab Emirates	576	762	781
United Kingdom	1,112	1,084	1,084
USA	4,924	4,078	4,600
Total (incl. others)	40,716	41,869	48,530

* Excluding specie and gold.

Exports†	2006	2007	2008*
Australia	7,076	8,023	9,994
Belgium	627	538	507
Canada	553	538	512
China, People's Republic	1,875	1,953	2,539
Fiji	371	340	n.a.
France	387	406	n.a.
Germany	882	754	895
Hong Kong	560	584	700
Indonesia	613	777	1,005
Italy	513	461	n.a.
Japan	3,556	3,364	3,615
Korea, Republic	1,358	1,328	1,359
Malaysia	497	651	950
Mexico	424	600	n.a.
Netherlands	n.a.	401	509
Philippines	512	667	734
Saudi Arabia	411	528	729
Singapore	540	687	863
Taiwan	768	772	750
Thailand	438	567	826
United Kingdom	1,694	1,640	1,672
USA	4,540	4,211	4,383
Venezuela	n.a.	359	655
Total (incl. others)	34,634	36,557	42,915

* Provisional figures.
† Including re-exports, but excluding specie and gold.

Transport

RAILWAYS
(traffic, year ending 30 June)

	2000/01	2001/02	2002/03
Freight ('000 metric tons)	14,461	14,330	14,822
Passengers ('000)	12,714	12,521	12,300*

* Excludes passengers on the Tranz Scenic network.

Source: Tranz Rail Ltd, Wellington.

ROAD TRAFFIC
(vehicles licensed at June)

	2005	2006	2007
Passenger cars	2,211,791	2,254,669	2,300,094
Taxis	8,172	8,011	8,069
Buses and service coaches	15,671	16,486	17,198
Trailers and caravans	408,982	420,289	435,633
Motorcycles and mopeds	47,999	57,684	65,658
Tractors	26,521	27,124	27,510
Trucks	399,843	408,757	417,886

Source: Land Transport New Zealand.

SHIPPING

Merchant Fleet
(registered at 31 December)

	2005	2006	2007
Number of vessels	174	171	174
Displacement (grt)	215,705	206,573	210,208

Source: Lloyd's Register-Fairplay, *World Fleet Statistics*.

Vessels Handled
(international, '000 grt)

	1993	1994	1995
Entered	37,603	39,700	48,827
Cleared	35,128	37,421	42,985

Source: UN, *Statistical Yearbook*.

International Sea-borne Freight Traffic
('000 metric tons, year ending 30 June)

	2004/05	2005/06	2006/07*
Goods loaded	21,894	21,840	22,986
Goods unloaded	19,164	18,119	18,499

* Provisional.

CIVIL AVIATION
(domestic and international traffic on scheduled services)

	2002	2003	2004
Kilometres flown (million)	180	164	176
Passengers carried ('000)	11,285	10,334	11,305
Passenger-km (million)	23,323	23,280	24,710
Total metric ton-km (million)	2,787	3,203	3,307

Source: UN, *Statistical Yearbook*.

Tourism

VISITOR ARRIVALS

Country of residence	2006	2007	2008
Australia	903,504	950,206	976,200
China, People's Republic	105,716	120,804	112,398
Germany	59,353	59,765	62,300
Japan	136,401	121,652	102,482
Korea, Republic	111,361	99,453	79,061
United Kingdom	294,812	292,717	285,094
USA	225,629	216,027	212,410
Total (incl. others)	2,421,561	2,465,680	2,458,503

Tourism receipts ($NZ million): 5,911 in 2006; 6,147 in 2007; 5,947 in 2008.

Source: partly Tourism Research Council, Wellington.

NEW ZEALAND

Communications Media

	2005	2006	2007
Telephones ('000 main lines in use)	1,729	1,790	1,706
Mobile cellular telephones ('000 subscribers)	3,530	3,818	4,245
Personal computers ('000 in use)	1,924	n.a.	n.a.
Internet users ('000)	2,754	3,200	3,360
Broadband subscribers ('000)	331.0	576.1	940.0

Television receivers ('000 in use): 2,130 in 2001.

Radio receivers ('000 in use): 3,750 in 1997.

Facsimile machines ('000 in use, year ending 31 March 1996): 65.

Daily newspapers: 23 (circulation 739,000 copies) in 2004.

Non-daily newspapers: 2 (circulation 311,380 copies) in 2002.

Book production (1999): 4,800 titles.

Sources: partly International Telecommunication Union; UNESCO, *Statistical Yearbook*; UN, *Statistical Yearbook*.

Education

(July 2007, unless otherwise indicated)

	Institutions	Teachers (full-time equivalent)	Students
Early childhood services	4,479	11,485[1]	190,907[2]
Primary schools[3]	2,047	26,469[1]	439,287
Composite schools[4]	147	2,550[1]	47,735
Secondary schools[5]	352	20,398[1]	270,085
Special schools	47	1,104[1]	2,799
Polytechnics	20[6]	4,331	206,965
Colleges of education	4[6]	301[7]	70,487
Universities	8[6]	7,758	146,931
Wananga[8]	3[6]	669	42,352
Private training establishments receiving government grants	522[6]	4,177[6]	59,158[9]

[1] Teachers employed in state schools at 1 April 2007.
[2] Includes children on the regular roll of the Correspondence School, kindergartens, playcentres, Te Kohanga Reo, Early Childhood Development Unit funded playgroups, Early Childhood Development Unit funded Pacific Islands language groups, education and care centres (incl. home-based childcare).
[3] Primary schools include Full Primary Years 1–8, Contributing Years 1–6, Intermediate Years 7–8.
[4] Composite schools provide both primary and secondary education (includes area schools and the Correspondence School).
[5] Secondary schools include Years 7–15, Years 9–15.
[6] 2003 figure.
[7] 2006 figure.
[8] Tertiary institutions providing polytechnic and university level programmes specifically for Maori students, with an emphasis on Maori language and culture.
[9] 2004 figure.

Source: Ministry of Education, Wellington.

Directory

The Constitution

New Zealand has no written constitution. The political system is closely modelled on that of the United Kingdom (with an element of proportional representation introduced to the legislature in 1996). As in the United Kingdom, constitutional practice is an accumulation of convention, precedent and tradition. A brief description of New Zealand's principal organs of government is given below:

HEAD OF STATE

Executive power is vested in the monarch and is exercisable in New Zealand by the monarch's personal representative, the Governor-General.

In the execution of the powers and authorities vested in him or her, the Governor-General must be guided by the advice of the Executive Council.

EXECUTIVE COUNCIL

The Executive Council consists of the Governor-General and all the Ministers. Two members, exclusive of the Governor-General or the presiding member, constitute a quorum. The Governor-General appoints the Prime Minister and, on the latter's recommendation, the other Ministers.

HOUSE OF REPRESENTATIVES

Parliament comprises the Crown and the House of Representatives. At the 1996 general election, a system of mixed member proportional representation was introduced. The House of Representatives comprises 122 members: 70 electorate members (seven seats being reserved for Maoris) and 52 members chosen from party lists. They are designated 'Members of Parliament' and are elected for three years, subject to the dissolution of the House before the completion of their term.

Everyone over the age of 18 years may vote in the election of members for the House of Representatives. Since August 1975 any person, regardless of nationality, ordinarily resident in New Zealand for 12 months or more and resident in an electoral district for at least one month is qualified to be registered as a voter. Compulsory registration of all electors except Maoris was introduced at the end of 1924; it was introduced for Maoris in 1956. As from August 1975, any person of the Maori race, which includes any descendant of such a person, may enrol on the Maori roll for the particular Maori electoral district in which that person resides.

By the Electoral Amendment Act 1937, which made provision for a secret ballot in Maori elections, Maori electors were granted the same privileges, in the exercise of their vote, as general electors.

In local government the electoral franchise is the same.

The Government

Head of State: HM Queen ELIZABETH II (acceded to the throne 6 February 1952).

Governor-General and Commander-in-Chief: Sir ANAND SATYANAND (assumed office 23 August 2006).

CABINET
(April 2009)

Prime Minister and Minister for Tourism: JOHN KEY.

Deputy Prime Minister, Minister of Finance and of Infrastructure: BILL ENGLISH.

Minister for Economic Development and of Energy and Resources: GERRY BROWNLEE.

Minister of Justice, for State-Owned Enterprises and of Commerce: SIMON POWER.

Minister of Health and of State Services: TONY RYALL.

Minister for the Environment, for Climate Change Issues and for the Accident Compensation Corporation: Dr NICK SMITH.

Minister of Police, of Corrections and of Veterans' Affairs: JUDITH COLLINS.

Minister of Education and for Tertiary Education: ANNE TOLLEY.

NEW ZEALAND

Attorney-General and Minister for Treaty of Waitangi Negotiations and for Arts, Culture and Heritage: CHRISTOPHER FINLAYSON.

Minister of Agriculture, for Biosecurity and of Forestry: DAVID CARTER.

Minister of Foreign Affairs and for Sport and Recreation: MURRAY MCCULLY.

Minister of Trade and of Conservation: TIM GROSER.

Minister of Defence and of Research, Science and Technology: Dr WAYNE MAPP.

Minister of Transport and for Communications and Information Technology: STEVEN JOYCE.

Minister for Courts, of Pacific Island Affairs and for Disarmament and Arms Control: GEORGINA TE HEUHEU.

Minister for Social Development and Employment, for Disability Issues and of Youth Affairs: PAULA BENNETT.

Minister for Ethnic Affairs and of Women's Affairs: PANSY WONG.

Minister of Fisheries and of Housing: PHIL HEATLEY.

Minister of Immigration and of Broadcasting: Dr JONATHAN COLEMAN.

Minister of Labour and for Food Safety: KATE WILKINSON.

MINISTERS OUTSIDE CABINET

Minister of Internal Affairs and for Land Information: Dr RICHARD WORTH.

Minister for Building and Construction, of Customs, of Statistics and of Small Business: MAURICE WILLIAMSON.

Minister of Civil Defence, for Senior Citizens and for Racing: JOHN CARTER.

SUPPORT PARTY MINISTERS

Minister of Local Government and for Regulatory Reform: RODNEY HIDE.

Minister of Consumer Affairs: HEATHER ROY.

Minister of Maori Affairs: Dr PITA SHARPLES.

Minister for the Community and Voluntary Sector: TARIANA TURIA.

Minister of Revenue: PETER DUNNE.

MINISTRIES AND GOVERNMENT DEPARTMENTS

Department of the Prime Minister and Cabinet: Executive Wing, Parliament Bldgs, Wellington; tel. (4) 817-9700; fax (4) 499-2109; e-mail admin@dpmc.govt.nz; internet www.dpmc.govt.nz.

Ministry of Agriculture and Forestry: 25 The Terrace, POB 2526, Wellington; tel. (4) 894-0100; fax (4) 894-0720; e-mail info@maf.govt.nz; internet www.maf.govt.nz.

Department of Building and Housing: Level 6, 86 Customhouse Quay, POB 10-729, Wellington; tel. (4) 494-0260; fax (4) 494-0290; e-mail info@dbh.govt.nz; internet www.dbh.govt.nz.

Ministry of Civil Defence and Emergency Management: Level 9, 22 The Terrace, POB 5010, Wellington; tel. (4) 473-7363; fax (4) 473-7369; e-mail emergency.management@dia.govt.nz; internet www.civildefence.govt.nz.

Department of Conservation: POB 10420, Wellington 6143; tel. (4) 471-0726; fax (4) 381-3057; e-mail enquiries@doc.govt.nz; internet www.doc.govt.nz.

Ministry of Consumer Affairs: POB 1473, Wellington 6140; tel. (4) 474-2750; fax (4) 473-9400; e-mail mcainfo@mca.govt.nz; internet www.consumeraffairs.govt.nz.

Ministry for Culture and Heritage: POB 5364, Wellington; tel. (4) 499-4229; fax (4) 499-4490; e-mail info@mch.govt.nz; internet www.mch.govt.nz.

Ministry of Defence: POB 12703, Molesworth St, Wellington 6144; tel. (4) 496-0999; fax (4) 496-0859; e-mail info@defence.govt.nz; internet www.defence.govt.nz.

Ministry of Economic Development: POB 1473, 33 Bowen St, Wellington; tel. (4) 472-0030; fax (4) 473-4638; e-mail info@med.govt.nz; internet www.med.govt.nz.

Ministry of Education: 45–47 Pipitea St, POB 1666, Thorndon, Wellington 6011; tel. (4) 463-8000; fax (4) 463-8001; e-mail enquiries.national@minedu.govt.nz; internet www.minedu.govt.nz.

Ministry for the Environment: POB 10362, Wellington 6143; tel. (4) 439-7400; fax (4) 439-7700; e-mail information@mfe.govt.nz; internet www.mfe.govt.nz.

Ministry of Fisheries: ASB Bank House, 101–103 The Terrace, POB 1020, Wellington; tel. (4) 470-2600; fax (4) 819-4601; e-mail info@fish.govt.nz; internet www.fish.govt.nz.

Ministry of Foreign Affairs and Trade: Private Bag 18901, Wellington 5045; tel. (4) 439-8000; fax (4) 439-8505; e-mail enquiries@mfat.govt.nz; internet www.mfat.govt.nz.

Ministry of Health: POB 5013, Wellington; tel. (4) 496-2000; fax (4) 496-2340; e-mail emailmoh@moh.govt.nz; internet www.moh.govt.nz.

Department of Internal Affairs: POB 805, Wellington 6140; tel. (4) 495-7200; e-mail info@dia.govt.nz; internet www.dia.govt.nz.

Ministry of Justice: Vogel Centre, 16 Kate Sheppard Place, POB 180, Wellington; tel. (4) 918-8800; fax (4) 918-8820; e-mail reception@justice.govt.nz; internet www.justice.govt.nz.

Department of Labour: POB 3705, Wellington; tel. (4) 915-4400; fax (4) 915-4015; e-mail info@dol.govt.nz; internet www.dol.govt.nz.

Ministry of Maori Development (Te Puni Kokiri): POB 3943, Wellington 6140; tel. (4) 819-6000; fax (4) 819-6299; e-mail info@tpk.govt.nz; internet www.tpk.govt.nz.

Ministry of Pacific Island Affairs: POB 833, Wellington 6140; tel. (4) 473-4493; fax (4) 473-4301; e-mail contact@mpia.govt.nz; internet www.mpia.govt.nz.

Ministry of Research, Science and Technology: POB 5336, Wellington 6145; tel. (4) 917-2900; fax (4) 471-1284; e-mail info@morst.govt.nz; internet www.morst.govt.nz.

Ministry of Social Development: POB 1556, Wellington 6140; tel. (4) 916-3300; fax (4) 918-0099; e-mail information@msd.govt.nz; internet www.msd.govt.nz.

State Services Commission: POB 329, Wellington 6140; tel. (4) 495-6600; fax (4) 495-6686; e-mail commission@ssc.govt.nz; internet www.ssc.govt.nz.

Statistics New Zealand (Tatauranga Aotearoa): POB 2922, Wellington 6140; tel. (4) 931-4600; fax (4) 931-4030; e-mail info@stats.govt.nz; internet www.stats.govt.nz.

Ministry of Tourism: 33 Bowen St, POB 5640, Wellington; tel. (4) 498-7440; fax (4) 498-7445; e-mail info@tourism.govt.nz; internet www.tourism.govt.nz.

Ministry of Transport: POB 3175, Wellington 6140; tel. (4) 439-9000; fax (4) 439-9001; e-mail info@transport.govt.nz; internet www.transport.govt.nz.

Treasury: POB 3724, Wellington 6140; tel. (4) 472-2733; fax (4) 473-0982; e-mail info@treasury.govt.nz; internet www.treasury.govt.nz.

Ministry of Women's Affairs: POB 10-049, Wellington; tel. (4) 915-7112; fax (4) 916-1604; e-mail mwa@mwa.govt.nz; internet www.mwa.govt.nz.

Ministry of Youth Development: POB 1556, Wellington 6143; tel. (4) 916-3300; fax (4) 918-0091; e-mail mydinfo@myd.govt.nz; internet www.myd.govt.nz.

Legislature

HOUSE OF REPRESENTATIVES

Speaker: LOCKWOOD SMITH.

General Election, 8 November 2008

Party	Number of party votes	% of votes	Party seats	List seats	Total seats
NZ National Party	1,053,398	44.93	41	17	58
NZ Labour Party	796,880	33.99	21	22	43
Green Party	157,613	6.72	—	9	9
ACT New Zealand	85,496	3.65	1	4	5
Maori Party	55,980	2.39	5	—	5
Progressive Party	21,241	0.91	1	—	1
United Future NZ	20,497	0.87	1	—	1
Total (incl. others)	2,356,536	100.00	70	52	122

Election Commission

Electoral Commission of New Zealand: POB 3050, Wellington 6140; tel. (4) 474-0670; fax (4) 474-0674; e-mail info@elections.govt.nz; internet www.elections.org.nz; independent; Pres. Justice ANDREW MCGECHAN; Chief Exec. Dr HELENA CATT.

Political Organizations

In September 2008 20 political parties were registered.

ACT New Zealand: 309 Broadway, POB 99-651, Newmarket, Auckland; tel. (9) 523-0470; fax (9) 523-0472; e-mail info@voteact

.org.nz; internet www.act.org.nz; f. 1994; supports free enterprise, tax reform and choice in education and health; Pres. GARRY MALLETT; Leader RODNEY HIDE.

Green Party of Aotearoa—New Zealand: POB 11-652, Wellington; tel. (4) 801-5102; fax (4) 801-5104; e-mail greenparty@greens.org.nz; internet www.greens.org.nz; f. 1989; fmrly Values Party, f. 1972; Co-Leaders JEANETTE FITZSIMONS, RUSSEL NORMAN.

Maori Party: POB 50-271, Porirua; tel. (4) 471-9900; fax (4) 499-7269; e-mail hekeretari2@maoriparty.com; internet www.maoriparty.org; f. 2004; Co-Leaders Dr PITA SHARPLES, Hon. TARIANA TURIA; Pres. Dr WHATARANGI WINIATA.

NZ Democrats for Social Credit: POB 18-907, New Brighton, Christchurch 8641; tel. and fax (3) 382-9544; fax (3) 382-9544; e-mail democrats@democrats.org.nz; internet www.democrats.org.nz; f. 1953; est. as Social Credit Political League; subsequently known as New Zealand Democratic Party Inc; liberal; Pres. NEVILLE AITCHISON; Leader STEPHNIE DE RUYTER.

New Zealand First: Parliament Bldgs, Wellington; tel. (4) 471-9292; fax (4) 472-8557; e-mail info@nzfirst.org.nz; internet www.nzfirst.org.nz; f. 1993 by fmr National Party mems; Leader WINSTON PETERS; Pres. GEORGE GROOMBRIDGE.

New Zealand Labour Party: Fraser House, POB 784, Wellington; tel. (4) 384-7649; fax (4) 384-8060; e-mail office@labourparty.org.nz; internet www.labour.org.nz, www.labourparty.org.nz; f. 1916; advocates an organized economy guaranteeing an adequate standard of living to every person able and willing to work; Pres. ANDREW LITTLE; Parl. Leader PHIL GOFF; Gen. Sec. MIKE SMITH.

New Zealand National Party: 14th Floor, Willbank House, 57 Willis St, POB 1155, Wellington 6001; tel. (4) 472-5211; fax (4) 478-1622; e-mail hq@national.org.nz; internet www.national.org.nz; f. 1936; centre-right; supports private enterprise and competitive business, together with maximum personal freedom; Pres. JUDY KIRK; Parl. Leader JOHN KEY.

Progressive Party: POB 33-243, Christchurch 8030; tel. (3) 377-7679; fax (3) 377-7673; e-mail contact@progressive.org.nz; internet www.progressive.org.nz; f. 2002 as the Progressive Coalition to contest the general election; name changed as above April 2004; Leader JIM ANDERTON; Gen. Sec. PHIL CLEARWATER.

United Future New Zealand (UFNZ): Bowen House, Parliament Bldgs, Wellington; tel. (4) 471-9410; e-mail unitedfuture@parliament.govt.nz; internet www.unitedfuture.org.nz; f. 1995; est. by four mems of National Party, two mems of Labour Party and leader of Future New Zealand; Leader PETER DUNNE; Pres. DENISE KRUM.

Other parties that contested the 2008 election included the Alliance, the Aotearoa Legalise Cannabis Party, the Family Party, Libertarianz, the Kiwi Party, the New Zealand Pacific Party, the Republic of New Zealand Party and the Workers' Party.

Diplomatic Representation

EMBASSIES AND HIGH COMMISSIONS IN NEW ZEALAND

Argentina: Sovereign Assurance House, 14th Floor, 142 Lambton Quay, POB 5430, Lambton Quay, Wellington; tel. (4) 472-8330; fax (4) 472-8331; e-mail enzel@arg.org.nz; internet www.arg.org.nz; Ambassador PEDRO R. HERRERA.

Australia: 72–76 Hobson St, Thorndon, POB 4036, Wellington; tel. (4) 473-6411; fax (4) 498-7135; e-mail nzinbox@dfat.gov.au; internet www.australia.org.nz; High Commissioner PAUL O'SULLIVAN.

Brazil: Level 9, Deloitte House, 10 Brandon St, Wellington 6011; tel. (4) 473-3516; fax (4) 473-3517; e-mail brasemb@brazil.org.nz; internet www.brazil.org.nz; Ambassador (vacant).

Canada: Level 11, 125 The Terrace, POB 8047, Wellington; tel. (4) 473-9577; fax (4) 471-2082; e-mail wlgtn@international.gc.ca; internet www.wellington.gc.ca; High Commissioner PAMELA DEACON (acting).

Chile: 19 Bolton St, POB 3861, Wellington; tel. (4) 471-6270; fax (4) 472-5324; e-mail echile@embchile.co.nz; internet www.embchile.co.nz; Ambassador LUIS LILLO.

China, People's Republic: 2–6 Glenmore St, Kelburn, Wellington; tel. (4) 472-1382; fax (4) 499-0419; e-mail administration@chinaembassy.org.nz; internet www.chinaembassy.org.nz; Ambassador ZHANG LIMIN.

Cuba: 35 Hobson St, Thorndon, Wellington; tel. (4) 472-3748; fax (4) 473-2958; e-mail embajada@xtra.co.nz; Ambassador JOSÉ LUIS ROBAINA GARCÍA.

Fiji: 31 Pipitea St, Thorndon, POB 3940, Wellington; tel. (4) 473-5401; fax (4) 499-1011; e-mail viti@paradise.net.nz; internet www.fiji.org.nz; High Commissioner CAMA TUILOMA (acting).

France: Sovereign House, 13th Floor, 34–42 Manners St, POB 11-343, Wellington; tel. (4) 384-2555; fax (4) 384-2579; e-mail amba.france@actrix.co.nz; internet www.ambafrance-nz.org; Ambassador MICHEL LEGRAS.

Germany: 90–92 Hobson St, POB 1687, Wellington; tel. (4) 473-6063; fax (4) 473-6069; e-mail german.embassy@iconz.co.nz; internet www.wellington.diplo.de; Ambassador JÖRG HANS ZIMMERMANN.

Greece: 5–7 Willeston St, 10th Floor, POB 24-066, Wellington; tel. (4) 473-7775; fax (4) 473-7441; e-mail info@greece.org.nz; Ambassador EVANGELOS DAMIANAKIS.

Holy See: Apostolic Nunciature, 112 Queen's Drive, Lyall Bay, POB 14-044, Wellington 6241; tel. (4) 387-3470; fax (4) 387-8170; e-mail nuntius@ihug.co.nz; Apostolic Nuncio Most Rev. CHARLES D. BALVO (Titular Archbishop of Castello).

India: 180 Molesworth St, POB 4045, Wellington 6015; tel. (4) 473-6390; fax (4) 499-0665; e-mail hicomind@hicomind.org.nz; internet www.hicomind.org.nz; High Commissioner K. P. ERNEST.

Indonesia: 70 Glen Road, Kelburn, POB 3543, Wellington; tel. (4) 475-8698; fax (4) 475-9374; e-mail info@indonesianembassy.org.nz; internet www.indonesianembassy.org.nz; Ambassador AMRIS HASSAN.

Iran: POB 14733, Kilbirnie, Wellington; tel. (4) 386-2983; fax (4) 386-3065; e-mail info@iranembassy.org.nz; internet www.iranembassy.org.nz; Ambassador MORTEZA RAHMANI-MOVAHED.

Italy: 34–38 Grant Rd, Thorndon, Wellington 6011; tel. (4) 473-5339; fax (4) 472-7255; e-mail ambasciata.wellington@esteri.it; internet www.ambwellington.esteri.it/ambasciata_wellington; Ambassador Dr GIOACCHINO TRIZZINO.

Japan: Majestic Centre, Levels 18–19, 100 Willis St, POB 6340, Marion Sq., Wellington 6141; tel. (4) 473-1540; fax (4) 471-2951; e-mail japan.emb@eoj.org.nz; internet www.nz.emb-japan.go.jp; Ambassador TOSHIHIRO TAKAHASHI.

Korea, Republic: ASB Bank Tower, Level 11, 2 Hunter St, POB 11-143, Wellington; tel. (4) 473-9073; fax (4) 472-3865; e-mail info@koreanembassy.org.nz; internet www.koreanembassy.org.nz; Ambassador NOH KWANG-IL.

Malaysia: 10 Washington Ave, Brooklyn, POB 9422, Wellington; tel. (4) 385-2439; fax (4) 385-6973; e-mail mwwelton@xtra.co.nz; internet www.kln.gov.my/perwakilan/wellington; High Commissioner Dato' HASNUDIN HAMZAH.

Mexico: AMP Chambers, Level 2, 185–187 Featherston St, POB 11-510, Wellington; tel. (4) 472-0555; fax (4) 496-3559; e-mail mexico@xtra.co.nz; internet www.sre.gob.mx/nuevazelandia; Chargé d'affaires a.i. LUIS ENRIQUE FRANCO.

Netherlands: Investment House, 10th Floor, cnr Featherston and Ballance Sts, POB 840, Wellington; tel. (4) 471-6390; fax (4) 471-2923; e-mail wel@minbuza.nl; internet www.netherlandsembassy.co.nz; Ambassador ANNELIES E. BOOGAERDT.

Pakistan: 182 Onslow Rd, Khandallah, Wellington 6035; tel. (4) 479-0026; fax (4) 479-4315; e-mail pakhcwellington@xtra.co.nz; High Commissioner MUNAWAR SAEED BHATTI.

Papua New Guinea: 279 Willis St, POB 197, Wellington; tel. (4) 385-2474; fax (4) 385-2477; e-mail pngnz@globe.net.nz; internet www.pngnz.org/highcom; High Commissioner BERNARD NAROKOBI.

Peru: Cigna House, Level 8, 40 Mercer St, POB 2566, Wellington; tel. (4) 499-8087; fax (4) 499-8057; e-mail embassy.peru@xtra.co.nz; internet www.embassyofperu.org.nz; Ambassador CARLOS ZAPATA.

Philippines: 50 Hobson St, Thorndon, Wellington 6011; tel. (4) 472-9848; fax (4) 472-5170; e-mail embassy@wellington-pe.co.nz; internet www.philembassy.org.nz; Ambassador Dr BIENVENIDO V. TEJANO.

Poland: 17 Upland Rd, Kelburn, POB 10211, Wellington; tel. (4) 475-9453; fax (4) 475-9458; e-mail polishembassy@xtra.co.nz; internet poland.org.nz; Ambassador LECH MASTALERZ.

Russia: 57 Messines Rd, Karori, Wellington; tel. (4) 476-6113; fax (4) 476-3843; e-mail info@rus.co.nz; internet www.rus.co.nz; Ambassador ANDREY ALEKSEEVICH TATARINOV.

Samoa: 1A Wesley Rd, Kelburn, POB 1430, Wellington; tel. (4) 472-0953; fax (4) 471-2479; e-mail shc@paradise.net.nz; High Commissioner ASI TUIATAGA J. F. BLAKELOCK.

Singapore: 17 Kabul St, Khandallah, POB 13140, Wellington; tel. (4) 470-0850; fax (4) 479-4066; e-mail singhc_wlg@sgmfa.gov.sg; internet www.mfa.gov.sg/wellington; High Commissioner (vacant).

Switzerland: Panama House, 22 Panama St, POB 25004, Wellington; tel. (4) 472-1593; fax (4) 499-6302; e-mail wel.vertretung@eda.admin.ch; internet www.eda.admin.ch/wellington; Ambassador Dr BEAT NOBS.

Thailand: 2 Cook St, Karori, POB 17-226, Wellington; tel. (4) 476-8616; fax (4) 476-3677; e-mail information@thaiembassynz.org.nz; internet www.thaiembassynz.org.nz; Ambassador OUM MAOLANON.

NEW ZEALAND
Directory

Turkey: 15–17 Murphy St, Level 8, POB 12-248, Wellington; tel. (4) 472-1292; fax (4) 472-1277; e-mail turkem@xtra.co.nz; Chargé d'affaires a.i. KEMALETTIN ERUYGUR.

United Kingdom: 44 Hill St, POB 1812, Wellington; tel. (4) 924-2888; fax (4) 473-4982; e-mail ppa.mailbox@fco.gov.uk; internet ukinnewzealand.fco.gov.uk; High Commissioner GEORGE FERGUSSON.

USA: 29 Fitzherbert Terrace, POB 1190, Wellington; tel. (4) 462-6000; fax (4) 499-0490; internet newzealand.usembassy.gov; Chargé d'affaires Dr DAVID KEEGAN.

Viet Nam: Level 21, Grand Plimmer Tower, 2–6 Gilmer Terrace, Wellington; tel. (4) 473-5912; fax (4) 473-5913; e-mail embassyvn@paradise.net.nz; Ambassador VUONG HAI NAM.

Judicial System

The Judicial System of New Zealand comprises a Supreme Court, a Court of Appeal, a High Court and District Courts, all of which have civil and criminal jurisdiction, and the specialist courts, the Employment Court, the Family Court, the Youth Court and the Maori Land Court. Until the establishment of the Supreme Court on 1 January 2004, final appeal was to the Judicial Committee of the Privy Council in the United Kingdom. After 1 January 2004 the Supreme Court replaced the Privy Council as the final appellate court. The right to appeal to the Supreme Court was granted only if the Court was satisfied that the case involved a matter of general or public importance or commercial significance, or in order to correct or prevent a substantial miscarriage of justice.

The Court of Appeal hears appeals from the High Court and from District Court Jury Trials, although it does have some original jurisdiction. Its decisions are final, except in cases that may be appealed to the Supreme Court. Appeals regarding convictions and sentences handed down by the High Court or District Trial Courts are by leave only.

The High Court has jurisdiction to hear cases involving crimes, admiralty law and civil matters. It hears appeals from lower courts and tribunals, and reviews administrative actions.

District Courts have an extensive criminal and civil law jurisdiction. They hear civil cases, while Justices of the Peace can hear minor criminal and traffic matters. The Family Court, which is a division of the District Courts, has the jurisdiction to deal with dissolution of marriages, adoption, guardianship applications, domestic actions, matrimonial property, child support, care and protection applications regarding children and young persons, and similar matters.

The tribunals are as follows: the Employment Tribunal (administered by the Department of Labour), Disputes Tribunal, Complaints Review Tribunal, Residential Tenancies Tribunal, Waitangi Tribunal, Environment Court, Deportation Review Tribunal and Motor Vehicles Disputes Tribunal.

In criminal cases involving indictable offences (major crimes), the defendant has the right to a jury. In criminal cases involving summary offences (minor crimes), the defendant may elect to have a jury if the sentence corresponding to the charge is three months or greater.

Attorney-General: CHRISTOPHER FINLAYSON.

Chief Justice: Dame SIAN ELIAS.

THE SUPREME COURT

Judges: Dame SIAN ELIAS, PETER BLANCHARD, ANDREW PATRICK CHARLES TIPPING, JOHN MCGRATH, WILLIAM WILSON.

THE COURT OF APPEAL

President: WILLIAM YOUNG.

Judges: SUSAN GLAZEBROOK, ROBERT GRANT HAMMOND, ROBERT CHAMBERS, MARK O'REGAN, BRUCE ROBERTSON, TERENCE ARNOLD, ELLEN FRANCE, DAVID BARAGWANATH.

THE HIGH COURT

Permanent Judges: Chief Justice Dame SIAN ELIAS (ex officio), Chief High Court Judge ANTHONY RANDERSON, HUGH WILLIAMS, LOWELL GODDARD, GRAHAM PANCKHURST, LESTER CHISHOLM, WARWICK GENDALL, JUDITH POTTER, JOHN WILD, RODNEY HANSEN, JOHN PRIESTLEY, RONALD YOUNG, RHYS HARRISON, PAUL HEATH, GEOFFREY VENNING, PATRICK KEANE, JOHN FOGARTY, ALAN MACKENZIE, FORREST MILLER, MARK COOPER, HELEN WINKELMANN, CHRISTOPHER ALLAN, PATRICIA COURTNEY, SIMON FRANCE, RAYNOR ASHER, GRAHAM LANG, DENIS CLIFFORD, PAMELA ANDREWS, LYNTON STEVENS, JILLIAN MALLON, PETER WOODHOUSE, AILSA DUFFY, ROBERT ANDREW DOBSON, CHRISTINE FRENCH, EDWIN WYLIE, JOSEPH WILLIAMS.

Religion

CHRISTIANITY

Te Runanga Whakawhanaunga i Nga Hahi o Aotearoa (Maori Council of Churches in New Zealand): Private Bag 11903, Ellerslie, Auckland; tel. (9) 525-4179; fax (9) 525-4346; f. 1982; four mem. churches; Administrator TE RUA GRETHA.

The Anglican Communion

The Anglican Church in Aotearoa, New Zealand and Polynesia comprises Te Pihopatanga o Aotearoa and eight dioceses (one of which is Polynesia). In 1996 the Church had an estimated 631,764 members in New Zealand.

Primate of the Anglican Church in Aotearoa, New Zealand and Polynesia, and Bishop of Aotearoa: Rt Rev. WILLIAM BROWN TUREI, POB 568, Gisborne 4040; tel. (6) 867-88561; fax (9) 377-6962; e-mail browntmihi@xtra.co.nz.

General Secretary and Treasurer of the Anglican Church in Aotearoa, New Zealand and Polynesia: JACKIE PEARSE, POB 87-188, Meadowbank, Auckland 1742; tel. (9) 521-4439; fax (9) 521-4490; e-mail gensec@ang.org.nz; internet www.anglican.org.nz.

The Roman Catholic Church

For ecclesiastical purposes, New Zealand comprises one archdiocese and five dioceses. At 31 December 2006 there were an estimated 496,086 adherents.

Bishops' Conference

New Zealand Catholic Bishops' Conference, Catholic Centre, 22–30 Hill St, POB 1937, Wellington 6140; tel. (4) 496-1747; fax (4) 496-17461; e-mail adickinson@nzcbc.org.nz; internet www.catholic.org.nz.

f. 1974; Pres. Most Rev. DENIS BROWNE (Bishop of Hamilton); Sec. Archbishop JOHN A. DEW (Archbishop of Wellington); Exec. Officer ANNE DICKINSON.

Archbishop of Wellington: Most Rev. JOHN A. DEW, Catholic Centre, 22–30 Hill St, POB 1937, Wellington; tel. (4) 496-1766; fax (4) 496-1728; e-mail j.dew@wn.catholic.org.nz; internet www.wn.catholic.org.nz.

Other Christian Churches

Baptist Churches of New Zealand: 473 Great South Rd, POB 12149, Penrose, Auckland; tel. (9) 526-0333; fax (9) 526-0334; e-mail info@baptist.org.nz; internet www.baptist.org.nz; f. 1882; 22,456 mems; Pres. MERRILYN WITHERS; Nat. Leader Rev. RODNEY MACANN.

Congregational Union of New Zealand: 8C Kirrie Dr., Te Atatu South, Auckland; tel. and fax (9) 837-2220; fax (9) 620-8291; e-mail cunz@xtra.co.nz; internet www.congregational.org.nz; f. 1884; 600 mems, 14 churches; Sec. ROGER FROST; Chair. PETER ECCLES.

Methodist Church of New Zealand: Connexional Office, POB 931, Christchurch 8140; tel. (3) 366-6049; fax (3) 364-9439; e-mail info@methodist.org.nz; internet www.methodist.org.nz; 18,548 mems; Gen. Sec. Rev. JILL VAN DE GEER.

Presbyterian Church of Aotearoa New Zealand: Level 1, Terralink House, 275–283 Cuba St, POB 9049, Wellington; tel. (04) 801-6000; fax (04) 801-6001; e-mail info@presbyterian.org.nz; internet www.presbyterian.org.nz; 30,000 mems; Moderator Rev. Dr GRAHAM REDDING; Assembly Convenor Rev. RHYS PEARSON.

There are several Maori Churches in New Zealand, with a total membership of over 30,000. These include the Ratana Church of New Zealand, Ringatu Church, Church of Te Kooti Rikirangi, Absolute Maori Established Church, Destiny Church and United Maori Mission. The Antiochian Orthodox Church, the Assemblies of God, the Greek Orthodox Church of New Zealand, the Liberal Catholic Church and the Society of Friends (Quakers) are also active.

BAHÁ'Í FAITH

National Spiritual Assembly of the Bahá'ís of New Zealand: POB 21-551, Henderson, Auckland 1231; tel. (9) 837-4866; fax (9) 837-4898; e-mail admin@bahaiorg.nz; internet www.bahai.org.nz; f. 1957; CEO MURRAY R. SMITH.

The Press

NEWSPAPERS AND PERIODICALS

Principal Dailies

In 2006 there were 28 daily newspapers in New Zealand.

NEW ZEALAND

Ashburton Guardian: 119–205 Burnett St, POB 77, Ashburton; tel. (3) 307-7967; fax (3) 307-0777; e-mail enquiries@theguardian.co.nz; internet www.ashburtonguardian.co.nz; f. 1879; morning; Mon.–Sat.; Man. Editor JOHN SCHALCH; circ. 5,459 (2008).

Bay of Plenty Times: 108 Durham St, Private Bag 12002, Tauranga; tel. (7) 577-7770; fax (7) 578-0047; e-mail editor@bopp.co.nz; internet www.bayofplentytimes.co.nz; f. 1872; evening; Mon.–Sat.; Gen. Man. SIMON ELLIS; Editor LAURA FRANKLIN; circ. 21,903 (2008).

The Daily Post: 1143 Hinemoa St, POB 1442, Rotorua; tel. (7) 348-6199; fax (7) 346-0153; e-mail daily@dailypost.co.nz; internet www.dailypost.co.nz; f. 1885; evening; Gen. Man. GREG ALEXANDER; Editor SCOTT INGLIS; circ. 10,526 (2008).

Dominion Post: Dominion Post House, 40 Boulcott St, POB 3740, Wellington; tel. (4) 474-0222; fax (4) 474-0584; e-mail editor@dompost.co.nz; internet www.dompost.co.nz; f. 2002; est. by merger of *The Evening Post* and *The Dominion*; morning; Mon.–Sat.; Gen. Man. PAUL ELENIO; Editor TIM PANKHURST; circ. 92,055 (2008).

Gisborne Herald: 64 Gladstone Rd, POB 1143, Gisborne; tel. (6) 869-0600; fax (6) 869-0644; e-mail info@gisborneherald.co.nz; internet www.gisborneherald.co.nz; f. 1874; evening; Man. Dir MICHAEL MUIR; Editor IAIN GILLIES; circ. 8,466 (2008).

Greymouth Star: 3 Werita St, POB 3, Greymouth; tel. (3) 768-7121; fax (3) 768-6205; internet www.greystar.co.nz; f. 1866; Mon.–Fri. (evening); Sat (morning); Gen. Man. JOHN GOULDING; Editor PAUL MADGWICK; circ. 4,306.

Hawke's Bay Today: 113 Karamu Rd, POB 180, Hastings; tel. (6) 873-0800; fax (6) 873-0812; e-mail editor@hbtoday.co.nz; internet www.hbtoday.co.nz; f. 1999; evening; conservative; Gen. Man. MATTHEW SHERRY; Editor NATALIE GAULD; circ. 25,706 (2008).

Manawatu Standard: 57–64 The Square, POB 3, Palmerston North; tel. (6) 356-9009; fax (6) 350-9545; e-mail editor@msl.co.nz; internet www.manawatustandard.co.nz; f. 1880; evening; Gen. Man. CRAIG NASH; Editor BERNADETTE COURTNEY; circ. 18,611 (2008).

Marlborough Express: 62–66 Arthur St, POB 242, Blenheim; tel. (3) 577-2950; fax (3) 577-2952; e-mail lanced@marlexpress.co.nz; internet www.marlboroughexpress.co.nz; f. 1866; Gen. Man. ROGER G. ROSE; Editor LANCE DODD; circ. 10,007 (2008).

The Nelson Mail: 15 Bridge St, POB 244, Nelson; tel. (3) 548-7079; fax (3) 546-2802; e-mail mailbox@nelsonmail.co.nz; internet www.stuff.co.nz/nelsonmail; f. 1866; evening; Gen. Man. CRAIG DENNIS; Editor BILL MOORE; circ. 16,920 (2008).

New Zealand Herald: 46 Albert St, POB 32, Auckland; tel. (9) 379-5050; fax (9) 373-6414; internet www.nzherald.co.nz; f. 1863; morning; CEO MARTIN SIMONS; Editor-in-Chief TIM MURPHY; circ. 180,939 (2008).

The Northern Advocate: 88 Robert St, POB 210, Whangarei; tel. (9) 470-2899; fax (9) 470-2869; e-mail daily@northernadvocate.co.nz; internet www.northernadvocate.co.nz; f. 1875; evening; 6 a week; Gen. Man. TONY VERDON; Editor CRAIG COOPER; circ. 14,167 (2008).

Oamaru Mail: 80 Thames St, POB 343, Oamaru; tel. (3) 434-9970; fax (3) 434-9723; e-mail news@oamarumail.co.nz; f. 1876; Mon.–Fri.; morning; Gen. Man. TONY NEILSON; Editor BARRY CLARKE; circ. 3,157 (2008).

Otago Daily Times: 52 Stuart St, POB 517, Dunedin; tel. (3) 477-4760; fax (3) 474-7422; e-mail odt.editorial@alliedpress.co.nz; internet www.odt.co.nz; f. 1861; morning; 6 a week; Man. Dir JULIAN C. S. SMITH; Editor ROBIN CHARTERIS; circ. 40,668 (2008).

The Press: 22 Cathedral Sq., Private Bag 4722, Christchurch 8140; tel. (3) 379-0940; fax (3) 364-8496; e-mail letters@press.co.nz; internet www.press.co.nz; f. 1861; morning; Gen. Man. ANDREW BOYLE; Editor ANDREW HOLDEN; circ. 85,053 (2008).

Southland Times: 67 Esk St, POB 805, Invercargill; tel. (3) 218-1909; fax (3) 218-4349; e-mail letters@stl.co.nz; internet www.southlandtimes.co.nz; f. 1862; morning; Gen. Man. GARETH CODD; Editor FRED TULETT; circ. 28,809 (2008).

Taranaki Daily News: 49–65 Currie St, POB 444, New Plymouth; tel. (6) 759-0800; fax (6) 758-4653; e-mail jonathan.mackenzie@tnl.co.nz; internet www.stuff.co.nz/dailynews; f. 1857; morning; Gen. Man. MIKE BREWER; Editor JONATHAN MACKENZIE; circ. 25,578 (2008).

Timaru Herald: 52 Bank St, POB 42, Timaru; tel. (3) 684-4129; fax (3) 688-6399; e-mail editor@timaruherald.co.nz; internet www.timaruherald.co.nz; f. 1864; morning; Gen. Man. CHRIS MCAUSLIN; Editor DAVE WOOD; circ. 14,062 (2008).

Waikato Times: Private Bag 3086, Hamilton; tel. (7) 849-6180; fax (7) 849-9554; e-mail editor@waikatotimes.co.nz; internet www.stuff.co.nz/waikatotimes; f. 1872; evening; independent; Gen. Man. ANDREW BOYLE; Editor BRYCE JOHNS; circ. 41,245 (2008).

Wairarapa Times-Age: Cnr Perry St and Chapel St, POB 445, Masterton; tel. (6) 370-0933; fax (6) 370-0959; internet www.times-age.co.nz; f. 1892; evening; 6 a week; Gen. Man. WENDY MORRISON; Editor DAVE SAUNDERS; circ. 7,283 (2008).

Wanganui Chronicle: 59 Taupo Quay, POB 433, Wanganui; tel. (6) 349-0710; fax (6) 349-0721; e-mail news@wanganuichronicle.co.nz; internet www.wanganuichronicle.co.nz; f. 1856; morning; Gen. Man. ANDY JARDEN; Editor KIM GILLESPIE; circ. 11,785.

Weeklies and Other Newspapers

Best Bets: 155 New North Rd, Eden Terrace, POB 1327, Auckland; tel. (9) 302-1300; fax (9) 366-4565; e-mail alan.caddy@best-bets.co.nz; Sun. and Thur.; horse-racing, trotting and greyhounds; Editor ALAN CADDY; circ. 10,000.

The Star: 293 Tuam St, POB 1467, Christchurch; tel. (3) 379-7100; fax (3) 366-0180; e-mail star.reporters@starcanterbury.co.nz; internet www.starcanterbury.co.nz; f. 1868; fmrly Christchurch Star; 2 a week; Chief Reporter BOB COTTON; circ. 118,170.

Herald on Sunday: 58 Albert St, POB 32, Auckland; tel. (9) 373-9323; fax (9) 373-9372; internet www.heraldonsunday.co.nz; f. 2004; Editor SHAYNE CURRIE.

MG Business: Freepost 5003, POB 20-034 Bishopdale, Christchurch; tel. (3) 358-3219; fax (3) 358-4490; internet www.mgpublications.co.nz/mercantile; f. 1876; fmrly Mercantile Gazette; fortnightly; Mon; economics, finance, management, stock market, politics; Editor BILL HORSLEY; circ. 16,300.

The National Business Review: Citigroup Centre, Level 14, 23 Customs St East, POB 1734, Auckland; tel. (9) 307-1629; fax (9) 307-5129; e-mail editor@nbr.co.nz; internet www.nbr.co.nz; f. 1970; weekly; Editor-in-Chief NEVIL GIBSON; circ. 12,873.

New Zealand Gazette: New Zealand Gazette Office, Dept of Internal Affairs, POB 805, Wellington 6140; tel. (4) 470-2930; fax (4) 470-2932; e-mail gazette@parliament.govt.nz; internet www.gazette.govt.nz; official government publication; f. 1840; weekly; Man. PATRICK GEDDES; circ. 1,000.

New Zealand Truth Weekly: Truth Publications Ltd, POB 9613, Newmarket, Auckland 1149; tel. (9) 909-3660; fax (9) 373-5410; e-mail editor@truth.co.nz; internet www.truth.co.nz; f. 1905; Friday; local news and features, TV and entertainment, sports; owned by Truth Publications Ltd; Editor WAYNE BUTLER; circ. 24,000.

North Shore Times: POB 33-235, Takapuna, Auckland; tel. (9) 489-4189; fax (9) 486-6700; e-mail janet.ainsworth@snl.co.nz; 3 a week; Man. JANET AINSWORTH; Editor PETER ELEY; circ. 75,000.

Sunday News: POB 1327, Auckland; tel. (9) 302-1300; fax (9) 358-3003; e-mail editor@sunday-news.co.nz; internet www.sundaynews.co.nz; Man. Editor MITCHELL MURPHY; circ. 113,422.

Sunday Star-Times: 155 New North Rd, Eden Terrace, POB 1327, Auckland; tel. (9) 302-1300; fax (9) 309-0258; e-mail editor@star-times.co.nz; internet www.stuff.co.nz/sunday-star-times; f. 1994 by merger; Editor CATE BRETT; circ. 182,314 (2007).

Taieri Herald: 137 Gordon Rd, POB 105, Mosgiel; tel. (3) 489-7123; fax (3) 489-7668; e-mail kate.tucholski@stl.co.nz; f. 1962; weekly; Regional Man. KATE TUCHOLSKI; circ. 12,309 (2006)0.

Wairarapa News: Media House, 89 Chapel St, POB 902, Masterton; tel. (6) 370-5690; fax (6) 370-5691; e-mail editor@wainews.co.nz; f. 1869; Editor WALT DICKSON; circ. 19,920 (2006).

Other Periodicals

AA Directions: POB 5, Auckland 1010; tel. (9) 966-8800; fax (9) 966-8975; e-mail editor@aa.co.nz; internet www.aa.co.nz/Online; quarterly; official magazine of The New Zealand Automobile Association; Editor KATHRYN WEBSTER; circ. 546,968.

Architecture New Zealand: AGM Publishing Ltd, Private Bag 99-915, Newmarket, Auckland; tel. (9) 846-4068; fax (9) 846-8742; e-mail john.walsh@agm.co.nz; internet www.agm.co.nz; f. 1987; every 2 months; Man. Dir IAN CLOSE; Editor JOHN WALSH; circ. 8,500 (2008).

Australian Women's Weekly (NZ edition): Private Bag 92-512, Wellesley St, Auckland; tel. (9) 308-2945; fax (9) 302-0667; e-mail aww@acpmagazines.co.nz; monthly; Editor LEONIE BARLOW; circ. 73,739 (2008).

Dairying Today: POB 3855, Auckland; tel. (9) 913-9627; fax (9) 307-0122; e-mail sudeshk@ruralnews.co.nz; internet www.ruralnews.co.nz; fortnightly; Editor SUDESH KISSUN; circ. 26,792 (2007).

Fashion Quarterly: ACP Media Centre, Private Bag 92-512, Auckland; tel. (9) 308-2735; fax (9) 302-0667; e-mail fq@acpmedia.co.nz; f. 1982; 5 a year; Editor FIONA HAWTIN; circ. 21,378 (2008).

Grapevine: Private Bag 92-124, Auckland; tel. (9) 813-4956; fax (9) 813-4957; e-mail info@grapevine.org.nz; internet www.grapevine.org.nz; 4 issues a year; family magazine; Editor JOHN COONEY; circ. 160,000.

Home New Zealand: ACP Media Centre, cnr Fanshawe and Beaumont Sts, Private Bag 92-512, Auckland; tel. (9) 308-2700; f. 1936; fmrly *NZ Home and Entertaining*; bimonthly; design, architecture, lifestyle; Editor JEREMY HANSEN; circ. 16,331 (2008).

NEW ZEALAND

Info-Link: AGM Publishing Ltd, Private Bag 99-915, Newmarket, Auckland; tel. (9) 846-4068; fax (9) 846-8742; e-mail infolink@agm.co.nz; internet www.info-link.co.nz; quarterly; Publrs PARUL SHEOPURI, REBECCA WOOD; circ. 19,303 (2008).

Inwood Magazine: POB 17124, Greenlane, Auckland 1546; tel. (9) 269-4531; fax (9) 535-7295; e-mail info@inwoodmag.com; internet www.inwoodmag.com; f. 1993; monthly; forestry; Publr TONY NEILSON; circ. 8,000.

Landfall: Otago University Press, POB 56, Dunedin; tel. (3) 479-8807; fax (3) 479-8385; e-mail landfall@otago.ac.nz; internet www.otago.ac.nz/press/landfall; f. 1947; 2 a year; new fiction, poetry, biographical and critical essays, cultural commentary; circ. 1,200.

Mana Magazine: POB 1101, Rotorua; tel. (7) 349-0260; fax (7) 349-0258; e-mail editor@manaonline.co.nz; internet www.manaonline.co.nz; Maori news magazine; Editor DEREK FOX.

New Idea New Zealand: 48 Greys Ave, 4th Floor, Auckland; tel. (9) 979-2726; fax (9) 979-2721; weekly; women's interest; Editor HAYLEY MCLARIN; circ. 52,251 (2008).

New Zealand Dairy Exporter: 8 Weld St, POB 529, Feilding; tel. (6) 323-7104; fax (6) 323-7101; e-mail glenys@dairymag.co.nz; internet www.dairymag.co.nz; f. 1925; monthly; Editor GLENYS CHRISTIAN; circ. 22,739.

New Zealand Gardener: POB 6341, Wellesley St, Auckland; tel. (4) 909-6800; e-mail mailbox@nzgardener.co.nz; internet www.nzgardener.co.nz; f. 1944; monthly; Editor LYNDA HALLIMAN; circ. 40,456.

New Zealand Horse and Pony: POB 12965, Penrose, Auckland; tel. (9) 634-1800; fax (9) 634-2948; e-mail editor@horse-pony.co.nz; internet www.horse-pony.co.nz; f. 1959; monthly; Editor ROWAN DIXON; circ. 12,700.

New Zealand Management: Wellesley St, POB 5544, Auckland; tel. (9) -8400; fax (9) 968-0126; e-mail editor@management.co.nz; internet www.management.co.nz; f. 1954; monthly; business; Editor ELLEN READ; circ. 12,000.

New Zealand Medical Journal: Department of Surgery, Christchurch Hospital, POB 4345, Christchurch; tel. (3) 364-1277; fax (3) 364-1683; e-mail nzmj@cdhb.govt.nz; internet www.nzma.org.nz/journal; f. 1887; publ. by New Zealand Medical Asscn; online publication; articles free to non-subscribers 6 months after publication; 20 a year; Editor Prof. FRANK A. FRIZELLE; circ. 5,000.

New Zealand Science Review: POB 1874, Wellington; tel. (021) 487-284; e-mail editor@nzas.rsnz.org; internet nzas.rsnz.org/publish.html; f. 1942; 4 a year; reviews, policy and philosophy of science; Editor ALLEN PETREY.

New Zealand Woman's Day: Wellesley St, Private Bag 92-512, Auckland; tel. (9) 308-2700; fax (9) 357-0978; e-mail wdaynz@acpmagazines.co.nz; weekly; Editor SARAH HENRY; circ. 116,202.

New Zealand Woman's Weekly: POB 90-119, Auckland Mail Centre, Auckland; tel. (9) 373-9400; fax (9) 373-9405; e-mail editor@nzww.co.nz; internet www.nzww.co.nz; f. 1932; Mon.; women's issues and general interest; Editor SIDO KITCHIN; circ. 90,144.

Next: Level 4, cnr Fanshawe and Beaumont Sts, Westhaven, Private Bag 92-512, Auckland 1036; tel. (9) 308-2773; fax (9) 377-6725; e-mail next@acpmagazines.co.nz; internet www.acpmedia.co.nz; f. 1991; monthly; home and lifestyle; owned by ACP Media; Editor BRENDA WARD; circ. 54,804 (2008).

North & South: Wellesley St, Private Bag 92-512, Auckland; tel. (9) 308-2700; fax (9) 308-9498; e-mail northsouth@acpmedia.co.nz; f. 1986; monthly; current affairs and lifestyle; Editor VIRGINIA LARSON; circ. 31,185.

NZ Catholic: POB 147-000, Ponsonby, Auckland 1034; tel. (9) 360-3067; fax (9) 360-3065; e-mail contact@nzcatholic.org.nz; internet www.nzcatholic.org.nz; f. 1996; fortnightly; Roman Catholic; Man. Editor GAVIN ABRAHAM; circ. 6,700.

NZ House and Garden: 317 New North Rd, Eden Terrace, Auckland; tel. (9) 909-6700; fax (9) 909-6802; e-mail sally.duggan@nzhouseandgarden.co.nz; internet www.nzhouseandgarden.co.nz; monthly; Editor KATE COUGHLAN; circ. 49,231.

NZ Listener: POB 90-783, Victoria St West, Auckland 1142; tel. (9) 373-9400; fax (9) 373-9406; e-mail submissions@listener.co.nz; internet www.listener.co.nz; f. 1939; weekly; current affairs and entertainment; Editor PAMELA STIRLING; Publr and Chief Exec. RICK NEVILLE; circ. 73,404.

Otago Southland Farmer: POB 105, Mosgiel; tel. (3) 489-7123; fax (3) 489-7668; e-mail newspapersales@stl.co.nz; fortnightly; Editor TAM MATANGI; circ. 22,180 (2008).

Pacific Wings: POB 138, Amberley; tel. (3) 233-8368; fax (3) 982-3595; e-mail editor@pacificwingsmagazine.com; internet www.pacificwingsmagazine.com; f. 1932; monthly; Editor ROB NEIL; circ. 20,000.

PC World: POB 6813, Wellesley St, Auckland; tel. (9) 377-9902; fax (9) 377-4604; e-mail ted.gibbons@ffxbusinessgroup.co.nz; internet pcworld.co.nz; f. 1988; monthly; Editor TED GIBBONS; circ. 14,482 (2008).

Prodesign: AGM Publishing Ltd, Private Bag 99-915, Newmarket, Auckland; tel. (9) 846-2722; fax (9) 846-8742; e-mail michael.barrett@agm.co.nz; f. 1993; every 2 months; publ. of the Designers' Institute of New Zealand; Editor MICHAEL BARRETT; circ. 8,000.

PSA Journal: PSA House, 11 Aurora Terrace, POB 3817, Wellington 6015; tel. (4) 917-0333; fax (4) 917-2051; e-mail enquiries@psa.org.nz; internet www.psa.org.nz; f. 1913; 4 a year; journal of the NZ Public Service Asscn; circ. 52,000.

Reader's Digest: POB 90-487, Mail Service Centre, Auckland; e-mail editor@readersdigest.co.nz; internet www.readersdigest.co.nz; f. 1950; monthly; Editor TONY SPENCER-SMITH; circ. 91,145 (2008).

RSA Review: RNZRSA National Headquarters, POB 27248, Wellington 6030; tel. (6) 384-7994; fax (6) 385-3325; e-mail subscribe@rnzrsa.org.nz; internet www.rsa.org.nz; quarterly; official magazine of the Royal New Zealand Returned and Services' Asscn; Editor BARRY ALLISON; circ. 95,000.

Rural News: POB 3855, Auckland; tel. (9) 307-0399; fax (9) 307-0122; e-mail editor@ruralnews.co.nz; fortnightly; Editor HAMISH CARNACHAN; circ. 81,811 (2007).

Spanz: POB 9049, Wellington; tel. (4) 801-6000; fax (4) 801-6001; e-mail amanda@presbyterian.org.nz; internet www.presbyterian.org.nz; f. 1987; bi-monthly; magazine of Presbyterian Church; circ. 21,500.

Straight Furrow: c/o Rural Press, POB 4233, Auckland; tel. (9) 524-1177; fax (9) 524-1170; e-mail straightfurrow@ruralpress.com; internet www.straightfurrow.co.nz; f. 1933; weekly; Group Editor JEFF SMITH; circ. 85,000.

Time New Zealand: POB 198, Auckland 1015; fax (9) 366-4706; internet www.time.com; weekly; circ. 23,970 (2008).

TV Guide (NZ): 317–319 New North Rd, Eden Terrace, POB 6341, Auckland; tel. (9) 909-6902; fax (9) 909-6912; e-mail julie.eley@tv-guide.co.nz; internet www.stuff.co.nz/entertainment/tv; f. 1986; weekly; Editor JULIE ELEY; circ. 171,962 (2008).

UNANewZ: UN Asscn of NZ, POB 24494, Wellington 6142; tel. (4) 496-9638; fax (4) 473-2339; e-mail office@unanz.org.nz; internet www.unanz.org.nz; f. 1946; every 2 months; Pres. ANTONY VALLYON.

NEWS AGENCIES

New Zealand Press Association: Newspaper House, 93 Boulcott St, POB 1599, Wellington 6015; tel. (4) 498-7366; fax (4) 498-7367; e-mail editor@nzpa.co.nz; internet www.nzpa-online.co.nz; f. 1879; non-political; Editor NICK BROWN.

South Pacific News Service Ltd (Sopacnews): Lambton Quay, POB 5026, Wellington; tel. and fax (3) 472-8329; e-mail farthing@deepsouth.co.nz; f. 1948; Man. Editor NEALE MCMILLAN.

PRESS COUNCIL

New Zealand Press Council: The Terrace, 79 Boulcott St, POB 10879, Wellington; tel. (4) 473-5220; fax (4) 471-1785; e-mail presscouncil@asa.co.nz; internet www.presscouncil.org.nz; f. 1972; Chair. BARRY PATERSON; Sec. M. E. MAJOR.

PRESS ASSOCIATIONS

Commonwealth Press Union (New Zealand Section): POB 1066, Wellington; tel. (4) 472-6223; fax (4) 471-0987; Sec. LINCOLN GOULD.

Newspaper Publishers' Association of New Zealand (Inc): Newspaper House, 93 Boulcott St, POB 1066, Wellington 6015; tel. (4) 472-6223; fax (4) 471-0987; e-mail npa@npa.co.nz; internet www.npa.co.nz; f. 1898; 31 mems; Pres. M. MUIR; CEO (vacant); Corporate Services Man. R. PATETE (acting).

Publishers

Auckland University Press: Private Bag 92-019, University of Auckland, Auckland; tel. (9) 373-7528; fax (9) 373-7465; e-mail aup@auckland.ac.nz; internet www.auckland.ac.nz/aup; f. 1966; scholarly press; Dir SAM ELWORTHY.

The Caxton Press Ltd: 113 Victoria St, POB 25-088, Christchurch 8013; tel. (3) 366-8516; fax (3) 365-7840; e-mail peter@caxton.co.nz; internet www.caxton.co.nz; f. 1935; human and general interest, local and NZ history, tourist publs; Man. Dir BRUCE BASCAND.

Dunmore Publishing Ltd: POB 250-80, Wellington 6146; tel. (4) 472-2705; fax (4) 471-0604; e-mail books@dunmore.co.nz; internet www.dunmore.co.nz; f. 1975; non-fiction, educational; Publrs MURRAY GATENBY, SHARMIAN FIRTH.

Hachette New Zealand Ltd: POB 100-749, North Shore Mail Centre, Auckland 0745; tel. (9) 478-1000; fax (9) 478-1010; e-mail admin@hachette.co.nz; f. 1971; fmrly Hachette Livre NZ Ltd; Man. Dir KEVIN CHAPMAN.

HarperCollins Publishers (New Zealand) Ltd: POB 1, Shortland St, Auckland 1140; tel. (9) 443-9400; fax (9) 443-9403; e-mail editors@harpercollins.co.nz; internet www.harpercollins.co.nz; f. 1888; general and educational; CEO JIM DEMETRIOU (acting); Man. Dir TONY FISK.

Learning Media Ltd: POB 3293, Wellington; tel. (4) 472-5522; fax (4) 472-6444; e-mail info@learningmedia.co.nz; internet www.learningmedia.co.nz; f. 1947 as School Publications; state-owned enterprise; contract publishing, professional devt services, and educational products in a range of media and languages; Chief Exec. DAVID GLOVER.

Legislation Direct: POB 12357, Wellington 6144; tel. (4) 568-0005; fax (4) 568-0003; e-mail Ldorders@legislationdirect.co.nz; internet www.legislationdirect.co.nz; general publishers and leading distributor of government publs; fmrly Govt Printing Office/GP Publications; Publications Man. WENDY CAYLOR.

LexisNexis NZ Ltd: Level 1, 181 Wakefield St, POB 472, Wellington 6140; tel. (4) 385-1479; fax (4) 385-1598; internet www.lexisnexis.co.nz; legal; Gen. Man. DARRYN KEILLER.

McGraw-Hill Book Co, New Zealand Ltd: Private Bag 11904, Ellerslie, Auckland 1005; tel. (9) 526-6200; fax (9) 526-6216; e-mail cservice_auckland@mcgraw-hill.com; internet www.mcgraw-hill.com.au; f. 1974; educational; Man. Dir MURRAY ST LEGER.

New Zealand Council for Educational Research: POB 3237, Wellington 6140; tel. (4) 384-7939; fax (4) 384-7933; e-mail sales@nzcer.org.nz; internet www.nzcer.org.nz; f. 1934; scholarly, research monographs, educational, academic, periodicals; Chair. PETER ALLEN; Dir ROBYN BAKER.

Otago University Press: POB 56, Dunedin; tel. (3) 479-8807; fax (3) 479-8385; e-mail university.press@otago.ac.nz; internet www.otago.ac.nz/press; f. 1958; publishes titles on New Zealand, the Pacific and Asia, with special emphasis on history, literature, the arts and natural and social sciences; also educational titles and journals; Publr WENDY HARREX.

Pearson Education New Zealand Ltd: Private Bag 102-902, North Shore City, Auckland 0745; tel. (9) 414-9980; fax (9) 414-9981; e-mail customer.service@pearsonnz.co.nz; internet www.pearsoned.co.nz; f. 1968; fmrly Addison Wesley Longman; educational; Dirs ROSEMARY STAGG, P. FIELD.

Penguin Group (NZ) Ltd: Private Bag 102-902, North Shore Mail Centre, Auckland 0745; tel. (9) 442-7400; fax (9) 442-7401; e-mail publishing@penguin.co.nz; internet www.penguin.co.nz; f. 1973; Publ. Dir GEOFF WALKER; Man. Dir TONY HARKINS.

Wendy Pye Ltd: Private Bag 17-905, Greenlane, Auckland; tel. (9) 525-3575; fax (9) 525-4205; e-mail admin@sunshine.co.nz; internet www.sunshinebooks.com.au; children's fiction and educational; Man. Dir WENDY PYE.

Random House New Zealand Ltd: Private Bag 102-950, North Shore Mail Centre, Auckland; tel. (9) 444-7197; fax (9) 444-7524; e-mail admin@randomhouse.co.nz; internet www.randomhouse.co.nz; f. 1977; general; Chair. MICHAEL MOYNAHAN; Man. Dir KAREN FERNS.

Victoria University Press: POB 600, Wellington; tel. (4) 463-3680; fax (4) 463-6581; e-mail victoria-press@vuw.ac.nz; internet www.victoria.ac.nz/vup; f. 1970; Publr FERGUS BARROWMAN.

PUBLISHERS' ASSOCIATION

Book Publishers' Association of New Zealand Inc: Private Bag 102902, North Shore City, Auckland 0745; tel. (9) 480-2711; fax (9) 479 8356; e-mail admin@bpanz.or.nz; internet www.bpanz.org.nz; f. 1977; Dir ANNE DE LAUTOUR.

Broadcasting and Communications

TELECOMMUNICATIONS

CallPlus: Level 4, 110 Symonds St, POB 108-109, Auckland; tel. (9) 915-7575; e-mail info@callplus.co.nz; internet www.callplus.co.nz; f. 1996; 100% New Zealand owned; full-service telecommunications co; CEO MARTIN WYLIE.

Compass Communications Ltd: POB 2533, Auckland; tel. (9) 965-2200; fax (9) 965-2270; internet www.compass.net.nz; f. 1995; CEO KARIM HUSSONA.

Kordia: Level 4, Fidelity House, 81 Carlton Gore Rd, Auckland 1023; tel. (9) 916-6400; fax (9) 916-6402; internet www.kordiasolutions.com; fmrly known as THL Group; name changed as above 2006; telecommunications, broadcasting and converged solutions; operates in New Zealand and Australia; Chair. WAYNE BROWN; CEO GEOFF HUNT.

Telecom Corpn of New Zealand Ltd: Telecom House, 8 Hereford St, Auckland 1011; tel. (4) 801-9000; fax (4) 385-3469; internet www.telecom.co.nz; Chair. WAYNE BOYD; Chief Exec. PAUL REYNOLDS.

Telecommunications Users Association of New Zealand (TUANZ): POB 331014, Takapuna North Shore Mail Centre 0740; tel. (9) 488-1888; fax (9) 489-9515; e-mail bernice@tuanz.org.nz; internet www.tuanz.org.nz; f. 1986; non-profit asscn representing corporate telecommunications users; Chair. CHRIS O'CONNELL; CEO ERNIE NEWMAN; 500 corporate mems.

TelstraClear: Private Bag 92-143, Auckland 1142; tel. (9) 913-9150; fax (9) 982-6232; internet www.telstraclear.co.nz; f. 1990 as Clear Communications Ltd; merged with TelstraSaturn Ltd 2001; owned by Australian telecommunications co Telstra; business solutions, local and toll services, enhanced internet, etc.; Chair. DAVID THODEY; CEO Dr ALLAN FREETH.

Vodafone New Zealand Ltd: POB 7281, Wellesley St, Auckland 1141; tel. (9) 355-2007; fax (9) 962-9300; internet www.vodafone.co.nz; fmrly Bell South; cellular network; CEO RUSSELL STANNERS.

Woosh Wireless Ltd: 11–15 Railway St, POB 9635, Newmarket, Auckland; tel. (9) 940-0111; fax (9) 520-3447; internet www.woosh.com; f. 1999 as Walker Wireless Ltd; name changed as above 2003; provides internet and telephony services; Chair. ROD INGLIS; CEO KEVIN WILEY.

WorldxChange Communications Ltd: Level 9, Tower Two, 55–65 Shortland St, POB 3296, Auckland; tel. (9) 950-1300; e-mail service@wxc.co.nz; internet www.wxc.co.nz; CEO CECIL ALEXANDER.

Regulatory Authority

Telecommunications Policy Section, Ministry of Economic Development: 33 Bowen St, POB 1473, Wellington; tel. (4) 472-0030; fax (4) 473-4638; e-mail info@med.govt.nz; internet www.med.govt.nz.

BROADCASTING

In December 1995 Radio New Zealand Commercial (RNZC) and New Zealand Public Radio Ltd (NZPR) became independent entities, having assumed responsibility for, respectively, the commercial and non-commercial activities of Radio New Zealand. RNZC was sold to the New Zealand Radio Network Consortium in 1996, and NZPR, which remained a Crown-owned company, assumed the name of its now-defunct parent company, to become Radio New Zealand Ltd. In late 1999 there were 190 radio stations broadcasting on a continuous basis, of which 170 were operating on a commercial basis.

Radio

Radio Broadcasters' Association (NZ) Inc: POB 3762, Auckland; tel. (9) 378-0788; fax (9) 378-8180; e-mail janine@rba.co.nz; internet www.rba.co.nz; represents commercial radio industry; Exec. Council Chair. JOHN MCELHINNEY; Exec. Dir DAVID INNES; 13 mems.

Radio New Zealand Ltd: RNZ House, 155 The Terrace, POB 123, Wellington; tel. (4) 474-1999; fax (4) 474-1459; e-mail rnz@radionz.co.nz; internet www.radionz.co.nz; f. 1936; Crown-owned entity, operating non-commercial national networks: Radio New Zealand National and Radio New Zealand Concert; parliamentary broadcasts on AM Network; Radio New Zealand News and Current Affairs; the short-wave service, Radio New Zealand International; and Radio New Zealand Sound Archives; Chair. CHRISTINE GRICE; Dep. Chair. ALISON TIMMS.

The Radio Network of New Zealand Ltd: 54 Cook St, Private Bag 92-198, Auckland; tel. (9) 373-0000; e-mail enquiry@radionetwork.co.nz; internet www.radionetwork.co.nz; operates 129 commercial stations, reaching 1.4m. people; Chief Exec. JOHN MCELHINNEY.

Television

Television New Zealand (TVNZ) Ltd: Television Centre, 100 Victoria St West, POB 3819, Auckland; tel. (9) 916-7000; e-mail news@tvnz.co.uk; fax (9) 916-7934; internet www.tvnz.co.nz; f. 1960; the television service is responsible for the production of programmes for five TV networks: TV One, TV2, TVNZ Sport Extra, TVNZ 6 and TVNZ 7; networks are commercial all week and transmit in colour; channels broadcast 24 hours a day, seven days a week, and reach 99.9% of the population; Chair. Sir JOHN ANDERSON; CEO RICK ELLIS.

Maori Television: 9–15 Davis Crescent, POB 113-017, Newmarket, Auckland; tel. (9) 539-7000; fax (9) 539-7199; e-mail info@maoritelevision.com; internet www.maoritelevision.com; f. 2003; operates two stations; Te Reo station, launched in early 2008, broadcasts Maori-language programmes for 3 hrs daily; Maori Television station broadcasts Maori- and English-language programmes for 7.5 hrs daily; Chair. GARRY MURIWAI; CEO JIM MATHER.

Private Television

Auckland Independent Television Services Ltd: POB 1629, Auckland.

Sky Network Television Limited: 10 Panorama Rd, POB 9059, Newmarket, Auckland; tel. (9) 579-9999; fax (9) 579-0910; internet www.skytv.co.nz; f. 1990; UHF service on seven channels, satellite service; 720,919 subscribers (Dec. 2007); Chair. PETER MACOURT; CEO JOHN FELLET.

TV3 Network Services Ltd: Symonds St, Private Bag 92-624, Auckland; tel. (9) 377-9730; fax (9) 366-5949; internet www.tv3.co.nz; f. 1989; operated by MediaWorks NZ; Man. Dir RICK FRIESEN.

Finance

(cap. = capital; res = reserves; dep. = deposits; m. = million; br(s). = branch(es); amounts in New Zealand dollars)

BANKING

Central Bank

Reserve Bank of New Zealand (RBNZ): 2 The Terrace, POB 2498, Wellington; tel. (4) 472-2029; fax (4) 473-8554; e-mail rbnz-info@rbnz.govt.nz; internet www.rbnz.govt.nz; f. 1933; res 1,578.7m., dep. 15,851.4m. (June 2007); Gov. ALAN BOLLARD; Chair. Dr ARTHUR GRIMES.

Registered Banks

As a result of legislation that took effect in 1987, several foreign banks were incorporated into the domestic banking system.

ANZ National Bank Ltd: Level 14, ANZ Tower, 215–229 Lambton Quay, Wellington; tel. (4) 496-7123; fax (4) 494-4000; internet www.anz.com/nz; f. 1979; subsidiary of Australia and New Zealand Banking Group Ltd of Melbourne, Australia; fmrly ANZ Banking Group (New Zealand) Ltd; name changed as above 2004 following merger with National Bank of New Zealand Ltd; cap. 9,817m., res 889m., dep. 277,039m. (Sept. 2007); Chair. Sir DRYDEN SPRING; Chief Exec. GRAHAM HODGES; 143 brs and sub-brs.

ASB Bank Ltd: ASB Bank Centre, 135 Albert Sts, POB 35, Auckland 1010; tel. (9) 306-3000; fax (9) 358-3511; e-mail helpdesk@asbbank.co.nz; internet www.asbbank.co.nz; f. 1847; est. as Auckland Savings Bank, name changed 1988; cap. 2,113m., res 278m., dep. 48,776m. (June 2007); Chair. G. J. JUDD; Man. Dir CHARLES PINK; 138 brs.

Bank of New Zealand (BNZ): BNZ Tower, 125 Queen St, Auckland; tel. (9) 302-4955; fax (9) 375-9537; internet www.bnz.co.nz; f. 1861; owned by National Australia Bank; cap. 1,451m., res 26m., dep. 50,911m. (Sept. 2007); Chair. JOHN WALLER; Man. Dir and CEO ANDREW THORBURN; 179 domestic brs and 1 overseas br.

Citibank NA (USA): Citibank Centre, Level 11, 23 Customs Street East, POB 3429, Auckland; tel. (9) 307-1902; fax (9) 308-9928; internet www.citibank.com.au; CEO ANDREW AU; 2 brs.

Deutsche Bank New Zealand: Level 11, ASB Bank Centre, Wellesley St, POB 6900, Auckland; tel. (9) 351-1000; fax (9) 351-1001; e-mail christine.cutler@db.com; internet www.deutsche-bank.co.nz; f. 1986; fmrly Bankers Trust New Zealand; Chair. JOSEPH ACKERNMAN.

Hongkong and Shanghai Banking Corporation Ltd (Hong Kong): 1 Queen St, Level 9, POB 5947, Auckland; tel. (9) 918-8688; fax (9) 918-8797; internet www.hsbc.co.nz; CEO DAVID JAMES GRIFFITHS; 6 brs.

Kiwibank Ltd: Private Bag 39888, Wellington; tel. (4) 473-1133; fax (4) 462-7996; internet www.kiwibank.co.nz; f. 2001; 100% New Zealand-owned; savings bank for small depositors; Chair. JIM BOLGER; Chief Exec. SAM KNOWLES.

Rabobank (New Zealand): POB 38-396, Wellington Mail Centre, Wellington; tel. (4) 819-2700; fax (4) 819-2706; e-mail wellington.enquiry@rabobank.com; internet www.rabobank.co.nz; f. 1996; full subsidiary of Rabobank Nederland; Chair. WILLIAM P. GURRY; CEO BRUCE DICK.

TSB Bank Ltd: POB 240, New Plymouth; tel. (6) 968-3810; fax (6) 968-3815; internet www.tsbbank.co.nz; f. 1850; dep. 2,870m. (March 2008); Chair. ELAINE GILL; Man. Dir KEVIN RIMMINGTON; 17 brs.

Westpac New Zealand: 188 Quay St, Auckland; tel. (9) 912-8000; fax (4) 498-1350; e-mail customer_support@westpac.co.nz; internet www.westpac.co.nz; acquired Trust Bank New Zealand; New Zealand division of Westpac Banking Corpn (Australia); Chair. PETER WILSON; CEO GAIL KELLY; 196 brs.

Association

New Zealand Bankers' Association: POB 3043, Wellington 6140; tel. (4) 802-3358; fax (4) 473-1698; e-mail nzba@nzba.org.nz; internet www.nzba.org.nz; f. 1891; Chief Exec. (vacant).

STOCK EXCHANGES

Dunedin Stock Exchange: POB 298, Dunedin; tel. (3) 477-5900; Chair. E. S. EDGAR; Sec. R. P. LEWIS.

New Zealand Exchange Ltd (NZX): Level 2, NZX Centre, 11 Cable St, POB 2959, Wellington 6140; tel. (4) 472-7599; fax (4) 496-2893; e-mail info@nzx.com; internet www.nzx.com; Chair. ANDREW HARMOS; CEO MARK WELDON (acting).

Supervisory Body

New Zealand Securities Commission: POB 1179, Wellington 6011; tel. (4) 472-9830; fax (4) 472-8076; e-mail seccom@seccom.govt.nz; internet www.seccom.govt.nz; f. 1979; Chair. JANE DIPLOCK.

INSURANCE

ACE Insurance NZ Ltd: POB 734, Auckland 1140; tel. (9) 377-1459; fax (9) 303-1909; e-mail michael.poole@ace-ina.com; internet www.aceinsurance.co.nz; Man. Dir RICHARD PARKINSON.

AMI Insurance Ltd: 29–35 Latimer Sq., POB 2116, Christchurch 8001; tel. (3) 371-9000; fax (3) 371-8314; internet www.ami.co.nz; f. 1926; Chair. KERRY G. L. NOLAN; CEO JOHN B. BALMFORTH.

Atradius: POB 2404, Auckland 1140; tel. (9) 302-4560; fax (9) 353-1244; e-mail info.nz@atradius.com; internet www.atradius.com/nz; fmrly known as Gerling NCM; name changed as above following acquisition by Deutsche Bank and Swiss Re; trade credit insurance services.

AXA New Zealand Ltd: POB 1692, Wellington; tel. (4) 474-4500; fax (4) 472-5069; internet www.axa.co.nz; Chair. RICK ALLERT; CEO RALPH STEWART.

BNZ Life Insurance Ltd: POB 1299, Wellington; tel. (4) 382-2577; fax (4) 474-6883; internet www.bnz.co.nz; Chair. JOHN WALLER; Man. Dir and CEO ANDREW THORBURN.

Farmers' Mutual Group: POB 1943, Palmerston North 4440; tel. (6) 356-9456; fax (6) 356-4603; e-mail contact@fmg.co.nz; internet fmg.co.nz; comprises Farmers' Mutual Finance Ltd and other cos; insurance investment and financial services for the New Zealand rural sector; Chair. GREG GENT.

ING Life (NZ) Ltd: Private Bag 92131, Victoria St West, Auckland 1142; tel. (9) 442-4800; fax (9) 442-4801; e-mail clientservices@inglife.co.nz; internet www.inglife.co.nz; operates ANZ- and The National Bank-branded insurance policies; CEO HELEN TROUP; Man. Dir, Insurance NAOMI BALLANTYNE.

New Zealand Insurance: IAG House, 151 Queen St, Private Bag 92130, Auckland 1030; tel. (9) 309-7000; fax (9) 309-7097; internet www.nzi.co.nz; owned by Insurance Australia Group New Zealand Ltd; Head KARL ARMSTRONG.

New Zealand Local Government Insurance Corporation Ltd (Civic Assurance): Civic Assurance House, 114–118 Lambton Quay, POB 5521, Wellington; tel. (4) 978-1250; fax (4) 978-1260; e-mail info@civicassurance.co.nz; internet www.civicassurance.co.nz; f. 1960; local govt insurance provider; fire, motor, all risks, accident; Chair. BRIAN TAYLOR; Chief Exec. TIM SOLE.

QBE Insurance (International) Ltd: Level 6, AMP Centre, 29 Customs St West, POB 44, Auckland; tel. (9) 366-9920; fax (9) 308-8526; internet www.qbe.co.nz/New-Zealand/Insurance; f. 1890; Gen. Man. ROSS CHAPMAN.

Sovereign Ltd: Private Bag Sovereign, Auckland Mail Centre 1142; tel. (9) 487-9000; fax (9) 487-8003; e-mail enquire@sovereign.co.nz; internet www.sovereign.co.nz; f. 1989; life insurance and investment.

State Insurance Ltd: POB 3233, Wellington 6140; tel. (9) 969-1150; fax (4) 476-9664; internet www.state.co.nz; f. 1905; mem. NRMA Insurance Group; Man. Dir T. C. SOLE.

Tower Insurance Ltd: Level 11, Tower Centre, 22 Fanshawe St, POB 90347, Auckland; tel. (9) 369-2000; fax (9) 369-2129; internet www.tower.co.nz; f. 1873; fmrly National Insurance Co of New Zealand; Chair. TONY GIBBS; Group Man. Dir ROB FLANNAGAN.

Associations

Insurance Council of New Zealand: Perpetual Trust House, Level 7, 111–115 Customhouse Quay, POB 474, Wellington; tel. (4) 472-5230; fax (4) 473-3011; e-mail icnz@icnz.org.nz; internet www.icnz.org.nz; Chief Exec. CHRISTOPHER RYAN.

Investment Savings and Insurance Association of New Zealand Inc: City Chambers, Cnr Johnston and Featherston Sts, POB 1514, Wellington; tel. (4) 473-8730; fax (4) 471-1881; e-mail isi@isi.org.nz; internet www.isi.org.nz; f. 1996 from Life Office Asscn and Investment Funds Asscn; represents cos that act as manager, trustee, issuer, insurer, etc. of managed funds, life insurance and superannuation; Chair. SEAN CARROLL; Chief Exec. VANCE ARKINSTALL.

NEW ZEALAND

Trade and Industry

GOVERNMENT AGENCY

New Zealand Trade and Enterprise: POB 2878, Wellington 6140; tel. (4) 816-8100; fax (4) 816-8101; e-mail info@nzte.govt.nz; internet www.nzte.govt.nz; f. 2003; national government development agency with global network of 48 offices; provides businesses, organizations and investors with access to quality New Zealand goods and services and acts as a gateway to partnerships with New Zealand businesses and to investment opportunities in New Zealand; CEO TIM GIBSON; Chair. PHIL LOUGH.

CHAMBERS OF COMMERCE

Auckland Regional Chamber of Commerce and Industry: POB 47, Auckland 1140; tel. (9) 309-6100; fax (9) 309-0081; e-mail mbarnett@chamber.co.nz; internet www.chamber.co.nz; CEO MICHAEL BARNETT; Chair. JOHN LINDSAY.

Canterbury Employers' Chamber of Commerce: 57 Kilmore St, POB 359, Christchurch 8140; tel. (3) 366-5096; fax (3) 379-5454; e-mail info@cecc.org.nz; internet www.cecc.org.nz; f. 1859; formed through merger of Employers' Fed. and Chamber of Commerce; employment and business support services including legal consultancy and international trade advice, business performance and training, networking and advocacy; Chief Exec. PETER TOWNSEND; Pres. ALLAN POLLARD.

Otago Chamber of Commerce Inc: Ground Floor, Burns House, 10 George St, POB 5173, Dunedin; tel. (3) 479-0181; fax (3) 477-0341; e-mail office@otagochamber.co.nz; internet www.otagochamber.co.nz; f. 1861; CEO J. A. CHRISTIE; Pres. M. WILLIS.

Wellington Regional Chamber of Commerce: 28th Level, Majestic Centre, 100 Willis Street, Wellington; tel. (4) 914-6500; fax (4) 914-6524; e-mail info@wellingtonchamber.co.nz; internet www.wellingtonchamber.co.nz; f. 1856; Chief Exec. CHARLES FINNY; Pres. JO BRANSGROVE; 1,000 mems.

INDUSTRIAL AND TRADE ASSOCIATIONS

Employers' and Manufacturers' Association (Central Inc): 2nd Floor, Lumley House, 3–11 Hunter St, Wellington, POB 1087, Wellington 6140; tel. (4) 473-7224; fax (4) 473-4501; e-mail ema@emacentral.org.nz; internet www.emacentral.org.nz; f. 1997 by merger of Wellington Manufacturers' Asscn and Wellington Regional Employers' Asscn; CEO PAUL WINTER; 2,200 mems.

Employers' and Manufacturers' Association (Northern Inc): 159 Khyber Pass Rd, Grafton, Private Bag 92066, Auckland; tel. (9) 367-0900; fax (9) 367-0902; e-mail ema@ema.co.nz; internet www.ema.co.nz; f. 1886; fmrly Auckland Manufacturers' Asscn; Chief Exec. ALASDAIR THOMPSON; Pres. GRAHAM MOUNTFORT; 5,000 mems.

ENZA: POB 56, Auckland; tel. (9) 573-8700; fax (9) 573-8879; e-mail info@enza.co.nz; internet www.enza.co.nz; f. 1956; owned by Turners and Growers Ltd; fmrly New Zealand Apple and Pear Marketing Board; export apples, pears and kiwifruit; creates new apple varieties; Man. Dir JEFF WESLEY; Gen. Man. SNOW HARDY.

Federated Farmers of New Zealand (Inc): POB 715, Wellington; tel. (4) 473-7269; fax (4) 473-1081; e-mail receptionwgton@fedfarm.org.nz; internet www.fedfarm.org.nz; f. 1946; Pres. DON NICOLSON; CEO CONOR ENGLISH; 16,000 mems.

Horticulture New Zealand: POB 10232, Wellington 6143; tel. (4) 472-3795; fax (4) 471-2861; internet www.hortnz.co.nz; formed through merger of New Zealand Fruitgrowers' Federation, New Zealand Berryfruit Federation and New Zealand Vegetable and Potato Growers' Federation; 7,000 mems; Pres. and Chair. ANDREW FENTON; CEO PETER SILCOCK.

Kiwifruit New Zealand (KNZ): POB 4683, Mt Maunganui South 3149; tel. (7) 572-3685; fax (7) 572-5934; e-mail richard.procter@knz.co.nz; f. 2000; Chair. Sir BRIAN ELWOOD.

Meat and Wool New Zealand: POB 121, Wellington 6140; tel. (4) 473-9150; fax (4) 474-0800; e-mail help@meatandwoolnz.com; internet www.meatandwoolnz.com; Chair. MIKE PETERSEN; CEO Dr SCOTT CHAMPION.

Meat Industry Association of New Zealand (Inc) (MIA): Level 13, PricewaterhouseCoopers Bldg, 113–119 The Terrace, POB 345, Wellington 6140; tel. (4) 473-6465; fax (4) 499-5924; e-mail info@mia.co.nz; internet www.mia.co.nz; Chair. W. J. (BILL) FALCONER; CEO TIM RITCHE.

National Beekeepers' Association of New Zealand (Inc): 10 Nikau Lane, RD 3, Otaki 5583; tel. (6) 362-6301; fax (6) 362-6302; e-mail secretary@nba.org.nz; internet www.nba.org.nz; f. 1913; 400 mems; Pres. GARY GOODWIN; Sec. JO SCOTT.

New Zealand Animal By-Products Exporters' Association: 11 Longhurst Terrace, POB 12-222, Christchurch; tel. (3) 332-2895; fax (3) 332-2825; 25 mems; Sec. J. L. NAYSMITH.

Directory

New Zealand Council of Wool Exporters Inc: POB 2857, Christchurch; tel. (3) 353-1049; fax (3) 374-6925; e-mail cwe@woolexport.net; internet www.woolexport.net; f. 1893; Exec. Man. R. H. F. NICHOLSON; Pres. JOHN HENDERSON.

The New Zealand Forest Owners' Association: POB 1208, Wellington; tel. (4) 473-4769; fax (4) 499-8893; e-mail nzfoa@nzfoa.org.nz; internet www.nzfoa.org.nz; Pres. PETER BERG; Chief Exec. DAVID RHODES.

New Zealand Fruit Wine and Cider Makers Inc: POB 912, New Plymouth; tel. and fax (6) 769-9009; fax (6) 769-9009; e-mail admin@fruitwines.co.nz; internet www.fruitwines.co.nz; f. 1987; 30 mems; Chair. MARK ATKIN; Exec. Officer CHRISTINE GARNHAM.

New Zealand Manufacturers' and Exporters' Association (MEA): POB 13-152, Armagh, Christchurch 8141; tel. (3) 353-2540; fax (3) 353-2549; e-mail cma@cma.org.nz; internet www.mea.org.nz; f. 2007; formed by merger of Canterbury Manufacturers' Association and New Zealand Engineers' Federation; CEO JOHN WALLEY; Pres. GORDON SUTHERLAND.

New Zealand Meat Board: Level 13, PriceWaterhouseCoopers Tower, 113–119 The Terrace, POB 121, Wellington; tel. (4) 473-9150; fax (4) 474-0801; e-mail info@nzmeatboard.org; internet www.nzmeatboard.org; f. 1922; Chair. MIKE PETERSEN; Sec. A. DOMETAKIS; 10 mems.

New Zealand Pork Industry Board (New Zealand Pork): POB 4048, Wellington 6140; tel. (4) 917-4750; fax (4) 385-8522; e-mail info@pork.co.nz; internet www.pork.co.nz; f. 1937; Chair. C. TRENGROVE; CEO S. McIVOR.

New Zealand Retailers' Association Inc: Willbank House, 8th Floor, 57 Willis St, Wellington; tel. (4) 472-3733; fax (4) 472-1071; e-mail bhellberg@retail.org.nz; internet www.retail.org.nz; direct membership 6,000; Pres. BILL WALLACE; CEO JOHN ALBERTSON.

New Zealand Seafood Industry Council: Private Bag 24-901, Wellington; tel. (4) 385-4005; fax (4) 384-2727; e-mail info@seafood.co.nz; internet www.seafood.co.nz; CEO OWEN SYMMANS; Chair. DAVID SHARP.

New Zealand Timber Industry Federation: 2–8 Maginnity St, POB 308, Wellington; tel. (4) 473-5200; fax (4) 473-6536; e-mail inquiries@nztif.co.nz; internet www.nztif.co.nz; 350 mems; Exec. Dir W. S. COFFEY.

Registered Master Builders' Federation (Inc): 234 Wakefield St, Level 6, POB 1796, Wellington; tel. (4) 385-8999; fax (4) 385-8995; internet www.masterbuilder.org.nz; Chief Exec. WARWICK QUINN.

EMPLOYERS' ORGANIZATION

Business New Zealand: Lumley House, Level 6, 3–11 Hunter St, POB 1925, Wellington; tel. (4) 496-6555; fax (4) 496-6550; e-mail admin@businessnz.org.nz; internet www.businessnz.org.nz; f. 2001; Chief Exec. PHIL O'REILLY.

UTILITIES

Energy Efficiency and Conservation Authority (EECA): Vector House, Level 8, 44 The Terrace, POB 388, Wellington; tel. (4) 470-2200; fax (4) 499-5330; e-mail info@eeca.govt.nz; internet www.eeca.govt.nz; f. 2000; Chair. ROGER SUTTON; Chief Exec. MIKE UNDERHILL.

Electricity

Electricity Commission: Level 7, ASB Bank Tower, 2 Hunter St, POB 10041, Wellington; tel. (4) 460-8860; fax (4) 460-8879; e-mail info@electricitycommission.govt.nz; internet www.electricitycommission.govt.nz; f. 2003; independent; regulatory body supervising electricity sector; Chair. DAVID CAYGILL.

Bay of Plenty Electricity Ltd: 52 Commerce St, POB 404, Whakatane; tel. (7) 922-2700; fax (7) 307-0922; e-mail enquiries@bopelec.co.nz; internet www.bopelec.co.nz; f. 1995; generation, purchase and supply of electricity and natural gas; Commercial Man. CHRIS POWER; CEO DAVID BULLEY.

Contact Energy Ltd: Harbour City Tower, Level 1, 29 Brandon St, POB 10742, Wellington; tel. (4) 449-4001; fax (4) 499-4003; e-mail help@contact-energy.co.nz; internet www.contactenergy.co.nz; f. 1996; generation of electricity, wholesale and retail of energy; transferred to the private sector in 1999; Chair. GRANT KING; CEO DAVID BALDWIN.

Genesis Power Ltd: 602 Great South Rd, POB 17-188, Greenlane 1546, Auckland; tel. (9) 580-2094; fax (9) 580-4891; internet www.genesisenergy.co.nz; f. 1999; state-owned; generation and retail of electricity and gas; Chair. BRIAN CORBAN; Chief Exec. ALBERT BRANTLEY.

The Marketplace Co Ltd (M-CO): Level 2, 10 Brandon St, POB 5422, Wellington; tel. (4) 473-5240; fax (4) 473-5247; e-mail info@nz.m-co.com; internet www.nz.m-co.com; administers wholesale electricity market; Chief Exec. CARL HANSEN.

Meridian Energy Ltd: POB 2128, Christchurch; tel. (3) 353-9500; fax (3) 353-9501; internet www.meridianenergy.co.nz; state-owned; generation and retail of electricity; Chair. WAYNE BOYD; Chief Exec. TIM LUSK.

Mighty River Power Ltd: Level 14, 23–29 Albert St, POB 90-399, Auckland; tel. (9) 308-8200; fax (9) 308-8209; e-mail enquiries@mightyriver.co.nz; internet www.mightyriverpower.co.nz; f. 1999; electricity generation and retail; cos include Vector Electricity; Chair. CAROLE DURBIN; Chief Exec. DOUG HEFFERMAN.

Nova Energy Ltd: POB 10-141, Wellington 6143; tel. (4) 472-6263; fax (4) 472-6264; e-mail info@novaenergy.co.nz; internet www.novaenergy.co.nz; fmrly Nova Gas Ltd; supplier of electricity, gas, LPG and solar energy; Group Gas Man. HAMISH TWEEDIE.

Todd Energy Ltd: 95 Customhouse Quay, POB 3141, Wellington; tel. (4) 471-6555; fax (4) 472-2474; e-mail energy@toddenergy.co.nz; internet www.toddenergy.co.nz; Man. Dir and CEO RICHARD TWEEDIE.

Transpower New Zealand Ltd: Level 7, Transpower House, 96 The Terrace, POB 1021, Wellington; tel. (4) 495-7000; fax (4) 495-7100; internet www.transpower.co.nz; manages national grid; Chair. WAYNE BROWN; Chief Exec. PATRICK STRANGE.

TrustPower Ltd: Private Bag 12-023, Tauranga Mail Centre, Tauranga 3143, Auckland; tel. (7) 574-4754; fax (7) 574-4803; e-mail trustpower@trustpower.co.nz; internet www.trustpower.co.nz; f. 1920 as Tauranga Electric Power Board; independent generator; Chair. Dr BRUCE HARKER; CEO KEITH TEMPEST.

Vector Electricity Ltd: POB 99-882, Newmarket, Auckland; tel. (9) 303-0626; fax (9) 978-7799; internet www.vectorelectricity.co.nz; owned by Vector Ltd; fmrly Mercury Energy Ltd; operates power networks in Auckland, Manukau and Papakura; Group CEO SIMON MACKENZIE.

Gas

Bay of Plenty Electricity Ltd: see Electricity, above.

E-gas Ltd: Level 13, Forsyth Barr House, cnr Lambton Quay and Johnston St, POB 2577, Wellington; tel. (4) 499-4964; fax (4) 499-4965; e-mail info@e-gas.co.nz; internet www.e-gas.co.nz; supplier of natural gas.

Genesis Energy Ltd: see Electricity, above.

NGC Holdings Ltd: Level 8, NGC Bldg, 44 The Terrace, Private Bag 39-980, Wellington Mail Centre, Wellington; tel. (4) 462-8700; fax (4) 462-8600; internet www.ngc.co.nz; f. 1992; fmrly Natural Gas Corpn Holdings Ltd; name changed as above 2002; purchase, processing and transport of natural gas; wholesale and retail sales; Chair. MICHAEL STIASSNY; Chief Exec. BRYAN CRAWFORD.

Nova Energy Ltd: See Electricity, above.

Vector Gas Ltd: 101 Carlton Gore Rd, Newmarket, Auckland; tel. (9) 978-7788; fax (9) 978-7799; e-mail info@vectorgas.co.nz; internet www.vectorgas.co.nz; distribution of natural gas in Auckland.

Wanganui Gas Ltd: 179 Hill St, POB 32, Wanganui; tel. (6) 349-0909; fax (6) 345-4931; e-mail enquiries@wanganuigas.co.nz; internet www.wanganuigas.co.nz; f. 1879; supplier of gas on North Island; Chair. CHARLES POYNTER; Chief Exec. TREVOR GOODWIN.

Water

Waste Management NZ Ltd: 86 Lunn Ave, Mt Wellington, Private Bag 14-919, Auckland; tel. (9) 527-1300; fax (9) 570-1417; internet www.wastemanagement.co.nz; f. 1985; waste collection, recovery and disposal; liquid waste collection and processing; recycling; Man. Dir GREGG CAMPBELL; Regional Man. KEVIN BONNIFACE.

Watercare Services Ltd: Private Bag 92521, Wellesley St, Auckland 1141; tel. (9) 539-7300; fax (9) 539-7334; e-mail info@water.co.nz; internet www.watercare.co.nz; f. 1993; provides water and waste water services in the Auckland area; Chair. GRAEME HAWKINS; Chief Exec. MARK FORD.

TRADE UNIONS

In December 2000 a total of 134 unions were in operation; 318,519 workers belonged to a union.

New Zealand Council of Trade Unions: Education House, West Block, 178 Willis St, POB 6645, Wellington 6141; tel. (4) 385-1334; fax (4) 385-6051; e-mail helen@nzctu.org.nz; internet www.union.org.nz; f. 1937; present name since 1987; affiliated to ITUC; 40 affiliated unions with more than 350,000 mems; Pres. HELEN KELLY; Sec. PETER CONWAY.

Principal Affiliated Unions

Association of Staff in Tertiary Education (ASTE)/Te Hau Takitini o Aotearoa: POB 27141, Wellington; tel. (4) 801-5098; fax (4) 385-8826; e-mail enquiry@aste.ac.nz; internet www.aste.ac.nz; 3,500 mems; Nat. Sec. SHARN RIGGS.

Central Amalgamated Workers Union (CAWU): 307 Willis St, POB 27-291, Wellington; tel. (4) 384-4049; fax (4) 801-7306; e-mail info@cawu.org.nz; internet www.cawu.org.nz; Sec. HAROLD LEWIS.

FinSec Finance and Information Workers Union: POB 27-355, Wellington; tel. (4) 385-7723; fax (4) 385-2214; e-mail union@finsec.org.nz; internet www.finsec.org.nz; Pres. SUE BORASTON; Sec. ANDREW CASIDY.

Maritime Union of New Zealand: POB 27004, Wellington; tel. (4) 385-0792; fax (4) 384-8766; e-mail trevor.hanson@muno.org.nz; internet www.munz.org.nz; 2,800 mems; Sec. TREVOR HANSON.

New Zealand Dairy Workers Union, Inc: Freepost 538, POB 9046, Hamilton; tel. (7) 839-0239; fax (7) 838-0398; e-mail nzdwu@nzdwu.org.nz; internet www.nzdwu.org.nz; f. 1992; 7,000 mems; Sec. JAMES RITCHIE; Pres. SINCLAIR WATSON.

New Zealand Educational Institute (NZEI) (Te Riu Roa): POB 466, Wellington; tel. (4) 384-9689; fax (4) 385-1772; e-mail nzei@nzei.org.nz; internet www.nzei.org.nz; f. 1883; Pres. FRANCES NELSON; Sec. PAUL GOULTER.

New Zealand Engineering, Printing & Manufacturing Union (EPMU): POB 14-277, Kilbirnie, Wellington; tel. (4) 387-4681; fax (4) 387-4673; e-mail andrew.little@epmu.org.nz; internet www.epmu.org.nz; Sec. ANDREW LITTLE.

New Zealand Meat Workers and Related Trades Union: POB 13-048, Armagh, Christchurch; tel. (3) 366-5105; fax (3) 379-7763; e-mail nzmeatworkersunion@clear.net.nz; internet www.nzmeatworkersunion.co.nz; 13,788 mems; Pres. M. NAHU; Gen. Sec. DAVID EASTLAKE.

New Zealand Nurses' Organisation: POB 2128, Wellington 6140; tel. (4) 499-9533; fax (4) 382-9993; e-mail nurses@nzno.org.nz; internet www.nzno.org.nz; 38,000 mems; CEO GEOFF ANNALS.

New Zealand Post Primary Teachers' Association: POB 2119, Wellington; tel. (4) 384-9964; fax (4) 382-8763; e-mail enquiries@ppta.org.nz; internet www.ppta.org.nz; Pres. KATE GAINSFORD; Gen. Sec. KEVIN BUNKER.

New Zealand Public Service Association (PSA): PSA House, 11 Aurora Terrace, POB 3817, Wellington 1; tel. (4) 917-0333; fax (4) 917-2051; e-mail enquiries@psa.org.nz; internet www.psa.org.nz; 56,000 mems; Pres. PAULA SCHOLES.

Rail & Maritime Transport Union Inc: POB 1103, Wellington; tel. (4) 499-2066; fax (4) 471-0896; e-mail tvalster@rmtunion.org.nz; internet www.rmtunion.org.nz; 4,100 mems; Pres. J. KELLY; Sec. W. BUTSON.

Service and Food Workers' Union: Private Bag 68-914, Newton, Auckland 1145; tel. (9) 375-2680; fax (9) 375-2681; e-mail info@sfwu.org.nz; internet www.sfwu.org.nz; 23,000 mems; Pres. BARBARA WYETH; Sec. JOHN RYALL.

Tertiary Education Union (TEU): POB 11-767, Wellington; tel. (4) 803-3999; fax (4) 801-4799; e-mail teu@teu.ac.nz; internet www.teu.ac.nz; fmrly Association of University Staff; 6,000 mems; Nat. Pres. TOM RYAN.

Other Unions

Manufacturing & Construction Workers Union: Manners St, POB 6287, Wellington; tel. (4) 385-8264; fax (4) 384-8007; e-mail m.c.union@tradeshall.org.nz; Gen. Sec. GRAEME CLARKE.

National Distribution Union (NDU): 120 Church St, Private Bag 92-904, Onehunga, Auckland; tel. (9) 622-8355; fax (9) 622-8353; e-mail ndu@nduunion.org.nz; internet www.nduunion.org.nz; 18,500 mems; Pres. BILL ANDERSEN; Sec. MIKE JACKSON; Vice-Pres. DENNIS DAWSON.

New Zealand Building Trades Union: Manners St, POB 11-356, Wellington; tel. (4) 385-1178; fax (4) 385-1177; Pres. P. REIDY; Sec. ASHLEY RUSS.

New Zealand Seafarers' Union: Marion Square, POB 9288, Wellington; tel. (4) 385-9288; fax (4) 384-9288; e-mail admin@seafarers.org.nz; f. 1993; Pres. DAVE MORGAN.

Transport

RAILWAYS

There were 3,898 km of railways in New Zealand in 2003, of which more than 500 km were electrified.

Toll New Zealand: Smales Farm, Cnr Northcote Rd and Taharoto Drive, Takapuna, Auckland; tel. (4) 498-3000; fax (4) 498-3259; e-mail freight@tollnz.co.nz; internet www.toll.co.nz; fmrly Toll Rail Ltd; acquired Tranz Rail Ltd 2003; 3,898 km of railway; Gen. Man. GARY TAYLOR.

ROADS

In 2006 there were a total of 93,576 km of maintained roads in New Zealand, including 11,065 km of state highways and motorways.

New Zealand Transport Agency: Victoria Arcade, 44 Victoria St, Private Bag 6995, Wellington 6141; tel. (4) 894-5400; fax (4) 894-6100; e-mail info@nzta.govt.nz; internet www.nzta.govt.nz; f. 2008; formed by merger of Land Transport NZ and Transit NZ; Crown entity charged with contributing to an integrated, safe, responsive and sustainable land transport system; Chair. BRIAN ROCHE; Chief Exec. GEOFF DANGERFIELD.

SHIPPING

There are 13 main seaports, of which the most important are Auckland, Tauranga, Wellington, Lyttleton (the port of Christchurch) and Port Chalmers (Dunedin). In December 2007 the New Zealand merchant fleet comprised 174 vessels, with a total displacement of 210,208 grt.

Principal Companies

Maersk New Zealand: The CPO, Level 3, 12 Queen St, Auckland; tel. (9) 359-3499; fax (9) 359-3488; e-mail nezcsedir@maersk.com; internet www.maerskline.com; f. 1928; CEO EIVIND KOLDING.

Sofrana Unilines NZ Ltd: 396–404 Queen St, POB 3614, Auckland; tel. (9) 356-1400; fax (9) 356-1429; e-mail info@sofrana.co.nz; internet www.sofrana.co.nz; Chair DIDIER LEROUX; Man. Dir BENOIT MARCENAC.

Other major shipping companies operating services to New Zealand include Blue Star Line (NZ) Ltd and Columbus Line, which link New Zealand with Australia, the Pacific Islands, South-East Asia and the USA.

CIVIL AVIATION

There are international airports at Auckland, Christchurch and Wellington.

Civil Aviation Authority of New Zealand: Aviation House, 10 Hutt Rd, Petone, POB 31-441, Lower Hutt; tel. (4) 560-9400; fax (4) 569-2024; e-mail info@caa.govt.nz; internet www.caa.govt.nz; Dir of Civil Aviation STEVE DOUGLAS.

Principal Airlines

Air Nelson: Private Bag 32, Nelson 7030; tel. (3) 547-8700; fax (3) 547-8788; internet www.airnewzealand.com; f. 1979; owned by Air New Zealand; changed to present name 1986; operates services throughout New Zealand; Gen. Man. JOHN HAMBLETON.

Air New Zealand: Air New Zealand Contact Centre, Private Bag 93537, Takapuna, North Shore City 0740; tel. (9) 357-3000; fax (9) 366-2401; e-mail investor@airnz.co.nz; internet www.airnewzealand.co.nz; f. 1942; privatized in 1989, recapitalized by govt 2001; 80% govt-owned; services to Australia, the Pacific Islands, Asia, Europe and North America, as well as regular daily services to 25 cities and towns in New Zealand; Chair. JOHN PALMER; CEO ROB FYFE.

Pacific Blue Airlines (NZ) Ltd: internet www.flypacificblue.com; f. 2003; wholly owned subsidiary of Australian Virgin Blue; domestic services and services to Pacific Islands; CEO TONY MARKS.

Tourism

New Zealand's principal tourist attractions are its mountains, lakes, forests, volcanoes, hot springs and beaches. The sector makes a substantial contribution to the country's economy, and receipts from tourism totalled an estimated $NZ5,947m. in 2008. In that year New Zealand received almost 2.5m. international visitors. The majority of visitors are from Australia, the United Kingdom and the USA.

Tourism New Zealand: POB 95, Wellington; tel. (4) 462-8000; fax (4) 915-3817; e-mail reception@tnz.govt.nz; internet www.newzealand.com; f. 1901; responsible for marketing of New Zealand as a tourism destination; offices in Auckland, Wellington and Christchurch; 13 offices overseas; Chair. GEORGE MUIR; Chief Exec. GEORGE HICKTON.

NEW ZEALAND'S DEPENDENT TERRITORIES

New Zealand's two Dependent Territories are the Ross Dependency, which is situated in Antarctica, and Tokelau, located in the Pacific Ocean.

ROSS DEPENDENCY

The Ross Dependency comprises the sector of Antarctica between 160°E and 150°W (moving eastward) and the islands lying between those degrees of longitude and south of latitude 60°S. It has been administered by New Zealand since 1923 and has a total area of 750,310 sq km (289,700 sq miles), comprising a land area of 413,540 sq km and an ice shelf of 336,770 sq km. The Territory rises to a height of 3,794 m above sea-level at the peak of the volcano, Mount Erebus.

Scott Base was established in 1957 on Ross Island, and in the following year the Ross Dependency Research Committee was formed to supervise New Zealand activity on the Territory. In 1968 a new scientific station was set up at Lake Vanda, about 130 km (80 miles) west of Scott Base. In 1986 traces of petroleum were discovered in the Territory, more than 600 m below the sea-bed. The Ross Dependency Research Committee was disbanded in 1995.

Legislation approved in the mid-1990s consolidated measures aimed at conserving the region's flora and fauna (which includes 18 species of penguin, six species of seal and several rare species of whale) included in the Antarctic Treaty (see p. 591), and reinforced the Convention for the Conservation of Antarctic Marine Living Resources. Since 1997 New Zealand has conducted exploratory fishing for toothfish in the Ross Sea. In April 2006 it was announced that an Estonian summer-only research station was to be built at Edmonson Point South, 350 km north-west of Scott Base, to provide facilities for six personnel. Following a visit by the New Zealand Minister of Research, Science and Technology in November 2006, new proposals, including emphasis on the provision of renewable energy resources and the encouragement of greater investment in scientific projects in the territory, were announced.

TOKELAU

Introductory Survey

Location, Climate, Language, Religion, Flag, Capital

Tokelau consists of three atolls (Atafu, Nukunonu and Fakaofo), which lie about 480 km (300 miles) north of Samoa, in the Pacific Ocean. The annual average temperature is 28°C (82°F), July being the coolest month and May the warmest; rainfall is heavy but inconsistent. The principal language is Tokelauan (a Polynesian language), although English is also widely spoken. The population is almost entirely Christian, with 67% adhering to the Congregational Christian Church of Samoa (a Protestant denomination) and 30% to the Roman Catholic Church. The New Zealand flag (see p. 3364) is used in the Territory. Tokelau has no capital, each atoll having its own administrative centre. However, the seat of government, the Office of the Tokelau Council for Ongoing Government (formerly the Council of Faipule) is recognized as 'the capital' and is rotated on a yearly basis among the three atolls.

Recent History

The Tokelau (formerly Union) Islands became a British protectorate in 1877. At the request of the inhabitants, the United Kingdom annexed the islands in 1916 and included them within the Gilbert and Ellice Islands Colony (now Kiribati and Tuvalu). The British Government transferred administrative control of the islands to New Zealand by legislation enacted in 1925, effective from February 1926. The group was officially designated the Tokelau Islands in 1946, and sovereignty was transferred to New Zealand by legislation of 1948, effective from January 1949. From 1962 until the end of 1971 the High Commissioner for New Zealand in Western Samoa (now Samoa) was also the Administrator of the Tokelau Islands. In November 1974 the administration of the Tokelau Islands was transferred to the Ministry of Foreign Affairs in New Zealand. In 1976 the Tokelau Islands were officially redesignated Tokelau.

New Zealand has undertaken to assist Tokelau towards increased self-government and economic self-sufficiency. The Territory was visited by the UN Special Committee on Decolonization in 1976 and 1981, but on both occasions the mission reported that the people of Tokelau did not wish to change the nature of the existing relationship between Tokelau and New Zealand. This opinion was reiterated by an emissary of the General Fono, the Territory's highest advisory body, in 1987, and by the Official Secretary in 1992. In June 1987, however, in a statement to the UN Special Committee, Tokelau had expressed a desire to achieve a greater degree of political autonomy, while maintaining its relationship with New Zealand. A report by the UN Special Committee in 2002 listed Tokelau as one of 16 dependent territories it was seeking to encourage towards independence. However, a UN decolonization mission which visited the islands in September of that year was told that the majority of Tokelauans wanted to remain part of New Zealand and that the Territory was far too dependent on that country to change its status.

In December 1980 New Zealand and the USA signed a treaty whereby a US claim to Tokelau, dating from 1856, was relinquished. At the same time New Zealand abandoned a claim, on behalf of Tokelau, to Swains Island, which had been administered by the USA since 1925 as part of American Samoa. The treaty was ratified in August 1983, although there was some dissent in Tokelau.

In 1989 Tokelau supported efforts by the South Pacific Forum to impose a regional ban on drift-net fishing (which was believed to have resulted in a serious depletion in tuna stocks). In November New Zealand prohibited drift-net fishing within Tokelau's exclusive economic zone (which extends to 200 nautical miles (370 km) from the islands' coastline). At the annual meeting of the Pacific Islands Forum (formerly the South Pacific Forum) in August 2002 New Zealand endorsed Tokelau's membership of the Forum Fisheries Agency.

In 1989 a UN report on the 'greenhouse effect' (the heating of the earth's atmosphere as a result of pollution) listed Tokelau as one of the island groups that would completely disappear beneath the sea in the 21st century, unless drastic action were taken.

A programme of constitutional change, agreed in 1992 and formalized in January 1994, provided for a more defined role for Tokelau's political institutions, as well as for their expansion. A process of relocating the Tokelau Public Service (hitherto based in Apia, Western Samoa, now Samoa) to the Territory began in 1994, and by 1995 all government departments, except Transport and Communications and part of the Administration and Finance Department, had been transferred to Tokelauan soil. However, the Tokelau Apia Liaison Office (formerly the Office for Tokelau Affairs) was to remain in Western Samoa, owing to that country's more developed communications facilities.

The development of Tokelau's institutions at a national level prompted renewed interest in the islands' prospects for greater internal autonomy. In June 1994 the General Fono adopted a National Strategic Plan, which gave details of Tokelau's progression (over the next five to 10 years) towards increased self-determination and, possibly, free association with New Zealand. The executive and administrative powers of the Administrator were formally transferred, in that year, to the General Fono and, when the Fono was not in session, to the Council of Faipule (cabinet). A draft constitution was subsequently drawn up. In May 1996 the New Zealand House of Representatives approved the Tokelau Amendment Bill, granting the General Fono the power to enact legislation, to impose taxes and to declare public holidays, effective from 1 August 1996 (although New Zealand was to retain the right to legislate for Tokelau). A visit to the islands by the Prime Minister of Tuvalu in mid-1996, for the signing of a mutual co-operation agreement (covering shipping, trade and fisheries), was widely interpreted as an indication of Tokelau's increased autonomy. A further co-operation agreement was established in March 2003, following a five-day visit to the islands by the Prime Minister of Samoa. Tokelau's traditional leaders agreed a framework for annual meetings with the Samoan Government to discuss issues of concern and mutual benefit in what was regarded as a sign of the growing relationship between the two parties.

Following electoral reforms introduced in the latter half of the 1990s, delegates were, for the first time, elected to the General Fono for a three-year term in January 1999; they had previously been nominated by each Taupulega (Island Council or Council of Elders). As part of the same reform process, the number of delegates to the General Fono was reduced from 27 to 18. At the elections two of the Territory's Faipule (political leaders) were re-elected, while the remaining Faipule and three Pulenuku (village mayor) posts were secured by new candidates. At elections in January 2002 all three incumbent Faipule and one Pulenuku were re-elected to office; two new Pulenuku were elected. In January 2005 the three Faipule were again re-elected, along with one of the Pulenuku; two new Pulenuku were chosen.

Mounting fears among islanders that, despite their wishes, New Zealand was seeking to loosen its ties with Tokelau, led the New Zealand Minister of Foreign Affairs and Trade to state in April 2000 that his country would not impose independence on the Territory and that any change in its political status would only occur with the consent of Tokelauans. In early 2001 the head of the Tokelau Public Service Commission, Aleki Silau, reiterated the islanders' reluctance to renounce New Zealand citizenship, and emphasized that both sides had until 2010 to reach a decision. A mission from the UN Special Committee on Decolonization visited the islands in September 2002 (see above). Under legislation approved in 1999, management of the islands' public service was formally transferred to Tokelau in July 2001. In July 2003 responsibility for the islands' budget was transferred to the General Fono. In October of that year a number of constitutional changes were instituted. The Council of Faipule was renamed the Tokelau Council for Ongoing Government, henceforth to comprise the three Faipule and the three Pulenuku. In the following month New Zealand's Governor-General, Dame Sylvia Cartwright, made an official visit to Tokelau to sign the Principles of Partnership agreement. The document was described by New Zealand's Minister of Foreign Affairs, Phil Goff, as a step closer to decolonization for the islands. Goff reiterated that the final decision on Tokelau's future would be made by its inhabitants, although he also confirmed that he expected the islands to adopt a system of self-government in free association with New Zealand, similar to that existing in Niue and the Cook Islands. In March 2004 it was announced that new powers were to be granted to the three atolls' Taupulega, giving them greater control over local affairs. In May a senior government member reiterated the view that, despite the ambition of New Zealand and the UN for Tokelau to achieve self-determination, the islanders themselves were extremely reluctant to change their status. In June the Administrator's powers were formally transferred from the General Fono to the three Taupulega, as part of the Modern House of Tokelau Project.

In mid-August 2004 New Zealand's Prime Minister, Helen Clark, made an official visit to Tokelau (the first such visit in more than 20 years). During the visit Clark announced the provision of a grant worth some US $0.3m. towards improvements for boat access to the islands and a review of the islands' communications infrastructure. The Prime Minister also expressed her confidence that the islanders would vote in favour of free association with New Zealand when the issue was finally put to a referendum. In early November leaders from Tokelau travelled to New Zealand for a series of meetings with the latter's Minister of Foreign Affairs, Phil Goff, following which certain elements to be included in a treaty of free association with New Zealand were agreed upon. However, contrary to the New Zealand Government's expectations, at a referendum on the issue of the future status of Tokelau held between 11 and 15 February 2006 the requisite two-thirds' majority in favour of the proposed change to free association with New Zealand was not received: 349 votes were cast in favour of greater self-government, while 232 voters wanted Tokelau to remain a Dependent Territory. The referendum was observed by several international organizations, including representatives of the UN. The result was regarded as a major set-back for the New Zealand Government. However, in June 2006 it was announced that the General Fono had agreed to the holding of another referendum on the issue of Tokelau's status. In November regional inter-governmental groups, led by the Secretariat of the Pacific Community (see p. 391), began a fact-finding operation in Tokelau. The mission aimed to identify the islands' particular needs and priorities and to formulate a three-year strategy. In February 2007, following similar visits to the Tokelauan communities in Hawaii, American Samoa and New Zealand, an official delegation from Tokelau travelled to Samoa in order to discuss with expatriate Tokelauans the various issues relating to the next referendum. It was emphasized that if they wished to participate in the second referendum, Tokelauans resident overseas would be required to return to the islands three months prior to the poll. In March the Faipule of Fakaofo, Kolouei O'Brien, declared that if the requisite majority in favour of greater autonomy were to be secured at the next referendum then Tokelau would wish to enter immediate negotiations with the USA regarding the return of Swains Island, which had remained part of American Samoa (see above).

In October 2006 David Payton replaced Neil Walter as Tokelau's Administrator. The decision to appoint a New Zealand diplomat to the position gave rise to some controversy, and it was suggested that the appointment indicated a lack of confidence in the people of Tokelau and their ability to manage their own affairs.

At the second referendum on Tokelau's status, conducted in October 2007, the level of participation was reported to be almost 100%; UN officials were again present as observers. However, support for self-government was not sufficient to produce the requisite two-thirds' majority, with 246 out of 692 voters rejecting the proposal. There was speculation about the influence of Tokelauans living in New Zealand, although expatriates were not permitted to cast a vote. Prime Minister Clark pledged her Government's 'ongoing friendship and support'. Elections to the General Fono were held on 18–19 January 2008, when 20 delegates were elected. In the same month one new Faipule was elected to office and two incumbent Faipule were re-elected, while three new Pulenuku were also chosen.

In February 2005, meanwhile, all three atolls were struck by Cyclone Percy, which caused widespread damage to infrastructure, homes and crops. Nukunonu was subjected to severe flooding as a result of the storm. The New Zealand Government approved some $NZ0.5m. in emergency aid in the form of food supplies and temporary shelter (to be shipped from Samoa) and the restoration of essential services.

Tokelau was badly affected by an outbreak of influenza in March 2009. About 150 people, mostly children, were reported to have been taken ill, with several requiring hospital treatment. Owing to the islands' isolation, the level of immunity to the virus was low. As the authorities attempted to limit the spread of the illness, sick islanders were urged to stay at home. Schools were closed and public gatherings were cancelled.

New Zealand is responsible for the external relations of Tokelau. Strong links are maintained with Samoa, the people of which the Tokelauans are closely related. There is considerable co-operation in health and education matters.

Government

The administration of Tokelau is the responsibility of the Minister of Foreign Affairs and Trade of New Zealand, who is empowered to appoint an Administrator to the Territory. In practice, most of the Administrator's powers are delegated to the Official Secretary, who heads the Tokelau Apia Liaison Office, as well as to the General Fono and the Tokelau Council for Ongoing Government (formerly the Council of Faipule). Each atoll has its own Taupulega (Island Council or Council of Elders), which comprises the heads of family groups together with two elected members, the Faipule and the Pulenuku. The Faipule represents the atoll in its dealings with the administering power and the public service, and presides over the Council and the court. The Pulenuku is responsible for the administration of village affairs. The Faipule and the Pulenuku are democratically elected by universal adult suffrage every three years. The three Faipule, who hold ministerial portfolios and along with the three Pulenuku form the six-member Tokelau Council for Ongoing Government, choose one of their number to hold the title Ulu-O-Tokelau (Head of Tokelau) for a term of one year. The Ulu-O-Tokelau chairs sessions of the territorial assembly, the General Fono. The General Fono is a meeting of 20 delegates, who are elected by universal adult suffrage for a three-year term (including the three Faipule and the three Pulenuku) and who represent the entire Territory. There are two or three meetings of the General Fono each year, which may take place on any of the atolls.

Economic Affairs

According to estimates by the UN Development Programme (UNDP), in 1982 Tokelau's gross national product (GNP) was US $1.2m., equivalent to US $760 per head. Gross domestic product (GDP) was estimated at US $1.5m. in 1993. During 1996–2004 the population increased at an average rate of 0.8% per year.

Agriculture (including fishing) is, excluding copra production, of a basic subsistence nature. Coconuts (the source of copra) are the only cash crop, for which there is an increasingly limited market. Pulaka, breadfruit, papayas, the screw-pine (*Pandanus*) and bananas are cultivated as food crops. Livestock comprises pigs, ducks and other poultry. Ocean and lagoon fish and shellfish are staple constituents of the islanders' diet. In early 2004 the Secretariat of the Pacific Community produced a fisheries management plan for Tokelau. The plan, which was to be implemented in mid-2004, focused on community-based activities and included the increased exploitation of the islands' giant-clam resources. A five-year development plan for the fisheries sector was drafted for 2006–10. Meanwhile, the sale to foreign fleets of fishing licences permitting them to operate in Tokelau's exclusive economic zone (EEZ) provides an important, albeit fluctuating, source of income (see below).

The industrial sector has been constrained by a lack of resources. Manufacturing comprises mainly the production of handicrafts, notably woven items such as mats. However, the opening on Atafu, in 1990, of a factory processing highly priced yellowfin tuna provided another important source of income. The principal markets for the product were New Zealand and Japan.

Energy is provided by diesel-powered generators, the fuel for which is imported via Samoa. With funding from New Zealand, a major power project was initiated in 2002. The implementation of this scheme, which was ultimately to supply all three atolls with a more reliable source of electricity, was scheduled for completion in 2006. In the longer term, greater emphasis was to be given to renewable forms of energy, particularly solar power. In conjunction with the Governments of New Zealand and France, UNDP and UNESCO, in 2003 Tokelau embarked on a programme aimed at utilizing the territory's solar energy potential for grid-connected power generation.

The tourism sector is limited, having remained undeveloped owing to the lack of air services and the difficulty of access. There is just one recognized hotel, on the central atoll of Nukunonu. Fewer than 30 tourists visited the islands in 2001. Since 1982 the General Fono has levied a tax on the salaries of public servants who are unavailable for the community service labour levy. Public salaries and employment account for the single largest item of government expenditure (about one-third in the early 1990s). Following the purchase by a Dutch entrepreneur of the islands' internet domain address '.tk' in 2001, more than 1.6m. names had been registered to the facility by 2007. Although the Government's precise earnings from Dot TK were not disclosed, the services of this joint venture with Teletok, the islands' communications company, were reported to be proving highly lucrative. The establishment of Dot TK was believed to have increased annual government revenue by about 10%. Furthermore, the attendant upgrading of Tokelau's communications infrastructure, including a broadband connection via satellite, greatly enhanced the islanders' own information technology facilities. In March 2007, however, a leading information technology publication reported that '.tk' was the most insecure web domain in the world. A content-filtering system was subsequently installed, in an attempt to reduce the risks. Furthermore, in March 2008 an international software security company reported that, along with Niue, in per caput terms Tokelau was one of the world's worst offenders with regard to the relaying of unsolicited e-mails.

Imports to the value of $NZ1.7m. were purchased in 2002. The principal imports in that year were food and live animals (which cost 55.2% of total imports), mineral fuels (11.6%) and miscellaneous manufactured goods (11.0%).

In 1999/2000 there was a budgetary deficit of $NZ0.9m. Tokelau's budget for 2001/02 was to include at least $NZ4.2m. from New Zealand and an estimated $NZ1.7m. to be obtained from local revenues such as fisheries licensing, duty, taxes, philatelic sales, freight charges and interest earned. Tokelau assumed responsibility for the management of its own budgetary affairs in 2003. Since then most of New Zealand's bilateral assistance has been transferred directly to the Territory's budget, thereby enabling Tokelau to finance its recurrent expenditure on services such as transport, education and health. Local revenue was estimated to have reached about $NZ2m. in 2005. Receipts from EEZ fees rose from $NZ286,000 in 2004 to an estimated $NZ569,000 in 2005. Fees from shipping, radio excises and customs duties have provided another source of revenue; local receipts from such duties increased from $NZ372,000 in 2004 to an estimated $NZ388,000 in 2005. The sale of postage stamps and souvenir coins (which are legal tender, although New Zealand currency is in general use) also makes a significant contribution to the Territory's income. Receipts from this source increased from $NZ54,000 in 2004 to an estimated $NZ70,000 in 2005. Some revenue is provided by remittances from Tokelauans working abroad, mainly in New Zealand. Official development assistance from New Zealand was projected to reach $NZ17.13m. in 2008/09. In addition to its links to New Zealand, Tokelau maintains a bilateral development assistance plan with Australia, focused upon human resource development.

Tokelau is a member of the Pacific Community (see p. 391), and, as a Dependent Territory of New Zealand, has been represented by that country in the Pacific Islands Forum (see p. 393) and other international organizations. In October 2005 Tokelau was granted observer status at the Pacific Islands Forum.

Tokelau's agricultural development has been constrained by the lack of suitable cultivable soil and by the adverse effects of inclement weather. In February 2005 Cyclone Percy caused serious destruction on the islands, coinciding with 'king tides' that flooded the Territory resulting in widespread damage. Moreover, the Territory's small size, remote location, lack of land-based resources and the population's continuing migration to New Zealand have severely hindered economic development. In September 2002 renewed proposals were announced for the construction of wharves and improved access for shipping to facilitate the export of fish. The construction of an airport, to encourage tourism, has been intermittently considered. It was hoped that Tokelau would derive greater benefits from its fisheries resources as a result of a plan initiated by the Secretariat of the Pacific Community in 2004 (see above). The Tokelau International Trust Fund (TITF) was established in the early 21st century, with assistance from New Zealand and with the aim of enhancing the Territory's long-term self-reliance. By early 2006 the assets of this inter-generational fund had exceeded $NZ25m. Australia and the United Kingdom also contributed to the TITF, along with Tokelau itself. Following New Zealand's contribution of $NZ15m. in November 2008, the assets of the TITF totalled $NZ52m. A three-year Economic Support Arrangement was implemented under the direction of the New Zealand Government during 2007–10, with a projected total budget of $NZ43m. Areas targeted for development included transport, communications, education and health. Under the Administrative Assistance scheme (part of the Principles of Partnership agreement—see Recent History), the limited capacity of the Tokelau Public Service is supplemented by the resources of various New Zealand government departments. In early 2009 the islands' activities were disrupted by a serious outbreak of influenza, which was reported to have affected 10% of the population.

Education

Education is provided free of charge, and is compulsory between the ages of five and 14 years. The provision of an additional year for 15-year-olds is rotated among the Territory's three schools every five years. Government expenditure on education in 1998/99 totalled $NZ0.8m. (equivalent to 18% of total budgetary expenditure). The New Zealand Department of Education provides advisory services and some educational equipment. Scholarships are awarded for secondary and tertiary education and vocational training in Samoa, Fiji, Niue, Tonga and New Zealand. In 2004 a total of 53 Tokelauans over the age of 15 years were studying overseas under the Tokelau Sponsorship Scheme (34 in Samoa, 12 in New Zealand and seven in Fiji). In 2003 there were some 176 Tokelauan pupils enrolled at the Samoa Secondary School. Australia also provides scholarships for Tokelauan students to study in Australia or at regional academic institutions. There were a total of 358 pupils enrolled in primary and secondary education and 54 teachers on the islands in 2003.

Public Holidays

2009: 1 January (New Year's Day), 6 February (Waitangi Day, anniversary of 1840 treaty), 10–13 April (Easter), 25 April (ANZAC Day, anniversary of 1915 landing at Gallipoli), 2 June (Queen's Official Birthday), 26 October (Labour Day), 25 December (Christmas Day), 26 December (Boxing Day).

2010: 1 January (New Year's Day), 6 February (Waitangi Day, anniversary of 1840 treaty), 2–5 April (Easter), 25 April (ANZAC Day, anniversary of 1915 landing at Gallipoli), 1 June (Queen's Official Birthday), 27 October (Labour Day), 25 December (Christmas Day), 26 December (Boxing Day).

Weights and Measures

The metric system is in force.

Statistical Survey

Source (unless otherwise indicated): Tokelau Apia Liaison Office, POB 805, Apia, Samoa; tel. 20822; fax 21761; e-mail f.aukuso@clear.net.nz.

AREA AND POPULATION

Area: Atafu 3.5 sq km; Nukunonu 4.7 sq km; Fakaofo 4.0 sq km; Total 12.2 sq km (4.7 sq miles).

Population: 1,537 (males 761, females 776) at census of 11 October 2001; 1,466 (males 736, females 730) at census of 19 October 2006. *By Atoll* (2006 census): Atafu 524; Nukunonu 426; Fakaofo 483; Total 1,466 (incl. 33 usually resident on Samoa).

Density (2006 census): 120.2 per sq km.

Births and Deaths (1996): Birth rate 33.1 per 1,000; Death rate 8.2 per 1,000. *2003:* Live births 24.

Life Expectancy (years at birth, 1996, official estimates): Males 68; Females 70. Source: Ministry of Foreign Affairs and Trade, Wellington.

Economically Active Population (2001 census, persons aged 15 years and over): Construction 78; Retail trade 12; Hotels and restaurants 4; Transport 7; Communications 20; Village services 182; Public administration 59; Education 53; Medical 23; Total 438. *2006 Census:* Total in paid employment 375.

HEALTH AND WELFARE
Key Indicators

Access to Water (% of households, 2004): 88.
Access to Sanitation (% of households, 2004): 78.
For sources and definitions, see explanatory note on p. vi.

AGRICULTURE, ETC.

Crop Production (metric tons, 2007, FAO estimates): Coconuts 3,000; Roots and tubers 300; Bananas 15.
Livestock (year ending September 2007, FAO estimates): Pigs 1,000; Chickens 5,000.
Livestock Products (metric tons, 2007, FAO estimates): Pig meat 20; Chicken meat 5; Hen eggs 8.
Fishing (metric tons, live weight, 2006, FAO estimate): Total catch 200.
Source: FAO.

INDUSTRY

Production (1990, estimate): Electric energy 300,000 kWh.

FINANCE

Currency and Exchange Rates: New Zealand currency is legal tender. Tokelau souvenir coins have also been issued. New Zealand currency: 100 cents = 1 New Zealand dollar ($NZ); *Sterling, US Dollar and Euro Equivalents* (31 December 2008): £1 sterling = $NZ2.5200; US $1 = $NZ1.7286; €1 = $NZ2.4057; $NZ100 = £39.68 = US $57.85 = €41.57. *Average Exchange Rate* ($NZ per US $): 1.5421 in 2006; 1.3607 in 2007; 1.4227 in 2008.

Budget ($NZ, year ending 30 June 1998): *Revenue:* Local 734,950; New Zealand subsidy 4,600,000; Total 5,334,950. *Expenditure:* Total 5,208,449.

Overseas Aid (projection, $NZ '000, 2002/03): Official development assistance from New Zealand 8,100 (of which Budget support 4,750, Projects and training 2,650). *2008/09* (projection) Total development assistance from New Zealand $NZ17.13m. Source: Ministry of Foreign Affairs and Trade, Wellington.

EXTERNAL TRADE

Principal Commodities ($NZ, 2002): *Imports:* Food and live animals 923,766; Mineral fuels, lubricants, etc. 194,779; Animal and vegetable oils, fats and waxes 50,012; Chemicals and related products 45,429; Manufactured goods 183,488; Total (incl. others) 1,673,389.

COMMUNICATIONS MEDIA

Radio Receivers (1997, estimate): 1,000 in use.

EDUCATION

Schools (1999): 3 (one school for all levels on each atoll).
Teachers (2003): Primary 31; Secondary 23.
Pupils (2003): Primary 182; General secondary 176.
Students Overseas (1999): Secondary 22; Tertiary 20.

Directory

The Constitution

Tokelau is administered under the authority of the Tokelau Islands Act 1948 and subsequent amendments and regulations. The Act declared Tokelau (then known as the Tokelau Islands) to be within the territorial boundaries of New Zealand. The Administrator is the representative of the Crown and is responsible to the Minister of Foreign Affairs and Trade in the New Zealand Government. The office of Administrator is normally held conjointly with that of New Zealand's Secretary of Foreign Affairs and Trade, but provision is made for the offices to be held separately. Most of the powers of the Administrator are delegated to the Tokelau Apia Liaison Office, the General Fono and the Tokelau Council for Ongoing Government (formerly the Council of Faipule). The chief representative of the Administrator (and the Crown) on each atoll is the highest elected official, the Faipule, who exercises executive, political and judicial powers. The three Faipule, who hold ministerial portfolios and along with the three Pulenuku (Village Mayors) form the six-member Tokelau Council of Faipule, act as the representatives of the Territory in dealings with the administration and at international meetings, and choose one of their number to hold the title Ulu-O-Tokelau (Head of Tokelau) for a term of one year. The Ulu-O-Tokelau chairs sessions of the territorial assembly, the General Fono. The General Fono is a meeting of 20 delegates (including the Faipule and the Pulenuku from each atoll), representing the entire Territory. There are three or four meetings each year, which take place on the atoll of the Ulu-O-Tokelau. The General Fono is the highest advisory body and the administration must consult it about all policy affecting the Territory. The assembly has responsibility for the territorial budget and has the power to enact legislation, to impose taxes and to declare public holidays. There are a number of specialist committees, such as the Budget Committee and the Law Committee.

Tokelau is an association of three autonomous atoll communities. Local government consists of the Faipule, the Pulenuku and the Taupulega (Island Council or Council of Elders). The Faipule, the Pulenuku and delegates to the General Fono are elected every three years on the basis of universal adult suffrage (the age of majority being 21). The Faipule represents the atoll community, liaises with the administration and the Tokelau Public Service, acts as a judicial commissioner and presides over meetings of the Taupulega. The Pulenuku is responsible for the administration of village affairs, including the maintenance of water supplies and the inspection of plantations, and, in some instances, the resolution of land disputes (practically all land is held by customary title, by the head of a family group, and may not be alienated to non-Tokelauans). The Taupulega is the principal organ of local government. The Taupulega also appoints the Failautuhi (Island Clerk), to record its meetings and transactions. The Taupulega in Atafu consists of the Faipule, the Pulenuku and the head of every family group; in Nukunonu it consists of the Faipule, the Pulenuku, the elders of the community and the nominated heads of extended families; in Fakaofo it consists of the Faipule, the Pulenuku and the elders (meetings of all the heads of family groups take place only infrequently).

The Government
(April 2009)

Administrator: DAVID PAYTON (took office October 2006).

FAIPULE

The title of Ulu-O-Tokelau (Head of Tokelau) is held on a one-year rotational basis by each Faipule in turn. At elections in January 2008, one new Faipule was elected to office and two incumbent Faipule were re-elected.

Faipule of Fakaofo: FOUA TOLOA.
Faipule of Nukunonu: PIO TUIA.
Faipule of Atafu: KURESA NASAU.

PULENUKU

At elections in January 2008, three new Pulenuku were elected to office.

Pulenuku of Fakaofo: OTINIELU TUUMULI.
Pulenuku of Nukunonu: LINO ISAIA.
Pulenuku of Atafu: NOUATA TUFOUA.

GOVERNMENT OFFICES

Tokelau Apia Liaison Office/Ofiha o Fehokotakiga Tokelau Ma Apia: POB 865, Apia, Samoa; tel. 20822; fax 21761; e-mail maka@lesamoa.net; responsible for transport, accounting and consular functions; Gen. Man. FALANI AUKUSO.

The Tokelau Public Service has seven departments, divided among the three atolls, with a supervising administrative official located in each village. Two departments are established on each atoll, while the seventh department, the Office of the Tokelau Council for Ongoing Government (formerly the Council of Faipule), rotates on a yearly basis in conjunction with the position of Ulu-O-Tokelau. Management of the Tokelau Public Service was formally transferred to Tokelau in July 2001.

Legislature

GENERAL FONO

The General Fono, or territorial assembly, is a meeting of delegates representing the Territory, and includes the Faipule and Pulenuku; it is the highest advisory body and must be consulted by the administration about all policy affecting the Territory. The General Fono has responsibility for the territorial budget and has the power to enact legislation, impose taxes and declare public holidays. The assembly is elected by universal suffrage and, since the legislative elections of 2002, the number of representatives from each atoll has been determined by its proportion of the total population. Members of the General Fono elect a Chairman, and hold between three and four sessions a year on the Ulu-O-Tokelau's atoll. At the elections held on 18–19 January 2008, 20 delegates were elected.

Judicial System

Tokelau's legislative and judicial systems are based on the Tokelau Islands Act 1948 and subsequent amendments and regulations. The Act provided for a variety of British regulations to continue in force and, where no other legislation applies, the law of England and Wales in 1840 (the year in which British sovereignty over New Zealand was established) was to be applicable. New Zealand statute law applies in Tokelau only if specifically extended there. In 1986 legislation formalized the transfer of High Court civil and criminal jurisdiction from Niue to New Zealand. Most cases are judged by the Commissioner established on each atoll, who has limited jurisdiction in civil and criminal matters. Commissioners are appointed by the New Zealand Governor-General, after consultation with the elders of the atoll.

Commissioner of Fakaofo: PENEHE TULAFONO.
Commissioner of Nukunonu: IOANE TUMUA.
Commissioner of Atafu: SALASOPA SEMU IUPATI.

Religion

On Atafu almost all inhabitants are members of the Tokelau Congregational Christian Church, on Nukunonu all are Roman Catholic, while both denominations are represented on Fakaofo. In the late 1990s some 70% of the total population adhered to the Congregational Christian Church, and 30% to the Roman Catholic Church.

CHRISTIANITY

Roman Catholic Church

The Church is represented in Tokelau by a Mission, established in 1992. There were an estimated 500 adherents at 31 December 2006.
Superior: Mgr PATRICK EDWARD O'CONNOR, Catholic Mission, Nukunonu, Tokelau (via Apia, Samoa); tel. 4160; fax 3146; e-mail dr.tovite@clear.net.n3.

Broadcasting and Communications

Each atoll has a radio station to broadcast shipping and weather reports. Radio-telephone provided the main communications link with other areas until the late 1990s. A new telecommunications system established at a cost of US $2.76m. (US $1m. of which was provided by New Zealand) and operating through an earth station, linked to a communications satellite, on each atoll, became operational in 1997. A new weekly radio programme, called Vakai, broadcast by Samoa Broadcasting Service to Tokelau's three atolls, began in October 2004.

TELECOMMUNICATIONS

Telecommunications Tokelau Corporation (TeleTok): Fenuafala, Fakaofo; tel. 3100; fax 3108; e-mail apvitale@clear.net.nz; f. 1996; govt-owned; Gen. Man. AUKUSITINO VITALE.

Finance

There are no banks in operation in Tokelau; however, the Office of Tokelau Affairs provides a facility for deposits and withdrawals, and pays interest on accounts. Commercial and other banking facilities are available in Apia, Samoa.

Trade and Industry

A village co-operative store was established on each atoll in 1977. These stores are operated by village management committees, which work with the public service administration to reduce the costs of imported goods. Most imports are purchased from Samoa, with an increasing amount coming from New Zealand and Fiji. Local industries include copra production, woodwork and plaited craft goods, and the processing of tuna. Electricity is provided by diesel generators based in the village on each atoll.

Transport

There are no roads or motor vehicles. Unscheduled inter-atoll voyages, by sea, are forbidden because the risk of missing landfall is too great. Passengers and cargo are transported by vessels that anchor off shore, as there are no harbour facilities. A scheme to provide wharves (primarily to facilitate the export of fish) was proposed in September 2002. Most shipping links are with Samoa, but a monthly service from Fiji was introduced in 1986. The vessel *Forum Tokelau*, operated by Pacific Forum Line, began a monthly service between Tokelau and Apia, Samoa, in mid-1997. A New Zealand-funded inter-atoll vessel commenced service in 1991, providing the first regular link between the atolls for 40 years. Plans to construct an airstrip on each atoll were postponed in 1987 in favour of the development of shipping links. Proposals for the introduction of air links have encountered resistance from the island communities.

NEW ZEALAND'S ASSOCIATED STATES

New Zealand's two Associated States are the self-governing Cook Islands and Niue, both of which are situated in the Pacific Ocean.

THE COOK ISLANDS

Introductory Survey

Location, Climate, Language, Religion, Flag, Capital

The 13 inhabited and two uninhabited islands of the Cook Islands are located in the southern Pacific Ocean and lie between American Samoa, to the west, and French Polynesia, to the east. The islands extend over about 2m. sq km (more than 750,000 sq miles) of ocean, and form two groups: the Northern Cooks, which are all atolls and include Pukapuka, Rakahanga and Manihiki, and the Southern Cooks, including Aitutaki, Mangaia and Rarotonga, which are all volcanic islands. From December to March the climate is warm and humid, with the possibility of severe storms; from April to November the climate is mild and equable. The average annual rainfall on Rarotonga is 2,012 mm (79 ins). The official languages are English and Cook Islands Maori. The principal religion is Christianity, with about 70% of the population adhering to the Cook Islands Congregational Christian Church. The islands' flag (proportions 1 by 2) displays 15 five-pointed white stars (representing the islands of the group) on a royal blue field, with the United Kingdom's Union Flag as a canton in the upper hoist. The capital is Avarua, on Rarotonga.

Recent History

The first Europeans to visit the islands were members of a British expedition, led by Capt. James Cook (after whom the islands are named), in 1773. The Cook Islands were proclaimed a British protectorate in 1888, and a part of New Zealand in 1901.

On 4 August 1965 the Cook Islands became a self-governing Territory in free association with New Zealand. The people are New Zealand citizens. Sir Albert Henry, leader of the Cook Islands Party (CIP), was elected Premier in 1965 and re-elected in 1971, 1974 and March 1978. However, in July 1978, following an inquiry into alleged electoral malpractice, the Chief Justice disallowed votes cast in the elections to the Legislative Assembly (later renamed Parliament) by Cook Islands expatriates who had been flown from New Zealand, with their fares paid from public funds. The amended ballot gave a majority to the Democratic Party (DP), and its leader, Dr (later Sir) Thomas Davis, was sworn in as Premier by the Chief Justice. In August 1979 Sir Albert Henry was convicted of conspiracy to defraud, and was formally stripped of his knighthood.

In May 1981 the Cook Islands' Constitution was amended to increase the membership of Parliament from 22 to 24, and to extend the parliamentary term from four to five years. In March 1983 Sir Thomas Davis lost power to the CIP, under Geoffrey (later Sir Geoffrey) Henry, cousin of the former Premier. However, with one seat already subject to re-election, Henry's majority of three was reduced by the death of one CIP member of Parliament and the transfer of allegiance to the DP by another. Henry resigned in August, and a general election in November returned the DP to power under Davis. In August 1984 Davis announced wide-ranging government changes, with three of the seven posts going to members of the CIP, to form a coalition Government, with Henry as Deputy Prime Minister. In mid-1985, however, Davis dismissed Henry, who had endorsed an unsuccessful motion expressing no confidence in the Government, and Henry's supporters withdrew from the coalition. Henry's successor as Deputy Prime Minister was Dr (later Sir) Terepai Maoate, one of four CIP members who continued to support the Davis Government, in defiance of the CIP central committee.

Davis was forced to resign as Prime Minister in July 1987, after a parliamentary motion expressing no confidence in his administration was approved. He was succeeded by Dr Pupuke Robati, a member of the Cabinet and a leading figure in the DP. Geoffrey Henry again became Prime Minister following a general election victory for the CIP in January 1989. The defection in mid-1990 of a member of Parliament from the DP to the CIP provided the latter with 15 seats in Parliament and thus the minimum two-thirds' majority support necessary to amend the Constitution. In August 1991 a constitutional amendment was approved to increase the number of members of Parliament to 25 and, at an election to the newly created seat, a CIP candidate was successful. The amendment also provided for an increase in the number of cabinet members from seven to nine (including the Prime Minister).

At a general election in March 1994 the CIP increased its majority, winning 20 seats in Parliament; the DP secured three seats and the Alliance Party (established in 1992 by Norman George, the former DP parliamentary whip, who had been expelled from the party following a dispute over spending) two. Davis, who failed to win a seat, subsequently resigned as leader of the DP. A referendum held simultaneously revealed that a majority of the electorate favoured retaining the current name (69.8% of voters) and national anthem (80.2%), while 48.5% favoured the retention of the flag of the Cook Islands. (At subsequent by-elections the CIP lost two seats and the DP and Alliance Party each gained one seat.)

A financial scandal was narrowly averted following reports that during 1994 the Government had issued loan guarantees for foreign companies worth more than $NZ1,200m. (the island's total revenue for 1994/95 was estimated at $NZ50m.). An investigation into the affair by the New Zealand Reserve Bank found that the Government had not been guilty of fraud, but rather had been coerced into the activity by unscrupulous foreign business interests. However, the affair led many investors to remove their funds from the islands, provoking a financial crisis that resulted in Henry's decision in mid-1995 to withdraw the Cook Islands dollar from circulation, and to implement a programme of retrenchment measures. The crisis deepened during 1995 as new allegations emerged, and Henry's Government was severely criticized by New Zealand for failing to cooperate with an official inquiry into accusations of fraud and tax evasion involving several New Zealand companies. Henry maintained that the islands' bank secrecy laws prevented the disclosure of information relating to financial transactions. The situation deteriorated further when it was revealed that the Government had defaulted on a debt of some US $100m. to an Italian bank. In response to pressure from New Zealand, and in an attempt to restore a degree of financial stability to the islands, Henry (whose management of the crisis had been questioned both by his own party and by the opposition) announced a severe restructuring programme in April 1996. The measures included a 50% reduction in the pay of public sector workers, the closure of almost all diplomatic missions overseas, a 60% reduction in the number of government departments and ministries, and the privatization of the majority of government-owned authorities. A marked increase in 1995/96 in the emigration rate and a decline in the number of Cook Islanders returning to the islands following a period of residency overseas was attributed to the austere economic conditions created by the financial crisis.

In August 1997 Parliament approved the Outer Islands Local Government Act, providing for a new budgetary system to allocate funds for projects in the outer islands and for increased powers for local authorities, with the aim of reducing significantly central government administration of the outer islands. As part of the plan, three new government bodies were elected in April 1998.

Henry's administration continued to attract controversy, with the announcement in December 1997 of the closure of the Ministry of Public Works, Survey, Housing, Water Supply and Environment Services for exceeding its budget. The minister responsible, Tihina Tom Marsters, resigned in protest at the closure, which resulted in the loss of more than 100 public servants' jobs, problems with the supply of utilities (particularly water) and the suspension of several development projects.

At legislative elections in June 1999 the CIP won 11 of the 25 seats in Parliament, the Democratic Alliance Party (DAP, a grouping that included the DP) 10 seats and the New Alliance Party (NAP, formerly the Alliance Party) four seats. Sir Geoffrey Henry of the CIP was reappointed Prime Minister and formed a new Cabinet, following the establishment of a political coalition with the NAP; the leader of the NAP, Norman George, became Deputy Prime Minister. However, three members of the CIP subsequently left the party to form a coalition with the DAP, in protest at the alliance with the NAP, and at the end of July Henry resigned and was replaced by a 'rebel' CIP member, Dr Joe Williams. Williams was confirmed as the new Prime Minister by 13 votes to 12 in a vote of confidence by the Parliament. Williams' appointment provoked a public protest in Rarotonga, exacerbated by general discontent at the nomination of a Prime Minister whose parliamentary constituency was outside the Cook Islands (having been elected to the seat reserved for non-resident voters). Electors also voted in a referendum on whether the parliamentary term should be reduced from five years to four. The shorter term was favoured by 63% of voters, and thus narrowly failed to receive the support of the two-thirds' majority required to amend the

Constitution. The result of the contest for the Pukapuka seat, which had been won by former Prime Minister Inatio Akaruru by just one vote, was challenged by the DAP. The matter was taken to the Court of Appeal, which subsequently declared the result invalid, stripping the Government of its one-seat majority. A by-election was held in late September 1999 to decide the Pukapuka seat; however, the result was again said to be invalid and a further by-election was scheduled. The Government became a minority administration in mid-October when the Prime Minister dismissed his deputy, Norman George, along with the Minister of Education, following their defection to the opposition. Despite the appointment of three new ministers, Williams failed to regain a majority in Parliament. In November Williams resigned, shortly before a vote of no confidence was to be tabled against him by Dr Terepai Maoate, now the leader of the opposition DAP. Maoate won the vote by 14 votes to 11 and was appointed Prime Minister, forming a new coalition Government with the NAP. He subsequently reappointed Norman George to the post of Deputy Prime Minister.

Maoate dismissed Norman George in July 2001 on the grounds that he was attempting to undermine him; this was the second time that George had lost the position of Deputy Prime Minister. He was replaced by Dr Robert Woonton. However, Woonton strongly criticized Maoate's leadership in the same month. In late 2001 the rift between the Prime Minister and his Cabinet widened. Woonton announced his resignation, which Maoate refused to accept. This led to a motion of no confidence in the Prime Minister, which he only narrowly survived. In February 2002 Maoate's leadership was again challenged: 15 of the 25 members of Parliament voted against him in a second motion of no confidence. He was therefore replaced by Robert Woonton. In an extensive ministerial reorganization Sir Geoffrey Henry returned to the Cabinet as Deputy Prime Minister. Woonton declared his priorities to be the encouragement of emigrant workers to return to the islands through income tax incentives and an ambitious redevelopment plan for the capital, Avarua.

The Government's decision not to name a senior civil servant in the Prime Minister's office who had been arrested and charged with fraud in August 2002 led to accusations of secrecy by the opposition. Criticism of the Government's position increased in the following month with the introduction of new media laws (which many observers believed would serve to suppress opposition to government policy), particularly when a government official stated his desire for 'Zimbabwe-style legislation to stop inaccurate reporting'.

In November 2002 Parliament approved a constitutional amendment abolishing the requirement for electoral candidates to reside in the islands for a qualifying period of three months. This action was widely interpreted as a way of retaining the overseas voters' parliamentary seat for the CIP leader, Dr Joe Williams, who lived permanently in New Zealand. In the same month the CIP and the DP formed a coalition government (the fifth such coalition since the previous election) which left Norman George, who had been recently dismissed from his position in the Cabinet, as the sole opposition member of Parliament. The Government's action prompted a demonstration outside the parliament building by some 150 people, organized by a recently formed organization, the Group for Political Change. The protesters claimed that the virtual absence of an opposition constituted an erosion of democracy and appealed to the Prime Minister to commit to an early general election. However, in late January 2003 the CIP was ousted from the coalition. The continued political manoeuvring was widely denounced, particularly among the business community, for creating a climate of instability in the islands. Public dissatisfaction with the situation resulted in the presentation of a petition to Government in March signed by a significant percentage of the population. The petition called for a number of political reforms including a reduction in the number of members of Parliament, the introduction of a shorter parliamentary term and the abolition of the overseas seat. Moreover, businessman Teariki Heather announced the formation of a new political party, the Cook Islands National, in the same month. In September 2003 legislation was approved providing for the abolition of the overseas seat and for a referendum (to be held concurrently with the next general election) on a proposal to shorten the parliamentary term from five years to four.

In November 2003 Dr Terepai Maoate, who had been appointed Deputy Prime Minister earlier in the year, and the Minister of Justice, Tangata Vavia, resigned following an unsuccessful attempt by Maoate to propose a motion of no confidence in the Government. The Government was the focus of further criticism in December when about 200 people marched through Avarua to protest at the granting of a residency permit to New Zealander Mark Lyon. The protesters claimed that Lyon, a wealthy businessman with recent convictions for weapons possession and a reputation for behaviour deemed disrespectful to island traditions, was not a suitable candidate for residency in the islands. Moreover, the demonstrators demanded the resignation of the Prime Minister and his chief adviser, Norman George, over the matter, stating that the islands should not be obliged to host undesirable characters, regardless of their ability to finance important business projects.

The reputation of the public service suffered a reversal in November 2003 when the former Chief of Staff in the Office of the Prime Minister, Edward Drollet, was convicted on seven charges of receiving secret commissions and one of forgery and was sentenced to more than two years' imprisonment.

At a general election in September 2004 the DP won 14 of the 24 seats, the CIP secured nine and an independent candidate won the remaining seat. Prime Minister Robert Woonton regained his seat by only four votes, amid accusations that he had secured the support of some voters through bribery. In the concurrent referendum 82.3% of participating voters indicated their support for the shortening of the parliamentary term from five years to four. The period immediately after the election was characterized by political manoeuvring and the initiation of several legal cases challenging the outcome in a number of constituencies. In mid-November Woonton announced that his party was to form a coalition government with the CIP. This decision was widely opposed within the DP, whose leadership questioned its legality, and prompted the resignation of the Deputy Prime Minister, Aunty Mau Munokoa. Further controversy was caused by the appointment of the defeated former MP, Norman George, to the position of Speaker. In mid-December, with the DP effectively divided over Woonton's actions, Jim Marurai, of the minority Democratic Tumu Party, was elected Prime Minister and a governing coalition was formed between his party and the CIP. It was understood that Marurai would serve as Prime Minister for the first two years of the parliamentary term and would then be replaced by Sir Geoffrey Henry of the CIP. However, in August 2005 Henry was dismissed and replaced by DP leader Dr Terepai Maoate. In September two further CIP cabinet ministers were dismissed and replaced by DP members. Marurai declared that the coalition had been dissolved, claiming that the action followed threats to his leadership.

The islands suffered considerable damage in February and March 2005 when five cyclones struck in just over four weeks. The resultant damage to housing, infrastructure and crops was estimated at $NZ25m. A rehabilitation programme was implemented, and in October 2005 discussions took place between Jim Marurai and the Prime Minister of New Zealand, Helen Clark, regarding the progress made. The islands' economic situation was also discussed.

In October 2005 Peri Vaevae Pare, the Minister of Health and Internal Affairs, whose other portfolios included social services, was suspended from office pending police investigations into allegations of fraud. In November he was convicted on three charges of intent to defraud and gain pecuniary advantage, each conviction carrying a maximum sentence of five years' imprisonment. In early 2006 the Prime Minister requested the formal resignation of the suspended Minister, who was subsequently replaced. Dr Terepai Maoate continued as Deputy Prime Minister, retaining responsibility for the finance portfolio, while Wilkie Rasmussen remained responsible for foreign affairs. In March Robert Woonton, who had previously been appointed as the islands' High Commissioner to New Zealand, was dismissed from that post, following allegations that he had been involved in an attempt to oust the islands' Government. In July a by-election victory for the opposition CIP gave it a parliamentary majority, prompting the Queen's Representative, Sir Frederick Goodwin, to dissolve the legislature and to call an early election. Votes on a motion of no confidence in Prime Minister Marurai and a motion in favour of his replacement by Sir Geoffrey Henry, submitted at a parliamentary session following the decision, were invalidated by the dissolution of Parliament. Marurai retained the role of Prime Minister in an interim capacity pending the election, which was scheduled for September. Henry announced his retirement as leader of the CIP in August.

Provisional results of the election, held on 26 September 2006, indicated that the DP had secured 15 of the 24 parliamentary seats and the CIP seven, with one seat being taken by an independent candidate. Henry Puna, who had succeeded Sir Geoffrey Henry as leader of the CIP, failed to retain his seat. A by-election to resolve the tied result in the remaining constituency resulted in victory for the CIP candidate in November. In the following month it was announced that a by-election would also be held in Titikaveka after the eligibility of the winning candidate, Robert Wigmore of the DP, was called into question. Wigmore won the Titikaveka by-election in February 2007, thus taking the final result of the 2006 election to 15 seats for the DP and eight for the CIP, along with one independent. Jim Marurai, who had returned to the DP, thus retained the position of Prime Minister, although Maoate continued as leader of the DP. In August 2007 Wilkie Rasmussen, the cabinet member responsible for foreign affairs, among other portfolios, was elected deputy leader of the DP, having left the CIP prior to the 2006 election.

In April 2007 a proposal for legislation to regulate the media, presented by Deputy Prime Minister Maoate, provoked a public debate about the freedom of the press; the subsequent formation of a monitoring body by the industry itself was reportedly linked to the indefinite postponement of the legislation. Meanwhile, in July a report by the Fiji-based Pacific Institute of Advanced Studies in

Development and Governance on seven Pacific island nations gave the Cook Islands the highest rating in the area of good governance.

Preparations for the 2009 South Pacific Mini Games, which were to be hosted by the islands in September of that year, attracted considerable media attention in 2007–08, with the Ministry of Finance and Economic Management warning against the acceptance of a grant from the People's Republic of China to finance the construction of a sports complex, maintaining that it would neither be cost-effective nor serve the long-term economic interests of the islands. In February 2008 the Government took a loan of US $10.2m. from China, the bulk of which was to fund preparations for the Mini Games; the decision resulted in threats of legal action from the local Chamber of Commerce. In March 2009 China agreed to provide a further loan of nearly US $28m., of which $11m. was to be allocated to the construction of the sports stadium and the remainder was to finance infrastructure projects. The announcement prompted further demands for a public inquiry from the opposition, which claimed that the Cook Islands could not afford to repay such a large loan. The Deputy Prime Minister, Sir Terepai Maoate, who was also responsible for the finance portfolio, was alleged to have stated that repayments would be made with New Zealand aid; however, a New Zealand government official was reported as stating that such requests for aid were likely to be rejected. Meanwhile, preparations for the Mini Games were marred by allegations of financial mismanagement, and in March 2009 the Government announced an audit into the finances of Pacific Mini Games Company, the enterprise responsible for organizing the event.

Brian Donnelly was appointed to replace John Bryan as New Zealand's High Commissioner to the Cook Islands, taking office in February 2008. In August, however, Brian Donnelly was himself compelled to resign owing to poor health, and was replaced in December by Tia Barrett.

As the rate of emigration from the islands continued to increase, in late 2000 it was announced that some 1,400 residents had left the islands during that year (compared with 641 in the previous year). This resulted in a reduction in the population of the islands to its lowest level in more than 50 years, the majority of the loss being from the outer islands, and prompted the Government to campaign in Australia and New Zealand to encourage former citizens to return to the Cook Islands. Private-sector businesses, many of which had experienced difficulties in recruiting workers in sufficient numbers, were also involved in the campaign. At the census of 2001 the resident population was recorded at only 14,990. In August 2002 the Government announced that it would allocate US $23,350 for the campaign.

In early 2000 the islands of Penrhyn, Pukapuka, Rakahanga and Manihiki expressed their desire to become fully devolved and to take sole control over areas such as administration, public expenditure and justice. In response, the Government pledged gradually to phase out the Ministry of Outer Islands Development, as well as the post of Government Representative in the outer islands. In December of that year an additional US $2m. in funding under the Cotonou agreement was designated for projects on the outer islands.

A reported increase in the number of Russian nationals opening accounts in the Cook Islands led to allegations in early 1999 that the islands' 'offshore' financial centre was being used extensively by criminal organizations for 'laundering' the proceeds of their activities. The claims were vigorously denied by officials in the sector. However, in June 2000 the naming of the islands by the Paris-based Financial Action Task Force (FATF, see p. 430) as one of a number of countries and territories that had failed to co-operate in regional efforts to combat money-laundering, along with the islands' identification by the Organisation for Economic Co-operation and Development (OECD, see p. 358) as a tax 'haven' that lacked financial transparency, led to increased international pressure on the Government to implement stricter controls over its 'offshore' financial centre. Consequently, legislation was approved in August of that year providing for the creation of the Money Laundering Authority and the introduction of new regulations aimed at reducing criminal activity in the sector. In February 2005 the Cook Islands were finally removed from the FATF list of non-co-operative countries and territories. However, in April 2009 the OECD included the Cook Islands on its so-called 'grey list' of countries that, while committed to the internationally agreed tax standard, had yet to implement substantial measures to combat tax evasion. In response, the Government stated that priority would be given to enacting the necessary legislative amendments, and requested assistance from the Group of 20 (G20, see p. 430) leading industrial countries. In February the Government introduced legislation into Parliament to abolish 'offshore' banks in the Cook Islands, arguing that the cost of regulating such organizations outweighed any financial benefits that they brought to the country. Parliament was due to vote on the proposed legislation in late May. Meanwhile, since 2004 the Wall Street Banking Corporation Bank (WSBC Bank) had been engaged in litigation with the Cook Islands Financial Supervisory Commission over the issue of its operating licence, which was finally revoked in April 2009. The WSBC Bank had links to a New Zealand financial services company, WSD Global Markets, which was being investigated by the New Zealand Serious Fraud Office in connection with suspected money-laundering activities.

In August 1985 eight members of the South Pacific Forum (subsequently restyled the Pacific Islands Forum, see p. 393), including the Cook Islands, signed a treaty on Rarotonga, designating a 'nuclear-free' zone in the South Pacific. The treaty imposed a ban on the manufacture, testing, storage and use of nuclear weapons, and the dumping of nuclear waste, in the region.

In January 1986, following the rift between New Zealand and the USA in respect of the ANZUS (see p. 437) security arrangements, Sir Thomas Davis declared the Cook Islands a neutral country, because he considered that New Zealand (which has control over the islands' defence and foreign policy) was no longer in a position to defend the islands. The proclamation of neutrality meant that the Cook Islands would not enter into a military relationship with any foreign power, and, in particular, would prohibit visits by US warships. Visits by US naval vessels were allowed to resume by Henry's Government. In November 2007 the Cook Islands and the USA signed agreements on maritime surveillance and anti-trafficking measures. In October 1991 the Cook Islands signed a treaty of friendship and co-operation with France, covering economic development, trade and surveillance of the islands' exclusive economic zone (EEZ). The establishment of closer relations with France was widely regarded as an expression of the Cook Islands Government's dissatisfaction with existing arrangements with New Zealand. However, relations deteriorated considerably when the French Government resumed its programme of nuclear-weapons testing at Mururoa Atoll in September 1995. Henry was fiercely critical of the decision and dispatched a *vaka* (traditional voyaging canoe) with a crew of Cook Islands' traditional warriors to protest near the test site. The tests were concluded in January 1996. Full diplomatic relations with France were established in early 2000. Meanwhile, the islands established diplomatic relations at ambassadorial level with the People's Republic of China in July 1997. In November 1998 Henry made an official visit to China, during which the two countries signed a bilateral trade agreement and each conferred the status of 'most favoured nation' on the other. Henry stated that the move constituted a further attempt by his Government to reduce the islands' dependence on New Zealand. During her visit to the islands in June 2001, Helen Clark, the New Zealand Prime Minister, stated that if the Cook Islands desired complete independence, and membership of international organizations, the process would not be obstructed by New Zealand. However, Cook Islanders would then be obliged to renounce their New Zealand citizenship.

In September 2008 the Cook Islands became a member of the International Maritime Organization (IMO) after securing the approval of two-thirds of the organization's members. As a result, the Cook Islands became eligible for IMO funding and assistance. In the same month the Cook Islands Government submitted a claim to the UN to extend its seabed boundaries by 777,000 sq km. The application, the first such claim to be lodged by a Pacific island nation, was motivated by the Government's desire to gain access to potential reserves of petroleum and gas, mineral deposits and other marine resources.

Government

The Cook Islands is an internally self-governing state in free association with New Zealand, which is responsible for the Cook Islands' external affairs and defence (although the Territory has progressively assumed control over much of its foreign policy). Executive authority is vested in the British monarch, who is Head of State, and is exercised through her official representative; a representative of the New Zealand Government (redesignated High Commissioner in 1994) resides on Rarotonga. Executive government is carried out by the Cabinet, consisting of the Prime Minister and between five and seven other ministers. The Cabinet is collectively responsible to the Parliament, which is formed of 24 members (decreased from 25 in 2004, following the abolition of the seat for a member chosen by non-resident voters) who are elected by universal adult suffrage every four years (reduced from five years by a referendum in 2004). The House of Ariki, which comprises up to 15 members who are hereditary chiefs, can advise the Government, but has no legislative powers. The Koutu Nui is a similar body, comprising sub-chiefs. Each of the main islands, except Rarotonga, has an elected island council, and a government representative who is appointed by the Prime Minister.

Economic Affairs

In 2007, according to official sources, the Cook Islands' gross domestic product (GDP), measured at current prices, totalled an estimated $NZ286.7m. GDP, measured at average 2000 prices, increased, in real terms, at an estimated average annual rate of 4.5% in 2000–07. In 2007 GDP per head was estimated at $NZ10,438. During 2000–07, it was estimated, the population increased at an average annual rate of about 1.7%. According to the Asian Development Bank (ADB), compared with the previous year overall GDP rose by 1.3% in 2007 and by 1.1% in 2008.

According to provisional estimates by the ADB, agriculture (including forestry and fishing) contributed 11.9% of GDP in 2007. In 2005 the sector engaged 28.6% of the economically active population, according to FAO estimates. The real GDP of the agricultural sector increased by an average of 4.1% per year in 2000–07. Compared with the previous year, the sector's GDP declined by 3.7% in 2006 and increased by an estimated 9.1% in 2007. Cash crops include coconuts and tropical fruits such as mangoes, pineapples, bananas and papayas. Cassava, sweet potatoes and vegetables are cultivated as food crops. Pigs and poultry are the main livestock kept. The sale of fishing licences to foreign fleets provides an important source of income. Revenue from the export of fresh and chilled fish reached $NZ3.1m. in 2007, providing 45.2% of export earnings. Pearl oyster farming is also an important industry. Receipts from pearl exports totalled $NZ2.1m. (equivalent to 30.3% of total export earnings) in 2007.

Industry (comprising mining and quarrying, manufacturing, construction and utilities) provided 9.4% of GDP in 2007, according to provisional figures. The sector engaged 13.3% of employees in 2001. Industrial GDP increased, in real terms, at an average rate of 6.8% per year during 2000–07. Compared with the previous year, the industrial sector's GDP increased by 1.5% in 2006 and (according to official estimates) by under 7.5% in 2007.

The manufacturing sector engaged 6.0% of employees in 2001. The manufacturing and mining sectors together accounted for an estimated 3.6% of GDP in 2007. The real GDP of manufacturing and mining increased at an average rate of 6.7% per year during 2000–07. Compared with the previous year the two sectors' combined GDP decreased by 8.5% in 2006 and increased by an estimated 10.9% in 2007. Industrial activities include fruit-processing, brewing, the manufacture of garments and handicrafts. In 1997 the Government signed an agreement with a consortium of Norwegian companies to mine cobalt, nickel, manganese and copper by extracting mineral-rich nodules found in the islands' exclusive economic zone (EEZ) between Aitutaki and Penrhyn. Construction contributed an estimated 3.7% of GDP in 2007 and engaged 5.9% of the employed labour force in 2001.

The islands depend on imports for their energy requirements. Mineral fuels and lubricants accounted for 22.6% of total imports in 2007. Tax rebates on the purchase of solar panels and water tanks by homeowners were under consideration in 2008. It was also reported in 2008 that the Government intended to increase fuel storage capacity on the islands.

Service industries contributed an estimated 78.7% to GDP in 2007. The sector engaged 79.5% of the employed labour force in 2001. The GDP of the services sector increased, in real terms, at an average annual rate of 4.5% in 2000–07. Compared with the previous year, the GDP of the sector rose by 1.2% in 2006 and decreased by an estimated 0.8% in 2007. Tourism expanded considerably from the late 1980s, and generated revenue of an estimated US $NZ90m. in 2006. Visitor arrivals rose from 92,351 in 2006 and to an estimated 97,077 in 2007, but were reported to have declined in 2008. The restaurants and hotels sector contributed an estimated 15.8% of GDP in 2007, while this sector (together with wholesale and retail trade) engaged 32.6% of the employed labour force in 2001. 'Offshore' banking, introduced to the islands in 1982, expanded rapidly, with more than 2,000 international companies registered by 1987. In 2009, however, legislation to abolish offshore banks awaited approval by Parliament (see Recent History). The financial and business services sector provided an estimated 7.1% of GDP in 2007 and engaged 5.4% of the employed labour force (including persons occupied in the real estate sector) in 2001. Significant revenue is provided by remittances from emigrants from the islands (who outnumber the residents of the islands).

In 2007 the cost of imports rose to $NZ237.1m., while export revenue reached only $NZ7.0m., thus resulting in a trade deficit of more than $NZ230.1m. According to the ADB, the deficit on the current account of the balance of payments steadily decreased from US $21m., equivalent to 11.5% of GDP, in 2005 to US $10m. (4.5% of GDP) in 2008. The principal exports in 2007 were fresh and chilled fish and pearls. The principal imports in that year were machinery and transport equipment (accounting for 26.5% of total import costs), mineral fuels and lubricants (22.6%), food and live animals (19.0%), and basic manufactures (11.3%). The principal source of imports in 2007 was New Zealand (66.4% of the total). In the same year, Japan and New Zealand were the principal markets for exports (30.1% and 15.5% respectively).

In the financial year ending June 2006 the overall budgetary deficit was estimated at $NZ2.7m. Development assistance is provided mainly by New Zealand and Australia. In mid-2004 New Zealand and Australia agreed to combine their programmes of aid to the Cook Islands in order to improve their effectiveness. In 2008/09 aid to the Cook Islands from Australia was projected at $A5.1m. and New Zealand allocated aid of $NZ11.0m. The islands were also to receive €3.3m. per year between 2008 and 2013 (to be spent on improvements to the environment, water supply and sanitation, including waste disposal) under the Cotonou Agreement with the European Union. It was estimated by the ADB that the islands' external debt at the end of 2001 amounted to some US $53m. The cost of debt-servicing in that year was equivalent to 3.5% of the value of exports of goods and services. By 2004 the total debt stood at an estimated US $66m. The annual rate of inflation in Rarotonga averaged 3.3% in 2000–07. Consumer prices rose by an average of 2.5% in 2007 and by 7.8% in 2008. The ADB estimated the unemployment rate to be 13.1% of the labour force in 2001.

The Cook Islands is a member of the Pacific Community (see p. 391) and the Pacific Islands Forum (see p. 393) and an associate member of the UN Economic and Social Commission for Asia and the Pacific (ESCAP, see p. 36). In 1999 the Cook Islands were granted observer status at the Lomé Conventions with the European Union (subsequently superseded by the Cotonou Agreement, see p. 311).

From the 1990s development plans sought to expand the economy of the Cook Islands by stimulating investment in the private sector, developing the infrastructure and promoting 'offshore' financial activities. However, following continued international criticism of the operations of the offshore sector, in 2009 such financial institutions were in the process of being abolished. A major challenge for the Government in the early 21st century was that of delivering basic services to the outer islands. The dramatic increase in tourist arrivals gave rise to concerns that the Cook Islands, and Rarotonga in particular, were unable to sustain such rapid development. Reports indicated that waste disposal and energy provision were inadequate in relation to the demands of the large numbers of visitors and that pollution was increasing; fears for the islands' traditional culture were also expressed. The National Sustainable Development Plan and the Infrastructure Master Plan, the latter to encompass a 20-year period, were announced in 2007. These long-term programmes envisaged substantial capital expenditure. Nevertheless, the economy remained largely dependent on tourism and, in an effort to maintain numbers of incoming tourists from the USA, in March 2007 the Government began subsidizing Air New Zealand flights on the Los Angeles–Rarotonga route. In 2008, however, mainly owing to the higher costs of aviation fuel and to the global economic deceleration, the number of tourist arrivals decreased. Reports of an outbreak of dengue fever also had a negative impact on the tourism sector in that year. In December it was reported that, in addition to the sum of $NZ2.9m. already allocated, a further subsidy of $NZ5.0m. was to be given by the Cook Islands Government to Air New Zealand, in order to ensure the continuation of the carrier's vital service to Rarotonga. Tenders for the upgrading of Rarotonga airport were under consideration in late 2008. The deterioration in the global economy was also expected to lead to a decline in remittances from islanders employed overseas. The sharp increase in international prices for petroleum and other essential commodities, along with higher housing costs, contributed to the islands' inflationary pressures in 2008 and curtailed consumer demand. The ADB projected GDP growth of 1.0% in 2009.

Education

Free secular education is compulsory for a period of 10 years between six and 15 years of age. Primary education, from the age of five, lasts for six years. Secondary education, beginning at 11 years of age, comprises two cycles, each of three years. In 1998 there were 28 primary schools and 23 secondary schools, with a total of 144 primary school teachers and 129 teachers at secondary level. In 2004/05 enrolment at primary school level included 79.7% of pupils in the relevant age-group, while enrolment at secondary level included 72.2% of pupils. In 2007 there were 463 pupils enrolled in pre-primary education, 1,968 in primary education and 1,915 in secondary education. Tertiary education is provided at a teacher-training college, a nursing school and through an apprenticeship scheme. Under the New Zealand Training Scheme, the New Zealand Government offers overseas scholarships in New Zealand, Fiji, Papua New Guinea, Australia and Samoa for secondary and tertiary education, career-training and short-term in-service training. There is an extension centre of the University of the South Pacific (based in Fiji) in the Cook Islands.

Public Holidays

2009: 1 January (New Year's Day), 2 January (Second day of New Year), 10–13 April (Easter), 25 April (ANZAC Day, anniversary of 1915 landing at Gallipoli), 10 May (Mothers' Day), 1 June (Queen's Official Birthday), 4 August (Constitution Day), 26 October (Cook Islands Gospel Day), 25 December (Christmas Day), 26 December (Boxing Day).

2010: 1 January (New Year's Day), 2 January (Second day of New Year), 2–5 April (Easter), 25 April (ANZAC Day, anniversary of 1915 landing at Gallipoli), 9 May (Mothers' Day), 7 June (Queen's Official Birthday), 4 August (Constitution Day), 26 October (Cook Islands Gospel Day), 25 December (Christmas Day), 26 December (Boxing Day).

Weights and Measures
The metric system is in force.

Statistical Survey

Sources (unless otherwise stated): Ministry of Finance and Economic Management, POB 41, Rarotonga; tel. 29511; fax 21511; e-mail info@stats.gov.ck; internet www.spc.int/prism/country/ck/stats; Prime Minister's Department, Government of the Cook Islands, Avarua, Rarotonga; tel. 29300; fax 22856.

AREA AND POPULATION

Area: 236.7 sq km (91.4 sq miles).

Population: 18,027 (males 9,303, females 8,724) at census of 1 December 2001; 19,569 (males 9,932, females 9,637) at census of 1 December 2006 (preliminary). *Resident Population:* 14,990 (males 7,738, females 7,252) at 2001 census. *By Island* (2006 census, preliminary): Rarotonga (including the capital, Avarua) 14,153; Aitutaki 2,194; Atiu 572; Mangaia 654; Manihiki 351; Mauke 393; Mitiaro 219; Nassau 71; Palmerston (Avarua) 63; Penrhyn (Tongareva) 251; Pukapuka 507; Rakahanga 141. *Cook Island Maoris Resident in New Zealand* (census of 6 March 2001): 52,569. *2007* (mid-year estimate): 21,100 (provisional).

Density (mid-2007): 85.3 per sq km.

Principal Town (UN population estimate at mid-2003, incl. suburbs): Avarua (capital) 12,507. Source: UN, *World Urbanization Prospects: The 2003 Revision.*

Births, Marriages and Deaths (2007): Registered live births 287 (birth rate 13.6 per 1,000); Registered marriages 786 (marriage rate 37.3 per 1,000); Registered deaths 82 (death rate 3.9 per 1,000).

Life Expectancy (years at birth, WHO estimates): 73.0 (males 75.0; females 71.0) in 2006. Source: WHO, *World Health Statistics.*

Economically Active Population (resident population aged 15 years and over, 2001 census): Agriculture, hunting, forestry and fishing 427; Mining and quarrying 3; Manufacturing 357; Electricity, gas and water 79; Construction 347; Trade, restaurants and hotels 1,938; Transport, storage and communications 587; Financing, insurance, real estate and business services 323; Community, social and personal services 1,867; *Total employed* 5,928 (males 3,386, females 2,542); Unemployed 892 (males 449, females 443); *Total labour force* 6,820 (males 3,835, females 2,985).

HEALTH AND WELFARE
Key Indicators

Total Fertility Rate (children per woman, 2006): 3.0.

Under-5 Mortality Rate (per 1,000 live births, 2006): 19.

Physicians (per 1,000 head, 2004): 1.2.

Hospital Beds (per 1,000 head, 2005): 6.3.

Health Expenditure (2006): US $ per head (PPP): 566.

Health Expenditure (2006): % of GDP: 4.5.

Health Expenditure (2006): public (% of total): 91.4.

Access to Water (% of persons, 2006): 95.

For sources and definitions, see explanatory note on p. vi.

AGRICULTURE, ETC.

Principal Crops (metric tons, 2007, FAO estimates, unless otherwise indicated): Cassava 1,500; Sweet potatoes 700; Coconuts 2,000 (unofficial figure); Tomatoes 700; Watermelons 75; Guavas, mangosteens and mangoes 300; Papayas 800; Bananas 60; Oranges 100. *Aggregate Production* (metric tons, may include official, semi-official or estimated data): Roots and tubers 4,700; Vegetables (incl. melons) 2,277; Fruits (excl. melons) 1,325.

Livestock (head, year ending September 2007, FAO estimates): Cattle 125; Pigs 32,200; Goats 1,010; Poultry 20,000; Horses 305.

Livestock Products (metric tons, 2007, FAO estimates): Hen eggs 20; Pig meat 555; Chicken meat 35.

Forestry ('000 cu m, 2007, FAO estimate): Roundwood removals (excl. bark) 5.

Fishing (metric tons, live weight, 2006): Albacore 2,559; Yellowfin tuna 277; Bigeye tuna 291; Total catch (incl. others) 3,773.

Source: FAO.

INDUSTRY

Electric Energy (million kWh): 30 in 2005; 32 in 2006; 33 in 2007.

FINANCE

Currency and Exchange Rates: New Zealand currency is legal tender. In mid-1995 it was announced that the Cook Islands dollar (formerly the local currency, at par with the New Zealand dollar) was to be withdrawn from circulation. New Zealand currency: 100 cents = 1 New Zealand dollar ($NZ); for details of exchange rates, see Tokelau.

Budget ($NZ '000, year ending 30 June 2007): *Revenue:* Total revenue 81,955 (Tax 69,685, Other current 6,630, Capital 5,640). (Note: Revenue excludes grants of 21,271) *Expenditure:* Total expenditure 92,767 (Current 81,279, Capital 11,489). Source: Asian Development Bank.

Overseas Aid ($NZ '000): Official development assistance from New Zealand 8,870 in 2004/05; 8,000 in 2006/07, 11,000 in 2008/09 (provisional). Source: Ministry of Foreign Affairs and Trade, Wellington.

Cost of Living (Consumer Price Index for Rarotonga, average of quarterly figures; base: December 2006 = 100): All items 96.57 in 2005; 99.82 in 2006; 102.23 in 2007.

Gross Domestic Product ($NZ '000 at constant 2000 prices): 215,968 in 2005; 217,487 in 2006; 220,250 in 2007.

Gross Domestic Product by Economic Activity ($NZ '000 in current prices, 2007, provisional): Agriculture, forestry and fishing 34,952; Mining, quarrying and manufacturing 10,430; Electricity, gas and water 6,208; Construction 10,879; Wholesale and retail trade 64,729; Restaurants and hotels 46,364; Transport and communications 36,549; Finance and business services 20,664; Ownership of dwellings 18,245; Public administration 36,248; Other community, social and personal services 7,780; *Sub-total* 293,048; *Less* Imputed bank service charge 6,336; *GDP in purchasers' values* 286,711.

EXTERNAL TRADE

Principal Commodities ($NZ '000, 2007): *Imports c.i.f.:* Food and live animals 44,980; Mineral fuels, lubricants, etc. 53,521; Chemicals 10,538; Basic manufactures 26,766; Machinery and transport equipment 62,789; Miscellaneous manufactured articles 22,686; Total (incl. others) 237,124. *Exports f.o.b.:* Fish, fresh or chilled 3,141; Pearls 2,109; Total (incl. others) 6,951.

Principal Trading Partners ($NZ '000, 2007): *Imports:* Australia 14,803; Fiji 42,663; Japan 5,212; New Zealand 157,554; USA 12,049; Total (incl. others) 237,124. *Exports:* Australia 258; Japan 2,094; New Zealand 1,080; USA 582; Total (incl. others) 6,951.

TRANSPORT

Road Traffic (registered vehicles, April 1983): 6,555. *New Motor Vehicles Registered* (Rarotonga, 2007): Motorcycles 1,047; Cars and jeeps 355; Vans and pick-ups 163; Trucks and buses 65; Others 18; *Total* 1,648.

Shipping: *Merchant Fleet* (registered at 31 December 2007): 93 vessels, displacement 178,329 grt (Source: Lloyd's Register-Fairplay, *World Fleet Statistics*); *International Sea-borne Freight Traffic* ('000 metric tons, estimates): Goods unloaded 32.6 (2001); Goods loaded 9; Goods unloaded 32 (1990) (Source: UN, *Monthly Bulletin of Statistics*).

Civil Aviation (2007): *Aircraft Movements:* 844 departures. *Freight Traffic* (metric tons): Goods loaded 159; Goods unloaded 1,270.

TOURISM

Foreign Tourist Arrivals: 88,405 in 2005; 92,351 in 2006; 97,077 in 2007.

Tourist Arrivals by Place of Residence (2007, provisional): Australia 12,445; Canada 2,636; Europe 15,317; New Zealand 58,931; USA 4,343; Total (incl. others) 97,077.

Tourism Revenue (US $ million, incl. passenger transport): 72 in 2004; 91 in 2005; 90 in 2006. Source: World Tourism Organization.

COMMUNICATIONS MEDIA

Radio Receivers (1997): 14,000 in use*.

Television Receivers (1997): 4,000 in use*.

Telephones (main lines, 2002): 6,000 in use†.

Mobile Cellular Telephones (2002): 1,499 subscribers†.

Facsimile Machines (1990): 230 in use‡.

Internet Users (2002): 3,600.

Daily Newspaper (1996): 1; circulation 2,000*.

NEW ZEALAND'S ASSOCIATED STATES

Non-daily Newspaper (1996): 1; circulation 1,000*.
* Source: UNESCO, *Statistical Yearbook*.
† Source: International Telecommunication Union.
‡ Source: UN, *Statistical Yearbook*.

EDUCATION

Pre-primary (2007, unless otherwise indicated): 26 schools (1998); 31 teachers (2000); 463 pupils.

Primary (2007, unless otherwise indicated): 28 schools (1998); 144 teachers (2000); 1,968 pupils.

Secondary* (1998, unless otherwise indicated): 23 schools; 129 teachers; 1,915 pupils (2007).

Higher (1980): 41 teachers; 360 pupils†.
* Includes high school education.
† Source: UNESCO, *Statistical Yearbook*.

Directory

The Constitution

On 4 August 1965 a new Constitution was proclaimed, whereby the people of the Cook Islands have complete control over their own affairs in free association with New Zealand, but they can at any time move into full independence by a unilateral act if they so wish.

Executive authority is vested in the British monarch, who is Head of State, and exercised through an official representative. The New Zealand Government also appoints a representative (from 1994 redesignated High Commissioner), resident on Rarotonga.

Executive powers are exercised by a Cabinet consisting of the Prime Minister and between five and seven other ministers including a Deputy Prime Minister. The Cabinet is collectively responsible to Parliament.

Legislation approved in September 2003 resulted in the abolition of the seat for one member elected by voters living overseas and consequently Parliament consists of 24 members elected by universal suffrage and presided over by the Speaker. Moreover, as a result of a referendum held concurrently with the general election of September 2004, the parliamentary term was shortened from five years to four. The House of Ariki comprises up to 15 members who are hereditary chiefs; it can advise the Government, particularly on matters relating to land and indigenous people, but has no legislative powers. The Koutu Nui is a similar body composed of sub-chiefs, which was established by an amendment in 1972 of the 1966 House of Ariki Act.

Each of the main islands, except Rarotonga (which is divided into three tribal districts or *vaka*), has an elected mayor and a government representative who is appointed by the Prime Minister. In January 2000 it was announced that the post of Government Representative in the outer islands was to be phased out over two years.

The Government

Queen's Representative: Sir FREDERICK GOODWIN.
New Zealand High Commissioner: TIA BARRETT.

CABINET
(April 2009)

Prime Minister, Minister of Information and Technology, Education, National Human Resources, Office of the Head of State, Police and Public Service Commission: JIM MARURAI.

Deputy Prime Minister, Minister of Finance and Economic Development, Financial Intelligence Unit, Public Expenditure and Review Committee, Ombudsman, Attorney-General, Business, Trade and Investment Board, Commerce Commission, National Superannuation, House of Ariki and Koutu Nui, Health, Broadcasting, Pearl Authority and Minerals, Natural Resources and Mines: Sir TEREPAI MAOATE.

Minister of Foreign Affairs and Immigration, Tourism Cook Islands, Cultural Development and Marine Resources: WILKIE RASMUSSEN.

Minister of Internal Affairs, National Environment Services, Youth and Sport, Punanganui Market and Non-Government Organizations: NGAMAU ('AUNTY MAU') MUNOKOA.

Minister of Infrastructure and Planning, Transport, Cook Islands Investment Corporation and Energy: TANGATA VAVIA.

Minister of Agriculture, Justice and Parliamentary Services: KETE IOANE.

GOVERNMENT OFFICES

Office of the Queen's Representative: POB 134, Titikaveka, Rarotonga; tel. 29311.

Office of the Prime Minister: Government of the Cook Islands, Private Bag, Avarua, Rarotonga; tel. 25494; fax 20856; e-mail coso@pmoffice.gov.ck; internet www.pmoffice.gov.ck.

Office of the Public Service Commissioner: POB 24, Rarotonga; tel. 29421; fax 21321; e-mail epati@psc.gov.ck.

New Zealand High Commission: 1st Floor, Philatelic Bureau Bldg, Takuvaine Rd, POB 21, Avarua, Rarotonga; tel. 22201; fax 21241; e-mail nzhraro@oyster.net.ck.

Ministries

Ministry of Agriculture: POB 96, Rarotonga; tel. 28711; fax 21881; e-mail cimoa@oyster.net.ck.

Ministry of Cultural Development: POB 8, Rarotonga; tel. 20725; fax 23725; e-mail parts@culture.gov.ck; internet www.culture.gov.ck.

Ministry of Education: Tereora, Nikao, Rarotonga; tel. 29357; fax 28357; e-mail cieducat@oyster.net.ck; internet www.education.gov.ck.

Ministry of Energy: POB 72, Rarotonga; tel. 24484; fax 24483; e-mail punanga@energy.gov.ck.

Ministry of Finance and Economic Management: POB 120, Rarotonga; tel. 22878; fax 23877; e-mail etuatina@mfem.gov.ck; internet www.mfem.gov.ck.

Ministry of Foreign Affairs and Immigration: POB 105, Rarotonga; tel. 29347; fax 21247; e-mail secfa@mfai.gov.ck.

Ministry of Health: POB 109, Rarotonga; tel. 22664; fax 22670; e-mail soh1@health.gov.ck; internet www.health.gov.ck.

Ministry of Internal Affairs: POB 98, Rarotonga; tel. 29370; fax 23608; e-mail secintaff@intaff.gov.ck.

Ministry of Justice: POB 111, Rarotonga; tel. 29410; fax 29610; e-mail offices@justice.gov.ck.

Ministry of Marine Resources: POB 85, Rarotonga; tel. 28721; fax 29721; e-mail I.Bertram@mmr.gov.ck.

Ministry of Island Administration: POB 383, Rarotonga; tel. 20321; fax 24321; e-mail otheniel@omia.gov.ck.

Ministry of Transport: POB 61, Rarotonga; tel. 28810; fax 28816; e-mail transport@oyster.net.ck.

National Environment Service: POB 371, Rarotonga; tel. 21256; fax 22256; e-mail resources@environment.org.ck; internet www.environment.org.ck.

Advisory Chambers

House of Ariki: POB 13, Rarotonga; tel. 26500; fax 21260; Pres. ADA RONGOMATANE ARIKI.

Koutu Nui: POB 13, Rarotonga; tel. 29317; fax 21260; e-mail nvaloa@parliament.gov.ck; Pres. TETIKA MATAIAPO DORICE REID.

Legislature

PARLIAMENT

Parliamentary Service
POB 13, Rarotonga; tel. 26500; fax 21260; e-mail nvaloa@parliament.gov.ck.

Speaker: MAPU TAIA.
Clerk of Parliament: NGA VALOA.

General Election, 26 September 2006*

Party	Seats
Democratic Party (DP)	15
Cook Islands Party (CIP)	8
Independent	1
Total	**24**

* A by-election held on 28 November 2006 in the constituency of Akaoa, where the seat had been tied at the poll of 26 September, was won by the Cook Islands Party. A second by-election was held in Titikaveka on 7 February 2007, following a court ruling that the winning Democratic Party candidate had been ineligible to contest the election; the Democratic Party candidate was re-elected.

Political Organizations

Cook Islands Labour Party: Rarotonga; f. 1988; anti-nuclear; Leader RENA ARIKI JONASSEN.
Cook Islands Party (CIP): Rarotonga; f. 1965; Leader HENRY PUNA; Deputy Leader TUPOU FAIREKA.
Democratic Party (DP): POB 73, Rarotonga; tel. 21224; e-mail demo1@oyster.net.ck; f. 1972; Pres. MAKIUTI TONGIA; Leader Sir TEREPAI MAOATE; Deputy Leader WILKIE RASMUSSEN.

Judicial System

High Court

Avarua, Rarotonga; e-mail offices@justice.gov.ck.
The judiciary comprises the Privy Council, the Court of Appeal and the High Court.
   The High Court exercises jurisdiction in respect of civil, criminal and land titles cases on all the islands, except for Mangaia, Pukapuka and Mitiaro, where disputes over land titles are settled according to custom. The Court of Appeal hears appeals against decisions of the High Court. The Privy Council, sitting in the United Kingdom, is the final appellate tribunal for the country in civil, criminal and land matters.

Attorney-General: Sir TEREPAI MAOATE.
Solicitor-General: TINGIKA ELIKANA.
Chief Justice of the High Court: DAVID ARTHUR RHODES WILLIAMS.
Judges of the High Court: GLENDYN CARTER, COLIN NICHOLSON, HETA HINGSTON, CHRISTINE GRICE.

Religion

CHRISTIANITY

The principal denomination is the Cook Islands (Congregational) Christian Church, to which about 58% of the islands' population belong, according to figures recorded in the census conducted in 1996.

Religious Advisory Council of the Cook Islands: POB 763, Rarotonga; tel. 23778; fax 21767; e-mail tpere@oyster.net.ck; f. 1972; six mem. churches; Pres. Pastor TUTAI PERE.

The Roman Catholic Church

The Cook Islands form the diocese of Rarotonga, suffragan to the archdiocese of Suva (Fiji). At 31 December 2006 the diocese contained an estimated 2,519 adherents. The Bishop participates in the Catholic Bishops' Conference of the Pacific, based in Suva.

Bishop of Rarotonga: Rt Rev. STUART FRANCE O'CONNELL, Catholic Diocese, POB 147, Avarua, Rarotonga; tel. 20817; fax 29817; e-mail sbish@oyster.net.ck.

The Anglican Communion

The Cook Islands are within the diocese of Polynesia, part of the Church of the Province of New Zealand. The Bishop of Polynesia is resident in Fiji.

Protestant Churches

Cook Islands Christian Church: Takamoa, POB 93, Rarotonga; tel. 26452; 11,193 mems (1986); Pres. Rev. TANGIMETUA TANGATATUTA; Gen. Sec. WILLIE JOHN.
Seventh-day Adventists: POB 31, Rarotonga; tel. 22851; fax 22852; e-mail umakatu@oyster.net.ck; 732 mems (1998); Pres. UMA KATU.

Other churches active in the islands include the Assembly of God, the Church of Latter-day Saints (Mormons), the Apostolic Church, the Jehovah's Witnesses and the Baptist Church.

BAHÁ'Í FAITH

Administrative Committee of the Bahá'ís of Cook Islands: POB 1, Rarotonga; tel. 20658; e-mail nsacooks@bahai.org.ck; mems resident in six localities; Sec. DIANE SCOTT.

The Press

Cook Islands Herald: POB 126, Tutakimoa, Rarotonga; e-mail bestread@ciherald.co.ck; internet www.ciherald.co.ck; weekly; Publr GEORGE PITT.
Cook Islands News: POB 15, Rarotonga; tel. 22999; fax 25303; e-mail editor@cookislandsnews.com; internet www.cinews.co.ck; f. 1954; est. by Govt; transferred to private ownership in 1989; daily; mainly English; Editor JOHN WOODS; circ. 2,100.
Cook Islands Star: POB 798, Rarotonga; tel. 29965; e-mail jason@oyster.net.ck; fortnightly; Chief Reporter JASON BROWN.

Broadcasting and Communications

TELECOMMUNICATIONS

Telecom Cook Islands Ltd: POB 106, Avarua, Rarotonga; tel. 29680; fax 26174; e-mail sales@telecom.co.ck; internet www.telecom.co.ck; CEO STUART DAVIES.

BROADCASTING

Radio

Cook Islands Broadcasting Corpn (CIBC): POB 126, Avarua, Rarotonga; tel. 29460; fax 21907; f. 1989; est. to operate new television service, and radio service of former Broadcasting and Newspaper Corpn; state-owned; Gen. Man. EMILE KAIRUA.
Radio Cook Islands: tel. 20100; e-mail tunein@radio.co.ck; internet www.radio.co.ck; broadcasts in English and Maori 18 hours daily.
KC Radio: POB 521, Avarua, Rarotonga; tel. 23203; f. 1979; est. as Radio Ikurangi; commercial; operates station ZK1ZD; broadcasts 18 hours daily on FM; Man. Dir and Gen. Man. DAVID SCHMIDT.

Television

Cook Islands Broadcasting Corpn (CIBC): see Radio
Cook Islands TV (CITV): POB 126, Rarotonga; tel. 29460; fax 21907; f. 1989; operated by Elijah Communications; broadcasts nightly, in English and Maori, from 5 p.m. to 10.15 p.m; 10 hours of local programmes per week; remainder provided by Television New Zealand.

Finance

(cap. = capital; dep. = deposits; m. = million; brs = branches)

Financial Supervisory Commission: POB 594, Avarua, Rarotonga; tel. 20798; fax 21798; e-mail Inquire@fsc.gov.ck; internet www.fsc.gov.ck; f. 1981 as Cook Islands Monetary Board, name changed as above in 2003; supervises banks and insurance cos; licenses trustee cos; registers international companies, limited liability cos, trusts, financial institutions, etc.; Commissioner LORRAINE ALLAN; Chair. TREVOR CLARKE.
Trustee Companies Association (TCA): Rarotonga; controlling body for the 'offshore' financial sector; Sec. LOU COLVEY.

BANKING

Legislation was adopted in 1981 to facilitate the establishment of 'offshore' banking operations.

Development Bank

Bank of the Cook Islands (BCI): POB 113, Avarua, Rarotonga; tel. 29341; fax 29343; e-mail cash@bci.co.ck; f. 2003; formed when Cook Islands Development Bank merged with Cook Islands Savings Bank; 100% state-owned; finances development projects in all areas of the economy and helps islanders establish small businesses and industries by providing loans and management advisory assistance; Man. Dir VAINE ARIOKA; 10 brs throughout the Cook Islands.

Commercial Banks

ANZ Cook Islands: 1st Floor, Development Bank Bldg, POB 907, Avarua, Rarotonga; tel. 21750; fax 21760; e-mail murphyp@anz.co.uk; internet www.anz.com/cookislands; Gen. Man. PHIL HAYNES.
Banktec Cook Islands Ltd: Level 2, Kids 'n Action Bldg, Nikao, Rarotonga; tel. 23086; fax 23096; e-mail info@banktecgroup.com; internet www.banktecgroup.com; f. 1993 as First Trading Bank Ltd; named changed as above in 2005; 70% owned by Financial Community Partnership Inc, Panamá City, 15% owned by L. F. Vareas, 15% owned by J. L. Bado; cap. US $10.0m., dep. US $5.2m. (Dec. 2006); Resident Dir FACUNDO SEIGAL.
Westpac Banking Corpn (Australia): Main Rd, POB 42, Avarua, Rarotonga; tel. 22014; fax 20802; e-mail bank@westpac.co.ck; internet www.westpac.co.ck/pacific; Man. TERRY SMITH.

INSURANCE

Cook Islands Insurance: POB 44, Rarotonga.

Trade and Industry

GOVERNMENT AGENCIES

Cook Islands Development Investment Board: Private Bag, Avarua, Rarotonga; tel. 24296; fax 24298; e-mail cidib@oyster.net.ck; f. 1996; est. as replacement for Development Investment Council; promotes, monitors and regulates foreign investment, promotes international trade, advises the private sector and Government and provides training in business skills; CEO MARK SHORT.

Cook Islands Investment Corporation: Rarotonga; tel. 29391; fax 29381; e-mail ciic@oyster.net.ck; f. 1998; manages government assets and shareholding interests; Chair. JOHN SHORT; CEO JOHN TINI.

Cook Islands Public Service Commission: POB 24, Rarotonga; tel. 29421; fax 21321; e-mail epati@psc.gov.ck; Commissioner NAVY EPATI; CEO RUSSELL THOMAS.

Cook Islands Trading Corporation (CITC): Private Bag 1, Avarua, Rarotonga; tel. 22000; fax 20857; e-mail shop@citc.co.ck; internet kiaorana.net/citc; f. 1891; principal importer, distributor, wholesaler and retailer of products in the Cook Islands; Exec. Chair. TREVOR CLARKE; Gen. Man. GAYE WHITTA.

CHAMBER OF COMMERCE

Chamber of Commerce: POB 242, Rarotonga; tel. 20925; fax 20969; e-mail chamber@commerce.co.ck; internet www.cookislandschamber.org; f. 1956; represents the private sector in the Cook Islands; Pres. STEVE ANDERSON.

INDUSTRIAL AND TRADE ASSOCIATION

Pearl Guild of the Cook Islands: POB 257, Rarotonga; tel. 21902; fax 21903; e-mail trevon@oyster.net.ck; f. 1994; monitors standards of quality within the pearl industry and develops marketing strategies; Pres. TREVON BERGMAN.

UTILITIES

Electricity

Te Aponga Uira O Tumutevarovaro (TAUOT) (Rarotonga Electricity Authority): POB 112, Rarotonga; tel. 20054; fax 21944; Chair. TAMARII TUTANGATA.

Water

Water Supply Department: POB 102, Arorangi, Rarotonga; tel. 20034; fax 21134.

TRADE UNIONS

Airport Workers' Association: Rarotonga Int. Airport, POB 90, Rarotonga; tel. 25890; fax 21890; f. 1985; Pres. NGA JESSIE; Gen. Sec. (vacant).

Cook Islands Industrial Union of Waterside Workers: Avarua, Rarotonga.

Cook Islands Workers' Association (CIWA): POB 403, Avarua, Rarotonga; tel. 24422; fax 24423; e-mail ciwa@oyster.net.ck; largest union in the Cook Islands; Pres. ANTHONY TURUA; Gen. Sec. TUAINE MAUNGA; 700 mems (2006).

Transport

ROADS

On Rarotonga a 33-km sealed road encircles the island's coastline. A partly sealed inland road, parallel to the coastal road and known as the Ara Metua, is also suitable for vehicles. In February 2006 it was announced that construction of a cyclone-proof road, which would encompass the flood-prone area west of Rarotonga airport, was to be initiated with aid from the People's Republic of China. Roads on the other islands are mainly unsealed.

SHIPPING

The main ports are on Rarotonga (Avatiu), Penrhyn, Mangaia and Aitutaki. The Cook Islands National Line operates a three-weekly cargo service between the Cook Islands, Tonga, Samoa and American Samoa. In August 2002 the Government approved proposals to enlarge Avatiu Harbour. The project received additional funding from the Ports Authority and from New Zealand. In October 2008 plans further to upgrade Avatiu Wharf, to enable large ships to berth in the harbour, were endorsed by the Government. The Asian Development Bank (ADB, see p. 191) agreed to lend US $15.5m. for the three-year project, expected to begin in September 2009.

Apex Maritime: POB 378, Rarotonga; tel. 27651; fax 21138.

Cook Islands National Line: POB 264, Rarotonga; tel. 20374; fax 20855; 30% govt-owned; operates three fleet cargo services between the Cook Islands, Niue, Samoa, Norfolk Island, Tonga and New Zealand; Dirs CHRIS VAILE, GEORGE ELLIS.

Cook Islands Shipping Ltd: POB 2001, Arorangi, Rarotonga; tel. 24905; fax 24906.

Ports Authority: POB 84, Rarotonga and Aitutaki; tel. 21921; fax 21191; e-mail info@ports.co.ck; internet www.ports.co.ck; Gen. Man. ANDREW MCBIRNEY.

Reef Shipping Company: Rarotonga; e-mail reef@reefship.co.nz; operates services between Rarotonga and Aitutaki.

Taio Shipping Ltd: Teremoana Taio, POB 2001, Rarotonga; tel. 24905; fax 24906.

Triad Maritime (1988) Ltd: Rarotonga; fax 20855.

CIVIL AVIATION

An international airport was opened on Rarotonga in 1974. Air New Zealand is among the airlines operating services between Rarotonga and other airports in the region. Air Pacific (Fiji) began a twice-weekly service between Nadi and Rarotonga in June 2000, and in August of that year Air New Zealand began a direct service from Rarotonga to Los Angeles, USA.

Airport Authority, Cook Islands: POB 90, Rarotonga; tel. 25890; fax 21890; e-mail aaci@airport.gov.ck; f. 1986; CEO JOE NGAMATA.

Air Rarotonga: POB 79, Rarotonga; tel. 22888; fax 23288; e-mail admin@airraro.co.ck; internet www.airraro.com; f. 1978; privately owned; operates internal passenger and cargo services and charter services to Niue and French Polynesia; Man. Dir EWAN F. SMITH.

Tourism

Tourism is the most important industry in the Cook Islands and, according to provisional estimates, there were 97,019 foreign tourist arrivals in 2007, compared with 25,615 in 1984. Of total foreign visitors in 2007, an estimated 60.8% came from New Zealand, 12.9% from Australia and 15.6% from Europe. There were 1,874 beds available at hotels and similar establishments in the islands in 1999. Most of the tourist facilities are to be found on Rarotonga and Aitutaki, but the outer islands also offer attractive scenery. Revenue from tourism was estimated at some US $90m. in 2006.

Cook Islands Tourism Corporation: POB 14, Rarotonga; tel. 29435; fax 21435; e-mail tourism@cookislands.gov.ck; internet www.cookislands.travel; Chair. DES EGGELTON; CEO JOHN DEAN.

NIUE

Introductory Survey

Location, Climate, Language, Religion, Flag, Capital

Niue is a coral island, located in the Pacific Ocean, about 480 km (300 miles) east of Tonga and 930 km (580 miles) west of the southern Cook Islands. Rainfall occurs predominantly during the hottest months, from December to March, when the average temperature is 27°C (81°F). Average annual rainfall is 7,715mm (298 ins). Niuean, a Polynesian language, and English are spoken. The population is predominantly Christian, with 66% belonging to the Ekalesia Niue, a Protestant church, in 1991. Niue's flag (proportions 1 by 2) is yellow, bearing, in the upper hoist corner, the United Kingdom's Union Flag with a yellow five-pointed star on each arm of the cross of St George and a slightly larger yellow five-pointed star on a blue disc in the centre of the cross. Some 30% of the population resides in Alofi, which is the capital and administrative centre of Niue. Plans to relocate the capital to Fonuakula on the upper plateau of the island were announced following the widespread devastation caused by Cyclone Heta in January 2004.

Recent History

The first Europeans to discover Niue were members of a British expedition, led by Capt. James Cook, in 1774. Missionaries visited the island throughout the 19th century, and in 1900 Niue was declared a British protectorate. In 1901 Niue was formally annexed to New Zealand as part of the Cook Islands, but in 1904 it was granted a separate administration.

In October 1974 Niue attained 'self-government in free association with New Zealand'. Niueans retain New Zealand citizenship, and a sizeable resident Niuean community exists in New Zealand. The 1991 population census revealed an 11.5% decrease since 1986, and many more Niueans live in New Zealand than on Niue. Robert (from 1982, Sir Robert) Rex, who had been the island's political leader since the early 1950s, was Niue's Premier when it became self-governing, and retained the post at three-yearly general elections in 1975–90.

The migration of Niueans to New Zealand has been a cause of concern, and in October 1985 the Government of New Zealand announced its intention to review its constitutional relationship with Niue, with the express aim of preventing further depopulation of the island. In 1987 a six-member committee, comprising four New Zealanders and two Niueans, was formed to examine Niue's economic and social conditions, and to consider the possibility of the island's reversion to the status of a New Zealand-administered territory.

At the 1987 general election all except three of the 20 members of the Niue Assembly were re-elected. The newly founded Niue People's Action Party (NPAP) secured one seat. The NPAP, Niue's only political party, criticized the Government's economic policy, and in particular its apparent inability to account for a substantial amount of the budgetary aid received from New Zealand. A declared aim of the party was to persuade Niueans residing in New Zealand to invest in projects on Niue.

In April 1989 the New Zealand Auditor-General issued a report which was highly critical of the Niuean Government's use of aid money from New Zealand, in particular Rex's preferential treatment of public servants in the allocation of grants. In June Young Vivian, leader of the unofficial NPAP opposition in the Niue Assembly, proposed a motion expressing no confidence in the Government, which was defeated by 13 votes to seven. In November proposed legislation which included the replacement of New Zealand's Governor-General by a Niuean citizen was rejected by the Niue Assembly, owing to the implications for relations with New Zealand.

At the 1990 general election candidates of the NPAP and its sympathizers won 12 of the 20 seats. Earlier disagreements in the NPAP leadership, however, allowed Rex to secure the support of four members previously opposed to his Government. Rex therefore remained Premier.

The announcement in mid-1991 by the New Zealand Government that it was to reduce its aid payments to Niue by about $NZ1m. (a decrease of some 10% on the average annual allocation) caused considerable concern on the island. More than one-quarter of the paid labour force on Niue were employed by the Niue Government, and, following the reduction in aid in July, about 150 (some 25%) lost their jobs. Members of the Government subsequently travelled to New Zealand to appeal against the decision and to request the provision of redundancy payments for the dismissed employees. Their attempts failed, however, with the New Zealand Government reiterating its claim that aid had been inefficiently used in the past.

In December 1992 Sir Robert Rex died, and Young Vivian (who had been serving as acting Premier at the time of Rex's death) was unanimously elected Premier by the Government. Legislative elections took place in February 1993, and in the following month the Niue Assembly elected Frank Lui, a former cabinet minister, as Premier. Lui, who defeated Young Vivian by 11 votes to nine, announced a new Cabinet following the election; among the new Premier's stated objectives were the development of tourism and further plans to encourage Niueans resident in New Zealand to return to the island.

In March 1994 Vivian proposed an unsuccessful motion of no confidence in the Government, and a further attempt by the opposition to introduce a similar motion was invalidated in the High Court in October on a procedural matter. However, during the ensuing debate, the Minister of National Planning and Economic Development, Sani Lakatani, resigned in order to join the opposition as its deputy leader, thus leaving the Government with only 10 official supporters in the Niue Assembly. Subsequent opposition demands for the intervention of the Governor-General of New Zealand in dissolving the legislature, in preparation for a fresh general election, were rejected, and, despite Lui's assurance that an early election would take place in order to end the atmosphere of increasing political uncertainty, polls were not held until February 1996. The Premier and his three cabinet ministers were re-elected to their seats, although support among the electorate for candidates of the Niue People's Party (NPP, as the NPAP had been renamed in 1995) and independents appeared fairly equally divided; in one village the result was decided by the toss of a coin when both candidates received an equal number of votes. Frank Lui was re-elected by the Niue Assembly as Premier, defeating Robert Rex, Jr (son of Niue's first Premier) by 11 votes to nine.

The issue of Niue's declining population continued to cause concern, particularly when provisional census figures, published in late 1997, revealed that the island's population was at its lowest recorded level. The Government expressed disappointment that its policy of encouraging Niueans resident in New Zealand to return to the island had failed and announced its intention to consider introducing more lenient immigration laws in an attempt to increase the population.

At a general election on 19 March 1999 Lui lost his seat and subsequently announced his retirement from politics. The Minister of Finance, Aukuso Pavihi, also failed to be re-elected. On 29 March Sani Lakatani, leader of the NPP, was elected Premier by the new Assembly, defeating O'Love Jacobsen by 14 votes to six. Lakatani's stated priority as Premier was to increase Niue's population to at least 3,000; he claimed that the sharp decline in the number of residents constituted a threat to the island's self-governing status.

It was reported in May 1999 that New Zealand was to phase out aid to Niue by 2003; New Zealand's aid programme to the island had been reduced by $NZ250,000 annually over the previous five years. However, doubts were expressed over the legality of the New Zealand Government's action, and it was suggested that New Zealand was required by law to provide financial assistance under the 1974 act that established Niue as a self-governing state.

In December 1999 a motion of no confidence in Lakatani was proposed by a number of opposition ministers, in protest at the Government's plans to fund a new national airline (Coral Air Niue). The result of the vote was inconclusive, with an equal number of votes cast for and against the motion. The proposed airline did not materialize, and the Government lost $NZ400,000 of its initial investment in the project. The New Zealand Government subsequently criticized officials in Niue for failing to secure a business plan or feasibility study for the proposed airline.

In late 1999 allegations made by a foreign news agency that Niue was being used by criminal organizations for 'laundering' the proceeds of their illegal activities were strongly denied by Lakatani. However, the naming of the island in a report by the Financial Action Task Force (FATF, see p. 430) in June 2000 as one of a number of countries and territories that had failed to co-operate in regional efforts to combat money-laundering led the Government to suspend the issue of any further 'offshore' banking licences until stricter regulations governing the financial sector had been introduced. In early 2001 the USA imposed sanctions on Niue (including a ban on transactions with US banks), claiming that the island had not implemented all the recommendations of the report. Lakatani appealed directly to President George W. Bush to end the embargo, which he said was having a devastating effect on Niue's economy. The Government stressed its commitment to meeting international requirements in its financial sector but claimed that it was having difficulty doing so, given its limited legal resources. Moreover, the Premier expressed strong disapproval that a nation as powerful as the USA should choose to inflict such hardship on a small, economically-vulnerable island, and urged other Pacific islands targeted by the report to unite in protest against such impositions. In June 2001 the Government engaged a US law firm in an effort to persuade two banks, Chase Manhattan and Bank of New York, to remove their bans on the transfer of some $NZ1m. to Niue via the business registry in Panama that the Government used for its 'offshore' tax activity.

Having failed to meet an FATF deadline in August 2001, in February 2002 Niue pledged to repeal its 'offshore' banking legislation. Premier Sani Lakatani was also considering closing down international business registrations based in Niue. The FATF announced in April 2002 that, in view of the island's commitment to improving the transparency of its tax and regulatory systems, the organization was to remove Niue from its list of non-co-operative territories; the decision was duly implemented in October. The bank-licensing legislation was repealed in June.

In December 2001 the Alliance of Independents, a new political party led by Frank Lui, was formed to contest the forthcoming general election. The party's spokesperson, O'Love Jacobsen, announced that the Alliance would campaign for a direct air link to New Zealand and for increased spending on public health.

At the general election, held on 20 April 2002, all 20 incumbent members were returned to the Niue Assembly. Independent candidate Toke Talagi polled the highest number of votes (445), but overall the NPP was victorious. However, despite having polled the second-highest number of votes (428), Sani Lakatani did not command the general support of his party, and faced a leadership challenge from his deputy, Young Vivian. Following several days of lobbying within the NPP, Vivian was chosen as Premier. Vivian announced that the party had the support of 10 elected members, having formed a coalition with several independents associated with Toke Talagi. Lakatani was appointed Deputy Premier, however, later that year and following a period of ill health, the former Premier indicated that he might withdraw from politics.

In July 2003 Niue's only formal political party, the Niue People's Party, was dissolved as a result of ongoing disagreement among its membership and the failure of several projects (the most prominent of which was the attempted establishment of Coral Air Niue, see above). Opposition member Terry Coe expressed satisfaction with the news, stating that he hoped that party politics would cease henceforth in Niue. Observers also commented that Robert Rex (Niue's widely respected first Premier) had strongly opposed party politics, believing it to cause rifts in families and communities.

In September 2003 the opposition expressed concern that too many government members were travelling overseas on business, and that a significant amount of public money was being used to fund these trips. At the time of the statement seven of the Niue Assembly's 20 members (including two cabinet ministers) were absent on engagements overseas. In the same month it was announced that Niue was to receive US $90,000 from the People's Republic of China in order to build new accommodation for the 300 delegates and visitors who were expected to visit the island for the Pacific Islands Forum (see p. 393) summit meeting in 2004. The meeting was relocated, however, following the widespread devastation of the island by a cyclone in early 2004 (see below).

In October 2003 Niue's Premier issued a statement inviting the residents of Tuvalu (whose continued existence on those islands was increasingly threatened by rising sea levels) to migrate to Niue. The Government of Tuvalu subsequently requested that Niue produce a memorandum of understanding giving formal details of this invitation and of the rights that Tuvaluans would enjoy on Niue. Further discussions between officials from the two Governments took place in June 2005.

In early January 2004 Niue was devastated by Cyclone Heta. Damage caused by the storm, which was described as the worst in the island's recent history, included the destruction of many buildings, the loss of most food crops, the death of two people and serious injury of several others, and extensive damage to Niue's infrastructure, communications and coral reef. Relief supplies were sent from New Zealand as part of an initial aid programme worth some US $3.5m. It was estimated that US $23m. would be needed for a rebuilding programme to be carried out over a five-year period. The destruction of Alofi was so severe that the Government announced plans to relocate the island's capital to Fonuakula on the upper plateau. However, fears for the continued feasibility of the island were expressed by some observers, who suggested that many Niueans might exercise their right to take up residency in New Zealand, leaving the community on Niue unviable. As work began to repair or rebuild some 300 homes under the Government's New Niue or Niue Foou recovery plan, it was announced that renewed efforts would be made to attract expatriate Niueans back to the island. Plans for a fish-processing plant, as well as a number of new agricultural projects, were expected to provide some employment opportunities. In October 2004 New Zealand's Prime Minister Helen Clark made an official visit to Niue to celebrate the 30-year anniversary of the island's attainment of self-governing status. She urged expatriate Niueans to return to the island and support efforts to regenerate its infrastructure and economy. She also announced a programme to introduce the Niuean language into the education curriculum from pre-school level onwards by 2006, as part of Taoga Niue, an initiative aimed at preserving traditional customs and cultural practices on the island. The Halavaka ke he Monuina Arrangement (HkhMA), a bilateral agreement signed in October 2004, aimed to facilitate closer co-operation between the various government agencies of Niue and New Zealand. The arrangement represented a major shift in New Zealand's approach to the management of its relationship with Niue. In addition, Clark confirmed that $NZ6m. was to be made available to rebuild the hospital destroyed by Cyclone Heta. The new hospital, located at Kaimiti, opened in March 2006. In April of that year New Zealand and France agreed jointly to finance the construction of a government administration building on Niue.

In March 2000, meanwhile, a Niue-New Zealand joint consultative committee met, for the first time, in Alofi to consider the two sides' future constitutional relationship. Later that year the committee proposed to conduct a survey of islanders' views and to consider all options, from reintegration with New Zealand to full independence. A meeting of the joint committee took place in March 2001 in Wellington at which the issues of New Zealand aid and reciprocal immigration laws were discussed, as well as options for Niue's future constitutional status. In early 2001 Hima Takelesi was appointed Niue's first High Commissioner to New Zealand. New Zealand remained committed to annual assistance of $NZ6.3m. in the years 2001–03. At New Zealand's 2001 census, a total of 20,148 Niueans were recorded as resident in New Zealand. Discussions took place in Wellington in March 2003 between the New Zealand Prime Minister, Helen Clark, and Niue's Premier, Young Vivian. Topics debated included budgetary assistance, a review of the island's development plan and the continued migration of islanders from the territory to New Zealand.

The Government conducted a survey in September 2004 to assess the current population of the island. However, its apparent reluctance to release the information prompted speculation that more people had left Niue than official reports had previously indicated. When its findings were made public in October some observers disputed the figure of 1,550 (which many believed was higher than the reality, in order to attract more favourable levels of economic assistance). A local newspaper conducted a similar survey and estimated a resident population of some 1,300. In July 2005 the Premier announced that efforts to attract Niueans back to the island, notably by promoting the farming and fisheries sectors, were to be increased. The people of Niue were also to be granted better access to health care following an agreement concluded in November 2005 between the Niue Ministry for Health and the Counties Manukau District Health Board of New Zealand. The agreement was expected to facilitate the referral of Niuean patients to New Zealand.

In November 2004 Niue's High Commissioner to New Zealand, Hima Takelesi, announced his intention to return to the island to stand for parliament in the forthcoming elections. His stated motivation was a desire to form a stronger partnership with the 20,000 Niueans resident in New Zealand, in an attempt to ensure that Niue retained its current status and did not become incorporated into New Zealand. At the election, held on 30 April 2005, Takelesi succeeded in securing a seat in the Niue Assembly. Candidates in two constituencies (one of whom was the Minister of Finance) received equal numbers of votes. The allocation of the seat was eventually determined by the procedure of drawing names out of a hat. Young Vivian was re-elected Premier several days later, defeating O'Love Jacobsen by 17 votes to three. Vivian's stated priorities for the new Assembly included ongoing efforts to increase Niue's population (see above), the clearing of some 350 derelict homes and continued efforts to increase economic prospects for the island. Moreover, in June Vivian announced his intention to propose political reforms to the legislature, including an increase in the parliamentary term from three years to five years and an increase in the number of cabinet ministers from four to six members.

In February 2006 Anton Ojala replaced Kurt Meyer as New Zealand High Commissioner to Niue; Ojala was in turn replaced by Brian Smythe in January 2008. In February 2007, in an attempt to ease its financial difficulties, the Government announced a 10% decrease in public servants' salaries, along with a reduction in working hours for certain employees and decreases in local grants. In the following month a parliamentary motion of no confidence submitted by the opposition against Premier Vivian, in protest at the Government's alleged financial mismanagement, failed to garner enough votes to succeed. Niue's financial problems were again highlighted in late 2007, when a member of the opposition reported that the island's financial secretary had admitted the Government's bankruptcy.

On 7 June 2008 a general election was held, with 11 of the 20 parliamentary seats being contested. Three new members were elected to the Niue Assembly, including Togia Sioneholo, hitherto the Secretary of Justice, who defeated Hima Takelesi, the former High Commissioner to New Zealand. On 26 June 2008 Toke Talagi, a former Minister of Finance, was elected Premier by 14 parliamentary votes to five, thereby succeeding the incumbent Young Vivian. Talagi assumed responsibility for numerous ministerial portfolios, including planning, economic development, finance, external affairs and environment. O'Love Jacobsen was allocated the portfolios of health and women's affairs, among others. Togia Sioneholo received the justice portfolio, along with other responsibilities. Pokotoa Sipeli was appointed Minister of Agriculture, Forestry and Fisheries, Posts and Telecommunications and Administrative Services. The new Premier declared that his immediate priority was to address the island's economic situation.

In February 2009, after a delay of almost two years, modified legislation providing for the introduction of a new consumption tax, which would be applicable to visitors to the island, was finally approved by the Niue Assembly. Owing to its likely impact on low-income families, the controversial tax had encountered widespread opposition within the Assembly, and in early 2009 led to the drafting of a motion of no confidence in the Government.

Following almost 10 years of technical and political consultations, Niue and the USA signed a maritime boundary treaty in May 1997, delineating the precise boundary between the territorial waters of Niue and American Samoa. In October 2006 Niue agreed to join the Regional Assistance Mission to Solomon Islands (RAMSI), with the deployment of two Niuean police officers to Solomon Islands. In August 2008 Niue hosted the annual summit meeting of the Pacific Islands Forum, at which the Niue Declaration on Climate Change was endorsed.

The New Zealand Minister of Foreign Affairs, Murray McCully, visited Niue in January 2009. The Government of Niue hoped that New Zealand might provide financial assistance for the reopening of a fish-processing plant, which had closed in 2007 and resulted in many job losses (see Economic Affairs).

Government

Niue enjoys self-government in free association with New Zealand. The New Zealand Government, however, remains responsible for the island's defence and external affairs. Executive government is carried out by the Premier and three other ministers. Legislation is the responsibility of the Niue Assembly, which has 20 members (14 village representatives and six elected on a common roll), but New Zealand, if called upon to do so by the Assembly, will also legislate for the island. There is a New Zealand representative in Niue, whose status was upgraded to that of High Commissioner in 1993.

Economic Affairs

Niue's gross domestic product (GDP) was estimated at $NZ17.3m. in 2003, when GDP per head was estimated at $NZ10,048. The population decreased at an average annual rate of 2.3% in 1991–2001.

Agriculture, forestry and fishing contributed 23.3% of GDP in 2003. According to the census of 2006, the sector engaged 15.9% of the employed labour force. Two-thirds of the land surface is uncultivable, but many households practise subsistence gardening. The principal crops are coconuts, taro, yams, cassava and sweet potatoes. A taro export scheme was successfully introduced in the early 1990s, and production of the crop increased by more than 500% in 1993. Exports of taro, principally to New Zealand, contributed nearly 93% of total export earnings in 2003, being facilitated by a new regular shipping service. Plans to increase the production of vanilla as an export crop were discussed in 2003, but the promising crop was destroyed by the cyclone of early 2004. The reintroduction of vanilla cultivation, as well as that of organic nonu (or noni, a fruit renowned for its medicinal properties), for export was initiated during 2004 as part of the Government's post-cyclone recovery programme. Honey is also produced for export. Pigs, poultry, goats and beef cattle are raised, mainly for local consumption. An island development plan for 2003 included proposals to develop Niue's fishing industry by employing a fleet of used Korean fishing vessels. The construction of a fish-processing factory at Amanau was completed in 2004. It was estimated that the new plant might raise $NZ9m. annually in revenue. Fishing licences to five New Zealand vessels and four Samoan vessels were issued. However, a series of problems resulted in operational difficulties. Operations were suspended in 2007. In early 2009 Niue continued to hope that the plant, an important source of employment for islanders, might resume activities with financial support from New Zealand.

Industry (including mining, manufacturing, construction and utilities) contributed only 2.8% of GDP in 2003 but engaged 17.1% of the labour force in 2006. The manufacturing sector has been very limited, accounting for only 1.5% of GDP in 2003. A noni juice factory also opened in October 2004. Exploration for deposits of uranium continued on the island in 2005, but in November it was announced that no commercially viable resources had been identified. The extensive damage caused by Cyclone Heta led to much activity in the construction sector from early 2004, as rebuilding programmes commenced.

The island remains dependent upon imported diesel fuel for its energy requirements. In collaboration with the international environmentalist group Greenpeace, in December 2005 Niue confirmed its commitment to the development of wind power, hoping to become one of the first locations in the world to be completely reliant on renewable energy sources. A major fire at the island's main electricity-generating plant in May 2006 seriously disrupted power supplies. In April 2009 Niue signed a memorandum of understanding on the Pacific Petroleum Project, a regional initiative that aimed to reduce the energy costs of the Pacific islands through collective negotiations for the bulk procurement of petroleum supplies.

The services sector contributed 73.9% of GDP in 2003. The sector engaged 66.9% of the labour force in 2006. The Government is the most important employer, engaging 512 members of the paid labour force in December 2004, when an estimated 269 people were employed in the private sector. Tourism has begun to make a significant contribution to the economy, and the sector recovered well from the damage caused by the cyclone of January 2004. Tourist arrivals by air increased from 3,463 in 2007 to an estimated 4,750 in 2008. Receipts from tourism amounted to US $0.9m. in 2006. In October 2005 it was announced that Air New Zealand was to begin a weekly service between Auckland and Niue. An 'offshore' financial centre was established in the mid-1990s but, amid accusations that Niue had allowed criminal organizations to 'launder' their funds, in February 2005 the virtual closure of the centre was announced. From the 1990s various other attempts to secure new sources of revenue in Niue included the leasing of the island's telecommunications facilities to foreign companies for use in specialist telephone services. However, this enterprise (which earned the island an estimated $NZ1.5m. per year) caused considerable controversy when it was revealed that Niue's telephone code had been made available to companies offering personal services considered indecent by the majority of islanders. The sale of the internet domain name '.nu' yielded significant revenue but proved similarly controversial (see below).

Niue records an annual trade deficit, with imports generally far exceeding exports. The principal exports in 1993 were root crops (which provided 87.1% of total export earnings), coconuts (1.9%), honey and handicrafts. The principal imports were foodstuffs (which constituted 28.0% of the total cost of imports), electrical goods (11.8%), motor vehicles (10.6%) and machinery (5.4%). Niue's most significant exports normally include taro, coconuts, honey and vanilla. New Zealand is the island's main trading partner. The value of New Zealand's exports to Niue totalled an estimated $NZ11.6m. in 2004, while that country's imports from Niue were worth less than $NZ0.3m.

The budget for 2006/07 was projected to balance at $NZ23.4m., with budgetary support of $NZ6.9m. from New Zealand. The Niue Government envisaged budgetary expenditure of $NZ16.7m. for 2008/09. Total development assistance from New Zealand was raised to $NZ16.7m. in 2008/09. In addition, an aid programme totalling $NZ20m. over five years was announced in late 2004. A trust fund was established with $NZ10m. from New Zealand and Australia. By mid-2005 the trust fund's assets stood at $NZ12m. In May 2006 it was announced that, in response to a request from the Premier of Niue, New Zealand had agreed to provide advance funding equivalent to almost US $190,000 in budgetary support. The annual rate of inflation averaged 3.9% in 2000–07. Compared with the previous year, consumer prices increased by 6.8% in 2007. The unemployment rate was estimated at 13.8% of the labour force in 2001.

Niue is a member of the Pacific Community (see p. 391) and the Pacific Islands Forum (see p. 393), and an associate member of the UN Economic and Social Commission for Asia and the Pacific (ESCAP, see p. 36). In 2000 Niue became a signatory of the Cotonou Agreement (see p. 311) with the European Union (EU).

Niue's entire economy was severely affected by Cyclone Heta, which struck the island in January 2004 causing extensive damage to housing, crops and infrastructure. The subsequent recovery programme, known as New Niue or Niue Foou, emphasized rebuilding works and included the fish-processing plant at Amanau and the establishment of an industrial park at Fonuakula. New Zealand assisted Niue's post-cyclone recovery programme and was also providing funding in areas such as government housing. In April 2007 the Niue Development Bank signed an agreement with the European Investment Bank, which was to allocate €2m. to the improvement of the island's infrastructure, including projects in the areas of agriculture, fisheries, mining, commerce, tourism and energy. In addition to the revenue derived from the leasing of telecommunications facilities to overseas companies (see above), Niue's earnings from the sale of its internet domain name '.nu' led to further controversy when a report published in July 2004 claimed that the island was hosting some 3m. pages of pornographic material via its .nu domain. In March 2008, furthermore, an international software security company reported that, along with Tokelau, in per caput terms Niue had become one of the world's worst offenders with regard to the relaying of unsolicited e-mails. Upon taking office in June 2008, Premier Toke Talagi stated that his immediate intention was to focus on the economy of Niue. The priorities of his administration were to be the control of government expenditure and the creation of new sources of revenue. In April 2009 a controversial new consumption tax entered into effect (see Recent History). Levied at a rate of 12.5%, the tax on goods and services was expected to make a substantial contribution to government revenue. Revised tax legislation was also implemented. The new Government identified the tourism sector as a potential source of higher income. In 2008 Niue hosted the annual meeting of the Pacific Islands Forum. Two other important meetings, that of the Forum Fisheries Agency and that of FAO delegates, were convened in Niue in May 2009.

Education

Education is provided free of charge, and is compulsory for 10 years between five and 16 years of age. The school-leaving age was raised from 14 to 16 in 1998. Primary education, from the age of five, lasts for six years, and is followed by six years of secondary education. In 2004/05 estimated enrolment at primary school level was equivalent to 86% of pupils of the relevant age-group, while enrolment at secondary level was equivalent to 99% of pupils. In 2006 a total of 212 children were enrolled in pre-primary and primary schools. A total of 191 pupils were enrolled in secondary education in the same year. A number of school-leavers take up tertiary education, mainly in the Pacific region and, to a lesser extent, in New Zealand. There is an extension centre of the University of the South Pacific in Niue. An estimated 50 students were engaged in tertiary education in 1991. A private medical school opened in 2000 but subsequently closed. A private university offering online information technology and business management courses opened in late 2003. In 2002 10.2% of total government expenditure was allocated to education. A long-term programme between Niue and the Dunedin College of Education, funded by New Zealand, concluded at the end of 2005.

Public Holidays

2009: 1 January (New Year's Day), 2 January (Commission Day), 6 February (Waitangi Day, anniversary of 1840 treaty), 10–13 April (Easter), 25 April (ANZAC Day, anniversary of 1915 landing at Gallipoli), 1 June (Queen's Official Birthday), 16 October (Constitution Day celebrations), 26 October (Peniamina's Day), 25 December (Christmas Day), 26 December (Boxing Day).

2010: 1 January (New Year's Day), 2 January (Commission Day), 6 February (Waitangi Day, anniversary of 1840 treaty), 2–5 April (Easter), 25 April (ANZAC Day, anniversary of 1915 landing at

Gallipoli), 7 June (Queen's Official Birthday), 16 October (Constitution Day celebrations), October (Peniamina's Day), 25 December (Christmas Day), 26 December (Boxing Day).

Weights and Measures
The metric system is in force.

Statistical Survey

Source (unless otherwise indicated): Statistics Unit, Economics, Planning, Development Office, Government of Niue, POB 95, Alofi; tel. and fax 4219; fax 4148; e-mail statsniue@mail.gov.nu; internet www.spc.int/prism/country/nu/stats/.

AREA AND POPULATION

Area: 261.5 sq km (100.9 sq miles).

Population: 1,788 at census of 7 September 2001; 1,625 (males 802, females 823) at census of September 2006. An estimated 22,473 Niueans lived in New Zealand at the time of the 2006 census.

Density (at September 2006): 6.2 per sq km.

Ethnic Groups (2001 census, declared ethnicity): Niuean 1,399; Caucasian 81; Pacific Islander 182; Niuean/Caucasian 28; Niuean/Pacific Islander 42; Asian 4.

Principal Villages (estimated population at 2006 census): Alofi (capital) 581; Hakupu 162; Avatele 164.

Births, Marriages and Deaths (2001 census): Crude birth rate 18.5 per 1,000; Death rate 7.8 per 1,000. *2003:* Live births 9; Marriages 3; Deaths 9. *2004* (including Niueans temporarily resident in New Zealand): Live births 18; Marriages 14; Deaths 18. *2006:* Birth rate 16 per 1,000; Death rate 9.2 per 1,000.

Life Expectancy (years at birth, WHO estimates): 69.9 (males 63.7; females 77.9) in 2006. Source: WHO, *World Health Statistics*.

Immigration and Emigration (2007): Arrivals 5,131; Departures 5,250.

Economically Active Population (2006 census, persons aged 15 years and over): Agriculture, forestry and fishing 119; Mining, electricity, gas, water and construction 61; Manufacturing 67; Trade, restaurants and hotels 84; Transport, storage and communications 43; Finance, real estate, business activities 33; Public administration 180; Education and health 117; Community, social and personal services. 43; *Total employed* 747. Note: Figures exclude subsistence workers. **Paid Employment** (December 2004): Government sector 512 (males 294, females 218); Private sector (estimates) 269 (males 143, females 126).

HEALTH AND WELFARE
Key Indicators

Total Fertility Rate (children per woman, 2006): 2.6.
Under-5 Mortality Rate (per 1,000 live births, 2006): 42.
Physicians (per 1,000 head, 2004): 2.0.
Hospital Beds (per 1,000 head, 2006): 4.9.
Health Expenditure (2006): US $ per head (PPP): 298.
Health Expenditure (2006): % of GDP: 13.6.
Health Expenditure (2006): public (% of total): 98.6.

For sources and definitions, see explanatory note on p. vi.

AGRICULTURE, ETC.

Principal Crops (metric tons, 2007, FAO estimates): Taro 3,300; Sweet potatoes 260; Yams 130; Coconuts 2,600; Bananas 80; Lemons and limes 130. *Aggregate Production* ('000 metric tons, may include official, semi-official or estimated data): Vegetables (incl. melons) 130; Fruits (excl. melons) 210.

Livestock (year ending September 2007, FAO estimates): Cattle 115; Pigs 2,100; Chickens 15,000.

Livestock Products (metric tons, 2007, FAO estimates): Pig meat 65; Chicken meat 18; Cows' milk 55; Hen eggs 12; Honey 7.

Forestry (cu m, 1985): Roundwood removals 613; Sawnwood production 201.

Fishing (metric tons, live weight, 2006, FAO estimate): Total catch 203.

Source: FAO.

INDUSTRY

Production (2005): Electric energy 3 million kWh. Source: UN, *Industrial Commodity Statistics Yearbook*.

FINANCE

Currency and Exchange Rates: 100 cents = 1 New Zealand dollar ($NZ). For details, see Tokelau.

Budget ($NZ '000, year ending 30 June 2006, provisional): Internal revenue 14,206; New Zealand budgetary support 6,953; *Total revenue* 21,159; Recurrent expenditure 21,417; Capital 90; *Total expenditure* 21,507. *2006/07* ($NZ '000, forecasts): Internal revenue 16,499; New Zealand budgetary support 6,915; Total revenue 23,414; Recurrent expenditure 23,364; Capital projects 50; Total expenditure 23,414.

Overseas Aid ($NZ '000, 2008/09, provisional): Official development assistance from New Zealand 16,690. Source: Ministry of Foreign Affairs and Trade, Wellington.

Cost of Living (Consumer Price Index, average of quarterly figures; base: July–Sept. 2003 = 100): All items 104.0 in 2005; 106.4 in 2006; 113.6 in 2007.

Gross Domestic Product ($NZ '000 in current prices): 16,711 in 2001; 16,245 in 2002; 17,252 in 2003.

Gross Domestic Product by Economic Activity ($NZ '000 in current prices, 2003): Agriculture, forestry and fishing 4,062; Mining and quarrying −12; Manufacturing 268; Electricity, gas and water 201; Construction 36; Trade 2,181; Restaurants and hotels 566; Transport, storage and communications 1,395; Financial and business services, real estate, etc. 1,434; Public administration 6,800; Other community, social and personal services 519; *Sub-total* 17,450; *Less* Imputed bank service charge 215; *GDP at factor cost* 17,235; Indirect taxes 970; *Less* Subsidies 953; *GDP in purchasers' values* 17,252.

EXTERNAL TRADE

Principal Commodities (trade with New Zealand only, $NZ '000, 2004): *Imports c.i.f.:* Animals and animal products 523; Prepared foodstuffs 1,196; Mineral products 1,842; Chemical products 560; Plastics and rubber 399; Wood and wood products 717; Base metals and articles thereof 1,714; Machinery, mechanical appliances and electrical equipment 2,100; Miscellaneous manufactured articles 1,528; Total (incl. others) 11,574. *Exports f.o.b.:* Prepared foodstuffs 39; Machinery, mechanical appliances and electrical equipment 153; Optical, photographic and medical instruments, etc. 50; Total (incl. others) 264.

Principal Trading Partners ($NZ '000, 2004): *Imports c.i.f.:* New Zealand 11,574; Total (incl. others) 11,859. *Exports f.o.b.:* New Zealand 264.

TRANSPORT

Road Traffic (2001 census): Passenger cars 323; Motorcycles 134; Vans 170; Trucks 74; Pick-ups 76; Buses 11.

International Shipping: *Ship Arrivals* (1989): Yachts 20; Merchant vessels 22; Total 42. *Freight Traffic* (metric tons, 1989, official estimates): Unloaded 3,410; Loaded 10.

Civil Aviation: *Passengers* (1992): Arrivals 3,500; Departures 3,345. *Freight Traffic* (metric tons, 1992): Unloaded 41.6; Loaded 15.7.

TOURISM

Foreign Tourist Arrivals (by air): 2,793 in 2005; 3,008 in 2006; 3,463 in 2007.

Tourist Arrivals by Country of Residence (2007): Australia 371; New Zealand 2,517; United Kingdom 82; USA 177; Total (incl. others) 3,463.

Tourism Receipts (US $ million, incl. passenger transport): 1.0 in 2004; 1.2 in 2005; 0.9 in 2006. Source: World Tourism Organization.

COMMUNICATIONS MEDIA

Telephones (2002): 1,000 main lines in use.
Mobile Cellular Telephones (2001 census): 225 units in use*.
Radio Receivers (2006 census): 373 per 1,000 persons.
Television Receivers (2006 census): 519 per 1,000 persons.
Personal Computers (2001 census): 77 in use.
Internet Users (2002): 900.
Daily Newspaper (2004): 1.

Non-daily Newspaper (2004): 1†.
* Source: International Telecommunication Union.
† Source: UNESCO.

EDUCATION

Pre-primary and Primary (2006): 1 school; 212 pupils (males 104, females 108); 20 teachers (males 3, females 17).

Secondary (2006): 1 school; 191 pupils (males 102, females 89); 31 teachers (males 9, females 22).

Source: Department of Education, Niue.

Directory

The Constitution

In October 1974 Niue gained self-government in free association with New Zealand. The latter, however, remains responsible for Niue's defence and external affairs and will continue economic and administrative assistance. Executive authority in Niue is vested in the British monarch as sovereign of New Zealand but exercised through the government of the Premier, assisted by three ministers. Legislative power is vested in the Niue Assembly or Fono Ekepule, which comprises 20 members (14 village representatives and six elected on a common roll), but New Zealand, if requested to do so by the Assembly, will also legislate for the island. There is a New Zealand representative in Niue, the High Commissioner, who is charged with liaising between the Governments of Niue and New Zealand.

The Government

New Zealand High Commissioner: BRIAN SMYTHE.
Secretary to Government: RICHARD HIPA.

CABINET
(April 2009)

Premier, Chairman of the Cabinet and Minister responsible for the Premier's Department, Civil Aviation, Crown Law Office, Planning, Economic Development and Statistics, External Affairs, Niue Public Service Commission, Finance, Customs and Revenue, Government Assets, Police and National Security, Environment, Meteorological Services and Climate Change, Tourism, Immigration and Population, Private Sector Development, and Youth and Sports: TOKE TUFUKIA TALAGI.

Minister of Agriculture, Forestry and Fisheries, Post and Telecommunications, and Administrative Services: POKOTOA SIPELI.

Minister of Health, Public Works, Women's Affairs and the Niue Power Corporation: O'LOVE JACOBSEN.

Minister of Community Affairs, Justice, Lands and Survey, Education, Shipping and Bulk Fuel: TOGIA SIONEHOLO.

GOVERNMENT OFFICES

All ministries are in Alofi.

Office of the New Zealand High Commissioner: POB 78, Tapeu, Alofi; tel. 4022; fax 4173.

Office of the Secretary to Government: POB 40, Alofi; tel. 4220; fax 4232; e-mail secgov.premier@mail.gov.nu.

Legislature

ASSEMBLY

The Niue Assembly or Fono Ekepule has 20 members (14 village representatives and six members elected on a common roll). The most recent general election was held on 7 June 2008.
Speaker: ATAPANA SIAKIMOTU.

Political Organization

Alliance of Independents: Alofi; f. 2001; Leader FRANK LUI; Spokesperson O'LOVE JACOBSEN.

Judicial System

The Chief Justice of the High Court and the Land Court Judge visit Niue quarterly. In addition, lay justices are locally appointed and exercise limited criminal and civil jurisdiction. Appeals against High Court judgments are heard in the Court of Appeal of Niue. Established in 1992, sessions of the Court of Appeal of Niue are usually held in the New Zealand capital of Wellington. In April 2009, however, for the first time the four New Zealand judges heard various cases, including several land disputes, on Niue itself.

The High Court: exercises civil and criminal jurisdiction; Registrar JUSTIN KAMUPALA.

The Land Court: is concerned with litigation over land and titles.

Land Appellate Court

Hears appeals over decisions of the Land Court.
Chief Justice: HETA HINGSTON.

Religion

About 63% of the population belong to the Ekalesia Niue, a Protestant organization, which had 1,093 adherents at the time of the 2001 census. Within the Roman Catholic Church, which had 128 adherents (equivalent to 7.4% of the population) in 2001, Niue forms part of the diocese of Tonga. The Church of Jesus Christ of Latter-day Saints (Mormon—which had 158 adherents in 2001), the Seventh-day Adventists, the Jehovah's Witnesses and the Church of God of Jerusalem are also represented.

Ekalesia Niue: Head Office, POB 25, Alofi; tel. 4195; fax 4352/4010; e-mail ekalesia.niue@niue.nu; f. 1846; est. by London Missionary Society, became Ekalesia Niue in 1966; Pres. Rev. MATAGI VILITAMA; Gen. Sec. Rev. ARTHUR PIHIGIA.

The Press

Niue Business News: 20 Lautamina Rd, Mutalau 110175; tel. 3317; e-mail sioneholof@gmail.com; internet www.niuebusinessnews.com; electronic; previously publ. in print as *Niue Economic Review*; non-profit organization; volunteer-based.

Niue Star: weekly; Niuean and English; publ. in Alofi until destruction of office by Cyclone Heta in 2004; operations transferred to Auckland, New Zealand; Publr MIKE JACKSON; circ. 800.

Broadcasting and Communications

TELECOMMUNICATIONS

In 2003 Niue became the first location in the world to have a national wireless internet system allowing access from anywhere on the island by means of solar-powered aerials attached to coconut palms.

Director of Posts and Telecommunications: POB 37, Alofi; tel. 4000; fax 4010.

Telecom Niue: POB 37, Alofi; tel. 4002; Dir TULI HEKA (acting).

BROADCASTING

Radio

Broadcasting Corporation of Niue: POB 68, Alofi; tel. 4026; fax 4217; operates television service and radio service; govt-owned; Chair. NEAL MORRISSEY; CEO TREVOR TIAKIA; Gen. Man. PATRICK LINO.

Radio Sunshine: broadcasts in English and Niuean between 6 a.m. and 10 p.m. Mon.–Sat.

Television

Broadcasting Corporation of Niue: see Radio.
Television Niue broadcasts in English and Niuean six days a week from 5 p.m. to 11 p.m.

Finance

DEVELOPMENT BANK

Niue Development Bank: POB 34, Alofi; tel. 4335; fax 4290; e-mail devbank@niue.nu; f. 1993; govt-owned; began operations July 1994; Gen. Man. ANGELA TUHIPA.

COMMERCIAL BANK

Bank South Pacific Ltd: POB 76, Main St, Alofi; tel. 4220; fax 4043; e-mail bsp@niue.nu; internet www.bsp.com.pg/niue/niue; acquired from Westpac Banking Corpn in Sept. 2004; Man. REX YAWANE.

Trade and Industry

GOVERNMENT AGENCIES

Business Advisory Service: Alofi; tel. 4228.

Office of Economic Affairs, Planning and Development, Statistics and Trade and Investment: POB 42, Alofi; tel. 4148; e-mail business.epdsu@mail.gov.nu; responsible for planning and financing activities in the agricultural, tourism, industrial sectors, business advisory and trade and investment.

CHAMBER OF COMMERCE

Niue Chamber of Commerce: POB 160, Alofi; tel. 4399; fax 4010; e-mail chamber@niue.nu; internet www.niuechamber.com; SONYA TALAGI.

UTILITIES

Niue Power Corporation: POB 198, Alofi; tel. 4119; fax 4385; e-mail gm.npc.@mail.gov.nu; Gen. Man. SPEEDO HETUTU.

TRADE UNION

Public Service Association: Alofi.

Transport

ROADS

There are 123 km of all-weather roads and 106 km of access and plantation roads. A total of 788 motor vehicles were registered in 2001. The road network was extensively damaged by Cyclone Heta in January 2004. In mid-2004 it was estimated that some 48 km of sealed roads were clear and in good condition.

SHIPPING

The best anchorage is an open roadstead at Alofi, the largest of Niue's 14 villages. Work to extend a small wharf at Alofi began in mid-1998 with US assistance. The New Zealand Shipping Corporation operates a monthly service between New Zealand, Nauru and Niue. Fuel supplies are delivered by a tanker (the *Pacific Explorer*) from Fiji. In December 2002 the Government signed an agreement with Reef Shipping Ltd to provide a service to New Zealand every three to four weeks.

CIVIL AVIATION

Hanan International Airport has a total sealed runway of 2,350 m, following the completion of a 700 m extension in 1995, with New Zealand assistance. In 2005 Air New Zealand began a weekly service between Auckland and Niue.

Tourism

Niue has a small but significant tourism industry (specializing in holidays based on activities such as diving, rock-climbing, caving and game fishing), which has benefited from an increase in the frequency of flights between the island and New Zealand. Niue's tourist industry made a good recovery from the extensive damage caused by Cyclone Heta in January 2004. The Matavai Resort provides the main tourist facilities. A total of 3,463 people arrived by air to visit Niue in 2007. In that year some 73% of visitors were from New Zealand. The number of arrivals rose to 4,750 in 2008.

Niue Tourism Office: POB 42, Alofi; tel. 4224; fax 4225; e-mail niuetourism@mail.gov.nu; internet www.niueisland.com; Dir of Tourism IDA TALAGI-HEKESI.

NICARAGUA

Introductory Survey

Location, Climate, Language, Religion, Flag, Capital

The Republic of Nicaragua lies in the Central American isthmus, bounded by the Pacific Ocean to the west and by the Caribbean Sea to the east. Its neighbours are Honduras, to the north, and Costa Rica, to the south. The climate is tropical, with an average annual temperature of 25.5°C (78°F). The rainy season extends from May to October. The national language is Spanish, although English is also spoken on the Caribbean coast. Almost all of the inhabitants profess Christianity, and the great majority are Roman Catholics. The national flag (proportions 3 by 5) has three equal horizontal stripes, of blue, white and blue, with the state emblem (a triangle enclosing a dark blue sea from which rise five volcanoes, in green, surmounted by a Phrygian cap from which extend white rays and, at the top, a rainbow, all encircled by the words, in gold capitals, 'República de Nicaragua' and 'América Central') in the centre of the white stripe; the same flag without the state emblem is an alternative version of the civil flag. The capital is Managua.

Recent History

Nicaragua was under Spanish rule from the 16th century until 1821. It then became part of the Central American Federation until 1838. From 1927 US troops were based in Nicaragua at the request of the Government, which was opposed by a guerrilla group, led by Augusto César Sandino. In 1933, following the establishment of the National Guard (commanded by Gen. Anastasio Somoza García), the US troops left Nicaragua. Sandino was assassinated in 1934, but some of his followers ('Sandinistas') continued actively to oppose the new regime. Somoza seized power in a coup in 1935 and took office as President in 1936. Apart from a brief interlude in the late 1940s, Somoza remained as President until September 1956, when he was assassinated. However, the Somoza family continued to dominate Nicaraguan politics until 1979.

In 1962 the left-wing Frente Sandinista de Liberación Nacional (FSLN—Sandinista National Liberation Front) was formed with the object of overthrowing the Somozas by revolution. Gen. Anastasio Somoza Debayle, son of the former dictator, became President in May 1967, holding office until April 1972. The Congreso Nacional (National Congress) was dissolved, and a triumvirate ruled until Gen. Somoza was re-elected President in September 1974. In January 1978 the murder of Pedro Joaquín Chamorro Cardenal, the leader of the opposition coalition and the editor of *La Prensa* (the country's only independent newspaper), provoked violent demonstrations against the Government.

In June 1979 the FSLN announced the formation of a provisional Junta of National Reconstruction. With the FSLN in command of many towns and preparing for the final onslaught on Managua, President Somoza resigned and left the country on 17 July 1979. (He was assassinated in Paraguay in September 1980.) After the Sandinistas had gained control of the capital, the Junta and its Provisional Governing Council took power on 20 July as the Government of National Reconstruction. The 1974 Constitution was abrogated, and the bicameral Congreso Nacional dissolved. The National Guard was disbanded and replaced by the Ejército Popular Sandinista (EPS—Sandinista People's Army), officially established in August. In that month the Junta issued a 'Statute on Rights and Guarantees for the Citizens of Nicaragua', providing for basic personal freedoms and restoring freedom of the press and broadcasting. Civil rights were restored in January 1980.

On taking office, the Junta had issued a Basic Statute, providing for the creation of an appointed Council of State to act as an interim legislature. In March 1981 Commdr Daniel Ortega Saavedra was appointed Co-ordinator of the Junta and of its new consultative body, the Council of Government.

By 1981 discontent at the postponement of elections and the increasing hegemony of the Sandinistas had led to the creation of counter-revolutionary forces ('Contras'), who were mostly members of the former National Guard and operated from camps in Honduras. Meanwhile, relations between the US and Nicaraguan Governments had seriously deteriorated, culminating in the suspension of US economic aid in April. In the same year the US Government donated US $10m. in support of the Contras, while covert operations by the US Central Intelligence Agency (CIA) attempted to destabilize the Sandinista regime. In March 1982 the Sandinista Government declared a state of emergency. However, the intensity of attacks by the Fuerzas Democráticas Nicaragüenses (FDN), anti-Sandinista guerrillas based in Honduras, increased. A Contra group, the Alianza Revolucionaria Democrática (ARDE), was also established in Costa Rica, led by Edén Pastora Gómez, a prominent figure in the revolution who had become disillusioned with the Sandinistas. In December the Sandinistas reaffirmed their support for the initiatives of the 'Contadora group' (Colombia, Mexico, Panama and Venezuela), which was attempting to find peaceful solutions to the disputes involving Central America, and adopted a more conciliatory approach towards the opposition.

In June 1984 talks commenced between the Nicaraguan and US Governments in order to foster the peace negotiations proposed by the Contadora group. However, although the Sandinistas agreed in September to sign a peace agreement, the USA rejected the agreement on the grounds that the forthcoming Nicaraguan elections would not be fairly conducted. In June 1985 the US Congress voted to allocate US $27m. in non-military aid to the Contras. None the less, the Nicaraguan Government reaffirmed its desire to resume negotiations with the USA. Concurrently, however, the civil conflict escalated, and clashes along Nicaragua's borders with Costa Rica and Honduras became increasingly frequent. In July thousands of Miskito Indians, who had allied themselves with the Contras in the early 1980s, began to return to their ancestral homelands in northern Nicaragua, following talks with the Government concerning autonomy for the region.

A presidential election and elections to a constituent assembly were held on 4 November 1984. The assembly was to draw up a constitution within two years of taking office. In August the Government had restored the majority of the civil rights that had been suspended in September 1982, in order to permit parties to campaign without restrictions. In the presidential ballot the FSLN candidate, Ortega, received 67% of the votes cast, and the party won 61 of the 96 seats in the National Constituent Assembly, which replaced the Council of State. Ortega's new Government and the National Constituent Assembly were inaugurated in January 1985.

In August 1986 the US Congress approved assistance for the Contras worth US $100m. In November the US Government disclosed that funds accruing from its clandestine sales of military equipment to Iran had been used to support the Contras.

In January 1987 a new Constitution was promulgated; on the same day, however, civil liberties, guaranteed in the Constitution, were again suspended by the renewal of the five-year-old state of emergency.

In February 1987 the Governments of Costa Rica, El Salvador, Guatemala and Honduras approved a peace plan for Nicaragua, largely based on earlier Contadora proposals, but placing greater emphasis on democratization, including the ending of the state of emergency. Following some modification, in August the peace plan was signed by the Presidents of the five nations, in Guatemala. In accordance with the plan's requirements, a four-member National Commission for Reconciliation was created in Nicaragua in August: it was chaired by Cardinal Miguel Obando y Bravo, the Archbishop of Managua, a leading critic of the Government. In January 1988 the Government ended the state of emergency, and consented to participate directly in negotiations with the Contras. In March negotiations between representatives of the Government and the Contras resulted in agreement on a 60-day cease-fire (with effect from 1 April), as a prelude to detailed peace negotiations (this was later unilaterally extended by the Government until November 1989). The Government agreed to the gradual release of political prisoners and to the participation of the Contras in domestic political dialogue and, eventually, in elections. In August 1988 the US Senate approved the provision of US $27m. in humanitarian aid for the Contras. As the hope of further military aid diminished, the Contras retreated into Honduras.

In February 1989 the five Central American Presidents met in El Salvador to discuss the reactivation of the regional peace plan. At the meeting it was agreed that, in return for the dismantling of Contra bases in Honduras, there would be moves towards greater democracy in Nicaragua. These included a pledge to hold a general election, open to opposition parties, by February 1990. A number of electoral reforms were introduced: Contra rebels were to be permitted to return to vote, on condition that they relinquished their armed struggle under a proposed demobilization plan. In June 1989 the Unión Nacional Opositora (UNO) was formed by 14 opposition parties of varying political views: the UNO was to present a joint presidential candidate and a single programme in the forthcoming elections.

In August 1989 the five Central American Presidents met in Tela, Honduras, where they signed an agreement providing for the voluntary demobilization, repatriation or relocation of the Contra forces within a 90-day period. To facilitate this process, an International Commission of Support and Verification (CIAV) was established by the UN and the Organization of American States (OAS, see p. 373). Following mediation (conducted by former US President Jimmy Carter), the Government concluded an agreement with the leaders of the Miskito Indians of the Caribbean coast. The rebels agreed to renounce their armed struggle and to join the political process. Meanwhile, the UNO designated Violeta Barrios de Chamorro (the owner and director of *La Prensa* since the assassination of her husband, Pedro Chamorro, in 1978) as its presidential candidate in the forthcoming election. Daniel Ortega was nominated as the candidate of the FSLN.

In November 1989 President Ortega declared the ending of the cease-fire with the Contras, on the grounds that the rebels had made insufficient progress in implementing the Tela agreement and disbanding their forces stationed in Honduras. In response, the UN Security Council established the UN Observer Group in Central America (ONUCA) to monitor compliance with the Tela agreement, to prevent cross-border incursions by rebels and to assist in supervising the forthcoming Nicaraguan elections.

The elections proceeded on 25 February 1990, resulting in an unexpected victory for Chamorro, who obtained some 55% of votes in the presidential election, while Ortega received 41%. Foreign observers confirmed the conduct of the polls to have been free and fair. After the elections, the Sandinista Government decreed an immediate cease-fire. The President-elect pledged to 'depoliticize' the military and security forces, and urged the Contra rebels to disband and return to civilian life. However, the UNO had not secured a sufficient majority of seats in the Asamblea Nacional to make amendments to the Constitution. In the interim period before the transfer of power on 25 April 1990, Ortega introduced a number of reforms. A General Amnesty and National Reconciliation Law was adopted: this was designed to pre-empt retaliatory measures against outgoing officials and to quash legal proceedings against those who had committed politically motivated crimes against the State since 1979.

On 19 April 1990 a cease-fire was agreed by the Contras and the Sandinista armed forces. The Contras agreed to surrender their weapons by 10 June, and to assemble in 'security zones' supervised by UN troops. A transitional agreement between the outgoing Sandinista Government and the newly elected UNO coalition provided for a reduction in the strength of the security forces and their subordination to civilian authority. Upon taking office President Chamorro assumed the post of Minister of National Defence, but allowed the previous minister, Gen. Humberto Ortega Saavedra, temporarily to retain the post of Chief of the EPS: this provoked considerable controversy within the UNO and the Contra leadership. However, in return for a commitment from the Contras to sign the demobilization accords, the Government agreed to the establishment of a special police force, composed of former Contra rebels, in order to guarantee security within the demobilization zones. Demobilization of the Contra rebels was officially concluded on 27 June, signifying the end of 11 years of civil war in Nicaragua.

On assuming office, the UNO Government immediately attempted to reverse much Sandinista policy. The suspension of the civil service law in May 1990 provoked a public sector strike, which paralysed the country. Chamorro was forced to concede wage increases of 100% and the establishment of a joint commission of trade union and government representatives to revise the civil service law. In July another general strike, involving 100,000 workers, was held in support of demands for wage increases and also in protest at the implementation of legislation allowing the restoration to private ownership of land that had been nationalized and redistributed under the Sandinista regime. Once again the Government made concessions, including a wage increase and the suspension of the programme to privatize land. The agreement was condemned by the Vice-President, Virgilio Godoy Reyes, who accused Chamorro of capitulating too readily to the demands of the FSLN. In October the Government announced the formation of a National Agrarian Commission to study problems of land distribution and illegal land seizures. The commission was to include members of the trade unions and former Contras. In mid-1991, however, the emergence of groups of rearmed Contra rebels (known as Re-contras) became apparent with the reported occupation of several cities in the northern province of Jinotega. The Re-contras' stated aim was to publicize the grievances of thousands of demobilized Contras in the north of the country who had not received land and aid promised them under the terms of the Government's resettlement plan.

In August 1991 a National Security Commission was established to disarm civilians. In the same month the FSLN-operated Radio Sandino acknowledged the existence of groups of rearmed Sandinistas (Re-compas), claiming that these had been formed to counter the military operations of the Re-contras. The phased disarmament of the Re-contras and the Re-compas began in January 1992. However, in April groups of the former combatants began joining forces to form the Revueltos, demanding land and credit promised to them prior to demobilization. In May the Government allocated 800 plots of land outside the capital to the Revueltos, as a gesture of its intention to address the groups' grievances. However, rebel activity continued in 1992–94, despite successive government ultimatums requiring the rebels to disarm or face military intervention. In February 1994, following the mediation of Cardinal Obando y Bravo and the OAS, a peace agreement was signed that provided for the demobilization of a prominent Re-contra group, the Frente Norte 3-80, by mid-April, in return for which the rebels were granted an amnesty and the right to be incorporated into the national police force. Nevertheless, violent incidents involving further groups of Re-contras continued in northern and central Nicaragua. In response the Government deployed security forces to combat the rebels' activities, which, it asserted, were criminal and not related to legitimate demands for land.

In June 1991 the FSLN withdrew indefinitely its 39 deputies from the Asamblea Nacional, in protest against the introduction by conservative deputies of a draft bill revoking two laws concerning redistribution of property. The so-called *piñata* laws had been introduced by the FSLN in March 1990, immediately prior to the transfer of power to the Chamorro administration. They guaranteed the property rights of the thousands of people who had benefited from the land expropriation that had been conducted by the Sandinistas. In August 1991 the legislature approved the abrogation of the *piñata* laws, but in the following month President Chamorro vetoed parts of the bill that she deemed to be unconstitutional. In response, right-wing supporters of Vice-President Godoy accused Chamorro of yielding to pressure exerted by the Sandinistas. Disagreement over the property issue had by now led to the alienation by Chamorro of the majority of UNO deputies, and the legislature only narrowly failed to overturn the veto in December. In July, meanwhile, the first congress of the FSLN appointed Daniel Ortega to the newly created post of General Secretary.

In April 1992 an announcement by Antonio Lacayo Oyanguren (son-in-law of Violeta Chamorro and widely considered to be the principal architect of government policy) that the Government was seeking 'fundamental agreements' with the FSLN served to fuel the anger of right-wing and liberal members of the UNO, who accused both Lacayo and Chamorro of being in league with the Sandinistas. In May the US Congress suspended the release of US $116m. in aid to Nicaragua, on the grounds that the Nicaraguan Government had failed to compensate US citizens for land expropriated under the Sandinista regime. In September Chamorro signed decrees establishing a property ombudsman's office and other provisions to expedite the processing of property claims. In addition, the President signed an agreement specifying that all unjustly confiscated property would be returned (or the rightful owners compensated).

A serious legislative crisis arose in September 1992, when the President of the Asamblea Nacional, Alfredo César, convened the legislature in the absence of the deputies of the FSLN and the

Grupo de Centro (GC—a group of eight dissident UNO deputies who had maintained their allegiance to the Government, thus depriving the UNO of its parliamentary majority), recruiting substitute deputies in order to elect new legislative authorities. Chamorro subsequently announced that no laws approved by the legislature would be promulgated until the assembly recognized a Supreme Court decision ruling César's actions to be unconstitutional and declaring all subsequent rulings by the legislature null and void. In late December Chamorro ordered the army to occupy the assembly building and appointed a provisional administration to manage parliamentary affairs pending the election of new legislative authorities. In January 1993 Chamorro announced a cabinet reorganization. Excluded from the new Government, the UNO declared itself an opposition party, as the Alianza Política Opositora (APO), expelling four member parties for their involvement with the GC. The APO continued to boycott the Asamblea Nacional and to demand the expulsion of Sandinistas from the Government.

In October 1993 unprecedented discussions between the APO and the FSLN resulted in a joint demand for a complete restructuring of the Government's economic policy. In addition, it was agreed that Humberto Ortega should resign as Chief of the EPS as soon as a new law regulating the armed forces was enacted. Constitutional issues were also discussed, with the APO proposing the election of a constituent assembly, while the FSLN favoured the implementation of partial constitutional reform by the incumbent legislature. In late October the APO and the FSLN signed an agreement providing for the implementation of partial constitutional reforms, on condition that a consensus was reached on the substance of the reforms by the end of November (subsequently extended to mid-December). The APO stipulated that it would support the reforms only on condition that its parliamentary majority be restored (through the dismissal of the GC deputies and their replacement by APO members) and that it gain control of the legislative authorities. However, divisions within the APO resulted in the Unión Demócrata Cristiana (UDC), the Movimiento Democrático Nicaragüense (MDN) and the Alianza Popular Conservadora (APC) breaking away from the alliance. The Asamblea Nacional reconvened in January 1994, and a new working alliance, including the FSLN, the GC, the UDC, the MDN and the APC, elected new legislative authorities. The APO subsequently abandoned its boycott of the legislature.

In February 1994 a widening division within the FSLN became apparent when Daniel Ortega founded the Izquierda Democrática Sandinista, an internal faction comprising what were termed 'orthodox revolutionaries' and intended to maintain the party's role as a revolutionary force; the faction declared support for 'all forms of struggle', aims not shared by the party's 'renewalist' faction, led by Sergio Ramírez Mercado. In May, following internal elections, the orthodox faction of the party secured control of the party's national directorate and of the party assembly, the Asamblea Sandinista, which subsequently approved a policy of opposition to the Government.

In November 1994 the Asamblea Nacional approved amendments to some 67 of the Constitution's 202 articles, which adjusted the balance of authority in favour of the legislature. In particular, the Government would be required to seek legislative approval for external loans, debt negotiations and international trade agreements. A further amendment, prohibiting close relatives of a serving President from contesting the presidential election, was widely considered to be intended specifically to prevent Lacayo, Chamorro's son-in-law and Minister of the Presidency, from securing presidential office at the next election, due in 1996. Other reforms included a reduction in the presidential and legislative terms, from six to five years, and the withdrawal of the absolute ban on presidential re-election, although consecutive terms remained prohibited. The amendments were deemed illegal by the FSLN leadership but won the support of 32 of the 39 deputies in the FSLN bloc, reflecting the seemingly irreconcilable division within the party. Amendments were also introduced enshrining civilian authority over the depoliticized security forces. The EPS was thenceforth referred to as the Ejército de Nicaragua (Nicaraguan Army).

In January 1995 the disunity within the FSLN finally resulted in members of the renewalist faction forming a separate political party, the Movimiento Renovador Sandinista (MRS). In the following month the constitutional amendments were signed and submitted to Chamorro for approval within 15 days. However, following Chamorro's refusal to promulgate the reforms, on 24 February the Asamblea Nacional released the amendments for publication, thereby enacting them. Chamorro condemned the decision as unconstitutional. In June a resolution to the dispute was achieved by the signing of a political accord between the Government and the legislature. Under the terms of the agreement, many of the amendments intended to reduce presidential authority were to be moderated. Legislation defining the interpretation and implementation of the amendments was approved by the Asamblea Nacional in July, and was subsequently promulgated by Chamorro.

Presidential and legislative elections were held on 20 October 1996. Arnoldo Alemán Lacayo of the Partido Liberal Constitucionalista (PLC), the presidential candidate of the Alianza Liberal (an electoral alliance comprising mainly liberal parties), secured 51% of the votes, while Ortega won 38%. However, although international observers declared the ballot to have been generally free and fair, the FSLN and several other parties disputed the result as fraudulent. Many of the provisional results were subsequently revised and, while the Consejo Supremo Electoral (CSE—Supreme Electoral Tribunal) acknowledged the existence of serious anomalies, it maintained that these had been insufficient to affect the overall outcome of the poll. The Alianza Liberal also won the largest number of seats (42) in the Asamblea Nacional, although it failed to gain a majority. The FSLN obtained 35 seats. The day before Alemán took office, in January 1997, the FSLN boycotted the newly inaugurated Asamblea Nacional in protest at the decision of the CSE to conduct an open ballot (rather than a secret vote) to elect the legislative authorities.

In November 1999 the Comptroller-General, Agustín Jarquín, was arrested on charges of committing fraud against the State. Jarquín, a vigorous critic of corruption in the Government, had launched numerous investigations into corrupt practices by members of the Alemán administration, the most notable of which had resulted in the publication of a report revealing that Alemán had increased his personal wealth by 900% during his terms of office as Mayor of Managua and as President, and that he had failed to declare these assets to the Office of the Comptroller-General, as required by law. Following his detention, Jarquín supporters alleged that the accusations made against him were politically motivated. Representatives of donor nations and multilateral organizations expressed concern over the case, and both Germany and Sweden suspended funding for various projects as a result of Jarquín's detention. In December Jarquín was acquitted of the charges against him, and formally renewed the corruption charges against Alemán.

In June 1999 the Government and the FSLN reached an agreement to begin negotiations on constitutional and electoral reform. This co-operation prompted the formation of an anti-Ortega faction within the FSLN. In July these dissident Sandinistas, in alliance with former Contras and various minor right-wing and centre-right parties, protested in Managua against the pact. In January 2000 a series of constitutional reforms came into force. The principal amendments included a reduction in the proportion of votes necessary for a President to be elected outright from 45% to 35%, thus increasing the likelihood of an FSLN victory. In return, Alemán was guaranteed a seat in the Asamblea Nacional after leaving office, thus making him virtually immune from prosecution. Other reforms included the restructuring of the judiciary, electoral authorities and the Office of the Comptroller-General—which was to be headed by a five-member board, thereby effectively removing the threat to the Alemán administration of Jarquín.

In January 2001 the Vice-President, Enrique Bolaños Geyer, resigned his position and announced his presidential candidacy, representing the PLC. If elected, Bolaños pledged to investigate legislative corruption and to reduce civil service salaries. Ortega, who was the FSLN nominee, sought to reassure the electorate that he had renounced the more militaristic policies of his past, pledging to demilitarize the border with Costa Rica and to return property belonging to US citizens confiscated by his Government during the 1980s. Nevertheless, Ortega proved to be a controversial choice of candidate. From 1998 his step-daughter, Zoilamérica Narváez Murillo, had made accusations of sexual abuse against him, and Bolaños, his main opponent, made much of the FSLN's links with the Cuban regime of Fidel Castro Ruz and with the Libyan leader, Col Muammar al-Qaddafi.

Presidential and legislative elections took place on 4 November 2001, amid tight security. The final results of the presidential poll gave Bolaños 56% of votes cast, while Ortega secured 42%. The PLC also won a majority of votes (53%) in the elections to the Asamblea Nacional, securing 47 seats; the FSLN won 43 seats and the PCN the remaining two. In the weeks following the election the FSLN made allegations of electoral irregularities. Three FSLN magistrates on the seven-member electoral council objected to the party's allocation of seats in the Asamblea Nacional and resigned their positions in protest. However, the complaint was rejected by the Supreme Constitutional Court.

Bolaños took office on 10 January 2002. Almost immediately he encountered opposition from within his own party, when members of the PLC rejected his preferred candidate for President of the Asamblea Nacional, Jaime Cuadra, and voted with the majority in favour of former President Alemán. In March the Attorney-General announced that former President Alemán was to face charges of fraud and embezzlement relating to the state television company, Sistema Nacional de Televisión Canal 6 (SNTV Canal 6). In the months that followed President Bolaños made several attempts to remove Alemán's congressional immunity. However, internal divisions within the PLC (which had divided into pro-Alemán and pro-Bolaños factions) meant that the President lacked the votes necessary to have the motion approved. As President of the Asamblea Nacional, Alemán obstructed approval of the budget and several reforms to the tax system which the Government needed to introduce in order to negotiate credit from the IMF. In August thousands of protesters marched through Managua to demand an end to the former head of state's immunity.

In September 2002 several of Alemán's relatives and former members of his Government were convicted of 'laundering' some US $100m. from state communications, infrastructure, insurance and petroleum enterprises. One week later Alemán, who faced the same charges, suspended a parliamentary session at which the removal of his congressional immunity was to be discussed. The following day FSLN members joined the Bolaños faction of the PLC to vote in favour of Alemán's dismissal. Cuadra was installed as President of the Asamblea and a new legislative commission, comprising supporters of Bolaños, was formed to determine whether Alemán's immunity should be revoked. The former President's financial assets in Panama and those of his family in the USA were frozen while investigations into the charges were made. The USA also suspended Alemán's right to enter its territory; several members of his family and former administration had already fled the country. In December the Asamblea Nacional approved a motion revoking Alemán's congressional immunity by a narrow majority; the former President was immediately put under house arrest.

In October 2002 Bolaños himself became the subject of allegations of fraud. In response to charges filed with the Supreme Court, that he and his Vice-President, José Rizo Castellón, had used an illegal fund controlled by Alemán to finance his 2001 electoral campaign, Bolaños promised to renounce his presidential immunity at a date named by his prosecutors. In November Bolaños and Rizo were formally charged with embezzling US $4.1m. from public funds.

Alemán's arrest further deepened divisions within the PLC. In January 2003 Bolaños's veto of parts of the budget, in order to comply with conditions stipulated by the IMF for Nicaragua to qualify for financial assistance and debt relief, was opposed by both the pro-Alemán faction of the PLC and the FSLN (the Sandinistas had supported the President in his attempts to remove Alemán). In March the pro-Alemán faction of the PLC officially announced that it was in opposition to the Government, in protest at the Government's alliance with the FSLN. The departure of the deputies left Bolaños with the unconditional support of only nine PLC members in the Asamblea (although six members of the Alemán faction later declared their allegiance to the President).

In June 2003 the pro-Alemán faction of the PLC formed an alliance with the FSLN in order successfully to approve in the legislature the appointment of nine Supreme Court judges with FSLN or pro-Alemán sympathies. The PLC faction believed that the appointments would increase the likelihood that Alemán would be acquitted of the charges against him. Nevertheless, in August an FSLN-appointed Supreme Court judge ruled that the cost of keeping Alemán under house arrest was too great, and the former President was incarcerated. However, in November Alemán was returned to house arrest, allegedly following an agreement between the pro-Alemán faction of the PLC and the FSLN. In return for the support of the FSLN in the release of Alemán, the PLC agreed to support FSLN attempts to postpone municipal elections to 2006, and to replace the country's presidential system with a parliamentary one. The Supreme Court ruling was strongly opposed by many traditionalist members of the FSLN and damaged Ortega's standing within the party. The move provoked a strong reaction from the international community, particularly the USA, which declared Ortega and Alemán to be discredited figures who ought to have no further role in Nicaraguan politics. Concern was also expressed at opposition efforts to impeach President Bolaños on charges of electoral fraud. The USA suspended US $4.9m. in aid for judicial reform, and threatened to obstruct Nicaragua's access to the IMF debt-reduction programme.

In December 2003 Alemán was found guilty of charges of money-laundering, fraud and theft of state funds and was sentenced to 20 years' imprisonment. He was also fined US $17m. Owing to ill health, however, he was to serve his prison term under house arrest. The trial was considered to be a test of Nicaragua's judiciary and the outcome was welcomed by the international community. In the same month the alliance between the FSLN and the dissident PLC members collapsed, following the latter's insistence that the release of Alemán was essential if the pact were to continue. One week later the pro-Alemán PLC deputies joined with the pro-Bolaños faction of the party to approve the budget for 2004, essential to gain IMF funding. In January 2004 the two factions of the ruling party attempted a fragile truce in order to select a new directorate of the Asamblea. The new legislative President, Carlos Noguera Pastora, was an Alemán supporter, while the six remaining seats were divided evenly between the two factions of the party. In December a court of appeal acquitted Alemán of the charge of appropriating some US $1.5m. from SNTV Canal 6. However, he continued to serve his sentence for money-laundering under house arrest.

In March 2004 the Asamblea began to debate a series of measures proposed by President Bolaños. The proposed reforms included the introduction of an independently appointed judiciary, adoption of a five-year national budget and reform of the electoral system. The proposed judicial reform prompted protests in the Asamblea from judges. Bolaños declared he was willing to engage in all-party dialogue on his proposals. Throughout most of 2004 the PLC- and FSLN-dominated Asamblea blocked the reform proposals, although in October the creation of an independent judicial council to appoint judges did receive legislative approval.

Also in March 2004 President Bolaños, Vice-President Rizo and 31 other senior members of the PLC were accused of illegal campaign-financing during the previous presidential election. Seven PLC members were arrested, including party president Jorge Castillo Quant. In October the Comptroller-General, Juan Gutiérrez, requested that President Bolaños be removed from power and fined two months' salary for withholding information regarding the financing of his 2001 election campaign. Supporters of the President claimed the request was politically motivated, as the office of the Comptroller-General was controlled by the FSLN and the anti-Bolaños faction of the PLC. At the invitation of Bolaños, a delegation arrived from the OAS to investigate the Comptroller-General's findings. Following a meeting with the OAS representatives, Ortega agreed to withdraw FSLN support for the initiation of impeachment proceedings against the President until after the November municipal elections.

The FSLN won a decisive victory in the local elections of 7 November 2004, securing control of 84 of the 151 municipalities, including Managua. The following day a two-thirds' majority in the Asamblea Nacional voted in support of constitutional reform legislation limiting presidential powers. The reforms would require the President to seek legislative ratification for key appointments such as ministers, ambassadors, the chief prosecutor and banking superintendent, and would enable the Asamblea to remove officials deemed to be incompetent. A further reform provided for the transfer of control of the state energy, water and telecommunications services from the President to one regulatory body, the Surperintendencia de Servicios Públicos (Sisep). In December President Bolaños appealed to the Supreme Court of Justice, contending that the reforms, supported by the FSLN and the PLC, would engender irreconcilable tension between the Government and the legislature. Furthermore, Bolaños asserted that the legislation was unconstitutional and that such an attempt to redefine the powers of the executive and legislative branches of government exceeded the remit of the Asamblea Nacional. In January 2005 the Central American Court of Justice (CCJ) ruled that ratification of the controversial constitutional amendments should be suspended. None the less, one week later the Asamblea approved the legislation. In mid-January, two days before the legislation was due to come into effect, the Presidents of El Salvador, Guatemala and Honduras issued a joint statement of support for President Bolaños. Following further negotiations between factions supporting Bolaños, Ortega and Alemán, the President agreed to promulgate the controversial reforms in return for a pledge from the opposition that it would work towards a consensus with the executive on such matters as the budget and social security reform. Nevertheless, in March the CCJ declared the constitutional reforms to be illegal, ruling that they could only be approved by a specially convened constituent assembly. On the same day the Supreme Court declared the reforms valid.

In July 2005 Alemán was released on probation for the remainder of his sentence, allegedly for health reasons. The Court of Appeal overruled the decision three days later, ordering that he return to house arrest. However, Alemán's probation was upheld in August by the Supreme Court of Justice, thereby permitting the former President to travel within the province of Managua and to participate in political activities. The Supreme Court of Justice also ratified the constitutional amendment to restrict presidential powers, which had been approved by the Asamblea Nacional in January. Ernesto Leal, the Secretary to the Presidency, criticized the ruling, asserting that the executive would adhere to the CCJ ruling that declared the reforms to be illegal.

Meanwhile, accusations against Bolaños and his associates of illegal campaign-financing during the 2001 elections persisted. In early September 2005 seven Central American heads of state gathered in Managua to demonstrate their support for Bolaños. None the less, later that month the Asamblea Nacional removed the immunity from prosecution of three ministers and three deputy ministers.

Dissension over the proposed constitutional reforms impeded the Government's legislative agenda, including efforts to gain approval for the proposed Dominican Republic-Central American Free Trade Agreement (DR-CAFTA, comprising Nicaragua, Costa Rica, the Dominican Republic, El Salvador, Guatemala, Honduras and the USA). In early October 2005 the US Assistant Secretary of State publicly criticized the PLC-FSLN legislative pact and proposed the implementation of DR-CAFTA without Nicaragua. This intervention, combined with ongoing mediation by the OAS, was widely seen as instrumental in resolving the political crisis: in October the FSLN withdrew its opposition to DR-CAFTA and the following day the proposed free trade agreement was approved by the Asamblea Nacional. In addition, Ortega and Bolaños reached an agreement to delay the implementation of the constitutional reforms until the end of Bolaños' mandate in January 2007; legislation providing for this postponement was subsequently adopted. In October the Asamblea Nacional rejected a proposal to remove Bolaños' immunity from prosecution, and the charges against the ministers whose immunity had been lifted in September were dismissed in December.

Presidential and legislative elections took place on 5 November 2006. Ortega, who had sought to distance himself from the more extreme Sandinista policies of the 1980s and had pledged to respect free enterprise, protect private property and encourage investment, was elected to the presidency with 38.0% of the votes cast. Eduardo Montealegre Rivas of the Alianza Liberal Nicaragüense (ALN), a recently founded party composed primarily of dissident former PLC members opposed to Alemán, secured 28.3%, while former Vice-President Rizo, a close ally of Alemán, took 27.1% on behalf of the PLC. Under the electoral reforms that took effect in January 2000 (reducing the proportion of votes necessary for a President to be elected outright from 45% to 35%), a second round of voting was not required. The poor performance of the MRS candidate, Edmundo Jarquín, who, with 6.3%, obtained a substantially lower share of the vote than most polls had predicted, suggested that Ortega's moderate tone prior to the elections had succeeded in persuading dissident Sandinistas to return to the FSLN. The FSLN also became the largest party in the Asamblea Nacional, winning 38 seats; the PLC took 25 seats (compared with 47 in the 2001 elections), the ALN 22 and the MRS the remaining five elective seats. Montealegre and Bolaños were both awarded supplementary legislative seats, in accordance with electoral rules. An estimated 16,000 domestic and international observers monitored the elections, with the OAS mission concluding that the process had generally been conducted peacefully and transparently. An estimated 69% of the electorate participated in the poll.

Ortega took office on 10 January 2007. His new Cabinet included Samuel Santos López, mayor of Managua during Ortega's previous period in office, as Minister of Foreign Affairs, Ana Isabel Morales Mazún as Minister of the Interior and Alberto Guevara Obregón as Minister of Finance and Public Credit. Ortega's wife, Rosario Murillo Zambrana, was appointed to the newly created cabinet position of Co-ordinator of the Communication and Citizenship Council, in which role she was to be responsible for all government publicity. Later that month the President issued a decree more than halving his own salary and substantially lowering those of government ministers and other senior officials. In late January the Asamblea Nacional adopted amendments to legislation on the organization and duties of the executive. Proposed by Ortega, and supported by the PLC, these 'urgent' reforms gave the President greater control over the police force and the military (consequently reducing the powers of the Ministers of the Interior and of National Defence) and allowed the President to create 'Citizen Power Councils' by decree. Amid concerns regarding the potential power of these Councils, which were intended to encourage direct democracy by co-ordinating the work of non-governmental organizations and public institutions on a regional and local level, opposition parties insisted that they should be purely consultative and not assume any of the functions of government ministries.

Also in late January 2007 the legislature approved the further postponement, for one year, of the constitutional amendments limiting presidential powers that had been due to take effect that month. A special commission, comprising seven deputies, was designated in February by the four parties represented in the legislature to draft new constitutional reform legislation. The ALN advocated a reduction in the number of deputies and an increase in the percentage of the vote required to secure an outright win in a presidential election, while the FSLN was in favour of allowing a President to serve two consecutive terms. In January 2008 the Supreme Court annulled the law postponing the implementation of the constitutional reforms, although it also declared invalid the majority of the reforms themselves, including the transfer of control of utilities to Sisep. However, it did not annul the law requiring the President to seek legislative approval of key appointments, with the result that this reform duly entered into force.

Meanwhile, in January 2007 Ortega announced the creation of a National Commission for Reconciliation and Peace, which was to lead efforts to resolve issues arising from the civil war. The commission, subsequently renamed the Commission for Verification, Reconciliation, Peace and Justice, was formally constituted in May under the chairmanship of Cardinal Obando y Bravo (who had retired as Archbishop of Managua in 2005). Its stated remit was to continue the work of the commission established following the peace accords of 1987, ensuring that former combatants and victims of the war had received land and compensation as stipulated in the accords.

The national prison service granted Alemán complete freedom of movement within Nicaragua in March 2007. Montealegre claimed that the decision to ease the restrictions on the former President (who had been released on probation in July 2005, but hitherto confined to Managua) had been made on the orders of Ortega, in a joint attempt by the FSLN and the PLC to ensure that the country's liberal factions remained divided. Alemán's status continued to be exploited by the Government throughout 2007 to ensure PLC support for its programme. In December the Managua Appeals Court ordered that Alemán should return to house arrest, but the order was overturned in March 2008, ensuring that he would remain at liberty. In January 2009 Alemán was definitively absolved from his conviction by the Supreme Court.

In September 2007 the Asamblea Nacional approved a law to prevent the proposed Citizen Power Councils from forming any part of the executive branch of government, ensuring that they would perform a purely consultative role and would not receive any state funding. However, this law was vetoed by Ortega, and, despite further motions against the decree by the Asamblea, in December the Supreme Court ruled in favour of the President's veto. In the mean time, the Citizen Power Councils were created by presidential decree on 29 November, and inaugurated in a public ceremony in Managua on the following day. Ortega assumed the role of President of the Councils, and his wife, Murillo, that of General Co-ordinator. Opposition parties continued to voice strong criticism of the Councils, which they claimed would serve to consolidate the power and influence of the FSLN in local affairs.

Events surrounding the municipal elections of November 2008 caused substantial tension between the FSLN and its opponents. In April the Government announced its decision to postpone the elections in the Región Autónoma Atlántico Norte (RAAN) until 2009, due to the damage caused by 'Hurricane Felix' in September 2007. Anti-Government protesters claimed that the FSLN was acting to avoid an electoral defeat in the autonomous region, and riots led to two deaths in Bilwi. In June 2008 the CSE revoked the legal status of two political parties for administrative reasons, provoking criticism that the PLC-FSLN legislative pact remained in place and continued to pose a threat to multi-party democracy. The CSE, comprised of seven magistrates, all of whom were aligned with either the FSLN or the PLC, voted to ban the MRS on the grounds that it had failed to present the necessary documentation, and the Partido Conservador (PC) for failing to nominate candidates in 80% of municipalities. In the elections, which were held on 9 November, the FSLN secured 105 of the 146 contested mayoralties, including that of Managua, while the PLC took 37. However, allegations of widespread fraud, supported by the discovery of burned and discarded ballots, undermined the results. A recount in Managua was negotiated, but demands that it be monitored by independent observers were rejected, and the recount confirmed the victory of the FSLN candidate, Alexis Argüello. Standing in opposition to Argüello was former presidential candidate Eduardo Montealegre, whose movement, Vamos con Eduardo (VCE), had formed a political alliance with the PLC in March 2008 after the CSE had disqualified Montealegre from the presidency of the ALN due to irregularities that had allegedly taken place in 2006. The PLC-VCE alliance, supported by the monitoring authority Etica y Transparencia (which the Government had refused to accredit), maintained that Montealegre was the rightful mayor of Managua. Despite riots and demonstrations across Nicaragua, a bill proposed by the PLC to annul the November elections failed to generate sufficient support in the Asamblea Nacional. At the end of November the Asamblea Nacional was suspended by its President, René Núñez Téllez, due to the prevailing election crisis. The Asamblea reconvened in January 2009 and re-elected Núñez as President, further decreasing the likelihood of the elections being annulled. In the same month the PLC candidates elected in the municipal elections refused to attend their inauguration ceremonies in an attempt to avoid legitimizing the allegedly fraudulent results. Confidence in the electoral system was undermined further when Roberto Rivas, the President of the CSE, was accused of tax fraud in February 2009.

Full military relations between Nicaragua and the USA, suspended since 1980, were re-established in May 2001. In 2003 the Government resisted pressure from the USA to destroy its stockpile of surface-to-air missiles, claiming that a certain number were necessary for defence against terrorism. However, in March 2004 it was reported that the Government had agreed to destroy one-half of the 2,000 weapons. In November President Bolaños announced that about one-half of the remaining surface-to-air missiles (an estimated 1,334) would be destroyed within 18 months. However, in the following month the opposition-controlled Asamblea approved legislation granting it authority to decide on the acquisition and disposal of armaments. The measure formed part of the controversial reforms intended to curtail President Bolaños' powers (see above). Although Bolaños vetoed the legislation, this was overridden in February 2005 by the PLC-FSLN parliamentary bloc. The issue gathered momentum in the previous month following reports in a US newspaper that Nicaraguan missiles were being sold to would-be terrorists. The outgoing Commander-in-Chief of the Armed Forces, Gen. Javier Carrión, rejected the reports; however, on 18 February two men were convicted of selling a surface-to-air missile on the 'black' (parallel, illegal) market. As a result, the Government pledged to destroy 79% of the remaining stockpile of missiles. However, dissatisfaction with a lack of progress on the issue prompted the US Administration to suspend military aid to Nicaragua in April–October. In July 2007 President Ortega—who had hitherto favoured the retention of all 1,051 missiles unless other Central American countries also agreed to reduce the size of their armed forces—proposed the destruction of 651 missiles, leaving 400 for the purposes of national defence, in exchange for military helicopters and medical equipment from the USA. Talks between the two countries concerning the destruction of the missiles took place in late 2007 and 2008, although no agreement had been reached by early 2009.

In June 1995, prompted by frequent disputes concerning fishing rights in the Gulf of Fonseca, Nicaragua signed an accord with Honduras providing for the visible demarcation of each country's territorial waters. Despite this agreement, in December the Honduran Government issued an official protest to Nicaragua at what it claimed to be the illegal seizure of Honduran fishing vessels by a Nicaraguan naval patrol in Honduran waters. In May 1997 a further incident, in which Nicaraguan and Honduran naval patrols exchanged fire following the seizure by the Nicaraguan navy of Honduran fishing boats, gave renewed impetus to the demarcation issue. However, the demarcation process did not begin until May 1998. In December 1999, following further confrontations, Nicaragua initiated proceedings at the International Court of Justice (ICJ, see p. 22) in The Hague, Netherlands, to determine the maritime delimitation in the Gulf of Fonseca. In that month a dispute arose prompting Nicaragua to sever commercial ties with, and impose import taxes on, Honduras, in direct contravention of Central American free trade undertakings (Nicaragua also imposed similar tariffs on Colombia, thereby violating commitments entered into with the World Trade Organization). Following mediation by the OAS, in January 2000 Nicaragua ended its trade sanctions against Honduras, and in March both countries signed an accord committing them to observe a maritime exclusion zone in the Caribbean and to reduce troop numbers on their common border. In addition, both countries agreed to submit all issues pertaining to maritime space in the Caribbean Sea to the ruling of the ICJ. An agreement was also made to mount co-ordinated naval patrols in the Gulf of Fonseca. However, shortly after conflict again ensued over a small islet in the disputed territory, which Nicaragua claimed had been occupied by the Honduran armed forces. Furthermore, in February 2001 the Minister of Defence, José Adán Guerra, accused Honduras of violating the March 2000 accords by carrying out military exercises in the area and, in the following month, Nicaragua submitted documentation to the ICJ contesting the treaty. Nicaragua also refused to participate in the joint patrol of the Gulf of Fonseca. In March 2001 delegates from both Governments attended OAS-sponsored discussions in Washington, DC, USA. In June Nicaragua and Honduras concluded a confidence-building agreement, which provided for OAS observers to monitor the actions of army and navy forces on both sides of the common border. None the less, in August the Nicaraguan Government claimed that Honduras was planning to launch an attack on its border. In July 2002 the situation further deteriorated when the Nicaraguan Government announced plans to sell oil-drilling rights in the disputed area. In November 2006, however, during a visit to Honduras, President-elect Ortega surprised the Honduran President, Manuel Zelaya, and the Nicaraguan Government by proposing the joint development of the disputed area. The Nicaraguan Minister of National Defence, Avil Ramírez, warned Ortega against making remarks that might jeopardize Nicaragua's claims before the ICJ. The ICJ conducted public hearings on the dispute in March 2007 and in October ruled on a revised maritime border approximately mid-way between the two countries. Both the Nicaraguan and Honduran Governments declared themselves satisfied with the ruling.

In 1997 relations with Costa Rica became strained when, following a change in that country's immigration policy, it began deporting Nicaraguans who were residing illegally in the country. Remittances from Nicaraguans in Costa Rica represented a significant contribution to the Nicaraguan economy, averaging US $240m.–$300m. per year. In February 1999 Costa Rica offered one-year renewable residence permits to registering illegal Nicaraguan immigrants. Further antagonism had developed between the two countries in July 1998 when Nicaragua prohibited Costa Rican civil guards from carrying arms while navigating the San Juan river, which forms the border between the two countries. According to a long-standing treaty, the river, which is Nicaraguan territory, was only to be used by Costa Rica for commercial purposes. Following protests by Costa Rica, agreement was reached allowing for that country's civil guard to carry arms on the river while under escort by the Nicaraguan authorities. In August, however, following concerted pressure by opposition parties, the media and the Roman Catholic Church in Nicaragua, which accused the Government of surrendering part of the nation's sovereignty, Nicaragua annulled the accord. In June 2000 both Governments agreed a procedure that would allow armed Costa Rican police officers to patrol the river. In October 2001 President Alemán further announced that Costa Rican guards could patrol the river, providing they had first obtained permission from his Government, but rejected Costa Rica's submission of the dispute to the ICJ. In September 2002 the two countries appeared to have made some progress towards resolving the dispute when Nicaragua agreed to discontinue the fees charged to Costa Ricans crossing the river in exchange for the abolition of charges levied on visas and tourist permits required by Nicaraguans to enter Costa Rica. Costa Rica also announced that it would relinquish plans to refer the matter to the ICJ. In October bilateral discussions began on the Nicaraguan Government's plans to sell oil-exploration rights in an area of the Caribbean Sea and Pacific Ocean claimed by Costa Rica. Failure to agree on the issue within the stipulated three years prompted Costa Rica, in September 2005, to refer the matter to the ICJ. In response, President Bolaños recalled the Nicaraguan ambassador to Costa Rica, ordered the troops patrolling the border area to prohibit the passage of armed Costa Rican police officers, and imposed a 35% tariff on Costa Rican imports. Furthermore, in November the Nicaraguan Government declared an interest in reclaiming the province of Guanacaste, annexed by Costa Rica in 1825. Bilateral relations deteriorated further in February 2006 when Nicaragua brought a case before the Inter-American Commission on Human Rights accusing the Costa Rican authorities of tolerating xenophobia and discrimination against immigrants, citing the violent deaths of two Nicaraguan immigrants in late 2005 as evidence of this. The Commission dismissed the case in March 2007.

In November 2001 a dispute with Colombia arose after a Nicaraguan fishing vessel was captured allegedly in Colombian waters. The Colombian authorities charged the crew with violating its sovereignty and misappropriating its natural resources. It was the third time in that year that a Nicaraguan vessel had been apprehended in Colombian waters. In the following month Nicaragua presented a request to the ICJ that its claim over territorial waters in the Caribbean Sea and around the islands of San Andrés and Providencia be recognized. In July 2003 the Colombian Minister of Foreign Affairs formally objected to the ICJ's involvement in the case. The ICJ dismissed Nicaragua's claim to the San Andrés archipelago in December 2007, although it had yet to rule on jurisdiction of the other disputed waters. In early March 2008 Nicaragua briefly suspended diplomatic relations with Colombia in protest at that country's recent military incursion into Ecuador, during which a senior member of the Fuerzas Armadas Revolucionarias de Colombia—Ejército del Pueblo (FARC) was killed; however, relations were restored shortly afterwards. In July Ortega again angered the Colombian Government by offering to hold talks with the FARC.

Developing strong regional relations appeared to be a priority for Ortega following his election as President: he toured four other Central American countries in late November 2006, before visiting the leaders of Cuba and Venezuela, with whom he already had close links. At the same time, Ortega adopted a conciliatory approach towards the USA, stating that he would seek to foster a 'respectful' bilateral relationship, and in late November the US Assistant Secretary of State for Western Hemisphere Affairs, Thomas Shannon, held talks with the President-elect in Managua. None the less, on taking office Ortega sought to strengthen relations with other left-wing administrations in Latin America. His close ties to the Presidents of Bolivia and Venezuela were evident at his inauguration, on 10 January 2007, and on the following day he confirmed Nicaragua's participation in the Bolivarian Alternative for the Americas (Alternativa Bolivariana para América Latina y el Caribe—ALBA), which had been devised by Venezuela as an alternative model to the US-promoted Free Trade Area of the Americas and was also supported by Bolivia and Cuba. Furthermore, Ortega signed a number of economic agreements with the Venezuelan President, Lt-Col (retd) Hugo Rafael Chávez Frías, who pledged substantial financial assistance to Nicaragua, including the construction of a petroleum refinery, capable of processing 100,000–150,000 barrels of oil per day, and the provision of low-interest loans for impoverished Nicaraguans living in rural areas. A few days later Ortega met the Iranian President, Mahmoud Ahmadinejad, who visited Nicaragua during a tour of Latin America. The two leaders announced plans to open embassies in their respective countries and signed a co-operation agreement, which provided for Iranian investment in various projects aimed at improving the Nicaraguan economy and reducing poverty. Ortega dismissed suggestions that such alliances would damage Nicaragua's relations with the USA. In March a joint Nicaraguan-Venezuelan committee was formed to advance plans for bilateral co-operation, particularly in the energy sector. Venezuela was to supply Nicaragua with 10,000 barrels of petroleum per day at preferential rates and 32 electricity generators to alleviate severe energy shortages. Speaking at the launch of the joint committee in Managua, Ortega compared ALBA favourably with DR-CAFTA, praising the former's focus on the principles of social justice. In June Ortega met President Ahmadinejad in Iran, as part of a tour that also included Cuba, Algeria and Libya, and in August Ortega and the Iranian Minister of Energy signed a further series of accords in Managua, under the terms of which Iran would invest in a number of infrastructure projects in Nicaragua in exchange for the establishment of trade links.

The dispute regarding the results of the municipal elections of November 2008 put a strain on international relations: in that month the European Union and the USA both suspended budgetary aid to Nicaragua due to the country's failure to resolve the dispute. The opposition's ongoing refusal to accept the FSLN victory as legitimate meant that funds remained withheld in March 2009. Earlier in the year Ortega had expressed suspicions about international aid, accusing non-governmental organizations operating in Nicaragua of embezzlement, subversion and destabilizing the administration.

Government

Executive power is vested in the President, who is elected by popular vote for a five-year term. The President is assisted by a Vice-President and an appointed Cabinet. Legislative power is held by the Asamblea Nacional (National Assembly), elected by universal adult suffrage, under a system of proportional representation, for a five-year term.

Defence

As assessed at November 2008, the armed forces were estimated to total 12,000 (army 10,000, navy 800, air force 1,200). Compulsory military service was abolished in April 1990. In 1995 the armed forces were renamed the Ejército de Nicaragua, following a constitutional amendment removing their Sandinista affiliation. The defence budget for 2008 totalled 809m. gold córdobas.

Economic Affairs

In 2007, according to estimates by the World Bank, Nicaragua's gross national income (GNI), measured at average 2005–07 prices, was US $5,519m., equivalent to $980 per head (or $2,520 per head on an international purchasing-power parity basis). During 2000–07 the population increased at an average annual rate of 1.3%, while gross domestic product (GDP) per head increased, in real terms, by an average of 2.0% per year. Nicaragua's GDP increased, in real terms, by an average of 3.4% per year in 2000–07; GDP increased by 4.2% in 2007.

Agriculture (including forestry and fishing) contributed an estimated 18.2% of GDP in 2007 and engaged 34.1% of the employed work-force in 2005. The principal cash crops are coffee (which accounted for 18.7% of export earnings in 2008), groundnuts, sugar cane and beans. Maize, rice and beans are the principal food crops. Production of shellfish became increasingly important in the 1990s, and by 2000 shrimps and lobsters accounted for some 17.4% of export earnings, although this decreased to 2.7% by 2008. Meat and meat products accounted for 14.2% of export earnings in that year. According to the World Bank, agricultural GDP increased at an average annual rate of 3.2% during 2000–07; the sector's GDP increased by 4.2% in 2007.

Industry (including mining, manufacturing, construction and power) engaged 18.3% of the employed labour force in 2005 and provided an estimated 27.7% of GDP in 2007. According to the World Bank, industrial GDP increased by an average of 4.1% per year during 2000–07; it increased by 4.2% in 2007.

Mining contributed an estimated 1.1% of GDP in 2007 and engaged an estimated 0.3% of the employed labour force in 2005. Nicaragua has workable deposits of gold, silver, copper, lead, antimony, zinc and iron; its non-metallic minerals include limestone, gypsum, bentonite and marble. In 2008 gold accounted for 5.3% of export earnings. The GDP of the mining sector increased at an average annual rate of 0.2% in 2000–07; however, the sector's GDP decreased by 3.4% in 2006 and by an estimated 8.8% in 2007.

Manufacturing contributed some 17.7% of GDP in 2007 and engaged 12.4% of the employed labour force in 2005. The principal branches of manufacturing were food products, beverages and tobacco (about 67% of the total), machinery and metal products and petroleum derivatives and rubber products. The *maquila*, or assembly, sector expanded rapidly in the early

1990s, although growth slowed in the early 2000s. The principal products were clothing, footwear, aluminium frames and jewellery. Manufacturing GDP increased, according to the World Bank, by an average of 5.0% per year in 2000–07; the sector's GDP grew by 4.2% in 2007.

Energy is derived principally from imported petroleum, although two hydroelectric plants in the department of Jinotega account for one-10th of the electrical energy generated in the country. Imports of mineral fuels and lubricants comprised 23.1% of the total value of imports in 2008. In that year Nicaragua produced an estimated 3,327.4 GWh of electrical energy.

The services sector contributed an estimated 54.1% of GDP in 2007 and engaged 47.6% of the employed labour force in 2005. The tourism sector expanded throughout the 1990s; in 2006 annual income totalled US $237m., with arrivals put at 773,398, an 8.6% increase on the previous year's figures. According to the World Bank, the GDP of the services sector increased by an average of 4.3% per year in 2000–07; the sector grew by 9.7% in 2007.

In 2007 Nicaragua recorded a visible trade deficit of approximately US $1,803.8m., and there was a deficit of $1,045.7m. on the current account of the balance of payments. In 2008 the principal source of imports (an estimated 20.7%) was the USA; other major suppliers were Nicaragua's partners in the Central American Common Market (CACM—Costa Rica, El Salvador, Guatemala and Honduras, see p. 211), as well as Venezuela and Mexico. The USA was also the principal market for exports (an estimated 29.5%) in 2008; other notable purchasers were the countries of the CACM, Mexico and Canada. The principal exports in 2008 were coffee, meat and groundnuts. The principal imports were non-durable consumer goods, primary materials and intermediate goods for industry and crude petroleum.

In 2008 Nicaragua recorded a budgetary deficit of an estimated 1,438.0m. gold córdobas, according to central bank figures. At the end of 2006 Nicaragua's total external debt was US $4,391m., of which $3,425m. was long-term public debt. The cost of servicing external debt in that year was equivalent to 4.1% of the value of goods and services. In 2001–07 the average annual rate of increase in consumer prices was 7.9%. Consumer prices increased by an annual average of 11.1% in 2007. An estimated 5.2% of the labour force was unemployed in 2006.

Nicaragua is a member of the CACM (see p. 211), which aims eventually to liberalize intra-regional trade, and of the Inter-American Development Bank (IDB, see p. 318). Negotiations towards a free trade agreement, to be known as the Central American Free Trade Agreement, were concluded between El Salvador, Guatemala, Honduras, Nicaragua and the USA in December 2003. The agreement entailed the gradual elimination of tariffs on most industrial and agricultural products over the next 10 and 20 years, respectively. Ratification of the Dominican Republic-Central American Free Trade Agreement (DR-CAFTA, as the agreement was restyled in 2004) was finally approved by the Nicaraguan legislature on 10 October 2005. DR-CAFTA was inaugurated in April 2006.

In the early 2000s Nicaragua remained the second-poorest country in Latin America (after Haiti), heavily dependent on international aid, despite advances made since 1990 in reducing inflation and the fiscal deficit and in increasing foreign reserves. In 2003 Nicaragua became the 10th country to qualify for debt alleviation under the World Bank's heavily indebted poor countries (HIPC) initiative, making it eligible for some US $4,500m. in loans in early 2004; in 2005 it was among 18 countries to be granted 100% debt relief on multilateral debt incurred prior to 2005 agreed by the Group of Eight (G8) leading industrialized nations, subject to the approval of the lenders. This cancellation was approved by the IMF in December, and totalled some $201m. ($132m., excluding the remaining HIPC funding). Although the Government of Enrique Bolaños succeeded in meeting IMF criteria for inclusion in the HIPC initiative, the fiscal and trade deficits remained high, and considerable social deprivation continued. The administration of Daniel Ortega, which took office in January 2007, pledged to promote fiscal prudence and ongoing reconciliation with the USA, although closer relations with Iran and Venezuela were pursued. A focus on social policies resulted in a reduction in maternal mortality rates, greater school enrolment (and an increase in literacy) and better access to safe water. Programmes were initiated to stimulate agricultural productivity, with microcredits offered to small-scale farmers, while in early 2008 the minimum wage was increased by 15%. Meanwhile, the legislative impasse that followed disputed municipal elections in November 2008 (see Recent History) threatened to lead to a decline in donor support, and in December the USA withheld disbursement of some $62m. in development aid. The economy remained vulnerable to external shocks, including natural disasters and fluctuations in the international price of commodities (notably petroleum imports). It was anticipated that the economy would be adversely affected by the global financial crisis, not least because of a projected decline in income from exports (particularly textiles sales to the USA) and remittances from workers abroad (estimated at some $807m. in 2008). Indeed, the value of exports in the first two months of 2009 was some 19% lower than it had been in the corresponding period in 2008, with those destined for the USA (Nicaragua's principal trading partner) declining in value by 33%. The Government anticipated GDP growth of 1.1%–2.1% in 2009, compared with 3.9% in 2008.

Education

Primary and secondary education have been provided free of charge since 1979. Primary education, which is officially compulsory, begins at seven years of age and lasts for six years. Secondary education, beginning at the age of 13, lasts for up to five years, comprising a first cycle of three years and a second of two years. In 2005/06 enrolment at primary schools included 89.8% of the relevant age-group. Secondary enrolment in that year included 43.4% of children in the relevant age-group. There are many commercial schools and eight universities. In 2003 a total of 103,577 students attended universities and other higher education institutes. In that year public expenditure on education accounted for 15.0% of total government expenditure.

Public Holidays

2009: 1 January (New Year's Day), 9 April (Maundy Thursday), 10 April (Good Friday), 1 May (Labour Day), 30 May (Mothers' Day, afternoon only), 19 July (Liberation Day), 1 and 10 August (Managua local holidays), 14 September (Battle of San Jacinto), 15 September (Independence Day), 2 November (All Souls' Day, afternoon only), 8 December (Immaculate Conception), 25 December (Christmas Day).

2010: 1 January (New Year's Day), 1 April (Maundy Thursday), 2 April (Good Friday), 1 May (Labour Day), 30 May (Mothers' Day, afternoon only), 19 July (Liberation Day), 1 and 10 August (Managua local holidays), 14 September (Battle of San Jacinto), 15 September (Independence Day), 2 November (All Souls' Day, afternoon only), 8 December (Immaculate Conception), 25 December (Christmas Day).

Various local holidays are also observed.

Weights and Measures

The metric system is officially used, although some Spanish and local units are also in general use.

Statistical Survey

Sources (unless otherwise stated): Banco Central de Nicaragua, Carretera Sur, Km 7, Apdos 2252/3, Zona 5, Managua; tel. 265-0500; fax 265-2272; e-mail bcn@cabcn.gob.ni; internet www.bcn.gob.ni; Instituto Nacional de Estadísticas y Censos (INEC), Las Brisas, Frente Hospital Fonseca, Managua; tel. 266-2031; internet www.inec.gob.ni.

Area and Population

AREA, POPULATION AND DENSITY

Area (sq km)	
Land	120,340
Inland water	10,034
Total	130,373*
Population (census results)	
25 April 1995	4,357,099
28 May–11 June 2005	
Males	2,534,491
Females	2,607,607
Total	5,142,098
Population (official estimates at mid-year)	
2006	5,522,606
2007	5,595,538
Density (per sq km) at mid-2007	42.9

* 50,337 sq miles.

ADMINISTRATIVE DIVISIONS
(land area only, population at mid-2007)

	Area (sq km)	Population	Density (per sq km)	Capital
Departments:				
Chinandega	4,822.4	408,495	84.7	Chinandega
León	5,138.0	390,775	76.1	León
Managua	3,465.1	1,347,123	388.8	Managua
Masaya	610.8	321,268	526.0	Masaya
Carazo	1,081.4	174,578	161.4	Jinotepe
Granada	1,039.7	187,449	180.3	Granada
Rivas	2,161.8	166,367	77.0	Rivas
Estelí	2,229.7	215,308	96.6	Estelí
Madriz	1,708.2	144,711	84.7	Somoto
Nueva Segovia	3,491.3	227,215	65.1	Ocotal
Jinotega	9,222.4	367,695	39.9	Jinotega
Matagalpa	6,803.9	501,602	73.7	Matagalpa
Boaco	4,176.7	163,381	39.1	Boaco
Chontales	6,481.3	168,859	26.1	Juigalpa
Río San Juan	7,540.9	103,961	13.8	San Carlos
Autonomous Regions:				
Atlántico Norte (RAAN)	32,819.7	370,517	11.3	Bilwi
Atlántico Sur (RAAS)	27,546.3	336,233	12.2	Bluefields
Total	120,339.5	5,595,538	46.5	—

PRINCIPAL TOWNS
(population at 2005 census)

Managua (capital)	937,489	Chinandega	121,793
León	174,051	Estelí	112,084
Masaya	139,582	Granada	105,171
Matagalpa	133,416	Tipitaga	101,685

BIRTHS AND DEATHS
(annual averages, UN estimates)

	1990–95	1995–2000	2000–05
Birth rate (per 1,000)	35.4	30.1	26.3
Death rate (per 1,000)	6.5	5.6	5.0

Source: UN, *World Population Prospects: The 2008 Revision*.

2001: Registered births 103,593 (19.9 per 1,000); Registered deaths 10,071 (1.9 per 1,000).

2002: Registered births 103,643 (19.4 per 1,000); Registered deaths 10,830 (2.0 per 1,000).

2003 (estimates): Live births 102,676; Deaths 14,630 (Source: UN, *Demographic Yearbook*).

Life expectancy (years at birth, WHO estimates): 71.4 (males 68.4; females 74.4) in 2006 (Source: WHO, *World Health Statistics*).

EMPLOYMENT
(population aged 10 years and over, 2005 census)

	Male	Female	Total
Agriculture, forestry and fishing	537,209	33,611	570,820
Mining and quarrying	5,005	503	5,508
Manufacturing	118,919	89,074	207,993
Electricity, gas and water	3,830	954	4,784
Construction	86,574	2,182	88,756
Trade, restaurants and hotels	166,863	150,580	317,443
Transport and communications	60,346	5,338	65,684
Financial services	7,104	7,320	14,424
Government services	150,992	232,220	383,212
Other activities	9,817	7,109	16,926
Total employed	1,146,659	528,891	1,675,550

Health and Welfare

KEY INDICATORS

Total fertility rate (children per woman, 2006)	2.8
Under-5 mortality rate (per 1,000 live births, 2006)	36
HIV/AIDS (% of persons aged 15–49, 2007)	0.2
Physicians (per 1,000 head, 2003)	0.40
Hospital beds (per 1,000 head, 2005)	0.9
Health expenditure (2006): US $ per head (PPP)	251
Health expenditure (2006): % of GDP	7.8
Health expenditure (2006): public (% of total)	54.7
Access to water (% of persons, 2006)	79
Access to sanitation (% of persons, 2006)	48
Human Development Index (2006): ranking	120
Human Development Index (2006): value	0.699

For sources and definitions, see explanatory note on p. vi.

NICARAGUA

Agriculture

PRINCIPAL CROPS
('000 metric tons)

	2005	2006	2007
Rice, paddy	316.7	316.0	302.7
Maize	555.6	501.9	569.9
Sorghum	91.3	73.2	90.3
Cassava (Manioc)	119.4	105.0*	115.0*
Sugar cane	3,816.6	4,505.0	4,875.0
Beans, dry	211.9	179.7	189.4
Groundnuts, in shell	121.5	102.0	116.7
Oil palm fruit*	60.0	60.0	62.5
Bananas	49.9	42.6	47.1
Plantains*	44.5	42.0	42.0
Oranges*	72.0	72.0	72.0
Pineapples*	49.0	50.0	51.0
Coffee, green	95.5	55.3	81.8

* FAO estimate(s).

Aggregate production ('000 metric tons, may include official, semi-official or estimated data): Total cereals 964 in 2005, 891 in 2006, 963 in 2007; Total roots and tubers 157 in 2005, 144 in 2006, 155 in 2007; Total vegetables (incl. melons) 35 in 2005, 36 in 2006, 36 in 2007; Total fruits (excl. melons) 228 in 2005, 207 in 2006, 212 in 2007.

Source: FAO.

LIVESTOCK
('000 head, year ending September)

	2003	2004	2005*
Cattle	3,500	3,400†	3,500
Pigs*	121	122	123
Goats*	7	7	7
Horses*	260	265	268
Asses, mules or hinnies*	56	57	57
Poultry*	16,000	16,500	18,000

* FAO estimates.
† Unofficial figure.

2006–07: Figures assumed to be unchanged from 2005 (FAO estimates).

Source: FAO.

LIVESTOCK PRODUCTS
('000 metric tons)

	2005	2006	2007
Cattle meat	76.0	84.3	90.0*
Pig meat	6.6	6.8	7.0
Horse meat*	2.1	2.1	2.1
Chicken meat	70.6	83.6	87.5
Cows' milk	614.1	633.7	646.2
Hen eggs	20.4	21.1	21.5

* FAO estimate(s).

Source: FAO.

Forestry

ROUNDWOOD REMOVALS
('000 cubic metres, excl. bark, FAO estimates)

	2005	2006	2007
Sawlogs, veneer logs and logs for sleepers	93	93	93
Fuel wood	5,948	5,975	6,003
Total	6,041	6,068	6,096

Source: FAO.

SAWNWOOD PRODUCTION
('000 cubic metres, incl. railway sleepers, FAO estimates)

	2004	2005	2006
Coniferous	24.0	19.5	19.5
Broadleaved	42.8	34.6	34.6
Total	66.8	54.1	54.1

2007: Production assumed to be unchanged from 2006 (FAO estimates).

Source: FAO.

Fishing

('000 metric tons, live weight)

	2004	2005	2006
Capture	19.3	30.9	33.3
Snooks	1.1	1.3	1.6
Snappers	2.4	4.6	3.1
Yellowfin tuna	3.9	7.3	7.6
Common dolphinfish	0.4	0.4	0.3
Caribbean spiny lobsters	4.3	3.8	3.6
Penaeus shrimp	3.0	4.5	2.5
Aquaculture	7.9	10.0	11.2
Whiteleg shrimp	7.9	9.6	10.9
Total catch	27.2	40.9	44.5

Source: FAO.

Mining

(estimates)

	2004	2005	2006
Gold (kg)	4,315	3,674	3,395
Silver (kg)	2,950	2,999	2,929
Gypsum and anhydrite (metric tons)	36,466	36,456	42,191

Source: US Geological Survey.

Industry

SELECTED PRODUCTS
('000 barrels, unless otherwise indicated)

	2006	2007	2008*
Liquid gas	178	185	110
Motor spirit	774	721	714
Kerosene	211	239	201
Diesel	1,486	1,515	1,398
Fuel oil	2,691	2,633	2,305
Bitumen (asphalt)	73	92	74
Electric energy (million kWh)	3,137.2	3,208.8	3,327.4

* Preliminary figures.

Cement ('000 metric tons, estimates): 820 in 2004; 820 in 2005 (Source: US Geological Survey).

Finance

CURRENCY AND EXCHANGE RATES

Monetary Units
100 centavos = 1 córdoba oro (gold córdoba).

Sterling, Dollar and Euro Equivalents (31 December 2008)
£1 sterling = 28.395 gold córdobas;
US $1 = 19.848 gold córdobas;
€1 = 27.623 gold córdobas;
1,000 gold córdobas = £34.56 = $50.38 = €36.20.

Average Exchange Rate (gold córdobas per US dollar)
2006 17.5700
2007 18.4485
2008 19.3719

Note: In February 1988 a new córdoba, equivalent to 1,000 of the former units, was introduced, and a uniform exchange rate of US $1 = 10 new córdobas was established. Subsequently, the exchange rate was frequently adjusted. A new currency, the córdoba oro (gold córdoba), was introduced as a unit of account in May 1990 and began to be circulated in August. The value of the gold córdoba was initially fixed at par with the US dollar, but in March 1991 the exchange rate was revised to $1 = 25,000,000 new córdobas (or 5 gold córdobas). On 30 April 1991 the gold córdoba became the sole legal tender.

BUDGET
(million gold córdobas)

Revenue*	2006	2007†	2008†
Taxation	16,262.2	18,984.2	21,730.3
Income tax	4,780.2	5,746.0	n.a.
Value-added tax	6,806.3	8,025.3	n.a.
Taxes on petroleum products	1,846.1	2,107.6	n.a.
Taxes on imports	972.2	1,093.3	n.a.
Other revenue	1,251.4	1,594.6	1,737.8
Total	17,513.6	20,578.8	23,468.0

Expenditure‡	2006	2007†	2008†
Compensation of employees	6,117.4	7,247.3	9,050.6
Goods and services	2,600.8	2,526.5	4,832.9
Interest payments	1,684.4	1,579.8	1,447.4
Current transfers	5,904.1	3,863.8	4,498.8
Capital transfers	3,160.4	3,211.3	3,528.7
Social security contributions	422.0	528.7	18.5
Other expenditure	1,189.7	1,166.5	1,654.9
Total	17,918.4	20,124.0	25,031.8

* Excluding grants received (million gold córdobas): 3,692.2 in 2006; 3,912.1 in 2007 (preliminary); 3,573.9 in 2008 (preliminary).
† Preliminary figures.
‡ Excluding net acquisition of non-financial assets (million gold córdobas): 3,224.5 in 2006; 3,926.2 in 2007 (preliminary); 3,448.1 in 2008 (preliminary).

INTERNATIONAL RESERVES
(excluding gold, US $ million at 31 December)

	2005	2006	2007
IMF special drawing rights	0.31	0.39	0.12
Foreign exchange	727.50	921.50	1,103.20
Total	727.81	921.89	1,103.32

Source: IMF, *International Financial Statistics*.

MONEY SUPPLY
(million gold córdobas at 31 December)

	2005	2006	2007
Currency outside banks	3,808.0	4,401.3	5,537.2
Demand deposits at commercial banks	1,973.8	2,231.8	3,250.8
Total money (incl. others)	5,784.7	6,634.9	8,790.5

Source: IMF, *International Financial Statistics*.

COST OF LIVING
(Consumer Price Index; base: 1999 = 100)

	2005	2006	2007
Food	149.0	162.5	188.9
Clothing	117.8	122.3	129.5
Rent, fuel and light	156.0	175.0	189.7
All items (incl. others)	147.4	160.9	178.8

Source: ILO.

NATIONAL ACCOUNTS
(million gold córdobas at current prices)

Expenditure on the Gross Domestic Product

	2005	2006*	2007†
Government final consumption expenditure	9,581.7	11,502.2	13,080.4
Private final consumption expenditure	71,610.5	81,208.3	94,858.1
Increase in stocks	1,330.5	474.0	2,470.0
Gross fixed capital formation	23,193.7	27,114.8	31,093.6
Total domestic expenditure	105,716.4	120,299.3	141,502.1
Exports of goods and services	23,613.6	29,501.8	35,083.5
Less Imports of goods and services	47,805.5	56,793.8	70,942.1
GDP in purchasers' values	81,524.4	93,007.3	105,643.5
GDP at constant 1994 prices	31,623.9	32,858.2	34,090.7

* Preliminary figures.
† Estimates.

Gross Domestic Product by Economic Activity

	2005	2006*	2007†
Agriculture, hunting, forestry and fishing	13,690.8	15,429.8	17,888.2
Mining and quarrying	900.1	1,083.8	1,119.8
Manufacturing	13,361.5	15,073.4	17,452.1
Electricity, gas and water	2,254.9	2,712.6	2,970.7
Construction	4,654.2	5,333.5	5,764.2
Wholesale and retail trade	11,254.3	12,631.2	14,444.9
Transport and communications	4,424.2	5,022.7	5,857.8
Finance, insurance and business services	3,568.7	4,254.8	5,555.0
Real estate	6,373.7	6,988.8	7,766.5
Other private services	5,813.5	6,479.6	7,195.0
Government services	9,106.2	10,895.3	12,530.1
Sub-total	75,402.0	85,905.4	98,544.3
Net taxes on products	9,762.0	11,528.1	13,289.2
Less Imputed bank service charge	3,639.6	4,426.3	6,190.0
GDP in purchasers' values	81,524.4	93,007.3	105,643.5

* Preliminary figures.
† Estimates.

NICARAGUA

BALANCE OF PAYMENTS
(US $ million)

	2005	2006	2007
Exports of goods f.o.b.	1,654.1	2,033.9	2,313.2
Imports of goods f.o.b.	−2,956.1	−3,450.5	−4,117.0
Trade balance	−1,302.0	−1,416.6	−1,803.8
Exports of services	308.5	341.0	372.1
Imports of services	−448.2	−477.7	−555.8
Balance on goods and services	−1,441.7	−1,553.3	−1,987.5
Other income received	22.7	41.4	48.2
Other income paid	−172.7	−169.9	−182.8
Balance on goods, services and income	−1,591.7	−1,681.8	−2,122.1
Current transfers (net)	857.4	1,003.3	1,074.6
Current balance	−734.3	−678.5	−1,045.7
Capital (net)	299.8	348.0	418.1
Direct investment from abroad	241.1	286.8	381.7
Portfolio investment	−7.8	−9.6	−12.2
Other investment assets	−182.3	5.3	−163.8
Other investment liabilities	132.0	232.5	284.1
Net errors and omissions	−57.4	−151.5	42.9
Overall balance	−308.8	33.0	−96.7

Source: IMF, *International Financial Statistics*.

External Trade

PRINCIPAL COMMODITIES
(US $ million)

Imports c.i.f.	2006	2007	2008
Consumer goods	970.3	1,072.5	1,255.9
Non-durable consumer goods	748.7	843.5	1,009.1
Durable consumer goods	221.6	229.0	246.8
Petroleum, mineral fuels and lubricants	689.8	813.4	1,000.2
Crude petroleum	366.0	403.5	503.1
Mineral fuels and lubricants	323.8	409.9	497.1
Intermediate goods	804.9	1,009.5	1,226.3
Primary materials and intermediate goods for agriculture and fishing	84.6	113.9	172.2
Primary materials and intermediate goods for industry	553.7	678.5	808.5
Construction materials	166.7	217.2	245.7
Capital goods	556.1	695.2	846.0
For agriculture and fishing	31.2	35.6	44.0
For industry	312.1	405.5	536.7
For transport	212.8	254.0	265.3
Miscellaneous	5.2	7.2	9.4
Total	3,026.4	3,597.8	4,337.8

Exports f.o.b.	2006	2007	2008
Coffee	207.2	188.1	278.3
Groundnuts	43.0	56.0	90.2
Cattle on hoof	39.3	42.2	26.8
Beans	37.0	39.9	79.8
Bananas	9.6	9.9	9.6
Lobster	40.0	46.8	39.5
Fresh fish	13.2	14.1	14.0
Shrimp	48.6	46.1	48.3
Tobacco (leaf)	8.2	4.8	5.4
Gold	55.3	61.4	78.2
Meat and meat products	148.0	179.5	210.7
Refined sugars, etc.	60.3	74.3	50.4
Cheese	34.5	49.7	66.2
Wood products	7.3	6.3	4.9
Chemical products	31.0	49.6	63.8
Refined petroleum	13.8	10.1	15.7
Porcelain products	11.4	12.1	10.0
Total (incl. others)	1,049.9	1,224.8	1,488.7

PRINCIPAL TRADING PARTNERS
(US $ million)

Imports c.i.f.	2006	2007	2008
Canada	27.3	27.5	37.9
Costa Rica	261.1	303.9	341.1
Ecuador	75.2	136.0	107.0
El Salvador	157.6	172.4	229.3
Germany	41.4	42.6	50.8
Guatemala	198.3	222.8	264.6
Honduras	75.9	108.4	135.3
Japan	111.4	121.5	124.3
Mexico	395.4	492.8	361.7
Panama	10.5	16.0	19.7
Spain	36.6	36.9	46.9
Sweden	11.7	21.0	19.3
Taiwan	16.6	15.4	21.0
USA	634.9	781.3	899.9
Venezuela	220.9	255.8	625.2
Total (incl. others)	3,026.4	3,597.8	4,337.8

Exports f.o.b.	2006	2007	2008
Belgium	32.5	25.2	28.6
Canada	45.3	69.4	75.0
Costa Rica	59.8	87.6	102.97
El Salvador	149.3	168.1	217.2
France	7.5	10.3	12.6
Germany	30.5	24.0	26.8
Guatemala	48.2	65.6	74.9
Honduras	98.1	111.1	101.4
Italy	9.7	11.3	14.6
Mexico	48.5	57.9	78.9
Spain	34.6	43.3	43.3
USA	339.7	353.6	439.0
Total (incl. others)	1,049.9	1,224.8	1,488.7

Transport

RAILWAYS
(traffic)

	1990	1991	1992
Passenger-km (million)	3	3	6

Freight ton-km (million): 4 in 1985.

Source: UN, *Statistical Yearbook*.

ROAD TRAFFIC
(motor vehicles in use)

	2002	2003	2004
Cars	83,168	86,020	94,998
Buses and coaches	6,947	13,782	16,139
Lorries and vans	111,797	120,408	136,674
Motorcycles and mopeds	28,973	42,153	47,547

Source: IRF, *World Road Statistics*.

SHIPPING
Merchant fleet
(registered at 31 December)

	2005	2006	2007
Number of vessels	28	28	28
Total displacement ('000 grt)	5.7	5.7	5.7

Source: Lloyd's Register-Fairplay, *World Fleet Statistics*.

NICARAGUA

International Sea-Borne Freight Traffic
('000 metric tons)

	1997	1998	1999
Imports	1,272.7	1,964.7	1,180.7
Exports	329.3	204.5	183.6

Total freight traffic ('000 metric tons): 2,215.9 in 2000; 2,363.0 in 2001; 2,093.8 in 2002.

CIVIL AVIATION
(traffic on scheduled services)

	1998	1999	2000
Kilometres flown (million)	1.2	0.8	0.8
Passengers carried ('000)	52	59	61
Passenger-km (million)	93	67	72
Freight ton-km (million)	n.a.	0.5	0.5

Source: UN Economic Commission for Latin America and the Caribbean.

Tourism

TOURIST ARRIVALS BY COUNTRY OF ORIGIN

	2004	2005	2006
Canada	15,586	18,068	22,200
Costa Rica	99,674	108,598	92,308
El Salvador	88,103	100,574	113,793
Guatemala	48,990	58,019	67,510
Honduras	126,916	139,134	150,146
Panama	13,563	17,591	20,905
USA	131,865	147,331	168,939
Total (incl. others)	614,782	712,444	773,398

Tourism receipts (US $ million, incl. passenger transport): 196 in 2004; 210 in 2005; 237 in 2006.

Source: World Tourism Organization.

Communications Media

	2004	2005	2006
Telephones ('000 main lines in use)	214.5	220.9	247.9
Mobile cellular telephones ('000 subscribers)	738.6	1,119.4	1,830.2
Personal computers ('000 in use)	200	220	n.a.
Internet users ('000)	125.0	140.0	155.0
Broadband subscribers ('000)	5.0	10.5	19.0

2007: Mobile cellular telephones ('000 subscribers) 2,122.8.
Radio receivers ('000 in use): 1,240 in 1997.
Television receivers ('000 in use): 350 in 2000.
Daily newspapers: 4 in 1996 (average circulation 135,000 copies).
Sources: UNESCO, *Statistical Yearbook*; International Telecommunication Union.

Education

(2005/06, unless otherwise indicated)

	Institutions*	Teachers	Males	Females	Total
Pre-primary	5,980	8,536	106,235	103,715	209,950
Primary	8,251	29,039	498,530	467,676	966,206
Secondary: general	1,249	12,569	202,234	223,484	425,718
Tertiary: university level	35	3,630†	47,683‡	51,222‡	98,905‡
Tertiary: other higher	73	210†	1,902‡	2,770‡	4,672‡

* 2002/03 figures.
† 2001/02 figure.
‡ 2003/04 figure.

Sources: UNESCO, *Statistical Yearbook*; Ministry of Education, Culture and Sports.

Adult literacy rate (UNESCO estimates): 80.5% (males 79.7%; females 81.4%) in 2007 (Source: UNESCO Institute for Statistics).

Directory

The Constitution

Shortly after taking office on 20 July 1979, the Government of National Reconstruction abrogated the 1974 Constitution. On 22 August 1979 the revolutionary junta issued a 'Statute on Rights and Guarantees for the Citizens of Nicaragua', providing for the basic freedoms of the individual, religious freedom and freedom of the press and abolishing the death penalty. The intention of the Statute was formally to re-establish rights that had been violated under the deposed Somoza regime. A fundamental Statute took effect from 20 July 1980 and remained in force until the Council of State drafted a political constitution and proposed an electoral law. A new Constitution was approved by the National Constituent Assembly on 19 November 1986 and promulgated on 9 January 1987. Amendments to the Constitution were approved by the Asamblea Nacional (National Assembly) in July 1995 and January 2000. The following are some of the main points of the Constitution.

Nicaragua is an independent, free, sovereign and indivisible state. All Nicaraguans who have reached 16 years of age are full citizens.

POLITICAL RIGHTS

There shall be absolute equality between men and women. It is the obligation of the State to remove obstacles that impede effective participation of Nicaraguans in the political, economic and social life of the country. Citizens have the right to vote, to be elected at elections and to offer themselves for public office. Citizens may organize or affiliate with political parties, with the objective of participating in, exercising or vying for power. The supremacy of civilian authority is enshrined in the Constitution.

SOCIAL RIGHTS

The Nicaraguan people have the right to work, to education and to culture. They have the right to decent, comfortable and safe housing, and to seek accurate information. This right comprises the freedom to seek, receive and disseminate information and ideas, both spoken and written, in graphic or any other form. The mass media are at the service of national interests. No Nicaraguan citizen may disobey the law or prevent others from exercising their rights and fulfilling their duties by invoking religious beliefs or inclinations.

LABOUR RIGHTS

All have a right to work, and to participate in the management of their enterprises. Equal pay shall be given for equal work. The State shall strive for full and productive employment under conditions that guarantee the fundamental rights of the individual. There shall be an eight-hour working day, weekly rest, vacations, remuneration for national holidays and a bonus payment equivalent to one month's salary, in conformity with the law.

EDUCATION

Education is an obligatory function of the State. Planning, direction and organization of the secular education system is the responsibility of the State. All Nicaraguans have free and equal access to education. Private education centres may function at all levels.

LEGISLATIVE POWER

The Asamblea Nacional exercises Legislative Power through representative popular mandate. The Asamblea Nacional is composed of 90 representatives elected by direct secret vote by means of a system of proportional representation, of which 70 are elected at regional level and 20 at national level. The number of representatives may be increased in accordance with the general census of the population, in conformity with the law. Representatives shall be elected for a period of five years. The functions of the Asamblea Nacional are to draft and approve laws and decrees; to decree amnesties and pardons; to consider, discuss and approve the General Budget of the Republic; to elect judges to the Supreme Court of Justice and the Supreme Electoral Council; to fill permanent vacancies for the Presidency or Vice-Presidency; and to determine the political and administrative division of the country.

EXECUTIVE POWER

The Executive Power is exercised by the President of the Republic (assisted by the Vice-President), who is the Head of State, Head of Government and Commander-in-Chief of the Defence and Security Forces of the Nation. The election of the President (and Vice-President) is by equal, direct and free universal suffrage in a secret ballot. Should a single candidate in a presidential election fail to secure the necessary 35% of the vote to win outright in the first round, a second ballot shall be held. Close relatives of a serving President are prohibited from contesting a presidential election. The President shall serve for a period of five years and may not serve for two consecutive terms. All outgoing Presidents are granted a seat in the Asamblea Nacional.

JUDICIAL POWER

The Judiciary consists of the Supreme Court of Justice, Courts of Appeal and other courts of the Republic. The Supreme Court is composed of at least seven judges, elected by the Asamblea Nacional, who shall serve for a term of six years. The functions of the Supreme Court are to organize and direct the administration of justice. There are 12 Supreme Court justices, appointed for a period of seven years.

LOCAL ADMINISTRATION

The country is divided into regions, departments and municipalities for administrative purposes. The municipal governments shall be elected by universal suffrage in a secret ballot and will serve a six-year term. The communities of the Atlantic Coast have the right to live and develop in accordance with a social organization that corresponds to their historical and cultural traditions. The State shall implement, by legal means, autonomous governments in the regions inhabited by the communities of the Atlantic Coast, in order that the communities may exercise their rights.

The Government

HEAD OF STATE

President: José Daniel Ortega Saavedra (took office 10 January 2007).

Vice-President: Jaime René Morales Carazo.

CABINET
(April 2009)

Minister of Foreign Affairs: Samuel Santos López.

Minister of the Interior: Ana Isabel Morales Mazún.

Secretary-General of Defence with Ministerial Rank: Ruth Esperanza Tapia Roa.

Minister of Finance and Public Credit: Alberto José Guevara Obregón.

Minister of Development, Industry and Trade: Dr Orlando Solórzano Delgadillo.

Minister of Labour: Jeannette Chávez Gómez.

Minister of the Environment and Natural Resources: Juana Argeñal.

Minister of Transport and Infrastructure: Pablo Fernando Martínez Espinoza.

Minister of Agriculture and Forestry: Ariel Bucardo Rocha.

Minister of Health: Dr Guillermo González.

Minister of Education, Culture and Sports: Dr Miguel de Castilla Urbina.

Minister of the Family: María Isabel Muñoz (acting).

Minister of Energy and Mines: Emilio Rappaccioli.

Secretary to the Presidency: Salvador Vanegas Guido.

Co-ordinator of the Communication and Citizenship Council: Rosario Murillo Zambrana.

MINISTRIES

Office of the President: Casa Presidencial, Managua; e-mail daniel@presidencia.gob.ni; internet www.presidencia.gob.ni.

Ministry of Agriculture and Forestry: Km 8½, Carretera a Masaya, Managua; tel. 276-0200; e-mail prensa@magfor.gob.ni; internet www.magfor.gob.ni.

Ministry of Defence: De los semáforos el Redentor, 4 c. arriba, donde fue la casa 'Ricardo Morales Aviles', Managua; tel. 222-2201; fax 222-5439; internet www.midef.gob.ni.

Ministry of Development, Industry and Trade: Edif. Central, Km 6, Carretera a Masaya, Apdo 8, Managua; tel. 278-8702; fax 270-095; internet www.mific.gob.ni.

Ministry of Education, Culture and Sports: Complejo Cívico Camilo Ortega Saavedra, Managua; tel. 265-1451; e-mail rivash@mecd.gob.ni; internet www.mined.gob.ni.

Ministry of Energy and Mines: Hospital Bautista, 1 c. al oeste, 1 c. al norte; tel. 222-5576; e-mail info@mem.gob.ni; internet www.mem.gob.ni.

Ministry of the Environment and Natural Resources: Km 12½, Carretera Norte, Apdo 5123, Managua; tel. 233-1111; fax 263-1274; e-mail jargenal@marena.gob.ni; internet www.marena.gob.ni.

Ministry of the Family: Managua; tel. 278-1620; e-mail webmaster@mifamilia.gob.ni; internet www.mifamilia.gob.ni.

Ministry of Finance and Public Credit: Frente a la Asamblea Nacional, Apdo 2170, Managua; tel. 222-6530; fax 222-6430; e-mail webmaster@mhcp.gob.ni; internet www.hacienda.gob.ni.

Ministry of Foreign Affairs: Del Cine González al sur sobre Avda Bolívar, Managua; tel. 244-8000; fax 228-5102; e-mail despacho.ministro@cancilleria.gob.ni; internet www.cancilleria.gob.ni.

Ministry of Health: Complejo Nacional de Salud 'Dra Concepción Palacios', costado oeste Colonia Primero de Mayo, Apdo 107, Managua; tel. 289-7164; e-mail secretaria@minsa.gob.ni; internet www.minsa.gob.ni.

Ministry of the Interior: Apdo 68, Managua; tel. 228-2284; fax 222-2789; e-mail webmaster@migob.gob.ni; internet www.migob.gob.ni.

Ministry of Labour: Estadio Nacional, 400 m al norte, Apdo 487, Managua; tel. 228-2028; fax 228-2103; e-mail info@mitrab.gob.ni; internet www.mitrab.gob.ni.

Ministry of Transport and Infrastructure: Frente al Estadio Nacional, Apdo 26, Managua; tel. 228-2061; fax 222-5111; e-mail webmaster@mti.gob.ni; internet www.mti.gob.ni.

President and Legislature

PRESIDENT

Election, 5 November 2006

Candidate	Votes	% of total
José Daniel Ortega Saavedra (FSLN)	930,862	37.99
Eduardo Montealegre Rivas (ALN)	693,391	28.30
José Rizo Castellón (PLC)	664,225	27.11
Edmundo Jarquín Calderón (MRS)	154,224	6.29
Edén Pastora Gómez (AC)	7,200	0.29
Total	**2,449,902**	**100.00**

ASAMBLEA NACIONAL
(National Assembly)

Asamblea Nacional
Avda Bolívar, Contiguo a la Presidencia de la República, Managua; e-mail webmaster@correo.asamblea.gob.ni; internet www.asamblea.gob.ni.

President: René Núñez Téllez.

First Vice-President: Luis Roberto Callejas.

Second Vice-President: Oscar Moncada Reyes.

Third Vice-President: Juan Ramón Jiménez.

NICARAGUA

Election, 5 November 2006

Party	Votes	% of total	Seats
Frente Sandinista de Liberación Nacional (FSLN)	1,837,901	37.47	38
Partido Liberal Constitucionalista (PLC)	1,355,594	27.63	25
Alianza Liberal Nicaragüense (ALN)	1,279,859	26.09	22
Movimiento Renovador Sandinista (MRS)	405,149	8.26	5
Alternativa por el Cambio (AC)	27,135	0.55	—
Total	**4,905,638***	**100.00**	**90†**

* Each elector had two votes: one for representatives at regional level (for which there were 70 seats) and one for representatives at national level (20 seats). The total number of votes cast at regional level was 2,487,448, while at national level 2,418,190 votes were cast.

† In addition to the 90 elected members, supplementary seats in the Asamblea Nacional are awarded to the unsuccessful candidates at the presidential election who were not nominated for the legislature but who received, in the presidential poll, a number of votes at least equal to the average required for one of the 70 legislative seats decided at a regional level. On this basis, the ALN obtained one additional seat in the Asamblea Nacional. A legislative seat is also awarded to the outgoing President, bringing the total number of seats in the Asamblea Nacional to 92.

Election Commission

Consejo Supremo Electoral (CSE): Iglesia Las Palmas, 1 c. al sur, Apdo 2241, Managua; tel. 268-7948; e-mail info@cse.gob.ni; internet www.cse.gob.ni; Pres. ROBERTO RIVAS REYES.

Political Organizations

Alianza Liberal Nicaragüense (ALN): Managua; fmrly Movimiento de Salvación Liberal; adopted current name in 2006; formed alliance with Partido Conservador (q.v.) ahead of 2006 elections; supporters of Eduardo Montealegre formed the Vamos con Eduardo movement in 2008; Pres. ELISEO NÚÑEZ HERNÁNDEZ.

Alianza por la República (APRE): Casa 211, Col. Los Robles, Funeraria Monte de los Olivos 1.5 c. al norte, Managua; f. 2004 by supporters of President Enrique Bolaños Geyer; Pres. MIGUEL LÓPEZ BALDIZÓN.

   Movimiento Democrático Nicaragüense (MDN): Casa L-39, Ciudad Jardín Bnd, 50 m al sur, Managua; tel. 243-898; f. 1978; Leader ROBERTO SEQUEIRA GÓMEZ.

   Partido Social Cristiano (PSC): Ciudad Jardín, Pizza María, 1 c. al lago, Managua; tel. 222-026; f. 1957; 42,000 mems; Pres. ABEL REYES.

Alternativa por el Cambio (AC): Managua; f. as Alternativa Cristiana; fmr faction of Frente Sandinista de Liberación Nacional (q.v.); name changed as above in 2006; Pres. Dr ORLANDO J. TARDENCILLA ESPINOZA.

Camino Cristiano Nicaragüense (CCN): Managua; Pres. GUILLERMO ANTONIO OSORNO MOLINA.

Frente Sandinista de Liberación Nacional (FSLN) (Sandinista National Liberation Front): Costado oeste Parque El Carmen, Managua; tel. and fax 266-8173; internet www.fsln.org.ni; f. 1960; led by a 15-mem. directorate; embraces Izquierda Democrática Sandinista 'orthodox revolutionary' faction, led by Daniel Ortega Saavedra; leads Nicaragua Triunfa electoral alliance; 120,000 mems; Gen. Sec. JOSÉ DANIEL ORTEGA SAAVEDRA.

Movimiento Renovador Sandinista (MRS): Tienda Katty 1 c. abajo, Apdo 24, Managua; tel. 250-9461; fax 278-0268; e-mail info@partidomrs.com; internet www.partidomrs.com; f. 1995; fmr faction of Frente Sandinista de Liberación Nacional (q.v.); legal status annulled by the Consejo Supremo Electoral in June 2008; Pres. ENRIQUE SÁENZ.

Movimiento de Unidad Cristiana (MUC): Managua; mem. of Convergencia Nacional alliance; Pres. Pastor DANIEL ORTEGA REYES.

Partido Conservador (PC): Colegio Centroamérica, 500 m al sur, Managua; tel. 267-0484; e-mail contactenos@partidoconservador.org.ni; f. 1992 following merger between Partido Conservador Demócrata and Partido Socialconservadurismo; formed alliance with Alianza Liberal Nicaragüense (q.v.) ahead of 2006 elections; legal status annulled by the Consejo Supremo Electoral in June 2008; Pres. AZALIA AVILÉS.

Partido Indígena Multiétnico (PIM): Residencial Los Robles, de Farmacentro 1 c. al este, 80 varas al sur, Managua; Pres. CARLA WHITE HODGSON.

Partido Liberal Constitucionalista (PLC): Semáforos Country Club 100 m al este, Apdo 4569, Managua; tel. 278-8705; fax 278-1800; f. 1967; Pres. JORGE CASTILLO QUANT; Nat. Sec. Dr NOEL RAMÍREZ SÁNCHEZ.

Partido Liberal Independiente (PLI): Ciudad Jardín, H-4, Calle Principal, Managua; tel. 244-3556; fax 248-0012; f. 1944; Leader VIRGILIO GODOY REYES.

Partido Liberal Nacionalista (PLN): Managua; f. 1913; Pres. CONSTANTINO VELÁSQUEZ ZEPEDA.

Partido Movimiento de Unidad Costeña (PAMUC): Bilwi Puerto Cabeza; Pres. KENNETH SERAPIO HUNTER.

Partido Neo-Liberal (Pali): Cine Dorado, 2 c. al sur, 50 m arriba, Managua; tel. 266-5166; f. 1986; Pres. Dr RICARDO VEGA GARCÍA.

Partido Resistencia Nicaragüense (PRN): Edif. VINSA, frente a Autonica, Carretera Sur, Managua; tel. and fax 270-6508; e-mail salvata@ibw.com.ni; f. 1993; nationalist party; Pres. SALVADOR TALAVERA ALANIZ.

Partido Socialista (PS): Hospital Militar, 100 m al norte, 100 m al oeste, 100 m al sur, Managua; tel. 266-2321; fax 266-2936; f. 1944; social democratic party; Sec.-Gen. Dr GUSTAVO TABLADA ZELAYA.

Partido Unionista Centroamericano (PUCA): Cine Cabrera, 1 c. al este, 20 m al norte, Managua; tel. 227-472; f. 1904; Pres. BLANCA ROJAS ECHAVERRY.

Unión Demócrata Cristiana (UDC): De Iglesia Santa Ana, 2 c. abajo, Barrio Santa Ana, Apdo 3089, Managua; tel. 266-2576; f. 1976 as Partido Popular Social Cristiano; name officially changed as above in Dec. 1993; mem. of Convergencia Nacional alliance; Pres. AGUSTÍN JARQUÍN ANAYA.

Yatama (Yapti Tasba Masraka Nanih Aslatakanka): Of. de Odacan, Busto José Martí, 1 c. al este y $^1/_2$ c. al norte, Managua; tel. 228-1494; Atlantic coast Miskito org.; mem. of FSLN-led electoral alliance, Nicaragua Triunfa; Leader BROOKLYN RIVERA BRYAN.

Diplomatic Representation

EMBASSIES IN NICARAGUA

Argentina: Semáforos de Villa Fontana, 2 c. abajo, 1 al sur, 1 abajo, 75 varas oeste, Casa 133, Apdo 703, Managua; tel. 283-7066; fax 270-2343; e-mail embargentina@cablenet.com.ni; Chargé d'affaires a.i. NICOLÁS SERGIO REBOK.

Brazil: Km $7^3/_4$, Carretera Sur, Quinta los Pinos, Apdo 264, Managua; tel. 265-0035; fax 265-2206; e-mail ebrasil@ibw.com.ni; Ambassador FLAVIO HELMOLD MACIEIRA.

Chile: Entrada principal los Robles, 1 c. abajo, 1 c. al sur, Apdo 1289, Managua; tel. 278-0619; fax 270-4073; e-mail echileni@cablenet.com.ni; Ambassador NATACHA MOLINA GARCÍA.

China (Taiwan): Optica Matamoros, 2 c. abajo, $^1/_2$ c. al lago, Carretera a Masaya, Planes de Altamira, Apdo 4653, Managua; tel. 277-1333; fax 267-4025; e-mail nic@mofa.gov.tw; internet www.roc-taiwan.org.ni; Ambassador WU CHIN-MU.

Colombia: 2da Entrada a las Colinas, 1 c. arriba, $^1/_2$ c. al lago, Casa 97, Apdo 1062, Managua; tel. 276-2149; fax 276-0644; e-mail emanagua@cancilleria.gov.co; Ambassador ANTONIO GONZÁLEZ CASTAÑO.

Costa Rica: Reparto las Colinas, Prado Ecuestre 304, 1°, Managua; tel. 276-1352; fax 276-0115; e-mail infembcr@cablenet.com.ni; Ambassador ANTONIO TACSAN LAM.

Cuba: Carretera a Masaya, 3a Entrada a las Colinas, 400 varas arriba, 75 al sur, Managua; tel. 276-0742; fax 276-0166; e-mail embacuba@embacuba.net.ni; internet embacu.cubaminrex.cu/nicaragua; Ambassador LUIS HERNÁNDEZ OJEDA.

Denmark: De la Plaza España, 1 c. abajo, 2 c. al lago, $^1/_2$ c. abajo, Apdo 4942, Managua; tel. 268-0250; fax 266-8095; e-mail mgaambu@um.dk; internet www.ambmanagua.um.dk; Ambassador SØREN VØHTZ.

Dominican Republic: Reparto Las Colinas, Prado Ecuestre 100, con Curva de los Gallos, Apdo 614, Managua; tel. 276-2029; fax 276-0654; e-mail embdom@alfanumeric.com.ni; Ambassador PEDRO BLANDINO.

Ecuador: De los Pipitos $1^1/_2$ c. abajo, Apdo C-33, Managua; tel. 268-1098; fax 266-8081; e-mail ecuador@ibw.com.ni; Ambassador ANTONIO PRECIADO BEDOYA.

El Salvador: Reparto Las Colinas, Avda del Campo y Pasaje Los Cerros 142, Apdo 149, Managua; tel. 276-0712; fax 276-0711; e-mail embelsa@cablenet.com.ni; internet www.embelsanica.org.ni; Ambassador ALFREDO FRANCISCO UNGO RIVAS LAGUARDIA.

NICARAGUA

Directory

Finland: Sucursal Jorge Navarro, Apdo 2219, Managua; tel. 266-3415; fax 266-3416; e-mail sanomat.mgu@formin.fi; internet www.finlandia.org.ni; Ambassador ELIJA ROTINEN.

France: Iglesia el Carmen 1½ c. abajo, Apdo 1227, Managua; tel. 222-6210; fax 268-5630; e-mail info@ambafrance-ni.org; internet www.ambafrance-ni.org; Ambassador THIERRY PIERRE FRAYSSÉ.

Germany: Bolonia, de la Rotonda El Güegüense, 1½ c. al lago, contiguo a Optica Nicaragüense, Apdo 29, Managua; tel. 266-3917; fax 266-7667; e-mail alemania@cablenet.com.ni; internet www.managua.diplo.de; Ambassador BETINA KERN.

Guatemala: Km 11½, Carretera a Masaya, Apdo E-1, Managua; tel. 279-9609; fax 279-9610; e-mail embnic@minex.gob.gt; Ambassador EDGAR RUANO NAJARRO.

Holy See: Apostolic Nunciature, Km 10.8, Carretera Sur, Apdo 506, Managua; tel. 265-8657; fax 265-7416; e-mail nuntius@cablenet.com.ni; Apostolic Nuncio Most Rev. HENRYK JÓZEF NOWACKI (Titular Archbishop of Blera).

Honduras: Reparto Las Colinas, Prado Ecuestre 298, frente a Residencia de la Embajada de China (Taiwán), Apdo 321, Managua; tel. 276-2406; fax 276-1998; e-mail embhonduras@cablenet.com.ni; Ambassador JORGE ALBERTO MILLA REYES.

Iran: Del Club Terraza, 300 m al este, de la principal entrada de las Cumbres, 3 c. al sur, No E4, Managua; Chargé d'affaires a.i. AKBAR ESMAEIL POUR.

Italy: Rotonda El Güegüense, 1 c. al norte, Apdo 2092, ½ c. abajo, Managua 4; tel. 266-2961; fax 266-3987; e-mail embitaliasegr@cablenet.com.ni; internet www.ambmanagua.esteri.it; Ambassador OMBRETTA PACILIO.

Japan: Plaza España, 1 c. abajo y 1 c. al lago, Bolonia, Apdo 1789, Managua; tel. 266-8668; fax 266-8566; e-mail embjpnic@cablenet.com.ni; internet www.ni.emb-japan.go.jp; Ambassador SHINICHI SAITO.

Korea, Republic: De la Plaza España, 3 c. abajo, 500 m al sur, casa A-45, Managua; tel. 254-8107; fax 254-8131; e-mail hrlee92@mofat.go.kr; Ambassador LEE SANG-PAL.

Libya: Mansión Teodolinda, 1 c. al sur, ½ c. abajo, Managua; tel. (2) 66-8540; fax (2) 66-8542; e-mail ofilibia@ibw.com.ni; Sec. of the People's Bureau ABDULLAH MUHAMMAD MATOUG.

Mexico: Contiguo a Optica Matamoros, Km 4½, Carretera a Masaya, Apdo 834, Managua; tel. 278-1859; fax 278-2886; e-mail embamex@turbonett.com.ni; Ambassador RAÚL LÓPEZ-LIRA NAVA.

Netherlands: Calle Erasmus de Rotterdam, Carretera a Masaya km 5, del Colegio Teresiano 1 c. al sur, 1 c. abajo, Apdo 3688, Managua; tel. 276-8630; fax 276-0399; e-mail mng@minbuza.nl; internet www.embajadaholanda-nic.com; Ambassador LAMBERTUS CHRISTIAAN GRIJNS.

Norway: Plaza España, Apdo 2090, Correo Central, Managua; tel. 266-4199; fax 266-3303; e-mail emb.managua@mfa.no; internet www.noruega.org.ni; Chargé d'affaires a.i. OLE ØVERAAS.

Panama: Casa 93, Reparto Mántica, del Cuartel General de Bomberos 1 c. abajo, Apdo 1, Managua; tel. 266-2224; fax 266-8633; e-mail embdpma@ibw.com.ni; Ambassador MIGUEL LECARO BÁRCENAS.

Peru: Las Cumbres, Casa D-13, contiguo a la Residencia del diputado Wilfredo Navarro Moreira, Apdo 211, Managua; tel. 266-8677; fax 266-1408; e-mail peru1@cablenet.com.ni; Ambassador HARRY GERARDO MORRIS ABARCO.

Russia: Reparto Las Colinas, Calle Vista Alegre 214, Entre Avda Central y Paseo del Club, Apdo 249, Managua; tel. 276-0374; fax 276-0179; e-mail rossia@ibw.com.ni; Ambassador IGOR SERGEEVICH KONDRASHEV.

Spain: Avda Central 13, Las Colinas, Apdo 284, Managua; tel. 276-0966; fax 276-0937; e-mail embespni@correo.mae.es; internet www.mae.es/embajadas/managua; Ambassador ANTONIO PÉREZ-HERNÁNDEZ TORRA.

USA: Km 5½, Carretera Sur, Apdo 327, Managua; tel. 252-7100; fax 252-7300; e-mail consularmanagua@state.gov; internet managua.usembassy.gov; Ambassador ROBERT CALLAHAN.

Venezuela: Costado norte de la Iglesia Santo Domingo, Las Sierritas, Casa 27, Apdo 406, Managua; tel. (2) 72-0267; fax (2) 72-2265; e-mail embaveznica@cablenet.com.ni; Ambassador SERGIO RODRÍGUEZ GELFENSTEIN.

Judicial System

The Supreme Court

Km 7½, Carretera Norte, Managua; tel. 233-0083; fax 233-0581; e-mail webmaster@csj.gob.ni; internet www.poderjudicial.gob.ni.

Deals with both civil and criminal cases, acts as a Court of Cassation, appoints Judges of First Instance, and generally supervises the legal administration of the country.

President: Dr JOSÉ MANUEL MARTÍNEZ SEVILLA.
Vice-President: Dr RAFAEL SOLÍS CERDA.
Attorney-General: Dr HERNÁN ESTRADA.

Religion

All religions are tolerated. Almost all of Nicaragua's inhabitants profess Christianity, and the great majority belong to the Roman Catholic Church. The Moravian Church predominates on the Caribbean coast.

CHRISTIANITY

The Roman Catholic Church

Nicaragua comprises one archdiocese, six dioceses and the Apostolic Vicariate of Bluefields. At 31 December 2006 adherents represented an estimated 82.7% of the total population.

Bishops' Conference

Conferencia Episcopal de Nicaragua, Ferretería Lang 1 c. al norte, 1 c. al este, Zona 3, Las Piedrecitas, Apdo 2407, Managua; tel. 266-6292; fax 266-8069; e-mail cen@tmx.com.ni.

f. 1975; statute approved 1987; Pres. LEOPOLDO JOSÉ BRENES SOLÓRZANO (Archbishop of Managua).

Archbishop of Managua: LEOPOLDO JOSÉ BRENES SOLÓRZANO, Arzobispado, Apdo 2008, Managua; tel. 276-0129; fax 276-0130; e-mail mob@unica.edu.ni.

The Anglican Communion

Nicaragua comprises one of the five dioceses of the Iglesia Anglicana de la Región Central de América.

Bishop of Nicaragua: Rt Rev. STURDIE W. DOWNS, Apdo 1207, Managua; tel. 222-5174; fax 222-6701; e-mail episcnic@tmx.com.ni.

Protestant Churches

Baptist Convention of Nicaragua: Apdo 2593, Managua; tel. 225-785; fax 224-131; f. 1917; 135 churches, 20,000 mems (2006); Pres. ABEL MENDOZA; Sec. DALIA NAVARRETE.

The Moravian Church in Nicaragua: Iglesia Morava, Bilwi; tel. and fax 282-2222; 199 churches, 83,000 mems; Leader Rt Rev. JOHN WILSON.

The Nicaraguan Lutheran Church of Faith and Hope: Apdo 151, Managua; tel. 266-4467; fax 266-4609; e-mail luterana@turbonett.com.ni; f. 1994; 7,000 mems (2007); Pres. Rev. VICTORIA CORTEZ RODRÍGUEZ.

The Press

NEWSPAPERS AND PERIODICALS

Bolsa de Noticias: Col. Centroamérica 852, Apdo VF-90, Managua; tel. 270-0546; fax 277-4931; e-mail prensa@bolsadenoticias.com.ni; internet www.grupoese.com.ni/BolsadeNoticias; f. 1974; daily; Dir MARÍA ELSA SUÁREZ GARCÍA.

Confidencial: De Pharoahs Casino, 2 c. abajo, 2 c. al sur, Managua; tel. 277-5134; fax 270-7017; e-mail revista@confidencial.com.ni; internet www.confidencial.com.ni; weekly; political analysis; Editor CARLOS F. CHAMORRO.

La Gaceta, Diario Oficial: Semáforos de Plaza Inter, 1 c. arriba, 1½ c. al lago, Managua; tel. 228-3791; e-mail lagaceta@ibw.com.ni; f. 1912; morning; official.

Novedades: Pista P. Joaquín Chamorro, Km 4, Carretera Norte, Apdo 576, Managua; daily; evening.

Nuevo Diario: Pista P. Joaquín Chamorro, Km 4, Carretera Norte, Apdo 4591, Managua; tel. 249-1190; fax 249-0700; e-mail info@elnuevodiario.com.ni; internet www.elnuevodiario.com.ni; f. 1980; morning; daily; independent; Dir DANILO AGUIRRE SOLÍS; circ. 45,000.

El Observador Económico: Antiguo Hospital el Retiro, 2 c. al lago, Apdo 2074, Managua; tel. 266-8708; fax 266-8711; e-mail info@elobservadoreconomico.com; internet www.elobservadoreconomico.com; Dir-Gen. ALEJANDRO MARTÍNEZ CUENCA.

La Prensa: Km 4½, Carretera Norte, Apdo 192, Managua; tel. 249-8405; fax 249-6926; e-mail info@laprensa.com.ni; internet www.laprensa.com.ni; f. 1926; morning; daily; independent; Pres. JAIME CHAMORRO CARDENAL; Editor EDUARDO ENRÍQUEZ; circ. 30,000.

Prensa Proletaria: Managua; tel. 222-594; fortnightly; official publ. of the Movimiento de Acción Popular Marxista-Leninista.

NICARAGUA

Revista Encuentro: Universidad Centroamericana, Apdo 69, Managua; tel. 278-3923; fax 267-0106; e-mail ucapubli@ns.uca.edu.ni; internet www.uca.edu.ni:8080/encuentro; f. 1968; termly; academic publ. of the Universidad Centroamericana; Dir JORGE ALBERTO PÉREZ HUETE.

Revista Envío: Edif. Nitlapán, 2°, Campus Universidad Centroamericana, Managua; tel. 278-2557; fax 278-1402; e-mail info@envio.org.ni; internet www.envio.org.ni; f. 1981; 11 a year; political analysis; edns in Spanish, English and Italian; Dir JUAN RAMIRO JIMÉNEZ; Chief Editor MARÍA LÓPEZ VIGIL.

Revista 7 Días: Altamira de lo Vicky, 5½ al lago, Managua; e-mail 7dias@ibw.com.ni; internet www.7dias.com.ni.

Tiempos del Mundo: Apdo 3525, Managua; tel. 270-3418; fax 270-3419; e-mail tiempos@tdm.com.ni; f. 1996; weekly; Gen. Man. TAKUYA ISHII; circ. 5,000.

La Tribuna: Detrás del Banco Mercantil, Plaza España, Apdo 1469, Managua; tel. 266-9282; fax 266-5167; e-mail tribuna@latribuna.com.ni; f. 1993; morning; daily; Dir HAROLDO J. MONTEALEGRE; Gen. Man. MARIO GONZÁLEZ.

Trinchera de la Noticia: Managua; tel. 240-0114; e-mail info@trinchera.com.ni; internet www.trinchera.com.ni; daily; Dir EMILIO NÚÑEZ.

Visión Sandinista: Costado este, Parque El Carmen, Managua; tel. and fax 268-1565; internet www.vsandinista.com; f. 1980; weekly; official publ. of the Frente Sandinista de Liberación Nacional; Dir MAYRA REYES SANDOVAL.

Association

Unión de Periodistas de Nicaragua (UPN): Apdo 4006, Managua; tel. 271-2436; e-mail uperiodistasnic@yahoo.com; internet www.aquinicaragua.com/periodistas2.html; Pres. ROBERTO LARIOS.

Publishers

Academia Nicaragüense de la Lengua: Calle Central, Reparto Las Colinas, Apdo 2711, Managua; f. 1928; languages; Dir JORGE EDUARDO ARELLANO.

Editora de Arte SA: 53 Reparto Los Robles III, Managua; tel. 278-5854; e-mail editarte@editarte.com.ni; internet www.editarte.com.ni.

Editorial Nueva Nicaragua: Paseo Salvador Allende, Km 3½, Carretera Sur, Apdo 073, Managua; fax 266-6520; f. 1981; Pres. Dr SERGIO RAMÍREZ MERCADO; Dir-Gen. ROBERTO DÍAZ CASTILLO.

Editorial Unión: Avda Central Norte, Managua; travel.

Librería Hispanoamericana (HISPAMER): Costado este de la UCA, Apdo A-221, Managua; e-mail hispamer@hispamer.com.ni; internet www.hispamer.com.ni; f. 1991.

UCA Publicaciónes: Rectoría de la Universidad Centroamericana, Apdo 69, Managua; tel. 278-3923; fax 267-0106; e-mail ucapubli@ns.uca.edu.ni; internet www.uca.edu.ni/publicaciones; academic publishing dept of the Universidad Centroamericana.

Universidad Nacional Agraria: Km 12½ Carretera Norte, Apdo 453, Managua; tel. 233-1950; e-mail info@una.edu.ni; internet www.una.edu.ni; sciences.

Broadcasting and Communications

TELECOMMUNICATIONS

Regulatory Body

Instituto Nicaragüense de Telecomunicaciones y Correos (Telcor): Edif. Telcor, Avda Bolívar diagonal a Cancillería, Apdo 2264, Managua; tel. 222-7350; fax 222-7554; e-mail mgutierrez@telcor.gob.ni; internet www.telcor.gob.ni; Exec. Pres. ORLANDO CASTILLO.

Major Service Providers

Claro: Villafontana 2°, Apdo 232, Managua; tel. 277-3057; fax 270-2128; internet www.claro.com.ni; f. 2006 by merger of ALO PCS (f. 2002) and Empresa Nicaragüense de Telecomunicaciones (Enitel, f. 1925); subsidiary of América Móvil, SA de CV (Mexico); Chair. PATRICIO SLIM DOMIT; CEO DANIEL HAJJ ABOUMRAD.

Telefónica Móviles Nicaragua: Km 6½, Carretera a Masaya, Managua; tel. 277-0731; internet www.movistar.com.ni; fmrly BellSouth; owned by Grupo Telefónica Móviles (Spain); mobile cellular telephone provider; Vice-Pres. HUMBERTO PATO-VINUESA; Gen. Man. MARÍA JOSEFINA PERALTA.

BROADCASTING

Radio

La Nueva Radio Ya: Pista de la Resistencia, Frente a la Universidad Centroamericana, Managua; tel. 278-8336; fax 278-8334; e-mail info@nuevaya.com.ni; internet www.nuevaya.com.ni; f. 1990 as Radio Ya; restyled as above in 1999; operated by Entretenimiento Digital, SA; Dir-Gen. DENNIS SCHWARTZ.

Radio Católica: Altamira D'Este 621, 3°, Apdo 2183, Managua; tel. 278-0836; fax 278-2544; e-mail oramos@radiocatolica.org; internet www.radiocatolica.org; f. 1961; controlled by Conferencia Episcopal de Nicaragua; Dir Fr ROLANDO ÁLVAREZ; Gen. Man. ALBERTO CARBALLO MADRIGAL.

Radio Corporación, Gadea y Cía: Ciudad Jardín Q-20, Apdo 24242, Managua; tel. 249-1619; fax 244-3824; e-mail rc540@radio-corporacion.com; internet www.radio-corporacion.com; f. 1995; Gen. Man. FABIO GADEA MANTILLA; Asst Man. CARLOS GADEA MANTILLA.

Radio Estrella: Sierritas de Santo Domingo, Frente al Cementerio, Apdo UNICA 104, Managua; tel. 276-0241; fax 276-0062; e-mail radiosm@radioestrelladelmar.com; internet www.radioestrelladelmar.com.

Radio Mundial: 36 Avda Oeste, Reparto Loma Verde, Apdo 3170, Managua; tel. 266-6767; fax 266-4630; f. 1948; commercial; Dir-Gen. ALMA ROSA ARANA HARTIG.

Radio Nicaragua: Villa Fontana, Contiguo a Enitel, Apdo 4665, Managua; tel. 227-2330-1; fax 267-1448; e-mail director@radionicaragua.com.ni; internet www.radionicaragua.com.ni; f. 1960; govt station; Dir-Gen. ALBERTO CARBALLO MADRIGAL.

Radio Ondas de Luz: Costado Sur del Hospital Bautista, Apdo 607, Managua; tel. and fax 249-7058; internet www.radioondasdeluz.org; f. 1959; religious and cultural station; Pres. GUILLERMO OSORNO MOLINA; Dir EDUARDO GUTIÉRREZ NARVÁEZ.

Radio Sandino: Paseo Tiscapa Este, Contiguo al Restaurante Mirador, Apdo 4776, Managua; tel. 228-1330; fax 262-4052; internet www.lasandino.com.ni; f. 1977; station controlled by the Frente Sandinista de Liberación Nacional; Pres. RAFAEL ORTEGA MURILLO.

Radio Segovia: Ocotal, Nueva Segovia; tel. 732-2870; fax 732-2271; e-mail info@radiosegovia.net; internet www.radiosegovia.net; f. 1980; commercial.

Radio Tiempo: Reparto Pancasan 217, 7°, Apdo 2735, Managua; tel. 278-2540; f. 1976; Dir DANILO LACAYO LANZAS.

Radio Universidad: Avda Card, 3 c. abajo, Apdo 2883, Managua; tel. 278-4743; fax 277-5057; f. 1984; Dir LUIS LÓPEZ RUIZ.

There are some 50 other radio stations.

Television

Canal 4: Montoya, 1 c. al sur, 2 c. arriba, Managua; tel. 228-1310; fax 222-4067; internet www.multinoticias.tv.

Nicavisión, Canal 12: Bolonia Dual Card, 1 c. abajo, ½ c. al sur, Apdo 2766, Managua; tel. 266-0691; fax 266-1424; f. 1993; Dir MARIANO VALLE PETERS.

Televicentro de Nicaragua, SA, Canal 2: Casa del Obrero, 6½ c. al sur, Apdo 688, Managua; tel. 268-2222; fax 266-3688; internet www.canal2.com.ni; f. 1965; Pres. OCTAVIO SACASA RASKOSKY; Gen. Man. ALEJANDRO SACASA PASOS.

Televisión Internacional, Canal 23: Casa L-852, Col. Centroamérica, Managua; tel. 268-7466; fax 266-0625; e-mail canal23@ibw.com.ni; f. 1993; Pres. CÉSAR RIGUERO.

Televisora Nicaragüense, SA (Telenica 8): De la Mansión Teodolinda, 1 c. al sur, ½ c. abajo, Bolonia, Apdo 3611, Managua; tel. 266-5021; fax 266-5024; internet www.telenica.com.ni; f. 1989; Pres. CARLOS A. BRICEÑO LOVO.

Ultravisión de Nicaragua, SA: Casa 567, Rotonda los Cocos, Altamira, Managua; tel. 277-3524; Pres. CRISEYDA OLIVAS VEGA.

Finance

(cap. = capital; res = reserves; dep. = deposits; m. = million; amounts in gold córdobas)

BANKING

All Nicaraguan banks were nationalized in July 1979. Foreign banks operating in the country are no longer permitted to secure local deposits. All foreign exchange transactions must be made through the Banco Central or its agencies. Under a decree issued in May 1985, the establishment of private exchange houses was permitted. In 1990 legislation allowing for the establishment of private banks was enacted.

NICARAGUA

Supervisory Authority

Superintendencia de Bancos y de Otras Instituciones Financieras: Edif. SIBOIF, Km 7, Carretera Sur, Apdo 788, Managua; tel. 265-1555; fax 265-0965; e-mail correo@sibiof.gob.ni; internet www.superintendencia.gob.ni; f. 1991; Supt Dr VICTOR M. URCUYO VIDAURRE.

Central Bank

Banco Central de Nicaragua: Carretera Sur, Km 7, Apdos 2252/3, Zona 5, Managua; tel. 255-7171; fax 265-0561; e-mail bcn@bcn.gob.ni; internet www.bcn.gob.ni; f. 1961; bank of issue and govt fiscal agent; cap. and res 293.8m., dep. 40,436.3m. (Dec. 2006); Pres. Dr ANTENOR ROSALES BOLAÑOS; Gen. Man. JOSÉ DE JESÚS ROJAS RODRÍGUEZ.

Private Banks

Banco de América Central (BAC): Km 4½, Carretera a Masaya, Managua; tel. 274-4444; fax 274-4620; e-mail serviciocliente@bac.com.ni; internet www.bancodeamericacentral.com; f. 1991; total assets 10,516m. (1999); Pres. CARLOS PELLAS CHAMORRO; Gen. Man. CARLOS MATUS TAPIA.

Banco de Crédito Centroamericano (BANCENTRO): Edif. BANCENTRO, Km 4½ Carretera a Masaya, Managua; tel. 278-2777; fax 278-6001; e-mail info@bancentro.com.ni; internet www.bancentro.com.ni; f. 1991; total assets 282m. (2005); Pres. ROBERTO J. ZAMORA LLANES; Gen. Man. CARLOS A. BRICEÑO RÍOS.

Banco Uno, SA: Plaza España, Rotonda el Güegüense 20 m al oeste, Managua; tel. 278-7171; fax 277-3154; e-mail info@bancouno.com.ni; internet www.bancouno.com.ni; dep. 2,372m. (Dec. 2002); fmrly Banco de la Exportación (BANEXPO), present name adopted in Nov. 2002; acquired by Citibank in 2007; Dir ADOLFO ARGÜELLO LACAYO.

STOCK EXCHANGE

Bolsa de Valores de Nicaragua: Edif. Oscar Pérez Cassar, Centro BANIC, Km 5½, Carretera Masaya, Apdo 121, Managua; tel. 278-3830; fax 278-3836; e-mail info@bolsanic.com; internet bolsanic.com; f. 1993; Pres. Dr RAÚL LACAYO SOLÓRZANO; Gen. Man. GERARDO ARGÜELLO LEIVA.

INSURANCE

State Company

Instituto Nicaragüense de Seguros y Reaseguros (INISER): Centro Comercial Camino de Oriente, Km 6, Carretera a Masaya, Apdo 1147, Managua; tel. (2) 66-6772; fax (2) 66-5636; e-mail iniser@iniser.com.ni; internet www.iniser.com.ni; f. 1979 to assume the activities of all the pre-revolution national private insurance cos; Exec. Pres. EDUARDO HALLESLEVENS; Vice-Pres GUILLERMO JIMÉNEZ, JUAN JOSÉ UBEDA.

Private Companies

Aseguradora Mundial Nicaragua: Edif. Invercasa, 1°, Managua; tel. 276-8890; fax 278-6358; e-mail lucia.ramirez@amundial.com.ni; internet www.amundial.com.ni; Pres. ORLANDO EDMUNDO SÁNCHEZ AVILÉS; Gen. Man. LUCÍA RAMÍREZ.

Metropolitana Compañía de Seguros, SA: Reparto Serrano Plaza El Sol, 400 m al norte, Managua; tel. 276-9000; fax 276-9002; e-mail metroseg@metroseg.com; internet www.metroseg.com; Pres. Dr LEONEL ARGÜELLO RAMÍREZ; Sec. HORACIO ARGÜELLO CARAZO.

Seguros América, SA: Centro BAC, Km 5½ Carretera a Masaya, Apdo 6114, Managua; tel. 274-4200; fax 274-4202; e-mail sergioulvert@segamerica.com.ni; internet www.segurosamerica.com.ni; f. 1996; Pres. CARLOS F. PELLAS CHAMORRO; Man. SERGIO ULVERT SÁNCHEZ.

Seguros Lafise, SA: Centro Financiero Lafise, Km 5½ Carretera a Masaya, Managua; tel. 270-3505; fax 270-3558; e-mail seguros@seguroslafise.com.ni; internet www.seguroslafise.com.ni; fmrly Seguros Centroamericanos (Segurossa); Pres. ROBERTO ZAMORA LLANES; Gen. Man. CLAUDIO TABOADA RODRÍGUEZ.

Trade and Industry

GOVERNMENT AGENCIES

Empresa Nicaragüense de Alimentos Básicos (ENABAS): Salida a Carretera Norte, Apdo 1041, Managua; tel. 248-1640; e-mail direccion.administrativa@enabas.gob.ni; internet www.enabas.gob.ni; f. 1979; controls trading in basic foodstuffs; Exec. Dir MIGUEL ÁNGEL DÍAZ RODRIGUEZ.

Directory

Instituto de Desarrollo Rural (IDR) (Institute of Rural Development): B3, Camino de Oriente, Apdo 3593, Managua; tel. 255-8777; e-mail divulgacion@idr.gob.ni; internet www.idr.gob.ni; f. 1995; Dir JUANA MARÍA BÜSCHTING.

Instituto Nicaragüense de Apoyo a la Pequeña y Mediana Empresa (INPYME): De la Shell Plaza el Sol, 1 c. al sur, 300 m abajo, Apdo 449, Managua; tel. 278-7836; e-mail bcantillo@inpyme.gob.ni; internet www.inpyme.gob.ni; supports small and medium-sized enterprises; Exec. Dir MARÍA LIDIA ESPINALES.

Instituto Nicaragüense de Tecnología Agropecuaria (INTA): Col. Centroamérica, contiguo al Distrito 5, Managua; tel. 227-2290; fax 278-0373; e-mail bayserfe@inta.gob.ni; internet www.inta.gob.ni; f. 1993; Dir-Gen. Dr BAYARDO SERRANO.

Instituto de la Vivienda Urbana y Rural (INVUR): Managua; tel. 266-9774; e-mail gmartinez@invur.gob.ni; internet www.invur.gob.ni; housing devt; Pres. JUDITH SILVA.

DEVELOPMENT ORGANIZATIONS

Asociación de Productores y Exportadores de Nicaragua (APEN): Del Hotel Intercontinental, 2 c. al sur y 2 c. abajo, Bolonia, Managua; tel. 26-6053; fax 266-5160; internet www.apen.org.ni; Pres. ENRIQUE ZAMORA LLANES.

Cámara de Industrias de Nicaragua: Rotonda el Güegüense, 300 m al sur, Apdo 1436, Managua; tel. 266-8847; fax 266-1891; e-mail cadin@cadin.org.ni; internet www.cadin.org.ni; Pres. MARIO AMADOR RIVAS; Vice-Pres. ALFREDO MARÍN XIMÉNEZ.

Cámara Nacional de la Mediana y Pequeña Industria (CONAPI): Plaza 19 de Julio, Frente a la UCA, Apdo 153, Managua; tel. 278-4892; fax 267-0192; e-mail conapi@nicarao.org.ni; Pres. FLORA VARGAS LOAISIGA; Gen. Man. URIEL ARGEÑAL C.

Cámara Nicaragüense de la Construcción (CNC): Bolonia de Aval Card, 2 c. abajo, 50 varas al sur, Managua; tel. 226-3363; fax 266-3327; e-mail camara@construccion.org.ni; internet www.construccion.org.ni; f. 1961; construction industry; Pres. MARIO ZELAYA BLANDÓN; Vice-Pres. BENJAMIN LANSAS SOMARRIBA.

Instituto Nicaragüense de Fomento Municipal (INIFOM): Edif. Central, Carretera a la Refinería, entrada principal residencial Los Arcos, Apdo 3097, Managua; tel. and fax 266-6050; e-mail eduardo.centeno@infom.gob.ni; internet www.inifom.gob.ni; Pres. EDUARDO CENTENO GADEA.

CHAMBERS OF COMMERCE

Cámara de Comercio de Nicaragua (CACONIC): Rotonda El Güegüense 400 m al sur, 20 m al oeste, Managua; tel. 268-3505; fax 268-3600; e-mail comercio@caconic.org.ni; internet www.caconic.org.ni; f. 1892; 530 mems; Pres. ERNESTO PORTA BALLADERES; Exec. Dir EDUARDO FONSECA.

Cámara de Comercio Americana de Nicaragua: Semáforos ENEL Central, 500 m al sur, Apdo 2720, Managua; tel. 267-3099; fax 267-3098; e-mail amcham@ns.tmx.com.ni; internet www.amchamni.org; f. 1974; Pres. ROGER ARTEAGA CANO.

Cámara Oficial Española de Comercio de Nicaragua: Restaurante la Marseilleisa, ½ c. arriba, Los Robles, Apdo 4103, Managua; tel. 278-9047; fax 278-9088; e-mail camacoesnic@cablenet.com.ni; internet www.camacoesnic.com.ni; Pres. JOSÉ DE LA JARA AHLERS; Sec.-Gen. MARÍA AUXILIADORA MIRANDA DE GUERRERO.

EMPLOYERS' ORGANIZATIONS

Asociación de Café Especiales de Nicaragua (ACEN): Managua; tel. 254-7549; fax 254-2486; internet www.acen.org.ni; coffee producers and exporters; Pres. JOSÉ BARCENAS LEVI; Sec. JUAN CARLOS MUNGUIA.

Consejo Superior de la Empresa Privada (COSEP): De Telcor Zacarías Guerra, 1 c. abajo, Apdo 5430, Managua; tel. 276-3333; fax 276-1666; e-mail cosep@cablenet.com.ni; internet www.cosep.org.ni; f. 1972; private businesses; consists of Cámara de Industrias de Nicaragua (CADIN), Unión de Productores Agropecuarios de Nicaragua (UPANIC), Cámara de Comercio, Cámara de la Construcción, Confederación Nacional de Profesionales (CONAPRO), Instituto Nicaragüense de Desarrollo (INDE); mem. of Coordinadora Democrática Nicaragüense; Pres. Dr JOSÉ ADÁN AGUERRI; Sec. Dr ORESTES ROMERO ROJAS.

Instituto Nicaragüense de Desarrollo (INDE): Col. Los Robles, del Hotel Colón 1 c. al sur, Managua; tel. 270-8258; fax 270-9866; e-mail inde@inde.org.ni; internet www.inde.org.ni; f. 1963; private business org.; 650 mems; Pres. ALONSO CHAMORRO ARGEÑAL.

Unión Nacional de Agricultores y Ganaderos (UNAG): Managua; tel. 266-2135; e-mail afo@unag.org.ni; internet www.unag.org.ni; f. 1981; Pres. ALVARO FIALLOS OYANGUREN.

Unión de Productores Agropecuarios de Nicaragua (UPANIC): Reparto San Juan No 300, detrás del Gimnasio Hércules, Managua; tel. 251-0340; fax 251-0307; e-mail upanic@ibw.com.ni;

NICARAGUA

internet www.upanic.org.ni; private agriculturalists' asscn; Pres. Manuel Alvarez Solórzano.

UTILITIES
Regulatory Bodies

Comisión Nacional de Energía: Del Hospital Bautista 1 c. abajo, 120 varas al lago, Apdo CJ-159, Managua; tel. 222-5576; Exec. Pres. Ernesto Espinoza Maradiaga.

Instituto Nicaragüense de Acueductos y Alcantarillados (INAA): De la Mansión Teodolinda, 3 c. al sur, Bolonia, Apdo 1084, Managua; tel. 266-7882; fax 266-7917; e-mail inaa@inaa.gob.ni; internet www.inaa.gob.ni; f. 1979; water regulator; Exec. Pres. Carlos Schutze Sugrañes.

Instituto Nicaragüense de Energía (INE): Edif. Petronic, 4°, Managua; tel. 222-4864; fax 228-3104; e-mail jhernandez@ine.gob.ni; internet www.ine.gob.ni; Pres. José David Castillo Sánchez.

Electricity

Empresa Nicaragüense de Electricidad (ENEL): Ofs Centrales, Pista Juan Pablo II y Avda Bolívar, Managua; tel. 277-4160; fax 267-2683; e-mail relapub@ibw.com.ni; internet www.enel.gob.ni; responsible for planning, organization, management, administration, research and development of energy resources; split into a transmission co, 2 distribution businesses and 4 generation cos in 1999; Pres. Emilio Rappaccioli Baltodano.

Empresa Nacional de Transmisión Eléctrica, SA (ENATREL): Intersección Bolívar y Pista Juan Pablo II, Managua; tel. 277-4159; fax 267-4379; internet www.enatrel.gob.ni; operates the electricity transmission network; Exec. Pres. Salvador Mansell Castrillo; Pres. Emilio Rappaccioli Baltodano.

GECSA: electricity generation co; 79 MW capacity thermal plant; almost obsolete and therefore difficult to privatize, GECSA was likely to be retained for emergency purposes.

GEOSA: electricity generation co; 112 MW capacity thermal plant; sold to Coastal Power International (USA) in Jan. 2002.

HIDROGESA: electricity generation co; 94 MW capacity hydroelectric plant; privatized in 2002; however, sale annulled in July 2003 owing to alleged irregularities.

ORMAT Momotombo Power Co: Momotombo; internet www.ormat.com; f. 1999 on acquisition of 15-year concession to rehabilitate and operate Momotombo power plant; subsidiary of ORMAT International, Inc; CEO Lucien Y. Bronicki; 30 MW capacity geothermal plant.

Unión Fenosa DISSUR y DISNORTE: Managua; e-mail accionistasuf@ni.unionfenosa.com; internet www.disnorte-dissur.com.ni; electricity distribution co; privatized in 2000; distributes some 1460 GWh (DISSUR 658 GWh, DISNORTE 802 GWh); Dir Danilo Lacayo Rappaccioli.

Water

Empresa Nicaragüense de Acueductos y Alcantarillados Sanitarios (ENACAL): 5 Km Carretera Sur 505, Asososca; tel. 266-7875; e-mail ccomunicacion@enacal.com.ni; internet www.enacal.com.ni; Exec. Pres. Ruth Herrera Montoya.

TRADE UNIONS

Asociación Nacional de Educadores de Nicaragua (ANDEN): Managua; e-mail anden@guegue.com.ni; Sec.-Gen. José Antonio Zepeda; 19 affiliates, 15,000 mems.

Asociación de Trabajadores del Campo (ATC) (Association of Rural Workers): Apdo A-244, Managua; tel. 278-4576; fax 278-4575; e-mail atcnic@ibw.com.ni; internet www.movimientos.org/cloc/atc-ni; f. 1977; Gen. Sec. Edgardo García; 52,000 mems.

Central Sandinista de Trabajadores (CST): Iglesia del Carmen, 1 c. al oeste, ½ c. al sur, Managua; tel. 265-1096; fax 240-1285; Sec.-Gen. Roberto González Gaitán; 40,000 mems.

Central de Trabajadores de Nicaragua (CTN) (Nicaraguan Workers' Congress): De la Iglesia del Carmen, 1 c. al sur, ½ c. arriba y 75 varas al sur, Managua; tel. 268-3061; fax 265-2056; f. 1962; mem. of Coordinadora Democrática Nicaragüense; Sec.-Gen. Carlos Humbes.

Confederación de Acción y Unidad Sindical (CAUS) (Confederation for Trade Union Action and Unity): Semáforos de Rubenia, 2 c. abajo y 2 c. al lago, Barrio Venezuela, Managua; tel. and fax 244-2587; f. 1973; trade-union wing of Partido Comunista de Nicaragua; Sec.-Gen. Emilio Márquez.

Confederación General de Trabajadores Independientes (CGT(I)) (Independent General Confederation of Labour): Centro Comercial Nejapa, 1 c. arriba y 3 c. al lago, Managua; tel. 222-5195; fax 228-7505; f. 1953; Sec.-Gen. Nilo M. Salazar Aguilar; 4,843 mems (est.) from six federations with 40 local unions, and six non-federated local unions.

Confederación de Unificación Sindical (CUS) (Confederation of United Trade Unions): Casa Q3, del Colegio la Tenderi 2½ c. arriba, Ciudad Jardín, Managua; tel. 248-3681; fax 240-1330; f. 1972; affiliated to the Inter-American Regional Organization of Workers, etc.; mem. of Coordinadora Democrática Nicaragüense; Sec.-Gen. José Espinoza.

Enrique Schmidt Cuadra Federation (FESC): Managua; e-mail fschmidt@tmx.com.ni; communications and postal workers' union.

Federación de Trabajadores Nicaragüenses (FTN): workers' federation; Leader Domingo Pérez.

Federación de Trabajadores de la Salud (FETSALUD) (Federation of Health Workers): Optica Nicaragüense, 2 c. arriba ½ c. al sur, Apdo 1402, Managua; tel. and fax 266-3065; e-mail fntsid@ibw.com.ni; Sec.-Gen. Isidro Iglesias; 25,000 mems.

Federación de Transportadores de Carga de Nicaragua (FETRACANIC) (Cargo Transport Workers' Federation of Nicaragua): Avda del Ejército del Arbolito, 2½ c. al sur, Casa 410, Managua; tel. 266-5255; fax 254-7381; Pres. José Francisco Guerra Cabrera.

Frente Nacional de los Trabajadores (FNT) (National Workers' Front): Residencial Bolonia, de la Optica Nicaragüense, 2 c. arriba, 30 varas al sur, Managua; tel. and fax 266-3065; e-mail prensa@fnt.org.ni; internet www.fnt.org.ni; f. 1979; affiliated to Frente Sandinista de Liberación Nacional; Leader Dr Gustavo Porras Cortés.

Unión Nacional de Caficultores de Nicaragua (UNCAFENIC) (National Union of Coffee Growers of Nicaragua): Reparto San Juan, Casa 300, Apdo 3447, Managua; tel. 278-3382; fax 772-3330; Pres. Freddy Torres.

Unión Nacional de Empleados (UNE): Managua; e-mail cocentrafemenino@xerox.com.ni; f. 1978; public sector workers' union; Sec.-Gen. Domingo Pérez; 18,000 mems.

Transport

RAILWAYS

There are no functioning railways. The state-owned rail operator, Ferrocarril de Nicaragua, which formerly operated a network of 287 km, ceased operations in 1994, and the only remaining private line closed in 2001.

ROADS

In 2004 there were an estimated 18,669 km of roads, of which 5,117 km were highways and 6,123 km were secondary roads. Of the total, only some 9,000–10,000 km were accessible throughout the entire year. Some 8,000 km of roads were damaged by 'Hurricane Mitch', which struck in late 1998. The Pan-American Highway runs for 384 km in Nicaragua and links Managua with the Honduran and Costa Rican frontiers and the Atlantic and Pacific Highways, connecting Managua with the coastal regions.

SHIPPING

Corinto, Puerto Sandino and San Juan del Sur, on the Pacific, and Puerto Cabezas, El Bluff and El Rama, on the Caribbean, are the principal ports. Corinto deals with about 60% of trade. In 2001 the US-based company Delasa was given a 25-year concession to develop and modernize Puerto Cabezas port. It was to invest some US $200m.

Empresa Portuaria Nacional (EPN): Residencial Bolonia, de la Optica Nicaragüense ½ c. al norte, 1 c. al oeste, Managua; tel. 266-3039; fax 266-3488; e-mail epn_puertos@epn.com.ni; internet www.epn.com.ni; Pres. Virgilio Silva Mungüia.

CIVIL AVIATION

The principal airport is the Augusto Sandino International Airport, in Managua. There are some 185 additional airports in Nicaragua.

Empresa Administradora de Aeropuertos Internacionales (EAAI): POB 5179, 11 Km Carretera Norte, Managua; tel. 233-1624; fax 263-1072; e-mail czamora@eaai.com.ni; internet www.eaai.com.ni; autonomous govt entity; operates Managua International Airport and three national airports: Bluefields, Puerto Cabezas and Corn Island; Pres. Danilo Lacayo Rappaccioli; Gen. Man. Orlando Castillo Guerrero.

La Costeña: Managua International Airport, Managua; tel. 263-2142; fax 263-1281; e-mail info@lacostena.com.ni; internet www.lacostena.com.ni; Gen. Man. Alfredo Caballero.

Tourism

In 2006 tourist arrivals totalled 773,398, while receipts from tourism totalled US $237m.

Instituto Nicaragüense de Turismo (INTUR): Del Hotel Crowne Plaza, 1 c. al sur, 1 c. al oeste, Apdo 5088, Managua; tel. 254-5191; fax 222-6610; e-mail promocion@intur.gob.ni; internet www.intur.gob.ni; f. 1998; Pres. María Nelly Rivas Blanco; Sec.-Gen. Ian Coronel.

Asociación Nicaragüense de Agencias de Viajes y Turismo (ANAVYT): Edif. Policlínica Nicaragüense, Reparto Bolonia, Apdo 1045, Managua; tel. 266-9742; fax 266-4474; e-mail aeromund@cablenet.com.ni; f. 1966; Pres. Ana María Rocha C.

Cámara Nacional de Turismo (CANATUR): Contiguo al Ministerio de Turismo, Apdo 2105, Managua; tel. 278-9971; e-mail direccion@canaturnicaragua.org; internet www.canaturnicaragua.org; f. 1976; Exec. Dir Grethel Collins.

NIGER

Introductory Survey

Location, Climate, Language, Religion, Flag, Capital

The Republic of Niger is a land-locked country in western Africa, with Algeria and Libya to the north, Nigeria and Benin to the south, Mali and Burkina Faso to the west, and Chad to the east. The climate is hot and dry, with an average temperature of 29°C (84°F). The official language is French, but numerous indigenous languages, including Hausa (spoken by about one-half of the population), Tuareg, Djerma and Fulani, are also used (the 1991 sovereign National Conference identified 10 'national' languages). Some 95% of the population are Muslims, the most influential Islamic groups being the Tijaniyya, the Senoussi and the Hamallists. Most of the remainder of the population follow traditional beliefs, and there is a small Christian minority. The national flag (proportions 6 by 7) has three equal horizontal stripes, of orange, white and green, with an orange disc in the centre of the white stripe. The capital is Niamey.

Recent History

Formerly a part of French West Africa, Niger became a self-governing member of the French Community in December 1958 and was granted independence on 3 August 1960. Hamani Diori, leader of the Parti progressiste nigérien (the local section of the Ivorian-dominated Rassemblement démocratique africain) and Prime Minister since December 1958, became Head of State. Diori was elected President in November 1960, and re-elected in 1965 and 1970. Close links were maintained with France.

The Sahelian drought of 1968–74 was particularly damaging to the Nigerien economy and was a major factor in precipitating a military coup in April 1974. Diori was arrested, and Lt-Col (later Maj.-Gen.) Seyni Kountché, the armed forces Chief of Staff, became President. The new administration, headed by a Conseil militaire suprême (CMS), suspended the Constitution; the legislature was replaced by a consultative Conseil national de développement (CND), and political activity was banned. Kountché obtained the withdrawal of French troops and reduced French influence over the exploitation of Niger's deposits of uranium (which France had initiated in 1968).

From 1977 the proportion of army officers in the Government was progressively reduced. Senior members of Diori's administration and other political prisoners were released in 1978, and in 1980 Diori was released from prison, although he was kept under house arrest. In January 1983 a civilian, Oumarou Mamane, was appointed to the newly created post of Prime Minister. In November Mamane, who in August had been appointed President of the CND, was replaced as premier by Hamid Algabid.

A draft 'national charter' was approved by a reported 99.6% of voters in a referendum in June 1987. In November Kountché died while undergoing medical treatment in France, and Col (later Brig.) Ali Saïbou, the army Chief of Staff, was inaugurated as Chairman of the CMS and Head of State. In July 1988 Mamane (who had been replaced as President of the CND in September 1987) was reinstated as Prime Minister, and the CND was given the task of drafting a new constitution. In August 1988 Brig. Saïbou formed a new ruling party, the Mouvement national pour la société de développement (MNSD).

In May 1989 an MNSD congress elected a Conseil supérieur d'orientation nationale (CSON) to succeed the CMS. The draft Constitution was endorsed by a reported 99.3% of voters in a referendum in September. At elections in December Saïbou (as President of the CSON and the sole candidate) was confirmed as President of the Republic, for a seven-year term, by 99.6% of those who voted, while 99.5% of voters endorsed a single list of CSON-approved deputies to a new, 93-member Assemblée nationale. In March 1990 a prominent industrialist, Aliou Mahamidou, was appointed Prime Minister in an extensive government reorganization. In November Saïbou announced that a multi-party political system would be established. A national conference on political reform was to be convened in mid-1991, and multi-party national elections would take place in 1992.

In March 1991 the armed forces Chief of Staff announced that the armed forces were to distance themselves from the MNSD—Nassara (as the MNSD had been restyled) with immediate effect. In July Saïbou resigned as Chairman of the MNSD—Nassara, in preparation for the National Conference, which was convened in Niamey later that month and attended by about 1,200 delegates, including representatives of the organs of state, 24 political organizations, the military and civil society. It declared itself sovereign, voting to suspend the Constitution and dissolve the legislature. Saïbou would remain in office as Head of State on an interim basis, but the Conference would supervise the exercise of his (now largely ceremonial) powers. The Government was dissolved in September, and in October the Conference appointed Cheiffou Amadou to head a transitional Council of Ministers, which was intended to hold office until the inauguration of democratically elected institutions, now scheduled for early 1993. Prior to the conclusion of the Conference, in November 1991, its President, André Salifou, was designated Chairman of a 15-member interim legislative body, the Haut conseil de la République (HCR), which was, *inter alia*, to supervise the drafting of a new constitution.

The new Constitution was approved by 89.8% of those who voted in a referendum held on 26 December 1992. The MNSD—Nassara won the greatest number of seats (29) at elections to the 83-member Assemblée nationale, held on 14 February 1993 and contested by 12 political parties, but was prevented from resuming power by the rapid formation, following the elections, of the Alliance des forces de changement (AFC) by six parties with a total of 50 seats in the legislature. Principal members of the AFC were the Convention démocratique et sociale—Rahama (CDS), the Parti nigérien pour la démocratie et le socialisme—Tarayya (PNDS), and the Alliance nigérienne pour la démocratie et le progrès social—Zaman Lahiya (ANDP). At the first round of the presidential election, held on 27 February and contested by eight candidates, Col (retd) Mamadou Tandja, Saïbou's successor as leader of the MNSD—Nassara, won the greatest proportion of votes cast (34.2%). He and his nearest rival, Mahamane Ousmane (the leader of the CDS, with 26.6%), proceeded to a second round on 27 March, at which Ousmane was elected President by 55.4% of voters; his inauguration took place on 16 April. Ousmane appointed Mahamadou Issoufou of the PNDS as Prime Minister. Despite an attempt by the MNSD—Nassara to block the appointment, in May Moumouni Adamou Djermakoye of the ANDP became President of the Assemblée nationale.

The new regime's efforts to curb public expenditure, combined with the effects of the 50% devaluation of the CFA franc in January 1994, provoked considerable disquiet among workers and students. In September the PNDS withdrew from the AFC, and Issoufou resigned the premiership, in protest at the perceived transfer of certain prime ministerial powers to the President. A new minority Government, led by Souley Abdoulaye of the CDS, failed to withstand a parliamentary motion of 'no confidence' proposed by the MNSD—Nassara and the PNDS in October. Ousmane therefore dissolved the Assemblée nationale.

At legislative elections held in mid-January 1995 the MNSD—Nassara won 29 seats and subsequently led a 43-strong majority group in the Assemblée nationale. Although the CDS increased its representation to 24 seats, the AFC secured only 40 seats. Ousmane declined to accept the new majority's nominee to the premiership, Hama Amadou (the Secretary-General of the MNSD—Nassara), instead appointing another member of that party, Amadou Aboubacar Cissé, a former official of the World Bank. The MNSD—Nassara and its allies announced that they would not co-operate with his administration, and Cissé was expelled from the party. Meanwhile, Issoufou was elected President of the Assemblée nationale. In February the legislature approved a motion of censure against Cissé, and Ousmane accepted the nomination of Amadou as Prime Minister. This political 'cohabitation' encountered serious difficulties, as the President and Prime Minister disputed their respective competencies, in particular with regard to a proposed programme for the reorganization and privatization of state enterprises, which Ousmane opposed. Following several months of industrial unrest, Ousmane's rejection of the Government's draft budget, in January 1996, resulted in a new impasse in relations.

On 27 January 1996 the elected organs of state were overthrown by the military. The coup leaders, who formed a Conseil de salut national (CSN), chaired by Col (later Brig.-Gen.) Ibrahim Baré Maïnassara, armed forces Chief of Staff since March 1995 and a former aide-de-camp to Kountché, asserted that their seizure of power had been necessitated by Niger's descent into political chaos. The CSN annulled the Constitution and dissolved the Assemblée nationale, while political parties were suspended. A national forum was to be convened to consider the revision of the Constitution and the electoral code, and to determine a timetable for a return to civilian rule. The CSN appointed Boukary Adji, the Deputy Governor of the Banque centrale des états de l'Afrique de l'ouest as Prime Minister. Adji's transitional Government, named in February 1996, was composed entirely of civilians although military officers were appointed to regional governorships.

Two consultative bodies were established to prepare for the restoration of civilian government, the advisory Conseil des sages and the co-ordinating committee of the national forum. The National Forum for Democratic Renewal, which was convened in April 1996, adopted revisions to the Constitution that aimed to guarantee greater institutional stability, essentially by conferring executive power solely on the President. In April Ousmane, Amadou and Issoufou accompanied Maïnassara to northern Niger to celebrate National Concord Day, on the first anniversary of the signing of the peace agreement with the Tuareg movement (see below).

The revised Constitution was approved by some 92.3% of the votes cast at a referendum on 12 May 1996 (about 35% of the electorate participated). The ban on political activity was lifted shortly afterwards. Voting in the presidential election commenced, as scheduled, on 7 July 1996, but was quickly halted in several areas where preparations were incomplete: polling took place in these areas on 8 July. Shortly before the end of voting the authorities announced the dissolution of the Commission électorale nationale indépendante (CENI), citing its alleged obstruction of the electoral process. A new commission was appointed to collate the election results and, according to provisional results announced by that body, Maïnassara won the election, with some 52.2% of the votes cast; Ousmane secured 19.8% and Tandja 15.7%. The Supreme Court validated the election results on 21 July and Maïnassara was installed as President on 7 August. A new Government, with Adji as Prime Minister, also included Abdoulaye and Cissé. Members of the CDS, the MNSD—Nassara and the PNDS who had accepted government posts were subsequently expelled from these parties.

In August 1996 the legislative elections, which had been scheduled for September, were postponed until 10 November. The Conseil des sages recommended a further delay, pending the resolution of difficulties, including the threatened boycott by the main opposition parties, now grouped in a Front pour la restauration et la défense de la démocratie (FRDD). The Government agreed to permit opposition access to the state media and to rescind the ban (in force since the presidential election) on public meetings and demonstrations, and in October announced the further postponement of the legislative elections, to 23 November, and the restoration of the CENI, with the same composition as that which had overseen the 1995 election. The commission's prerogatives were, however, amended, and the FRDD responded that it would not participate in the forthcoming poll unless the CENI was reinstated with its original powers and the presidential election annulled.

The legislative elections proceeded on 23 November 1996, contested by 11 parties and movements. According to official results, the pro-Maïnassara Union nationale des indépendants pour le renouveau démocratique (UNIRD) won 52 of the Assemblée nationale's 83 seats. International observers pronounced themselves satisfied with the organization and conduct of the election. (The Supreme Court later annulled the results in three constituencies won by the UNIRD, on the grounds of fraud.) A new Government was formed, with Cissé as Prime Minister.

In January 1997 an unauthorized opposition demonstration in Niamey degenerated into clashes with the security forces. Some 62 people were arrested, among them Ousmane, Tandja and Issoufou, who were to be tried by the recently restored State Security Court. In response to opposition claims that neither the Constitution nor the penal code made provision for the Court (which had been in existence under the Kountché regime), the Government cited constitutional provisions that ensured the continued validity of laws in force at the time of the promulgation of the Constitution, unless specifically repealed. Nine days later, following clashes in Zinder and a further protest in Niamey, the opposition leaders were released, reportedly on Maïnassara's direct order. The FRDD rejected an invitation by the President to participate in a government of national unity, demanding the dissolution of the Assemblée nationale and the holding of free and fair elections.

In November 1997 Maïnassara dismissed the entire Government and subsequently appointed Ibrahim Hassane Maiyaki, hitherto Minister of Foreign Affairs and Co-operation, as Prime Minister.

In February 1998 three parties of the presidential group, including the ANDP, formed the Alliance des forces démocratiques et sociales (AFDS). However, the AFDS subsequently protested against its perceived marginalization in the political process and in the state media, observing that the alliance was increasingly associated with the opposition. Clashes in Tahoua in April between the security forces and FRDD activists, who were demanding Maïnassara's resignation, were followed by violent protests by the FRDD in Maradi and in Zinder. In July the Government and the FRDD and the AFDS signed an agreement that was intended to facilitate opposition participation in the local elections. Revisions to electoral procedures and institutions were outlined, while the equal access of all political groups to the state media and the freedom to demonstrate were to be guaranteed. However, following a dispute over the President of the CENI, in October the CENI postponed voting until February 1999. Elections took place on 7 February, but due to overt irregularities the CENI recommended that by-elections be held in affected areas; voting was to be rerun at some 4,000 polling stations nation-wide.

On 9 April 1999 Maiyaki made a broadcast to the nation, announcing the death of Maïnassara in an 'unfortunate accident' at a military airbase in Niamey. The Prime Minister stated that the defence and security forces would continue to be the guarantors of republican order and national unity, and announced the dissolution of the Assemblée nationale, as well as the temporary suspension of all party political activity. Despite the official explanation for his death, it was generally perceived that members of the presidential guard had assassinated Maïnassara in a *coup d'état*. Although members of the Assemblée nationale initially rejected its dissolution, on 11 April the Constitution was suspended and its institutions dissolved. The February local elections were annulled. A military Conseil de réconciliation nationale (CRN), under the chairmanship of Maj. Daouda Mallam Wanké (hitherto head of the presidential guard), was to exercise executive and legislative authority during a nine-month transitional period, prior to the restoration of elected civilian institutions. Wanké immediately signed an ordinance on interim political authority, which was to function as a constitutional document during the transitional period. Maiyaki was reappointed as Prime Minister of the transitional Government on 12 April; a new Council of Ministers was named shortly afterwards. Moussa Moumouni Djermakoye, who had been succeeded as armed forces Chief of Staff by Lt-Col Soumara Zanguina, became Minister of National Defence. In July, in a minor reshuffle, the Minister of the Interior and Territorial Administration, Lt-Col Moumouni Boureima, was appointed armed forces Chief of Staff, while Zanguina became an adviser to the Head of State.

The new draft Constitution was submitted to referendum on 18 July 1999, when it was approved by 89.6% of those who voted (about one-third of the registered electorate). The Constitution envisaged a balance of powers between the President, the Government and the legislature, but, none the less, vested strong powers in the Head of State, who was to be politically liable only in the case of high treason. The Government, under a Prime Minister appointed by the President, was to be responsible to the Assemblée nationale, which would be competent to remove the Prime Minister by vote of censure. A clause in the Constitution guaranteeing all those involved in the military take-overs of 1996 and 1999 immunity from prosecution provoked controversy and was condemned by Amnesty International, in a report in September, as undermining the rule of law. The report was regarded as particularly significant in that it published the testimony of a witness who alleged that Maïnassara had been killed by the presidential guard under Wanké's command. The Wanké regime continued to assert that Maïnassara's death had been accidental, and that a commission of inquiry into the death had been ordered in response to a complaint lodged by the late President's family.

Voting at the presidential election, which was contested by seven candidates, took place on 17 October 1999, and was considered both by the CENI and by independent observers to have been largely transparent and peaceful. Mamadou Tandja, of the MNSD—Nassara, won 32.3% of the votes cast, followed by Issoufou, of the PNDS, with 22.8%, and Ousmane, of the CDS, with 22.5%. The rate of participation by voters was 43.7%. Tandja and Issoufou proceeded to a second round on 24 November. Having secured the support of Ousmane, Tandja was elected President, with 59.9% of the votes cast. About 39% of the registered electorate voted. The MNSD—Nassara was similarly successful in the concurrent elections to the Assemblée nationale, winning 38 of the 83 seats; the CDS took 17, the PNDS 16, the pro-Maïnassara Rassemblement pour la démocratie et le progrès—Djamaa (RDP) eight and the ANDP four. Tandja, who had served in the CMS under Kountché and was Minister of the Interior in the early 1990s, was inaugurated as President on 22 December. Hama Amadou was subsequently appointed Prime Minister, and a new Council of Ministers was named in January 2000.

In January 2000 the Assemblée nationale adopted draft amnesty legislation, as provided for in the Constitution. The amnesty was opposed by the RDP, and many activists of the party joined a demonstration in February to denounce the legislation and to demand an international inquiry into the death of Maïnassara. In March 12 opposition parties, led by the PNDS, formed a coalition, the Coordination des forces démocratiques (CFD). Similarly, 17 parties loyal to the President, most notably the MNSD—Nassara and the CDS, formed the Alliance des forces démocratiques (AFD). In May Col Bourahima Moumouni was appointed armed forces Chief of Staff. None the less, rumours persisted of dissent within the army. In July the ANDP withdrew from the opposition CFD alliance and joined the AFD, thereby increasing the Government's parliamentary majority by four seats. Explaining his party's shift in allegiances, the leader of the ANDP, Moumouni Adamou Djermakoye, accused the CFD of intolerance and of failing to ease social tensions.

In late July 2002 a mutiny broke out at a barracks in Diffa. The mutineers arrested several officers, the mayor of Diffa and the regional governor, and took control of a radio station to broadcast their demands for improved pay and conditions, including the payment of wage arrears. The Government declared a state of emergency in Diffa and dispatched troops to bring the rebellion, which continued for 10 days, to a halt. A further uprising, at a barracks to the east of Diffa, was also rapidly quashed. In early August, meanwhile, a military uprising broke out in Niamey, although government forces quickly restored order in the capital. By mid-September special security measures in the Diffa region had been relaxed. Amadou claimed that the rebellion in Diffa had been intended to serve as a distraction, while a *coup d'état* was being prepared in Niamey.

Tandja implemented a major government reorganization in November 2002, as a result of which the position of allies of Prime Minister Amadou was reportedly strengthened. At the end of December the Assemblée nationale approved legislation providing for the creation of a special military tribunal to try those accused of involvement in the rebellion earlier in the year (a total of 268 arrests were reported); elements within the opposition alleged that the legislation violated several articles of the Constitution. However, many soldiers were reportedly released during 2003, owing to a lack of evidence, and the three highest-ranking officers arrested were provisionally freed in February 2004. (Six of the mutineers were awarded custodial sentences at a military tribunal in early 2006.)

In mid-October 2003 the Council of Ministers announced proposals to increase the number of deputies in the Assemblée nationale from 83 to 113, in order to reflect the growth in the population recorded between the national censuses of 1988 and 2001. A minor government reshuffle was effected later in October 2003. Also in that month the Council of Ministers approved the abolition of the State Security Court.

In mid-February 2004 Rhissa Ag Boula, a former Tuareg rebel leader (see below), was dismissed as Minister of Tourism and Crafts, following allegations that he was implicated in the murder of an MNSD—Nassara activist earlier in the year; he was subsequently arrested and charged with complicity in the murder. Meanwhile, another former Tuareg rebel leader, Mohamed Anako, was appointed as Minister-delegate at the Ministry of the Economy and Finance, responsible for the Taxation of Local Communities and the Informal Sector.

In the first round of the presidential election, held on 16 November 2004, Tandja won 40.67% of votes cast, followed by Issoufou, who received 24.60% and both, therefore, proceeded to a second round of voting, while the four eliminated candidates (representing the CDS, the newly formed Rassemblement social-démocratique—Gaskiya, the ANDP and the RDP) all urged their supporters to transfer their allegiance to Tandja. In the second round of voting, held on 4 December, Tandja was victorious, receiving 65.53% of votes cast. (Turn-out in the first round was reported to be 48.5% of registered voters, declining slightly, to 45.0%, in the second round.) At elections to the newly enlarged 113-seat Assemblée nationale, held concurrently with the second round of voting in the presidential election, the MNSD—Nassara won the largest number of seats, obtaining 47, while allied pro-presidential parties secured a further 41 seats. An opposition coalition formed around the PNDS, which also comprised the Parti nigérien pour l'autogestion (PNA), the Parti progressiste nigérien pour le rassemblement démocratique africain (PPN-RDA), the Union pour la démocratie et la République (UDR) and the Union nigérienne des indépendants (UNI), won a total of 25 seats. Ousmane was subsequently re-elected as President of the Assemblée nationale, 13 seats in which, in accordance with legislation adopted in 2001, were reserved for women. Later in December President Tandja announced the formation of a new Government, in which Amadou remained as Prime Minister.

In mid-March 2005 up to 20,000 people were reported to have participated in demonstrations in Niamey against the recent introduction of a 19% value-added tax on basic commodities. The demonstration was organized by an alliance of some 30 groups, including trade unions, human rights organizations and consumer movements known as the Coalition contre la vie chère (CCVC). In the following week, after the Government refused to authorize a second protest march, the CCVC staged a one-day strike, which halted most activity in the capital. The authorities subsequently agreed to hold talks with the CCVC, although they emphasized that the tax would not be withdrawn. However, before the proposed meeting, five leaders of the Coalition were arrested and accused of establishing an unauthorized association and plotting against state security. The radio station Alternative FM, which had broadcast interviews with prominent supporters of the CCVC, was also closed by police, prompting protests from international press freedom groups. (The director of the station, Moussa Tchangari, was among those arrested.) During a further one-day strike, held a few days later, protesters erected barricades and burned tyres in Maradi and Tahoua, leading to more arrests. A third strike was suspended by the Coalition in early April in the hope that a compromise could be reached with the Government. The five leaders of the CCVC were subsequently released and, following negotiations between the Government and the leadership of the CCVC, agreement was reached on numerous concessions; notably flour and milk were to be exempted from the tax, and special arrangements were to be made to limit the effect of the tax on the cost of water and electricity.

None the less, public discontent with the Government arose again in mid-2005 over severe food shortages, which had largely resulted from a poor harvest in 2004, when low rainfall had been combined with an invasion of locusts. According to the Ministry of Agricultural Development, there was a shortfall of more than 223,000 metric tons of grain, representing the country's largest deficit for more than 20 years. In early June up to 2,000 people marched through Niamey in protest at the Government's failure to respond adequately to the crisis and in support of opposition-backed demands for the distribution of free food. The Government, which had been supplying cereals at subsidized prices in the most stricken areas, appealed for international assistance (the response to a UN appeal for Niger, launched in late 2004, had been extremely limited), but insisted that it did not have the resources to distribute free food and instead announced plans to 'loan' grain to farmers most at risk until they could reimburse the Government after the harvest later in the year. As people reportedly began fleeing to Nigeria, government ministers and officials contributed financially to efforts to alleviate the crisis. In mid-July the UN World Food Programme appealed for further international aid for Niger.

In June 2006 it was revealed that some 1,118,000m. francs CFA were missing from government accounts and two cabinet ministers suspected of the embezzlement of European Union (EU, see p. 255) funds targeted at the education sector were dismissed: Hamani Harouna, the Minister of Basic Education and Literacy, was replaced by Dr Ousmane Samba Mamadou, while Mahamane Kabaou assumed responsibility for the public health portfolio in place of Ari Ibrahim. In September more than 30 people were arrested on suspicion of fraud and corruption involving education sector funding, and in October Harouna was charged with corruption and the misappropriation of funds.

President Tandja effected a major government reorganization in March 2007, in which the number of ministers was increased from 26 to 31. Although the key portfolios remained largely unchanged, both the Minister for Agricultural Development, Labo Moussa, and the Minister for Secondary and Higher Education, Research and Technology, Ousmane Galadima, were removed from office. Two new ministerial posts were created, to assume responsibility for education and anti-desertification, and for relations with institutions of the Republic. In May the Government was dissolved following a vote of 'no confidence' in the Assemblée nationale, supported by 62 of the 113 deputies. The administration denied any involvement in corruption and the embezzlement of public funds. The following month President Tandja named Seyni Oumarou as Prime Minister, an appointment which drew considerable criticism from opposition members. Oumarou was nevertheless sworn in and he later announced a new Council of Ministers in which many key portfolios remained unchanged, although Jidda Hamadou assumed the national defence portfolio while Dagra Mahamadou was appointed Minister of Justice, Attorney-General.

In December 2007 two French journalists working for the Franco-German broadcasting network Arte Television were arrested near Niamey for an alleged breach of national security. The two men had officially entered Niger to investigate avian influenza, although the authorities claimed that they were illegally reporting on Tuareg rebels; they were released in January 2008. The arrests followed the expulsion from Niger of a French documentary film-maker, François Bergeron, in September 2007, after he was accused of having links with the Mouvement des Nigeriens pour la justice (MNJ—see below). Two Nigerien journalists had also been arrested and imprisoned in late 2007: Ibrahim Manzo Diallo was released in February 2008 but Moussa Kaka was held until October that year. In a further crackdown on the media in April the private radio station Sahara FM was closed down by the media regulatory authority, after it had broadcast testimonies from victims of attacks by the Nigerien military. In January the director of an independent radio station had been killed when a land mine exploded under his car in Niamey, although it was not clear who was responsible.

Despite being considered a potential candidate to succeed Tandja as President, former Prime Minister Hama Amadou was arrested and charged with corruption in June 2008. Around 100 people protested outside the High Court of Justice in response to his arrest and were dispersed by police, who fired tear gas into the crowd; in October several thousand demonstrators took to the streets of Niamey to call for his release. Amadou denied the charges against him, claiming that they were part of a campaign to prevent him running in the presidential elections, scheduled for December 2009. Meanwhile, in August 2008 the Minister of Transport and Civil Aviation, Kindo Hamani, was dismissed and replaced by Amadou Nouhou. In January 2009 Issoufou Bako was appointed Minister of Education and Anti-desertification.

There was a further demonstration in the capital in mid-December 2008, as thousands of people appealed for the extension of President Tandja's term in office, and a change to the Constitution to allow the President to serve beyond the two-term limit stipulated therein. There were reports of similar rallies taking place elsewhere in the country, and there were also counter-demonstrations the following week. In March 2009 Tandja announced that, although he would be willing to remain in power after the end of his second term, he would not amend the Constitution in order to do so.

Ethnic unrest followed the return to northern Niger, during the late 1980s, of large numbers of Tuareg nomads who had migrated to Libya and Algeria in the early 1980s to escape the Sahelian drought. It was widely believed that the perceived failure of the Saïbou administration to assist in the rehabilitation of returnees was a significant factor contributing to the subsequent Tuareg uprising. In January 1992 the transitional authorities intensified security measures in the north and, for the first time, formally acknowledged that there was a rebellion in the country. Rhissa Ag Boula, the leader of the rebel Front de libération de l'Aïr et l'Azaouad (FLAA), subsequently stated that the Tuareg rebels were seeking to achieve the establishment of a federal system of governance. Although the Government and the FLAA concluded a truce agreement in May, violence swiftly resumed. In August the security forces launched a major offensive against rebel Tuareg groups. Military authority was reinforced in October by the appointment of senior members of the security forces to northern administrative posts. In November, none the less, a commission that had been appointed by the transitional Government recommended a far-reaching programme of decentralization, according legal status and financial authority to local communities. In December the Government announced the release from custody of 57 Tuaregs.

In January 1993 five people were killed in a Tuareg attack on a meeting of the MNSD—Nassara attended by Mamadou Tandja (who was Minister of the Interior at the time of the suppression of the Tchin-Tabaraden raid) in the northern town of Abala. Later in January 81 Tuaregs were released from detention, and a Minister of State for National Reconciliation, whose main responsibility would be to seek a solution to the Tuareg issue, was appointed to the Government. In March, following Algerian mediation, Ag Boula (who was based in Algeria) agreed that the FLAA would observe a truce for the duration of the campaign for the second round of the presidential election. Shortly afterwards Tuareg representatives in Niamey signed a similar (French-brokered) agreement. In April the outgoing transitional Government and the FLAA agreed to extend the truce indefinitely; the remaining Tuareg prisoners were subsequently released from detention, and the rebels released their hostages.

In mid-1993 a three-month truce agreement between representatives of the Government and the Tuaregs, which provided for the demilitarization of the north, and envisaged negotiations on the Tuaregs' political demands, was signed in Paris, France. However, a new group, the Armée révolutionnaire de libération du nord-Niger (ARLN), emerged to denounce the truce, and supporters of the truce (led by Mano Dayak, the Tuareg signatory to the agreement) broke away from the FLAA to form the Front de libération de Tamoust (FLT): Ag Boula and the remainder of the FLAA stated that they could not support any agreement that contained no specific commitment to discussion of federalism. In September the FLT and the Government agreed to extend the truce for a further three months. Although the FLAA and the ARLN refused to sign the accord, in October they joined with the FLT in a Coordination de la résistance armée (CRA), with the aim of presenting a cohesive programme in future negotiations.

Despite an escalation of violence during May 1994 negotiations took place in Paris in June. Tentative agreement was reached on the creation of ethnically based autonomous regions, each of which was to have its own elected assembly and governor to function in parallel with the organs of central government. Despite renewed unrest, in September the CRA presented Nigerien government negotiators with a plan for the restoration of peace. Formal negotiations resumed, with mediation by the Burkinabè President, Blaise Compaoré, as well as representatives of France and Algeria, in Ouagadougou (Burkina Faso) in October. A new peace accord resulted, emphasizing that Niger was 'unitary and indivisible', while proposing the establishment of elected assemblies or councils for territorial communities, which would be responsible for the implementation of economic, social and cultural policies. A renewable three-month truce was to take immediate effect, to be monitored by French and Burkinabè military units. By the time of the conclusion of the Ouagadougou agreement the number of deaths since the escalation of the Tuareg rebellion in late 1991 was officially put at 150. A commission was established in January 1995 to consider the administrative reorganization of the country.

Ag Boula, who had withdrawn from the CRA, and refused to participate in the decentralization committee, in protest at alleged delays in the implementation of the provisions of the October 1994 agreement, emerged as the leader of the Tuareg delegation (now renamed the Organisation de la résistance armée—ORA) at negotiations in Ouagadougou in March 1995. In April it was announced that a lasting peace agreement had been reached. Demobilized rebels were to be integrated into the Nigerien military and public sector; particular emphasis was to be placed on the economic, social and cultural development of the north, and the Government undertook to support the decentralization process. There was to be a general amnesty for all parties involved in the Tuareg rebellion and its suppression, and a day of national reconciliation was to be instituted in memory of the victims of the conflict. The peace agreement was formally signed by Ag Boula and a representative of the Nigerien Government on 24 April 1995, one day before the cease-fire took effect.

Meanwhile, there was increasing ethnic unrest in the Lake Chad region of south-east Niger, where several thousand (mainly Toubou) Chadian refugees had settled since the overthrow of President Hissène Habré in late 1990. The Front démocratique du renouveau (FDR) emerged in October 1994 to demand increased autonomy for the Toubou population of the south-east. In November, in compliance with a request by the UN, Niger established a committee whose stated aim was to disarm militias and to combat arms-trafficking, which was reportedly well-established in the Agadez and Lake Chad regions. A Comité spécial de la paix (CSP) was inaugurated in May 1995, and a military observer group, comprising representatives of Burkina and France, was deployed in the north in July. The Prime Minister approved an amnesty in that month, and all Tuareg prisoners were reported to have been released shortly afterwards. The peace process was undermined, however, by evidence that Dayak and other Tuareg groups in a revived CRA were making common cause with the FDR in demanding autonomy for their respective regions. In October clashes in the north-east involving rebel Tuaregs and the armed forces were attributed to elements of the CRA. In the same month bilateral and international donors pledged some 18,700m. francs CFA in support of a two-year emergency programme for the development of the north. In December Dayak was one of three leading CRA members to be killed in an air crash. In January 1996 the new leader of the FLT (and acting leader of the CRA), Mohamed Akotai, indicated that his movement favoured inter-Tuareg reconciliation and a dialogue with the Government.

Following the *coup d'état* of January 1996, the CSN expressed its commitment to the peace process. The new administration, the ORA and the CRA all expressed the view that direct contacts between the military and the Tuareg movements would expedite the peace process. In March the Nigerien authorities, the office of the UN High Commissioner for Refugees (UNHCR) and the Governments of Algeria and Burkina signed agreements on refugee repatriation. Shortly afterwards the CRA, including the FDR, affirmed its recognition of the April 1995 agreement, and announced that it would observe a unilateral truce for one month, while negotiations continued. In April 1996 the Government and the CRA signed an agreement formalizing the latter's adherence to the peace process. The following month the ORA and the CRA agreed to establish a joint committee to co-ordinate their activities and to represent their interests in negotiations. In July the CSP and the resistance movements recommended measures aimed at curbing ongoing insecurity in northern areas. In September joint peace-keeping patrols of the Nigerien armed forces and former rebels were inaugurated in the north.

In late September 1996 Ag Boula announced that the ORA no longer considered itself bound by the peace treaty. The authorities asserted that this abandonment of the 1995 accord was linked primarily to the arrest of ORA members in connection with the diversion, some months previously, of a large consignment of cigarettes bound for the north. In an apparent gesture of reconciliation, the detainees were released at the end of October 1996, and the ORA surrendered the consignment to the authorities. In November it was reported that a new group had emerged from among the ORA and the CRA; led by Mohamed Anako, the Union des forces de la résistance armée (UFRA) affirmed its commitment to the peace accord. Following a meeting between Maïnassara and Ag Boula in January 1997, and assurances regarding the implementation of provisions of the 1995 accord, the ORA declared its renewed support; it was announced, moreover, that the FLAA and FLT would establish a joint patrol aimed at combating insecurity and banditry, and other measures intended to facilitate the reintegration of former rebels proceeded.

Insecurity persisted, none the less, particularly in the east. Violent clashes were reported in March 1997, involving several hundred soldiers and Toubou rebels: the FDR protested that the operation was endangering the peace accord. In July, however, the FDR announced its withdrawal from the peace process, stating that Nigerien and Chadian military units had attacked one of its bases; the FDR reported that 17 members of the armed forces had been killed in clashes with its fighters. The Nigerien authorities denied that any engagement had taken place. The conclusion of the disarmament process was officially celebrated in Tchin-Tabaraden in late October. The armed forces subsequently undertook an offensive against positions held by rebel groups. In November a peace accord, known as the Algiers addendum protocol, providing for an immediate cease-fire, was signed in Algeria between the Nigerien Government, the UFRA and the Forces armées révolutionnaires du Sahara (FARS), which comprised both Toubou and Arab elements. In March 1998 the ORA and CRA surrendered their weapons stocks at Agadez. Meanwhile, Ag Boula was appointed as Minister-delegate responsible for Tourism in December 1997.

In June 1998 it was reported that the last units of the UFRA had disarmed at a ceremony near Agadez. A peace agreement was signed with the FDR in August. Following the death of President Maïnassara, in April 1999, the military CRN gave assurances that the peace process would be continued. Ag Boula was promoted to the rank of minister in the transitional Government, while Anako was appointed as special adviser to Wanké. Ag Boula retained his ministerial post in the new Government of Hama Amadou, formed in January 2000. In June the final groups of fighters from the UFRA and other movements participating in the peace process were disarmed near Agadez, prior to their intended integration into the national forces. Concerns remained, however, that progress still had to be made in the implementation of moves towards greater administrative decentralization, as well as regarding the delayed fulfilment of quotas for Tuaregs in military formations. In late September more than 1,200 guns, surrendered by the disarmed factions, were ceremoniously burned in Agadez, in the presence of President Mamadou Tandja, leaders of other West African nations and UN representatives. At the ceremony, Anako announced the dissolution of several of the rebel groups and militias. In September 2001 Chahayi Barkaye, the leader of the FARS, the principal rebel group to have refused disarmament, was killed in heavy fighting with Nigerien soldiers near the Libyan border.

In February 2004 Ag Boula was dismissed from his ministerial post and detained on a charge of complicity in the murder of an MNSD—Nassara activist (in order to maintain Tuareg representation in the Government, Anako was appointed as a Minister-delegate at the Ministry of the Economy and Finance). The Government subsequently denied rumours that elements of FLAA had resumed insurgent activities in the north; however, following a clash with government forces in October, in which five people were reported to have died, Ag Boula's brother, Mohammed Ag Boula, claimed responsibility for the attack during an interview with French radio broadcaster Radio France Internationale, citing the failure of the Government to implement the 1995 peace agreements, and the continuing detention of certain former insurgents, as motivation for the attack. Also in late 2004 four government soldiers were taken hostage in northern Niger; once more, Mohammed Ag Boula declared responsibility for the action, as the leader of a revived FLAA. Following mediation by the Libyan authorities, the hostages were released, after some five months in captivity, in February 2005; Rhissa Ag Boula was released from prison one month later where he had been awaiting trial. The authorities reportedly denied Ag Boula's release was linked to that of the hostages, although Mohamed Ag Boula had previously refused to free the kidnapped soldiers while his brother remained in detention. In July 2008 Rhissa Ag Boula (who had fled to France following his release) was convicted for the murder of the MNSD—Nassara activist and sentenced to death *in absentia*.

In February 2007 a lesser known Tuareg rebel group, the MNJ, claimed responsibility for an attack on a military base north of Niamey, prompting concerns that ethnic unrest was once again increasing. Further attacks were reported throughout mid-2007, including an assault on a military post in which some 15 government soldiers were believed to have been killed. Despite repeated demands from the rebel group for fairer distribution of revenue generated by mining the uranium resources of the northern region, the Government refused to enter into negotiations, insisting that the attacks were not considered to be a rebellion. However, by August the situation had worsened with the number of Tuareg attacks increasing, and in that month President Tandja declared a three-month state of emergency in the region and granted additional powers of arrest to the security forces. Meanwhile, residents fled the towns of northern Niger as the rebel group used landmines to block roads and prevent the delivery of food supplies.

The MNJ claimed that it was behind an attack on the town of Tanhout in January 2008, in which seven soldiers were reported to have been killed and several more captured; the civilian administrator of the town was also taken prisoner. There was further violence in March when Tuareg gunmen attacked a vehicle that was transporting uranium to a port in Benin, killing one civilian, and in the same month the Nigerien armed forces launched an offensive against the MNJ in the north. It was claimed that 10 rebels were killed and many more wounded; however, the MNJ denied this. In May the army announced that it had killed a further 11 Tuareg rebels in a new operation against rebel bases in the north (the MNJ again denied this claim, stating that it was civilians who were killed), while President Tandja issued a decree extending the state of emergency declared in August 2007. In June 2008 there were reports that four French executives working for the nuclear power company, Areva, had been kidnapped by Tuareg rebels: they were held for just four days before being handed over to the International Committee of the Red Cross. In the following month further clashes between government forces and the MNJ resulted in the death of a senior member of that organization, Mohamed Acherif.

In August 2008 a government spokesman falsely claimed that the Tuareg rebels had agreed to cease hostilities after holding peace talks with Libyan Revolutionary Leader Col Muammar al-Qaddafi. Nevertheless, a senior MNJ member stated that the rebels were willing to engage in peace talks with the Government, on the condition that they were conducted outside Niger. Despite this development there were reports in October that MNJ forces had attacked an army convoy near the town of Arlit, and in December another Tuareg rebel organization, the Front des forces de redressement (FFR), claimed responsibility for the kidnapping of a Canadian diplomat, Robert Fowler; the FFR, however, later retracted its claim. An Algerian-based rebel group styled al-Qa'ida in the Islamic Maghreb (previously known as the Groupe salafiste pour la prédication et le combat—GSPC, see below) then claimed that it had Fowler in captivity, and in March 2009 demanded the return of 20 of its members detained in Mali and elsewhere, as a condition for his release and that of several other Western hostages. Meanwhile, in the same month, numerous members of the MNJ split from the group to form the Front patriotique du Niger, which sought to enter into negotiations with the Government to restore peace. Days later al-Qaddafi appealed to all Tuareg rebels in Niger and Mali to end their armed struggle, and in April the Government dispatched a senior security official to Libya for mediation with the rebels, demonstrating a softening of the Government's stance towards the rebellion.

In foreign affairs, there was a notable deterioration in relations with the USA in the immediate aftermath of the 1996 presidential election in Niger. The assumption of power by the CRN in April 1999, following the death of Maïnassara, was condemned by the USA, France and Niger's other Western creditors. Relations with the USA improved following the reinstallation of an elected Government; in February 2000 Niger's Minister of Foreign Affairs, Co-operation and African Integration visited Washington, DC, and in March the USA announced an end to the sanctions imposed after Maïnassara's death. In August President Tandja met President Bill Clinton and other US representatives in Abuja, Nigeria, where the USA announced increased support for Niger in areas including food security, the promotion of democracy, education and health care.

Countries of the region with which Maïnassara had forged close relations also condemned the military take-over of April 1999: Libya notably denounced the new regime, although relations between the CRN and the Libyan Government had normalized by the end of the year. In December the two countries signed an agreement envisaging the establishment of a joint company to distribute oil and liquefied natural gas; it was also agreed to expedite the establishment of a joint company for petroleum exploration and production. On a visit to Agadez in early July, Libyan leader Col Muammar al-Qaddafi pledged support for the Tuareg peace process. In November Libya pledged to grant financial support for several construction and development projects in Niger. Meanwhile, some 1,000 Nigerien citizens were repatriated from Libya in October, following instances of inter-ethnic violence between Libyan Arabs and black Africans in that country. On 24 April 2006, the 11th anniversary of the signing of the peace agreement, President Tandja announced that a rehabilitation programme was to be launched to assist more than 3,000 former Tuareg rebels. On surrendering their weapons in 1995 the rebels were forced onto barren land in the north of the country, but, with funds from the project amounting to 850m. francs CFA, it was hoped that the Tuaregs would develop prosperous farming and agricultural communities. Following a meeting in April 2009 between the Libyan Secretary for Public Security, Gen. Abd al-Fattah Yunis al-Abaidi, and Nigerien Minister of the Interior, Albadé Abouba, the two countries agreed to establish a joint organization to combat organized crime, narcotics trafficking and illegal migration through their common borders.

The EU suspended all assistance to Niger in the aftermath of the military take-over in April 1999 and made its resumption dependent on a full investigation into Maïnassara's death; the CRN subsequently stated that its report had been lodged with organizations including the EU, and EU aid recommenced in June 2000. France also suspended military and civilian co-operation with Niger in April 1999. Following a visit to France by Mamadou Tandja in January 2000, when the newly installed Nigerien President met President Jacques Chirac and Prime Minister Lionel Jospin, the resumption of French co-operation was formalized, with the announcement of exceptional assistance principally to allow payment of outstanding salaries in the public sector. Chirac visited Niger in October 2003, when he praised 'the return of democratic life' to the country.

In May 2000 a long-term dispute between Niger and Benin regarding the ownership of a number of small islands along their common border at the Niger river escalated, reportedly following the sabotage of a Beninois administrative building on the island of Lété, apparently by Nigerien soldiers. A meeting between representatives of the two Governments failed to resolve the dispute, which was subsequently referred to the Organization of African Unity (OAU, now the African Union, see p. 172) for arbitration. Further clashes between rival groups of farmers were reported on Lété in late August. In April 2002 the two Governments officially ratified an agreement (signed in 2001) to refer the issue of ownership of the islands to the International Court of Justice (ICJ) in The Hague, Netherlands, for arbitration. Benin and Niger filed confidential written arguments with the Court, and in November 2003 a five-member chamber formed to consider the case held its first public sitting. Both countries subsequently submitted counter-arguments, and a third written pleading was submitted by both parties in December of that year. The public hearings in the case took place before the Chamber of the ICJ in March 2005. Meanwhile, in late 2004 Nigerien traders and haulage contractors boycotted Cotonou port in Benin in reaction to the shooting of two Nigerien citizens by Beninois gendarmes in the city in September. The boycott was ended in January 2005 following a visit to Niamey by the Beninois Minister of Foreign Affairs and African Integration, Rogatien Biaou, during which he announced that the Beninois Government would compensate the victims' families. In July 2005 the ICJ issued a final ruling to the effect that 16 of the 25 disputed islands, including Lété, belonged to Niger; the Governments of both countries announced their acceptance of the ruling.

In June 2001 Niger and Nigeria announced that joint border patrols of their common frontier would be instigated, in order to combat increasing cross-border crime and smuggling in the region. It was reported that the introduction of *Shari'a* law in several northern Nigerian states, from 2000, had been instrumental in encouraging Nigerian criminal gangs to operate from within Niger. Further concerns regarding regional security were raised in early 2004, when Islamic militants belonging to the GSPC reportedly attacked a group of tourists in northern Niger. In March clashes between the militants and Chadian and Nigerien troops reportedly resulted in the deaths of some 43 GSPC fighters in northern Niger. It was reported in that month that the Governments of Algeria, Chad, Mali and Niger were to reinforce security co-operation in the regions of their common borders. In January 2005 President Tandja was elected Chairman of the Economic Community of West African States (see p. 243); paramount among the organization's concerns during the first months of his chairmanship were common agricultural policy and the political crises in Côte d'Ivoire and Togo. In June Niger, Algeria, Chad, Mali and Nigeria were among nine North and West African countries that participated in US-led military exercises aimed at increasing co-operation in combating cross-border banditry and militancy in the region.

In October 2006 the Government announced that it was to forcibly remove some 150,000 Mahamid Arabs from eastern Niger and return them to their native Chad. Several thousand Chadians had crossed the border into Niger during the 1970s to escape widespread drought, which had caused outbreaks of violence in their homeland. During the 1980s thousands more fled to Niger when conflict escalated into civil war in Chad. Mahamid communities continued to establish themselves in the Diffa region, but there followed complaints of deteriorating relations between the Mahamids and the local population, and it was feared that the Chadians' presence posed a serious threat to national security. UNHCR responded with claims that the Mahamid communities did not hold refugee status and stipulated that it be ensured that those forced to leave would not become victims of discrimination on their return to Chad. The Niger authorities then reversed the earlier decision, stating instead that the Mahamids would be asked to move to land better suited to their agricultural needs. In late October several thousand Nigeriens protested against that ruling, threatening that they would be forced to take action to protect their land and property if the Mahamids were not returned to Chad. The Nigerien Government subsequently announced that only those who did not have the required documents would be sent back; according to the census of 2001, the majority of the Arab community held identity cards issued by the local authorities.

Government

Following the death of President Ibrahim Baré Maïnassara, in April 1999, a military Conseil de réconciliation nationale (CRN) was established, under the chairmanship of Maj. Daouda Mallam Wanké, to exercise executive and legislative authority during a nine-month transitional period prior to the restoration of elected organs of government. A new constitution was approved in a national referendum in July 1999. The Constitution of the Fifth Republic, promulgated on 9 August, envisages a balance of powers between the President, Government and legislative Assemblée nationale. The President, who is elected by universal adult suffrage, is Head of State, and is accorded 'broad ordinary and arbitral powers'. The Government, under a Prime Minister appointed by the President, is responsible to the Assemblée nationale, which is competent to remove the Prime Minister by vote of censure. The Assemblée nationale is similarly elected by direct adult suffrage. The new President and legislature were inaugurated in December 1999.

For the purposes of local administration, Niger comprises seven regions and the municipality of Niamey. A reorganization of Niger's administrative structures, with the aim of devolving increased autonomy to local and regional authorities, was undertaken in the second half of the 1990s.

Defence

As assessed at November 2008, Niger's armed forces totalled 5,300 men (army 5,200; air force 100). Paramilitary forces numbered 5,400 men, comprising the gendarmerie (1,400), the republican guard (2,500) and the national police force (1,500). Conscription to the armed forces is selective and lasts for two years. Budgetary expenditure on defence in 2007 was estimated at 22,000m. francs CFA.

Economic Affairs

In 2007, according to estimates by the World Bank, Niger's gross national income (GNI), measured at average 2005–07 prices, was US $3,992m., equivalent to $280 per head (or $630 on an international purchasing-power parity basis). During 2000–07, it was estimated, the population increased at an average annual rate of 3.5%, while gross domestic product (GDP) per head decreased, in real terms, by an average of 0.6% per year. Overall GDP increased, in real terms, at an average annual rate of 4.2% in 2000–07; growth was 3.2% in 2007.

Agriculture (including hunting, forestry and fishing) contributed 43.9% of GDP in 2007. In that year, according to official figures, 2.0% of the labour force were employed in the sector. The principal cash crops are cow-peas, onions, groundnuts and cotton. The principal subsistence crops are millet and sorghum. Niger is able to achieve self-sufficiency in basic foodstuffs in non-drought years. Agricultural production in northern Niger in 2004/05 was severely affected by drought and by the swarms of locusts that invaded the Sahel region from mid-2004, resulting in a grain deficit of 223,487 tons for that agricultural year. However, by 2006 a surplus had been re-established. The effects of drought and locust invasion were also thought to have caused significant damage to pasture land: livestock-rearing in Niger is especially important among the nomadic population, and live animals intended chiefly for food accounted for 13.2% of total export earnings in 2007, constituting the second most important source of export revenue, after uranium. Major anti-desertification and reafforestation programmes are in progress. According to the World Bank, agricultural GDP increased by an average of 7.0% per year in 2000–03. Agricultural GDP increased by 6.0% in 2003.

Industry (including mining, manufacturing, construction and power) contributed 14.9% of GDP in 2007. Some 40.6% of the labour force were employed in industrial activities in that year. According to the World Bank, industrial GDP increased by an average of 3.1% per year in 2000–03; growth was 4.0% in 2003.

Mining contributed 5.2% of GDP in 2007, but employed only 0.8% of the labour force in that year. Niger is among the world's foremost producers of uranium (the fifth largest, after Canada, Australia, Kazakhstan and Russia in 2007), although the contribution of uranium-mining to the domestic economy has declined, as production costs have exceeded world prices for the mineral. In 2007 exports of uranium accounted for 63.2% of total export earnings. In addition, gypsum, coal, salt and cassiterite are also extracted, and commercial exploitation of gold (previously mined on a small scale) at the Samira Hill mine began in 2004, with production of 79,300 oz of gold in 2007. In that year the Government awarded the US firm Caracal Gold Burkina two permits for gold exploration in western Niger. According to the IMF, the GDP of the mining sector increased at an average annual rate of 2.3% in 1998–2005; mining GDP increased by an estimated 3.8% in 2005.

Manufacturing contributed 5.6% of GDP and employed 25.7% of the labour force in 2007. The processing of agricultural products (groundnuts, cereals, cotton and rice) constitutes the principal activity. Some light industries, including a textiles plant, a brewery and a cement works, supply the internal market. According to the World Bank, manufacturing GDP increased by an average of 3.9% per year in 2000–03. Manufacturing GDP increased by 5.1% in 2003.

The domestic generation of electricity (almost entirely thermal) provides a little less than one-half of Niger's electrical energy requirements, much of the remainder being imported from Nigeria. Construction of a hydroelectric installation at Kandadji, on the Niger, is planned. Imports of mineral fuels accounted for 17.0% of the value of merchandise imports in 2007.

The services sector contributed 41.2% of GDP and employed 57.3% of the labour force in 2007. The GDP of the sector increased by an average of 3.6% per year in 2000–03, according to the World Bank; growth was 3.1% in 2003.

In 2007 Niger recorded a visible trade deficit of an estimated 107,000m. francs CFA, while there was a deficit of 181,100m. francs CFA on the current account of the balance of payments. France was Niger's principal source of imports in 2007, supplying 18.9%; other major suppliers were the USA, Côte d'Ivoire and the People's Republic of China. The principal markets for exports in that year were France (44.0%), Japan, Switzerland-Liechtenstein, Nigeria and the USA. The principal exports in 2007 were uranium (most of which is purchased by France) and live animals. The principal imports in that year were food and live animals (18.0% of total imports, of which around one-half was accounted for by cereals and cereal preparations), machinery and transport equipment, refined petroleum products, and medicinal and pharmaceutical products.

Niger's overall budget deficit for 2007 was estimated at 20,500m. francs CFA (equivalent to 1.0% of GDP). Niger's total external debt was US $805m. at the end of 2006, of which $703m. was long-term public debt. Consumer prices increased by an annual average of 1.8% during 2000–07. Consumer prices increased by less than 0.1% in 2007. Some 64,987 people were registered as unemployed in 2001.

Niger is a member of numerous regional organizations, including the Economic Community of West African States (see p. 243), the West African organs of the Franc Zone (see p. 316), the Conseil de l'Entente (see p. 425), the Lake Chad Basin Commission (see p. 427), the Liptako–Gourma Integrated Development Authority (see p. 427), the Niger Basin Authority (see p. 427) and the Permanent Inter-State Committee on Drought Control in the Sahel (see p. 428).

Niger is one of the world's poorest countries, and has consistently been among the lowest ranking countries in the United Nations Development Programme's Human Development Report, while literacy levels are also among the lowest in the world. Niger's narrow export base, which is dominated by uranium, and political instability have adversely affected economic performance, and most major creditors withdrew support after the military take-over that followed the death of President Maïnassara in 1999. Following the restoration of civilian rule, France resumed aid and debt relief to Niger in early 2000, and in December the IMF and the World Bank announced that Niger would receive US $890m. in debt-service relief under the enhanced framework of the initiative for heavily indebted poor countries. In July 2005 Niger was among 18 countries to be granted 100% debt relief on multilateral debt by the Group of Eight leading industrialized nations (G8), while a new three-

NIGER

year Poverty Reduction and Growth Facility became effective in June 2008, worth a total of $35.3m. An impressive agricultural harvest, with a 25% increase in production, supported growth during the first half of 2008, while economic activity was aided by significant public and private sector investment in mining, telecommunications and the transport infrastructure. Despite the negative impact of the global financial crisis, GDP growth was estimated at 9.5% in 2008. Nevertheless, the increasing international prices of food and fuel led to rising inflation levels in that year, with the IMF estimating an 8.3% increase in consumer prices over the year. More positively, however, inflationary pressure eased towards the end of 2008, and the rate was projected to decline, to 3.5%, in 2009. Meanwhile, in early 2009 the UN International Fund for Agricultural Development provided $16m. to support the second phase of a rural rehabilitation and development project in the Maradi region, benefiting rural communities. The IMF stated in March 2009 that the economic outlook for the year remained favourable, with public investment in irrigation, roads and electricity generation deemed vital to future growth.

Education

Education is available free of charge, and is officially compulsory for eight years between the ages of seven and 15 years. Primary education begins at the age of seven and lasts for six years. Secondary education begins at the age of 13 years and comprises a four-year cycle followed by a three-year cycle. According to UNESCO estimates, primary enrolment in 2005/06 included 43.4% of children in the appropriate age-group (boys 49.8%; girls 36.6%). Secondary enrolment in that year included only 9.4% of the relevant age-group (boys 11.5%; girls 7.3%). The Abdou Moumouni University (formerly the University of Niamey) was inaugurated in 1973, and the Islamic University of Niger, at Say (to the south of the capital), was opened in 1987. Some 8,710 students were enrolled at those institutions in 2005/06. In December 2001 the Assemblée nationale approved legislation providing for the introduction of teaching in all local languages, with the aim of improving the literacy rate. Expenditure on education in 2000 was 32,500m. francs CFA, representing 15.5% of total spending.

Public Holidays

2009: 1 January (New Year's Day), 9 March* (Mouloud, Birth of the Prophet), 13 April (Easter Monday), 24 April (National Concord Day), 1 May (Labour Day), 3 August (Independence Day), 20 September* (Id al-Fitr, end of Ramadan), 27 November* (Tabaski, Feast of the Sacrifice), 18 December (Republic Day and Islamic New Year).

2010: 1 January (New Year's Day), 26 February* (Mouloud, Birth of the Prophet), 5 April (Easter Monday), 24 April (National Concord Day), 1 May (Labour Day), 3 August (Independence Day), 10 September* (Id al-Fitr, end of Ramadan), 16 November* (Tabaski, Feast of the Sacrifice), 7 December* (Islamic New Year), 18 December (Republic Day).

* These holidays are dependent on the Islamic lunar calendar and may vary by one or two days from the dates given.

Weights and Measures

The metric system is in force.

Statistical Survey

Source (unless otherwise stated): Institut national de la Statistique, Immeuble sis à la Rue Sirba, derrière la Présidence de la république, BP 720, Niamey; tel. 20-72-35-60; fax 20-72-21-74; e-mail insniger@ins.ne; internet www.stat-niger.org.

Area and Population

AREA, POPULATION AND DENSITY

Area (sq km)	1,267,000*
Population (census results)	
20 May 1988	7,248,100
20 May 2001	
Males	5,516,588
Females	5,543,703
Total	11,060,291
Population (official estimates at mid-year)	
2006	13,044,973
2007	13,475,457
2008	14,296,815
Density (per sq km) at mid-2008	11.3

* 489,191 sq miles.

ETHNIC GROUPS
(2001 census, Nigerien citizens only)

	Population	%
Hausa	6,069,731	55.36
Djerma-Sonraï	2,300,874	20.99
Tuareg	1,016,883	9.27
Peulh	935,517	8.53
Kanouri-Manga	513,116	4.68
Toubou	42,172	0.38
Arab	40,085	0.37
Gourmantché	39,797	0.36
Others	5,951	0.05
Total	**10,964,126**	**100.00**

ADMINISTRATIVE DIVISIONS
(mid-year estimates, 2008)

Agadez	437,210	Niamey (city)	1,033,295
Diffa	446,651	Tahoua	2,524,514
Dosso	1,921,202	Tillabéri	2,396,411
Maradi	2,865,219	Zinder	2,672,314

PRINCIPAL TOWNS
(population at 2001 census)

Niamey (capital)	707,951	Agadez	78,289
Zinder	170,575	Tahoua	73,002
Maradi	148,017	Arlit	69,435

Mid-2007 (incl. suburbs, UN estimate): Niamey 915,000 (Source: UN, *World Urbanization Prospects: The 2007 Revision*).

BIRTHS AND DEATHS
(annual averages, UN estimates)

	1990–95	1995–2000	2000–05
Birth rate (per 1,000)	55.3	54.0	52.2
Death rate (per 1,000)	22.7	20.5	17.4

Source: UN, *World Population Prospects: The 2008 Revision*.

2006: Birth rate 49.4 per 1,000; Death rate 14.1 per 1,000 (Source: African Development Bank).

2007: Birth rate 49.0 per 1,000; Death rate 13.8 per 1,000 (Source: African Development Bank).

Life expectancy (years at birth, WHO estimates): 42.2 (males 41.7; females 43.1) in 2006 (Source: WHO, *World Health Statistics*).

NIGER

EMPLOYMENT
('000 persons at 31 December)

	2005	2006	2007*
Agriculture, hunting, forestry and fishing	59	60	72
Mining and quarrying	21	24	29
Manufacturing	845	846	907
Electricity, gas and water	71	71	79
Construction	380	411	421
Trade, restaurants and hotels	592	678	704
Transport, storage and communications	312	319	342
Financing, insurance, real estate and business services	195	196	205
Community, social and personal services	650	666	775
Total	**3,125**	**3,271**	**3,535**

* Provisional figures.

2001 census (persons aged 10 years and over): Total employed 4,015,951 (males 2,706,910, females 1,309,041), Unemployed 64,987 (males 49,437, females 15,550), Total labour force 4,080,938 (males 2,756,347, females 1,324,591).

Health and Welfare

KEY INDICATORS

Total fertility rate (children per woman, 2006)	7.3
Under-5 mortality rate (per 1,000 live births, 2006)	253
HIV/AIDS (% of persons aged 15–49, 2007)	0.8
Physicians (per 1,000 head, 2004)	0.03
Hospital beds (per 1,000 head, 1998)	0.12
Health expenditure (2006): US $ per head (PPP)	27
Health expenditure (2006): % of GDP	4.0
Health expenditure (2006): public (% of total)	52.7
Access to water (% of persons, 2006)	42
Access to sanitation (% of persons, 2006)	7
Human Development Index (2006): ranking	174
Human Development Index (2006): value	0.370

For sources and definitions, see explanatory note on p. vi.

Agriculture

PRINCIPAL CROPS
('000 metric tons)

	2005	2006	2007
Wheat	9.0*	7.8	6.6†
Rice, paddy	59.9	78.4	70.0
Millet	2,652	3,009	2,782
Sorghum	944	929	975
Potatoes†	4.2	4.2	4.2
Sweet potatoes†	45	42	45
Cassava (Manioc)†	120	118	120
Sugar cane†	220	218	220
Cow peas, dry	586.1	712.0	1,001
Groundnuts, with shell	139.1	152.6	147.7
Sesame seed	40†	44	35†
Cottonseed	10*	10†	10†
Cabbages and other brassicas†	120	120	120
Lettuce and chicory†	40	40	40
Tomatoes†	100	106	105
Chillies and peppers, green†	17	17	17
Onions, dry	322	320†	330†
Garlic†	8	8	8
Beans, green†	24	23	23
Carrots and turnips†	18	18	18
Dates†	7.8	7.8	7.8
Tobacco, unmanufactured†	1.0	0.8	1.0

* Unofficial figure.
† FAO estimate(s).

Aggregate production ('000 metric tons, may include official, semi-official or estimated data): Total cereals 3,649 in 2005, 4,004 in 2006, 3,816 in 2007; Total roots and tubers 1692 in 2005, 164 in 2006, 169 in 2007; Total vegetables (incl. melons) 700 in 2005, 701 in 2006, 710 in 2007; Total pulses 608 in 2005, 734 in 2006, 1,023 in 2007.

Source: FAO.

LIVESTOCK
('000 head, year ending September, FAO estimates)

	2005	2006	2007
Cattle	2,430	2,344	2,360
Sheep	4,900	4,700	4,750
Goats	7,700	7,300	7,400
Pigs	40	40	40
Horses	106	106	106
Asses	580	n.a.	n.a.
Camels	439	427	430
Chickens	25,000	25,000	25,000

Source: FAO.

LIVESTOCK PRODUCTS
('000 metric tons, FAO estimates)

	2005	2006	2007
Game meat	15	15	15
Horse meat	0.5	0.7	0.7
Goat meat	31.2	27.0	28.0
Sheep meat	17.6	16.5	16.0
Chicken meat	28.4	28.6	29.0
Hen eggs	10.5	10.5	10.5

Source: FAO.

Forestry

ROUNDWOOD REMOVALS
('000 cubic metres, excl. bark, FAO estimates)

	2005	2006	2007
Industrial wood	411	411	411
Fuel wood	8,806	9,010	9,218
Total	**9,217**	**9,421**	**9,629**

Source: FAO.

SAWNWOOD PRODUCTION
('000 cubic metres, incl. railway sleepers, FAO estimates)

	1991	1992	1993
Total (all broadleaved)	0	1	4

1994–2007: Figures assumed to be unchanged from 1993 (FAO estimates).
Source: FAO.

Fishing

(metric tons, live weight)

	2004	2005	2006
Capture (freshwater fishes)	51,466	50,018	29,835
Aquaculture	40	40	40
Total catch	**51,506**	**50,058**	**29,875**

Source: FAO.

NIGER

Mining

('000 metric tons, unless otherwise indicated)

	2005	2006	2007
Hard coal	182.1	176.3	171.3
Tin (metric tons)*†	14.0	13.0	n.a.
Uranium (metric tons)*	3,093	3,431	3,154
Gold (kg)	4,962	2,615	2,649
Gypsum	17.4	13.0	n.a.

* Data refer to the metal content of ore.
† Artisanal production only.

Industry

SELECTED PRODUCTS
('000 metric tons, unless otherwise indicated)

	2003	2004	2005
Raw sugar ('000 metric tons)*	15	10	10
Cement	63.7	59.2	83.4
Soap	10.4	10.2	9.4
Textile fabrics (million metres)	5.6	4.0	2.0
Beer ('000 bottles)	116.5	103.5	94.9
Electric energy (million kWh)†	245	247	250

* Estimates from International Sugar Organization (London).
† Source: UN, *Industrial Commodity Statistics Yearbook*.

Source: mostly IMF, *Niger: Selected Issues and Statistical Appendix* (January 2007).

Finance

CURRENCY AND EXCHANGE RATES

Monetary Units
100 centimes = 1 franc de la Communauté financière africaine (CFA).

Sterling, Dollar and Euro Equivalents (31 December 2008)
£1 sterling = 687.113 francs CFA;
US $1 = 471.335 francs CFA;
€1 = 655.957 francs CFA;
10,000 francs CFA = £14.55 = $21.22 = €15.24.

Average Exchange Rate (francs CFA per US $)
2006 522.890
2007 479.267
2008 447.805

Note: An exchange rate of 1 French franc = 50 francs CFA, established in 1948, remained in force until January 1994, when the CFA franc was devalued by 50%, with the exchange rate adjusted to 1 French franc = 100 francs CFA. This relationship to French currency remained in effect with the introduction of the euro on 1 January 1999. From that date, accordingly, a fixed exchange rate of €1 = 655.957 francs CFA has been in operation.

BUDGET
('000 million francs CFA)

Revenue*	2006	2007†	2008‡
Tax revenue	203.8	233.2	255.8
International trade	95.8	100.7	100.7
Non-tax revenue	38.5	71.2	149.0
Annexed budgets and special accounts	4.9	4.6	2.6
Total	247.2	309.0	407.4

Expenditure	2006	2007†	2008‡
Current expenditure	174.2	239.4	301.2
Wages and salaries	68.0	72.2	86.3
Materials and supplies	47.4	61.7	71.5
Subsidies and transfers	43.5	58.3	105.3
Interest	4.9	7.1	7.4
Capital expenditure	202.3	236.6	263.3
Total	376.6	476.0	564.5

* Excluding grants received ('000 million francs CFA, estimates): 898.6 in 2006; 146.5 in 2007; 146.2 in 2008 (provisional).
† Estimates.
‡ Provisional figures.

Source: IMF, *Niger: 2008 Article IV Consultation and First Review Under the Three-Year Arrangement Under the Poverty Reduction and Growth Facility, and Request for Waivers and Modification of Performance Criteria - Staff Report; Staff Supplement; Public Information Notice and Press Release on the Executive Board Discussion; and Statement by the Executive Director for Niger* (February 2009).

INTERNATIONAL RESERVES
(US $ million at 31 December, excl. gold)

	2005	2006	2007
IMF special drawing rights	0.3	0.1	0.1
Reserve position in IMF	12.3	13.0	13.6
Foreign exchange	236.9	357.8	579.3
Total	249.5	370.9	593.0

2008: IMF special drawing rights 1.5; Reserve position in IMF 13.3.
Source: IMF, *International Financial Statistics*.

MONEY SUPPLY
('000 million francs CFA at 31 December)

	2005	2006	2007
Currency outside banks	108.1	133.1	133.3
Demand deposits at deposit money banks*	81.4	90.0	134.5
Checking deposits at post office	2.5	1.8	1.4
Total money (incl. others)*	192.2	225.4	269.3

* Excluding the deposits of public enterprises of an administrative or social nature.

Source: IMF, *International Financial Statistics*.

COST OF LIVING
(Consumer Price Index for Niamey, annual averages; base: 2000 = 100)

	2005	2006	2007
Food	120.7	118.4	117.6
Clothing	102.6	100.0	99.8
Rent	106.2	107.5	108.1
All items (incl. others)	113.5	113.5	113.6

Source: ILO.

2008 (Consumer Price Index for Niamey, annual averages; base: 2000 = 100): All items 126.5 (Source: IMF, *International Financial Statistics*).

NATIONAL ACCOUNTS
('000 million francs CFA at current prices)

Expenditure on the Gross Domestic Product

	2005	2006	2007
Government final consumption expenditure	280.2	286.2	364.9
Household final consumption expenditure	1,324.4	1,412.7	1,440.5
Gross fixed capital formation	384.6	430.2	473.8
Changes in stocks	25.8	19.5	6.7
Total domestic expenditure	2,015.0	2,148.6	2,285.9
Exports of goods and services	304.2	320.9	389.3
Less Imports of goods and services	542.2	563.1	640.4
GDP in market prices	1,777.0	1,906.4	2,034.8
GDP at constant 1987 prices	1,167.9	1,235.7	1,276.5

NIGER

Gross Domestic Product by Economic Activity

	2005	2006	2007
Agriculture, hunting, forestry and fishing	754.3	817.2	829.9
Mining and quarrying	35.7	40.1	98.2
Manufacturing	98.4	102.6	106.6
Electricity, gas and water supply	19.6	24.6	26.0
Construction	41.6	47.5	50.7
Wholesale and retail trade	260.4	273.9	290.8
Transport	115.1	124.1	134.9
Public administration and defence; compulsory social security	181.5	198.0	204.9
Other services	136.0	140.2	148.1
Sub-total	1,642.5	1,768.2	1,890.1
Taxes, *less* subsidies, on products	134.5	138.2	144.7
GDP at market prices	1,777.0	1,906.4	2,034.8

Source: IMF, *Niger: Selected Issues and Statistical Appendix* (February 2009).

BALANCE OF PAYMENTS
('000 million francs CFA)

	2005	2006	2007
Exports of goods f.o.b.	258.0	273.5	341.0
Imports of goods f.o.b.	−394.8	−391.3	−448.0
Trade balance	−136.8	−117.8	−107.0
Services (net)	−101.2	−124.4	−144.1
Balance on goods and services	−238.0	−242.2	−251.1
Income (net)	−5.0	0.6	−16.6
Balance on goods, services and income	−243.0	−241.6	−267.7
Private unrequited transfers (net)	43.5	41.6	42.8
Public unrequited transfers (net)	52.4	43.9	43.8
Current balance	−147.1	−156.2	−181.1
Capital account (net)	81.0	887.7	153.6
Direct investment (net)	18.3	26.9	61.0
Portfolio investment (net)	22.0	−2.0	4.9
Other investment (net)	49.3	−645.8	34.2
Net errors and omissions	−8.3	−9.4	—
Overall balance	15.2	101.2	72.6

Source: IMF, *Niger: Selected Issues and Statistical Appendix* (February 2009).

External Trade

PRINCIPAL COMMODITIES
(distribution by SITC, US $ million)

Imports c.i.f.	2005	2006	2007
Food and live animals	200.6	183.9	172.8
Dairy products and birds' eggs	17.3	25.1	15.7
Milk and cream	16.8	24.8	15.4
Milk and cream, preserved, concentrated or sweetened	16.5	24.3	15.0
Cereals and cereal preparations	126.1	100.5	94.6
Rice, semi-milled or wholly milled	93.6	64.0	50.9
Rice, semi-milled or milled (unbroken)	92.8	63.5	50.9
Sugar, sugar preparations and honey	24.6	21.2	22.2
Beverages and tobacco	18.5	22.0	27.6
Cigarettes	15.8	19.0	24.5
Crude materials (inedible) except fuel	40.8	50.4	61.2
Textile fibres (not wool tops) and their wastes (not in yarn)	26.3	34.7	40.6
Bulk textile waste, old clothing, traded in bulk or in bales	26.1	34.5	40.4
Mineral fuels, lubricants, etc., (incl. electric current)	107.6	124.3	162.4
Petroleum, petroleum products, etc.	96.8	108.6	145.7

Imports c.i.f.—*continued*	2005	2006	2007
Petroleum products, refined	94.5	106.9	144.5
Animal and vegetable oils, fats and waxes	31.4	30.0	22.9
Fixed vegetable oils and fats	28.3	27.9	20.4
Palm oil	22.9	23.4	15.9
Chemicals and related products	54.6	82.5	120.1
Medicinal and pharmaceutical products	19.5	36.3	75.4
Basic manufactures	108.5	122.4	124.4
Textile yarn, fabrics, made-up articles, etc.	26.9	22.3	20.6
Cotton fabrics, woven (not incl. narrow or special fabrics)	11.9	13.3	13.6
Machinery and transport equipment	141.1	193.2	215.8
Telecommunications, sound recording and reproducing equipment	18.9	30.6	25.6
Road vehicles	51.5	59.5	87.3
Passenger motor vehicles (excl. buses)	21.6	21.7	28.3
Miscellaneous manufactured articles	32.2	51.5	46.8
Total (incl. others)	735.6	860.2	957.8

Exports f.o.b.	2005	2006	2007
Food and live animals	61.5	72.2	62.4
Live animals chiefly for food	32.9	38.7	34.2
Animals of the bovine species (incl. buffaloes), live	19.5	20.1	18.1
Sheep and goats, live	12.0	13.7	12.0
Fish, crustaceans and molluscs, and preparations thereof	2.2	0.5	0.5
Vegetables and fruit	24.5	25.9	17.6
Vegetables, fresh or simply preserved; roots and tubers	24.1	25.3	17.1
Other fresh or chilled vegetables	22.5	23.8	15.0
Beverages and tobacco	4.6	4.2	3.5
Cigarettes	4.4	3.9	3.3
Crude materials (inedible) except fuels	162.0	164.8	312.1
Textile fibres (not wool tops) and their wastes (not in yarn)	10.1	10.3	12.3
Ores and concentrates of uranium and thorium	149.3	152.0	298.8
Basic manufactures	10.5	12.6	9.2
Fabrics, woven, 85% plus of cotton, bleached, dyed, etc., or otherwise finished	8.7	9.4	8.5
Total (incl. others)	347.7	329.7	473.1

Source: UN, *International Trade Statistics Yearbook*.

PRINCIPAL TRADING PARTNERS
(US $ million)

Imports c.i.f.	2005	2006	2007
Argentina	8.5	12.7	6.5
Belgium	12.2	22.4	25.2
Benin	37.4	42.5	23.0
Brazil	21.1	19.0	26.1
Burkina Faso	10.4	9.4	9.5
Cameroon	16.1	4.8	9.1
China, People's Republic	40.1	107.3	66.3
Côte d'Ivoire	66.7	55.4	75.5
France (incl. Monaco)	116.4	132.3	180.9
Germany	10.8	12.2	28.8
Ghana	13.2	14.7	13.6
India	28.6	40.0	30.5
Italy	9.1	8.4	12.2
Japan	22.8	32.6	46.7
Malaysia	5.8	12.9	14.2

Imports c.i.f.—continued	2005	2006	2007
Netherlands	7.2	16.0	23.0
Nigeria	40.1	52.3	45.4
Pakistan	29.2	16.4	18.6
South Africa	13.8	12.9	13.5
Thailand	25.2	6.8	7.5
Togo	37.0	20.2	36.7
United Kingdom	7.4	23.6	44.3
USA	39.5	86.5	86.5
Viet Nam	20.0	8.9	3.3
Total (incl. others)	735.6	860.2	957.8

Exports f.o.b.	2005	2006	2007
Algeria	0.4	0.4	0.2
Belgium	6.2	6.7	1.8
Benin	6.5	6.4	2.4
Brazil	—	2.0	3.4
Burkina Faso	2.1	2.5	0.4
Cameroon	3.3	0.3	—
China, People's Republic	1.2	3.8	3.9
Côte d'Ivoire	8.6	7.8	9.2
France (incl. Monaco)	107.5	114.9	208.4
Germany	—	2.8	0.6
Ghana	13.6	14.4	9.4
India	0.1	1.0	1.1
Japan	41.1	44.5	66.6
Libya	0.7	0.9	0.1
Mali	1.2	0.5	0.1
Netherlands	1.2	0.9	1.6
Nigeria	49.7	48.6	40.5
South Africa	1.0	1.4	2.7
Spain	10.1	8.1	14.1
Switzerland-Liechtenstein	64.6	32.5	59.0
Thailand	0.1	2.1	3.9
Togo	8.5	5.2	0.6
United Kingdom	0.4	1.9	0.6
USA	10.7	11.1	27.3
Total (incl. others)	347.7	329.7	473.1

Source: UN, *International Trade Statistics Yearbook*.

Transport

ROAD TRAFFIC
(estimates, motor vehicles in use)

	1994	1995	1996
Passenger cars	38,610	37,620	38,220
Lorries and vans	13,160	14,100	15,200

Source: IRF, *World Road Statistics*.

CIVIL AVIATION
(traffic on scheduled services)*

	1999	2000	2001
Kilometres flown (million)	3	3	1
Passengers carried ('000)	84	77	46
Passenger-km (million)	235	216	130
Total ton-km (million)	36	32	19

* Including an apportionment of the traffic of Air Afrique.
Source: UN, *Statistical Yearbook*.

Tourism

FOREIGN TOURIST ARRIVALS BY ORIGIN*

	2004†	2005	2006
Africa	38,000	37,926	36,199
America	2,500	3,150	4,223
Asia	1,500	2,835	3,017
Europe	14,500	17,649	16,893
France	12,000	14,588	13,971
Total (incl. others)	57,000	63,451	60,332

* Figures refer to arrivals at national borders.
† Rounded figures.

Receipts from tourism (US $ million, excl. passenger transport): 31 in 2004; 43 in 2005; 35 in 2006.

Source: World Tourism Organization.

Communications Media

	2004	2005	2006
Telephones ('000 main lines in use)	24.1	24.0	n.a.
Mobile cellular telephones ('000 subscribers)	148.3	299.9	483.0
Personal computers ('000 in use)*	9	10	n.a.
Internet users ('000)*	24.0	24.0	40
Broadband subscribers	100	200	200

* Estimates.
2006: Internet users ('000) 40.0.
Television receivers ('000 in use): 395 in 2000.
Radio receivers ('000 in use): 680 in 1997.
Facsimile machines (number in use): 327 in 1995.
Daily newspapers: 1 (average circulation 2,000 copies) in 1996; 1 (average circulation 2,000 copies) in 1997; 1 (average circulation 2,000 copies) in 1998.
Non-daily newspapers: 5 (average circulation 14,000 copies) in 1996.
Books published (first editions): titles 5; copies ('000) 11 in 1991.

Sources: UNESCO, *Statistical Yearbook*; UNESCO Institute for Statistics; UN, *Statistical Yearbook*; International Telecommunication Union.

Education

(2005/06, unless otherwise indicated)

	Institutions	Teachers	Students
Pre-primary	347	914	24,287
Primary	8,301*	28,163	1,126,075
Secondary	367	4,130	210,626
Tertiary*	7	278	4,953
University	1	284	8,710

* 2004/05 figure(s).
Adult literacy rate (UNESCO estimates): 30.4% (males 44.3%; females 16.4%) in 2007 (Source: UNESCO Institute for Statistics).

Directory

The Constitution

The Constitution of the Fifth Republic, promulgated on 9 August 1999, envisages a balance of powers between the President, Government and legislative Assemblée nationale. The President, who is elected by universal adult suffrage, is Head of State, and is accorded 'broad ordinary and arbitral powers'. The Government, under a Prime Minister appointed by the President, is responsible to the Assemblée nationale, which is competent to remove the Prime Minister by vote of censure. The Assemblée nationale is similarly elected by direct adult suffrage. The new President and legislature were inaugurated in December 1999.

Enshrined in the Constitution is a clause granting immunity from prosecution for all those involved in the *coups d'état* of January 1996

NIGER

and April 1999. Legislation to this effect was adopted by the Assemblée nationale in January 2000.

Among regulatory bodies provided for in the Constitution are the Conseil supérieur de la communication, responsible for the broadcasting and communications sector, and the Conseil supérieur de la défense nationale, which advises the Head of State on defence matters.

The Government

HEAD OF STATE

President: Col (retd) MAMADOU TANDJA (inaugurated 22 December 1999, re-elected 4 December 2004).

COUNCIL OF MINISTERS
(April 2009)

Prime Minister: SEYNI OUMAROU.
Minister of State, Minister of the Interior, Public Security and Decentralization: ALBADÉ ABOUBA.
Minister of Foreign Affairs and Co-operation: AÏCHATOU MINDAOUDOU.
Minister of the Economy and Finance: ALI MAHAMANE LAMINE ZEINE.
Minister of Agricultural Development: MOUSSA MAHAMANE.
Minister of Youth and Sports: MOUSSA ABDOURAHAMANE SEYDOU.
Minister of Town Planning, Living Conditions and the Land Register: AÏSSA DIALLO ABDOULAYE.
Minister of Mines and Energy: MOHAMED ABDOULAHI.
Minister of Secondary and Higher Education, Research and Technology: Prof. SIDIKOU OUMAROU.
Minister of Communication, Spokesperson for the Government: MOHAMED BEN OMAR.
Minister of the Civil Service and Labour: KANDA SIPTEY.
Minister of Culture, the Arts and Leisure, responsible for the Promotion of Entrepreneurship in the Arts: OUMAROU HADARY.
Minister of Population and Social Reform: BOUKARI ZILA MAHAMADOU.
Minister of National Education: Dr OUSMANE SAMBA MAMADOU.
Minister of Equipment: LAMIDO MOUMOUNI HAROUNA.
Minister responsible for Relations with State Institutions: SALIFOU MADOU KELZOU.
Minister of the Environment and Anti-desertification: ISSOUFOU BAKO.
Minister of National Competitiveness and the Reduction of the High Cost of Living: ABDOU DAOUDA.
Minister responsible for Religious Affairs and Humanitarian Action: LABO ISSAKA.
Minister of Trade, Industry and Normalization: HALIDOU BADJE.
Minister of Justice, Keeper of the Seals: DAGRA MAHAMADOU.
Minister of Animal Resources: ISSIAH KATO.
Minister of National Defence: JIDDA HAMADOU.
Minister of Public Health: ISSA LAMINE.
Minister of Tourism and Crafts: AMADOU AISSA SIDDO.
Minister of Transport and Civil Aviation: AMADOU NOUHOU.
Minister of Land Settlement and Community Development: SADÉ SOULEY.
Minister of Water Resources: AMINOU TASSIOU.
Minister for the Promotion of Young Entrepreneurs and the Reform of Public Enterprises: SALOU GOBI.
Minister of Vocational and Technical Training: MAIZAMA HADIZA.
Minister for the Promotion of Women and the Protection of Children: BARRY BIBATA NIANDOU.
Minister of African Integration and Nationals Living Abroad: SEYDOU HACHIMOU.

MINISTRIES

Office of the President: BP 550, Niamey; tel. 20-72-23-80; fax 20-72-33-96; internet www.presidence.ne.
Office of the Prime Minister: BP 893, Niamey; tel. 20-72-26-99; fax 20-73-58-59.
Ministry of Agricultural Development: BP 12091, Niamey; tel. 20-73-35-41; fax 20-73-20-08.
Ministry of Animal Resources: BP 12091, Niamey; tel. 20-73-79-59; fax 20-73-31-86.
Ministry of Basic Education and Literacy: BP 557, Niamey; tel. 20-72-28-33; fax 20-72-21-05; e-mail scdameb@intnet.ne.
Ministry of Capital Works: BP 403, Niamey; tel. 20-73-53-57; fax 20-72-21-71.
Ministry of the Civil Service and Labour: BP 11107, Niamey; tel. 20-73-22-31; fax 20-73-61-69; e-mail sani.yakouba@caramail.com.
Ministry of Culture, the Arts and Communication: BP 452, Niamey; tel. 20-72-28-74; fax 20-73-36-85.
Ministry of the Economy and Finance: BP 389, Niamey; tel. 20-72-23-74; fax 20-73-59-34.
Ministry of Equipment: Niamey.
Ministry of Foreign Affairs and Co-operation: BP 396, Niamey; tel. 20-72-29-07; fax 20-73-52-31.
Ministry of the Interior, Public Security and Decentralization: BP 622, Niamey; tel. 20-72-32-62; fax 20-72-21-76.
Ministry of Justice: BP 466, Niamey; tel. 20-72-31-31; fax 20-72-37-77.
Ministry of Land Settlement and Community Development: BP 403, Niamey; tel. 20-73-53-57; fax 20-72-21-71.
Ministry of Mines and Energy: BP 11700, Niamey; tel. 20-73-45-82; fax 20-73-27-59.
Ministry of National Defence: BP 626, Niamey; tel. 20-72-20-76; fax 20-72-40-78.
Ministry of Population and Social Reform: BP 11286, Niamey; tel. 20-72-23-30; fax 20-73-61-65.
Ministry of Privatization and the Restructuring of Enterprises: Immeuble CCCP, BP 862, Niamey; tel. 20-73-27-50; fax 20-73-59-91; e-mail ccpp@intnet.ne.
Ministry of Professional and Technical Training: BP 628, Niamey; tel. 20-72-26-20; fax 20-72-40-40.
Ministry for the Promotion of Women and the Protection of Children: BP 11286, Niamey; tel. 20-72-23-30; fax 20-73-61-65.
Ministry of Public Health and the Fight against Epidemics: BP 623, Niamey; tel. 20-72-28-08; fax 20-73-35-70.
Ministry of Secondary and Higher Education, Research and Technology: BP 628, Niamey; tel. 20-72-26-20; fax 20-72-40-40; e-mail mesnt@intnet.ne.
Ministry of Tourism and Crafts: BP 480, Niamey; tel. 20-73-65-22; fax 20-72-23-87; internet www.niger-tourisme.com.
Ministry of Town Planning, Living Conditions and the Land Register: BP 403, Niamey; tel. 20-73-53-57; fax 20-72-21-71.
Ministry of Trade, Industry and the Promotion of the Private Sector: BP 480, Niamey; tel. 20-73-29-74; fax 20-73-21-50; e-mail nicom@intnet.ne.
Ministry of Transport: BP 12130, Niamey; tel. 20-72-28-21; fax 20-73-36-85.
Ministry of Water Resources, the Environment and Anti-desertification: BP 257, Niamey; tel. 20-73-47-22; fax 20-72-40-15.
Ministry of Youth, Sports and the Games of La Francophonie: BP 215, Niamey; tel. 20-72-32-35; fax 20-72-23-36.

President and Legislature

PRESIDENT

Presidential Election, First Round, 16 November 2004

Candidate	Votes	% of votes
Mamadou Tandja (MNSD—Nassara)	991,764	40.67
Mahamadou Issoufou (PNDS)	599,792	24.60
Mahamane Ousmane (CDS)	425,052	17.43
Cheiffou Amadou (RSD)	154,732	6.34
Moumouni Adamou Djermakoye (ANDP)	147,957	6.07
Hamid Algabid (RDP)	119,153	4.89
Total	**2,438,450**	**100.00**

Second Round, 4 December 2004

Candidate	Votes	% of votes
Mamadou Tandja (MNSD—Nassara)	1,509,905	65.53
Mahamadou Issoufou (PNDS)	794,397	34.47
Total	**2,304,302**	**100.00**

LEGISLATURE

Assemblée nationale

pl. de la Concertation, BP 12234, Niamey; tel. 20-72-27-38; fax 20-72-43-08; e-mail an@assemblee.ne; internet www.assemblee.ne.
President: El Hadj MAHAMANE OUSMANE.

General Election, 4 December 2004

Party	Seats
Mouvement national pour la société de développement—Nassara (MNSD—Nassara)	47
Parti nigérien pour la démocratie et le socialisme—Tarayya (PNDS)	25*
Convention démocratique et social—Rahama (CDS)	22
Rassemblement social-démocratique—Gaskiya (RSD)	7
Rassemblement pour la démocratie et le progrès—Jama'a (RDP)	6
Alliance nigérienne pour la démocratie et le progrès social—Zaman Lahiya (ANDP)	5
Parti Social Démocrate du Niger—Alheri	1
Total	**113**

*Including eight seats won by parties running in coalition with the PNDS, namely the Parti nigérien pour l'autogestion (PNA), the Parti progressiste nigérien pour le rassemblement démocratique africain (PPN—RDA), the Union pour la démocratie et la République (UDR) and the Union nigérienne des indépendants (UNI).

Election Commission

Commission électorale nationale indépendante (CENI): Niamey; Chair. HAMIDOU MOUMOUNI.

Political Organizations

In early 2008 there were some 24 political parties registered in Niger, of which the following were among the most prominent:

Alliance nigérienne pour la démocratie et le progrès social—Zaman Lahiya (ANDP): Quartier Abidjan, Niamey; tel. 20-74-07-50; fmrly mem. of opposition Coordination des forces démocratiques (CFD); joined pro-Govt Alliance des forces démocratiques (AFD) in 2002; Leader Col (retd) MOUMOUNI ADAMOU DJERMAKOYE.

Alliance pour la démocratie et le progrès—Zumunci (ADP): Niamey; tel. 20-73-67-57; e-mail adp@zumunci.com; internet www.adpzumunci.com; f. 1992; Chair. ISSOUFOU BACHAR.

Convention démocratique et social—Rahama (CDS): BP 11973, Niamey; tel. 20-74-19-85; f. 1991; supports Govt of Hama Amadou; mem. of Alliance des forces démocratiques (AFD); Pres. MAHAMANE OUSMANE.

Mouvement national pour la société de développement—Nassara (MNSD—Nassara): rue Issa Beri 30, cnr blvd de Zarmaganda, porte 72, BP 881, Niamey; tel. 20-73-39-07; fax 20-72-41-74; e-mail presi@mnsd-nassara.org; internet www.mnsd.ne; f. 1988; sole party 1988–90; restyled as MNSD—Nassara in 1991; Chair. Col (retd) MAMADOU TANDJA; Pres. SEYNI OUMAROU.

Parti nigérien pour l'autogestion—al Umat (PNA): Quartier Zabarkian, Niamey; tel. 20-72-33-05; f. 1997; contested legislative elections in Dec. 2004 in coalition with the PNDS; Leader SANOUSSI JACKOU.

Parti nigérien pour la démocratie et le socialisme—Tarayya (PNDS): pl. Toumo, Niamey; tel. 20-74-48-78; f. 1990; mem. of Coordination des forces démocratiques (CFD); Sec.-Gen. MAHAMADOU ISSOUFOU.

Parti progressiste nigérien—Rassemblement démocratique africain (PPN—RDA): Quartier Sonni, Niamey; tel. 20-74-16-70; associated with the late Pres. Diori; mem. of Coordination des forces démocratiques (CFD); contested legislative elections in Dec. 2004 in coalition with the PNDS; Chair. ABDOULAYE DIORI.

Parti social-démocrate nigérien—Alheri (PSDN): tel. 20-72-28-52; Pres. LABO ISSAKA.

Rassemblement pour la démocratie et le progrès—Djamaa (RDP): pl. Toumo, Niamey; tel. 20-74-23-82; party of late Pres. Maïnassara; Chair. HAMID ALGABID; Sec.-Gen. MAHAMANE SOULEY LABI.

Rassemblement social-démocratique—Gaskiya (RSD): Quartier Poudrière, Niamey; tel. 20-74-00-90; f. 2004 following split in the CDS; Pres. CHEIFFOU AMADOU.

Rassemblement pour un Sahel vert—Ni'ima (RSV): BP 12515, Niamey; tel. and fax 20-74-11-25; e-mail agarba_99@yahoo.com; f. 1991; Pres. ADAMOU GARBA.

Union pour la démocratie et le progrès—Amici (UDP): supports Govt of Hama Amadou; mem. of Alliance des forces démocratiques (AFD); Leader ABDOULAYE TONDI.

Union pour la démocratie et le progrès social—Amana (UDPS): represents interests of Tuaregs; mem. of Coordination des forces démocratiques (CFD); Chair. RHISSA AG BOULA.

Union pour la démocratie et la République—Tabbat (UDR): Quartier Plateau, Niamey; f. 2002; contested legislative elections in Dec. 2004 in coalition with the PNDS; Pres. AMADOU BOUABACAR CISSÉ.

Union des forces populaires pour la démocratie et le progrès—Sawaba (UFPDP): Niamey; tel. 20-73-51-38; Leader IBRAHIM BAOUA SOULEY.

Union des Nigeriens indépendants (UNI): Quartier Zabarkan, Niamey; tel. 20-74-23-81; contested legislative elections in Dec. 2004 in coalition with the PNDS; Leader AMADOU DJIBO.

Union des patriotes démocratiques et progressistes—Shamuwa (UPDP): Niamey; tel. 20-74-12-59; Chair. Prof. ANDRÉ SALIFOU.

Union des socialistes nigériens—Talaka (USN): f. 2001 by mems of the UFPDP; Leader ISSOUFOU ASSOUMANE.

Diplomatic Representation

EMBASSIES IN NIGER

Algeria: route des Ambassades-Goudel, BP 142, Niamey; tel. 20-72-35-83; fax 20-72-35-93; Ambassador HAMID BOUKRIF.

Benin: BP 11544, Niamey; tel. 20-72-28-60; Ambassador TAÏROU MAMADOU DJAOUGA.

Chad: POB 12820, Niamey; tel. 20-75-34-64; fax 20-72-43-61; Ambassador YOUSSOUF MBODOU MBAMI.

China, People's Republic: BP 873, Niamey; tel. 20-72-32-83; fax 20-72-32-85; e-mail embchina@intnet.ne; Ambassador CHEN GONGLAI.

Cuba: rue Tillaberi, angle rue de la Cure Salée, face lycée Franco-Arabe, Plateau, BP 13886, Niamey; tel. 20-72-46-00; fax 20-72-39-32; e-mail embacuba@niger.cubaminrex.cu; Ambassador ROBERTO RODRÍGUEZ PENA.

Egypt: Terminus Rond-Point Grand Hôtel, BP 254, Niamey; tel. 20-73-33-55; fax 20-73-38-91; Ambassador MOHAMED MAHMOUD MOUSTAFA EL-ASHMAWI.

France: route de Tondibia, Quartier Yantala, BP 10660, Niamey; tel. 20-72-24-32; fax 20-72-25-18; e-mail webmestre@mail.com; internet www.ambafrance-ne.org; Ambassador ALAIN HOLLEVILLE.

Germany: 71 ave du Général de Gaulle, BP 629, Niamey; tel. 20-72-35-10; fax 20-72-39-85; e-mail amb-all-ny@web.de; Ambassador RÜDIGER JOHN.

Iran: 11 rue de la Présidence, BP 10543, Niamey; tel. 20-72-21-98; fax 20-72-28-10; Ambassador MOHAMMAD AMIN NEJAD.

Korea, Democratic People's Republic: Niamey; Ambassador PAK SONG IL.

Libya: route de Goudel, BP 683, Niamey; tel. 20-72-40-19; fax 20-72-40-97; e-mail boukhari@intnet.ne; Ambassador BOUKHARI SALEM HODA.

Morocco: ave du Président Lubke, face Clinique Kaba, BP 12403, Niamey; tel. 20-73-40-84; fax 20-73-80-27; e-mail ambmang@intnet.ne; Ambassador TAYEB RAOUF.

Nigeria: rue Goudel, BP 11130, Niamey; tel. 20-73-24-10; fax 20-73-35-00; e-mail embnig@intnet.ne; Ambassador Dr YAKUBU KWARI.

Pakistan: 90 rue YN 001, ave des Zarmakoye, Yantala Plateau, BP 10426, Niamey; tel. 20-75-32-57; fax 20-75-32-55; e-mail parepniamey@yahoo.com; internet www.brain.net.pk/~farata/; Ambassador (vacant).

Saudi Arabia: route de Tillabery, BP 339, Niamey; tel. 20-75-32-15; fax 20-75-24-42; e-mail neemb@mofa.gov.sa; Ambassador ABDUL KAREEM MOHAMMAD AL-MALIKI.

USA: rue des Ambassades, BP 11201, Niamey; tel. 20-73-31-69; fax 20-73-55-60; e-mail NiameyPASN@state.gov; internet niamey.usembassy.gov; Ambassador BERNADETTE MARY ALLEN.

Judicial System

The Supreme Court was dissolved following the death of President Ibrahim Baré Maïnassara in April 1999, but was re-established

NIGER

Directory

following the return to constitutional order later in that year. In accordance with the Constitution of the Fifth Republic, promulgated in August 1999, a Constitutional Court was established to replace the former Constitutional Chamber of the Supreme Court.

High Court of Justice: Niamey; internet www.assemblee.ne/organes/hjc.htm; competent to indict the President of the Republic and all other state officials (past and present) in relation to all matters of state, including high treason; comprises seven perm. mems and three rotating mems; Pres. OUMAROU CISSE.

Supreme Court: Niamey; tel. 20-74-26-36; comprises three chambers; in 2002 the Government announced proposals to replace the Supreme Court with three separate courts: a Court of Cassation, a Council of State and an Audit Court; Pres. MAMADOU MALLAM AOUMI; Vice-Pres. SALIFOU FATIMATA BAZEYE; Pres. of the Administrative Chamber DILLE RABO; Pres. of the Judicial Chamber (vacant); Pres. of the Chamber of Audit and Budgetary Discipline SIKKOSO MORY OUSMANE; Prosecutor-Gen. MAHAMANE BOUKARY.

Constitutional Court: BP 10779, Niamey; tel. 20-72-30-81; fax 20-72-35-40; e-mail cconstit@intnet.ne; f. 1999; comprises a President, a Vice-President and five Councillors; Pres. SANI KOUTOUBI; Vice-Pres. ABDOU HASSAN.

Courts of First Instance: located at Niamey (with sub-divisions at Dosso and Tillabéri), Maradi, Tahoua (sub-divisions at Agadez, Arlit and Birni N'Konni) and Diffa (sub-division at Diffa).

Labour Courts: function at each Court of the First Instance and sub-division thereof.

Religion

It is estimated that some 95% of the population are Muslims, 0.5% are Christians and the remainder follow traditional beliefs.

ISLAM

The most influential Islamic groups in Niger are the Tijaniyya, the Senoussi and the Hamallists.

Association Islamique du Niger: BP 2220, Niamey; tel. 20-74-08-90; Dir CHEIKH OUMAROU ISMAEL.

CHRISTIANITY

The Roman Catholic Church

Niger comprises two dioceses, directly responsible to the Holy See. The Bishops participate in the Bishops' Conference of Burkina Faso and Niger (based in Ouagadougou, Burkina Faso). At 31 December 2006 there were an estimated 19,150 adherents in Niger.

Bishop of Maradi: Rt Rev. AMBROISE OUÉDRAOGO, Evêché, BP 447, Maradi; tel. and fax 20-41-03-30; fax 20-41-13-86; e-mail evechemi@intnet.ne.

Bishop of Niamey: Rt Rev. MICHEL CHRISTIAN CARTATÉGUY, Evêché, BP 10270, Niamey; tel. 20-73-32-59; fax 20-73-80-01; e-mail cartateguymi@voila.fr; internet www.multimania.com/cathoniger.

The Press

The published press expanded considerably in Niger after 1993, when the requirement to obtain prior authorization for each edition was lifted, although legislation continued to require that a copy of each publication be deposited at the office of the Procurator of the Republic. For the most part, however, economic difficulties have ensured that few publications have maintained a regular, sustained appearance. The following were among those newspapers and periodicals believed to be appearing regularly in early 2005:

L'Action: Quartier Yantala, Niamey; tel. 96-96-92-22; e-mail action_ne@yahoo.fr; internet www.tamtaminfo.com/action.pdf; f. 2003; fortnightly; popular newspaper intended for youth audience; Dir of Publication BOUSSADA BEN ALI; circ. 2,000 (2003).

L'Alternative: BP 10948, Niamey; tel. 20-74-24-39; fax 20-74-24-82; e-mail alter@intnet.ne; internet www.alternative.ne; f. 1994; weekly; in French and Hausa; Dir MOUSSA TCHANGARI; Editor-in-Chief ABDRAMANE OUSMANE.

Anfani: Immeuble DMK, rue du Damagaram, BP 2096, Niamey; tel. 20-74-08-80; fax 20-74-00-52; e-mail anfani@intnet.ne; f. 1992; 2 a month; Editor-in-Chief IBBO DADDY ABDOULAYE; circ. 3,000.

As-Salam: BP 451, Niamey; tel. 20-74-29-12; e-mail assa_lam@yahoo.fr; monthly; Dir IBBO DADDY ABDOULAYE.

Le Canard Déchainé: BP 383, Niamey; tel. 93-92-66-64; satirical; weekly; Dir of Publication ABDOULAYE TIÉMOGO; Editor-in-Chief IBRAHIM MANZO.

Le Canard Libéré: BP 11631, Niamey; tel. 20-75-43-52; fax 20-75-39-89; e-mail canardlibere@caramail.com; satirical; weekly; Dir of Publication TRAORÉ DAOUDA AMADOU; Editorial Dir OUMAROU NALAN MOUSSA.

Le Démocrate: 21 rue 067, NB Terminus, BP 11064, Niamey; tel. 20-73-24-25; e-mail le_democrate@caramail.com; internet www.tamtaminfo.com/democrate.pdf; weekly; independent; f. 1992; Dir of Publication ALBERT CHAÏBOU; Editor-in-Chief OUSSEINI ISSA.

Les Echos du Sahel: Villa 4012, 105 Logements, BP 12750, Niamey; tel. and fax 20-74-32-17; e-mail ecosahel@intnet.ne; f. 1999; rural issues and devt; quarterly; Dir IBBO DADDY ABDOULAYE.

L'Enquêteur: BP 172, Niamey; tel. 93-90-18-74; e-mail lenqueteur@yahoo.fr; fortnightly; Publr TAHIROU GOURO; Editor IBRAHIM SOULEY.

Haské: BP 297, Niamey; tel. 20-74-18-44; fax 20-73-20-06; e-mail webmaster@planetafrique.com; internet www.haske.uni.cc; f. 1990; weekly; also Haské Magazine, quarterly; Dir CHEIKH IBRAHIM DIOP.

La Jeune Académie: BP 11989, Niamey; tel. 20-73-38-71; e-mail jeune.academie@caramail.com; monthly; Dir ABDOULAYE HASSOUMI GARBA.

Journal Officiel de la République du Niger: BP 116, Niamey; tel. 20-72-39-30; fax 20-72-39-43; f. 1960; fortnightly; govt bulletin; Man. Editor BONKOULA AMINATOU MAYAKI; circ. 800.

Libération: BP 10483, Niamey; tel. 96-97-96-22; f. 1995; weekly; Dir BOUBACAR DIALLO; circ. 1,000 (2003).

Matinfo: BP 11631, Niamey; tel. 20-75-43-52; fax 20-75-39-89; e-mail matinfo@caramail.com; daily; independent; Dir DAOUDA AMADOU TRAORÉ.

Nigerama: BP 11158, Niamey; tel. 20-74-08-09; e-mail anpniger@intnet.ne; quarterly; publ. by the Agence Nigérienne de Presse.

L'Opinion: BP 11116, Niamey; tel. 20-74-09-84; e-mail lopinion@dounia.ne; Dir ALZOUMA ZAKARI.

Le Regard: Niamey; tel. 20-73-84-07; e-mail le_regard@usa.net; Dir MAHAMADOU TOURÉ.

Le Républicain: Nouvelle Imprimerie du Niger, pl. du Petit Marché, BP 12015, Niamey; tel. 20-73-47-98; fax 20-73-41-42; e-mail webmasters@republicain-niger.com; internet www.republicain-niger.com; f. 1991; weekly; independent; Dir of Publication MAMANE ABOU; circ. 2,500.

La Roue de l'Histoire: Zabarkan, rue du SNEN, BP 5005, Niamey; tel. 20-74-05-69; internet www.tamtaminfo.com/roue.pdf; weekly; Propr SANOUSSI JACKOU; Dir ABARAD MOUDOUR ZAKARA.

Le Sahel Quotidien: BP 13182, ONEP, Niamey; tel. 20-73-34-87; fax 20-73-30-90; f. 1960; publ. by Office National d'Edition et de Presse; daily; Dir IBRAHIM MAMANE TANTAN; Editor-in-Chief ALASSANE ASOKOFARE; circ. 5,000; also Sahel-Dimanche, Sundays; circ. 3,000.

Sauyi: BP 10948, Niamey; tel. 20-74-24-39; fax 20-74-24-82; e-mail sarji@alternative.ne; fortnightly; Hausa; publ. by Groupe Alternative; Hausa; rural interest; Dir SAÏDOU ARJI.

Stadium: BP 10948, Niamey; tel. 20-74-08-80; e-mail kiabba@yahoo.fr; sports; 2 a month; Dir ABDOU TIKIRÉ.

Le Témoin: BP 10483, Niamey; tel. 96-96-58-51; e-mail istemoin@yahoo.fr; internet www.tamtaminfo.com/temoin.pdf; 2 a month; Dir of Publication IBRAHIM SOUMANA GAOH; Editors AMADOU TIÉMOGO, MOUSSA DAN TCHOUKOU, I. S. GAOH; circ. 1,000 (2005).

Ténéré Express: BP 13600, Niamey; tel. 20-73-35-76; fax 20-73-77-75; e-mail tenerefm@intnet.ne; daily; independent; current affairs; Dir ABDOULAYE MOUSSA MASSALATCHI.

La Tribune du Peuple: Niamey; tel. 20-73-34-28; e-mail tribune@intnet.ne; f. 1993; weekly; Man. Editor IBRAHIM HAMIDOU.

Le Trophée: BP 2000, Niamey; tel. 20-74-12-79; e-mail strophee@caramail.com; sports; 2 a month; Dir ISSA HAMIDOU MAYAKI.

NEWS AGENCIES

Agence Nigérienne de Presse (ANP): BP 11158, Niamey; tel. 20-74-08-09; e-mail anpniger@intnet.ne; f. 1987; state-owned; Dir YAYE HASSANE.

Sahel—Office National d'Edition et de Presse (ONEP): BP 13182, Niamey; tel. 20-73-34-86; f. 1989; Dir ALI OUSSEÏNI.

Publishers

La Nouvelle Imprimerie du Niger (NIN): pl. du Petit Marché, BP 61, Niamey; tel. 20-73-47-98; fax 20-73-41-42; e-mail imprim@intnet.ne; f. 1962 as Imprimerie Nationale du Niger; govt publishing house; brs in Agadez and Maradi; Dir MAMAN ABOU.

Réseau Sahélien de Recherche et de Publication: Niamey; tel. 20-73-36-90; fax 20-73-39-43; e-mail resadep@ilimi.uam.ne; press of the Université Abdou Moumouni; Co-ordinator BOUREIMA DIADIE.

NIGER

Directory

Broadcasting and Communications

REGULATORY AUTHORITY

Conseil Supérieur de la Communication (CSC): Plateau, Niamey; tel. 20-72-23-56; comprises 15 mems; Pres. MARIAMA KEÏTA.

TELECOMMUNICATIONS

Celtel Niger (Zain): Route de l'Aéroport, BP 11922, Niamey; tel. 20-73-23-46; fax 20-73-23-85; e-mail info.ne@zain.com; internet www.ne.zain.com; f. 2001 to operate mobile cellular telecommunications network in Niamey and Maradi; owned by Zain Group (Kuwait); Dir-Gen. JEAN-LÉON BONNECHÈRE.

Société Nigérienne des Télécommunications (SONITEL): BP 208, Niamey; tel. 20-72-29-98; fax 20-72-24-78; e-mail sonitel@intnet.ne; internet www.intnet.ne; f. 1998; 51% jtly owned by ZTE Corpn (People's Republic of China) and Laaico (Libya), 46% state-owned; Dir-Gen. MOUSSA BOUBACAR.

Sahel Com: BP 208, Niamey; f. 2002; mobile cellular telecommunications in Niamey.

Telecel Niger: Niamey; tel. 20-74-44-44; e-mail telecel@telecelniger.com; internet www.telecelniger.com; f. 2001 to operate mobile cellular telecommunications network, initially in Niamey and western regions, expanding to cover Maradi and Zinder by 2003, and Tahoua and Agadez by 2004; 68% owned by Orascom Telecom (Egypt); Dir HIMA SOULEY.

BROADCASTING

Radio

Independent radio stations have been permitted to operate since 1994, although the majority are concentrated in the capital, Niamey. In 2000 the first of a network of rural stations, RURANET, which were to broadcast mainly programmes concerned with development issues, mostly in national languages, was established. Several local radio stations, funded by the Agence intergouvernementale de la francophonie, were expected to commence operations in the early 2000s.

Anfani FM: blvd Nali-Béro, BP 2096, Wadata, Niamey; tel. 20-74-08-80; fax 20-74-00-52; e-mail anfani@intnet.ne; private radio station, broadcasting to Niamey, Zinder, Maradi and Diffa; Dir ISMAËL MOUTARI.

Office de Radiodiffusion-Télévision du Niger (ORTN): BP 309, Niamey; tel. 20-72-31-63; fax 20-72-35-48; internet www.telesahel.org/ortne; f. 1967; state broadcasting authority; Dir-Gen. YAYÉ HAROUNA.

La Voix du Sahel: BP 361, Niamey; tel. 20-72-22-02; fax 72-35-48; e-mail ortny@intnet.ne; f. 1958; govt-controlled radio service; programmes in French, Hausa, Djerma, Kanuri, Fulfuldé, Tamajak, Toubou, Gourmantché, Boudouma and Arabic; Dir IBRO NA-ALLAH AMADOU.

Ténéré FM: BP 13600, Niamey; tel. 20-73-65-76; fax 20-73-46-94; e-mail tenerefm@intnet.ne; f. 1998; Dir ABIBOU GARBA; Editor-in-Chief SOULEYMANE ISSA MAÏGA.

Ruranet: Niamey; internet membres.lycos.fr/nigeradio; f. 2000; network of rural radio stations, broadcasting 80% in national languages, with 80% of programmes concerned with devt issues; 31 stations operative in April 2002.

La Voix de l'Hémicycle: BP 12234, Niamey; f. 2002 as the radio station of the Assemblée nationale; broadcasts parliamentary debates and analysis for 15 hours daily in French and national languages to Niamey and environs.

Sudan FM: Dosso; auth. 2000; private radio station; Dir HIMA ADAMOU.

Television

Office de Radiodiffusion-Télévision du Niger (ORTN): see Radio

Tal TV: BP 309, Niamey; f. 2001; broadcasts 72 hours of programmes each week.

Télé-Sahel: BP 309, Niamey; tel. 20-72-31-55; fax 20-72-35-48; govt-controlled television service; broadcasts daily from 13 transmission posts and six retransmission posts, covering most of Niger; Dir-Gen. ABDOU SOULEY.

Télévision Ténéré (TTV): BP 13600, Niamey; tel. 20-73-65-76; fax 20-73-77-75; e-mail tenerefm@intnet.ne; f. 2000; independent broadcaster in Niamey; Dir ABIBOU GARBA.

The independent operator, Télé Star, broadcasts several international or foreign channels in Niamey and environs, including TV5 Monde, Canal Horizon, CFI, RTL9, CNN and Euro News.

Finance

(cap. = capital; res = reserves; dep. = deposits; m. = million; brs = branches; amounts in francs CFA)

BANKING

Central Bank

Banque centrale des états de l'Afrique de l'ouest (BCEAO): BP 487, Niamey; tel. 20-72-24-91; fax 20-73-47-43; HQ in Dakar, Senegal; f. 1962; bank of issue for the mem. states of the Union économique et monétaire ouest-africaine (UEMOA, comprising Benin, Burkina Faso, Côte d'Ivoire, Guinea-Bissau, Mali, Niger, Senegal and Togo); cap. and res 1,148,589m., total assets 5,099,908m. (Dec. 2005); Gov. PHILIPPE-HENRI DACOURY-TABLEY; Dir in Niger ABDOULAYE SOUMANA; brs at Maradi and Zinder.

Commercial Banks

Bank of Africa—Niger (BOA-Niger): Immeuble BOA, rue du Gawèye, BP 10973, Niamey; tel. 20-73-36-20; fax 20-73-38-18; e-mail information@boaniger.com; internet www.boaniger.com; f. 1994 to acquire assets of Nigeria International Bank Niamey; 42.6% owned by African Financial Holding; cap. 1,950m., res 1,194m., total assets 70,542m. (Dec. 2007); Pres. PAUL DERREUMAUX; Dir-Gen. MAMADOU SÉNÉ; 5 brs.

Banque Atlantique Niger: BP 375, Rond Point Liberté, Niamey; tel. 20-73-98-88; fax 20-73-98-91; e-mail ban@banqueatlantique.net; internet www.banqueatlantique.net; f. 2005; 73% owned by Atlantic Financial Group, Lomé; total assets US $ 19.5m. (Dec. 2006); Chair. KONE DOSSONGUI; Man. Dir AMADOU MOUSTAPHA DIOUF.

Banque Commerciale du Niger (BCN): rue du Combattant, BP 11363, Niamey; tel. 20-73-39-15; fax 20-73-21-63; e-mail info@bcn.ne; internet www.bcn-niger.com; f. 1978; 83.15% owned by Libyan Arab Foreign Bank, 16.85% state-owned; cap. and res 1,477m., total assets 14,618m. (Dec. 2003); Administrator IBRAHIM MAJDOUB NAJI (acting).

Banque Internationale pour l'Afrique au Niger (BIA—Niger): ave de la Mairie, BP 10350, Niamey; tel. 20-73-31-01; fax 20-73-35-95; e-mail bia@intnet.ne; internet www.bianiger.com; f. 1980; 35% owned by Groupe Belgolaise (Belgium); cap. 2,800m., res 1,905m., dep. 58,108m. (Dec. 2005); Pres. AMADOU HIMA SOULEY; Dir-Gen. DANIEL HASSER; 11 brs.

Banque Islamique du Niger pour le Commerce et l'Investissement (BINCI): Immeuble El Nasr, BP 12754, Niamey; tel. 20-73-27-30; fax 20-73-47-35; e-mail binci@intnet.ne; f. 1983; fmrly Banque Masraf Faisal Islami; 33% owned by Dar al-Maal al-Islami (Switzerland), 33% by Islamic Development Bank (Saudi Arabia); cap. 1,810m., total assets 7,453m. (Dec. 2003); Pres. ABDERRAOUF BENESSAÏAH; Dir-Gen. AISSANI OMAR.

Ecobank Niger: blvd de la Liberté, angle rue des Bâtisseurs, BP 13804, Niamey; tel. 20-73-71-81; fax 20-73-72-04; e-mail ecobankni@ecobank.com; internet www.ecobank.com; f. 1999; 99.85% owned by Ecobank Transnational Inc, Lomé; total assets 38,256m. (Dec. 2005); Chair. IBRAHIM IDDI ANGO; Dir-Gen. MOUKARAMOU CHANOU.

Société Nigérienne de Banque (SONIBANK): ave de la Mairie, BP 891, Niamey; tel. 20-73-45-69; fax 20-73-46-93; e-mail sonibanq@intnet.ne; internet www.sonibank.net; f. 1990; 25% owned by Société Tunisienne de Banque; cap. 2,000m., res 6,101m., dep. 82,686m. (Dec. 2007); Pres. ILLA KANÉ; Dir-Gen. MOUSSA HAITOU; 6 brs.

Development Banks

Caisse de Prêts aux Collectivités Territoriales (CPCT): route Torodi, BP 730, Niamey; tel. 20-72-34-12; fax 20-72-30-80; f. 1970; 100% state-owned (94% by organs of local govt); cap. and res 744m., total assets 2,541m. (Dec. 2003); Administrator ABDOU DJIBO (acting).

Crédit du Niger (CDN): 11 blvd de la République, BP 213, Niger; tel. 20-72-27-01; fax 20-72-23-90; e-mail cdb-nig@intnet.ne; f. 1958; 54% state-owned, 20% owned by Caisse Nationale de Sécurité Sociale; transfer to full private ownership pending; cap. and res 1,058m., total assets 3,602m. (Dec. 2003); Administrator ABDOU DJIBO (acting).

Fonds d'Intervention en Faveur des Petites et Moyennes Entreprises Nigériennes (FIPMEN): Immeuble Sonara II, BP 252, Niamey; tel. 20-73-20-98; f. 1990; state-owned; cap. and res 124m. (Dec. 1991); Chair. AMADOU SALLA HASSANE; Man. Dir IBRAHIM BEIDARI.

Savings Bank

Office National de la Poste et de l'Epargne: BP 11778, Niamey; tel. 20-73-24-98; fax 20-73-35-69; fmrly Caisse Nationale d'Epargne; Chair. Mme PALFI; Man. Dir HASSOUME MATA.

NIGER

STOCK EXCHANGE

Bourse Régionale des Valeurs Mobilières (BRVM): c/o Chambre de Commerce et d'Industrie du Niger, pl. de la Concertation, BP 13299, Niamey; tel. 20-73-66-92; fax 20-73-69-47; e-mail imagagi@brvm.org; internet www.brvm.org; f. 1998; national branch of BRVM (regional stock exchange based in Abidjan, Côte d'Ivoire, serving the member states of UEMOA); Man. IDRISSA S. MAGAGI.

INSURANCE

Agence d'Assurance du Sahel: BP 10661, Niamey; tel. 20-74-05-47.

Agence Nigérienne d'Assurances (ANA): pl. de la Mairie, BP 423, Niamey; tel. 20-72-20-71; f. 1959; cap. 1.5m.; owned by L'Union des Assurances de Paris; Dir JEAN LASCAUD.

Caren Assurance: BP 733, Niamey; tel. 20-73-34-70; fax 20-73-24-93; e-mail carenas@intnet.ne; insurance and reinsurance; Dir-Gen. IBRAHIM IDI ANGO.

Leyma—Société Nigérienne d'Assurances et de Réassurances (SNAR—Leyma): BP 426, Niamey; tel. 20-73-57-72; fax 20-73-40-44; f. 1973; restructured 2001; Pres. AMADOU HIMA SOULEY; Dir-Gen. GARBA ABDOURAHAMANE.

La Nigérienne d'Assurance et de Réassurance: BP 13300, Niamey; tel. 20-73-63-36; fax 20-73-73-37.

Union Générale des Assurances du Niger (UGAN): rue de Kalley, BP 11935, Niamey; tel. 20-73-54-06; fax 20-73-41-85; f. 1985; cap. 500m.; Pres. PATHÉ DIONE; Dir-Gen. MAMADOU TALATA; 7 brs.

Trade and Industry

GOVERNMENT AGENCIES

Cellule de Coordination de la Programme de Privatisation: Immeuble Sonibanque, BP 862, Niamey; tel. 20-73-29-10; fax 20-73-29-58; responsible for co-ordination of privatization programme; Co-ordinator IDÉ ISSOUFOU.

Office des Eaux du Sous-Sol (OFEDES): BP 734, Niamey; tel. 20-74-01-19; fax 20-74-16-68; govt agency for the maintenance and devt of wells and boreholes; Pres. DJIBO HAMANI.

Office du Lait du Niger (OLANI): BP 404, Niamey; tel. 20-73-23-69; fax 20-73-36-74; f. 1971; devt and marketing of milk products; transferred to majority private ownership in 1998; Dir-Gen. M. DIENG.

Office National de l'Energie Solaire (ONERSOL): BP 621, Niamey; tel. 20-73-45-05; govt agency for research and devt, commercial production and exploitation of solar devices; Dir ALBERT WRIGHT.

Office National des Ressources Minières du Niger (ONAREM): Rond-Point Kennedy, BP 12716, Niamey; tel. 20-73-59-28; fax 20-73-28-12; f. 1976; govt agency for exploration, exploitation and marketing of all minerals; Pres. MOUDY MOHAMED; Dir-Gen. A. A. ASKIA.

Office des Produits Vivriers du Niger (OPVN): pl. du petit Marché, BP 474, Niamey; tel. 20-73-44-43; fax 20-73-24-68; e-mail opvn@opvn.net; internet www.opvn.net; govt agency for developing agricultural and food production; Dir-Gen. ADAMOU CHAIFOU.

Riz du Niger (RINI): BP 476, Niamey; tel. 20-71-13-29; fax 20-73-42-04; f. 1967; cap. 825m. francs CFA; 30% state-owned; transfer to 100% private ownership proposed; production and marketing of rice; Pres. YAYA MADOUGOU; Dir-Gen. M. HAROUNA.

DEVELOPMENT ORGANIZATIONS

Agence Française de Développement (AFD): 203 ave du Gountou-Yéna, BP 212, Niamey; tel. 20-72-33-93; fax 20-72-26-05; e-mail afdniamey@groupe-afd.org; internet www.afd.fr; Country Dir FRANÇOIS GIOVALUCCHI.

Mission Française de Coopération et d'Action Culturelle: BP 494, Niamey; tel. 20-72-20-66; administers bilateral aid from France; Dir JEAN BOULOGNE.

SNV (Société Néerlandais de Développement): ave des Zarmakoye, BP 10110, Niamey; tel. 20-75-36-33; fax 20-75-35-06; e-mail snvniger@snv.ne; internet www.snv.ne; present in Niger since 1978; projects concerning food security, agriculture, the environment, savings and credit, marketing, water and communications; operations in Tillabéri, Zinder and Tahoua provinces.

CHAMBERS OF COMMERCE

Chambre de Commerce d'Agriculture, d'Industrie et d'Artisanat du Niger: BP 209, Niamey; tel. 20-73-22-10; fax 20-73-46-68; e-mail cham209n@intnet.ne; internet www.ccaian.org; BP 201, Agadez; tel. 20-44-01-61; BP 91, Diffa; tel. 20-54-03-92; BP 79, Maradi; tel. 20-41-03-76; BP 172, Tahoua; tel. 20-61-03-84; BP 83, Zinder; tel. 20-51-00-78; f. 1954; comprises 80 full mems and 40 dep. mems; Pres. IBRAHIM IDI ANGO; Sec.-Gen. SADOU AISSATA.

INDUSTRIAL AND TRADE ORGANIZATIONS

Centre Nigérien du Commerce Extérieur (CNCE): pl. de la Concertation, BP 12480, Niamey; tel. 20-73-22-88; fax 20-73-46-68; f. 1984; promotes and co-ordinates all aspects of foreign trade; Dir AÏSSA DIALLO.

Société Nationale de Commerce et de Production du Niger (COPRO-Niger): Niamey; tel. 20-73-28-41; fax 20-73-57-71; f. 1962; monopoly importer of foodstuffs; cap. 1,000m. francs CFA; 47% state-owned; Man. Dir DJIBRILLA HIMA.

EMPLOYERS' ORGANIZATIONS

Syndicat des Commerçants Importateurs et Exportateurs du Niger (SCIMPEXNI): Chambre de Commerce, d'Agriculture, d'Industrie et d'Artisanat du Niger, Niamey; tel. 20-73-33-17; Pres. M. SILVA; Sec.-Gen. INOUSSA MAÏGA.

Syndicat National des Petites et Moyennes Entreprises et Industries Nigériennes (SYNAPEMEIN): Chambre de Commerce, d'Agriculture, d'Industrie et d'Artisanat du Niger, Niamey; tel. 20-73-50-97; Pres. ALZOUMA SALEY; Sec.-Gen. HASSANE LAWAL KADER.

Syndicat Patronal des Entreprises et Industries du Niger (SPEIN): BP 415, Niamey; tel. 20-73-24-01; fax 20-73-47-07; f. 1994; Pres. AMADOU OUSMANE; Sec.-Gen. NOUHOU TARI.

UTILITIES

Electricity

Société Nigérienne d'Electricité (NIGELEC): 46 ave du Gen. de Gaulle, BP 11202, Niamey; tel. 20-72-26-92; fax 20-72-32-88; e-mail nigelec@intnet.ne; f. 1968; 95% state-owned; 51% transfer to private ownership proposed; production and distribution of electricity; Dir-Gen. IBRAHIM FOUKORI.

Water

Société d'Exploitation des Eaux du Niger (SEEN): blvd Zarmaganda, BP 12209, Niamey; tel. 20-72-25-00; fax 20-73-46-40; fmrly Société Nationale des Eaux; 51% owned by Veolia Environnement (France); production and distribution of drinking water; Pres. ABARY DAN BOUZOUA SOULEYMENE; Dir-Gen. SEYNI SALOU.

TRADE UNION FEDERATIONS

Confédération des Travailleurs du Niger (CTN): Niamey; Sec.-Gen. ISSOUFOU SEYBOU.

Entente des Travailleurs du Niger (ETN): Bourse du Travail, BP 388, Niamey; tel. and fax 20-73-52-56; f. 2005 by merger of Confédération Nigérienne du Travail, Union Generale des Travailleurs du Niger and Union des Syndicats des Travailleurs du Niger.

Transport

ROADS

Niger is crossed by highways running from east to west and from north to south, giving access to neighbouring countries. A road is under construction to Lomé, Togo, via Burkina Faso, and the 428-km Zinder–Agadez road, scheduled to form part of the Trans-Sahara Highway, has been upgraded. Niger and Algeria appealed jointly in mid-1998 for international aid to fund construction of the Trans-Sahara Highway, development of which was suspended in the mid-1990s because of the conflict in northern Niger. In 2006 there were 18,550 km of classified roads, of which 3,803 km were paved.

Société Nationale des Transports Nigériens (SNTN): BP 135, Niamey; tel. 20-72-24-55; fax 20-74-47-07; e-mail stratech@intnet.ne; f. 1963; operates passenger and freight road-transport services; 49% state-owned; Chair. MOHAMED ABDOULAHI; Man. Dir BARKE M. MOUSTAPHA.

RAILWAYS

There are as yet no railways in Niger.

Organisation Commune Bénin-Niger des Chemins de Fer et des Transports (OCBN): BP 38, Niamey; tel. 20-73-27-90; f. 1959; 50% owned by Govt of Niger, 50% by Govt of Benin; manages the Benin-Niger railway project (begun in 1978); also operates more than 500 km within Benin (q.v.); extension to Niger proposed; transfer to private ownership proposed; Dir-Gen. FLAVIEN BALOGOUN.

INLAND WATERWAYS

The River Niger is navigable for 300 km within the country. Access to the sea is available by a river route from Gaya, in south-western Niger, to the coast at Port Harcourt, Nigeria, between September and March. Port facilities at Lomé, Togo, are used as a commercial outlet for land-locked Niger.

Niger-Transit (NITRA): Zone Industrielle, BP 560, Niamey; tel. 20-73-22-53; fax 20-73-26-38; f. 1974; 48% owned by SNTN; customs agent, freight-handling, warehousing, etc.; manages Nigerien port facilities at Lomé, Togo; Pres. OUMAROU ALI BEÏOLI; Man. Dir SADE FATIMATA.

Société Nigérienne des Transports Fluviaux et Maritimes (SNTFM): Niamey; tel. 20-73-39-69; river and sea transport; cap. 64.6m. francs CFA; 99% state-owned; Man. Dir BERTRAND DEJEAN.

CIVIL AVIATION

There are international airports at Niamey (Hamani Diori), Agadez (Mano Dayak) and Zinder, and major domestic airports at Diffa, Maradi and Tahoua.

Air Continental: Niamey; f. 2003 to replace Air Niger International (f. 2002); 60% owned by private Nigerian interests, 20% by private Nigerien interests, 5% by Govt of Niger; regional and international services.

Air Inter Afrique: Niamey; tel. 20-73-85-85; fax 20-73-69-73; f. 2001; operates services within West Africa; CEO CHEIKH OUSMANE DIALLO.

Air Inter Niger: Agadez; f. 1997 to operate services to Tamanrasset (Algeria).

Niger Air Continental: Niamey; e-mail info@nigeraircontinental.com; f. 2003.

Nigeravia: BP 10454, Niamey; tel. 20-73-30-64; fax 20-74-18-42; e-mail nigavia@intnet.ne; internet www.nigeravia.com; f. 1991; operates domestic, regional and international services; Pres. and Dir-Gen. JEAN SYLVESTRE.

Sahel Airlines: rue de Rivoli, BP 10154, Niamey; tel. 20-73-65-71; fax 20-73-65-33; e-mail sahelair@intnet.ne.

Société Nigérienne des Transports Aériens (SONITA): Niamey; f. 1991; owned by private Nigerien (81%) and Cypriot (19%) interests; operates domestic and regional services; Man. Dir ABDOULAYE MAIGA GOUDOUBABA.

Tourism

The Aïr and Ténéré Nature Reserve, covering an area of 77,000 sq km, was established in 1988. Tourism was hampered by insecurity in the north and east during the 1990s. However, the number of foreign arrivals at hotels and similar establishments increased from 39,190 in 1997 to 42,433 in 1999, when tourism receipts amounted to US $24m. In 2006 some 60,332 tourists entered Niger, while receipts from tourism totalled $35m.

Centre Nigerien de Promotion Touristique (CNPT): ave de Président H. Luebke, BP 612, Niamey; tel. 20-73-24-47; fax 20-73-28-07; e-mail CNPT2@yahoo.fr; internet www.maisontourism-niger.com; Dirs BOULOU AKANO, IBRAHIM HALIDOU, KIEPIW TOYÉ FANTA.

NIGERIA

Introductory Survey

Location, Climate, Language, Religion, Flag, Capital

The Federal Republic of Nigeria is a West African coastal state on the shores of the Gulf of Guinea, with Benin to the west, Niger to the north, Chad to the north-east, and Cameroon to the east and south-east. The climate is tropical in the southern coastal areas, with an average annual temperature of 32°C (90°F) and high humidity. It is drier and semi-tropical in the north. Average annual rainfall is more than 2,500 mm (98 ins) in parts of the south-east, but in certain areas of the north is as low as 600 mm (24 ins). In 1963 the most widely spoken languages were Hausa (20.9%), Yoruba (20.3%), Ibo (16.6%) and Fulani (8.6%). English is the country's official language. In 1963 the principal religious groups were Muslims (47.2%) and Christians (34.5%), while 18% of the total population followed animist beliefs. The national flag (proportions 1 by 2) has three equal vertical stripes, of green, white and green. The capital is Abuja, to which the Federal Government was formally transferred in December 1991; however, many non-government institutions remained in the former capital, Lagos.

Recent History

The territory of present-day Nigeria, except for the section of former German-controlled Cameroon (see below), was conquered by the United Kingdom, in several stages, during the second half of the 19th century and the first decade of the 20th century. The British dependencies of Northern and Southern Nigeria were merged into a single territory in 1914, administered largely by traditional native rulers, under the supervision of the colonial authorities. In 1947 the United Kingdom introduced a new Nigerian Constitution, establishing a federal system of government, based on three regions: Northern, Western and Eastern. The federal arrangement was an attempt to reconcile religious and regional tensions, and to accommodate Nigeria's diverse ethnic groups, notably the Ibo (in the east), the Yoruba (in the west) and the Hausa and Fulani (in the north). The Northern Region, which was predominantly Muslim, contained about one-half of Nigeria's total population.

In 1954 the federation became self-governing, and the first federal Prime Minister, Alhaji Abubakar Tafawa Balewa (a Muslim northerner), was appointed in August 1957. A constitutional conference, convened in 1958, agreed that Nigeria should become independent in 1960, and elections to an enlarged federal legislature took place in December 1959. The Northern People's Congress (NPC), which was politically dominant in the north, became the single largest party in the new legislature, although lacking an overall majority. Tafawa Balewa (a prominent member of the NPC) continued to head a coalition government of the NPC and the National Council for Nigeria and the Cameroons (NCNC), which attracted most support in the Eastern Region.

On 1 October 1960, as scheduled, the Federation of Nigeria achieved independence, initially as a constitutional monarchy. In June 1961 the northern part of the UN Trust Territory of British Cameroons was incorporated into Nigeria's Northern Region as the province of Sardauna, and in August 1963 a fourth region, the Mid-Western Region, was created by dividing the existing Western Region. On 1 October a revised Constitution was adopted, and the country was renamed the Federal Republic of Nigeria, although it remained a member of the Commonwealth. Dr Nnamdi Azikiwe of the NCNC took office as Nigeria's first President (then a non-executive post).

In January 1966 Balewa's civilian Government was overthrown by junior army officers (mainly Ibos from the Eastern Region). The Commander-in-Chief of the Armed Forces, Maj.-Gen. Johnson Aguiyi-Aronsi (an Ibo), formed a Supreme Military Council, suspended the Constitution and imposed emergency rule. In July Aguiyi-Aronsi was killed in a further coup, staged by northern troops, and power was transferred to the Chief of Army Staff, Lt-Col (later Gen.) Yakubu Gowon, a Christian northerner. Gowon subsequently reintroduced the federal system, which had been suppressed after the January coup.

In early 1967 there was a rapid deterioration in relations between the Federal Government and the military Governor of the Eastern Region, Lt-Col Chukwuemeka Odumegwu Ojukwu, following a dispute between the federal and regional authorities concerning the distribution of petroleum revenues. The increasing tensions in Nigeria's federal structure prompted Gowon to propose the replacement of the four existing regions by 12 states. On 30 May Ojukwu announced the secession of the Eastern Region from the Federation, and proclaimed its independence as the Republic of Biafra. Fighting between the forces of Biafra and the Federal Government began in July; federal forces eventually suppressed the rebellion in December 1969, following Ojukwu's departure into exile, and Biafran forces formally surrendered in January 1970. Meanwhile, the proposed 12-state structure replaced the four federal regions in April 1968.

Increasing opposition to Gowon's regime culminated in his overthrow on 29 July 1975. Gowon was replaced as Head of State by Brig. (later Gen.) Murtala Ramat Muhammed, hitherto Federal Commissioner for Communications, who, in October, announced a detailed timetable for a transition to civilian rule. In February 1976, however, Muhammed was assassinated during an unsuccessful coup attempt. Power was immediately assumed by Lt-Gen. (later Gen.) Olusegun Obasanjo, the Chief of Army Staff, who promised to fulfil his predecessor's programme for the restoration of civilian rule.

In March 1976 the number of states was increased from 12 to 19, and it was announced that a new federal capital was to be constructed near Abuja, in central Nigeria. In September 1978 a new Constitution was promulgated, and the state of emergency, in force since 1966, was ended. At the same time the 12-year ban on political activity was revoked. Elections took place in July 1979 to a new bicameral National Assembly (comprising a Senate and a House of Representatives), and for State Assemblies and State Governors. The National Party of Nigeria (NPN), which included many prominent members of the former NPC, received the most widespread support in all the elections. The NPN's presidential candidate, Alhaji Shehu Shagari (who had served as an NPC federal minister prior to 1966 and as a federal commissioner in 1970–75), was elected to the new post of executive President in August 1979. He took office on 1 October, whereupon the military regime transferred power to the newly elected civilian authorities and the new Constitution came into effect.

On 31 December 1983 the civilian Government was deposed in a bloodless military coup, led by Maj.-Gen. Muhammadu Buhari, who had been Federal Commissioner for Petroleum in 1976–78. The Government was replaced by a Supreme Military Council (SMC), headed by Buhari; the National Assembly was dissolved, and all political parties were banned. Hundreds of politicians, including former President Shagari, were arrested on charges of corruption, and legislation that severely restricted the freedom of the press was introduced.

On 27 August 1985 Buhari's administration was deposed in a bloodless coup, led by Maj.-Gen. (later Gen.) Ibrahim Babangida, the Chief of Army Staff and a member of the SMC. A new military administration, the Armed Forces Ruling Council (AFRC), was established, with Babangida as President. The decree on press censorship was revoked, and a number of journalists and other political detainees were released. (Shagari and 17 other former government officials were released in July 1986, having been acquitted of corruption charges.) In December 1985 the AFRC suppressed a coup attempt by disaffected army officers; 10 of the alleged conspirators were later executed.

In February 1986 Babangida's announcement that Nigeria had been accepted as a full member of the Organization of the Islamic Conference (OIC, see p. 382) prompted concern in the non-Muslim sector of the population at increasing 'Islamization' in Nigeria. In July 1987 Babangida announced details of a programme to transfer power to a civilian government on 1 October 1992. The ban on party politics was to be revoked in 1989, and a maximum of two associations were to be approved to contest elections. In August 1987 the Government established a National Electoral Commission (NEC); in September the number of states was increased to 21. In May 1988 a Constituent Assembly, comprising 450 members elected by local government and 117 members nominated by the AFRC, commenced preparation of a draft constitution. The progress of the Constituent

Assembly was impeded, however, by controversy over the proposed inclusion of Islamic (*Shari'a*) courts in the new document.

In April 1989 the Constituent Assembly presented a draft Constitution to Babangida. In May Babangida announced the end of the prohibition on political parties, and the new Constitution (which was scheduled to take effect on 1 October 1992) was promulgated. Only 13 of the existing parties managed to fulfil the requirements for registration by the stipulated date in July 1989. In September the NEC submitted six political associations to the AFRC; in October, however, it was decided to dissolve all the newly formed political parties, on the grounds that they were too closely associated with discredited former parties. In their place, the AFRC created two new organizations, the Social Democratic Party (SDP) and the National Republican Convention (NRC), provoking widespread criticism.

Following the completion of registration for membership of the SDP and the NRC, party executives were elected for each state in July 1990, replacing government-appointed administrators. Later in August Babangida replaced nine government ministers, and the position of Chief of General Staff, held by Vice-Adm. (later Adm.) Augustus Aikhomu, was replaced by the office of Vice-President (to which Aikhomu was immediately appointed). Babangida subsequently announced plans to reduce substantially the size of the armed forces.

In October 1990 the Movement for the Survival of the Ogoni People (MOSOP) was formed to co-ordinate opposition to the exploitation of petroleum reserves in territory of the Ogoni ethnic group (Ogoniland), in the south-central Rivers State, by the Shell Petroleum Development Co of Nigeria. Following a demonstration, organized by MOSOP in protest at environmental damage resulting from petroleum production, it was reported that security forces had killed some 80 Ogonis.

In September 1991, in an apparent attempt to relieve ethnic tensions, nine new states were created, increasing the size of the federation to 30 states. On 12 December the Federal Government was formally transferred from Lagos to Abuja, the new federal capital. In January 1992 Babangida formed a new Council of Ministers, in which several portfolios were restructured. In the same month the Government announced that elections to a bicameral National Assembly, comprising a 593-member House of Representatives and a 91-member Senate, would take place on 7 November, and would be followed by a presidential election on 5 December. The formal installation of a civilian government (and the implementation of the new Constitution) was consequently scheduled for 2 January 1993, rather than, as previously planned, on 1 October 1992.

In May 1992 some 300 people were reported to have been killed in renewed violence between the Hausa ethnic group (which was predominantly Muslim) and the Kataf (predominantly Christian) in Kaduna. Shortly afterwards the Government announced that all organizations with religious or ethnic interests were to be prohibited. Later in May further rioting occurred in Lagos, following the arrest of the Chairman of the Campaign for Democracy (CD—an informal alliance of Nigerian human rights organizations, which had been established in late 1991), Dr Beko Ransome-Kuti, who had accused the Government of deliberately provoking unrest in order to delay the transition to civilian rule. In June several human rights activists, including Ransome-Kuti, were released, pending their trial (which was later deferred) on charges of conspiring to incite the previous month's riots.

At elections to the bicameral National Assembly, which had been brought forward to 4 July 1992, the SDP secured a majority in both chambers, with 52 seats in the Senate and 314 seats in the House of Representatives, while the NRC won 37 seats in the Senate and 275 seats in the House of Representatives. The formal inauguration of the National Assembly, due to take place on 27 July, was, however, postponed until 5 December, the stipulated date for the presidential election, prompting concern at the AFRC's apparent reluctance to relinquish legislative power.

Voting in primary elections for presidential candidates took place in September 1992. In October, however, shortly before a final round of voting was due to take place, Babangida suspended the primary elections, pending the outcome of an investigation by the NEC into alleged incidents of electoral malpractice. Later that month, following a report by the NEC that confirmed malpractice, Babangida announced that the leaders of the NRC and the SDP were to be removed from office.

In November 1992 Babangida postponed the presidential election until 12 June 1993. On 2 January Babangida announced that the 23 prospective presidential candidates who had contested the discredited primary elections were to be prohibited from political activity during the transitional period: new candidates were to be nominated at a series of party congresses, to be conducted at ward, local government, state and national level.

On 5 December 1992 Babangida inaugurated the National Assembly. On 2 January 1993 the AFRC and the Council of Ministers were dissolved, and a civilian Transitional Council and the National Defence and Security Council (which comprised the President, Vice-President, the heads of the armed forces and senior members of the Transitional Council) were formally installed. The Chairman of the Transitional Council, Chief Ernest Adegunle Shonekan, was officially designated Head of Government (although supreme power was vested in the NDSC and the President), while Aikhomu retained the post of Vice-President. In accordance with the new programme for the transition to civilian rule, party congresses to select presidential candidates were conducted in February–March; the NRC elected Alhaji Bashir Othman Tofa and the SDP Chief Moshood Kastumawo Olawale Abiola to contest the presidential election.

In June 1993 the Association for a Better Nigeria (ABN), a newly formed pro-Babangida pressure group, obtained an interim injunction in the Abuja High Court prohibiting the NEC from conducting the presidential election, pending an appeal by the ABN for the extension of military rule until 1997. The NEC, however, announced that the injunction was invalid, and that the election would take place as scheduled. Owing, in part, to confusion caused by the court action, only about 30% of the registered electorate voted in the presidential election, which took place on 12 June. Initial results indicated that Abiola had secured the majority of votes in 11 of 15 states. Shortly afterwards, however, the ABN obtained a further injunction suspending the promulgation of the election results. Nevertheless, later in June the CD released election results (which it claimed to be official) indicating that Abiola had secured the majority of votes in 19 states, and Tofa in 11; Abiola subsequently proclaimed himself President. Amid increasing tension, the Abuja High Court declared the election results to be invalid, on the grounds that the NEC had failed to comply with the ruling that had cancelled the poll.

On 23 June 1993, in what it claimed was an effort to uphold the judicial system, the NDSC annulled the results of the presidential election, suspended the NEC and halted all proceedings pertaining to the election. Babangida subsequently announced that the poll had been marred by widespread irregularities (despite reports by international observers that voting had been conducted fairly), but insisted that he remained committed to the transition to civilian rule on 27 August. The SDP and the NRC were to select two new presidential candidates, under the supervision of a reconstituted NEC. The annulment of the election attracted widespread international criticism, particularly from the USA and the United Kingdom, which announced the imposition of military sanctions against Nigeria. In July the NDSC announced that a new presidential election was to take place on 14 August. Legal proceedings initiated by Abiola in the Lagos Supreme Court, in an attempt to uphold his claim to the presidency, were abandoned after Babangida introduced legislation that prohibited any legal challenges to the annulment of the election.

At the end of July 1993 Babangida announced that an Interim National Government (ING) was to be established, on the grounds that there was insufficient time to permit the scheduled transition to civilian rule on 27 August. In August the CD continued its campaign of civil disobedience in protest at the annulment of the election, appealing for a three-day general strike (which was widely observed in the south-west of the country, where Abiola received most popular support). Later in August Babangida resigned; on 27 August a 32-member interim Federal Executive Council (FEC), headed by Shonekan, was installed, while the transitional period for the return to civilian rule was extended to 31 March 1994. Supporters of democracy criticized the inclusion in the ING of several members of the now-dissolved NDSC, including Gen. Sani Abacha, who was appointed to the new post of Vice-President.

At the end of August 1993 the CD staged a further three-day strike, while the Nigerian Labour Congress (NLC) and the National Union of Petroleum and Natural Gas Workers (NUPENG) also announced industrial action in support of the installation of a civilian administration, headed by Abiola. The combined strike action resulted in a severe fuel shortage and the suspension of most economic activity. Following the establishment of the ING, Shonekan pledged his commitment to the democratic process and, in an effort to restore order, initiated negotiations with the NLC and effected the release of several journalists and prominent members of the CD.

In September 1993 a series of military appointments, which included the nomination of Lt-Gen. Oladipo Diya to the office of Chief of Defence Staff, effectively removed supporters of Babangida from significant posts within the armed forces, thereby strengthening Abacha's position. Later in September the NRC and SDP agreed to a new timetable whereby local government elections and a presidential election would take place concurrently in February 1994. The CD subsequently announced the resumption of strike action in support of demands for the installation of Abiola as President, and Ransome-Kuti and other prominent members were again arrested.

On 17 November 1993, following a meeting with senior military officials, Shonekan resigned as Head of State and immediately transferred power to Abacha (confirming widespread speculation that the latter had effectively assumed control of the Government following Babangida's resignation). On the following day Abacha dissolved all state institutions that had been established under the transitional process, replaced the State Governors with military administrators, prohibited political activity (thereby proscribing the NRC and the SDP), and announced the formation of a Provisional Ruling Council (PRC), which was to comprise senior military officials and principal members of a new FEC. He insisted, however, that he intended to relinquish power to a civilian government, and pledged to convene a conference with a mandate to determine the constitutional future of the country. Restrictions on the media were revoked. On 21 November Abacha introduced legislation that formally restored the 1979 Constitution and provided for the establishment of the new government organs. In an apparent attempt to counter domestic and international criticism, several prominent supporters of Abiola, including Kingibe, and four former members of the ING were appointed to the PRC and FEC, which were installed on 24 November. Abacha subsequently removed 17 senior military officers who were believed to be loyal to Babangida. In the same month the NLC agreed to abandon strike action after the Government acted to limit the increase in the price of petroleum products.

In December 1993 the United Kingdom announced that member nations of the European Union (EU, see p. 255) were to impose further sanctions against Nigeria, including restrictions on the export of armaments. In April 1994 the Government announced a programme for the establishment of a National Constitutional Conference (NCC), which was to submit recommendations, including proposals for a new draft constitution, to the PRC in October. The ban on political activity was to end in January 1995. In May 1994 a new pro-democracy organization, comprising former politicians, retired military officers and human rights activists, the National Democratic Coalition (NADECO), demanded that Abacha relinquish power by the end of that month and urged a boycott of the NCC. In the same month the leader of MOSOP, Ken Saro-Wiwa, was arrested in connection with the deaths, during political violence, of four Ogoni traditional leaders. Saro-Wiwa was alleged to have incited his supporters to commit the murders.

In June 1994 a number of prominent opposition members, including Ransome-Kuti, were also arrested after the CD urged a campaign of civil disobedience, supported by NADECO. Following a public gathering, at which he declared himself Head of State and President of a parallel government, Abiola was arrested by security forces. He was arraigned before a special High Court in Abuja in July and charged with treason, although his trial was repeatedly adjourned as a consequence of legal action challenging the jurisdiction of the special High Court in Abuja with regard to an offence that had been allegedly committed in Lagos.

In January 1995 the NCC, which had been scheduled to complete the preparations for a draft constitution in October 1994, adjourned until March 1995, prompting increasing concern that its protracted deliberations served to prolong the tenure of the military administration. The trial of Saro-Wiwa and a further 14 Ogoni campaigners, on charges of complicity in the murder of the four Ogoni traditional leaders, commenced in mid-January; the defendants were to challenge the legitimacy of the government-appointed Special Military Tribunal, at Port Harcourt. In February the Federal Court of Appeal dismissed Abiola's legal action challenging the jurisdiction of the High Court in Abuja.

In February 1995 Abacha dissolved the FEC, after a number of ministers announced their intention of engaging in political activity in the forthcoming transitional period. In March some 150 military officials were arrested, and the authorities subsequently confirmed reports of a conspiracy to overthrow the Government. The arrest of the former Head of State, Olusegun Obasanjo, and his former deputy, Maj.-Gen. (retd) Shehu Musa Yar'Adua, together with other prominent critics of the Government, prompted international protests. In mid-March Abacha appointed a new, 36-member FEC. In May more than 40 people, including Obasanjo, Yar'Adua and Ransome-Kuti, were arraigned before a Special Military Tribunal in Lagos, in connection with the alleged coup attempt in March.

In late June 1995 the NCC submitted a draft Constitution to Abacha, who rescinded the ban on political activity; a programme for transition to civilian rule was to be announced on 1 October. (A number of political organizations subsequently emerged, in response to the removal of the ban.) At the end of June it was reported that Yar'Adua and a further 13 military officers had been sentenced to death for conspiring to overthrow the Government, while several other defendants, including Obasanjo and Ransome-Kuti, received custodial terms. The Government subsequently confirmed that a total of 43 had been convicted in connection with the coup attempt, prompting protests and appeals for clemency from the international community. On 1 October, however, Abacha officially commuted the death sentences to terms of imprisonment and reduced the custodial sentences (although he did not withdraw the capital charges against Abiola). At the same time he announced the approval of the new Constitution (which was due to be formally endorsed later that year) and the adoption of a three-year programme for transition to civilian rule, whereby a new President was to be inaugurated on 1 October 1998, following elections at local, state and national level. (The duration of the transitional period was received with disapproval by the international community.)

At the end of October 1995 Saro-Wiwa and a further eight Ogoni activists were sentenced to death by the Special Military Tribunal in Port Harcourt, having been convicted of involvement in the murder of the four Ogoni leaders in May 1994; six defendants were acquitted. Although the defendants were not implicated directly in the incident, the nine convictions were based on the premise that the MOSOP activists had effectively incited the killings. An international campaign against the convictions and numerous appeals for clemency ensued. However, on 10 November the nine convicted Ogonis were executed, prompting immediate condemnation by the international community. Nigeria was suspended from the Commonwealth, and threatened with expulsion if the Government failed to restore democracy within a period of two years. Later that month the EU reaffirmed its commitment to existing sanctions that had been imposed in 1993 (notably an embargo on the export of armaments and military equipment to Nigeria), and extended visa restrictions to civilian members of the administration. The Governments of the USA, South Africa and the EU member nations recalled their diplomatic representatives from Nigeria in protest at the executions. The Nigerian Government condemned the imposition of sanctions and, in turn, withdrew its diplomatic representatives from the USA, South Africa and the EU member countries.

In December 1995 Abacha approved the establishment of a number of committees, including the National Electoral Commission of Nigeria (NECON), to implement the transitional programme. NECON subsequently divided the country into seven regions (rather than six, as originally envisaged), prior to local government elections in early 1996. Later in December the Commonwealth Ministerial Action Group (CMAG—comprising the ministers with responsibility for foreign affairs of eight member countries), which had been established at the summit meeting in November, met to discuss further measures to be taken if the Nigerian Government failed to restore democracy, and announced that five of the ministers were to visit Nigeria to initiate negotiations with the military administration. In January 1996 the Government refused the Commonwealth delegation permission to visit Nigeria, and demanded that the decision to suspend Nigeria be reviewed. At the end of January the Government announced that the new Constitution would be formally adopted in 1998, upon the completion of the transitional period (rather than in late 1995).

In March 1996 local government elections were contested, on a non-party basis, as part of the transitional programme; although opposition leaders had urged a boycott, NECON claimed that a high level of voter participation had been recorded. In April, following the Government's continued refusal to enter into negotiations with CMAG regarding human rights issues and the restoration of democracy, the Commonwealth proposed to adopt a number of sanctions against Nigeria.

In June 1996 Nigerian officials met CMAG in an attempt to avert the threatened imposition of sanctions against Nigeria; the Nigerian delegation demanded that Nigeria be readmitted to the Commonwealth in exchange for the Government's adoption of the programme for transition to civilian rule by October 1998. The Commonwealth dismissed the programme as unsatisfactory, but remained divided regarding the adoption of consequent measures. It was finally agreed that the Commonwealth would suspend the adoption of sanctions, but that the situation would subsequently be reviewed. Canada, however, announced its opposition to this decision and unilaterally imposed a number of sanctions (similar to those already adopted by the EU). In September 1996 CMAG agreed that the Commonwealth delegation would visit Nigeria, despite conditions imposed by the military authorities, which insisted that it would not be permitted access to opposition activists or political prisoners.

In June 1996 legislation governing the formation of political parties was promulgated. Five of 15 political organizations that applied for registration were granted legal status in September. NADECO condemned the disqualification of the remaining 10 parties, which were subsequently dissolved by decree; it was widely believed that the associations that had been granted registration were largely sympathetic towards the military administration. In October Abacha announced the creation of a further six states, increasing the total size of the federation to 36 states.

In early 1997 escalating tension between the Ijaw and Itsekiri ethnic groups in the town of Warri, in south-western Nigeria, severely disrupted operations in the region of the Niger Delta by the Shell Petroleum Development Company of Nigeria. In March a demonstration by members of the Ijaw ethnic group in Warri precipitated violent clashes. Protesters seized Shell installations and took about 100 employees hostage, in an attempt to force the Government to accede to their demands. The disruption in petroleum production resulted in a national fuel shortage, effectively suspending the transportation system in much of the country. Further attacks on Shell installations were reported in May. Later that month the authorities established a commission of inquiry to investigate the cause of the unrest and submit recommendations for restoring order in the region. Persistent attacks by Ijaw activists against petroleum installations resulted in the imposition of a state of emergency at the end of December 1998.

At a summit meeting of the Commonwealth Heads of Government, which took place in Edinburgh, United Kingdom, in October 1997, Nigeria's suspension from the organization was extended for an additional year; it was further indicated that the country would be expelled from the Commonwealth if Abacha reneged on his pledge to restore democratic rule by 1 October 1998. The Government had announced a new electoral timetable: elections to the State Assemblies were to take place in December 1997, followed by elections to the National Assembly on 25 April 1998, and presidential and gubernatorial elections on 1 August of that year (although it was maintained that the new elected organs of government would be installed by 1 October 1998). Elections to the state legislatures, which were contested by the five registered parties, took place accordingly on 6 December 1997; the United Nigeria Congress Party (UNCP) won 637 of the 970 contested seats, securing a majority in 29 of the 36 State Assemblies. The other four parties (the Congress for National Consensus, the Democratic Party of Nigeria, the Grassroots Democratic Movement and the National Centre Party of Nigeria) subsequently attributed the electoral success of the UNCP to malpractice on the part of the authorities, and threatened to withdraw from the remainder of the electoral process. In mid-December Abacha nominated a new FEC, in which most of the ministers who had served in the previous administration were replaced.

Later in December 1997, following reports of a bomb attack at the presidential wing of the airport at Abuja, the Government announced that an attempted coup had been thwarted. However, there was widespread speculation that government claims of a coup attempt were a pretext for the removal of a number of army officers who were perceived to be a threat to Abacha. The incident also served to divert attention from the death in detention of Yar'Adua earlier that month. In April all five registered parties voted separately to nominate Abacha as the sole presidential candidate; Abacha was therefore to contest the presidential election in August unopposed.

On 8 June 1998 Abacha died unexpectedly from heart failure. The PRC designated the Chief of Defence Staff, Maj.-Gen. Abdulsalami Abubakar, as Abacha's successor, and on 9 June he was inaugurated as Head of State (having been promoted to the rank of General). Abubakar pledged to continue the Abacha Government's scheduled transition to civilian rule. In mid-June Abubakar ordered the release of about 26 political prisoners, including Obasanjo (ostensibly on grounds of ill health). In July, following discussions with UN officials, the authorities agreed to release Abiola from detention. Shortly after his release, however, Abiola collapsed and subsequently died. Violent rioting ensued, amid widespread speculation that the authorities were responsible for Abiola's death. Although an autopsy confirmed that he had died of heart failure, it was indicated that his period in detention had contributed to his poor health. Later in July Abubakar announced that the transition to civilian rule would be completed on 29 May 1999 (rather than 1 October 1998). The Government annulled the results of the elections that had previously been conducted, and dissolved the five authorized political parties, NECON and other electoral bodies. In August a new, 31-member FEC, which included a number of civilians, was appointed to remain in office pending the formal transition to civilian rule; an Independent National Electoral Commission (INEC) was also established. Later that month the INEC announced that local government elections would take place on 5 December 1998 and state legislative elections on 9 January 1999, followed by elections to a bicameral national legislature on 20 February and a presidential election on 27 February. On 7 September 1998 the Government published the draft Constitution that had been submitted by the NCC in June 1995. Abubakar announced that all charges against Nigerian exiles abroad had been abandoned.

Some 25 new political organizations submitted applications for registration to the INEC. The commission provisionally approved nine political associations, notably the People's Democratic Party (PDP), which principally comprised former opponents of the Abacha administration. In October 1998 CMAG recommended that Commonwealth member states end sanctions against Nigeria, in preparation for the country's readmission to the Commonwealth. At the end of that month, in response to the democratization measures undertaken by the Government, the EU ended a number of sanctions against Nigeria (while maintaining the embargo on the export of armaments).

In January 1999 several prominent members of former administrations announced that they intended to seek nomination to contest the forthcoming presidential election. In early February the All Nigeria People's Party (ANPP) and the Alliance for Democracy (AD), which, despite the stated opposition of the INEC, had established an electoral alliance, nominated a joint candidate, Samuel Oluyemisi Falae (a former Minister of Finance in the Babangida administration). Later that month Obasanjo (who had joined the PDP in October 1998) was elected as the presidential candidate of that party. At the elections to the bicameral legislature, which took place on 20 February, the PDP secured 215 seats in the 360-member House of Representatives and 66 seats in the 109-member Senate. (Voting in the Niger Delta region was postponed, owing to continued unrest, and a further by-election for the vacant seat to the National Assembly took place in March.)

On 27 February 1999 Obasanjo was elected to the presidency with 62.8% of votes cast. The Constitution was promulgated on 5 May and Obasanjo was formally inaugurated as President on 29 May; on the same day Nigeria was readmitted as a full member of the Commonwealth. On 3 June the inaugural session of the National Assembly took place. Obasanjo nominated a new Cabinet, principally comprising members of the PDP, which was approved by the Senate later that month. He also undertook a reorganization of the armed forces, removing more than 150 military officers who had served under the Abacha Government.

The Christian Association of Nigeria threatened to initiate a legal challenge to the introduction of Islamic *Shari'a* law, announced in Kano and Zamfara States in December 1999 and January 2000, respectively, on the grounds that it contravened the principle of secularity enshrined in the Constitution. In February a demonstration by Christians in the northern town of Kaduna in protest at the proposed imposition of *Shari'a* in Kaduna State precipitated violent hostilities between Muslims and Christians, in which more than 300 people were killed;

government troops eventually suppressed the unrest and a curfew was imposed in the town. However, more than 50 people were killed in further clashes between Christians and Muslims in the south-eastern towns of Aba and Umuahia, which ensued in reprisal for the violence in the north. By the end of the month thousands of Christians had fled the north of the country, fearing possible retaliatory massacres. At an emergency meeting at the end of February, chaired by Obasanjo, the Governors of the 18 northern states agreed, in the interests of peace, to withdraw the new legislation introducing Shari'a law, and to revert to the provisions for Shari'a in the existing penal code, in accordance with the federal Constitution. However, the Governors of a number of the states subsequently announced that they would not comply with the federal government order, but would proceed with the implementation of Shari'a law. In March religious rioting in Niger State (where the adoption of the Shari'a law had been declared) was reported. In May some 150 people were killed in further clashes between Christians and Muslims in Kaduna; government troops were again deployed in the town to restore order. In early June Obasanjo reorganized the Cabinet, following media criticism of a number of ministers.

In August 2000, following persistent dissension between the executive and the legislature over the issue of government corruption, the President of the Senate was removed from office and charged with misusing public funds. In the same month Shari'a law was formally adopted in the northern states of Katsina, Jigawa and Yobe (to enter into effect later that year). In September the Governor of Borno State also announced the adoption of Shari'a. Although the Governors of most of these states had declared that Christians would be exempt from the provisions of Shari'a, social segregation of men and women and the application of punishments stipulated under Islamic law had been widely implemented in Zamfara and Kano States. In view of the violence in Kaduna State, the Governor announced that the form of Shari'a to be introduced in the state was to be modified to allow Islamic courts to exist in conjunction with special courts upholding secular laws.

At the end of January 2001 Obasanjo replaced 10 members of the Cabinet in an extensive reorganization, following widespread criticism of the Government's failure to resolve economic and social difficulties. In late March the Governors of Nigeria's 17 southern states, meeting in Benin City, urged that the Constitution be amended to provide for greater government decentralization, including the right for states to establish separate security forces. In April Obasanjo replaced the heads of the three branches of the armed forces.

In mid-June 2001 religious and ethnic unrest in northern and central Nigeria intensified; some 1,000 people were killed in fighting between Christians and Muslims in Bauchi (which had become the 10th northern state to adopt Shari'a law). In early 2002 the death sentence imposed on a woman in northern Sokoto State, who had been convicted in October 2001 under Shari'a law on charges of adultery, attracted increasing international attention. Following pressure from the international community, in March the Minister of Justice urged the 12 State Governors who had adopted Shari'a law to discontinue its strict enforcement, on the grounds that it contravened the Constitution for reasons of discrimination (applying only to Muslims). A Court of Appeal subsequently overturned the sentence against the convicted woman, ruling that there was insufficient evidence to justify the death penalty. However, the Governors of several northern states insisted that they would continue to implement Shari'a.

In April 2002 the Federal Government reached an agreement with Abacha's relatives and business associates, whereby Swiss banks were to return state funds appropriated by the former President, and the Nigerian authorities were to abandon legal proceedings against several members of Abacha's family. Also in April Obasanjo announced that he intended to seek a second term in office, while the former Head of State, Muhammadu Buhari, stated that he planned to contest the forthcoming presidential election on behalf of the ANPP. In June the INEC announced that, of 24 political parties that had applied for official registration, only three had been recognized (increasing the total number of legal associations to six). In June, after a longstanding dispute between Obasanjo and the Senate over control of public finances, the President survived an impeachment attempt by the upper chamber. In August the House of Representatives adopted by an overwhelming majority a resolution demanding that Obasanjo resign from office or face impeachment, on charges of mismanagement and abuse of power. Obasanjo refused to comply with the resolution, and at the end of that month the PDP voted in favour of drafting a list of charges against the President.

In August 2002 the Shari'a Court of Appeal in Katsina State upheld a sentence of death by stoning imposed in March against a woman, Amina Lawal, who had been convicted for having extramarital sexual intercourse. The case attracted international outrage, and the Minister of Justice announced that the Federal Government was opposed to the death sentence. (A further appeal against the sentence was submitted at federal level.) In the same month a Shari'a court in Jigawa State imposed a death sentence against a man who had been convicted for rape of a minor. In October the Federal Government announced that it would not permit executions under Shari'a law.

In December 2002 the INEC granted registration to a further 24 political associations, after the Supreme Court upheld an appeal by five opposition parties against their exclusion, and ordered less restrictive regulations for legalization. Later that month the Commission announced that legislative elections were to be conducted on 12 April 2003, followed by a presidential election on 19 April and elections to regional Houses of Assembly on 3 May. In January Obasanjo was formally elected as the presidential candidate of the PDP. A further 18 political leaders subsequently announced their intention to contest the presidential election. In March further clashes between members of the Ijaw and Itsekiri ethnic group near Warri forced the suspension of the operations of a number of international petroleum companies; government troops were dispatched to the region to suppress the violence.

Incidences of violence and malpractice were reported during the federal legislative elections on 12 April 2003. The PDP emerged with an overwhelming majority in both legislative chambers (213 seats in the House of Representatives and 73 in the Senate), while the ANPP was the only other party to secure significant representation (95 seats in the House of Representatives and 28 in the Senate). At the presidential election on 19 April (the first to be organized by civilian authorities for 19 years), Obasanjo was elected for a second term by 61.9% of the valid votes cast, while Buhari received 32.2% of votes. Opposition leaders, notably Buhari, contested the results, claiming that widespread electoral malpractice had been perpetrated, and indicated that violent protests might ensue. International monitors, although generally satisfied with the organization of the elections, declared that irregularities had taken place, particularly in the region of the Niger Delta. At gubernatorial elections, which also took place on 19 April, the PDP gained eight state governorships from the ANPP and AD, losing only one (that of Kano). Later that month Obasanjo criticized a statement by EU monitors, who claimed that they had obtained evidence of electoral malpractice perpetrated in 13 states. Meanwhile, at the end of April four offshore petroleum rigs, operated by a US enterprise, Transocean, in the Niger Delta were seized by protesting Nigerian employees, who took hostage 97 foreign national workers. Military naval forces were dispatched to the region. Following negotiations between officials of NUPENG, the NLC and Transocean, all hostages were airlifted from the rigs.

Obasanjo officially dissolved the Federal Government on 21 May 2003. He was sworn in on 29 May (after a legal challenge against his inauguration by Buhari was rejected by the federal Court of Appeal), and in early June began to nominate ministers to his new administration. In mid-July Obasanjo finally inaugurated the new, 40-member Federal Government, which included the hitherto Vice-President of the World Bank, Dr Ngozi Okonja-Iweala, as the Minister of Finance and the Economy (an appointment that reflected the authorities' stated intention to eliminate corruption and implement economic reforms).

In September 2003 the Shari'a Court of Appeal in Katsina State overturned the sentence of death by stoning imposed on Lawal, on the grounds that procedural irregularities had discredited the previous judgment. The case had attracted international protests on Lawal's behalf. Meanwhile, legislation to repeal the death penalty was under debate at the National Assembly; the proposed abrogation was strongly opposed by the Muslim community, which perceived it as an infringement of Shari'a law.

In early April 2004 the Government announced that some 20 army officials had been arrested, following the discovery of a conspiracy to seize power, believed to have been instigated by a former head of security in the Abacha administration, Maj. Hama al-Mustapha. (In October three senior military officers, including al-Mustapha, were charged with planning to overthrow the

Government with an attack on the presidential helicopter.) Later in April reports emerged of severe clashes between Christian and Muslim tribes in farming villages on the border of Plateau State, reportedly as a result of land ownership disputes; by early May it was estimated that a total of 650 people, mainly Muslims, had been killed in the fighting. Muslims subsequently rioted in Kano in reprisal for the deaths; the Christian Association of Nigeria announced that 600 Christians had been killed and that a further 30,000 had fled from the region. Later in May Obasanjo dispatched security forces to restore order and imposed emergency powers in Plateau State, replacing the Governor with a former military officer and dissolving its legislature. (In November Obasanjo ended the state of emergency imposed in Plateau State and reinstated the elected Governor, who, however, had been detained in London, on suspicion of financial malpractice.)

In September 2004 renewed hostilities between the Ijaw and Ijekiri in the Niger Delta prompted further concern on the part of the authorities, particularly after an Ijaw militia, the Niger Delta People's Volunteer Force (NDPVF), threatened a campaign to disrupt petroleum supplies by attacking installations. Consequently, the Government announced a further substantial increase in the price of fuel in that month, prompting the NLC to organize a general strike in October. Further planned strike action by the NLC and allied organizations was suspended in November, after the Government agreed to a reduction in the price. Following a peace accord between the Government and the activists, reached in October, fighting in the region declined significantly. However, Ijaw militia had failed to disarm by the scheduled date at the end of December, and a campaign of peaceful protests was threatened, on the grounds that the Government had not complied with the terms of the agreement.

In February 2005 a three-month national conference, comprising 400 government appointed delegates, was convened to decide on political reform, including possible constitutional amendments, prior to the elections in 2007; however, the conference was boycotted by the opposition and was refused funding by the legislature. At the end of March the Government introduced new legislation permitting the establishment of unions independent of the NLC and prohibiting strikes in essential service sectors, with the aim of restricting the influence of the Congress.

In September 2005 tension increased in the Niger Delta region, following the arrest of the leader of the NDPVF; Mujahid Dokubo-Asari had threatened to continue hostilities unless his demands that the Ijaw people of the region be granted self-determination were met. Petroleum installations, which had temporarily closed, resumed operations after Dokubo-Asari urged his supporters to maintain civil order. In October he was officially charged with treason before the Abuja Federal High Court. Later that month the leader of the Movement for the Actualization of the Sovereign State of Biafra (MASSOB), Chief Ralph Uwazurike, was arrested and subsequently charged with treason (on the grounds that he had attempted to overthrow the Federal Government). In December Obasanjo placed defence and security personnel in the region on alert, following a petroleum pipeline explosion, in which several people were killed. Protests by members of MASSOB against the arrest of their leader ended in clashes, in which some 20 people were killed.

In January 2006 four foreign nationals employed by companies subcontracted by the Shell Petroleum Development Co were seized by militants in Bayelsa State; a hitherto unknown organization, the Movement for the Emancipation of the Niger Delta (MEND), claimed responsibility for taking the hostages. Following the explosion of a further petroleum pipeline, Shell suspended production from that offshore field (equivalent to one-tenth of the country's total output). MEND demanded that the Shell Petroleum Development Co pay US $1,500m. in compensation for environmental damage and release from custody Dokubo-Asari and the Governor of Bayelsa State, Diepreye Alamaieyeseigha, who had been arrested in the United Kingdom and charged with financial malpractice. (Dokubo-Asari was released in June 2007; Alamaieyeseigha was given a two-year custodial sentence in August but released several days later.) At the end of January 2006 MEND announced the release of the hostages on humanitarian grounds, but maintained that it would continue attacks in the Niger Delta region and seized a further nine foreign nationals employed by a subcontracted US enterprise, Willbros. Six of the hostages were released one week later, while the remaining three (two US and one British national) were released in late March. Also in February a High Court in Port Harcourt ruled that the Shell Petroleum Development Co pay $1,500m. in compensation to the Ijaw population in the Niger Delta for environmental damage, in compliance with a decision by the National Assembly in 2000.

The situation worsened during mid-2006 and in June five Nigerian soldiers were killed in a raid by MEND on a petroleum installation. In August Obasanjo ordered the establishment of a joint operation between the armed forces and the police to patrol the Niger Delta region and respond to reports of kidnapping; at least 12 oil workers had been taken hostage during that month. Shortly after the operation commenced it was reported that the security forces had opened fire in the region, forcing civilians to flee from the area. Concerns were raised that the order from the President would aggravate an already volatile situation; in October the number of kidnappings multiplied and the disturbances led to the reduction of petroleum production by some 25%.

In early 2006 the Nigerian Constitutional Committee conducted a series of public debates on proposed amendments to the Constitution, which would allow Obasanjo to seek a third term in office. In April relations between Obasanjo and the Vice-President, Alhaji Atiku Abubakar (who had protested at the proposals to end the constitutional restriction on two presidential terms), significantly deteriorated. In May the National Assembly rejected the proposals, thus preventing Obasanjo from contesting the 2007 presidential election.

In the months leading up to the presidential and legislative elections, scheduled to be held on 14 and 21 April 2007, several government reorganizations were effected. In June 2006 Obasanjo reassigned Okonja-Iwealato to the foreign affairs portfolio amid concerns over the durability of the Government's financial management and economic reforms, while the hitherto Minister of Solid Mineral Development, Obiageli Ezekwesili, assumed responsibility for education. Okonja-Iwealato resigned from the new position in August, having been dismissed from her role as head of the economic reform team; Prof. Joy Ogwu replaced her at the Ministry of Foreign Affairs. In early November Prof. Babalola Borishade was dismissed as Minister of Aviation and replaced by Femi Fani-Kayode, hitherto the Minister of Culture and Tourism. Further changes to the Government were carried out in mid-January 2007 when almost one-third of the ministries were dissolved or merged to simplify the administration's structure and improve its efficiency ahead of the forthcoming elections. Three new appointments were made during the reorganization, including that of Thomas I. Aguiyi-Ironsi to the defence portfolio.

With Obasanjo prohibited from contesting the presidential election, Abubakar emerged as the primary presidential candidate. However, his relationship with the President had become increasingly strained and Obasanjo strongly opposed Abubakar's candidacy. In September 2006 Obasanjo submitted a report to the Senate containing allegations of fraudulent activity involving Abubakar, who was subsequently indicted by the Economic and Financial Crimes Commission (EFCC), which had been established by Obasanjo in 2004. As Vice-President, Abubakar held immunity against prosecution unless impeached. Later in September 2006 he was suspended from the PDP for three months; although he retained his position as Vice-President, the suspension prevented him from seeking nomination from the PDP to stand as its presidential candidate. Abubakar continually denied the allegations against him, and it subsequently emerged that he would represent the Action Congress (AC), a new party formed in September by the merger of several minor political parties, in the presidential election. Abubakar was disqualified from contesting the election by the INEC in mid-March 2007, owing to his indictment for corruption, but following a number of legal challenges, his candidature was confirmed by a Supreme Court ruling on 16 April.

The presidential election was expected to be a historical landmark for Nigeria; for the first time in the country's history power was to be transferred between democratically elected civilian leaders. However, polling was marred by violent incidents that followed gubernatorial and state assembly elections, which were held on 14 April 2007. According to provisional results of the state elections, the PDP secured control of 28 states, the ANPP five, while the AC and the Progressive People's Alliance each took the largest number of votes in one state. The results in the remaining two states were declared void, owing to voter irregularities.

Provisional results of the presidential election, which was held concurrently with those to the National Assembly as scheduled on 21 April 2007, released by the INEC indicated that the PDP candidate, Alhaji Umaru Musa Yar'Adua (the younger brother of the late Maj.-Gen. (retd) Shehu Musa Yar'Adua, former Vice-

President in Obasanjo's military Government during the 1960s), had secured a decisive victory, receiving 70.00% of the votes cast. Buhari, who contested the election as the candidate of the ANPP, was his closest rival with 18.65% of the ballots, while Abubakar secured 7.25%. Yar'Adua was sworn in as President on 29 May. Despite claims by the INEC that the elections had been successfully held, international observers cast doubt on the credibility of the polls as reports emerged that no voting took place in some states due to delays in the distribution of ballot papers. Provisional results of elections to the National Assembly indicated that the PDP had increased its majority in both the House of Representatives and the Senate, winning 258 seats and 78 seats, respectively. The ANPP secured 64 seats in the lower house and 22 seats in the upper chamber.

Opposition parties challenged the outcome of the presidential election, demanding that the results be annulled and that an interim Government be established. However, members of the Senate insisted that to cancel the election results would be unconstitutional. Meanwhile, shortly after the presidential election Ezekwesili announced her resignation as Minister of Education, to take effect on 27 April 2007. Ezekwesili assumed a new role at the World Bank as Regional Vice-President responsible for Africa and was replaced by Dr Sayyadi Abba Ruma, hitherto the Minister of State for Education. In June the House of Representatives elected for the first time a woman, Patricia Etteh, to the position of Speaker. However, following allegations regarding the misappropriation of funds, Etteh resigned in November, and was replaced by Dimeji Bankole.

President Yar'Adua named a new Cabinet in August 2007, which included Mahmud Yayale Ahmed as Minister of Defence, Ojo Maduekwe as Minister of Foreign Affairs and Shamsudeen Usman as Minister of Finance; in October four more ministers were sworn in, having received approval from the Senate. Yar'Adua assumed responsibility for the petroleum resources portfolio, as Obasanjo had before him, and pledged to continue with reforms to the energy sector that had commenced under the previous administration. Furthermore the new President ordered investigations, which commenced in August, into the award of numerous petroleum and gas contracts. (Yar'Adua also established a 22-member electoral reform panel to address issues that led to the violence triggered by the April elections.)

Following the election of Yar'Adua in April 2007, Buhari and Abubakar had instigated legal proceedings to have the results of the ballot annulled. However, at a final hearing in Abuja in February 2008 five judges dismissed the case, citing insufficient grounds for overruling the result. The two defeated candidates announced their intention to appeal against the decision in the Supreme Court. By this time eight State Governors had had their appointments nullified by the Court of Appeal and in April the elections of the Governors of Bayelsa and Sokoto States were also ruled invalid. In May the elections were repeated in those states, with the PDP candidates winning both. A gubernatorial by-election was held in Adamawa State in April which was also won by the PDP candidate, Murtala Nyako; the INEC insisted that the election was peaceful and transparent, although the opposition AC disputed this. Further court rulings in February 2009 nullified gubernatorial elections in Ondo State and Ekiti State on the basis that they did not comply with electoral law.

In March 2008 the PDP elected the party's former General Secretary, Col Dr Vincent Ogbulafor, as its new Chairman. In the same month the human rights group Amnesty International issued a report condemning Nigeria's criminal justice system: according to the report at least 65% of prisoners in the country had never been convicted of a crime, and abuse of prisoners' rights was systematic, with widespread use of torture and severe overcrowding in prisons.

In mid-August 2008 Yar'Adua announced an overhaul of the command structure of the armed forces, replacing the Chief of Defence Staff, Gen. Andrew Owoye Azazi, with Air Marshall Paul Dike; the chiefs of staff of the army, navy and air force were also removed, although intense media speculation that the changes were effected as a result of a perceived threat to the Government were denied by the presidency. In September there was further speculation that Yar'Adua was to step down as President owing to ill health; furthermore, it was also falsely reported that he had died while receiving medical treatment in Saudi Arabia. In the same month Yar'Adua approved the restructuring of several government departments, including the creation of a new Ministry of Niger Delta Affairs and the division of the Ministry of Energy into two separate ministries, namely the Ministry of Power and the Ministry of Petroleum. He also dismissed the Secretary to the Government of the Federation, Baba Gana Kingibe, following suggestions in the media that he planned to challenge for the presidency. A total of eight ministers and 12 ministers of state were removed from the Cabinet in November in preparation for the major reorganization of the structure of the federal ministries. In the following month Yar'Adua named his new Government, in which only three members of the outgoing administration retained their positions. The new Cabinet featured 19 new appointees: most notably, Dr Rilwanu Lukman (the Secretary-General of the Organization of the Petroleum Exporting Countries, see p. 386 in 1995–2000), was appointed Minister of Petroleum and Dr Shettima Mustapha was named as the new Minister of Defence, while Chief Ufot Ekaette, a former Secretary to the Government of the Federation, was awarded responsibility for the Niger Delta affairs portfolio.

Meanwhile, in late November 2008 there was significant unrest in the Plateau State town of Jos; violent clashes between Christian and Muslim groups resulted in the deaths of some 400 people, while thousands more were displaced. The rioting followed a dispute over local elections in mid-November (the first for some 10 years) at which the PDP defeated the largely Muslim-supported ANPP, and swiftly escalated into sectarian violence, as rival gangs fought in the streets, property was looted and churches and mosques were set alight. A report published by Human Rights Watch in early 2009 claimed that police had carried out summary executions of some 90 youths while suppressing the disturbances.

Unrest continued in the Niger Delta region throughout 2007 with numerous kidnappings and abductions reported, and in the months preceding the elections there had also been an escalation of attacks on oil installations and several car bombings in Port Harcourt; by mid-February some 52 hostages had been taken, the majority of whom had links to the petroleum sector. President Yar'Adua had indicated that his administration would give special priority to the problems of the Niger Delta and intensive discussions commenced with the newly elected Governors from the region. However, in August a cease-fire negotiated by the Nigerian Government and MEND in May broke down and further abductions and disruptions to petroleum production were reported during late 2007 and early 2008.

In January 2008 MEND confirmed reports that foreign mercenaries were operating in the Niger Delta, where they were helping to train younger members of the organization, and urged the UN to intervene in the region to prevent a full-scale war. In February Henry Okah and Edward Atatah, the leaders of MEND, were extradited from Angola, where they had been arrested in September 2007 on weapons charges; reports that Okah had been shot dead while in custody in Nigeria were later proven to be false, and in March 2008 treason charges were filed against both men. MEND claimed responsibility for four separate attacks on oil installations and pipelines in April 2008, and further attacks on installations owned by Royal Dutch Shell Plc in May. The company was reportedly forced to halt production equivalent to some 169,000 barrels per day as a result, and in June shut down production at its facility in the offshore Bonga oil field, after it was attacked. Despite declaring a unilateral cease-fire in June, rebels attacked a military camp in the following month, leading to a retaliatory raid by Nigerian security forces on the village of Agge in August. In mid-September the Nigerian military carried out a large-scale bombardment of a MEND position in Rivers State, prompting the declaration of an 'oil war' by the rebels: after a week of intensified attacks on oil installations, MEND declared another cease-fire. However, there was a resumption of hostilities in early 2009 after rebels affiliated to MEND launched an assault on an oil platform and kidnapped six crew members. On 31 January MEND officially ended its cease-fire in response to a military attack on one of its bases; attacks on oil and gas installations continued, and there was an increase in the number of foreign nationals and oil workers being kidnapped in the region, leading to a two-day strike by workers at the French company Total, who were concerned about the continuing unrest and insecurity.

Nigeria has taken a leading role in African affairs and is a prominent member of the Economic Community of West African States (ECOWAS, see p. 243) and other regional organizations. The Nigerian Government has contributed a significant number of troops to the ECOWAS Monitoring Group (ECOMOG, see p. 246), which was deployed in Liberia from August 1990 in response to the conflict between government forces and rebels in that country (see the chapter on Liberia). In 1993 Nigerian troops were dispatched to Sierra Leone, in response to a formal request by the Sierra Leonean Government for military assistance to repulse attacks by rebels in that country. Following the completion of the transition to civilian rule in Nigeria in May 1999, a phased withdrawal of Nigerian troops from Sierra Leone commenced. By the end of April 2000 all Nigerian troops belonging to ECOMOG had left Sierra Leone; however, Nigeria continued to contribute troops to the UN Mission in Sierra Leone (UNAMSIL). In September an official visit to Nigeria by the US President, Bill Clinton, the first by a US Head of State since 1978, provided for a number of new trade and development initiatives. After further full-scale conflict in Liberia in mid-2003 (see the chapter on Liberia), the Liberian President, Charles Taylor, finally accepted an offer of asylum from Obasanjo, following pressure from the international community, and took up residence in Calabar, in south-eastern Nigeria, in early August. Some 1,500 Nigerian troops, which were deployed in the country, under an ECOWAS mandate, at the end of August, were instrumental in restoring peace and were incorporated into the replacement contingent, the UN Mission in Liberia (UNMIL, see p. 86), on 1 October. In October the Nigerian Government strongly protested at the US authorities' approval of a reward of some US $2m. for the arrest of Taylor (who had been indicted by the Special Court established in Sierra Leone to try war crime suspects). In March 2006 Nigeria announced that it had received a formal request from the new Liberian Government (see chapter on Liberia) to extradite Taylor to the Special Court. Obasanjo agreed to return him to the Liberian authorities, but failed to comply with demands by the Chief Prosecutor of the Special Court and the USA to take him into custody. Taylor fled from his residence in Calabar, but was apprehended two days later in Borno State, near the border with Cameroon, and dispatched to Liberia, from where he was immediately extradited by UNMIL peace-keepers to the Special Court.

In 1991 the Nigerian Government claimed that Cameroonian security forces had annexed several Nigerian fishing settlements in Cross River State (in south-eastern Nigeria), following a longstanding border dispute, based on a 1913 agreement between Germany and the United Kingdom that ceded the Bakassi peninsula in the Gulf of Guinea (a region with significant petroleum reserves) to Cameroon. Subsequent negotiations between Nigerian and Cameroonian officials in an effort to resolve the dispute achieved little progress. In December 1993 some 500 Nigerian troops were dispatched to the region, in response to a number of incidents in which Nigerian nationals had been killed by Cameroonian security forces. Later that month the two nations agreed to establish a joint patrol at the disputed area, and to investigate the cause of the incidents. In February 1994, however, the Nigerian Government increased the number of troops deployed in the region. Later in February the Cameroonian Government announced that it was to submit the dispute for adjudication by the UN, the Organization of African Unity (OAU, now the African Union, see p. 172) and the International Court of Justice (ICJ), and requested military assistance from France. Subsequent reports of clashes between Cameroonian and Nigerian forces in the region prompted fears of a full-scale conflict between the two nations.

In February 1996 renewed hostilities between Nigerian and Cameroonian forces in the Bakassi region resulted in several casualties. Later that month, however, Nigeria and Cameroon agreed to refrain from further military action, and delegations from the two countries resumed discussions, with mediation by President Gnassingbe Eyadéma of Togo, in an attempt to resolve the dispute. In March the ICJ ruled that Cameroon had failed to provide sufficient evidence to support its contention that Nigeria had instigated the border dispute, and ordered both nations to cease military operations in this respect, to withdraw troops to former positions, and to co-operate with a UN investigative mission that was to be dispatched to the region. In April, however, clashes continued, with each Government accusing the other of initiating the attacks. Although tension in the region remained high, diplomatic efforts to avoid further conflict increased in May; in that month a Cameroonian delegation visited Nigeria, while Abacha accepted an invitation to attend an OAU summit meeting, which was to be convened in Yaoundé in July. The UN investigative mission visited the Bakassi region in September. In May 1997 the Cameroonian Government denied further allegations by Nigeria that it had initiated hostilities; the UN requested that the Togolese President continue mediation efforts. Further clashes between Nigerian and Cameroonian forces were reported in December 1997 and February 1998. In March the Nigerian Government contested the jurisdiction of the ICJ to rule on the Bakassi issue, on the grounds that the two countries had agreed to settle the dispute through bilateral negotiations. In June, however, the Court pronounced that it had the necessary jurisdiction.

In October 2002 the ICJ finally ruled that the disputed Bakassi region was part of Cameroon, under the terms of the 1913 agreement. Obasanjo criticized the decision, in support of strong opposition expressed by the Nigerian majority inhabitants of the peninsula, although he subsequently pledged to abide by the ruling. In August 2003, following UN mediation, Nigeria and Cameroon finally adopted a framework agreement for the implementation of the ICJ's judgment; all military and administrative personnel were to be withdrawn from the Bakassi region, and a commission, comprising Nigerian, Cameroonian and UN officials, was to resolve outstanding issues for the redemarcation of boundaries between the two countries, in a process that was expected to continue for up to three years. In December the Nigerian Government ceded control of some 33 villages on its north-eastern border to Cameroon, but sovereignty over the disputed territory with petroleum resources remained under discussion by the commission. However, the Nigerian Government announced that the transfer of authority in the peninsula, scheduled for September 2004, had been postponed, citing technical difficulties in the final redemarcation of the joint border. Following a meeting in May 2005 between Obasanjo and the Head of State of Cameroon, conducted in Geneva, Switzerland, under the aegis of the UN Secretary-General, it was announced that the two sides had agreed to draft a new programme for Nigeria's withdrawal from the Bakassi peninsula. On 12 June 2006 an accord was signed, according to which Nigeria agreed to withdraw troops from the peninsula within 60 days, and on 14 August Nigerian troops left the peninsula. Although the peninsula would remain under Nigerian control during the interim period, a full transfer of the Bakassi peninsula was to be completed by June 2008. The situation remained calm during October 2006 as steady progress was made in the demarcation of the border between the countries and agreement was reached on the relocation of 13 villages. However, in November 2007 21 Cameroonian soldiers were reported to have been killed by Nigerian troops, raising concerns that the security of the region was under threat. The Nigerian authorities denied involvement in the attack and local sources blamed a faction of MEND; however, a group styling itself the Liberators of the Southern Cameroons later claimed responsibility, claiming that the soldiers had been implicated in illegal arms trading with Nigerian forces. Meanwhile, that same month the Nigerian Senate approved a motion to declare the handover of the Bakassi peninsula to be illegal and that no Nigerian territory could be ceded without amendments to the Constitution.

An agreement was reached in March 2008 which finalized the position of the two countries' long-disputed maritime boundary in the Gulf of Guinea, and the transfer of the Bakassi peninsula to Cameroon was scheduled for August that year. There was further violence in the peninsula in June, when five Cameroonian troops and a local government official, Felix Morfan, were abducted and later killed; soldiers from both Nigeria and Cameroon stationed there were placed on high alert, although it was not clear who was responsible for the murders. In the following month Nigerian gunmen opened fire on a Cameroonian security patrol in Bakassi: the attack was launched by the Niger Delta Defence and Security Council (NDDSC), a rebel group seeking to prevent the agreed transfer of the Bakassi peninsula from proceeding as planned. It was reported that two NDDSC members were captured in the attack, although the group denied this. The NDDSC claimed responsibility for a further attack on a Cameroon military post in the same month, in which the Cameroonian military claimed to have killed 10 of the rebels and captured another eight, while one of its soldiers was killed. There were also reports in July that another militant group, the Bakassi Freedom Fighters, had merged its forces with the NDDSC in a final attempt to disrupt the handover scheduled for the following month. None the less, on 14 August the transfer was finally completed with an official flag-exchange ceremony that, for security reasons, took place in the city of Calabar, over 100 miles from the peninsula. In October the NDDSC stated that it had been involved in an attack on Cameroonian soldiers in the Bakassi peninsula, insisting that it would continue to fight even though Bakassi had been returned to Cameroon; the group demanded the release of the two rebels captured earlier in the year, as well as compensation for Nigerians who had been forced to leave Bakassi. The clash occurred one week after the two countries had agreed to co-ordinate efforts to protect their land and sea borders from raids by militant groups and pirates.

In mid-February 2007, following a meeting in Abuja, Nigeria signed a pact with Benin and Togo aimed at promoting peace and stability between the three countries and which provided for the establishment of a body to be known as the Nigeria–Benin–Togo Co-prosperity Zone. The three countries also announced the implementation of the ECOWAS Protocol on Free Movement of Persons and the Right of Residence and Establishment, and an early warning system for conflict prevention.

Government

Under the terms of the Constitution of the Federal Republic of Nigeria, which entered into effect on 31 May 1999, executive power is vested in the President, who is the Head of State. The President, who is elected for a term of four years (and is restricted to two mandates), nominates a Vice-President and a Cabinet, subject to confirmation by the Senate. Legislative power is vested in the bicameral National Assembly, comprising a 360-member House of Representatives and a 109-member Senate, which is elected by universal suffrage for a four-year term. Nigeria is a federation of 36 states, comprising 774 local government areas. The executive power of a state is vested in the Governor of that state, who is elected for a four-year term, and the legislative power in the House of Assembly of that state.

Defence

As assessed at November 2008, Nigeria's total armed forces numbered 80,000 (army 62,000, navy 8,000 and air force 10,000). There was also a paramilitary force of 82,000. Military service is voluntary. Expenditure on defence by the Federal Government in 2008 was budgeted at ₦158,000m.

Economic Affairs

In 2007, according to estimates by the World Bank, Nigeria's gross national income (GNI), measured at average 2005–07 prices, was US $137,091m., equivalent to $930 per head (or $1,770 per head on an international purchasing-power parity basis). During 2000–07, it was estimated, the population increased, in real terms, at an average annual rate of 2.5%, while gross domestic product (GDP) per head rose by 3.6%. Overall GDP increased, in real terms, at an average annual rate of 6.2% in 2000–07; growth was 6.3% in 2007.

Agriculture (including hunting, forestry and fishing) contributed an estimated 33.1% of GDP in 2007. An estimated 58.6% of the employed labour force were engaged in the sector in 2005. The principal cash crops are cocoa (which accounted for only 0.3% of total merchandise exports in 2006), rubber and oil palm. Staple food crops include cassava, yams, maize, millet, taro, rice and sorghum. Timber production, the raising of livestock (principally goats, sheep, cattle and poultry), and artisanal fisheries are also important. According to the African Development Bank (AfDB), agricultural GDP increased at an average annual rate of 4.8% in 2000–07. Growth in agricultural GDP was 4.5% in 2007.

Industry (including mining, manufacturing, construction and power) engaged an estimated 3.4% of the employed labour force in 2005, and contributed an estimated 35.7% of GDP in 2007. According to the AfDB, industrial GDP increased at an average annual rate of 3.7% in 2000–07. It declined by 0.4% in 2006, but increased by 3.2% in 2007.

Mining contributed an estimated 31.2% of GDP in 2007, although the sector engaged just 0.1% of the employed labour force in 2005. The principal mineral is petroleum, of which Nigeria is Africa's leading producer (providing an estimated 92.9% of total export earnings in 2007). In addition, Nigeria possesses substantial deposits of natural gas and coal. In late 1999 the Nigerian Government commenced exports of liquefied natural gas, and by 2004 natural gas accounted for 8.8% of earnings. A 678-km pipeline, which would transport natural gas from the Escravos field, in Delta State, to Benin, Togo and Ghana, commenced operations in April 2007. Tin and iron ore are also mined, while there are plans to exploit deposits of uranium. The GDP of the mining sector was estimated by the IMF to have declined by an average of 0.1% per year in 1997–2001; mining GDP increased by 0.6% in 2001.

Manufacturing contributed an estimated 2.7% of GDP in 2007, and engaged about 1.8% of the employed labour force in 2005. The principal sectors are food-processing, brewing, petroleum-refining, iron and steel, motor vehicles (using imported components), textiles, cigarettes, footwear, pharmaceuticals, pulp and paper, and cement. According to the AfDB, manufacturing GDP increased at an average annual rate of 7.3% in 2000–07. Manufacturing GDP increased by 3.5% in 2007.

Energy is derived principally from natural gas, which provided some 53.6% of electricity in 2005, and hydroelectric power (33.8%); petroleum provided 12.7%. Mineral fuels comprised 1.8% of the value of merchandise imports in 2007.

The services sector contributed an estimated 31.1% of GDP in 2007, and engaged 38.0% of the employed labour force in 2005. According to the AfDB, the GDP of the services sector increased at an average annual rate of 9.6% in 2000–07. The GDP of the services sector increased by 2.0% in 2007.

In 2007 Nigeria recorded a trade surplus of US $33,138m., and there was a surplus of $21,972m. on the current account of the balance of payments. In 2007 the principal source of imports (15.1%) was the USA; the other major supplier was the United Kingdom. The USA was also the principal market for exports (46.6%) in that year; the other significant purchaser was Brazil. The principal export in 2007 was petroleum. The principal imports in 2007 were machinery and transport equipment, food and live animals, and chemicals and related products.

Nigeria's overall budget surplus for 2007 was an estimated ₦35,000m., equivalent to around 0.2% of GDP. The country's external debt totalled US $7,693m. at the end of 2006, of which $3,800m. was long-term public debt. In 2005 the cost of debt-servicing was equivalent to 15.8% of the value of exports of goods and services. The annual rate of inflation averaged 7.3% in 2000–07; consumer prices increased by 5.3% in 2007. An estimated 4.5% of the labour force were unemployed at the end of 1997.

Nigeria is a member of the African Development Bank (see p. 170), of the Economic Community of West African States (see p. 243), which aims to promote trade and co-operation in West Africa, and of OPEC.

Nigeria is one of Africa's most powerful economies, but despite considerable agricultural and mineral resources, political instability has severely impeded economic reform, and it is classified as a low-income country by the World Bank. Although high levels of external debt caused concern in the early 2000s, through government reform policies, support from the IMF and the cancellation of debt by the 'Paris Club', by early 2007 it was estimated that Nigeria's external debt had been reduced to just 3.0% of GDP. From 2006 an escalation of unrest in the Niger Delta region, with a series of attacks against petroleum pipelines and seizures of foreign nationals as hostages, threatened national stability. Militant groups in the region continued to demand the withdrawal of all foreign enterprises exploiting the country's resources, and the violence resulted in the temporary closure of an offshore field and a 25% reduction in oil production (valued at some ₦70,000m.) in the three years from 2006. Moreover, the downturn in production further exacerbated the country's energy shortage, and many regions were subject to frequent blackouts. A number of refineries were scheduled to commence production in 2008 and 2009, and in the long-term, the Government envisaged processing 50% of the economy's energy needs in Nigeria, thus reducing the reliance on imports. Meanwhile, the West African Gas Pipeline became operational in April 2007, delivering 16.4m. cu m of gas per day to Benin, Ghana and Togo. Although in mid-2009 the Nigerian economy appeared to be relatively unharmed by the global economic slowdown and the long-term effect was expected to be limited, the global price of oil had fallen sharply, from US $140 per barrel in June 2008 to around $40 in early 2009, and there were concerns that inward investment to the country would reduce. The IMF predicted that GDP growth would still amount to 8.1% in 2009. However, corruption remained a serious concern, and the ongoing petroleum protests caused widespread disruption to the petroleum industry, upon which Nigeria's economy was heavily reliant.

Education

Education is partly the responsibility of the state governments, although the Federal Government has played an increasingly important role since 1970. Primary education begins at six years of age and lasts for six years. Secondary education begins at 12 years of age and lasts for a further six years, comprising two three-year cycles. Education to junior secondary level (from six to 15 years of age) is free and compulsory. According to UNESCO estimates, in 2005/06 63% of children in the relevant age-group (males 68%; females 59%) were enrolled in primary education, while the comparable ratio for secondary enrolment in that year was 26% (males 28%; females 23%). In 2005 724,856 students were enrolled at Nigerian universities. Expenditure on education by the Federal Government in 2005 was ₦82,797m., equivalent to 5.0% of total expenditure in the federal budget.

NIGERIA

Public Holidays

2009: 1 January (New Year's Day), 9 March* (Mouloud, Birth of the Prophet), 10–13 April (Easter), 1 October (National Day), 20 September* (Id al-Fitr, end of Ramadan), 27 November* (Id al-Kabir, Feast of the Sacrifice), 25–26 December (Christmas).

2010: 1 January (New Year's Day), 26 February* (Mouloud, Birth of the Prophet), 2–5 April (Easter), 10 September* (Id al-Fitr, end of Ramadan), 1 October (National Day), 16 November* (Id al-Kabir, Feast of the Sacrifice), 25–26 December (Christmas).

* These holidays are dependent on the Islamic lunar calendar, and may vary by one or two days from the dates given.

Weights and Measures

The metric system is in force.

Statistical Survey

Sources (unless otherwise stated): National Bureau of Statistics, Plot 762, Independence Avenue, Central Business District, PMB 127, Garki, Abuja; tel. (9) 2731085; fax (9) 2731084; internet www.nigerianstat.gov.ng; Central Bank of Nigeria, Central Business District, PMB 187, Garki, Abuja; tel. (9) 61639701; fax (9) 61636012; e-mail info@cenbank.org; internet www.cenbank.org.

Area and Population

AREA, POPULATION AND DENSITY

Area (sq km)	909,890*
Population (census results)	
28–30 November 1991†	88,992,220
21–27 March 2006 (provisional)	
Males	71,709,859
Females	68,293,683
Total	140,003,542
Density (per sq km) at March 2006	157.2

* 351,310 sq miles.
† Revised 15 September 2001.

Population (UN estimates at mid-year): 147,722,000 in 2007; 151,212,000 in 2008 (Source: UN, *World Population Prospects: The 2008 Revision*).

STATES
(2006 census, provisional)

	Area (sq km)	Population	Density (per sq km)	Capital
Abia	4,900	2,833,999	578	Umuahia
Adamawa	38,700	3,168,101	82	Yola
Akwa Ibom	6,900	3,920,208	568	Uyo
Anambra	4,865	4,182,032	860	Awka
Bauchi	49,119	4,676,465	95	Bauchi
Bayelsa	9,059	1,703,358	188	Yenogoa
Benue	30,800	4,219,244	137	Makurdi
Borno	72,609	4,151,193	57	Maiduguri
Cross River	21,787	2,888,966	133	Calabar
Delta	17,108	4,098,391	240	Asaba
Ebonyi	6,400	2,173,501	340	Abakaliki
Edo	19,187	3,218,332	168	Benin City
Ekiti	5,435	2,384,212	439	Ado-Ekiti
Enugu	7,534	3,257,298	432	Enugu
Gombe	17,100	2,353,879	138	Gombe
Imo	5,288	3,934,899	744	Owerri
Jigawa	23,287	4,348,649	187	Dutse
Kaduna	42,481	6,066,562	143	Kaduna
Kano	20,280	9,383,682	463	Kano
Katsina	23,561	5,792,578	246	Katsina
Kebbi	36,985	3,238,628	88	Birnin Kebbi
Kogi	27,747	3,278,487	118	Lokoja
Kwara	35,705	2,371,089	66	Ilorin
Lagos	3,671	9,013,534	2,455	Ikeja
Nassarawa	28,735	1,863,275	65	Lafia
Niger	68,925	3,950,249	57	Minna
Ogun	16,400	3,728,098	227	Abeokuta
Ondo	15,820	3,441,024	218	Akure
—continued	Area (sq km)	Population	Density (per sq km)	Capital
Osun	9,026	3,423,535	379	Oshogbo
Oyo	26,500	5,591,589	211	Ibadan
Plateau	27,147	3,178,712	117	Jos
Rivers	10,575	5,185,400	490	Port Harcourt
Sokoto	27,825	3,696,999	241	Sokoto
Taraba	56,282	2,300,736	41	Jalingo
Yobe	46,609	2,321,591	50	Damaturu
Zamfara	37,931	3,256,846	86	Gusau
Federal Capital Territory (Abuja)	7,607	1,405,201	185	Abuja
Total	**909,890**	**140,003,542**	**157**	—

PRINCIPAL TOWNS
(unrevised census of November 1991)

Lagos (federal capital)*	5,195,247	Enugu	407,756
Kano	2,166,554	Oyo	369,894
Ibadan	1,835,300	Warri	363,382
Kaduna	933,642	Abeokuta	352,735
Benin City	762,719	Onitsha	350,280
Port Harcourt	703,421	Sokoto	329,639
Maiduguri	618,278	Okene	312,775
Zaria	612,257	Calabar	310,839
Ilorin	532,089	Katsina	259,315
Jos	510,300	Oshogbo	250,951
Aba	500,183	Akure	239,124
Ogbomosho	433,030	Bauchi	206,537

* Federal capital moved to Abuja (population 107,069) in December 1991.

Mid-2007 ('000 incl. suburbs, UN estimates): Lagos 9,466; Kano 3,140; Ibadan 2,628; Kaduna 1,442; Benin City 1,190; Port Harcourt 1,020; Ogbomosho 951; Maiduguri 896; Zaria 889 (Source: UN, *World Urbanization Prospects: The 2007 Revision*).

BIRTHS AND DEATHS
(annual averages, UN estimates)

	1990–95	1995–2000	2000–05
Birth rate (per 1,000)	45.2	43.5	41.8
Death rate (per 1,000)	19.7	18.8	17.4

Source: UN, *World Population Prospects: The 2008 Revision*.

Life expectancy (years at birth, WHO estimates): 48.4 (males 47.6; females 49.1) in 2006 (Source: WHO, *World Health Statistics*).

NIGERIA

EMPLOYMENT
('000 persons aged 14 years and over)

	2003	2004	2005
Agriculture, hunting, forestry and fishing	27,840	28,439	37,487
Mining and quarrying	66	67	89
Manufacturing	820	836	1,173
Electricity, gas and water	410	422	551
Construction	260	267	353
Wholesale and retail trade; repairs of motor vehicles and motorcycles and personal and household articles	93	97	134
Hotels and restaurants	87	89	125
Transport, storage and communications	400	411	537
Financial intermediation	270	275	363
Real estate, renting and business activities	59	60	78
Public administration, defence and compulsory social security	4,900	5,039	6,547
Education	8,430	8,760	12,239
Health and social welfare	280	291	383
Other community, social and personal service activities	2,885	2,942	3,874
Total employed	46,800	47,993	63,932

Health and Welfare

KEY INDICATORS

Total fertility rate (children per woman, 2006)	5.5
Under-5 mortality rate (per 1,000 live births, 2006)	191
HIV/AIDS (% of persons aged 15–49, 2007)	3.1
Physicians (per 1,000 head, 2003)	0.28
Hospital beds (per 1,000 head, 2004)	0.5
Health expenditure (2006): US $ per head (PPP)	50
Health expenditure (2006): % of GDP	4.1
Health expenditure (2006): public (% of total)	30.1
Access to water (% of persons, 2006)	47
Access to sanitation (% of persons, 2006)	30
Human Development Index (2006): ranking	154
Human Development Index (2006): value	0.499

For sources and definitions, see explanatory note on p. vi.

Agriculture

PRINCIPAL CROPS
('000 metric tons)

	2005	2006	2007
Wheat	66	71	70*
Rice, paddy	3,567	4,042	4,677*
Maize	5,957	7,100	7,800*
Millet	7,168	7,705	7,700*
Sorghum	9,178	9,866	1,050*
Potatoes	776	838	843†
Sweet potatoes	3,205	3,462	3,490†
Cassava	41,565	45,721	45,750†
Taro (Coco yam)	5,068	5,473	5,485†
Yams	34,000	36,720	37,150†
Sugar cane	914	987	1,029†
Cow peas, dry	2,815	3,040	3,150†
Cashew nuts	594	636	660†
Kolanuts†	85	86	88†
Soybeans	565	605	617†
Groundnuts, with shell	3,478	3,825	3,836†
Coconuts	209	225	230†
Oil palm fruit†	8,500	8,300	8,500†
Sesame seed	100*	100*	100†
Melonseed	451	483	489†
Tomatoes†	890	896	898
Chillies and peppers, green†	721	722	723
Onions and shallots, green†	221	221	225
Onions, dry†	616	616	618
Carrots and turnips†	238	240	243

—continued	2005	2006	2007
Okra†	731	731	733
Maize, green†	577	577	579
Plantains	2,591	2,785	2,800†
Citrus fruits†	3,250	3,300	3,325
Guavas, mangoes and mangosteens†	731	732	734
Pineapples†	890	895	900
Papayas†	756	759	765
Cocoa beans	441	485	500*
Ginger	125	134	138†
Tobacco, unmanufactured†	15	14	14
Natural rubber†	142	143	143

* Unofficial figure.
† FAO estimate(s).

Aggregate production ('000 metric tons, may include official, semi-official or estimated data): Total cereals 26,031 in 2005, 28,884 in 2006, 30,850 in 2007; Total roots and tubers 84,614 in 2005, 92,214 in 2006, 92,718 in 2007; Total vegetables (incl. melons) 9,176 in 2005, 9,654 in 2006, 9,869 in 2007; Total fruits (excl. melons) 9,619 in 2005, 8,471 in 2006, 8,524 in 2007.

Source: FAO.

LIVESTOCK
('000 head, year ending September)

	2005	2006*	2007*
Horses*	206	207	208
Asses	1,050	n.a.	n.a.
Cattle	15,875	16,066	16,259
Camels*	18	19	19
Pigs*	6,650	6,690	6,730
Sheep*	23,500	23,500	23,994
Goats*	28,500	28,300	28,583
Chickens	150,700	158,400	166,500

* FAO estimates.

Source: FAO.

LIVESTOCK PRODUCTS
('000 metric tons, FAO estimates)

	2005	2006	2007
Cattle meat	260.9	284.1	287.5
Sheep meat	100.2	103.4	105.6
Goat meat	147.7	147.4	148.8
Pig meat	209.5	209.5	212.0
Chicken meat	218.8	221.8	233.1
Game meat	120	120	121
Cows' milk	239	463	468
Hen eggs	500	526	553

Source: FAO.

Forestry

ROUNDWOOD REMOVALS
('000 cubic metres, excluding bark, FAO estimates)

	2005	2006	2007
Sawlogs, veneer logs and logs for sleepers	7,100	7,100	7,100
Pulpwood	39	39	39
Other industrial wood	2,279	2,279	2,279
Fuel wood	61,274	61,629	62,000
Total	70,692	71,047	71,418

Source: FAO.

NIGERIA

SAWNWOOD PRODUCTION
('000 cubic metres, including railway sleepers)

	1995	1996	1997
Broadleaved (hardwood)	2,356	2,178	2,000

1998–2007: Broadleaved (hardwood) production as in 1997.
Source: FAO.

Fishing

('000 metric tons, live weight)

	2004	2005	2006
Capture	465.3	523.2	552.3
Tilapias	22.9	31.8	30.5
Elephant snout fishes	19.5	18.6	18.7
Torpedo-shaped catfishes	9.6	16.2	14.9
Sea catfishes	20.5	21.2	23.5
West African croakers	14.1	10.7	12.5
Sardinellas	71.4	65.8	72.7
Bonga shad	14.7	19.8	22.6
Southern pink shrimp	11.4	12.4	11.9
Other shrimps and prawns	11.5	16.2	16.1
Aquaculture	44.0	56.4	84.6
Total catch	509.2	579.5	636.9

Source: FAO.

Mining

(metric tons, unless otherwise indicated)

	2005	2006	2007
Coal, bituminous	8,000	530,000	530,000
Kaolin*	93,000	100,000	100,000
Gypsum*	150,000	169,000	579,000
Crude petroleum ('000 barrels)	923,500	869,197	803,000
Natural gas (million cu m)	57,369	57,754	68,404
Tin concentrates*†	1,300	1,400	180

* Estimates.
† Metal content.
Source: US Geological Survey.

Industry

SELECTED PRODUCTS
('000 metric tons, unless otherwise indicated)

	2001	2002	2003
Palm oil*	903	908	915
Raw sugar*†	40	40	40
Wheat flour*†	1,564	1,730	1,598
Beer of barley*†	956	1,171	1,170
Beer of sorghum*†	698	760	794
Plywood ('000 cubic metres)*†	55	55	55
Wood pulp*†	23	23	23
Paper and paperboard*†	19	19	19
Liquefied petroleum gas ('000 barrels)†	1,000	2,300	2,000
Motor spirit—petrol ('000 barrels)†	24,400	22,400	20,000
Kerosene ('000 barrels)†	12,500	11,800	12,000
Gas-diesel (distillate fuel) oil ('000 barrels)†	18,900	18,800	19,000
Residual fuel oils ('000 barrels)†	21,500	17,200	17,000
Cement†	2,400	2,100	2,100
Tin metal—unwrought (metric tons)†	25	25	25
Electric energy (million kWh)‡	15,453	21,544	20,183

* Source: FAO.
† Estimates.
‡ Source: UN, *Industrial Commodity Statistics Yearbook*.

2004 (million kWh): Electric energy 20,224 (Source: UN, *Industrial Commodity Statistics Yearbook*).

Source (unless otherwise indicated): US Geological Survey.

2004 ('000 barrels, estimates): Motor spirit–petrol 4,600; Kerosene 4,900; Gas-diesel (distillate fuel) oil 8,800; Residual fuel oils 12,400 (Source: US Geological Survey).

2005 ('000 barrels, estimates): Motor spirit–petrol 14,800; Kerosene 10,100; Gas-diesel (distillate fuel) oil 15,800; Residual fuel oils 19,200 (Source: US Geological Survey).

2006 ('000 barrels, estimates): Motor spirit–petrol 8,500; Kerosene 6,100; Gas-diesel (distillate fuel) oil 9,400; Residual fuel oils 14,400 (Source: US Geological Survey).

2007 ('000 barrels, estimates): Motor spirit–petrol 2,450; Kerosene 2,550; Gas-diesel (distillate fuel) oil 4,645; Residual fuel oils 6,670 (Source: US Geological Survey).

Finance

CURRENCY AND EXCHANGE RATES

Monetary Units
100 kobo = 1 naira (₦).

Sterling, Dollar and Euro Equivalents (30 September 2008)
£1 sterling = 211.883 naira;
US $1 = 117.726 naira;
€1 = 168.384 naira;
1,000 naira = £4.72 = $8.49 = €5.94.

Average Exchange Rate (naira per US $)
2005   131.274
2006   128.652
2007   125.808

FEDERAL BUDGET
(₦ '000 million)

Revenue	2006	2007*	2008†
Petroleum revenue	2,166	1,734	2,411
Crude receipts, cash calls (net) and derivation	926	683	1,105
Profit tax and royalty	989	851	1,153
Non-petroleum revenue	258	476	484
Import and excise duties	80	111	131
Companies' income tax	114	156	182
Value-added tax	31	42	51
Total	2,424	2,211	2,895

NIGERIA

Expenditure	2006	2007*	2008†
Recurrent expenditure	1,169	1,471	1,600
Goods and services	888	1,139	1,210
Personnel and pension	665	864	943
Overhead cost	223	275	267
Interest payments	187	208	203
Transfers	94	141	188
Capital expenditure	495	705	850
Total	1,664	2,176	2,451

* Estimates.
† Projected.

Source: IMF, *Nigeria: 2007 Article IV Consultation - Staff Report; Staff Supplement and Statement; Public Information Notice on the Executive Board Discussion; and Statement by the Executive Director for Nigeria* (February 2008).

INTERNATIONAL RESERVES
(US $ million at 31 December)

	2005	2006	2007
Total*	28,280	42,299	51,334

* Almost exclusively foreign exchange, and excluding gold reserves (687,000 troy ounces each year).

Source: IMF, *International Financial Statistics*.

MONEY SUPPLY
(₦ '000 million at 31 December)

	2005	2006	2007
Currency outside banks	563.2	690.8	732.9
Demand deposits at commercial banks	953.2	1,114.2	2,429.7
Total money (incl. others)	1,523.4	1,823.1	3,164.4

Source: IMF, *International Financial Statistics*.

COST OF LIVING
(Consumer Price Index; base: May 2003 = 100)

	2005	2006	2007
Food (excl. beverages)	144.2	152.2	155.0
Alcoholic beverages, tobacco and kola	122.3	138.7	158.5
Clothing (incl. footwear)	119.1	129.4	140.5
Rent, fuel and light	158.0	184.7	203.2
Household goods and maintenance	125.7	133.0	145.3
Medical care and health	126.0	141.4	142.5
Transport	125.4	142.8	170.2
Education	144.6	151.0	173.0
All items (incl. others)	143.6	155.5	163.8

NATIONAL ACCOUNTS
(₦ '000 million at current prices)

Expenditure on the Gross Domestic Product

	2005	2006*	2007*
Government final consumption expenditure	1,003.1	1,283.4	1,672.1
Private final consumption expenditure	10,258.6	12,254.3	14,065.5
Increase in stocks }	1,781.2	2,272.8	3,150.3
Gross fixed capital formation }			
Total domestic expenditure	13,042.9	15,810.5	18,887.9
Exports of goods and services	4,664.8	6,184.6	8,323.3
Less Imports of goods and services	2,813.2	3,772.3	4,624.4
GDP in purchasers' values	14,894.5	18,222.8	22,586.7
GDP in constant 1990 prices	560.2	602.4	722.2

* Provisional.

Gross Domestic Product by Economic Activity

	2005	2006*	2007*
Agriculture, hunting, forestry and fishing	4,773.2	5,940.2	7,574.4
Mining and quarrying	5,682.2	7,010.2	7,138.4
Crude petroleum	5,664.9	6,982.9	7,101.2
Manufacturing	412.7	478.5	619.2
Electricity, gas and water	29.4	42.6	50.8
Construction	215.8	250.3	349.7
Wholesale and retail trade	1,868.3	2,741.8	3,906.7
Hotels and restaurants	46.1	57.6	80.5
Transport, storage and communications	426.7	609.5	1,103.2
Finance, insurance	130.8	296.7	385.0
Real estate and business services	712.8	808.6	1,234.2
Government services	148.1	168.8	204.5
Other community, social and personal services	126.3	159.7	202.3
Sub-total	14,572.2	18,564.6	22,848.9
Taxes, less subsidies, on products†	322.3	−341.8	−262.2
GDP in purchasers' values	14,894.5	18,222.8	22,586.7

* Provisional.
† Data obtained as residuals.

BALANCE OF PAYMENTS
(US $ million)

	2004	2005	2007*
Exports of goods f.o.b.	34,766	48,069	65,086
Imports of goods f.o.b.	−15,009	−17,288	−31,948
Trade balance	19,757	30,781	33,138
Exports of services	3,336	4,164	1,682
Imports of services	−5,973	−7,321	−14,118
Balance on goods and services	17,120	27,624	20,702
Other income received	157	705	2,581
Other income paid	−2,689	−7,437	−19,327
Balance on goods, services and income	14,588	20,892	3,955
Current transfers received	2,273	3,329	18,168
Current transfers paid	−21	−18	−151
Current balance	16,840	24,202	21,972
Capital account (net)	36	23	—
Direct investment abroad	—	—	−468
Direct investment from abroad	1,874	2,013	6,087
Portfolio investment assets	178	2,869	−138
Portfolio investment liabilities	—	—	5,640
Other investment assets	−7,301	−15,786	−7,400
Other investment liabilities	−7,812	−12,682	1,438
Net errors and omissions	4,676	9,758	−18,095
Overall balance	8,491	10,397	9,035

* Data for 2006 was not available.

Source: IMF, *International Financial Statistics*.

External Trade

PRINCIPAL COMMODITIES
(₦ '000 million)

Imports c.i.f.	2005	2006	2007
Food and live animals	364.0	498.7	777.1
Beverages and tobacco	8.4	14.4	31.0
Crude materials, inedible (excluding fuels)	29.7	29.0	49.1
Mineral fuels	99.7	84.3	73.5
Chemicals and related products	249.2	473.1	684.7
Basic manufactures	302.2	497.9	942.0
Machinery and transport equipment	556.7	1,208.1	1,427.1
Miscellaneous manufactured articles	166.3	105.7	123.7
Total (incl. others)	1,779.6	2,922.2	4,127.7

NIGERIA

Statistical Survey

Exports f.o.b.	2005	2006	2007
Crude petroleum	6,252.9	7,006.6	6,395.2
Total (incl. others)	6,621.3	7,555.1	6,881.5

PRINCIPAL TRADING PARTNERS
(₦ '000 million)*

Imports c.i.f.	2004	2005	2006
Belgium	67.4	91.6	149.4
Brazil	21.5	25.7	58.6
China, People's Repub.	147.9	244.7	403.3
France (incl. Monaco)	64.4	125.9	128.7
Germany	148.6	84.8	163.2
Greece	10.6	23.9	18.3
Hong Kong	17.2	25.6	33.7
India	43.5	49.3	141.6
Indonesia	6.9	9.3	14.0
Italy	28.4	23.6	99.7
Japan	39.0	62.9	96.6
Korea, Repub.	37.1	30.0	77.9
Netherlands	47.1	60.5	90.1
Russia	28.2	n.a.	28.6
Singapore	11.2	15.5	45.9
South Africa	65.7	32.2	51.5
Spain	93.9	14.9	24.3
Switzerland	17.2	16.6	27.1
Thailand	19.8	13.9	28.1
United Kingdom	206.0	151.0	344.6
USA	174.2	361.0	455.2
Total (incl. others)	1,575.6	1,779.6	2,922.2

Exports f.o.b.	2004	2005	2006
Brazil	410.2	561.8	319.5
Cameroon	57.1	71.9	136.4
Canada	112.6	149.9	291.7
Chile	47.3	16.0	n.a.
China, People's Repub.	70.5	46.7	0.5
Côte d'Ivoire	85.7	111.5	273.3
France (incl. Monaco)	227.3	340.8	427.5
Germany	50.8	136.0	0.5
Ghana	85.7	111.5	273.3
India	542.3	894.0	703.2
Indonesia	126.3	177.4	—
Italy	83.5	108.4	187.4
Korea, Repub.	55.5	81.1	268.3
Netherlands	54.7	6.9	195.0
Peru	8.3	6.6	73.5
Portugal	70.0	86.8	93.2
Senegal	43.8	75.2	—
South Africa	78.7	110.7	135.9
Spain	334.5	534.4	603.0
USA	2,201.8	2,703.1	3,400.6
Total (incl. others)	5,129.0	6,621.3	7,555.1

* Imports by country of consignment; exports by country of destination.

2007: *Imports:* Brazil 142.3; Canada 5.5; France 158.6; Germany 201.2; Italy 105.1; Japan 95.4; Netherlands 129.5; Spain 28.7; United Kingdom 218.4; USA 623.6; Total (incl. others) 4,127.7. *Exports:* Brazil 441.2; Canada 141.0; France 251.4; Germany 159.9; Italy 74.5; Japan 45.8; Netherlands 22.3; Spain 91.6; United Kingdom 36.1; USA 3,207.7; Total (incl. others) 6,881.5.

Transport

RAILWAYS
(traffic)

	1995	1996	1997
Passenger-km (million)	161	170	179
Freight ton-km (million)	108	114	120

Source: UN, *Statistical Yearbook*.

ROAD TRAFFIC
(estimates, motor vehicles in use)

	1995	1996
Passenger cars	820,069	885,080
Buses and coaches	1,284,251	903,449
Lorries and vans	673,425	912,579
Motorcycles and mopeds	481,345	441,651

Source: IRF, *World Road Statistics*.

1997 ('000 vehicles): Passenger cars 52.3; Commercial vehicles 13.5 (Source: UN *Statistical Yearbook*).

SHIPPING

Merchant Fleet
(registered at 31 December)

	2005	2006	2007
Number of vessels	339	350	379
Displacement ('000 grt)	358.1	363.3	407.7

Source: Lloyd's Register-Fairplay, *World Fleet Statistics*.

International Sea-borne Freight Traffic
(estimates, '000 metric tons)

	1991	1992	1993
Goods loaded	82,768	84,797	86,993
Goods unloaded	10,960	11,143	11,346

Source: UN Economic Commission for Africa, *African Statistical Yearbook*.

CIVIL AVIATION
(traffic on scheduled services)

	2002	2003	2004
Kilometres flown (million)	6	12	12
Passengers carried ('000)	512	520	540
Passenger-km (million)	522	638	683
Total ton-km (million)	57	61	64

Source: UN, *Statistical Yearbook*.

Tourism

ARRIVALS BY NATIONALITY*

Country	2004	2005	2006
Benin	374,491	393,215	432,537
Cameroon	102,008	107,108	117,818
Chad	81,026	85,077	93,584
France	58,925	61,871	68,058
Germany	57,475	60,348	66,383
Ghana	19,701	20,686	22,755
Italy	62,470	65,593	72,152
Liberia	102,287	107,401	118,141
Niger	591,103	620,658	642,724
Sudan	60,044	63,046	69,350
Total (incl. others)	2,646,411	2,778,365	3,055,800

* Figures refer to arrival at frontiers of visitors from abroad, including same-day visitors (excursionists).

Tourism receipts (US $ million, incl. passenger transport): 49 in 2004; 46 in 2005; 51 in 2006.

Source: World Tourism Organization.

Communications Media

	2005	2006	2007
Telephones ('000 main lines in use)	1,223.3	1,688.0	1,579.7
Mobile cellular telephones ('000 in use)	18,587.0	32,322.2	40,395.6
Personal computers ('000 in use)	867	n.a.	n.a.
Internet users ('000)	5,000	8,000	10,000
Broadband subscribers	500	n.a.	n.a.

Radio receivers ('000 in use): 23,500 in 1997.

Television receivers ('000 in use): 12,000 in 2001.

Book production (titles, including pamphlets): 1,314 in 1995.

Daily newspapers: 25 (estimated average circulation 2,760,000 copies) in 1998.

Sources: International Telecommunication Union; UNESCO Institute for Statistics.

Education

(2005)

	Institutions	Teachers	Males	Females	Total
Primary	50,741	594,192	11,712,479	9,239,339	20,951,818
Secondary	11,010	156,635	3,079,832	2,342,779	5,422,611
Poly/Monotechnic	178	16,499	n.a.	n.a.	237,708
University	80	23,535	n.a.	n.a.	724,856

Adult literacy rate (UNESCO estimates): 72.0% (males 80.1%; females 64.1%) in 2007 (Source: UNESCO Institute for Statistics).

Directory

The Constitution

The Constitution of the Federal Republic of Nigeria was promulgated on 5 May 1999, and entered into force on 31 May. The main provisions are summarized below:

PROVISIONS

Nigeria is one indivisible sovereign state, to be known as the Federal Republic of Nigeria. Nigeria is a Federation, comprising 36 States and a Federal Capital Territory. The Constitution includes provisions for the creation of new States and for boundary adjustments of existing States. The Government of the Federation or of a State is prohibited from adopting any religion as a state religion.

LEGISLATURE

The legislative powers of the Federation are vested in the National Assembly, comprising a Senate and a House of Representatives. The 109-member Senate consists of three Senators from each State and one from the Federal Capital Territory, who are elected for a term of four years. The House of Representatives comprises 360 members, representing constituencies of nearly equal population as far as possible, who are elected for a four-year term. The Senate and House of Representatives each have a Speaker and Deputy Speaker, who are elected by the members of the House from among themselves. Legislation may originate in either the Senate or the House of Representatives, and, having been approved by the House in which it originated by a two-thirds majority, will be submitted to the other House for approval, and subsequently presented to the President for assent. Should the President withhold his assent, and the bill be returned to the National Assembly and again approved by each House by a two-thirds majority, the bill will become law. The legislative powers of a State of the Federation will be vested in the House of Assembly of the State. The House of Assembly of a State will consist of three or four times the number of seats that the State holds in the House of Representatives (comprising not less than 24 and not more than 40 members).

EXECUTIVE

The executive powers of the Federation are vested in the President, who is the Head of State, the Chief Executive of the Federation and the Commander-in-Chief of the Armed Forces of the Federation. The President is elected for a term of four years and must receive not less than one-quarter of the votes cast at the election in at least two-thirds of the States in the Federation and the Federal Capital Territory. The President nominates a candidate as his associate from the same political party to occupy the office of Vice-President. The Ministers of the Government of the Federation are nominated by the President, subject to confirmation by the Senate. Federal executive bodies include the Council of State, which advises the President in the exercise of his powers. The executive powers of a State are vested in the Governor of that State, who is elected for a four-year term and must receive not less than one-quarter of votes cast in at least two-thirds of all local government areas in the State.

JUDICIARY

The judicial powers of the Federation are vested in the courts established for the Federation, and the judicial powers of a State in the courts established for the State. The Federation has a Supreme Court, a Court of Appeal and a Federal High Court. Each State has a High Court, a *Shari'a* Court of Appeal and a Customary Court of Appeal. Chief Judges are nominated on the recommendation of a National Judicial Council.

LOCAL GOVERNMENT

The States are divided into 768 local government areas. The system of local government by democratically elected local government councils is guaranteed, and the Government of each State will ensure their existence. Each local government council within the State will participate in the economic planning and development of the area over which it exercises authority.

Federal Government

HEAD OF STATE

President, Commander-in-Chief of the Armed Forces and Minister responsible for Petroleum Resources: Alhaji UMARU MUSA YAR'ADUA (inaugurated 29 May 2007).

Vice-President: Dr GOODLUCK EBELE JONATHAN.

CABINET
(April 2009)

Attorney-General and Minister of Justice: MICHAEL KAASE AONDOAKAA.

Minister of Agriculture and Water Resources: SYADDI ABBA RUMA.

Minister of Aviation: BABATUNDE OMOTOBA.

Minister of Commerce and Industry: Chief ACHIKE UDENWA.

Minister of Culture and Tourism: BELLO J. GADA.

Minister of Defence: Dr SHETTIMA MUSTAPHA.

Minister of Education: Dr SAM EGWU.

Minister of the Environment: JOHN OGAR ODEY.

Minister of the Federal Capital Territory: M. A. ALIRO.

Minister of Finance: Dr MANSUR MUHKTAR.

Minister of Foreign Affairs: OJO MADUEKWE.

Minister of Health: Prof. BABATUNDE OTSOTIMEHIN.

Minister of Information and Communication: Prof. DORA AKUNYILI.

Minister of the Interior: Maj. Gen. (retd) GODWIN ABBE.

Minister of Labour: ADETOKUNBOH KAYODE.

Minister of Mines and Steel Development: DEZIANI ALLISON-MADUEKE.

Minister of Niger Delta Affairs: Chief UFOT EKAETTE.

Minister of Petroleum: Dr RILWANU LUKMAN.

NIGERIA

Minister of Police Affairs: Dr IBRAHIM LAME.
Minister of Power: Dr LANRE BABALOLA.
Minister of Science and Technology: Dr A. B. ZAKU.
Minister of Special Duties: A. KAZAURE.
Minister of Transport: Alhadji IBRAHIM BIO.
Minister of Women's Affairs: SALAMATU H. SULAIMAN.
Minister of Works and Housing: Dr HASSAN M. LAWAL.
Minister of Youth Development: AKINLABI OLASUNKANMI.
Minister, Deputy Chairman of the National Planning Commission: Dr SHAMSUDEEN USMAN.
Minister, Chairman of the National Sports Commission: S. M. NDANUSA.

There were, in addition, 13 Ministers of State.

MINISTRIES

Office of the Head of State: New Federal Secretariat Complex, Shehu Shagari Way, Central Area District, Abuja; tel. (9) 5233536.
Ministry of Agriculture and Water Resources: Area 11, Secretariat Complex, Garki, PMB 135, Abuja; tel. (9) 3141931; e-mail aruma@nigeria.gov.ng.
Ministry of Aviation: New Federal Secretariat Complex, Shehu Shagari Way, Central Area District, PMB 146, Abuja; tel. (9) 5237487.
Ministry of Commerce and Industry: Area 1, Secretariat Complex, Garki, PMB 88, Abuja; e-mail fmi@fmind.gov.ng; tel. (9) 2341662.
Ministry of Culture and Tourism: Phase II Federal Secretariat, Block A, 1st Floor, Shehu Shagari Way, Abuja; tel. (9) 2348311; fax (9) 23408297; e-mail akayode@nigeria.gov.ng; internet www.visit-nigeria.gov.ng.
Ministry of Defence: Ship House, Central Area, Abuja; tel. (9) 2340534; fax (9) 2340714; e-mail mamed@nigeria.gov.ng.
Ministry of Education: New Federal Secretariat Complex, Shehu Shagari Way, Central Area District, PMB 146, Abuja; tel. (9) 5237838; e-mail enquires@fme.gov.ng; internet www.fme.gov.ng.
Ministry of Energy: Annex 3, Federal Secretariat Complex, Shehu Shagari Way, Central Area, PMB 278, Garki, Abuja; tel. (9) 5239462; fax (9) 5236652; e-mail info@mpr.gov.ng.
Ministry of the Environment: Federal Secretariat Towers, Shehu Shagari Way, Central Area, PMB 468, Garki, Abuja; tel. (9) 5234014; fax (9) 5211847; e-mail haloa@nigeria.gov.ng; internet www.environmentnigeria.org.
Ministry of the Federal Capital Territory: Kapital St, off Obafemi Awolowo St, Garki Area 11, PMB 25, Garki, Abuja; tel. (9) 2341525; fax (9) 3143859; e-mail presunit@fct.gov.ng; internet www.fct.gov.ng.
Ministry of Finance: Ahmadu Bello Way, Central Area, PMB 14, Garki, Abuja; tel. (9) 2346290; e-mail susman@nigeria.gov.ng; internet www.fmf.gov.ng.
Ministry of Foreign Affairs: Maputo St, Zone 3, Wuse District, PMB 130, Abuja; tel. (9) 5230570; e-mail omaduekwe@nigeria.gov.ng; internet www.mfa.gov.ng.
Ministry of Health: New Federal Secretariat Complex, Ahmadu Bello Way, Central Business District, PMB 083, Garki, Abuja; tel. (9) 5238362; e-mail agrange@nigeria.gov.ng.
Ministry of Information and Communication: New Federal Secretariat Complex, Shehu Shagari Way, Central Area District, PMB 1278, Abuja; tel. (9) 5237183; e-mail jodey@nigeria.gov.ng.
Ministry of the Interior: Area 1, Secretariat Complex, Garki, PMB 16, Abuja; tel. (9) 2341934; fax (9) 2342426; e-mail gabbe@nigeria.gov.ng; internet www.fmia.gov.ng.
Ministry of Justice: New Federal Secretariat Complex, Shehu Shagari Way, Central Area, PMB 192, Garki, Abuja; tel. (9) 5235208; fax (9) 5235194.
Ministry of Labour: New Federal Secretariat Complex, Shehu Shagari Way, Central Area, PMB 04, Garki, Abuja; tel. (9) 5235980; e-mail hlawal@nigeria.gov.ng.
Ministry of Mines and Steel Development: New Federal Secretariat Complex, Shehu Shagari Way, Central Area, PMB 107, Garki, Abuja; tel. (9) 5235830; fax (9) 5235831.
Ministry of Niger Delta Affairs: Abuja.
Ministry of Petroleum: Abuja.
Ministry of Power: Abuja.
Ministry of Science and Technology: New Federal Secretariat Complex, Shehu Shagari Way, Central Area, PMB 331, Garki, Abuja; tel. (9) 5233397; fax (9) 5235204.
Ministry of Special Duties: Abuja.
Ministry of Transport: Dipcharima House, Central Business District, off 3rd Ave, PMB 0336, Garki, Abuja; tel. (9) 2347451; fax (9) 2347453; e-mail info@fmt.gov.ng; internet www.fmt.gov.ng.
Ministry of Women's Affairs: New Federal Secretariat Complex, Shehu Shagari Way, Central Area, PMB 229, Garki, Abuja; tel. (9) 5237112; fax (9) 5233644; e-mail sbungudu@nigeria.gov.ng; internet www.fmwa.gov.ng.
Ministry of Works and Housing: Mabushi District, Garki, Abuja; tel. (9) 2346550; fax (9) 2340174.
Ministry of Youth Development: Federal Secretariat, Phase II, Shehu Shagari Way, PMB 229, Abuja; tel. (9) 5237112; fax (9) 5233644; e-mail aolasunkanmi@nigeria.gov.ng.
National Planning Commission: Old Central Bank Bldg, 4th Floor, Garki, PMB 234, Abuja; e-mail info@nigerianeconomy.com; internet www.npc.gov.ng.
National Sports Commission: New Federal Secretariat Complex, Shehu Shagari Way, Maitama, Abuja; tel. (9) 5235905; fax (9) 5235901; e-mail agimba@nigeria.gov.ng.

President and Legislature

PRESIDENT

Election, 21 April 2007*

Candidate	Votes	% of votes
Umaru Musa Yar'Adua (People's Democratic Party)	24,784,227	70.00
Muhammadu Buhari (All Nigeria People's Party)	6,607,419	18.65
Atiku Abubakar (Action Congress)	2,567,798	7.25
Orji Uzor Kalu (Progressive People's Alliance)	608,833	1.72
Attahiru Dalhatu Bafarawa (Democratic People's Party)	289,324	0.82
Dim Chukwuemeka Odumegwu-Ojukwu (All Progressive Grand Alliance)	155,947	0.44
Christopher Pere Ajuwa (Alliance for Democracy)	89,511	0.25
Chris O. Okotie (Fresh Democratic Party)	74,049	0.21
Others†	248,100	0.70
Total	**35,425,208**	**100.00**

* Provisional results released by the Independent National Election Commission.
† There were 16 other candidates.

NATIONAL ASSEMBLY

House of Representatives

Speaker of the House of Representatives: DIMEJI BANKOLE.
Election, 14 April 2007

Party	Seats
People's Democratic Party	258
All Nigeria People's Party	64
Action Congress	32
Progressive People's Alliance	3
Alliance for Democracy	1
Others	1
Total	**359***

* One seat remained vacant.

Senate

Speaker of the Senate: DAVID MARK.
Election, 14 April 2007

Party	Seats
People's Democratic Party	78
All Nigeria People's Party	22
Action Congress	6
All Nigeria People's Party	1
Alliance for Democracy	1
Others	1
Total	**109**

NIGERIA

Election Commission

Independent National Electoral Commission (INEC): Plot 436 Zambezi Cres., Maitama District, PMB 0184, Garki, Abuja; tel. (9) 2224632; e-mail contact@inecnigeria.org; internet www.inecnigeria.org; f. 1998; Chair. Prof. MAURICE IWU.

Political Organizations

Following the death of the military Head of State in June 1998, the existing authorized political parties were dissolved. The Government established a new Independent National Electoral Commission (INEC), which officially approved three political parties to contest elections in February 1999. Prior to legislative and presidential elections in April 2003, three political associations were granted registration in June 2002, as were a further 24 in December. According to INEC, by mid-2007 51 parties were registered.

Action Congress (AC): 16 Bissau St, Wuse Zone 6, Abuja; tel. (9) 2730102; e-mail mail@actioncongressng.org; internet actioncongressng.org; f. 2006 by a merger of the Alliance for Democracy, the Justice Party, the Advanced Congress of Democrats and several minor parties; Chair. Chief BISI AKANDE; Nat. Sec. Dr USMAN BUGAJE.

   Alliance for Democracy (AD): Plot 2096, Bumbona Close, Zone 1, Wuse, Abuja; tel. (9) 5239357; e-mail info@alliancefordemocracy.org; f. 1998; Chair. MOJISOLUWA AKINFEWA.

   Justice Party (JP): 2nd Ave, Gwarimpa, Abuja; tel. 8057764363; Chair. RALPH OBIOHA.

   Advanced Congress of Democrats (ACD): Plot 882, Emeka Ampoku St, Area 11, Garki, Abuja; tel. 8044107989; Chair. ALEXIS ANIELO.

All Nigeria People's Party (ANPP): Bassan Plaza, Plot 759, Central Business Area, Abuja; tel. (9) 2347556; f. 1998; Chair. Alhaji Dr MODU SHERIF.

All Progressive Grand Alliance (APGA): 41b Libreville Cres., Wuse 11, Abuja; tel. 8035903910; regd June 2002; Chair. VICTOR C. UMEH.

Democratic People's Party (DPP): 1st Floor, Labour House, Central Business District, Abuja; tel. (9) 2343345; Chair. Lt-Gen. JEREMIAH USENI.

Fresh Democratic Party: 4 Park Close, Aguyi Ironsi St, Maitma, Abuja; Chair. Rev. CHRIS OKOTIE.

Movement for the Actualization of the Sovereign State of Biafra (MASSOB): Okwe, Imo; f. 1999; Leader Chief RALPH UWAZURIKE.

Movement for the Emancipation of the Niger Delta (MEND): f. 2005; main Ijaw militant group operating in the Niger Delta; Leader Maj.-Gen. GODSWILL TAMUNO.

Movement for the Survival of the Ogoni People (MOSOP): 27 Odu St, Ogbunabali, Port Harcourt; tel. (84) 230250; f. 1990 to organize opposition to petroleum production in Ogoni territory; Pres. LEDUM MITEE.

National Conscience Party (NCP): 18 Phase 1 Low Cost Housing Estate, Lake City Ave, Gwagwalada, Abuja; tel. (9) 4937279; internet www.nigeriancp.net; Leader GANI FAWEHINMI; Chair. OSAGIE OBAYUWANA.

National Democratic Party (NDP): POB 8196, Abuja; tel. (9) 6703366; e-mail info@ndpnigeria.com; internet www.ndpnigeria.com; regd June 2002; Chair. Alhaji ALIYU HABU FARI.

Niger Delta People's Volunteer Force (NDPVF): prominent Ijaw militant group operating in the Niger Delta; Leader Alhaji MUJAHID DOKUBO-ASARI.

People's Democratic Party (PDP): Wadata Plaza, Michael Okpara Way, Zone 5, Wuse, Abuja; tel. (9) 5232589; e-mail info@peopledemocraticparty.org; internet www.peopledemocraticparty.org; f. 1998 by fmr opponents of the Govt of Gen. Sani Abacha; supports greater federalism; ruling party; Chair. Dr AMADU ALI GCON.

People's Redemption Party (PRP): City Plaza, Area 11, Garki, Abuja; tel. 8033495403; regd Dec. 2002; Chair. Alhaji ABDULKADIR B. MUSA.

People's Salvation Party (PSP): 441 Oron St, Wuse Zone 1, Abuja; tel. (9) 5235359; regd Dec. 2002; Chair. Alhaji LAWAL MAITURARE.

Progressive People's Alliance (PPA): 52, Libreville St, Wuse 11, Abuja; Chair. Alhadji SULEIMAN AHMED.

United Nigeria People's Party (UNPP): Plot 1467, Safana Close, Garki 11, Abuja; tel. (9) 2340091; regd June 2002; Chair. MALLAM SALEH JAMBO.

Directory

Diplomatic Representation

EMBASSIES AND HIGH COMMISSIONS IN NIGERIA

Algeria: Plot 203, Etim Inyang Cres., POB 55238, Falomo, Lagos; tel. (1) 612092; fax (1) 2624017; Ambassador EL-MIHOUB MIHOUBI.

Angola: 5 Kasumu Ekomode St, Victoria Island, POB 50437, Falomo Ikoyi, Lagos; tel. (9) 4135121; fax (9) 4134082; Ambassador EVARISTO DOMINGOS KIMBA.

Argentina: 2 Abubakar Koko Cres., Asokoro District, Abuja; tel. (9) 3148680; fax (9) 3148683; e-mail enige@mrecic.gov.ar; Chargé d'affaires a.i. JORGE HORACIO INSAUSTI.

Australia: 5th Floor, Oakland Centre, 48 Aguiyi Ironsi St, Maitama, Abuja; PMB 5152, Abuja; tel. (9) 4135226; fax (9) 4135227; e-mail ahc.abuja@dfat.gov.au; internet www.nigeria.embassy.gov.au; High Commissioner JEFF HART.

Austria: Plot 9, Usuma St, Maitama, Abuja; tel. (9) 4130772; fax (9) 4612715; e-mail abuja-ob@bmeia.gv.at; Ambassador Dr PETER CHRISTIAN FELLNER.

Belgium: 9 Usuma St, Maitama, Abuja; tel. (9) 4131859; fax (9) 4132015; e-mail abuja@diplobel.fed.be; internet www.diplomatie.be/abuja; Ambassador DIRK VAN EECKHOUT.

Benin: 4 Abudu Smith St, Victoria Island, POB 5705, Lagos; tel. (1) 2614411; fax (1) 2612385; Ambassador PATRICE HOUNGAVOU.

Brazil: Plot 324, Diplomatic Dr., Zone Central, Area District, Abuja; tel. (9) 4618688; fax (9) 4618687; Ambassador ALBERTO FERREIRA GUIMARAES.

Bulgaria: 10 Euphrates St, cnr Aminu Kano Cres., Maitama, Abuja; tel. (9) 4130034; fax (9) 4132741; e-mail bulgarian@nigtel.com; Ambassador (vacant).

Burkina Faso: No. 4, Freetown St, off Ademola Adetokunbo Cres., Wuse II, Abuja; tel. (9) 4130491; fax (9) 4130492; e-mail ebfn@nova.net.ng; Ambassador DRAMANE YAMÉOGO.

Cameroon: 5 Elsie Femi Pearse St, Victoria Island, PMB 2476, Lagos; tel. (1) 2612226; fax (1) 7747510; High Commissioner ANDRÉ E. KENDECK MANDENG.

Canada: 15 Bobo St, Maitama, POB 5144, Abuja; tel. (9) 4139910; fax (9) 4139932; e-mail abuja@international.gc.ca; internet nigeria.gc.ca; High Commissioner CAROLINE CHRÉTIEN.

Chad: 2 Goriola St, Victoria Island, PMB 70662, Lagos; tel. (1) 2622590; fax (1) 2618314; Ambassador MAHAMAT HABIB DOUTOUM.

China, People's Republic: Plot 302–303, Central Area, Abuja; tel. (9) 4618661; fax (9) 4618660; e-mail chinaemb_ng@mfa.gov.cn; internet ng.china-embassy.org; Ambassador XU JIANGUO.

Congo, Republic: Ambassador PIERRE NGUIA.

Côte d'Ivoire: 3 Abudu Smith St, Victoria Island, POB 7786, Lagos; tel. (1) 610936; fax (1) 2613822; e-mail cotedivoire@micro.com.ng; Ambassador AMIDOU DIARRA.

Cuba: Plot 339, Diplomatic Zone, Area 10, Garki, Abuja; tel. (9) 2348934; fax (9) 2348942; e-mail cubabuja1@linkserve.com; Ambassador ELIO SAVÓN OLIVA.

Czech Republic: Plot 1223, Gnassingbé Eyadéma St, Asokoro District, POB 4628, Abuja; tel. (9) 3141245; fax (9) 3141248; e-mail abuja@embassy.mzv.cz; internet www.mzv.cz/abuja; Ambassador JAROSLAV SIRO.

Egypt: Plot 3319, Barada Close, off Amazon St, Maitama, Abuja; tel. (9) 4136091; fax (9) 4132602; Ambassador MOHAMED ASHRAF HARBY SALAMA.

Equatorial Guinea: Plot 199, Cadastral Zone A, Blue Plaza St, A7 off Parakou Cres., Wuse II, Abuja; tel. and fax (9) 5239993; Ambassador HERIBETO MIKO MBENGONO.

Ethiopia: 19 Ona Cres., Maitama, POB 2488, Abuja; tel. (1) 4131691; fax (1) 4131692; e-mail etabuja@primair.net; Ambassador YOHANESS GENDA.

Finland: Maputo St Wuse, Zone 3, PMB 5140, Abuja; tel. (9) 3147256; fax (9) 3147252; e-mail sanomat.aba@formin.fi; Ambassador ANNELI VUORINEN.

France: 37 Udi Hills St, Abuja; tel. (9) 8077098730; fax (9) 5235482; e-mail sec-amb.abuja.amba@diplomatie.fr; internet www.ambafrance-ng.org; Ambassador JEAN-MICHEL DUMOND.

Gabon: 8 Norman Williams St, SW Ikoyi, POB 5989, Lagos; tel. (1) 2684673; fax (1) 2690692; Ambassador CORENTIN HERVO-AKENDENGUE.

The Gambia: 162 Awolowo Rd, SW Ikoyi, POB 873, Lagos; tel. (1) 682192; High Commissioner ANGELA COLLEY.

Germany: 9 Lake Maracaibo Close, off Amazon St, Maitama, Abuja; tel. (9) 4130962; fax (9) 4130949; e-mail info@abuja.diplo.de; internet www.abuja.diplo.de; Ambassador JOACHIM CHRISTOPH SCHMILLEN.

Ghana: 21–25 King George V Rd, POB 889, Lagos; tel. (1) 2630015; fax (1) 2630338; High Commissioner (vacant).

NIGERIA

Greece: No. 6, Takum Close, Wuse II, Abuja; tel. (9) 4139433; fax (9) 4139435; e-mail grembabuja@mfa.gr; internet gremb.abj@mfa.gr; Ambassador HARALAMBOS DAFARANOS.

Guinea: No. 349, Central Business District, opp. United Nations Premises, POB 591, Abuja; tel. (9) 2349144; fax (9) 4133407; Ambassador CHEICK ABDOUL CAMARA.

Holy See: Pope John Paul II Cres., Maitama, PMB 541, Garki, Abuja; tel. (9) 4138381; fax (9) 4136653; e-mail nuntiusabj@hotmail.com; Apostolic Nuncio Most Rev. RENZO FRATINI (Titular Archbishop of Botriana).

Hungary: Plot 1685, Jose Marti Cres., Asokoro, Abuja; tel. (1) 3141180; fax (1) 3141177; e-mail huemblgs@nova.net.ng; internet www.mfa.gov.hu/emb/abuja; Ambassador Dr FERENC KATÓ.

India: 15 Rio Negro Close, off Yedseram St, Maitama, Abuja; tel. (9) 4132323; fax (9) 4132324; e-mail hoc.abuja@mea.gov.in; internet www.hicomindlagos.com; High Commissioner HARIHARA SUBRAMANIAM VISWANATHAN.

Indonesia: 5B Anifowoshe St, Victoria Island, POB 3473, Marina, Lagos; tel. (1) 2614601; fax (1) 2613301; e-mail unitkomigs@hyperia.com; Ambassador NURHADI DJAZULI.

Iran: 2 Udi St, Maitama, Abuja; tel. (1) 5238048; fax (1) 5237785; e-mail irembassy_abuja@yahoo.com; Ambassador JAWAD TORKABADI.

Ireland: Plot 415, Negro Cres., Maitama District, Abuja; tel. (9) 4131751; fax (9) 4131805; e-mail abujaembassy@dfa.ie; internet www.embassyofireland.org.ng; Ambassador KYLE O'SULLIVAN.

Israel: Plot 12, Mary Slessor St, Asokoro, POB 10924, Abuja; tel. (9) 3143170; fax (9) 3143177; e-mail info@abuja.mfa.gov.il; internet abuja.mfa.gov.il; Ambassador MOSHE RAM.

Italy: 21st Cres., off Constitution Ave, Central Business District, Abuja; tel. (9) 4614722; fax (9) 4614709; e-mail ambasciata.abuja@esteri.it; internet www.ambabuja.esteri.it; Ambassador MASSIMO BAISTROCCHI.

Jamaica: Plot 77, Samuel Adedoyin Ave, Victoria Island, POB 75368, Lagos; tel. (1) 2611085; fax (1) 2610047; High Commissioner ROBERT MILLER (acting).

Japan: Plot 585 Bobo St, Maitama, PMB 5070, Abuja; tel. (9) 4138898; fax (9) 4137667; Ambassador AKIO TANAKA.

Kenya: 18 Yedseram St, Maitama, PMB 5160, Abuja; tel. (9) 4139155; fax (9) 4139157; e-mail abuja@mfa.go.ke; High Commissioner DANIEL MEPUKORI KOIKAI.

Korea, Democratic People's Republic: Plot 350, Central Area, Cadastral Zone, AO, POB 407, Garki, Abuja; tel. (9) 2347200; fax (9) 2347199; Ambassador RI CHAN HO.

Korea, Republic: Plot 934, Idejo St, Victoria Island, POB 4668, Lagos; tel. (1) 2615353; Ambassador KIE DONG-LEE.

Liberia: 3 Idejo St, Plot 162, off Adeola Odeku St, Victoria Island, POB 70841, Lagos; tel. (1) 2618899; Ambassador Prof. JAMES TAPEH.

Libya: Plot 1591, Mike Okoye Cl., off George Sowemimo St, Asokoro Ext., POB 435, Garki, Abuja; tel. (9) 3148356; fax (9) 3148354; Ambassador Eng. MANSOUR O. OSMAN.

Malaysia: 2 Pechora Close, Maitama PMB 5217, Abuja; tel. (9) 4133918; fax (9) 413 3922; e-mail malabuja@kln.gov.my; High Commissioner NIK MUSTAFA KAMAL NIK.

Morocco: 5 Mary Slessor St, Asokoro, Abuja; tel. (9) 3141961; fax (9) 3141959; e-mail mcherkaoui45@yahoo.fr; Ambassador MUSTAPHA CHERQAOUI.

Namibia: Plot 1738 T. Y., Danyuma St, Cadasdral Zone, Asokoro, Abuja; tel. (9) 3142740; fax (9) 3142743; e-mail namibiahighcomabuja@yahoo.com; Ambassador DAVID SMITH.

Netherlands: 21st Cres., off Constitution Ave, Central Business District, Abuja; tel. (9) 4611200; fax (9) 4611240; e-mail abj@minbuza.nl; internet nigeria.nlembassy.org; Ambassador ARIE VAN DER WIEL.

Niger: 15 Adeola Odeku St, Victoria Island, PMB 2736, Lagos; tel. (1) 2612300; Ambassador MOUSSA ELHADJI IBRAHIM.

Norway: 54 T.Y. Danjuma St, Asokoro, Abuja; tel. (9) 3149127; fax (9) 3149309; e-mail emb.abuja@mfa.no; internet www.emb-norway.com.ng; Ambassador TORE NEDREBO.

Pakistan: 4 Molade Okoya-Thomas St, Victoria Island, POB 2450, Lagos; tel. (1) 613909; fax (1) 614822; Ambassador KHALID DURRANI.

Philippines: 16 Lake Chad Cres., cnr Kainji St, Maitama, Abuja; tel. (9) 4133649; fax (9) 4133650; Ambassador MASARANGA R. UMPA.

Poland: 16 Ona Cres., Maitama, Abuja; tel. (9) 4138280; fax (9) 4138281; e-mail poembabu@linkserve.com; internet www.abuja.polemb.net; Ambassador GRZEGORZ WALINSKI.

Portugal: 27B Gana St, Maitama, Abuja; tel. (9) 4137211; fax (9) 4137214; e-mail portemb@rosecom.net; Ambassador MARIA DE FÁTIMA DE PINA PERESTRELLO.

Romania: Nelson Mandela St, No. 76, Plot 498, Asokoro, Abuja; tel. (9) 3142304; fax (9) 3142306; e-mail secretary@romnig.com; internet www.romnig.com; Ambassador MARIAN PARJOL.

Russia: 5 Walter Carrington Cres., Victoria Island, POB 2723, Lagos; tel. (1) 2613359; fax (1) 4619994; Ambassador ALEXANDER DIMITRIEVICH POLYAKOV.

Saudi Arabia: Plot 347H, off Adetokunbo Ademola Cres., Wuse 2, Abuja; tel. (9) 4131880; fax (9) 4134906; Ambassador ANWAR A. ABD-RABBUH.

Senegal: 14 Kofo Abayomi Rd, Victoria Island, PMB 2197, Lagos; tel. (1) 2611722; Ambassador AMADOU THIALAW DIOP.

Serbia: 11, Rio Negro Close, off Yedseram St, Cadastral Zone A6, Maitama District, Abuja; tel. (9) 4139492; fax (9) 4130078; e-mail mail@ambnig.com; Ambassador DRAGAN MRAOVIĆ.

Sierra Leone: Plot 308 Mission Rd, opp Ministry of Defence (Ship House), Diplomatic Zone, Central Business District, Abuja; tel. (9) 2349332; fax (9) 2349890; e-mail slhcnig@yahoo.com; High Commissioner AMIRA BAYOH.

Slovakia: POB 1290, Lagos; tel. (1) 2621585; fax (1) 2612103; e-mail obeo.sk@micro.com.ng; Ambassador VASIL HUDÁK.

Somalia: Plot 1270, off Adeola Odeka St, POB 6355, Lagos; tel. (1) 2611283; Ambassador M. S. HASSAN.

South Africa: 71 Usuma St, Maitama, Abuja; tel. (9) 4133776; fax (9) 4133829; e-mail sahcabuja@yahoo.co.uk; High Commissioner B. SIFINGO.

Spain: Plot 611, 8 Bobo Close, Maitama, PMB 5120, Abuja; tel. (9) 4137091; fax (9) 4137095; e-mail embespng@mail.mae.es; Ambassador ÁNGEL LOSADA FERNÁNDEZ.

Sudan: 2B Kofo Abayomi St, Victoria Island, POB 2428, Lagos; tel. (1) 2615889; Ambassador AHMED ALTIGANI SALEH.

Sweden: PMB 569, Garki, Abuja; tel. (9) 8746913; fax (9) 3143398; e-mail ambassaden.abuja@foreign.ministry.se; internet www.swedenabroad.com/abuja; Ambassador PER LINDGÄRDE.

Switzerland: 157 Adetokumbo Ademola Cres., Wuse II, Abuja; tel. (9) 4131081; fax (9) 4131089; e-mail abu.vertretung@eda.admin.ch; internet www.eda.admin.ch/abuja; Ambassador (vacant).

Syria: 25 Kofo Abayomi St, Victoria Island, Lagos; tel. (1) 2615860; Chargé d'affaires a.i. MUSTAFA HAJ-ALI.

Tanzania: 15 Yedseram St, Maitama, PMB 5125, Wuse, Abuja; tel. (9) 4132313; fax (9) 4132314; e-mail tanabuja@lytos.com; High Commissioner CISCO MTIRO (acting).

Thailand: Plot 766, Panama St, Cadastral Zone A6, Maitama, Abuja; e-mail thaiabj@mfa.go.th; Ambassador N. SATHAPORN.

Togo: 96 Awolowo Rd, SW Ikoyi, POB 1435, Lagos; tel. (1) 2617449; Ambassador FOLI-AGBENOZAN TETTEKPOE.

Trinidad and Tobago: 3A Tiamiyu Savage St, Victoria Island, POB 6392, Marina, Lagos; tel. (1) 2612087; fax (1) 612732; High Commissioner Dr VICTORIA MENDEZ-CHARLES.

Turkey: 3 Okunola Martins Close, Ikoyi, POB 56252, Lagos; tel. (1) 2691140; fax (1) 2693040; e-mail turkemb@infoweb.abs.net; Ambassador ÖMER SAHINKAYA.

Ukraine: Plot 1273, Parakou Cres., off Nairobi St, Wuse II, Abuja; tel. (9) 5239577; fax (9) 5239578; e-mail emb_ng@mfa.gov.ua; internet www.mfa.gov.ua/nigeria; Ambassador OLEH M. SKOROPAD.

United Kingdom: 19 Torren Close, off Mississippi St, Shehu Shagari Way, Maitama, Abuja; tel. (9) 4132010; fax (9) 4133552; e-mail information.abuja@fco.gov.uk; internet www.ukinnigeria.com; High Commissioner ROBERT DEWAR.

USA: 7 Plot 1075, Diplomatic Dr., Central District Area, Abuja; tel. (9) 4614000; fax (9) 4614036; e-mail ircabuja@state.gov; internet abuja.usembassy.gov; Ambassador ROBIN RENEE SANDERS.

Venezuela: Plot 1361 Hon, Justice Sowemino St, Asokoro District, Abuja; tel. (9) 3140900; fax (9) 3140903; e-mail evenigeria@yahoo.com; Ambassador BORIS ENRÍQUEZ MARTÍNEZ.

Zambia: 351 Mission Rd, Central Area District, Garki, Abuja; tel. (9) 4618605; fax (9) 4618602; e-mail zambiahc@yahoo.com; High Commissioner GODFREY C. MUSONDA.

Zimbabwe: Abuja; tel. (9) 4611322; fax (9) 4611327; Ambassador Dr JOHN SHUMBA MVUNDURA.

Judicial System

Supreme Court
Three Arms Complex, Central District, PMB 308, Abuja; tel. (9) 2346594.

Consists of a Chief Justice and up to 15 Justices, appointed by the President, on the recommendation of the National Judicial Council (subject to the approval of the Senate); has original jurisdiction in any dispute between the Federation and a State, or between States, and hears appeals from the Federal Court of Appeal.

Chief Justice: IDRIS LEGBO KUTIGI.

NIGERIA

Court of Appeal: consists of a President and at least 35 Justices, of whom three must be experts in Islamic (*Shari'a*) law and three experts in Customary law.

Federal High Court: Chief Judge ABDULLAHI MUSTAPHA.

Each State has a **High Court**, consisting of a Chief Judge and a number of judges, appointed by the Governor of the State on the recommendation of the National Judicial Council (subject to the approval of the House of Assembly of the State). If required, a state may have a **Shari'a Court of Appeal** (dealing with Islamic civil law) and a **Customary Court of Appeal**. **Special Military Tribunals** have been established to try offenders accused of crimes such as corruption, drugs-trafficking and armed robbery; appeals against rulings of the Special Military Tribunals are referred to a **Special Appeals Tribunal**, which comprises retired judges.

Religion

ISLAM

According to the 2003 Nigeria Demographic and Health Survey, Muslims comprised 50.5% of the total population.

Spiritual Head: Col MUHAMMADU SA'AD ABUBAKAR (the Sultan of Sokoto).

CHRISTIANITY

According to the 2003 Nigeria Demographic and Health Survey, 48.2% of the population were Christians.

Christian Council of Nigeria: 139 Ogunlana Dr., Surulere, POB 2838, Lagos; tel. (1) 7923495; f. 1929; 15 full mems and six assoc. mems; Pres. Rt Rev. ROGERS O. UWADI; Gen. Sec. Rev. IKECNUKWU OKORIE.

The Anglican Communion

Anglicans are adherents of the Church of the Province of Nigeria, comprising 61 dioceses. Nigeria, formerly part of the Province of West Africa, became a separate Province in 1979; in 1997 it was divided into three separate provinces. The Church had an estimated 10m. members in 1990.

Archbishop of Province I and Bishop of Lagos: Most Rev. EPHRAIM A. ADEMOW, Archbishop's Palace, 29 Marina, POB 13, Lagos; tel. (1) 2635681; fax (1) 2631264.

Archbishop of Province II and Bishop of Awka: Most Rev. MAXWELL ANIKWENWA, Bishopscourt, Ifite Rd, POB 130, Awka.

Archbishop of Province III and Bishop of Abuja: Most Rev. PETER JASPER AKINOLA, Archbishop's Palace, POB 212, ADCP, Abuja; fax (9) 5230986; e-mail abuja@anglican.skannet.com.ng.

General Secretary: Ven. SAMUEL B. AKINOLA, 29 Marina, POB 78, Lagos; tel. (1) 2635681; fax (1) 2631264.

The Roman Catholic Church

Nigeria comprises nine archdioceses, 41 dioceses and two Apostolic Vicariates. At 31 December 2006 the total number of adherents represented an estimated 15.6% of the population.

Catholic Bishops' Conference of Nigeria
6 Force Rd, POB 951, Lagos; tel. (1) 2635849; fax (1) 2636670; e-mail cathsec1@infoweb.abs.net.

f. 1976; Pres. Most Rev. FELIX ALABA ADEOSIN JOB (Archbishop of Ibadan); Sec.-Gen. of Secretariat Rev. Fr MATTHEW HASSAN KUKAH.

Archbishop of Abuja: Most Rev. JOHN O. ONAIYEKAN, Archdiocesan Secretariat, POB 286, Garki, Abuja; tel. (9) 2340661; fax (9) 2340662; e-mail onaiyekan7@hotmail.com.

Archbishop of Benin City: Most Rev. RICHARD ANTHONY BURKE, Archdiocesan Secretariat, POB 35, Benin City, Edo; tel. (52) 253787; fax (52) 255763; e-mail cadobc@infoweb.abs.net.

Archbishop of Calabar: Most Rev. JOSEPH EDRA UKPO, Catholic Secretariat, PMB 1044, 1 Bishop Moynagh Ave, Calabar, Cross River; tel. (87) 231666; fax (87) 239177; e-mail archdical@yahoo.com.

Archbishop of Ibadan: Most Rev. FELIX ALABA JOB, Archbishop's House, PMB 5057, 8 Bale Latosa Rd, Onireke, Ibadan, Oyo; tel. (22) 2413544; fax (22) 2414855; e-mail archdiocese.ibadan@skannet.com.

Archbishop of Jos: Most Rev. IGNATIUS AYAU KAIGAMA, Archdiocesan Secretariat, 20 Joseph Gomwalk Rd, POB 494, Jos, Plateau; tel. (73) 452878; fax (73) 451547; e-mail josarch@hisen.org.

Archbishop of Kaduna: Most Rev. MATTHEW MAN-OSO NDAGOSO, Archbishop's House, 71 Tafawa Balewa Way, POB 248, Kaduna; tel. (62) 246076; fax (62) 240026; e-mail catholickad@email.com.

Archbishop of Lagos: Cardinal ANTHONY OLUBUNMI OKOGIE, Archdiocesan Secretariat, 19 Catholic Mission St, POB 8, Lagos; tel. (1) 2635729; fax (1) 2633841; e-mail arclagos@yahoo.com.

Archbishop of Onitsha: Most Rev. VALERIAN OKEKE, Archdiocesan Secretariat, POB 411, Onitsha, Anambra; tel. (46) 413298; fax (46) 413913; e-mail secretariat@onitsha-archdiocese.org.

Archbishop of Owerri: Most Rev. ANTHONY JOHN VALENTINE OBINNA, Villa Assumpta, POB 85, Owerri, Imo; tel. (83) 250115; fax (83) 230760; e-mail owcatsec@owerriarchdiocese.org.

Other Christian Churches

Brethren Church of Nigeria: c/o Kulp Bible School, POB 1, Mubi, Adamawa; f. 1923; 100,000 mems; Gen. Sec. Rev. JINATU WAMDEO.

Church of the Lord (Aladura): Anthony Village, Ikorodu Rd, POB 308, Ikeja, Lagos; tel. (1) 4964749; f. 1930; 1.1m. mems; Primate Dr E. O. A. ADEJOBI.

Lutheran Church of Christ in Nigeria: POB 21, Numan, Adamawa; tel. (75) 772330; fax (75) 625093; e-mail nemuelbabba@hotmail.com; Pres. Archbishop NEMUEL A. BABBA; 1.7m. mems (2009).

Lutheran Church of Nigeria: POB 49, Obot Idim Ibesikpo, Uyo, Akwa Ibom; tel. and fax (85) 201848; f. 1936; Pres. Most Rev. CHRISTIAN EKONG; 135,000 mems (2009).

Methodist Church Nigeria: Wesley House, 21–22 Marina, POB 2011, Lagos; tel. (1) 2702563; fax (1) 2702710; 483,500 mems; Patriarch Rev. Dr SUNDAY OLA KAKINDE.

Nigerian Baptist Convention: Baptist Bldg, PMB 5113, Ibadan; tel. (2) 2412267; fax (2) 2413561; e-mail baptconv@nigerianbaptist.org; internet nigerianbaptist.org; 3.5m. mems; Pres. Rev. Dr REUBEN I. CHUGA; Gen. Sec. Dr S. ADEMOLA ISHOLA.

The Presbyterian Church of Nigeria: 26–29 Ehere Rd, Ogbor Hill, POB 2635, Aba, Imo; tel. (82) 222551; f. 1846; 1m. mems; Moderator Rt Rev. Dr UBON B. USUNG; Synod Clerk Rev. Dr BENEBO F. FUBARA-MANUEL.

The Redeemed Church of Christ, the Church of the Foursquare Gospel, the Qua Iboe Church and the Salvation Army are prominent among numerous other Christian churches active in Nigeria.

AFRICAN RELIGIONS

The beliefs, rites and practices of the people of Nigeria are very diverse, varying between ethnic groups and between families in the same group.

The Press

DAILIES

Daily Champion: Isolo Industrial Estate, Oshodi-Apapa, Lagos; fax (1) 4526011; e-mail letters@champion-newspapers.com; internet www.champion-newspapers.com; Editor AUGSTEN ADAMU.

Daily Independent: Independent Newspapers Ltd, Block 5, Plot 7D, Wempco Rd, Ogba, Lagos; tel. (1) 4962136; e-mail newseditor@independentngonline.com; internet www.independentngonline.com; f. 2001; Editor IKECHUKWU AMAECHI.

Daily Times: Daily Times of Nigeria Ltd, Lateef Jakande Rd, Agidingbi, PMB 21340, Ikeja, Lagos; tel. and fax (1) 8510385; e-mail info@dailytime-nigeria.com; internet www.dailytimes-nigeria.com; f. 1925; 60% govt-owned; Editor-in-Chief STANLEY EGBOCHUKU; circ. 400,000.

Daily Trust: 20 Mafemi Crescent, Off Solomon Lar Way, Utako, Abuja; tel. (9) 6726241; internet www.dailytrust.com; f. 2001; Editor MAHMUD JEGA.

Evening Times: Daily Times of Nigeria Ltd, Lateef Jakande Rd, Agidingbi, PMB 21340, Ikeja, Lagos; tel. and fax (1) 8510385; Man. Dir Dr ONUKA ADINOYI-OJO; Editor CLEMENT ILOBA; circ. 20,000.

The Guardian: Rutam House, Isolo Expressway, Isolo, PMB 1217, Oshodi, Lagos; tel. (1) 4524111; fax (1) 4524080; e-mail editday@ngrguardiannews.com; internet www.ngrguardiannews.com; f. 1983; independent; Editor-in-Chief EMEKA IZEZE; Editor DEBO ADESINA; circ. 80,000.

Leadership: 8 Umuozu Close, off Samuel Ladoke Akintola Blvd, Garki II, Abuja; tel. (9) 2345055; fax (9) 2345360; e-mail info@leadershipnigeria.com; internet leadershipnigeria.com.

The Nation: 27B Fatai Atere Way, Matori, Mushin, Lagos; tel. (1) 8168361; e-mail info@thenationonlineng.com; internet www.thenationonlineng.com; f. 2006; Editor GBENGA OMOTOSO.

National Daily: internet www.nationaldailyngr.com; f. 2006; Exec. Editor SYLVESTER EBHODAGHE; circ. 50,000.

New Nigerian: Ahmadu Bello Way, POB 254, Kaduna; tel. (62) 245220; fax (62) 245221; e-mail webmaster@newnigerian1.com; internet www.newnigeriannews.com; f. 1965; govt-owned; Chair. Prof. TEKENA TAMUNO; Editor MALAM TUKUR ABDULRAHMAN; circ. 80,000.

NIGERIA

Nigerian Observer: The Bendel Newspaper Corpn, 24 Airport Rd, POB 1334, Benin City; tel. (52) 240050; e-mail info@nigerianobservernews.com; internet nigerianobservernews.com; f. 1968; Editor TONY IKEAKANAM; circ. 150,000.

Nigerian Tide: Rivers State Newspaper Corpn, 4 Ikwerre Rd, POB 5072, Port Harcourt; internet www.thetidenews.com; f. 1971; Editor AUGUSTINE NJOAGWUANI; circ. 30,000.

Nigerian Tribune: African Newspapers of Nigeria Ltd, Imalefalafi St, Oke-Ado, POB 78, Ibadan; tel. (2) 2312844; e-mail correspondence@nigerian-tribune.com; internet www.nigerian-tribune.com; f. 1949; Editor FOLU OLAMITI; circ. 109,000.

Post Express: 7 Warehouse Rd, PMB 1186, Apapa, Lagos; tel. (1) 5453351; fax (1) 5453436; e-mail postexpress@nova.net.ng; internet www.postexpresswired.com; Publr Chief S. ODUWU; Man. Dir Dr STANLEY MACEBUH.

The Punch: 1 Olu Aboderin St, Onipetesi, PMB 21204, Ikeja, Lagos; tel. (1) 7748081; e-mail editor@punchontheweb.com; internet www.punchng.com; f. 1976; Editor-in-Chief ADEMOLA OSINUBI; circ. 150,000.

The Sun: 2 Coscharis St, Kirikiri Industrial Layout, Apapa, PMB 21776 Ikeja, Lagos; tel. (1) 5875560; fax (1) 5875561; e-mail thesun@sunnewsonline.com; internet www.sunnewsonline.com; f. 2003; Editor FEMI ADESINA.

This Day: 35 Creek Rd, Apapa, Lagos; tel. 8022924721; fax (1) 4600276; e-mail info@thisdayonline.com; internet www.thisdayonline.com; f. 1995; Editor-in-Chief NDUKA OBAIGBENA.

Vanguard: Kirikiri Canal, PMB 1007, Apapa; e-mail vanguard@linkserve.com.ng; internet www.vanguardngr.com; f. 1984; Editor FRANK AIGBOGUN.

SUNDAY NEWSPAPERS

Sunday New Nigerian: Ahmadu Bello Way, POB 254, Kaduna; tel. (62) 245220; fax (62) 213778; e-mail auduson@newnigerian.com; internet www.newnigerian.com; f. 1981; weekly; Editor TAWEY ZAKKA; circ. 120,000.

Sunday Observer: PMB 1334, Bendel Newspapers Corpn, 18 Airport Rd, Benin City; f. 1968; Editor T. O. BORHA; circ. 60,000.

Sunday Punch: Kudeti St, PMB 21204, Ikeja, Lagos; tel. (1) 4964691; fax (1) 4960715; f. 1973; Editor DAYO WRIGHT; circ. 150,000.

Sunday Sketch: Sketch Publishing Co Ltd, PMB 5067, Ibadan; tel. (2) 414851; f. 1964; govt-owned; Editor OBAFEMI OREDEIN; circ. 125,000.

Sunday Standard: Plateau Publishing Co Ltd, Owerri-Egbu Rd, PMB 1095, Owerri; tel. (83) 230099; f. 1978; sponsored by Imo State Govt; Editor EDUBE WADIBIA.

Sunday Sun: PMB 1025, Okoro House, Factory Lane, off Upper Mission Rd, New Benin.

Sunday Tide: 4 Ikwerre Rd, POB 5072, Port Harcourt; f. 1971; Editor AUGUSTINE NJOAGWUANI.

Sunday Times: Daily Times of Nigeria Ltd, New Isheri Rd, Agidingbi, PMB 21340, Ikeja, Lagos; tel. (1) 4900850; f. 1953; 60% govt-owned; Editor DUPE AJAYI; circ. 100,000.

Sunday Tribune: Imalefalafi St, POB 78, Oke-Ado, Ibadan; tel. (2) 2310886; Editor WALE OJO.

Sunday Vanguard: Kirikiri Canal, PMB 1007, Apapa; Editor DUPE AJAYI.

WEEKLIES

Business Times: Daily Times of Nigeria Ltd, New Isheri Rd, Agidingbi, PMB 21340, Ikeja, Lagos; tel. (1) 4900850; f. 1925; 60% govt-owned; Editor GODFREY BAMAWO; circ. 22,000.

Gboungboun: Sketch Publishing Co Ltd, New Court Rd, PMB 5067, Ibadan; tel. (2) 414851; govt-owned; Yoruba; Editor A. O. ADEBANJO; circ. 80,000.

The Independent: Bodija Rd, PMB 5109, Ibadan; f. 1960; English; Roman Catholic; Editor Rev. F. B. CRONIN-COLTSMAN; circ. 13,000.

Irohin Imole: 15 Bamgbose St, POB 1495, Lagos; f. 1957; Yoruba; Editor TUNJI ADEOSUN.

Irohin Yoruba: 212 Broad St, PMB 2416, Lagos; tel. (1) 410886; f. 1945; Yoruba; Editor S. A. AJIBADE; circ. 85,000.

Lagos Life: Guardian Newspapers Ltd, Rutam House, Isolo Expressway, Isolo, PMB 1217, Oshodi, Lagos; f. 1985; Editor BISI OGUNBADEJO; circ. 100,000.

Lagos Weekend: Daily Times of Nigeria Ltd, New Isheri Rd, Agidingbi, PMB 21340, Ikeja, Lagos; tel. (1) 4900850; f. 1965; 60% govt-owned; news and pictures; Editor SAM OGWA; circ. 85,000.

The News: 27 Acme Rd, Agidingbi, PMB 21531, Ikeja, Lagos; tel. (1) 7939286; e-mail info@thenewsng.com; internet thenewsng.com; independent; Editor-in-Chief JENKINS ALUMONA.

Newswatch: 3 Billingsway Rd, Oregun, Lagos; tel. (1) 7619660; e-mail newswatch@newswatchngr.com; internet www.newswatchngr.com; f. 1985; English; CEO RAY EKPU; Editor-in-Chief DAN AGBESE.

Nigerian Radio/TV Times: Nigerian Broadcasting Corpn, POB 12504, Ikoyi.

Sporting Records: Daily Times of Nigeria Ltd, New Isheri Rd, Agidingbi, PMB 21340, Ikeja, Lagos; tel. (1) 4900850; f. 1961; 60% govt-owned; Editor CYRIL KAPPO; circ. 10,000.

Technology Times: Suite B316, 81 Ikeja Plaza, Mobolaji Bank Anthony Way, Ikeja, Lagos; tel. (1) 8968161; e-mail info@technologytimesng.com; internet www.technologytimesng.com.

Tempo: 26 Ijaiye Rd, PMB 21531, Ogba, Ikeja, Lagos; tel. (1) 920975; fax (1) 4924998; e-mail ijc@linkserve.com.ng; news magazine.

Times International: Daily Times of Nigeria Ltd, 3–7 Kakawa St, POB 139, Lagos; f. 1974; Editor Dr HEZY IDOWU; circ. 50,000.

Truth (The Muslim Weekly): 45 Idumagbo Ave, POB 418, Lagos; tel. (1) 2668455; f. 1951; Editor S. O. LAWAL.

ENGLISH-LANGUAGE PERIODICALS

Afriscope: 29 Salami Saibu St, PMB 1119, Yaba; monthly; African current affairs.

The Ambassador: PMB 2011, 1 peru-Remo, Ogun; tel. (39) 620115; quarterly; Roman Catholic; circ. 20,000.

Benin Review: Ethiope Publishing Corpn, PMB 1332, Benin City; f. 1974; African art and culture; 2 a year; circ. 50,000.

Economic Confidential: Abuja; e-mail info@economicconfidential.com; internet www.economicconfidential.com; f. 2007; monthly; Editor DONATUS ETUKUDO.

Financial Standard: 2 IPM Ave, CBD, Alausa-Ikeja, Lagos; tel. (1) 4934894; fax (1) 4934891; internet www.financialstandardnews.com; f. 1999; Mon.–Fri.; circ. 60,000.

Headlines: Daily Times of Nigeria Ltd, New Isheri Rd, Agindingbi, PMB 21340, Ikeja, Lagos; f. 1973; monthly; Editor ADAMS ALIU; circ. 500,000.

Home Studies: Daily Times Publications, 3–7 Kakawa St, Lagos; f. 1964; 2 a month; Editor Dr ELIZABETH E. IKEM; circ. 40,000.

Insight: 3 Kakawa St, POB 139, Lagos; quarterly; contemporary issues; Editor SAM AMUKA; circ. 5,000.

Journal of the Nigerian Medical Association: 3–7 Kakawa St, POB 139, Apapa; quarterly; Editor Prof. A. O. ADESOLA.

Lagos Education Review: Faculty of Education, University of Lagos Akoka, Lagos; tel. (1) 5820396; fax (1) 4932669; e-mail dajeyalemi@unilag.edu.ng; f. 1978; 2 a year; African education; Editor Prof. DURO AJEYALEMI.

The Leader: 19A Assumpta Press Ave, Industrial Layout, PMB 1017, Owerri, Imo; tel. (83) 230932; fortnightly; Roman Catholic; Editor Rev. KEVIN C. AKAGHA.

Management in Nigeria: Plot 22, Idowu Taylor St, Victoria Island, POB 2557, Lagos; tel. (1) 2615105; fax (1) 614116; e-mail nim@rcl.nig.com; quarterly; journal of Nigerian Inst. of Management; Editor Rev. DEJI OLOKESUSI; circ. 25,000.

Marketing in Nigeria: Alpha Publications, Surulere, POB 1163, Lagos; f. 1977; monthly; Editor B. O. K. NWELIH; circ. 30,000.

Modern Woman: 47–49 Salami Saibu St, Marina, POB 2583, Lagos; f. 1964; monthly; Man. Editor TOUN ONABANJO.

The New Nation: 52 Iwaya Rd, Onike, Yaba, Surulere, POB 896, Lagos; tel. (1) 5863629; monthly; news magazine.

Nigeria Magazine: Federal Dept of Culture, PMB 12524, Lagos; tel. (1) 5802060; f. 1927; quarterly; travel, cultural, historical and general; Editor B. D. LEMCHI; circ. 5,000.

Nigerian Businessman's Magazine: 39 Mabo St, Surulere, Lagos; monthly; Nigerian and overseas commerce.

Nigerian Journal of Economic and Social Studies: Nigerian Economic Society, c/o Dept of Economics, University of Ibadan; tel. (2) 8700395; e-mail banayochukwu@yahoo.co.uk; internet www.nigerianeconomicsociety.org; f. 1957; 3 a year; Editor Prof. BEN AIGBOKHAN.

Nigerian Journal of Science: University of Ibadan, POB 4039, Ibadan; e-mail iyifawole@yahoo.com; publ. of the Science Asscn of Nigeria; f. 1966; 2 a year; Editor Prof. I. FAWOLE; circ. 1,000.

Nigerian Worker: United Labour Congress, 97 Herbert Macaulay St, Lagos; Editor LAWRENCE BORHA.

The President: New Breed Organization Ltd, Plot 14 Western Ave, 1 Rafiu Shitty St, Alaka Estate, Surulere, POB 385, Lagos; tel. (1) 5802690; fax (1) 5831175; fortnightly; management; Chief Editor CHRIS OKOLIE.

Quality: Ultimate Publications Ltd, Oregun Rd, Lagos; f. 1987; monthly; Editor BALA DAN MUSA.

Radio-Vision Times: Western Nigerian Radio-Vision Service, Television House, POB 1460, Ibadan; monthly; Editor ALTON A. ADEDEJI.

Savanna: Ahmadu Bello University Press Ltd, PMB 1094, Zaria; tel. (69) 550054; e-mail abupl@wwlkad.com; f. 1972; 2 a year; Editor Prof. J. A. ARIYO; circ. 1,000.

Spear: Daily Times of Nigeria Ltd, New Isheri Rd, Agidingbi, PMB 21340, Ikeja, Lagos; tel. (1) 4900850; f. 1962; monthly; family magazine; Editor COKER ONITA; circ. 10,000.

Technical and Commercial Message: Surulere, POB 1163, Lagos; f. 1980; 6 a year; Editor B. O. K. NWELIH; circ. 12,500.

Today's Challenge: PMB 2010, Jos; tel. (73) 52230; f. 1951; 6 a year; religious and educational; Editor JACOB SHAIBY TSADO; circ. 15,000.

Woman's World: Daily Times of Nigeria Ltd, New Isheri Rd, Agidingbi, PMB 21340, Ikeja, Lagos; monthly; Editor TOYIN JOHNSON; circ. 12,000.

VERNACULAR PERIODICALS

Abokiyar Hira: Albah International Publishers, POB 6177, Bompai, Kano; f. 1987; monthly; Hausa; cultural; Editor BASHARI F. FOUKBAH; circ. 35,000.

Gaskiya ta fi Kwabo: Ahmadu Bello Way, POB 254, Kaduna; tel. (62) 201420; f. 1939; 3 a week; Hausa; Editor ABDUL-HASSAN IBRAHIM.

NEWS AGENCIES

Independent Media Centre (IMC): POB 894, Benin City; e-mail nigeriaimc@yahoo.com; internet www.nigeria.indymedia.org.

News Agency of Nigeria (NAN): Independence Avenue, Central Business District, PMB 7006, Garki, Abuja; tel. (9) 6703672; e-mail nanhq@nanngr.com; internet www.nannewsngr.com; f. 1976; state-owned; Man. Dir OLUREMI OYO; Editor-in-Chief DIPO OGBEDE.

Publishers

Africana First Publishers Ltd: Book House Trust, 1 Africana-First Dr., PMB 1639, Onitsha; tel. (46) 485031; f. 1973; study guides, general science, textbooks; Chair. RALPH O. EKPEH; Man. Dir J. C. ODIKE.

Ahmadu Bello University Press: PMB 1094, Zaria; tel. (69) 550054; f. 1972; history, Africana, social sciences, education, literature and arts; Man. Dir SA'IDU HASSAN ADAMU.

Albah International Publishers: 100 Kurawa, Bompai-Kano, POB 6177, Kano City; f. 1978; Africana, Islamic, educational and general, in Hausa; Chair. BASHARI F. ROUKBAH.

Aromolaran Publishing Co Ltd: POB 1800, Ibadan; tel. (2) 715980; f. 1968; educational and general; Man. Dir Dr ADEKUNLE AROMOLARAN.

Cross Continent Press Ltd: 25 Egbeyemi Rd, Ilupeju, POB 282, Yaba, Lagos; tel. and fax (1) 7746348; e-mail crosscontinent@yahoo.com; f. 1974; general, educational and academic; Man. Dir Dr T. C. NWOSU.

Daar Communications PLC: Daar Communications Centre, Kpaduma Hills, off Gen. T. Y. Danjuma St, Asokoro, Abuja; tel. (9) 3144802; fax (9) 3300512; broadcasting and information services; Man. Dir LADI LAWAL.

Daystar Press: Daystar House, POB 1261, Ibadan; tel. (2) 8102670; f. 1962; religious and educational; Man. PHILLIP ADELAKUN LADOKUN.

ECWA Productions Ltd: PMB 2010, Jos; tel. (73) 52230; f. 1973; religious and educational; Gen. Man. Rev. J. K. BOLARIN.

Ethiope Publishing Corpn: Ring Rd, PMB 1332, Benin City; tel. (52) 243036; f. 1970; general fiction and non-fiction, textbooks, reference, science, arts and history; Man. Dir SUNDAY N. OLAYE.

Evans Brothers (Nigeria Publishers) Ltd: Jericho Rd, PMB 5164, Ibadan; tel. (2) 2414394; fax (2) 2410757; f. 1966; general and educational; Chair. Dr ADEKUNLE OJORA; Man. Dir GBENRO ADEGBOLE.

Fourth Dimension Publishing Co Ltd: 16 Fifth Ave, City Layout, PMB 01164, Enugu; tel. (42) 459969; fax (42) 456904; e-mail nwankwov@infoweb.abs.net; internet www.fdpbooks.com; f. 1977; periodicals, fiction, verse, educational and children's; Chair. ARTHUR NWANKWO; Man. Dir V. U. NWANKWO.

Gbabeks Publishers Ltd: POB 37252, Ibadan; tel. (62) 2315705; e-mail gbabeks@hotmail.com; f. 1982; educational and technical; Man. Dir TAYO OGUNBEKUN.

HEBN Publishers PLC: 1 Ighodaro Rd, Jericho, PMB 5205, Ibadan; tel. (2) 2412268; fax (2) 2411089; e-mail info@hebnpublishers.com; internet www.hebnpublishers.com; f. 1962; educational, law, medical and general; Chair. AIGBOJE HIGO; Man. Dir AYO OJENIYI.

Heritage Books: The Poet's Cottage, Artistes Village, Ilogbo-Eremi, Badagry Expressway, POB 610, Apapa, Lagos; tel. (1) 5871333; f. 1971; general; Chair. NAIWU OSAHON.

Ibadan University Press: Publishing House, University of Ibadan, PMB 16, IU Post Office, Ibadan; tel. (2) 400550; e-mail iup-unibadan@yahoo.com; f. 1951; scholarly, science, law, general and educational; Dir F. A. ADESANOYE.

Ilesanmi Press Ltd: Akure Rd, POB 204, Ilesha; tel. 2062; f. 1955; general and educational; Man. Dir G. E. ILESANMI.

John West Publications Ltd: Plot 2, Block A, Acme Rd, Ogba Industrial Estate, PMB 21001, Ikeja, Lagos; tel. (1) 4925459; f. 1964; general; Man. Dir Alhaji L. K. JAKAUDE.

Literamed Publications Ltd (Lantern Books): Plot 45, Alausa Bus-stop, Oregun Industrial Estate, Ikeja, PMB 21068, Lagos; tel. (1) 7901129; fax (1) 7936521; e-mail information@lantern-books.com; internet www.lantern-books.com; f. 1969; children's, medical and scientific; Chair. O. M. LAWAL-SOLARIN.

Longman Nigeria Ltd: 52 Oba Akran Ave, PMB 21036, Ikeja, Lagos; tel. (1) 4978925; fax (1) 4964370; e-mail longman@linkserve.com; f. 1961; general and educational; Man. Dir J. A. OLOWONIYI.

Macmillan Nigeria Publishers Ltd: Ilupeju Industrial Estate, 4 Industrial Ave, POB 264, Yaba, Lagos; tel. (1) 4962185; e-mail macmillan@hotmail.com; internet www.macmillan.nigeria.com; f. 1965; educational and general; Exec. Chair. J. O. EMANUEL; Man. Dir Dr A. I. ADELEKAN.

Minaj Systems Ltd: Ivie House, 4–6 Ajose Adeogun St, POB 70811, Victoria Island, Lagos; tel. (1) 2621168; fax (1) 2621167; e-mail minaj@minaj.com; broadcasting, printing and publishing; Chair. Chief MIKE NNANYE I. AJEGBO.

Northern Nigerian Publishing Co Ltd: Gaskiya Bldg, POB 412, Zaria; tel. (69) 332087; fax (69) 331348; internet www.nnpchausa.com; f. 1966; general, educational and vernacular texts; Gen. Man. MAHMUD BARAU BAMBALE.

NPS Educational Publishers Ltd: Trusthouse, Ring Rd, off Akinyemi Way, POB 62, Ibadan; tel. (2) 316006; f. 1969; academic, scholarly and educational; CEO T. D. OTESANYA.

Nwamife Publishers: 10 Ibiam St, Uwani, POB 430, Enugu; tel. (42) 338254; f. 1971; general and educational; Chair. FELIX C. ADI.

Obafemi Awolowo University Press Ltd: Obafemi Awolowo University, Ile-Ife; tel. (36) 230284; f. 1968; educational, scholarly and periodicals; Man. Dir AKIN FATOKUN.

Obobo Books: The Poet's Cottage, Artistes Village, Ilogbo-Eremi, Badagry Expressway, POB 610, Apapa, Lagos; tel. and fax (1) 5871333; e-mail theendofknowledge@yahoo.com; internet www.theendofknowledge.com; f. 1981; children's books; Editorial Dir BAKIN KUNAMA.

Ogunsanya Press Publishers and Bookstores Ltd: SW9/1133 Orita Challenge, Idiroko, POB 95, Ibadan; tel. (2) 310924; f. 1970; educational; Man. Dir Chief LUCAS JUSTUS POPO-OLA OGUNSANYA.

Onibonoje Press and Book Industries (Nigeria) Ltd: Felele Layout, Challenge, POB 3109, Ibadan; tel. (2) 313956; f. 1958; educational and general; Chair. G. ONIBONOJE; Man. Dir J. O. ONIBONOJE.

Spectrum Books Ltd: Spectrum House, Ring Rd, PMB 5612, Ibadan; tel. (2) 2310058; fax (2) 2318502; e-mail admin1@spectrumbooksonline.com; internet www.spectrumbooksonline.com; f. 1978; educational and fiction; Chair. JOOP BERKHOUT; Man. Dir SINA OKEOWO.

University of Lagos Press: University of Lagos, POB 132, Akoka, Yaba, Lagos; tel. (1) 825048; e-mail library@rcl.nig.com; university textbooks, monographs, lectures and journals; Man. Dir S. BODUNDE BANKOLE.

University Press Ltd: Three Crowns Bldg, Eleyele Rd, Jericho, PMB 5095, Ibadan; tel. (2) 2411356; fax (2) 2412056; e-mail unipress@skannet.com.ng; f. 1978; associated with Oxford University Press; educational; Man. Dir WAHEED O. OLAJIDE.

University Publishing Co: 11 Central School Rd, POB 386, Onitsha; tel. (46) 210013; f. 1959; primary, secondary and university textbooks; Chair. E. O. UGWUEGBULEM.

Vanguard Media Ltd: Vanguard Ave, off Mile 2/Apapa Expressway, Kirikiri Canal; tel. (1) 5871200; fax (1) 5872662; e-mail vanguard@linkserve.com.ng; Publr SAM AMUKA.

Vista Books Ltd: 59 Awolowo Rd, S. W. Ikoyi, POB 282, Yaba, Lagos; tel. (1) 7746348; e-mail vista-books@yahoo.com; f. 1991; general fiction and non-fiction, arts, children's and educational; Man. Dir Dr T. C. NWOSU.

West African Book Publishers Ltd: Ilupeju Industrial Estate, 28–32 Industrial Ave, POB 3445, Lagos; tel. (1) 7754518; fax (1) 2799127; e-mail w_bookafricapubl@hotmail.com; internet www.wabp.com; f. 1963; textbooks, children's, periodicals and general; Chair. B. A. IDRIS-ANIMASHAUN; Man. Dir FOLASHADE B. OMO-EBOH.

NIGERIA

PUBLISHERS' ASSOCIATION

Nigerian Publishers Association: Book House, NPA Permanent Secretariat, Jericho G.R.A., POB 2541, Ibadan; tel. (2) 2413396; f. 1965; Pres. S. B. BANKOLE.

Broadcasting and Communications

TELECOMMUNICATIONS

Nigerian Communications Commission (NCC): Plot 423, Aguiyi Ironsi St, Maitama, Abuja; tel. (9) 4617000; fax (9) 4617514; e-mail ncc@ncc.gov.ng; internet www.ncc.gov.ng; f. 1932 as an independent regulatory body for the supply of telecommunications services and facilities; Chair. Alhaji AHMED JODA; CEO ERNEST C. A. NDUKWE.

Globacom Nigeria Ltd: Abuja; e-mail customercare@gloworld.com; internet www.gloworld.com; f. 2003; Chair. Dr MIKE ADENUGA, Jr; 9m. subscribers (2007).

Intercellular Nigeria Ltd: UBA House, 57, Marina, PMB 80078, Victoria Island, Lagos; tel. (1) 4703010; fax (1) 2643014; internet www.intercellular-ng.com; f. 1993; internet and international telephone services; 70% owned by Sudatel (Sudan); CEO ARVID KNUTSEN.

Motophone Ltd: C. & C. Towers, Plot 1684, Sanusi Fafumwa St, Victoria Island, Lagos; tel. (1) 2624168; fax (1) 2620079; e-mail motophone@hyperia.com; internet www.motophone.com; f. 1990; Man. Dir ERIC CHAMCHOUM.

MTN Nigeria Communications Ltd: Churchgate Towers, 5th Floor, Plot 30, Africabank St, Victoria Island, Lagos; tel. 8032005638; fax 8039029636; e-mail info@mtnnigeria.net; internet www.mtnonline.com; f. 2001; CEO AHMAD FARROUKH.

Multi-Links Telecommunication Ltd: 231 Adeola Odeku St, Victoria Island, POB 3453, Marina, Lagos; tel. (1) 7740000; fax (1) 7912345; internet www.multilinks.com; f. 1994; CEO and Man. Dir D. J. RAMAIYA.

Nigerian Mobile Telecommunications Ltd (M-TEL): 2 Bissau St, off Herbert Macaulay Way, Wuse Zone 6, Abuja; tel. (9) 5233031; internet www.mtelnigeria.com; f. 1996; Chair. OLULADE ADEGBOYEGA.

Nigerian Telecommunications (NITEL): 2 Bissau St, off Herbert Macaulay Way, Wuse Zone 6, Abuja; tel. (9) 5233021; Chair. Dr MARTINS IGBOKWE.

Starcomms: Starcomms House, Plot 1261 Bishop Kale Close, off Saka Tinubu St, Victoria Island, Lagos; tel. (1) 8041234; e-mail customerservice@starcomms.com; internet www.starcomms.com; f. 1999; Chair. PAUL EDWARDS; CEO MAHER QUBAIN.

Telnet (Nigeria) Ltd: Plot 242, Kofo Abayomi St, Victoria Island, POB 53656, Falomi Ikoyi, Lagos; tel. (1) 2611729; fax (1) 2619945; e-mail contact@iteco.com; internet www.telnetng.com; f. 1985; telecommunications engineering and consultancy services; Man. Dir GBENGA ODUJINRIN.

Zain Nigeria: Plot L2, Banana Island, Foreshore Estate, Ikoyi, Lagos; tel. 8021900000; fax (1) 3200477; e-mail customercare.ng@zain.com; internet www.ng.zain.com; f. 2000; fmrly Celtel Nigeria; CEO ADEBAYO WASIU LIGALI.

BROADCASTING

Regulatory Authority

National Broadcasting Commission: Plot 807, Ibrahim Taiwo Rd, Asokoro District, POB 5747, Garki, Abuja; tel. (9) 3147527; fax (9) 3147522; e-mail infonbc@nbc.gov.ng; internet www.nbc.gov.ng; Dir-Gen. Eng. YOMI BOLARINWA.

Radio

Federal Radio Corpn of Nigeria (FRCN): Radio House, PMB 452, Garki, Abuja; tel. (9) 2345230; fax (9) 2346486; e-mail info@radionigeria.net; internet www.radionigeria.net; f. 1976; controlled by the Fed. Govt and divided into five zones: Lagos (English); Enugu (English, Igbo, Izon, Efik and Tiv); Ibadan (English, Yoruba, Edo, Urhobo and Igala); Kaduna (English, Hausa, Kanuri, Fulfulde and Nupe); Abuja (English, Hausa, Igbo and Yoruba); Dir-Gen. YUSUF NUHU.

Imo Broadcasting Corpn: 14 Savage Cres., Enugu, Imo; tel. (42) 250327; operates one radio station in Imo State.

Voice of Nigeria (VON): 6th and 7th Floor, Radio House, Garki, Abuja; tel. (9) 2344017; fax (9) 2346970; e-mail info@voiceofnigeria.org; internet www.voiceofnigeria.org; f. 1990; controlled by the Fed. Govt; external services in English, French, Arabic, Ki-Swahili, Hausa and Fulfulde; Dir-Gen. Alhaji ABUBAKAR BOBBOYI JIJIWA.

Menage Holding's Broadcasting System Ltd: Umuahia, Imo; commenced broadcasting Jan. 1996; commercial.

Ray Power Radio 100.5 FM: Abeokuta Express Way, Ilapo, Alagbado, Lagos; tel. (1) 2644814; fax (1) 2644817; 100% owned by DAAR Communications Ltd; commenced broadcasting Sept. 1994; commercial; Chair. Chief ALEOGHO DOKPESI.

Television

Nigerian Television Authority (NTA): Television House, Area 11, Garki, PMB 13, Abuja; tel. (9) 2345907; fax (9) 2345914; internet www.nta.com.ng; f. 1976; controlled by the Fed. Govt; operates a network of 31 terrestrial broadcasters, which share national programming but also broadcast local programmes; also operates c. 70 regional channels; Chair. YAKUBULL HUSSAINI; Dir-Gen. Dr TONNIE IREDIA.

Africa Independent Television (AIT): Kpaduma Hill, off T. Y. Danjuma, Asokoro Extension, Abuja; e-mail feedback@daargroup.com; internet www.daargroup.com; f. 1994; 100% owned by DAAR Communications Ltd; Exec. Chair. Dr ALEOGHO DOKPESI.

Minaj Broadcast International (MBI): Minaj Media Group, 130/132, Ladipo St, Matori, Mushin, POB 70811, Victoria Island, Lagos; tel. (01) 4529203; fax (01) 4528500; e-mail info@minajmedia.com; internet www.minajmedia.com; provides free-to-air services.

Murhi International Television (MITV): MITV Plaza, Ikeja Central Business District, Obafemi Awolowo Way, Alausa, Lagos; tel. (1) 4931271; fax (1) 4931272; e-mail mitv@murhi-international.com.

Finance

(cap. = capital; res = reserves; dep. = deposits; m. = million; brs = branches; amounts in naira)

BANKING

At the end of 2003 the Nigerian banking system included a total of 89 deposit banks (with 3,300 branches); of these, 11 were estimated by the Central Bank to be insolvent and 24 marginally solvent.

Central Bank

Central Bank of Nigeria: Central Business District, Cadestral Zone, PMB 0187, Garki, Abuja; tel. and fax (9) 61639701; fax (9) 61636012; e-mail info@cenbank.org; internet www.cenbank.org; f. 1958; bank of issue; cap. 5,000m., res 320,165m., dep. 4,971,643m. (Dec. 2006); Gov. Prof. CHUKWUMA C. SOLUDO; 23 brs.

Commercial Banks

Afribank Nigeria Ltd: 51–55 Broad St, PMB 12021, Lagos; tel. (1) 2641566; fax (1) 2664890; e-mail info@afribank.com; internet www.afribank.net; f. 1969 as International Bank for West Africa Ltd; cap. 2,554.2m., res 25,741.8m., dep. 142,894.3m. (March 2007); Chair. Alhaji ALIYU K. BELGORE; Man. Dir and CEO SEBASTIAN ADIGWE; 137 brs.

Allstates Trust Bank PLC: Allstates Centre, Plot 1675, Oyin Jolayemi St, POB 73018, Victoria Island, Lagos; tel. (1) 4618445; fax (1) 2612206; e-mail enquiry@allstatesbankng.com; internet www.allstatesbankng.com; cap. 2,476.8m. (Sept. 2001); Man. Dir DUATE PATMORE IYABI.

Citizens' International Bank Ltd: 243 Ahmadu Bello Way, Victoria Island, Lagos; tel. (1) 2601030; fax (1) 2615138; e-mail info@citizensbankng.com; internet www.citizensbankng.com; f. 1990; cap. 619.8m., res 1,809.6m., dep. 31,496.3m. (March 2002); Chair. Chief JOYCE D. U. IFEGWU.

Diamond Bank PLC: Plot 1261, Adeola Hopewell St, Victoria Island, POB 70381, Lagos; tel. (1) 2701500; fax (1) 2619728; e-mail info@diamondbank.com; internet www.diamondbank.com; f. 2005 by merger with Lion Bank of Nigeria PLC; cap. 4,700m., res. 49,191.9m., dep. 226,378.7m. (April 2007); Man. Dir and CEO EMEKA ONWUKA.

Ecobank Nigeria Ltd: 2 Ajose Adeogun St, Victoria Island, POB 72688, Lagos; tel. (1) 2626638; fax (1) 2616568; e-mail ecobank.ng@ecobank.com; internet www.ecobank.com; f. 1989; cap. 10,827.1m., res 16,327.6m., dep. 84,040.5m. (Dec. 2006); Chair. OMO-OBA ODIMAYO; Man. Dir O. OSIBODU; 23 brs.

First Bank of Nigeria PLC: Samuel Asabia House, 35 Marina, POB 5216, Lagos; tel. (1) 2665900; fax (1) 2669073; e-mail fbn@firstbank-nig.com; internet www.firstbanknigeria.com; f. 1894 as Bank of British West Africa; cap. 5,238m., res. 72,113m., dep. 596,275m. (March 2007); Chair. UMAR ABDUL MUTALLAB; CEO and Man. Dir JACOBS M. AJEKIGBE; 302 brs.

Intercontinental Bank Ltd: Danmole St, Plot 999C, Adela Odeku, Victoria Island, Lagos; tel. (1) 2622940; fax (1) 2622981; e-mail corporateaffairs@intercontinentalbankplc.com; internet www.intercontinentalbankplc.com; cap. 5,361.8m., res 139,975.9m., dep. 457,295m. (Feb. 2007); Chair. Dr RAYMOND C. OBIERI; 42 brs.

NIGERIA

Nigeria International Bank Ltd: Commerce House, 11 Idowu Taylor St, Victoria Island, POB 6391, Lagos; tel. (1) 2622000; fax (1) 2618916; internet www.citibanknigeria.com; f. 1984; cap. 2,793.8m., res 31,019.2m., dep. 61,956.3m. (Dec. 2006); Chair. Chief CHARLES S. SANKEY; 4 brs.

Oceanic Bank International PLC: Plot 270, Ozumba Mbadiwe Ave, Waterfront Plaza, Victoria Island, Lagos; tel. (1) 2705010; fax (1) 2705066; e-mail info@oceanicbanknigeria.com; internet www.oceanicbanknigeria.com; f. 1990; name changed as above June 2005; cap. 5,821m., res. 200,641m., dep. 739,767m. (Sept. 2007); Man. Dir and CEO Dr C. A. IBRU.

Omegabank (Nigeria) PLC: 1 Engineering Close, PMB 80134, off Idowu Taylor, Victoria Island, Lagos; tel. (1) 2622580; fax (1) 2620761; e-mail omegabank@omegabankplc.com; internet www.omegabankplc.com; f. 1982 as Owena Bank plc; name changed 2001; 30% owned by Ondo State Govt; cap. 2,896.4m., res 208.0m., dep. 11,676.8m. (Dec. 2001); Chair. Chief ANTHONY ADENIYI; CEO Rev. Dr SEGUN AGBETUYI.

Stanbic IBTC Bank PLC: I.B.T.C. Place, Walter Carrington Cres., POB 71707, Victoria Island, Lagos; tel. (1) 2626520; fax (1) 2626541; internet www.ibtc-lagos.com; f. 1989 as Investment Banking & Trust Co Ltd; name changed as above 2008 following merger with Stanbic Bank (Nigeria) Ltd; cap. 6,028.6m., res 25,486.9m., dep. 57,073.3m. (March 2006); Chair. Chief OLUDOLAPO IBUKUN AKINKUGBE; CEO ALEDO A. PETERSIDE; 57 brs.

Sterling Bank: Sterling Towers, 20 Marina, POB 12735, Lagos; tel. (1) 2702300; fax (1) 2633294; e-mail tradeservices@sterlingbankng.com; internet www.sterlingbankng.com; f. 2005 following merger of Indo-Nigerian Bank Ltd, Magnum Trust Bank, NAL Bank PLC, NBM Bank and Trust Bank of Africa Ltd; cap. 5,276.4m., res. 21,043.0m., dep. 75,026.4m. (Sept. 2006); Chair. Alhaji ADEGUNWA (acting); Man. Dir RAZACK ADEYEMI ADEOLA.

Union Bank of Nigeria Ltd: 36 Marina, PMB 2027, Lagos; tel. (1) 2630361; fax (1) 2669873; e-mail info@unionbankng.com; internet www.unionbankng.com; f. 1969 as Barclays Bank of Nigeria Ltd; cap. 101,049m., res 1,493m., dep. 482,382m. (March 2007); Chair. Prof. MUSA G. YAKUBU; CEO G. A. T. OBOH; 235 brs.

United Bank for Africa (Nigeria) Ltd: UBA House, 57 Marina, PMB 12002, Lagos; tel. (1) 2807822; fax (1) 2644760; e-mail cic@ubagroup.com; internet www.ubagroup.com; f. 1961; cap. 5,748m., res 159,073m., dep. 897,651m. (Sept. 2007); Chair. KAYODE SOFOLA SAN; Man. Dir TONY O. ELUMELU; 428 brs.

Unity Bank PLC: Plot 785, Herbert Macaulay Way, Central Business District, POB 52463, Abuja; tel. (9) 4616700; fax (1) 2693256; e-mail nbm@nbmbank.com; internet www.unitybankng.com; f. 2005; cap. 21,752.9m., res. 9,015.0m., dep. 79,683.5m. (June 2006); Man. Dir and CEO Alhaji FALALU BELLO.

Wema Bank Ltd: Wema Towers, PMB 12862, 54 Marina, Lagos; tel. (1) 2668043; fax (1) 2669236; e-mail info@wemabank.com; internet www.wemabank.com; f. 1945; cap. 5,035.0m., res 19,781.7m., dep. 125,476.0m. (March 2007); Chair. Alhaji OLAPADE MOHAMMED; Man. Dir ADEBISI OMOYENI; 146 brs.

Zenith Bank PLC: Plot 84, Ajose Adeogun St, Victoria Island, POB 75315, Lagos; tel. (1) 2788000; fax (1) 2618212; e-mail enquiry@zenithbank.com; internet www.zenithbank.com; f. 1990; name changed as above in 2004; cap. 4,632.7m., res. 108,200.6m., dep. 572,761.5m. (June 2007); Man. Dir JIM OVIA.

Merchant Banks

FBN (Merchant Bankers) Ltd: 9/11 Macarthy St, Onikan, POB 12715, Lagos; tel. (1) 2600880; fax (1) 2633600; e-mail bisioni@fbnmb.com; internet www.fbnmb.com; cap. 1,000m. (2003); Chair. JACOBS MOYO AJEKIGBE.

Fidelity Bank PLC: 2 Kofo Abayomi St, Victoria Island, Lagos; tel. (1) 2610408; fax (1) 2610414; e-mail info@fidelitybankplc.com; internet www.fidelitybankplc.com; f. 1988; cap. 8,231.8m., res 21,525.2m., dep. 176,681.3m. (June 2007); Chair. Chief CHRISTOPHER EZEH; CEO REGINALD IHEJIAHI; 20 brs.

First City Monument Bank Ltd: Primrose Tower, 17A Tinubu St, POB 9117, Lagos; tel. (1) 2665944; fax (1) 2665126; e-mail fcmb@fcmb-ltd.com; internet www.fcmb-ltd.com; internet www.fcmb-ltd.com; f. 1983; cap. 4,751.2m., res 26,217.6m., dep. 203,627.5m. (April 2007); Chair. Dr JONATHAN LONG; 12 brs.

Development Banks

Bank of Industry (BOI) Ltd: BOI House, 63/71 Broad St, Lagos; tel. (1) 2665528; fax (1) 2665286; e-mail info@boi-ng.com; f. 1964 as the Nigerian Industrial Development Bank Ltd to provide medium and long-term finance to industry, manufacturing, non-petroleum mining and tourism; name changed as above Oct. 2001; cap. 6,585.1m., dep. 3,500m. (Dec. 2005); Man. Dir Dr LAWRENCE OSS-AFIANA; 8 brs.

Guaranty Trust Bank PLC: The Plural House, Plot 1669, Oyin Jolayemi St, PMB 75455, Victoria Island, Lagos; tel. (1) 2622650; fax (1) 2622698; e-mail corpaff@gtbplc.com; internet www.gtbplc.com; f. 1990; cap. 4,000m., res 43,433.2m., dep. 295,281m. (Feb. 2007); Chair. OWELLE GILBERT CHIKELU.

Nigerian Agricultural, Co-operative and Rural Development Bank Ltd (NACB): Yakubu Gowoh, PMB 2155, Kaduna; tel. (62) 243590; fax (62) 245012; e-mail nacb@infoweb.abs.net; f. 1973 for funds to farmers and co-operatives to improve production techniques; name changed as above Oct. 2000, following merger with People's Bank of Nigeria; cap. 1,000m. (2002); Chair. Alhaji ISA TATA YUSUF; Man. Dir Alhaji UMAR BABALE GIREI; 200 brs.

Bankers' Association

Chartered Institute of Bankers of Nigeria: PC 19 Adeola Hopewell St, POB 72273, Victoria Island, Lagos; tel. (1) 2617924; fax (1) 4618930; e-mail cibn@cibnnigeria.org; internet www.cibnnigeria.org; Chair. JOHNSON O. EKUNDAYO; CEO Dr UJU M. OGUBUNKA.

STOCK EXCHANGE

Securities and Exchange Commission (SEC): Mandilas House, 96–102 Broad St, PMB 12638, Lagos; f. 1979 as govt agency to regulate and develop capital market and to supervise stock exchange operations; Dir-Gen. MUSA AL-FAKI.

Nigerian Stock Exchange: Stock Exchange House, 2–4 Customs St, POB 2457, Lagos; tel. (1) 2660287; fax (1) 2668724; e-mail nse@nigerianstockexchange.com; internet www.nigerianstockexchange.com; f. 1960; Pres. Dr OBA OTUDEKO; Dir-Gen. Dr NDI OKEREKE-ONYIUKE; 6 brs.

INSURANCE

In early 2005 more than 450 registered insurance companies were operating in Nigeria. Since 1978 they have been required to reinsure 20% of the sum insured with the Nigeria Reinsurance Corpn.

Insurance Companies

African Alliance Insurance Co Ltd: 112 Broad St, POB 2276, Lagos; tel. (1) 7227666; fax (1) 2660943; e-mail info@africanallianceinsurance.com; internet www.africanallianceinsurance.com; f. 1960; life assurance and pensions; Man. Dir WISDOM PHILLIPS; 30 brs.

Aiico International Insurance (AIICO): AIICO Plaza, Plot PC 12, Afribank St, Victoria Island, POB 2577, Lagos; tel. (1) 2610651; fax (1) 2617433; e-mail info@aiicoplc.com; internet www.aiicoplc.com; CEO M. E. HANSEN.

Ark Insurance Group: Glass House, 11A Karimu Kotun St, Victoria Island, POB 3771, Marina, Lagos; tel. (1) 2615826; fax (1) 2615850; e-mail ark@nova.net.ng; internet www.nigeriaweb.com/ark; Chair. F. O. AWOGBORO.

Continental Reinsurance Co Ltd: Reinsurance House, 11th Floor, 46 Marina, POB 2401, Lagos; tel. (1) 2665350; fax (1) 2665370; CEO ADEYEMO ADEJUMO.

Cornerstone Insurance Co PLC: POB 75370, Victoria Island, Lagos; tel. (1) 2631832; fax (1) 2633079; e-mail marketing@cornerstone.com.ng; internet www.cornerstone.com; f. 1991; Chair. CLEMENT O. BAIYE.

Equity Indemnity Insurance Co Ltd: POB 1514, Lagos; tel. (1) 2637802; fax (1) 2637479; e-mail equity@infoweb.abs.net; f. 1991; Chair. Prof. O. A. SERIKI.

Great Nigeria Insurance Co Ltd: 8 Omo-Osaghie St, off Obafemi Awolono Rd, Ikoyi S/W, Ikoyi, Lagos; tel. (1) 2695805; fax (1) 2693483; e-mail info@greatinsure-ng.com; internet www.greatinsure-ng.com; f. 1960; all classes; Man. Dir M. A. SIYANBOLA.

Guinea Insurance Co Ltd: Guinea Insurance House, 21 Nnandi Azikiwe St, POB 1136, Lagos; tel. (1) 2665201; f. 1958; all classes; CEO AYO BAMMEKE.

Industrial and General Insurance Co Ltd: Plot 741, Adeola Hopewell St, POB 52592, Falomo, Lagos; tel. (1) 2625437; fax (1) 2621146; Chair. Y. GOWON.

Kapital Insurance Co Ltd: 116 Hadejia Rd, POB 2044, Kano; tel. (64) 645666; fax (64) 636962; CEO MOHAMMED GAMBO UMAR.

Law Union and Rock Insurance Co of Nigeria Ltd: 88–92 Broad St, POB 944, Lagos; tel. (1) 2663526; fax (1) 2664659; fire, accident and marine; 6 brs; CEO S. O. AKINYEMI.

Leadway Assurance Co Ltd: NN 28–29 Constitution Rd, POB 458, Kaduna; tel. (62) 200660; fax (62) 236838; f. 1970; all classes; Man. Dir OYEKANMI ABIODUN HASSAN-ODUKALE.

Lion of Africa Insurance Co Ltd: St Peter's House, 3 Ajele St, POB 2055, Lagos; tel. (1) 2600950; fax (1) 2636111; f. 1952; all classes; Man. Dir G. A. ALEGIEUNO.

National Insurance Corpn of Nigeria (NICON): 5 Customs St, POB 1100, Lagos; tel. (1) 2640230; fax (1) 2666556; f. 1969; all classes; cap. 200m.; Chair. JOHN IRIATA ABUHME; 28 brs.

N.E.M. Insurance Co (Nigeria) Ltd: 22A Borno Way, Ebute, POB 654, Lagos; tel. (1) 5861920; all classes; Chair. Alhaji Dr ALIYU MOHAMMED; Man. Dir J. E. UMUKORO.

Niger Insurance Co Ltd: 47 Marina, POB 2718, Lagos; tel. (1) 2664452; fax (1) 2662196; all classes; Chair. P. M. G. SOARES; 6 brs.

Nigeria Reinsurance Corpn: 46 Marina, PMB 12766, Lagos; tel. (1) 2667049; fax (1) 2668041; e-mail info@nigeriare.com; internet www.nigre.com; all classes of reinsurance; Man. Dir T. T. MIRILLA.

Nigerian General Insurance Co Ltd: 1 Nnamdi Azikiwe St, Tirubu Square, POB 2210, Lagos; tel. (1) 2662552; e-mail odua@odua.com; f. 1951; all classes; Chair. O. O. OKEYODE; Man. Dir J. A. OLANIHUN; 15 brs.

Phoenix of Nigeria Assurance Co Ltd: Mandilas House, 96–102 Broad St, POB 12798, Lagos; tel. (1) 2661160; fax (1) 2662883; e-mail phoenixassce@alpha.linkserve.com; f. 1964; all classes; cap. 10m.; Chair. A. A. OJORA; Man. Dir A. A. AKINTUNDE; 5 brs.

Prestige Assurance Co (Nigeria) Ltd: 19 Ligali Ayorinde St, Victoria Island, POB 650, Lagos; tel. (1) 3204681; fax (1) 3204684; e-mail prestigeassurance@yahoo.co.uk; f. 1952; all classes except life; Chair. Chief C. S. SANKEY; Man. Dir N. S. R. CHANDRAPRASAD.

Royal Exchange Assurance (Nigeria) Group: New Africa House, 31 Marina, POB 112, Lagos; tel. (1) 2663120; fax (1) 2664431; all classes; Chair. Alhaji MUHTAR BELLO YOLA; Man. Dir JONAH U. IKHIDERO; 6 brs.

Sun Insurance Office (Nigeria) Ltd: Unity House, 37 Marina, POB 2694, Lagos; tel. (1) 2661318; all classes except life; Man. Dir A. T. ADENIJI; 6 brs.

United Nigeria Insurance Co Ltd (UNIC): 53 Marina, POB 588, Lagos; tel. (1) 2663201; fax (1) 2664282; f. 1965; all classes except life; CEO E. O. A. ADETUNJI; 17 brs.

Unity Life and Fire Insurance Co Ltd: 25 Nnamdi Azikiwe St, POB 3681, Lagos; tel. (1) 2662517; fax (1) 2662599; all classes; Man. Dir R. A. ODINIGWE.

West African Provincial Insurance Co: WAPIC House, 119 Awolowo Rd, POB 55508, Falomo-Ikoyi, Lagos; tel. (1) 2672770; fax (1) 2693838; e-mail wapic@alpha.linkserve.com; Man. Dir D. O. AMUSAN.

Insurance Association

Nigerian Insurance Association: Nicon House, 1st Floor, 5 Customs St, POB 9551, Lagos; tel. (1) 2640825; f. 1971; Chair. J. U. IKHIDERO.

Trade and Industry

GOVERNMENT AGENCIES

Bureau of Public Enterprises: Secretariat of the National Council on Privatization, 1 Osun Cres., off Ibib Way, Maitama District, PMB 442, Garki, Abuja; tel. (9) 4134636; fax (9) 4134657; e-mail bpe@bpeng.org; internet www.bpeng.org; Dir-Gen. Mallam NASIR AHMAD EL-RUFAI.

Corporate Affairs Commission: Area 11, Garki, Abuja; tel. (9) 2342917; fax (9) 2342669; e-mail info@cac.gov.ng; internet www.cac.gov.ng; Sec. HENRIEITA O. M. TALABI.

National Council on Privatisation: Bureau of Public Enterprises, NDIC Bldg, Constitution Ave, Central Business District, PMB 442, Garki, Abuja; tel. (9) 5237405; fax (9) 5237396; e-mail bpegen@micro.com.ng; internet www.bpe.gov.ng.

Nigeria Export Processing Zones Authority: 2 Zambezi Cres., Cadastral Zone A6, off Aguiyi Ironsi St, Maitama, PMB 037, Garki-Abuja; tel. (9) 2343059; fax (9) 2343061; e-mail info@nepza.com; internet www.nepza.com; Man. Dir SINA A. AGBOLUAJE.

DEVELOPMENT ORGANIZATIONS

Benin–Owena River Basin Development Authority: 24 Benin-Sapele Rd, PMB 1381, Obayantor, Benin City; tel. (52) 254415; f. 1976 to conduct irrigation; Gen. Man. Dr G. E. OTEZE.

Chad Basin Development Authority: Dikwa Rd, PMB 1130, Maiduguri; tel. (76) 232015; f. 1973; irrigation and agriculture-allied industries; Chair. MOHAMMED ABALI; Gen. Man. Alhaji BUNU S. MUSA.

Cross River Basin Development Authority: 32 Target Rd, PMB 1249, Calabar; tel. (87) 223163; f. 1977; Gen. Man. SIXTUS ABETIANBE.

Federal Institute of Industrial Research, Oshodi (FIIRO): Blind Center St, by Cappa Bus Stop, off Agege Motor Rd, Oshodi, Ikeja, PMB 21023, Lagos; tel. (1) 4701846; fax (1) 4525880; e-mail info@fiiro-ng.org; internet www.fiiro-ng.org; f. 1956; plans and directs scientific research for industrial and technological development; provides tech. assistance and information to industry; specializes in foods, minerals, textiles, natural products and industrial intermediates; Dir-Gen. Dr O. OLATUNJI.

Industrial Training Fund: Miango Rd, PMB 2199, Jos, Plateau; tel. and fax (73) 461887; e-mail dp@itf-nigeria.com; internet www.itf-nigeria.com; f. 1971 to promote and encourage skilled workers in trade and industry; Dir-Gen. Prof. OLU E. AKEREJOLA.

Kaduna Industrial and Finance Co Ltd: Investment House, 27 Ali Akilu Rd, PMB 2230, Kaduna; tel. (62) 240751; fax (62) 240754; e-mail kadunainvestment@yahoo.com; f. 1989; provides devt finance; Chair. HARUNA ZEGO AZIZ; Man. Dir and CEO DAHIRU MOHAMMED.

Kwara State Investment Corpn: 109–112 Fate Rd, PMB 1344, Ilorin, Kwara; tel. (31) 220510.

Lagos State Development and Property Corpn: 1 Town Planning Way, Ilupeju, Lagos; tel. (1) 4972243; e-mail isdpc@isdpc.com; internet www.isdpc.com; f. 1972; planning and devt of Lagos; Gen. Man. O. R. ASHAFA.

New Nigerian Development Co Ltd: 18/19 Ahmadu Bello Way, Ahmed Talib House, PMB 2120, Kaduna; tel. (62) 249355; fax (62) 245482; e-mail nndc@skannet.com.ng; f. 1949; owned by the Govts of 19 northern States; investment finance; 8 subsidiaries, 83 assoc. cos; Chair. Prof. HALIDU IBRAHIM ABUBAKAR.

Niger Delta Development Commission: 6 Olumeni St, Port Harcourt; internet www.nddconline.org; f. 1976; Man. Dir GODWIN OMENE.

Nigerian Enterprises Promotion Board: 15–19 Keffi St, Ikoyi, Lagos; tel. (1) 2680929; f. 1972 to promote indigenization; Chair. MINSO GADZAMA.

Northern Nigeria Investments Ltd: 4 Waff Rd, POB 138, Kaduna; tel. (62) 239654; fax (62) 230770; f. 1959 to identify and invest in industrial and agricultural projects in 16 northern States; cap. p.u. 20m.; Chair. Alhaji ABUBAKAR G. ADAMU; Man. Dir GIMBA H. IBRAHIM.

Odu'a Investment Co Ltd: Cocoa House, PMB 5435, Ibadan; tel. (2) 417710; fax (2) 413000; f. 1976; jtly owned by Ogun, Ondo and Oyo States; Man. Dir Alhaji R. S. ARUNA.

Plateau State Water Resources Development Board: Jos; incorporates the fmr Plateau River Basin Devt Authority and Plateau State Water Resources Devt Board.

Projects Development Institute: Emene Industrial Layout, Proda Rd, POB 01609, Enugu; tel. (42) 451593; fax (42) 457691; e-mail proda@rmrdc.nig.com; f. 1977; promotes the establishment of new industries and develops industrial projects utilizing local raw materials; Dir BASIL K. C. UGWA.

Raw Materials Research Development Council: Plot 427, Aguiyi, Ironsi St, Maitama, Abuja; tel. (9) 5237417.

Rubber Research Institute of Nigeria: PMB 1049, Benin City; tel. 8033197241; e-mail rubberresearchnig@yahoo.com; f. 1961; conducts research into the production of rubber and other latex products; Exec. Dir M.U.B. MOKWUNYE.

Trans Investments Co Ltd: Bale Oyewole Rd, PMB 5085, Ibadan; tel. (2) 416000; f. 1986; initiates and finances industrial and agricultural schemes; Gen. Man. M. A. ADESIYUN.

CHAMBERS OF COMMERCE

Nigerian Association of Chambers of Commerce, Industry, Mines and Agriculture: 8A Oba Akinjobi Way, PMB 12816, Lagos; tel. (1) 4964727; fax (1) 4964737; e-mail contact@naccima.com; internet www.naccima.com; Pres. Dr IGNATIUS ADAJI; Dir-Gen. L. O. ADEKUNLE.

Aba Chamber of Commerce and Industry: UBA Bldg, Ikot Expene Rd/Georges St, POB 1596, Aba; tel. (82) 352084; fax (82) 352067; internet abachamber@yahoo.com; f. 1971; Pres. Chief KALU OMOJI KALU.

Abeokuta Chamber of Commerce and Industry: 29 Kuto Rd, Ishabo, POB 937, Abeokuta; tel. (39) 241230; Pres. Chief S. O. AKINREMI.

Abuja Chamber of Commerce, Industry, Mines & Agriculture: International Trade Fair Complex, KM8, Airport Road, PMB 86, Garki, Abuja; tel. (9) 6707428; fax (9) 2348808; e-mail abuccima@hotmail.com; Pres. Sir PETER OKOLO.

Adamawa Chamber of Commerce and Industry: c/o Palace Hotel, POB 8, Jimeta, Yola; tel. (75) 255136; Pres. Alhaji ISA HAMMANYERO.

Akure Chamber of Commerce and Industry: 57 Oyemekun Rd, POB 866, Akure; tel. (34) 242540; f. 1984; Pres. ADEDEJI OMISAMI.

Awka Chamber of Commerce and Industry: 220 Enugu Rd, POB 780, Awka; tel. (45) 550105; Pres. Lt-Col (retd) D. ORUGBU.

NIGERIA   *Directory*

Bauchi Chamber of Commerce and Industry: 96 Maiduguri Rd, POB 911, Bauchi; tel. (77) 42620; f. 1976; Pres. Alhaji MAGAJI MU'AZU.

Benin Chamber of Commerce, Industry, Mines and Agriculture: 10 Murtala Muhammed Way, POB 2087, Benin City; tel. (52) 255761; Pres. C. O. EWEKA.

Benue Chamber of Commerce, Industry, Mines and Agriculture: 71 Ankpa Qr Rd, PMB 102344, Makurdi; tel. (44) 32573; Chair. Col (retd) R. V. I. ASAM.

Borno Chamber of Commerce and Industry: Grand Stand, Ramat Sq., off Central Bank, PMB 1636, Maiduguri; tel. (76) 232832; e-mail bsumar@hotmail.com; f. 1973; Pres. Alhaji MOHAMMED RIJYA; Sec.-Gen. BABA SHEHU BUKAR.

Calabar Chamber of Commerce and Industry: Desan House Bldg, 38 Ndidem Iso Rd, POB 76, Calabar, Cross River; tel. (87) 221558; 92 mems; Pres. Chief TAM OFORIOKUMA.

Enugu Chamber of Commerce, Industry and Mines: International Trade Fair Complex, Abakaliki Rd, POB 734, Enugu; tel. (42) 250575; fax (42) 252186; e-mail eccima@infoweb.abs.net; internet www.enuguchamber.com; f. 1963; Dir EMEKA OKEREKE.

Franco-Nigerian Chamber of Commerce: Big Leaf House, 7 Oyin Jolayemi St, POB 70001, Victoria Island, Lagos; tel. (1) 4611201; fax (1) 4613501; e-mail fncci@ccife.org; internet franco-nigerian.com; f. 1985; Chair. MARCEL HOCHET; Gen. Man. AKIN AKINBOLA.

Gongola Chamber of Commerce and Industry: Palace Hotel, POB 8, Jimeta-Yola; tel. (75) 255136; Pres. Alhaji ALIYU IBRAHIM.

Ibadan Chamber of Commerce and Industry: Commerce House, Ring Rd, Challenge, PMB 5168, Ibadan; tel. (2) 317223; Pres. JIDE ABIMBOLA.

Ijebu Chamber of Commerce and Industry: 51 Ibadan Rd, POB 604, Ijebu Ode; tel. (37) 432880; Pres. DOYIN DEGUN.

Ikot Ekpene Chamber of Commerce and Industry: 47 Aba Rd, POB 50, Ikot Ekpene; tel. (85) 400153; Pres. G. U. EKANEM.

Kaduna Chamber of Commerce, Industry and Agriculture: 24 Waff Rd, POB 728, Kaduna; tel. (62) 211216; fax (62) 214149; Pres. Alhaji MOHAMMED SANI AMINU.

Kano Chamber of Commerce, Industry, Mines and Agriculture: Zoo Rd, POB 10, Kano City, Kano; tel. (64) 666936; fax (64) 667138; Pres. MALLAM U. J. KIRU.

Katsina Chamber of Commerce and Industry: 1 Nagogo Rd, POB 92, Katsina; tel. (65) 31014; Pres. ABBA ALI.

Kwara Chamber of Commerce, Industry, Mines and Agriculture: Kwara Hotel Premises, Ahmadu Bello Ave, POB 1634, Ilorin; tel. (31) 223069; fax (31) 224131; e-mail kwaccima@yahoo.com; internet www.kwaccima.com; Pres. Alhaji JANI IBRAHIM; Dir-Gen. ABDULSALAAM A. JIMOH.

Lagos Chamber of Commerce and Industry: Commerce House, 1 Idowu Taylor St, Victoria Island, POB 109, Lagos; tel. (1) 2705386; fax (1) 2701009; e-mail inform@micro.com.ng; f. 1888; 1,267 mems; Pres. Chief OLUSOLA FALEYE.

Niger Chamber of Commerce and Industry: Trade Fair Site, POB 370, Minna; tel. (66) 223153; Pres. Alhaji U. S. NDANUSA.

Nnewi Chamber of Commerce, Industry, Mines and Agriculture: 31A Nnobi Rd, POB 1471, Nnewi, Anambra State; tel. (70) 35187662; f. 1987; Pres. PRINCE EMEKA AYABAZU.

Osogbo Chamber of Commerce and Industry: Obafemi Awolowo Way, Ajegunle, POB 870, Osogbo, Osun; tel. (35) 231098; Pres. Prince VICTOR ADEMLE.

Owerri Chamber of Commerce and Industry: OCCIMA Secretariat, 123 Okigwe Rd, POB 1439, Owerri; tel. (83) 234849; Pres. Chief OKEY IKORO.

Oyo Chamber of Commerce and Industry: POB 67, Oyo; Pres. Chief C. A. OGUNNIYI.

Plateau State Chambers of Commerce, Industry, Mines and Agriculture: POB 74, 21A Nassarawa Rd, Jos; tel. (73) 453918; f. 1976; Pres. Chief M. E. JACDOMI.

Port Harcourt Chamber of Commerce, Industry, Mines and Agriculture: Alesa Eleme, POB 585, Port Harcourt; tel. (84) 239536; f. 1952; Pres. Chief S. I. ALETE.

Remo Chamber of Commerce and Industry: 7 Sho Manager Way, POB 1172, Shagamu; tel. (37) 640962; Pres. Chief S. O. ADEKOYA.

Sapele Chamber of Commerce and Industry: 144 New Ogorode Rd, POB 154, Sapele; tel. (54) 42323; Pres. P. O. FUFUYIN.

Sokoto Chamber of Commerce and Industry: 12 Racecourse Rd, POB 2234, Sokoto; tel. (60) 231805; Pres. Alhaji ALIYU WAZIRI BODINGA.

Umahia Chamber of Commerce: 44 Azikiwe Rd, Umahia; tel. (88) 223373; fax (88) 222299; Pres. GEORGE AKOMAS.

Uyo Chamber of Commerce and Industry: 141 Abak Rd, POB 2960, Uyo, Akwa Ibom; Pres. Chief DANIEL ITA-EKPOTT.

Warri Chamber of Commerce, Industry, Mines and Agriculture (WACCIMA): Block 1, Edewor Shopping Centre, Warri/Sapele Rd, PMB 302, Warri; tel. (53) 253709; fax (53) 254875; e-mail info@waccima.com; f. 1963; Pres. AUSTIN E. EGBEGBADIA.

INDUSTRIAL AND TRADE ASSOCIATIONS

Nigerian Export Promotion Council: Plot 40, Blantyre St, Wuse 2, Abuja; tel. (9) 5230930; fax (9) 5230931; internet www.nepcng.com; f. 1976; Chair. Alhaji ISIAKA ADELEKE.

Nigerian Investment Promotion Commission (NIPC): Plot 1181, Agyuiyi-Ironsi St, Maitama District, Abuja; tel. (9) 4138026; fax (9) 4138021; e-mail nipc@nipc-nigeria.org; internet www.nipc-nigeria.org; Chair. FELIX O. A. OHIWEREI; Exec. Sec. Alhaji MUSTAFA BELLO.

EMPLOYERS' ORGANIZATIONS

Association of Advertising Practitioners of Nigeria: 3 William St, off Sylvia Cres., POB 50648, Anthony Village, Lagos; tel. (1) 4970842.

Chartered Institute of Bankers: Plot PC 19, Adeola Hopewell St, POB 72273, Victoria Island, Lagos.

Institute of Chartered Accountants of Nigeria: Plot 16, Professional Layout Centre, Idowu Taylor St, Victoria Island, POB 1580, Lagos; tel. (1) 2622394; fax (1) 4627048; e-mail info.ican@ican.org.ng; internet www.ican-ngr.org; f. 1965; CEO and Registrar OLUTOYIN ADEPATE.

Nigeria Employers' Consultative Association: Commercial House, 1–11 Commercial Ave, POB 2231, Yaba, Lagos; tel. (1) 800360; fax (1) 860309; f. 1957; Pres. Chief R. F. GIWA.

Nigerian Institute of Architects: 2 Idowu Taylor St, Victoria Island, POB 178, Lagos; tel. (1) 2617940; fax (1) 2617947; internet niarchitects.org; f. 1960; Pres. E. C. CHUKWUKA.

Nigerian Institute of Building: 24 Road 37, Gwarinpa Housing Estate, Abuja; tel. (1) 7935719; fax (1) 7935719; e-mail niob@niobuilding.org; internet www.niobuilding.org; f. 1967; Pres. DOLA ARILESERE.

Nigerian Institution of Estate Surveyors and Valuers: Flat 2B, Dolphin Scheme, Ikoyi, POB 2325, Lagos; tel. (1) 2673131; fax (1) 2694314; e-mail niesv@nova.net.ng; Pres. NWEKE UMEZURUIKE.

Nigerian Society of Engineers: National Engineering Centre, off National Mosque-Labour Rd, Central Business Area, Abuja; tel. (9) 6735096; e-mail nsehqr@linkserve.com; internet www.nse.org.ng; Pres. KASHIM A. ALI.

UTILITIES
Electricity

Power Holding Company of Nigeria (PHCN): Plot 1071, Area 3, Garki, Abuja; tel. (1) 5231938; f. 1972 as National Electric Power Authority, by merger of the Electricity Corpn of Nigeria and the Niger Dams Authority; renamed as above April 2005; assets were to be diverted to six generating companies and 11 distribution companies, prior to privatization; CEO HUSEIN LABO.

Gas

Nigeria Liquefied Natural Gas Co Ltd (NLNG): C. & C. Towers, Plot 1684, Sanusi Fafunwa St, Victoria Island, PMB 12774, Marina, Lagos; tel. (1) 2624190; fax (1) 2616976; internet www.nigerialng.com; Man. Dir Dr CHRIS HAYNES.

TRADE UNIONS
Federation

Nigerian Labour Congress (NLC): Labour House, Plot 820/821, Central Business District, Abuja; tel. (9) 6276042; fax (9) 6274342; e-mail gsec@nlcng.org; internet www.nlcng.org; f. 1978; comprised 36 affiliated industrial unions in 2009; Pres. ABDULWAHED OMAR.

Principal Unions

Amalgamated Union of Public Corpns, Civil Service, and Technical and Recreational Services Employees: 9 Aje St, PMB 1064, Yaba, Lagos; tel. (1) 5863722; Sec.-Gen. SYLVESTER EJIOFOR.

National Union of Journalists: Lagos; Pres. LANRE OGUNDIPE; Sec. MOHAMMED KHALID.

National Union of Petroleum Workers and Natural Gas (NUPENG): 9 Jibowu St, off Ikorodu Rd, Yaba, Lagos; tel. (1) 8770277; fax (1) 3425310; e-mail headoffice@nupeng.org; internet nupeng.org; f. 1977; Sec.-Gen. ELIJAH OKOUGBO.

NIGERIA

Nigerian Union of Civil Engineering, Construction, Furniture and Woodworkers: 51 Kano St, Ebute Metta, PMB 1064, Lagos; tel. (1) 5800263.

Nigerian Union of Mine Workers: 95 Enugu St, POB 763, Jos; tel. (73) 52401.

Petroleum and Gas Senior Staff Association of Nigeria (PENGASSAN): U. M. Okoro House, 288 Ikorodu Rd, Anthony, Lagos; tel. (1) 2790715; fax (1) 2790717; e-mail headoffice@pengassan.org; internet www.pengassan.org; f. 1978; Gen. Sec. M. A. OLOWOSHILE.

Transport

RAILWAYS

There are about 3,505 km of mainly narrow-gauge railways. The two principal lines connect Lagos with Nguru and Port Harcourt with Maiduguri.

Nigerian Railway Corpn: PMB 1037, Ebute-Metta, Lagos; tel. (1) 7747320; fax (1) 5831367; e-mail info.nrc@nrc-ng.org; internet www.nrc-ng.org; f. 1955; restructured in 1993 into three separate units: Nigerian Railway Track Authority; Nigerian Railways; and Nigerian Railway Engineering Ltd; Man. Dir MAZI NWANKWO.

ROADS

In 2004 the Nigerian road network totalled 193,200 km, including 15,688 km of highways and 18,719 km of secondary roads; some 9,660 km were paved.

Nigerian Road Federation: Ministry of Transport, National Maritime Agency Bldg, Central Area, Abuja; tel. (9) 5237053.

INLAND WATERWAYS

National Inland Waterways Authority (NIWA): PMB 1004, Adankolo, Lokoja, Kogi State; tel. (58) 2220965; f. 1997; responsible for all navigable waterways; Man. Dir YAKUBU ZUBAIRU.

SHIPPING

The principal ports are the Delta Port complex (including Warri, Koko, Burutu and Sapele ports), Port Harcourt and Calabar; other significant ports are situated at Apapa and Tin Can Island, near Lagos. The main petroleum ports are Bonny and Burutu.

Nigerian Maritime Administration and Safety Agency (NIMASA): f. 2007 following merger of National Maritime Authority and Joint Maritime Labour Industrial Council; Dir-Gen. Dr ADE DOSUNMU.

Nigerian Ports Authority: Olusegun Obasanjo Way, Plot 126, Central Business District, Garki, Abuja; tel. (9) 2347920; fax (9) 2347930; e-mail telnpo@infoweb.abs.net; internet www.nigeria-ports.com; f. 1955; CEO Chief ADEBAYO SARUMI.

Nigerian Green Lines Ltd: Yinka Folawiyo Plaza, 38 Yinka Folawiyo Ave (fmrly Warehouse Rd), Apapa; tel. (1) 5450436; fax (1) 5450204; f. 1972; Yinka Folawiyo Group; 2 vessels totalling 30,751 grt; Chair. Alhaji W. I. FOLAWIYO.

Nigeria Unity Line: Maritime Complex, 34 Creek Rd, PMB 1175, Apapa, Lagos; tel. (1) 5804808; fax (1) 5804807; e-mail nul@hyperia.com; f. 1995 following the dissolution of the Nigerian National Shipping Line; govt-owned; Chair. Chief A. R. DIKIBO.

Association

Nigerian Shippers Council: 4 Park Lane, Apapa, Lagos; tel. (1) 5452307; fax (1) 5452906; e-mail info@shipperscouncil.com; internet www.shipperscouncil.com; CEO Capt. ADAMU A. BIU.

CIVIL AVIATION

The principal international airports are at Lagos (Murtala Mohammed Airport), Kano, Port Harcourt and Abuja. There are also 14 airports for domestic flights.

Federal Airports Authority of Nigeria (FAAN): Murtala Mohammed Airport, PMB 21607, Ikeja, Lagos; tel. (1) 4970335; fax (1) 4970342; e-mail contact@faannigeria.org; internet www.faannigeria.org; Chair. Capt. E. UKEJE; CEO RICHARD AISUEBEOGUN.

Principal Airlines

Arik Air: Murtala Mohammed Airport, POB 10468, Ikeja, Lagos; tel. (1) 2799900; fax Fax : (1) 4975940; e-mail info@arikair.com; internet www.arikair.com; f. 2002; Man. Dir MICHAEL MCTIGHE.

Virgin Nigeria: 3rd Floor Ark Towers Plot 17, Ligali Ayorinde St Victoria Island Extension, Ikeja, Lagos; tel. (1) 4600505; e-mail commercial@virginnigeria.com; internet www.virginnigeria.com; f. Sept. 2004; private flag carrier; 51% owned by Nigerian institutional investors and 49% by Virgin Atlantic; scheduled domestic regional and international services; CEO CONRAD CLIFFORD.

Tourism

Potential attractions for tourists include fine coastal scenery, dense forests, and the rich diversity of Nigeria's arts. A total of 3,055,800 tourists visited Nigeria in 2006. Receipts from tourism amounted to US $51m. in that year.

Nigerian Tourism Development Corpn: Old Federal Secretariat, Area 1, Garki, PMB 167, Abuja; tel. (9) 2342764; fax (9) 2342775; e-mail ntdc@metrong.com; internet www.nigeria.tourism.com; Chair. Prince ADESUYI HAASTRUP; CEO OMOTAYO OMOTOSHO.

NORWAY

Introductory Survey

Location, Climate, Language, Religion, Flag, Capital

The Kingdom of Norway forms the western part of Scandinavia, in northern Europe. It is bordered to the east by Sweden and, within the Arctic Circle, by Finland and Russia. A long, indented coast faces the Atlantic Ocean. Norway exercises sovereignty over the Svalbard archipelago, Jan Mayen island and the uninhabited dependencies of Bouvetøya and Peter I Øy. Dronning Maud Land, in Antarctica, is also a Norwegian dependency. Norway's climate is temperate on the west coast but colder inland. Average temperatures range from −2°C (28°F) to 8°C (46°F). There are two forms of the Norwegian language, which are officially recognized as equal. About 80% of children in schools use the older form, *Bokmål*, as their principal language, whereas only 20% use the newer form, *Nynorsk* (Neo-Norwegian). Lappish is also spoken by the Sámi population, in northern Norway. Almost all of the inhabitants profess Christianity: the Evangelical Lutheran Church is the established religion, with about 81% of the population professing adherence in early 2009. The civil flag (proportions 8 by 11) has a dark blue cross, bordered with white, on a red background, the upright of the cross being to the left of centre; the state flag (16 by 27) displays the same cross, but forms a triple swallow-tail at the fly. The capital is Oslo.

Recent History

Norway, formerly linked to the Swedish crown, declared its independence in 1905. The union with Sweden was peacefully dissolved and the Norwegians elected their own monarch, Prince Karl of Denmark, who took the title of King Håkon VII. He reigned until his death in 1957, and was succeeded by his son, Olav V. Olav's son, Crown Prince Harald (who had acted as regent since May 1990, when his father suffered a stroke), became King Harald V upon Olav's death in January 1991.

During the Second World War Norway was occupied by German forces between 1940 and 1945. Norway abandoned its traditional policy of neutrality after the war, joining the North Atlantic Treaty Organization (NATO, see p. 351) in 1949. Norway was also a founder member of the Nordic Council (see p. 440) in 1952 and of the European Free Trade Association (EFTA, see p. 426) in 1960.

Det norske Arbeiderparti (DnA—Norwegian Labour Party) governed from 1935 to 1965, except for the period of German occupation, when a pro-Nazi 'puppet' regime was administered by Vidkun Quisling, and an interlude of one month in 1963. Norway applied for membership of the European Community (EC, now European Union—EU, see p. 255) in 1962, and again in 1967. A general election to the Storting (parliament) in September 1965 resulted in a defeat for the DnA Government of Einar Gerhardsen, who had been Prime Minister almost continuously since 1955. His administration was replaced in October 1965 by a non-socialist coalition under Per Borten, leader of the Senterpartiet (Sp—Centre Party). However, in March 1971 Borten resigned, following revelations that he had deliberately disclosed confidential details of Norway's negotiations with the EC. He was succeeded by a minority DnA Government, led by Trygve Bratteli. The terms of Norway's entry into the EC were agreed in December 1971, and a preliminary Treaty of Accession was signed in January 1972. In September, however, a consultative referendum on the agreed terms produced a 53.3% majority against entering the EC. The application was withdrawn, and Bratteli resigned in October. A coalition of Venstre (Liberals), the Sp and the Kristelig Folkeparti (KrF—Christian Democrats' Party) formed a new minority Government, with Lars Korvald of the KrF as Prime Minister.

Following the general election of September 1973, Bratteli formed another minority DnA Government, dependent on the support of a socialist alliance known from 1975 as the Socialistisk Venstreparti (SV—Socialist Left Party). In January 1976 Odvar Nordli replaced Bratteli as Prime Minister. Nordli resigned in February 1981, citing reasons of ill health, and was succeeded by Gro Harlem Brundtland. At the general election in September DnA lost support to centre-right groups. In October a minority administration, led by Kåre Willoch, became Norway's first Høyre (Conservative) Government since 1928. In June 1983 a coalition of Høyre with the Sp and the KrF was formed, with 79 of the 165 parliamentary seats. Willoch's Government was returned to power, although lacking an overall majority in the Storting, following the general election in September 1985. In May 1986 Willoch resigned when the Storting narrowly rejected a proposal to increase taxation on petrol. The Norwegian Constitution did not permit a general election before the expiry of the Storting's term (due in 1989). Brundtland accepted an invitation by the King to form a minority DnA administration. The new Government devalued the krone by 12%, and a revised budget was approved by the Storting in June 1986.

At the general election in September 1989 both DnA and Høyre lost support to more radical parties. The SV gained nine seats, to achieve a total of 17 seats. The Fremskrittspartiet (FrP—Progress Party) increased its representation from two to 22 seats, despite attracting allegations of racism during the election campaign. Brundtland's Government resigned in October, following an agreement made by Høyre, the Sp and the KrF to form a coalition. The new Government, led by Jan Syse of Høyre, controlled only 62 seats in the Storting and was dependent upon the support of the FrP. Also in September 1989 the Sámi (Lapps) of northern Norway elected 39 representatives for a new Sameting (Consultative Assembly), to be based in Karasjok. This followed an amendment to the Constitution the previous year, which recognized the Sámi as an indigenous people and an ethnic minority. There was considerable support among the Sámi for a degree of autonomy, in order to protect their traditional way of life. The Sámi had officially ceased to exist by 1900, with their culture and language being declared illegal, but by 2000 they had formed a joint council comprising Sámi populations in Norway, Sweden, Finland and Russia, and received a parliament building, opened in November by King Harald V. The issue of land rights, however, remained unresolved. This was aggravated by the discovery, in 2001, of substantial platinum deposits in Finnmark, an area to which the Sámi laid claim.

While Høyre had supported EC membership since 1988, the Sp remained strongly opposed to it. In October 1990 the Government announced that the Norwegian krone was to be linked to the European Currency Unit (ECU). Later in that month the coalition collapsed, following disagreement between Høyre and the Sp regarding Norwegian demands in the negotiations between EFTA and the EC on the creation of a joint European Economic Area (EEA). In November DnA formed another minority Government, led by Brundtland.

In October 1991 agreement was finally reached on the terms of the EEA treaty, including arrangements whereby EC countries were to be allowed to take extra quotas of fish from Norwegian waters, while Norwegian fish products were to have increased access to EC markets. Many Norwegians remained opposed to membership of the EC, fearing, in particular, that government subsidies to remote rural and coastal communities would no longer be permitted. The EEA treaty was ratified by the Storting in October 1992. (The treaty entered into effect on 1 January 1994.) A proposal by Brundtland to apply for EC membership was endorsed by the Storting in November 1992, and an application was duly submitted.

At the September 1993 general election DnA increased its representation in the Storting, from 63 to 67 seats. The Sp (which opposed EC membership) increased its total from 11 to 32 seats, thereby becoming the second largest party in the Storting, while Høyre won only 28 seats, compared with 37 at the previous election.

Negotiations on Norway's entry to the EU, as the EC had been restyled, were concluded in March 1994. However, at a national referendum held on 27–28 November (shortly after Sweden and Finland had voted to join the Union), 52.4% of voters rejected EU membership. The success of the campaign opposing Norway's entry to the EU was attributed to several factors: in particular, farmers feared the impact of an influx of cheaper agricultural goods from the EU, and fisheries workers feared that fish stocks would be severely depleted if EU boats were granted increased access to Norwegian waters. There was also widespread concern that national sovereignty would be compromised by the transfer to the EU of certain executive responsibilities.

At local elections held in September 1995, DnA received 31% of the votes cast (compared with 37% at the 1993 general election), Høyre obtained 20% and the Sp 12%. The right-wing FrP, which had campaigned for more stringent policies on law and order, also won 12% of the vote, compared with 6% at the general election.

In October 1996 Brundtland resigned as Prime Minister and was succeeded by Thorbjørn Jagland, who had replaced Brundtland as DnA leader in November 1992. Jagland pledged to continue the previous Government's cautious fiscal policy. By the end of the year, however, the Government's credibility had been seriously undermined, after Terje Röd-Larsen, the newly appointed Minister of National Planning, and Grete Faremo, the Minister of Petroleum and Energy, were forced to resign, following, respectively, allegations of financial irregularities and abuse of power.

A general election was conducted on 16 September 1997, at which DnA attracted the largest level of support, winning 35.0% of the votes cast (65 seats), ahead of the FrP with 15.3% (25 seats), Høyre 14.3% (23 seats) and the KrF 13.7% (25 seats). In October Jagland resigned, honouring a pre-election pledge to stand down should DnA fail to secure at least the 36.9% of popular support that it attracted at the 1993 poll. Kjell Magne Bondevik, the parliamentary leader of the KrF, had organized an alliance of the KrF, the Sp and Venstre (with representation totalling 42 seats), and was invited to form a coalition government on that basis. The new Council of State was dominated by the KrF. There was some uncertainty regarding the durability of the Government after the Prime Minister took more than three weeks' leave from his post from the end of August 1998, owing to depression. Bondevik was reported to have been under intense pressure as a result of recent economic instability, largely attributable to the sharp decline in international prices for petroleum; this had notably necessitated the postponement of the introduction of a scheme, promoted by Bondevik, to give financial support to parents choosing to look after children aged between one and two years at home. In November, furthermore, the Government was obliged to abandon proposed tax increases in order to secure the support of the FrP (and thus parliamentary approval) for the 1999 budget. At local elections held in September, electoral support for DnA and the three coalition partners declined further, while the most significant gains were made by the FrP, which campaigned on an anti-immigration platform and received the third largest share of the vote.

On 9 March 2000 Bondevik resigned following his defeat in a confidence motion in the Storting by 81 votes to 71. The vote was called to resolve a dispute over government plans to postpone the construction of gas-fired power plants pending the introduction of new technology to render them pollution-free. Bondevik recommended that Jens Stoltenberg, who had replaced Jagland as leader of DnA in February, be approached to form a single-party minority government. Stoltenberg duly took office as Prime Minister on 17 March. The new Council of State included Jagland as Minister of Foreign Affairs. The new Government pledged to reform the public sector, resume the country's privatization programme, forge stronger links with Europe and continue Norway's role as a mediator in international peace negotiations.

At a general election conducted on 10 September 2001, DnA received only 24.3% of the valid votes cast (its poorest electoral performance since 1909), attaining 43 seats. Høyre secured 21.2% of the votes cast (38 seats), the FrP 14.7% (26 seats), the SV 12.5% (23 seats) and the KrF 12.4% (22 seats). DnA formed a minority Government, but was unable to attract enough political support to hold a majority in the Storting. Stoltenberg consequently resigned on 17 October, and DnA was replaced in government by a minority centre-right coalition comprising Høyre, the KrF and Venstre, with Bondevik as Prime Minister. The coalition gained a majority in the Storting with the informal support of the FrP.

In February 2003 the Government announced its decision to expel Mullah Krekar, the leader of the Kurdish guerrilla organization Ansar al-Islam, who was suspected by both the USA and the UN of having links to terrorism, and possibly to the Islamist al-Qa'ida (Base) organization. However, Krekar, who had stated that he would not leave Norway voluntarily, was not taken into custody or otherwise compelled to leave the country. The following month the Government announced that the case merited further investigation, and that the launch of the US-led military action in Iraq that month posed difficulties for his repatriation, effectively granting Krekar the right to remain in the country for a further two months. A request from Jordan for him to be extradited for drugs offences was also to be investigated. Krekar was eventually detained following an appearance on Dutch television during which he stated that Ansar al-Islam had suicide bombers ready to attack US citizens, but did not remain in custody for long. Krekar was arrested again in December and charged with plotting the murder of his political rivals in Iraq in 2000–01, and was imprisoned in January 2004 while prosecutors investigated the charges against him. Despite the prosecutors' efforts to keep Krekar in custody, he was freed by the Lagmannsrett (Court of Appeal) in February. The charges against Krekar were withdrawn in June owing to insufficient evidence. In 2005 Krekar's expulsion was further delayed pending a guarantee from the Iraqi authorities that he would not face the death penalty. (Norwegian law forbids extradition to countries with the death penalty.) In November 2007 the Høyesterett (Supreme Court) upheld the decision to expel Krekar. However, in April 2008 it was reported that the Government had failed to reach an agreement with the Iraqi authorities over his extradition and that Krekar was to be allowed to remain in Norway indefinitely.

In December 2003 the Storting adopted legislation introducing a minimum quota of 40% for female board members for all publicly owned enterprises and public limited-liability companies in the private sector. The rules applying to publicly owned companies took effect in January 2004, but private companies were given until July 2005 to achieve the desired gender representation voluntarily before the legislation would be enforced. In December 2005 the Government concluded that the gender representation requirements would not be reached on a voluntary basis and approved the entry into force of the legislation as regards public limited-liability companies in the private sector from January 2006. Companies were initially given until the end of 2007 to meet the requirements set by the legislation, but this was subsequently extended to late February 2008. By January 2008 more than 80% of companies had complied with the legislation, giving Norway the highest proportion of female directors in the world, at 36%. Informal gender quotas have operated in Norway since 1981, since when some 40% of government posts have been held by women.

In 2004 Norway introduced transitional rules aimed at limiting (for an initial period of two years) the entry of migrant workers from the eight Central and Eastern European countries that joined the EU on 1 May. While Norway was not itself a member of the EU, it nevertheless had commitments arising from its membership of the EEA and the EU's Schengen Agreement.

Local elections were held on 15 September 2003, at which the participation rate was the lowest since the Second World War. DnA secured the largest share of the vote. The KrF performed particularly poorly, receiving just one-half as much support as it had done at the 2001 general election. The biggest gains were made by the SV and the FrP, which achieved its best result in 30 years. In January 2004 Valgerd Svarstad Haugland resigned as Chairperson of the KrF; however, she retained her post as the Minister of Culture and Church Affairs. The Minister of Health, Dagfinn Høybråten, was unanimously elected to replace her as leader of the KrF. In February Jan Petersen announced his decision to step down as Chairman of Høyre after 10 years in this post, while remaining Minister of Foreign Affairs. Erna Solberg replaced him as party leader in May.

A general election was held on 12 September 2005, at which DnA received 32.7% of the votes cast and won 61 of the 169 seats in the enlarged Storting, thus retaining its position as the largest parliamentary party. DnA contested the election at the head of a centre-left alliance also comprising the SV (which secured 15 seats, with 8.8% of the votes cast) and the Sp (11 seats, with 6.5%). The FrP won 22.1% of the votes cast (38 seats), while Høyre secured 14.1% (23 seats), the KrF 6.8% (11 seats) and Venstre 5.9% (10 seats). Some 77.1% of the electorate participated in the election. DnA, the SV and the Sp subsequently formed the first majority Government since 1985, led by Stoltenberg, which was sworn into office in mid-October. The new coalition Government's programme included proposals to increase welfare spending, raise taxes and eradicate social inequality.

In January 2006 the Government announced that the State Pension Fund would henceforth no longer invest in companies whose activities 'violate fundamental humanitarian principles', including those involved in the production of nuclear weapons. Also in January, a tax was introduced on milk and juice cartons in an attempt to persuade producers and consumers to recycle more of their refuse. The tax was to be removed once recycling levels reached 95%.

The FrP elected its parliamentary leader, Siv Jensen, as party Chairperson in May 2006, replacing Carl Hagen, who had held the post for 28 years. During late 2006 Jensen commenced informal discussions with Høyre regarding co-operation between the two parties prior to the next general election, which was due in September 2009, and the possible formation of a right-wing coalition government thereafter.

In late September 2006 Dag Terje Andersen, of DnA, succeeded party colleague Odd Eriksen as Minister of Trade and Industry. At a DnA party conference held in April 2007, Stoltenberg announced that the Government intended to reduce Norway's emissions of carbon dioxide by 30% (from 1990 levels) by 2020 and to achieve a reduction in emissions world-wide equivalent to 100% of Norwegian emissions by 2050, mainly through a system of trading in emissions with other countries. In January 2008 this date was brought forward to 2030 after the Government reached an agreement with three opposition parties to set a more ambitious target.

In September 2007 Odd Roger Enoksen resigned as Minister of Petroleum and Energy. The appointment of his successor, the leader of the Sp, Aslaug Haga, created Norway's first female-majority government; with 10 of the 19 ministerial positions occupied by women. A minor government reorganization took place in October and included new appointments by the SV, following significant losses for the party in nation-wide local elections in September, which were widely attributed to popular disenchantment with the SV members of the Cabinet. Helen Bjørnøy and Øystein Djupedal, responsible for the environment and education portfolios, respectively, were removed from the Cabinet. In the same reorganization, DnA's Manuela Ramin-Osmundsen, who had previously led the Norwegian Directorate of Immigration, was appointed Minister of Children and Equality. In February 2008, however, Ramin-Osmundsen left the Cabinet, following media allegations of favouritism over her decision to appoint a government lawyer, Ida Hjort Kraby, as children's ombudsman. Stoltenberg, who initially offered his support to Ramin-Osmundsen, announced her dismissal from the Cabinet after it emerged that she had withheld information from the Prime Minister. Ramin-Osmundsen had acknowledged that she knew Hjort Kraby, but denied that they were close friends. However, the media subsequently documented professional and social links between the two women dating back 20 years. She was succeeded later that month by Anniken Huitfeldt. Hjort Kraby subsequently resigned from the post of children's ombudsman.

In June 2008 Haga resigned both as Minister of Petroleum and Energy and as leader of the Sp, citing ill health, following media accusations of tax irregularities in connection with the letting of a holiday home. Stoltenberg subsequently effected a reorganization of the Council of State. The Sp's Terje Riis-Johansen, hitherto Minister of Agriculture and Food, was appointed as Minister of Petroleum and Energy, while Lars Peder Brekk, who had been appointed as interim leader of the Sp, assumed the portfolio formerly held by Riis-Johansen. In September the Minister of Transport and Communications, Liv Signe Navarsete, was elected as leader of the Sp.

In March 1999 the Storting approved compensation valued at US $57.5m. for the country's Holocaust victims and their descendants. The programme was to include compensation for plundered property, as well as funding for contemporary Jewish community projects. In October 2001 a lawsuit was brought against the Norwegian Government by surviving victims of the Nazi *Lebensborn* (Source of Life) project. The survivors, children of German soldiers and Norwegian women, were conceived during the Nazi occupation of Norway in the Second World War as part of a scheme to create a 'master race'. They alleged that, following the liberation of Norway, they and their mothers were subjected to systematic abuse and discrimination, and that the Government not only allowed this abuse to occur, but also attempted to conceal it. The lawsuit was rejected on the grounds that the alleged offences occurred too long ago to be brought to court. However, in late 2002 the Storting's Justice Committee recommended that the Government 'make amends'. In March 2007 the European Court of Human Rights rejected as inadmissible a lawsuit against the Norwegian Government brought by a group of 159 *Lebensborn* survivors.

During 1993 the Norwegian Government was instrumental in conducting secret negotiations between the Israeli Government and the Palestine Liberation Organization (PLO), which led to agreement on Palestinian self-rule in certain areas occupied by Israel. Norway won international acclaim for its role in furthering peace in the Middle East through these negotiations, and continued to be involved in the advancement of the peace process in the late 1990s and first half of the 2000s.

In February 2000 Norway extended its role as an international mediator, agreeing to broker negotiations between the Sri Lankan Government and Tamil separatists in an attempt to end the 17-year conflict. A cease-fire agreement was signed by the two parties in February 2002, supervised by the Norwegian-led Sri Lanka Monitoring Mission (SLMM). However, the SLMM's activities were terminated in January 2008, following an escalation of violence in the country and the Government's withdrawal from the cease-fire agreement.

In April 2001 Norway agreed to host peace negotiations between the Philippine Government and the Philippine dissident communist alliance, the National Democratic Front. These formal negotiations stalled in 2004 and in 2005, and had not resumed by early 2009, although Norway continued to act as a mediator between the two parties. Representatives of both parties held informal discussions in Oslo in November 2008. However, the talks collapsed without agreement owing to the Philippine Government's insistence upon a cease-fire as a precondition for the resumption of formal negotiations.

Norway declared an exclusive economic zone extending to 200 nautical miles (370 km) from its coastline in 1977, and also unilaterally established a fisheries protection zone around its territory of Svalbard. The declaration of an economic zone around Jan Mayen island in 1980 led to agreements with Iceland, in 1980 and 1981, over conflicting claims to fishing and mineral rights. A similar dispute with Denmark, acting for Greenland, was not resolved, and in 1988 Denmark requested arbitration by the International Court of Justice, in The Hague, Netherlands, which gave its judgment on the delimitation of the disputed zones in June 1993 (see under Jan Mayen). During 1994 incidents were reported between vessels of the Norwegian coastguard and Icelandic fishing boats, within the economic zone surrounding the Norwegian island of Spitsbergen (see under Svalbard). In October 2005 Norway detained two Russian vessels that were illegally transferring fish within the same zone.

Following a moratorium on commercial whaling, adopted by the International Whaling Commission (IWC, see p. 418) in 1982 with effect from 1986, Norway continued to hunt small numbers of whales ostensibly for the purpose of scientific research. Norway registered an objection to the moratorium on hunting minke whales, claiming that (according to the findings of the IWC's scientific commission) this species was plentiful enough to allow whaling on a sustainable basis and that many Norwegian coastal communities depended on whaling for their existence. In 1992 the Norwegian Government declared that it would allow the resumption of commercial hunting of minke whales in 1993, as it was not bound by the moratorium, having reserved its position when the ban was introduced. In December 2005 the Norwegian Government announced an increase in its quota for minke whales from 797 in 2005 to 1,052 in 2006, the highest quota since 1993. The narrow approval, at an IWC meeting in June 2006, of a Norwegian-backed resolution for an eventual resumption of commercial whaling provoked strong protests from countries opposed to whaling. Although the vote was not binding, it was considered to represent a further step towards a return for the IWC to a role of setting limits for the capture of whales, rather than one of protection.

In January 2002, following the US-led military campaign against the Taliban and al-Qa'ida militants in Afghanistan in 2001, Norway contributed 180 troops to the International Security Assistance Force (ISAF), deployed in the Afghan capital, Kabul, and at Bagram airbase to help maintain security in the area. In January 2004, at the request of the Loya Jirga (the Afghan Grand Assembly) the Norwegian troops extended their mission in Afghanistan until August of that year. Norway also contributed special forces troops from its Naval Ranger Command and the Norwegian Army's Ranger Command to the US-led operation 'Enduring Freedom', the main aim of which was to combat al-Qa'ida's terrorist network in Afghanistan. In August 2004 the mandate of Norway's ISAF troops in northern Afghanistan was extended indefinitely. In January 2006 Norway withdrew almost all its remaining troops from 'Enduring Freedom' and instead increased its commitment to ISAF. In February 2009

575 Norwegian troops were stationed in Afghanistan. The Government confirmed that there were no plans to increase this number, following the US announcement of the deployment of an additional 17,000 US troops and pleas for NATO allies to expand their commitment to Afghanistan.

In January 2008 the Minister of Foreign Affairs, Jonas Gahr Støre, visited Kabul as part of a Norwegian delegation. During the trip, Taliban militants attacked the hotel in which the delegation was staying, killing six people. Norway subsequently closed its embassy in Kabul; it remained closed in April 2009.

In July 2003 Norway sent 150 soldiers from the Telemark Engineer Squadron to Iraq to help British troops south of Basra repair roads and bridges and to clear land mines, following the success of the US-led military action in removing the regime of Saddam Hussain earlier in the year. Norway had not supported the war, and insisted that its troops were in Iraq as part of a humanitarian 'stabilizing force' mandated by the UN Security Council Resolution 1483, and that they would remain separate from peace-keeping forces dispatched by the USA, the United Kingdom, Denmark and Poland. In December the Storting voted to extend the troops' presence in Iraq by at least six months. Norway withdrew its troops from Iraq in mid-2004. However, a small number of staff officers, who were attached to a Polish brigade, remained until late December 2005.

From 1999 Norway contributed 520 troops to the KFOR peace-keeping mission in Kosovo, consisting of a mechanized infantry battalion and a smaller rapid reaction force that was specially trained in riot control. In 2004 Norway increased its contribution to KFOR, sending four helicopters and support personnel. By January 2009 Norway's contribution had been reduced to 22 troops.

Government

Norway is a constitutional monarchy. Legislative power is held by the Storting (parliament), with 165 members elected for four years by universal adult suffrage, on the basis of proportional representation. For the consideration of legislative proposals, the Storting divides itself into two chambers by choosing one-quarter of its members to form the Lagting (upper house), the remainder forming the Odelsting (lower house). Executive power is nominally held by the monarch, but is, in effect, exercised by the Statsråd (Council of State), led by the Prime Minister. The Council is appointed by the monarch in accordance with the will of the Storting, to which the Council is responsible. Norway comprises 19 counties (*fylker*) and 430 municipalities (*kommuner*).

Defence

Norway is a member of the North Atlantic Treaty Organization (NATO, see p. 351), and became an associate member of Western European Union (WEU, see p. 442) in 1992. Every male is liable for 12 months' national service at the age of 19. Periodical refresher programmes are also compulsory until the age of 44. As assessed at November 2008, the total strength of the armed forces was 21,100 (including 8,375 conscripts): army 7,500 (3,950 conscripts), navy 3,150 (1,250 conscripts), air force 2,700 (1,250 conscripts), home guard 750 (325 conscripts) and central support, administration and command 7,000 (conscripts 1,600). There is also a mobilization reserve of about 45,190 (army 270, navy 320, home guard 44,250 and central support 350). The defence budget for 2008 was projected at 31,500m. kroner.

In November 2004 the European Union (EU, see p. 255) ministers responsible for defence agreed to create a number of 'battlegroups' (each comprising about 1,500 troops), which could be deployed at short notice to crisis areas around the world. The EU battlegroups, two of which were to be ready for deployment at any one time, following a rotational schedule, reached full operational capacity from 1 January 2007. In December 2004 the Storting gave qualified approval for Norway's participation, with Finland and Sweden, in a joint Nordic battlegroup, which was subsequently joined by Estonia and Ireland.

Economic Affairs

In 2007, according to estimates by the World Bank, Norway's gross national income (GNI), measured at average 2005–07 prices, was US $360,036m., equivalent to $76,450 per head (or $53,320 per head on an international purchasing-power parity basis). During 2000–07, it was estimated, the population increased by an average of 0.7% per year, while gross domestic product (GDP) per head increased, in real terms, by an average of 1.8% per year. Norway's overall GDP increased, in real terms, at an average annual rate of 2.5% in 2000–07. Real GDP increased by 2.0% in 2008, according to provisional figures.

The contribution of agriculture (including hunting, forestry and fishing) to GDP in 2007 was estimated at 1.4%. In 2008 the agricultural sector engaged 2.8% of the employed labour force. Around 3.4% of the land surface is cultivated, and the most important branch of the sector is livestock-rearing. Fish farming has been intensively developed by the Government since the early 1970s. The fishing industry provided an estimated 4.4% of total export revenue in 2007. In 2006 Norway produced some 626,400 metric tons of farmed salmon. Agricultural GDP increased at an average annual rate of 3.7% during 2000–06. Agricultural GDP increased by 7.5% in 2008.

Industry (including mining, manufacturing, construction, power and public utilities) contributed an estimated 43.5% of GDP in 2007, and engaged 21.0% of the employed labour force in 2008. During 2000–06 industrial GDP increased, in real terms, at an average annual rate of 0.7%. Industrial GDP (including service activities incidental to the oil and gas sector) increased by 1.4% in 2008.

Mining (including gas and petroleum extraction) provided an estimated 26.1% of GDP in 2007, and engaged 1.5% of the employed labour force in 2004. Extraction of petroleum and natural gas dominates the sector, accounting for 25.9% of GDP in 2007 and 1.7% of employment in 2008. Norway possesses substantial reserves of petroleum and natural gas (exports of petroleum and petroleum products accounted for 43.6% of total export earnings in 2007). Most of the reserves are located off shore. During 1995–2005 the production of crude petroleum from fields on the Norwegian continental shelf decreased at an average annual rate of 0.6%, while output of natural gas grew at an average rate of 11.8% per year, according to the Norwegian Petroleum Directorate. Norway's other mineral reserves include iron ore, iron pyrites, copper, lead and zinc. A large terminal to pump natural gas via a 1,200-km pipeline to the United Kingdom was completed in Aukra, on the island of Gossa, in 2007. In December 2003 the Government announced that it was to open the hitherto unexplored Barents Sea for petroleum and gas extraction; three exploratory wells were drilled in 2004–05. In March 2006 the Government announced that it was to allow further prospecting in the Barents Sea, but that drilling was to be prohibited until 2010 in a 50-km coastal zone (including the Lofoten Islands) in order to protect the environment and fish stocks.

Manufacturing contributed an estimated 9.9% of GDP in 2007, and employed 11.3% of the working population in 2008. In 2006 the most important branches of manufacturing were food products, transport equipment (including ships and oil platforms), metals and metal products, electrical and optical equipment, chemicals and chemical products, and pulp and paper products. During 2000–2006 manufacturing GDP increased, in real terms, by an average of 2.6% per year. Manufacturing GDP increased by 3.0% in 2008.

In 2005, according to provisional figures, some 98.9% of Norway's installed capacity of electric energy was produced by hydroelectric power schemes; domestic energy demands are easily supplied, and Norway has exported hydroelectricity since 1993. Norway's extensive reserves of petroleum and natural gas are mainly exploited for sale to foreign markets, since the domestic market is limited.

The services sector contributed an estimated 55.1% of GDP in 2007, and engaged 76.2% of the employed labour force in the 2008. The GDP of the services sector increased, in real terms, by an average of 2.8% per year during 2000–05; it grew by 3.3% in 2008.

Although shipbuilding has declined since the early 1970s, Norway remains a leading shipping nation. The establishment of the Norwegian International Ship Register in 1987 allowed an expansion of the merchant fleet by more than 300%, in terms of gross tonnage. At 31 December 2007 the combined displacement of the merchant fleet totalled 18.2m. grt, of which the Norwegian International Ship Register accounted for 14.7m. grt.

In 2007, according to IMF figures, Norway recorded a visible trade surplus of US $60,217m., and there was a surplus of $60,459m. on the current account of the balance of payments. In 2007 the EU provided 68.7% of imports and took 81.1% of exports; fellow members of the European Free Trade Association (EFTA, see p. 426) accounted for 1.3% of Norway's imports and 0.9% of exports in the same year. The principal source of imports in 2007 was Sweden (providing 14.6% of the total), followed by Germany (13.6%), the United Kingdom (6.8%) and Denmark

(6.4%); the principal market for exports was the United Kingdom (taking 26.0%), followed by Germany (12.7%), the Netherlands (10.2%) and France (8.5%). In 2007 the principal exports were petroleum and petroleum products (accounting for 43.6% of total exports), natural gas (21.0%), basic manufactures (12.0%, notably aluminium), and machinery and transport equipment (9.1%); the principal imports were machinery and transport equipment (39.8%), basic manufactures (17.0%), miscellaneous manufactured articles (14.3%), and chemicals and related products (8.8%).

In 2008 Norway recorded an overall surplus of 477,500m. kroner in the general budget (equivalent to some 18.8% of GDP in purchasers' values). At the end of 2007 Norway's gross external debt was equivalent to 52.0% of GDP. General government debt was equivalent to 51.0% of GDP in 2007. During 2000–08 the average annual rate of inflation was 1.9%; consumer prices increased by 3.8% in 2008. The rate of unemployment was 3.1% in February 2009, according to official sources.

In addition to its membership of EFTA, Norway is a member of the European Economic Area (EEA), the Nordic Council (see p. 440) and the Nordic Council of Ministers (see p. 440). Although Norway is not a member of the EU, it joined the EU's Schengen Agreement (see p. 285) on the abolition of border controls in May 1999 (Denmark, Finland and Sweden—all EU members—had already joined in 1996) by virtue of its membership in the Nordic passport union.

The Norwegian economy, which is highly dependent on its hydrocarbons sector (Norway is the world's second largest petroleum exporter), experienced a sustained expansion during the 1990s, leading to virtually full employment, as well as rises in real incomes. It maintained a stable exchange rate during this period and a prudent fiscal position, reinvesting a substantial proportion of petroleum revenues abroad through the State Petroleum Fund, partly in preparation for future increased demands on pensions and also to offer a degree of protection to the economy against fluctuations in the petroleum sector. In the first years of the 21st century a strong policy framework underpinned enviable prosperity and a high degree of social equity in Norway. Norway's traditionally high social cohesiveness and solidarity ensured that the use of the petroleum wealth benefited people at all levels of society, and would continue to benefit future generations well after the petroleum itself was depleted. Continued rises in productivity and significant levels of inward migration, notably from Poland and the Baltic states, contributed to low inflation, although rapid employment growth, leading to an increasingly tight labour market, resulted in higher wage growth in 2007. Strong economic expansion during 2004–07, not least because of high international prices for petroleum and gas, led to considerable increases in real disposable income and investment in housing; however, in 2008 the economy slowed, with GDP growth of just 2.0%. The economy was expected to contract by 1.7% in 2009, as it suffered the adverse effects of the global financial crisis. There was a notable fall in exports (by both value and volume), as well as in private consumption, the decline in house prices accelerated and unemployment was expected to reach at least 3.5% in 2009 (from 2.5% in 2008). In January 2009 the Government announced fiscal measures designed to stimulate economic growth, which included a significant increase in public spending, principally on infrastructure projects, as well as reductions in the level of taxation for businesses. The following month the Government further announced the creation of two separate funds to supply credit to financial institutions and small businesses.

Education

Compulsory education begins at six years of age and lasts for 10 years. Elementary education is divided into a four-year lower stage (*barnetrinnet*), for children aged six to 10 years, a three-year intermediate stage (*mellomtrinnet*), for children aged 10 to 13 years, and a three-year upper stage (*ungdomstrinnet*), from the age of 13. A pupil may then transfer to an upper secondary school for a course lasting three years. Primary enrolment in 2006 included 98% of children (males 98%; females 98%) in the relevant age-group, while the comparable ratio for secondary enrolment was 97% (males 96%; females 97%). From the second half of 2002 adults who had not completed compulsory education, or who wished to refresh their competence, were given a statutory right to lower-secondary education. This also applied to special education. With effect from the 2000/01 academic year, everyone had the right to upper-secondary education. Upon completion of a three-year course in general and technical areas of study at an upper secondary school, a pupil may seek admission to one of Norway's four universities or other colleges. From 2000 persons from the age of 25 years had the right to be assessed for admittance to higher education based on non-formal learning. A broader system of higher professional education has been organized on a regional basis, including colleges of education and technology. At 1 October 2006 86,366 students were enrolled at universities and their equivalent. Expenditure on education by all levels of government in 2008 was estimated at 127,190m. kroner (equivalent to 13.3% of total government expenditure).

Public Holidays

2009: 1 January (New Year's Day), 9 April (Maundy Thursday), 10 April (Good Friday), 13 April (Easter Monday), 1 May (Labour Day), 17 May (Constitution Day), 21 May (Ascension Day), 1 June (Whit Monday), 25–26 December (Christmas).

2010: 1 January (New Year's Day), 1 April (Maundy Thursday), 2 April (Good Friday), 5 April (Easter Monday), 1 May (Labour Day), 13 May (Ascension Day), 17 May (Constitution Day), 24 May (Whit Monday), 25–26 December (Christmas).

Weights and Measures

The metric system is in force.

NORWAY

Statistical Survey

Sources (unless otherwise stated): Statistics Norway, Kongensgt. 6, Oslo; tel. 21-09-00-00; fax 21-09-49-73; e-mail biblioteket@ssb.no; internet www.ssb.no; Nordic Statistical Secretariat (Copenhagen), *Yearbook of Nordic Statistics*.

Area and Population

AREA, POPULATION AND DENSITY

Area (sq km)
Land	304,280
Inland water	19,522
Total	323,802*

Population (census results)
3 November 1990	4,247,546
3 November 2001	
Males	2,240,281
Females	2,280,666
Total	4,520,947

Population (official estimates at 1 January)
2007	4,681,134
2008	4,737,171
2009	4,799,252
Density (per sq km) at 1 January 2009†	15.8

* 125,020 sq miles.
† Excluding inland water.

COUNTIES
(1 January 2009)

	Land area (sq km)*	Population†	Density (per sq km)
Østfold	3,887	268,584	69.1
Akershus	4,579	527,625	115.2
Oslo	426	575,475	1,350.9
Hedmark	26,082	190,071	7.3
Oppland	23,787	184,288	7.7
Buskerud	13,797	254,634	18.5
Vestfold	2,147	229,134	106.7
Telemark	13,854	167,548	12.1
Aust-Agder	8,312	107,359	12.9
Vest-Agder	6,677	168,233	25.2
Rogaland	8,590	420,574	49.0
Hordaland	14,551	469,681	32.3
Sogn og Fjordane	17,680	106,457	6.0
Møre og Romsdal	14,590	248,727	17.0
Sør-Trøndelag	17,830	286,729	16.1
Nord-Trøndelag	20,777	130,708	6.3
Nordland	36,074	235,380	6.5
Troms	24,884	155,553	6.3
Finnmark	45,757	72,492	1.6
Total	304,280	4,799,252	15.8

* Excluding inland waters, totalling 19,522 sq km.
† Estimates.

PRINCIPAL TOWNS
(estimated population of urban settlements at 1 January 2008)

Oslo (capital)	560,484	Bodø	46,049
Bergen	247,746	Sandefjord	42,333
Stavanger/Sandnes*	181,623	Ålesund	41,833
Trondheim	165,191	Larvik	41,723
Fredrikstad/ Sarpsborg*	123,029	Arendal	40,701
Porsgrunn/Skien*	85,050	Tønsberg	38,393
Kristiansand	78,919	Haugesund	32,956
Tromsø	65,286	Moss	29,073
Drammen	60,145	Hamar	27,976

* From 1 January 1999 continuous urban settlements are merged to one settlement.

BIRTHS, MARRIAGES AND DEATHS

	Registered live births		Registered marriages*		Registered deaths†	
	Number	Rate (per 1,000)	Number	Rate (per 1,000)	Number	Rate (per 1,000)
2000	59,234	13.2	25,356	5.6	44,002	9.8
2001	56,696	12.6	22,967	5.1	43,981	9.7
2002	55,434	12.3	24,069	5.3	44,465	9.8
2003	56,458	12.4	22,361	4.9	42,478	9.3
2004	56,951	12.4	22,354	4.9	41,200	9.0
2005	56,756	12.3	22,392	4.9	41,232	8.9
2006	58,545	12.6	21,721	4.7	41,253	8.9
2007	58,459	12.5	23,471	5.0	41,954	9.0

* Where bridegroom is resident in Norway.
† Including deaths of residents temporarily abroad.

Life expectancy (years at birth, WHO estimates): 80.5 (males 78.1; females 82.7) in 2006 (Source: WHO, *World Health Statistics*).

IMMIGRATION AND EMIGRATION

	2005	2006	2007
Immigrants	40,148	45,776	61,774
Emigrants	21,709	22,053	22,122

ECONOMICALLY ACTIVE POPULATION
('000 persons aged 16 to 74 years)*

	2006	2007	2008
Agriculture, fishing and forestry	75	70	70
Oil and gas extraction, etc.	31	35	42
Manufacturing and other mining	273	282	286
Electricity, gas and water	16	17	18
Construction	167	180	183
Trade, restaurants and hotels	419	425	430
Transport and communications	156	158	156
Financing, insurance, real estate and business services	311	324	345
Public administration and defence	142	154	162
Education	193	215	220
Health and social work	469	476	502
Other services	100	108	109
Total employed	2,354	2,443	2,524
Unemployed	85	63	66
Total labour force	2,439	2,506	2,590
Males	1,292	1,323	n.a.
Females	1,147	1,183	n.a.

* Figures are annual averages, based on quarterly sample surveys.

Health and Welfare

KEY INDICATORS

Total fertility rate (children per woman, 2006)	1.8
Under-5 mortality rate (per 1,000 live births, 2006)	4
HIV/AIDS (% of persons aged 15–49, 2007)	0.1
Physicians (per 1,000 head, 2006)	3.8
Hospital beds (per 1,000 head, 2006)	4.1
Health expenditure (2006): US $ per head (PPP)	4,521
Health expenditure (2006): % of GDP	8.7
Health expenditure (2006): public (% of total)	83.6
Human Development Index (2006): ranking	2
Human Development Index (2006): value	0.968

For sources and definitions, see explanatory note on p. vi.

Agriculture

PRINCIPAL CROPS
('000 metric tons)*

	2005	2006	2007†
Wheat	395.4	389.7	380.0
Barley	589.3	552.4	580.0
Rye	34.8	28.4	30.0
Oats	279.0	258.4	260.0
Potatoes	316.6	376.0	380.0
Rapeseed	11.2	10.7	12.0
Cabbages and other brassicas	33.5	31.9	30.0
Tomatoes	13.3	11.7	12.0
Cucumbers and gherkins	13.3	13.7	13.5
Onions and shallots, green	19.1	19.1	20.0
Carrots and turnips	44.7	40.9	40.0
Apples	10.9	15.0	15.0

* Figures refer to holdings with at least 0.5 ha of agricultural area in use.
† FAO estimates.

Aggregate production ('000 metric tons, may include official, semi-official or estimated data): Total cereals 1,298 in 2005, 1,229 in 2006, 1,250 in 2007; Total roots and tubers 317 in 2005, 376 in 2006, 380 in 2007; Total vegetables (incl. melons) 184 in 2005, 167 in 2006, 169 in 2007; Total fruits (excl. melons) 26 in 2005, 30 in 2006, 30 in 2007.

Source: FAO.

LIVESTOCK
('000 head)*

	2005	2006	2007†
Horses	30.0	31.0	30.5
Cattle	933.7	920.4	930.0
Sheep	2,423.0	2,356.2	2,400.0
Goats	73.1	72.5	73.0
Pigs	824.2	827.5	830.0
Chickens	3,415	3,316	3,350

* Figures refer to holdings with at least 0.5 ha of agricultural area in use.
† FAO estimates.

Source: FAO.

LIVESTOCK PRODUCTS
('000 metric tons)

	2005	2006	2007†
Cattle meat	87.4	87.6	88.0
Sheep meat	26.0	25.2	26.0
Pig meat	112.8	116.3	120.0
Chicken meat	49.9	55.3	55.0
Cows' milk	1,565.7	1,553.5	1,550.0
Goats' milk	22.5	21.2	22.0
Hen eggs	50.7	50.5	50.5
Honey	1.5	1.3	1.3
Wool, greasy	5.1	4.9	5.0

* FAO estimates.
Source: FAO.

Forestry

ROUNDWOOD REMOVALS
('000 cubic metres, excl. bark)

	2005	2006	2007
Sawlogs, veneer logs and logs for sleepers	4,850	3,719	4,353
Pulpwood	3,615	3,538	3,830
Other industrial wood	25	26	29
Fuel wood	1,177	2,511	2,253
Total	9,667	9,794	10,465

Source: FAO.

SAWNWOOD PRODUCTION
('000 cubic metres, incl. railway sleepers)

	2005	2006	2007
Coniferous (softwood)	2,300	2,361	2,374
Broadleaved (hardwood)	26	28	28
Total	2,326	2,389	2,402

Source: FAO.

Fishing

('000 metric tons, live weight)

	2004	2005	2006
Capture	2,524.5	2,393.0	2,255.5
Atlantic cod	230.7	226.0	220.8
Saithe (Pollock)	211.3	230.7	256.8
Blue whiting (Poutassou)	958.8	738.6	642.5
Sandeels (Sandlances)	48.7	17.3	5.8
Capelin	49.1	67.3	2.0
Atlantic herring	616.2	748.1	710.6
Atlantic mackerel	157.4	119.7	122.0
Aquaculture	636.8	661.8	708.8
Atlantic salmon	563.8	586.5	626.4
Total catch	3,161.3	3,054.8	2,964.3

* FAO estimate.

Note: Figures exclude aquatic plants ('000 metric tons, wet weight, capture): 148.3 in 2004; 153.9 in 2005; 145.4 in 2006. Also excluded are aquatic mammals, recorded by number rather than by weight. The number of minke whales caught was: 544 in 2004; 639 in 2005; 545 in 2006. The number of harp seals caught was: 9,895 in 2004; 17,771 in 2005; 13,390 in 2006. The number of hooded seals caught was: 4,851 in 2004; 3,826 in 2005; 3.647 in 2006.

Source: FAO.

Mining

('000 metric tons, unless otherwise indicated, estimates)

	2004	2005	2006†
Coal (all grades)	300	300	300
Crude petroleum (million barrels)	1,024	964	1,017
Iron ore*	408	420†	400

* Metal content of ore.
† Estimate(s).
Source: US Geological Survey.

Natural gas (million cu m, excl. flared or recycled): 78,465 in 2004; 84,963 in 2005; 87,613 in 2006; 89,682 in 2007 (Source: BP, *Statistical Review of World Energy 2008*).

NORWAY

Industry

SELECTED PRODUCTS
('000 metric tons, unless otherwise indicated)

	2004	2005	2006
Margarine	43.6	42.4	n.a.
Mechanical wood pulp (dry weight)*	1,783	1,684	1,536
Chemical wood pulp (dry weight)*	563	597	600
Particle board ('000 cu m)*	383	366	382
Paper and paperboard*	2,294	2,223	2,109
Kerosene ('000 barrels)	4,774	5,771	5,800†
Naphthas ('000 barrels)	8,741	10,017	10,000†
Gas-diesel (distillate fuel) oil ('000 barrels)	45,765	50,121	50,000†
Residual fuel oil ('000 barrels)	13,823	11,806	12,000†
Cement	1,870	1,900	1,850†
Ferro-silicon (75% basis)	300	165	80†
Other ferro-alloys	15	60	60†
Crude steel	695	701	679†
Nickel (refined): primary	71.4	84.9	82.0†
Copper (refined): primary and secondary	36	39	40†
Aluminium (refined): primary	1,321.7	1,376.5	1,422.0†
Aluminium (refined): secondary	348.7	362.4	349.2†
Zinc (refined): primary	140.9	151.3	160.7†
Electric energy (million kWh)	110,598	138,108	n.a.

* Source: FAO.
† Estimated or unofficial figure.

Sources (unless otherwise indicated): UN, *Industrial Commodity Statistics Yearbook*; US Geological Survey.

Finance

CURRENCY AND EXCHANGE RATES

Monetary Units
100 øre = 1 Norwegian krone (plural: kroner).

Sterling, Dollar and Euro Equivalents (31 December 2008)
£1 sterling = 10.205 kroner;
US $1 = 7.0000 kroner;
€1 = 9.7419 kroner;
100 Norwegian kroner = £9.80 = $14.29 = €10.26.

Average Exchange Rate (kroner per US $)
2006   6.4133
2007   5.8614
2008   5.6400

GENERAL BUDGET
(million kroner)

Revenue	2005	2006	2007
Taxation*	845,680	948,622	982,570
Taxes on income, profits and wealth*	433,589	493,950	492,636
Social security contributions	173,846	189,223	206,032
Value-added tax and investment levy	153,138	172,066	187,203
Property income	204,650	261,453	271,835
Interest	61,296	80,185	95,564
Other current transfers	8,315	8,553	9,644
Other transfers	6,904	6,866	7,821
Operating surplus	1,068	696	892
Capital transfers*	1,768	2,063	2,576
Total	1,061,482	1,221,386	1,267,516

Expenditure†	2005	2006	2007
General public services	77,903	90,805	93,116
Defence	28,720	32,665	34,940
Public order and safety	15,069	16,165	17,203
Economic affairs	68,044	70,455	73,935
Environmental protection	3,610	3,956	4,149
Housing and community amenities	3,887	4,646	4,983
Health	132,897	140,618	151,904
Recreation, culture and religion	19,076	20,195	22,626
Education	107,306	113,546	120,180
Social protection	311,426	329,425	348,435
Total	767,938	822,476	871,471
Current	748,302	798,029	843,376
Capital	19,636	24,448	28,095

* Inheritance and gift taxes are excluded from tax revenue and are treated as capital transfers.
† Excluding lending minus repayments.

2008 ('000 million kroner): Total revenue 1,434.9; Total expenditure 957.4.

INTERNATIONAL RESERVES
(excluding gold, US $ million at 31 December)

	2006	2007	2008
IMF special drawing rights	453.2	367.5	436.6
Reserve position in IMF	207.0	178.0	299.1
Foreign exchange	56,181.4	60,294.1	50,223.6
Total	56,841.6	60,839.6	50,959.4

Source: IMF, *International Financial Statistics*.

MONEY SUPPLY
(million kroner at 31 December)

	2001	2002	2003
Currency outside banks	42,100	40,410	41,687
Demand deposits at commercial and savings banks	616,023	671,850	706,246
Total money (incl. others)	658,123	712,260	747,933

Demand deposits at commercial and savings banks (million kroner at 31 December): 700,074 in 2004; 791,120 in 2005; 923,210 in 2006.

Source: IMF, *International Financial Statistics*.

COST OF LIVING
(Consumer Price Index; base: 1998 = 100)

	2004	2005	2006
Food	106.4	108.0	109.6
Alcoholic beverages and tobacco	123.6	126.7	129.1
Housing, fuel and power	130.0	132.2	140.2
Clothing and footwear	74.1	70.7	68.2
Furnishings and household equipment	100.4	100.0	98.5
Health	126.3	129.8	134.4
Transport	115.8	120.8	124.8
Communications	82.8	82.2	83.3
Recreation and culture	105.7	106.5	107.0
Education	141.5	143.4	146.6
Restaurants and hotels	122.3	124.3	128.3
Other goods and services	119.9	122.1	120.9
All items (incl. others)	113.3	115.1	117.7

2007: All items 118.6.
2008: All items 123.1.

NORWAY

Statistical Survey

NATIONAL ACCOUNTS
(million kroner at current prices)

National Income and Product

	2005	2006*	2007*
Compensation of employees	810,715	882,807	972,634
Operating surplus	705,199	803,718	800,702
Domestic factor incomes	1,515,914	1,686,525	1,773,336
Consumption of fixed capital	247,889	269,502	293,045
Gross domestic product (GDP) at factor cost	1,763,803	1,956,027	2,066,381
Indirect taxes	213,768	238,196	254,167
Less Subsidies	31,855	32,494	31,855
GDP in purchasers' values	1,945,716	2,161,729	2,288,693
Net factor income from abroad	13,450	−5,447	9,851
Gross national product (GNP)	1,959,166	2,156,282	2,298,544
Less Consumption of fixed capital	247,889	269,502	293,045
National income in market prices	1,711,277	1,886,780	2,005,499
Other current transfers abroad (net)	−17,157	−14,541	−14,948
National disposable income	1,694,121	1,872,239	1,990,551

* Provisional.

Expenditure on the Gross Domestic Product

	2005	2006*	2007*
Government final consumption expenditure	387,186	415,377	447,067
Private final consumption expenditure	826,215	883,221	946,374
Increase in stocks	46,461	60,650	43,727
Gross fixed capital formation	365,564	409,130	474,289
Total domestic expenditure	1,625,426	1,768,378	1,911,457
Exports of goods and services	868,352	1,005,483	1,062,715
Less Imports of goods and services	548,062	612,133	685,479
GDP in purchasers' values	1,945,716	2,161,728	2,288,693
GDP at constant 2005 prices	1,945,716	1,994,924	2,065,062

* Provisional.

Gross Domestic Product by Economic Activity

	2005	2006*	2007*
Agriculture, hunting and forestry	13,961	13,518	15,332
Fishing and fish farming	12,593	15,053	13,265
Petroleum and gas extraction	447,660	537,050	527,109
Other mining and quarrying	3,720	3,850	4,752
Manufacturing	169,563	186,009	200,942
Electricity, gas and water	44,685	52,972	48,631
Construction	76,802	87,767	104,020
Wholesale and retail trade; repair of motor vehicles	140,952	148,673	163,901
Hotels and restaurants	22,262	24,108	27,871
Transport, storage and communications†	133,524	139,017	146,690
Financing, insurance, real estate and business services	235,861	259,923	294,793
Private services in households	74,284	76,781	75,409
Public administration and defence	76,051	82,346	89,502
Education	76,456	80,183	84,996
Health and social work	149,122	159,994	176,099
Other social and personal services	54,452	58,970	63,241
Sub-total	1,731,948	1,926,212	2,036,555
Value-added tax and investment levy	153,138	172,065	187,203
Other taxes on products (net)	60,630	66,131	66,964
Statistical discrepancy	—	−2,681	−2,029
GDP in purchasers' values	1,945,716	2,161,728	2,288,693

* Figures are provisional.
† Including transportation of petroleum and gas by pipeline.

BALANCE OF PAYMENTS
(US $ million)

	2005	2006	2007
Exports of goods f.o.b.	104,011	122,789	137,297
Imports of goods f.o.b.	−55,094	−62,933	−77,026
Trade balance	48,917	59,856	60,271
Exports of services	29,928	33,328	40,592
Imports of services	−29,182	−31,957	−39,758
Balance on goods and services	49,664	61,227	61,105
Other income received	24,557	30,988	39,273
Other income paid	−22,586	−31,610	−37,272
Balance on goods, services and income	51,635	60,606	63,106
Current transfers received	3,458	3,304	3,554
Current transfers paid	−6,090	−5,587	−6,201
Current balance	49,003	58,323	60,459
Capital account (net)	−290	−146	−163
Direct investment abroad	−21,823	−21,170	−12,500
Direct investment from abroad	5,209	6,617	3,788
Portfolio investment assets	−38,107	−113,451	−68,808
Portfolio investment liabilities	32,321	39,463	44,283
Other investment assets	−38,085	−29,143	−47,671
Other investment liabilities	21,791	78,994	50,243
Net errors and omissions	−5,508	−14,012	−28,586
Overall balance	4,511	5,475	1,045

Source: IMF, *International Financial Statistics*.

OFFICIAL ASSISTANCE TO DEVELOPING COUNTRIES
(million kroner)

	2001	2002	2003
Bilateral assistance	7,901	8,493	9,646
Technical assistance	1,140	1,551	1,878
Investments	532	412	378
Sector-related project and programme aid	3,510	3,496	3,310
Non-sector related project and programme aid	2,357	3,132	3,983
Associated financing	9	69	—
Loan assistance	—	—	—
Norfund	61	57	96
Multilateral assistance	3,374	4,400	4,107
Contributions to multilateral organizations	273	—	—
Humanitarian relief work	273	—	—
Administration	595	652	704
Total official development assistance	11,870	13,545	14,457

2004 (million kroner): Bilateral assistance 6,932; Multilateral-bilateral assistance 2,629; Multilateral assistance 4,463; Administration 793; Total official development assistance 14,817.

2005 (million kroner): Bilateral assistance 7,850; Multilateral-bilateral assistance 4,053; Multilateral assistance 5,157; Administration 885; Total official development assistance 17,946.

2006 (million kroner): Bilateral assistance 8,487; Multilateral-bilateral assistance 4,127; Multilateral assistance 5,283; Administration 1,053; Total official development assistance 18,950.

2007 (million kroner, provisional figures): Bilateral assistance 10,338; Multilateral-bilateral assistance 5,436; Multilateral assistance 4,968; Administration 1,098; Total official development assistance 21,840.

External Trade

(Note: Figures include all ships bought and sold but exclude trade in military supplies under defence agreements.)

PRINCIPAL COMMODITIES
(distribution by SITC, million kroner)

Imports c.i.f.*	2005	2006	2007
Food and live animals	18,292	20,811	24,280
Crude materials (inedible) except fuels	27,178	31,208	42,582
Metalliferous ores and metal scrap	17,544	21,952	31,837
Mineral fuels, lubricants, etc. (incl. electric current)	15,441	19,203	20,301
Petroleum, petroleum products, etc.	12,960	14,110	17,061
Chemicals and related products	34,497	38,466	41,463
Basic manufactures	61,372	70,084	79,728
Metal manufactures	13,741	17,562	20,195
Machinery and transport equipment	141,206	165,130	186,650
Machinery specialized for particular industries	13,814	18,203	19,762
General industrial machinery, equipment and parts	20,762	21,372	24,890
Office machines and automatic data-processing equipment	15,926	16,734	16,420
Telecommunications and sound equipment	14,119	16,771	18,956
Other electrical machinery, apparatus, etc.	17,548	20,897	24,226
Road vehicles and parts†	37,061	41,845	47,998
Other transport equipment†	13,877	18,564	22,583
Miscellaneous manufactured articles	54,355	61,035	67,120
Clothing and accessories (excl. footwear)	11,900	12,662	13,358
Total (incl. others)	357,656	411,684	468,633

* Equipment imported directly to the Norwegian sector of the continental shelf is excluded.
† Excluding tyres, engines and electrical parts.

Exports f.o.b.	2005	2006	2007
Food and live animals	33,903	37,470	38,697
Fish and fish preparations*	31,257	34,667	35,919
Mineral fuels, lubricants, etc. (incl. electric current)	453,643	531,930	531,237
Petroleum, petroleum products, etc.	331,950	362,976	355,131
Gas (natural and manufactured)	117,117	164,401	171,182
Chemicals and related products	31,747	35,282	39,925
Basic manufactures	68,271	83,365	97,963
Non-ferrous metals	36,876	51,949	61,858
Machinery and transport equipment	55,571	66,291	74,028
Miscellaneous manufactured articles	15,369	17,230	19,611
Total (incl. others)	668,760	782,950	813,600

* Including crustaceans and molluscs.

PRINCIPAL TRADING PARTNERS
(million kroner)

Imports c.i.f.	2005	2006	2007
Belgium	9,155.6	9,523.6	9,670.0
Canada	9,088.1	11,074.7	20,433.5
China, People's Repub.	20,040.1	23,467.2	28,313.2
Denmark	26,166.7	28,378.9	30,020.5
Finland	11,254.1	13,171.6	17,203.5
France	14,192.6	16,202.3	17,007.7
Germany	48,040.3	55,368.2	63,571.2
Ireland	5,721.1	5,740.1	5,559.5
Italy	11,743.8	13,981.9	15,424.7
Japan	11,325.4	11,076.5	10,342.3
Korea, Republic	3,670.7	6,045.1	4,334.6
Netherlands	14,124.6	16,788.4	17,409.5
Poland	6,175.1	8,134.1	9,751.9
Russia	8,298.9	9,992.2	11,459.5
Spain	8,120.1	9,282.6	10,121.3
Sweden	51,546.8	61,707.0	68,572.2
Switzerland	3,676.9	4,486.8	4,963.9
Taiwan	3,390.8	3,806.8	4,242.8
United Kingdom	25,991.8	26,357.3	32,075.9
USA	17,983.2	21,878.1	22,374.2
Total (incl. others)	357,656.5	411,683.6	468,663.4

Exports f.o.b.	2005	2006	2007
Belgium	16,465.2	19,639.3	20,328.7
Canada	25,256.9	24,256.2	23,279.6
China, People's Repub.	5,854.2	10,948.9	9,492.6
Denmark	23,715.2	27,481.4	25,578.0
Finland	8,470.3	12,182.2	9,948.4
France	62,091.3	64,609.1	69,248.0
Germany	84,301.6	96,385.4	103,401.4
Ireland	11,938.2	13,830.0	12,835.3
Italy	19,086.8	24,682.2	23,796.0
Japan	6,555.7	7,650.3	7,703.2
Korea, Republic	5,084.9	4,740.8	7,132.6
Netherlands	66,446.1	80,383.9	83,052.4
Spain	16,152.1	16,941.2	18,607.1
Sweden	43,575.4	50,292.6	51,954.1
United Kingdom	167,490.7	209,483.1	211,504.4
USA	43,806.7	44,750.3	49,686.5
Total (incl. others)	668,759.5	782,949.9	813,600.1

Transport

STATE RAILWAYS
(traffic)

	1999	2000	2001
Passengers carried ('000)	50,019	50,773	49,396
Goods carried ('000 metric tons)	8,229	7,959	8,190
Passenger-km (million)	2,668	2,635	2,536
Freight ton-km (million)	2,456	2,399	2,451

2002: Passenger-km (million) 2,543; Net ton-km (million) 3,019 (Source: UN, *Statistical Yearbook*).
2003: Passenger-km (million) 2,474; Net ton-km (million) 2,627 (Source: UN, *Statistical Yearbook*).
2004: Passenger-km (million) 2,657; Net ton-km (million) 2,804 (Source: UN, *Statistical Yearbook*).

NORWAY

ROAD TRAFFIC
(motor vehicles registered at 31 December)

	2005	2006	2007
Passenger cars (incl. station wagons and ambulances)	2,028,909	2,084,193	2,154,837
Buses	28,783	26,954	25,205
Vans	302,956	331,052	361,911
Combined vehicles	79,705	73,904	67,020
Goods vehicles, etc.	82,778	83,609	84,742
Tractors	231,630	234,243	237,484
Special purpose vehicles	8,361	8,255	8,208
Motorcycles	109,338	116,875	126,207
Snow scooters	55,776	58,327	61,145
Mopeds	148,161	151,670	156,287

SHIPPING

Merchant Fleet
(registered at 31 December)

	2005	2006	2007
Number of vessels	2,068	2,078	2,088
Total displacement ('000 grt)	17,531.9	18,222.3	18,156.0

Note: Figures include vessels on the Norwegian International Ship Register.
Source: Lloyd's Register-Fairplay, *World Fleet Statistics*.

International Sea-borne Freight Traffic*
('000 metric tons)

	1998	1999	2000
Goods loaded	154,116	151,116	160,080
Goods unloaded	27,264	25,788	23,400

* Figures exclude transit traffic (other than Swedish iron ore), packing and re-export.

Source: UN, *Monthly Bulletin of Statistics*.

CIVIL AVIATION
(traffic on scheduled services)*

	2002	2003	2004
Kilometres flown (million)	129	127	128
Passengers carried ('000)	13,699	12,806	12,277
Passenger-km (million)	10,546	10,506	10,321
Total ton-km (million)	1,231	1,211	1,199

* Including an apportionment (2/7) of the international services of Scandinavian Airlines System (SAS), operated jointly with Denmark and Sweden.

Source: UN, *Statistical Yearbook*.

Tourism

VISITOR ARRIVALS BY COUNTRY OF ORIGIN*

	2004	2005	2006
Denmark	640,198	619,111	587,565
Finland	60,602	62,168	67,295
France	216,437	210,224	205,741
Germany	738,372	810,092	746,031
Italy	146,398	141,938	163,982
Japan	123,364	124,710	122,132
Netherlands	291,182	296,252	285,178
Spain	177,292	197,514	243,163
Sweden	503,087	531,157	526,764
United Kingdom	577,751	602,449	651,545
USA	320,953	316,340	316,954
Total (incl. others)	4,596,218	4,761,074	4,914,019

* Non-residents staying in all types of accommodation establishments.

Tourism receipts (US $ million, incl. passenger transport): 3,531 in 2004; 3,959 in 2005; 4,251 in 2006.

Source: World Tourism Organization.

Communications Media

	2005	2006	2007
Telephones ('000 main lines in use)	2,129	2,055	1,988
Mobile cellular telephones ('000 subscribers)	4,754.5	5,007.7	5,191.6
Personal computers ('000 in use)	2,630	n.a.	n.a.
Internet users ('000)	2,702	3,792	1,800
Broadband subscribers ('000)	991.3	1,278.3	1,436.1

Source: International Telecommunication Union.

Television receivers (2000): 3,000,000 in use.
Radio receivers (1997): 4,030,000 in use*.
Books published (1999): 4,985 titles†.
Daily newspapers (2002): 61; net circulation ('000 copies) 2,201‡.

* Source: UNESCO, *Statistical Yearbook*.
† Source: UN, *Statistical Yearbook*.
‡ Issued at least 6 times a week.

Education
(incl. Svalbard, 1 October 2003)

	Institutions	Teachers*	Students
Pre-primary	5,924	58,422†	205,172
Primary and lower secondary	3,209	65,376	617,577
Upper secondary	462	26,618	218,089
Colleges of higher education	59	6,313	130,148
Universities and their equivalent	11	9,553	79,611

* Full-time.
† Of the total, 19,422 were trained as pre-school teachers.

Directory

The Constitution

The Constitution was promulgated on 17 May 1814.

According to the Constitution, Norway is a 'free, independent, indivisible, inalienable Realm'; its form of government a 'limited and hereditary monarchy'. (In May 1990 the law of succession, which stipulated that a male heir should have precedence in succeeding to the throne, was amended to permit men and women an equal right to the throne. The previous law would still apply to those born before 1990.) The Evangelical Lutheran Church is the established religion of the State.

Executive power is vested in the monarch, legislative power in the Storting (parliament), and judicial power in the Judicature.

EXECUTIVE POWER

The monarch exercises power through the Statsråd (Council of State). The Statsråd is composed of a Prime Minister and not fewer than seven other Councillors of State, more than one-half of whom must profess the established religion. The business to be dealt with in the Statsråd is prepared by the various executive Ministries, each with a Councillor of State at its head. These executive departments conduct the administrative work of the country.

The Government submits the budget estimates and introduces bills in the Storting.

Formally, the monarch appoints the Government, but since the introduction of the parliamentary system in 1884 it is the practice for the monarch to act in accordance with the will of the Storting.

LEGISLATIVE POWER

The Storting is elected quadrennially by universal suffrage. All Norwegian citizens aged 18 years and over are eligible to vote and every qualified voter who has resided in Norway for at least 10 years is eligible to stand for election. In 2005 the Storting was expanded from 165 seats to 169, 150 of which are elected directly, with the remaining 19 (one for each constituency) being allocated by proportional representation among parties receiving a minimum of 4% of the votes cast. The members of the Storting elect one-quarter of their own body to constitute the Lagting (upper house); the other three-quarters compose the Odelsting (lower house). All bills must first be introduced in the Odelsting, either by the Government through a Councillor of State or by a member of the Odelsting. Should the bill be approved by the Odelsting, it is sent to the Lagting, which may adopt it or return it with amendments. If a bill is approved twice by the Odelsting and rejected on both occasions by the Lagting, it is submitted to the entire Storting and decided by a two-thirds majority. When a bill has thus been approved, it must receive royal assent in the Statsråd.

Bills for the revision of the Constitution must be introduced in the first, second or third session after a new election. However, only the Storting, after the next election, has the power to decide whether the proposed alteration should be adopted. Bills relating to the Constitution are dealt with only by the united Storting. For the adoption of a bill of this nature, a two-thirds majority is required, and the measure becomes law without royal assent.

The Storting votes all state expenditure and determines state revenue, taxes, customs tariffs and other duties; the Odelsting exercises control over government administration, government appointments and so forth.

The Storting prepares its business through its committees and settles such business, with the exception of bills, in plenum. The Councillors of State may attend the Storting, having the right of speech, but not of voting.

The Storting determines the duration of each session. It is opened and prorogued by the monarch each year. The Storting cannot be dissolved either by the monarch or by its own resolution until the expiry of the quadrennial period for which it has been elected.

Note: In September 1989 the Sámi (Lapps) of northern Norway elected 39 representatives to a new Sameting (Consultative Assembly). The Sameting is elected quadrennially and is based in the town of Karasjok, in Finnmark.

The Government

HEAD OF STATE

Sovereign: HM King HARALD V (succeeded to the throne 17 January 1991; sworn in 21 January 1991).

COUNCIL OF STATE
(Statsråd)
(April 2009)

A majority Government, comprising Det norske Arbeiderparti (DnA), the Sosialistisk Venstreparti (SV) and the Senterpartiet (Sp).

Prime Minister: JENS STOLTENBERG (DnA).
Minister of Finance: KRISTIN HALVORSEN (SV).
Minister of Transport and Communications: LIV SIGNE NAVARSETE (Sp).
Minister of Foreign Affairs: JONAS GAHR STØRE (DnA).
Minister of Research and Higher Education: TORA AASLAND (SV).
Minister of Local Government and Regional Development: MAGNHILD MELTVEIT KLEPPA (Sp).
Minister of Defence: ANNE-GRETE STRØM-ERICHSEN (DnA).
Minister of the Environment and Development Co-operation: ERIK SOLHEIM (SV).
Minister of Agriculture and Food: LARS PEDER BREKK (Sp).
Minister of Labour and Social Inclusion: DAG TERJE ANDERSEN (DnA).
Minister of Justice and the Police: KNUT STORBERGET (DnA).
Minister of Trade and Industry: SYLVIA KRISTIN BRUSTAD (DnA).
Minister of Culture and Church Affairs: TROND GISKE (DnA).
Minister of Health and Care Services: BJARNE HÅKON HANSSEN (DnA).
Minister of Government Administration and Reform: HEIDI GRANDE RØYS (SV).
Minister of Petroleum and Energy: TERJE RIIS-JOHANSEN (Sp).
Minister of Children and Equality: ANNIKEN HUITFELDT (DnA).
Minister of Education: BÅRD VEGAR SOLHJELL (SV).
Minister of Fisheries and Coastal Affairs: HELGA PEDERSEN (DnA).

MINISTRIES

Office of the Prime Minister: Akersgt. 42, POB 8001 Dep., 0030 Oslo; tel. 22-24-90-90; fax 22-24-95-00; e-mail postmottak@smk.dep.no; internet www.regjeringen.no/smk.

Ministry of Agriculture and Food: Akersgt. 59 (R5), POB 8007 Dep., 0030 Oslo; tel. 22-24-90-90; fax 22-24-95-55; e-mail postmottak@lmd.dep.no; internet www.regjeringen.no/lmd.

Ministry of Children and Equality: Akersgt. 59, POB 8036 Dep., 0030 Oslo; tel. 22-24-90-90; fax 22-24-95-15; e-mail postmottak@bld.dep.no; internet www.regjeringen.no/bld.

Ministry of Culture and Church Affairs: Akersgt. 59, POB 8030 Dep., 0030 Oslo; tel. 22-24-78-39; fax 22-24-95-50; e-mail postmottak@kkd.dep.no; internet www.regjeringen.no/kkd.

Ministry of Defence: Glacisgt. 1, POB 8126 Dep., 0032 Oslo; tel. 23-09-80-00; fax 23-09-60-75; e-mail postmottak@fd.dep.no; internet www.regjeringen.no/fd.

Ministry of Education and Research: Akersgt. 44, POB 8119 Dep., 0032 Oslo; tel. 22-24-90-90; fax 22-24-95-44; e-mail postmottak@kd.dep.no; internet www.regjeringen.no/kd.

Ministry of the Environment: Myntgt. 2, POB 8013 Dep., 0030 Oslo; tel. 22-24-90-90; fax 22-24-95-60; e-mail postmottak@md.dep.no; internet www.regjeringen.no/md.

Ministry of Finance: Akersgt. 40, POB 8008 Dep., 0030 Oslo; tel. 22-24-90-90; fax 22-24-95-10; e-mail postmottak@fin.dep.no; internet www.regjeringen.no/fin.

Ministry of Fisheries and Coastal Affairs: Grubbegt. 1, POB 8118 Dep., 0032 Oslo; tel. 22-24-90-90; fax 22-24-95-85; e-mail postmottak@fkd.dep.no; internet www.regjeringen.no/fkd.

Ministry of Foreign Affairs: 7 juni pl. 1, POB 8114 Dep., 0032 Oslo; tel. 22-24-36-00; fax 22-24-95-80; e-mail post@mfa.no; internet www.regjeringen.no/ud; also incl. Ministry of International Development.

Ministry of Government Administration and Reform: Akersgt. 59, POB 8004 Dep., 0030 Oslo; tel. 22-24-90-90; fax 22-24-95-16; e-mail postmottak@fad.dep.no; internet www.regjeringen.no/fad.

Ministry of Health and Care Services: Einar Gerhardsens pl. 3, POB 8011 Dep., 0030 Oslo; tel. 22-24-90-90; e-mail postmottak@hod.dep.no; internet www.regjeringen.no/hod.

Ministry of Justice and the Police: Akersgt. 42, POB 8005 Dep., 0030 Oslo; tel. 22-24-51-04; e-mail postmottak@jd.dep.no; internet www.regjeringen.no/jd.

Ministry of Labour and Social Inclusion: Einar Gerhardsens pl. 3, POB 8019 Dep., 0030 Oslo; tel. 22-24-90-90; fax 22-24-87-11; e-mail postmottak@aid.dep.no; internet www.regjeringen.no/aid.

Ministry of Local Government and Regional Development: Akersgt. 59, POB 8112 Dep., 0032 Oslo; tel. 22-24-90-90; e-mail postmottak@krd.dep.no; internet www.regjeringen.no/krd.

Ministry of Petroleum and Energy: Einar Gerhardsens pl. 1, POB 8148 Dep., 0033 Oslo; tel. 22-24-90-90; fax 22-24-95-96; e-mail postmottak@oed.dep.no; internet www.regjeringen.no/oed.

Ministry of Trade and Industry: Einar Gerhardsens pl. 1, POB 8014 Dep., 0030 Oslo; tel. 22-24-90-90; fax 22-24-01-30; e-mail postmottak@nhd.dep.no; internet www.regjeringen.no/nhd.

Ministry of Transport and Communications: Akersgt. 59 (R5), POB 8010 Dep., 0030 Oslo; tel. 22-24-90-90; fax 22-24-95-71; e-mail postmottak@sd.dep.no; internet www.regjeringen.no/sd.

Legislature

Storting

Karl Johansgt. 22, 0026 Oslo; tel. 23-31-30-50; fax 23-31-38-17; e-mail info@stortinget.no; internet www.stortinget.no.

President: THORBJØRN JAGLAND.
Vice-President: CARL I. HAGEN.

NORWAY

The Storting (Stortinget) has 169 members, one-quarter of whom sit as the upper house, the Lagting (Lagtinget), and the rest as the lower house, the Odelsting (Odelstinget).

President of the Lagting: INGE LØNNING.
Vice-President: OLA T. LÅNKE.
President of the Odelsting: BERIT BRØRBY.
Vice-President: OLAV GUNNAR BALLO.

General Election, 12 September 2005

Party	Votes	% of votes	Seats
Det norske Arbeiderparti (DnA)	862,671	32.69	61
Fremskrittspartiet (FrP)	582,014	22.05	38
Høyre (H)	372,046	14.10	23
Sosialistisk Venstreparti (SV)	233,049	8.83	15
Kristelig Folkeparti (KrF)	179,109	6.79	11
Senterpartiet (Sp)	171,036	6.48	11
Venstre (V)	156,101	5.92	10
Rød Valgallianse (RV)	32,364	1.23	—
Kystpartiet (KP)	21,947	0.83	—
Pensjonistpartiet (Pp)	13,568	0.51	—
Others	15,039	0.57	—
Total	**2,638,944**	**100.00**	**169**

Political Organizations

Fremskrittspartiet (FrP) (Progress Party): Karl Johans gt. 25, 0159 Oslo; tel. 23-13-54-00; fax 23-13-54-01; e-mail frp@frp.no; internet www.frp.no; f. 1973 as Anders Langes Parti; present name adopted 1977; anti-tax; favours privatization, the diminution of the welfare state and less immigration; Chair. SIV JENSEN; Sec.-Gen. GEIR ALMÅSVOLD MO.

Høyre (H) (Conservative): Stortingsgt. 20, POB 1536 Vika, 0117 Oslo; tel. 22-82-90-00; fax 22-82-90-80; e-mail politikk@hoyre.no; internet www.hoyre.no; f. 1884; aims to promote economic growth and sound state finances, achieve a property-owning democracy, and to uphold democratic govt, social security, private property, private initiative and personal liberty; 67,000 mems; Leader ERNA SOLBERG; Sec.-Gen. TROND REIDAR HOLE.

Kristelig Folkeparti (KrF) (Christian Democratic Party): Øvre Slottsgt. 18–20, POB 478 Sentrum, 0105 Oslo; tel. 23-10-28-00; fax 23-10-28-10; e-mail krf@krf.no; internet www.krf.no; f. 1933; aims to promote a democratic policy based on Christian values; Chair. DAGFINN HØYBRÅTEN; Sec.-Gen. KNUT H. JAHR.

Kystpartiet (Coastal Party): Kanalveien 107, 5068 Bergen; tel. 55-29-25-70; e-mail post@kystpartiet.no; internet www.kystpartiet.no; nationalist; Leader KJELL IVAR VESTÅ; Sec. HILDUR LARSEN.

Miljøpartiet De Grønne (Green Party of Norway): POB 9124, Grønland, 0133 Oslo; tel. 23-10-95-43; e-mail gronne@gronne.no; internet www.mdg.no; f. 1988; Principal Speakers SONDRE LINDHOLM BÅTSTRAND, JAN HANNA ELISE MARCUSSEN.

Norges Kommunistiske Parti (NKP) (Communist Party of Norway): Helgesensgt. 21, POB 9288 Grønland, 0134 Oslo; tel. 22-71-60-44; fax 22-71-79-07; e-mail nkp@nkp.no; internet www.nkp.no; f. 1923; Chair. ZAFER GÖZET; Sec. KNUT HARTMANN OLSEN.

Det norske Arbeiderparti (DnA) (Norwegian Labour Party): Youngstorget 2A, 5th floor, POB 8743, 0028 Oslo; tel. 24-14-40-00; fax 24-14-40-01; e-mail post@arbeiderpartiet.no; internet www.arbeiderpartiet.no; f. 1887; social democratic; 48,589 mems (2009); Leader JENS STOLTENBERG; Gen. Sec. MARTIN KOLBERG.

Pensjonistpartiet (Pensioners' Party): Møllergt. 6, 0179 Oslo; tel. 45-28-90-10; fax 22-42-77-00; e-mail post@pensjonistpartiet.no; internet www.pensjonistpartiet.no; Leader RAGNAR DAHL; Sec. ØYSTEIN NESS.

Rødt: Osterhausgt. 27, 0183 Oslo; tel. 22-98-90-50; fax 22-98-90-55; e-mail raudt@raudt.no; internet roedt.no; f. 2007 by merger of Rød Valgallianse (Red Electoral Alliance) and Arbeidernes Kommunistparti (Workers' Communist Party); left-wing group; Leader TORSTEIN DAHLE; Sec. BETH HARTMANN.

Senterpartiet (Sp) (Centre Party): Akersgt. 35, 3rd Floor, POB 1191 Sentrum, 0107 Oslo; tel. 23-69-01-00; fax 23-69-01-01; e-mail epost@senterpartiet.no; internet www.senterpartiet.no; f. 1920 as the Bondepartiet (Farmers' Party), name changed 1959; advocates a decentralized society that will secure employment and diversified settlements in all parts of the country; opposes Norwegian membership of the EU; encourages the devt of an ecologically balanced society; Leader LIV SIGNE NAVARSETE; Sec.-Gen. IVAR EGEBERG.

Sosialistisk Venstreparti (SV) (Socialist Left Party): Akersgt. 35, 0158 Oslo; tel. 21-93-33-00; fax 21-93-33-01; e-mail post@sv.no; internet www.sv.no; f. 1975 by merger of the Socialist People's Party, the Democratic Socialists and other socialist forces united previously in the Socialist Electoral League; advocates non-alignment and socialism independent of international centres, based on workers' control, decentralized powers, gender equality and ecological principles; Chair. KRISTIN HALVORSEN; Sec. SILJE SCHEI TVEITDAL.

Venstre (V) (Liberal): Møllergt. 16, 0179 Oslo; tel. 22-40-43-50; fax 22-40-43-51; e-mail venstre@venstre.no; internet www.venstre.no; f. 1884; in 1988 reunited with Det Liberale Folkepartiet (Liberal Democratic Party, f. 1972); advocates the promotion of national and democratic progress on the basis of the present system by gradual economic, social and cultural reforms; Leader LARS SPONHEIM; Sec.-Gen. TERJE BREIVIK.

Diplomatic Representation

EMBASSIES IN NORWAY

Afghanistan: Kronprinsensgt. 17, 0251 Oslo; tel. 22-83-84-10; fax 22-83-84-11; e-mail info@afghanemb.com; internet www.afghanistanembassy.no; Ambassador JAVID LODIN.

Algeria: Inkognitogt. 35, 0265 Oslo; tel. 22-55-75-31; fax 25-55-75-30; e-mail ambalgoslo@live.fr; Ambassador BOUBAKEUR OGAB.

Argentina: Drammensvn 39, 0244 Oslo; tel. 22-55-24-49; fax 22-44-16-41; e-mail enoru@online.no; internet www.argentour.com/embajada; Ambassador JUAN MANUEL ORTIZ DE ROSAS.

Austria: Thomas Heftyesgt. 19–21, 0244 Oslo; tel. 22-54-02-00; fax 22-55-43-61; e-mail oslo-ob@bmeia.gv.at; Ambassador Dr LORENZ GRAF.

Belgium: Drammensvn 103D, 0244 Oslo; tel. 23-13-32-20; fax 23-13-32-32; e-mail oslo@diplobel.org; internet www.diplomatie.be/oslo; Ambassador CHRISTIAN MONNOYER.

Bosnia and Herzegovina: Bygdøy allé 10, POB 2407 Solli, 0201 Oslo; tel. 22-54-09-63; fax 22-55-27-50; e-mail gkbih@gkbih.com; internet www.gkbih.com; Ambassador ELMA KOVAČEVIĆ.

Brazil: Sigurd Syrsgt. 4, 0244 Oslo; tel. 22-54-07-30; fax 22-44-39-64; e-mail brasil@brasil.no; internet www.brasil.no; Ambassador SÉRGIO EDUARDO MOREIRA LIMA.

Bulgaria: Tidemandsgt. 11, 0244 Oslo; tel. 22-55-40-40; fax 22-55-40-24; e-mail bulgemb@online.no; internet www.mfa.bg/oslo; Ambassador NIKOLA KARADIMOV.

Canada: Wergelandsvn 7, 0244 Oslo; tel. 22-99-53-00; fax 22-99-53-01; e-mail oslo@international.gc.ca; internet www.canada.no; Ambassador JILLIAN STIRK.

Chile: Meltzersgt. 5, 0244 Oslo; tel. 22-44-89-55; fax 22-44-24-21; e-mail embassy@chile.no; internet www.chile.no; Ambassador ROBERTO EDUARDO ALONSO BUDGE.

China, People's Republic: Tuengen allé 2B, Vinderen, 0244 Oslo; tel. 22-49-20-52; fax 22-92-19-78; e-mail webmaster@chinese-embassy.no; internet www.chinese-embassy.no; Ambassador GAO JIAN.

Colombia: Oscarsgt. 34, 0258 Oslo; tel. 23-12-01-50; fax 23-12-01-51; e-mail eoslo@cancilleria.gov.co; Chargé d'affaires a.i. SANTIAGO SALCEDO BUITRAGO.

Costa Rica: Skippergt. 33, 8th Floor, 0154 Oslo; tel. 22-42-58-23; fax 22-33-04-08; e-mail embassy@costarica.no; internet www.costarica.no; Ambassador Dr CLAUDIO BOGANTES ZAMORA.

Croatia: Drammensvn 82, 0244 Oslo; tel. 23-01-40-50; fax 23-01-40-60; e-mail croemb.oslo@mvpei.hr; Ambassador DOBROSLAV SILOBRČIĆ.

Cuba: Oscarsgt. 78B, 0244 Oslo; tel. 23-08-32-60; fax 23-08-32-61; e-mail enoruega@online.no; internet www.embacuba.no; Ambassador REGERIO SANTANA.

Czech Republic: Fritznersgt. 14, 0244 Oslo; tel. 22-12-10-31; fax 22-55-33-95; e-mail oslo@embassy.mzv.cz; internet www.mzv.cz/oslo; Ambassador LUBOŠ NOVÝ.

Denmark: Olav Kyrresgt. 7, 0244 Oslo; tel. 22-54-08-00; fax 22-55-46-34; e-mail oslamb@um.dk; internet www.amboslo.um.dk; Ambassador THEIS TRUELSEN.

Egypt: Drammensvn 90A, 0244 Oslo; tel. 23-08-42-00; fax 22-56-22-68; e-mail information@egypt-embassy.no; internet www.egypt-embassy.no; Ambassador TAMER ABD AL-AZIZ A. KHALIL.

Estonia: Parkvn 51A, 0244 Oslo; tel. 22-54-00-70; fax 22-54-00-71; e-mail embassy.oslo@mfa.ee; internet www.estemb.no; Ambassador ARTI HILPUS.

Finland: Thomas Heftyesgt. 1, 0244 Oslo; tel. 22-12-49-00; fax 22-12-49-49; e-mail sanomat.osl@formin.fi; internet www.finland.no; Ambassador PETER STENLUND.

NORWAY

France: Drammensvn 69, 0244 Oslo; tel. 23-28-46-00; fax 23-28-46-70; e-mail ambafrance.oslo@diplomatie.gouv.fr; internet www.ambafrance-no.org; Ambassador BRIGITTE COLLET.

Germany: Oscarsgt. 45, 0244 Oslo; tel. 23-27-54-00; fax 22-44-76-72; e-mail info@oslo.diplo.de; internet www.oslo.diplo.de; Ambassador ROLAND MAUCH.

Greece: Nobelsgt. 45, 0244 Oslo; tel. 22-44-27-28; fax 22-56-00-72; e-mail gremb.osl@mfa.gr; Ambassador ANTONIOS VLAVIANOS.

Guatemala: Drammensvn 126B, 0277 Oslo; tel. 22-55-60-04; fax 22-55-60-47; e-mail guatemala@embajada.no; Ambassador JUAN LEÓN ALVORADO.

Hungary: Sophus Liesgt. 3, 0244 Oslo; tel. 22-55-24-18; fax 22-44-76-93; e-mail mission.osl@kum.hu; internet www.mfa.gov.hu/kulkepviselet/no; Ambassador LAJOS BOZI.

Iceland: Stortingsgt. 30, 0244 Oslo; tel. 23-23-75-30; fax 22-83-07-04; e-mail emb.oslo@mfa.is; internet www.island.no; Ambassador Dr SIGRIÐUR DÚNA KRISTMUNDSDÓTTIR.

India: Niels Juelsgt. 30, 0244 Oslo; tel. 24-11-59-10; fax 24-11-59-12; e-mail amb.oslo@mea.gov.in; internet www.indemb.no; Ambassador BANBIT A. ROY.

Indonesia: Fritznersgt. 12, 0244 Oslo; tel. 22-12-51-30; fax 22-12-51-31; e-mail kbrioslo@online.no; internet www.indonesia-oslo.no; Chargé d'affaires a.i. MANSYUR PANGERAN.

Iran: Drammensvn 88E, 0244 Oslo; tel. 23-27-29-60; fax 22-55-49-19; e-mail iremb@iran-embassy-oslo.no; internet www.iran-embassy-oslo.no; Chargé d'affaires a.i. MAJID RAMEZANI.

Iraq: Torgbygget rom 301, Nydalsvn 33, 0484 Oslo; tel. 21-52-02-17; fax 21-52-01-71; e-mail oslemb@iraqmfamail.com; Chargé d'affaires FADHIL SALIH JASIM MAROFA.

Ireland: Haakon VIIs gt. 1, 0244 Oslo; tel. 22-01-72-00; fax 22-01-72-01; e-mail osloembassy@dfa.ie; internet www.embassyofireland.no; Ambassador GERALD F. ANSBRO.

Israel: Parkvn 35, POB 534 Skøyen, 0214 Oslo; tel. 21-01-95-00; fax 21-01-95-30; e-mail israel@oslo.mfa.gov.il; internet oslo.mfa.gov.il; Ambassador MICHAEL ELIGAL.

Italy: Inkognitogt. 7, 0244 Oslo; tel. 23-08-49-00; fax 22-44-34-36; e-mail ambasciata.oslo@esteri.it; internet www.amboslo.esteri.it; Ambassador ROSA ANNA CONIGLIO PAPALIA.

Japan: Wergelandsveien 15, 0244 Oslo; tel. 22-99-16-00; fax 22-44-25-05; e-mail info@japan-embassy.no; internet www.no.emb-japan.go.jp; Ambassador HISAO YAMAGUCHI.

Kazakhstan: Nedre Vollgt. 3, 0158 Oslo; tel. 22-42-06-40; fax 22-42-06-42; e-mail kazak@online.no; internet www.kazembassy.no; Chargé d'affaires a.i. MARAT T. YESENBAYEV.

Korea, Republic of: Inkognitogt. 3, 0244, Oslo; tel. 22-54-70-90; fax 22-56-14-11; e-mail kornor@mofat.go.kr; internet nor.mofat.go.kr; Ambassador BYUNG-KOO CHOI.

Latvia: Bygdøy allé 76, POB 3163 Elisenberg, 0208 Oslo; tel. 22-54-22-80; fax 22-54-64-26; e-mail embassy.norway@mfa.gov.lv; Ambassador ANDRIS SEKACIS.

Lithuania: Dronningensgt. 3, 0244 Oslo; tel. 22-12-92-00; fax 22-12-92-01; e-mail amb.no@urm.lt; internet no.mfa.lt; Ambassador ALFONTAS EIDINTAS.

Morocco: Holtegt. 28, 0355 Oslo; tel. 23-19-71-50; fax 23-19-71-51; e-mail oslosifam@yahoo.com; Ambassador BOUCHAÂB YAHDIH.

Netherlands: Oscarsgt. 29, 0244 Oslo; tel. 23-33-36-00; fax 23-33-36-01; e-mail nlgovosl@online.no; internet www.netherlands-embassy.no; Ambassador RONALD VAN ROEDEN.

Pakistan: Eckersbergsgt. 20, 0244 Oslo; tel. 23-16-60-80; fax 22-55-50-97; e-mail info@pakistanembassy.no; internet www.pakistanembassy.no; Ambassador RAB NAWAZ KHAN.

Philippines: Nedre Vollgt. 4, 0158 Oslo; tel. 22-41-74-00; fax 22-41-74-01; e-mail ambassador@philembassy.no; internet www.philembassy.no; Ambassador ELIZABETH BUENSUCESO.

Poland: Olav Kyrres pl. 1, 0244 Oslo; tel. 24-11-08-50; fax 22-44-48-39; e-mail ambassador@oslo.polemb.net; internet www.oslo.polemb.net; Ambassador WOJCIECH LUDWIK KOLAŃCZYK.

Portugal: Josefinesgt. 37, 0244 Oslo; tel. 23-33-28-50; fax 22-56-43-55; e-mail portuguese.embassy@scosl.dgaccp.pt; Ambassador JOÃO DE LIMA PIMENTEL.

Romania: Oscarsgt. 51, 0244 Oslo; tel. 22-44-15-12; fax 22-43-16-74; e-mail embassy@romanianembassy.no; internet oslo.mae.ro; Ambassador Dr CRISTIAN ISTRATE.

Russia: Drammensvn 74, 0244 Oslo; tel. 22-55-32-78; fax 22-55-00-70; e-mail rembassy@online.no; internet www.norway.mid.ru; Ambassador SERGEI V. ANDREYEV.

Serbia: Drammensvn 105, 0244 Oslo; tel. 23-08-68-58; fax 22-55-29-92; e-mail ambasada@serbianembassy.no; internet www.serbianembassy.no; Ambassador VLADISLAV MLADENOVIĆ.

Slovakia: Thomas Heftyesgt. 24, 0244 Oslo; tel. 22-04-94-70; fax 22-04-94-74; e-mail slovakr@online.no; internet www.oslo.mfa.sk; Ambassador DUŠAN ROZBORA.

South Africa: Drammensvn 88C, POB 2822 Solli, 0204 Oslo; tel. 23-27-32-20; fax 22-44-39-75; e-mail info@saemboslo.no; internet www.saemboslo.no; Ambassador BERYL ROSE SISULU.

Spain: Oscarsgt. 35, 0244 Oslo; tel. 22-92-66-90; fax 22-55-98-22; e-mail embespno@mail.mae.es; internet www.maec.es/embajadas/oslo; Ambassador FERNANDO ALVARGONZÁLEZ SAN MARTÍN.

Sri Lanka: Nedre Vollgt. 3, 0158 Oslo; tel. 23-31-70-80; fax 23-31-70-90; e-mail embakont@online.no; internet www.srilanka.no; Ambassador ESALA RUWAN WEERAKOON.

Sudan: Holtegt. 28, 0355 Oslo; tel. 22-60-33-55; fax 22-69-83-44; e-mail sudanembassy@sudanoslo.com; Ambassador ILHAM I. M. AHMED.

Sweden: Nobelsgt. 16, 0244 Oslo; tel. 24-11-42-00; fax 22-55-15-96; e-mail ambassaden.oslo@foreign.ministry.se; internet www.swedenabroad.com/oslo; Ambassador MICHAEL SAHLIN.

Switzerland: Bygdøy allé 78, 0244 Oslo; tel. 22-43-05-90; fax 22-44-63-50; e-mail osl.vertretung@eda.admin.ch; internet www.eda.admin.ch/oslo; Ambassador DENIS FELDMEYER.

Thailand: Eilert Sundtsgt. 4, 0244 Oslo; tel. 22-12-86-75; fax 22-04-99-69; e-mail thaioslo@online.no; internet www.thaiembassy.no; Ambassador JULLAPONG NONSRICHAI.

Tunisia: Fridtjof Nansenspl. 9, 0160 Oslo; tel. 22-41-72-01; fax 22-41-72-04; e-mail at.oslo@online.no; Chargé d'affaires NABIL AMMAR.

Turkey: Halvdan Svartesgt. 5, 0244 Oslo; tel. 22-12-87-50; fax 22-55-62-63; e-mail postmaster@oslo-turkish-embassy.com; Ambassador HAYATI GÜVEN.

Ukraine: Arbinsgt. 4, 0253 Oslo; tel. 22-83-55-60; fax 22-83-55-57; e-mail embassy@ukremb.no; internet www.mfa.gov.ua/norway; Ambassador OLEKSANDR H. TSVYETKOV.

United Kingdom: Thomas Heftyesgt. 8, 0264 Oslo; tel. 23-13-27-00; fax 23-13-27-41; e-mail britemb@online.no; internet www.britain.no; Ambassador DAVID POWELL.

USA: Henrik Ibsensgt. 48, 0244 Oslo; tel. 22-44-85-40; fax 22-43-07-77; e-mail oslo@usa.no; internet www.usa.no; Ambassador BENSON K. WHITNEY.

Venezuela: Drammensvn 82, POB 2820 Solli, 0204 Oslo; tel. 22-43-06-60; fax 22-43-14-70; e-mail consulado@venezuela.no; Chargé d'affaires a.i. EDUARDO SPADARO ALVÁREZ.

Judicial System

The judicial system in Norway is organized on three levels. The courts of first instance are the District (Herredsrett) and City (Byrett) Courts. The country is divided into 93 judicial areas, most of which are served by one professional judge and one or two deputies (in the major cities the number of judges ranges from three to 52). The Court of Appeal (Lagmannsrett) consists of six jurisdictions, each with between 10 and 52 judges, and two divisions (Appeals and Criminal Divisions). The Supreme Court (Høyesterett) sits in Oslo and decides cases in the last instance. The Court, which is served by 19 judges appointed by the Crown and presided over by a Chief Justice, is competent to try all factual and legal aspects of cases in civil and criminal cause. In criminal cases, however, the competence of the Court is limited to questions concerning the application of the law, the nature of the penalty, and procedural errors of the lower courts. Appeals to the Supreme Court may not be based on errors in the assessment of evidence in connection with the question of guilt.

SUPREME COURT

Høyesterett

Høyesteretts pl., POB 8016 Dep., 0030 Oslo; tel. 22-03-59-00; fax 22-33-23-55; e-mail post@hoyesterett.no; internet www.hoyesterett.no. f. 1815; pronounces judgment in the final instance; hears both civil and criminal cases, and has jurisdiction in all areas of law; composed of 18 ordinary justices of the Supreme Court and one Chief Justice; individual cases are heard by five justices—in some instances cases are heard by all of the justices sitting in plenary session; works in two parallel and equal divisions; Supreme Court justices also sit on the Appeals Selection Committee of the Supreme Court, which is classed as a separate court; cases brought before the Appeals Selection Committee are heard by three justices; any matter brought before the Supreme Court must initially be considered by the Appeals Selection Committee; justices sit in both divisions of the Supreme Court and on the Appeals Selection Committee in accordance with a rota system.

Chief Justice of the Supreme Court: TORE SCHEI.

NORWAY

Justices of the Supreme Court: LIV GJØLSTAD, KETIL LUND, KARENANNE GUSSGARD, STEINAR TJOMSLAND, KIRSTI COWARD, EILERT STANG LUND, HANS FLOCK, MAGNUS MATNINGSDAL, KARIN MARIA BRUZELIUS, JENS EDVIN A. SKOGHØY, KARL ARNE UTGÅRD, INGER-ELSE STABEL, OLE BJØRN STØLE, TORIL MARIE ØIE, BÅRD TØNDER, CLEMENT ENDRESEN, HILDE INDREBERG, ARFINN BÅRDSEN, AAGE THOR FALKANGER.

COURTS OF APPEAL

Agder Lagmannsrett (Court of Appeal in Skien): Statens hus, Gjerpensgt. 16, 3708 Skien; tel. 35-54-05-00; fax 35-52-10-09; e-mail agder.lagmannsrett@domstol.no; internet www.domstol.no/agder; Presiding Judge ASBJØRN NES HANSEN.

Borgarting Lagmannsrett (Court of Appeal in Oslo): Keysersgt. 13, POB 8017 Dep., 0030 Oslo; tel. 21-55-80-00; fax 21-55-80-38; e-mail borgadm@domstol.no; internet www.domstol.no/borgarting; Presiding Judge NILS ERIK LIE.

Eidsivating Lagmannsrett (Court of Appeal in Hamar): Hamar tinghus, Østregt. 41, 2326 Hamar; tel. 62-55-06-00; fax 62-55-06-20; e-mail eidsivating.lagmannsrett@domstol.no; internet www.domstol.no/elag; Presiding Judge ODD JARL PEDERSEN.

Frostating Lagmannsrett (Court of Appeal in Trondheim): Trondheim tinghus, Munkegt. 20, 7004 Trondheim; tel. 73-54-24-60; fax 73-54-24-84; e-mail frostating.lagmannsrett@domstol.no; internet www.frostating.no; Presiding Judge KJELL BUER.

Gulating Lagmannsrett (Court of Appeal in Bergen): Bergen tinghus, Tårnpl. 2, POB 7414, 5020 Bergen; tel. 55-69-95-00; fax 55-69-95-01; e-mail gulating@domstol.no; internet www.domstol.no/gulating; Presiding Judge BJØRN SOLBAKKEN.

Hålogaland Lagmannsrett (Court of Appeal in Tromsø): Fridtjof Nansens pl. 17, POB 2511, 9271 Tromsø; tel. 77-66-00-35; fax 77-66-00-60; e-mail halogaland.lagmannsrett@domstol.no; internet www.domstol.no/halogaland; Presiding Judge ARILD O. EIDESEN.

CIVIL COURTS

In each municipality there is a Conciliation Board (Forliksråd) consisting of three lay members elected by the municipal council for four years. With a few exceptions, no case may be taken to a court of justice without a prior attempt at mediation by a Conciliation Court. In addition to mediation, the Conciliation Court has a judicial capacity and is intended to settle minor cases in a simple manner without great expense to the parties involved.

The ordinary lower courts are the District and City Courts, which decide all cases not adjudicated upon by the Conciliation Court, and they also act as courts of appeal from judgments given in the Conciliation Court. During the main hearing, the court is generally convened with only one professional judge, but each of the parties may request that the court be convened with two lay judges, in addition to the professional judge. When the court finds it advisable, it may also summon lay judges on its own initiative.

Judgments delivered in the District and City Courts may be taken, on appeal, to the Court of Appeal or to the Supreme Court. In the Court of Appeal cases are judged by three professional judges, but, if requested by one of the parties, lay judges may be summoned.

CRIMINAL COURTS

The criminal courts are: the Court of Examination and Summary Jurisdiction (Forhørsretten), the District and City Courts, the Court of Appeal and the Supreme Court. In the Court of Examination and Summary Jurisdiction the professional judge presides alone, but in the District and City Courts two lay judges also sit. Following the implementation of a major reform in 1995, all criminal cases now begin in a District or City Court. The gravest offences were previously tried directly before a jury in the Court of Appeal and the possibilities for appeal were thus limited. Now, however, the issue of guilt can be appealed to the Court of Appeal in all cases. (Such cases are tried either by three professional judges, and four lay judges with equal votes, or by three professional judges and a jury of 10 members. For a guilty verdict to be upheld in the latter case, at least seven members of the jury must support the original decision of the lower court. In other cases appeal is directly to the Supreme Court.) The maximum penalty permissible under Norwegian law is 21 years of imprisonment.

OMBUDSMAN

The office of Parliamentary Ombudsman was established in 1962. An Ombudsman is elected by the Storting after every general election for a four-year term (with the possibility of re-election). The Ombudsman is accessible to all citizens, and attempts to ensure against the public administration committing any injustice to the individual citizen. The Ombudsman does not cover private legal affairs, and does not have the right to reverse an official decision, but his pronouncements are normally complied with.

Sivilombudsmannen—Stortingets ombudsmann for forvaltningen (Parliamentary Ombudsman for Public Administration): Akersgt. 8, 6th Floor, POB 3 Sentrum, 0101 Oslo; tel. 22-82-85-00; fax 22-82-85-11; e-mail postmottak@sivilombudsmannen.no; internet www.sivilombudsmannen.no; Ombudsman ARNE FLIFLET.

Religion

CHRISTIANITY

Citizens are considered to be members of the National Church unless they explicitly associate themselves with another denomination; around 80.7% of the population (3,874,823 persons) nominally belonged to the Church at January 2009, although actual church attendance is low. Other Protestant Christian denominations accounted for some 4.5% of the population. There are a very small number of Orthodox Christians in Norway.

The National Church

Church of Norway

The Church Synod, Rådhusgt. 1-3, POB 799 Sentrum, 0106 Oslo; tel. 23-08-12-00; fax 23-08-12-01; e-mail post.kirkeradet@kirken.no; internet www.kirken.no.

The Evangelical Lutheran Church, constituted as the State Church; there are 11 dioceses, 105 archdeaconries, 620 clerical districts and 1,285 parishes. The highest representative body of the Church is the Synod, summoned for the first time in 1984. At January 2009 3,874,823 persons (around 80.7% of the population) belonged to the State Church.

Bishop of Oslo: OLE CHRISTIAN MÆLEN KVARME.
Bishop of Borg: HELGA HAUGLAND BYFUGLIEN.
Bishop of Hamar: SOLVEIG FISKE.
Bishop of Tunsberg: LAILA RIKSAASEN DAHL.
Bishop of Agder and Telemark: OLAV SKJEVESLAND.
Bishop of Stavanger: ERNST ODDVAR BAASLAND.
Bishop of Bjørgvin: HALVOR NORDHAUG.
Bishop of Møre: INGEBORG SYNØVE MIDTTØMME.
Bishop of Nidaros: TOR SINGSAAS.
Bishop of Sør-Hålogaland: TOR BERGER JØRGENSEN.
Bishop of Nord-Hålogaland: PER OSKAR KJØLAAS.

The Roman Catholic Church

For ecclesiastical purposes, Norway comprises the diocese of Oslo and the territorial prelatures of Tromsø and Trondheim. The diocese and the prelatures are directly responsible to the Holy See. At 31 December 2006 there were an estimated 62,934 adherents in Norway, equivalent to about 1.3% of the population. The Bishop of Oslo participates in the Scandinavian Episcopal Conference (based in Västra Frölunda, Sweden).

Bishop of Oslo: Rt Rev. BERNT IVAR (MARKUS) EIDSVIG, Oslo Katolske Bispedømme, Akersvn 5, POB 8270, 0177 Oslo; tel. 23-21-95-00; fax 23-21-95-01; e-mail okb@katolsk.no; internet www.katolsk.no.

Other Churches

Church of England: St Edmund's Anglican Church, Møllergt. 30, Oslo; tel. 22-69-22-14; e-mail j-heil@online.no; internet www.osloanglicans.net; 1,800 mems (2008); also in Stavanger, Bergen and Trondheim; part of the Diocese of Gibraltar in Europe; Chaplain Rev. Canon JANET HEIL.

Evangelical Lutheran Free Church of Norway: POB 23, Bekkelagshøgda, 1109 Oslo; tel. 22-74-86-00; fax 22-74-86-01; e-mail post@frikirken.no; internet www.frikirken.no; f. 1877; c. 19,308 mems (2006); Chair. of Synod ARNFINN LØYNING.

Norwegian Baptist Union: Micheletsvei 62C, 1368 Stabekk; tel. 67-10-35-60; fax 67-10-35-69; e-mail post@baptist.no; f. 1860; 9,500 mems (2008); Gen. Sec. MAGNAR MAELAND.

Pinse Bevegelsen i Norge (Pentecostal Movement): POB 6717, St Olavs pl., 0130 Oslo; tel. 22-11-43-00; fax 22-11-43-43; e-mail jeppestol@pinsebevegelsen.no; internet www.pinsebevegelsen.no; 39,492 mems (2006).

United Methodist Church: POB 2744 St Hanshaugen, 0131 Oslo; tel. 23-33-27-00; fax 23-33-27-01; e-mail post@metodistkirken.no; internet www.metodistkirken.no; f. 1856; 12,000 mems (2008); Council Dir GUNNAR BRADLEY.

In 2008 there were 14,856 Jehovah's Witnesses in Norway and 5,117 Seventh-day Adventists.

OTHER RELIGIONS

In 2008 there were 83,684 Muslims, 11,038 Buddhists, 4,566 Hindus, 2,537 Sikhs and 850 Jews in Norway.

The Press

The principle of press freedom is safeguarded in the Norwegian Constitution. There is no law specifically dealing with the Press. Editors bear wide responsibility in law for the content of their papers, especially regarding such matters as libel. Although a journalist is legally entitled to conceal his source he may be required to disclose this information under penalty of imprisonment, but such instances are rare. A three-member Council of Conduct gives judgments in cases of complaint against a paper or of disputes between papers. It has no powers of enforcement but its judgments are highly respected. The Press Association has a Code of Ethics aimed at maintaining the standards and reputation of the profession.

The Eastern region dominates press activity. Oslo dailies are especially influential throughout this area, and four of these—*Aftenposten*, *Dagsavisen*, *Dagbladet* and *Verdens Gang*—have a national readership. Nevertheless, in Norway's other major cities the large local dailies easily lead in their own districts. In 2007 the most popular newspapers were *Verdens Gang* (Oslo), *Aftenposten* (Oslo), *Dagbladet* (Oslo), *Bergens Tidende* (Bergen) and *Adresseavisen* (Trondheim), with a combined average circulation of almost 900,000.

PRINCIPAL NEWSPAPERS
(circulation figures refer to the year 2007, unless otherwise indicated)

Ålesund

Sunnmørsposten: POB 123, 6001 Ålesund; tel. 70-12-00-00; fax 70-12-46-42; e-mail redaksjon@smp.no; internet www.smp.no; f. 1882; Liberal; Editor HARALD KJØLÅS; circ. 33,712.

Arendal

Agderposten: POB 8, 4801 Arendal; tel. 37-00-37-00; fax 37-00-38-38; e-mail agderposten@agderposten.no; internet www.agderposten.no; f. 1874; independent; Editor STEIN GAUSLAA; circ. 23,746.

Bergen

Bergens Tidende: Krinkelkroken 1, POB 7240, 5020 Bergen; tel. 55-21-45-02; fax 55-21-48-48; e-mail webmaster@bt.no; internet www.bergens-tidende.no; f. 1868; Editor HANS ERIK MATRE; circ. 87,668.

Bergensavisen: Chr. Michelsensgt. 4, POB 824 Sentrum, 5807 Bergen; tel. 55-23-50-00; fax 55-31-00-30; e-mail nyhet@ba.no; internet www.ba.no; f. 1927; independent, social democratic; Editor-in-Chief OLAV BERGO; circ. 29,311.

Dagen: POB 76/77, 5002 Bergen; tel. 55-31-17-55; fax 55-31-71-06; f. 1919; religious daily; Editor FINN JARLE SÆLE; circ. 9.033.

Billingstad

Budstikka: POB 133, 1376 Billingstad; tel. 66-77-00-00; fax 66-77-00-60; e-mail redaksjonen@budstikka.no; internet www.budstikka.no; f. 1898; 6 a week; fmrly *Asker og Baerums Budstikke*; Conservative; Editor ANDREAS GJØLME; circ. 29,660.

Bodø

Avisa Nordland: Storgt. 38, 8002 Bodø; tel. 75-50-50-00; fax 75-50-50-60; e-mail kundeservice@an.no; internet www.an.no; f. 1910; Labour; Editor JAN-ELRIK HANSSEN; circ. 23,959.

Drammen

Drammens Tidende: POB 7033, 3007 Drammen; tel. 32-20-40-00; fax 32-20-40-61; e-mail redaksjonen@dt.no; internet www.dt.no; f. 1832 and 1883; Conservative daily; Dir FINN GRUNDT; Editor HANS ARNE ODDE; circ. 40,954.

Fredrikstad

Fredrikstad Blad: POB 143, 1606 Fredrikstad; tel. 46-80-77-77; e-mail tips@f-b.no; internet www.f-b.no; f. 1889; Conservative; Editor ERLING OMVIK; circ. 23,442.

Gjøvik

Oppland Arbeiderblad: POB 24, 2801 Gjøvik; tel. 61-18-93-00; fax 61-17-98-56; e-mail redaksjonen@oa.no; internet www.oa.no; f. 1924; daily; Labour; Editor-in-Chief JENS OLAI JENSSEN; circ. 27,173.

Hamar

Hamar Arbeiderblad: Torggt. 51, POB 333, 2301 Hamar; tel. 62-51-96-99; fax 62-51-96-18; e-mail post@ha-nett.no; internet www.ha-nett.no; f. 1925; daily; Labour; Editor ROLV AMDAL; circ. 27,363.

Harstad

Harstad Tidende: Storgt. 11, POB 85, 9481 Harstad; tel. 77-01-80-00; fax 77-01-80-05; e-mail redaksjonen@ht.no; internet www.ht.no; f. 1887; Conservative; Editor BÅRD MICHALSEN; circ. 13,503.

Haugesund

Haugesunds Avis: POB 2024, 5504 Haugesund; tel. 52-72-00-00; fax 52-72-04-44; e-mail redaksjonen@haugesunds-avis.no; internet www.h-avis.no; f. 1895; independent; Editor-in-Chief TONNY NUNDAL; circ. 33,013.

Hønefoss

Ringerikes Blad: POB 68, 3502 Hønefoss; tel. 32-17-95-00; fax 32-17-95-01; e-mail redaksjonen@ringblad.no; internet www.ringblad.no; f. 1845; independent; Editor TORE ROLAND; circ. 12,694.

Kongsvinger

Glåmdalen: POB 757, 2204 Kongsvinger; tel. 62-88-25-00; fax 62-88-25-01; e-mail redaksjon@glomdalen.no; internet www.glomdalen.no; f. 1926; daily; Labour; Editor ROLF NORDBERG; circ. 19,848.

Kristiansand

Fædrelandsvennen: POB 369, 4664 Kristiansand; tel. 38-11-30-00; fax 38-11-30-01; e-mail fep@fvn.no; internet www.fvn.no; f. 1875; daily; Liberal independent; Editor FINN HOLMER-HOVEN; circ. 41,326.

Lillehammer

Gudbrandsdølen Dagningen: POB 954, 2604 Lillehammer; tel. 61-22-10-00; fax 61-26-09-60; e-mail redaksjonen@gd.no; internet www.gd.no; f. 1841 and 1894; independent; Editor-in-Chief KRISTIAN SKULLERUD; circ. 26,723.

Lillestrøm

Romerikes Blad: POB 235, 2001 Lillestrøm; tel. 63-80-50-50; fax 63-80-50-60; e-mail redaksjonen@rb.no; internet www.rb.no; f. 1913; Labour; Editor-in-Chief THOR WOJE; circ. 43,238.

Molde

Romsdals Budstikke: POB 2100, 6402 Molde; tel. 71-25-00-00; fax 71-25-00-11; e-mail redaksjon@r-b.no; internet www.rbnett.no; f. 1843; Conservative independent; Editor NILS-KRISTIAN MYHRE; circ. 18,205.

Moss

Moss Avis: POB 248/250, 1530 Moss; tel. 69-20-50-00; fax 69-20-50-02; e-mail jan.tollefsen@moss-avis.no; internet www.moss-avis.no; f. 1876; Liberal/Conservative independent; Editor JAN TOLLEFSEN; circ. 15,304.

Oslo

Aftenposten: POB 1 Sentrum, 0051 Oslo; tel. 22-86-30-00; fax 22-42-63-25; e-mail aftenposten@aftenposten.no; internet www.aftenposten.no; f. 1860; Conservative independent; Editor-in-Chief HANS ERIK MATRE; circ. morning 250,179, evening 131,089.

Akers Avis/Groruddalen Budstikke: POB 100 Grorud, 0905 Oslo; tel. 22-91-88-20; e-mail redaksjonen@groruddalen.no; internet www.groruddalen.no; fax 22-16-01-05; f. 1928; 2 a week; non-political; Editor HJALMAR KIELLAND; circ. 15,171.

Dagbladet: POB 1184 Sentrum, 0107 Oslo; tel. 22-31-06-00; fax 22-31-05-10; e-mail annb@dagbladet.no; internet www.dagbladet.no; f. 1869; daily; Editor-in-Chief ANNE AASHEIM; circ. 135,611.

Dagens Næringsliv: POB 1182 Sentrum, 0107 Oslo; tel. 22-00-11-90; fax 22-00-10-70; e-mail redaksjonen@dn.no; internet www.dn.no; Editor SVEIN-THORE GRAN; circ. 81,391.

Dagsavisen: POB 1183 Sentrum, 0107 Oslo; tel. 22-72-60-00; fax 22-64-92-82; e-mail abonnement@dagsavisen.no; internet www.dagsavisen.no; f. 1884; Labour; Editor-in-Chief ARVID JACOBSEN; circ. 31,403.

Nationen: POB 9390 Grønland, 0135 Oslo; tel. 21-31-00-00; fax 21-31-00-90; e-mail hans.eldegard@nationen.no; internet www.nationen.no; f. 1918; daily; Centre; Editor-in-Chief TOVE LIE; circ. 15,871.

Verdens Gang (VG): Akersgt. 55, POB 1185 Sentrum, 0107 Oslo; tel. 22-00-00-00; fax 22-42-68-70; e-mail redaksjonen@vg.no;

internet www.vg.no; f. 1945; independent; Editor-in-Chief TORRY PEDERSEN; circ. 309,610.

Vårt Land: POB 1180 Sentrum, 0107 Oslo; tel. 22-31-03-10; fax 22-31-03-05; e-mail sentral@vl.no; internet www.vl.no; f. 1945; independent, religious daily; Editor HELGE SIMONNES; circ. 27,146.

Sandefjord

Sandefjords Blad: POB 143, 3201 Sandefjord; tel. 33-42-00-00; fax 33-46-29-91; e-mail redaksjonen@sb.no; internet www.sb.no; f. 1861; Conservative; Editor LEIF MAGNE FLEMMEN; circ. 14,260.

Sarpsborg

Sarpsborg Arbeiderblad: POB 83, 1701 Sarpsborg; tel. 69-11-11-11; fax 69-11-11-00; e-mail redaksjonen@sa.no; internet www.sa.no; f. 1929; independent; Editor EIRIK MOE; circ. 15,016.

Skien

Telemarksavisa AS: POB 2833, Kjørbekk, 3702 Skien; tel. 35-58-55-00; fax 35-52-82-09; e-mail redaksjonen@ta.no; internet www.ta.no; f. 1921; independent; Editor OVE MELLINGEN; circ. 22,346.

Varden: POB 2873 Kjørbekk, 3702 Skien; tel. 35-54-30-00; fax 35-52-83-23; e-mail info@varden.no; internet www.varden.no; f. 1874; Conservative; Editor MAJ-LIS STORDAL; circ. 27,341.

Stavanger

Stavanger Aftenblad: POB 229, 4001 Stavanger; tel. 05150; fax 51-89-30-05; e-mail redaksjonen@aftenbladet.no; internet www.aftenbladet.no; independent; f. 1893; Editor-in-Chief TOM HETLAND; circ. 68,010.

Steinkjer

Trønder-Avisa: Hamnegt., 7738 Steinkjer; tel. 74-12-12-00; fax 74-12-13-13; e-mail redaksjonen@t-a.no; internet www.t-a.no; Centre/Liberal; Editor ARVE LØBERG; circ. 23,268.

Tønsberg

Tønsbergs Blad: POB 2003, Postterminalen, 3103 Tønsberg; tel. 33-37-00-00; fax 33-37-30-10; e-mail redaksjonen@tb.no; internet www.tb.no; f. 1870; Conservative; Editor-in-Chief HÅKON BORUD; circ. 30,354.

Tromsø

Nordlys: Rådhusgt. 3, POB 2515, 9272 Tromsø; tel. 77-62-35-00; fax 77-62-35-01; e-mail firmapost@nordlys.no; internet www.nordlys.no; f. 1902; Labour; Editor HANS KRISTIAN AMUNDSEN; circ. 27,647.

Trondheim

Adresseavisen: 7003 Trondheim; tel. 07200; fax 72-50-15-16; e-mail redaksjon@adresseavisen.no; internet www.adressa.no; f. 1767; Editor ROLF DYRNES SVENDSEN; circ. 79,789.

POPULAR PERIODICALS

Allers: Stenersgt. 2, 0107 Oslo; tel. 21-30-10-00; fax 21-30-12-04; e-mail allersredaktion@afj.no; family weekly; Editor-in-Chief ORY BJØRHOVDE; circ. 123,578.

Bedre Helse: 0441 Oslo; tel. 22-58-53-37; fax 22-58-58-79; e-mail bedrehelse@hm-media.no; internet www.bedrehelse.com; health; Editor INGVILD HAGEN; circ. 35,000 (2007).

Bonytt: 0441 Oslo; tel. 22-58-56-90; fax 22-58-05-85; e-mail bonytt@hm-media.no; internet www.klikk.no/bonytt; home and furnishing; 14 a year; Editor ANNA KOLBERG; circ. 68,000 (2003).

Byavisa: Munkegt. 66E, 7011 Trondheim; tel. 73-95-49-00; fax 73-99-05-60; e-mail redaksjonen@byavisa.no; internet www.byavisa.no; f. 1996; weekly; Editor-in-Chief PAUL JOSTEIN AUNE; circ. 82,000.

Familien: 0441 Oslo; tel. 22-58-57-00; fax 22-58-07-64; e-mail abo-familien@hm-media.no; internet www.familien.no; family fortnightly; Editor-in-Chief IVAR MOE; circ. 151,303 (2002).

Foreldre & Barn: 0441 Oslo; tel. 22-58-50-50; fax 22-58-05-80; e-mail foreldreogbarn@hm-media.no; internet www.foreldreogbarn.no; 11 a year; for parents of young children; Editor EDDA ESPELAND; circ. 59,210 (2000).

Foreldremagasinet: Gullhaugvn 1, 0483 Oslo; POB 5001 Majorstuen, 0301 Oslo; tel. 22-58-55-39; e-mail vibeke.ostelie@hm-media.no; for parents; circ. 20,470 (2000).

Henne: POB 1169 Sentrum, 0107 Oslo; tel. 21-30-10-00; e-mail nettredaksjonen@henne.no; internet www.henne.no; women's; Editor-in-Chief ELLEN ARNSTAD; circ. 45,586.

Hjemmepc: Sandakervn 114B, 0483 Oslo; POB 5001 Majorstuen, 0301 Oslo; tel. 22-58-55-14; e-mail hjemmepc@hm-media.no; internet www.hjemmepc.no; home computers; Editor-in-Chief HALLVARD LUNDE; circ. 28,963 (2003).

Hjemmet: 0441 Oslo; tel. 22-58-50-00; fax 22-58-05-70; e-mail hjemmet@hm-media.no; internet www.hm-media.no; family weekly; Editor-in-Chief LISE HANSEN; circ. 228,313 (2004).

Hytteliv: 0441 Oslo; tel. 22-58-50-00; fax 22-58-58-59; e-mail hytteliv@hm-media.no; internet www.klikk.no/produkthjemmesider/hytteliv; f. 1972; 9 a year; for second-home owners; Editor TURID RØSTE; circ. 55,000 (2000).

I form: Trim.no AS, 6789 Loen; tel. 22-37-30-50; fax 91-38-59-26; e-mail redaksjonen@trim.no; internet www.iform.no; monthly; health and fitness; Editor-in-Chief JENS HENNEBERG; circ. 46,551.

Jærbladet: POB 23, 4349 Bryne; tel. 51-77-99-00; fax 51-48-37-40; internet redaksjon@jbl.no; internet www.jbl.no; 3 days a week; independent; Editor IVAR RUSDAL; circ. 12,477.

KK (Kvinner og Klær): POB 1169 Sentrum, 0107 Oslo; Stenersgt. 2, Oslo; tel. 21-30-10-00; fax 22-63-61-02; e-mail leserservice@kk.no; internet www.kk.no; women's weekly; Editor-in-Chief JUNE TRØNNES HANSSEN; circ. 88,158.

Mann: 0441 Oslo; tel. 22-58-50-00; fax 22-58-05-69; e-mail post@mann.no; internet www.mann.no; men's magazine; Editor-in-Chief ROGER GROENDALEN; circ. 20,000.

Mat & Drikke: Sandakerveien 24D, 0473 Oslo; tel. 90-04-64-40; e-mail olav@matogdrikke.no; internet www.matogdrikke.no; 7 a year; food and wine; Editor-in-Chief LINDAN SANNUM; circ. 23,032.

Norsk Ukeblad: Gullhaugvn 1, 0441 Oslo; tel. 22-58-53-00; fax 22-58-05-69; e-mail nu-tips@hm-media.no; internet www.norskukeblad.no; family weekly; Editor-in-Chief MAJ-LIS STORDAL; circ. 178,119 (2000).

Det Nye: 0441 Oslo; tel. 22-58-50-00; fax 22-58-58-09; e-mail detnye@hm-media.no; internet www.detnye.com; for young women; 14 a year; Editor-in-Chief KRISTIN MA BERG; circ. 72,000.

Programbladet: POB 1151 Sentrum, 0107 Oslo; tel. 22-31-03-10; fax 22-31-04-55; e-mail elins@programbladet.no; internet www.programbladet.no; f. 1946; radio and television weekly; Editor TORGEIR SOLLIEN; circ. 65,000.

Se og Hør: POB 1164 Sentrum, 0128 Oslo; tel. 22-41-51-80; fax 22-41-51-70; f. 1978; news weekly (radio and TV); Editors-in-Chief KNUT HÅVIK, ODD J. NELVIK; circ. 366,887.

TOPP: POB 481 Sentrum, 0107 Oslo; tel. 21-30-12-28; e-mail vilvite@topp.no; internet www.topp.no; monthly; for young people aged between 10 and 17 years; Editors ODD J. NELVIK, KNUT HÅVIK; circ. 48,011.

Vi Menn: 0441 Oslo; tel. 22-58-50-00; fax 22-58-05-71; e-mail vimenn@hm-media.no; internet www.vimenn.no; f. 1951; men's weekly; publ. by Hjemmet Mortensen; Editor-in-Chief ALEXANDER OEYSTAA; circ. 88,700.

SPECIALIST PERIODICALS

Alt om Fiske: Sandakerveien 116, 0484 Oslo; tel. 22-58-50-00; fax 22-58-59-59; e-mail fiske@hm-media.no; internet www.klikk.no/altomfiske; angling; circ. 22,906 (2005); Chief Editor JON LENÆS.

Barnemagasinet BAM: 0441 Oslo; Gullhaugvn 1, 0483 Oslo; tel. 23-00-81-80; fax 23-00-81-89; e-mail postmaster@bam.no; internet www.bam.no; for expectant and new parents; three additional titles, *BAM Gravid*, *BAM Nyfødt* and *BAM Spedbarn*; circ. 80,000 (2000).

Batmagasinet: POB 1169 Sentrum, 0107 Oslo; tel. 21-30-10-00; fax 21-30-12-59; e-mail hans.due@afj.no; internet www.batmagasinet.no; f. 1985; owned by Aller Norge AS; 12 a year; boating, powerboats; Editor HANS DUE; circ. 22,500.

Bil: POB 9247 Vaterland, 0134 Oslo; tel. 23-03-66-00; fax 23-03-66-40; e-mail bil@bilforlaget.no; internet www.bilnorge.no; 10 a year; motoring; Editor KJELL-MAGNE AALBERGSJØ; circ. 51,388.

Bondebladet: POB 9367 Grønland, 0135 Oslo; tel. 21-31-44-00; fax 21-31-44-01; e-mail post@bondebladet.no; internet www.bondebladet.no; f. 1974; weekly; farming; Editor JON LAURITZEN; circ. 85,593.

Familiens Grønne Gleder: 0441 Oslo; Gullhaugvn 1, 0483 Oslo; tel. 22-58-55-13; fax 22-58-05-06; e-mail aud.haugvik@hm-media.no; gardening; circ. 55,000 (2004).

Fjell og Vidde: Den Norske Turistforening, Youngstorget 1, 0181 Oslo; tel. 40-00-18-68; fax 22-42-64-27; e-mail redaksjonen@turistforeningen.no; internet www.turistforeningen.no; f. 1967; 6 a year; organ of The Norwegian Mountain Touring Asscn; Editor HELLE ANDRESEN; circ. 131,000.

Fotball: Sørkedalsvn 10A, 0301 Oslo; tel. 22-96-15-00; fax 22-96-13-52; 8 a year; for football players and spectators; Editor ØYVIND STEEN JENSEN; circ. 98,655.

Gravid: Gullhaugvn 1, 0483 Oslo; POB 5001 Majorstuen, 0301 Oslo; tel. 22-58-55-00; fax 22-58-05-80; e-mail gravid@hm-media.no; internet www.gravid.no; for pregnant women; circ. 15,301 (2000).

NORWAY

Hagen for alle: POB 433, Sentrum, 0103 Oslo; tel. 22-40-12-00; e-mail post@hagenforalle.no; internet www.hagenforalle.no; monthly; gardening; Editor ARILD SANDGREN; circ. 30,000.

Hundesport: POB 163 Bryn, 0611 Oslo; tel. 21-60-09-00; fax 21-60-09-01; e-mail hundesport@nkk.no; internet www.nkk.no; monthly; for dog-owners; circ. 60,000.

IngeniørNytt AS: POB 164, 1332 Østerås; Nils Lassons vei 5, 1359 Eiksmarka; tel. 67-16-34-99; fax 67-16-34-55; e-mail post@ingeniornytt.no; internet www.ingeniornytt.no; every 2 weeks; engineering, architecture; circ. 65,000.

Jakt & Fiske: POB 94, 1378 Nesbru; tel. 66-79-22-00; fax 66-90-15-87; e-mail jaktogfiske@njff.no; internet www.jaktogfiske.info; monthly; hunting and angling; Editor VIGGO KRISTIANSEN; circ. 76,710.

Jakt, Hund & Våpen: Gullhaugvn 1, 0483 Oslo; POB 5001 Majorstuen, 0301 Oslo; tel. 22-58-55-34; e-mail inger.storodegard@hm-media.no; hunting; circ. 25,908 (2000).

Kampanje: Sandakerv. 116, 0483 Oslo; tel. 22-58-50-00; fax 22-15-40-86; e-mail redaksjon@kampanje.com; internet www.kampanje.com; marketing and media; Editor-in-Chief GLENN Ø. STØLDAL; circ. 11,340 (2000).

Kapital: POB 444 Vinderen 0319 Oslo; tel. 23-29-65-50; fax 23-29-65-51; e-mail wenchew@kapital.no; internet www.hegnar.no; fortnightly; business, management; Editor-in-Chief FINN ØYSTEIN BERGH; circ. 40,000.

Kommuniké: POB 9202, 0134 Oslo; tel. 21-03-36-00; fax 21-03-36-50; f. 1936; 9 a year; organ of Norwegian Confederation of Municipal Employees; Editor AUDUN HOPLAND; circ. 54,000.

Kontor & Finans: POB 14 Røa, 0701 Oslo; tel. 22-52-44-60; fax 22-52-24-80; e-mail ergjerts@sn.no; f. 1977; quarterly; business; Editor THOR O. SANDBERG; circ. 100,000.

LINUXmagasinet: POB 7183 Majorstuen, 0307 Oslo; tel. 23-36-82-00; fax 23-36-82-01; e-mail redaksjonen@linmag.no; internet www.linmag.no; Linux operating system, open-source software; 5 a year; Editor-in-Chief SVEIN ERIK TOSTERUD; circ. 8,000.

Motor: POB 494 Sentrum, 0105 Oslo; tel. 22-34-15-55; fax 22-34-14-90; e-mail redaksjonen@motor.no; internet www.motor.no; monthly; motoring, travel and leisure; Editor SVEIN OLA HOPE; circ. 400,000.

Norsk Hagetidend: POB 53 Manglerud, 0612 Oslo; tel. 23-03-16-00; fax 23-03-16-01; e-mail postkasse@hageselskapet.no; internet www.hageselskapet.no; f. 1885; monthly; gardening; Editor BERGLJOT GUNDERSEN; circ. 41,878.

Norsk Landbruk: POB 9303 Grønland, 0135 Oslo; tel. 21-31-44-00; fax 21-31-44-92; e-mail norsk.landbruk@tunmedia.no; internet www.norsklandbruk.no; f. 1882; 22 a year; agriculture, horticulture and forestry; Editor-in-Chief MARIANNE RØHME; circ. 16,172.

Okonomisk Rapport: POB 290 Skøyen, 0213 Oslo; tel. 22-40-41-00; fax 22-40-41-01; e-mail rapport@orapp.no; internet www.orapp.no; business; circ. 24,946 (2000).

PCPro: Sandakervn 114B, 0441 Oslo; POB 5001 Majorstuen, 0301 Oslo; tel. 22-58-59-34; e-mail pcpro@hm-media.no; internet www.pcpro.no; f. 2000; 8 a year; computing; circ. 25,000; Editor-in-Chief KJETIL ENSTAD.

Seilmagasinet: POB 253, 1379 Nesbru; tel. 66-77-40-60; fax 66-77-40-61; e-mail morten.jensen@seilmagasinet.no; internet www.seilmagasinet.no; f. 1975; publ. by MediaNavigering A/S; 10 a year; sailing; Editor MORTEN JENSEN; circ. 14,000.

SKOGeieren: POB 1438 Vika, 0115 Oslo; tel. 22-01-05-50; fax 22-83-40-47; e-mail anders.hals@skog.no; f. 1914; 12 a year; forestry; Editor ANDERS HALS; circ. 46,100.

Snø og Ski: Kongevn 5, 0787 Oslo; tel. 22-92-32-00; fax 22-92-32-50; quarterly; winter and summer sports; Editor KRISTIN MOE KROHN; circ. 42,000.

Teknisk Ukeblad (Technology Review Weekly): POB 5844 Majorstuen, 0308 Oslo; tel. 23-19-93-00; fax 23-19-93-01; e-mail redaksjonen@tu.no; internet www.tu.no; f. 1854; technology, industry, management, marketing and economics journal; Editor-in-Chief TOMMY RUDIHAGEN; circ. 93,542.

Tidsskriftet Sykepleien: POB 456 Sentrum, 0104 Oslo; tel. 22-04-33-04; fax 22-04-33-756; internet www.sykepleien.no; f. 1912; 21 a year; health personnel, nursing; Editor-in-Chief BARTH THOLENS; circ. 69,000.

Tips: Gullhaugvn 1, 0483 Oslo; POB 5001 Majorstuen, 0301 Oslo; tel. 22-58-50-00; fax 22-58-59-19; e-mail firmapost@tips.as; internet www.tips.as; football and betting; circ. 20,000 weekdays, 18,000 weekend (2000).

Utdanning: POB 9191 Grønland, 0134 Oslo; tel. 24-14-20-00; fax 24-14-22-85; e-mail redaksjonen@utdanning.ws; internet www.utdanning.ws; f. 1934; fmrly *Norsk Skoleblad*; weekly; teaching; Editor KNUT HOVLAND; circ. 129,423.

Utsyn: Sinsenvn 25, 0572 Oslo; tel. 22-00-72-00; fax 22-00-72-02; e-mail utsyn@nlm.no; internet www.utsyn.no; 25 a year; organ of Norsk Luthersk Misjonssamband (Norwegian Lutheran Mission); circ. 17,000.

Vi Menn Båt: 0441 Oslo; Gullhaugvn 1, 0483 Oslo; tel. 22-58-50-00; fax 22-58-05-66; e-mail inger.storodegord@hm-media.no; internet www.vimenn.no; f. 1992; 7 a year; boats; Editor MORTEN MUNCH ERICHSEN; circ. 77,000 (2004).

Vi Menn Bil: 0441 Oslo; Gullhaugvn 1, 0483 Oslo; tel. 22-58-50-00; fax 22-58-05-66; e-mail wiggo.frantzen@hm-media.no; internet www.vimenn.no; f. 1996; 10 a year; cars; Editor MORTEN MUNCH ERICHSEN.

Vi Menn Fotball: Gullhaugvn 1, 0483 Oslo; POB 5001 Majorstuen, 0301 Oslo; tel. 22-58-55-15; e-mail erika-o.asker@hm-media.no; internet www.vimenn.no; football; circ. 30,000 (2000).

Villmarksliv: 0441 Oslo; tel. 22-58-50-00; fax 22-58-59-59; e-mail knut.brevik@hm-media.no; internet www.villmarksliv.no; f. 1972; monthly; angling, hunting, photography; Editor-in-Chief KNUT BREVIK; circ. 45,600 (2006).

NEWS AGENCIES

Bulls Pressetjeneste A/S: Ebbellsgt. 3, 0179 Oslo; tel. 22-98-26-60; fax 22-20-49-78; e-mail info@bulls.no; internet www.bulls.no; Man. PAUL E. VATNE.

A/S Norsk Telegrambyrå (NTB) (Norwegian News Agency): Akersgt. 55, POB 6817 St Olavs pl., 0130 Oslo; tel. 22-03-44-00; fax 22-20-12-29; e-mail ntb@ntb.no; internet www.ntb.no; f. 1867; Editor-in-Chief PÅL BJERKETVEDT.

PRESS ASSOCIATIONS

Mediebedriftenes Landsforening (Norwegian Media Businesses' Asscn): Tollbugt. 27, 0157 Oslo; tel. 22-86-12-00; fax 22-42-26-11; e-mail info@mediebedriftene.no; internet www.mediebedriftene.no; Man. Dir ARVID SAND.

Den Norske Fagpresses Forening (Specialized Press Asscn): Akersgt. 41, 0158 Oslo; tel. 24-14-61-00; fax 24-14-61-10.

Norsk Journalistlag (Norwegian Union of Journalists): Torggt. 5, 5th Floor, POB 8793 Youngstorget, 0028 Oslo; tel. 22-05-39-50; fax 22-41-33-70; e-mail nj@nj.no; internet www.nj.no; f. 1946; Sec.-Gen. JAHN-ARNE OLSEN; 8,770 mems (2004).

Norsk Presseforbund (Norwegian Press Asscn): Rådhusgt. 17, POB 46 Sentrum, 0101 Oslo; tel. 22-40-50-40; fax 22-40-50-55; e-mail np@presse.no; internet www.presse.no; f. 1910; asscn of newspapermen, editors and journalists; Pres. KJETIL HAANES; Sec.-Gen. PER EDGAR KOKKVOLD.

Publishers

Andresen & Butenschøn A/S: POB 1153 Sentrum, 0107 Oslo; tel. 23-13-92-40; fax 22-33-58-05; e-mail abforlag@abforlag.no.

Antropos Forlag: Josefinesgt. 12, 0351 Oslo; tel. 22-46-03-74; e-mail forlag@antropos.no; internet www.antropos.no.

H. Aschehoug & Co (W. Nygaard): Sehestedsgt. 3, POB 363 Sentrum, 0102 Oslo; tel. 22-40-04-00; fax 22-20-63-95; e-mail epost@aschehoug.no; internet www.aschehoug.no; f. 1872; general non-fiction, fiction, reference, children's, educational, textbooks; Man. Dir WILLIAM NYGÅRD.

Boksenteret Erik Pettersen & Co A/S: Krusesgt. 11, POB 3125 Elisenberg, 0207 Oslo; tel. 22-54-07-00; fax 22-54-07-07; e-mail bs@boksenteret.no; internet www.boksenteret.no; f. 1999; illustrated, non-fiction, craft, DIY; Man. Dir ERIK PETTERSEN.

Bokvennen Forlag: POB 9017, 0133 Oslo; tel. 22-19-14-25; fax 22-19-14-26; e-mail post@bokvennen.no; internet www.vidarforlaget.no; f. 1989; fiction, essays, biographies; Mans MORTEN CLAUSSEN, JAN M. CLAUSSEN.

F. Bruns Bokhandel og Forlag A/S: Kongensgt. 10–14, 7005 Trondheim; tel. 73-51-00-22; fax 73-50-93-20; f. 1873; local history, technology; Publr FRIDTHJOV BRUN.

Cappelen Akademisk Forlag: POB 350 Sentrum, 0055 Oslo; tel. 21-61-65-00; fax 21-61-72-83; e-mail cafinfo@cappelen.no; internet www.cappelendamm.no; f. 1946; textbooks for universities and colleges, social sciences, law, economics, medicine, health and nursing, educational science, psychology; Publr ESTER MOEN.

Cappelen Damm AS: Mariboesgt. 13, POB 350 Sentrum, 0101 Oslo; tel. 21-61-65-00; fax 22-36-50-40; e-mail web@cappelen.no; internet www.cappelendamm.no; f. 1829; general, educational, popular science, fiction, maps, children's, encyclopaedias; Man. Dir PIP HALLÉN.

Eide Forlag A/S: POB 6050 Postterminalen, 5892 Bergen; tel. 55-38-88-00; fax 55-38-88-01; e-mail post@eideforlag.no; internet www

NORWAY

.eideforlag.no; f. 1880; general, children's, textbooks, fiction, non-fiction; Publrs ARNO VIGMOSTAD, ARNSTEIN BJORKE.

Forlaget Fag og Kultur A/S: St Olavsgt. 12, 0165 Oslo; tel. 23-30-24-00; fax 23-30-24-04; e-mail firmapost@fagogkultur.no; internet www.fagogkultur.no; f. 1987; reference; Man. Dir MARI ETTRE OLSEN.

Fagbokforlaget: POB 6050, Postterminalen, 5892 Bergen; tel. 55-38-88-00; fax 55-38-88-01; e-mail fagbokforlaget@fagbokforlaget.no; internet www.fagbokforlaget.no; f. 1992; general and scientific; Publrs ARNO VIGMOSTAD, ARNSTEIN BJORKE.

Falken Forlag: Helgesens gt. 21, 0553 Oslo; tel. 22-35-54-00; e-mail falkenforlag@falkenforlag.no; internet www.falkenforlag.no; f. 1946; fiction, non-fiction; Publr KIRSTI KRISTIANSEN.

Fonna Forlag: POB 6912 St Olavs pl., 0130 Oslo; tel. 22-20-13-03; fax 22-20-12-01; e-mail fonna@fonna.no; internet www.fonna.no; f. 1934; limited co; general, fiction; Man. Dir ARNT ÅRNES.

Fono Forlag AS: Billingstadsletta 30, POB 169, 1376 Billingstad; tel. 66-84-64-90; fax 66-84-75-07; e-mail mail@fonoforlag.no; internet www.fonoforlag.no; f. 1991; audio books; Gen. Man. HALVOR HANEBORG.

Frifant Forlag A/S: Leinvn 10, 1453 Bjørnemyr; tel. 66-91-29-40; fax 66-91-29-41; e-mail frifor@online.no; internet www.frifant.no; f. 1997.

Genesis Forlag: POB 83, 2027 Kjeller; tel. 63-80-30-99; fax 63-81-69-22; e-mail genesis@genesis.no; internet www.genesis.no; f. 1996; Dir SVEIN ANDERSEN.

John Grieg Forlag A/S: Spelhaugen 20, 5147 Bergen; tel. 55-16-13-44; fax 66-16-13-44; e-mail post@grieg1721.no; internet www.grieg1721.no; f. 1721; children's, art, education, aquaculture; Publr SVEIN SKOTHEIM.

Gyldendal Akademisk: Kristian IVs gt. 13, POB 6730 St Olavs pl., 0130 Oslo; tel. 22-03-43-00; fax 22-03-43-05; e-mail akademisk@gyldendal.no; internet www.gyldendal.no/akademisk; f. 1992; university textbooks; Man. Dir FREDRIK NISSEN.

Gyldendal Norsk Forlag A/S: Sehestedsgt. 4, POB 6860 St Olavs pl., 0130 Oslo; tel. 22-03-41-00; fax 22-03-41-05; internet www.gyldendal.no; f. 1925; general, non-fiction, fiction, biography, religion, cookery, school and university textbooks, children's, manuals; Man. Dir BJØRGUN HYSING.

Hjemmet Mortensen A/S: 0441 Oslo; tel. 22-58-50-00; fax 22-58-50-68; e-mail firmapost@hm-media.no; internet www.hm-media.no; f. 1941; fiction, non-fiction, children's; Man. Dir ANNE BRITT BERENSTEN.

Imprintforlaget A/S: POB 2336 Solli, 0201 Oslo; tel. 23-13-69-30; fax 23-13-69-39; e-mail imprint@imprint.no; internet www.imprint.no; imprints: Omnipax, Pegasus, Unipax; Publr BJØRN SMITH-SIMONSEN.

InfoMediaHuset A/S: POB 382 Sentrum, 0250 Oslo; tel. 21-03-70-01; fax 21-03-70-01; e-mail post@infomediahuset.no; internet infomediahuset.com; f. 1844 as Elanders Forlag; present name adopted 2003; legislation, catalogues; Publr AINA THORSTENSEN.

Kolibri Forlag A/S: POB 44 Øvre Ullern, 0311 Oslo; tel. 92-45-25-29; e-mail post@kolibriforlag.no; internet www.kolibriforlag.no; f. 1982; fantasy, non-fiction, cookery, children's, humour, leisure; Publr ELSE LILL BJØNNES.

Kolon Forlag: Sehestedsgt. 4, POB 6860 St Olavs pl., 0130 Oslo; tel. 22-03-42-02; fax 22-03-41-05; e-mail kolon@gyldendal.no; internet www.kolonforlag.no; f. 1995; modern Norwegian poetry and fiction; Publr BJØRN AAGENÆS.

Kunnskapsforlaget: Gullhaug Torg 1, POB 4432 Nydalen, 0403 Oslo; tel. 22-02-22-00; fax 22-02-22-99; e-mail resepsjonen@kunnskapsforlaget.no; internet www.kunnskapsforlaget.no; f. 1975; reference books, encyclopaedias, dictionaries, atlases, electronic reference titles; Man. Dir KRISTENN EINARSSON.

Libretto Forlag: Kristian 4 gt. 15, 0164 Oslo; tel. 22-20-42-80; fax 22-20-42-81; e-mail post@librettoforlag.no; internet www.librettoforlag.no; f. 1990; children's, gift books and handbooks; Publr TOM THORSTEINSEN.

Lunde Forlag A/S: Sinsenvn 25, 0572 Oslo; tel. 22-00-73-50; fax 22-00-73-73; e-mail post@lundeforlag.no; internet www.lundeforlag.no; f. 1905; religious, general, fiction, children's; Dir TORLEIF BELT.

Luther Forlag: Grensen 3, 0159 Oslo; tel. 22-00-87-80; fax 22-00-87-81; e-mail postkasse@lutherforlag.no; internet www.lutherforlag.no; religious, fiction, general; Dir ASLE DINGSTAD.

Lydbokforlaget A/S: Søreggen 2, 7224 Melhus; tel. 72-85-60-70; fax 72-85-60-90; e-mail info@lydbokforlaget.no; internet www.lydbokforlaget.no; f. 1987; owned by H. Aschehoug & Co (33%), Gyldendal Norsk Forlag (33%) and Stiftergruppen (34%).

Messel Forlag: Øvre Vollgate 15, 0158 Oslo; tel. 22-42-14-20; e-mail info@messelforlag.no; internet www.messelforlag.no; f. 1992; Pub. Dir ANNE-GRETHE MESSEL.

NKI Forlaget: Hans Burumsvn 30, POB 111, 1319 Bekkestua; tel. 67-58-88-00; fax 67-58-19-02; f. 1972; textbooks for secondary and technical schools and colleges; Publr JAN B. THOMSEN.

Norsk Bokreidingslag: POB 6045, 5892 Bergen; tel. 55-30-18-99; fax 55-32-03-56; e-mail post@bodonihus.no; internet www.bokreidingslaget.no; f. 1939; fiction, folklore, linguistics, cultural history; Man. FROYDIS LEHMANN.

Det Norske Samlaget: Jens Bjelkesgt. 12, POB 4672 Sofienberg, 0506 Oslo; tel. 22-70-78-00; fax 22-68-75-02; e-mail det.norske@samlaget.no; internet www.samlaget.no; f. 1868; fiction, non-fiction, poetry, children's, textbooks; Man. Dir TOVE LIE.

Forlaget Oktober A/S: Kr. Augustsgt. 11, POB 6848 St Olavs pl., 0130 Oslo; tel. 23-35-46-20; fax 23-35-46-21; e-mail oktober@oktober.no; internet www.oktober.no; f. 1970; fiction, politics, social and cultural books; Publr GEIR BERDAHL.

Orion Forlag: Skippergt 33, 0154 Oslo; tel. 24-15-50-90; fax 24-15-50-99; e-mail orion@orionforlag.no; internet www.orionforlag.no; f. 1994; Man. Dir GUNN ELIN SCHMIDT.

Pantagruel Forlag A/S: POB 2370 Solli, 0201 Oslo; tel. 23-27-28-10; e-mail alle@pantagruel.no; internet www.pantagruel.no; Pub. Dir ALEXANDER ELGURÉN.

Pax Forlag A/S: Huitfeldtgt. 15, POB 2336 Solli, 0201 Oslo; tel. 23-13-69-00; fax 23-13-69-19; e-mail pax@pax.no; internet www.pax.no; f. 1964; fiction, non-fiction, feminism, social sciences; Man. Dir BJØRN SMITH-SIMONSEN.

Sambåndet Forlag AS: Vetrlidsalm. 1, 5014 Bergen; tel. 55-31-79-63; fax 55-31-09-44; e-mail vestlandskes.bokhandel@vestbok.no; f. 1945; religion, children's, poetry; Dir TARALD UELAND.

Schibsted Forlagene AS: POB 6974 St Olavs pl., 0130 Oslo; tel. 24-14-68-00; fax 24-14-68-01; e-mail schibstedforlag@schibstedforlag.no; internet www.schibstedforlag.no; f. 2004 by merger of Chr. Schibsteds Forlagene A/S (f. 1839) and other units within Schibsted Group; reference, biographies, handbooks, children's, food and drink, sports, foreign language, guides, fiction, comics; Publishing Dir TOR ERIK SOLBERG.

Skolebokforlaget A/S: Stortingsgt. 30, 0161, Oslo; tel. 22-83-77-05; fax 22-83-38-32; f. 1979; educational; Man. Dir HANS B. BUTENSCHØN; Editor SVERRE MØRKHAGEN.

Snøfugl Forlag: POB 95, 7221 Melhus; tel. 72-87-24-11; fax 72-87-10-13; e-mail snoefugl@online.no; internet www.snoefugl.no; f. 1972; fiction, general; Man. ASMUND SNØFUGL.

Solum Forlag A/S: Hoffsvn 18, POB 140 Skøyen, 0212 Oslo; tel. 22-50-04-00; fax 22-50-14-53; e-mail info@solumforlag.no; internet www.solumforlag.no; f. 1973; fiction, human sciences, general; Man. Dir KNUT ENDRE SOLUM.

Spartacus Forlag A/S: POB 2587 Solli, 0203 Oslo; tel. 22-44-56-70; fax 22-44-46-50; e-mail post@spartacus.no; internet www.spartacus.no; f. 1989.

Spektrum Forlag AS: Rosencrantzgt. 22, 0160 Oslo; tel. 22-00-82-60; fax 85-03-64-78; e-mail post@spektrum-forlag.no; internet www.spektrum-forlag.no; f. 1992; Pub. Dir CYRUS BRANTENBERG.

Stabenfeldt A/S: Sothammargeilen 3, 4029 Stavanger; tel. 51-84-54-00; fax 51-84-54-90; f. 1920; general fiction, adventure, reference; Man. Dir JENS OTTO HANSEN.

Tell Forlag A/S: Nilsemarka 5C, 1390 Vollen; tel. 66-78-09-18; fax 66-90-05-72; e-mail tell@tell.no; internet www.tell.no; f. 1987; textbooks and educational books; Man. TELL-CHR. WAGLE.

Tiden Norsk Forlag: Sehestedsgt. 4, POB 6704 St Olavs pl., 0130 Oslo; tel. 23-32-76-60; fax 23-32-76-97; e-mail tiden@tiden.no; internet www.tiden.no; f. 1933; literary fiction, crime, thrillers, fantasy, non-fiction; Pub. Dir RICHARD AARØ.

Tun Forlag A/S: Schweigaardsgt. 34A POB 9303 Grønland, 0135 Oslo; tel. 21-31-44-00; e-mail post@tunforlag.no; internet www.boktunet.no; f. 2005; agriculture, hunting, fishing, outdoor, handicrafts, culture, horses, dogs; Man. HEIDI JANNICKE ANDERSEN.

Universitetsforlaget AS: Sehestedsgt. 3, POB 508 Sentrum, 0105 Oslo; tel. 24-14-75-00; fax 24-14-75-01; e-mail post@universitetsforlaget.no; internet www.universitetsforlaget.no; f. 1950; publishers to the Universities of Oslo, Bergen, Trondheim and Tromsø and various learned societies; school books, university textbooks, specialized journals; Man. Dir SVEIN SKARHEIM.

Verbum Forlag: Bernhard Getzgt. 3, POB 6624 St Olavs pl., 0129 Oslo; tel. 22-93-27-21; fax 22-93-27-27; e-mail verbumforlag@verbumforlag.no; internet www.verbumforlag.no; f. 1820; Christian literature; Man. TURID BARTH PETTERSEN.

Forlaget Vett & Viten AS: Nye Vakås Vn. 56, POB 203, 1379 Nesbru; tel. 66-84-90-40; fax 66-98-39-99; e-mail vv@vettviten.no; internet www.vettviten.no; f. 1987; medical, technical and engineering textbooks; Publr JAN LIEN.

NORWAY

Wigestrand Forlag A/S: POB 621, 4003 Stavanger; tel. 51-51-76-10; fax 51-51-76-40; e-mail forlag@wigestrand.no; internet www.wigestrand.no; Publr ØYVIND WIGESTRAND.

PUBLISHERS' ASSOCIATION

Den norske Forleggerforening (Norwegian Publishers' Asscn): Øvre Vollgt. 15, 0158 Oslo; tel. 22-00-75-80; fax 22-33-38-30; e-mail dnf@forleggerforeningen.no; internet www.forleggerforeningen.no; f. 1895; Chair. GEIR BERDAHL; Man. Dir PER CHRISTIAN OPSAHL; 52 mem. firms.

Broadcasting and Communications

REGULATORY AUTHORITY

Post- og Teletilsynet (Norwegian Post and Telecommunications Authority): Nygård 1, POB 93, 4791 Lillesand; tel. 22-82-46-00; fax 22-82-46-40; e-mail firmapost@npt.no; internet www.npt.no; f. 1987; issues and supervises regulations, concessions and licences; expanded to incorporate postal matters in 1997; Dir-Gen. WILLY JENSEN.

TELECOMMUNICATIONS

NetCom AS: Sandakervn 140, 0485 Oslo; tel. 92-40-50-50; internet www.netcom.no; f. 1990; mobile cellular telecommunications; owned by TeliaSonera AB (Sweden); Man. Dir AUGUST BAUMANN.

Network Norway AS: Grensevn 92, 0663 Oslo; tel. 51-84-64-00; fax 23-40-43-01; e-mail 09060@networknorway.no; internet www.networknorway.no; f. 2005; mobile cellular telecommunications and broadband internet services; Man. Dir ARILD E. HUSTAD.

Norkring AS: Telenor Broadcast, 1331 Fornebu; tel. 67-89-20-00; fax 67-89-36-11; internet www.norkring.no; f. 1996; owned by Telenor Broadcast Holding A/S; Dir TORBJOERN TEIGEN.

Telenor ASA: Snarøyvn 30, 1331 Fornebu; tel. 67-89-00-00; e-mail infomaster@telenor.no; internet www.telenor.no; offers fixed-line telecommunications, broadband internet and digital television services; 53.97% stake owned by Ministry of Trade and Industry; CEO JON FREDRIK BAKSAAS.

    djuice: Snarøyvn 30, 1331 Fornebu; tel. 81-07-70-00; fax 67-89-00-00; e-mail infomaster@telenor.com; internet www.djuice.no; mobile cellular telecommunications; subsidiary of Telenor ASA.

Tele2 Norge AS: Brynsengfaret 6B, 0667 Oslo; tel. 21-31-90-00; fax 21-31-91-00; internet www.tele2.no; f. 1998; fixed-line and mobile cellular telecommunications services, also broadband internet access; subsidiary of Tele2 AB (Sweden); Man. Dir HAAKON DYRNES.

BROADCASTING

Radio

Norsk Rikskringkasting (NRK) (Norwegian Broadcasting Corpn): Bj. Bjørnsons pl. 1, 0340 Oslo; tel. 23-04-70-00; fax 23-04-75-75; e-mail info@nrk.no; internet www.nrk.no; autonomous public corpn; operates three national services (including a youth programme), 18 regional services (including one in the language of the Sámi—Lappish) and an international service, Radio Norway International; Chair. of Govs HALLVARD BAKKE; Dir-Gen. HANS-TORE BJERKAAS; CEO (Broadcasting) ANNIKA BIØRNSTAD.

P4—Radio Hele Norge ASA: Serviceboks, 2626 Lillehammer; tel. 61-24-84-44; fax 61-24-84-45; e-mail p4@p4.no; internet www.p4.no; f. 1993; private commercial station; Man. Dir KALLE LISBERG.

Radio Norge: Kråkerøyvn 2 POB 144, 1601 Fredrikstad; tel. 69-70-76-00; fax 69-70-76-01; e-mail redaksjonen@radionorge.com; internet www.radionorge.com; f. 2004 as Kanal24; present name adopted 2008; 77% stake owned by SBS Radio Norge AS; Man. Dir BENTE KLEMETSDAL.

Television

Digital terrestrial broadcasting began in 2007. Analogue signals were due to be discontinued by the end of 2009.

Canal Digital Norge AS: POB 1036, 3905 Porsgrunn; fax 81-53-20-30; internet www.canaldigital.no; digital satellite and cable television services; also broadband internet access; owned by Telenor ASA; Man. Dir SVEIN ERIK DAVIDSEN.

Norsk Rikskringkasting (NRK) (Norwegian Broadcasting Corpn): Dir of Television ANNIKA BIØRNSTAD.

RiksTV AS: Økernvn 145, POB 393, Økern, 0513 Oslo; tel. 22-88-37-90; fax 22-88-37-91; e-mail post@rikstv.no; internet www.rikstv.no; f. 2005; a digital terrestrial, cable and satellite television service, offering up to 26 channels; co-owned by NRK, Telenor Broadcast Holding and TV 2 Gruppen; Man. Dir ESPEN THORSBY.

Directory

TV-2: Nøstegaten 72, POB 7222, 5020 Bergen; tel. 02255; fax 21-00-60-03; e-mail 02255@tv2.no; internet www.tv2.no; f. 1992; private commercial station; Man. Dir ALF HILDRUM; Dir of Programmes NILS KETIL ANDRESEN.

TV Norge AS: Biskop Gunnerus gt. 6, POB 11, Sentrum, 0101 Oslo; tel. 21-02-20-00; fax 22-05-10-00; e-mail tvnorge@tvnorge.no; internet www.tvnorge.no; private commercial television channel; owned by ProSiebenSat1 (Germany); Dir-Gen. MORTEN SKOTLAND HANSEN; Dir of Programmes EIVIND LANDSVERK.

Finance

In 2008 there were 18 commercial banks (comprising the major banks, some large regional banks and a number of smaller regional and local banks) and 121 savings banks.

Kredittilsynet (Financial Supervisory Authority of Norway): Østensjøvn 43, POB 100 Bryn, 0611 Oslo; tel. 22-93-98-00; fax 22-63-02-26; e-mail post@kredittilsynet.no; internet www.kredittilsynet.no; f. 1986; finance inspectorate; Dir-Gen. BJØRN SKOGSTAD AAMO.

BANKING

(cap. = capital; res = reserves; dep. = deposits; m. = million; brs = branches; amounts in kroner)

Central Bank

Norges Bank: Bankplassen 2, POB 1179 Sentrum, 0107 Oslo; tel. 22-31-60-00; fax 22-41-31-05; e-mail central.bank@norges-bank.no; internet www.norges-bank.no; f. 1816; holds the exclusive right of note issue; cap. and res 56,548m., dep. 2,304,252m. (Dec. 2007); Chair. of Supervisory Bd MARY KVIDAL; Gov. SVEIN GJEDREM; 12 brs.

Principal Commercial Banks

Bank 1 Oslo AS: Hammersborggt. 2, POB 778 Sentrum, 0106 Oslo; tel. 21-02-50-50; fax 21-02-50-51; e-mail bank1@sparebank1.no; internet www.oslo.sparebank1.no; f. 1898; present name adopted 2000; cap. 291m., res 671m., dep. 15,647m. (Dec. 2006); CEO TORBJØRN VIK; Chair. ELDAR MATHISEN; 10 brs.

DnB NOR Bank ASA: Aker Brygge, Stranden 21, 0021 Oslo; tel. 91-50-30-00; fax 24-02-53-00; internet www.dnbnor.no; f. 2004 by merger of Den norske Bank ASA and Union Bank of Norway; cap. 17,514m., res 43,659m., dep. 1,038,936m. (Dec. 2007); Chair. ANNE CARINE TANUM; Pres. and CEO RUNE BJERKE; 187 brs.

Fokus Bank ASA: Søndregt. 13-15, 7466 Trondheim; tel. 72-88-20-11; fax 72-88-20-61; e-mail fokus@fokus.no; internet www.fokus.no; f. 1987 by merger of Böndernes Bank A/S, Buskerudbanken A/S, Forretningsbanken A/S and Vestlandsbanken; present name adopted 1996; owned by Danske Bank A/S (Denmark); Chair. SØREN MØLLER NIELSEN; Man. Dir THOMAS BORGEN; 55 brs.

Nordea Bank Norge ASA: Middelthunsgt. 17, POB 1166 Sentrum, 0107 Oslo; tel. 22-48-50-00; fax 22-48-47-49; internet www.nordea.no; fmrly Christiania Bank og Kreditkasse ASA; present name adopted 2001; part of Nordea Bank Group (Sweden); cap. 2,597m., res −160m., dep. 337,178m. (Dec. 2007); Group Pres. and CEO CHRISTIAN CLAUSEN; Senior Exec., Norway GUNN WÆRSTED; 130 brs.

Nordlandsbanken ASA: Molov. 16, 8002 Bodø; tel. 91-50-89-00; fax 75-55-87-89; e-mail post@nordlandsbanken.no; internet www.nordlandsbanken.no; f. 1893; owned by DnB NOR Bank ASA; cap. 625m., res 814m., dep. 25,623m. (Dec. 2007); Chair. PÅL SKOE; CEO MORTEN STØVER; 16 brs.

Principal Savings Banks

Sparebank 1 Nord-Norge: Storgt. 65, POB 6800, 9298 Tromsø; tel. 91-50-22-44; fax 77-62-25-71; e-mail 02244@snn.no; internet www.snn.no; f. 1989 as Sparebanken Nord-Norge, following merger of Sparebanken Nord and Tromsø Sparebank; present name adopted 2008; cap. 800m., dep. 48,579m. (Dec. 2006); Chair. KJELL OLAV PETTERSEN; CEO HANS OLAV KARDE; 81 brs.

Sparebank 1 SMN: Sondregt. 4, 7467 Trondheim; tel. 73-58-51-11; fax 73-58-64-50; e-mail smn@smn.no; internet www.smn.no; f. 1823 as Trondhjems Sparebank; fmrly Sparebanken Midt-Norge; present name adopted 2008; cap. 1,349m., res 3,032m., dep. 61,912m. (Dec. 2007); Chair. PER AXEL KOCHE; Man. Dir FINN HAUGAN; 56 brs.

SpareBank 1 SR-Bank: Bjergsted Terrasse 1, 4001 Stavanger; tel. 91-50-20-02; fax 51-53-54-67; e-mail sr-kundeservice@sr-bank.no; internet www.sr-bank.no; f. 1839 as Egersund Sparebank; merged with 22 savings banks in 1976; present name adopted 2007; cap. 1,131m., res 2,667m., dep. 72,269m. (Dec. 2006); CEO TERJE VAREBERG; 52 brs.

Sparebanken Hedmark: Strandgt. 15, 2302 Hamar; tel. 62-51-20-00; fax 62-53-29-75; e-mail konsern@sparebanken-hedmark.no; internet www.sparebanken-hedmark.no; f. 1845; cap. 3,587m.,

NORWAY

Directory

dep. 30,566m. (Dec. 2006); Chair. RICHARD H. HEIBERG; Man. Dir HARRY KONTERUD; 29 brs.

Sparebanken Møre: Keiser Wilhelmsgt. 29–33, POB 121, 6002 Ålesund; tel. 70-11-30-00; fax 70-12-26-70; e-mail sparebanken .more@sbm.no; internet www.sbm.no; f. 1985; cap. 627m., res 1,417m., dep. 19.800m. (Dec. 2006); CEO OLAV-ARNE FISKERSTRAND; 31 brs.

Sparebanken Pluss: Rådhusgt. 7–9, POB 200, 4662 Kristiansand; tel. 38-17-35-00; fax 38-17-35-04; e-mail firmapost@ sparebankenpluss.no; internet www.sparebankenpluss.no; f. 1824; merged with four savings banks in 1987; dep. 19,254m., total assets 21,542m. (Dec. 2006); Chair. JENS FREUCHEN; Man. Dir STEIN HANNEVIK.

Sparebanken Sør: Vestervn. 1, POB 602, 4800 Arendal; tel. 37-02-50-00; fax 37-02-19-36; e-mail international@sor.no; internet www .sor.no; f. 1825; cap. and res 2,039m., dep. 23,400m. (Dec. 2006); Chair. ALICIA JERVELL; Man. Dir MORTEN KRAFT; 27 brs.

Sparebanken Vest: Kaigt. 4, 5016 Bergen; tel. 91-50-55-55; fax 55-21-73-50; e-mail sparebanken.vest@spv.no; internet www.spv.no; f. 1823 as Bergens Sparebank; merger 1982 of 25 savings banks; cap. 250m., res 3,230m., dep. 53,519m. (Dec. 2006); Man. Dir STEIN KLAKEGG; 59 brs.

Bankers' Associations

Finansnaeringens Hovedorganisasjon (FNH) (Norwegian Financial Services Asscn): Hansteensgt. 2, POB 2473 Solli, 0202 Oslo; tel. 23-28-42-00; fax 23-28-42-01; e-mail fnh@fnh.no; internet www.fnh.no; f. 2000 by merger of Den norske Bankforening (Norwegian Bankers' Asscn) and Norges Forsikringsforbund (Norwegian Insurance Asscn); 53 mems; Chair. IDAR KREUTZER; Man. Dir ARNE SKAUGE.

Sparebankforeningen i Norge (Savings Banks Asscn): Universitetsgt. 8, St Olavs pl., POB 6772, 0130 Oslo; tel. 22-11-00-75; fax 22-36-25-33; e-mail firmapost@sparebankforeningen.no; internet www .sparebankforeningen.no; f. 1914; Pres. TERJE VAREBERG (Sparebank 1 SR-Bank); Man. Dir ARNE HYTTNES; 121 mems.

STOCK EXCHANGE

Oslo Børs: Tollbugt. 2, POB 460 Sentrum, 0105 Oslo; tel. 22-34-17-00; fax 22-34-19-25; e-mail pe@oslobors.no; internet www.oslobors .no; f. 1819; 5.8% owned by NASDAQ OMX; part of an alliance (Nordic Exchanges—NOREX) with the Copenhagen (Denmark), Helsinki (Finland), Reykjavík (Iceland) and Stockholm (Sweden) stock exchanges, launched 1999; Pres. and CEO BENTE A. LANDSNES.

INSURANCE

Assuranceforeningen Skuld: POB 1376 Vika, 0114 Oslo; tel. 22-00-22-00; fax 22-42-42-22; e-mail osl@skuld.com; internet www .skuld.com; f. 1897; mutual, shipowners' protection and indemnity; Chair. ERIK GLØERSEN; Pres. and CEO DOUGLAS JACOBSOHN.

Gjensidige NOR Forsikring: Drammensvn 228, POB 276, 1326 Lysaker; tel. 22-96-80-00; fax 22-96-92-00; e-mail epost@ gjensidigenor.no; internet www.gjensidigenor.no; f. 1847; merged with Forenede Norge Forsikring and Forenede Skadeforsikring in 1993; Pres. HELGE KVAMME; CEO LARS AUSTIN.

Nordea Liv AS: POB 7078, 5020 Bergen; tel. 22-48-50-00; fax 55-17-33-80; internet www.nordealink.no; f. by merger of Norske Liv AS and Vesta Liv AS; life insurance; Dir JØRUND VANDVIK.

Uni Storebrand: Håkon VIIs gt. 10, POB 1380 Vika, 0114 Oslo; tel. 22-31-50-50; e-mail international@storebrand.no; internet www .storebrand.no; f. 1991 by merger of Storebrand (f. 1947) and Uni Forsikring (f. 1984); group includes life, non-life and international reinsurance operations; taken over by govt administrators in 1992 and new holding co (Uni Storebrand New) formed, following suspension of payments to creditors; CEO IDAR KREUTZER.

TrygVesta: Folke Bernadottesvei 50, 5020 Bergen; tel. 89-56-35-21; internet www.trygvesta.com; f. 1884; f. as Vesta; bought by Tryg-Baltica in 1999; current name adopted 2002; includes Skadeforsikringsselskapet Vesta A/S (general insurance), Vesta Liv A/S (life insurance), Vesta Finans A/S (financial services); Chair. MIKAEL OLUFSEN; CEO STINE BOSS.

Vital Insurance: Folke Bernadottesvei 40, 5020 Bergen; tel. 55-17-70-00; fax 55-17-86-99; e-mail kundesenter@vital.no; internet www .vital.no; f. 1990 by a merger between NKP Forsikring and Hygea; life and pension insurance; Dir-Gen. TOM RATHKE.

Insurance Association

Finansnaeringens Hovedorganisasjon (FNH) (Norwegian Financial Services Asscn): (see Bankers' Associations, above).

Trade and Industry

GOVERNMENT AGENCY

Innovasjon Norge (Innovation Norway): Akersgt. 13, POB 448 Sentrum, 0104 Oslo; tel. 22-00-25-00; fax 22-00-25-01; e-mail post@ invanor.no; internet www.invanor.no; f. 2004 to replace Norges Turistråd (Norwegian Tourist Board), Norges Eksportråd (Norwegian Trade Council), Statens nærings- og distriktsutviklingsfond (SND-Industrial and Regional Development Fund) and Statens Veiledningskontor for Oppfinnere (SVO-Government Consultative Office for Inventors); state-owned; operates in all Norwegian counties and more than 30 countries world-wide; Pres. KJELL A. STOREIDE; Man. Dir GUNN OVESEN.

CHAMBERS OF COMMERCE

Bergen Chamber of Commerce and Industry: POB 843, Sentrum, 5807 Bergen; tel. 55-55-39-00; fax 55-55-39-01; e-mail firmapost@bergen-chamber.no; internet www.bergen-chamber.no; f. 1915; Pres. EGIL HERMAN SJURSEN; Man. Dir MARIT WARNCKE.

Oslo Chamber of Commerce: Drammensvn 30, POB 2874 Solli, 0230 Oslo; tel. 22-12-94-00; fax 22-12-94-01; e-mail mail@chamber .no; internet www.chamber.no; Man. Dir LARS-KÅRE LEGERNES.

INDUSTRIAL AND TRADE ASSOCIATION

Norges Skogeierforbund (Norwegian Forest Owners' Fed.): Roald Amundsensgt. 6, POB 1438 Vika, 0115 Oslo; tel. 23-00-07-50; fax 22-42-16-90; e-mail nsf@skog.no; internet www.skog.no; f. 1913; aims to promote the economic and technical interests of the forest owners, a general forest policy in the interests of private ownership and co-operation between the affiliated asscns; Man. Dir GUDBRAND KVAAL; 38,000 mems.

EMPLOYERS' ASSOCIATIONS

Næringslivets Hovedorganisasjon (Confederation of Norwegian Business and Industry): Middelthunsgt. 27, POB 5250 Majorstua, 0303 Oslo; tel. 23-08-80-00; fax 23-08-80-01; e-mail firmapost@nho .no; internet www.nho.no; f. 1989; rep. org. for industry, crafts and service industries; Pres. JENS ULLTVEIT-MOE; Dir-Gen. FINN BERGSEN, Jr; c. 18,500 mems who must also belong to one of the 21 affiliated national asscns, chief among which are the following:

Bensinforhandlernes Bransjeforening (BBF) (Petrol Retailers' Organization): POB 5488, Majorstua, 0305 Oslo; tel. 23-08-87-50; fax 23-08-87-51; e-mail bbf@nho.no; internet www .bensinforhandlerne.no; Man. Dir JAN CARHO; 700 mems.

Energibedriftenes Landsforening (EBL) (Electricity Industry Asscn): Sørkedalsveien 6, POB 7184 Majorstua, 0307 Oslo; tel. 23-08-89-00; fax 23-08-89-01; e-mail ebl@ebl.no; internet www.ebl .no; Dir-Gen. STEINAR BYSVEEN.

Fiskeri—og Havbruksnæringens Landsforening (FHL) (Fish and Aquaculture Industries): POB 5471 Majorstua, 0305 Oslo; tel. 23-08-87-30; fax 23-08-87-31; e-mail firmapost@fhl.no; internet www.fhl.no; Dir-Gen. GEIR ANDREASSEN.

NHO Grafisk (Fed. of Graphic Arts Enterprises): Tollbugt. 27, 0369, POB 5495, Majorstua, 0305 Oslo; tel. and fax 23-08-78-70; e-mail hh@nhografisk.no; internet www.nhografisk.no; f. 1906; fmrly Visuell Kommunikasjon Norge; Man. Dir PÅL STEPHENSEN; 240 mems.

NHO Håndverk (Fed. of Craft Industries): POB 5250, Majorstua, 0303 Oslo; tel. 23-08-87-60; fax 23-08-87-63; e-mail handverk@nho .no; internet www.hbl.no; Man. Dir HARRY BJERKENG.

NHO Luftfart (Norwegian Aviation Industry): POB 5474 Majorstua, 0305 Oslo; tel. 23-08-85-70; fax 23-08-85-71; e-mail nholuftfart@nho.no; internet www.nholuftfart.no; Dir TORBJØRN LOTHE.

NHO Mat og Drikke (Fed. of Norwegian Food and Drink Industry): POB 5472 Majorstua, 0305 Oslo; tel. 23-08-87-00; fax 23-08-87-20; e-mail firmapost@nhomd.no; internet www.nhomatodrikke .no; Dir-Gen. KNUT MARONI.

NHO Reiseliv (Norwegian Hospitality Asscn): POB 5465 Majorstua, Essendropsgt. 6, 0305 Oslo; tel. 23-08-86-20; fax 23-08-86-21; e-mail firmapost@nhoreiseliv.no; internet www.nhoreiseliv.no; f. 1997 as Reiselivsbedriftenes Landsforening; present name adopted 2006; Dir-Gen. KNUT ALMQUIST.

NHO Service (Fed. of Service Industries): POB 5473, Majorstua, 0305 Oslo; tel. 23-08-86-50; fax 23-08-86-59; e-mail firmapost@sbl .no; internet www.nhoservice.no; Admin. Dir PETTER FURULUND.

Norges Bilbransjeforbund (NBF) (Asscn of Norwegian Motor Car Dealers and Services): Drammensvn 97, POB 2804 Solli, 0204 Oslo; tel. 22-54-21-00; fax 22-44-10-56; e-mail firmapost@nbf.no; internet www.nbf.no; f. 1962; Admin. Dir SYVER LEIVESTAD.

NORWAY

Norsk Industri (Fed. of Norwegian Industries): POB 7072 Majorstuen, 0306 Oslo; Oscars gt. 20, 0352 Oslo; tel. 22-59-00-00; fax 22-59-00-01; e-mail post@norskindustri.no; internet www.norskindustri.no; f. 2005 by merger of Teknologibedriftenes Landsforening (Fed. of Norwegian Manufacturing Industries) and Prosessindustriens Landsforening (Fed. of Norwegian Process Industries); Chair. RASMUS SUNDE; Man. Dir STEIN LIER-HANSEN; c. 2,000 mems.

Skogbrukets Landsforening (SL) (Forestry Asscn): Essendropsgt. 6, 0368 Oslo; POB 5496, Majorstuen 0305 Oslo; tel. 23-08-86-80; fax 23-08-86-75; e-mail firmapost@skogbruk.no; internet www.skogbruk.no; f. 1928; Man. Dir HAAVARD ELSTRAND.

Transportbedriftenes Landsforening (TL) (Fed. of Norwegian Transport Cos): POB 5477 Majorstuen, 0305 Oslo; tel. 23-08-86-00; fax 23-08-86-01; e-mail tl@transport.no; internet www.transport.no; Dir-Gen. SIRI BERGH.

Bryggeri- og Drikkevareforeningen (Norwegian Breweries and Soft Drink Producers): POB 7087 Majorstua, 0306 Oslo; tel. 23-08-86-96; fax 22-60-30-04; e-mail info@bryggeriforeningen.no; internet www.bryggeri-ogdrikkevareforeningen.no; f. 1901; Man. Dir HALFDAN KVERNELAND OLAFSSON; 21 mems.

Entreprenørforeningen—Bygg og Anlegg (General Contractors): POB 5485 Majorstua, 0305 Oslo; tel. 23-08-75-00; fax 23-08-75-30; e-mail firmapost@ebanett.no; internet www.ebanett.no; Admin. Dir ØIVIND SERERGREN; 220 mems.

Handels- og Servicenæringens Hovedorganisasjon (HSH) (Federation of Commercial and Service Enterprises): Henrik Ibsensgt. 90, POB 2900 Solli, 0230 Oslo; tel. 22-54-17-00; fax 22-06-09-30; e-mail info@hsh-org.no; internet www.hsh-org.no; f. 1990 by merger; 10,400 mem. cos; Pres. CARL OTTO LØVENSKIOLD.

Oljeindustriens Landsforening (OLF) (Oil Industry): Vassbotnen 1, POB 8065, 4068 Stavanger; tel. 51-84-65-00; fax 51-84-65-01; e-mail firmapost@olf.no; internet www.olf.no; Admin. Dir PER TERJE VOLD.

TBL Møbel- og Innredning (Asscn of Norwegian Furnishing Industries): POB 7072 Majorstuen, 0306 Oslo; tel. 22-59-00-00; fax 22-59-00-01; e-mail tbl@tbl.no; Exec. Man. EGIL SUNDET.

Treforedlingsindustriens Bransjeforening (TFB) (Pulp and Paper): Oscarsgt. 20, POB 7772 Majorstuen, 0306 Oslo; tel. 22-59-00-51; fax 23-08-78-99; e-mail mb@norskindustri.no; Chair. PER A. SOERLIE; 23 mems.

UTILITIES

Electricity

Bergenshalvøens Kommunale Kraftselskap AS (BKK): Kokstadvegen 37, POB 7050, 5020 Bergen; tel. 55-12-70-00; fax 55-12-70-01; e-mail firmapost@bkk.no; internet www.bkk.no; f. 1920; production, distribution and supply of electricity; supplies customers throughout western Norway; 49.9% stake owned by Statkraft AS, 37.75% owned by Bergen city council, 12.35% owned by 16 other municipalities; Chair. MARTIN SMITH-SIVERTSEN; CEO ATLE NETELAND.

Fjordkraft AS: Folke Bernadottes Vei 38, POB 3507, Fyllingsdalen, 5845 Bergen; tel. 06-11-0; fax 33-46-63-73; internet www.fjordkraft.no; electricity supplier; owned by BKK, Skagerak Energi and Statkraft; Man. Dir SVERRE GJESSING; c. 325,000 customers.

Hafslund ASA: Drammensvn 144, 0277 Oslo; tel. 22-43-50-00; internet www.hafslund.no; f. 1898; electrical generation (nine hydroelectric plants), sales, distribution, safety, installation, security and network infrastructure; Pres. and CEO CHRISTIAN BERG; Chair. CHRISTIAN BRINCH.

Lyse Energi AS: Breiflåtvn 18, Mariero, 4017 Stavanger; tel. 51-90-80-00; internet www.lyse.no; production, distribution and supply of electricity; also supplier of natural gas and telecommunications services; owned by 16 municipalities in south Rogaland (incl. Stavanger city council); Chair. IVAR RUSDAL; Man. Dir EIMUND NYGAARD.

Nordkraft AS: Teknologivn 2, 8517 Narvik; tel. 76-96-10-00; fax 76-94-10-67; e-mail post@nordkraft.no; internet www.nordkraft.no; f. 2006 by merger of Nordkraft AS and Narvik Energi AS; production of electricity (hydroelectric power plants and wind-power farms); 50.01% stake owned by Narvik municipal council, 33.33% owned by DONG Energy A/S (Denmark); Chair. SIGVE NILS STOKLAND; Man. Dir OLAF ANDREAS LARSEN.

Salten Kraftsamband AS (SKS): Eliasbakken 7, 8205 Fauske; tel. 75-40-22-00; e-mail firmapost@sks.no; internet www.sks.no; production, distribution and supply of electricity nation-wide; 40% stake owned by Bodø municipal council, 23.7% by DONG Energy A/S (Denmark); Man. Dir LEIF FINSVEEN.

Statnett SF: Husebybakken 28B, POB 5192 Majorstua, 0302 Oslo; tel. 22-52-70-00; fax 22-52-70-01; e-mail firmapost@statnett.no; internet www.statnett.no; f. 1992; national power grid co; supervises and co-ordinates the operation of the entire Norwegian power system, also operates own transmission lines and submarine cables, as well as sub-stations and switching stations; state-owned co under the jurisdiction of the Ministry of Petroleum and Energy; Pres. and CEO ODD AUKE LONT.

Trondheim Energi AS: 7005 Trondheim; tel. 73-96-10-11; fax 73-96-11-90; e-mail informasjon@trondheimenergi.no; internet www.trondheimenergi.no; f. 1901 as Trondheim Energiverk; present name adopted 2007; production and supply of electricity in Sør-Trøndelag; owned by Statkraft AS; Chair. JON BRANDSAR.

Ustekveikja Energi AS: Geilovegen 68, 3580 Geilo; tel. 32-08-70-00; fax 32-08-70-10; e-mail post@ustekveikja.no; internet www.ustekveikja.no; f. 1992; producer and retailer of electricity; supplies customers throughout Norway; Man. Dir BJØRN SKARET.

Other major production and distribution companies include Agder Energi AS, Akershus Energi AS, Bodø Energi AS, Fredrikstad Energi AS, Haugeland Kraft AS, HelgelundsKraft AS, Istad AS, Oppland Energi AS, Østfold Energi AS, Skagerrak Energi AS, Sira-Kvina Kraftselskap, Troms Kraft AS, TrønderEnergi AS and Vest-Agder Energiverk.

Water

Responsibility for water supply in Norway lies with the municipalities.

TRADE UNIONS

National Confederations

Landsorganisasjonen i Norge (LO) (Norwegian Confederation of Trade Unions): Folkets Hus, Youngstorget 11, 0181 Oslo; tel. 23-06-10-50; fax 23-06-17-43; e-mail inter@lo.no; internet www.lo.no; f. 1899; Pres. ROAR FLÅTHEN; 860,000 mems in 21 affiliated unions (2009).

Unio (Confed. of Unions for Professionals): Stortingsgt 2, 0158 Oslo; tel. 22-70-88-50; fax 22-70-88-50; e-mail post@unio.no; internet www.unio.no; f. 2001; Pres. ANDERS FOLKESTAD; 280,979 mems in 10 affiliated unions (Jan. 2009).

Yrkesorganisasjonenes Sentralforbund (YS) (Confed. of Vocational Unions): Brugt. 19, 0134 Grønland, Oslo; tel. 21-01-36-00; fax 21-01-37-20; e-mail post@ys.no; internet www.ys.no; f. 1977; Pres. TORE EUGEN KVALHEIM; 213,288 mems in 22 affiliated unions (July 2008).

Principal Affiliated Unions

Delta (Public- and Private-Sector Services Union): Brugt. 19, POB 9202, 0134 Oslo; tel. 21-01-36-00; fax 21-01-36-50; e-mail post@delta.no; internet www.delta.no; affiliated to YS; Pres. GUNN OLANDER; 61,590 mems (July 2008).

EL & IT Forbundet (Electricians and Information Technology Workers): Youngstorget 11, 0181 Oslo; tel. 23-06-34-00; fax 23-06-34-01; e-mail firmapost@elogit.no; internet www.elogit.no; f. 1999 by merger of Tele- og Dataforbundet (TD) and Norsk Elektriker- og Kraftstasjonsforbundet (NEKF); affiliated to LO; Pres. HANS OLAV FELIX; 37,000 mems.

Fagforbundet (Norwegian Union of Municipal and General Employees): POB 7003, Keysersgt 15, 0165 Oslo; tel. 23-06-40-00; fax 23-06-40-01; e-mail servicetorget@fagforbundet.no; internet www.fagforbundet.no; f. 2003; affiliated to LO; Pres. JAN DAVIDSEN; 305,000 mems.

Fellesforbundet (The Norwegian United Federation of Trade Unions): Lilletorget 1, 0184 Oslo; tel. 23-06-31-00; fax 23-06-31-01; e-mail fellesforbundet@fellesforbundet.no; internet www.fellesforbundet.no; f. 1988; affiliated to LO; Pres. ARVE BAKKE; 162,000 mems.

Fellesorganisasjonen (FO) (Social Educators and Social Workers): Mariboesgt. 13, POB 4693 Sofienberg, 0506 Oslo; tel. 23-06-11-70; fax 23-06-11-14; e-mail kontor@fo.no; internet www.fo.no; f. 1992; affiliated to LO; Pres. RANDI REESE; 24,000 mems.

Finansforbundet (Financial Services Union): Schweigaards gt. 14, 5th Floor, 0185 Oslo; tel. 22-05-63-00; fax 22-17-06-90; e-mail post@finansforbundet.no; internet www.finansforbundet.no; f. 2000 by merger of 3 separate unions; affiliated to YS; Pres. JORUN BERLAND; 37,388 mems (July 2008).

Handel og Kontor i Norge (Commercial and Office Employees): Youngstorget 11, 0181 Oslo; tel. 22-03-11-80; fax 22-03-12-06; internet www.handelogkontor.no; f. 1908; affiliated to LO; Pres. STURE ARNTZEN; 62,000 mems.

Industri Energi (IE): Youngstorget 11, 0181 Oslo; tel. 23-06-22-30; fax 22-03-13-60; e-mail oslopost@industrienergi.no; internet www.industrienergi.no; f. 2006 by merger of Norsk Olje- og Petrokjemisk Fagforbund (Norwegian Oil and Petrochemical Industry Union) and Norsk Kjemisk Industriarbeiderforbund (Norwegian Chemical Industry Union); affiliated to LO; Pres. LEIF SANDE; 55,000 mems.

NORWAY

LO Stat (Government Employees): Møllergt. 10, 0179 Oslo; tel. 23-06-10-53; fax 22-42-00-75; e-mail lostat@lostat.no; internet www.lostat.no; f. 1939 as Statstjenestemannskartellet; present name adopted 1996; affiliated to LO; Pres. MORTEN ØYE; 105,867 mems.

Norsk Arbeidsmandsforbund (Norwegian General Workers): Grubbegt. 6, POB 8704, Youngstorget, 0028 Oslo; tel. 23-06-10-50; fax 23-06-10-92; e-mail norsk@arb-mand.no; internet www.arbeidsmandsforbundet.no; f. 1895; affiliated to LO; Pres. ERNA C. HAGENSEN; 34,000 mems.

Norsk Næring- og Nytelsesmiddelforbund (NNN) (Norwegian Food and Allied Workers): Arbeidersamfunnets pl. 1, 0181 Oslo; POB 8719 Youngstorget, 0028 Oslo; tel. 23-10-29-60; fax 23-10-29-61; e-mail firmapost@nnn.no; internet www.nnn.no; f. 1923; affiliated to LO; Pres. JAN-EGIL PEDERSEN; 30,556 mems (Dec. 2008).

Norsk Post- og Kommunikasjonsforbund (Postkom) (Norwegian Union of Postal and Communications Workers): Møllergt. 10, 0179 Oslo; tel. 23-06-22-50; e-mail postkom@postkom.no; internet www.postkom.no; f. 2000; affiliated to LO; Pres. ODD-CHRISTIAN ØVERLAND; 22,000 mems.

Norsk Sjømannsforbund (Norwegian Seamen): Maritimt Hus, Rosenkrantz gt. 15-17, 0125 Oslo; POB 2000, Vika, 0125 Oslo; tel. 22-82-58-00; fax 22-33-66-18; e-mail firmapost@sjomannsunion.no; internet www.sjomannsforbundet.no; f. 1910; affiliated to LO; Pres. JACQUELINE SMITH; 11,500 mems.

Norsk Sykepleierforbund (Norwegian Nurses' Union): Tollbugt 22, POB 456, Sentrum, 0104 Oslo; tel. 22-04-33-04; fax 22-04-32-99; e-mail post@sykepleierforbundet.no; internet www.sykepleierforbundet.no; f. 1912; affiliated to Unio; Pres. LISBETH NORMANN; 87,083 mems (Jan. 2009).

Norsk Tjenestemannslag (Norwegian Civil Service Union): Møllergt. 10, 0179 Oslo; tel. 23-06-15-99; fax 23-06-15-55; e-mail post@ntl.no; internet www.ntl.no; f. 1947; affiliated to LO; Pres. TURID LILLEHEIE; 47,000 mems.

Norsk Transportarbeiderforbund (Norwegian Transport Workers): Hammersborg Torg 3, 0179 Oslo; tel. 23-06-27-40; fax 22-20-50-89; e-mail ntf@transportabeider.no; internet www.transportarbeider.no; f. 1896; affiliated to LO; Pres. PER ØSTVOLD; 20,000 mems.

Utdanningsforbundet (Union of Education): Hausmannsgt 17, 0182 Oslo; tel. 24-14-20-00; fax 24-14-21-00; e-mail post@utdanningsforbundet.no; internet www.utdanningsforbundet.no; f. 2002 by merger of the Norwegian Union of Teachers (Norsk Lærerlag) and the Teachers' Union of Norway (Lærerforbundet); affiliated to Unio; Pres. HELGA HJETLAND; 146,543 mems (Jan. 2009).

Transport

RAILWAYS

In 2008 there were 4,087 km of state railways (standard gauge), of which 2,599 km were electrified.

Jernbaneverket (JBV) (Norwegian National Rail Administration): POB 4350, 2308 Hamar; tel. 22-45-50-00; fax 22-45-54-99; e-mail dsft@jbv.no; internet www.jernbaneverket.no; f. 1996; manages railway infrastructure; Dir-Gen. ELISABETH ENGER.

Norges Statsbaner AS (NSB) (Norwegian State Railways): Prinsensgt. 7–9, 0048 Oslo; tel. 23-15-00-00; fax 23-15-33-00; internet www.nsb.no; f. 1854 as private line; govt-owned; Chair. INGEBORG MOEN BORGERUD; CEO EINAR ENGER.

ROADS

In 2006 there were 92,863 km of public roads in Norway, of which 717 km were motorways and 27,274 km were national main roads. In 2005 a new bridge linking Norway and Sweden was opened in Svinesund.

Vegdirektoratet: Brynsengfaret 6A, POB 8142 Dep., 0033 Oslo; tel. 22-07-35-00; fax 22-07-37-68; e-mail firmapost@vegvesen.no; internet www.vegvesen.no; f. 1864; Dir TERJE MOE GUSTAVSEN.

SHIPPING

At 31 December 2007 the Norwegian merchant fleet numbered 2,088 vessels, with a combined displacement of 18.2m. grt. The total includes vessels on the Norwegian International Ship Register (established in 1987), which numbered 565 vessels at 31 December 2007, with a combined displacement of 14.7m. grt. The Norwegian-controlled fleet represents some 5% of the world's total fleet.

Port Authorities

Ålesund Port Authority: Ålesund Havn KF, Skansekaia, 6002 Ålesund; tel. 70-16-34-00; fax 70-16-34-01; e-mail post@alesund.havn.no; internet www.alesund.havn.no.

Bergen: Bergen & Omland Havnevesen, Slottsgt. 1, 5003 Bergen; tel. 55-56-89-50; fax 55-56-89-86; e-mail bergen.havn@bergen-kommune.telemax.no; internet www.bergenhavn.no; Harbour Master GUNVALD ISAKSEN.

Bodø Port Authority: Bodø Havnevesen, POB 138, 8001 Bodø; tel. 75-58-15-80; fax 75-58-39-90; e-mail firmapost@bodo-havnevesen.no; Harbour Master TERJE DOKSRØD.

Borg Harbour Port Authority: Borg Havnevesen, Oravn 27, POB 1205 Gamle, 1631 Fredrikstad; tel. 69-35-89-00; fax 69-35-89-20; e-mail borghavnevesen@borghavn.of.no; Port Capt. SVEN-JAN JOHANSEN.

Flekkefjord Port Authority: Flekkefjord Havnevesen, Eschebrygga, 4400 Flekkefjord; tel. 38-32-89-90; fax 38-32-89-91; e-mail post@flekkefjord.kommune.no; internet flekkefjord.kommune.no; Harbour Master HELGE NILSEN.

Flora Hamn og Næring KF Port Authority: POB 17, 6901 Florø; tel. 57-75-67-40; fax 57-74-09-16; e-mail hamn@flora.kommune.no; internet www.flora.kommune.no; Harbour Master NILS ARILD HOVLAND.

Grenland Port Authority: Grenland Havnevesen, POB 20, 3951 Brevik; tel. 35-93-10-00; fax 35-93-10-11; e-mail ghv@grenland-havn.no; internet www.port.of.grenland.com; Port Capt. TORJUS JOHNSEN.

Halden Port Authority: Halden Havnevesen, Wiels Pass 4, 1771 Halden; tel. 69-17-48-30; fax 69-17-46-83; e-mail post@haldenhavn.no; internet www.haldenhavn.no; Harbour Master ØYVIND JOHANNESSEN.

Hammerfest Port Authority: Hammerfest Havnevesen, POB 123, 9615 Hammerfest; tel. 78-40-74-00; fax 78-40-74-01; e-mail harbour@hammerfest.havn.no; internet www.hammerfesthavn.no; f. 1828; Harbour Master ROLL STIANSEN.

Haugesund Port Authority: Karmsund Interkommunale Havnevesen, Garpaskjaerskaien, POB 186, 55001 Haugesund; tel. 52-70-37-50; fax 52-70-37-69; e-mail post@karmsund-havn.no; internet www.karmsund-havn.no.

Horten Port Authority: Borre Havnevesen, POB 167, 3192 Horten; tel. 33-03-17-17; fax 33-04-47-27; tel. horten.havnevesen@horten.kommune.no; internet www.hortenhavn.no; Harbour Master HANS CHRISTIAN GUNNENG.

Kirkenes Port Authority: Municipality of Sør-Varanger, Rådhusplassen, POB 406, 9915 Kirkenes; tel. 78-97-74-99; fax 78-97-75-89; e-mail post@kirkenes-havn.no; internet www.kirkenes-havn.no.

Kopervik Port Authority: Karmsund Havnevesen, POB 134, 4291 Kopervik; tel. 52-84-43-00; fax 52-84-43-10; e-mail postmattak@karmsund-havn.no; internet www.karmsund-havn.no; Harbour Master O. E. MAELAND.

Kragerø Port Authority: Board of Harbour Commissioners, POB 158, 3791 Kragerø; tel. 35-98-17-50; fax 35-99-13-34; e-mail post@kragero-havnevesen.no; Harbour Master Capt. BORGAR F. THORSEN.

Kristiansand Port Authority: Kristiansand Havn KF, Gravane 4, 4661 Kristiansand; tel. 38-00-60-00; fax 38-02-70-99; e-mail post@kristiansand-havn.no; internet www.kristiansand-havn.no; Port Dir STEIN E. HAARTVEIT.

Kristiansund Port Authority: Kristiansund og Nordmøre Havn IKS, Kaibakken 1, 6509 Kristiansund; tel. 40-00-65-04; fax 71-67-14-83; e-mail info@knhavn.no; internet www.knhavn.no; Harbour Master JAN OLAV BJERKESTRAND.

Larvik Port Authority: Larvik Havn KF, POB 246 Sentrum, Havnegt. 5, 3251 Larvik; tel. 33-16-57-50; fax 33-16-57-59; e-mail post@larvik.havn.no; internet www.larvik.havn.no; Port Dir JAN FREDRIK JONAS.

Malm Port Authority: Fosdalens Bergverks Aktie, 7720 Malm; tel. 74-15-71-00; fax 74-15-78-76; Agent OLAV VAARDAL.

Mandal Port of Agder Port Authority: Mandal Havnevesen KF, POB 905, 4509 Mandal; tel. 40-00-51-52; fax 38-26-34-76; e-mail mandalhavn@mandal.kommune.no; internet www.mandal-kommune.no/mandalhavn; Harbour Master JONNY O. HANSEN.

Mongstad Port Authority: Statoil Mongstad, 5954 Mongstad; tel. 56-34-40-00; fax 56-34-47-29; e-mail jja@statoilhydro.com; internet www.statoilhydro.com/mongstad; Port Capt. JON M. JAKOBSEN.

Mosjøen Port Authority: Mosjøen Havnevesen, Mosjøen 8663; tel. 75-10-18-70; fax 75-10-18-71; e-mail torbjorn.jorgensen@vefsn.kommune.no; Port Man. GUNNAR JOHANSEN.

Moss Port Authority: Moss Havnevesen, Moss Maritime Centre, POB 118, 1501 Moss; tel. 69-20-87-00; fax 69-20-87-01; e-mail firmapost@moss-havn.no; internet www.moss-havn.no; Harbour Master REIDAR MAGNUS HANSEN.

Narvik Port Authority: Narvik Havn KF, POB 627, 8508 Narvik; tel. 76-95-03-70; fax 76-95-03-84; e-mail post@narvikhavn.no; internet www.portofnarvik.com; Port Man. RUNE J. ARNØY.

Odda Port Authority: Odda Havnevesen, Opheimsgt 31, 5750 Odda; tel. 53-64-84-00; fax 53-64-12-92; e-mail svenn.berglie@odda.kommune.no; Harbour Master OLAV BJØERKE.

NORWAY

Orkanger Port Authority: Orkanger Havnevesen, 7300 Orkanger; tel. 72-48-00-09; fax 72-48-10-03; e-mail tom.hamborg@orkdal.kommune.no; Port Man. TOM HAMBORG.

Oslo Port Authority: Oslo Havnevesen, POB 230 Sentrum, 0103 Oslo 1; tel. 81-50-06-06; fax 23-49-26-01; e-mail postmottak@havnevesenet.oslo.kommune.no; internet www.ohv.oslo.no; Port Dir ANNE SIGRID HAMRAN.

Risør Port Authority: Risør Havnekontor, 4950 Risør; tel. 37-15-05-00; fax 37-15-00-58; Agent KJELL SKARHEIM.

Sandefjord Port Authority: Sandefjord Havnevesen, Tollbugt. 5, 3200 Sandefjord; tel. 33-45-60-38; fax 33-46-26-13; e-mail info@visitsandefjord.com; internet www.cruisesandefjord.com; Harbour Master LEIF ALLUM.

Sauda Port Authority: Sauda Havnekontor, 4200 Sauda; tel. 52-78-62-21; fax 52-78-39-68; Harbour Master HARALD HALVORSEN LOELAND.

Stavanger Port Authority: Stavanger Interkommunale Havn IKS, Nedre Strandgt. 51, 4005 Stavanger; tel. 51-50-12-00; fax 51-50-12-22; e-mail info@stavanger.havn.no; internet www.stavanger.havn.no; Port Dir BJØRN HELGOY.

Tønsberg Port Authority: Tønsberg Havnevesen, Nedre Langgate 36, 3126 Tønsberg; tel. 33-35-45-00; fax 33-33-26-75; e-mail tonsberg.havn@tonsberg.havn.no; internet www.tonsberghavn.no; Harbour Master PER SVENNAR.

Tromsø Port Authority: Tromsø Havnevesen, POB 392, 9254 Tromsø; tel. 77-66-18-50; fax 77-66-18-51; e-mail adm@tromso.havn.no; internet www.tromso.havn.no; f. 1827; Port Capt. HALVAR PETTERSEN.

Trondheim Port Authority: Trondheim Havn, Pirsenteret, 7462 Trondheim; tel. 73-99-17-00; fax 73-99-17-17; fax firmapost@trondheim.havn.no; internet www.trondheim.havn.no; Port Capt. SIGURD KLEIVEN.

Vardø Port Authority: Vardø Havn KF, POB 50, 9951 Vardø; tel. 78-98-72-76; fax 78-98-78-28; tel. vardhavn@online.no; internet www.vardoport.no; Harbour Master INGOLF ERIKSEN.

Shipping Organizations

Nordisk Skibsrederforening (Nordisk Defence Club): Kristinelundvn 22, POB 3033 Elisenberg, 0207 Oslo; tel. 22-13-56-00; fax 22-43-00-35; e-mail post@nordisk.no; internet www.nordisk.no; f. 1889; Pres. MORTEN WERRING; Man. Dir GEORG SCHEEL.

Norges Rederiforbund (Norwegian Shipowners' Asscn): POB 1452 Vika, 0116 Oslo; tel. 22-40-15-00; fax 22-40-15-15; e-mail post@rederi.no; internet www.rederi.no; f. 1909; Dir-Gen. STURLA HENRIKSEN.

Norsk Skipsmeglerforbund (Norwegian Shipbrokers' Asscn): Fr. Nansens pl. 9, 0160 Oslo; tel. 22-20-14-85; fax 22-42-74-13; e-mail mail@shipbroker.no; internet www.shipbroker.no; f. 1919; Pres. THOMAS G. ROED; Gen. Man. GRETE C. NOER; 141 mems.

Det Norske Veritas (DNV): Veritasvn 1, POB 300, 1322 Høvik; tel. 67-57-99-00; f. 1864; global provider of services for managing risk; acts on behalf of 130 national maritime authorities; CEO HENRIK O. MADSEN.

Rederienes Landsforening (Federation of Norwegian Coastal Shipping): Essendropsgt. 6, POB 5201 Majorstua, 0302 Oslo; tel. 23-08-85-60; fax 23-08-85-61; e-mail rlf@rlf.no; internet www.rlf.no; Admin. Dir HARALD THOMASSEN.

Principal Companies

Actinor Shipping ASA: Rådhusgt. 27, 0158 Oslo; tel. 22-42-78-30; fax 22-42-72-04; Pres. ALF OLSEN.

Bergshav Management AS: POB 8, 4891 Grimstad; tel. 37-25-63-00; fax 37-25-63-01; e-mail mgmt@bergshav.com; internet www.bergshav.com; Chair. ATLE BERGSHAVEN.

Bona Shipping AS: Rådhusgt. 27, POB 470 Sentrum, 0105 Oslo; tel. 22-31-00-00; fax 22-31-00-01; internet www.bona.no; Pres. RAGNAR BELCK-OLSEN.

BW Gas ASA: Drammensvn 106, POB 2800 Solli, 0204 Oslo; tel. 22-12-05-05; fax 22-12-05-00; e-mail bwgas@bwgas.com; internet www.bwgas.com; f. 1935; fmrly Bergesen d.y. ASA; Chair. MORTEN SIG. BERGESEN; Man. Dir SVEIN ERIK AMUNDSEN.

Grieg Shipping A/S: POB 781, 5804 Bergen; tel. 55-57-66-00; fax 55-57-68-55; internet www.grieg.no; Chair. ELISABETH GRIEG.

Leif Høegh & Co ASA: Wergelandsvn 7, POB 2596 Solli, 0203 Oslo; tel. 22-86-97-00; fax 22-20-14-08; e-mail ihc@hoegh.no; internet www.hoegh.no; f. 1927; vessels for the transport of liquefied gas, ores and other bulk materials, car and ro-ro ships and reefers; world-wide services; Chief Exec. THOR J. GUTTORMSEN; Chair. WESTYE HØEGH.

Jahre-Wallem AS: Strandpromenaden 9, POB 271, 3201 Sandefjord; tel. 33-48-44-44; fax 33-48-44-43; e-mail jawa@jawa.no; Dir HENRIK LIAN.

Jebsens Management A/S: POB 4145 Dreggen, 5015 Bergen; tel. 55-31-03-20; fax 55-31-72-70; f. 1929; services in Scandinavia, and to Europe, Far East, Australia, the Americas; Owner ATLE JEBSEN.

Torvald Klaveness & Co AS: Harbitzalleen 2A, POB 182 Skøyen, 0212 Oslo; tel. 22-52-60-00; fax 22-50-67-31; e-mail management@klaveness.com; internet www.klaveness.com; Chair. TOM ERIK KLAVENESS; Man. Dir TROND HARALD KLAVENESS.

Knutsen OAS Shipping A/S: Smedasundet 40, POB 2017, 5504 Haugesund; tel. 52-70-40-00; fax 52-70-40-40; e-mail firmapost@knutsenoas.com; internet www.knutsenoas.com; Man. JENS ULLTVEIT MOE.

A/S J. Ludwig Mowinckels Rederi: Bradbenken 1, POB 4070 Dreggen, 5835 Bergen; tel. 55-21-63-00; fax 55-21-63-05; e-mail mailbox@jlmr.no; internet www.jlmr.no; f. 1898; tankers and cargo services; Man. Dir BØRGE ROSENBERG.

Norbroker Shipping & Trading A/S: POB 34, 4401 Flekkefjord; Strandgt. 36, 4400 Flekkefjord; tel. 38-32-61-00; fax 38-32-61-01; e-mail drycargo@norbroker.no; internet www.norbroker.no; Man. Dir ARNT IVAR BJOERNELI.

Odfjell ASA: Conrad Mohrsveg 29, 5892 Bergen; POB 6101 Postterminalen, 5892 Bergen; tel. 55-27-00-00; fax 55-28-47-41; e-mail bgo.mail@odfjell.com; internet www.odfjell.no; f. 1916; transportation and storage of liquid chemicals; Chair. BERNT DANIEL ODFJELL.

Fred.Olsen Marine Services AS: Prinsensgt. 2B, POB 374 Sentrum, 0101 Oslo; tel. 22-34-11-00; fax 22-42-13-14; e-mail foms@foms.no; internet www.fredolsen-marine.com; Man. Dir LEIF LAURITZEN.

OSM Ship Management AS: POB 69, 4661 Kristiansand; tel. 38-04-12-00; fax 38-04-12-01; e-mail osm.krs@osm.no; internet www.osm.no; part of OSM Group; frmly Rasmussen Maritime Services AS; Man. Dir OIVIND STAERK.

Det Stavangerske Dampskibsselskab: POB 848, 4004 Stavanger; tel. 51-84-56-00; fax 51-84-56-01; e-mail mail@dsd-shipping.no; tel. www.dsd-shipping.no; Chair. HENRIK AGER-HANSSEN.

Uglands Rederi A/S: POB 128, 4891 Grimstad; tel. 37-29-26-00; fax 37-04-47-22; e-mail jjuc@jjuc.no; internet www.jjuc.no; f. 1930; part of J. J. Ugland Cos (f. 1996; group of cos with shipping interests; tankers, bulk carriers, crane vessel, barges).

A. Wilhelmsen Gruppen AS: Beddingen 8, Aker Brygge, POB 1583 Vika, 0118 Oslo; tel. 22-01-42-00; fax 22-01-43-72; e-mail thagen@awilco.no; Chair. ARNE WILHELMSEN; Man. Dir KNUT INGER NOSSEN.

Wilh. Wilhelmsen ASA: Strandvn 20, POB 33, 1324 Lysaker; tel. 67-58-40-00; fax 67-58-40-80; e-mail ww@wilhelmsen.com; internet www.wilhelmsen.com; f. 1861; regular fast freight services worldwide; Chair. WILHELM WILHELMSEN; Man. Dir INGAR SKAUG.

CIVIL AVIATION

In 2008 there were 46 airports in Norway, the principal international airport being Gardermoen Airport, 47 km north of Oslo.

Avinor AS: POB 150, 2061 Gardermoen; Oslo Atrium, Christian Fredrikspl. 6, 0154 Oslo; tel. 81-53-05-50; fax 67-03-00-01; e-mail post@avinor.no; internet www.avinor.no; f. 2003; state-owned; owns and operates 46 airports in Norway and responsible for air traffic control services; Chair. INGE K. HANSEN; CEO SVERRE QUALE.

Luftfartstilsynet (Civil Aviation Authority): POB 243, 8001 Bodø; tel. 75-58-50-00; fax 75-58-50-05; e-mail postmottak@caa.no; internet www.caa.no; f. 2000; independent administrative body under the Ministry of Transport and Communications; Dir-Gen. HEINE RICHARDSEN.

Principal Airlines

SAS Norge ASA: 0800 Oslo; tel. 64-81-77-00; fax 67-58-78-77; internet www.sas.no; f. 2004 as SAS Braathens; present name adopted 2007; wholly-owned subsidiary of the Scandinavian Airlines System (SAS) Group; Gen. Man. OLA H. STRAND.

Scandinavian Airlines System (SAS): Head Office: Snaröyvn 57, 0080 Oslo; tel. 64-81-60-50; e-mail cr@sas.no; internet www.sas.no; f. 1946; the national carrier of Denmark, Norway and Sweden; consortium owned two-sevenths by SAS Danmark A/S, two-sevenths by SAS Norge ASA and three-sevenths by SAS Sverige AB; parent org. 50% owned by the Govt and 50% by private shareholders; SAS group includes the consortium and the subsidiaries in which the consortium has a majority or otherwise controlling interest; the Board consists of two members from each of the parent cos and the chairmanship rotates among the three national chairmen on an annual basis; strategic alliance with Lufthansa (Germany) formed in 1995; Chair. FRITZ H. SCHUR; Pres. and CEO MATS JANSSON.

Norwegian Air Shuttle ASA: Oksenøyvn 10A, POB 115, 1330 Fornebu; tel. 67-59-30-00; fax 67-59-30-01; e-mail post@norwegian.no; internet www.norwegian.no; f. 1966; present name since 1993; low-cost carrier, offering flights to domestic and European destinations; CEO BJØRN KJOS.

NORWAY

Widerøes Flyveselskap AS: Langstranda 6, POB 257, 8001 Bodø; tel. 75-51-35-00; fax 75-51-35-81; e-mail kundservice@wideroe.no; internet www.wideroe.no; f. 1934; subsidiary of Scandinavian Airlines System (SAS) Group; scheduled domestic service and flights to destinations in Denmark, Russia, Sweden and the United Kingdom; Pres. and CEO LARS KOBBERSTAD.

Tourism

Norway is a popular resort for tourists who prefer holidays in rugged, peaceful surroundings. It is also a centre for winter sports. In 2006 receipts from tourism amounted to US $4,251m., compared with $3,959m. in the previous year. In 2006 visitor arrivals totalled 4.9m.

Innovasjon Norge (Innovation Norway): Akersgt 13, POB 448 Sentrum, 0104 Oslo; tel. 22-00-25-00; fax 22-00-25-01; e-mail post@invanor.no; internet www.visitnorway.com; f. 2004 to replace Norges Turistråd (Norwegian Tourist Board), Norges Eksportråd (Norwegian Trade Council), Statens nærings- og distriktsutviklingsfond (SND-Industrial and Regional Development Fund) and Statens Veiledningskontor for Oppfinnere (SVO-Government Consultative Office for Inventors); state-owned; operates in all Norwegian counties and more than 30 countries world-wide; Pres. KJELL A. STOREIDE; Man. Dir GUNN OVESEN.

NORWEGIAN EXTERNAL TERRITORIES
SVALBARD

Introductory Survey

Location and Climate
The Svalbard archipelago is the northernmost part of the Kingdom of Norway. It lies in the Arctic Sea, 657 km north of mainland Norway, between latitudes 74°N and 81°N and longitudes 10°E and 35°E, comprising a total area of 61,022 sq km (23,561 sq miles). The group consists of nine principal islands, Spitsbergen (formerly Vestspitsbergen), the main island, Kvitøya, Edgeøya, Barentsøya, Nordaustlandet, Prins Karls Forland, Kong Karls Land, Hopen and Bjørnøya (Bear Island), some 204 km to the south of the main island, together with numerous small islands. Mild Atlantic winds lessen the severity of the Arctic climate, but almost 60% of the land area is covered with glaciers. Average temperatures range from −16°C (3°F) to 6°C (43°F), and precipitation in the lowlands averages some 200 mm per year.

History and Government
The existence of Svalbard has probably been known since Viking exploration in the 12th century. There were conflicting claims to sovereignty by Britain, the Netherlands and Denmark-Norway in the 17th century, when the area was an important centre for whale hunting, but interest subsequently lapsed until the early years of the 20th century, when coal deposits were discovered. On 9 February 1920 14 nations signed a treaty recognizing Norwegian sovereignty over Svalbard. International rights of access and economic exploitation were agreed, but the use of the islands for bellicose purposes and the construction of fortifications were expressly forbidden.

Svalbard has been part of the Kingdom of Norway since it was formally incorporated in 1925. The territory is administered by a Sysselmann (Governor), resident at Longyearbyen, on Spitsbergen, which is the administrative centre of the archipelago. The Sysselmann is responsible to the Polar Department of the Ministry of Justice and the Police. The Norwegian Polar Institute acts in an advisory capacity to the administration. Svalbard lies within the same judicial jurisdiction as the city of Tromsø.

In accordance with the Svalbard Treaty of 1920, the Norwegian Government prescribed a mining code in 1925, regulating all mineral prospecting and exploitation in the islands and their territorial waters extending to 4 nautical miles (7.4 km). The Mining Code is administered by a Commissioner of Mines.

In 1941 the population was evacuated by Allied forces for the duration of the war, and three years later the USSR, to which Svalbard was of considerable strategic interest, unsuccessfully sought Norway's agreement to a revision of the 1920 treaty whereby part of the archipelago would become a Soviet-Norwegian condominium. Russia currently maintains a helicopter station and a mobile radar station adjoining its coal-mining settlement at Barentsburg on Spitsbergen. Russia (and, before it, the USSR) has refused to recognize Norway's unilateral declaration of a fisheries protection zone around Svalbard from 1977.

In June 1994 vessels of the Norwegian coastguard severed the nets of Icelandic fishing boats that were alleged to be fishing within the fisheries protection zone. The Icelandic Government subsequently withdrew its boats from the zone; in August, however, Norway claimed that an Icelandic boat had opened fire on a Norwegian coastguard vessel.

Particularly since a Royal Decree of 1971, the Norwegian administration has endeavoured to protect the flora, fauna and environment of Svalbard. The protected areas, which total 39,815 sq km of land, or 64% of the land area, and 76,293 km of sea, include seven national parks, the most recently created (September 2005) being at Indre Wijdefjorden in northern Spitsbergen. From April 2007 visitors to Svalbard were required to pay an 'environment fee', the income from which was to be added to the territory's environmental protection fund.

Apart from a small permanent research station established by Poland, only Norway and Russia maintain permanent settlements on Svalbard. In order to continue Norwegian occupation of Svalbard, thus ensuring its future as a Norwegian territory and protecting it from potential, rival claims for sovereignty, notably from Russia, in 2000 the Svalbard administration proposed the opening of a new coal mine on Spitsbergen to exploit newly discovered reserves. Svalbard has also been promoted as a centre for scientific research; at the end of 2000 there were more than 20 scientific stations from foreign countries on the islands. In January 2004 representatives of the Norwegian Ministry of Foreign Affairs met with Russia's Deputy Minister of Foreign Affairs to discuss possible bilateral co-operation in Svalbard, in the areas of energy, fisheries and environmental protection. In February 2008 the Svalbard Global Seed Vault was inaugurated by the Norwegian Prime Minister, Jens Stoltenberg. Established at a depth of 130 m in the permafrost of a mountain at Longyearbyen, the vault was designed to store up to 4.5m. seed samples from around the world, in order to preserve biological diversity for future generations.

In November 2001 Norwegians resident on Spitsbergen conducted, for the first time, an election for a local council. The new Longyearbyen Council (Longyearbyen Lokalstyre) replaced the incumbent Svalbard Council, which had been partly appointed by the state-owned mining company, Store Norske Spitsbergen Kulkompani. The new 15-seat Council was to exercise only limited power in issues relating to health, education and the Church, which would all continue to be controlled by the state. The rate of participation in the local election was only 51.5% of the electorate; a multi-party grouping won eight seats on the Council, while Det norske Arbeiderparti (DnA—Norwegian Labour Party) secured six seats; Høyre (Conservative) took the remaining seat.

Elections to the Longyearbyen Council were held in October 2003. DnA won 44.6% of the votes cast and six seats on the Council, while the multi-party grouping won five seats, with 31.0% of the votes cast. The Fremskrittspartiet (FrP—Progress Party) and Høyre each won two seats, respectively receiving 12.3% and 12.1% of the votes cast. The Council's mandate was increased from two to four years.

At elections to the Council held in October 2007 DnA won 44.4% of the votes cast and seven seats on the Council. The multi-party grouping won 26.9% of the votes cast and four seats, while Høyre received 17.7% of the votes and three seats. The FrP failed to secure any seats. The rate of voter participation was recorded at just 40.3% of the electorate.

Social and Economic Affairs
The total population in January 2009 was 2,565, of whom 2,085 were resident in Norwegian settlements (including 293 foreign nationals), 470 in Russian settlements and 10 in the Polish settlement. There are limited recreational, transport, financial and educational facilities on Svalbard. There are hospitals in the capital, Longyearbyen (which had a population of 2,075 in March 2007), and in Barentsborg.

Coal is the islands' main product. In 2006 2,419,745 metric tons were shipped from mines on Svalbard (2,331,605 tons from Norwegian mines). The Norwegian state-owned coal company Store Norske Spitsbergen Grubekompani (SNSG) directly employs some 230 people. Until 1989 Store Norske Spitsbergen Kulkompani (SNSG's parent company) operated many local services and provided most of the infrastructure, but in that year these functions were assumed by the state company Svalbard Samfunnsdrift, which employed 140 people in 1998. By 1998 the number of people employed in the Norwegian mines had declined to 201 (from 358 in 1991), but the number increased again, to 265, in 2004. SNSG's most productive mine, at Svea Nord, about 60 km from Longyearbyen, was opened in 2001 to exploit significant newly discovered reserves of coal. The coal was of high calorific value (1,200 kilocalories per kilo more than usual) and therefore burnt more cleanly than normal coal. Svea is extremely well-placed for exporting coal to Europe, as it is located only 10 km from the port; the mine is linked to the port by road, and in 2004 a conveyor belt was constructed to transport the coal directly to the ships. A second Norwegian coal-mining camp, Gruve 7, some 15 km from Longyearbyen, is used largely to supply a coal-burning power station, which provides electricity for Longyearbyen. Russia had only one camp on Svalbard in early 2009, at Barentsburg; in 2006 88,140 tons of coal were produced at Barentsburg and shipped to Russia. Barentsburg, located about 40 km south-west of Longyearbyen, with a population of almost 500 in March 2007, has its own coal-fired power station. Mining activity at a second Russian settlement, Pyramiden, was largely discontinued in 1998, and the town was subsequently abandoned.

Deep drillings for petroleum have been carried out by Norwegian and other companies, but no commercial results have been reported. Svalbard's other mineral resources include reserves of phosphate, asbestos, iron ore, anhydrite, limestone and various sulphides.

Tourism has been encouraged on Svalbard; cruise ships make stops at the islands and there is also a small industry in skiing and trekking across the wilderness. In 2006 visitors spent a total of 83,049 nights in Svalbard. The services sector has grown substantially in recent years, particularly in the areas of education and research. Many jobs are connected to Norwegian government organizations, such as Statsbygg, the state-owned building agency, and Longyearbyen Elementary and High School.

For 2005 the Svalbard budget was 195.2m. kroner, of which 135.9m. kroner was a direct subsidy from the Norwegian state budget. Svalbard raises some revenue from the sale of hunting and fishing licences.

Statistical Survey

Source: Statistics Norway, Kongensgt. 6, Oslo; tel. 21-09-00-00; fax 21-09-49-73; e-mail biblioteket@ssb.no; internet www.ssb.no.

AREA AND POPULATION

Area: 61,020 sq km (23,561 sq miles).

Population (1 January 2009): 2,565 (Norwegian settlements 2,085—including 293 foreign nationals, Russian settlements 470, Polish settlement 10).

Density (1 January 2009): 0.04 per sq km.

Economically Active Population (2003): Mining and quarrying 233; Manufacturing 8; Construction 194; Wholesale and retail trade 107; Hotels and restaurants 100; Transport and storage 177; Supporting and auxiliary transport activities 120; Public administration 147; Education, health and social work 133; Other community, social and personal service activities 15; *Total* 1,234.

MINING

Coal Shipments ('000 metric tons): 2,991.2 (Norwegian mines 2,859.1) in 2004; 1,863 (Norwegian mines 1,768.3) in 2005; 2,419.7 (Norwegian mines 2,331.6) in 2006.

FINANCE

(Norwegian currency is used)

Budget (million kroner, 2005): Estimated revenue 195.2 (incl. direct grant of 135.9 from central Govt); Budgeted expenditure 195.2.

TRANSPORT

Road Traffic (vehicles registered at 31 December 2004): Passenger cars 930; Buses 41; Goods vehicles 394; Mopeds and motorcycles 130; Snow scooters 1,468.

Civil Aviation (2004, metric tons unless otherwise specified): Passengers (number) 86,232; Goods received 641; Goods sent 42; Mail received 412; Mail sent 54.

TOURISM

Overnight Stays (Longyearbyen): 77,926 in 2004; 76,570 in 2005; 83,049 in 2006.

EDUCATION

(2006, unless otherwise indicated)

Pre-primary: Schools 2; Teachers 29; Pupils 106.
Primary and Lower Secondary: Schools 1; Pupils 198.
Upper Secondary (2004): Schools 1; Pupils 55.

Directory

The Government

(April 2009)

ADMINISTRATION

Governor (Sysselmann): PER SEFLAND.
Commissioner of Mines: PER ZAKKEN BREKKE.

OFFICES

Office of the Governor: Kontoret til Sysselmannen på Svalbard, POB 633, 9171 Longyearbyen, Svalbard; tel. 79-02-43-00; fax 79-02-11-66; e-mail firmapost@sysselmannen.no; internet www.sysselmannen.no.

Ministry of Justice and the Police (Polar Affairs Department): Akersgt. 42, POB 8005 Dep., 0030 Oslo; tel. 22-24-56-01; fax 22-24-95-30; e-mail postmottak@jd.dep.no; responsible for the administration of Svalbard and Jan Mayen, and for the Norwegian Antarctic dependencies.

Norsk Polarinstitutt på Svalbard (Norwegian Polar Institute in Svalbard): Forskningsparken, POB 505, 9171 Longyearbyen, Svalbard; tel. 79-02-26-00; fax 79-02-26-04; e-mail post@npolar.no; internet npweb.npolar.no; f. 1928 as Norges Svalbard- og Ishavsundersøkelser; adopted present name and expanded functions in 1948; branch of Norwegian Polar Institute, Tromsø; mapping and research institute; responsible for advising Govt on matters concerning Svalbard, Jan Mayen and the Antarctic dependencies; monitors and investigates environment of the territories; organizes regular Antarctic research expeditions; establishes and maintains aids to navigation in Svalbard waters; Dir JAN-GUNNAR WINTHER.

Norsk Polarinstitutts Forskningsstasjon (Norwegian Polar Institute Research Station): Sverdrupstasjonen, 9173 Ny-Ålesund, Svalbard; tel. 79-02-74-00; fax 79-02-70-02; permanent research base in Svalbard.

LONGYEARBYEN COUNCIL

Longyearbyen Lokalstyre: POB 350, 9171 Longyearbyen, Svalbard; tel. 79-02-21-50; fax 79-02-21-51; e-mail postmottak@lokalstyre.no; internet www.lokalstyre.no; f. 2002; first locally elected body in Svalbard; replaced Svalbard Council; 15 mems; Leader KJELL MORK.

Svalbard, as an integral part of the Kingdom of Norway, has provision for its Norwegian inhabitants to participate in the national elections. For judicial matters Svalbard lies in the jurisdiction of the Nord-Troms District Court (based in Tromsø). The state Evangelical Lutheran Church provides religious services.

Press

There is only one newspaper published in the Svalbard archipelago.

Svalbardposten: POB 503, 9171 Longyearbyen, Svalbard; tel. 79-02-47-00; fax 79-02-47-01; e-mail post@svalbardposten.no; internet www.svalbardposten.no; f. 1948; weekly; Editor-in-Chief BIRGER AMUNDSEN; circ. 3,380 (2004).

Finance

Norwegian currency is used. Most banking facilities are available.

Sparebank 1 Nord-Norge: POB 518, 9171 Longyearbyen, Svalbard; tel. 79-02-29-10; fax 79-02-29-11; e-mail kundesenter@snn.no; internet www.snn.no; savings bank.

Trade and Industry

Bydrift Longyearbyen A/S: Vei 227, POB 475, 9171 Longyearbyen, Svalbard; tel. 79-02-23-00; fax 79-02-23-01; e-mail bydrift@lokalstyre.no; internet www.lokalstyre.no; state-owned; operates most local services, incl. utilities, and undertakes infrastructure devt; Admin. Dir IVAR UNDHEIM.

Store Norske Spitsbergen Kulkompani A/S (SNSK): 9171 Longyearbyen, Svalbard; tel. 79-02-52-00; fax 79-02-18-41; e-mail firmapost@snsk.no; internet www.snsk.no; state-owned; develops the Store Norske group's proprietary and coal mining rights on Svalbard, with the exception of the Svea area; Chair. BÅRD MIKKELSEN; CEO BJØRN ARNESTAD.

Store Norske Spitsbergen Grubekompani A/S (SNSG): f. 2002; manages all assets, rights, contractual obligations and liabilities in connection with the Svea Nord mine, responsible for coal production and sales in Longyearbyen and Svea, and for exploration at both its own and SNSK's claims; 230 employees.

Store Norske Boliger A/S: f. 2002; manages the group's accommodation in Longyearbyen and some of the accommodation in Svea.

Transport

In 1975 an airport was opened near Longyearbyen. SAS operates services to Oslo, via Tromsø, up to six times per week. There are air strips at Ny-Ålesund and Svea, and a Russian helicopter facility at Barentsburg. Apart from helicopters, and a fixed-wing service between Longyearbyen and Ny-Ålesund, internal traffic is little developed.

AIRPORT

Svalbard Lufthavn: POB 550, 9170 Longyearbyen, Svalbard; tel. 79-02-38-00; fax 79-02-38-01; e-mail ole.m.rambech@avinor.no; internet www.avinor.no/lufthavn/svalbard; f. 1975; owned by Avinor; Man. OLE M. RAMBECH.

Tourism

Svalbard Reiseliv AS: 9171 Longyearbyen, Svalbard; tel. 79-02-55-50; fax 79-02-55-51; e-mail info@svalbard.net; internet www.svalbard.net; f. 2001; represents and promotes tourism-related enterprises in Svalbard; produces brochures for tourists and collates statistics.

JAN MAYEN

The lofty volcanic island of Jan Mayen is located in the Arctic Ocean, some 910 km west-north-west of Bodø on the Norwegian mainland, 610 km north-north-east of Iceland and 480 km east of Greenland (Denmark). The island is 53 km in length and has a total area of 377 sq km (145 sq miles). The highest point is the summit of Mt Beerenberg, which is an active volcano (2,277 m above sea level). The climate is severe, cold and usually misty.

The sea north and west of Jan Mayen (which was frequented by various whalers and hunters for a brief period in the 17th century) has been an important area for sealing by Norwegians since the mid-19th century. Partly to assist their navigation, the Norwegian Meteorological Institute instigated activities on the island in the early 20th century. In 1922 Jan Mayen was declared annexed by the Institute, and on 8 May 1929 Norwegian sovereignty was proclaimed by Royal Decree. The island was made an integral part of the Kingdom of Norway by the Jan Mayen Act of 1930. Jan Mayen is not included in the Svalbard Treaty.

The island has no known exploitable mineral resources and is largely barren. Fishing in the surrounding waters is intermittently productive. In September 1970 there was a violent volcanic eruption on the island, the first since the early 19th century. In the course of the first few days of the eruption a huge glacier melted and millions of cubic metres of ice disappeared as steam. Lava poured into the sea and formed about 3.5 sq km of new land. The last volcanic eruption on the island occurred in 1985. The island's main use remains as a meteorological, navigational and radio station.

During the Second World War Jan Mayen remained the only part of Norway under Norwegian rule, following the German invasion of the mainland. Despite some conflict, the Norwegian Government and its allies maintained the strategic meteorological station and established a radio-locating station on the island during the war.

In 1946 a new base was established at Nordlaguna, both as a meteorological and a coastal radio station. As a result of a North Atlantic defence co-operation exercise in 1959–60, a long-range navigation (LORAN) network was established, with one base on Jan Mayen. At the same time, it was decided to build an airstrip near the new LORAN C base, and in 1962 the personnel of the weather and coastal radio services also moved to the same area.

Following negotiations with Iceland in 1980, the Norwegian Government declared an economic zone extending for 200 nautical miles (370 km) around the coast of Jan Mayen. In 1981 a further agreement was made with Iceland, regarding mineral and fishing rights. A dispute with Denmark, acting on behalf of Greenland, concerning the delimitation of maritime economic zones between Greenland and Jan Mayen was referred by Denmark to the International Court of Justice (based in The Hague, Netherlands) in 1988. The Court delivered its judgment in June 1993, deciding that 57% of the disputed area belonged to Norway. A subsequent accord on maritime delimitation, agreed between the Governments of Norway, Greenland and Iceland in November 1997, established the boundaries of a 1,934-sq km area of Arctic sea that had been excluded from the terms of the 1993 settlement.

The commanding officer in charge of the LORAN C base is the chief administrative official of the island. The officer is responsible for the 15–25 inhabitants (who usually remain on the island for only one year at a time), and is accountable to the Chief of Police for Salten district (headquartered in Bodø), and the Ministry of Justice and the Police (as in Svalbard). The commander may grant permission for visits of not more than 24 hours. For longer visits, the Chief of Police or the Ministry must approve the application. Visits are normally allowed only for scientific purposes and only if private provision has been made for transport. There is no public transport or accommodation on Jan Mayen.

Station Commander: KRISTIAN RUBACH, LORAN C Base, 8099 Jan Mayen; tel. 32-17-79-00; fax 32-17-79-01; e-mail janmayen@www.jan-mayen.no; internet www.jan-mayen.no.

Chief of Police (Salten district): TONE VANGEN, Kongensgt. 81, POB 1023, 8006 Bodø; tel. 75-54-58-00; e-mail post.salten@politiet.no.

For the Ministry of Justice and the Police and the Norsk Polarinstitutt (Norwegian Polar Institute), see under Svalbard.

NORWEGIAN DEPENDENCIES

Norway's so-called 'Antarctic' dependencies are all uninhabited and were acquired as a result of Norwegian whaling interests in the region since the 1890s. The three territories are dependencies of the Kingdom of Norway, and are administered by the Polar Affairs Department of the Ministry of Justice and the Police, with the advice of the Norsk Polarinstitutt (Norwegian Polar Institute: for details, see under Svalbard) and the assistance of the Ministry of the Environment.

Bouvetøya

Bouvetøya (Bouvet Island) is a volcanic island in the South Atlantic Ocean, some 2,400 km south-west of the Cape of Good Hope (South Africa) and 1,600 km north of Antarctica. The island lies north of the Antarctic Circle (it is not, therefore, encompassed by the terms of the Antarctic Treaty). Bouvetøya has an area of 49 sq km, but about 93% of the surface is covered by ice. The climate is maritime antarctic, with a mean annual temperature of −1°C and a persistent heavy fog.

Regular landings on the island occurred only as part of Norwegian Antarctic expeditions in the 1920s and 1930s. Bouvetøya was claimed for Norway in 1927, placed under its sovereignty in 1928, and declared a Norwegian dependency in 1930. A Royal Decree of 1971 declared the entire island to be a nature reserve. An automatic weather station was established in 1977, and the island is regularly visited by Norwegian scientific expeditions.

Dronning Maud Land

Dronning Maud Land (Queen Maud Land) is that sector of the Antarctic continent lying between the longitudes of 20°W (adjoining the British Antarctic Territory to the west) and 45°E (neighbouring the Australian Antarctic Territory). The territory is, in area, several times the size of Norway, and 98% of its surface is covered by ice. The climate is severe, the usual temperature always being below 0°C and, in the winter months of mid-year, falling to −60°C on the coast and −88°C inland. The territory's coast is divided into five named sectors (the exact delimitations of which, and of the territory as a whole, have varied at different periods): Kronprinsesse Märtha Kyst (Crown Princess Märtha Coast), Prinsesse Astrid Kyst, Prinsesse Ragnhild Kyst, Prins Harald Kyst and Kronprins Olav Kyst.

The first Norwegian territorial claims in Antarctica were made in 1929, following many years of Norwegian involvement in the exploration and survey of the continent. Further claims were made in 1931 and 1936–37. These claims were formalized by the Norwegian authorities, and the land placed under their sovereignty, only in 1939. The extent of Dronning Maud Land then received its current limits, between the British and Australian claims. Norway now follows a policy which upholds its claim to sovereignty but supports the pattern of international co-operation, particularly that established under the terms of the Antarctic Treaty (see p. 591) (signed in 1959), to which the Kingdom of Norway is an original signatory. There are six wintering stations, staffed by personnel of various nationalities, in Dronning Maud Land.

Peter I Øy

Peter I Øy (Peter I Island) is located in the Bellingshausen Sea, some 450 km north of Antarctica and more than 1,800 km south-west of Chile, the nearest inhabited territory. It covers an area of some 156 sq km, 95% of which is covered by ice. The island lies within the Antarctic Circle and the area covered by the terms of the Antarctic Treaty. The first recorded landing on the island was not made until 1929, by a Norwegian expedition, which then claimed the island. A Royal Proclamation placed Peter I Øy under Norwegian sovereignty in 1931, and the island was declared a dependency in 1933. Few landings have been made since, but in 1987 the Norsk Polarinstitutt (Norwegian Polar Institute) conducted a relatively long survey and established an automatic weather station on the island.

OMAN

Introductory Survey

Location, Climate, Language, Religion, Flag, Capital

The Sultanate of Oman occupies the extreme east and south-east of the Arabian peninsula. It is bordered to the west by the United Arab Emirates (UAE), Saudi Arabia and Yemen. A detached portion of Oman, separated from the rest of the country by UAE territory, lies at the tip of the Musandam peninsula, on the southern shore of the Strait of Hormuz. Oman has a coastline of more than 1,600 km (1,000 miles) on the Indian Ocean, and is separated from Iran by the Gulf of Oman. In Muscat average annual rainfall is 100 mm and the average temperature varies between 21°C (70°F) and 35°C (95°F). Rainfall is heavier on the hills of the interior, and the south-western province of Dhofar is the only part of Arabia to benefit from the summer monsoon. The official language is Arabic. Islam is the official religion. The majority of the population are Ibadi Muslims; there are also Sunni Muslim, Hindu and Christian minorities. The national flag (proportions 1 by 2) has three equal horizontal stripes, of white, red and green, with a vertical red stripe at the hoist. In the upper hoist is a representation, in white, of the state emblem, two crossed swords and a dagger (*khanjar*), surmounted by a belt. The capital is Muscat.

Recent History

Officially known as Muscat and Oman until 1970, the Sultanate has had a special relationship with the United Kingdom since the 19th century. Full independence was confirmed by a treaty of friendship with the United Kingdom on 20 December 1951, although the armed forces and police retain some British officers on loan service. Sultan Said bin Taimur succeeded his father in 1932 and maintained a strictly conservative and isolationist rule until July 1970, when he was overthrown by his son in a bloodless palace coup. The new Sultan, Qaboos bin Said as-Said, then began a liberalization of the regime, and spending on development was increased.

A Consultative Assembly (comprising representatives of the Government, the private sector and the regions, appointed by the Sultan) was created in 1981, in order to advise Sultan Qaboos on economic and social development. In November 1990 it was announced that the Assembly was to be replaced by a Consultative Council (Majlis ash-Shoura), comprising regional representatives, which was intended to extend participation by Omani citizens in national affairs. A selection process was duly announced whereby representatives of each of the country's 59 districts (*wilayat*—increased to 61 in 2006) would nominate three candidates; the nominations would then be submitted to the Deputy Prime Minister for Legal Affairs, who, with the Sultan's approval, would choose one representative for each district to join the new Majlis. No government official or civil servant would be eligible for election to the new body. The President of the Majlis ash-Shoura would be appointed by royal decree; other executive officers and committee members would be designated by, and from among, the local delegates. Although the role of the Majlis was strictly advisory, government ministers were to be obliged to submit reports to the assembly and to answer any questions addressed to them. The Majlis was formally established by royal decree in November 1991 and was convened in January 1992, when its members were sworn in for a three-year term. In 1994 membership of the Majlis was increased from 59 to 80, to include an additional member for any district with 30,000 or more inhabitants. For the first time women were nominated as candidates in six regions in and around the capital; two women were subsequently appointed to the enlarged Majlis.

In mid-1994 the Government was reported to be employing stringent measures to curb an apparent rise in Islamist militancy in Oman. In August the security forces arrested more than 200 members of an allegedly foreign-sponsored Islamist organization, including two junior ministers, university lecturers, students and soldiers. Most were later released, but in November several of those against whom charges had been brought were sentenced to death, having been found guilty of conspiracy to foment sedition; the Sultan subsequently commuted the death sentences to terms of imprisonment. In November 1995 139 prisoners were released, under a general amnesty granted by Sultan Qaboos.

In November 1996 Sultan Qaboos issued a decree promulgating a Basic Statute of the State, a constitutional document defining for the first time the organs and guiding principles of the state. The Statute provided for a Council of Oman (Majlis Oman), to be composed of the Majlis ash-Shoura and a new State Council (Majlis ad-Dawlah). The latter was to be appointed from among prominent Omanis, and would liaise between the Government and the people of Oman. It was subsequently reported that 23 senior government ministers had resigned as directors of public joint-stock companies, in accordance with a stipulation in the Basic Statute that ministers should not abuse their official position for personal gain. In December a Defence Council was established by royal decree, comprising the Minister of the Royal Court, the heads of the armed and police forces, and the chief of internal security. The Basic Statute defined a process of succession to the Sultan, requiring that the ruling family determine a successor within three days of the throne's falling vacant, failing which the Defence Council would confirm the appointment of a successor predetermined by the Sultan.

Voting was organized in October 1997 to select candidates for appointment to the Majlis ash-Shoura. Women from all regions were permitted to seek nomination. Of a total of 736 candidates, 164 were chosen, from whom the Sultan selected the 82 members of the newly expanded Majlis in November. The two female members of the outgoing Majlis were returned to office. In December Sultan Qaboos issued a decree appointing the 41 members of the Majlis ad-Dawlah, which was reportedly dominated by former politicians, business leaders and academics. A further decree established the Majlis Oman, which was formally inaugurated by the Sultan on 27 December.

The elections to the Majlis ash-Shoura held on 14 September 2000 were the first in which members were directly elected rather than appointed by the Sultan. However, voting rights were restricted to prominent business leaders, intellectuals, professionals and tribal chiefs. Of a total of 541 candidates, 21 of whom were women, 83 (including two women) were elected to the (again expanded) Majlis. The number of eligible voters had tripled, to some 150,000, since the previous election; according to official figures, an estimated 90% of the electorate participated in the poll. A new Majlis ad-Dawlah was appointed in October, and the Majlis Oman convened for its second term on 4 November.

From late 2000 the Government intensified measures aimed at reducing the number of expatriates in Oman's labour force, a process termed 'Omanization'. In April 2001 more than 100 suspected illegal immigrants were detained by the Omani authorities, who announced that all foreign nationals employed illegally in the country and who had not supplied the correct documentation within a period of two months would be liable to deportation. About 130 alleged illegal immigrants were reportedly arrested in September.

In March 2003 Sultan Qaboos issued a decree establishing a Public Authority for Craft Industries. The President of the Authority, Sheikha Aisha bint Khalfan bin Jumiel as-Siyabiah, was given the rank of Minister, and thus became the first female to be appointed to that level of government. Elections to the Majlis ash-Shoura were held on 4 October, for which voting rights were granted to all Omani citizens over 21 years of age—some 820,000 people. Few changes to the composition of the Majlis resulted from the elections. A total of 506 candidates, 15 of them women, stood for election to the 83-seat assembly. While the electoral process was described by observers as fair and open, the turn-out was a disappointing 32% of the electorate. Critics of the elections claimed that tribal loyalties had guided the decision-making of most voters, resulting in a predictable set of results—a situation that was exacerbated by the lack of legislative power wielded by council members. Only two female candidates secured election to the Majlis, both of whom were already serving members. A royal decree issued in October extended the term of office for members of both the Majlis ash-Shoura and the Majlis ad-Dawlah from three to four years. In November a new Majlis ad-Dawlah was appointed, with an expanded membership of 57 (including eight women); membership of the Majlis was subsequently increased to 59 (nine of whom were women) and then again, to 70 (see below).

Sultan Qaboos announced a limited reorganization of the Council of Ministers in February 2004. A further decree signed in March appointed Dr Rawya bint Saud bin Ahmad al-Busaidiyah as Minister of Higher Education (the first female member of the Council of Ministers) and Sheikh Yahya bin Mahfoudh al-Mantheri as President of the Majlis ad-Dawlah. Following further cabinet changes implemented in May, in June the Sultan created by royal decree a Ministry of Tourism; another woman, Rajha bint Abd al-Amir bin Ali, was appointed as the new minister. A third woman was appointed to the Council of Ministers as part of a limited reorganization in October, when Dr Sharifah bint Khalfan bin Nasser al-Yahiyaia was given the role of Minister of Social Development.

In May 2005 30 suspected Islamist militants were sentenced to prison terms ranging from one to 20 years for allegedly planning a series of attacks on a cultural and trade festival in Muscat, with the supposed aim of overthrowing the regime. However, in the following month Sultan Qaboos pardoned all those convicted. Although Oman has remained free from acts of terrorism, the convictions raised concerns that militant Islamism was flourishing in the country. In October 31 Omanis were sentenced to prison terms on charges including bribery and forgery, thus apparently signalling that the Government was keen to combat administrative corruption. Several high-ranking government officials were reportedly among those convicted. Meanwhile, as permitted by the approval of a press and broadcasting law in 2004, the country's first private radio stations received licences in 2005 and began broadcasting in 2007. (The law also allowed the establishment of private television stations.) Although Omanis can, against the wishes of the state, receive private broadcasts from foreign broadcasters, this represented a significant concession to reformist elements in society. Nevertheless, despite such reforms, the views of two popular writers, Abdullah ar-Riyami and Muhammad al-Harthy, were reportedly suppressed in the media after they had criticized the Government in 2004; in 2005 ar-Riyami was arrested and detained for a week without charges being brought. Also in 2005 Taiba al-Mawali, a former member of the Majlis ash-Shoura, was sentenced to 18 months' imprisonment for writing articles that were critical of the Government's treatment of the suspected Islamist militants (see above); she served six months of her sentence before being released.

'Cyclone Gonu' struck the eastern coast of Oman in June 2007, causing the deaths of some 50 people and widespread destruction to the region's infrastructure. Much of the country, including Muscat, suffered severe flooding, and some hydrocarbon installations were damaged by the storm, which was said to have been the worst in the Arabian peninsula's history. The estimated cost of the damage in Oman was reported to be around US $3,900m.

In September 2007 Sultan Qaboos carried out a further reorganization of the Council of Ministers, which included the creation of new Ministries of Fisheries and of Environment and Climate Affairs. A Public Authority for Electricity and Water was also established to plan and supervise the development of Oman's utilities. The same female ministers remained in charge of the higher education, tourism and social development portfolios after the reshuffle. Sheikh Ahmad bin Muhammad al-Issai was appointed as President of the Majlis ash-Shoura, elections to which were held on 27 October. Membership of the Majlis was increased from 83 to 84. The polls were contested by 632 candidates, 21 of them women; however, none of the contested seats were secured by women. The majority of elected members of the new Majlis ash-Shoura were reported to be tribal leaders or businessmen. The conduct of the ballot was assessed by independent observers to have been free and fair, and turn-out of some 62.7% was recorded. A new Majlis ad-Dawlah, comprising 70 members, was appointed on 5 November.

A report issued by the US Department of State in June 2008, which classified Oman as one of the countries failing to tackle the problem of human trafficking, led to forceful protests from the Omani authorities. Sultan Qaboos issued a new law in early December which for the first time specifically targeted human trafficking, and specified prison sentences of up to 15 years and fines of up to RO 100,000 for those convicted of the crime. Meanwhile, in November a new National Commission for Human Rights was established; the body, which was described as 'autonomous', was to be attached to the Majlis ad-Dawlah, whose members are directly appointed by the Sultan.

An agreement on the demarcation of Oman's border with Yemen, which had been the subject of a lengthy dispute with the former People's Democratic Republic of Yemen, was signed in October 1992 and ratified in December; demarcation was completed in June 1995. In July 1996 Oman withdrew an estimated 15,000 troops from the last of the disputed territories on the Yemeni border, in accordance with the 1992 agreement, and in May 1997 the border demarcation maps were signed in Muscat. Several bilateral economic co-operation accords were announced in September 1998, and a free trade zone was subsequently established near the border at Al-Mazyona. Oman and Yemen agreed in October 2001 to extend co-operation between their hydrocarbon industries. Having signed a preliminary border accord in June 2002, Oman and the UAE also reached agreement on the final delineation of their mutual land borders in July 2008. Both countries expressed the hope that the agreement would enhance economic co-operation and facilitate development in the previously contested border areas.

In response to the invasion of Kuwait by Iraq in August 1990, Oman, together with the other members of the Co-operation Council for the Arab States of the Gulf (Gulf Co-operation Council—GCC, see p. 229), gave its support to the deployment of a US-led defensive force in Saudi Arabia. The Omani Government expressed the view that the imposition of international economic sanctions would compel Iraq to withdraw from Kuwait. In November there was evidence that Oman was attempting to mediate in the crisis when the Iraqi Minister of Foreign Affairs, Tareq Aziz, visited Oman. By the mid-1990s Oman's stance regarding the continuation of economic sanctions against Iraq appeared ambivalent: Oman and Qatar were, notably, absent from talks held in March 1995 between the US Secretary of State, Warren Christopher, and other GCC members to discuss the issue. In November 1997 and again in early 1998 Oman stated its opposition to possible military action to force Iraq to submit to inspections of its weapons capabilities by the UN Special Commission (UNSCOM, see the chapter on Iraq), maintaining that the UN should remove the economic sanctions against Iraq once UNSCOM had been permitted to complete its task.

Although the Omani Government was swift to condemn the September 2001 suicide attacks in New York and Washington, DC, it expressed concern that the US-led military campaign in Afghanistan against the al-Qa'ida (Base) network of Osama bin Laden (held by the USA to be principally responsible for the attacks) and the Taliban regime should not be extended to target any Arab state, notably Iraq. Street demonstrations were held in October by Omani students protesting against the war in Afghanistan. During an official visit to Oman by the US Secretary of Defense, Donald Rumsfeld, in that month, it was reported that the USA was to supply Oman with 12 F-16 fighter aircraft and other advanced weaponry, at a cost of some US $1,120m. From 2002 Oman opposed attempts led by the USA, as part of its 'war on terror', to garner international support for a military offensive against the Iraqi regime of Saddam Hussain, and advocated a diplomatic solution to the escalating crisis. In March 2003, as the US-led force began assaults on targets in Iraq, Sultan Qaboos appealed for a swift curtailment of the conflict, which he described as 'unjustified' and 'illegitimate'. Frequent anti-war protests were held in Oman during March and April.

In April 1994 the Israeli Deputy Minister of Foreign Affairs, Yossi Beilin, participated in talks in Oman. This constituted the first official visit by an Israeli government member to an Arab Gulf state since Israel's declaration of independence in 1948. In September 1994, moreover, Oman and the other GCC member states announced the partial ending of their economic boycott of Israel. In December the Israeli Prime Minister, Itzhak Rabin, made an official visit to Oman to discuss the Middle East peace process, and in February 1995 it was announced that low-level diplomatic relations were to be established between Oman and Israel. An Omani trade office was opened in Tel-Aviv in August 1996, despite concerns that bilateral relations would be undermined by the uncompromising stance adopted by the new Israeli Government of Binyamin Netanyahu. In March 1997 ministers responsible for foreign affairs of the countries of the League of Arab States (the Arab League, see p. 344) recommended, in condemnation of Israeli settlement policy, the suspension of involvement in multilateral negotiations with Israel, a reassertion of the primary economic boycott and the ending, by means of closing representative offices in Tel-Aviv, of efforts to normalize bilateral relations. In April Oman prohibited Israeli participation at a Muscat trade fair. Oman attended the Middle East and North Africa economic conference in Doha, Qatar, in November, despite a boycott by most Arab League and GCC members in response to the perceived failure of Israel (which was represented at the conference) to comply with its obligations under the Middle East peace process. In October 2000, in view of the deepening crisis in Israeli–Palestinian relations, Oman closed both its trade office in Tel-Aviv and the Israeli trade office in Muscat. Oman hosted the annual summit meeting of GCC heads of state in December 2001, at the close of which a statement was issued blaming Israel for the collapse of the peace process and expressing support for the Palestinian leadership. Demonstrations have subsequently taken place in Muscat to demand an end to Israeli military incursions into Palestinian territory. Nevertheless, the Israeli Vice-Prime Minister and Minister of Foreign Affairs, Tzipi Livni, held discussions with Oman's Minister Responsible for Foreign Affairs, Yousuf bin al-Alawi bin Abdullah, during a visit to Qatar in April 2008.

The 29th Annual Summit of the Supreme Council of the GCC was held in Muscat on 29–30 December 2008. The foremost topics on the agenda were the Gulf's impending monetary union and the regional impact of the global financial crisis. The Council approved a monetary union agreement covering the legislative and institutional framework of the union, and reaffirmed its commitment to ratify the agreement and introduce a single currency by 1 January 2010—a target that was seen by most commentators as extremely ambitious given the complexity of the project and the unfavourable economic climate. However, since 2006 Oman had made clear its intention to abstain from a single currency, preferring to maintain the rial's pegging to the US dollar. The Government did not rule out joining such a currency at a later date, but was adamant that joining by 2010 would jeopardize the Sultanate's ongoing development plans. The agenda of the Muscat summit was, to an extent, overshadowed by the Israeli military operation against Islamic Resistance Movement (Hamas) targets in the Gaza Strip, which was launched on 27 December (see the chapters on Israel and the Palestinian Autonomous Areas). The GCC Supreme Council, in its final communiqué, strongly condemned the 'brutal Israeli aggression', and called for a cessation of hostilities and a lifting of the Israeli blockade on Gaza, which had been in place since January 2008.

Negotiations between Oman and the USA concerning a bilateral free trade agreement (FTA) took place in March–October 2005, and the deal was signed following their conclusion. Ratification of the legislation by both Omani and US institutions was confirmed in late 2006, and the FTA came into force on 1 January 2009. The FTA followed similar agreements between the USA and Bahrain, Israel, Jordan and Morocco, with a view to establishing a wider free trade area across the Middle East. The development of US-Omani relations was expected to displease the Saudi Government, which had previously argued that the GCC should negotiate a trade deal as a single body and in 2004 claimed that the FTA with Bahrain contravened the GCC's external tariff agreement. Meanwhile, Oman's close ties with Iran are a potential source of disagreement with the USA, since Oman supports the right of the Iranian regime to pursue the peaceful development of nuclear energy and opposes any use of military force against Iran—a proposal that apparently remained under consideration by the US Administration throughout 2008, but which appeared somewhat less likely with the inauguration of Barack Obama as US President in January 2009. Oman and Iran were engaged in negotiations concerning a joint venture to develop Iran's Kish gasfield, at an estimated cost of more than US $9,000m., throughout 2008 and early 2009. The proposed deal, which was first announced in June 2007, would involve Oman providing finance for the project in exchange for a guaranteed gas supply of 1,000m. cu ft per day. Sayyid Fahd bin Mahmoud as-Said, Oman's Deputy Prime Minister, led a high-level delegation to the Iranian capital, Tehran, in April 2008 for talks on bilateral relations, including the Kish development project. During the visit Iranian President Mahmoud Ahmadinejad described Iranian-Omani ties as a model for all relations in the region.

Sultan Qaboos arrived in Libya in mid-August 2008 for his first official visit to the North African state. The Sultan held talks with Libyan leader Col Muammar al-Qaddafi on the enhancement of bilateral relations, and on regional and international affairs. During the visit the establishment of a joint Libyan-Omani Investment Company, with initial capital of US $500m., was announced. The company, which was to be based in the Libyan capital, Tripoli, was expected to explore opportunities for investment in industry, tourism, real estate and banking projects in both countries. Dr Manmohan Singh, the Prime Minister of India, visited Oman in early November for a two-day state visit—the first by an Indian premier for more than a decade. Since the establishment of an India-Oman Joint Commission in 1995 bilateral relations have progressed considerably, with the signing of several agreements on trade and defence co-operation. During Prime Minister Singh's visit two significant memorandums of understanding were signed: one concerning labour co-operation and another on the establishment of an India-Oman Joint Investment Fund, with initial capital of $100m. and the potential to expand eventually to $1,500m.

Government

The Basic Statute of the State, which was promulgated by Royal Decree on 6 November 1996, defines Oman's organs of government. The Sultan, who is Head of State, is empowered to promulgate and ratify legislation. He is assisted in formulating and implementing the general policy of the state by a Council of Ministers. Members of the Council of Ministers are appointed by the Sultan, who presides, or may appoint a Prime Minister to preside, over the Council. There is no legislature. However, a Majlis ash-Shoura (Consultative Council) is now elected for four years at national polls. Voters were previously nominated within the country's *wilayat*, or districts, with the franchise effectively limited to prominent business leaders, intellectuals, professionals and tribal chiefs; with effect from elections held in October 2003, however, voting rights were granted to all Omani citizens over 21 years of age. The Majlis is composed of one representative from each *wilaya* with fewer than 30,000 inhabitants, and two from each *wilaya* with 30,000 or more inhabitants. The Majlis ash-Shoura elected in October 2007 comprised 84 members. A Majlis ad-Dawlah (State Council) is appointed by the Sultan from among prominent Omanis; currently it comprises 70 members, who also serve a four-year term of office. The two Councils together comprise the Majlis Oman (Council of Oman).

Oman comprises four governorates and five regions, which are subdivided into 61 *wilayat*; each *wilaya* has its own governor (*wali*).

Defence

As assessed in November 2008, the Omani armed forces numbered 42,600 (including about 2,000 expatriate personnel): army 25,000; navy 4,200; air force 5,000; royal household 6,400. Paramilitary forces numbered 4,400: tribal home guard (*firqat*) 4,000; police coastguard 400. Military service is voluntary. Government expenditure on defence was budgeted at RO 1,230m. in 2007.

Economic Affairs

In 2005, according to estimates by the World Bank, Oman's gross national income (GNI), measured at average 2003–05 prices, was US $27,887m., equivalent to $11,120 per head (or $19,740 per head on an international purchasing-power parity basis). During 2000–07, it was estimated, the population increased at an average annual rate of 1.1%, while real gross domestic product (GDP) per head increased, in real terms, by an average of 3.7% per year during 2000–05. Overall GDP increased, in real terms, at an average annual rate of 4.6% in 2000–05; growth was 7.7% in 2007, according to provisional official figures.

Agriculture (including fishing) contributed 1.3% of GDP in 2007, and engaged 32.4% of the labour force in 2005, according to FAO. The major crops are dates, tomatoes, watermelons, bananas and other fruits. The production of frankincense, formerly an important export commodity, has been revived. Livestock and fishing are also important. The real GDP of the agricultural sector increased by an average of 0.4% annually in 2000–07. Real agricultural GDP expanded by 3.7% in 2007, according to official figures.

Industry (including mining and quarrying, manufacturing, construction and power) provided 58.8% of GDP in 2007, and employed 27.9% of the working population in 2003. According to the World Bank, real industrial GDP declined by an average of 0.1% annually in 2000–04. The sector's real GDP decreased by 1.0% in 2004.

The mining sector contributed 44.9% of GDP in 2007, and engaged 2.8% of the employed labour force in 2003. The principal mineral reserves are petroleum and natural gas, which together provided around 44.6% of GDP in 2007. There were proven petroleum reserves of 5,600m. barrels at the end of 2007, sufficient to maintain output at that year's levels—which averaged an estimated 718,000 barrels per day (b/d)—for just over 21 years. Exports of Omani crude petroleum provided 58.4% of total export earnings in 2007. Natural gas is also an important mineral resource; there were proven reserves of some 690,000m. cu m at the end of 2007, sustainable for about 28 years at that year's production levels (output in 2007 totalled 24,100m. cu m). Budgetary revenue from petroleum and natural gas contributed some 75.8% of the total in 2007. Chromite, gold, silver, salt, marble, gypsum and limestone are also mined, and the exploitation of coal deposits is planned. The GDP of the mining sector (including petroleum activities) declined at an average annual rate of 2.9% in 2000–07; mining GDP (including petroleum activities) decreased by an estimated 1.6% in 2007.

Manufacturing contributed 9.9% of GDP in 2007, and engaged 8.2% of the employed labour force in 2003. The most important branches of the sector are petroleum-refining, construction materials, cement production and copper-smelting. Assembly industries, light engineering and food-processing are being encouraged at industrial estates in Muscat, Sohar and Salalah. Completion in 2000 of a US $9,000m. liquefied natural gas plant at Sur reduced domestic demand for petroleum and also produced a surplus for export. The GDP of the manufacturing sector increased, in real terms, at an average rate of 11.6% annually in 2000–07. The sector's real GDP grew by an estimated 6.5% in 2007, according to official figures.

Energy is derived almost exclusively from domestic supplies of natural gas (which accounted for 82.0% of electricity produced in 2005) and petroleum. Imports of fuel products comprised just 3.5% of total imports in 2007.

Services provided 39.9% of GDP in 2007, and engaged 64.0% of the employed population in 2003. With the Government seeking to diversify Oman's petroleum-dependent economy, the construction of several large-scale tourism projects have been initiated in recent years. Pre-eminent among these was Al-Madina az-Zarqa (Blue City) resort, the plans for which were announced in June 2005, and which was expected to cost US $15,000m. and to take some 15 years to complete. The Government intends to increase the contribution of tourism to GDP to 5% by 2020. The GDP of the services sector increased, in real terms, at an average rate of 8.3% per year during 2000–07. Real services GDP expanded by an estimated 12.7% in 2007, according to official figures.

In 2007 Oman recorded a visible trade surplus of US $10,380m., and there was a surplus of $1,918m. on the current account of the balance of payments. In 2007 the principal sources of imports were the UAE and Japan (which supplied, respectively, 26.5% and 15.8% of Oman's imports). India, the USA and Germany were also important suppliers. The most important market for non-petroleum exports in 2007 was the UAE (taking 47.7%). India, Saudi Arabia and Iran were also important markets for non-petroleum exports. Petroleum and natural gas is, by far, the principal export category, comprising 75.9% of the total in 2007. Live animals and animal products made the most notable contribution to export revenue of all non-oil exports of Omani origin in the same year. The principal imports in 2007 were machinery and transport equipment (accounting for 51.5% of total imports), basic manufactures, food and live animals, and chemicals.

Oman recorded an estimated overall budgetary surplus of RO 40m. in 2007 (equivalent to some 0.3% of GDP in that year). At the end of 2006 Oman's total external debt was US $4,819m., of which $819m. was long-term public debt. The cost of debt-servicing in that year was equivalent to 1.3% of the total value of exports of goods and services. Annual inflation increased by an average of 1.2% in 2000–07, and consumer prices grew by an average of 5.0% in 2007. Although Oman has traditionally relied on a high level of immigrant labour (non-Omanis accounted for 57.6% of the employed labour force in 2003), employment opportunities for young Omanis declined in the early 1990s and, according to census results, unemployment among Omanis stood at 11.9% in 1993; the figure was estimated at 12%–15% in 2006, although unemployment in rural areas was assumed to be far greater.

Oman is a member of the Arab Fund for Economic and Social Development (see p. 183), the Islamic Development Bank (see p. 340) and the Arab Monetary Fund (see p. 184). It was a founder member of the Co-operation Council for the Arab States of the Gulf (the Gulf Co-operation Council—GCC, see p. 229), and of the Indian Ocean Rim Association for Regional Co-operation (see p. 427). Oman is not a member of the Organization of the Petroleum Exporting Countries (OPEC, see p. 386) nor of the Organization of Arab Petroleum Exporting Countries (OAPEC, see p. 379), but it generally respects OPEC's policies regarding levels of petroleum production and pricing. Oman was admitted to the World Trade Organization (WTO, see p. 410) in November 2000. In preparation for admittance to the WTO, the Government abolished import fees, raised the limit on foreign ownership of local industries from 49% to 70% (effective from 1 January 2001) and authorized 100% foreign ownership in banking, insurance and brokerage firms (from 1 January 2003). The GCC's six members established a unified regional customs tariff in January 2003, and the organization has undertaken to establish a single market and currency no later than January 2010. The economic convergence criteria for the proposed monetary union were agreed at a GCC summit in Abu Dhabi, the UAE, in December 2005. However, it was announced in February 2007 that the Omani authorities had decided to withdraw their participation from the project, owing to concerns regarding the convergence criteria. In January 2008 the GCC launched its common market.

Oman's limited petroleum reserves and fluctuations in the price of petroleum have necessitated a series of five-year development plans to diversify the country's economic base, in particular through the expansion of the private sector. Nevertheless, several foreign oil companies have been brought in to explore Oman's territorial waters, in the hope of increasing oil and gas reserves. According to the Ministry of Oil and Gas in early 2007, petroleum production was expected to reach 1m. b/d by 2012. However, production levels continued to decline following a peak of 961,000 b/d in 2001. Despite efforts to diversify the economy, the Government continued to allocate large sums of expenditure to the hydrocarbons sector to reverse this trend, with output projected by the Ministry to rise to 805,000 b/d in 2009 from 757,000 b/d in 2008. Oman has had to invest heavily in enhanced oil recovery techniques, increasing the cost of production while global oil prices have declined. The state-owned Petroleum Development Oman announced in early 2008 that, in anticipation of a rapid increase in demand for energy (which was forecast to rise by as much as 170% by 2016), it planned to make significant improvements to its existing infrastructure. Meanwhile, under the seventh Development Plan (2006–10), emphasis was to be placed on the development of the non-petroleum sector (with gas-based industry and tourism being notable targets), and the expansion of the privatization programme (begun in 1994). Under the Plan, the Government aimed to achieve annual GDP growth of at least 3% and to maintain low annual rates of inflation; GDP increased by some 7.7% in 2007, but inflation had reportedly reached double figures by mid-2008. The previous Plan (2001–05) had sought, in particular, to create more jobs for Omani nationals and to limit the employment of expatriates in certain fields, under the so-called 'Omanization' policy. Omanis were now reported to constitute at least 95% of employees in the banking sector, with similar rates close to being achieved in health, education and government services. To coordinate the nascent tourism industry, the Government established a Ministry of Tourism in June 2004; however, although the sector benefited from foreign investment, it represented only an estimated 0.9% of GDP in 2008. The Government had targeted the tourism sector as an area for job creation and to reduce the reliance on the petroleum industry, aiming for a 3% contribution to GDP and 30m. incoming tourists by 2020. Some US $3,000m. was allocated to developing the sector's infrastructure, including the construction of six airports and the expansion of Muscat International and Salalah airports. Meanwhile, the implementation of a bilateral free trade agreement with the USA in January 2009 was expected significantly to increase trading opportunities for Omani businesses. Oman's budget surplus reached a record high in 2008, although falling international oil prices and the impact of the global financial crisis led to forecasts of a fiscal deficit equivalent to 7% of GDP in 2009.

Education

In 1970 there were only three schools, with a total of 909 pupils. By 2007/08 there were 1,052 schools at the primary, preparatory and secondary levels, as well as 174 private kindergartens and schools regulated by the Ministry of Education; in total, 553,236 students were in state education (at the primary–secondary level) and 22,959 in private education in that year. According to the Basic Statute, the state endeavours to make education available to all; it provides public education and encourages the establishment of private educational institutions. However, education is still not compulsory. Primary education begins at six years of age and lasts for six years. The next level of education, divided into two equal stages, lasts for a further six years. In 1998/99 a new system, comprising 10 years of basic education and two extra years of secondary education, dependent on attainment, was introduced in 17 schools; it was to be imple-

OMAN

mented gradually throughout the country. Primary enrolment in 2006/07 included 72.7% of children in the relevant age-group, while secondary enrolment included 78.6% of children in the relevant age-group. In 2007/08 there were six teacher-training colleges, five technical colleges, 16 institutes of health and four vocational institutes, together with the College of Shari'a and Law, the Academy of Tourism and Catering and the College of Banking and Financial Studies. Oman's first national university, named after Sultan Qaboos, was opened in late 1986, and had 14,722 students in 2007/08. There are four private universities and several private technical colleges. In the 2007 budget, RO 572.7m. (10.3%) of current and investment expenditure was allocated to the Ministries of Education and Higher Education by the central Government.

Public Holidays

2009: 9 March* (Mouloud, Birth of the Prophet), 19 July* (Leilat al-Meiraj, Ascension of the Prophet), 22 August* (Ramadan begins), 20 September* (Id al-Fitr, end of Ramadan), 18 November (National Day), 19 November (Birthday of Sultan Qaboos), 27 November* (Id al-Adha, Feast of the Sacrifice), 18 December* (Muharram, Islamic New Year).

2010: 26 February* (Mouloud, Birth of the Prophet), 8 July* (Leilat al-Meiraj, Ascension of the Prophet), 11 August* (Ramadan begins), 10 September* (Id al-Fitr, end of Ramadan), 16 November* (Id al-Adha, Feast of the Sacrifice), 18 November (National Day), 19 November (Birthday of Sultan Qaboos), 7 December* (Muharram, Islamic New Year).

* These holidays are dependent on the Islamic lunar calendar and may vary by one or two days from the dates given.

Weights and Measures

The imperial, metric and local systems are all used, although the metric system was officially adopted in 1974.

Statistical Survey

Sources (unless otherwise stated): Information and Publication Centre, Ministry of National Economy, POB 506, Muscat 113; tel. 24604285; fax 24698467; e-mail mone@omantel.net.om; internet www.mone.gov.om; Central Bank of Oman, POB 1161, 44 Mutrah Commercial Centre, Ruwi 112; tel. 24702222; fax 24788995; e-mail cboccr@omantel.net.om; internet www.cbo-oman.org.

Area and Population

AREA, POPULATION AND DENSITY

Area (sq km)	309,500*
Population (census results)	
1 December 1993†	2,018,074†
1 December 2003	
Males	1,313,239
Females	1,027,576
Total	2,340,815‡
Population (official estimates at mid-year)	
2005	2,509,000
2006	2,577,000
2007	2,743,000
Density (per sq km) at mid-2007	8.9

* 119,500 sq miles.
† Comprising 1,483,226 Omani nationals and 534,848 non-Omanis.
‡ Comprising 1,781,558 Omani nationals and 559,257 non-Omanis.

Mid-2008 ('000, UN estimate): 2,651 (Source: UN, *World Population Prospects: The 2006 Revision*).

ADMINISTRATIVE DIVISIONS
(population at mid-2007)

	Area (sq km)*	Population	Density (per sq km)
Muscat Governorate	3,900	786,000	201.5
Al-Batinah Region	12,500	736,000	58.9
Musandam Governorate	1,800	34,000	18.9
Adh-Dhahira Region	44,000	148,000	3.4
Ad-Dakhliya Region	31,900	299,000	9.3
Ash-Sharqiya Region	36,400	355,000	9.8
Al-Wosta Region	79,700	27,000	0.3
Dhofar Governorate	99,300	260,000	2.6
Al-Buraymi Governorate	n.a.	98,000	n.a.
Total	**309,500**	**2,743,000**	**8.9**

* Area data predate the creation, from Adh-Dhahira Region, of Al-Buraymi Governorate in October 2006.

Note: Figures for area and population are rounded, and totals may not be equal to the sum of components as a result.

PRINCIPAL TOWNS
(population at 2003 census)

Salalah	156,530	Nizwa	68,785
Suhar	104,312	Al-Buraymi	67,963
Ibri	97,429	Sur	66,785
Ar-Rustaq	74,224	Muscat (capital)	24,893

Source: Thomas Brinkhoff, *City Population* (internet www.citypopulation.de).

Mid-2007 ('000, incl. suburbs, UN estimate): Muscat 620 (Source: UN, *World Urbanization Prospects: The 2007 Revision*).

BIRTHS AND DEATHS
(Omani nationals only, official estimates)

	2005	2006	2007
Birth rate (per 1,000)	24.8	24.2	25.0
Death rate (per 1,000)	2.5	n.a.	n.a.

Life expectancy (years at birth, provisional): 72.0 (males 70.4; females 73.6) in 2007.

EMPLOYMENT
(persons aged 15 years and over, 2003 census)

	Omanis	Non-Omanis	Total
Agriculture and fishing	14,210	43,904	58,114
Mining and quarrying	11,998	8,117	20,115
Manufacturing	13,831	45,661	59,492
Electricity, gas and water	1,826	2,219	4,045
Construction	10,128	108,129	118,257
Trade, hotels and restaurants	24,999	84,158	109,157
Transport, storage and communications	17,202	10,472	27,674
Finance, insurance and real estate	12,657	12,543	25,200
Public administration and defence	144,699	18,043	162,742
Other community, social and personal services	54,923	83,299	138,222
Activities not adequately defined	5,973	7,633	13,606
Total employed	**312,446**	**424,178**	**736,624**
Males	258,655	364,337	622,992
Females	53,791	59,841	113,632

Mid-2005 (estimates in '000): Agriculture, etc. 317; Total labour force 977 (Source: FAO).

OMAN

Health and Welfare

KEY INDICATORS

Total fertility rate (children per woman, 2006)	3.1
Under-5 mortality rate (per 1,000 live births, 2006)	11
HIV/AIDS (% of persons aged 15–49, 2003)	0.1
Physicians (per 1,000 head, 2005)	1.7
Hospital beds (per 1,000 head, 2006)	2.1
Health expenditure (2006): US $ per head (PPP)	382
Health expenditure (2006): % of GDP	2.3
Health expenditure (2006): public (% of total)	84.0
Access to water (% of persons, 2002)	79
Access to sanitation (% of persons, 2002)	89
Human Development Index (2006): ranking	53
Human Development Index (2006): value	0.839

For sources and definitions, see explanatory note on p. vi.

Agriculture

PRINCIPAL CROPS
('000 metric tons)

	2005	2006	2007*
Sorghum	9.5	8.8	8.9
Potatoes	5.9	5.4	5.5
Tomatoes	39.4	40.4	41.0
Onions, dry	5.4	4.2	4.5
Watermelons*	27.0	27.0	27.0
Bananas	26.7	26.0	26.0
Lemons and limes	6.2	5.9	6.0
Mangoes, mangosteens and guavas	7.7	6.9	6.4
Dates	247.3	258.7	260.0
Papayas	1.4	1.4	1.4

* FAO estimates.

Aggregate production ('000 metric tons, may include official, semi-official or estimated data): Total cereals 15.1 in 2005, 14.2 in 2006, 14.5 in 2007; Total roots and tubers 5.9 in 2005, 5.4 in 2006, 5.5 in 2007; Total vegetables (incl. melons) 206.1 in 2005, 204.9 in 2006, 206.7 in 2007; Total fruits (excl. melons) 289.3 in 2005, 298.9 in 2006, 299.8 in 2007.

Source: FAO.

LIVESTOCK
('000 head, year ending September)

	2005	2006	2007*
Asses, mules or hinnies	29*	n.a.	n.a.
Cattle	302	308	310
Camels	117	120	120
Sheep	351	358	360
Goats	1,557	1,598	1,600
Chickens*	4,500	4,200	4,200

* FAO estimate(s).
Source: FAO.

LIVESTOCK PRODUCTS
('000 metric tons)

	2005	2006	2007*
Cattle meat*	4.2	4.2	4.2
Camel meat*	6.6	6.8	6.8
Sheep meat*	10.8	11.0	11.0
Goat meat	22.5	23.0	23.5
Chicken meat*	5.8	5.9	5.9
Cows' milk	46.0	47.0	47.0
Sheep's milk*	4.0	4.0	4.0
Goats' milk*	84.7	85.0	85.0
Hen eggs*	9.5	9.0	9.0

* FAO estimates.
Source: FAO.

Fishing

('000 metric tons, live weight)

	2004	2005	2006
Capture	165.1	150.6	154.0
Groupers	5.9	4.2	4.8
Emperors (Scavengers)	10.3	8.0	8.9
Porgies and seabreams	8.2	6.3	6.8
Hairtails and cutlassfishes	3.5	4.8	5.7
Demersal percomorphs	6.5	8.0	6.8
Indian oil sardine	34.9	40.2	36.2
Longtail tuna	7.8	7.5	7.9
Yellowfin tuna	24.3	15.9	18.0
Indian mackerel	5.8	5.2	5.1
Carangids	3.2	2.5	2.8
Sharks, rays, skates, etc.	5.6	5.1	5.6
Cuttlefish and bobtail squids	11.8	9.8	11.0
Aquaculture	0.5	0.2	0.1*
Total catch	165.5	150.7	154.1*

* FAO estimate.
Source: FAO.

Mining

('000 metric tons, unless otherwise indicated, estimates)

	2004	2005	2006
Crude petroleum (million barrels)	285.4	282.6	269.2*
Natural gas (dry, million cu m)	17,000	17,390	21,754
Chromium	18.6	34.0	67.0*
Gold (kg)	211	384	144*
Marble	163.8	220.9	220.0*
Salt	12.4	10.9	11.0*
Gypsum	103.0	133.1	130.0*

* Provisional.
Source: US Geological Survey.

Industry

SELECTED PRODUCTS
('000 barrels, unless otherwise indicated, estimates)

	2004	2005	2006
Jet fuel and kerosene	1,407	1,770	2,339
Motor spirit (petrol)	5,215	5,436	5,078
Gas-diesel (distillate fuel) oils	6,442	7,089	6,750
Residual fuel oils	14,247	15,445	14,947
Electric energy (million kWh)	11,499	12,648	13,585

Source: mainly US Geological Survey.

Electric energy (million kWh): 14,443 in 2007.

Finance

CURRENCY AND EXCHANGE RATES

Monetary Units
1,000 baiza = 1 rial Omani (RO).

Sterling, Dollar and Euro Equivalents (31 December 2008)
£1 sterling = 560.5 baiza;
US $1 = 384.5 baiza;
€1 = 535.1 baiza;
10 rials Omani = £17.84 = $26.01 = €18.69.

Exchange Rate: Since January 1986 the official exchange rate has been fixed at US $1 = 384.5 baiza (1 rial Omani = $2.6008).

BUDGET
(RO million)

Revenue	2005	2006	2007*
Petroleum revenue (net)	3,161.9	3,225.9	3,678.2
Gas revenues	393.6	613.5	810.9
Other current revenue	888.3	1,073.4	1,344.9
Taxes and fees	337.2	357.2	528.5
Income tax on enterprises	79.0	85.4	187.1
Customs duties	88.5	114.6	159.6
Non-tax revenue	551.1	716.2	816.4
Electricity	14.0	—	—
Surplus from public authorities	7.6	5.4	5.9
Income from government investments	302.0	369.6	393.3
Capital revenue	35.0	49.0	66.2
Capital repayments	31.7	18.1	20.4
Total	**4,510.5**	**4,979.9**	**5,920.6**

Expenditure	2005	2006	2007*
Current expenditure	3,179.4	3,531.0	3,857.5
Defence and national security	1,404.2	1,549.6	1,663.4
Civil ministries	1,531.9	1,735.0	1,898.7
Investment expenditure	966.5	1,199.5	1,697.3
Share of PDO expenditure†	249.5	322.5	476.9
Participation and subsidies	61.7	205.6	325.6
Total	**4,207.6**	**4,936.1**	**5,880.4**

* Preliminary figures.
† Referring to the Government's share of current and capital expenditure by Petroleum Development Oman.

INTERNATIONAL RESERVES
(US $ million at 31 December)

	2005	2006	2007
Gold (national valuation)	0.3	0.4	0.5
IMF special drawing rights	14.8	16.7	18.7
Reserve position in IMF	34.6	27.2	19.6
Foreign exchange	4,308.7	4,970.2	9,485.1
Total	**4,358.4**	**5,014.4**	**9,523.9**

Source: IMF, *International Financial Statistics*.

MONEY SUPPLY
(RO million at 31 December)

	2005	2006	2007
Currency outside banks	383.2	470.9	563.4
Demand deposits at commercial banks	750.4	756.9	1,353.5
Total money	**1,133.6**	**1,227.8**	**1,916.9**

Source: IMF, *International Financial Statistics*.

COST OF LIVING
(Consumer Price Index for Muscat; base: 2000 = 100)

	2005	2006	2007
Food, beverages and tobacco	102.7	108.7	119.0
Textiles, clothing and footwear	99.2	98.8	99.1
Rent, electricity, water and fuel	97.4	98.7	106.1
All items (incl. others)	**100.2**	**103.5**	**108.7**

NATIONAL ACCOUNTS
(RO million in current prices)

Expenditure on the Gross Domestic Product

	2004	2005	2006*
Government final consumption expenditure	2,031.8	2,289.0	2,457.2
Private final consumption expenditure	4,198.0	4,258.6	5,326.8
Gross fixed capital formation	1,958.1	2,130.2	2,545.7
Total domestic expenditure	**8,187.9**	**8,677.8**	**10,329.7**
Exports of goods and services	5,424.0	7,472.0	8,651.0
Less Imports of goods and services	4,087.0	4,260.0	5,243.0
GDP in purchasers' values	**9,524.9**	**11,889.8**	**13,737.7**
GDP at constant 1988 prices	6,694.7	7,095.8	7,609.2

* Provisional.

Gross Domestic Product by Economic Activity

	2005	2006	2007
Agriculture and fishing	184.7	195.9	204.9
Mining and quarrying	5,809.0	6,595.2	7,067.0
Crude petroleum	5,362.8	6,082.1	6,437.5
Natural gas	421.8	489.4	595.8
Non-petroleum	24.4	23.7	33.7
Manufacturing	983.1	1,421.7	1,557.9
Electricity and water	143.6	151.3	163.5
Construction	292.1	349.5	470.7
Wholesale and retail trade	1,240.9	1,478.9	1,948.6
Hotels and restaurants	86.7	103.2	114.2
Transport, storage and communications	684.0	847.1	1,046.5
Financial intermediation	374.8	451.6	552.9
Real estate	343.1	352.9	377.3
Public administration and defence	926.1	922.8	1,017.4
Other services	986.0	1,069.4	1,232.1
Sub-total	**12,054.0**	**13,939.6**	**15,753.0**
Less Financial intermediation services indirectly measured	252.7	316.4	387.2
Gross value added in basic prices	**11,801.3**	**13,623.1**	**15,365.8**
Taxes on imports	88.5	114.6	146.3
GDP in purchasers' values	**11,889.8**	**13,737.7**	**15,512.0**

BALANCE OF PAYMENTS
(US $ million)

	2005	2006	2007
Exports of goods f.o.b.	18,692	21,586	24,723
Imports of goods f.o.b.	−8,029	−9,880	−14,343
Trade balance	**10,663**	**11,706**	**10,380**
Exports of services	754	931	1,163
Imports of services	−3,255	−3,847	−4,996
Balance on goods and services	**8,163**	**8,790**	**6,546**
Other income received	830	1,549	2,026
Other income paid	−1,801	−2,464	−2,985
Balance on goods, services and income	**7,193**	**7,875**	**5,587**
Current transfers paid	−2,257	−2,788	−3,670

OMAN

Statistical Survey

—continued	2005	2006	2007
Current account	4,935	5,087	1,918
Capital account (net)	−16	−96	827
Direct investment abroad	−234	−328	−568
Direct investment from abroad	1,688	1,622	2,376
Portfolio investment assets	−437	−1,495	775
Portfolio investment liabilities	479	806	2,056
Other investment assets	−3,226	−6,050	−5,135
Other investment liabilities	292	2,620	2,880
Net errors and omissions	−673	41	1,159
Overall balance	2,809	2,206	6,287

Source: IMF, *International Financial Statistics*.

External Trade

PRINCIPAL COMMODITIES
(RO million)

Imports c.i.f. (distribution by SITC)*	2005	2006	2007
Food and live animals	340.3	382.1	509.1
Beverages and tobacco	31.2	32.9	42.5
Crude materials (inedible) except fuels	88.5	123.0	114.5
Minerals, fuels, lubricants, etc.	141.0	139.2	214.4
Chemicals and related products	284.6	280.6	395.6
Basic manufactures	569.1	799.4	1,283.5
Machinery and transport equipment	1,637.4	2,085.0	3,165.3
Miscellaneous manufactured articles	198.3	239.4	340.8
Commodities not elsewhere classified	78.8	80.2	32.6
Total (incl. others)	3,394.2	4,190.1	6,144.2

Exports f.o.b.	2005	2006	2007
Petroleum and natural gas	6,047.8	6,720.3	7,211.7
Crude petroleum	5,071.1	5,528.3	5,553.5
Refined petroleum	88.3	47.4	466.0
Natural gas	888.4	1,144.6	1,192.2
Non-oil and -gas exports	1,139.1	1,579.2	2,294.0
Live animals and animal products	99.4	92.4	103.9
Mineral products	50.5	216.1	450.1
Total†	7,186.9	8,299.5	9,505.7

* Excluding unrecorded imports (RO million): 55.1 in 2005; 54.3 in 2006; 17.3 in 2007.
† Including re-exports (RO million): 583.8 in 2005; 766.7 in 2006; 1,003.3 in 2007.

PRINCIPAL TRADING PARTNERS
(RO million)

Imports c.i.f.	2005	2006	2007
Australia	70.0	83.2	121.8
Bahrain	59.2	34.6	56.3
Belgium	38.3	54.1	57.2
China, People's Republic	81.8	141.7	183.4
France	71.4	73.6	149.2
Germany	232.9	212.0	325.8
India	153.3	222.2	400.1
Italy	67.7	86.8	144.9
Japan	534.0	724.0	969.1
Korea, Republic	109.0	147.7	212.6
Netherlands	59.4	83.7	131.2
Saudi Arabia	97.5	144.8	149.7
Singapore	32.9	49.2	42.2
United Arab Emirates	898.3	1,083.7	1,625.2
United Kingdom	147.8	142.1	181.7
USA	208.8	219.3	354.8
Total (incl. others)	3,394.0	4,190.1	6,144.2

Exports f.o.b.*	2004	2005	2006
Belgium	14.6	6.0	16.8
China, People's Republic	15.2	14.7	16.2
Germany	10.3	9.8	9.7
Hong Kong	21.5	18.1	23.5
India	14.0	78.2	134.6
Iran	87.8	52.0	83.0
Iraq	20.1	15.4	15.5
Jordan	27.2	24.3	6.0
Kenya	0.9	1.3	1.3
Kuwait	15.8	15.6	16.9
Libya	10.8	11.9	17.1
Pakistan	11.1	9.6	18.0
Qatar	17.0	27.0	43.2
Saudi Arabia	85.8	99.5	85.7
Singapore	15.0	11.3	12.7
Syria	12.6	14.4	7.9
Tanzania	4.6	3.8	3.1
United Arab Emirates	357.0	510.9	752.6
United Kingdom	26.2	27.1	37.0
USA	34.1	22.2	20.7
Yemen	27.6	28.7	29.2
Total (incl. others)	958.5	1,139.1	1,579.2

* Excluding petroleum exports.

2007: India 185.7; Iran 129.2; Iraq 22.2; Saudi Arabia 96.8; United Arab Emirates 1,081.0; Yemen 39.7. Total exports (incl. others) 2,294.0.

Transport

ROAD TRAFFIC
(registered vehicles at 31 December)

	2001	2002	2003
Private cars	309,217	335,771	284,902
Taxis	20,901	23,639	23,761
Commercial	132,920	140,270	109,118
Government	27,788	29,175	14,861
Motorcycles	5,195	5,436	3,977
Diplomatic	1,274	1,386	561
Other	23,631	24,625	7,320
Total	520,926	560,302	444,500

SHIPPING

Merchant Fleet
(registered at 31 December)

	2005	2006	2007
Number of vessels	31	33	36
Total displacement ('000 grt)	18.7	20.3	24.1

Source: Lloyd's Register-Fairplay, *World Fleet Statistics*.

International Sea-borne Freight Traffic
('000 metric tons, unless otherwise specified)

	2004	2005	2006
Port Sultan Qaboos:			
Goods loaded onto vessels ('000 US shipping tons)	1,180	1,226	1,298
Goods unloaded from vessels ('000 US shipping tons)	5,415	5,748	6,967
Goods loaded onto launches	154	346	9,065
Goods unloaded from launches	63,535	40,997	36,263
Port Salalah:			
Goods loaded	1,070	1,185	1,691
Goods unloaded	464	603	617
Mina al-Fahal Coastal Area			
Petroleum loaded	36,889	36,759	31,993
Petroleum products unloaded	328	417	1,231

CIVIL AVIATION
(aircraft movements, passengers and cargo handled at Seeb International Airport)

	2004	2005	2006
International flights:			
flights (number)	35,803	44,408	42,087
passengers ('000)	3,187	3,778	4,460
goods handled (metric tons)	65,917	75,332	96,493
Domestic flights:			
flights (number)	7,819	8,373	7,814
passengers ('000)	274	292	318
goods handled (metric tons)	1,234	1,231	1,415

Tourism

FOREIGN TOURIST ARRIVALS*

Country of nationality	2004	2005	2006
Bahrain	26,536	37,586	37,360
Egypt	20,276	16,775	14,867
France	23,495	26,621	36,669
Germany	78,129	112,276	125,285
India	106,456	116,375	110,841
Kuwait	15,564	12,775	14,574
Netherlands	11,408	12,084	13,849
Pakistan	16,506	18,743	15,993
Saudi Arabia	31,066	33,256	25,597
Switzerland	17,203	26,498	38,295
Tanzania	7,828	2,725	441
United Arab Emirates	103,317	94,902	95,334
United Kingdom	92,887	135,197	219,485
USA	26,910	12,064	33,775
Total (incl. others)	908,466	989,390	1,306,128

* Figures refer to international arrivals at hotels and similar establishments.

Tourism receipts (US $ million, incl. passenger transport): 604 in 2004; 599 in 2005; 743 in 2006.

Source: World Tourism Organization.

Communications Media

	2005	2006	2007
Telephones ('000 main lines in use)	265.2	269.7	268.1
Mobile cellular telephones ('000 subscribers)	1,333.2	1,818.0	2,500.0
Personal computers ('000 in use)	118	n.a.	n.a.
Internet users ('000)	285	319	340
Broadband subscribers ('000)	8.3	18.8	18.9

Daily newspapers (number): 6 in 2004.

Non-daily newspapers and other periodicals (number): 23 in 2004.

Television receivers (number in use): 1,430,000 in 2000.

Radio receivers (number in use): 1,400,000 in 1997.

Facsimile machines (number in use): 6,356 in 1997.

Book production (number of titles): 7 in 1996; 136 in 1998; 12 in 1999.

Sources: mainly UNESCO, *Statistical Yearbook*, and International Telecommunication Union.

Education

(state schools, 2007/08 unless otherwise indicated)

	Institutions	Teachers	Pupils/Students Males	Females	Total
Pre-primary*	5	529	4,973	4,456	9,429
Basic†		26,499	143,869	139,268	283,137
General†:					
Grades 1–6	1,052	2,873	26,657	26,321	52,978
Grades 7–9		5,305	42,448	39,640	82,088
Grades 10–12		9,186	70,680	64,353	135,033
Higher‡§	34	1,608	12,282	11,004	23,286
University	1	1,074	7,542	7,180	14,722

* 2005/06.
† The Basic education system began to replace the General education system from 1998/99.
‡ Comprising six teacher-training colleges, the College of *Shari'a* and Law, five technical colleges, the Academy of Tourism and Catering, the College of Banking and Financial Studies, 16 institutes of health and four vocational-training centres.
§ 2004/05.

Adult literacy rate (UNESCO estimates): 84.4% (males 89.4%; females 77.5%) in 2007 (Source: UNESCO Institute for Statistics).

Directory

The Constitution

The Basic Statute of the State was promulgated by royal decree on 6 November 1996, as Oman's first document defining the organs and guiding principles of the State.

Chapter 1 defines the State and the system of government. Oman is defined as an Arab, Islamic and independent state with full sovereignty. Islamic law (*Shari'a*) is the basis for legislation. The official language is Arabic. The system of government is defined as Sultani (Royal), hereditary in the male descendants of Sayyid Turki bin Said bin Sultan. Article 6 determines the procedure whereby the Sultan is designated.

Chapter 2 defines the political, economic, social, cultural and security principles of the State. Article 11 (economic principles) includes the stipulation that 'All natural resources and revenues therefrom shall be the property of the State which will preserve and utilize them in the best manner taking into consideration the requirements of the State's security and the interests of the national economy'. The constructive and fruitful co-operation between public and private activity is stated to be the essence of the national economy. Public property is inviolable, and private ownership is safeguarded. Article 14 (security principles) provides for a Defence Council to preserve the safety and defence of the Sultanate.

Chapter 3 defines public rights and duties. Individual and collective freedoms are guaranteed within the limits of the law.

Chapter 4 concerns the Head of State, the Council of Ministers, Specialized Councils and financial affairs of the State. Article 41 defines the Sultan as Head of State and Supreme Commander of the Armed Forces. The article states that 'His person is inviolable. Respect for him is a duty and his command must be obeyed. He is the symbol of national unity and the guardian of its preservation and protection'. The Sultan presides over the Council of Ministers, or may appoint a person (Prime Minister) to preside on his behalf. Deputy Prime Ministers and other Ministers are appointed by the Sultan. The Council of Ministers and Specialized Councils assist the Sultan in implementing the general policy of the State.

Chapter 5 comprises a single Article (58). This states that the Council of Oman shall consist of the Majlis ash-Shura (Consultative Council) and the Majlis ad-Dawlah (State Council). The jurisdiction, terms, sessions, rules of procedure, membership and regulation of each shall be determined by the law.

Chapter 6 concerns the judiciary. Articles 59 and 60 state that the supremacy of the law shall be the basis of governance, and enshrine the dignity, integrity, impartiality and independence of the judiciary. Article 66 provides for a Supreme Council of the judiciary.

Chapter 7 defines the general provisions pertaining to the application of the Basic Statute.

The Government

HEAD OF STATE

Sultan: Qaboos bin Said as-Said (assumed power on 23 July 1970, after deposing his father).

COUNCIL OF MINISTERS
(April 2009)

Prime Minister and Minister of Foreign Affairs, Defence and Finance: Sultan Qaboos bin Said as-Said.
Deputy Prime Minister for the Council of Ministers: Sayyid Fahd bin Mahmoud as-Said.
Personal Representative of the Sultan: Sayyid Thuwaini bin Shihab as-Said.
Minister of National Economy, Supervisor of the Finance Ministry and Deputy Chairman of the Financial Affairs and Energy Resources Council: Ahmad bin Abd an-Nabi Macki.
Minister Responsible for Defence Affairs: Sayyid Badr bin Saud bin Hareb al-Busaidi.
Minister of Legal Affairs: Muhammad bin Ali bin Nasir al-Alawi.
Minister of Oil and Gas: Dr Muhammad bin Hamad bin Saif ar-Rumhi.
Minister of Justice: Sheikh Muhammad bin Abdullah bin Zahir al-Hinai.
Minister of Awqaf (Religious Endowments) and Religious Affairs: Sheikh Abdullah bin Muhammad bin Abdullah as-Salimi.
Minister Responsible for Foreign Affairs: Yousuf bin al-Alawi bin Abdullah.
Minister of Information: Hamad bin Muhammad bin Muhsin ar-Rashdi.
Minister of Housing: Sheikh Saif bin Muhammad ash-Shabaibi.
Minister of Education: Yahya bin Saud bin Mansoor as-Sulaimi.
Minister of Higher Education: Dr Rawya bint Saud bin Ahmad al-Busaidiyah.
Minister of Heritage and Culture: Sayyid Haitham bin Tariq as-Said.
Minister of Tourism: Dr Rajha bint Abd al-Amir bin Ali.
Minister of Social Development: Dr Sharifah bint Khalfan bin Nasser al-Yahiyaia.
Minister of Manpower: Abdullah bin Nasser al-Bakri.
Minister of Sports Affairs: Eng. Ali bin Massoud bin Ali as-Sinaidi.
Minister of Transport and Communications: Dr Khamis bin Mubarak bin Isa al-Alawi.
Minister of the Interior: Sayyid Saud bin Ibrahim bin Saud al-Busaidi.
Minister of Commerce and Industry: Maqbool bin Ali bin Sultan.
Minister of Agriculture: Sheikh Salim bin Hilal al-Khalili.
Minister of Fisheries: Sheikh Muhammad bin Ali al-Qatabi.
Minister of Environment and Climate Affairs: Sayyid Hamoud bin Faisal al-Busaidi.
Minister of Health: Dr Ali bin Muhammad bin Mousa.
Minister of Regional Municipalities and Water Resources: Sheikh Abdullah bin Salem bin Amer ar-Rawas.
Minister of the Civil Service: Sheikh Muhammad bin Abdullah al-Harthi.
Minister of State and Governor of Muscat: Sayyid al-Mutassim bin Hamoud al-Busaidi.
Minister of State and Governor of Dhofar: Sheikh Muhammad bin Marhoud al-Mamari.
Minister of the Diwan of the Royal Court: Sayyid Ali bin Hamoud bin Ali al-Busaidi.
Minister of the Royal Office: Maj.-Gen. Ali bin Majid al-Ma'amari.

MINISTRIES

Diwan of the Royal Court: POB 632, Muscat 113; tel. 24738711; fax 24739427.
Ministry of Agriculture: POB 3738, Ruwi 112; tel. 24700896; fax 24707939; e-mail info@maf.gov.om; internet www.maf.gov.om.
Ministry of Awqaf (Religious Endowments) and Religious Affairs: POB 3232, Ruwi 112; tel. 24696870; e-mail info@mara.gov.om; internet www.maraoman.net.
Ministry of the Civil Service: POB 3994, Ruwi 112; tel. 24696000; fax 24601365; internet www.mocs.gov.om.
Ministry of Commerce and Industry: POB 550, Muscat 113; tel. 24774290; fax 24817238; e-mail info@mocioman.gov.om; internet www.mocioman.gov.om.
Ministry of Defence: POB 113, Muscat 113; tel. 24312605; fax 24702521.
Ministry of Education: POB 3, Muscat 113; tel. 24773181; fax 24704465; e-mail moe@moe.gov.om; internet www.moe.gov.om.
Ministry of Environment and Climate Affairs: POB 323, Muscat 113; tel. 24696464; fax 24692553.
Ministry of Finance: POB 506, Muscat 113; tel. 24738201; fax 24737028; e-mail info@mof.gov.om; internet www.mof.gov.om.
Ministry of Fisheries: POB 467, Muscat 113; tel. 24696338; fax 24605634.
Ministry of Foreign Affairs: POB 252, Muscat 113; tel. 24699453; fax 24696141; e-mail info@mofa.gov.om; internet www.mofa.gov.om.
Ministry of Health: POB 393, Muscat 113; tel. 24600527; fax 24602647; e-mail moh@moh.gov.om; internet www.moh.gov.om.
Ministry of Heritage and Culture: POB 668, Muscat 113; tel. 24641300; fax 24641331; e-mail info@mhc.gov.om; internet www.mhc.gov.om.
Ministry of Higher Education: POB 82, Ruwi 112; tel. 24755999; e-mail press@mohe.gov.om; internet www.mohe.gov.om.
Ministry of Housing: POB 1491, Ruwi 112; tel. 24603906; fax 24699180.
Ministry of Information: POB 600, Muscat 113; tel. 24603222; fax 24693770; e-mail omanet@omantel.net.om; internet www.omanet.om.
Ministry of the Interior: POB 127, Ruwi 112; tel. 24602244; fax 24696660; internet www.moi.gov.om.
Ministry of Justice: POB 354, Ruwi 112; tel. 24697699; e-mail webmaster@moj.gov.om; internet www.moj.gov.om.
Ministry of Legal Affairs: POB 578, Ruwi 112; tel. 24605802; fax 24605697; internet www.mola.gov.om.
Ministry of Manpower: POB 413, Muscat 113; tel. 24816739; fax 24816234; internet www.manpower.gov.om.
Ministry of National Economy: POB 881, Muscat 100; tel. 24698900; fax 24698467; e-mail mone@omantel.net.om; internet www.mone.gov.om.
Ministry of Oil and Gas: POB 551, Muscat 113; tel. 24603333; fax 24696972.
Ministry of the Royal Office: POB 2227, Ruwi 112; tel. 24600841.
Ministry of Regional Municipalities and Water Resources: POB 461, Muscat 112; tel. 24692550; fax 24694015; e-mail admin@mrmwr.gov.om; internet www.mrmwr.gov.om.
Ministry of Sports Affairs: POB 211, Muscat 113; tel. 24755240; fax 24704558; e-mail feedback@sportsoman.com; internet www.sportsoman.com.
Ministry of Tourism: Madinat as-Sultan Qaboos, POB 200, Muscat 115; tel. 24588700; fax 24588880; e-mail info@omantourism.gov.om; internet www.mot.gov.om.
Ministry of Transport and Communications: POB 338, Ruwi 112; tel. 24697870; fax 24696817; e-mail dgroads@omantel.net.om; internet www.motc.gov.om.

MAJLIS OMAN
(Council of Oman)

Majlis ash-Shoura
(Consultative Council)

President: Sheikh Ahmad bin Muhammad al-Issai.

The Majlis ash-Shoura was established by royal decree in November 1991. Initially, members of the Majlis were appointed by the Sultan from among nominees selected at national polls, but from the September 2000 elections, members were directly elected. Two representatives are appointed from four candidates in each *wilaya* (province) of more than 30,000 inhabitants, and one from two candidates in each *wilaya* of fewer than 30,000 inhabitants. Members of the Majlis are appointed for a single four-year term of office. The Majlis elected in October 2007 comprised 84 members. The Majlis is an advisory body, the duties of which include the review of all social and economic draft laws prior to their enactment; public-service ministries are required to submit reports and answer questions regarding their performance, plans and achievements. The President of the Majlis ash-Shoura is appointed by royal decree.

Majlis ad-Dawlah
(State Council)

President: Sheikh Yahya bin Mahfoudh al-Mantheri.

The Majlis ad-Dawlah was established in December 1997, in accordance with the terms of the Basic Statute of the State. Like the Majlis

OMAN

ash-Shoura, it is an advisory body, whose function is to serve as a liaison between the Government and the people of Oman. Its members are appointed by the Sultan for a four-year term. A new Majlis, comprising 70 members, was appointed in November 2007.

Political Organizations

There are no political organizations in Oman.

Diplomatic Representation

EMBASSIES IN OMAN

Algeria: POB 216, Muscat 115; tel. 24694945; fax 24694419; e-mail afcongem@omantel.net.om; Ambassador TAYEB SAADI.

Austria: Villa No. 898, Way No. 3013, POB 2070, Ruwi 112; tel. 24694127; fax 24699265; e-mail maskat-ob@bmeia.gv.at; Ambassador Dr ANDREAS KARABACZEK.

Bahrain: POB 66, Madinat Qaboos, Al-Khuwair; tel. 265683901; fax 265664190; e-mail bahraine@omantel.net.om; Ambassador FOUAD SALMAN AL-MUAWDA.

Bangladesh: St 664, Bldg 5903, POB 3959, Ruwi 112; tel. 24567379; fax 24567502; e-mail bania@omantel.net.om; Ambassador MUHAMMAD ABD AL-HANNAN.

Brazil: c/o Intercontinental Hotel, Suite 317/318, Al-Kharijiya St, Shatti al-Qurum; Chargé d'affaires SERGIO TAM.

Brunei: Shatti al-Qurum, St 3050, Villa 4062, POB 91, Ruwi 112; tel. 24603533; fax 24605910; e-mail kbopuni@omantel.net.om; Ambassador Haji MUHARRAM BIN Haji PIAH.

China, People's Republic: Al-Ansherah St, Way No. 1507, House No. 465, Madinat Alalam, POB 315, Muscat 112; tel. 24696698; fax 24602322; e-mail chinaemb_om@mfa.gov.cn; Ambassador PAN WEIFANG.

Egypt: Jamiat ad-Dowal al-Arabiya St, Diplomatic City, Al-Khuwair, POB 2252, Ruwi 112; tel. 24600411; fax 24603626; e-mail egyembmuscat@hotmail.com; Ambassador IZZADIN FAHMY MAHMOUD.

France: Diplomatic City, Al-Khuwair, POB 208, Madinat Qaboos 115; tel. 24681800; fax 24681843; e-mail diplofr1@omantel.net.om; internet www.ambafrance-om.org; Ambassador MALIKA BERAK.

Germany: POB 128, Ruwi 112; tel. 24832482; fax 24835690; e-mail info@maskat.diplo.de; internet www.maskat.diplo.de; Ambassador KLAUS GEYER.

India: POB 1727, Ruwi 112; tel. 24684500; fax 24698291; e-mail indiamct@omantel.net.om; internet www.indemb-oman.org; Ambassador ANIL WADHWA.

Iran: Diplomatic Area, Jamiat ad-Dowal al-Arabiya St, POB 3155, Ruwi 112; tel. 24696944; fax 24696888; e-mail iranembassy@hotmail.com; internet www.iranembassy.gov.om; Ambassador MORTEZA RAHIMI ZARCHI.

Iraq: Shatti al-Qurum, Way 3025, House No. 1073, POB 262, Muscat 115; tel. 24603642; fax 24602026; e-mail musemb@iraqmofamail.net; internet www.iraqem.com; Ambassador ABD AR-RASOUL KADHIM MUHAMMAD J. ALOUSH.

Italy: Shatti al-Qurum, Way No. 3034, House No. 2697, POB 3727, Ruwi 112; tel. 24693727; fax 24695161; e-mail ambasciata.mascate@esteri.it; internet www.ambmascate.esteri.it; Ambassador CESARE CAPITANI.

Japan: Shatti al-Qurum, Villa No. 760, Way No. 3011, Jamiat ad-Dowal al-Arabiya St, POB 3511, Ruwi 112; tel. 24601028; fax 24698720; internet www.oman.emb-japan.go.jp; Ambassador SEIJI MORIMOTO.

Jordan: Diplomatic City, Arab League St, POB 70, Al-Adhaiba 130; tel. 24692760; fax 24692762; e-mail embhkjom@omantel.net.om; Ambassador MAZIN MIDHAT JUMAH.

Korea, Republic: POB 377, Madinat Qaboos 115; tel. 24691490; fax 24691495; e-mail emboman@mofat.go.kr; Ambassador CHO SUNG-HWAN.

Kuwait: Al-Khuwair Diplomatic Area, Arab League St, Block No. 13, Bldg No. 58, POB 1798, Ruwi 112; tel. 24699626; fax 24604732; e-mail muscat@mofa.gov.kw; Ambassador SHAMLAN AR-ROUMI.

Lebanon: Shatti al-Qurum, Way No. 3019, Villa No. 1613, Al-Harthy Complex, POB 67, Muscat 118; tel. 24695844; fax 24695633; e-mail lebanon1@omantel.net.om; Ambassador AFIF AYYUB.

Malaysia: Shatti al-Qurum, Villa No. 1611, Way No. 3019, POB 3939, Ruwi 112; tel. 24698329; fax 24605031; e-mail mwmuscat@omantel.net.om; internet www.kln.gov.my/perwakilan/muscat; Ambassador Dato MUHAMMAD ZAMRI MUHAMMAD KASSIM.

Morocco: Shatti al-Qurum, Villa No. 2443, Way No. 3030, POB 3125, Ruwi 112; tel. 24696152; fax 24601114; e-mail sifamamu@omantel.net.om; Ambassador Dr NOUREDDINE BENOMAR.

Netherlands: Shatti al-Qurum, Way No. 3017, Villa No. 1366, POB 3302, Ruwi 112; tel. 24603706; fax 24603778; e-mail mus@minbuza.nl; internet www.mfa.nl/mus; Ambassador STEFAN VAN WERSCH.

Pakistan: POB 1302, Ruwi 112; tel. 24603439; fax 24697462; e-mail parepmuscat@gmail.com; Ambassador SOHAIL AMIN.

Philippines: POB 420, Madinat Qaboos 115; tel. 24605140; fax 24605176; e-mail muscatpe@omantel.net.om; Ambassador ACMAD D. OMAR.

Qatar: Diplomatic City, Jamiat ad-Dowal al-Arabiya St, Al-Khuwair, POB 802, Muscat 113; tel. 24691152; fax 24691156; Ambassador ABDULLAH BIN MUHAMMAD BIN KHALID AL-KHATIR.

Russia: Shatti al-Qurum, Way No. 3032, Surfait Compound, POB 80, Ruwi 112; tel. 24602894; fax 24604189; e-mail rusoman@omantel.net.om; Ambassador Dr SERGEI E. EVANOV.

Saudi Arabia: Diplomatic City, Jamiat ad-Dowal al-Arabiya St, POB 1411, Ruwi 112; tel. 24601744; fax 24603540; e-mail omemb@mofa.gov.sa; Ambassador ABD AL-AZIZ BIN SULAIMAN AT-TURKI.

Somalia: Mumtaz St, Villa Hassan Jumaa Baker, POB 1767, Ruwi 112; tel. 24564412; fax 24564965; e-mail danjsiad@omantel.net.om; Ambassador Gen. ISMA'IL QASIM NAJI.

South Africa: Al-Harthy Complex, POB 231, Muscat 118; tel. 24694791; fax 24694792; e-mail southae@omantel.net.om; internet www.saembassymuscat.gov.om; Ambassador YOUSEF SALOJI.

Sri Lanka: POB 95, Madinat Qaboos 115; tel. 24697841; fax 24697336; e-mail lankaemb@omantel.net.om; Ambassador MUDIYANSELAGE MAHINDA RANARJA.

Spain: Shatti al-Qurum, Way No. 2834, House No. 2573, POB 3492, Ruwi 112; tel. 24691101; fax 24698969; e-mail emb.mascate@mae.es; Ambassador TOMÁS RODRÍGUEZ-PANTOJA MÁRQUEZ.

Sudan: Diplomatic City, Al-Khuwair, POB 3971, Ruwi 112; tel. 24697875; fax 24699065; e-mail suanimt@gto.net.om; Ambassador ASHAFEA AHMAD MUHAMMAD.

Syria: Madinat Qaboos, Al-Ensharah St, Villa No. 201, POB 85, Muscat 115; tel. 24697904; fax 24603895; e-mail syria@omantel.net.om; internet www.syrianembassy.gov.om; Ambassador FAROUK MAHMOUD QADDOUR.

Thailand: Shatti al-Qurum, Villa No. 1339, Way No. 3017, POB 60, Ruwi 115; tel. 24602683; fax 24605714; e-mail thaimct@omantel.net.om; Ambassador VORAVEE WIRASAMBAN.

Tunisia: Al-Ensharah St, Way No. 1507, POB 220, Muscat 115; tel. 24603486; fax 24697778; Ambassador HAMMOUDA RIHANI.

Turkey: Shatti al-Qurum, Bldg No. 3270, St No. 3042, POB 47, Mutrah 115; tel. 24697050; fax 24697053; e-mail turemmus@omantel.net.om; Ambassador ENGIN TÜRKER.

United Arab Emirates: Diplomatic City, Al-Khuwair, POB 551, Muscat 111; tel. 24600302; fax 24604182; e-mail uaeoman@omantel.net.om; Ambassador MUHAMMAD ALI ABD AR-RAHMAN AL-OSAIMI.

United Kingdom: POB 185, Mina al-Fahal 116; tel. 24609000; fax 24609010; e-mail enquiries.muscat@fco.gov.uk; internet www.britishembassy.gov.uk/oman; Ambassador Dr NOEL GUCKIAN.

USA: Jamiat ad-Dowal al-Arabiya St, Madinat Qaboos, POB 202, Muscat 115; tel. 24643400; fax 24699771; e-mail answersom@state.gov; internet oman.usembassy.gov; Ambassador GARY A. GRAPPO.

Yemen: Shatti al-Qurum, Area 258, Way No. 2840, Bldg No. 2981, POB 105, Madinat Qaboos 115; tel. 24600815; fax 24605008; Ambassador ABD AR-RAHMAN KHAMIS UBAID.

Judicial System

Oman's Basic Statute guarantees the independence of the judiciary. The foundation for the legal system is *Shari'a* (Islamic law), which is the basis for family law, dealing with matters such as inheritance and divorce. Separate courts have been established to deal with commercial disputes and other matters to which *Shari'a* does not apply.

Courts of the First Instance are competent to try cases of criminal misdemeanour; serious crimes are tried by the Criminal Courts; the Court of Appeal is in Muscat. There are district courts throughout the country. Special courts deal with military crimes committed by members of the armed and security forces.

The Basic Statute provides for a Supreme Council to supervise the proper functioning of the courts.

An Administrative Court, to review the decisions of government bodies, was instituted in April 2001.

The office of Public Prosecutor was established in 1999, and the first such appointment was made in June 2001.

Religion

ISLAM

The majority of the population (estimated at 89.2% in 2001) are Muslims, of whom approximately three-quarters are of the Ibadi sect and about one-quarter are Sunni Muslims.

Grand Mufti of Oman: Sheikh AHMAD BIN HAMAD AL-KHALILI.

HINDUISM

According to 2001 estimates, 6.0% of the population are Hindus.

CHRISTIANITY

According to 2001 estimates, 2.9% of the population are Christians.

Protestantism

The Protestant Church in Oman: POB 1982, Ruwi 112; tel. 24702372; fax 24789943; e-mail pcomct@omantel.net.om; internet 76.12.38.165/occ2003/skur/history.htm; joint chaplaincy of the Anglican Church and the Reformed Church of America; four interdenominational churches in Oman, at Ruwi and Ghala in Muscat, at Sohar and at Salalah; Senior Pastor Rev. Dr EDWARD SCHREUR.

The Roman Catholic Church

A small number of adherents, mainly expatriates, form part of the Apostolic Vicariate of Arabia. The Vicar Apostolic is resident in the United Arab Emirates.

The Press

Article 31 of Oman's Basic Statute guarantees the freedom of the press, printing and publishing, according to the terms and conditions specified by the law. Published matter 'leading to discord, harming the State's security or abusing human dignity or rights' is prohibited.

NEWSPAPERS

Oman: POB 3002, Ruwi 112; tel. 24699689; fax 24697443; e-mail editor@omandaily.com; internet www.omandaily.com; daily; Arabic; publ. by Oman Establishment for Press, News, Publication and Advertising; Editor-in-Chief ABDULLAH BIN NASSER AR-RAHBI; circ. 26,000.

Ash-Shabiba (Youth): POB 2998, Ruwi 112; tel. 24814373; fax 24811722; e-mail editor@shabiba.com; internet www.shabiba.com; f. 1993; daily; Arabic; culture, leisure and sports; publ. by Muscat Press and Publishing House SAOC; Editor-in-Chief AHMAD BIN ESSA AZ-ZEDJALI; circ. 15,000.

Al-Watan (The Nation): POB 463, Muscat 113; tel. 24491919; fax 24491280; e-mail alwatan@omantel.net.om; internet www.alwatan.com; f. 1971; daily; Arabic; Editor-in-Chief MUHAMMAD BIN SULAYMAN AT-TAI; circ. 40,000.

English Language

Oman Daily Observer: POB 3002, Ruwi 112; tel. 24699647; fax 24600362; e-mail editor@omanobserver.com; internet www.omanobserver.com; f. 1981; daily; publ. by Oman Establishment for Press, News, Publication and Advertising; Chair. ABDULLAH BIN NASSER AR-RAHBI; Editor IBRAHIM BIN SAIF AL-HAMDANI; circ. 22,000.

Oman Tribune: POB 463, Muscat 113; tel. 24491919; fax 24498444; e-mail eomantribune@omantribune.com; internet www.omantribune.com; f. 2004; Founder and Chair. MUHAMMAD BIN SULAYMAN AT-TAI; Editor-in-Chief ABD AL-HAMID BIN SULAYMAN AT-TAI.

Times of Oman: POB 770, Ruwi 112; tel. 24811953; fax 24813153; e-mail online@timesofoman.com; internet www.timesofoman.com; f. 1975; daily; publ. by Muscat Press and Publishing House SAOC; Founder, Chair. and Editor-in-Chief ESSA BIN MUHAMMAD AZ-ZEDJALI; Man. Dir ANIS BIN ESSA AZ-ZEDJALI; circ. 34,000.

TheWeek: POB 2616, Ruwi 112, Muscat; tel. 24799388; fax 24793316; e-mail theweek@apexstuff.com; internet www.theweek.co.om; f. 2003; weekly; free; publ. by Apex Press and Publishing; CEO and Man. Editor MOHANA PRABHAKAR; circ. 50,743 (copies per week).

PERIODICALS

Al-Ain as-Sahira (The Vigilant Eye): Royal Oman Police, POB 302, Mina' al-Fahl 116; tel. 24569270; fax 24567161; internet www.rop.gov.om; quarterly magazine of Royal Oman Police; Editor-in-Chief Col ABDULLAH BIN ALI AL-HARTHI.

Alam Aliktisaad Wala'mal (World of Economy and Business): POB 3305, Ruwi 112; tel. 24700896; fax 24707939; f. 2007; monthly; Arabic; business magazine; publ. by United Press and Publishing LLC.

Al-'Aqida (The Faith): POB 1001, Ruwi 112; tel. 24701000; fax 24709917; weekly illustrated magazine; Arabic; political; Editor SAID AS-SAMHAN AL-KATHIRI; circ. 10,000.

Business Today: POB 2616, Ruwi 112; tel. 24799388; fax 24793316; e-mail editorial@apexstuff.com; internet www.businesstoday.co.om; monthly; publ. by Apex Press and Publishing; Man. Editor MOHANA PRABHAKAR.

The Commercial: POB 2002, Ruwi 112; tel. 24704022; fax 24795885; e-mail omanad@omantel.net.om; f. 1978; monthly; Arabic and English; business news; Man. MUHAMMAD AYOOB; Chief Editor ALI BIN ABDULLAH AL-KASBI; circ. 10,000.

Al-Ghorfa (The Chamber): POB 1400, Ruwi 112; tel. 24703082; fax 24708497; e-mail alghorfa@chamberoman.com; internet www.chamberoman.com; f. 1978; bi-monthly; English and Arabic; business; publ. by Oman Chamber of Commerce and Industry; Editor HAMOOD HAMAD AL-MAHROUQ; circ. 10,500.

Al-Jarida ar-Rasmiya (Official Gazette): POB 578, Ruwi 112; tel. 24605802; fax 24605697; f. 1972; fortnightly; publ. by Ministry of Legal Affairs.

Jund Oman (Soldiers of Oman): Ministry of Defence, POB 113, Muscat 113; tel. 24613615; fax 24613369; f. 1974; monthly; Arabic; illustrated magazine of the Ministry of Defence; Supervisor Chief of Staff of the Sultan's Armed Forces.

Al-Mar'a (Woman): United Media Services, POB 3305, Ruwi 112; tel. 24700896; fax 24707939; e-mail almara@umsoman.com; internet www.almaraonline.com; monthly; Arabic and English; women's interest; publ. by United Press and Publishing LLC.

Al-Markazi (The Central): POB 1161, Ruwi 112; tel. 24702222; fax 24707913; e-mail cboccr@omantel.net.om; internet www.cbo-oman.org; f. 1975; bi-monthly economic magazine; Arabic and English; publ. by Central Bank of Oman; Editor-in-Chief HAIDER BIN ABD AR-REDHA AL-LAWATI.

An-Nahda (The Renaissance): POB 979, Muscat 113; tel. 24563104; fax 24563106; weekly illustrated magazine; Arabic; political and social; Editor TALEB SAID AL-MEAWALY; circ. 10,000.

Nizwa: POB 855, 117 Wadi Kabir; tel. 24601608; fax 24694254; e-mail nizwa99@nizwa.com; internet www.nizwa.com; f. 1994; quarterly; Arabic; literary and cultural; publ. by Oman Establishment for Press, News, Publication and Advertising; Editor-in-Chief SAIF AR-RAHBI.

Oman Economic Review: POB 3305, Ruwi 112; tel. 24700896; fax 24707939; e-mail editor@oeronline.com; internet www.oeronline.com; f. 1998; monthly; English; business news; publ. by United Press and Publishing LLC; Editor-in-Chief Sayyid TARIK BIN SHABIB; circ. 25,000.

Oman Today: POB 2616, Ruwi 112; tel. 24799388; fax 24793316; e-mail editorial@apexstuff.com; internet www.omantoday.co.om; f. 1981; monthly; English; leisure and sports; publ. by Apex Press and Publishing; Man. Editor MOHANA PRABHAKAR; circ. 20,000.

Al-Omaniya (Omani Woman): POB 3303, Ruwi 112; tel. 24792700; fax 24707765; f. 1982; monthly; Arabic; Editor AIDA BINT SALIM AL-HUJRI; circ. 10,500.

Risalat al-Masjid (The Mosque Message): POB 6066, Muscat; tel. 24561178; fax 24560607; issued by Diwan of the Royal Court Protocol Dept (Schools and Mosques Section); Editor JOUMA BIN MUHAMMAD BIN SALEM AL-WAHAIBI.

Al-Usra (The Family): POB 440, Mutrah 114; tel. 24794922; fax 24795348; e-mail admeds@omantel.net.om; f. 1974; fortnightly; Arabic; socio-economic illustrated magazine; Chief Editor SADEK ABDOWANI; circ. 15,000.

NEWS AGENCY

Oman News Agency: Ministry of Information, POB 3659, Ruwi 112; tel. 24698891; fax 24699657; e-mail onaoman@omantel.net.om; internet www.omannews.gov.om; f. 1986; Dir-Gen. and Editor-in-Chief MAJID BIN MUHAMMAD BIN FARAJ AR-ROWAS.

Publishers

Apex Press and Publishing: POB 2616, Ruwi 112, Muscat; tel. 24799388; fax 24793316; e-mail editorial@apexstuff.com; internet www.apexstuff.com; f. 1980; art, history, trade directories, maps, leisure and business magazines, and guidebooks; publs incl. TheWeek (English weekly), Business Today (business monthly), Oman Today (leisure monthly); Pres. SALEH M. TALIB AZ-ZAKWANI; Man. Editor MOHANA PRABHAKAR.

Dar al-Usra: POB 440, Mutrah 114; tel. 24794922; fax 24795348; e-mail alusra@omantel.net.om.

OMAN

Muscat Press and Publishing House SAOC: POB 770, Ruwi 112; tel. 24811953; fax 24813153; publs incl. Times of Oman (English daily) and Ash-Shabiba (Arabic daily); Chair. ESSA MUHAMMAD AZ-ZEDJALI; CEO AHMAD BIN ESSA AZ-ZEDJALI.

National Publishing and Advertising LLC: POB 3112, Ruwi 112; tel. 24793098; fax 24708445; e-mail advertising@npaoman.com; internet www.npaoman.com; f. 1987; Man. ASHOK SUVARNA.

Oman Establishment for Press, News, Publication and Advertising (OEPNPA): POB 974, Al-Qurum, Muscat 113; tel. 24699170; f. 1996 as Oman Newspaper House; responsible for publication of Oman (Arabic daily), Oman Daily Observer (English language), Nizwa and Money Works (magazines), and the Oman News Agency; three regional offices in Dhofar, Nizwa and Sohar; Chair. ABDULLAH BIN NASSER AR-RAHBI.

United Press and Publishing LLC (UPP): POB 3305, Ruwi 112; tel. 24700896; fax 24707939; internet www.renaissanceoman.com; f. 1995; part of Renaissance Services SAOG; publishes Alam al-Iqtisad (Arabic monthly) and Oman Economic Review (English monthly); Gen. Man. SANDEEP SEHGAL.

Broadcasting and Communications

TELECOMMUNICATIONS

Regulatory Authority

Telecommunications Regulatory Authority: POB 579, Ruwi 112; tel. 24574300; fax 24565464; e-mail traoman@tra.gov.om; internet www.tra.gov.om; f. 2002 to oversee the privatization of Omantel (see below) and to set tariffs and regulate the sale of operating licences; Chair. MUHAMMAD BIN NASSER AL-KHUSAIBI.

Service Providers

Oman Telecommunications Company SAOC (Omantel): POB 789, Ruwi 112; tel. 24631417; fax 24697066; e-mail info@omantel.net.om; internet www.omantel.net.om; f. 1999 as successor to the General Telecommunications Organization; provider of fixed-line, mobile and internet services; held a monopoly on fixed-line services until 2008; state-owned, but undergoing privatization; Chair. Eng. SULTAN BIN HAMDOUN AL-HARTHI; Exec. Pres. Eng. MUHAMMAD BIN ALI AL-WAHAIBI.

Oman Mobile Telecommunications Company LLC (Oman Mobile): POB 694, Al-Azaiba 130; tel. 24474000; e-mail enquiry@omanmobile.om; internet www.omanmobile.om; f. 2004; subsidiary of Omantel; Chair. Eng. SULTAN BIN HAMDOUN AL-HARTHI.

Nawras: POB 874, Muscat 111; tel. 95011500; fax 95011555; e-mail customerservice@nawras.om; internet www.nawras.om; f. 2004; mobile telephone operator; awarded Oman's second fixed-line licence Nov. 2008; Chair. Sheikh SALIM BIN MUSTAHIL AL-MA'ASHANI; CEO ROSS CORMACK.

BROADCASTING

The Law on Private Radio and Television Stations, enacted in 2004, provided for the establishment of private broadcasters for the first time.

Radio

Sultanate of Oman Radio: Ministry of Information, POB 600, Muscat 113; tel. 24602058; fax 24601393; e-mail feedback_rd@oman-radio.gov.om; internet www.oman-radio.gov.om; f. 1970; operates four services: General Arabic Channel, Ash-Shabab Channel (youth service), English language FM service, Holy Koran Channel; Dir-Gen. NASSER SULAYMAN AS-SAIBANI.

The first private radio licences were issued in 2005, and broadcasts began in 2007 with the launch of Hala FM (Arabic, entertainment and music) and Hi FM (English, entertainment and music). A third private station, Al-Wisal FM, began broadcasting in Arabic in 2008.

Television

Sultanate of Oman Television: Ministry of Information, POB 600, Muscat 113; tel. 24603222; fax 24605032; e-mail feedback_tv@oman-tv.gov.om; internet www.oman-tv.gov.om; began broadcasting in 1974; programmes broadcast via Arabsat and Nilesat satellite networks.

Finance

(cap. = capital; res = reserves; dep. = deposits; m. = million; brs = branches; amounts in rials Omani)

BANKING

At the end of August 2008 there were 17 commercial banks (seven local and 10 foreign) and two specialized banks, with a total network of 410 domestic branch offices operating throughout Oman.

Central Bank

Central Bank of Oman: POB 1161, 44 Mutrah Commercial Centre, Ruwi 112; tel. 24702222; fax 24788995; e-mail cboccr@omantel.net.om; internet www.cbo-oman.org; f. 1974; cap. 400.0m., res 575.5m., dep. 2,053.7m. (Dec. 2007); 100% state-owned; Exec. Pres. HAMOUD SANGOUR AZ-ZADJALI; 2 brs.

Commercial Banks

Ahli Bank SAOG: POB 545, Mina al-Fahal 116; tel. 24577000; fax 24568001; e-mail info@ahlibank-oman.com; internet www.ahlibank-oman.com; f. 1997 as Alliance Housing Bank, renamed as above 2008; privately owned; cap. 184.8m., res 3.4m., dep. 152.1m. (Dec. 2007); Chair. Sayyid KHALID HAMAD HAMOOD AL-BUSAIDI; CEO ABD AL-AZIZ AL-BALUSHI; 8 brs.

Bank Dhofar SAOG: POB 1507, Ruwi 112; tel. 24790466; fax 24797246; e-mail info@bankdhofar.com; internet www.bankdhofar.com; f. 1990 as Bank Dhofar al-Omani al-Fransi SAOG; renamed as above in 2004 after merger with Majan International Bank SAOC; cap. 53.0m., res 31.0m., dep. 768.0m. (Dec. 2007); Chair. Eng. ABD AL-HAFIDH SALIM RAJAB AL-AUJAILI; CEO KRIS BABICCI; 50 brs.

BankMuscat SAOG: POB 134, Ruwi 112; tel. 24768888; fax 24785572; e-mail banking@bkmuscat.com; internet www.bankmuscat.com; f. 1993 by merger as Bank Muscat Al-Ahli Al-Omani; renamed Bank Muscat International in 1998, and as above in 1999; merged with Commercial Bank of Oman Ltd SAOG in 2000 and with Industrial Bank of Oman in 2002; 88.8% owned by Omani shareholders; cap. 83.2m., res 165.8m., dep. 2,371.7m. (Dec. 2006); Chair. Sheikh ABD AL-MALEK BIN ABDULLAH AL-KHALILI; CEO ABD AR-RAZAK ALI ISSA; 95 brs in Oman, 1 br. abroad.

Bank Sohar SAOG: POB 44, Hay al-Mina, Muttrah 114; tel. 24730000; fax 24793972; e-mail info@banksohar.net; internet www.banksohar.net; f. 2007; 32.5% owned by Oman Govt, 12% by Al Ghadir Al Arabia LLC, 55.5% by various Omani shareholders; cap. 50m., res 1.8m., dep. 362.5m. (Dec. 2007); Chair. Sheikh HILAL HAMOOD AL-MAMARI; CEO NANI JAVERI.

National Bank of Oman SAOG (NBO): POB 751, Ruwi 112; tel. 24778000; fax 24778585; e-mail ask@nbo.co.om; internet www.nbo.co.om; f. 1973; 100% Omani-owned; cap. 80.0m., res 101.2m., dep. 833.9m. (Dec. 2006); Chair. OMAR HUSSAIN AL-FARDAN (acting); CEO ANDREW MCGREGOR DUFF; 52 brs in Oman, 6 brs abroad.

Oman Arab Bank SAOC: POB 2010, Ruwi 112; tel. 24706265; fax 24797736; e-mail mktoab@omantel.net.om; internet www.omanab.com; f. 1984; purchased Omani European Bank SAOG in 1994; 51% Omani-owned, 49% by Arab Bank PLC (Jordan); cap. 48.0m., res 32.0m., dep. 539.0m. (Dec. 2007); Chair. RASHAD MUHAMMAD AZ-ZUBAIR; CEO ABD AL-QADER ASKALAN; 38 brs.

Oman International Bank SAOG: POB 1727, Muscat 111; tel. 24682500; fax 24682800; e-mail oibgm@omantel.net.om; internet www.oiboman.com; f. 1984; 100% Omani-owned; cap. 75.5m., res 25.9m., dep. 782.3m. (Dec. 2006); Chair. REEM BINT OMAR AZ-ZAWAWI; Gen. Man. DOUGLAS EMMETT; 82 brs in Oman, 4 brs abroad.

Development Banks

Oman Development Bank SAOC: POB 3077, Ruwi 112; tel. 24812507; fax 24813100; e-mail customer.care@odboman.net; internet www.odboman.net; f. 1977; absorbed Oman Bank for Agriculture and Fisheries in 1997; short-, medium- and long-term finance for devt projects in industry, agriculture and fishing; state-owned; cap. 40.0m., res 4.9m., total assets 60.2m. (Dec. 2007); Chair. Sheikh YAQOOB BIN HAMAD AL-HARTHY; Gen. Man. SAMIR BIN BECHIR AS-SAID; 9 brs.

Oman Housing Bank SAOC: POB 2555, Ruwi 112; tel. 24704444; fax 24704071; e-mail ohb@ohb.co.om; internet www.ohb.co.om; f. 1977; long-term finance for housing devt; 100% state-owned; cap. 30.0m., res 44.5m., total assets 176.5m. (Dec. 2007); Chair. DARWISH ISMAIL ALI AL-BULUSHI; Gen. Man. ADNAN HAIDAR DARWISH AZ-ZA'ABI; 9 brs.

STOCK EXCHANGE

Muscat Securities Market (MSM): POB 3265, Muscat 112; tel. 24823600; fax 24815776; e-mail msm.info.news@msm.gov.om; internet www.msm.gov.om; 221 cos listed (Jan. 2009); f. 1989; Chair.

OMAN

Hassan bin Ali Jawad al-Lawati; Dir-Gen. Ahmad Saleh al-Marhoon.

Supervisory Body

Capital Market Authority (CMA): POB 3359, Ruwi 112; tel. 24823224; fax 24817471; e-mail info_cma@msm.gov.om; internet www.omancma.org; f. 1998 to regulate capital market and insurance sector; Chair. Maqbool bin Ali bin Sultan (Minister of Commerce and Industry); Exec. Pres. Yahya bin Said Abdullah al-Jabri.

INSURANCE

In 2007 there were 17 licensed insurance companies operating in Oman. Of these, 10 were local firms and the remainder were branches of non-resident companies.

Al-Ahlia Insurance Co SAOG: POB 1463, Ruwi 112; tel. 24709441; fax 24797151; e-mail aaic@alahliaoman.com; internet www.alahliaoman.com; f. 1985; cap. 6.0m., total assets 63.1m. (June 2008); Chair. Sayyid Khalid Hamad Hamood al-Busaidi; Gen. Man. A. R. Srinivasan.

Dhofar Insurance Co SAOG: POB 1002, Ruwi 112; tel. 24705305; fax 24793641; e-mail dhofar@dhofarinsurance.com; internet www.dhofarinsurance.com; f. 1989; cap. 20.0m. (Dec. 2007); Chair. Sheikh Salim bin Mubarak ash-Shanfari; CEO Taher T. al-Heraki.

Falcon Insurance Co SAOC: POB 2279, Ruwi 112; tel. 24660900; fax 24565323; e-mail ficins@omantel.net.om; f. 1977 as Al-Ittihad al-Watani; assoc. co of Al Anwar Holdings SAOG; cap. 5.4m.; Gen. Man. Michael Jan Wright.

Al Madina Gulf Insurance Co SAOC: POB 1805, Athaiba 130; tel. 24771888; fax 24771899; e-mail contact@amgioman.com; internet www.amgioman.com; f. 2006; cap 10m. (Dec. 2006); CEO Ravi Shankar.

Muscat Insurance Co SAOC: POB 72, Ruwi 112; tel. 24478897; fax 24481847; e-mail mic@muscatlife.com; internet www.omzest.com/mic.htm; f. 1995 as Muscat Insurance Co SAOG, restructured in 1999 as Muscat National Holding Co SAOG (parent co), Muscat Insurance Company SAOC and Muscat Life Assurance Company SAOC; subsidiary of Omar Zawawi Establishment (OMZEST); Gen. Man. Andrew M. Woodward; Asst Gen. Man. Philip K. Philip.

National Life and General Insurance Co SAOC: POB 798, Wadi Kabir 117; tel. 24730999; fax 24795222; e-mail natlife@nlicgulf.com; internet www.nlicgulf.com; f. 1983; sudsidiary of Oman National Investment Corpn Holding SAOG; Gen. Man. S. Venkatachalam.

Oman Qatar Insurance Co SAOC: POB 3660, Ruwi 112; tel. 24700067; fax 24700815; e-mail contact@oqic.com; internet www.qatarinsurance.com/net_oman.htm; subsidiary of Qatar Insurance Co; Gen. Man. Thomas M. Devasia.

Oman United Insurance Co SAOG: POB 1522, Ruwi PC 112; tel. 24477300; fax 24477323; e-mail enquiry@ouic.com.om; internet www.ouic-oman.com; f. 1985; cap. 10.0m., total assets 65.4m. (Dec. 2007); Chair. and Acting CEO Said Salim bin Nassir al-Busaidi.

Royal and Sun Alliance Oman (RSA Oman): POB 889, Muscat 100; tel. 24478318; fax 24482296; e-mail rsaoman@om.royalsun.com; internet www.rsa.com.om; f. 2004; 67% owned by Royal and Sun Alliance Group (RSA); CEO Sanjeev Jha.

Trade and Industry

GOVERNMENT AGENCY

Omani Centre for Investment Promotion and Export Development (OCIPED): POB 25, Al-Wadi Kabir 117, Muscat; tel. 24812344; fax 24810890; e-mail info@ociped.com; internet www.ociped.com; f. 1996; promotes investment to Oman and the devt of non-oil Omani exports; Chair. Maqbool bin Ali bin Sultan (Minister of Commerce and Industry); Exec. Pres. Salem bin Nasser al-Ismaily.

CHAMBER OF COMMERCE

Oman Chamber of Commerce and Industry: POB 1400, Ruwi 112; tel. 24763700; fax 24708497; e-mail occi@chamberoman.com; internet www.chamberoman.com; f. 1973; Chair. Khalil bin Abdullah bin Muhammad al-Khonji; 142,881 mems (Sep. 2008).

STATE HYDROCARBONS COMPANIES

National Gas Co SAOG: POB 95, Rusayl 124; tel. 24446073; fax 24446307; e-mail info@nationalgasco.net; internet www.nationalgasco.net; f. 1979; bottling of liquefied petroleum gas; Chair. Sheikh Khalid Ahmad Sultan al-Hosni; Gen. Man. Pradyot Kumar Bagchi; 158 employees.

Oman Gas Co SOAC (OGC): POB 799, Al-Khuwair 133; tel. 24681600; fax 24681678; e-mail info@oman-gas.com.om; internet www.oman-gas.com.om; f. 1999; govt-owned (80% Ministry of Oil and Gas; 20% Oman Oil Co SAOC); operates gas network and builds pipelines to supply power plants and other industries in Oman; Chair. Dr Muhammad bin Hamad bin Saif ar-Rumhi (Minister of Oil and Gas); CEO Yousuf bin Muhammad al-Ojaili.

Oman LNG LLC: POB 560, Mina al-Fahal 116; tel. 24609999; fax 24609900; e-mail info@omanlng.co.om; internet www.omanlng.com; f. 1992; 51% state-owned; Royal Dutch Shell 30%; manages 6.6m. metric-tons-per-year liquefied natural gas plant at Qalhat; manufacturing, shipping and marketing; Chair. Nasser bin Khamis al-Jashmi; CEO and Gen. Man. Dr Brian Buckley; 225 employees.

Oman Oil Co SAOC (OOC): POB 261, al-Harthy Complex, Ruwi 118; tel. 24573100; fax 24573101; e-mail info@oman-oil.com; internet www.oman-oil.com; f. late 1980s to invest in foreign commercial enterprises and oil trading operations; 100% state-owned; Chair. Maqbool bin Ali bin Sultan (Minister of Commerce and Industry); CEO Ahmad al-Wahaibi.

Oman Refineries and Petrochemicals Co LLC (ORPC): POB 3568, Ruwi 112; tel. 24561200; fax 24561384; internet www.orpc.co.om; f. 2007 after merger of Oman Refinery Co (f. 1982) and Sohar Refinery Co LLC; production of light petroleum products; production capacity 222,000 b/d (2008); 75% owned by Oman Govt, 25% by Oman Oil Co SAOC; Chair. Dr Muhammad bin Hamad bin Saif ar-Rumhi (Minister of Oil and Gas); CEO Dr Adil bin Abd-al Aziz al-Kindy; 355 employees.

Petroleum Development Oman LLC (PDO): POB 81, Muscat 113; tel. 24678111; fax 24677106; e-mail external-affairs@pdo.co.om; internet www.pdo.co.om; incorporated in Sultanate of Oman since 1980 by royal decree as limited liability co; 60% owned by Oman Govt, 34% by Royal Dutch Shell; exploration and production of crude oil and gas; crude oil production (2007) averaged 561,000 b/d from over 100 fields, linked by a pipeline system to terminal at Mina al-Fahal, near Muscat; gas production (2007) totalled 63.3m. cu m/d; Chair. Dr Muhammad bin Hamad bin Saif ar-Rumhi (Minister of Oil and Gas); Man. Dir John Malcolm; 5,000 employees.

Qalhat LNG SAOC: POB 514, Al-Khuwair 133; tel. 24574004; fax 24574090; e-mail info@qalhatlng.co.om; internet www.qalhatlng.co.om; f. 2003; production of LNG; 46.8% owned by Oman Govt, 36.8% by Oman LNG LLC, 16.4% by foreign investors; Chair. Sheikh al-Fadhil bin Muhammad al-Harthy; CEO Harib al-Kitani.

UTILITIES

As part of its privatization programme, the Omani Government is divesting the utilities on a project-by-project basis. Private investors have already been found for several municipal wastewater projects, desalination plants and regional electricity providers.

Supervisory Body

Public Authority for Electricity and Water (PAEW): POB 106, Ruwi 112; tel. 24601464; fax 24601672; e-mail dg-project@paew.gov.om; internet www.paew.gov.om; f. 2007 following the restructuring of the former Ministry of Housing, Electricity and Water; plans and supervises devt of the utilities in Oman; Chair. Muhammad bin Abdullah bin Muhammad al-Mahrouqi.

Electricity

Authority for Electricity Regulation: POB 954, Al-Khuwair 133; tel. 24609700; fax 24609701; e-mail enquiries@aer-oman.org; internet www.aer-oman.org; f. 2004 to regulate and facilitate the privatization of the electricity and related water sector; Chair. Dr Saleh Muhammad al-Alawi; Exec. Dir John Cuneen.

Electricity Holding Co SAOC (EHC): POB 850, Mina al-Fahal 116; tel. 24559203; fax 24559288; e-mail ehcoman@omantel.net.om; internet www.ehcoman.com; f. 2005; state-owned; established to hold Govt's ownership in nine utility cos and to facilitate the commercial restructuring of the sector; Ar-Rusail Power Co was privatized in 2007; of the remaining eight successor cos, six are currently scheduled for privatization; Chair. Muhammad bin Abdullah bin Muhammad al-Mahrouqi; CEO Karl Matacz.

Principal subsidiaries of the EHC include:

Muscat Electricity Distribution Co SAOC (MEDC): POB 3732, Al-Ghubrah 112; tel. 24588600; fax 24588666; e-mail medc@medcoman.com; internet www.medcoman.com; f. 2005; responsible for all distribution in the Governorate of Muscat; Chair. Eng. Saleh al-Farsi; Gen. Man. Eng. Zahir al-Abri.

Oman Electricity Transmission Co SAOC (OETC): POB 1224, Al-Hamriya 131; tel. 24573221; fax 24573222; e-mail webmaster@omangrid.com; internet www.omangrid.com; f. 2003; owns and operates the Main Interconnected System, which covers the north of Oman and accounts for 90% of the Sultanate's electricity transmission; scheduled for privatization by 2010; Chair. Irshad Mousa al-Lawati; Gen. Man. Ali al-Hadabi.

Oman Power and Water Procurement Co SAOC: POB 1388, Ruwi 112; e-mail vacancies@omanpwp.com; internet www.omanpwp.co.om; f. 2003; responsible for forecasting and managing the supply and demand of electricity and water; Chair. SULTAN BIN HAMDOUN AL-HARTHI; CEO ALASTAIR DE REUCK.

Other subsidiaries of the EHC are: Majan Electricity Co, Mazoon Electricity Co, Rural Areas Electricity Co, Wadi Jizzi Power Co, Al-Ghubrah Power and Desalination Co.

Water

Ministry of Regional Municipalities and Water Resources: (see The Government); assesses, manages, develops and conserves water resources.

Oman Power and Water Procurement Co SAOC: see Electricity.

Oman Wastewater Services Co SAOC (Haya Water): POB 1047, Al-Khuwair 133; tel. 24590544; fax 24693418; e-mail customerservice@omanwsc.com; internet www.owsc.com.om; f. 2002; devt and operation of a wastewater system in the Governorate of Muscat; govt-owned; CEO OMAR KHALFAN AL-WAHAIBI.

Transport

RAILWAYS

There are no railways in Oman, although plans for a regional rail network, connecting Oman with member countries of the Co-operation Council for the Arab States of the Gulf (or Gulf Co-operation Council—GCC), were under discussion in 2009.

ROADS

A network of adequate graded roads links all the main centres of population and only a few mountain villages are inaccessible by off-road vehicles. In 2007 there were 48,874 km of roads, of which 1,087 km were dual carriageways and a further 19,074 km were asphalted roads. Several large-scale road-building projects were under way in 2007–08, including the construction of a 56-km partial ring-road around Muscat, at a cost of some US $342m. Plans for a new 240-km Batinah coastal road linking Barka and Sohar with Khatmat Malaha on the border with the UAE were finalized in 2008; phase one of the construction was expected to commence in early 2009.

Directorate-General of Roads: Ministry of Transport and Communications, POB 338, Ruwi 112; tel. 24697870; fax 24696817; e-mail dgroads@omantel.net.om; internet www.motc.gov.om/en/edgr/edgr.html; Dir-Gen. of Roads Sheikh MUHAMMAD BIN HILAL AL-KHALILI.

Oman National Transport Co SAOG (ONTC): POB 620, Muscat 113; tel. 24490046; fax 24490152; e-mail info@ontcoman.com; internet www.ontcoman.com; f. 1972; re-established in 1984; operates local, regional and long-distance bus services from Muscat; Chair. MAJID SAID SALIM AR-RUWAHI; Gen. Man. MAJID AL-MANDHRY.

SHIPPING

Port Sultan Qaboos (Mina Sultan Qaboos), at the entrance to the Persian (Arabian) Gulf, was built in 1974 to provide nine deep-water berths varying in length from 250 ft to 750 ft (76 m to 228 m), with draughts of up to 43 ft (13 m), and three berths for shallow-draught vessels drawing 12 ft to 16 ft (3.7 m to 4.9 m) of water. A total of 12 new berths have been opened and two of the existing berths have been upgraded to a container terminal capable of handling 60 containers per hour. The port also has a 3,000-metric-ton-capacity cold store which belongs to the Oman Fisheries Co. In the 1990s Port Sultan Qaboos underwent a further upgrade and expansion. In 2007 1,856 ships visited the port and 4.7m. tons of cargo were handled. Plans to expand capacity further were put on hold in mid-2008 as bidders for the project estimated that the cost would significantly exceed the Government's projection of US $390m.

The oil terminal at Mina al-Fahal can also accommodate the largest super-tankers on offshore loading buoys. Similar facilities for the import of refined petroleum products exist at Mina al-Fahal. Mina Raysut, near Salalah (now known as Salalah port), has been developed into an all-weather port, and, in addition to container facilities, has four deep-water berths and two shallow berths. The port is currently undergoing transformation into a free trade zone. During 2007 1,500 ships called at Salalah and the port handled a reported 2.8m. TEUs. Two further deep-water berths had been completed by the end of 2008, increasing the port's capacity to some 3m. TEUs per year, and plans for three more container berths were at the design stage in early 2009. Loading facilities for smaller craft exist at Sohar and Khasab (both of which are being expanded), Khaboura, Sur, Marbet, Ras Al Hadd, Al-Biaa, Masirah and Salalah. A major redevelopment of the port at Duqm, on the Gulf of Masirah, was announced in 2007. In 2008 the authorities announced that the project would be significantly expanded to provide: deep-water berths of −18 m; a deepened approach channel; breakwaters expanded to 7.7 km; a new dry dock for ships of up to 400,000 tonnes; and a new ship repair yard. The project is expected to be completed by 2012 and has been allocated an initial RO 700m. in government investment.

Directorate-General of Ports and Maritime Affairs: POB 684, Ruwi 112; tel. 24685994; fax 24685992; e-mail dgpma@omantel.net.om; Dir-Gen. Eng. QASSIM ASH-SHIZAWI.

National Ferries Co SAOC: POB 911, Al-Kuwair 113; tel. 24698910; fax 24698477; e-mail nfc.reservations@gmail.com; operates a high-speed, passenger and vehicle ferry service between Muscat and Khasab, on the Strait of Hormuz; govt-owned; Chair. MEHDI AL-ABDUWANI.

Oman Shipping Co SAOC (OSC): Al-Harthy Complex, POB 104, Muscat 118; tel. 24400900; fax 24400922; e-mail info@omanship.co.om; internet www.omanship.co.om; f. 2003; owns and operates a fleet of over 30 vessels; transportation of liquefied natural gas, crude petroleum and petrochemical products; subsidiaries include: Oman Charter Co, Duqm Maritime Transportation Co, Liwa Maritime Transportation Co, Energy Spring LNG Carrier SA, Oasis LNG Carrier SA; govt-owned (Ministry of Finance 80%, Oman Oil CoSAOC 20%); Chair. AHMAD BIN ABD AN-NABI MACKI (Minister of National Economy).

Port Services Corpn SAOG (PSC): POB 133, Muscat 113; tel. 24714000; fax 24714007; e-mail mktg@pscoman.com; internet www.pscoman.com; f. 1976; responsible for management of Port Sultan Qaboos; cap. RO 7.9m. (2007); jointly owned by the Govt of Oman and private shareholders; Exec. Pres. SAUD BIN AHMAD AN-NAHARI.

Salalah Port Services Co SAOG (SPS): POB 105, Muscat 118; tel. 24600586; fax 24601003; e-mail info@salalahport.com; internet www.salalahport.com; port authority for Salalah port; CEO MARTIJN VAN DE LINDE.

CIVIL AVIATION

Domestic and international flights operate from Muscat International Airport (known as Seeb International Airport prior to February 2008). In 2007 4.1m. passengers passed through the airport; however, it was planned to increase annual passenger capacity to 12.5m. over a 25-year period. Oman's second international airport, at Salalah, was completed in 1978; in 2007 337,452 passengers passed through the airport. Both Seeb and Salalah were effectively privatized in October 2001. Responsibility for the management and refurbishment of the airports passed to Oman Airports Management Company (OAMC), 75% of which was owned by foreign investors and 25% by the Omani Government; however, following the failure of the Government successfully to agree financial terms for the privatization and ongoing development of the airports with OAMC, the 25-year contract was cancelled in October 2004 and Seeb and Salalah airports were returned to state control. OAMC continues to manage and operate Oman's airports, but it is now a wholly government-owned entity. Plans for substantial development and expansion of both international airports to provide additional terminals and increase passenger handling capacity were announced as part of the Government's seventh Development Plan in 2006. There are also airports at Sur, Masirah, Khasab and Diba, with six further airports planned for Sohar, Duqm, Ras Al Hadd, Adam, Haima and Shaleem. Three new private airfields, owned and operated by Petroleum Development Oman, were opened in 2008 at Marmul, Qarn Alam and Fahud.

Directorate-General of Civil Aviation and Meteorology: POB 1, CPO Muscat International Airport, Muscat 111; tel. 24519356; fax 24519880; internet www.met.gov.om; Dir-Gen. Eng. AHMAD BIN SAID BIN SALIM AR-RAWAHY.

Oman Air SAOC: POB 58, Muscat International Airport 111; tel. 24531111; fax 24765121; e-mail wycallcenter@omanair.aero; internet www.omanair.aero/wy; f. 1993 as a subsidiary of Oman Aviation Services Co (f. 1981), whole corpn renamed Oman Air 2008; cap. RO 50m.; state-owned; air-charter, maintenance, handling and catering; operators of Oman's domestic and international commercial airline; carried over 1.5m. passengers in 2007; Chair. AHMAD BIN ABD AN-NABI MACKI (Minister of National Economy); CEO PETER HILL.

Oman Airports Management Co SOAC: POB 1707, Muscat 111; tel. 24518030; fax 24518088; e-mail oamcinfo@omanairports.com; f. 2002; operates Muscat International and Salalah airports; originally 75% owned by private investors; 100% owned by Oman Govt since 2004; Chair. Dr KHAMIS BIN MUBARAK BIN ISA AL-ALAWI (Minister of Transport and Communications); CEO GEORGE BELLEW.

OMAN

Tourism

Tourism, introduced in 1985, is strictly controlled. Oman's attractions, apart from the capital itself, include Nizwa, ancient capital of the interior, Dhofar and the forts of Nakhl, Rustaq and Al-Hazm. The country also possesses an attractive and clean environment, including around 1,700 km of sandy beaches. The tourism sector has been undergoing a period of intensive investment and development in recent years, overseen by the Oman Tourism Development Company (Omran). The emphasis has been on the development of extensive luxury resorts in areas of outstanding natural beauty. By mid-2008 there were some 9,000 hotel rooms, with plans for a further 9,000 by 2015. In 2006 there were 1,306,128 visitor arrivals in Oman, and tourism receipts totalled US $743m.

Directorate-General of Tourism: Madinat as-Sultan Qaboos, POB 200, Muscat 115; tel. 24588700; fax 24588880; e-mail info@omantourism.gov.om; internet www.omantourism.gov.om; Dir-Gen. MUHAMMAD ALI SAID.

Oman Tourism Development Co (Omran): POB 479, Muttrah 114; tel. 24773700; fax 24793929; e-mail enquiries@omran.om; internet www.omran.om; f. 2005; CEO WAEL BIN AHMAD AL-LAWATI.

PAKISTAN

Introductory Survey

Location, Climate, Language, Religion, Flag, Capital

The Islamic Republic of Pakistan lies in southern Asia, bordered by India to the east and by Afghanistan and Iran to the west. It has a short frontier with the People's Republic of China in the far north-east. The climate is dry and generally hot, with an annual average temperature of 27°C (80°F), except in the mountains, which have very cold winters. Temperatures in Karachi are generally between 13°C (55°F) and 34°C (93°F), with negligible rainfall. The principal languages are Punjabi (the language usually spoken in 44.2% of households in 1998), Pushto (Pashtu) (15.4%), Sindhi (14.1%) and Saraiki (10.5%). Urdu (7.6%) is the national language, and English is extensively used. The state religion is Islam, embracing about 97% of the population, the remainder being mainly Hindus or Christians. The national flag (proportions 2 by 3) has a vertical white stripe at the hoist, while the remainder is dark green, with a white crescent moon and a five-pointed star in the centre. The capital is Islamabad.

Recent History

Pakistan was created in August 1947 by the partition of the United Kingdom's former Indian Empire into the independent states of India and Pakistan, in response to demands by elements of the Muslim population in the subcontinent for the establishment of a specifically Islamic state. Pakistan originally comprised two distinct regions: East Pakistan and West Pakistan, separated by some 1,600 km (1,000 miles) of Indian territory, and united only by a common religion. Although the majority of the population lived in the smaller East Pakistan, political and military power was concentrated in the west, where the Muslim League was the dominant political movement. The leader of the Muslim League, Muhammad Ali Jinnah, popularly known as Quaid-i-Azam ('Great Leader'), became the first Governor-General of Pakistan but died in 1948. The country, formerly a dominion with the British monarch as Head of State, became a republic on 23 March 1956, when Pakistan's first Constitution was promulgated. At the same time Maj.-Gen. Iskander Mirza became Pakistan's first President.

Pakistan came under military rule in early October 1958, when President Mirza abrogated the Constitution, declared martial law, dismissed the national and provincial governments and dissolved all political parties. In late October, however, Gen. (later Field Marshal) Muhammad Ayub Khan, the Martial Law Administrator appointed by Mirza, removed Mirza from office and became President himself. Ayub Khan's autocratic but modernizing regime lasted until March 1969, when he was forced to resign following widespread unrest. Gen. Agha Muhammad Yahya Khan, the Commander-in-Chief of the Army, replaced him, and martial law was reimposed.

In December 1970 the country's first general election was held for a national assembly. Sheikh Mujibur Rahman's Awami League, which advocated autonomy for East Pakistan, won almost all the seats in the east (thus gaining an absolute majority in the National Assembly), while the Pakistan People's Party (PPP), led by Zulfikar Ali Bhutto, won a majority of seats in the west. Following the failure of negotiations to achieve a coalition government of the two parties, on 23 March 1971 East Pakistan declared its independence as the People's Republic of Bangladesh. Civil war immediately broke out, as Pakistani troops clashed with Bengali irregular forces. In December the Indian army intervened in the conflict to support the Bengalis, and the Pakistani army was forced to withdraw, thus permitting Bangladesh to establish firmly its independence. In the truncated Pakistan that remained in the west Yahya Khan resigned, military rule was ended, and Bhutto became the new President.

A new Constitution, which came into effect in August 1973, provided for a parliamentary system of government. Bhutto became executive Prime Minister, while Fazal Elahi Chaudry, hitherto Speaker of the National Assembly, became constitutional President. The PPP won an overwhelming majority of seats in elections to the National Assembly in March 1977. However, the opposition Pakistan National Alliance (PNA) accused the PPP of widespread electoral malpractice and launched a nation-wide campaign of civil disobedience. An estimated 1,000 people died in subsequent clashes between troops and demonstrators, and some 40,000 people were arrested. In July the armed forces intervened in the crisis: Bhutto was deposed in a bloodless military coup and a martial law regime was instituted, with Gen. Mohammad Zia ul-Haq, the Army Chief of Staff, as Chief Martial Law Administrator. President Chaudry remained in office as Head of State. Bhutto was subsequently charged with instigating the murder of a PPP dissident and a member of the dissident's family in 1974. He was sentenced to death in March 1978 and executed in April 1979.

In September 1978 President Chaudry resigned and Gen. Zia became President. General elections were postponed several times by the military administration, and in October 1979 Gen. Zia announced an indefinite postponement of the polls. Opposition to the military regime was severely suppressed, particularly after new martial law orders were adopted in May 1980. In March 1981 nine political parties formed an opposition alliance, the Movement for the Restoration of Democracy (MRD), which advocated an end to military rule and a return to a parliamentary system of government. Several opposition politicians were subsequently interned or placed under house arrest. In August 1983 the MRD, led by the PPP, launched a civil disobedience campaign to press for the restoration of parliamentary democracy on the basis of the 1973 Constitution. The campaign enjoyed considerable support in Sindh province, where anti-Government protests resulted in numerous deaths. However, there was limited popular support elsewhere in the country, and the campaign ended in December 1983. Many political leaders and activists, including Benazir Bhutto (daughter of the former President and herself a leading PPP activist), were subsequently imprisoned or went into exile.

Gen. Zia's regime zealously pursued a policy of 'Islamization' of the country's institutions, including the enforcement of Islamic penal codes, and the introduction of Islamic economic principles, such as interest-free banking. In December 1984 a referendum was held, which sought affirmation of the Islamization process and, indirectly, endorsement of a further five-year term for Gen. Zia. The referendum was boycotted by the MRD, but, according to official figures, 98% of those participating supported the proposal. However, there were widespread allegations of electoral malpractice.

In February 1985 a general election was held for a national assembly, followed shortly afterwards by elections to four provincial assemblies. The elections were held on a non-party basis, but widespread dissatisfaction with the regime was indicated by the defeat of several of Zia's cabinet ministers and close supporters. The largest two groupings in the new National Assembly were formed by a faction of the Pakistan Muslim League (PML, the successor to the Muslim League), known as the Pagara Group, and former members of the PPP. In late March Gen. Zia appointed Muhammad Khan Junejo, a member of the PML (Pagara Group), as Prime Minister, and an almost entirely civilian Cabinet was formed.

In October 1985 the National Assembly approved changes to the Constitution (the 'Eighth Amendment'), proposed by Gen. Zia, which introduced a powerful executive presidency and indemnified all actions of the military regime during the previous eight years. On 30 December Gen. Zia announced the repeal of martial law and the restoration of the Constitution (as amended in October). The military courts were dissolved, and military personnel were removed from civilian posts, with the exception of Gen. Zia, who remained as President and head of the armed forces. Junejo retained the post of Prime Minister in a new Cabinet. However, the MRD continued to demand the restoration of the unamended 1973 Constitution. In April 1986 its cause was strengthened by the return from exile of Benazir Bhutto, who travelled throughout the country holding political rallies which attracted thousands of supporters. She demanded the resignation of President Zia and the holding of a free general election, open to all political parties. In May Benazir Bhutto and her mother, Nusrat Bhutto, were elected as Co-Chairwomen of the PPP. In August the Government adopted a less tolerant approach towards the MRD by banning all rallies scheduled for

Independence Day and by detaining hundreds of opposition members, including Benazir Bhutto. The arrests provoked violent anti-Government demonstrations in a number of cities.

In late 1986 violent clashes occurred in Karachi, Quetta and Hyderabad as a result of disputes between rival ethnic groups (primarily between the Pathans, originally from the North-West Frontier Province—NWFP—and Afghanistan, and the Urdu-speaking Mohajirs, who migrated from India when the subcontinent was partitioned in 1947). The violence was most severe in Karachi, where some 170 people were killed in December. The rise of ethnic communalism in Pakistan was reflected in the results of local elections held throughout the country in November 1987. The party of the Mohajirs, the Mohajir Qaumi Movement (MQM), won the majority of seats in Karachi and was also successful in other urban areas of Sindh province. Nationwide the government-supported PML received the majority of votes, while the PPP won less than 20% of total seats.

In May 1988, in accordance with the authority vested in him through the Eighth Amendment, President Zia dismissed the Prime Minister and his Cabinet, and dissolved the National Assembly and the four provincial assemblies. Zia became head of an interim administration, which was to govern until a general election was held. In July Zia announced that the elections to the National Assembly and the provincial assemblies would be held in November. However, on 17 August 1988 President Zia was killed in an air crash in eastern Pakistan. Subsequent speculation that the cause of the crash was sabotage was not officially confirmed. The Chairman of the Senate, Ghulam Ishaq Khan, was appointed acting President, and an emergency National Council (composed of senior military officers, the four provincial governors and four federal ministers) was appointed to take charge of government.

Despite the imposition of a state of emergency after the death of Zia, the general election took place, as scheduled, in November 1988. In the elections to the National Assembly the PPP won 93 of the 207 directly elected seats, and was the only party to secure seats in each of Pakistan's four provinces. The Islamic Democratic Alliance (IDA), a grouping of nine Islamic and right-wing parties (including the PML), gained 54 seats, with the remaining seats going to independents and candidates representing seven smaller parties. However, the PPP did not achieve such a high level of support in the elections to the provincial assemblies, held three days later. The PPP was able to form coalition governments in Sindh and the NWFP, but the IDA took power in Punjab, the most populous province. At the federal level, a coalition Government was formed by the PPP and the MQM, which together had a working majority in the National Assembly (the MQM had 14 seats). Benazir Bhutto, the leader of the PPP, was appointed Prime Minister on 1 December, thus becoming the first female leader of a Muslim country. The state of emergency was repealed on the same day. A new Cabinet was formed, and later in December an electoral college (comprising the Senate, the National Assembly and the four provincial assemblies) elected Ghulam Ishaq Khan as President.

Benazir Bhutto's attempts, in early 1989, to repeal the Eighth Amendment to the Constitution, which severely constrained her powers as Prime Minister, were unsuccessful. Moreover, the fragile coalitions that the PPP had formed in the provincial assemblies soon came under pressure. In April the coalition Government formed by the PPP and the Awami National Party (ANP) in the NWFP collapsed. In May the coalition with the MQM in Sindh province also failed, following renewed ethnic conflict in the region. In the same month the opposition was strengthened by the formation of an informal parliamentary grouping, the Combined Opposition Party (COP), comprising the IDA, the ANP, Jamiat-e-Ulema-e-Islam (JUI) and the Pakistan Awami Ittehad. In October the Government suffered a serious reversal when the MQM withdrew its parliamentary support for the PPP and transferred it to the opposition, claiming that the PPP had failed to honour any of the promises made in the original co-operation agreement between the two parties. In November a parliamentary motion of no confidence, proposed by the COP against the Government, was narrowly defeated. In January 1990 the COP organized a campaign to undermine the Government, accusing it of corruption, political bribery and mismanagement. Rallies and demonstrations in Sindh province culminated in violence between supporters of the PPP and the MQM; in May about 100 people were killed during violent clashes between police and demonstrators in the region. Calm was temporarily restored by the deployment of army units.

By mid-1990 the initial popularity of the PPP Government appeared to have declined considerably: the maintenance of law and order had worsened; no significant new legislation had been introduced; the economic situation was deteriorating; and there were widespread allegations of corruption against high-ranking officials. On 6 August the President, in accordance with his constitutional powers, dissolved the National Assembly, dismissed the Prime Minister and her Cabinet and declared a state of emergency. He also announced that a general election would take place in late October. The President alleged that the ousted Government had violated the Constitution, accusing it of corruption, nepotism and incompetence. Ghulam Mustafa Jatoi, the leader of the COP in the National Assembly, was appointed acting Prime Minister in an interim Government. The four provincial assemblies were also dissolved, and 'caretaker' Chief Ministers appointed. Benazir Bhutto claimed that the dissolution of her administration was illegal and strongly denied the various charges made against her Government. At the end of August several of Benazir Bhutto's former ministers were arrested, and in the following month she herself was indicted on more than 10 charges of corruption and abuse of power. In early October Benazir Bhutto's husband, Asif Ali Zardari, was arrested on charges of extortion, kidnapping and financial irregularities (he was later acquitted on all counts).

At the general election, which took place, as scheduled, on 24 October 1990, the IDA doubled its representation in the National Assembly, leaving it only four seats short of an absolute majority, while the People's Democratic Alliance (PDA, an electoral alliance comprising the PPP and three smaller parties) suffered a heavy defeat. Support for the PPP also declined in the provincial elections, where it unexpectedly lost control of its traditional stronghold in Sindh and fared badly elsewhere. Regional and ethnic parties continued to expand their influence, notably the MQM in urban areas of Sindh, and the ANP in the NWFP. On 6 November Mohammad Nawaz Sharif, the leader of the IDA and the former Chief Minister of Punjab, was elected as the new Prime Minister. He officially ended the three-month-long state of emergency, and appointed a new Cabinet, which included several ministers who had served under President Zia. Nawaz Sharif promised that one of the Government's major priorities was to establish lasting peace in Sindh, where ethnic conflict and general lawlessness continued to prevail. However, it was alleged that the Government's subsequent campaign of suppression in the province, in response to numerous local murders and kidnappings, was aimed primarily at supporters of the PPP, hundreds of whom were arrested. In January 1991 the IDA won 19 of the 25 by-elections for seats in the National Assembly and the provincial assemblies, and in March won a decisive majority in elections to 42 seats in the Senate.

In May 1991 the National Assembly adopted legislation imposing the incorporation of *Shari'a*, the Islamic legal code, in Pakistan's legal system. The Assembly also adopted legislation providing for the Islamization of the educational, economic and judicial systems. Benazir Bhutto criticized the legislation as being extreme and fundamentalist, while the right-wing JUI claimed that the new law's provisions were not stringent enough.

The fundamentalist Jamaat-e-Islami Pakistan (JIP) left the IDA in May 1992, in protest at the Government's decision to support the new moderate *mujahidin* Government in Kabul, Afghanistan. The JIP accused the Government of abandoning the extremist Afghan guerrilla leader, Gulbuddin Hekmatyar, and also of failing to effect the full Islamization of Pakistan.

In response to continuing violence in Sindh, the Government launched 'Operation Clean-up' in May 1992, whereby the army was to apprehend criminals and terrorists, and seize unauthorized weapons. A violent clash between two factions of the MQM (the majority Altaf faction and the small breakaway Haqiqi faction) in Karachi in June provided the armed forces with the opportunity to suppress the extremist elements within the MQM. More than 500 people were arrested; caches of arms were located and seized; and 'torture cells', allegedly operated by the MQM, were discovered. The leader of the MQM (A), Altaf Hussain, accused the Government of attempting to crush the MQM through the military operation. In protest, 12 of the 15 MQM members in the National Assembly and 24 of the 27 members in the Sindh assembly resigned their seats. However, the Government repeatedly gave assurances that the operations were against criminals, and not specifically against the MQM.

In mid-November 1992 the PDA intensified its campaign of political agitation and was now supported by the majority of the components of the newly formed opposition National Democratic

Alliance (NDA), including the National People's Party (NPP—which had been expelled from the IDA in March). However, the large-scale demonstrations and marches organized by Benazir Bhutto were ruthlessly suppressed by the Government. By mid-December tensions between the Government and opposition had eased considerably, and in January 1993, in an apparently conciliatory move on the part of Nawaz Sharif's administration, Benazir Bhutto was elected Chairperson of the National Assembly's Standing Committee on Foreign Affairs. Shortly after Benazir Bhutto had accepted the nomination, her husband was released on bail.

In March 1993 a growing rift between the Prime Minister and the President became evident when the Government initiated discussions regarding proposed modifications to the provisions of the Eighth Constitutional Amendment, which afforded the President the power to dismiss the Government and dissolve assemblies, and to appoint judicial and military chiefs. In late March three cabinet ministers resigned in protest at Nawaz Sharif's nomination as President of the PML (Junejo Group), to succeed Muhammad Khan Junejo (who had died earlier that month), and voiced their support for Ghulam Ishaq Khan in his political struggle with the Prime Minister. In a seemingly final attempt at reconciliation, the Cabinet unanimously decided, in early April, to nominate Ghulam Ishaq Khan as the PML's candidate for the forthcoming presidential election. By mid-April, however, a total of eight ministers had resigned from the Cabinet in protest at Nawaz Sharif's continued tenure of the premiership. On 18 April the President dissolved the National Assembly and dismissed the Prime Minister and his Cabinet, accusing Nawaz Sharif of 'maladministration, nepotism and corruption'. However, the provincial assemblies and governments remained in power, despite demands by the PDA and the NDA for their dissolution. A member of the dissolved National Assembly, Mir Balakh Sher Mazari, was sworn in as acting Prime Minister. It was announced that elections to the National Assembly would be held on 14 July. In late April a broadly-based interim Cabinet, including Benazir Bhutto's husband, was sworn in. In early May the PML (Junejo Group) split into two factions: one led by Nawaz Sharif, the other by Hamid Nasir Chattha (with the support of the President).

On 26 May 1993, in an historic and unexpected judgment, the Supreme Court ordered that the National Assembly, the Prime Minister and the Cabinet (dismissed in April) should be restored to power immediately, stating that President Khan's order had been unconstitutional. The President agreed to honour the Court's ruling, and the National Assembly and Nawaz Sharif's Government were reinstated with immediate effect. On the following day Nawaz Sharif's return to power was consolidated when he won a vote of confidence in the National Assembly. A few days later, however, there was renewed political turmoil following the dissolution, through the machinations of supporters of the President, of the provincial assemblies in Punjab and the NWFP. Lacking effective authority in each of the four provinces, Nawaz Sharif resorted to the imposition of federal government's rule on Punjab through a resolution passed by the National Assembly in late June. However, the Punjab provincial government refused to obey the federal Government's orders, claiming that they subverted provincial autonomy, prompting the Government to threaten the imposition of a military administration. Meanwhile, an All Parties Conference (APC), including, among others, Benazir Bhutto and the Chief Ministers of Punjab and the NWFP, convened in Lahore to pass a resolution, urging the President to dissolve the legislature, dismiss Nawaz Sharif's Government and hold fresh elections. In early July the Chief of Army Staff, following an emergency meeting of senior army officers, acted as an intermediary in talks between the President and Prime Minister in an attempt to resolve the political crisis. Benazir Bhutto, supported by her APC collaborators, announced a 'long march' on 16 July, with the intention of laying siege to the federal capital and forcing Nawaz Sharif to resign. Fearing the outbreak of serious violence, the army persuaded Benazir Bhutto to postpone the march, reportedly assuring her that both the President and the Prime Minister would resign and that a general election would be held under a neutral administration. On 18 July, in accordance with an agreement reached under the auspices of the army, both Khan and Nawaz Sharif resigned from their posts, the federal legislature and the provincial assemblies were dissolved, the holding of a general election in October was announced, and neutral administrations were established at both federal and provincial level. As specified in the Constitution, Khan was succeeded by the Chairman of the Senate, Wasim Sajjad Jan, who was to hold the presidency for the remaining tenure of the deposed President. A small, apolitical Cabinet was sworn in, headed by Moeenuddin Ahmad Qureshi, a former Executive Vice-President of the World Bank, as interim Prime Minister.

The general election, held in early October 1993 under military supervision, was widely considered to have been fair, although the turn-out, which some officials estimated to be less than 50%, was disappointing. The polling was closely contested between the PML faction led by Nawaz Sharif—PML (Nawaz—N)—and the PPP (the MQM boycotted the elections to the National Assembly, claiming systematic intimidation by the army, but took part in the provincial assembly elections a few days later). However, neither of the two leading parties won an outright majority in the federal elections, and in the provincial elections an outright majority was only achieved by the PPP in Sindh. Following intensive negotiations with smaller parties and independents in the National Assembly, on 19 October Benazir Bhutto was elected to head a coalition Government. On the following day a PPP-led coalition assumed control of the provincial administration in Punjab (traditionally a PML stronghold). However, the provincial governments in the NWFP and in Balochistan were headed by alliances led by the PML (N).

In November 1993 the PPP's candidate, the newly appointed Minister of Foreign Affairs, Sardar Farooq Ahmad Khan Leghari, was elected President, having secured 274 votes (62% of the total) in the electoral college. The incumbent acting President, Wasim Sajjad Jan, who stood as the candidate of the PML (N), obtained 168 votes (38%). On assuming office, Leghari stated that he intended to end his political ties with the PPP and that he hoped for the early repeal or modification of the controversial Eighth Constitutional Amendment.

In February 1994 the President dismissed the Chief Minister and government of the NWFP, suspended the provincial legislature and imposed governor's rule, following the thwarted introduction of a vote of no confidence against the PML (N)-led coalition by the PPP. The PPP consolidated its hold on federal power in March by winning the majority of the contested seats in elections to the Senate. In April a PPP member was elected as Chief Minister of the newly revived provincial government in the NWFP; the opposition alliance boycotted the proceedings.

September 1994 witnessed an upsurge in political unrest when Nawaz Sharif organized a nation-wide general strike; in response, the Government arrested hundreds of PML supporters. In November the Government was confronted with a series of uprisings staged by heavily-armed tribesmen in the mountainous regions of Malakand and Swat demanding the enforcement of *Shari'a*. The fundamentalist revolt was suppressed by paramilitary forces (but only after the deaths of several hundred people), and the *Shari'a* measures were implemented in the tribal areas. By the end of the year, however, the police and paramilitary forces appeared to be losing control of Karachi, which was riven by rapidly escalating ethnic and criminal violence; nearly 170 people were killed in the city in December alone, following the lengthy 'Operation Clean-up' and the withdrawal of the army in the previous month. Much of the violence stemmed from the bloody rivalry between the opposing factions of the MQM, while other killings were linked to drugs mafias and to sectarian disputes between Sunni and Shi'a Muslims.

In early 1995, despite the arrest of large numbers of suspected Islamist militants, there was an upsurge in religious violence between Sunni and Shi'a Muslims in Karachi. In March the murder of two US consular officials by unidentified gunmen in the troubled Sindh capital provoked international condemnation. There was no respite from the violence in the following months, and by June the security forces had lost control of large areas of Karachi to MQM activists. Negotiations between representatives of the MQM (A) and government officials in mid-1995 proved fruitless and it was estimated that during 1995 almost 2,000 people (including about 250 members of the security forces) were killed as a result of the political and ethnic violence in Karachi. In September of that year the growing political instability in Pakistan was underlined by the arrest of nearly 40 army officers on suspicion of plotting to overthrow the Government and to establish an Islamist fundamentalist state. In November 18 people were killed when a car bomb exploded at the Egyptian embassy in Islamabad; within hours of the attack three militant Islamist groups in Egypt had claimed responsibility for the bombing. During the previous year the Pakistani Government had been co-operating with Egypt in attempts to apprehend and extradite members of illegal Islamist militant organizations operating in the NWFP or across the border in Afghanistan. (In 1993–95 the Pakistan authorities, concerned at the country's growing reputation as a refuge for Islamist extremists, expelled more than 2,000 Arabs, the majority of whom were reported to have been involved in the civil war in Afghanistan.) Acts of violence and terrorism in Pakistan continued throughout late 1995 and early 1996.

A new political force emerged in Pakistan in early 1996 when the popular former international cricketer Imran Khan (of late a prominent benefactor of charitable causes) established a political reform movement, known as the Tehrik-e-Insaf (Movement for Justice), to oppose Benazir Bhutto's administration.

In March 1996 the Supreme Court in Karachi ruled that the Government no longer had the exclusive mandate to appoint judges to the higher courts; these appointments would, in future, be required to have the consent of the Chief Justices of the High Courts and the Chief Justice of Pakistan. This ruling aroused considerable controversy since it deprived the executive of substantial authority within the national judicial system.

The Government's popularity was undermined by the necessary introduction of an austere budget, including the introduction of new taxes, in mid-June 1996, in an attempt to reduce the budget deficit. The volatile political situation was intensified by a bomb explosion at Lahore airport in late July, a series of debilitating public-sector strikes and by a resurgence of violence in Karachi. In addition, the appointment of the Prime Minister's unpopular husband, Asif Ali Zardari, as Minister of Investment, as part of a cabinet expansion in July, aroused much controversy and criticism. At the end of that month the Government's position appeared even less secure when about 16 opposition parties, including the PML (N), the MQM and the JIP, established an informal alliance with a one-point agenda: to oust Prime Minister Bhutto and her Government. Pakistan was thrown into further political turmoil in mid-September following the fatal shooting of Benazir Bhutto's estranged brother, Mir Murtaza Bhutto, in a gun battle with police in Karachi. A number of opposition politicians accused the Prime Minister and her husband of complicity in the killing, while Benazir Bhutto implied in a number of public statements that she believed that the President and the army were to blame. In 1995 Mir Murtaza Bhutto had established a rival faction of the PPP, known as the PPP (Shaheed Bhutto Group), charging his sister's Government with corruption and misrule; however, the breakaway faction attracted no substantial support and posed little threat to the Prime Minister. Meanwhile, growing discord between Benazir Bhutto and President Leghari was becoming more apparent.

Amid mounting public discontent, President Leghari dismissed Prime Minister Benazir Bhutto and her Government and dissolved the National Assembly on 5 November 1996 (the state assemblies were dissolved over the following week), citing as justification the deteriorating law and order situation, severe economic problems, widespread corruption, disregard for judicial authority and the violation of various constitutional provisions. A former Speaker of the National Assembly, Malik Meraj Khaled, who claimed no affiliation to any political party, was named as acting Prime Minister and an interim Cabinet was appointed. Following the dismissal of her Government, it was reported that several leading members of Benazir Bhutto's PPP, including her husband, had been arrested. In mid-November the President promulgated a decree providing for a five-year disqualification from public office of politicians (with the exception of the President and members of the judiciary and armed forces) involved in corruption and abuses of power. At the end of December the JIP announced its intention to boycott the forthcoming general election, accusing the 'caretaker' Government of failing in its much-vaunted anti-corruption drive. Sectarian violence between Sunni and Shi'a Muslims escalated in January 1997, culminating in a bomb blast outside a district court in Lahore, which killed 25 people, including the leader of the Sunni extremist group Sipah-e-Sahaba Pakistan. Meanwhile, in early January the President instituted an official advisory role for the military, with the formation of a 10-member Council of Defence and National Security (CDNS), which was to advise the Government on a broad range of issues from national security to the economy. The President chaired the new body, which comprised the Prime Minister, four senior cabinet ministers, the Chairman of the Joint Chiefs of Staff and the three armed services chiefs, and could refer any matter to it without previously consulting the Prime Minister. In response to this unexpected development, many political parties, including the PPP, but with the notable exception of the PML (N), accused the President of an unconstitutional usurpation of authority. However, the Government insisted that the role of the CDNS would be purely advisory.

The general election, which was held on 3 February 1997, was marred by an extremely low turn-out (an estimated 30%–40%). The PML (N) won a decisive victory, obtaining 134 of the 204 directly elective seats in the National Assembly (voting in three seats was deferred until a later date), while the PPP was routed, both at federal and state level, winning only 18 seats. The MQM emerged as the country's third political force (obtaining 12 seats), while Imran Khan's Tehrik-e-Insaf failed to win a single seat. Nawaz Sharif was sworn in as Prime Minister on 17 February and a small Cabinet was appointed the following week. In March the PML (N) and its allies secured a two-thirds' majority in the 87-seat Senate following elections for about one-half of the seats.

Nawaz Sharif's political authority was strengthened considerably in April 1997, when both the National Assembly and the Senate voted unanimously to repeal the major components of the 1985 Eighth Constitutional Amendment, thereby divesting the President of the power to appoint and dismiss the Prime Minister and Cabinet, to dissolve the legislature, to order a national referendum on any national issue, and to appoint provincial Governors, the Chairman of the Joint Chiefs of Staff and the three armed forces chiefs (these functions and appointments were, in future, to be carried out subject to mandatory advice from the Prime Minister). The President thus became a largely ceremonial figure whose main executive role was the appointment of judges. President Leghari was reported to have 'willingly agreed' to the constitutional changes.

In July 1997 Asif Ali Zardari was formally charged with ordering the killing of Mir Murtaza Bhutto; 21 other former officials were simultaneously charged with murder and conspiracy in the death. In September the Swiss police ordered four banks in Geneva to 'freeze' the accounts of Benazir Bhutto and her family after Pakistan's Accountability Commission alleged that up to US $80m. had been illegally transferred to them. In January 1998 the British authorities, at the request of the Pakistani Government, ordered the seizure of documents relating to assets and bank accounts of Benazir Bhutto in the United Kingdom. In March the Sindh High Court issued an arrest warrant for the leader of the PPP on a charge of misuse of power during her final term in office as Prime Minister. In April the High Court in Lahore ordered that all assets belonging to Benazir Bhutto, her husband and her mother be 'frozen' as the government investigation into allegations of corruption continued.

Meanwhile, in the latter half of 1997 a serious rift developed between Nawaz Sharif and the Chief Justice of the Supreme Court, Sajjad Ali Shah, over the appointment of new judges to the Court. In early November, however, a compromise was reached between the Supreme Court and the Government, allowing the former to appoint five new judges while confirming the right of the legislature to determine the total number of judges. Yet, despite this outcome, the crisis was not over, and later that month the Supreme Court charged Nawaz Sharif and five other officials with contempt for slandering the Court and defying its orders in the previous month. The Prime Minister, who, if found guilty, was liable to be disqualified from office, denied the charges. However, the Chief Justice was forced to adjourn Nawaz Sharif's trial in late November, when thousands of the Prime Minister's supporters stormed the Supreme Court in Islamabad. The constitutional crisis came to a dramatic end on 2 December when the Chief Justice was suspended from office by rebel members of the Supreme Court; on the same day President Leghari also stood down from office. The Chairman of the Senate, Wasim Sajjad Jan, assumed the position of acting President. It was widely speculated that the army, in tacitly supporting the Prime Minister, had exerted considerable influence in resolving the constitutional impasse. Nawaz Sharif strengthened his hold on power on 31 December when his nominee and fellow Punjabi, Mohammad Rafiq Tarar (a personal acquaintance of the Prime Minister and a former Supreme Court judge), won the presidential election by a record margin (winning more than 80% of the total votes cast by the electoral college).

In January 1998 sectarian violence erupted again in Lahore when at least 24 Shi'a Muslims were massacred by a clandestine Sunni group. In response, the Government approved measures to control illicit weapons in an attempt to curb terrorism. (A controversial anti-terrorist law had been passed in August 1997, giving the security forces extensive powers of arrest and enabling the Government to ban any group or association without parliamentary approval.) However, in late February 1998 two Iranian engineers were murdered by unidentified terrorists in Karachi, and in the following month more than 20 people were killed in two bomb explosions on passenger trains in Lahore.

Despite the temporary public euphoria and heightened popularity of the Prime Minister arising from the conduct of the controversial nuclear tests in May 1998 (see below), the repercussions (particularly the international sanctions) left Pakistan in dire financial straits. In late August the Prime Minister introduced the Fifteenth Constitutional Amendment Bill to the National Assembly, seeking to replace Pakistan's legal code with *Shari'a*. Nawaz Sharif attempted to allay fears of a move towards Islamist extremism by promising to uphold women's rights and to safeguard minorities. The Bill was passed in the National Assembly in October; it was denounced by human rights activists as 'regressive'.

The Government suffered a severe reverse in late October 1998 when the Muttahida Qaumi Movement—MQM (A)—(formerly known as the Mohajir Qaumi Movement) withdrew its support for the PML (N)-led provincial administration in Sindh. On 30 October the provincial legislature was suspended and the troubled province was placed under governor's rule in an effort to curb the violence. In November the Prime Minister announced the establishment of anti-terrorist military courts in Karachi (which were designed to dispense rapid and punitive justice), and the suspension of civil rights in Sindh.

In April 1999 the Lahore High Court found Benazir Bhutto (now in self-imposed exile abroad) and her husband guilty of corruption; they were each sentenced to five years' imprisonment, their property was confiscated and they were jointly fined US \$8.6m. The verdict automatically removed the former Prime Minister and Asif Ali Zardari (who was already in prison serving a separate sentence) from their seats in the National Assembly and Senate, respectively.

Meanwhile, in early January 1999 the Prime Minister escaped an apparent assassination attempt when a bomb exploded near his country residence in Punjab, killing four people. The following day there was an upsurge in sectarian violence in the province when unidentified gunmen murdered 17 worshippers in a Shi'a mosque near Multan. Sindh became the focus of political attention later in the month when the Supreme Court declared unlawful the central Government's decision (made in November 1998) to remove the powers of the Speaker and Deputy Speaker of the suspended Sindh assembly. In mid-February 1999 the Supreme Court ruled that military trials could not be used for cases against civilians, thus sparing 14 people from death sentences imposed in the military tribunals in Sindh and effectively barring the establishment of military courts throughout the country (as the Government had proposed). The Supreme Court ordered the transfer of the cases to civilian anti-terrorist courts.

A dangerous escalation in the Kashmir crisis between Pakistan and India in mid-1999 (see below) and the former's effective defeat in the face of almost universal condemnation and diplomatic isolation appeared to represent a major turning point in the fortunes of the PML Government. Although Nawaz Sharif attempted to ensure that any blame attached to the episode would be diverted to the army, many of his opponents in Pakistan declared that his seeming haste to concede defeat and to agree to a Pakistani withdrawal in the face of US pressure constituted a national 'betrayal'. In mid-September Nawaz Sharif's position looked increasingly precarious following the formation of a Grand Democratic Alliance by 19 conservative and centrist opposition parties, including the PPP, the MQM (A) and the ANP, which demanded the Prime Minister's immediate resignation. The various Islamist parties, including the JIP, also stepped up their anti-Government protests and rallies throughout the country. However, the opposition was weakened to some extent by the fact that Benazir Bhutto was unwilling to return to Pakistan for fear of being arrested.

Events took a dramatic turn on 12 October 1999, when, shortly after Nawaz Sharif's announcement of a decision to dismiss the Chief of Army Staff and Chairman of the Joint Chiefs of Staff Committee, Gen. Pervez Musharraf, the army chief flew back from an official tour in Sri Lanka and promptly organized a bloodless military coup in Islamabad. Nawaz Sharif and his Government were overthrown, and the deposed Prime Minister was placed under house arrest. On 15 October Gen. Musharraf assumed the position of Chief Executive, declared a nation-wide state of emergency and suspended the Constitution, the National Assembly, the Senate, the four provincial legislatures and all political officials, with the exception of the President and judiciary. He also ensured, by means of a Provisional Constitution Order, that his actions could not be challenged by any court of law, thus imposing virtual martial law. On 18 October the Commonwealth Ministerial Action Group (CMAG) condemned the coup and demanded a time-frame for the restoration of democracy; Pakistan was suspended from participation in meetings of the Commonwealth with immediate effect (it was not readmitted to full membership until May 2004). Meanwhile, on 22 October 1999 Gen. Musharraf appointed four new provincial governors, and on 26 October he installed a three-member Cabinet (which was later expanded) and named the members of a National Security Council (NSC), which was expected to be the supreme executive body of the country.

Following his seizure of power, Gen. Musharraf attempted to win over international opinion by portraying himself as a moderate, liberal leader. He was aided in this respect by the fact that the majority of the Pakistani people appeared to support the army's coup (it was a widely-held opinion that the military had no provincial bias and represented all levels of society—rather than purely the landed élite). Although expressing regret at Pakistan's effective suspension from the Commonwealth, the military regime was more concerned with the reaction of the USA and international financial organizations to the coup. The US Government's initial relations with the new administration in Pakistan appeared cautious but conciliatory. Gen. Musharraf promised an eventual return to civilian rule and announced wide-ranging measures to tackle corruption, loan defaulters, tax evasion, regional instability and religious extremism. The new regime's stated major priority was the revival of the almost bankrupt economy.

In November 1999 Nawaz Sharif and six other senior officials (including Mohammad Shahbaz Sharif, the brother of the ousted Prime Minister and the former Chief Minister of Punjab) were arrested on charges of criminal conspiracy, hijacking (a charge that carried the maximum penalty of the death sentence), kidnapping and attempted murder in relation to the alleged refusal of landing rights to the commercial aircraft carrying Gen. Musharraf from Sri Lanka to Karachi on 12 October; the aircraft ran precariously low on fuel before troops loyal to the army chief seized control of the airport and permission to land was finally granted (although the aircraft was rerouted to Nawabshah). The military authorities also charged Nawaz Sharif and his brother in November with corruption and non-repayment of bank loans. Later that month a new law was enacted barring politicians from holding public office for 21 years if found guilty of corruption or of defaulting on loans. The bill also allowed for the establishment of special courts to conduct trials within 30 days and gave the newly formed National Accountability Bureau far-reaching powers of investigation.

In early April 2000 Nawaz Sharif was sentenced to life imprisonment on charges of terrorism and hijacking, despite the prosecution having demanded the maximum penalty of the death sentence; in addition to the life sentence, all of the former Prime Minister's property in Pakistan was to be confiscated by the State. The six other defendants were acquitted. In May Nawaz Sharif's trial on charges of corruption opened; two months later the deposed Prime Minister was convicted and sentenced to 14 years' imprisonment, and barred from holding public office for 21 years. In August the Chief Executive issued a decree disqualifying those convicted of criminal offences and of terrorist acts from holding public office. The decision was viewed by many as a ban on convicted political leaders, notably former Prime Ministers Benazir Bhutto and Nawaz Sharif. In October the Karachi High Court upheld Nawaz Sharif's conviction and sentence for hijacking, but sustained the deposed Prime Minister's appeal against a conviction for terrorism.

Meanwhile, in late January 2000 Gen. Musharraf was accused of undemocratic conduct and of attempting to erode the independence of the judiciary when he dismissed the country's Chief Justice, Saiduzzaman Siddiqui, together with five other judges of the Supreme Court, following their refusal to swear allegiance to the military regime under a new oath. In May Gen. Musharraf's regime was strengthened by a unanimous decision by the pro-military Supreme Court to validate the October 1999 coup as having been necessary to spare the country from chaos and bankruptcy. At the same time, the Court announced that the Chief Executive should name a date not later than 90 days before the expiry of the three-year period from 12 October 1999 for the holding of elections to the National Assembly, the provincial assemblies and the Senate. Gen. Musharraf stated that he would comply with the Supreme Court ruling regarding the restoration of democracy.

In July 2000 Gen. Musharraf issued a decree to revive the Islamic provisions of the suspended Constitution and to incorporate them in the Provisional Constitution Order, thereby supporting a ban on the passing of any law that conflicted with Islamic principles. In mid-August the NSC was reconstituted and redefined as the supreme executive body, comprising the three chiefs of staff and the Ministers of Foreign Affairs, of Interior, of Finance and of Commerce.

In late 2000 former leaders Nawaz Sharif and Benazir Bhutto, together with the heads of 16 other smaller political parties, agreed to form the Alliance for the Restoration of Democracy (ARD), with the aim of ending military rule and accelerating a return to democracy. The new alliance superseded the PPP-led Grand Democratic Alliance. On 10 December Nawaz Sharif was unexpectedly released from prison and sent into exile in Saudi Arabia, with his wife and 17 other members of his family. The Government announced that the deposed Prime Minister had been granted a 'presidential pardon' and had been permitted to leave the country to seek medical treatment. In return, Nawaz Sharif relinquished his personal and business assets worth approximately Rs 500m., promised not to return to Pakistan for 10 years, and agreed not to take part in Pakistani politics for 21 years. The deal, reportedly negotiated by a member of the Saudi Arabian royal family, weakened Nawaz Sharif's prospects as a serious opponent to the Chief Executive, and adversely affected the credibility of Gen. Musharraf's campaign against political corruption.

In early April 2001 the Supreme Court ordered that Benazir Bhutto's conviction for corruption be set aside and a retrial held. Later that month the Court concluded that the verdict had been politically motivated. Meanwhile, Bhutto and her husband faced further charges of corruption. In May a warrant was issued for Bhutto's arrest on her return to Pakistan. However, owing to her continued exile in Dubai (United Arab Emirates), in June she was sentenced, *in absentia*, to three years' imprisonment for failing to appear in court to answer these latest corruption allegations; this criminal conviction effectively disqualified Bhutto from holding further public office in Pakistan.

In late December 2000 the first phase of local elections was held. According to the Government, the turn-out reached 43.5%. However, the opposition PPP claimed that less than 20% of the electorate had participated, attributing the low turn-out to the ban on political parties. Of a total of 20,076 seats, 33% were reserved for female candidates, but few women were able or willing to participate. The next three phases of local elections took place in March, May and July 2001. Although the elections were conducted on a non-party basis, it was believed that the majority of candidates were sponsored by either the PML (N) or the PPP. Elections to the 40-member legislative assembly for Azad Kashmir also took place in early July. Meanwhile, Musharraf insisted that a ban on party political activity in public would be maintained until after the forthcoming parliamentary elections, and opposition attempts at organizing pro-democracy rallies in March and May were suppressed by the authorities, who detained thousands of ARD supporters prior to the planned demonstrations.

On 20 June 2001 Gen. Musharraf unexpectedly assumed the presidency, having dismissed Mohammad Rafiq Tarar (who had reportedly refused to resign from the post). Musharraf immediately issued a formal dissolution of both houses of the federal legislature (which had been suspended since October 1999) in preparation for the elections. In August Musharraf confirmed that elections to the four provincial legislatures and to the bicameral federal parliament would be conducted between 1 and 11 October 2002, thereby providing for the full restoration of democratic institutions by 12 October (the deadline established by the Supreme Court). Musharraf also announced that certain 'checks and balances' would be contained in constitutional amendments to be promulgated before June 2002; these were expected to include enhanced presidential powers and an advisory executive role for the military.

In response to a continuing escalation in sectarian and ethnically motivated violence, in June 2001 the Government approved new legislation to tackle terrorist activity. Earlier in the month Musharraf had complained that Pakistan's growing reputation as a centre for militant religious intolerance and fundamentalism was having a detrimental effect on the country's international standing and on its economic prospects. In August Musharraf appealed for greater tolerance and understanding and announced an immediate ban on the activities of two militant Islamist groups: the Sunni Lashkar-e-Jhangvi and the Shi'a Sipah-e-Mohammad.

As one of only three states to have recognized the legitimacy of the Taliban administration in Afghanistan, and as the most significant trading partner and political associate of the regime, Pakistan's support was crucial to the efforts of the US-led anti-terrorism coalition in the aftermath of the 11 September 2001 terrorist attacks on the US mainland, and Musharraf was left in little doubt that his refusal to co-operate with the campaign to apprehend those members of the al-Qa'ida (Base) organization held responsible for the attacks would result in Pakistan's increased economic and political isolation. Therefore, Musharraf's political opponents in the PML and PPP appeared to accept his declaration of co-operation with US requests for shared intelligence and use of air space with resignation. However, large-scale popular opposition to the President's decision was inevitable, particularly in the NWFP bordering Afghanistan, which was home to large numbers of Pakhtoon (Pashtun) Pakistanis who were fiercely opposed to any assault on the Pashtun-dominated Taliban. Despite Musharraf's insistence that the US-led activities in the region did not represent an attack on Islam, protests against the action spread throughout the country, and on 21 September a grouping of more than 30 Pakistani militant Islamist organizations, known as the Afghan Defence Council (ADC), organized an opposition campaign of demonstrations and nation-wide industrial action. There was further opposition to Pakistan's support for the intervention in Afghanistan from within the armed forces and the Inter-Services Intelligence (ISI) agency, both having enjoyed particularly close links with the Taliban. In early October, having extended indefinitely his term of office as Chief of Army Staff, Musharraf implemented a radical reorganization of the military high command and the intelligence service, replacing a number of senior personnel with known sympathies for the country's militant Islamist cause, including Lt-Gen. Mahmood Ahmed, head of the ISI. However, popular protests against co-operation with the US-led coalition continued. None the less, Musharraf's resolve remained firm (strengthened, in part, by the promise of financial recognition of his political support from the USA and the European Union—EU), and despite the uncompromising response of the security forces to sporadic rioting, an attempt to capture the Jacobabad airbase in Sindh province (which was providing logistical support to US forces) by some 5,000 demonstrators, and an opposition rally attended by around 20,000 protesters in Karachi, there were surprisingly few casualties. In early November the leaders of the JUI and the JIP were detained following allegations that they were continuing to promote anti-Government activities and demonstrations. Earlier in the month a Qatar-based Arab satellite television channel, Al-Jazeera, had broadcast details of a new communication from Osama bin Laden, the Saudi-born leader of the al-Qa'ida organization, in which he issued a renewed call to *jihad* against non-Muslims and urged Pakistanis to rise up and overthrow Musharraf's administration for its part in the US-led campaign. Bin Laden's exhortations were particularly resonant in the border regions of the NWFP and Balochistan, where reports were emerging of large numbers of armed local tribesmen crossing the border as willing recruits for the Taliban. By mid-November there were believed to be significant numbers of Pakistanis fighting in Afghanistan (and reports that supply lines were being maintained into north-western Pakistan), rekindling long-standing animosity with the anti-Taliban forces of the United National Islamic Front for the Salvation of Afghanistan (commonly known as the United Front or Northern Alliance), which—much to the alarm of Musharraf—made impressive territorial gains in Afghanistan (with the support of the US-led coalition) in early November. By mid-November the United Front had taken Kabul (the Afghan capital), leaving Musharraf to concentrate his efforts in attempting to convince the international community of the need for plural (including Pashtun, perhaps even moderate Taliban) representation in any interim administration in Afghanistan. As the rout of Taliban forces in Afghanistan continued in December and the USA intensified its bombardment of suspected al-Qa'ida positions in the Tora Bora region of southern Afghanistan, Pakistan reinforced security personnel along its north-western border (believed to number some 125,000 by the end of 2001) in order to intercept fleeing combatants. Many ethnic Pashtuns (both Pakistani and Afghan) were believed to have evaded capture on the border and escaped into north-western

Pakistan. Violent exchanges between Pakistani security forces and intercepted (mostly Arab) al-Qa'ida fighters in the border regions resulted in a number of casualties on both sides.

Meanwhile, relations with India had become openly hostile as a result of the deteriorating security situation in Kashmir and the increasingly violent activities of Pakistan's militant Islamist groups in India (see below). Following intense international pressure (particularly from the USA) to address the continuing security risk presented by these groups, in December 2001 the security forces began to detain some of their most prominent members, financial assets were 'frozen' and offices closed down. Moreover, in January 2002 Musharraf announced an indefinite ban on the activities of five predominantly separatist groups (Tehrik-e-Nifaz-e-Shariat-e-Mohammadi, Sipah-e-Sahaba Pakistan, Jaish-e-Mohammed, Tehrik-e-Jafria and Lashkar-e-Taiba) and plans to reform the country's system of *madrassa* religious schools, many of which were accused of promoting extremism and theocracy. Musharraf's counter-terrorism initiative and new moderate vision drew plaudits from the international community, but the murder of US journalist Daniel Pearl (see below) and several subsequent sectarian attacks, mainly on Shi'a Muslims, appeared to undermine the success of Musharraf's rhetoric. Nevertheless, in mid-June it was announced that the Government had approved an ordinance for the registration of *madrassas*, according to which only *madrassas* that were registered by the Madrassa Education Board within the next six months would be allowed to operate.

During early 2002 Musharraf reiterated his commitment to returning the country to democracy, beginning with the parliamentary elections scheduled for October. In early April the Government approved a plan to hold a national referendum seeking endorsement for Musharraf's term of office as President to be extended by five years and approval of the Government's political and economic programme. Opposition parties and the independent Human Rights Commission of Pakistan condemned the decision as unconstitutional and illegal and resolved to boycott the vote; however, on 27 April the Supreme Court ruled that the referendum was legitimate, allowing the poll to take place three days later. According to official figures, 98% of those participating supported the proposal. However, there were widespread allegations of gross irregularities and fraud. The Government claimed that the turn-out was 70%, but opposition parties and independent monitors estimated that it was only about 5%. In late June Musharraf dismissed the head of the political wing of the ISI and chief organizer of the presidential referendum, Maj.-Gen. Ehtesam Zamir, after being forced to admit that his referendum victory had been fraudulent. In an attempt to reduce the political influence wielded by feudal landowning families, on 24 June the President issued a Chief Executive's Order stipulating that all candidates for future elections to federal and provincial legislatures should hold a university degree. Several days later Musharraf announced a set of radical proposals for constitutional reform. The suggested reforms were strongly criticized by political parties, constitutional experts and human rights groups for attempting to remodel Pakistan's prime ministerial system into a presidential one and to undermine the authority of any elected government. Among the changes put forward by Musharraf were proposals to reduce the parliamentary term from five years to four, to lower the voting age from 21 years to 18 years, to restrict the number of terms premiers or provincial chief ministers could hold in office to two, and to disqualify those members of the legislature who had criminal convictions, had defaulted on loans or had absconded. The last two amendments were widely considered to be aimed at preventing former Prime Ministers Benazir Bhutto and Nawaz Sharif from returning to office. Furthermore, in early July Musharraf issued a decree barring former premiers and chief ministers from seeking a third term in office. Several days later Musharraf announced that elections to the federal and provincial legislatures would be held on 10 October.

Instead of presenting the proposed constitutional amendments before the next legislature, on 21 August 2002 President Musharraf unilaterally enacted the Legal Framework Order (LFO), which introduced 29 amendments to the Constitution (including those listed above) and validated all the military decrees approved since the coup in 1999. The amendments were to take effect from 12 October 2002. As a result, the President's powers were enlarged and the military was ensured influence in decision-making beyond the parliamentary elections in October. One of the most significant amendments, the permanent establishment of an NSC, which would include Musharraf in his capacity as President and Chief of Army Staff, as well as the three other armed forces chiefs, the Prime Minister, the provincial chief ministers, the leader of the parliamentary opposition and Speakers of both houses of the federal legislature, was also authorized. The NSC would provide consultation to the elected government on strategic issues. The President was also restored the right to dissolve the National Assembly, and to dismiss the Prime Minister and Cabinet; furthermore, he was given the authority to override parliamentary majorities and provincial assemblies in order to appoint a Prime Minister and provincial governors himself if necessary. The amendments allowed the President to appoint Supreme Court judges and to extend his term in office. The changes were heavily criticized by the PML (N) and PPP. However, Musharraf insisted that a formal role for the military in governing the country was necessary to ensure a stable transition to democracy and to forestall a potential military coup. According to the LFO, the size of the National Assembly would be increased to 342 members, with 60 seats reserved for women and 10 seats reserved for non-Muslims. The Senate would consist of 100 members. The PML (N) and Pakistan People's Party Parliamentarians (PPPP—see below) were permitted to take part in the elections.

Meanwhile, in late July 2002 Benazir Bhutto was re-elected as leader of the PPP. However, the decree barring parties from contesting an election if any of its office-holders have a criminal conviction prompted the PPP in early August to create the PPPP under new leadership to contest the forthcoming general elections. At the same time Shahbaz Sharif was elected leader of the PML (N). Bhutto's plans to return to the political arena were thwarted in late August when election officials in Sindh province rejected her candidacy in the National Assembly elections, owing to her criminal conviction. In response, Nawaz Sharif withdrew his nomination papers (although they had been accepted by the Election Commission), reportedly in solidarity with Bhutto. In mid-September Shahbaz Sharif was disqualified from entering the general election for defaulting on a bank loan. Meanwhile, a pro-Musharraf faction of the PML, the Quaid-e-Azam group, was reportedly receiving covert support from the Government.

On 9 October 2002 Musharraf declared that he was relinquishing the title of Chief Executive. The following day elections for the National Assembly and provincial assemblies took place. In elections to the National Assembly the PML (Quaid-e-Azam—Q) won 77 of the 272 directly elective seats (25.7% of the vote). The PPPP won 25.8% of the vote, but only 63 seats. A surprising outcome was the success of the Muttahida Majlis-e-Amal (MMA), an alliance of six Islamist parties, in securing 45 seats (11.3% of the vote). The PML (N) won only 14 seats (9.4% of the vote). According to the Election Commission, the turn-out at the election was 41.8%; voting to five seats was deferred to a later date. The PML (Q)'s strong performance had been expected, since Musharraf had publicly voiced his support for the party during the election campaign. Opposition parties, independent analysts and the Human Rights Commission of Pakistan claimed that the army had provided financial and other support to the PML (Q), while hampering other parties' campaign efforts. Meanwhile, Benazir Bhutto claimed that the election had been rigged. EU election monitors reported that the poll was 'seriously flawed'. The emergence of the MMA as a third political force suggested that a significant proportion of the population objected to Musharraf's support for the US-led military action against the Taliban and al-Qa'ida in Afghanistan, and the ongoing campaign against al-Qa'ida in Pakistan. PPPP and PML (N) leaders considered the religious alliance's success to be a result of the military Government's attempts to prevent their parties from achieving power. However, many observers held the opinion that the army and ISI sponsored the MMA in an attempt to convince the West that continued military rule was necessary to contain the religious parties, to gain further concessions from the USA, and to ensure support from the new Government for aggressive policies towards India, particularly over the Kashmir issue. On 31 October the 60 seats reserved for women and 10 for non-Muslims were allocated by the Election Commission. The three leading parties entered intensive and protracted negotiations on forming a governing coalition: the PML (Q) and PPPP each attempted to gain the support of the MMA. However, the parties failed to reach common ground; neither the PML (Q) or PPPP was able to persuade the MMA to withdraw its candidate for prime minister. By mid-November the parties had yet to reach a compromise; nevertheless, the National Assembly convened and elected a Speaker and Deputy Speaker. Shortly beforehand, the

President revived the 1973 Constitution, which had been in abeyance since he assumed power in 1999—it was believed that the Constitution incorporated the controversial LFO—and took an oath to begin his new five-year term as President. On 21 November the PML (Q) candidate, Zafarullah Khan Jamali, was elected Prime Minister by the National Assembly. Jamali's victory ensured a PML (Q)-led, pro-army Government with a slim majority, which was sworn in two days later. Meanwhile, Musharraf agreed to transfer power to the elected Government, but emphasized that he would continue to carry out his 'important role'.

The MMA won a majority in the provincial elections in the NWFP in October 2002 and formed a provincial government in late November, with Muhammad Akram Durrani elected Chief Minister. In Balochistan the MMA and PML (Q) formed a coalition government led by a PML (Q) Chief Minister, while the PML (Q) assumed power in Punjab. The PPPP emerged as the single largest party in the Sindh assembly, but failed to form a coalition government despite support from the MMA. Eventually, in mid-December the PML (Q), MMA and several smaller parties agreed to a power-sharing arrangement with Ali Mohammad Maher, a PML (Q) representative, as Chief Minister. The delay in forming the new federal and provincial governments meant that the Senate elections were not held until 25–27 February 2003. Some 88 of the 100 seats in the Senate were elected by the four provincial assemblies. The remaining 12 seats were chosen by the National Assembly from a list of candidates provided by the Federally Administered Tribal Areas (FATA) and the federal capital. The PML (Q) secured 34 seats, making it the largest single party in the Senate. The Senate convened on 12 March. The PML (Q) candidate, Mian Mohammad Soomro, was elected unopposed as Chairman of the Senate after the eight opposition parties boycotted the vote in protest at the President's LFO and the alleged military interference in the Senate elections.

At the end of April 2003 the National Assembly suspended its session, following a month of disruption caused by opposition parties. The MMA, PPPP and other opposition parties had refused to allow Musharraf to address the legislature (a constitutional requirement before it could begin to legislate) and repeatedly demanded that the President submit the LFO to approval by the National Assembly; however, the President, mindful of the fact that the amendments would not secure the two-thirds' majority required for constitutional change, refused to accede to this demand. A joint committee formed by the Government and opposition to discuss the LFO failed to reach an agreement and the consultations collapsed. In June the opposition presented a motion of no confidence in the Speaker of the National Assembly, Chaudhry Amin Hussain, following his ruling that Musharraf's constitutional amendments were valid and that the legislature should function according to them. The opposition argued that Hussain had contravened the 1973 Constitution (which it regarded as the only legitimate Constitution) by ruling in favour of the LFO, and, as a result, the Speaker no longer had the right to the confidence of the Assembly. However, when the Deputy Speaker ruled that the vote would be by secret ballot, the opposition refused to participate and the motion collapsed. None the less, the opposition's campaign of boycott and agitation of parliamentary proceedings continued. Tensions between the MMA and Musharraf increased after an election tribunal barred an MMA legislator from office on educational grounds. Members of the Islamist coalition who did not hold a degree were eventually permitted by Musharraf to stand as candidates, but the tribunal ruled against this exemption, prompting further protests by the MMA. The National Assembly reconvened on 20 August 2003, after having being forced to suspend its session for more than two months.

Meanwhile, in early June 2003 the legislative assembly in the NWFP unanimously voted in favour of legislation to implement *Shari'a* throughout the province (the NWFP Government had already issued a directive requiring civil servants to pray twice a day and introduced legislation forbidding male doctors to examine women). In response to the bill, which gave Islamic law precedence over secular provincial law, Musharraf dismissed two senior NWFP officials—the chief secretary and police chief—for failing to secure law and order in the provincial capital of Peshawar against attacks by militant Islamists. During a visit to the NWFP later that month Musharraf warned against the adoption of Taliban-style Islam, promoting instead the practice of 'tolerant, progressive and civilized' Islam. However, in July a journalist was sentenced to life imprisonment for blasphemy in Peshawar.

In September 2003 the Cabinet unanimously endorsed a modified version of the LFO. Although the PML (N) and PPPP appeared to be willing to compromise regarding their opposition to the measures, the MMA remained dissatisfied and negotiations between the Government and opposition continued. Finally, in December Musharraf announced seven further concessionary amendments to the LFO, including his commitment to resign as Chief of Army Staff by December 2004. On 29 December 2003 the National Assembly passed the Constitution (Seventeenth Amendment) Bill, which comprised the seven modifications. The opposition ARD boycotted the parliamentary proceedings, dismissing the concessions as 'cosmetic'. According to the Bill, which became law on 31 December following the Senate's approval, the existing NSC, which had been inactive since its creation one year previously, disbanded. A new NSC was to be established by an act of parliament, rather than be incorporated into the Constitution by the LFO. Furthermore, while the President would have the right to dismiss the National Assembly, he would be obliged to refer the matter to the Supreme Court within 15 days. Despite the concessions, Musharraf retained most of the special powers that he had awarded himself in 2002. In early January 2004 the federal and provincial legislatures passed votes of confidence in Musharraf, allowing him to complete his five-year term as President (which was due to expire in 2007). In April 2004 the National Assembly passed an item of legislation on the establishment of the NSC amid strong protest by opposition members. The Council was to comprise the President, the Prime Minister, the Chairman of the Senate, the Speaker of the National Assembly, the leader of the parliamentary opposition, the provincial chief ministers and the three other chiefs of armed forces. The new Chief of Army Staff (who was to be appointed in late 2004 following Musharraf's resignation from the position) would also be a member. The NSC law, approved by the Senate several days later, gave the armed forces a formal, albeit supervisory, role in civilian politics for the first time in Pakistan's history.

In the mean time, in late September 2003 the leader of the ARD, Nawabzada Nasrullah Khan, died; he was replaced by Makhdoom Javed Hashmi, the acting President of the PML (N), in early October. In late October, however, Hashmi was arrested on charges of inciting mutiny after circulating a letter at a press conference criticizing the military's involvement in politics that he claimed was written by junior army officers. The authorities asserted that the letter, which was also critical of President Musharraf and his alliance with the USA, was a forgery. Hashmi was convicted of inciting mutiny in the army, forgery and defamation in mid-April 2004 and was sentenced to up to seven years' imprisonment. The PML (N) condemned the verdict, claiming that it proved that the judiciary was under the control of Musharraf. Meanwhile, in December 2003 the President of the MMA and leader of Jamiat-e-Ulema-e-Pakistan, Maulana Shah Ahmed Noorani Siddiqui, died. Amir Qazi Hussain Ahmad was appointed President of the MMA in an acting capacity. In the same month, in a landmark judgment, the Supreme Court ruled that all adult Muslim women were able to marry anyone of their own free will, with or without the consent of their father or guardian (*wali*). The ruling supported a similar judgment declared by the Federal Shari'a Court in 1981 and overturned 1997 rulings by the Lahore High Court that a marriage without the consent of the *wali* was invalid.

In mid-August 2003 Asif Ali Zardari was acquitted of all charges relating to the 1998 murder of Sajjad Hussain, the former Chairman of Pakistan Steel Mills. However, earlier that month Zardari and Benazir Bhutto were convicted by a Swiss investigative judge in Geneva of money-laundering and receiving bribes from two Swiss companies in 1995. Bhutto and her husband each received a suspended six-month prison sentence and a fine of US $50,000. They were also ordered to repay the Pakistani Government $11.9m. (The Lahore High Court had convicted Bhutto and Zardari in the same case in 1999—see above, but the Supreme Court had overturned the verdict two years later, concluding that it had been politically motivated, and had ordered a retrial by a state accountability court.) However, in early November 2003 a court in Geneva quashed the prison sentences and fines following an appeal by Benazir Bhutto and her husband. At the same time, opposition parties in Pakistan held widespread protests on the seventh anniversary of Zardari's arrest to demand his release from prison. Zardari, now largely considered a political prisoner, was implicated in 14 pending criminal cases, but had been convicted on only one corruption charge (in September 2002). Meanwhile, Bhutto faced further corruption cases in Pakistan, Switzerland, the United Kingdom and the USA. In June 2004 Bhutto was indicted by a Geneva court on a new, more serious charge of 'money-laundering by profession', relating to alleged commissions and bribes that she had received from Swiss companies in the 1990s. In September the Lahore High Court overturned Zardari's corruption conviction following an appeal. However, Zardari remained in custody owing to another pending case against him. In November the Supreme Court ordered that Zardari be released on bail, following eight years of imprisonment. His freedom initially appeared to be short-lived, as he was rearrested the following month upon his arrival in Islamabad; a judge in Karachi had cancelled bail as Zardari had allegedly failed to attend a hearing into a 1996 murder case in which he was accused of involvement. However, later in that month the decision was overturned and Zardari's bail was restored. In June 2005 Zardari suffered a major heart attack and was admitted to a hospital in Dubai. In September an arrest warrant was issued for him, after he failed to attend a court hearing in Rawalpindi related to ongoing corruption allegations against him. In the same month Bhutto testified at a Geneva court in relation to the money-laundering charges against her and her husband. In November the former Prime Minister was acquitted by a court in Karachi of corruption charges against her. Later in that month Bhutto claimed that President Musharraf had offered to abandon all remaining charges against her, on the condition that she declined to contest elections scheduled for 2007; she asserted that she was unable to accept the condition.

Attacks by suspected militant Islamists on Western targets, meanwhile, continued to take place in 2003. Although Musharraf decided not to support the USA in its attempt to gain UN endorsement of the planned military campaign to remove the regime of Saddam Hussain in Iraq in March, the President was condemned by some sectors of the Pakistani community for not opposing the war in stronger terms. In November Musharraf proscribed six militant Islamist groups under the 1997 Anti-Terrorist Act. Three of the organizations—Islami Tehrik-e-Pakistan (formerly Tehrik-e-Jafria-e-Pakistan), Millat-e-Islamia Pakistan (formerly Sipah-e-Sahaba) and Khudam ul-Islam (formerly Jaish-e-Mohammed)—had disregarded an earlier ban by changing their names, thus bringing into question the President's commitment to curbing militant activity. The activities of Jamiat ul-Furqan, Jamiat ul-Ansar (formerly Harakat ul-Mujahideen) and Hizb-ut-Tahrir were also proscribed. Jamaat-ud-Dawa (considered by some to be the new identity for the banned Lashkar-e-Taiba movement) was placed under surveillance. Some commentators doubted the effectiveness of Musharraf's approach to militant Islamism, claiming that the groups would continue to receive covert support from the army and judiciary. Indeed, in December 2003 the President narrowly escaped two assassination attempts by suspected Islamist militants near his residence in Rawalpindi. No one was hurt in the first suicide bomb attack, but the second killed at least 17 people and injured about 50 others. Islamist militants had reportedly been greatly angered by the Government's agreement to enter negotiations with India (see below), and by Musharraf's decision to allow the UN International Atomic Energy Agency (IAEA, see p. 113) to investigate the sale of Pakistani nuclear technology to Iran, the Democratic People's Republic of Korea (North Korea) and Libya (see below). It was suggested that al-Qa'ida, which in September had issued a death threat to Musharraf, blaming him for the arrest of hundreds of its members, was responsible for organizing the attacks. There was also speculation that the extremists had infiltrated Musharraf's security apparatus in order to gain secret information on his travel plans. Notably, among those sentenced to death in 2005 for their part in the assassination attempts were five junior members of the Pakistani armed forces.

From mid-2003 the frequency and scale of sectarian attacks increased. In June gunmen shot dead 11 Shi'a Muslims and wounded nine others in Quetta; 18 members of Millat-e-Islamia Pakistan were arrested on suspicion of involvement in the attacks. In the following month a suicide bomb attack took place in a Shi'a mosque also in Quetta, killing at least 50 worshippers and injuring more than 60; the Sunni militant organization Lashkar-e-Jhangvi claimed responsibility for the attack. In early October seven Shi'a Muslims were killed in a gun attack in Karachi by Sunni militants. The Government held a group called 313, a newly formed alliance of Lashkar-e-Jhangvi, Harakat ul-Mujahideen and Harakat ul-Jihad al-Islami, responsible for the attack, claiming that its motives were sectarian and anti-Government. On 6 October the legislator and leader of Millat-e-Islamia Pakistan, Maulana Azam Tariq, was assassinated in Islamabad; a previously unknown Shi'a group, Fedayim Imam Mahdi, claimed responsibility for the attack. The shooting provoked riots in Islamabad and the city of Jhang: Sunni militants, vowing revenge, burnt down a Shi'a shrine and cinema in the capital and a Shi'a mosque in Tariq's home city, Jhang. The leader of the Shi'a extremist Islami Tehrik-e-Pakistan, Allama Sajid Ali Naqvi, was arrested in mid-November, in connection with Tariq's murder. Sectarian strife continued to afflict Quetta: in March 2004 more than 40 Shi'a Muslims were killed and more than 150 injured after Sunni extremists attacked a Shi'a procession during a religious ceremony to commemorate the holy day of Ashoura.

In December 2003 the Minister of Information and Media Development, Sheikh Rashid Ahmad, admitted that the authorities were investigating allegations that Pakistan had transferred nuclear technology to other countries, and that Dr Abdul Qadeer Khan, the founder of Pakistan's nuclear weapons programme, and two other nuclear scientists were being questioned. The Government was under tremendous pressure from the USA and IAEA, which had recently concluded that Iran had been supplied with designs for nuclear equipment that originated from Pakistan, to investigate the accusations. However, the authorities were quick to deny any official involvement, suggesting that 'rogue' individuals motivated by personal greed were to blame. Khan was reportedly placed under house arrest and in late January 2004 was removed from his post as scientific adviser to the Prime Minister. On 4 February, in a dramatic development, Khan confessed on television that during the past 15 years he had provided Iran, North Korea and Libya with designs and technology to develop nuclear weapons (he had already signed a detailed confession). He apologized, asked for forgiveness, and took full responsibility for his actions; he also denied any government involvement and absolved the military and his fellow scientists. Dr Khan's plea for clemency was granted two days later by Musharraf. The President announced that he and the Cabinet had taken into account the nuclear scientist's services to the country before coming to their decision and that Khan would remain under strict surveillance. Musharraf also refused to allow independent investigators to continue their inspection, provoking speculation that the authorities were trying to protect the Pakistani military. It was widely acknowledged that prosecuting Dr Khan would have led to unrest throughout the country (he had been long revered as the 'father' of Pakistan's nuclear bomb and had the status of a national hero) and political problems (there were fears that if put on trial the scientist would provide evidence that incriminated Pakistani leaders and generals). Musharraf countered allegations that he might have been involved in the sale of weapons, claiming that he tried to curb the proliferation after becoming suspicious three years previously by forcing Khan's retirement from his post as head of the Khan Research Laboratories, and that he delayed holding an investigation into the matter owing to the scientist's popularity and privileged position. He also stated that he was only able to take action once the USA had provided him with enough information in October 2003. Musharraf attempted to evade allegations that Khan was ideologically motivated by attributing the scientist's activities to personal gain. However, military analysts continued to doubt that Khan was solely responsible, declaring that it was unlikely that the transfer of nuclear materials could have been conducted without the knowledge and involvement of at least parts of the military. Meanwhile, two former chiefs of army staff, retired Gen. Mirza Aslam Beg and retired Gen. Jehangir Karamat, were questioned and exonerated of any wrongdoing. Musharraf stated that Pakistan would continue to co-operate with the IAEA but would not allow IAEA inspectors to monitor its nuclear programmes. In November 2004 the Supreme Court rejected a petition that Khan be released from house arrest on the grounds of ill health. In February 2005 the Government denied a report in the US magazine *Time* that Khan had also sold nuclear technology to Saudi Arabia and Egypt.

In the first half of 2004 violence between Sunni and Shi'a Muslims in Karachi escalated. In early May the Shi'a Hyderi mosque was attacked by a suicide bomber, resulting in the deaths of 16 people. Later that month a senior Sunni cleric and known Taliban supporter, Mufti Nizamuddin Shamzai, was assassinated. In an apparent revenge attack, another Shi'a mosque in the centre of the city was bombed, killing 16 people and prompting an outbreak of rioting in the city. In June the Chief Minister of Sindh, Sardar Ali Mohammed Maher, was forced to resign as a result of Karachi's deteriorating law and order situation; he was replaced by Dr Arbab Ghulam Rahim. In the same month at least 10 people were killed following an attack on the motorcade of the commander of the Karachi army corps, Lt-Gen. Ahsan Saleem Hayat. Shortly afterwards it was announced that 10 suspected members of al-Qa'ida had been apprehended in the city; they allegedly confessed to having participated in Lt-Gen. Hayat's attempted assassination. The men were charged with terrorist offences in September. Meanwhile, in August several more explosions occurred in Karachi.

In the mean time, in June 2004 Prime Minister Jamali tendered his resignation, having been placed under considerable pressure to do so by Musharraf. The President was reportedly frustrated at the weakness of Jamali's Government and, in particular, its apparent inability to curb sectarian violence in Pakistan. Later in the same month Musharraf's nominee, Chaudhry Shujaat Hussain, President of the newly formed PML (which had been created following the merger of several factions of the PML and the Sindh Democratic Alliance in the previous month), was elected to serve as interim Prime Minister. It was reported that Minister of Finance Shaukat Aziz was Musharraf's choice to serve in the post permanently, but, as Aziz was a Senator, he would first need to be elected to the House of Representatives. In July Aziz survived an assassination attempt by an alleged suicide bomber in the town of Attock in Punjab, one of the two constituencies that he was contesting in forthcoming by-elections. In late August, following victories in both constituencies, Aziz was elected as Prime Minister and leader of the house by the National Assembly and, on the following day, was formally sworn in to his new office. In the following month a new Cabinet was appointed, which included the 20 members of Chaudhry Shujaat Hussain's interim Government and incorporated an additional 13 members. Aziz retained the finance portfolio, while Aftab Ahmad Khan Sherpao became Minister of the Interior and Rao Sikander Iqbal continued as Minister of Defence.

In October 2004 the National Assembly approved legislation enabling Musharraf to retain his dual role as President and Chief of Army Staff, contrary to his December 2003 pledge that he would resign from his military position by the end of 2004. The opposition protested that the bill was unconstitutional and condemned it strongly, although the Speaker curtailed debate on the issue. The Government claimed that the ongoing terrorist threat necessitated Musharraf's retention of both roles, a claim supported by the state assemblies of Punjab and Sindh, both of which passed motions requesting that Musharraf remain as army chief. In November, having been approved by the Senate, the bill was signed into law by its Chairman, Mian Mohammad Soomro, who was acting President while Musharraf was out of the country. In December Musharraf formally confirmed that he intended to retain his military position until the end of his presidential term, in 2007. In March 2005 the MMA orchestrated marches throughout the country to protest against Musharraf's actions; its supporters also observed a series of nation-wide strikes, culminating in a general strike in early April. However, this received only limited support. Later that month the Supreme Court dismissed all petitions challenging Musharraf's dual role as unconstitutional. In May it was announced that Musharraf would definitely seek re-election as President following the expiry of his term of office in 2007; the opposition denounced his decision.

Meanwhile, in late 2004 and early 2005 outbreaks of sectarian violence intensified in frequency. In October in Multan two bombs exploded at a Sunni Muslim rally, held to commemorate the first anniversary of the assassination of Maulana Azam Tariq, killing at least 40 people. Minister of the Interior Sherpao subsequently announced that he would order provincial governments to ban all religious gatherings apart from prayers at mosques. There was speculation that the bombing was revenge for a suicide attack on a Shi'a mosque in Sialkot in Punjab earlier in that month, in which an estimated 30 people lost their lives. Meanwhile, in Karachi another prominent Sunni religious leader, Mufti Muhammad Jamil, was assassinated and, on the following day, a suicide bomber attacked a Shi'a mosque in Lahore. In December at least 11 people died when a bomb exploded next to an army vehicle at a market in Quetta; the separatist Balochistan National Army claimed responsibility for the attack, but denied that it had intended to kill civilians, declaring that members of the armed forces were its target. In March 2005 a bomb explosion at a Sufi Muslim shrine, sacred to both Sunni and Shi'a Muslims, in the town of Fatehpur resulted in the deaths of at least 50 pilgrims. Four suspects, believed to be members of the banned Sunni Millat-e-Islamia Pakistan group, were subsequently arrested in connection with the attack. In May a suicide bombing at a Sufi shrine in Islamabad killed at least 20 people. Later in the same month an attack on a Shi'a mosque in Karachi resulted in five deaths.

In January 2005 claims that military personnel had raped and assaulted a female doctor employed by Pakistan Petroleum Ltd in Balochistan precipitated an outbreak of violence in the province, which had become increasingly lawless throughout late 2004. Bugti tribesmen clashed with security forces at the Sui gas processing plant, causing severe damage to the plant and to three gas pipelines and affecting gas supplies throughout the country (the Sui gas field accounted for some 45% of total gas production in Pakistan). In response to an appeal by the provincial government, the federal Government dispatched army and paramilitary troops to protect the gas field, resulting in a temporary cessation of the unrest in Sui. However, later in the month three bombs exploded in the provincial capital, Quetta. The violence in the province was seen to some extent to be indicative of local resentment at the federal Government's exploitation of its mineral wealth. It was feared that further clashes between the army and local rebels would encourage Balochi nationalist sentiment. In February a spate of bomb attacks took place in various different areas of Balochistan as the violence continued. Responsibility for several of the attacks was claimed by the Balochistan Liberation Army (BLA), an insurgent group operating in the province. In March more than 60 civilians died during clashes between security forces and tribesmen in the area as the conflict intensified. Following an attack on a military convoy, a stand-off ensued between the two sides, with tribal leader and President of the Jamhuri Watan Party, Nawab Akbar Bugti, refusing to compromise in the tribesmen's struggle to secure political autonomy and a greater share of revenue from Balochistan's gas reserves. Following talks between Bugti and a government delegation that included former Prime Minister Chaudhry Shujaat Hussain, an agreement was reached to defuse the crisis. The process of implementing the agreement, which included the withdrawal of troops by both sides, began in April. Meanwhile, later in March a bomb exploded at a Muslim shrine in the town of Usa Mohammad, killing 35 people. Sporadic unrest continued throughout 2005, intensifying again during a visit by President Musharraf to the province in December of that year. The violence continued into 2006: in August Bugti was killed in clashes between government forces and tribesmen, triggering a spate of strikes and civil unrest. Preliminary talks were initiated between the Government and Baluch nationalists in December. However, in July 2007 the spokesman of the Balochistan provincial government was shot dead, and in November it was reported that Mir Balaach Marri, who was alleged to be the leader of the BLA, had been killed.

In the mean time, the issue of religious extremism continued to resonate in Pakistani society. In July 2005, following the discovery that at least two of the four British Muslim suicide bombers who had attacked the transport network in London, United Kingdom, in that month had previously visited Pakistan and had allegedly received instruction at one of the country's many *madrassas*, President Musharraf announced the implementation of a more stringent policy to prevent the spread of Islamic extremism. Hundreds of suspected Islamist militants were arrested and several *madrassas* suspected of being involved in extremism were raided. However, Musharraf stressed that he did not believe that the British bombers had been radicalized in Pakistan. In August the National Assembly gave its assent to legislation requiring all *madrassas* to register with the Government and to submit annual reports. The schools were also barred from encouraging militancy and propagating religious hatred. Furthermore, all foreign students studying at *madrassas* in Pakistan were to be expelled. Meanwhile, President Musharraf filed a petition with the Supreme Court objecting to certain sections of legislation passed in the previous month by the provincial assembly of the NWFP. The new laws made provision for 'morality police' in the province, who would enforce prayer attendance, discourage singing and dancing and practise strict media censorship. The legislation had been proposed by the conservative religious alliance the MMA, which dominated the province's assembly. The Supreme Court subsequently ruled that sections of the law relating to the powers of an Islamic *Mohtasib* (moral guardian), which had been established by the bill, were unconstitutional. The increasing dominance of the MMA and its implementation of guidelines to govern social behaviour, in line with Islamic values, provided an indication of the increasing 'Talibanization' of some sections of Pakistani society.

During August–October 2005 local government elections took place over several stages. Although political parties were theoretically prohibited from participating in the elections, the political allegiances of most candidates were widely known. The polls were marred by violence and intimidation in many areas; in particular, the exercise of the franchise by women and the candidature of some for office attracted controversy, with repolling ordered in several areas as a result of complaints that women had been prevented from voting. Overall, the results indicated a decline in support for religious parties, with more moderate parties reported to have won a majority of seats in Punjab and Sindh. Meanwhile, in the NWFP and Balochistan support for the MMA had apparently decreased significantly. However, the results of the polls were called into question by widespread allegations of malpractice and corruption.

In October 2005 a huge earthquake, the epicentre of which was in the town of Balakot, in the NWFP, devastated Azad Kashmir and much of the NWFP, resulting in the deaths of more than 81,000 people and leaving many thousands homeless. The response of the Government and armed forces to the disaster attracted criticism for its tardiness and lack of co-ordination, although the logistical challenge of delivering relief to many of the remote areas affected was considerable. Furthermore, the aid committed by international donors in the aftermath of the earthquake was reportedly criticized as inadequate by President Musharraf. At a meeting of donors held in November in Islamabad, a total of US $5,800m. was pledged by the international community for the relief and reconstruction effort, exceeding the Government's target. However, most of the aid donated was intended for the long-term effort, and funds for immediate humanitarian relief remained slow to arrive. Although relief efforts focused on reconstruction in 2006, it was estimated by the Government that only 17% of the 400,000 homes affected by the earthquake had been rebuilt, and in October Musharraf appealed for further aid from foreign donors.

In February 2006 widespread protests occurred across Pakistan, as demonstrators gathered to condemn the publication of cartoons of the Prophet Mohammed in a Danish newspaper in September 2005. Although the demonstrations began peacefully and on a relatively small scale, they became increasingly violent in some areas, resulting in several deaths. The MMA exploited the protests to increase public opposition to President Musharraf, whose Government had condemned the cartoons but who was widely perceived to be allied with the West. The protests culminated in the withdrawal of the Danish ambassador from the country.

In March 2006 elections took place for one-half of the seats in the Senate; Mohammad Mian Soomro was subsequently re-elected as Chairman. Legislative decisions were the subject of much public debate in 2006 and the first half of 2007. In November 2006 the federal legislature passed the Women's Protection Bill, which amended the *Hudood* ordinance, giving civil courts jurisdiction in rape cases and revoking the death penalty for extra-marital sexual intercourse. Religious groups voiced their opposition to the bill, arguing that it was 'un-Islamic', while others demanded the abolition of the *Hudood* ordinance in its entirety. In December the Supreme Court issued a delaying order against the *Hasba* (Accountability) Bill, which had been approved by the NWFP provincial assembly in July 2005 to regulate the application of Islamic values, on the grounds that it breached human rights. In March 2007 Musharraf suspended the Chief Justice of the Supreme Court, Iftikhar Mohammad Chaudhry—who was widely recognized for his independent stance on controversial issues and for his investigations into human rights violations—on charges of abuse of office. This controversial action provoked the holding of large-scale, violent demonstrations by the legal community and the resignation of several senior judicial officials. The authorities' decision to dispatch riot police to contain the protests precipitated further unrest and strengthened the protesters' cause in the eyes of ordinary citizens. The escalation in anti-Government sentiment among the general public led many observers to question the solidity of Musharraf's power base. In mid-May Chaudhry arrived in Karachi to address a political rally organized by his supporters, but was unable to leave the airport because the roads into the city were blocked. Demonstrations in Karachi subsequently escalated into violent clashes between supporters of the Government and the opposition, resulting in some 41 fatalities. The campaign to reinstate Chaudhry appeared to have succeeded when the Supreme Court voted to restore him to the position of Chief Justice in July.

Sectarian violence and terrorist attacks continued to pose a threat to internal security and stability in 2006 and 2007. In April 2006 a suicide bombing at a religious gathering of approximately 10,000 Sunni Muslims in Karachi resulted in the deaths of at least 58 people. In January 2007 a bomb explosion in Peshawar, immediately prior to the commencement of a Shi'a religious procession, killed at least 14 people, including several police officers. The incident followed a suicide attack at a hotel in Islamabad the previous day, when the bomber and a security officer were killed and several people were wounded. In the following month the provincial Minister for Social Welfare for Punjab and PML member, Zill-e-Huma, was assassinated in Gujranwala; her attacker, who was arrested at the scene of the crime, objected to women's involvement in politics on the grounds that it was 'un-Islamic'. In April a suicide bombing at a public meeting in Charsadda, NWFP, resulted in at least 22 fatalities; the federal Minister of the Interior, Aftab Ahmad Khan Sherpao, who appeared to have been the target of the attack, sustained injuries. A bomb explosion at a hotel in Peshawar in mid-May killed some 24 people and injured several more.

In 2007 the growing prominence of religious leaders of the Lal Masjid (Red Mosque) in central Islamabad posed a further threat to the Government's attempts to stabilize the security situation. Members of the Lal Masjid and its two *madrassas*, who demanded the imposition of *shari'a* law, had been involved in increasingly overt challenges to authority, issuing a *fatwa* (Islamic edict) against Minister of Tourism Nilofar Bakhtyar and even abducting security officers and alleged prostitutes. The religious extremism advocated by the mosque was rejected by protesters who took part in demonstrations in major cities in April. Matters came to a head in July with violent clashes between paramilitary forces and occupants of the large Lal Masjid compound; although some 1,500 students reportedly surrendered and the imam, Maulana Abdul Aziz, was taken into custody, the imam's brother and a contingent of students remained until negotiations collapsed and security forces invaded the compound. It was later estimated that some 100 people, many of them Lal Masjid followers, had been killed, but some estimates put the death toll much higher. The siege aggravated anti-Government sentiment in certain quarters, and resulted in a spate of retaliatory attacks in Islamabad, the NWFP and elsewhere, exacerbating an already deteriorating security situation. The rise of another radical cleric in the Swat valley, NWFP, in late 2007 opened up a new front in the Government's struggles against militancy.

Meanwhile, conjecture about the possible return to Pakistan of two former prime ministers, Benazir Bhutto and Nawaz Sharif, intensified. In August 2007 the Supreme Court decided that, regardless of the terms of his exile agreement, Sharif was entitled to return to the country; however, upon his arrival in Islamabad in the following month, Sharif was sent back to Saudi Arabia, prompting a legal challenge to the deportation. There were reports of negotiations between Musharraf and Bhutto about the latter's re-entry into domestic politics as the former apparently searched for an alternative power base. Bhutto's conditions for working with Musharraf were said to include the President's resignation from the army and the withdrawal of corruption charges against herself and others. In early October Musharraf passed the 'national reconciliation' ordinance, giving Bhutto and other politicians immunity from prosecution under charges brought during 1986–99. Despite the absence of a conclusive agreement, Bhutto entered Pakistan later that month. She was greeted by hundreds of thousands of supporters in Karachi, but fears for her safety were confirmed when a bomb attack on her procession resulted in approximately 139 fatalities. Bhutto herself was unharmed.

On 6 October 2007 Musharraf was re-elected as President by the incumbent national and provincial legislatures, securing 671 votes against the eight received by Wajihuddin Ahmed. Members of the MMA, the PML (N) and other parties of the All Parties Democratic Movement opposition grouping had resigned from the National Assembly in protest prior to the ballot, while the PPP abstained from the vote. Just before the vote, the Supreme Court had ruled that the victor could not be declared until the legality of the election had been confirmed pending legal challenges from the opposition, a decision that was not expected until later in the month. The Supreme Court was also expected to rule on the legality of the national reconciliation ordinance. In early November the presiding judge estimated that a decision would not be made before the middle of the month. On 3 November Musharraf declared a state of emergency and suspended the Constitution, citing, among other contributing factors, the deteriorating law and order situation and the judiciary's interference in government affairs. Immediate measures included the dismissal of Chief Justice Chaudhry and the swearing in of Abdul Hameed Dogar as his replacement. Members of the judiciary were reportedly among those detained, together with lawyers, opposition figures and human rights activists who had taken part in demonstrations to protest against the imposition of emergency measures. Meanwhile, the police force was accorded special powers, and the broadcasting of private and international television channels was suspended. The National Assembly was dissolved on 15 November, and the Chairman of the Senate, Mohammad Mian Soomro, was sworn in to lead an interim government the following day. The Punjab, Balochistan and Sindh provincial legislatures were subsequently dissolved, the provincial assembly of NWFP having been dissolved in early October. On 20 November the Chief Election Commissioner confirmed that parliamentary and provincial assembly elections would be held on 8 January 2008. Gen. Musharraf resigned as Chief of Army Staff on 28 November 2007, following the Supreme Court's dismissal, on 22 November, of the final legal challenge to Musharraf's re-election as President, thus facilitating Musharraf's inauguration as civilian head of state (which duly took place on 29 November). Meanwhile, also on 22 November, the Commonwealth Ministerial Action Group on the Harare Declaration suspended Pakistan from the Councils of the Commonwealth. Musharraf revoked the state of emergency on 15 December.

A power-sharing agreement between Musharraf and Bhutto had appeared increasingly unlikely as Bhutto called for Musharraf's resignation as Chief of Army Staff in the aftermath of his declaration of a state of emergency. PPP supporters joined the ranks of opposition members detained under the emergency measures, and Bhutto herself was placed under temporary house arrest to prevent her participation in political rallies. In mid-November 2007 Bhutto had announced an end to the negotiations, demanded Musharraf's resignation from the post of President as well as the head of the military, and indicated a willingness to consider the formation of a coalition government with other opposition parties. Nawaz Sharif was permitted to return to Pakistan at the end of November, following the reported intervention of the King of Saudi Arabia. In late December, as the country prepared for elections, Bhutto was killed in a suicide bomb attack on a PPP rally in Rawalpindi. The cause of death was initially unclear, with conflicting reports from different quarters: some claimed she had been shot, while others asserted that she had died as a result of the explosion, which killed some 20 others (in February 2008 British detectives corroborated the results of a domestic investigation, which concluded that Bhutto had died from a head injury caused by the force of the bomb blast, and in February 2009 the UN Secretary-General, Ban Ki-Moon, announced the formation of an independent commission of inquiry into the assassination). The Government, which declared three days of mourning, was criticized for not arranging adequate security measures, and some voiced suspicion about the perpetrators' possible links to sections of the Government or the intelligence establishment, a claim that Musharraf vehemently denied. According to officials, Baitullah Mehsud, an extremist from the FATA, and al-Qa'ida were involved in the attack. News of the assassination provoked rioting in several cities, resulting in more than 45 deaths. On 30 December 2007 19-year-old Bilawal Bhutto Zardari was named to succeed his mother as leader of the PPP following the completion of his university studies, with Asif Ali Zardari assuming the role in an interim capacity. In January 2008 the Election Commission of Pakistan announced that legislative elections, hitherto scheduled for 8 January, would be postponed until February.

At the legislative elections, which were held on 18 February 2008, the PPPP—established by the PPP in 2002 in order to meet electoral requirements—secured a total of 121 general and reserved seats in the National Assembly. The PML (N) won 91 seats, while the PML, which supported Musharraf, took just 54 seats. Turn-out was estimated at some 45% of the electorate. The PML was also defeated in all of the provincial assemblies except Balochistan. On 9 March 2008 the PPP and the PML (N) announced a coalition agreement, the terms of which reportedly included the reinstatement of judges dismissed in November 2007 and the entry of the latter party into the new cabinet. A coalition Government was consequently sworn in on 31 March, under the premiership of Yousaf Raza Gilani of the PPP, who had formally assumed the post of Prime Minister on 25 March. The new Cabinet included 11 members of the PPP, nine from the PML (N), two from the ANP, one from a faction of the JUI and one independent member of the National Assembly from the FATA (in late 2008 members of the Pakistan Muslim League—Functional (PML—F) and the Balochistan National Party—Awami (BNP—A) also held ministerial posts). Among the new holders of the most important government positions, Chaudhry Ahmed Mukhtar of the PPP was appointed Minister of Defence, Shah Mehmud Qureshi of the PPP became Minister of Foreign Affairs, while Muhammad Ishaq Dar of the PML (N) took the finance portfolio. Shortly after assuming office, Gilani ordered the release of several judges arrested in November 2007. With popular and political support for President Musharraf severely diminished, there was much speculation about his future role. Following the reinstallation of a democratically elected government, the Commonwealth readmitted Pakistan as a full member in May 2008.

The fragility of the new coalition Government was demonstrated almost immediately, when a disagreement over the reinstatement of the dismissed judges necessitated prolonged negotiations between the PPP and the PML (N) in April–May 2008. The PML (N), which made no secret of its wish to unseat President Musharraf, was believed to be anxious to return Chaudhry and the other judges to their positions, while the PPP was hesitant, perhaps fearing the consequences of their reinstatement. In the absence of a resolution, in mid-May the PML (N) announced the withdrawal of its ministers from the Cabinet, although Nawaz Sharif gave an assurance of his party's continuing support for the coalition in the legislature. Prime Minister Gilani and PPP leader Zardari initially refused to accept the resignations, but ministerial portfolios were subsequently reallocated to incumbent cabinet members. Later in the month, Zardari put forward plans for numerous amendments to the Constitution, one of which was the restriction of the President's executive powers, including the right to dissolve the legislature and make military and provincial appointments; these, it was proposed, would be reassigned to the Prime Minister. In June pressure on Musharraf to step down from the presidency increased, but he denied that his resignation was imminent. A campaign instigated by lawyers to reinstate the judges was gaining momentum and targeting the President, with thousands of people participating in a march from Lahore to Islamabad. The PPP also adopted a more uncompromising stance, suggesting that it would name his replacement. In mid-August Pervez Musharraf finally announced his resignation as President, prompted by the prospect of impending impeachment proceedings initiated by the PPP and the PML (N). He denied charges of violation of the Constitution and gross misconduct, but recognized that the proceedings could lead to further instability in the country. The Chairman of the Senate, Mohammad Mian Soomro, was appointed President in an acting capacity, pending the parliamentary election of a successor.

Later in August 2008 the PPP presented Zardari as its nominee for the presidency. Several corruption charges against Zardari had been dismissed in the preceding months, and in April he had been acquitted in two separate murder cases. In late August money-laundering charges against him in Switzerland were also withdrawn. At the presidential election held on 6 September, Zardari secured a majority of votes in the federal and provincial legislatures, defeating the PML (N) candidate, former Chief Justice of the Supreme Court Saeeduzzaman Siddiqui, by 481 votes to 153; a third candidate, Mushahid Hussain Syed, supported by the PML (Q), received only 44 votes. Zardari was sworn in on 9 September. In early November Prime Minister Gilani effected a cabinet reorganization, allocating the finance and revenue and economic affairs portfolios to Shaukat Tareen, an independent, and the interior portfolio to PPP member Rehman Malik. The appointments of Hazar Khan Bijarani as Minister of Education and Israrullah Zehri as Minister of Postal Services provoked outrage in some quarters, as both had been involved in women's rights controversies. The rift between the PPP and the PML (N) appeared to widen in February 2009, when the Supreme Court upheld a verdict barring Nawaz Sharif and his brother, Muhammad Shahbaz Sharif, from elected office. The latter was dismissed from his position as Chief Minister of

Punjab, and governor's rule was imposed in the province. Nawaz Sharif protested against the ruling, claiming that Zardari was behind the decision and reiterating his demand for the reinstatement of the judges. In mid-March, in an apparent attempt to defuse the political crisis and to end the agitation by the lawyers and PML (N) activists that threatened to destabilize the country, the Government agreed to reinstate Chaudhry as Chief Justice. In response, Nawaz Sharif called off a 'long march' protest that was heading for Islamabad. At the end of the month, in a further conciliatory move, President Zardari lifted central rule in Punjab and the Supreme Court restored Muhammad Shahbaz Sharif as Chief Minister of the province.

These political crises took place against a background of increasing instability in Pakistan. As fighting and bombings continued in the NWFP and FATA, there were concerns about the expanding power base of the militants. The emergence of the Tehrik-e-Taliban Pakistan, or the so-called Pakistani Taliban, reportedly led by Baitullah Mehsud, was a disturbing development for the Government. In his capacity as new Prime Minister, Yousaf Raza Gilani vowed to tackle terrorism, but he also declared a willingness to negotiate with militants on the condition of the cessation of violence; talks between the Government and Baitullah Mehsud reportedly followed. Receiving particular media attention was the situation in the Swat valley, where the provincial government was reported to have signed a peace agreement with pro-Taliban radicals in May 2008. However, sporadic fighting continued, as did attacks on girls' schools. In February 2009 a further cease-fire agreement was announced, under the terms of which large parts of the NWFP's Malakand Division (which includes the Swat valley, Lower Dir and Buner) would be brought under *Shari'a* law. However, in late April government forces launched a fresh offensive against the Taliban militants who—in violation of the peace agreement—were attempting to expand their power base southwards into Buner (only around 100 km from Islamabad). In early May it was reported that thousands of civilians were fleeing their homes in the Swat valley as the peace agreement between the Taliban militants and the government troops appeared to have collapsed, with increasingly frequent violent clashes (centred around the town of Mingora) and rising casualties on both sides. In mid-May the UN reported that around 830,000 civilians had been forced to flee their homes since April to escape the violence and appealed for immediate international humanitarian aid.

Meanwhile, numerous attacks took place in major cities in 2008 and 2009. A suicide bombing at the Lahore High Court in January 2008, on the day of a scheduled protest by the lawyers' movement, led to some 24 deaths. In June 2008 a car bomb exploded outside the Danish embassy in Islamabad, resulting in eight or more fatalities. In the following month, a suicide bombing was carried out at an anti-Musharraf protest in Islamabad on the anniversary of the Lal Masjid encounter; some 20 deaths resulted, include those of several police officers. Another attack took place at a military munitions factory near Islamabad in August, killing 67 people. The death toll for a large-scale bombing at the Marriott hotel in Islamabad in September was estimated at 54, with hundreds injured. In early March 2009 members of the visiting Sri Lankan cricket team were shot at by a group of attackers in Lahore; six police officers and a driver were killed. Towards the end of the month a suicide bomber caused the deaths of at least 50 people in a crowded mosque near the town of Jamrud in the FATA, and a few days later a group of gunmen laid siege to a police academy near Lahore, as a result of which eight policemen were killed and around 100 injured.

In foreign relations Pakistan has traditionally pursued a policy of maintaining close links with Islamic states in the Middle East and Africa and with the People's Republic of China, while continuing to seek aid and assistance from the USA. Pakistan's controversial nuclear programme prompted the USA to terminate development aid in April 1979, but, as a result of the Soviet invasion of Afghanistan in December of that year, military and economic assistance was renewed in 1981. However, increased concern about Pakistan's ability to develop nuclear weapons and its refusal to sign the Treaty on the Non-Proliferation of Nuclear Weapons led to the suspension of military and economic aid by the US Government again in 1990 (under the Pressler Amendment). In February 1992 the Pakistani Government admitted for the first time that Pakistan had nuclear-weapons capability, but added that it had 'frozen' its nuclear programme at the level of October 1989, when its capabilities were insufficient to produce a nuclear device. In September 1995 the US Senate voted in favour of the Brown Amendment, which allowed a limited resumption of defence supplies to Pakistan. The Brown Amendment (which was ratified by the US President, Bill Clinton, in January 1996) also deleted the Pressler Amendment requirements for economic sanctions, thus paving the way for the resumption of US economic aid to Pakistan. In August 1996 the first consignment of US military equipment released by the US Government after a six-year delay arrived in Pakistan. In December 1998 Prime Minister Nawaz Sharif held talks with President Clinton in the US capital in an attempt to gain support for Pakistan's ailing economy and to persuade the US leader further to ease sanctions imposed on Pakistan following nuclear tests carried out by the latter in May (see below). During 1998–99 the USA lifted some of the sanctions imposed on Pakistan and India, while reiterating requests that the two countries sign the Comprehensive Test Ban Treaty (CTBT) and exercise restraint in their respective missile development programmes to ensure peace in South Asia. During 2000 US foreign policy appeared to favour closer co-operation with India at the expense of improved relations with Pakistan. However, Pakistan's strategic importance to US efforts to dismantle the Taliban regime in Afghanistan and thus apprehend members of the al-Qa'ida terrorist organization held responsible for the devastating attacks on New York and Washington, DC, USA, in September 2001 resulted in attempts by the USA to promote Pakistan's political rehabilitation in the Western international community. Although in September the US Government withdrew sanctions imposed on Pakistan in May 1998, and Gen. Musharraf was warmly received on official visits to the USA in November 2001 and February 2002, a 1990 suspension order on the delivery to Pakistan of 28 US F-16 fighter aircraft was not lifted, to the evident disappointment of the Pakistani President.

Despite the international acclaim that greeted Musharraf's public declaration of his commitment to the eradication of militant religious extremism in January 2002, US concerns persisted about the proliferation of armed fundamentalist groups in Pakistan's border regions, and the possibility of their assisting scattered al-Qa'ida units to regroup in these areas. A US journalist, Daniel Pearl, was abducted in Karachi in January by a previously unknown group called the National Movement for the Restoration of Pakistani Sovereignty; the group made a number of demands in exchange for his safe return, including the release of all Pakistani nationals captured by US forces in Afghanistan and transported (together with other suspected al-Qa'ida members) to a detention centre at the US military base in Guantánamo Bay, Cuba. Despite the prompt arrest by the Pakistani authorities of a British-born militant Islamist, Ahmed Omar Saeed Sheikh, who was believed to have organized the kidnapping, it soon emerged that Pearl had been murdered by his abductors. Confounding speculation that suspects in the case would be extradited for trial in the USA, in March Saeed Sheikh and three alleged accomplices appeared in a specially instituted anti-terrorism court in Karachi on charges of kidnapping, murder and terrorism. The men were convicted of the charges in mid-July; Saeed Sheikh was sentenced to death and his co-defendants were each sentenced to life imprisonment. Following an anti-US grenade attack on the Protestant International Church in Islamabad in March, in which five people (including the wife and daughter of a US diplomat) were killed, Musharraf dismissed five senior police officers for what he considered a serious lapse in security. It was widely believed that intelligence proceeding from Pakistani investigations to discover the identities of the assailants was a crucial factor in the arrest of Abu Zubaydah, one of al-Qa'ida's most senior commanders, by officers of the US Federal Bureau of Investigation (FBI) in Faisalabad at the end of March. However, it was reported that several prominent Islamic clerics and at least 1,300 of their supporters who had been detained in late 2001 were released in early April 2002. In early May a suicide bomber killed 14 people, the majority of whom were French engineers, in Karachi. (Three men were convicted on charges of conspiracy relating to the suicide bombing and sentenced to death in June 2003; two of the men were reportedly members of the banned Islamist Harakat ul-Jihad-al-Islami and Harakat ul-Mujahideen.) Another attack occurred in mid-June 2002 outside the US consulate in Karachi, killing 12 people. One month later two Pakistani members of the al-Alami faction of Harakat ul-Mujahideen claimed responsibility for the attack on the US consulate as well as other attacks on Western targets. In September Pakistani security forces arrested 12 alleged members of al-Qa'ida in Karachi, including the Yemeni-born Ramzi Binalshibh, a principal suspect in the attacks on the USA on 11 September 2001. The USA took custody of Binalshibh and four other al-Qa'ida suspects.

In an apparent breakthrough in the campaign against religious extremism, the alleged operations chief of the al-Qa'ida network, Khalid Sheikh Mohammed, who was suspected of having planned the attacks on the USA in September 2001, was arrested in Rawalpindi in March 2003. It was hoped that the suspect, who was promptly taken into US custody, would provide information on the identity and whereabouts of al-Qa'ida cells in Pakistan and elsewhere in the world. Two other suspected Islamist militants were also arrested. The ISI's involvement in the arrest of the alleged militants suggested that the intelligence agency was genuinely attempting to curb militant activity. Furthermore, in early March the ISI declared that since 11 September 2001 Pakistan had arrested 442 suspected foreign militants, of whom 346 had been handed over to US custody. However, the discovery of Mohammed in a house owned by an army officer's brother raised questions about links between al-Qa'ida and the Pakistani military. Furthermore, the proprietor's prominent role in the Jamaat-e-Islami generated speculation about that political party's connections with al-Qa'ida. Later in March 2003 Pakistan, influenced by widespread large-scale protest marches against US-led military action to remove the regime of Saddam Hussain in Iraq, stated that it would not support the USA in this action. In the same month the USA removed all remaining sanctions imposed on Pakistan after the 1999 military coup and in early April 2003 agreed to waive a total of US $1,000m. in debt, in recognition of Pakistan's efforts in the 'war on terror'. Later that month security forces arrested 10 allegedly senior members of the terrorist network and seized a large quantity of weapons in Peshawar. During Musharraf's visit to the USA in June, the Pakistani President hoped to secure further pledges of co-operation, economic aid and possibly military sales in return for his support. Indeed, the US President, George W. Bush, offered an aid package of $3,000m. in financial and military assistance over the next five years. However, the Bush Administration declined to cancel a further $1,800m. debt, owing to reservations over whether enough was being done by the Pakistan authorities to curb militant activity and to prevent the infiltration of separatist militants into Indian-controlled Kashmir. There were also concerns expressed regarding Islamist fundamentalism in Pakistani politics, the country's incomplete return to democratic rule and Pakistan's nuclear weapons programme (the USA had already placed a symbolic two-year ban on trade with Khan Research Laboratories following allegations that the latter had assisted North Korea in supplying nuclear designs).

In early October 2003 Pakistani forces arrested 18 suspected militants in South Waziristan in the FATA. The offensive followed reports of increased militant activity in the region, particularly in conservative Pashtun areas where Taliban members were known to enjoy support. At least eight Taliban and al-Qa'ida suspects were killed during the operation; it was later reported that the majority of the dead were of foreign origin. Later that month the armed forces arrested a further 40 people, including tribal elders who were accused of sheltering al-Qa'ida suspects. However, despite the apparent attempts to combat Taliban activity in the tribal areas, there were claims that Pakistani troops continued to allow Taliban movement across the Afghan–Pakistani border and that senior Taliban members were openly living in Quetta in Balochistan. In January 2004 Musharraf, during a speech to the Pakistani legislature, attempted to reassure the USA and the rest of the world that Pakistan was committed to defeating militant Islamism. While an army operation in South Waziristan earlier that month largely failed, by the end of January seven al-Qa'ida suspects and the Taliban former governor of Baghis province in Afghanistan, had been arrested. The search for suspected militants remained focused on South Waziristan, where the USA believed bin Laden and other al-Qa'ida leaders were receiving shelter. Several thousand Pakistani troops were deployed to force al-Qa'ida fugitives across the border into Afghanistan, where US soldiers were active (US troops were not permitted to operate from Pakistani soil). In late February, following the expiry of a deadline for tribal leaders to hand over Islamist fugitives, the army launched another attack, this time arresting 58 suspects. Pakistan's concerted efforts were largely in response to the USA's restraint over the nuclear proliferation scandal (see above). However, the reluctance by Pakistani troops to attack Afghanistan's former rulers threatened to affect Musharraf's relations with the US Administration. Nevertheless, the USA remained anxious not to destabilize the Pakistani President, who was facing growing domestic opposition owing to his support for the 'war on terror'.

Meanwhile, fighting between Pakistani troops and militants in March 2004 resulted in the deaths of more than 100 people, including the al-Qa'ida intelligence chief, Abdullah. Many other militants were believed to have evaded capture and escaped. The army subsequently offered a temporary amnesty to both the militants and those tribesmen sheltering them. However, by the 30 April deadline only five tribesmen had surrendered. Meanwhile, during a visit to Pakistan in March, the US Secretary of State announced that, in recognition of the close military relations between the two countries, the USA had decided to designate Pakistan a 'major non-North Atlantic Treaty Organization (NATO) ally'. Shortly afterwards President Bush announced that all remaining US sanctions against Pakistan would be lifted. However, concerns continued to be expressed by the USA that more progress was not being made in the campaign against al-Qa'ida. Renewed fighting in June, after a period of calm in Waziristan, resulted in the deaths of 72 people, including the popular Waziri tribal leader and former Taliban commander Nek Mohammed. In the following month it was announced that several suspected al-Qa'ida members, including the Tanzanian Ahmed Khalfan Ghailani, who was wanted in connection with the 1998 bombing of US embassies in Kenya and Tanzania, had been arrested in the town of Gujrat in Punjab. Ghailani was later placed in the custody of the USA. In August 2004 the Government announced that it had thwarted a militant plot to carry out several attacks in Islamabad, and had subsequently arrested at least 12 al-Qa'ida suspects. Meanwhile, the authorities in the United Arab Emirates had arrested Qari Saifullah Akhtar, who was believed to be one of bin Laden's chief advisers and the leader of Harakat ul-Jihad-al-Islami, and extradited him to Pakistan. Akhtar was suspected of having been involved in the plots to assassinate President Musharraf in December 2003.

In the mean time military operations continued in Waziristan, although it was believed that the death of Nek Mohammed had strengthened local resistance to the army campaign. The fighting escalated in September 2004 and officials claimed that, as a result of intensified military pressure, al-Qa'ida fighters were being driven out of the area, possibly leaving for Iraq. In the same month it was announced that police had killed a prominent al-Qa'ida figure, Amjad Hussain Farooq, during a gun battle in Nawabshah, north of Karachi. Farooq was believed to have planned the failed assassination attempts on Musharraf in December 2003 and to have been involved in both the murder of Daniel Pearl and in several bombings in Karachi in 2002. In February 2005 the army announced that it had concluded a peace agreement with five tribal leaders in South Waziristan under which, in exchange for an amnesty, the leaders had pledged that they would not fight the Pakistani army or support Taliban and al-Qa'ida fighters in the area. In the same month, in a move indicative of the improved relations between the two countries, the USA revived the deal that it had suspended in 1990 to supply Pakistan with F-16 fighter aircraft. The agreement constituted part of a US $3,000m., five-year assistance programme. Following the devastating earthquake of October 2005, however, the purchase of the aircraft was postponed, in order that the funds could be allocated instead to the reconstruction effort. Meanwhile, in May it was announced that Abu Faraj al-Libbi, reported to be the operational head of al-Qa'ida in Pakistan, had been captured in the city of Mardan in the NWFP. A further 20 suspected al-Qa'ida operatives were arrested in the following weeks. Al-Libbi was subsequently transferred into US custody for interrogation.

In January 2006 several civilians were killed in a US air-strike on a house in a village near the border with Afghanistan that intelligence sources claimed was being visited by Ayman al-Zawahiri, a leading al-Qa'ida figure. However, it subsequently emerged that Al-Zawahiri had not been present at the house. In March President Bush visited Pakistan, although his one-night stay was overshadowed somewhat by a visit that he had made to India several days previously, during which a landmark nuclear co-operation agreement had been announced. Shortly before his arrival in Pakistan, a suicide bomb attack on the US consulate in Karachi resulted in the deaths of three people, including a US diplomat.

In April 2006 President Musharraf was reported to have acknowledged the increase in extremism in Waziristan and other border areas. In September the signing of a peace accord by the Government and tribal leaders in North Waziristan prompted criticism from international observers for what was seen as a strategy of appeasement: under the terms of the agreement the Government was to downgrade its military presence in the area in exchange for a cessation of rebel offensives against the army and across the border with Afghanistan. In October some 80 people were killed in an army attack on a *madrassa* in the Bajaur region of the FATA bordering Afghanistan; the army's contention that the victims were militants who were using the school as a training facility conflicted with accounts by locals who claimed that they were innocent students. In an apparent act of retaliation, at least 42 army troops were killed in a suicide bombing at an army base in Dargai, NWFP, in November. However, in March 2007 the Government signed a peace agreement with tribal elders in Bajaur under which the latter confirmed that they would not provide refuge to foreign militants, while the Government, on its part, was obliged to consult tribal elders before launching operations in the region. In late March fighting erupted between Uzbek militants in the area and local tribesmen; by the beginning of April it was estimated that the violence had resulted in approximately 200 fatalities. In July Baitullah Mehsud (a militant later accused of involvement in Benazir Bhutto's assassination in December, see above), along with a group of tribal leaders, declared an end to the cease-fire in North Waziristan. Clashes between militants and security forces resulted in many deaths in North and South Waziristan in 2007 and 2008. Accounts of attacks by unmanned US aircraft ('drones') in the FATA and cross-border incursions served to strain relations between Pakistan and the USA, with the former demanding the latter respect its sovereignty. The reportedly high civilian death toll was also perceived to have a counter-productive effect on public sentiment. The new US President, Barack Obama, who took office in January 2009, emphasized his 'commitment to a strong partnership' with Pakistan in February, including an increase in the provision of non-military aid. However, there was no abatement in the frequency of the unpopular US 'drone' attacks in north-west Pakistan in the first few months of 2009, as the USA continued its struggle against the Islamist militants who were based in that area.

Relations with Afghanistan were strained during the 1980s and early 1990s, as rebel Afghan tribesmen (*mujahidin*) used areas inside Pakistan (notably the city of Peshawar) as bases for their activities. In early 1988 there were an estimated 3.2m. Afghan refugees in Pakistan, most of them in the NWFP. The presence of the refugees prompted cross-border attacks against *mujahidin* bases by Soviet and Afghan government troops. In 1988 Pakistan signed the Geneva Accords on the withdrawal of Soviet troops from Afghanistan, which included agreements on the voluntary repatriation of Afghan refugees from Pakistan. Following the withdrawal of Soviet troops from Afghanistan in 1989, Pakistan maintained its support for the guerrillas' cause, while denying accusations by the Afghan Government that it was taking an active military part in the conflict, or that it was acting as a conduit for arms supplies to the *mujahidin*. The Pakistani Government welcomed the overthrow of the Afghan regime by the guerrillas in April 1992 and supported the interim coalition Government that was formed to administer Afghanistan pending the holding of free elections. However, relations between Pakistan and Afghanistan deteriorated in 1994. The turbulence and increasing anti-Pakistan feeling in Afghanistan threatened not only to result in an extension of the violence into the Pakhtoon (Pashtun) areas of the NWFP, but also obstructed the trade route from the Central Asian republics of the former USSR to the Arabian Sea at Karachi. The situation worsened in September 1995 when the Pakistani embassy in Kabul was ransacked and burned down by a mob of about 5,000 Afghans protesting at Pakistan's alleged active support for the Islamist Taliban militia. In the following month the Afghan ambassador to Pakistan was expelled from the country. Following the capture of Kabul by Taliban troops in September 1996 and their assumption of power, the Pakistani Government issued a statement in which it recognized the Taliban militia as the new Afghan Government.

In December 1999 there were signs of distinct changes in Pakistan's policy towards Afghanistan. Following the imposition of UN-mandated sanctions on Afghanistan the previous month for refusing to hand over the terrorist suspect bin Laden, Pakistan appeared to be exerting pressure on the Taliban to accede to Western demands by closing down a number of Afghan banking operations in Pakistan. The Pakistani Government continued to offer financial and diplomatic support to the Taliban, although Gen. Musharraf repeatedly and strongly denied giving military assistance. However, allegations regarding the involvement of Pakistan's special forces in the Taliban campaign grew following the latter's successful offensive in August–September 2000. The Pakistani Government agreed to implement the UN sanctions imposed on Afghanistan in January 2001, but announced that it would attempt to mitigate the effect of the restrictions, warning of a steep increase in refugee numbers and a worsening of the civil war. The failure of (somewhat unconvincing) attempts by senior Pakistani military officers to persuade the Taliban administration to comply with US demands that bin Laden and members of his al-Qa'ida terrorist organization thought to be resident in Afghanistan should be handed over to the US authorities to answer charges of responsibility for the September 2001 terrorist attacks on the US mainland, ultimately resulted in a US-led military campaign to remove the Taliban from power. Despite considerable opposition from ethnic Pashtuns in north-western Pakistan and from elements of the armed forces who had spent years consolidating relations with the Taliban regime (the majority of which was composed of Pashtuns), Musharraf was forced to co-operate with the US-led coalition to avoid potentially devastating economic and political isolation. Long-standing enmity between the Pakistani Government and the tribes of the United Front, arising from Pakistani sponsorship of the Taliban regime, was exacerbated by the participation of Pakistani nationals in the armed resistance to the United Front's renewed military campaign (supported by the international coalition) to recapture Afghanistan (see above). As the United Front continued to make impressive territorial gains in Afghanistan, culminating in the capture of the capital, Kabul, in mid-November, the Pakistani Government announced the closure of all Taliban consular offices in Pakistan, including the embassy in Islamabad. It was hoped that the broad-based ethnicity of the Afghan Interim Administration (which included Pashtun representatives) installed in December would help to foster improved relations between the Pakistani authorities and the tribes of the United Front.

Publicly, Musharraf supported Hamid Karzai and the new Afghan Transitional Administration. However, Afghan officials were convinced that the Pakistani ISI was giving sanctuary to senior Taliban members and other anti-Afghan government military commanders, such as Gulbuddin Hekmatyar. In mid-February 2003 the Pakistani and Afghan military intelligence services held talks in Rome, Italy, in an attempt to resolve deep-rooted differences. Some two months later, during an official visit to Pakistan, President Karzai urged the Pakistani Government to assist in curbing cross-border attacks by militant Islamists. Relations were strained when Pakistan delivered a formal protest to Afghanistan in June over the dumping of the bodies of some 21 Taliban fighters on its territory; the Afghan authorities were forced to recover the bodies after Pakistani border guards discovered that the dead were, in fact, not Pakistani, but Afghan citizens. One month later, in a seemingly well-planned operation, the Pakistani embassy in Afghanistan was stormed and raided by hundreds of Afghans in protest against alleged incursions by Pakistani border troops into Afghan territory. The crowds were dispersed by Afghan police; Karzai apologized for the incident to the Pakistani President and promised to pay compensation. In January 2004 the Pakistani Prime Minister paid his first ever official visit to Afghanistan; the two countries agreed to work together to combat cross-border infiltration. In August Karzai visited Islamabad, where he held talks with Musharraf, who insisted that Taliban and al-Qa'ida militants operating in the NWFP and Balochistan would not be permitted to use the areas as bases from which to disrupt the Afghan presidential election, which was scheduled to take place in October. In March 2005, during a visit by Karzai, who had secured victory in the presidential election, the improvement in bilateral relations was illustrated when the two countries agreed to establish bus services linking Peshawar with the Afghan city of Jalalabad and Quetta with the Afghan city of Qandahar. However, in mid-2005 relations became strained again, when Afghan police apprehended three Pakistani men suspected of having plotted to kill the outgoing US ambassador to Afghanistan. The Afghan Government accused Pakistan of failing to prevent Taliban insurgents hiding in the border regions from perpetrating an increasing number of attacks in its southern and eastern provinces. In response, Musharraf assured Karzai of his continued co-operation in the battle against terrorism. However, questions continued as to the extent of Pakistan's commitment to preventing the resurgence of the Taliban.

In September 2005 additional Pakistani troops were deployed along the border with Afghanistan in order to prevent disruption of the Afghan legislative elections that were to take place in that month. Bilateral relations deteriorated further in 2006 when Karzai gave Musharraf a list of militants believed to be hiding in Pakistan; Musharraf responded by claiming that the Afghan Government's intelligence on the militants was out of date and accused Karzai of being unaware of security issues in his own country. In late 2006 the announcement of Pakistan's plans to lay landmines and construct a series of fences along sections of the Afghan–Pakistani border to prevent insurgents based in Pakistan from launching cross-border raids, while also reducing drugs-smuggling from Afghanistan, elicited a negative response from Karzai, who complained that the strategy (which had originally been proposed by Musharraf in 2005) was divisive. Preparatory work on the fence carried out by Pakistani officials in March 2007 raised further protests from the Afghan Government, which argued that the demarcation of the border was in dispute, but construction continued. Meanwhile, following talks held in Kabul between Karzai and the Pakistani Prime Minister, Shaukat Aziz, in January 2007, the latter announced that the two countries were to establish a *Jirga* Commission, which would be headed by the Pakistani Minister of the Interior and would work towards combating cross-border terrorism (the Commission met for the first time in March). The two leaders also agreed to accelerate the repatriation process for the Afghan refugees remaining in Pakistan. In February 2008 the Pakistani ambassador to Afghanistan was abducted by suspected Taliban militants in the Khyber Agency in Pakistan; he was released unharmed in mid-May. In late February 2009 the new US Secretary of State, Hillary Rodham Clinton, hosted a meeting with the foreign ministers of Pakistan and Afghanistan in Washington, DC, and announced that these trilateral negotiations would be held on a regular basis to discuss mutually strategic issues.

Drought conditions in the region contributed to a new influx of Afghan refugees in early 2001 (there were estimated to be more than 2m. refugees in Pakistan in March), placing renewed strain on limited resources and threatening to exacerbate the country's deteriorating economy and security situation. Military operations by the US-led anti-terrorism coalition in Afghanistan in October resulted in a fresh exodus of refugees. Although Pakistan had officially closed its border with Afghanistan in late September, it was estimated that as many as 80,000 refugees had illegally crossed into Pakistan before the Government approved plans at the end of October to reopen the border to allow the inflow of up to 300,000 of the most vulnerable refugees; the measure constituted part of an agreement with the office of the UN High Commissioner for Refugees (UNHCR) that was to include the establishment of 15 new camps. According to UNHCR, by April 2002 (following the decisive defeat of Taliban forces in most of Afghanistan) repatriation offices in Pakistan were processing the return of as many as 50,000 Afghan refugees each week. At the end of 2002 UNHCR announced that more than 1.5m. Afghan refugees in Pakistan had returned to their homeland, surpassing all expectations; a further 400,000 returned in 2003 and approximately 384,000 in 2004. In early 2005 the Pakistani Government and UNHCR launched a census intended to determine how many Afghan refugees remained in Pakistan, in order to aid the development of policies to assist them. According to reports, between early 2002 and April 2007 more than 3m. refugees had returned to Afghanistan from Pakistan. In early 2009 around 2.1m. registered Afghan refugees were believed to be resident in Pakistan.

Relations with India have dominated Pakistan's foreign policy since the creation of the two states in 1947. Relations deteriorated during the late 1970s and early 1980s, owing to Pakistan's programme to develop nuclear weapons, and as a result of major US weapons deliveries to Pakistan. The other major contentious issue between the two states was the disputed region of Kashmir, where, since 1949, a cease-fire line, known as the Line of Control (LoC), has separated Indian-controlled Kashmir (the state of Jammu and Kashmir) and Pakistani Kashmir, which comprises Azad (Free) Kashmir and the Northern Areas. While Pakistan demanded that the sovereignty of the region be decided in accordance with earlier UN resolutions (which advocated a plebiscite in both parts of the region), India argued that a solution should be reached through bilateral negotiations.

Relations between Pakistan and India reached a crisis in late 1989, when the outlawed Jammu and Kashmir Liberation Front (JKLF) and several other Muslim groups in Indian-controlled Kashmir intensified their campaigns of terrorism, strikes and civil unrest, in support of demands for an independent Kashmir or unification with Pakistan. In response, the Indian Government dispatched troops to Jammu and Kashmir. By early February 1990 it was officially estimated that about 80 people (mostly civilians) had been killed in resulting clashes between troops and protesters. The opposition parties in Pakistan organized nation-wide strikes, to express their sympathy for the Muslims in Jammu and Kashmir, and urged the Government to adopt more active measures regarding the crisis.

In December 1990 discussions were held between the Ministers of External Affairs of Pakistan and India, at which an agreement not to attack each other's nuclear facilities was finalized, but no solution was found to the Kashmiri problem. Further high-level talks held between the two countries during the first half of the 1990s made no progress in resolving the crisis, and skirmishes between Pakistani and Indian troops along the border in Kashmir continued. In December 1994 Pakistan was successful in securing the passage of a resolution condemning reported human rights abuses by Indian security forces in Kashmir at the summit meeting of the Organization of the Islamic Conference held in Casablanca, Morocco. (In the same month Pakistan's decision to close down its consulate in Mumbai (Bombay), amid claims of Indian support for acts of terrorism in Karachi, provided a further indication of the growing rift between the two countries.) In February 1995 (and again in February 1996) Benazir Bhutto's Government organized a nation-wide general strike to express solidarity with the independence movement in Jammu and Kashmir and to protest against alleged atrocities carried out by the Indian forces. In January 1996 relations between the two countries deteriorated when the Pakistani Government accused the Indian forces of having launched a rocket attack on a mosque in Azad Kashmir, which killed 20 people. The Indian authorities claimed that the deaths had been caused by misfired Pakistani rockets. Tensions between Pakistan and India were also exacerbated in early 1996 by allegations that each side was on the verge of conducting nuclear tests. Later that year, India's holding of state assembly elections in Jammu and Kashmir (described as 'farcical' by Benazir Bhutto) and its refusal to sign the CTBT did nothing to encourage an improvement in relations between Islamabad and New Delhi. Despite the resumption in March 1997 of bilateral talks (which had been suspended since 1994), both at official and at ministerial level, little progress was made during the course of the year to ease tension between the two countries.

In April 1998 Pakistan provoked stern condemnation from the recently elected right-wing Government in India following its successful test-firing of a new intermediate-range missile (capable of reaching deep into Indian territory). The arms race escalated dramatically and to potentially dangerous proportions in the following month when India conducted five underground nuclear test explosions. The test programme was condemned world-wide, and the USA imposed economic sanctions against India. The US President, Bill Clinton, and the UN Security Council urged Pakistan to show restraint in not carrying out its own retaliatory test explosions. However, at the end of May Pakistan carried out six underground atomic test explosions. In early June the Pakistani Government ordered a 50% reduction in public expenditure in an attempt to mitigate the effects of the resultant economic sanctions imposed by various foreign countries, including the USA. Immediately after the nuclear tests, India and Pakistan announced self-imposed moratoriums on further testing and engaged themselves in intense diplomatic activity. In September, however, the Pakistani Minister of Foreign Affairs categorically stated that Pakistan would not sign the CTBT until all of the sanctions were lifted and other legitimate concerns addressed.

Indo-Pakistani talks at foreign secretary level regarding Kashmir and other issues were resumed in Islamabad in October 1998. In February 1999 relations appeared to improve considerably when the Indian Prime Minister, Atal Bihari Vajpayee, made an historic journey (inaugurating the first passenger bus service between India and Pakistan) over the border to Lahore. Following his welcome by the Pakistani Prime Minister, the two leaders held a summit meeting (the first to be conducted in Pakistan for 10 years), at the end of which they signed the Lahore Declaration, which, with its pledges regarding peace and nuclear security, seemed designed to allay world-wide fears of a nuclear 'flashpoint' in South Asia. However, the contentious subject of Jammu and Kashmir was largely avoided. Concern over the escalating arms race in South Asia again heightened in April, following a series of ballistic missile tests carried out first by India and subsequently by Pakistan (however, both countries appeared to have adhered to the procedures incorporated in the Lahore Declaration, by informing each other of their test plans well in advance).

In May 1999 the Kashmir conflict intensified to reach what was termed a 'near-war situation' following the reported infiltration of 600–900 well-armed Islamist militants, reinforced by regular Pakistani troops, across the LoC into the area around Kargil in the Indian-held sector of Kashmir. It was widely believed that the incursion of the guerrillas had been planned months in advance by the Pakistani army and intelligence agents; however, the Pakistani Government claimed that it had no direct involvement whatsoever with the Islamist insurgents. In response, the Indian troops launched a series of airstrikes against the militants at the end of the month, a move that represented a serious provocation to Pakistan since it constituted the first peacetime use of air power in Kashmir. Within days tensions were heightened when a militant Kashmiri group claimed responsibility for shooting down an Indian helicopter gunship and Pakistani troops destroyed two Indian fighter aircraft, which had reportedly strayed into Pakistani airspace. Artillery exchanges increased along the LoC (with both sides suffering heavy casualties) and reports of the massing of troops and evacuation of villages along the international border aroused considerable concern. In early July, however, Indian military dominance combined with US diplomatic pressure prompted Nawaz Sharif's precipitate visit to Washington, DC, in the USA for talks with President Clinton. The resultant Washington Declaration effectively ended the Kargil crisis through the Pakistan leader's agreement to the withdrawal of all 'intruders' from Indian-controlled Kashmir. In August there was renewed tension between Pakistan and India when India shot down a Pakistani naval reconnaissance aircraft near Pakistan's border with Gujarat, killing all 16 personnel on board; Pakistan retaliated the following day by opening fire on Indian military aircraft in the same area.

In October–November 1999 there was a notable increase in terrorist incidents in Kashmir, and Indian and Pakistani forces were reported to have resumed skirmishes across the LoC. Relations between the two countries worsened in early November after the success of Vajpayee in promoting an official condemnation of the new Pakistani military regime by the Commonwealth heads of government, following the military coup in Pakistan in mid-October. In December the Indian Government stated that it would not resume dialogue with Pakistan until the latter halted 'cross-border terrorism'.

In late December 1999 the Kashmir conflict came to international attention when five Islamist fundamentalists hijacked an Indian Airlines aircraft and held its passengers captive at Qandahar airport in southern Afghanistan for one week. Among the hijackers' demands was the release from Indian prisons of 36 Muslim militants who supported the Kashmiri separatist movement. Under increasing domestic pressure to prioritize the safety of the hostages, the Indian Government agreed to release three of the prisoners in exchange for the safe return of the captive passengers and crew. Despite Indian accusations of complicity, the Pakistani Government denied any links with the hijackers. In late March 2000 the US President's recent visit to the region appeared to have failed to bring Pakistan and India any closer together when Gen. Musharraf's offer of peace talks regarding Kashmir was firmly rejected by the Indian Government (which still seemed deeply suspicious of the Pakistani Chief Executive). India continued to demand that Pakistan cease 'cross-border terrorism' as a precondition for negotiations, while Pakistan repeatedly denied arming and funding militants.

In mid-August 2000 Pakistan renewed its offer to resume negotiations, despite claims of increased violence on the part of the Indian army against separatists. However, the impasse in relations remained unchanged and there was an escalation of violent incidents in the region. In November the Indian Government declared the suspension of combat operations against Kashmiri militants during the Muslim holy month of Ramadan. The unilateral cease-fire began at the end of November (and was subsequently extended, at intervals, until the end of May); however, Indian security forces were authorized to retaliate if fired upon. The majority of national parties and foreign governments supported the cessation of hostilities, although the Pakistani authorities described the cease-fire as 'meaningless' without simultaneous constructive dialogue. The moderate All-Party Hurriyat Conference in Indian-administered Kashmir welcomed the development and offered to enter negotiations with Pakistani authorities in order to prepare for tripartite discussions. However, the Hizbul Mujahideen and other militant groups in Pakistan-administered Kashmir rejected the offer of talks and continued their campaign of violence, extending their activities as far as the Red Fort in Old Delhi, where three people were shot dead in December. In mid-January 2001 the Indian High Commissioner to Pakistan visited Gen. Musharraf. This meeting signified the first high-level contact since the military coup in Pakistan in 1999. The two officials urged an early resumption of negotiations on the Kashmir question.

Relations with India appeared to improve following the earthquake in Gujarat in January 2001, when Pakistan offered humanitarian relief to India and the leaders of the two countries thus established contact. In May Prime Minister Vajpayee issued an unexpected invitation to Gen. Musharraf to attend bilateral negotiations in Agra in July. However, hopes for a significant breakthrough on the issue of Kashmir were frustrated by the failure of the two leaders to agree to a joint declaration at the conclusion of the dialogue; the divergent views of the two sides on the priority issue in the dispute (cross-border terrorism according to India, and Kashmiri self-determination in the opinion of Pakistan) appeared to be more firmly entrenched than ever. Tension with India was heightened considerably following a guerrilla-style attack on the state assembly building in Srinagar on 1 October. An estimated 38 people (including two of the four assailants) were killed and around 70 were wounded in the attack and in the subsequent confrontation with security forces. The Indian Government attributed responsibility for the attack to the Pakistan-based Jaish-e-Mohammed and Lashkar-e-Taiba groups. Tensions were exacerbated later in the month when Gen. Musharraf rejected official Indian requests to ban the activities of the organizations in Pakistan, although he did publicly condemn the attack.

On 13 December 2001 five armed assailants gained access to the grounds of the Indian union Parliament in New Delhi and attempted to launch an apparent suicide attack on the parliament building. Although no parliamentary deputies were hurt in the attack, nine people were killed and some 25 were injured in the botched assault; the five assailants were also killed in the attack. The Indian authorities again attributed responsibility for the attack to the Jaish-e-Mohammed and Lashkar-e-Taiba groups, and suggested that the assailants appeared to be of Pakistani origin. Pakistan, which had been among the numerous countries to express immediate condemnation of the attack, demanded concrete proof to support the allegations made by the Indian Government, while the US Administration urged the Indian authorities to exercise restraint in their response. Tensions between India and Pakistan continued to mount when Mohammed Afzal, a member of Jaish-e-Mohammed arrested in Kashmir on suspicion of complicity in the incident, admitted his involvement and alleged publicly that Pakistani security and intelligence agencies had provided support to those directly responsible for the attack. India recalled its High Commissioner from Islamabad and announced that overground transport services between the two countries would be suspended from 1 January 2002. As positions were reinforced with troops and weapons (including missiles) on both sides of the LoC, there was considerable international concern that such brinkmanship might propel the two countries (each with nuclear capabilities) into renewed armed conflict. Mindful of the potential detriment to security at Pakistan's border with Afghanistan that could result from escalated conflict in Kashmir, the USA applied increased pressure on the beleaguered Pakistan Government (already facing vociferous domestic opposition to its accommodation of US activities in Afghanistan) to adopt a more conciliatory attitude towards India's security concerns, and in late December the Pakistani authorities followed the US Government's lead in 'freezing' the assets of the two groups held responsible for the attack by India. Although the leaders of the two groups were later detained by the Pakistani authorities (who arrested some 80 suspected militants in the last week of December), the Indian Government continued to dismiss much of the Pakistani response as superficial and demanded that the two leaders be extradited (together with 20 other named Pakistan-based militants) to stand trial in India.

It had been hoped that tensions between the two countries might be defused by renewed dialogue between Vajpayee and Musharraf at a summit meeting of the South Asian Association for Regional Co-operation (SAARC, see p. 397) convened in Nepal in the first week of January 2002, but contacts between the two men were minimal, and troops on both sides of the LoC continued to exchange gunfire in the days following the conference. However, on 12 January Musharraf yielded to relentless international pressure by publicly condemning the activities of militant extremists based in Pakistan and announcing the introduction of a broad range of measures to combat terrorist activity and religious zealotry, including the proscription of five extremist organizations (among them Jaish-e-Mohammed and Lashkar-e-Taiba). However, in mid-May suspected Islamist militants attacked an Indian army camp in Jammu and Kashmir, killing more than 30 people. In response, India expelled Pakistan's High Commissioner from New Delhi. Indo-Pakistani relations deteriorated further following the assassination of Abdul Ghani Lone, the leader of the moderate All-Party Hurriyat Conference on 21 May, by suspected Islamist militants. India accused the Pakistani Government of supporting the extremists. Despite US attempts to calm tensions, artillery fire was exchanged along the LoC. More than 1m. soldiers were mobilized on both sides of the border as the two countries appeared once more to be on the brink of war. Pakistan would not rule out first use of nuclear weapons, and India declared that it would be prepared to go to war if its neighbour refused to halt 'cross-border terrorism'. In mid-June, following intense diplomatic efforts by British and US officials, the threat of conflict appeared to diminish. India lifted its ban on Pakistani commercial aircraft flying over its territory and prepared to appoint a new High Commissioner to Pakistan, in response to Pakistani pledges to halt cross-border infiltration. However, the killing of 27 Hindu civilians by suspected Islamist militants in Jammu in mid-July disrupted attempts to restore diplomatic relations between India and Pakistan, and the Indian Government decided to delay the appointment of a new High Commissioner to Pakistan. Both countries conducted 'routine' ballistic-missile tests in early October. In mid-October the Indian Minister of Defence stated that India would withdraw a large number of troops from the international border with Pakistan; however, the number of troops along the LoC would remain unchanged. Pakistan reciprocated the announcement shortly afterwards. India's gradual removal of troops began in late October; Pakistan responded by withdrawing a portion of its troops in November. President Musharraf dismissed elections in Jammu and Kashmir in September–October as a 'sham' and 'farcical'.

Relations with India deteriorated in early 2003. Tensions were exacerbated by India conducting its latest set of 'routine' ballistic-missile tests without advance warning (Pakistan responded in kind), the violence in Kashmir and India's new military agreement with Russia. Diplomatic relations between Pakistan and India were severed in February amid allegations of espionage and the funding of terrorism. Nevertheless, in mid-April, during a visit to Jammu and Kashmir, Vajpayee offered to enter dialogue with Pakistan; the Pakistani Prime Minister, Zafarullah Khan Jamali, welcomed the decision and formally invited Vajpayee to visit Pakistan. In early May the two neighbours agreed to restore diplomatic relations and civil aviation links. Two months later the bus service between Lahore and New Delhi was renewed. However, India continued to insist on a complete cessation of cross-border infiltration by militant Islamists as a precondition for direct peace talks.

In mid-August 2003 President Musharraf proposed a cease-fire along the LoC, but wanted India to reciprocate by reducing its armed personnel in the Srinagar valley and by ending the alleged atrocities committed by the Indian armed forces. India refused Musharraf's offer and continued to hold Pakistan-based militants responsible for the recent rise in attacks in Jammu and Kashmir. However, in October a series of confidence-building measures (including more transport links) announced by the Indian Government was met with a cautious welcome on the part of Pakistan, and on 23 November Pakistani Prime Minister Jamali announced a unilateral cease-fire along the LoC. India reciprocated the gesture, but reserved the right to fire at so-called 'infiltrators'. At midnight on 25–26 November a cease-fire came into effect. In mid-December the chances of a peace agreement between India and Pakistan improved after Musharraf declared that Pakistan was prepared to cede a long-standing demand for a UN-sponsored plebiscite for the Kashmiri people; India welcomed the initiative. At the same time, Indian and Pakistani officials signed a three-year agreement on the restoration from mid-January 2004 of a passenger and freight train service between New Delhi and Lahore. Direct aviation links were resumed on 1 January 2004. In late December 2003 it was reported that, since the implementation of the cease-fire, separatist-related violence in Jammu and Kashmir had declined. Meanwhile, in November President Musharraf banned six Islamist militant groups (three of which had been banned in 2002 but had re-emerged under different names—see above), closed down their offices and 'froze' their bank accounts.

At the ground-breaking SAARC summit meeting in Islamabad in early January 2004, Musharraf assured Vajpayee that he would not permit any territory under Pakistan's control to be used to support terrorism; in return Vajpayee agreed to begin negotiations on all bilateral issues, including Kashmir, in February. Meanwhile, Islamist militants who were unhappy with what they perceived as a betrayal by Musharraf continued their violent campaign. Indian and Pakistani senior officials opened discussions in Islamabad in mid-February; a timetable for future dialogue was established. In June several rounds of discussions took place between Indian and Pakistani officials in New Delhi. In a joint statement issued at the end of the month, both sides stressed their renewed commitment to reaching a negotiated final settlement on the Kashmir issue and agreed to restore their diplomatic missions to full strength and, in principle, to reopen their respective consulates in Mumbai and Karachi. An agreement was also reached that each country would, in future, notify the other of any forthcoming missile tests. In September Pakistan and India held their first, official, ministerial-level talks in more than three years in New Delhi. As a result, the two sides again agreed to implement a series of confidence-building measures, including the restoration of bilateral transport links.

In November 2004 Pakistan welcomed a move by India to reduce the number of Indian troops deployed in Jammu and Kashmir. Despite the holding of a number of high-level talks in late 2004, tensions between the two countries resurfaced in early 2005 when each side accused the other of violating the cease-fire along the LoC. However, in February, following talks at foreign minister level, the two countries agreed to open a bus service across the LoC, linking Srinagar with Muzaffarabad. Despite militant threats of disruption, and several attacks on the proposed route, the service opened in early April. Plans were also announced to reopen the consulates in Mumbai and Karachi. However, in March India made clear its disapproval of the US decision to supply Pakistan with F-16 fighter aircraft, stating its concerns that the deal would exacerbate security tensions in the region. In mid-April Musharraf travelled to India for the first time since 2001 and met with Manmohan Singh in Delhi for further peace talks; the two leaders subsequently issued a statement referring to the peace process as 'irreversible' and agreeing to improve trade and transport links over the LoC.

In October 2005 the devastating consequences of the massive earthquake centred in Azad Kashmir had significant implications for the ongoing peace process. In the aftermath of the disaster, Pakistan accepted an Indian offer of aid. Following a series of negotiations, the two countries subsequently agreed to open a number of crossing points on the LoC, in order to permit the reunification of divided families. However, continued fears on the part of both countries that the other would take advantage of the situation to conduct military surveillance hampered prospects for more extensive co-operation. Despite speculation that many militants operating in the area had been killed by the earthquake, sporadic separatist violence continued. In February 2006 a second rail link was opened between the two countries, linking the town of Khokrapar in Sindh with the Indian town of Munabao in Rajasthan.

In March 2006 the peace process advanced further when Manmohan Singh proposed, during the launch of a new bus service linking the two countries, that they sign a treaty of friendship, peace and security, a suggestion welcomed by the Pakistani Government. However, the proposal was criticized for separating the resolution of the Kashmir dispute from other issues affecting the bilateral relationship. It was subsequently agreed that trade links would be further developed, as part of efforts to restore normal relations through the improvement of economic and commercial ties. Relations became temporarily strained in the aftermath of the Mumbai train bombings in July, when, despite Musharraf's condemnation of the atrocities, Singh suggested the perpetrators had links to Pakistan. Bilateral peace talks were postponed but the two leaders agreed to resume negotiations in September. In November, during foreign secretary-level talks, the two countries agreed to form an intelligence-sharing panel to combat terrorism; the panel's first meeting took place in Islamabad in March 2007.

The Indian Minister of External Affairs, Pranab Mukherjee, travelled to Pakistan in January 2007 amid relative optimism about the resolution of outstanding issues such as Kashmir; further rounds of talks on the issue were scheduled to be held later that year. The explosions on the Delhi–Lahore Samjhauta Express train in February, which claimed 68 lives, were widely believed to have been a deliberate attempt to sabotage negotiations between Pakistan and India. Fighting across the LoC in late July 2008 threatened to destabilize relations between the two countries, with India accusing Pakistan of the most 'serious violation' of the cease-fire yet. In July a suicide bombing at the Indian embassy in Kabul, Afghanistan, resulted in more than 40 fatalities; the Indian Government intimated that the plot had originated in Pakistan. In the aftermath of the November Mumbai attacks, when more than 170 people were killed in co-ordinated offensives against public targets, including two hotels, a hospital, a railway station and a Jewish centre, the Indian Government suggested that the perpetrators were all from Pakistan. The Pakistani authorities initially issued a denial, but subsequently conceded that the sole gunman captured alive was indeed a Pakistani citizen. Moreover, in February 2009, in an unexpected turnaround, a senior official of the Pakistan Government publicly admitted that the Mumbai attacks had been partly planned in Pakistan and stated that six suspects belonging to Lashkar-e-Taiba had been arrested. The Indian Government described this groundbreaking admission as a 'positive development' and demanded that the suspects be extradited to India; however, Pakistan insisted that any prosecutions be carried out internally.

Relations with Bangladesh deteriorated in September 2000 when, at the UN Millennium Summit meeting in the USA, the Bangladeshi Prime Minister condemned the Pakistani military leadership, ostensibly as part of a general request for the UN to take action against undemocratic changes of government. Gen. Musharraf subsequently cancelled forthcoming meetings with the Prime Minister of Bangladesh. A diplomatic row ensued over who was responsible for the events during Bangladesh's war of liberation, culminating in the withdrawal of the Pakistani Deputy High Commissioner to Bangladesh in November. In July 2002 Pakistani President Pervez Musharraf paid a visit to Bangladesh, during which he expressed regret for the atrocities committed by Pakistani troops during the 1971 war. In February 2006 Prime Minister Khaleda Zia visited Pakistan to hold talks with her Pakistani counterpart, Shaukat Aziz; the latter hailed the visit, during which the two sides signed four memorandums of understanding on trade, agriculture, tourism, and standardization and quality control, as a turning point in bilateral relations.

Pakistan withdrew from the Commonwealth in January 1972, in protest at the United Kingdom's role in the East Pakistan crisis. Pakistan recognized Bangladesh in February 1974, but attempts to rejoin the Commonwealth in the late 1970s and early 1980s were thwarted by India. However, in January 1989 India announced that it would no longer oppose Pakistan's application to rejoin the organization, and in July, during an official visit to the United Kingdom by Benazir Bhutto, Pakistan was formally invited to rejoin the Commonwealth, which it did on 1 October 1989. However, in October 1999 Pakistan was suspended from participation in meetings of the Commonwealth. In September 2003 the CMAG agreed to maintain Pakistan's suspension from participation in meetings, as it was not convinced that democracy had been completely restored in the country. However, in May 2004 the CMAG agreed to restore fully Pakistan's Commonwealth membership, stating that it had decided that the country had consolidated the progress made towards democracy following the October 2002 general election, owing to President Musharraf's statement that he would step down as Chief of Army Staff by the end of 2004 and the subsequent legislative vote of confidence in his leadership. In February 2005 the CMAG criticized Musharraf for reneging on his pledge to become a civilian president and insisted that he must relinquish his military role by 2007. Following Musharraf's imposition of a state of emergency and suspension of the Constitution in November 2007, the CMAG once again suspended Pakistan from participation in meetings. However, full membership was restored in May 2008 as a result of the restoration of democratic government in February.

In early 1992 the Economic Co-operation Organization (ECO, see p. 249), comprising Pakistan, Iran and Turkey, was reactivated, and by the end of the year had been expanded to include Afghanistan, Azerbaijan and the five Central Asian, mainly Muslim, republics of the former USSR; the 'Turkish Republic of Northern Cyprus' joined ECO in 1993. Trade delegations from Turkey and the new republics visited Pakistan, and an agreement for the restoration and construction of highways in Afghanistan, to link Pakistan with these republics, was signed. In 1995 Pakistan, the People's Republic of China, Kazakhstan and Kyrgyzstan signed a transit trade agreement, restoring Pakistan's overland trade route with Central Asia, through China. During a commemorative visit to Pakistan by the Chinese Premier, organized in May 2001 to celebrate 50 years of bilateral relations, the two countries concluded a number of agreements on technical and economic co-operation. Bilateral relations were consolidated and further co-operation agreements were signed during an official visit to China made by Gen. Musharraf in December. Meanwhile, in March Pakistan's Chasma Nuclear Power Plant in Punjab province, which had been built in the 1990s with substantial assistance from the Chinese National Nuclear Corporation, was opened. In early January 2002 it was reported that China had supplied several dozen fighter aircraft and air defence missiles to Pakistan. In November 2002 President Musharraf made another visit to China during which various Sino-Pakistani agreements were concluded, including a US $500m. loan to Pakistan, a trade agreement and an extradition treaty. In May 2004 the two countries signed an agreement to construct a second nuclear power plant at Chasma (scheduled to be completed by 2010). Relations between Pakistan and China were further strengthened by the signing of a Treaty of Friendship, Co-operation and Good-Neighbourly Relations in April 2005 and of a landmark free-trade agreement in November 2006. It was hoped that the latter accord would lead to the tripling of bilateral trade (to around $15,000m. per year) within five years. In April 2008 the Pakistani navy took delivery of the first of four advanced Chinese-constructed frigates that had been ordered in 2005. The new Pakistani President, Asif Ali Zardari, made China the destination of his first official state visit in October, during which it was reported that the two countries agreed to expand their nuclear co-operation. In February 2003, meanwhile, President Musharraf visited Moscow, the first official visit by a Pakistani head of state to the Russian capital in 33 years. In April 2007, during the holding of official talks in Islamabad, the prime ministers of Pakistan and Russia pledged further to strengthen bilateral ties, particularly in the fields of trade and the economy. In March 2009 the two countries agreed to establish a Pakistan-Russia Business Forum.

Government

The President is a constitutional Head of State, who is normally elected for five years by an electoral college, comprising the Federal Legislature and the four provincial assemblies. The former consists of a lower and upper house.

Pakistan comprises four provinces (each with an appointed Governor and provincial government), the federal capital of Islamabad and the Federally Administered Tribal Areas (FATA).

According to the 2002 Legal Framework Order and the 2003 Seventeenth Constitutional Amendment Act, the number of seats in the lower house of the Federal Legislature, called the National Assembly, was increased from 217 to 342, with 272 members directly elected (on the basis of adult suffrage), 60 seats reserved for women and 10 for non-Muslims. The term of the National Assembly was reduced to four years. The size of the upper house, called the Senate, was increased to 100 seats (from 87). The provincial assemblies directly elect 88 members—of whom 16 have to be women and a further 16 technocrats (including *ulema*, Muslim legal scholars)— and the remaining 12 members are elected by the Federally Administered Tribal Areas and federal capital. The term of the Senate is six years, with one-half of the membership being renewed every three years. The Prime Minister is elected by the National Assembly and he/she and the other ministers in the Cabinet are responsible to it. The powers of the President were greatly enhanced by the constitutional amendments (see The Constitution).

The establishment of a National Security Council (NSC) was endorsed in 2004, giving the armed forces a formal, albeit supervisory, role in civilian politics for the first time in Pakistan's history. The NSC was to comprise the President, the Prime Minister, the Chairman of the Senate, the Speaker of the National Assembly, the leader of the parliamentary opposition, the provincial chief ministers and the four armed forces chiefs. The new body was to provide consultation to the elected government on strategic issues. In February 2009 the Government announced that the NSC was to be abolished.

Defence

As assessed at November 2008, the armed forces totalled 617,000: 550,000 in the army, 22,000 in the navy and 45,000 in the air force. Active paramilitary forces numbered up to 304,000 (including a National Guard of 185,000 men). The projected defence budget for 2008 was Rs 296,000m. at the federal level. Military service is voluntary.

Economic Affairs

In 2007, according to estimates by the World Bank, Pakistan's gross national income (GNI), measured at average 2005–07 prices, was US $141,009m., equivalent to $870 per head (or $2,570 per head on an international purchasing-power parity basis). During 2000–07, it was estimated, the population increased at an average annual rate of 2.3%, while gross domestic product (GDP) per head increased, in real terms, by an average of 3.1% per year. Overall GDP increased, in real terms, at an average annual rate of 5.5% in 2000–07. According to the Asian Development Bank (ADB), growth reached 5.8% in 2005/06, 6.8% in 2006/07 and 5.8% in 2007/08.

Agriculture (including forestry and fishing) contributed an estimated 20.4% of GDP in the year ending 30 June 2008. An estimated 43.6% of the employed labour force was engaged in the sector at 30 June 2007. The principal cash crops are cotton (which accounted for around 17.7% of export earnings in 2007/08) and rice; sugar cane, wheat and maize are also major crops. Fishing and leather production provide significant export revenues. During 2000–07 agricultural GDP increased at an average annual rate of 2.5%; according to the ADB, it rose by 6.3% in 2005/06, by 3.7% in 2006/07 and by 1.5% in 2007/08.

Industry (including mining, manufacturing, power and construction) engaged an estimated 21.0% of the employed labour force at 30 June 2007, and provided an estimated 26.6% of GDP in 2007/08. During 2000–07 industrial GDP increased by an average of 7.2% per year. According to the ADB, industrial GDP grew by 4.1% in 2005/06, by 8.0% in 2006/07 and by 4.6% in 2007/08.

Mining and quarrying contributed an estimated 3.1% of GDP in 2007/08, and, according to the ILO, engaged 0.1% of the employed labour force at 30 June 2007. Petroleum and petroleum products are the major mineral exports. Limestone, rock salt, gypsum, silica sand, natural gas and coal are also mined. In addition, Pakistan has reserves of graphite, copper and manganese. The GDP of the mining sector increased at an average annual rate of 7.6% during 1999/2000–2006/07; mining GDP grew by 14.6% in 2006/07, compared with the previous year, and by an estimated 21.8% in 2007/08.

Manufacturing contributed an estimated 19.1% of GDP in 2007/08, and engaged about 13.5% of the employed labour force at 30 June 2007. The most important sectors include the manufacture of textiles, food products, automobiles and electrical goods and also petroleum refineries. During 2000–07 manufacturing GDP increased at an average annual rate of 9.7%; according to official figures, manufacturing GDP rose by 10.0% in 2005/06 and by 8.4% in 2006/07.

Energy is derived principally from natural gas (providing 44.0% of the total electrical energy supply in 2005), hydroelectric power (32.9%) and petroleum (20.3%). Imports of mineral fuels, lubricants, etc. comprised about 30.8% of the cost of total imports in 2007/08.

Services engaged 35.4% of the employed labour force at 30 June 2007, and provided an estimated 53.0% of GDP in 2007/08. The combined GDP of the service sectors increased at an average rate of 6.4% per year in 2000–07. According to the ADB, the GDP of services expanded by 6.5% in 2005/06, by 7.6% in 2006/07 and by 8.2% in 2007/08.

According to the International Monetary Fund (IMF), Pakistan recorded a visible trade deficit of US $10,640m. in 2007 and there was a deficit of $8,295m. on the current account of the balance of payments. Remittances from Pakistanis working abroad declined substantially during the 1990s, and by 2000/01 had levelled off to about $1,087m. The flow of remittances recovered significantly, however, during the 2000s and increased from $4,600m. in 2005/06, to $5,490m. in 2006/07 and to a record $6,451m. in 2007/08. The principal source of imports in 2007/08 was Saudi Arabia (which provided 13.4% of the total), and the principal market for exports was the USA (19.5%). Other major trading partners were the People's Republic of China, the United Arab Emirates, Japan, Kuwait and Germany. The principal exports in 2007/08 were garments and hosiery, cotton fabrics, yarn and thread, and rice. The principal imports were mineral fuels and lubricants, machinery and transport equipment, and chemicals and related products.

For the financial year ending 30 June 2006 there was a budgetary deficit of Rs 173,661m. (equivalent to approximately 2.4% of GDP). For 2006/07 there was an estimated deficit of Rs 140,893m. According to the ADB, Pakistan's total external debt was US $44,467m. at the end of 2008. The cost of debt-servicing in that year was equivalent to 12.3% of earnings from exports of goods and services. During 1996–2006 the average annual rate of inflation was 6.0%; according to the ADB, consumer prices rose by 7.9% in 2005/06, by 7.8% in 2006/07 and by 12.0% in 2007/08. About 5.3% of the labour force was estimated to be unemployed at 30 June 2007.

Pakistan is a member of the South Asian Association for Regional Co-operation (SAARC, see p. 397), of the ADB (see p. 191), of the UN Economic and Social Commission for Asia and the Pacific (ESCAP, see p. 36) and of the Colombo Plan (see p. 425). Pakistan is also a founder member of the Islamic Financial Services Board.

During the 1990s economic growth was constrained by poor investment in manufacturing and inadequate agricultural production, while widespread corruption and inefficient revenue management (particularly in the collection and administration of taxes) undermined attempts to address worsening levels of poverty and deteriorating infrastructure and social services. However, the Musharraf administration that took office in 1999 demonstrated renewed commitment to radical economic reform. In December of that year the IMF agreed to extend a US $1,320m. Poverty Reduction and Growth Facility (PRGF) to Pakistan, in support of a three-year social and economic reform programme, which was implemented during October 2001–September 2004. Despite the economic repercussions of the terrorist attacks on the USA in September 2001, the prolonged drought, and regional and domestic security problems, Pakistan made substantial progress in implementing the programme's crucial objectives, which were: increased potential for economic growth; improved social provisions; and reduced vulnerability to external factors. The economy experienced steady growth, while foreign-exchange reserves increased sharply, owing to an improved trade balance, increased remittances from Pakistanis working abroad and a current-account surplus. Encouraged by the IMF's extension of the PRGF, in December 2001 the 'Paris Club' of creditor governments agreed to reschedule Pakistan's entire bilateral debt stock of $12,500m. In 2003 Pakistan's privatization programme was accelerated. In 2003/04 the Government pledged to use 90% of the proceeds from privatization to pay off some of its foreign debt; the remaining 10% would help to alleviate poverty. In 2005 the Government's privatization programme accelerated significantly, the most significant divestment being the sale of a controlling 26% stake in Pakistan Telecommunications (Pvt) Ltd (PTCL) in June to Dubai-based Emirates Telecommunications. In 2004/05, driven primarily by the manufacturing, financial and agricultural sectors, GDP expanded by 9.0%, its fastest rate of expansion for 20 years. Despite fears that the political strife, domestic and regional security concerns, bureaucratic obstacles, corruption and inadequate infrastructure would continue to deter potential investors, foreign direct investment (FDI) increased substantially in the latter half of the first decade of the 2000s; in 2005/06 FDI more than doubled, compared with the previous year, to reach $3,450m. and rose by a further 45.7% to a total of $5,026m. in 2006/07. However, over the same period levels of foreign debt rose steadily. In early 2007 total external debt reached $38,420m., mainly owing to the inflow of international loans following the 2005 earthquake, and by the end of 2008 the figure had increased to $44,467m. In mid-2008 negotiations on the proposed Iran-Pakistan-India (IPI) gas pipeline were nearing completion; the project was expected to provide much-needed energy in the region, particularly in Pakistan, where an energy crisis was imminent. Meanwhile, the trade gap increased by a massive 57.5%, from $9,711m. in 2006/07 to $15,295m. in 2007/08. Over the same period the current-account deficit rose from 4.8% of GDP to 8.4% of GDP. The economy revealed other signs of weakening in 2007–08, particularly amid the political strife and violence following the assassination of Benazir Bhutto in December 2007. Increases in food prices, continuing energy shortages and poor export figures for textiles and rice—especially significant considering the ongoing global rice shortages—negatively affected GDP growth, which for the year ending 30 June 2009 was projected to reach 2.8%. The threat to Pakistan's economic stability was somewhat alleviated by the implementation of an

PAKISTAN

IMF-supported stabilization programme in November 2008. The programme, with its stringent fiscal and monetary policies, aimed to lower the current-account deficit, strengthen foreign exchange reserves and reduce the burgeoning rate of inflation. However, at the same time, the programme of economic austerity was expected to result in lower rates of growth over the short to medium term. According to the ADB, GDP was projected to increase by only 2.8% in 2008/09.

Education

Universal free primary education is a constitutional right, but education is not compulsory. Primary education begins at five years of age and lasts for five years. Secondary education, beginning at the age of 10, is divided into two stages, of three and four years, respectively. In 2005/06 enrolment at primary schools included 65.6% of children in the relevant age-group (73.5% of boys; 57.3% of girls), while in 2006/07 enrolment at secondary level included an estimated 32.2% of pupils of the relevant age (36.5% of boys; 27.7% of girls). In 2006/07 it was estimated that there were 17,043,000 children enrolled at primary schools (including mosque schools), and 7,820,000 at middle and secondary schools. All institutions, except missions and an increasing number of private schools and universities, are nationalized. There are 120 universities and degree-awarding institutions. Development expenditure on science and technology and education and training in 2001/02 was projected at Rs 4,343.3m. (only 3.3% of the Government's total development spending.)

Public Holidays

2009: 19 January*† (Ashoura), 9 March* (Eid-i-Milad-un-Nabi, Birth of the Prophet), 23 March (Pakistan Day, proclamation of republic in 1956), 1 May (Labour Day), 14 August (Independence Day), 22 August* (Ramadan begins), 6 September (Defence of Pakistan Day), 11 September (Anniversary of Death of Quaid-i-Azam), 20 September* (Id al-Fitr, end of Ramadan), 9 November (Allama Iqbal Day), 27 November* (Id al-Adha, Feast of the Sacrifice), 18 December* (Muharram, Islamic New Year), 25 December (Birthday of Quaid-i-Azam), 27 December*† (Ashoura).

2010: 26 February* (Eid-i-Milad-un-Nabi, Birth of the Prophet), 23 March (Pakistan Day, proclamation of republic in 1956), 1 May (Labour Day), 14 August (Independence Day), 11 August* (Ramadan begins), 6 September (Defence of Pakistan Day), 10 September* (Id al-Fitr, end of Ramadan), 11 September (Anniversary of Death of Quaid-i-Azam), 9 November (Allama Iqbal Day), 16 November* (Id al-Adha, Feast of the Sacrifice), 7 December* (Muharram, Islamic New Year), 16 December* (Ashoura), 25 December (Birthday of Quaid-i-Azam).

* These holidays are dependent on the Islamic lunar calendar and may vary by one or two days from the dates given.

† This festival occurs twice (in the Islamic years AH 1430 and AH 1431) within the same Gregorian year.

Weights and Measures

The metric system has been officially introduced. Also in use are imperial and local weights, including:

1 maund = 82.28 lb (37.32 kg).
1 seer = 2.057 lb (933 grams).
1 tola = 180 grains (11.66 grams).

Statistical Survey

Sources (unless otherwise stated): Federal Bureau of Statistics, 5-SLIC Building, F-6/4, Blue Area, Islamabad; fax (51) 9203233; e-mail statpak@isb.paknet.com.pk; internet www.statpak.gov.pk/depts/index.html; State Bank of Pakistan, Karachi; internet www.sbp.org.pk.

Area and Population

AREA, POPULATION AND DENSITY*

Area (sq km)	796,095†
Population (census results)	
1 March 1981	84,253,644
2 March 1998	
Males	68,873,686
Females	63,478,593
Total	132,352,279
Population (official estimates at 1 January)	
2006	155,360,000
2007	158,170,000
2008	160,970,000
Density (per sq km) at 1 January 2008	202.2

* Excluding data for the disputed territory of Jammu and Kashmir. The Pakistani-held parts of this region are known as Azad ('Free') Kashmir, with an area of 11,639 sq km (4,494 sq miles) and a population of 1,980,000 in 1981, and Northern Areas (including Gilgit and Baltistan), with an area of 72,520 sq km (28,000 sq miles) and a population of 562,000 in 1981. Also excluded are Junagardh and Manavadar. The population figures exclude refugees from Afghanistan (estimated to number 900,000 in late 2007).

† 307,374 sq miles.

ADMINISTRATIVE DIVISIONS
(population at 1998 census)

	Area (sq km)	Population	Density (per sq km)
Provinces:			
Balochistan	347,188	6,565,885	18.9
North-West Frontier Province	74,522	17,743,645	238.1
Punjab	205,345	73,621,290	358.5
Sindh	140,913	30,439,893	216.0
Federally Administered Tribal Areas	27,221	3,176,331	116.7
Federal Capital Territory:			
Islamabad	906	805,235	888.8
Total	**796,095**	**132,352,279**	**166.3**

PRINCIPAL TOWNS
(population at 1998 census)

Karachi	9,339,023	Bahawalpur	408,395
Lahore	5,143,495	Sukkur	335,551
Faisalabad (Lyallpur)	2,008,861	Jhang Maghiana (Jhang Sadar)	293,366
Rawalpindi	1,409,768	Shekhupura	280,263
Multan	1,197,384	Larkana	270,283
Hyderabad	1,166,894	Gujrat	251,792
Gujranwala	1,132,509	Mardan	245,926
Peshawar	982,816	Kasur	245,321
Quetta	565,137	Rahimyar Khan	233,537
Islamabad (capital)	529,180	Sahiwal	208,778
Sargodha	458,440	Okara	201,815
Sialkot	421,502		

Mid-2007 ('000, incl. suburbs, UN estimates): Karachi 12,130; Lahore 6,577; Faisalabad (Lyallpur) 2,617; Rawalpindi 1,858; Multan 1,522; Gujranwala 1,513; Hyderabad 1,459; Peshawar 1,303; Islamabad 780; Quetta 768 (Source: UN, *World Urbanization Prospects: The 2007 Revision*).

PAKISTAN

BIRTHS AND DEATHS
(annual averages, UN estimates)

	1990–95	1995–2000	2000–05
Birth rate (per 1,000)	37.8	34.0	31.7
Death rate (per 1,000)	9.8	8.5	7.6

Source: UN, *World Population Prospects: The 2008 Revision*.

2006 (preliminary): Crude birth rate 26.1 per 1,000; crude death rate 7.1 per 1,000 (Source: Ministry of Finance, *Economic Survey, 2007/08*).

Life expectancy (years at birth, WHO estimates): 62.7 (males 61.9; females 63.5) in 2006 (Source: WHO, *World Health Statistics*).

ECONOMICALLY ACTIVE POPULATION
('000 persons aged 10 years and over, excl. armed forces, at 30 June)

	2005	2006	2007
Agriculture, hunting, forestry and fishing	18,431	20,364	20,780
Mining and quarrying	29	43	52
Manufacturing	5,881	6,499	6,454
Electricity, gas and water	287	308	360
Construction	2,496	2,880	3,127
Wholesale and retail trade, and restaurants and hotels	6,336	6,886	6,872
Transport, storage and communication	2,455	2,697	2,569
Financing, insurance, real estate and business services	453	518	544
Community, social and personal services	6,427	6,739	6,868
Activities not adequately defined	21	18	25
Total employed	42,816	46,952	47,651
Unemployed	3,566	3,103	2,680
Total labour force	46,382	50,055	50,331
Males	38,081	39,974	39,925
Females	8,301	10,081	10,406

Source: ILO.

Health and Welfare

KEY INDICATORS

Total fertility rate (children per woman, 2006)	3.6
Under-5 mortality rate (per 1,000 live births, 2006)	97
HIV/AIDS (% of persons aged 15–49, 2007)	0.1
Physicians (per 1,000 head, 2005)	0.80
Hospital beds (per 1,000 head, 2005)	0.12
Health expenditure (2006): US $ per head (PPP)	51
Health expenditure (2006): % of GDP	2.0
Health expenditure (2006): public (% of total)	16.4
Access to water (% of persons, 2006)	90
Access to sanitation (% of persons, 2006)	58
Human Development Index (2006): ranking	139
Human Development Index (2006): value	0.562

For sources and definitions, see explanatory note on p. vi.

Agriculture

PRINCIPAL CROPS
('000 metric tons)

	2005	2006	2007
Wheat	21,612	21,277	23,520
Rice, paddy	8,321	8,137	8,300*
Barley	92	88	83
Maize	3,110	2,971	3,240*
Millet	221	212	210†
Sorghum	153	180	200*
Potatoes	2,025	1,568	2,622
Sugar cane	44,666	44,666	54,752
Sugar beet	121	93	72†
Beans, dry	130	154	172*
Chick peas	868	480	842

—continued	2005	2006	2007
Groundnuts, with shell	69	59	60†
Sunflower seed	328	348	560*
Rapeseed	347	350	384
Tomatoes	432	468	470†
Cauliflower and broccoli	206	209	209†
Pumpkins, squash and gourds	247	254	255†
Onions, dry	1,765	2,056	2,100†
Carrots and turnips	242	244	250†
Okra	109	112	112†
Watermelons	353	393	395†
Cantaloupes and other melons	236	263	265†
Bananas	163	155	155†
Oranges	1,721	1,721	1,721†
Tangerines, mandarins, clementines and satsumas	639*	639	640†
Lemons and limes	98*	98	99†
Apples	351	350	350†
Apricots	197	190	190†
Peaches and nectarines	70	72	72†
Plums and sloes	60	61	61†
Guavas, mangoes and mangosteens	1,674	2,243	2,250†
Dates	497	507	510†
Pimento and allspice	123	62	130*
Tobacco, unmanufactured	101	113	126

* Unofficial figure.
† FAO estimate.

Aggregate production ('000 metric tons, may include official, semi-official or estimated data): Total cereals 33,508 in 2005, 32,864 in 2006, 35,553 in 2007; Total roots and tubers 2,493 in 2005, 2,048 in 2006, 3,122 in 2007; Total vegetables (incl. melons) 5,042 in 2005, 5,449 in 2006, 5,509 in 2007; Total fruits (excl. melons) 5,236 in 2005, 6,379 in 2006; 6,137 in 2007.

Source: FAO.

LIVESTOCK
('000 head, year ending September)

	2005	2006	2007
Cattle	24,200	25,500	29,600
Buffaloes	26,300	28,400	27,300
Sheep	24,900	25,400	26,500
Goats	56,700	61,900	53,800
Horses	313	339	300
Asses, mules or hinnies	4,450	n.a.	n.a.
Camels	736	738	900
Chickens*	169,000	176,000	182,000
Ducks*	3,500	3,500	3,500

* FAO estimates.

Source: FAO.

LIVESTOCK PRODUCTS
('000 metric tons)

	2005	2006	2007
Cattle meat	465	486	562
Buffalo meat	540	571	551
Sheep meat	162	172	179
Goat meat	370	392	350
Chicken meat	384	463	514
Cows' milk	9,082	9,404	11,000
Buffaloes' milk	19,884	21,136	21,500
Sheep's milk	31	31	31
Goats' milk	675	676	699
Hen eggs	400.0*	425.7†	452.0†
Other poultry eggs†	7.2	7.2	7.2
Wool, greasy	40.7	41.0	41.0†

* Unofficial figure.
† FAO estimate(s).

Source: FAO.

PAKISTAN

Forestry

ROUNDWOOD REMOVALS
('000 cubic metres, excl. bark)

	2005	2006	2007*
Sawlogs, veneer logs and logs for sleepers	1,950	1,961	1,961
Pulpwood	50	50	50
Other industrial wood	820	859	859
Fuel wood	26,500	26,124*	26,353
Total	29,320	28,994	29,223

* FAO estimate(s).
Source: FAO.

SAWNWOOD PRODUCTION
('000 cubic metres, incl. railway sleepers)

	2004	2005	2006
Coniferous (softwood)	420	432	432
Broadleaved (hardwood)	840	856	881
Total	1,260	1,288	1,313

2007: Production assumed to be unchanged from 2005 (FAO estimates).
Source: FAO.

Fishing

('000 metric tons, live weight)

	2004	2005	2006
Capture	479.8	434.5	489.4
Freshwater fishes	93.7	94.6	140.0
Sea catfishes	30.4	26.3	28.7
Croakers and drums	16.9	15.9	14.7
Largehead hairtail	25.6	23.2	23.5
Indian oil sardine	34.3	31.5	31.0
Other clupeoids	19.5	16.4	16.9
Jacks and crevalles	6.0	3.3	4.9
Requiem sharks	18.9	12.3	10.7
Skates, rays and mantas	11.1	9.9	8.9
Aquaculture	76.7*	80.6	121.8
Total catch	556.4*	515.1	611.2

* FAO estimate.
Source: FAO.

Mining

('000 metric tons, unless otherwise indicated)

	2005/06	2006/07	2007/08*
Barite	50	45	50
Chromite	67	107	110
Limestone	18,390	23,053	32,616
Gypsum	601	589	850
Rock salt	1,859	1,865	1,849
Coal	3,857	3,329	4,074
Crude petroleum (million barrels)	24	24	25
Natural gas (million cu ft)	1,400,000	1,413,000	1,454,000

* Provisional.

Industry

SELECTED PRODUCTS
('000 metric tons, unless otherwise indicated, year ending 30 June)

	2005/06	2006/07	2007/08
Cotton cloth (million sq m)	904	978	1,016
Cotton yarn	2,546	2,846	2,915
Refined sugar	2,960	3,527	4,733
Vegetable ghee	1,152	1,180	1,120
Cement	18,564	22,739	26,751
Urea	4,806	4,733	4,925
Superphosphate	161	149	158
Sulphuric acid	94	96	103
Soda ash	319	331	365
Caustic soda	219	242	248
Chlorine gas	18	17	18
Cigarettes ('000 million)	64	66	67
Ammonium nitrate	328	331	344
Nitrophosphate	182	326	330
Pig-iron	768	1,009	993
Paper and paperboard	477	465	443
Tractors (number)	49,439	54,610	53,607
Bicycles ('000)	590	486	536
Motor tyres and tubes ('000)	13,106	17,304	16,617
Bicycle tyres and tubes ('000)	15,491	15,602	13,467
Electric energy (million kWh)	94,030	97,753	n.a.

Finance

CURRENCY AND EXCHANGE RATES

Monetary Units
100 paisa = 1 Pakistani rupee.

Sterling, Dollar and Euro Equivalents (31 December 2008)
£1 sterling = 115.31 rupees;
US $1 = 79.10 rupees;
€1 = 110.08 rupees;
1,000 Pakistani rupees = £8.67 = $12.64 = €9.08.

Average Exchange Rate (Pakistani rupees per US $)
2006 60.271
2007 60.739
2008 70.408

CENTRAL GOVERNMENT BUDGET
(million rupees, year ending 30 June)

Revenue	2005/06	2006/07*	2007/08†
Tax revenue	715,712	839,598	1,030,547
Income and corporate taxes‡	215,500	305,000	388,000
Other direct taxes	9,500	15,619	20,250
Excise duty	56,500	72,000	91,000
Sales tax‡	286,500	311,000	375,000
Taxes on international trade	136,000	134,000	154,000
Other taxes revenue	11,712	1,979	2,297
Non-tax revenue (incl. surcharges)	306,992	374,445	337,592
Total	1,022,704	1,214,043	1,368,139

Expenditure	2005/06	2006/07*	2007/08†
Current expenditure	918,789	1,033,532	1,056,349
General public service	563,673	634,761	881,657
Defence‡	241,062	252,631	275,000
Economic affairs	67,572	91,222	78,941
Development expenditure	153,434	200,616	297,311
Capital expenditure	124,140	130,334	155,373
Total	1,196,364	1,364,482	1,509,032

* Revised estimates.
† Budget estimates.
‡ Exclusively federal.

PAKISTAN

INTERNATIONAL RESERVES
(US $ million, last Thursday of the year)

	2006	2007	2008
Gold*	1,273	1,645	1,709
IMF special drawing rights	216	215	183
Foreign exchange	11,328	13,829	7,011
Total	12,817	15,689	8,903

* Revalued annually, in June, on the basis of London market prices.

Source: IMF, *International Financial Statistics*.

MONEY SUPPLY
(million rupees, last Thursday of the year)

	2005	2006	2007
Currency outside banks	732,011	874,597	1,008,186
Demand deposits at scheduled banks	1,571,500	1,821,017	2,216,451
Total money*	2,306,838	2,700,412	3,229,783

* Including also private-sector deposits at the State Bank.

Source: IMF, *International Financial Statistics*.

COST OF LIVING
(Consumer Price Index; base: 2000/01 = 100; year ending 30 June)

	2005/06	2006/07	2007/08
Food, beverages and tobacco	134.4	148.2	174.4
Clothing and footwear	117.6	123.7	133.8
Rent	132.4	141.2	154.5
Fuel and lighting	137.1	149.4	158.5
All items (incl. others)	131.6	141.9	158.9

Source: Ministry of Finance, *Economic Survey 2007/08*.

NATIONAL ACCOUNTS
(million rupees at current prices, year ending 30 June)

Expenditure on the Gross Domestic Product

	2005/06	2006/07	2007/08*
Government final consumption expenditure	824,300	796,204	926,101
Private final consumption expenditure	5,720,225	6,549,875	8,346,206
Increase in stocks	121,971	139,571	167,651
Gross fixed capital formation	1,565,838	1,857,628	2,090,540
Total domestic expenditure	8,232,334	9,343,278	11,530,498
Exports of goods and services	1,161,257	1,231,025	1,267,078
Less Imports of goods and services	1,770,386	1,851,088	2,319,382
Gross domestic product (GDP) in market prices	7,623,205	8,723,215	10,478,194
GDP at constant 1999/2000 prices	5183,371	5,495,127	5,822,128

* Provisional figures.

Gross Domestic Product by Economic Activity

	2005/06	2006/07	2007/08*
Agriculture, forestry and fishing	1,457,222	1,698,000	2,016,950
Mining and quarrying	219,682	251,725	306,696
Manufacturing	1,370,793	1,566,123	1,892,778
Electricity and gas distribution	153,338	165,154	158,617
Construction	179,885	213,655	277,141
Wholesale and retail trade	1,262,001	1,433,337	1,760,491
Transport, storage and communications	908,409	1,029,582	1,174,090
Banking and insurance	364,320	451,573	582,620
Ownership of dwellings	184,812	206,166	235,838
Public administration and defence	404,628	475,871	577,554
Community, social and personal services	653,437	766,208	923,324
GDP at factor cost	7,158,527	8,257,394	9,906,099
Indirect taxes	569,077	617,104	718,667
Less Subsidies	104,399	151,283	146,572
GDP in market prices	7,623,205	8,723,215	10,478,194

* Provisional figures.

Source: Ministry of Finance, *Economic Survey 2007/08*.

BALANCE OF PAYMENTS
(US $ million)

	2005	2006	2007
Exports of goods f.o.b.	15,432	17,049	18,121
Imports of goods f.o.b.	−21,773	−26,696	−28,761
Trade balance	−6,341	−9,647	−10,640
Exports of services	3,678	3,506	3,758
Imports of services	−7,508	−8,418	−8,764
Balance on goods and services	−10,171	−14,559	−15,646
Other income received	658	864	1,357
Other income paid	−3,172	−3,995	−5,092
Balance on goods, services and income	−12,685	−17,691	−19,381
Current transfers received	9,169	11,030	11,215
Current transfers paid	−90	−89	−129
Current balance	−3,606	−6,750	−8,295
Capital account (net)	202	345	176
Direct investment abroad	−44	−109	−98
Direct investment from abroad	2,201	4,273	5,333
Portfolio investment assets	19	−4	5
Portfolio investment liabilities	906	1,973	2,083
Other investment assets	126	−242	−106
Other investment liabilities	871	1,545	2,791
Net errors and omissions	−200	520	238
Overall balance	475	1,551	2,127

Source: IMF, *International Financial Statistics*.

External Trade

Note: Data exclude trade in military goods.

PRINCIPAL COMMODITIES
(million rupees, year ending 30 June)

Imports c.i.f. (excl. re-imports)	2005/06	2006/07	2007/08
Food and live animals	103,890.2	82,331.1	121,756.6
Mineral fuels, lubricants, etc.	414,113.7	469,508.4	773,199.2
Animal and vegetable oils, fats and waxes	50,332.0	62,400.9	115,459.7
Chemicals and related products	250,349.8	268,607.9	364,136.3
Basic manufactures	200,619.4	206,482.0	238,769.1
Machinery and transport equipment	498,388.5	548,969.3	602,387.0
Total (incl. others)	1,711,158.4	1,851,805.9	2,512,071.7

PAKISTAN

Exports f.o.b. (excl. re-exports)	2005/06	2006/07	2007/08
Rice	69,325.1	68,285.9	117,088.1
Raw cotton	4,079.7	3,047.8	4,426.1
Leather, leather manufactures and dressed furskins	17,504.5	21,640.9	26,026.3
Carpets and rugs	15,248.0	13,923.9	13,295.4
Cotton fabrics, cotton yarn and thread	209,008.2	209,542.5	207,918.5
Petroleum and related products	49,438.4	n.a.	n.a.
Garments and hosiery	226,837.0	230,027.9	236,221.0
Synthetic textiles	11,990.6	n.a.	n.a.
Sports goods	20,560.1	17,482.8	19,012.9
Total (incl. others)	984,840.6	1,029,311.7	1,196,637.6

PRINCIPAL TRADING PARTNERS
(million rupees, year ending 30 June)

Imports c.i.f. (excl. re-imports)	2005/06	2006/07	2007/08
Australia	14,611	17,984	32,589
Belgium	21,137	13,617	14,946
Canada	19,242	29,982	31,297
China, People's Republic	161,991	214,275	294,684
France	20,380	25,399	30,776
Germany	70,424	73,073	79,950
Hong Kong	9,800	11,714	11,797
India	48,072	74,938	106,872
Indonesia	45,379	51,333	73,998
Iran	26,942	24,596	34,654
Italy	31,353	32,977	34,639
Japan	110,175	105,484	114,510
Korea, Republic	36,915	40,699	42,567
Kuwait	101,935	104,850	188,502
Malaysia	42,405	57,319	96,935
Netherlands	14,940	14,894	22,282
Saudi Arabia	179,258	211,751	336,590
Singapore	27,735	29,225	48,764
Switzerland	28,231	19,488	23,475
Thailand	38,924	36,201	37,259
Turkey	11,302	9,283	9,742
United Arab Emirates	203,923	167,907	214,561
United Kingdom	48,194	42,383	48,373
USA	99,220	139,453	153,278
Total (incl. others)	1,711,158	1,851,806	2,512,072

Exports f.o.b. (excl. re-exports)	2005/06	2006/07	2007/08
Afghanistan	63,671	45,686	71,974
Australia	7,362	7,462	8,689
Bangladesh	16,075	15,884	21,501
Belgium	19,266	21,833	25,743
Canada	12,510	12,222	12,347
China, People's Republic	27,773	34,927	43,164
France	20,155	20,988	22,905
Germany	41,142	42,527	51,255
Hong Kong	40,660	39,645	32,595
Italy	35,045	38,794	45,391
Japan	7,668	7,524	8,585
Korea, Republic	11,447	10,556	12,523
Netherlands	23,889	26,799	32,303
Saudi Arabia	19,710	17,530	23,981
Spain	24,876	28,231	33,992
Turkey	18,228	23,645	27,244
United Arab Emirates	78,587	83,990	130,549
United Kingdom	53,530	57,610	64,597
USA	250,990	253,584	232,758
Total (incl. others)	984,841	1,020,312	1,196,638

Source: Ministry of Finance, *Economic Survey, 2007/08*.

Transport

RAILWAYS
(year ending 30 June)

	2005/06	2006/07	2007/08
Passenger journeys ('000)	81,430	83,780	79,980
Passenger-km (million)	25,621	26,446	n.a.
Freight ('000 metric tons)	6,030	6,420	7,230
Net freight ton-km (million)	4,971	5,454	6,187

Source: Ministry of Finance, *Economic Survey, 2007/08*.

ROAD TRAFFIC
('000 vehicles in use, year ending 30 June)

	2005/06*	2006/07	2007/08*
Motorcycles and scooters	3,791.0	4,463.8	4,805.0
Passenger cars	1,999.2	1,682.2	1,811.0
Jeeps	65.7	85.4	92.0
Station wagons	140.8	169.1	182.0
Road tractors	822.3	877.8	945.0
Buses	103.6	108.4	117.0
Taxicabs	122.1	119.1	129.0
Rickshaws	77.8	79.0	85.0
Delivery vans and pick-ups	236.8	253.5	272.0
Trucks and tankers	160.4	182.1	196.0

* Estimates.

Source: Ministry of Finance, *Economic Survey, 2007/08*.

SHIPPING

Merchant Fleet
(displacement at 31 December)

	2005	2006	2007
Number of vessels	53	53	53
Total displacement ('000 grt)	397.6	414.6	349.0

Source: Lloyd's Register-Fairplay, *World Fleet Statistics*.

International Sea-borne Shipping
(port of Karachi, year ending 30 June)

	2005/06	2006/07	2007/08
Goods ('000 long tons):			
loaded	6,697	7,517	11,675
unloaded	25,573	23,329	25,517

Source: Ministry of Finance, *Economic Survey, 2007/08*.

CIVIL AVIATION
(PIA only, domestic and international flights, '000, year ending 30 June)

	2004/05	2005/06	2006/07
Kilometres flown	80,699	87,273	80,302
Passengers carried	5,132	5,828	5,732
Passenger-km ('000)	13,634	15,260	15,124

Source: Ministry of Finance, *Economic Survey, 2007/08*.

Tourism

FOREIGN TOURIST ARRIVALS
('000)

Country of nationality	2005	2006	2007
Afghanistan	77.6	84.9	80.5
Canada	23.0	30.8	36.5
China, People's Republic	29.6	36.4	30.4
Germany	24.7	27.3	23.9
India	59.6	70.2	48.2
Japan	14.1	14.4	11.0
United Kingdom	248.6	275.1	275.5
USA	121.6	126.2	121.9
Total (incl. others)	648.0	897.6	839.5

Receipts from tourism (US $ million, incl. passenger transport): 765 in 2004; 828 in 2005; 899 in 2006.

Source: partly World Tourism Organization.

Communications Media

	2005	2006	2007
Television receivers (number in use)*	7,047,308	7,971,882	9,003,882
Telephones ('000 main lines in use)	5,227.8	5,240.0	4,940.4
Mobile cellular telephones ('000 subscribers)	12,771.2	34,506.6	78,852.9
Internet users ('000)	10,500	12,000	17,500
Broadband subscribers ('000)	44.6	56.6	128.7
Daily newspapers:			
number	438	370	437
average circulation	7,889,639	8,208,874	9,934,951
Other newspapers and periodicals:			
number	1,559	1,094	1,383
average circulation	2,196,295	2,438,008	3,797,835

Radio receivers ('000 in use): 13,500 in 1997.

Facsimile machines ('000 in use): 268 in 1998.

* Estimates as at 30 June; includes Azad Kashmir and Northern Areas.

Sources: partly UNESCO, *Statistical Yearbook*; International Telecommunication Union.

Education

(2007/08, provisional, unless otherwise indicated)

	Institutions	Teachers	Students
Primary*	158,781	444,400	16,970,000
Middle	43,319	335,800	5,640,000
Secondary	25,875	394,800	2,460,000
of which secondary vocational institutes	3,121	14,679	263,000
Higher:			
arts and science colleges	3,592	75,774	983,000
professional	1,329	23,558	377,767
universities/degree-awarding institutes	120	46,893	666,639

* Including mosque schools.

Source: Ministry of Finance, *Economic Survey 2007/08*.

Adult literacy rate (UNESCO estimates): 54.9% (males 68.7%; females 40.2%) in 2007 (Source: UNESCO Institute for Statistics).

Directory

The Constitution

The Constitution was promulgated on 10 April 1973, and amended on a number of subsequent occasions (see Amendments, below). Several provisions were suspended following the imposition of martial law in 1977. The (amended) Constitution was restored on 30 December 1985. The Constitution was placed in abeyance on 15 October 1999 following the overthrow of the Government in a military coup. The Constitution, incorporating a Legal Framework Order, was revived on 15 November 2002.

GENERAL PROVISIONS

The Preamble upholds the principles of democracy, freedom, equality, tolerance and social justice as enunciated by Islam. The rights of religious and other minorities are guaranteed.

The Islamic Republic of Pakistan consists of four provinces—Balochistan, the North-West Frontier Province, Punjab and Sindh—and the tribal areas under federal administration. The provinces are autonomous units.

Fundamental rights are guaranteed and include equality of status (women have equal rights with men), freedom of thought, speech, worship and the press and freedom of assembly and association. No law providing for preventive detention shall be made except to deal with persons acting against the integrity, security or defence of Pakistan. No such law shall authorize the detention of a person for more than one month.

PRESIDENT

The President is Head of State and acts on the advice of the Prime Minister. He is elected by an electoral college, comprising the two chambers of the Federal Legislature and the four Provincial Assemblies, to serve for a term of five years. He must be a Muslim. The President may be impeached for violating the Constitution or gross misconduct.

FEDERAL LEGISLATURE

The Federal Legislature consists of the President, a lower and an upper house. The lower house, called the National Assembly, has 272 members elected directly for a term of five years, on the basis of universal suffrage (for adults over the age of 21 years), plus 60 female members and 10 members representing minorities. The upper house, called the Senate, has 87 members who serve for six years, with one-half retiring every three years. Each Provincial Assembly is to elect 19 Senators. The tribal areas are to return eight members and the remaining three are to be elected from the Federal Capital Territory by members of the Provincial Assemblies.

There shall be two sessions of the National Assembly and Senate each year, with not more than 120 days between the last sitting of a session and the first sitting of the next session.

The role of the Senate in an overwhelming majority of the subjects shall be merely advisory. Disagreeing with any legislation of the National Assembly, it shall have the right to send it back only once for reconsideration. In case of disagreement in other subjects, the Senate and National Assembly shall sit in a joint session to decide the matter by a simple majority.

GOVERNMENT

The Constitution provides that bills may originate in either house, except money bills. The latter must originate in the National Assembly and cannot go to the Senate. A bill must be passed by both houses and then approved by the President, who may return the bill and suggest amendments. In this case, after the bill has been reconsidered and passed, with or without amendment, the President must give his assent to it.

PROVINCIAL GOVERNMENT

In the matter of relations between Federation and Provinces, the Federal Legislature shall have the power to make laws, including laws bearing on extra-territorial affairs, for the whole or any part of Pakistan, while a Provincial Assembly shall be empowered to make laws for that Province or any part of it. Matters in the Federal Legislative List shall be subject to the exclusive authority of the Federal Legislature, while the Federal Legislature and a Provincial Assembly shall have power to legislate with regard to matters referred to in the Concurrent Legislative List. Any matter not referred to in either list may be subject to laws made by a Provincial Assembly alone, and not by the Federal Legislature, although the latter shall have exclusive power to legislate with regard to matters not referred to in either list for those areas in the Federation not included in any Province.

Four provisions seek to ensure the stability of the parliamentary system. First, the Prime Minister shall be elected by the National Assembly and he and the other Ministers shall be responsible to it. Secondly, any resolution calling for the removal of a Prime Minister shall have to name his successor in the same resolution, which shall be adopted by not less than two-thirds of the total number of members of the lower house. The requirement of a two-thirds' majority is to remain in force for 15 years or three electoral terms, whichever is more. Thirdly, the Prime Minister shall have the right to seek dissolution of the legislature at any time even during the pendency of a no-confidence motion. Fourthly, if a no-confidence motion is defeated, such a motion shall not come up before the house for the next six months.

All these provisions for stability shall apply *mutatis mutandis* to the Provincial Assemblies also.

A National Economic Council, to include the Prime Minister and a representative from each province, shall advise the Provincial and Federal Governments.

There shall be a Governor for each Province, appointed by the President, and a Council of Ministers to aid and advise him, with a Chief Minister appointed by the Governor. Each Province has a provincial legislature consisting of the Governor and Provincial Assembly.

The executive authorities of every Province shall be required to ensure that their actions are in compliance with the Federal laws which apply in that Province. The Federation shall be required to consider the interests of each Province in the exercise of its authority in that Province. The Federation shall further be required to afford every Province protection from external aggression and internal disturbance, and to ensure that every Province is governed in accordance with the provisions of the Constitution.

To further safeguard the rights of the smaller provinces, a Council of Common Interests has been created. Comprising the Chief Ministers of the four provinces and four Central Ministers to decide upon specified matters of common interest, the Council is responsible to the Federal Legislature. The constitutional formula gives the net proceeds of excise duty and royalty on gas to the province concerned. The profits on hydroelectric power generated in each province shall go to that province.

OTHER PROVISIONS

Other provisions include the procedure for elections, the setting up of an Advisory Council of Islamic Ideology and an Islamic Research Institute, and the administration of tribal areas.

AMENDMENTS

Amendments to the Constitution shall require a two-thirds' majority in the National Assembly and the Senate.

In 1975 the Constitution (Third Amendment) Bill abolished the provision that a State of Emergency may not be extended beyond six months without the approval of the National Assembly and empowered the Government to detain a person for three months instead of one month.

In July 1977, following the imposition of martial law, several provisions, including all fundamental rights provided for in the Constitution, were suspended.

An amendment of September 1978 provided for separate electoral registers to be drawn up for Muslims and non-Muslims.

In October 1979 a martial law order inserted a clause in the Constitution establishing the supremacy of military courts in trying all offences, criminal and otherwise.

On 26 May 1980 the President issued a Constitution Amendment Order, which amended Article 199, debarring High Courts from making any order relating to the validity of effect of any judgment or sentence passed by a military court or tribunal granting an injunction; from making an order or entering any proceedings in respect of matters under the jurisdiction or cognizance of a military court or tribunal, and from initiating proceedings against the Chief Martial Law Administrator or a Martial Law Administrator.

By another amendment of the Constitution, the Federal Shari'a Court was to replace the Shari'a Benches of the High Courts. The Shari'a Court, on the petition of a citizen or the Government, may decide whether any law or provision of law is contrary to the injunction of Islam as laid down in the Holy Koran and the Sunnah of the Holy Prophet.

In March 1981 the Government promulgated Provisional Constitution Order 1981, whereby provision is made for the appointment of one or more Vice-Presidents, to be appointed by the Chief Martial Law Administrator, and a Federal Advisory Council (*Majlis-i-Shura*) consisting of persons nominated by the President. All political parties not registered with the Election Commission on 13 September 1979 were to be dissolved and their properties made forfeit to the Federal Council. Any party working against the ideology, sovereignty or security of Pakistan may be dissolved by the President.

The proclamation of July 1977, imposing martial law, and subsequent orders amending the Constitution and further martial law regulations shall not be questioned by any court on any grounds.

All Chief Justices and Judges shall take a new oath of office. New High Court benches for the interior of the provinces shall be set up and retired judges are debarred from holding office in Pakistan for two years. The powers of the High Courts shall be limited for suspending the operation of an order for the detention of any person under any law providing for preventative detention, or release of any person on bail, arrested under the same law.

The Advisory Council of Islamic Ideology, which was asked by the Government to suggest procedures for the election and further Islamization of the Constitution, recommended non-party elections, separate electorates, Islamic qualifications for candidates and a federal structure with greater devolution of power by changing the present divisions into provinces.

Under the Wafaqi Mohtasib Order 1982, the President appointed a Wafaqi Mohtasib (Federal Ombudsman) to redress injustice committed by any government agency.

In March 1985 the President, Gen. Zia ul-Haq, promulgated the Revival of the 1973 Constitution Order, which increased the power of the President by amendments such as those establishing a National Security Council, powers to dismiss the Prime Minister, the Cabinet and provincial Chief Ministers, to appoint judicial and military chiefs, and to call elections, and indemnity clauses to ensure the power of the President. The Constitution was then revived with the exception of 28 key provisions relating to treason, subversion, fundamental rights and jurisdiction of the Supreme Court. In October 1985 the Constitution (Eighth Amendment) Bill became law, incorporating most of the provisions of the Revival of the 1973 Constitution Order and indemnifying all actions of the military regime. In December the enactment of the Political Parties (Amendment) Bill allowed political parties to function under stringent conditions (these conditions were eased in 1988). In December Gen. Zia lifted martial law and restored the remainder of the Constitution.

In March 1987 the Constitution (Tenth Amendment) Bill reduced the minimum number of working days of the National Assembly from 160 days to 130 days.

In April 1997 the Constitution (Thirteenth Amendment) Bill repealed the main components of the Eighth Constitutional Amendment, thus divesting the President of the power to appoint and dismiss the Prime Minister and Cabinet, to dissolve the legislature, to order a national referendum, and to appoint provincial Governors, the Chairman of the Joint Chiefs of Staff and the three armed forces chiefs (these functions and appointments were, in future, to be carried out subject to a mandatory advice from the Prime Minister).

In October 1998 the Constitution (Fifteenth Amendment) Bill replaced the country's existing legal code with full *Shari'a*; the bill remained to be ratified by the Senate.

Following the overthrow of the Government in a military coup on 12 October 1999, the Constitution was placed in abeyance on 15 October. On the same day a Provisional Constitution Order was promulgated, according to which executive power was transferred to a National Security Council, under the leadership of a Chief Executive. A federal Cabinet, which was to aid and advise the Chief Executive in the exercise of his functions, was to be appointed by the President on the advice of the Chief Executive. The President was to act on, and in accordance with, the advice of the Chief Executive. The National Assembly, Senate and the Provincial Assemblies were suspended and the Chairman and Deputy Chairman of the Senate ceased to hold office.

PAKISTAN

In July 2000 the Chief Executive issued a decree to revive the Islamic principles of the suspended Constitution and to incorporate them in the Provisional Constitution Order.

On 20 June 2001 the Proclamation of Emergency (Amendment) Order 2001 was promulgated, according to which the Chief Executive assumed the office of President of Pakistan. The National Assembly, Senate and Provincial Assemblies were dissolved with immediate effect. The Speaker and Deputy Speaker of the National Assembly and Provincial Assemblies ceased to hold office with immediate effect. The President later announced that elections to federal and provincial legislatures would be held on 10 October 2002 (see Recent History).

On 21 August 2002 the Legal Framework Order 2002 was promulgated, which sanctioned the President's 29 amendments to the Constitution, including the restoration of Article 58 (2-B), which authorized the President to dissolve the National Assembly (the article was also amended to allow the President to appoint provincial governors in consultation with the Prime Minister), the restoration of Article 243, which gave the President power to appoint the Chairman of the Joint Chiefs of Staff Committee and the three armed forces chiefs and the power to establish the National Security Council to provide consultation to the elected government on strategic matters. Other amendments included the extension of the President's term in office and role as Chief of Army Staff for five years from the date of the election (10 October 2002). The terms of the National Assembly and Senate were to be decreased to four and five years, respectively, and the number of seats in each house to be increased to 342 and 100, respectively. Part III of the Legal Framework Order sanctioned an amendment to Article 71: a Mediation Committee would be established in instances where the Senate disagrees with legislation of the National Assembly, or vice versa. The Mediation Committee would formulate an agreed item of legislation and place it separately before each house for consideration. According to the amendments, the Prime Minister would continue to have the right to seek dissolution of the legislature at any time, but not during the pendency of a no-confidence motion. Ten Orders endorsed by Musharraf since the establishment of military rule were placed in 'Schedule Six', and therefore could not be altered, repealed or amended without the approval of the President. Constitutional protection was thereby awarded to the offices of the National Accountability Bureau and the Governor of the State Bank of Pakistan. Other provisions granted constitutional protection included the lowering of the voting age from 21 to 18 years, the Political Parties' Order, the Local Government Ordinances and the autonomy of the Election Commission. The 1973 Constitution, incorporating the Legal Framework Order, was revived on 15 November 2002.

In late December 2003 the legislature passed the Constitution (Seventeenth Amendment) Bill, comprising several amendments to the 2002 Legal Framework Order (in passing this Bill the legislature also endorsed for the first time the validity of the Legal Framework Order). The Bill allowed the President to remain as Chief of Army Staff until 31 December 2004, when he would have to relinquish his military role. The President also retained the right to dissolve the legislature (on the recommendation of the Prime Minister); the matter would then have to be referred to the Supreme Court within 15 days. The Bill endorsed the lowering of the minimum national voting age to 18 years, and accepted the revised composition of the Senate, National Assembly and provincial assemblies, and clauses relating to political parties.

In April 2004 the legislature approved the National Security Council Bill. This enabled the formation, under the protection of the Constitution, of the National Security Council (NSC), a 13-member council chaired by the President and composed of nine civilian politicians and four members of the military. The Council was to serve as a forum for consultation with the Government on matters of national security. Critics protested that the Bill institutionalized the role of the military in national government. In February 2009 the Government announced that the NSC was to be abolished.

The Government

HEAD OF STATE

President: ASIF ALI ZARDARI (sworn in 9 September 2008).

CABINET
(April 2009)

Following the general election held on 18 February 2008, a coalition Government was formed, comprising members of the Pakistan People's Party (PPP), the Pakistan Muslim League—Nawaz (PML—N), the Awami National Party (ANP) and the Jamiat-e-Ulema-e-Islam—Fazl (JUI—F), along with one independent member of the National Assembly from the Federally Administered Tribal Areas. In May the PML (N) withdrew its ministers from the Cabinet, and in August the party pulled out of the coalition. In late 2008 the Pakistan Muslim League—Functional (PML—F) and the Balochistan National Party—Awami (BNP—A) also had representatives in the coalition.

Prime Minister: YOUSAF RAZA GILANI.
Minister of Commerce: MAKHDOOM AMIN FAHIM (PPP).
Minister of Communications: Dr ARBAB ALAMGIR KHAN (PPP).
Minister of Defence: CHAUDHRY AHMED MUKHTAR (PPP).
Minister of Defence Production: ABDUL QAYYUM KHAN JATOI (PPP).
Minister of Education: Mir HAZAR KHAN BIJARANI (PPP).
Minister of the Environment: HAMEEDULLAH JAN AFRIDI.
Minister of Finance and Revenue, and of Economic Affairs: SHAUKAT TAREEN (Ind.).
Minister of Food and Agriculture: NAZAR MUHAMMAD GONDAL (PPP).
Minister of Foreign Affairs: SHAH MEHMUD QURESHI (PPP).
Minister of Health: Mir AIJAZ HUSSAIN JAKHRANI (PPP).
Minister of Housing and Works: REHMATULLAH KAKAR (JUI—F).
Minister of Human Rights: SYED MUMTAZ ALAM GILLANI (PPP).
Minister of Industries and Production: MANZOOR AHMAD WATTOO (PPP).
Minister of Inter-provincial Co-ordination: RAZA RABBANI (PPP).
Minister of the Interior: REHMAN MALIK (PPP).
Minister of Investment: WAQAR AHMED KHAN (Ind.).
Minister of Kashmir Affairs and Northern Areas (KANA) and of Information and Broadcasting: QAMARUZ ZAMAN KAIRA (PPP).
Minister of Labour and Manpower: SYED KHURSHEED AHMED SHAH (PPP).
Minister of Law and Justice: FAROOQ H. NAIK (PPP).
Minister of Livestock and Dairy Development: HUMAYUN AZIZ KURD (PPP).
Minister of Local Government and Rural Development: Justice (retd) ABDUL RAZZAQ A. THAHIM (PML—F).
Minister of Minorities: SHAHBAZ BHATTI (PPP).
Minister of Narcotics Control: Nawabzada KHAWAJA MUHAMMAD KHAN HOTI (ANP).
Minister of National Security: Maj.-Gen. (retd) MAHMUD ALI DURRANI (Ind.).
Minister of Parliamentary Affairs: Dr ZAHEERUDDIN BABAR AWAN (PPP).
Minister of Planning and Development: MAKHDOOM SHAHABUDDIN (PPP).
Minister of Population Welfare: FIRDOUS ASHIQ AWAN (PPP).
Minister of Postal Services: ISRARULLAH ZEHRI (BNP—A).
Minister of Privatization: SYED NAVEED QAMAR (PPP).
Minister of Railways: Haji GHULAM AHMAD BILOUR (ANP).
Minister of Religious Affairs: SYED HAMID SAEED KAZMI (PPP).
Minister of Social Welfare and Special Education: SAMINA KHALID GHURKI (PPP).
Minister of Special Initiatives: LAL MUHAMMAD KHAN.
Minister of Sports: PIR AFTAB HUSSAIN SHAH JILANI.
Minister of States and Frontier Regions: NAJMUDDIN KHAN (PPP).
Minister of the Textile Industry: RANA MOHAMMAD FAROOQ SAEED KHAN (PPP).
Minister for Tourism: Maulana ATTA-UR-REHMAN.
Minister of Water and Power: RAJA PERVAIZ ASHRAF (PPP).
Minister of Youth Affairs: SHAHID HUSSAIN BHUTTO (PPP).
Minister of Zakat and Ushr: NOOR-UL-HAQ QADRI (Ind.).

MINISTRIES

Office of the President: Aiwan-e-Sadr, Islamabad; tel. (51) 9206060; fax (51) 9208046; internet www.presidentofpakistan.gov.pk.

Office of the Prime Minister's Secretariat: Cabinet Secretariat, Cabinet Division, Islamabad; tel. (51) 925190512; e-mail contact@cabinet.gov.pk; internet www.cabinet.gov.pk.

Ministry of Commerce: Block A, Pakistan Secretariat, Islamabad; tel. (51) 9201816; fax (51) 9205241; e-mail naveed@commerce.gov.pk; internet www.commerce.gov.pk.

PAKISTAN

Ministry of Culture, Minorities, Sports and Youth Affairs: NFCH, 12th Floor, Green Tower, Blue Area, F-6/3, Islamabad; tel. (51) 9206127; fax (51) 9224697; internet www.heritage.gov.pk.

Ministry of Defence: Pakistan Secretariat, No. II, Rawalpindi 46000; tel. (51) 9271107; fax (51) 9271113; e-mail tahir@mod.gov.pk.

Ministry of Education: Block D, Pakistan Secretariat, Islamabad; tel. (51) 9212020; fax (51) 9202851; e-mail pak@yahoo.com; internet www.moe.gov.pk.

Ministry of Environment, Local Government and Rural Development: Block 4, Old Naval Headquarters, Civic Centre, G-6, Melody, Islamabad; tel. (51) 9224291; fax (51) 9202211; e-mail minister@moenv.gov.pk; internet www.moenv.gov.pk.

Ministry of Finance: Block Q, Pakistan Secretariat, Islamabad; tel. (51) 9201941; fax (51) 9202640; e-mail webmaster@finance.gov.pk; internet www.finance.gov.pk.

Ministry of Food, Agriculture and Livestock: Block B, Pakistan Secretariat, Islamabad; tel. (51) 9203307; fax (51) 9210616.

Ministry of Foreign Affairs: Constitution Ave, Islamabad; tel. (51) 9210335; fax (51) 9207600; e-mail sadiq@mofa.gov.pk; internet www.mofa.gov.pk.

Ministry of Health: Block C, Pakistan Secretariat, Islamabad; tel. (51) 9213933; fax (51) 9203944; e-mail minister@health.gov.pk; internet www.health.gov.pk.

Ministry of Housing and Works: Block B, Pakistan Secretariat, Islamabad; tel. (51) 9214121; fax (51) 9209125; e-mail minister@housing.gov.pk; internet www.pha.gov.pk.

Ministry of Industries, Production and Special Initiatives: Block A, Pakistan Secretariat, Islamabad; tel. (51) 9212164; fax (51) 9205130; e-mail info@moip.gov.pk; internet www.moip.gov.pk.

Ministry of Information and Broadcasting: Cyber Wing, 4th Floor, Cabinet Block, Pakistan Secretariat, Islamabad; tel. (51) 9206176; fax (51) 9201350; e-mail webmaster@infopak.gov.pk; internet www.infopak.gov.pk.

Ministry of Information Technology and Telecommunications: 4th Floor, Evacuee Trust Bldg, Aga Khan Rd, F-5/1, Islamabad; tel. (51) 9201990; fax (51) 9205233; e-mail minister@moitt.gov.pk; internet www.moitt.gov.pk.

Ministry of the Interior: Block R, Room 404, Pakistan Secretariat, Islamabad; tel. (51) 9212026; fax (51) 9202624; e-mail info@interior.gov.pk; internet www.interior.gov.pk.

Ministry of Kashmir Affairs and Northern Areas (KANA): Block R, Pakistan Secretariat, Islamabad; tel. (51) 9208442; fax (51) 9207084; e-mail minister@moka.gov.pk; internet www.moka.gov.pk.

Ministry of Labour, Manpower and Overseas Pakistanis: Block B, Pakistan Secretariat, Islamabad; tel. (51) 9210077; fax (51) 9203462.

Ministry of Law, Justice and Human Rights: Block R, Pakistan Secretariat, Islamabad; tel. and fax (51) 9211278.

Ministry of Local Government and Rural Development: Pakistan Secretariat, Islamabad; tel. (51) 9202080; fax (51) 9201165; e-mail minister@lgrd.gov.pk; internet www.lgrd.gov.pk.

Ministry of Petroleum and Natural Resources: 3rd Floor, Block A, Pakistan Secretariat, Islamabad; tel. (51) 9210220; fax (51) 9213180; e-mail minister@mpnr.gov.pk; internet www.mpnr.gov.pk.

Ministry of Planning and Development: Block P, Pakistan Secretariat, Islamabad; tel. (51) 9204926; fax (51) 9202704; internet www.mopd.gov.pk.

Ministry of Population Welfare: Jamil Mohsin Mansion, Civic Centre, G-6, Islamabad 44000; tel. (51) 9207383; fax (51) 9201408; e-mail minister@mopw.gov.pk; internet www.mopw.gov.pk.

Ministry of Privatisation and Investment: 5-A, EAC Bldg, Constitution Ave, Islamabad 44000; tel. (51) 9205146; fax (51) 9203076; e-mail info@privatisation.gov.pk; internet www.privatisation.gov.pk.

Ministry of Railways: Block D, Pakistan Secretariat, Islamabad; tel. (51) 9218515; fax (51) 9210247; e-mail minister@railways.gov.pk; internet www.railways.gov.pk.

Ministry of Religious Affairs, Zakat and Ushr: G-6, Civic Centre, Islamabad; tel. (51) 9214856; fax (51) 9205833; e-mail minister@mra.gov.pk; internet www.mra.gov.pk.

Ministry of Scientific and Technological Research: 4th Floor, Evacuee Trust Complex, Aga Khan Rd, F-5/1, Islamabad; tel. (51) 9208026; fax (51) 9204541; e-mail minister@most.gov.pk; internet www.most.gov.pk.

Ministry of States and Frontier Regions (SAFRON): Islamabad; tel. 9211405; fax 9218772; e-mail minister@safron.gov.pk.

Ministry of the Textiles Industry: 2nd Floor, FBC Bldg, Attaturk Ave, G-5/2, Islamabad; tel. (51) 9212799; fax (51) 9214015; e-mail minister@textile.gov.pk; internet www.textile.gov.pk.

Ministry of Tourism: Green Trust Towers, 7th Floor, Jinnah Ave, Blue Area, Islamabad 44000; tel. (51) 9203772; fax (51) 9207427; e-mail secretary@tourism.gov.pk; internet www.tourism.gov.pk.

Ministry of Water and Power: Block A, 15th Floor, Shaheed-e-Millat, Pakistan Secretariat, Islamabad; tel. (51) 9212442; fax (51) 9224825; e-mail fminister@mowp.gov.pk; internet www.mowp.gov.pk.

Ministry of Women's Development, Social Welfare and Special Education: State Life Bldg, 1st Floor, No. 5, Blue Area, China Chowk, F-6/4, Islamabad; tel. (51) 9206328; fax (51) 9201083; e-mail secretary@moya.gov.pk.

Federal Legislature

SENATE

The Legal Framework Order, promulgated by the President in August 2002, increased the number of seats in the Senate from 87 to 100. Eighty-eight of the members are elected by the four provincial legislatures; eight are chosen by representatives of the Federally Administered Tribal Areas; and four by the federal capital. Its term of office is six years, but one-half of the membership is renewed after three years. The most recent election was held on 6 March 2006.

Chairman: FAROOQ HAMEED NAIK.

Deputy Chairman: JAN MOHAMMAD KHAN JAMALI.

Distribution of Seats, March 2006

	Seats
Pakistan Muslim League (Quaid-e-Azam Group)	38
Muttahida Majlis-e-Amal*	17
Pakistan People's Party Parliamentarians	9
Muttahida Qaumi Movement	6
Pakistan Muslim League (Nawaz Group)	4
Pakistan People's Party (Sherpao Group)	3
Pakhtoonkhwa Milli Awami Party	3
Awami National Party	2
Balochistan National Party (Awami)	1
Balochistan National Party (Maingal)	1
Jamhuri Watan Party	1
Jamiat-e-Ulema-e-Islam (F)	1
National Alliance†	1
Pakistan Muslim League (Functional Pir Pagara Group)	1
Independents	12
Total	**100**

* Coalition comprising Jamaat-e-Islami Pakistan, Jamiat-e-Ulema-e-Pakistan, Jamiat-e-Ulema-e-Islam (S), Jamiat-e-Ulema-e-Islam (F), Islami Tehreek Pakistan and Jamiat Ahl-e-Hadith.
† Coalition comprising the National People's Party, the Millat Party, the Sindh National Front, the Sindh Democratic Alliance and the National Awami Party.

NATIONAL ASSEMBLY

In accordance with the Legal Framework Order (LFO), which was promulgated by the President in August 2002, the number of seats in the National Assembly increased from 217 to 342, with 60 seats reserved for women and 10 for non-Muslims. Also incorporated in the LFO was a reduction in the National Assembly's term of office by one year to four.

Speaker: Dr FEHMIDA MIRZA.

Deputy Speaker: FAISAL KARIM KUNDI.

General Election, 18 February 2008

	Seats
Pakistan People's Party Parliamentarians	87
Pakistan Muslim League (Nawaz Group)	67
Pakistan Muslim League	42
Muttahida Qaumi Movement	19
Awami National Party	10
Muttahida Majlis-e-Amal	5
Pakistan Muslim League (Functional Group)	4
Balochistan National Party (Awami)	1
National People's Party	1
Pakistan People's Party (Sherpao Group)	1
Independents and others	29
Reserved	70
Vacant	6
Total	**342**

PAKISTAN

Provincial Governments
(April 2009)

Pakistan comprises the four provinces of Sindh, Balochistan, Punjab and the North-West Frontier Province, plus the federal capital and Federally Administered Tribal Areas.

BALOCHISTAN
(Capital—Quetta)

Governor: Nawab ZULFIQAR ALI MAGSI.

Chief Minister: Nawab MOHAMMAD ASLAM RAISANI.

Legislative Assembly: 65 seats (Pakistan Muslim League—Quaid-e-Azam Group 20, Pakistan People's Party Parliamentarians 11, Muttahida Majlis-e-Amal 10, Balochistan National Party—Awami 7, Awami National Party 4, National Party 1, independents 10, vacant 2).

NORTH-WEST FRONTIER PROVINCE
(Capital—Peshawar)

Governor: OWAIS AHMED GHANI.

Chief Minister: AMIR HAIDER KHAN HOTI.

Legislative Assembly: 124 seats (Awami National Party 46, Pakistan People's Party Parliamentarians 30, Muttahida Majlis-e-Amal 14, Pakistan Muslim League—Nawaz 9, Pakistan People's Party—Sherpao 7, Pakistan Muslim League—Quaid-e-Azam Group 6, independents 9, vacant 3).

PUNJAB
(Capital—Lahore)

Governor: SALMAN TASEER.

Chief Minister: MUHAMMAD SHAHBAZ SHARIF.

Legislative Assembly: 371 seats (Pakistan Muslim League—Nawaz 165, Pakistan People's Party Parliamentarians 106, Pakistan Muslim League—Quaid-e-Azam Group 86, Pakistan Muslim League—Functional 4, Muttahida Majlis-e-Amal 2, independents 2, vacant or withheld 6).

SINDH
(Capital—Karachi)

Governor: Dr ISHRATUL EBAD KHAN.

Chief Minister: SYED QAIM ALI SHAH.

Legislative Assembly: 168 seats (Pakistan People's Party Parliamentarians 90, Muttahida Qaumi Movement 51, Pakistan Muslim League—Quaid-e-Azam Group 10, Pakistan Muslim League—Functional 9, Awami National Party 2, National People's Party 2, vacant, withheld and others 4).

Election Commission

Election Commission of Pakistan: Secretariat, Election House, Constitution Ave, G-5/2, Islamabad; e-mail info@ecp.gov.pk; internet www.ecp.gov.pk; independent; Chief Election Commr Justice HAMID ALI MIRZA.

Political Organizations

Some 49 parties, issued with election symbols by the Election Commission, contested the general election on 18 February 2008.

All Jammu and Kashmir Muslim Conference: f. 1948; advocates the holding of a free plebiscite in the whole of Kashmir; Leader Sardar ATTIQ AHMED KHAN.

Awami Muslim League (AML): Lav Haveli, Rawalpindi; tel. (51) 5554242; fax (51) 5772708; e-mail info@aml.org.pk; internet www.aml.org.pk; f. 2008; Pres. SHEIKH RASHID AHMED.

Awami National Party (ANP) (People's National Party): Bacha Khan Markaz, Pajagi Rd, Peshawar; tel. (91) 2246851-3; fax (91) 2252406; e-mail info@awaminationalparty.org; internet www.awaminationalparty.org; f. 1986 by the merger of the National Democratic Party, the Awami Tehrik (People's Movement) and the Mazdoor Kissan (Labourers' and Peasants' Party); federalist and nationalist; the Pakhtoonkhawa Qaumi Party merged with the ANP in February 2006, followed by the National Awami Party Pakistan in June of the same year; Pres. ASFANDYAR WALI KHAN.

Awami Qiyadat Party (People's Leadership Party): 88 Race Course Rd, St 3, Rawalpindi Cantt; f. 1995; Chair. Gen. (retd) MIRZA ASLAM BEG.

Balochistan National Party (Awami) (BNP—A): Quetta; Leader SYED EHSAN SHAH; Pres. ISRARULLAH ZEHRI.

Balochistan National Party (Maingal) (BNP—M): Quetta; e-mail bnpwebadmin@balochistan.net; Leader Sardar MOHAMMAD AKHTAR MAINGAL.

Jamaat-e-Islami Pakistan (JIP): Mansoorah, Multan Rd, Lahore 54570; tel. (42) 5419520; fax (42) 5419505; e-mail uroobah@gmail.com; internet www.jamaat.org; f. 1941; seeks the establishment of Islamic order through adherence to teaching of Maulana MAUDUDI, founder of the party; revivalist; right-wing; mem. of Muttahida Majlis-e-Amal (United Action Front); Chair. Amir QAZI HUSSAIN AHMAD; Sec.-Gen. SYED MUNAWAR HASAN; c. 5m. mems (2005).

Jamhuri Watan Party (Bugti) Balochistan: Bugti House, Dera Bugti; Pres. Nawab TALAL AKBAR KHAN BUGTI.

Jamiat-e-Ulema-e-Islam (JUI): Jamia al-Maarf, al-Sharia, Dera Ismail Khan; f. 1950; mem. Muttahida Majlis-e-Amal alliance; advocates adoption of a constitution in accordance with (Sunni) Islamic teachings; split into factions led by Maulana Fazlur Rehman (JUI—F) and Sami ul-Haq (JUI—S).

Jamiat-e-Ulema-e-Pakistan (JUP): Burns Rd, Karachi; f. 1948; mem. Muttahida Majlis-e-Amal alliance; advocates progressive (Sunni) Islamic principles and enforcement of Islamic laws in Pakistan; Pres. Dr ABUL KHAIR MOHAMMAD ZUBAIR (acting); Gen. Sec. QARI ZAWWAR BAHADUR.

Millat Party: 21-E/3, Gulberg III, Lahore; tel. (42) 5757805; fax (42) 5756718; e-mail millat@lhr.comsats.net.pk; advocates 'true federalism'; Chair. FAROOQ AHMAD KHAN LEGHARI.

Muttahida Qaumi Movement (MQM): 494/8 Azizabad, Federal Area B, Karachi; tel. (21) 6313690; fax (21) 6329955; e-mail mqm@mqm.org; internet www.mqm.org; f. 1984 as Mohajir Qaumi Movement; name changed to Muttahida Qaumi Movement in 1997; associated with the All Pakistan Muttahida Students' Organization (f. 1978 as the All Pakistan Mohajir Students' Organization; name changed July 2006); represents the interests of Muslim, Urdu-speaking immigrants (from India) in Pakistan; seeks the designation of Mohajir as fifth nationality (after Sindhi, Punjabi, Pathan and Balochi); aims to abolish the prevailing feudal political system and to establish democracy; Founder and Leader ALTAF HUSSAIN; Pres. AFTAB SHEIKH.

National Party: Faiz Arbab Saryab Rd, Quetta; f. 2003 following merger of Balochistan National Movement and Balochistan National Democratic Party; Chair. Dr ABDUL HAYAI BALOCH.

National People's Party (NPP): 18 Khayaban-e-Shamsheer, Defence Housing Authority, Phase V, Karachi; tel. (21) 5854522; fax (21) 5873753; f. 1986; centre left-wing party advocating a just, democratic welfare state for Pakistan; breakaway faction from PPP; Chair. GHULAM MUSTAFA JATOI; Parl. Leader Dr IBRAHIM KHAN.

Pakhtoonkhwa Milli Awami Party: Leader MEHMOOD KHAN ACHAKZAI.

Pakistan Awami Tehreek (PAT): 365-M Model Town, Lahore; tel. (42) 5169111; fax (42) 5169114; e-mail info@pat.com.pk; internet www.pat.com.pk; Pres. SAHIBZADA MISKEEN FAIZ UR REHMAN KHAN DURANI; Sec.-Gen. Dr ANWAAR AKHTAR.

Pakistan Democratic Party (PDP): f. 1969; advocates democratic and Islamic values; Pres. NAWABZADA MANSOOR AHMED KHAN.

Pakistan Muslim League (PML): PML House, F-7/3, Islamabad; internet www.pakistanmuslimleague.info; f. 2004 following merger of PML Quaid-e-Azam Group, PML (Junejo), PML (Functional), PML (Zia-ul-Haq Shaheed), PML (Jinnah) and the Sindh Democratic Alliance; PML (Functional) subsequently split from party; Pres. CHAUDHRY SHUJAAT HUSSAIN; Sec.-Gen. Sen. MUSHAHID HUSSAIN SYED.

Pakistan Muslim League—Functional (PML—F): Islamabad; merged with PML Quaid-e-Azam Group, PML (Junejo), PML (Zia-ul-Haq Shaheed), PML (Jinnah) and the Sindh Democratic Alliance in 2004 but subsequently split from party; Leader PIR PAGARA.

Pakistan Muslim League—Nawaz (PML—N): House No. 20-H, St 10, F-8/3, Islamabad; tel. (51) 2852662; e-mail pmlisb@hotmail.com; internet www.pmln.org.pk; f. 1993 as faction of Pakistan Muslim League (Junejo); Leader NAWAZ SHARIF; Pres. SHAHBAZ SHARIF; Chair. RAJA ZAFARUL HAQ.

Pakistan People's Party (PPP): 8, St 19, F-8/2, Islamabad; tel. (51) 2255264; fax (51) 228274l; e-mail ppp@comsats.net.pk; internet www.ppp.org.pk; formed Pakistan People's Party Parliamentarians (PPPP) 2002 in order to meet electoral requirements; advocates Islamic socialism, democracy and a non-aligned foreign policy; Leaders BILAWAL BHUTTO ZARDARI, ASIF ALI ZARDARI.

Pakistan People's Party (Shaheed Bhutto Group): 71 Clifton, Karachi; f. 1995 as a breakaway faction of the PPP; Chair. GHINWA BHUTTO; Sec.-Gen. Dr MUBASHIR HASAN.

Punjabi Pakhtoon Ittehad (PPI): f. 1987 to represent the interests of Punjabis and Pakhtoons in Karachi; Pres. MALIK MIR HAZAR KHAN.

Sindh National Front (SNF): Pres. MUMTAZ BHUTTO.

Sindh Taraqi Passand Party (STPP): Leader Dr QADIR MAGSI.

Tehreek-e-Insaf (Movement for Justice): Central Secretariat, H-07, Parliament Lodges, Islamabad; tel. (51) 2270744; fax (51) 2873893; e-mail info@insaf.org.pk; internet www.insaf.org.pk; f. 1996; Leader IMRAN KHAN; Sec.-Gen. A. M. SHAHID ZULFIQAR.

Diplomatic Representation

EMBASSIES AND HIGH COMMISSIONS IN PAKISTAN

Afghanistan: 8, St 90, G-6/3, Islamabad 44000; tel. (51) 2824505; fax (51) 2824504; e-mail contact@islamabad.mfa.gov.af; internet www.islamabad.mfa.gov.af; Ambassador MOHAMMAD ANWAR ANWARZAI.

Algeria: 107, St 9, E-7, POB 1038, Islamabad; tel. (51) 2653793; fax (51) 2820912; Ambassador AHMED BENFLIS.

Argentina: 60, Street 1, F-6/3, POB 1015, Islamabad; tel. (51) 8438120; fax (51) 2825564; e-mail epaki@mrecic.gov.ar; internet www.pakistan.embajada-argentina.gov.ar; Ambassador RODOLFO MARTIN-SARAVIA.

Australia: Diplomatic Enclave 1, Constitution Ave and Isphani Rd, G-5/4, POB 1046, Islamabad; tel. (51) 8355500; fax (51) 2820112; e-mail consular.islm@dfat.gov.au; internet www.pakistan.embassy.gov.au; High Commissioner ZORICA MCCARTHY.

Austria: 13, St 1, F-6/3, POB 1018, Islamabad 44000; tel. (51) 2279237; fax (51) 2828366; e-mail islamabad-ob@bmeia.gv.at; Ambassador Dr MICHAEL STIGELBAUER.

Azerbaijan: House 14, St 87, G-6/3, Atatürk Ave, Islamabad; tel. (51) 2829345; fax (51) 2820898; e-mail azeremb@isb.paknet.com.pk; internet www.azembassy.com.pk; Ambassador Dr EYNULLA YADALLA OGLU MADATLI.

Bahrain: House 5, St 83, G-6/4, Islamabad; tel. (51) 2831060; fax (51) 2206732; Ambassador MOHAMMED EBRAHIM MOHAMMED ABD AL-QADIR.

Bangladesh: 1, St 5, F-6/3, Islamabad; tel. (51) 2279267; fax (51) 2279266; e-mail bdhcisb@dsl.net.pk; internet www.bdhcpk.org; High Commissioner YASMEEN MURSHED.

Belgium: 14, St 17, F-7/2, Islamabad; tel. (51) 2652635; fax (51) 2652631; e-mail islamabad@diplobel.fed.be; internet www.diplomatie.be/islamabad; Ambassador KINT CHRISTIAN-HAUS.

Bosnia and Herzegovina: 195, Street 10, E-7, Islamabad; tel. (51) 2654018; fax (51) 2654017; e-mail ambassador@bosnianembassypakistan.org; internet www.bosnianembassypakistan.org; Ambassador DAMIR DZANKO.

Brazil: 23, Street 19, F-6/2, Islamabad; tel. (51) 2279690; fax (51) 2823034; e-mail brasembp@isb.compol.com; Ambassador CARLOS EDUARDO SETTE CAMARA DA FONSECA COSTA.

Brunei: House 5, St 6, F-6/3, Islamabad; tel. (51) 2879636; fax (51) 2823688; e-mail islamabad.pakistan@mfa.gov.bn; High Commissioner Pehin Dato' Haji Panglima Col (retd) Haji ABDUL JALIL BIN Haji AHMAD.

Bulgaria: Plot No. 6-11, Diplomatic Enclave, Ramna 5, POB 1483, Islamabad; tel. (51) 2279196; fax (51) 2279195; e-mail bul@isd.wol.net.pk; Ambassador ROUMEN PIRONCTHEV.

Canada: Diplomatic Enclave, Sector G-5, POB 1042, Islamabad; tel. (51) 27291007; fax (51) 2279110; e-mail isbad@international.gc.ca; internet www.international.gc.ca/missions/pakistan; High Commissioner RANDOLPH MANK.

China, People's Republic: Ramna 4, Diplomatic Enclave, Islamabad; tel. (51) 2877279; fax (51) 2279600; e-mail chinaemb_pk@mfa.gov.cn; internet pk.china-embassy.org; Ambassador LUO ZHAOHUI.

Cuba: House 37, School Rd, F-6/2, Islamabad; tel. (51) 2824077; fax (51) 2824076; e-mail embacubapakistan@yahoo.com; Ambassador GUSTAVO MACHÍN GÓMEZ.

Czech Republic: 49, St 27, Shalimar F-6/2, POB 1335, Islamabad; tel. (51) 2274304; fax (51) 2825327; e-mail islamabad@embassy.mzv.cz; internet www.mzv.cz/islamabad; Ambassador PAVOL SEPELAK.

Denmark: House No. 16, Street 21, F-6/2, POB 1118, Islamabad; tel. (51) 2824722-; fax (51) 2823483; e-mail isbamb@um.dk; internet www.ambislamabad.um.dk; Ambassador ANDERS C. HOUGAARD HOUGAARS.

Egypt: 38–51, UN Blvd, Diplomatic Enclave, Ramna 5/4, POB 2088, Islamabad; tel. (51) 2209072; fax (51) 2279552; Ambassador MAGDY MAHMOUD HELMY AMER.

Eritrea: 28, St No. 33, F-8/1, Islamabad; tel. (51) 2816131; fax (51) 2816133; Ambassador ABDUL MOHAMED HEGGI.

Finland: House No. 11, St 90, G-6/3, Islamabad; tel. (51) 2828426; fax (51) 2828427; e-mail finnemb@isd.wol.net.pk; Ambassador OSMO LIPONNEN.

France: Diplomatic Enclave 1, Ramna 5, Islamabad; tel. (51) 2011414; fax (51) 2011400; e-mail ambafra@isb.comsats.net.pk; internet www.ambafra-pk.org; Ambassador DANIEL JOUANNEAU.

Germany: Ramna 5, Diplomatic Enclave, POB 1027, Islamabad 44000; tel. (51) 2279430; fax (51) 2279436; e-mail info@isla.diplo.de; internet www.islamabad.diplo.de; Ambassador Dr MICHAEL KOCH.

Greece: 33A, School Rd, F-6/2, Islamabad; tel. (51) 2822558; fax (51) 8358985; e-mail gremb.isl@mfa.gr; internet www.grembpak.mfa.gr; Ambassador PETROS MAVROIDIS.

Holy See: Apostolic Nunciature, St 5, G-5, Diplomatic Enclave 1, POB 1106, Islamabad 44000; tel. (51) 2278218; fax (51) 2820847; e-mail vatipak@dsl.net.pk; Apostolic Nuncio Most Rev. ADOLFO TITO YLLANA (Titular Archbishop of Montecorvino).

Hungary: 12, Margalla Rd, F-6/3, POB 1103, Islamabad; tel. (51) 2823352; fax (51) 2825256; e-mail hungemb@comsats.net.pk; internet www.mfa.gov.hu/emb/islamabad; Ambassador BELA FAZEKAS.

India: G-5, Diplomatic Enclave, Islamabad; tel. (51) 2206950; fax (51) 2823102; e-mail hoc.islamabad@mea.gov.in; internet www.india.org.pk; High Commissioner SHARAT SABHARWAL.

Indonesia: St 5, G-5/4, Diplomatic Enclave 1, POB 1019, Islamabad; tel. (51) 2826390; fax (51) 2832013; e-mail unitkom@kbri-islamabad.go.id; internet www.kbri-islamabad.go.id; Ambassador IBNU PRISPERMANA.

Iran: Plot No. 222, 238, St 2, F-5/1, Islamabad; tel. (51) 2276270; fax (51) 2824839; Ambassador MASHALLAH SHAKERI.

Iraq: 57, St 48, F-8/4, Islamabad; tel. (51) 2253734; fax (51) 2253688; e-mail iraqiya@sat.net.pk; Ambassador KAIS SUBHI AL-YACOUBI.

Italy: 54 Margalla Rd, F-6/3, POB 1008, Islamabad; tel. (51) 2828982; fax (51) 2829026; e-mail segreteria.ambislamabad@esteri.it; internet www.italian-embassy.org.ae/Ambasciata_Islamabad; Ambassador VINCENZO PRATI.

Japan: Plot No. 53-70, Ramna 5/4, Diplomatic Enclave 1, Islamabad 44000; tel. (51) 2279320; fax (51) 2279340; e-mail japanemb@comsats.net.pk; internet www.pk.emb-japan.go.jp; Ambassador CHIHIRO ATSUMI.

Jordan: 99, Main Double Rd, F-10/1, Islamabad; tel. (51) 2297383; fax (51) 2211630; e-mail islamabad@fm.gov.jo; Ambassador SALEH JAWARNEH.

Kazakhstan: House 11, St 45, F-8/1, Islamabad; tel. (51) 2262926; fax (51) 2262806; e-mail embkaz@isb.comsats.net.pk; Ambassador BAKHITBEK SHABARKAYE.

Kenya: 8A, Embassy Rd, F-6/4, POB 2097, Islamabad; tel. (51) 2876024; fax (51) 2876027; e-mail kenreppk@apollo.net.pk; High Commissioner MISHI MASIKA MWATSAHU.

Korea, Democratic People's Republic: House 9, St 18, F-8/2, Islamabad; tel. and fax (51) 2252756; Ambassador RI YONG HWAN.

Korea, Republic: Block 13, St 29, G-5/4, Diplomatic Enclave 2, POB 1087, Islamabad; tel. (51) 2279380; fax (51) 2279411; e-mail emb-pk@mofat.go.kr; internet pak-islamabad.mofat.go.kr/eng/index.jsp; Ambassador SHIN UN.

Kuwait: Plot Nos 1, 2 and 24, University Rd, G-5, Diplomatic Enclave, POB 1030, Islamabad; tel. (51) 2297411; fax (51) 2829487; Ambassador AZIZ RAHIUM ALEDHANI.

Kyrgyzstan: House 163, Street 36, F-10/1, Islamabad; tel. (51) 2212196; fax (51) 2212169; e-mail kyrgyzembassy@dsl.net.pk; Ambassador NURLAN T. AITMURZAYEV.

Lebanon: House 6, Street 27, F-6/2, Islamabad; tel. (51) 2278338; fax (51) 2826410; e-mail lebemb@comsats.net.pk; Ambassador WAFIC MUHAMMAD REHAIME.

Libya: House 736, Margalla Rd, F-10/2, Islamabad; tel. (51) 2214348; fax (51) 2290093; Ambassador IBRAHIM AL-ABID MUKHTAR.

Malaysia: House 34, St 56, F-7/4, Islamabad; tel. (51) 2279570; fax (51) 2824761; e-mail malislamb@kln.gov.my; internet www.kln.gov.my/perwakilan/islamabad; High Commissioner AHMAD SHAHIZAN ABD SAMAD.

Maldives: Islamabad; High Commissioner ADAM HASSAN.

Mauritius: House 13, St 26, F-6/2, POB 1084, Islamabad; tel. (51) 2824657; fax (51) 2824656; e-mail mauripak@dsl.net.pk; High Commissioner ABDOOL RASCHID MEERUN.

Morocco: 6, Gomal Rd, E-7, POB 1179, Islamabad; tel. (51) 2654744; fax (51) 2654741; e-mail sifamapak@morocco-embassy.com.pk; internet www.morocco-embassy.com.pk; Ambassador MOHAMMAD RIDA EL FASSI.

Myanmar: 240, St 51, F-10/4, Islamabad; tel. (51) 2114148; fax (51) 2114149; e-mail embassy_myanmar@yahoo.com; Ambassador U TIN OO.

Nepal: 4, St 21, Atatürk Ave, F-7/2, Islamabad; tel. (51) 2854696; fax (51) 2854722; e-mail nepem@isb.comsats.net.pk; Ambassador BAL BAHADUR KUNWAR.

PAKISTAN

Netherlands: 2nd Floor, PIA Bldg, Blue Area, Islamabad; tel. (51) 2004444; fax (51) 2279512; e-mail isl@minbuza.nl; internet www.mfa.nl/isl-en; Ambassador TJEERD FEICO DE ZWAAN.

Nigeria: 132–135, Diplomatic Enclave 1, Isphani Rd, G-5/4, POB 1075, Islamabad; tel. (51) 2823542; fax (51) 2824104; e-mail nigeria@isb.comsats.net.pk; High Commissioner RIDHWAN A. MUSTAPHA.

Norway: 25, St 19, F-6/2, Islamabad; tel. (51) 2254955; fax (51) 2255074; e-mail emb.islamabad@mfa.no; internet www.norway.org.pk; Ambassador HANNE MELDGAARD.

Oman: 53, St 48, F-8/4, POB 1194, Islamabad; tel. (51) 2254955; fax (51) 2255074; Ambassador MOHAMMAD BIN SAID BIN MOHAMMAD AL-LAWATI.

Philippines: 20C, Collage Rd, F-7/2, Islamabad; tel. (51) 2653661; fax (51) 2655078; e-mail isdpe@isb.comsats.net.pk; Ambassador JAIME J. YAMBAO.

Poland: St 24, G-5/4, Diplomatic Enclave 2, POB 1032, Islamabad; tel. (51) 2600847; fax (51) 2825442; e-mail polemb@dsl.net.pk; internet www.islamabad.polemb.net; Ambassador Dr KRZYSTOF DEBNICKI.

Portugal: 40A, Main Margalla Rd, F-7/2, Islamabad; tel. (51) 2279530; fax (51) 2652492; e-mail portugal@isb.paknet.com.pk; Ambassador Dr ANTONIO JOSÉ M. SANTOS BRAGA.

Qatar: 20, Khayaban-e-Iqbal, F-6/3, Islamabad; tel. (51) 2270833; fax (51) 2270207; e-mail islamabad@mofa.gov.qa; Ambassador HAMAD ALI AL-HENZAB.

Romania: 13, St 88, G-6/3, Islamabad; tel. (51) 2826514; fax (51) 2826515; e-mail romania@isb.comsats.net.pk; Chargé d'affaires a.i. BOGDAN TRIFU.

Russia: Khayaban-e-Suhrawardy, Diplomatic Enclave, Ramna 4, Islamabad; tel. (51) 2278670; fax (51) 2826552; e-mail russia2@comsats.net.pk; internet www.pakistan.mid.ru; Ambassador BUDNIK ANDREY.

Saudi Arabia: 14, Hill Rd, F-6/3, Islamabad; tel. (51) 2600900; fax (51) 2278816; Ambassador ALI S. AWADH ASSERI.

Somalia: 17, St 60, F-8/4, Islamabad; tel. (51) 2854733; fax (51) 2854733; Ambassador AHMED ABDIRAHMAN SHEIKH NUR.

South Africa: House No. 48, Margalla Rd, Khayaban-e-Iqbal, F-8/2, Islamabad; tel. (51) 2262354; fax (51) 2250114; e-mail xhosa@isb.comsats.net.pk; internet www.southafrica.org.pk; High Commissioner DANIEL JABULANI MAVIMBELA.

Spain: St 6, G-5, Diplomatic Enclave 1, POB 1144, Islamabad; tel. (51) 2088777; fax (51) 2088774; e-mail embspain@dsl.net.pk; Ambassador JOSÉ MARÍA ROBLES FRAGA.

Sri Lanka: 315C, Khayaban-e-Iqbal, F-7/2, Islamabad; tel. (51) 2828723; fax (51) 2828751; e-mail srilanka@dsl.net.pk; High Commissioner Dr WIJERATNE BANDARA DORAKUMBURE.

Sudan: 1A, St 32, F-8/1, Islamabad; tel. (51) 2263926; fax (51) 2264404; e-mail sudanipk@isb.compol.com; Ambassador DAFAA ALLAH EL-HAJ ALI.

Sweden: 32, St 3, Margalla Rd, F-6/3, Islamabad; tel. (51) 2828712; fax (51) 2825284; e-mail ambassaden.islamabad@foreign.ministry.se; internet www.swedenabroad.com/Start___28997.aspx; Chargé d'affaires a.i. JÖRGEN LINDSTRÖM.

Switzerland: St 6, G-5/4, Diplomatic Enclave, POB 1073, Islamabad; tel. (51) 2279291; fax (51) 2279286; e-mail isl.vertretung@eda.admin.ch; internet www.eda.admin.ch/islamabad; Ambassador MARKUS PETER.

Syria: 30 Hill Rd, F-6/3, Islamabad; tel. (51) 2279470; fax (51) 2279472; Ambassador Dr RIAD ISMAT.

Tajikistan: House 90, Main Double Rd, F-10/1, Islamabad; tel. (51) 2101254; fax (51) 2299710; e-mail tajemb_islamabad@inbox.ru; Ambassador ZUBAYDULLO ZUUBAYDOV.

Thailand: 10, St 33, F-8/1, Islamabad; tel. (51) 2280909; fax (51) 5837422; e-mail thaiemb@dslplus.net.pk; internet www.mfa.go.th/web/1330.php?depid=231; Ambassador SUKHO PIROMNAM.

Tunisia: 221, St 21, E-7, Islamabad; tel. (51) 2827869; fax (51) 2653564; Ambassador ZOUHEIR DHAOUADI.

Turkey: 58 Atatürk Ave, G-6/3, Islamabad; tel. (51) 2278748; fax (51) 2278752; e-mail turkemb@dsl.net.pk; internet www.turkishembassy.org.pk; Ambassador RAUF ENGIN SOYSAL.

Turkmenistan: House 22A, Nazim-Ud-Din Rd, F-7/1, Islamabad; tel. (51) 2274913; fax (51) 2278790; e-mail turkmen@comsats.net.pk; Ambassador SAPOR BERDINIYAZOV.

Ukraine: 20, St 18, F-6/2, Islamabad; tel. (51) 2274732; fax (51) 2274643; e-mail emb_pk@mfa.gov.ua; Ambassador Dr IHOR PASKO.

United Arab Emirates: Plot No. 1-22, Quaid-e-Azam University Rd, Diplomatic Enclave, POB 1111, Islamabad; tel. (51) 2279052; fax (51) 2279063; e-mail uaeempk@isb.paknet.pk; Ambassador ALI SAIF SULTAN AL-AWANI.

United Kingdom: Diplomatic Enclave, Ramna 5, POB 1122, Islamabad; tel. (51) 2012000; fax (51) 2823439; e-mail bhcmedia@isb.comsats.net.pk; internet www.britainonline.org.pk; High Commissioner ROBERT BRINKLEY.

USA: Diplomatic Enclave, Ramna 5, POB 1048, Islamabad; tel. (51) 2080000; fax (51) 2276427; e-mail webmasterisb@state.gov; internet islamabad.usembassy.gov; Ambassador ANNE WOODS PATTERSON.

Uzbekistan: 2, St 21, E-7, Kaghan Rd, Islamabad; tel. (51) 2821146; fax (51) 2261739; e-mail uzbekemb@isb.comsats.net.pk; internet www.pakistan.mfa.uz; Ambassador OYBEK A. USMANOV.

Vietnam: House 10A, Street 31, F-6/1, Islamabad; tel. (51) 2850581; fax (51) 2850582; Chargé d'affaires a.i. NGUYEN QUANG THUC.

Yemen: 90 Main Double Rd, Sector F-10/2, Islamabad; tel. (51) 2102448; fax (51) 2102417; e-mail yemen22@isb.apollo.net.pk; Ambassador ABDO ALI ABDUL RAHMAN.

Judicial System

A constitutional amendment bill was passed in the National Assembly in October 1998 replacing the country's existing legal code with full Islamic *Shari'a*. However, the bill remained to be approved by the Senate.

SUPREME COURT

Chief Justice: IFTIKHAR CHAUDHRY.
Attorney-General: MALIK MUHAMMAD QAYYUM.

Federal Shari'a Court

Chief Justice: HAZIQ-UL-KHAIRI.
Federal Ombudsman: Justice JAVED SADIQ MALIK.
Federal Tax Ombudsman: Justice MUNIR A. SHEIKH.

Religion

ISLAM

Islam is the state religion. The majority of the population are Sunni Muslims, while estimates of the Shi'a sect vary between 5% and 20% of the population. Only about 0.001% are of the Ahmadi sect.

CHRISTIANITY

About 3% of the population are Christians.

National Council of Churches in Pakistan: 32-B, Shahrah-e-Fatima Jinnah, POB 357, Lahore 54000; tel. (42) 7592167; fax (42) 7569782; e-mail nccp@lhr.comsats.net.pk; internet nccpakistan.pk.org; f. 1949; four mem. bodies, 14 assoc. mems; Gen. Sec. VICTOR AZARIAH.

The Roman Catholic Church

For ecclesiastical purposes, Pakistan comprises two archdioceses, four dioceses and one apostolic prefecture. At 31 December 2007 there were an estimated 1,139,333 adherents in the country.

Bishops' Conference: Pakistan Catholic Bishops' Conference, St 55, F-8/4, Kaghan Rd, Islamabad 44000; tel. (42) 6366137; fax (42) 6368336; e-mail cbcp2000@isb.comsats.net.pk; internet www.pcbcsite.org; f. 1976; Pres. Most Rev. LAWRENCE J. SALDANHA (Archbishop of Lahore); Sec.-Gen. Rt Rev. ANTHONY LOBO (Bishop of Islamabad-Rawalpindi).

Archbishop of Karachi: Most Rev. EVARIST PINTO, St Patrick's Cathedral, Shahrah-e-Iraq, Karachi 74400; tel. (21) 7781533; fax (21) 7781532.

Archbishop of Lahore: Most Rev. LAWRENCE J. SALDANHA, Sacred Heart Cathedral, 1 Mian Mohammad Shafi Rd, POB 909, Lahore 54000; tel. (42) 6366137; fax (42) 6368336; e-mail info@archdioceselahore.org; internet www.archdioceselahore.org.

Protestant Churches

Church of Pakistan: Moderator Rt Rev. Dr ALEXANDER JOHN MALIK (Bishop of Lahore), Bishopsbourne, Cathedral Close, The Mall, Lahore 54000; tel. (42) 7233560; fax (42) 7221270; e-mail bishop_lahore@hotmail.com; f. 1970 by union of the fmr Anglican Church in Pakistan, the United Methodist Church in Pakistan, the United Church in Pakistan (Scots Presbyterians) and the Pakistani Lutheran Church; eight dioceses; c. 700,000 mems (1993); Gen. Sec. HUMPHREY PETERS.

Presbyterian Church of Pakistan: Gujranwala Theological Seminary, Civil Lines, POB 13, Gujranwala; tel. (431) 259512; fax (431) 258314; e-mail kamil65@gjr.paknet.com.pk; f. 1961; c. 340,000 mems

PAKISTAN

(1989); Moderator Rev. Dr ARTHUR JAMES; Sec. Rev. Dr MAGSOOD KAMIL.

Other denominations active in the country include the Associated Reformed Presbyterian Church and the Pakistan Salvation Army.

HINDUISM

Hindus comprise about 1.8% of the population.

BAHÁ'Í FAITH

National Spiritual Assembly: 56, H-8/4, Islamabad; tel. (51) 4444699; fax (51) 4444691; e-mail nsapakistan@cyber.net.pk; internet www.bahai.org; f. 1956; Gen. Sec. Prof. MEHRDAD YOSUF.

The Press

The Urdu press comprises almost 800 newspapers, with *Daily Jang*, *Daily Khabrain*, *Nawa-i-Waqt* and *Jasarat* among the most influential. The daily newspaper with the largest circulation is *Daily Jang*. Although the English-language press reaches only a small percentage of the population, it is influential in political, academic and professional circles. The four main press groups in Pakistan are Jang Publications (the *Daily Jang*, *The News*, the *Daily News* and the weekly *Akhbar-e-Jehan*), the Dawn or Herald Group (the *Dawn*, and the monthly *Herald* and *Spider*), the Khabrain Group (the *Daily Khabrain* and the English language daily *The Post*) and the Nawa-i-Waqt Group (the *Nawa-i-Waqt*, *The Nation* and the weekly *Family*).

PRINCIPAL DAILIES

Islamabad

Al-Akhbar: 44, St 2, I-10/3, Islamabad; tel. (51) 4438862; fax (51) 4438860; e-mail alakabar@dsl.net.pk; Urdu; also publ. in Muzaffarabad; Editor GHULAM AKBAR.

Daily Khabrain: 12 Lawrence Rd, Lahore; tel. (42) 111-55-88-55; fax (42) 6314658; e-mail khabrain@khabrain.com; internet www.khabrain.com; Urdu; Editor and Proprietor ZIA SHAHID.

The Nation: Nawa-i-Waqt House, Zero Point, Islamabad; tel. (51) 2202641; fax (51) 2202645; e-mail editor@nation.com.pk; internet www.nation.com.pk; English; Man. Dir and Editor-in-Chief MAJID NIZAMI; circ. 15,000.

Pakistan Observer: Al-Akbar House, Markaz G-8, Islamabad 44870; tel. (51) 2852027; fax (51) 2262258; e-mail observer@pakobserver.net; internet www.pakobserver.net; f. 1988; English; independent; Editor-in-Chief ZAHID MALIK.

Karachi

Aghaz: 11 Japan Mansion, Preedy St, Sadar, Karachi 74400; tel. (21) 2720228; fax (21) 2722125; e-mail ex101@hotmail.com; f. 1962; evening; Urdu; Chief Editor MOHAMMAD ANWAR FAROOQI; circ. 65,000.

Amn: Deen Muhammad Wafai Rd, opposite NED City Campus, Karachi; tel. (21) 2634451; fax (21) 2634454; e-mail amn@cyber.net.pk; Urdu; Editor AJMAL DEHLVI.

Awami Awaz: 2nd Floor, New Central Block No. 2, Hockey Stadium, Liaquat Barracks, off Shahrah-e-Faisal, Karachi; tel. (21) 5672949; fax (21) 5672946; e-mail awamiawaz@hotmail.com; Man. Editor Dr KHAIR MUHAMMAD JUNO.

Barsat: 246/D-6, PECHS, Karachi; tel. (21) 4535228; fax (21) 4535227; Editor MUHAMMAD SALEEM DAUDPOTA.

Beopar: 205 Alfalah Court, I. I. Chundrigar Rd, Karachi; tel. (21) 2636442; fax (21) 2630784; e-mail beopar@yahoo.com.

Business Daily: 13th Floor, Chapal Plaza, Hasrat Mohani Rd, Karachi; tel. (21) 2429445; fax (21) 2429450; Editor TAUQIR MOHAJIR.

Business Recorder: Recorder House, 53 Business Recorder Rd, Karachi 74550; tel. (21) 2250071; fax (21) 2228644; e-mail ed.khi@br-mail.com; internet www.brecorder.com; f. 1965; English; Editor WAMIQ A. ZUBERI; Editor-in-Chief M. A. ZUBERI.

Daily Awam: Printing House, I. I. Chundrigar Rd, POB 52, Karachi; tel. (21) 2637111; fax (21) 2636066; e-mail awam@awam.com.pk; f. 1994; evening; Urdu; Editor-in-Chief Mir SHAKIL-UR-RAHMAN.

Daily Beopar: 205 Alfalah Court, I. I. Chundrigar Rd, Karachi; tel. (21) 2636442; fax (21) 2630784; Urdu; Man. Editor YOUNUS RIAZ.

Daily Express: 5 Expressway, off Korangi Rd, Karachi; tel. (21) 5800051-6; fax (21) 58000510; Urdu; Editor TAHIR NAJMI.

Daily Intekhab: Liaison Office, 3rd Floor, Mashhoor Mahal Bldg, Kucha Haji Usman, off I. I. Chundrigar Rd, Karachi; tel. (21) 2634518; fax (21) 2631092; e-mail intekhab@comsats.net.pk; Urdu; also publ. from Hub (Balochistan) and Quetta; Man. Editor NARGIS BALOCH; Publr and Exec. Editor ANWAR SAJIDI.

Directory

Daily Jang: HQ Printing House, I. I. Chundrigar Rd, POB 52, Karachi; tel. (21) 2637111; fax (21) 2636066; e-mail jangkarachi@janggroup.com.pk; internet www.jang.com.pk; f. 1940; morning; Urdu; also publ. in Quetta, Rawalpindi, Lahore and London; Editor-in-Chief Mir SHAKIL-UR-RAHMAN; combined circ. 750,000.

Daily Khabar: A-8 Sheraton Centre, F. B. Area, Karachi; tel. (21) 210059; Urdu; Exec. Editor FAROOQ PARACHA; Editor and Publr SAEED ALI HAMEED.

Daily Mohasaba: Imperial Hotel, M. T. Khan Rd, Karachi; tel. (21) 519448; Urdu; Editor TALIB TURABI.

Daily Naya Akhbar: Zia Shahid Printer and Publisher, Muzammil Press, 1301, Mehmoodabad No. 6, Masjid-e-Awais Qarni, Block 7, Karachi; tel. (21) 111-55-88-55; fax (21) 5382271; CEO ZIA SHAHID; Editor AMTNAN SHAHID.

Daily News: Al-Rahman Bldg, I. I. Chundrigar Rd, Karachi; tel. (21) 2637111; fax (21) 2634395; e-mail dailynews@janggroup.com.pk; f. 1962; evening; English; Editor S. M. FAZAL; circ. 50,000.

Daily Public: Falak Printing Press, 191 Altaf Hussain Rd, New Challi, Karachi; tel. (21) 5687522; Man. Editor INQUILAB MATRI; Editor ANWAR SANROY.

Daily Sindh Sujag: Suite 414, 6th Floor, Amber Medical Centre, M. A. Jinnah Rd, Karachi; tel. (21) 2700252; fax (21) 2700249; e-mail sindhsujag786@yahoo.com; Sindhi; political; Editor NASIR DAD BALOCH.

Daily Special: Ahbab Printers, Beauty House, nr Regal Chowk, Abdullah Haroon Rd, Sadar, Karachi; tel. (21) 7771655; fax (21) 7722776; Urdu; Editor MOHAMMAD AT-TAYYAB.

Daily Times: Plot No. SR 5/12/1, 2nd Floor, Nelson Chamber, I. I. Chundrigar Rd, Karachi; tel. (21) 2213822; fax (21) 2213874; e-mail yousaf@dailytimes.com.pk; internet www.dailytimes.com.pk; Resident Editor YOUSAF RAFIQ.

Dawn: Haroon House, Dr Ziauddin Ahmed Rd, POB 3740, Karachi 74200; tel. (21) 111444777; fax (21) 5683801; e-mail editor@dawn.com; internet www.dawn.com; f. 1947; English; also publ. from Islamabad, Rawalpindi and Lahore; Chief Exec. HAMEED HAROON; Editor ABBAS NASIR; circ. 110,000 (weekdays), 125,000 (Sundays).

Deyanet: 4th Floor, Al Warid Centre, off I. I. Chundrigar Rd, Karachi; tel. (21) 2631556; fax (21) 2631888; Urdu; also publ. in Sukkur and Islamabad; Editor NAJMUDDIN SHAIKH.

The Finance: 903–905 Uni Towers, I. I. Chundrigar Rd, Karachi; tel. (21) 2411665; fax (21) 2422560; e-mail tfinance@super.net.pk; English; Chief Editor S. H. SHAH.

Financial Daily: 11-C, Jami Commercial St No. 11, Phase VII, DHA, Karachi; tel. (21) 5311893-5; e-mail info@thefinancialdaily.com; internet thefinancialdaily.com; publ. by Data Research & Communications.

Financial Post: Bldg No. 106/C, 11 Commercial St, Phase II, Extension, Defence Housing Authority, Karachi; tel. (21) 5381626; fax (21) 5802760; e-mail fpost@gerrys.net; internet www.dailyfpost.com; f. 1994; English; Chief Editor and CEO QUDSIA K. KHAN; Publr WAJID JAWAD.

Hilal-e-Pakistan: Court View Bldg, 2nd Floor, M. A. Jinnah Rd, POB 3737, Karachi 74200; tel. (21) 2624997; fax (21) 2624996; Sindhi; Editor MOHAMMAD IQBAL DAL.

Jago: Karachi; tel. (21) 2635544; fax (21) 2628137; f. 1990; Sindhi; political; Editor AGHA SALEEM.

Janbaz: 9th Floor, Uni Tower, I. I. Chundrigar Rd, Karachi; tel. (21) 2411665; fax (21) 2422560; Editor ALI AKHBAR RIZVI.

Jasarat: 3rd Floor, Syed House, I. I. Chundrigar Rd, Karachi 74200; tel. (21) 2630391; fax (21) 2629344; e-mail jasarat@cyber.net.pk; f. 1970; Urdu; Editor ATHAR HASHMI; circ. 50,000.

Jurat: Jurat House, off I. I. Chundrigar Rd, Karachi; tel. (21) 2637641-4; fax (21) 2637640; Editor MUKHTAR AAQIL.

The Leader: Block 5, 609, Clifton Centre, Clifton, Karachi 75600; tel. (21) 5820801; fax (21) 5872206; e-mail info@theleader.com.pk; f. 1958; English; independent; Man. Editor MUNIR M. LADHA; circ. 7,000.

Mazdur: Spencer Bldg, I. I. Chundrigar Rd, Karachi 2; f. 1984; Urdu; Editor MOHAMMAD ANWAR BIN ABBAS.

Millat: 3rd Floor, Saify Market, Shahrah-e-Liaquat, New Challi, Karachi; tel. (21) 2219022; fax (21) 2211764; e-mail editor@millat.com; internet www.millat.com; f. 1946; Gujarati; independent; Editor INQUILAB MATRI; circ. 22,550.

Mohasib: Karachi; fax (21) 2632763; Urdu; also publ. from Abbotabad; Chief Editor ZAFAR MAJAZI; Editor NAEEM AHMAD.

The Nation: Block-I, Hockey Stadium, off Khayaban-e-Shamsher, Phase V, Defence Housing Authority, Karachi; tel. (21) 5846622; fax (21) 5848892; e-mail editor@nation.com.pk; internet www.nation.com.pk; English; Editor ARIF NIZAMI.

The News International: Al-Rahman Bldg, I. I. Chundrigar Rd, POB 52, Karachi; tel. (21) 2630611; fax (21) 2418343; e-mail

PAKISTAN

thenewskarachi@thenews.com.pk; f. 1990; English; also publ. from Lahore and Rawalpindi/Islamabad; Editor-in-Chief Mir SHAKIL-UR-RAHMAN; Editor TALAT ASLAM.

Qaumi Akhbar: 14 Ramzan Mansion, Dr Bilmoria St, off I. I. Chundrigar Rd, Karachi; tel. (21) 2633381; fax (21) 2635774; f. 1988; Urdu; offices in Islamabad; Editor ILYAS SHAKIR.

Savera: 108 Adam Arcade, Shaheed-e-Millat Rd, Karachi; tel. (21) 419616; Urdu; Editor RUKHSANA SAHAM MIRZA.

Sindh Tribune: No. 246-D/6, PECHS, Karachi; tel. (21) 4535227; fax (21) 4432680; English; political; Editor YOUSUF SHAHEEN.

The Times of Karachi: Al-Falah Chambers, 9th Floor, Abdullah Haroon Rd, Karachi; tel. (21) 7727740; e-mail iqbalmir@yahoo.com; evening; English; independent; city news; Editor Mir IQBAL AZIZ.

Ummat: Room Nos 1–3, VIP Block IV, Hockey Club of Pakistan Stadium, Liaquat Barracks, Karachi; tel. (21) 5655270; fax (21) 5655275; Editor NASEER HASHMI.

Lahore

Daily Pakistan: 41 Jail Rd, Lahore; tel. (42) 7576301; fax (42) 7586251; f. 1990; Urdu; Chief Editor MUJIBUR RAHMAN SHAMI.

Daily Times: Media Times (Pvt) Ltd, 41-N, Industrial Area, Gulberg II, Lahore; tel. (42) 5878614; fax (42) 5878620; e-mail editor@dailytimes.com.pk; internet www.dailytimes.com.pk; Editor NAJAM SETHI.

Daily Wifaq: 6A Warris Rd, Lahore; tel. (42) 6367467; e-mail wifaqtimes@yahoo.com; Urdu; also publ. in Rawalpindi, Sargodha and Rahimyar Khan; Editor MUTAHHIR WAQAR; circ. 50,000.

Mahgribi Pakistan: Lahore; tel. (42) 53490; Urdu; also publ. in Bahawalpur and Sukkur; Editor M. SHAFAAT.

The Nation: NIPCO House, 4 Sharah-e-Fatima Jinnah, POB 1815, Lahore 54000; tel. (42) 6367580; fax (42) 6367005; e-mail editor@nation.com; internet www.nation.com.pk; f. 1986; English; Chair. MAJEED NIZAMI; Editor ARIF NIZAMI; circ. 52,000.

Nawa-i-Waqt (Voice of the Time): 4 Sharah-e-Fatima Jinnah, Lahore 54000; tel. (42) 6367580; fax (42) 6367005; internet www.nawaiwaqt.com.pk; f. 1940; English, Urdu; also publ. edns in Karachi, Islamabad and Multan; Editor MAJID NIZAMI; combined circ. 560,000.

The Sun International: 15-L, Gulberg III, Ferozepur Rd, Lahore; tel. (42) 5883540; fax (42) 5839951; Editor MAHMOOD SADIQ.

Tijarat: 14 Abbot Rd, opp. Nishat Cinema, Lahore; tel. (42) 6312462; fax (42) 6362767; Urdu; Editor JAMIL ATHAR.

Rawalpindi

Daily Asas: Asas Plaza, B-27, Murree Road, Rawalpindi; tel. (51) 111272711; fax (51) 4428315; e-mail info@dailyasas.com.pk; internet www.dailyasas.com.pk; f. 1993; also printed from Islamabad, Lahore, Karachi and Faisalabad; Editor DANISH IFTIKHAR.

Daily Jang: Murree Rd, Rawalpindi; tel. (51) 5962444; fax (51) 5962277; internet www.jang.com.pk; f. 1940; also publ. in Quetta, Karachi, Lahore and London; Urdu; independent; Editor Mir JAVED REHMAN; circ. (Rawalpindi) 65,000.

Daily Wifaq: Mohallah Waris Khan 604, Murree Rd, Rawalpindi; tel. (51) 553979; e-mail dailywifaq@hotmail.com; f. 1959; also publ. in Lahore, Sargodha and Rahimyar Khan; daily publ. in Urdu, monthly magazine in English *The Times*; Editor MUSTAFA SADIQ.

The News: Al-Rehman Bldg, Murree Rd, Rawalpindi; tel. (51) 5962444; fax (51) 5962277; e-mail thenews@isb.comsats.net.pk; internet www.jang-group.com; f. 1991; also publ. in Lahore and Karachi; English; independent; Chief Editor Mir SHAKIL-UR-RAHMAN.

Other Towns

Aftab: Opposite WASA Office, Bagh Langay Khan Rd, Multan; tel. (61) 4546080; fax (61) 4786083; e-mail aftabmultan@aftabdaily.com; Sindhi; Editor ASAD MUMTAZ SEYAL.

Al Falah: Al Falah House, Al Falah Bazar, nr State Life Bldg, Mall Rd, Peshawar; tel. (91) 5853694; f. 1939; Urdu and Pashtu; Editor SYED BADRUDDIN SHAH.

Al-Jamiat-e-Sarhad: Kocha Gilania Chakagali, Karimpura Bazar, Peshawar; tel. (91) 2567757; e-mail sagha@brain.net.pk; f. 1941; Urdu and Pashtu; Propr and Chief Editor S. M. HASSAN GILANI.

Balochistan Times: Jinnah Rd, Quetta; Editor SYED FASIH IQBAL.

Basharat: Peshawar; Urdu; general; also publ. in Islamabad; Chief Editor ANWAR-UL-HAQ; Editor KHALID ATHER.

Daily Awaz: Peshawar; political; Man. Editor ALI RAZA MALIK.

Daily Business Report: Railway Rd, Faisalabad; tel. (41) 2642131; fax (41) 2621207; f. 1948; Editor ABDUL RASHID GHAZI; circ. 26,000.

Daily Ibrat Hyderabad: Ibrat Building, Gadi Khata, Hyderabad; tel. (22) 2728571; fax (22) 2784300; e-mail ibrat@hyd.paknet.com.pk; internet www.dailyibrat.com; Sindhi; Man. Editor Qazi ASAD ABID.

Daily Khadim-e-Waten: B-2, Civil Lines, Hyderabad; Editor MUSHATAQ AHMAD.

Daily Rehber: 17-B East Trust Colony, Bahawalpur; tel. (621) 884664; fax (621) 874032; e-mail rehberbwp@yahoo.co.uk; f. 1951; Urdu; Chief Editor AKHTER HUSSAIN ANJUM; circ. 250,000.

Daily Sarwan: 11-EGOR Colony, Hyderabad; tel. (221) 781382; Sindhi; Chief Editor GHULAM HUSSAIN.

Daily Shabaz: Peshawar; tel. (521) 220188; fax (521) 216483; Urdu; organ of the Awami National Party; Chief Editor Begum NASEEM WALI KHAN.

Frontier Post: 32 Stadium Rd, Peshawar; tel. (521) 79174; fax (521) 76575; e-mail editor@frontierpost.com.pk; f. 1985; English; left-wing; also publ. in Lahore; closed down temporarily in January 2001, reopened in June; Editor-in-Chief REHMAT SHAH AFRIDI; Editor MUZAFFAR SHAH AFRIDI.

Jihad: 15A Islamia Club Bldg, Khyber Bazar, Peshawar; tel. (521) 210522; e-mail jehad@pes.comsats.net.pk; also publ. in Karachi, Rawalpindi, Islamabad and Lahore; Editor SHARIF FAROOQ.

Kaleem: Shahi Bazar, Thalla, POB 88, Sukkur; tel. (71) 5622086; fax (71) 5622087; e-mail kaleemsukkur@yahoo.com; Urdu; Editor SHAHID MEHR SHAMSI.

Kavish: Sindh Printing and Publishing House, Civil Lines, POB 43, Hyderabad; Chief Editor MUHAMMAD AYUB QAZI; Publr/Editor ASLAM A. QAZI.

Nawai Asma'n: Mubarak Ali Shah Rd, Peshawar; tel. and fax (221) 21925; Urdu, Sindhi and Pashtu; Chief Editor DOST MUHAMMAD.

The News: Qaumi Printing Press, Peshawar; English; Editor KHURSHID AHMAD.

Punjab News: Iftikhar Heights, Aminpur Bazar, POB 419, Faisalabad; tel. (41) 633102; fax (41) 615731; e-mail imranlateef1@hotmail.com; f. 1968; Chief Editor and Publr Sheikh Sultan MAHMOOD; circ. 10,000.

Sindh Guardian: Tulsi Das Rd, POB 300, Hyderabad; tel. and fax (221) 21926; English; Chief Editor DOST MUHAMMAD.

Sindh News: Garikhata, Hyderabad; tel. (221) 20793; fax (221) 781867; Editor Kazi SAEEED AKBER.

Sindh Observer: POB 43, Garikhata, Hyderabad; tel. (221) 27302; English; Editor ASLAM AKBER KAZI.

Sindhu: Popular Printers, Ibrat Bldg, Garhhi Khata, Hyderabad; tel. (221) 783571; fax (221) 783570; Sindhi; political.

Watan: 10 Nazar Bagh Flat, Peshawar.

Zamana: Jinnah Rd, Quetta; tel. (81) 71217; Urdu; Editor SYED FASIH IQBAL; circ. 5,000.

SELECTED WEEKLIES

Akhbar-e-Jehan: Printing House, off I. I. Chundrigar Rd, Karachi; tel. (21) 2634368; fax (21) 2635693; e-mail editor-in-chief@akhbar-e-jehan.com; internet www.akhbar-e-jehan.com; f. 1967; Urdu; independent; illustrated family magazine; Editor-in-Chief Mir JAVED RAHMAN; circ. 285,000.

Amal: Shah Qabool Colony, POB 185, Peshawar; tel. (91) 5704673; e-mail maab_kaifi@hotmail.com; f. 1958; Urdu, Pashtu and English; Chief Editor F. M. ZAFAR KAIFI; Publr MUNAZIMA MAAB KAIFI.

Chatan: Chatan Bldg, 88 McLeod Rd, Lahore; tel. (42) 6311336; fax (42) 6374690; f. 1948; Urdu; Editor MASUD SHORISH.

Family Magazine: 4 Shara-i-Fatima Jinnah, Lahore 54000; tel. (42) 6367551; fax (42) 6367583; circ. 100,000.

The Friday Times: 72-F. C. C. Gulberg IV, Lahore; tel. (42) 5673510; fax (42) 5751025; e-mail tft@lhr.comsats.net.pk; internet www.thefridaytimes.com; independent; Editor/Owner NAJAM SETHI.

Hilal: Hilal Rd, Rawalpindi 46000; tel. (51) 56134605; fax (51) 565017; f. 1951; Friday; Urdu; illustrated armed forces; Editor MUMTAZ IQBAL MALIK; circ. 90,000.

Insaf: P/929, Banni, Rawalpindi 46000; tel. and fax (51) 5550903; e-mail insafrwp@isb.paknet.com.pk; f. 1955; Editor Mir WAQAR AZIZ.

Lahore: Galaxy Law Chambers, 1st Floor, Room 1, Turner Rd, Lahore 5; f. 1952; Editor SAQIB ZEERVI; circ. 8,500.

Memaar-i-Nao: 39 KMC Bldg, Leamarket, Karachi; Urdu; labour magazine; Editor M. M. MUBASIR.

The Muslim World: 49-B, Block 8, Gulshan-e-Iqbal, Karachi 75300; POB 5030, Karachi 74000; tel. (21) 4960738; fax (21) 466878; English; current affairs.

Nairang Khayal: 8 Mohammadi Market, Rawalpindi; f. 1924; Urdu; Chief Editor Sultan RASHK.

Nida-i-Millat: 4 Sharah-e-Fatima Jinnah, Lahore 54000.

Noor Jehan Weekly: 32A National Auto Plaza, POB 8833, Karachi 74400; tel. and fax (21) 7723946; f. 1948; Urdu; film journal; Editor KHALID CHAWLA.

Pak Kashmir: Pak Kashmir Office, Soikarno Chowk, Liaquat Rd, Rawalpindi; tel. (51) 74845; f. 1951; Urdu; Editor M. MUSADDIQ ABBASI.

Pakistan and Gulf Economist: 1st Floor, 20-C, Sunset Lane 9, Phase 2 Extension, D. H. A., Karachi 75500; tel. (21) 5883967; fax (21) 5883295; e-mail information@pakistaneconomist.com; internet www.pakistaneconomist.com; f. 1960; English; Editor ALI HAIDER GOKAL; circ. 30,000.

Parsi Sansar and Loke Sevak: 8 Mehrabad, 5 McNeil Rd, Karachi 75530; tel. and fax (21) 5656217; e-mail organ@cyber.net.pk; f. 1909; English and Gujarati; Editor MEHERJI P. DASTUR.

Parwaz: Madina Office, Bahawalpur; Urdu; Editor MUSTAQ AHMED.

Qalandar: Peshawar; f. 1950; Urdu; Editor M. A. K. SHERWANI.

Shahab-e-Saqib: Shahab Saqib Rd, Maulana St, Peshawar; f. 1950; Urdu; Editor S. M. RIZVI.

Takbeer: A-1, 3rd Floor, 'Namco Centre', Campbell St, Karachi 74200; tel. (21) 2626613; fax (21) 2627742; e-mail irfanfaruqi@usa.com; f. 1984; Urdu; Sr. Exec. IRFAN KALIM FAROOQ; circ. 70,000.

Tarjaman-i-Sarhad: Peshawar; Urdu and Pashtu; Editor MOHAMMAD SHAFI SABIR.

Times of Kashmir: P/929, Banni, Rawalpindi 46000; tel. (51) 5550903; fax (51) 4411348; e-mail insafrwp@isb.paknet.com.pk; f. 1982; English; Editor Mir IQBAL AZIZ.

Ufaq: 44H, Block No. 2, PECHS, Karachi; tel. (21) 437992; f. 1978; Editor WAHAJUDDIN CHISHTI; circ. 2,000.

SELECTED PERIODICALS

Aadab Arz: 190 N. Ghazali Rd, Saman Abad, Lahore 54500; tel. (42) 7582449; monthly; Editor KHALID BIN HAMID.

Aalami Digest: B-1, Momin Sq., Rashid Minhas Rd, Gulshan-e-Iqbal, Karachi; monthly; Urdu; Editor ZAHEDA HINA.

Akhbar-e-Watan: 68-C, 13th Commercial St, Phase-II, Extension Defence, Karachi; tel. (21) 5886071; fax (21) 5890179; e-mail akhbarewatan@hotmail.com; f. 1977; monthly; Urdu; cricket; Man. Editor MUNIR HUSSAIN; circ. 63,000.

Albalagh Darul Uloom: Korangi Rd, Karachi; monthly; Editor MOHAMMED TAQI USMANI.

Al-Ma'arif: Institute of Islamic Culture, Club Rd, Lahore 54000; tel. (42) 6363127; f. 1950; quarterly; Urdu; Dir and Editor-in-Chief Dr RASHID AHMAD JALLANDHRI.

Anchal: 24 Saeed Mansion, I. I. Chundrigar Rd, Karachi; monthly.

Archi Times: B-34, Block 15, Gulshan-e-Iqbal, Karachi; tel. (21) 4977652; fax (21) 4967656; e-mail architimes@cyber.net.pk; internet www.archpresspk.com; f. 1986; monthly; English; architecture; Editor MURTAZA SHIKOH.

Architecture and Interiors: B-34, Block 15, Gulshan-e-Iqbal, Karachi; tel. (21) 4977652; fax (21) 4967656; e-mail aplusi@cyber.net.pk; internet www.archpresspk.com; f. 2001; quarterly; English; Editor MUTJUBA HUSSAIN; Man. Editor MURTUZA SHIKOH.

Asia Travel News: 101 Muhammadi House, I. I. Chundrigar Rd, Karachi 74000; tel. (21) 2424837; fax (21) 2420797; fortnightly; travel trade, tourism and hospitality industry; Editor JAVED MUSHTAQ.

Auto Times: 5 S. J. Kayani Shaheed Rd, off Garden Rd, Karachi; tel. (21) 713595; fortnightly; English; Editor MUHAMMAD SHAHZAD.

Bachoon Ka Risala: 108–110 Adam Arcade, Shaheed-e-Millat Rd, Karachi; tel. (21) 419616; monthly; Urdu; childrens; Editor RUKHSANA SEHAM MIRZA.

Bagh: 777/18 Federal B Area, POB 485, Karachi; tel. (21) 449662; monthly; Urdu; Editor RAHIL IQBAL.

Bayyenat: Jamia Uloom-e-Islamia, Binnori Town, Karachi 74800; tel. (21) 4927233; f. 1962; monthly; Urdu; religious and social issues.

Beauty: Plot No. 4-C, 14th Commercial St, Defence Housing Authority, Phase II Extension, Karachi; tel. (21) 5805391; fax (21) 5896269; e-mail riazmansuri@hotmail.com; f. 2000; bi-monthly; English; Chief Editor RIAZ AHMED MANSURI.

Beemakar (Insurer): 58 Press Chambers, I. I. Chundrigar Rd, Karachi; e-mail tahakn@cyber.net.pk; f. 1990; monthly; Urdu; Man. Editor SHAMSHAD AHMAD; Editor AYAZ KHAN.

Chand: 190 N. Ghazali Rd, Saman Abad, Lahore 54500; tel. (42) 7582449; monthly; Editor MASOOD HAMID.

The Cricketer: Plot No. 4-C, 14th Commercial St, Defence Housing Authority, Phase II Extension, Karachi; tel. (21) 5805391; fax (21) 5896269; e-mail riazmansuri@hotmail.com; f. 1972; monthly; English/Urdu; Chief Editor RIAZ AHMED MANSURI.

Dastarkhuan: Plot No. 4-C, 14th Commercial St, Defence Housing Authority, Phase II Extension, Karachi; tel. (21) 5805391; fax (21) 5896269; e-mail riazmansuri@hotmail.com; f. 1998; monthly; Urdu; Chief Editor RIAZ AHMED MANSURI.

Defence Journal: SMS Block, Defence Hockey Stadium, Phase-V, Karachi; tel. (21) 5843502; fax (21) 5843416; e-mail defjrnl@pathfinder9.com; internet www.defencejournal.com; f. 1975; monthly; English; Editor-in-Chief IKRAM SEHGAL; circ. 10,000.

Dentist: 70/7, Nazimabad No. 3, Karachi 18; f. 1984; monthly; English and Urdu; Editor NAEEMULLAH HUSAIN.

Dosheeza: 108–110 Adam Arcade, Shaheed-e-Millat Rd, Karachi; tel. (21) 4930470; fax (21) 4934369; monthly; Urdu; Editor RUKHSANA SEHAM MIRZA.

Duniya-e-Tibb: Eveready Chambers, 2nd Floor, Mohd Bin Qasim Rd, off I. I. Chundrigar Rd, POB 1385, Karachi 1; tel. (21) 2630985; fax (21) 2637624; e-mail mcm@digicom.net.pk; f. 1986; monthly; Urdu; modern and Asian medicine; Editor QUTUBUDDIN; circ. 12,000.

Economic Review: Al-Masiha, 3rd Floor, 47 Abdullah Haroon Rd, POB 7843, Karachi 74400; tel. (21) 7728963; fax (21) 7728957; f. 1969; monthly; economic, industrial and investment research; Editor AHMAD MUHAMMAD KHAN.

Engineering Horizons: 13-J, Markaz F-7, Islamabad 44000; tel. (51) 2650174; fax (51) 2650943; e-mail islamabad@engghorizons.com; internet www.engghorizons.com; f. 1988; monthly; English; Chief Editor IMTIAZ SHEIKH.

Engineering Review: 305 Spotlit Chambers, Dr Billimoria St, off I. I. Chundrigar Rd, POB 807, Karachi 74200; tel. (21) 2632567; fax (21) 2639378; e-mail engineeringreview@yahoo.com; internet www.engineeringreview.com.pk; f. 1975; fortnightly; English; circ. 5,000.

Film Asia: 68-C, 13th Commercial St, Phase-II, Extension Defence, Karachi; tel. (21) 5886071; fax (21) 5890179; e-mail akhbarewatan@hotmail.com; f. 1973; monthly; film, television, fashion, art and culture; Man. Editor MUNIR HUSSAIN; circ. 38,000.

Good Food: Plot No. 4-C, 14th Commercial St, Defence Housing Authority, Phase II Extension, Karachi; tel. (21) 5805391; fax (21) 5896269; e-mail riazmansuri@hotmail.com; f. 1997; bi-monthly; English; Chief Editor RIAZ AHMED MANSURI.

Hamdard-i-Sehat: Institute of Health and Tibbi Research, Hamdard Foundation Pakistan, Nazimabad, Karachi 74600; tel. (21) 6616001; fax (21) 6611755; e-mail hfp@hamdardfoundation.org; internet www.hamdardfoundation.org; f. 1933; monthly; Urdu; Editor-in-Chief SADIA RASHID; circ. 13,000.

Hamdard Islamicus: Hamdard Foundation Pakistan, Nazimabad, Karachi 74600; tel. (21) 6620949-54; fax (21) 6611755; e-mail hfp@hamdardfoundation.org; internet hamdardfoundation.org; f. 1978; quarterly; English; Editor-in-Chief SADIA RASHID; Dir-Gen. FURQAN AHMAD SHAMSI; circ. 750.

Hamdard Medicus: Hamdard Foundation Pakistan, Nazimabad, Karachi 74600; tel. (21) 6620949-54; fax (21) 6611755; e-mail hfp@hamdardfoundation.org; internet hamdardfoundation.org; f. 1957; quarterly; English; Editor-in-Chief SADIA RASHID; Dir-Gen. FURQAN AHMAD SHAMSI; circ. 1,000.

Hamdard Naunehal: Hamdard Foundation Pakistan, Nazimabad, Karachi 74600; tel. (21) 6620949-54; fax (21) 6611755; e-mail hfp@hamdardfoundation.org; internet hamdardfoundation.org; f. 1952; monthly; Urdu; Editor MASOOD AHMAD BARAKATI; Dir-Gen. FURQAN AHMAD SHAMSI; circ. 34,000.

The Herald: Haroon House, Dr Ziauddin Ahmed Rd, Karachi 74200; tel. (21) 5670001; fax (21) 5683188; e-mail letters.herald@dawn.com; internet www.dawn.com/herald; f. 1970; monthly; English; Editor ARIFA NOOR; circ. 38,000.

Hikayat: 26 Patiala Ground, Link McLeod Rd, Lahore; monthly; Editor SHAHID JAMIL; circ. 25,000.

Islamic Studies: Islamic Research Institute, Faisal Masjid Campus, POB 1035, Islamabad 44000; tel. (51) 850751; fax (51) 250821; e-mail amzia555@apollo.net.pk; f. 1962; quarterly; English, Urdu (Fikro-Nazar) and Arabic (Al Dirasat al-Islamiyyah) edns; Islamic literature, religion, history, geography, language and the arts; Editor Dr ZAFAR ISHAQ ANSARI (acting); circ. 3,000.

Jamal: Institute of Islamic Culture, 2 Club Rd, Lahore 54000; tel. (42) 6363127; f. 1950; annual; English; Dir and Editor-in-Chief Dr JULUNDHRI RASHEED.

Journal of the Pakistan Historical Society: Bait al-Hikmah, Hamdard University, Muhammad Bin Qasim Ave, Karachi, 74700; tel. (21) 6616001; fax (21) 6611755; e-mail phs@hamdard.edu.pk; f. 1953; quarterly; English; Editor Dr ANSAR ZAHID KHAN; circ. 700.

Khel-Ke-Duniya: 6/13 Alyusaf Chamber, POB 340, Karachi; tel. (21) 216888.

Khwateen Digest: Urdu Bazar, M. A. Jinnah Rd, Karachi; monthly; Urdu; Editor MAHMUD RIAZ.

Kiran: 37 Urdu Bazar, M. A. Jinnah Rd, Karachi; tel. (21) 216606; Editor MAHMUD BABAR FAISAL.

Leather News: Iftikhar Chambers, opp. UNI Plaza, Altaf Hussain Rd, POB 4323, Karachi 74000; fax (21) 2631545; f. 1989; Editor ABDUL RAFAY SIDDIQI.

PAKISTAN

Ma'arif Feature: D-35, Block 5, Federal 'B' Area, Karachi 75950; tel. (21) 6349840; fax (21) 6361040; e-mail irak63@gmail.com; f. 1999; journal of the Islamic Research Acad; fortnightly; Urdu; Editor SYED SHAHID HASHMI.

Medical Variety: 108–110 Adam Arcade, Shaheed-e-Millat Rd, Karachi; tel. (21) 419616; monthly; English; Editor RUKHSANA SEHAM MIRZA.

Muslim World Business: 20 Sasi Arcade, 4th Floor, Main Clifton Rd, POB 10417, Karachi 6; tel. (21) 534870; f. 1989; monthly; English; political and business; Editor-in-Chief MUZAFFAR HASSAN.

Naey-Ufaq: 24 Saeed Mansion, I. I. Chundrigar Rd, Karachi; fortnightly.

NGM Communication: POB 3540, Post Mall, Gulberg, Lahore 54660; tel. (42) 5879524; e-mail anjeeam@yahoo.com; internet www.geocities.com/anjeeam; f. 1980; owned by Nizam Nizami; English; lists newly released Pakistani publications on the internet; updated weekly; Editor GHUFRAN NIZAMI.

Pakistan Journal of Applied Economics: Applied Economics Research Centre, University of Karachi, POB 8403, Karachi 75270; tel. (21) 9261541; fax (21) 9261545; e-mail pjae@aerc.edu.pk; internet www.aerc.edu.pk; twice a year; Editor MUHAMMAD SABIHUDDIN BUTT.

Pakistan Journal of Scientific and Industrial Research: Pakistan Council of Scientific and Industrial Research, Scientific Information Centre, PCSIR Laboratories Campus, off University Rd, Karachi 75280; tel. (21) 4651740; fax (21) 4651738; e-mail pcsir@cyber.net.pk; f. 1958; bi-monthly; English; Exec. Editor Dr KANIZ FIZZA AZHAR; circ. 1,000.

Pakistan Management Review: Pakistan Institute of Management, Management House, Shahrah Iran, Clifton, Karachi 75600; tel. (21) 9251711; e-mail pimkhi@pim.com.pk; internet www.pim.com.pk; f. 1960; quarterly; English; Editor IQBAL A. QAZI.

Pasban: Faiz Modh Rd, Quetta; fortnightly; Urdu; Editor MOLVI MOHD ABDULLAH.

Phool: 23 Queen's Rd, Lahore 54000; tel. (42) 6314099; fax (42) 6309661; e-mail editor@phool.com; internet www.phool.com.pk; f. 1989; monthly; children's; Chief Editor MAJID NIZAMI; Editor MUHAMMAD SHOAIB MIRZA; circ. 50,000.

Progress: 4th Floor, PIDC House, Dr Ziauddin Ahmed Rd, Karachi 75530; tel. (21) 111-568-568; fax (21) 5680005; e-mail h_saquib@ppl.com.pk; f. 1956; monthly; publ. by Pakistan Petroleum Ltd; Editor and Publr NUSRAT NASARULLAH; Chief Exec./Man. Dir S. MUNSIF RAZA.

Qaumi Digest: 50 Lower Mall, Lahore; tel. (42) 7225143; fax (42) 7233261; monthly; Editor MUJIBUR REHMAN SHAMI.

Sabrang Digest: 47–48 Press Chambers, I. I. Chundrigar Rd, Karachi 1; tel. (21) 211961; f. 1970; monthly; Urdu; Editor SHAKEEL ADIL ZADAH; circ. 150,000.

Sach-Chee Kahaniyan: 108–110 Adam Arcade, Shaheed-e-Millat Rd, Karachi; tel. (21) 4930470; fax (21) 4934369; monthly; Urdu; Editor RUKHSANA SEHAM MIRZA.

Sayyarah: Aiwan-e-Adab, Urdu Bazar, Lahore 54000; tel. (42) 7321842; f. 1962; monthly; Urdu; literary; Man. Editor HAFEEZ-UR-RAHMAN AHSAN.

Sayyarah Digest: 244, Main Market Riwaz Garden, Lahore 54000; tel. (42) 7245412; fax (42) 7325080; e-mail sayyaradigest@brain.com.pk; f. 1963; monthly; Urdu; Chief Editor AMJAD RAUF KHAN; Editor KAMRAN AMJAD KHAN; circ. 40,000.

Science Magazine: Science Book Foundation, Haji Bldg, Hassan Ali Efendi Rd, Karachi; tel. (21) 2625647; monthly; Urdu; Editor QASIM MAHMOOD.

Seep: Alam Market, Block No. 16, Federal B Area, Karachi; quarterly; Editor NASIM DURRANI.

Show Business: 108–110 Adam Arcade, Shaheed-e-Millat Rd, POB 12540, Karachi; tel. (21) 419616; monthly; Urdu; Editor RUKHSANA SEHAM MIRZA.

Sindh Quarterly: 36D Karachi Administrative Co-operative Housing Society, off Shaheed-e-Millat Rd, Karachi 75350; tel. (21) 4531988; f. 1973; Editor SAYID GHULAM MUSTAFA SHAH.

Smash: Plot No. 4-C, 14th Commercial St, Defence Housing Authority, Phase II Extension, Karachi; tel. (21) 5805391; fax (21) 5896269; e-mail riazmansuri@hotmail.com; f. 2000; monthly; English; Chief Editor RIAZ AHMED MANSURI.

Spider: Haroon House, Dr Ziauddin Ahmed Rd, Karachi 74200; tel. (21) 111-444-777; fax (21) 5681544; e-mail reba@spider.tm; internet www.spider.tm; f. 1998; internet monthly; Editor REBA SHAHID; CEO HAMEED HAROON.

Sports International: Arshi Market, Firdaus Colony, Nazimabad, Karachi 74600; tel. (21) 6602171; fax (21) 6683768; e-mail ibp-khi@cyber.net.pk; f. 1972; fortnightly; Urdu and English; Chief Editor KANWAR ABDUL MAJEED; Editor RAHEEL MAJEED.

Taj: Jamia Tajia, St 13, Sector 14/B, Buffer Zone, Karachi 75850; monthly; Editor BABA M. ATIF SHAH ANWARI ZAHEENI TAJI.

Talimo Tarbiat: Ferozsons (Pvt) Ltd, 60 Shahrah-e-Quaid-e-Azam, Lahore 54000; tel. (42) 6301196; fax (42) 6369204; e-mail support@ferozsons.com.pk; f. 1941; children's monthly; Urdu; Publr and Editor ZAHEER SALAM; circ. 50,000.

Textile Times: Arshi Market, Firdaus Colony, Nazimabad, Karachi 74600; tel. (21) 6683768; e-mail ibp-khi@cyber.net.pk; f. 1993; monthly; English; Chief Editor KANWAR ABDUL MAJEED; Exec. Editor RAHEEL MAJEED KHAN.

Trade Chronicle: Iftikhar Chambers, Altaf Hussain Rd, POB 5257, Karachi 74000; tel. (21) 2631587; fax (21) 2635007; e-mail arsidiqi@ptcl.net; f. 1953; monthly; English; trade, politics, finance and economics; Editor ABDUL RAB SIDDIQI; circ. 6,000.

Trade Link International: Zahoor Mansion, Tariq Rd, Karachi; monthly; English; Man. Editor M. IMRAN BAIG; Editor IKRAMULLAH QUREISHI.

TV Times: Plot No. 4-C, 14th Commercial St, Defence Housing Authority, Phase II Extension, Karachi; tel. (21) 5805391; fax (21) 5896269; e-mail rmansuri@fascom.com; f. 1987; monthly; English; Chief Editor RIAZ AHMED MANSURI.

UNESCO Payami: 30 UNESCO House, Sector H-8/1, Islamabad; tel. (51) 434196; fax (51) 431815; monthly; Urdu; publ. by Pakistan National Commission for UNESCO; Editor Dr MUNIR A. ABRO.

Urdu Digest: 21-Acre Scheme, Samanabad, Lahore 54500; tel. (42) 7589957; fax (42) 7563646; e-mail urdudigest42@hotmail.com; monthly; Urdu; Editor ALTAF HASAN QURESHEE.

Voice of Islam: Jamiatul Falah Bldg, Akbar Rd, Saddar, POB 7141, Karachi 74400; tel. (21) 7721394; f. 1952; monthly; Islamic Cultural Centre magazine; English; Editor Prof. ABDUL QADEER SALEEM; Man. Editor Prof. WAQAR ZUBAIRI.

Wings: 101 Muhammadi House, I. I. Chundrigar Rd, Karachi 74000; tel. (21) 2412591; fax (21) 2420797; monthly; aviation and defence; English; Editor and Publr JAVED MUSHTAQ.

Women's Own: Plot No. 4-C, 14th Commercial St, Defence Housing Authority, Phase II Extension, Karachi; tel. (21) 5805391; fax (21) 5896269; e-mail riazmansuri@hotmail.com; f. 1987; monthly; English; Chief Editor RIAZ AHMED MANSURI.

Yaqeen International: Darut Tasnif (Pvt) Ltd, Main Hub River Rd, Mujahidabad, Karachi 75760; tel. (21) 2814432; fax (21) 2811304; e-mail daruttasnif@yaqeendtl.com; f. 1952; English and Arabic; Islamic organ; Editor Dr HAFIZ MUHAMMAD ADIL.

Yaran-e-Watan: Overseas Pakistanis Foundation, Shahrah-e-Jamhuriate, G-5/2, POB 1470, Islamabad 44000; tel. (51) 9224518; fax (51) 9211613; e-mail yw@opf.org.pk; f. 1982; monthly; Urdu; publ. by the Overseas Pakistanis Foundation; Editor TANVIR HUSSAIN.

Youth World International: 104/C Central C/A, Tariq Rd, Karachi; tel. (21) 442211; f. 1987; monthly; English; Editor SYED ADIL EBRAHIM.

NEWS AGENCIES

Agence France Press: House 90, Ataturk Ave, G-6/3, Islamabad; tel. (51) 2822738; fax (51) 2822203; Bureau Chief JEAN-HERVÉ DEILLER.

Associated Press of Pakistan (APP): 18 Mauve Area, Zero Point, G-7/1, POB 1258, Islamabad; tel. (51) 2203073; fax (51) 2203074; e-mail news@app.com.pk; internet app.com.pk; f. 1948; Dir-Gen. FAZALUR REHMAN MALIK.

International News Network (INN): Suite 803, 8th Floor, Regal Trade Sq., Saddar, Karachi; tel. (21) 7767810; fax (21) 2767810; Chief Editor MUHAMMAD AKRAM.

Kyodo News Agency (Japan): House 31, St 28, F-10/1, Islamabad; tel. (51) 2291577; fax (51) 2297031; Bureau Chief KIMURA KAZUHIRO.

National News Agency (NNA): 491-C, Margalla Town, Islamabad 45510; tel. (51) 2840896; fax (51) 2841746; e-mail nnaisb@yahoo.com; f. 1990; Chief Editor SUHAIL ILYAS.

News Network International: 2nd Floor, Redco Plaza, Islamabad 44000; tel. (51) 2874344; fax (51) 2826289; e-mail nni2005@isb.paknet.com.pk; internet www.nni-news.com; f. 1992; independent international news agency; news in Arabic, Urdu and English; provides services to 435 newspapers and radio and television channels in South Asia, Europe, the Middle East, the Far East and the USA; Editor-in-Chief QAISAR JAVED; Editor MUHAMMAD TAHIR KHAN.

Pakistan—International Press Agency (PPA): 6, St 39, G-6/2, Islamabad 44000; tel. (51) 2279830; fax (51) 2272405; e-mail khalidathar@hotmail.com; f. 1991; Urdu; Chief Editor KHALID ATHAR.

Pakistan Press International (PPI): Press Centre, Shahrah Kamal Ataturk, POB 541, Karachi; tel. (21) 2630562; fax (21)

PAKISTAN

2631275; e-mail owais.ali@attglobal.net; f. 1956; pvt ltd co; Chair. OWAIS ASLAM ALI.

Sharp Eye: 111 Lytton Rd, Qurtaba Chowk, Lahore; tel. (42) 7313401; fax (42) 7313404; e-mail editor@sharpeye.com.pk; internet www.sharpeye.com.pk; Chief Editor MIAN MUHAMMAD AZHAR AMIN.

United Press of Pakistan (Pvt) Ltd (UPP): 1 Victoria Chambers, Haji Abdullah Haroon Rd, Karachi 74400; tel. (21) 2822738; fax (21) 5682694; e-mail pnrupp2000@yahoo.com; f. 1949; Chair. KHURSHID ABDUL HAFIZ; 5 brs.

Voice of America (VOA): House 1, St 89, G-6/3, Islamabad; tel. (51) 2278784; fax (51) 2277349.

PRESS ASSOCIATIONS

All Pakistan Newspaper Employees Confederation: Karachi Press Club, M. R. Kayani Rd, Karachi; f. 1976; confed. of all press industry trade unions; Pres. MAZHAR ABBAS; Sec.-Gen. PERVAIZ SHAUKAT.

All Pakistan Newspapers Society: 32 Farid Chambers, Abdullah Haroon Rd, POB 74400, Karachi 3; tel. (21) 5671256; fax (21) 5671310; e-mail theapns@gmail.com; internet www.apns.com.pk; f. 1949; Pres. MUJEEB-UR-RAHMAN SHAMI; Sec.-Gen. JABBAR KHATTAK.

Council of Pakistan Newspaper Editors: c/o United Press of Pakistan, 1 Victoria Chambers, Haji Abdullah Haroon Rd, Karachi 74400; tel. and fax (21) 5682694; f. 1957; Pres. SYED FASEIH IQBAL; Sec.-Gen. WAMIQ A. ZUBERI.

Federal Union of Journalists: Press Club, M. R. Keyani Rd, Karachi; Pres. HUMA ALI; Sec. MAZHAR ABBAS.

Pakistan Press Foundation: Press Centre, Shahrah Kamal Ataturk, Karachi 74200; tel. (21) 2633215; fax (21) 2631275; e-mail aboutus@pakistanpressfoundation.org; internet www.pakistanpressfoundation.org; f. 1967; independent media research and training centre for promotion of press freedom; Sec.-Gen. OWAIS ASLAM ALI.

Publishers

Alhamra Publishing: Al-Babar Centre, Office 6, 1st Floor, F-8 Markaz, Islamabad 44000; tel. (51) 2818033; fax (51) 2855150; e-mail contact@alhamra.com; internet www.alhamra.com; f. 2000; publs broad range of subjects incl. fiction, literary criticism, languages, history, education and religion in Urdu and English translations; Man. Dir SHAFIQ NAZ.

Anjuman Taraqqi-e-Urdu Pakistan: D-159, Block 7, Gulshan-e-Iqbal, Karachi 75300; tel. (21) 461406; f. 1903; literature, religion, textbooks, Urdu dictionaries, literary and critical texts; Pres. AFTAB AHMED KHAN; Hon. Sec. JAMIL UDDIN AALI.

Camran Publishers: Jalaluddin Hospital Bldg, Circular Rd, Lahore; f. 1964; general, technical, textbooks; Propr ABDUL HAMID.

Chronicle Publications: Iftikhar Chambers, Altaf Hussain Rd, POB 5257, Karachi 74000; tel. (21) 2631587; fax (21) 2635007; e-mail arsidiqi@ptcl.net; f. 1953; reference, directories, religious books; Dir ABDUL RAUF SIDDIQI.

Dasnavi Book House: Book St, G-6, Mazang Rd, Lahore; tel. (42) 2231518; e-mail bookhome@hotmail.com.

Economic and Industrial Publications: Al-Masiha, 3rd Floor, 47 Abdullah Haroon Rd, POB 7843, Karachi 74400; tel. (21) 7728963; fax (21) 7728434; f. 1965; industrial, economic and investment research.

Elite Publishers Ltd: D-118, SITE, Karachi 75700; tel. (21) 2573435; fax (21) 2564720; e-mail elite@elite.com.pk; internet www.elite.com.pk; f. 1951; general commercial printing and packaging; Chair. AHMED MIRZA JAMIL; Chief Exec. KHALID JAMIL.

Ferozsons (Pvt) Ltd: 60 Shahrah-e-Quaid-e-Azam, Lahore; tel. (42) 111-626-262; fax (42) 6369204; e-mail support@ferozsons.com.pk; internet www.ferozsons.com.pk; f. 1894; general books, school books, periodicals, maps, atlases, stationery products; Man. Dir ZAHEER SALAM; Dir (Business Development) MUQEET SALAM.

Fiction House: 18, Mozang House, Lahore; publs quarterly social science journal Tareekh.

Frontier Publishing Co: 22, Urdu Bazar, Lahore; tel. (42) 7247310; fax (42) 7247323; e-mail azam.fpc@gmail.com; internet www.fpcpk.com; f. 1951; academic and general; Dirs AZAM MUHAMMAD, AMIR MUHAMMAD.

Sh. Ghulam Ali and Sons (Pvt) Ltd: 14 Lawrence Rd, Lahore 54000; tel. (42) 7352908; fax (42) 6315478; e-mail info@ghulamali.com.pk; internet www.ghulamali.com.pk; f. 1887; general, religion, technical, textbooks; Dirs NIAZ AHMAD, ASAD NIAZ.

Harf Academy: G/307, Amena Plaza, Peshawar Rd, Rawalpindi.

Idara Taraqqi-i-Urdu: S-1/363 Saudabad, Karachi 27; f. 1949; general literature, technical and professional books and magazines; Propr IKRAM AHMED.

Ilmi Kitab Khana: Kabeer St, Urdu Bazar, Lahore; tel. (42) 7248129; f. 1948; technical, professional, historical and law; Propr Haji SARDAR MOHAMMAD.

INAYAT Sons: YMCA Bldg, 16 The Mall, Lahore 54000; tel. (42) 8401335; fax (42) 7231896; e-mail general@inayatsons.com; internet www.inayatsons.com; f. 1971; Propr S. PERVEZ.

Indus Publications: 25 Fared Chambers, Abdullah Haroon Rd, Karachi; tel. (21) 5660242; e-mail muzaffar_indus@hotmail.com; f. 1959; printers, publishers and importers of books; Dir AATIF SAFDAR.

Islamic Book Centre: 25B Masson Rd, POB 1625, Lahore 54000; tel. (42) 6361803; fax (42) 6360955; e-mail lsaeed@paknetl.ptc.pk; religion in Arabic, Urdu and English; Islamic history, textbooks, dictionaries and reprints; Propr and Man. Dir SUMBLEYNA SAJID SAEED.

Islamic Publications (Pvt) Ltd: 3 Court St, Lower Mall, Lahore 54000; tel. (42) 7248676; fax (42) 7214974; e-mail islamicpak@hotmail.com; internet www.islamicpak.com.pk; f. 1959; Islamic literature in Urdu and English; Man. Dir Prof. MUHAMMAD AMIN JAVED; Gen. Man. AMANAT ALI.

Jamiatul Falah Publications: Jamiatul Falah Bldg, Akbar Rd, Saddar, POB 7141, Karachi 74400; tel. (21) 7721394; f. 1952; Islamic history and culture; Pres. MUZAFFAR AHMED HASHMI; Sec. Prof. SHAHZADUL HASAN CHISHTI.

Kazi Publications: 121 Zulqarnain Chambers, Ganpat Rd, POB 1845, Lahore; tel. (42) 7311359; fax (42) 7350805; e-mail kazipublications@hotmail.com; internet www.brain.net.pk/~kazip; f. 1978; Islamic literature, religion, law, biographies; Propr/Man. MUHAMMAD IKRAM SIDDIQI; Chief Editor MUHAMMAD ASIM BILAL.

Lark Publishers: Urdu Bazar, Karachi 1; f. 1955; general literature, magazines; Propr MAHMOOD RIAZ.

Liberty Books (Pvt) Ltd: 3 Rafiq Plaza, M. R. Kayani Rd, Saddar, Karachi; tel. (21) 5656567; fax (21) 5684319; e-mail info@libertybooks.com; internet www.libertybooks.com; f. 1980.

Lion Art Press (Pvt) Ltd: 112 The Mall, Lahore 54000; tel. (42) 6304444; fax (42) 6367728; e-mail lionart786@hotmail.com; f. 1919; general publs in English and Urdu; Chief Exec. KHALID A. SHEIKH; Dir ASMA KHALID.

Maktaba Darut Tasnif: Main Hub River Rd, Mujahidabad, Karachi 75760; tel. (21) 2814432; fax (21) 2811307; e-mail daruttasnif@yaqeendtl.com; f. 1951; Koran Majeed and Islamic literature; Dir ABDUL BAQI FAROOQI.

Malik Sirajuddin & Sons: 48-C, Lower Mall, Lahore 54000; tel. (42) 7225809; fax (42) 7224586; e-mail sirajco@brain.net.pk; f. 1905; general, religion, law, textbooks; Man. MALIK ABDUL ROUF.

Malik Sons: Karkhana Bazar, Faisalabad.

Medina Publishing Co: M. A. Jinnah Rd, Karachi 1; f. 1960; general literature, textbooks; Propr HAKIM MOHAMMAD TAQI.

Mehtab Co: Ghazni St, Urdu Bazar, Lahore; tel. (42) 7120071; fax (42) 7353489; e-mail shashraf@brain.net.pk; f. 1978; Islamic literature; Propr SHAHZAD RIAZ SHEIKH.

Mohammad Hussain and Sons: 17 Urdu Bazar, Lahore 2; tel. (42) 7244114; f. 1941; religion, textbooks; Partners MOHAMMAD HUSSAIN, AZHAR ALI SHEIKH, PERVEZ ALI SHEIKH.

Sh. Muhammad Ashraf: 7 Aibak Rd, New Anarkali, Lahore 7; tel. (42) 7353171; fax (42) 7353489; e-mail shashraf@brain.net.pk; f. 1923; books in English on all aspects of Islam; Man. Dir SHAHZAD RIAZ SHEIKH.

National Book Service: 22 Urdu Bazar, Lahore; tel. (42) 7247310; fax (42) 7247323; e-mail fpc_pak@hotmail.com; internet www.fpcpk.com; f. 1950; academic and primary, secondary and ELT school books; Execs MUHAMMAD ARIF, MUHAMMAD AMIR, MUHAMMAD ASIM.

Oxford University Press: Plot No. 38, Sector 15, Korangi Industrial Area, Karachi; tel. (21) 4265945; fax (21) 5071586; e-mail oup.pk@oup.com; internet www.oup.com.pk; academic, educational and general; Man. Dir AMEENA SAIYID.

Pakistan Law House: Pakistan Chowk, POB 90, Karachi 1; tel. (21) 2212455; fax (21) 2627549; e-mail plh_law_house@hotmail.com; internet www.pakistanlawhouse.com; f. 1950; importers and exporters of legal books and reference books; Man. K. NOORANI.

Pakistan Publishing House: Victoria Chambers 2, A. Haroon Rd, Karachi 75400; tel. (21) 5681457; fax (21) 2627549; e-mail danyalbooks@hotmail.com; f. 1959; Propr HOORI NOORANI; Gen. Man. AAMIR HUSSEIN.

Paramount Books: 152/0, Block 2, PECHS, Karachi 75400; tel. (21) 4310030; fax (21) 4553772; e-mail info@paramountbooks.com.pk; internet www.paramountbooks.com.pk.

PAKISTAN
Directory

Pioneer Book House: M. A. Jinnah Rd, Karachi; tel. (21) 2628739; internet www.pioneerbookhouse.com; agent for state and federal govt publications; periodicals, gazettes, maps and reference works in English, Urdu and other regional languages.

Premier Bookhouse: Shahin Market, Room 2, Anarkali, POB 1888, Lahore; tel. (42) 7321174; Islamic and law.

Publishers United (Pvt) Ltd: c/o Gulam Ali Medicine Market, Chowk Lohari Gate, POB 1689, Lahore 54000; tel. (42) 6361306; fax (42) 6316015; e-mail smalipub2@hotmail.com; f. 1950; Islamic studies, history, art, archaeology, literature, Oriental studies, genealogy, scientific, medical, humanities and social sciences; Man. Dir ASAD NIAZ.

Punjab Religious Books Society: Anarkali, Lahore 2; tel. (42) 54416; educational, religious, law and general; Gen. Man. A. R. IRSHAD; Sec. NAEEM SHAKIR.

Reprints Ltd: 16 Bahadur Shah Market, M. A. Jinnah Rd, Karachi; f. 1983; Pakistani edns of foreign works; Chair. A. D. KHALID; Man. Dir AZIZ KHALID.

Royal Book Co: BG-5, Rex Centre, Basement, Fatima Jinnah Rd, Karachi 75530; tel. (21) 5653418; e-mail royalbook@hotmail.com.

Sang-e-Meel Publications: 25 Lower Mall, Lahore 54000; tel. (42) 7220100; fax (42) 7245101; e-mail smp@sang-e-meel.com; internet www.sang-e-meel.com; f. 1962; Marketing and Sales Exec. ALI KAMRAN.

Say Publishing (Pvt) Ltd: SAI-3, Shahnawaz Arcade, Shahid-e-Millat Rd, Karachi; tel. (21) 4129552; e-mail saybooks@gerry.net.

Sindhi Adabi Board (Sindhi Literary and Publishing Organization): Hyderabad; tel. (221) 771276; e-mail bookinfo@sindhiadabiboard.org; internet www.sindhiadabiboard.org; f. 1951; history, literature, culture of Sindh; in Sindhi, Urdu, English, Persian and Arabic; translations into Sindhi, especially of literature and history; chaired by Minister of Education and Literacy, Sindh; Sec. INAM SHEIKH.

Taj Co Ltd: Qissa Khani Bazar, Peshawar; tel. (91) 2580245; fax (91) 2580247; internet www.tajcom.com; f. 1929; religious books; Man. Dir A. H. KHOKHAR.

The Times Press (Pvt) Ltd: C-18, Al-Hilal Society, off University Rd, Karachi 74800; tel. (21) 4932931; fax (21) 4935602; e-mail timekhi@cyber.net.pk; internet www.timespress.8m.com; f. 1948; printers, publishers and stationery manufacturers, incl. security printing (postal stationery and stamps); registered publishers of Koran, school textbooks, etc.; Dir S. M. MINHAJUDDIN.

Tooba Publishers: 85 Sikandar Block, Allama Iqbal Town, Lahore; tel. (42) 5410185; e-mail haroonkallem@hotmail.com; f. 1983; poetry; Man. HAROON KALEEM USMANI.

Urdu Academy Sind: Main Urdu Bazar, M. A. Jinnah Rd, Karachi; tel. (21) 2628655; fax (21) 2625992; e-mail urduacademy@cyber.net .pk; f. 1947; brs in Hyderabad and Lahore; academic, reference, general and textbooks; Man. Dir AZIZ KHALID.

Vanguard Books (Pvt) Ltd: 72-FCC, Gulberg IV, Lahore; tel. (42) 5763510; fax (42) 5751025; e-mail vbl@brain.net.pk; Chief Exec. NAJAM SETHI.

West-Pak Publishing Co (Pvt) Ltd: 17 Urdu Bazar, Lahore; tel. (42) 7230555; fax (42) 7120077; e-mail pakcompany@hotmail.com; f. 1932; textbooks and religious books; Chief Exec. SYED AHSAN MAHMUD.

GOVERNMENT PUBLISHING HOUSE

Government Publications: Office of the Deputy Controller, Stationery and Forms, nr Old Sabzi Mandi, University Rd, Karachi 74800; tel. (21) 9231989; publ. Gazette of Pakistan; Dep. Controller MUHAMMAD AMIN BUTT.

PUBLISHERS' ASSOCIATION

Pakistan Publishers' and Booksellers' Association: 6 Gunpat Rd, Lahore; tel. (42) 7722043; Chair. MALIK MAZHAR MEHDI; Sec. ZUBAIR SAEED.

Broadcasting and Communications

TELECOMMUNICATIONS

Since 2000 the mobile cellular telephone industry has expanded significantly in Pakistan. In January 2004 the Government approved legislation providing for enhanced competition in the industry. In 2007 there were 78.9m. mobile cellular telephone subscribers nationwide (compared with 34.5m. in 2006).

Pakistan Telecommunication Authority (PTA): F-5/1, Islamabad 44000; tel. (51) 2878143; fax (51) 2878155; e-mail administration@pta.gov.pk; internet www.pta.gov.pk; f. 1997; regulatory authority; Chair. Dr MOHAMMAD YASEEN; Dir-Gen. CH. MOHAMMAD DIN.

Burraq Telecom (Pvt) Ltd: Plot 94A, St 7, Sector I-10/3, Islamabad; tel. (51) 111-287-727; fax (51) 2112380; e-mail info@burraqtel.com .pk; internet www.burraqtel.com.pk; f. 2004; CEO SADIQ YOUSAF YALMAZ.

Carrier Telephone Industries (Pvt) Ltd: 1-9/2 Industrial Area, POB 1098, Islamabad 44000; tel. (51) 4434981; fax (51) 4449581; e-mail niamatullah.khan.ext@siemens.com; internet www.ctipak .com.pk; f. 1969; Man. Dir MALIK MOHAMMAD AMIN.

Callmate Telips Telecom Ltd: 99-CF, 1/5 Clifton, Karachi; tel. (21) 5867696; fax (21) 5833006; e-mail info@cttelecom.net; internet www .cttelecom.net; f. 2003; telecommunications services.

CMPak Ltd: 68E, Jinnah Ave, Blue Area, Islamabad 44000; tel. (51) 2271105; fax (51) 2271111; private mobile telephone co; acquired from Millicom, Luxembourg, by China Mobile Communications Corpn in Feb. 2007; co name changed from Paktel Ltd to CMPak Ltd in May 2007; CEO GUO YONG HONG.

Instaphone: 75 East, Fazal-ul-Haq Rd, Blue Area, POB 1681, Islamabad; tel. (51) 2277400; fax (51) 111-501501; internet www .instaphone.com; private mobile telephone co; CEO SHAHID FEROZ.

Megatech Communications (Pvt) Ltd: 47 Banglore Town, off Tipu Sultan Rd, Karachi 75350; tel. (21) 4528954; fax (21) 4533768; e-mail info@megatech.com.pk; internet www.megatech.com.pk; f. 1992; supplier of new digital telephone systems integrated with ISDN/BRI.

Mobilink: 42 Kulsum Plaza, 1st Floor, Blue Area, Islamabad; tel. (21) 2273984-9; fax (21) 2826999; e-mail customercare@mobilink .net; internet www.mobilinkgsm.com; subsidiary of Orascom Telecom; Pres. and CEO ZOUHAIR ABDUL KHALIQ.

National Telecommunication Corporation: NTC Building, F-5/1, Islamabad; tel. (51) 9206450; e-mail infohr@ntc.net.pk; internet www.ntc.net.pk; f. 1996 by government; Chair. NOOR-UD-DIN BAQAI.

Pakistan Telecommunications (Pvt) Ltd (PTCL): Block E, G-8/4, Islamabad 44000; tel. (51) 4844463; fax (51) 4843991; e-mail info@ptcl.net.pk; internet www.ptcl.com.pk; f. 1990; 74% state-owned; 26% owned by Etisalat (United Arab Emirates); Chair. HIFZ-UR-REHMAN; Pres. and CEO WALID IRSHAID.

TeleCard Ltd: 7th Floor, World Trade Centre, 10 Khayaban-e-Roomi, Block 5, Clifton, Karachi 75600; tel. (21) 111-222-124; e-mail customerservices@telecard.com.pk; internet www.telecard.com.pk; Chief Exec. SHAHID FIROZ.

Telenor: 13-K, Moaiz Centre, F-7 Markaz, Islamabad; tel. (51) 111-345-700; fax (51) 2651923; internet www.telenor.com.pk; f. 2004; private mobile telephone co; Pres. and CEO TORE JOHNSEN.

Telephone Industries of Pakistan (TIP): Khanpur Rd, Haripur 22630, NWFP; tel. (995) 611469; fax (995) 610490; e-mail mdtip@tip .org.pk; internet www.tip.org.pk; f. 1952; mfrs of telecommunications equipment.

Ufone: 13-B, F-7 Markaz, Jinnah Super Market, Islamabad; fax (51) 111-333-100; e-mail customercare@ufonegsm.net; internet www .ufone.com; f. 2001; subsidiary of Pakistan Telecommunications (Pvt) Ltd; private mobile telephone co; Pres. and Chief Exec. ABDUL AZIZ.

Warid Telecom (Pvt) Ltd: 9th Floor, EFU Bldg, Jail Rd, Lahore; e-mail customerservice@waridtel.com; internet www.waridtel.com; owned by Abu Dhabi Group; CEO MARWAN ZAWAYDEH.

Wateen Telecom (Pvt) Ltd: POB 3527, Lahore; fax (21) 4324096; e-mail info@wateen.com; internet www.wateen.com; subsidiary of the Abu Dhabi Group, UAE; mobile and fixed line telephone services; internet, television and multimedia provider; CEO TARIQ MALIK.

RADIO

Pakistan Broadcasting Corporation: National Broadcasting House, Constitution Ave, Islamabad 4400; tel. (51) 9208306; fax (51) 9223827; e-mail info@radio.gov.pk; internet www.radio.gov.pk; f. 1947 as Radio Pakistan; national broadcasting network of 33 stations; home service 24 hrs daily in 17 languages and dialects; external services 11 hrs daily in 15 languages; world service 11.49 hrs daily in two languages; 80 news bulletins daily; Dir-Gen. ASHFAQ GONDAL; Programme Dir NAYYAR MEHMOOD.

Pakistan Broadcasting Foundation: Planning and Development, Headquarters, Constitution Ave, Islamabad; tel. (51) 9216942; fax (51) 9204363.

Azad Kashmir Radio: Muzaffarabad; state-owned; Station Dir MASUD KASHFI; Dep. Controller (Eng.) SYED AHMED.

Capital FM: Islamabad; f. 1995; privately owned; broadcasts music and audience participation shows 24 hrs daily.

CityFM89: Penthouse, Anum Empire, Block 7 & 8, KCHS, Karachi; tel. (21) 4390155; fax (21) 4390160; e-mail info@cityFM89.com; internet cityfm89.com; f. 2004; owned by Kohinoor Airwaves (Pvt)

PAKISTAN

Ltd; broadcasts in Karachi, Lahore, Islamabad and Faisalabad; Chief Operating Officer NERMEEN CHINOY.

FM-100: Karachi; tel. (21) 2630611; fax (21) 2629311; music station; broadcasts in Karachi, Lahore and Islamabad.

TELEVISION

ARY One World: 6th Floor, Madina City Mall, Abdullah Haroon Rd, Saddar, Karachi; tel. (21) 5212815; fax (21) 5655700; internet www.thearynews.com.

ATV Shalimar Television Network Channel (Shalimar Recording and Broadcasting Co Ltd): 36, Sector H-9, POB 1246, Islamabad; tel. (51) 9257396; fax (51) 4434830; e-mail contact@srbc.com.pk; internet www.srbc.com.pk; f. 1976 as Shalimar Recording Co; 92.81% state-owned, 7.19% privately owned; 20 terrestrial stations throughout Pakistan; Man. Dir and CEO FAZAL-UR-REHMAN MALIK; Gen. Man. TARIQ MAJID.

CNBC Pakistan: Techno City Corporate Tower, 17/F Altaf Hussain Rd, Karachi; tel. (21) 2270850; fax (21) 2270852; internet www.cnbcpakistan.com.

Geo TV: I. I. Chundrigar Rd, Jang Building, Karachi; tel. (21) 2628614; fax (21) 2636937; e-mail distribution@geo.tv; internet www.geo.tv; f. 2003; Pakistan's first private broadcasting network; broadcasts in Urdu; operates four channels; Pres. IMRAN ASLAM.

HUM TV: Plot 10/11, Hassan Ali St, Karachi; tel. (21) 5374258; fax (21) 2628840.

Indus TV Network: 2nd Floor, Shafi Court, Civil Lines, Mereweather Rd, Karachi; tel. (21) 5693801; fax (21) 5693813; internet www.indus.tv; f. 2000; Pakistan's first independent satellite channel; CEO GHAZANFAR ALI.

Pakistan Television Corpn Ltd: Federal TV Complex, Constitution Ave, POB 1221, Islamabad; tel. (51) 9208651; fax (51) 9211184; e-mail md@ptv.com.pk; internet ptv.com.pk; f. 1964; transmits 24 hrs daily; four channels; Chair. SYED ANWAR MEHMOOD; Man. Dir ARSHAD KHAN.

SAMAA TV: Techno City Corporate Tower, Karachi; tel. (21) 111262275; fax (21) 2270848; internet www.samaa.tv.

WAQT Television: NIPCO House, 4 Sharah Fatimah Jinnah, Lahore; tel. (42) 6367551; fax (42) 6367616.

Finance

(cap. = capital; auth. = authorized; p.u. = paid up; res = reserves; dep. = deposits; m. = million; brs = branches; amounts in rupees unless otherwise stated)

BANKING

In January 1974 all domestic banks were nationalized. In December 1990 the Government announced that it intended to transfer the five state-owned commercial banks to private ownership. By late 1991 the majority of shares in the Muslim Commercial Bank Ltd and the Allied Bank of Pakistan Ltd had been transferred to private ownership. In 1991 the Government granted 10 new private commercial bank licences, the first since banks were nationalized in 1974. In June 2002 the Supreme Court reversed its 1999 ruling that ordered the Government to abolish charging interest. Interest charges, known as *riba*, are forbidden under Islamic law. The ruling would have required all financial institutions to adopt the Islamic style of banking. In late 2002 the State Bank of Pakistan gave banks three options for the launching of Islamic banking: to establish an independent Islamic bank; to open subsidiaries of existing commercial banks; and to establish new branches to carry out Islamic banking operations.

Central Bank

State Bank of Pakistan: Central Directorate, I. I. Chundrigar Rd, POB 4456, Karachi 2; tel. (21) 9212400; fax (21) 9217234; e-mail info@sbp.org.pk; internet www.sbp.org.pk; f. 1948; bank of issue; controls and regulates currency and foreign exchange; cap. 100m., res 76,067m., dep. 392,506m. (June 2005); Gov. SYED SALIM RAZA; 17 brs.

Commercial Banks

Allied Bank Ltd: Central Office, Main Clifton Rd, Bath Island, Karachi; tel. (21) 5370499; fax (21) 5370500; e-mail aftab.manzoor@abl.com.pk; internet www.abl.com.pk; f. 1942 as Australasia Bank Ltd; name changed as above 2005; cap. 5,386.4m., res 7,520.6m., dep. 267,466.8m. (Dec. 2007); 49% state-owned; Pres. and Chief Exec. MOHAMMAD AFTAB MANZOOR; Chair. MOHAMMAD NAEEM MUKHTAR; 741 brs in Pakistan.

Arif Habib Bank Ltd: 2A, R. Y. 16, Old Queens Rd, Karachi; tel. (21) 111-124-725; fax (21) 2463553; e-mail kamalkhan@arifhabibbank.com; internet www.arifhabibbank.com; f. 2006; cap. 4,500.0m., res

Directory

1,608.8m., dep. 9,464.8m. (Dec. 2007); President and CEO HUSAIN LAWAI.

Askari Bank Ltd: AWT Plaza, The Mall, POB 1084, Rawalpindi; tel. (51) 9272289; fax (51) 9273180; e-mail president@askaribank.com.pk; internet www.askaribank.com.pk; f. 1992; cap. 3,006.5m., res 2,997.3m., dep. 145,663.8m. (Dec. 2007); Chair. Lt-Gen. ZAVED ZIA; Pres. and Chief Exec. MUHAMMAD RIYAZUL HAQUE; 98 brs.

Atlas Bank Ltd: 3rd Floor, Federation House, Abdullah Shah Ghazi Rd, Clifton, Karachi; tel. (21) 111–333–225; fax (21) 5877197; e-mail info@atlasbank.com.pk; internet www.atlasbank.com.pk; President and CEO ABDUL AZIZ RAJKOTWALA.

Bank Al Habib Ltd: Mackinnons Bldg, I. I. Chundrigar Rd, Karachi; tel. (21) 2412421; fax (21) 2419752; e-mail info@bankalhabib.com; internet www.bankalhabib.com; f. 1991; cap. 3,681.1m., res 2,839.5m., dep. 114,818.9m. (Dec. 2007); Chief Exec. and Man. Dir ABBAS D. HABIB; 103 brs.

Bank Alfalah Ltd: BA Bldg, I. I. Chundrigar Rd, POB 6773, Karachi; tel. (21) 2416811; fax (21) 2424901; e-mail figroup@bankalfalah.com; internet www.bankalfalah.com; f. 1992 as Habib Credit and Exchange Ltd; name changed as above 1998; cap. 6,500.0m., res 4,868.0m., dep. 277,312.1m. (Dec. 2006); 61.66% owned by Abu Dhabi Consortium, 20% public, 12.60% non-residents, 5.19% employees and execs, 0.55% dirs; Chair SHEIKH HAMDAN BIN MUBARAK AL NAHAYAN; 231 brs.

The Bank of Khyber: 24 The Mall, Peshawar; tel. (521) 111-959-595; fax (915) 278146; e-mail bokforex@psh.paknet.com.pk; internet www.bok.com.pk; f. 1991; cap. 2,000.9m., res 924.1m., dep. 19,227.0m. (Dec. 2006); 51% state-owned; 49% public shareholders; the main branch in Peshawar began Islamic banking operations in June 2003; Man. Dir BILAL MUSTAFA; 29 brs.

The Bank of Punjab: BOP Tower, 10-B, Block-E-II, Main Blvd, Gulberg-III, POB 2254, Lahore; tel. (42) 5783711; fax (42) 5783713; e-mail sajjad.hussain@bop.com.pk; internet www.bop.com.pk; f. 1989; cap. 4,230.4m., res 10,880.1m., dep. 191,968.9m. (Dec. 2007); 51% owned by provincial govt; Chair. JAVED MEHMOOD; Pres. SAJJAD HUSSAIN; 271 brs.

Faysal Bank Ltd: ST-02, Faysal House, 4th Floor, FIG, Main Shahrah-e-Faisal, Karachi; tel. (21) 2795306; fax (21) 2793131; e-mail fbl@faysalbank.com; internet www.faysalbank.com; f. 1995; merged with Al-Faysal Investment Bank Ltd 2002; cap. 5,296.4m., res 9,378.4m., dep. 112,063.3m. (Dec. 2007); Pres. and CEO NAVED A. KHAN; 107 brs.

Habib Bank Ltd: 22 Habib Bank Plaza, I. I. Chundrigar Rd, Karachi 75650; tel. (21) 2411530; fax (21) 2411556; e-mail zmahmood@hblpak.com; internet www.habibbankltd.com; f. 1941; cap. 6,900m., res 27,030.1m., dep. 546,716.4m. (Dec. 2007); transferred to private sector Feb. 2004; 51% owned by Agha Khan Fund for Economic Development (United Kingdom), 41% by State Bank of Pakistan and 8% by Government and National Bank of Pakistan; Pres. ZAKIR MAHMOOD; 1,437 brs in Pakistan; 39 foreign brs.

Habib Metropolitan Bank Ltd: Mezzanine Floor, Spencer's Bldg, I. I. Chundrigar Rd, POB 1289, Karachi; tel. (21) 2638080; fax (21) 2630404; e-mail info@hmb.com.pk; internet www.hmb.com.pk; f. 1992; fmrly Metropolitan Bank; merged with Habib Bank AG Zurich in 2006; cap. 5,018.4m., res 6,439.9m., dep. 124,276.4m. (Dec. 2007); Pres. and Chief Exec. KASSIM PAREKH; Exec. Dir MOHAMADALI R. HABIB; 82 brs.

JS Bank Ltd: 1st Floor, Shaheen Commercial Complex, Dr Ziauddin Ahmed Rd, Karachi 74200; tel. (21) 2635208; fax (21) 2631803; e-mail info@jsbl.com; internet www.jsbl.com; f. 2006; cap. 5,106.3m., res 59,542.0m., dep. 14,406.1m. (Dec. 2007); Pres. NAVEED QAZI.

KASB Bank Ltd: Business and Finance Centre, I. I. Chundrigar Rd, Karachi 74000; tel. (21) 2446800; fax (21) 9217588; e-mail international@kasb.com; internet www.kasbbank.com; f. 1995 as Platinum Commercial Bank Ltd; name changed as above 2003; cap. 3,107.0m., res 1,184.5m., dep. 34,010.9m. (Dec. 2007); Pres. and CEO MUNEER KAMAL; 35 brs.

Khushhali Bank: 94 West, 4th Floor, Jinnah Ave, Blue Area, POB 3111, Islamabad; tel. (51) 111-092-092; fax (51) 9206080; internet www.khushhalibank.com.pk; cap. 1,705.0m., res 15,023.4m. (Dec. 2004); Pres. GHALIB NISHTAR.

MCB Bank Ltd: MCB Tower, I. I. Chundrigar Rd, POB 4976, Karachi 74000; tel. (21) 2270075; fax (21) 2270076; e-mail atif.bajwa@mcb.com.pk; internet www.mcb.com.pk; f. 1947; cap. 6,282.8m., res 43,706.2m., dep. 302,577.1m. (Dec. 2007); Chair. Mian MUHAMMAD MANSHA; Pres. and CEO ATIF ASLAM BAJWA; 1,057 brs in Pakistan, 4 brs abroad.

Mybank Ltd: 10th Floor, Business & Finance Centre, I. I. Chundrigar Rd, Karachi; tel. (21) 111-692-265; fax (21) 2471951; e-mail president@mybankltd.com; internet mybankltd.com; f. 1991; fmrly Bolan Bank Ltd; cap. 5,063m., res 878m., dep. 30,153m. (Dec. 2007); Chair. IQBAL ALIMOHAMED; Pres. and CEO MUHAMMAD BILAL SHEIKH; 60 brs.

PAKISTAN

National Bank of Pakistan (NBP): NBP Bldg, I. I. Chundrigar Rd, POB 4937, Karachi 2; tel. (21) 9212208; fax (21) 9212774; e-mail nbp@nbp.com.pk; internet www.nbp.com.pk; f. 1949; cap. 8,154.3m., res 62,839.1m., dep. 598,969.3m. (Dec. 2007); 100% state-owned; Pres. SYED ALI RAZA; 1,491 brs in Pakistan and 22 brs abroad.

NIB Bank Ltd: Muhammadi House, I. I. Chundrigar Rd, Karachi; tel. (21) 2420333; fax (21) 2472258; e-mail info@nibpk.com; internet www.nibpk.com; f. 2003; cap. 36,044.2m., res 691.3m., dep. 118,781.4m. (Dec. 2007); Pres. and CEO Khawaja IQBAL HASSAN; 27 brs.

PICIC Commercial Bank Ltd: Spencer Bldg, I. I. Chundrigar Rd, POB 572, Karachi 74200; tel. (21) 2638817; fax (21) 2639760; e-mail info@picicbank.com.pk; internet www.picicbank.com.pk; f. 1994 as Schön Bank Ltd; name changed to Gulf Commercial Bank Ltd in 1998; 60% shares and full management of bank acquired by PICIC in February 2001, name changed to above in June 2001; controlling 63.36% stake acquired by NIB Bank (subsidiary of Tamasek Holdings, Singapore) in June 2007 in preparation for proposed full merger with NIB later that year; cap. 2,734.9m., res 867.5m., dep. 59,148.3m. (Dec. 2005); Chair. FRANCES A. ROZARIO; Pres. and CEO KHAWAJA IQBAL HASSAN; 129 brs.

Royal Bank of Scotland (RBS) Pakistan: 16 Abdullah Haroon Rd, Karachi; tel. (21) 5683097; fax (21) 5683432; e-mail info@rbs.com.pk; internet www.rbs.com.pk; fmrly ABN AMRO Bank Pakistan Ltd; Chair. MUHAMMAD AURANGZEB; CEO SHEHZAD NAQVI; 80 brs.

Samba Bank Ltd: 5th & 6th Floor, Sidco Avenue Centre, Maulana Deen Mohammad Wafai Rd, Karachi 74000; tel. (21) 111-999-333; internet www.cresbank.com; f. 2002 as Crescent Commercial Bank Ltd; Pres. and CEO SHEHZAD NAQVI; Chair. SYED SAJJAD RAZVI; 18 brs.

Saudi Pak Commercial Bank Ltd: Saudi Pak Bldg, I. I. Chundrigar Rd, Karachi; tel. (21) 2460475; e-mail president@spcb.com.pk; internet www.saudipakbank.com; f. 1994 as Prudential Commercial Bank; acquired by Saudi Pak Industrial and Agricultural Investment Co (Pvt) Ltd in 2001; cap. 5,001,8.m., res 1,298.2m., dep. 42,373.7m. (Dec. 2007); Chair. MUNNAWAR HAMID; Pres. and CEO AZMAT TARIN; 38 brs.

Soneri Bank Ltd: 87 Shahrah-e-Quaid-e-Azam, POB 49, Lahore; tel. (42) 6368142; fax (42) 6368138; e-mail main.lahore@soneribank.com; internet www.soneribank.com; f. 1991; cap. 4,114.2m., res 2,257.5m., dep. 66,015.6m. (Dec. 2007); Chair. ALAUDDIN FEERASTA; Pres. and CEO SAFAR ALI K. LAKHANI; 69 brs.

Standard Chartered Bank (Pakistan) Ltd: 3rd Floor, Main Br., POB 5556, I. I. Chundrigar Rd, Karachi; tel. (21) 2450288; fax (21) 2414914; e-mail badar.kazmi@pk.standardchartered.com; internet www.standardchartered.com/pk; f. 2006; cap. 38,715.9m., res 785.0m., dep. 161,138.2m. (Dec. 2006); Pres. and CEO BADAR KAZMI; 144 brs.

United Bank Ltd: State Life Bldg, No. 1, I. I. Chundrigar Rd, POB 4306, Karachi 74000; tel. (21) 2417021; fax (21) 2413492; e-mail president@ubl.com.pk; internet www.ubl.com.pk; f. 1959; cap. 8,093.8m., res 18,674.0m., dep. 407,717.2m. (Dec. 2007); privatized in 2002; Pres. and CEO ATIF BOKHARI; 1,040 brs in Pakistan and 15 brs abroad.

Leasing Banks (*Modarabas*)

The number of leasing banks (*modarabas*), which conform to the strictures placed upon the banking system by *Shari'a* (the Islamic legal code), rose from four in 1988 to about 45 in 2002. The following are among the most important *modarabas* in Pakistan.

Asian Leasing Corporation Ltd: 85-B Jail Rd, Gulberg, POB 3176, Lahore; tel. (42) 484417; fax (42) 484418.

Atlas Lease Ltd: Ground Floor, Federation House, Shahrah-e-Firdousi, Main Clifton, Karachi 75600; tel. (21) 5866817; fax (21) 5870543; e-mail all@atlasgrouppk.com; Chair. YUSUF H. SHIRAZI.

B. R. R. International Modaraba: 1500 ASaima Trade Towers, I. I Chundrigar Rd, Karachi 74000; tel. (21) 2271874; fax (21) 2271912; e-mail brr@cyber.net.pk; internet www.firstdawood.com/brr.

Dadabhoy Leasing Co Ltd: 5th Floor, Maqbool Commercial Complex, JCHS Block, Main Shahrah-e-Faisal, Karachi; tel. (21) 4548171; fax (21) 4547301; Man. (Finance) MOHAMMAD AYUB.

English Leasing Ltd: D-16, Block 3, Clifton, Scheme 5, Karachi; tel. (21) 5810453; fax (21) 5375770; e-mail info@engl.com.pk; internet www.engl.com.pk; Chair. ASIM MAHBOOB SHEIKH.

First Habib Bank Modaraba: 18 Habib Bank Plaza, I. I. Chundrigar Rd, Karachi 75650; tel. (21) 2635949; fax (21) 2627373; e-mail wazir@habibmodaraba.com; internet www.habibmodaraba.com; f. 1991; wholly owned subsidiary of Habib Bank Ltd; Chair. WAZIR HUSAIN JAFREE; CEO MUHAMMAD SHOAIB.

Orix Leasing Pakistan Ltd: Overseas Investors Chamber of Commerce Bldg, Talpur Rd, Karachi 74000; tel. (21) 2425896; fax (21) 2425897; e-mail olp@orixpakistan.com; internet www.orixpakistan.com; f. 1986; cap. US $10m. (June 2004); Chief Exec. HUMAYUN MURAD.

Directory

Pakistan Industrial and Commercial Leasing Ltd: 504 Park Ave, 24-A, Block 6, PECHS, Shahrah-e-Faisal, Karachi 75210; tel. (21) 4551045; fax (21) 4520655; e-mail picl@super.net.pk; internet www.piclltd.com; f. 1987; Exec. Chair. ZAHEERUL HAQUE.

Standard Chartered Modaraba: Standard Services of Pakistan (Pvt) Ltd, Standard Bank Bldg, I. I. Chundrigar Rd, POB 5556, Karachi 74000; tel. (21) 2450566; fax (21) 2422821; e-mail contact@scmodaraba.com; internet www.scmodaraba.com; fmrly First Grindlays Modaraba; Man. Dir SYED ZAHIR MEHDI.

Islamic Banks

BankIslami Pakistan Ltd: 11th Floor, Executive Tower One, Dolmen City, Marine Dr., Block 4, Clifton, Karachi; tel. (21) 111-247-111; fax (21) 5378373; e-mail info@bankislami.com.pk; internet www.bankislami.com.pk; CEO HASSAN BILGRAMI.

Dawood Islamic Bank Ltd: Trade Centre, I. I. Chundrigar Rd, Karachi; tel. (21) 2272440; fax (21) 2272460; e-mail nikolaus.schwarz@dawoodislamic.com; internet www.dawoodislamic.com; Pres. and CEO NIKOLAUS SCHWARZ.

Dubai Islamic Bank Pakistan Ltd: Hassan Chambers, Plot DC-7, Block 7, Clifton, Karachi; tel. (21) 5368556; fax (21) 5821071; e-mail saad.zaman@dib.ae; internet www.dibpak.com; CEO SAAD ZAMAN.

Emirates Global Islamic Bank Ltd: Shopping Arcade, Karachi Sheraton Hotel and Towers, Club Rd, Karachi; tel. (21) 5633418; fax (21) 5633427; e-mail feedback@egibl.com; internet www.egibl.com; sponsored by Emirates Investment Group LLC, UAE, and Saudi Arabian investors; Pres. and CEO SYED TARIQ HUSSAIN.

Meezan Bank Ltd: 2nd Floor, PNSC Bldg, Moulvi Tamizuddin Khan Rd, Karachi 74000; tel. (21) 5610582; fax (21) 5610375; e-mail info@meezanbank.com; internet www.meezanbank.com; f. 1997 as Al-Meezan Investment Bank; became commercial bank 2002 and name changed as above; cap. 2,036.6m., res 988.0m., dep. 26,011.7m. (Dec. 2005); Pres. and CEO IRFAN SIDDIQUI; Gen. Man. ARIFUL ISLAM; 37 brs.

Co-operative Banks

In 1976 all existing co-operative banks were dissolved and given the option of becoming a branch of the appropriate Provincial Co-operative Bank, or of reverting to the status of a credit society.

Federal Bank for Co-operatives: State Bank Bldg, G-5/2, POB 1218, Islamabad; tel. (51) 9204518; fax (51) 9204534; f. 1976; owned jtly by the fed. Govt, the prov. govts and the State Bank of Pakistan; provides credit facilities to each of six prov. co-operative banks and regulates their operations; they in turn provide credit facilities through co-operative socs; supervises policy of prov. co-operative banks and of multi-unit co-operative socs; assists fed. and prov. govts in formulating schemes for development and revitalization of co-operative movement; carries out research on rural credit, etc.; Man. Dir M. AFZAL HUSSAIN; four regional offices.

Investment Banks

Asset Investment Bank Ltd: Rm 1-B, 1st Floor, Ali Plaza, Khayaban-e-Quaid-e-Azam, Blue Area, Islamabad; tel. (51) 2270625; fax (51) 2272506; Chief Exec. SYED NAVEED ZAIDI.

Atlas Investment Bank Ltd: 3rd Floor, Federation House, Abdullah shah Ghazi Rd, Main Clifton, Karachi; tel. (21) 111-333-225; fax (21) 5870543; e-mail info@atlasbank.com.pk; internet www.atlasbank.com.pk; 15% owned by Bank of Tokyo-Mitsubishi UFJ Ltd; Chair. YUSUF H. SHIRAZI; CEO AZIZ RAJKOTWALA.

Escorts Investment Bank Ltd: Escorts House, 26 Davis Rd, Lahore; tel. (42) 6371931; fax (42) 6375950; e-mail mailmanager@escortsbank.net; internet escortsbank.net; Pres. and CEO RASHID MANSUR.

IGI Investment Bank Ltd: 7th Floor, The Forum, Suite 701–703, 4-20, Block 9, Khayaban-e-Jami, Clifton, Karachi; tel. (21) 111-234-234; fax (21) 111-567-567; e-mail contact.center@igi.com.pk; internet www.igiinvestmentbank.com.pk; Man. Dir and CEO SAMIR AHMED.

Orix Investment Bank Pakistan Ltd: 2nd Floor, Islamic Chamber of Commerce Bldg, St 2/A, Block 9, Clifton, Karachi 75600; tel. (21) 5861266; fax (21) 5868862; e-mail oibpl@orixbank.com; internet www.orixbank.com; f. 1995; Man. Dir and CEO NAIM FAROOQUI.

Development Finance Organizations

Bankers' Skill Development Centre: Hamilton Court, 1st Floor, Suite 206/A, G-1, Main Clifton Rd, Block 7, Karachi 75600; tel. (21) 5306244; fax (21) 5306245; Pres. and CEO Dr AHSAN H. KHAN.

First MicroFinanceBank Ltd: President's Secretariat, 62-C, 25th Commercial St, Tauheed Commercial Area, DHA Phase V, Karachi; tel. (21) 5822432; fax (21) 5822434; e-mail information@mfb.com.pk; internet www.mfb.com.pk; Pres. and CEO HUSSAIN TEJANY.

First Women Bank Ltd: S.T.S.M. Foundation Bldg, CL-10/20/2 Beaumont Rd, Civil Lines, Karachi 75530; tel. (21) 111-676-767; fax

(21) 5657756; e-mail info@fwbl.com.pk; internet www.fwbl.com.pk; f. 1989; cap. and res 590m., dep. 8,690m. (Dec. 2004); Pres. ZARINE AZIZ; 38 brs.

House Building Finance Corpn: Finance and Trade Centre, 3rd Floor, Shahrah-e-Faisal, Karachi 74400; tel. (21) 9202314; fax (21) 9202360; e-mail info@hbfc.com.pk; internet www.hbfc.com.pk; provides loans for the construction and purchase of housing units; Man. Dir and CEO AZHAR A. JAFFRI.

Industrial Development Bank of Pakistan: State Life Bldg No. 2, Wallace Rd, off I. I. Chundrigar Rd, POB 5082, Karachi 74000; tel. (21) 9213601-10; fax (21) 9213644; e-mail idbp@idbp.com.pk; internet www.idbp.com.pk; f. 1961; provides credit facilities for small and medium-sized industrial enterprises in the private sector; 100% state-owned; Chair. and Man. Dir JAMAL NASIM; 19 brs.

Investment Corpn of Pakistan: NBP Bldg, 5th Floor, I. I. Chundrigar Rd, POB 5410, Karachi 74400; tel. (21) 9212360; fax (21) 9212388; e-mail icp@paknet3.ptc.pk; f. 1966 by the Govt to encourage and broaden the base of investments and to develop the capital market; Man. Dir ISTIQBAL MEHDI; 10 brs.

Khushhali Bank: 94W, 4th Floor, Jinnah Ave, Blue Area, Islamabad 44000; tel. (51) 111-092-092; internet www.khushhalibank.com.pk; f. 2000 by the Govt under the Asian Development Bank's microfinance sector development programme; provides micro-loans to the poor and finances reforms in the micro-finance sector; cap. 1,705m. (Aug. 2000); Pres. GHALIB NISHTAR.

National Investment Trust Ltd: NBP Bldg, 6th Floor, I. I. Chundrigar Rd, POB 5671, Karachi; tel. (21) 2419061; fax (21) 2430623; e-mail info@nit.com.pk; internet www.nit.com.pk; f. 1962; an open-ended mutual fund, mobilizes domestic savings to meet the requirements of growing economic development and enables investors to share in the industrial and economic prosperity of the country; 67,000 Unit holders (1999/2000); Man. Dir TARIQ IQBAL KHAN.

Network Microfinance Bank Ltd: 202 Azayam Plaza, opp. FTC Bldg, SMCHS, Shahrah-e-Faisal, Karachi; fax (21) 4311722; e-mail nmb@networkmicrobank.com; internet www.networkmicrobank.com; Pres. and CEO M. MOAZZAM KHAN.

Pak Oman Microfinance Bank Ltd: 2nd Floor, Tower C, Finance and Trade Centre, Shahrah-e-Faisal, Karachi; tel. (21) 5630941; fax (21) 5630999; e-mail info@pomicro.com; internet www.pomicro.com; f. 2005; Pres. and CEO MUNAWAR SULEMAN.

Pakistan Industrial Credit and Investment Corpn Ltd (PICIC): State Life Bldg No. 1, I. I. Chundrigar Rd, POB 5080, Karachi 74000; tel. (21) 2414220; fax (21) 2419100; f. 1957 as an industrial development bank to provide financial assistance in both local and foreign currencies, for the establishment of new industries in the private sector and balancing modernization, replacement and expansion of existing industries; merchant banking and foreign exchange activities; total assets 33,949m., cap. 2,736m., res 4,188m. (June 2005); held 97.9% and 2.1% by local and foreign investors respectively; Man. Dir MOHAMMAD ALI KHOJA; Chair. ALTAF M. SALEEM; 19 brs.

Pakistan Kuwait Investment Co (Pvt) Ltd: Tower 'C', 4th Floor, Finance and Trade Centre, Shahrah-e-Faisal, POB 901, Karachi 74000; tel. (21) 5630901; fax (21) 5630939; e-mail info@pkic.com; internet www.pkic.com; jt venture between the Govt and Kuwait to promote investment in industrial and agro-based enterprises; Man. Dir SHAMSUL HASAN.

Pak-Libya Holding Co (Pvt) Ltd: Finance and Trade Centre, 5th Floor, Tower 'C', Shahrah-e-Faisal, POB 10425, Karachi 74400; tel. (21) 111-111-115; fax (21) 5630665; e-mail paklibya@paklibya.com.pk; internet www.paklibya.com.pk; jt venture between the Govts of Pakistan and Libya to promote industrial investment in Pakistan; Chair. RAMADAN A. HAGGIAGI; Man. Dir KAMAL UDDIN KHAN.

Saudi Pak Industrial and Agricultural Investment Co (Pvt) Ltd: Saudi Pak Tower, 61-A Jinnah Ave, Islamabad; tel. (51) 2273514; fax (51) 2273508; e-mail saudipak@saudipak.com; internet www.saudipak.com; f. 1981 jtly by Saudi Arabia and Pakistan to finance industrial and agro-based projects and undertake investment-related activities in Pakistan; cap. 2,000m., res 732m., dep. 5,900m. (March 2001); CEO MUHAMMAD RASHID ZAHIR; Chair. ABDULLAH T. AL-THENAYAN; 1 br.

SME Bank Ltd: Jang Plaza, 2nd Floor, 40 Fazal-ul-Haq Rd, Blue Area, POB 1587, Islamabad; tel. (51) 9217000; fax (51) 9217001; e-mail info@smebank.org; internet www.smebank.org; formed through merger of Regional Development Finance Corpn (RDFC) and Small Business Finance Corpn (SBFC); provides loans for small businesses; Pres. and CEO R. A. CHUGHTAI.

Zarai Taraqiati Bank Ltd (ZTBL): 1 Faisal Ave, POB 1400, Islamabad; tel. (51) 9252805; fax (51) 9252737; e-mail contactus@ztbl.com.pk; internet www.ztbl.com.pk; f. 1961; provides credit facilities to agriculturists (particularly small-scale farmers) and cottage industrialists in the rural areas and for allied projects; 100% state-owned; Pres. MUHAMMAD ZAKA ASHRAF; 24 zonal offices and 342 brs.

Banking Associations

Investment Banks Association of Pakistan: 7th Floor, Shaheen Commercial Complex, Dr Ziauddin Ahmed Rd, POB 1345, Karachi; tel. (21) 2631396; fax (21) 2630678; internet www.ibap.biz; Chair. RASHID MANSUR.

Modaraba Association of Pakistan: 6th Floor, Progressive Centre, 30–A, Block 6, PECHS, Shahrah-e-Faisal, Karachi; tel. (21) 4322439; fax (21) 4322440; internet www.modarabas.com.pk; Chair. MUHAMMAD SHOAIB.

Pakistan Banks' Association: D-126, Block 4, Clifton, Karachi, Karachi 2; tel. (21) 5822986; fax (21) 5823418; e-mail pba@pakistanbanks.org; internet www.pakistanbanks.org; Chair. M. YOUNAS KHAN; Sec. A. GHAFFAR K. HAFIZ.

Banking Organizations

Banking Mohtasib Pakistan: Secretariat, 5th Floor, Shaheen Complex, POB 604, M. R. Kiyani Rd, Karachi; tel. (21) 9217334; fax (21) 9217375; e-mail info@bankingmohtasib.gov.pk; internet www.bankingmohtasib.gov.pk; resolves public grievances against banks and disputes between banking institutions; offices in Quetta, Lahore, Rawalpindi and Peshawar; Banking Ombudsman AZHAR HAMID.

Pakistan Banking Council: Habib Bank Plaza, I. I. Chundrigar Rd, Karachi; tel. (21) 227121; fax (21) 222232; f. 1973; acts as a co-ordinating body between the nationalized banks and the Ministry of Finance; Chair. MUHAMMAD ZAKI; Sec. Mir WASIF ALI.

Pakistan Development Banking Institute: 4th Floor, Sidco Ave Centre, Stratchen Rd, Karachi; tel. (21) 5688049; fax (21) 5688460.

STOCK EXCHANGES

Securities and Exchange Commission of Pakistan: NIC Bldg, 63 Jinnah Ave, Blue Area, Islamabad 44000; tel. (51) 9218585; fax (51) 9204915; e-mail enquiries@secp.gov.pk; internet www.secp.gov.pk; oversees and co-ordinates operations of exchanges and registration of companies; registration offices in Faisalabad (356-A, 1st Floor, Al-Jamil Plaza, People's Colony, Small D Ground, Faisalabad; tel. (41) 713841), Karachi (No. 2, 4th Floor, State Life Building, North Wing, Karachi; tel. (21) 2415855), Lahore (3rd and 4th Floors, Associated House, 7 Egerton Rd, Lahore; tel. (42) 9202044), Multan (61 Abdali Rd, Multan; tel. (61) 542609), Peshawar (Hussain Commercial Bldg, 3 Arbab Rd, Peshawar), Quetta (382/3, IDBP House, Shahrah-e-Hall, Quetta; tel. (81) 844138) and Sukkur (B-30, Sindhi Muslim Housing Society, Airport Rd, Sukkur; tel. (71) 30517); Chair. RAZI-UR-RAHMAN KHAN.

Islamabad Stock Exchange (Guarantee) Ltd: 4th Floor, Stock Exchange Bldg, 101E Faz-ul-haq Rd, Blue Area, Islamabad; tel. (51) 2275045; fax (51) 2275044; e-mail ise@ise.com.pk; internet www.ise.com.pk; f. 1991; 103 mems; Chair. SHAHARYAR AHMAD; Sec. YOUSUF H. MAKHDOOMI.

Karachi Stock Exchange (Guarantee) Ltd: Stock Exchange Bldg, Stock Exchange Rd, Karachi 74000; tel. (21) 111-001-122; fax (21) 2410825; e-mail info@kse.com.pk; internet www.kse.com.pk; f. 1947; 200 mems, 654 listed cos (Jan. 2007); Chair. KAMRAN Y. MIRZA; Man. Dir ADNAN AFRIDI.

Lahore Stock Exchange (Guarantee) Ltd: Lahore Stock Exchange Bldg, 19 Khayaban-e-Aiwan-e-Iqbal, POB 1315, Lahore 54000; tel. (42) 6368000; fax (42) 6368484; e-mail secretary@lahorestock.com; internet www.lahorestock.com; f. 1970; 511 listed cos, 151 mems; Chair. ARIF SAEED; Man. Dir/CEO MIAN SHAKEEL ASLAM.

National Commodity Exchange Ltd: 9th Floor, PIC Towers, 32-A Lalazar Drive, M. T. Khan Rd, Karachi; tel. (21) 111-623-623; fax (21) 5611263; e-mail info@ncel.com.pk; internet www.ncel.com.pk; f. 2002; online commodity futures exchange; regulated by Securities and Exchange Commission of Pakistan; Chair. SHAUKAT TARIN; Man. Dir ASSIM JANG.

Central Depository Co: CDC House, 99-B, Block B, S. M. C. H. Society, Main Shahrah-e-Faisal, Karachi 74400; tel. (21) 2416774; fax (21) 4326016; e-mail info@cdcpak.com; internet www.cdcpakistan.com; f. 1993 to manage and operate Central Depository System of the financial services industry; CEO HANIF JAKHURA.

INSURANCE

In 1995 legislation came into effect allowing foreign insurance companies to operate in Pakistan.

Insurance Division: Securities and Exchange Commission, 4th Floor, NIC Bldg, Jinnah Ave, Islamabad; tel. (51) 9207091; fax (51) 9204915; e-mail enquiries@secp.gov.pk; internet www.secp.gov.pk;

PAKISTAN

Directory

under the Ministry of Finance; Commissioner of Insurance TARIQ A. HUSSAIN; Exec. Dir S. GULREZ YAZDANI.

Life Insurance

American Life Insurance Co (Pakistan) Ltd: 13th Floor (Level 16), Block 4, Scheme 5, Clifton, Karachi 75600; tel. (21) 111-111-711; fax (21) 5290042; e-mail alico@cyber.net.pk; internet www.alico.com.pk; Chair. and CEO ARIF SULTAN MUFTI.

EFU Life Assurance Ltd: 37-K, Block 6, PECHS, Karachi; tel. (21) 111-338-111; fax (21)4535079; e-mail info@efulife.com; internet www.efulife.com; f. 1932; Chair. SAIFUDDIN N. ZOOMKAWALA; Man. Dir and CEO TAHER G. SACHAK.

Postal Life Insurance Organization: 2nd and 3rd Floors, Karachi GPO Bldg, I. I. Chundrigar Rd, Karachi; tel. (21) 9211102; e-mail gmplikar@paknet.pk.com; f. 1884; life and group insurance; Gen. Man. SHAHAR YARUDDIN.

State Life Insurance Corpn of Pakistan: State Life Bldg No. 9, Dr Ziauddin Ahmed Rd, POB 5725, Karachi 75530; tel. (21) 111-111-888; fax (21) 9202868; e-mail dhasp@statelife.com.pk; internet www.statelife.com.pk; f. 1972; life and group insurance and pension schemes; Chair. SHAHID AZIZ SIDDIQI.

General Insurance

ACE Insurance Ltd: 6th Floor, NIC Bldg, Abbasi Shaheed Rd, off Shahrah-e-Faisal, Karachi; tel. (21) 5681320; fax (21) 5683935; e-mail zehra.naqvi@acegroup.com; internet www.ace-ina.com; f. 1948; Chief Exec. ZEHRA NAQVI.

Adamjee Insurance Co Ltd: Adamjee House, 6th Floor, I. I. Chundrigar Rd, POB 4850, Karachi 74000; tel. (21) 2410145; fax (21) 2412627; e-mail info@adamjeeinsurance.com; internet www.adamjeeinsurance.com; f. 1960; Man. Dir MUHAMMAD ALI ZEB.

Agro General Insurance Co Ltd: Room No. 416–418, 4th Floor, Continental Trade Centre, Block 8, Main Clifton Rd, Karachi; tel. (21) 5302902-06; fax (21) 5302913; e-mail agiho@cyber.net.pk; f. 1987; Man. Dir and CEO M. JALILULLAH.

AIG Pakistan New Hampshire Insurance Co: 7th Floor, Dawood Centre, M. T. Khan Rd, Karachi 75530; tel. (21) 111-111-244; fax (21) 5634022; e-mail info-pakistan@aig.com; internet www.aigpakistan.com; f. 1869; Country Man. GOKTUG GUR.

Alpha Insurance Co Ltd: State Life Bldg No. 1B–1C, 2nd Floor, off I. I. Chundrigar Rd, POB 4359, Karachi 74000; tel. (21) 2416041; fax (21) 2419968; internet www.alphainsurance.com.pk; f. 1952; Chair. IQBAL M. QURESHI; Man. Dir V. C. GONSALVES; 9 brs.

Amicus Insurance Co Ltd: F-50, Block 7, Feroze Nana Rd, Bath Island, POB 3971, Karachi; tel. (21) 5831082; fax (21) 5870220; f. 1991; Chair. M. IRSHAD UDDIN.

Asia Insurance Co Ltd: 19C and 19D, Block L, Gulberg III, Ferozepur Rd, Lahore; tel. (42) 5858532; fax (42) 5865579; e-mail asiains@nexlinx.net.pk; f. 1979; Chief Exec. ZAFAR IQBAL SHEIKH.

Askari General Insurance Co Ltd: 4th Floor, AWT Plaza, The Mall, POB 843, Rawalpindi; tel. (51) 9272425; fax (51) 9272424; e-mail agicoho@agico.com.pk; internet www.agico.com.pk; f. 1995; Pres. and Chief Exec. MOHAMMAD HUSSAIN HIRJI.

Business and Industrial Insurance Co Ltd: 65 East Pak Pavilions, 1st Floor, Fazal-e-Haq Rd, Blue Area, Islamabad; tel. (51) 2278757; fax (51) 2271914; e-mail biic.ltd@yahoo.com; f. 1995; Chair. and Chief Exec. Mian MUMTAZ ABDULLAH.

Capital Insurance Co Ltd: Office 222, 5th Floor, Mega Tower, 63-B Main Blvd, Gulberg-II, Lahore; tel. (42) 5777527; fax (42) 5777548; e-mail info@capital-insurance.net; internet www.capital-insurance.net; f. 1998; CEO M. B. MANAF; Chair. MUHAMMAD SADIQUE LONE.

Central Insurance Co Ltd: Dawood Centre, 5th Floor, M. T. Khan Rd, POB 3988, Karachi 75530; tel. (21) 5686001; fax (21) 5680218; e-mail info.cic@dawoodgroup.com; internet www.ceninsure.com; f. 1960; owned by the Dawood Group; Chief Exec. VIQUAR SIDDIQI.

Century Insurance Co Ltd: 11th Floor, Lakson Square Bldg No. 3, Sarwar Sheheed Rd, POB 4895, Karachi 74200; tel. (21) 5698000; fax (21) 5671665; e-mail info@cicl.com.pk; internet www.cicl.com.pk; f. 1988; Chair. and Chief Exec. IQBALALI LAKHANI; Man. Dir and CEO TINKU IRFAN JOHNSON.

CGU Inter Insurance PLC: 74/1-A, Lalazar, M. T. Khan Rd, POB 4895, Karachi 74000; tel. (21) 5611802; fax (21) 5611456; f. 1861; general and life insurance; Gen. Man. ABDUR RAHIM; 3 brs.

Commerce Insurance Co Ltd: 11 Shahrah-e-Quaid-e-Azam, POB 1132, Lahore 54000; tel. (42) 7325330; fax (42) 7230828; f. 1992; Chief Exec. SYED MOIN-UD-DIN.

Co-operative Insurance Society of Pakistan Ltd: Co-operative Insurance Bldg, Shahrah-e-Quaid-e-Azam, POB 147, Lahore; tel. (42) 7352306; fax (42) 7352794; f. 1949; Chief Exec. and Gen. Man. CH. AKHTAR MAHMOOD.

Credit Insurance Co Ltd: Asmat Chambers, 68 Mazang Rd, Lahore; tel. (42) 6316774; fax (42) 6368868; f. 1995; Chief Exec. MUHAMMAD IKHLAQ BUTT.

Crescent Star Insurance Co Ltd: Nadir House, I. I. Chundrigar Rd, POB 4616, Karachi 74000; tel. (21) 2415471; fax (21) 2415474; internet www.cstar.com.pk; f. 1957; Man. Dir MUNIR I. MILLWALA.

Dadabhoy Insurance Co Ltd: Maqbool Commercial Complex, JCHS Block, Main Shahrah-e-Faisal, Karachi; tel. (21) 4545704; fax (21) 4548625; f. 1983; Chief Exec. USMAN DADABHOY.

Delta Insurance Co Ltd: 101 Baghpatee Bldg, Altaf Hussain Rd, New Challi, Karachi; tel. (21) 2632297; fax (21) 2422942; f. 1991; Man. Dir SYED ASIF ALI.

East West Insurance Co Ltd: 310, EFU House, M. A. Jinnah Rd, POB 6693, Karachi 74000; tel. (21) 2311662; fax (21) 2311667; e-mail info@eastwestlifeco.com; internet www.eastwestlifeco.com; f. 1983; Man. Dir and Chief Exec. MAHEEN YUNUS.

EFU General Insurance Ltd: EFU House, M. A. Jinnah Rd, Karachi 74000; tel. (21) 2313471; fax (21) 2310450; e-mail info@efuinsurance.com; internet www.efuinsurance.com; f. 1932; Man. Dir and Chief Exec. SAIFUDDIN N. ZOOMKAWALA.

Excel Insurance Co Ltd: 38/C-1, Block 6, PECH Society, Shahrah-e-Faisal, Karachi 75400; tel. (21) 111-777-666; fax (21) 4548076; e-mail eicl@cyber.net.pk; f. 1991; Man. Dir GHULAM H. ALI MOHAMMAD.

Gulf Insurance Co Ltd: Gulf House, 1-A Link McLeod Rd, Patiala Grounds, Lahore; tel. (42) 7312028; fax (42) 7234987; f. 1988; Chief Exec. S. ARIF SALAM.

Habib Insurance Co Ltd: Insurance House, 6 Habib Sq., M. A. Jinnah Rd, POB 5217, Karachi 74000; tel. (21) 2424038; fax (21) 2421600; e-mail info@habibinsurance.net; internet www.habibinsurance.net; f. 1942; Chair. HAMID D. HABIB; Man. Dir and Chief Exec. ALI RAZA D. HABIB.

IGI Insurance Ltd: 7th Floor, The Forum, Suite 701–713m G-20, Block 9, Khayaban-e-Jami, Clifton, Karachi 75600; tel. (21) 5301726-8; fax (21) 5301729; e-mail contact.center@igi.com.pk; internet www.igi.com.pk; Chief Operating Officer S. KHALID YUSUF.

Ittefaq General Insurance Co Ltd: H-16 Murree Rd, Rawalpindi; tel. (51) 5771333; f. 1982; Chief Exec. and Man. Dir Dr SYED ISHTIAQ HUSSAIN SHAH.

Jupiter Insurance Co Ltd: 4th Floor, Finlay House, I. I. Chundrigar Rd, POB 4655, Karachi 74000; tel. (21) 2426070; fax (21) 2427660; e-mail jicl20@cyber.net.pk; f. 1994; Chief Exec. MAHMUD HASAN.

Muslim Insurance Co Ltd: 3 Bank Sq., Shahrah-e-Quaid-e-Azam, POB 1219, Lahore; tel. (42) 7320542; fax (42) 7234742; e-mail fariq.rohilla@mickhi.atlasgrouppk.com; f. 1935; Chief Exec. S. C. SUBJALLY.

National General Insurance Co Ltd: 401-B, Satellite Town, nr Commercial Market, Rawalpindi; tel. (51) 4427818; fax (51) 4427361; f. 1969; Gen. Man. F. A. JAFFERY.

National Insurance Corpn: NIC Bldg, Abbasi Shaheed Rd, Karachi 74400; tel. (21) 9202741; fax (21) 9202779; e-mail info@nicl.com.pk; internet www.nicl.com.pk; govt-owned; sole govt insurance co; Chair. and CEO MUHAMMAD AYYAZ NIAZI.

New Jubilee Insurance Co Ltd: 2nd Floor, Jubilee Insurance House, I. I. Chundrigar Rd, POB 4795, Karachi 74000; tel. (21) 2416022; fax (21) 2416728; e-mail nji@cyber.net.pk; internet www.nji.com.pk; f. 1953; Man. Dir TAHIR AHMED.

North Star Insurance Co Ltd: 37–38 Basement, Sadiq Plaza, 69 The Mall, Lahore 54000; tel. (42) 6314308; fax (42) 6375366; e-mail northstarins@hotmail.com; f. 1995; Chief Exec./Man. Dir M. RAFIQ CHAUDHRY.

Orient Insurance Co Ltd: 2nd Floor, Dean Arcade, Block No. 8, Kahkeshan, Clifton, Karachi; tel. (21) 5865327; fax (21) 5865724; f. 1987; Man. Dir FAZAL REHMAN.

Pak Equity Insurance Co Ltd: M. K. Arcade, 32 Davis Rd, Lahore; tel. (42) 6361536; fax (42) 6365959; f. 1984; Chief Exec. CH. ATHAR ZAHOOR.

Pakistan General Insurance Co Ltd: 3 Bank Sq., Shahrah-e-Quaid-e-Azam, POB 1364, Lahore; tel. (42) 7323569; fax (42) 7230634; f. 1948; Chair. CH. AZFAR MANZOOR; Pres. and CEO CH. ZAHOOR AHMAD.

Pakistan Guarantee Insurance Co Ltd: Al-Falah Court, 3rd and 5th Floors, I. I. Chundrigar Rd, POB 5436, Karachi 74000; tel. (21) 2636111; fax (21) 2638740; f. 1965; Chief Exec. SHAKIL RAZA SYED.

Pakistan Reinsurance Co Ltd: PRC Towers, 32A Lalazar Dr., M. T. Khan Rd, POB 4777, Karachi 74000; tel. (21) 9202908; fax (21) 9202921; e-mail prcl@pakre.org.pk; internet www.pakre.org.pk; Chair. RUKHSANA SALEEM.

PICIC Insurance Ltd: 8th Floor, Shaheen Complex, M. R. Kiyani Rd, Karachi; tel. (21) 2219550; fax (21) 2219561; e-mail info@

picicinsurance.com; internet www.picicinsurance.com; Man. Dir and CEO AHMED SALAHUDDIN.

Premier Insurance Co of Pakistan Ltd: 2-A State Life Bldg, 5th Floor, Wallace Rd, off I. I. Chundrigar Rd, POB 4140, Karachi 74000; tel. (21) 2416331; fax (21) 2416572; e-mail info@pil.com.pk; internet www.pil.com.pk; f. 1952; Chair. ZAHID BASHIR; CEO FAKHIR A. RAHMAN.

Prime Insurance Co Ltd: 505–507, Japan Plaza, M. A. Jinnah Rd, POB 1390, Karachi; tel. (21) 7770801; fax (21) 7725427; f. 1989; Chief Exec. ABDUL MAJEED.

Progressive Insurance Co Ltd: 2nd Floor, Sasi Arcade, Block 7, Main Clifton Rd, Clifton, Karachi; tel. (21) 5823560; fax (21) 5823561; f. 1989; Man. Dir and CEO ABDUL MAJEED.

Raja Insurance Co Ltd: Panorama Centre, 5th Floor, 256 Fatimah Jinnah Rd, POB 10422, Karachi 4; tel. (21) 5670619; fax (21) 5681501; f. 1981; Chair. RAJA ABDUL RAHMAN; Man. Dir Sheikh HUMAYUN SAYEED.

Reliance Insurance Co Ltd: Reliance Insurance House, 181-A, Sindhi Muslim Co-operative Housing Society, POB 13356, Karachi 74400; tel. (21) 4539415; fax (21) 4539412; e-mail reli-ins@cyber.net.pk; internet www.relianceins.com; Chief Exec. and Man. Dir ABDUL RAZAK AHMED.

Royal Exchange Assurance: P&O Plaza, I. I. Chundrigar Rd, POB 315, Karachi 74000; tel. (21) 2635141; fax (21) 2631369; Man. (Pakistan) Dr MUMTAZ A. HASHMI.

Saudi Pak Insurance Co Ltd: 2nd Floor, State Life Bldg, No. 2A, Wallace Rd, Karachi; tel. (21) 2418430; fax (21) 2417885; e-mail info@saudipakinsurance.com.pk; internet www.saudipakinsurance.com.pk; Man. Dir and CEO Capt. AZHAR EHTESHAM AHMED.

Seafield Insurance Co Ltd: 86-Q, Block 2, Allama Iqbal Rd, PECHS, Karachi; tel. (21) 4527592; fax (21) 4527593; e-mail sifcpk89@hotmail.com; f. 1989; Man. Dir ADNAN HAFEEZ.

Security General Insurance Co Ltd: Nishat House, 53A Lawrence Rd, Lahore; tel. (42) 6279192; fax (42) 6303466; e-mail sgicl@hotmail.com; f. 1996; Man. Dir SYED JAWAD GILLANI.

Shaheen Insurance Co Ltd: 10th Floor, Shaheen Complex, M. R. Kayani Rd, Karachi 74200; tel. (21) 2630370; fax (21) 2626674; e-mail sihifc@cyber.net.pk; internet www.shaheeninsurance.com; f. 1996; Chief Exec. SHEHRAYAR AKBAR RAJA.

Silver Star Insurance Co Ltd: Silver Star House, 2nd Floor, 5 Bank Sq., POB 2533, Lahore 54000; tel. (42) 7324488; fax (42) 7229966; e-mail info@silverstarinsurance.com; internet www.silverstarinsurance.com; f. 1984; Man. Dir and Chief Exec. ZAHIR MUHAMMAD SADIQ; Chair. CHAUDHRY MUHAMMAD SADIQ.

Trakker Direct Insurance Ltd: 172-B, 2nd Floor, Najeeb Centre, Block 2, P.E.C.H.S., Karachi; tel. (21) 4322555; fax (21) 4322515; e-mail insurance@trakkerdirect.com; internet www.trakkerdirect.com; CEO ALI JAMEEL.

UBL Insurers Ltd: 8th Floor, State Life Bldg, No. 2, Wallace Rd, off I. I. Chundrigar Rd, Karachi; tel. (21) 111–845–111; fax (21) 2463117; e-mail khalid.hamid@ublinsurers.com; internet www.ublinsurers.com; CEO and Man. Dir KHALID HAMID.

Union Insurance Co of Pakistan Ltd: Adamjee House, 9th Floor, I. I. Chundrigar Rd, Karachi; tel. (21) 2416171; fax (21) 2420174; e-mail unionins@cyber.net.pk; Pres. NISHAT RAFFIQ.

United Insurance Co of Pakistan Ltd: Nizam Chambers, 5th Floor, Shahrah-e-Fatima Jinnah, POB 532, Lahore; tel. (42) 6361471; fax (42) 6375036; e-mail uicp@xcess.net.pk; internet www.theunitedinsurance.com; f. 1959; Chair. and CEO M.A. SHAHID.

Universal Insurance Co Ltd: Universal Insurance House, 63 Shahrah-e-Quaid-e-Azam, POB 539, Lahore; tel. (42) 7353458; fax (42) 7230326; e-mail tuic@nexlinx.net.pk; internet www.uic.com.pk; f. 1958; Chief Exec. Begum ZEB GAUHAR AYUB KHAN; Man. Dir SARDAR KHAN.

Insurance Associations

Insurance Association of Pakistan: 1713–1715, 17th Floor, Saima Trade Tower A, I. I. Chundrigar Rd, POB 4932, Karachi 74000; tel. (21) 2277165; fax (21) 2277170; e-mail iapho@cyber.net.pk; internet www.iap.net.pk; f. 1948; mems comprise 32 non-life insurance cos and 4 life insurance cos; establishes rules for insurance in the country; regional office in Lahore; Chair. FAKHIR RAHMAN; Sec. N. A. USMANI.

Pakistan Insurance Institute: Shafi Court, 2nd Floor, Mereweather Rd, Karachi 4; f. 1951 to encourage insurance education; Chair. MOHAMMAD CHOUDHRY.

Trade and Industry

GOVERNMENT AGENCIES

Alternative Energy Development Board (AEDB): 3, St 8, F-8/3, Islamabad; tel. (51) 9262947; fax (51) 9205790; e-mail support@aedb.org; internet www.aedb.org; f. 2003; mandate incl. development of national plans and policies, undertaking promotion and dissemination of activities in field of renewable energy technologies, facilitation of power generation projects using alternative or renewable energy resources; CEO ARIF ALAUDDIN.

Board of Investment (BOI): Government of Pakistan, Atatürk Ave, Sector G-5/1, Islamabad; tel. (51) 9204339; fax (51) 9215554; e-mail secretary@pakboi.gov.pk; internet www.pakboi.gov.pk; operates under the presidency of the Prime Minister of Pakistan and chairmanship of the Minister of Privatisation and Investment; Chair. WAQAR AHMED KHAN; Sec. TARIQ IQBAL PURI.

Central Board of Revenue: Constitution Ave, G-5, Islamabad; tel. (51) 9207545; fax (51) 9207540; e-mail helpline@cbr.gov.pk; internet www.cbr.gov.pk; tax authority; Chair. M. ABDULLAH YUSUF.

Corporate and Industrial Restructuring Corpn: 13-C-II, M. M. Alam Rd, Gulberg III, Lahore; tel. (42) 5871532; fax (42) 5761650; e-mail info@circ-gov.com.

Earthquake Reconstruction and Rehabilitation Authority (ERRA): Prime Minister's Secretariat (Public), Constitution Ave, Islamabad; tel. (51) 9201254; fax (51) 9209525; e-mail chairman@erra.gov.pk; internet www.erra.gov.pk; f. 2005; Chair. ALTAF SALEEM.

Electronic Government Directorate: 10-D, 3rd Floor, Taimur Chambers, Blue Area West, Islamabad; tel. (51) 9205992; fax (51) 9205981; e-mail contact@e-government.gov.pk; internet www.pakistan.gov.pk/e-government-directorate; f. 2002; fmrly the Information Technology Commission; subsidiary department of the Ministry of Information Technology and Telecommunications; Dir-Gen. of Projects SYED RAZA ABBAS SHAH.

Engineering Development Board: 5-A, Constitution Ave, SEDC Bldg (STP), Sector F-5/1, Islamabad 44000; tel. (51) 9205595; fax (51) 9203584; e-mail ceo@edb.gov.pk; internet www.engineeringpakistan.com; CEO ASAD ELAHI.

Environmental Protection Agency: 311 Margalla Rd, F-11/3, Islamabad 44000; tel. (51) 9267621; fax (51) 9267625; e-mail greenlib@isb.paknet.com.pk; internet www.environment.gov.pk; Dir-Gen. ASIF S. KHAN.

Export Processing Zones Authority (EPZA): Landhi Industrial Area Extension, Mehran Highway, Landhi, Karachi 75150; tel. (21) 5082008; fax (21) 5082009; e-mail info@epza.gov.pk; internet www.epza.gov.pk; Chair. KAMRAN MIRZA.

Family Planning Association of Pakistan (Rahnuma—FPAP): 3-A Temple Rd, Lahore 54000; tel. (42) 111-223-366; fax (42) 6368692; e-mail info@fpapak.org; internet www.fpapak.org; f. 1953; executes diversified community uplift programmes and activities; Pres. Begum SURAYYA JABEEN; CEO SYED KAMAL SHAH.

Geological Survey of Pakistan: Sariab Rd, POB 15, Quetta; tel. (81) 9211032; fax (81) 9211018; e-mail qta@gsp.gov.pk; internet www.gsp.gov.pk; Dir-Gen. MIRZA TALIB HASAN; Asst Dir MOHSIN ANWAR KAZIM.

Higher Education Commission: H-9, Islamabad; tel. (51) 9040305; fax (51) 9290120; e-mail info@hec.gov.pk; internet www.hec.gov.pk; Exec. Dir Dr S. SOHAIL H. NAQVI.

Intellectual Property Organization of Pakistan (IPO-PAKISTAN): House 23, St 87, Ataturk Ave (West), G-6/3, Islamabad; tel. (51) 9208587; fax (51) 9208157; e-mail info@ipo.gov.pk; internet www.ipo.gov.pk; f. 2005; Chair. PERVAIZ KAUSAR.

National Accountability Bureau: Atatürk Ave, G-5/2, Islamabad; tel. (51) 111-622-622; fax (51) 9214502; e-mail infonab@nab.gov.pk; internet www.nab.gov.pk.

National Aliens Registration Authority (NARA): C-82, Block 2, Clifton, Karachi; tel. (21) 9251083; f. 2001; registers all foreign nationals who wish to work in Pakistan.

National Commission for Human Development: 14th Floor, Shaheed-e-Millat Secretariat, Jinnah Ave, Islamabad; tel. (51) 9216200; fax (51) 9216164; e-mail info@nchd.org.pk; internet www.nchd.org.pk; f. 2002.

National Database and Registration Authority (NADRA): State Bank of Pakistan Bldg, Shahrah-e-Jamhuriat, G-5/2, Islamabad; tel. (51) 9201120; e-mail info@nadra.gov.pk; internet www.nadra.gov.pk.

National Economic Council: supreme economic body; the governors and chief ministers of the four provinces and fed. ministers in charge of economic ministries are its mems; sr fed. and provincial officials in the economic field are also associated; Chair. Prime Minister.

National Electric Power Regulatory Authority (NEPRA): (see Utilities).

National Energy Conservation Centre (ENERCON): ENERCON Bldg, G-5/2, Islamabad; tel. (51) 9206005; fax (51) 9206004; e-mail ferts@enercon.gov.pk; internet www.enercon.gov.pk; Man. Dir FARIDULLAH KHAN.

National Highway Authority (NHA): (see Transport: Roads).

National Housing Authority: Prime Minister's Office, Islamabad; tel. (51) 9202279; fax (51) 9217813; e-mail info@nhagov.pk; internet www.nhagov.pk; Dir-Gen. TALIT MIYAN.

National Tariff Commission: State Life Bldg, No. 5, Blue Area, Jinnah Ave, POB 1689, Islamabad 44000; tel. (51) 9202839; fax (51) 9221205; e-mail ntc@ntc.gov.pk; internet www.ntc.gov.pk; f. 1990; Chair. M. IKRAM ARIF.

National Testing Service (NTS): 402, St 34, I-8/2, Islamabad; tel. (51) 9258478; fax (51) 9258480; e-mail support@nts.org.pk; internet www.nts.org.pk; conducts assessment programs for students at all educational levels; facilitates employment and career development through subject testing.

Oil and Gas Regulatory Authority: Tariq Chambers, Civic Centre, G-6, Islamabad; tel. (51) 9221715; fax (51) 9221714; e-mail secretary@ogra.org.pk; internet www.ogra.org.pk; regulates oil and gas sector.

Pakistan Electronic Media Regulatory Authority: Islamabad; tel. (51) 9202174; fax (51) 9219634; e-mail info@pemra.gov.pk; internet www.pemra.gov.pk; f. 2002; Chair. IFTIKHAR RASHID; Dir-Gen. RANA ALTAF MAJID.

Pakistan National Accreditation Council (PNAC): Ministry of Scientific and Technological Research, 4th Floor, Evacuee Trust Complex, Aga Khan Rd, F-5/1, Islamabad; tel. (51) 9222310; fax (51) 9222312; e-mail info@pnac.org.pk; internet www.pnac.org.pk; f. 1998; Dir-Gen. ABDUL RASHID KHAN.

Pakistan Software Export Board (Guarantee) Ltd: 2nd Floor, Evacuee Trust Complex, F-5/1, Aga Khan Rd, Islamabad; tel. (51) 9204074; fax (51) 9204075; e-mail info@pseb.org.pk; internet www.pseb.org.pk; Man. Dir YTALIB BALOCH.

Pakistan Standards and Quality Control Authority (PSQCA): Pakistan Secretariat, Block 77, Karachi 74400; tel. and fax (21) 9206290; fax (21) 9206263; e-mail psqcadg@super.net.pk; internet www.psqca.com.pk; f. 1996; regulates standards in industry; Dir-Gen. ABDUL GHAFFAR SOOMRO.

Pakistan Stone Development Co: I. C. C. I. Bldg, 2nd Floor, Mauve Area, G-8/A, Islamabad; tel. (51) 9263465; fax (51) 9263464; internet www.pasdec.org; f. 2006; promotes devt of marble and granite sector; Chair. IHSANULLAH KHAN.

Pakistan Telecommunication Authority: (see Telecommunications).

Pakistan Tobacco Board: 46-B Office Enclave, Phase-V, Hayatabad, POB 188, Peshawar; tel. (91) 9217156; fax (91) 9217149; e-mail mail@ptb.gov.pk; internet www.ptb.gov.pk; f. 1968; regulates, controls and promotes the export of tobacco and related products, and fixes grading standards; Chair. Maj. SAHIBZADA MUHAMMAD KHALID; Research and Devt Dir MOHAMMAD TARIQ.

Privatisation Commission: Experts Advisory Cell Bldg, 5A Constitution Ave, Islamabad 44000; tel. (51) 9205146; fax (51) 9203076; e-mail info@privatisation.gov.pk; internet www.privatisation.gov.pk; supervised by Ministry of Privatisation and Investment.

Sindh Privatisation Commission: Sindh Secretariat, 4-A, Block 15, Court Rd, Karachi; tel. (21) 9202077; fax (21) 9202071; e-mail spcsecretary@yahoo.com; Sec. SYED ZULFIQAR ALI SHAH.

Sustainable Development Policy Institute (SDPI): 20 Hill Rd, F-6/3, Islamabad; tel. (51) 2278134; fax (51) 2278135; e-mail main@sdpi.org; internet www.sdpi.org; f. 1992; Chair. H. U. BEG.

Trade Development Authority of Pakistan (TDAP): Finance and Trade Centre, Block A, 5th Floor, POB 1293, Shahrah-e-Faisal, Karachi 75200; tel. (21) 1114441; fax (21) 9206487; e-mail tdap@tdap.gov.pk; internet www.tdap.gov.pk; f. 1963 as Export Promotion Bureau (EPB) affiliated to the Ministry of Commerce; Trade Development Authority was established in Nov. 2006 by an Ordinance of President Musharraf to assume all functions fmrly dispatched by the EPB; Chair. TARIQ IKRAM; Sec. ZAFAR MAHMOOD.

Trading Corporation of Pakistan: 4th and 5th Floors, Finance and Trade Centre, Main Shahrah-e-Faisal, Karachi 75530; tel. (21) 9202947-9; fax (21) 9202722; e-mail tcp@tcp.gov.pk; internet www.tcp.gov.pk; f. 1967; Chair. MUHAMMAD SAEED.

Utility Stores Corporation of Pakistan: Plot No. 2039, G-7/F-7, POB 1339, Jinnah Ave, Blue Area, Islamabad; tel. (51) 9210976; fax (51) 9210982; e-mail usc_ho@yahoo.com; internet www.usc.com.pk; f. 1971; Man. Dir MUHAMMAD ARIF KHAN.

DEVELOPMENT ORGANIZATIONS

Balochistan Development Authority: Civil Secretariat, Block 7, Quetta; tel. (81) 9202491; created for economic devt of Balochistan; exploration and exploitation of mineral resources; development of infrastructure, water resources, etc.

Capital Development Authority: G-7/4, Islamabad; tel. (51) 9252638; fax (51) 9252612; e-mail info@cda.gov.pk; internet www.cda.gov.pk; Chair. TARIQ MAHMOOD KHAN.

Center for International Private Enterprise (Pakistan) (CIPE): Glass Tower, Suite 214–15, 2 Ft 3, adjacent to PSO House, Main Clifton Rd, Karachi 75530; tel. (21) 5656993; e-mail pakistan@cipe.org; internet www.cipe.org; international org.; affiliate of US Chamber of Commerce and key member of National Endowment for Democracy; US Agency for international Development supports programs of CIPE; Country Dir M. MOIN FUDDA.

Council for Works and Housing Research (CWHR): F-40, SITE Hub River Rd, Karachi 75730; tel. (21) 2577236; fax (21) 2577235; e-mail cwhr@khi.comsats.net.pk; internet www.cwhr.gov.pk; f. 1964.

Faisalabad Industrial Estate Development & Management Co (FIEDMC): Faisalabad; tel. (41) 8523106; fax (41) 8522884; e-mail fiedmc@fiedmc.com.pk; internet www.fiedmc.com.pk; established by the Punjab state government under the Public Private Partnership system to promote devt of industrial estates; Chair. Mian MUHAMMAD LATIF; CEO KHURRAM IFTIKHAR.

Gwadar Development Authority: Governor House Rd, Gwadar; tel. and fax (86) 4211775; e-mail info@gda.gov.pk; internet www.gda.gov.pk; Dir-Gen. AHMAD BAKSH LEHRI.

Lahore Development Authority (LDA): LDA Plaza, 9th Floor, Egerton Rd, Lahore; tel. (42) 9201510; internet www.lda.gop.pk; f. 1975; Dir of Admin. ABDUL HAMEED CHAUDHRY.

Lasbella Industrial Estate Development Authority (LIEDA): Hub Industrial Trading Estate, Lasbella, Balochistan; tel. (853) 303361; fax (853) 302470; e-mail lieda@lieda.org.pk; est. under section 3 of Government of Balochistan Ordinance IX (1989); promotes devt of industrial concerns over 1,000 acre coastal Highway region; Man. Dir Col (retd) BASHIR AHMED NADIM.

Malir Development Authority: Main Northern By-Pass, Scheme No. 45, Taisar Town, Karachi; Dir-Gen. AMEERZADA KOHATI; Chair. SYED MUSTAFA KAMAL.

National Commission for Human Development: Shaheed-e-Millat Secretariat, 14th Floor, Jinnah Ave, Islamabad; tel. (51) 9216200; fax (51) 9216164; e-mail info@nchd.org.pk; internet www.nchd.org.pk; f. 2001 by presidential decree; facilitates programs towards achievement of the UNDP Millennium Development Goals; Chair. FARROKH K. CAPTAIN.

Pakistan Engineering Council: Ataturk Ave (East), G-5/2, Islamabad; tel. (51) 2829348; fax (51) 2276224; e-mail info@pec.org.pk; internet www.pec.org.pk; f. 1976; Chair. RUKHSANA ZUBERI.

Pakistan Gems & Jewellery Development Co (PGJDC): Regent Plaza Hotel and Convention Centre, M-3 Mezzanine Floor, Shahra-e-Faisal, Karachi; tel. (21) 5631394; fax (21) 5631398; e-mail info@pgjdc.org; internet www.pgjdc.org; f. 2006; est. as non-profit org. under Ministry of Industries, Production and Special Initiatives; subsidiary of Pakistan Industrial Devt Corpn; promotes devt of Pakistan's gem and jewellery industry; CEO FAWAD KHAN.

Pakistan Industrial Technical Assistance Centre (PITAC): 234 Maulana Jalaluddin Roomi Rd (old Ferozepur Rd), Lahore 54600; tel. (42) 9230699; fax (42) 9230589; e-mail info@pitac.gov.pk; internet www.pitac.gov.pk; f. 1962 by the Govt to provide prototype tooling facilities and spare parts to manufacturing industries and advanced training to industrial personnel in the fields of metal trades and tool engineering design and related fields; under Ministry of Industries, Production and Special Initiatives; provides human resource devt programmes; Chair. MANZAR SHAMIM; Gen. Man. Lt-Col (retd) KHAN M. NAZIR.

Pakistan Poverty Alleviation Fund: House No. 1, St 20, F-7/2, Islamabad; tel. (51) 111-000-102; fax (51) 2652246; e-mail info@ppaf.org.pk; internet www.ppaf.org.pk; f. 1997 by the Government; funded by the World Bank; works with non-governmental organizations and private-sector institutions to alleviate poverty; 68 partner orgs nationwide; Chief Exec. and Man. Dir KAMAL HAYAT.

Quetta Development Authority: Sarai Rd, Quetta; tel. (81) 9211069.

Sarhad Development Authority (SDA): PIA Bldg, Arbab Rd, POB 172, Peshawar; tel. (91) 9211608; fax (91) 9211605; e-mail sda.psh@ntc.net.pk; internet www.sda.org.pk; f. 1972; promotes industrial and commercial devt in the North-West Frontier Province; Chair. GHULAM DASTGIR AKHTAR.

Sindh Katchi Abadis Authority (SKAA): Maulana Din Muhammad Wafai Rd, Karachi 74200; tel. (21) 9211278; fax (21) 9211272; e-mail skaa@khi.compol.com; f. 1987; govt agency established to

PAKISTAN

regulate and improve slums in Pakistan's southern province; Dir-Gen. MIR NASIR ABBAS.

Small and Medium Enterprises Development Authority (SMEDA): 6th Floor, LDA Plaza, Egerton Rd, Lahore; tel. (42) 111-111-456; fax (42) 6304926; e-mail helpdesk@smeda.org.pk; internet www.smeda.org.pk; f. 1998; four brs; 18 regional business centres; CEO SHAHAB KHAWAJA.

CHAMBERS OF COMMERCE

The Federation of Pakistan Chambers of Commerce and Industry: Federation House, Main Clifton, POB 13875, Karachi 75600; tel. (21) 5873691; fax (21) 5874332; e-mail fpcci@cyber.net.pk; internet www.fpcci.com.pk; f. 1950; 163 mem. bodies; Pres. SULTAN AHMED CHAWLA; Sec.-Gen. and CEO M. A. LODHI.

Islamic Chamber of Commerce and Industry: St 2/A, Block 9, KDA Scheme 5, Clifton, Karachi 75600; tel. (21) 5874756; fax (21) 5870765; e-mail icci@icci-oic.org; internet www.iccionline.net; f. 1979; Pres. Sheikh SALEH BIN ABDULLAH KAMEL; Sec.-Gen. Dr MOSTAFA HODIEB.

Overseas Investors' Chamber of Commerce and Industry: Chamber of Commerce Bldg, Talpur Rd, POB 4833, Karachi 74000; tel. (21) 2426076; fax (21) 2427315; e-mail info@oicci.org; internet www.oicci.org; f. 1860 as the Karachi Chamber of Commerce, name changed to above in 1968; 175 mem. bodies; Pres. FARHAT ALI; Sec.-Gen. UNJELA SIDDIQI.

Principal Affiliated Chambers

Attock Chamber of Commerce and Industry: Rehman Villas, Attock; tel. (57) 2611776; fax (57) 2610888; Pres. MIRZA ABDUL REHMAN.

Bahawalpur Chamber of Commerce and Industry: 43-A/1, Tipu Shaheed Rd, Model Town A, Bahawalpur; tel. and fax (62) 2883192; fax (62) 2889283; e-mail info@bahawalpurchamber.com; internet www.bahawalpurchamber.com; Pres. CHAUDHRY MAHMOOD MAJEED.

Chaman Chamber of Commerce and Industry: Commerce House, Trunch Rd, Chaman; tel. (826) 613308; fax (826) 615376; e-mail Cccichaman@Yahoo.Com; Pres. Haji HAMEEDULLAH KHAN.

Dadu Chamber of Commerce and Industry: C-15, Larkana Rd, Dadu; tel. (25) 4610093; fax (25) 4610092; e-mail daduchamber@hotmail.com; Pres. OSMAN DADABHOY.

Dera Ghazi Khan Chamber of Commerce and Industry: Block 34, Khakwani House, Dera Ghazi Khan, Punjab; tel. (64) 9260503; fax (64) 9260507; Pres. Dr MUHAMMAD HARIS.

Faisalabad Chamber of Commerce and Industry: East Canal Rd, Canal Park, Faisalabad; tel. (41) 9230265; fax (41) 9230270; e-mail info@fcci.com.pk; internet www.fcci.com.pk; Pres. Mian HAMID JAVED; Vice-Pres. MIAN ZAFAR IQBAL.

Gujranwala Chamber of Commerce and Industry: Aiwan-e-Tijarat Rd, Gujranwala; tel. (55) 3256701; fax (55) 3254440; e-mail info@gcci.org.pk; internet www.gcci.org.pk; f. 1978; Pres. MUHAMMAD AKRAM; Sec. SYED ALI ASIM.

Gujrat Chamber of Commerce and Industry: 26-A, G. T. Rd, S.I.E. POB 169, Gujrat; tel. (4331) 523012; fax (4331) 523011; Pres. KHALID PERVAIZ URF JAVED BUTT.

Haripur Chamber of Commerce and Industry: Chamber House, GPO Rd, Haripur; tel. (995) 613364; fax (995) 614664; e-mail haripur-chamber@yahoo.com; internet www.hccl.com.pk; Pres. Haji FAKHAR-E-ALAM; Sec.-Gen. FAQIR MUHAMMAD KHAN.

Hyderabad Chamber of Commerce and Industry: Aiwan-e-Tijarat Rd, Saddar, POB 99, Hyderabad 71000; tel. (22) 2784972; fax (22) 2784977; e-mail hcci@muchomail.com; f. 1961; Pres. SHAFIQ AHMED QURESHI; Sec.-Gen. Dr MOHAMAD ALI MIAN.

Islamabad Chamber of Commerce and Industry: Aiwan-e-Sana't-o-Tijarat Rd, Mauve Area, Sector G-8/1, Islamabad; tel. (51) 2250526; fax (51) 2252950; e-mail icci@brain.net.pk; internet www.icci.com.pk; f. 1984; Pres. MIAN SHAUKAT MASUD; Sec.-Gen. MAJID SHABBIR.

Jhang Chamber of Commerce and Industry: Aamir Colony, Yousaf Shah Rd, Jhang; tel. (47) 7611780; fax (47) 7612371; e-mail jcci@paknet4.ptc.pk; Pres. Haji ABAD HUSSAIN KHOKHAR.

Jhelum Chamber of Commerce and Industry: G. T. Rd, Jhelum; tel. (544) 646532; fax (544) 646229; e-mail jhelumcci@gmail.com; internet www.jlmcci.com; f. 1993; Pres. RAJA MUHAMMAD ANWER; Sec. Capt. (retd) MUHAMMAD ZAMAN.

Karachi Chamber of Commerce and Industry: Aiwan-e-Tijarat Rd, off Shahrah-e-Liaquat, POB 4158, Karachi 74000; tel. (21) 9218001; fax (21) 9218010; e-mail info@karachichamber.com; internet www.karachichamber.com; f. 1959; 11,705 mems; Pres. ANJUM NISAR; Sec. MAZAHIR RIZVI.

Khanewal Chamber Of Commerce and Industry: Sadar Bazar, Jahanian, Khanewal; tel. (65) 563223; Pres. WAHEED SINDU.

Lahore Chamber of Commerce and Industry: 11 Shahrah-e-Aiwan-e-Tijarat, POB 597, Lahore; tel. (42) 6305538; fax (42) 6368854; e-mail sect@lcci.org.pk; internet www.lcci.org.pk; f. 1923; 8,000 mems; Pres. MIAN MUZAFFAR ALI; Sec.-Gen. MUHAMMAD YASEEN.

Larkana Chamber of Commerce and Industry: 21–23 Kenedy Market, POB 78, Larkana, Sindh; tel. (741) 457136; fax (741) 440709; e-mail president@larkanachamber.com; Pres. MASOOD AHMED SHAIKH.

Lasbela Chamber of Commerce and Industry: LIEDA Office Bldg, Ground Floor, Hub District, Lasbela, Balochistan; tel. (853) 303410; fax (853) 302431; e-mail lcci@gerrys.net; internet www.lasbelachamber.com; f. 1995; Pres. Dr MUHAMMAD ASLAM.

Mardan Chamber of Commerce and Industry: Saleem Manzil, Muqam Mandi, Malakand Rd, Mardan; tel. (37) 9230215; fax (37) 9230214; e-mail mrd_chamber@yahoo.com; Pres. NASEEM UR REHMAN.

Multan Chamber of Commerce and Industry: Shahrah-e-Aiwan-e-Tijarat-o-Sanat, Multan; tel. (61) 4517087; fax (61) 4570463; e-mail mccimultan@hotmail.com; internet www.mcci.org.pk; Pres. Mian ANIS AHMAD. SHEIKH; Sec. KHURRAM JAVED.

Okara Chamber of Commerce and Industry: 9 M. A. Jinnah Rd, Okara; tel. (44) 2551901; fax (44) 2552005; internet www.occi.org.pk; Pres. CH. SHAFQAT RASOOL.

Quetta Chamber of Commerce and Industry: Zarghoon Rd, POB 117, Quetta 87300; tel. (81) 2821943; fax (81) 2821948; e-mail qcci@hotmail.com; Pres. MOHAMMAD SIDDIQUE KAKAR; Sec. MUHAMMAD AHMED.

Rawalpindi Chamber of Commerce and Industry: 39 Mayo Rd, Civil Lines, Rawalpindi; tel. (51) 5110514; fax (51) 5111055; e-mail rcci@isd.wol.net.pk; internet www.rcci.org.pk; f. 1952; Pres. SYED ASSAD MASHADI; Sec. MUHAMMAD IFTIKHAR-UD-DIN.

SAARC Chamber of Commerce and Industry: House No. 397, St No. 64, I-8/3, Islamabad; tel. (51) 4860611; fax (51) 8316024; e-mail info@saarcchamber.com; internet www.saarcchamber.com; f. 1993; Pres. TARIQ SAEED.

Sahiwal Chamber of Commerce and Industry: Liaqat Rd, Sahiwal; tel. (40) 4221429; fax (4) 4221039; e-mail scciswl@brain.net.pk; Pres. SAFDAR RASHID.

Sargodha Chamber of Commerce and Industry: 80/2-A, Satellite Town, Sargodha 40100; tel. (48) 9230883; fax (48) 9230835; e-mail info@scci.pk; internet www.scci.pk; f. 1986; Pres. ABID RAFIQUE KHAWAJA; Sec.-Gen. KASHIF MUKHTAR SHEIKH.

Sarhad Chamber of Commerce and Industry: Sarhad Chamber House, Family Park, G. T. Rd, Peshawar; tel. (91) 9213314; fax (91) 9213316; e-mail sccip@brain.net.pk; internet www.scci.org.pk; f. 1958; 3,159 mems; Pres. SHARAFAT ALI MUBARAK; Sec. FAQIR MUHAMMAD.

Sheikhupura Chamber Of Commerce and Industry: Chamber House, Kot Abdul Malik, Sheikhupura; tel. (56) 7910313; fax (56) 7728125; Pres. SHAKEEL AHMED MUKHTAR.

Sialkot Chamber of Commerce and Industry: Shahrah-e-Aiwan-e-Sanat-o-Tijarat, POB 1870, Sialkot 51310; tel. (52) 4261881; fax (52) 4268835; e-mail directorrnd@scci.com.pk; internet www.scci.com.pk; f. 1982; 7,500 mems; Pres. HASSAN ALI BHATTI; Sec. NAWAZ AHMED TOOR.

South Punjab Women's Chamber of Commerce and Industry: 116, Metro Plaza, Qasim Rd, Multan; tel. (61) 4002389; fax (61) 4027621; e-mail spwcci@hotmail.com; Pres. ANEELA IFTIKHAR.

Sukkur Chamber of Commerce and Industry: Sukkur Chamber House, 1st Floor, opp. Mehran View Plaza, Bunder Rd, Sukkur; tel. (71) 5623938; fax (71) 5623059; e-mail info@sukkurcci.org.pk; internet www.sukkurcci.org.pk; Pres. SHAKEEL AHMED MUKHTAR; Sec. MIRZA IQBAL BEG.

INDUSTRIAL AND TRADE ASSOCIATIONS

Air Cargo Agents' Association of Pakistan: Suite 305, 3rd Floor, Fortune Centre, 45-A, Block 6, PECHS, Shahrah-e-Faisal, Karachi 75400; tel. (21) 4383501; fax (21) 4383502; e-mail acaap@pk.netsolir.com; Chair. JAMSHED QURESHI.

All Pakistan Cement Manufacturers' Association: House 27-28/3A FCC, Gulberg-IV, Lahore; tel. (42) 5871632; fax (42) 5874442; e-mail apcma@apcma.com; internet apcma.com; Chair. Maj.-Gen. (retd.) REHMAT KHAN.

All Pakistan Cloth Merchants' Association: 4th Floor, Hasan Ali Centre, Hussaini Cloth Market, nr Mereweather Tower, M. A. Jinnah Rd, Karachi; tel. (21) 2444274; fax (21) 2401423; e-mail pcma@cyber.net.pk; f. 1947; Chair. AHMED CHINOY; Sec.-Gen. RAFIQ KHAN.

PAKISTAN

All Pakistan Cotton Powerlooms' Association: P-79/3, Montgomery Bazaar, Faisalabad; tel. (41) 2612929; fax (41) 2613636; Chair. KHALID MAHMOOD CHEEMA.

All Pakistan Furniture Exporters' Association: Karachi; tel. (21) 5861963; Chair. TURHAN BAIG MOHAMMAD.

All Pakistan Textile Mills' Association (APTMA): APTMA House, 44A Lalazar, off Moulvi Tamizuddin Khan Rd, POB 5446, Karachi 74000; tel. (21) 111-700-000; fax (21) 5611305; e-mail aptma@cyber.net.pk; internet www.aptma.org.pk; f. 1959; Chair. TARIQ MEHMOOD.

Association of Builders and Developers of Pakistan: Abed House, St 1-1/D, Block 16, Gulistan-e-Jauhar, Karachi 75290; tel. (21) 4613645; fax (21) 4613645; e-mail info@abad.com.pk; internet www.abad.com.pk; f. 1972; Chair. BABAR MIRZA CHUGHTAI.

Cigarette Manufacturers' Association of Pakistan: Caesars Towers (opp. Aisha Bawany Academy), Rm 102, 1st Floor, Main Shahrah-e-Faisal, Karachi 75400; tel. and fax (21) 2789555; e-mail cmaofpak@cyber.net.pk; Sec. TARIQ FAROOQ.

Cotton Board: Dr Abbasi Clinic Bldg, 76 Strachan Rd, Karachi 74200; tel. (21) 215669; fax (21) 5680422; f. 1950; Dep. Sec. Dr MUHAMMAD USMAN.

Federal 'B' Area Association of Trade and Industry: ST-7, Block 22, Federal 'B' Area, Karachi 75950; tel. (21) 6340362; fax (21) 6360203; e-mail info@fbati.com; internet www.fbati.com; Chair. M. IDREES GIGI.

Karachi Cotton Association: The Cotton Exchange, I. I. Chundrigar Rd, Karachi; tel. (92) 2412570; fax (21) 2413035; e-mail kcapak@cyber.net.pk; internet www.kcapk.org; Chair. MOHAMMAD ATIF DADA; Sec. S. A. JAWED.

Korangi Association of Trade and Industry: ST-4/2, 1st Floor, Aiwan-e-Sanat, Sector 23, Korangi Industrial Area, Karachi 74900; tel. (21) 5061211; fax (21) 5061215; e-mail kati@cyber.net.pk; internet www.kati.com.pk; Chair. MIAN ZAHID HUSSAIN; Sec. NIHAL AKHTAR.

Management Association of Pakistan: 36-A/4, Lalazar, opp. Beach Luxury Hotel, Karachi 74000; tel. (21) 5610903; fax (21) 5611683; e-mail info@mappk.org; internet www.mappk.org; f. 1964; Pres. ASIF QADIR; Exec. Dir FAROOQ HASSAN.

Pakistan Advertising Association: Rm 318, 3rd Floor, Hotel Metropole, Club Rd, Karachi; tel. (21) 5671567; fax (21) 5671571; e-mail info@paa.com.pk; internet www.paa.com.pk; Chair. MANSOOR ALI ZAIDI; Sec. S. NAJMUL HASSAN.

Pakistan Agricultural Machinery and Implements Manufacturers' Association: Samundari Rd, Faisalabad; tel. (41) 714517; fax (41) 722721; e-mail iqra@fsd.comsats.net.pk.

Pakistan Arms and Ammunition Merchants' and Manufacturers' Association: Metropole Cinema Bldg, Rm 7, Abbot Rd, Lahore; tel. (42) 7239973; fax (42) 7230170; e-mail ssalimali@hotmail.com.

Pakistan Art Silk Fabrics and Garments Exporters' Association: 60, The Mall, Lahore; tel. (42) 6360919; fax (42) 6361291; e-mail pasfgea@hotmail.com; internet www.pasfgea.org; Chair. JAMIL MEHBOOB MAGOON; Sec.-Gen. IFTIKHAR AHMED KHAN.

Pakistan Association of Automotive Parts and Accessories Manufacturers: 501, 5th Floor, Mehdi Towers, SMCHS, Main Shahrah-e-Fasal, Karachi; tel. (21) 5412514; fax (42) 7237613; e-mail chairman@paapam.com; internet www.paapam.com; Chair. JAWAID SHAIKH.

Pakistan Association of Builders and Developers: Abad House, St 1/D, Block 16, Gulistan-e-Jauhar, Karachi; tel. (21) 4613645; fax (21) 4613648; e-mail info@abad.com.pk; internet abad.com.pk; Chair. BABAR MIRZA CHUGHTAI.

Pakistan Association of Printing and Graphic Arts: 214, Mashriq Centre, 2nd Floor, Staduim Rd, Karachi; tel. (21) 4920175; fax (21) 4926625; e-mail info@papgai.com.pk; internet www.papgai.com.pk; f. 1959; affiliated with the federation of Pakistan Chambers of Commerce and Industry; promotion and devt of the printing and graphic arts industry; Chair. ABDUL AZIZ GAUBA.

Pakistan Automotive Manufacturers' Association: 1st Floor, Block-C, Finance & Trade Centre, Sharah-e-Faisal, Karachi Karachi; tel. (21) 5630992; fax (21) 5630995; e-mail pamaftc@cyber.net.pk; internet www.pama.org.pk; Chair. ALI S. HABIB.

Pakistan Bedwear Exporters' Association: 245-1-V, Block 6, PECHS, Karachi; tel. (21) 4541149; fax (21) 4541192; e-mail bedwear@fascom.com; Chair. SHABIR AHMED; Sec. S. IFTIKHAR HUSSAIN.

Pakistan Beverage Manufacturers' Association: C, 1st Floor, Kiran Centre, M-28, Model Town Extension, Lahore; tel. (42) 5167306; fax (42) 5167316.

Pakistan Canvas and Tents Manufacturers' and Exporters' Association: 15/63, Shadman Commercial Market, Afridi Mansion, Lahore 3; tel. (42) 7577522; fax (42) 7578836; e-mail pctmea@wol.net.pk; internet www.pctmea.org; f. 1984; Chair. MALIK MUHAMMED SALEEM; Sec.-Gen. IJAZ HUSSAIN.

Pakistan Carpet Manufacturers' and Exporters' Association: 23–D, Block 6, PECHS, Shahrah-e-Faisal, Karachi; tel. (21) 4382728; fax (21) 4382739; e-mail pcmeaho@gerrys.net; Chair. ABDUL GHAFOOR SAJID.

Pakistan Chemicals and Dyes Merchants' Association: Chemicals and Dyes House, Rambharti St, Jodia Bazar, Karachi; tel. (21) 2432752; fax (21) 2430117; e-mail pcdma@super.net.pk; Chair. SHAUKAT RIAZ.

Pakistan Commercial Exporters of Towels Association: PCETA House, 7-H, Block 6, PECHS, Karachi; tel. (21) 4535757; fax (21) 4522372; e-mail pceta@cyber.net.pk; Chair. ALI ASHRAF KHAN.

Pakistan Cotton Fashion Apparel Manufacturers' and Exporters' Association: 5 & 6, Amber Court, 2nd Floor, Shahrah-e-Faisal, Shaheed-e-Millat Rd, Karachi 75350; tel. (21) 4522936; fax (21) 4546711; e-mail pcfa@cyber.net.pk; internet www.pcfa.pk; f. 1982; 650 mems; Chair. KHAWAJA M. USMAN.

Pakistan Cotton Ginners' Association: PCGA House, M.D.A. Rd, Multan; tel. (61) 4549815; fax (61) 4549817; e-mail pcga@pgca.org; internet www.pcga.org; Chair. MUHAMMAD AKRAM; Sec. AIJAZUDDIN GHAURI.

Pakistan Dairy Association: 11/19-B, Link Shami Rd, Lahore; tel. (42) 6680041; fax (42) 6682042; e-mail pakdairy@yahoo.com.

Pakistan Electronics Manufacturers' Association: 3rd Floor, Lakson Square Bldg 1, Sarwar Shaheed Rd, Karachi; tel. (21) 5658872; fax (21) 5620877; Chair. SARFRAZUDDIN.

Pakistan Engineering Council: Atatürk Ave (East), Sector G-5/2, Islamabad; tel. (51) 9206974; fax (51) 2276224; e-mail info@pec.org.pk; internet www.pec.org.pk; f. 1976; Chair. RUKSHANA ZUBERI.

Pakistan Film Producers' Association: Regal Cinema Bldg, Shahrah-e-Quaid-e-Azam, Lahore; tel. (42) 7322904; fax (42) 7241264; Chair. Mian AMJAD FARZEND; Sec. SAMI DEHLVI.

Pakistan Flour Mills' Association: 676, Shadman Colony-1, Lahore; tel. (42) 7596330; fax (42) 7573967; Chair. SYED ZAHOOR AHMAD AGHA.

Pakistan Footwear Manufacturers' Association: 6-F, Rehman Business Centre, 32-B-III, Gulberg III, Lahore 54660; tel. (42) 5750051; fax (42) 5780276; e-mail pfma@pakfootwear.org; internet www.pakfootwear.org; f. 1984; Chair. NASIR ANWAR; Sec. Col (retd) ARSHAD AYYAZ.

Pakistan Glass Manufacturers' Association: 52, West Wakeel Plaza, Islamabad; tel. (51) 2825045; fax (51) 5857692.

Pakistan Gloves Manufacturers' and Exporters' Association: PGMEA Bldg, Kashmir Rd, POB 1330, Sialkot; tel. (52) 4272959; fax (52) 4274860; e-mail pgmea@brain.net.pk; internet www.brain.net.pk/~pgmea; f. 1978; Chair. ARFAN ELAHI.

Pakistan Hardware Merchants' Association: 47 Nishtar Rd, Lahore 54000; tel. (42) 7631182; e-mail phmasbcircle@hotmail.com; internet www.phma.info; f. 1961; more than 1,500 mems; Chair. BASIT ALAVI; Sec. SYED ZAFRUN NABI.

Pakistan Hosiery Manufacturers' Association: PHMA House, 37-H, Block 6, PECHS, Karachi; tel. (21) 4544789; fax (21) 4543774; internet www.phmaonline.com; Chair. MUHAMMAD JAWED BILANI.

Pakistan Iron and Steel Merchants' Association: Mustafa Cloth Market, M. A. Jinnah Rd, Karachi; tel. (21) 2464567; fax (21) 2464568; Chair. AKBAR ABDULLAH.

Pakistan Jute Mills' Association: 18 D-E, 2 Gulberg III, Lahore 546600; tel. (42) 5774400; fax (42) 5774402; e-mail secretary@pjma.com.pk; internet www.pjma.com.pk; Chair. ABDUL KHALIQ.

Pakistan Knitwear and Sweaters Exporters' Association: Rms Nos 1014–1016, 10th Floor, Park Ave, Block 6, PECHS, Shahrah-e-Faisal, Karachi 95350; tel. (21) 4544035; fax (21) 4544039; Chair. RAFIQ H. GABOL.

Pakistan Leather Garments Manufacturers' and Exporters' Association: 60-C, Mezzanine Floor, 11th Commercial St, DHA Phase II (Extension), Karachi; tel. (21) 5387365; fax (21) 5388799; e-mail plgmea@cyber.net.pk; internet www.plgmea.com; f. 2001; Chair. FAWAD IJAZ KHAN.

Pakistan Paint Manufacturers' Association: St 6/A, Block 14, Federal 'B' Area, Karachi 38; tel. (21) 6321103; fax (21) 2560468; f. 1953; Chair. WASSIM A. KHAN; Sec. SYED AZHAR ALI.

Pakistan Petroleum Exploration and Production Companies' Association: 1 St 49, Sector F-6/4, Islamabad; tel. (51) 2823928; fax (51) 2276084; e-mail mail@ppepca.com; internet www.ppepca.com; f. 1995; Chair. JANOS FEHRER; Sec.-Gen. MAZHAR FAROOQ.

Pakistan Pharmaceutical Manufacturers' Association: 430–431, Hotel Metropole, Karachi; tel. (21) 5211773; fax (21) 5675608;

e-mail ppma@cyber.net.pk; internet www.ppma.org.pk; Chair. ZAHID SAEED.

Pakistan Plastic Manufacturers' Association: 2nd Floor, 8 Estate Ave, Karachi; tel. (21)6040111; fax (21) 4382739; e-mail pakppma@yahoo.com; Chair. SHAKEEL AHMED.

Pakistan Polypropylene Woven Sacks Manufacturers' Association: Karachi; Chair. SHOUKAT AHMED.

Pakistan Poultry Association: 219 Mashriq Centre, Block 14, Sir Shah Muhammad Suleman Rd, Gulshan-e-Iqbal, Karachi; tel. (21) 4940362; fax (21) 4940364; e-mail ppasee@cyber.net.pk.

Pakistan Pulp, Paper and Board Mills' Association: 402 Burhani Chambers, Abdullah Haroon Rd, Karachi 74400; tel. (21) 7726150; Chair. KAMRAN KHAN.

Pakistan Readymade Garments Manufacturers' and Exporters' Association: Shaheen View Bldg, Mezzanine Floor, Plot No. 18A, Block 6, PECHS, Shahrah-e-Faisal, Karachi; tel. (21) 4547912; fax (21) 4539669; e-mail info@prgmea.org; internet www.prgmea.org; Chair. JAMSHAID HANIF.

Pakistan Seafood Industries' Association: A-2, Fish Harbour, West Wharf, Karachi; tel. (21) 2311117; fax (21) 2310939; e-mail psiapk@hotmail.com.

Pakistan Ship Breakers' Association: 608, S. S. Chamber, Siemens Chowrangi, S.I.T.E., Karachi; tel. (21) 293958; fax (21) 256533.

Pakistan Silk and Rayon Mills' Association: Rms Nos 44, 48 & 49, Textile Plaza, 5th Floor, M. A. Jinnah Rd, Karachi 2; tel. (21) 2410288; fax (21) 2415261; e-mail ctech@edu.pk; f. 1974; Chair. KHALID AMIN.

Pakistan Small Units Powerlooms' Association: 2nd Floor, Waqas Plaza, Aminpura Bazar, POB 8647, Faisalabad; tel. (411) 627992; fax (411) 633567.

Pakistan Soap Manufacturers' Association: 148 Sunny Plaza, Hasrat Mohani Rd, Karachi 74200; tel. (21) 2218937; fax (21) 2634648; e-mail pakistansma@yahoo.com; Chair. MUHAMMAD KALI ZIA.

Pakistan Software Houses Association (PASHA): 172/P Najeeb Corner, 4th Floor, Block 2, PECHS, Karachi; tel. (21) 5418121; fax (21) 4547759; e-mail karachi@pasha.org.pk; internet www.pasha.org.pk; f. 1992; Pres. JEHAN ARA.

Pakistan Sports Goods Manufacturers' and Exporters' Association: 298–99 Shah Faisal Rd, Model Town, Sialkot 51310; tel. (52) 3256930; fax (52)3256920; e-mail psga@brain.net.pk; Chair. MOHAMMAD YOUNUS SONY.

Pakistan Steel Melters' Association: 30-S, Gulberg Centre, 84-D/1, Main Boulevard, Gulberg-III, Lahore; tel. (42) 5759284; fax (42) 5712028; e-mail steelmelters@angelfire.com; Chair. ILYAS AZIZ MALIK.

Pakistan Steel Re-rolling Mills' Association: Rashid Chambers, 6-Link McLeod Rd, Lahore 54000; tel. (42) 7227136; fax (42) 7231154; e-mail steel_re_rollers@hotmail.com; Chair. Mian TARIQ WAHEED.

Pakistan Sugar Mills' Association: 24D Rashid Plaza Mezzanine Floor, Jinnah Ave, Islamabad; tel. (51) 2270525; fax (51) 2274153; e-mail center@psmaonline.com; internet www.psmaonline.com; Chair. ISKANDAR M. KHAN; Sec.-Gen. K. ALI QAZILBASH.

Pakistan Tanners' Association: Plot No. 46-C, 21st Commercial St, Phase II Extension, Defence Housing Authority, Karachi 75500; tel. (21) 5880180; fax (21) 5880093; e-mail info@pakistantanners.org; internet www.pakistantanners.org; Chair. AGHA SAIDDAIN.

Pakistan Tea Association: Suite 307, Business Plaza, Mumtaz Hassan Rd, off I. I. Chundrigar Rd, Karachi; tel. (21) 2422161; fax (21) 2422209; e-mail pta@cyber.net.pk; Chair. HANIF JANOO.

Pakistan Textile Exporters Association: 30/7, Civil Lines, Faisalabad; tel. (41) 644750; fax (41) 617985; e-mail info@ptea.org; internet www.ptea.org; Chair. MUHAMMAD YOUSAF.

Pakistan Vanaspati Manufacturers' Association: 7, I-8/2, Main Service Rd, Islamabad; tel. (51) 2502004; fax (51) 4430125; Chair. ABDUL MAJID HAJI MOHAMMAD.

Pakistan Wool and Hair Merchants' Association: 27 Idris Chambers, Talpur Rd, Karachi; Pres. Mian MOHAMMAD SIDDIQ KHAN; Sec. KHALID LATEEF.

Pakistan Woollen Mills' Association: 25A, Davis Rd, Lahore 54000; tel. (42) 6307691; fax (42) 6306881; e-mail pwma@brain.net.pk; Chair. Mian MUZAFFAR ALI; Sec. MUHAMMAD RAHEEL CHOHAN.

Pakistan Yarn Merchants' Association: Rms Nos 802–803, Business Centre, 8th Floor, Dunolly Rd, Karachi 74000; tel. (21) 2410320; fax (21) 2424896; e-mail pakyarn@cyber.net.pk; internet www.pyma.com.pk; Chair. MOHAMMAD. ASHRAF GANDHI.

Rice Exports Association of Pakistan: 4th Floor, Sadiq Plaza, The Mall, Lahore; tel. and fax (42) 6280146; fax (42) 6280196; e-mail reap@cyber.net.pk; internet www.reap.com.pk; Chair. ABDUL RAHIM JANOO.

Towel Manufacturers' Association of Pakistan: 77-A, Block A, Sindhi Muslim Co-operative Housing Society, Karachi 74400; tel. (21) 111-360-360; fax (21) 4551628; e-mail tma@towelassociation.com; internet www.towelassociation.com; Chair. FEROZE ALAM LARI.

EMPLOYERS' ORGANIZATION

Employers' Federation of Pakistan: 2nd Floor, State Life Bldg No. 2, Wallace Rd, off I. I. Chundrigar Rd, POB 4338, Karachi 74000; tel. (21) 2411049; fax (21) 2439347; e-mail efpak@cyber.net.pk; internet www.efp.org.pk; f. 1950; Pres. ASHRAF WALI MOHAMMAD TABANI; Sec.-Gen. Prof. M. MATIN KHAN.

UTILITIES

Water and Power Development Authority (WAPDA): WAPDA House, Shahrah-e-Quaid-e-Azam, Lahore; tel. (42) 6366911; fax (42) 9202454; internet www.wapda.gov.pk; f. 1958 for devt of irrigation, water supply and drainage, building of replacement works under the World Bank-sponsored Indo-Pakistan Indus Basin Treaty; flood-control and watershed management; reclamation of waterlogged and saline lands; inland navigation; generation, transmission and distribution of hydroelectric and thermal power; partial transfer to private ownership carried out in 1996; Chair. MOHAMMAD SHAKEEL DURRANI.

Electricity

Kohinoor Energy Ltd: Near Tablighi Ijtima, PO Kohinoor Energy, Raiwind Bypass, Lahore; tel. (42) 5392317; fax (42) 5393415; e-mail info@kel.com.pk; internet www.kel.com.pk; f. 1994; jt venture of Saigols Group of Cos and Toyota Tsusho Corpn; Chair. M. NASEEM SAIGOL; CEO MUNEKI UDAKA.

National Electric Power Regulatory Authority (NEPRA): OPF Bldg, 2nd Floor, Shahrah-e-Jamhuriat, G-5/2, Islamabad 44000; tel. (51) 9207200; fax (51) 9210215; e-mail info@nepra.org.pk; internet www.nepra.org.pk; f. 1997; fixes the power tariff; Chair. Lt-Gen. (retd) SAEED UZ ZAFAR.

Hub Power Co Ltd (Hubco): Islamic Chamber Bldg, 3rd Floor, St 2/A, Block No. 9, Clifton, POB 13841, Karachi 75600; tel. (21) 5874677; fax (21) 5870397; e-mail info@hubpower.com; internet www.hubpower.com; f. 1991; supplies electricity; Chair. MOHAMMAD AHMED ZAINAL ALIREZA; Chief Exec. JAVED MAHMOOD.

Karachi Electric Supply Corpn Ltd (KESC): Aimai House, Abdullah Haroon Rd, POB 7197, Karachi; tel. (21) 5685492; fax (21) 5682408; internet www.kesc.com.pk; f. 1913; Chair. ABDUL AZIZ HAMEED AL-JOMAIH; CEO Lt-Gen. SYED MOHAMMAD AMJAD.

Kot Addu Power Co (KAPCO): 404 Siddiq Trade Centre, 72-Main Blvd, Gulberg, Lahore; tel. (42) 5781631; e-mail info@kapco.com.pk; fax (42) 5781636; internet www.kapco.com.pk; f. 1996; 46% owned by Pakistan Water and Power Development Authority; Chair. SHAKIL DURRANI.

National Power Construction Corpn (Pvt) Ltd: 9 Shadman II, Lahore 54000; tel. (42) 7566019; fax (42) 7566022; e-mail npcc@wol.net.pk; internet www.npcc.com.pk; f. 1974; execution of power projects on turnkey basis, e.g. extra high voltage transmission lines, distribution networks, substations, power generation plants, industrial electrification, external lighting of housing complexes, etc.; Chair. MUHAMMAD ISMAIL QURESHI; Man. Dir MUHAMMAD AJAZ MALIK; project office in Jeddah (Saudi Arabia).

Pakistan Atomic Energy Commission (PAEC): POB 1114, Islamabad; tel. (51) 9206384; fax (51) 9204908; e-mail feedback@paec.gov.pk; internet www.paec.gov.pk; responsible for harnessing nuclear energy for devt of nuclear technology as part of the nuclear power programme; operates Karachi Nuclear Power Plant—KANUPP (POB 3183, nr Paradise Point, Hawksbay Rd, Karachi 75400; tel. (21) 9202222; fax (21) 7737488; e-mail knpc@khi.comsats.net.pk) and Chashma Nuclear Power Plant (CHASNUPP) at Chashma District, Mianwali (tel. (459) 9224430; fax (0459) 241505; email chasnupp1@ntc.net.pk); building another nuclear power station at Chashma; establishing research centres, incl. Pakistan Institute of Nuclear Science and Technology (PINSTECH); promoting peaceful use of atomic energy in agriculture, medicine, industry and hydrology; searching for indigenous nuclear mineral deposits; training project personnel; Chair. ANSAR PARVEZ; Dir-Gen. (KANUPP) JAWED IQBAL; Dir-Gen. (CHASNUPP) SAFDER HABIB.

Pakistan Electric Power Co: WADPA House, Lahore; tel. (42) 9203846; fax (42) 9202402; e-mail info@pepco.gov.pk; internet www.pepco.gov.pk; f. 1998; Man. Dir FAZL AHMED KHAN.

Pakistan Nuclear Regulatory Authority (PNRA): POB 1912, Islamabad 44000; tel. (51) 9263017; fax (51) 9263007; e-mail officialmail@pnra.org; internet www.pnra.org; f. 2001 by presidential ordinance; Chair. JAMSHED AZIM HASHMI.

Private Power and Infrastructure Board (PPIB): 50 Nazimuddin Rd, F-7/4, Islamabad; tel. (51) 9205421; fax (51) 9217735; e-mail ppib@ppib.gov.pk; internet www.ppib.gov.pk; f. 1994; facilitates participation of private sector in national power generation; Man. Dir MOHAMMAD YOUSUF MEMON.

Quetta Electric Supply Co Ltd (QESCO): Zarghoon Rd, Quetta Cantt, Balochistan; tel. (81) 9202211; fax (81) 836554; e-mail qesco@qta.infolink.net.pk; internet www.qesco.com.pk; f. 1998; CEO MUHAMMAD KHATTAK.

Gas

Hydrocarbon Development Institute of Pakistan: Plot 18, Street 6, H-9/1, POB 1308, Islamabad; tel. (51) 9258301; fax (51) 9258310; e-mail info@hdip.com.pk; internet www.hdip.com.pk; f. 1975; re-established Jan. 2006 under Ministry of Petroleum and Natural Resources; national petroleum research and devt org.; provides consultancy and laboratory services to petroleum industry; Chair. ASIM HUSSAIN; Dir-Gen. and Chief Exec. HILAL A. RAZA.

Mari Gas Co Ltd (MGCL): 21 Mauve Area, 3rd Rd, Sector G-10/4, POB 1614, Islamabad; tel. (51) 111-410-410; fax (51) 2297686; e-mail info@marigas.com.pk; internet www.marigas.com.pk; 20% govt-owned; Chair. Lt-Gen. (retd) SYED ARIF HASSAN; Resident Gen. Man. Col (retd) AMJAD JAVED.

Oil and Gas Development Co Ltd (OGDCL): OGDC House, Blue Area, Islamabad; tel. (51) 9209882; fax (51) 9209859; f. 1961; became a publicly limited co in 1997; 85% govt-owned; plans, promotes, organizes and implements programmes for the exploration and devt of petroleum and gas resources, and the production, refining and sale of petroleum and gas; transfer to private ownership pending; Man. Dir and CEO SYED ZAHID HUSSAIN; 11,624 employees (Aug. 2005).

Oil and Gas Regulatory Authority: Tariq Chambers, Main Civic Centre, Islamabad; tel. (51) 9204516; e-mail registrar@ogra.org.pk; internet www.ogra.org.pk; f. 2002; Chair. (vacant); Vice-Chair. RASHID FAROOQ.

Pakistan Petroleum Ltd (PPL): PIDC House, 4th Floor, Dr Ziauddin Ahmed Rd, POB 3942, Karachi 75530, Sindh; tel. (21) 111-568-568; fax (21) 5680005; e-mail info@ppl.com.pk; internet www.ppl.com.pk; 78.4% govt-owned, 15.5% owned by private Pakistani shareholders and 6.1% owned by International Finance Corpn; Pakistan's largest producer of natural gas; cap. and res Rs 18,393m., sales Rs 10,732m. (July–Dec. 2004); Chief Exec./Man. Dir KHALID RAHMAN; 2,520 employees (2006).

Petroleum Institute of Pakistan (PIP): Federation House, 1st Floor, Street 28, Block V, Kehkashan, Clifton, Karachi 75600; tel. (21) 5378701; fax (21) 5378704; e-mail info@pip.org.pk; internet www.pip.org.pk; f. 1963; represents all sectors of the petroleum industry (incl. exploration, production, refining, marketing and natural gas); promotes and co-ordinates industry activities; mem. of the International Gas Union and World Petroleum Council; 25 Industrial Collective mems, over 860 individual industry mems; Chair. TARIQ KHAMISANI.

Sui Northern Gas Pipelines Ltd: Gas House, 21 Kashmir Rd, Lahore; tel. (42) 9201451; fax (42) 9201302; e-mail info@sngpl.com.pk; internet www.sngpl.com.pk; f. 1964; 36% state-owned; transmission and distribution of natural gas in northern Pakistan; sales Rs 107,897.3m. (2005/06); Chair. TARIQ IQBAL KHAN; Man. Dir ABDUL RASHID LONE.

Sui Southern Gas Co Ltd: 4B Sir Shah Suleman Rd, Block 14, Gulshan-e-Iqbal, Karachi 75000; tel. (21) 9231602; fax (21) 9231604; e-mail info@ssgc.com.pk; internet www.ssgc.com.pk; f. 1988; 70% state-owned; Chair. SALIM ABBAS JILANI; Man. Dir UMAIR KHAN.

Water

Faisalabad Development Authority (Water and Sanitation Agency) (FDA): Jail Rd, POB 229, Faisalabad; tel. (41) 9210053; fax (41) 9210054; e-mail wasa_fsd@yahoo.com; internet www.wasafsd.gov.pk; f. 1978; Man. Dir Dr ARSHAD MAHMOOD.

Karachi Water and Sewerage Board: 9th Mile, Karsaz, Shahrah-e-Faisal, Karachi; tel. (21) 9231882; fax (21) 9231814; e-mail mdkwsb@yahoo.co.uk; internet www.kwsb.gos.pk; f. 1983; Man. Dir FAZAL-UR-REHMAN.

Lahore Development Authority (Water and Sanitation Agency): 4-A Gulberg V, Jail Rd, Lahore; tel. (42) 5752483; fax (42) 5752960; internet www.lda.gop.pk; f. 1967; Dir-Gen. RAJA MUHAMMAD ABBAS.

TRADE UNIONS

National Trade Union Federation Pakistan: Bharocha Bldg, 2-B/6, Commercial Area, Nazimabad No. 2, Karachi 74600; tel. (21) 628339; fax (21) 6622529; e-mail ntuf@super.net.pk; f. 1999; 50 affiliated unions; covers following fields: steel, agriculture, textiles, garments, leather, automobiles, pharmaceuticals, chemicals, transport, printing, food, shipbuilding, engineering and power; Pres. MUHAMMAD RAFIQUE; Gen. Sec. SALEEM RAZA.

Pakistan Workers Federation (PWF): Bakhtiar Labour Hall, 28 Nisbet Rd, Lahore; tel. (42) 7229192; fax (42) 7239529; e-mail cpr@pwf.org.pk; internet www.pwf.org.pk; f. 2005 following the merger of the All Pakistan Federation of Trade Unions, Pakistan National Federation of Trade Unions and All Pakistan Federation of Labour; affiliated with the International Confederation of Free Trade Unions; 10 regional offices; Pres. CH. TALIB NAWAZ; Chair. MUHAMMAD AHMED; Gen. Sec. KHURSHID AHMED.

The principal affiliated federations are:

Muttahida Labour Federation: 24, Circular Bldg, Risala Rd, Hyderabad; c. 120,000 mems; Pres. KHAMASH GUL KHATTAK; Sec.-Gen. NABI AHMED.

National Labour Federation (NLF): 28, Circular Rd, Hyderabad; Pres. RANA MAHMOOD ALI KHAN.

Pakistan Central Federation of Trade Unions: 220 Al-Noor Chambers, M. A. Jinnah Rd, Karachi; tel. (21) 728891.

Pakistan Railway Employees' Union (PREM): City Railway Station, Karachi; tel. (21) 2415721; Divisional Sec. BASHIRUDDIN SIDDIQUI.

Pakistan Trade Union Federation: Khamosh Colony, Karachi; Pres. KANIZ FATIMA; Gen. Sec. SALEEM RAZA.

Pakistan Transport Workers' Federation: 110 McLeod Rd, Lahore; 17 unions; 92,512 mems; Pres. MEHBOOB-UL-HAQ; Gen. Sec. CH. UMAR DIN.

Other affiliated federations include: Pakistan Bank Employees' Federation, Pakistan Insurance Employees' Federation, Automobile, Engineering and Metal Workers' Federation, Pakistan Teachers Organizations' Council, Sarhad WAPDA Employees' Federation, and Balochistan Ittehad Trade Union Federation.

Transport

RAILWAYS

Pakistan Railways: Empress Rd, Lahore; tel. (42) 9201700; fax (42) 9201669; e-mail gmopr@pr.org.pk; internet www.pakrail.com; state-owned; 11,515 km of track and 7,791 route km; seven divisions (Karachi, Lahore, Multan, Quetta, Rawalpindi, Peshawar and Sukkur); Chair. MOHAMMAD KASHIF MURTAZA; Man. Dir JAVEED IQBAL.

ROADS

The total length of roads was 254,410 km (motorways 339 km, main 6,587 km, secondary 211,846 km, other roads 35,638 km) in 1999. By June 2004 the total length of roads had increased to 258,340 km, 64.7% of which were paved, including 9,031 km of highways and motorways.

Government assistance comes from the Road Fund, financed from a share of the excise and customs duty on sales of petrol and from development loans.

National Highways Authority: 27 Mauve Area, G-9/1, Islamabad; tel. (51) 9261111; fax (51) 9261075; e-mail info@nha.gov.pk; internet www.nha.gov.pk; f. 1991; jt venture between Govt and private sector; Chair. ALTAF AHMAD; Dir-Gen. ATHAR HUSSAIN KHAN.

Punjab Road Transport Board: Department of Transport, Pension Cell, 11A Egerton Rd, Lahore.

SHIPPING

In 1974 maritime shipping companies were placed under government control. The chief port is Karachi. A second port, Port Qasim, started partial operation in 1980. A third port, Port Gwadar, has been developed as a deep-water seaport; construction was completed in March 2005 and the port opened in March 2007. Another port, Port Pasni, which is situated on the Balochistan coast, was completed in 1988. In 1991 the Government amended the 1974 Pakistan Maritime Shipping Act to allow private companies to operate.

Mercantile Marine Dept: 70/4, Timber Pond, N. M. Reclamation, Keamari, Karachi 74000; tel. (21) 9263014; fax (21) 9263018; e-mail info@mercantilemarine.gov.pk; internet www.mercantilemarine.gov.pk; f. 1930; ensures safety of life and property at sea and prevention of marine pollution through implementation of national legislation and international conventions; Prin. Officer TARIQ SARDAR.

Ports and Shipping: Government of Pakistan, Plot No. 12, Misc. Area, Mai Kolachi Bypass, Karachi 74200; tel. (21) 9204191; e-mail contact@mops.gov.pk; internet www.mops.gov.pk; Dir-Gen. HASSAN ZAIDI.

Al-Hamd International Container Terminal (Pvt) Ltd: Plot No. 28, O & L Trans Lyari Quarters, Hawkesbay Rd, New Truck Stand, Karachi; tel. (21) 2352660; fax (21) 2351556; e-mail info@aictpk.com; internet www.aictpakistan.com; CEO HUSSAIN ISLAM; Gen. Man. Col (retd) SHAHZADA FARRUKH ZAMAN.

Engro Vopak Terminal Ltd: 1st Floor, Bahrai Complex 1, 24 M. T. Khan Rd, POB 5736, Karachi 74000; tel. (21) 7301213; fax (21) 730113; e-mail saqadri@engro.com; internet www.vopak.com; Man. SYED ATIQUDDIN QADRI.

Gwadar Port Authority: GPA Complex, Fish Harbour Rd, Gwadar 92100; tel. (864) 210073; fax (864) 210075; e-mail gwadarport@hotmail.com.

Karachi International Container Terminal (KICT): Administration Bldg, Berths 28–30, Dockyard Rd, West Wharf, Karachi 74000; tel. (21) 2316401; fax (21) 2313816; e-mail info@kictl.com; internet www.kictl.com; f. 1996; Chief Exec. ROGER L. HAWKE.

Karachi Port Trust (KPT): Eduljee Dinshaw Rd, Karachi 74000; tel. (21) 9214312; fax (21) 9214329; e-mail chairman@kpt.gov.pk; internet www.kpt.gov.pk; Chair. NASREEN HAQUE; Gen. Operations Man. Rear-Adm. AGHA DANISH; Sec. KHALID MOBIN ARSHAD.

Karachi Shipyard and Engineering Works Ltd: POB 4419, West Wharf, Dockyard Rd, Karachi 74000; tel. (21) 9214045; fax (21) 9214020; e-mail contact@karachishipyard.com.pk; internet www.karachishipyard.com.pk; f. 1953; building and repairing ships; general engineering; Man. Dir Vice-Adm. IFTIKHAR AHMED RAO.

Korangi Fisheries Harbour Authority: Ghashma Goth, Landhi, POB 15804, Karachi 75160; tel. (21) 5013315; fax (21) 5015096; e-mail kfha@sat.net.pk.

National Tanker Co (Pvt) Ltd (Pak): 15th Floor, PNSC Bldg, M. T. Khan Rd, Karachi 74000; tel. (21) 5611843; fax (21) 5610780; f. 1981 by the Pakistan National Shipping Corpn and the State Petroleum Refining and Petrochemical Corpn Ltd; aims to make Pakistan self-reliant in the transport of crude petroleum and petroleum products; Chief Exec. Vice-Adm. A. U. KHAN; Dep. Chief Exec. TURAB ALI KHAN.

Pakistan International Container Terminal Ltd: 2nd Floor, Business Plaza, Mumtaz Hussain Rd, Karachi 74000; tel. (21) 2855701; fax (21) 2855715; e-mail info@pict.com.pk; internet www.pictcntrtrack.com; Chair. Capt. HALEEM A. SIDDIQI; CEO Capt. ZAFAR IQBAL AWAN.

Pakistan National Shipping Corpn: PNSC Bldg, M. T. Khan Rd, POB 5350, Karachi 74000; tel. (21) 9203980; fax (21) 9203974; e-mail communication@pnsc.com.pk; internet www.pnsc.com.pk; f. 1979 by merger; state-owned; national flag carrier; undertakes global shipping operations; Chair. Vice-Adm. S. T. H. NAQVI; Sec. ZAINAB SULEMAN.

Port Qasim Authority (PQA): Bin Qasim, Karachi 75020; tel. (21) 9272111; fax (21) 4730108; e-mail webmaster@portqasim.org.pk; internet www.portqasim.org.pk; f. 1973; Chair. AFSAR DIN TALPUR; Sec. ANWAR MEHTAB ZAIDI.

Qasim International Container Terminal: Berths 5–7, Marginal Wharfs, POB 6425, Port Mohammad Bin Qasim, Karachi 75020; tel. (21) 4739100; fax (21) 4730021; e-mail info@qict.net; internet www.dpworldkarachi.com; f. 1994; CEO CHANGEZ NIAZI.

Associations

All Pakistan Shipping Association: 01-E, 1st Floor, Sattar Chambers, West Wharf Rd, Karachi; tel. (21) 2200742; fax (21) 2200743; e-mail apsa-pak@cyber.net.pk; Chair. MUHAMMAD F. QAISER.

Pakistan Ship Agents' Association: GSA House, 1st Floor, 19 Timber Pound, Keamari, Karachi 75620; tel. (21) 2850837; fax (21) 2851528; e-mail psaa@cyber.net.pk; internet www.shipezee.com/psaa; f. 1976; Chair. FAROUQ H. RAHIMTOOLA.

Terminal Association of Pakistan: 8th Floor, Adamjee House, I. I. Chundrigar Rd, Karachi 74000; tel. (21) 2417131; fax (21) 2416477; e-mail terasspak@cyber.net.pk; Chair. MOHAMMED KASIM HASHIM; Sec. AKHTAR SULTAN.

CIVIL AVIATION

Karachi, Lahore, Rawalpindi, Peshawar and Quetta have international airports. In April 2007 the first phase of construction for the development of a new international airport at Islamabad commenced following a series of postponements; the project was to cost an estimated Rs 35,000m. and would handle 6.5m. passengers annually upon completion.

In 1992 the Government ended the air monopoly held by the Pakistan International Airlines Corpn, and opened all domestic air routes to any Pakistan-based company.

Civil Aviation Authority: Terminal 1 Bldg, Karachi Airport, Karachi; tel. (21) 9242070; fax (21) 9242071; e-mail chief.hr@caapakistan.com.pk; internet www.caapakistan.com.pk; controls all the civil airports; Chair. Lt-Gen. (retd) SYED ATHAR ALI; Sec. KHURSHID ANWAR.

Air Blue Ltd: Ground Floor, Saudi Pak Bldg, Jinnah Ave, Islamabad; tel. (51) 111-247-258; e-mail writetous@airblue.com; internet www.airblue.com; f. 2004; Man. Dir SYED NASIR ALI.

Pakistan International Airlines Corpn (PIA): Jinnah International Airport, Karachi 75200; tel. (21) 9040000; fax (21) 4570419; e-mail info@piac.com.pk; internet www.piac.com.pk; f. 1954; merged with Orient Airways in 1955; 57.7% govt-owned; operates domestic services to 35 destinations and international services to 40 destinations in 31 countries; reduced number of weekly flights to Europe and the USA from 42 to 24 in March 2007 in response to proscriptive new European Union safety regulations; Chair. CHAUDHRY AHMED MUKHTAR; Man. Dir Capt. MOHAMMAD AIJAZ HAROON.

Shaheen Air International: Jinnah International Airport, Karachi 75200; tel. (21) 9242951; fax (21) 9242965; e-mail info@shaheenair.com; internet www.shaheenair.com; f. 1993; operates scheduled domestic services and international services to the Gulf region; Chair. and CEO KHALID M. SEHBAI.

Tourism

The Himalayan hill stations of Pakistan provide magnificent scenery, a fine climate and excellent opportunities for field sports, mountaineering, trekking and winter sports. The archaeological remains and historical buildings are also impressive.

In 2007 Pakistan received some 839,500 foreign visitors; receipts from tourism amounted to around US $899m. in 2006.

Pakistan Tourism Development Corpn: 32, St 48, Sector F-8/4, Islamabad 44000; tel. (51) 2850035; fax (51) 2850039; e-mail support@tourism.gov.pk; internet www.tourism.gov.pk; f. 1970; Chair. Maulana ATTA-UR-REHMAN; Man. Dir GHULAM IDREES KHAN.

Travel Agents' Association of Pakistan: 115, Central Hotel Bldg, Mereweather Rd, Karachi 75530; tel. (21) 5682748; fax (21) 5689469; e-mail taap@cyber.net.pk.

RELATED TERRITORIES

The status of Jammu and Kashmir has remained unresolved since the 1949 cease-fire agreement, whereby the area was divided into sectors administered by India and Pakistan separately. Pakistan administers Azad (Free) Kashmir and the Northern Areas as *de facto* dependencies, being responsible for foreign affairs, defence, coinage, currency and the implementation of UN resolutions concerning Kashmir.

AZAD KASHMIR

Area: 11,639 sq km (4,494 sq miles).

Population: 1,980,000 (1981 census).

Administration: Government is based on the Azad Jammu and Kashmir Interim Constitution Act of 1974. There are seven administrative districts: Bagh, Bhimber, Kotli, Mirpur, Muzaffarabad, Poonch and Sudhnuti.

Legislative Assembly: consists of 48 members: 40 directly elected and eight indirectly elected, including five women.

Azad Jammu and Kashmir Council: consists of the President of Pakistan as Chairman, the President of Azad Kashmir as Vice-Chairman, five members nominated by the President of Pakistan, six members by the Legislative Assembly, and, *ex officio*, the Pakistan Minister of Kashmir Affairs and Northern Areas.

President of Azad Kashmir: RAJA ZULQARNAIN KHAN.

Prime Minister: Sardar MOHAMMAD YAQOOB KHAN.

NORTHERN AREAS

Area: 72,520 sq km (28,000 sq miles).

Population: 562,000 (1981 census).

Administration: There are five administrative districts: Gilgit, Skardu, Diamir, Ghizer and Ghanche. The Northern Areas Council consists of 26 members (24 members are elected in a party-based election and two seats are reserved for women), headed by the federal Minister of Kashmir Affairs and Northern Areas.

PALAU

Introductory Survey

Location, Climate, Language, Religion, Flag, Capital

The Republic of Palau (also known as Belau) consists of more than 200 islands, in a chain about 650 km (400 miles) long, lying about 7,150 km (4,450 miles) south-west of Hawaii and about 1,160 km (720 miles) south of Guam. With the Federated States of Micronesia (q.v.), Palau forms the archipelago of the Caroline Islands. Palau is subject to heavy rainfall, and seasonal variations in precipitation and temperature are generally small. Palauan and English are the official languages. The principal religion is Christianity, much of the population being Roman Catholic. The flag (proportions 3 by 5) features a large golden disc (representing the moon), placed off-centre, towards the hoist, on a light blue background. The capital is Melekeok, on the island of Babeldaob.

Recent History

The Republic of Palau's independence, under the Compact of Free Association, in October 1994 marked the end of the Trust Territory of the Pacific Islands, of which Palau was the final component (for history up to 1965, see the chapter on the Marshall Islands). From 1965 there were increasing demands for local autonomy within the Trust Territory. In that year the Congress of Micronesia was formed, and in 1967 a commission was established to examine the future political status of the islands. In 1970 the commission declared Micronesians' rights to sovereignty over their own lands, self-determination, the right to their own constitution and to revoke any form of free association with the USA. In May 1977, after eight years of negotiations, US President Jimmy Carter announced that his Administration intended to adopt measures to terminate the trusteeship agreement by 1981. In the Palau District a referendum in July 1979 approved a proposed local Constitution, which came into effect on 1 January 1981, when the district became the Republic of Palau.

The USA signed the Compact of Free Association with the Republic of Palau in August 1982, and with the Marshall Islands and the Federated States of Micronesia in October. The trusteeship of the islands was due to end after the principle and terms of the Compacts had been approved by the respective peoples and legislatures of the new countries, by the US Congress and by the UN Security Council. Under the Compacts, the four countries (including the Northern Mariana Islands) would be independent of each other and would manage both their internal and foreign affairs separately, while the USA would be responsible for defence and security. In addition, the USA was to allocate some US $3,000m. in aid to the islands.

More than 60% of Palauans voted in February 1983 to support their Compact, but fewer than the required 75% approved changing the Constitution to allow the transit and storage of nuclear materials. A revised Compact, which contained no reference to nuclear issues, was approved by 66% of votes cast in a referendum in September 1984. However, the US Government had hoped for a favourable majority of 75% of the votes cast, which would have allowed the terms of the Compact to override the provisions of the Palau Constitution in the event of a conflict between the two.

In June 1985 President Haruo Remeliik of Palau was assassinated. Relatives of a rival candidate in the 1984 presidential election, Roman Tmetuchl, were convicted of the murder, but remained at liberty pending an appeal; this was upheld, on the grounds of unreliable evidence, by Palau's Supreme Court in August 1987. Lazarus Salii was elected President in September 1985.

In January 1986 representatives of the Palau and US administrations reached a preliminary agreement on a new Compact, whereby the USA consented to provide US $421m. in economic assistance to the islands. However, the proportion of votes in favour of the new Compact at a referendum in the following month was still less than that required for the constitutional ban on nuclear material to be waived. Both Salii and US President Ronald Reagan supported the terms of the Compact, arguing that a simple majority would suffice for its approval, as the USA had guaranteed that it would observe the constitutional ban on nuclear material.

In May 1986 the UN Trusteeship Council endorsed the US Administration's request for the termination of the existing trusteeship agreement with the islands. However, a writ was subsequently submitted to the Palau High Court, in which it was claimed that approval of the Compact with the USA was unconstitutional because it had failed to obtain the requisite 75% of votes. The High Court ruled in favour of the writ, but the Palau Government appealed against the ruling and in October the Compact was approved by the US Congress. At a new plebiscite in December, however, only 66% of Palauans voted in favour of the Compact. Ratification of the Compact thus remained impossible.

A fifth plebiscite on Palau's proposed Compact with the USA, in June 1987, again failed to secure the 75% endorsement required by the Constitution. Under alleged physical intimidation by pro-nuclear supporters of the Compact, the House of Delegates (the lower house of the Palau National Congress) agreed to a further referendum in August. In this referendum an amendment to the Constitution was approved, ensuring that a simple majority would henceforth be sufficient to approve the Compact. This was duly achieved in a further referendum in the same month. When a writ was entered with the Supreme Court challenging the legality of the decision to allow approval of the Compact by a simple majority, a campaign of arson and bombing followed, and one person was murdered.

In February 1988 a team from the US General Accounting Office travelled to Palau to investigate allegations of corruption and intimidation on the part of the Palau Government. Approval of the Compact by the US Congress was to be delayed until the investigators had published their findings. However, in April a ruling by Palau's Supreme Court invalidated the procedure by which the Compact had finally been approved by a simple majority in the previous August. Three government employees, including Salii's personal assistant, were imprisoned in April, after being found guilty of firing on the home of Santos Olikong, Speaker of Palau's House of Delegates. The attack was widely considered to have been prompted by Olikong's public opposition to the Compact.

In August 1988 Salii, the principal subject of the bribery allegations, apparently committed suicide. At an election in November Ngiratkel Etpison was elected President, with just over 26% of the total votes. Although Etpison advocated the proposed Compact and was supported by the pro-Compact Ta Belau Party, his closest challenger, Tmetuchl, opposed it and was supported by the anti-nuclear Coalition for Open, Honest and Just Government, which had demanded that a special prosecutor from the USA be dispatched to Palau to investigate alleged corruption and violent attacks against opponents of the Compact.

Only 60% of voters approved the proposed Compact at a seventh referendum in February 1990. In July the US Department of the Interior declared its intention to impose stricter controls on the administration of Palau, particularly in financial matters. In the following year the leader of Palau's Council of Chiefs (a presidential advisory body), Yutaka Gibbons, initiated proceedings to sue the US Government: his claim centred on demands for compensation for the extensive damage caused to Palau's infrastructure by US forces during the Second World War and the subsequent retardation of the economy, allegedly as a result of the US administration of the islands.

During 1991 the US authorities reopened investigations into the assassination of Remeliik in 1985. In March 1992 Palau's Minister of State, John Ngiraked, his wife, Emerita Kerradel, and Sulial Heinrick (already serving a prison sentence for another killing) were charged with Remeliik's murder. In March 1993 Ngiraked and Kerradel were found guilty of aiding and abetting the assassination of the President, while Heinrick was acquitted.

Legislative and presidential elections were held in November 1992. (The electoral system had been modified earlier in the year to include primary elections for the selection of two presidential candidates.) At the presidential election the incumbent Vice-President, Kuniwo Nakamura, narrowly defeated Johnson Toribiong to become President. A concurrent referendum endorsed a proposal that, in future polls, a simple majority be sufficient to approve the adoption of the Compact of Free Association. Some 62% of voters were in favour of the proposal, which was approved in 14 of Palau's 16 states. A further referendum on the proposed Compact took place in November 1993. Some 68.3% of participating voters approved the proposed Compact, giving the Government a mandate to proceed with its adoption. Nevertheless, opposition to the changes remained fierce, and in January 1994 two legal challenges were mounted that questioned the validity of the amendments and stated that the Compact's approval had been procured by coercion. The challenges failed, however, and on 1 October Palau achieved independence under the Compact of Free Association. At independence celebrations, Nakamura appealed to opponents of the Compact to support Palau's new status. He announced that his Government's principal concern was the regeneration of the country's economy, which he aimed to initiate with an economic programme financed by funds from the Compact. Palau was admitted to the UN in December 1994, and became a member of the IMF in December 1997.

A preliminary round of voting in the presidential election took place in September 1996; Kuniwo Nakamura secured 52.4% of total votes, Johnson Toribiong received 33.5%, and Yutaka Gibbons 14.2%. Nakamura and Toribiong were, therefore, expected to proceed to a second election due to take place in November. However, in late September a serious crisis struck Palau when the bridge linking the islands of Koror and Babeldaob collapsed, killing two people and injuring several others. The collapse of the bridge left the capital isolated from the international airport on Babeldaob, with disastrous economic repercussions for Palau, which was reliant on the route for all domestic and international communications. It was subsequently revealed that major repairs had recently been carried out on the bridge, at a cost of US $3.2m., and several reports implied that inappropriate changes made to its structure during the work were responsible for the disaster. Toribiong was harshly critical of Nakamura, who had commissioned the repair work, and demanded his resignation along with those of the public works officials involved. However, following the revelation that Toribiong's running-mate in the election for the vice-presidency was one of the officials involved in the work, Toribiong withdrew his candidacy from the second round of the presidential election. Yutaka Gibbons thus re-entered the contest by default; none the less, at the second round of the presidential poll, held concurrently with legislative elections on 5 November 1996, Nakamura was re-elected with 62.0% of total votes. Meanwhile, the Japanese Government offered to finance the construction of a new bridge linking Koror to Babeldaob; the work was completed in January 2002.

In October 1998 the Senate approved legislation providing for the establishment of an 'offshore' financial centre in Palau. The measure was strongly opposed by President Nakamura, who believed that it might attract criminal organizations seeking to 'launder' the proceeds of their illegal activities. In December 1999, following discussions with US government officials, Nakamura signed an executive order establishing a National Banking Review Commission, with the aim of maintaining a legally responsible banking environment in Palau: both the Bank of New York (of the USA) and Deutsche Bank (of Germany) had alleged that Palau's 'offshore' banks were facilitating money-laundering. The new body was given wide-ranging powers to examine banking operations in the country and to evaluate current banking regulations.

At the presidential election held on 7 November 2000, Thomas E. Remengesau, Jr, hitherto the Vice-President of Palau, was elected with 52% of the votes cast, defeating Senator Peter Sugiyama. Sandra Pierantozzi was elected as Vice-President. Remengesau was officially inaugurated on 19 January 2001. In July 2001 Remengesau introduced a formal resolution proposing the reduction of the legislature to a single chamber, to replace the existing House of Delegates and the Senate, claiming that a unicameral legislature would reduce bureaucracy. However, owing to a lack of legislative progress on the necessary constitutional changes, in early 2004 Remengesau endorsed a congressional resolution to conduct a popular referendum. The poll, which would first require the signatures of 25% of the electorate, was scheduled to take place in November. The proposals included the creation of a unicameral legislature and restrictions on legislators' terms of office; furthermore, it was proposed that Palauans resident in the USA be offered the opportunity of dual citizenship.

Despite President Remengesau's inauguration pledges to improve transparency in public office, there were several instances of fraudulent use of official funds in the early 2000s. In December 2002 the Speaker of the House of Delegates, Mario Gulibert, was arrested on charges relating to the alleged misuse of travel expenses (he was dismissed on unrelated charges in March 2004). In February 2003 the former Governor of Ngardmau state, Albert Ngirmekur, was fined and sentenced to six months' imprisonment following his impeachment for theft. In late 2003 President Remengesau was obliged to veto an attempt by legislators to eliminate the Office of the Special Prosecutor, which had conducted a number of investigations into alleged misuse of public funds. In February 2004, however, members of the National Congress under investigation for alleged misuse of expenses agreed to pay some US $250,000 on condition that the cases against them be withdrawn. In November the Senate overturned President Remengesau's veto of a bill to ease bank-licensing restrictions, although this decision was reversed in December, following the threat of international financial sanctions.

At the presidential election of 2 November 2004, President Remengesau was re-elected with 6,494 of the votes cast; his opponent, Polycarp Basilius, received 3,268 votes. Elias Camsek Chin was elected Vice-President. Following his re-election, Remengesau announced that the priorities of his new administration would include increasing government revenues, promoting economic diversification and tourism, and maintaining programmes of infrastructural development. Concurrent to the presidential election, voters also approved various amendments to the Constitution: to restrict members of the National Congress to three terms of four years, to permit dual US-Palauan citizenship, to provide for the joint election of the country's President and Vice-President as a team and to adjust congressional members' salaries. A proposal to create a unicameral legislature, however, was rejected. A plan to hold a constitutional convention was approved by 5,085 votes (some 53% of the votes cast), with 3,742 votes (some 39%) against the motion. In April 2005 16 state delegates and nine delegates-at-large were elected to the Constitutional Convention, which in mid-June ended its deliberations, following consultations with the general public and special-interest groups. The Convention concluded with 251 proposals, of which 22 were to be submitted for the electorate's consideration at a referendum to be held concurrently with the elections scheduled for 2008.

The issue of misuse of public funds was highlighted by several political developments in 2006–08. In March 2006 the legislature of Peleliu state approved a resolution to impeach Governor Jackson Ngiraingas on charges of treason, unlawful spending of state finances and the lodging of accusations, against President Remengesau and others, purporting to be on the state's behalf. In April Ngiraingas failed to gain the support of a majority in the state legislature to revoke the impeachment and was removed from office; he subsequently filed a civil suit, claiming that the allegations against him were false and not necessarily grounds for impeachment, and that his removal from office was unconstitutional. The Supreme Court invalidated the legislature's resolution in the following month, deciding that Ngiraingas had been denied due process. Meanwhile, in March the Ngardmau state legislature adopted a resolution to impeach Governor J. Schwartz Tudong. Tudong was accused of illegally spending state funds and making payments to himself without legal authority; a trial court later decided that it did not have the jurisdiction to rule on his appeal against the impeachment, and in May Akiko C. Sugiyama was elected to succeed him. In August Augustine Mesebeluu, the Speaker of the House of Delegates, was charged on numerous counts related to personal use of public finances (Mesebeluu later entered into settlement agreements to repay costs he had incurred during trips off the island). The closure of the Pacific Savings Bank, which went into receivership in late 2006, was followed by charges against the bank's President, Timothy Taunton, and other employees in 2007.

In October 2006 the relocation of Palau's seat of government from Koror to the new capital, Melekeok, on the island of Babeldaob, was marked with official ceremonies and celebrations. In March 2007 the President of the Senate, Johnny Reklai, was killed in a fishing accident. Joshua Koshiba was subsequently elected as his successor, but, following a successful legal appeal by some members of the Senate, Surangel Whipps replaced Koshiba. A special election to fill the Senate vacancy took place in May. By February 2008 three candidates, Whipps, Koshiba and Johnson Toribiong, had announced plans to contest the forthcoming presidential election, scheduled for November. Preparations for a review of the Compact with the USA, which was due to expire in 2009, were under way with the formation of the Palau Compact Review Commission; President Remengesau was reported to be eager to begin the negotiating process in order to allow Palauans the opportunity to vote on the issues in 2008. However, in 2007 the US Government reportedly indicated that aid to Palau would be terminated following the expiry of the Compact.

In June 2008 the US General Accountability Office (GAO) published an audit report examining Palau's financial accountability and the provisions of the Compact. The report judged that Palau had made progress in providing financial accountability and that the country had complied with most of the Compact's conditions. However, problems of internal control persisted.

Elections took place on 4 November 2008 for the 16 seats in the House of Delegates and 13 seats in the newly expanded Senate, along with the country's presidency. In the presidential contest (for which primary elections to determine the candidates had been held in September) Johnson Toribiong defeated Vice-President Elias Camsek Chin by a narrow margin, having obtained 5,040 of the votes cast, compared with the 4,828 received by Chin. The level of voter participation was 74%. Kerai Mariur was elected as the country's new Vice-President. President Toribiong took office in January 2009; Vice-President Mariur also assumed the role of Minister of Administration and of Finance. In the legislative elections several incumbents were re-elected to the House of Delegates and to the Senate. Despite a legal challenge, other members of the National Congress, including a number of long-serving Senators, were unable to stand for re-election owing to the implementation of a limit of a maximum of three terms of office. Outgoing President Thomas Remengesau was elected to a seat in the Senate, which included two women, who thus became the country's first female Senators. A total of 22 proposed constitutional amendments were submitted to the electorate in a concurrent referendum held on 4 November 2008, when voters endorsed a proposal henceforth to elect the President and Vice-President separately.

In March 2009 the Compact with the USA was extended for one year from the end of September, following a meeting in Washington, DC, between President Toribiong and US Secretary of State Hillary Clinton. Toribiong and Clinton announced that within that additional period the Compact was to be reviewed, prior to the implementation of a new long-term agreement.

In January 2009 the Speaker of the Koror state legislature, Timothy Uehara, was convicted of perjury and of misconduct in public office. Uehara was found to have subleased government properties and embezzled tenants' rental payments from the Koror State Public Lands Authority. In March he received a six-year prison sentence and a fine of US $10,000; however, he was to serve only one year of the prison sentence, with the remainder being suspended. In April the Governor of Melekeok State, Lazarus Kodep, was formally charged with misconduct. It was alleged that between 2003 and 2007 Kodep had used public funds to repay a personal bank loan.

In mid-1999 a delegation from Solomon Islands visited Palau to discuss the possibility of allowing Solomon Islanders to work in Palau, in an attempt to resolve the latter's severe labour shortage. In August 2001, however, the Government imposed a ban on the hiring of Indian and Sri Lankan workers, citing rising tensions and disputes with local employers which the Government claimed were largely due to religious differences. The ban was to remain in place until legislation to create official recruitment agencies in Palau had been approved. In July 2002 the Senate approved a bill that would amend the islands' immigration law in order to give greater authority over immigration affairs to the President of Palau. (Non-Palauan nationals were estimated to represent about 73% of the islands' population in 2003.) In March 2003 the Government introduced a measure to extend employment permits for foreign workers, which allowed a new maximum extension of two years. In April some 200 Chinese migrant employees of a failed clothing business were stranded on Palau and placed under house arrest. However, the migrants were subsequently repatriated, following diplomatic intervention from the People's Republic of China. In December 2006 the House of Delegates approved legislation banning the employment of Bangladeshi nationals in Palau, making an exception for those Bangladeshis already contracted to work in the country, who would be allowed to complete their terms.

Diplomatic relations were established, at ambassadorial level, with Taiwan in late 1999. The first Taiwanese ambassador to Palau was formally appointed in April 2000. Reports in December of that year that the Palau Government was considering establishing diplomatic relations with the People's Republic of China were denied, and President-elect Remengesau reaffirmed Palau's diplomatic relations with Taiwan. In early 2000, meanwhile, Palau and Taiwan signed an agreement pledging to develop bilateral projects in a number of areas, including agriculture, fisheries and tourism. In late January 2005 President Chen Shui-bian of Taiwan visited Palau to discuss economic co-operation and to strengthen bilateral political relations. President Remengesau travelled to Taiwan in May 2008 to attend the inauguration of President Ma Ying-jeou.

In October 2001 the Government sought to establish diplomatic relations with Malaysia and Indonesia in an attempt to facilitate the resolution of disputes about overlapping territorial boundaries, amid concern over increasing instances of illegal fishing in Palauan waters. (Palau introduced more stringent regulations to counter illegal fishing in 2002 and 2003.) Diplomatic relations with Indonesia were established in July 2007.

Palau maintains strong diplomatic links with Japan, which has been a leading source of tourist revenue since the 1980s. The Japanese Government provided US $25m. for the reconstruction of the Koror bridge (see above) and contributed to the construction of a new terminal building at Palau International Airport, which opened in May 2003. In June 2002 President Remengesau undertook his first state visit to the Republic of Korea. His itinerary incorporated visits to a number of infrastructural development projects.

In early 2009 Palau and the Philippines were in the process of defining their marine boundary. Discussions in March focused on claims to the extended continental shelf, that of the Philippines overlapping with seven other countries, including Palau.

Government

In October 1994 Palau, the last remaining component of the Trust Territory of the Pacific Islands (a United Nations Trusteeship administered by the USA), achieved independence under the Compact of Free Association. Administrative authority was transferred to the Government of Palau (with the USA retaining responsibility for the islands' defence—see below).

A locally drafted Constitution of the Republic of Palau entered into effect on 1 January 1981. Under the Constitution, executive authority is vested in the President, elected by direct suffrage for a four-year term. Legislative power is exercised by the Olbiil era Kelulau ('House of Whispered Decisions', or Palau National Congress), composed of the directly elected House of Delegates (comprising one Delegate from each of the 16 states of Palau) and the Senate (comprising 13 Senators after the elections of 2008). Members of the National Congress are elected for a four-year term.

Local governmental units are the municipalities and villages. Elected Magistrates and Councils govern the municipalities. Village government is largely traditional.

Defence

The USA is responsible for the defence of Palau, according to the Compact of Free Association implemented in October 1994, and has exclusive military access to its waters, as well as the right to operate two military bases on the islands.

Economic Affairs

In 2007, according to estimates by the World Bank, Palau's gross national income (GNI), measured at average 2005–07 prices, totalled US $167m., equivalent to $8,210 per head. During 2003–07, it was estimated, the population increased at an average annual rate of 0.8%, while gross domestic product (GDP) per head increased, in real terms, by an average of 3.2% per year. In 2000–07 overall GDP increased, in real terms, at an average annual rate of 1.7%. The Asian Development Bank (ADB) estimated that real GDP grew by 2.1% in 2007, before contracting by 1.0% in 2008.

Agriculture (including forestry and fishing) is mainly on a subsistence level, the principal crops being coconuts, root crops and bananas. Pigs and chickens are kept for domestic consumption. Eggs are produced commercially, and the introduction of cattle-ranching on Babeldaob was under consideration in the early 2000s. The agricultural sector engaged 7.8% of the employed labour force in 2005 and, according to provisional figures, provided 3.5% of GDP in 2007. Fishing licences are sold to foreign fleets, including those of Taiwan, the USA, Japan and the Philippines, although revenue from the sale of these licences totalled only US $76,000 in 2000/01, compared with $230,000 in

1994/95. Fish have traditionally been a leading export, accounting for almost $8.9m. of exports in 2004. According to the ADB, the agricultural sector's GDP expanded in real terms by 2.9% in 2006 and by 2.7% in 2007.

The industrial sector (including mining and quarrying, manufacturing, construction and utilities) engaged 18.7% of the employed labour force in 2005 and provided an estimated 20.7% of GDP in 2007, according to provisional figures. The only manufacturing activity of any significance is the production of garments; the sector has employed mainly non-resident workers. In 2005 manufacturing accounted for 2.3% of employment, but only 0.5% of GDP in 2007. Construction is the most important industrial activity, contributing 15.7% of GDP in 2007 and engaging 14.0% of the employed labour force in 2005. Electrical energy, output of which totalled 128m. kWh in 2005, is produced by two power plants at Aimeliik and Malakal. In July 2008 it was announced that the World Bank was to provide financial and technical assistance in the exploration for reserves of petroleum and gas in an area north-east of Babeldaob. According to the ADB, real growth in the industrial sector's GDP was 12.7% in 2006 and 19.8% in 2007.

Service industries dominate Palau's economy, providing some 73.5% of GDP in 2007, according to provisional results, and engaging 73.5% of the employed labour force in 2005. The Government is a significant employer within the sector, public administration engaging 17.7% of the total employed labour force in 2005. Tourism is an important source of foreign exchange. Receipts from tourism (including passenger transport) totalled US $90m. in 2006. The trade, hotels and restaurants sector engaged 17.1% of the employed labour force and provided 30.8% of GDP in 2005. However, visitor arrivals (mostly from Taiwan and Japan) declined from 84,566 in 2007 to 75,829 in 2008. The Micronesian Games were to be held in Palau in 2010. The real GDP of the services sector increased by 0.8% in 2006, but decreased by 1.5% in 2007, according to the ADB.

In the year ending September 2007 the visible trade deficit was provisionally estimated at US $81.2m. A surplus on the current account of the balance of payments, including grants, was estimated at $9.8m. in 2006/07, equivalent to 6.0% of GDP. Import costs were a provisional $91.3m. in that year, while revenue from exports totalled a provisional $10.1m. The principal sources of imports in 2005 were the USA (which supplied 32.3% of the total), Singapore (25.3%) and Guam (13.4%). The principal imports in 2004, according to the ADB, were machinery and transport equipment (40.7% of the total), mineral fuels and lubricants (25.8%) and food and live animals (9.3%).

The islands record a persistent budget deficit, which reached US $23.4m. in the year ending 30 September 2007. Financial assistance from the USA contributes a large part of the islands' external revenue. Furthermore, upon implementation of the Compact of Free Association with the USA in 1994, Palau became eligible for an initial grant of US $142m. and for annual aid of $23m. over a period until 2009. In March of that year the Compact was extended for a further 12 months (see Recent History). Palau's external debt was estimated by the ADB to have risen from $18m. in 2006 to $23m. in 2007. The cost of debt-servicing decreased to the equivalent of 1.0% of the value of exports of goods and services in 2007. The annual rate of inflation averaged 2.0% between 2000 and 2007. The inflation rate subsequently rose significantly, from 3.2% in 2007 to 12.0% in 2008. At the 2005 census 4.2% of the total labour force were unemployed.

Palau is a member of the Pacific Community (see p. 391) and of the Pacific Islands Forum (see p. 393); it is also an associate member of the UN Economic and Social Commission for Asia and the Pacific (ESCAP, see p. 36). In 1996 Palau joined representatives of the other countries and territories of Micronesia at a meeting in Hawaii, at which a new regional organization, the Council of Micronesian Government Executives, was established. The new body aimed to facilitate discussion of economic developments in the region. Palau was admitted to the IMF in late 1997. In December 2002 Palau requested to join the World Trade Organization (WTO, see p. 410), and in December 2003 the country became a member of the Asian Development Bank (ADB, see p. 191).

The economy of Palau has benefited greatly from the substantial aid payments from the US Government that followed the implementation of the Compact of Free Association in 1994. Grants from the USA have accounted for about 20% of GDP annually. The tourism sector has expanded rapidly since the 1980s. The contraction in real GDP in 2008 was attributed mainly to the decline in tourist arrivals, which decreased by 10% in comparison with the previous year. In addition to the less favourable global economic conditions prevailing in 2008, flight schedules from Taiwan (the source of 19% of visitors to Palau in that year) were disrupted by the cessation of operations by a Taiwanese carrier in May. China Airlines, based in Taipei, subsequently began a new service to Palau, replacing that of the failed airline. In February 2009 the Government of Taiwan provided a stimulus grant of $3.2m. to Palau, for the purposes of infrastructural improvements. Meanwhile, the rate of inflation increased significantly during 2008, reaching a high point of 16.8% in the third quarter, on a year-on-year basis. Inflationary pressures emanated largely from the higher costs of foodstuffs and fuel, but they were expected to ease in 2009. The ADB forecast that GDP would contract by around 2% in 2009. However, in the longer term much depended on the renegotiation of the terms of the Compact with the USA, rescheduled for 2009/10. Uncertainty continued with regard to future levels of discretionary federal grants from the USA. Palau's trust fund remained vulnerable to the volatility of global stock markets, and the value of the fund's assets were estimated to have decreased by 28% in 2008. The US General Accountability Office (GAO) suggested in its report of mid-2008 that the trust fund might be depleted soon after 2016. The GAO also drew attention to the need for fiscal reform and for an improvement in investment conditions, in order to encourage the growth of the private sector. The GAO also estimated that by the fiscal year ending in September 2009 total US aid to Palau since 1995 would have reached more than US $852m., with direct assistance under the Compact accounting for 48% of this.

Education

Education is compulsory for children between the ages of six and 14 years. In 1999/2000 enrolment at primary school level included 96.4% of pupils from the relevant age-group. In 2006/07 an estimated 2,683 pupils attended elementary school. There were 19 public elementary schools in 2006/07. After eight years of compulsory elementary education, a pupil may enrol in the government-operated high school or one of the five private (church-affiliated) high schools. In 2006/07 an estimated total of 1,309 pupils attended secondary school. The Micronesian Occupational College, based in Palau, provides two-year training programmes. Government spending on education in 1999/2000 totalled US $9.1m., equivalent to 10.7% of total budgetary expenditure.

Public Holidays

2009: 1 January (New Year's Day), 15 March (Youth Day), 5 May (Senior Citizens' Day), 1 June (Presidents' Day), 10 July (Constitution Day), 1 September (Labor Day), 1 October (Independence Day), 24 October (United Nations Day), 27 November (Thanksgiving), 25 December (Christmas).

2010: 1 January (New Year's Day), 14 March (Youth Day), 5 May (Senior Citizens' Day), 1 June (Presidents' Day), 10 July (Constitution Day), 1 September (Labor Day), 1 October (Independence Day), 23 October (United Nations Day), 25 November (Thanksgiving), 25 December (Christmas).

Weights and Measures

With certain exceptions, the imperial system is in force. One US cwt equals 100 lb; one long ton equals 2,240 lb; one short ton equals 2,000 lb. A policy of gradual voluntary conversion to the metric system is being undertaken.

Statistical Survey

Source (unless otherwise indicated): Office of Planning and Statistics, Ministry of Finance, POB 6011, Koror; tel. 767-1269; fax 767-5642; e-mail ops@palaugov.net; internet www.palaugov.net/stats/index.htm.

AREA AND POPULATION

Area: 508 sq km (196 sq miles); Babeldaob (Babeldaop, Babelthuap) island 409 sq km (158 sq miles).

Population: 19,129 at census of 15 April 2000; 19,907 (males 10,699, females 9,208) at census of 1 April 2005. *2008* (mid-year estimate): 20,279.

Density (mid-2008): 39.9 per sq km.

Principal Towns (population at 2005 census): Koror (capital) 10,743; Meyuns 1,153. Source: Thomas Brinkhoff, *City Population* (internet www.citypopulation.de).

Births and Deaths (2006): Registered live births 259 (birth rate 12.0 per 1,000); Registered deaths 144 (death rate 6.6 per 1,000).

Life Expectancy (years at birth, WHO estimates): 69.4 (males 67.9; females 71.0) in 2006. Source: WHO, *World Health Statistics*.

Economically Active Population (persons aged 16 years and over, 2005 census): Agriculture 451; Forestry and fishing 310; Mining 34; Manufacturing 225; Utilities and sanitary services 208; Construction 1,365; Transport and communications 561; Trade, restaurants, etc. 1,670; Finance, insurance and real estate 132; Public administration 1,734; Professional and related services 1,466; Private households 915; Other personal services 387; Other services 319; *Total employed* 9,777 (males 5,982, females 3,795); Unemployed 426 (males 232, females 194); *Total labour force* 10,203 (males 6,214, females 3,989).

HEALTH AND WELFARE
Key Indicators

Total Fertility Rate (children per woman, 2006): 2.5.

Under-5 Mortality Rate (per 1,000 live births, 2006): 11.

Physicians (per 1,000 head, 2000): 1.6.

Hospital Beds (per 1,000 head, 2006): 5.9.

Health Expenditure (2006): US $ per head (PPP): 1,084.

Health Expenditure (2006): % of GDP: 10.7.

Health Expenditure (2006): public (% of total): 92.5.

Access to Water (% of persons, 2006): 89.

Access to Sanitation (% of persons, 2006): 67.

For sources and definitions, see explanatory note on p. vi.

AGRICULTURE, ETC.

Fishing (metric tons, live weight, 2006): Marine fishes 962; Total catch (incl. others) 972 (FAO estimate). Source: FAO.

INDUSTRY

Production (2005): Electric energy 128 million kWh. Source: UN, *Industrial Commodity Statistics Yearbook*.

FINANCE

Currency and Exchange Rates: United States currency is used: 100 cents = 1 United States dollar (US $). *Sterling and Euro Equivalents* (31 December 2008): £1 sterling = US $1.4578; €1 = US $1.3917; US $100 = £68.60 = €71.85.

Budget (US $ million, year ending 30 September 2007, provisional): *Revenue:* Current revenue 38.0 (Taxes 29.8, Non-tax revenue 8.0); Grants 48.2; Total 86.2. *Expenditure:* Current expenditure 81.2; Capital expenditure 22.8; Net lending 5.5; Total 109.6. Source: Asian Development Bank.

Cost of Living (Consumer Price Index, average of quarterly figures; base: October–December 2004 = 100): 103.3 in 2005; 107.9 in 2006; 111.4 in 2007.

Gross Domestic Product (US $ '000 at current prices): 145,428 in 2005; 156,614 in 2006; 164,289 in 2007 (provisional). Source: Asian Development Bank.

Gross Domestic Product by Economic Activity (US $ '000 at current prices, 2007, provisional): Agriculture and fishing 5,597; Mining 180; Manufacturing 822; Electricity, gas and water 7,027; Construction 25,099; Trade 34,369; Transport and communications 12,655; Finance 6,188; Public administration 32,340; Other services 35,730; *Sub-total* 160,007; Import duties 7,367; *Less* Imputed bank service charges 3,087; *GDP in purchasers' values* 164,289. Source: Asian Development Bank.

Balance of Payments (US $ million, year ending September 2007, provisional): Exports of goods f.o.b. 10.1; Imports of goods f.o.b. −91.3; *Trade balance* −81.2; Services and income (net) 89.5; *Balance on goods, services and income* 8.3; Current transfers (net) 1.5; *Current balance* 9.8; Capital and financial account (net) 50.6; Net errors and omissions −65.7; *Overall balance* −5.3. Source: Asian Development Bank.

EXTERNAL TRADE

Principal Commodities (US $ '000): *Imports f.o.b.* (2004): Food and live animals 10,862; Beverages and tobacco 4,947; Mineral fuels, lubricants, etc. 30,061; Chemicals 5,772; Basic manufactures 8,597; Machinery and transport equipment 47,405; Miscellaneous manufactured articles 7,129; Total (incl. others) 116,499. *Exports* (2004/05): 13,414 (including trochus shells, tuna, copra and handicrafts). Source: Asian Development Bank, *Key Indicators of Developing Asian and Pacific Countries*.

Principal Trading Partners (US $ '000, year ending September 2004): *Imports:* Japan 8,531; Korea, Republic 5,411; Philippines 6,934; Singapore 29,885; Taiwan 5,343; USA (incl. Guam) 48,225; Total (incl. others) 107,280. *Exports:* Total 5,882.

TRANSPORT

International Shipping (1995): *Ship Arrivals:* 280. *Freight Traffic* (metric tons): Goods unloaded 64,034.

TOURISM

Tourist Arrivals: 78,252 in 2006; 84,566 in 2007; 75,829 in 2008.

Tourist Arrivals by Country of Residence (2008): Guam 1,572; Japan 29,632; Korea, Republic 14,081; Philippines 659; Taiwan 14,175; USA (mainland) 9,376; Total (incl. others) 75,829.

Tourism Receipts (US $ million, incl. passenger transport): 97 in 2004; 97 in 2005; 90 in 2006.

Source: World Tourism Organization.

COMMUNICATIONS MEDIA

Radio Receivers (1997): 12,000 in use.

Television Receivers (1997): 11,000 in use.

Telephones (2006): 7,000 main lines in use.

Mobile Cellular Telephones (2006): 8,300 subscribers.

Source: partly International Telecommunication Union.

EDUCATION

Pre-Primary (public institutions only, 2006/07): 13 schools; 30 teachers; 509 pupils.

Enrolment (2006/07): *Elementary:* Total 2,683 (Public 2,135, Private 548). *Secondary:* Total 1,309 (Public 810, Private 499).

Teachers (1999/2000, estimates): *Elementary:* 124. *Secondary:* 126.

Institutions (2006/07): *Elementary:* Total 21 (Public 19, Private 2). *Secondary:* Total 6 (Public 1, Private 5).

Tertiary (Palau Community College): 54 teachers (full-time and part-time, 2005/06); 545 students (at 2005 census).

Directory

The Constitution

In October 1994 Palau, the last remaining component of the Trust Territory of the Pacific Islands (a United Nations Trusteeship administered by the USA), achieved independence under the Compact of Free Association. Full responsibility for defence lies with the USA, which undertakes to provide regular economic assistance.

From 1986 the three polities of the Commonwealth of the Northern Mariana Islands, the Republic of the Marshall Islands and the Federated States of Micronesia ceased, de facto, to be part of the Trust Territory. In December 1990 the United Nations Security Council agreed formally to terminate the Trusteeship Agreement for all the territories except Palau. The agreement with Palau was finally terminated in October 1994.

The islands became known as the Republic of Palau when the locally drafted Constitution came into effect on 1 January 1981. The Constitution provides for a democratic form of government, with executive authority vested in the directly elected President and Vice-President. Presidential elections are held every four years. Legislative power is exercised by the Olbiil era Kelulau, the Palau National Congress, which is an elected body consisting of the Senate and the House of Delegates. The Senators represent geographical districts, determined by an independent reapportionment commission every eight years, according to population. The number of Senators was increased to 13 at the elections of 2008. The House of Delegates comprises 16 members, one elected to represent each of the 16 states of the Republic. The states are: Kayangel, Ngerchelong, Ngaraard, Ngardmau, Ngaremlengui, Ngiwal, Melekeok, Ngchesar, Ngatpang, Aimeliik, Airai, Koror, Peleliu, Angaur, Sonsorol and Tobi. Each state elects its own Governor and legislature.

The Government

HEAD OF STATE

President: JOHNSON TORIBIONG (took office 15 January 2009).

Vice-President and Minister of Administration and of Finance: KERAI MARIUR.

CABINET
(April 2009)

Minister of Health: Dr STEVENSON KUARTEI.

Minister of Public Infrastructure, Industries and Commerce: JACKSON NGIRAINGAS.

Minister of Natural Resources, Environment and Tourism: HARRY FRITZ.

Minister of Education: MASA-AKI EMESIOCHEL.

Minister of Community and Cultural Affairs: FAUSTINA K. REHUHER-MARUGG.

Minister of State: SANDRA S. PIERANTOZZI.

COUNCIL CHIEFS

The Constitution provides for an advisory body for the President, comprising the 16 highest traditional chiefs from the 16 states. The chiefs advise on all traditional laws and customs, and on any other public matter in which their participation is required.

Chairman: Ibedul YUTAKA GIBBONS (Koror).

GOVERNMENT OFFICES AND MINISTRIES

Office of the President: POB 6051, Koror, PW 96940; tel. 488-2403; fax 488-1662; e-mail pres@palaunet.com.

Department of the Interior, Office of Insular Affairs (OIA): OIA Field Office, POB 6031, Koror, PW 96946; tel. 488-2601; fax 488-2649; internet www.doi.gov/oia/Islandpages/palaupage.htm; Field Rep. (vacant); Co-ordinator HAURO WILLTER.

Ministry of Commerce and Trade: POB 1471, Ngerulmud, PW 96940; tel. 767-2111; fax 767-3207; e-mail mincat@palaunet.com.

Ministry of Community and Cultural Affairs: POB 100, Koror, PW 96940; tel. 767-1126; fax 767-3354; e-mail mcca@palaunet.com; internet www.palaugov.net/mincommunity.

Ministry of Education: POB 189, Koror, PW 96940; tel. 488-1464; fax 488-1465; e-mail moe@palaumoe.net; internet www.palaumoe.net.

Ministry of Finance: POB 6011, Koror, PW 96940; tel. 767-2501; fax 767-2168; e-mail stechitong@palaugov.net.

Ministry of Health: POB 6027, Koror, PW 96940; tel. 488-2552; fax 488-1211; e-mail moh@palau-health.net; internet www.palau-health.net.

Ministry of Justice: POB 3022, Koror, PW 96940; tel. 488-3198; fax 488-4567; e-mail justice@palaunet.com; internet www.palaugov.net/minjustice.

Ministry of Resources and Development: POB 100, Koror, PW 96940; tel. 767-2701; fax 767-3380; e-mail mrd@palaunet.com.

All national government offices were transferred from Koror to Melekeok in October 2006. Each state has its own administrative headquarters.

President and Legislature

PRESIDENT

At the presidential election held on 4 November 2008, Johnson Toribiong defeated his opponent, Elias Camsek Chin, by a narrow margin. Toribiong secured 5,040 votes, and Chin received 4,828.

OLBIIL ERA KELULAU
(Palau National Congress)

The Palau National Congress comprises two chambers, the Senate and the House of Delegates. The Senate has 13 elected members, and the House of Delegates consists of 16 elected members. The most recent election was held on 4 November 2008.

President of the Senate: MLIB TMETUCHL.

Vice-President of the Senate: KATHY KESOLEI.

Speaker of the House of Delegates: NOAH IDECHONG.

Vice-Speaker of the House of Delegates: ALEXANDER MEREP.

Election Commission

Palau Election Commission: POB 826, Koror, PW 96940; tel. 488-1554; fax 488-3327; Chair. SANTOS BORJA.

Political Organizations
(There are currently no active political parties in Palau)

Palau Nationalist Party: c/o Olbiil era Kelulau, Koror, PW 96940; inactive; Leader JOHNSON TORIBIONG.

Ta Belau Party: c/o Olbiil era Kelulau, Koror, PW 96940; inactive; Leader KUNIWO NAKAMURA.

Diplomatic Representation

EMBASSIES IN PALAU

China (Taiwan): WCTC Bldg, Of. 3F, POB 9087, Koror, PW 96940; tel. 488-8150; fax 488-8151; e-mail embrocb@palaunet.com; Ambassador MAGGIE TIEN.

Japan: POB 6050, Palau Pacific Resort, Arakebesang, Koror, PW 96940; tel. 488-6455; fax 488-6458; Ambassador (vacant).

Philippines: 2nd Flr, M. Ueki Bldg, Iyebukel Hamlet, POB 1497, Koror, PW 96940; tel. 488-5077; fax 488-6310; e-mail philkor@palaunet.com; Ambassador RAMONCITO MARIÑO.

USA: POB 6028, Koror, PW 96940; tel. 488-2920; fax 488-2911; e-mail usembassykoror@palaunet.com; internet palau.usembassy.gov; Chargé d'affaires MARK BEZNER.

Judicial System

The judicial system of the Republic of Palau consists of the Supreme Court (including Trial and Appellate Divisions), presided over by the Chief Justice, the National Court (inactive), the Court of Common Pleas and the Land Court.

Supreme Court of the Republic of Palau: POB 248, Koror, PW 96940; tel. 488-2182; fax 488-1597; e-mail cjngiraklsong@palaunet.com; Chief Justice ARTHUR NGIRAKLSONG.

Office of the Attorney-General: 1365 Koror, PW 96940; tel. 488-2481; fax 488-3329; e-mail agoffice@palaunet.com; internet www

.palaugov.net/minjustice/attrgeneral.html; Attorney-Gen. ERNESTINE RENGIIL.

Religion

The population is predominantly Christian, mainly Roman Catholic. The Assembly of God, Baptists, Seventh-day Adventists, the Church of Jesus Christ of Latter-day Saints (Mormons), and the Bahá'í and Modignai (or Modeknai) faiths are also represented.

CHRISTIANITY

The Roman Catholic Church

Palau forms part of the diocese of the Caroline Islands, suffragan to the archdiocese of Agaña (Guam). The Bishop, who is resident in Chuuk, Eastern Caroline Islands (see the Federated States of Micronesia), participates in the Catholic Bishops' Conference of the Pacific, based in Suva, Fiji.

MODIGNAI FAITH

Modignai Church: Koror, PW 96940; an indigenous, non-Christian religion; also operates a high school.

The Press

Moonshadow Publications: POB 9006, Koror, PW 96940; tel. 488-8655; fax 779-3440; e-mail jerome@palaunet.com; internet jerometemengil.synthasite.com; Publr JEROME TEMENGIL.

Palau Gazette: POB 100, Koror, PW 96940; tel. 488-3257; fax 488-1662; e-mail roppresoffice@palaunet.com; newsletter publ. by Govt; monthly; Publr ROMAN YANO.

Palau Horizon: POB 10207, Koror, PW 96940; tel. 488-4588; fax 488-4565; e-mail hprinting@palautelecoms.com; twice weekly; f. 1998; Publr ABED E. YOUNIS; circ. 1,500.

Roureur Belau: POB 477, Koror, PW 96940; tel. 488-6365; fax 488-4810; e-mail myu@palaunet.com; weekly; Publr CLIFFORD 'SPADE' EBAS.

Tia Belau (This is Palau): POB 477, Koror, PW 96940; tel. 488-6365; fax 488-4810; e-mail tiabelau@palaunet.com; internet www.tiabelau.com; f. 1992; weekly; English and Palauan; Editor RAOUL G. BRIONES; Publr MOSES ULUDONG; circ 1,500.

Broadcasting and Communications

TELECOMMUNICATIONS

Palau National Communications Corpn (PNCC): POB 99, Koror, PW 96940; tel. 587-9000; fax 587-1888; e-mail pncc@palaunet.com; internet www.palaunet.com; f. 1982; mem. of the Pacific Islands Broadcasting Asscn; telephone, internet and digital television operator; 24 hrs daily; Chair. LEILANI REKLAI; Gen. Man. RICHARD L. MISECH.

Palau Mobile Corpn (PMC): POB 8084, Koror, PW 96940; tel. 488-4088; fax 488-2111; e-mail marklin@palaumobile.com; internet www.palaumobile.com; mobile telephone operator.

BROADCASTING

Radio

High Adventure Ministries: POB 66, Koror, PW 96940; tel. 488-2162; fax 488-2163; e-mail hamadmin@palaunet.com; f. 1992; broadcasts religious material; Engineering Man. BENTLEY CHAN.

KRFM: Sure Save Store, Koror, PW 96940; tel. 488-1359; e-mail rudimch@palaunet.com.

T8AA (Eco Paradise): POB 279, Koror, PW 96940; tel. 488-2417; fax 488-1932; broadcasts news, entertainment and music; govt-owned.

WSZB Broadcasting Station: POB 279, Koror, PW 96940; tel. 488-2417; fax 488-1932; Station Man. ALBERT SALUSTIANO.

WWFM: POB 1327, Koror, PW 96940; tel. 488-4848; fax 488-4420; e-mail wwfm@palaunet.com; internet www.brouhaha.net/palau/wwfm.html; Man. ALFONSO DIAZ.

Television

PNCC Digital Television: POB 39, Koror, PW 96940; tel. 488-1490; fax 587-1888; internet www.palaunet.com; owned by the Palau National Communications Corpn; fmrly Island Cable Television.

STV-TV Koror: POB 2000, Koror, PW 96940; tel. 488-1357; fax 488-1207; broadcasts 12 hrs daily; Man. DAVID NOLAN; Technical Man. RAY OMELEN.

Finance

(cap. = capital; res = reserves; amounts in US dollars)

BANKING

Bank of Guam: POB 338, Koror, PW 96940; tel. 488-2696; fax 488-1384; internet www.bankofguam.com; Man. KATHERINE LUJAN.

Bank of Hawaii (USA): POB 340, Koror, PW 96940; tel. 488-2428; fax 488-2427; internet www.boh.com.

Bank Pacific: Lebuu St, Tngerongel Hamlet, Koror; tel. 488-5635; fax 488-4752; internet www.bankpacific.com; Sr Country Officer JOSEPH KOSHIBA.

National Development Bank of Palau: POB 816, Koror, PW 96940-0816; tel. 488-2578; fax 488-2579; e-mail ndbp@palaunet.com; f. 1982; cap. and res 11.5m. (Sept. 2002); 100% govt-owned; Pres. KALEB ADUI, Jr; Chair. NORIWO UBEDEI.

INSURANCE

Century Insurance Co: POB 318, Koror, PW 96940; tel. 488-8580; fax 488-8632; e-mail knakamura@palaunet.com.

Moylan's Insurance Underwriters Palau: POB 156, Koror, PW 96940; tel. 488-2765; fax 488-2744; e-mail palau@moylans.net; internet www.moylansinsurance.com; Branch Man. KENJI DENGOKL.

NECO Insurance Underwriters Ltd: POB 129, Koror, PW 96940; tel. 488-2325; fax 488-2880; e-mail necogroup@palaunet.com.

Poltalia National Insurance: POB 12, Koror, PW 96940; tel. 488-2254; fax 488-2834; e-mail psata@palaunet.com; f. 1974; Pres. and CEO EPHRAM POLYCARP.

Trade and Industry

CHAMBER OF COMMERCE

Palau Chamber of Commerce: POB 1742, Koror, PW 96940; tel. 488-3400; fax 488-3401; e-mail pcoc@palaunet.com; f. 1984; Pres. SURANGEL WHIPPS, Jr.

CO-OPERATIVES

These include the Palau Fishermen's Co-operative, Palau Boatbuilders' Asscn and the Palau Handicraft and Woodworkers' Guild. In 1990, of the 13 registered co-operatives, eight were fishermen's co-operatives, three consumers' co-operatives (only two in normal operation) and two farmers' co-operatives (one in normal operation).

DEVELOPMENT ORGANIZATION

Palau Conservation Society: POB 1811, Koror, PW 96940; tel. 488-3993; fax 488-3990; e-mail pcs@palaunet.com; internet www.palau-pcs.org; f. 1994; sustainable devt, environmental protection; Exec. Dir TIARE TURANG HOLM.

Transport

ROADS

Macadam and concrete roads are found in the more important islands. Other islands have stone and coral-surfaced roads and tracks. The Government is responsible for 36 km (22 miles) of paved roads and 25 km (15 miles) of coral- and gravel-surfaced roads. Most paved roads are located on Koror and are in a poor state of repair. A major project to construct a new 85-km (53-mile) road around Babeldaob began in 1999 and was completed in 2007. The project was funded with US $150m. from the Compact of Free Association.

SHIPPING

Most shipping in Palau is government-organized. However, the Micronesia Transport Line operates a service from Sydney (Australia) to Palau. A twice-weekly inter-island service operates between Koror and Peleliu. There is one commercial port at Malakal Harbor, which is operated by the privately owned Belau Transfer and Terminal Company.

CIVIL AVIATION

There is an international airport on Babeldaob. A new terminal building, construction of which was funded by a grant of US $16m. from Japan, opened in May 2003. Domestic airfields (former Japanese military airstrips) are located on Angaur and Peleliu. Continental Micronesia (Northern Mariana Islands and Guam) provides daily flights to Koror from Guam, and twice-weekly flights from Manila (Philippines). Cebu Pacific operates direct flights from Davao (Philippines) to Koror. In May 2008 China Airlines began operating charter flights between Taiwan and Palau, after the Far Eastern Air Transport Corpn suspended flights on that route. Palau Trans Pacific

PALAU

also operates from Taiwan. In July 2008 two South Korean carriers, Korean Air and Asiana Airlines, reached an agreement with the Palau Government, allowing for up to seven passenger flights and four cargo flights per week. Japan Airlines was to commence trial flights to Palau in October 2008 between the Japanese city of Haneda and Koror.

Rock Island Airlines: managed by Aloha Airlines (Hawaii).

Tourism

Tourism is becoming increasingly important in Palau. The islands are particularly rich in their marine environment, and the Government has implemented measures to conserve and protect these natural resources. The myriad Rock Islands, now known as the Floating Garden Islands, are a noted reserve in the lagoon to the west of the main group of islands. There were 959 hotel rooms in 2004. In 2008 Palau received 75,829 visitors, most of whom were from Taiwan and from Japan. Tourist revenue reached US $90m. in 2006. The Micronesian Games were to be held in Palau in 2010.

Belau Tourism Association: POB 9032, Koror, PW 96940; tel. 488-4377; fax 488-1725; e-mail bta@palaunet.com.

Palau Visitors' Authority: POB 256, Koror, PW 96940; tel. 488-2793; fax 488-1453; e-mail info@visit-palau.com; internet www.visit-palau.com; Man. Dir DARIN DE LEON.

PALESTINIAN AUTONOMOUS AREAS

Introductory Survey

Location, Climate, Language, Religion, Flag, Capital

The Palestinian Autonomous Areas are located in the West Bank and the Gaza Strip. (For a more detailed description of the location of the Palestinian territories, see Government, below.) The West Bank lies in western Asia, to the west of the Jordan river and the Dead Sea, with the State of Israel to the north, west and south. The Gaza Strip lies on the easternmost coast of the Mediterranean, with Israel to the north and east and Egypt to the south. The Interim Agreement of September 1995 (see below) provides for the creation of a corridor, or safe passage, linking the Gaza Strip with the West Bank. A 'southern' safe passage between Hebron and Gaza was opened in October 1999 (although it has been closed since October 2000). Including East Jerusalem, the West Bank covers an area of 5,655 sq km. Precipitation ranges between 600 mm and 800 mm on the Mount Hebron massif and 200 mm in the Jordan valley. Apart from the urban centres of Beit Lahm (Bethlehem) and Al-Khalil (Hebron) to the south, the majority of the Palestinian population is concentrated in the northern localities around Ram Allah (Ramallah), Nabulus (Nablus), Janin (Jenin) and Tulkarm. The Gaza Strip covers an area of 365 sq km. Annual average rainfall is 300 mm. The language of Palestinians in the West Bank and Gaza is Arabic. The majority of the Palestinian population are Muslims, with a Christian minority representing about 2% of the Palestinian population of the territories. This minority, in turn, represents about 45% of all Palestinian Christians. The national flag (proportion 1 by 2) comprises three equal horizontal stripes of black, white and green, with a red triangle with its base corresponding to the hoist. Gaza City is the main population centre and the centre of administration for the Palestinian (National) Authority (PA), appointed in May 1994. Ramallah is the PA's administrative centre in the West Bank. In November 1988 the Palestine National Council (PNC) proclaimed Jerusalem as the capital of the newly declared independent State of Palestine. Israel (q.v.) declares Jerusalem as its capital. In 1967 East Jerusalem was formally annexed by the Israeli authorities, although the annexation has never been recognized by the UN. The permanent status of Jerusalem remains subject to negotiation on so-called 'final status' issues under the Oslo accords (see Recent History).

Recent History

Until the end of the 1948 Arab–Israeli War, the West Bank formed part of the British Mandate of Palestine, before becoming part of the Hashemite Kingdom of Jordan under the Armistice Agreement of 1949. It remained under Jordanian sovereignty, despite Israeli occupation in 1967, until King Hussein of Jordan formally relinquished legal and administrative control on 31 July 1988. Under Israeli military occupation the West Bank was administered by a military government, which divided the territory into seven sub-districts. The Civil Administration, as it was later termed, did not extend its jurisdiction to the many Israeli settlements that were established under the Israeli occupation; settlements remained subject to the Israeli legal and administrative system. By October 2000 approximately 17.2% of the West Bank was under exclusive Palestinian jurisdiction and security control, although Israel retained authority over access to and from the zone; about 23.8% was under Israeli military control, with responsibility for civil administration and public order transferred to the PA; the remaining 59% was under Israeli occupation.

An administrative province under the British Mandate of Palestine, Gaza was transferred to Egypt after the 1949 armistice and remained under Egyptian administration until June 1967, when it was invaded by Israel. Following Israeli occupation the Gaza Strip, like the West Bank, became an 'administered territory'. Until the provisions of the Declaration of Principles on Palestinian Self-Rule (see below) began to take effect, the management of day-to-day affairs was the responsibility of the area's Israeli military commander. Neither Israeli laws nor governmental and public bodies—including the Supreme Court—could review or alter the orders of the military command to any great extent. In 2001 an estimated 42% of the Gaza Strip was under Israeli control, including Jewish settlements, military bases, bypass roads and a 'buffer zone' along the border with Israel. However, Israel withdrew its settlers and military personnel from Gaza in August–September 2005 (see below).

In accordance with the Declaration of Principles on Palestinian Self-Rule of 13 September 1993, and the Cairo Agreement on the Gaza Strip and Jericho of 4 May 1994, the Palestine Liberation Organization (PLO) assumed control of the Jericho area of the West Bank, and of the Gaza Strip, on 17 May 1994. In November and December 1995, under the terms of the Israeli-Palestinian Interim Agreement on the West Bank and the Gaza Strip concluded on 28 September 1995, Israeli armed forces withdrew from the West Bank towns of Nablus, Ramallah, Jenin, Tulkarm, Qalqilya and Bethlehem. (These three agreements and associated accords are referred to collectively as the 'Oslo accords', owing to the role played by Norwegian diplomacy in their negotiation.) In late December the PLO assumed responsibility in some 17 areas of civil administration in the town of Hebron, with a view to eventually assuming full responsibility for civil affairs in the 400 surrounding villages. However, despite a partial withdrawal from Hebron in January 1997, Israeli armed forces were to retain freedom of movement to act against potential hostilities there and also to provide security for some 400 Jewish settlers. Responsibility for security in the rest of Hebron (excluding access roads) passed to the Palestinian police force. Following the first phase of the redeployment and the holding, on its completion, of elections to a Palestinian Legislative Council and for a Palestinian executive president, Israel was to have completed a second redeployment from rural areas by July 1997. The Israeli occupation was to be maintained in military installations, Jewish settlements, East Jerusalem and the settlements around Jerusalem until the conclusion of 'final status' negotiations between Israel and the Palestinians, scheduled for May 1999.

Diplomatic developments within the context of the Oslo peace process led to a new timetable for Israeli redeployment which envisaged two phases, subsequent to the Hebron withdrawal, to be completed by October 1997 and August 1998. Discussions on 'final status' issues—borders, Jerusalem, Jewish settlements and Palestinian refugees—were to commence within two months of the signing of the agreement on Hebron. As guarantor of the Oslo accords, the USA undertook to obtain the release from Israeli custody of Palestinian prisoners, and to ensure that Israel continued to engage in negotiations for the establishment of a Palestinian airport in the Gaza Strip and for safe passage for Palestinians between the West Bank and Gaza. The USA also endeavoured to ensure that the Palestinians would continue to combat terrorism, complete the revision of the Palestinian National Charter (or PLO Covenant), adopted in 1964 and amended in 1968, and consider Israeli requests to extradite Palestinians suspected of involvement in attacks in Israel.

In February 1997 the Israeli Government of Binyamin Netanyahu announced the construction of a new Jewish settlement at Jabal Abu Ghunaim (Har Homa in Hebrew), near Beit Sahur, which would prejudice 'final status' negotiations concerning Jerusalem because it would effectively separate East Jerusalem from the West Bank. In response, the PA withdrew from 'final status' talks scheduled to commence in March. The start of construction work at Jabal Abu Ghunaim provoked rioting among Palestinians and a resumption of attacks by the military wing of the Islamic Resistance Movement (Hamas) on Israeli civilian targets. Israel responded by ordering a general closure of the West Bank and Gaza. Both the Jabal Abu Ghunaim construction and Israel's unilateral decision to redeploy its armed forces from only 9% of West Bank territory (announced in March) were regarded by many observers as a vitiation of both the Oslo and the subsequent post-Hebron agreements. Moreover, the Israeli newspaper *Ha'aretz* later reported that Israeli plans, evolved within the framework of the Oslo accords, to relinquish 90% of the West Bank had been revised to a 40% redeployment.

In June 1997 the US House of Representatives voted in favour of recognizing Jerusalem as the undivided capital of Israel and of transferring the US embassy to the city from Tel-Aviv. The vote (which was opposed by US President Bill Clinton) coincided with violent clashes between Palestinian civilians and Israeli troops in Gaza and Hebron. In July, on the eve of a scheduled visit by Dennis Ross, the US Special Co-ordinator to the Middle East, to reactivate negotiations between Israel and the PA, Hamas carried out a suicide bomb attack at a Jewish market in Jerusalem, in which 14 civilians were killed. Ross cancelled his visit and the Israeli Government immediately halted payment of tax revenues to the PA and closed the Gaza Strip and the West Bank. In the aftermath of the bombing the PA undertook a campaign to detain members of Hamas and another militant organization, Islamic Jihad. As a result of US diplomacy, Israeli and Palestinian officials agreed to resume negotiations focusing on the outstanding issues of the Oslo accords in October.

Meanwhile, the attempted assassination in Amman, Jordan, in September 1997, of Khalid Meshaal, the head of the Hamas political bureau there, provoked warnings of retaliation against Israel, even before official confirmation that agents of the Israeli security service, Mossad, had been responsible for the attack. In order to secure the release of its agents by the Jordanian authorities, Israel was obliged to free a number of Arab political prisoners, most notably Sheikh Ahmad Yassin, the founder and spiritual leader of Hamas, who had been sentenced to life imprisonment in Israel in 1989 for complicity in attacks on Israeli soldiers. The release of Sheikh Yassin into Jordanian custody was swiftly followed by his return, in October 1997, to Gaza.

It was reported in December 1997 that, under further US pressure, the Israeli Cabinet had agreed in principle to withdraw troops from an unspecified area of the West Bank. However, the Israeli Government subsequently reiterated that it would not conduct such a redeployment until the Palestinian leadership had fulfilled a series of conditions: these included the adoption of effective measures to counter terrorism, a reduction in the strength of its security forces from 40,000 to 24,000, and a revision of the Palestinian National Charter to recognize explicitly Israel's right to exist. Moreover, prior to a summit meeting in January 1998 between Clinton and Netanyahu in Washington, DC, the Israeli Cabinet issued a communiqué detailing 'vital and national interests' in the West Bank (amounting to some 60% of the entire territory) that it was not prepared to relinquish; the document asserted that Israel would, among other areas, retain control of the territory surrounding Jerusalem. In late January, however, direct contacts between Palestinian representatives and the Israeli Prime Minister collapsed.

In March 1998 it emerged that the USA planned to present new proposals regarding the withdrawal of Israeli armed forces from the West Bank at separate meetings in Europe between US Secretary of State Madeleine Albright and the PA President, Yasser Arafat, and Israeli Prime Minister Netanyahu. However, it was evident that, even if agreement could be reached on the extent of territory involved, the issue of whether a subsequent withdrawal should take place prior to the commencement of 'final status' talks remained far more contentious. The Israeli Cabinet rejected the new US initiative. Having persuaded Arafat to attend a conference in London, United Kingdom, based on the US initiative, during a visit to Gaza City on behalf of the European Union (EU), in early May the British Prime Minister, Tony Blair, hosted a summit meeting attended by Netanyahu, Arafat and Albright. At its conclusion the US Secretary of State invited Netanyahu and Arafat to attend a summit meeting with Bill Clinton in Washington, DC, to discuss the apparent US proposal that Israeli and Palestinian officials could proceed to 'final status' negotiations as soon as the scope of the next Israeli withdrawal from the West Bank had been agreed. In June details of the latest US initiative were unofficially disclosed in the Israeli press: Israel would be required to agree to 'no significant expansion' of Jewish settlements and to relinquish slightly more than 13% of West Bank territory over a period of 12 weeks, in exchange for increased Palestinian co-operation on security issues. The adoption by the Israeli Cabinet later that month of a plan to extend the boundaries of Jerusalem and construct homes there for a further 1m. people prompted accusations by the PA that it amounted to a de facto annexation of territories that were officially subject to 'final status' discussions.

On 7 July 1998 the UN General Assembly overwhelmingly approved a resolution to upgrade the status of the PLO at the UN. The new provision, which the USA and Israel had opposed, allowed the PLO to participate in debates, to co-sponsor resolutions, and to raise points of order during discussions of Middle East affairs.

On 19–22 July 1998 Israeli and Palestinian delegations held direct negotiations for the first time since March 1997, in order to discuss the US peace initiative disclosed in June. In September 1998 Netanyahu and Arafat met in Washington, DC, and agreed to participate in a peace conference in the USA in the following month. The summit meeting, also attended by President Clinton, commenced at the Wye Plantation, Maryland, USA, on 15 October 1998, and culminated in the signing, on 23 October, of the Wye River Memorandum, which was intended to facilitate the implementation of the Oslo accords. Under the terms of the Wye Memorandum, to be implemented within three months of its signing, Israel was to transfer a further 13.1% of West Bank territory from exclusive Israeli control to joint Israeli-Palestinian control. An additional 14% of the West Bank was to be transferred from joint Israeli-Palestinian control to exclusive Palestinian control. The Wye Memorandum also stipulated that: negotiations with regard to a third Israeli redeployment (under the terms of the Oslo accords) should proceed concurrently with 'final status' discussions; the PA should reinforce anti-terrorism measures and arrest 30 suspected terrorists; the strength of the Palestinian police force should be reduced by 25%; Israel should carry out the phased release of 750 Palestinian prisoners (including political detainees); the Palestine National Council (PNC) should annul those clauses of the PLO Covenant deemed to be anti-Israeli; Gaza International Airport was to become operational with an Israeli security presence; and an access corridor between the West Bank and the Gaza Strip should be opened. The Memorandum was endorsed by both the Israeli Cabinet and the Knesset (parliament) by mid-November. On 20 November Israel redeployed its armed forces from about 500 sq km of the West Bank (with the PA assuming responsibilty for all civil affairs and for security affairs in some 400 sq km); released some 250 (mainly non-political) Palestinian prisoners; and signed a protocol for the opening of Gaza International Airport. Israel retained the right to decide which airlines could use the airport, which was officially inaugurated by Arafat on 24 November.

However, implementation of the Wye Memorandum did not proceed smoothly. In December 1998, prior to a planned visit by Bill Clinton to Israel and the Gaza Strip, violent clashes erupted in the West Bank between Palestinians and Israeli security forces. One cause of the unrest was a decision by the Israeli Cabinet to suspend further releases of Palestinian prisoners under the terms of the Wye Memorandum, and its insistence that no Palestinians convicted of killing Israelis, nor members of Hamas or Islamic Jihad, would be released. On 14 December, meanwhile, in the presence of President Clinton, the PNC voted to annul articles of the Palestinian National Charter that were deemed to be anti-Israeli. However, at a summit meeting the following day between Clinton, Netanyahu and Arafat at the Erez checkpoint between Israel and the Gaza Strip, the Israeli Prime Minister reiterated Israel's stance regarding the release of Palestinian prisoners and further demanded that the Palestinians should honour their commitments by ceasing incitement to violence and formally relinquishing plans for a unilateral declaration of Palestinian statehood on 4 May 1999 (the original deadline as established by the Oslo accords). Netanyahu announced that Israel would not proceed with the second scheduled redeployment of its armed forces on 18 December 1998, and on 20 December the Israeli Cabinet voted to suspend implementation of the Wye Memorandum.

Palestinians reacted to the death of King Hussein of Jordan in February 1999 with public grief—about 65% of the kingdom's inhabitants are believed to be of Palestinian origin—especially in the West Bank, which King Hussein ruled for 15 years until June 1967. For Arafat, the death of Hussein was a major political reverse since the King had frequently supported him when the peace process with Israel appeared to be on the verge of collapse. Arafat subsequently surprised many Jordanians by proposing the establishment of a Palestinian-Jordanian confederation. The proposal (which had been put forward as part of a peace initiative in 1985, but was rejected by King Hussein) was not welcomed in Jordan, where it was considered to be premature while the West Bank was still largely under Israeli occupation.

President Arafat came under intense international pressure to postpone a unilateral declaration of Palestinian statehood, at least until after the Israeli elections scheduled for May 1999. In late April PLO chief negotiators Mahmud Abbas (also known as Abu Mazen) and Saeb Erakat (the Minister of Local Government) visited Washington, DC, in order to secure certain assurances from the USA in return for an extension of the 4 May deadline. Following a meeting of the Palestinian Central Council

(PCC), together with Hamas representatives, in Gaza, it was announced that a declaration on Palestinian statehood would be postponed until after the Israeli elections. The decision was applauded internationally, but provoked violent demonstrations among many Palestinians.

Meeting at Sharm esh-Sheikh, Egypt, on 4 September 1999, during a visit to the region by US Secretary of State Albright, Arafat and the new Israeli Prime Minister, Ehud Barak, signed the Sharm esh-Sheikh Memorandum (or Wye Two accords), outlining a revised timetable for implementation of the outstanding provisions of the original Wye agreement. Under the terms of the Memorandum, on 9 September Israel released some 200 Palestinian 'security' prisoners, and the following day Israel transferred a further 7% of the West Bank to PA control. A ceremonial opening of 'final status' negotiations between Israel and the PA was held at the Erez checkpoint on 13 September; shortly afterwards details emerged of a secret meeting between Barak and Arafat to discuss an agenda for such talks. However, in early October the Palestinians' chief negotiator and Minister of Culture and Information, Yasser Abd ar-Rabbuh, warned that the PA would boycott 'final status' talks unless Israel ended its settlement expansion programme. In mid-October Barak, also under pressure from left-wing groups in Israel, responded by dismantling 12 'settlement outposts' in the West Bank which he deemed to be illegal. Meanwhile, Israel released a further 151 Palestinian prisoners under the terms of Wye Two. The first 'safe passage' between the West Bank and Gaza was inaugurated on 25 October. Israel asserted that it would maintain almost complete control over the so-called 'southern route', which linked Hebron to the Erez checkpoint.

'Final status' negotiations between Israel and the PA commenced in Ramallah on 8 November 1999, following a summit meeting held earlier in the month in Oslo, Norway, between Arafat, Barak and Clinton. A further redeployment of Israeli armed forces from 5% of the West Bank, scheduled for 15 November, was postponed owing to disagreement over the areas to be transferred. In early December Palestinian negotiators walked out of the talks, following reports that settlement activity had intensified under Barak. Apparently in response to US pressure, the Israeli Prime Minister subsequently announced a halt to settlement construction until the close of negotiations regarding a framework agreement on 'final status'. In late December Arafat conducted talks in Ramallah with Barak, who became the first Israeli premier to hold peace discussions on Palestinian territory. At the end of the month Israel released some 26 Palestinian 'security' prisoners as a gesture of 'goodwill'. Israeli armed forces withdrew from a further 5% of the West Bank on 6–7 January 2000; however, Israel announced in mid-January that a third redeployment from 6.1% of the territory (scheduled to take place on 20 January) would be postponed until Barak had returned from revived peace talks with Syria in the USA. During a meeting with Arafat on his return from the USA (where talks on the Israeli-Syrian track had collapsed), Barak was reported to have proposed that the deadline for reaching a framework agreement be postponed for two months. The approval by the Israeli Cabinet of a withdrawal of its troops from a sparsely populated area of the West Bank led the PA to break off negotiations in early February. On 19–20 March Israel released 15 Palestinian 'security' prisoners, and the resumption of 'final status' talks was announced on 21 March. On the same day Israeli armed forces withdrew from a further 6.1% of the West Bank.

In mid-April 2000, following talks between Barak and Clinton in Washington, DC, Israel was said to have agreed to Palestinian demands for greater US involvement in future discussions. Moreover, the Israeli premier reportedly indicated that a Palestinian entity could be established in what was now PA-controlled territory—covering 60%–70% of the West Bank—although he refused to speak of a Palestinian 'state'. The third round of 'final status' talks between Israel and the PA opened at the Israeli port of Eilat on 30 April, at which Palestinian negotiators denounced a recent decision by the Israeli Government to construct 174 new Jewish homes in the West Bank. At crisis talks between Arafat and Barak in Ramallah in early May, mediated by Dennis Ross, Barak reportedly proposed the transfer to full PA control of three Palestinian villages close to Jerusalem, on condition that the third West Bank redeployment (scheduled to be implemented in June) be postponed. After PA negotiators admitted that the 13 May deadline for reaching a framework agreement would not be met, 'final status' talks were suspended. Moreover, on 21 May Israel suspended 'secret' talks being conducted between Israeli and Palestinian representatives in Stockholm, Sweden, after an Israeli child was seriously wounded in continuing violence in the West Bank. (The latest unrest came after Palestinians declared 15 May—the anniversary of the declaration of the State of Israel in 1948—to be a 'day of rage' and amid growing anger over the apparent unaccountability of the PA leadership.) The Israeli Government also reversed its decision to transfer the three Arab villages to PA control, demanding that Arafat take action to curb Palestinian unrest.

In early June 2000, following US diplomatic efforts, Israel released three Palestinian prisoners as a 'goodwill' gesture. On 21 June, two days prior to the scheduled date, the PA reportedly agreed to a postponement of the third redeployment of Israeli forces from the West Bank. The PCC convened on 2 July, and after two days of discussions stated that the PLO would declare a State of Palestine on or before 13 September. On 11 July Bill Clinton inaugurated a peace summit between Arafat and Barak at the US presidential retreat at Camp David, Maryland, with the aim of achieving a framework agreement on 'final status'. However, the talks ended without agreement on 25 July. Despite reported progress regarding the borders of a future Palestinian entity and the question of Palestinian refugees, disagreements over the future status of Jerusalem had been the principal obstacle to an accord. Israel was said to have offered the Palestinians municipal authority over certain parts of East Jerusalem, as well as access to the Islamic holy sites. PA officials, however, demanded full sovereignty over the holy sites (in particular the al-Aqsa Mosque and the Dome of the Rock), with East Jerusalem as the capital of a Palestinian state. Nevertheless, Israel and the PA pledged to continue peace negotiations and to avoid 'unilateral actions'—interpreted as Arafat's threat unilaterally to declare an independent Palestinian state. During a tour principally of Europe, the Middle East and Asia, intense pressure was exerted on Arafat not to announce the establishment of a Palestinian state on 13 September. The PCC convened in Gaza on 9–10 September and agreed to postpone the declaration of statehood for an indefinite period (although 15 November was reportedly designated as the new target date). Later in September negotiations between Israeli and PA officials resumed in the USA, and on 20 September an agreement was signed allowing for construction of the Gaza seaport to begin (although the work failed to progress owing to the worsening security situation).

From late September 2000 the West Bank and Gaza Strip became engulfed in what became known as the al-Aqsa *intifada* (uprising—the first *intifada* began at the end of 1987 and continued for some five years), as Palestinians demonstrated their frustration at the lack of progress in the Oslo peace process and at their failure to achieve statehood. The outbreak of violence was triggered by the visit of Ariel Sharon, leader of Israel's right-wing Likud party, to Temple Mount/Haram ash-Sharif in Jerusalem—the site of the al-Aqsa Mosque and the Dome of the Rock—on 28 September. Sharon's visit to the Islamic holy sites provoked violent protests and stone-throwing by Palestinians, to which Israeli security forces responded forcefully. The clashes spread rapidly to other Palestinian towns: by the end of October at least 140 people had died—all but eight of them Palestinians—and thousands had been wounded. In early October Arafat and Barak travelled to Paris, France, for negotiations led by the US Secretary of State, Madeleine Albright, but no agreement was reached on the composition of an international commission of inquiry into the causes of the violence. The Israeli authorities subsequently sealed off the borders of the West Bank and Gaza, and on 7 October the UN Security Council issued a resolution condemning the 'provocation carried out' at Temple Mount/Haram ash-Sharif and the 'excessive use of force' employed by the Israeli security forces against Palestinians. Meanwhile, Israel accused Arafat of failing to intervene to halt the violence, as members of Arafat's own Fatah movement joined Hamas and other militant groups in the quickly escalating *intifada*. In an attempt to prevent the crisis from developing into a major regional conflict, a US-sponsored summit meeting between Barak and Arafat was convened on 16–17 October at Sharm esh-Sheikh. At the close of the meeting US President Clinton announced that the Israeli and Palestinian leaders had agreed the terms of a 'truce' to halt the spiralling violence. The two sides had also reportedly agreed on the formation of a US-appointed committee to investigate the clashes. Barak, however, demanded that Arafat rearrest some 60 militant Islamists whom the PA had freed in early October. The League of Arab States (the Arab League, see p. 344) held an emergency summit meeting in the Egyptian capital on 21–

PALESTINIAN AUTONOMOUS AREAS

Introductory Survey

22 October, and issued a strong condemnation of Israel's actions towards the Palestinians. Barak responded by announcing that Israel was calling a 'time-out' in the peace process.

At the end of October 2000 Islamic Jihad claimed responsibility for a suicide bombing on an Israeli army post in Gaza, signalling a new campaign against Israeli forces by militant Palestinian organizations opposed to the Oslo process. Israel responded by launching air-strikes on Fatah military bases, and declared a new strategy of targeting leading officials of militant Islamist groups suspected of terrorist activities. On 1 November Arafat held a crisis meeting in Gaza with the Israeli Minister for Regional Co-operation, Shimon Peres; the two sides were reported to have agreed a 'cease-fire', based on the truce brokered in Egypt in October. The following day, however, a car bomb exploded in Jerusalem, for which Islamic Jihad claimed responsibility. In early November President Clinton appointed the five-member international commission of inquiry, to be chaired by former US Senator George Mitchell. Meeting with Clinton in the USA shortly afterwards, Arafat demanded that the USA support Palestinian requests for the establishment of a UN peace-keeping force in the self-rule areas (Barak was opposed to such a force). Israel imposed an economic blockade on the West Bank and Gaza in mid-November, and launched air-strikes against PA offices in Gaza later that month, in reprisal for the deaths of two people in the bombing of a school bus for Jewish settlers. At the end of November the Palestinians rejected a partial peace plan, announced by Barak, whereby Israel would withdraw its armed forces from additional West Bank territory provided that the PA agreed to postpone any discussion of the remaining 'final status' issues. In mid-December the US-led commission of inquiry began conducting investigations into the violence.

A further round of peace talks opened in mid-December 2000, at which Clinton was reported to have proposed a peace deal that included plans for a future Palestinian state covering the Gaza Strip and some 95% of the West Bank, as well as granting the Palestinians sovereignty over the Islamic holy sites in the Old City of Jerusalem. However, the US plan also required that Palestinians renounce the right of return for 3.7m. refugees, which the PA deemed unacceptable. The negotiations broke down in late December after two Israelis died in bombings by Palestinian militants in Tel-Aviv and the Gaza Strip. In January 2001 Israel confirmed its policy of assassinating local Palestinian officials who were regarded as endangering Israeli society, which it referred to as 'targeted killings'.

The election of Ariel Sharon to the Israeli premiership in early February 2001 provoked violent demonstrations by Palestinians, who held Sharon responsible—as Israel's Minister of Defence at that time—for the Phalangist massacre of Palestinian refugees in Lebanese camps in 1982 (see the chapters on Israel and Lebanon). Immediately after Sharon's election Palestinian militants carried out a car bombing in Jerusalem, and in mid-February a Palestinian bus driver launched an attack on Israeli soldiers and civilians in Tel-Aviv, killing nine people. Israel responded by again sealing off the Palestinian territories.

At the beginning of June 2001 21 Israelis were killed in a suicide bomb attack, apparently perpetrated by Hamas, at a Tel-Aviv nightclub. The PA agreed the following day to implement the recommendations listed in the final report of the international commission of inquiry under George Mitchell (the Sharm esh-Sheikh Fact-Finding Committee, or 'Mitchell Committee'), published in late May. The Mitchell Report recommended a freeze on Israeli settlement expansion; a clear statement by the PA demanding an end to Palestinian violence; an 'immediate and unconditional' end to the conflict and the disengagement of forces by both sides; and the resumption of security co-operation. Moreover, in mid-June the PA also agreed to an extended cease-fire brokered by the US Central Intelligence Agency (CIA) Director, George Tenet, although in early July both Hamas and Islamic Jihad formally announced that the cease-fire was ended. In late July Palestinian security forces in Gaza arrested a number of militants, including members of Fatah's military wing, the *tanzim*.

In August 2001 the PA rejected a demand by Israel for the arrest of seven alleged 'terrorists', who headed a 'most wanted' list of about 100 Palestinians suspected of involvement in attacks against Israeli targets. Soon afterwards Israel ordered its armed forces to occupy several PA offices including Orient House, the PA's de facto headquarters in East Jerusalem, following a Hamas suicide bombing which killed at least 15 Israelis at a restaurant in central Jerusalem. Israeli troops entered the West Bank town of Jenin in mid-August—the first Israeli reoccupation of territory transferred to full PA control under the terms of the Oslo accords. Palestinian officials called the action a 'declaration of war'. Later in the month Abu Ali Moustafa, the leader of the Popular Front for the Liberation of Palestine (PFLP), was assassinated by Israeli forces in the West Bank.

The unprecedented scale of the suicide attacks launched against New York and Washington, DC, on 11 September 2001—for which the USA held the al-Qa'ida (Base) network led by the Saudi-born militant Islamist Osama bin Laden principally responsible—precipitated efforts by the US Administration to encourage Israel and the PA to end the violence in the Palestinian territories, as President George W. Bush (who had been elected to the presidency in November 2000) sought to garner support for an international 'war on terror'. In mid-September 2001 Yasser Arafat, who had condemned the attacks in the strongest terms, declared that he had ordered militant Palestinian groups to halt their actions against Israelis, while Israel agreed to withdraw from PA-controlled areas of the West Bank. However, Sharon stated that his Government required 48 hours without violence prior to any resumption of peace talks. Arafat and Peres finally met in the Gaza Strip in late September, in an attempt to consolidate the cease-fire arrangements outlined in the Mitchell Report. However, on the first anniversary of the al-Aqsa *intifada* five Palestinians were shot dead by Israeli forces in Gaza, and retaliatory attacks between the two sides resumed.

President Bush disclosed for the first time in early October 2001 that the USA would accept the creation of a Palestinian state, on condition that Israel's existence was not threatened. The assassination in Jerusalem of Israel's ultra-nationalist Minister of Tourism, Rechavam Ze'evi, by three members of the PFLP—apparently in revenge for the murder of the PFLP leader in August—led Israel, in late October, to order its armed forces into six major West Bank towns. Shortly after Ze'evi's death Arafat banned all military factions of Palestinian political groups, and his security forces arrested several PFLP militants; however, the PA refused Israeli demands for their extradition. At least five Palestinians reportedly died in Beit Rima, near Ramallah, in a raid by Israeli forces searching for Ze'evi's assassins. Towards the end of October Israel stated that it would carry out a phased withdrawal from the six West Bank towns; however, its 'anti-terrorist' operation continued in Jenin and Tulkarm, and Israeli tanks continued to surround Ramallah.

Hamas claimed responsibility for a series of attacks in Jerusalem and Haifa over a 24-hour period in early December 2001, in which at least 25 Israelis were killed. Palestinian security forces subsequently claimed to have arrested more than 150 militants, mostly in Jenin, and also reportedly placed the spiritual leader of Hamas, Sheikh Ahmad Yassin, under house arrest. Meanwhile, an Israeli missile strike on Arafat's official residence in Gaza destroyed two of his helicopters, while in Ramallah Israeli tanks advanced to the edge of the presidential compound, where Arafat was then residing. The Israeli Prime Minister increasingly began to draw parallels between Israel's efforts to suppress the *intifada* and the USA's 'war on terror', describing the PA as a 'terror-supporting entity'. In mid-December Israel responded to an assault on a settlers' bus in the West Bank (in which some 10 Israelis died) by declaring the PA leader to be 'irrelevant', owing to his failure to prevent such attacks, and announced that it was severing all contacts with Arafat. The Israeli military launched air-raids across the West Bank and Gaza, reoccupied large areas of Ramallah and reinforced its military blockade of Arafat's headquarters; several Palestinian police officers and civilians were killed during the Israeli operations. Meanwhile, the USA again vetoed a proposed UN resolution calling for international observers to be deployed in the Palestinian areas. In a televised speech Arafat issued a strong condemnation of groups that carried out gun attacks and suicide bombings against Israelis, although Sharon insisted that Arafat would not be permitted to leave Ramallah until the PA arrested the perpetrators of Ze'evi's murder.

In January 2002 Arafat ordered an investigation into Israeli and US claims that the PA was complicit in a massive shipment of largely Iranian-produced weaponry—including *Katyusha* rockets, mortar shells and anti-tank missiles—which Israeli forces had intercepted in the Red Sea; the freighter, the *Karine A*, was apparently en route for the Gaza Strip to be used in attacks against Israeli targets. (In February Arafat finally accepted responsibility on behalf of his administration for the shipment.) Following a gun attack by members of another militant group, the Al-Aqsa Martyrs Brigades, that killed six guests at a bar mitzvah ceremony in Hadera, northern Israel, Sharon ordered tanks and armoured vehicles to tighten their blockade of Arafat's Ramallah headquarters (the President had effectively been under house arrest for several weeks), and also reoccupied Tulkarm in order to arrest known Palestinian 'terrorists'. Although the troops withdrew a day later, it was reported to be the largest military incursion since the start of the al-Aqsa *intifada*. Meanwhile, EU officials increasingly distanced themselves from the US position towards the conflict, reaffirming their support for Arafat as a crucial partner in the peace process. The EU also issued a formal complaint to Israel, listing EU-funded projects in the West Bank and Gaza that had undergone physical damage during recent military operations.

In early February 2002 Israel carried out the 'targeted killing' of at least four members of the radical Democratic Front for the Liberation of Palestine (DFLP) in the Gaza Strip. The violence came at a time of renewed efforts to restart peace negotiations. Ariel Sharon met leading PA representatives, while Shimon Peres held a series of discussions with the PLC Speaker, Ahmad Quray (also known as Abu Ala). However, Israeli officials were angered when a large number of Palestinian militants were freed during Israeli air-strikes on the PA's security headquarters in Nablus. Requests for calm by the UN and attempts by the EU to launch a new peace initiative in the second week of February—reportedly based on the convening of new elections to the PLC—failed to prevent an escalation of violence in the territories, particularly in Gaza. As Hamas appeared to be intensifying its attacks on Israelis by firing a new type of missile, the *Qassam-2*, against Jewish settlers, four Palestinian security officers died during incursions by the Israeli army into three Gazan towns. Israel also accelerated its military offensive in Hebron and Ramallah. In late February up to 30 Palestinians were reportedly killed in Israeli military operations across the West Bank and Gaza in retaliation for the shooting of six Israelis at an army checkpoint near Ramallah. The Israeli Cabinet subsequently agreed to withdraw its tanks from Arafat's compound in Ramallah, but refused to allow the Palestinian leader freedom of movement beyond the town: Sharon stated that the travel ban would remain in place despite the arrest by Palestinian security forces of three militants believed to have been responsible for Ze'evi's murder. The Israeli position led PA security officials to suspend recently resumed bilateral talks.

Gun battles raged across the West Bank, despite efforts by Crown Prince Abdullah of Saudi Arabia to promote his proposals for peace in the Middle East prior to a summit meeting of the Arab League Council, due to be held in Beirut, Lebanon, in March 2002. Abdullah's proposals centred on Arab recognition of the State of Israel and the normalization of diplomatic relations, in exchange for agreement by Israel to withdraw from all Arab land occupied since 1967 and on the establishment of a Palestinian state with East Jerusalem as its capital. Arafat announced that he would not attend the Beirut conference owing to threats by Sharon to prevent his return to the West Bank and Gaza. Meanwhile, in response to a suicide bombing by a Palestinian woman at an Israeli army checkpoint, Israel for the first time sent ground troops into two refugee camps in the West Bank which it claimed were centres of Islamist militancy: the Balata camp near Nablus and the camp at Jenin. Fierce fighting ensued, and the PA announced subsequently that it was suspending all contacts with the Israeli Government. The USA, meanwhile, urged Israel to show restraint, while UN and EU officials demanded an immediate Israeli withdrawal from the camps.

PA officials categorically rejected an offer made by Ariel Sharon in early March 2002 that Yasser Arafat should agree to go into voluntary exile. At the same time Israel refused to allow senior UN and EU diplomats to visit Arafat. A number of Palestinians were killed as Israeli forces entered Ramallah, Bethlehem and Tulkarm in an attempt to find those responsible for two attacks apparently perpetrated by the Al-Aqsa Martyrs Brigades, in which 20 Israelis had died. The US Secretary of State, Gen. Colin Powell, publicly criticized Sharon's declared aim of forcing the PA to return to peace talks by defeating them militarily. On 8 March five Jewish settler students were killed by Hamas gunmen in Gaza; an estimated 40 Palestinians died during the fierce fighting that ensued. Meanwhile, Sharon declared that Arafat had met the conditions required for his release after a fifth suspect in Ze'evi's murder was arrested by Palestinian security forces in the first week of March. However, after a suicide bombing in Jerusalem, killing 11 Israelis, and a shooting in Netanya in which two died, Israel's 'inner' Security Cabinet voted to intensify its military offensive. Tanks entered Qalqilya and the Jabalia refugee camp in Gaza (where 18 Palestinians, including four Hamas members, were reported to have been killed), while Arafat's headquarters in Gaza were destroyed by Israeli helicopters and gunboats.

On 11 March 2002 Israel announced that it was lifting its travel ban on Arafat, although the Palestinian leader would still not be permitted to travel abroad. The following day some 20,000 Israeli troops began a massive ground offensive in the Palestinian territories as part of a campaign to dismantle the 'infrastructure of terror'; hundreds of Palestinian men were detained for questioning, and several civilians died during the incursions. This was reported to be the largest Israeli operation against Palestinian militants since the 1982 invasion of Lebanon. Israeli forces again took control of most of Ramallah, with tanks coming to within a short distance of Arafat's presidential compound. On 12 March 2002 the UN Security Council adopted Resolution 1397, affirming its 'vision' of both Israeli and Palestinian states 'within secure and recognized borders'; the US-drafted resolution also demanded an immediate end to 'all acts of violence' by both sides, and called upon Israel and the Palestinians to co-operate in implementation of the Mitchell Report and George Tenet's recommendations. US special envoy to the Middle East Anthony Zinni returned to the region on the following day. Under pressure to withdraw as a 'goodwill' gesture to Zinni, the Israeli army later withdrew from Ramallah, Tulkarm and Qalqilya, although they continued to surround the towns. Following discussions between Zinni and Arafat, and US-brokered talks between Israeli and PA security officials in Jerusalem, Israel also agreed to redeploy its troops from Bethlehem and Beit Jala. After the security talks ended without agreement on 21 March, the Israeli Government again ordered troops into much of the West Bank and detained several alleged militants. A further suicide attack by the Al-Aqsa Martyrs Brigades, which killed three Israelis in central Jerusalem, prompted the USA to add the group to its list of proscribed terrorist organizations.

The Arab League summit proceeded in Beirut on 27–28 March 2002, in the notable absence of both President Hosni Mubarak of Egypt and King Abdullah of Jordan (the two leaders had apparently boycotted the meeting as a gesture of support for the PA President). Palestinian officials were angered when the Lebanese hosts refused to permit Arafat to address the session via a live satellite link from Ramallah: the Lebanese authorities had stated that they feared an Israeli disruption of such a broadcast. At the close of the conference the participating Arab states unanimously endorsed the Saudi peace initiative, which also included a clause calling for a 'just solution' to the question of Palestinian refugees. Israel rejected the plan, however, stating that its terms would lead to the destruction of the Jewish state.

The Israeli–Palestinian crisis deepened at the end of March 2002, following an attack by a Hamas suicide bomber at a hotel in the Israeli town of Netanya, where Jews were celebrating the festival of Passover; 30 people died as a result of the attack and some 140 were injured. Although Arafat personally condemned the bombing, and reportedly ordered the immediate arrest of four prominent West Bank militants, Sharon blamed the PA for its failure to prevent such attacks. In response to what was swiftly called the 'Passover massacre', Israel mobilized about 20,000 army reservists and convened an emergency cabinet meeting, at which 'extensive operational activity against Palestinian terrorism' was agreed. With Arafat effectively isolated at his compound in Ramallah, on 29 March Israeli armed forces began a huge campaign of incursions into West Bank towns—code-named 'Operation Defensive Shield'—with the declared aim of dismantling the Palestinian 'terrorist infrastructure' in order to prevent future suicide bombings against Israeli citizens. During the offensive Israeli forces entered and conducted house-to-house searches for militants in Ramallah, Bethlehem, Beit Jala, Qalqilya, Tulkarm, Jenin and Nablus. On 30 March the UN Security Council met in emergency session and demanded, in Resolution 1402, an immediate Israeli withdrawal from all towns that had been transferred to the PA under the Oslo accords. At the end of the month a Hamas suicide bomber from Jenin killed 15 Israelis at a café in Haifa. Sharon declared that Israel was 'at war', and his 'inner' Security Cabinet gave the army permission to broaden its offensive in the West Bank. Israeli armed forces reoccupied Ramallah and declared it to be a 'closed military area'; many Palestinians were reported to have been killed as a result of the invasion.

In early April 2002 Yasser Arafat again dismissed a suggestion by Sharon that the Palestinian leader should go into exile. On 2 April fighting between Israelis and Palestinians in Bethlehem escalated into a siege at the Church of the Nativity—believed to mark the site of Christ's birth. As many as 200 people—Palestinian civilians and priests as well as some 30 armed militants wanted by Israel—sought shelter from Israeli troops inside the church. On 3 April Israeli tanks entered Jenin and its refugee camp. By the following day Israel had effectively reoccupied all but two major towns (Jericho and Hebron) in the West Bank and detained more than 1,000 Palestinians; Bethlehem, like Ramallah, was declared a 'closed military area'. Israel prevented an EU delegation from holding discussions with Arafat, and George W. Bush demanded that Israel withdraw its forces immediately from Palestinian towns and implement the Tenet and Mitchell recommendations for a cease-fire. On 4 April Israeli troops reportedly withdrew from Nablus but entered Hebron. Israel also intensified its offensive in the Jenin refugee camp, the alleged base of several of the suicide bombers. According to PA reports, more than 80 Palestinians died during the first week of Israeli military operations in Jenin. The UN Security Council unanimously adopted a resolution (No. 1403) that demanded the implementation of Resolution 1402 (i.e. an Israeli withdrawal from Palestinian territories) 'without delay'. On 9 April 13 Israeli army reservists were killed in ambushes in the Jenin camp, and the following day, in response to the deaths of at least eight people in the Hamas suicide bombing of a bus near Haifa, Israel ruled out the prospect of further withdrawals from the West Bank.

During mid-April 2002 Palestinians made increasingly vocal allegations of an Israeli 'massacre' at the Jenin refugee camp—where many buildings had been destroyed by tanks and bulldozers—and claimed that Israeli armed forces were guilty of war crimes. Palestinian sources suggested that at least 100 Palestinians had died during the Israeli invasion; 23 Israelis were believed to have died. (In May the US-based Human Rights Watch issued a report stating that Israeli forces had been guilty of 'excessive force' and of war crimes in Jenin, but that there had been no massacre, findings echoed by a UN report released in August.) Meanwhile, although Israel's forces began to withdraw from some Palestinian-administered towns, a number of Palestinians were killed as Israeli tanks entered the Gazan town of Rafah. Also in mid-April Marwan Barghouthi, the Fatah leader in the West Bank (whom Israel also claimed was the commander of the Al-Aqsa Martyrs Brigades), was arrested by Israeli forces in Ramallah; his trial, on charges of leading Palestinian 'terrorist' groups in the West Bank and of orchestrating a number of suicide bombings against Israeli citizens, began in August. (Barghouthi claimed that the Israeli judiciary had no jurisdiction over him, as an elected member of the PLC.) Meanwhile, Sharon announced on 21 April 2002 that the first stage of Operation Defensive Shield had been completed; however, Israeli forces were to remain in Ramallah and Bethlehem. Some reports stated that more than 4,000 Palestinians were detained during the offensive, although many were subsequently released. According to the Palestine Red Crescent Society (PRCS), by the end of April at least 1,500 Palestinians had been killed, and more than 19,000 injured, since the start of the al-Aqsa *intifada* in September 2000. According to Israeli sources, more than 470 Israelis had been killed, and many more wounded, as a result of the violence.

Yasser Arafat was freed by the Israeli authorities on 1 May 2002. His release came after the USA secured an arrangement whereby Israel agreed to end its siege of Ramallah, including Arafat's headquarters, on condition that the PA leader handed over six prisoners sheltering in the presidential compound who were wanted by Israel in connection with 'terrorist' activities. In late April four of the prisoners were convicted of direct involvement in the assassination of Rechavam Ze'evi by an ad hoc Palestinian court inside the compound and variously sentenced to between one and 18 years' imprisonment. The other two detainees were the PFLP leader, Ahmad Saadat, and a militant implicated in the *Karine A* affair. In early May the six prisoners were moved from Ramallah to a gaol in Jericho, where they were to remain in 'international custody' under US and British guard. Despite Arafat's release, US President Bush declared that he was not yet willing to meet the Palestinian leader. Following protracted negotiations, the siege at the Church of the Nativity in Bethlehem finally came to an end, after more than five weeks, on 10 May, when 13 remaining militants were transferred under international guard to Cyprus pending their dispersal to permanent exile elsewhere in Europe. The agreement ending the siege envisaged that 26 other militants who were removed to the Gaza Strip should be tried by a Palestinian court there. It was reported in mid-June that Israel had begun construction of an electrified (later, partially concrete) 'security fence', which would eventually extend along the length of its border with the West Bank, in an attempt to prevent further suicide bombings. In response to a series of fatal suicide attacks against Israeli citizens by Palestinian militants in late June, Israel again ordered its armed forces into several towns in the West Bank and Gaza.

The Israeli Cabinet responded to the latest suicide bombing in Tel-Aviv in September 2002 by announcing that it would seek to 'isolate' Yasser Arafat. Sharon declared that Arafat had failed to arrest militant Islamists known to advocate violence against Israeli citizens, and Israeli forces began the systematic destruction of Arafat's compound in Ramallah while the Palestinian leader reportedly remained inside one of the office buildings. At the same time Israeli armed forces launched a series of incursions into the Gaza Strip, which increasingly became the focus of Israeli military operations. At the end of September the Israeli siege of Arafat's headquarters was brought to an end, after the UN Security Council had issued a resolution (No. 1435), demanding the immediate cessation of Israeli military actions in and around Ramallah.

The stalled peace process was temporarily revived by the publication of the 'roadmap' peace plan (sponsored by the Quartet group, comprising the USA, Russia, the UN and the EU) on 30 April 2003. The release of the roadmap, which had originally been agreed in December 2002, was conditional on the announcement of a new Palestinian Cabinet under Prime Minister Mahmud Abbas (see below). However, it also affirmed George W. Bush's pledge to focus attention on Israeli-Palestinian affairs following the successful US-led coalition's campaign during March–April 2003 to overthrow the regime of Saddam Hussain in Iraq. The roadmap envisaged an end to Israeli–Palestinian conflict and the establishment of a sovereign Palestinian state by 2005–06 (for further details, see the chapter on Israel). Broadly speaking, Palestinian responsibilities under the terms of the roadmap were restricted to a commitment to ending militant actions against Israeli targets and the establishment of a civilian and government infrastructure; otherwise, crucial issues concerning the Palestinian population, such as the borders of a future state, the status of refugees and Jerusalem, were to be decided during Israel's negotiations with Lebanon, Syria and other Arab states. Initially, Sharon objected to the issue of the right to return of Palestinian refugees and refused to consider the dismantling of Jewish settlements, but on 25 May 2003 the Israeli Cabinet accepted the terms of the roadmap. At the end of the month Sharon made the unprecedented acknowledgement that Israel was indeed in occupation of the Palestinian areas. In early June Sharon, Abbas and President Bush met in Aqaba, Jordan, to discuss the implementation of the roadmap, particularly the contentious issue of Jewish settlements.

Israeli troops had begun dismantling settlements in the West Bank in early June 2003, but this positive development in the peace process was overshadowed by a resumption of violence: on 10 June Israel attempted to kill the prominent Hamas leader, Abd al-Aziz ar-Rantisi, leading to a retaliatory suicide attack against a bus in Jerusalem, in which 16 people died. Subsequently, Israeli helicopter gunships attacked targets in Gaza. Twenty-six people were killed in the renewed fighting, and the USA condemned the attempted Israeli assassination of ar-Rantisi. Nevertheless, Israel continued to dismantle some Jewish settlements, to withdraw troops from certain areas of the West Bank and Gaza, and to release Palestinian prisoners. This latter development was not a condition of the roadmap, but was viewed as a 'goodwill' gesture to Mahmud Abbas, who was now apparently engaged in a power struggle with Yasser Arafat (see below). Some 400 prisoners were released in August, but excluded those members of Hamas and Islamic Jihad who had been involved in planning or executing attacks against Israeli targets. Along with Fatah, these two militant groups had declared a three-month cease-fire at the end of June. Following the cease-fire declaration, Israeli troops withdrew from key parts of northern and central Gaza and removed roadblocks from the arterial north–south highway. In July Bethlehem was handed over to Palestinian control. The successful implementation of the roadmap was threatened, however, by Israel's ongoing construction of a 'security fence' in the West Bank.

Construction of Israel's 'security fence' in the West Bank had begun in mid-2002. Ostensibly intended to act as a barrier against Palestinian militants who infiltrated Israel to carry out attacks, by mid-2003 Israel was being accused of seeking to annex Palestinian territory. However, construction of the barrier continued despite international criticism, and Israel also maintained its policy of targeting and killing Palestinian militant leaders. A senior commander of Islamic Jihad in Hebron was killed by Israeli forces on 14 August; on 19 August a suicide bomber killed 20 Israelis on a bus in Jerusalem, an attack for which both Hamas and Islamic Jihad claimed responsibility; and Israel raided militant targets in both the West Bank and Gaza Strip. The resumption of hostilities between Israel and the Palestinian militant groups effectively marked the end of the cease-fire declared in June. A prominent member of Hamas, Ismael Abu Shanab, was killed in an Israeli missile attack on 21 August; the following day Israel reimposed roadblocks on the main north–south highway in the Gaza Strip, a reversal of one of the first initiatives under the terms of the roadmap.

In September 2003 it was reported that the Israeli Cabinet had agreed in principle to the removal of Yasser Arafat as 'a total obstacle to peace'. It was not made clear whether Israel sought to eliminate Arafat or to send him into exile, and although the US Administration declared that it was opposed to either outcome, the USA vetoed a UN Security Council resolution on 16 September condemning Israel's new policy, on the grounds that the resolution did not condemn the actions of Palestinian militant groups. At the end of October Sharon denied that Israel had any intention of 'removing' Yasser Arafat from power. Earlier in the month the Israeli Cabinet had approved the next phase of the 'security fence', and although the new sections were not contiguous to those already built, they would completely enclose Jewish settlements in the West Bank.

Senior Palestinian and Israeli political figures launched a new peace plan in Geneva, Switzerland, in early December 2003. Yasser Abd ar-Rabbuh, the former Palestinian Minister of Information, and Yossi Beilin, Israel's former Minister of Justice, were the most prominent supporters of the so-called 'Geneva Accords', which did not have the official approval of either the Israeli or Palestinian administrations. The Geneva Accords outlined a two-state solution to the Israeli–Palestinian issue, including proposals that: Palestinians would receive compensation for giving up the right of return; most settlements in the West Bank and Gaza (except those neighbouring Jerusalem) would be dismantled; and Jerusalem (to become the capital of two states) would be divided administratively rather than physically.

On 19 December 2003 Israel declared that, unless the PA started disarming and disbanding Palestinian militant groups, it was prepared to initiate a 'disengagement plan', consisting of the accelerated construction of the 'security fence' in the West Bank and the physical separation of Israel from the Palestinian territories. In February 2004 Ariel Sharon announced in an interview published in *Ha'aretz* that a plan had been drawn up for the evacuation of all Jewish settlements in the Gaza Strip: this would reportedly affect 7,500 settlers in 17 settlements (although details of the plan were subsequently amended—see below). This news was welcomed by the recently appointed Palestinian Prime Minister, Ahmad Quray. On 14 March 10 Israelis were killed in a double suicide bombing at the southern Israeli port of Ashdod, an attack for which both Hamas and the Al-Aqsa Martyrs Brigades claimed responsibility. In retaliation for the attack Ariel Sharon and his inner 'Security Cabinet' ordered Israel's most high profile 'targeted killing'. On 22 March Israeli helicopter gunships in the Gaza Strip attacked the founder and spiritual leader of Hamas, Sheikh Ahmad Yassin, and his entourage as they left a mosque, killing the cleric and several others. Yassin's assassination prompted international condemnation, especially from Iran and from Arab countries, where mass protests took place. However, a UN Security Council resolution condemning the killing was vetoed by the USA, which criticized the absence of any reference to Hamas as a 'terrorist organization'. Immediately after Yassin's assassination, Abd al-Aziz ar-Rantisi was appointed to the leadership of Hamas in Gaza; however, ar-Rantisi himself was killed in a targeted airstrike by Israeli forces in Gaza City on 17 April. EU leaders condemned both of the 'targeted killings' as illegal and unjustified. Hamas did not disclose the identity of ar-Rantisi's successor and reportedly adopted a policy of 'collective leadership' in order to prevent future leaders of the organization from being victims of Israel's strategy. Khalid Meshaal apparently remained the head of the group's political bureau, based in Damascus, Syria. Meanwhile, details of Sharon's 'disengagement plan' were published in Israeli newspapers: it combined a complete Israeli withdrawal from the Gaza Strip, and evacuation of all Jewish settlements there, with the consolidation of six settlement blocs in the West Bank. In May the US Secretary of State, Gen. Colin Powell, urged Quray to consider an Israeli withdrawal from the Gaza Strip as a sign of progress towards Palestinian self-sufficiency, while expressing US opposition to the demolition of Palestinian houses there. In October the Israeli Knesset voted in favour of Sharon's proposal to dismantle all 21 settlements in Gaza, and four in the northern West Bank, entailing the eviction of about 9,000 Jewish settlers. The removal of settlements in Gaza was scheduled to commence in July 2005, but was later postponed until August (see below).

In May 2004 imprisoned Fatah leader Marwan Barghouthi was convicted by a Tel-Aviv court on five counts of murder and of leading a 'terrorist organization' which had launched Palestinian militant assaults on Israeli forces and settlers, although lack of evidence forced the court to acquit Barghouthi on 33 counts of resistance attacks. The court's verdict provoked strong criticism from the PA, which called the conviction 'illegal, immoral and unjust'. In early June Barghouthi was sentenced to five terms of life imprisonment and two additional 20-year terms.

Following a ruling by the Israeli Supreme Court, in June 2004 Israel altered the route of part of the 'security fence', including a 30-km section in a Palestinian village, Beit Sourik. In early July the International Court of Justice (ICJ) in the Hague, Netherlands, issued a non-binding ruling that the barrier breached international law and effectively constituted the annexation of Palestinian land. The ICJ urged Israel to remove sections of the fence and to pay compensation to affected Palestinians. Sharon rejected the court's recommendations, while the Palestinian leadership hoped that the decision would mobilize public opinion. In late July the UN General Assembly voted to demand that Israel comply with the ICJ ruling and take down the barrier (the USA voted against the resolution). Meanwhile, in August Sharon approved the construction of 1,000 new Jewish settlements in the West Bank.

In September 2004, following a double suicide bombing by Hamas in Beersheba, Israel, that killed 16 people, Israeli tanks and aircraft attacked a Hamas training camp in the centre of the Gaza Strip. In October the UN reported that 135 Palestinians had been killed and an estimated 95 homes destroyed following a 16-day Israeli military assault in northern and southern Gaza, prompted by a Hamas rocket that killed two children in Sderot, close to the border with Gaza. Following the death of Yasser Arafat in November (see below), Sharon expressed hope that the new Palestinian leadership would understand the need to end 'terrorist' attacks before relations between the two sides could be improved and outstanding issues resolved, and international leaders similarly looked forward to positive change, with US President Bush, urged by British Prime Minister Tony Blair, promising to redouble US efforts to assist in the creation of a Palestinian state, which he considered to be possible within four years.

Israel and Egypt agreed in early December 2004 that 750 Egyptian troops would be deployed along the country's border with Gaza in advance of Israel's planned withdrawal; however, Jewish settlers in Gaza vowed to resist eviction. In mid-December Mahmud Abbas issued a call (rejected by Hamas) for an end to the continuing use of violence in resistance to Israeli occupation, while in early January 2005, during the week of the Palestinian presidential election (see below), having earlier criticized Israeli offensives in Gaza as a ploy to disrupt the poll, he demanded that Israel release all Palestinian prisoners before they reached a political agreement. Abbas later strengthened his criticism of Israel, calling it 'the Zionist enemy' when Israeli armed forces responded to Palestinian mortar attacks by firing two shells into a field in Beit Lahiya, killing seven Palestinians. However, Abbas continued to express hopes of implementing the roadmap and of achieving peace with Israel in the event of his election to the Palestinian presidency. Israel announced that it would withdraw troops from Palestinian areas prior to the election, and that its military would remain outside towns in the West Bank and Gaza Strip for 72 hours. Towards the end of December Israel released 159 Palestinian prisoners as a gesture of 'goodwill' prior to the Palestinian election.

In mid-January 2005 the deaths of six Israelis in a Palestinian militant attack at the Karni crossing prompted Sharon to sever ties with the Palestinian leadership and to order the Israeli army to raid several areas of Gaza. Following a demand by the PLO leadership that Palestinians should cease all military action against Israel, Sharon called off the offensive and announced that Israel would co-operate on security issues, although he instructed his troops to prepare for a full-scale assault on an area in the northern Gaza Strip from where rockets were being fired on Israeli targets, and in late January Palestinian security forces were deployed in the area to prevent such attacks. Despite talks being held between Hamas, Islamic Jihad and other militant groups chaired by newly elected PA President Abbas, Hamas continued to insist on its right to retaliate against Israeli attacks and demanded that Israel released more than 7,000 Palestinian prisoners and end its policy of targeting militants before it would enter into negotiations.

Security talks between Palestinian and Israeli officials began in late January 2005, and, despite attacks on Palestinian police vehicles by Jewish settlers, an agreement was reached on the deployment of Palestinian security forces in the southern Gaza Strip within 24 hours to reduce attacks on Israeli targets. (By this time 2,500 Palestinian security forces were patrolling northern Gaza, on the orders of the new Palestinian President.) However, Hamas and Islamic Jihad dismissed an announcement by Israelis that 'targeted killings' of militants in areas where Palestinian security forces were successfully operating would stop. Later in the month the former Palestinian Minister of Security, Muhammad Dahlan, and the Israeli Minister of Defence, Lt-Gen. Shaul Mofaz, agreed to the withdrawal of Israeli troops and the deployment of PA security forces in the five West Bank towns of Ramallah, Qalqilya, Tulkarm, Jericho and Bethlehem.

Abbas and Sharon finally met in early February 2005 at a summit meeting held in Sharm esh-Sheikh, with Egypt's President Mubarak and King Abdullah of Jordan also in attendance. At the summit Abbas announced a Palestinian cease-fire and Sharon declared that Israeli military operations would end if Palestinian militant attacks stopped, emphasizing that Israel would not compromise in its fight against 'terrorism'; Sharon also agreed to release 500 Palestinian prisoners as a 'goodwill' gesture. However, although some Palestinian militant groups signed up to the cease-fire, Hamas asserted that it would not be bound by it, criticizing the fact that it had been negotiated unilaterally, and demanded that Israel cease all acts of aggression against Palestinians and release all Palestinian prisoners before agreeing to a formal cease-fire, although they apparently agreed to an informal 'truce'. Soon after the Sharm esh-Sheikh meeting, Israel permitted 56 deported Palestinians to return to the West Bank, and also transferred the bodies of 15 Palestinian bombers to the PA. The relative lull in violence was interrupted in late February by a suicide bomb attack by Islamic Jihad outside a nightclub in Tel-Aviv that killed four Israelis, halting Israeli plans to withdraw from the five West Bank towns. The Israeli army entered a West Bank village and arrested Palestinians suspected of involvement in the attack.

In early March 2005, at an international conference in support of the PA hosted by British Prime Minister Tony Blair in London, Abbas expressed his commitment to reforms and to a crackdown on militants, advocating renewed efforts to realize the objectives of the roadmap. Shortly afterwards it was reported that Palestinian militant groups had declared their readiness to cease attacks against Israelis, although this was denied by Hamas. In mid-March Israel officially surrendered Jericho to Palestinian security control, and also announced plans to remove all 24 outposts constructed since Sharon was elected to the premiership in February 2001, after a ministerial report condemned the illegal use of budget funds to develop the outposts. Although this development fulfilled a condition of the roadmap, it was criticized for the fact that not all of the 105 outposts, which were deemed by many to be illegal, would be dismantled. In late March 2005 Israeli forces withdrew from the West Bank town of Tulkarm.

Meanwhile, in late February 2005 Israel announced plans to alter the route of the 'security fence' so that it would cut out 7% of the territory of the West Bank instead of the 16% outlined in the original route. In mid-March the Israeli Government announced that the barrier (to be completed by the end of 2005) would divide the town of Bethlehem and also separate East Jerusalem and the settlement of Ma'aleh Edomin from the rest of the West Bank; the decision provoked protests by Palestinians, who demanded that the ICJ's recommendations be implemented and expressed concern at the unilateralism of the move and the negative impact that this could have on future peace talks with Israel.

Abbas travelled to Washington, DC, in May 2005 for his first meeting with President Bush since becoming President of the PA. Bush reportedly offered US $50m. in direct aid to the PA to develop the Gaza Strip after the Israeli withdrawal. The US President also urged Israel to dismantle illegal settlement outposts in the West Bank, to end the expansion of settlements and to ensure that Israel's 'security fence' did not become a 'political border'. Abbas later advocated the start of 'final status' negotiations with Israel after its disengagement from the Gaza Strip. Meanwhile, in accordance with the agreement reached by Abbas and Sharon in February at Sharm esh-Sheikh, the Israeli Government approved the release of 400 Palestinian prisoners. (A total of 398 prisoners were released in early June—two had chosen to remain in gaol.) Israel had released 500 prisoners shortly after the February summit meeting, but had delayed further releases, urging the PA to curb terrorism more effectively.

Following a series of Palestinian militant attacks on Israeli and Jewish targets (which the militants justified as retaliation for Israeli violations of the cease-fire), in late June 2005 Israel carried out raids across the West Bank and detained around 50 members of Islamic Jihad. The Israeli Minister of Defence, Lt-Gen. Shaul Mofaz, asserted that the PA's incompetence had prompted Israel to carry out the raids. Israel apparently readopted its policy of 'targeted assassinations' of militants, when it launched a missile strike on Gaza in a failed attempt to kill an Islamic Jihad activist. Palestinian Minister of the Interior and National Security Maj.-Gen. Nasser Yousuf declared a state of emergency in the Gaza Strip, and gave his forces permission to prevent militants from launching rocket and mortar attacks on targets in Israel. As clashes broke out between members of the Palestinian security services and Hamas militants, Israel carried out further air attacks on Hamas targets, killing seven fighters. Islamic Jihad claimed responsibility for a suicide bomb attack near a shopping mall in Netanya in mid-July that killed four Israelis. Israeli troops re-entered Tulkarm (military control and responsibility for security of which Israel had surrendered to the PA in March—see above), after it was reported that the suicide bomber had come from a nearby village. Meanwhile, Hamas launched a series of rocket attacks from Gaza, killing an Israeli woman and prompting Israel to carry out air-strikes on targets in Gaza used by the militant group. Abbas and Sharon held their second summit meeting since Abbas's election to the presidency in Jerusalem in late July, when Sharon again urged Abbas to rein in militants and suppress terrorism.

Although Israel's withdrawal from the Gaza Strip was accompanied by relatively little violence (see the chapter on Israel), in late August 2005 Israeli troops raided a refugee camp near Tulkarm, killing five Palestinians. Israel asserted that the five were suspected of involvement in two suicide bombings and had resisted arrest. In response, the Popular Resistance Committees claimed responsibility for firing a rocket that landed near Sderot. Israel completed its withdrawal from the Gaza Strip (according to the terms of its unilateral Disengagement Plan) ahead of schedule on 12 September, when the last Israeli forces left Gaza. Thousands of Palestinians entered the evacuated settlements and started to damage buildings and demolish synagogues. Although in July Israeli and Palestinian officials had reportedly agreed in principle to establish a 'safe passage' between the West Bank and Gaza Strip following the withdrawal, the status of Gaza's southern crossing into Egypt at Rafah was still disputed. Soon after it had completed the disengagement, Israel declared that the crossing would be closed for six months. Meanwhile, in late August Israel had approved the deployment of 750 Egyptian troops along Egypt's border with the Gaza Strip, having accepted Egypt's offer to deploy the troops in December 2004 (see above). In mid-November 2005, following intervention by US Secretary of State Condoleezza Rice, Israel reached an agreement with Palestinian officials to reopen the Rafah crossing later that month. The PA, assisted by European observers, was to manage the crossing, which Israeli, Palestinian and EU observers were to monitor remotely from a control centre via live television cameras.

In September 2005 21 people were killed when a Palestinian truck carrying rockets exploded during a Hamas parade in the Jabalia refugee camp in the Gaza Strip. Hamas accused Israel of having fired a missile at the truck from a remote-controlled drone aircraft; both Israel and the PA denied the accusation. However, Hamas responded by launching mortars into Sderot. The Israeli Government decided at an emergency meeting to permit the army to use any means necessary to suppress militants. Accordingly, the Israeli army stationed tanks and artillery batteries on Gaza's eastern and northern borders, began seizing Hamas and Islamic Jihad activists in the West Bank and readopted its policy of 'targeted killings', using air-strikes to kill militants in Gaza and to destroy a weapons store and weapons-production facilities, despite a pledge from Hamas to end attacks and return to

PALESTINIAN AUTONOMOUS AREAS

the cease-fire. In October Israeli security forces also killed two senior Islamic Jihad militants in Tulkarm and arrested five other members of the Tulkarm cell, which it believed to be responsible for the suicide attacks in Tel-Aviv in February and in Netanya in July. Islamic Jihad avenged the 'targeted killings' by launching a suicide bomb attack on a market in Hadera, resulting in the deaths of five Israelis. Israeli Prime Minister Ariel Sharon declared a 'broad and continuous' offensive against militant Islamist groups, and hours later the Israeli army launched an air-strike on a car carrying two senior Islamic Jihad militants in Gaza: eight Palestinians, mostly civilians, died. In December Islamic Jihad launched a further suicide attack on the shopping mall in Netanya that it had targeted in July, killing another five Israelis. Israel responded by arresting Palestinians thought to be associated with the bomber, and carrying out air-strikes to target further militants.

Israel reacted to Hamas's victory in the legislative elections held in January 2006 (see below) by declaring that it would not negotiate with a Palestinian authority that included 'an armed terrorist organization' which advocated Israel's destruction. US President Bush announced that his country would also refuse to deal with Hamas until it renounced its call to destroy Israel, and stated that the USA would consider halting aid to the Palestinians. At the end of the month the Quartet group announced that financial assistance to a future Palestinian administration would depend on the extent to which Hamas fulfilled the following conditions: that it renounce violence, respect agreements approved under the Fatah regime and recognize Israel's right to exist. Egypt and Jordan also demanded that the militant organization reject violence and accept Israel's existence. The head of Hamas's political bureau, Khalid Meshaal, announced that his organization could enter into a long-term truce with Israel, under certain conditions, including the return of Israel to its pre-1967 borders. However, Meshaal asserted that violent resistance of the occupation was legal.

Israel announced in mid-February 2006 that, in order to punish the new Palestinian regime until it renounced violence and recognized Israel's right to exist, it would stop collecting customs and tax revenues on Palestinians' behalf, and would ask foreign donors to cease all payments to the PA; however, it would permit the transfer of humanitarian aid to Palestinians. President Abbas announced that the PA faced a financial crisis, while Hamas asserted that Arab and Islamic countries would compensate for a reduction in aid from Israel and the West. Later in the month the EU, which—like Israel and the USA—considered Hamas to be a terrorist organization, announced that it was to give the PA US $140m.-worth of aid to save the interim administration from financial collapse. However, following the installation of the new Hamas-led Cabinet on 28 March, both the USA and the EU announced that they were withdrawing direct aid to the PA until Hamas fulfilled the three conditions placed on it by the Quartet group.

Meanwhile, as Israel continued to kill militants in the Palestinian territories following further missile strikes, it declared that, should Hamas resume attacks on Israel, all members of the organization would be deemed to be legitimate targets for assassinations, including Prime Minister-designate Ismail Haniya and future ministers. In March 2006 Israeli forces stormed the gaol in Jericho in which the Secretary-General of the PFLP, Ahmad Saadat, was being held prisoner, detaining him and other inmates suspected of involvement in attacks against Israel. US and British monitors had left the gaol immediately prior to the raid, ostensibly to protest against poor security arrangements there. A Palestinian high court had announced in 2002 that there was no evidence that Saadat had been involved in Rechavam Ze'evi's murder, and both President Abbas and Hamas had recently announced plans to release him, as he had been elected to the PLC at the elections in January 2006. Israel, however, still wished to interrogate Saadat in connection with the murder, and therefore resolved to detain him before the Palestinian authorities released him. The raid, in which two Palestinians were killed, provoked unrest throughout the territories. Palestinians set fire to the British Council building in Jericho in protest at perceived British collusion with the Israeli authorities, and gunmen briefly kidnapped 11 foreign workers. Palestinian factions urged schools and businesses to go on strike, and the PFLP vowed to avenge Saadat's capture, which President Abbas condemned as a crime and a humiliation for Palestinians. In April the Israeli Ministry of Justice announced that a pre-trial inquiry had not produced enough evidence to try Saadat for Ze'evi's murder, but that he would be tried for other security offences.

However, four other militant PFLP members detained with him were charged with the murder, among them the man accused of firing the shot.

Israel's new Government under Prime Minister Ehud Olmert, which was appointed in May 2006, was at this time pursuing plans to establish Israel's permanent borders, if necessary unilaterally, by 2010. Olmert's so-called Convergence Plan entailed the annexation of West Bank settlement blocs to Israel and the transfer of other, majority-Palestinian sections of the West Bank to full PA control. (Israel would retain the whole of Jerusalem under the plans.) The Israeli premier affirmed that Israel was, however, seeking to secure an internationally supported peace plan with Hamas, but that such a solution required the group to reject violence and adhere to peace agreements signed by Israel and the previous Fatah administration. Khalid Meshaal dismissed the Convergence Plan as allowing Israel to: illegally retain its possession of the largest section of the West Bank and its 'security fence'; reject concessions on the status of Jerusalem; and thwart the 'right of return' of Palestinian refugees.

In June 2006 Palestinians claimed that the shelling of a beach in the northern Gaza Strip, in which seven members of one family were killed while they were having a picnic, had been carried out by Israeli forces firing from gunboats. (The Israeli Prime Minister later declared that a technical failure had been to blame for the deaths, and issued an apology to the Palestinian authorities.) On 25 June Hamas militants from Gaza launched a cross-border raid, which resulted in the kidnapping of an Israeli soldier, Corporal Gilad Shalit; two other Israeli soldiers were killed during the raid, as were two of the militants. The following day Palestinian militant groups issued a statement demanding that Israel release all female Palestinian prisoners and prisoners under 18 years of age in exchange for Shalit. Israel responded by launching air-strikes on Gaza and entering the southern part of the Strip. Israel's military actions (code-named 'Operation Summer Rains') to seek to secure the release of Corporal Shalit in the Gaza Strip continued despite the conflict that began between Israel and Hezbollah in July (see the chapters on Israel and Lebanon). Several bridges and official buildings were bombed by the Israeli military, while the territory's only power plant was also destroyed, leaving thousands of Gazans without electricity or water. Palestinian officials denounced Israel for what they considered to be the 'collective punishment' of the Palestinian people. (A senior Hamas representative affirmed in early April 2008 that Shalit was still alive, but reiterated that this would not remain the case unless Israel agreed to release 350 Palestinian prisoners.)

On 29 June 2006 Israeli security forces arrested 64 senior Palestinian officials, including eight Hamas ministers from the Cabinet and 20 other parliamentarians, for questioning in relation to their alleged involvement in attacks against Israeli targets. On the following day an Israeli missile destroyed the offices of the Ministry of the Interior and Civil Affairs in Gaza City. On 2 July an Israeli air-strike destroyed the office of the Palestinian Prime Minister, Hamas's Ismail Haniya. The crisis continued to escalate during July, and many Palestinians died in the ensuing violence: it was estimated that Israeli troops killed more than 160 Palestinians in the period between late June and 23 July. Israel arrested the Speaker of the PLC, Dr Aziz Duweik, on 6 August, while some of the cabinet ministers arrested in June were released during subsequent weeks. Meanwhile, it became apparent that, following Israel's month-long conflict with Hezbollah in Lebanon and the ongoing military campaign in Gaza, Olmert had abandoned his plans for Israel to withdraw unilaterally from parts of the West Bank.

In November 2006 Israeli armed forces began a new military offensive in the town of Beit Hanoun, in northern Gaza. 'Operation Autumn Clouds' was aimed at destroying the infrastructure and weapons supplies used by Palestinian militants across the border in order to prevent the firing of rockets into Israel by the armed groups. It was reported that more than 50 Palestinians, including many civilians, were killed in the operation. A cease-fire between the sides was secured by President Abbas towards the end of the month, however, and Israel withdrew its troops from Gaza. Nevertheless, relations between Israel and the PA deteriorated once again in early 2007, after the truce was broken by militant Palestinian groups, who continued to launch large numbers of rockets against Israeli targets such as the town of Sderot. Two human rights organizations claimed that the number of Palestinians killed by Israeli security forces in the West Bank and Gaza had tripled in 2006. A report issued by the Israeli human rights organization B'Tselem in December put the death toll at 657 people (including 140 minors); of this total, B'Tselem assessed that more than 322 Palestinians were unarmed civilians. In May 2007 Amnesty International also reported that at least 650 Palestinians (including 120 minors) had been killed by Israeli troops in 2006, of whom more than 50% were civilians. The majority of fatalities had occurred in the Gaza Strip, following the intensification of Israeli bombardments of the territory from mid-2006. In mid-April 2007 Abbas and Olmert held discussions concerning a future Palestinian state and a possible prisoner exchange, in what was intended to be the first of a series of regular fortnightly meetings between the two leaders. However, in late April Hamas militants, announcing that they were ending the truce brokered in November 2006, resumed the firing of rockets into Israel from the Gaza Strip. Israel responded in May 2007 by conducting a series of air-strikes against alleged militant targets in Gaza; a number of Hamas legislators, ministers and local government officials were also detained by Israeli security forces.

Following the takeover of the Gaza Strip by militants of Hamas on 14 June 2007 and the subsequent naming of an Emergency Cabinet—consisting principally of independents and techno-crats—by President Abbas in the West Bank on 17 June (see below), on 24 June the Israeli Government agreed to transfer tax revenues to the PA that it had withdrawn following Hamas's election victory of January 2006. On 25 June 2007 a summit meeting was held in Sharm esh-Sheikh between Egypt's President Mubarak, King Abdullah of Jordan, Israeli Prime Minister Ehud Olmert and President Abbas, aimed at expressing solidarity with Abbas's newly appointed Emergency Cabinet in the West Bank. Olmert declared that Israel was to free 250 Palestinian security prisoners as a gesture of 'goodwill' to the Palestinian President; a final total of 255 (mainly Fatah-affiliated) prisoners were duly released on 20 July. In that month Israel also granted an amnesty for some 180 Fatah militants who were sought by the Israeli security forces in the West Bank, provided that the men renounced violence against Israel and handed themselves over to the PA.

Abbas held discussions with Olmert in Jericho on 6 August 2007—the first meeting between Israeli and Palestinian leaders on Palestinian territory since May 2000—in preparation for the US-sponsored Middle East peace meeting scheduled for November. The two leaders held further talks on 'fundamental issues' in late August and early September 2007. On 5 September Israel's Supreme Court issued a ruling that the route of a further section of the 'security fence' along Israel's boundary with the West Bank should be altered in order to improve the living conditions of Palestinians residing at the affected village of Bil'in; the villagers had been conducting regular protests against the Israeli barrier since it had separated their homes from the land they were cultivating. During 26–27 September the Israeli military took firm action against the continued launching by Palestinian militants of *Qassam* rockets against northern Israel by carrying out air raids and sending tanks into the north of the Gaza Strip; at least 12 Palestinians were reported to have died during the military campaign. Nevertheless, Israel released another 57 (mainly Fatah) Palestinian prisoners to the West Bank and 29 to the Gaza Strip on 1 and 2 October, respectively. In mid-October President Abbas for the first time outlined his specific demands with regard to the territory on which a future Palestinian state should be established: Abbas demanded that the state should cover 6,205 sq km (2,400 sq miles) of the West Bank and Gaza Strip—the exact amount of territory occupied by Israel in 1967. Towards the end of October 2007 the Israeli Government responded to the launching of missiles into northern Israel by Gazan militants by confirming a policy of reducing fuel and electricity supplies to Gaza, which it now classified as a 'hostile entity'. (An intervention by the Supreme Court prevented the authorities from phasing out electricity supplies until they could prove that this would not impede vital services such as hospitals and sanitation provision, although the fuel sanctions were permitted.)

An international peace meeting intended officially to relaunch the Middle East peace process was held in Annapolis, Maryland, USA, on 27 November 2007, with members of the Quartet group and the Arab League in attendance. Prior to the meeting the US Secretary of State, Condoleezza Rice, had stated that it must advance the prospect of Palestinians achieving statehood, and had affirmed that reaching a two-state solution between Israelis and Palestinians was one of the priorities of the Bush Administration. At the close of the Annapolis summit US President George W. Bush read a statement of 'joint understanding' between Ehud Olmert and Mahmud Abbas, who expressed their commitment to achieving a final settlement of the outstanding issues of contention between Israelis and Palestinians by the end of 2008. It was announced that: an Israeli-Palestinian steering committee would oversee 'vigorous, ongoing and continuous' negotiations between the two sides; the Israeli and Palestinian leaders would continue to meet on a fortnightly basis; and both Israel and the PA would comply with their obligations as agreed under the terms of the roadmap signed in 2003. However, on 4 December 2007 Palestinians complained that Israel had again contravened its obligations by issuing tenders for 307 new homes to be built at the Jabal Abu Ghunaim settlement in East Jerusalem; Rice warned the Israeli Government that such an expansion could jeopardize the newly restarted peace process. Moreover, Olmert appeared to indicate that Israel would not be required to conclude a peace treaty with the PA by the end of 2008 if it considered that the Palestinians had not met their security obligations; the Israeli leader was reported to have told his Cabinet that there was 'no commitment to a specific timetable' made at Annapolis. A Hamas spokesman reportedly responded to the Annapolis meeting by pledging that Palestinian 'resistance' to Israeli occupation would continue. Nevertheless, the Israeli authorities released a further 429 Palestinian prisoners (408 to the West Bank and 21 to Gaza—none of whom had been involved in attacks against Israelis) on 3 December 2007 as a further 'goodwill' gesture to President Abbas; most of those freed were Fatah members from the West Bank, with no Hamas or Islamic Jihad detainees on the list.

Meanwhile, on 2 December 2007 a court in Jerusalem sentenced a PFLP militant, Hamdi Koran, to a term of life imprisonment (and an additional 100 years in prison), after he was convicted of having assassinated the Israeli Minister of Tourism, Rechavam Ze'evi, in Jerusalem in October 2001 (see above), as well as involvement in other attacks against Israeli citizens. (Koran had been serving a sentence for the crime at a West Bank prison; however, when Western supervisors withdrew from the Jericho gaol and Israeli forces entered it in 2006, he was handed over to the Israeli legal system.)

The first session of the Israeli-Palestinian steering committee established at the Annapolis peace meeting was held on 12 December 2007. However, against the backdrop of increased violence between Israeli forces and Palestinian militants in the Gaza Strip, and following the announcement of Israel's proposed settlement expansion, the talks failed to achieve significant progress. An international donors' conference was held in Paris on 17 December, with 68 states and international instititutions in attendance. At the meeting donors pledged US $7,400m. in financial assistance to the PA; the funds were to ease the budgetary crisis and to assist with proposed development projects. Meanwhile, Israeli air-strikes against alleged militant targets in the Gaza Strip continued during December, with several members of Islamic Jihad believed to have fired rockets into Sderot being targeted. According to B'Tselem at the end of December, 344 Palestinians had been killed as a result of inter-factional violence in 2007—the highest number since the start of the second *intifada* in 2000.

The Palestinian death toll increased rapidly in early January 2008, as Israel intensified its military campaign in Gaza following a Palestinian rocket assault on the town of Ashkelon; Israeli officials explained the high number of casualties by claiming that militants were deliberately firing on Israeli security forces from civilian areas. By mid-January it was estimated that at least 100 Palestinians (mostly militants) had been killed by Israeli forces in Gaza since the Annapolis peace conference in November 2007. Nevertheless, B'Tselem reported at the end of 2007 that there had been a decline in the number of fatalities in the Israeli–Palestinian conflict in that year, compared with 2006: some 373 Palestinians were killed by Israeli troops during 2007, of whom 131 were estimated to be civilians and 53 minors; 290 of the deaths occurred in the Gaza Strip. During a visit to Israel and the West Bank in the second week of January 2008, US President Bush asserted that a future Palestinian state should be contiguous territory and not a 'Swiss cheese' of separate cantons; he also urged Israel to withdraw from Arab territory that its forces had occupied in 1967. Bush reiterated his demand that the PA dismantled the territories' militias.

On 17 January 2008 Israel imposed virtually a complete blockade on the Gaza Strip, which prompted vehement international criticism: the Israeli response to Palestinian violence targeted at its citizens was widely viewed as 'collective punishment' of the people of Gaza for the actions of a minority of militants. The blockade resulted in severe disruption to Gaza's electricity supplies, although Olmert did subsequently agree to allow some essential supplies into the Strip. None the less, on 23 January hundreds of thousands of Palestinians entered Egypt from Gaza in search of food, fuel and medical supplies, after Hamas militants had breached the Rafah crossing separating the two territories. (The crossing had been almost permanently closed since Hamas's takeover of the Strip in June 2007 because the Egyptian Government, as does Israel, refuses to recognize Hamas as the legitimate administration there.) Egyptian officials responded by offering their backing to a plan proposed by President Abbas which would allow for the PA, rather than Hamas, to assume control of the Egypt–Gaza border. Although the breaches in the border were repaired by 3 February 2008, there were reports of exchanges of gunfire between Egyptian security forces and Palestinian gunmen as tensions continued. The UN estimated that 700,000 Gazans (about 50% of the territory's population) had crossed the border into Egypt. On 4 February the Al-Aqsa Martyrs Brigades reportedly claimed responsibility for the first suicide bombing in Israel for more than a year, in the southern town of Dimona (in which an Israeli woman died), although a Hamas representative apparently alleged that militants from its Hebron branch had in fact carried out the attack. The Israeli Government implied that the perpetrator of the bombing, whom it believed to be Gazan, must have entered Israel via Egypt as a direct result of the border having been breached. As Israeli officials threatened a full-scale invasion of the Gaza Strip and also pledged to restart its policy of 'targeted killings' of Hamas and other militants, Olmert declared that he considered the status of Jerusalem to be the final 'core issue' to be negotiated by the two parties—a proposal that was rejected strongly by many Palestinians.

In early March 2008 a militant Palestinian, believed to be a resident of East Jerusalem, entered a Jewish religious college in West Jerusalem and shot dead eight students. As with the Dimona bombing, the issue of whether ultimate responsibility for the shooting could be attributed to Hamas was unclear: a spokesman for the militant group appeared to claim, and later deny, its involvement in the crime. Although the Israeli Government affirmed that it would not break off peace negotiations with the PA, the likelihood of a swift breakthrough in the peace process was again impeded when, shortly after the Jerusalem shooting, Olmert approved a plan to construct a further 330 homes for Jewish settlers in the West Bank. At the end of April 12 Palestinian militant factions (excluding Fatah and Hamas), meeting in Cairo under the auspices of the Egyptian Government, reportedly agreed to new proposals for a cease-fire to be reached with Israel; under the proposals, a cessation of violence was to be implemented gradually, beginning in the Gaza Strip and then being undertaken in the West Bank, provided that Israel also end its economic blockade of Gaza. Talks between Abbas and Olmert, under the terms agreed at Annapolis, had resumed earlier that month. However, with regard to a proposed cease-fire deal between Israel and Hamas, Olmert emphasized during discussions in Jerusalem with the Egyptian intelligence chief, Lt-Gen. Omar Suleiman, that Israel demanded an end to the weapons-smuggling by Palestinian militants into Gaza and the release of its abducted soldier, Corporal Gilad Shalit, in order for any sustainable truce to be realized. A Hamas spokesman subsequently rejected any linkage between Shalit's release and a period of calm, asserting that the organization required the release of 450 Palestinian prisoners in exchange for Shalit.

Following several violent incidents in previous weeks, in mid-June 2008 a formal cease-fire was finally agreed between Israel and Hamas representatives in the Gaza Strip, after lengthy negotiations led by Egyptian mediators. Israel was to end its economic blockade of the Strip and cease military action in the territory, on condition that Hamas militants and those of other Palestinian groups refrained from conducting any cross-border attacks on Israeli targets. The truce was to remain in place for at least six months, but to take effect in stages. Yet towards the end of June Israeli officials complained of a 'grave violation' of the cease-fire by Palestinian militants who had launched a rocket attack against the town of Sderot, and responded by closing Israel's border crossings into Gaza. The rocket attack was alleged to have been carried out by Islamic Jihad in retaliation for an Israeli military raid in the West Bank, which caused two Palestinian deaths. Hamas spokesmen asserted in early July that, since Israel was not abiding by terms of the recent truce, it had suspended bilateral negotiations concerning a proposed prisoner exchange involving the release of Corporal Shalit. In early July three Israelis were killed in Jerusalem by a Palestinian militant.

In late August 2008 the Israeli Government released 198 Palestinian prisoners as a gesture of 'goodwill' to President Abbas. The list included two of the longest-serving Palestinian detainees, who—contrary to Israel's usual policy of not freeing those with 'blood on their hands'—had been responsible for the deaths of two Israeli citizens in the 1970s.

In early November 2008 the first direct clashes between Israeli armed forces and Hamas militants since the cease-fire agreement of mid-June took place in the Gaza Strip. Israel launched a renewed military campaign in the territory and reimposed its blockade, while Hamas and Islamic Jihad fighters responded by firing rockets into northern Israel. Officials from the US Administration conceded at that time that it was no longer possible to achieve an Israeli-Palestinian peace agreement by the end of the year (as envisaged by the November 2007 Annapolis meeting). Nevertheless, at the first meeting held between Abbas and Olmert for two months, Olmert promised to free 250 Palestinian prisoners as a 'confidence-building measure' towards the Palestinian President. After a government committee agreed to the release of only 230 Palestinians, on 15 December a total of 227 prisoners (none of whom were from Hamas or Islamic Jihad) were freed. On 16 December the UN Security Council approved Resolution 1850, which reiterated its endorsement of a two-state solution to the Israeli–Palestinian conflict and affirmed that the peace process was 'irreversible'. The resolution urged all parties involved in the negotiations to intensify their efforts to achieve a comprehensive and lasting peace in the Middle East.

However, on 19 December 2008, following discussions with other Palestinian factions in the Gaza Strip, Hamas formally declared an end to its six-month truce with Israel, asserting that Israel had not adhered to its requirements under the terms of the agreement. Rocket and mortar attacks by Palestinian militants against towns in northern Israel followed, and Israel launched air-strikes against Gaza. On 27 December Olmert ordered a campaign of intensive air-strikes against targets in the Strip, as the first phase of its offensive code-named 'Operation Cast Lead', undertaken in response to the increased cross-border attacks. The principal targets initially appeared to be security headquarters and police stations, as well as the tunnels used by militants to smuggle weapons used to launch attacks against Israelis. At least 225 Palestinians were reported to have been killed on the first day of the Israeli military operation. On 27 December the Commissioner-General of the UN Relief and Works Agency for Palestine Refugees in the Near East (UNRWA) expressed horror at the extensive destruction and loss of life caused by the Israeli action and, while recognizing Israel's legitimate security concerns, urged the Israeli military to cease the bombardment and to respect all international conventions regarding the protection of non-combatants in times of conflict to which Israel is a signatory. Meeting on the following day the UN Security Council expressed 'serious concern at the escalation of the situation in Gaza' and urged an immediate halt to all violence. A statement issued by the US Administration, meanwhile, apportioned the blame for the situation on the 'completely unacceptable' attacks launched against Israelis by Hamas militants.

Having declared an 'all-out war against Hamas' on 29 December 2008, the Israeli Government sanctioned a wider campaign of air-strikes, which now targeted government offices (including the Ministry of the Interior), presidential buildings and the Islamic University in Gaza. On 31 December UNRWA stated that the ongoing Israeli bombardment had inflicted considerable damage on the Gaza Strip's already fragile public infrastructure, and that it had erased the territory's public service capacity. On 3 January 2009 Israel launched a major ground assault into the Strip. The declared aim of the operation, which effectively divided the enclave into two, was to guarantee the long-term security of Israel's citizens by preventing the continued firing of rockets and mortars by Hamas militants against towns in southern Israel; the Israeli military sought to destroy Hamas's infrastructure, weapons factories and supplies. Heavy fighting ensued in densely populated districts of Gaza City and other urban centres. There was condemnation from the international community on 6 January, when an Israeli mortar attack close to an UNRWA-administered school in the Jabalia refugee camp resulted in the deaths of 43 Palestinians; at that time around 25 UNRWA-run schools were serving as temporary shelters to Palestinians who had been displaced by the ongoing violence, and a further two of these had also come under attack. Soon afterwards UNRWA temporarily suspended its movements through Gaza (including food distribution activities) owing to Israeli air strikes on humanitarian convoys that had caused several fatalities. On 8 January the UN Security Council adopted Resolution 1860 demanding an immediate and durable cease-fire in Gaza, culminating in the full withdrawal of Israeli forces; the unimpeded provision throughout Gaza of food, fuel and medical treatment; improved international arrangements to prevent arms and ammunition smuggling; intra-Palestinian reconciliation; and renewed efforts to achieve a comprehensive long-term peace between Israel and Palestine. The USA abstained from the vote. Hostilities continued, however, and on 15 January UNRWA's Gaza field headquarters was struck and set alight by Israeli shells that reportedly contained incendiary white phosphorus; the UN Secretary-General protested strongly against the attack. On the same day Said Siyam, the Minister of the Interior and Civil Affairs in the Hamas administration, was killed, along with two members of his family, in an Israeli aerial attack on the Jabalia camp.

On 17 January 2009 the Israeli Government declared a unilateral cease-fire in its conflict with Hamas, with Prime Minister Olmert asserting that the objectives of 'Operation Cast Lead' had been achieved. Hours after the cease-fire entered into effect, on 18 January, Hamas also announced a week-long cessation of hostilities against Israeli targets, in order to permit Israel to withdraw its armed forces from the Gaza Strip; the Israeli withdrawal was completed on 21 January. UNRWA reported that by the time of the cease-fire 1,340 Palestinians had been killed (including 460 children and 106 women), and some 5,320 wounded (including 1,855 children and 795 women), during the 22-day Israeli offensive. In addition, thousands of Palestinian homes, commercial and industrial buildings had been destroyed by Israeli forces. Some 13 Israelis (including 10 soldiers) were reported to have died, and at least 680 to have been injured.

Sporadic clashes continued between Israeli armed forces and Hamas militants during late January–May 2009. Towards the end of January an Israeli soldier patrolling the border with Gaza became the first soldier to be reported killed since the end of 'Operation Cast Lead'. The Israeli's death in a militant bomb attack led the Israeli Government to order renewed military action against Hamas targets in Gaza, with at least one Palestinian also being killed.

In early 2009 international diplomatic efforts were conducted in the region with the aim of securing a more formal, permanent truce between Israel and Hamas, thereby ensuring that international arrangements would be put in place to prevent the smuggling of weapons into Gaza, and to allow for the unimpeded provision of humanitarian aid within Gaza and the subsequent reconstruction of the territory's infrastructure. On 18 January an international summit was held in Sharm esh-Sheikh, hosted by Egypt's President Mubarak and attended principally by leaders of European nations and the Arab League (including President Abbas). Delegates at the Sharm esh-Sheikh summit agreed to intensify efforts to provide much-needed humanitarian aid to Gaza's population, to support Egypt in its ongoing mediation between Hamas and Israel, and to maintain a dialogue with the Israeli Government. On 19–20 January, at an Arab Economic, Social and Development Summit taking place in Kuwait City, King Abdullah of Saudi Arabia warned Israel that the Arab League peace initiative originally proposed in 2002 would not remain on offer indefinitely; the King also denounced Israel's 'excessive use of force' in Gaza during 'Operation Cast Lead'. In mid-February 2009 the Israeli Government stated that, until the release of Corporal Gilat Shalit, who was still being held captive by Hamas, border crossings into Gaza would not be reopened and an official long-term cease-fire would not be concluded. International donors, convened in Sharm esh-Sheikh at the beginning of March, pledged some US $5,200m. in funds that were to provide humanitarian aid and rebuilding assistance for Gaza, as well as budgetary support to the PA.

Meanwhile, the inauguration of Barack Obama as US President on 20 January 2009 appeared, in the few weeks after his new Democrat-led Administration took office, to result in renewed efforts by the USA to engage constructively in efforts to resolve the Israeli–Palestinian situation, and indeed, wider Middle East conflict. In early March 2009 the new US Secretary of State, Hillary Clinton, declared her support for the creation of a Palestinian state in the West Bank and Gaza. However, at the end of March a new Israeli Government took office, under the premiership of Binyamin Netanyahu, who, shortly after his appointment as Prime Minister, stated that he would not endorse a two-state solution to the Israeli–Palestinian crisis.

Furthermore, the new Israeli Minister of Foreign Affairs, Avigdor Lieberman, declared at that time that decisions reached at the November 2007 Annapolis meeting had 'no validity'. In early April 2009 President Obama restated the US Administration's strong support for the commitments made at Annapolis; a meeting between Netanyahu and Obama was due to be held in mid-May. During April the UN Human Rights Council appointed a fact-finding team to investigate violations of human rights and humanitarian law committed in the context of the December 2008–January 2009 conflict in Gaza.

According to the PRCS, by the end of December 2008 (therefore excluding most of the duration of 'Operation Cast Lead') some 5,365 Palestinians had been killed, and 33,639 injured, since the start of the al-Aqsa *intifada* in September 2000.

Legislative elections took place on 20 January 1996, with the participation of some 79% of the estimated 1m. eligible Palestinian voters, selecting 88 deputies to the 89-seat PLC. (One seat was reserved for the president of the Council's executive body—the Palestinian President.) At the concurrent election for a Palestinian Executive President, Yasser Arafat defeated his only rival, Samiha Khalil, winning 88.1% of the votes cast, and took office as President on 12 February. Deputies returned to the PLC automatically became members of the PNC, the existing 483 members of which were subsequently permitted to return from exile by the Israeli authorities. The PLC held its first session in Gaza City on 7 March, electing Ahmad Quray as its Speaker. At the 21st session of the PNC, held in Gaza City on 22–24 April, the PNC voted to amend the Palestinian National Charter (or PLO Covenant) by annulling those clauses that sought the destruction of the State of Israel and those that were inconsistent with the agreement of mutual recognition concluded by Israel and the PLO in September 1993. At the close of its session the PNC elected a new Executive Committee, and in May 1996 President Arafat appointed a Palestinian Cabinet. The appointments were approved by the PLC in July.

In April 1997 Arafat's audit office disclosed evidence of the misappropriation by PA ministers of some US $326m. of public funds. The PA General Prosecutor, Khalid al-Qidram, resigned in response to the findings, and was reportedly placed under house arrest in June. In August the findings of a parliamentary committee appointed by Arafat to investigate the affair led to the resignation of the Cabinet. New appointments were made in early 1998, but the Cabinet resigned again in June, apparently in order to obstruct a second vote of no confidence in Arafat's leadership, in protest partly at alleged corruption within the PA. A new Cabinet was appointed by Arafat in August, but soon attracted criticism from officials of the principal international organizations granting funds to the PA. In November donors pledged aid worth more than $3,000m., to be disbursed over the next five years. In October 1998 the PA was again accused of financial mismanagement, after customs revenues amounting to some $70m. allegedly failed to be deposited at the PA treasury.

US officials reportedly confirmed in March 1998 that the CIA was assisting the Palestinian security forces in the spheres of espionage, information-gathering and interrogation, in an attempt to reassure the Israeli Government of the PA's ability to take effective action against groups involved in attacks on Israeli targets. (Under the terms of the Wye Memorandum—see above—the CIA was to monitor the PA's compliance with the security provisions of the accord.) In October the PA detained 11 journalists who had attempted to obtain an interview with the spiritual leader of Hamas, Sheikh Ahmad Yassin (who was subsequently placed under house arrest). In subsequent weeks several radio and television stations, as well as press offices, were closed down by the PA, and numerous journalists were imprisoned. There was also a marked increase in self-censorship in the state-controlled and pro-Government media. In May 2000 the chief news editor at the Voice of Palestine radio station, Fathi Barqawi, was arrested after publicly criticizing the PA's 'secret' talks with Israel in Sweden.

In January 1999 the PLC approved a motion urging an end to political detentions and the release of all those imprisoned on exclusively political charges; the motion further demanded the formation of a special committee to assess the case of every political prisoner in the Palestinian territories and to recommend prisoner releases. The committee was duly appointed in February, under the chairmanship of the Minister of Justice. Despite the release of 37 political prisoners by the PA, however, in late January Hamas and Islamic Jihad activists began a hunger strike in Jericho and Nablus, in protest at their continued detention without trial. In February some 3,000 protesters marched to the headquarters of the PA, whom they accused of 'subservience to Israel and the CIA'. In March a security agent and former member of Hamas's military wing was sentenced to death for the killing of a Palestinian intelligence officer in Rafah. The verdict provoked serious clashes between Palestinian police and protesters in the Gaza Strip, and Arafat was forced to curtail an official visit to Jordan to address the domestic security crisis. In November 20 leading Palestinian intellectuals (including members of the PLC) issued a joint statement in which they criticized alleged corruption, mismanagement and abuse of power within the PA, and accused Palestinian officials of ineffectiveness in the peace talks with Israel. An official crackdown on Arafat's critics was subsequently instigated, during which several of the document's signatories were detained or placed under house arrest (they were later released on bail). The establishment, announced in January 2000, of a Higher Council for Development under Arafat's chairmanship was welcomed by foreign donors as a major step towards ending corruption and mismanagement within the Palestinian administration.

In August 1999 a Palestinian national dialogue conference was held in Cairo, Egypt, between representatives of Fatah and the PFLP. Later in August Arafat and the Secretary-General of the DFLP, Nayef Hawatmeh, met, also in Cairo, for the first time since 1993. At the end of the month representatives of nine Palestinian political factions, meeting in Ramallah, agreed on an agenda for a comprehensive national dialogue; Hamas and Islamic Jihad, however, refused to participate. In September the PFLP's deputy leader, Abu Ali Moustafa, was permitted by the Israeli Government to return to the West Bank from exile in Jordan, in order to participate in reconciliation talks with Arafat. George Habash stepped down as leader of the PFLP in April 2000, and Abu Ali Moustafa was elected to lead the organization in July. (Following Moustafa's assassination in August 2001, Ahmad Saadat assumed the party leadership.)

The start of the al-Aqsa *intifada* by Palestinians in September 2000 (see above) moved some analysts to suggest that Arafat's influence over Palestinians might be waning, as other Fatah leaders began to pursue their own agendas and to speak out against the President: Marwan Barghouthi, in particular, was said to be attracting considerable support among Palestinians in the West Bank, where he was the regional leader of Fatah. In December a court in Nablus sentenced to death a Palestinian who had been convicted of collaborating with Israeli secret services in the assassination of a Hamas commander. The harsh sentence apparently signalled a change in policy by the PA, which in January 2001 carried out the executions, by firing squad, of two alleged collaborators. The Al-Aqsa Martyrs Brigades claimed responsibility for the assassination in mid-January of Hisham Mekki, the Chairman of Palestinian Satellite Television, director of the state broadcasting corporation and a close associate of Arafat. In August a group of Palestinians were sentenced to death, and at least 100 others arrested, on charges of having collaborated with Israeli security services in recent attacks against Hamas officials. In October three Palestinians were killed by security forces in Gaza during violent protests in support of Osama bin Laden. Although the al-Qa'ida leader claimed to have launched the previous month's suicide attacks against the USA partly in protest against Israel's occupation of Palestinian territory, the PA sought to distance itself from the atrocities.

A report published by Human Rights Watch in November 2001 accused the PA of systematic abuses of human rights since the start of the al-Aqsa *intifada*, citing incidences of arbitrary arrests and of detention without trial and torture of prisoners. When Sheikh Ahmad Yassin was placed under house arrest in December, hundreds of Hamas supporters demanded his release, resulting in clashes between Hamas gunmen and security forces. Fierce protests by militants also ensued in January 2002 when Palestinian security services in Ramallah arrested the PFLP leader, Ahmad Saadat. There were also an increasing number of 'vigilante killings': in February a crowd led by members of the security services entered a military court in Jenin and killed three defendants, two of whom had just been sentenced to death for the murder of a security official; and during one day in April 11 suspected collaborators were reportedly murdered by Palestinians in Tulkarm, Qalqilya and Bethlehem.

In early June 2002, following Arafat's release from Israeli house arrest in the previous month, the President implemented major government changes: membership of the Cabinet was reduced from 31 ministers to 21, with several ministries being either merged or abolished. Maj.-Gen. Abd ar-Razzaq al-Yahya was appointed Minister of the Interior—a position previously held by Arafat. Dr Salam Fayyad was named as the new Minister of Finance. The new Government was described as an interim administration, its main task to be the preparation and supervision of far-reaching reforms, including the organization of municipal elections towards the end of 2002 and of presidential and legislative elections by early 2003. The planned reforms would also include the streamlining of the Palestinian security services. Perhaps most importantly, draft legislation was prepared in order to create a new post of Prime Minister, to be responsible for the day-to-day administration of the PA. President Bush emphasized in late June 2002 that the USA would give its support to the creation of a 'provisional Palestinian state' if the PA undertook constitutional and judicial reforms. In September the entire Palestinian Cabinet resigned in order to prevent a vote of no confidence being brought in the legislature; a new administration was announced in the following month. Meanwhile, the PA President set 20 January 2003 as the day on which legislative and presidential elections were to be held. However, in December 2002 Arafat announced a postponement of the polls, claiming that it would be untenable to hold elections while Israel continued to occupy PA-controlled population centres in the West Bank and Gaza.

Palestinian representatives participated in a conference on reform of the Palestinian administration, held in London in January 2003, via a video link, after the Israeli Government refused to allow the delegates to attend the talks following a double suicide bombing in Tel-Aviv in which more than 20 Israelis died. At the conference, which was also attended by officials of the Quartet group and representatives from Jordan, Egypt and Saudi Arabia, it was agreed that a new draft Palestinian constitution would be presented within two weeks. In March the PLC endorsed a bill defining the role to be played by a future Palestinian Prime Minister, after having rejected amendments to the legislation proposed by Arafat according to which the President would retain authority over the appointment of cabinet ministers. In the proposed power-sharing arrangement, the President was reportedly to control security and foreign affairs and would also have the authority to appoint and dismiss a premier, while the Prime Minister would nominate ministers and retain responsibility for domestic affairs. Mahmud Abbas, the Secretary-General of the PLO Executive Committee, formally accepted the post of Prime Minister on 19 March; on 29 April the Palestinian legislature endorsed his appointment. A newly expanded Palestinian Cabinet was announced on that day, comprising 25 ministers under the premiership of Mahmud Abbas (who also became Minister of the Interior). Muhammad Dahlan was confirmed as the Minister of State for Security Affairs, while Dr Nabil Shaath was named as the Minister of External Affairs and Saeb Erakat as the Minister of Negotiation Affairs. The announcement of the new PA Cabinet prompted the publication of the Quartet-sponsored 'roadmap' peace plan (see above).

Ongoing tensions between Arafat and Abbas appeared to be the principal reason for the resignation of Saeb Erakat in May 2003. Erakat was regarded as an Arafat ally and had traditionally been at the forefront of Palestinian negotiations with Israel; however, his resignation was interpreted as a protest against his omission from the Palestinian delegation, which included Abbas, Muhammad Dahlan and the Speaker of the PLC, Ahmad Quray, scheduled to hold talks with Ariel Sharon and leading Israeli officials. Immediately following the Aqaba summit (see above), Abbas had engaged in a round of discussions with Hamas and Islamic Jihad to effect a cease-fire in attacks by those groups against Israeli targets; despite an early walk-out by Hamas, a truce was duly brought into effect at the end of June, with the support of Fatah. Abbas and Arafat continued to clash on the issue of security: after a meeting of the Fatah Central Committee in July, Abbas offered to resign, having been criticized for making too many concessions to Israel. In early August Palestinian security forces arrested 20 militants, mostly believed to belong to the Al-Aqsa Martyrs Brigades, who were sheltering in Arafat's Ramallah compound. Arafat's appointment of a new National Security Adviser, Brig.-Gen. Jibril Rajoub (who had been dismissed as commander of the Preventive Security Force in the West Bank in 2002), in late August, was interpreted as a snub to Abbas and Muhammad Dahlan: as head of the Palestinian National Security Council (PNSC), Rajoub would be de facto commander in the field of the Palestinian security forces. (Rajoub was reported to have resigned from the post in January 2005.)

Mahmud Abbas resigned as Prime Minister in September 2003, seemingly representing the culmination of his power struggle with Arafat over control of the Palestinian security apparatus. Arafat nominated PLC Speaker Quray to replace Abbas. Meanwhile, Saeb Erakat was reinstated as Minister of Negotiation Affairs, and it appeared that Arafat had effectively regained control of the PA. However, in October Yasser Arafat declared a state of emergency in the Palestinian territories, following Israel's continuing construction of the 'security fence' (see above) and the arrest of a key member of Islamic Jihad; he also announced the establishment of an eight-member Emergency Cabinet. Shortly after the formation of the Emergency Cabinet, Quray reportedly offered his resignation. In early November the PLC approved Ahmad Quray's first full Cabinet. Ministers who retained their portfolios from the previous administration under Mahmud Abbas included Dr Nabil Shaath as Minister of Foreign Affairs and Dr Salam Fayyad as Minister of Finance; notable new appointments included Hakam Balawi as Minister of the Interior and Nahid ar-Rayyis as Minister of Justice. Rafiq an-Natsheh was elected Speaker of the PLC (but was replaced by Rawhi Fattouh in March 2004).

In late November 2003 the EU initiated an investigation into claims that EU funding for the PA had been channelled to the Al-Aqsa Martyrs Brigades. An audit of the PA's finances carried out by the IMF in 2003 had estimated that in the period 1995–2000 nearly US $900m. had been diverted into accounts controlled by Yasser Arafat. Moreover, documents seized by Israeli forces during the reoccupation of Palestinian areas in 2001 reportedly revealed that some EU funds had been used by the Al-Aqsa Martyrs Brigades. In February 2004 Israeli soldiers raided banks in Ramallah in an operation to seize funds reputedly belonging to Palestinian militant groups. The Arab Bank and the Cairo-Amman Bank were among those raided, and it was later reported that nearly $9m. had been confiscated.

In December 2003 Quray held talks in Cairo with the principal militant organizations, including Fatah, Hamas, Islamic Jihad and the PFLP, in order to achieve a full cessation of attacks against Israeli targets. Several of the Palestinian groups rejected a total cease-fire, and a joint statement by all parties at the conclusion of the talks stated that while attacks against civilian targets inside Israel would cease, attacks would continue against Israeli military targets and Jewish settlements in the Palestinian areas. In February 2004 more than 300 members of Fatah resigned from the group in protest at alleged corruption and the failure to instigate reform, particularly with regard to elections to the organization's leadership, which had last been held in 1989.

Arafat's authority was further threatened in July 2004 by mass disorder in the Gaza Strip, in protest against PA corruption and incompetence, as well as a threat by Prime Minister Quray to bring about the collapse of the administration if his powers were not increased. In mid-July Arafat took measures against the growing anarchy in Gaza, discharging two senior security commanders, declaring a state of emergency and sending loyal troops to protect official buildings in Gaza. He also replaced the national police chief and the commander of general security forces in Gaza (the latter with his cousin, Musa Arafat), and amalgamated eight rival security forces into three, following internal pressure on Arafat to combat corruption and to reform the PA and its security services. However, Fatah members demanding reforms rejected those introduced by the President as 'superficial and unconvincing', and pressure on Arafat (especially from the Al-Aqsa Martyrs Brigades) apparently forced him to reverse his decision to appoint his cousin as head of security. In late July Quray reportedly announced his resignation (which was rejected by Arafat) after chaos erupted in Gaza following the kidnapping of the Palestinian police commander, a colonel in the PA security forces and four French aid workers. However, Quray later announced his intention to stay in office as caretaker Prime Minister, having, according to one of his ministers, urged Arafat to forgo some of his powers to prevent the PA from collapsing further. Yet Quray did little to combat the widespread poverty in the Palestinian territories—a principal cause of popular anger—nor to address the power struggle within the Fatah movement, and in August the Minister of Justice, Nahid ar-Rayyis, resigned, citing the ongoing disorder in Gaza.

It was announced on 11 November 2004 that Yasser Arafat, who had been undergoing treatment at a military hospital in France, had died. In accordance with Palestinian law, the Speaker of the PLC, Rawhi Fattouh, was sworn in as acting President, pending elections due to take place in the territories within 60 days. Mahmud Abbas assumed the chairmanship of the PLO, and Quray was chosen to head the PNSC in addition to taking charge of the administration of the PA. Farouk Kaddoumi was appointed leader of Fatah. In late November Abbas was nominated to contest the elections as Fatah's only candidate. In early December Hamas declared that it would not be fielding a candidate for the forthcoming election, which they urged voters to boycott, while Marwan Barghouthi registered as a candidate. Islamic Jihad also announced a boycott of the ballot. Palestinian election officials declared that a total of 10 candidates had qualified for registration, including a human rights activist, Mustafa Barghouthi, who was to stand as an independent. Marwan Barghouthi later withdrew from the campaign, following pressure on him to give Abbas the best chance of securing the presidency; it had been feared that, had Barghouthi won the ballot, Israel would have refused to negotiate with him due to his imprisonment.

The first municipal elections to be held in the West Bank since 1976 began on 23 December 2004, at which Hamas, participating in an election in the Palestinian territories for the first time, won 16 councils and Fatah secured nine, with the two movements to share the control of one municipality. At the local elections held in the Gaza Strip in late January 2005 Hamas secured control of seven of the 10 councils. The lack of support for Fatah was attributed to its association with corruption, while voters were encouraged by Hamas's provision of welfare and educational services and by its opposition to Israel.

The election to appoint a successor to Yasser Arafat was held in the West Bank, Gaza Strip and East Jerusalem on 9 January 2005. The Palestinian Central Elections Commission (CEC) asserted that the presence of Israeli forces in Jerusalem interfered with the voting process, forcing international observers to intervene. Moreover, polling centres remained open for an extra two hours because some citizens had difficulty locating them, and owing to problems with voter registration. Nevertheless, international observers considered the overall conduct of the election to have been free and fair. Final results showed that, from the seven candidates, Abbas had received 62.5% of votes cast and Mustafa Barghouthi 19.5%. The other candidates had all secured less than 4% of the votes. Abbas was sworn in as Executive President of the PA on 15 January.

In early February 2005 a Hamas militant attack on Israeli army outposts and settlements in the Gaza strip prompted Abbas to dismiss senior security commanders. Later in the month the PLC voted to approve a new Cabinet under Prime Minister Ahmad Quray. Dr Nabil Shaath was appointed Deputy Prime Minister and Minister of Information; Shaath's previous role as Minister of Foreign Affairs was assumed by Dr Nasser al-Kidwa, hitherto the Palestinian representative to the UN. Maj.-Gen. Nasr Yousuf became Minister of the Interior and National Security. Quray pledged the new administration's determination to heighten security and combat poverty. In March, after militants from the Fatah-affiliated Al-Aqsa Martyrs Brigades reportedly shot at the presidential compound in Ramallah, President Abbas removed the military chief in the West Bank and the Ramallah district commander, explaining that the security apparatus had failed and needed to be reorganized. In an effort to consolidate various (often rival) factions into a unified command, in the following month Abbas nominated four new heads of security forces in the West Bank and Gaza Strip, and ordered 10 senior officers to resign.

A reported 82% of eligible voters took part in a second round of municipal elections in the West Bank and Gaza Strip on 5 May 2005. According to official results, 45 of the 84 municipal districts contested were to be governed by councils with a majority of Fatah representatives (which took 56% of votes). Hamas, which had not participated in the presidential elections, took 23 councils (33% of votes), and left-wing and independent lists secured 16 councils. Later in the month the CEC declared that elections to the PLC, scheduled for July, would be delayed while the PLC ratified a new elections law, intended to replace the system of simple majority by which the 1996 general elections had been held, with a 'mixed' electoral system (see President and Legislature). The PLC ratified the new law in June 2005. In August Abbas issued a decree setting 25 January 2006 as the date for the legislative elections. A third round of municipal elections was held in 82 towns and villages in the West Bank on 29 September 2005. Fatah won a reported 54% of the votes, and Hamas took 26%. At local elections in some of the largest cities in the West Bank conducted on 15 December, Fatah secured 35% of the 414 contested seats, while Hamas won 26%. However, although

Fatah retained control of Ramallah, Hamas notably gained control of Nablus and Jenin.

In accordance with Palestinian elections law (which stipulates that officials intending to contest seats in elections to the PLC must resign their posts two months in advance of the ballot), various ministers were reported to have submitted their resignations in November 2005, including the Minister of Finance, Dr Salam Fayyad. Prime Minister Ahmad Quray also resigned in mid-December in order to be eligible to participate in the elections. Deputy Prime Minister and Minister of Information Dr Nabil Shaath was appointed to replace him; however, later in the month Quray declared that he would not take part in the poll, and returned to his former post.

Israel announced in late December 2005 that it would not allow Arabs in East Jerusalem to vote if Hamas participated in the forthcoming legislative elections. After PA officials threatened to postpone the elections, and amid international pressure, in mid-January 2006 Israel declared that it would allow a small number of Arabs in East Jerusalem to vote on 25 January, and that candidates from groups other than Hamas could campaign there. In the event, Hamas, competing as the Change and Reform list in order to avoid a ban on its direct participation, secured 74 of the 132 seats, and Fatah only 45. A large part of Change and Reform's election campaign had focused on the movement's social welfare programme and its strong stance against official corruption. Other groups, including the PFLP (contesting the poll as Martyr Abu Ali Moustafa) and independents, also achieved representation. Quray announced the resignation of his administration on 26 January.

The new PLC was inaugurated on 18 February 2006. Dr Aziz Duweik was appointed to replace Rawhi Fattouh as Speaker, and President Abbas called on Hamas to establish a new administration. Hamas subsequently held discussions with Abbas and other factions, including Fatah, concerning the possibility of forming a coalition administration of national unity, and nominated Ismail Haniya as Prime Minister. Haniya, who had led the organization's national list for the elections, had held senior positions within Hamas; imprisoned in Israeli gaols in 1987–89 for his participation in the first *intifada* and leading one of Hamas's security apparatuses, Haniya had survived an Israeli assassination attempt in 2003, five years after assuming control of Sheikh Ahmad Yassin's office. Hamas began to assert its authority at a PLC session in early March 2006 when it reversed legislation that the Fatah-led parliament had approved immediately prior to its dissolution. Fatah deputies walked out of the session, asserting that Hamas had no right to reverse their decisions. The new laws had given President Abbas further powers, apparently in an attempt to increase his authority and curb that of parliament, in anticipation of Hamas's domination of the legislature. One of the rulings had provided for the establishment of a constitutional court and granted Abbas the right to elect its members.

Hamas leaders continued their attempts to persuade Fatah to enter into an administration of national unity. However, in late March 2006, after weeks of discussions between the two factions, Fatah rejected Hamas's offer, and the Islamist organization decided to form a cabinet alone. One of the most important matters of dispute had been Hamas's rejection of bilateral Israeli-Palestinian agreements approved by the former legislature: Hamas considered that by recognizing these accords it would be accepting Israeli occupation of Palestinian territory. The PLC approved Hamas's proposed Cabinet on 28 March, and President Abbas inaugurated the new administration on the following day. Notable appointees included Nasser ash-Shaer as Deputy Prime Minister and Minister of Education and Higher Education, Mahmud az-Zahhar as Minister of Foreign Affairs and Said Siyam as Minister of the Interior and Civil Affairs.

In the weeks following the elections to the PLC, there were sporadic violent clashes between rival militias and security forces of Hamas and Fatah. The increased tensions in the Palestinian territories were aggravated by the decision by the USA and the EU to withdraw all direct aid to the PA until Hamas fulfilled the three conditions that the Quartet group had placed on it (see above). Nevertheless, in June 2006 Hamas and Fatah reportedly agreed to a joint political platform which contained implicit recognition of Israel's existence. The representatives approved a document drawn up in May by a group of Palestinian political prisoners in Israeli gaols, led by Marwan Barghouthi and fellow prisoner Sheikh Abd al-Khaliq an-Natsheh of Hamas, which detailed 18 points for a return to negotiations with Israel. The so-called 'prisoners' document' called for the formation of an administration of national unity in which all political parties that accepted the terms of the document would be represented, as well as the establishment of a 'unified resistance front' against Israeli occupation. Shortly afterwards Hamas endorsed the prisoners' document and agreed in principle to share power with Fatah in an administration committed to a two-state settlement and negotiations with Israel on the basis of an independent Palestinian state on territories occupied in 1967. (The group had been under intense pressure from President Abbas to accept the proposals or face a referendum.) However, the agreement was rejected by Hamas's military wing and the organization's political leaders in exile. Moreover, it failed to achieve the immediate resumption of foreign aid to the PA, which was urgently required in order to allow the authorities to begin paying workers' salaries.

In September 2006 a general strike was organized by public sector workers in protest against unpaid wages. In early November Arab ministers responsible for foreign relations, meeting in Cairo, pledged to increase levels of financial assistance given to the PA; Iran also gave funds to the Hamas-led administration in the following month. In mid-November it was announced that Fatah and Hamas had agreed to nominate Muhammad Shbeir, a former head of the Islamic University in Gaza, as Prime Minister in a coalition administration. However, despite lengthy discussions, it proved impossible for Shbeir to form a cabinet. On 8 February 2007 Fatah and Hamas—represented by President Abbas and Khalid Meshaal, respectively—signed an agreement to form a national unity administration; the accord followed two days of discussions in Mecca, Saudi Arabia, held at the invitation of King Abdullah. Although Hamas continued to reject an acceptance of Israel's right to exist, it was reported that the organization had agreed, for the first time, to 'respect and work to implement' the 'land-for-peace' proposal adopted at the Beirut summit in 2002 (see above).

Finally, on 17 March 2007 the PLC approved the composition of a new Cabinet, which replaced the former Hamas-dominated administration with a coalition of ministers from Hamas and Fatah, together with independents and representatives from the DFLP and the Palestinian People's Party. Hamas's Ismail Haniya retained the post of Prime Minister, while Azzam al-Ahmad, of Fatah, became Deputy Prime Minister. Three prominent ministries were allocated to independents: Hani Talab al-Qawasmeh was appointed Minister of the Interior, Dr Ziad Abu Amr Minister of Foreign Affairs and Dr Salam Fayyad Minister of Finance. At the end of March EU ministers responsible for foreign affairs, meeting in Germany, declared their support for the peace initiative revived in Saudi Arabia a few days previously, and announced that they would be willing to have contacts with non-Hamas members of the new Palestinian Cabinet. Israel declared that it would continue its boycott of the PA, however, until the new administration met the conditions demanded by the Quartet group. Having initially tendered his resignation in April, when it was rejected by President Abbas, in May al-Qawasmeh formally resigned as Minister of the Interior. His departure from the Cabinet appeared to demonstrate the divisions within the administration with regard to the difficult security issues facing the West Bank and Gaza. Prime Minister Haniya assumed the interior portfolio in an acting capacity.

Abbas announced in March 2007 that he had appointed Muhammad Dahlan as Secretary of the newly re-established PNSC, which in theory meant that he became general commander of the Palestinian security forces; Dahlan, however, was profoundly disliked by Hamas. Following several unsuccessful attempts to achieve a lasting cease-fire between the rival militias in the Palestinian territories, a new security plan to restore order in Gaza was announced by the Cabinet in May. Yet the factional fighting between gunmen from Hamas and Fatah continued, leading Abbas, speaking in June, on the anniversary of 40 years of Israeli occupation, to warn of the threat of a Palestinian civil war. In mid-2007 scores of Palestinians were killed in the violence, some of which even occurred within hospital buildings. On 12 June gun battles between Hamas and Fatah fighters intensified across the Gaza Strip. As Hamas began to demonstrate its military superiority, it seized control of the headquarters of security forces in the north and south of the Strip, before taking over Gaza City itself. At the same time Fatah militias in the West Bank stormed Hamas-controlled institutions, seeking revenge for the Islamist movement's takeover of the Strip. On 14 June Abbas dissolved the national unity Cabinet under Haniya's premiership, declared a state of emergency and appointed the independent Minister of Finance, Dr Salam Fayyad, as

Prime Minister. As a respected economist and former employee of the World Bank and the IMF, Fayyad had wide support in Israel, the USA and the EU. Meanwhile, Haniya sought to consolidate his power over Gaza by naming a new chief of security in the territory, Maj.-Gen. Said Fanouna.

An Emergency Cabinet, consisting principally of independents and technocrats, as well as one Fatah representative, was sworn in by President Abbas in Ramallah on 17 June 2007. Besides assuming the premiership, Fayyad also held charge of the finance portfolio, and, briefly, that of foreign affairs. (Riyad al-Maliki assumed responsibility for the latter from the beginning of September.) Fatah's Abd ar-Razzaq al-Yahya became Minister of the Interior and of Civil Affairs. The hope was that this administration would restore law and order throughout the Palestinian territories, but it became apparent that divisions between the Fatah-controlled West Bank and Hamas-administered Gaza Strip were widening. Abbas refused to enter into a dialogue with Hamas until it withdrew its militias from former Fatah positions in Gaza. Moreover, the President granted himself the power to take decisions without the endorsement of the PLC, where Hamas held a majority of the seats. Abbas also declared that he was outlawing Hamas's paramilitary wing and other militias associated with the Islamist group. On 18 June the USA and the EU, in a demonstration of support for President Abbas and his formation of an administration that excluded Hamas ministers, lifted their 15-month economic and political boycott of the PA. The Bush Administration additionally pledged assistance valued at some US $190m. to the Ramallah-based Cabinet.

Upon the expiry of the 30-day state of emergency, on 13 July 2007 President Abbas accepted the resignation of the Emergency Cabinet and appointed three new ministers to a reshuffled Cabinet, which was to function as a caretaker administration until either the PLC convened or new legislative elections were called. (Hamas was unwilling for a vote to be held in the PLC as, with so many of its legislators in Israeli detention, it would lose its parliamentary majority.) Hamas leaders again refused to recognize the legitimacy of this interim administration. On 4 July, three days after Israel began transferring US $117m. of withheld Palestinian taxes to the Fayyad administration, thousands of Palestinian civil servants began receiving their first full salaries since March 2006. However, the West Bank administration continued to withhold the salaries of thousands of civil servants in the Gaza Strip. On 19 July 2007, at the first meeting of the international Quartet group since the appointment of former British Prime Minister Tony Blair as its representative, members of the Quartet affirmed their joint refusal to deal with Hamas. Muhammad Dahlan resigned as National Security Adviser on 26 July, citing ill health; however, some reports alleged that Dahlan had been asked to resign after his security forces in Gaza had allowed Hamas militants to oust Fatah from power in Gaza (when Dahlan was undergoing medical treatment abroad). Nevertheless, the resignation was essentially a formality since President Abbas had dissolved the PNSC following Hamas's takeover of Gaza. In August Fayyad issued a statement outlining the conditions required for inter-Palestinian dialogue to begin: Hamas should renounce any claims to be the legal authority governing Gaza (although Fayyad did not insist on an annulment of the 2006 election results) and disband all armed militias. This demand apparently included the Hamas Executive Force, which was responsible for maintaining law and order in Gaza.

In October 2007 Haniya appeared to demonstrate a move towards reconciliation with Fatah, when he described Hamas's administration of the Gaza Strip as 'temporary'. In early November President Abbas hosted Hamas representatives for discussions at his Ramallah headquarters; it was hoped that there would soon be a resumption of complete negotiations with Abbas's faction, with a view to restoring Palestinian unity. However, Abbas's administration in the West Bank launched a major clampdown on the activities of Hamas-affiliated clerics in the territories, with a number of preachers being dismissed or arrested on charges of fomenting political unrest. Moreover, the third anniversary of the death of Yasser Arafat in November provoked a further outbreak of factional violence; eight Palestinians were reported to have died in clashes between rival Fatah and Hamas supporters in Gaza City. Abbas subsequently declared that the PA must bring an end to Hamas's control of Gaza.

In early March 2008 international aid organizations stated that the humanitarian crisis afflicting the Gazan population was the worst in the territory since 1967; in that month both the USA and the EU released to the PA the first instalments of funds pledged at the December 2007 donors' conference. In late March 2008 Hamas and Fatah signed a reconciliation agreement brokered by the Yemeni President, Ali Abdullah Saleh, and thus termed the San'a Declaration, which included a pledge to resume direct discussions between the feuding parties and affirmed the 'unity of the Palestinian people, territory and authority'. However, doubts were immediately expressed as to exactly what preconditions had been agreed, and productive dialogue was not pursued.

In late July 2008 a bomb exploded near the beach at Gaza City, killing five Hamas members and a child, and injuring 27 others. The Hamas-controlled security forces subsequently arrested up to 160 people associated with Fatah, which Hamas publicly blamed for the crime. Fatah, meanwhile, denied involvement and claimed that the atrocity had resulted from infighting within Hamas; an increase in numbers of Hamas members detained by Fatah-controlled PA security forces in the West Bank ensued. In mid-August Fatah and Hamas agreed to participate in a national committee aimed at calming the spate of politically-motivated arrests and facilitating the release of detainees.

In September 2008 Abbas declared that he would remain President beyond the formal expiry, on 8 January 2009, of his term of office, pending the organization of national elections. In early October 2008 it was reported that the Fatah and Hamas leaderships, as well as representatives of other Palestinian factions, had agreed to meet to discuss national reconciliation under mediation by Egyptian government officials. Later in October the Egyptian Government, following a series of consultations with relevant parties, released a draft proposal for achieving Palestinian national unity, urging the immediate formation of a united government that would have responsibility for rebuilding the Palestinian security forces and for organizing legislative and presidential elections, for which a date was to be scheduled without delay. Under the Egyptian proposal the currently Fatah- and Hamas-controlled security forces were to be managed at the national level and thereby removed from involvement in factional politics. In addition, any future peace deal reached by President Abbas with the Israeli Government was to be submitted to a national referendum or else presented to a restructured PLO that was to encompass Hamas and other factions opposed to the peace process. On 8 November, however, Hamas, alleging that politically-motivated arrests of its members were continuing to be ordered by the PA in the West Bank, announced its withdrawal from a conference that had been planned for the following day to discuss the Egyptian proposal.

The reconciliation process received new impetus in early 2009 in the aftermath of Israel's devastating 'Operation Cast Lead', targeted at Hamas's administration in the Gaza Strip (see above). As reports emerged that intra-Palestinian tensions were causing delays in transfers of aid to Gaza, and that many international donors considered it preferable to pledge assistance to a united government, it appeared that continuing political divisions might undermine urgently required reconstruction activities in the Strip. Under those circumstances it was also feasible that any faction seen not to be acting in the best collective interest might lose popular support. In late February representatives of Fatah, Hamas, and of 11 other Palestinian factions, met in Cairo to begin a newly arranged series of Egyptian-mediated negotiations, with the principal aims of pursuing reconciliation, and reaching agreement on the staging of elections and on the formation of a national unity coalition. Prior to the commencement of the talks the Fatah-controlled PA had released 40 Hamas members detained in the West Bank as a 'goodwill' gesture. Five negotiating committees were established at the February meeting, covering reconciliation; elections; the proposed interim government; security; and PLO-Hamas integration, and the participants also agreed to draft a new agreement to govern use of the Rafah crossing between Gaza and Egypt. In mid-March the parties to the negotiations jointly determined that concurrent presidential and legislative elections should be held by 25 January 2010. Progress on the formation of the planned national unity government, however, remained deadlocked over several contentious issues, including Fatah's and Hamas's conflicting perspectives on Israel's right to exist; on the use of state violence; and on the legitimacy of existing Israeli-Palestinian agreements.

At the beginning of April 2009 Dr Salam Fayyad, who had been intending to stand down as Prime Minister, announced that, at the request of President Abbas, he would remain in office until the conclusion of the ongoing Egyptian-mediated negotiations. At the end of April a new round of the talks ended without agreement, and with Hamas having rejected a compromise proposal, suggested by the Egyptian mediators, under which President Abbas would appoint, pending the January 2010 elections, a transitional government without Hamas representation. Under the Egyptian compromise proposal Hamas, with other militant factions, would form an advisory committee entitled to exert some influence over the decisions of the transitional government. The Egyptian intelligence chief, Lt-Gen. Omar Suleiman, was reported to have requested a final response to the Egyptian compromise proposal by the time the negotiations were reconvened. Shortly before the new round of talks, scheduled for 16 May 2009, President Abbas announced his readiness to swear in, within 48 hours, the newly proposed transitional government, reportedly under the premiership of Fayyad. President Abbas stated that he did not intend to abandon the reconciliation negotiations with Hamas, and promised that the planned transitional government without Hamas representation would be disbanded upon the conclusion of any Fatah-Hamas reconciliation agreement. Abbas also declared that a long awaited Fatah conference would be convened on 1 July to elect a new party leadership (the last party conference having been held in 1989). A Hamas official declared that the appointment of President Abbas's planned new transitional government would deepen intra-Palestinian divisions and imperil the impending new round of reconciliation negotiations. In response to demands from elements within Fatah that the formation of the new government should be delayed until the completion of the new round of negotiations, Abbas postponed its inauguration. At that time some of the Fatah membership was also strongly opposed to a decision by Abbas to locate the planned July Fatah conference in the West Bank, on the grounds that this could exclude participation by many Fatah members living in neighbouring countries who might be denied entry to the West Bank by Israel.

Government

In accordance with the Declaration of Principles on Palestinian Self-Rule and the Cairo Agreement on the Gaza Strip and Jericho (see Recent History), the PLO assumed control of the Jericho area of the West Bank and of the Gaza Strip on 17 May 1994. In November and December 1995, under the terms of the Israeli-Palestinian Interim Agreement on the West Bank and the Gaza Strip concluded in September 1995, Israeli armed forces withdrew from the West Bank towns of Nablus, Ramallah, Jenin, Tulkarm, Qalqilya and Bethlehem. In late December the PLO assumed responsibility in some 17 areas of civil administration in the town of Hebron. The Interim Agreement divided the West Bank into three zones: Areas A, B and C. As of July 1998, the PA had sole jurisdiction and security control in Area A (2% of the West Bank), but Israel retained authority over movement into and out of the area. In Area B (26% of the West Bank) the PA had some limited authority while Israel remained in control of security. Area C, the remaining 72% of the West Bank, was under Israeli military occupation. In accordance with the Wye Memorandum of October 1998 (see Recent History), Israel effected a further redeployment of its armed forces from approximately 500 sq km of West Bank territory in November. Of this, about 400 sq km became Area A territory and the remainder Area B territory. The Sharm esh-Sheikh Memorandum of September 1999 was intended to facilitate completion of outstanding commitments under agreements previously signed, as well as to enable the resumption of 'final status' negotiations with Israel. By October 2000 approximately 17.2% of the West Bank (Area A) was under sole Palestinian jurisdiction and security control, although Israel retained authority over access to and from the zone; about 23.8% (Area B) was under Israeli military control, with the PA responsible for civil administration and public order; the remaining 59% (Area C) remained under Israeli military occupation. Israel implemented its unilateral Disengagement Plan, according to which it dismantled Israeli military installations and settlements in the Gaza Strip, and withdrew from four settlements in the West Bank, in August–September 2005 (see Recent History). The total area of the territory over which the PA will eventually assume control, and the extent of its jurisdiction there, remain subject to 'final status' talks.

Defence

As assessed at November 2007, paramilitary forces in the Gaza Strip and in the areas of the West Bank where the PA has assumed responsibility for security totalled an estimated 56,000; however, figures for personnel strength in the various forces were impossible to confirm, owing to the uncertain situation in the Palestinian territories at that time. There is, *inter alia*, a Presidential Security Force, a Preventative Security Force, a Civil Defence Force and a Police Force. Units of the Palestine National Liberation Army (PNLA) have been garrisoned in various countries in the Middle East and North Africa; however, much of the PNLA's personnel strength has now been incorporated into the PA's various security forces. The public security and order budget of the Palestinian Autonomous Areas was estimated at US $433.9m. in 2004.

Economic Affairs

In 2005, according to estimates by the World Bank, the gross national income (GNI) of the West Bank and the Gaza Strip, measured at average 2003–05 prices, was US $4,452m., equivalent to $1,230 per head. During 2000–07, it was estimated, the population increased at an average annual rate of 3.9%, while in 2000–07 gross domestic product (GDP) per head decreased, in real terms, by an average of 5.1% per year. Overall GDP declined, in real terms, at an average annual rate of an estimated 1.4% in 2000–07; a decrease in real GDP of 2.5% was recorded in 2007.

Agriculture and fishing contributed 9.9% of the GDP of the West Bank and Gaza Strip in 2007, according to official figures. In 2007 agriculture (including hunting, forestry and fishing) engaged 15.6% of the employed Palestinian labour force. Citrus fruits are the principal export crop, and horticulture also makes a significant contribution to trade. Other important crops are tomatoes, cucumbers, olives and grapes. The livestock sector is also significant. Agricultural GDP decreased at an average annual rate of 3.5% during 2000–07. The GDP of the sector declined by 10.4% in 2007.

Industry (including mining, manufacturing, electricity and water supply, and construction) contributed 31.8% of GDP in the West Bank and Gaza Strip in 2007. The industrial sector engaged 23.8% of the employed labour force of the West Bank and Gaza in 2007. Construction alone accounted for 9.5% of GDP in 2007 and employed 10.9% of the working population in the same year. During 2000–07 industrial GDP decreased at an average rate of 5.6% annually. The sector's GDP contracted by 10.8% in 2007.

Mining and quarrying contributed 0.4% of GDP in the West Bank and Gaza Strip in 2007, and engaged 0.2% of the employed labour force in 2007. Two significant gasfields were discovered off the Gazan coast in 1999; however, the exploration and supply of this offshore gas is dependent upon agreement being reached with Israel, which is likely to be the principal purchaser.

Manufacturing contributed 19.2% of the GDP of the West Bank and Gaza Strip in 2007. In that year 12.3% of the employed labour force were engaged in the sector. Palestinian manufacturing is characterized by small-scale enterprises, which typically engage in food-processing and the production of textiles and footwear. The frequent closure of the West Bank and Gaza by the Israeli authorities has prompted the development of free trade industrial zones on the Palestinian side of the boundaries separating Israel from the territories: Israeli and Palestinian enterprises can continue to take advantage of low-cost Palestinian labour at times of closure, and the zones also benefit from tax exemptions and export incentives. Manufacturing GDP contracted at an average annual rate of 3.4% during 2000–07. The GDP of the sector decreased by 18.6% in 2007.

The energy sector (comprising electricity and water supply) accounted for an estimated 2.7% of GDP in the West Bank and Gaza Strip in 2007. Electricity, gas and water utilities together employed 0.3% of the employed labour force of the West Bank and Gaza in that year. In the West Bank, the Jerusalem District Electric Company supplies electric power to Jerusalem, Bethlehem, Jericho, Ramallah and Al-Birah, while the National Electric Company operates in the northern West Bank. The Israel Electric Corporation (IEC) was the only source of electricity to municipalities in the Gaza Strip prior to the establishment of the Palestine Electric Company in 1999, and Palestinian utility firms remain reliant on the purchase of electricity from the IEC.

In 2007 the services sector contributed 58.3% of GDP in the West Bank and Gaza Strip. Services engaged 60.6% of the employed labour force in that year. Although tourism previously contributed more than 10% of the GDP of the West Bank and Gaza, it has been all but halted by the ongoing violence in the territories. The GDP of the services sector increased at an average rate of 1.1% per year during 2000–07. Real GDP of the services sector grew by 7.3% in 2007.

PALESTINIAN AUTONOMOUS AREAS

In 2006, according to preliminary estimates, the West Bank and Gaza Strip recorded a visible trade deficit of US $2,703.5m. and a deficit of $538.4m. on the current account of the balance of payments. In the absence of seaport facilities and of an airport (Gaza International Airport was opened in November 1998 but has frequently been closed by the Israeli authorities), foreign trade (in terms of value) has been conducted almost exclusively with Israel since occupation. In 2006 Israel was the source of 72.5% of all imports and took 89.1% of all exports. Most Palestinian exports are of agricultural or horticultural products. One notable feature of this trade is that Palestinian goods have often been exported to Israel, and subsequently re-exported as originating in Israel. In 2006 imports (c.i.f.) from Israel alone were valued at $2,002.2m. and exports (f.o.b.) to Israel totalled $326.6m.

In 2004, according to official revised estimates, the PA recorded an overall budget deficit of US $790.1m. The annual rate of inflation in the West Bank and Gaza averaged 3.5% in 2000–07; consumer prices increased by an average of 2.8% in 2007. According to official estimates, some 23.6% of the labour force in the Palestinian territories (18.6% in the West Bank; 34.8% in Gaza) were unemployed in 2006. According to ILO, the overall rate of unemployment in 2007 was 21.6%.

The prospects for an improvement in economic conditions in the Palestinian Autonomous Areas, which remain highly dependent on Israel, are inextricably linked to the full implementation of the Oslo accords (see Recent History) and the outcome of 'final status' negotiations between the PA and Israel. Agriculture remains focused mainly on meeting local demand, although the sector supplies the bulk of Palestinian exports and there is proven demand for Palestinian products beyond the Israeli market. The expansion of Palestinian agriculture is also limited by problems with irrigation: access to water supplies is subject to 'final status' discussions. Economic conditions in the West Bank and Gaza have deteriorated markedly since 1993, largely as a result of frequent border closures enforced by the Israeli authorities in reprisal for terrorist attacks by militant Islamist groups. Such closures lead to an immediate rise in the rate of unemployment among Palestinians, raise transportation costs for Palestinian goods and, at times, halt trade entirely. The Oslo accords provide for the development of seaport facilities and for the opening of Gaza International Airport and of a safe passage linking the Gaza Strip with the West Bank.

Shortly after the militant Islamic Resistance Movement (Hamas) secured the highest number of seats at the legislative elections of January 2006, Israel again halted payments of tax and customs duties to the PA. Meanwhile, the USA and the EU declared that they were withdrawing direct aid to the PA. Every year since the creation of the PA in 1994, the EU had donated an estimated US $600m., and the USA some $400m. However, the USA pledged to increase by over 50% the amount of humanitarian aid it donated to the Palestinians via agencies not linked to the administration, to $245m. Nonetheless, in late 2008 the USA provided $150m. in budget aid to the PA. The EU asserted that its direct humanitarian aid to Palestinians, which included annual donations from individual states of some $262m., would not be affected by its decision to withdraw direct aid to the PA. At an international donors' conference in Stockholm, Sweden, in September 2006, donors pledged funds of $500m. to assist non-governmental bodies operating in the PA-controlled territories. Economic prospects in the West Bank and Gaza appeared improved following the formation, in March 2007, of a national unity administration, but the takeover of Gaza by Hamas militants in June resulted in a de facto separation between the emergency administration appointed by Fatah's President Abbas in the West Bank and a Hamas-led cabinet in the Gaza Strip. Abbas's establishment of a Cabinet that excluded ministers from Hamas did, however, result in the international embargo imposed on the West Bank in 2006 being lifted. The PA's Prime Minister in the West Bank, Dr Salam Fayyad, launched a three-year Palestinian Reform and Development Plan in late 2007, which was intended to stimulate the economy and to encourage private sector development. At an international donors' conference held in Paris in December, some $7,400m. was pledged in support to the PA, both to alleviate the budgetary crisis and to fund proposed development projects. There was further deterioration in the economy in 2008, with real GDP contracting by 3.7%. The Palestinian Central Bureau of Statistics forecast further contractions in 2009 following the Israeli offensive ('Operation Cast Lead') that targeted Hamas-administered Gaza in late 2008–early 2009, with exports expected to fall over that year by 8.2%; GDP per head to fall by 6.3%; and real GDP to fall by 3.6%. The cost of rebuilding infrastructure destroyed during 'Operation Cast Lead' was estimated at $1,100m. An international donors' conference, convened in Sharm esh-Sheikh, Egypt, at the beginning of March 2009, raised pledges totalling $5,200m., to finance humanitarian aid and rebuilding assistance for Gaza, as well as budgetary support to the PA. The IMF stated in early 2009 that the economic and humanitarian situation in the West Bank and Gaza had deteriorated significantly since the Palestinian Reform and Development Plan was initiated in December 2007, highlighting falls in GDP per head and rises in unemployment. Some economic sectors have proved resilient: analysts believe, for example, that the IT sector, which has grown in recent years, has the potential to make a significant contribution to the economy. Furthermore, the Palestinian Monetary Authority has made progress towards becoming a central bank, and it has been anticipated that it might be in a position to issue its own currency by 2010–12.

Education

In the West Bank the Jordanian education system is in operation. Services are provided by the Israeli Civil Administration, the UN Relief and Works Agency for Palestine Refugees in the Near East (UNRWA) and private, voluntary organizations, which provide all university and most community college education. There are 20 community and teacher training colleges in the West Bank, and six universities (including an open university). The Egyptian system of education operates in the Gaza Strip, where there are three universities and one teacher training college. Palestinian education has been severely disrupted since 1987, and more recently as a result of the al-Aqsa *intifada*, which began in late 2000. Since May 1994 the PA has assumed responsibility for education in Gaza and parts of the West Bank. According to UNESCO estimates, enrolment at primary schools in 2006/07 included 80.4% of pupils in the relevant age group, while 92.4% of children in the appropriate age group were enrolled at secondary schools. In 2007/08, according to the Palestinian Central Bureau of Statistics, 84,133 pupils attended 972 pre-primary schools, 957,831 pupils attended 1,615 primary schools and 140,126 students were enrolled at 815 secondary institutions. In 2007/08 167,984 students attended universities or equivalent third-level institutions.

Since 1950 UNRWA has provided education services to all Palestinian refugees, numbering 762,820 in the West Bank and 1,073,303 in the Gaza Strip in December 2008. The focus of UNRWA's education programme is basic primary and junior secondary schooling, offered free of charge to all refugee children and youth in accordance with local systems. In 2008/09 UNRWA operated 94 schools in the West Bank and 221 in the Gaza Strip, providing education to 56,384 pupils in the West Bank and to 198,860 pupils in Gaza. In addition, UNRWA operated five vocational training centres in the West Bank and Gaza. In 2009 UNRWA budgeted some US $150.3m. for expenditure on education in the Palestinian territories.

Public Holidays

2009: 9 March* (Mouloud/Yum an-Nabi, Birth of Muhammad), 19 July* (Leilat al-Meiraj, Ascension of Muhammad), 20 September* (Id al-Fitr, end of Ramadan), 15 November (Independence Day), 27 November* (Id al-Adha, Feast of the Sacrifice).

2010: 26 February* (Mouloud/Yum an-Nabi, Birth of Muhammad), 8 July* (Leilat al-Meiraj, Ascension of Muhammad), 10 September* (Id al-Fitr, end of Ramadan), 15 November (Independence Day), 16 November* (Id al-Adha, Feast of the Sacrifice).

*These holidays are dependent on the Islamic lunar calendar and may vary by one or two days from the dates given.

Christian holidays are observed by the Christian Arab community.

Weights and Measures

The metric system is in force, although local weights and measures are also used.

PALESTINIAN AUTONOMOUS AREAS

Statistical Survey

Source (unless otherwise indicated): Palestinian Central Bureau of Statistics (PCBS), POB 1647, Ramallah; tel. (2) 2406340; fax (2) 2406343; e-mail diwan@pcbs.gov.ps; internet www.pcbs.gov.ps.

Note: Unless otherwise indicated, data include East Jerusalem, annexed by Israel in 1967.

Area and Population

AREA, POPULATION AND DENSITY

Area (sq km)	6,020*
Population (census of 9 December 1997)†	2,895,683
Population (census of 1 December 2007, preliminary figures)	
Males	1,908,432
Females	1,853,214
Total	3,761,646
Density (per sq km) at 1 December 2007	624.9

* 2,324 sq miles. The total comprises: West Bank 5,655 sq km (2,183 sq miles); Gaza Strip 365 sq km (141 sq miles).

† Figures include an estimate of 210,209 for East Jerusalem and an adjustment of 83,805 for estimated underenumeration. The total comprises 1,873,476 (males 951,693, females 921,783) in the West Bank (including East Jerusalem) and 1,022,207 (males 518,813, females 503,394) in the Gaza Strip. The data exclude Jewish settlers. According to official Israeli estimates, the population of Israelis residing in Jewish localities in the West Bank (excluding East Jerusalem) and Gaza Strip was 243,900 at 31 December 2004 (West Bank 235,700, Gaza Strip 8,200). The withdrawal of Israeli settlers residing in Jewish localities in the Gaza Strip was completed in September 2005 (see Recent History).

Note: Official projected estimates of a total world-wide Palestinian population of 10,094,565 at 31 December 2006 included 1,134,293 Palestinians resident in Israel and 2,799,440 resident in Jordan.

GOVERNORATES
(census of 1 December 2007, preliminary results)

	Area (sq km)	Population*	Density (per sq km)
West Bank			
Janin (Jenin)	583	256,212	439.5
Tubas	402	48,771	121.3
Tulkarm	246	158,213	643.1
Qalqilya	166	91,046	548.5
Salfeet	204	59,464	291.5
Nabulus (Nablus)	605	321,493	531.4
Ram Allah (Ramallah) and Al-Birah	855	278,018	325.2
Al-Quds (Jerusalem)†	345	362,521	1,050.8
Ariha (Jericho) and Al-Aghwar	593	41,724	70.4
Beit Lahm (Bethlehem)	659	176,515	267.9
Al-Khalil (Hebron)	997	551,130	552.8
Gaza Strip			
North Gaza	61	270,245	4,430.2
Gaza	74	496,410	6,708.2
Deir al-Balah	58	205,534	3,543.7
Khan Yunus (Khan Yunis)	108	270,979	2,509.1
Rafah	64	173,371	2,708.9
Total	6,020	3,761,646	624.9

* Figures exclude Jewish settlers.
† Figures refer only to the eastern sector of the city.

PRINCIPAL LOCALITIES
(estimated population at mid-2002, excluding Jewish settlers)

West Bank			
Al-Quds (Jerusalem)	242,081*	Adh-Dhahiriya	25,348
Al-Khalil (Hebron)	147,291	Ar-Ram and Dahiyat	
Nabulus (Nablus)	121,344	al-Bareed	23,038
		Ram Allah	
Tulkarm	41,109	(Ramallah)	22,493
Qalqilya	39,580	Halhul	19,345
Yattah (Yatta)	38,023	Dura	19,124
Al-Birah	34,920	Ariha (Jericho)	18,239
Janin (Jenin)	32,300	Qabatiya	17,788
Beit Lahm (Bethlehem)	26,847		

Gaza Strip			
Ghazzah (Gaza)	361,651	Beit Lahya	50,576
Khan Yunus (Khan Yunis)	110,677	Deir al-Balah	43,593
Jabalyah (Jabalia)	104,620	Bani Suhaylah	28,761
Rafah	62,452	Beit Hanun	27,341
An-Nuseirat	56,449	Tel as-Sultan Camp	21,477
		Al-Maghazi Camp	21,278

* The figure refers only to the eastern sector of the city.

Mid-2007 (incl. suburbs, UN estimate): Ramallah 67,000 (Source: UN, *World Urbanization Prospects: The 2007 Revision*).

BIRTHS AND DEATHS
(official estimates)*

	2004	2005	2006
Live births:			
West Bank	63,136	61,194	52,265
Gaza Strip	48,109	48,245	48,588
Deaths:			
West Bank	5,658	5,507	4,712
Gaza Strip	4,371	4,138	4,490

* Excluding Jewish settlers.

Birth rate (official estimates per 1,000): 39.6 in 2002; 38.8 in 2003; 38.1 in 2004.

Death rate (official estimates per 1,000): 4.3 in 2002; 4.2 in 2003; 4.1 in 2004.

MARRIAGES
(number registered)

	2005	2006	2007
West Bank	16,706	16,380	18,576
Gaza Strip	12,170	11,853	14,109

Marriage rate (rates per 1,000, official estimates): West Bank: 7.0 in 2005; 6.7 in 2006; 7.9 in 2007. Gaza Strip: 8.8 in 2005; 8.2 in 2006; 10.0 in 2007.

ECONOMICALLY ACTIVE POPULATION
(persons aged 15 years and over)

	2005	2006	2007
Agriculture, hunting, forestry and fishing	92,310	107,024	103,721
Mining and quarrying	1,377	2,237	1,542
Manufacturing	80,874	80,543	81,964
Electricity and gas	2,366	2,500	2,230
Construction	81,644	73,905	72,722
Wholesale and retail trade	110,110	114,662	116,408
Hotels and restaurants	12,813	13,492	13,407
Transport, storage and communications	36,134	38,242	37,404
Financial intermediation	3,513	4,503	4,214
Real estate, renting and business activities	10,492	11,217	11,380
Public administration and defence	92,977	98,922	99,584
Education	60,743	67,704	68,034
Health and social work	22,804	24,400	24,525
Services	17,462	19,426	20,594
Extra-territorial organizations and bodies	7,186	7,221	7,411
Households with employed persons	133	348	182
Unclassified	—	30	298
Total employed	632,939	666,375	665,620
Unemployed	194,458	206,150	183,689
Total labour force	827,397	872,525	849,309
Males	n.a.	721,153	691,695
Females	n.a.	151,372	157,615

Source: ILO.

Health and Welfare

KEY INDICATORS

Total fertility rate (children per woman, 2005)	5.6
Under-5 mortality rate (per 1,000 live births, 2004)	24
Physicians (per 1,000 head, 2005, official estimate)	1.62
Hospital beds (per 1,000 head, 2006, official estimate)	1.4
Access to water (% of persons, 2006)	89
Access to sanitation (% of persons, 2006)	80
Human Development Index (2006): ranking	106
Human Development Index (2006): value	0.731

For other sources and definitions, see explanatory note on p. vi.

Agriculture

PRINCIPAL CROPS
('000 metric tons)

	2005	2006	2007*
Wheat	44.7	39.4	40.0
Barley	22.2	13.9	22.0
Potatoes	54.8	65.5	66.0
Sweet potatoes	5.0	8.8	9.0
Olives	137.8	137.8	141.0
Cabbages and other brassicas	18.3	25.3	26.0
Tomatoes	212.1	207.2	205.0
Cauliflowers and broccoli	20.9	27.4	30.0
Cucumbers and gherkins	132.1	150.0	153.0
Aubergines (Eggplants)	56.0	56.3	56.5
Onions, dry	36.2	40.8	46.0
Watermelons	16.5	15.6	16.0
Grapes	66.2	52.5	56.0
Plums and sloes	6.5	8.4	8.4
Oranges	37.7	36.3	35.0
Tangerines, mandarins, clementines and satsumas	7.2	8.2	8.4
Lemons and limes	12.9	18.1	18.0
Grapefruit and pomelos	1.6	1.8	1.8
Bananas	9.8	8.0	8.0
Strawberries	6.0	5.3	5.7

* FAO estimates.

Aggregate production ('000 metric tons, may include official, semi-official or estimated data): Total cereals 68.2 in 2005, 55.0 in 2006, 63.5 in 2007; Total roots and tubers 62.3 in 2005, 77.7 in 2006, 79.1 in 2007; Total vegetables (incl. melons) 628.5 in 2005, 670.9 in 2006, 689.2 in 2007; Total fruits (excl. melons) 179.7 in 2005, 159.8 in 2006, 162.7 in 2007.

Source: FAO.

LIVESTOCK
('000 head)

	2005	2006	2007*
Cattle	33.7	36.3	39.0
Sheep	803.2	793.9	785.0
Goats	371.2	387.1	404.0
Chickens*	11,300	11,600	11,900

* FAO estimates.
Source: FAO.

LIVESTOCK PRODUCTS
('000 metric tons)

	2005	2006	2007*
Cattle meat	5.2	4.6*	5.1
Chicken meat	69.1	53.6	69.0
Goat meat*	4.5	4.6	4.8
Sheep meat*	11.9	12.9	12.7
Cows' milk	99.5	102.6	115.0
Hen eggs	37.4†	37.9*	38.5

* FAO estimate(s).
† Unofficial figure.

Source: FAO.

Fishing

GAZA STRIP
(metric tons, live weight)

	2004	2005	2006*
Bogue	29	27	15
Jack and horse mackerels	82	88	50
Sardinellas	2,080	928	500
Chub mackerel	113	82	45
Cuttlefish and bobtail squids	66	73	40
Total catch (incl. others)	2,951	1,805	1,000

* FAO estimates.
Source: FAO.

Finance

CURRENCY AND EXCHANGE RATES

Monetary Units

At present there is no domestic Palestinian currency in use. The Israeli shekel, the Jordanian dinar and the US dollar all circulate within the West Bank and the Gaza Strip.

BUDGET OF THE PALESTINIAN AUTHORITY
(US $ million, estimates)

Revenue	2002	2003*	2004†
Domestic revenue	185	259	298
Revenue clearances‡	150	442	508
Total	335	701	806

Expenditure	2002	2003*	2004†
Central administration	141.8	128.0	109.2
Public security and order	310.4	392.1	433.9
Financial affairs	292.5	352.2	410.7
Foreign affairs	13.8	17.2	25.6
Economic development	35.8	39.8	43.1
Social services	340.5	432.9	526.6
Cultural and information services	25.4	29.2	32.8
Transport and communication services	10.4	12.1	14.2
Total	1,170.6	1,403.5	1,596.1

* Revised estimates.
† Provisional figures.
‡ Figures refer to an apportionment of an agreed pool of selected tax revenues arising as a result of the de facto customs union between Israel and the Palestinian territories. Israel is the collecting agent for these receipts and periodically makes transfers to the Palestinian Authority.

Source: Ministry of Finance, Ramallah.

COST OF LIVING
(Consumer Price Index; base: 1996 = 100)

	2005	2006	2007
Food	137.3	144.0	150.8
Beverages and tobacco	162.7	168.1	176.9
Textiles, clothing and footwear	129.5	130.3	129.3
Housing	158.4	163.0	166.2
All items (incl. others)	146.8	152.3	156.4

PALESTINIAN AUTONOMOUS AREAS

NATIONAL ACCOUNTS*
Expenditure on the Gross Domestic Product
(US $ million at constant 2004 prices)

	2005	2006	2007
Final consumption expenditure	5,609.1	5,722.1	6,086.4
Households	4,579.6	4,662.6	4,848.8
Non-profit institutions serving households	197.0	189.8	238.1
General government	832.5	869.7	999.5
Gross capital formation	1,275.5	1,420.2	1,159.1
Gross fixed capital formation	1,257.1	1,393.6	1,135.2
Changes in inventories	18.4	26.6	23.9
Total domestic expenditure	6,884.6	7,142.3	7,245.5
Exports of goods and services	613.3	678.3	748.1
Less Imports of goods and services	2,863.5	3,201.5	3,321.3
GDP in purchasers' values	4,634.4	4,619.1	4,672.3

Gross Domestic Product by Economic Activity
(US $ million at current prices)

	2005	2006	2007
Agriculture and fishing	720.8	718.0	745.0
Mining and quarrying	48.7	41.6	32.1
Manufacturing	1,537.5	1,680.6	1,436.6
Electricity and water supply	273.1	188.5	202.2
Construction	693.3	676.4	708.8
Wholesale and retail trade	706.7	750.0	803.3
Transport, storage and communications	412.6	455.5	460.0
Financial intermediation	263.5	228.0	265.5
Real estate, renting and business services	494.4	488.7	422.0
Community, social and personal services	102.0	96.2	93.8
Hotels and restaurants	103.4	112.7	108.4
Education	416.5	375.3	444.7
Health and social work	201.4	165.8	217.3
Public administration and defence	1,078.7	959.6	1,164.8
Households with employed persons	1.8	2.9	3.6
Other services	351.6	372.7	386.5
Gross value added	7,406.0	7,312.5	7,494.6
Taxes on imports	635.0	641.9	755.4
GDP in purchasers' values	8,041.0	7,954.4	8,250.0

* Referring to the West Bank and Gaza Strip, but excluding that part of Jerusalem annexed in 1967.

BALANCE OF PAYMENTS
(US $ million, preliminary estimates)

	2004	2005	2006
Exports of goods f.o.b.	404.4	411.6	451.4
Imports of goods f.o.b.	−2,769.9	−3,049.5	−3,154.9
Trade balance	−2,365.5	−2,638.0	−2,703.5
Exports of services	181.4	265.3	263.7
Imports of services	−489.8	−487.4	−559.8
Balance on goods and services	−2,674.0	−2,860.1	−2,999.6
Other income received (net)	426.1	573.3	646.2
Balance on goods, services and income	−2,247.9	−2,286.8	−2,353.4
Current transfers (net)	764.6	1,179.8	1,815.0
Current balance	−1,483.3	−1,107.1	−538.4
Capital account (net)	670.3	422.2	275.0
Direct investment abroad (net)	99.7	37.8	−115.9
Portfolio investment (net)	61.9	2.4	−8.4
Other investment (net)	587.0	616.5	771.9
Net errors and omissions	91.7	2.6	−361.9
Overall balance	27.4	−25.7	22.3

External Trade

PRINCIPAL COMMODITIES
(US $ million)

Imports c.i.f.	2004	2005	2006
Food and live animals	470.3	452.1	464.7
Beverages and tobacco	108.7	102.4	125.1
Crude materials (inedible) except fuels	47.9	62.0	51.8
Mineral fuels, lubricants, etc.	660.1	718.3	942.4
Animal and vegetable oils and fats	20.8	20.3	20.6
Chemicals and related products	201.8	222.9	199.0
Basic manufactures	449.6	491.4	413.5
Machinery and transport equipment	281.6	433.5	329.3
Miscellaneous manufactured articles	132.4	147.5	153.1
Commodities not classified elsewhere	0.0	17.4	59.3
Total	2,373.2	2,666.8	2,758.7

Exports f.o.b.	2004	2005	2006
Food and live animals	35.9	36.2	38.8
Beverages and tobacco	17.2	14.3	10.0
Crude materials (inedible) except fuels	11.1	13.2	18.5
Mineral fuels, lubricants, etc.	10.5	12.2	3.3
Animal and vegetable oils and fats	9.9	12.3	13.7
Chemicals and related products	29.4	28.9	35.2
Basic manufactures	122.7	129.8	155.4
Machinery and transport equipment	14.8	18.5	22.1
Miscellaneous manufactured articles	61.1	66.8	69.6
Other commodities and transactions	0.0	3.3	0.0
Total	312.7	335.4	366.7

Source: UN, *International Trade Statistics Yearbook*.

PRINCIPAL TRADING PARTNERS
(US $ million)

Imports c.i.f.	2004	2005	2006
China, People's Republic	88.7	110.9	114.3
Egypt	29.9	32.2	31.4
France (incl. Monaco)	23.4	30.3	24.2
Germany	33.3	54.2	38.7
Israel	1,747.9	1,872.9	2,002.2
Italy	45.5	39.8	31.8
Japan	12.0	47.0	87.1
Jordan	34.0	35.1	33.0
Spain	26.1	28.2	24.9
Sweden	19.1	26.3	42.9
Thailand	4.9	49.1	9.4
Turkey	116.7	120.7	92.5
United Kingdom	21.1	21.5	16.0
USA	39.5	31.9	21.6
Total (incl. others)	2,373.2	2,666.8	2,758.7

Exports f.o.b.	2004	2005	2006
Algeria	1.1	2.5	3.5
Israel	281.1	290.6	326.6
Jordan	11.9	17.5	23.0
Netherlands	3.1	5.4	0.0
Saudi Arabia	2.4	2.1	2.1
United Arab Emirates	1.7	1.2	2.4
USA	1.6	4.1	2.4
Total (incl. others)	312.7	335.4	366.7

Source: UN, *International Trade Statistics Yearbook*.

Transport

ROAD TRAFFIC
(registered motor vehicles holding Palestinian licence, 2006)

	West Bank	Gaza Strip
Private cars	36,323	42,372
Taxis	7,432	3,392
Buses	950	219
Trucks and commercial cars	12,013	10,788
Motorcycles and mopeds	29	219
Tractors	615	1,416

Tourism

ARRIVALS OF VISITORS AT HOTELS*

	2004	2005	2006
Total	100,184	131,908	151,801†

* Including Palestinians.
† Preliminary.

2005: Total guest nights in hotels 350,220 (Palestinians 98,862; European Union members 109,347; Israelis 30,400; Asians 49,179).

2006: Total guest nights in hotels 383,603 (Palestinians 52,309; European Union members 142,980; Israelis 44,602; Asians 47,421).

2007: Total guest nights in hotels 673,458.

Communications Media

	2005	2006	2007
Telephones ('000 main lines in use)	349.0	341.3	350.4
Mobile cellular telephones ('000 subscribers)	1,094.6	821.8	1,025.9
Personal computers ('000 in use)	169	n.a.	n.a.
Internet users ('000)	243	266	356
Broadband subscribers ('000)	7.7	25.9	55.6

Source: International Telecommunication Union.

Book production (1996): 114 titles; 571,000 copies (Source: UNESCO, *Statistical Yearbook*).

Daily newspapers (titles): 2 in 2004.

Non-daily newspapers (titles): 11 in 2004.

Education

(2007/08, unless otherwise indicated)

	Institutions	Teachers	Students
Pre-primary	972	3,285	84,289
Primary	1,615	43,560	957,831
Secondary	815		140,126
Higher: universities, etc.	11*	4,527	167,984
other	23*		

*2006/07.

Adult literacy rate (persons aged 15 and over, official estimates): 93.5% (males 97.1%; females 89.8%) in 2006.

Directory

Administration

PALESTINIAN NATIONAL AUTHORITY

Appointed in May 1994, the Palestinian National Authority (PNA), generally known internationally as the Palestinian Authority (PA), has assumed some of the civil responsibilities formerly exercised by the Israeli Civil Administration in the Gaza Strip and parts of the West Bank.

Executive President: MAHMUD ABBAS (assumed office 15 January 2005).

CABINET
(April 2009)

Following the seizure of control by militants of the Islamic Resistance Movement (Hamas) in the Gaza Strip, on 14 June 2007 President Mahmud Abbas dissolved the national unity administration under the premiership of Ismail Haniya of Hamas and appointed Dr Salam Fayyad, an independent, as Prime Minister. An Emergency Cabinet, consisting principally of independents (Ind.), as well as one representative of the Fatah movement, was sworn in on 17 June. Upon the expiry of the 30-day state of emergency, on 13 July President Abbas appointed three new ministers to the Cabinet, which was to function as a caretaker administration under Fayyad's premiership. Hamas refused to recognize the legitimacy of this interim administration, as it had the Emergency Cabinet.

Prime Minister and Minister of Finance: Dr SALAM KHALED ABDULLAH FAYYAD (Ind.).
Minister of the Interior and of Civil Affairs: ABD AR-RAZZAQ AL-YAHYA (Fatah).
Minister of Foreign Affairs and of Information: Dr RIYAD NAJIB AL-MALIKI (Ind.).
Minister of Local Government: ZIAD ABDULLAH AL-BANDAK (Ind.).
Minister of Tourism and Antiquities, and of Women's Affairs: KHOULOUD IHADEB DAIBES (Ind.).
Minister of National Economy, of Public Works and Housing, and of Telecommunications and Information Technology: MUHAMMAD KAMAL IBRAHIM HASSOUNEH (Ind.).
Minister of Education and Higher Education, and of Culture: LAMIS AL-ALAMI (Ind.).
Minister of Planning and of Labour: Dr SAMIR ABDULLAH (Ind.).
Minister of Health: Dr FATHI ABDULLAH ABU MUGHLI (Ind.).
Minister of Awqaf (Religious Endowments): Dr TALEB ABU SHA'AR (Ind.).
Minister of Transport: Dr MASHHOUR MUHAMMAD ABU DAQQA (Ind.).
Minister of Prisoners' Affairs: ASHRAF EID AL-AJRAMI (Ind.).
Minister of Social Affairs and Agriculture: MAHMUD SIDQI AL-HABBASH (Ind.).
Minister of Justice: Dr ALI AHMAD SALIM KHASHAN (Ind.).
Minister of Youth and Sports: TAHANI SULAYMAN MAHMUD ABU DAQQA (Ind.).

MINISTRIES

Office of the President: Ramallah.
Ministry of Agriculture: POB 197, Ramallah; tel. (2) 2961080; fax (2) 2961212; e-mail moa@planet.edu.
Ministry of Awqaf (Religious Endowments): POB 17412, Jerusalem; tel. (2) 6282085; fax (2) 2986401.
Ministry of Civil Affairs: Ramallah; tel. (2) 2987336; fax (2) 2987335.
Ministry of Culture: POB 147, Ramallah; tel. (2) 2986205; fax (2) 2986204.
Ministry of Education and Higher Education: POB 576, Al-Masioun, Ramallah; POB 5285, Al-Wihda St, Gaza; tel. (2) 2983200; fax (2) 2983222; e-mail irp@mohe.gov.ps; tel. (8) 2866809; fax (8) 2865909; e-mail hope@hally.net; internet www.moehe.gov.ps.
Ministry of Environmental Affairs: POB 3841, Ramallah; Ath-Thawra St, Gaza; tel. (2) 2403495; fax (2) 2403494; e-mail menawb@gov.ps; tel. (7) 2822000; fax (7) 2847198; e-mail environment@gov.ps; internet www.mena.gov.ps.
Ministry of Finance: POB 795, Sateh Marhaba, Al-Birah/Ramallah; POB 4007, Gaza; tel. (2) 2400650; fax (2) 2400595; tel. (8)

PALESTINIAN AUTONOMOUS AREAS

2826188; fax (8) 2820696; e-mail cbomof@palnet.com; internet www.mof.gov.ps.

Ministry of Foreign Affairs: POB 1336, Ramallah; POB 4017, Gaza; tel. (2) 2405040; fax (2) 2403772; tel. (8) 2829260; fax (8) 2868971; e-mail mofapal@gmail.com; internet www.mofa.gov.ps.

Ministry of Health: POB 14, al-Mukhtar St, Nablus; POB 1035, Abu Khadra Center, Gaza; tel. (9) 2384772; fax (9) 2384777; e-mail moh@gov.ps; tel. (8) 2829173; fax (8) 2826295; internet www.moh.gov.ps.

Ministry of Industry: POB 2073, Ramallah; POB 4053, Gaza; tel. (2) 2987641; fax (2) 2987640; tel. (8) 2826463; fax (8) 2824884; e-mail industry_wb@gov.ps.

Ministry of Information: Al-Masyoun Area, Ramallah; tel. (2) 2954042; fax (2)2954043; e-mail minfo@minfo.gov.ps; internet www.minfo.gov.ps.

Ministry of the Interior: Gaza; tel. (8) 2829185; fax (8) 2862500.

Ministry of Jerusalem Affairs: POB 20479, Jerusalem; tel. (2) 6273330; fax (2) 6286820.

Ministry of Justice: POB 267, Ramallah; POB 1012, Gaza; tel. (2) 2987661; fax (2) 2974491; e-mail info@moj.gov.ps; internet www.moj.gov.ps.

Ministry of Labour: POB 350, Al-Irsal St, Ramallah; tel. (2) 2900375; fax (2) 2900607; e-mail info@mol.pna.org; internet www.mol.gov.ps.

Ministry of Local Government: POB 731, Albaloo, Al-Birah/Ramallah; Gaza; tel. (2) 2401092; fax (2) 2401091; tel. (8) 2820272; fax (8) 2828474; e-mail info@molg.gov.ps; internet www.molg.gov.ps.

Ministry of National Economy: Umm ash-Sharayet, Ramallah; Maqqusi Bldg, An-Nasser St, Gaza; tel. (2) 2981218; fax (2) 2981207; tel. (8) 2874146; fax (8) 2874145; e-mail info@met.gov.ps; internet www.met.gov.ps.

Ministry of Planning: POB 4557, Al-Birah/Ramallah; POB 4017, Gaza; tel. (2) 2973010; fax (2) 2973012; tel. (8) 2828825; fax (8) 2830509; e-mail mop@gov.ps; internet www.mop.gov.ps.

Ministry of Public Works and Housing: Gaza; tel. (8) 2829232; fax (8) 2823653; e-mail mopgaza@palnet.com.

Ministry of Social Affairs: POB 3525, Ramallah; tel. (2) 2986181; fax (2) 2985239; e-mail msa@hally.net; internet www.mosa.gov.ps.

Ministry of Supply: Gaza; tel. (8) 2824324; fax (8) 2826430.

Ministry of Telecommunications and Information Technology: Ramallah; Gaza; tel. (2) 2409354; fax (2) 2409352; tel. (8) 2829171; fax (8) 2824555; e-mail mdiwan@mtit.gov.ps; internet www.mtit.gov.ps.

Ministry of Tourism and Antiquities: POB 534, Manger St, Bethlehem; Gaza; tel. (2) 2741581; fax (2) 2743753; tel. (7) 2824866; fax (7) 2824856; e-mail mota@visit-palestine.com; internet www.visit-palestine.com.

Ministry of Transport: POB 399, Ramallah; tel. (2) 2986945; fax (2) 2986943.

Ministry of Women's Affairs: Al-Birah/Ramallah; tel. (2) 2403315; e-mail contactus@mowa.ps; internet www.mowa.gov.ps.

Ministry of Youth and Sports: POB 52, Irsal St, Ramallah; POB 1416, Rimal Izz ed-Din Qassam St, Gaza; tel. (2) 2985983; fax (2) 2985991; tel. (8) 2826668; fax (8) 2822736; e-mail youth@p-ol.com; internet www.mys.gov.ps.

President and Legislature

PRESIDENT

Election, 9 January 2005

Candidates	Votes	%
Mahmud Abbas (Fatah)	501,448	62.52
Mustafa Barghouthi (Ind.)	156,227	19.48
Tayseer Khalid (DFLP)	26,848	3.35
Abd al-Halim al-Ashqar (Ind.)	22,171	2.76
Bassam es-Salhi (PPP)	21,429	2.67
As-Said Baraka (Ind.)	10,406	1.30
Abd al-Karim Shbeir (Ind.)	5,717	0.71
Invalid votes	57,831	7.21
Total	**802,077**	**100.00**

PALESTINIAN LEGISLATIVE COUNCIL

Speaker: Dr AHMAD BAHAR (acting).

General Election, 25 January 2006

	Seats		
Parties, Lists and Coalitions	Majority system	Proportional system	Total
Change and Reform*	29	45	74
Fatah	28	17	45
Martyr Abu Ali Moustafa†	3	0	3
The Third Way	2	0	2
The Alternative‡	2	0	2
Independent Palestine§	2	0	2
Independents	0	4	4
Total	**66**	**66**	**132**

* The Islamic Resistance Movement (Hamas) contested the elections as Change and Reform.
† The Popular Front for the Liberation of Palestine contested the elections as Martyr Abu Ali Moustafa.
‡ Electoral list comprising the Palestinian Democratic Union, the Coalition of the Democratic Front (representing the Democratic Front for the Liberation of Palestine) and the Palestinian People's Party.
§ Coalition comprising independents and representatives of the Palestinian National Initiative.

On 18 June 2005 the Palestinian Legislative Council (PLC) had approved a new election law, adopting a 'mixed' electoral system for forthcoming legislative polls: the system combined a 'majority system' and a system of proportional representation. Under the majority system, according to which candidates were elected to 66 of the PLC's 132 seats, the Palestinian territories were divided into 16 electoral districts (11 in the West Bank and five in the Gaza Strip), and candidates contested seats allocated to their district in proportion to the size of its population. The remaining 66 deputies were elected to the PLC by the system of proportional representation, under which the Palestinian enclaves were treated as one electoral district, and voters chose between nation-wide lists of political organizations and coalitions ('party lists'). Six of the seats were reserved for Christians. All deputies elected to the PLC automatically became members of the Palestine National Council (see the Palestine Liberation Organization).

Election Commission

Central Elections Commission (CEC): POB 2319, Qasr al-Murjan Bldg, Al-Balou, nr Jawwal Circle, Ramallah; tel. (2) 2969700; fax (2) 2969712; e-mail info@elections.ps; internet www.elections.ps; f. 2002; independent; comprises nine mems, appointed by the Exec. Pres. of the PA; Chair. Dr HANNA NASIR; Sec.-Gen. Dr RAMI HAMDALLAH.

Political Organizations

Alliance of Palestinian Forces: f. 1994; 10 members representing the PFLP, the DFLP, the PLF, the PPSF, the Palestine Revolutionary Communist Party and the PFLP—GC; opposes the Declaration of Principles on Palestinian Self-Rule signed by Israel and the PLO in September 1993, and subsequent agreements concluded within its framework (the 'Oslo accords'). The PFLP and DFLP left the Alliance in 1996. The **Fatah Revolutionary Council**, headed by Sabri Khalil al-Banna, alias 'Abu Nidal', split from Fatah in 1973. Its headquarters were formerly in Baghdad, Iraq, but the office was closed down and its staff expelled from the country by the Iraqi authorities in November 1983; a new base was established in Damascus, Syria, in December. Al-Banna was readmitted to Iraq in 1984, having fled Syria. With 'Abu Musa' (whose rebel Fatah group is called **Al-Intifada** or 'Uprising'), Abu Nidal formed a joint rebel Fatah command in February 1985, and both had offices in Damascus until June 1987, when those of Abu Nidal were closed by the Syrian Government. Forces loyal to Abu Nidal surrendered to Fatah forces at the Rashidiyeh Palestinian refugee camp near Tyre, northern Lebanon, in 1990. Abu Nidal was reportedly found dead in Baghdad in August 2002.

Arab Liberation Front (ALF): Ramallah; f. 1969; fmrly supported by Iraq's Arab Baath Socialist Party under the leadership of former President Saddam Hussain; member of the PLO; opposes Oslo accords; Sec.-Gen. RAKAD SALIM (imprisoned in 2002).

Democratic Front for the Liberation of Palestine (DFLP) (Al-Jabha ad-Dimuqratiyya li-Tahrir Filastin): Damascus, Syria; tel. (11) 4448993; fax (11) 4442380; Ramallah; tel. (2) 2954438; fax (2)

2980401; e-mail dflp-palestine@dflp-palestine.org; internet www.dflp-palestine.org; f. 1969 following split with PFLP; Marxist-Leninist; contested Jan. 2006 legislative elections on The Alternative electoral list as the Coalition of the Democratic Front; Sec.-Gen. NAIF HAWATMEH (Damascus).

Fatah (Harakat at-Tahrir al-Watani al-Filastin—Palestine National Liberation Movement): e-mail fateh@fateh.net; internet www.fateh.net; f. 1957; militant group which became the single largest Palestinian organization and strongest faction in both the administration and Palestinian Legislative Council until the legislative elections of Jan. 2006; leadership is nominally shared by the members of the Central Committee, who were elected at Fatah's Fifth General Conference on 8 August 1989; however, some of those elected to the Central Committee have since died; it was announced in May 2009 that the Sixth General Conference would be held on 1 July; Chair. of Central Cttee FAROUK KADDOUMI (Tunis, Tunisia).

Islamic Jihad (Al-Jihad al-Islami): Damascus, Syria; f. 1979–80 by Palestinian students in Egypt; militant Islamist; opposed to the Oslo accords; Sec.-Gen. RAMADAN ABDULLAH SHALLAH.

Islamic Resistance Movement (Hamas—Harakat al-Muqawama al-Islamiyya): Gaza; Damascus, Syria; f. 1987; originally welfare organization Mujama (f. 1973) led by the late Sheikh AHMAD YASSIN (killed by Israeli forces in March 2004); militant Islamist; opposes the Oslo accords and does not recognize the PA as the sole national authority in the Palestinian territories; following the killing by Israeli forces of Hamas's leader in the Gaza Strip, Abd al-Aziz ar-Rantisi, in April 2004, the group announced that it was adopting a policy of 'collective leadership'; contested Jan. 2006 legislative elections as Change and Reform; Head of Political Bureau KHALID MESHAAL (Damascus); Gen. Commdr of military wing, Izz ad-Din al-Qassam Brigades, MUHAMMAD DEIF (in hiding from the Israeli authorities since 1992, though presumed to be in Gaza).

Palestine Liberation Front (PLF): f. 1977 following split with PFLP—GC; the PLF split into three factions in the early 1980s, all of which retained the name PLF; one faction (Leader MUHAMMAD 'ABU' ABBAS) was based in Tunis, Tunisia, and Baghdad, Iraq, and remained nominally loyal to Yasser Arafat; the second faction (Leader TALAAT YAQOUB) belonged to the anti-Arafat National Salvation Front and opened offices in Damascus, Syria, and Libya; a third group derived from the PLF was reportedly formed by its Central Cttee Secretary, ABD AL-FATTAH GHANIM, in June 1986; the factions of Yaqoub and Ghanim were reconciled in early 1985; at the 18th session of the PNC a programme for the unification of the PLF was announced, with Yaqoub (died November 1988) named as Secretary-General and Abu Abbas appointed to the PLO Executive Committee, while unification talks were held. The merging of the two factions was announced in June 1987, with Abu Abbas becoming Deputy Secretary-General. Abu Abbas was apprehended by US-led coalition forces in Iraq in April 2003, and reportedly died of natural causes in March 2004 while still in US custody; Sec.-Gen. ABU NIDAL AL-ASHQAR.

Palestine Liberation Organization (PLO) (Munazzimat at-Tahrir al-Filastiniyya): Negotiations Affairs Dept, POB 4120, Ramallah; tel. (2) 2963741; fax (2) 2963740; internet www.nad-plo.org; f. 1964; the supreme organ of the PLO is the Palestine National Council (PNC; Pres. SALIM AZ-ZA'NUN), while the PLO Executive Committee (Chair. MAHMUD ABBAS; Sec.-Gen. FAROUK KADDOUMI) deals with day-to-day business. Fatah (the Palestine National Liberation Movement) joined the PNC in 1968, and all the guerrilla organizations joined the Council in 1969. In 1973 the Palestinian Central Council (PCC; Chair. SALIM AZ-ZA'NUN) was established to act as an intermediary between the PNC and the Executive Committee. The Council meets when the PNC is not in session and approves major policy decisions on its behalf; Chair. MAHMUD ABBAS.

Palestine Revolutionary Communist Party (PRCP) (Al-Hizb ash-Shuyu'i ath-Thawri al-Filastini): principally based in Lebanon; promotes armed struggle in order to achieve its aims; Sec.-Gen. ARABI AWAD.

Palestinian Democratic Union (FIDA): POB 247, Ramallah; fax (2) 2954071; e-mail fida@palnet.com; internet www.fida.ps; f. 1990 following split from the DFLP; contested Jan. 2006 legislative elections on The Alternative electoral list; Leader YASSER ABD AR-RABBUH; Sec.-Gen. SALEH RA'FAT.

Palestinian National Initiative (Al-Mubadara): Ramallah; tel. (5) 9293006; e-mail almubadara@almubadara.org; internet www.almubadara.org; f. 2002; seeks peaceful resolution of conflict with Israel through establishment of an independent, unified, viable and democratic Palestinian state, with East Jerusalem as its capital; advocates reform of internal political structures, and aims to fight corruption and injustice, and to uphold citizens' rights; contested Jan. 2006 legislative elections as part of the Independent Palestine coalition; Sec.-Gen. Dr MUSTAFA BARGHOUTHI.

Palestinian People's Party (PPP) (Hezb ash-Sha'ab): Ramallah; tel. (2) 2963593; fax (2) 2963592; e-mail shaab@palpeople.org; internet www.palpeople.org; f. 1921 as Palestine Communist Party; adopted current name in 1991; admitted to the PNC at its 18th session in 1987; contested Jan. 2006 legislative elections on The Alternative electoral list; Sec.-Gen. BASSAM ES-SALHI.

Palestinian Popular Struggle Front (PPSF) (Jabhat an-Nidal ash-Sha'biyya al-Filastiniyya): f. 1967; has reportedly split into two factions which either support or oppose the PA; the pro-PA faction (Leader SAMIR GHOSHEH) is based in the West Bank; the anti-PA faction (Leader KHALID ABD AL-MAJID) is based in Damascus, Syria.

Popular Front for the Liberation of Palestine (PFLP) (Al-Jabha ash-Sha'biyya li-Tahrir Filastin): Damascus, Syria; internet www.pflp.ps; f. 1967; Marxist-Leninist; publ. Democratic Palestine (English; monthly); contested Jan. 2006 legislative elections as Martyr Abu Ali Moustafa; Sec.-Gen. AHMAD SAADAT (imprisoned in 2002).

Popular Front for the Liberation of Palestine—General Command (PFLP—GC): Damascus, Syria; f. 1968 following split from the PFLP; pro-Syrian; Leader AHMAD JIBRIL.

Popular Front for the Liberation of Palestine—National General Command: Amman, Jordan; split from the PFLP—GC in 1999; aims to co-operate with the PA; Leader ATIF YUNUS.

As-Saiqa (Thunderbolt, or Vanguard of the Popular Liberation War): f. 1968; Syrian-backed; pan-Arab; opposed to the Oslo accords; Sec.-Gen. ISSAM AL-QADI.

The formation of the **Right Movement for Championing the Palestinian People's Sons** by former members of Hamas was announced in April 1995. The movement, based in Gaza City, was reported to support the PA. The **Al-Aqsa Martyrs Brigades**, consisting of a number of Fatah-affiliated activists, emerged soon after the start of the al-Aqsa *intifada* in September 2000, and have carried out attacks against Israeli targets in Israel, the West Bank and Gaza Strip.

Diplomatic Representation

Countries with which the PLO maintains diplomatic relations include:

Afghanistan, Albania, Algeria, Angola, Austria, Bahrain, Bangladesh, Benin, Bhutan, Botswana, Brunei, Bulgaria, Burkina Faso, Burundi, Cambodia, Cameroon, Cape Verde, Central African Republic, Chad, China (People's Rep.), Comoros, Congo (Dem. Rep.), Congo (Rep.), Costa Rica, Cuba, Cyprus, Czech Republic, Djibouti, Egypt, Equatorial Guinea, Ethiopia, Gabon, Gambia, Ghana, Guinea, Guinea-Bissau, Hungary, India, Indonesia, Iran, Iraq, Jordan, Korea (Dem. People's Rep.), Kuwait, Laos, Lebanon, Libya, Madagascar, Malaysia, Maldives, Mali, Malta, Mauritania, Mauritius, Mongolia, Morocco, Mozambique, Nepal, Nicaragua, Niger, Nigeria, Norway, Oman, Pakistan, Philippines, Poland, Qatar, Romania, Russia, Rwanda, São Tomé and Príncipe, Saudi Arabia, Senegal, Serbia, Seychelles, Sierra Leone, Somalia, Sri Lanka, Sudan, Swaziland, Sweden, Tanzania, Togo, Tunisia, Turkey, Uganda, the United Arab Emirates (UAE), Uzbekistan, Vanuatu, the Vatican City, Viet Nam, Yemen, Zambia and Zimbabwe.

The following states, while they do not recognize the State of Palestine, allow the PLO to maintain a regional office: Belgium, Brazil, France, Germany, Greece, Italy, Japan, the Netherlands, Portugal, Spain, Switzerland and the United Kingdom.

Judicial System

In the Gaza Strip, the West Bank towns of Jericho, Nablus, Ramallah, Jenin, Tulkarm, Qalqilya, Bethlehem and Hebron, and in other, smaller population centres in the West Bank, the PA has assumed limited jurisdiction with regard to civil affairs. However, the situation is confused owing to the various and sometimes conflicting legal systems which have operated in the territories occupied by Israel in 1967: Israeli military and civilian law; Jordanian law; and acts, orders-in-council and ordinances that remain from the period of the British Mandate in Palestine. Religious and military courts have been established under the auspices of the PA. In February 1995 the PA established a Higher State Security Court in Gaza to decide on security crimes both inside and outside the PA's area of jurisdiction; and to implement all valid Palestinian laws, regulations, rules and orders in accordance with Article 69 of the Constitutional Law of the Gaza Strip of 5 March 1962.

General Prosecutor of the PA: AHMAD AL-MOGHANI.

Religion

The vast majority of Palestinians in the West Bank and Gaza are Muslims, while a small (and declining) minority are Christians of the Greek Orthodox and Roman Catholic rites.

ISLAM

The PA-appointed Grand Mufti of Jerusalem and the Palestinian Lands is the most senior Muslim cleric in the Palestinian territories.

Mufti of Jerusalem: Sheikh MUHAMMAD AHMAD HUSSEIN.

CHRISTIANITY

The Roman Catholic Church

Latin Rite

The Patriarchate of Jerusalem covers Israel and the Occupied Territories, the Palestinian Autonomous Areas, Jordan and Cyprus. At 31 December 2006 there were an estimated 78,215 adherents.

Patriarchate of Jerusalem: Patriarcat Latin, POB 14152, Jerusalem 91141; tel. (2) 6282323; fax (2) 6271652; e-mail chancellery@latinpat.org; internet www.lpj.org; Patriarch His Beatitude Archbishop FOUAD TWAL; Vicar-General for Jerusalem KAMAL HANNA BATHISH (Titular Bishop of Jericho); Vicar-General for Israel GIACINTO-BOULOS MARCUZZO (Titular Bishop of Emmaus Nicopolis).

Melkite Rite

The Greek-Melkite Patriarch of Antioch and all the East, of Alexandria and of Jerusalem (GRÉGOIRE III LAHAM) is resident in Damascus, Syria.

Patriarchal Vicariate of Jerusalem: Patriarcat Grec-Melkite Catholique, POB 14130, Porte de Jaffa, Jerusalem 91141; tel. (2) 6282023; fax (2) 6289606; e-mail gcpjer@p-ol.com; about 3,300 adherents (31 December 2006); Protosyncellus Archim. Archbishop GEORGES MICHEL BAKAR.

The Greek Orthodox Church

The Patriarchate of Jerusalem contains an estimated 260,000 adherents in Israel and the Occupied Territories, the Palestinian Autonomous Areas, Jordan, Kuwait, the UAE and Saudi Arabia.

Patriarchate of Jerusalem: POB 14518, Jerusalem 91145; tel. (2) 6274941; fax (2) 6282048; e-mail secretariat@jerusalem-patriarchate.info; internet www.jerusalem-patriarchate.info; Patriarch THEOPHILOS III.

The Press

NEWSPAPERS

Al-Ayyam: POB 1987, Al-Ayyam St, Commercial Area, Ramallah; tel. (2) 2987341; fax (2) 2987342; e-mail info@al-ayyam.com; internet www.al-ayyam.ps; f. 1995; weekly; Arabic; publ. by Al-Ayyam Press, Printing, Publishing and Distribution Co; Editor-in-Chief AKRAM HANIYA.

Al-Ayyam al-Arabi: POB 1987, Al-Ayyam St, Commercial Area, Ramallah; tel. 2-2987341; fax 2-2987342; e-mail info@al-ayyam.com; internet www.al-ayyam.com; f. 1995; daily; Arabic; publ. by Al-Ayyam Press, Printing, Publishing and Distribution Co; Editor-in-Chief AKRAM HANIYA.

Filastin ath-Thawra (Palestine of the Revolution): fmrly publ. in Beirut, but resumed publication from Cyprus in November 1982; weekly newspaper of the PLO; Arabic.

Al-Hadaf (The Target): e-mail alhadaf@alhadafmagazine.com; internet www.alhadafmagazine.com; f. 1969 in Beirut, Lebanon; weekly; Arabic; organ of the Popular Front for the Liberation of Palestine.

Al-Hayat al-Jadidah: POB 1822, Ramallah; tel. (2) 2407251; fax (2) 2407250; e-mail info1@alhayat-j.com; internet www.alhayat-j.com; f. 1994; weekly; Arabic; Editor NADIL AMR.

Al-Hourriah (Liberation): POB 11488, Damascus, Syria; tel. (1) 6319455; fax (1) 6319125; e-mail hourriah@hotmail.com; internet www.alhourriah.org; Arabic; organ of the Democratic Front for the Liberation of Palestine; publ. in Beirut (Lebanon) and Damascus; Editor-in-Chief HAMADEH MUTASIM.

Al-Istiqlal (Independence): Ath-Thawra St, Gaza City; e-mail alesteqlal@p-i-s.com; weekly; Arabic; organ of Islamic Jihad; Sec. TAWFIQ AS-SAYYID SALIM.

Palestine Times: POB 4195, Al-Birah, Ramallah; tel. (2) 599399033; fax (2) 22972277; e-mail palestimes@ptimes.org; internet www.ptimes.org; f. 2006; monthly; English; privately owned; independent; Editor-in-Chief AHMAD KARMAWI; circ. 5,000; temporary closure in May 2007.

Al-Quds (Jerusalem): POB 19788, Jerusalem; tel. (2) 5833501; fax (2) 5856937; e-mail info@alquds.com; internet www.alquds.com; Arabic; independent; pro-PA; supports peace negotiations; reportedly has largest circulation of all Palestinian newspapers; daily; Editor MAHER AL-ALAMI.

Ar-Risala (Letter): Gaza City; weekly; Arabic; affiliated with the Islamic Resistance Movement (Hamas); Editor-in-Chief GHAZI HAMAD.

Al-Watan: Gaza City; weekly; Arabic; supports Hamas.

PERIODICALS

Filastin (Palestine): Gaza City; e-mail adel@falasteen.com; internet www.falasteen.com; f. 1994; weekly; Arabic; pro-Hamas, banned from publication and distribution in the West Bank; Editor-in-Chief MUSTAFA AS-SAWWAF.

The Jerusalem Times: POB 20185, 19 Nablus Rd, Jerusalem; tel. (2) 6264883; fax (2) 6287893; e-mail webmaster@jerusalem-times.net; internet www.jerusalem-times.net; f. 1994; weekly; English; independent; Chair. of Bd SHUKRI BISHARA; Publr HANNA SINIORA; Man. Editor SAMI KAMAL.

Al-Karmel Magazine: POB 1887, Ramallah; tel. (2) 2965934; fax (2) 2987374; e-mail editor@alkarmel.org; internet www.alkarmel.org; f. 1981 in Beirut, Lebanon; literature; Editor-in-Chief MAHMOUD DARWISH.

Madar: Madar—al-Markaz al-Filastini lil-Dirasat al-Israiliyah, Ramallah; publ. by Madar—The Palestinian Centre for Israeli Studies; political; Editor SALMAN NATOUR.

Palestine Report: Jerusalem Media and Communications Centre, POB 25047, 7 Nablus Rd, Jerusalem 97300; tel. (2) 5838266; fax (2) 5836837; e-mail jmcc@jmcc.org; internet www.jmcc.org; f. 1990; weekly; English; current affairs; publ. by the Jerusalem Media and Communications Centre; Man. Dir OMAR KARMI; Editor-in-Chief JOHARAH BAKER.

The Youth Times: Orabi Bldg, 2 Ramallah St, Jerusalem; tel. (2) 2426280; fax (2) 2426281; e-mail pyalara@pyalara.org; internet www.pyalara.org; f. 1998; monthly; Arabic and English; publ. by the Palestinian Youth Association for Leadership and Rights Activation; Editor-in-Chief HANIA BITAR.

NEWS AGENCY

Wikalat Anbaa' Filastiniya (WAFA, Palestine News Agency): POB 5300, Gaza City; tel. (8) 2824036; fax (8) 2824046; e-mail edit@wafa.ps; internet www.wafa.ps; official PLO news agency; Editor ZIAD ABD AL-FATTAH.

Publishers

Al-Ayyam Press, Printing, Publishing and Distribution Co: POB 1987, Ramallah; tel. (2) 2987341; fax (2) 2987342; e-mail info@al-ayyam.com; internet www.al-ayyam.com; f. 1995; publishes Al-Ayyam al-Arabi daily newspaper, Al-Ayyam weekly newspaper, books and magazines.

Beit Al-Maqdes for Publishing and Distribution: Ramallah; history, politics, fiction, children's.

Centre for Palestine Research and Studies (CPRS): POB 132, Nablus; tel. (9) 2380383; fax (9) 2380384; f. 1993; history, politics, strategic studies and economics; Dir SAID KANAAN.

Ogarit Centre for Publishing and Distribution: Ramallah; non-fiction, children's.

Broadcasting and Communications

TELECOMMUNICATIONS

Palestine Telecommunications Co PLC (PalTel): POB 1570, Nablus; tel. (9) 2390108; fax (9) 2350140; e-mail paltel@palnet.net; internet www.paltel.ps/index.php; f. 1995; privately owned monopoly; launched cellular telephone service (Palcel, now Jawwal) in 1999; Chair. SABIH MASRI; Gen. Man. MUHAMMAD HEAJAWI.

Palestine Cellular Co (Jawwal): POB 3999, Al-Birah; tel. (2) 2402440; fax (2) 2968636; e-mail atyourservice@jawwal.ps; internet www.jawwal.ps/index.php; f. 1999; 100% owned by PalTel; 700,000 subscribers (May 2006), representing some 55% of the Palestinian mobile (cellular) telecommunications market; CEO AMMAR AKER.

BROADCASTING

Palestinian Broadcasting Co (PBC): POB 984, Al-Birah/Ramallah; tel. (2) 2959894; fax (2) 2959893; e-mail pbcinfo@pbc.gov.ps;

internet www.pbc.gov.ps; f. 1994; state-controlled; Chair. BASEM ABU SUMAYA.

Sawt Filastin (Voice of Palestine): c/o Police HQ, Jericho; tel. (2) 921220; f. 1994; official radio station of the PA; broadcasts in Arabic from Jericho and Ramallah; Dir RADWAN ABU AYYASH.

Palestine Television: f. 1994; broadcasts from Ramallah and Gaza City; broadcasts online on JumpTV; Dir RADWAN ABU AYYASH.

Finance

(cap. = capital; res = reserves; dep. = deposits; brs = branches; m. = million)

BANKING

The Palestine Monetary Authority (PMA) is the financial regulatory body in the Palestinian Autonomous Areas, and is expected to evolve into the Central Bank of Palestine. Three currencies circulate in the Palestinian economy—the Jordanian dinar, the Israeli shekel and the US dollar—and the PMA currently has no right of issue. According to the PMA, there were 21 banks with a network of more than 180 branches operating in the West Bank and Gaza in mid-2008.

Palestine Monetary Authority (PMA): Nablus Rd, Ramallah; tel. (2) 2415250; fax (2) 2409922; e-mail info@pma.ps; internet www.pma-palestine.org; f. 1994; began licensing, inspection and supervision of the Palestinian and foreign commercial banks operating in the Gaza Strip and the Jericho enclave in the West Bank in July 1995; assumed responsibility for 13 banks in the Palestinian territories over which the Central Bank of Israel had hitherto exercised control in Dec. 1995; Gov. Dr JIHAD AL-WAZIR.

National Banks

Bank of Palestine PLC: POB 471, Court St, Ain Misbah, Ramallah; tel. (2) 2965010; fax (2) 2964703; e-mail info@bankofpalestine.com; internet www.bankofpalestine.com; f. 1960; cap. US $59.8m., res $12.4m., dep. $737.3m. (Dec. 2007); Chair. and Gen. Man. Dr HANI HASHEM SHAWA; 31 brs and sub-brs in West Bank and Gaza.

Commercial Bank of Palestine PLC: POB 1799, Michael Tanous Bldg, Alawda St, Ramallah; tel. (2) 2954141; fax (2) 2953888; e-mail cbp@cbpal.palnet.com; internet www.cbpal.com; f. 1992; total assets US $73m.; Pres. MAHMOUD ZUHDI MALHAS; Gen. Man. Dr ANIS AL-HAJJEH; 5 brs.

Palestine International Bank: Al-Birah/Ramallah; tel. (2) 2983300; fax (2) 2983344; e-mail issam@ias.intranets.com; internet www.pibank.net; f. 1997; cap. US $20m.; Chair. OSAMA MUHAMMAD KHADIR; 4 brs.

Investment Banks

Arab Palestinian Investment Bank: POB 1260, Al-Harji Bldg, Ramallah; tel. (2) 2987126; fax (2) 2987125; e-mail apibank@palnet.com; f. 1996; Arab Bank of Jordan has a 51% share; cap. US $15m.; Dir ABD AL-MAJID SHOMAN; Gen. Man. BESHARA DABBAH.

Palestine Investment Bank PLC: POB 3675, Al-Helal St, Al-Birah/Ramallah; tel. (2) 2407880; fax (2) 2407887; e-mail info@pinvbank.com; internet www.pinvbank.com; f. 1995 by the PA; some shareholders based in Jordan and the Gulf states; cap. US $60m.; provides full commercial and investment banking services throughout the West Bank and Gaza; Chair. ABD AL-QADER AHMAD QADI; Man. ZAKARIA GHAWANMEH; 9 brs and 2 rep. offices.

Al-Quds Bank for Development and Investment (Quds Bank): POB 2471, Ramallah; tel. (2) 2961750; fax (2) 2961754; e-mail quds@qudsbank.ps; internet www.alqudsbank.ps; f. 1995; merchant bank; cap. p.u. US $50m.; Gen. Man. AZZAM A. SHAWWA; Dep. Gen. Man. GHAZI A. MUSLEH; 8 brs and 12 offices.

Islamic Banks

Arab Islamic Bank: POB 631, Nablus St, Al-Birah/Ramallah; tel. (2) 2407060; fax (2) 2407065; e-mail aib@arabislamicbank.com; internet www.arabislamicbank.com; f. 1995; cap. US $38.4m., res $1.5m., dep. $284.4m. (June 2008); Chair. WALID T. FAKHOURI; Gen. Man. ATIYEH A. SHANANIER; 8 brs.

Palestine Islamic Bank: POB 1244, Omar al-Mukhtar St, Gaza City; tel. (8) 2827360; fax (8) 2825269; e-mail info@islamicbank.ps; internet www.islamicbank.ps; f. 1996; Chair. and Gen. Man. ABDULLAH HASSAN HUSRI.

STOCK EXCHANGE

Palestine Securities Exchange (PSE): POB 128, 3rd Floor, Al-Qaser Bldg, Nablus; tel. (9) 2345555; fax (9) 2341341; e-mail habulibdeh@p-s-e.com; internet www.p-s-e.com; f. 1997; privatization scheduled for 2009 or later; Chair. and CEO Dr HASSAN ABU LIBDEH.

INSURANCE

A very small insurance industry exists in the West Bank and Gaza.

Ahleia Insurance Group Ltd (AIG): POB 1214, Al-Jalaa Tower, Remal, Gaza; tel. (8) 2824035; fax (8) 2824015; e-mail info@aig.ps; internet www.aig.ps; f. 1994; Chair. and CEO Dr MUHAMMAD AS-SABAWI; 11 brs.

Arab Insurance Establishment Co Ltd (AIE): POB 166, Al-Qasr St, Nablus; tel. (9) 2341040; fax (9) 2341033; e-mail info@aie.com.ps; internet aie.com.ps; f. 1975; Chair. WALID ALOUL.

National Insurance Co: POB 1819, 34 Municipality St, Al-Birah/Ramallah; tel. (2) 2983800; fax (2) 2407460; e-mail nic@nic-pal.com; internet www.nic-pal.com; f. 1992; Chair. MUHAMMAD MAHMOUD MASROUJI; Gen. Man. AZIZ MAHMOUD ABD AL-JAWAD; 8 brs.

DEVELOPMENT FINANCE ORGANIZATIONS

Arab Palestinian Investment Co Ltd: POB 2396, Kharaz Center, Yafa St, Industrial Zone, Ramallah; tel. (2) 2981060; fax (2) 2981065; e-mail apic@apic.com.jo; internet www.apic-pal.com; f. 1995; headquarters in Amman, Jordan; Chair. and CEO TAREK OMAR AGGAD.

Jerusalem Real Estate Investment Co: POB 1876, Ramallah; tel. (2) 2965215; fax (2) 2965217; e-mail jrei@palnet.com; f. 1996; Chair. NIZAR ABD AR-RAHIM MUNIB JARDANEH.

Palestine Development & Investment Co (PADICO): POB 316, Nablus; tel. (9) 2384480; fax (9) 2384355; e-mail padico@padico.com; internet www.padico.com; f. 1993; 12 subsidiary and affiliate cos; Chair. MUNIB R. AL-MASRI; CEO Dr SAMIR HULILEH.

Palestine Real Estate Investment Co (Aqaria): POB 4049, Gaza; tel. (8) 2824815; fax (8) 2824845; e-mail aqaria@rannet.com; internet www.aqaria.com; f. 1994; Chair. NABIL SARRAF; Vice-Chair. OMAR AL-ALAMI.

Palestinian Economic Council for Development and Reconstruction (PECDAR): POB 54910, Dahiyat al-Barid, Jerusalem; tel. (2) 2974300; fax (2) 2974331; e-mail info@pecdar.pna.net; internet www.pecdar.org; privately owned; Pres. Dr MUHAMMAD SHTAYYEH.

Trade and Industry

CHAMBERS OF COMMERCE

Federation of Chambers of Commerce, Industry and Agriculture: tel. (2) 2344923; fax (2) 2344924; e-mail fpccia@palnet.com; internet www.pal-chambers.org; f. 1989; 14 chambers, 32,000 mems.

Bethlehem Chamber of Commerce and Industry: POB 59, Bethlehem; tel. (2) 2742742; fax (2) 2764402; e-mail bcham@palnet.com; internet www.pal-chambers.org/chambers/bethlehem.html; f. 1952; 2,500 mems; Chair. of Bd SAMIR HAZBOUN.

Gaza Chamber of Commerce, Industry and Agriculture: POB 33, Sabra Quarter, Gaza; tel. and fax (8) 2864588; e-mail gazacham@palnet.com; internet www.gazacham.ps; f. 1954; Chair. MUHAMMAD QUDWAH; Man. Dir BASSAM MORTAJA; 14,000 mems.

Hebron Chamber of Commerce and Industry: POB 272, Hebron; tel. (2) 2228218; fax (2) 2227490; e-mail info@hebroncci.org; internet www.hebroncci.org; f. 1954; Chair. HASHEM NATSHEH; 7,350 mems.

Jenin Chamber of Commerce, Industry and Agriculture: Jenin; tel. (4) 2501107; fax (4) 2503388; e-mail jencham@hally.net; internet www.pal-chambers.org/chambers/jenin.html; f. 1953; 3,800 mems.

Jericho Chamber of Commerce, Industry and Agriculture: POB 91, Jericho 00970; tel. (2) 2323313; fax (2) 2322394; e-mail jericho@pal-chambers.org; internet www.pal-chambers.org/chambers/jericho.html; f. 1953; 400 mems; Chair. HAJ MANSOUR SALAYMEH; Sec.-Gen. SELMI HAMAD.

Jerusalem Arab Chamber of Commerce and Industry: POB 19151, Jerusalem 91191; tel. (2) 2344923; fax (2) 2344914; e-mail chamber@jerusalemchamber.org; internet www.jerusalemchamber.org; f. 1936; 2,050 mems; Chair. AHMAD HASHEM ZUGHAYAR; Dir AZZAM ABU SAUD.

Nablus Chamber of Commerce and Industry: POB 35, Nablus; tel. (9) 2380335; fax (9) 2377605; e-mail nabluschamber@gmail.com; internet www.pal-chambers.org/chambers/nablus.html; f. 1941; Pres. MA'AZ NABULSI; Dir TAJ ED-DIN BITAR; 7,000 mems.

Palestinian-European Chamber of Commerce: Jerusalem; tel. (2) 894883; Chair. HANNA SINIORA.

Qalqilya Chamber of Commerce, Industry and Agriculture: POB 13, Qalqilya; tel. (9) 2941473; fax (9) 2940164; e-mail chamberq@hally.net; internet www.pal-chambers.org/chambers/qalqilya.html; f. 1972; 1,068 mems.

PALESTINIAN AUTONOMOUS AREAS

Ramallah Chamber of Commerce and Industry: POB 256, Al-Birah/Ramallah; tel. (2) 2955052; fax (2) 2984691; e-mail info@ramallahcci.org; internet www.ramallahcci.org; f. 1950; Chair. MUHAMMAD AHMAD AMIN; Vice-Chair. YOUSUF ASH-SHARIF; 4,100 mems.

Salfeet Chamber of Commerce, Industry and Agriculture: Salfit; tel. and fax (9) 2515970; e-mail salfeetchamber@hotmail.com; internet www.salfeetchamber.org; f. 1997; Chair. FOUAD AWAD.

Tulkarm Chamber of Commerce, Industry and Agriculture: POB 51, Tulkarm; tel. (9) 2671010; fax (9) 2675623; e-mail tulkarm@palnet.com; internet www.tulkarmchamber.org; f. 1945; 2,000 mems; Chair. SHUKRI AHMAD JALLAD.

TRADE AND INDUSTRIAL ORGANIZATIONS

Palestinian General Federation of Trade Unions (PGFTU): POB 1216, Nablus; tel. (9) 2385136; fax (9) 2384374; e-mail pgftu@pgftu.org; internet www.pgftu.org; f. 1965; Sec.-Gen. SHAHER SAED.

Union of Industrialists: POB 1296, Gaza; tel. (8) 2866222; fax (8) 2862013; Chair. MUHAMMAD YAZIJI.

UTILITIES

Electricity

Palestinian Energy Authority (PEA): POB 3591, Nablus St, Al-Birah/Ramallah; POB 3041, Gaza; tel. (2) 2986190; fax (2) 2986191; tel. (8) 2821702; fax (8) 2824849; e-mail pea@palnet.com; internet pea-pal.tripod.com; f. 1994; Chair. Dr ABD AR-RAHMAN T. HAMAD.

Jerusalem District Electricity Co (JDECO): POB 19118, 15 Salah ed-Din St, Jerusalem; tel. (2) 6269333; fax (2) 6282441; e-mail info@jdeco.net; internet www.jdeco.net.

National Electric Co (NEC): West Bank; f. 2000.

Palestine Electric Co (PEC): POB 1336, Gaza; tel. (8) 2823800; fax (8) 2823297; e-mail info@pec-gpgc.com; internet www.pec-gpgc.com; f. 1999; 33% state-owned; Chair. SAID KHOURY; CEO WALID SALMAN.

Water

Palestinian Water Authority (PWA): POB 1438, Gaza; tel. (8) 2827520; fax (8) 2822697; e-mail pwa@pwa-gaza.org; internet www.pwa-gaza.org; f. 1995; Dir Eng. NABIL ASH-SHARIF.

Transport

ROADS

In 2006, according to estimates by the International Road Federation, the Palestinian territories had 5,147 km of paved roads, of which 535 km were highways or main roads, 438 km were secondary roads and 4,175 km were other roads.

CIVIL AVIATION

Palestinian Civil Aviation Authority (PCAA): Yasser Arafat International Airport, POB 4043, Rafah, Gaza; tel. and fax (8) 2827844; e-mail abuhalib@gaza-airport.org; internet www.gaza-airport.org; f. 1994; Gaza International Airport (renamed as above after Arafat's death in Nov. 2004) was formally inaugurated in November 1998 to operate services by Palestinian Airlines (its subsidiary), Egypt Air and Royal Jordanian Airline; Royal Air Maroc began to operate services to Amman, Abu Dhabi, Cairo, Doha, Dubai, Jeddah, Istanbul and Larnaca, and intends to expand its network to Europe; the airport was closed by the Israeli authorities in February 2001 and the runway seriously damaged by Israeli air-strikes in late 2001 and early 2002; Dir-Gen. SALMAN ABU HALIB; Admin. Man. JAMAL AL-MASHHARAWI.

Palestinian Airlines: POB 4043, Gaza; tel. (8) 2822800; fax (8) 2821309; e-mail commercial@palairlines.com; internet www.palairlines.com; f. 1994; state-owned; Dir-Gen. Capt. MANSOUR IBRAHIM; Exec. Dir YASSER IRQAYEQ.

Tourism

Although the tourism industry in the West Bank was virtually destroyed as a result of the 1967 Arab–Israeli War, by the late 1990s the sector was expanding significantly, with a number of hotels being opened or under construction. Much of the tourism in the West Bank centres around the historical and biblical sites of Jerusalem and Bethlehem. However, the renewed outbreak of Israeli–Palestinian conflict in the West Bank and Gaza Strip from late 2000, as well as the recent increase in inter-Palestinian violence, has generally prevented the recovery of the tourism industry.

Ministry of Tourism and Antiquities: See Administration.

NET—Near East Tourist Agency: POB 19015, 30 Mount of Olives Rd, Jerusalem 91190; tel. (2) 5328720; fax (2) 5328701; internet new.netours.com; f. 1964; CEO SAMI ABU DAYYEH; Man. STEVE USTIN.

PANAMA

Introductory Survey

Location, Climate, Language, Religion, Flag, Capital

The Republic of Panama is a narrow country situated at the southern end of the isthmus separating North and South America. It is bounded to the west by Costa Rica and to the east by Colombia in South America. The Caribbean Sea is to the north, and the Pacific Ocean to the south. Panama has a tropical maritime climate (warm, humid days and cool nights). There is little seasonal variation in temperatures, which average 23°C–27°C (73°F–81°F) in coastal areas. The rainy season is from April until December. Spanish is the official language. Almost all of the inhabitants profess Christianity, and some 83% are Roman Catholics. The national flag (proportions 2 by 3) is composed of four equal rectangles: on the top row the quarter at the hoist is white, with a five-pointed blue star in the centre, while the quarter in the fly is red; on the bottom row the quarter at the hoist is blue, and the quarter in the fly is white, with a five-pointed red star in the centre. The capital is Panamá (Panama City).

Recent History

Panama was subject to Spanish rule from the 16th century until 1821, when it became independent as part of Gran Colombia. Panama remained part of Colombia until 1903, when it declared its separate independence with the support of the USA. In that year the USA purchased the concession for construction of the Panama Canal, which was opened in 1914. The 82-km Canal links the Atlantic and Pacific Oceans, and is a major international sea route. Under the terms of the 1903 treaty between Panama and the USA concerning the construction and administration of the Canal, the USA was granted ('in perpetuity') control of a strip of Panamanian territory, called the Canal Zone, extending for 8 km on either side of the Canal route. The treaty also established Panama as a protectorate of the USA. In exchange for transferring the Canal Zone, Panama was to receive an annuity from the USA. The terms of this treaty and its successors have dominated relations between Panama and the USA since 1903.

In 1939 a revised treaty with the USA ended Panama's protectorate status. A new Constitution for Panama was adopted in 1946. Following a period of rapidly changing governments, the 1952 presidential election was won by Col José Antonio Remón, formerly Chief of Police. During his term of office, President Remón negotiated a more favourable treaty with the USA, whereby the annuity payable to Panama was increased. In January 1955, however, before the treaty came into force, Remón was assassinated. He was succeeded by José Ramón Guizado, hitherto the First Vice-President, but, less than two weeks after assuming power, the new President was implicated in the plot to assassinate Remón. Guizado was removed from office and later imprisoned. Remón's Second Vice-President, Ricardo Arias Espinosa, then completed the presidential term, which expired in 1956, when Ernesto de la Guardia was elected President. The next presidential election was won by Roberto Chiari, who held office in 1960–64, and his successor was Marco Aurelio Robles (1964–68). During this period there were frequent public demands for the transfer to Panama of sovereignty over the Canal Zone.

The presidential election of May 1968 was won by Dr Arnulfo Arias Madrid, the candidate supported by the coalition Unión Nacional (which included his own Partido Panameñista). Dr Arias had been President in 1940–41 and 1949–51, but both terms had ended in his forcible removal from power. He took office for a third term in October 1968 but, after only 11 days, he was deposed by the National Guard (Panama's only military body), led by Col (later Brig.-Gen.) Omar Torrijos Herrera, who accused him of planning to establish a dictatorship. The Asamblea Nacional (National Assembly) was dissolved, and political activity suspended. Political parties were banned in February 1969.

In August 1972 elections were held to a new legislative body, the 505-member Asamblea Nacional de Corregidores (National Assembly of Community Representatives). In October the Asamblea conferred extraordinary powers on Gen. Torrijos as Chief of Government for six years.

In February 1974 representatives of Panama and the USA concluded an agreement on principles for a new treaty whereby the USA would surrender its jurisdiction over the Canal Zone. Discontent arising from the Government's handling of subsequent protracted negotiations, combined with deteriorating living standards, culminated in student riots in 1976. Intensified talks in 1977 resulted in two new Canal treaties, which were approved by voters at a referendum in October. The treaties became effective from October 1979. Panama assumed control of the former Canal Zone, which was abolished. Administration of the Canal was placed under the control of a joint Panama Canal Commission until the end of 1999. US military forces in Panama were to remain until 2000, and the USA was to be entitled to defend the Canal's neutrality thereafter.

In August 1978 elections were held to the Asamblea Nacional de Corregidores; in October the new representatives elected Dr Arístides Royo Sánchez to be President for a six-year term. Gen. Torrijos resigned as Chief of Government, but continued in the post of Commander of the National Guard, and effectively retained power until his death in an air crash in July 1981. President Royo failed to gain the support of the National Guard, and in July 1982 he was forced to resign by Col Rubén Darío Paredes, who had ousted Col Florencio Flores as Commander-in-Chief in March. The Vice-President, Ricardo de la Espriella, was installed as President, and, under the direction of Col Paredes, promoted business interests and pursued a foreign policy more favourable to the USA.

In April 1983 a series of amendments to the Constitution were approved by referendum. However, in spite of new constitutional measures to limit the power of the National Guard, de facto power remained with the armed forces, whose position was strengthened by a decision in September to unite all security forces within one organization (subsequently known as the National Defence Forces). In June Paredes was succeeded as Commander-in-Chief by Brig. (later Gen.) Manuel Antonio Noriega Morena. In February 1984 Dr Jorge Illueca, hitherto the Vice-President, became Head of State after the sudden resignation of President de la Espriella, who was believed to have been ousted from power by the National Defence Forces.

Elections to the presidency and the legislature (the new 67-member Asamblea Legislativa—Legislative Assembly) took place in May 1984. Despite allegations of extensive electoral fraud, Dr Nicolás Ardito Barletta, the candidate of the Partido Revolucionario Democrático (PRD) who received the electoral support of the armed forces, was eventually declared President-elect, narrowly defeating Arias Madrid, standing as candidate of the Partido Panameñista Auténtico (PPA). However, as a result of protracted opposition to his economic policies, Ardito was unable to secure a political base to support his administration, and in September 1985 he resigned. Ardito claimed that his resignation had been prompted by the deterioration in his relations with the legislature and with the National Defence Forces, although there was considerable speculation that he had been forced to resign by Gen. Noriega, to prevent a public scandal over the alleged involvement of the National Defence Forces in the murder of Dr Hugo Spadafora, a former deputy minister under Torrijos and a leading critic of Noriega. Ardito was succeeded as President in September by Eric Arturo Delvalle, formerly First Vice-President.

In June 1986 US sources alleged that Noriega was involved in the trafficking of illegal drugs and weapons and in the transfer of proceeds from these activities through Panamanian banks. In addition, Noriega was implicated in the sale of US national security information and restricted technology to Cuba. There were also renewed allegations of his involvement in the murder of Dr Spadafora and in electoral fraud during the 1984 presidential election. Strikes and demonstrations in support of demands for Noriega's dismissal resulted in violent clashes with the National Defence Forces. Following this outbreak of violence, the US Senate approved a resolution urging the establishment of democracy in Panama, the suspension of Noriega and the holding of an independent investigation into the allegations against him. The Panamanian Government responded by accusing the USA of interfering in Panamanian affairs, and a wave of anti-US sentiment was unleashed, including an attack on the US embassy building by protesters in July 1987. The USA subsequently suspended economic and military aid to Panama and downgraded its official links with the country. Protests against Noriega continued, in an atmosphere of mounting political and economic insecurity.

In February 1988 Noriega was indicted by two US Grand Juries on charges of drugs-smuggling and racketeering. President Delvalle subsequently dismissed Noriega from his post, following his refusal to resign voluntarily. However, leading members of the ruling coalition and the National Defence Forces united in support of their Commander-in-Chief, and on the following day the Asamblea Legislativa voted to remove President Delvalle from office because of his 'failure to abide by the Constitution'. The Minister of Education, Manuel Solís Palma, was appointed acting President. Delvalle refused to accept his dismissal, and the US Administration affirmed its support for the ousted President by declining to recognize the new leadership. Delvalle, who went into hiding, became the figurehead of the USA's attempts to oust Noriega, and at the end of the month, following Delvalle's demand that the US Government impose an economic boycott on Panama, US courts authorized a 'freeze' on some US $50m. of Panamanian assets held in US banks. This move, coupled with a general strike organized by the Cruzada Civilista Nacional (a broadly based opposition grouping led by the business sector) after Delvalle's dismissal, brought economic chaos to Panama, prompting the closure of all banks for more than two months.

In March 1988 a coup attempt by the chief of police, Col Leónidas Macías, was thwarted by members of the National Defence Forces loyal to Noriega. The attempted coup represented the first indication of opposition to Noriega from within the security forces. The Government announced a state of emergency (which was revoked in April) and the suspension of civil rights. Negotiations between Noriega and a representative of the US Administration, during which the USA was reported to have proposed the withdrawal of charges against Noriega in exchange for his retirement and departure into exile before the elections scheduled for 1989, ended acrimoniously in late March. The US Administration subsequently reinforced economic sanctions against Panamanian interests.

Presidential, legislative and municipal elections were held on 7 May 1989. The presidential candidate of the pro-Government electoral alliance, the Coalición de Liberación Nacional (COLINA), was Carlos Duque Jaén, the leader of the PRD and a close associate of Noriega. Guillermo Endara Galimany of the PPA was the presidential candidate of the opposition alliance, the Alianza Democrática de Oposición Civilista (ADOC). The election campaign was dominated by accusations of electoral malpractice, and, following the voting, both ADOC and COLINA claimed victory, despite indications from exit polls and unofficial sources that ADOC had received between 50% and 75% of votes cast. A group of international observers declared that the election had been conducted fraudulently. A delay in announcing the results was interpreted by the opposition as an attempt by the Government to falsify the outcome. Endara declared himself President-elect; in subsequent demonstrations crowds clashed with the National Defence Forces, and many members of the opposition, including Endara and other leaders, were severely beaten. On 10 May the election results were annulled by the Electoral Tribunal, which cited US interference.

On 31 August 1989, following intervention by the Organization of American States (OAS, see p. 373), Panama's General State Council announced the appointment of a provisional Government and a 41-member Legislative Commission to preserve 'institutional order'. The holding of elections was to be considered within six months, but this was to be largely dependent upon the cessation of US 'hostilities' and the withdrawal of US economic sanctions. On 1 September Francisco Rodríguez, a known associate of Noriega, was inaugurated as President, and Carlos Ozores Typaldos as Vice-President. The USA immediately severed diplomatic relations with Panama. In October an attempted coup, led by middle-ranking officers seeking to replace Noriega at the head of the de facto military dictatorship, was suppressed by forces loyal to Noriega.

In November 1989 the Asamblea Nacional de Corregidores was provisionally restored. This body, now numbering 510 members, was intended to fulfil a consultative and (limited) legislative function. Noriega was elected as its 'national coordinator'. In December the Asamblea adopted a resolution declaring Noriega to be Head of State and 'leader of the struggle for national liberation', and announced that a state of war existed with the USA. On 20 December a US military offensive ('Operation Just Cause'), involving some 24,000 troops, was launched against Noriega and the headquarters of the National Defence Forces from US bases within Panama. The objects of the assault were swiftly brought under US control, although sporadic attacks on US bases by loyalist forces continued for several days, and Noriega eluded capture long enough to take refuge in the residence of the Papal Nuncio in Panama. On 21 December Endara, who had been installed as Head of State in a ceremony attended by a Panamanian judge at the Fort Clayton US military base only hours before the invasion, was officially inaugurated as President. President Endara declared that the Panamanian judicial system was inadequate to try Noriega. Following his surrender to US forces in January 1990, Noriega was immediately transported to the USA and arraigned on several charges of involvement in drugs-trafficking and money-laundering operations. (Noriega, who claimed the status of a prisoner of war, refused to recognize the right of jurisdiction of a US court.) In April 1992 Noriega was found guilty on eight charges of conspiracy to manufacture and distribute cocaine; he was sentenced to 40 years' imprisonment.

International criticism of the USA's military operation was widespread, although the Administration cited the right to self-defence, under Article 51 of the UN Charter, as a legal justification for armed intervention, and US President George Bush asserted that military action was necessary for the protection of US citizens, the protection of the Panama Canal, support for Panama's 'democratically elected' officials and the pursuit of an indicted criminal. According to the US Government, 'Operation Just Cause' resulted in about 500 Panamanian casualties, but a total of at least 1,000 Panamanian deaths was estimated by the Roman Catholic Church and other unofficial sources; 26 US troops were killed, and more than 300 wounded, during the invasion.

Following the appointment of a new Cabinet (comprising members of the ADOC alliance) in December 1989, the Endara administration declared itself to be a 'democratic Government of reconstruction and national reconciliation'. Shortly afterwards the Electoral Tribunal revoked its annulment of the May elections and announced that ADOC had obtained 62% of the votes cast in the presidential election, according to copies of incomplete results (covering 64% of total votes) that had been held in safe keeping by the Bishops' Conference of the Roman Catholic Church. In February 1990 the composition of the Asamblea Legislativa was announced, based on the same documentation, with 51 seats awarded to ADOC and six to COLINA; fresh elections were to be held for nine seats that could not be reliably allocated. The National Defence Forces were officially disbanded, and a new, 'non-political' Public Force was created.

Although the overthrow of Noriega immediately released US $375m. in assets that had previously been withheld by the US Government, the new administration inherited serious economic difficulties. The cost of 'Operation Just Cause', in terms of damage and lost revenues alone, was estimated to be at least $2,000m. Although the Bush Administration agreed to provide aid amounting to more than $1,000m., the US Congress was slow to approve the appropriation of funds. In April 1990 the USA revoked the economic restrictions that had been imposed two years previously, and in May Congress approved financial assistance to Panama totalling $420m. Disbursement of a substantial tranche was to be dependent upon the successful negotiation of a Mutual Legal Assistance Treaty between the two countries, whereby the US authorities sought to gain greater access to information amassed by Panama City's 'offshore' international finance centre, in order to combat the illegal laundering of money.

Accusations from public and political opponents that the security forces had not been adequately purged following the ousting of Noriega were seemingly justified by a succession of coup attempts during the early 1990s. Meanwhile, growing public concern at the Government's failure to restore civil and economic order was reflected in the results of elections held in January 1991 for the nine seats in the Asamblea Legislativa that had not been awarded by the Electoral Tribunal following the elections of May 1989 (see above). Member parties of the former electoral alliance COLINA, which had supported the previous regime, secured five of the contested seats, while parties represented in the governing alliance secured only four seats. President Endara's recently formed Partido Arnulfista (PA, formerly a faction of the PPA) failed to secure a single seat. Serious concern had been expressed at the increasing level of influence exerted by the US Government over the President, particularly when it became known that in July 1990 the Government had accepted US funds to establish, by decree, a 100-strong Council for Public Security, which would maintain close links with the US Central Intelligence Agency.

Long-standing political differences within the Government reached a crisis in March 1991 when one of the parties in the ruling coalition, the Partido Demócrata Cristiano (PDC), initiated proceedings to impeach Endara for involving the US armed forces in suppressing an uprising in December 1990 (a technical violation of the 1977 Panama Canal Treaty). Although the proposal was dismissed by the Asamblea Legislativa, Endara and his supporters strongly criticized leaders of the PDC and dismissed the five PDC members of his Cabinet.

In October 1991 and February 1992 two further alleged coup attempts were immediately suppressed, and resulted in the detention of several more members of the former National Defence Forces, and the creation, in March 1992, of a presidential police force to be directly responsible to the Head of State. In November, however, the President suffered a serious political reverse, when proposals for more than 50 reforms (including the constitutional abolition of the armed forces and the creation of the post of ombudsman to protect the rights of Panamanian citizens) were rejected by 64% of voters in a referendum.

The acquittal, in September 1993, of seven former soldiers tried for involvement in the 1985 assassination of Dr Spadafora provoked widespread public outrage. Noriega was tried in connection with the affair *in absentia* and, in October 1993, was found guilty and sentenced to 20 years' imprisonment for ordering his murder. Further convictions followed in 1994 for the 1989 murder of an army major who had led an unsuccessful military coup and in 2001 for corruption charges. In April 2009 the US federal Court of Appeal ruled that Noriega could be extradited to France, where he had been convicted *in absentia* on money-laundering charges in 1999.

A presidential election was held in May 1994. Ernesto Pérez Balladares, the candidate of the Pueblo Unido alliance (that included the PRD), won a narrow victory ahead of Mireya Moscoso de Gruber (the widow of former President Arias Madrid). Moscoso was the nominee of the Alianza Democrática, a grouping of the PA with the Partido Liberal (PL), the Partido Liberal Auténtico (PLA), the Unión Democrática Independiente and the Partido Nacionalista Popular (PNP). The failure of the Pueblo Unido alliance to secure a majority in the legislature was reflected in the broad political base of Pérez Balladares' proposed cabinet, announced in May. Post-electoral political manoeuvring resulted in the creation of the Alianza Pueblo Unido y Solidaridad, Pérez Balladares' electoral alliance having secured the additional support of the Partido Solidaridad in the Asamblea. Pérez Balladares assumed the presidency on 1 September 1994. A new Cabinet, installed on the same day, included former members of the PA and the PDC who had been obliged to resign their party membership in order to take up their cabinet posts.

In May 1996 the credibility of the Government was damaged by the discovery that a private Panamanian bank (Banaico, which had collapsed earlier in the year), in whose activities senior PRD members were implicated, had been a centre for money-laundering. In June, moreover, the position of President Pérez Balladares was undermined by reports that an alleged drugs-trafficker had contributed some US $51,000 to his 1994 presidential campaign. Pérez Balladares was forced to admit that his campaign fund had 'unwittingly' received the payment; the Procurator-General subsequently announced a thorough investigation into the origin of the 1994 campaign funds.

At a presidential election conducted in May 1999, Mireya Moscoso de Gruber, the candidate of the Unión por Panamá alliance (comprising the PA, Movimiento Liberal Republicano Nacionalista—MOLIRENA, Movimiento de Renovación Nacional and Cambio Democrático), was elected with 45% of the votes, ahead of Martín Torrijos Espino, son of former dictator Omar Torrijos, the candidate of the Nueva Nación alliance (comprising the PRD, the Partido Solidaridad, the Partido Liberal Nacional—PLN—and the Movimiento Papa Egoró—MPE), who secured 38%. However, the Unión por Panamá failed to secure a majority in the concurrent legislative election. Moscoso assumed the presidency on 1 September. A new Cabinet, installed on the same day, included members of the Partido Solidaridad, the PLN, the PDC and the Partido Renovación Civilista (PRC), each of which had abandoned their respective electoral alliances in order to form a 'Government of national unity', thereby giving Moscoso a narrow majority in the legislature. However, in August of the following year the governing coalition lost its narrow legislative majority after the PRD and the PDC formed an alliance. The effective legislative impasse was ended in February 2002 following the defection of three opposition deputies.

On 31 December 1999 the USA officially relinquished ownership of the Canal to Panama. In early 2000 a five-year canal-modernization project was initiated. In February the Government negotiated a counter-narcotics agreement with the USA.

Following the discovery of human remains in a former military barracks in Tocumen, in December 2000 President Moscoso announced the establishment of a Truth Commission, headed by Alberto Santiago Almanza Henríquez, to investigate 'disappearances' during the military dictatorships of 1968–89. Following excavations in 12 separate areas, the Commission reported in October 2001 that 72 of the 189 people believed to have 'disappeared' had been killed or tortured by state forces. In March 2004 the Asamblea approved the establishment of a Special Prosecutor's Office to investigate crimes committed during the military dictatorships; in February 2006 the Special Prosecutor announced that four officers who served in the military regimes were prepared to offer anonymous testimonies against former colleagues.

President Moscoso's administration encountered problems in the wake of an agreement signed in February 2002, which provided for US authorities to join the Panamanian National Maritime Service in patrolling its territorial waters, in an attempt to control the illegal trade in narcotics. The agreement was strongly criticized by opposition members. However, in September a number of defections from the opposition to the governing coalition gave Moscoso a working majority in the Asamblea for the first time since taking office. An additional accord, which provided the USA with increased powers to inspect Panama's financial and tax records as part of its campaign against money-laundering, provoked protests from opposition parties. In April of that year Panama was removed from the Organisation for Economic Co-operation and Development's (OECD) list of 'un-co-operative tax havens' after the Government committed to making its financial sector more transparent. In January 2004 the country's bank auditors, the Unidad de Análisis Financiero, identified 392 bank accounts that it suspected were being used for money-laundering purposes. They included 40 accounts associated with the former President of Nicaragua Arnoldo Alemán Lacayo, and a further 14 connected to the former Guatemalan President Alfonso Portillo Cabrera.

In September 2003 President Moscoso dismissed Juan Jované as Director of the social security fund, the Caja de Seguro Social (CSS), after he had refused to agree on a balanced budget with the other members of the CSS board. The CSS had been running at a loss for years, and, according to the Government, would go bankrupt without reform. In a subsequent television appearance, however, Jované alleged that he had been removed to allow for the privatization of the CSS. Furthermore, he claimed that the Government was intending to compel the CSS to purchase US $500m. of government debt, in order to finance the PA's re-election campaign. In mid-September CSS employees, trade union members and students marched through the capital to protest at Jované's dismissal. Moscoso subsequently signed a declaration pledging not to sell off the CSS. Nevertheless, a second march took place and in late September an umbrella trade union organization, the Frente Nacional por la Defensa de la Seguridad Social (FRENADESSO), held a 24-hour general strike.

Presidential and legislative elections took place in May 2004, in which 76.9% of the electorate participated. Martín Torrijos Espino, the candidate of the PRD (which contested the elections as part of the Patria Nueva electoral alliance with the Partido Popular), won the presidential ballot, winning 47.4% of the votes cast. Former President Endara, representing the Partido Solidaridad, came second with 30.9% of the ballot. The PA's presidential candidate, former Minister of Foreign Affairs José Miguel Alemán (officially the representative of the Visión de País electoral alliance, comprising the PA, MOLIRENA and the PLN), attracted only 16.4% of the votes cast. The Patria Nueva also performed well in the concurrently held elections to the enlarged, 78-seat Asamblea Legislativa: the party won 43.9% of the votes cast and secured a total of 43 seats, 42 of which were won by the PRD. The PA obtained 19.3% of the ballot and 16 seats, while the Partido Solidaridad received 15.7% of the votes cast and nine seats. Torrijos assumed office on 1 September.

In August 2004, just prior to the end of her mandate, President Moscoso pardoned and released four prisoners sought by the authorities in Cuba for allegedly plotting to assassinate the Cuban leader Fidel Castro Ruz in 2000. The men had been found guilty by a Panamanian court in April 2004 of illegal possession of weapons and sentenced to varying terms of imprisonment. The Venezuelan Government also had been attempting to extradite one of the men, Luis Posada Carriles, in connection with the bombing of a Cuban aeroplane in 1976.

Even before he assumed the presidency, Torrijos was successful in bringing about several constitutional amendments. In July 2004 his proposed reform of the Asamblea Legislativa received legislative approval. The number of parliamentary seats in the legislature—which was renamed the Asamblea Nacional (National Assembly)—was to be reduced to 71 (from 78) from 2009. Furthermore, deputies voted to end parliamentary immunity from prosecution and to transfer the authority to ratify constitutional amendments from the legislature to a constituent assembly. President Torrijos also pledged to address the problem of official corruption. One week after Torrijos' Government took office, Panama's ambassador to Cuba, Abraham Bárcenas, who had been recalled at the end of the previous month, was arrested as part of an investigation into the alleged sale of Panamanian visas to Cuban citizens. Then, in November the Government announced that corruption charges had been filed against former Minister of Finance and the Treasury Norberto Delgado. His successor, Ricaurte Vázquez Morales, criticized the former administration's fiscal management, and stated that the fiscal deficit was an estimated 5.4% of gross domestic product, rather than the 2.7% announced by his predecessor. Fiscal reform legislation was submitted to the Asamblea in January 2005 that proposed, *inter alia*, to reduce the public sector work-force by 12% over five years and to revise methods of corporate taxation. Despite opposition from business associations and trade unions, the legislation was approved at the end of the month.

In October 2004 some 5,000 people participated in a protest march organized by FRENADESSO, the social organization established to resist privatization of the CSS. The new Government denied intentions to fully privatize the CSS, but emphasized the need for reform in light of the institution's estimated deficit of between US $2,500m. and $3,000m. Proposed social security reforms included an increase in the retirement age, a reduction in retirement benefits and the transfer of some pensions into private funds. Despite further protests and industrial action co-ordinated by FRENADESSO in May 2005, the pension reforms were approved by the Asamblea Nacional in early June. However, they included a number of concessions, including proportional pensions for those who failed to make sufficient contributions, and the reduction in the proposed pensionable retirement age for women from 62 years of age to 60 (hitherto 57). None the less, industrial unrest continued, and one week later medical workers joined the ongoing strike. In late June the Government partially suspended implementation of the new law, and a revised series of measures (which maintained the retirement age for women at 57 years of age and increased the minimum qualifying number of monthly pension contributions from 180 to just 240—rather than 300 as initially suggested) was voted into law in December.

In April 2006 the Autoridad del Canal de Panamá (ACP) announced plans to expand the Canal's capacity to allow the passage of larger commercial container vessels, by constructing a third set of locks at either end of the waterway. The projected cost of US $5,250m. to build the wider locks was to be funded by toll revenues and loans totalling an estimated $2,270m. President Torrijos pledged to hold a national debate and an eventual referendum on the ACP's proposals. While widely considered to be vital to the future of the Canal and therefore the country's commercial sector, concerns were raised relating to the environmental consequences of the expansion and the possible relocation of farmers in communities bordering the Canal. Environmental groups criticized the high volume of water that would be required. However, the ACP countered that an estimated 60% of the water was to be recycled, using a system of overspill reservoirs. At the end of the month Héctor Alemán and Vázquez Morales, previously Ministers of the Interior and Justice and of the Economy and Finance, respectively, were appointed co-ordinators of the national debate. (In mid-April 2007 Vázquez Morales also stood down as Chairman of the ACP. He was subsequently replaced by Dani Kuzniecky.) Responsibility for the interior and justice was subsequently assumed by Olga Gólcher, while the economy and finance portfolio was transferred to Carlos Vallarino, hitherto Minister of Public Works. Vallarino was succeeded at the public works ministry by Benjamín Colamarco. In mid-July 2006, in the second of three scheduled debates, the Asamblea Nacional overwhelmingly approved the ACP's plan to expand the canal. At the referendum duly conducted on 22 October, the project was approved by a clear majority of 78.3% of those voting. However, voter participation was much lower than expected, at just 43.3% of the electorate. A ceremony to launch the project took place in September 2007. In March 2009 contractors were invited to submit bids to undertake the design and construction of the two new locks. It was anticipated that work on enlarging the canal, which would not disrupt normal operations, would be completed in 2014.

Allegations of corruption in public institutions continued to be a problem for the Government in 2006. In mid-July the head of the counter-terrorism and counter-narcotics police unit, Franklin Brewster, died from poisoning. Following an investigation by the Public Prosecutor's office, in collaboration with the US Federal Bureau of Investigation, in November three police officers were arrested on suspicion of contaminating Brewster's food with pesticide. Shortly prior to his assassination Brewster had launched an investigation into possible links between drugs-traffickers and the police force.

A number of deaths from poisoning by CSS-manufactured medicines in late 2006 led to demands for the resignation of the Minister of Public Health, Camilo Alleyne, together with the other members of the CSS board of directors. In mid-October the Government announced that a poisonous industrial alcohol had been detected in four remedies manufactured by the CSS. In November President Torrijos announced that an independent standards agency was to be established to oversee the manufacture of prescription drugs. In mid-January 2007 the Government announced that compensation was to be paid to the families of confirmed and suspected victims. By March the death toll had risen to 353, with more non-fatal cases. Human rights activists and members of the opposition demanded the resignation of Alleyne, who was eventually replaced by Rosario Turner in a major cabinet reorganization in September.

In mid-February 2008 a construction worker participating in a demonstration in Colón against poor working conditions was shot dead by police. In response, the construction workers' union, the Sindicato Unico Nacional de Trabajadores de la Industria de la Construcción y Similares (SUNTRACS), staged several days of nation-wide protests, in which some 40,000 members participated. Some 500 workers were arrested during the demonstrations. Following the protests, the Government approved legislation intended to improve health and safety standards in the construction industry, although SUNTRACS also demanded the resignation of Rolando Mirones, the chief of police, and the Minister of the Interior and Justice, Daniel Delgado Diamante, which was not forthcoming. Mirones eventually resigned in May, but Torrijos' choice of former soldier Jaime Ruiz as his replacement provoked criticism that the appointment of a military official was a constitutional violation.

The Asamblea Nacional approved legislation aimed at improving internal security in May 2008. The Government claimed the new law introduced a more hard-line stance against crime, increasing maximum prison sentences, and recognizing 37 new offences. In the following month the legislature, in which the President's PRD enjoyed a majority, granted Torrijos temporary powers to introduce security reforms by decree. The reforms included the creation of a single national intelligence and security service (SENIS—Servicio Nacional de Inteligencia y Seguridad), a proposal that met with widespread opposition owing to fears that the agency would wield excessive power. The Constitution was also amended to validate Ruiz's position as chief of police. FRENADESO (Frente Nacional por la Defensa de los Derechos Económicos y Sociales, as FRENADESSO had been restyled) mobilized over 15,000 people in marches in the capital and other cities on 14 August to protest both the SENIS decree and rising living costs. Despite the widespread opposition, Torrijos approved the security reforms the following week. Nevertheless, civil unrest continued with a national strike on 5 September; as well as protesting the security laws, strikers also demanded a 20% salary increase and a halt to price increases.

Cabinet changes continued throughout Torrijos' final year in power. In April 2008 the Minister of Housing, Balbina Herrera Araúz, resigned in order to contest the PRD candidacy for the

2009 presidential election, and was replaced by Gabriel Diez. Rubén Arosemena, Minister of the Presidency, and Belgis Castro, Minister of Education, also resigned to stand as deputies, and were replaced by Dilio Arcia Torres and Salvador Rodríguez, respectively. The most significant dismissal was that of the Minister of the Interior and Justice, Delgado, in late October following allegations by a national newspaper that, as a lieutenant in the national guard in 1970, he had murdered a corporal. Delgado admitted the killing, but claimed that the case was a police matter and had already been investigated; however, he volunteered to step down from his position temporarily in order to clear his name. Torrijos announced another reorganization of ministerial portfolios in November, however, which included the permanent replacement of Delgado by Arcia (whose post as Minister of the Presidency was filled by Rafael Mezquita), along with several other changes. Shortly after, Jaime Ruiz was replaced as chief of police by Francisco Troya. Meanwhile, in September Herrera secured the PRD's presidential candidacy. Her campaign was damaged in March 2009 by allegations that Colombian financier David Murcia Guzmán, who was in gaol for fraud, had contributed US $3m. to Herrera's presidential campaign, and the same amount to the party's Panama City mayoral candidate, Roberto Velásquez.

The presidential election, which was held on 3 May 2009, was won decisively by Ricardo Martinelli Berrocal on behalf of the Alianza por el Cambio, which included his own Cambio Democrático party and the Partido Panameñista. Martinelli secured 60.0% of valid votes cast, according to provisional results, while Herrera, representing the PRD-led Un País para Todos alliance, obtained 37.7%; former President Endara, of the Vanguardia Moral de la Patria, took just 2.3%. According to partial results of the concurrent legislative elections, the Alianza por el Cambio won an overall majority in the Asamblea Nacional with at least 37 of the 71 seats (reduced from 78), while Un País para Todos was to hold at least 23 seats. Martinelli, whose campaign had concentrated on crime and poverty reduction, was scheduled to take office on 1 July.

In July 1997, in the light of the increasing number of incursions by Colombian guerrillas and paramilitary groups into Panamanian territory, the Government deployed more than 1,200 members of the security forces to Darién Province to secure the border with Colombia. In previous months Colombian paramilitary members were reported to have forcibly occupied several settlements in the area while in pursuit of guerrillas who had taken refuge over the border. Following discussions between Pérez Balladares and his Colombian counterpart, Andrés Pastrana Arango, an agreement on improved co-operation concerning border security was reached. In June 1999, following further incursions by Colombian guerrillas into Darién Province, Panama and Colombia reached agreement on the strengthening of military patrols on both sides of the countries' joint border. However, in October 2000 one person was killed and 12 people were injured when Colombian paramilitaries attacked the town of Nazaret.

In October 1993 President Endara signed a protocol to establish Panama's membership of the Central American Parliament (Parlacen), a regional political forum with its headquarters in Guatemala. Later in the month Endara, together with the five Presidents of the member nations of the Central American Common Market (CACM, see p. 211), signed a protocol to the 1960 General Treaty on Central American Integration, committing Panama to fuller economic integration in the region. However, at a meeting of Central American Presidents, convened in Costa Rica in August 1994, Pérez Balladares (attending as an observer) stated that his administration considered further regional economic integration to be disadvantageous to Panama, owing to the differences between Panama's services-based economy and the reliance on the agricultural sector of the other Central American states. Negotiations on a free trade agreement with El Salvador were concluded in March 2002. Although Panama was excluded from the negotiations towards a Dominican Republic-Central American Free Trade Agreement (DR-CAFTA) with the USA, a bilateral free trade agreement with the USA was finally signed in June 2007. However, the accord had still to be ratified by the US legislature, and further negotiations on labour laws were also to be held. Panama has observer status within the Andean Community of Nations (see p. 178).

Government

Legislative power is vested in the unicameral Asamblea Nacional (National Assembly), which was known as the Asamblea Legislativa (Legislative Assembly) until 2004 and which replaced the Asamblea Nacional de Corregidores (National Assembly of Community Representatives) in 1984 (except for its brief reintroduction in late 1989), with a total of 71 members elected for five years by universal adult suffrage. Executive power is held by the President, also directly elected for a term of five years, assisted by two elected Vice-Presidents and an appointed Cabinet. Panama is divided into nine provinces and three autonomous Indian Reservations. Each province has a governor, appointed by the President.

Defence

In 1990, following the overthrow of Gen. Manuel Noriega, the National Defence Forces were disbanded and a new Public Force was created. This numbered 12,000 men, as assessed at November 2008, comprising the National Police (11,000 men), the National Air Service (400 men) and the National Maritime Service (an estimated 600 men). Budgeted security expenditure for 2006 was estimated at US $226m.

Economic Affairs

In 2007, according to estimates by the World Bank, Panama's gross national income (GNI), measured at average 2005–07 prices, was US $18,423m., equivalent to $5,510 per head (or $10,610 on an international purchasing-power parity basis). During 2000–07, it was estimated, the population increased at an average annual rate of 1.8%, while gross domestic product (GDP) per head increased, in real terms, by an average of 4.0% per year. Overall GDP increased, in real terms, at an average annual rate of 5.9% in 2000–07; according to official estimates, growth was 9.2% in 2008.

Agriculture (including hunting, forestry and fishing) contributed an estimated 6.5% of GDP in 2006 and engaged some 14.7% of the employed labour force in 2007. Rice, maize and beans are cultivated as subsistence crops, while the principal cash crops are bananas (which accounted for an estimated 8.6% of total export earnings in 2008), melons, sugar cane and coffee. Cattle-raising, tropical timber and fisheries (particularly shrimps and yellowfin tuna for export) are also important. The banana sector was adversely affected by industrial action and poor weather conditions in the early 2000s. The end of the European Union's (EU, see p. 255) quota system on banana imports from 2006 was predicted to boost the sector. In the 1990s, in an attempt to diversify the agricultural sector, new crops such as oil palm, cocoa, coconuts, various winter vegetables and tropical fruits were introduced. Fish exports increased steadily from the 1990s. In 2008 exports of yellowfin tuna and fish fillet accounted for an estimated 8.4% of export revenue. Agricultural GDP increased by an average of 4.8% annually during 2000–07; the sector increased by an estimated 2.1% in 2008.

Industry (including mining, manufacturing, construction and power) contributed an estimated 16.3% of GDP in 2006 and engaged 19.3% of the employed labour force in 2007. According to World Bank figures, industrial GDP increased at an average annual rate of 2.8% during 2000–07; the sector's GDP increased by an estimated 14.2% in 2008.

Mining contributed an estimated 1.2% of GDP in 2006 and engaged 0.3% of the employed labour force in 2007. Panama has significant deposits of copper and coal. The GDP of the mining sector increased by an estimated average of 16.9% per year in 2004–08; the sector expanded by an estimated 29.8% in 2008.

Manufacturing contributed an estimated 7.0% of GDP in 2006 and engaged an estimated 8.7% of the employed labour force in 2007. The most important sectors, measured by output in producers' prices, were refined petroleum products, food-processing, beverages, and cement, lime and plaster. Manufacturing GDP increased by an average of 0.7% annually during 2000–07; the sector increased by an estimated 3.8% in 2008.

The country's topography and climate make it ideal for hydroelectric power, and in 2005 approximately 63.9% of Panama's total output of electricity was water-generated. A new hydroelectric project on the Bonyic river, costing US $49m., was approved in 2004. Petroleum accounted for the most of the remainder (35.7%) of the country's generating capacity. In 2007 imports of mineral products accounted for 19.4% of the value of merchandise imports.

Panama's economy is dependent upon the services sector, which contributed an estimated 77.3% of GDP in 2006 and engaged 66.0% of the employed labour force in 2007. The Panama Canal contributed an estimated 6.3% of the country's GDP in that year. Panama is an important 'offshore' financial centre, and in 2006 financial, property and business services contributed an estimated 26.4% of GDP. Important contributions to the economy are also made by trade in the Colón Free Zone (CFZ—in which some 1,800 companies were situated in 2005, and which contributed an estimated 8.4% of GDP the following year), and by the registration of merchant ships under a 'flag of convenience' in Panama. The tourism sector also increased steadily from the last decade of the 20th century. In 2006 income from tourism totalled US $1,450m., compared with $1,108m. in the previous year. According to the World Bank, the GDP of the services sector increased by an average of 6.6% per year in 2000–07; the sector grew by an estimated 8.8% in 2008.

In 2007 Panama recorded a visible trade deficit of US $3,182.2m., and there was a deficit of $1,422.4m. on the current account of the balance of payments. According to preliminary figures, in 2008 the principal source of imports (29.6%) was the USA, which was also the principal market for exports (38.0%). Other major trading partners are Costa Rica, the People's Republic of China, Japan, Mexico and Spain. The principal exports in 2007 were fresh and frozen fish and fillets, melons and bananas. The principal imports in that year were machinery and apparatus, mineral products, and transport materials.

In 2007 there was an estimated overall budgetary surplus of 636.9m. balboas (equivalent to 3.3% of GDP). Panama's external debt at the end of 2006 was US $9,989m., of which $7,774m. was long-term public debt. In that year the cost of debt-servicing was equivalent to 24.7% of the value of exports of goods and services. Annual inflation averaged 3.1% in 2002–08; consumer prices increased by 4.2% in 2007 and by 8.8% in 2008. Some 9.1% of the labour force were unemployed in August 2006.

Panama is a member of the Inter-American Development Bank (IDB, see p. 318). In September 1997 Panama joined the World Trade Organization (WTO, see p. 410). In March 2002 Panama concluded a free trade agreement with El Salvador. In August 2003 a free trade accord between Panama and Taiwan was concluded. In December 2006 negotiations towards a free trade agreement with the USA were finally concluded. The accord would remove 90% of tariffs on Panamanian–US trade, with the remaining 10% to be eliminated over the next 10 years; however, by April 2009 the agreement had still to be ratified by the US Congress. A free trade agreement with Chile was concluded in December 2007, while a similar accord with Guatemala was scheduled to enter into effect in June 2009.

Following the cession to Panamanian control of the Panama Canal at the end of 1999, the waterway was operated as a profit-making venture, providing the Government with a considerable source of funds. Nevertheless, the administration of President Martín Torrijos Espino, which took office in September 2004, confronted the problems of high unemployment and widespread poverty (affecting an estimated 40% of the population). In October 2006 plans to expand the Canal (at a cost of US $5,250m.) were approved. The upgrade would create some 7,000 jobs and lead to a considerable expansion in the construction sector. Once finished, the Canal was expected to increase GDP growth by 1%–2% per year until 2025. Following the introduction of a fiscal adjustment programme in 2005, designed to reduce the deficit by increasing the tax yield, rationalizing public spending and reducing expenditure on salaries, the Asamblea Nacional approved the Fiscal Responsibility Law in May 2008 in order to limit the deficit to 1% of GDP for the non-financial public sector, excluding the Panama Canal Authority, and achieve a debt target of 40% of GDP by 2015. It was hoped that implementation of these reforms would help the Torrijos Government secure financing, on favourable terms, for the planned Canal expansion. In December 2008 the Government received $2,300m. in funding for the project from five multilateral agencies and affirmed that it was on course to complete the expansion in 2014; bidding opened in March 2009. Strong growth in 2006–07 was driven primarily by foreign investment, the expansion of the construction and financial sectors and increasing Canal traffic. However, foreign debt remained a problem, as did the current account deficit and rising inflation. According to official estimates, the economy grew by an impressive 9.2% in 2008, but growth was expected to slow to a still robust 7.8% in 2009.

Education

The education system is divided into elementary, secondary and university schooling, each of six years' duration. Education is free up to university level, and is officially compulsory for six years between six and 15 years of age. In 2006/07 some 61.4% of children aged 4–5 years were enrolled at pre-primary schools (males 61.7%; females 61.0%). Primary education begins at the age of six, and secondary education, which comprises two three-year cycles, at the age of 12. The enrolment at primary schools of children in the relevant age-group was 98.5% (males 98.8%; females 98.2%) in 2005/06, and secondary enrolment was 64.2% (males 61.0%; females 67.5%) in the same year. There are four public universities, with regional centres in the provinces, and 11 private ones, including one specializing in distance learning. Budgetary expenditure on education by the central Government in 2007 totalled a preliminary 639m. balboas (equivalent to 18.5% of total current expenditure).

Public Holidays

2009: 1 January (New Year's Day), 12 January (National Martyrs' Day), 23–24 February (Carnival), 25 February (Ash Wednesday), 9 April (Maundy Thursday), 10 April (Good Friday), 1 May (Labour Day), 1 July (Presidential Inauguration), 15 August (Foundation of Panama City, Panama City only)*, 11 October (Revolution Day), 1 November (National Anthem Day)*, 2 November (Day of the Dead), 3 November (Independence from Colombia), 4 November (Flag Day)*, 5 November (Independence Day, Colón only), 10 November (First Call for Independence), 28 November (Independence from Spain), 8 December (Immaculate Conception, Mothers' Day), 25 December (Christmas).

2010: 1 January (New Year's Day), 9 January (National Martyrs' Day), 15–16 February (Carnival), 17 February (Ash Wednesday), 1 April (Maundy Thursday), 2 April (Good Friday), 1 May (Labour Day), 14 August (Foundation of Panama City, Panama City only)*, 11 October (Revolution Day), 1 November (National Anthem Day)*, 2 November (Day of the Dead), 3 November (Independence from Colombia), 4 November (Flag Day)*, 5 November (Independence Day, Colón only), 10 November (First Call for Independence), 29 November (Independence from Spain), 8 December (Immaculate Conception, Mothers' Day), 25 December (Christmas).

* Official holiday: banks and government offices closed.

Weights and Measures

Both the metric and the imperial systems of weights and measures are in use.

PANAMA

Statistical Survey

Sources (unless otherwise stated): Dirección de Estadística y Censo, Contraloría General de la República, Avda Balboa y Federico Boyd, Apdo 5213, Panamá 5; tel. 210-4800; fax 210-4801; e-mail cgrdec@contraloria.gob.pa; internet www.contraloria.gob.pa; Ministry of the Economy and Finance, Edif. Ogawa, Vía España, Apdo 5245, Panamá 5; e-mail webmaster@mef.gob.pa; internet www.mef.gob.pa.

Note: The former Canal Zone was incorporated into Panama on 1 October 1979.

Area and Population

AREA, POPULATION AND DENSITY

Area (sq km)	75,517*
Population (census results)	
13 May 1990	2,329,329
14 May 2000	
Males	1,432,566
Females	1,406,611
Total	2,839,177
Population (official estimates at mid-year)	
2006	3,283,959
2007	3,339,781
2008	3,395,346
Density (per sq km) at mid-2008	45.0

* 29,157 sq miles.

ADMINISTRATIVE DIVISIONS
(official estimates at mid-2008)

Province	Population	Capital (and population)*
Bocas del Toro	113,180	Bocas del Toro (12,996)
Chiriquí	418,518	David (143,320)
Coclé	232,557	Penonomé (82,716)
Colón	243,115	Colón (209,035)
Comarca Emberá	9,432	—
Comarca Kuna Yala	37,212	—
Comarca Ngöbe-Buglé	143,189	—
Darién	45,325	Chepigana (31,128)
Herrera	111,647	Chitré (48,538)
Los Santos	90,259	Las Tablas (26,904)
Panamá	1,725,293	Panamá (861,977)
Veraguas	225,619	Santiago (83,577)
Total	3,395,346	—

* Population of district in which capital is located.
Note: Population figures include the former Canal Zone.

PRINCIPAL TOWNS
(population at 2000 census)

Panamá (Panama City, capital)	463,093	Pacora	57,232
San Miguelito	291,769	Santiago	55,146
Tocumen	81,250	La Chorrera	54,823
David	76,481	Colón	52,286
Nuevo Arraiján	63,753	Changuinola	45,063
Puerto Armuelles	60,102	Pedregal	45,033

Mid-2007 ('000, incl. suburbs, UN estimate): Panama City 1,281 (Source: UN, *World Urbanization Prospects: The 2007 Revision*).

BIRTHS, MARRIAGES AND DEATHS

	Registered live births		Registered marriages*		Registered deaths	
	Number	Rate (per 1,000)†	Number	Rate (per 1,000)†	Number	Rate (per 1,000)†
2000	64,839	22.7	10,430	3.9	11,841	4.1
2001	63,900	21.3	9,687	3.6	12,442	4.1
2002	61,671	20.2	9,558	3.1	12,428	4.1
2003	61,753	19.8	10,310	3.3	13,248	4.3
2004	62,743	19.8	10,290	3.2	13,475	4.2
2005	63,645	19.7	10,512	3.3	14,180	4.4
2006	65,764	20.0	10,747	3.3	14,358	4.4
2007	67,364	20.2	11,516	3.4	14,775	4.4

* Excludes tribal Indian population.
† Based on official mid-year population estimates.

Life expectancy (years at birth, WHO estimates): 76.1 (males 73.9; females 78.5) in 2006 (Source: WHO, *World Health Statistics*).

ECONOMICALLY ACTIVE POPULATION
('000 persons aged 15 years and over, August of each year)

	2005	2006	2007
Agriculture, hunting and forestry	176.8	183.1	176.5
Fishing	9.5	9.9	9.8
Mining and quarrying	1.0	2.3	3.6
Manufacturing	104.3	105.2	109.6
Electricity, gas and water supply	7.7	8.4	8.1
Construction	91.1	102.8	122.4
Wholesale and retail trade; repair of motor vehicles, motorcycles and personal and household goods	226.9	229.6	240.7
Hotels and restaurants	69.6	64.5	69.5
Transport, storage and communications	91.3	90.8	91.9
Financial intermediation	24.3	26.4	28.8
Real estate, renting and business activities	61.7	62.6	67.0
Public administration and defence; compulsory social service	69.4	70.3	79.6
Education	64.9	62.7	65.3
Health and social work	47.6	48.3	50.6
Other community, social and personal service activities	71.6	68.0	63.8
Private households with employed persons	70.0	74.9	76.1
Extra-territorial organizations and bodies	0.6	0.8	0.7
Total employed	1,188.3	1,210.7	1,264.0
Unemployed	136.8	121.4	92.0
Total labour force	1,325.1	1,332.1	1,355.9

Source: ILO.

PANAMA

Health and Welfare

KEY INDICATORS

Total fertility rate (children per woman, 2006)	2.6
Under-5 mortality rate (per 1,000 live births, 2006)	23
HIV/AIDS (% of persons aged 15–49, 2007)	1.0
Physicians (per 1,000 head, 2000)	1.5
Hospital beds (per 1,000 head, 2005)	2.4
Health expenditure (2006): US $ per head (PPP)	721
Health expenditure (2006): % of GDP	7.3
Health expenditure (2006): public (% of total)	68.8
Access to water (% of persons, 2006)	92
Access to sanitation (% of persons, 2006)	74
Human Development Index (2006): ranking	58
Human Development Index (2006): value	0.832

For sources and definitions, see explanatory note on p. vi.

Agriculture

PRINCIPAL CROPS
('000 metric tons)

	2005	2006*	2007*
Rice, paddy	235.2	280.0	280.0
Maize	89.1	70.0	73.0
Sugar cane	1,766.1	1,770.0	1,800.0
Watermelons	71.9	72.0	72.0
Cantaloupes and other melons	102.9	130.0	130.0
Bananas	439.2	440.0	440.0
Plantains	108.8	95.2	95.2
Oranges	41.9	42.0	42.0
Coffee, green	13.2	13.5	14.3
Tobacco, unmanufactured*	2.4	2.6	2.8

* FAO estimates.

Aggregate production ('000 metric tons, may include official, semi-official or estimated data): Total cereals 334.3 in 2005, 360.3 in 2006, 363.8 in 2007; Total roots and tubers 91.8 in 2005, 91.8 in 2006, 94.5 in 2007; Total vegetables (incl. melons) 291.3 in 2005, 272.6 in 2006, 274.0 in 2007; Total fruits (excl. melons) 672.9 in 2005, 641.0 in 2006, 624.4 in 2007.

Source: FAO.

LIVESTOCK
('000 head, year ending September)

	2005	2006*	2007*
Horses*	180	185	190
Asses, mules or hinnies*	4	n.a.	n.a.
Cattle*	1,564	1,600	1,650
Pigs	286	290	300
Goats*	6	6	6
Chickens*	14,623	14,535	15,000
Ducks*	225	230	235
Turkeys*	35	35	40

* FAO estimates.
Source: FAO.

LIVESTOCK PRODUCTS
('000 metric tons)

	2005	2006*	2007*
Cattle meat	57.0	57.0	57.0
Pig meat	21.3	21.0	21.5
Chicken meat	94.6	85.2	85.3
Cows' milk	181.0	187.0	187.0
Hen eggs	28.1	21.0	21.0

* FAO estimates.
Source: FAO.

Statistical Survey

Forestry

ROUNDWOOD REMOVALS
('000 cubic metres, excluding bark)

	2005	2006	2007
Sawlogs, veneer logs and logs for sleepers	64	69	83
Other industrial wood	1	1	1
Fuel wood*	1,205	1,189	1,173
Pulp wood*	90	90	90
Total*	**1,360**	**1,349**	**1,347**

* FAO estimates.
Source: FAO.

SAWNWOOD PRODUCTION
('000 cubic metres, incl. railway sleepers)

	2003	2004	2005*
Total (all broadleaved)	27	30	30

* FAO estimate.
2006–07: Production assumed to be unchanged from 2005 (FAO estimate).
Source: FAO.

Fishing

('000 metric tons, live weight)

	2004	2005	2006
Capture	208.8	220.3	226.8
Snappers and jobfishes	5.0	11.0	8.8
Pacific thread herring	45.5	32.0	30.3
Pacific anchoveta	47.0	59.5	53.4
Skipjack tuna	18.8	39.2	56.7
Yellowfin tuna	33.8	36.1	37.9
Bigeye tuna	10.4	11.4	11.9
Marine fishes	25.9	10.9	8.7
Aquaculture	7.0	7.8	8.7
Whiteleg shrimp	6.5	7.1	8.1
Total catch	**215.9**	**228.1**	**235.6**

Note: Figures exclude crocodiles. The number of spectacled caimans caught was: 15,850 in 2004; 4,696 in 2005; 2,210 in 2006.
Source: FAO.

Industry

SELECTED PRODUCTS
('000 metric tons, unless otherwise indicated)

	2005	2006	2007*
Salt	20	19	20
Sugar	157	168	164
Beer (million litres)	167	180	195
Wines and spirits (million litres)	13	12	13
Evaporated, condensed and powdered milk	23	21	19
Fish oil	4	7	7
Footwear ('000 pairs)	10	8	14
Electricity (million kWh, net)	5,546	5,731	6,156

* Preliminary.

Finance

CURRENCY AND EXCHANGE RATES

Monetary Units
100 centésimos = 1 balboa (B).

Sterling, Dollar and Euro Equivalents (31 December 2008)
£1 sterling = 1.458 balboas;
US $1 = 1.000 balboas;
€1 = 1.392 balboas;
100 balboas = £68.60 = $100.00 = €71.85.

Exchange Rate: The balboa's value is fixed at par with that of the US dollar.

BUDGET
(consolidated general government budget, '000 balboas)

Revenue	2005	2006	2007*
Central government revenue	3,438,186	3,783,081	4,433,157
Current revenue	2,328,211	3,158,010	3,682,164
Tax revenue	1,378,673	1,813,549	2,132,803
Direct taxes	708,181	1,020,263	1,134,342
Income tax	583,901	878,407	985,184
Taxes on property and inheritance	88,037	91,715	109,316
Educational insurance	36,243	50,141	39,842
Indirect taxes	670,492	793,286	998,461
Non-tax revenue	866,506	1,281,780	1,460,182
Panama Canal	200,000	334,181	463,414
Transfers from balance of public sector	2,626	2,522	2,754
Other current revenue	83,032	62,681	89,179
Surplus on cash account	22,265	12,564	357
Capital revenue	1,087,710	612,507	750,636
Decentralized institutional revenue	1,796,600	1,971,100	2,369,000
Department of social security	1,388,900	1,494,300	—
University of Panama	114,800	116,900	—
State enterprises	1,412,000	1,683,800	2,150,300
Non-financial	532,300	568,200	792,000
Financial	879,700	1,115,600	1,358,300
Municipalities	101,400	111,600	129,500
Total revenue	**6,748,200**	**7,549,600**	**9,081,900**

Expenditure	2005	2006	2007*
Central government expenditure	3,408,186	3,772,692	4,432,114
Current expenditure	3,020,194	3,041,525	3,462,913
National Assembly	45,245	50,722	56,305
State treasury	34,122	38,106	40,688
Ministry of the Presidency	41,299	51,863	60,607
Ministry of the Interior and Justice	210,398	224,806	247,908
Ministry of Foreign Affairs	30,807	33,498	39,326
Ministry of Social Development	15,507	16,774	15,384
Ministry of the Economy and Finance	154,515	138,825	112,053
Ministry of Education	533,327	594,516	639,408
Ministry of Commerce and Industry	37,067	33,050	29,660
Ministry of Public Works	22,454	36,003	26,439
Ministry of Agricultural Development	33,755	39,280	42,792
Ministry of Public Health	358,734	473,234	598,101
Ministry of Labour and Social Welfare	8,719	7,197	8,649
Ministry of Housing	11,177	12,147	13,627
Judiciary	36,553	40,474	43,068
Ombudsman	42,244	45,581	49,486

Expenditure—continued	2005	2006	2007*
Electoral tribunal	23,237	32,247	29,031
Other expenditures of administration	11,148	11,314	11,478
Debt-servicing	1,333,411	1,115,816	1,362,504
Education fund	36,475	46,072	639,408
Ministerial development expenditure	387,992	731,167	969,201
Decentralized institutional expenditure	1,617,900	1,745,100	1,996,800
Department of social security	1,261,100	1,312,600	—
State enterprises	1,316,400	1,623,800	1,896,300
Municipalities	94,000	102,400	119,800
Total	**6,436,500**	**7,244,000**	**8,445,000**

* Preliminary figures.

Note: Totals may not be equal to the sum of component parts, owing to partial rounding.

INTERNATIONAL RESERVES
(US $ million at 31 December*)

	2005	2006	2007
IMF special drawing rights	1.1	1.3	0.9
Reserve position in IMF	17.0	17.8	18.7
Foreign exchange	1,192.5	1,315.9	1,915.4
Total	**1,210.5**	**1,335.0**	**1,935.1**

* Excludes gold, valued at US $476,000 in 1991–93.

Note: US treasury notes and coins form the bulk of the currency in circulation in Panama.

Source: IMF, *International Financial Statistics*.

MONEY SUPPLY
(million balboas at 31 December)

	2005	2006	2007
Demand deposits at commercial banks	1,810.8	2,519.2	2,933.6
Total money (incl. others)	1,906.3	2,610.3	3,053.9

Source: IMF, *International Financial Statistics*.

COST OF LIVING
(Consumer Price Index, base: 2000 = 100)

	2005	2006	2007
Food (incl. beverages)	105.6	107.0	114.2
Rent, fuel and light	104.0	109.3	114.3
Clothing (incl. footwear)	97.1	96.3	94.9
All items (incl. others)	103.3	105.9	110.3

Source: ILO.

PANAMA

Statistical Survey

NATIONAL ACCOUNTS

National Income and Product
(million balboas at current prices)

	2005	2006	2007*
Compensation of employees	5,122.5	5,675.5	6,282.2
Operating surplus	6,006.0	6,391.2	7,482.1
Net mixed income	1,996.2	2,207.8	2,544.9
Domestic factor incomes	13,124.7	14,274.5	16,309.2
Consumption of fixed capital	1,060.4	1,254.0	1,354.8
Gross domestic product (GDP) at factor cost	14,185.1	15,528.5	17,664.0
Indirect taxes	1,366.3	1,770.5	1,995.5
Less Subsidies	86.7	162.0	174.1
GDP in purchasers' values	15,464.7	17,137.0	19,485.4
Less Net factor income paid to the rest of the world	1,436.5	1,546.0	1,745.9
Gross national product	14,028.2	15,591.0	17,739.5
Less Consumption of fixed capital	1,060.4	1,254.0	1,354.8
National income in market prices	12,967.8	14,337.0	16,384.7
Other current transfers from abroad (net)	165.6	153.7	150.3
National disposable income	13,133.4	14,490.7	16,535.0

* Provisional figures.

Expenditure on the Gross Domestic Product
(million balboas at current prices)

	2005	2006	2007*
Government final consumption expenditure	2,033.8	2,116.3	2,236.3
Private final consumption expenditure	9,597.2	10,445.6	11,701.4
Increase in stocks	237.7	200.0	221.0
Gross fixed capital formation	2,601.3	3,134.9	4,357.5
Total domestic expenditure	14,470.0	15,896.8	18,516.2
Exports of goods and services	11,674.2	13,146.6	15,586.5
Less Imports of goods and services	10,679.5	11,906.4	14,617.3
GDP in purchasers' values	15,464.7	17,137.0	19,485.4
GDP at constant 1996 prices	14,041.2	15,238.6	16,997.6

* Provisional figures.

Gross Domestic Product by Economic Activity
(million balboas at constant 1996 prices)

	2006	2007*	2008†
Agriculture, hunting, forestry and fishing	1,039.1	1,056.4	1,119.7
Mining and quarrying	159.5	195.7	254.1
Manufacturing	1,066.7	1,125.7	1,168.5
Electricity, gas and water	447.6	488.6	513.5
Construction	704.0	846.9	1,101.2
Wholesale and retail trade, repair of vehicles, motorcycles and other household goods	2,274.0	2,465.1	2,638.4
Hotels and restaurants	433.2	493.9	539.8
Transport, storage and communications	2,920.9	3,427.2	3,965.1
Financial intermediation	1,187.1	1,416.3	1,449.4
Renting, real estate and business services	2,401.3	2,583.4	2,734.3
General government services	1,231.8	1,272.7	1,321.0
Social services and private education and health	243.7	258.2	264.9

—continued	2006	2007*	2008†
Other community, social and personal services	448.4	499.8	532.8
Private households with employed persons	111.3	114.2	117.2
Sub-total	14,668.6	16,244.1	17,719.9
Less Financial intermediation services indirectly measured	374.3	379.7	337.1
Gross value added in basic prices	14,294.3	15,864.4	17,382.8
Import duties and other taxes, less subsidies	944.3	1,133.2	1,175.3
GDP in market prices	15,238.6	16,997.6	18,558.1

* Provisional figures.
† Estimates.

BALANCE OF PAYMENTS
(US $ million)*

	2005	2006	2007
Exports of goods f.o.b.	7,375.2	8,478.1	9,338.4
Imports of goods f.o.b.	−8,933.0	−10,190.0	−12,520.6
Trade balance	−1,557.8	−1,711.9	−3,182.2
Exports of services	3,231.3	3,938.0	4,924.4
Imports of services	−1,811.4	−1,727.7	−2,106.7
Balance on goods and services	−137.9	498.4	−364.5
Other income received	1,054.8	1,403.0	1,875.7
Other income paid	−2,180.4	−2,680.7	−3,186.8
Balance on goods, services and income	−1,263.5	−779.3	−1,675.6
Current transfers received	338.2	388.4	416.4
Current transfers paid	−96.5	−135.9	−163.2
Current balance	−1,021.8	−526.8	−1,422.4
Capital account (net)	15.8	15.2	43.7
Direct investment from abroad	917.6	2,497.9	1,907.2
Portfolio investment assets	−1,102.8	−748.0	−1,084.1
Portfolio investment liabilities	545.7	254.9	450.0
Other investment assets	−334.4	−3,781.8	−4,998.4
Other investment liabilities	2,014.0	2,152.2	6,499.2
Net errors and omissions	−357.9	308.1	−775.3
Overall balance	676.2	171.7	619.9

* Including the transactions of enterprises operating in the Colón Free Zone.

Source: IMF, *International Financial Statistics*.

External Trade

PRINCIPAL COMMODITIES
('000 balboas)

Imports c.i.f.	2005	2006	2007
Food and live animals	531,893	556,660	737,830
Mineral products	787,357	919,126	1,331,529
Chemicals and chemical products	456,809	522,161	643,643
Plastics, rubber and articles thereof	176,076	210,454	282,982
Textiles and articles thereof	155,792	169,953	223,895
Metals and manufactures of metal	272,669	388,368	530,211
Machinery and apparatus	772,351	878,577	1,415,090
Transport materials	434,684	531,824	813,776
Total (incl. others)	4,152,847	4,817,655	6,869,921

PANAMA

Exports f.o.b.*	2006	2007	2008†
Sugar	21,285	17,637	15,149
Bananas	109,437	111,615	98,581
Melons	166,431	202,523	213,994
Pineapples	36,922	42,855	36,503
Coffee	13,363	16,303	15,399
Shellfish	50,239	56,367	40,624
Fresh and frozen fish and fillets (incl. yellowfin tuna)	250,148	286,820	346,923
Meat from cattle	14,246	11,636	13,161
Standing cattle	30,590	16,429	—
Total (incl. others)	1,021,820	1,126,799	1,144,714

* Including re-exports.
† Preliminary.

PRINCIPAL TRADING PARTNERS*
('000 balboas)

Imports c.i.f.†	2006	2007	2008‡
Brazil	150,047	140,703	140,287
China, People's Republic	166,844	358,725	454,489
Colombia	169,910	192,109	273,287
Costa Rica	246,243	326,226	456,434
El Salvador	59,077	72,337	93,479
Germany	56,828	87,350	125,669
Guatemala	84,859	107,372	149,789
Japan	229,243	328,945	385,101
Korea, Republic	165,674	267,671	263,459
Mexico	173,017	212,027	312,727
Netherlands Antilles§	488,250	489,156	n.a.
Peru	n.a.	69,029	107,067
Spain	73,925	106,958	142,145
USA	1,295,624	2,079,584	2,683,075
Venezuela	51,504	55,401	n.a.
Total (incl. others)	4,817,655	6,869,921	9,050,168

Exports f.o.b.	2006	2007	2008‡
Belgium-Luxembourg	38,646	42,347	11,688
China, People's Republic	13,449	68,032	49,113
Colombia	18,813	19,138	12,142
Costa Rica	45,608	57,101	65,983
Dominican Republic	16,030	13,440	16,960
El Salvador	9,305	8,022	7,521
Guatemala	33,018	16,712	8,147
Honduras	17,914	20,923	17,152
Hong Kong	n.a.	5,337	n.a.
India	n.a.	7,791	6,671
Italy	26,384	18,309	29,598
Mexico	10,453	9,252	8,901
Netherlands	68,306	114,640	122,756
Nicaragua	17,248	12,879	13,462
Portugal	11,731	13,076	n.a.
Puerto Rico	13,871	9,045	13,062
Spain	83,435	55,792	56,926
Sweden	56,856	62,150	62,689
Taiwan	23,664	38,920	46,665
United Kingdom	34,650	61,239	61,326
USA	393,512	391,402	435,116
Total (incl. others)	1,021,820	1,126,799	1,144,714

* Including trade with the Colón Free Zone (CFZ) ('000 balboas): *Imports:* 573,479 in 2006; 714,614 in 2007; 840,454 in 2008 (preliminary). *Exports:* 16,341 in 2006; 20,229 in 2007; 19,748 in 2008 (preliminary).
† Including imports to the Petroleum Free Zone ('000 balboas): 162,690 in 2006; 360,009 in 2007; 1,365,296 in 2008 (preliminary).
‡ Preliminary.
§ Curaçao only.

Transport

RAILWAYS
(traffic)

	2002*	2003	2004
Passenger-km (million)	35,693	52,324	53,377
Freight ton-km (million)	20,665	41,863	52,946

* Panama Railway only.
Source: UN, *Statistical Yearbook*.

ROAD TRAFFIC
(motor vehicles in use)

	2000	2001	2002
Cars	223,433	219,372	224,504
Buses and coaches	16,865	15,558	16,371
Lorries and vans	75,454	73,139	74,247

Source: IRF, *World Road Statistics*.

SHIPPING

Merchant Fleet
(registered at 31 December)

	2005	2006	2007
Number of vessels	6,838	7,183	7,605
Total displacement ('000 grt)	141,821.7	154,964.6	168,165.5

Source: Lloyd's Register-Fairplay, *World Fleet Statistics*.

International Sea-borne Freight Traffic
('000 metric tons)

	2001	2002	2003
Goods loaded	108,456	110,556	99,516
Goods unloaded	84,864	99,288	76,152

Panama Canal Traffic

	2005/06	2006/07	2007/08
Transits	14,194	14,721	14,702
Cargo ('000 long tons)	211,606.2	208,216.6	209,714.3

Source: Panama Canal Authority.

CIVIL AVIATION
(traffic on scheduled services)

	2005	2006	2007
Kilometres flown (million)	55	67	81
Passenger-km (million)	5,206	6,078	7,940
Total ton-km (million)	37	36	36

Source: UN Economic Commission for Latin America and the Caribbean, *Statistical Yearbook*.

Tourism

VISITOR ARRIVALS BY COUNTRY OF ORIGIN
(arrivals at Tocumen International Airport)

	2004	2005	2006
Argentina	10,108	11,629	14,230
Canada	16,911	19,660	29,392
Chile	7,406	8,150	9,985
Colombia	93,510	108,628	129,418
Costa Rica	21,459	25,455	31,248
Dominican Republic	5,923	7,396	9,049
Ecuador	22,391	25,903	35,024
El Salvador	8,031	9,279	11,545
France	6,881	7,289	9,396
Germany	4,222	4,745	6,275
Guatemala	12,400	14,349	17,361

PANAMA

—continued	2004	2005	2006
Honduras	6,027	6,584	8,143
Italy	5,198	6,617	10,584
Jamaica	4,629	5,593	6,890
Mexico	24,532	29,280	34,507
Nicaragua	5,304	6,056	7,332
Peru	11,508	12,592	15,416
Puerto Rico	8,129	8,625	10,585
Spain	9,569	10,838	12,267
USA	140,062	160,288	191,094
Venezuela	16,249	18,892	23,113
Total (incl. others)	498,415	576,050	703,745

Tourism receipts (US $ million, incl. passenger transport): 903 in 2004; 1,108 in 2005; 1,450 in 2006.

Source: World Tourism Organization.

Communications Media

	2005	2006	2007
Telephones ('000 main lines in use)	470.5	488.3	491.9
Mobile cellular telephones ('000 subscribers)	1,748.7	2,174.5	2,391.9
Personal computers ('000 in use)	147	n.a.	n.a.
Internet users ('000)	371.1	502.6	525.2
Broadband subscribers ('000)	17.6	33.1	34.6

Radio receivers ('000 in use): 815 in 1997.

Television receivers ('000 in use): 550 in 2000.

Daily newspapers: 8 in 2004.

Sources: UNESCO, *Statistical Yearbook*; UN, *Statistical Yearbook*; International Telecommunication Union.

Education

(2006/07 unless otherwise indicated, provisional)

			Students		
	Institutions*	Teachers	Males	Females	Total
Pre-primary	1,662	5,270	49,798	47,059	96,857
Primary	3,116	18,183	230,841	215,335	446,176
Secondary	442	16,847	128,212	132,482	260,694
General	n.a.	13,574	105,765	111,938	217,703
Vocational	n.a.	3,273	22,447	20,544	42,991
Tertiary†	24	11,528	51,129	79,709	130,838

* 2001/02 figures.
† 2005/06.

Sources: Ministry of Education; UNESCO, *Statistical Yearbook*; UNESCO Institute for Statistics.

Adult literacy rate (UNESCO estimates): 93.4% (males 94.0%; females 92.8%) in 2007 (Source: UNESCO Institute for Statistics).

Directory

The Constitution

Under the terms of the amendments to the Constitution, implemented by the adoption of Reform Acts No. 1 and No. 2 in October 1978, and by the approval by referendum of the Constitutional Act in April 1983, the 67 (later 78) members of the unicameral Asamblea Legislativa (Legislative Assembly) are elected by popular vote every five years. Executive power is exercised by the President of the Republic, who is also elected by popular vote for a term of five years. Two Vice-Presidents are elected by popular vote to assist the President. The President appoints the Cabinet. The armed forces are barred from participating in elections. In July 2004 further amendments to the Constitution were adopted, including a reduction (to 71) in the number of members of the Asamblea from 2009, the abolition of parliamentary immunity from prosecution, and the creation of a constitutional assembly to consider future changes to the Constitution.

The Government

HEAD OF STATE

President: MARTÍN TORRIJOS ESPINO (took office 1 September 2004).
First Vice-President: SAMUEL LEWIS NAVARRO.
President-elect: RICARDO A. MARTINELLI BERROCAL (scheduled to take office 1 July 2009).

THE CABINET
(April 2009)

Minister of the Interior and Justice: DILIO ARCIA TORRES.
Minister of Foreign Affairs: SAMUEL LEWIS NAVARRO.
Minister of Public Works: BENJAMÍN COLAMARCO.
Minister of the Economy and Finance: HÉCTOR ALEXANDER.
Minister of Agricultural Development: OLMEDO ESPINO.
Minister of Commerce and Industry: GISELA ALVAREZ DE PORRAS.
Minister of Health: Dr ROSARIO TURNER.
Minister of Labour and Social Welfare: EDWIN ANTONIO SALAMÍN JAÉN.
Minister of Education: SALVADOR RODRÍGUEZ.
Minister of Housing: GABRIEL DIEZ.
Minister of the Presidency: RAFAEL MEZQUITA.
Minister of Social Development: MARÍA DEL CARMEN ROQUEBERT LEÓN.
Minister of Canal Affairs: DANIEL KUZNIECKY.

MINISTRIES

Office of the President: Palacio Presidencial, Valija 50, Panamá 1; tel. 227-4062; fax 227-0076; internet www.presidencia.gob.pa.

Ministry of Agricultural Development: Edif. 576, Calle Manuel E. Melo, Altos de Curundú, Apdo 5390, Panamá 5; tel. 507-0600; e-mail infomida@mida.gob.pa; internet www.mida.gob.pa.

Ministry of Commerce and Industry: El Paical, 3°, Avda Ricardo J. Alfaro, Plaza Edison, Apdo 9658, Panamá 4; tel. 560-0600; fax 560-0663; e-mail uti@mici.gob.pa; internet www.mici.gob.pa.

Ministry of the Economy and Finance: Edif. Ogawa, Vía España, Apdo 5245, Panamá 5; tel. 507-7008; e-mail webmaster@mef.gob.pa; internet www.mef.gob.pa.

Ministry of Education: Edif. Poli y Los Rios, Avda Justo Arosemena, Calles 26 y 27, Apdo 0816-04049, Panamá 3; tel. 511-4400; fax 262-9087; e-mail meduca@meduca.gob.pa; internet www.meduca.gob.pa.

Ministry of Foreign Affairs: Altos de Ancón, Complejo Narciso Garay, Panamá 4; tel. 511-4100; e-mail prensa@mire.gob.pa; internet www.mire.gob.pa.

Ministry of Health: Apdo 2048, Panamá 1; tel. and fax 512-9202; e-mail saludaldia@minsa.gob.pa; internet www.minsa.gob.pa.

PANAMA

Ministry of Housing: Avda Ricardo J. Alfaro, Edif. Plaza Edison, 4°, Apdo 5228, Panamá 5; tel. 579-9200; e-mail webmaster@mivi.gob.pa; internet www.mivi.gob.pa.

Ministry of the Interior and Justice: Avda Central, entre calle 2 y 3, San Felipe, Apdo 1628, Panamá 1; tel. 512-2000; fax 512-2126; e-mail informa@gobiernoyjusticia.gob.pa; internet www.gobiernoyjusticia.gob.pa.

Ministry of Labour and Social Welfare: Avda Ricardo J. Alfaro, Plaza Edison, 5°, Apdo 2441, Panamá 3; tel. 560-1100; e-mail mitrabs2@sinfo.net; internet www.mitradel.gob.pa.

Ministry of the Presidency: Palacio de Las Garzas, Corregimiento de San Felipe, Apdo 2189, Panamá 1; tel. 527-9600; e-mail ofasin@presidencia.gob.pa; internet www.presidencia.gob.pa.

Ministry of Public Works: Edif. 1019, Curundú, Zona 1, Apdo 1632, Panamá 1; tel. 507-9600; e-mail info@mop.gob.pa; internet www.mop.gob.pa.

Ministry of Social Development: Avda Ricardo J. Alfaro, 4°, Plaza Edison, Apdo 680-50, El Dorado, Panamá; tel. 500-6000; e-mail mides@mides.gob.pa; internet www.mides.gob.pa.

President and Legislature

PRESIDENT

Election, 3 May 2009, provisional results

Candidate	Votes	% of valid votes
Ricardo A. Martinelli Berrocal (Alianza por el Cambio*)	948,360	59.98
Balbina Herrera Araúz (Un País para Todos†)	595,891	37.69
Guillermo Endara Galimany (Vanguardia Moral de la Patria)	36,810	2.33
Total valid votes	**1,581,061**	**100.00**

* Electoral alliance comprising Cambio Democrático, el Partido Panameñista, el Movimiento Liberal Republicano Nacionalista and the Unión Patriótica.
† Electoral alliance comprising the Partido Revolucionario Democrático, the Partido Popular and the Partido Liberal.

ASAMBLEA NACIONAL
(National Assembly)

President: Raúl Rodríguez Araúz.

General Election, 3 May 2009, partial results

Affiliation/Party	% of votes	Seats
Alianza por el Cambio		
Partido Panameñista	24.1	19
Cambio Democrático	23.4	12
Unión Patriótica	6.4	4
Movimiento Liberal Republicano Nacionalista	3.4	2
Un País para Todos		
Partido Revolucionario Democrático	34.6	22
Partido Popular	2.6	1
Partido Liberal	0.9	—
Vanguardia Moral de la Patria	2.0	1
Others	2.6	2
Total	**100.0**	**71***

* Eight seats were yet to be apportioned at mid-May 2009.

Election Commission

Tribunal Electoral: Avda Ecuador y Justo Arosemena, Edif. Dirección Superior, Apdo 5281, Panamá 5; tel. 207-8000; e-mail secretaria-general@tribunal-electoral.gob.pa; internet www.tribunal-electoral.gob.pa; f. 1956; independent; Pres. Erasmo Pinilla Castillero.

Political Organizations

Cambio Democrático (CD): Parque Lefevre, Plaza Carolina, arriba de la Juguetería del Super 99, Panamá; tel. 217-2643; fax 217-2645; e-mail cambio.democratico@hotmail.com; formally registered 1998; contested the 2009 elections as part of the Alianza por el Cambio; Pres. Ricardo A. Martinelli Berrocal; Sec.-Gen. Giacomo Tamburelli.

Movimiento Liberal Republicano Nacionalista (MOLIRENA): Calle Venezuela, Casa No 5, entre Vía España y Calle 50, Panamá; tel. 213-5928; fax 265-6004; internet www.molirenaonline.com; formally registered 1982; conservative; contested the 2009 elections as part of the Alianza por el Cambio; Pres. Sergio González Ruiz.

Partido Panameñista (PP): Avda Perú y Calle 38E, No 37–41, al lado de Casa la Esperanza, Apdo 9610, Panamá 4; tel. 227-1267; f. 1990 by Arnulfista faction of the Partido Panameñista Auténtico as Partido Arnulfista (PA); name changed as above in Jan. 2005; contested the 2009 elections as part of the Alianza por el Cambio; Pres. Juan Carlos Varela.

Partido Popular: Avda Perú, frente al Parque Porras, Apdo 6322, Panamá 5; tel. 227-3204; fax 227-3944; e-mail pdc@cwpanama.net; f. 1960 as Partido Demócrata Cristiano; name changed as above in 2001; contested the 2009 elections as part of the Un País para Todos alliance; Pres. Camilo Brenes.

Partido Revolucionario Democrático (PRD): Calle 42 Bella Vista, entre Avda Perú y Avda Cuba, bajando por el teatro Bella Vista, Panamá 9; tel. 225-1050; e-mail prdpanama@yahoo.com; f. 1979; supports policies of late Gen. Omar Torrijos Herrera; combination of Marxists, Christian Democrats and some business interests; contested the 2009 elections as part of the Un País para Todos alliance; Pres. Balbina Herrera Araúz; Sec.-Gen. Martín Torrijos Espino.

Unión Patriótica (UP): Panamá; f. 2007 following merger of Partido Liberal Nacional and Partido Solidaridad; contested the 2009 elections as part of the Alianza por el Cambio; Pres. José Raul Mulino.

Vanguardia Moral de la Patria (VMP): Vía España, esq. con Vía Porras, Panamá; tel. 212-7300; f. 2004; Pres. Guillermo Endara; Gen. Sec. Dr John Hoger Castrellón.

Diplomatic Representation

EMBASSIES IN PANAMA

Argentina: Edif. del Banco de Iberoamérica, 7°, Avda 50 y Calle 53, Apdo 1271, Panamá 1; tel. 264-6561; fax 269-5331; e-mail embargen@c-com.net.pa; Ambassador Jorge Alberto Arguindegui.

Belize: Villa de la Fuente 1, F-32, Calle 22, POB 0819-12255, Panamá; tel. 236-3762; fax 236-4132; e-mail nmusag@cwpanama.net; Ambassador Alma Musa.

Bolivia: Calle Eric Arturo del Valle, Bella Vista 1, Panamá; tel. 269-0274; fax 264-3868; e-mail emb_bol_pan@cwpanama.net; Ambassador Edgar Soliz Morales.

Brazil: Edif. El Dorado, 1°, Calle Elvira Méndez y Avda Ricardo Arango, Urb. Campo Alegre, Apdo 4287, Panamá 5; tel. 263-5322; fax 269-6316; e-mail embrasil@embrasil.org.pa; Ambassador Eduardo Prisco Paraíso Ramos.

Canada: Edif. World Trade Center, Galería Comercial, 1°, Urb. Marbella, Apdo 0832-2446, Panamá; tel. 264-7115; fax 263-8083; e-mail panam@international.gc.ca; internet www.dfait-maeci.gc.ca/panama; Ambassador Patricia Langan-Torell.

Chile: Edif. Banco de Boston, 11°, Calle Elvira Méndez y Vía España, Apdo 7341, Panamá 5; tel. 223-9748; fax 263-5530; e-mail echilepa@cw.panama.net; internet www.embachilepanama.com; Ambassador Juan de Dios Gutiérrez Soto.

China (Taiwan): Edif. Torre Hong Kong Bank, 10°, Avda Samuel Lewis, Panamá; tel. 223-3424; fax 269-8757; e-mail embchina@cableonda.net; Ambassador Shen-Yeaw Ko.

Colombia: Edif. World Trade Center, Of. 1802, Calle 53, Urb. Marbella, Panamá; tel. 264-9644; fax 223-1134; e-mail epanama@minrelext.gov.co; Ambassador Gina Benedetti de Vélez.

Costa Rica: Edif. Plaza Omega, 3°, Calle Samuel Lewis, Apdo 8963, Panamá; tel. 264-2980; fax 264-4057; e-mail embarica@cwp.net.pa; Ambassador Ekhart Peters Seveers.

Cuba: Avda Cuba y Ecuador 33, Apdo 6-2291, Bellavista, Panamá; tel. 227-5277; fax 225-6681; e-mail embacuba@cableonda.net; Ambassador Carlos Eloy García Trápaga.

Dominican Republic: Casa 40A, Calle 75, Apdo 6250, Panamá 5; tel. 270-3884; fax 270-3886; e-mail embajdom@sinfo.net; Ambassador Virgilio Augusto Alvarez Bonilla.

Ecuador: Edif. Torre 2000, 6°, Calle 50, Marbella, Bellavista, Panamá; tel. 264-2654; fax 223-0159; e-mail eecuador@cwpanama.net; Ambassador Elsa Beatriz Villacís Roca.

Egypt: Calle 55, No 15, El Cangrejo, Apdo 7080, Panamá 5; tel. 263-5020; fax 264-8406; Ambassador Reda Halim Fahmy Ibrahim.

PANAMA

El Salvador: Edif. Metrópolis, 4°, Avda Manuel Espinosa Batista, Panamá; tel. 223-3020; fax 264-1433; e-mail embasalva@cwpanama.net; Ambassador GERARDO SOL MIXCO.

France: Plaza de Francia 1, Las Bovedas, San Felipe, Apdo 869, Panamá 1; tel. 211-6200; fax 211-6201; e-mail pierre_henri.guignard@diplomatie.gouv.fr; internet www.ambafrance-pa.org; Ambassador PIERRE HENRI GUIGNARD.

Germany: Edif. World Trade Center, 20°, Calle 53E, Marbella, Apdo 0832-0536, Panamá 5; tel. 263-7733; fax 223-6664; e-mail germpanama@cwp.net.pa; internet www.panama.diplo.de; Ambassador BORUSSO VON BLÜCHER.

Guatemala: Edif. Altamira, Of. 925, Vía Argentina, El Cangrejo, Corregimiento de Bella Vista, Panamá 9; tel. 269-3475; fax 223-1922; Ambassador STELLA RIEGER DE GARCÍA-GRANADOS.

Haiti: Edif. Dora Luz, 2°, Calle 1, El Cangrejo, Apdo 442, Panamá 9; tel. 269-3443; fax 223-1767; Chargé d'affaires a.i. BOCCHIT EDMOND.

Holy See: Punta Paitilla, Avda Balboa y Vía Italia, Apdo 4251, Panamá 5 (Apostolic Nunciature); tel. 269-2102; fax 264-2116; e-mail nuncio@cableonda.net; Apostolic Nuncio Most Rev. ANDRÉS CARRASCOSA COSO (Titular Archbishop of Elo).

Honduras: Edif. Bay Mall, 1°, Avda Balboa 112, Apdo 8704, Panamá 5; tel. 264-5513; fax 224-5513; e-mail ehpan@cableonda.net; Ambassador JUAN ALFARO POSADAS.

India: Avda Federico Boyd y Calle 51, Bella Vista, Apdo 8400, Panamá 7; tel. 264-3043; fax 264-2855; e-mail indempan@c-com.net.pa; internet www.indempan.org; Ambassador VISHNU NAMDEO HADE (designate).

Israel: Panamá; tel. 208-4700; fax 208-4755; Ambassador YOAD MAGEN.

Italy: Torre Banco Exterior, 25°, Avda Balboa, Apdo 2369, Panamá 9; tel. 225-8950; fax 227-4906; e-mail ambpana.mail@esteri.it; internet www.ambpanama.esteri.it; Ambassador PLACIDO VIGO.

Japan: Calle 50 y 60E, Obarrio, Apdo 1411, Panamá 1; tel. 263-6155; fax 263-6019; e-mail taiship2@cwpanama.net; internet www.panama.emb-japan.go.jp; Ambassador MAKOTO MISAWA.

Korea, Republic: Edif. Plaza, planta baja, Calle Ricardo Arias y Calle 51E, Campo Alegre, Apdo 8096, Panamá 7; tel. 264-8203; fax 264-8825; e-mail panama@mofat.go.kr; Ambassador GWANG-KEUN KIM.

Libya: Avda Balboa y Calle 32 (frente al Edif. Atalaya), Apdo 6-894 El Dorado, Panamá; tel. 227-3342; fax 227-3886; Chargé d'affaires a.i. ABDULMAJID MILUD SHAHIN.

Mexico: Edif. Torre ADR, 10°, Avda Samuel Lewis y Calle 58, Urb. Obarrio, Corregimiento de Bella Vista, Panamá; tel. 263-4900; fax 263-5446; e-mail embamexpan@cwpanama.net; internet www.sre.gob.mx/panama; Ambassador YANERIT CRISTINA MORGAN SOTOMAYOR.

Nicaragua: Quarry Heights, 16°, Ancón, Apdo 772, Zona 1, Panamá; tel. 211-2113; fax 211-2116; e-mail embapana@sinfo.net; Ambassador ANTENOR ALBERTO FERREY PERNUDI.

Paraguay: Edif. Galerías Balboa, 3°, Of. 45, Avda Balboa y Aquilino de la Guardia, Bella Vista, Panamá; tel. 263-4782; fax 269-4247; e-mail embapar_pa@cwpanama.net; Chargé d'affaires a.i. EDUARDO MANUEL INSFRÁN SALDÍVAR.

Peru: Edif. World Trade Center, 12°, Calle 53, Urb. Marbella, Apdo 4516, Panamá 5; tel. 223-1112; fax 269-6809; e-mail embaperu@pananet.com; Ambassador JOSÉ BARBA CABALLERO.

Russia: Torre IBC, 10°, Avda Manuel Espinosa Batista, Apdo 6-4697, El Dorado, Panamá; tel. 264-1408; fax 264-1588; e-mail emruspan@sinfo.net; Ambassador EVGENY ROSTISLAVOVICH VORONIN.

Spain: Calle 53 y Avda Perú (frente a la Plaza Porras), Apdo 1857, Panamá 1; tel. 227-5122; fax 227-6284; e-mail embesppa@correo.mae.es; Ambassador JOSÉ MANUEL LÓPEZ-BARRÓN DE LABRA.

United Kingdom: MMG Tower, 4°, Calle 53, Urb. Marbella, Apdo 0816-07946, Panamá 1; tel. 269-0866; fax 263-5138; e-mail britemb@cwpanama.net; internet www.ukinpanama.fco.gov.uk; Ambassador RICHARD AUSTEN.

USA: Avda Balboa y Calle 38, Apdo 6959, Panamá 5; tel. 207-7000; fax 227-1964; e-mail panamaweb@state.gov; internet panama.usembassy.gov; Ambassador BARBARA J. STEPHENSON.

Uruguay: Edif. Los Delfines, Of. 8, Avda Balboa, Calle 50E Este, Apdo 8898, Panamá 5; tel. 264-2838; fax 264-8908; e-mail urupanam@cwpanama.net; Ambassador FRANCISCO HEBER PURIFICATTI GAMARRA.

Venezuela: Torre Hong Kong Bank, 5°, Avda Samuel Lewis, Apdo 661, Panamá 1; tel. 269-1014; fax 269-1916; e-mail embvenp@c-com.net.pa; Ambassador JORGE LUIS DURÁN CENTENO.

Viet Nam: 52 José Gabriel Duque, La Cresta, Apdo 12434-6A, El Dorado, Panamá; tel. 264-2551; fax 265-6056; e-mail embavinapa@cwpanama.net; Ambassador HOANG CONG THUY.

Judicial System

The judiciary in Panama comprises the following courts and judges: Corte Suprema de Justicia (Supreme Court of Justice), with nine judges appointed for a 10-year term; 10 Tribunales Superiores de Distrito Judicial (High Courts) with 36 magistrates; 54 Jueces de Circuito (Circuit Judges) and 89 Jueces Municipales (Municipal Judges).

Panama is divided into four judicial districts and has seven High Courts of Appeal. The first judicial district covers the provinces of Panamá, Colón, Darién and the region of Kuna Yala and contains two High Courts of Appeal, one dealing with criminal cases, the other dealing with civil cases. The second judicial district covers the provinces of Coclé and Veraguas and contains the third High Court of Appeal, located in Penonomé. The third judicial district covers the provinces of Chiriquí and Bocas del Toro and contains the fourth High Court of Appeal, located in David. The fourth judicial district covers the provinces of Herrera and Los Santos and contains the fifth High Court of Appeal, located in Las Tablas. Each of these courts deals with civil and criminal cases in their respective provinces. There are two additional special High Courts of Appeal. The first hears maritime, labour, family and infancy cases; the second deals with anti-trust cases and consumer affairs.

Corte Suprema de Justicia
Edif. 236, Calle Culebra, Ancón, Apdo 1770, Panamá 1; tel. 262-9833; e-mail prensa@organojudicial.gob.pa; internet www.organojudicial.gob.pa.

President of the Supreme Court of Justice: HARLEY JAMES MITCHELL DALE.

Procurator-General: ANA MATILDE GÓMEZ DE RUILOBA.

Religion

The Constitution recognizes freedom of worship and the Roman Catholic Church as the religion of the majority of the population.

CHRISTIANITY

The Roman Catholic Church

For ecclesiastical purposes, Panama comprises one archdiocese, five dioceses, the territorial prelature of Bocas del Toro and the Apostolic Vicariate of Darién. At 31 December 2006 Roman Catholics represented some 82.8% of the population.

Bishops' Conference
Conferencia Episcopal de Panamá, Secretariado General, Apdo 870933, Panamá 7; tel. 223-0075; fax 223-0042; internet www.iglesia.org.pa.

f. 1958; statutes approved 1986; Pres. Mgr JOSÉ LUIS LACUNZA MAESTROJUAN (Bishop of David).

Archbishop of Panamá: Most Rev. JOSÉ DIMAS CEDEÑO DELGADO, Arzobispado Metropolitano, Calle 1a Sur Carrasquilla, Apdo 6386, Panamá 5; tel. 261-0002; fax 261-0820; e-mail ascen4@keops.utp.ac.pa.

The Baptist Church

The Baptist Convention of Panama (Convención Bautista de Panamá): Apdo 0816-01761, Panamá 5; tel. and fax 259-5485; e-mail convencionbautistadepanama@hotmail.com; f. 1959; Pres. FRANCISCO MEDINA; Sec. ESMERALDA DE TUY; 7,573 mems.

The Anglican Communion

Panama comprises one of the five dioceses of the Iglesia Anglicana de la Región Central de América.

Bishop of Panama: Rt Rev. JULIO MURRAY, Edif. 331A, Calle Culebra, Apdo R, Balboa; tel. 212-0062; fax 262-2097.

BAHÁ'Í FAITH

National Spiritual Assembly of the Bahá'ís: Apdo 815-0143, Panamá 15; tel. 231-1191; fax 231-6909; e-mail panbahai@cwpanama.net; internet www.pa.bahai.org; mems resident in 529 localities; Nat. Sec. EMELINA RODRÍGUEZ.

The Press

DAILIES

Crítica Libre: Vía Fernández de Córdoba, Apdo B-4, Panamá 9A; tel. 261-0575; fax 230-0132; e-mail esotop@epasa.com; internet www.critica.com.pa; f. 1925; morning; Pres. ROSARIO ARIAS DE GALINDO; Dir JUAN PRITSIOLAS; circ. 40,000.

PANAMA

DIA a DIA: Vía Ricardo J. Alfaro, al lado de la USMA, Apdo B-4, Panamá 9A; tel. 230-7777; fax 230-2279; e-mail editor.diaadia@epasa.com; internet www.diaadia.com.pa; Pres. Francisco Arias V.; Gen. Man. Ramón R. Vallarino A.

La Estrella de Panamá: Calle Alejandro Duque, Vía Transistmica y Frangipani, Panamá; tel. 227-0555; fax 227-1026; e-mail laestre@estrelladepanama.com; internet www.estrelladepanama.com; f. 1853; morning; Pres. Ebrahim Asvat; Editor Gerardo Berroa; circ. 10,000.

El Panamá América: Vía Ricardo J. Alfaro, al lado de la USMA, Apdo 0834-02787, Panamá 9A; tel. 230-7777; fax 230-7773; e-mail director@epasa.com; internet pa-digital.com.pa; f. 1925; morning; independent; affiliated to Interamerican Press Assen; Pres. Francisco Arias V.; Dir Guido Rodríguez Lugari; circ. 25,000.

La Prensa: Avda 12 de Octubre y Calle C, Hato Pintado, Pueblo Nuevo, Apdo 0819-05620, Panamá; tel. 222-1222; fax 221-7328; e-mail editor@prensa.com; internet www.prensa.com; f. 1980; morning; independent; Pres. Ricardo Alberto Arias; Editor Fernando Berguido; circ. 38,000.

El Siglo: Calle 58 Obarrio, Panamá; tel. 264-3921; fax 269-6954; e-mail redaccion@elsiglo.com; internet www.elsiglo.com; f. 1985; morning; acquired by Geo-Media, SA, in 2001; Pres. Dr Nivia Rossana Castrellón; Editor Octavio Cogley; circ. 30,000.

PERIODICALS

Dirección de Estadística y Censo: Avda Balboa y Federico Boyd, Apdo 0816-01521, Panamá 5; tel. 210-4800; fax 210-4801; e-mail cie_dec@contraloria.gob.pa; internet www.contraloria.gob.pa/dec; f. 1941; published by the Contraloría General de la República; statistical survey in series according to subjects; Controller-Gen. Carlos A. Vallarino R.; Dir of Statistics and Census Dimas Quiel.

FOB Colón Free Zone: Apdo 0819-06908, El Dorado, Panamá; tel. 225-6638; fax 225-0466; e-mail focusint@sinfo.net; internet www.colonfreezone.com; annual; bilingual trade directory; publ. by Focus Publications (Int.), SA; Editor Israel Arguedas; circ. 60,000.

Focus Panamá: 742 Calle 2A, Perejil, Panamá; tel. 225-6638; fax 225-0466; e-mail focusint@sinfo.net; internet www.focuspublicationsint.com; f. 1970; 2 a year; publ. by Focus Publications; visitors' guide; separate English and Spanish editions; Dir Kenneth J. Jones; circ. 100,000.

Informativo Industrial: Apdo 6-4798, El Dorado, Panamá 1; tel. 230-0482; fax 230-0805; monthly; organ of the Sindicato de Industriales de Panamá; Pres. Gaspar García de Paredes.

Mi Diario, La Voz de Panamá: Avda 12 de Octubre y Calle C, Hato Pintado, Pueblo Nuevo, Apdo 0819-05620, Panamá; tel. 222-9000; fax 222-9090; e-mail midiario@midiario.com; internet www.midiario.com; f. 2003 by La Prensa (q.v.); Dir Lorenzo Ábrego.

Revista SIETE: Vía Ricardo J. Alfaro, al lado de la USMA, Apdo B-4, Panamá 9A; tel. 230-7777; fax 230-1033; e-mail revista.siete@epasa.com; internet www.epasa.com/siete; weekly; Editor Nayla G. Montenegro.

PRESS ASSOCIATION

Sindicato de Periodistas de Panamá: Avda Gorgas 287, Panamá; tel. 214-0163; fax 214-0164; e-mail sindiperpana@yahoo.com; f. 1949; Sec.-Gen. Filemón Medina Ramos.

Publishers

Editora Panamá América (EPASA): Vía Ricardo J. Alfaro, al lado de la USMA, Apdo B-4, Panamá 9A; tel. 230-7777; fax 230-0136; e-mail gerente.general@epasa.com; internet www.epasa.com; Pres. Francisco Arias V.; Gen. Man. Ramón R. Vallarino A.

Editora Sibauste, SA: Panamá; tel. 229-4577; fax 229-4582; e-mail esibauste@cwpanama.net; Editor Denis de Sibauste.

Editorial Universitaria: Vía José de Fábrega, Panamá; tel. 264-2087; f. 1969; history, geography, law, sciences, literature.

Focus Publications: Apdo 6-3287, El Dorado, Panamá; tel. 225-6638; fax 225-0466; e-mail focusint@sinfo.net; internet www.focuspublicationsint.com; f. 1970; guides, trade directories, yearbooks and maps; Gen. Man. Kenneth J. Jones.

Ruth Casa Editorial: Edif. Los Cristales, Of. No 6, Calle 38 y Avda Cuba, Apdo 2235, Zona 9A, Panamá; e-mail webmaster@forumdesalternatives.org; internet www.forumdesalternatives.org/Ruth_publicaciones.htm; Pres. François Houtart.

GOVERNMENT PUBLISHING HOUSE

Editorial Mariano Arosemena: Instituto Nacional de Cultura, Apdo 662, Panamá 1; tel. 211-4000; fax 211-4016; e-mail comunicacion@inac.gob.pa; internet www.inac.gob.pa; f. 1974; division of National Institute of Culture; literature, history, social sciences, archaeology; Dir Leslie Mock.

Broadcasting and Communications

REGULATORY AUTHORITY

Autoridad Nacional de los Servicios Públicos: Vía España, Edif. Office Park, Apdo 4931, Panamá 5; tel. 278-4500; fax 278-4600; e-mail webmaster@ersp.gob.pa; f. 1996 as Ente Regulador de los Servicios Públicos; name changed as above in 2006; state regulator with responsibility for television, radio, telecommunications, water and electricity; Deputy Dir Horacio Hoquee.

TELECOMMUNICATIONS

Dirección Nacional de Medios de Comunicación Social: Avda 7A Central y Calle 3A, Apdo 1628, Panamá 1; tel. 262-3197; fax 262-9495.

Major Service Providers

Cable & Wireless Panama: Box 0834-00659, Panamá; e-mail cwp@cwpanama.com; internet www.cwpanama.com.pa; 49% govt-owned, 49% owned by Cable & Wireless; major telecommunications provider; Pres. Jorge Nicolau.

Movistar: Edif. Magna, Area Bancaria, Calle 51 Este y Manuel M. Icaza, Panamá; tel. 265-0955; internet www.movistar.com.pa; f. 1996 as BellSouth Panamá, SA; acquired by Telefónica Móviles, SA (Spain) in Oct. 2004; name changed as above in April 2005; mobile telephone services; Gen. Man. Claudio Hidalgo.

Optynex Telecom, SA: Edif. Aliado, 2°, Calle 50 y 56, Urb. Obarrio, Apdo 0832-2650, Panamá; tel. 380-0000; fax 380-0099; e-mail info@optynex.com; internet www.optynex.com; f. 2002; Gen. Man. Eric Meyer.

BROADCASTING

Radio

In 2004 there were 109 AM (Medium Wave) and 181 FM stations registered in Panama. Most stations are commercial.

La Mega 98.3 FM: Casa 35, Calle 50 y 77 San Francisco, Panamá; tel. 270-3242; fax 226-1021; e-mail ventas@lamegapanama.com; internet www.lamegapanama.com; f. 2000.

Omega Stereo: Calle G, El Cangrejo 3, Panamá; e-mail omegaste@omegastereo.com; internet www.omegastereo.com; f. 1981; Pres. Guillermo Antonio Adames.

RPC Radio: Avda 12 de Octubre, Panamá; tel. 390-6700; e-mail mtalessandria@medcom.com.pa; internet www.rpcradio.com; f. 1949; broadcasts news, sports and commentary; Man. María Teresa Alessandría.

SuperQ: Edif. Dominó, Via España, Panamá; tel. 263-5298; fax 263-0362; e-mail info@superqpanama.com; internet www.superqpanama.com; f. 1984; Pres. G. Aris De Icaza.

WAO 97.5: Edif. Plaza 50, 2°, Calle 50 y Vía Brasil, Panamá; tel. 223-8348; fax 223-8351; Gen. Man. Rogelio Campos.

Television

In 2005 there were 133 authorized television channels broadcasting in Panama.

Fundación para la Educación en la Televisión—FETV (Canal 5): Vía Ricardo J. Alfaro, Apdo 0819-02874, Panamá; tel. 230-8000; fax 230-1955; e-mail comentarios@fetv.org; internet www.fetv.org; f. 1992; Pres. José Dimas Cedeño Delgado; Dir Manuel Santiago Blanquèr i Planells; Gen. Man. Teresa Wong de Fong.

Medcom: Avda 12 de Octubre, Hato Pintado, Apdo 0827-00116, Panamá 8; tel. 390-6802; fax 390-6895; e-mail murrutia@medcom.com.pa; internet www.rpctv.com; f. 1998 by merger of RPC Televisión (Canal 4) and Telemetro (Canal 13); commercial; also owns Cable Onda 90 and RPC Radio; Pres. Fernando Eleta; CEO Nicolás González-Revilla.

Sistema Estatal de Radio y Televisión (Canal 11): Curundu, Panamá; tel. 507-1500; e-mail contactenos@sertv.gob.pa; internet www.sertv.gob.pa; f. 1978 as Radio y Televisión Educativa; was restructured and assumed present name in 2005; educational and cultural; Dir-Gen. Carlos Aguilar Navarro.

Televisora Nacional—TVN (Canal 2): Vía Bolívar, Apdo 6-3092, El Dorado, Panamá; tel. 279-3700; fax 236-2987; e-mail tvn@tvn-2.com; internet www.tvn-2.com; f. 1962; Dir Jaime Alberto Arias.

PANAMA *Directory*

Broadcasting Association

Asociación Panameña de Radiodifusión: Apdo 7387, Estafeta de Paitilla, Panamá; tel. 263-5252; fax 226-4396; Pres. ALESSIO GRONCHI; Vice-Pres. RICARDO A. BUSTAMANTE.

Finance

(cap. = capital; res = reserves; dep. = deposits; m. = million; br.(s) = branch(es); amounts in balboas, unless otherwise stated)

BANKING

Superintendencia de Bancos (Banking Superintendency): Torre HSBC, 18°, Apdo 2397, Panamá 1; tel. 206-7800; fax 264-9422; internet www.superbancos.gob.pa; f. 1970 as Comisión Bancaria Nacional (National Banking Commission); licenses and controls banking activities within and from Panamanian territory; Comisión Bancaria Nacional superseded by Superintendencia de Bancos in June 1998 with enhanced powers to supervise banking activity; Supt OLEGARIO BARRELIER CHIARI.

National Bank

Banco Nacional de Panamá: Torre BNP, Vía España, Apdo 5220, Panamá 5; tel. 263-5151; fax 269-0091; e-mail bnpvalores@cwp.net.pa; internet www.banconal.com.pa; f. 1904; govt-owned; cap. 500.0m., res 1.1m., dep. 4,089.3m. (Dec. 2007); Chair. ARTURO MELO SARASQUETA; Gen. Man. JUAN RICARDO DE DIANUOS; 53 brs.

Savings Bank

Caja de Ahorros: Vía España y Calle Thays de Pons, Apdo 1740, Panamá 1; tel. 205-1000; fax 269-3674; e-mail atencionalcliente@cajadeahorros.com.pa; internet www.cajadeahorros.com.pa; f. 1934; govt-owned; cap. 150.7m., res 47.9m., dep. 170.9m. (Dec. 2006); Pres. ROGELIO ALEMÁN; Gen. Man. SERGIO ALTAMIRANDA; 37 brs.

Domestic Private Banks

Banco Continental de Panamá, SA: Calle 50 y Avda Aquilino de la Guardia, Apdo 135, Panamá 9A; tel. 215-7000; fax 215-7134; e-mail bcp@bcocontinental.com; internet www.bbvabancocontinental.com; f. 1972; merged with Banco Internacional de Panamá in 2002; took over Banco Atlántico (Panamá), SA in 2006; cap. 126.7m., res 29.0m., dep. 3,079.8m. (Dec. 2006); Chair. PEDRO BRESCIA CAFFERATA; Gen. Man. EDUARDO TORRES-LLOSA VILLACORTA; 36 brs.

Banco Cuscatlán de Panamá: Edif. Panabank, Casa Matriz, Calle 50, Apdo 1828, Panamá 1; tel. 208-8300; fax 269-1537; e-mail gerencia@panabank.com; internet www.bancocuscatlan.com/panama; f. 1983; acquired Banco Panamericano (Panabank) in 2004; acquired by Citi in 2007; Chair. MAURICIO SAMAYOA; Gen. Man. GUIDO J. MARTINELLI, Jr.

Banco General, SA: Calle Aquilino de la Guardia, Apdo 4592, Panamá 5; tel. 227-3200; fax 265-0210; e-mail info@bgeneral.com; internet www.bgeneral.com; f. 1955; purchased Banco Comercial de Panamá (BANCOMER) in 2000; cap. 300.0m., res 14.8m., dep. 2,504.6m. (Dec. 2006); Chair. and CEO FEDERICO HUMBERT; Exec. Vice-Pres. and Gen. Man. RAÚL ALEMÁN Z.; 36 brs.

Banco Panameño de la Vivienda (BANVIVIENDA): Casa Matriz-Bella Vista, Avda Chile y Calle 41, Apdo 8639, Panamá 5; tel. 227-4020; fax 227-5433; e-mail bpvger@pty.com; internet www.banvivienda.com; f. 1981; cap. 12.4m., dep. 128.0m., total assets 150.3m. (2004); Pres. ORLANDO SÁNCHEZ AVILES; 3 brs.

Banco Pichincha Panamá: Edif. PH Parque Urraca, entre Avda Federico Boyd y Avda Balboa, Panamá; tel. 264-6323; fax 264-6129; e-mail banco@pichinchapanama.com; internet wwwp2.pichinchapanama.com; f. 2006; Gen. Man. FRANCISCO JAVIER LEJARRAGA LÓPEZ DE ARROYABE.

Banco Universal: Edif. Miguel A. Brenes, Calle B Norte y Avda 1ra, Apdo 0426-00564, David, Chiriquí; tel. 775-4394; fax 775-2308; e-mail cosorio@bancouniversal.com; internet www.bancouniversal.com; f. 1970 as Asociación Chiricana de Ahorros y Préstamos para la Vivienda; present name adoptado 1994; Pres. JOSÉ ISAAC VIRZI LÓPEZ; Gen. Man. CARLOS RAÚL BARRIOS ICAZA.

Global Bank Corporation: Torre Global Bank, Calle 50, Apdo 55-1843, Paitilla, Panamá; tel. 206-2000; fax 263-3518; e-mail global@pan.gbm.net; internet www.globalbank.com.pa; f. 1994; Pres. LAWRENCE MADURO; Gen. Man. JORGE VALLARINO S.

Multibank: Edif. Prosperidad, planta baja, Vía España 127, Apdo 8210, Panamá 7; tel. 269-0188; fax 264-4014; e-mail banco@grupomulticredit.com; internet www.multibank.com.pa; f. 1990 as Multi Credit Bank; current name adopted 2008; total assets 536.1m. (Dec. 2005); Pres. ALBERTO S. BTESH; Gen. Man. RAFAEL SÁNCHEZ GARRÓS.

Primer Banco del Istmo, SA: Edif. Banco del Istmo, Calle 77 Este y 50, San Francisco, Panamá; tel. 270-0015; fax 270-1952; internet www.banistmo.com; f. 1984 as Banco del Istmo; current name adopted in 2000 following merger of Primer Grupo Nacional and Banco del Istmo; merged with Banco de Latinoamerica in 2002; acquired by HSBC in July 2006; cap. US $692.2m., dep. $4,343.7m. (Dec. 2006); Chair. SAMUEL LEWIS GALINDO; CEO ALBERTO VALLARINO CLÉMENT.

Towerbank International Inc: Edif. Tower Plaza, Calle 50 y Beatriz M. de Cabal, Apdo 6-6039, Panamá; tel. 269-6900; fax 269-6800; e-mail towerbank@towerbank.com; internet www.towerbank.com; f. 1971; cap. 34.8m., res –90.8m., dep. 371.1m. (Dec. 2006); Pres. FRED KARDONSKI; Gen. Man. JOSÉ CAMPA.

Foreign Banks

Principal Foreign Banks with General Licence

BAC International Bank (Panamá), Inc (USA): Edif. BAC Credomatic, Calle Aquilino de la Guardia, Apdo 6-3654, Panamá; tel. 213-0822; fax 269-3879; e-mail infobac@pa.bac.net; internet www.bac.net/panama; f. 1995; Chair. CARLOS PELLAS; Gen. Man. RODOLFO TABASH.

BANCAFE (Panamá), SA (Colombia): Avda Manuel María Icaza y Calle 52E, No 18, Apdo 384, Panamá 9A; tel. 264-6066; fax 263-6115; e-mail info@bancafe-pa.com; internet www.bancafe-pa.com; f. 1966 as Banco Cafetero; current name adopted in 1995; Pres. JORGE CASTELLANOS RUEDA; Gen. Man. JAIME DE GAMBOA GAMBOA; 2 brs.

Banco Aliado, SA: Calle 50 y 56, Urb. Obarrio, 0831-2109 Paitilla, Panamá; tel. 302-1555; fax 302-1556; e-mail bkaliado@bancoaliado.com; internet www.bancoaliado.com; f. 1992; Pres. MOISÉS CHREIM; Gen. Man. ALEXIS A. ARJONA.

Banco Bilbao Vizcaya Argentaria (Panama), SA (Spain): Torre BBVA, Avda Balboa, Apdo 8673, Panamá 5; tel. 227-0973; fax 227-3663; e-mail fperezp@bbvapanama.com; internet www.bbvapanama.com; f. 1982; cap. 28.7m., res 56.6m., dep. 907.8m. (Dec. 2006); Chair. MANUEL UBIRÍA PASTOR; Gen. Man. FELIX PEREZ PARRA; 15 brs.

Banco Delta, SA (BMF): Edif. Torre Delta, planta baja, Vía España 122 y Calle Elvira Méndez, Apdo 0816-00548, Panamá; tel. 340-0000; fax 340-0076; internet www.bandelta.com; f. 2006; Gen. Man. ARIEL ANTONIO SANMARTÍN MÉNDEZ.

Banco Internacional de Costa Rica, SA: Casa Matriz, Calle Manuel M. Icaza 25, Apdo 0816-07810, Panamá 1; tel. 208-9500; fax 208-9581; e-mail informacion@bicaspan.net; internet www.bicsa.com; f. 1976; Gen. Man. FEDERICO CARRILLO ZURCHER.

Banco Latinoamericano de Exportaciones (BLADEX) (Multinational): Casa Matriz, Calles 50 y Aquilino de la Guardia, Apdo 6-1497, El Dorado, Panamá; tel. 210-8500; fax 269-6333; e-mail infobla@blx.com; internet www.blx.com; f. 1979; groups together 254 Latin American commercial and central banks, 22 international banks and some 3,000 New York Stock Exchange shareholders; cap. US $280.0m., res $97.8m., dep. $3,265.6m. (Dec. 2006); CEO JAIME RIVERA; Chair. GONZALO MENÉNDEZ DUQUE.

Citibank Panamá (USA): Plaza Panama Bldg, Calle 50, Apdo 555, Panamá 9A; tel. 210-5900; fax 210-5901; internet www.citibank.com.pa; f. 1904; Gen. Man. FRANCISCO CONTO; 4 brs.

Credicorp Bank, SA: Plaza Credicorp Bank, Nicanor de Obarrio, Calle 50, Apdo 833-0125, Panamá; tel. 210-1111; fax 210-0412; internet www.credicorpbank.com; f. 1992; cap. 24.1m., res –0.5m., dep. 340.3m. (Dec. 2006); Pres. RAYMOND HARARI; Gen. Man. MAX J. HARARI.

HSBC Bank (Panama), SA: Plaza HSBC, Calle Aquilino de La Guardia, Urb. Marbella, Panamá; tel. 263-5855; fax 263-6009; e-mail hsbcpnm@sinfo.net; internet www.pa.hsbc.com; dep. 477m. (1999); in 2000 it acquired the 11 br. operations of the Chase Manhattan Bank, with assets of US $752m. (2000); Gen. Man. JOSEPH L. SALTERIO; 3 brs.

Stanford Bank (Panamá), SA: Torre Generali, 19°, Avda Samuel Lewis y Calle 54, Urb. Obarrio, Panamá; tel. 208-7300; fax 263-4165; e-mail sbpanama@stanfordeagle.com; internet www.stanfordbankpanama.com; f. 2003; taken over by the Superintendencia de Bancos de Panamá in 2009; Pres. and Gen. Man. JUAN FERNANDO POSADA CORPAS.

Principal Foreign Banks with International Licence

Austrobank Overseas (Panamá), SA: Torre Morgan y Morgan, planta baja, Calle 53, Este Marbella, Apdo 6-3197, El Dorado, Panamá; tel. 223-4455; fax 264-6918; internet www.austrobank.com; f. 1995; Gen. Man. GUILLERMO WILLIS.

Banco Agrícola (Panamá), SA: Edif. Global Bank, 17°, Local E y F, Calle 50, Apdo 6-2637, Panamá; tel. 263-5762; fax 263-5626; e-mail info@bancoagricola.com; internet www.bancoagricolapanama.com; f. 2002; Exec. Pres. JOSÉ ROBERTO ORELLANA MILLA.

PANAMA

Banco de la Nación Argentina: Edif. World Trade Center 501, Calle 53, Urb. Marbella, Panamá; tel. 269-4666; fax 269-6719; e-mail bnapanama@bna.com.pa; internet www.bna.com.ar; f. 1977; Gen. Man. JUAN CARLOS FABREGA.

Banco de Occidente (Panama), SA: Edif. American International, Calle 50 y Aquilino de la Guardia, Apdo 6-7430, El Dorado, Panamá; tel. 263-8144; fax 269-3261; internet www.bancoccidente.com.pa; f. 1982; cap. US $6.3m., res $6.0m., dep. $199.0m. (Dec. 2002); Gen. Man. OSCAR LUNA GORDILLO.

Banco del Pacífico (Panama), SA: Calle Aquilino de la Guardia y Calle 52, Apdo 6-3100, El Dorado, Panamá; tel. 263-5833; fax 263-7481; e-mail bpacificopanama@pacifico.fin.ec; internet www.bancodelpacifico.com.pa; f. 1980; Pres. ANA ESCOBAR.

Bancolombia (Panama), SA: Plaza Marbella, Calle Aquilino de la Guardia y Calle 47, Apdo 0816-03320, Panamá; tel. 263-6955; fax 269-1138; e-mail mdebetan.bicpma@mail.bic.com.co; internet www.bancolombiapanama.com; f. 1973; current name adopted in 1999; cap. US $14.0m., res $3.8m., dep. $1,171.9m. (Dec. 2006); Gen. Man. MARÍA ISABEL URIBE RAMÍREZ.

FPB International Bank Inc: Ofs. A y C, 16°, Calle 50 y Aquilino de la Guardia, Panamá; tel. 210-6600; fax 263-0919; f. 2005; Gen. Man. JOSÉ APARECIDO PAULUCCI.

GNB Sudameris Bank, SA: Area Bancaria, Calle Manuel María Icaza 19, Panamá; tel. 206-6900; fax 206-6901; internet www.gnbsudameris.com; f. 1970; Gen. Man. ANGELMIRO CASTILLO H.

Popular Bank Ltd Inc: Apdo 0816-00265, Panamá; tel. 269-4166; fax 269-1309; e-mail gversari@bpt.com.pa; internet www.popularbank.com.pa; f. 1983 as Banco Popular Dominicano (Panama), SA; current name adopted in 2003; cap. 24.4m., res 11.3m., dep. 372.3m. (Dec. 2006); Pres. RAFAEL A. RODRÍGUEZ; Gen. Man. GIANNI VERSARI.

Banking Association

Asociación Bancaria de Panamá (ABP): Torre Hong Kong Bank, 15°, Avda Samuel Lewis, Apdo 4554, Panamá 5; tel. 263-7044; fax 223-5800; e-mail abp@orbi.net; internet www.asociacionbancaria.com; f. 1962; 79 mems; Pres. ALEXIS A. ARJONA.

STOCK EXCHANGE

Bolsa de Valores de Panamá: Edif. Vallarino, planta baja, Calles Elvira Méndez y 52, Apdo 87-0878, Panamá; tel. 269-1966; fax 269-2457; e-mail bvp@pty.com; internet www.panabolsa.com; f. 1960; Pres. RICARDO ARANGO; Gen. Man. ROBERTO BRENES PÉREZ.

INSURANCE

Arca Internacional de Reaseguros, SA: Edif. Bolsa de Valores, 1°, Avda Federico Boyd, Frente al Restaurante Rinos, Panamá; tel. 300-2858; fax 300-2859; f. 1996; Gen. Man. CARLOS G. DE LA LASTRA.

Aseguradora Ancón, SA: Avda Samuel Lewis y Calle 54, Urb. Obarrio, Panamá; tel. 210-8700; fax 210-8790; e-mail info@asegurancon.com; internet www.asegurancon.com; f. 1992; Pres. TOBIAS CARRERO NACAR; Gen. Man. CARLOS G. CHAMORRO.

Aseguradora Mundial, SA: Edif. Aseguradora Mundial, Avda Balboa y Calle 41, Apdo 8911, Panamá 5; tel. 207-6600; fax 207-8787; e-mail info@mundial.com; internet www.amundial.com; f. 1937; general; Pres. ORLANDO EDMUNDO SÁNCHEZ AVILES.

ASSA Cía de Seguros, SA: Edif. ASSA, Avda Nicanor de Obarrio (Calle 50), Apdo 0816-01622, Panamá 5; tel. 300-2772; fax 300-2729; e-mail assamercadeo@assanet.com; internet www.assanet.com; f. 1973; Pres. STANLEY MOTTA.

Assicurazioni Generali, Spa: Torre Generali, Avda Samuel Lewis y Calle 54, Urb. Obarrio, Apdo 0816-02206, 507 Panamá; tel. 206-9100; fax 206-9101; e-mail mercadeo@generali.com.pa; internet www.generali.com.pa; f. 1977; Gen. Man. GABRIEL R. DE OBARRIO, III.

Cía Interoceánica de Seguros, SA: Plaza Margella, Frente Banco HSBC, Calle Alquilino de la Guardia, Panamá; tel. 205-0700; fax 264-7668; e-mail info@interoceanica.com; internet www.interoceanica.com; f. 1978; Gen. Man. SALVADOR MORALES BACA.

Empresa General de Seguros, SA: Edif. Bancomer, Enre Piso, Calles 50 y 53, Panamá; tel. 269-1896; fax 264-1107; internet www.asecomer.com; f. 1987; Gen. Man. LUIS E. BANDERA.

HSBC Seguros (Panamá), SA (CONASE): Edif. HSBC, No 62, Calle 50, Apdo 5303, Panamá 5; tel. 205-0300; fax 223-1146; e-mail ines.m.arosemena@hsbc.com.pa; f. 1957 as Cía Nacional de Seguros, SA; current name adopted July 2007; Pres. JOSEPH SALTERIO.

Internacional de Seguros, SA: Avda Cuba y Calles 35 y 36, Apdo 1036, Panamá 1; tel. 227-4000; e-mail conase@conase.net; internet www.iseguros.com; f. 1910; Pres. RICHARD A. FORD.

Mitsui Sumitomo Insurance Co Ltd: Of. 701, 7°, Plaza Credicorp Bank Panamá, Panamá; tel. 210-0133; fax 210-0122; internet www.msilm.com; f. 1979; Gen. Man. TA KASHI MORIMOTO.

Provincial Re Panamá, SA: Edif. Alexandra, Of. 3A, Avda Octavio de Icaza, Panamá; tel. 260-5078; fax 260-5055; f. 1984; Gen. Man. FRANK CASTAGNET.

QBE del Istmo Cía de Reaseguros, Inc: Costa del Este, Avda Paseo del Mar y Calle Vista del Pacífico, Apdo 51, Panamá; tel. 301-0610; fax 223-0479; internet www.istmore.com; f. 1979; Pres. and CEO RAMÓN E. FERNÁNDEZ.

La Seguridad de Panamá, Cía de Seguros, SA: Edif. American International, Calle 50, esq. Aquilino de la Guardia, Apdo 5306, Panamá 5; tel. 263-6700; f. 1986; Gen. Man. MARIELA OSORIO.

Trade and Industry

Colón Free Zone (CFZ): Avda Roosevelt, Apdo 1118, Colón; tel. 445-1033; fax 445-2165; e-mail zonalibre@zolicol.org; internet www.zonalibredecolon.com.pa; f. 1948 to manufacture, import, handle and re-export all types of merchandise; some 1,800 companies were established in 2005; well-known international banks operate in the CFZ, where there are also customs, postal and telegraph services; the main exporters to the CFZ are Japan, the USA, Hong Kong, Taiwan, the Republic of Korea, Colombia, France, Italy and the United Kingdom; the main importers from the CFZ are Brazil, Venezuela, Mexico, Ecuador, the Netherlands Dependencies, Bolivia, the USA, Chile, Argentina and Colombia; the total area of the CFZ was 485.3 ha; Gen. Man. NILDA IRIS QUIJANO.

CHAMBERS OF COMMERCE

American Chamber of Commerce and Industry of Panama: POB 0843-00152, Panamá; tel. 301-3881; fax 301-3882; e-mail amcham@panamcham.com; internet www.panamcham.com; Pres. THOMAS H. KENNA; Exec. Dir DAVID HUNT.

Cámara de Comercio, Industrias y Agricultura de Panamá: Avda Cuba y Ecuador 33A, Apdo 74, Panamá 1; tel. 207-3440; fax 207-3422; e-mail presidencia@panacamara.com; internet www.panacamara.com; f. 1915; Pres. JOSÉ RAMÓN VARELA C.; Exec. Dir RAFAEL ZUÑIGA BRID; 1,300 mems.

Cámara Oficial Española de Comercio: Calle 33E, Apdo 1857, Panamá 1; tel. 225-1487; fax 225-0626; internet www.caespan.com.pa; Pres. NOEL RIANDE; Sec. MARICARMEN DE AMAYA.

INDUSTRIAL AND TRADE ASSOCIATIONS

Asociación Panameña de Exportadores (APEX): Edif. Ricardo Galindo Quelquejeu, Avda Ricardo J. Alfaro, Panamá; tel. 230-0169; e-mail apex@cableonda.net; internet www.apexpanama.org; f. 1971; export asscn; Pres. MÁXIMO GALLARDO.

Cámara Panameña de la Construcción: Calle Aquilino de la Guardia No 19, Apdo 0816-02350, Panamá 5; tel. 265-2500; fax 265-2571; e-mail informacion@capac.org; internet www.capac.org; represents interests of construction sector; Pres. WALTER C. MEDRANO.

Corporación Azucarera La Victoria: Transístmica, San Miguelito; tel. 229-4794; state sugar corpn; scheduled for transfer to private ownership; Dir Prof. ALEJANDRO VERNAZA.

Corporación para el Desarrollo Integral del Bayano: Avda Balboa, al lado de la estación del tren, Estafeta El Dorado, Panamá 2; tel. 232-6160; f. 1978; state agriculture, forestry and cattle-breeding corpn.

Dirección General de Industrias: Edif. Plaza Edison, 3°, Apdo 9658, Panamá 4; tel. 360-0720; govt body which undertakes feasibility studies, analyses and promotion; Dir-Gen. LUCÍA FUENTES DE FERGUSON; Nat. Dir of Business Devt FRANCISCO DE LA BARRERA.

Sindicato de Industriales de Panamá: Vía Ricardo J. Alfaro, Entrada Urb. Sara Sotillo, Apdo 6-4798, Estafeta El Dorado, Panamá; tel. 230-0169; fax 230-0805; e-mail sip@cableonda.net; internet www.industriales.org; f. 1945; represents and promotes activities of industrial sector; Pres. VALERIO DE SANCTIS.

EMPLOYERS' ORGANIZATIONS

Asociación Panameña de Ejecutivos de Empresas (APEDE): Avda Ricardo Arango, Calle 53, Obarrio, Panamá; tel. 263-5133; fax 263-1071; e-mail apede@sinfo.net; internet www.apede.org; Pres. ROBERTO ALFARO ESTRIPEAUT.

Consejo Nacional de la Empresa Privada (CONEP): Avda Morgan, Balboa, Ancón, Casa 302, Apdo 1276, Panamá 1; tel. 211-2672; fax 211-2694; e-mail conep1@cwpanama.net; internet www.conep.org.pa; Pres. SEVERO SOUSA.

UTILITIES

Regulatory Authority

Autoridad Nacional de los Servicios Públicos: see Broadcasting and Communications—Regulatory Authority.

PANAMA

Electricity

The partial divestment of generation and distribution services was completed in December 1998. The restructuring of the state-owned Instituto de Recursos Hidráulicos y Electrificación (IRHE) resulted in the sale of four generation and three distribution companies. However, transmission operations remained under state control.

AES Panama: Panamá; internet www.aes.com; f. 1998 upon acquisition by AES Corpn of 49% interest in Empresa de Generación Electrica Bayano and Empresa de Generación Electrica Chiriqui; operates three hydroelectric facilities in Bayano (248 MW), Estí (120 MW) and Chiriqui (90 MW) and one 43-MW thermal facility; Pres. PAUL HANRAHAN.

Elektra Noreste, SA: Edif. Hatillo, Torre A, entre Avda Cuba y Justo Arosemena, Apdo 0833-0202, Plaza Panamá, Panamá; tel. 323-7100; internet www.elektra.com.pa; electricity distribution; Gen. Man. JAVIER PARIENTE.

Empresa de Transmisión Eléctrica, SA (ETESA): Plaza Sun Tower, 3°, Avda Ricardo J. Alfaro, Panamá; tel. 501-3800; fax 501-3506; e-mail info@etesa.com.pa; internet www.etesa.com.pa; f. 1998; state-owned transmission co; Pres. RICAURTE VÁZQUEZ; Gen. Man. ISAAC CASTILLO.

Unión FENOSA—EDEMET EDECHI: Albrook, Panamá; internet www.ufpanama.com; f. 1998 by acquisition from IRHE of Empresa de Distribución Eléctrica Metro Oeste (EDEMET) and Empresa de Distribución Eléctrica Chiriquí (EDECHI) by Unión FENOSA, Spain; Pres. SALVADOR GABARRÓ.

Water

Instituto de Acueductos y Alcantarillados Nacionales (IDAAN) (National Waterworks and Sewage Systems Institute): Apdo 5234, Panamá; tel. 523-8570; e-mail consultas@idaan.gob.pa; internet www.idaan.gob.pa; Exec. Dir JAVIER CARDOZE.

TRADE UNIONS

Central General Autónoma de Trabajadores de Panamá (CGTP): Casa 15, Calle 3a Perejil, Vía España, Panamá; tel. 269-9741; fax 223-5287; e-mail srivera@cwpanama.net; internet www.cgtp.org.pa; fmrly Central Istmeña de Trabajadores; Sec.-Gen. MARIANO E. MENA.

Confederación Nacional de Unidad Sindical Independiente (CONUSI): 0421B Calle Venado, Ancón, Apdo 830344, Zona 3, Panamá; tel. 212-3865; fax 212-2565; e-mail conusipanama@hotmail.com; Sec.-Gen. GABRIEL E. CASTILLO C.

Confederación de Trabajadores de la República de Panamá (CTRP) (Confederation of Workers of the Republic of Panama): Calle 31, entre Avdas México y Justo Arosemena 3-50, Apdo 0816-03647, Panamá 5; tel. 225-0293; fax 225-0259; e-mail ctrp@cableonda.net; f. 1956; admitted to ITUC/ORIT; Sec.-Gen. GUILLERMO PUGA; 62,000 mems from 13 affiliated groups.

Consejo Nacional de Trabajadores Organizados (CONATO) (National Council of Organized Labour): Edif. 777, 2°, Balboa-Ancón, Panamá; tel. and fax 228-0224; e-mail conato@cwpanama.net; Co-ordinator JOSÉ PEDROZA; 150,000 mems.

Convergencia Sindical: Casa 2490, Balboa-Ancón, Calle Bomparte Wise, Apdo 0815-00863, Panamá 4; tel. and fax 314-1615; e-mail conversind@cwpanama.net; f. 1995; Sec.-Gen. VICTOR MANUEL TORRES.

Federación Nacional de Asociaciones de Empleados y Servidores Públicos (FENASEP) (National Federation of Associations of Public Employees): Galerías Alvear, 2°, Of. 301, Vía Argentina, Apdo 66-48, Zona 5, Panamá; tel. and fax 269-1316; e-mail fenasep@sinfo.net; f. 1984; Sec.-Gen. LEANDRO AVILA.

A number of unions exist without affiliation to a national centre.

Transport

RAILWAYS

In 1998 there was an estimated 485 km of track in Panama. In 2000 a US $75m. project to modernize the line between the ports at either end of the Panama Canal began. In July 2001 the 83-km transisthmian railway, originally founded in 1855, reopened.

Ferrocarril Nacional de Chiriquí: Apdo 12B, David City, Chiriquí; tel. 775-4241; fax 775-4105; 126 km linking Puerto Armuelles and David.

Panama Canal Railway Company: Edif. T-376, Corozal Oeste, Apdo 0843-02448, Balboa Ancón, Panamá; tel. 317-6070; fax 317-6061; e-mail info@panarail.com; internet www.panarail.com; private investment under 50-year govt concession; 83 km linking Panama City and Colón, running parallel to Panama Canal; operation on concession by Kansas City Southern (KS, USA) and Mi-Jack Products (IL, USA); modernization programme completed in 2001; operates daily passenger and cargo service; Marketing Dir THOMAS KENNA.

ROADS

In 2004 there were an estimated 11,985 km of roads, of which some 4,387 km were paved. The two most important highways are the Pan-American Highway and the Boyd-Roosevelt, or Trans-Isthmian, linking Panama City and Colón. The Pan-American Highway to Mexico City runs for 545 km in Panama and was being extended towards Colombia. There is also a highway to San José, Costa Rica.

SHIPPING

The Panama Canal opened in 1914. In 1984 more than 4% of all the world's sea-borne trade passed through the waterway. It is 82 km long, and ships take an average of eight hours to complete a transit. In 2007 some 14,721 transits were recorded. The Canal can accommodate ships with a maximum draught of 12 m, beams of up to approximately 32.3 m (106 ft) and lengths of up to about 290 m (950 ft), roughly equivalent to ships with a maximum capacity of 65,000–70,000 dwt. In 2000 a five-year modernization project was begun. The project included: a general improvement of facilities; the implementation of a satellite traffic-management system; the construction of a bridge; and the widening of the narrowest section of the Canal, the Culebra Cut (which was completed in 2001). Plans were also announced to construct a 203-ha international cargo-handling platform at the Atlantic end of the Canal, including terminals, a railway and an international airport. Terminal ports are Balboa, on the Pacific Ocean, and Cristóbal, on the Caribbean Sea.

Autoridad del Canal de Panamá (ACP): Administration Bldg, Balboa, Ancón, Panamá; tel. 272-7602; fax 272-7693; e-mail info@pancanal.com; internet www.pancanal.com; f. 1997; manages, operates and maintains the Panama Canal; succeeded the Panama Canal Commission, a US govt agency, on 31 December 1999, when the waterway was ceded to the Govt of Panama; the ACP is the autonomous agency of the Govt of Panama; there is a Board of 11 mems; Chair. DANIEL KUZNIECKY; Administrator ALBERTO ALEMÁN ZUBIETA; Dep. Administrator JOSÉ BARRIOS NG.

Autoridad Marítima de Panamá: Edif. 5534, Diablo Heights, Ancón, Apdo 8062, Panamá 7; tel. 232-5528; fax 232-5527; e-mail ampadmin@amp.gob.pa; internet www.amp.gob.pa; f. 1998 to unite and optimize the function of all state institutions with involvement in the maritime sector; Administrator FERNANDO SOLORZANO.

Panama City Port Authority and Foreign Trade Zone 65: Apdo 15095, Panamá; FL 32406, USA; tel. 767-3220; e-mail wstubbs@portpanamacityusa.com; internet www.portpanamacityusa.com; Chair. JOSEPH K. TANNEHILL; Exec. Dir WAYNES STUBBS.

There are deep-water ports at Balboa and Cristóbal (including general cargo ships, containers, shipyards, industrial facilities); Coco Solo (general cargo and containers); Bahía Las Minas (general bulk and containers); Vacamonte (main port for fishing industry); Puerto Armuelles and Almirante (bananas); Aguadulce and Pedregal (export of crude sugar and molasses, transport of fertilizers and chemical products); and Charco Azul and Chiriquí Grande (crude petroleum).

The Panamanian merchant fleet was the largest in the world in December 2007, numbering 7,605 vessels with total displacement of 168.2m. gross registered tons. In November 2000 construction was completed on the largest container terminal in Latin America, in Balboa.

CIVIL AVIATION

Tocumen (formerly Omar Torrijos) International Airport, situated 19 km (12 miles) outside Panamá (Panama City), is the country's principal airport and is served by many international airlines. A project to expand the airport's facilities, at a cost of US $20m., was completed in 2006. The France Airport in Colón and the Rio Hato Airport in Coclé province have both been declared international airports. There are also 11 smaller airports in the country.

Aerolíneas Pacífico Atlántico, SA (Aeroperlas): Apdo 6-3596, El Dorado, Panamá; tel. 315-7500; fax 315-0331; e-mail info@aeroperlas.com; internet www.aeroperlas.com; f. 1970; fmrly state-owned, transferred to private ownership in 1987; operates scheduled regional and domestic flights to 16 destinations; initiated international flights in 2000; Pres. GEORGE F. NOVEY; Gen. Man. EDUARDO STAGG.

Air Panama: Marcos A. Gelabert Airport, Panamá; tel. 316-9000; e-mail info@flyairpanama.com; internet www.flyairpanama.com; operates flights throughout Panama and to Costa Rica; Pres. GEORGE NOVEY.

Compañía Panameña de Aviación, SA (COPA): Avda Justo Arosemena 230 y Calle 39, Apdo 1572, Panamá 1; tel. 227-2522; fax 227-1952; e-mail proquebert@mail.copa.com.pa; internet www.copaair.com; f. 1947; scheduled passenger and cargo services from Panamá (Panama City) to Central America, South America, the

PANAMA

Caribbean and the USA; Chair. ALBERTO MOTTA; CEO PEDRO O. HEILBRON.

Tourism

Panama's attractions include Panamá (Panama City), the ruins of Portobelo and 800 sandy tropical islands, including the resort of Contadora, one of the Pearl Islands in the Gulf of Panama, and the San Blas Islands, lying off the Atlantic coast. In 2006 the number of visitor arrivals at Tocumen International Airport stood at 703,745. Income from tourism was some US $1,450m. in 2006. In 2003 there were some 16,766 hotel rooms in Panama.

Asociación Panameña de Agencias de Viajes y Turismo (APAVIT): Edif. Balmoral, Vía Argentina, diagonal a la Universidad de Panamá, Panamá; tel. 264-9171; fax 264-5355; e-mail apavit@cableonda.net; f. 1957; Pres. ERNESTO REINA.

Autoridad de Turismo Panamá (IPAT): Centro de Convenciones ATLAPA, Vía Israel, Apdo 4421, Panamá 5; tel. 526-7000; fax 526-7100; e-mail gerencia@atp.gob.pa; internet www.atp.gob.pa; f. 1960; Dir-Gen. RUBÉN BLADES.

PAPUA NEW GUINEA

Introductory Survey

Location, Climate, Language, Religion, Flag, Capital

The Independent State of Papua New Guinea lies east of Indonesia and north of the north-eastern extremity of Australia. It comprises the eastern section of the island of New Guinea (the western section being Papua (West Papua), formerly Irian Jaya, which forms part of Indonesia) and about 600 smaller islands, including the Bismarck Archipelago (mainly New Britain, New Ireland and Manus) and the northern part of the Solomon Islands (mainly Bougainville and Buka). The climate is hot and humid throughout the year, with an average maximum temperature of 33°C (91°F) and an average minimum of 22°C (72°F). Rainfall is high on the coast but lower inland: the annual average varies from about 1,000 mm (40 ins) to 6,350 mm (250 ins). There are more than 800 native languages, but Pidgin and, to a lesser extent, standard English are also spoken, and, together with Motu, are the official languages in Parliament. More than 90% of the population profess Christianity. The national flag (proportions 3 by 4) is divided diagonally from the upper hoist to the lower fly: the upper portion displays a golden bird of paradise in silhouette on a red ground, while the lower portion has five white five-pointed stars, in the form of the Southern Cross constellation, on a black ground. The capital is Port Moresby.

Recent History

Papua New Guinea was formed by the merger of the Territory of Papua, under Australian rule from 1906, with the Trust Territory of New Guinea, a former German possession which Australia administered from 1914, first under a military Government, then under a League of Nations mandate, established in 1921, and later under a trusteeship agreement with the UN. During the Second World War, parts of both territories were occupied by Japanese forces from 1942 to 1945.

A joint administration for the two territories was established by Australia in July 1949. The union was named the Territory of Papua and New Guinea. A Legislative Council was established in November 1951 and was replaced by a House of Assembly, with an elected indigenous majority, in June 1964. The territory was renamed Papua New Guinea in July 1971. It achieved internal self-government in December 1973 and full independence on 16 September 1975, when the House of Assembly became the National Parliament.

Michael Somare, who from 1972 served as Chief Minister in an interim coalition Government, became Prime Minister on independence. He remained in office until 1980, despite widespread allegations of inefficiency in government ministries and of discrimination against the Highland provinces. The first elections since independence were held in mid-1977, following which Somare's Pangu (Papua New Guinea Unity) Pati formed a governing coalition, first with the People's Progress Party (PPP) and later with the United Party (UP).

In March 1980 the Government lost a vote of confidence, the fourth in 15 months, and Sir Julius Chan, the leader of the PPP and a former Deputy Prime Minister, succeeded to the premiership. Somare became Prime Minister again following a general election in June 1982. In 1983 the Somare Government effected a constitutional change to provide the central authorities with greater control of the provincial governments as a means of preventing abuse of their powers. As a result, between 1983 and 1991 a total of nine provincial governments were suspended by the central Government for alleged maladministration.

In March 1985 a motion expressing no confidence in Somare's Government was introduced in Parliament by Chan, who nominated Paias Wingti (hitherto Deputy Prime Minister and a member of the Pangu Pati) as alternative Prime Minister. Somare quickly formed a coalition, comprising the ruling Pangu Pati, the National Party (NP) and the Melanesian Alliance (MA), and the no confidence motion was defeated. Fourteen Members of Parliament (MPs) who had supported the motion were expelled from the Pangu Pati, and subsequently formed a new political party, the People's Democratic Movement (PDM), under the leadership of Wingti.

In August 1985 the NP withdrew from Somare's coalition Government, and in November Chan presented another motion of no confidence, criticizing Somare's handling of the economy. Somare was defeated and Wingti took office as Prime Minister of a new five-party coalition Government (comprising the PDM, the PPP, the NP, the UP and the MA), with Chan as Deputy Prime Minister.

At the mid-1987 election to the National Parliament Somare's Pangu Pati won 26 of the 109 elective seats, while Wingti's PDM obtained 18. However, by forming a coalition with minor parties, Wingti succeeded in securing a parliamentary majority and was re-elected Prime Minister. In July 1988 Wingti was defeated in a no confidence motion, proposed by Rabbie Namaliu, who had replaced Somare as leader of the Pangu Pati. As a result, Namaliu took office as Prime Minister and announced a new coalition Government, comprising members of the Pangu Pati and five minor parties: the People's Action Party (PAP), the MA, the NP, the League for National Advancement (LNA) and the Papua Party. In August Ted Diro, the leader of the PAP, was acquitted on a charge of perjury by the Supreme Court (having been accused of illegally appropriating funds for his party). An amendment to the Constitution, whereby a motion expressing no confidence in the Prime Minister could not be proposed until the premier had completed 18 months in office, was approved by Parliament in August 1990 and incorporated into the Constitution in July 1991.

In September 1991 a leadership tribunal found Ted Diro, the leader of the PAP, guilty of 81 charges of misconduct in government office. However, the Governor-General, Sir Serei Eri, refused to ratify the tribunal's decision and reinstated Diro as Deputy Prime Minister, despite recommendations that he be dismissed. A constitutional crisis subsequently arose, during which a government envoy was sent to the United Kingdom to request that the monarch dismiss Eri, but in early October the resignation of the Governor-General was announced; this was followed shortly afterwards by that of Diro.

In 1992 the Government continued to be troubled by allegations of corruption and misconduct (notably bribery and misuse of public funds). Campaigning for the 1992 general election began amid serious fighting among the various political factions, which led to rioting, in April, by some 10,000 supporters of rival candidates. At the election in June a total of 59 members of the legislature (including 15 ministers) lost their seats. The final result gave the Pangu Pati 22 of the 109 elective seats, while the PDM secured 15. Independent candidates won a total of 31 seats. Paias Wingti of the PDM was subsequently elected Prime Minister by the National Parliament, defeating Rabbie Namaliu of the Pangu Pati by a single vote. Wingti formed a coalition Government, comprising PDM, PPP and LNA members, as well as several independents. As part of the new administration's anti-corruption policy, Wingti suspended six provincial governments for financial mismanagement in October, and threatened to abolish the entire local government system.

In early 1993 a resurgence of tribal violence, mainly in the Enga Province, resulted in the deaths of more than 100 people. This development, together with a continued increase in violent crime throughout the country (despite the implementation in 1991 of severe measures to combat crime, including the introduction of the death penalty and the tattooing of the foreheads of convicted criminals) prompted the National Parliament to approve a new internal security act in May 1993. The measures, which included an amendment of the legal system that required defendants accused of serious crimes to prove their innocence, rather than be proven guilty, were criticized by the opposition as oppressive. In May 1994 the Supreme Court nullified six of the 26 sections of the act (most of which concerned the extension of police powers), denouncing them as unconstitutional.

In September 1993 Prime Minister Wingti announced his resignation to Parliament. The Speaker immediately requested nominations for the premiership, and Wingti was re-elected unopposed with 59 of the 109 votes. According to the Constitution (as amended in 1991), a motion of no confidence in the Prime Minister could not be presented for at least 18 months, and

Wingti claimed that his action had been necessary in order to secure a period of political stability for the country. However, opposition members described the events as an abuse of the democratic process, and several thousand demonstrators gathered in the capital to demand Wingti's resignation. In December the National Court rejected a constitutional challenge from the opposition to Wingti's re-election, but in August 1994 the Supreme Court declared Wingti's re-election in September 1993 invalid. Wingti did not contest the ensuing parliamentary vote for a new Prime Minister, in which Sir Julius Chan of the PPP defeated the Speaker, Bill Skate, by 66 votes to 32; Chris Haiveta, the leader of the Pangu Pati, was appointed Deputy Prime Minister.

The abolition of the directly elected provincial government system, as proposed by Wingti, was rejected by Chan's Government, although there was still considerable support among members of the opposition for the planned changes and, as a result, it was decided that Parliament would vote on a series of motions to amend the Constitution accordingly; the first of these was approved in March 1995. However, in June the Pangu Pati withdrew its support for the reforms, and considerable opposition to the proposals was expressed by the provincial governments. Nevertheless, the controversial legislation was approved later that month on condition that Chan lent his support to several opposition amendments to be considered later in the year. Chan subsequently dismissed six ministers for failing to vote for the legislation and effected a major reorganization of portfolios. The new regional authorities, comprising national politicians and selected local councillors and led by appointed governors, were appointed in that month. Wingti resigned as parliamentary leader of the opposition in order to assume the post of Governor in the Western Highlands Province, and was replaced by another PDM member, Roy Yaki.

The involvement of mercenaries to counter the secessionist movement on the island of Bougainville in early 1997 (see below) led to a period of extreme instability throughout the country, culminating in Chan's temporary resignation and the appointment of John Giheno as acting Prime Minister for about two months. The atmosphere of political uncertainty was exacerbated by serious outbreaks of violence in the weeks preceding the legislative election (which had been set for mid-June). The Government imposed a dusk-to-dawn curfew and a nationwide ban on the sale of alcohol. Many senior politicians, including Giheno and Wingti, failed to secure re-election at the polls. Outbreaks of violence were reported in several Highlands constituencies as the results were declared. A period of intense political manoeuvring followed the election, as various members sought to form coalitions and groupings in an attempt to achieve a majority in Parliament. In July Bill Skate of the People's National Congress (PNC), who was the former Speaker and Governor of the National Capital District, was elected Prime Minister, defeating Sir Michael Somare (who had established a new party—the National Alliance—in 1996) by 71 votes to 35. Skate was supported by a coalition of the PNC, PDM, PPP, Pangu Pati and independent members. A new Government was appointed in late July 1997, and extensive changes in the functional responsibilities of ministries were announced.

In September 1997 the Government declared a national disaster following a prolonged period of drought. By December more than 1,000 people had died. Several countries and organizations that had provided relief funds during the disaster were highly critical of the Government's management of the aid it received. The Minister for Finance, Roy Yaki, was dismissed, in part for his role in the affair, and responsibility for the administration of relief funds was subsequently transferred from the Department of Finance to the Department of Provincial Affairs. In March 1998 (when the drought was deemed to have ended following heavy rainfall) it was revealed that less than one-half of the relief aid received had been deployed to help the victims of the disaster.

In mid-November 1997 Silas (later Sir Silas) Atopare was appointed Governor-General, defeating Sir Getake Gam, head of the Evangelical Lutheran Church, by 54 votes to 44 in the legislature. A serious political scandal erupted in late November, following allegations of corruption against the Prime Minister. The accusations centred on a videotape broadcast on Australian television, which appeared to show Skate arranging bribes and boasting of his strong connections with criminal elements in Port Moresby. The Prime Minister dismissed his recorded comments (and the resultant allegations) stating that he had been drunk at the time of filming. Several senior politicians, including Somare, demanded his resignation over the affair. Meanwhile, Skate dismissed the leaders of the Pangu Pati and the PPP (Chris Haiveta and Andrew Baing, respectively), his coalition partners, accusing them of conspiring against him. The situation intensified with the resignation of seven Pangu Pati members from the Government in early December, and the announcement that the Pangu Pati and the PPP would join the opposition. However, the PPP rejoined the Government shortly afterwards, having voted to replace Baing as leader of the party with Michael Nali. Similarly, four Pangu Pati ministers rejoined the Government, thereby restoring Skate's majority in the National Parliament. A major ministerial reorganization was subsequently announced, in which Nali was appointed Deputy Prime Minister.

In April 1998 the Prime Minister announced the formation of a new political grouping, the Papua New Guinea First Party (which absorbed the PNC, the Christian Country Party and several other minor parties); Skate also effected a ministerial reorganization. However, the Government's majority was subsequently undermined, following a series of decisions by the Court of Disputed Returns during mid-1998, which declared the election in 1997 of seven government MPs to be null and void. Furthermore, in June 1998 the Pangu Pati officially joined the opposition, thereby reducing the Government's representation to 61 members in the National Parliament. Rumours of a forthcoming motion of no confidence in the Prime Minister prompted the establishment of a new pro-Skate coalition in the National Parliament in late July 1998. In the same month Skate announced a number of major reforms in the structure of the Government and an extensive ministerial reorganization. In October the PPP left the governing coalition and, in a subsequent ministerial reorganization, the party's leader, Nali, was replaced as Deputy Prime Minister by Iairo Lasaro.

In late 1998 there was a series of scandals relating to the various serious misdemeanours of a number of provincial governors. Moreover, outbreaks of tribal fighting continued to cause problems (particularly in the Highlands) in 1998–99. A serious conflict in the Eastern Highlands in early 1999 involved villagers using rocket launchers and grenades, and resulted in numerous deaths. In mid-1999 a state of emergency was declared in the Southern Highlands, following serious disturbances provoked by the death of a former provincial Governor, Dick Mune, in a road accident.

The establishment of a new political party, the PNG Liberal Party, in May 1999 by the Speaker, John Pundari (relaunched in June as the Advance PNG Party—APP), encouraged rumours of a forthcoming vote of no confidence against the Prime Minister. In early June, as part of a government reorganization, Skate dismissed the PDM leader, Sir Mekere Morauta, and three other PDM ministers, replacing them with four Pangu Pati members, including Haiveta. Later that month both the PDM and the United Resource Party (URP) announced their decision to withdraw completely from the coalition Government, following the resignation of nine government ministers. Both parties were expected to support the APP, in an attempt to subject the Prime Minister to a vote of no confidence. In early July, however, Skate unexpectedly resigned, but declared that he would remain in power in an acting capacity, pending the appointment of a new Prime Minister. The opposition alliance announced Morauta as their candidate for the premiership. Skate claimed that the APP had pledged support for the Government, thereby ensuring that it would have a sufficient majority to defeat any motion of no confidence. At the opening session of the National Parliament in mid-July, Lasaro, the incumbent Prime Minister's nominee, defeated the opposition candidate, Bernard Narokobi of the PDM, by 57 votes to 45, to become Speaker. However, on the next day Morauta was elected Prime Minister by an overwhelming majority, following his nomination by Pundari, who had transferred his allegiance from Skate, having refused to accept the latter's nomination of himself as candidate for the premiership. Lasaro immediately resigned as Speaker, and Narokobi was elected unopposed to the position. Morauta subsequently appointed a new coalition Government, with Pundari as Deputy Prime Minister.

In early August 1999 Sir Mekere Morauta, a former Governor of the central bank, presented a 'mini-budget', in an attempt to combat various economic problems which, he claimed, were a consequence of the previous Government's mismanagement. In October legislation was drafted to prevent ministers transferring political allegiances. In early December the Prime Minister expelled the APP from the coalition Government and dismissed Pundari from his post as Deputy Prime Minister, claiming that this constituted a further move towards the restoration of political stability. (Pundari was rumoured to have conspired with the opposition leader, Skate, to oust the Prime Minister.) Pundari was replaced by the former Minister of Works and deputy leader of the PDM, Mao Zeming. Following Pundari's sudden dismissal, four small political parties within the governing coalition—the National Alliance, the People's National Party, the Melanesian Alliance and the Movement for Greater Autonomy—joined to form the People's National Alliance. Also in that month, Skate (who had been charged with attempted fraud during his term in office as Governor of the National Capital District Commission), announced that his party, the PNC, which had 10 MPs, was to join the coalition Government; in May he assumed leadership of the party. Later in December, the resignation of the Minister of Agriculture and Livestock, Ted Diro, prompted Morauta to carry out a government reorganization.

Morauta dismissed three ministers in March 2000, on the grounds that they had allegedly conspired to introduce a parliamentary motion of no confidence in the Prime Minister. The parliamentary strength of the ruling coalition was increased to 76 MPs in April, following the readmission of the APP to government, including the appointment of Pundari to the post of Minister of Lands and Physical Planning. In an attempt to increase government stability, Morauta proposed legislation in August that would restrict the ability of MPs to change their party allegiance within a parliamentary session. Moreover, Morauta also announced the adjournment of Parliament between January and July 2001, the only period during which votes of no confidence could be tabled. (The Constitution forbade such votes in the 18 months following the election of a Prime Minister, and in the 12 months prior to a general election.) In November, however, a revolt by 25 government MPs (including six cabinet ministers) prevented a vote on the so-called Political Parties Integrity Bill. The rebellion prompted a major cabinet reorganization, in which all of the ministers involved in the revolt, including the Deputy Prime Minister, Mao Zeming, were dismissed. Further changes to the composition of the cabinet were made in December, notably the dismissal of Michael Somare, the Minister for Foreign Affairs and Trade, following which Morauta secured the parliamentary approval of the bill. The Prime Minister claimed that the introduction of the new legislation represented the most important constitutional change in Papua New Guinea since independence and would greatly enhance the political stability of the country, as it required MPs who wished to change party allegiance to stand down and contest a by-election.

Allegations of corruption and mismanagement resulted in the suspension of four provincial governments (Western Province, Southern Highlands, Enga and the National Capital District—NCD) in late 2000 and early 2001. The central Government claimed that a failure to deliver services had resulted from the misuse of public funds. Moreover, in January 2001 the Minister for Provincial and Local Government, Iairo Lasaro, was arrested for the alleged misappropriation of public funds, and in mid-March Bill Skate was charged with the same crime, having been acquitted earlier in the month of conspiring to defraud an insurance company (the trial was to be abandoned in December 2001 owing to lack of evidence).

A Commonwealth report into the Papua New Guinea Defence Force, published in January 2001, recommended reducing the number of army personnel by one-third. Subsequent plans by the Government to make more than 2,000 soldiers redundant (equivalent to some 50% of the entire Defence Force) resulted in a revolt at the Port Moresby barracks in March. It was believed that senior officers had helped to distribute weapons to the rebels, who demanded the resignation of the Prime Minister and the transfer of power to an interim administration. The rebellion ended two weeks later with an amnesty for the soldiers involved, during which hundreds of looted weapons were surrendered. In March 2002 another rebellion by soldiers protesting against the proposed reductions in defence personnel took place at the Moem barracks on the northern coast. The leader of the rebellion, Nebare Dege, was sentenced to 15 years' imprisonment in December.

In April 2001 the Advance PNG Party, led by John Pundari, was dissolved and merged with the PDM, led by the Prime Minister. In May, following a minor ministerial reorganization in March, Morauta expelled the National Alliance from the ruling coalition and dismissed the party's ministers (including Bart Philemon, Minister for Foreign Affairs) from the National Executive Council, accusing Somare, the party's leader, of attempting to destabilize the Government. In late June, following several days of protests against the Government's economic reforms, police used tear gas to disperse hundreds of demonstrators outside the Prime Minister's office in Port Moresby. In a separate incident, four students were killed and several injured when riot police allegedly entered the premises of the University of Papua New Guinea and opened fire. A temporary curfew was imposed, and a Commission of Inquiry was established; in December relatives of one of the dead students began legal action against the police force.

In October 2001 the Prime Minister effected another reallocation of ministerial portfolios. At the end of the month, furthermore, the Minister for Foreign Affairs, John Pundari, was dismissed. His removal from office followed his criticism of the Government's participation in Australia's 'Pacific Solution', whereby 216 refugees, who had attempted to enter Australia by boat, were being housed in a former military prison on Manus Island. In December negotiations with Australia were under way to accommodate a further 1,000 asylum-seekers, and Australia had requested the Government to hold the refugees for an additional six months, although no formal agreement was made. In January 2002 the Government decided to accept 784 additional asylum-seekers. It was understood that they were to remain only until their asylum claims were processed. The agreement with Australia to accommodate the asylum-seekers on Manus Island was extended for a further 12 months in October 2002 and was to provide for the housing of an additional 1,000 people. The camp remained open, despite the Australian Government's announcement in August 2003 that it intended to close the facility. In early 2004 it was revealed that the sole occupant of the camp was a Palestinian refugee who had been held in solitary confinement for almost seven months at a cost of more than US $3m.

A legislative election was held in mid-2002. Voting commenced on 15 June and was to extend over a two-week period. However, many polling stations failed to open as scheduled, amid reports of the theft of ballot papers and subsequent strike action by electoral staff. Some 25 people were killed and dozens injured in election-related violence, much of which occurred in the Highlands provinces as a result of disputes between clan-based candidates. A Commonwealth inquiry was subsequently planned to investigate the events surrounding the election, which was described as the worst in the country's history. In the final results, announced in August, six seats in the Highlands provinces remained vacant where voting had been unable to proceed (elections for these seats were held in April and May 2003). Of the 103 seats determined, Somare's National Alliance won 19 and Morauta's PDM secured 12. Independent candidates won 17 seats, with the remainder divided among a large number of minor parties, many of which had been formed specifically to contest the election.

On 5 August 2002 Sir Michael Somare was elected unopposed as Prime Minister, receiving 88 parliamentary votes. Bill Skate, who had played an important part in Somare's campaign, was elected Speaker. After appointing a 28-member Cabinet (which was dominated by 19 newly elected MPs), Somare began his third term as Prime Minister, pledging to restore stability, halt the privatization programme and reduce expenditure. Instability within the parliamentary opposition in late 2002 resulted in the dismissal of Morauta as leader of the opposition in December.

In June 2003 the Government submitted proposals for a number of changes to the political system, including a mandatory general election following the approval of a no confidence motion and stricter rules governing the switching of party allegiances among members of the National Parliament. In late 2003 the Government proposed legislation that would extend the period during which a new government should be exempt from votes of no confidence, from 18 months to three years. Both attempts to introduce these constitutional changes were unsuccessful, despite government inducements of some US $25,000 for members of the National Parliament to support the proposals.

In mid-September 2003 Sir Albert Kipalan defeated Sir Paulias Matane by a single vote in the final poll to elect a new Governor-General. Kipalan was expected to take up the position in mid-November, when the term of the incumbent, Sir Silas Atopare, expired. However, questions concerning possible irregularities in the procedure arose in the following week, casting doubt on the validity of the election, and the Supreme Court subsequently declared it to be defective and invalid. Speaker Bill Skate was appointed acting Governor-General until a new election could be arranged. At the poll, which was duly held in early December, Sir Pato Kakaraya was the successful candidate. However, Kipalan, who had also contested the election, challenged the result and was granted a legal injunction against Kakaraya's inauguration, which had been due to take place in late January 2004. In March the Supreme Court declared the election of Sir Pato Kakaraya to be null and void. Somare consequently ordered the recall of the National Parliament in order that a new election to the post could be organized. Following four rounds of voting Sir Paulias Matane, a former Minister of Foreign Affairs, was narrowly elected Governor-General in late May and, when the Supreme Court had dismissed an injunction against his appointment by Kakaraya, was duly sworn in in the following month.

In May 2004 Somare dismissed Deputy Prime Minister Moses Maladina, together with all the PNC members of the Cabinet who had refused to support proposed government legislation and who were believed to be planning a vote of no confidence in the Government. Meanwhile, ongoing fears about increasing gun ownership were highlighted in early August, when the National Parliament was adjourned for a period of three months after both the Government and the opposition expressed concern over the number of legislators who were reported to be bringing firearms into the National Parliament building. In early 2005 Somare announced a reorganization of cabinet portfolios which included the appointment of his son, Arthur, to the role of Minister for National Planning and Monitoring. In February 2006, however, Arthur Somare resigned from his cabinet position following allegations of misappropriation of public funds; he was referred to the Public Prosecutor for failing to submit annual statements on time and to account for the application of local grants. The Minister for Forestry, Patrick Pruaitch, was appointed to the post in an acting capacity. In a reallocation of portfolios in early April, Pruaitch also assumed responsibility for the finance portfolio, which was removed from Bart Philemon, who nevertheless remained as Minister for Treasury. Mark Maipakai, hitherto Minister of Justice, was appointed Minister for Housing and Urban Resettlement, being replaced in the former position by Bire Kimisopa. Kimisopa had previously served as Minister for Internal Security, a post to which Alphonse Willie was appointed. A major reorganization of the National Executive Council was carried out in July; five cabinet ministers, including the Minister for Treasury, Bart Philemon, and the Minister for Defence, Mathew Gubag, were dismissed. Sir Michael Somare himself took the foreign affairs portfolio from Rabbie Namaliu, who became Minister for Treasury, while Arthur Somare, whose case with the Public Prosecutor was still pending, was reappointed to the cabinet as Minister for State Enterprise, Communication and Information. In November Prime Minister Somare assigned the foreign affairs portfolio to Paul Tiensten.

In early 2007 the Prime Minister announced further cabinet changes, including the appointment of Michael Nali as Minister for Commerce and Industry and Nick Kuman as Minister for Culture and Tourism. In late February Martin Aini, the Minister for Defence, was dismissed by Somare, reportedly for reasons related to the Julian Moti affair (see below).

Meanwhile, in April 2006 it was reported that the Public Prosecutor had found enough evidence to justify the establishment of a leadership tribunal to investigate alleged misconduct on the part of Puka Temu, the Minister for Lands and Physical Planning, and Andrew Baing, the Deputy Leader of the Opposition. In February 2007 a tribunal was formed to examine allegations of misconduct against Melchior Pep, who had previously served as Minister for Correctional and Administrative Services. In May 2007 a leadership tribunal recommended the dismissal of Sir Moi Avei, the former Deputy Prime Minister who had subsequently held the cabinet portfolio of petroleum and energy, over charges of financial misconduct; however, a final decision was postponed pending his appeal.

In June 2007 the Minister for Commerce and Industry, Michael Nali, and the Minister for Culture and Tourism, Nick Kuman, resigned in order to contest the next legislative election as PNC candidates. Polling took place, under a new 'limited preferential voting' system, in relatively peaceful circumstances between 30 June and 15 July, although there were some fatalities. The National Alliance ultimately secured 27 of the 109 seats, with its nearest rival, the PNG Party, winning only eight. Following coalition negotiations with several smaller parties including the PAP, the Pangu Pati and the URP, along with additional support from independents, Sir Michael Somare was re-elected as Prime Minister in mid-August; Sir Mekere Morauta became leader of the opposition soon after. In late August the composition of the new National Executive Council was announced. The National Alliance, from which a total of 13 ministers were taken, was allocated important portfolios: Puka Temu was appointed Deputy Prime Minister and Minister for Lands, Physical Planning and Mining, while Patrick Pruaitch assumed responsibility for the finance and treasury portfolio, and a new appointee to the cabinet, Sam Abal, became Minister for Foreign Affairs and Trade. Bob Dadae of the UP was appointed Minister for Defence, and Allan Marat of the Melanesian Labour Party (MLP) received the justice portfolio. Other parties represented included the PAP and the PNC. Somare announced his intention to expand the National Executive Council from 28 ministers to 35, in order fully to represent the composition of the governing coalition; the cost of the additional ministers was reported to have been estimated at US $1m. In early 2008 Somare's proposals for the creation of five new ministries were criticized by the opposition. The Minister for Education, Michael Laimo, was forced to relinquish his portfolio when a court invalidated the election result in his parliamentary constituency in February; Somare assumed responsibility for education in an acting capacity. In October it was reported that Laimo's opponent had secured his seat in the recount of the ballot papers. Meanwhile, relations with Taiwan came under international scrutiny in May 2008, when two senior members of the Taiwanese Government were forced to resign over a major funding controversy involving the use of intermediaries to secure the diplomatic recognition of Papua New Guinea. The affair, which highlighted the practice of so-called 'chequebook diplomacy', prompted Somare to issue a denial of any involvement.

Controversy surrounding the role of foreign interests in the exploitation of the country's natural resources re-emerged in early 2005 when a group representing landowners near the Porgera gold mine protested at the mysterious deaths of villagers while panning for alluvial gold near the mine. The group claimed that several local people had been shot dead by Porgera security personnel and their bodies removed and that others had been seriously assaulted. Mine officials denied the allegations, stating that most of the deaths had been caused by falling rocks or other accidents, and that any shootings by their security guards had been carried out in self-defence. The opposition leader, Peter O'Neill, demanded an official inquiry into the deaths, which by early May had reached 29, with many others having been seriously assaulted. Violent incidents between miners and villagers living near the Porgera mine continued sporadically. In May 2009 villagers reportedly claimed that their homes had been destroyed by security personnel who had been sent to the mine in the previous month, to quell alleged tribal warfare and halt illegal mining activities. A spokesman for people living near the mine stated that 309 homes had been burned down, with more than 1,000 villagers affected. Also in May, violence between local workers and foreign employees over the issue of labour conditions broke out at the Chinese-owned Ramu nickel mine, forcing it to close temporarily.

Tribal conflicts, principally between the Ujimap and Wagia tribes, broke out near Mendi, the capital of Southern Highlands Province, in December 2001. It was alleged that national and local politicians, along with tribal leaders, had made little effort to end the fighting, which had originated in a dispute over the governorship of the province in 1997; furthermore, many were dissatisfied at the election of Tom Tomiape as Governor, in late November 2001, and at the widespread political corruption and deteriorating public services in the province. Tomiape's election was ruled invalid by the Supreme Court in December, and Wambi Nondi was appointed acting Governor. A brief ceasefire was brokered in early January 2002 and an independent peace commission was established in February, headed by Francis Awesa, a local businessman. By early 2002 more than 120 people had been killed since the onset of the fighting.

Ethnic and tribal violence continued in several regions of the country during 2003. Eight people were killed in fighting near Port Moresby in May, and 17 died during inter-clan violence involving more than 1,000 people in Enga Province in July. Further killings led to rioting in the following month and to an appeal by the Governor of the province for those responsible to be hanged. In early 2004 eight villagers were killed in Enga Province in further tribal conflicts, and by mid-2004 ethnic violence in Morobe, Chimbu and East Highlands Provinces had resulted in many more deaths, including those of several children. Concerns regarding the conduct of the national police force in tackling such conflicts intensified following an incident in August when a confrontation between security personnel and a group of youths in Enga Province resulted in police setting fire to an entire village, shooting dead a villager and injuring several others, and killing domestic animals. Earlier in the year the former Commander-in-Chief of the Defence Force, Jerry Singirok, stated his belief that the marked increase in ownership of illegal firearms, particularly in the Highlands region, was the single most significant problem in Papua New Guinea. Ethnic violence continued in 2005 with at least 10 people being killed in February in an incident in Enga Province prompted by the incorrect allocation of a village magistrate's allowance. Some 5,000 villagers were left homeless following fighting in Chimbu Province in April. Further violence during the year, particularly in the Highlands provinces, resulted in many more deaths. In one outbreak of fighting in July, resulting from a land dispute, an estimated 7,000 guns were believed to have been used and police officers declined to intervene as they were considerably less well-armed. In another incident fuel shortages prevented police from attending a serious tribal conflict in which many people were killed. A report published in July 2005 claimed that the majority of illegal firearms in circulation in the country originated from Papua New Guinea Defence Force or police stocks. Another report released in early 2006 confirmed that many of the weapons used in these inter-tribal conflicts had been bought or stolen from the security forces, who appeared to be unable or unwilling to intervene in such incidents, while home-made shotguns were increasingly being replaced by more sophisticated weaponry.

In early August 2006 a state of emergency was declared in Southern Highlands Province in response to allegations of financial mismanagement and corruption within the regional administration; the provincial Government was later suspended. In February 2007 the central Government extended the state of emergency for a further nine months, but in the following month the Supreme Court annulled the Government's decision, maintaining that conditions in the Southern Highlands Province did not warrant such extreme measures.

In November 2007 Cyclone Guba struck Papua New Guinea, causing major floods that resulted in the deaths of at least 163 people and the displacement of thousands more. A state of emergency was declared in Oro province, the worst-affected region. In December of the following year the northern coast was hit by tidal waves, which affected an estimated 75,000 people.

Meanwhile, a reported increase in murders involving allegations of sorcery was a source of concern for officials in 2008. In January 2009 the police estimated that as many as one-half of all the murders in the country in the previous year were linked to accusations of 'black magic', which, according to human rights organizations, frequently led to the persecution of innocent individuals.

From the late 1980s the status of the province of Bougainville was increasingly questioned, becoming an issue that developed into civil unrest and a long-term national crisis. In April 1988 landowners on the island of Bougainville submitted claims for financial compensation for land that had been mined by the Australian-owned Bougainville Copper Ltd since 1972. When no payment was forthcoming, acts of sabotage were perpetrated in late 1988 by the Bougainville Revolutionary Army (BRA), led by Francis Ona, a former mine surveyor and landowner, and the mine was obliged to suspend operations. Members of the national security forces were deployed in the area and production at the mine recommenced in December, but a curfew was imposed after further violence in January 1989.

The BRA increasingly favoured secession from Papua New Guinea for Bougainville (and for North Solomons Province as a whole), together with the closure of the mine until their demands for compensation and secession had been met. In May 1989, as the violent campaign on the island intensified, the mine was forced once more to suspend production, and in June the Papua New Guinea Government declared a state of emergency on Bougainville, sending 2,000 security personnel to the island. In September a minister in the Bougainville provincial government, who had been negotiating an agreement with Bougainville landowners to increase their share of mining royalties from 5% to 20%, was shot dead. The signing of the accord, due to take place the following day, was postponed indefinitely. In early 1990 the owners of Bougainville Copper Ltd completed a full withdrawal and Australian nationals were evacuated by their Government.

In March 1990 the Government negotiated a cease-fire with the BRA and withdrew its security forces; later in that month it imposed an economic blockade on Bougainville, now under the control of the BRA. The blockade was intensified in May, when banking, telecommunications and public services on the island were suspended. Also in May, Ona proclaimed Bougainville's independence and declared himself interim President. The unilateral declaration of independence was immediately dismissed by the central Government as unconstitutional and invalid. Negotiations between the BRA and the Government in July resulted in the BRA representatives agreeing to defer implementation of the May declaration of independence and to hold further discussions on the political status of the island. The Government agreed to end the blockade, and to restore essential services to the island. However, violence between the BRA and armed forces restarted in September, leading to many reported deaths, after the Government sent troops to take control of Buka, claiming Buka islanders had petitioned for help.

In January 1991 further negotiations between representatives of the Papua New Guinea Government and of Bougainville in Honiara, the capital of Solomon Islands, resulted in the 'Honiara Accord'. The Papua New Guinea Government agreed not to station its security forces on Bougainville if the BRA disbanded and surrendered all prisoners and weapons to a multinational peace-keeping force. The Bougainville secessionists were guaranteed immunity from prosecution. However, the agreement made no provision for any change in the political status of Bougainville, and by early March it appeared to have failed. Government troops launched a further attack on Bougainville in April. In June Col Leo Nuia was dismissed from his post as Commander of the Papua New Guinea Defence Force, after admitting that his troops had committed atrocities during fighting on Bougainville in early 1990. Further allegations of human rights abuses and summary executions of BRA members and sympathizers by government troops prompted Namaliu to announce plans for an independent inquiry into the claims. (The report, published in late 1996, identified numerous problems contributing to a lack of discipline among the troops, and recommended a thorough reorganization of the country's armed forces.)

Fighting continued throughout 1991 and the situation deteriorated further in early 1992 when, in an attempt to force the Government to end its economic blockade of the island, the BRA intercepted and set fire to a supply ship, and held its crew hostage. As a result, all shipping and air services to Bougainville were suspended, and in October government troops began a major offensive against rebel-held areas of Bougainville. Violence on the island intensified in early 1993, and allegations of atrocities and violations of human rights by both sides were widely reported.

Talks between government representatives and Bougainville secessionists in Honiara during 1994 led to the signing of a cease-fire agreement in September. Under the terms of the agreement, a regional peace-keeping force, composed of troops from Fiji, Vanuatu and Tonga, was deployed in October (with the Governments of Australia and New Zealand in a supervisory role) and the economic blockade of Bougainville was ended. In the following month Prime Minister Chan and a group of non-BRA Bougainville leaders signed the Charter of Mirigini, which provided for the establishment of a transitional Bougainville government. The BRA declared its opposition to the proposed authority, reiterating its goal of outright secession.

In April 1995, following the suspension of the Bougainville provincial government, Theodore Miriong, a former legal adviser to Ona, was sworn in as Premier of a 32-member transitional administration. Three seats reserved for the BRA leaders, Ona, Kauona and Joseph Kabui (a former Premier of North Solomons Province), remained vacant, as the rebels urged their supporters to reject the new administration. The murder of several more members of the security forces in March 1996 led the Government to abandon all talks with the secessionists and to reimpose a military blockade on Bougainville. An escalation of violence in mid-1996 culminated in a major military offensive against rebel-held areas in June. By August it was estimated that some 67,000 Bougainvilleans were taking refuge in 59 government 'care centres'. In the same month defence forces arrested Miriong, accusing him of incitement regarding the killing of 13 government soldiers at an army camp. In October Miriong was assassinated by unidentified gunmen, later found by an official inquiry to be a group of government soldiers, assisted by pro-Government civilians (known as 'resistance fighters'). Meanwhile, Gerard Sinato was elected as the new Premier of the Bougainville Transitional Government.

In late 1996 there was an increase in violence by the BRA, with government troops and 'resistance fighters' becoming involved in a series of attacks on civilians (for which both sides denied responsibility). The Red Cross temporarily suspended its operations on the island following an attack on one of its vehicles.

In February 1997, in response to unofficial reports, Prime Minister Chan confirmed that a company based in the United Kingdom, Sandline International (a subsidiary of Executive Outcomes, a supplier of private armed forces in Africa), had been commissioned to provide military advice and training for soldiers on Bougainville. Subsequent reports of mercenary activity on the island and of the large-scale purchase of military equipment and of weapons provoked condemnation from numerous international sources. The situation developed into a major crisis in mid-March when the Commander of the Defence Force, Brig.-Gen. (later Maj.-Gen.) Jerry Singirok, announced that the mercenaries (most of whom were from South Africa) had been captured by the armed forces and were being detained while arrangements were made for their deportation. Singirok demanded the immediate resignation of Chan, but denied that his actions constituted a coup attempt. On the following day the Prime Minister dismissed Singirok, replacing him with Col Alfred Aikung. However, the armed forces rejected the new leadership, remaining loyal to Singirok. Popular support for the army's stance became increasingly vocal, as several thousand demonstrators rampaged through the streets of the capital, looting and clashing with security forces. The contract with Sandline International was suspended and the remaining mercenaries left the country. Aikung was replaced as Commander of the Defence Force by Col Jack Tuat. However, demands for the Prime Minister's resignation intensified. Following large-scale demonstrations, an (unsuccessful) parliamentary motion of no confidence and the appeals of military, political and religious leaders, as well as the Governor-General, Chan resigned from office, along with the Deputy Prime Minister and the Minister for Defence. John Giheno, the erstwhile Minister for Mining and Petroleum, was subsequently elected acting Prime Minister.

In June 1997 an inquiry into the mercenary affair concluded that Chan had not been guilty of misconduct and, as a result (despite Giheno's stated intention to continue as acting Prime Minister until a general election had taken place), Chan announced his immediate resumption of his former position. Shortly after resuming office, Chan again provoked controversy by re-appointing Col Leo Nuia to the position of Commander of the Defence Force (see above).

A second inquiry into the mercenary affair, begun following the election of a new Government and based on broader criteria, concluded in September 1998 that former Deputy Prime Minister Chris Haiveta had been the beneficiary of corrupt payments from Sandline, and upheld the first inquiry's finding that Chan had not been guilty of any wrongdoing. In the same month an international tribunal ruled that the Government owed $A28m. to Sandline in outstanding payments under the mercenary contract. Meanwhile, government soldiers reacted angrily to the prosecution of military leaders involved in the operation to oust Sandline mercenaries from Bougainville in March. Nuia was imprisoned in his barracks by members of the Defence Force, while Maj. Walter Enuma, who was being held while awaiting trial on charges of 'raising an illegal force', was freed by rebel soldiers.

Throughout 1997 talks were held at the Burnham army base in New Zealand between secessionists and representatives of the Bougainville Transitional Government, which concluded in October with the signing of the 'Burnham Truce'. Both sides agreed to a series of interim measures, which included refraining from acts of armed confrontation pending a formal meeting of government and secessionist leaders in early 1998. The Prime Ministers of both Papua New Guinea and Solomon Islands made an extended visit to Bougainville in December 1997 to demonstrate their united support for the truce; however, Ona, who appeared to be becoming increasingly marginalized within the BRA, refused to give his support. Further talks held at Lincoln University in Christchurch, New Zealand, in January 1998 resulted in the 'Lincoln Agreement', providing for an extension to the truce, the initiation of a disarmament process and the phased withdrawal of government troops from the island. The Prime Minister also issued a public apology for the mistakes of successive administrations during the conflict, which was estimated to have resulted in the deaths of some 20,000 people.

A permanent cease-fire agreement was signed in Arawa on 30 April 1998. Ona declined to take part in the ceremony, reiterating his opposition to the peace agreement. In June government troops were withdrawn from Arawa, and reconstruction projects on Bougainville were initiated.

In August 1998 more than 2,000 representatives from different groups in Bougainville met in Buin (in the south of the island) to discuss their response to the 'Burnham Truce'. In the resultant 'Buin Declaration' the islanders stated their united aspiration for independence through peaceful negotiation. In October the National Parliament voted to amend the Constitution to allow the Bougainville Reconciliation Government to replace the Bougainville Transitional Government. The new authority came into existence on 1 January 1999, following the renewed suspension of the Bougainville provincial government, and at its first sitting elected Sinato and Kabui as its co-leaders. In April an agreement signed by Bougainville and Papua New Guinea government representatives (although not acknowledged by the BRA), known as the Matakana and Okataina Understanding, reaffirmed both sides' commitment to the cease-fire, while undertaking to discuss options for the political future of the island. Elections to the Bougainville People's Congress (BPC, formerly the Bougainville Reconciliation Government) were held in early May 1999, and were reported to have proceeded smoothly. At the first session of the BPC, Kabui was elected President by an overwhelming majority, securing 77 of the 87 votes, thus defeating his former co-leader, Sinato, who received only 10 votes. Kabui subsequently appointed 29 members to the Congressional Executive Council. Ona refused Kabui's offer to join the BPC. At a subsequent session of the Council, Kabui announced his intention to campaign for independence for Bougainville. In response, Prime Minister Bill Skate stated that, although there was no possibility of independence (as this was not provided for in the Constitution), Parliament would consider terms for greater autonomy for the island. In August the suspension of the Bougainville provincial government was extended for a further six months in an attempt to find a peaceful resolution to the autonomy issue. Following a visit to the province, the Minister for Bougainville Affairs and for Foreign Affairs, Sir Michael Somare (as he had become), stated that the Government was willing to grant the island a greater degree of autonomy. Somare proposed that Bougainville be self-governing in all matters except foreign affairs, defence and policing, all of which would remain the responsibility of the central Government. The proposal was welcomed by members of the BPC, although they also announced their intention not to surrender their weapons until the Government had agreed to hold a referendum on independence.

In October 1999 a Supreme Court ruling declared the suspension of the Bougainville provincial government illegal on technical grounds. On 9 December the provincial government was formally recognized, in theory: in effect, however, the provincial government comprised only four members—the Bougainville Regional Member of Parliament, John Momis, who thus became Governor-elect (although he agreed not to exercise his powers for the time being) and the three other Bougainville parliamentarians. Further talks regarding the future status of Bougainville between Somare and members of the BPC, the BRA and elders of the island took place in December 1999 and March 2000, and an agreement was subsequently signed. Known as the Loloata Understanding, this allowed for the eventual holding of a referendum on independence, once full autonomy had been implemented, and the formal establishment of the Bougainville Interim Provincial Government (BIPG), composed of an Executive Council and a 25-member Provincial Assembly (including the four original members).

At the end of March 2000 the Provincial Assembly and the Executive Council were sworn in by the Governor-General. Six seats were left vacant in the Provincial Assembly for other Bougainville officials such as Kabui and Ona; however, Kabui stated that, rather than joining the BIPG, he would await the establishment of a fully autonomous government (which he hoped would be in place by early 2001). In May 2000 the Office of Bougainville Affairs was renamed the Office of Peace and Reconstruction. In July Somare approved an allocation of K200,000, as part of a scheme co-ordinated by the United Nations Development Programme (UNDP), to facilitate the collection and disposal of weapons held by dissident groups. Uncertainties regarding the proposed date of a referendum, as well as concerns about renewed Australian funding of the Papua New Guinea Defence Force troops stationed on Bougainville and the BRA's failure to begin disarmament, continued to delay the progress of negotiations. Following a further round of peace talks in November, Kabui confirmed that he had secured an agreement from Somare that a future referendum would include a legally binding option of independence, although disagreement over how soon the vote should be held persisted. In the following month Somare was abruptly dismissed from his ministerial position and replaced by Bart Philemon; Morauta believed Somare was impeding the progress of the Political Parties Integrity Bill (see above).

In February 2001 agreement on the terms of the referendum was finally reached following the intervention of the Australian Minister for Foreign Affairs. The agreement stated that the referendum would be held in 10–15 years' time and would contain the option of independence. In the interim the provincial government was to be granted increased autonomy and the BRA would be expected to disarm. Despite a temporary breakdown in negotiations, in early May commanders of the BRA and the Bougainville Resistance Force (BRF, a militia that was allied to the Government during the civil conflict on Bougainville) signed an agreement to surrender their weapons. In late June Moi Avei, who had replaced Philemon as Minister for Bougainville Affairs in May, announced that negotiations had resulted in a comprehensive agreement on autonomy for the island, with the Government ceding to demands that Bougainville be accorded its own system of criminal law and an autonomous police force. It was also agreed that the Papua New Guinea Defence Force's jurisdiction on the island would be strictly limited. On 30 August the Government and island leaders signed the Bougainville Peace Agreement in Arawa. Although he signed the accord, which was still to be approved by the National Parliament, Toroama stated that the BRA would campaign for the referendum to be held in three–five years' time and would continue to seek full independence. (Francis Ona did not attend the signing ceremony; he died in July 2005.)

Weapons disposal by the BRA and BRF began in early December 2001, and the UN Observer Mission on Bougainville (UNOMB) formally acknowledged the Bougainville Peace Agreement later in that month. In January 2002 the National Parliament unanimously endorsed the Organic Law enacting the Bougainville Peace Agreement, along with a bill containing the requisite constitutional amendment. A second vote, held in late March, ratified the legislation, and the Papua New Guinea Defence Force began its withdrawal from Bougainville. The withdrawal of troops was completed in late December.

In August 2003 the Government of Papua New Guinea formally announced its plan for autonomy in Bougainville, allowing provincial authorities to proceed with the establishment of a constitution and the eventual organization of elections for an autonomous government leader and local assembly. In March 2004 the BIPG approved legislation providing for its merger with the BPC to establish the Bougainville Constituent Assembly (BCA), which was finally convened later that month to consider the third and final draft of the proposed constitution. In mid-December the Government of Papua New Guinea finally approved Bougainville's Constitution, and the UN agreed to extend its Observer Mission by a further six months to cover the period of the forthcoming election. Elections for the President of the new Autonomous Bougainville Government (ABG) and for the 39 members of the first local assembly began on 20 May 2005 and continued for two weeks to allow islanders, some of whom had to travel for several days on foot or by canoe, sufficient time to reach the polling stations. Despite some attempts by armed rebels to disrupt the election process, it was deemed to have been largely successful. Joseph Kabui was declared to be Bougainville's first President, with 37,928 votes, defeating several other candidates (the closest of whom, former Governor John Momis, received 23,861 votes). The inauguration of the autonomous assembly took place on 14 June and was attended by most members of the Cabinet, as well as by several foreign dignitaries. Kabui appointed his 10-member cabinet several days later.

The leader of the Observer Mission left Papua New Guinea at the beginning of August 2005. Also in August the Government announced its commitment to ensuring that a referendum on the independence of Bougainville be carried out by 2020. In March 2006 the ABG requested UN assistance in the ongoing efforts to resolve peacefully the issue of five former Fijian soldiers who, it was reported, were training a militia group in the south-west of Bougainville, under direction from alleged fraudster and self-proclaimed 'King of Me'ekamui', Noah Musingku. In May clashes in Buin and Siwai between police and activists reportedly linked to Musingku raised fears of a renewed civil conflict. It was reported that a Me'ekamui rebel faction had joined Musingku, who had retreated to Tonu in Siwai and erected a roadblock in the area. In June the Bougainville police affirmed that the authorities were negotiating with Musingku's supporters, and in the following month the Fijian High Commission in Papua New Guinea confirmed its participation in discussions to repatriate the Fijian fugitives, who remained at Musingku's camp but had allegedly requested safe passage out. Following further discussions, Musingku and local chiefs submitted to the ABG proposals for local development in the area, and at the end of October Musingku declared his willingness to begin containing his group's weapons. At the beginning of November, however, the Bougainville Freedom Fighters (BFF), a group of former combatants from Buin and Siwai aligned with the ABG, conveyed its dissatisfaction with the negotiation process and speed of disarmament. Later in that month the BFF reportedly carried out an offensive against Musingku's base, resulting in the deaths of four of his bodyguards and injuring Musingku, who apparently escaped to Siwai with the Fijian fugitives. It later emerged that the Bougainville police had formed part of the offensive, but Tsiamalili refuted suggestions that the ABG had been involved. The Fijian members of Musingku's group were, according to the latter, refusing to leave the area without the millions of dollars in salaries promised to them by Musingku, and did not surrender until February 2007, when they were charged with 'raising an illegal force' at a Buka court. Four of these members were released in February 2008 owing to lack of evidence; two others reportedly remained with Musingku. Meanwhile, the 'Me'ekamui Government of Unity' organization was said to have entered into an agreement with the ABG in August 2007, signalling a new phase of co-operation.

In September 2000 a group of landowners from Bougainville initiated legal action in a US court against Rio Tinto, the operator of the Panguna copper mine between 1972 and 1988. The group was reported to be suing the company for the environmental and social damage caused by its activities, including health problems experienced by workers and islanders living near the mine. Moreover, their case alleged that the company had effectively transformed the Papua New Guinea Defence Force into its own private army and was therefore responsible for the deaths of some 15,000 civilians in military action and a further 10,000 as a result of the economic blockade on the island. In 2007 the US Ninth Court of Appeals upheld the Bougainville residents' right to sue, and the case was continuing in early 2009. A committee was established by the provincial Government in late 2005 to work on reopening the mine following an overwhelming vote in favour of the proposal.

In early June 2008 Joseph Kabui, the President of Bougainville, died of a heart attack. John Tabinaman was appointed as his temporary replacement, pending the scheduling of an election. Although it was initially proposed that a new president be chosen by the Bougainville Assembly, a by-election was held in December, at which James Tanis, an unsuccessful opponent of Kabui in the first presidential election in 2005, secured victory. However, the election process was criticized, as the electoral rolls were alleged to be incorrect. In January 2009 Tanis was sworn in, and in mid-February it was reported that as part of his policy of reconciliation, he was attending discussions with Musingku and working towards the resolution of the Panguna issue. Discussions between Somare and Tanis in February resulted in statements reaffirming both leaders' commitment to peace.

In 1984 more than 9,000 refugees crossed into Papua New Guinea from the Indonesian province of Irian Jaya (officially known as Papua from January 2002), as a consequence of operations by the Indonesian army against Melanesian rebels of the pro-independence Organisasi Papua Merdeka (Free Papua Movement—OPM). For many years relations between Papua New Guinea and Indonesia had been strained by the conflict in Irian Jaya, not least because the independence movement drew sympathy from many among the largely Melanesian population of Papua New Guinea. A new border treaty was signed in October 1984, and attempts were made to repatriate the refugees, based on assurances by the Indonesian Government that there would be no reprisals against those who returned. In October 1985 representatives of the Papua New Guinea and Indonesian Governments signed a treaty providing for the settlement of disputes by consultation, arbitration and 'other peaceful means'. However, the treaty provoked strong criticism among opposition politicians in Papua New Guinea, who claimed that it effectively precluded the censure of any violation of human rights in Irian Jaya. In 1988 the Government condemned the incursions by Indonesian soldiers into Papua New Guinea, in search of OPM members, and the resultant violence and killings, as a breach of bilateral accords, and affirmed that Papua New Guinea would not support Indonesia in its attempt to suppress the OPM. In late 1995 the Indonesian consulate in the border town of Vanimo was attacked by OPM rebels and a subsequent increase in Indonesian troops along the border was reported. Violent confrontations resulted in the killing of several rebels and security personnel and the kidnapping by OPM activists of some 200 villagers. Australia urged the Papua New Guinea Government to accept several thousand refugees living in camps along the border, and in May 1996 the Government announced that 3,500 Irian Jayans would be allowed to remain in Papua New Guinea on condition that they were not involved in OPM activities. In mid-1998, on an official visit to Indonesia, Prime Minister Bill Skate signed a memorandum of understanding on bilateral relations, which was expected to provide the basis for closer co-operation in political, economic and defence matters. Under the terms of the agreement, troop numbers along the border were increased in March 1999. In May of that year 11 Javanese people were taken hostage and three people were reported to have been killed by OPM rebels in the West Sepik Province of Papua New Guinea. The hostages were later released as a result of the intervention of Papua New Guinea security forces. The OPM subsequently demanded an inquiry into the operation leading to the release of the hostages, after its communications director was allegedly shot dead at a border post. During 2000 hundreds of refugees were voluntarily repatriated to Indonesia (including more than 600 in a major operation in early September), although approximately 7,000 were believed to remain in Papua New Guinea in September. In late 2000 it was reported that Indonesian security forces had made some 400 incursions into Papua New Guinea in the previous two months while pursuing separatists. In December the border with Irian Jaya was officially closed.

In January 2003 the Papua New Guinea Government denied a number of security breaches, which were reported to have occurred along its border with Indonesia. Concerns grew following a dramatic increase in the numbers of Indonesian troops along the border, from some 150 in late 2002 to a reported 1,500 in early 2003. In late January the Government of Papua New Guinea ordered its security forces to arrest OPM rebels believed to be staying in refugee camps along the border, following complaints from the Indonesian authorities that rebels based there were carrying out operations in the province of Papua. The Government also confirmed in April that it had been unable to persuade more than 400 Papuans living in a camp near the border town of Vanimo to return to Indonesia, despite assurances that their safety would not be at risk. In July 2004 it was announced that Vanuatu would host a series of negotiations between the Indonesian authorities and Papuan separatists. In January 2009 it was reported that 700 West Papuans would voluntarily return to Indonesia, although observers were sceptical about their reasons for departing.

In regional affairs, relations with Australia have been affected by various developments. In December 2003, following the apparent success of the intervention in Solomon Islands earlier in the year, Australia announced the deployment of some 250 of its security personnel to different regions of Papua New Guinea, as part of plans for a five-year operation costing US $325m., aimed at restoring order to troubled areas of the country. Moreover, the Australian Government was to send up to 70 officials to Papua New Guinea to take up senior public roles in the spheres of finance, justice, public sector management, immigration, border security and transport safety. The agreement, known as the Enhanced Co-operation Program (ECP), was officially concluded in June 2004 and incorporated a total aid 'package' worth US $690m. Prime Minister Somare had initially been reluctant to accept Australia's expanded role in the country, fearing that it would erode national sovereignty, but had been obliged to reconsider when the Australian Prime Minister, John Howard, implied that aid payments to Papua New Guinea were dependent on the country's co-operation. A report by the Australian Strategic Policy Institute, published in December 2004, claimed that Papua New Guinea risked economic and social collapse. It urged the Australian Government to intervene further in the country by radically increasing the amount of aid it provided and by taking control of some aspects of government, particularly immigration. Research by the organization indicated that government and state institutions had become too weak to prevent drugs and weapons smuggling, human trafficking and money-laundering activities, operated by international criminal groups, which had relocated to Papua New Guinea from South-East Asia in recent years. Furthermore, an investigation carried out by Australian journalists, the results of which were published in early 2005, alleged that Chinese mafia groups had infiltrated the highest levels of Papua New Guinea's police force. According to the report, the corruption of the country's authorities was facilitating serious criminal activities that posed a threat to the national security of Australia. It was also believed that the criminals had been recruiting Port Moresby's notorious 'raskol' gangs (groups of heavily armed, disaffected young men responsible for much of the violent crime in the capital) to commit armed robberies, assaults and other crimes in support of their activities.

The ECP suffered a serious reversal in May 2005 when Papua New Guinea's Supreme Court ruled that the deployment of Australian security personnel in the country was unconstitutional (principally because they had been given immunity from prosecution). Personnel began to return to Australia shortly after the ruling. Relations between the two countries had deteriorated in March when Prime Minister Sir Michael Somare had been subjected to a security search at Brisbane airport. A demonstration by more than 7,000 people in Lae, demanding an apology from Australia for the incident and accusing that country's authorities of showing contempt and disrespect for Papua New Guinea, took place in the following month. In October, following revisions to the ECP, it was announced that Australia was to commit as many as 40 police officers to assist the local forces in a renewed attempt to curb the increasing levels of violence and crime in the country. The dispatch of the new police component was part of the revised ECP. In February 2006 an internal police investigation that had begun in 2003 revealed that as many as 66 police officers had been implicated in corrupt activities, such as receiving funds from Asian crime syndicates.

Relations between the two countries became increasingly strained towards the end of 2006 over the extradition of the newly appointed Solomon Islands Attorney-General, Julian Moti, who was wanted by the authorities in Australia on a child molestation charge (see the chapter on Australia). Moti had been arrested in Port Moresby in September, but escaped to Solomon Islands at the beginning of October, reportedly on an aircraft of the Papua New Guinea Defence Force. Prime Minister Somare denied any knowledge of the operation, which he described as setting a 'dangerous precedent'. Australia subsequently imposed a ban on ministerial exchanges with Papua New Guinea and ministerial-level travel to Australia. At the end of the month the Papua New Guinea Government recalled its High Commissioner to Australia, Charles Lepani, for consultations, amid fears that the dispute would intensify. In November it was reported that the Papua New Guinea Chief Secretary, the Commander of the Defence Force and the acting Police Commissioner had been suspended, ostensibly owing to the Moti affair. Meanwhile, Prime Minister Somare indicated that, according to the findings of an investigation into the incident, Moti's arrest might not have followed correct procedures; both Papua New Guinean and Australian officials were implicated. The newly appointed Minister for Foreign Affairs, Paul Tiensten, declared his aim of restoring normal relations with Australia. The progress of a Papua New Guinea Defence Force inquiry was closely scrutinized by both countries in early 2007. In February, following a testimony that Somare had given instructions to fly Moti out to Solomon Islands, the inquiry issued a summons to the Prime Minister, prompting him to criticize it for exceeding its jurisdiction. Somare's dismissal of the Minister for Defence, Martin Aini, who had established the board of inquiry and admitted that the Prime Minister had exerted pressure on him to disband it, prompted further speculation over Somare's involvement. In September 2007 the National Court overruled Somare's attempt to dismiss the inquiry's conclusions. According to media sources, the report alleged that Somare had given the order to fly Moti out of the country and was therefore liable to prosecution. In October the new Minister for Defence, Bob Dadae, rejected the findings of the report on the basis that the 'composition of the board was not legally constituted'. Relations between Papua New Guinea and Australia appeared to improve when the latter removed its ban on contact between ministers of the two countries in September. The new Australian Prime Minister, Kevin Rudd, paid a three-day visit to Papua New Guinea in March 2008.

In April 2009 Prime Minister Somare embarked upon a visit to Australia for discussions on both political and business issues. At a press conference given by Somare and the Australian Prime Minister, Kevin Rudd criticized the distribution of Australia's aid in Papua New Guinea, stating that too much aid was being spent on the engagement of consultants. Somare refuted Rudd's claim, maintaining that resources were being devoted to areas where funding was most needed.

From 1990 relations with Solomon Islands were overshadowed by the conflict on Bougainville. Solomon Islands (the inhabitants of which are culturally and ethnically very similar to Bougainville islanders) protested against repeated incursions by Papua New Guinea defence forces into Solomon Islands' territorial waters, while the Papua New Guinea Government consistently accused Solomon Islands of harbouring members of the BRA and providing them with supplies. Despite several attempts during the 1990s to improve the situation between the two countries (including an agreement by Solomon Islands in 1993 to close the BRA office in the capital, Honiara), relations remained tense. In April 1997 the Solomon Islands Government announced that it was considering the initiation of proceedings against the Papua New Guinea Government concerning the latter's attempted use of mercenaries on Bougainville (see above). In June of that year Papua New Guinea and Solomon Islands concluded a maritime border agreement, following several years of negotiations. The purpose of the agreement (which took effect in January 1998) was not only to delineate the sea boundary between the two countries but also to provide a framework for co-operation in matters of security, natural disaster, customs, quarantine, immigration and conservation. In March 2000 relations between Papua New Guinea and Solomon Islands were further strengthened following the opening of a Solomon Islands High Commission in Port Moresby. In March 2004 the two countries signed a number of treaties and agreements relating to the management of their common border area.

Concerns were expressed in mid-2003 that the rebel Solomon Islands leader Harold Keke (alleged to be responsible for a campaign of terror in Solomon Islands) was recruiting new members for his Guadalcanal Liberation Force in Bougainville and strengthening his links with the BRA. These fears were exacerbated by sightings of Keke in Buka and Bougainville and attacks against journalists who had reported on the activities of Keke's supporters (including the stockpiling of weapons) along the border between Papua New Guinea and Solomon Islands. However, in August the Governor of Bougainville, John Momis, officially stated that he did not believe that any link existed between Keke and the BRA. In that month Keke surrendered and was arrested by the regional peace-keeping force in Solomon Islands.

Diplomatic relations with the People's Republic of China were established in 1976. In February 2004 Prime Minister Sir Michael Somare led a delegation of 80 officials (the largest such group Papua New Guinea had ever sent on a state visit) to China. Almost one-half of the delegates were representatives from the mining sector, who were hoping to secure agreements with Chinese interests relating to petroleum, gas and other mineral developments in Papua New Guinea.

In March 1988 Papua New Guinea signed an agreement with Vanuatu and Solomon Islands to form the Melanesian Spearhead Group, which was subsequently joined by Fiji. The grouping was dedicated to the preservation of Melanesian cultural traditions and to achieving independence for the French Overseas Territory of New Caledonia. In March 2007 the members of the Melanesian Spearhead Group signed a constitution. In 1989 Papua New Guinea increased its links with South-East Asia, signing a Treaty of Amity and Co-operation with the Association of South East Asian Nations (ASEAN, see p. 194).

By the early 21st century various environmental concerns were increasingly being expressed. Fears that rising sea-levels might have very serious consequences for Pacific islanders intensified in May 2003 when an emergency operation was undertaken to save the inhabitants of Carteret and Mortlock islands, near Bougainville. Food supplies were sent to the islands, the 2,000 inhabitants of which were reported to be suffering from starvation and health problems related to poor diet, since the failure of their crops, which had been flooded by sea water. However, the islanders were reluctant to accept a government proposal to relocate them to Bougainville, fearing the loss of their distinct Polynesian culture and way of life. In September 2008 it was reported that the proposed relocation of families was finally to commence in phases in 2009. The country was beset by a series of severe floods in late 2003 and early 2004 which affected some 5,000 people in Morobe Province and more than 10,000 in West Highlands Province.

The growing exploitation of Papua New Guinea's natural resources led to much anxiety about the impact of the operations of numerous foreign business interests on the environment. Activity in the forestry sector increased dramatically in the early 1990s, and an official report published in 1994 indicated that the current rate of logging was three times the sustainable yield of the country's forests. However, attempts to introduce new regulations to govern the industry were strongly opposed by several Malaysian logging companies with operations in the country. In early 2000, however, environmentalists welcomed a commitment by the Papua New Guinea Government to impose a moratorium on all new forestry licences and to review all existing licences. Concern continued among conservation organizations as the Government failed to enforce laws promoting sustainable forestry activity, which if upheld were deemed sufficient to ensure the long-term survival of the forestry sector. Conservationists hoped that pressure from consumers in the destination countries might lead to a reduction in illegal logging.

Considerable environmental damage has also resulted from the exploitation of the country's extensive mineral resources. In 1989 the Government gave Ok Tedi Mining Ltd (OTML), the owners of a gold and copper mine, permission to discharge 150,000 metric tons of toxic waste per day into the Fly River. In 1994 6,000 people living in the region began a compensation claim against the Australian company operating the mine for damage caused by the resultant pollution. A settlement worth some $A110m. was reached in an Australian court in 1995 (and a further settlement worth $A400m. for the establishment of a containment system was concluded in mid-1996), despite opposition from the Papua New Guinea Government, which feared that such action might adversely affect the country's prospects of attracting foreign investment in the future. Similar claims were initiated by people living near the Australian-controlled Porgera gold-mine in early 1996 for pollution of the Strickland River system, as well as by landowners near the Kutubu oilfield. The results of an independent study into the effects of mining activities by OTML, published in mid-1999, showed that damage to the environment might be greater than originally believed. The results of an independent review, carried out by the World Bank and published in March 2000, recommended the closure of the mine on environmental grounds, but also emphasized the potentially damaging impact of the mine's early closure on both the local economy and world copper markets. In October 2001 BHP Billiton, the Australian operator, announced its withdrawal from the OTML venture and in early 2002 it transferred its 52% stake in the company to a development fund called the PNG Sustainable Development Programme Ltd. In early 2006 the managing director of OTML acknowledged that mining operations had caused major damage to the Ok Tedi and Fly River systems, resulting in flooding and forest die-back. Furthermore, the toxic effects of this waste were now believed to be threatening supplies of ground and drinking water.

Government

Executive power is vested in the British monarch (the Head of State), represented locally by the Governor-General, who is appointed on the proposal of the National Executive Council (the Cabinet) in accordance with the decision of the National Parliament by simple majority vote. The Governor-General acts on the advice of the National Executive Council, which is led by the Prime Minister. The Prime Minister is appointed and dismissed by the Head of State on the proposal of the National Parliament. Legislative power is vested in the unicameral National Parliament, with 109 members elected by universal adult suffrage for a term of five years. The National Executive Council is responsible to the National Parliament. The local government system underwent extensive reform in 1995, when the directly elected provincial governments were replaced by new regional authorities, composed of members of the National Parliament and local councillors, and led by an appointed Governor. The National Capital District (NCD) has its own governing body. Papua New Guinea comprises 20 provinces.

In January 2005 the National Government approved the final draft of the proposed Constitution for the province of Bougainville, and elections for the President of the new autonomous Government and for the 39 members of the House of Representatives commenced in May (see Recent History). In mid-June the new President was duly sworn in and the House of Representatives was inaugurated.

Defence

As assessed at November 2008, Papua New Guinea's national Defence Force numbered an estimated 3,100, comprising an army of 2,500, a navy of 400 and an air force of 200. In addition, 38 troops from Australia were stationed in the country for training purposes. Military service is voluntary. Budget estimates for 2008 allocated K101m. to defence.

Economic Affairs

In 2007, according to estimates by the World Bank, Papua New Guinea's gross national income (GNI), measured at average 2005–07 prices, was US $5,400m., equivalent to $850 per head (or $1,870 per head on an international purchasing-power parity basis). During 2000–07, it was estimated, the population increased at an average annual rate of 2.3%, while gross domestic product (GDP) per head remained constant in real terms. Overall GDP increased, in real terms, at an average annual rate of 2.4% in 2000–07. According to the Asian Development Bank (ADB), real GDP increased by 6.2% in 2007 and 7.2% in 2008.

Agriculture (including hunting, forestry and fishing) contributed 35.1% of GDP in 2007. In mid-2005, according to FAO, the sector engaged an estimated 71.4% of the labour force. The principal cash crops are oil palm (palm oil accounting for 4.8% of export earnings in 2007) and coffee (coffee beans accounting for 2.9% of export earnings in 2007). Other significant crops are cocoa and coconuts (for the production of copra and coconut oil), rubber, tea and vanilla. Roots and tubers, vegetables, bananas and melons are grown as food crops. Forestry is an important activity, and Papua New Guinea is one of the world's largest exporters of unprocessed tropical timber. Exports of forest products accounted for almost 4.6% of total export earnings in 2007, when revenue reached US $631m., compared with $527m. in the previous year. However, there is serious concern about the environmental damage caused by extensive logging activity in the country. The sale of fishing licences to foreign fleets has provided a substantial source of revenue. Most of the tuna caught by foreign operators is shipped directly overseas. During 2000–06, according to figures from the World Bank, agricultural GDP increased at an average annual rate of 0.5%. According to the ADB, the GDP of the agricultural sector expanded by 3.8% in 2007 and by 5.0% in 2008.

Industry (including mining, manufacturing, construction and power) contributed an estimated 44.4% of GDP in 2007. During 2000–06 industrial GDP decreased by an average of 2.5% per year, according to figures from the World Bank. The ADB estimated that industrial GDP increased by 7.6% in 2007 and by 7.8% in 2008.

Mining and quarrying provided an estimated 27.2% of GDP in 2007. Copper (which accounted for an estimated 30.1% of the country's total export revenue in 2007), gold (26.5%) and crude petroleum (21.5%) are the sector's major exports. Other mineral deposits include cobalt, nickel, silver, chromite and quartz. The country's largest petroleum refinery, at Napa Napa, began production in 2004. Papua New Guinea also has substantial reserves of natural gas. Construction of a 700-km pipeline from Southern Highlands to the capital of Port Moresby was expected to commence in 2010, part of a liquefied natural gas project (LNG), which was scheduled for completion in 2013/14 (see below). The GDP of the mining sector was estimated to have expanded at an average annual rate of 2.8% during 2003–07, inceasing by 4.1% in the latter year.

Manufacturing contributed an estimated 5.9% of GDP in 2007. The sector is limited, employing only 1.1% of the working population in 2000. The principal branches of manufacturing are food products, beverages, tobacco, wood products, metal products, machinery and transport equipment. Several fish canneries were established in the 1990s and exports of canned tuna were expected to increase significantly, following the signing of a new quota agreement with the European Union (EU) in March 2003. A major tuna-loining plant in Wewak, processing 110 metric tons of fish per day, provides direct employment for 1,900 people. According to the World Bank, during 2000–06 manufacturing GDP increased by an average of 2.6% per year. Compared with the previous year, the sector's GDP expanded by 4.0% in 2007, according to figures from the ADB.

Energy is derived principally from hydroelectric power, which in 2000 accounted for more than 50% of electricity supplies. Output of electric energy reached 1,399m. kWh in 2004. However, more than 90% of the population are estimated to have no access to electricity, and in early 2009, with assistance from the ADB, the Government was in the process of formulating a new development plan for the country's power sector. In 2004 fuel imports accounted for 16.7% of the value of total merchandise imports.

The services sector contributed an estimated 20.5% of GDP in 2007, according to the ADB. Tourism is an expanding industry, although political instability and reports of widespread violent crime have had a detrimental effect on the sector. Total foreign visitor arrivals were reported to have increased from 104,122 in 2007 to 114,182 in 2008. Tourism receipts were worth an estimated US $3.7m. in 2005. The GDP of the services sector increased at an average annual rate of 2.8% in 2000–06, according to figures from the World Bank. The sector's GDP expanded by 9.4% in 2007 and by 9.2% in 2008, according to the ADB.

In 2007 Papua New Guinea recorded a visible trade surplus of K6,282m., and a surplus of K550m. on the current account of the balance of payments. In 2007 the principal source of imports (51.2%) was Australia; other major suppliers were Singapore (11.5%), the People's Republic of China (7.6%), Japan, Indonesia, New Zealand, the and the USA. In that year Australia was also the principal market for exports (26.1%), followed by Japan (9.3%), China and Germany. The principal exports were copper, gold, crude petroleum, forestry products, palm oil, coffee beans and cocoa. The principal imports included machinery and transport equipment, basic manufactures, food and live animals, miscellaneous manufactured articles, chemicals and mineral fuels.

The budget for 2008 (excluding grants from abroad) projected a surplus of K999.1m. The ADB calculated that, if adjusted to take account of trust funds, this surplus was equivalent to 12% of GDP. The 2009 budget envisaged expenditure of K7,600m., of which K2,590m. was allocated to the development budget. Papua New Guinea receives grants for budgetary aid from Australia. In 2008/09 official development assistance from Australia was projected at $A389.4m., while New Zealand's allocation of aid totalled $NZ23.0m. According to the ADB, Papua New Guinea's external debt totalled US $1,061m. at the end of 2008. In 2007 the cost of debt-servicing was equivalent to 2.3% of the value of exports of goods and services. A large informal sector supports the majority of the population. At the census of 2000, 2.8% of the registered labour force were reported to be unemployed. In urban areas, however, the unemployment rate was estimated at some 70%. In the rural areas underemployment remained a serious problem. The annual rate of inflation averaged 7.0% in 2000–06. Consumer prices increased by only 0.9% in 2007 but by 10.8% in 2008.

Papua New Guinea is a member of Asia-Pacific Economic Cooperation (APEC, see p. 185), the Asian Development Bank (ADB, see p. 191), the Colombo Plan (see p. 425), the Pacific Community (see p. 391), the Pacific Islands Forum (see p. 393), the UN Economic and Social Commission for Asia and the Pacific (ESCAP, see p. 36), the World Trade Organization (WTO, see p. 410), the International Cocoa Organization (see p. 422) and the International Coffee Organization (see p. 422). Papua New Guinea is also a member of the Melanesian Spearhead Group, which among other benefits provides for free trade among member countries (the others being Fiji, Solomon Islands and Vanuatu).

Papua New Guinea's development has been impeded by the lack of infrastructure and its vulnerability to extreme climatic conditions. The Government's Medium Term Development Strategy for 2005–10 focused on improvements to the transport network. The plan also stressed the importance of wider opportunities for the generation of income within the agricultural sector, and the improvement of the country's basic education and health services, with emphasis on the prevention of HIV/AIDS. In May 2007 it was announced that the EU was to allocate US $159m. to various development projects in Papua New Guinea, over a six-year period commencing in 2008. Foreign investment has often been discouraged by the country's high levels of crime and associated security costs. In March 2008, however, following several years of relative political stability and an improvement in the management of public finances, Papua New Guinea was categorized by a leading international ratings agency, for the first time, as a stable destination for foreign investment. The country's long-term prospects were also greatly enhanced by plans for a major LNG project and export facility (see above), which were to be developed in collaboration with an international consortium. Meanwhile, the economy remained highly susceptible to fluctuations in world commodity prices. Plans to revitalize the coffee industry, encompassing the period 2008–18, were to be implemented, in an attempt to counter the weakening of global coffee prices and the changes in the country's climatic conditions of recent years. In the Highlands region crops of both coffee and tea were damaged by heavy flooding in early 2009. Between 2006 and mid-2008 the strength of prices for gold, copper, petroleum and timber was very advantageous to

PAPUA NEW GUINEA

Papua New Guinea, while the Government also benefited from an increase in its revenue from taxes on the mining sector. However, the steep decline in international commodity prices in the latter part of 2008 had a major impact on the economy. The inflation rate rose sharply in 2008, mainly owing to the higher costs of fuel and foodstuffs, but inflationary pressures were expected to ease in 2009. Having expanded by more than 7% in 2008, the highest rate of growth for a decade, GDP was forecast by the ADB to increase by 4.0% in 2009.

Education

Education is not compulsory. Primary education, available at community schools, begins at seven years of age and lasts for six years. Secondary education, beginning at the age of 13, lasts for up to six years (comprising two cycles, the first of four years, the second two). Originally, schooling was free; fees and charges for equipment were introduced, although the 2002 budget provided for the reinstatement of free education. In 2002/03 enrolment at pre-primary schools was equivalent to 59% of pupils in the relevant age-group (males 61%; females 57%). In the same year enrolment at primary schools was equivalent to 75.4% of children in the relevant age-group (80% of boys; 70% of girls) and secondary enrolment was equivalent to 25.8% of children in the relevant age-group (boys 29%; girls 23%). Tertiary education is provided by the University of Papua New Guinea and the University of Technology. There are also teacher-training colleges and higher institutions, which cater for specific professional training, such as a medical school, which had a total enrolment of 656 students in early 2005. Budget allocations for 2006 granted K43m. to the education sector. In February 2006 it was announced that the European Union was to grant a total of K156m. over the next six years in support of education and training in Papua New Guinea. The Government hoped that this would enable it to provide universal primary education by 2015 and to eliminate gender disparities.

Public Holidays

2009: 1 January (New Year's Day), 10–13 April (Easter), 8 June (Queen's Official Birthday), 23 July (Remembrance Day), 16 September (Independence Day and Constitution Day), 25 December (Christmas Day), 26 December (Boxing Day).

2010: 1 January (New Year's Day), 2–5 April (Easter), 9 June (Queen's Official Birthday), 23 July (Remembrance Day), 16 September (Independence Day and Constitution Day), 25 December (Christmas Day), 26 December (Boxing Day).

Weights and Measures

The metric system is in force.

Statistical Survey

Source (unless otherwise stated): Papua New Guinea National Statistical Office, POB 337, Waigani, NCD; tel. 3011200; fax 3251869; e-mail pmaime@nso.gov.pg; internet www.nso.gov.pg.

Area and Population

AREA, POPULATION AND DENSITY

Area (sq km)	462,840*
Population (census results)	
11 July 1990†	3,607,954
9 July 2000	
Males	2,691,744
Females	2,499,042
Total	5,190,786
Population (UN estimates at mid-year)‡	
2006	6,270,000
2007	6,423,000
2008	6,577,000
Density (per sq km) at mid-2008	14.2

* 178,704 sq miles.
† Excluding North Solomons Province (estimated population 154,000).
‡ Source: UN, *World Population Prospects: The 2008 Revision*.

PRINCIPAL TOWNS
(census of 9 July 2000, provisional)

Port Moresby (capital)	254,158	Mount Hagen	27,782
Lae	78,038	Madang	27,394
Arawa	36,443	Kokopo/Vunamami	20,262

Source: Thomas Brinkhoff, *City Population* (internet www.citypopulation.de).

Mid-2007 (incl. suburbs, UN estimate): Port Moresby 299,000 (Source: UN, *World Urbanization Prospects: The 2007 Revision*).

BIRTHS AND DEATHS
(2003)

Registered live births 192,817; Registered deaths 7,054. Registration is incomplete (Source: UN, *Population and Vital Statistics Report*).

Birth rate (per 1,000): 36.7 in 1990–95; 36.9 in 1995–2000; 34.1 in 2000–05.
Death rate (per 1,000): 10.6 in 1990–95; 10.0 in 1995–2000; 8.7 in 2000–05
(Source: UN, *World Population Prospects: The 2008 Revision*).

Life expectancy (years at birth, WHO estimates): 61.8 (males 60.2; females 63.6) in 2006 (Source: WHO, *World Health Statistics*).

ECONOMICALLY ACTIVE POPULATION
(census of 9 July 2000, persons aged 10 years and over)

Agriculture, hunting and forestry	1,666,247
Fishing	30,024
Mining and quarrying	9,282
Manufacturing	25,557
Electricity, gas and water	2,208
Construction	48,312
Wholesale and retail trade; repair of motor vehicles, motorcycles and personal and household goods	353,186
Hotels and restaurants	4,395
Transport, storage and communications	24,513
Financial intermediation	3,670
Real estate, renting and business activities	27,459
Public administration and defence; compulsory social security	32,043
Education	27,118
Health and social work	12,341
Other community, social and personal service activities	31,409
Private households with employed persons	15,523
Extra-territorial organizations and bodies	163
Activities not adequately defined	31,284
Total employed	2,344,734
Unemployed	68,623
Total labour force	2,413,357
Males	1,256,887
Females	1,156,470

Source: ILO.

Mid-2005 (estimates in '000): Agriculture, etc. 2,032; Total labour force 2,844 (Source: FAO).

Health and Welfare

KEY INDICATORS

Total fertility rate (children per woman, 2006)	4.0
Under-5 mortality rate (per 1,000 live births, 2006)	73
HIV/AIDS (% of persons aged 15–49, 2007)	1.5
Physicians (per 1,000 head, 2000)	0.05
Hospital beds (per 1,000 head, 1990)	4.0
Health expenditure (2006): US $ per head (PPP)	134
Health expenditure (2006): % of GDP	3.2
Health expenditure (2006): public (% of total)	82.7
Access to water (% of persons, 2006)	40
Access to sanitation (% of persons, 2006)	45
Human Development Index (2006): ranking	149
Human Development Index (2006): value	0.516

For sources and definitions, see explanatory note on p. vi.

Agriculture

PRINCIPAL CROPS
('000 metric tons)

	2005	2006	2007
Sweet potatoes	520*	520*	520†
Cassava (Manioc)	125*	125*	125†
Yams	290*	290*	290†
Taro (Cocoyam)	260*	260*	260†
Sugar cane	450*	450*	450†
Coconuts	651†	660*	677*
Oil palm fruit*	1,300	1,350	1,400
Pineapples*	20	20	20
Bananas*	900	870	870
Coffee, green	76.1	46.9†	75.4†
Cocoa beans†	47.8	51.1	50.3
Tea*	9	9	9
Natural rubber	4.0†	4.5†	4.7*

* FAO estimates.
† Unofficial figures.

Aggregate production ('000 metric tons, may include official, semi-official or estimated data): Total cereals 11.3 in 2005, 11.3 in 2006, 12.3 in 2007; Total oil crops 434 in 2005, 495 in 2006, 529 in 2007; Total vegetables (incl. melons) 501 in 2005, 501 in 2006, 501 in 2007; Total fruits (excl. melons) 1,866 in 2005, 890 in 2006, 890 in 2007.

Source: FAO.

LIVESTOCK
('000 head, year ending September)

	2005*	2006*	2007
Horses*	2	2	2
Cattle*	92	93	94
Pigs*	1,800	1,800	1,800
Sheep*	7	7	7
Goats*	3	3	3
Chickens	4,000	4,000	4,000†

* FAO estimates.
† Unofficial figure.
Source: FAO.

LIVESTOCK PRODUCTS
('000 metric tons, FAO estimates)

	2004	2005	2006
Cattle meat	3.1	3.1	3.2
Pig meat	68	68	68
Chicken meat	5.7	5.7	5.7
Game meat	320	330	330
Hen eggs	4.8	4.8	4.8

2007: Production assumed to be unchanged from 2006 (FAO estimates).
Source: FAO.

Forestry

ROUNDWOOD REMOVALS
('000 cubic metres, excluding bark)

	2000	2001	2002*
Sawlogs, veneer logs and logs for sleepers	2,064	1,611	1,611
Pulpwood	120	97	97
Fuel wood*	5,533	5,533	5,533
Total	7,717	7,241	7,241

* FAO estimates.

2003–07: Annual production assumed to be unchanged from 2002 (FAO estimates).
Source: FAO.

SAWNWOOD PRODUCTION
('000 cubic metres, including railway sleepers)

	2001	2002	2003
Coniferous (softwood)	—	10	10*
Broadleaved (hardwood)	40	60	50†
Total	40	70	60*

* FAO estimate.
† Unofficial figure.

2004–07: Production assumed to be unchanged from 2003 (FAO estimates).
Source: FAO.

Fishing

('000 metric tons, live weight of capture)

	2004	2005	2006
Mozambique tilapia*	2.3	2.3	2.3
Other freshwater fishes*	6.7	6.7	6.7
Sea catfishes*	1.9	1.9	1.9
Skipjack tuna	172.4	166.3	159.0
Yellowfin tuna	24.4	44.9	49.5
Total catch (incl. others)*	253.2	287.2	274.7

* FAO estimates.

Note: Figures exclude crocodiles, recorded by number rather than weight. The number of estuarine crocodiles caught was: 11,043 in 2004; 10,750 in 2005; 10,135 in 2006. The number of New Guinea crocodiles caught was: 40,358 in 2004; 20,082 in 2005; 22,351 in 2006. Figures also exclude shells (metric tons, FAO estimates) 0.4 in 2004; 0.4 in 2005; 0.4 in 2006.
Source: FAO.

Mining

	2004	2005	2006
Petroleum, crude ('000 barrels)	15,495	17,113	17,300*
Copper ('000 metric tons)†	173.4	193.0	194.4
Silver (metric tons)†	55.6	51.1	50.0*
Gold (metric tons)†	73.7	68.5	50.0*

* Estimate.
† Figures refer to metal content of ore.

Source: US Geological Survey.

PAPUA NEW GUINEA

Industry

SELECTED PRODUCTS
('000 metric tons)

	2003	2004	2005
Beer of barley	40*	39*	45†
Palm oil ('000 metric tons)	326*	345*	350†
Raw sugar ('000 metric tons)*	51	46	46

* Unofficial figure(s).
† FAO estimate.

Electric energy (million kWh): 1,398 in 2003; 1,399 in 2004.

Wood products ('000 cu m, excl. furniture): 1,611 in 2003.

Sources: FAO; UN, *Industrial Commodity Statistics Yearbook*; Asian Development Bank, *Key Indicators of Developing Asian and Pacific Countries*.

Finance

CURRENCY AND EXCHANGE RATES

Monetary Units
100 toea = 1 kina (K).

Sterling, Dollar and Euro Equivalents (28 November 2008)
£1 sterling = 4.025 kina;
US $1 = 2.625 kina;
€1 = 3.340 kina;
100 kina = £24.84 = $38.10 = €29.94.

Average Exchange Rate (kina per US $)
2005 3.1020
2006 3.0567
2007 2.9654

Note: The foregoing information refers to the mid-point exchange rate of the central bank. In October 1994 it was announced that the kina would be allowed to 'float' on foreign exchange markets.

BUDGET
(million kina)

Revenue*	2006	2007	2008†
Taxation	4,944.7	5,853.9	5,516.8
Personal tax	907.0	1,006.9	1,053.7
Company tax	2,497.1	3,057.6	2,711.5
Other direct tax	419.4	426.8	376.8
Import duties	90.4	135.8	132.7
Excise duties	408.1	455.1	467.8
Export tax	162.6	155.2	155.2
Goods and services tax	401.1	557.5	600.8
Other indirect tax	59.1	59.0	18.3
Non-tax revenue	428.8	411.0	487.5
Dividends	339.3	290.7	388.3
Interest revenue/fees	0.6	0.5	5.0
Other internal revenue	88.9	119.8	94.2
Total	5,373.5	6,264.9	6,004.3

Expenditure‡	2006	2007	2008†
Recurrent expenditure	3,018.8	3,501.8	3,640.3
National departmental	1,665.9	2,098.3	2,262.2
Provincial governments	811.6	794.8	777.8
Interest payments	307.0	370.1	373.5
Foreign	119.9	117.9	98.2
Domestic	187.1	252.2	275.3
Other grants and expenditure	234.3	238.6	226.8
Development expenditure	1,554.1	1,327.5	1,887.1
National projects	1,243.3	1,062.0	1,509.7
Provincial projects	310.8	265.5	377.4
Additional priority expenditure	1,207.0	405.7	1,476.0
Supplementary budget	—	1,321.1	—
Total	5,779.9	6,556.1	7,003.4

* Excluding grants received from abroad (million kina): 914.6 in 2006; 721.0 in 2007; 1,123.7 in 2008 (forecast).
† Forecasts.
‡ Excluding net lending (million kina): −4.2 in 2006; −4.1 in 2007; −4.0 in 2008 (forecast).

Source: Bank of Papua New Guinea, Port Moresby.

INTERNATIONAL RESERVES
(US $ million at 31 December)

	2005	2006	2007
Gold (national valuation)	30.65	26.76	32.84
IMF special drawing rights	0.03	0.06	0.09
Reserve position in IMF	0.63	0.66	0.69
Foreign exchange	717.45	1,399.96	2,052.92
Total	748.76	1,427.44	2,086.54

Source: IMF, *International Financial Statistics*.

MONEY SUPPLY
(million kina at 31 December)

	2006	2007	2008
Currency outside banks	519.82	607.52	604.52
Demand deposits at deposit money banks	3,222.51	4,176.11	4,776.28
Total money (incl. others)	3,745.15	4,786.34	5,383.52

Source: IMF, *International Financial Statistics*.

COST OF LIVING
(Consumer Price Index; base: 1977 = 100)

	2005	2006	2007
Food	784.1	826.0	831.3
Clothing and footwear	480.5	480.8	514.1
Rent, fuel and power	328.6	361.8	374.2
All items (incl. others)	795.9	814.7	822.2

Source: Bank of Papua New Guinea, Port Moresby.

NATIONAL ACCOUNTS
(million kina at current prices)

National Income and Product

	2004	2005	2006
Compensation of employees	2,450.5	2,491.1	2,550.9
Operating surplus	9,163.8	10,505.1	11,994.5
Domestic factor incomes	11,614.3	12,996.2	14,545.4
Consumption of fixed capital	828.9	876.7	985.0
Gross domestic product (GDP) at factor cost	12,443.2	13,872.9	15,530.4
Indirect taxes / Less Subsidies	1,016.3	1,221.8	1,366.2
GDP in purchasers' values	13,459.3	15,094.7	16,896.5
Net factor income from abroad	−1,408.8	−1,670.0	−2,462.0
Gross national product	12,050.7	13,424.7	14,434.6
Less Consumption of fixed capital	828.9	876.7	985.0
National income in market prices	11,221.8	12,548.0	13,449.6

Source: Bank of Papua New Guinea, Port Moresby.

Expenditure on the Gross Domestic Product

	2004	2005	2006
Government final consumption expenditure	2,237.6	2,437.6	2,837.6
Private final consumption expenditure	7,047.5	7,239.2	7,959.0
Increase in stocks	580.2	150.0	350.0
Gross fixed capital formation	2,294.3	2,489.3	2,302.6
Total domestic expenditure	12,159.6	12,316.1	13,449.2
Exports of goods and services	9,143.4	11,245.7	13,986.2
Less Imports of goods and services	7,843.7	8,467.1	10,538.9
GDP in purchasers' values	13,459.3	15,094.7	16,896.5
GDP at constant 1998 prices	8,299.1	8,625.2	8,823.1

Source: Bank of Papua New Guinea, Port Moresby.

PAPUA NEW GUINEA

Gross Domestic Product by Economic Activity
(unofficial estimates)

	2005	2006	2007
Agriculture, hunting, forestry and fishing	5,684.0	5,822.9	6,342.9
Mining and quarrying	3,555.2	4,685.6	4,927.7
Manufacturing	942.5	999.5	1,070.6
Electricity, gas and water	284.4	301.7	320.1
Construction	1,245.8	1,437.2	1,720.3
Wholesale and retail trade	944.6	1,021.3	1,136.1
Transport, storage and communications	317.0	326.2	396.3
Finance, insurance, real estate and business services*	449.0	501.8	542.7
Community, social and personal services (incl. defence)	1,427.2	1,521.4	1,629.7
Sub-total	14,849.7	16,617.6	18,086.4
Import duties, *less* subsidies	413.4	433.2	464.5
GDP in purchasers' values	15,263.2	17,050.8	18,550.9

* Including services of owner-occupied dwellings.
Source: Asian Development Bank.

BALANCE OF PAYMENTS
(million kina)

	2005	2006	2007
Exports of goods f.o.b.	10,291	12,851	14,079
Imports of goods f.o.b.	−4,732	−6,084	−7,797
Trade balance	5,559	6,667	6,282
Exports of services	938	965	1,069
Imports of services	−3,621	−4,519	−5,409
Balance on goods and services	2,876	3,113	1,942
Other income received	81	215	310
Other income paid	−1,751	−2,677	−2,444
Balance on goods, services and income	1,206	651	−192
Current transfers received	1,092	999	1,219
Current transfers paid	−290	−396	−477
Current balance	2,009	1,354	550
Capital account (net)	101	135	113
Direct investment abroad	−20	−3	−23
Direct investment from abroad	104	−21	284
Portfolio investment assets	82	382	1,210
Portfolio investment liabilities	−6	7	—
Financial derivatives assets	−6	−35	−274
Other investment assets	−2,108	766	26
Other investment liabilities	139	−613	−335
Net errors and omissions	−1	−14	41
Overall balance	296	1,958	1,592

Source: Bank of Papua New Guinea, Port Moresby.

External Trade

PRINCIPAL COMMODITIES
(US $ million)

Imports f.o.b.*	2002	2003	2004
Food and live animals	176.8	192.4	237.3
Meat and meat preparations	32.9	34.8	40.8
Cereals and cereal preparations	81.4	94.6	122.7
Rice	53.2	61.5	90.8
Milled or semi-milled rice	23.5	20.5	88.6
Mineral fuels, lubricants and related materials	153.9	173.2	264.5
Petroleum and petroleum products	150.0	169.9	262.1
Chemicals and related products	90.6	109.6	128.9
Basic manufactures	239.2	233.6	247.5
Iron and steel	35.5	39.2	41.2
Manufactures of other metals	100.1	82.0	80.2

Imports f.o.b.*—*continued*	2002	2003	2004
Machinery and transport equipment	399.9	454.3	541.6
Power-generating machinery and equipment	36.1	51.2	57.1
Machinery specialized for particular industries	89.5	90.6	123.6
General industrial machinery and equipment	84.3	92.4	102.4
Electrical machinery, apparatus and appliances, etc.	40.3	46.7	48.1
Road vehicles and parts†	63.2	68.1	101.0
Motor vehicles for goods transport	24.0	24.2	43.1
Other transport equipment and parts†	27.9	46.4	52.8
Miscellaneous manufactured articles	90.3	100.7	102.6
Total (incl. others)	1,186.0	1,302.4	1,567.2

Exports f.o.b.	2002	2003	2004
Food and live animals	206.3	285.0	280.4
Coffee, tea, cocoa and spices, etc.	127.9	193.2	192.0
Crude materials, inedible, except fuels	588.8	1,107.2	753.3
Cork and wood	96.4	54.3	167.6
Metalliferous ores and metal scrap	478.9	1,043.4	572.8
Ores and concentrates of precious metals	263.2	645.0	91.3
Mineral fuels, lubricants and related materials	367.8	459.3	543.1
Crude petroleum and oils obtained from bituminous materials	367.7	458.1	513.3
Animal and vegetable oils, fats and waxes	107.0	146.5	140.2
Palm oil	86.0	122.8	113.2
Gold, non-monetary, unwrought or semi-manufactured	278.7	143.9	880.7
Total (incl. others)	1,625.1	2,260.2	2,722.2

* Figures include migrants' and travellers' dutiable effects, but exclude military equipment and some parcel post.
† Data on parts exclude tyres, engines and electrical parts.
Source: UN, *International Trade Statistics Yearbook*.

2005 (million kina): *Imports c.i.f.:* Total 4,732. *Exports f.o.b.:* Gold 2,834; Crude petroleum 2,283; Copper 2,498; Forestry products 476; Coffee beans 471; Palm oil 391; Cocoa 199; Total (incl. others) 10,168 (Source: Asian Development Bank).

2006 (million kina): *Imports c.i.f.:* Total 6,084. *Exports f.o.b.:* Gold 3,091; Crude petroleum 2,989; Copper 4,330; Forestry products 527; Coffee beans 337; Palm oil 430; Cocoa 204; Total (incl. others) 12,752 (Source: Asian Development Bank).

2007 (million kina): *Imports c.i.f.:* Total 7,603. *Exports f.o.b.:* Gold 3,672; Crude petroleum 2,984; Copper 4,173; Forestry products 631; Coffee beans 408; Palm oil 672; Cocoa 261; Total (incl. others) 13,866 (Source: Asian Development Bank).

PRINCIPAL TRADING PARTNERS
(US $ million)

Imports c.i.f.	2005	2006	2007
Australia	1,103.2	1,228.1	1,533.7
China, People's Republic	73.1	139.0	228.0
Indonesia	54.0	67.9	77.3
Japan	87.5	102.5	153.3
Korea, Republic	18.6	17.8	20.5
Malaysia	84.4	85.9	107.5
New Zealand	79.2	80.1	97.0
Singapore	271.0	296.7	344.8
Thailand	38.7	57.0	66.3
USA	60.8	48.2	72.3
Total (incl. others)	2,018.3	2,360.4	2,996.5

PAPUA NEW GUINEA

Exports f.o.b.	2005	2006	2007
Australia	1,506.6	1,895.3	1,892.3
China, People's Republic	281.3	356.1	457.3
Germany	207.1	242.4	244.4
India	65.4	80.8	96.4
Indonesia	45.4	56.1	73.0
Italy	37.9	59.1	86.8
Japan	449.9	511.7	677.5
Philippines	104.5	158.3	188.9
United Kingdom	98.2	67.6	63.8
USA	56.6	80.1	104.4
Total (incl. others)	5,235.8	6,268.1	7,251.5

Note: Data reflect the IMF's direction of trade methodology and, as a result, the totals may not be equal to those presented for trade in commodities.

Source: Asian Development Bank.

Transport

ROAD TRAFFIC
('000 vehicles in use)

	1999	2000	2001
Passenger cars	18.8	24.9	24.9
Commercial vehicles	87.0	87.8	87.8

Source: UN, *Statistical Yearbook*.

SHIPPING
Merchant Fleet
(registered at 31 December)

	2005	2006	2007
Number of vessels	116	118	125
Total displacement ('000 grt)	81.4	85.0	85.2

Source: Lloyd's Register-Fairplay, *World Fleet Statistics*.

International Sea-borne Freight Traffic

	1997	1998	1999
Cargo unloaded ('000 metric tons)	2,208.6	2,209.0	2,062.8
Cargo loaded ('000 metric tons)	735.9	823.3	788.1

Source: Papua New Guinea Harbours Board, *Monthly Shipping Register Form*.

CIVIL AVIATION
(traffic on scheduled services)

	2002	2003	2004
Kilometres flown (million)	18	11	12
Passengers carried ('000)	1,235	691	763
Passenger-km (million)	1,175	576	667
Total ton-km (million)	133	76	84

Source: UN, *Statistical Yearbook*.

Tourism

FOREIGN TOURIST ARRIVALS

Country of origin	2004	2005	2006
Australia	32,290	36,662	40,654
Canada	586	660	978
Germany	1,172	597	818
Japan	3,474	5,401	3,966
Malaysia	2,106	2,443	3,155
New Zealand	1,858	2,386	2,868
Philippines	2,657	3,344	3,781
United Kingdom	1,581	1,476	1,781
USA	4,748	5,709	6,224
Total (incl. others)	59,013	69,251	77,731

Receipts from tourism (US $ million, incl. passenger transport): 5.9 in 2004; 3.7 in 2005.

Source: World Tourism Organization.

Communications Media

	2004	2005	2006
Telephones ('000 main lines in use)	64	64	62
Mobile cellular telephones ('000 subscribers)	48	75	100
Personal computers ('000 in use)	367	367	n.a.
Internet users ('000)	90	105	110

2007: Telephones ('000 main lines in use) 60; Mobile cellular telephones ('000 subscribers) 300.

Daily newspapers (1996): 2 (combined circulation 65,000 copies).

Radio receivers (1997): 410,000 in use.

Television receivers (2001): 110,000 in use.

Facsimile machines (1994): 795 in use.

Sources: UNESCO, *Statistical Yearbook*; International Telecommunication Union.

Education

(2005/06, unless otherwise indicated)

	Institutions*	Teachers	Students
Pre-primary	29	2,697	95,121†
Primary	2,790	14,860	532,250
Secondary	n.a.	8,420‡	173,214‡
Tertiary§	n.a.	815	13,761

* 1994/95 figures.
† 2001/02 figure.
‡ 2002/03 figure.
§ 1998/99 figures.

Sources: National Department of Education, *The State of Education in PNG* (March 2001); UN, *Statistical Yearbook for Asia and the Pacific*; UNESCO Institute for Statistics.

Adult literacy rate (UNESCO estimates): 57.8% (males 62.1%; females 53.4%) in 2007 (Source: UNESCO Institute for Statistics).

Directory

The Constitution

The present Constitution came into effect on 16 September 1975, when Papua New Guinea became independent. The main provisions of the Constitution are summarized below:

PREAMBLE

The national goals of the Independent State of Papua New Guinea are: integral human development, equality and participation in the development of the country, national sovereignty and self-reliance, conservation of natural resources and the environment and development primarily through the use of Papua New Guinean forms of social, political and economic organization.

BASIC HUMAN RIGHTS

All people are entitled to the fundamental rights and freedoms of the individual whatever their race, tribe, place of origin, political opinion, colour, creed or sex. The individual's rights include the right to freedom, life and the protection of the law, freedom from inhuman treatment, forced labour, arbitrary search and entry, freedom of

PAPUA NEW GUINEA

conscience, thought, religion, expression, assembly, association and employment, and the right to privacy. Papua New Guinea citizens also have the following special rights: the right to vote and stand for public office, the right to freedom of information and of movement, protection from unjust deprivation of property and equality before the law.

THE NATION
Papua New Guinea is a sovereign, independent state. There is a National Capital District which shall be the seat of government.

The Constitution provides for various classes of citizenship. The age of majority is 19 years.

HEAD OF STATE
Her Majesty the Queen of the United Kingdom of Great Britain and Northern Ireland is Queen and Head of State of Papua New Guinea. The Head of State appoints and dismisses the Prime Minister on the proposal of the National Parliament and other ministers on the proposal of the Prime Minister. The Governor-General and Chief Justice are appointed and dismissed on the proposal of the National Executive Council. All the privileges, powers, functions, duties and responsibilities of the Head of State may be exercised or performed through the Governor-General.

Governor-General
The Governor-General must be a citizen who is qualified to be a member of Parliament or who is a mature person of good standing who enjoys the respect of the community. No one is eligible for appointment more than once unless Parliament approves by a two-thirds' majority. No one is eligible for a third term. The Governor-General is appointed by the Head of State on the proposal of the National Executive Council in accordance with the decision of Parliament by simple majority vote. He may be dismissed by the Head of State on the proposal of the National Executive Council in accordance with a decision of the Council or of an absolute majority of Parliament. The normal term of office is six years. In the case of temporary or permanent absence, dismissal or suspension he may be replaced temporarily by the Speaker of the National Parliament until such time as a new Governor-General is appointed.

THE GOVERNMENT
The Government comprises the National Parliament, the National Executive and the National Judicial System.

National Parliament
The National Parliament, or the House of Assembly, is a single-chamber legislature of members elected from single-member open or provincial electorates. The National Parliament has 109 members elected by universal adult suffrage. The normal term of office is five years. There is a Speaker and a Deputy Speaker, who must be members of Parliament and must be elected to these posts by Parliament. They cannot serve as government ministers concurrently.

National Executive
The National Executive comprises the Head of State and the National Executive Council. The Prime Minister, who presides over the National Executive Council, is appointed and dismissed by the Head of State on the proposal of Parliament. The other ministers, of whom there shall be not fewer than six nor more than a quarter of the number of members of the Parliament, are appointed and dismissed by the Head of State on the proposal of the Prime Minister. The National Executive Council consists of all the ministers, including the Prime Minister, and is responsible for the executive government of Papua New Guinea.

National Judicial System
The National Judicial System comprises the Supreme Court, the National Court, Local Courts and Village Courts. The judiciary is independent.

The Supreme Court consists of the Chief Justice, the Deputy Chief Justice and the other judges of the National Court. It is the final court of appeal. The Chief Justice is appointed and dismissed by the Head of State on the proposal of the National Executive Council after consultation with the minister responsible for justice. The Deputy Chief Justice and the other judges are appointed by the Judicial and Legal Services Commission. The National Court consists of the Chief Justice, the Deputy Chief Justice and no fewer than four nor more than six other judges.

The Constitution also makes provision for the establishment of the Magisterial Service and the establishment of the posts of Public Prosecutor and the Public Solicitor.

THE STATE SERVICES
The Constitution establishes the following State Services which, with the exception of the Defence Force, are subject to ultimate civilian control.

National Public Service
The Public Service is managed by the Department of Personnel Management which is headed by a Secretary, who is appointed by the National Executive Council on a four-year contract.

Police Force
The Police Force is subject to the control of the National Executive Council through a minister and its function is to preserve peace and good order and to maintain and enforce the law.

Papua New Guinea Defence Force
The Defence Force is subject to the superintendence and control of the National Executive Council through the Minister of Defence. The functions of the Defence Force are to defend Papua New Guinea, to provide assistance to civilian authorities in a civil disaster, in the restoration of public order or during a period of declared national emergency.

The fourth State Service is the Parliamentary Service.

The Constitution also includes sections on Public Finance, the office of the Auditor-General, the Public Accounts Commission and the declaration of a State of National Emergency.

The Government

HEAD OF STATE
Queen: HM Queen ELIZABETH II.

Governor-General: Sir PAULIAS MATANE (sworn in 29 June 2004).

NATIONAL EXECUTIVE COUNCIL
(April 2009)

Prime Minister and Acting Minister for Education: Sir MICHAEL SOMARE.

Deputy Prime Minister and Minister for Lands, Physical Planning and Mining: Dr PUKA TEMU.

Minister of State assisting the Prime Minister: PHILEMON EMBEL.

Minister for Agriculture and Livestock: JOHN HICKEY.

Minister for Commerce and Industry: GABRIEL KAPRIS.

Minister for Communications and Information: PATRICK TAMMUR.

Minister for Community Development, Women, Religion and Sports: Dame CAROL KIDU.

Minister for Correctional Services: TONY AIMO.

Minister for Culture and Tourism: CHARLES ABEL.

Minister for Defence: BOB DADAE.

Minister for Environment and Conservation: BENNY ALLAM.

Minister for Finance and Treasury: PATRICK PRUAITCH.

Minister for Fisheries: BEN SEMRI.

Minister for Foreign Affairs, Trade and Immigration: SAM ABAL.

Minister for Forestry: BELDEN NAMAH.

Minister for Health and HIV/AIDS: SASA ZIBE.

Minister for Higher Education, Research, Science and Technology: MICHAEL OGIO.

Minister for Housing and Urban Development: ANDREW KUMBAKOR.

Minister for Inter-Government Relations: JOB POMAT.

Minister for Internal Security: SANI RAMBE.

Minister for Justice: Dr ALLAN MARAT.

Minister for Labour and Industrial Relations: MARK MAIPAKAI.

Minister for National Planning and District Development: PAUL TIENSTEN.

Minister for Petroleum and Energy: WILLIAM DUMA.

Minister for Public Enterprise: ARTHUR SOMARE.

Minister for Public Service: PETER O'NEILL.

Minister for Works, Transport and Civil Aviation: DON POLYE.

PAPUA NEW GUINEA

GOVERNMENT DEPARTMENTS AND OFFICES

Office of the Prime Minister: POB 639, Waigani, NCD; tel. 3276525; fax 3273943; e-mail pmsoffice@pm.gov.pg; internet www.pm.gov.pg/pmsoffice/PMsoffice.nsf.

Department of Agriculture and Livestock: POB 417, Konedobu 125; tel. 3231848; fax 3230563; e-mail dalit@daltron.com.pg; internet www.agriculture.gov.pg.

Department of the Attorney-General: POB 591, Waigani, NCD; tel. 3230138; fax 3230241.

Department of Communications and Information: POB 1122, Waigani, NCD; tel. 3250148; fax 3250412; e-mail homerang2003@yahoo.com.

Department of Community Development: POB 7354, Boroko, NCD; internet www.pngfamilies.gov.pg.

Department of Defence: Murray Barracks, Free Mail Bag, Boroko 111, NCD; tel. 3242480; fax 3256117; internet www.defence.gov.pg.

Department of Education: POB 446, Waigani, NCD 131, Fin Corp Haus; tel. 3013555; fax 3254648.

Department of Environment and Conservation: POB 6601, Boroko 111, Kamul Ave, Waigani, NCD; tel. 3011607; fax 3011691.

Department of Family and Church Affairs: Ori Lavi Haus, Nita St, POB 7354, Boroko, NCD; tel. 3254566; fax 3251230.

Department of Finance: POB 710, Waigani, Vulupindi Haus, NCD; tel. 3288000; fax 3289000; internet www.finance.gov.pg.

Department of Fisheries and Marine Resources: POB 2016, Port Moresby; tel. 3271799; fax 3202074.

Department of Foreign Affairs and Trade: POB 422, Waigani 131, NCD; tel. 3156047; fax 3254263.

Department of Health: POB 3991, Boroko, Aopi Centre, Waigani Drive, Waigani; tel. 3254648; fax 3013555; internet www.health.gov.pg.

Department of Housing and Urban Resettlement: POB 1550, Boroko, NCD; tel. 3247200; fax 3259918.

Department of Inter-Government Relations: Somare Haus, Independence Drive, Waigani, POB 1287, Boroko, NCD; tel. 3011002; fax 3250553; e-mail paffairs@dalton.com.pg; internet www.dplga.gov.pg.

Department of Justice: Port Moresby; internet www.justice.gov.pg.

Department of Labour and Industrial Relations: POB 5644, Boroko, NCD; tel. 3217408; fax 3214085.

Department of Lands and Physical Planning: Aopi Centre, Tower 2, Levels 2, 3 and 4, Waigani Drive, Boroko, NCD; tel. 3013206; fax 3013205; e-mail onnoj@lands.gov.pg; internet www.lands.gov.pg.

Department of Mining: Private Mailbag, Port Moresby Post Office, Port Moresby 121; tel. 3227600; fax 3213701; internet www.mineral.gov.pg.

Department of National Planning and Monitoring: Port Moresby.

Department of Personnel Management: POB 519, Wards Strip, Waigani, NCD; tel. 3276422; fax 3250520; e-mail perrtsiamalili@dpm.gov.pg.

Department of Petroleum and Energy: POB 1993, Port Moresby, NCD; tel. 3224200; fax 3224222; e-mail joseph_gabut@petroleum.gov.pg.

Department of Police: Police Headquarters, POB 85, Konedobu, NCD; tel. 3226100; fax 3226113; internet www.rpngc.gov.pg.

Department of Social Welfare and Development, Youth and Women: Maori Kiki Bldg, 2nd Floor, POB 7354, Boroko, NCD; tel. 3254967; fax 3213821.

Department of State: Haus To Makala, 5th Floor, Post Office, Wards Strip, Waigani, NCD; tel. 3276758; fax 3214861.

Department of Transport and Civil Aviation: POB 1489, Port Moresby; tel. 3222580; fax 3200236.

Department of Treasury: POB 542, Waigani 131, NCD; tel. 3128817; fax 3128844; internet www.treasury.gov.pg.

Department of Works and Implementation: POB 1489, Port Moresby 121; tel. 3222500; fax 3200236; internet www.works.gov.pg.

Correctional Service: POB 6889, Boroko, NCD III; tel. 3231437; fax 3230407; e-mail rsikani@hq.cs.gov.pg.

National Forest Authority: POB 5055, Boroko, Frangipani St, Hohola, Port Moresby; tel. 3277800; fax 3254433.

Office of Information and Communication: Somare Foundation Bldg, 8th Floor, Independence Drive, Waigani; tel. 3250148; fax 3250412; e-mail hiduhu@datec.com.pg; internet www.communication.gov.pg.

Office of Peace and Reconstruction (fmrly Office of Bougainville Affairs): Morauta Haus, POB 343, Waigani 131, NCD; tel. 3276760; fax 3258038.

Legislature

NATIONAL PARLIAMENT

The unicameral legislature has 109 elective seats: 89 representing open constituencies and 20 representing provincial constituencies. There is constitutional provision for up to three nominated members.

Speaker: JEFFREY MARUS.

General Election, 30 June–15 July 2007 (provisional results)

Party	Seats
National Alliance	28
Papua New Guinea Party	8
People's Action Party	6
Pangu Pati	5
People's Democratic Movement	5
People's National Congress	5
People's Progress Party	5
United Resource Party	5
New Generation Party	4
Rural Development Party	4
People's Party	3
Melanesian Liberal Party	2
People's Labour Party	2
PNG Country Party	2
United Party	2
Melanesian Alliance Party	1
National Advance Party	1
Pipol First Party	1
PNG Conservative Party	1
PNG Labour Party	1
PNG National Party	1
Independents	16
Invalidated	1
Total	**109**

Note: in many cases party affiliations were subject to review in the immediate aftermath of the election.

Autonomous Region

BOUGAINVILLE ASSEMBLY

In late March 2004 the Bougainville Interim Provincial Government (BIPG) approved legislation to establish the Bougainville Constituent Assembly (BCA). The organization, which was composed of the members of both the BIPG and the Bougainville People's Congress (BPC), was convened for the first time on 30 March 2004, to approve the third and final draft of the proposed Constitution for Bougainville. Following its consideration by the Bougainville Constitutional Commission in August, in November the BCA recommended the proposed Constitution to the National Government, which approved the document in January 2005. Elections for the 39 seats of the new autonomous assembly and for the President of the incoming autonomous Government took place over a period of two weeks commencing on 20 May 2005. Joseph Kabui was elected as President of the new Government, winning 54.7% of the total votes cast, defeating his nearest rival, John Momis (34.4%), and three other candidates. Kabui held office until his death in June 2008. The House of Representatives was inaugurated on 14 June 2005. Nick Peniai was appointed as the Assembly's Speaker.

President: JAMES TANIS.

Election Commission

Election Commission of Papua New Guinea: POB 5348, Boroko NCD, Port Moresby; tel. 3258187; fax 3258650; e-mail info@pngec.gov.pg; internet www.pngec.gov.pg; Electoral Commr ANDREW TRAWEN.

Political Organizations

Bougainville Revolutionary Army (BRA): f. 1988; demands full independence for island of Bougainville; Leader ISMAEL TOROAMA.

PAPUA NEW GUINEA

Christian Democratic Party: Leader Dr BANARE BUN.
Melanesian Alliance (MA): Port Moresby; tel. 3277635; f. 1978; socialist; Chair. Sir MOI AVEI; Gen. Sec. FABIAN WAU KAWA.
Melanesian Labour Party: Port Moresby; Leader PAUL MONDIA.
Movement for Greater Autonomy: Manus Province; Leader STEPHEN POKAWIN.
National Alliance: c/o National Parliament, Port Moresby; f. 1996; est. to combat corruption in public life; Pres. SIMON KAIWI; Parliamentary Leader Sir MICHAEL SOMARE.
National Party (NP): Private Bag, Boroko, NCD; f. 1979; fmrly People's United Front; Leader MICHAEL MEL.
New Generation Party: c/o National Parliament, Port Moresby; Leader BART PHILEMON.
Pangu Pati (Papua New Guinea Unity): POB 289, Waigani, NCD; tel. 3277628; fax 3277611; f. 1968; urban- and rural-based; Leader ANDREW KUMBAKOR; Deputy Leader PHILEMON EMBEL.
Papua New Guinea Party: f. 2007; Leader Sir MEKERE MORAUTA.
People's Action Party (PAP): Boroko, NCD; tel. 3251343; f. 1985; Leader (vacant).
People's Democratic Movement (PDM): POB 972, Boroko, NCD; f. 1985; merged with Advance PNG Party in 2001; Leader PAIAS WINGTI.
People's National Congress (PNC): c/o National Parliament, Port Moresby; Leader PETER O'NEILL.
People's National Party: Port Moresby.
People's Party: Leader PETER IPATAS.
People's Progress Party (PPP): POB 6030, Boroko, NCD; f. 1970; Parliamentary Leader JULIUS CHAN; Nat. Pres. ALEX ANISI; Gen. Sec. EMOS DANIELS.
Rural Development Party: Leader MOSES MALADINA.
United Party: c/o National Parliament, Port Moresby; Leader BOB DADAE.
United Resource Party (URP): Port Moresby; f. 1997; aims to secure greater representation in Government for resource owners; Leader TIM NEVILLE.

Other parties that contested the 2007 election included the Melanesian Liberal Party, the National Advance Party, the People's Labour Party, the Pipol First Party, the PNG Conservative Party, the PNG Country Party, the PNG Labour Party and the PNG National Party.

Diplomatic Representation

EMBASSIES AND HIGH COMMISSIONS IN PAPUA NEW GUINEA

Australia: Godwit Rd, Waigani, NCD; tel. 3259333; fax 3256647; internet www.png.embassy.gov.au; High Commissioner CHRIS MORAITIS.
China, People's Republic: POB 1351, Boroko, NCD; tel. 3259836; fax 3258247; internet www.chinaembassy.org.pg; Ambassador WEI RUIXING.
Fiji: Defence House, 4th Floor, Champion Parade, Port Moresby, NCD; tel. 3211914; fax 3217220; e-mail rakaie@fijihighcom.org.pg; High Commissioner Ratu ISOA TIKOCA.
France: Defens Haus, 6th Floor, Cnr of Hunter St and Champion Parade, POB 1155, Port Moresby; tel. 3215550; fax 3215549; e-mail ambfrpg@global.net.pg; internet www.ambafrance-pg.org; Ambassador PATRICK BOURSIN.
Holy See: POB 98, Port Moresby; tel. 3256021; fax 3252844; e-mail nunciaturepng@datec.net.pg; Apostolic Nuncio Archbishop FRANCISCO MONTECILLO PADILLA.
India: Lot 20, Section 8, Unit 2, Tanatana St, Boroko, POB 86, Waigani, NCD; tel. 3254757; fax 3253138; e-mail hcipom@datec.net.pg; High Commissioner S. P. MANN.
Indonesia: 1–2/410 Kiroki St, Sir John Guise Dr., Waigani, NCD; tel. 3253116; fax 3253544; e-mail kbripom@daltron.com.pg; Ambassador BOM SOEJANTO.
Japan: Cuthbertson House, Cuthbertson St, POB 1040, Port Moresby; tel. 3211800; fax 3214868; Ambassador HASHIME NISHIYAMA.
Korea, Republic: POB 381, POM, 4th Floor, Pacific MMI Bldg, Sec. 21, Allotments 2 and 3, Champion Parade, Granville, Port Moresby; tel. 3215822; fax 3215828; e-mail hkkim68@mofat.go.kr; internet png.mofat.go.kr; Ambassador HAN WON-JUNG.
Malaysia: POB 1400, Pacific View Apts, Units 201/203, 2nd Floor, Pruth St, Korobosea, Port Moresby; tel. 3252076; fax 3252784; e-mail malpmresby@kln.gov.my; internet www.kln.gov.my/perwakilan/portmoresby; Chargé d'affaires NUR AZMAN ABDUL RAHIM.

New Zealand: Waigani Crescent, POB 1051, Waigani, NCD; tel. 3259444; fax 3250565; e-mail nzhcpom@dg.com.pg; High Commissioner NIELS HOLM.
Philippines: POB 5916, Boroko, NCD; tel. 3256414; fax 3231803; e-mail pompe@datec.met.pg; Ambassador SHIRLEY HO-VICARIO.
Solomon Islands: Port Moresby; e-mail sihicomm@daltron.com.pg; High Commissioner BERNARD BATA'ANISIA.
United Kingdom: Kiroki St, Locked Bag 212, Waigani 131, NCD; tel. 3251677; fax 3253547; e-mail ukinpng@datec.net.pg; internet www.ukinpng.fco.gov.uk; High Commissioner DAVID DUNN.
USA: Douglas St, POB 1492, Port Moresby; tel. 3211455; fax 3211593; e-mail png@state.gov; internet portmoresby.usembassy.gov; Ambassador LESLIE V. ROWE.

Judicial System

The Supreme Court is the highest judicial authority in the country, and deals with all matters involving the interpretation of the Constitution, and with appeals from the National Court. The National Court has unlimited jurisdiction in both civil and criminal matters. All National Court Judges (except acting Judges) are Judges of the Supreme Court. District Courts are responsible for civil cases involving compensation, for some indictable offences and for the more serious summary offences, while Local Courts deal with minor offences and with such matters as custody of children under the provision of Custom. There are also Children's Courts, which judge cases involving minors. Appeal from the District, Local and Children's Courts lies to the National Court. District and Local Land Courts deal with disputes relating to Customary land, and Warden's Courts with civil cases relating to mining. In addition, there are other courts with responsibility for determining ownership of government land and for assessing the right of Customary landowners to compensation. Village Courts, which are presided over by Magistrates with no formal legal qualification, are responsible for all Customary matters not dealt with by other courts.

Supreme Court of Papua New Guinea
POB 7018, Boroko, NCD; tel. 3245700; fax 3234492; internet www.pngjudiciary.gov.pg; Chief Justice Sir SALAMO INJIA.
Attorney-General: Dr ALLAN MARAT.

Religion

The belief in magic or sorcery is widespread, even among the significant proportion of the population that has adopted Christianity (nominally 97% in 1990). Pantheism also survives. There are many missionary societies.

CHRISTIANITY

Papua New Guinea Council of Churches: POB 1015, Boroko, NCD; tel. 3259961; fax 3251206; f. 1965; seven mem. churches; Chair. EDEA KIDU; Gen. Sec. SOPHIA W. R. GEGEYO.

The Anglican Communion

Formerly part of the Province of Queensland within the Church of England in Australia (now the Anglican Church of Australia), Papua New Guinea became an independent Province in 1977. The Anglican Church of Papua New Guinea comprises five dioceses and had 246,000 members in 2000.

Archbishop of Papua New Guinea and Bishop of Aipo Rongo: Most Rev. JAMES AYONG, POB 893, Mount Hagen, Western Highlands Province; tel. 5421131; fax 5421181; e-mail acpnghgn@global.net.pg.
General Secretary: MARTIN GARDHAM, POB 673, Lae, Morobe Province; tel. 4724111; fax 4721852; e-mail acpng@global.net.pg.

The Roman Catholic Church

For ecclesiastical purposes, Papua New Guinea comprises four archdioceses and 15 dioceses. At 31 December 2006 there were 1,776,359 adherents.

Catholic Bishops' Conference of Papua New Guinea and Solomon Islands
POB 398, Waigani, NCD; tel. 3259577; fax 3232551; e-mail cbc@dg.com.pg; internet www.catholicpng.org.pg; f. 1959; Pres. Most Rev. FRANCESCO SAREGO (Bishop of Goroka); Gen. Sec. LAWRENCE STEPHENS.
Archbishop of Madang: Most Rev. WILLIAM KURTZ, Archbishop's Residence, POB 750, Madang 511; tel. 8522599; fax 8522596; e-mail Kurtz_caom@global.net.pg.

PAPUA NEW GUINEA

Archbishop of Mount Hagen: Most Rev. MICHAEL MEIER, Archbishop's Office, POB 54, Mount Hagen, Western Highlands Province 281; tel. 5421285; fax 5422128; e-mail archdios@online.net.pg.

Archbishop of Port Moresby: Most Rev. Sir BRIAN BARNES, Archbishop's House, POB 1032, Boroko, NCD 111; tel. 3251192; fax 3256731; e-mail archpom@daltron.com.pg.

Archbishop of Rabaul: Most Rev. KARL HESSE, Archbishop's House, POB 357, Kokopo 613, East New Britain Province; tel. 9829384; fax 9828404; e-mail abkhesse@online.net.pg.

Other Christian Churches

Baptist Union of Papua New Guinea Inc: POB 705, Mount Hagen, Western Highlands Province; tel. 5522364; fax 5522402; e-mail bupng@global.net.pg; f. 1976; Gen. Sec. JOHN KAENKI; 48,000 mems.

Evangelical Lutheran Church of Papua New Guinea: Bishop Rt Rev. WESLEY KIGASUNG, POB 80, Lae, Morobe Province; tel. 4723711; fax 4721056; e-mail bishop.admin@global.net.pg; f. 1956; Sec. ISAAC TEO; 900,000 mems.

Gutnius Lutheran Church of Papua New Guinea: Bishop Rev. DAVID P. PISO, POB 111, 291 Wabag, Enga Province; tel. 5471280; fax 5471235; e-mail dpisoglc@online.net.pg; f. 1948; Gen. Sec. RICHARD R. MOSES; 138,000 mems.

Papua New Guinea Union Mission of the Seventh-day Adventist Church: POB 86, Lae, Morobe Province 411; tel. 4721488; fax 4721873; Pres. Pastor WILSON STEPHEN; Sec. Pastor BRADLEY RICHARD KEMP; 200,000 adherents.

The United Church in Papua New Guinea: POB 1401, Port Moresby; tel. 3211744; fax 3214930; e-mail ucpng@daltron.com.pg; f. 1968; formed by union of the Methodist Church in Melanesia, the Papua Ekalesia and United Church, Port Moresby; Moderator Rev. SAMSON LOWA; 600,000 mems; Gen. Sec. Rev. SIULANGI KAVORA.

BAHÁ'Í FAITH

National Spiritual Assembly: Private Mail Bag, Boroko, NCD; tel. 3250286; fax 3236474.

ISLAM

In 2000 the Muslim community in Papua New Guinea numbered about 1,500, of whom approximately two-thirds were believed to be expatriates. The religion was introduced to the island in the 1970s. The first mosque there was opened in late 2000 at Poreporena Highway, Hohola, Port Moresby; Imam KHALID ARAI (acting).

The Press

There are numerous newspapers and magazines published by government departments, statutory organizations, missions, sporting organizations, local government councils and regional authorities. They are variously in English, Tok Pisin (Pidgin), Motu and vernacular languages.

Ailans Nius: POB 1239, Rabaul, East New Britain Province; weekly.

Foreign Affairs Review: Dept of Foreign Affairs, Central Government Offices, Kumul Ave, Post Office, Wards Strip, Waigani, NCD; tel. 3271401; fax 3254886.

Hailans Nius: Mount Hagen, Western Highlands Province; weekly.

Lae Nius: POB 759, Lae, Morobe Province; 2 a week.

The National: POB 6817, Boroko, NCD; tel. 3246888; fax 3246868; e-mail national@thenational.com.pg; internet www.thenational.com.pg; f. 1993; daily; Editor DANIEL KORIMBAU; circ. 30,000.

Papua and New Guinea Education Gazette: Dept of Education, PSA Haus, POB 446, Waigani, NCD; tel. 3272413; fax 3254648; monthly; Editor J. OBERLENTER; circ. 8,000.

Papua New Guinea Post-Courier: POB 85, Port Moresby; tel. 3091000; fax 3212721; e-mail postcourier@ssp.com.pg; internet www.postcourier.com.pg; f. 1969; daily; English; published by News Corpn; Gen. Man. TONY YIANNI; Editor OSEAH PHILEMON; circ. 25,044.

Sunkamap Times: POB 322, Buka, Bougainville, North Solomons Province; e-mail stephen@viscom.co.nz; internet www.viscom.co.nz/SunkamapTimes; monthly; f. 2004; community newsletter.

Wantok (Friend) Niuspepa: POB 1982, Boroko, NCD; tel. 3252500; fax 3252579; e-mail word@global.net.pg; f. 1970; weekly in New Guinea Pidgin; mainly rural readership; Publr ANNA SOLOMON; Editor NEVILLE CHOI; circ. 10,000.

Publishers

Gordon and Gotch (PNG) Pty Ltd: POB 107, Boroko, NCD; tel. 3254855; fax 3250950; e-mail ggpng@online.net.pg; f. 1970; books, magazines and stationery; Gen. Man. PETER G. PORTER.

Scripture Union of Papua New Guinea: POB 280, University, Boroko, NCD; tel. and fax 3253987; f. 1966; religious; Chair. RAVA TAVIRI.

Word Publishing Co Pty Ltd: POB 1982, Boroko, NCD; tel. 3252500; fax 3252579; e-mail word@global.net.pg; f. 1982; 60% owned by the Roman Catholic Church, 20% by Evangelical Lutheran, 10% by Anglican and 10% by United Churches; Gen. Man. JEREMY BURGESS.

Broadcasting and Communications

TELECOMMUNICATIONS

Office of Information and Communication: POB 639, Waigani; tel. 3250148; fax 3250412; e-mail hiduhu@datec.com.pg; internet www.communication.gov.pg; Dir-Gen. HENAO IDUHU.

Digicel (PNG) Ltd: POB 1618, Port Moresby, NCD; e-mail customercarepng@digicelgroup.com; internet www.digicelpng.com; GSM services; CEO JOHN MANGOS.

Pacific Mobile Communications Company Ltd: POB 6973, Boroko, NCD; tel. 3232555; fax 3232554; e-mail pmc@tiare.net.pg; internet www.pacificmobile.com.pg; Chair. Dr FLORIAN GUBON.

Papua New Guinea Radiocommunications and Telecommunications Technical Authority (Pangtel): POB 8444, Boroko, NCD; tel. 3258633; fax 3256868; e-mail licensing@pangtel.gov.pg; internet www.pangtel.gov.pg; f. 1997; CEO CHARLES PUNAHA.

Telikom PNG Pty Ltd: POB 736, Port Moresby, NCD; tel. 1881234; fax 3004321; e-mail webadmin@telikompng.com.pg; internet www.telikompng.com.pg; Chair. GEREA AOPI; CEO PETER LOKO (acting).

In 2006 Green Communications (GreenCom), an Indonesian company, acquired a licence to expand into Papua New Guinea. The new venture was reportedly due to become operational in early 2009.

BROADCASTING

Radio

National Broadcasting Corporation of Papua New Guinea: POB 1359, Boroko, NCD; tel. 3255233; fax 3256296; e-mail info@nbc.com.pg; internet www.nbc.com.pg; f. 1973; commercial and free govt radio programmes services; broadcasting in English, Melanesian, Pidgin, Motu and 30 vernacular languages; Chair. CHRIS RANGATIN; Man. Dir Dr KRISTOFFA NINKAMA.

Kalang Service (FM): POB 1359, Boroko, NCD; tel. 3255233; commercial radio co established by National Broadcasting Commission; Chair. CAROLUS KETSIMUR.

Nau FM/Yumi FM: POB 774, Port Moresby; tel. 3201996; fax 3201995; f. 1994; Gen. Mans MARK ROGERS, JUSTIN KILI.

Television

EM TV: POB 443, Boroko, NCD; tel. 3257322; fax 3254450; e-mail emtv@emtv.com.pg; internet www.emtv.com.pg; f. 1988; operated by Media Niugini Pty Ltd; Gen. Man. GLENN ARMSTRONG.

Media Niugini Pty Ltd: POB 443, Boroko, NCD; tel. 3257322; fax 3254450; e-mail emtv@emtv.com.pg; internet www.emtv.com.pg; f. 1987; owned by Fijity Ltd; Gen. Man. GLENN ARMSTRONG.

Finance

(cap. = capital; res = reserves; dep. = deposits; m. = million; brs = branches; amounts in kina unless otherwise stated)

BANKING

Central Bank

Bank of Papua New Guinea: Douglas St, POB 121, Port Moresby; tel. 3227200; fax 3211617; e-mail info@bankpng.gov.pg; internet www.bankpng.gov.pg; f. 1973; bank of issue since 1975; sold to Bank of South Pacific in 2002; cap. 74.0m., res 525.7m., dep. 3,740.7m. (Dec. 2006); Gov. WILSON KAMIT; Deputy Gov. BENNY POPOITAI.

Commercial Banks

Australia and New Zealand Banking Group (PNG) Limited: Defens Haus, 3rd Floor, cnr of Champion Parade and Hunter St, POB 1152, Port Moresby; tel. 3211079; fax 3223302; e-mail cshdpg@anz.com; internet www.anz.com/Png; f. 1976; Chair. R. G. LYON; Man. Dir GARRY TUNSTALL; 11 brs.

PAPUA NEW GUINEA

Bank of South Pacific Ltd: POB 78, Allotment 12–13, Sect. 5, Cnr Douglas and Musgrave Sts, Granville, Port Moresby; tel. 3211999; fax 3211954; e-mail servicebsp@bsp.com.pg; internet www.bsp.com.pg; f. 1974; acquired from National Australia Bank Ltd by Papua New Guinea consortium (National Investment Holdings, now BSP Holdings Ltd) in 1993; merged with Papua New Guinea Banking Corpn in 2002; cap. 212.2m., res 36.4m., dep. 3,779.2m. (Dec. 2006); Chair. NOREO BEANGKE; Man. Dir GARTH MCILWAIN; 35 brs.

Finance Corpn Ltd (FinCorp): Aopi Centre, Ground Floor, Waigani Dr., Port Moresby, NCD 121; tel. 3232399; fax 3230167; e-mail sales@fincorp.com.pg; internet www.fincorp.com.pg; Chair. KERENGA KUA; Man. Dir and CEO TONY WITHAM; 5 brs.

Maybank (PNG) Ltd: Cnr Waigani Rd and Islander Dr., POB 882, Waigani, NCD; tel. 3258028; fax 3256128; e-mail maybankpom@datec.net.pg; f. 1995; CEO OOI SAY HOOI.

Westpac Bank—PNG—Ltd: Deloitte Tower, 9th Floor, Douglas St, POB 706, Port Moresby; tel. 3220888; fax 3220841; e-mail westpacpng@westpac.com.au; internet www.westpac.com.pg; f. 1910; est. as Bank of New South Wales, present name since 1982; 93.5% owned by Westpac Banking Corpn (Australia); cap. 5.8m., res 24.9m., dep. 864.5m. (Sept. 2006); Man. Dir ROSS HAMMOND; 15 brs.

Development Bank

National Development Bank (NDB): POB 686, Waigani, NCD; tel. 3247500; fax 3259817; e-mail rbank@devbank.com.pg; internet www.ndb.com.pg; f. 1967; est. as Agriculture Bank of Papua New Guinea; later known as Rural Development Bank of Papua New Guinea; name changed as above in 2007; statutory govt agency; Chair. WILLIAM LAMUR; Man. Dir RICHARD MARU; 18 brs.

Savings and Loan Societies

Registry of Savings and Loan Societies: Bank of Papua New Guinea, Financial System Supervision Dept, POB 121, Port Moresby; tel. 3227200; fax 3214548; 21 savings and loan societies; 205,205 mems (2007); total funds 631.2m., loans outstanding 27.2m., investments 359m. (Dec. 2007); Man. ELIZABETH GIMA.

STOCK EXCHANGE

Port Moresby Stock Exchange (POMSoX) Ltd: Level 4, Defens Haus, POB 1531, Port Moresby; tel. 3201980; fax 3201981; e-mail pomsox@pomsox.com.pg; internet www.pomsox.com.pg; f. 1999; Chair. GEREA AOPI; Gen. Man. VINCENT IVOSA.

INSURANCE

Capital Life Insurance Co: POB 1972, Port Moresby, NCD; tel. 3234036; fax 3232533; e-mail cilc@daltron.com.pg; f. 1993; fmrly Pan Asia Pacific Assurance (PNG).

Kwila Insurance Corpn: POB 1457, Boroko, NCD; tel. 3258811; fax 3112867; internet www.kwilainsurance.com.pg; f. 1977; Gen. Man. JASON R. MCILVENA.

Pacific MMI Insurance Ltd: POB 331, Port Moresby, NCD; tel. 3214077; fax 3214837; e-mail enquiries@pacificmmi.com; internet www.pacificmmi.com; f. 1998; fmrly Niugini Insurance Corpn Ltd; jt venture; general and life insurance; financial services; Chair. Dr JOHN MUA; Man. Dir WAYNE DORGAN.

There are branches of several Australian and United Kingdom insurance companies in Port Moresby, Rabaul, Lae and Kieta.

Trade and Industry

GOVERNMENT AGENCIES

Investment Promotion Authority (IPA): POB 5053, Boroko, NCD 111; tel. 3217311; fax 3212819; e-mail biepd@ipa.gov.pg; internet www.ipa.gov.pg; f. 1992; est. following reorganization of National Investment and Development Authority; statutory body responsible for the promotion of foreign investment; recommends priority areas for investment to the Govt; also co-ordinates investment proposals; Man. Dir IVAN POMALEU.

Privatization Commission: POB 45, Konedobu, NCD; tel. 3212977; fax 3213134; internet www.ipbc.com.pg; f. 1999; est. to oversee transfer of state-owned enterprises to private ownership; Exec. Chair. BEN MICAH.

DEVELOPMENT ORGANIZATIONS

CDC Capital Partners Ltd: CDC Haus, 2nd Floor, POB 907, Port Moresby; tel. 3212944; fax 3212867; e-mail png@cdc.com.pg; internet www.cdcgroup.com; fmrly Commonwealth Development Corpn; Man. Dir ASHLEY EMBERSON-BAIN.

Industrial Centres Development Corporation: POB 1571, Boroko, NCD; tel. 3232913; fax 3231109; e-mail henlytaka@hotmail.com; internet www.icdc.gov.pg; f. 1990; promotes foreign investment in non-mining sectors through establishment of manufacturing facilities.

CHAMBERS OF COMMERCE

Lae Chamber of Commerce Inc: POB 265, Lae, Morobe Province; tel. 4722340; fax 4726038; e-mail lcci@global.net.pg; internet www.lcci.org.pg; Pres. ALAN MCLAY.

Papua New Guinea Chamber of Commerce and Industry: POB 1621, Port Moresby; tel. 3213057; fax 3210566; e-mail pngcci@global.net.pg; internet www.pngcci.org.pg; Pres. MICHAEL MAYBERRY; CEO (vacant).

Papua New Guinea Chamber of Mines and Petroleum: POB 1032, Port Moresby; tel. 3212988; fax 3217107; e-mail conf@pngchamberminpet.com.pg; internet www.pngchamberminpet.com.pg; Exec. Dir GREG ANDERSON; Pres. PETER BOTTEN.

Port Moresby Chamber of Commerce and Industry: POB 1764, Port Moresby; tel. 3213077; fax 3214203; e-mail pomcci@global.net.pg; internet www.pomcci.org.pg/pres.html; Pres. DAVID CONN.

INDUSTRIAL AND TRADE ASSOCIATIONS

Cocoa Board of Papua New Guinea: POB 532, Rabaul, East New Britain Province; tel. 9829083; fax 9828712; e-mail l.tautea@global.net.pg; f. 1974; Chair. JIMMY SIMITAB; CEO LAVATAU TAUTEA.

Coffee Industry Corpn Ltd: POB 137, Goroka, Eastern Highlands Province; tel. 7321266; fax 7321214; e-mail cicgka@daltron.com.pg; internet www.coffeecorp.org.pg; CEO RICKY MITIO.

Fishing Industry Association (PNG) Inc: POB 5860, Boroko, NCD; tel. 3258222; fax 3258994; e-mail netshop1@daltron.com.pg; Chair. MAURICE BROWNJOHN.

Forest Industries Association: POB 229, Waigani, NCD; internet www.fiapng.com; Pres. ANTHONY HONEY; CEO ROBERT TATE.

Higaturu Oil Palms Pty Ltd: POB 28, Popondetta, Oro Province; tel. 3297177; fax 3297137; f. 1976; jtly owned by the Commonwealth Development Corpn (UK) and the Papua New Guinea Govt; major producer of palm oil and cocoa; Gen. Man. RICHARD CASKIE.

Kokonas Indastri Korporesen (KIK): POB 81, Port Moresby; tel. 3211133; fax 3214257; e-mail info@kik.com.pg; regulates and markets all copra and coconut products in Papua New Guinea; represents producers; fmrly Copra Marketing Board of Papua New Guinea (f. 1950s); name changed as above 2002; govt-owned; Chair. JOE ARARUA; Man. Dir TORE OVASURU.

Manufacturers' Council of Papua New Guinea: POB 598, Port Moresby; tel. 3259512; fax 3230199; e-mail pngmade@global.net.pg; Chair. WAYNE GOLDING; CEO BRUCE REVILLE.

Mineral Resources Development Corporation: POB 1076, Port Moresby; tel. 3255822; fax 3252633; Man. Dir FRANCIS KAUPA.

Morobe Produce Marketing Ltd: POB 3434, Lae 411, Morobe Province; tel. 4724144; fax 4725186; f. 1982; owned by Gerard Kananimara; handles distribution of fruit and vegetables throughout the country.

National Fisheries Authority: POB 2016, Port Moresby; tel. 3212643; fax 3202061; e-mail nfa@fisheries.gov.pg; internet www.fisheries.gov.pg; Man. Dir TONY LEWIS; Dep. Man. Dir MICHAEL BATTY.

National Housing Corpn (NHC): POB 1550, Boroko, NCD; tel. 3247000; fax 3254363; Man. Dir GABRIEL TOVO.

New Britain Palm Oil Ltd: POB 389, Kimbe, West New Britain; tel. 9852177; fax 9852178; e-mail info@nbpol.com.pg; internet www.nbpol.com.pg; f. 1967; 80% owned by Kulim (Malaysia), 20% owned by Govt, employees and local producers; major producer of palm oil, coffee trader and exporter, supplier of high quality oil palm seed; Chair. ANTONIO DE CASTRO; CEO NICK THOMPSON.

Palm Oil Producers Association: Port Moresby; Exec. Sec. ALLAN MAINO.

Papua New Guinea Contractor Association: POB 2289, Boroko, NCD; tel. 3202239; formed by construction cos for the promotion of education, training and professional conduct in the construction industry; Pres. ROY THORPE.

Papua New Guinea Forest Authority: POB 5055, Boroko, NCD; tel. 3277800; fax 3254433; e-mail info_general@pngfa.gov.pg; internet www.forestry.gov.pg; Man. Dir KANAWI POURU; Chair. JOSEPH LELANG.

Papua New Guinea Growers Association: POB 14, Kokopo, East New Britain Province 613; tel. 9829123; fax 9829264; e-mail growers@global.net.pg; Pres. PAUL ARNOLD; Exec. Dir DAVID LOH.

Papua New Guinea Holdings Corpn: POB 131, Port Moresby; fax 3217545; f. 1992; responsible for managing govt privatization programme; Chair. MICHAEL MEL; Man. Dir PETER STEELE.

PAPUA NEW GUINEA

Papua New Guinea Log Carriers Association: f. 1993.

Pita Lus National Silk Institute: Kagamuga, Mount Hagen, Western Highlands Province; f. 1978; govt silk-producing project.

Rural Industries Council: Chair. PETER COLTON.

UTILITIES

Electricity

PNG Power Ltd (PPL): POB 1105, Boroko, NCD; tel. 3243200; fax 3250072; e-mail marketing@pngpower.com.pg; internet www.pngpower.com.pg; prev. PNG Electricity Commission (Elcom); Commission privatized and name changed to above in 2002; undertakes regulatory role on behalf of Consumer and Competition Commission; Chair. SARI MASO (acting); Chief Exec. TONY KOIRI (acting).

Water

Eda Ranu (Our Water): POB 1084, Waigani, NCD; tel. 3122100; fax 3122190; e-mail info@edaranu.com.pg; internet www.edaranu.com.pg; fmrly Port Moresby Water Supply Company; Gen. Man. BILLY IMAR.

PNG Waterboard: POB 2779, Boroko, NCD; tel. 3235700; fax 3236317; e-mail pamini@pngwater.com.pg; f. 1986; govt-owned; operates 17 water supply systems throughout the country; Man. Dir PATRICK AMINI.

TRADE UNIONS

Papua New Guinea Trade Unions Congress (PNGTUC): POB 4279, Boroko, NCD; tel. 3257642; fax 3257890; e-mail tucl@daltron.com.pg; Pres. GASPER LAPAN; Gen. Sec. JOHN PASKA; 52 affiliates, 76,000 mems.

The following are among the major trade unions:

Bougainville Mining Workers' Union: POB 777, Panguna, North Solomons Province; tel. 9958272; Pres. MATHEW TUKAN; Gen. Sec. ALFRED ELISHA TAGORNOM.

Central Province Building and Construction Industry Workers' Union: POB 265, Port Moresby.

Central Province Transport Drivers' and Workers' Union: POB 265, Port Moresby.

Employers' Federation of Papua New Guinea: POB 6057, Boroko; tel. 3258266; fax 3258272; e-mail information@efpng.org.pg; internet www.efpng.org.pg; f. 1963; Pres. JOHN GORDON JEFFERY; Exec. Dir FLORENCE WILLIE.

National Federation of Timber Workers: Madang; f. 1993; Gen. Sec. MATHIAS KENUANGI (acting).

Papua New Guinea Communication Workers' Union: Pres. BOB MAGARU; Gen. Sec. EMMANUEL KAIRU.

Papua New Guinea National Doctors' Association: Pres. Dr BOB DANAYA; 225 mems.

Papua New Guinea Teachers' Association: POB 1027, Waigani, NCD; tel. 3262588; fax 321514; f. 1971; Pres. TOMMY HECKO; Gen. Sec. MURRAY PAIVA; 20,049 mems.

Papua New Guinea Waterside Workers' and Seamen's Union: POB 76, Kimbe 621; tel. 9835603; f. 1979; an amalgamation of four unions; Sec. DOUGLAS GADEBO.

Police Association of Papua New Guinea: tel. 3214172; f. 1964; Pres. ROBERT ALI; 4,596 mems.

Port Moresby Council of Trade Unions: POB 265, Boroko, NCD; Gen. Sec. JOHN KOSI.

Port Moresby Miscellaneous Workers' Union: POB 265, Boroko, NCD.

Printing and Kindred Industries Union: Port Moresby.

Public Employees' Association: POB 965, Boroko, NCD; tel. 3252955; fax 3252186; f. 1974; Pres. NAPOLEON LIOSI; Gen. Sec. JACK N. KUTAL; 28,000 mems.

Transport

There are no railways in Papua New Guinea. The capital city, Port Moresby, is not connected by road to other major population centres. Therefore, air and sea travel are of particular importance.

ROADS

In 2000 there were an estimated 19,600 km of roads in Papua New Guinea, of which 3.5% were paved.

National Roads Authority: Lae, Morobe Province; f. 2004; statutory authority; maintains the road network, particularly the Highlands Highway; Chair. ALLAN MCLAY.

SHIPPING

Papua New Guinea has 16 major ports and a coastal fleet of about 300 vessels.

Papua New Guinea Harbours Board: POB 671, Port Moresby; tel. 3211400; fax 3211546; Chair. TIMOTHY BONGA.

PNG Ports Corporation Ltd: POB 273, Madang; tel. 3211400; fax 3211546; e-mail Casper.Petrus@pngharbours.com.pg; internet www.pngports.com.pg; CEO BRIAN RICHES.

Port Authority of Kieta: POB 149, Kieta, North Solomons Province; tel. 9956066; fax 9956255; Port Man. CHARLES TARURAVA.

Port Authority of Lae: POB 563, Lae, Morobe Province; tel. 4723464; fax 4723543; Port Man. SAKEUS GEM.

Port Authority of Port Moresby: POB 671, Port Moresby; tel. 211400; fax 3211546; Gen. Man. BEN PUKAI.

Port Authority of Rabaul: POB 592, Rabaul, East New Britain Province; tel. 9821533; fax 9821535; Port Man. JOHN TUNGAPIK.

Shipping Companies

Coastal Shipping Co Ltd: Sulphur Creek Rd, POB 423, Rabaul, East New Britain Province; tel. 9821746; fax 9821734; e-mail coastco@global.net.pg; f. 1967; Man. Dir HENRY CHOW.

Lutheran Shipping: POB 789, Madang; tel. 8522577; fax 8522180; e-mail finance.luship@global.net.pg.

Morehead Shipping Pty Ltd: POB 1908, Lae, Morobe Province; tel. 4423602.

New Guinea Australia Line Pty Ltd: POB 145, Port Moresby; tel. 3212377; fax 3214879; e-mail ngal@daltron.com.pg; f. 1970; operates regular container services between Australia, Papua New Guinea, Singapore, Indonesia, Vanuatu, Tuvalu and Solomon Islands; Chair. (vacant); Gen. Man. GEOFFREY CUNDLE.

P & O Maritime Services (PNG) Ltd: MMI House, 3rd Floor, Champion Parade, POB 1403, Port Moresby; tel. 3229200; fax 3229251; e-mail jhulse@pom.popng.com.pg; owned by P & O (Australia); Country Man. JOHN HULSE.

Papua New Guinea Shipping Corporation Pty Ltd: POB 634, Port Moresby; tel. 3220290; fax 3212815; e-mail shipping@steamships.com.pg; f. 1977; owned by Steamships Trading Co Ltd; provides a container/break-bulk service to Australia and the Pacific islands; Chair. CHRISTOPHER PRATT; Man. Dir JOHN DUNLOP.

South Sea Lines Proprietary Ltd: POB 5, Lae, Morobe Province; tel. 4423455; fax 4424884; Man. Dir R. CUNNINGHAM.

Western Tug & Barge Co P/L: POB 1403, Port Moresby; tel. 3229290; fax 3229251; ship-owning division of P & O PNG; operates 24 vessels.

CIVIL AVIATION

There is an international airport, Jackson's Airport, at Port Moresby, and there are more than 400 other airports and airstrips throughout the country. International services from Lae and Mount Hagen airports began in 1999.

Air Niugini: POB 7186, Boroko, NCD; tel. 3259000; fax 3273482; e-mail airniugini@airniugini.com.pg; internet www.airniugini.com.pg; f. 1973; govt-owned national airline; operates scheduled domestic cargo and passenger services within Papua New Guinea and international services to Australia, Fiji, Solomon Islands, Philippines, Hong Kong, Singapore and Japan; Chair. JIM TJOENG; CEO WASANTHA KUMARASIRI.

Airlines PNG: POB 170, NCD, Port Moresby; tel. 3252011; fax 3252219; e-mail apng@apng.com; internet www.apng.com; f. 1984 as Milne Bay Air (MBA); operates domestic scheduled and charter services; Chair. SIMON WILD; Gen. Man. JOHN FITZGERALD.

National Aviation Services: Boroko, NCD; f. 2005; provides services between all small airstrips in Central, Oro, Gulf and Western provinces, primarily for the transport of agricultural products from producers to markets; Operations Man. GILBERT YENBARI; Propr and CEO TED DIRO.

Tourism

Despite Papua New Guinea's spectacular scenery and abundant wildlife, tourism makes only a small contribution to the economy. Visitor arrivals rose from an estimated 104,122 in 2007 to 114,182 in 2008. The industry earned an estimated US $3.7m. in 2005.

PNG Tourism Promotion Authority: POB 1291, Port Moresby; tel. 3200211; fax 3200223; e-mail info@pngtourism.org.pg; internet www.pngtourism.org.pg; CEO PETER VINCENT.

Tour Operators Association (TOAPNG): tel. 3200211; fax 3200223; e-mail toapng@pngtourism.org.pg; internet www.toa.org.pg; f. 2006; Pres. MICHAEL BULEAU; Treas. AARON HAYES.

PARAGUAY

Introductory Survey

Location, Climate, Language, Religion, Flag, Capital

The Republic of Paraguay is a land-locked country in central South America. It is bordered by Bolivia to the north, by Brazil to the east, and by Argentina to the south and west. The climate is sub-tropical. Temperatures range from an average maximum of 34.3°C (93.7°F) in January to an average minimum of 14°C (51°F) in June. The official languages are Spanish and Guaraní, the latter, an indigenous Indian language, being spoken by the majority of the population. Almost all of the inhabitants profess Christianity, and some 92% adhere to the Roman Catholic Church, the country's established religion. There is a small Protestant minority. The national flag (proportions 3 by 5) has three equal horizontal stripes, of red, white and blue. It is the only national flag with a different design on each side, having a varying emblem in the centre of the white stripe: the obverse side bears the state emblem (a white disc with a red ring bearing the words 'República del Paraguay', in yellow capitals, framing a blue disc with the five-pointed 'May Star', in yellow, surrounded by a wreath, in green), while the reverse side carries the seal of the Treasury (a white disc with a red ribbon bearing the words 'Paz y Justicia' in yellow capitals above a lion supporting a staff, surmounted by the red 'Cap of Liberty'). The capital is Asunción.

Recent History

Paraguay, ruled by Spain from the 16th century, achieved independence in 1811. In 1865 Paraguay was involved in a disastrous war against Brazil, Argentina and Uruguay (the Triple Alliance), resulting in the loss of more than one-half of its population. Paraguay also suffered heavy losses in the Chaco Wars of 1928–30 and 1932–35 against Bolivia, but won a large part of the disputed territory when the boundary was fixed in 1938. Gen. Higinio Morínigo established an authoritarian regime in 1940, but the return of a number of political exiles in 1947 precipitated a civil war in which supporters of the right-wing Asociación Nacional Republicana—Partido Colorado (ANR—PC, commonly known as the Partido Colorado) defeated the Liberals and the Partido Revolucionario Febrerista, leading to the overthrow of Gen. Morínigo in June 1948. A period of great instability ensued. In May 1954 Gen. Alfredo Stroessner Mattiauda, the Army Commander-in-Chief, assumed power in a military coup. He nominated himself for the presidency, as the Colorado candidate, and was elected unopposed in July to complete the term of office of his predecessor, Federico Chávez. In 1955 Stroessner assumed extensive powers, and established a state of siege. Regular purges of the Partido Colorado membership, together with the mutual co-operation of the ruling party, the armed forces and the business community, enabled Stroessner to become the longest-serving dictator in South America: he was re-elected President, by large majorities, at five-yearly elections in 1958–88.

In February 1978 President Stroessner revoked the state of siege in all areas except Asunción. The assassination of the former Nicaraguan dictator, Gen. Anastasio Somoza Debayle, in Asunción in September 1980, however, caused President Stroessner to doubt the security of his own position, and the state of siege was reimposed throughout the country; harassment of leaders of the political opposition and of peasant and labour groups continued. The leader of the Partido Demócrata Cristiano, Luis Alfonso Resck, was expelled from the country in June 1981, and Domingo Laíno, leader of the Partido Liberal Radical Auténtico (PLRA), was deported in December 1982. After Ronald Reagan took office as President of the USA in 1981, Paraguay encountered less pressure from the US Administration to curb abuses of human rights, and the use of torture against detainees reportedly became widespread once more. It was estimated at this time that more than 60% of all Paraguayans resided outside the country.

The majority of opposition parties boycotted the presidential and legislative elections of February 1983, enabling Stroessner to obtain more than 90% of the votes cast in the presidential poll, and in August he formally took office for a further five-year term. In May 1983 the Government instigated a campaign of repression against students and trade unionists. In February 1984 opposition parties organized demonstrations in Asunción for the first time in 30 years.

Divisions over Stroessner's continuance in office led to factionalism within the Partido Colorado in the mid-1980s. In April 1987 Stroessner announced that the state of siege was to be ended, since extraordinary security powers were no longer necessary to maintain peace. (Later in the month Laíno was finally allowed to return to Paraguay.) However, the suppression of civil liberties and of political activity continued under the new penal code that replaced the state of siege. The level of participation in the 1988 presidential election (which took place simultaneously with legislative elections) was reported to be 93% of eligible voters, and it was announced that Stroessner had received 89% of the votes cast. However, opposition leaders (who had urged voters to boycott the elections) complained of electoral malpractice, and denounced Stroessner's re-election as fraudulent.

On 3 February 1989 Gen. Stroessner was overthrown in a coup led by Gen. Andrés Rodríguez, the second-in-command of the armed forces. Stroessner was allowed to leave for exile in Brazil, as Gen. Rodríguez assumed the presidency (in a provisional capacity) and appointed a new Council of Ministers. The interim President pledged to respect human rights and to strengthen links with neighbouring countries. At the presidential election in May Rodríguez, the candidate of the Partido Colorado, was confirmed as President. The Partido Colorado also won the largest number of seats in both the Cámara de Diputados (Chamber of Deputies) and the Senado (Senate—48 and 24, respectively). Despite widespread allegations of electoral fraud, all parties agreed to respect the results.

In July 1989 the Cámara ratified the San José Pact on Human Rights, adopted by the Organization of American States (OAS, see p. 373) in 1978. In August 1989 the Congreso Nacional (National Congress—comprising the Cámara de Diputados and the Senado) initiated judicial proceedings against former government officials for violations of human rights. Following the repeal, in August 1989, of laws that had provided a basis for political repression under the Stroessner regime, the PCP was formally legalized. In November 1990, however, Rodríguez vetoed congressional proposals for the establishment of a legislative commission to investigate alleged violations of human rights.

Divisions within the Partido Colorado became evident at its annual convention in December 1989, when the 'Tradicionalistas' attempted to elect new party officials drawn exclusively from their own membership. The newly emerged Coloradismo Democrático faction, led by Blas Riquelme (a vice-president of the party at that time), succeeded in obtaining a judicial annulment of all decisions of the convention. The political crisis led to the resignation of the entire Council of Ministers. However, Rodríguez subsequently reappointed all but one of the outgoing ministers to their former posts. In February 1990 a new electoral code was adopted; this banned party affiliation for serving members of the armed forces and the police, and reformed procedures for the election of party officials.

Paraguay's first direct municipal elections took place in May 1991. Although the Partido Colorado secured control of a majority of municipalities, the important post of mayor of Asunción was won by a relatively unknown candidate, Carlos Filizzola, the representative of a new centre-left coalition, Asunción Para Todos (APT). Defeat in the capital precipitated mutual recriminations within the increasingly fragmented Partido Colorado.

In August 1991 the Congreso Nacional approved proposals for a complete revision of the 1967 Constitution. In anticipation of the elections to a National Constituent Assembly, President Rodríguez and military leaders made concerted efforts to forge unity within the Partido Colorado, with the result that the party's three main factions, the 'Renovadores', the 'Democráticos' and the 'Autónomos', were persuaded to present a single list of candidates, under the title 'Tradicionalistas'. In the December elections the Partido Colorado won 55% of the votes cast, thus securing an overwhelming majority of the Assembly's 198 seats. The PLRA won 27% of the votes, while Constitución Para Todos, formed as a result of APT's success in the municipal elections, won 11% of the votes. The new body was convened in January 1992.

In November 1991 new legislation, drafted by President Rodríguez in co-operation with military leaders, was approved by the Congreso Nacional. The law appeared to guarantee the autonomy of the armed forces, and the definition of the role of the military was expanded to include responsibility, at the request of the Head of State, for civil defence and internal order. Apparently in contradiction of the 1990 electoral code, no restrictions were placed on political activities by serving members of the armed forces. Provision was made for the President to delegate the functions of Commander-in-Chief of the Armed Forces to a senior military officer (with the Head of State retaining only ceremonial powers as the military commander). Opposition parties protested that, should the new legislation be entrenched in the new Constitution, the armed forces would remain a 'parallel' political force, following the transition to civilian rule.

On 20 June 1992 the new Constitution was promulgated before the Constituent Assembly. Under the new Constitution, the President and the Vice-President (a new post) were to be elected by a simple majority of votes. The Constituent Assembly had ostensibly disregarded the November 1991 military legislation by confirming the President as Commander-in-Chief of the Armed Forces and excluding officers on active duty from participating directly in politics. Other significant changes in the Constitution included the abolition of the death penalty and the granting of the right to unionize and to strike to public sector employees (excluding the armed forces and police).

In August 1992, following the party's first direct internal elections, Riquelme was appointed President of the Partido Colorado. However, serious divisions within the party persisted. An internal election, conducted in December, to select the party's presidential candidate was declared to have been won by Luis María Argaña (who had resigned the position in 1992), the candidate of the far right. However, the candidate believed to be favoured by Rodríguez, Juan Carlos Wasmosy, refused to recognize the result, claiming that the vote had been fraudulent. An electoral tribunal failed to resolve the issue, and, following intense pressure and alleged death threats by both factions, several members of the tribunal resigned. Party leaders organized an extraordinary national convention in February 1993, at which a new electoral tribunal was to be chosen. Wasmosy was eventually confirmed as the presidential candidate of the Partido Colorado. The decision was denounced by Argaña, whose supporters threatened to resign *en masse* from the party.

At the general election of May 1993 Wasmosy was elected President with 40% of the votes cast, ahead of Laíno and Guillermo Caballero Vargas of the Partido Encuentro Nacional (PEN). However, the Partido Colorado failed to gain a majority in either the Cámara or the Senado. Moreover, the faction of the Partido Colorado led by Argaña, the Movimiento de Reconciliación Colorada (MRC), negotiated with the PLRA and the PEN to exclude supporters of the President-elect from appointment to important posts in the Congreso Nacional. Wasmosy was inaugurated as President on 15 August. The opposition expressed some concern over the composition of his first Council of Ministers, many of whom had served in the administrations of Rodríguez and Stroessner. Despite Wasmosy's apparent desire to restrict the influence of the military (he notably appointed a civilian to the post of Minister of National Defence), the designation of Gen. Lino César Oviedo Silva as Commander of the Army provoked further criticism, since, prior to the elections, Oviedo had publicly stated that the army would not accept an opposition victory.

A preliminary agreement on a 'governability pact' between the Government and the opposition, initiated in an attempt to facilitate the implementation of a coherent economic and legislative programme, was signed in October 1993, and this, in turn, facilitated an agreement between the Government and the legislature towards resolving the controversial question of judicial reform. Under the latter agreement, the two were to appoint members of the Supreme Court and the Supreme Electoral Tribunal by consensus. (The new members of the Supreme Court, enlarged from five to nine justices in accordance with the 1992 Constitution, were eventually elected in April 1995). In January 1994 Riquelme resigned as President of the Partido Colorado, following disagreements with Wasmosy. By early 1995 speculation concerning unrest in the armed forces, prompted by Wasmosy's recent uncompromising manipulation of the ranks of the military high command, and by a reported clash of interests between the President and Gen. Oviedo, had reached such a level that Wasmosy was forced to issue a public statement discounting the possibility of a military coup. In February Wasmosy announced a further reorganization of the military high command, thus consolidating his position of authority.

In May 1995 an investigation into corruption at the Central Bank revealed the existence of an illegal 'parallel' financial system involving a network of institutions, including the Central Bank. The investigation precipitated the collapse of the system and a severe liquidity crisis. In December the Government issued an emergency decree extending the powers of intervention of the Central Bank, with the aim of resolving the financial crisis and restoring confidence in the banking sector. By late December the Central Bank had disbursed almost US $400m. of reserves in order to contain the liquidity crisis, which had resulted in the closure of several financial institutions.

In April 1996 a serious confrontation arose between President Wasmosy and Gen. Oviedo, with the result that a military coup was only narrowly averted. Following an attempt by Oviedo to postpone the internal elections of the Partido Colorado, Wasmosy accused Oviedo of contravening the ban on political activity by serving members of the military, and, on 22 April, demanded his resignation as Commander of the Army. When Oviedo refused to resign, Wasmosy promptly announced his dismissal, naming Gen. Oscar Rodrigo Díaz Delmas as his successor. Oviedo rejected the decision, and installed himself at the army headquarters in Asunción, from where he issued demands for Wasmosy's resignation and threatened, with the support of the army, violently to overthrow the Government. Wasmosy took refuge in the US embassy building. The following day, in a demonstration of popular support for Wasmosy, thousands rallied outside the presidential palace. Declarations of support were also issued by the Commanders of the Navy and the Air Force, and by the Congreso Nacional. External pressure for Wasmosy to resist the overthrow of democratic rule came from the USA, which immediately suspended military aid, and from neighbouring South American countries, and was sufficient to prompt Wasmosy to seek a compromise: in return for his retirement from military service, Oviedo was given the position of Minister of Defence. However, the measure was condemned by the legislature, which threatened to initiate impeachment proceedings against Wasmosy should Oviedo be appointed. Public opinion was also strongly opposed to the appointment, and on 25 April, following Oviedo's retirement from military service and his replacement by Gen. Díaz, Wasmosy withdrew the offer of the defence portfolio. Despite fears of an outright coup, Oviedo accepted the final outcome of the dispute and announced that, as a private citizen, he would now dedicate himself to the political campaign of the Partido Colorado.

In late April 1996 the internal elections of the Partido Colorado resulted in victory for Argaña, the leader of the MRC faction, who was appointed President of the party. In May Oviedo announced the creation of a new faction of the Partido Colorado, the Unión Nacional de Colorados Eticos (UNACE). In that month, in an effort to purge the armed forces of officers sympathetic to Oviedo, Wasmosy announced the retirement of some 20 high-ranking officers, including the Commander of the First Army Corps and the Chief of Staff of the Army. In June Oviedo was placed under house arrest on charges of insurrection and insubordination with respect to the events of April. In July Oviedo's assets were seized and the order for his detention was revised from house arrest to preventative imprisonment. This development provoked protest by Oviedo's supporters, who rallied outside the Congreso Nacional to demand his release. Wasmosy continued to reorganize the military hierarchy, replacing several senior officers. In August an appeal court acquitted Oviedo of the charge of insurrection, ruling that there was insufficient evidence to suggest that he had made military preparations to overturn the constitutional order. In December 1996 Oviedo was acquitted of the lesser charge of insubordination.

In August 1997 Juan Carlos Galaverna, a Colorado senator and prominent supporter of Argaña, presented a motion to the Senado seeking the impeachment of President Wasmosy on the grounds that he had contravened the Constitution by attempting to influence the outcome of the forthcoming Partido Colorado primary election; Wasmosy denied the allegations. Although the impeachment motion was unsuccessful, it illustrated the extent of division between rival factions of the Partido Colorado in advance of the forthcoming general election. In September Oviedo succeeded in securing the Partido Colorado's presidential nomination, defeating Wasmosy's preferred candidate, Carlos

Facetti Masulli, and Argaña himself, in the party's primary. However, Argaña's faction, which effectively controlled the party's executive board, refused to accept the outcome of the ballot, claiming that it had been fraudulent, and presented a legal challenge to the result.

In October 1997 Wasmosy issued an executive order for the 'disciplinary arrest', for a period of 30 days, of Oviedo; the grounds for the detention was contempt of the President and Commander-in-Chief of the Armed Forces, after Oviedo had publicly accused Wasmosy of corruption. In December, following a ruling by the Supreme Court endorsing the arrest order, Oviedo surrendered to the military authorities. He completed his 30-day period of confinement on 11 January 1998; however, a special military tribunal, established by Wasmosy to investigate the events of the coup attempt led by Oviedo in April 1996, ordered that he be detained indefinitely pending the results of the investigation. In March the tribunal found Oviedo guilty of crimes committed against the order and security of the armed forces, and also of sedition, and sentenced him to 10 years' imprisonment. In the following month the Supreme Court ratified the military tribunal's decision, and the Supreme Electoral Tribunal consequently annulled Oviedo's presidential candidacy. In accordance with the law, the candidacy of the Partido Colorado was assumed by Raúl Cubas Grau, hitherto the vice-presidential nominee; Argaña was to be the new candidate for the vice-presidency.

The presidential election of 10 May 1998 resulted in victory for Cubas Grau, who secured some 55% of the votes cast, ahead of Laíno, the candidate of the Alianza Democrática (an electoral alliance comprising the PLRA and the PEN), who received 44% of the votes. Colorado candidates were also most successful at legislative elections and at elections for provincial administrators held concurrently. Cubas Grau's election campaign had emphasized his support for his long-time political ally, Oviedo. Prior to the inauguration of the new administration, in July Vice-President-elect Argaña (a staunch opponent of Oviedo) concluded an informal political pact involving his faction of the Partido Colorado and the opposition PLRA and PEN, effectively depriving Cubas Grau of a congressional majority, while in early August President Wasmosy implemented a comprehensive reorganization of the military high command, which promoted the interests of many of Oviedo's military opponents.

Cubas Grau duly took office on 15 August 1998, and a new Council of Ministers, largely composed of supporters of Oviedo, was sworn in on the same day. On 18 August, deliberately circumventing a new law restricting presidential pardons, Cubas Grau issued a decree commuting Oviedo's prison sentence to time already served. On the following day the Congreso Nacional voted to condemn the decree and to initiate proceedings to impeach the President for unconstitutional procedure. (A successful impeachment would have resulted in the elevation of Oviedo's severest critic, Vice-President Argaña, to the presidency.) The new President's confrontational stance (and the release of Oviedo) also provoked dissent among his own supporters and associates; Cubas Grau's brother, Carlos, resigned the industry and commerce portfolio in the new Council of Ministers later that month. In December the Argaña faction-controlled central apparatus of the Partido Colorado expelled Oviedo from the party. While the Congreso Nacional was unable to muster the two-thirds' majority support necessary to impeach President Cubas Grau, the country remained in effective political deadlock, prompting serious concerns in the business community that the country's mounting economic difficulties would not be addressed.

In March 1999, however, the political impasse ended dramatically. On 23 March Vice-President Argaña was assassinated, prompting nation-wide speculation that Oviedo was behind the attack, and galvanizing the Congreso Nacional sufficiently to secure the support of the two-thirds' majority needed to initiate Cubas Grau's impeachment. Increasing tensions were exacerbated three days later by the killing of seven protesters who were demonstrating in Asunción in support of demands for the resignation of the President, in the light of Argaña's assassination. On 28 March Cubas Grau resigned the presidency and sought refuge in Brazil, while Oviedo crossed the border to Argentina. (In February 2002 Cubas Grau surrendered to the Paraguayan authorities to face trial for the killings of the protesters and was placed under house arrest until June 2003, when he was released without the charges against him having been dismissed.) In early April the judicial authorities ordered the arrest of Oviedo for involvement in the death of Argaña, after three of his close collaborators were identified as the assassins. (In October 2000 Maj.-Gen. Reinaldo Servin, Constantino Rodas and Pablo Vera Esteche were sentenced to long prison terms for their roles in the assassination.) However, the Argentine Government rejected Paraguay's request for extradition, resulting in a rapid deterioration in the relationship between the two countries. Oviedo left Argentina in early December in order to avoid being extradited by the new Argentine Government of Fernando de la Rúa.

Meanwhile, in accordance with the terms of the Constitution, in the absence of the elected President and Vice-President, the President of the Congreso Nacional, the pro-Argaña Colorado senator Luis González Macchi, was swiftly installed as head of state. He announced the composition of a multi-party Government of National Unity at the end of March 1999. In late April, following careful scrutiny of the articles of the Constitution, the Supreme Court ruled that González Macchi should serve the remainder of Cubas Grau's presidential term (scheduled to expire in 2003). The Court also ruled that an election to select a new Vice-President should be conducted. Hoping to consolidate the new Government, González Macchi announced that his own party would not present a vice-presidential candidate. However, prominent figures within the Partido Colorado decided to contest the election none the less, precipitating tension with the PLRA, which had effectively been promised the post. Meanwhile, factionalism within the PLRA placed increasing strains on the Government of National Unity. Events culminated in February 2000 when PLRA members voted to withdraw from the ruling coalition, depriving the Government of a legislative majority. The Partido Colorado's remaining coalition partner, the PEN, was, furthermore, divided over its continuing participation in the Government.

In May 1999 González Macchi forcibly retired more than 100 army officers, including several high-ranking supporters of Oviedo. By mid-November another 45 senior commanders, who were thought to be supporters of Oviedo, had been replaced. However, the reorganization did not prevent a coup attempt, in May 2000, by rebellious soldiers thought to be sympathetic to Oviedo. It was swiftly defeated by the Government (most army brigades and the air force remained loyal to the President), which declared a 30-day nation-wide state of emergency, assuming extraordinary powers that resulted in the arrest of more than 70 people, mostly members of the security forces. Oviedo denied any involvement with the coup, but in June he was arrested by Brazilian police in Foz do Iguaçu, near the Brazilian border with Paraguay. In March 2001 the Brazilian Chief Prosecutor ruled that Oviedo could be extradited, but in December the Supreme Court rejected the ruling, stating that Oviedo was a victim of political persecution, and released him from imprisonment.

The initial popularity of the Government of National Unity collapsed as thousands of peasants, assembled by rural organizations, mobilized on several occasions during 1999 to protest against the Government's lack of action on rural issues. In response to the protests, in November the Government offered a US $168m. rescue package for the agricultural and livestock sector, mostly for debt-refinancing schemes. In March 2000 the Government announced a scheme to assist 250,000 small farmers. However, by the end of the month there were an estimated 10,000 smallholders camped outside the Congreso building. (The protest continued until March 2001, when government concessions were eventually secured.) Strikes were undertaken by power and telecommunications workers and by public sector workers during March and June 2000, respectively. However, the Government insisted it would continue with its 'state restructuring' programme. In mid-November the Congreso Nacional approved legislation allowing for the sale of the state railway, water and telecommunications companies.

At the vice-presidential election, which was finally held on 13 August 2000, the 53-year Colorado monopoly on power was ended when Félix Argaña, son of the late Vice-President, was narrowly defeated (by less than 1% of the votes cast) by the PLRA candidate, Julio César Franco. The election of Franco, whose candidacy was endorsed by Oviedo, increased the divisions within the Partido Colorado and resulted in the resignation of the Minister of National Defence, Nelson Argaña, another son of the late Vice-President.

A corruption scandal in early May 2001 forced the President of the Central Bank, Washington Ashwell, to resign over his alleged involvement in the fraudulent transfer of US $16m. to a US bank account. An opposition attempt to impeach the President over his alleged involvement in the fraud was defeated by the Cámara de Diputados in August. In September several thousand protesters marched in Asunción to demand the resignation of González Macchi. In April 2002 González Macchi was formally charged with involvement in the corruption scandal.

In late January 2002 the credibility of the Government was further undermined after two leaders of the left-wing party Movimiento Patria Libre (MPL) alleged that they had been illegally detained for 13 days and tortured by the police, with the knowledge of government ministers, as part of an investigation into a kidnapping case. In response to the allegations, in early February the head of the national police force and his deputy, as well as the head of the judicial investigations department, were dismissed. Following sustained public and political pressure the Minister of the Interior and the Minister of Justice and Labour resigned soon afterwards, although both protested their innocence. In addition, the national intelligence agency, the Secretaría Nacional de Informaciones, was disbanded. The Cámara de Diputados issued a statement assigning some responsibility for the detention of the MPL leaders to the President and the Attorney-General, and describing the event as 'state terrorism'.

Throughout 2002 an alliance of farmers, trade unions and left-wing organizations staged mass protests throughout the country to call for an end to the Government's free market policies and to protest at widely perceived government corruption. In response to the mounting opposition, in June the Government suspended its planned privatization of the state telecommunications company, Corporación Paraguaya de Comunicaciones (COPACO). Nevertheless, the protests continued as the economic situation worsened, prompting González Macchi to declare a state of emergency in July, which was lifted two days later after clashes between anti-Government protesters and security forces resulted in two fatalities.

In December 2002 the Cámara de Diputados voted in favour of the impeachment of President González Macchi on five charges of corruption. In an attempt to avoid the charges, González Macchi offered to resign early from office, immediately following the presidential election due in April 2003 (his term of office officially ended in August of that year). However, in February 2003 the Senado voted narrowly against impeachment. Proceedings began against González Macchi in mid-2004 on charges relating to the May 2001 embezzlement scandal; in February 2005 further charges were brought against him for misuse of public funds and irregularities connected to the sale of two state-owned banks. He was found guilty on charges of embezzlement and false testimony and, despite appealing against the verdict, was sentenced to eight years' imprisonment in December 2006.

Legislative and presidential elections were held on 27 April 2003. The Colorado candidate, Nicanor Duarte Frutos, won 37% of the votes cast in the presidential ballot, compared with the 24% attracted by the PLRA candidate and former Vice-President, Julio César Franco, who had resigned in October 2002 in order to contest the election. A businessman, Pedro Nicolás Fadul Niella, of the Patria Querida movement, came third with 21% of the votes, while Guillermo Sánchez Guffanti of UNACE (which had disassociated itself from the Partido Colorado and been renamed the Unión Nacional de Ciudadanos Eticos) attracted 13% of the ballot. However, the Partido Colorado secured only 37 of the 80 seats in the Cámara de Diputados (thus losing its majority in the chamber) and 16 of the 45 seats in the Senado. At his inauguration on 15 August 2003, President Duarte reiterated his election pledges to reduce corruption, improve the public finances and restore the country's international credibility. A number of well-regarded technocrats were appointed to the Council of Ministers, notably including the new Minister of Finance, Dionisio Borda. On taking office, Duarte announced his intention to effect wide-ranging judicial reform; to this effect, in October the Congreso reached consensus on impeachment proceedings against six Supreme Court judges suspected of corruption. Four of the judges resigned during the impeachment process, which finally resulted in the indictment of the remaining two judges in December. However, despite hopes that political influence in the selection of new judges might be avoided, two of the six new Supreme Court judges appointed in March 2004 were Colorado supporters.

In June 2004 Oviedo returned voluntarily from Brazil. On arrival, he was taken to a military prison to serve the remainder of his 10-year sentence for organizing the attempted coup in 1996 against the Government of President Wasmosy. Oviedo was also to be tried on other charges still pending against him. In October, however, Oviedo was provisionally acquitted of having organized the failed coup attempt of May 2000, and in January 2005 charges against him relating to a discovered arms cache were dismissed. In March the Supreme Court ruled that Oviedo would nevertheless have to serve out his prison sentence. Throughout the rest of 2005 demonstrations against his detention were staged by his supporters.

In October 2004 the kidnap and murder of an 11-year-old child provoked a vociferous public outcry against the perceived deterioration of security in Paraguay. In response, President Duarte dismissed the Minister of the Interior, Orlando Fiorotto Sánchez (who was replaced by Attorney-General Nelson Mora), and the head of the national police, Umberto Núñez. In February 2005 Mora was himself dismissed—in addition to some 50 senior members of the police force—following the discovery of the body of Cecilia Cubas under a house in a suburb of Asunción. Cubas, the daughter of former President Raúl Cubas Grau, had been kidnapped in the previous September. In advance of the police inquiry, President Duarte held the MPL responsible for the killing and subsequently supported claims made by the Colombian President, Alvaro Uribe Vélez, that the MPL had been assisted by the Fuerzas Armadas Revolucionarias de Colombia—Ejército del Pueblo (FARC). Twelve of the 15 people charged with involvement in the kidnap and murder of Cecilia Cubas, all of whom were members or sympathizers of the MPL, were found guilty in November 2006.

Throughout 2003 and 2004 strikes, roadblocks, marches and illegal land occupations were organized by farmers and indigenous groups in protest at a range of government policies, including agrarian reform and privatizations. In response to the continuing civil unrest, in September 2004 the Government signed an agreement to distribute some 13,000 ha of land in six western departments to landless peasants; however, the main peasant grouping, the Federación Nacional Campesina (FNC), maintained its demand for the redistribution of some 100,000 ha of land. Illegal land occupations and other protests continued in late 2004 and 2005, resulting in the arrest of hundreds of protesters and several fatalities. In February 2005 President Duarte announced the creation of a three-year security plan, which included a greater role of the armed forces in policing rural areas. The plan was publicly opposed in Asunción by some 5,000 rural activists in March.

In November 2005 President Duarte announced plans to reform the Constitution in order to allow for presidential re-election. At that time, Duarte was also seeking re-election to the leadership of the Partido Colorado, which he had ceded on taking office as President. However, opposition groups argued that it was unconstitutional for the President to hold any additional public office, and in December a motion to impeach President Duarte was proposed in the Cámara de Diputados by the opposition Patria Querida. The proposal was defeated, receiving only 39 votes in favour (a minimum two-thirds' majority, or 53 votes, was required to pass an impeachment motion). In January 2006 the Supreme Electoral Tribunal rejected criminal charges against President Duarte, brought by the leader of the Frente Colorado faction, Luis Talavera, for attempting to hold two public offices, although the Court ruled that it would be unconstitutional for Duarte to hold another office concurrently with the presidency of the Republic.

In February 2006, nevertheless, Duarte won a convincing victory in the Partido Colorado leadership election, defeating his rival Osvaldo Domínguez Dibb, who represented the pro-Stroessner ('Stronista') faction of the party. In March the Supreme Court overturned the Supreme Electoral Tribunal's earlier ruling that forbade the President of the Republic from holding an additional office; as a result, Duarte assumed the leadership of his party. He simultaneously announced a proposed referendum on whether to amend the Constitution to allow presidential re-election. In response to the Supreme Court's ruling, opposition groups again initiated impeachment proceedings against Duarte, as well as against the five judges of the Court's Constitutional Panel. Faced with such resistance, the following day Duarte resigned from the party presidency.

In February 2007 a group of more than 30 social and labour organizations joined the principal opposition parties in signing an accord to form the Concertación Nacional (CN). The new coalition announced its intention to present a single candidate in the presidential election in 2008 in the hope of providing an effective challenge to the Partido Colorado. In July six of the eight political parties in the CN, including the PLRA and the PEN, announced their support for Fernando Lugo Méndez, a popular former Roman Catholic bishop known for his frequent pronouncements on social justice and his work with deprived communities, who had retired from the priesthood in late 2006 in order to become more actively involved in politics. However, Patria Querida and UNACE rejected the nomination of Lugo, arguing that it contravened the February accord's requirement to hold a primary election to select the opposition candidate, and both parties subsequently withdrew from the CN. As a result, in September Lugo founded the Alianza Patriótica para el Cambio (APC) to support his candidacy. Earlier in September Oviedo, who had previously declared his intention to stand in the election, was granted conditional release from gaol by a military tribunal. In the following month the Supreme Court acquitted Oviedo of involvement in the 1996 coup attempt, thereby making him eligible to stand for the presidency, and he was declared the UNACE candidate in January 2008. There was speculation that Oviedo's release and acquittal had been orchestrated by the Government in order to divide the opposition. Meanwhile, a primary election held by the Partido Colorado in December 2007 to determine its presidential candidate resulted in a very narrow victory for President Duarte's nominee, former Minister of Education and Culture Blanca Ovelar. However, the result was contested by the defeated candidate, former Vice-President Luis Castiglioni (who had resigned the vice-presidency in October in order to contest the election), amid allegations of malpractice, causing damaging divisions within the party. Ovelar was not declared the winner of the primary contest until late January 2008.

At the presidential election, held on 20 April 2008, Lugo won a comfortable victory, securing 40.9% of votes cast, against 30.6% for Ovelar. Oviedo won 21.9% of votes, while Pedro Fadul, again representing Patria Querida, obtained just 2.4%. In the concurrent legislative elections the Partido Colorado narrowly retained its status as the largest party in both chambers of the Congreso Nacional, securing 30 of the 80 seats in the Cámara de Diputados and 15 out of 45 seats in the Senado. The PLRA (the largest party in Lugo's APC) obtained 27 seats in the lower house and 14 in the upper, while UNACE won 15 and nine seats, respectively. In order to achieve a working majority in the Congreso, Lugo secured the support of UNACE and the 'Nicanorista' faction of the Partido Colorado, the latter comprising supporters of President Duarte. However, the stability of the new legislature was threatened by a dispute regarding the fact that Duarte had been elected to a seat in the Senado, in apparent contravention of the Constitution (which granted former Presidents a non-voting seat for life in the chamber, but prohibited a serving President from exercising any additional public office). In an attempt to assume his elective seat on the appointed date of 1 July, on 23 June Duarte submitted his resignation as President, nearly two months before his term in office was due to expire. However, a session of the Senado that was convened on the following day to consider the President's resignation was boycotted by the PLRA and other senators opposed to his election to the chamber; it thus failed to achieve a quorum, and Duarte was forced to remain in office.

President Lugo was inaugurated on 15 August 2008. His cabinet included four representatives of different factions of the PLRA (in addition to the Vice-President, Federico Franco Gómez) and a number of non-affiliated ministers, notably including Dionisio Borda as Minister of Finance, a position he had previously held from 2003–06 under Duarte. In the first month of Lugo's presidency the dispute over Duarte's senatorial seat continued to disrupt relations between the new Government and the Congreso Nacional. On 26 August an inquorate session of the Senado chaired by the chamber's pro-Duarte President, Enrique González Quintana of UNACE, swore Duarte into office as an elected senator, but later the same day the PLRA Vice-President of the Senado, in defiance of González Quintana, chaired a session dominated by anti-Duarte senators that swore the former President's nominated alternate, Jorge Céspedes, into the same seat. The impasse, which appeared to indicate an inability of Lugo's allies to co-operate, was ended in early September after Lugo publicly accused Duarte and Oviedo, along with González Quintana and other senior political figures, of plotting a coup to overthrow the new Government. Although Duarte and Oviedo both strongly denied Lugo's allegations, UNACE subsequently relinquished its support for Duarte; on 4 September Céspedes was legitimately sworn in as a senator and Duarte was afforded the honorary position of senator for life.

One of Lugo's main campaign pledges was to initiate a process of land reform. In the months following the elections of April 2008, peasants organized by the Mesa Coordinadora Nacional de Organizaciones Campesinas staged a series of land invasions, demanding that the President-elect promise to carry out a comprehensive land redistribution programme. The demonstrations intensified in October, when one person was killed in a violent confrontation between police and peasants occupying an agricultural estate in Alto Paraná. In the same month the government body responsible for rural development, the Instituto Nacional del Desarrollo Rural y de la Tierra, declared that it would no longer allow foreigners to acquire land in Paraguay; the large proportion of land in foreign (especially Brazilian) ownership was a major source of tension between landowners and landless peasants. In late October the Government announced the purchase of some 22,000 ha from 11 Brazilian farmers in the department of San Pedro for redistribution to landless families; none the less, protests by peasants continued, and were countered in December with demonstrations by large landowners. In January 2009 the Government announced the first stage of its land reform programme, which concentrated on rural development and did not include any redistributive measures. The FNC continued to demand a major programme of redistribution, and the federation's annual demonstration in Asunción in March was attended by some 10,000 people protesting against the slow pace of reform.

President Lugo carried out a cabinet reorganization in mid-April 2009, replacing the Ministers of Industry and Commerce, Justice and Labour, Agriculture and Livestock, and Education and Culture. The appointment of the new ministers, all four of whom were members of the PLRA, was interpreted as an attempt to ensure the continued support of that party for the Government's legislative programme. Later in April Héctor Lacognata was appointed Minister of Foreign Affairs in place of Alejandro Hamed Franco, who had reportedly submitted his resignation in the previous month. None the less, public confidence in Lugo's presidency was damaged in April by the President's admission that he was the father of a two-year-old son, made after the child's mother presented a paternity suit against him. Two other women subsequently alleged that Lugo had fathered children by them during his time as Bishop of San Pedro; a prominent PLRA senator publicly urged Lugo to resign in response to the scandal.

In March 1991 the Presidents and Ministers of Foreign Affairs of Argentina, Brazil, Uruguay and Paraguay signed a formal agreement in Asunción creating a common market of the 'Southern Cone' countries, the Mercado Común del Sur (Mercosur, see p. 405). The agreement allowed for the dismantling of trade barriers between the four countries, and entered into full operation in 1995. In mid-2006 President Duarte announced that his Government was to seek engagement for Paraguay in other free trade agreements aside from Mercosur.

Paraguay's relations with the USA were strained in late 2006 when the Government of Paraguay announced that US military personnel operating in that country would no longer enjoy immunity from prosecution. Unlike other Mercosur countries, Paraguay had signed an agreement with the USA in 2005 protecting US soldiers from extradition to the International Criminal Court. The decision by Paraguay not to renew this agreement prompted the USA to announce the withdrawal of humanitarian and medical services that it had been providing to people living in remote, rural areas of Paraguay.

In late 2006 the US Government reported that it intended to encourage greater co-operation between Paraguay, Argentina and Brazil in monitoring terrorist activity in the so-called triple frontier area. The Paraguayan border town of Ciudad del Este was believed to generate some 30% of the country's entire tax revenue from customs, much of which was known to come from illegal trade in arms, drugs and counterfeit goods. There was evidence that proceeds from illegal dealings, such as these, were funding the activities of terrorist groups in the area.

Following Fernando Lugo's accession to the presidency in August 2008, relations with Brazil appeared likely to be dominated by the new President's stated commitment to renegotiate the treaty governing the Itaipú hydroelectric project on the border between Brazil and Paraguay. The treaty, signed in 1973 and which was due to expire in 2023, apportioned to each country one-half of the electricity produced by the project, and bound each country to sell to the other any surplus (in the case of Paraguay, some 95% of its share) at the cost of production. In December the Brazilian Minister of Foreign Affairs, Celso Amorim, rejected Paraguay's demands for the right to sell its surplus energy on the open market and for a pardon of some US $19,000m. of debt resulting from the scheme, declaring that they were 'unrealistic'.

PARAGUAY

Government

Under the 1992 Constitution, legislative power is held by the bicameral Congreso Nacional (National Congress), whose members serve for five years. The Senado (Senate) has 45 members, and the Cámara de Diputados (Chamber of Deputies) 80 members. Elections to the legislature are by universal adult suffrage. Executive power is held by the President, directly elected for a single term of five years at the same time as the legislature. The President of the Republic governs with the assistance of a Vice-President and an appointed Council of Ministers. Paraguay is divided into 17 departments, each administered by an elected governor.

Defence

As assessed at November 2008, the armed forces totalled 10,650 (including 2,550 conscripts). There was an army of 7,600 and an air force of 1,100. The navy, which is largely river-based, had 1,950 men, including 900 marines and a naval air force of 100. There is also a 14,800-strong paramilitary police force, including 4,000 conscripts. Military service, which is compulsory, lasts for 12 months in the army and for two years in the navy. The defence budget for 2008 totalled 576,000m. guaraníes.

Economic Affairs

In 2007, according to estimates by the World Bank, Paraguay's gross national income (GNI), measured at average 2005–07 prices, was US $10,225m., equivalent to $1,670 per head (or $4,380 per head on an international purchasing-power parity basis). During 2000–07, it was estimated, the population increased at an average annual rate of 2.0%, while gross domestic product (GDP) per head decreased, in real terms, by an average of 1.4% per year. Overall GDP increased, in real terms, at an average annual rate of 1.4% in 2000–07; GDP increased by 4.6% in 2007.

According to preliminary figures, agriculture (including forestry, hunting and fishing) contributed an estimated 24.2% of GDP in 2007. In November–February 2006/07 31.2% of the economically active population were employed in the sector. The principal cash crop is soybeans, which accounted for an estimated 33.9% of total export revenue in 2008. Other significant crops are sugar cane, cassava, sunflowers, cotton, wheat and maize. Timber and wood manufactures provided an estimated 2.5% of export revenues in 2008. The raising of livestock (particularly cattle and pigs) is also important. Meat accounted for an estimated 14.0% of export earnings in 2008. According to the World Bank, agricultural GDP increased at an average annual rate of 5.0% in 2000–07; real agricultural GDP increased by 4.0% in 2007.

According to provisional figures, industry (including mining, manufacturing, construction and power) contributed an estimated 22.0% of GDP in 2007 and employed 17.2% of the working population in November–February 2006/07. Industrial GDP increased by an average of 1.9% per year in 2000–07; the sector increased by 3.6% in 2007.

Paraguay has almost no commercially exploited mineral resources, and the mining sector employed only 0.1% of the labour force in 2004 and contributed a provisional 0.1% of GDP in 2007. Production is confined to gypsum, kaolin and limestone. However, foreign companies have been involved in exploration for gold and petroleum deposits, and deposits of natural gas were discovered in 1994.

Manufacturing contributed a provisional 14.1% of GDP in 2007, and, including the mining sector, employed 10.7% of the working population in November–February 2006/07. The main branch of manufacturing (in terms of value added) was production of food and beverages. The other principal sectors were wood and wood products, handicrafts, paper, printing and publishing, hides and furs, and non-metallic mineral products. Manufacturing GDP increased at an average annual rate of 1.3% in 2000–06. However; the real GDP of this sector declined by 1.2% in 2007, according to official estimates.

Energy is derived almost completely from hydroelectric power. Imports of mineral fuels comprised an estimated 15.4% of the value of total merchandise imports in 2008. Ethyl alcohol (ethanol), derived from sugar cane, is widely used as a component of vehicle fuel.

The services sector contributed a provisional 53.8% of GDP in 2007, and engaged 51.5% of the working population in November–February 2006/07. Paraguay traditionally serves as an entrepôt for regional trade. The GDP of the services sector increased by an average of 3.2% per year in 2000–07; the sector increased by 8.6% in 2007.

In 2007 Paraguay recorded a visible trade deficit of US $545m., and there was a deficit of $126.1m. on the current account of the balance of payments. According to preliminary figures, in 2008 the principal source of registered imports was the People's Republic of China (27.7%); other major suppliers in that year were Brazil and Argentina. Uruguay was the principal market for registered exports in that year (a preliminary 17.4% of total exports); other notable purchasers were Argentina and Brazil. The principal exports in 2008 were, according to preliminary estimates, soybeans and vegetable oils. The principal imports were motors, general industrial machinery equipment and parts, mineral fuels, transport equipment, and chemical products.

In 2007 there was, according to IMF projections, a central government budget surplus of 593m. guaraníes (equivalent to 1.0% of GDP). Paraguay's total external debt was US $3,426m. at the end of 2006, of which $2,235m. was long-term public debt. In that year the cost of debt-servicing was equivalent to 6.8% of the total value of exports of goods and services. Annual inflation averaged 8.7% in 2000–07; consumer prices increased by an average of 8.7% in 2007. An estimated 6.7% of the labour force were unemployed in November–February 2006/07.

Paraguay is a member of the Inter-American Development Bank (IDB, see p. 318), of the Latin American Integration Association (ALADI, see p. 342), of the Latin American Economic System (SELA, see p. 427) and of the Mercado Común del Sur (Mercosur, see p. 405). In December 2004 Paraguay was one of 12 countries that were signatories to the agreement, signed in Cusco, Peru, creating the South American Community of Nations (Comunidad Sudamericana de Naciones), intended to promote greater regional economic integration. It had been anticipated that the new entity, to be styled after the EU, would become operational by 2007; however, by April 2009 implementation of the necessary legal frameworks, to achieve the integrated structure envisaged, remained incomplete. A constitutive treaty for the community—referred to as the Union of South American Nations (UNASUR) since its reinvention at the first South American Energy Summit of 16 April 2007—was signed by heads of state in Brasília, Brazil, in May 2008, with full functionality of economic union tentatively scheduled for 2019.

In the early years of the 21st century the Government relied on external loans, particularly from the IMF, to keep the economy afloat. In March 2005 the IMF gave a broadly positive assessment of the Government's economic management, while encouraging further structural reform. Government revenues increased significantly in both 2005 and 2006, owing to improved tax collection and a widening of the tax base. While in 2006 the IMF renewed its praise of Paraguay's continued fiscal prudence, government expenditure increased in 2007 and 2008 as a result of additional subsidies to the country's ailing cotton industry, increased spending on health, education and social security and a 20% wage increase for government employees. The Government successfully reduced its debt burden by some US $6,200m. in 2006 after Argentina agreed to forgive one-half of the debt owed on the Yacyretá power plant. GDP was estimated to have increased by 4.6% in 2007, driven by increased soy production, high soy prices and greater export demand for the crop, the latter in spite of a strongly performing currency against the US dollar. According to the Banco Central del Paraguay, total exports increased by 77% in 2007, compared with 24% for imports. However, the current account deficit remained high at 26% of GDP for that year, while inflationary pressures continued to cause concern. The economy grew by 5.5% in 2008, but the rate was projected to slow to 4.2% in 2009 as the increasingly severe global economic crisis began to stifle demand for Paraguayan exports. This was compounded by a drought in late 2008 and early 2009 which drastically curtailed soybean production. More positively, inflation started to decline and the banking system, according to the IMF, was relatively stable.

Education

Education is, where possible, compulsory for six years, to be undertaken between six and 12 years of age, but there are insufficient schools, particularly in the remote parts of the country. Primary education begins at the age of six and lasts for six years. Secondary education, beginning at 12 years of age, lasts for a further six years, comprising two cycles of three years each. In 2005 enrolment at primary schools included 94.3% of the relevant age-group, while enrolment at secondary schools included 57.4% of the relevant age-group. There are 12 universities in Paraguay. Public expenditure by all levels of governm-

PARAGUAY

nent on education was equivalent to 10.0% of total government spending in 2004, according to UNESCO estimates.

Public Holidays

2009: 1 January (New Year's Day), 2 March (for Heroes' Day), 9 April (Maundy Thursday), 10 April (Good Friday), 1 May (Labour Day), 15 May (Independence Day), 12 June (Peace of Chaco), 17 August (for Founding of Asunción), 29 September (Battle of Boquerón), 8 December (Immaculate Conception), 25 December (Christmas Day).

2010: 1 January (New Year's Day), 1 March (Heroes' Day), 1 April (Maundy Thursday), 2 April (Good Friday), 3 May (for Labour Day), 15 May (Independence Day), 14 June (for Peace of Chaco), 16 August (for Founding of Asunción), 29 September (Battle of Boquerón), 8 December (Immaculate Conception), 25 December (Christmas Day).

Weights and Measures
The metric system is in force.

Statistical Survey

Sources (unless otherwise stated): Dirección General de Estadística, Encuestas y Censos, Naciones Unidas, esq. Saavedra, Fernando de la Mora, Zona Norte; tel. (21) 51-1016; fax (21) 50-8493; internet www.dgeec.gov.py; Banco Central del Paraguay, Avda Federación Rusa y Marecos, Casilla 861, Barrio Santo Domingo, Asunción; tel. (21) 61-0088; fax (21) 60-8149; e-mail ccs@bcp.gov.py; internet www.bcp.gov.py; Secretaría Técnica de Planificación, Presidencia de la República, Iturbe y Eligio Ayala, Asunción.

Area and Population

AREA, POPULATION AND DENSITY

Area (sq km)	406,752*
Population (census results)	
26 August 1992	4,152,588
28 August 2002	
Males	2,627,831
Females	2,555,249
Total	5,183,080
Population (UN estimates at mid-year)†	
2006	6,015,000
2007	6,127,000
2008	6,238,000
Density (per sq km) at mid-2008	15.3

* 157,048 sq miles.
† Source: UN, *World Population Prospects: The 2008 Revision*.

DEPARTMENTS
(census of August 2002)

	Area (sq km)	Population	Density (per sq km)	Capital
Alto Paraguay (incl. Chaco)	82,349	13,250	0.2	Fuerte Olimpo
Alto Paraná	14,895	559,769	37.6	Ciudad del Este
Amambay	12,933	115,320	8.9	Pedro Juan Caballero
Asunción	117	510,910	4,366.8	—
Boquerón (incl. Nueva Asunción)	91,669	43,480	0.5	Doctor Pedro P. Peña
Caaguazú	11,474	443,311	38.6	Coronel Oviedo
Caazapá	9,496	139,080	14.6	Caazapá
Canindeyú	14,667	140,250	9.6	Salto del Guairá
Central	2,465	1,362,650	552.8	Asunción
Concepción	18,051	178,900	9.9	Concepción
Cordillera	4,948	233,170	47.1	Caacupé
Guairá	3,846	178,130	46.3	Villarrica
Itapúa	16,525	459,480	27.8	Encarnación
Misiones	9,556	102,230	10.7	San Juan Bautista
Ñeembucú	12,147	76,730	6.3	Pilar
Paraguarí	8,705	224,850	25.8	Paraguarí
Presidente Hayes	72,907	82,030	1.1	Pozo Colorado
San Pedro	20,002	319,540	16.0	San Pedro
Total	406,752	5,183,080	12.7	—

PRINCIPAL TOWNS
(population at 2002 census, incl. rural environs)

Asunción (capital)	510,910	Lambaré	119,830
Ciudad del Este*	222,109	Fernando de la Mora	113,990
San Lorenzo	203,150	Caaguazú	100,132
Luque	185,670	Encarnación	97,000
Capiatá	154,520	Pedro Juan Caballero	88,530

* Formerly Puerto Presidente Stroessner.

Mid-2007 ('000, incl. suburbs, UN estimate): Asunción 1,870 (Source: UN, *World Urbanization Prospects: The 2007 Revision*).

BIRTHS, MARRIAGES AND DEATHS

	Live births		Marriages		Deaths	
	Number	Rate (per 1,000)	Number	Rate (per 1,000)	Number	Rate (per 1,000)
2002	46,012	8.3	16,100	2.9	19,416	3.5
2003	45,669	8.0	17,717	3.1	19,593	3.4
2004	49,857	8.6	17,763	3.1	20,283	3.5
2005	51,444	8.7	19,826	3.4	17,360	2.9

Note: Rates were derived from estimates of mid-year population.

Life expectancy (years at birth, WHO estimates): 74.9 (males 72.3; females 77.8) in 2006 (Source: WHO, *World Health Statistics*).

PARAGUAY

ECONOMICALLY ACTIVE POPULATION
(household survey, August–December 2000)

	Males	Females	Total
Agriculture, hunting, forestry and fishing	689,825	212,497	902,322
Mining and quarrying	2,500	—	2,500
Manufacturing	186,322	99,864	286,186
Electricity, gas and water	10,432	3,300	13,732
Construction	107,340	—	107,340
Trade, restaurants and hotels	281,928	306,039	587,967
Transport, storage and communications	62,788	11,461	74,249
Financing, insurance, real estate and business services	55,836	28,950	84,786
Community, social and personal services	174,747	326,571	501,318
Activities not adequately described	208	—	208
Total employed	1,571,926	988,682	2,560,608

2004 (household survey, persons aged 10 years and over, September–December): Agriculture, hunting, forestry and fishing 852,077; Mining and quarrying 2,388; Manufacturing industries 289,702; Electricity, gas and water 16,360; Construction 114,027; Trade, restaurants and hotels 584,331; Transport and communications 95,484; Financing, insurance, etc. 72,153; Community, social and personal services 533,852; Activities not adequately described 238; *Total employed* 2,560,612 (males 1,561,745, females 998,867); Unemployed 201,847 (males 95,872, females 105,975); *Total labour force* 2,762,459 (males 1,657,617, females 1,104,842). **2005** (household survey, persons aged 10 years and over, October–December): Agriculture, hunting, forestry and fishing 847,161; Mining and quarrying 5,711; Manufacturing industries 248,035; Electricity, gas and water 17,263; Construction 140,872; Trade, restaurants and hotels 583,346; Transport and communications 95,622; Financing, insurance, etc. 98,969; Community, social and personal services 580,729; *Total employed* 2,617,708; Unemployed 162,102; *Total labour force* 2,779,810. **2006/07** (household survey, persons aged 10 years and over, November–February): Agriculture, hunting, forestry and fishing 797,677; Manufacturing industry (including mining and quarrying) 271,905; Electricity, gas and water 18,714; Construction 149,445; Trade, restaurants and hotels 584,255; Transport and communications 98,931; Financing, insurance, etc. 84,028; Community, social and personal services 548,057; Activities not adequately described 628; *Total employed* 2,553,640; Unemployed 182,006; *Total labour force* 2,735,646.

Health and Welfare

KEY INDICATORS

Total fertility rate (children per woman, 2006)	3.2
Under-5 mortality rate (per 1,000 live births, 2006)	22
HIV/AIDS (% of persons aged 15–49, 2007)	0.6
Physicians (per 1,000 head, 2002)	1.11
Hospital beds (per 1,000 head, 2006)	1.3
Health expenditure (2006): US $ per head (PPP)	342
Health expenditure (2006): % of GDP	7.6
Health expenditure (2006): public (% of total)	38.3
Access to water (% of persons, 2006)	77
Access to sanitation (% of persons, 2006)	70
Human Development Index (2006): ranking	98
Human Development Index (2006): value	0.752

For sources and definitions, see explanatory note on p. vi.

Agriculture

PRINCIPAL CROPS
('000 metric tons)

	2005	2006	2007*
Wheat	630	620*	675
Rice, paddy	102	126	132
Maize	830	1,100	1,003
Sorghum	17	25	35
Sweet potatoes	135	165	166
Cassava (Manioc)	4,785	4,800	5,100
Sugar cane	3,820	3,200	3,400
Beans, dry	67	70	78
Soybeans (Soya beans)	3,988	3,800	3,900
Oil palm fruit*	126	126	130
Sunflower seed	65	68	75
Tomatoes	69	88	90
Onions, dry*	27	27	29
Carrots and turnips	21	24	27
Watermelons*	115	115	118
Cantaloupes and other melons*	29	29	29
Bananas	48	45	46
Oranges	188	183	190
Tangerines, mandarins, clementines and satsumas	19	19	19
Grapefruit and pomelos	38	38	39
Guavas, mangoes and mangosteens*	29	29	29
Pineapples	57	72	73
Maté	74	86	88

* FAO estimate(s).

Aggregate production ('000 metric tons, may include official, semi-official or estimated data): Total cereals 1,579 in 2005, 1,871 in 2006, 1,845 in 2007; Total roots and tubers 4,921 in 2005, 4,967 in 2006, 5,267 in 2007; Total vegetables (incl. melons) 312 in 2005, 330 in 2006, 342 in 2007; Total fruits (excl. melons) 452 in 2005, 433 in 2006, 445 in 2007.

Source: FAO.

LIVESTOCK
('000 head, year ending September)

	2004	2005	2006
Cattle	9,622	9,838	9,983
Horses*	360	360	360
Pigs	1,507	1,600*	1,600*
Sheep	525	500*	500*
Goats	159	155*	155*
Chickens*	17,000	17,000	17,000
Ducks*	730	730	730
Geese and guinea fowls*	95	95	95
Turkeys*	105	105	105

* FAO estimate(s).

2007: Cattle 10,000,000 (FAO estimate); otherwise figures assumed to be unchanged from 2006 (FAO estimates).

Source: FAO.

LIVESTOCK PRODUCTS
('000 metric tons, FAO estimates)

	2005	2006	2007
Cattle meat	215	215	220
Pig meat	106	98	99
Chicken meat	37	37	37
Cows' milk	372	372	375
Hen eggs	100	100	100

Source: FAO.

Forestry

ROUNDWOOD REMOVALS
('000 cubic metres, excluding bark, FAO estimates)

	2005	2006	2007
Sawlogs, veneer logs and logs for sleepers	3,515	3,515	3,515
Other industrial wood	529	529	529
Fuel wood	6,047	6,149	6,252
Total	10,091	10,193	10,296

Source: FAO.

SAWNWOOD PRODUCTION
('000 cubic metres, including railway sleepers)

	1995	1996	1997
Total (all broadleaved)	400	500	550

1998–2007: Annual production as in 1997 (FAO estimates).
Source: FAO.

Fishing

('000 metric tons, live weight, FAO estimates)

	2004	2005	2006
Capture	22.0	21.0	20.0
Characins	7.8	7.5	7.0
Freshwater siluroids	10.8	10.3	10.0
Other freshwater fishes	3.4	3.2	3.0
Aquaculture	2.1	2.1	2.1
Total catch	24.1	23.1	22.1

Source: FAO.

Industry

SELECTED PRODUCTS
('000 metric tons)

	2005	2006	2007
Soya bean oil	232*	269*	300†
Total sugars†	118	119	n.a.
Hydraulic cement‡§	550	600	600

* Unofficial figure.
† FAO estimate(s).
‡ Data from US Geological Survey.
§ Estimates.

Source (unless otherwise indicated): FAO.

Finance

CURRENCY AND EXCHANGE RATES

Monetary Units
  100 céntimos = 1 guaraní (G).

Sterling, Dollar and Euro Equivalents (28 November 2008)
  £1 sterling = 7,484.0 guaraníes;
  US $1 = 4,880.0 guaraníes;
  €1 = 6,210.8 guaraníes;
  100,000 guaraníes = £13.36 = $20.49 = €16.10.

Average Exchange Rate (guaraníes per US dollar)
  2005   6,178.0
  2006   5,635.5
  2007   5,030.3

BUDGET
('000 million guaraníes)

Revenue	2005	2006	2007
Taxation	5,471	6,295	7,019
Corporate taxes	967	1,009	1,229
Excises	1,007	1,049	1,310
Value-added tax	2,372	2,786	3,318
Import duties	843	938	853
Non-tax revenue and grants	2,946	3,262	3,794
Capital revenues	2	31	25
Total	8,419	9,588	10,837

Expenditure	2005	2006	2007
Current expenditure	6,231	7,138	7,964
Goods and services	546	674	704
Wages and salaries	3,334	3,857	4,360
Interest payments	560	519	515
Transfers	1,771	2,067	2,366
Pensions and benefits	1,126	1,207	1,264
Other	19	22	19
Capital expenditure and net lending	1,860	2,185	2,280
Net lending	−24	99	132
Statistical discrepancy	−39	−216	—
Total	8,052	9,107	10,244

Source: IMF, *Paraguay: Sixth and Final Review Under the Stand-By Arrangement—Staff Report; Staff Statement; Press Release on the Executive Board Discussion; Statement by the Executive Director for Paraguay* (August 2008).

INTERNATIONAL RESERVES
(excl. gold, US $ million at 31 December)

	2006	2007	2008
IMF special drawing rights	137.82	43.65	44.19
Reserve position in IMF	32.31	33.94	33.08
Foreign exchange	1,531.52	2,384.29	2,767.29
Total	1,701.65	2,461.88	2,844.56

Source: IMF, *International Financial Statistics*.

MONEY SUPPLY
('000 million guaraníes at 31 December)

	2006	2007	2008
Currency outside banks	2,987.15	3,804.17	3,997.14
Demand deposits at commercial banks	3,579.42	5,495.71	6,163.49
Total money (incl. others)	6,703.92	9,473.95	10,198.01

Source: IMF, *International Financial Statistics*.

COST OF LIVING
(Consumer Price Index for Asunción; base: 2000 = 100)

	2005	2006	2007
Food (incl. beverages)	156.2	182.5	213.2
Housing (incl. fuel and light)	145.5	155.7	159.7
Clothing (incl. footwear)	128.6	137.1	141.5
All items (incl. others)	149.5	165.4	178.8

Source: ILO.

PARAGUAY

NATIONAL ACCOUNTS
('000 million guaraníes at current prices)

Expenditure on the Gross Domestic Product

	2005	2006*	2007*
Final consumption expenditure	39,079.8	44,373.3	52,257.7
Households†	34,069.8	38,512.2	45,592.4
General government	5,010.0	5,861.1	6,665.3
Gross capital formation	9,128.0	10,269.6	11,095.9
Total domestic expenditure	48,207.8	54,642.9	63,353.6
Exports of goods and services	23,636.1	28,067.9	31,323.0
Less Imports of goods and services	25,674.6	30,440.7	33,164.9
GDP in purchasers' values	46,169.3	52,270.1	61,511.7
GDP at constant 1994 prices	15,666.3	16,346.3	17,451.6

* Preliminary figures.
† Including non-profit institutions serving households.

Gross Domestic Product by Economic Activity

	2005	2006	2007*
Agriculture, hunting, forestry and fishing	9,756.2	10,560.0	13,533.4
Mining and quarrying	55.5	65.7	68.9
Manufacturing	6,414.8	7,141.2	7,901.7
Construction	2,132.6	2,457.5	3,269.5
Electricity and water	940.9	1,024.7	1,048.0
Trade	9,093.4	10,859.9	11,982.5
Transport and communications	3,547.6	3,959.2	4,863.5
Financial intermediation	1,095.5	1,352.7	1,540.0
Government services	4,186.8	4,827.2	5,640.0
Real estate, renting and business activities	1,647.1	1,868.6	2,073.3
Hotels and restaurants	492.7	563.5	659.0
Other services	2,721.5	2,903.9	3,263.4
Gross value added in basic prices	42,084.4	47,584.0	55,843.2
Net taxes on products	4,084.9	4,686.0	5,668.4
GDP in market prices	46,169.3	52,270.1	61,511.7

* Preliminary figures.

BALANCE OF PAYMENTS
(US $ million)

	2005	2006	2007
Exports of goods f.o.b.	3,351.8	4,409.2	5,463.2
Imports of goods f.o.b.	−3,814.3	−5,022.2	−6,008.3
Trade balance	−462.5	−613.0	−545.0
Exports of services	692.8	809.0	853.5
Imports of services	−343.4	−383.8	−462.9
Balance on goods and services	−113.1	−187.8	−154.5
Other income received	205.7	301.0	318.7
Other income paid	−263.5	−320.2	−411.4
Balance on goods, services and income	−170.9	−206.9	−247.2
Current transfers received	225.3	430.0	374.8
Current transfers paid	−1.5	−4.0	−1.5
Current balance	52.9	219.1	126.1
Capital account (net)	20.0	30.0	28.0
Direct investment abroad	−6.4	−4.0	−7.6
Direct investment from abroad	53.5	182.9	196.4
Other investment assets	386.5	106.7	483.8
Other investment liabilities	−132.4	−109.0	−33.6
Net errors and omissions	−210.8	−42.9	−168.1
Overall balance	163.2	382.7	625.0

Source: IMF, *International Financial Statistics*.

External Trade
(excl. border trade)

PRINCIPAL COMMODITIES
(US $ million, preliminary)

Imports f.o.b.	2006	2007	2008
Food and live animals	192.7	233.9	363.0
Beverages and tobacco	129.9	157.4	209.3
Mineral fuels	691.1	715.1	1,307.7
Chemical products	328.7	378.2	496.2
Road vehicles	139.5	186.6	335.5
Transport equipment and accessories	302.7	405.8	738.0
Electrical appliances	125.4	144.6	189.3
Motors, general industrial machinery equipment and parts	1,347.0	2,050.9	2,508.4
Total (incl. others)	4,614.4	5,662.8	8,470.7

Exports f.o.b.	2007	2008
Meat and derivatives	368.0	621.4
Cereals	376.2	378.5
Oleaginous seeds	890.3	1,502.5
Vegetable oils	211.2	592.6
Flour	218.7	562.6
Wood and wooden products	116.0	111.3
Cotton fibres	47.1	19.2
Total (incl. others)	2,784.7	4,433.7

PRINCIPAL TRADING PARTNERS
(US $ '000)

Imports c.i.f.	2004	2005	2006*
Argentina	619,344	639,188	715,757
Brazil	821,008	883,944	1,052,630
Chile	35,592	38,208	73,063
China, People's Republic	439,401	667,440	1,416,641
France	35,523	38,137	39,431
Germany	44,832	50,683	125,406
Japan	86,710	93,401	435,161
Korea, Republic	26,918	35,453	86,575
Malaysia	10,779	30,539	65,134
Switzerland-Liechtenstein	64,621	136,981	176,183
Taiwan	33,898	53,711	64,613
USA	108,055	169,299	331,904
Uruguay	61,272	52,987	59,095
Venezuela	6,075	5,697	139,922
Total (incl. others)	2,657,707	3,251,429	5,254,271

Exports f.o.b.	2004	2005	2006*
Argentina	101,844	107,304	168,498
Brazil	312,498	325,528	327,983
Cayman Islands	173,736	169,329	180,228
Chile	29,567	64,787	130,835
Germany	14,202	13,865	19,438
Italy	24,565	16,335	21,198
Japan	18,144	18,479	24,699
Netherlands	33,148	47,194	41,661
Peru	19,807	19,606	27,841
Russia	41,216	101,084	227,802
Switzerland-Liechtenstein	66,661	14,565	34,127
USA	52,211	51,561	62,376
Uruguay	451,211	479,290	420,243
Total (incl. others)	1,626,584	1,687,823	1,906,367

* Preliminary figures.

2007 (US $ '000, preliminary): *Imports:* Argentina 799,692; Brazil 1,587,833; China, People's Republic 1,566,789; Uruguay 73,720; Total (incl. others) 5,662,759. *Exports:* Argentina 551,785; Brazil 557,925; China, People's Republic 26,279; Uruguay 264,221; Total (incl. others) 2,784,728.

2008 (US $ '000, preliminary): *Imports:* Argentina 1,215,638; Brazil 2,262,402; China, People's Republic 2,346,400; Uruguay 100,408; Total (incl. others) 8,470,668. *Exports:* Argentina 712,026; Brazil 619,979; China, People's Republic 93,155; Uruguay 771,779; Total (incl. others) 4,433,706.

Transport

RAILWAYS
(traffic)

	1988	1989	1990
Passengers carried	178,159	196,019	125,685
Freight (metric tons)	200,213	164,980	289,099

Source: UN, *Statistical Yearbook*.

Passenger-kilometres: 3.0 million per year in 1994–96.

Freight ton-kilometres: 5.5 million in 1994.

Source: UN Economic Commission for Latin America and the Caribbean.

ROAD TRAFFIC
(vehicles in use)

	1999	2000
Cars	267,587	274,186
Buses	8,991	9,467
Lorries	41,329	42,992
Vans and jeeps	134,144	138,656
Motorcycles	6,872	8,825

Source: Organización Paraguaya de Cooperación Intermunicipal.

SHIPPING

Merchant Fleet
(registered at 31 December)

	2005	2006	2007
Number of vessels	43	43	45
Total displacement ('000 grt)	44.3	44.1	49.3

Source: Lloyd's Register-Fairplay, *World Fleet Statistics*.

CIVIL AVIATION
(traffic on scheduled services)

	2004	2005	2006
Kilometres flown (million)	6.9	7.3	7.2
Passenger-km (million)	433.4	500.6	480.7

Source: UN Economic Commission for Latin America and the Caribbean, *Statistical Yearbook*.

Tourism

ARRIVALS BY NATIONALITY

	2004	2005	2006
Argentina	197,563	209,130	194,532
Brazil	48,985	56,036	98,480
Chile	7,282	9,941	14,238
Germany	6,336	7,622	9,324
Uruguay	6,692	9,287	10,295
USA	12,012	13,044	13,044
Total (incl. others)	309,287	340,845	388,465

Tourism receipts (US $ million, incl. passenger transport): 87 in 2004; 96 in 2005; 111 in 2006.

Source: World Tourism Organization.

Communications Media

	2005	2006	2007
Telephones ('000 main lines in use)	320.3	331.1	453.8
Mobile cellular telephones ('000 subscribers)	1,887.0	3,232.8	4,330.0
Personal computers ('000 in use)	460	n.a.	n.a.
Internet users ('000)	200	260	280
Broadband subscribers ('000)	5.6	16.0	49.0

Television receivers ('000 in use): 1,200 in 1997.

Radio receivers ('000 in use): 925 in 1997.

Facsimile machines (number in use): 1,691 in 1992.

Daily newspapers: 5* in 1996 (average circulation 213,000* copies).

Non-daily newspapers: 2 in 1988 (average circulation 16,000* copies).

Book production: 152 titles (incl. 23 pamphlets) in 1993.

* Estimate.

Sources: UNESCO, *Statistical Yearbook*; UN, *Statistical Yearbook*; International Telecommunication Union.

Education

(2004/05, unless otherwise indicated)

	Institutions*	Teachers	Students
Pre-primary schools	4,071	5,671†	148,085
Primary	7,456	33,434†	933,995
Secondary	2,149	44,440†	529,309
Tertiary: university level	111	1,844‡	156,167§

* 1999.
† 2003/04.
‡ 1999/2000.
§ Estimate.

Source: partly UNESCO Institute for Statistics.

Adult literacy rate (UNESCO estimates): 93.7% (males 94.4%; females 93.1%) in 2007 (Source: UNESCO Institute for Statistics).

Directory

The Constitution

A new Constitution for the Republic of Paraguay came into force on 22 June 1992, replacing the Constitution of 25 August 1967.

FUNDAMENTAL RIGHTS, DUTIES AND FREEDOMS

Paraguay is an independent republic whose form of government is representative democracy. The powers accorded to the legislature, executive and judiciary are exercised in a system of independence, equilibrium, co-ordination and reciprocal control. Sovereignty resides in the people, who exercise it through universal, free, direct, equal and secret vote. All citizens over 18 years of age and resident in the national territory are entitled to vote.

All citizens are equal before the law and have freedom of conscience, travel, residence, expression, and the right to privacy. The freedom of the press is guaranteed. The freedom of religion and ideology is guaranteed. Relations between the State and the Catholic Church are based on independence, co-operation and autonomy. All citizens have the right to assemble and demonstrate peacefully. All public and private sector workers, with the exception of the Armed

PARAGUAY

Forces and the police, have the right to form a trade union and to strike. All citizens have the right to associate freely in political parties or movements.

The rights of the indigenous peoples to preserve and develop their ethnic identity in their respective habitat are guaranteed.

LEGISLATURE

The legislature (Congreso Nacional—National Congress) comprises the Senado (Senate) and the Cámara de Diputados (Chamber of Deputies). The Senado is composed of 45 members, the Cámara of 80 members, elected directly by the people. Legislation concerning national defence and international agreements may be initiated in the Senado. Departmental and municipal legislation may be initiated in the Cámara. Both chambers of the Congreso are elected for a period of five years.

GOVERNMENT

Executive power is exercised by the President of the Republic. The President and the Vice-President are elected jointly and directly by the people, by a simple majority of votes, for a period of five years. They may not be elected for a second term. The President and the Vice-President govern with the assistance of an appointed Council of Ministers. The President participates in the formulation of legislation and enacts it. The President is empowered to veto legislation sanctioned by the Congreso, to nominate or remove ministers, to direct the foreign relations of the Republic, and to convene extraordinary sessions of the Congreso. The President is Commander-in-Chief of the Armed Forces.

JUDICIARY

Judicial power is exercised by the Supreme Court of Justice and by the tribunals. The Supreme Court is composed of nine members who are appointed on the proposal of the Consejo de la Magistratura, and has the power to declare legislation unconstitutional.

The Government

HEAD OF STATE

President: FERNANDO ARMINDO LUGO MÉNDEZ (took office 15 August 2008).
Vice-President: LUIS FEDERICO FRANCO GÓMEZ.

COUNCIL OF MINISTERS
(April 2009)

Minister of the Interior: RAFAEL FILIZZOLA.
Minister of Foreign Affairs: HÉCTOR LACOGNATA.
Minister of Finance: DIONISIO BORDA.
Minister of Industry and Commerce: FRANCISCO RIVAS.
Minister of Public Works and Communications: EFRAÍN ALEGRE.
Minister of National Defence: Gen. (retd) LUIS BAREIRO SPAINI.
Minister of Public Health and Social Welfare: ESPERANZA MARTÍNEZ.
Minister of Justice and Labour: HUMBERTO BLASCO.
Minister of Agriculture and Livestock: ENZO CARDOZO.
Minister of Education and Culture: LUIS ALBERTO RIART.

MINISTRIES

Office of the President: Palacio de los López, Asunción; internet www.presidencia.gov.py.

Ministry of Agriculture and Livestock: Presidente Franco 472, Asunción; tel. (21) 44-9614; fax (21) 49-7965; e-mail secretariagral@mag.gov.py; internet www.mag.gov.py.

Ministry of Education and Culture: 15 de Agosto, esq. Gral Díaz y Eduardo V. Haedo, Edif. del ex-BNT, Asunción; tel. (21) 44-3078; fax (21) 44-3919; internet www.mec.gov.py.

Ministry of Finance: Chile 128, esq. Palmas, Asunción; tel. (21) 44-0010; e-mail info@hacienda.gov.py; internet www.hacienda.gov.py.

Ministry of Foreign Affairs: Palma y 14 de Mayo, Palacio Benigno López, Asunción; tel. (21) 49-3928; e-mail webmaster@mre.gov.py; fax (21) 49-3910; internet www.mre.gov.py.

Ministry of Industry and Commerce: Avda Marescal López 3333, esq. Dr Wiss, Villa Morra, Casilla 2151, Asunción; tel. (21) 20-4638; fax (21) 616-3000; e-mail msalcedo@mic.gov.py; internet www.mic.gov.py.

Ministry of the Interior: Chile 1002, esq. Manduvira, Asunción; tel. (21) 415-2000; fax (21) 44-6448; e-mail ministro@mdi.gov.py; internet www.mdi.gov.py.

Ministry of Justice and Labour: Avda J. G. Rodríguez de Francia y Estados Unidos, Asunción; tel. (21) 49-3209; fax (21) 20-8469; e-mail prensa@mjt.gov.py; internet www.mjt.gov.py.

Ministry of National Defence: Avda Mariscal López, esq. Vicepresidente Sánchez y 22 de Septiembre, Asunción; tel. (21) 21-0052; fax (21) 21-1815; e-mail ministro@mdn.gov.py; internet www.mdn.gov.py.

Ministry of Public Health and Social Welfare: Avda Pettirossi, esq. Brasil, Asunción; tel. (21) 20-4601; fax (21) 20-6700; internet www.mspbs.gov.py.

Ministry of Public Works and Communications: Oliva y Alberdi, Asunción; tel. (21) 414-9000; fax (21) 44-4421; e-mail comunicaciones@mopc.gov.py; internet www.mopc.gov.py.

President and Legislature

PRESIDENT

Election, 20 April 2008

Candidate	Votes	% of votes
Fernando Armindo Lugo Méndez (APC)	766,502	40.90
Blanca Ovelar de Duarte (ANR—PC)	573,995	30.63
Gen. (retd) Lino César Oviedo Silva (UNACE)	411,034	21.93
Pedro Nicolás Fadul Niella (PPQ)	44,060	2.35
Others	12,233	0.65
Total	1,874,127*	100.00

* Including 38,485 blank and 27,818 invalid ballots.

CONGRESO NACIONAL
(National Congress)

President of the Senado and the Congreso Nacional: ENRIQUE GONZÁLEZ QUINTANA (UNACE).

President of the Cámara de Diputados: ENRIQUE BUZARQUIS CÁCERES (PLRA).

General Election, 20 April 2008

	Seats	
Party	Cámara de Diputados	Senado
Asociación Nacional Republicana—Partido Colorado	30	15
Partido Liberal Radical Auténtico	27	14
Unión Nacional de Ciudadanos Eticos	15	9
Partido Patria Querida	3	4
Others	5	3
Total	80	45

Election Commission

Tribunal Superior de Justicia Electoral (TSJE): Avda Eusebio Ayala 2759 y Santa Cruz de la Sierra, Casilla 1209, Asunción; tel. and fax (21) 618-0217; e-mail protocolo@tsje.gov.py; internet www.tsje.gov.py; f. 1995; Pres. Dr JUAN MANUEL MORALES SOLER.

Political Organizations

Alianza Patriótica para el Cambio (APC): República Argentina, esq. Fernando de la Mora, Asunción; tel. (21) 55-9400; f. 2007 to support the presidential campaign of Fernando Lugo Méndez; alliance of parties and other orgs; mems incl. Partido Liberal Radical Auténtico, Partido Encuentro Nacional, Partido Demócrata Cristiano, Partido Democrático Progresista, Partido País Solidario and Partido Revolucionario Febrerista.

Asociación Nacional Republicana—Partido Colorado (ANR—PC): Casa de los Colorados, 25 de Mayo 842, Asunción; tel. (21) 44-4137; fax (21) 49-7857; internet www.anr.org.py; f. 19th century; factions include Movimiento Vanguardia Colorada, led by LUIS CASTIGLIONI; Pres. LILIAN SAMANIEGO.

Partido Comunista Paraguayo (PCP): Asunción; internet www.pcparaguay.org; f. 1928; banned 1928–46, 1947–89; Sec.-Gen. ANANÍAS MAIDANA.

PARAGUAY

Partido Demócrata Cristiano (PDC): Dupuis 962 y Colón, Asunción; tel. (21) 42-0434; e-mail info@pdc.org.py; internet www.pdc.org.py; f. 1960; 20,500 mems; Pres. GERARDO ROLÓN POSE.

Partido Democrático Progresista (PDP): 25 de Mayo y Brasil, Asunción; Pres. RAFAEL FILIZZOLA.

Partido Encuentro Nacional (PEN): 370 Avda Senador Long, Asunción; tel. (21) 60-3935; fax (21) 61-0699; e-mail parenac@pla.net.py; f. 1991; Pres. JOSÉ BURRÓ.

Partido Frente Amplio: Antequera 764, esq. Fulgencio R. Moreno, Asunción; tel. (21) 44-1389; Sec.-Gen. VÍCTOR BAREIRO ROA.

Partido Humanista Paraguayo: Fulgencio R. Moreno 584, esq. Paraguari, Asunción; tel. (21) 44-2625; f. 1985; recognized by the Tribunal Superior de Justicia Electoral in March 1989; campaigns for the protection of human rights and environmental issues; Gen. Sec. NICOLÁS SERVÍN.

Partido Liberal Radical Auténtico (PLRA): Iturbe 936, entre Manuel Domínguez y Teniente Fariña, Asunción; tel. (21) 49-8442; fax (21) 49-8443; e-mail prensa@plra.org.py; internet www.plra.org.py; f. 1978; centre party; 806,000 mems; Pres. ANTONIO GUSTAVO CARDOZO.

Partido País Solidario: Avda 5, esq. Méjico, Asunción; tel. (21) 39-1271; e-mail presidencia@paissolidario.org.py; internet www.paissolidario.org.py; f. 2000; mem. of Socialist International; Pres. Dr CARLOS FILIZZOLA PALLARÉS; Vice-Pres. JORGE GIUCICH.

Partido Patria Libre (PPL): 15 de Agosto 1939, Asunción; tel. (21) 37-2384; socialist.

Partido Patria Querida (PPQ): 469 Padre Cardozo, Asunción; tel. 21-3300; e-mail info@patriaquerida.org; internet www.patriaquerida.org; f. 2002; recognized by the Tribunal Superior de Justicia Electoral in March 2004; Leader PEDRO NICOLÁS FADUL NIELLA.

Partido Popular Tekojojá: Carios, esq. Médicos del Chaco, Asunción; tel. and fax (21) 55-4104; e-mail tekojoja@tekojoa.org.py; internet www.tekojoja.org.py; f. 2006 to support the presidential campaign of Fernando Lugo Méndez; left-wing, mainly comprising social and indigenous groups; Pres. SIXTO PEREIRA; Sec. FIDELINA ROJAS.

Partido Revolucionario Febrerista (PRF): Casa del Pueblo, Manduvira 552, Asunción; tel. (21) 49-4041; e-mail partyce@mixmail.com; internet www.prfparaguay.org; f. 1951; social democratic party; mem. of Socialist International; Pres. NILS CANDIA GINI.

Partido de los Trabajadores (PT): Asunción; f. 1989; Socialist.

Partido de la Unidad Popular (PUP): Azara 2843, esq. Rodó, Asunción; tel. (21) 21-5059; recognized by the Tribunal Superior de Justicia Electoral in March 2004; Pres. JUAN DE DIOS ACOSTA MENA.

Unión Nacional de Ciudadanos Eticos (UNACE): Eusebio Ayala 4135, esq. Corrales, Asunción; e-mail loviedo@unace.org.py; internet www.unace.org.py; f. 1996 as Unión Nacional de Colorados Eticos, a faction of the Partido Colorado; f. as political party under current name in 2002; left-wing; Pres. Gen. (retd) LINO CÉSAR OVIEDO SILVA.

OTHER ORGANIZATIONS

Federación Nacional Campesina (FNC): Nangariry 1196, esq. Cacique Cará Cará, Asunción; tel. (21) 51-2384; grouping of militant peasants' orgs; Sec.-Gen. ODILÓN ESPÍNOLA; Asst Sec.-Gen. MARCIAL GÓMEZ.

Frente en Defensa de los Bienes Públicos y el Patrimonio Nacional: Asunción; left-wing grouping of orgs opposed to privatization; Co-ordinator GABRIEL ESPÍNOLA.

Frente Nacional de Lucha por la Soberanía y la Vida: Asunción; left-wing grouping of orgs campaigning for agrarian reform and opposed to privatization; Co-ordinator LUIS AGUAYO.

Diplomatic Representation

EMBASSIES IN PARAGUAY

Argentina: Avda España, esq. Avda Perú, Casilla 757, Asunción; tel. (21) 21-2320; fax (21) 21-1029; e-mail embarpy@supernet.com.py; internet www.embajada-argentina.org.py; Ambassador RAFAEL EDGARDO ROMÁ.

Bolivia: Campos Cervera 6421, Asunción; tel. (21) 61-4984; fax (21) 60-1999; e-mail embolivia.asuncion@personaldata.net.py; Ambassador FREDDY MARCEL QUEZADA GAMBARTE.

Brazil: Col Irrazábal, esq. Eligio Ayala, Casilla 22, Asunción; tel. (21) 21-4466; fax (21) 21-2693; e-mail parbrem@embajadabrasil.org.py; internet www.embajadabrasil.org.py; Ambassador EDUARDO DOS SANTOS.

Chile: Capital Emilio Nudelman 351, esq. Campos Cervera, Asunción; tel. (21) 61-3855; fax (21) 66-2755; e-mail echilepy@conexion.com.py; Ambassador CRISTIÁN MAQUIEIRA ASTABURUAGA.

China (Taiwan): Avda Mariscal López 1143 y Vicepresidente Sánchez, Casilla 503, Asunción; tel. (21) 21-3362; fax (21) 21-2373; e-mail embroc01@rieder.net.py; internet www.taiwanembassy.org/py; Ambassador DAVID C. Y. HU.

Colombia: Coronel Brizuela 3089, esq. Ciudad del Vaticano, Asunción; tel. (21) 22-9888; fax (21) 22-9703; e-mail easuncio@cancilleria.gov.co; Ambassador MAURICIO GONZÁLEZ LÓPEZ.

Costa Rica: Shopping del Sol 13104, Avda Antonio Mena Porta, casi Dr Manuel Peña, Asunción; tel. and fax (21) 29-7158; e-mail embarica@tigo.com.py; Ambassador ESTEBAN ARIAS MONGE.

Cuba: Luis Morales 757, esq. Luis León y Luis Granado, Barrio Jara, Asunción; tel. (21) 22-2763; fax (21) 21-3879; e-mail embacuba@cmm.com.py; internet www.embacuba.org.py; Ambassador ADOLFO CURBELLO CASTELLANOS.

Ecuador: Dr Bestard 861, esq. Juan XXIII, Barrio Manorá, Casilla 13162, Asunción; tel. (21) 61-4814; fax (21) 61-4813; e-mail mecuapy@conexion.com.py; Ambassador JULIO CÉSAR PRADO ESPINOSA.

France: Avda España 893 y Padre Pucheu, Casilla 97, Asunción; tel. (21) 21-2449; fax (21) 21-1690; e-mail chancellerie@ambafran.gov.py; internet www.ambafran.gov.py; Ambassador GILLES BIENVENU.

Germany: Avda Venezuela 241, Casilla 471, Asunción; tel. (21) 21-4009; fax (21) 21-2863; e-mail info@asuncion.diplo.de; internet www.asuncion.diplo.de; Ambassador DIETMAR BLAAS.

Holy See: Ciudad del Vaticano 350, casi con 25 de Mayo, Casilla 83, Asunción (Apostolic Nunciature); tel. (21) 21-5139; fax (21) 21-2590; e-mail nunciatura@tigo.com; Apostolic Nuncio Most Rev. ORLANDO ANTONINI (Titular Archbishop of Formia).

Italy: Quesada 5871 con Bélgica, Asunción; tel. (21) 61-5620; fax (21) 61-5622; e-mail archivio.assunzione@esteri.it; internet www.embajadadeitalia.org.py; Ambassador GIOVANNI MAROCCO.

Japan: Avda Mariscal López 2364, Casilla 1957, Asunción; tel. (21) 60-4616; fax (21) 60-6901; e-mail embajaponpy@rieder.net.py; internet www.py.emb-japan.go.jp; Ambassador KAZUO WATANABE.

Korea, Republic: Avda Rep. Argentina Norte 678, esq. Pacheco, Casilla 1303, Asunción; tel. (21) 60-5606; fax (21) 60-1376; e-mail paraguay@mofat.go.kr; internet pry.mofat.go.kr; Ambassador JOO TECK KIM.

Lebanon: San Francisco 629, esq. República Siria y Juan de Salazar, Asunción; tel. 22-9375; fax 23-2012; e-mail embajadadelibano@tigo.com.py; Ambassador FARES EID.

Mexico: Avda España 1428, casi San Rafael, Casilla 1184, Asunción; tel. (21) 618-2000; fax (21) 618-2500; e-mail embamex@embamex.com.py; internet www.embamex.com.py; Ambassador ERNESTO CAMPOS TENORIO.

Panama: Carmen Soler 3912 y Radio Operadores del Chaco, Asunción; tel. and fax (21) 21-1091; e-mail embapana@gmail.com.py; Ambassador GONZALO MONCADA LUNA.

Peru: Feliciano Marecos 441, casi Agustín Barrios y España, Manorá, Casilla 433, Asunción; tel. (21) 60-0226; fax (21) 60-7327; e-mail embperu@embperu.com.py; Ambassador ENRIQUE PALACIOS REYES.

Spain: Edif. S. Rafael, 5° y 6°, Yegros 437, Asunción; tel. (21) 49-0686; fax (21) 44-5394; e-mail embesppy@correo.mae.es; internet www.mae.es/embajadas/asuncion; Ambassador MIGUEL ANGEL CORTIZO NIETO.

Switzerland: Edif. Parapití, 4°, Ofs 419–423, Juan E. O'Leary 409 y Estrella, Casilla 552, Asunción; tel. (21) 44-8022; fax (21) 44-5853; e-mail asu.vertretung@eda.admin.ch; internet www.eda.admin.ch/asuncion; Ambassador EMANUEL JENNI.

USA: Avda Mariscal López 1776, Casilla 402, Asunción; tel. (21) 21-3715; fax (21) 21-3728; e-mail paraguayusembassy@state.gov; internet asuncion.usembassy.gov; Ambassador LILIANA AYALDE.

Uruguay: Guido Boggiani 5832, 3°, Asunción; tel. (21) 66-4244; fax (21) 60-1335; e-mail uruasun@embajadauruguay.com.py; internet www.embajadauruguay.com.py; Ambassador JUAN ENRIQUE FISCHER.

Venezuela: Mariscal Estigarribia 1023 con Estados Unidos, Asunción; tel. (21) 66-4682; fax (21) 66-4683; e-mail bolivar@embaven.org.py; internet www.embaven.org.py; Ambassador NORA MARGARITA URIBE TRUJILLO.

Judicial System

The Corte Suprema de Justicia (Supreme Court of Justice) is composed of nine judges appointed on the recommendation of the Consejo de la Magistratura (Council of the Magistracy).

PARAGUAY

Corte Suprema de Justicia: Palacio de Justicia, Asunción; internet www.pj.gov.py; Ministers Dr ANTONIO FRETES (President), Dr CÉSAR ANTONIO GARAY ZUCCOLILLO (First Vice-President), Dra ALICIA BEATRIZ PUCHETA DE CORREA (Second Vice-President), Dr VÍCTOR MANUEL NÚÑEZ, Dr SINDULFO BLANCO, Dr JOSÉ RAÚL TORRES KIRMSER, Dr MIGUEL O. BAJAC, Dr JOSÉ V. ALTAMIRANO AQUINO; one vacancy.

Attorney-General: RUBÉN CANDIA AMARILLA.

Under the Supreme Court are the Courts of Appeal, the Tribunal of Jurors and Judges of First Instance, the Judges of Arbitration, the Magistrates (Jueces de Instrucción), and the Justices of the Peace.

Religion

The Roman Catholic Church is the established religion, although all sects are tolerated.

CHRISTIANITY

The Roman Catholic Church

For ecclesiastical purposes, Paraguay comprises one archdiocese, 11 dioceses and two Apostolic Vicariates. At 31 December 2006 there were an estimated 5,603,950 adherents in the country, representing about 91% of the total population.

Bishops' Conference

Conferencia Episcopal Paraguaya, Calle Alberdi 782, Casilla 1436, 1209 Asunción; tel. (21) 49-0920; fax (21) 49-5115; e-mail cep@infonet.com.py; internet www.episcopal.org.py.

f. 1977, statutes approved 2000; Pres. Most Rev. EUSTAQUIO PASTOR CUQUEJO VERGA (Archbishop of Asunción).

Archbishop of Asunción: Most Rev. EUSTAQUIO PASTOR CUQUEJO VERGA, Arzobispado, Avda Mariscal López 130 esq. Independencia Nacional, Casilla 654, Asunción; tel. (21) 44-5551; fax (21) 44-4150; e-mail asa@pla.net.py.

The Anglican Communion

Paraguay constitutes a single diocese of the Iglesia Anglicana del Cono Sur de América (Anglican Church of the Southern Cone of America). The Presiding Bishop of the Church is the Bishop of Northern Argentina.

Bishop of Paraguay: Rt Rev. JOHN ELLISON, Iglesia Anglicana, Avda España casi Santos, Casilla 1124, Asunción; tel. (21) 20-0933; fax (21) 21-4328; e-mail iapar@sce.cnc.una.py.

The Baptist Church

Baptist Evangelical Convention of Paraguay: Casilla 1194, Asunción; tel. (21) 22-7110; fax (21) 21-0588; e-mail cebp@sce.cnc.una.py; internet www.ublaonline.org/paises/paraguay.htm; Exec. Sec. AUGUSTO VEGA.

BAHÁ'Í FAITH

National Spiritual Assembly of the Bahá'ís of Paraguay: Eligio Ayala 1456, Apdo 742, Asunción; tel. (21) 22-5747; e-mail bahai@highway.com.py; internet www.bahai.org.py; Sec. MIRNA LLAMOSAS DE RIQUELME.

The Press

DAILIES

ABC Color: Yegros 745, Apdo 1421, Asunción; tel. (21) 49-1160; fax (21) 415-1310; e-mail azeta@abc.com.py; internet www.abc.com.py; f. 1967; independent; Propr ALDO ZUCCOLILLO; circ. 45,000.

La Nación: Avda Zavala Cué entre 2da y 3ra, Fernando de la Mora, Asunción; tel. (21) 51-2520; fax (21) 51-2535; e-mail redaccion@lanacion.com.py; internet www.lanacion.com.py; f. 1995; Dir ALEJANDRO DOMÍNGUEZ WILSON-SMITH; circ. 10,000.

Noticias: Avda Artigas y Avda Brasilia, Casilla 3017, Asunción; tel. (21) 29-2721; fax (21) 29-2716; e-mail alebluth@diarionoticias.com; f. 1985; independent; Dir ALEJANDRO BLUTH; circ. 20,000.

Popular: Avda Mariscal López 2948, Asunción; tel. (21) 60-3401; fax (21) 60-3400; e-mail popular@mm.com.py; internet www.diariopopular.com.py; Dir JAVIER PIROVANO PEÑA; circ. 28,000.

Ultima Hora: Benjamín Constant 658, Asunción; tel. (21) 49-6261; fax (21) 44-7071; e-mail ultimahora@uhora.com.py; internet www.ultimahora.com; f. 1973; independent; Dir OSCAR AYALA BOGARÍN; circ. 30,000.

PERIODICALS

Acción: CEPAG, Vicepresidente Sánchez 612, casi Azara, Asunción; tel. (21) 23-3541; e-mail revistaaccion@cepag.org.py; internet www.montoya.com.py/revista_accion.php; f. 1923; monthly; published by the Centro de Estudios Paraguayos Antonio Guasch (CEPAG—Jesuit org.); Dir JOSÉ MARÍA BLANCH.

Revista Zeta: Eligio Ayala 2002, esq. Gral Bruguez, Asunción; tel. (21) 61-3392; fax (21) 61-3393; e-mail zeta@revistazeta.com.py; internet www.revistazeta.com.py; f. 2000; monthly; general interest; Dir ZUNI CASTIÑEIRA.

TeVeo: Santa Margarita de Youville 250, Santa María, Asunción; tel. (21) 67-2079; fax (21) 21-1236; e-mail sugerencias@teveo.com.py; internet www.teveo.com.py; weekly; society.

NEWS AGENCY

Información Pública Paraguay (IP Paraguay): Palacio de los López, Asunción; e-mail ipparaguay@gmail.com; internet www.ipparaguay.com.py; f. 2009; attached to the Office of the President.

Jaku'éke Paraguay—Agencia Nacional de Noticias: Itapúa y Río Monday, Asunción; tel. (21) 29-7806; fax (21) 28-1950; internet www.jakueke.com; f. 2002; independent.

Publishers

La Colmena, SA: Asunción; tel. (21) 20-0428; Dir DAUMAS LADOUCE.

Dervish SA, Editorial: Avda Mariscal López 1735, CP 1584, Asunción; tel. (21) 21-1729; fax (21) 22-2580; e-mail dervish@dervish.com.py; f. 1989; Co-ordinator JORGELINA MIGLIORISI; Vice-Pres. and Dir JANINE GIANI PATTERSON.

Ediciones Diálogo: Brasil 1391, Asunción; tel. (21) 20-0428; f. 1957; fine arts, literature, poetry, criticism; Man. MIGUEL ANGEL FERNÁNDEZ.

Ediciones Nizza: Eligio Ayala 1073, Casilla 2596, Asunción; tel. (21) 44-7160; medicine; Pres. Dr JOSÉ FERREIRA MARTÍNEZ.

Editorial Comuneros: Cerro Corá 289, Casilla 930, Asunción; tel. (21) 44-6176; fax (21) 44-4667; e-mail rolon@conexion.com.py; f. 1963; social history, poetry, literature, law; Man. OSCAR R. ROLÓN.

Librería Intercontinental: Caballero 270, Calle Mariscal, Estigarribia, Asunción; tel. (21) 49-6991; fax (21) 44-8721; e-mail agatti@libreriaintercontinental.com.py; internet www.libreriaintercontinental.com.py; political science, law, literature, poetry; Dir ALEJANDRO GATTI VAN HUMBEECK.

R. P. Ediciones: Eduardo Víctor Haedo 427, Asunción; tel. (21) 49-8040; Man. RAFAEL PERONI.

ASSOCIATION

Cámara Paraguaya del Libro: Nuestra Señora de la Asunción 697, esq. Eduardo Víctor Haedo, Asunción; tel. (21) 44-4104; fax (21) 44-7053; Pres. PABLO LEÓN BURIAN; Sec. EMA DE VIEDMA.

Broadcasting and Communications

REGULATORY AUTHORITY

Comisión Nacional de Telecomunicaciones (CONATEL): Edif. San Rafael, 2°, Yegros 437 y 25 de Mayo, Asunción; tel. (21) 44-0020; fax (21) 49-8982; e-mail presidencia@conatel.gov.py; internet www.conatel.gov.py; Pres. JORGE ANTONIO SEALL SASIAIN.

TELECOMMUNICATIONS

Claro (AMX Paraguay, SA): Avda Mariscal López 1730, Asunción; tel. (21) 249-9000; fax (21) 249-9099; internet www.claro.com.py; subsidiary of América Móvil, SA de CV (Mexico); fmrly CTI Móvil; mobile cellular telephone services.

Corporación Paraguaya de Comunicaciones, SA (COPACO): Edif. Morotí, 1°–2°, esq. Gen. Bruguez y Teodoro S. Mongelos, Casilla 2042, Asunción; tel. (21) 20-3800; fax (21) 20-3888; e-mail infoweb@copaco.com.py; internet www.copaco.com.py; fmrly Administración Nacional de Telecomunicaciones (ANTELCO); adopted current name in Dec. 2001 as part of the privatization process; privatization suspended in June 2002; Pres. ARNULFO RECALDE.

BROADCASTING

Radio

Radio Arapysandú: Avda Mariscal López y Capitán del Puerto San Ignacio, Misiones; tel. (82) 2374; fax (82) 2206; f. 1982; AM; Dir HECTOR BOTTINO.

PARAGUAY

Radio Asunción: Avda Artígas y Capitán Lombardo 174, Asunción; tel. and fax (21) 28-2662; fax (21) 28-2661; e-mail radioasuncion@cmm.com.py; internet www.radioasuncion.com.py; AM; Propr MIGUEL GERÓNIMO FERNÁNDEZ; Dir-Gen. BIBIANA LANDO MEYER.

Radio Cáritas: Kubitschek 661 y Azara, Asunción; tel. (21) 21-3570; fax (21) 20-4161; e-mail pedroportillo@caritas.com.py; internet www.caritas.com.py; f. 1936; station of the Archdiocese of Asunción and the Universidad Católica Nuestra Señora de la Asunción; AM; Dir-Gen. JORGE BAZÁN; Dir of Operations PEDRO PORTILLO.

Radio Cardinal: Comendador Nicolás Bó 1334 y Guaraníes, Casilla 2532, Lambaré, Asunción; tel. (21) 31-0555; fax (21) 31-0557; e-mail info@cardinal.com.py; internet www.cardinal.com.py; f. 1991; AM and FM; Pres. ALFREDO CHENA; Man. ANDREA BITTAR.

Radio City: Edif. Líder III, Antequera 652, 9°, Asunción; tel. (21) 44-3324; fax (21) 44-4367; e-mail direccion@fmradiocity.com; internet www.fmradiocity.com; f. 1950; FM; Dir GREGORIO RAMAN MORALES.

Radio Concepción: Coronel Panchito López 241, entre Schreiber y Profesor Guillermo A. Cabral, Casilla 78, Concepción; tel. (31) 42318; fax (31) 42254; f. 1963; AM; Dir SERGIO E. DACAK.

Radio Emisoras del Paraguay, SRL: Teniente Martínez Ramella 1355, Calle Avda Eusebio Ayala, Asunción; tel. (21) 22-0132; e-mail administracion@emisorasparaguay.com.py; internet www.desdeparaguay.com/emisoras; FM; Dir FRANCISCO JAVIER BOSCARINO BÁEZ.

Radio Guairá: Presidente Franco 788 y Alejo García, Villarica; tel. (541) 42130; fax (541) 42385; e-mail administracion@fmguaira.com; internet www.fmguaira.com; f. 1950; AM and FM; Dir LÍDICE RODRÍGUEZ DE TRAVERSI.

Radio Itapiru SRL: Avda San Blás esq. Coronel Julián Sánchez, Ciudad del Este; tel. (61) 57-2206; fax (61) 57-2210; internet www.radioitapiru.com; f. 1969; AM and FM; Dir-Gen. FABIÁN ARANDA.

Radio La Voz de Amambay: 14 de Mayo y Cerro León, Pedro Juan Caballero, Amambay; tel. (36) 72537; f. 1959; AM and FM; Gen. Man. DANIEL ROLÓN DANTAS P.

Radio Nacional del Paraguay: Blas Garay 241 y Iturbe, Asunción; tel. (21) 39-0374; fax (21) 39-0376; f. 1957; AM and FM; Dir TEODOSO FERMÍN ESPINOSA.

Radio Ñandutí: Choferes del Chaco y Carmen Soler, Asunción; tel. (21) 60-4308; fax (21) 60-6074; e-mail prensaam@holdingderadio.com.py; internet www.nanduti.com.py; f. 1962; FM; Dir HUMBERTO LEÓN RUBÍN.

Radio Nuevo Mundo: Coronel Romero 1181 y Flórida, San Lorenzo, Asunción; tel. (21) 58-6258; fax (21) 58-2424; f. 1972; AM; Dir JULIO CÉSAR PEREIRA BOBADILLA.

Radio Primero de Marzo: Avda General Perón y Concepción, Casilla 1456, Asunción; tel. (21) 31-1564; fax (21) 33-3427; internet www.780am.com.py; AM and FM; Dir-Gen. ANGEL R. GUERREÑOS.

Radio Santa Mónica FM: Avda Boggiani y Herrera, 3°, Asunción; tel. (21) 50-7501; fax (21) 50-9494; f. 1973; FM; Dir RICARDO FACCETTI.

Radio Uno: Avda Mariscal López 2948, Asunción; tel. (21) 61-2151; internet www.radiouno.com.py; f. 1968 as Radio Chaco Boreal; AM; Dir JAVIER MARÍA PIROVANO SILVA.

Radio Venus: Avda República Argentina y Souza, Asunción; tel. (21) 61-0151; fax (21) 60-6484; e-mail 105.1@venus.com.py; internet www.venus.com.py; f. 1987; FM; Dir ANGEL AGUILERA.

Radio Ysapy: Independencia Nacional 1260, 1°, Asunción; tel. (21) 44-4037; e-mail secretaria@radioysapy.com.py; internet www.radioysapy.com.py; FM; Dir JOSÉ TOMÁS CABRIZA SALVIONI.

Television

Paravision: Belgica 4498, casi Mariscal López, Asunción; tel. (21) 66-4380; e-mail info@paravision.com.py; internet www.paravision.com.py.

Red Guaraní (Canal 2): Complejo Textilia, General Santos 1024, casi Concordia, Asunción; tel. (21) 20-5444; e-mail oescobar@redguarani.com.py; internet www.redguarani.com.py; Exec. Dir Dr ARNOLDO WIENS; Gen. Man. OSCAR ESCOBAR.

Sistema Nacional de Televisión Cerro Corá—Canal 9 (SNT): Avda Carlos A. López 572, Asunción; tel. (21) 42-4222; fax (21) 48-0230; e-mail snt@snt.com.py; internet www.snt.com.py; f. 1965; commercial; Dir Gen. ISMAEL HADID.

Teledifusora Paraguaya—Canal 13: Comendador Nicolás Bó y Guaraníes, Lambaré, Asunción; tel. (21) 33-2823; fax (21) 33-1695; e-mail prensa@rpc.com.py; internet www.rpc.com.py; f. 1981; Pres. ALFREDO CHENA; Dir-Gen. GUSTAVO CUBILLA.

Telefuturo (TV Acción, SA): Andrade 1499 y O'Higgins, Asunción; tel. (21) 618-4000; fax (21) 618-4166; e-mail telefuturo@telefuturo.com.py; internet www.telefuturo.com.py; Gen. Man. MARCO GALANTI.

Finance

(cap. = capital; res = reserves; dep. = deposits; m. = million; brs = branches; amounts in guaraníes, unless otherwise indicated)

BANKING

Superintendencia de Bancos: Edif. Banco Central del Paraguay, Avda Federación Rusa y Avda Marecos, Barrio Santo Domingo, Asunción; tel. (21) 60-8011; fax (21) 60-8149; e-mail supban@bcp.gov.py; internet www.bcp.gov.py/supban; Supt EDGAR ANDRÉS LEGUIZAMON CARMONA.

Central Bank

Banco Central del Paraguay: Avda Federación Rusa y Cabo 1° Marecos, Casilla 861, Barrio Santo Domingo, Asunción; tel. (21) 61-0088; fax (21) 60-8149; e-mail webmaster@bcp.gov.py; internet www.bcp.gov.py; f. 1952; cap. 828,145m., res 454,695m., dep. 4,605,137m. (Dec. 2005); Pres. JORGE RAÚL CORVALÁN MENDOZA; Gen. Man. JORGE AURELIO VILLALBA LEGUIZAMON.

Development Banks

Banco Nacional de Fomento: Independencia Nacional y 25 de Mayo, Asunción; tel. (21) 44-4440; fax (21) 44-6056; e-mail correo@bnf.gov.py; internet www.bnf.gov.py; f. 1961 to take over the deposit and private banking activities of the Banco del Paraguay; Pres. AGUSTÍN SILVERA ORUE; Sec.-Gen. CÉSAR LEONARDO FURIASSE ROLÓN; 52 brs.

Crédito Agrícola de Habilitación (CAH): Caríos 362 y Willam Richardson, Asunción; tel. (21) 569-0100; fax (21) 55-4956; e-mail info@cah.gov.py; internet www.cah.gov.py; f. 1943; Pres. JOSÉ MARCELO BRUSTEIN ALEGRE.

Fondo Ganadero: Avda Mariscal López 1669 esq. República Dominicana, Asunción; tel. (21) 22-7288; fax (21) 22-7378; e-mail info@fondogan.gov.py; internet www.fondogan.gov.py; f. 1969; govt-owned; Pres. JUAN FERNANDO PERONI.

Commercial Banks

Banco Amambay, SA: Avda Aviadores del Chaco, entre San Martín y Pablo Alborno, Asunción; tel. (21) 60-8831; fax (21) 60-8813; e-mail bcoama@bancoamambay.com.py; internet www.bancoamambay.com.py; f. 1992; cap. US $8.2m., res $5.1m., dep. $125.7m. (Dec. 2007); Pres. and Gen. Man. HUGO PORTILLO SOSA; 6 brs.

Banco Bilbao Vizcaya Argentaria Paraguaya, SA: Yegros 435 y 25 de Mayo, Casilla 824, Asunción; tel. (21) 49-2072; fax (21) 44-8103; e-mail bbva.paraguay@bbva.com.py; internet www.bbva.com.py; f. 1961 as Banco Exterior de España, SA; present name adopted in 2000; cap. 40,052m., res 149,069m., dep. 1,912,815m. (Dec. 2006); Pres. VICENTE LUIS BOGLIOLO DEL RÍO; 5 brs.

Banco Continental, SAECA: Estrella 621, Casilla 2260, Asunción; tel. (21) 44-2002; fax (21) 44-2001; e-mail contil@connexion.com.py; internet www.bancontinental.com.py; f. 1980; cap. US $4.2m., res $2.5m., dep. $44.6m. (Dec. 2001); Pres. CARLOS ESPÍNOLA; 28 brs.

Interbanco, SA: Oliva 349, esq. Chile y Alberdi, Asunción; tel. (21) 49-4992; fax (21) 41-71372; e-mail interban@conexion.com.py; internet www.interbanco.com.py; f. 1978; owned by Unibanco (Brazil); cap. 21,739m., res 176,386m., dep. 2,234,925m. (Dec. 2006); Pres. CLAUDIO YAMAGUTI; 17 brs.

Sudameris Bank, SAECA: Independencia Nacional y Cerro Corá, Casilla 1433, Asunción; tel. (21) 44-8670; fax (21) 44-4024; e-mail gerencia@sudameris.com.py; internet www.sudamerisbank.com.py; f. 1961; savings and commercial bank; cap. 142,991m., surplus and res 20,824m., dep. 837,319m. (Dec. 2006); Chair. CONOR MCENROY; Vice-Chair. and Gen. Man. JUAN LUIS KOSTNER; 8 brs.

Banking Associations

Asociación de Bancos del Paraguay: Jorge Berges 229, esq. Estados Unidos, Asunción; tel. (21) 21-4951; fax (21) 20-5050; e-mail abp.par@pla.net.py; mems: Paraguayan banks and foreign banks with brs in Asunción; Pres. VICENTE LUIS BOGLIOLO DEL RÍO.

Cámara de Bancos Paraguayos: 25 de Mayo, esq. 22 de Setiembre, Asunción; tel. (21) 22-2373; fax (21) 20-5050; Pres. MIGUEL ANGEL LARREINEGABE.

STOCK EXCHANGE

Bolsa de Valores y Productos de Asunción, SA: 15 de Agosto 640, esq. General Díaz y Víctor Haedo, Asunción; tel. (21) 44-2445; fax (21) 44-2446; internet www.bvpasa.com.py; f. 1977; Pres. RODRIGO CALLIZO LÓPEZ.

PARAGUAY   *Directory*

INSURANCE

Supervisory Authority

Superintendencia de Seguros: Edif. Banco Central del Paraguay, 1°, Federación Rusa y Sargento Marecos, Asunción; tel. (21) 619-2637; fax (21) 619-2542; e-mail dmarti@bcp.gov.py; internet www.bcp.gov.py; Supt DIEGO ARTURO MARTÍNEZ SÁNCHEZ.

Principal Companies

La Agrícola SA de Seguros Generales: Mariscal López 5377 y Concejal Vargas, Asunción; tel. (21) 60-9509; fax (21) 60-9606; e-mail sagricola@tigo.com.py; f. 1982; general; Pres. CARLOS ALBERTO LEVI SOSA.

ALFA SA de Seguros y Reaseguros: Yegros 944 esq. Tte Fariña, Asunción; tel. (21) 44-9992; fax (21) 44-9991; e-mail alfa.seg@conexion.com.py; Pres. NICOLÁS SARUBBI ZAYAS.

Aseguradora del Este SA de Seguros: Avda República Argentina 778, entre Pacheco y Souza, Asunción; tel. (21) 60-5015; e-mail dcespedes@aesaseguros.com.py; Pres. VÍCTOR ANDRÉS RIBEIRO ESPÍNOLA.

Aseguradora Paraguaya, SA (ASEPASA): Israel 309 esq. Rio de Janeiro, Casilla 277, Asunción; tel. (21) 21-5086; fax (21) 22-2217; e-mail asepasa@asepasa.com.py; internet www.asepasa.com.py; f. 1976; life and risk; Pres. and Gen. Man. GERARDO TORCIDA CONEJERO.

Aseguradora Yacyretá SA de Seguros y Reaseguros: Oliva 685, esq. Juan E. O'Leary y 15 de Agosto, Asunción; tel. (21) 45-2374; fax (21) 44-5070; e-mail spalomar@yacyreta.com.py; internet www.yacyretasa.com; f. 1980; Pres. OSCAR HARRISON JACQUET; Vice-Pres. NORMAN HARRISON PALEARI; Gen. Man. EDUARDO BARRIOS PERINI; 5 brs.

Atalaya SA de Seguros Generales: Independencia Nacional 565, 1°, esq. Azara y Cerro Corá, Asunción; tel. (21) 49-2811; fax (21) 49-6966; e-mail ataseg@telesurf.com.py; f. 1964; general; Pres. KARIN M. DOLL.

Cenit de Seguros, SA: Ayolas 1082, esq. Ibáñez del Campo, Asunción; tel. (21) 49-4972; fax (21) 44-9502; e-mail cenitsa@rieder.net.py; Pres. OSCAR CÁCERES CARDOZO.

Central SA de Seguros: Edif. Betón I, 1° y 2°, Eduardo Víctor Haedo 179, Independencia Nacional, Casilla 1802, Asunción; tel. (21) 49-4654; fax (21) 49-4655; e-mail censeg@conexion.com.py; f. 1977; general; Pres. MIGUEL JACOBO VILLASANTI; Gen. Man. Dr FÉLIX AVEIRO.

El Comercio Paraguayo SA Cía de Seguros Generales: Alberdi 453 y Oliva, Asunción; tel. (21) 49-2324; fax (21) 49-3562; e-mail elcomercioparaguayo@elcomercioparaguayo.com.py; internet www.elcomercioparaguayo.com.py; f. 1947; life and risk; Dir VICTORIA MARTÍNEZ DE ELIZECHE.

La Consolidada SA de Seguros y Reaseguros: Chile 719 y Eduardo Víctor Haedo, Casilla 1182, Asunción; tel. (21) 49-5174; fax (21) 44-5795; internet www.consolidada.com.py; f. 1961; life and risk; Pres. JUAN CARLOS DELGADILLO ECHAGÜE.

Fénix SA de Seguros y Reaseguros: Iturbe 823 y Fulgencio R. Moreno, Asunción; tel. (21) 49-5549; fax (21) 44-5643; e-mail fenixsa@pla.net.py; internet www.fenixseguros.com.py; Pres. VÍCTOR MARTÍNEZ YARYES.

Garantía SA de Seguros y Reaseguros: 25 de Mayo 640, Asunción; tel. (21) 44-3748; fax (21) 49-0678; e-mail garantia@rieder.net.py; Pres. GERALDO CRISTALDO JURE.

Grupo General de Seguros y Reaseguros, SA: Edif. Grupo General, Jejuí 324 y Chile, 2°, Asunción; tel. (21) 49-7897; fax (21) 44-9259; e-mail general_de_seguros@ggeneral.com.py; Pres. JORGE OBELAR LAMAS.

La Independencia de Seguros y Reaseguros, SA: Edif. Parapatí, 1°, Juan E. O'Leary 409, esq. Estrella, Casilla 980, Asunción; tel. (21) 44-7021; fax (21) 44-8996; e-mail liseguros@laindependencia.com.py; f. 1965; general; Pres. EDMUNDO EMILIO RICHER BÉCKER.

Intercontinental SA de Seguros y Reaseguros: Iturbe 1047 con Teniente Fariña, Altos, Asunción; tel. (21) 49-2348; fax (21) 49-1227; e-mail intercontinentalseguros@flash.com.py; f. 1978; Pres. Dr JUAN MÓDICA LUCENTE; Gen. Man. LUIS SANTACRUZ.

Mapfre Paraguay, SA: Avda Mariscal López 910 y General Aquino, Asunción; tel. (21) 44-1983; fax (21) 49-7441; e-mail sac@mapfre.com.py; internet www.mapfre.com.py; Pres. LUIS MARÍA ZUBIZARRETA.

La Meridional Paraguaya SA de Seguros: Iturbe 1046, Teniente Fariña, Asunción; tel. (21) 44-9827; fax (21) 49-8826; e-mail meridian@conexion.com.py; Pres. TITO LIVIO MUJICA VARELA.

La Paraguaya SA de Seguros: Estrella 675, 7°, Asunción; tel. (21) 49-1367; fax (21) 44-8235; e-mail lps@laparaguaya.com.py; internet www.laparaguaya.com.py; f. 1905; life and risk; Pres. JUAN BOSCH BEYNEN.

Patria SA de Seguros y Reaseguros: General Santos 715 esq. Siria, Asunción; tel. (21) 22-5250; fax (21) 21-4001; e-mail patria@tigo.com.py; f. 1967; general; Pres. Dr ERNESTO GOBERMAN.

El Productor SA de Seguros y Reaseguros: Ind. Nacional 811 esq. Fulgencio R. Moreno, 8°, Asunción; tel. (21) 49-1577; fax (21) 49-1599; e-mail ncabanas@elproductor.com.py; Pres. REINALDO PAVÍA MALDONADO.

Regional SA de Seguros y Reaseguros: Roque González 390 y Dr Hassler, Asunción; tel. (21) 61-0692; fax (21) 22-4447; e-mail regisesa@itacom.com.py; Pres. JUAN A. DIAZ DE VIVAR PRIETO.

Rumbos SA de Seguros: Estrella 851, Ayolas, Casilla 1017, Asunción; tel. (21) 44-9488; fax (21) 44-9492; e-mail rumbos@conexion.com.py; f. 1960; general; Pres. MIGUEL A. LARREINEGABE LESME; Man. Dir ROBERTO GÓMEZ VERLANGIERI.

La Rural SA de Seguros: Avda Mariscal López 1082, esq. Mayor Bullo, Casilla 21, Asunción; tel. (21) 49-1917; fax (21) 44-1592; e-mail larural@larural.com.py; internet www.larural.com.py; f. 1920; general; Pres. JUAN CARLOS MANEGLIA; Gen. Man. EDUARDO BARRIOS PERINI.

Seguros Chaco SA de Seguros y Reaseguros: Mariscal Estigarribia 982, Casilla 3248, Asunción; tel. (21) 44-7118; fax (21) 44-9551; e-mail seguroschaco@pla.net.py; f. 1977; general; Pres. EMILIO VELILLA LACONICH; Exec. Dir ALBERTO R. ZARZA TABOADA.

Seguros Generales, SA (SEGESA): Edif. SEGESA, 1°, Oliva 393 esq. Alberdi, Casilla 802, Asunción; tel. (21) 49-1362; fax (21) 49-1360; e-mail segesa@conexion.com.py; f. 1956; life and risk; Pres. CÉSAR AVALOS.

El Sol del Paraguay, Cía de Seguros y Reaseguros, SA: Cerro Corá 1031, Asunción; tel. (21) 49-1110; fax (21) 21-0604; e-mail elsol@elsol.com.py; internet www.elsol.com.py; f. 1978; Pres. MIGUEL ANGEL BERNI CENTURIÓN; Vice-Pres. CAROLINA VEGA DE ONETTO.

Universo de Seguros y Reaseguros, SA: Edif. de la Encarnación, 9°, 14 de Mayo esq. General Díaz, Casilla 788, Asunción; tel. (21) 44-8530; fax (21) 44-7278; f. 1979; Pres. ZENÓN AGÜERO MIRANDA.

Insurance Association

Asociación Paraguaya de Cías de Seguros: 15 de Agosto, esq. Lugano, Casilla 1435, Asunción; tel. (21) 44-6474; fax (21) 44-4343; e-mail apcs@activenet.com.py; f. 1963; Pres. Dr EMILIO VELILLA LACONICH; Gen. Man. RUBÉN RAPPENECKER COSCIA.

Trade and Industry

GOVERNMENT AGENCIES

Instituto Nacional de Tecnología, Normalización y Metrología (INTN): Avda General Artigas 3973 y General Roa, Casilla 967, Asunción; tel. (21) 29-0160; fax (21) 29-0266; e-mail intn@intn.gov.py; internet www.intn.gov.py; national standards institute; Dir-Gen. OSCAR SALAZAR YARYES.

Instituto de Previsión Social: Constitución y Luis Alberto de Herrera, Casilla 437, Asunción; tel. (21) 22-5719; fax (21) 22-3654; internet www.ips.gov.py; f. 1943; responsible for employees' welfare and health insurance scheme; Pres. Dr AMADO GIL PESSAGNO.

DEVELOPMENT ORGANIZATIONS

Secretaría Técnica de Planificación: Edif. AYFRA, 3°, Presidente Franco y Ayolas, Asunción; tel. (21) 45-0422; fax (21) 49-6510; e-mail webmarketing@stp.gov.py; govt body responsible for overall economic and social planning; Minister CARLOS SÁNCHEZ LEÓN.

Alter Vida (Centro de Estudios y Formación para el Ecodesarrollo): Itapúa 1372, esq. Primer Presidente y Río Monday, Barrio Trinidad, Asunción; tel. (21) 29-8842; fax (21) 29-8845; e-mail info@altervida.org.py; internet www.altervida.org.py; f. 1985; ecological devt; Exec. Dir VÍCTOR BENÍTEZ INSFRÁN.

Centro de Información y Recursos para el Desarrollo (CIRD): Asunción; tel. (21) 22-6071; fax (21) 21-2540; e-mail cird@cird.org.py; internet www.cird.org.py; f. 1988; information and resources for devt orgs; Exec. Pres. AGUSTÍN CARRIZOSA.

Centro de Cooperación Empresarial y Desarrollo Industrial (CEDIAL): Edif. UIP, 2°, Cerro Corá 1038, esq. Estados Unidos y Brasil, Asunción; tel. and fax (21) 23-0047; e-mail cedial@cedial.org.py; internet www.cedial.org.py; f. 1991; promotes commerce and industrial devt; Gen. Man. HERNÁN RAMÍREZ.

Instituto Nacional de Desarrollo Rural y de la Tierra (INDERT): Tacuary 276, Asunción; tel. (21) 44-0578; fax (21) 44-6534; f. 1963 as Instituto de Bienestar Rural; adopted current name in 2004; responsible for rural welfare and colonization; Pres. ALBERTO ALDERETE.

Instituto Paraguayo de Artesanía (IPA): Asunción; tel. (21) 61-4896; fax (21) 60-0035; internet ipa@artesania.gov.py; f. 2004;

promotes handicraft industries; Pres. FREDDY GERARDO OLMEDO COLMAN.

Instituto Paraguayo del Indígena (INDI): Don Bosco 745, Casilla 1575, Asunción; tel. (21) 49-3737; fax (21) 44-7154; e-mail pres@indi.gov.py; internet www.indi.gov.py; f. 1981; responsible for welfare of Indian population; Pres. (vacant).

Red de Inversiones y Exportaciones (REDIEX): Avda Mariscal López 3333, Asunción; tel. and fax (21) 66-5112; e-mail info@rediex.gov.py; internet www.rediex.gov.py; replaced ProParaguay in 2007; responsible for promoting investment in Paraguay and the export of national products; Dir GUILLERMO ALCARAZ.

Red Rural de Organizaciones Privadas de Desarrollo: Manuel Domínguez 1045, entre Brasil y Estados Unidos, Asunción; tel. (21) 22-9740; e-mail redrural@redrural.org.py; internet www.redrural.org.py; f. 1989; co-ordinating body for rural devt orgs; Gen. Co-ordinator IDALINA GÓMEZ HANSEN; Sec. HEBE GONZÁLEZ.

CHAMBERS OF COMMERCE

Cámara Nacional de Comercio y Servicios de Paraguay: Estrella 540 esq. 14 de Mayo y 15 de Agosto, Asunción; tel. (21) 49-3321; fax (21) 44-0817; e-mail info@ccparaguay.com.py; internet www.ccparaguay.com.py; f. 1898; fmrly Cámara y Bolsa de Comercio; adopted current name 2002; Pres. BELTRÁN MACCHI SALIN; Gen. Man. MIGUEL RIQUELME OLAZAR.

Cámara de Comercio Paraguayo-Americana (Paraguayan-American Chamber of Commerce): 25 de Mayo 2090, esq. Mayor Bullo, Asunción; tel. (21) 22-2160; fax (21) 22-1926; e-mail pamcham@pamcham.com.py; internet www.pamcham.com.py; f. 1981; c. 120 mem. cos; Exec. Dir GERALD MCCULLOCH.

Cámara de Comercio Paraguayo-Arabe: Próceres de Mayo 296, esq. Ana Díaz, Asunción; tel. 22-7197; fax 21-3240; Pres. MOHAMED RAHAL.

Cámara de Comercio Paraguayo-Británico: Avda Boggiani 5848, Asunción; tel. 61-2611; fax 60-5007; e-mail britcham@conexion.com.py; Pres. RONALD BURNETT.

Cámara de Comercio Paraguayo-Chileno: Guido Spano 1687, Asunción; tel. and fax 66-3085; e-mail ccpch@quanta.com.py; Pres. GUSTAVO OLMEDO SISUL.

Cámara de Comercio Paraguayo-Francesa (CCPF): Yegros 837, 1°, Of. 12, CP 3009, Asunción; tel. 49-7852; fax 44-6324; e-mail info@ccpf.com.py; internet www.ccpf.com.py; Pres. HUMBERT SOLENTE; Man. IRIS FELIU DE FLEITAS.

AGRICULTURAL, INDUSTRIAL AND EMPLOYERS' ORGANIZATIONS

Asociación de Empresas Financieras del Paraguay (ADEFI): Edif. Ahorros Paraguayos, Torre II, 6°, Of. 05, General Díaz 471, Asunción; tel. (21) 44-8298; fax (21) 49-8071; e-mail adefi@conexion.com.py; internet www.adefi.org.py; f. 1975; grouping of financial cos; Pres. MILCIADES FRETES RUBIANI.

Asociación Paraguaya de la Calidad: Luis Alberto de Herrera 195, 19°, Asunción; tel. (21) 44-7348; fax (21) 45-0705; e-mail apc@apc.org.py; internet www.apc.org.py; f. 1988; grouping of cos to promote quality of goods and services; Pres. SANTIAGO LLANO.

Asociación de Productores de Soja, Oleaginosas y Cereales del Paraguay (APS): Asunción; soya and grain producers' asscn; Pres. CLAUDIA RUSER.

Asociación Rural del Paraguay (ARP): Ruta Transchaco, Km 14, Mariano Roque Alonso; tel. (21) 75-4412; e-mail ania@arp.org.py; internet www.arp.org.py; grouping of agricultural cos and farmers; Pres. JUAN NÉSTOR NÚÑEZ.

Cámara Paraguaya de Exportadores de Cereales y Oleaginosas (CAPECO): Avda Brasilia 840, Asunción; tel. (21) 20-8855; fax (21) 21-3971; internet www.capeco.org.py; f. 1980; grain exporters' asscn; Pres. JOSÉ BOGARÍN ACOSTA.

Centro de Importadores del Paraguay (CIP): Avda Brasilia 1947, casi Artigas, Asunción; tel. (21) 29-9800; e-mail cip@cip.org.py; internet www.cip.org.py; f. 1939; importers' asscn; Pres. MAX HABER NEUMANN; Man. JULIO SÁNCHEZ LASPINA.

Federación de la Producción, Industria y Comercio (FEPRINCO): Edif. Union Club, Palma 751, 3°, esq. O'Leary y Ayolas, Asunción; tel. (21) 44-6634; fax (21) 44-6638; e-mail feprinco@quanta.com.py; org. of private-sector business execs; Pres. MIGUEL ÁNGEL CARRIZOSA GALLIANO.

Unión Industrial Paraguaya (UIP): Cerro Corá 1038, entre Estados Unidos y Brasil, Casilla 782, Asunción; tel. (21) 21-2556; fax (21) 21-3360; e-mail uip@uip.org.py; internet www.uip.org.py; f. 1936; org. of business entrepreneurs; Pres. GUSTAVO VOLPE.

UTILITIES

Electricity

Administración Nacional de Electricidad (ANDE): Avda España 1268, Asunción; tel. (21) 21-1001; fax (21) 21-2371; e-mail luis_rojas@ande.gov.py; internet www.ande.gov.py; f. 1949; national electricity board; Pres. SIXTO EUSEBIO AMARILLA FERNÁNDEZ; Sec.-Gen. LUIS RAMÓN ROJAS IBARRA.

Entidad Binacional Yacyretá: General Díaz 831 esq. Ayolas y Montevideo, Edif. Héroes de Marzo, Asunción; tel. and fax (21) 44-5611; internet www.eby.gov.py; owned jtly by Paraguay and Argentina; operates the hydroelectric dam at Yacyretá on the Paraná river, completed in 1998; installed capacity of 3,200 MW; 14,673 GWh of electricity produced in 2007; Dir (Paraguay) CARLOS MANUEL CARDOZO FLORENTÍN.

Itaipú Binacional: Centro Administrativo, Ruta Internacional Km 3.5, Avda Señor Rodríguez 150, Ciudad del Este; tel. (61) 599-8989; e-mail itaipu@itaipu.gov.br; internet www.itaipu.gov.py; f. 1974; jtly owned by Paraguay and Brazil; hydroelectric power station on Brazilian-Paraguayan border; 94,685 GWh of electricity produced in 2008; Dir-Gen. (Paraguay) CARLOS MATEO BALMELLI.

Water

Empresa de Servicios Sanitarios del Paraguay, SA (ESSAP): José Berges 516, entre Brasil y San José, Asunción; tel. (21) 21-0330; fax (21) 21-2624; e-mail secretaria@essap.com.py; internet www.essap.com.py; fmrly Corporación de Obras Sanitarias (CORPO-SANA); responsible for public water supply, sewage disposal and drainage; privatization plans suspended in 2002; Pres. EMILIANO INSFRÁN ROLÓN.

TRADE UNIONS

Central Nacional de Trabajadores (CNT): Piribebuy 1078, Asunción; tel. (21) 44-4084; fax (21) 49-2154; e-mail cnt@telesurf.com.py; Sec.-Gen. EDUARDO OJEDA; 120,840 mems (2007).

Central de Sindicatos de Trabajadores del Estado Paraguayo (Cesitep): Asunción; comprises public sector workers; Pres. REINALDO BARRETO MEDINA.

Central Unitaria de Trabajadores (CUT): San Carlos 836, Asunción; tel. (21) 44-3936; fax (21) 44-8482; f. 1989; Pres. ALAN FLORES; Sec.-Gen. JORGE ALVARENGA.

Confederación Paraguaya de Trabajadores (CPT): Yegros 1309–33 y Simón Bolívar, Asunción; tel. (21) 44-4921; fax (21) 20-5070; e-mail sixto10@telesurf.com.py; f. 1951; Pres. SIXTO ALONSO MENDOZA; Sec.-Gen. PATROCINIO CARMONA; 43,500 mems from 189 affiliated groups.

Coordinadora Agrícola de Paraguay (CAP): Asunción; farmers' org.; Pres. HÉCTOR CRISTALDO.

Organización de Trabajadores de Educación del Paraguay (OTEP): Avda del Pueblo 845 con Ybyra Pyta, Barrio Santa Lucía, Lambaré; tel. and fax (21) 55-5525; e-mail otepsn@highway.com.py.

Transport

RAILWAYS

Ferrocarriles del Paraguay, SA (FEPASA): México 145, Casilla 453, Asunción; tel. (21) 44-3273; fax (21) 44-2733; e-mail ferroca@rieder.net.py; internet www.ferrocarriles.com.py; f. 1854; state-owned since 1961; restructured in 2002 and scheduled for privatization; 376 km of track; Pres. LAURO MANUEL RAMÍREZ LÓPEZ.

ROADS

In 1999 there were an estimated 29,500 km of roads, of which 14,986 km were paved. The Pan-American Highway runs for over 700 km in Paraguay and the Trans-Chaco Highway extends from Asunción to Bolivia.

SHIPPING

Administración Nacional de Navegación y Puertos (ANNP) (National Shipping and Ports Administration): Colón y El Paraguayo Independiente, Asunción; tel. (21) 49-5086; fax (21) 49-7485; e-mail gciacomercial@annp.gov.py; internet www.annp.gov.py; f. 1965; responsible for ports services and maintaining navigable channels in rivers and for improving navigation on the Paraguay and Paraná rivers; Pres. ALBINO GONZÁLEZ.

Ocean Shipping

Compañía Paraguaya de Navegación de Ultramar, SA: Presidente Franco 625, 2°, Casilla 77, Asunción; tel. (21) 49-2137; fax (21)

PARAGUAY

44-5013; f. 1963 to operate between Asunción, US and European ports; 10 vessels; Exec. Pres. JUAN BOSCH B.

Navemar S.R.L.: B. Constant 536, 1°, Casilla 273, Asunción; tel. (21) 49-3122; 5 vessels.

Transporte Fluvial Paraguayo S.A.C.I.: Edif. de la Encarnación, 13°, 14 de Mayo 563, Asunción; tel. (21) 49-3411; fax (21) 49-8218; e-mail tfpsaci@tm.com.py; Admin. Man. DANIELLA CHARBONNIER; 1 vessel.

CIVIL AVIATION

The major international airport, Aeropuerto Internacional Silvio Pettirossi, is situated 15 km from Asunción. A second international airport, Aeropuerto Internacional Guaraní, 30 km from Ciudad del Este, was inaugurated in 1996.

National Airlines

Transportes Aéreos del Mercosur (TAM Mercosur): Aeropuerto Internacional Silvio Pettirossi, Hangar TAM/ARPA, Luque, Asunción; tel. (21) 49-1039; fax (21) 64-5146; e-mail tammercosur@uninet.com.py; internet www.tam.com.py; f. 1963 as Líneas Aéreas Paraguayas (LAP); name changed as above in 1997; services to destinations within South America; 80% owned by TAM Linhas Aéreas (Brazil); Pres. MIGUEL CANDIA.

Aerolíneas Paraguayas (ARPA): Terminal ARPA, Aeropuerto Internacional Silvio Pettirossi, Asunción; tel. (21) 21-5072; fax (21) 21-5111; f. 1994; domestic service; wholly owned by Transportes Aéreos del Mercosur (TAM Mercosur).

Tourism

Tourism is undeveloped, but, with recent improvements in infrastructure, efforts were being made to promote the sector. Tourist arrivals in Paraguay in 2006 totalled 388,465 (of whom some 50% came from Brazil). In 2006 tourism receipts were US $111m.

Secretaría Nacional de Turismo: Palma 468, Asunción; tel. (21) 49-4110; fax (21) 49-1230; e-mail ministra@senatur.gov.py; internet www.senatur.gov.py; f. 1998; Exec. Sec. LIZ ROSANNA CRÁMER CAMPOS.

PERU

Introductory Survey

Location, Climate, Language, Religion, Flag, Capital

The Republic of Peru lies in western South America, bordered by Ecuador and Colombia to the north, by Brazil and Bolivia to the east, and by Chile to the south. Peru has a coastline of more than 2,300 km (1,400 miles) on the Pacific Ocean. The climate varies with altitude, average temperatures being about 11°C (20°F) lower in the Andes mountains than in the coastal plain. The rainy season is between October and April, with heavy rainfall in the tropical forests. Temperatures in Lima are usually between 13°C (55°F) and 28°C (82°F). The three official languages are Spanish, Quechua and Aymará. Almost all of the inhabitants profess Christianity, and the great majority are adherents of the Roman Catholic Church. The civil flag (proportions 2 by 3) has three equal vertical stripes, of red, white and red. The state flag additionally has the national coat of arms (a shield divided into three unequal segments: red, with a golden cornucopia spilling coins of yellow and white at the base, blue, with a yellow vicuña in the dexter chief, and white, with a green tree in the sinister chief; all surmounted by a green wreath, and framed by branches of palm and laurel, tied at the bottom with a red and white ribbon) in the centre of the white stripe. The capital is Lima.

Recent History

Following independence from Spain, declared in 1821 and finally achieved in 1824, Peruvian politics were characterized by alternating periods of civilian administration and military dictatorship. In the early 1920s opposition to the dictatorial regime of President Augusto Bernardino Leguía resulted in the creation of the Alianza Popular Revolucionaria Americana (APRA), Peru's oldest political party to command mass support. The party, founded as a nationalist revolutionary movement, was formally established in Peru as the Partido Aprista Peruano (PAP) in 1930, when Leguía was deposed and the party's founder (and its leader for more than 50 years), Dr Víctor Raúl Haya de la Torre, returned from enforced exile in Mexico. A long-standing tradition of hostility developed between the Apristas and the armed forces, and the party was banned in 1931–45, and again in 1948–56.

During 1945–63 political power shifted regularly between the armed forces and elected government. In 1948 Dr José Luis Bustamente y Rivera was deposed by Gen. Manuel Odría, following a right-wing military rebellion. Odría established a military junta which governed until 1950, when the General was elected unopposed to the presidency, and subsequently appointed a cabinet composed of military officers and civilians. In 1956 Odría was succeeded by Dr Manuel Prado y Ugartache (who had been President in 1939–45). An inconclusive presidential election in 1962 precipitated military intervention, and power was assumed by Gen. Ricardo Pérez Godoy, at the head of a military junta. In March 1963, however, Pérez was supplanted by his second-in-command, Gen. Nicolás Lindley López.

Fernando Belaúnde Terry, the joint candidate of his own Acción Popular (AP) party and the Partido Demócrata Cristiano, was elected President in June 1963. An increase in internal disturbances in predominantly Indian areas resulted in the temporary suspension of constitutional guarantees in 1965–66 and an intensive military campaign of counter-insurgency. Lack of congressional support for the Government contributed to a succession of ministerial crises which, together with continuing internal unrest, prompted renewed military intervention in October 1968, when Gen. Juan Velasco Alvarado assumed the presidency, dissolved Congress and appointed a military cabinet.

Despite the re-emergence of internal disturbances and dissension within the armed forces, Velasco retained power until August 1975, when he was overthrown and replaced by Gen. Francisco Morales Bermúdez. In July 1977 President Morales announced plans for the restoration of civilian rule. Accordingly, a national election was conducted in June 1978 to select the members of a constituent assembly, which was to draft a new constitution in preparation for presidential and congressional elections. In the election, PAP emerged as the largest party, and in July the assembly elected the 83-year-old Dr Haya de la Torre to be its President. The new Constitution, adopted in July 1979, provided for elections by universal adult suffrage, and extended the franchise to the sizeable illiterate population.

The presidential contest of May 1980 was won decisively by Belaúnde. At the same time, the AP won an outright majority in the Cámara de Diputados (Chamber of Deputies) and also secured the greatest representation in the Senado (Senate). The new organs of state were inaugurated in July, when the new Constitution became fully effective. While Belaúnde sought to liberalize the economy and to reverse many of the agrarian and industrial reforms implemented under Velasco, much of his term of office was dominated by the increasing threat to internal stability posed by the emergence, in the early 1980s, of the Maoist rebel group Sendero Luminoso (SL—Shining Path). The situation deteriorated following the uncompromising response of the armed forces to terrorist activity in a designated emergency zone, which extended to 13 provinces (primarily in the departments of Ayacucho, Huancavelica and Apurímac) by mid-1984, and a dramatic increase in violent deaths and violations of human rights was reported.

At elections in April 1985 Alan García Pérez (the candidate for PAP) received 46% of the total votes in the presidential poll, while PAP secured a majority in both houses (the Cámara and the Senado) of the Congreso (legislature). García's victory was ensured in May, prior to a second round of voting, when his closest opponent, Dr Alfonso Barrantes Lingán (of the left-wing Izquierda Unida coalition), withdrew his candidature. At his inauguration in July, García announced that his Government's priorities would be to arrest Peru's severe economic decline and to eradicate internal terrorism.

Despite PAP successes at municipal elections in 1986, widespread opposition to the Government's economic programme was manifested in a succession of well-supported general strikes in 1987 and 1988. Government plans in 1987 for the nationalization of Peru's banks and private financial and insurance institutions encountered considerable opposition from the financial sector, and prompted the creation of Libertad, a 'freedom movement' expressing opposition to the plans (which were subsequently modified), which was established under the leadership of a well-known writer, Mario Vargas Llosa. The authority of the García administration was further undermined by persistent rumours of military unrest, by allegations of links between members of the Government and the right-wing paramilitary 'death squad', the Comando Rodrigo Franco, and by the continuing terrorist activities of the SL and a resurgence of activity by the Movimiento Revolucionario Túpac Amaru (MRTA) guerrilla group, in northeast Peru. In addition, the Government was criticized by international human rights organizations for its methods of combating political violence.

General elections took place on 8 April 1990, despite the attempts of the SL to disrupt the elections with another 'armed strike' and a campaign of bombing and looting. In the presidential poll Vargas Llosa, the candidate of the centre-right Frente Democrático (FREDEMO) alliance (established in 1988 by the AP, Libertad and the Partido Popular Cristiano), obtained the largest percentage of the total votes cast, followed by a hitherto little-known agronomist, Alberto Fujimori, the candidate of the Cambio 90 group of independents. In a second round of voting, conducted on 10 June, Fujimori emerged as the successful candidate, having attracted late support from left-wing parties and from PAP. Following his inauguration in July, Fujimori announced the composition of a new centre-left Council of Ministers, with Juan Carlos Hurtado Miller, a member of the AP, as President of the Council (prime minister) and Minister of Economy and Finance.

Proposals for economic readjustment announced in August 1990 abolished subsidies for consumers, thereby increasing prices by more than 3,000% for petrol and by as much as 600% for basic foods. Although these economic reforms secured Peru's rehabilitation within the international financial community, they provoked widespread opposition and industrial unrest (as well as the resignation of Hurtado). In November 1991, despite public and congressional dissent, Fujimori took advantage of a 150-day period of emergency legislative powers (granted to him in June in order that the country's potentially destabilizing economic and security problems might be addressed) to issue a series of economic decrees that represented a continuation of policies concerning the elimination of state monopolies of telecommunications, postal networks and railways, the opening to private investment of the power sector, the privatization of schools and a reform of the health and social security services.

On 5 April 1992 Fujimori announced the immediate suspension of the 1979 Constitution and the dissolution of the Congreso, pending a comprehensive restructuring of the legislature. The President maintained that the reform of the Congreso was essential in order to eradicate 'corruption and inefficiency', to enable him to implement a programme of 'pacification' of the nation by combating terrorism and drugs-trafficking, and also fully to implement free-market economic policies. In the interim an Emergency and National Reconstruction Government would govern the country, and legislative power would be exercised by the President, with the approval of the Council of Ministers. Fujimori also announced a reform of the judiciary. The constitutional coup (or 'autogolpe') was implemented with the full cooperation and support of the armed forces. On the following day the President of the Council of Ministers, Alfonso de los Heros Pérez Albela, resigned in protest, and was replaced by Oscar de la Puente; most government ministers, however, elected to remain in office. Members of the dissolved parliament declared Fujimori to be incapable of continuing in office, although an attempt to establish Máximo San Román, the First Vice-President, as the head of an alternative 'constitutional government' was undermined by a lack of domestic and international support. Moreover, while Fujimori's actions prompted outrage from politicians, the judiciary and the media, popular reaction to the 'autogolpe' was less hostile. Bolstered by demonstrations of public support for his actions, Fujimori dismissed 13 of Peru's 28 Supreme Court judges, whom he accused of corruption, and detained several prominent opposition party figures. The President of the central bank was also removed from office, as were 134 judges. The Organization of American States (OAS, see p. 373) deplored Fujimori's actions, and dispatched a mission to attempt to effect a reconciliation between the legislature and the executive. Later in April Fujimori announced that congressional elections would be conducted in February 1993.

The threat posed to Fujimori's programme of radical reform by economic constraints resulting from the suspension of international financial aid to Peru prompted the revision of the timetable for a return to democracy, and in June 1992 Fujimori confirmed that national elections would be conducted in October to a unicameral constituent congress, which would then draft a new constitution. The President also announced that, pending approval of a new document, the 1979 Constitution would be reinstated without certain articles that might 'impede the progress of the Government'.

A 'National Dialogue for Peace and Development', comprising a series of discussions with representatives of the political opposition and with the public, sought to identify important issues for future consideration by the new Congreso Constituyente Democrático (CCD). Elections to the CCD, conducted on 22 November 1992 and attended by OAS observers, were a qualified success for pro-Government parties. An electoral coalition of Cambio 90 and the Nueva Mayoría (a new independent party supported by many former cabinet ministers), headed by Fujimori's former Minister of Energy and Mines, Jaime Yoshiyama Tanaka (who was subsequently elected President of the CCD), secured 44 of the 80 congressional seats. The only significant opposition party not to boycott the elections, the Partido Popular Cristiano, took eight seats. In December, at the inaugural meeting of the CCD, Yoshiyama identified its immediate aims as the restoration of the autonomy of the judiciary, the eradication of terrorism, the generation of employment and of favourable conditions for foreign investment, and the projection of an enhanced national image abroad. In January 1993, having formally reinstated the 1979 Constitution, the CCD confirmed Fujimori as constitutional Head of State. Following the resignation of de la Puente's Government in July, Alfonso Bustamante y Bustamante was appointed prime minister in August.

The final text of the draft Constitution, which enhanced presidential powers and provided for the establishment of a unicameral legislature, was approved by the CCD in September 1993. Among the text's most controversial articles were the introduction of the death penalty for convicted terrorists and a provision permitting a President of the Republic to be re-elected for a successive five-year term of office. At a national referendum held on 31 October—the first occasion on which such popular consultation had been sought in Peru—the Constitution was narrowly approved, by an overall 52% of the votes cast. The Constitution was promulgated on 29 December, at a ceremony boycotted by opposition members of the CCD.

In a presidential election conducted on 9 April 1995, Fujimori secured an unexpected outright victory over his closest opponent, Javier Pérez de Cuéllar de la Guerra (the former UN Secretary-General and the candidate of the Unión por el Perú—UPP), obtaining 64% of the total votes. In concurrent legislative elections, Fujimori's coalition movement, Cambio 90-Nueva Mayoría, also secured an absolute majority in the unicameral Congreso. The composition of the new Government, installed following Fujimori's inauguration in July, was largely unaltered. Efraín Goldenberg, who had succeeded Bustamante as prime minister in February 1994, was replaced by Dante Córdova Blanco.

In June 1995 legislation was approved by the Congreso granting an amnesty to all members of the military, police and intelligence forces who had been convicted of human rights violations committed since 1980 in the internal conflict against separatist violence; ostensibly, the legislation was to promote national reconciliation, although it was also widely thought to have been introduced by the President in order to consolidate his relationship with the military leadership. The legislation attracted broad criticism from opposition parties, and internationally. In August an international warrant was issued for the arrest of former President Alan García, who had been accused of receiving bribes and other corrupt practices during his term of office.

In April 1996 the sudden resignation of the President of the Council of Ministers demonstrated the extent of disunity within the Government, particularly over economic policy. Alberto Pandolfi Arbulu was appointed premier, and the Government's privatization programme was accelerated. Meanwhile, Fujimori was attempting to formulate legislation that would allow him to stand for election for a third presidential term. A congressional committee approved a new 'interpretation' of the Constitution in August (on the grounds that Fujimori was first elected under the 1979 Constitution), and the legislation was approved by the Congreso later in that month (with a boycott of the vote by the majority of opposition politicians). In January 1997 the Constitutional Court ruled the new interpretation of the Constitution to be invalid.

On 17 December 1996 MRTA activists launched an assault on the residence of the Japanese ambassador in Lima, and detained by force more than 500 people attending an evening reception. Among those taken hostage were the Peruvian Ministers of Foreign Affairs and of Agriculture, at least nine foreign ambassadors and other diplomatic personnel, leading police and security officials and representatives of the business community. The MRTA activists' demands included the release of all 458 MRTA prisoners in detention in Peru, safe passage to an area in Peru's central highlands, greater economic assistance to the country's poorest people and payment of a 'war tax'. On 27 December Fujimori declared a state of emergency in Lima. On 22 April 1997 Peruvian troops launched an unexpected assault on the ambassador's residence, ending the MRTA siege. Two soldiers and all 14 of the MRTA activists were killed in the operation, and one of the 72 remaining hostages died of heart failure. President Fujimori presented the assault as a measure of his Government's uncompromising stance against terrorism; it was later alleged that some of the MRTA members might have been killed after having surrendered to army officers.

Fujimori's immediate hopes for election to a third presidential term were encouraged in February 1998 by the Supreme Court's announcement that it could foresee no significant obstacle to Fujimori's candidature in 2000. However, a final decision on his eligibility was to be decided by the Jurado Nacional Electoral (JNE—National Electoral Board). The Government was accused of further supporting the subversion of normal judicial processes in March, when the Congreso approved a new law severely reducing the regulatory powers of the National Council of the Judiciary. The legislation prompted the resignation of all seven members of the Council, and the cancellation, by the World Bank, of a substantial loan to the Peruvian Government, intended for judicial reform projects.

There was further evidence of the President's circumvention of the traditional role of the judiciary in May 1998 when Fujimori introduced draconian anti-crime legislation by decree (subsequently approved by the Congreso) seeking to extend the extreme powers and penalties employed in recent successful anti-terrorism initiatives to other areas of criminal activity. Among the provisions of the new law were plans to increase the powers of military tribunals to try civilians. Despite appeals by international observers and opposition groups for greater judicial independence and respect for human rights, in December the Congreso voted to extend the period of judicial reorganization initiated by Fujimori's administration for a further two-year period.

Fujimori's popularity continued to wane during 1998 (the ruling party chose not to field candidates for local elections conducted in October, as a consequence), and the President's attempts to consolidate his position and reassert his authority resulted in repeated changes to the Council of Ministers. In April 1999 the entire Council of Ministers resigned, amid a rift over corruption allegations against officials at the state customs authority. Another mass cabinet resignation followed in October, in accordance with the law requiring public officials intending to stand for election to resign their posts six months before the April 2000 polls. Alberto Bustamante Belaúnde was appointed to lead a new cabinet.

Meanwhile, Fujimori's continuing efforts to secure support for a third presidential term were encouraged by the defeat in the Congreso, in September 1998, of an opposition proposal to decide the question of Fujimori's eligibility by a national referendum. Opposition to Fujimori's possible re-election was vociferously expressed when a broad range of labour unions and political parties participated in April 1999 in a one-day general strike. However, this, together with a demonstration involving some 20,000 people in October, failed to prevent the announcement in December of Fujimori's candidature on behalf of the Perú 2000 alliance (a new movement formed to support the incumbent's re-election campaign). On 1 January 2000 the JNE, which was dominated by Fujimori's supporters, ratified his registration as a candidate in response to a legal challenge issued by the political opposition. The election board's rationale was that although the Constitution did not permit a President to serve three terms, Fujimori had only served one term under the current Constitution, as amended in 1993, and therefore was eligible for re-election. The ruling precipitated further street protests. Allegations of electoral fraud and campaign misconduct were widespread. Accusations by opposition leaders included government manipulation of the media to deny them equal access, the use of state resources to promote Fujimori's campaign, and alleged falsification of more than 1m. signatures by members of Perú 2000 to register Fujimori's candidacy. Opposition plans to reach a consensus on a single candidate to challenge Fujimori did not materialize, and in January 2000 seven opposition candidates registered to stand for election to the presidency.

The general election proceeded on 9 April 2000. During the vote count opposition candidates and international observers alleged that the ballot was marred by fraud. US officials issued increasingly strong statements stressing the need for a second round of voting as the only credible proof of legitimacy. At the final count Fujimori officially received 49.9% of the votes cast and Alejandro Toledo (the first presidential candidate of Amerindian descent) 40.2%. In the congressional elections Perú 2000 won 52 of the 120 seats, while Perú Posible (PP), which supported Toledo, won 29 seats. The JNE resisted both domestic and external pressure for a postponement of the second round (scheduled for 28 May), in order to correct irregularities noted in the first round. In response, Toledo withdrew his candidature one week before the election and urged his supporters to spoil their votes in protest. Violent incidents, including the firebombing of the presidential palace, followed the JNE decision. The OAS and US-based Carter Center suspended monitoring of the election, citing difficulties with the computer system for tabulating votes. Amid further mass demonstrations, Fujimori contested the election effectively unopposed (although the JNE ruled that Toledo remained a candidate and refused to remove his name from the ballot papers), taking 51% of the total votes; Toledo received 18%. Excluding spoiled (30%) and blank (1%) papers, the incumbent was thus returned to office with 74% of the valid votes cast. The result was denounced as invalid by the political opposition and by the US Government (though it later moderated its position, describing the outcome as imperfect). Fujimori's inauguration on 28 July was accompanied by violent protests in Lima.

In September 2000 a major political scandal erupted after the disclosure of a video that allegedly showed Vladimiro Montesinos, the head of the national intelligence service and a close ally of the President, bribing an opposition member of the Congreso. In response Fujimori declared that new elections would be held, in which he would not participate. He also announced that the national intelligence service would be disbanded. At the same time, 10 Perú 2000 deputies defected to the opposition, thus depriving Fujimori of his majority in the legislature. Demonstrations, led by Toledo, demanded the immediate resignation of Fujimori and the arrest of Montesinos, who fled to Panama. On 5 October the Congreso approved OAS-mediated proposals paving the way for power to be transferred from Fujimori to his successor in mid-2001, as well as the disbandment of the Congreso to make way for a newly elected legislature. Later in the month Fujimori announced the replacement of the most senior commanders of the armed forces.

In late October 2000 the political crisis deepened when Montesinos returned from Panama, after failing to obtain political asylum there. His apparent impunity supported the widely held view that the armed forces were protecting him. At the same time, the first Vice-President, Francisco Tudela, resigned in protest at government attempts to make new elections conditional upon an amnesty for those in the armed forces accused of human rights violations. Further OAS-sponsored negotiations between opposition groups and the Government led to the announcement that new elections would be held on 8 April 2001, without any conditions attached. An investigation into Montesinos's activities was launched, with charges ranging from corruption to torture and murder. In mid-November the Congreso voted to replace its pro-Fujimori President, Martha Hildebrandt Pérez Treviño, with Valentín Paniagua Corazao, effectively giving the opposition control of the legislature. The following day Fujimori travelled to Japan, from where, on 20 November, he resigned the presidency. The Congreso, however, refused to accept the resignation, and instead voted to dismiss Fujimori.

On 22 November 2000 Paniagua was appointed interim President. A new cabinet was sworn in three days later, which included Javier Pérez de Cuéllar as prime minister and Minister of Foreign Affairs. The aims of the interim Government, the mandate of which would last until 28 July 2001, included the achievement of a balanced budget and the strengthening of democracy. Several days later the new Minister of Defence, Walter Ledesma Rebaza, announced the decision to retire 13 generals who were known to be associates of Montesinos. A congressional commission, established in the same month to investigate the activities of Montesinos, uncovered hundreds of secret videotapes that seemed to compromise the integrity of judges, politicians, military officers, businessmen and bishops. In early December it was announced that the commission's investigations were to extend to Fujimori. In mid-December it was announced that Fujimori had taken up Japanese citizenship and was thus, in effect, protected from the threat of extradition from Japan. Nevertheless, in February 2001 corruption charges were formally filed against him. Furthermore, in August the Congreso voted unanimously to lift Fujimori's constitutional immunity and issued an international warrant for his arrest on the charge of dereliction of duty. Further charges of embezzlement and illicit enrichment were subsequently filed against the former President. However, the Japanese Government proved unresponsive to diplomatic pressure and stated that it had no intention of allowing Fujimori's extradition. In June 2005 the Japanese authorities rejected a further extradition request for Fujimori, citing a lack of further evidence to justify its approval.

In June 2001 Montesinos was arrested in Venezuela. He was sent back to Peru and, in July 2002, sentenced to nine years' imprisonment on charges relating to 'usurpation of power'. However, investigating judges subsequently brought a further 80 indictments against him, including murder, bribery and the illegal sale of weapons and narcotics. Following his first public trial in February 2003, Montesinos was convicted on corruption charges and sentenced to a further five years' imprisonment. In June 2004 Montesinos was found guilty of bribing newspaper editors to support Fujimori's re-election attempt in 2000, and was sentenced to a further 15 years' imprisonment. (In January 2005 eight newspaper chiefs were sentenced to five years in gaol after being convicted of receiving payments from Montesinos.) In August 2005 the trial began of Montesinos and 56 alleged members of the Colina group on charges of involvement in the disappearances of 36 people under the administration of President Fujimori. In September 2006 Montesinos received another gaol term of 20 years after being convicted of arms-trafficking.

In January 2001, only a few days after corruption charges against him were ruled to have expired under the statute of limitations former President Alan García Pérez returned to Peru to launch his campaign for the forthcoming presidential election. The first round of the election was held on 8 April, following a bitter campaign. Toledo won 37% of the votes cast, while García attracted 26% of the ballot and Lourdes Flores Nano of the Unidad Nacional alliance 24%. In concurrently held elections to the 120-seat Congreso, no party secured a majority: PP took 45 seats, PAP 27 and the Unidad Nacional 17, while the right-wing Frente Independiente Moralizador (FIM) won 12 seats. Election monitors declared the election process to have been open and fair. In the second round of the presidential election, held on 3 June, Toledo won with 53% of the vote. Toledo was inaugurated on 28 July. A broad-based 15-member cabinet was appointed, headed by lawyer Roberto Dañino and with Pedro Pablo Kuczynski as Minister of Economy and Finance. The new Government promised to create more jobs, to reduce poverty and to put an end to the corruption of the Fujimori regime. In the previous month a congressional commission implicated 180 people in corruption scandals that took place during Fujimori's presidencies, including Gen. Walter Chacón Málaga, the recently appointed head of the armed forces.

However, the popularity of the Toledo Government declined sharply after only a few months in power, as high expectations were not matched by an increase in economic prospects. In September and October 2001 popular protests erupted throughout Peru as workers demanded more jobs and improvements to transport infrastructure and health care. Hundreds of former public sector workers protested in central Lima in January 2002 to demand their jobs back, and in February cotton producers and fishery workers staged demonstrations to demand more government aid. The protests proliferated, and in June, following a week of violent demonstrations in protest at government plans to privatize two regional electricity companies in Arequipa, the Minister of the Interior, Fernando Rospigliosi Capurro, resigned and the privatization process was suspended indefinitely. An extensive cabinet reorganization was carried out in July, in which the Secretary-General of PP, Luis Solari, replaced Dañino as prime minister and Kuczynski was succeeded as Minister of Economy and Finance by Javier Silva Ruete. Nevertheless, popular dissatisfaction continued, and in January 2003 difficulties in the reform of the police service led to the resignation of the Minister of the Interior, Gino Costa Santolaya. He was succeeded by Alberto Sanabría Ortiz, a leading member of PP. In the same month the ruling party's congressional majority was reduced after five PP deputies resigned from the party in order to form a new movement, Perú Ahora.

In January 2003 a constitutional tribunal ruled that anti-terrorism legislation adopted by the Fujimori administration had violated the Constitution. In order to alleviate the potential pressure on the judiciary, and to prevent the release of large numbers of alleged terrorists, the Congreso granted President Toledo exceptional temporary powers to legislate by decree on security issues. In February the Government announced that all military sentences passed during Fujimori's presidency were to be annulled. The courts would have 60 days to decide whether to release convicted individuals or commit them for retrial. In March anti-terrorism legislation received congressional approval.

In February 2003 coca growers staged demonstrations to demand the suspension of the Government's coca-eradication policy. The demonstrations escalated after a coca growers' federation leader, Nelson Palomino La Serna, was imprisoned on terrorism charges. At the end of the month the Government announced that some US $3,000m. was to be invested in a coca-eradication plan by 2020. Following 11 days of protests, a temporary truce was declared between the coca growers and the Government, although the Government refused to release Palomino La Serna and pledged to continue with its eradication strategy. Following 20 days of further negotiations, the Government agreed to give $11m. in direct aid to farmers affected by the eradication efforts. In April thousands of coca growers began a protest march towards Lima to demand subsidies for alternative crops and an increase in the amount of coca that could legally be grown. Following a meeting with the coca leaders, on 23 April President Toledo signed into law a decree that pledged that the eradication programme would be gradual and that the Government would discuss policy with the growers. Nevertheless, civil unrest continued; in May public sector workers began a series of demonstrations against salary levels and conditions, and farmers also continued to mount protests. Outbreaks of violence during these demonstrations prompted the President to declare a state of emergency in 12 of the country's 25 regions. In June the Government acquiesced to teachers' demands, and in July the Congreso approved a series of limited fiscal measures intended to pay for the wage increases.

In 2003 and 2004 a rapid succession of government changes reflected President Toledo's deteriorating public credibility. Following the resignation of the entire Council of Ministers in June 2003, the President appointed Beatriz Merino Lucero, previously the head of the tax inspection service, as President of the Council. Merino Lucero proved popular, although she was obliged to resign in December following reports of nepotistic practices during her previous career and opposition allegations relating to her personal life. Carlos Ferrero Costa, a former President of the Congreso and a leading member of PP, was appointed to succeed her. In February 2004 Ferrero Costa effected a wide-ranging cabinet reorganization, appointing a number of independent technocrats. A notable inclusion in the new cabinet was Pedro Pablo Kuczynski, who was reappointed Minister of Economy and Finance. Furthermore, the reallocation of portfolios removed members of the FIM from the Government; nevertheless, the FIM pledged to continue its legislative alliance with PP.

Throughout 2004 President Toledo, his family and his advisers were implicated in several major scandals. In January a purported recording was made public of his former legal adviser, César Almeyda, meeting with an associate of Vladimiro Montesinos. Almeyda was placed under house arrest at the end of January, but was cleared of any wrongdoing in June. Almeyda had been director of the national intelligence service until April 2003, when he had been forced to resign after being accused of authorizing the illegal use of surveillance technology. He was replaced by Adm. (retd) Alfonso Panizzo; however, in September Panizzo also tendered his resignation after it emerged that the intelligence agency had been spying on journalists investigating corrupt practices in public office. Panizzo's successor, Gen. (retd) Daniel Mora, held the post until March 2004, when the revelation that the agency had been compiling a dossier on Minister of the Interior Fernando Rospigliosi Capurro forced his resignation. In late March Toledo announced that the national intelligence agency was to be abolished. A government committee was immediately formed to oversee the establishment of a successor body, the Agencia de Inteligencia Estratégica. In early May Rospigliosi Capurro himself was forced to resign from the Government, having been held responsible for the authorities' inability to quell violent disturbances in the southern region of Puno, which had culminated in late April in the lynching of a local mayor. Javier Reátegui was named as the new Minister of the Interior.

In July 2004 the President's sister, Margarita Toledo, was ordered by a judge not to leave the country pending investigations into an alleged large-scale forging of signatures in 1999 in order to register PP for the 2000 legislative elections. Toledo and her husband were placed under house arrest in January 2005. A special congressional commission was established to investigate the case. Meanwhile, in July 2004 President Toledo granted investigators authority to probe bank accounts held in Peru and abroad by himself and his wife, Eliane Karp, following media accusations that they had accepted bribes. In mid-July a general strike was held in protest at, *inter alia*, the perceived corruption of the Toledo administration and its failure to fulfil electoral promises, as well as at the proposed free trade agreement with the USA and the Government's failure to act upon the findings of the Truth Commission (see below). Then, in late July, PP suffered another major set-back when its candidate for the presidency of the Congreso, Luis Solari, was defeated by Antero Flores-Aráoz of the Unidad Nacional. In early May a congressional committee concluded that Toledo and his associates had violated electoral law by forging signatures to register PP for the 2000 legislative elections. However, on 20 May the Congreso decided, by 57 to 47 votes, not to impeach President Toledo. In February 2006 the Supreme Court issued a ruling ending Margarita Toledo's house arrest; however, the charges of electoral fraud against her remained. Having left office in July, former President Toledo was charged in December in connection with the forgery case; he denied all allegations against him.

Meanwhile, on 1 January 2005 about 200 members of an ultra-nationalist grouping, the Movimiento Etnocacerista (allied to the Movimiento Nacionalista Peruana), forcibly occupied a police station in the southern province of Andahuaylas, taking 21 people hostage. President Toledo declared a state of emergency in the province and troops were dispatched to the region. The uprising, which resulted in the death of seven people, including four police officers, was primarily intended to force the resignation of President Toledo, whom the group accused of incompetence, corruption, acquiescence to foreign interests and the debasement of the armed forces. On 3–4 January the insurgents and their leader, Maj. (retd) Antauro Igor Humala Tasso, surrendered to the police; all were arrested on terrorism charges. In response to public dissatisfaction with the authorities' handling of events, Reátegui resigned as Minister of the Interior; he was succeeded by Félix Murazzo, the former head of the national police.

In August 2005, following the resignation of the Minister of Foreign Affairs, Manuel Rodrígues Cuadros, President Toledo appointed the outspoken FIM leader, Fernando Olivera, to succeed him. However, Olivera's appointment caused dissent within the Council of Ministers (ostensibly over Olivera's approval of the legalization of coca cultivation for traditional use in the province of Cusco), and prompted the resignation of the prime minister, Ferrero Costa. Three days after his appointment, Olivera resigned as Minister of Foreign Affairs. President Toledo was forced to effect a major cabinet reorganization. The appointment of Pedro Pablo Kuczynski, hitherto Minister of Economy and Finance, as President of the Council of Ministers received broad congressional and popular approval, although Toledo's approval ratings remained low for the remainder of the year.

In November 2005 Fujimori was arrested on his arrival in Santiago, Chile, where he had arrived unannounced from Japan via Mexico. It was believed that the former President, who had announced his intention to contest the presidential election scheduled for April 2006, had planned to conduct his election campaign from Chile. Immediately following Fujimori's arrest, the Peruvian authorities informally requested that Chile extradite him to Peru to face charges pending against him. An extradition petition was formally submitted to the Chilean Government in January 2006. Fujimori was released on bail in May. In November a Peruvian judge issued a new international arrest warrant for Fujimori on the charge that he ordered the killing of 20 members of the SL during a prison riot in May 1992. In September 2007, following a ruling by the Chilean Supreme Court, Fujimori was extradited to Peru on seven charges. In December the former President went on trial before the Supreme Court in Lima on four of those charges: namely, responsibility for the killing of 15 civilians in Barrios Altos in 1991, and of nine students and a professor at Lima's La Canuta university in 1992, by an assassination squad known as the Colina group (see below); and the abductions of a journalist and a businessman, also in 1992. In April 2009 Fujimori was convicted of all four charges and sentenced to 25 years' imprisonment. The trial, which was praised by international human rights organizations for its rigour and fairness, was the first of a Latin American President in his own country on charges of human rights violations.

Presidential and legislative elections were held on 9 April 2006. A left-wing nationalist candidate, Lt-Col (retd) Ollanta Humala Tasso, who was the nominee of a coalition of his own party, the Partido Nacionalista Peruano (PNP), and the UPP, won the first round of the presidential ballot with 30.6% of valid votes, while former President García, representing PAP, secured 24.3%. The candidate of the conservative Unidad Nacional, Lourdes Flores Nano, came third with 23.8%. A high turn-out, of 88.7%, was recorded. In the concurrently held legislative elections the UPP emerged as the largest party in the new Congreso, winning 45 of the 120 seats, while PAP took 36 seats, the Unidad Nacional 17 and the Alianza por el Futuro (a coalition of Cambio 90 and Nueva Mayoría) 13. At a second round of presidential voting, held on 4 June, García defeated Humala, securing 52.6% of the votes cast. By portraying himself as a moderate who had learned from past errors, García had succeeded in attracting sufficient numbers of votes from those who had supported Flores in the first round, despite concerns regarding the policies he had pursued during his previous period in office (1985–90). Moreover, fears that Humala's intention to increase state control over Peru's natural resources would damage the economy had been heightened by the controversial endorsement of his candidacy by the Venezuelan President, Hugo Chávez Frías, which had provoked considerable diplomatic tensions (see below).

García took office on 28 July 2006. At his inauguration the new President focused on the need to reduce poverty, announcing plans to lower administrative expenses, including his own salary and those of members of the Congreso and other officials, and to invest some US $1,600m. in rural areas to improve public infrastructure and the provision of education and health care. Nine independents were appointed to the new 16-member Council of Ministers, including Luis Carranza Ugarte, a former director of the central bank, as Minister of Economy and Finance, and Antonio García Belaúnde, a senior diplomat, as Minister of Foreign Affairs. Jorge del Castillo Gálvez, the Secretary-General of PAP and a close ally of García, was designated President of the Council of Ministers.

Although the UPP-PNP coalition had secured the largest number of seats in the legislature, divisions within the alliance became apparent soon after the elections, with the UPP favouring the adoption of a less confrontational approach towards García's administration. In late June 2006 Carlos Torres Caro and two other deputies withdrew from the coalition to form the Partido Demócrata Peruano, and in mid-August the UPP announced that it had severed ties with Humala and the PNP, leaving PAP as the largest bloc in the Congreso. Humala suffered a further set-back in late August, when he was formally charged with human rights abuses based on allegations of murder and torture by counter-insurgency troops under his command at a military base in the department of San Martín in 1992; the former army officer denied any involvement in rights violations, claiming that the charges were a form of political persecution. In late December Humala was also charged with rebellion in relation to his alleged involvement in the uprising at a police station in Andahuaylas in January 2005 (led by his imprisoned brother, Antauro). Meanwhile, he formed a new alliance, the Gran Alianza Nacionalista Peruana (Gran Perú), with the aim of uniting the regional and local movements that had supported his candidacy in the presidential election.

In August 2006 the Congreso endorsed the Government's five-year programme, which was dominated by measures to alleviate poverty. A social welfare fund was to be established to finance projects in the High Andes and the Amazon (where Humala had received strong support in the presidential election), while, under the 'Sierra Exportadora' initiative, US $102m. was to be spent over five years on cultivating 150,000 hectares of land in the Andes, with the aim of producing 730,000 metric tons of agricultural goods for export and creating 300,000 jobs. However, critics expressed doubt about the viability of the 'Sierra Exportadora' project, questioning the agricultural capacity of the area concerned. In November García announced funding for 2007 of some $900m. for 11 social welfare programmes.

Non-governmental organizations (NGOs) expressed strong opposition to legislation, approved by the Congreso in November 2006, that would force them to provide details of their funding and activities to a government agency, the Agencia Peruana de Cooperación Internacional (APCI), which would monitor their work to ensure that it was compatible with the Government's development policy. The Government relied on the support of the Unidad Nacional and the Alianza por el Futuro, as well as PAP, to secure the adoption of the controversial legislation, which it insisted was intended to promote transparency. Minor amendments to the legislation were adopted in early December, reducing the APCI's control over NGOs that received all their funding from abroad, without aid from the state.

President García suffered his first congressional defeat in January 2007, when the legislature rejected his proposal to apply the death penalty to those convicted of terrorism. Although the Constitution provided for the death penalty to be imposed in cases of treason in times of war or of terrorism, the penal code did not allow capital punishment for acts of terrorism. García declared that he would seek a referendum on the issue as, according to opinion polls, 80% of the public supported his proposal. However, other senior PAP officials considered that such a vote would contravene the Constitution, which prohibited referendums on initiatives that would suppress a fundamental right, such as the right to life.

Pilar Mazzetti, the independent Minister of the Interior, resigned in February 2007, following accusations of corruption relating to the overpriced purchase of 469 police cars. Her replacement by Luis Alva Castro, a PAP veteran who had served as prime minister in 1985–87, prompted criticism from the PNP and the Unidad Nacional, which asserted that another unaffiliated minister should have been appointed. In May the Minister of Agriculture, Juan José Salazar García, was also forced to resign after acting against the Government's counter-narcotics policy (see below); he was replaced by Ismael Benavides Ferreyros.

The Government's reputation was damaged by widespread social unrest in several of the country's regions in July 2007. An indefinite strike, initiated in early July by teachers protesting against the introduction of a controversial education law, later escalated into a two-day general strike organized by the Confederación General de Trabajadores del Perú (CGTP), during which one person was killed in Satipo. The army was mobilized to support the police in maintaining order. Later that month—following the end of the teachers' 15-day strike, as it became—the Government issued a number of decrees intended to restrict future unrest, including one prohibiting regional presidents and mayors from participating in strikes.

President García replaced six members of his cabinet in December 2007. Among other appointments, Antero Flores-Aráoz replaced Allan Wagner Tizón as Minister of Defence and Rosario Fernández Figueroa substituted María Zavala Valladares as Minister of Justice. It was announced that Wagner was to head the Peruvian delegation to the International Court of Justice (ICJ) in its maritime border dispute with Chile (see below). In May 2008 García appointed Antonio Brack Egg, a well-known ecologist, to the newly created post of Minister of the Environment.

Civil unrest and violence continued in various parts of the country during 2008. In February a strike by farmers protesting against the Government's agricultural policies resulted in four deaths in Ayacucho. In June miners went on strike in Moquegua in protest at a new law that would have reduced the revenue received by the regional government from mining royalties; some 28 people were injured during the demonstrations, and a number of police officers were taken hostage by protesters while attempting to break up a roadblock. The 10-day strike was ended after the Government reached an agreement with the regional authorities regarding the distribution of mining revenues. A nation-wide one-day general strike, organized by the CGTP and supported by the PNP, was held in early July in protest at the Government's economic policies and the rising cost of living, although the violence that the authorities had anticipated was largely absent. In August a state of emergency was declared in several provinces after members of 65 indigenous groups erected roadblocks and picketed energy installations in protest against two decrees, promulgated earlier in the month by President García, relating to the sale of native land. The protesters claimed that the new laws, which allowed indigenous communities to sell their land if more than 50% of the community voted in favour of the sale (rather than a two-thirds' majority, as was previously the case), would have put large areas of the Amazon rainforest at risk of development by energy companies. Despite strong opposition from the Government, which argued that the development of hydrocarbons resources in the Amazon basin would increase investment in rural areas, the controversial decrees were revoked by the Congreso in late August.

In October 2008 a series of tape recordings emerged that appeared to indicate that a senior official of Perupetro, the government agency responsible for the development of the petroleum industry, had accepted bribes in exchange for the awarding of exploration contracts to a small Norwegian company, Discover Petroleum. The Minister of Energy and Mines, Juan Valdivia Romero, resigned in response to the allegations, as did the head of the state oil company, Petroperú, César Gutiérrez, who was also implicated in the scandal. Three days later, on 10 October, the entire Council of Ministers tendered its resignation, following allegations that the prime minister, del Castillo, had been involved in the affair. García subsequently appointed the President of the north-western region of Lambayeque, Yehude Simon Munaro, as prime minister, and he was sworn in on 14 October along with a new Council of Ministers that included 10 members of del Castillo's cabinet and six new appointees. It was thought that the appointment of Simon, a left-winger who had been imprisoned under the Fujimori Government for supposed links to the MRTA (for which he was subsequently pardoned), would help to diminish tension between the Government and the regions in the wake of further strikes and protests in early October. Among the new cabinet appointments was Remigio Hernani Meloni as Minister of the Interior; however, Hernani subsequently received criticism for his confrontations with senior police officers, as well as for a number of perceived failures of the police force. In February 2009 he was replaced by a PAP congresswoman, Mercedes Cabanillas Bustamante, who immediately promised measures to reform the police. Meanwhile, in July 2008 Carranza had resigned as Minister of Economy and Finance for personal reasons, and had been replaced by Luis Valdivieso Montano; however, in January 2009 García dismissed Valdivieso and reappointed Carranza to his former role.

In the early 1990s the SL intensified its attacks against government and military targets, strategic power installations, commercial enterprises and rural defence groups. Following Fujimori's 'autogolpe' of April 1992 (effected partly in response to continuing congressional opposition to his efforts to expand the role of the armed forces), considerable concern was expressed by human rights organizations that the security forces would be permitted an increasing degree of autonomy. In September 1992 government forces succeeded in capturing the SL's founder and leader, Abimael Guzmán Reynoso, together with 20 prominent SL members. Guzmán was tried by a military court, where he was found guilty of treason and sentenced to life imprisonment. The SL, however, remained highly active, and in early 1993 was held responsible for the assassination of 20 candidates campaigning in local elections, and for attacks on rural communities that had formed self-defence militia units. The Government actively pursued its offensive against terrorist organizations in the mid-1990s, and publicized the detention of leading members of the SL, the MRTA and the dissident SL 'Sendero Rojo' faction (which advocated a continuation of the armed struggle). In 1999 Oscar Ramírez Durand (alias 'Comrade Feliciano'), the leader of Sendero Rojo, was captured and sentenced to life imprisonment.

The SL emerged again in 2001, with at least 31 deaths attributed to the terrorist organization in that year. In March 2002, three days before the US President, George W. Bush, was due to visit Peru, the first such visit by a serving US head of state, a car bomb killed 10 people and injured at least 40 more near the US embassy in Lima. The attack was attributed to a radical wing of the SL, and did not herald an immediate return to a sustained campaign of terrorism. In June 2003 the Government attributed the abduction of 60 pipeline construction workers in the Ayacucho region to the remnants of the SL; the hostages were subsequently released unharmed. In November the kidnappers' alleged leader, Jaime Zuñiga Córdova, was captured by security forces. In November 2004 a retrial of Guzmán and 16 other SL militants began in a civilian court after the Constitutional Court ruled that their convictions by military court in 1992 were invalid. The retrial was subsequently suspended for 30 days following the resignation, at the request of the state prosecutor, of two of the three judges. President Toledo's announcement in late November 2004, in advance of the verdict, that none of the defendants would go free also contributed to the collapse of the retrial soon afterwards. In September 2005, however, the retrial of Guzmán began anew. Guzmán and his former second-in-command, Elena Iparraguirre, were both sentenced to life imprisonment in October 2006, while the 10 other defendants being retried received prison sentences ranging between 24 and 35 years.

Meanwhile, in December 2005 13 police officers were killed in ambushes by SL guerrillas in rural provinces known to be centres of coca cultivation and cocaine production. It was believed that the SL was increasingly turning away from its ideological struggle in favour of protecting the illegal drugs trade, from which it allegedly derived a substantial part of its funding. In January 2006 President Toledo announced the establishment of a new police unit to combat the resurgence of the SL. Eight people, including five police officers, were killed in December in an ambush mounted against a coca eradication operation near the town of Machente in Ayacucho. The Government dispatched some 500 commandos to the area, and eight alleged SL rebels were subsequently arrested. A month earlier the Minister of Defence had announced the deployment of 1,500 special troops to combat terrorism and drugs-trafficking in the regions of Ayacucho and Huancayo, in co-ordination with military personnel already stationed at bases in that area. An attack on a police station in Ocobamba, Apurímac, by some 50–80 armed men in November 2007, which resulted in the death of a police officer, was blamed by the Government on SL members involved in the drugs trade. Increased military operations in the wake of the attack resulted in the killing, later that same month, of a senior SL commander, Mario Epifanio Espíritu Acosta. In August 2008 the army launched an offensive in the area of the Apurímac-Ene valley aimed at defeating the larger of the two remaining SL contingents in Peru; none the less, attacks by the guerrilla group in the area intensified. In October the SL inflicted its most deadly attack on the army in 11 years when it ambushed a military convoy in a coca-producing area in Huancavelica: it was reported that 13 soldiers from an anti-terrorist unit and at least three civilians were killed in the attack. Despite some apparent advances by the army during the following months, in April 2009 two co-ordinated ambushes by the SL in the Huanta province of Ayacucho resulted in the deaths of another 13 soldiers.

The Peruvian Government attracted criticism from human rights organizations for its methods in achieving the apparent subjugation of the terrorist movements in the 1990s. In July 1999 Peru withdrew from the jurisdiction of the Inter-American Court of Human Rights (IACHR, see p. 374), a branch of the OAS, after the court ruled the previous month that new trials should be held for four Chilean MRTA activists who were serving life sentences. However, in January 2001, apparently as part of its effort to improve the country's international image, the Congreso approved Peru's return to the jurisdiction of the IACHR. In March, one week after the IACHR ruled that a military amnesty law approved in 1995 was incompatible with the American Convention on Human Rights, two former intelligence generals were arrested on charges of involvement in the early 1990s with the right-wing Colina death squad. In September 2001 the Attorney-General charged Fujimori with responsibility for two mass killings by the Colina group that took place in the early 1990s, for which crimes he was subsequently tried and convicted (see above). In November 2006 the IACHR ruled that the Peruvian state was responsible for the killings of 41 suspected members of the SL during an assault by the security forces on a prison in 1992, and ordered the current Government to pay compensation totalling some US $20m. to relatives of the deceased and to survivors who were injured during the attack. President García later declared that the Government would challenge the ruling. In a separate case, the court also held the state responsible for the abduction and subsequent summary execution by Colina of 10 civilians at La Canuta university (which constituted one of the charges against Fujimori); compensation of $1.8m. was to be paid to the victims' relatives. The opposition PNP suggested that the President's efforts to restore the death penalty in early 2007 (see above) were intended to undermine the authority of the IACHR ahead of the court's ruling on human rights cases dating from García's first term in office (1985–90).

In January 2001 a Truth Commission, composed of church leaders and civil and military representatives, was established to investigate the impact of the campaign against the guerrilla groups in the 1980s and 1990s. The Commission conducted some 17,000 interviews, and initially secured the support of the Peruvian army (although the navy refused to co-operate). In August 2003 the body presented its findings, which estimated the number of deaths during the conflict at some 69,000, twice the previous official total, with some 6,000 individuals reported as 'disappeared'. Nevertheless, despite the report's conclusion that the SL was responsible for the greater part of the killings, its conclusions were criticized by elements of the Roman Catholic Church, the military and PAP. In November President Toledo publicly apologized for the state's actions during the period and announced a US $817m. plan to improve social conditions in the regions most affected by the violence.

In February 1990, in Cartagena, Colombia, the Presidents of Peru, Colombia, Bolivia and the USA signed the Cartagena Declaration, pledging the intensification of efforts to combat the consumption, production and trafficking of illegal drugs. However, commitments to fund subsequent anti-drugs schemes in Peru were suspended by the US Administration as a result of international criticism of the Peruvian Government's record on human rights and its flouting of accepted democratic processes. In January 1996 responsibility for combating the drugs trade was transferred from the military to the national police force, following a series of allegations that army officers had themselves been involved in illegal trafficking. A new bilateral agreement to combat the drugs trade was signed with the USA in July. Following the approval of the Andean Trade Promotion and Drug Eradication Act by the US Congress in August 2002, it was announced that Peru qualified for expanded US benefits and trade preferences. In March 2003 a new US $3,000m. development strategy for the regions of Peru affected by coca cultivation was announced; the plans envisaged the reforestation of 1m. hectares of arable land judged to be capable of producing coca, and the replanting of some 500,000 ha with alternative crops.

The Government also envisaged that the new initiatives would lead to the creation of some 2.5m. jobs by 2020, with the complete elimination of coca in the area under illegal cultivation (which totalled approximately 24,600 ha). However, in February 2005 it was reported that US funding to the Andean region for drugs eradication would prioritize Colombia over Bolivia and Peru, which were to receive some 16% less in 2005 (Peru's funding would total some $115m. and $97m. in 2005 and 2006, respectively). There was speculation that the reduction of funding to Peru reflected the US Administration's disappointment with the lack of progress made by the Toledo Government in coca eradication. In that same month Nils Ericsson, head of the Comisión Nacional para el Desarrollo y Vida sin Drogas (Devida—Peru's anti-narcotics agency), announced that some 17,000 ha of coca had been planted in 2004, exceeding the quantities eradicated, and that cocaine production had increased by 13% in the previous year, to 160 metric tons. In October 2005 Ericsson announced that international funding for Peru's counter-narcotics operations in 2006 would be some $10m. less than in the previous year. In September 2006 Rómulo Pizarro Tomasio, Minister of the Interior under Toledo, replaced Ericsson as head of Devida. Pizarro announced that García's new Government intended to increase the state's presence in coca-producing areas and to extend crop-replacement programmes. However, US funding for drugs eradication continued to decline, with a total of only $66m. proposed for 2007/08. In March 2007, following protests in the province of Tocache by coca growers who claimed that crops destined for sale to the state coca company were being destroyed by the authorities, the Minister of Agriculture, Juan José Salazar, agreed to suspend coca eradication in the province for 10 days and provide compensation for those whose crops had been mistakenly destroyed. Salazar subsequently proposed a shift in Peru's counter-narcotics policy, to focus more on combating the production and smuggling of cocaine rather than the eradication of coca. Salazar provoked further controversy in May by signing an agreement with coca producers in the Cusco region that committed the Government to re-evaluating its membership of the Vienna Convention on Narcotic Drugs (ratified by Peru in November 1991, and which required that the authorities implement measures to control coca production). Following Salazar's resignation over the issue later that month, the new Minister of Agriculture, Ismael Benavides, signalled that his ministry would avoid involvement in coca eradication, stating that it was the sole responsibility of Devida.

Meeting in Caracas, Venezuela, in May 1991, the Presidents of the five South American nations comprising the Andean Group (now the Andean Community of Nations, see p. 178) formalized their commitment to the full implementation of an Andean free trade area by the end of 1995, to be achieved by a gradual reduction in tariffs and other trade barriers. An agreement to restructure the Group into the Andean Community, thus strengthening regional integration, was signed in March 1996 in Trujillo. In June 1997 the Peruvian Government announced plans to abolish tariffs on some 2,500 goods entering Peru from within the Community (with immediate effect), and its intention to remove tariffs on a further 3,500 goods (including more than 600 deemed 'sensitive') by 2005. Peru was admitted as an associate member of the Southern Common Market (Mercosur—Mercado Común del Sur, see p. 405) in August 2003. In August 2002 the US Andean Trade Promotion and Drug Eradication Act (ATPDEA) came into operation, which awarded Peru significant new tariff reductions on exports to the USA, including clothing and manufactures. In late February 2008 the ATPDEA was renewed for a further 10 months. Peru also concluded a free trade agreement with the USA in December 2005, in spite of vociferous opposition from left-wing and indigenous groups. The free trade agreement was ratified by the Peruvian Congreso in June 2006, and by the US House of Representatives and Senate in November and December 2007, respectively.

A long-standing border dispute with Ecuador over the Cordillera del Cóndor descended into armed conflict in January 1981. A cease-fire was declared a few days later, under the auspices of the guarantors (Argentina, Brazil, Chile and the USA) of the Rio de Janeiro Protocol of 1942, which had awarded the area, affording access to the Amazon river basin, to Peru. However, the Protocol had never been recognized by Ecuador, and, despite mutual efforts to achieve a constructive dialogue, the matter continued to be a source of tension and recurrent skirmishes between the two countries. In January 1995 serious fighting broke out. In February representatives of both countries, meeting in Brazil under the auspices of the Rio de Janeiro Protocol guarantors, approved a provisional cease-fire. Following further negotiations, on 17 February both countries signed the Itamaraty Peace Declaration. Foreign affairs ministers from both countries, meeting in Uruguay at the end of the month, signed the Montevideo Declaration, which ratified the Itamaraty agreement. The withdrawal of forces from the disputed border area was achieved by mid-May. None the less, reports of further armed clashes prompted requests from both countries for an extension of the observer mission. Agreement on the delimitation of a demilitarized zone in the disputed Cenepa river region came into effect on 1 August. In September Fujimori agreed to reopen the border with Ecuador for commercial purposes, and in November both countries agreed to pursue further confidence-building measures. In October 1996 the Ministers of Foreign Affairs of both countries, meeting in Chile under the auspices of the guarantor countries, signed the Santiago Agreement, which was to provide a framework for a settlement of the border issue.

Following further negotiations, in early 1998 a number of commissions were established to examine specific aspects of a potential agreement between Peru and Ecuador, including a trade and navigation treaty and the fixing of frontier markers on the ground in the Cordillera del Cóndor. Talks culminated in the signing of an accord in Brasília, Brazil, in October by the Ministers of Foreign Affairs of Peru and Ecuador in the presence of the two countries' Presidents and of six other regional leaders. The accord confirmed Peru's claim regarding the delineation of the border, but granted Ecuador navigation and trading rights on the Amazon and its tributaries and the opportunity to establish two trading centres in Peru (although this was not to constitute sovereign access). Moreover, Ecuador was given 1 sq km of territory, as private property, at Tiwintza in Peru, where many Ecuadorean soldiers, killed during the conflict in 1995, were buried. Both countries were committed to establishing ecological parks along the border, where military personnel would not be allowed access. Although considerable opposition to the accord was expressed in Peru, notably in the town of Iquitos, international reaction was very favourable and resulted in several offers of finance from multilateral agencies for cross-border development projects. The Presidents of Peru and Ecuador met in May 1999 at the Peru–Ecuador frontier to mark the placing of the last boundary stone on the border.

In January 1992 the Presidents of Peru and Bolivia concluded an agreement whereby Bolivia would be granted access to the Pacific Ocean via the Peruvian port of Ilo (which would be jointly developed as a free zone). In return, Bolivia agreed to help facilitate Peruvian access to the Atlantic Ocean (through Brazil) by way of the Bolivian town of Puerto Suárez. In August 2004, following negotiations on economic integration, the Presidents of Peru and Bolivia signed a declaration of intent to create a special zone in Ilo for the exportation of Bolivian gas.

The support of President Chávez for Humala in the presidential election of 2006 severely strained Peru's relations with Venezuela. In late April Chávez threatened to sever diplomatic ties with Peru if García won the election. In response, President Toledo criticized Chávez for interfering in Peru's domestic affairs and withdrew Peru's ambassador from Venezuela, prompting Chávez to recall the Venezuelan ambassador from Peru a few days later. Full diplomatic relations were restored in February 2007, with the exchange of new ambassadors, following talks between Presidents García and Chávez in the previous month. The establishment in March 2008 of a congressional committee to investigate the 'Casas del Alba'—ostensibly humanitarian organizations founded in previous months by Peruvian supporters of Chávez—once again strained relations between the two countries. Venezuela strongly denied allegations by the Peruvian Government that the offices, named after Chávez's regional integration project, the Alternativa Bolivariana para las Américas (ALBA), were funded by the Venezuelan Government as a means of promoting 'Bolivarian' ideology in Peru. Nevertheless, in March 2009 a report published by the congressional committee concluded that both Venezuela and Bolivia, another ALBA member country, had interfered in Peru's internal affairs through the Casas del Alba; the report recommended that the Congreso close all 146 Casas del Alba and submit formal protests to the Governments of Venezuela and Bolivia. Relations with Venezuela were further impaired in April by the Peruvian Government's decision to grant asylum to the Venezuelan opposition leader and former presidential candidate, Manuel Rosales, who had taken refuge in Peru after being charged with corruption offences in his home country. Venezuela recalled its ambassador in response to the incident.

Peru's relations with Chile, which had been strained during Toledo's presidency, improved significantly after García took office in July 2006. In August the two countries agreed to expand the scope of a bilateral economic agreement reached in 1998 by including provisions related to cross-border investment and trade in services. It was hoped that this would eventually lead to the conclusion of a free trade agreement. García also urged the Chilean Government to rejoin the Andean Community as an associate member (which it did in November 2006), and an agreement on military co-operation was reached in October. Notwithstanding these advances, an ongoing dispute over maritime boundaries was rekindled in August 2007 by the Peruvian Government's publication of an official map that restated the country's long-standing claim to some 37,900 sq km of the Pacific Ocean controlled by Chile. The move prompted the Chilean Government, which maintained that the issue had already been resolved by previous bilateral treaties, to recall its ambassador for consultations. In January 2008 Peru presented an application to the ICJ for adjudication on the disputed border.

Government

A new Constitution, drafted by the Congreso Constituyente Democrático, was approved by a national referendum on 31 October 1993, and was promulgated on 29 December. Under the terms of the Constitution, executive power is vested in the President, who is elected for a five-year term by universal adult suffrage and is eligible for re-election for a successive term of office. Two Vice-Presidents are also elected. The President governs with the assistance of an appointed Council of Ministers. Legislative power is vested in a single chamber Congreso, elected for five years by a single national list system. For administrative purposes, Peru comprises 25 regions, which are subdivided into 195 provinces; the provinces are further subdivided into districts.

Defence

Military service is selective and lasts for two years. As assessed at November 2008, the armed forces numbered 114,000 men: an army of 74,000, a navy of 23,000 and an air force of 17,000. Paramilitary police forces numbered 77,000. There were 188,000 army reserves. The 2008 budget allocated 4,150m. new soles for defence and domestic security.

Economic Affairs

In 2007, according to estimates by the World Bank, Peru's gross national income (GNI), measured at average 2005–07 prices, was US $96,241m., equivalent to $3,450 per head (or $7,240 per head on an international purchasing-power parity basis). During 2000–07, it was estimated, the population increased by an average of 1.2% per year, while gross domestic product (GDP) per head increased, in real terms, at an average annual rate of 4.1%. Overall GDP increased, in real terms, at an average annual rate of 5.3% in 2000–07; growth was 9.8% in 2008.

Agriculture (including forestry and fishing) contributed 6.6% of GDP in 2007, and the sector engaged 9.3% of the economically active population residing in urban areas. Rice, maize and potatoes are the principal food crops. The principal cash crop is coffee. Peru is the world's leading producer of coca, and the cultivation of this shrub, for the production of the illicit drug cocaine, reportedly generated revenue of US $1,500m.–$2,500m. per year. Undeclared revenue from the export of coca is believed to exceed revenue from legal exports. Fishing, particularly for the South American pilchard and the anchoveta, provides another important source of revenue, and the fishing sector contributed an estimated 0.7% of GDP in 2007. Fishing accounted for 7.7% of the total value of exports in 2008. During 2000–07 agricultural GDP (including fishing) increased at an average annual rate of 3.5%; the sector's GDP increased by 6.7% in 2008.

Industry (including mining, manufacturing, construction and power) provided 37.0% of GDP and employed 42.1% of the working population in 2007. During 2000–07 industrial GDP increased by an average of 5.4% per year; industrial GDP increased by 9.8% in 2008.

Mining (including hydrocarbon extraction) contributed 12.5% of GDP and employed 14.1% of the urban working population in 2007. The sector's contribution to GDP increased following the start of operations of the Camisea natural gas export pipeline in August 2004 (mining contributed 6.9% of GDP in 2003). Production of natural gas rose sharply from 2005 onwards, reaching 119,955.8m. cu ft in 2008 (representing a 27% increase on the previous year). Copper output increased by 16.4% in 2007, and

Health and Welfare

KEY INDICATORS

Total fertility rate (children per woman, 2006)	2.5
Under-5 mortality rate (per 1,000 live births, 2006)	25
HIV/AIDS (% of persons aged 15–49, 2007)	0.5
Physicians (per 1,000 head, 1999)	1.2
Hospital beds (per 1,000 head, 2004)	0.9
Health expenditure (2006): US $ per head (PPP)	300
Health expenditure (2006): % of GDP	4.3
Health expenditure (2006): public (% of total)	57.1
Access to water (% of persons, 2006)	84
Access to sanitation (% of persons, 2006)	70
Human Development Index (2006): ranking	79
Human Development Index (2006): value	0.788

For sources and definitions, see explanatory note on p. vi.

Agriculture

PRINCIPAL CROPS
('000 metric tons)

	2005	2006	2007
Wheat	178.5	191.1	181.4
Rice, paddy	2,468.4	2,468.4	2,455.8
Barley	193.1	191.7	200.0*
Maize	1,240.8	1,230.0	1,361.7
Potatoes	3,289.7	3,235.3	3,388.1
Sweet potatoes	184.4	194.7	195.0*
Cassava (Manioc)	1,004.5	945.0	1,100.0*
Sugar cane	6,804.1†	7,245.8	8,246.4
Beans, dry	71.7	82.9	81.8
Oil palm fruit	199.9	190.0*	190.0*
Cabbages	18.7	24.1	27.0*
Asparagus	206.0	246.5	283.5
Tomatoes	159.2	168.6	180.0*
Pumpkins, squash and gourds	83.2	86.5*	87.5*
Chillies and peppers, green	8.1	8.1	8.5*
Onions, dry	493.3	576.6	580.0*
Garlic	54.9	73.5	75.0*
Peas, green	80.4	86.4	86.5*
Broad beans, dry	52.9	57.0	58.0*
Carrots and turnips	148.7	187.8	195.0*
Maize, green	351.3	361.7	380.0*
Plantains	1,697.1	1,772.2	1,837.4
Oranges	334.5	334.5*	335.0*
Tangerines, mandarins clementines and satsumas	171.3	171.3*	172.0*
Lemons and limes	225.8	226.0*	227.0*
Apples	139.3	139.3*	145.0*
Grapes	196.5	196.5*	200.0*
Watermelons	54.6	65.1	67.5*
Guavas, mangoes and mangosteens	239.3	239.3*	245.0*
Avocados	103.4	113.2	120.0*
Pineapples	203.9	221.2	225.0*
Papayas	171.1	171.1*	175.0*
Coffee, green	175.0	258.3	230.0

* FAO estimate.
† Unofficial figure.

Aggregate production ('000 metric tons, may include official, semi-official or estimated data): Total cereals 4,132 in 2005, 4,163 in 2006, 4,252 in 2007; Total roots and tubers 4,760 in 2005, 4,812 in 2006, 4,960 in 2007; Total vegetables (incl. melons) 1,991 in 2005, 2,228 in 2006, 2,326 in 2007; Total fruits (excl. melons) 3,826 in 2005, 3,716 in 2006, 3,814 in 2007.

Source: FAO.

LIVESTOCK
('000 head, year ending September)

	2005	2006*	2007*
Horses*	730	730	730
Asses, mules or hinnies*	910	n.a.	n.a.
Cattle	5,241	5,300	5,300
Pigs	3,005	3,005	3,000
Sheep	14,822	14,822	15,000
Goats	1,957	1,957	2,000
Chickens	99,255	99,500	100,000

* FAO estimates.
Source: FAO.

LIVESTOCK PRODUCTS
('000 metric tons)

	2005	2006	2007*
Cattle meat	153.1	161.8	165.0
Sheep meat	33.7	33.9	35.0
Pig meat	102.9	107.9	108.0
Chicken meat	733.2	789.6	800.0
Cows' milk	1,329.7	1,428.9	1,500.0
Hen eggs	182.3	202.4	205.0
Wool, greasy	10.9	10.9*	11.0

* FAO estimate(s).
Source: FAO.

Forestry

ROUNDWOOD REMOVALS
('000 cubic metres, excluding bark)

	2005	2006	2007
Sawlogs, veneer logs and logs for sleepers	1,438	1,657	1,833*
Other industrial wood	304	147	161
Fuel wood	7,364	7,454	7,454*
Total	9,106	9,258	9,448

* FAO estimate.
Source: FAO.

SAWNWOOD PRODUCTION
('000 cubic metres, including railway sleepers)

	2005	2006	2007
Coniferous (softwood)	7	16	16*
Broadleaved (hardwood)	736	840	932
Total	743	856	948

* FAO estimate.
Source: FAO.

Fishing

('000 metric tons, live weight)

	2004	2005	2006
Capture	9,604.5	9,388.7	7,017.5
Chilean jack mackerel	187.4	80.7	277.6
Anchoveta (Peruvian anchovy)	8,808.5	8,655.5	5,935.3
Jumbo flying squid	270.4	291.1	434.3
Aquaculture	22.1	26.2	28.4
Total catch	9,626.8	9,414.8	7,045.9

Note: Figures exclude aquatic plants ('000 metric tons, all capture): 7.4 in 2004; 5.0 in 2005; 3.4 in 2006.

Source: FAO.

Mining

('000 metric tons, unless otherwise indicated, preliminary figures)*

	2006	2007	2008
Crude petroleum ('000 barrels)	42,187.2	41,562.2	43,930.4
Natural gas (million cubic feet)	62,691.1	94,485.5	119,955.8
Copper	818.5	952.8	1,036.7
Lead	288.4	303.0	317.7
Molybdenum	16.5	16.1	16.1
Tin	33.4	33.9	33.9
Zinc	1,029.9	1,236.1	1,371.5
Iron ore	4,861.2	5,185.3	5,243.3
Gold (kg)	197.0	165.4	174.7
Silver (kg)	3,263.0	3,291.9	3,465.4

* Figures for metallic minerals refer to metal content only.

Industry

SELECTED PRODUCTS
('000 metric tons, unless otherwise indicated)

	2005	2006	2007
Canned fish	55.5	107.3	84.3
Wheat flour	1,034	1,088	1,056
Raw sugar	695.0	805.1	910.1
Beer ('000 hectolitres)	7,916	9,634	10,535
Motor spirit (petrol, '000 barrels)*	8,968	12,777†	n.a.
Kerosene ('000 barrels)*	2,501	960†	n.a.
Distillate fuel oils ('000 barrels)*	15,287	17,598†	n.a.
Residual fuel oils ('000 barrels)*	20,740	14,713†	n.a.
Portland cement	4,535	5,052	5,335
Crude steel*	510	510†	n.a.
Copper (refined)	189.5	205.7	188.4
Zinc (refined)	164.7	177.5	162.7
Electric energy (million kWh)	25,509.9	27,402.5	29,856.5

* Source: US Geological Survey.
† Estimate.

Finance

CURRENCY AND EXCHANGE RATES

Monetary Units
100 céntimos = 1 nuevo sol (new sol).

Sterling, Dollar and Euro Equivalents (31 December 2008)
£1 sterling = 4.577 new soles;
US $1 = 3.140 new soles;
€1 = 4.369 new soles;
100 new soles = £21.85 = $31.85 = €22.89.

Average Exchange Rate (new soles per US $)
2006   3.2738
2007   3.1280
2008   2.9244

Note: On 1 February 1985 Peru replaced its former currency, the sol, by the inti, valued at 1,000 soles. A new currency, the nuevo sol (equivalent to 1m. intis), was introduced in July 1991.

CENTRAL GOVERNMENT BUDGET
(million new soles, preliminary figures)

Revenue	2006	2007	2008
Taxation	45,485	52,454	58,242
Taxes on income, profits, etc.	18,414	22,847	24,146
Taxes on imports (excl. VAT)	2,847	2,198	1,911
Value-added tax	21,517	25,258	31,583
Domestic	11,982	13,586	15,749
Imports	9,535	11,672	15,834
Excises	4,042	4,291	3,461
Fuel duty	2,399	2,419	1,457
Other taxes	3,369	3,848	4,371
Less Refunds	4,704	5,989	7,230
Other current revenue	7,229	8,659	9,716
Capital revenue	361	385	394
Total	53,076	61,497	68,352

Expenditure	2006	2007	2008
Current non-interest expenditure	37,252	42,292	46,160
Compensation of employees	12,553	13,017	13,873
Goods and non-labour services	10,192	10,130	10,939
Transfers	14,506	19,145	21,348
Pensions	4,027	4,077	n.a.
National savings fund	2,564	2,648	n.a.
Municipal compensation fund	2,410	2,806	n.a.
Interest payments	5,413	5,525	5,128
Internal	1,117	1,279	1,814
External	4,297	4,247	3,314
Capital expenditure	6,008	7,206	8,785
Gross capital formation	4,779	5,878	6,869
Total	48,673	55,023	60,073

General Budget (million new soles, preliminary figures): *2006:* Total revenue 60,416 (current 60,055, capital 361); Total expenditure 54,912 (current non-interest 40,833, capital 8,485, interest payments 5,593). *2007:* Total revenue 69,842 (current 69,456, capital 386); Total expenditure 59,538 (current non-interest 43,504, capital 10,100, interest payments 5,934). *2008:* Total revenue 78,105 (current 77,710, capital 395); Total expenditure 70,078 (current non-interest 49,264, capital 15,065, interest payments 5,749).

INTERNATIONAL RESERVES
(US $ million at 31 December)

	2006	2007	2008
Gold	705.9	927.8	982.6
IMF special drawing rights	0.9	3.7	9.0
Foreign exchange	16,732.4	26,852.7	30,262.5
Total	17,439.2	27,784.2	31,254.1

Source: IMF, *International Financial Statistics*.

MONEY SUPPLY
(million new soles at 31 December)

	2006	2007	2008
Currency outside banks	11,796	14,985	17,508
Demand deposits at commercial and development banks	16,791	25,586	28,221
Total money (incl. others)	32,694	43,983	48,430

Source: IMF, *International Financial Statistics*.

COST OF LIVING
(Consumer Price Index, Lima metropolitan area; base: 2000 = 100)

	2005	2006	2007
Food (incl. beverages)	107.6	110.2	113.0
Rent	120.3	123.3	124.5
Electricity, gas and other fuels	129.7	132.5	132.9
Clothing (incl. footwear)	107.5	109.1	111.9
All items (incl. others)	110.1	112.3	114.3

Source: ILO.

PERU

NATIONAL ACCOUNTS
(million new soles at current prices)

Expenditure on the Gross Domestic Product

	2006	2007	2008
Government final consumption expenditure	28,810	30,707	33,784
Private final consumption expenditure	186,644	206,347	237,598
Increase in stocks	2,503	5,628	3,736
Gross fixed capital formation	58,077	71,332	95,468
Total domestic expenditure	276,034	314,014	370,586
Exports of goods and services	86,234	96,925	102,295
Less Imports of goods and services	60,013	75,209	100,021
GDP in purchasers' values	302,255	335,730	372,861
GDP at constant 1994 prices	160,145	174,329	191,479

Gross Domestic Product by Economic Activity

	2005	2006	2007
Agriculture, hunting and forestry	15,135	17,107	18,220
Fishing	2,041	2,099	2,183
Mining and quarrying	23,139	35,248	38,413
Manufacturing	39,077	44,234	48,811
Electricity and water	5,379	5,656	6,011
Construction	14,214	17,122	20,395
Wholesale and retail trade	32,726	37,845	42,200
Restaurants and hotels	9,811	10,520	11,659
Transport and communications	20,075	22,772	28,622
Government services	19,249	20,970	22,194
Finance	6,117	7,163	8,393
Insurance	1,645	1,658	1,709
Real estate and renting	7,112	7,408	7,713
Business services	19,568	21,577	24,027
Health, private	4,715	5,123	5,454
Education, private	9,204	9,926	10,667
Other services	9,131	9,824	10,732
Gross value added at basic prices	238,338	276,251	307,403
Import duties	3,143	2,847	2,198
Other taxes on products	20,172	23,158	26,129
GDP in purchasers' values	261,653	302,255	335,730

BALANCE OF PAYMENTS
(US $ million)

	2005	2006	2007
Exports of goods f.o.b.	17,368	23,800	27,956
Imports of goods f.o.b.	−12,082	−14,866	−19,599
Trade balance	5,286	8,934	8,356
Exports of services	2,289	2,647	3,343
Imports of services	−3,123	−3,428	−4,270
Balance on goods and services	4,452	8,153	7,429
Other income received	625	1,033	1,567
Other income paid	−5,701	−8,616	−9,985
Balance on goods, services and income	−624	570	−989
Current transfers received	1,781	2,194	2,504
Current transfers paid	−10	−10	−10
Current balance	1,148	2,755	1,505
Capital account (net)	−123	−127	−134
Direct investment from abroad	2,579	3,467	5,343
Portfolio investment assets	−818	−1,993	−520
Portfolio investment liabilities	2,579	155	3,955
Other investment assets	−1,084	8	−30
Other investment liabilities	−3,233	−541	546
Net errors and omissions	362	−503	−322
Overall balance	1,411	3,221	10,343

Source: IMF, *International Financial Statistics*.

External Trade

PRINCIPAL COMMODITIES
(distribution by SITC, US $ million)

Imports c.i.f.	2005	2006	2007
Food and live animals	1,158.1	1,249.6	1,723.5
Cereals and cereal preparations	514.5	555.3	874.4
Mineral fuels, lubricants and related materials	2,471.1	2,959.7	3,829.1
Petroleum, petroleum products and related materials	2,471.1	2,959.7	3,829.1
Chemicals and related products	2,012.6	2,333.8	2,982.0
Plastics in primary forms	551.8	640.7	869.1
Basic manufactures	1,928.4	2,461.4	3,143.0
Iron and steel	507.9	770.9	1,101.3
Machinery and transport equipment	3,541.5	4,732.9	6,234.6
Machinery specialized for particular industries	500.4	738.4	1,070.3
General industrial machinery, equipment, etc.	621.6	759.3	1,077.6
Telecommunications, sound recording and reproducing equipment	659.5	857.3	963.6
Road vehicles	652.9	981.9	1,516.6
Miscellaneous manufactured articles	835.9	965.6	1,149.4
Total (incl. others)	12,501.8	15,311.6	20,493.8

Exports f.o.b.	2005	2006	2007
Food and live animals	2,729.8	3,278.1	3,571.8
Fish, crustaceans, molluscs and preparations thereof	326.7	433.6	488.3
Coffee	306.1	514.9	426.9
Crude materials	4,114.9	6,676.8	9,363.9
Iron ore and concentrates	216.1	256.0	285.4
Copper ores and concentrates	1,410.0	2,863.8	4,600.5
Lead ores and concentrates	312.4	449.6	649.4
Zinc ores and concentrates	683.2	1,759.3	2,318.6
Molybdenum ores and concentrates (excl. roasted)	1,149.4	847.1	984.1
Mineral fuels and lubricants	1,595.9	1,901.8	2,409.6
Petroleum, petroleum products and related materials	1,508.2	1,875.3	2,407.5
Basic manufactures	3,482.3	5,550.3	5,386.5
Non-ferrous metals	2,976.7	4,923.2	4,633.4
Copper	2,130.1	3,540.4	2,947.1
Miscellaneous manufactured articles	1,381.2	1,553.6	1,804.6
Total (incl. others)	17,114.3	23,764.9	27,800.1

Source: UN, *International Trade Statistics Yearbook*.

2008 (US $ million, preliminary): Total imports 28,439; Total exports 31,529.

PERU

PRINCIPAL TRADING PARTNERS
(US $ million)

Imports c.i.f.	2005	2006	2007
Argentina	724.5	802.4	1,127.1
Brazil	1,028.4	1,597.2	1,885.6
Canada	210.4	292.4	336.1
Chile	615.6	864.0	883.6
China, People's Republic	1,057.9	1,583.7	2,476.0
Colombia	772.6	950.7	991.5
Ecuador	914.2	1,092.1	1,515.5
France (incl. Monaco)	146.5	172.2	184.1
Germany	400.9	506.6	698.6
Italy	195.3	227.7	371.0
Japan	445.6	563.7	792.8
Korea, Republic	347.5	391.6	523.3
Mexico	363.9	518.8	756.7
Nigeria	115.1	271.5	292.6
Spain	193.4	255.8	290.7
United Kingdom	96.7	105.2	143.3
USA	2,220.1	2,515.7	3,626.8
Venezuela	528.3	544.9	227.2
Total (incl. others)	12,501.8	15,311.6	20,493.8

Exports f.o.b.	2005	2006	2007
Belgium	227.0	509.5	558.3
Bolivia	154.9	189.5	223.9
Brazil	453.2	814.5	934.6
Canada	1,021.8	1,611.6	1,834.2
Chile	1,129.4	1,429.9	1,694.3
China, People's Republic	1,860.9	2,268.7	3,034.7
Colombia	346.6	505.8	616.6
Ecuador	295.0	327.3	379.1
Germany	515.0	812.3	928.5
Italy	389.0	777.9	817.3
Japan	604.5	1,230.8	2,181.6
Korea, Republic	227.4	548.5	887.9
Mexico	332.1	390.4	269.9
Netherlands	534.7	737.8	630.8
Panama	265.2	337.5	397.2
Spain	558.1	765.8	982.5
Switzerland-Liechtenstein	786.3	1,687.6	2,335.3
United Kingdom	232.9	331.3	229.6
USA	5,257.3	5,707.5	5,383.4
Venezuela	298.5	412.0	765.3
Total (incl. others)	17,114.3	23,764.9	27,800.1

Source: UN, *International Trade Statistics Yearbook*.

Transport

RAILWAYS
(traffic)*

	2003	2004	2005
Passenger-km (million)	103	119	126
Freight ton-km (million)	1,117	1,147	1,115

* Including service traffic.

Source: UN, *Statistical Yearbook*.

ROAD TRAFFIC
(motor vehicles in use)

	2002	2003	2004
Passenger cars	781,751	812,978	824,613
Buses and coaches	44,576	44,486	43,919
Lorries and vans	425,679	415,206	418,884
Motorcycles	231,148	248,395	268,125

Source: IRF, *World Road Statistics*.

Statistical Survey

SHIPPING
Merchant Fleet
(registered at 31 December)

	2005	2006	2007
Number of vessels	727	749	751
Total displacement ('000 grt)	227.2	235.3	272.5

Source: Lloyd's Register-Fairplay, *World Fleet Statistics*.

International Sea-borne Freight Traffic
('000 metric tons)

	2004*	2005*	2006
Goods loaded	6,600	6,800	6,329
Goods unloaded	10,100	8,900	9,490

* Approximate figures extrapolated from monthly averages.

Source: UN, *Monthly Bulletin of Statistics*.

CIVIL AVIATION
(traffic on scheduled services)

	2005	2006	2007
Kilometres flown (million)	67	47	60
Passenger-km (million)	5,298	5,752	6,472
Total ton-km (million)	139	112	149

Source: UN Economic Commission for Latin America and the Caribbean, *Statistical Yearbook*.

Tourism

ARRIVALS BY NATIONALITY

	2004	2005	2006
Argentina	46,035	56,232	63,543
Bolivia	65,906	71,718	84,068
Brazil	33,327	43,291	44,092
Canada	25,610	33,933	40,007
Chile	301,024	338,629	415,106
Colombia	39,026	48,365	53,639
Ecuador	110,294	100,808	111,239
France	43,848	52,050	53,518
Germany	34,846	42,565	42,663
Italy	24,296	27,258	26,755
Japan	27,326	32,553	33,925
Mexico	23,510	27,961	28,168
Spain	43,023	58,785	62,289
United Kingdom	43,023	58,719	59,876
USA	243,790	293,241	297,317
Total (incl. others)	1,276,639	1,486,502	1,634,745

Tourism receipts (US $ million, incl. passenger transport): 1,169 in 2004; 1,371 in 2005; 1,586 in 2006.

Source: World Tourism Organization.

Communications Media

	2005	2006	2007
Telephones ('000 main lines in use)	2,250.9	2,400.6	2,673.4
Mobile cellular telephones ('000 subscribers)	5,583.4	8,772.2	15,417.2
Personal computers ('000 in use)	2,800	n.a.	n.a.
Internet users ('000)	4,600.0	6,497.6	7,636.4
Broadband subscribers ('000)	352.6	484.9	570.2

Television receivers ('000 in use): 3,800 in 2000.

Radio receivers ('000 in use): 6,650 in 1997.

Facsimile machines ('000 in use, estimate): 15 in 1995.

Book production (titles): 612 in 1996.

Daily newspapers: 73 in 2004.

Sources: UNESCO, *Statistical Yearbook*; International Telecommunication Union.

Education

(2007 unless otherwise indicated, incl. adult education)

	Institutions	Teachers	Pupils
Nursery	19,373	51,385	934,792
Primary	36,006	192,358	3,960,510
Secondary	11,423	162,942	2,536,350
Higher: universities*	78	33,177	435,637
Higher: other tertiary	1,112	28,172	393,952
Special	458	3,620	23,406
Vocational	2,240	13,900	301,993

* Figures for 2000.

Source: Ministerio de Educación del Perú.

Adult literacy rate (UNESCO estimates): 90.5% (males 95.2%; females 85.8%) in 2007 (Source: UNESCO Institute for Statistics).

Directory

The Constitution

In 1993 the Congreso Constituyente Democrático (CCD) began drafting a new constitution to replace the 1979 Constitution. The CCD approved the final document in September 1993, and the Constitution was endorsed by a popular national referendum that was conducted on 31 October. The Constitution was promulgated on 29 December 1993.

EXECUTIVE POWER

Executive power is vested in the President, who is elected for a five-year term of office by universal adult suffrage; this mandate is renewable once. The successful presidential candidate must obtain at least 50% of the votes cast, and a second round of voting is held if necessary. Two Vice-Presidents are elected in simultaneous rounds of voting. The President is competent to initiate and submit draft bills, to review laws drafted by the legislature (Congreso) and, if delegated by the Congreso, to enact laws. The President is empowered to appoint ambassadors and senior military officials without congressional ratification, and retains the right to dissolve parliament if two or more ministers have been censured or have received a vote of 'no confidence' from the Congreso. In certain circumstances the President may, in accordance with the Council of Ministers, declare a state of emergency for a period of 60 days, during which individual constitutional rights are suspended and the armed forces may assume control of civil order. The President appoints the Council of Ministers.

LEGISLATIVE POWER

Legislative power is vested in a single-chamber Congreso (removing the distinction in the 1979 Constitution of an upper and lower house) consisting of 120 members. The members of the Congreso are elected for a five-year term by universal adult suffrage. The Congreso is responsible for approving the budget, for endorsing loans and international treaties and for drafting and approving bills. It may conduct investigations into matters of public concern, and question and censure the Council of Ministers and its individual members. Members of the Congreso elect a Standing Committee, to consist of not more than 25% of the total number of members (representation being proportional to the different political groupings in the legislature), which is empowered to make certain official appointments, approve credit loans and transfers relating to the budget during a parliamentary recess, and conduct other business as delegated by parliament.

ELECTORAL SYSTEM

All citizens aged 18 years and above, including illiterate persons, are eligible to vote. Voting in elections is compulsory for all citizens aged 18–70, and is optional thereafter.

JUDICIAL POWER

Judicial power is vested in the Supreme Court of Justice and other tribunals. The Constitution provides for the establishment of a National Council of the Judiciary, consisting of nine independently elected members, which is empowered to appoint judges to the Supreme Court. An independent Constitutional Court, comprising seven members elected by the Congreso for a five-year term, may interpret the Constitution and declare legislation and acts of government to be unconstitutional.

The death penalty may be applied by the Judiciary in cases of terrorism or of treason (the latter in times of war).

Under the Constitution, a People's Counsel is elected by the Congreso with a five-year mandate, which authorizes the Counsel to defend the constitutional and fundamental rights of the individual. The Counsel may draft laws and present evidence to the legislature.

According to the Constitution, the State promotes economic and social development, particularly in the areas of employment, health, education, security, public services and infrastructure. The State recognizes a plurality of economic ownership and activity, supports free competition, and promotes the growth of small businesses. Private initiative is permitted within the framework of a social market economy. The State also guarantees the free exchange of foreign currency.

The Government

HEAD OF STATE

President: ALAN GABRIEL LUDWIG GARCÍA PÉREZ (took office 28 July 2006).

First Vice-President: LUIS GIAMPIETRI ROJAS.

Second Vice-President: LOURDES MENDOZA DEL SOLAR.

COUNCIL OF MINISTERS
(April 2009)

President of the Council of Ministers: YEHUDE SIMON MUNARO.

Minister of Foreign Affairs: JOSÉ ANTONIO GARCÍA BELAÚNDE.

Minister of Defence: ANTERO FLORES-ARÁOZ.

Minister of the Interior: MERCEDES CABANILLAS BUSTAMANTE.

Minister of Justice: ROSARIO FERNÁNDEZ FIGUEROA.

Minister of Economy and Finance: LUIS CARRANZA UGARTE.

Minister of Labour and Employment: JORGE VILLASANTE ARANÍBAR.

Minister of International Trade and Tourism: MERCEDES ARÁOZ FERNÁNDEZ.

Minister of Transport and Communications: ENRIQUE JAVIER CORNEJO RAMÍREZ.

Minister of Housing, Construction and Sanitation: NIDIA RUTH VILCHEZ YUCRA.

Minister of Health: OSCAR UGARTE UBILLÚS.

Minister of Agriculture: CARLOS LEYTON MUÑOZ.

Minister of Energy and Mines: PEDRO SÁNCHEZ GAMARRA.

Minister of Production: ELENA CONTERNO MARTINELLI.

Minister of Education: JOSÉ ANTONIO CHANG ESCOBEDO.

Minister for the Advancement of Women and Social Development: CARMEN VILDOSO CHIRINOS.

PERU

Minister of the Environment: Antonio Brack Egg.

MINISTRIES

Office of the President of the Council of Ministers: Avda 28 de Julio 878, Miraflores, Lima; tel. (1) 6109800; fax (1) 4449168; e-mail webmaster@pcm.gob.pe; internet www.pcm.gob.pe.

Ministry for the Advancement of Women and Social Development: Jirón Camaná 616, Lima 1; tel. (1) 6261600; fax (1) 4261665; e-mail postmaster@mimdes.gob.pe; internet www.mimdes.gob.pe.

Ministry of Agriculture: Avda Salaverry s/n, Jesús María, Lima 11; tel. (1) 6135800; e-mail postmaster@minag.gob.pe; internet www.minag.gob.pe.

Ministry of Defence: Avda Arequipa 291, Lima 1; tel. (1) 6191600; e-mail webmaster@mindef.gob.pe; internet www.mindef.gob.pe.

Ministry of Economy and Finance: Jirón Junín 339, 4°, Circado de Lima, Lima 1; tel. (1) 3115930; e-mail postmaster@mef.gob.pe; internet www.mef.gob.pe.

Ministry of Education: Avda Van De Velde 160, cuadra 33 Avda Javier Prado Este, San Borja, Lima 41; tel. (1) 4353900; fax (1) 4370471; e-mail postmaster@minedu.gob.pe; internet www.minedu.gob.pe.

Ministry of Energy and Mines: Avda Las Artes Sur 260, San Borja, Apdo 2600, Lima 41; tel. (1) 6188700; internet www.minem.gob.pe.

Ministry of the Environment: Avda Guardia Civil 205, San Borja, Lima; tel. (1) 2255370; fax (1) 2255369; internet www.minam.gob.pe.

Ministry of Foreign Affairs: Jirón Lampa 535, Lima 1; tel. (1) 6232400; e-mail informes@rree.gob.pe; internet www.rree.gob.pe.

Ministry of Health: Avda Salaverry 801, Jesús María, Lima 11; tel. (1) 3156600; e-mail webmaster@minsa.gob.pe; internet www.minsa.gob.pe.

Ministry of Housing, Construction and Sanitation: Avda Paseo de la República 3361, San Isidro, Lima; tel. (1) 2117930; e-mail webmaster@vivienda.gob.pe; internet www.vivienda.gob.pe.

Ministry of the Interior: Plaza 30 de Agosto 150, San Isidro, Lima 27; tel. (1) 2242406; fax (1) 2242405; e-mail ofitel@mininter.gob.pe; internet www.mininter.gob.pe.

Ministry of International Trade and Tourism: Calle 1 Oeste 50, Urb. Corpac, San Isidro, Lima 27; tel. (1) 5136106; fax (1) 2243362; e-mail webmaster@mincetur.gob.pe; internet www.mincetur.gob.pe.

Ministry of Justice: Scipión Llona 350, Miraflores, Lima 18; tel. (1) 4404310; e-mail webmaster@minjus.gob.pe; internet www.minjus.gob.pe.

Ministry of Labour and Employment: Avda Salaverry 655, cuadra 8, Jesús María, Lima 11; tel. (1) 3157214; fax (1) 4230741; e-mail webmaster@mintra.gob.pe; internet www.mintra.gob.pe.

Ministry of the Presidency: Avda Paseo de la República 4297, Lima 1; tel. (1) 4465886; fax (1) 4470379; internet www.peru.gob.pe.

Ministry of Production: Calle 1 Oeste 60, Urb. Corpac, San Isidro, Lima 27; tel. (1) 6162222; e-mail portal@produce.gob.pe; internet www.produce.gob.pe.

Ministry of Transport and Communications: Avda Jirón Zorritos 1203, Lima 1; tel. (1) 6185800; internet www.mtc.gob.pe.

Regional Presidents
(April 2009)

Amazonas: Oscar Ramiro Altamirano Quispe.
Ancash: César Joaquín Alvarez Aguilar.
Apurímac: David Abraham Salazar Morote.
Arequipa: Juan Manuel Guillén Benavides.
Ayacucho: Isaac Ernesto Molina Chávez.
Cajamarca: Jesús Coronel Salirrosas.
Callao: Alexander Martín Kouri Bumachar.
Cusco: Hugo Eulogio Gonzales Sayán.
Huancavelica: Luis Federico Salas Guevara Schultz.
Huánuco: Jorge Espinoza Egoávil.
Ica: Rómulo Triveño Pinto.
Junín: Vladimiro Huaroc Portocarrero.
La Libertad: José Humberto Murgia Zannier.
Lambayeque: Nery Enni Saldarriaga de Kroll.
Lima: Nelson Oswaldo Chui Mejía.
Loreto: Yván Enrique Vásquez Valera.
Madre de Dios: Santos Kaway Komori.
Moquegua: Jaime Alberto Rodríguez Villanueva.
Pasco: Félix Rivera Serrano.
Piura: César Trelles Lara.
Puno: Pablo Hernán Fuentes Guzmán.
San Martín: César Villanueva Arévalo.
Tacna: Hugo Froilán Ordoñez Salazar.
Tumbes: Wilmer Florentino Dios Benites.
Ucayali: Jorge Velásquez Portocarrero.

President and Legislature

PRESIDENT

Election, 9 April and 4 June 2006

Candidate	First round % of votes	Second round % of votes
Alan Gabriel Ludwig García Pérez (PAP)	24.32	52.63
Lt-Col (retd) Ollanta Moisés Humala Tasso (UPP*)	30.62	47.38
Lourdes Flores Nano (Unidad Nacional)	23.81	—
Martha Gladys Chávez Cossío de Ocampo (Alianza por el Futuro)	7.43	—
Valentín Paniagua Corazao (Frente de Centro)	5.75	—
Humberto Lay Sun (Restauración Nacional)	4.38	—
Others	3.68	—
Total	**100.00**	**100.00**

* In coalition with the Partido Nacionalista Peruano.

CONGRESO

President: Angel Javier Velásquez Quesquén (PAP).

General Election, 9 April 2006

Parties	% of votes	Seats
Unión por el Perú (UPP)	21.15	45
Partido Aprista Peruano (PAP)	20.59	36
Unidad Nacional	15.33	17
Alianza por el Futuro	13.09	13
Frente de Centro	7.07	5
Perú Posible (PP)	4.11	2
Restauración Nacional	4.02	2
Others	14.64	
Total	**100.00***	**120**

* Excluding 1,682,768 blank votes and 2,188,789 spoiled votes.

Election Commission

Oficina Nacional de Procesos Electorales (ONPE): Jirón Washington 1894, Lima 1; tel. (1) 4170630; e-mail informes@onpe.gob.pe; internet www.onpe.gob.pe; f. 1995; independent; Nat. Dir Dra Magdalena Chú Villanueva.

Political Organizations

Acción Popular (AP): Paseo Colón 218, Lima 1; tel. and fax (1) 3321965; e-mail webmaster@accionpopular.pe; internet www.accionpopular.pe; f. 1956; 1.2m. mems; liberal; contested the presidential and legislative elections of April 2006 as part of the Frente de Centro coalition; Pres. Víctor Andrés García Belaúnde; Sec.-Gen. Mesías Guevara Amasifuen.

Alianza por el Futuro (AF): Lima; f. 2005 as a coalition of Cambio 90 and Nueva Mayoría in order to contest the 2006 presidential and legislative elections; supporters of fmr President Fujimori; Leader Keiko Fujimori.

Alianza para el Progreso: Avda de la Policía 643, Jesús María, Lima; tel. (1) 4601251; internet www.app-peru.org.pe; f. 2001; Founder and Pres. César Acuña Peralta; Sec.-Gen. Juan Pablo Horna Santa Cruz.

Cambio 90 (C90): Avda Jorge Aprile 312, San Borja; tel. (1) 3461853; f. 1990; part of Alianza por el Futuro coalition formed with Nueva Mayoría in order to contest the 2006 presidential and legislative elections; Sec.-Gen. Andrés Reggiardo Sayán.

Coordinadora Nacional de Independientes (CNI): Domingo Elías 1450, Surquillo, Lima; tel. (1) 2411884; fax (1) 4455968; f. 2003;

PERU

contested the presidential and legislative elections of April 2006 as part of the Frente de Centro coalition; Pres. GONZALO GERMAN AGUIRRE ARRIZ.

Frente de Centro: Avda Paseo de la República 3920, Miraflores, Lima; f. 2005 as a coalition of Acción Popular, Somos Perú and the Coordinadora Nacional de Independientes in order to contest the presidential and legislative elections of April 2006; Presidential Candidate VALENTÍN PANIAGUA CORAZAO.

Movimiento Nueva Izquierda (MNI): Jirón Miró Quesada 360, Lima; tel. (1) 4264640; internet www.mni.org.pe; f. 1997; left-wing; Pres. NÍLVER LÓPEZ AMES.

Nueva Mayoría: Martier 655, San Borja, Lima 41; tel. (1) 2249924; f. 1992; part of Alianza por el Futuro coalition formed with Cambio 90 in order to contest the presidential and legislative elections of April 2006; Pres. MARTHA GLADYS CHÁVEZ COSSÍO DE OCAMPO; Sec.-Gen. DEMETRIO PATSIAS MELLA.

Partido Aprista Peruano (PAP): Avda Alfonso Ugarte 1012, Lima 5; tel. (1) 4281736; internet www.apra.org.pe; f. in Mexico 1924, in Peru 1930; legalized 1945; democratic left-wing party; Pres. ALAN GABRIEL LUDWIG GARCÍA PÉREZ; Sec.-Gen. MAURICIO MULDER BEDOYA; 700,000 mems.

Partido Comunista Peruano (PCP): Plaza Ramón Castilla 67, Lima; tel. and fax (1) 3306106; e-mail unidad@ec-red.com; internet www.pcp.miarroba.com; f. 1928; Pres. JORGE DEL PRADO.

Partido Justicia Nacional: Avda Arequipa 1799, Lince, Lima; tel. (1) 4723744; e-mail info@justicianacional.com; internet www.justicianacional.com; f. 2003; Pres. JAIME SALINAS LÓPEZ-TORRES.

Partido Nacionalista Peruano: Avda Arequipa 3410, Lima 27; tel. (1) 4223592; internet www.partidonacionalistaperuano.com; f. 2005 to support presidential candidacy of Lt-Col (retd) Ollanta Moisés Humala Tasso; contested the 2006 elections in coalition with the Unión por el Perú; Pres. Lt-Col (retd) OLLANTA MOISÉS HUMALA TASSO.

Partido Popular Cristiano (PPC): Avda Alfonso Ugarte 1484, Lima; tel. (1) 4238723; fax (1) 4238721; e-mail estflores@terra.com.pe; internet www.ppc.pe; f. 1967; 250,000 mems; Pres. LOURDES FLORES NANO; Sec.-Gen. RAÚL CASTRO STAGNARO.

Partido Socialista: Plaza Bolognesi 590, Breña, Lima 5; tel. (1) 3305558; internet www.socialista.org.pe; f. 2002 as Partido Democrático Descentralista; contested the 2006 election; Presidential Candidate JAVIER DIEZ CANSECO.

Partido Verde: Avda Jorge Chávez 654, 4°, Lima 33; tel. (1) 96437268; e-mail alternativaverde@verdes.org.pe; internet www.verdes.org.pe; ecologist; Pres. ALEX GONZÁLEZ.

Perú Posible (PP): Avda Faustino Sánchez Carrión, Jesús María, Lima 11; tel. (1) 4602493; fax (1) 2612418; e-mail sgpp@mixmail.com; internet www.peruposible.org.pe; f. 1994; Leader ALEJANDRO TOLEDO MANRIQUE; Sec.-Gen. GILBERTO DÍAZ PERALTA.

Proyecto País: Nicolás de Piérola 917, Of. 211, Plaza San Martín, Lima; tel. (1) 3312696; fax (1) 2222785; e-mail info@proyectopais.org.pe; internet www.proyectopais.org.pe; f. 1998; Leader MARCO ANTONIO ARRUNATEGUI CEVALLOS.

Renovación Nacional: Jirón Tacna 3321, San Martín de Porres, Lima; tel. (1) 5673798; f. 1992; Sec.-Gen. WILDER RUIZ SILVA.

Restauración Nacional: Jirón Lampa 974, Cercado de Lima; tel. (9) 7566117; internet www.restauracionnacional.org; f. 2005; evangelical Christian party; Pres. HUMBERTO LAY SUN; Sec.-Gen. JUAN DAVID PERRY.

Sí Cumple: Lima; tel. (1) 4266451; f. 2003; supporters of fmr President Fujimori; Sec.-Gen. LUIS DELGADO APARICIO.

Solidaridad Nacional (SN): Amador Merino Reyna 140, San Isidro, Lima 27; tel. (1) 4213348; e-mail fsandoval@psn.org.pe; internet www.psn.org.pe; f. 1999; centre-left; Pres. LUIS CASTAÑEDA LOSSIO; Sec.-Gen. MARCO ANTONIO PARRA SÁNCHEZ.

Somos Perú (SP): Mariscal Las Heras 393, Lince, Lima 14; tel. (1) 4714484; e-mail postmaster@somosperu.org.pe; internet www.somosperu.org.pe; f. 1998; contested the April 2006 elections as part of the Frente de Centro coalition; Pres. ALBERTO ANDRADE CARMONA; Sec.-Gen. YURI VILELA SEMINARIO.

Unidad Nacional: Calle Ricardo Palma 1111, Miraflores, Lima; tel. (1) 2242773; f. 2000; centrist alliance comprising Partido Popular Cristiano and Solidaridad Nacional; Leader LOURDES FLORES NANO.

Unión por el Perú (UPP): Pablo de Olavide 270, San Isidro, Lima; tel. (1) 4403227; e-mail ivega@partidoupp.org; f. 1994; ind. movt; contested 2006 elections in coalition with Partido Nacionalista Peruano, led by Lt-Col (retd) Ollanta Moisés Humala Tasso; Pres. Dr ALDO ESTRADA CHOQUE; Sec.-Gen. JOSÉ VEGA ANTONIO.

ARMED GROUPS

Movimiento Nacionalista Peruano (MNP) (Movimiento Etnocacerista): Pasaje Velarde 188, Of. 204, Lima; tel. (1) 3311074; e-mail movnacionalistaperuano@yahoo.es; internet mnp.tripod.com.pe; ultra-nationalist paramilitary group; Pres. Dr ISAAC HUMALA NÚÑEZ; Leader of paramilitary wing Maj. (retd) ANTAURO IGOR HUMALA TASSO (arrested Jan. 2005 following an armed uprising in Andahuaylas).

Sendero Luminoso (Shining Path): f. 1970; began armed struggle 1980; splinter group of PCP; active in the Apurímac-Ene and Upper Huallaga valleys; advocated the policies of the late Mao Zedong and his radical followers, including the 'Gang of Four' in the People's Republic of China; from the mid-2000s it became increasingly involved in the illegal drugs trade; founder Dr ABIMAEL GUZMÁN REYNOSO (alias 'Comandante Gonzalo'—arrested Sept. 1992); leaders VÍCTOR QUISPE PALOMINO (alias 'Comrade José'—commander of the Apurímac-Ene contingent), 'COMRADE ARTEMIO' (identified as Filomeno Cerrón Cardoso—commander of the Upper Huallaga contingent).

Diplomatic Representation

EMBASSIES IN PERU

Algeria: Miguel de Cervantes 504–510, San Isidro, Lima; tel. 421-7582; fax 421-7580; e-mail embarg@embajadadeargelia.com; Ambassador ABDELKADER RIAME.

Argentina: Arequipa 121, Lima 1; tel. (1) 4339966; fax (1) 4330769; e-mail embajada@terra.com.pe; Ambassador DARIO PEDRO ALESSANDRO.

Austria: Avda República de Colombia 643, 5°, San Isidro, Lima 27; tel. (1) 4420503; fax (1) 4428851; e-mail lima-ob@bmeia.gv.at; Ambassador GEORG WOUTSAS.

Belgium: Avda Angamos Oeste 380, Miraflores, Lima 18; tel. (1) 2417566; fax (1) 2416379; e-mail lima@diplobel.org; internet www.diplomatie.be/lima; Ambassador MARIE-LOUISE VANHERK.

Bolivia: Los Castaños 235, San Isidro, Lima 27; tel. (1) 4402095; fax (1) 4402298; e-mail jemis@emboli.attla.com.pe; Ambassador FRANZ SOLANO CHUQUIMIA.

Brazil: Avda José Pardo 850, Miraflores, Lima; tel. (1) 5120830; fax (1) 4452421; e-mail embajada@embajadabrasil.org.pe; internet www.embajadabrasil.org.pe; Ambassador JORGE D'ESCRAGNOLLE TAUNAY, Filho.

Canada: Calle Bolognesi 228, Miraflores, Lima; tel. (1) 3193200; fax (1) 4464912; e-mail lima@international.gc.ca; internet www.dfait-maeci.gc.ca/peru; Ambassador RICHARD LECOQ.

Chile: Avda Javier Prado Oeste 790, San Isidro, Lima; tel. (1) 7102121; fax (1) 7102223; e-mail embajada@embachileperu.com.pe; Ambassador FAVIO VIO UGARTE.

China, People's Republic: Jirón José Granda 150, San Isidro, Apdo 375, Lima 27; tel. (1) 2220841; fax (1) 4429467; e-mail chinaemb_pe@mfa.gov.cn; internet www.embajadachina.org.pe; Ambassador GAO ZHENGYUE.

Colombia: Avda J. Basadre 1580, San Isidro, Lima 27; tel. (1) 4410954; fax (1) 4419806; e-mail emperu@embajadacolombia.org.pe; Ambassador ÁLVARO PAVA CAMELO.

Costa Rica: Baltazar La Torre 828, San Isidro, Lima; tel. (1) 2642999; fax (1) 2642799; e-mail costarica.peru@hotmail.com; Ambassador SARA FAIGENZICHT WEISLEDER.

Cuba: Coronel Portillo 110, San Isidro, Lima; tel. (1) 2642053; fax (1) 2644525; e-mail embacuba@ecuperu.minrex.gov.cu; internet embacu.cubaminrex.cu/peru; Ambassador LUIS DELFÍN PÉREZ OSORIO.

Czech Republic: Baltazar La Torre 398, San Isidro, Lima 27; tel. (1) 2643374; fax (1) 2641708; e-mail lima@embassy.mzv.cz; internet www.mfa.cz/lima; Ambassador VĚRA ZEMANOVÁ.

Dominican Republic: Calle Tudela y Varela 360, San Isidro, Lima; tel. (1) 4219765; fax (1) 4219763; e-mail embdomperu@terra.com.pe; Ambassador RAFAEL JULIÁN CEDANO.

Ecuador: Las Palmeras 356 y Javier Prado Oeste, San Isidro, Lima 27; tel. (1) 2124171; fax (1) 4220711; e-mail embajada@mecuadorperu.org.pe; internet www.mecuadorperu.org.pe; Ambassador DIEGO RIBADENEIRA ESPINOSA.

Egypt: Avda Jorge Basadre 1470, San Isidro, Lima 27; tel. (1) 4402642; fax (1) 4402547; e-mail emb-egypt@amauta.rcp.net.pe; Ambassador HESHAN MOHAMED ABBAS.

El Salvador: Avda Javier Prado 2108, San Isidro, Lima 27; tel. (1) 4403500; fax (1) 2212561; e-mail embajadasv@terra.com.pe; Ambassador RAÚL SOTO-RAMÍREZ.

Finland: Avda Víctor Andrés Belaúnde 147, Edif. Real Tres, Of. 502, San Isidro, Lima; tel. (1) 2224466; fax (1) 2224463; e-mail sanomat.lim@formin.fi; internet www.finlandiaperu.org.pe; Ambassador PEKKA ORPANA.

France: Avda Arequipa 3415, Lima 27; tel. (1) 2158400; fax (1) 2158410; e-mail france.consulat@ambafrance-pe.org; internet www

PERU

.ambafrance-pe.org; Ambassador CÉCILE MOUTON-BRADY DE POZZO DI BORGO.

Germany: Avda Arequipa 4210, Miraflores, Lima 18; tel. (1) 2125016; fax (1) 4226475; e-mail kanzlei@embajada-alemana.org.pe; internet www.embajada-alemana.org.pe; Ambassador CHRISTOPH MÜLLER.

Greece: Avda Principal 190, 6°, Urb. Santa Catalina, Lima 13; tel. (1) 4761548; fax (1) 4761329; e-mail emgrecia@terra.com.pe; Ambassador IONNIS PAPADOPOULOS.

Guatemala: Inca Ripac 309, Jesús María, Lima 11; tel. (1) 4602078; fax (1) 4635885; e-mail embperu@minex.gob.gt; Ambassador LUIS PEDRO QUEZADA CÓRDOVA.

Holy See: Avda Salaverry, 6a cuadra, Lima 11 (Apostolic Nunciature); tel. (1) 4319436; fax (1) 4315704; e-mail nunciaturaperu@inbox.com; Apostolic Nuncio Most Rev. BRUNO MUSARÒ (Titular Archbishop of Abari).

Honduras: Avda Las Camelias 491, Of. 202, San Isidro, Lima; tel. (1) 4228111; fax (1) 2211677; internet www.embhonpe.org; Ambassador JUÁN JOSÉ CUEVA MEMBREÑO.

India: Avda Salaverry 3006, San Isidro, Lima 27; tel. (1) 4602289; fax (1) 4610374; e-mail hoc@indembassy.org.pe; internet www.indembassy.org.pe; Ambassador APPUNNI RAMESH.

Indonesia: Avda Las Flores 334, San Isidro, Lima; tel. (1) 2220308; fax (1) 2222684; e-mail kbrilima@indonesia-peru.org.pe; internet www.indonesia-peru.org.pe; Ambassador I GDE DJELANTIK.

Israel: Edif. El Pacifico, 6°, Plaza Washington, Natalio Sánchez 125, Santa Beatriz, Lima; tel. (1) 4334431; fax (1) 4338925; e-mail info@lima.mfa.gov.il; internet lima.mfa.gov.il; Ambassador WALID MANSOUR.

Italy: Avda Giuseppe Garibaldi 298, Apdo 0490, Lima 11; tel. (1) 4632727; fax (1) 4635317; e-mail segretaria@italembperu.org.pe; internet www.italembperu.org.pe; Chargé d'affaires a.i. FRANCESCO TAFURI.

Japan: Avda San Felipe 356, Apdo 3708, Jesús María, Lima 11; tel. (1) 2181130; fax (1) 4630302; internet www.pe.emb-japan.go.jp; Ambassador SHUICHIRO MEGATA.

Korea, Democratic People's Republic: Los Nogales 227, San Isidro, Lima; tel. (1) 4411120; fax (1) 4409877; e-mail embcorea@hotmail.com; Ambassador RI MUN GYU.

Korea, Republic: Avda Principal 190, 7°, Urb. Santa Catalina, La Victoria, Lima; tel. (1) 4760815; fax (1) 4760950; e-mail peru@mofat.go.kr; internet per.mofat.go.kr; Ambassador HAN BYUNG-KIL.

Malaysia: Avda Daniel Hernández 350, San Isidro, Lima 27; tel. (1) 4220297; fax (1) 2210786; e-mail mallima@kln.gov.my; internet www.kln.gov.my/perwakilan/lima; Ambassador AHMAD IZLAM BIN IDRIS.

Mexico: Avda Jorge Basadre 710, esq. Los Ficus, San Isidro, Lima; tel. (1) 2211100; fax (1) 4404740; e-mail info@mexico.org.pe; internet www.mexico.org.pe; Ambassador ANTONIO GUILLERMO VILLEGAS VILLALOBOS.

Morocco: Calle Manuel Ugarte y Morosco 790, San Isidro, Lima; tel. (1) 2643323; fax (1) 2640006; e-mail sifamlim@chavin.rcp.net.pe; internet www.embajadamarruecoslima.com; Ambassador OUMAMA AOUAD.

Netherlands: Torre Parque Mar, 13°, Avda José Larco 1301, Miraflores, Lima; tel. (1) 2139800; fax (1) 2139805; e-mail info@nlgovlim.com; internet www.nlgovlim.com; Ambassador BAREND VAN DER HEIJDEN.

Nicaragua: Avda Alvarez Calderón 738, San Isidro, Lima; tel. (1) 4223892; fax (1) 4223895; e-mail embanic@telefonica.net.pe; Ambassador TOMÁS WIGBERTO BORGE MARTÍNEZ.

Panama: Avda Alvarez Calderón 738, San Isidro, Lima 27; tel. (1) 4413652; fax (1) 4419323; e-mail panaemba@amauta.rcp.net.pe; Ambassador ROBERTO DÍAZ HERRERA.

Paraguay: Alcanfores 1286, Miraflores, Lima; tel. (1) 4474762; fax (1) 4442391; e-mail embaparpe@terra.com.pe; Chargé d'affaires a.i. FELIPE JARA AGÜERO.

Poland: Apdo 180174, Miraflores, Lima 18; tel. (1) 4713920; fax (1) 4714813; e-mail wojciech@amauta.rcp.net.pe; Ambassador PRZEMYSŁAW MARZEC.

Portugal: Calle Antequera 777, 3°, San Isidro, POB 3692, Lima 100; tel. (1) 4409905; fax (1) 4429655; e-mail limaportugal@hotmail.com; Ambassador NUNO BESSA LÓPES.

Romania: Avda Jorge Basadre 690, San Isidro, Lima; tel. (1) 4224587; fax (1) 4210609; e-mail ambrom@terra.com.pe; Ambassador ȘTEFAN COSTIN.

Russia: Avda Salaverry 3424, San Isidro, Lima 27; tel. (1) 2640036; fax (1) 2640130; e-mail embrusa@amauta.rcp.net.pe; internet www.embajada-rusa.org; Ambassador MIKHAIL G. TROYANSKII.

Serbia: Carlos Porras Osores 360, Apdo 18-0392, San Isidro, Lima 27; Apdo 0392, Lima 18; tel. (1) 4212423; fax (1) 4212427; e-mail yugoembperu@amauta.rcp.net.pe; Ambassador GORAN MESIĆ.

South Africa: Edif. Real Tres, Avda Víctor Andres Belaúnde 147, Of. 801, Lima 27; tel. (1) 4409996; fax 4223881; e-mail general.peru@foreign.gov.za; Ambassador ALBERT LESLIE MANLEY.

Spain: Jorge Basadre 498, San Isidro, Lima 27; tel. (1) 2125155; fax (1) 4410084; e-mail embesppe@correo.mae.es; internet www.mae.es/embajadas/lima; Ambassador FRANCISCO JAVIER SANDOMINGO NÚÑEZ.

Switzerland: Avda Salaverry 3240, San Isidro, Lima 27; tel. (1) 2640305; fax (1) 2641319; e-mail lana.llosa@eda.admin.ch; internet www.eda.admin.ch/lima; Ambassador PETER MÜLLER.

Thailand: Avda Los Incas 255, San Isidro, Lima 27; tel. (1) 2216442; fax (1) 4229895; Ambassador UDOMPHOL NINNAD.

Ukraine: José Dellepiani 470, San Isidro, Lima; tel. (1) 2642884; fax (1) 2642892; e-mail emb_pe@mfa.gov.ua; internet www.mfa.gov.ua/peru; Chargé d'affaires a.i. OLEKSIY V. LYASHENKO.

United Kingdom: Torre Parque Mar, 22°, Avda José Larco 1301, Miraflores, Lima; tel. (1) 6173000; fax (1) 6173100; e-mail belima@fco.gov.uk; internet www.ukinperu.fco.gov.uk; Ambassador CATHERINE NETTLETON.

USA: Avda La Encalada 17, Surco, Lima 33; tel. (1) 4343000; fax (1) 6182397; internet lima.usembassy.gov; Ambassador PETER MICHAEL McKINLEY.

Uruguay: José D. Anchorena 84, San Isidro, Lima; tel. (1) 2640099; fax (1) 2640112; e-mail uruinca@embajada-uruguay.com; Ambassador JUAN JOSÉ ARTEAGA SÁENZ DE ZUMARÁN.

Venezuela: Avda Arequipa 298, Lima; tel. (1) 4334511; fax (1) 4331191; Ambassador Vice-Adm. ARMANDO JOSÉ LAGUNA LAGUNA (recalled in April 2009).

Judicial System

The Supreme Court consists of a President and 17 members. There are also Higher Courts and Courts of First Instance in provincial capitals. A comprehensive restructuring of the judiciary was implemented during the late 1990s.

SUPREME COURT

Corte Suprema
Palacio de Justicia, 2°, Avda Paseo de la República, Lima 1; tel. (1) 4284457; fax (1) 4269437; internet www.pj.gob.pe.

President: Dr JAVIER VILLA STEIN.

Attorney-General: Dra GLADYS MARGOT ECHAÍZ RAMOS.

Religion

CHRISTIANITY

The Roman Catholic Church

For ecclesiastical purposes, Peru comprises seven archdioceses, 18 dioceses, 11 territorial prelatures and eight Apostolic Vicariates. At 31 December 2006, according to Vatican estimates, 87.5% of the country's population were adherents of the Roman Catholic Church.

Bishops' Conference
Conferencia Episcopal Peruana, Jirón Estados Unidos 838, Apdo 310, Lima 100; tel. (1) 4631010; fax (1) 4636125; e-mail sgc@iglesiacatolica.org.pe; internet www.iglesia.org.pe; f. 1981; Pres. HÉCTOR MIGUEL CABREJOS VIDARTE (Archbishop of Trujillo).

Archbishop of Arequipa: JAVIER AUGUSTO DEL RIO ALBA, Arzobispado, Moral San Francisco 118, Apdo 149, Arequipa; tel. (54) 234094; fax (54) 242721; e-mail arzobispadoaqp@planet.com.pe.

Archbishop of Ayacucho or Huamanga: LUIS ABILIO SEBASTIANI AGUIRRE, Arzobispado, Jirón 28 de Julio 148, Apdo 30, Ayacucho; tel. and fax (64) 812367; e-mail arzaya@mail.udep.edu.pe.

Archbishop of Cusco: JUAN ANTONIO UGARTE PÉREZ, Arzobispado, Herrajes, Hatun Rumiyoc s/n, Apdo 148, Cusco; tel. (84) 225211; fax (84) 222781; e-mail arzobisp@terra.com.pe.

Archbishop of Huancayo: PEDRO RICARDO BARRETO JIMENO, Arzobispado, Jirón Puno 430, Apdo 245, Huancayo; tel. (64) 234952; fax (64) 239189; e-mail arzohyo@hotmail.com.

Archbishop of Lima: Cardinal JUAN LUIS CIPRIANI THORNE, Arzobispado, Jirón Carabaya, Plaza Mayor, Apdo 1512, Lima 100; tel. (1) 4275980; fax (1) 4271967; e-mail arzolim@terra.com.pe; internet www.arzobispadodelima.org.

Archbishop of Piura: JOSÉ ANTONIO EGUREN ANSELMI, Arzobispado, Libertad 1105, Apdo 197, Piura; tel. and fax (74) 327561; e-mail ocordova@upiura.edu.pe.

PERU

Archbishop of Trujillo: HÉCTOR MIGUEL CABREJOS VIDARTE, Arzobispado, Jirón Mariscal de Orbegozo 451, Apdo 42, Trujillo; tel. (44) 256812; fax (44) 231473; e-mail arztrujillo@terra.com.pe.

The Anglican Communion

The Iglesia Anglicana del Cono Sur de América (Anglican Church of the Southern Cone of America), formally inaugurated in April 1983, comprises seven dioceses, including Peru. The Presiding Bishop of the Church is the Bishop of Northern Argentina.

Bishop of Peru: Rt Rev. HAROLD WILLIAM GODFREY, Apdo 18-1032, Miraflores, Lima 18; tel. and fax (1) 4229160; e-mail diocesisperu@anglicanperu.org; internet www.peru.anglican.org.

The Methodist Church

There are an estimated 4,200 adherents of the Iglesia Metodista del Perú.

President: Rev. JORGE BRAZO CABALLERO, Baylones 186, Lima 5; Apdo 1386, Lima 100; tel. (1) 4245970; fax (1) 4318995; e-mail iglesiamp@computextos.com.pe; internet www.iglesiametodista.org.pe.

Other Protestant Churches

Among the most popular are the Asamblea de Dios, the Iglesia Evangélica del Perú, the Iglesia del Nazareno, the Alianza Cristiana y Misionera and the Iglesia de Dios del Perú.

BAHÁ'Í FAITH

National Spiritual Assembly of the Bahá'ís of Peru: Horacio Urteaga 827, Jesús María, Apdo 11-0209, Lima 11; tel. (1) 4316077; fax (1) 4333005; e-mail bahai@pol.com.pe; mems resident in 220 localities.

The Press

DAILIES

Lima

El Bocón: Jirón Jorge Salazar Araoz 171, Urb. Santa Catalina, Apdo 152, Lima 1; tel. (1) 6908090; fax (1) 6908127; internet www.elbocon.com.pe; f. 1994; football; Editorial Dir JORGE ESTÉVES ALFARO; circ. 90,000.

El Comercio: Empresa Editora 'El Comercio', SA, Jirón Antonio Miró Quesada 300, Lima; tel. (1) 3116310; fax (1) 4260810; e-mail editorweb@comercio.com.pe; internet www.elcomercioperu.com.pe; f. 1839; morning; Editor JUAN CARLOS LUJÁN; Dir-Gen. FRANCISCO MIRÓ QUESADA G.; circ. 150,000 weekdays, 220,000 Sundays.

Expreso: Jirón Antonio Elizalde 753, Lima; tel. (1) 6124000; fax (1) 6124024; e-mail luis.garciamiro@expreso.com.pe; internet www.expreso.com.pe; f. 1961; morning; conservative; Dir LUIS GARCÍA MIRÓ; circ. 100,000.

Extra: Jirón Libertad 117, Miraflores, Lima; tel. (1) 4447088; fax (1) 4447117; e-mail extra@expreso.com.pe; f. 1964; evening edition of Expreso; Dir CARLOS SÁNCHEZ; circ. 80,000.

Gestión: Miró Quesada 247, 8°, Lima 1; tel. (1) 3116370; fax (1) 3116500; e-mail gestion2@diariogestion.com.pe; internet www.gestion.pe; f. 1990; Gen. Editor JULIO LIRA; Gen. Man. ERNESTO CORTES ROJAS; circ. 131,200.

Ojo: Jirón Jorge Salazar Araoz 171, Urb. Santa Catalina, Apdo 152, Lima; tel. (1) 4709696; fax (1) 4761605; internet www.ojo.com.pe; f. 1968; morning; Editorial Dir AGUSTÍN FIGUEROA BENZA; circ. 100,000.

El Peruano (Diario Oficial): Avda Alfonso Ugarte 873, Lima 1; tel. (1) 3150400; fax (1) 4245023; e-mail gbarraza@editoraperu.com.pe; internet www.elperuano.com.pe; f. 1825; morning; official State Gazette; Dir DELFINA BECERRA GONZÁLEZ; circ. 27,000.

Perú 21: Jirón Miró Quesada 247, 6°, Lima; tel. (1) 3116500; fax (1) 3116391; e-mail director@peru21.com; internet www.peru21.com; independent; Editors CLAUDIA IZAGUIRRE, MANUEL TUMI.

La República: Jirón Camaná 320, Lima 1; tel. (1) 7116000; fax (1) 2511029; e-mail otxoa@larepublica.com.pe; internet www.larepublica.pe; f. 1982; left-wing; Dir GUSTAVO MOHME SEMINARIO; circ. 50,000.

Arequipa

Arequipa al Día: Santa Marta 103, Arequipa; tel. (54) 215515; fax (54) 217810; internet www.ucsm.edu.pe/arequipa; f. 1991; Dir CARLOS MENESES CORNEJO; Editor-in-Chief ENRIQUE ZAVALA CONCHA.

Correo de Arequipa: Calle Bolívar 204, Arequipa; tel. (54) 235150; e-mail diariocorreo@epensa.com.pe; internet www.correoperu.com.pe; Dir ALDO MARIÁTEGUI; circ. 70,000.

El Pueblo: Sucre 213, Arequipa; tel. and fax (54) 205086; internet www.elpueblo.com.pe; f. 1905; morning; independent; Pres. DANIEL MACEDO GUTIÉRREZ; Dir CARLOS MENESES CORNEJO; circ. 70,000.

Chiclayo

La Industria: Tacna 610, Chiclayo; tel. (74) 237952; fax (74) 227678; f. 1952; Dir JULIO ALBERTO ORTIZ CERRO; circ. 20,000.

Cusco

El Diario del Cusco: Centro Comercial Ollanta, Avda El Sol 346, Cusco; tel. (84) 229898; fax (84) 229822; e-mail buzon@diariodelcusco.com; internet www.diariodelcusco.com; morning; independent; Exec. Pres. WASHINTON ALOSILLA PORTILLO; Gen. Man. JOSÉ FERNANDEZ NÚÑEZ.

Huacho

El Imparcial: Avda Grau 203, Huacho; tel. (34) 2392187; fax (34) 2321352; e-mail elimparcial1891@hotmail.com; f. 1891; evening; Dir ADÁN MANRIQUE ROMERO; circ. 5,000.

Huancayo

Correo de Huancayo: Jirón Cusco 337, Huancayo; tel. (64) 235792; fax (64) 233811; evening; Editorial Dir RODOLFO OROSCO.

La Opinión Popular: Huancayo; tel. (64) 231149; f. 1922; Dir MIGUEL BERNABÉ SUÁREZ OSORIO.

Ica

La Opinión: Avda Los Maestros 801, Apdo 186, Ica; tel. (56) 235571; f. 1922; evening; independent; Dir GONZALO TUEROS RAMÍREZ.

La Voz de Ica: Castrovirreyna 193, Ica; tel. and fax (56) 232112; e-mail lavozdeica1918@infonegocio.net.pe; f. 1918; Dir ATILIO NIERI BOGGIANO; Man. MARIELLA NIERI DE MACEDO; circ. 4,500.

Pacasmayo

Diario Ultimas Noticias: 2 de Mayo 33, Pacasmayo; tel. and fax (44) 523022; e-mail escribanos@ultimasnoticiasdiario.com; internet www.ultimasnoticiasdiario.com; f. 1973; morning; independent; Editor MARÍA DEL CARMEN BALLENA RAZURI; circ. 3,000.

Piura

Correo: Zona Industrial Manzana 246, Lote 6, Piura; tel. (74) 321681; fax (74) 324881; Editorial Dir ROLANDO RODRICH ARANGO; circ. 12,000.

El Tiempo: Ayacucho 751, Piura; tel. (74) 325141; fax (74) 327478; e-mail lmhelguero@eltiempo.com.pe; internet www.eltiempo.com.pe; f. 1916; morning; independent; Dir LUZ MARÍA HELGUERO; circ. 18,000.

Tacna

Correo: Jirón Hipólito Unanue 636, Tacna; tel. (54) 711671; fax (54) 713955; Editorial Dir RUBÉN COLLAZOS ROMERO; circ. 8,000.

Trujillo

La Industria: Gamarra 443, Trujillo; tel. (44) 295757; fax (44) 427761; e-mail phidalgo@laindustria.com; internet www.laindustria.com; f. 1895; morning; independent; Dir ERNESTO BARREDA ARIAS; circ. 8,000.

PERIODICALS AND REVIEWS

Caretas: Jirón Huallaya 122, Portal de Botoneros, Plaza de Armas, Lima 1; Apdo 737, Lima 100; tel. (1) 4289490; fax (1) 4262524; e-mail info@caretas.com.pe; internet www.caretas.com.pe; weekly; current affairs; Dir MARCO ZILERI DOUGALL; circ. 90,000.

Cosas: Calle Recaveren 111, Miraflores, Lima 18; tel. (1) 2023000; fax (1) 4473776; internet www.cosasperu.com; weekly; society; Editor ELIZABETH DULANTO.

Debate: Apdo 671, Lima 100; tel. (1) 2425656; fax (1) 4455946; f. 1980; every 2 months; Editor GONZALO ZEGARRA-HUILANDVICH.

Debate Agrario: Avda Salaverry 818, Lima 11; tel. (1) 4336610; fax (1) 4331744; e-mail fegurenl@cepes.org.pe; f. 1987 by Centro Peruano de Estudios Sociales; every 4 months; rural issues; Dir FERNANDO EGUREN L.

Gente Peru: Calle Las Margaritas, San Eugenio, Lince, Lima 14; tel. (1) 2217997; fax (1) 4413646; internet www.genteinternacional.com; f. 1958; weekly; circ. 25,000; Dir HÉCTOR ESCARDÓ.

Hora del Hombre: Lima; tel. (1) 4220208; f. 1943; monthly; cultural and political journal; illustrated; Dir JORGE FALCÓN.

PERU

Industria Peruana: Los Laureles 365, San Isidro, Apdo 632, Lima 27; f. 1896; monthly publication of the Sociedad de Industrias; Editor ROLANDO CELI BURNEO.

Lima Times: Pasaje Los Pinos 156, Of. B6, Miraflores, Apdo 531, Lima 100; tel. (1) 4469120; fax (1) 4467888; e-mail perutimes@ amauta.rcp.net.pe; f. 1975; monthly; travel, cultural events, general news on Peru; English; Editor ELEANOR GRIFFIS DE ZÚÑIGA; circ. 10,000.

Mercado Internacional: Lima; tel. (1) 4445395; business.

Monos y Monadas: Lima; tel. (1) 4773483; f. 1981; fortnightly; satirical; Editor NICOLÁS YEROVI; circ. 17,000.

Oiga: Pedro Venturo 353, Urb. Aurora, Miraflores, Lima; tel. (1) 4475851; internet www.oigaenlinea.com; weekly; right-wing; circ. 60,000.

Ollanta: e-mail ollantaprensa@yahoo.com; internet ollantaprensa .tripod.com.pe; fortnightly; published by the Movimiento Nacionalista Peruano (MNP—'Movimiento Etnocacerista').

Onda: Jorge Vanderghen 299, Miraflores, Lima; tel. (1) 4227008; f. 1959; monthly cultural review; Dir JOSÉ ALEJANDRO VALENCIA-ARENAS; circ. 5,000.

Orbita: Parque Rochdale 129, Lima; tel. (1) 4610676; weekly; f. 1970; Dir LUZ CHÁVEZ MENDOZA; circ. 10,000.

Perú Económico: Apdo 671, Lima 100; tel. (1) 2425656; fax (1) 4455946; internet www.apoyopublicaciones.com/perueconomico; f. 1978; monthly.

The Peruvian Times: Paseo de la República 291, Of. 702, Lima 1; tel. (1) 4284069; fax (1) 4467888; e-mail egriffis@peruviantimes.com; internet www.peruviantimes.com; f. 1912 as The Andean Report; adopted current name in 2007; weekly, online only; general news, analysis and features; English; Publr ELEANOR GRIFFIS; circ. 1,000.

QueHacer: León de la Fuente 110, Lima 17; tel. (1) 6138300; fax (1) 6138308; e-mail qh@desco.org.pe; internet www.desco.org.pe/ quehacer; f. 1979; 6 a year; supported by Desco research and devt agency; Editor-in-Chief MARTÍN PAREDES; Dir ABELARDO SÁNCHEZ-LEÓN; circ. 5,000.

Revista Agraria: Avda Salaverry 818, Lima 11; tel. (1) 4336610; fax (1) 4331744; internet www.cepes.org.pe/revista/agraria.htm; f. 1987 by Centro Peruano de Estudios Sociales; monthly review of rural problems; Dir FERNANDO EGUREN; circ. 100,000.

Runa: Lima; f. 1977; monthly; review of the Instituto Nacional de Cultura; Dir MARIO RAZZETO; circ. 10,000.

Semana Económica: Juan de la Fuente 625, Miraflores, Lima 18; tel. (1) 2130600; fax (1) 4445240; e-mail analistas@ apoyopublicaciones.com; internet www.semanaeconomica.com; f. 1985; weekly; Editor GONZALO ZEGARRA MULANOVICH.

Unidad: Jirón Lampa 271, Of. 703, Lima; tel. (1) 4270355; weekly; Communist; Dir GUSTAVO ESTEVES OSTOLAZA; circ. 20,000.

Vecino: Avda Petit Thouars 1944, Of. 15, Lima 14; tel. (1) 4706787; f. 1981; fortnightly; supported by Yunta research and urban publishing institute; Dirs PATRICIA CÓRDOVA, MARIO ZOLEZZI; circ. 5,000.

NEWS AGENCY

Andina—Agencia de Noticias Peruana: Jirón Quilca 556, Lima; tel. (1) 3306341; fax (1) 4312849; e-mail bbecerra@editoraperu.com .pe; internet www.andina.com.pe; f. 1981; state-owned; Pres. MARÍA DEL PILAR TELLO LEYVA; Dir of Media DELFINA BECERRA GONZÁLEZ.

PRESS ASSOCIATIONS

Asociación Nacional de Periodistas del Perú: Jirón Huancavélica 320, Apdo 2079, Lima 1; tel. (1) 4270687; fax (1) 4278493; internet www.anp.org.pe; f. 1928; 8,800 mems; Pres. ROBERTO MARCOS MEJÍA ALARCÓN.

Federación de Periodistas del Perú (FPP): Avda Abancay 173, 3°, Lima; tel. (1) 4261806; e-mail fpp@omco.org; internet www.omco .org/fpp; f. 1950; Pres. JESÚS GERMÁN LLANOS CASTILLO.

Publishers

Asociación Editorial Bruño: Avda Arica 751, Breña, Lima 5; tel. (1) 4237890; fax (1) 4240424; e-mail federico@brunoeditorial.com.pe; internet www.brunoeditorial.com.pe; f. 1950; educational; Man. FEDERICO DÍAZ PINEDO.

Biblioteca Nacional del Perú: Avda de la Poesia 160, San Borja, Lima 41; tel. (1) 5136900; fax (1) 5137060; e-mail contactobnp@bnp .gob.pe; internet www.bnp.gob.pe; f. 1821; general non-fiction, directories; Dir HUGO NEIRA SAMANAZ.

Colección Artes y Tesoros del Perú: Calle Centenario 156, Urb. Las Laderas de Melgarejo, La Molina, Lima 12; tel. (1) 3493128; fax (1) 3490579; e-mail acarulla@bcp.com.pe; f. 1971; Dir ALVARO CARULLA.

Ediciones Médicas Peruanas, SA: Lima; f. 1965; medical; Man. ALBERTO LOZANO REYES.

Editora Normas Legales, SA: Angamos Oeste 526, Miraflores, Lima; tel. and fax (1) 4861410; e-mail ventas@normaslegales.com; internet www.normaslegales.com; law textbooks; Man. JAVIER SANTA MARÍA SILVE.

Editorial Book City: Calle José R. Pizarro 1260 (espalda cuadra 11 de La Mar), Pueblo Libre, Lima; tel. (1) 2613266; general interest, juvenile, reference and literature; Man. MIRTHA YI YANG.

Editorial Colegio Militar Leoncio Prado: Avda Costanera 1541, La Perla, Callao; f. 1946; textbooks and official publications; Man. OSCAR MORALES QUINA.

Editorial Cuzco, SA: Calle 5 Marzo, Jirón Lote 3, Urb. Las Magnolias, Surco, Lima; tel. (1) 4453261; e-mail ccuzco@camaralima.org .pe; law; Man. SERGIO BAZÁN CHACÓN.

Editorial D.E.S.A.: General Varela 1577, Breña, Lima; f. 1955; textbooks and official publications; Man. ENRIQUE MIRANDA.

Editorial Desarrollo, SA: Ica 242, 1°, Apdo 3824, Lima; tel. and fax (1) 4286628; f. 1965; business administration, accounting, auditing, industrial engineering, English textbooks, dictionaries, and technical reference; Dir LUIS SOSA NÚÑEZ.

Editorial Horizonte: Avda Nicolás de Piérola 995, Lima 1; tel. (1) 4279364; fax (1) 4274341; e-mail damonte@terra.com.pe; f. 1968; social sciences, literature, politics; Man. HUMBERTO DAMONTE.

Editorial Labrusa, SA: Los Frutales Avda 670-Ate, Lima; tel. (1) 4358443; fax (1) 4372925; f. 1988; literature, educational, cultural; Gen. Man. ADRIÁN REUILLA CALVO; Man. FEDERICO DÍAZ TINEO.

Editorial Milla Batres, SA: Lima; f. 1963; history, literature, art, archaeology, linguistics and encyclopaedias on Peru; Dir-Gen. CARLOS MILLA BATRES.

Editorial Navarrete SRL-Industria del Offset: Manuel Tellería 1842, Apdo 4173, Lima; tel. (1) 4319040; fax (1) 4230991; Man. LUIS NAVARRETE LECHUGA.

Editorial Océano Peruana, SA: Avda Salaverry 2890, San Isidro, Lima; tel. (1) 2613999; fax (1) 4618628; e-mail ocelibros@oceano.com .pe; general interest and reference.

Editorial Peisa: Avda 2 de Mayo 1285, San Isidro, Lima; tel. (1) 4410473; fax (1) 2215988; e-mail burtech@yahoo.com; internet www .peisa.com.pe; fiction and scholarly; Man. BENJAMIN URTECHO.

Editorial Salesiana: Avda Brasil 218, Apdo 0071, Lima 5; tel. (1) 4235225; internet www.libreriasalesiana.com; f. 1918; religious and general textbooks; Man. Dir Dr FRANCESCO VACARELLO.

Editorial Santillana: Avda Primavera 2160, Santiago de Surco, Lima; tel. (1) 3134000; fax (1) 3134001; e-mail santillana@santillana .com.pe; internet www.gruposantillana.com.pe; literature, scholarly and reference; Man. ANA CECILIA HALLO.

Editorial Universo, SA: Lima; f. 1967; literature, technical, educational; Pres. CLEMENTE AQUINO; Gen. Man. Ing. JOSÉ A. AQUINO BENAVIDES.

Fundación del Banco Continental para el Fomento de la Educación y la Cultura (EDUBANCO): Avda República de Panamá 3055, San Isidro, Apdo 4687, Lima 27; tel. (1) 2111000; fax (1) 2112479; f. 1973; Pres. PEDRO BRESCIA CAFFERATA; Man. FERNANDO PORTOCARRERO.

Industrial Gráfica, SA: Jirón Chavín 45, Breña, Lima 5; fax (1) 4324413; f. 1981; Pres. JAIME CAMPODONICO V.

INIDE: Van de Velde 160, Urb. San Borja, Lima; f. 1981; owned by National Research and Development Institute; educational books; Editor-in-Chief ANA AYALA.

Librerías ABC, SA: Avda Paseo de la República 3440, Local B-32, Lima 27; tel. (1) 4422900; fax (1) 4224901; f. 1956; history, Peruvian art and archaeology; Man. Dir HERBERT H. MOLL.

Librería San Pablo: Jirón Callao 198, Lima 1; tel. (1) 3795336; fax (1) 4593842; e-mail admlima@paulinas.org.pe; internet www .paulinas.org.pe; f. 1981; religious and scholastic texts; Man. Sister MARÍA GRACIA CAPALBO.

Librería Studium, SA: Lima; tel. (1) 4326278; fax (1) 4325354; f. 1936; textbooks and general culture; Man. Dir EDUARDO RIZO PATRÓN RECAVARREN.

Pablo Villanueva Ediciones: Lima; f. 1938; literature, history, law, etc.; Man. AUGUSTO VILLANUEVA PACHECO.

Pontificia Universidad Católica del Perú: Fondo Editorial, Avda Universitaria 1801, San Miguel, Lima 32; tel. (1) 6262650; fax (1) 6262913; e-mail feditor@pucp.edu.pe; internet www.pucp.edu .pe; Dir-Gen. ANA PATRICIA ARÉVALO MAJLUF.

Sociedad Bíblica Peruana, AC: Avda Petit Thouars 991, Apdo 14-0295, Lima 100; tel. (1) 4336608; fax (1) 4336389; internet www

PERU   *Directory*

.casadelabiblia.org; f. 1821; Christian literature and bibles; Gen. Sec. PEDRO ARANA-QUIROZ.

Universidad Nacional Mayor de San Marcos: Of. General de Editorial, Avda República de Chile 295, 5°, Of. 508, Lima; tel. (1) 4319689; internet www.unmsm.edu.pe; f. 1850; textbooks, education; Man. Dir JORGE CAMPOS REY DE CASTRO.

PUBLISHING ASSOCIATION

Cámara Peruana del Libro: Avda Cuba 427, esq. Jesús María, Apdo 10253, Lima 11; tel. (1) 4729516; fax (1) 2650735; e-mail cp-libro@amauta.rep.net.pe; internet www.cpl.org.pe; f. 1946; 102 mems; Pres. CARLOS A. BENVIDES AGUIJE; Exec. Dir LOYDA MORÁN BUSTAMANTE.

Broadcasting and Communications

TELECOMMUNICATIONS

Regulatory Authorities

Dirección General de Regulación y Asuntos Internacionales de Telecomunicaciones: Avda Jirón Zorritos 1203, Lima 1; tel. (1) 6185800; Dir-Gen. PATRICIA CARREÑO FERRÉ.

Instituto Nacional de Investigación y Capacitación de Telecomunicaciones (INICTEL): Avda San Luis 1771, esq. Bailetti, San Borja, Lima 41; tel. (1) 3461808; fax (1) 3464354; e-mail informes@inictel.gob.pe; internet www.inictel.gob.pe; Pres. MANUEL ADRIANZEN.

Organismo Supervisor de Inversión Privada en Telecomunicaciones (OSIPTEL): Calle de la Prosa 136, San Borja, Lima 41; tel. (1) 2251313; fax (1) 4751816; e-mail sid@osiptel.gob.pe; internet www.ospitel.gob.pe; f. 1993; established by the Peruvian Telecommunications Act to oversee competition and tariffs, to monitor the quality of services and to settle disputes in the sector; Pres. Dr GUILLERMO THORNBERRY VILLARÁN.

Major Service Providers

Claro Perú: Lima; internet www.claro.com.pe; f. 2005; owned by América Móvil, SA de SV (Mexico); mobile cellular telecommunications services; Gen. Dir HUMBERTO CHÁVEZ.

Telefónica MoviStar: Juan de Arona 786, San Isidro, Lima; tel. (1) 9817000; internet www.telefonicamoviles.com.pe; f. 1994; 98% bought by Telefónica Móviles, SA (Spain) in 2000; mobile telephone services; 1.8m. customers.

Telefónica del Perú, SA: Avda Arequipa 1155, Santa Beatriz, Lima 1; tel. (1) 2101013; fax (1) 4705950; e-mail mgarcia@tp.com.pe; internet www.telefonica.com.pe; Pres. ANTONIO CARLOS VALENTE.

Telmex: Torre Parque Mar, Avda Larco 1301, Miraflores, Lima; tel. (1) 6105555; internet www.telmex.com/pe.

BROADCASTING

Regulatory Authorities

Asociación de Radio y Televisión del Perú (AR&TV): Avda Roma 140, San Isidro, Lima 27; tel. (1) 4703734; Pres. HUMBERTO MALDONADO BALBÍN; Dir DANIEL LINARES BAZÁN.

Coordinadora Nacional de Radio: San Felipe 943, Jesús María, Lima 11; tel. (1) 4725252; fax (1) 4715808; e-mail postmaster@cnr.org.pe; internet www.cnr.org.pe; f. 1978; Pres. HUGO RAMÍREZ HUAMÁN; Exec. Dir JORGE ACEVEDO ROJAS.

Instituto Nacional de Comunicación Social: Jirón de la Unión 264, Lima; Dir HERNÁN VALDIZÁN.

Unión de Radioemisoras de Provincias del Perú (UNRAP): Mariano Carranza 754, Santa Beatriz, Lima 1.

State Corporation

Instituto Nacional de Radio y Televisión Peruana (IRTP): Avda Paseo de la República 1110, Lima 1; tel. (1) 471-8200; internet www.irtp.com.pe; f. 1996; Exec. Pres. ALFONSO SALCEDO RUBIO; runs the following stations:

   Radio Nacional del Perú: Avda Petit Thouars 447, Santa Beatriz, Lima 1; tel. (1) 4331404; fax (1) 4338952; internet www.radionacional.com.pe; state broadcaster; Man. FELIPE TOMÁS GRANADOS VÁSQUEZ.

   Televisión Nacional del Perú (TV Perú): Lima; tel. (1) 6190707; internet www.tnp.gob.pe; f. 1958 as Radio y Televisión Peruana; state broadcaster; 22 stations; Commercial Man. RODOLFO RUSCA LEVANO.

Radio

Radio Agricultura del Perú, SA—La Peruanísima: Casilla 625, Lima 11; tel. (1) 4246677; e-mail radioagriculturadelperu@yahoo.com; internet www.laperuanisima.com; f. 1963; Gen. Man. LUZ ISABEL DEXTRE NÚÑEZ.

Radio América: Montero Rosas 1099, Santa Beatriz, Lima 1; tel. (1) 2653841; fax (1) 2653844; f. 1943; Dir-Gen. KAREN CROUSILLAT.

Cadena Peruana de Noticias: Gral Salaverry 156, Miraflores, Lima; tel. (1) 4461554; fax (1) 4457770; e-mail webmastercpn@gestion.com.pe; internet www.cpnradio.pe; f. 1996; Pres. MANUEL ROMERO CARO; Gen. Man. OSCAR ROMERO CARO.

Radio Cutivalú, La Voz del Desierto: Jirón Ignacio de Loyola 300, Urb. Miraflores, Castilla, Piura; tel. (73) 343370; internet www.radiocutivalu.org; f. 1986; Pres. FRANCISCO MUGUIRO IBARRA; Dir RODOLFO AQUINO RUIZ.

Emisoras 'Cruz del Perú': Victorino Laynes 1402, Urb. Elio, Lima 1; tel. (1) 4521028; Pres. FERNANDO CRUZ MENDOZA; Gen. Man. MARCO CRUZ MENDOZA M.

Emisoras Nacionales: León Velarde 1140, Lince, Lima 1; tel. (1) 4714948; fax (1) 4728182; Gen. Man. CÉSAR COLOMA R.

Radio Inca del Perú: Pastor Dávila 197, Lima; tel. (1) 2512596; fax (1) 2513324; f. 1951; Gen. Man. ABRAHAM ZAVALA CHOCANO.

Radio Panamericana: Paseo Parodi 340, San Isidro, Lima 27; tel. (1) 4226787; fax (1) 4221182; internet www.radiopanamericana.com; f. 1953; Dir RAQUEL DELGADO DE ALCÁNTARA.

Radio Programas del Perú (GRUPORPP): Avda Paseo de la República 3866, San Isidro, Lima; tel. (1) 2150200; fax 2150264; Pres. HUGO DELGADO NACHTIGAL; Gen. Man. MANUEL DELGADO PARKER.

Radio Santa Rosa: Jirón Camaná 170, Apdo 206, Lima; tel. (1) 4277488; fax (1) 4269219; f. 1958; Dir P. JUAN SOKOLICH ALVARADO.

Sonograbaciones Maldonado: Mariano Carranza 754, Santa Beatriz, Lima; tel. (1) 4715163; fax (1) 4727491; Pres. HUMBERTO MALDONADO B.; Gen. Man. LUIS HUMBERTO MALDONADO.

Television

América Televisión, Canal 4: Jirón Montero Rosas 1099, Santa Beatriz, Lima; tel. (1) 2657361; fax (1) 2656979; e-mail web@americatv.com.pe; internet www.americatv.com.pe; Gen. Man. MARISOL CROUSILLAT.

ATV, Canal 9: Avda Arequipa 3570, San Isidro, Lima 27; tel. (1) 2118800; fax (1) 4427636; e-mail jdewerpe@atv.com.pe; internet www.atv.com.pe; f. 1983; Gen. Man. MARCELLO CÚNEO LOBIANO.

Frecuencia Latina, Canal 2: Avda San Felipe 968, Jesús María, Lima; tel. (1) 2191000; fax (1) 2656660; internet www.frecuencialatina.com.pe; Pres. BARUCH IVCHER.

Global Televisión, Canal 13: Gen. Orbegoso 140, Breña, Lima; tel. (1) 3303040; fax (1) 4238202; f. 1989; Pres. GENARO DELGADO PARKER; Gen. Man. RAFAEL LEGUÍA.

Nor Peruana de Radiodifusión, SA: Avda Arequipa 3520, San Isidro, Lima 27; tel. (1) 403365; fax (1) 419844; f. 1991; Dir FRANCO PALERMO IBARGUENGOITIA; Gen. Man. FELIPE BERNINZÓN VALLARINO.

Panamericana Televisión SA, Canal 5: Avda Alejandro Tirado 217, Santa Beatriz, Lima; tel. (1) 4113201; fax (1) 4703001; internet www.24horas.com.pe; Pres. RAFAEL RAVETTINO FLORES; Gen. Man. FREDERICO ANCHORENA VÁSQUEZ.

Cía Peruana de Radiodifusión, Canal 4 TV: Mariano Carranza y Montero Rosas 1099, Santa Beatriz, Lima; tel. (1) 4728985; fax (1) 4710099; f. 1958; Dir JOSÉ FRANCISCO CROUSILLAT CARREÑO.

RBC Televisión, Canal 11: Avda Manco Cápac 333, La Victoria, Lima; tel. (1) 4310169; fax (1) 4331237; Pres. FERNANDO GONZÁLEZ DEL CAMPO; Gen. Man. JUAN SÁENZ MARÓN.

Cía de Radiodifusión Arequipa SA, Canal 9: Centro Comercial Cayma, R2, Arequipa; tel. (54) 252525; fax (54) 254959; f. 1986; Dir ENRIQUE MENDOZA NÚÑEZ; Gen. Man. ENRIQUE MENDOZA DEL SOLAR.

Uranio, Canal 15: Avda Arequipa 3570, 6°, San Isidro, Lima; e-mail agamarra@atv.com.pe; Gen. Man. ADELA GAMARRA VÁSQUEZ.

Finance

In April 1991 a new banking law was introduced, relaxing state control of the financial sector and reopening the sector to foreign banks (which had been excluded from the sector by a nationalization law promulgated in 1987).

BANKING

(cap. = capital; res = reserves; dep. = deposits; m. = million; brs = branches; amounts in new soles unless otherwise indicated)

Superintendencia de Banca y Seguros: Los Laureles 214, San Isidro, Lima 27; tel. (1) 2218990; fax (1) 4417760; e-mail mostos@sbs.gob.pe; internet www.sbs.gob.pe; f. 1931; Supt FELIPE TAM FOX; Sec.-Gen. NORMA SOLARI PRECIADO.

Central Bank

Banco Central de Reserva del Perú: Jirón Antonio Miró Quesada 441-445, Lima 1; tel. (1) 4267041; fax (1) 4273091; e-mail webmaster@bcrp.gob.pe; internet www.bcrp.gob.pe; f. 1922; refounded 1931; cap. 295.7m., res 110.3m., dep. 39,030.5m. (Dec. 2006); Chair. JULIO VELARDE FLORES; Gen. Man. RENZO ROSSINI MIÑÁN; 7 brs.

Other Government Banks

Banco de la Nación: Avda Canaval y Moreyra 150, San Isidro, Lima 1; tel. (1) 4405858; fax (1) 4223451; e-mail imagen@bn.com.pe; internet www.bn.com.pe; f. 1966; cap. 866.5m., res 336.4m., dep. 10,928.0m. (Dec. 2006); conducts all commercial banking operations of official govt agencies; Exec. Pres. HUMBERTO ORLANDO MENESES ARANCIBIA; Gen. Man. JULIO DEL CASTILLO VARGAS; 391 brs.

Corporación Financiera de Desarrollo (COFIDE): Augusto Tamayo 160, San Isidro, Lima 27; tel. (1) 6154000; fax (1) 4423374; e-mail postmaster@cofide.com.pe; internet www.cofide.com.pe; f. 1971; also owners of Banco Latino; Pres. AURELIO LORET DE MOLA BÖHME; Gen. Man. MARCO CASTILLO TORRES; 11 brs.

Commercial Banks

Banco de Comercio: Avda Paseo de la República 3705, San Isidro, Lima; tel. (1) 5136000; fax (1) 4405458; e-mail postmaster@bancomercio.com.pe; internet www.bancomercio.com; f. 1967; fmrly Banco Peruano de Comercio y Construcción; cap. 54.6m., res 0.3m., dep. 548.8m. (Dec. 2005); Chair. WILFREDO JESÚS LAFOSSE QUINTANA; Gen. Man. CARLOS ALBERTO MUJICA CASTRO; 23 brs.

Banco de Crédito del Perú: Calle Centenario 156, Urb. Las Laderas de Melgarejo, Apdo 12-067, Lima 12; tel. (1) 3132000; internet www.viabcp.com; f. 1889; cap. 1,286.5m., res 1,037.9m., dep. 37,071.7m., total assets 43,713.7m. (Dec. 2007); Pres. and Chair. DIONISIO ROMERO SEMINARIO; 217 brs.

Banco Interamericano de Finanzas, SA: Avda Rivera Navarrete 600, San Isidro, Lima 27; tel. (1) 6133000; fax (1) 2212489; e-mail gchang@bif.com.pe; internet www.bif.com.pe; f. 1991; cap. 156.3m., res 11.7m., dep. 2,813.1m. (Dec. 2007); Pres. FRANCISCO ROCHE; Gen. Man. and CEO JUAN IGNACIO DE LA VEGA; 37 brs.

BBVA Banco Continental: Avda República de Panamá 3055, San Isidro, Lima 27; tel. (1) 2111000; fax (1) 2111788; internet www.bbvabancocontinental.com; f. 1951; merged with BBVA of Spain in 1995; 92.01% owned by Holding Continental, SA; cap. 852.9m., res 369.6m., dep. 16,445.2m. (Dec. 2006); Pres. and Chair. PEDRO BESCIA CAFFERATA; Gen. Man. JOSÉ ANTONIO COLOMER GUIU; 190 brs.

INTERBANK (Banco Internacional del Perú): Carlos Villarán 140, Urb. Santa Catalina, Lima 13; tel. (1) 2192347; fax (1) 2192336; e-mail krubin@intercorp.com.pe; internet www.interbank.com.pe; f. 1897; commercial bank; cap. 478.6m., res 117.6m., dep. 8,691.7m. (Dec. 2007); Chair. and Pres. CARLOS RODRÍGUEZ-PASTOR; Gen. Man. JORGE FLORES ESPINOZA; 90 brs.

Scotiabank Perú, SAA: Avda Dionisio Derteano 102, San Isidro, Apdo 1235, Lima; tel. (1) 2116060; fax (1) 4407945; e-mail scotiaenlinea@scotiabank.com.pe; internet www.scotiabank.com.pe; f. 2006 by merger of Banco Sudamericano (owned by Scotiabank, Canada) and Banco Wiese Sudameris; cap. 502.6m., res 1,353.6m., dep. 10,671.7m. (Dec. 2006); Chair. JIM MEEK; Vice-Pres. and CEO CARLOS GONZÁLEZ-TABOADA.

Banking Association

Asociación de Bancos del Perú: Calle 41, No 975, Urb. Córpac, San Isidro, Lima 27; tel. (1) 6123333; fax (1) 6123316; e-mail estudioseconomicos@asbanc.com.pe; internet www.asbanc.com.pe; f. 1929; refounded 1967; Pres. OSCAR JOSÉ RIVERA; Gen. Man. ENRIQUE ARROYO RIZO PATRÓN.

STOCK EXCHANGE

Bolsa de Valores de Lima: Pasaje Acuña 106, Lima 100; tel. (1) 6193333; fax (1) 4267650; internet www.bvl.com.pe; f. 1860; Pres. ROBERTO HOYLE.

Regulatory Authority

Comisión Nacional Supervisora de Empresas y Valores (CONASEV): Santa Cruz 315, Miraflores, Lima; tel. (1) 6106300; fax (1) 6106325; e-mail cendoc@conasev.gob.pe; internet www.conasev.gob.pe; f. 1968; regulates the securities and commodities markets; responsible to Ministry of Economy and Finance; Pres. NAHIL LILIANA HIRSH CARRILLO.

INSURANCE

ACE Seguros, SA: Avda Paseo de la República 3587, 10°, San Isidro, Lima; tel. (1) 4428228; fax (1) 422717; Chair. and CEO EVAN G. GREENBERG.

Interseguro Cía de Seguros de Vida, SA: Avda Pardo y Aliaga 640, 4°, San Isidro, Lima; tel. (1) 6114730; fax (1) 2223222; e-mail juan.vallejo@intercorp.com.pe; f. 1998; life; Pres. FELIPE MORRIS GUERINONI; Gen. Man. JUAN CARLOS VALLEJO BLANCO.

Invita Seguros de Vida, SA: Torre Wiese, Canaval y Moreyra 532, San Isidro, Lima; tel. (1) 2222222; fax (1) 2211683; e-mail dcosta@invita.com.pe; internet www.invita.com.pe; f. 2000; life; fmrly Wiese Aetna, SA; Pres. CARIDAD DE LA PUENTE WIESE; Gen. Man. JAVIER FREYRE TRIVELLI.

Mapfre Perú Cía de Seguros: Avda 28 de Julio 873, Miraflores, Apdo 323, Lima 100; tel. (1) 2137373; fax (1) 2433131; e-mail fmarco@mapfreperu.com; internet www.mapfreperu.com; f. 1994; general; fmrly Seguros El Sol, SA; Pres. RENZO CALDA GIURATO.

Pacífico, Cía de Seguros y Reaseguros: Avda Juan de Arona 830, San Isidro, Lima 27; tel. (1) 5184000; fax (1) 5184295; e-mail arodrigo@pps.com.pe; internet www.pacificoseguros.com; f. 1943; general; Pres. DIONISIO ROMERO SEMINARIO; Gen. Man. DAVID SAETTONE WATMOUGH.

La Positiva Cía de Seguros y Reaseguros, SA: San Francisco 301, Arequipa; tel. (54) 214130; fax (54) 214939; e-mail jaimep@lapositiva.com.pe; internet www.lapositiva.com.pe; f. 1947; Pres. JUAN MANUEL PEÑA ROCA; Gen. Man. GUILLERMO ZARAK.

Rimac Internacional, Cía de Seguros: Las Begonias 475, 3°, San Isidro, Lima; tel. (1) 4218383; fax (1) 4210570; e-mail jortecho@rimac.com.pe; internet www.rimac.com.pe; f. 1896; acquired Seguros Fénix in 2004; Pres. Ing. PEDRO BRESCIA CAFFERATA; Gen. Man. PEDRO FLECHA ZALBA.

SECREX, Cía de Seguro de Crédito y Garantías: Avda Angamos Oeste 1234, Miraflores, Lima; Apdo 0511, Lima 18; tel. (1) 4424033; fax (1) 4423890; e-mail ciaseg@secrex.com.pe; internet www.secrex.com.pe; f. 1980; Pres. Dr RAÚL FERRERO COSTA; Gen. Man. JUAN A. GIANNONI MURGA.

Insurance Association

Asociación Peruana de Empresas de Seguros (APESEG): Arias Araguez 146, Miraflores, Lima 18; tel. (1) 4442294; fax (1) 4468538; e-mail rda@apeseg.org.pe; internet www.apeseg.org.pe; f. 1904; Pres. RENZO CALDA GIURATO; Gen. Man. RAÚL DE ANDREA DE LAS CARRERAS.

Trade and Industry

GOVERNMENT AGENCIES

Agencia de Promoción de la Inversión Privada (ProInversión): Avda Paseo de la República 3361, 9°, San Isidro, Lima 27; tel. (1) 6121200; fax (1) 2212942; e-mail gvillegas@proinversion.gob.pe; internet www.proinversion.gob.pe; f. 2002 to promote economic investment; Dir CAYETANA ALJOVÍN GAZZANI; Gen. Sec. ITALO BIZERRA OSORIO.

Empresa Nacional de la Coca, SA (ENACO): Avda Arequipa 4528, Miraflores, Lima; tel. (1) 4423746; fax (1) 4471667; e-mail jjara@enaco.com.pe; internet www.enaco.com.pe; f. 1949; agency with exclusive responsibility for the purchase and resale of legally produced coca and the promotion of its derivatives; Pres. JULIO BALTAZAR JARA LADRÓN DE GUEVARA; Gen. Man. RAÚL CAMPANA RAMOS.

Fondo Nacional de Compensación y Desarrollo Social (FONCODES): Avda Paseo de la República 3101, San Isidro, Lima; tel. (1) 4212102; fax (1) 4214128; e-mail consultas@foncodes.gob.pe; internet www.foncodes.gob.pe; f. 1991; responsible for social devt and eradicating poverty; Exec. Dir CARLOS GERARDO ARANA VIVAR.

Instituto Nacional de Recursos Forestales (INRENA): Calle Diecisiete 355, Urb. El Palomar, Lima; tel. (1) 2243298; fax (1) 2243218; e-mail gerencia.general@inrena.gob.pe; internet www.inrena.gob.pe; f. 1992; promotes sustainable devt of Amazon rainforest; Pres. JOSÉ LUIS CAMINO IVANISSEVICH; Gen. Man. FRANCISCO MARCELINO PALEMINO GARCÍA.

Perupetro: Luis Aldana 320, San Borja, Lima; tel. (1) 6171800; fax (1) 4754860; e-mail mcobena@perupetro.com.pe; internet www.perupetro.com.pe; f. 1993; responsible for promoting investment in hydrocarbon exploration and exploitation; Chair. DANIEL SABA DE ANDREA; CEO RONALD EGUSQUIZA.

DEVELOPMENT ORGANIZATIONS

ACP Inversiones y Desarrollo: Avda Domingo Orue 165, Surquillo, Lima 34; tel. (1) 2220202; fax (1) 2224166; e-mail accion@accion.org.pe; f. 1969; promotes economic, social and cultural devt through improvements in service provision.

Asociación de Exportadores (ADEX): Javier Prado Este 2875, San Borja, Lima 41; Apdo 1806, Lima 1; tel. (1) 6183333; fax (1) 6183355; e-mail prensa@adexperu.org.pe; internet www.adexperu.org.pe; f. 1973; exporters' asscn; Pres. LUIS VEGA MONTEFERRI; Gen. Man. FERNANDO FERREYROS CANNOCK; 600 mems.

Asociación Kallpa para la Promoción Integral de la Salud y el Desarrollo: Jirón Rospigliosi 105, Barranco, Lima 4; tel. (1) 4455521; fax (1) 2429693; e-mail postmast@kallpa.org.pe; internet www.kallpa.org.pe; health devt for youths; Pres. ARIELA LUNA FLORES.

Asociación Nacional de Centros de Investigación, Promoción Social y Desarrollo: Pablo Bermúdez 234, Jesús María, Lima; tel. (1) 4411063; fax (1) 4411227; e-mail postmaster@anc.org.pe; internet www.anc.org.pe; umbrella grouping of devt orgs; Pres. LUIS SIRUMBAL; Exec. Dir FEDERICO ARNILLAS L.

Asociación para la Naturaleza y Desarrollo Sostenible (ANDES): Calle Ruinas 451, Cusco; tel. (8) 4245021; e-mail andes@andes.org.pe; internet www.andes.org.pe; devt org. promoting the culture, education and environment of indigenous groups; Exec. Dir CESAR ARGUMEDO.

Sociedad Nacional de Industrias (SNI) (National Industrial Association): Los Laureles 365, San Isidro, Apdo 632, Lima 27; tel. (1) 6164444; fax (1) 6164433; e-mail sni@sni.org.pe; internet www.sni.org.pe; f. 1896; comprises permanent commissions covering various aspects of industry including labour, integration, fairs and exhibitions, industrial promotion; its Small Industry Cttee groups over 2,000 small enterprises; Pres. EDUARDO FARAH; Gen. Man. FEDERICO DE APARICI; 90 dirs (reps of firms); 2,500 mems; 60 sectorial cttees.

    Centro de Desarrollo Industrial (CDI): Los Laureles 365, San Isidro, Lima; tel. (1) 2158888; fax (1) 2158877; e-mail cdi@sni.org.pe; internet www.cdi.org.pe; f. 1986; supports industrial devt and programmes to develop industrial cos; Exec. Dir LUIS TENORIO PUENTES.

CHAMBERS OF COMMERCE

Cámara de Comercio de Lima (Lima Chamber of Commerce): Avda Giuseppe Garibaldi 396, Jesús María, Lima 11; tel. (1) 4633434; fax (1) 2191777; e-mail secreceex@camaralima.org.pe; internet www.camaralima.org.pe; f. 1888; Pres. PETER DE BERNHARD ANDERS MOORES; 5,500 mems.

Cámara Nacional de Comercio, Producción y Servicios (PERUCAMARAS): Gregorio Escobedo 396, Jesús María, Lima 11; tel. (1) 2191580; fax (1) 2191586; e-mail cnadministracion@perucam.com; internet www.perucam.com; national asscn of chambers of commerce; Pres. GUILLERMO VEGA ALVEAR; Gen. Man. MÓNICA M. WATSON ARAMBURÚ.

There are also Chambers of Commerce in Arequipa, Cusco, Callao and many other cities.

EMPLOYERS' ORGANIZATIONS

Asociación Automotriz del Perú: Dos de Mayo 299, Apdo 1248, San Isidro, Lima 27; tel. (1) 4404119; fax (1) 4428865; e-mail aap@aap.org.pe; internet www.aap.org.pe; f. 1926; asscn of importers of motor cars and accessories; 360 mems; Pres. ARMANDO NEGRI PIÉROLA; Gen. Man. ENRIQUE PRADO REY.

Asociación de Ganaderos del Perú (Association of Stock Farmers of Peru): Pumacahua 877, 3°, Jesús María, Lima; f. 1915; Gen. Man. Ing. MIGUEL J. FORT.

Confederación Nacional de Instituciones Empresariales Privadas (CONFIEP): Pasaje Acuña 106, Lima; e-mail postmaster@confiep.org.pe; internet www.confiep.org.pe; f. 1984; federation of 20 employers' orgs; Pres. JAIME CÁCERES SAYAN.

Consejo Nacional del Café: Lima; reps of govt and industrial coffee growers; Pres. ENRIQUE ALDAVE.

Sociedad Nacional de Minería y Petróleo: Francisco Graña 671, Magdalena del Mar, Lima 17; tel. (1) 4601600; fax (1) 4601616; e-mail postmaster@snmpe.org.pe; internet www.snmpe.org.pe; f. 1940; asscn of cos involved in mining, petroleum and energy; Pres. HANS FLURY.

Sociedad Nacional de Pesquería (SNP): Javier Prado Oeste 2442, San Isidro, Lima 27; tel. (1) 2612970; fax (1) 2617912; e-mail snpnet@snp.org.pe; internet www.snp.org.pe; f. 1952; private sector fishing interests; Pres. RAÚL ALBERTO SÁNCHEZ SOTOMAYOR; Gen. Man. RICHARD INURRITEGUI BAZÁN.

STATE HYDROCARBONS COMPANY

Petroperú (Petróleos del Perú, SA): Avda Enrique Canaval Moreyra 150, Lima 27; tel. (1) 2117800; fax (1) 6145000; internet www.petroperu.com; f. 1969; state-owned petroleum-refining co; Pres. LUIS REBOLLEDO SOBERÓN.

UTILITIES

Regulatory Authority

Gerencia Adjunta de Regulación Tarifaria (GART): Avda Canadá 1470, San Borja, Lima 41; tel. (1) 2240487; fax (1) 2240491; internet www2.osinerg.gob.pe/gart.htm; autonomous agency controlling tariffs.

Electricity

Distriluz: Edif. Torre el Pilar, 13°, Avda Camino Real 348, San Isidro, Lima 27; tel. (1) 2115500; e-mail central@distriluz.com.pe; internet www.distriluz.com.pe; operates 4 energy distribution cos: Enosa, Ensa, Hidrandina and Electrocentro; Dir FERNANDO ROSSINELLI UGARELLI.

Electroperú: Prolongación Pedro Miotta 421, San Juan de Miraflores, Lima 29; tel. (1) 2170600; fax (1) 2170621; internet www.electroperu.com.pe; state-owned; Pres. LUIS ALEJANDRO BEDOYA WALLACE; Gen. Man. RAÚL TENGAN MATSUTAHARA.

Sociedad Eléctrica del Sur-Oeste, SA (SEAL): Consuelo 310, Arequipa; tel. (54) 212946; fax (54) 213296; e-mail seal@sealperu.com; internet www.sealperu.com; f. 1905; Pres. MAURICIO CHIRINOS CHIRINOS; Gen. Man. JOSÉ OPORTO VARGAS.

TRADE UNIONS

The right to strike was restored in the Constitution of July 1979. In 1982 the Government recognized the right of public employees to form trade unions.

Central Unica de Trabajadores Peruanos (CUTP): Lima; f. 1992; Pres. JULIO CÉSAR BAZÁN; includes:

    Confederación General de Trabajadores del Perú (CGTP): Plaza 2 de Mayo 4, Lima 1; tel. (1) 4242357; e-mail cgtp@cgtp.org.pe; internet www.cgtp.org.pe; f. 1968; Pres. CARMELA SIFUENTES INOSTROZA; Sec.-Gen. MARIO HUAMÁN RIVERA.

Confederación Intersectorial de Trabajadores Estatales (CITE) (Union of Public Sector Workers): Lima; tel. (1) 4245525; f. 1978; Sec.-Gen. ALAVARO COLE; Asst Sec. OMAR CAMPOS; 600,000 mems.

Confederación Nacional de Trabajadores (CNT): Avda Iquitos 1198, Lima; tel. (1) 4711385; affiliated to the PPC; c. 12,000 mems; Sec.-Gen. ANTONIO GALLARDO EGOAVIL.

Confederación de Trabajadores del Perú (CTP): Jirón Ayacucho 173, CP 3616, Lima 1; tel. (1) 4261310; e-mail ctp7319@hotmail.com; affiliated to PAP; Sec.-Gen. ELÍAS GRIJALVA ALVARADO.

Federación de Empleados Bancarios (FEB) (Union of Bank Employees): Jirón Miró Quesada 260, 7°, Lima; tel. (1) 7249570; e-mail febperu@terra.com.pe; Sec.-Gen. HÉCTOR PÉREZ PÉREZ.

Federación Nacional de Trabajadores Mineros, Metalúrgicos y Siderúrgicos (FNTMMS) (Federation of Peruvian Mineworkers): Jirón Callao 457, Of. 311, Lima; tel. (1) 4277554; Sec.-Gen. PEDRO ESCATE SULCA; 70,000 mems.

Movimiento de Trabajadores y Obreros de Clase (MTOC): Lima.

Sindicato Unitario de los Trabajadores en la Educación del Perú (SUTEP) (Union of Peruvian Teachers): Camaná 550, Lima; tel. (1) 4276677; fax (1) 4268692; e-mail suteperu@yahoo.es; internet www.sutep.org.pe; f. 1972; Sec.-Gen. LUIS MUÑOZ.

Independent unions, representing an estimated 37% of trade unionists, include the Comité para la Coordinación Clasista y la Unificación Sindical, the Confederación de Campesinos Peruanos (CCP) and the Confederación Nacional Agraria (Pres. MIGUEL CLEMENTE ALEGRE).

Confederación Nacional de Comunidades Industriales (CONACI): Lima; co-ordinates worker participation in industrial management and profit-sharing.

The following agricultural organizations exist:

Confederación Nacional de Productores Agropecuarios de las Cuencas Cocaleras del Perú (CONPACCP): Lima; coca-growers' confederation; Sec.-Gen. NELSÓN PALOMINO.

Consejo Unitario Nacional Agrario (CUNA): f. 1983; represents 36 farmers' and peasants' orgs; including:

    Confederación Campesina del Perú (CCP): radical left-wing; Pres. ANDRÉS LUNA VARGAS; Sec. HUGO BLANCO.

    Organización Nacional Agraria (ONA): org. of dairy farmers and cattle breeders.

Transport

RAILWAYS

In 2006 there were some 1,691 km of track.

Ministry of Transport and Communications: see section on The Government (Ministries).

Consorcio Ferrocarriles del Perú: in July 1999, following the privatization of the state railway company, Empresa Nacional de Ferrocarriles (ENAFER), the above consortium won a 30-year concession to operate the following lines:

Empresa Minera del Centro del Perú SA—División Ferrocarriles (Centromín-Perú SA) (fmrly Cerro de Pasco Railway): Edif. Solgas, Avda Javier Prado Este 2175, San Borja, Apdo 2412, Lima 41; tel. (1) 4761010; fax (1) 4769757; acquired by Enafer-Perú in 1997; 212.2 km; Pres. Hernán Barreto; Gen. Man. Guillermo Guanilo.

Ferrocarril Transandino, SA (Southern Railway): Avenida Tacna y Arica 200, Arequipa; tel. (54) 215350; fax (54) 231603; internet www.ferrocarriltransandino.com; 915 km open; operates Ferrocarril del Sur y Oriente; also operates steamship service on Lake Titicaca; Man. Rómulo Guidino.

Ferrovías Central Andina, SA: Avda José Galvez Barrenechea 566, 5°, San Isidro, Lima; tel. (1) 2266363; e-mail ferroviasperu@fcca.com.pe; internet www.ferroviasperu.com.pe; f. 1999; operates Ferrocarril del Centro del Perú.

Tacna–Arica Ferrocarril (Tacna–Arica Railway): Avda Aldarracín 484, Tacna; 62 km open.

Private Railways

Ferrocarril Ilo–Toquepala–Cuajone: Apdo 2640, Lima; 219 km open, incl. five tunnels totalling 27 km; owned by the Southern Peru Copper Corpn for transporting copper supplies and concentrates only; CEO Oscar González Rocha; Gen. Dir, Operations Mauricio Peró.

Ferrocarril Supe–Barranca–Alpas: Barranca; 40 km open; Dirs Carlos García Gastañeta, Luis G. Miranda.

ROADS

There were an estimated 78,000 km of roads in Peru, of which approximately 30% were paved or semi-paved. The most important highways are: the Pan-American Highway (3,008 km), which runs southward from the Ecuadorean border along the coast to Lima; Camino del Inca Highway (3,193 km) from Piura to Puno; Marginal de la Selva (1,688 km) from Cajamarca to Madre de Dios; and the Trans-Andean Highway (834 km), which runs from Lima to Pucallpa on the River Ucayali via Oroya, Cerro de Pasco and Tingo María.

SHIPPING

Most trade is through the port of Callao, but there are 13 deep-water ports, mainly in northern Peru (including Salaverry, Pacasmayo and Paita) and in the south (including the iron-ore port of San Juan). There are river ports at Iquitos, Pucallpa and Yurimaguas, aimed at improving communications between Lima and Iquitos, and a further port is under construction at Puerto Maldonado.

Agencia Naviera Maynas, SA: Avda San Borja Norte 761, San Borja, Lima 41; tel. (1) 4752033; fax (1) 4759680; e-mail lima@navieramaynas.com.pe; f. 1996; Pres. R. Usseglio D.; Gen. Man. Roberto Melgar B.

Asociación Marítima del Perú: Avda Javier Prado Este 897, Of. 33, San Isidro, Apdo 3520, Lima 27; tel. and fax (1) 4221904; internet www.asmarpe.org.pe; f. 1957; asscn of 20 int. and Peruvian shipping cos; Pres. Juan José Salmón Balestra; Gen. Man. Guillermo E. Acosta Rodríguez.

Empresa Nacional de Puertos, SA (Enapu): Avda Contralmirante Raygada 110, Callao; tel. (1) 4299210; fax (1) 4691010; e-mail enapu@inconet.net.pe; internet www.enapu.com.pe; f. 1970; govt agency administering all coastal and river ports; Gen. Man. Jose Pablo Mejía Gonzalo.

Consorcio Naviero Peruano, SA: Avda República de Colombia 643, 7° y 8°, San Isidro, Lima 27; tel. (1) 4116500; fax (1) 4116599; e-mail cnp@cnpsa.com; internet www.cnpsa.com; f. 1959.

Naviera Humboldt, SA: Edif. Pacífico–Washington, 9°, Natalio Sánchez 125, Apdo 3639, Lima 1; tel. (1) 4334005; fax (1) 4337151; e-mail postmast@sorcomar.com.pe; internet www.humboldt.com.pe; f. 1970; cargo services; Pres. Augusto Bedoya Camere; Man. Dir Luis Freire R.

Naviera Universal, SA: Calle 41 No 894, Urb. Corpac, San Isidro, Apdo 10307, Lima 100; tel. (1) 4757020; fax (1) 4755233; Chair. Herbert C. Buerger.

Petrolera Transoceánica, SA (PETRANSO): San Isidro, Lima 27; tel. (1) 5139300; fax (1) 5139322; e-mail petranso@petranso.com; internet www.petranso.com; Gen. Man. Juan Villarán.

CIVIL AVIATION

Of Peru's 294 airports and airfields, the major international airport is Jorge Chávez Airport near Lima. Other important international airports are Coronel Francisco Secada Vignetta Airport, near Iquitos, Velasco Astete Airport, near Cusco, and Rodríguez Ballón Airport, near Arequipa.

Corporación Peruana de Aeropuertos y Aviación Comercial: Aeropuerto Internacional Jorge Chávez, Callao; tel. (1) 7081000; fax (1) 5745578; e-mail sugerencias@corpac.gob.pe; internet www.corpac.gob.pe; f. 1943; Pres. Walter Hugo Tello Castillo; Gen. Man. Luis Felipe Vallejo Leigh.

Domestic Airlines

Aero Condor: Juan de Arona 781, San Isidro, Lima; tel. (1) 4425215; fax (1) 2215783; internet www.aerocondor.com.pe; domestic services; Pres. Carlos Palacín Fernández.

LAN Perú, SA: Lima; tel. (1) 2138200; internet www.lan.com; f. 1999; operations temporarily suspended in Oct. 2004; Exec. Vice-Pres. Enrique Cueto P.

Star Perú: Avda Comandante Espinar 331, Miraflores, Lima 18; tel. (1) 7059000; fax (1) 3324789; e-mail atencionalcliente@starperu.com; internet www.starperu.com; f. 1997; operates services to eight domestic destinations; Gen. Man. Román Kasianov.

Tourism

Tourism is centred on Lima, with its Spanish colonial architecture, and Cusco, with its pre-Inca and Inca civilization, notably the 'lost city' of Machu Picchu. Lake Titicaca, lying at an altitude of 3,850 m above sea level, and the Amazon jungle region to the north-east are also popular destinations. From the mid-1990s there was evidence of a marked recovery in the tourism sector, which had been adversely affected by health and security concerns. In 2006 Peru received 1,634,745 visitors. Receipts from tourism in 2006 generated US $1,586m.

Comisión de Promoción del Perú (PromPerú): Edif. Mitinci, Calle Uno Oeste, 13°, Urb. Corpac, San Isidro, Lima 27; tel. (1) 2243279; fax (1) 2243323; e-mail postmaster@promperu.gob.pe; internet www.peru.info; f. 1993; Head of Tourism María del Pilar Lazarte Conroy; Gen. Man. María M. Seminario Marón.

THE PHILIPPINES

Introductory Survey

Location, Climate, Language, Religion, Flag, Capital

The Republic of the Philippines lies in the western Pacific Ocean, east of mainland South-East Asia. The island of Borneo is to the south-west, and New Guinea to the south-east. The principal islands of the Philippine archipelago are Luzon, in the north, and Mindanao, in the south. Between these two (which together account for 66% of the country's area) lie the 7,000 islands of the Visayas. The climate is maritime and tropical. It is generally hot and humid, except in the mountains. There is abundant rainfall, and the islands are frequently in the path of typhoons. At the 1995 census there were 102 languages; the most frequently used were Tagalog (by 29.3% of the population), Cebuano (21.2%), Ilocano (9.3%), Hiligaynon (Ilongo—9.1%) and Bicol (5.7%). Filipino, based on Tagalog, is the native national language. English is widely spoken, and Spanish is used in some communities. In 1991 94.2% of the population were Christians (84.1% Roman Catholics, 6.2% belonged to the Philippine Independent Church (Aglipayan) and 3.9% were Protestants). In 1990 an estimated 4.6% of the population were Muslims. The national flag (proportions 1 by 2) has two equal horizontal stripes, of blue and red, with a white triangle, enclosing a yellow 'Sun of Liberty' (with eight large and 16 small rays) and three five-pointed yellow stars (one in each corner), at the hoist. The capital is Manila, on the island of Luzon.

Recent History

The Philippines became a Spanish colony in the 16th century. During the Spanish–American War, the independence of the Philippines was declared on 12 June 1898 by Gen. Emilio Aguinaldo, leader of the revolutionary movement, with the support of the USA. Under the Treaty of Paris, signed in December 1898, Spain ceded the islands to the USA. A new Constitution, ratified by plebiscite in May 1935, gave the Philippines internal self-government and provided for independence after 10 years. During the Second World War the islands were occupied by Japanese forces from 1942, but, after Japan's surrender in 1945, US rule was restored. The Philippines became an independent republic on 4 July 1946, with Manuel Roxas as its first President. A succession of Presidents, effectively constrained by US economic interests and the Filipino land-owning class, did little to help the peasant majority or to curb disorder and political violence.

At elections in November 1965 the incumbent President, Diosdado Macapagal of the Liberal Party (LP), was defeated by Ferdinand Marcos of the Nacionalista Party (NP). Rapid development of the economy and infrastructure followed. President Marcos was re-elected in 1969. His second term was characterized by civil unrest and economic difficulties. During the early 1970s there was also an increase in guerrilla activity, by the New People's Army (NPA), the armed wing of the outlawed (Maoist) Communist Party of the Philippines (CPP), in the north of the country, and by the Moro National Liberation Front (MNLF), a Muslim separatist movement, in the south.

In September 1972, before completing the (then) maximum of two four-year terms of office, President Marcos declared martial law in order to deal with subversive activity and to introduce drastic reforms. The bicameral Congress was suspended, opposition leaders were arrested, the private armies of the landed oligarchs were disbanded, stringent press censorship was introduced, and Marcos began to rule by decree. In November a new Constitution was approved by a constitutional convention, and in January 1973 it was ratified by Marcos. It provided for a unicameral National Assembly and a Constitutional President, with executive power held by a Prime Minister, to be elected by the legislature. Transitional provisions gave the incumbent President the combined authority of the presidency (under the 1935 Constitution) and the premiership, without any fixed term of office. Under martial law, the definitive provisions of the new Constitution remained in abeyance.

A referendum in July 1973 approved Marcos's continuation in office beyond his elected term. Referendums in February 1975 and October 1976 approved the continuation of martial law and the adoption of constitutional amendments, including a provision for the formation of an interim assembly. In December 1977 a fourth referendum approved the extension of Marcos's presidential term.

Criticism of President Marcos became more widespread after November 1977, when a sentence of death was imposed by a military tribunal on the principal opposition leader, Benigno Aquino, Jr (a former senator and Secretary-General of the LP, who had been detained since 1972), for alleged murder, subversion and the possession of firearms. Marcos allowed a stay of execution, and conceded some relaxation of martial law in 1977. Elections to the interim National Assembly took place in April 1978. Opposition parties were allowed to participate, but the pro-Government Kilusang Bagong Lipunan (KBL—New Society Movement), founded in 1978 by Marcos and former members of the NP, won 151 of the Assembly's 165 elective seats. The Assembly was inaugurated in June, when Marcos was also confirmed as Prime Minister. Martial law remained in force, and Marcos retained the power to legislate by decree. Local elections held in January 1980 resulted in decisive victories for the KBL. In May Aquino was released from prison to undergo medical treatment in the USA, where he renewed his opposition to Marcos's regime.

In January 1981 martial law was ended, although Marcos retained most of his former powers. A referendum in April approved constitutional amendments that permitted Marcos to renew his presidential mandate by direct popular vote and to nominate a separate Prime Minister. In June, amid allegations of electoral malpractice, Marcos was re-elected President for a six-year term. In April 1982 the United Nationalist Democratic Organization (UNIDO), an alliance of opposition groups, formed an official coalition: it included Lakas ng Bayan (the People's Power Movement, founded by Aquino in 1978) and the Pilipino Democratic Party (PDP), which merged to form PDP-Laban in 1983.

In August 1983 Aquino, returning from exile in the USA, was shot dead on arrival at Manila airport. Rolando Galman, the alleged communist assassin, was killed immediately by military guards. A commission of inquiry, nominated by the Government, concluded that Aquino's murder had been a military conspiracy. However, the Supreme Court announced in December 1985 that the evidence submitted to the commission was inadmissible, acquitted the 26 military personnel who had been accused of conspiring to murder Aquino and upheld the Government's assertion that the assassin was Galman.

Aquino's death proved to be a turning-point in Philippine politics, uniting the opposition in its criticism of Marcos. At elections to the National Assembly in May 1984, public participation was high, and, after numerous accusations by the opposition of electoral fraud and corruption by Marcos, the opposition won 59 of the 183 elective seats.

In November 1985, in response to US pressure, Marcos announced that a presidential election would be held in February 1986, 18 months earlier than scheduled. Corazon Aquino, the widow of Benigno Aquino, was chosen as the UNIDO presidential candidate, in spite of her lack of political experience. More than 100 people were killed in violence during the election campaign. Vote-counting was conducted by the government-controlled National Commission on Elections (Comelec) and by the independent National Citizens' Movement for Free Elections (Namfrel). Allegations of electoral fraud and irregularities, apparently perpetrated by supporters of Marcos, were substantiated by international observers. The National Assembly declared Marcos the winner of the presidential election, with 10.8m. votes, compared with 9.3m. for Aquino, according to figures from Comelec. According to Namfrel figures (based on 69% of the total votes), Aquino was in the lead. Marcos immediately announced the resignation of the Cabinet, and declared his intention to establish a council of presidential advisers. Aquino rejected an offer to participate in the council.

Later in February 1986 Lt-Gen. (later Gen.) Fidel Ramos, the acting Chief of Staff of the Armed Forces, and Juan Ponce Enrile, the Minister of National Defense, along with about 300 troops, established a rebel headquarters in the Ministry of National

Defense (later moving to the police headquarters), stating that they no longer accepted Marcos's authority and asserting that Aquino was the rightful President. Attempts by forces loyal to Marcos to attack the rebels were foiled by large unarmed crowds, which gathered to protect them at the instigation of the Catholic Archbishop of Manila, Cardinal Jaime Sin. Troops supporting Ramos subsequently secured control of the government broadcasting station. Rival ceremonies were held, at which both Marcos and Aquino were sworn in as President. However, later the same day, under US pressure, Marcos agreed to withdraw, and left the Philippines for Hawaii.

President Aquino appointed her Vice-President, Salvador Laurel (the President of UNIDO), to be Prime Minister and Minister of Foreign Affairs, while Enrile retained the post of Minister of National Defense. Ramos was appointed Chief of Staff of the Armed Forces. At the end of February 1986 Aquino ordered the controversial release of all political prisoners, including communist leaders. In March the Government announced the restoration of habeas corpus, the abolition of press censorship and the suspension of local government elections (scheduled for May). The Government also secured the resignation of all Justices of the Supreme Court, as well as the resignation of Comelec members. Aquino announced that the 1973 Constitution was to be replaced by an interim document, providing for the immediate abolition of the National Assembly and for the inauguration of a provisional government, with the President being granted emergency powers. The post of Prime Minister was temporarily abolished, and in May a commission was appointed to draft a new constitution.

In March 1986 military leaders pledged their loyalty to Aquino. The Government then began to implement a programme of military reform, in accordance with the demands of officers of the Rebolusyonaryong Alyansang Makabayan (RAM—Nationalist Revolutionary Alliance—also known as the Reform the Armed Forces Movement), who had supported the February revolution. In September the Supreme Court ordered the retrial of the members of the military who had earlier been acquitted of the murder of Benigno Aquino. In September 1990 a special court convicted 16 members of the armed forces of the murder of both Aquino and Galman.

In July 1986 an abortive coup took place in Manila, led by Arturo Tolentino, a former Minister of Foreign Affairs and Marcos's vice-presidential candidate, and a group of 300 pro-Marcos troops. One of the principal reasons for military dissatisfaction was the new Government's conciliatory attitude towards communist insurgents. In June the Government had announced that formal negotiations for a cease-fire agreement would begin with representatives of the National Democratic Front (NDF), a left-wing group that included the CPP and the NPA (estimated to number 25,000–30,000 members). In October, however, increasing pressure from Enrile and the RAM prompted Aquino to threaten the insurgents with open warfare if a solution were not reached by the end of November. In late November a group of army officers attempted to gain control of several military camps and to replace Aquino with Nicanor Yniguez, a former Speaker of the National Assembly. The rebellion was quelled by Ramos and troops loyal to Aquino; Enrile was dismissed from the Cabinet. In January 1987 a further coup attempt by 500 disaffected soldiers was suppressed by forces loyal to Aquino, and an attempt by Marcos to return to the Philippines was thwarted by US officials.

In February 1987 a new Constitution was approved by 76% of voters in a national plebiscite. The new Constitution gave President Aquino a mandate to rule until 30 June 1992, and established an executive presidency (see Government, below). All members of the armed forces swore an oath of allegiance to the new Constitution. An order followed disbanding all 'fraternal organizations' (such as the RAM) within the armed forces, because they 'encouraged divisiveness'. Elections to the bicameral Congress of the Philippines took place on 11 May 1987, at which more than 83% of the electorate participated. Aquino's Lakas ng Bayan coalition secured 180 of the 200 elective seats in the House of Representatives and 22 of the 24 seats in the Senate.

In August 1987 Ramos and troops loyal to Aquino averted a serious coup attempt, when rebel officers (led by Col Gregorio Honasan, an officer closely associated with Enrile) occupied the army headquarters, and captured a radio and television station. In the intense fighting that ensued in Manila and Cebu, 53 people were killed. Honasan and his supporters fled, successfully evading capture until December. (However, Honasan escaped from detention in April 1988.) In December 1990 a military court sentenced 81 members of the armed forces to prison terms of up to 32 years for their part in the rebellion.

In October 1988 former President Marcos and his wife, Imelda, were indicted in the USA and charged with the illegal transfer into the country of some US $100m. that had allegedly been obtained by embezzlement and racketeering. In November thousands of civilian supporters of Marcos entered Manila and distributed leaflets demanding a military rebellion to overthrow Aquino, before being dispersed by the armed forces. In February 1989 Laurel (who had formally dissociated himself from Aquino) began to campaign for Marcos to be permitted to return to the Philippines. In May Marcos's NP was revived, with Laurel as President and Enrile as Secretary-General.

In September 1989 the Philippine Government began the first of 35 planned civil suits against Marcos *in absentia* on charges of corruption. However, the former President died in Hawaii at the end of September. The Supreme Court prohibited the return of Marcos's body. Imelda Marcos was acquitted of charges of fraud and of the illegal transfer of stolen funds into the USA in New York in July 1990.

In December 1989 an abortive coup was staged by members of two élite military units, in collusion with the now illicit RAM and officers loyal to Marcos. President Aquino subsequently addressed a rally of 100,000 supporters, accusing Laurel and Enrile (who were both included in an eight-member provisional junta named by the rebels) of involvement in the coup attempt. At the end of August 1990 Aquino expressed willingness to hold discussions both with dissident troops (who had perpetrated a series of bombings of allegedly corrupt businesses owned by US interests or associated with the Aquino Government) and with communist rebels (who had unilaterally declared a cease-fire in Manila and in northern areas affected by an earthquake in July), in an effort to achieve a general reconciliation. Opposition leaders, including Enrile (who had been charged with rebellion), were also invited to attend. In early September Aquino belatedly suspended offensives against the NPA in the affected areas. However, later in that month the NPA ended the truce. The dissident members of the armed forces also continued their campaign to destabilize the Government.

In July 1991 Ramos resigned as Secretary of National Defense in order to contest the presidential election (scheduled for 1992). Having failed to secure the nomination of the ruling party, Laban ng Demokratikong Pilipino (LDP, formed in 1988 by members of pro-Government parties), Ramos, with Aquino's endorsement, resigned from the LDP and registered a new party, EDSA-LDP, with the support of 25 former LDP members of Congress. (EDSA was the popular acronym for the Epifanio de los Santos Avenue, the main site of the February 1986 uprising.) The party, which subsequently altered its title to Lakas ng EDSA, formed an alliance with the National Union of Christian Democrats to become Lakas-NUCD. The Roman Catholic Church extended its support to the LDP's candidate, Ramon Mitra, and criticized Ramos, a Protestant, for his involvement in the Marcos regime.

In February 1992 a prominent human rights organization, Amnesty International, published a report accusing the Aquino administration of acquiescence in violations of human rights by the armed forces. The report alleged that 550 extrajudicial killings had taken place during 1988–91. The armed forces denied the report's findings. The NPA had killed 563 members of the armed forces between January and April 1991.

On 11 May 1992 elections took place to select the President, Vice-President, 12 senators, 200 members of the House of Representatives and 17,014 local officials. Fidel Ramos was elected to the presidency, winning 23.6% of the votes cast; his closest rivals were Miriam Defensor Santiago, a former Secretary of Agrarian Reform (with 19.7%), and Eduardo Cojuangco (Aquino's estranged cousin, whose wing of the NP had been renamed the Nationalist People's Coalition—NPC) (18.2%). The success of Ramos and the high level of support for Santiago was widely regarded as a rejection of traditional patronage party politics, since neither candidate was supported by a large-scale party organization. However, in the legislative elections the LDP (the only party that had local bases in every province) won 16 of the 24 seats in the Senate and 89 of the 200 elective seats in the House of Representatives.

Following his inauguration on 30 June 1992, President Ramos formed a new administration that included six members of the outgoing Government and many senior business executives. Despite his party's poor representation in Congress, Ramos managed to gain the support of the NPC, the LP and 55 defectors (now known as Laban) from the LDP, to form a 'rainbow coalition', comprising 145 of the 200 elected members of the House of Representatives. The Senate remained under the control of the LDP.

In July 1992 Ramos formed the Presidential Anti-Crime Commission (PACC), headed by Joseph Estrada, the Vice-President, to combat organized crime, particularly the increase in abduction for ransom. It emerged that members of the Philippine National Police (PNP) were largely responsible for the abductions, and in August the Chief of Police resigned. In April 1993, following a review of the PNP, Ramos ordered the discharge of hundreds of personnel. There was also a serious decline in public respect for the judiciary, following allegations that seven Supreme Court judges were accepting bribes from drugs-dealers and other criminal syndicates. In February Congress adopted legislation (which was signed into law in December) to reinstate the death penalty, which had been banned under the 1987 Constitution.

On assuming power, Ramos gave priority to persuading mutinous right-wing soldiers, communist insurgents and Muslim separatists to abandon their armed struggle. In July 1992 two communist leaders were conditionally released, and Ramos submitted to Congress an amnesty proclamation for about 4,500 members of the NPA, the MNLF and renegade former members of the armed forces who had already applied for amnesty. In August the National Unification Commission (NUC) was formed to consult rebel groups and formulate a viable amnesty programme. Later that month Ramos ordered the temporary release from prison of more communist leaders, including the Commander of the NPA, Romulo Kintanar, and the NDF Spokesman, Saturnino Ocampo, and also of 16 rebel soldiers. In the same month the Government began discussions with exiled representatives of the NDF in the Netherlands.

In September 1992 Ramos repealed anti-subversion legislation, in place since 1957, that proscribed the CPP. Nevertheless, the exiled leadership of the NDF issued a statement to the effect that the CPP would continue its armed struggle, although there was a widening division within the CPP over co-operation with the NUC. Jose Maria Sison, a founder member of the CPP who had been based in the Netherlands since his release from prison in 1986, resumed the party chairmanship in April 1992. However, his election to the leadership was not recognized by all party members. In December Sison accused his opponents, including Kintanar, of collusion with the Ramos administration.

In July 1993 the CPP's influential Manila-Rizal regional committee publicly broke away from the CPP Central Committee led by Sison. This followed the attempted dissolution by Sison of the region's leading committee and its armed unit, the Alex Boncayao Brigade (ABB), accused of factionalism and military excesses. The Manila-Rizal organization, which comprised about 40% of CPP members, was subsequently joined by the CPP regional committee of the Visayas. In October four communist leaders, including Kintanar, were expelled from the CPP and the NPA for refusing to recognize the authority of Sison.

Negotiations between the Government and the NDF in 1994–96 were marred by their failure to agree terms for the granting of immunity for NDF members and the arrest and subsequent release of a number of leading members of the organization. In March 1998 the Government and the NDF signed a Comprehensive Agreement on Respect for Human Rights and International Law, the first of four agreements that would complete the peace process.

In December 1992 seven military renegades, including Honasan, emerged from hiding to sign a preliminary agreement to take part in talks with the Government. Discussions between the NUC and representatives of the RAM and the Young Officers' Union (YOU—a progressive offshoot of the RAM, which was alleged to have played an important role in the December 1989 coup attempt) began in January 1993, but were subsequently suspended. In February 1994 it was announced that peace negotiations with the RAM and the YOU would remain suspended, pending the release of six military detainees. In the following month Ramos proclaimed a general amnesty for all rebels and for members of the security forces charged with offences committed during counter-insurgency operations, as recommended by the NUC; however, the amnesty did not include persons convicted of torture, arson, massacre, rape and robbery. The RAM rejected the amnesty on the grounds that it failed to address the causes of the rebellion, while Ocampo dismissed the proclamation as being biased against the communist rebels. Following agreement between the RAM and the Government during 1994 on certain government programmes and the issue of electoral reform, in 1995 formal negotiations resumed. In October the RAM and the YOU signed a peace agreement with the Government, which provided for the return of the rebels' military weapons within 90 days and the reintegration of members of the two organizations into the armed forces.

In September 1993, with the permission of President Ramos, Marcos's remains were returned to the Philippines, and a funeral service was conducted in the former President's native province of Ilocos Norte. Later in that month Imelda Marcos (who had returned to the Philippines in 1991, with Aquino's permission, to stand trial on charges of fraud and tax evasion) was convicted of corruption and sentenced to 18 years' imprisonment; she remained at liberty pending an appeal against the conviction. In February 1994 a court in Hawaii, awarded US $2,000m. in punitive damages to 10,000 Filipinos tortured under President Marcos's administration, following a court ruling in October 1992 that victims of abuses of human rights under the Marcos regime could sue his estate for compensation. Imelda Marcos announced that she would appeal against the decision. Further charges of embezzlement were filed against her in April and June 1994 and in September 1995.

On 8 May 1995 elections were held to contest 12 of the 24 seats in the Senate, the 204 elective seats in the House of Representatives, 76 provincial governorships and more than 17,000 local government positions. Prior to the elections, in which an estimated 80% of all eligible voters participated, more than 80 people were killed in campaign violence. The ruling coalition won the vast majority (about 70%) of seats in the House of Representatives and an electoral alliance between Lakas-NUCD and the LDP (Lakas-Laban) won nine of the 12 seats in the Senate. One of the three opposition seats was secured by Honasan, despite a campaign by Aquino against his candidacy. Imelda Marcos secured a seat in the House of Representatives, having been allowed to contest the election pending the outcome of her appeal, although she was not permitted to take her seat in Congress until November, following a ruling in her favour by the Supreme Court.

During 1995–97 Ramos's supporters campaigned to amend the constitutional stipulation that restricted the President to a single term of office; however, the Senate opposed the proposal. In September 1997 a rally organized by Cardinal Sin, to protest against any such constitutional change, was attended by more than 500,000 demonstrators. The rally was supported by Corazon Aquino as well as influential business executives, who attributed the rapid decline of the peso, in part, to the insecurity created by speculation regarding Ramos's ambitions for a second term of office. Prior to the rally Ramos finally stated categorically that he would not contest the presidential election.

The formation of an opposition grouping, the Laban ng Makabayang Masang Pilipino (LaMMP—Struggle of Nationalist Filipino Masses), to contest the elections scheduled for May 1998 was announced in June 1997. The LaMMP was composed of the Partido ng Masang Pilipino, led by Estrada, the LDP, led by Edgardo Angara (which had withdrawn from its alliance with Lakas-NUCD in February 1996), and the NCP, led by Ernesto Maceda. In December 1997 Estrada and Angara were formally endorsed as the LaMMP's presidential and vice-presidential candidates respectively. The campaign was characterized by an emphasis on personalities and scandals and failed to address substantive policy issues.

Elections to the presidency, the vice-presidency, the Senate, the House of Representatives, provincial governorships and local government positions took place on 11 May 1998; an estimated 80% of the electorate participated in the polls. Although an estimated 51 people were killed in pre-election violence (mostly in the southern province of Mindanao), the elections were considered relatively orderly and free. Estrada was elected to the presidency with 39.9% of the votes cast. His closest rival was the Lakas-NUCD candidate, Jose de Venecia (who was responsible for negotiations with both the Islamist separatists and the NDF), who secured 15.9% of the votes. The vice-presidency was won by Gloria Macapagal Arroyo (the daughter of former President Diosdado Macapagal), who had supported de Venecia's candidacy. According to Comelec, seven of the victorious senators were members of the LaMMP, while the other five were Lakas-NUCD candidates. However, Lakas-NUCD dominated the House of Representatives, winning 106 seats compared with only 66 for the LaMMP. In a development indicative of the weakness of the party system, many congressional members subsequently defected to Estrada's party, which was renamed Laban ng Masang Pilipino (Fight of the Filipino Masses).

President Estrada's election altered the situation for the family and former associates of Marcos. In June 1998 the Solicitor-General, Romeo de la Cruz, recommended that the Supreme Court acquit Imelda Marcos of charges of corruption. A ruling by the Supreme Court in January had upheld her appeal against one charge of corruption but dismissed an appeal against her conviction in 1993 on a second corruption charge, which carried a sentence of up to 12 years' imprisonment. She remained at liberty pending the reconsideration of the verdict by the court. However, Ramos dismissed de la Cruz and his appointed successor, and withdrew the Government's petition for acquittal. Marcos was, nevertheless, acquitted in October 1998, although numerous civil suits remained pending against her. In December Marcos announced plans to initiate a legal appeal to recover 500,000m. pesos in assets allegedly belonging to her late husband, claiming that he had entrusted the money to close associates who had refused to return it. The election of the Marcoses' daughter, Imee, to Congress and of their son, Ferdinand Jr, to the governorship of Ilocos Norte was indicative of the general rehabilitation of the Marcos family. Estrada favoured a negotiated settlement with the Marcos family to resolve the dispute over funds misappropriated by the former President and also gave his support to the burial of Marcos in the cemetery of National Heroes. However, popular outrage prompted Imelda Marcos to postpone the burial indefinitely in the national interest.

In January 1998 the Swiss Supreme Court ruled that the total sum of US $560m. of Marcos's wealth in Swiss bank accounts be released (to be disbursed by the Philippine courts). The Swiss Supreme Court rejected an appeal by the Marcos family in early April. Later in that month the Marcoses filed a new petition, requesting that the Swiss Federal Court review the case; this request was also rejected. In February 1999 the Marcos family agreed to pay a total of $150m. in damages to 9,539 victims of human rights abuses. In March the Philippines Supreme Court upheld a 1990 decision by the Bureau of Internal Revenue assessing the unpaid inheritance tax owed by the heirs of Ferdinand Marcos at 23,500m. pesos. (In July 2003 the Philippines Supreme Court ruled that the sum of approximately $658m. that had been held by Ferdinand Marcos in several Swiss bank accounts should be released to the Philippine Government.)

Joseph Estrada was inaugurated as President at the end of June 1998. In his inaugural address he reiterated campaign pledges to eradicate poverty and corruption, but also assured the business sector that he would continue Ramos's programme of economic reform. His new Cabinet, which elicited widespread approval, comprised members from a wide political and social spectrum, including wealthy ethnic Chinese business executives, former associates of Marcos, and allies from Estrada's career as mayor and senator, as well as former activists from the communist movement and left-wing non-governmental organizations (NGOs). Five members of Lakas-NUCD were allocated portfolios and Ramos accepted a post as Senior Adviser. However, Estrada was criticized for appointing friends and relatives to lucrative and influential positions. Additional concerns about a reversion to the Marcos era of 'cronyism' were raised by the return to prominence of former Marcos associates, some of whom had made substantial financial contributions to Estrada's presidential campaign fund.

In spite of widespread apprehension regarding his leadership abilities, Estrada was credited with several successes during his first year in office. His creation in July 1998 of the Presidential Anti-Organized Crime Task Force resulted in a dramatic reduction in kidnappings for ransom. The elimination of several large organized syndicates was achieved by granting autonomy from the PNP (which had been implicated in many incidents) to the head of the Task Force, Brig.-Gen. Panfilo Lacson. (However, Lacson's appointment attracted criticism from human rights organizations, owing to his conviction with other military officers in 1993 of the illegal detention and torture of anti-Government dissidents in the 1970s.) Estrada effectively abolished 'pork barrel' funds (state funds from which congress members financed projects in their constituencies), which had led to corruption and the reinforcement of patronage politics.

The strained relationship between President Estrada and former President Ramos deteriorated in March 1999 when the Senate Blue Ribbon Committee, which had been established to investigate anomalies in government and was led by a member of Estrada's party, Aquilino Pimentel, recommended the prosecution of Ramos and five members of his Cabinet for the misappli-

cation of public funds to celebrate the centennial anniversary of Philippine independence in June 1998. Obliged to justify his actions before a newly formed Independent Citizens' Committee, Ramos claimed that the accusations were politically motivated and designed to distract attention from investigations into misconduct by Estrada's friends and relatives. The Committee's final report recommended the indictment for corruption of the former Vice-President, Salvador Laurel, who had led the centennial celebration committee, and fines for Ramos and his Secretary of Finance, Salvador Enrique, for failing to prevent Laurel's abuses.

In late 1999 President Estrada's hitherto excellent popularity ratings began to decline amid increasing concern about 'cronyism' and corruption in his administration. In August Aquino and Cardinal Sin mobilized 100,000 demonstrators in a Rally for Democracy to protest particularly against government plans to amend the 1987 Constitution. Estrada's stated aim in amending the Constitution was to extend economic deregulation by altering the provisions limiting to 40% foreign ownership of land and public utilities. While in any case opposed to these proposals, critics feared the potential removal from the Constitution of the stipulation limiting the President to a single term of office. Later in August 1999 Estrada relaunched the ruling coalition, restyling it the Lapian ng Masang Pilipino (LAMP—Party of the Filipino Masses). Estrada's popularity was also adversely affected by his failure to fulfil his pledges to alleviate poverty. Little progress had been made with regard to land redistribution or 'food security' apart from the rehousing of 25,000 poor in Manila in the year to September.

Following a report by the World Bank in November 1999 alleging that 20% of the Philippine budget was lost to corruption, President Estrada pledged to intensify investigations of officials suspected of dishonesty. In the same month, in a further attempt to dispel criticism, Estrada established the EDSA People Power Commission to promote the ideals of the 1986 uprising; its 15 members included Aquino, Ramos and Estrada. Also in November, having achieved significant reductions in kidnappings for ransom in his previous post, Lacson was appointed to head the PNP. However, these measures proved inadequate to reverse a trend that was compounded by the unexpected resignation of the respected Secretary of Finance, Edgardo Espiritu, in January 2000 and his subsequent accusations of undue influence exerted by unelected associates of Estrada. Estrada responded to growing public dissatisfaction by announcing the reform of his administration. He dismissed his informal advisers, replacing them with a six-member Economic Co-ordinating Council to promote coherence in economic affairs, and recruited five eminent business leaders to act as an economic advisory council. The proposed constitutional reforms were suspended and replaced by plans to achieve economic liberalization through legislation. Estrada's attempts to improve his popularity were swiftly undermined by the testimony in January of the Chairman of the Securities and Exchange Commission (SEC), Perfecto Yasay, to a Senate Committee investigating possible illegal share trading. Yasay alleged that Estrada had pressed him to exonerate Estrada's close associate, Dante Tan, who was suspected of illegally manipulating the share price of BW Resources Corporation. Estrada denied the intervention, although he admitted telephoning Yasay four times in relation to the investigation. Despite frequent rumours of an impending coup attempt and a request for Estrada's resignation by Teofisto Guingona, the President of Lakas-NUCD, an attempt to mobilize anti-Estrada sentiment in a mass protest in April received very little support.

In October 2000 the Philippines was engulfed by a political crisis that arose as a result of allegations, made to an investigative committee of the Senate by the Governor of Ilocos Sur, Luis Singson, that President Estrada had accepted large sums of money as bribes from illegal gambling businesses. Despite the President's denial of these allegations, opposition parties announced their intention to begin the process of impeaching him. Earlier in the month Vice-President Gloria Arroyo had announced her resignation from the Cabinet, in which she served as Secretary of Social Welfare and Development. The fact that she did not relinquish the vice-presidency at the same time led to speculation that she was preparing to succeed Estrada in the event of his being forced out of office. Following her resignation from the Cabinet, Arroyo established an alliance of opposition parties.

In mid-November 2000 the House of Representatives endorsed the impeachment of the President after more than one-third of its members signed a petition favouring this action. Supporters of

Estrada condemned the impeachment proceedings as unconstitutional since they had not been submitted to a formal vote in the House of Representatives. (The Speaker of the House had ruled that such a vote was unnecessary because more than one-third of its members had signed the petition.) Estrada himself welcomed an impeachment trial in the Senate as an opportunity to prove his innocence, and he was formally summoned by the Senate. The legal action pursued by Estrada in order to force the Senate to dismiss the charges against him was unsuccessful, and at the beginning of December he pleaded not guilty to charges of bribery, corruption, betrayal of public trust and violation of the Constitution. However, the impeachment trial in the Senate was adjourned indefinitely in January 2001 after prosecutors failed to obtain the disclosure of bank records as evidence against him. This effective acquittal of the President provoked mass demonstrations against him. Estrada had lost the support of many members of his Cabinet, the police and the armed forces, and, in response to a request by Vice-President Gloria Arroyo, the Supreme Court declared the presidency to be vacant.

Gloria Arroyo was sworn in as President on 20 January 2001, and by the end of the month most of the positions in her new Cabinet had been filled. The new administration moved quickly to prevent Estrada, members of his family and his associates from leaving the Philippines and insisted that the former President would be prosecuted for his alleged crimes. However, the manner in which Arroyo had assumed the presidency exacerbated the continued political crisis and raised fears of an impending military *coup d'état*. Estrada continued to assert that he remained the legitimate Head of State and pledged to take legal action to regain the presidency. In March, however, the Supreme Court affirmed the legitimacy of Arroyo's office. In April Estrada was formally indicted for a number of alleged offences, including one of economic plunder, which was punishable by the death penalty. Estrada was arrested for the first time in mid-April and charged with corruption and perjury. At the beginning of May there was violent unrest in Manila when supporters of Estrada attempted to storm the presidential palace. Three members of the Senate were arrested for having allegedly conspired to bring down the Government, and President Arroyo declared a state of rebellion, which permitted her to deploy the armed forces to quell the unrest. Estrada, who had subsequently been rearrested, was removed to a detention centre outside Manila, having had his application for bail denied.

Legislative and local elections were held on 14 May 2001. Lakas-NUCD secured 87 seats in the House of Representatives, followed by the NPC with 62. The People Power Coalition (PPC)—a coalition of Lakas-NUCD, the LP and several smaller parties, which had been formed by President Arroyo to contest the election—won eight seats in the Senate, while allies of the Laban ng Demokratikong Pilipino-Puwersa ng Masa (LDP-PnM)—the opposition coalition formed to support Estrada—secured four. The remaining seat went to an independent candidate. President Arroyo thus succeeded in securing a majority in both chambers. As a result of violence throughout the election period, 83 people died. The elections were further marred by reports of widespread corruption.

In October 2001 Estrada's trial on charges of perjury and plunder finally commenced; he had refused to enter a plea to any of the charges against him. In November the Supreme Court rejected a legal challenge brought by Estrada against his trial and affirmed the constitutionality of the anti-plunder law under which he was being tried. After the suspension of two senior judges involved in the trial (one following complaints that cases under his remit were proceeding too slowly and the other following defence allegations that he lacked impartiality), the trial was adjourned and resumed in January 2002 in a special anti-graft court. In February Estrada instructed his entire legal team to resign in protest at what he alleged to be a prejudiced court. In July 2004 the court ruled that Estrada had not been guilty of money-laundering when he opened a bank account under a different name in 2000. A few days later the court approved Estrada's transfer from military detention to house arrest. In September 2007 Estrada was convicted of plunder, having misappropriated some US $80m. during his tenure of office, and sentenced to life imprisonment; he was found not guilty of the charge of perjury. He denounced the verdict as being a 'political decision'. However, after apparently agreeing not to seek political office, Estrada was pardoned by President Arroyo in October. The pardon, and in particular the swiftness with which it had been granted, provoked considerable controversy, prompting not only concern that it would undermine efforts to combat official corruption, but also speculation that it was politically motivated.

In October 2001 Jose Miguel Arroyo, the husband of the President, was investigated by the Senate over allegations that he had diverted funds from a state lottery in order to finance electoral campaigns for prospective senators. In the same month Imelda Marcos was rearrested on four charges of corruption, connected to the suspected plunder of the economy under the regime of her late husband, before being released on bail; she appeared in court in November and denied all the charges.

In June 2002 Senator John Osmeña defected to the opposition, depriving the PPC of its narrow majority in the Senate. Owing to the simultaneous absence abroad of another senator, proceedings in the Senate were suspended for almost two months. In October the Senate gave its assent to the Absentee Voting Bill, which rendered Filipino citizens living and working abroad eligible to vote in future legislative and presidential elections. The bill was enacted in February 2003. In November 2002 President Arroyo announced her intention to adopt a strict policy aimed at ending the corruption apparently endemic within the Government. In the following month the Director-General of the National Economic and Development Authority (NEDA), Dante Canlas, resigned from his post at the request of the President. Later in December the President announced that she did not intend to contest the presidential election scheduled to take place in 2004, claiming that her decision was motivated by a desire to spare the country further political division. She subsequently stated her intention to revive the Council of State, an advisory body originally established by her father, Diosdado Macapagal, during his time in power, while holding exploratory talks with leading members of the opposition with the possible aim of forming a 'government of national unity'.

In July 2003 approximately 350 disaffected members of the armed forces staged a mutiny, taking control of a shopping centre in the Manila commercial district of Makati. The rebels, who demanded the resignation of the President and the Secretary of National Defense, finally surrendered peacefully. While the Government claimed that the mutiny constituted an attempted *coup d'état*, those who had participated claimed that they were merely seeking a chance to air their grievances, which included, most notably, allegations that senior military personnel were guilty of systematic collusion with Muslim rebels in the south. Later in that month the head of military intelligence, Brig.-Gen. Victor Corpus, who had been accused of misconduct by the rebels, resigned. In the aftermath of the mutiny President Arroyo declared a nation-wide state of rebellion, which was removed in August. In that month charges were filed against more than 1,000 people in connection with the coup attempt. Senator Gregorio Honasan was charged with involvement, along with six of his associates. Meanwhile, Secretary of National Defense Angelo Reyes resigned, while denying the allegations of corruption; Eduardo Ermita was appointed as his successor in September. In November the criminal charges of planning a *coup d'état* that had been filed against 290 of those who had taken part in the July mutiny were abandoned; however, it was announced that the 31 officers believed to have led the mutiny would be tried by a civilian court. In addition, all 321 soldiers were to appear at a court martial on separate charges related to their involvement in the mutiny. Six of the leaders of the uprising publicly apologized to the President in September 2004. In May 2005 the court martial sentenced 184 of the soldiers to one year's confinement with hard labour, demotion in rank and forfeiture of two-thirds of their basic salaries for three–six months; the soldiers had pleaded guilty to lesser offences in exchange for the withdrawal of a mutiny charge against them. Charges against a number of others had already been dismissed, while the court martial of a further 67 soldiers and 29 suspected leaders of the mutiny continued. In April 2007 54 soldiers, mostly junior officers, were sentenced to seven years and six months in prison for their involvement in the mutiny; their sentences were reduced to four years in June, and they were later dishonourably discharged from the armed forces, before being released in December. Charges against several other officers were dismissed. In August, having pleaded guilty, 12 of the 29 officers believed to have led the mutiny were convicted of the charge of conduct unbecoming an officer by the court martial and ordered to be discharged from service. A further five officers changed their plea before the court martial to guilty of conduct unbecoming an officer in April 2008, and were similarly ordered to be discharged; two of the officers were additionally sentenced to seven-and-a-half years' imprisonment for conduct prejudicial to good order and military discipline. In June 11 other officers reversed their pleas to guilty before the court martial. Meanwhile, the civilian trial of the 29 officers on separate charges of mounting a coup was ongoing. In April, having changed their plea to guilty, two of the officers were sentenced to life imprisonment, while seven received prison terms ranging from six to 12 years; however, all nine were granted presidential pardons in May. The trial of the other officers continued in early 2009. (In November 2007 several of the defendants had briefly attempted to stage a further coup, but soon surrendered—see below.)

In October 2003, in a reversal of her statement of December 2002, President Arroyo announced that she did intend to contest the next presidential election, scheduled to take place in May 2004. Vice-President Teofisto Guingona resigned from Lakas-NUCD (which restyled itself as Lakas-Christian Muslim Democrats—Lakas-CMD—in 2003), in advance of the announcement, citing differences of principle, but he retained his cabinet position. In November 2003 Secretary of Finance Jose Isidro Camacho tendered his resignation; Under-Secretary Juanita Amatong was appointed to succeed him. In the same month two armed men occupied the air traffic control tower at the Ninoy Aquino International Airport in Manila, protesting against government corruption and prompting speculation concerning another coup attempt. Both men were shot dead by the police.

In December 2003 Secretary of Foreign Affairs Blas Ople died unexpectedly; Under-Secretary Delia Domingo-Albert was appointed as his successor. Meanwhile, in advance of the legislative and presidential elections to be held in May 2004, Senator Edgardo Angara, President of the opposition LDP, announced that his party had merged with the PDP-Laban Party and Estrada's Puwersa ng Masang Pilipino (PMP) to form the Koalisyon ng Nagkakaisang Pilipino (KNP—Coalition of the United Filipino). The KNP subsequently announced that it had nominated the film actor Fernando Poe, Jr, as its presidential candidate. Later in the same month, however, former chief of police Brig.-Gen. Panfilo Lacson stated his intention to stand as the official presidential candidate of the LDP, supported by another faction of the party, which was led by its Secretary-General, Agapito Aquino. The former Secretary of Education, Culture and Sports, Raul Roco, who had resigned in August 2002, secured the presidential nomination of Aksyon Demokratiko. The fifth presidential candidate to emerge was Eduardo Villanueva, the leader of the 'Jesus is Lord' Church, who was to represent the newly established Bangon Pilipinas (Rise Philippines). The incumbent President Arroyo formed a new coalition in support of her candidacy—the Koalisyon ng Katapatan at Karanasan sa Kinabukasan (K-4). The alliance consisted of Lakas-CMD, the LP, Reporma and Probinsya Muna Development Intiatives (PROMDI). The coalition replaced the PPC, which had effectively been disbanded following the withdrawal of its most important members.

On 10 May 2004 elections took place to select the President, Vice-President, 12 members of the Senate and 212 members of the House of Representatives, and also to choose more than 17,000 local officials. Almost 100 people were killed as a result of violence during the campaign period, despite the deployment of some 230,000 police officers and troops at polling stations throughout the country. Arroyo won a narrow victory in the presidential election, receiving 40.0% of the votes cast, compared with Poe's 36.5%. Poe refused to accept the result, alleging widespread fraud. Noli de Castro, representing Lakas-CMD, was elected to the vice-presidency. Lakas-CMD also performed well in the legislative elections, securing 93 of the 212 elective seats in the House of Representatives, while the NPC won 54 seats and the LP 34. Seven candidates of the K-4 coalition, dominated by Lakas-CMD, were elected to the Senate, with the remaining five seats taken by the KNP.

Having secured an electoral mandate for her presidency, Arroyo was sworn in for a second term of office at the end of June 2004. During her inauguration speech she pledged to curb corruption, to improve basic services and to reform the economy, notably promising to create 6m. new jobs during her six-year term. On the day before the ceremony police had dispersed several thousand supporters of Poe who were demonstrating against the Government in Manila and, in a separate incident, arrested four Muslims suspected of planning a bomb attack in the capital during the inauguration. In early July Angelo Reyes, a close ally of the President, returned to the Government as Secretary of the Interior and Local Government, following the resignation of Jose Lina from that position. Later in that month Poe and his defeated vice-presidential candidate, Loren Legarda, lodged separate complaints with the Supreme Court, demanding a recount of votes cast in more than 118,000 voting precincts on the grounds of massive electoral fraud. Poe died in December after suffering a stroke.

In mid-August 2004 Arroyo announced a cabinet reorganization, in which former Executive Secretary Alberto Romulo succeeded Delia Domingo-Albert as Secretary of Foreign Affairs, while Eduardo Ermita, hitherto Secretary of National Defense, replaced Romulo, and Avelino Cruz, the President's former chief legal adviser, was allocated the defence portfolio. The Government launched a medium-term development plan for 2004–10 in October. As well as setting various economic targets, the plan proposed a number of political reforms, some of which would require the amendment of the Constitution. Major changes envisaged included the introduction of a federal form of government and a unicameral parliamentary system; the revision of restrictive provisions on foreign ownership; and the reform of the electoral system.

In late 2004 and early 2005 a number of military officers were charged with corruption, as the authorities demonstrated their commitment to eradicating corruption in the armed forces. The most notorious case was that of Maj.-Gen. Carlos Garcia, the former comptroller of the armed forces, who was to answer charges relating to 143m. pesos in unexplained wealth that he had allegedly amassed. He went on trial before both a military court and the special anti-graft court in November 2004. (Garcia was sentenced to two years' hard labour by the military court in December 2005; in February 2009 the anti-graft court found him guilty of perjury and sentenced him to two years' imprisonment, but his trial on plunder charges was ongoing.)

In January 2005 the Secretary of Finance, Juanita Amatong, and the Secretary of Energy, Vicente Perez, resigned from office. The finance portfolio was allocated to Cesar Purisima, hitherto Secretary of Trade and Industry, who was replaced by Juan Santos. Perez agreed to remain in the post until the end of March, when he was succeeded by Raphael Lotilla.

In June 2005 a major political scandal arose over the issue of a recording of a telephone conversation held between President Arroyo and an election official while votes in the 2004 presidential poll were still in the process of being counted. Arroyo acknowledged that she had made an 'error of judgement' by speaking with an election official at that time, but strenuously denied having tried to influence the outcome of the poll. Secretary of Agriculture Arthur Yap tendered his resignation from the Cabinet at the end of the month in order to focus his efforts on contesting tax evasion charges filed against him following the purchase of property in Pasig City (he was reappointed in October 2006). Further resignations from the Cabinet followed in July 2005, in protest at what the departing ministers, who included Secretary of Finance Purisima, perceived to be the illegality of Arroyo's presidency. Later in that month Arroyo announced that Purisima's position was to be assumed by Margarito Teves. In September Congress formally rejected three separate impeachment cases against Arroyo, deeming the complaints too weak to stand up to legislative scrutiny. In January 2006 the influential 120-member Catholic Bishops' Conference urged that investigations into the allegations of alleged malpractice against Arroyo be continued since previous efforts were perceived to have been undermined by 'acts of evasion and obstruction of truth'. In February the National Bureau of Investigation announced that it had concluded its own investigation into the episode, since (because the recording of the conversation had been adjudged to have been tampered with) there was no longer any sound basis for continuing with the proceedings. In the same month an estimated 20,000 people marched through the capital to demand President Arroyo's resignation as they marked the 20th anniversary of the ousting of President Marcos. In March it was reported that members of the opposition were compiling evidence with which to file another impeachment complaint against Arroyo, regarding not only the vote-manipulation allegations but also accusations concerning the mismanagement of a sum of 728m. pesos that had been intended to fund a fertilizer scheme, which, it was claimed, had been misappropriated by Arroyo and her allies to help fund her presidential election campaign in 2004. A fresh impeachment motion against Arroyo was defeated in the House of Representatives in August 2006. A Senate inquiry into the vote-manipulation allegations commenced in September 2007; however, in December 2008 the Supreme Court barred the Senate from continuing its investigations because the chamber had not published its rules of procedure before initiating the inquiry. In February 2009 the

Senate Blue Ribbon Committee recommended the prosecution of former Under-Secretary of Agriculture Jocelyn Bolante and nine others in connection with the fertilizer scandal, but found no direct evidence to link Arroyo to the controversy.

Meanwhile, in February 2006 President Arroyo effected a minor reorganization of the Cabinet. Notable changes included the transfer of the Secretary of the Budget and Management, Romulo Neri, to the position of Director-General of NEDA, and the appointment of Rolando Andaya, Jr, as Neri's replacement. Ronaldo Puno was appointed to the position of Secretary of the Interior and Local Government in place of Angelo Reyes, who was transferred to the Department of the Environment and Natural Resources. In the same month the Presidential Anti-Graft Commission (PAGC) signed an agreement with the NGO Volunteers Against Crime and Corruption (VACC) that was intended to bolster the Government's efforts to address the problem of corruption. The VACC submitted the names of 10 senior government officials, thought to include one minister of cabinet rank, to be investigated through the new joint initiative. In the same month a minor explosion within the presidential palace compound at Malacañang led to rumours of a potential military coup. A statement purporting to be from a rebel military faction, the Young Officers' Union-new generation (YOUng), claimed responsibility for the explosion; however, the YOUng leadership distanced itself from the statement, and, furthermore, forensic tests revealed the blast to have been the result of an inadvertent chemical reaction, rather than of terrorist activity. In late February it was reported that an attempted military coup intended to displace the Arroyo Government had been averted after 14 junior army officers had confessed to their involvement in the plot. A few days later President Arroyo issued Presidential Proclamation 1017, the declaration of a state of emergency, in response to the 'clear threat' to the nation, a decision that attracted considerable censure from the opposition, the media and civil liberties groups, which criticized Arroyo for infringing upon public freedoms. Under the terms of martial law, the authorities were granted the right to arrest people without warrant and to detain suspects without charge for an extended period of time; public protests were also prohibited. One week after the military's announcement that the threat had been successfully countered, Arroyo removed the state of emergency. A Supreme Court hearing into the legality of Proclamation 1017 commenced in March. Only days after the start of proceedings Solicitor-General Alfredo Benipayo tendered his resignation, effective from the beginning of April, amid rumours that Arroyo was dissatisfied with his efforts. In the same month a special task force, comprising élite army units, was created in order to counter any further threats to the Government. In April a total of 49 people, including members of the legislature and the military, were charged with rebellion for their alleged involvement in the February coup plot. In May the Supreme Court ruled that President Arroyo's declaration of a state of emergency had been legal, but that several actions that had followed the declaration, including certain arrests, were unlawful. In June 2007 the Supreme Court dismissed charges of rebellion against six members of the legislature.

The Arroyo administration's campaign for constitutional amendments to transform the bicameral legislative system into a unicameral parliamentary system was the subject of intense debate during 2006. The Government chose to pursue reform through two possible channels: a people's initiative, involving the collection of signatures and the holding of a plebiscite; and the formation of a constituent assembly. In October, however, following Comelec's rejection of the people's initiative petition, the Supreme Court ruled that approach to be unconstitutional. Signalling the adoption of the alternative method of amending the Constitution, the Speaker of the House of Representatives, Jose de Venecia, proposed in November the adoption by the House of a resolution to become a constituent assembly, whereupon a new constitution would be approved by mid-December. The Speaker envisioned the postponement of elections from May 2007 to November and the completion of the transformation of the legislature after June 2010. The move encountered significant opposition from the Senate, which was effectively excluded from the reform process, the Catholic Bishops' Conference of the Philippines and large sections of the public, with plans for anti-Government demonstrations in several cities. Under considerable pressure, the reformists in the House of Representatives proposed the formation of a constitutional convention of elected delegates as an alternative means towards constitutional amendments, but, with the suspension of the original resolution and a loss of momentum, the initiative was abandoned.

In June 2006 President Arroyo ratified a law that abolished the death penalty. Avelino Cruz resigned as Secretary of National Defense in November; Arroyo assumed personal responsibility for the portfolio in December, pending the appointment of Hermogenes Ebdane in January 2007. In February Congress approved the Human Security Act, anti-terrorism legislation giving security officials powers of detention for a period of up to three days in the absence of a warrant or charge, and allowing access to suspicious financial accounts. Critics, including human rights organizations, opposition politicians and the Roman Catholic Church, expressed concern that the Act could be used to suppress legitimate political dissent.

The increasing occurrence of extra-judicial killings and human rights violations was highlighted in 2006 and 2007 by several independent reports. In February 2007 the UN Special Rapporteur on extra-judicial, summary or arbitrary executions, Philip Alston, contended that, although the highest level of Government recognized the gravity of the situation, the army was 'in a state of almost total denial of its need to respond effectively and authentically to the significant number of killings which have been convincingly attributed to them'. Also in February, an inquiry supported by the Government and led by Jose Melo, a retired judge, found links between sections of the military and politically motivated murders. As part of efforts to address the issue, the armed forces and the national police established their own human rights offices, and in March the Chief Justice designated 99 special tribunals to try cases of political killings, with the intention of giving priority to such cases. In late November Arroyo ordered the creation of a task force against political violence, comprising representatives of eight government departments and agencies. On the following day Alston's final report was released, in which he concluded that claims by the armed forces that extra-judicial killings of leftist activists were a result of internal purges within communist groups were 'strikingly unconvincing' and observed that no one had been convicted of these killings. Other victims identified by Alston included civil society leaders, human rights activists, trade unionists and advocates of land reform. While welcoming measures initiated by the Government to combat the problem, Alston noted that they had yet to succeed.

Legislative and local elections held on 14 May 2007 were marred by numerous reports of fraud, voter intimidation and violence; some 120 people had been killed in election-related violence since the beginning of the year. Polling in 13 towns in the province of Lanao del Sur on Mindanao was postponed owing to the threat of violence, finally taking place on 26 May, amid heightened security. Moreover, six days before the elections at least eight people were killed in a bomb attack in the city of Tacurong, on Mindanao, which the security forces attributed to the regional terrorist organization Jemaah Islamiah (JI). President Arroyo described the electoral process as 'good, relatively peaceful, free and fair'. However, opposition leaders claimed that her portrayal was dishonest, demanding that the national police force take full responsibility for the deaths.

In the elections for 12 of the 24 seats in the Senate, the pro-Arroyo TEAM (Together Everyone Achieves More) Unity coalition—including Lakas-CMD, Kabalikat ng Malayang Pilipino (KAMPI, founded in 1997 to support Arroyo) and the LDP—won three seats, while the Genuine Opposition (GO) coalition—including the LP, the PDP-Laban Party and the NP—won seven, giving a majority to opponents of President Arroyo. Notably elected for the GO was Antonio Trillanes IV, who remained in detention for his alleged role in the 2003 mutiny. The remaining two seats in the Senate were secured by independent candidates, one of whom was Gregorio Honasan, who was on bail accused of involvement in the same mutiny (the charges were dismissed in July 2007). None the less, supporters of Arroyo retained control of the House of Representatives, with parties belonging to TEAM Unity reportedly securing 168 elective seats compared with the GO's 44. Voter turn-out was estimated at 68% for the upper chamber and 70% for the lower chamber. Some 17,000 provincial and municipal posts, including 81 provincial governorships, were also contested on the same day.

Addressing the newly elected Congress in late July 2007, Arroyo focused on her Government's economic achievements and pledged to allocate more resources to reducing poverty and to ending the insurgencies in the south of the country. As some 3,000 protesters participated in anti-Government demonstrations outside the legislative building, the President also urged

Congress to adopt legislation aimed at curbing politically motivated killings and defended the Human Security Act, which came into force earlier in that month.

In late September 2007 President Arroyo suspended a US $329m. contract signed by the Government and the Chinese ZTE Corporation in April for the provision of a national broadband telecommunications network, amid claims that Philippine officials brokering the agreement had both solicited and offered bribes. Testifying before a Senate investigation into the allegations earlier in that month, the son of the Speaker of the House of Representatives, Jose de Venecia III, whose company had unsuccessfully bid for the broadband contract, and the former Director-General of NEDA, Romulo Neri, had both implicated the Chairman of Comelec, Benjamin Abalos, in the scandal. De Venecia III had also claimed that the President's husband, Jose Miguel Arroyo, had warned him not to pursue the project. Abalos and Jose Miguel Arroyo denied any wrongdoing. Meanwhile, additional troops were deployed in Manila after the Chief of Staff of the Armed Forces, Gen. Hermogenes Esperon, announced that several junior officers who were suspected of recruiting soldiers to join a plot to destabilize the Government had been suspended or reassigned. The contract with ZTE Corporation, whose bid had been substantially higher than those of rival companies, was cancelled in early October. In mid-October the House of Representatives began considering a new impeachment complaint against President Arroyo based on her alleged failure to act on the bribery accusations concerning Abalos, who had resigned earlier that month; the impeachment bid was dismissed in November owing to 'lack of substance'.

A bomb exploded outside the House of Representatives in mid-November 2007, killing four people, including Wahab Akbar, the suspected target, who represented the island of Basilan in the lower chamber. The attack was attributed to Abu Sayyaf, the Muslim secessionist group (see below) of which Akbar was allegedly a former member. Later in that month several military officers walked out of a court in Manila where they were being tried on charges of staging a coup in July 2003 (see above) and occupied a nearby hotel, from where, joined by other dissident soldiers, former Vice-President Teofisto Guingona and a number of Catholic priests, among others, they appealed to the armed forces to withdraw support for President Arroyo. More than 1,000 heavily armed troops were deployed to quash the rebellion. Having failed to inspire a mass uprising, the leaders of the mutiny, Senator Antonio Trillanes IV and Brig.-Gen. Danilo Lim, surrendered to the authorities after several hours, claiming that they were doing so in order to avoid casualties. Most of the rebels were detained, although three reportedly managed to evade capture. Several journalists covering the incident were also detained, but later released, and an overnight curfew was imposed in Manila. In early December Trillanes, Lim, Guingona and 33 others were charged with rebellion and incitement to rebellion; the charges against 18 civilians, including Guingona, were dismissed later in that month.

The controversy over the broadband contract with ZTE Corporation persisted in early 2008, as the Senate hearings into the affair continued, with further witnesses corroborating the bribery allegations. Jose de Venecia was removed from the position of Speaker of the House of Representatives in a vote in early February, after accusing President Arroyo and the Government of corruption. Prospero Nograles was immediately elected to replace him. Once a close alliance, de Venecia's relationship with Arroyo had recently been strained as a result of the allegations made by his son before the Senate inquiry. De Venecia resigned as President of Lakas-CMD in March; he was again succeeded in this post by Nograles. Meanwhile, in late February an estimated 10,000 people participated in a demonstration in Manila to demand the resignation of Arroyo over the corruption scandal, while more than 50 former government officials issued a joint statement also urging the President to leave office. Further protests followed, and at the end of the month former Presidents Aquino and Estrada addressed an anti-Government rally attended by some 15,000 people in the capital, while smaller demonstrations were held in other towns. Yielding to considerable pressure, notably from the Catholic Bishops' Conference, in early March Arroyo revoked a controversial executive order issued in September 2005 that prevented public officials from attending congressional hearings on alleged corruption in the Government unless permitted by the President. Meanwhile, it was announced that three alleged militants, believed to have links to Abu Sayyaf or JI, had been arrested on suspicion of plotting to bomb foreign embassies in Manila and to assassinate President Arroyo. In July 2008 it was announced that a human rights lawyer and four former military officers had been arrested in connection with a new plot to oust President Arroyo; however, all five were acquitted of the charges against them in early 2009.

Juan Ponce Enrile, considered to be an ally of Arroyo, was elected as President of the Senate in mid-November 2008, following the resignation of the incumbent, Manuel Villar, who had recently been embroiled in controversy over the funding of a road extension project and had lost the support of the majority of senators. (In September Villar, the President of the NP, had declared his intention to contest the presidential election due to be held in 2010.) In December 2008 the House of Representatives rejected a fourth impeachment complaint against Arroyo, which detailed various accusations of corruption and human rights abuses under her administration. The President's husband, Jose Miguel Arroyo, came under considerable pressure in early 2009 to appear before a Senate inquiry into corruption involving World Bank-funded public works projects, following allegations linking him to claims of collusion between government officials and contractors in bids for road development contracts; the scandal had emerged in January, when three Philippine and four Chinese companies were barred from tendering for future Bank-financed projects. In March the Office of the Ombudsman recommended that 17 former and current officials of the Department of Public Works and Highways, which was responsible for implementing the bidding process, be charged with corruption.

Constitutional reform was again under consideration in 2008–09. In April 2008 12 senators, led by Aquilino Pimentel, proposed a resolution on the formation of a constituent assembly to amend the Constitution by introducing a federal system of government, comprising 11 states and one administrative region centred on Manila, while retaining the presidency and a bicameral legislature; a concurrent resolution supporting Pimentel's initiative was filed in the House of Representatives in May. In mid-August the President expressed her support for federalism as a means of achieving stability in Mindanao. However, later in that month the House of Representatives' committee on constitutional amendments deferred a planned vote on the need for constitutional change, instead approving a motion to conduct nationwide public consultations on the issue. Opposition politicians pledged to challenge efforts to reform the Constitution before the expiry of Arroyo's term of office in 2010, alleging that the President's supporters in the legislature intended to attempt to extend her tenure or to introduce a parliamentary system of government (under which she could assume the premiership); Arroyo's administration rejected these claims. Meanwhile, there was also considerable disagreement over the interpretation of the Constitution regarding the convening of a constituent assembly, with some claiming that the required approval of three-quarters of the members of Congress had to be secured in separate votes in both chambers, while others maintained that a joint vote in the combined Congress was sufficient; the latter approach (which Luis Villafuerte, the President of KAMPI, was reportedly pursuing) would allow the House of Representatives to force through change, even if opposed by all 24 senators. In December all the members of the Senate signed a resolution stating that any attempt by the House to propose constitutional revisions unilaterally would be unconstitutional. Also that month several thousand opponents of constitutional reform, supported by former Presidents Aquino and Estrada, attended a rally in the Makati district of Manila. In February 2009 the House of Representatives' committee on constitutional amendments approved a resolution, drafted by Speaker Nograles, seeking to remove constitutional restrictions on foreign ownership of companies and land. Opponents of Nograles's proposal feared that once the process of reforming the Constitution's economic provisions began, more controversial amendments might follow. By the end of March 185 members of the House of Representatives were reported to be in favour of Villafuerte's resolution to form a constituent assembly to amend the Constitution, which was expected to be formally filed in the House in mid-April, when its contents would become publicly known. If effectively excluded from the constituent assembly, the Senate was likely to refer the matter to the Supreme Court for a ruling on whether the three-quarters' majority vote in Congress required to convene an assembly should be achieved by the two chambers voting jointly or separately.

Meanwhile, the Philippines continued to be affected by regional instability, owing to the activities of several insurgent groups, operational particularly in the central and southern areas of the country. Despite President Estrada's inclusion of former communist activists in the Government, the leadership of the NDF-CPP-NPA condemned his administration. In July 1998 Estrada approved the human rights agreement that had been reached by the NDF and the Ramos administration, and invited the exiled leadership of the NDF to the Philippines to resume peace negotiations. In February 1999, however, Estrada suspended peace talks with the communists following the NPA's abduction of three hostages. The Government also suspended the Joint Agreement on Safety and Immunity Guarantees, exposing NDF-CPP-NPA members to the risk of arrest. A total of five hostages were released by the NPA in April, although the communists continued to reject other conditions for negotiations.

In May 1999 the NDF withdrew from peace negotiations in response to the Senate's ratification of a defence treaty with the USA (see below). Estrada subsequently adopted a position of outright hostility towards the movement. However, the NDF-CPP-NPA were recruiting increasing numbers of members, who were disillusioned with the Estrada administration. In an attempt to divide the communist movement, Estrada entered into negotiations with several breakaway factions, but failed to make substantial progress. In January 2000 the Government suspended military operations against the communists to facilitate the release of two NPA hostages. In December Estrada announced that a peace agreement had been concluded with the Revolutionary Proletarian Army (RPA)-ABB. The agreement, which applied only to the central Philippines, was accompanied by a presidential amnesty for some political prisoners whose death sentences had been upheld by the Supreme Court, and by the release of an additional 235 political detainees. In the same month the NPA rejected an offer by the Government of a truce.

In April 2001 the Government of President Arroyo held peace talks with the NDF in Oslo, Norway. The talks were reported to have made some progress, with both sides agreeing to undertake confidence-building measures, including the release of political prisoners. Further discussions were held in May, but were suspended in June when the NDF was implicated in the assassination of Congressman Rodolfo Aguinaldo. In November a total of 28 people were killed on the island of Mindanao when fighting broke out between the NPA and government soldiers. However, despite the renewal of violence, exiled NDF members announced shortly afterwards that they had agreed to resume peace talks with the Government in Oslo in December. In the same month President Arroyo announced a temporary cease-fire with the NDF, following its offer to suspend hostilities for one month if the Government made a reciprocal gesture. However, the arrival of US troops in the Philippines in 2002 (see below) threatened further peace negotiations, as the NDF continued to oppose any US involvement in the country. In May President Arroyo called off further peace negotiations after a number of political assassinations occurred.

In August 2002 the USA added the CPP and the NPA to its list of international terrorist organizations and requested that the Government of the Netherlands cease benefit payments to all group members resident there. In the same month government representatives met with members of the NDF in Quezon City, with the intention of resuming peace talks. However, the Chairman of the CPP, Jose Maria Sison, continued to oppose any negotiations while President Arroyo remained in power. In October the Government formally designated the NDF a terrorist organization, while emphasizing that it remained willing to continue peace negotiations. In January 2003 police officials announced that they intended to charge Sison with involvement in several murders, including those of Aguinaldo and former NPA leader Romulo Kintanar (who was killed by unidentified gunmen in that month), and to seek his extradition to stand trial in the Philippines. In June fighting broke out between government troops and NPA rebels on the island of Samar and in July, following continued hostilities by the NPA, the Government announced that it intended to launch a military offensive in order to quell the insurgency. In January 2004 NPA rebels attacked a power station near Manila, causing eight deaths.

Peace negotiations between the Government and the NDF finally recommenced in Oslo in February 2004, despite ongoing clashes between the two sides. A third round of talks took place in Oslo in June. Negotiations were scheduled to resume in August, but were suspended after the NDF claimed that the Government was failing to meet its demands, including the implementation of measures to secure the removal of the CPP and the NPA from the USA's list of international terrorist organizations. Sporadic violence continued, and at the end of 2004 the armed forces announced that a total of 182 NPA members had been killed in clashes with government troops in that year and a further 910 had surrendered or been captured. In February 2005 14 NPA rebels and two government soldiers were killed in skirmishes in the town of Compostela, some 930 km south-east of Manila. Negotiations between the NDF and the Government resumed during the first half of 2005, but were abandoned by the former in August in response to the political scandal surrounding President Arroyo (see above). Discussions between the two sides resumed in September. However, hopes for a peaceable resolution to the ongoing conflict suffered a set-back in November, when at least nine soldiers were killed and approximately 20 were injured in an ambush near Calinog, in the province of Iloilo, which was alleged to have been carried out by NPA members. Furthermore, in January 2006 a group of suspected NPA members conducted a raid on a prison in Barangay Cuta, Iloilo, during which they released 14 detainees. Later in that month it was reported that Philippine troops had killed at least 18 NPA rebels during fierce clashes in Santa Ignacia, north of Manila. In October President Arroyo declared that she hoped that the NPA movement would be largely defeated by the time that her term expired in 2010. In May 2007 five police officers were killed on the island of Mindoro by a landmine believed to have been planted by the NPA. In August Sison was arrested in the Netherlands, where he remained in exile, on suspicion of ordering the assassinations of former associates Romulo Kintanar and Arturo Tabara in 2003 and 2004; he was released in September owing to lack of evidence. (The Dutch prosecution service subsequently conducted further investigations into the case, before concluding in March 2009 that there was still insufficient evidence to prosecute Sison.) Meanwhile, at the beginning of September 2007 the Philippines military filed charges with the Commission on Human Rights accusing Sison and 18 other members of the CPP and the NPA of the murder or attempted murder of six people. Shortly afterwards, in an effort to restart the stalled peace negotiations, Arroyo signed a proclamation offering amnesty to communist rebels who relinquished their weapons. However, the NPA continued its activities, raiding a mining project of a Swiss company in January 2008. In March at least one government soldier and seven NPA rebels were killed in fighting after the NPA attacked an army base in the province of Surigao del Sur, on Mindanao. Also in that month the army claimed to have secured control of an NPA base in the north of the country, following a week of fighting in which two soldiers died. In May it was reported that Philippine troops had killed three NPA militants in clashes on Mindanao. Continued sporadic violence resulted in further fatalities on both sides in the following months. Little progress appeared to have been made at two rounds of informal talks between the Government and the NDF held in Oslo in May and November, with the NDF reportedly rejecting the Government's demand for an indefinite cease-fire as a condition for the resumption of formal peace negotiations. In early December the military announced that five soldiers had been killed in an NPA attack on an army vehicle in the province of Surigao del Norte. Philippine troops captured an NPA base on Mindanao in February 2009, following fighting in which at least 11 rebels and five soldiers died.

During 1986 the Aquino Government conducted negotiations to seek a solution to the conflict with Muslim separatists in the south. A cease-fire was established with the MNLF in September, following an announcement by the Government that it would grant legal and judicial autonomy to four predominantly Muslim provinces in Mindanao. Further talks ensued, under the auspices of the Organization of the Islamic Conference (OIC, see p. 382), and on 5 January 1987 the MNLF signed an agreement to relinquish demands for complete independence in Mindanao, and to accept autonomy. In February 1988, however, the MNLF resumed its offensive against the Government, which had attempted to prevent the MNLF from gaining membership of the OIC (which would imply that the MNLF was regarded as representing an independent state). The 1987 Constitution granted eventual autonomy to Muslim provinces in Mindanao, which had been promised by President Marcos in 1976. In November 1989 a referendum was held, in the country's 13 southern provinces and nine cities in Mindanao, on proposed legislation that envisaged the autonomy of these provinces and cities, with direct elections to a unicameral legislature in each province; this contrasted with the MNLF's demand for autonomy in 23 provinces, to be granted without a referendum. Four provinces (Lanao del Sur, Maguindanao, Tawi-Tawi and Sulu) voted in favour of the government proposal, and formed the autonomous region of Muslim Mindanao.

In February 1990 the candidate favoured by Aquino, Zacaria Candao (formerly the legal representative of the MNLF), was elected to the governorship of Muslim Mindanao. In October the autonomous regional government was granted limited executive powers. The MNLF boycotted the election, on the grounds that the provisions for autonomy were more limited than those reached with Marcos in 1976. Under Ramos's programme of reconciliation, the MNLF participated in discussions with the NUC. In October 1992 the leader of the MNLF, Nur Misuari, agreed to return to the Philippines from exile in Libya to facilitate negotiations. In January 1993 talks were suspended, and violence in Mindanao escalated prior to the impending elections for the region's Governor and Assembly. At the elections, which took place on 25 March, a former ambassador, Lininding Pangandaman, was elected Governor, with the unofficial support of Ramos.

In April 1993 exploratory discussions in Jakarta, Indonesia, between Nur Misuari and representatives of the Philippine Government led to an agreement on the resumption of formal peace talks under the auspices of the OIC. Further exploratory talks took place in Saudi Arabia in June, prior to the first formal negotiations in October in Jakarta, where the MNLF demanded the creation of an autonomous Islamic state in the south, as agreed in 1976. In November 1993 the two sides signed a memorandum of understanding and an interim cease-fire was agreed.

The second round of formal peace negotiations between the Government and the MNLF took place in Jakarta in April 1994. Agreement was subsequently reached on government administration in the proposed autonomous region, Islamic law, education and revenue-sharing between Manila and the autonomous zones. In August 1995 Misuari agreed for the first time to a referendum (which was required under the Constitution) prior to the establishment of an autonomous zone, but demanded the immediate establishment of a provisional MNLF government to ensure that the referendum was conducted fairly.

In June 1996 it was announced that the MNLF and the Government had finally reached agreement on a proposal by Ramos for the establishment of a transitional administrative council, to be known as the Southern Philippines Council for Peace and Development (SPCPD), which was to derive powers from the Office of the President. The five-member SPCPD, which was to be headed by Misuari, was to co-ordinate peace-keeping and development efforts in 14 provinces and 10 cities in Mindanao, with the assistance of an 81-member Consultative Assembly and a religious advisory council. After a period of three years a referendum was to be conducted in each province and city to determine whether it would join the existing Autonomous Region of Muslim Mindanao (ARMM—the MNLF had abandoned its demands for autonomy in 23 provinces in Mindanao). In July government officials announced that, under the peace agreement, Muslims were to be allocated one cabinet post, and were to be granted representation in state-owned companies and constitutional commissions. In addition, Ramos offered to support the candidacy of Misuari in the forthcoming gubernatorial election in the ARMM. In early September the Government and the MNLF signed a final draft of the peace agreement in Jakarta. In the same month elections took place peacefully in the ARMM for the region's Governor and Assembly; Misuari, who, as agreed, contested the gubernatorial election with the support of Lakas-NUCD, was elected unopposed. In October it was announced that Misuari had been officially appointed Chairman of the SPCPD. In March 1997 more than 1,000 former members of the MNLF were integrated into the armed forces under the terms of the peace accord.

In August 2001, after some delay, the referendum was finally held. As a result, the city of Marawi and the province of Basilan elected to join the ARMM. However, 10 provinces and 13 cities rejected the offer of membership and the electoral turn-out was low. In November around 600 supporters of Governor Misuari (who had been dismissed from the leadership of the MNLF in April owing to his widespread unpopularity) led an armed uprising against military and police outposts on the island of Jolo, resulting in the deaths of more than 100 people. The violence was reportedly intended to prevent an election to the governorship of the ARMM, scheduled for late November, from taking place. By instigating the rebellion Misuari had violated the terms of his five-year peace accord with the Government, although he claimed that by holding an election the Government was itself breaking the terms of the agreement. Shortly afterwards President Arroyo suspended Misuari from his post. Later in November Misuari and six of his supporters were arrested by the Malaysian authorities for attempting to gain illegal entry into the country. On 26 November polls to elect a new governor, vice-governor and 44 regional legislators for the province were conducted. The turn-out was low, a fact partly attributed to the escalating military presence in the region. The next day government forces launched air strikes on MNLF insurgents who remained in Zamboanga City, killing 25 rebels and one civilian. As they attempted to flee, the rebels took several local residents hostage. The next day the hostages were released in return for the rebels' safe passage out of the city, thus bringing an end to the confrontation. In early December the President's favoured candidate, former MNLF member Farouk Hussein, was declared Governor. He immediately urged the establishment of peace in the troubled region and stated that he would seek to open a dialogue with the remaining followers of Misuari and other radical groups in the area, including Abu Sayyaf. In January 2002 Misuari was finally deported from Malaysia to stand trial in Manila on charges of inciting a rebellion; he subsequently refused to enter a plea to the charges against him. In January 2003 the four factions comprising the MNLF signed a declaration of unity in advance of the election of a new leadership; significantly, Misuari's name was excluded from the statement, preventing him from regaining the chairmanship of the group.

In February 2005 more than 500 MNLF rebels loyal to Misuari, led by Habier Malik, attacked government troops in several towns on the island of Jolo, in retaliation for a recent army assault, which military leaders insisted had been targeted at Abu Sayyaf (see below), rather than the MNLF; an estimated 30 soldiers and 70 MNLF fighters were killed in the ensuing clashes. Elections to the governorship and Regional Legislative Assembly of the ARMM took place in August; Zaldy Puti U. Ampatuan, the candidate of Lakas-CMD, was elected Governor. At least nine MNLF rebels were killed in April 2007 during an offensive by government troops on a base commanded by Malik, who was believed to be responsible for a recent attack on an army outpost in which two soldiers and a child had died; some 8,000 people reportedly fled the violence. The OIC appealed for both sides to cease fighting and to abide by the 1996 peace agreement, but the Chief of Staff of the Armed Forces, Gen. Hermogenes Esperon, maintained that the operation was not targeted at the MNLF, but rather at Malik and his followers, who had allegedly aligned themselves with Abu Sayyaf. Misuari, who remained under house arrest near Manila but was yet to be convicted, contested the Sulu gubernatorial election in May 2007, but was overwhelmingly defeated. In August President Arroyo insisted that efforts would be made to maintain the cease-fire with the MNLF, despite the apparent involvement of members of the group in clashes between the armed forces and Abu Sayyaf (see below).

Tripartite talks between the OIC, the Philippine Government and the MNLF were held in Jeddah, Saudi Arabia, in November 2007 with the aim of addressing complaints by the MNLF that the Government had failed fully to implement the 1996 agreement; a second round of discussions was held in Istanbul, Turkey, in February 2008. Meanwhile, there was disquiet among MNLF members over the accord being negotiated between the Government and the MILF (Moro Islamic Liberation Front—see below), amid fears that it would violate the group's own peace agreement. The appointment by the MNLF Central Committee of Muslimin Sema, hitherto Secretary-General of the group, as its Chairman was rejected by Misuari loyalists in April, prompting the OIC to express concern at the internal divisions within the group. Misuari was released from house arrest on bail later in that month. In May leaders of various factions of the MNLF, meeting in Libya, agreed to form a 'transitional leadership and unification committee', comprising six members, including Misuari and Sema, with the aim of resolving their differences. However, it later appeared that Misuari, who had sent two representatives to the meeting rather than attending himself, was unwilling to accept this arrangement. A third round of tripartite discussions, which was scheduled to be held in Manila in late May, was postponed indefinitely, reportedly as a result of the uncertainty over the leadership of the MNLF. Gubernatorial and regional legislative elections were held in the ARMM on 11 August; Ampatuan was re-elected Governor of the region. Later in that month, following a meeting with Sema, the Secretary of the Interior and Local Government, Ronaldo Puno, announced that a total of 5,000 former MNLF fighters had been integrated into the armed forces, and a further 1,600 into the police force. The third round of tripartite talks finally took place in Manila in March 2009, at which the Government and the MNLF agreed to form a joint legal panel to propose amendments to the 1996 agreement; the MNLF delegation was reportedly headed by Misuari and also included Sema. A fourth meeting was scheduled to be held in Damascus, Syria, in May 2009.

The MILF, an Islamist fundamentalist grouping demanding secession for Mindanao, which was formed as a breakaway movement from the MNLF in 1978, was covered by the government cease-fire agreed in January 1994 but was not a party to the peace talks. The grouping was widely suspected of having taken advantage of negotiations between the MNLF and the Government to strengthen its position, both by an accumulation of arms and the recruitment of young militants disaffected with the compliance of the MNLF. In April 1996 the Government and the MILF agreed to a cease-fire in North Cotabato.

In August 1996, for the first time, MILF and government officials met in Davao City for preliminary peace discussions. The MILF had rejected the peace agreement with the MNLF and continued to demand separatism for 23 provinces in Mindanao. Alternating hostilities and short-term cease-fires, together with a high incidence of abductions by the rebels, characterized relations between the Government and the MILF between late 1996 and late 1997. In November 1997 a further cease-fire agreement was signed in which so-called terrorist acts (including abduction and arson) were banned as well as public executions based on Islamic (Shari'a) law. However, when the leader of the MILF, Hashim Salamat, returned to the Philippines (after living in Libya for 20 years) in December, he announced that public executions would continue in defiance of the government ban. Despite further clashes between the MILF and the Government in January 1998, with mutual accusations of violations of the cease-fire agreement, peace negotiations continued in February when the MILF demanded recognition of 13 MILF camps in Mindanao as 'legitimate territories'. In March the two sides agreed to create a 'quick response team' to resolve conflicts and confrontations before they escalated into serious clashes. In October the MILF and the Government agreed to disclose the location of their forces to prevent accidental encounters. However, in January 1999, following a statement by the MILF advocating independence for Mindanao, Estrada conducted successive offensives against the MILF, causing the collapse of the 1997 cease-fire agreement. Up to 60 people were estimated to have died in the ensuing fighting and 90,000 residents were displaced. A new cease-fire was implemented at the end of January 1999 and at the beginning of February the Presidential Adviser, Robert Aventajado, was sent to Mindanao to meet Salamat inside an MILF camp. They agreed to the resumption of peace negotiations and to a meeting between Salamat and Estrada to re-establish goodwill between the two sides. However, Estrada cancelled the meeting, as a result of a dispute over its location and security considerations. In March Salamat and Nur Misuari met for the first time in 20 years in an attempt to promote the peace process.

Estrada continued to vacillate between supporting the economic development of Mindanao to eradicate insurrection and threatening to eliminate the rebels through military action. Negotiations between the Government and the MILF took place in October 1999, despite MILF protests at continued government attacks on MILF camps in Mindanao. Clashes between the Government and the MILF continued despite reports of a renewed cease-fire agreement in November. Formal peace negotiations, originally scheduled for December, finally commenced in January 2000 but failed to achieve substantial progress. In that month Estrada announced a new anti-insurgency programme, the National Peace and Development Plan, which aimed to remove the causes of insurgency in Mindanao, including poverty, injustice and disease. Peace talks resumed in March after negotiations scheduled for February were suspended owing to escalating violence, during which the Government claimed to have captured an important MILF base, Camp Omar. Several incendiary devices planted on buses in Mindanao in February, which resulted in nearly 50 civilian deaths, were attributed by government sources to the MILF, but the MILF claimed that the bombings were perpetrated by government agents in an attempt to justify the intensification of the military campaign against the MILF. At a second round of talks in March a protocol was signed with improved cease-fire provisions, whereby the Government agreed to recognize 39 MILF camps as 'safe areas' while the MILF representatives agreed to carry a government identity card during talks (which they had formerly claimed would represent a surrender of sovereignty). However, intense fighting took place between the MILF and government forces in March and April in Lanao del Norte and Maguindanao Provinces. The MILF, which captured a small town in Lanao del Norte, claimed the attacks were designed to pressure government forces into the immediate cessation of its offensive against the MILF in central Mindanao. The escalation of violence in Mindanao prompted Estrada to convene a meeting of the National Security Council in March.

In May 2000 the MILF was reported to have withdrawn from a section of the Narciso Ramos highway, a strategically significant route, which it had controlled for more than five years. The withdrawal appeared to augur well for the resumption of peace negotiations, although the Government held Islamist separatist movements responsible for bomb attacks in Manila and Mindanao in the same month. Peace negotiations between the Government and the MILF resumed later in May, and in June the MILF was reported to be assessing an improved offer of autonomy by the Government. However, the MILF subsequently rejected the extension of the deadline for its acceptance of this offer from 1 July to 15 December, owing to a stipulation that it should meanwhile abandon its pursuit of independence. In late June, following a major offensive, government forces captured the MILF's military headquarters at Abubakar. In December the MILF appeared to have resumed its armed struggle after an attack on government forces on Jolo island was attributed to the movement. Bomb explosions in Manila at the end of the month, in which 22 people died, were also blamed on the group. (In January 2009 three Muslim militants with alleged links to both the MILF and JI were sentenced to life imprisonment in connection with the bombings.)

The new Cabinet appointed by President Arroyo in January 2001 included two members who originated from Mindanao. The incoming President stated that she would seek to resume the peace negotiations with the MILF, and in February the Government's military campaign against the MILF ceased. The MILF welcomed the Government's offer to resume talks, although sporadic clashes between its forces and those of the Government continued throughout February. In late March the Government announced that it had reached an agreement with the MILF to resume peace negotiations, and appeared prepared to accept the MILF's condition that renewed talks should be held in an OIC member state. In April the MILF announced a unilateral cease-fire, declaring its intention to observe this until the conclusion of a peace agreement. In June government representatives initiated talks with the MILF in Libya, leading to the conclusion of a preliminary cease-fire agreement in July. Later in the same month a new round of peace talks commenced, and in August a further cease-fire agreement was signed. In the same month the MILF also reached an accord with the MNLF. In September sporadic fighting between the MILF and army troops on Mindanao, which led to the deaths of 15 rebels, threatened to undermine the peace process. However, in October the MILF signed a pact with the Government to safeguard the recent cease-fire agreement. In November 2001 the Pentagon Gang—formed in 2000 and mainly comprising renegade members of the MILF—kidnapped an Italian priest, Father Giuseppe Pierantoni, in northern Manila. The leader of the faction, Akiddin Abdusalem, was shot dead as he attempted to escape from custody after being captured by government troops. In January 2002 39 separatist MILF guerrillas surrendered to government forces and relinquished a large cache of weapons. In February the MILF announced that it was to hold a new series of discussions with the Government as the situation had been complicated by the arrival of US troops on the island of Basilan (see below). In April government troops finally secured the release of Father Pierantoni after conducting intensive operations against the Pentagon Gang.

In May 2002 the Government signed several new peace agreements with the MILF in Putrajaya, Malaysia. In December the MILF denied responsibility for an ambush on Mindanao that resulted in the deaths of 12 employees of a Canadian mining company, as well as for a bomb attack that killed 17 people in the same week; the group claimed that it continued to observe the cease-fire agreed upon in 2001. Meanwhile, President Arroyo succeeded in deterring the US Government from classifying the MILF as an international terrorist organization, citing concerns that the ongoing negotiation process might be undermined by such an action. In February 2003 peace negotiations broke down when government troops assumed control of the important MILF base of Pikit, on Mindanao, in violation of the cease-fire arrangement. The Government claimed that it had ordered the military action in an attempt to capture members of the Pentagon Gang, who it believed were being sheltered by the MILF. Although President Arroyo called a halt to the operation several days later and proposed a peace agreement, many rebels were believed to have been killed in the fighting that had resulted. Insurgency in the area continued to intensify, as the MILF refused to negotiate unless government troops withdrew from Pikit. A number of attacks occurred, the most serious of which took place in March when a bomb exploded near Davao Airport, resulting in the deaths of 23 people. Although the MILF denied responsibility for the attack, the police subsequently filed charges against 150 of its members; four of the group's leaders were charged with murder and warrants issued for their arrest. (Five alleged members of the MILF were arrested in late 2004 in connection with the bomb attack. One of those detained reportedly claimed to have been trained by a leader of JI.) In late March 2003 the MILF sent representatives for preliminary discussions with government officials in Malaysia and, in April, the Government declared that formal peace negotiations would restart, although with the exclusion of those indicted in connection with the March attack on Davao Airport, including MILF leader Hashim Salamat. However, shortly afterwards the MILF was responsible for several further outbreaks of violence in the area and, in May, the Government abandoned peace talks and renewed its military offensive against the organization. Later in that month the MILF declared a 10-day unilateral cease-fire in order, it claimed, to prepare the way for the renewal of negotiations, but the Government rejected the offer following the perpetration of further attacks by the MILF during the cease-fire period. Nevertheless, at the request of the Malaysian Government, the MILF extended the cease-fire by a further 10 days in June and, later in that month, Salamat announced that the group had renounced terrorism, an important precondition for any peace agreement. Despite this, the Government continued to take military action against the organization. However, in July it was announced that the two sides had finally concluded a peace agreement. In August it was reported that Hashim Salamat had died as a result of a heart attack in the previous month; he was replaced as Chairman by Murad Ebrahim.

Following exploratory talks in February 2004, formal peace negotiations were to take place in April, but were postponed owing to the May elections (see above). In late April the MILF protested against the arrest of four of its members on suspicion of collaborating with JI, claiming it contravened the cease-fire agreement. In July it was announced that the MILF had agreed to co-operate with the armed forces in operations against kidnapping gangs and JI elements based in Mindanao. A 60-member International Monitoring Team (IMT), led by Malaysia, was deployed in Mindanao in October to oversee the ongoing cease-fire between the government forces and the MILF. Further exploratory talks aimed at restarting the stalled formal peace negotiations were held in December; the two sides reportedly made progress on the contentious issue of ancestral domain. In mid-January 2005 at least six government soldiers were killed in an attack on an army outpost by MILF rebels. The Government stated that it regarded the attack, which had not been sanctioned by the MILF leadership, as an isolated incident. Exploratory talks between the two sides were conducted between February and December.

In March 2005 the Government and the MILF finally agreed to resume formal peace negotiations in Malaysia, which commenced in February 2006 at Port Dickson, near Kuala Lumpur. ARMM Governor Zaldy Puti U. Ampatuan called for the holding of a plebiscite to assist the efforts to resolve the contentious issue of ancestral domain. In early March, however, the Malaysian Government postponed the next round of talks, scheduled for 5–7 March, owing to the state of emergency imposed upon the Philippines by President Arroyo (see above), although negotiations were resumed in late March following the removal of martial law. In the same month rumours circulated of a failed attempt to oust Murad Ebrahim from the MILF leadership, but senior MILF members denied such reports. Also in March it was reported that at least 50 suspected members of the MILF had surrendered to the army in advance of the resumption of peace talks with the Government; however, a spokesman for the organization disputed that those who had surrendered were in any way associated with the MILF, alleging that they were instead affiliated to the MNLF. In June a bomb explosion in Mindanao resulted in several fatalities and precipitated clashes between local paramilitaries and MILF rebels after the latter was accused of responsibility for the attack; in the following month, however, the two sides agreed to a cease-fire. The MILF denied perpetrating further bomb attacks in Mindanao in October, but suspicions were raised about the group's links to JI and Abu Sayyaf. Several MILF members were reported to be among at least 47 prisoners who escaped during an attack on a prison in Mindanao by a group of around 25 armed men in February 2007; the MILF denied any involvement in the incident. An Italian priest, Father Giancarlo Bossi, was kidnapped in June in his parish on Mindanao by suspected renegade members of the MILF. In July clashes between some 300 rebels and a group of marines who were searching for the priest on Basilan resulted in the deaths of 14 marines, 10 of whom were beheaded. The MILF claimed that it had ambushed the soldiers in self-defence, but denied beheading them. Father Bossi was released later in that month on Mindanao. There was speculation that Abu Sayyaf members might have been involved in the kidnapping or the fighting.

In November 2007 the Government announced that the latest round of peace negotiations with the MILF in Malaysia had resulted in agreement on the demarcation of the land and maritime boundaries of a proposed new autonomous area on Mindanao, to be known as the Bangsamoro Juridical Entity (BJE). Although no details of the borders were disclosed, it was reported that the BJE would cover a larger area than the ARMM. Talks faltered in December, however, over continued disagreement on ancestral domain, with the MILF opposed to the Government's position that any agreement should be implemented through the 'constitutional process', i.e. by conducting a plebiscite in the villages to be added to the ARMM to create the proposed BJE. Apparently frustrated with the lack of progress in the negotiations, Malaysia withdrew 28 of its cease-fire monitors from the IMT in May 2008. Finally, in late July, retired Gen. Hermogenes Esperon, who had been appointed as Presidential Adviser on the Peace Process following his retirement as Chief of Staff of the Armed Forces in May, announced that the Government and the MILF had concluded a Memorandum of Agreement on Ancestral Domain (MOA-AD), which would be signed in a formal ceremony in Kuala Lumpur on 5 August. The accord envisaged the creation of the BJE by extending the ARMM to include a further 712 villages, subject to the approval of their residents in a plebiscite to be conducted within 12 months, and outlined the expanded political and economic powers to be devolved to the new entity. However, the MOA-AD provoked considerable controversy, particularly within predominantly Christian communities intended for inclusion in the BJE, and a protest against the accord held in Zamboanga City in early August was attended by an estimated 15,000 people. On 4 August, in response to a number of petitions challenging the constitutionality of the MOA-AD, the Supreme Court issued a temporary restraining order, preventing the signing ceremony from taking place on the following day.

Tensions in the south subsequently escalated, as MILF rebels reportedly occupied some 15 villages in North Cotabato, prompting renewed fighting with government troops, which led to the displacement of an estimated 160,000 people in the province and the deaths of at least two soldiers and more than 20 militants. By mid-August the armed forces had secured control of the occupied villages, and people began to return home. However, on 18 August brutal raids by MILF forces on several towns and villages in the provinces of Lanao del Norte and Sarangani left more than 30 civilians dead and forced thousands to flee the violence, while seven soldiers died in a MILF ambush of an army convoy in Lanao del Sur. The MILF leadership claimed that the three commanders held responsible for the attacks, Abdullah Macapaar, Umbra Kato and Aleem Pangalian, were 'renegades', but refused to surrender them to the armed forces. The Government declared the MOA-AD defunct a few days later, and in early September the President ordered the dissolution of the peace panel responsible for negotiating with the MILF and announced a new policy of promoting direct dialogue with local communities, stating that future negotiations with armed groups would focus on disarmament, demobilization and reintegration. The National Disaster Co-ordinating Council (NDCC) estimated that some 500,000 people had been displaced by the violence by the end of September. In October the Supreme Court ruled the MOA-AD to be unconstitutional (by a narrow margin of eight votes to seven), noting that its implementation would require constitutional amendments that the President did not have the authority to guarantee would be adopted and criticizing Esperon for failing to consult local government and communities about the proposed agreement. Malaysia withdrew altogether from the

IMT in November, although monitors from Brunei, Libya and Japan were to continue their participation. Despite the re-establishment of the government peace panel in December, talks with the MILF remained in abeyance in early 2009. Meanwhile, sporadic fighting between MILF rebels and government troops continued during late 2008 and was ongoing in early 2009. In February 2009, according to the NDCC, more than 112,000 of those displaced in August–September 2008 remained in camps, while a further 200,000 were believed to be residing with friends or relatives.

In early June 1994 the Government undertook a major offensive against Abu Sayyaf, which was held responsible for numerous attacks, principally on the islands of Jolo and Basilan, to the south of Mindanao. In retaliation for the capture by the armed forces of its base on Jolo, the group took a number of Christians hostage on Basilan, killing 15 of them. All but one of the remaining 21 hostages were released in mid-June, following the apparent payment of a ransom and the intercession of the MNLF. Later in June government troops captured the group's main headquarters in Basilan. In early August the group's remaining hostage was released, and the authorities announced that Abu Sayyaf had been 'eliminated'. In April 1995, however, the group was believed to be responsible for an attack on the town of Ipil, in Mindanao, in which as many as 100 people were killed. Some of the assailants were also believed to belong to a splinter group of the MNLF, the Islamic Command Council. Some 14 hostages were reportedly killed as the army pursued the rebels in their retreat from Ipil. Despite intense counter-insurgency measures by government troops, Abu Sayyaf perpetrated a further assault in Tungawan, south of Ipil, in which six civilians were killed. In April 1996 two bomb explosions in Zamboanga City were widely attributed to Abu Sayyaf or to other groups opposed to the peace negotiations between the Government and the MNLF. Abu Sayyaf subsequently denounced the MNLF's peace agreement with the Government. In December 1998 the leader of Abu Sayyaf, Abdurajat Abubakar Janjalani, was killed in an exchange of fire with government security forces.

In April 2000 armed Abu Sayyaf troops abducted 21 people, including 10 foreign tourists, from the island resort of Sipadan in Malaysia, and held them hostage on Jolo. One month earlier members of a separate Abu Sayyaf group had seized a number of Filipino hostages on the island of Basilan where, demanding the release of convicted Islamist terrorists held in US prisons, they had at the end of April managed to evade capture by government forces by which they had been besieged. The Government's military response to the hostage crisis remained largely ineffective, and a stalemate lasting several months ensued, punctuated by both formal and informal negotiations and a partially successful intervention, involving the payment of ransoms, by Libyan mediators. Although sporadic releases were secured, some hostages were also killed by their captors. In April 2001 President Arroyo declared 'all-out war' against Abu Sayyaf.

In May 2001 Abu Sayyaf rebels abducted 20 people, including three US tourists, from a holiday resort off the western island of Palawan. President Arroyo immediately ordered a military response, although the group threatened to kill the hostages if it was attacked. In early June the rebels succeeded in fleeing from under military siege; nine Filipino captives escaped as a result. Later in the same month the Government was forced to bring in a Malaysian mediator in order to avert the threatened execution of the three US hostages still being held. It was reported that one, Guillermo Sobero, had already been beheaded, although his body had not been found. In early July two Filipino hostages were released, but Abu Sayyaf stated that it intended to continue attacking US and European citizens until government forces had been withdrawn from the southern Philippines. Nadzmie Sabtulah, the rebel leader alleged to have planned the May abductions, was arrested, together with three other members of the group. However, Abu Sayyaf activities continued, and in August a group of Abu Sayyaf guerrillas raided the town of Lamitan on the island of Basilan, taking at least 36 hostages and beheading 10. The next day 11 hostages were released and soon afterwards 13 more were freed, following an armed raid by government troops. However, the military failed to capture any members of the Abu Sayyaf leadership and 21 hostages remained in captivity, leading to allegations of collusion between Abu Sayyaf and the Philippine military. Soon afterwards three Chinese nationals were abducted as they tried to negotiate the release of a Chinese engineer who had been held by the group since June 2001. Two of the Chinese hostages were later killed following a clash between the kidnappers and government forces in Sultan Kudurat province.

In October 2001 Abu Sayyaf was responsible for two explosions in Zamboanga City. Meanwhile, government soldiers were reported to have cornered the kidnappers and their hostages following two days of fighting, which had resulted in the deaths of 21 guerrillas. Shortly afterwards the group threatened to behead its two US hostages—Martin and Gracia Burnham—prior to President Arroyo's scheduled November visit to the USA unless the military halted its offensive. In late October an explosion in Zamboanga, which killed six people, was attributed to the group. In the following month a Canadian man was abducted by men claiming to be Abu Sayyaf separatists. Shortly afterwards the group released one hostage, followed one week later by a further seven. In December government troops succeeded in rescuing the Canadian man. Three hostages remained—the Burnhams and Ediborah Yap, a Filipino nurse. The military offensive against the guerrilla group was intensified by the arrival of US troops on Basilan in 2002. In April a series of bombs exploded in the southern city of General Santos, killing 15 people and prompting President Arroyo to declare a state of emergency in the area. The police later arrested five men in connection with the attacks. While the suspects were initially thought to be connected to the MILF, Abu Sayyaf claimed responsibility for the bombings. Shortly afterwards four men reported to be members of Abu Sayyaf were killed during a gun battle with police in the area. In June 2002 Gracia Burnham was rescued in a military operation, but her husband and Ediborah Yap were killed. Later in the same month it was reported that Aldam Tilao (alias Abu Sabaya), a senior member of the organization, had died during a gunfight at sea.

In July 2002 the joint US-Philippine military exercises that had been conducted on Basilan were formally concluded; President Arroyo subsequently ordered the redeployment of government forces to combat insurgency elsewhere in the country. Although it was thought that the exercises had achieved some success in defeating Abu Sayyaf, in August the group was responsible for the kidnapping of eight members of a Christian sect on Jolo; although two of the hostages were released, a further two were beheaded. Following the group's threat to perpetrate attacks in retaliation for the military offensive being conducted against it, in early October a bomb exploded in Zamboanga City, resulting in the deaths of three people, including a US soldier. Responsibility for the attack was attributed to Abu Sayyaf. Later in the same month two further explosions in Zamboanga, which led to the deaths of seven people, were also suspected to have been carried out by members of Abu Sayyaf, although there was speculation that JI members might also have been involved. The bombings followed the terrorist attack on the island of Bali, Indonesia, several days previously (see the chapter on Indonesia). Meanwhile, a bomb exploded on a bus in the capital, Manila, killing at least three people.

In January 2003 three government soldiers were killed during a battle with Abu Sayyaf rebels on the island of Jolo. In the following month further fighting broke out in advance of the resumption of counter-terrorism exercises between US and Philippine troops in the area. In late February President Arroyo imposed a 90-day deadline upon military commanders for the elimination of the threat posed by Abu Sayyaf. In May the final two members of the Christian sect captured in August 2002 were freed from captivity and, in June 2003, the last hostage to have been taken from Sipadan in April 2000 escaped. Meanwhile, the Government announced the establishment of a commission to investigate claims by former hostage Gracia Burnham that collusion had taken place between Abu Sayyaf and Philippine military forces during her time in captivity. In December 2003 it was announced that government forces had captured Galib Andang, alias 'Commander Robot', a senior Abu Sayyaf figure, following a gun battle in Sulu. Abu Sayyaf claimed responsibility for a bomb explosion in February 2004 that caused a fire on a passenger ferry in Manila Bay in which 116 were presumed to have died. In March the Government announced that it had apprehended six members of Abu Sayyaf, thought to have connections to JI, who were believed to have been planning a bomb attack on Manila; one of those detained also allegedly confessed to planting the bomb on the ferry. In April the armed forces claimed to have killed Hamsiraji Sali, a leading member of Abu Sayyaf for whose capture the USA had offered a reward of US $1m., following a gun battle on the island of Basilan. Also in April at least eight members of Abu Sayyaf were among 53 prisoners who escaped from a prison on Basilan, using smuggled firearms; within four days 34 of the prisoners had been killed or recaptured by the security forces. In August 17 members of Abu Sayyaf were sentenced to death, having been convicted of kidnapping Ediborah Yap, two other nurses and a general hospital worker in 2001; four of the defendants were among those who had escaped in April 2004 and were sentenced *in absentia*. Sitra Tilao, the sister of Aldam, was arrested in September for her alleged participation in the kidnapping operations of Abu Sayyaf. In October President Arroyo announced that six members of Abu Sayyaf had been charged with murder and attempted murder in connection with the ferry bombing in February; Redendo Dellosa and Alhamser Limbong had been arrested in March, but the other four remained at large. A bomb exploded in a market in General Santos in mid-December, killing 16 people and injuring 52. The police arrested five men in connection with the attack, for which Abu Sayyaf was suspected of being responsible.

In late January 2005 the armed forces commenced a major offensive against Abu Sayyaf. Some 30,000 people fled the heavy fighting that ensued in the following month on the island of Jolo between government troops and Abu Sayyaf members, joined by followers of former MNLF leader Nur Misuari. Meanwhile, in mid-February Abu Sayyaf claimed responsibility for three coordinated bomb explosions, in Manila, General Santos and Davao City, in which 12 people were killed and some 150 injured. Amid fears of further attacks, the Government increased security at airports, seaports, bus terminals and shopping centres. In mid-March the security forces quashed an uprising at a prison near Manila, killing at least 22 detainees, including the Abu Sayyaf leaders Nadzmie Sabtulah, Galib Andang and Alhamser Limbong, after the expiry of an ultimatum for the prisoners to surrender weapons that they had seized from guards. Abu Sayyaf subsequently threatened to retaliate for the deaths of its members.

In the southern Philippines in August 2005 three explosive devices were detonated in Zamboanga City, injuring 26 people. In the same month a bomb exploded on a ferry, injuring at least 30 people. The Philippine authorities attributed the attacks to Abu Sayyaf. In October two alleged Abu Sayyaf members were sentenced to death, together with a suspected member of JI, for their part in a bomb attack on a bus in Manila's financial district, which had killed four people in February. In November at least 23 alleged Abu Sayyaf members were killed, and dozens more wounded, in violent clashes with government troops on the island of Jolo. In February 2006, in another suspected Abu Sayyaf attack, an explosion near an army base that was being used by US troops killed one person and injured an estimated 28 others. In January 2007 the campaign against Abu Sayyaf seemed to have made significant progress when it was reported that Jainal Antel Sali, or Abu Sulaiman, a senior Abu Sayyaf leader wanted for his alleged involvement in the kidnapping of several tourists in 2001 (see above) and the bombing of a ferry in 2004, had been killed by government forces on Jolo island. In the same month DNA tests confirmed earlier reports that the leader of Abu Sayyaf, Khadafi Janjalani, had been killed in September 2006. Four Filipinos later received a US $10m. reward from the US authorities for providing information that led to the two killings. None the less, Abu Sayyaf militants remained active, decapitating seven Christians whom they had taken hostage on Jolo in April 2007, and sending the severed heads to military camps on the island. In June it emerged that Abu Sayyaf had chosen one of its founders, Yasser Igasan, to replace Janjalani as leader.

In mid-August 2007 President Arroyo ordered the temporary transfer of the headquarters of the armed forces to Zamboanga City and announced that a major offensive had been launched against Abu Sayyaf on Jolo and Basilan, following clashes on Jolo in which 26 soldiers and an estimated 31 militants died. Rogue elements of the MNLF were also reported to be involved in the fighting, which prompted some 24,000 people to flee their homes. Later in that month the armed forces claimed to have killed 42 members of Abu Sayyaf in an attack on a camp on Basilan. Clashes continued in the following months, with further casualties reported on both sides. Abu Sayyaf was also held responsible for a bomb explosion outside the House of Representatives in Manila in November, in which four people died. In early December 14 members of Abu Sayyaf were sentenced to life imprisonment for the May 2001 abduction of 20 people from a holiday resort off Palawan (see above). Later in that month government troops killed Mobin Abdurajak, a senior leader of Abu Sayyaf and brother-in-law of Khadafi Janjalani, who was wanted for the April 2000 abduction of 21 people from a Malaysian resort (see above). A Catholic priest who had reportedly been receiving death threats from Abu Sayyaf was abducted and killed on the island of Tawi-Tawi in January 2008. Two minor bomb explosions in Zamboanga City in April were attributed to Abu Sayyaf. A further bomb attack outside an air force base in Zamboanga City in late May killed two people and injured at least 22 others; the MILF rejected suggestions that its members had perpetrated the bombing jointly with Abu Sayyaf. In June three employees of the ABS-CBN Broadcasting Corporation and an academic were abducted on Jolo, allegedly by Abu Sayyaf militants, but were released within 10 days. It was announced in August that Ruben Pestano Lavilla, Jr, who was wanted for his alleged involvement in the ferry bombing in 2004, as well as several other bomb attacks, had been arrested in Bahrain and deported to the Philippines. Moreover, in November 2008 Sakirin Andalan Sali (alias Kirih-Kirih), an Abu Sayyaf commander suspected of involvement in the April 2000 abduction, was captured on Jolo, while Faidar Hadjadi (alias Abu Solomon), another senior member of the movement wanted for kidnapping, was killed during a gunfight with troops in Sulu.

Militants linked to Abu Sayyaf were suspected of being responsible for the abduction of three aid workers from the International Committee of the Red Cross (ICRC) on Jolo in mid-January 2009, of three teachers near Zamboanga City later in that month, and of a Sri Lankan peace advocate on Basilan in mid-February. In March 10 people were killed in fighting between troops and militants holding the three ICRC workers captive. Later in that month Abu Sayyaf threatened to behead one of the ICRC hostages if all troops had not been withdrawn from several villages on Jolo by 31 March. At least 800 of 1,000 soldiers subsequently retreated, although the Government insisted that a complete withdrawal would compromise the security of residents. At the end of that month, as the deadline imposed by the rebels approached, the Governor of Sulu imposed a state of emergency in the province. At the beginning of April one of the hostages was released. Another hostage escaped from captivity later in that month. The remaining hostage was believed to be still alive at the beginning of May, as officials sought to resume talks aimed at securing his release.

Meanwhile, at the end of November 1991 the US military formally transferred management of the Clark Air Base to the Philippines, in accordance with the Constitution's stipulation that foreign military bases should not be allowed in the country after 1991. In late December negotiations for an extended withdrawal period of US forces from Subic Bay naval base collapsed, owing principally to the USA's policy of refusing to confirm or deny the presence of nuclear weapons (prohibited from the Philippines under the 1987 Constitution) on board naval vessels. US personnel withdrew from Subic Naval Bay at the end of September 1992, and from the Cubi Point Naval Air Station towards the end of November.

In November 1994 the Philippine Government rejected draft proposals (presented by President Bill Clinton of the USA during a visit to the Philippines earlier in the month) intended to facilitate access for US naval vessels to ports in the Philippines. Relations between the USA and the Philippines improved, following the Chinese occupation of a reef in the Spratly Islands claimed by the Philippines (see below). A joint naval exercise between US and Philippine forces took place in July 1995 about 100 km from the Spratly Islands. In January 1998 the Philippine and US Governments signed a Visiting Forces Agreement (VFA), which provided legal status for US military visits to Philippine territory and for the holding of joint military exercises, pending ratification by the Senate. However, the powerful Catholic Church opposed the agreement and the communist guerrillas announced that they would terminate peace talks if the VFA were ratified; in September popular protests against the VFA took place. Owing to the intensification of the dispute with the People's Republic of China concerning the Spratly Islands, the Philippines signed an agreement with the USA in October to allow for the formal resumption of joint military exercises. The Senate ratified the VFA on 27 May. The first phase of joint military exercises between the USA and the Philippines, which took place in January 2000, provoked popular protests outside the US embassy against the return to the Philippines of US troops. In July Estrada visited the USA where he requested financial assistance to combat rebel movements in the Philippines.

Following the terrorist attacks on the USA in September 2001 (see the chapter on the USA) President Arroyo offered President

George W. Bush her unqualified support for the US campaign against terrorism. In October the President stated that she had volunteered logistical and intelligence assistance, the use of Philippine airspace, and the former US military bases at Clark and Subic Bay to the US Government. An offer of combat troops had also been made, pending congressional approval. In November President Arroyo left for the USA to address the UN General Assembly and to hold talks with President Bush. In return for the ongoing support of the Philippines in the US anti-terrorist campaign, the US President promised the country US $100m. in military assistance and further development aid for Mindanao. The funds included $39m. to aid the Government in its continuing war against Abu Sayyaf, which had proven links to the al-Qa'ida terrorist network thought to be responsible for the attacks on the USA. President Arroyo declined an offer of direct US military involvement, limiting its role to the provision of technical and financial assistance for the offensive.

In January 2002 it was reported that the US Government had sent 660 soldiers to the southern Philippines. While they would engage in joint training exercises with Philippine troops, they would not participate in any direct combat as this would contravene the Constitution. The deployment marked the first significant extension of the US 'war on terror' beyond Afghanistan. Despite some popular opposition to the deployment, President Arroyo's stance was considerably strengthened when she succeeded in winning support for the US military presence from the National Security Council, which accepted that it was authorized under the terms of the VFA. In February more than 20 people died following clashes in the city of Jolo between police and soldiers; a later bomb blast in the city killed a further five people. A second explosion in Zamboanga—serving as a temporary base for US servicemen—occurred on the same day. The incidents were attributed to opponents of the ongoing military exercises. President Arroyo was also severely criticized by many members of Congress over her decision to allow the deployment, with several claiming that the exercises were intended to conceal a US offensive against Abu Sayyaf. Her most outspoken critic was the Vice-President and Secretary of Foreign Affairs, Teofisto Guingona, whose stance was a decisive factor in his resignation from the foreign affairs portfolio in July of that year. In April President Arroyo sanctioned the deployment of hundreds more US troops to the region and extended the deadline for their departure, owing to the apparent success of the exercises in containing terrorist activities in the Philippines. The exercises were formally concluded at the end of July.

In late 2002 the US Government signed a five-year military agreement with the Philippines, pledging to extend co-operation between the armed forces of the two countries and to facilitate the movement of heavy equipment and logistical supplies. In January 2003 an advance deployment of US Special Forces troops arrived in Zamboanga to commence anti-terrorism training exercises. In February the USA announced that it intended to send a new deployment of soldiers to the island of Jolo, a stronghold of Abu Sayyaf; it specified, controversially, that the troops would assume a combat role for the first time. However, the Philippine Government stressed later that US forces would play an entirely non-combative role in any counter-terrorism exercises. In March the President stated that, owing to local opposition, military exercises would not be conducted on Jolo. In April a new joint exercise—'Balikatan 03-1'—was announced, to take place in north Luzon and south-west Sulu.

In May 2003 President Arroyo visited the USA. During her visit, US President George W. Bush designated the country as a Major Non-North Atlantic Treaty Organization (NATO) Ally (MNA), entitling it to increased US military co-operation and supplies of armaments. Later in that month the Government stated that it expected to receive a total of US $356m. in military assistance from the USA. In October President Bush visited the Philippines during a tour of the region and thanked the country for its continued co-operation in the US-led war on terrorism. Relations with the USA were strained in July 2004 by President Arroyo's decision to withdraw the small Philippine contingent from the US-led coalition forces in Iraq a month ahead of schedule in order to comply with the demands of militants who had taken a Filipino civilian hostage in the country. Nevertheless, joint US-Philippine military exercises continued throughout 2004, and in February 2005 officials from both countries met to plan the 28 exercises scheduled to take place in that year. In August bilateral trade discussions were held; issues discussed by the two countries included agriculture, trade and investment, intellectual property rights and telecommunications, with both the Philippines and the USA affirming that the negotiations had generated mutually beneficial results. During a visit to the USA in June 2008, President Arroyo was praised by President Bush for her efforts to counter terrorism. Arroyo returned to the USA in February 2009, when she held discussions with the new US Secretary of State, Hillary Clinton, on issues such as the international economic downturn and the insurgency in the southern Philippines, but did not meet Bush's successor as President, Barack Obama.

In May 2007 President Arroyo and the Australian Prime Minister, John Howard, signed a new security pact designed to assist the Philippines in its efforts to combat insurgents in the south of the country. Under the agreement, Australian special forces would train Philippine troops and joint counter-terrorism exercises would be organized.

Following his inauguration in mid-1992, President Ramos visited Brunei, Thailand, Malaysia, Singapore and Japan, demonstrating an increasing interest in regional relations. The Philippines' commitment to the Association of South East Asian Nations (ASEAN, see p. 194) also deepened. Relations with Malaysia were somewhat strained, owing to the Philippines' claim to the Malaysian state of Sabah, dating from 1962, before Sabah joined the Federation of Malaysia. Sabah was ruled by the Sultan of Sulu, in the southern Philippines, until 1878, when it was leased to what was to become the British North Borneo Company. The Malaysian Government continues to pay a nominal rent to the Sultan. Attempts by both Presidents Marcos and Aquino to abandon the claim were thwarted by the Senate. In August 1993 the Philippine and Malaysian ministers responsible for foreign affairs signed a memorandum creating a commission to address bilateral issues, including the Philippines' claim to Sabah. Following his inauguration in June 1998, Estrada pledged to continue Ramos's commitment to regional relations. At the ASEAN ministerial meeting in Manila in July, Domingo Siazon, Jr, whom Estrada had retained as Secretary of Foreign Affairs, joined his Thai counterpart in expressing support for 'constructive intervention' in member countries' internal affairs, in marked contrast to ASEAN's policy of non-interference hitherto. Later that year relations with Malaysia were strained by Estrada's public condemnation of the arrest and beating of the former Malaysian Deputy Prime Minister, Dato' Seri Anwar Ibrahim. Despite Malaysian opposition, Estrada held a private meeting with Anwar's wife, Wan Azizah Wan Ismail, during her visit to the Philippines in May 1999. In August 2001 President Arroyo visited Malaysia on her first overseas trip since assuming the presidency. In November, however, relations were jeopardized again when the Malaysian authorities detained rebel leader Nur Misuari for attempting to enter the country illegally. After some vacillation, Misuari was finally deported in January 2002 and relations remained cordial. However, in August the bilateral relationship deteriorated following the implementation of stringent new laws in Malaysia whereby all illegal immigrants remaining in the country risked harsh penalties and deportation. Many of those affected were Filipino workers. The Philippine Government filed a formal complaint against Malaysia over its treatment of the immigrants and sent an official delegation to investigate allegations of maltreatment. Malaysia subsequently suspended implementation of the legislation.

In late November 1999 an informal summit meeting took place of the leaders of ASEAN and of China, Japan and the Republic of Korea (collectively known as ASEAN + 3), the third such meeting in three years. It was formally agreed to hold annual East Asian summit meetings of all 13 nations and to strengthen present economic co-operation with the distant aim of forming an East Asian bloc, with a common market and monetary union. At the annual ASEAN summit meeting held in Laos in November 2004, it was agreed to transform the ASEAN + 3 summit meeting into the East Asia summit, with the long-term objective of establishing an East Asian Community. In January 2007 the Philippines hosted the 12th annual ASEAN summit meeting and the second East Asia summit in Cebu. In October 2008 the Philippines ratified the new ASEAN Charter, which codified the principles and purposes of the Association and came into effect in December of that year. Meanwhile, in September 2006 President Arroyo and the Japanese Prime Minister, Junichiro Koizumi, signed an economic partnership agreement, which would eliminate tariffs on almost 95% of trade and provide for the entry of more Filipino workers to Japan. The agreement was approved by the Japanese legislature in December, but did not enter into force until two years later, in December 2008; its ratification by the Philippine Senate was delayed until October of that year, following considerable controversy over concerns that it would allow Japan to export toxic waste to the Philippines (a claim denied by officials) and that provisions apparently granting Japanese investors rights almost equal to those of Filipinos would violate constitutional restrictions on foreign ownership.

In August 2001 Indonesian President Megawati Sukarnoputri visited the Philippines on her first overseas trip since assuming power. During her brief stay she met with President Arroyo, and the two leaders promised to assist each other in overcoming the separatist violence endemic in both their countries. In March 2002 bilateral relations threatened to become strained when the Philippine police filed charges against three Indonesian men who had been arrested at Manila Airport for illegal possession of explosives. One of those arrested was believed to be a member of the Majelis Mujahidin Indonesia (MMI—Indonesian Mujahidin Council), an extremist Islamist organization, and to have links to JI. The Indonesian Government was reported to have been angered by the arrests and stated that the detentions should not be used as a pretext to portray Indonesia as a haven for Islamist extremists. However, in early 2003 it was reported that Philippine rebels were engaged in smuggling arms to militant groups in Indonesia, despite increased anti-terrorism co-operation between the two countries. In October Fathur Rohman al-Ghozi, believed to be a senior Indonesian member of JI, was shot dead by government forces three months after his escape from a prison in Manila, where he had been detained following his conviction for illegal possession of explosives.

The Philippines contributed 1,000 troops to a UN multinational force to restore peace and security in East Timor (which became Timor-Leste upon its accession to independence in May 2002), following the violence that erupted after the East Timorese voted in a referendum for independence from Indonesia; the International Force for East Timor (Interfet) was deployed in the territory in September 1999. The transfer of military command from Interfet to the newly established UN Transitional Administration in East Timor (UNTAET) took place in February 2000; the military component of UNTAET was commanded by a Filipino, Gen. Jaime de los Santos. The two East Timorese independence leaders, José Alexandre (Xanana) Gusmão and José Ramos Horta, visited the Philippines in that month and held a meeting with President Estrada. The Philippines also participated in subsequent UN missions in Timor-Leste, most recently the UN Integrated Mission in Timor-Leste (UNMIT), which was established in August 2006. A number of bilateral agreements were signed in August 2008, during Ramos Horta's first state visit to the Philippines since taking office as President of Timor-Leste in May 2007.

Diplomatic relations were established with the People's Republic of China in 1975, at which time the Philippine Government recognized Taiwan as an 'inalienable' part of the People's Republic. However, conflicting claims to the Spratly Islands, in the South China Sea, were a source of tension between the Philippines and China. (Viet Nam, Brunei, Malaysia and Taiwan also claimed sovereignty over some or all of the islands.) In February 1989 Chinese and Philippine warships exchanged gunfire in the vicinity of the Spratly Islands, although it was later declared that the incident occurred as a result of 'confusion over rules of engagement'. Indonesia hosted six rounds of negotiations over the sovereignty of the Spratly Islands between January 1990 and October 1995; all parties agreed to reach a settlement by peaceful means and to develop jointly the area's natural resources. In December 1993 the Philippines and Malaysia agreed to co-operate on fishing rights for the disputed Spratly Islands in the area not claimed by the other four countries. Following a visit to Viet Nam (the first official visit by a Philippine Head of State to that country) in March 1994, Ramos appealed for the six countries with claims to the Spratly Islands to remove all armed forces from the area.

In May 1994 China made an official protest after the Philippine Government granted a permit to a US company to explore for petroleum off Palawan, in an area including part of the disputed territory of the Spratly Islands. In February 1995 the Philippine Government formally protested when it was revealed that Chinese armed forces had occupied a reef, Mischief Reef, which lay within the Philippines' 200-mile exclusive economic zone established by a UN Convention on the Law of the Sea. Tensions in the disputed region were exacerbated during March by the arrest, by the Philippine naval forces, of more than 60 Chinese fishermen, as well as the seizure of vessels and the destruction of territorial markers allegedly deployed by China. (Most of the fishermen were released in October and the remainder in January 1996.) Following two days of consultations in August 1995, however, the Chinese Government agreed for the first time to settle disputes in the South China Sea according to international law, rather than insisting that historical claims should take precedence. The Chinese and Philippine Governments issued a joint statement agreeing on a code of conduct to reduce the possibility of a military confrontation in the area. A similar agreement was signed with Viet Nam in November 1995. In March 1996 the Philippines and China agreed to co-operate in combating piracy, which was also a source of tension between the two countries as pirate vessels in the area often sailed under Chinese flags. Despite these agreements, sporadic tension continued during 1996–98.

In August 1998 the Philippines rejected an offer from China for the joint use of the Chinese structures on Mischief Reef. In the same month Philippine and US warships staged military exercises in the South China Seas. The Philippines lodged a diplomatic protest against China in November, claiming that China was extending its structures on Mischief Reef, in contravention of the mutually agreed code of conduct. China insisted that it was only reinforcing existing structures. Estrada ordered increased naval and air patrols around the Spratly Islands to block entry and exit to the reef. A further 20 Chinese fishermen were arrested by the Philippine navy in November accused of entering Philippine waters illegally. In January 1999 the National Security Council was convened for the first time in three years to discuss the Spratly Islands and Muslim unrest in Mindanao. The Philippines favoured a multilateral solution to the problems, whereas China opposed any external intervention. China rebuffed the Philippines' attempts to involve the UN through a meeting with the Secretary-General, Kofi Annan, in the USA and threatened to leave the Asia-Europe meeting in Berlin, Germany, if the Spratly issue were discussed. A meeting in Manila achieved little progress, with the Chinese dismissing a Philippine proposal for joint use of the facility, owing to the allegedly aggressive behaviour of the Philippine armed forces. In April the Philippines and Viet Nam agreed to joint military operations and leisure activities to reduce the risk of confrontation. In October, however, the Philippines lodged a protest at the Vietnamese embassy, following an incident in which Vietnamese forces had fired on a Philippine aircraft patrolling in the area of the Spratly Islands.

In November 1999 ASEAN officials agreed on a regional code of conduct drafted by the Philippines to prevent conflicts in the Spratlys. In the same month the Chinese Premier, Zhu Rongji, visited the Philippines, and he and Estrada agreed to strengthen co-operation between the two countries. However, China rejected the proposed regional code of conduct. In early 2000 China proposed a new draft code omitting previous references to a ban on construction on islands or atolls and excluded the Paracel Islands, which China had seized from Viet Nam in 1974. However, China did meet with all the ASEAN representatives to discuss the draft, a departure from its previously exclusively bilateral approach. In May 2000 Estrada made a visit to China, where he met President Jiang Zemin and signed a joint statement on the framework for co-operation between China and the Philippines.

In mid-2002 relations with China were jeopardized when the Secretary of Justice, Hernando Perez, demanded that the Chinese ambassador be expelled from the country. His request marked the culmination of a dispute regarding the fate of more than 100 Chinese fishermen, who had been arrested over the preceding months and accused of fishing illegally in Philippine waters. Perez accused the ambassador of reneging on an agreement whereby the fishermen would be freed on condition that they entered guilty pleas and paid fines; he claimed that the ambassador had attempted to coerce the Philippine Government into releasing the fishermen without penalty. Perez subsequently withdrew his expulsion demand and, shortly afterwards, the Chinese Minister of Defence, Chi Haotian, paid a goodwill visit to the country. In November 2002 the improvement in bilateral relations was demonstrated when a senior delegation from the Chinese Communist Party arrived in the Philippines. Also in that month a 'declaration on the conduct of parties in the South China Sea' was signed by the ministers responsible for foreign affairs of China and the ASEAN member states. In September 2004, during a three-day state visit by President Arroyo to China, her first foreign trip since her election, the two countries signed five bilateral agreements, including one to conduct joint marine research in the South China Sea. It was also agreed to explore the possibility of defence co-operation. In

March 2005 the national oil companies of the Philippines, China and Viet Nam signed a three-year agreement on undertaking joint research into petroleum resources in the South China Sea. In March 2006 the Chinese Government granted the Philippine administration US $3m. with which to establish a Chinese-language military training programme, in return for the Philippines' continued adherence to the 'One China' policy, which recognized Taiwan as an integral part of the People's Republic of China. The Chinese Government also donated engineering equipment and invited the Philippines to participate in joint naval exercises. In January 2007 the Chinese Premier, Wen Jiabao, spent two days in Manila, after attending the 10th ASEAN-China summit and other ASEAN-related meetings in Cebu. During his visit several bilateral accords were signed, most notably a framework agreement on expanding economic and trade co-operation. President Arroyo visited China in October, shortly after suspending a telecommunications contract with China's ZTE corporation, following allegations of bribery in the bidding process (see above). In talks with the Chinese President, Hu Jintao, Arroyo sought to ensure that the cancellation of the contract did not adversely affect bilateral relations. However, Arroyo's administration was subsequently forced to defend the propriety of other economic agreements with China, amid criticism from Philippine opposition parties. Tension over sovereignty in the South China Sea resurfaced in February 2009, when the Philippines adopted legislation seeking to define the country's maritime boundaries, which referred to the disputed Kalayaan group of islands (known as the Nansha islands by the Chinese) and the Scarborough Shoal (or Huangyan) as being part of a 'regime of islands under the Republic of the Philippines'; the Chinese Government denounced the territorial claims as being illegal and invalid.

Relations between the Philippines and Taiwan deteriorated in October 1999, following Estrada's termination of all flights between Taipei and Manila after a failure to settle a dispute over passenger quotas. The Philippine authorities demanded that two Taiwanese airlines reduce passengers from the previously agreed 9,600 per week to 3,000 per week, in order to protect the Philippine national airline's share of the market. Following negotiations it was agreed in January 2000 that flights would resume in February. However, a disagreement over the interpretation of the new arrangement arose: the Taiwanese authorities claimed that the new quota of 4,800 passengers per week applied only to the Manila–Taipei flights, whereas the Philippines sought to include the route between Manila and Kaohsiung. The Philippines again severed air links after only six weeks, despite Taiwanese threats of an investment boycott and curbs on Filipino workers in Taiwan. The dispute was finally resolved in September 2000 when the Philippines and Taiwan agreed to reinstate a bilateral accord concluded in 1996. The Philippines had reportedly accepted that Taiwanese airlines should be allowed to fly passengers on to other destinations after arrival in the Philippines.

Government

The Constitution, which was approved by a national referendum on 2 February 1987, provided for a bicameral Congress, comprising a Senate, with 24 members directly elected by universal suffrage (for a six-year term, with one-half of the membership being elected every three years), and a House of Representatives (with a three-year mandate), with a maximum of 250 members, one being directly elected from each legislative district: in addition, one-fifth of the total number of representatives was to be elected under a party list system from lists of nominees proposed by minority groups. The number of members in the House of Representatives was increased to 275 at the 2007 election.

The President is Head of State, Chief Executive of the Republic and Commander-in-Chief of the Armed Forces. The President is elected by the people for a six-year term, and is not eligible for re-election. The President cannot prevent the enactment of legislative proposals if they are approved by a two-thirds' majority vote in Congress. The President may declare martial law in times of national emergency, but Congress is empowered to revoke such actions at any time by a majority vote of its members. The President appoints a Cabinet and other officials, with the approval of the Commission on Appointments (drawn from members of both chambers of Congress).

Local government is by Barangays (citizens' assemblies), and autonomy is granted to any region where its introduction is endorsed in a referendum. The Autonomous Region of Muslim Mindanao (ARMM), granted autonomy in November 1989, has its own 24-seat Regional Legislative Assembly (RLA).

Defence

The total strength of the active armed forces as assessed at November 2008 was an estimated 106,000, comprising an army of 66,000, a navy of approximately 24,000 and an air force of 16,000. There were also reserve forces of 131,000. Paramilitary forces included the Citizens Armed Forces Geographical Units, which comprised about 40,000 men. The 2007 budget allocated an estimated 52,100m. pesos to defence.

Economic Affairs

In 2007, according to estimates by the World Bank, the Philippines' gross national income (GNI), measured at average 2005–07 prices, was US $142,623m., equivalent to $1,620 per head (or $3,730 per head on an international purchasing-power parity basis). During 2000–07, it was estimated, the population increased at an average annual rate of 2.1%, while gross domestic product (GDP) per head increased, in real terms, by an average of 2.9% per year. According to figures from the World Bank, overall GDP increased, in real terms, at an average annual rate of 5.0% in 2000–07. According to the Asian Development Bank (ADB), GDP increased by 7.2% in 2007 and by 4.6% in 2008.

Agriculture (including hunting, forestry and fishing) contributed 14.1% of GDP in 2007 and engaged 36.1% of the employed labour force in October of that year. Rice, maize and cassava are the main subsistence crops. None the less, the Philippines relies on substantial imports of rice to meet domestic demand. Amid fears of shortages, prompted by the restriction of exports by major rice-producing countries and a consequent increase in world prices for the commodity, in April 2008 the Government announced a 43,700m. pesos programme of investment in the agricultural sector, aimed at improving general food security and achieving self-sufficiency in rice by 2013. The principal crops cultivated for export are coconuts, sugar cane, bananas and pineapples. Livestock (mainly pigs, buffaloes, goats and poultry) and fisheries are important. According to the World Bank, agricultural GDP increased at an average annual rate of 3.7% during 2000–07. According to the ADB, agricultural GDP increased by 3.2% in 2008.

Industry (including mining, manufacturing, construction and power) contributed 31.3% of GDP in 2007 and engaged 15.1% of the employed labour force in October of that year. According to the World Bank, industrial GDP increased at an average annual rate of 3.5% in 2000–07. According to the ADB, industrial GDP increased by 5.0% in 2008.

Mining contributed 1.5% of GDP in 2007 and engaged 0.4% of the employed labour force in October of that year. Copper is the Philippines' leading mineral product; gold, silver, chromium, nickel and coal are also extracted. Commercial production of crude petroleum began in 1979. Production from a substantial natural gas field and petroleum reservoir, off the island of Palawan, commenced in 2001. According to figures from the ADB, mining GDP increased by an annual average of 11.9% in 2000–07. The GDP of the mining sector contracted by 6.0% in 2006 but expanded by 26.1% in 2007.

Manufacturing contributed 22.0% of GDP in 2007, and engaged 9.1% of the employed labour force in October of that year. The most important branches of manufacturing include food products and beverages, electronic products and components (mainly telecommunications equipment), petroleum products and chemicals. According to the World Bank, the GDP of the manufacturing sector increased by an annual average of 4.3% in 2000–07. Manufacturing GDP increased by 4.0% in 2007.

The energy sector's reliance on imported petroleum has decreased significantly, as new sources of power have become available. In 2005 coal accounted for 27.0% of the total amount of electrical energy produced, natural gas for 29.8%, hydroelectric power for 14.8% and petroleum for 10.9%. In January 2009, as part of the Government's long-term programme to increase the contribution of renewable sources to the electricity supply, plans to construct five biomass plants on the islands were announced. In 2007 petroleum and its products accounted for 15.2% of the value of total merchandise imports. The transfer to private ownership of various government holdings in the power sector continued.

The services sector contributed 54.6% of GDP in 2007, and engaged 48.8% of the employed labour force in October of that year. Remittances from Filipino workers abroad (estimated to total almost 9m. in 2008, with many being employed in the oil industry or as nurses in the USA and elsewhere) constitute the Government's principal source of foreign exchange and a substantial percentage of the country's GNI. Such remittances continued to increase in 2008, when they were estimated to have reached almost US $16,500m. However, the growth in remittances was likely to decelerate during 2009–10, owing to the projected contraction in the global economy. Although periodically affected by political unrest, tourism remains a significant sector of the economy, with receipts reaching $4,019m. in 2006. Arrivals rose from 1.9m. in 2003 to over 2.8m. in 2006. In the early 2000s the provision of business process outsourcing and attendant call-centre services was of increasing significance to the economy. Revenue from these activities was estimated to have increased by 48% between 2004 and 2006 alone. According to the World Bank, the GDP of the services sector increased at an average annual rate of 6.6% in 2000–07. According to the ADB, the GDP of the services sector increased by 4.9% in 2008.

In 2007 the Philippines recorded a visible trade deficit of US $8,211m., while there was a surplus of $6,301m. on the current account of the balance of payments. In 2007 the principal source of imports was the USA (accounting for 14.0% of the total); other significant suppliers were Japan (12.4%) Singapore (11.1%), the People's Republic of China and the Republic of Korea. The principal market for exports in that year was the USA (17.0%); other major purchasers were Japan (14.5%), Hong Kong and the People's Republic of China. The principal imports in 2007 were machinery and transport equipment (31.4%), mineral fuels, basic manufactures, chemical products and food and live animals. The principal exports in that year were machinery and transport equipment, which accounted for 39.1% of total exports.

The budgetary deficit for 2008 was estimated at 68,100m. pesos (compared with 12,600m. pesos in the previous year), equivalent to 1.0% of GDP. According to the ADB, the Philippines' external debt totalled US $53,482m. at the end of 2008; in that year the cost of servicing the debt was equivalent to 9.8% of the value of exports of goods and services. The annual rate of inflation averaged 5.1% in 2000–07. According to the ADB, consumer prices increased by 9.3% in 2008. In 2008, according to the ADB, 7.4% of the labour force were unemployed (compared with 11.8% in 2004).

The Philippines is a member of the World Trade Organization (WTO, see p. 410), the UN Economic and Social Commission for Asia and the Pacific (ESCAP, see p. 36), the Asian Development Bank (ADB, see p. 191), the Association of South East Asian Nations (ASEAN, see p. 194), Asia-Pacific Economic Co-operation (APEC, see p. 185) and the Colombo Plan (see p. 425). In January 1993 the establishment of an ASEAN Free Trade Area (AFTA) commenced; a reduction in tariffs to a maximum of 5% was originally to be implemented over 15 years but this was later advanced to 2003 before being formally initiated on 1 January 2002. In November 1999 the target date for zero tariffs in ASEAN was brought forward from 2015 to 2010.

The inauguration of President Gloria Arroyo in January 2001 and the inception of a programme of economic liberalization restored some stability to the Philippines. The Medium-Term Philippine Development Plan (MTPDP) for 2004–10 accorded priority to the creation of new jobs and reforms in the power sector. The economy performed well in 2007, partly owing to higher levels of foreign direct investment, estimated to total US $2,916m. in that year. Other favourable factors were the continued strength of export revenues and an increase in consumption growth. Furthermore, the rate of inflation declined to 2.8% in 2007, its lowest level for 27 years. However, growth decelerated in 2008, as the economy adjusted to higher consumer prices for oil and food supplies in the earlier part of the year and as global economic conditions deteriorated in the latter months of 2008. Foreign direct investment declined to an estimated $1,520m. in 2008. Increased turmoil on international financial markets was expected to impede the privatization programme (which had been a major objective of the Arroyo administration) in 2009, although the Philippines' banking sector did not appear to be notably exposed. The imposition by many countries of restrictions on exports of rice (see above) presented the Philippine authorities with considerable difficulties, and businesses operating in the food industry were subsequently forced to ration supplies of rice. Inflation rose steeply in 2008, reportedly reaching a high point of 12.4% in August, before subsequently easing. The implementation of a fiscal stimulus plan in January 2009 was likely to impose a further strain on government finances. The Philippine Economic Resiliency Plan (PERP), which envisaged total expenditure of 330,000m. pesos, was scheduled to draw around 160,000m. pesos from budgetary revenue, thereby providing for an increase in welfare payments to impoverished households. (Despite strong levels of economic growth in recent years, the incidence of poverty among Filipinos increased to 32.9% of the population in 2006, according to a government report.) Increased capital expenditure on public infrastructure projects was also projected, with the intention of significantly expanding employment opportunities. The rate of economic growth was expected to decline in 2009, as the decrease in global demand began to affect the Philippines' export revenues. Inflows of remittances from overseas workers were likely to be curtailed by unfavourable global conditions, and this in turn was expected to temper domestic consumption. The ADB forecast a GDP growth rate of 2.5% in 2009.

Education

Elementary education, beginning at seven years of age and lasting for six years, is officially compulsory, and is provided free of charge at public (government-administered) schools. In 2005/06 enrolment at pre-primary level included 44.5% of pupils from the relevant age-group (males 44%; females 45%). In 2004/05 enrolment at primary level included 93.0% of pupils in the relevant age-group (males 92%; females 94%). Secondary education begins at the age of 13 and lasts for five years: there is a common general curriculum for all students in the first two years, and more varied curricula in the third and fourth years, leading to either college or technical vocational courses. In 2005/06 enrolment at secondary level included 83% of pupils from the relevant age-group (males 78%; females 87%). Instruction is in both English and Filipino. In the same year enrolment at tertiary level included 28% of students from the relevant age-group (males 25%; females 31%). According to the UN Development Programme, in 2002 the annual expenditure per pupil was 7,590 pesos (US $138). The Government's budget for 2005 allocated 135,470m. pesos (15.1% of total national expenditure) to education, culture and training.

Public Holidays

2009: 1 January (New Year's Day), 25 February (EDSA Revolution Day), 9 April (Maundy Thursday), (Bataan Day, Araw ng Kagitingan), 10 April (Good Friday), 1 May (Labour Day), 12 June (Independence Day, anniversary of 1898 declaration), 24 June (Araw ng Maynila)*, 19 August (Quezon Day)†, 31 August (National Heroes' Day), 1 November (All Saints' Day), 30 November (Bonifacio Day), 25 December (Christmas Day), 30 December (Rizal Day), 31 December (Last Day of the Year).

2010: 1 January (New Year's Day), 25 February (EDSA Revolution Day), 1 April (Maundy Thursday), 2 April (Good Friday), 9 April (Bataan Day, Araw ng Kagitingan), 3 May (Labour Day), 14 June (Independence Day, anniversary of 1898 declaration), 24 June (Araw ng Maynila)*, 19 August (Quezon Day)†, 31 August (National Heroes' Day), 1 November (All Saints' Day), 30 November (Bonifacio Day), 25 December (Christmas Day), 30 December (Rizal Day), 31 December (Last Day of the Year).

* Observed only in Metro Manila.

† Observed only in Quezon City.

Weights and Measures

The metric system is in force.

THE PHILIPPINES

Statistical Survey

Source (unless otherwise stated): National Statistics Office, Solicarel 1, R. Magsaysay Blvd, Sta. Mesa, 1008 Metro Manila; tel. (2) 7160807; fax (2) 7137073; internet www.census.gov.ph.

Area and Population

AREA, POPULATION AND DENSITY

Area (sq km)	300,000*
Population (census results)	
1 May 2000	
Males	38,524,267
Females	37,979,810
Total	76,504,077
1 August 2007	88,574,614
Density (per sq km) at census of 1 August 2007	295.2

* 115,831 sq miles.

REGIONS
(population at 2007 census)

	Population
National Capital Region	11,553,427
Ilocos (Region I)	4,545,906
Cagayan Valley (Region II)	3,051,487
Central Luzon (Region III)	9,720,982
CALABARZON (Region IV-A)*	11,743,110
MIMAROPA (Region IV-B)*	2,559,791
Bicol (Region V)	5,109,798
Western Visayas (Region VI)	6,843,643
Central Visayas (Region VII)	6,398,628
Eastern Visayas (Region VIII)	3,912,936
Zamboanga Peninsula (Region IX)†	3,230,094
Northern Mindanao (Region X)	3,952,437
Davao (Region XI)‡	4,156,653
SOCCSKSARGEN (Region XII)§	3,829,081
Cordillera Administrative Region	1,520,743
Autonomous Region of Muslim Mindanao	4,120,795
Caraga	2,293,480
Total	88,574,614‖

* Southern Tagalog region prior to September 2001.
† Western Mindanao region prior to September 2001.
‡ Southern Mindanao region prior to September 2001.
§ Including area designated Central Mindanao region prior to September 2001.
‖ Total includes Filipinos in Philippine embassies, consulates and missions abroad (2,279 persons) and populations of areas of dispute between the National Capital Region and the province of Rizal (24,789 persons) and between the province of Davao Oriental and Surigao del Sur (4,555 persons).

PRINCIPAL TOWNS
(population at 2007 census)

Manila (capital)*	1,660,714		Bacolod City	499,497
Quezon City*	2,679,450		Muntinlupa City*	452,943
Caloocan City*	1,378,856		Marikina City	424,610
Davao City	1,363,337		Iloilo City	418,710
Cebu City	798,809		Pasay City*	403,064
Zamboanga City	774,407		Mandaue City	318,575
Pasig City*	617,301		Angeles City	314,493
Valenzuela City	568,928		Iligan City	308,046
Cagayan de Oro City	553,966		Mandaluyong City*	305,576
Parañaque City	552,660		Baguio City	301,926
Las Piñas City	532,330		Butuan City	298,378
Gen. Santos City	529,542		Cotabato City	259,153
Makati City*	510,383		Olongapo City	227,270

* Part of Metropolitan Manila.

BIRTHS, MARRIAGES AND DEATHS*

	Registered live births		Registered marriages		Registered deaths	
	Number	Rate (per 1,000)	Number	Rate (per 1,000)	Number	Rate (per 1,000)
1996	1,608,468	23.0	525,555	7.5	344,363	4.9
1997	1,653,236	23.1	562,808	7.9	339,400	4.7
1998	1,632,859	22.3	549,265	7.5	352,992	4.8
1999	1,613,335	21.6	551,445	7.4	347,989	4.7
2000	1,766,440	23.1	577,387	7.5	366,931	4.8
2001	1,714,093	22.0	559,162	7.2	381,834	4.9
2002	1,666,773	21.0	583,167	7.3	396,297	5.0
2003	1,669,442	20.6	593,553	7.3	396,331	4.9
2004	1,710,994	20.7	582,281	7.0	403,191	4.9

* Registration is incomplete. According to UN estimates, the average annual rates per 1,000 were: births 31.7 in 1990–95, 28.9 in 1995–2000, 26.4 in 2000–05; deaths 6.3 in 1990–95, 5.5 in 1995–2000, 5.0 in 2000–05 (Source: UN, *World Population Prospects: The 2008 Revision*).

Life expectancy (years at birth, WHO estimates): 67.5 (males 64.4; females 71.0) in 2006 (Source: WHO, *World Health Statistics*).

ECONOMICALLY ACTIVE POPULATION*
('000 persons aged 15 years and over, October)

	2005	2006	2007
Agriculture, hunting and forestry	10,763	10,619	10,763
Fishing	1,408	1,423	1,392
Mining and quarrying	116	134	136
Manufacturing	3,043	3,010	3,061
Electricity, gas and water	108	122	141
Construction	1,616	1,626	1,741
Wholesale and retail trade; repair of motor vehicles, motorcycles and personal and household goods	6,215	6,152	6,176
Hotels and restaurants	871	907	905
Transport, storage and communications	2,471	2,460	2,599
Financial intermediation	337	366	384
Real estate, renting and business activities	736	799	881
Public administration and defence; compulsory social security	1,494	1,518	1,568
Education	989	997	1,043
Health and social work	362	370	396
Other community, social and personal services	781	761	780
Private households with employed persons	1,561	1,619	1,701
Extra-territorial organizations and bodies	3	2	3
Total employed	32,875	32,886	33,671
Unemployed	2,619	2,625	2,248
Total labour force	35,494	35,511	35,919

* Figures refer to civilians only and are based on quarterly household surveys (excluding institutional households).

THE PHILIPPINES

Health and Welfare

KEY INDICATORS

Total fertility rate (children per woman, 2006)	3.3
Under-5 mortality rate (per 1,000 live births, 2006)	32
HIV/AIDS (% of persons aged 15–49, 2005)	<0.1
Physicians (per 1,000 head, 2004)	0.58
Hospital beds (per 1,000 head, 2006)	1.3
Health expenditure (2006): US $ per head (PPP)	223
Health expenditure (2006): % of GDP	3.3
Health expenditure (2006): public (% of total)	39.6
Access to water (% of persons, 2006)	93
Access to sanitation (% of persons, 2006)	78
Human Development Index (2006): ranking	102
Human Development Index (2006): value	0.745

For sources and definitions, see explanatory note on p. vi.

Agriculture

PRINCIPAL CROPS
('000 metric tons)

	2005	2006	2007
Rice, paddy	14,603	15,327	16,000
Maize	5,253	6,082	6,730
Potatoes	70	69	72*
Sweet potatoes	575	567	591*
Cassava (Manioc)	1,678	1,757	1,829*
Taro	110	112	117*
Yams	29	30	32*
Sugar cane	31,400*	24,345	25,300*
Beans, dry	27	26	27*
Groundnuts, with shell	28	29	30*
Coconuts	14,825	14,958	15,580
Oil palm fruit	226*	373	385*
Cabbages and other brassicas	91	91	95*
Tomatoes	174	176	183*
Pumpkins, squash and gourds	393	371	386*
Aubergines (Eggplants)	188	192	198*
Onions, dry	82	76	78*
Watermelons	115	117	120*
Bananas	6,298	6,795	7,000*
Grapefruit and pomelos	41	39	41*
Guavas, mangoes and mangosteens	1,003	937	975*
Avocados	38	26	27*
Pineapples	1,788	1,834	1,900*
Papayas	147	157	164*
Coffee, green	106	104	106*
Ginger	25	27	28*
Tobacco, unmanufactured	45	38	40*
Natural rubber	316	352	360*

* FAO estimate.

Aggregate production ('000 metric tons, may include official, semi-official or estimated data): Total cereals 19,856 in 2005, 21,409 in 2006, 22,730 in 2007; Total roots and tubers 2,478 in 2005, 2,606 in 2006, 2,713 in 2007; Total vegetables (incl. melons) 5,353 in 2005, 5,729 in 2006, 5,879 in 2007; Total fruits (excl. melons) 13,111 in 2005, 10,016 in 2006, 10,340 in 2007.

Source: FAO.

LIVESTOCK
('000 head, year ending 30 June)

	2005	2006	2007*
Cattle	2,489	2,525	2,650
Pigs	12,140	13,047	13,250
Buffaloes	3,327	3,358	3,365
Horses*	230	230	232
Goats	6,700*	3,736	3,850
Sheep*	30	30	30
Chickens	136,001	134,300	136,000
Ducks	10,439	11,147	12,000

* FAO estimate(s).

Source: FAO.

LIVESTOCK PRODUCTS
('000 metric tons)

	2005	2006	2007*
Cattle meat	172.8	166.8	170.0
Buffalo meat	77.1	74.0*	75.5
Pig meat	1,415.0	1,466.8	1,501.0
Chicken meat	649.5	643.1	638.0
Cows' milk	13.0†	12.0	12.5
Hen eggs*	522	520	530
Other poultry eggs*	72.0	72.0	73.0

* FAO estimate(s).
† Unofficial figure.

Source: FAO.

Forestry

ROUNDWOOD REMOVALS
('000 cubic metres, excl. bark)

	2005	2006	2007
Sawlogs, veneer logs and logs for sleepers*	345	539	543
Pulpwood	489	472	258
Other industrial wood*	2,295	2,295	2,295
Fuel wood*	12,950	12,821	12,698
Total	16,079	16,127	15,794

* FAO estimates.

Source: FAO.

SAWNWOOD PRODUCTION
('000 cubic metres, incl. railway sleepers)

	2005	2006	2007
Total (all broadleaved)	288	468	362

Source: FAO.

Fishing

('000 metric tons, live weight)

	2004	2005	2006
Capture	2,211.1	2,245.9	2,319.0
Scads (Decapterus)	418.5	392.9	377.2
Sardinellas	270.2	336.3	304.1
Frigate and bullet tunas	208.1	174.0	175.3
Skipjack tuna	143.1	143.1	164.3
Yellowfin tuna	120.1	95.2	115.5
Indian mackerel	77.3	85.6	89.1
Aquaculture	512.2	557.3	623.4
Nile tilapia	118.1	126.6	160.5
Milkfish	273.6	289.2	315.1
Total catch	2,723.4	2,803.2	2,942.4

Note: Figures exclude aquatic plants ('000 metric tons): 1,205.2 (capture 0.4, aquaculture 1,204.8) in 2004; 1,338.9 (capture 0.3, aquaculture 1,338.6) in 2005; 1,469.2 (capture 0.3, aquaculture 1,468.9) in 2006.

Source: FAO.

THE PHILIPPINES

Mining

('000 metric tons, unless otherwise indicated)

	2004	2005	2006
Coal	2,727	3,165	2,529
Crude petroleum ('000 barrels)	139	208	181
Chromium ore (gross weight)	42.1	38.1	46.7
Copper ore*	16.0	16.3	17.2
Salt (unrefined)	427.6	421.0	425.0†
Nickel ore*	17.0	26.6	58.9
Gold (metric tons)*	35.5	37.5	36.1
Silver (metric tons)*	9.3	19.2	23.5
Dolomite	1,408.9	874.7	900.0†
Limestone‡	20,959	21,236	21,000†

* Figures refer to the metal content of ores and concentrates.
† Estimate.
‡ Excludes limestone for road construction.

Source: US Geological Survey.

Industry

SELECTED PRODUCTS
('000 metric tons, unless otherwise indicated)

	2004	2005	2006
Plywood ('000 cubic metres)	386	314	317
Mechanical wood pulp*	38	38	38
Chemical wood pulp*	147	147	147
Paper and paperboard*	1,097	1,097	1,097
Jet fuels ('000 barrels)	45,800	46,000*	46,000*
Motor spirit—petrol ('000 barrels)	127,600	128,000*	128,000*
Kerosene ('000 barrels)	17,700	18,000*	18,000*
Distillate fuel oils ('000 barrels)*	170,000	170,000	170,000
Residual fuel oils ('000 barrels)	234,200	234,000*	234,000*
Liquefied petroleum gas	30,600	31,000*	31,000*
Cement	13,346	15,494	12,033
Smelter (unrefined) copper	120	170	162
Electric energy (million kWh)	55,957	56,568	56,784

* Estimate(s).

2007: Electric energy (million kWh) 59,612.

Sources: FAO; US Geological Survey; Asian Development Bank.

Finance

CURRENCY AND EXCHANGE RATES

Monetary Units
100 centavos = 1 Philippine peso.

Sterling, Dollar and Euro Equivalents (31 December 2008)
£1 sterling = 69.22 pesos;
US $1 = 47.49 pesos;
€1 = 66.08 pesos;
1,000 Philippine pesos = £14.45 = $21.06 = €15.13.

Average Exchange Rate (pesos per US $)
2006 51.314
2007 46.148
2008 44.475

Statistical Survey

GENERAL BUDGET
(million pesos)

Revenue*	2003	2004	2005†
Tax revenue	537,684	596,408	677,707
Taxes on net income and profits	243,735	278,848	319,102
Taxes on property	712	798	914
Taxes on domestic goods and services	186,784	203,779	225,041
General sales tax	82,444	93,727	109,094
Excises on goods	56,865	51,433	50,699
Taxes on international trade	106,453	112,983	132,650
Non-tax revenue	87,748	79,491	80,239
Bureau of the Treasury income	56,657	40,735	45,369
Fees and charges	29,375	22,993	24,643
Privatization	1,716	1,000	500
Other non-tax revenue	—	14,763	9,726
Total	**625,432**	**675,898**	**757,945**

Expenditure‡	2003	2004	2005†
Economic services	169,881	155,585	159,158
Agriculture	32,932	25,262	25,941
Natural resources and the environment	6,752	6,776	6,803
Trade and industry	2,722	2,833	3,020
Tourism	1,182	1,200	1,412
Power and energy	1,099	1,999	1,512
Water resources, development and flood control	7,007	6,180	6,471
Transport and communications	67,149	54,908	54,949
Other economic services	1,688	7,077	5,982
Allotment to local government units	49,350	49,350	53,068
Social services	237,532	247,888	254,297
Education, culture and training	128,995	133,321	135,470
Health	12,400	12,880	12,927
Social security, welfare and employment	39,096	38,381	40,080
Housing and community development	3,019	2,577	1,739
Land distribution	907	4,284	4,422
Other social services	945	4,275	3,558
Allotment to local government units	52,170	52,170	56,101
Defence	44,439	43,847	44,193
General public services	141,233	137,278	140,650
General administration	43,442	42,254	40,143
Public order and safety	52,565	53,213	54,290
Other general public services	5,746	2,331	3,763
Allotment to local government units	39,480	39,480	42,454
Interest payments	226,408	271,531	301,692
Total	**819,493**	**856,129**	**899,990**

* Excluding grants received (million pesos): 1,198 in 2003; 511 in 2004; 527 in 2005 (forecast).
† Forecasts.
‡ Excluding net lending (million pesos): 5,620 in 2003; 5,500 in 2004; 7,600 in 2005 (forecast).

2006 ('000 million pesos): Total revenue 979.6; Total expenditure 1,044.4 (Source: IMF, *International Financial Statistics*).

INTERNATIONAL RESERVES
(US $ million at 31 December)

	2006	2007	2008
Gold*	2,941	3,541	4,358
IMF special drawing rights	2	1	11
Reserve position in IMF	132	138	135
Foreign exchange	19,891	30,071	33,047
Total	**22,966**	**33,751**	**37,551**

* Valued at market-related prices.

Source: IMF, *International Financial Statistics*.

THE PHILIPPINES

MONEY SUPPLY
(million pesos at 31 December)

	2005	2006	2007
Currency outside banks	273,710	312,020	355,200
Demand deposits at commercial banks	336,410	446,350	511,222
Total money (incl. others)	620,220	772,300	880,510

Source: IMF, *International Financial Statistics*.

COST OF LIVING
(Consumer Price Index; base: 2000 = 100)

	2005	2006	2007
Food (incl. beverages and tobacco)	123.8	130.6	134.9
Fuel, light and water	156.2	176.4	182.1
Clothing (incl. footwear)	118.4	122.0	124.8
Housing and repairs	126.9	131.9	133.9
Services	148.5	161.7	166.2
Miscellaneous	117.1	120.6	122.5
All items	129.8	137.9	141.8

NATIONAL ACCOUNTS
('000 million pesos at current prices)

Expenditure on the Gross Domestic Product

	2005	2006	2007
Government final consumption expenditure	521.6	587.5	654.1
Private final consumption expenditure	3,773.0	4,226.1	4,615.8
Increase in stocks	10.6	30.1	980.0
Gross fixed capital formation	783.4	834.4	
Statistical discrepancy	575.7	430.1	450.2
Total domestic expenditure	5,664.4	6,108.2	6,700.1
Exports of goods and services	2,589.7	2,798.0	2,729.8
Less Imports of goods and services	2,816.2	2,873.6	2,778.6
GDP in purchasers' values	5,437.9	6,032.6	6,651.3
GDP at constant 1985 prices	1,210.5	1,276.4	1,370.0

Gross Domestic Product by Economic Activity

	2005	2006	2007
Agriculture, hunting, forestry and fishing	780.1	855.5	937.3
Mining and quarrying	63.6	75.6	99.3
Manufacturing	1,264.7	1,381.2	1,460.7
Electricity, gas and water	196.7	216.1	232.1
Construction	210.2	235.2	290.7
Wholesale and retail trade, restaurants and hotels	776.9	877.5	997.2
Transport, storage and communications	413.9	446.2	478.2
Financial intermediation	263.7	312.0	359.9
Real estate, renting and business activities	320.4	350.7	374.5
Public administration	405.8	452.6	481.9
Other services	742.0	830.2	939.5
GDP in purchasers' values	5,437.9	6,032.6	6,651.3

BALANCE OF PAYMENTS
(US $ million)

	2005	2006	2007
Exports of goods f.o.b.	40,263	46,526	49,512
Imports of goods f.o.b.	−48,036	−53,258	−57,723
Trade balance	−7,773	−6,732	−8,211
Exports of services	4,525	6,444	8,448
Imports of services	−5,865	−6,307	−7,371
Balance on goods and services	−9,113	−6,595	−7,134
Other income received	3,937	4,388	5,488
Other income paid	−4,231	−5,643	−6,030
Balance on goods, services and income	−9,407	−7,850	−7,676
Current transfers received	11,711	13,511	14,397
Current transfers paid	−320	−314	−420
Current balance	1,984	5,347	6,301
Capital account (net)	40	138	24
Direct investment abroad	−189	−103	−3,442
Direct investment from abroad	1,854	2,921	2,928
Portfolio investment assets	−145	−1,567	813
Portfolio investment liabilities	3,446	6,144	3,702
Financial derivatives assets	98	159	170
Financial derivatives liabilities	−141	−297	−458
Other investment assets	−4,791	−3,512	−4,852
Other investment liabilities	1,309	−2,394	4,154
Net errors and omissions	−1,803	−1,594	−633
Overall balance	1,662	5,242	8,707

Source: IMF, *International Financial Statistics*.

External Trade

PRINCIPAL COMMODITIES
(distribution by SITC, US $ million)

Imports c.i.f.	2005	2006	2007
Food and live animals	2,946.1	3,170.6	3,713.1
Mineral fuels, lubricants, etc.	6,536.7	8,299.7	9,883.0
Petroleum, petroleum products, etc.	5,967.8	7,606.4	8,834.2
Crude petroleum oils, etc.	3,894.2	5,172.3	5,832.0
Chemicals and related products	3,610.4	3,974.9	4,200.5
Basic manufactures	4,397.5	4,638.8	4,442.0
Textile yarn, fabrics, etc.	1,101.1	1,244.0	911.4
Machinery and transport equipment	28,608.9	30,365.0	18,233.1
Office machines and automatic data-processing equipment	4,010.0	3,891.5	3,489.7
Parts and accessories for office machines, etc.	3,794.3	3,598.7	3,200.3
Telecommunications and sound equipment	1,319.7	1,329.4	1,234.5
Other electrical machinery, apparatus, etc.	19,144.4	20,525.6	8,346.1
Thermionic valves, tubes, etc.	16,652.1	18,078.5	6,340.0
Electronic microcircuits	1,807.9	4,103.8	5,118.4
Parts for electronic microcircuits	14,548.0	13,566.9	934.9
Road vehicles and parts (excl. tyres, engines and electrical parts)	1,295.3	1,443.1	1,827.5
Miscellaneous manufactured articles	1,689.1	1,874.6	1,478.2
Total (incl. others)	49,487.4	54,078.0	57,995.7

THE PHILIPPINES   Statistical Survey

Exports f.o.b.	2005	2006	2007
Food and live animals	1,689.1	1,790.8	2,021.1
Basic manufactures	1,804.6	3,654.8	3,738.1
Machinery and transport equipment	30,691.1	32,947.5	19,714.0
Office machines and automatic data-processing equipment	7,816.4	8,177.5	5,802.5
Automatic data-processing machines and units	4,080.7	4,666.1	3,940.7
Digital automatic data processing machines and units thereof	661.0	1,352.7	1,250.0
Digital central storage units, separately consigned	2,638.4	2,484.1	2,082.6
Parts and accessories for data-processing machines	3,600.3	3,370.0	1,729.1
Telecommunications and sound equipment	970.0	941.6	996.8
Other electrical machinery, apparatus, etc.	19,189.8	21,227.5	10,535.2
Thermionic valves, tubes, etc.	15,005.3	16,973.1	7,416.6
Diodes, transistors, etc.	6,592.6	7,885.9	1,860.6
Electronic microcircuits	7,640.3	8,324.2	4,970.8
Road vehicles and parts (excl. tyres, engines and electrical parts)	1,610.4	1,560.6	1,808.1
Miscellaneous manufactured articles	4,190.0	4,865.9	2,844.0
Clothing and accessories (excl. footwear)	2,287.1	2,624.3	1,493.5
Unclassified transactions and commodities	60.0	537.8	17,729.9
Total (incl. others)	41,254.7	47,410.1	50,465.7

Source: UN, *International Trade Statistics Yearbook*.

PRINCIPAL TRADING PARTNERS
(US $ million)

Imports f.o.b.	2005	2006	2007
China, People's Republic	3,134.1	3,869.4	4,232.9
Hong Kong	2,021.4	2,197.0	2,325.8
Japan	8,464.2	7,676.9	7,219.1
Korea, Republic	2,386.1	3,332.3	3,403.9
Malaysia	1,850.0	2,183.0	2,370.1
Netherlands	421.0	426.1	482.0
Singapore	3,864.6	4,556.3	6,411.3
Thailand	1,678.7	2,179.7	2,402.5
USA	9,340.4	8,698.7	8,115.3
Total (incl. others)	49,487.4	54,078.0	57,995.7

Exports f.o.b.	2005	2006	2007
China, People's Republic	4,077.0	4,627.7	5,749.5
Hong Kong	3,340.7	3,706.0	5,803.5
Japan	7,206.1	7,918.3	7,304.1
Korea, Republic	1,391.3	1,422.8	1,783.7
Malaysia	2,458.9	2,621.4	2,506.7
Netherlands	4,032.6	4,769.2	4,149.5
Singapore	2,706.9	3,505.0	3,138.7
Thailand	1,169.2	1,324.7	1,403.0
USA	7,444.1	8,697.6	8,601.4
Total (incl. others)	41,254.7	47,410.1	50,465.7

Source: UN, *International Trade Statistics Yearbook*.

Transport

RAILWAYS
(traffic)

	2002	2003	2004
Passenger-km (million)	93	83	84
Freight ton-km ('000)	63	69	76

Source: UN, *Statistical Yearbook*.

ROAD TRAFFIC
(registered motor vehicles)

	2005	2006	2007
Passenger cars	788,408	792,373	751,092
Utility vehicles	1,633,856	1,618,101	1,602,619
Sports utility vehicles (SUVs)	157,938	172,794	192,991
Buses	30,977	29,144	30,159
Trucks	266,915	285,901	281,261
Motorcycles and mopeds*	2,157,737	2,409,363	2,647,574
Trailers	23,922	23,898	24,356

* Including tricycles.

Source: Land Transportation Office, Manila.

SHIPPING
Merchant Fleet
(registered at 31 December)

	2005	2006	2007
Number of vessels	1,866	1,840	1,768
Total displacement (grt)	5,199,088	5,072,004	5,066,182

Source: Lloyd's Register-Fairplay, *World Fleet Statistics*.

International Sea-borne Shipping
(freight traffic)

	1994	1995	1996
Vessels ('000 net registered tons):			
entered	53,453	61,298	n.a.
cleared	53,841	61,313	n.a.
Goods ('000 metric tons):			
loaded	14,581	16,658	15,687
unloaded	38,222	42,418	51,830

CIVIL AVIATION
(traffic on scheduled services)

	2002	2003	2004
Kilometres flown (million)	79	75	82
Passengers carried ('000)	6,449	6,435	7,388
Passenger-km (million)	14,216	13,904	15,739
Total ton-km (million)	1,755	1,729	1,929

Source: UN, *Statistical Yearbook*.

Tourism

FOREIGN TOURIST ARRIVALS

Country of residence	2004	2005	2006
Australia	89,175	96,465	101,313
Canada	64,537	72,853	80,507
China, People's Republic	39,581	107,456	133,585
Germany	45,092	50,411	51,402
Hong Kong	162,381	107,195	96,296
Japan	382,307	415,456	421,808
Korea, Republic	378,602	489,465	572,133
Singapore	60,253	69,435	81,114
Taiwan	115,182	122,946	114,955
United Kingdom	56,770	63,002	68,490
USA	478,091	528,493	567,355
Total (incl. others)*	2,291,352	2,623,084	2,843,345

* Including Philippines nationals residing abroad.

Tourism receipts (US $ million, incl. passenger transport): 2,390 in 2004; 2,755 in 2005; 4,019 in 2006.

Source: World Tourism Organization.

THE PHILIPPINES

Communications Media

	2005	2006	2007
Telephones ('000 main lines in use)	3,367.3	3,633.2	n.a.
Mobile cellular telephones ('000 subscribers)	34,779	42,869	51,795
Personal computers ('000 in use)	3,684	n.a.	n.a.
Internet users ('000)	4,615	5,000	5,300
Broadband subscribers ('000)	123	n.a.	968

Radio receivers ('000 in use): 11,500 in 1997.

Television receivers ('000 in use): 13,500 in 2001.

Facsimile machines (estimated number in use): 50,000 in 1995.

Book production (titles, excluding pamphlets): 1,380 in 1999.

Daily newspapers: 42 (with average circulation of 4,712,000 copies) in 1997.

Non-daily newspapers: 47 (with average circulation of 199,000 copies) in 1997.

Sources: International Telecommunication Union; UN, *Statistical Yearbook*; UNESCO, *Statistical Yearbook*.

Education

(2006/07, estimates, unless otherwise stated)

	Institutions	Teachers	Pupils
Pre-primary	41,949*	343,646†	961,397
Primary schools			13,145,210
Secondary schools	8,287*	128,191†	6,363,002
University and other tertiary education‡	1,538	113,716	2,420,856

* 2005/06 figures.
† Excluding private education.
‡ 2003/04 figures.

Sources: Department of Education, Culture and Sports; Commission on Higher Education.

Adult literacy rate (UNESCO estimates): 93.4% (males 93.1%; females 93.7%) in 2007 (Source: UNESCO Institute for Statistics).

Directory

The Constitution

A new Constitution for the Republic of the Philippines was ratified by national referendum on 2 February 1987. Its principal provisions are summarized below:

BASIC PRINCIPLES

Sovereignty resides in the people, and all government authority emanates from them; war is renounced as an instrument of national policy; civilian authority is supreme over military authority.

The State undertakes to pursue an independent foreign policy, governed by considerations of the national interest; the Republic of the Philippines adopts and pursues a policy of freedom from nuclear weapons in its territory.

Other provisions guarantee social justice and full respect for human rights; honesty and integrity in the public service; the autonomy of local governments; and the protection of the family unit. Education, the arts, sport, private enterprise, and agrarian and urban reforms are also promoted. The rights of workers, women, youth, the urban poor and minority indigenous communities are emphasized.

BILL OF RIGHTS

The individual is guaranteed the right to life, liberty and property under the law; freedom of abode and travel, freedom of worship, freedom of speech, of the press and of petition to the Government are guaranteed, as well as the right of access to official information on matters of public concern, the right to form trade unions, the right to assemble in public gatherings, and free access to the courts.

The Constitution upholds the right of habeas corpus and prohibits the intimidation, detention, torture or secret confinement of apprehended persons.

SUFFRAGE

Suffrage is granted to all citizens over 18 years of age, who have resided for at least one year previously in the Republic of the Philippines, and for at least six months in their voting district. Voting is by secret ballot.

LEGISLATURE

Legislative power is vested in the bicameral Congress of the Philippines, consisting of the Senate and the House of Representatives, with a maximum of 274 members (subsequently increased to 299). All members shall make a disclosure of their financial and business interests upon assumption of office, and no member may hold any other office. Provision is made for voters to propose laws, or reject any act or law passed by Congress, through referendums.

The Senate shall be composed of 24 members; Senators are directly elected for six years by national vote, and must be natural-born citizens, at least 35 years of age, literate and registered voters in their district. They must be resident in the Philippines for at least two years prior to election, and no Senator shall serve for more than two consecutive terms. One-half of the membership of the Senate shall be elected every three years. No treaty or international agreement may be considered valid without the approval, by voting, of at least two-thirds of members.

A maximum of 250 Representatives (increased to 275 at the 2007 election) may sit in the House of Representatives. Its members may serve no more than three consecutive three-year terms. Representatives must be natural-born citizens, literate, and at least 25 years of age. Each legislative district may elect one representative; the number of legislative districts shall be determined according to population and shall be reapportioned following each census. Representatives must be registered voters in their district, and resident there for at least one year prior to election. In addition, one-fifth of the total number of representatives shall be elected under a party list system from lists of nominees proposed by indigenous, but non-religious, minority groups (such as the urban poor, peasantry, women and youth).

The Senate and the House of Representatives shall each have an Electoral Tribunal which shall be the sole judge of contests relating to the election of members of Congress. Each Tribunal shall have nine members, three of whom must be Justices of the Supreme Court, appointed by the Chief Justice. The remaining six members shall be members of the Senate or of the House of Representatives, as appropriate, and shall be selected from the political parties represented therein, on a proportional basis.

THE COMMISSION ON APPOINTMENTS

The President must submit nominations of heads of executive departments, ambassadors and senior officers in the armed forces to the Commission on Appointments, which shall decide on the appointment by majority vote of its members. The President of the Senate shall act as ex-officio Chairman; the Commission shall consist of 12 Senators and 12 members of the House of Representatives, elected from the political parties represented therein, on the basis of proportional representation.

THE EXECUTIVE

Executive power is vested in the President of the Philippines. Presidents are limited to one six-year term of office, and Vice-Presidents to two successive six-year terms. Candidates for both posts are elected by direct universal suffrage. They must be natural-born citizens, literate, at least 40 years of age, registered voters and resident in the Philippines for at least 10 years prior to election.

The President is Head of State and Chief Executive of the Republic. Bills (legislative proposals) that have been approved by Congress shall be signed by the President; if the President vetoes the bill, it may become law when two-thirds of members in Congress approve it.

The President shall nominate and, with the consent of the Commission on Appointments, appoint ambassadors, officers of the armed forces and heads of executive departments.

The President is Commander-in-Chief of the armed forces and may suspend the writ of habeas corpus or place the Republic under martial law for a period not exceeding 60 days when, in the Presi-

THE PHILIPPINES

dent's opinion, public safety demands it. Congress may revoke either action by a majority vote.

The Vice-President may be a member of the Cabinet; in the event of the death or resignation of the President, the Vice-President shall become President and serve the unexpired term of the previous President.

THE JUDICIARY

The Supreme Court is composed of a Chief Justice and 14 Associate Justices, and may sit *en banc* or in divisions comprising three, five or seven members. Justices of the Supreme Court are appointed by the President, with the consent of the Commission on Appointments, for a term of four years. They must be citizens of the Republic, at least 40 years of age, of proven integrity, and must have been judges of the lower courts, or engaged in the practice of law in the Philippines, for at least 15 years.

The Supreme Court, sitting *en banc*, is the sole judge of disputes relating to presidential and vice-presidential elections.

THE CONSTITUTIONAL COMMISSIONS

These are the Civil Service Commission and the Commission on Audit, each of which has a Chairman and two other Commissioners, appointed by the President (with the approval of the Commission on Appointments) to a seven-year term; and the Commission on Elections, which enforces and administers all laws pertaining to elections and political parties. The Commission on Elections has seven members, appointed by the President (and approved by the Commission on Appointments) for a seven-year term. The Commission on Elections may sit *en banc* or in two divisions.

LOCAL GOVERNMENT

The Republic of the Philippines shall be divided into provinces, cities, municipalities and barangays. The Congress of the Philippines shall enact a local government code providing for decentralization. A region may become autonomous, subject to approval by a majority vote of the electorate of that region, in a referendum. Defence and security in such areas will remain the responsibility of the national Government.

ACCOUNTABILITY OF PUBLIC OFFICERS

All public officers, including the President, Vice-President and members of Congress and the Constitutional Commissions, may be removed from office if impeached for, or convicted of, violation of the Constitution, corruption, treason, bribery or betrayal of public trust.

Cases of impeachment must be initiated solely by the House of Representatives, and tried solely by the Senate. A person shall be convicted by a vote of at least two-thirds of the Senate, and will then be dismissed from office and dealt with according to the law.

SOCIAL JUSTICE AND HUMAN RIGHTS

The Congress of the Philippines shall give priority to considerations of human dignity, the equality of the people and an equitable distribution of wealth. The Commission on Human Rights shall investigate allegations of violations of human rights, shall protect human rights through legal measures, and shall monitor the Government's compliance with international treaty obligations. It may advise Congress on measures to promote human rights.

AMENDMENTS OR REVISIONS

Proposals for amendment or revision of the Constitution may be made by:
  i) Congress (upon a vote of three-quarters of members);
  ii) A Constitutional Convention (convened by a vote of two-thirds of members of Congress);
  iii) The people, through petitions (signed by at least 12% of the total number of registered voters).

The proposed amendments or revisions shall then be submitted to a national plebiscite, and shall be valid when ratified by a majority of the votes cast.

MILITARY BASES

Foreign military bases, troops or facilities shall not be allowed in the Republic of the Philippines following the expiry, in 1991, of the Agreement between the Republic and the USA, except under the provisions of a treaty approved by the Senate, and, when required by Congress, ratified by the voters in a national referendum.

The Government

HEAD OF STATE

President: GLORIA MACAPAGAL ARROYO (assumed office 20 January 2001; inaugurated for second term 30 June 2004).

Vice-President: NOLI DE CASTRO.

CABINET
(April 2009)

Executive Secretary: EDUARDO ERMITA.
Secretary of Agrarian Reform: NASSER C. PANGANDAMAN.
Secretary of Agriculture: ARTHUR C. YAP.
Secretary of the Budget and Management: ROLANDO G. ANDAYA.
Secretary of Education: JESLI A. LAPUS.
Secretary of Energy: ANGELO REYES.
Secretary of the Environment and Natural Resources: JOSE LIVIOKO ATIENZA, Jr.
Secretary of Finance: MARGARITO B. TEVES.
Secretary of Foreign Affairs: ALBERTO G. ROMULO.
Secretary of Health: FRANCISCO T. DUQUE III.
Secretary of the Interior and Local Government: RONALDO V. PUNO.
Secretary of Justice: RAUL M. GONZALES.
Secretary of Labor and Employment: MARIANITO D. ROQUE.
Secretary of National Defense: GILBERTO C. TEODORO, Jr.
Secretary of Public Works and Highways: HERMOGENES E. EBDANE, Jr.
Secretary of Science and Technology: ESTRELLA F. ALABASTRO.
Secretary of Social Welfare and Development: ESPERANZA CABRAL.
Secretary of Tourism: JOSEPH 'ACE' DURANO.
Secretary of Trade and Industry: PETER B. FAVILA.
Secretary of Transportation and Communications: LEANDRO R. MENDOZA.
Director-General of the National Economic and Development Authority: RALPH B. RECTO.
Presidential Spokesman and Press Secretary: JESUS G. DUREZA.

There are a further 16 officials of cabinet rank.

MINISTRIES

Office of the President: New Executive Bldg, Malacañang Palace Compound, J. P. Laurel St, San Miguel, Metro Manila; tel. (2) 7356201; fax (2) 9293968; e-mail opnet@ops.gov.ph; internet www.opnet.ops.gov.ph.

Office of the Vice-President: PNB Financial Center, 7th Floor, President Diosdado Macapagal Blvd, Pasay City, Metro Manila; tel. (2) 8333311; fax (2) 8312618; e-mail vp@ovp.gov.ph; internet www.ovp.gov.ph.

Department of Agrarian Reform: DAR Bldg, Elliptical Rd, Diliman, Quezon City, Metro Manila; tel. (2) 9287031; fax (2) 9292527; e-mail info@dar.gov.ph; internet www.dar.gov.ph.

Department of Agriculture: DA Bldg, 4th Floor, Elliptical Rd, Diliman, Quezon City, Metro Manila; tel. (2) 9288741; fax (2) 9277152; e-mail admin@da.gov.ph; internet www.da.gov.ph.

Department of the Budget and Management: DBM Bldg, Gen. Solano St, San Miguel, Metro Manila; tel. (2) 7354807; fax (2) 7357814; e-mail dbmtis@dbm.gov.ph; internet www.dbm.gov.ph.

Department of Education, Culture and Sports: DepED Complex, Meralco Ave, Pasig City, 1600 Metro Manila; tel. (2) 6321361; fax (2) 6388634; internet www.deped.gov.ph.

Department of Energy: Energy Center, Merritt Rd, Fort Bonifacio, Taguig, Metro Manila; tel. (2) 8441021; fax (2) 8442495; e-mail v_perez@doe.gov.ph; internet www.doe.gov.ph.

Department of the Environment and Natural Resources: DENR Bldg, Visayas Ave, Diliman, Quezon City, 1100 Metro Manila; tel. (2) 9296626; fax (2) 9204352; e-mail web@denr.gov.ph; internet www.denr.gov.ph.

Department of Finance: DOF Bldg, Roxas Blvd, cnr Pablo Ocampo St, 1004 Metro Manila; tel. (2) 4041774; fax (2) 5219495; e-mail hotline@dof.gov.ph; internet www.dof.gov.ph.

Department of Foreign Affairs: DFA Bldg, 2330 Roxas Blvd, Pasay City, 1330 Metro Manila; tel. (2) 8344000; fax (2) 8321597; e-mail webmaster@dfa.gov.ph; internet www.dfa.gov.ph.

Department of Health: San Lazaro Compound, Rizal Ave, Santa Cruz, 1003 Metro Manila; tel. (2) 7438301; fax (2) 7431829; e-mail info@doh.gov.ph; internet www.doh.gov.ph.

Department of the Interior and Local Government: A. Francisco Gold Condominium II, Epifanio de los Santos Ave, cnr Mapagmahal St, Diliman, Quezon City, 1100 Metro Manila; tel. (2) 9250349; fax (2) 9250386; e-mail dilgmail@dilg.gov.ph; internet www.dilg.gov.ph.

Department of Justice: Padre Faura St, Ermita, Metro Manila; tel. (2) 5216264; fax (2) 5211614; e-mail sechbp@info.com.ph; internet www.doj.gov.ph.

THE PHILIPPINES

Department of Labor and Employment: DOLE Executive Bldg, 7th Floor, Muralla Wing, Muralla St, Intramuros, 1002 Metro Manila; tel. (2) 5273000; fax (2) 5272121; e-mail osec@dole.gov.ph; internet www.dole.gov.ph.

Department of National Defense: DND Bldg, 3rd Floor, Camp Aguinaldo, Quezon City, 1100 Metro Manila; tel. (2) 9113300; fax (2) 9116213; e-mail webmaster@dnd.gov.ph; internet www.dnd.gov.ph.

Department of Public Works and Highways: DPWH Bldg, Bonifacio Drive, Port Area, Metro Manila; tel. (2) 3043000; fax (2) 5275635; e-mail pid@dpwh.gov.ph; internet www.dpwh.gov.ph.

Department of Science and Technology: DOST Compound, Gen. Santos Ave, Bicutan, Taguig, 1631 Metro Manila; tel. (2) 8372071; fax (2) 8373161; e-mail efa@dost.gov.ph; internet www.dost.gov.ph.

Department of Social Welfare and Development: Batasang Pambansa, Constitution Hills, Quezon City, Metro Manila; tel. (2) 9318101; fax (2) 9318191; e-mail eicabral@dswd.gov.ph; internet www.dswd.gov.ph.

Department of Tourism: Rm 317, DOT Bldg, T. M. Kalaw St, 1000 Metro Manila; tel. (2) 5251805; fax (2) 5256538; e-mail ejarquejr@tourism.gov.ph; internet www.wowphilippines.com.ph.

Department of Trade and Industry: Industry and Investments Bldg, 385 Sen. Gil J. Puyat Ave, Buendia, Makati City, 1200 Metro Manila; tel. (2) 8953611; fax (2) 8956487; e-mail mis@dti.dti.gov.ph; internet www.dti.gov.ph.

Department of Transportation and Communications: Columbia Tower, 17th Floor, Ortigas Ave, Mandaluyong City, 1555 Metro Manila; tel. and fax (2) 7238235; e-mail aksyonagad@dotc.gov.ph; internet www.dotc.gov.ph.

National Economic and Development Authority (NEDA—Department of Socio-Economic Planning): NEDA-sa-Pasig Bldg, 12 St Josemaria Escriva St, Pasig City, 1605 Metro Manila; tel. (2) 6313747; fax (2) 6313282; e-mail info@neda.gov.ph; internet www.neda.gov.ph.

Philippine Information Agency (Office of the Press Secretary): PIA Bldg, Visayas Ave, Diliman, Quezon City, Metro Manila; tel. (2) 9204339; fax (2) 9815025; e-mail pia@ops.gov.ph; internet www.pia.gov.ph.

President and Legislature

PRESIDENT

Election, 10 May 2004

Candidate	Votes	% of votes
Gloria Macapagal Arroyo (Lakas-CMD)	12,905,808	39.99
Fernando Poe, Jr (KNP)	11,782,232	36.51
Panfilo Lacson (LDP)	3,510,080	10.88
Raul S. Roco (Aksyon Demokratiko)	2,082,762	6.45
Eduardo Villanueva (Bangon Pilipinas)	1,988,218	6.16
Total*	32,269,100	100.00

*Total may not be equal to sum of components, owing to rounding.

THE CONGRESS OF THE PHILIPPINES

Senate

President of the Senate: JUAN PONCE ENRILE.

Elections for 12 of the 24 seats were held on 14 May 2007. The TEAM Unity coalition won three seats and the Genuine Opposition (GO) coalition won seven, giving a majority to opponents of President Arroyo. Two seats were secured by independent candidates.

House of Representatives

Speaker of the House: PROSPERO NOGRALES.

General Election, 14 May 2007

	Seats
Lakas ng EDSA-Christian Muslim Democrats (Lakas-CMD)	70
Kabalikat ng Malayang Pilipino (KAMPI)	47
Nationalist People's Coalition (NPC)	26
Liberal Party (LP)	16
Nacionalista Party (NP)	6
PDP-Laban Party	4
Others	106
Total	**275**

Note: The distribution of seats in the House of Representatives was yet to be completed and confirmed. The total includes members of minority and cause-orientated groups allocated seats under the party list elections, which also took place on 14 May 2007.

Autonomous Region

MUSLIM MINDANAO

The Autonomous Region of Muslim Mindanao (ARMM) originally comprised the provinces of Lanao del Sur, Maguindanao, Tawi-Tawi and Sulu. The Region was granted autonomy in November 1989. Elections took place in February 1990, and the formal transfer of limited executive powers took place in October of that year. In August 2001 a plebiscite was conducted in 11 provinces and 14 cities in Mindanao to determine whether or not they would become members of the ARMM. The city of Marawi and the province of Basilan subsequently joined the Region. Elections for the 21 seats of the Regional Legislative Assembly (RLA) were held on 26 November 2001. Elections for the expanded 24-seat RLA took place on 8 August 2005. A total of six candidates contested the concurrent gubernatorial election; Zaldy Puti U. Ampatuan, the candidate of Lakas ng EDSA-Christian Muslim Democrats (Lakas-CMD), won an estimated 63.7% of the votes cast, defeating Mahid Mutilan of the Ompia Party, a Muslim grouping, and Ibrahim Paglas of the Liberal Party, who received 24.3% and 11.8% of the votes respectively.

Governor: Datu ZALDY PUTI U. AMPATUAN (took office 30 September 2005).

Vice-Governor: ANSARUDDIN-ABDULMALIK A. ADIONG.

Election Commission

Commission on Elections (COMELEC): Postigo St, Intramuros, 1002 Metro Manila; tel. (2) 527-5581; e-mail asd@comelec.gov.ph; internet www.comelec.gov.ph; f. 1940; Chair. JOSE MELO.

Political Organizations

Akbayan (Citizens' Action Party): 101 Matahimik St, Teacher's Village West, Quezon City, 1101 Metro Manila; tel. (2) 4336933; fax (2) 9252936; e-mail secretariat@akbayan.org; internet www.akbayan.org; f. 1998; left-wing party list; Pres. RONALD LLAMAS; Sec.-Gen. ARLENE SANTOS.

Aksyon Demokratiko (Democratic Action Party): 16th Floor, Strata 2000 Bldg, Emerald Ave, Ortigas Center, Pasig City, 1600 Metro Manila; tel. (2) 6385381; fax (2) 6343072; e-mail senator@raulroco.com; internet 203.115.161.138/library/raulroco/aksyond/aksyond.htm; f. 1997; est. to support presidential candidacy of RAUL ROCO; joined Alyansa ng Pag-asa in 2003 to contest 2004 elections; Chair. SULPICIO ROCO; Pres. HERMINIO AQUINO.

Bangon Pilipinas (Rise Philippines): 8th Floor, Dominion Bldg, 833 Arnaiz Ave, Legaspi Village, Makati City, 1200 Metro Manila; tel. (2) 8113355; fax (2) 8111110; e-mail feedback@bangonpilipinas.org; internet www.bangonpilipinasonline.org; Pres. EDUARDO VILLANUEVA.

Bayan Muna (People First): 153 Scout Rallos St, Kamuning, Quezon City, 1103 Metro Manila; tel. (2) 4251045; fax (2) 9213473; e-mail information@bayanmuna.net; internet www.bayanmuna.net; f. 1999; Pres. SATURNINO OCAMPO; Chair. Dr REYNALDO LESACA, Jr.

Kabalikat ng Malayang Pilipino (KAMPI): 7th Floor, LTA Bldg, 118 Perea St, Legaspi St, Makati City, Metro Manila; tel. (2) 8171316; fax (2) 8121138; internet kampi.ph; f. 1997; Chair. EMIGDIO TANJUACTO; Pres. LUIS VILLAFUERTE.

Kilusan para sa Pambansang Pagpapanibago (BAGO): Metro Manila; f. 1997; est. to support presidential candidacy of SANTIAGO F. DUMLAO, Jr; Chair. EDUARDO D. BONDOC.

Kilusang Bagong Lipunan (KBL) (New Society Movement): Metro Manila; f. 1978 by Pres. MARCOS and fmr mems of the Nacionalista Party; Chair. FERDINAND 'BONG BONG' MARCOS, Jr.

Laban ng Demokratikong Pilipino (LDP) (Fight of Democratic Filipinos): c/o House of Representatives, Metro Manila; f. 1987; reorg. 1988 as an alliance of Lakas ng Bansa and a conservative faction of the PDP-Laban Party; mem. of Lapian ng Masang Pilipino (LAMP) until Jan. 2001; split into two factions, led by EDGARDO ANGARA and AGAPITO AQUINO, to contest 2004 elections; Angara faction joined Koalisyon ng Nagkakaisang Pilipino (KNP) in Dec. 2003 to support presidential candidacy of FERNANDO POE, Jr; Aquino faction supported presidential candidacy of PANFILO LACSON; Pres. EDGARDO ANGARA.

Lakas ng EDSA (Power of EDSA)-Christian Muslim Democrats (Lakas-CMD): c/o House of Representatives, Metro Manila; f. 1992; est. as alliance to support the presidential candidacy of Gen. FIDEL V. RAMOS; formed alliance with UMDP to contest 1998 and 2001 elections; fmrly Lakas-National Union of Christian Democrats (Lakas-NUCD); name changed as above in 2003; joined Koalisyon

THE PHILIPPINES

ng Katapatan at Karanasan sa Kinabukasan (K-4) in 2003; Pres. PROSPERO NOGRALES; Sec.-Gen. HEHERSON ALVAREZ.

Liberal Party (LP): 2nd Floor, Matrinco Bldg, Chino Roces Ave, Makati City, 1231 Metro Manila; tel. (2) 8937483; fax (2) 8930218; e-mail liberalpartyphils@gmail.com; internet www.liberalparty.ph; f. 1946; represents centre-liberal opinion of the fmr Nacionalista Party, which split in 1946; joined Koalisyon ng Katapatan at Karanasan sa Kinabukasan (K-4) in Jan. 2004 to contest 2004 elections; Chair. FRANKLIN M. DRILON; Pres. MANUEL ROXAS II.

Nacionalista Party (NP): Metro Manila; tel. (2) 854418; fax (2) 865602; internet www.nacionalistaparty.com; Pres. MANUEL VILLAR.

Nationalist People's Coalition (NPC): 8 Bouganvilla St, cnr Balete Dr., Mariana, Quezon City, 1112 Metro Manila; tel. (2) 5847518; fax (2) 5848691; e-mail npcparty@gmail.com; internet npcparty.org; f. 1991; breakaway faction of the Nacionalista Party; mem. of Lapian ng Masang Pilipino (LAMP) from 1997 until Jan. 2001; Chair. FAUSTINO DY, Jr; Pres. FRISCO SAN JUAN.

Partido Demokratiko Sosyalista ng Pilipinas (PDSP) (Philippine Democratic Socialist Party): 45 Melchor St, Varsity Hills, Quezon City, Metro Manila; tel. and fax (2) 4161325; fax 9286678; e-mail secretariat@pdsp.net; internet pdsp.net; f. 1981; formed by mems of the Batasang Pambansa allied to the Nacionalista (Roy faction), Pusyon Visaya and Mindanao Alliance parties; joined People Power Coalition (PPC) in Feb. 2001; Chair. NORBERTO GONZALES.

Partido ng Bayan (New People's Alliance): f. May 1986; formed by JOSE MARIA SISON (imprisoned in 1977–86), the head of the Communist Party of the Philippines (CPP); militant left-wing nationalist group.

Partido ng Manggagawang Pilipino (PMP) (Filipino Workers' Party): e-mail pinoy_bolshevik@yahoo.com; internet manggagawangpilipino.tripod.com; f. 2002; est. by fmr supporters of the CPP (see below).

Partido para sa Demokratikong Reporma-Lapiang Manggagawa Coalition (Reporma): c/o House of Representatives, Metro Manila; joined People Power Coalition (PPC) in Feb. 2001; Leader RENATO DE VILLA.

PDP-Laban Party: c/o House of Representatives, Metro Manila; f. Feb. 1983; est. following merger of Pilipino Democratic Party (f. 1982 by fmr mems of the Mindanao Alliance) and Laban (Lakas ng Bayan—People's Power Movement, f. 1978 and led by BENIGNO S. AQUINO, Jr, until his assassination in Aug. 1983); centrist; formally dissolved in Sept. 1988, following the formation of the LDP, but a faction continued to function as a political movement; Pres. JEJOMAR BINAY; Chair. AQUILINO PIMENTEL.

People's Reform Party (PRP): c/o House of Representatives, Metro Manila; f. 1991; formed by MIRIAM DEFENSOR SANTIAGO to support her candidacy in the 1992 presidential election; joined Koalisyon ng Katapatan at Karanasan sa Kinabukasan (K-4) to contest 2004 elections to Senate; Pres. MIRIAM DEFENSOR SANTIAGO.

Probinsya Muna Development Initiatives (PROMDI): 7 Pasteur St, Lahug, Cebu City; tel. (32) 2326692; fax (32) 2313609; e-mail emro@cebu.pw.net.ph; f. 1997; joined People Power Coalition (PPC) to contest 2001 elections; Leader EMILIO ('LITO') OSMEÑA.

Puwersa ng Masang Pilipino (PMP): Metro Manila; mem. of Lapian ng Masan Pilipino (LAMP) from 1997 until Jan. 2001; joined Koalisyon ng Nagkakaisang Pilipino (KNP) to contest 2004 elections; Leader JOSEPH EJERCITO ESTRADA; Pres. HORACIO MORALES, Jr.

Sandigan ng Lakas at Demokrasya ng Sambayanan (SANLAKAS) (Upholder of People's Power and Democracy): 150K 6th St, Barangay East Kamias, Quezon City, Metro Manila; tel. (2) 4338377; fax (2) 4262422; e-mail sanlakas1@yahoo.com; internet www.geocities.com/sanlakasonline; leftist multi-sectoral; Pres. and Chair. WILSON FORTALEZA.

TEAM Unity: coalition of parties incl. supporters of Pres. Gloria Arroyo; founded to contest 2007 elections, mems include Kabalikat ng Malayang Pilipino (KAMPI), Laban ng Demokratikong Pilipino (LDP), Lakas ng EDSA (Power of EDSA)-Christian Muslim Democrats (Lakas-CMD) and Partido Demokratiko Sosyalista ng Pilipinas (PDSP).

United Muslim Democratic Party (UMDP): Mindanao; moderate Islamic party; formed an electoral alliance with Lakas-NUCD for the election to the House of Representatives in May 2001.

United Negros Alliance (UNA): Negros Occidental.

The following organizations are, or have been, in conflict with the Government:

Abu Sayyaf (Bearer of the Sword): Mindanao; radical Islamic group seeking the establishment of an Islamic state in Mindanao; breakaway grouping of the MILF; est. strength 1,500 (2000); Leader YASSER IGASAN.

Alex Boncayao Brigade (ABB): communist urban guerrilla group, fmrly linked to CPP, formed alliance with Revolutionary Proletarian Party in 1997; est. strength 500 (April 2001); Leader NILO DE LA CRUZ.

Islamic Command Council (ICC): Mindanao; splinter group of MNLF; Leader MELHAM ALAM.

Maranao Islamic Statehood Movement: Mindanao; f. 1998; armed grouping seeking the establishment of an Islamic state in Mindanao.

Mindanao Independence Movement (MIM): Mindanao; claims a membership of 1m.; Leader REUBEN CANOY.

Moro Islamic Liberation Front (MILF): Camp Abubakar, Lanao del Sur, Mindanao; aims to establish an Islamic state in Mindanao; comprises a faction that broke away from the MNLF in 1978; its armed wing, the Bangsa Moro Islamic Armed Forces, has c. 12,500 armed regulars; Chair. Al-Haj MURAD EBRAHIM.

Moro Islamic Reform Group: Mindanao; breakaway faction from MNLF; est. strength of 200 in 2000.

Moro National Liberation Front (MNLF): internet mnlf.net; seeks autonomy for Muslim communities in Mindanao; signed a peace agreement with the Govt in Sept. 1996; its armed wing, the Bangsa Moro Army, comprised an est. 10,000 mems in 2000; Chair. and Pres. of Cen. Cttee Dr NUR MISUARI.

Moro National Liberation Front—Islamic Command Council (MNLF—ICC): Basak, Lanao del Sur; f. 2000; Islamist separatist movement committed to urban guerrilla warfare; breakaway faction from MNLF.

National Democratic Front (NDF): a left-wing alliance of 14 mem. groups; Chair. MARIANA OROSA; Spokesman GREGORIO ROSAL.

The NDF includes:

Communist Party of the Philippines (CPP): f. 1968; breakaway faction of the Partido Komunista ng Pilipinas (PKP, f. 1930); legalized Sept. 1992; in July 1993 the Metro Manila-Rizal and Visayas regional committees, controlling 40% of total CPP membership (est. 15,000 in 1994), split from the Central Committee; Chair. JOSE MARIA SISON; Gen. Sec. BENITO TIAMZON.

New People's Army (NPA): f. 1969 as the military wing of the CPP; based in central Luzon, but operates throughout the Philippines; est. strength 9,500; Leader JOVENCIO BALWEG; Spokesman GREGORIO ROSAL.

Revolutionary Proletarian Party: Metro Manila; f. 1996; comprises mems of the Metro Manila-Rizal and Visayas regional committees, which broke away from the CPP in 1993; has a front organization called the Bukluran ng Manggagawang Pilipino (Association of Filipino Workers); Leader ARTURO TABARA.

Rajah Solaiman Movement (RSM): Mindanao; f. 2002; radical Islamic group seeking to establish an Islamic state in the Philippines; predominantly composed of converts to Islam.

Diplomatic Representation

EMBASSIES IN THE PHILIPPINES

Argentina: 8th Floor, Liberty Center, 104 H. V. de la Costa St, Salcedo Village, Makati City, 1227 Metro Manila; tel. (2) 8453218; fax (2) 8453220; e-mail embarfil@eastern.com.ph; Ambassador ISMAEL MARIO SCHUFF.

Australia: 23rd Floor, Tower II, RCBC Plaza, 6819 Ayala Ave, Makati City, 1200 Metro Manila; tel. (2) 7578100; fax (2) 7578268; e-mail public-affairs-MNLA@dfat.gov.au; internet www.australia.com.ph; Ambassador ROD SMITH (designate).

Austria: Prince Bldg, 4th Floor, 117 Rada St, Legaspi Village, Makati City, 1200 Metro Manila; tel. (2) 8179191; fax (2) 8134238; e-mail manila-ob@bmaa.gv.at; Ambassador HERBERT JÄGER.

Bangladesh: Universal-Re Bldg, 2nd Floor, 106 Paseo de Roxas, Legaspi Village, Makati City, Metro Manila; tel. (2) 8175001; fax (2) 8164941; Ambassador (vacant).

Belgium: Multinational Bancorporation Center, 9th Floor, 6805 Ayala Ave, Makati City, Metro Manila; tel. (2) 8451869; fax (2) 8452076; e-mail manila@diplobel.org; internet www.diplomatie.be/manila; Ambassador GRÉGOIRE VARDAKIS.

Brazil: 16th Floor, Liberty Center, 104 H. V. de la Costa St, Salcedo Village, Makati City, 1227 Metro Manila; tel. (2) 8453651; fax (2) 8453676; e-mail brascom@info.com.ph; internet www.brasemb.org.ph; Ambassador ALCIDES G. R. PRATES.

Brunei: Bank of the Philippine Islands Bldg, 11th Floor, Ayala Ave, cnr Paseo de Roxas, Makati City, 1227 Metro Manila; tel. (2) 8162836; fax (2) 8916646; Ambassador EMALEEN ABDUL RAHMAN TEO.

Cambodia: Unit 7A, 7th Floor, Country Space One Bldg, Sen. Gil J. Puyat Ave, Makati City, Metro Manila; tel. (2) 8189981; fax (2)

THE PHILIPPINES

8189983; e-mail phnompenhpe@ezecom.com.kh; Ambassador IN MAY.

Canada: Floors 6–8, Tower 2, RCBC Plaza, 6819 Ayala Ave, Makati City, 1200 Metro Manila; tel. (2) 8579000; fax (2) 8431082; e-mail manil@dfait-maeci.gc.ca; internet www.dfait-maeci.gc.ca/manila; Ambassador ROBERT DESJARDINS.

Chile: 17th Floor, Liberty Center, 104 H. V. de la Costa St, cnr Leviste St, Salcedo Village, Makati City, 1227 Metro Manila; tel. (2) 8433461; fax (2) 8431976; e-mail echileph@meridiantelekoms.net; internet www.embachileph.com; Ambassador OVID HARASICH.

China, People's Republic: 4896 Pasay Rd, Dasmariñas Village, Makati City, Metro Manila; tel. (2) 8443148; fax (2) 8452465; e-mail chinaemb_ph@mfa.gov.cn; internet ph.chineseembassy.org; Ambassador LIU JIANCHAO.

Cuba: 101 Aguirre St, cnr Trasierra St, Cacho-Gonzales Bldg Penthouse, Legaspi Village, Makati City, Metro Manila; tel. (2) 8171192; fax (2) 8164094; Ambassador RAMÓN ALONSO MEDINA.

Czech Republic: 30th Floor, Rufino Pacific Tower, 6784 Ayala Ave, 1200 Makati City, Metro Manila; tel. (2) 8111155; fax (2) 8111020; e-mail manila@embassy.mzv.cz; internet www.mzv.cz/manila; Ambassador JAROSLAV LUDVA.

Egypt: 2229 Paraiso St, cnr Banyan St, Dasmariñas Village, Makati City, Metro Manila; tel. (2) 8439232; fax (2) 8439239; Ambassador SALWA MOUFID KAMEL MAGARIOUS.

Finland: 21st Floor, BPI Buendia Center, Sen. Gil J. Puyat Ave, Makati City, Metro Manila; tel. (2) 8915011; fax (2) 8914106; e-mail sanomat.mni@formin.fi; internet www.finland.ph; Ambassador HEIKKI HANNIKAINEN.

France: Pacific Star Bldg, 16th Floor, Makati Ave, cnr Sen. Gil J. Puyat Ave, 1200 Makati City, Metro Manila; tel. (2) 8576900; fax (2) 8576951; e-mail consulat@ambafrance-ph.org; internet www.ambafrance-ph.org; Ambassador THIERRY BORJA DE MOZOTA.

Germany: 25th Floor, Tower 2, RCBC Plaza, 6819 Ayala Ave, Makati City, Metro Manila; tel. (2) 7023000; fax (2) 7023015; e-mail manila-ob@bmeia.gv.at; internet www.manila.diplo.de; Ambassador CHRISTIAN-LUDWIG WEBER-LORTSCH.

Holy See: 2140 Taft Ave, POB 3364, 1099 Metro Manila (Apostolic Nunciature); tel. (2) 5210306; fax (2) 5211235; e-mail nuntiusp@info.com.ph; Apostolic Nuncio Most Rev. EDWARD J. ADAMS (Titular Archbishop of Scalia).

India: 2190 Paraiso St, Dasmariñas Village, POB 2123, Makati City, Metro Manila; tel. (2) 8430101; fax (2) 8158151; e-mail amb@embindia.org.ph; internet www.embindia.org.ph; Ambassador Shri RAJEET MITTER.

Indonesia: 185 Salcedo St, Legaspi Village, Makati City, Metro Manila; tel. (2) 8925061; fax (2) 8925878; e-mail bidpen_manila@yahoo.com; internet www.kbrimanila.org.ph; Ambassador Dr IRZAN TANJUNG.

Iran: 2224 Paraiso St, cnr Pasay Rd, Dasmariñas Village, Makati City, Metro Manila; tel. (2) 8884757; fax (2) 8884777; e-mail mrouzbehani@gmail.com; Ambassador ALI MOJTABA ROUZBEHANI.

Israel: Trafalgar Plaza, 23rd Floor, 105 H. V. de la Costa St, Salcedo Village, Makati City, 1227 Metro Manila; tel. (2) 8940441; fax (2) 8941027; e-mail info@manila.mfa.gov.il; internet manila.mfa.gov.il; Ambassador ZVI VAPNI.

Italy: Zeta II Bldg, 6th Floor, 191 Salcedo St, Legaspi Village, Makati City, Metro Manila; tel. (2) 8924531; fax (2) 8171436; e-mail informazioni.manila@esteri.it; internet www.ambmanila.esteri.it; Ambassador RUBENS ANNA FEDELE.

Japan: 2627 Roxas Blvd, Pasay City, 1300 Metro Manila; tel. (2) 5515710; fax (2) 5515780; e-mail jicc-mnl@japanembassy.ph; internet www.ph.emb-japan.go.jp; Ambassador MAKOTO KATSURA.

Korea, Republic: Pacific Star Bldg, 10th Floor, Sen. Gil J. Puyat Ave, cnr Makati Ave, Makati City, 1226 Metro Manila; tel. (2) 8116139; fax (2) 8116148; internet phl.mofat.go.kr; Ambassador HONG JONG-KI.

Kuwait: 1230 Acacia Rd, Dasmariñas Village, Makati City, Metro Manila; tel. (2) 8876880; fax (2) 8876666; Ambassador BADER NASSER AL-HOUTI.

Laos: 34 Lapu-Lapu St, Magallanes Village, Makati City, Metro Manila; tel. and fax (2) 8525759; Ambassador LEUANE SOMBOUNKHAN.

Libya: 1644 Dasmariñas St, cnr Mabolo St, Dasmariñas Village, Makati City, Metro Manila; tel. (2) 8177331; fax (2) 8177337; e-mail lpbmanila@skynet.net; Chargé d'affaires a.i. SADEK A. A. OMAN.

Malaysia: 107 Tordesillas St, Salcedo Village, Makati City, 1200 Metro Manila; tel. (2) 8640761; fax (2) 8640727; e-mail mwmanila@indanet.com; internet www.kln.gov.my/perwakilan/manila; Ambassador AHMAD RASIDI HAZIZI.

Mexico: 150 Legaspi St, G. C. Corporate Plaza, Legaspi Village, Makati City, Metro Manila; tel. (2) 8122211; fax (2) 8927635; e-mail embmxfil@info.com.ph; internet portal.sre.gob.mx/filipinaseng/; Ambassador TOMAS JAVIER CALVILLO UNNA.

Myanmar: Xanland Center, 4th Floor, 152 Amorsolo St, Legaspi Village, Makati City, Metro Manila; tel. (2) 8931944; fax (2) 8928866; e-mail embmyanmnl@mindgate.net; Ambassador U HIN TUN.

Netherlands: Equitable PCI Bank Tower, 26th Floor, 8751 Paseo de Roxas, Makati City, Metro Manila; tel. (2) 7866666; fax (2) 7866600; e-mail man@minbuza.nl; internet www.netherlandsembassy.ph; Ambassador ROBERT BRINKS.

New Zealand: BPI Buendia Center, 23rd Floor, Sen. Gil J. Puyat Ave, POB 3228, MCPO, Makati City, Metro Manila; tel. (2) 8915358; fax (2) 8915357; e-mail nzmanila@nxdsl.com.ph; internet www.nzembassy.com/philippines; Ambassador ANDREW MATHESON.

Nigeria: 2211 Paraiso St, Dasmariñas Village, Makati City, 1221 Metro Manila; POB 3174, MCPO, Makati City, 1271 Metro Manila; tel. (2) 8439866; fax (2) 8439867; e-mail embassy@nigeriamanila.org; internet www.nigeriamanila.org; Chargé d'affaires a.i. NDUBUISI V. AMAKU.

Norway: Petron Mega Plaza Bldg, 21st Floor, 358 Sen. Gil J. Puyat Ave, Makati City, 1209 Metro Manila; tel. (2) 8863245; fax (2) 8863384; e-mail emb.manila@mfa.no; internet www.norway.ph; Ambassador STÅLE TORSTEIN RISA.

Pakistan: Alexander House, 6th Floor, 132 Amorsolo St, Legaspi Village, Makati City, Metro Manila; tel. (2) 8172776; fax (2) 8400229; e-mail pakrepmanila@yahoo.com; internet www.cpsctech.org/~pkembphil; Ambassador MUHAMMAD NAEEM KHAN.

Palau: Marbella Condominium II, Unit 101, Ground Floor, 2071 Roxas Blvd, Malate, Manila; tel. (2) 5221982; fax (2) 5210402; e-mail rop_piembassy@yahoo.com; Ambassador RAMON RECHEBEI.

Panama: 10th Floor, MARC 2000 Tower, 1973 Taft Ave and San Andres St, cnr Quirino Ave, Malate, 1004 Metro Manila; tel. (2) 5212790; fax (2) 5215755; e-mail panaembassy@i-manila.com.ph; Ambassador JUAN FELIPE PITTY.

Papua New Guinea: 3rd Floor, Corinthian Plaza Condominium Bldg, cnr Paseo de Roxas and Gamboa St, Makati City, Metro Manila; tel. (2) 8113465; fax (2) 8113466; e-mail kundumnl@pngembmnl.com.ph; Ambassador DAMIEN DOMINIC GAMIANDU.

Portugal: 17th Floor, Units C and D, Trafalgar Plaza, 105 H. V. de la Costa St, Salcedo Village, Makati City, Metro Manila; tel. (2) 8483789; fax (2) 8483791; Charge d'affaires a.i. LUÍS BRITO CAMARA.

Qatar: 1398 Cabellero St, cnr Lumbang St, Dasmariñas Village, Makati City, Metro Manila; tel. (2) 8874944; fax (2) 8876406; e-mail gemanila2000@yahoo.com; Ambassador ABDULLAH AHMED YOUSIF AL-MUTAWA.

Romania: 1216 Acacia Rd, Dasmariñas Village, Makati City, Metro Manila; tel. (2) 8439014; fax (2) 8439063; e-mail amaron@zpdee.net; Ambassador VALERIU GHEORGHE.

Russia: 1245 Acacia Rd, Dasmariñas Village, Makati City, Metro Manila; tel. (2) 8930190; fax (2) 8109614; e-mail RusEmb@i-manila.com.ph; Ambassador VITALIY VOROBIEV.

Saudi Arabia: Saudi Embassy Bldg, 389 Sen. Gil J. Puyat Ave Ext., Makati City, Metro Manila; tel. (2) 8564444; fax (2) 8953493; e-mail phemb@mofa.gov.sa; internet www.saudiembassy.com.ph; Ambassador MOHAMMAD AMEEN WALI.

Singapore: 505 Rizal Drive, Bonifacio, 1634 Taguig City, Metro Manila; tel. (2) 8569922; fax (2) 8569932; e-mail singemb_mnl@sgmfa.gov.sg; internet www.mfa.gov.sg/manila; Ambassador A. SELVERAJAH.

Spain: 27/F Equitable Bank Tower, 8751 Paseo de Roxas, 1226 Metro Manila; tel. (2) 8176676; fax (2) 8174892; e-mail emb.manila@mae.es; Ambassador LUIS ARIAS ROMERO.

Sri Lanka: 2260 Avocado Ave, Dasmariñas Village, Makati City, Metro Manila; tel. and fax (2) 8439813; e-mail srilanka@bronline.com; Ambassador (vacant).

Switzerland: Equitable Bank Tower, 24th Floor, 8751 Paseo de Roxas, Makati City, 1226 Metro Manila; tel. (2) 7579000; fax (2) 7573718; e-mail man.vertretung@eda.admin.ch; internet www.eda.admin.ch/manila; Ambassador PETER SUTTER.

Thailand: 107 Rada St, Legaspi Village, Makati City, 1229 Metro Manila; tel. (2) 8154220; fax (2) 8154221; e-mail thaimnl@pacific.net.ph; Ambassador KULKUMUT SINGHARA NA AYUDHYA.

Turkey: 2268 Paraiso St, Dasmariñas Village, Makati City, Metro Manila; tel. (2) 8439705; fax (2) 8439702; Ambassador ADNAN BASAGA.

United Arab Emirates: Renaissance Bldg, 2nd Floor, 215 Sakedo St, Legaspi Village, Makati City, Metro Manila; tel. (2) 8173906; fax (2) 8183577; Ambassador MOHAMMED EBRAHIM ABDULLAH AL-JOWAID.

United Kingdom: Locsin Bldg, 15th–17th Floors, 6752 Ayala Ave, cnr Makati Ave, Makati City, 1226 Metro Manila; tel. (2) 5808700; fax (2) 8197206; e-mail uk@info.com.ph; internet www.ukinthephilippines.fco.gov.uk; Ambassador PETER BECKINGHAM.

THE PHILIPPINES

USA: 1201 Roxas Blvd, 1000 Metro Manila; tel. (2) 5286300; fax (2) 5223242; e-mail manila1@pd.state.gov; internet manila.usembassy.gov; Ambassador KRISTIE A. KENNEY.

Venezuela: Unit 17A, Multinational Bancorporation Center, 6805 Ayala Ave, Makati City, Metro Manila 1226; tel. (2) 8452841; fax (2) 8452866; e-mail venezemb@info.com.ph; Chargé d'affaires a.i. MANUEL VICENTE PÉREZ ITURBE.

Viet Nam: 670 Pablo Ocampo St, Malate, Metro Manila; tel. (2) 5216843; fax (2) 5260472; e-mail vnembph@yahoo.com; internet www.vietnamembassy-philippines.org; Ambassador VU XUAN TRUONG.

Judicial System

The February 1987 Constitution provides for the establishment of a Supreme Court comprising a Chief Justice and 14 Associate Justices; the Court may sit *en banc* or in divisions of three, five or seven members. Justices of the Supreme Court are appointed by the President from a list of a minimum of three nominees prepared by a Judicial and Bar Council. Other courts comprise the Court of Appeals, Regional Trial Courts, Metropolitan Trial Courts, Municipal Courts in Cities, Municipal Courts and Municipal Circuit Trial Courts. There is also a special court for trying cases of corruption (the Sandiganbayan). The Office of the Ombudsman (Tanodbayan) investigates complaints concerning the actions of public officials.

SUPREME COURT

Taft Ave, cnr Padre Faura St, Ermita, 1000 Metro Manila; tel. (2) 5268123; e-mail infos@supremecourt.gov.ph; internet www.supremecourt.gov.ph.

Chief Justice: REYNATO S. PUNO.

COURT OF APPEALS

Consists of a Presiding Justice and 68 Associate Justices.

Presiding Justice: CONRADO M. VASQUEZ, Jr.

Islamic *Shari'a* courts were established in the southern Philippines in July 1985 under a presidential decree of February 1977. They are presided over by three district magistrates and six circuit judges.

Religion

According to the results of the 2000 census, 81.1% of the population were Roman Catholics and 11.6% belonged to other Christian denominations. The Islamic community constituted 5% of the population, Buddhists accounted for 0.1%, while indigenous and other religious traditions comprised a further 1.7%. Atheists and persons who did not state a religious preference accounted for 0.5%.

CHRISTIANITY

Sangguniang Pambansa ng mga Simbahan sa Pilipinas (National Council of Churches in the Philippines): 879 Epifanio de los Santos Ave, West Triangle, Quezon City 1104, Metro Manila; tel. (2) 9293745; fax (2) 9267076; e-mail library@nccphilippines.org; internet www.nccphilippines.org; f. 1963; 10 mem. churches, 10 assoc. mems; Gen. Sec. REX R. B. REYES, Jr.

The Roman Catholic Church

For ecclesiastical purposes, the Philippines comprises 16 archdioceses, 55 dioceses, six territorial prelatures, one military ordinate and seven apostolic vicariates. At 31 December 2006 approximately 80.8% of the population were adherents.

Catholic Bishops' Conference of the Philippines (CBCP) 470 General Luna St, Intramuros, 1076 Metro Manila; tel. (2) 5274054; fax (2) 5279634; e-mail cbcp@info.com.ph; internet www.cbcponline.org.

f. 1945 statutes approved 1952; Pres. Most Rev. ANGEL N. LAGDAMEO (Archbishop of Jaro).

Archbishop of Caceres: Most Rev. LEONARDO Z. LEGASPI, Archbishop's House, Elias Angeles St, POB 6085, 4400 Naga City; tel. (54) 4738483; fax (54) 4732800.

Archbishop of Cagayan de Oro: Most Rev. ANTONIO J. LEDESMA, Archbishop's Residence, POB 113, 9000 Misamis Oriental, Cagayan de Oro City; tel. (8822) 8571357; fax (8822) 726304; e-mail orochan@cdo.weblinq.com.

Archbishop of Capiz: Most Rev. ONESIMO C. GORDONCILLO, Chancery Office, POB 44, 5800 Roxas City; tel. (36) 6215595; fax (36) 6211053.

Archbishop of Cebu: Cardinal RICARDO J. VIDAL, Archbishop's Residence, cnr P. Gomez St and P. Burgos St, POB 52, 6000 Cebu City; tel. (32) 2541861; fax (32) 2530123; e-mail adelito@skynet.net.

Directory

Archbishop of Cotabato: Most Rev. ORLANDO B. QUEVEDO, Archbishop's Residence, 154 Sinsuat Ave, POB 186, 9600 Cotabato City; tel. (64) 4212918; fax (64) 4211446.

Archbishop of Davao: Most Rev. FERNANDO R. CAPALLA, Archbishop's Residence, 247 Florentino Torres St, POB 80418, 8000 Davao City; tel. (82) 2275992; fax (82) 2279771; e-mail bishop-davao68@yahoo.com.

Archbishop of Jaro: Most Rev. ANGEL N. LAGDAMEO, Archbishop's Residence, Jaro, 5000 Iloilo City; tel. (33) 3294442; fax (33) 3293197; e-mail abpjaro@skynet.net.

Archbishop of Lingayen-Dagupan: Most Rev. OSCAR V. CRUZ, Archbishop's House, 2400 Pangasinan, Dagupan City; tel. (75) 5235357; fax (75) 5221878; e-mail oscar@rezcom.com.

Archbishop of Lipa: Most Rev. RAMON C. ARGÜELLES, Archbishop's House, St Lorenzo Ruiz Rd, Lipa City, 4217 Batangas; tel. (43) 7562572; fax (43) 7560005; e-mail chancery@batangas.net.ph.

Archbishop of Manila: Most Rev. GAUDENCIO B. ROSALES, Arzobispado, 121 Arzobispo St, Intramuros, POB 132, 1099 Metro Manila; tel. (2) 5273956; fax (2) 5276159; e-mail chancery@pldtdsl.net; internet www.rcam.org.

Archbishop of Nueva Segovia: Most Rev. ERNESTO A. SALGADO, Archbishop's House, Vigan, 2700 Ilocos Sur; tel. (77) 7222018; fax (77) 7221591.

Archbishop of Ozamis: Most Rev. JESUS A. DOSADO, Archbishop's House, POB 2760, Rizal Ave, Banadero, 7200 Ozamis City; tel. (65) 5212771; fax (65) 5211574.

Archbishop of Palo: Most Rev. JOSE S. PALMA, Archdiocesan Chancery, Bukid Tabor, Palo, 6501 Leyte; POB 173, Tacloban City, 6500 Leyte; tel. (53) 3232213; fax (53) 3235607; e-mail rcap@mozcom.com.

Archbishop of San Fernando (Pampanga): Most Rev. PACIANO B. ANICETO, Chancery Office, San José, San Fernando, 2000 Pampanga; tel. (45) 9612819; fax (45) 9616772; e-mail rca@pamp.pworld.net.ph.

Archbishop of Tuguegarao: Most Rev. DIOSDADO A. TALAMAYAN, Archbishop's House, Rizal St, Tuguegarao, 3500 Cagayan; tel. (78) 8441663; fax (78) 8462822; e-mail dtalamayan-32@yahoo.com.

Archbishop of Zamboanga: Most Rev. ROMULO G. VALLES, Sacred Heart Center, POB 1, Justice R. T. Lim Blvd, 7000 Zamboanga City; tel. (62) 9927668; fax (62) 9932808; e-mail aofzam@yahoo.com.ph.

Other Christian Churches

Convention of Philippine Baptist Churches: POB 263, 5000 Iloilo City; tel. (33) 3290621; fax (33) 3290618; e-mail gensec@iloilo.net; f. 1935; Gen. Sec. Rev. Dr NATHANIEL M. FABULA; Pres. DONATO ENABE.

Episcopal Church in the Philippines: 275 E. Rodriguez Sr Ave, Quezon City, 1102 Metro Manila; POB 10321, Broadway Centrum, Quezon City, 1102 Metro Manila; tel. (2) 7228481; fax (2) 7211923; e-mail ecpnational@yahoo.com.ph; internet www.episcopalchurchphilippines.org; f. 1901; six dioceses; Prime Bishop Most Rev. EDWARD MALECDAN.

Iglesia Evangélica Metodista en las Islas Filipinas (Evangelical Methodist Church in the Philippines): Beulah Land, Iemelif Center, Greenfields 1, Subdivision, Marytown Circle, Novaliches, Quezon City, 1123 Metro Manila; tel. (2) 9356519; fax (2) 4185017; e-mail admin@iemelif.org; internet www.iemelif.org; f. 1909; 40,000 mems (2003); Gen. Supt Bishop NATHANAEL P. LAZARO.

Iglesia Filipina Independiente (Philippine Independent Church): POB 2484, 1000 Metro Manila; tel. (2) 5212794; fax (2) 5213932; e-mail gensec@ifi.ph; internet www.ifi.ph; f. 1902; 34 dioceses; 6.0m. mems; Obispo Maximo (Supreme Bishop) Most Rev. GODOFREDO J. DAVID.

Iglesia ni Cristo: 1 Central Ave, New Era, Quezon City, 1107 Metro Manila; tel. (2) 9814311; fax (2) 9811111; f. 1914; 2m. mems; Exec. Minister Brother ERAÑO G. MANALO.

Lutheran Church in the Philippines: 4461 Old Santa Mesa, 1008 Metro Manila; POB 507, 1099 Metro Manila; tel. (2) 7157084; fax (2) 7142395; internet www.lutheranphilippines.org; f. 1946; Pres. Rev. JAMES CERDEÑOLA.

Union Church of Manila: cnr Legaspi St and Rada St, Legaspi Village, Makati City, Metro Manila; tel. (2) 8126062; fax (2) 8172386; e-mail ucmweb@unionchurch.ph; internet www.unionchurch.ph; Senior Pastor Rev. STEVE RUESTCHLE.

United Church of Christ in the Philippines: 877 Epifanio de los Santos Ave, West Triangle, Quezon City, Metro Manila; POB 718, MCPO, Ermita, 1099 Metro Manila; tel. (2) 9240215; fax (2) 9240207; e-mail uccpnaof@manila-online.net; internet www.uccp.ph; f. 1948; 900,000 mems (1996); Gen. Sec. Rev. ELIEZER PASCUA (Bishop).

Among other denominations active in the Philippines are the Iglesia Evangélica Unida de Cristo and the United Methodist Church.

ISLAM

Some 14 different ethnic groups profess the Islamic faith in the Philippines. Mindanao and the Sulu and Tawi-Tawi archipelago, in the southern Philippines, are predominantly Muslim provinces, but there are 10 other such provinces, each with its own Imam, or Muslim religious leader. More than 500,000 Muslims live in the north of the country (mostly in, or near to, Manila).

Islamic Da'wah Council of the Philippines (IDCP): Suite 400, FUBC Bldg, Escolta, Metro Manila; tel. (2) 2458456; fax (2) 2415142; e-mail idcp@edsamail.com.ph; internet www.idcp-ph.org; f. 1982; federation of 95 mem. orgs; Pres. ABDUL RAHAM R. T. LINZAG.

BAHÁ'Í FAITH

National Spiritual Assembly: 1070 A. Roxas St, cnr Bautista St, Singalong Subdiv., Malate, 1004 Metro Manila; POB 4323, 1099 Metro Manila; tel. (2) 5240404; fax (2) 5232449; e-mail nsaphil@greendot.com.ph; mems resident in 129,949 localities; Chair. ALFREDO RAMIREZ; Sec.-Gen. MA ADORACION NEWMAN.

The Press

The Office of the President implements government policies on information and the media. Freedom of the press and freedom of speech are guaranteed under the Constitution.

METRO MANILA
Dailies

Abante: 167 Liberty Bldg, Roberto S. Oca St, Port Area, Manila; tel. (2) 5276722; fax (2) 5280147; e-mail abante@abante-tonite.com; internet www.abante.com.ph; morning; Filipino and English; Editor NICOLAS QUIJANO, Jr; circ. 417,000.

Abante Tonite: 301 BF Condominium, cnr of Solana and A. Soriano Sts, Intramuros, 1002 Metro Manila; tel. (2) 5276722; fax (2) 5280147; e-mail tonite@abante-tonite.com; internet www.abante-tonite.com; afternoon; Filipino and English; Man. Editor NICOLAS QUIJANO, Jr; circ. 277,000.

Ang Pilipino Ngayon: 202 Railroad St, cnr 13th St, Port Area, Metro Manila; tel. (2) 401871; fax (2) 5224998; Filipino; Publr and Editor JOSE M. BUHAIN; circ. 286,452.

Balita: Liwayway Publishing Inc, 2249 China Roces Ave, Makati City, Metro Manila; tel. (2) 8193101; fax (2) 8175167; internet www.balita.org; f. 1972; morning; Filipino; Editor MARCELO S. LAGMAY; circ. 151,000.

Daily Tribune: Penthouse Suites, GLC Bldg, T. M. Kalaw St, cnr A. Mabini St, Ermita, Metro Manila; tel. (2) 5215511; fax (2) 5215522; e-mail nco@tribune.net.ph; internet www.tribune.net.ph; f. 2000; English; Publr and Editor-in-Chief NINEZ CACHO-OLIVARES.

Malaya: 371 Bonifacio Drive, Port Area, 1018 Metro Manila; tel. (2) 5277651; fax (2) 5271839; e-mail apm_malaya@yahoo.com; internet www.malaya.com.ph; f. 1983; English; Editor JOY C. DE LOS REYES; circ. 175,000.

Manila Bulletin: Bulletin Publishing Corpn, cnr Muralla and Recoletos Sts, Intramuros, POB 769, Metro Manila; tel. (2) 5278121; fax (2) 5277510; e-mail bulletin@mb.com.ph; internet www.mb.com.ph; f. 1900; English; Publr HERMOGENES P. POBRE; Editor-in-Chief CHRIS J. ICBAN, Jr; circ. 265,000.

Manila Standard Today: Leyland Bldg, 21st St, cnr Railroad St, Port Area, Metro Manila; tel. (2) 5278351; fax (2) 5246649; e-mail mst@manilastandardtoday.com; internet www.manilastandardtoday.com; f. 1987; morning; English; Editor-in-Chief JOJO ROBLES; circ. 96,000.

Manila Times: 371A Bonifacio Drive, Port Area, Metro Manila; tel. (2) 5245664; fax (2) 5216897; e-mail newsboy1@manilatimes.net; internet www.manilatimes.net; f. 1945; morning; English; Publr and Editor-in-Chief FRED DELA ROSA.

People's Journal: 6th Floor, Universal-Re Bldg, 106 Paseo de Roxas, cnr Perea and Gallardo Sts, Legaspi Village, Makati City, Metro Manila; tel. (2) 5278421; fax (2) 5274627; English and Filipino; Editor AUGUST B. VILLANUEVA; circ. 219,000.

People's Taliba: 6th Floor, Universal-Re Bldg, 106 Paseo de Roxas, cnr Perea and Gallardo Sts, Legaspi Village, Makati City, Metro Manila; tel. (2) 5278121; fax (2) 5274627; Filipino; Editor BENJAMIN DEFENSOR; circ. 229,000.

People's Tonight: 6th Floor, Universal-Re Bldg, 106 Paseo de Roxas, cnr Perea and Gallardo Sts, Legaspi Village, Makati City, Metro Manila; tel. (2) 5278421; fax (2) 5274627; internet www.journal.com.ph; f. 1978; English and Filipino; Editor FERDIE RAMOS; circ. 500,000.

Philippine Daily Inquirer: Philippine Daily Inquirer Bldg, Chico Roces Ave, cnr Mascardo St and Yague St, Pasong Tamo, Makati City, 1220 Metro Manila; tel. (2) 8978808; fax (2) 8974793; e-mail feedback@inquirer.com.ph; internet www.inquirer.com.ph; f. 1985; English; Chair. MARIXI R. PRIETO; Editor-in-Chief LETTY JIMENEZ-MAGSANOC; circ. 250,000.

Philippine Herald-Tribune: V. Esguerra II Bldg, 140 Amorsolo St, Legaspi Village, Makati City, Metro Manila; tel. (2) 853711; f. 1987; Christian-orientated; Pres. AMADA VALINO.

Philippine Star: 13th and Railroad Sts, Port Area, Metro Manila; tel. (2) 5276856; fax (2) 5276851; e-mail philippinestar@hotmail.com; internet www.philstar.com; f. 1986; Editor BOBBY DE LA CRUZ; circ. 275,000.

Tempo: Bulletin Publishing Corpn, Recoletos St, cnr Muralla St, Intramuros, Metro Manila; tel. (2) 5278121; fax (2) 5277534; internet www.tempo.com.ph; f. 1982; English and Filipino; Editor BEN RODRIGUEZ; circ. 230,000.

Today: Independent Daily News, 55 Paseo de Roxas, Makati City, 1225 Metro Manila; tel. (2) 8940644; fax (2) 8131417; e-mail today@impactnet.com; f. 1993; Editor-in-Chief TEODORO L. LOCSIN, Jr; Man. Editor LOURDES MOLINA-FERNANDEZ; circ. 106,000.

United Daily News: 812 and 818 Benavides St, Binondo, Metro Manila; tel. (2) 2447171; f. 1973; Chinese; Editor-in-Chief CHUA KEE; circ. 85,000.

Selected Periodicals
Weeklies

Bannawag: Liwayway Bldg, 2249 Pasong Tamo, Makati City, Metro Manila; tel. (2) 8193101; fax (2) 8175167; f. 1934; Ilocano; Editor DIONISIO S. BULONG; circ. 42,900.

Bisaya: Liwayway Bldg, 2249 Pasong Tamo, Makati City, Metro Manila; tel. (2) 8193101; fax (2) 8175167; f. 1934; Cebu-Visayan; Editor EDGAR S. GODIN; circ. 90,000.

Liwayway: Liwayway Bldg, 2249 Pasong Tamo, Makati City, Metro Manila; tel. (2) 8193101; fax (2) 8175167; f. 1922; Filipino; Editor RODOLFO SALANDANAN; circ. 102,400.

Panorama: Manila Bulletin Publishing Corpn, POB 769, cnr Muralla and Recoletos Sts, Intramuros, Metro Manila; tel. and fax (2) 5277509; e-mail panorama@mb.com.ph; internet www.mb.com.ph; f. 1968; English; Editor RANDY V. URLANDA; circ. 239,600.

Philippine Starweek: 13th St, cnr Railroad St, Port Area, Metro Manila; tel. (2) 5277901; fax (2) 5275819; e-mail starweek@pacific.net.ph; internet www.philstar.com; English; Editor JOSEPH NACINO; circ. 268,000.

SELECTED PROVINCIAL PUBLICATIONS

The Aklan Reporter: 1227 Rizal St, Kalibo, Panay, Aklan; tel. (33) 3181; f. 1971; weekly; English and Aklanon; Editor ROMAN A. DE LA CRUZ; circ. 3,500.

Baguio Midland Courier: 16 Kisad Rd, POB 50, Baguio City; tel. (74) 4422444; fax (74) 4439485; e-mail admin@baguiomidlandcourier.com.ph; internet www.baguiomidlandcourier.com.ph; English and Ilocano; Editor CECILE C. AFABLE; circ. 6,000.

Bayanihan Weekly News: Bayanihan Publishing Co, P. Guevarra Ave, Santa Cruz, Laguna; tel. (645) 1001; f. 1966; Mon.; Filipino and English; Editor ARTHUR A. VALENOVA; circ. 1,000.

Bohol Chronicle: 56 B. Inting St, Tagbilaran City, 6300 Bohol; tel. and fax (32) 4113100; e-mail bohol-rd@mozcom.com; internet www.boholchronicle.com; f. 1954; 2 a week; English and Cebuano; Editor and Publr ZOILO DEJARESCO; circ. 5,500.

The Bohol Times: 100 Gallares St, Tagbilaran City, 6300 Bohol; tel. (38) 4112961; fax (38) 4112656; e-mail boholtimes@yahoo.com; Publr Dr LILIA A. BALITE; Editor-in-Chief SALVADOR D. DIPUTADO.

The Kapawa News: L. V. Moles and Jose Abad Santos Sts, Tangub, POB 365, 6100 Bacolod City; tel. and fax (34) 4441941; e-mail LM-Kapawa@eudoramail.com; f. 1966; weekly; Sat.; Hiligaynon and English; Publr HENRY G. DOBLE; circ. 2,000.

Mindanao Star: 44 Kolambagohan-Capistrano St, Cagayan de Oro City; weekly; Editor ROMULFO SABAMAL; circ. 3,500.

Mindanao Times: UMBN Bldg, Ponciano Reyes St, Davao City, Mindanao; tel. 2273252; e-mail timesmen@mozcom.com; internet www.mindanaotimes.com.ph; daily; Publr JOSEFINA SAN PEDRO; Editor-in-Chief AMALIA CABUSAO; circ. 5,000.

Pagadian Times: 0519 Alano St, Pagadian City, 7016; tel. (62) 2151504; fax (62) 2141721; e-mail pedelu@lasialink.com; f. 1969; weekly; English; Publr PEDE G. LU; Editor REMAI ALEJADS; circ. 7,000.

Sorsogon Today: 2903 Burgos St, East District, 4700 Sorsogon; tel. and fax (56) 4215306; fax (56) 2111340; e-mail sortoday@yahoo.com; f. 1977; weekly; Publr and CEO MARCOS E. PARAS, Jr; circ. 2,250.

Sun Star Cebu: Sun Star Bldg, 3rd Floor, cnr of P. del Rosario St and P. Cui St, Cebu City; tel. (32) 2546100; fax (32) 2537256; e-mail centralnewsroom@sunstar.com.ph; internet www.sunstar.com.ph/

THE PHILIPPINES

cebu; f. 1982; daily; English; Editor-in-Chief PACHICO A. SEARES; Gen. Man. JULIUS NERI.

The Tribune: Maharlika Highway, 2301 Cabanatuan City, Luzon; f. 1960; weekly; English and Filipino; Editor and Publr ORLANDO M. JARLEGO; circ. 8,000.

The Valley Times: Daang Maharlika, San Felipe, Ilagan, Isabela; f. 1962; weekly; English; Editor AUREA A. DE LA CRUZ; circ. 4,500.

The Visayan Tribune: 1973 Mezzanine Floor, Masonic Temple Bldg, Plaza Libertad 5000, Iloilo City; f. 1959; weekly; English; Editor HERBERT L. VEGO; circ. 5,000.

The Voice of Islam: Davao City; tel. (82) 81368; f. 1973; monthly; English and Arabic; official Islamic news journal; Editor and Publr NASHIR MUHAMMAD AL'RASHID AL HAJJ.

The Weekly Negros Gazette: Broce St, San Carlos City, 6033 Negros Occidental; f. 1956; weekly; Editor NESTORIO L. LAYUMAS, Sr; circ. 5,000.

NEWS AGENCY

Philippines News Agency: PIA Bldg, 2nd Floor, Visayas Ave, Diliman, Quezon City, Metro Manila; tel. (2) 9206551; fax (2) 9206566; e-mail bert.panganiban@gmail.com; internet www.pna.gov.ph; f. 1973; Gen. Man. VITTORIO V. VITUG; Exec. Editor RUBEN B. CAL.

PRESS ASSOCIATION

National Press Club of the Philippines: National Press Club Bldg, Magallanes Drive, Intramuros, 1002 Metro Manila; tel. (2) 3010521; fax (2) 3010522; e-mail ad-nationalpressclub@yahoo.com; f. 1952; Pres. ANTONIO ANTONIO; Vice-Pres. ALICE H. REYES; 1,405 mems.

Publishers

Abiva Publishing House Inc: Abiva Bldg, 851 Gregorio Araneta Ave, Quezon City, 1113 Metro Manila; tel. (2) 7120245; fax (2) 7120486; e-mail mmrabiva@i-manila.com.ph; internet www.abiva.com.ph; f. 1937; reference and textbooks; Pres. JORGE GARCIA.

Ateneo de Manila University Press: Bellarmine Hall, Ateneo de Manila University, Katipunan Ave, Loyola Heights, Quezon City, Metro Manila; tel. (2) 4265984; fax (2) 4265909; e-mail unipress@admu.edu.ph; internet www.ateneopress.org; f. 1972; literary, textbooks, humanities, social sciences, reference books on the Philippines; Dir MARICOR E. BAYTION.

Bookman, Inc: 373 Quezon Ave, Quezon City, 1114 Metro Manila; tel. (2) 7124818; fax (2) 7124843; e-mail bookman@info.com.ph; f. 1945; textbooks, reference, educational; Pres. LINA PICACHE-ENRIQUEZ; Exec. Vice-Pres. MARIETTA PICACHE-MARTINEZ.

Capitol Publishing House, Inc: 13 Team Pacific Bldg, Jose C. Cruz St, cnr F. Legaspi St, Barrio Ugong, Pasig City, Metro Manila; tel. (2) 6712662; fax (2) 6712664; e-mail cacho@mozcom.com; f. 1947; Gen. Man. MANUEL L. ATIENZA.

Heritage Publishing House: 33 4th Ave, cnr Main Ave, Cubao, Quezon City, POB 3667, Metro Manila; tel. (2) 7216218; fax (2) 7220468; e-mail heritage@skydsl.com.ph; art, anthropology, history, political science; Pres. MARIO R. ALCANTARA; Man. Dir GEORGE B. ALCANTARA.

The Lawyers' Co-operative Publishing Co Inc: 1071 Del Pan St, Makati City, 1206 Metro Manila; tel. (2) 5634073; fax (2) 5642021; e-mail lawbooks@info.com.ph; f. 1908; law, educational; Pres. ELSA K. ELMA.

Liwayway Publishing Inc: 2249 Chino Roces Ave, Makati City, Metro Manila; tel. (2) 8193101; fax (2) 8175167; magazines and newspapers; Pres. RENE G. ESPINA; Chair. DIONISIO S. BULONG.

Mutual Books Inc: 429 Shaw Blvd, Mandaluyong City, Metro Manila; tel. (2) 7257538; fax (2) 7213056; f. 1959; textbooks on accounting, management and economics, computers and mathematics; Pres. ALFREDO S. NICDAO, Jr.

Reyes Publishing Inc: Mariwasa Bldg, 4th Floor, 717 Aurora Blvd, Quezon City, 1112 Metro Manila; tel. (2) 7221827; fax (2) 7218782; e-mail reyespub@skyinet.net; f. 1964; art, history and culture; Pres. LOUIE REYES.

SIBS Publishing House Inc: Phoenix Bldg, 927 Quezon Ave, Quezon City, Metro Manila; tel. (2) 3764041; fax (2) 3764034; e-mail sibsbook@sibs.com.ph; internet www.sibs.com.ph; f. 1996; science, language, religion, literature and history textbooks; Pres. CARMEN MIMETTE M. SIBAL.

Sinag-Tala Publishers Inc: GMA Lou-Bel Plaza, 6th Floor, Chino Roces Ave, cnr Bagtikan St, San Antonio Village, Makati City, 1203 Metro Manila; tel. (2) 8971162; fax (2) 8969626; e-mail stpi@info.com.ph; internet www.sinagtala.com; f. 1972; educational textbooks; business, professional and religious books; Man. Dir LUIS A. USON.

University of the Philippines Press: Epifanio de los Santos St, U. P. Campus, Diliman, Quezon City, 1101 Metro Manila; tel. (2) 9252930; fax (2) 9282558; e-mail mricana@eee.upd.edu.ph; f. 1965; literature, history, political science, sociology, cultural studies, economics, anthropology, mathematics; Dir MARIA LUISA T. CAMAGAY.

Vibal Publishing House Inc: 1253 G. Araneta Ave, cnr Maria Clara St, Talayan, Quezon City, Metro Manila; tel. (2) 7122722; fax (2) 7118852; e-mail inquire@vibalpublishing.com; internet www.vibalpublishing.com; f. 1955; linguistics, social sciences, mathematics, religion; Pres. and Publr ESTHER A. VIBAL.

PUBLISHERS' ASSOCIATIONS

Philippine Educational Publishers' Asscn: 84 P. Florentino St, Quezon City, 1104 Metro Manila; tel. (2) 7402698; fax (2) 7115702; e-mail dbuhain@pldtdsl.net; Pres. DOMINADOR D. BUHAIN.

Publishers' Association of the Philippines Inc: 4th Floor, Dominga Bldg, 2113 Pasong Tamo, cnr de la Rosa St, Makati City, Metro Manila; tel. (2) 8191215; fax (2) 8931690; f. 1974; mems comprise all newspaper, magazine and book publrs in the Philippines; Pres. KERIMA P. TUVERA; Exec. Dir ROBERTO M. MENDOZA.

Broadcasting and Communications

TELECOMMUNICATIONS

National Telecommunications Commission (NTC): NTC Bldg, BIR Rd, East Triangle, Diliman, Quezon City, 1104 Metro Manila; tel. (2) 9244042; fax (2) 9217128; e-mail ntc@ntc.gov.ph; internet www.ntc.gov.ph; f. 1979; supervises and controls all private and public telecommunications services; Commr RUEL V. CANOBAS.

BayanTel: BayanTel Corporate Center, Maginhawa St, cnr Malingap St, Teacher's Village East, Quezon City, 1101 Metro Manila; tel. (2) 4493000; fax (2) 4492174; e-mail bayanserve@bayantel.com.ph; internet www.bayantel.com.ph; 359,000 fixed lines (1999); Chair. OSCAR M. LOPEZ; Pres. and CEO EUGENIO L. LOPEZ III.

Bell Telecommunications Philippines (BellTel): Pacific Star Bldg, 3rd and 4th Floors, Sen. Gil J. Puyat Ave, cnr Makati Ave, Makati City, Metro Manila; tel. (2) 8400808; fax (2) 8915618; e-mail info@belltel.ph; internet www.belltel.ph; f. 1997; Pres. EDGARDO REYES.

Capitol Wireless Inc: Dolmar Gold Tower, 6th Floor, 107 Carlos Palanca, Jr, St, Legaspi Village, Makati City, Metro Manila; tel. (2) 8159961; fax (2) 8941141; Pres. EPITACIO R. MARQUEZ.

Digital Telecommunications Philippines Inc (DIGITEL): 110 Eulogio Rodriguez, Jr, Ave, Bagumbayan, Quezon City, 1110 Metro Manila; tel. and fax (2) 6330000; e-mail support@digitelone.com; internet www.digitelone.com; provision of fixed line telecommunications services; 484,036 fixed lines (1998); Chief Exec. RICARDO J. ROMULO; Pres. JOHN GOKONGWEI.

Domestic Satellite Philippines Inc (DOMSAT): Solid House Bldg, 4th Floor, 2285 Pasong Tamo Ext., Makati City, 1231 Metro Manila; tel. (2) 8105917; fax (2) 8671677; Pres. SIEGFRED MISON.

Globe Telecom (GMCR) Inc: Globe Telecom Plaza, 57th Floor, Pioneer St, cnr Madison St, 1552 Mandaluyong City, Metro Manila; tel. (2) 7302701; fax (2) 7302586; e-mail custhelp@globetel.com.ph; internet www.globe.com.ph; 700,000 fixed and mobile telephone subscribers (1999); Pres. and CEO GERARDO C. ABLAZA, Jr.

Philippine Communications Satellite Corpn (PhilcomSat): 12th Floor, Telecoms Plaza, 316 Sen. Gil J. Puyat Ave, Makati City, Metro Manila; tel. (2) 8158406; fax (2) 8159287; Pres. MANUEL H. NIETO.

Philippine Global Communications, Inc (PhilCom): 8755 Paseo de Roxas, Makati City, 1259 Metro Manila; tel. (2) 8451101; fax (2) 8189720; e-mail helpdesk@philcom.com; internet www.philcom.com; Chair. WILLY N. OCIER; CEO SALVADOR M. CASTILLO.

Philippine Long Distance Telephone Co: Ramon Cojuangco Bldg, Makati Ave, POB 2148, Makati City, Metro Manila; tel. (2) 8889090; fax (2) 8446654; e-mail media@pldt.com.ph; internet www.pldt.com.ph; f. 1928; monopoly on overseas telephone service until 1989; transferred to private sector in 2007; Chair. MANUEL V. PANGILINAN; Pres. and CEO NAPOLEON L. NAZARENO.

Smart Communications, Inc (SCI): SMART Tower, 6799 Ayala Ave, Makati City, 1226 Metro Manila; tel. (2) 8881111; fax (2) 8488830; e-mail customercare@smart.com.ph; internet www.smart.com.ph; 20.8m. subscribers (2005); Pres. and CEO NAPOLEON L. NAZARENO.

Pilipino Telephone Corpn (Piltel): SMART Tower, 25th Floor, 6799 Ayala Ave, Makati City, 1200 Metro Manila; tel. (2) 8913888; fax (2) 8171121; subsidiary of Smart Communications, Inc; major

THE PHILIPPINES
Directory

cellular telephone provider; 400,000 subscribers (1999); Chair. Manuel V. Pangilinan; Pres. and CEO Napoleon L. Nazareno.

BROADCASTING
Radio

Banahaw Broadcasting Corpn: Broadcast City, Capitol Hills, Diliman, Quezon City, 3005 Metro Manila; tel. (2) 9329949; fax (2) 9318751; 14 stations; Station Man. Betty Livioco.

Bureau of Broadcast Services (BBS) (Philippine Broadcasting Service): Office of the Press Sec., Philippine Information Agency Bldg, 4th Floor, Visayas Ave, Diliman, Quezon City, 1100 Metro Manila; tel. (2) 9203931; fax (2) 9200461; e-mail mpangilinan@pbs.ops.gov.ph; internet www.pbs.gov.ph; f. 1952 as Philippine Broadcasting Service; govt-operated; 32 radio stations; Dir John S. Manalili.

Cebu Broadcasting Co: c/o Manila Broadcasting Co, Philippine Information Agency Bldg, 4th Floor, Visayas Ave, Quezon City, 1100 Metro Manila; tel. (2) 9203931; fax (2) 9242745; Chair. Hadrian Arroyo.

Far East Broadcasting Co Inc: POB 1, Valenzuela, 0560 Metro Manila; 62 Karuhatan Rd, Karuhatan, Valenzuela City, 1441 Metro Manila; tel. (2) 2921152; fax (2) 2925790; e-mail info@febc.org.ph; internet www.febc.org.ph; f. 1948; 18 stations; operates a classical music station, eight domestic stations and an overseas service in 64 languages throughout Asia; Pres. Dan Andrew Cura.

Filipinas Broadcasting Network: Legaspi Towers 200, Room 306, Paseo de Roxas, Makati City, Metro Manila; tel. (2) 8176133; fax (2) 8177135; Gen. Man. Diana C. Gozum.

GMA Network Inc: GMA Network Center, EDSA cnr Timog Ave, Diliman, Quezon City, 1103 Metro Manila; tel. and fax (2) 9287021; e-mail yourgmafamily@gmanetwork.com; internet www.igma.tv; f. 1950; fmrly Republic Broadcasting System Inc; transmits nation-wide through 44 television stations; Chair., Pres. and CEO Felipe L. Gozon; Exec. Vice-Pres. Gilberto R. Duavit, Jr.

Manila Broadcasting Co: Philippine Information Agency Bldg, 4th Floor, Visayas Ave, Quezon City, 1100 Metro Manila; tel. (2) 9203931; fax (2) 9242745; internet www.dagupan.com/dwidfm/mbc.htm; f. 1946; affiliate of Philippine Broadcasting Service; 10 stations; Pres. Ruperto Nicdao, Jr; Gen. Man. Eduardo L. Montilla.

Nation Broadcasting Corpn: NBC Tower, Epifanio de los Santos Ave, Guadalupe, Makati City, 1200 Metro Manila; tel. (2) 8195673; fax (2) 8197234; e-mail radio@philexport.com; internet philexport.org/philradio/network/nbchome.htm; f. 1963; 31 stations; Pres. Francis Lumen.

Newsounds Broadcasting Network Inc: Florete Bldg, Ground Floor, 2406 Nobel, cnr Edison St, Makati City, 3117 Metro Manila; tel. (2) 8430116; fax (2) 8173631; 10 stations; Gen. Man. E. Billones; Office Man. Herman Basbano.

Pacific Broadcasting System: c/o Manila Broadcasting Co, Philippine Information Agency Bldg, 4th Floor, Visayas Ave, Quezon City, 1100 Metro Manila; tel. (2) 9203931; fax (2) 9242745; Pres. Ruperto Nicdao, Jr; Vice-Pres. Rodolfo Arce.

PBN Broadcasting Network: Ersan Bldg, 3rd Floor, 32 Quezon Ave, Quezon City, Metro Manila; tel. (2) 7120190; fax (2) 7438162; e-mail pbnbroadcasting@yahoo.com; internet www.pbnbicol.com; f. 1958; Chair. Jorge D. Bayona.

Philippine Federation of Catholic Broadcasters: 2307 Pedro Gil, Santa Ana, POB 3169, Metro Manila; tel. (2) 5644518; fax (2) 5637316; e-mail nomm.xh@gmail.com; f. 1965; all 48 radio stations are united by the Dream Satellite; Pres. Rev. Francis Lucas.

Radio Philippines Network, Inc: Broadcast City, Capitol Hills, Diliman, Quezon City, Metro Manila; tel. (2) 9318627; fax (2) 984322; f. 1969; seven TV stations, 14 radio stations; Pres. Edgar San Luis; Gen. Man. Felipe G. Medina.

Radio Veritas Asia: Buick St, Fairview Park, POB 2642, Quezon City, Metro Manila; tel. (2) 9390011; fax (2) 9381940; e-mail rveritas-asia@rveritas-asia.org; internet www.rveritas-asia.org; f. 1969; Catholic short-wave station, broadcasts in 17 languages; Pres. and Chair. Archbishop Gaudencio B. Rosales; Gen. Man. Fr Roberto M. Ebisa (SVD).

UM Broadcasting Network: cnr P Reyes and Palma Gil Sts, Davao City; tel. (82) 2279535; fax (82) 2217824; e-mail umbndvo@mozcom.com; internet www.radyoukay.com.ph; Exec. Vice-Pres. Willy Torres.

Vanguard Radio Network: J & T Bldg, Room 208, Santa Mesa, Metro Manila; tel. (2) 7161233; fax (2) 7160899; Pres. Manuel Galvez.

Television

In July 1991 there were seven originating television stations and 105 replay and relay stations. The seven originating stations were ABS-CBN (Channel 2), PTV4 (Channel 4), ABC (Channel 5), GMA (Channel 7), RPN (Channel 9), IBC (Channel 13) and SBN (Channel 21). The following are the principal operating television networks:

ABC Development Corpn: APMC Bldg, 136 Amorsolo St, cnr Gamboa St, Legaspi Village, Makati City, Metro Manila; tel. (2) 8923801; fax (2) 8128840; CEO Edward U. Tan.

ABS-CBN Broadcasting Corpn: ABS-CBN Broadcasting Center, Sgt E. Esguerra Ave, cnr Mother Ignacia Ave, Quezon City, 1103 Metro Manila; tel. (2) 9244101; fax (2) 9215888; e-mail feedback_web@abs-cbn.com; internet www.abs-cbn.com; Chair. Eugenio Lopez III; Gen. Man. Federico M. Garcia.

AMCARA Broadcasting Network: ABS-CBN Broadcasting Centre, Mother Ignacia St, cnr Sgt Esguerra Ave, Quezon City, 1103 Metro Manila; tel. (2) 4152272; fax (2) 4121259; e-mail studio23@abs.pinoycentral.com; internet www.studio23.tv; Man. Dir Leonardo P. Katigbak.

Banahaw Broadcasting Corpn: Broadcast City, Capitol Hills, Quezon City, 3005 Metro Manila; tel. (2) 9329949; fax (2) 9318751; Station Man. Betty Livioco.

Channel V Philippines: Sagittarius Bldg, 6th Floor, H. V. de la Costa St, Salcedo Village, Makati City, Metro Manila; tel. (2) 8173747; fax (2) 8184192; e-mail channelv@i-next.net; Pres. Joel Jimenez; Gen. Man. Mon Alcaraz.

GMA Network, Inc: GMA Network Center, Timog Ave, cnr Epifanio de los Santos Ave, Diliman, Quezon City, 1103 Metro Manila; tel. and fax (2) 9287021; internet www.igma.tv; f. 1950; transmits nation-wide through 45 VHF and 2 affiliate stations and in Asia, Australia and Hawaii through Measat-2 satellite; Chair., Pres. and CEO Felipe L. Gozon; Exec. Vice-Pres. Gilberto R. Duavit, Jr.

Intercontinental Broadcasting Corpn: Broadcast City Complex, Capitol Hills, Diliman, Quezon City, Metro Manila; tel. (2) 9318781; fax (2) 9318743; 19 stations; Pres. and Chair. Boots Anson-Roa.

People's Television Network Inc (PTV4): Broadcast Complex, Visayas Ave, Quezon City, Metro Manila; tel. (2) 9206514; fax (2) 9204342; f. 1992; public television network; Chair. Lourdes I. Illustre.

Radio Mindanao Network: State Condominium, 4th Floor, 1 Salcedo St, Legaspi Village, Makati City, Metro Manila; tel. (2) 8120530; fax (2) 8163680; e-mail sales@rmn.com.ph; internet www.rmn.com.ph; f. 1952; owns and operates 50 radio and television stations; Chair. Henry Canoy; Pres. Eric S. Canoy.

Radio Philippines Network, Inc: Broadcast City, Capitol Hills, Diliman, Quezon City, Metro Manila; tel. (2) 9315080; fax (2) 9318627; 7 primary TV stations, 14 relay stations; Pres. Edgar San Luis; Gen. Man. Felipe G. Medina.

Rajah Broadcasting Network, Inc (RJ TV 29): Save a Lot Bldg, 3rd Floor, 2284 Pasong Tamo Ext., Makati City, Metro Manila; tel. (2) 8932360; fax (2) 8933404; e-mail rjofc@compass.com; f. 1993; Gen. Man. Bea J. Colamonici.

Southern Broadcasting Network, Inc: Suite 2902, Jollibee Plaza, Ortigas Center, Emerald Ave, Pasig City, Metro Manila; tel. (2) 6363286; fax (2) 6363288; e-mail gemceo@sbnphilippines.net; Pres. and CEO Teofilo A. Henson; Vice-Pres. Linnie Mayoralgo.

United Broadcasting Network: FEMS Tower 1, 11th Floor, 1289 Zobel Roxas, cnr South Superhighway, Malate; tel. (2) 5216138; fax (2) 5221226; Gen. Man. Joseph Hodreal.

Broadcasting Association

Kapisanan ng mga Brodkaster sa Pilipinas (KBP) (Association of Broadcasters in the Philippines): LTA Bldg, 6th Floor, 118 Perea St, Legaspi Village, Makati City, 1226 Metro Manila; tel. (2) 8151990; fax (2) 8151989; e-mail kbp@pacific.net.ph; internet www.kbp.org.ph; f. 1973 in order to regulate the broadcasting industry, elevate standards, disseminate govt information and strengthen relations with advertising industry; Chair. Butch S. Canoy, Jr; Pres. Herman Basbano.

Finance

(cap. = capital; res = reserves; dep. = deposits; m. = million; brs = branches; amounts in pesos, unless otherwise stated)

BANKING

Legislation enacted in 1993 provided for the establishment of a new monetary authority, the Bangko Sentral ng Pilipinas, to replace the Central Bank of the Philippines. In 1994 legislation providing for the establishment in the Philippines of additional foreign bank branches was enacted. By the end of 2002 the number of foreign banks had increased to 13; at that time some 44 principal commercial banks were operating in the Philippines.

Central Bank

Bangko Sentral ng Pilipinas (Central Bank of the Philippines): A. Mabini St, cnr Pablo Ocampo St, Malate, 1004 Metro Manila; tel. (2) 5247011; fax (2) 5231252; e-mail bspmail@bsp.gov.ph; internet www.bsp.gov.ph; f. 1993; cap. 10,000m., surplus and res 164,419.5m., dep. 661,015.1m. (Dec. 2007); Gov. AMANDO M. TETANGCO, Jr; 18 brs.

Principal Commercial Banks

Allied Banking Corpn: 6754 Allied Bank Centre, Ayala Ave, cnr Legaspi St, Makati City, 1200 Metro Manila; tel. (2) 8187961; fax (2) 8160921; e-mail info@alliedbank.com.ph; internet www.alliedbank.com.ph; f. 1977; cap. 495.3m., res 9,679.5m., dep. 123,681.4m. (Dec. 2006); Chair. PANFILO O. DOMINGO; Pres. REYNALDO A. MACLANG; 285 brs.

Banco de Oro Unibank Inc: 12 ADB Ave, Mandaluyong City, 1550 Metro Manila; tel. (2) 6366060; fax (2) 6317810; e-mail investor-relations@bdo.com.ph; internet www.bancodeoro.com.ph; f. 1996; fmrly known as Banco de Oro Universal Bank; name changed as above following merger with Equitable PCI Bank in 2007; acquired 1st e-Bank June 2003; Chair. TERESITA T. SY; Pres. NESTOR V. TAN; 185 brs.

Bank of Commerce: Phil First Bldg, 6764 Ayala Ave, Makati City, 1226 Metro Manila; tel. (2) 8120000; fax (2) 8300437; e-mail mscallangan@bankcom.com.ph; internet www.bankcom.com.ph; f. 1983; fmrly Boston Bank of the Philippines; merged with Traders Royal Bank 2001; cap. 2,050.2m., dep. 55,039.1m. (Dec. 2006); Chair. ANTONIO COJUANGCO; Pres. and CEO RAUL B. DE MESA; 38 brs.

Bank of the Philippine Islands: BPI Bldg, Ayala Ave, cnr Paseo de Roxas, POB 1827, MCC, Makati City, 0720 Metro Manila; tel. (2) 8910000; fax (2) 8910170; e-mail expressonline@bpi.com.ph; internet www.bpiexpressonline.com; f. 1851; merged with Far East Bank and Trust Co in April 2000; merged with DBS Bank Philippines, Inc, 2001; cap. 27,043m., res 6,805m., dep. 473,798m. (Dec. 2006); Pres. and Dir AURELIO R. MONTINOLA III; Chair. JAIME ZOBEL DE AYALA; 896 local brs; 1 overseas br.

China Banking Corpn: CBC Bldg, 8745 Paseo de Roxas, cnr Villar St, Makati City, 1226 Metro Manila; tel. (2) 8855555; fax (2) 8920220; e-mail online@chinabank.com.ph; internet www.chinabank.com.ph; f. 1920; cap. 7,708m., res 3,470.8m., dep. 141,557m. (Dec. 2007); Chair. GILBERT U. DEE; Pres. and CEO PETER S. DEE; 196 brs.

Development Bank of the Philippines: DBP Bldg, Makati Ave, cnr Sen. Gil J. Puyat Ave, Makati City, 1200 Metro Manila; tel. (2) 8189511; fax (2) 8934311; e-mail info@devbankphil.com.ph; internet www.devbankphil.com.ph; f. 1947 as the Rehabilitation Finance Corpn; govt-owned; provides medium- and long-term loans for strategic devt projects; cap. 38,105m., dep. 70,606m. (Dec. 2007); Chair. PATRICIA A. SANTO TOMAS; Pres. and CEO REYNALDO G. DAVID; 77 brs.

East West Banking Corpn: 20th Floor, PBCOM Tower, 6795 Ayala Ave, cnr Herrera St, Salcedo Village, Makati City, 1226 Metro Manila; tel. (2) 8150233; fax (2) 3250412; e-mail service@eastwestbanker.com; internet www.eastwestbanker.com; f. 1994; Chair. JONATHAN T. GOTIANUN; Pres. and CEO ANTONIO C. MONCUPA, Jr; 20 brs.

Export and Industry Bank, Inc (Exportbank): Exportbank Plaza, Chino Roces Ave, cnr Sen. Gil J. Puyat Ave, Makati City, 1200 Metro Manila; tel. (2) 8789100; fax (2) 8780000; e-mail expertinfo@exportbank.com.ph; internet www.exportbank.com.ph; merged with Urban Bank, Inc, 2002; cap. 4,787m., dep. 12,479m. (June 2007); Chair. JAIME GONZALEZ; Pres. NILO PACHECHO, Jr.

Land Bank of the Philippines: LandBank Plaza, 1598 M. H. del Pilar St, cnr J. Quintos St, Malate, 1004 Metro Manila; tel. (2) 5220000; fax (2) 5288580; e-mail landbank@mail.landbank.com; internet www.landbank.com; f. 1963; specialized govt bank with universal banking licence; cap. 11,971m., res 22,217m., dep. 269,470m. (Dec. 2006); Chair. GARY B. TEVES; Pres. and CEO GILDA E. PICO; 323 brs.

Manila Banking Corpn: Manila Bank Bldg, 6772 Ayala Ave, Makati City, 1226 Metro Manila; tel. (2) 7516000; fax (2) 8645016; internet www.manilabank.com; f. 1999; cap. 531m., res 2,288m., dep. 6,704m. (Dec. 2006); Pres. BENJAMIN J. YAMBAO; Chair. LUIS B. PUYAT.

Maybank Philippines Inc: Legaspi Towers 300, Pablo Ocampo St, cnr Roxas Blvd, Malate, 1100 Metro Manila; tel. (2) 5237777; fax (2) 5218514; e-mail mayphil@maybank.com.ph; internet www.maybank2u.com.my/philippines/index.shtml; f. 1961; cap. 3,679m., res −1,151m., dep. 10,861m. (Dec. 2006); Chair. Tan Sri MOHAMED BASIR BIN AHMAD; Pres. and CEO ONG SEET JOON; 45 brs.

Metropolitan Bank and Trust Co (Metrobank): Metrobank Plaza, Sen. Gil J. Puyat Ave, Makati City, 1200 Metro Manila; tel. (2) 8988000; fax (2) 8176248; e-mail metrobank@metrobank.com.ph; internet www.metrobank.com.ph; f. 1962; acquired Global Business Bank (Globalbank) 2002; cap. 36,145.4m., res 19,140.9m., dep. 590,989.8m. (Dec. 2007); Chair. ANTONIO S. ABACAN; Pres. ARTHUR TY, Jr; 344 local brs, 6 overseas brs.

Philippine Bank of Communications: PBCOM Tower, 6795 Ayala Ave, cnr V. A. Rufino St, 1226 Makati City; tel. (2) 8307000; fax (2) 8182598; e-mail info@pbcom.com.ph; internet www.pbcom.com.ph; f. 1939; merged with AsianBank Corpn in 1999; cap. 8,259.9m., res 1,502.2m., dep. 44,477.8m. (Dec. 2006); Chair. ENRIQUE LUY; Pres. and CEO ROMAN AZANZA; 64 brs.

Philippine National Bank (PNB): PNB Financial Center, President Diosdado Macapagal Blvd, Pasay City, 1300 Metro Manila; tel. (2) 8916040; fax (2) 8331245; e-mail cmcd@pnb.com.ph; internet www.pnb.com.ph; f. 1916; partially transferred to the private sector in 1996 and 2000; 10.93% govt-owned; cap. 22,930m., res 4,330m., dep. 181,667m. (Dec. 2005); Chair. FLORENCIA G. TARRIELA; Pres. and CEO OMAR BYRON T. MIER; 324 local brs, 5 overseas brs.

Philippine Veterans Bank: PVB Bldg, 101 V. A. Rufino St, cnr de la Rosa St, Legaspi Village, Makati City, Metro Manila; tel. (2) 7515000; fax (2) 7518577; e-mail corpcomm@veteransbank.com.ph; internet www.veteransbank.com.ph; cap. 4,200m., assets 29,600m. (Dec. 2006); Chair. EMMANUEL V. DE OCAMPO; Pres. and CEO RICARDO A. BALBIDO, Jr; 45 brs.

Philtrust Bank (Philippine Trust Co): Philtrust Bank Bldg, United Nations Ave, cnr San Marcelino St, Ermita, 1045 Metro Manila; tel. (2) 5249061; fax (2) 5217309; e-mail ptc@bancnet.net; f. 1916; cap. 5,000m., res 89m., dep. 48,832m. (Dec. 2006); Pres. ANTONIO H. OZAETA; Chair. EMILIO T. YAP; 42 brs.

Rizal Commercial Banking Corpn: Yuchengco Tower, RCBC Plaza, 6819 Alaya Ave, Makati City, 0727 Metro Manila; tel. (2) 8949000; fax (2) 8949958; e-mail customercontact@rcbc.com; internet www.rcbc.com; f. 1960; cap. 7,384.6m., res 10,841.2m., dep. 185,269.2m. (Dec. 2006); Chair. HELEN Y. DEE; Pres. and Dir FRANCISCO S. MAGSAIO, Jr; 287 brs.

Security Bank Corpn: 6776 Ayala Ave, Makati City, 0719 Metro Manila; tel. (2) 8949577; fax (2) 8911079; e-mail herrera@securitybank.com.ph; internet www.securitybank.com; f. 1951; fmrly Security Bank and Trust Co; cap. 3,293.5m., res 5,250.4m., dep. 99,127.3m. (Dec. 2006); Pres. and CEO ALBERTO S. VILLAROSA; Chair. FREDERICK Y. DY; 114 brs.

Union Bank of the Philippines: SSS Makati Bldg, Ayala Ave, cnr V. A. Rufino St, Makati City, 1200 Metro Manila; tel. (2) 8920011; fax (2) 8938593; e-mail online@unionbankph.com; internet www.unionbankph.com; f. 1982; cap. 19,895m. (Dec. 2006), res 6,442m. (Dec. 2002), dep. 115,982m. (Dec. 2006); Chair. and CEO JUSTO A. ORTIZ; Pres. VICTOR B. VALDEPEÑAS; 111 brs.

United Coconut Planters' Bank: UCPB Bldg, 7907 Makati Ave, Makati City, 0728 Metro Manila; tel. (2) 8119000; fax (2) 8119706; e-mail crc@ucpb.com; internet www.ucpb.com; f. 1963; cap. 1,484.8m., res 9,135.5m., dep. 79,974.2m. (Dec. 2005); Chair. CARLOS C. EJERCITO; Pres. and CEO RAMON Y. SY; 178 brs.

United Overseas Bank Philippines: 17th Floor, Pacific Star Bldg, Sen. Gil J. Puyat Ave, cnr Makati Ave, Makati City, Metro Manila; tel. (2) 8788686; fax (2) 8115917; e-mail crd@uob.com.ph; internet www.uob.com.ph; f. 1999; cap. 5,000m., res −3,904m., dep. 10,382m. (Dec. 2007); Pres. and CEO EMMANUEL MANGOSING; 67 brs.

Rural Banks

Small private banks have been established with the assistance of the Government in order to promote the rural economy. Their principal objectives are to provide credit facilities on reasonable terms and, in co-operation with other agencies of the Government, to give advice on management.

Thrift Banks

Thrift banks mobilize small savings and provide loans to lower income groups. The thrift banking system comprises savings and mortgage banks, stock savings and loan associations and private development banks.

Development Bank

Pampanga Development Bank: MacArthur Highway, Dolores San Fernando, Pampanga, Luzon; tel. (45) 9612786; fax (45) 9633931; e-mail pdb@ag.triasia.net; originally Agribusiness Development Bank; name changed as above 1995; cap. 75.0m., res 4.3m., dep. 125.8m. (Dec. 2006); Pres. JOSE ERIBERTO H. SUAREZ.

Islamic Bank

Al-Amanah Islamic Investment Bank of the Philippines: 10th Floor, Telecoms Plaza Bldg, 316 Sen. Gil Puyat Ave, Makati City, Metro Manila; tel. (2) 8164258; fax (2) 8195249; e-mail al-amanah@pldtdsl.net; internet www.islamicbank.com.ph; f. 1989; Chair. and CEO ALI B. SANGKI.

THE PHILIPPINES   *Directory*

Banking Associations

Bankers Association of the Philippines: Sagittarius Cond. Bldg, 11th Floor, H. V. de la Costa St, Salcedo Village, Makati City, Metro Manila; tel. (2) 8103858; fax (2) 8103860; internet www.bap.org.ph; Pres. Cesar E. A. Virata; Exec. Dir Leonilo G. Coronel.

Bankers Institute of the Philippines, Inc (BAIPhil): TRB Tower, Paseo de Roxas, Makati City, Metro Manila; tel. (2) 8325890; e-mail secretariat@baiphil.org; internet www.baiphil.org; f. 1941 under the name National Asscn of Auditors and Comptrollers; name changed to Bank Administration Institute in 1968, and as above in 2001; Pres. Lydia King.

Chamber of Thrift Banks: Cityland 10 Condominium Tower 1, Unit 614, H. V. de la Costa St, Salcedo Village, Makati City, Metro Manila; tel. (2) 8126974; fax (2) 8127203; Pres. Dionisio C. Ong.

Offshore Bankers' Association of the Philippines, Inc: MCPO 3088, Makati City, 1229 Metro Manila; tel. (2) 8103554; Chair. Teresita Malabanan.

Rural Bankers' Association of the Philippines: RBAP Bldg, A. Soriano, Jr, Ave, cnr Arzobispo St, Intramuros, Manila; tel. (2) 5272968; fax (2) 5272980; e-mail info@rbap.org; internet www.rbap.org; Pres. Tomas Gomez IV.

STOCK EXCHANGES

Securities and Exchange Commission: SEC Bldg, Epifanio de los Santos Ave, Greenhills, Mandaluyong City, Metro Manila; tel. (2) 5840923; fax (2) 5845293; e-mail mis@sec.gov.ph; internet www.sec.gov.ph; f. 1936; Chair. Fe B. Barin.

Philippine Stock Exchange: Philippine Stock Exchange Center, Exchange Rd, Ortigas Center, Pasig City, 1605 Metro Manila; tel. (2) 6887600; fax (2) 6345113; e-mail piac@pse.com.ph; internet www.pse.com.ph; f. 1994 following the merger of the Manila and Makati Stock Exchanges; 237 listed cos (Dec. 2005); Chair. Jose C. Vitug; Pres. Francisco Ed. Lim.

INSURANCE

At the end of 2000 a total of 156 insurance companies were authorized by the Insurance Commission to transact in the Philippines. Foreign companies were also permitted to operate in the country.

Principal Domestic Companies

Ayala Life Assurance Inc: Ayala Life Bldg, 6786 Ayala Ave, Makati City, Metro Manila; tel. (2) 8885433; fax (2) 8180171; e-mail customer.service@ayalalife.com.ph; internet www.ayalalife.com.ph; Chair. Xavier Loinaz; Pres. Emilio de Quiros.

BPI/MS Insurance Corpn: Ayala Life-FGU Center, 11th Floor, 6811 Ayala Ave, Makati City, 1226 Metro Manila; tel. (2) 8409000; fax (2) 8409099; e-mail insure@bpims.com; internet www.bpims.com; f. 2002 as result of merger of FGU Insurance Corpn and FEB Mitsui Marine Insurance Corpn; jt venture of Bank of the Philippine Islands and Sumitomo Insurance Co (Japan); cap. 731m. (2006), sales 2,140m.; Chair. Aurelio R. Montinola III; Pres. Noriaki Hamanaka.

Central Surety & Insurance Co: UniversalRe Bldg, 2nd Floor, 106 Paseo de Roxas, Legaspi Village, Makati City, 1200 Metro Manila; tel. (2) 8174931; fax (2) 8170006; f. 1945; bonds, fire, marine, casualty, motor car; Pres. Fermin T. Castañeda.

Commonwealth Insurance Co: 10th Floor, 1st e-Bank Tower, 8737 Paseo de Roxas, Makati City, Metro Manila; tel. (2) 8187626; fax (2) 8138575; internet www.cic.com.ph; f. 1935; Pres. Mario Noche.

Co-operative Insurance System of the Philippines: CISP Bldg, 80 Malakas St, Diliman, Quezon City, Metro Manila; tel. (2) 9240388; fax (2) 9240471; Chair. Leonida V. Chavez; Pres. Ambrosio M. Rodriguez.

Domestic Insurance Co of the Philippines: 5th Floor, Champ Bldg, Anda Circle, Bonifacio Drive, Port Area, Manila; tel. (2) 5278181; fax (2) 5273052; e-mail gdicp@skyinet.net; f. 1946; cap. 10m.; Pres. and Chair. Mar S. Lopez.

Empire Insurance Co: Prudential Life Bldg, 2nd Floor, 843 Arnaiz Ave, Legaspi Village, Makati City, 1229 Metro Manila; tel. (2) 8159561; fax (2) 8152599; e-mail empire_ins_co@yahoo.com; f. 1949; fire, bonds, marine, accident, motor car, extraneous perils; Pres. and CEO Jose Ma G. Santos.

Equitable Insurance Corpn: Equitable Bank Bldg, 4th Floor, 262 Juan Luna St, Binondo, POB 1103, Metro Manila; tel. (2) 2430291; fax (2) 2415768; e-mail info@equitableinsurance.com.ph; internet www.equitableinsurance.com.ph; f. 1950; fire, marine, casualty, motor car, bonds; Pres. Nora T. Go; Exec. Vice-Pres. Antonio C. Ocampo.

Insular Life Assurance Co Ltd: Insular Life Corporate Center, Insular Life Drive, Filinvest Corporate City, Alabang, 1781 Muntinlupa City; tel. (2) 7711818; fax (2) 7711717; e-mail headofc@insular.com.ph; internet www.insularlife.com.ph; f. 1910; members' equity 15,300m. (Dec. 2007); Chair. and CEO Vicente R. Ayllón.

Makati Insurance Co Inc: BPI Buendia Center, 19th Floor, Sen. Gil J. Puyat Ave, Makati City, 1200 Metro Manila; tel. (2) 8459576; fax (2) 8915229; f. 1965; non-life; Pres. and Gen. Man. Jaime L. Darantinao; Chair. Octavio V. Espiritu.

Malayan Insurance Co Inc: Yuchengco Tower, 4th Floor, 484 Quintin Paredes St, Binondo, 1099 Metro Manila; tel. (2) 2428888; fax (2) 2412188; e-mail malayan@malayan.com; internet www.malayan.com; f. 1949; cap. 100m. (1998); insurance and bonds; Pres. Yvonne S. Yuchengco; Chair. Adelita Vergel de Dios.

Manila Surety & Fidelity Co Inc: 66 P. Florentino St, Quezon City, Metro Manila; tel. (2) 7122251; fax (2) 7124129; f. 1945; cap. p.u. 50m., members' equity 85m. (Dec. 2003); Pres. Maria Lourdes V. Peña; Vice-Pres. Maria Editha Peña-Lim; 4 brs.

Metropolitan Insurance Co: Ateneum Bldg, 3rd Floor, Leviste St, Salcedo Village, Makati City, Metro Manila; tel. (2) 8108151; fax (2) 8162294; f. 1933; non-life; Pres. Jose M. Periquet, Jr; Exec. Vice-Pres. Roberto Abad.

National Life Insurance Co of the Philippines: National Life Insurance Bldg, 6762 Ayala Ave, Makati City, Metro Manila; tel. (2) 8100251; fax (2) 8178718; f. 1933; Pres. Benjamin L. de Leon; Sr Vice-Pres. Douglas McLaren.

National Reinsurance Corpn of the Philippines: AXA Life Center, 18th Floor, Sen. Gil J. Puyat Ave, cnr Tindalo St, Makati City, 1200 Metro Manila; tel. (2) 7595801; fax (2) 7595886; e-mail nrcp@nrcp.com.ph; internet www.nrcp.com.ph; f. 1978; Chair. Winston F. Garcia; Pres. and CEO Roberto B. Crisol.

Paramount Life and General Insurance Corpn: Sage House, 14th and 15th Floors, 110 V. A. Rufino St, Legaspi Village, Makati City, 1229 Metro Manila; tel. (2) 8127956; fax (2) 8131140; e-mail insure@paramount.com.ph; internet www.paramount.com.ph; f. 1950; fmrly Paramount General Insurance Corpn; name changed to Paramount Union Insurance Corpn in 2001; name changed as above in 2002; fire, marine, casualty, motor car; Chair. Patrick L. Go; Pres. George T. Tiu.

Philippine American Life and General Insurance Co (Philamlife): Philamlife Bldg, United Nations Ave, Metro Manila; POB 2167, 0990 Metro Manila; tel. (2) 5269258; fax (2) 5269253; e-mail philamwebmaster@aig.com; internet www.philamlife.com.ph; Pres. Jose Cuisia.

Pioneer Insurance and Surety Corpn: Pioneer House Makati, 108 Paseo de Roxas, Legaspi Village, Makati City, 1229 Metro Manila; tel. (2) 812777; fax (2) 8171461; e-mail info@pioneer.com.ph; internet www.pioneer.com.ph; f. 1954; cap. 3,300m. (2007); Pres. and CEO David C. Coyukiat.

Rizal Surety and Insurance Co: Prudential Life Bldg, 3rd Floor, 843 Arnaiz Ave, Legaspi Village, Makati City, Metro Manila; tel. (2) 8159561; fax (2) 8152599; e-mail rizalsic@mkt.weblinq.com; f. 1939; fire, bond, marine, motor car, accident, extraneous perils; Chair. and Pres. S. Corpus.

Standard Insurance Co Inc: Standard Insurance Tower, 999 Pedro Gil St, cnr F. Agoncillo St, Metro Manila; tel. (2) 5223230; fax (2) 5261479; f. 1958; Chair. Lourdes T. Echauz; Pres. Ernesto Echauz.

Sterling Insurance Co: Zeta II Annex Bldg, 6th Floor, 191 Salcedo St, Legaspi Village, Makati City, Metro Manila; tel. (2) 8925787; fax (2) 8183630; f. 1960; fmrly Dominion Insurance Corpn; name changed as above Nov. 2001; fire, marine, motor car, accident, engineering, bonds; Pres. Rafael Gallaga.

Tico Insurance Co Inc: Trafalgar Plaza, 7th Floor, 105 H. V. de la Costa St, Salcedo Village, Makati City, 1227 Metro Manila; tel. (2) 8140143; fax (2) 8140150; f. 1937; fmrly Tabacalera Insurance Co Inc; Chair. and Pres. Carlos Catholico.

UCPB General Insurance Co Inc: 25th Floor, LKG Tower, 6801 Ayala Ave, Makati City, Metro Manila; tel. (2) 8070355; fax (2) 8501086; e-mail ucpbgen@ucpbgen.com; internet www.ucpbgen.com; f. 1963; non-life; Pres. Isabelo P. Africa; Chair. Julita S. Manahan.

Universal Reinsurance Corpn: Ayala Life Bldg, 9th Floor, 6786 Ayala Ave, Makati City, Metro Manila; tel. (2) 7514977; fax (2) 8173745; f. 1949; life and non-life; Chair. Jaime Augusto Zobel de Ayala II; Pres. Herminia S. Jacinto.

Regulatory Body

Insurance Commission: 1071 United Nations Ave, Metro Manila; tel. and fax (2) 5238461; e-mail pubassist_ic@yahoo.com.ph; internet www.insurance.gov.ph; regulates the private insurance industry by, among other things, issuing certificates of authority to insurance companies and intermediaries and monitoring their financial solvency; Commr Eduardo T. Malinis.

THE PHILIPPINES   *Directory*

Trade and Industry

GOVERNMENT AGENCIES

Board of Investments: 385 Sen. Gil J. Puyat Ave, Makati City, 1200 Metro Manila; tel. (2) 8976682; fax (2) 8953641; e-mail OSAC@boi.gov.ph; internet www.boi.gov.ph; Chair. PETER B. FAVILA.

Bureau of Domestic Trade (BDT): Trade and Industry Bldg, 2nd Floor, 361 Sen. Gil J. Puyat Ave, Makati City, Metro Manila; tel. (2) 8904877; fax (2) 8904858; e-mail morbeta@yahoo.com; Dir MEYNARD R. ORBETA.

Cagayan Economic Zone Authority: Westar Bldg, 7th Floor, 611 Shaw Blvd, Pasig City, 1603 Metro Manila; tel. (2) 6365776; fax (2) 6313997; e-mail info@ceza.gov.ph; internet www.ceza.gov.ph; CEO JOSÉ MARI PONCE.

Clark Development Corpn: Bldg 2122, C. P. Garcia St, cnr E. Quirino St, Clark Field, Pampanga; tel. (2) 5999000; fax (2) 5994602; e-mail info@clark.com.ph; internet www.clark.com.ph; Pres. and CEO LIBERATO P. LAUS.

Industrial Technology Development Institute: DOST Compound, Gen. Santos Ave, Bicutan, Taguig, 1631 Metro Manila; tel. (2) 8372071; fax (2) 8373167; e-mail adiv@dost.gov.ph; Dir Dr NUNA E. ALMANZOR.

Maritime Industry Authority (MARINA): PPL Bldg, 1000 United Nations Ave, cnr San Marcelino St, Ermita, Metro Manila; tel. (2) 5238651; fax (2) 5242746; e-mail feedback@marina.gov.ph; internet www.marina.gov.ph; f. 1974; development of inter-island shipping, overseas shipping, shipbuilding and repair, and maritime power; Administrator VICENTE T. SUAZO, Jr.

National Tobacco Administration: NTA Bldg, Scout Reyes St, cnr Panay Ave, Quezon City, Metro Manila; tel. (2) 3743987; fax (2) 3742505; e-mail ntamis@ph.inter.net; internet www.geocities.com/miscsdnta; f. 1987; Administrator CARLITOS S. ENCARNACION.

Philippine Coconut Authority (PCA): PCA R & D Bldg, Elliptical Rd, Diliman, Quezon City, 1100 Metro Manila; tel. (2) 9284501; fax (2) 9216173; e-mail pca_ofad@yahoo.com.ph; internet www.pca.da.gov.ph; f. 1972; Chair. ARTHUR C. YAP; Administrator OSCAR G. GARIN.

Philippine Council for Advanced Science and Technology Research and Development (PCASTRD): DOST Main Bldg, Gen. Santos Ave, Bicutan, Taguig, 1631 Metro Manila; tel. (2) 8377522; fax (2) 8373168; e-mail pcastrd@dost.gov.ph; internet www.pcastrd.dost.gov.ph; f. 1987; Exec. Dir Dr REYNALDO V. EBORA.

Philippine Economic Zone Authority: Roxas Blvd, cnr San Luis St, Pasay City, Metro Manila; tel. (2) 5513454; fax (2) 8916380; e-mail info@peza.gov.ph; internet www.peza.gov.ph; Dir-Gen. LILIA B. DE LIMA.

Privatization and Management Office: Department of Finance, 104 Gamboa St, Legaspi Village, Makati City, 1229 Metro Manila; tel. (2) 8932383; fax (2) 8933453; e-mail pmo@eastern.com.ph; f. 2002; formed to handle the privatization of govt assets; succeeded Asset Privatization Trust; Chief Exec. RENATO V. VALDECANTOS.

Subic Bay Metropolitan Authority: SBMA Center, Bldg 229, Waterfront Rd, Subic Bay Freeport Zone, 2222 Zambales; tel. (47) 2524000; fax (47) 2524216; e-mail webteam@sbma.com; internet www.sbma.com; Chair. FELICIANO G. SALONGA; CEO and Admin. ARMAND C. ARREZA.

DEVELOPMENT ORGANIZATIONS

Bases Conversion Development Authority: 2nd Floor, Bonifacio Technology Center, 31st St, Crescent Park West, Bonifacio Global City, Taguig, 1634 Metro Manila; tel. (2) 8166666; fax (2) 8160996; e-mail bcda@bcda.gov.ph; internet www.bcda.gov.ph; f. 1992; est. to facilitate the conversion, privatization and development of fmr military bases; Chair. ALOYSIUS R. SANTOS; Pres. and CEO NARCISO L. ABAYA.

Bureau of Land Development: DAR Bldg, Elliptical Rd, Diliman, Quezon City, Metro Manila; tel. (2) 9287031; fax (2) 9260971; Dir EUGENIO B. BERNARDO.

Bureau of Small and Medium Business Development: Oppen Bldg, 3rd Floor, 349 Sen. Gil J. Puyat Ave, Makati City, Metro Manila; tel. and fax (2) 8967916; e-mail bsmbd@mnl.sequel.net; initiates and implements programmes and projects addressing the specific needs of SMEs in areas concerning entrepreneurship, institutional development, productivity improvement, organization, financing and marketing; Dir MEYNARDO R. ORBETA.

Capital Market Development Council (CMDC): Unit 310, Atrium Bldg, Makati Ave, Makati City, POB 1125, Metro Manila; tel. (2) 8114185; e-mail cmdc_phil@yahoo.com; internet cmdc-phil.net; Chair. DAVID L. BALANGUE.

Co-operatives Development Authority: 5th Floor, Benlor Bldg, 1184 Quezon Ave, Quezon City, Metro Manila; tel. (2) 3736894; fax (2) 3712077; e-mail cda.oed@gmail.com; internet www.cda.gov.ph; Chair. LECIRA V. JUAREZ; Exec. Dir NIEL A. SANTILLAN.

National Development Co (NDC): NDC Bldg, 8th Floor, 116 Tordesillas St, Salcedo Village, Makati City, Metro Manila; tel. (2) 8404898; fax (2) 8404862; e-mail info@ndc.gov.ph; internet www.ndc.gov.ph; f. 1919; govt-owned corpn engaged in the organization, financing and management of subsidiaries and corpns, incl. commercial, industrial, mining, agricultural and other enterprises assisting national economic devt; also jt industrial ventures with other ASEAN countries; Chair. PETER FAVILA; Gen. Man. LOURDES F. RUBUENO.

Philippine National Oil Co (PNOC): Energy Complex, Bldg 6, 6th Floor, Merritt Rd, Fort Bonifacio, Makati City, Metro Manila; tel. (2) 8126209; fax (2) 8152747; internet www.pnoc.com.ph; f. 1973; state-owned energy development agency mandated to ensure stable and sufficient supply of oil products and to develop domestic energy resources; Chair. ANGELO T. REYES; Pres. and CEO ANTONIO M. CAILAO.

Southern Philippines Development Authority: Basic Petroleum Bldg, 104 Carlos Palanca, Jr, St, Legaspi Village, Makati City, Metro Manila; tel. (2) 8183893; fax (2) 8183907; Chair. ROBERTO AVENTAJADO; Manila Rep. GERUDIO 'KHALIQ' MADUENO.

CHAMBERS OF COMMERCE AND INDUSTRY

Cebu Chamber of Commerce and Industry: CCCI Center, cnr 11th and 13th Ave, North Reclamation Area, Cebu City 6000; tel. (32) 2321421; fax (32) 2321422; e-mail m@cebuchamber.com.ph; internet www.cebubusinesswebportal.com; f. 1921; Pres. EDWARD S. GAISANO.

Federation of Filipino-Chinese Chambers of Commerce and Industry Inc: Federation Center, 6th Floor, Muelle de Binondo St, POB 23, Metro Manila; tel. (2) 2419201; fax (2) 2422361; e-mail ffcccii@yahoo.com; internet www.ffcccii.com.ph; Pres. JOHN K. TAN.

Philippine Chamber of Coal Mines (Philcoal): Rm 1007, Princeville Condominium, S. Laurel St, cnr Shaw Blvd, 1552 Mandaluyong City; tel. (2) 5330518; fax (2) 5315513; f. 1980; Exec. Dir BERTRAND GONZALES.

Philippine Chamber of Commerce and Industry: 3rd Floor, ECC Bldg, 355 Senator Gil Puyat Ave, Makati City, Metro Manila; tel. (2) 8964549; fax (2) 8991727; e-mail pcci@philippinechamber.com; internet www.philippinechamber.com; f. 1977; Chair. MIGUEL B. VARELA; Pres. EDGARDO LACSON.

Philippine Chamber of Mines: Rm 809, Ortigas Bldg, Ortigas Ave, Pasig City, 1605 Metro Manila; tel. (2) 6354123; fax (2) 6354160; e-mail comp@pldtdsl.net; f. 1975; Chair. ARTEMIO F. DISINI; Pres. BENJAMIN PHILIP G. ROMUALDEZ.

FOREIGN TRADE ORGANIZATIONS

Bureau of Export Trade Promotion: New Solid Bldg, 5th–8th Floors, 357 Sen. Gil J. Puyat Ave, Makati City, 1200 Metro Manila; tel. (2) 8990133; fax (2) 8904707; e-mail betpod@dti.gov.ph; internet tradelinephil.dti.gov.ph; Dir FERNANDO P. CALA II.

Bureau of Import Services: Oppen Bldg, 3rd Floor, 349 Sen. Gil J. Puyat Ave, Makati City, Metro Manila; tel. (2) 8905418; fax (2) 8957466; e-mail bis@dti.gov.ph; Exec. Dir ALEXANDER B. ARCILLA.

Garments and Textile Export Board (GTEB): New Solid Bldg, 2nd and 3rd Floors, 357 Sen. Gil J. Puyat Ave, Makati City, Metro Manila; tel. (2) 8904810; fax (2) 8904653; e-mail gtebebs@dti.gov.ph; manages and supervises the garment textile quota system; Exec. Dir FELICITAS R. AGONCILLO REYES.

Philippine International Trading Corpn (PITC): National Development Company, 5th Floor, 116 Tordesillas St, Salcedo Village, 1227 Metro Manila; tel. (2) 8189801; fax (2) 8920782; e-mail pitc@info.com.ph; internet pitc.gov.ph; f. 1973; state trading company to conduct international marketing of general merchandise, industrial and construction goods, raw materials, semi-finished and finished goods, and bulk trade of agri-based products; also provides financing, bonded warehousing, shipping, cargo and customs services; Chair. PETER B. FAVILA; Pres. and CEO JORGE MENDOZA JUDAN.

INDUSTRIAL AND TRADE ASSOCIATIONS

Beverage Industry Association of the Philippines: SMPC Bldg, 23rd Floor, St Francis St, Mandaluyong City, Metro Manila; tel. (2) 6346840; fax (2) 6318672; e-mail rbkmlo@mnl.sequel.net; Pres. HECTOR GUBALLA.

Chamber of Automotive Manufacturers of the Philippines (CAMPI): Suite 1206, 12th Floor, Jollibee Plaza, San Miguel Ave, Ortigas Center, Pasig City, Metro Manila; tel. (2) 6329733; fax (2) 6315313; e-mail campi@pacific.net.ph; Pres. ELIZABETH LEE.

Construction Industry Authority of the Philippines (CIAP): Jupiter I Bldg, 4th Floor, Jupiter St, Makati City, Metro Manila; tel.

THE PHILIPPINES
Directory

(2) 8979336; e-mail pocb@skynet.net; Officer-in-Charge KATHERINE T. DELA CRUZ.

Cotton Development Administration (CODA): Agricultural Training Institute, 1st Floor, Elliptical Rd, Diliman, Quezon City, 1100 Metro Manila; tel. (2) 9208878; fax (2) 9209238; e-mail coda_ho2003@yahoo.com; internet www.coda.da.gov.ph; Administrator Dr EUGENIO D. ORPIA, Jr.

Federation of Philippine Industries (FPI): Suite 701, Atlanta Center, Annapolis St, Greenhills, San Juan, Metro Manila; tel. (2) 7223409; fax (2) 7229737; e-mail fpi@philonline.com; internet www.fpi.ph; f. 1991; Chair. MENELEO J. CARLOS, Jr; Pres. JESUS L. ARRANZA.

Fiber Industry Development Authority: Asiatrust Bank Annex Bldg, 1424 Quezon Ave, Quezon City, Metro Manila; tel. (2) 3737489; fax (2) 3737494; e-mail fibernetwk@yahoo.com; internet fida.da.gov.ph; Administrator CECILIA GLORIA J. SORIANO.

Philippine Association of Electrical Industries: Banks of the Philippines Bldg, Suite 702, Plaza Cervantes, Binondo, Metro Manila; tel. and fax (2) 2421144; Pres. RICARDO SY.

Philippine Fisheries Development Authority: 2nd Floor, PCA Annex Bldg, 1 Elliptical Rd, Diliman, Quezon City, 1109 Metro Manila; tel. (2) 9258472; fax (2) 9256138; e-mail oagm@pfda.gov.ph; internet pfda.da.gov.ph; f. 1976; Gen. Man. PETRONILO B. BUENDIA.

Philippine Liquefied Petroleum Gas Association: 218 San Vicente St, Binondo, Metro Manila; tel. (2) 2412668; fax (2) 6337781; f. 1966; Pres. JOSELITO ASENTERO.

Semiconductor and Electronic Industries in the Philippines (SEIPI): Unit 902, RCBC Plaza, Tower 2, Sen. Gil J. Puyat Ave, Makati City, Metro Manila; tel. (2) 8449028; fax (2) 8449037; e-mail philippine.electronics@seipi.org.ph; internet www.seipi.org.ph; Pres. ERNESTO B. SANTIAGO.

EMPLOYERS' ORGANIZATIONS

Employers' Confederation of the Philippines (ECOP): ECC Bldg, 2nd Floor, 355 Sen. Gil J. Puyat Ave, Makati City, Metro Manila; tel. (2) 8904845; fax (2) 8958623; e-mail ecop@webquest.com; internet www.ecop.org.ph; f. 1975; Chair. MIGUEL B. VARELA; Pres. SERGIO ORTIZ-LUIS, Jr.

Filipino Shipowners' Association: Victoria Bldg, Room 503, 429 United Nations Ave, Ermita, 1000 Metro Manila; tel. (2) 5227318; fax (2) 5243164; e-mail filiship@info.com.ph; internet www.filipinoshipowners.com.ph; f. 1950; 24 mems, including 6 assoc. mems; Chair. CARLOS C. SALINAS; Exec. Sec. AUGUSTO Y. ARREZA, Jr.

Philippine Cement Manufacturers Corporation (PHILCEMCOR): Corporal Cruz, cnr E. Rodriguez Jr Ave, Bagong Ilog, Pasig City, Metro Manila; tel. (2) 6717585; fax (2) 6717588; e-mail alfiler@info.com.ph; Pres. FELIX ENRICO R. ALFILER.

Philippine Coconut Producers' Federation, Inc: Wardley Bldg, 2nd Floor, 1991 Taft Ave, cnr San Juan St, Pasay City, 1300 Metro Manila; tel. (2) 5230918; fax (2) 5211333; e-mail cocofed@pworld.net.ph; Pres. MARIA CLARA L. LOBREGAT.

Philippine Retailers' Association: Unit 2610, Jollibee Plaza, Emerald Ave, Ortigas Center, Pasig City; tel. (2) 6874180; fax (2) 6360825; e-mail pra@philretailers.com; internet www.philretailers.com; f. 1976; Pres. BIENVENIDO V. TANTOCO III.

Philippine Sugar Millers' Association Inc: 1402 Security Bank Centre, 6776 Ayala Ave, Makati City, 1226 Metro Manila; tel. (2) 8911138; fax (2) 8911144; e-mail psma@psma.com.ph; internet www.psma.com.ph; f. 1922; Chair. JULIO O. SY; Pres. PEDRO E. ROXAS.

Textile Mills Association of the Philippines, Inc (TMAP): Ground Floor, Alexander House, 132 Amorsolo St, Legaspi Village, Makati City, 1229 Metro Manila; tel. (2) 8186601; fax (2) 8183107; e-mail tmap@pacific.net.ph; f. 1956; 11 mems; Pres. HERMENEGILDO C. ZAYCO; Chair. JAMES L. GO.

Textile Producers' Association of the Philippines, Inc: Downtown Center Bldg, Room 513, 516 Quintin Paredes St, Binondo, Metro Manila; tel. (2) 2411144; fax (2) 2411162; Pres. GO CUN UY; Exec. Sec. ROBERT L. TAN.

UTILITIES

Energy Regulatory Commission: Pacific Center Bldg, San Miguel Ave, Ortigas Center, Pasig City, 1600 Metro Manila; tel. (2) 9145000; fax (2) 6315818; e-mail info@erc.gov.ph; internet www.erc.gov.ph; Chair. and CEO ZENAIDA CRUZ-DUCUT; Exec. Dir FRANCIS SATURNINO C. JUAN.

Electricity

Davao Light and Power Co: 163–5 C. Bangoy, Sr, St, Davao City 8000; tel. (82) 2212191; fax (82) 2212105; e-mail davaolight@davao-online.com; internet www.davaolight.com; the country's third largest electric utility with a peak demand of 175 MW in 2000.

Manila Electric Co (Meralco): Lopez Bldg, 2nd Floor, Meralco Center, Ortigas Ave, Pasig City, 0300 Metro Manila; tel. (2) 6312222; fax (2) 6315591; e-mail finplan.inv.relations@meralco.com.ph; internet www.meralco.com.ph; f. 1903; supplies electric power to Manila and seven provinces in Luzon; largest electricity distributor, supplying 54% of total consumption in 2000; privatized in 1991, 34% govt-owned; Chair. and CEO MANUEL M. LOPEZ; Pres. JOSE P. DE JESUS.

National Power Corpn (NAPOCOR): Quezon Ave, cnr BIR Rd, Quezon City, Metro Manila; tel. (2) 9213541; fax (2) 9212468; e-mail webmaster@napocor.gov.ph; internet www.napocor.gov.ph; f. 1936; state-owned corpn supplying electric and hydroelectric power throughout the country; partially privatized in 2007; Pres. FROILAN TAMPINCO.

Gas

First Gen Corpn: Benpres Bldg, 3rd Floor, Exchange Rd, cnr Meralco Ave, Pasig City, Metro Manila; tel. (2) 6343428; fax (2) 6352737; e-mail info@firstgen.com.ph; internet www.firstgen.com.ph; major interests in power generation and distribution; Chair. OSCAR M. LOPEZ; Pres. FEDERICO R. LOPEZ.

Water

Regulatory Authority

Metropolitan Waterworks and Sewerage System: 4th Floor, Administration Bldg, MWSS Complex, 489 Katipunan Rd, Balara, Quezon City, 1105 Metro Manila; tel. (2) 9223757; fax (2) 9212887; e-mail info@mwss.gov.ph; internet www.mwss.gov.ph; govt regulator for water supply, treatment and distribution within Metro Manila; Administrator DIOSDADO ALLADO.

Distribution Companies

Davao City Water District: Km 5, Jose P. Laurel Ave, Bajada, 8000 Davao City; tel. (82) 2219400; fax (82) 2264885; e-mail dcwd@davao-water.gov.ph; internet www.davao-water.gov.ph; f. 1973; public utility responsible for the water supply of Davao City; Chair. EDUARDO A. BANGAYAN; Gen. Man. Eng. RODORA N. GAMBOA.

Manila Water: Administration Bldg, 2nd Floor, MWSS Compound, 489 Katipunan Rd, Balara, Quezon City, 1105 Metro Manila; tel. (2) 9281223; fax (2) 9223761; e-mail info@manilawateronline.com; internet www.manilawater.com; f. 1997 following the privatization of Metro Manila's water services; responsible for water supply to Manila East until 2023; Pres. ANTONINO T. AQUINO.

Maynilad Water: MWSS Compound, Katipunan Rd, Balara, Quezon City, Metro Manila; tel. (2) 4353583; fax (2) 9223759; internet www.mayniladwater.com.ph; f. 1998 following the privatization of Metro Manila's water services; responsible for water supply, sewage and sanitation services for Manila West until 2021; Pres. FIORELLO R. ESTUAR.

Metropolitan Cebu Water District: Magallanes St, cnr Lapulapu St, 6000 Cebu City; tel. (32) 2548434; fax (32) 2545391; e-mail mcwd@cvis.net.ph; internet www.mcwd.gov.ph; f. 1974; public utility responsible for water supply and sewerage of Cebu City and surrounding towns and cities; Chair. JUAN SAUL F. MONTECILLO; Gen. Man. ARMANDO H. PAREDES.

TRADE UNION FEDERATIONS

In 1986 the Government established the Labor Advisory Consultation Committee (LACC) to facilitate communication between the Government and the powerful labour movement in the Philippines. The LACC granted unions direct recognition and access to the Government, which, under the Marcos regime, had been available only to the Trade Union Congress of the Philippines (KMP-TUCP). The KMP-TUCP refused to join the Committee.

In May 1994 a new trade union alliance, the Caucus for Labor Unity, was established; its members included the KMP-TUCP and three groups that had dissociated themselves from Kilusang Mayo Uno (see Independent Labour Federations).

Katipunang Manggagawang Pilipino (KMP-TUCP) (Trade Union Congress of the Philippines): TUCP Training Center Bldg, TUCP-PGEA Compound, Masaya St, cnr Maharlika St, Diliman, Quezon City, 1101 Metro Manila; tel. (2) 9247551; fax (2) 9219758; e-mail secrtucp@tucp.org.ph; internet www.tucp.org.ph; f. 1975; 1.0m. mems; Pres. DEMOCRITO T. MENDOZA; Gen. Sec. ERNESTO F. HERRERA; 39 affiliates, incl.:

Associated Labor Union for Metalworkers (ALU—METAL): TUCP-PGEA Compound, Diliman, Quezon City, 1101 Metro Manila; tel. (2) 9222575; fax (2) 9247553; e-mail alumla@info.com.ph; 29,700 mems; Pres. DEMOCRITO T. MENDOZA.

Associated Labor Union for Textile Workers (ALU—TEXTILE): TUCP-PGEA Compound, Elliptical Rd, Diliman, Quezon City, 1101 Metro Manila; tel. (2) 9222575; fax (2) 9247553; e-mail alumla@info.com.ph; 41,400 mems; Pres. DEMOCRITO T. MENDOZA.

THE PHILIPPINES

Associated Labor Unions (ALU—TRANSPORT): 1763 Tomas Claudio St, Baclaran, Parañaque, Metro Manila; tel. (2) 8320634; fax (2) 8322392; 49,500 mems; Pres. ALEXANDER O. BARRIENTOS.

Associated Labor Unions—Visayas Mindanao Confederation of Trade Unions (ALU—VIMCONTU): ALU Bldg, Quezon Blvd, Port Area, Elliptical Rd, cnr Maharlika St, Diliman, Quezon City, 1101 Metro Manila; tel. (2) 9222185; fax (2) 9247553; e-mail alumla@info.com.ph; f. 1954; 350,000 mems; Pres. DEMOCRITO T. MENDOZA.

Associated Professional, Supervisory, Office and Technical Employees Union (APSOTEU): TUCP-PGEA Compound, Elliptical Rd, Diliman, Quezon City, 1101 Metro Manila; tel. (2) 9222575; fax (2) 9247553; e-mail alumla@info.com.ph; Pres. CECILIO T. SENO.

Association of Independent Unions of the Philippines: Vila Bldg, Mezzanine Floor, Epifanio de los Santos Ave, Cubao, Quezon City, Metro Manila; tel. (2) 9224652; Pres. EMMANUEL S. DURANTE.

Association of Trade Unions (ATU): Antwel Bldg, Room 1, 2nd Floor, Santa Ana, Port Area, Davao City; tel. (82) 2272394; 2,997 mems; Pres. JORGE ALEGARBES.

Confederation of Labor and Allied Social Services (CLASS): Doña Santiago Bldg, TUCP Suite 404, 1344 Taft Ave, Ermita, Metro Manila; tel. (2) 5240415; fax (2) 5266011; f. 1979; 4,579 mems; Pres. LEONARDO F. AGTING.

Federation of Agrarian and Industrial Toiling Hands (FAITH): Kalayaan Ave, cnr Masigla St, Diliman, Quezon City, Metro Manila; tel. (2) 9225244; 220,000 mems; Pres. RAYMUNDO YUMUL.

Federation of Consumers' Co-operatives in Negros Oriental (FEDCON): Bandera Bldg, Cervantes St, Dumaguete City; tel. (32) 2048; Chair. MEDARDO VILLALON.

Federation of Unions of Rizal (FUR): Suite 307, Buenavista Bldg, 3rd Floor, 82 Quirino Ave, cnr Rivera St, Parañaque City, Metro Manila; tel. and fax (2) 8320110; 10,853 mems; Officer-in-Charge EDUARDO ASUNCION.

Lakas sa Industriya ng Kapatirang Haligi ng Alyansa (LIKHA): 32 Kabayanihan Rd Phase IIA, Karangalan Village, Pasig City, Metro Manila; tel. and fax (2) 6463234; e-mail jbvlikha@yahoo.com; Pres. JESUS B. VILLAMOR.

National Association of Free Trade Unions (NAFTU): Rm 404, San Luis Terrace, T. M. Kalaw St, Ermita, Metro Manila; tel. (2) 598705; 7,385 mems; Pres. JAIME RINCAL.

National Congress of Unions in the Sugar Industry of the Philippines (NACUSIP): 7431A Yakal St, Barangay San Antonio, Makati City, Metro Manila; tel. and fax (2) 8437284; e-mail nacusip@compass.com.ph; 32 affiliated unions and 57,424 mems; Nat. Pres. ZOILO V. DELA CRUZ, Jr.

National Mines and Allied Workers' Union (NAMAWU): Unit 201, A. Dunville Condominium, 1 Castilla St, cnr Valencio St, Quezon City, Metro Manila; tel. (2) 7265070; fax (2) 4155582; 13,233 mems; Pres. ROBERTO A. PADILLA.

Pambansang Kilusan ng Paggawa (KILUSAN): TUCP-PGEA Compound, Elliptical Rd, Diliman, Quezon City, 1101 Metro Manila; tel. (2) 9284651; 13,093 mems; Pres. AVELINO V. VALERIO; Sec.-Gen. IGMIDIO T. GANAGANA.

Philippine Agricultural, Commercial and Industrial Workers' Union (PACIWU): 5 7th St, Lacson, Bacolod City; fax (2) 7097967; Pres. ZOILO V. DELA CRUZ, Jr.

Philippine Federation of Labor (PFL): FEMII Bldg, Suite 528, Aduana St, Intramuros, Metro Manila; tel. (2) 5271686; fax (2) 5272838; 8,869 mems; Pres. ALEJANDRO C. VILLAVIZA.

Philippine Federation of Teachers' Organizations (PFTO): BSP Bldg, Room 112, Concepcion St, Ermita, Metro Manila; tel. (2) 5275106; Pres. FEDERICO D. RICAFORT.

Philippine Government Employees' Association (PGEA): TUCP-PGEA Compound, Elliptical Rd, Diliman, Quezon City, Metro Manila; tel. (2) 6383541; fax (2) 6375764; e-mail eso_pgea@hotmail.com; f. 1945; 65,000 mems; Pres. ESPERANZA S. OCAMPO.

Philippine Integrated Industries Labor Union (PIILU): Mendoza Bldg, Room 319, 3rd Floor, Pilar St, Zamboanga City; tel. (992) 2299; f. 1973; Pres. JOSE J. SUAN.

Philippine Labor Federation (PLF): ALU Bldg, Quezon Blvd, Port Area, Cebu City; tel. (32) 71219; fax (32) 97544; 15,462 mems; Pres. CRISPIN B. GASTARDO.

Philippine Seafarers' Union (PSU): TUCP-PGEA Compound, Elliptical Rd, Diliman, Quezon City, 1101 Metro Manila; tel. (2) 9222575; fax (2) 9247553; e-mail psumla@info.com.ph; f. 1984; 10,000 mems; Pres. DEMOCRITO T. MENDOZA; Gen. Sec. ERNESTO F. HERRERA.

Philippine Transport and General Workers' Organization (PTGWO—D): Cecilleville Bldg, 3rd Floor, Quezon Ave, Quezon City, Metro Manila; tel. (2) 4115811; fax (2) 4115812; f. 1953; 33,400 mems; Pres. VICTORINO F. BALAIS.

Port and General Workers' Federation (PGWF): Capilitan Engineering Corpn Bldg, 206 Zaragoza St, Tondo, Manila; tel. 208959; Pres. FRANKLIN D. BUTCON.

Public Services Labor Independent Confederation (PSLINK): 15 Clarion Lily St, Congressional Ave, Quezon City, 1100 Metro Manila; tel. (2) 9244710; fax (2) 9281090; e-mail annie.geron@pslink.org; internet www.pslink.org; f. 1987 as Public Sector Labor Integrative Center; 35,108 mems; Pres. JARAH HAMJAH; Gen. Sec. ANNIE ENRIQUEZ-GERON.

United Sugar Farmers' Organization (USFO): SPCMA Annex Bldg, 3rd Floor, 1 Luzuriaga St, Bacolod City; Pres. BERNARDO M. REMO.

Workers' Alliance Trade Unions (WATU): Delta Bldg, Room 300, Quezon Ave, cnr West Ave, Quezon City, Metro Manila; tel. (2) 9225093; fax (2) 975918; f. 1978; 25,000 mems; Pres. TEMISTOCLES S. DEJON, Sr.

INDEPENDENT LABOUR FEDERATIONS

The following organizations are not affiliated to the KMP-TUCP:

Associated Marine Officers and Seamen's Union of the Philippines (AMOSUP): Seaman's Centre, cnr Cabildo and Sta Potenciana Sts, Intramuros, Metro Manila; tel. (2) 5278491; fax (2) 5273534; e-mail s_center@amosup.org; internet www.amosup.org; f. 1960; 23 affiliated unions with 55,000 mems; Pres. GREGORIO S. OCA.

Federation of Free Workers (FFW): FFW Bldg, 1943 Taft Ave, Malate, Metro Manila; tel. (2) 5219435; fax (2) 4006656; internet www.ffw.org.ph; f. 1950; affiliated to International Trade Union Confederation (ITUC); 300 affiliated local unions and 400,000 mems; Pres. ALLAN S. MONTANO.

Kilusang Mayo Uno (KMU): 63 Narra St, Barangay Claro, Quezon City, 1102 Metro Manila; tel. (2) 4210986; fax (2) 4210768; e-mail obrero@kilusangmayouno.org; internet www.kilusangmayouno.org; f. 1980; Chair. ELMER LABOG; Sec.-Gen. WILSON BALDONAZA.

Lakas ng Manggagawa Labor Center: Rm 401, Femii Bldg Annex, A. Soriano St, Intramuros, Metro Manila; tel. and fax (2) 5280482; a grouping of 'independent' local unions; Chair. OSCAR M. ACERSON.

Manggagawa ng Komunikasyon sa Pilipinas (MKP): 22 Libertad St, Mandaluyong City, Metro Manila; tel. (2) 5313701; fax (2) 5312109; f. 1951; Pres. PETE PINLAC.

National Confederation of Labor: Suite 402, Carmen Bldg, Ronquillo St, cnr Evangelista St, Quiapo, Metro Manila; tel. and fax (2) 7334474; f. 1994 by fmr mems of Kilusang Mayo Uno; Pres. ANTONIO DIAZ.

Philippine Social Security Labor Union (PSSLU): Carmen Bldg, Suite 309, Ronquillo St, Quiapo, Metro Manila; f. 1954; Nat. Pres. ANTONIO B. DIAZ; Nat. Sec. OFELIA C. ALAVERA.

Samahang Manggagawang Pilipino (SMP) (National Alliance of Teachers and Office Workers): Fersal Condominium II, Room 33, 130 Kalayaan Ave, Quezon City, 1104 Metro Manila; tel. and fax (2) 9242299; Pres. ADELISA RAYMUNDO.

Solidarity Trade Conference for Progress: Rizal Ave, Dipolog City; tel. and fax (65) 2124303; Pres. NICOLAS E. SABANDAL.

Trade Unions of the Philippines and Allied Services (TUPAS): Med-dis Bldg, Suites 203–204, Solana St, cnr Real St, Intramuros, Metro Manila; tel. (2) 493449; affiliated to the World Fed. of Trade Unions; 280 affiliated unions and 75,000 mems; Nat. Pres. DIOSCORO O. NUÑEZ; Sec.-Gen. VLADIMIR R. TUPAZ.

Transport

RAILWAYS

The railway network is confined mainly to the island of Luzon.

Light Rail Transit Authority (Metrorail): Adm. Bldg, LRTA Compound, Aurora Blvd, Pasay City, Metro Manila; tel. (2) 8530041; fax (2) 8316449; e-mail lrtamain@lrta.gov.ph; internet www.lrta.gov.ph; managed and operated by Light Rail Transit Authority (LRTA); electrically driven mass transit system; Line 1 (15 km, Baclaran to Monumento) began commercial operations in Dec. 1984; Line 2 (13.8 km, Santolan to Recto) became fully operational in Oct. 2004; Line 1 South Extension (12 km, Baclaran to Bacoot) planned; Administrator MELQUIADES A. ROBLES.

Philippine National Railways: PNR Management Center, Torres Bugallon St, Kalookan City, 1408 Metro Manila; tel. (2) 3190041; fax (2) 3190169; e-mail info@pnr.gov.ph; internet www.pnr.gov.ph;

THE PHILIPPINES

f. 1887; govt-owned; northern line services run from Manila to Caloocan, 6 km (although the track extends to San Fernando, La Union) and southern line services run from Manila to Legaspi, Albay, 479 km; Chair. MICHAEL T. DEFENSOR; Gen. Man. MANUEL D. ANDAL.

ROADS

In 2003 there were 200,037 km of roads in the Philippines, of which 28,266 km were highways and 49,782 km were secondary roads; an estimated 42,419 km of the network were paved. Bus services provided the most widely used form of inland transport.

Department of Public Works and Highways: Bonifacio Drive, Port Area, Metro Manila; tel. (2) 5274111; fax (2) 5275635; e-mail soriquez.florante@dpwh.gov.ph; internet www.dpwh.gov.ph; responsible for the construction and maintenance of roads and bridges; Sec. HERMOGENES E. EBDANE, Jr.

Land Transportation Franchising and Regulatory Board: East Ave, Diliman, Quezon City, Metro Manila; tel. (2) 4262505; fax (2) 4262515; internet www.ltfrb.gov.ph; f. 1987; Chair. ALBERTO SUANSING.

Land Transportation Office (LTO): East Ave, Quezon City, 1100 Metro Manila; tel. (2) 9219072; fax (2) 9219071; e-mail ltombox@lto.gov.ph; internet www.lto.gov.ph; f. 1987; plans, formulates and implements land transport rules and regulations, safety measures; registration of motor vehicles; issues licences; Exec. Dir BELLA G. BERMUNDO; Asst Sec. ANNELI R. LONTOC.

SHIPPING

In 2000 there were 102 national and municipal ports, 20 baseports, 58 terminal ports and 270 private ports. The eight major ports are Manila, Cebu, Iloilo, Cagayan de Oro, Zamboanga, General Santos, Polloc and Davao.

Pangasiwaan ng Daungan ng Pilipinas (Philippine Ports Authority): Bonifacio Dr., South Harbour, Port Area, 1018 Metro Manila; tel. (2) 5274856; fax (2) 5274853; e-mail info@ppa.com.ph; internet www.ppa.com.ph; f. 1977; supervises all ports within the Philippine Ports Authority port system; Gen. Man. OSCAR M. SEVILLA.

Philippine Shippers' Bureau (PSB): Trade and Industry Bldg, 5th Floor, 361 Sen. Gil J. Puyat Ave, Makati City, Metro Manila; tel. and fax (2) 8904880; e-mail psb@dti.gov.ph; shipping facilitator for international and domestic trade; promotes and protects the interests of shippers, exporters, importers and domestic traders; Dir PEDRO VICENTE C. MENDOZA.

Domestic Lines

Aboitiz Transport System Inc: 12th Floor, Times Plaza Bldg, United Nations Ave, cnr Taft Ave, Ermita, Metro Manila; tel. (2) 5287171; internet www.atsc.com; f. 1996 following the merger of William Lines, Aboitiz Shipping and Carlos A. Gothong Lines; fmrly WG & A Philippines; passenger and cargo inter-island services; Chair. JON RAMON ABOITIZ; Pres. ENRIQUE M. ABOITIZ.

Albar Shipping and Trading Corpn: 2649 Molave St, cnr East Service Rd, United Hills Village, Parañaque, 1713 Metro Manila; tel. (2) 8232391; fax (2) 8233046; e-mail info@albargroup.com.ph; internet www.albargroup.com.ph; f. 1974; manning agency (maritime), trading, ship husbanding; Chair. AKIRA S. KATO; Pres. JOSE ALBAR G. KATO.

Candano Shipping Lines, Inc: Victoria Bldg, 6th Floor, 429 United Nations Ave, Ermita, 2802 Metro Manila; tel. (2) 5238051; fax (2) 5211309; f. 1953; inter-island and Far East chartering, cargo shipping; Pres. and Gen. Man. JOSE CANDANO.

Delsan Transport Lines Inc: Magsaysay Center Bldg, 520 T. M. Kalaw St, Ermita, Metro Manila; tel. (2) 5219172; fax (2) 2889331; Pres. VICENTE A. SANDOVAL; Gen. Man. CARLOS A. BUENAFE.

Eastern Shipping Lines, Inc: ESL Bldg, 54 Anda Circle, Port Area, POB 4253, 2803 Metro Manila; tel. (2) 5277841; fax (2) 5273006; e-mail eastship@skyinet.net; f. 1957; services to Japan; Pres. ERWIN L. CHIONGBIAN; Exec. Vice-Pres. ROY L. CHIONGBIAN.

Loadstar Shipping Co Inc: Loadstar Bldg, 1294 Romualdez St, Paco, 1007 Metro Manila; tel. (2) 5238381; fax (2) 5218061; Pres. and Gen. Man. TEODORO G. BERNARDINO.

Lorenzo Shipping Corpn: 20th Floor, Times Plaza Bldg, United Nations Ave, cnr Taft Ave, Ermita, Metro Manila; tel. (2) 5672180; fax (2) 5672030; internet www.lorenzoshipping.com; Pres. Capt. ROMEO L. MALIG.

Luzteveco (Luzon Stevedoring Corpn): Magsaysay Bldg, 520 T.M. Kalaw St, Ermita, Metro Manila; f. 1909; two brs; freight-forwarding, air cargo, world-wide shipping, broking, stevedoring, salvage, chartering and oil drilling support services; Pres. JOVINO G. LORENZO; Vice-Pres. RODOLFO B. SANTIAGO.

National Shipping Corpn of the Philippines: Knights of Rizal Bldg, Bonifacio Drive, Port Area, Metro Manila; tel. (2) 473631; fax (2) 5300169; services to Hong Kong, Taiwan, Korea, USA; Pres. TONY CHOW.

Negros Navigation Co Inc: Pier 2, North Harbor, Metro Manila; tel. and fax (2) 2454395; e-mail gcabalo@negrosnavigation.ph; internet www.negrosnavigation.ph; Chair. and CEO SULFICIO O. TAGUD.

Philippine Pacific Ocean Lines Inc: Delgado Bldg, Bonifacio Drive, Port Area, POB 184, Metro Manila; tel. (2) 478541; Vice-Pres. C. P. CARANDANG.

Philippine President Lines, Inc: PPL Bldg, 1000–1046 United Nations Ave, POB 4248, Metro Manila; tel. (2) 5249011; fax (2) 5251308; trading world-wide; Chair. EMILIO T. YAP; Pres. ENRIQUE C. YAP.

Sulpicio Lines, Inc: Don Sulpicio Go Bldg, Sulpicio Go St, Reclamation Area, POB 137, Cebu City 6000; tel. (32) 2325361; fax (32) 2321216; internet www.sulpiciolines.com; Chair. ENRIQUE S. GO; Man. Dir CARLOS S. GO.

Sweet Lines Inc: Pier 6, North Harbor, Metro Manila; tel. (2) 201791; fax (2) 205534; f. 1937; Pres. EDUARDO R. LOPINGCO; Exec. Vice-Pres. SONNY R. LOPINGCO.

Transocean Transport Corpn: Magsaysay Bldg, 8th Floor, 520 T. M. Kalaw St, Ermita, POB 21, Metro Manila; tel. (2) 506611; Pres. and Gen. Man. MIGUEL A. MAGSAYSAY; Vice-Pres. EDUARDO U. MANESE.

United Philippine Lines, Inc: UPL Bldg, Santa Clara St, Intramuros, POB 127, Metro Manila; tel. (2) 3380087; fax (2) 5271603; e-mail mailadmin@uplines.net; internet www.uplines.net; services world-wide; Pres. FERNANDO V. LISING.

CIVIL AVIATION

In addition to the international airports in Metro Manila (Ninoy Aquino International Airport), Cebu (Mactan International Airport), Angeles City (Clark International Airport) and Olongapo City (Subic Bay International Airport), there are five alternative international airports: Laoag City, Ilocos Norte; Davao City; Zamboanga City; Gen. Santos (Tambler) City; and Puerto Princesa City, Palawan. There are also numerous domestic and private airports. By late 2006 the development of new airports in Silay City, Iloilo City and Bohol was under way.

Civil Aviation Authority: MIA Rd, Pasay City, Metro Manila; tel. (2) 8799104; fax (2) 8340143; e-mail director_gen@ato.gov.ph; internet www.ato.gov.ph; implements govt policies for the development and operation of a safe and efficient aviation network; Dir-Gen. NILO C. JATICO.

Civil Aeronautics Board: Airport Rd, Pasay City, Metro Manila; tel. (2) 8337259; fax (2) 8336911; e-mail tmanalac@cab.gov.ph; internet www.cab.gov.ph; exercises general supervision and regulation of, and jurisdiction and control over, air carriers, their equipment facilities and franchise; Exec. Dir TOMAS T. MAÑALAC.

Manila International Airport Authority (MIAA): NAIA Complex, Pasay City, Metro Manila; tel. (2) 8322938; fax (2) 8331180; e-mail gm@miaa.gov.ph; internet www.miaa.gov.ph; Gen. Man. ALFONSO G. CUSI.

Air Philippines: R1 Hangar, APC Gate 1, Andrews Ave, Nichols, Pasay City, Metro Manila; tel. (2) 8517601; fax (2) 8517922; e-mail info@airphilippines.com.ph; internet www.airphils.com; f. 1995; domestic and regional services; Chair. DOMINGO T. CHUA; Pres. EDILBERTO R. MEDINA.

Asian Spirit: G & A Bldg, 3rd Floor, 2303 Don Chino Roces Ave, Makati City, Metro Manila; tel. (2) 8403811; fax (2) 8130183; e-mail info@asianspirit.com; internet www.asianspirit.com; Man. ANTONIO BUENDIA.

Cebu Pacific Air: Robinsons Equitable Tower, 16th Floor, ADB Ave, Cnr Poveda Rd, Ortigas Center, Pasig City, Metro Manila; tel. (2) 7020888; fax (2) 6379170; e-mail customerservice@cebupacificair.com; internet www.cebupacificair.com; f. 1995; domestic and international services; Chair. RICARDO J. ROMULO; Pres. and CEO LANCE Y. GOKONGWEI.

Grand Air: Mercure Hotel, Philippines Village Airport Compound, 8th Floor, Pasay City, 1300 Metro Manila; tel. (2) 8313001; fax (2) 8917682; f. 1994; Pres. REBECCA PANLILI.

Philippine Airlines Inc (PAL): PAL Corporate Communications Dept, PAL Center, Ground Floor, Legaspi St, Legaspi Village, Makati City, 0750 Metro Manila; tel. (2) 8558888; fax (2) 8557888; e-mail webmgr@pal.com.ph; internet www.philippineairlines.com; f. 1941; in Jan. 1992 67% of PAL was transferred to the private sector; operates domestic, regional and international services to destinations in the Far East, Australasia, the Middle East, the USA and Canada; Chair. and CEO LUCIO TAN.

THE PHILIPPINES

Tourism

Tourism, although intermittently affected by political unrest, remains an important sector of the economy. In 2006 arrivals totalled 2,843,345. Tourist receipts, including passenger transport, totalled US $4,019m. in 2006.

Philippine Convention and Visitors' Corpn: Legaspi Towers, 4th Floor, 300 Roxas Blvd, 1004 Metro Manila; tel. (2) 5259318; fax (2) 5253314; e-mail pcvcnet@dotpcvc.gov.ph; internet www.dotpcvc.gov.ph; Chair. JOSEPH H. DURANO; Exec. Dir DANIEL G. CORPUZ.

Philippine Tourism Authority: Department of Tourism Bldg, T. M. Kalaw St, Teodoro F. Valencia Circle, Ermita, 1000 Metro Manila; tel. (2) 5247141; fax (2) 5218113; e-mail info@philtourism.gov.ph; internet www.philtourism.com; Gen. Man. and CEO MARK T. LAPID.

POLAND

Introductory Survey

Location, Climate, Language, Religion, Flag, Capital

The Republic of Poland is situated in eastern Europe, bounded to the north by the Baltic Sea and an exclave of the Russian Federation (Kaliningrad Oblast), to the north-east by Lithuania, to the east by Belarus, to the south-east by Ukraine, to the west by Germany, and to the south by the Czech Republic and Slovakia. The climate is temperate in the west but continental in the east. Poland has short summers and cold, snowy winters. Temperatures in Warsaw are generally between $-6°C$ ($21°F$) and $24°C$ ($75°F$). Most of the inhabitants profess Christianity: more than 95% are adherents of the Roman Catholic Church, but there are numerous other denominations. The official language is Polish, spoken by almost all of the population, and there is a small German-speaking community. The national flag (proportions 5 by 8) has two equal horizontal stripes of white and red. The capital is Warsaw (Warszawa).

Recent History

Poland, partitioned since the 18th century, was declared an independent republic on 11 November 1918, at the end of the First World War. The country was ruled by a military regime from 1926 until 1939, when Poland was invaded by both Germany and the USSR and partitioned between the two powers. After Germany declared war on the USSR in June 1941, its forces occupied the whole of Poland until they were expelled by Soviet troops in March 1945.

At the end of the Second World War a pro-communist 'Polish Committee of National Liberation', established under Soviet auspices in July 1944, was transformed into a Provisional Government. Under the Potsdam Agreement, signed by the major Allied powers in 1945, the former German territories lying east of the rivers Oder and Neisse (which now comprise one-third of Poland's total area) came under Polish sovereignty, while Poland's frontier with the USSR was shifted westward. These border changes were accompanied by a major resettlement of the population in the affected areas.

Non-communist political groups suffered severe intimidation during national elections in January 1947, in which the communist-led 'democratic bloc' claimed victory. A People's Republic was established in February, with the Polish Workers' Party (PPR), led by Władysław Gomułka, as the dominant group. Gomułka's reluctance to implement certain aspects of Soviet economic policies, notably the collectivization of agriculture, led to his dismissal as First Secretary of the PPR in 1948. In December of that year the PPR merged with the Polish Socialist Party to form the Polish United Workers' Party (PZPR). Two other parties, the United Peasants' Party (ZSL) and the Democratic Party (SD), were permitted to remain in existence, but were closely controlled by the PZPR, and Poland effectively became a one-party state.

In 1956 mass demonstrations, provoked by food shortages, were suppressed by security forces. In the ensuing political crisis, Gomułka was returned to office, despite Soviet opposition. In 1964–70 limited economic reforms were implemented. In December 1970 a sharp rise in food prices led to strikes and demonstrations in the Baltic port of Gdańsk and in other cities. Many demonstrators were killed or injured in clashes with the police and army, and Gomułka was forced to resign as First Secretary of the PZPR; he was succeeded by Edward Gierek.

In July 1980 an increase in meat prices prompted widespread labour unrest, and shipyard employees in the Baltic ports, notably at Gdańsk, demanded the right to form free trade unions. Following negotiations, the Government finally granted permission to establish several self-governing trade unions, under the guidance of Solidarity, the organization involved in the Gdańsk strike, which was led by a local worker, Lech Wałęsa. In September, as labour unrest continued, Gierek was replaced as First Secretary of the PZPR by Stanisław Kania. Under the growing influence of Solidarity (which claimed an estimated 10m. members in 1981), strikes continued throughout the country, and in February Józef Pińkowski resigned as Chairman of the Council of Ministers. He was succeeded by Gen. Wojciech Jaruzelski, Minister of Defence (a post he retained) since 1968. Despite further concessions to Solidarity, the crisis persisted, forcing Kania's resignation in October; he was succeeded by Jaruzelski, who thus held the leading posts in both the PZPR and the Government.

On 13 December 1981 martial law was imposed throughout Poland. A governing Military Council of National Salvation, led by Jaruzelski, was established; all trade union activity was suspended, and Wałęsa and other Solidarity leaders were detained. Violent clashes between workers and security forces ensued, and thousands of protesters were arrested. Sporadic disturbances continued in 1982, particularly in response to legislation abolishing all trade unions. Wałęsa was released in November, and in December martial law was suspended and some other prisoners were freed. (During 1982 about 10,000 prisoners had been detained, and at least 15 demonstrators killed.) In July 1983 martial law was formally ended; the Military Council of National Salvation was dissolved, and an amnesty was declared for most political prisoners and activists. In October Wałęsa was awarded the Nobel Peace Prize.

In July 1984, to mark the 40th anniversary of the Polish communist regime, some 35,000 detainees were granted amnesty. In August US sanctions (imposed following the declaration of martial law) were relaxed. However, the murder, in October, of Fr Jerzy Popiełuszko, a well-known pro-Solidarity Roman Catholic priest, provoked renewed unrest. In February 1985 four officers from the Ministry of Internal Affairs were found guilty of the murder, and received lengthy prison sentences. (The case was subsequently reopened; two generals, accused of directing the murder, were acquitted in August 1994, but the verdict was overturned in March 1996.)

Legislative elections took place in October 1985. New regulations gave voters a choice of two candidates for 410 of the 460 seats in the Sejm (Assembly), the remaining 50 deputies being elected unopposed on a national list. Solidarity appealed to voters to boycott the poll, and subsequently disputed the Government's claim that 79% of the electorate had participated. In November Jaruzelski resigned as Chairman of the Council of Ministers, in order to become President of the Council of State (Head of State). He was succeeded by Prof. Zbigniew Messner, hitherto a Deputy Chairman of the Council of Ministers.

In December 1986, in an effort to increase support for the regime, Jaruzelski established a 56-member Consultative Council, which was attached to the Council of State and comprised mainly non-PZPR members. Nevertheless, public discontent intensified in 1987. Solidarity activists attempted to disrupt the official May Day celebrations in several cities, and in June there were violent clashes between police and protesters during a visit by Pope John Paul II to his native country. Significant price rises were imposed in early 1988, prompting widespread protests, and the May Day celebrations were again disrupted. In August a strike by coal workers rapidly spread to other sectors, leading to the most serious industrial unrest since 1981.

The Messner Government resigned in September 1988. Dr Mieczysław Rakowski, Deputy Chairman in 1981–85, was appointed Chairman of a new Council of Ministers, which included several non-PZPR members and younger, reformist politicians. However, the Government's announcement that the Lenin Shipyard in Gdańsk was to be closed provoked further strike action. By April 1989 agreement had been reached on the restoration of legal status to Solidarity, as well as on the holding of elections to a new, bicameral legislature, the Zgromadzenie Narodowe (National Assembly). Solidarity and other non-communist groups were to be permitted to contest all the seats in a new upper chamber, the Senat (Senate), which would have a limited right of veto over the lower chamber, the Sejm. Just 35% of the seats in the Sejm were to be subject to free elections, with the remainder open only to candidates of the PZPR and its associate organizations. A new post of executive President was also to be introduced. The necessary amendments to the Constitution were duly approved by the Sejm. In May the Roman Catholic Church was accorded legal status.

Elections to the new legislature took place on 4 and 8 July 1989, with 62% of eligible voters participating in the first round, but only 25% in the second. In the elections to the Senat, the Solidarity Citizens' Committee, the electoral wing of the trade union movement, secured all but one of the 100 seats. In the elections to the 460-member Sejm, Solidarity secured all the 161 seats that it was permitted to contest, and the other 299 seats were divided between the PZPR (173 seats), its allied parties—the ZSL (76) and the SD (27)—and members of Roman Catholic organizations (23).

The new legislature narrowly elected Jaruzelski, unopposed, to the post of executive President. He was replaced as First Secretary of the PZPR by Rakowski. Jaruzelski accepted Wałęsa's proposal of a coalition of Solidarity, the SD and the ZSL. The appointment of Tadeusz Mazowiecki, a newspaper editor and moderate member of Solidarity, as Chairman of the Council of Ministers, was approved by the Sejm on 24 August 1989, thus ending almost 45 years of exclusive communist rule in Poland. A Solidarity-dominated administration was formed in September.

The new Government's programme of radical political and economic reforms emphasized the creation of democratic institutions and the introduction of a market economy. In December 1989 the legislature voted to rename the country the Republic of Poland, and the national symbols of pre-communist Poland were reintroduced. In January 1990 the PZPR was dissolved to allow the establishment of a new left-wing party, Social Democracy of the Republic of Poland (SdRP). Local elections held in May were the first entirely free elections in Poland for more than 50 years. Candidates of the Solidarity Citizens' Committee won more than 41% of the seats, while nominally independent candidates secured 38%. By mid-1990 tension had developed between Wałęsa, who advocated an acceleration of economic reform and privatization, and the more cautious Mazowiecki.

In September 1990 Jaruzelski agreed to resign, to permit a direct presidential election to take place. In the first round, held on 25 November, Mazowiecki was placed third. Wałęsa and an émigré business executive, Stanisław Tymiński, proceeded to a second round of voting on 9 December, at which Wałęsa won 74.3% of the votes cast. Wałęsa resigned the chairmanship of Solidarity (he was replaced in February 1991 by Marian Krzaklewski), and in December 1990 was inaugurated as President for a five-year term. Jan Krzysztof Bielecki, a reformist economist, became Prime Minister. The new regime rapidly encountered challenges to its reform programme. In May 1991 Solidarity organized a nation-wide day of strikes and demonstrations, in protest at the Government's economic policies.

Legislative elections took place on 27 October 1991, with the participation of 43.2% of the electorate. Some 29 parties won representation in the Sejm. The party with the largest number of deputies (62) was Mazowiecki's Democratic Union (UD). The Democratic Left Alliance (SLD), an electoral coalition of the SdRP and the All Poland Trade Unions' Alliance, won 60 seats. The UD was also the largest single party in the Senat, with 21 seats, while Solidarity returned 11 senators. After Bronisław Geremek of the UD failed to form a government, Wałęsa nominated Jan Olszewski of the Centre Alliance (PC) as Prime Minister. Criticism of his economic programme by the President and the withdrawal of two parties from the coalition negotiations caused Olszewski to submit his resignation. However, this was rejected by the Sejm, which proceeded, in December, to approve a new centre-right Council of Ministers, incorporating members of the PC, the Peasant Alliance and the Christian-National Union (ZChN).

In June 1992, following controversy regarding government attempts to expose alleged communist conspirators, the Sejm approved a motion of no confidence in the Olszewski Government. After the failure of Waldemar Pawlak, the leader of the Polish People's Party (PSL), to form a government, the appointment of Hanna Suchocka of the UD was approved by the Sejm. Her new Government, a seven-party coalition dominated by the UD and the ZChN, was immediately challenged by a month-long strike by 40,000 workers at a copper plant in Legnica, supported by several transport and power workers' unions. In December an interim 'Small Constitution' entered into effect, pending a comprehensive revision of the 1952 Constitution. A motion of no confidence in the Suchocka administration, proposed by the Solidarity group after the failure of negotiations between the Government and striking teachers and health workers, was narrowly approved by the Sejm in May 1993. Wałęsa refused to accept Suchocka's resignation; instead, he dissolved the Sejm, scheduling new elections to both houses of parliament for September. The electoral code was amended, in order to achieve greater political stability, with a new stipulation that a party (with the exception of organizations representing national minorities) must secure at least 5% of the total votes cast (8% in the case of an electoral alliance) in order to achieve parliamentary representation.

The general election held on 19 September 1993 resulted in victory for parties of the left, as voters demonstrated their dissatisfaction with the recent economic reforms. The SLD and the PSL, both dominated by former communists and their allies, won, respectively, 171 and 132 seats in the Sejm, and 37 and 36 seats in the Senat. The two parties, which together won 35.8% of the total votes in the elections to the Sejm, benefited from the new law to secure more than 65% of the seats in the lower chamber. The UD took 74 seats in the Sejm (with 10.6% of the votes cast) and four in the Senat, while Solidarity won 10 seats in the Senat (although none in the Sejm). Wałęsa's Non-Party Bloc for Reform, established in June, won 16 seats in the Sejm and two seats in the Senat. Almost 35% of the votes cast in elections to the Sejm were for parties that received fewer than 5% of the total votes, notably the PC and the ZChN, and therefore secured no representation; the rate of participation by voters was 52.1%.

In October 1993 Pawlak formed a coalition Government, dominated by members of his PSL and the SLD. The new Prime Minister expressed his commitment to a continuation of market-orientated reforms, but pledged new measures to alleviate their adverse social effects. In early 1994 the Deputy Prime Minister and Minister of Finance, Marek Borowski (of the SLD), resigned. In February at least 20,000 people took part in a Solidarity-led demonstration in Warsaw, to demand increased government investment in the public sector and improved measures to combat unemployment. Solidarity began a nation-wide programme of strike action in March.

In January 1995 Wałęsa refused to endorse legislation to increase rates of personal income tax; however, he was obliged to approve the legislation after his actions were ruled to be unconstitutional. Relations between the Government and the President deteriorated sharply in February, when Wałęsa threatened to dissolve parliament if the Prime Minister did not resign. Further conflict was averted by Pawlak's departure, and in March Józef Oleksy, a member of the SLD and hitherto Marshal (Speaker) of the Sejm, took office as Prime Minister.

The first round of the 1995 presidential election took place on 5 November. The two leading candidates, Aleksander Kwaśniewski, the Chairman of the SdRP (and formerly a leading member of the PZPR), and Wałęsa proceeded to a second round on 19 November, when Kwaśniewski achieved a narrow victory, with 51.7% of the votes cast. On taking office on 23 December, Kwaśniewski asserted his commitment to the further integration of Poland into Western institutions and to the continuation of policies of economic liberalization. Following Kwaśniewski's election, the ministers responsible for foreign affairs, the interior and national defence (all effectively presidential appointees) submitted their resignations. The outgoing Minister of Internal Affairs, Andrzej Milczanowski, claimed that Oleksy had acted on behalf of Soviet (and subsequently Russian) espionage agents since the 1980s; although Oleksy vehemently denied the charges, he resigned as Prime Minister in January 1996 (he was fully exonerated in an official report published in October). He was subsequently elected Chairman of the SdRP, replacing Kwaśniewski, who had resigned his party membership following his election as President. Włodzimierz Cimoszewicz (the deputy leader of the SLD and hitherto deputy Marshal of the Sejm) was appointed as Prime Minister in February.

In June 1996 the Government's decision to file for bankruptcy for the loss-making Gdańsk shipyard prompted Solidarity-led demonstrations. Also in that month some 25 centre-right political parties, including Solidarity, the PC and the ZChN, established Solidarity Electoral Action (AWS) to contest the 1997 parliamentary elections. In September 1996 the Prime Minister dismissed Jacek Buchacz as Minister of Foreign Economic Relations, prompting his party, the PSL, to withdraw from government negotiations on proposed administrative reforms. Talks resumed at the end of September, after Cimoszewicz conceded that he had reneged on the coalition accord. Agreement was subsequently reached on the distribution of ministerial portfolios, whereby the PSL was accorded responsibility for the new Ministry of the Treasury, while the SLD secured the Ministry of Internal Affairs and Administration and the new Ministry of the Economy.

On 2 April 1997 the legislature adopted a new Constitution, which was approved by 52.7% of the votes cast by some 42.9% of the electorate in a national referendum on 25 May. Right-wing parties, notably AWS and the Movement for the Reconstruction of Poland (ROP), had opposed the Constitution, which slightly reduced presidential powers and committed Poland to a social market economy based on the freedom of economic activity and private ownership. The new Constitution came into force on 17 October.

In the general election of 21 September 1997, AWS secured 201 seats in the Sejm (with 33.8% of the valid votes cast) and 51 in the Senat, while the SLD won 164 seats in the Sejm (with 27.1% of the votes) and 28 in the Senat. The PSL retained only 27 seats in the Sejm and three in the Senat. The rate of voter participation was 48%. Krzaklewski, the leader of AWS, subsequently initiated coalition talks with the economically liberal Freedom Union (UW) and the ROP, which had won, respectively, 60 and six seats in the Sejm, and eight and five in the Senat. Jerzy Buzek (a member of Solidarity since its formation in 1980) was nominated as Prime Minister in mid-October. Following lengthy negotiations, AWS and the UW signed a coalition agreement later that month, despite some opposition from the ZChN and the PC (both members of AWS). A new Council of Ministers was subsequently appointed, which included Leszek Balcerowicz, leader of the UW, as Deputy Prime Minister, Minister of Finance and Chairman of the Economic Committee. In November the Sejm approved the new Government's programme, which prioritized rapid integration with the North Atlantic Treaty Organization (NATO, see p. 351) and the European Union (EU, see p. 255), and accelerated privatization and government reform. Shortly afterwards, the Social Movement of Solidarity Electoral Action, which was to replace Solidarity within AWS, applied for registration as a new political party. In December Wałęsa officially formed the Christian Democratic Party of the Third Republic.

In July 1998 a new structure of local and regional government was approved, which reduced the number of voivodships (provinces) from 48 to 16. Local elections were held in the 16 new voivodships in October. In nine voivodships, the opposition SLD was returned as the largest party, although the governing AWS-UW coalition won the largest number of seats overall, and secured control of the seven remaining voivodships. Meanwhile, the Government's programme of industrial restructuring continued to provoke public unrest, as well as discord among the governing parties. Railway workers took industrial action in June, and in July around 10,000 farmers attended a demonstration in Warsaw, to demand increased government protection for the agricultural sector. There was further unrest by farmers in August and December 1998, and in February 1999, when it was announced that the leader of the Self-Defence Trade Union (which had organized the protests), Andrzej Lepper, was to stand trial for having organized illegal road blocks. Meanwhile, the approval, in July 1998, of the divestment of the Gdańsk shipyard (which was completed in September), had prompted six AWS deputies to withdraw their support for the Government. (In preceding weeks nine other deputies had also left the ruling coalition.) In December a strike by coal miners over imminent changes to the pensions system spread to more than 50 mines, and resulted in government concessions; industrial unrest also affected the steel, armaments and railway sectors.

In June 1998 the Sejm adopted a resolution condemning the communist regime imposed on post-war Poland by the USSR; the resolution, which was opposed by the SLD, held the PZPR responsible for offences committed during the communist period. In late September the Sejm approved legislation granting access for Polish citizens to files compiled on them by the security services during the communist era.

During March 1999 the Prime Minister undertook a major government reorganization, in preparation for a significant reform of state administration, which took effect in April. The Secretary-General of the UW resigned in protest at the appointment of two ministers. In September a new political organization, the Alliance of Polish Christian Democrats (PPChD), was officially founded; members included the PC (a member of the governing AWS) and the Party of Christian Democrats (PChD).

During May 1999 farmers resumed their protests against agricultural policy. In June a protest in Warsaw by workers from a weapons factory in the central town of Radom resulted in violent clashes between the police and demonstrators. Farmers joined demonstrations against the low price of grain in August; an estimated 80 people were injured when violence erupted between police and farmers in northern Poland. Protests against the economic slowdown and the implementation of government reforms in education, health and pensions provision culminated, in September 1999, in a march through Warsaw by some 35,000 agricultural and industrial workers (as well as leaders from the opposition SLD and PSL parties).

During September 1999 Buzek came under growing criticism from leading members of his governing coalition, who accused him of weak leadership. At the beginning of the month the Deputy Prime Minister and Minister of Internal Affairs and Administration, Janusz Tomaszewski, announced his resignation. A minor government reorganization took place in early October, and AWS and the UW renewed their coalition agreement for a further two years. In late October the Government reached a compromise with miners' representatives from Solidarity regarding the restructuring of the industry, following protests in the capital. It was announced in December that Solidarity was to withdraw from political activities and become an 'organization of employees'; the movement's voting rights within AWS were transferred to the Social Movement of Solidarity Electoral Action. In January 2000 Lepper announced the formation of the Self-Defence Party of the Republic of Poland (SRP), an anti-Government party incorporating elements of several farmers' organizations and trade unions, under his leadership.

In mid-May 2000 the ruling coalition entered a serious crisis, when the Prime Minister suspended the Government of Warsaw's central commune (a coalition of the UW and the SLD) and replaced it with an AWS-affiliated commissioner. At the end of May the UW announced its withdrawal from the coalition, in protest at the blocking of Balcerowicz's proposals for economic reform by AWS deputies. Negotiations aimed at maintaining the coalition collapsed in early June, and Buzek subsequently formed a minority AWS Government. In August the treasury minister, Emil Wąsacz, was dismissed, following controversy surrounding his privatization policies.

In the presidential election, held on 8 October 2000, Kwaśniewski was re-elected, with 53.9% of the valid votes cast. The second-placed candidate, an independent former foreign minister, Andrzej Olechowski, secured 17.3% of the votes; Krzaklewski obtained 15.6%, Lepper 3.1% and Wałęsa just 1.0%. The rate of participation by the electorate was 61.1%. Wałęsa subsequently announced that he was to retire from politics. Krzaklewski resigned as leader of AWS in January 2001, and was succeeded by Prime Minister Buzek. (Krzaklewski remained Chairman of Solidarity until September 2002.) Meanwhile, Balcerowicz resigned the leadership of the UW, and became President of the central bank in December 2000.

In January 2001 Olechowski, together with the Marshal of the Sejm, Maciej Plazyński of AWS, and a Vice-Marshal of the Senat, Donald Tusk of the UW, founded a new political movement, the Civic Platform (PO). Kwaśniewski signed a new electoral law at the end of April, introducing a new method for the calculation of voting under the system of proportional representation. Following the enactment of the law, legislative elections were scheduled for 23 September. Thereafter, significant political realignment took place, and in May AWS was restructured as Solidarity Electoral Action of the Right (AWSP), in alliance with the ROP. At the end of May the traditionalist Roman Catholic, nationalist League of Polish Families (LPR), which opposed Polish membership of the EU, was registered as a party. In August the legislature rejected an austerity plan proposed by the Minister of Finance, Jarosław Bauc, in an attempt to address the predicted deficit in the budget for 2002, and in late August Buzek announced Bauc's dismissal.

The legislative elections took place as scheduled, on 23 September 2001, with a rate of voter participation of 46.3%. Neither AWSP nor the UW received the requisite 8% of the votes to obtain seats in the Sejm, although both parties contested the elections to the Senat as part of the Blok Senat 2001 (also comprising the PO, Law and Justice—PiS and the ROP), which won 15 of the 100 seats. Right-wing support was, instead, divided between PiS, which obtained 44 seats in the Sejm, and the LPR, which secured 38 seats in the Sejm and two seats in the Senat. Another party elected to the Sejm for the first time was the SRP, which took 53 seats in the Sejm (with 10.2% of the votes) and two seats in the Senat, and which also opposed accession to the EU. An electoral coalition of the SLD and the Union of Labour (UP) won 216 seats in the Sejm (with 41.0% of the votes) and 75 seats in the Senat, but failed to achieve an overall majority. The PO, which received 65 seats in the Sejm (with 12.7% of the votes), rejected an initial proposal to form a coalition with the SLD-UP. Instead, on 9 October the SLD and the UP signed a coalition agreement with the PSL, which had obtained 42 seats in the elections to the

Sejm (with 9.0% of the votes) and four seats in the Senat. The leader of the SLD, Leszek Miller, was sworn in as Prime Minister and Chairman of the European Integration Committee on 19 October; the PSL's leader, Jarosław Kalinowski, and the leader of the UP, Marek Pol, were appointed as Deputy Prime Ministers. Miller pledged to revive economic progress and announced that a referendum on entry to the EU would be held in mid-2003.

In May 2001 Andrzej Lepper was sentenced to 16 months' imprisonment, after being found guilty of charges associated with the farmers' blockades of 1998–99. In November 2001 Lepper was dismissed as a Vice-Marshal of the Sejm, and in January 2002 he was fined for having insulted the President. In the following month he was charged with seven counts of slander. In March, on appeal, Lepper's prison sentence was reduced to a suspended one-year term. Government changes in July included the resignation of Marek Belka as Minister of Finance; Grzegorz Kołodko subsequently assumed the post (which he had previously held in 1994–97), and in December survived a vote of no confidence in the Sejm.

Meanwhile, on 27 October 2002 local elections were held, in which the ruling SLD-UP coalition won 33.7% of the votes cast; the SRP won 18.0% of the votes and the LPR secured 16.4%. A second round of voting took place on 10 November. In January 2003 the Prime Minister reorganized the Government, consolidating the Ministries of the Economy and of Labour into a new Ministry of the Economy, Labour and Social Policy, under Jerzy Hausner. On 1 March Miller expelled the junior coalition partner, the PSL, from the Government, after it voted with opposition deputies against new tax legislation in the Sejm. In mid-March the Sejm rejected a motion, proposed by the LPR, to dissolve parliament. The following day the SLD-UD coalition formed a parliamentary alliance with the Peasant Democratic Party (PLD), although it remained 13 seats short of a majority. Meanwhile, public dissatisfaction at the state of the economy and the high rate of unemployment was expressed by frequently violent demonstrations led by the Solidarity trade union.

In June 2003 Miller transferred responsibility for economic policy from the Ministry of Finance to Hausner's Ministry of the Economy, Labour and Social Policy, prompting the resignation of the Deputy Prime Minister and Minister of Finance, Kołodko. Hausner was then appointed a Deputy Prime Minister (retaining his previous portfolio), and Andrzej Raczko became Minister of Finance. The Government subsequently won a vote of confidence in the Sejm. On 20 January 2004 Miller appointed Deputy Chairman of the SLD and former premier Józef Oleksy as Deputy Prime Minister and Minister of Internal Affairs and Administration, in an apparent attempt to reduce tensions within the party. The following day Miller dismissed Piotr Czyżewski as Minister of the Treasury, reportedly owing to his failure to implement the privatization of state-owned companies; he was replaced by Zbigniew Kaniewski.

In late January 2004 the PLD withdrew its support for the ruling coalition, thereby reducing the Government's majority in parliament. Following increasing divisions within the SLD, in mid-February Miller announced that he was to resign as Chairman of the party, but retain the premiership, to enable him to focus on Poland's planned accession to the EU on 1 May (see below). At a party congress on 6 March Krzysztof Janik was elected as the new party Chairman. None the less, in late March more than 20 deputies, led by Marek Borowski, announced that they were to defect from the SLD in order to establish a new party, Polish Social Democracy (SDPL); Borowski subsequently resigned as Marshal of the Sejm. On 26 March Miller acknowledged the loss of support for his leadership and announced that he would resign as Prime Minister on 2 May. Three days later President Kwaśniewski nominated former Minister of Finance Belka (latterly Director of Economic Policy in the US-led Coalition Provisional Authority in Iraq) to head a new government; Belka announced that he intended to retain key ministers, including Hausner, who had devised a controversial economic austerity programme for 2004–07, which some observers believed had contributed to Miller's loss of popular support. The lengthy investigation into a media bribery scandal that had emerged in late 2002 had also eroded the credibility of Miller's Government. In early April 2004 Miller, who had consistently denied the charges, was exonerated by a parliamentary investigative commission. In late April Oleksy (who had been widely regarded as a potential candidate for the premiership) was elected as the new Marshal of the Sejm.

Miller resigned on 2 May 2004, as planned, and Belka's Government, principally composed of SLD members and independents, took office, pending approval by the Sejm. Isabela Jaruga-Nowacka, who had been elected one week earlier to replace Marek Pol as the leader of the UP, was appointed as a Deputy Prime Minister. In mid-May, however, the Sejm rejected Belka's nomination, forcing the resignation of the new Government. The Sejm failed to propose a new candidate for the premiership within the requisite two weeks, and Kwaśniewski duly renominated Belka. In late June the Sejm approved Belka's appointment by 236 votes to 215, thus averting early elections. In order to secure the support of the SDPL, Belka agreed to hold a further confidence vote in October to confirm his mandate to govern.

In July 2004 the Minister of Finance, Andrzej Raczko, resigned to become Poland's representative at the IMF; he was succeeded by Mirosław Gronicki. In August the Government abandoned some elements of its economic austerity programme in order to secure political support for the majority of its proposals. In September the Minister of Justice, Marek Sadowski, resigned, after media reports suggested that he had abused his position as a judge and later as a government minister (both of which granted him immunity from prosecution) to avoid investigation into a road accident in which he had been involved in 1995.

In October 2004 Belka narrowly won the scheduled vote of confidence in the Sejm, by 234 votes to 218. Ahead of the vote Belka had announced to the lower chamber that Poland would begin reducing its 2,500-strong military contingent in Iraq (see below) from early 2005. Krzysztof Pater resigned as Minister of Social Policy in November, after the Sejm rejected austerity measures on corporate social insurance and pensions. Deputy Prime Minister Jaruga-Nowacka subsequently assumed additional responsibility for social policy.

In December 2004, at a congress of the SLD, Oleksy was elected Chairman of the party, defeating Krzysztof Janik in a second round of voting. The election increased tension within the SLD, which was suffering a decline in popularity, and Janik and his allies announced plans to form an opposition faction within the party. A few days later, following several years of investigations, the Vetting Court ruled that Oleksy had concealed his collaboration with the communist-era military intelligence services; Oleksy, who strongly refuted the charges against him, announced that he would appeal against the Court's verdict. In response to mounting pressure, Oleksy resigned as Marshal of the Sejm, and in early January 2005 Włodzimierz Cimoszewicz, hitherto Minister of Foreign Affairs, was elected as his replacement. Adam Rotfeld assumed the foreign affairs portfolio.

In early February 2005 Hausner resigned from the SLD, after the party's national council voted against holding early legislative elections in June, but announced his intention to retain his ministerial positions. In early March, however, in response to increasing pressure, particularly from the SLD, Hausner tendered his resignation as Deputy Prime Minister and Minister of the Economy and Labour. Jacek Piechota was appointed to the position of Minister of the Economy and Labour. In late February Hausner and Władysław Frasyniuk, the leader of the UW, announced plans to create a new centrist political organization: the Democratic Party (PD) held its founding congress in May. Amid speculation that he was to join the new party, in March Belka urged the Sejm to dissolve itself to allow early elections to take place, as the minority Government lacked sufficient support in the Sejm to approve proposed budget reforms. In early May, however, the Sejm voted to reject three motions submitted by opposition parties for its dissolution, and President Kwaśniewski rejected Belka's resignation, tendered on 6 May, stating that the Government should remain in office until the forthcoming legislative elections. Meanwhile, Jaruga-Nowacka resigned from the leadership of the UP. In late May Wojciech Olejniczak was elected as Chairman of the SLD, succeeding Józef Oleksy. Olejniczak was replaced as Minister of Agriculture and Rural Development by Jerzy Pilarczyk. In June Belka made public his police file, in response to allegations that he had collaborated with the communist security services.

In the legislative elections, which took place on 25 September 2005, with a rate of participation of 40.5% of the electorate, the conservative PiS obtained the largest number of seats in both the Sejm (taking 155 of the 460 seats, with 27.0% of the votes) and the Senat (with 49 of the 100 available). The centre-right PO won 133 seats in the Sejm (with 24.1% of the votes) and 34 seats in the Senat, whereas the incumbent SLD received just 55 seats in the Sejm (with 11.3% of the votes cast). Two days later the leader of

PiS, Jarosław Kaczyński, announced that he did not intend to lead the new government, and instead proposed Kazimierz Marcinkiewicz for the premiership, while Kaczyński's twin brother, Lech, the PiS Mayor of Warsaw, was to contest the forthcoming presidential election.

After a first round of voting in the presidential election, conducted on 9 October 2005, PO leader Donald Tusk (who obtained 36.3% of the votes) and Lech Kaczyński (33.1%) progressed to a second round on 23 October. Kaczyński emerged as the winner in the 'run-off' poll, with 54.0% of the votes. The rate of participation by the electorate was 49.7% in the first round and 51.0% in the second. Kaczyński was inaugurated as President on 23 December.

Although PiS and the more economically liberal PO, as the two principal parties of the centre-right, had been widely expected to negotiate a coalition government, the parties were unable to agree on the distribution of senior positions, and on 31 October 2005 Marcinkiewicz was appointed as Prime Minister of a minority Government, comprising nine members of PiS and eight independents. Stefan Meller, a diplomatist, became Minister of Foreign Affairs, and non-affiliated ministers were also appointed to the treasury, finance and economy portfolios. Bogdan Borusewicz, an independent, was appointed Marshal of the Senat, and Marek Jurek, of PiS, became Marshal of the Sejm. On 10 November the Government won a motion of confidence in the Sejm, by 272 to 187 votes, with the support of smaller rightist parties (the SRP, the LPR and the PSL).

In January 2006 the Minister of the Treasury, Andrzej Mikosz, resigned, following media allegations that his wife had been involved in financial misdemeanours in 2002; he was replaced by Wojciech Jasinski in mid-February 2006. Also in January Teresa Lubinska was removed from her position as Minister of Finance; she was succeeded by Zyta Gilowska, an independent (formerly aligned with the PO), who also became Deputy Prime Minister. In mid-February President Kaczyński confirmed that he would not schedule early legislative elections, despite the failure of the Senat to approve the budget by the constitutional deadline of 31 January (it was adopted by the Senat on 1 February). In late April PiS signed a coalition agreement with the SRP and the LPR. Stefan Meller subsequently resigned as Minister of Foreign Affairs, in protest at the Government's decision to co-operate with the SRP. Several new ministers were appointed to the Government on 5 May, giving the Government a majority in the Sejm for the first time. The leaders of both the SRP and LPR were awarded with deputy prime ministerial positions, with Lepper additionally gaining responsibility for agriculture and rural development, while the leader of the LPR, Roman Giertych, also became the Minister of National Education.

In June 2006 Gilowska resigned from the Council of Ministers following the opening of an investigation into claims, which she denied, that she had lied about collaborating with the secret services during the communist era. (Former members of the Soviet-backed secret services were eligible to hold public office, but falsely denying such links was considered a serious offence.) Gilowska was replaced as Minister of Finance by Pawel Wojciechowski. In early July, however, Marcinkiewicz tendered his resignation, reportedly owing to disagreements with Jarosław Kaczyński over economic policy, as a result of which the entire Government was constitutionally obliged to resign. Shortly afterwards President Kaczyński nominated his twin brother as Marcinkiewicz's replacement; this appointment was subsequently approved by the Sejm, and Jarosław Kaczyński was formally sworn into office on 14 July, together with his new Council of Ministers, to which only one change had been made—the replacement of Wojciechowski with Stanisław Kluza, hitherto Deputy Minister of Finance. However, Kluza remained in the position only until September, when Gilowska was reappointed as Deputy Prime Minister and Minister of Finance, having been cleared of the accusations levied against her. Also in September President Kaczyński removed Lepper from the Government, following several policy disagreements. In response, the SRP withdrew from the ruling coalition, thereby ending its parliamentary majority. However, in October, a few days prior to a planned parliamentary vote on an opposition-initiated motion for the legislature to dissolve itself and force elections three years earlier than anticipated, Lepper's dismissal was retracted and the alliance between PiS and the SRP revived.

Also in October 2006 both pro- and anti-Government rallies were held in Warsaw, following the broadcast in late September of a video purporting to show an aide of Prime Minister Kaczyński attempting to buy the support of a member of the opposition. The Prime Minister rejected demands that he resign and insisted that his aide had been engaged in legitimate political bargaining. In local elections held in the following month, PiS performed robustly overall, but crucially lost the mayoralty of Warsaw, which was secured by the PO's Hanna Gronkiewicz-Waltz, a former Governor of the central bank, who defeated Marcinkiewicz.

In January 2007 Stanisław Wielgus, the newly appointed Archbishop of Warsaw, succumbed to widespread pressure to resign, shortly before he was to be formally inaugurated. Wielgus's decision followed rumours that he had co-operated with the secret services in the 1970s, allegations that Wielgus had initially denied but which, in a highly damaging reversal, he had subsequently admitted to be true. In March new legislation entered into effect, dramatically expanding the remit of existing procedures intended to prevent those who had formerly collaborated with the communist-era secret services from acceding to positions of power. Previously, only those holding public office (approximately 30,000 people) had been required to declare whether or not they had co-operated with the secret services; henceforth, this was also to include, *inter alia*, teachers, journalists and state company executives, increasing the number to whom the law applied to as many as 700,000 people, who were given until 15 May to submit their declarations; furthermore, those found not to have divulged any past collaboration would be liable to a ban against practising their profession for up to 10 years, and even those who openly admitted to having assisted the secret services could be dismissed. This so-called lustration law deeply divided opinion among the Polish population. In May the Constitutional Tribunal ruled that the legislation was unconstitutional.

In February 2007 the Minister of National Defence, Radosław Sikorski, tendered his resignation, following policy differences with Prime Minister Kaczyński; he was replaced by a former head of the presidential chancellery, Aleksander Szczygło. In the same month Ludwik Dorn resigned the internal affairs portfolio (while initially retaining the post of Deputy Prime Minister), owing to a disagreement with the Prime Minister. A former Prosecutor-General, Janusz Kaczmarek, became the new Minister of Internal Affairs and Administration. Andrzej Krawczyk, foreign policy adviser to the President, was dismissed in March, owing to his alleged collaboration with the communist-era secret services in 1982. (Although Krawczyk denied the accusation and was exonerated by a court in the same month, the President refused to rescind the dismissal.) In April Dorn was elected Marshal of the Sejm, replacing Marek Jurek who had recently resigned after the chamber's failure to adopt a constitutional amendment enforcing stricter legislation on abortion. Jurek also resigned from PiS to form a new party, the Right of the Republic (PR), which was to emphasize pro-life and other traditionalist Christian policies. In May Przemysław Gosiewski was appointed as a Deputy Prime Minister. In early July Prime Minister Kaczyński again removed Lepper from his government post, on the grounds that he was under investigation for corrupt practice in the designation of agricultural land. The Minister of Sports was also dismissed, after allegations of corruption. Lepper announced that his SRP would provisionally remain in the Government, after deputies threatened to divide the party. However, on 13 August President Kaczyński dismissed the remaining SRP representatives and the LPR members from the Government, thereby ending the ruling coalition; they were replaced by PiS representatives on an interim basis, and it was announced that early legislative elections were to be organized. Proposals that received widespread publicity at this time, for the merger of the LPR and the SRP, failed to come to fruition.

On 7 September 2007 the Sejm voted to dissolve itself and elections to both parliamentary chambers were officially scheduled for 21 October. Prime Minister Kaczyński dismissed all 15 government ministers to prevent a motion of no confidence planned by the PO; they were subsequently reappointed on an interim basis. At the elections to the Sejm, conducted on 21 October, the PO obtained 209 seats, receiving 41.5% of the votes cast, with PiS receiving 166 seats (32.1% of the votes); an SLD-led coalition, known as Left and Democrats (LiD), secured 53 seats (13.2% of the votes), and the PSL 31 seats (8.9% of the votes). The rate of participation was recorded at 53.8% of the electorate. Neither the LPR nor SRP obtained legislative representation. Later in October Giertych resigned from the leadership of the LPR (which had contested the elections in a coalition with the PR). On 5 November Prime Minister Kaczyński submitted the resignation of his minority Government. On 9 November

President Kaczyński nominated Tusk, as leader of PO, as Prime Minister. Tusk reached a coalition agreement with the PSL; together, the PO and the PSL held 240 seats in the 460-member Sejm (and thus required the support of the LiD for the approval of motions that required a two-thirds' majority). The new PO-PSL Government was approved by 238 of the votes cast in the Sejm. Although Jarosław Kaczyński won a vote of confidence in his leadership of PiS at a party congress in December, increasing divisions within the party became apparent with the defection of three deputies from the PiS faction in the Sejm.

In early September 2008 trial began of Gen. (retd) Wojciech Jaruzelski and seven other former communist officials, on charges relating to the imposition of martial law in 1981; the repressive measures undertaken against the Solidarity movement were believed to have resulted in the deaths of some 100 people. Also in September 2008 the Government announced a financial plan to prevent the bankruptcy of three major shipyards, situated at Gdynia, Gdańsk and Szczecin, following an investigation by the European Commission into the alleged long-term misuse of state aid by the Polish authorities to support the shipyards, in contravention of EU regulations. However, in November the European Commission issued a decision ordering the Government to sell the assets of the Gdynia and Szczecin shipyards by the end of May 2009 in order that the Government reimburse some €2,300m. in aid.

After 1991 close relations were retained with the Czech Republic, Hungary and Slovakia through the structures of the Visegrad Group and the Central European Free Trade Agreement, and also with other countries of the Baltic region. In 1991–92 Poland established diplomatic relations with the former republics of the USSR, developing particularly strong links with Ukraine. In May 1997 the Polish and Ukrainian Presidents signed a declaration of reconciliation, which included the condemnation of the killing of tens of thousands of Poles by Ukrainian nationalists in 1942–43, and of the 'Wisła Operation' of 1947, in which more than 100,000 Ukrainians were forcibly deported from their homes in south-east Poland. During 1998 and early 1999 Poland sought to reassure Ukraine (as well as Russia) that good relations and mutual co-operation between their two countries would continue following Poland's entry into NATO in March 1999 and its eventual membership of the EU. In November and December 2004 President Kwaśniewski mediated in negotiations in Ukraine (q.v.) aimed at resolving a political crisis that had resulted from a disputed presidential election in that country. Following a new election in December, Kwaśniewski attended the inauguration of the new President of Ukraine, Viktor Yushchenko, in January 2005.

All former Soviet combat troops had been withdrawn from Poland by November 1992, and the last remaining Russian military presence was withdrawn in September 1994. Relations between Poland and Russia deteriorated after Poland acceded to NATO in 1999. However, tensions eased in July 2000, when President Kwaśniewski became the first Polish head of state to pay an official visit to Moscow since the collapse of communist rule; relations improved further in January 2002, when Russian President Vladimir Putin made an official visit to Poland. However, the Polish Government continued to oppose Russia's plans to construct a natural gas pipeline to Slovakia through Poland, bypassing Ukraine, as it feared that the project threatened adversely to affect Polish-Ukrainian relations. Relations were also perceived to have deteriorated following President Kwaśniewski's mediation in Ukraine in late 2004 (see above). In 2005 Poland expressed concern at plans to construct a North European Natural Gas Pipeline between Russia and Germany, under the Baltic Sea, effectively bypassing Poland. Relations suffered a marked deterioration in late 2005, when Russia imposed a ban on imports of meat and other agricultural products from Poland, ostensibly owing to health and sanitation concerns, but which Poland claimed was a politically motivated decision. Following Russia's continued refusal to lift the ban, in November 2006 the Polish Government vetoed the commencement of EU negotiations on a new strategic partnership agreement with Russia. In April 2007 Prime Minister Kaczyński announced that Poland would retract its veto only when Russia had removed the import restrictions. This stance was supported by the President of the European Commission, José Manuel Durão Barroso, following an inspection of Polish meat-processing plants by a team of EU and Russian experts, which had indicated that Russian health concerns were unfounded. Shortly after his installation as premier in November (see above), Donald Tusk announced that Poland was to end its objections to the initiation of negotiations on Russia's entry to the Organisation for Economic Co-operation and Development (OECD), which was required for membership of the World Trade Organization (WTO). In December the Russian Government announced its decision to end the embargo on meat imports from Poland. In January 2008 the Polish Minister of Defence announced that US officials had agreed to hold discussions on a possible US commitment to support Polish air defences in exchange for the proposed deployment in Poland of US anti-missile interceptors as part of the US national missile defence system. It was reported that the Polish Minister of Foreign Affairs, Radosław Sikorski, when meeting his Russian counterpart, Sergei Lavrov, in Moscow later that month, had agreed that his Government would consult the Russian leadership regarding the installation of the interceptor units. However, Sikorski, during a visit to Washington, DC, at the end of January, accused Russia of threatening to aim nuclear missiles at Poland in the event that it agreed to host the units. In March Poland announced that it was prepared to accept Russian inspections of any future US anti-missile installations on its territory. At a NATO summit meeting, which took place in Bucharest, Romania, in early April, member states endorsed the US plans to position missile defence bases in Poland and the Czech Republic. In early July Sikorski visited Washington, DC, the USA, for further discussions on the proposed US military installation in Poland; it was subsequently announced that negotiations on a treaty providing for the base were being finalized. On 20 August a formal treaty was signed in Warsaw between Sikorski and US Secretary of State Condoleezza Rice, providing for the installation of 10 US anti-missile interceptors, and guaranteeing the permanent stationing of missiles on Polish territory. The announcement, which followed Russian military action in Georgia earlier that month (see the chapter on Russia), prompted immediate protests by the Russian Government; in early September Lavrov, during a visit to Warsaw, reiterated that the missile installation presented a threat to Russian security (despite assurances by the US Administration that the planned defence system was intended to counter possible attacks, principally, from Iran). In early September Russian President Dmitrii Medvedev announced that the Russian Government would respond by stationing short-range missiles in the bordering Russian exclave of Kaliningrad Oblast. However, following the election of US President Barack Obama in November, the new US Administration indicated in early 2009 that it would review security policy, including the planned missile defence system; Sikorski subsequently expressed the hope that implementation of the programme would proceed according to the treaty. Meanwhile, in late January, in response to Obama's election, the Russian authorities announced that the proposal to deploy missiles to Kaliningrad had been suspended.

On 1 October 2003 the Polish Government introduced visa requirements for Belarusian, Moldovan, Russian and Ukrainian citizens, in accordance with EU policy, although simplified visa arrangements had been agreed for residents of the Russian exclave of Kaliningrad. In July 2005 the offices of the Union of Poles in Belarus were seized by the Belarusian authorities, and the newly elected leadership replaced, apparently owing to fears that the organization might participate in the eventual overthrow of the regime of Belarusian President Alyaksandr Lukashenka. Meanwhile, Polish journalists in Belarus were compelled to pay large fines, after protesting at the suppression by the authorities of the country's main Polish-language newspaper. In late July Poland recalled its ambassador to Belarus, and appealed to the EU for assistance in protecting the Polish minority there. The Polish ambassador returned to Belarus in October. Tensions arose again prior to the presidential election held in Belarus in March 2006. Polish journalists and a number of Polish parliamentarians were refused entry to Belarus, and a former Polish ambassador to Belarus was imprisoned for 15 days after participating in an unauthorized protest demonstration; in late March Belarus briefly recalled its ambassador to Poland.

In November 1990 Poland and Germany signed a border treaty confirming their post-1945 borders, and in June 1991 the two countries signed a treaty of 'good neighbourliness and friendly co-operation'. Poland welcomed the announcement made by the German Government in February 1999 of the establishment of a compensation fund for over 2m. Poles who were employed as forced labour in German companies during the Second World War. Following a campaign by Polish veteran groups, in May Polish and German representatives began complex negotiations regarding the payment of compensation by several leading German firms. In mid-December a compensation agreement was signed, whereby DM 10,000m. was to be paid by German companies into a compensation fund; however, payments were subject to delays. The German Chancellor, Gerhard Schröder, attended a ceremony in Warsaw in August 2004 to mark the 60th anniversary of the city's failed uprising against the Nazi occupation, becoming the first German leader to participate in such an event. In September, however, a resolution adopted by the Sejm urging Germany to pay reparations for the Nazi invasion of Poland in 1939 threatened to strain relations between the two countries. Both the German and Polish Governments rejected the resolution, which was regarded as a response to demands from groups of Germans for the restitution of ancestral property lost when Poland's borders shifted westward at the end of the Second World War. In November 2004, at a joint press conference following talks in Kraków, Belka and Schröder announced that a joint commission had concluded that there was no legal basis for compensation claims to be filed. The two leaders each appointed a special adviser to co-ordinate bilateral relations. In January 2005 the German President, Horst Köhler, attended a ceremony in Poland to commemorate the 60th anniversary of the liberation of the Nazi concentration camp at Oświęcim (Auschwitz). In August an exhibition devoted to the expulsion of Germans from Eastern Europe in the aftermath of the Second World War provoked outrage in Poland, the Government of which argued that it sought to rewrite history by portraying Germany as the victim of the war; the acting Mayor of Warsaw, former Prime Minister Marcinkiewicz, cancelled a planned visit to Berlin in protest.

Andrzej Byrt, the Polish ambassador to Germany, was dismissed following his public criticism of President Kaczyński for the latter's angry response to satirical comments published about him and his brother in a German newspaper in July 2006. President Kaczyński failed to attend a tripartite summit with German Federal Chancellor Angela Merkel and French President Jacques Chirac, ostensibly owing to ill health, but his withdrawal was widely interpreted as an implicit rebuff to his German counterpart, who had ignored his demands that action be taken against the German newspaper in question. In March 2007 Merkel met President Kaczyński during an official visit to Poland. In December the new Prime Minister, Donald Tusk, met Merkel in Berlin in an effort to improve bilateral relations; issues discussed included the proposed construction of the North European Natural Gas Pipeline between Russia and Germany (see above).

Poland joined the Council of Europe (see p. 236) in November 1991. In December Poland signed an association agreement with the European Community (now EU), and in April 1994 made a formal application for membership of the EU; accession negotiations began in March 1998. In December 2002 Poland, and nine other countries, were formally invited to join the EU from May 2004. In February 2003 the Government reached agreement with the EU on farm subsidies. A national referendum on EU membership took place in June 2003, at which some 77% of the votes cast by 58.9% of the electorate were in favour of accession. Poland became a full member of the EU on 1 May 2004, as scheduled. On 13 June the first elections to the European Parliament to be held in Poland were marked by a very low rate of voter participation, of 20.9%. The PO secured 15 of the 54 seats available, while the LPR won 10 seats, PiS seven seats and the SRP six seats. The ruling SLD-UP coalition took only five seats. In December 2007, following the approval of legislation in the Sejm in August, Poland, together with eight other nations, implemented the EU's Schengen Agreement on freedom of travel, effectively removing border controls between those states subject to the Agreement. On 9 April 2008 President Kaczyński approved a law permitting him to ratify the EU's Lisbon Treaty (signed in December 2007), after a compromise agreement securing the parliamentary support of PiS had permitted the Treaty's endorsement in both the Sejm and the Senate earlier that month. However, at the end of June, following a referendum in Ireland that resulted in rejection of the Treaty, Kaczyński indicated that he would suspend finalization of the ratification process until a resolution was reached in Ireland.

Poland, in common with other central and eastern European countries, regarded membership of NATO as a priority in guaranteeing regional security. In January 1994 Poland announced that it was to join that organization's 'Partnership for Peace' programme, and a defence co-operation agreement was duly signed with NATO in March. In May Poland was granted associate partnership status in Western European Union (see p. 442). In July 1997 Poland, together with the Czech Republic and Hungary, was officially invited to commence negotiations on potential membership of NATO. A protocol providing for the accession of the three states was signed in December, and Poland, the Czech Republic and Hungary secured full membership of NATO on 12 March 1999. The Polish Government strongly supported the US-led military campaign to remove from power the regime of the Iraqi President, Saddam Hussain, in early 2003, and Poland was subsequently offered the opportunity to manage one of three reconstruction zones in Iraq, under overall US command. In September the USA transferred responsibility for security in an area of central Iraq to a 9,500-strong multinational force led by Poland, which contributed some 2,500 troops. In early 2005 Poland reduced its military contingent in Iraq to 1,700 troops, following elections there. Although the Polish Minister of Defence announced in April that the country's troops would be withdrawn from Iraq by the end of that year, the new Government elected in September retracted this decision. Following his installation as Prime Minister in November 2007, Donald Tusk announced the withdrawal of the remaining 900 Polish troops in Iraq, despite the continued opposition of President Kaczyński; the Polish contingent in Iraq left the country, as scheduled, in October 2008. In March 2009 Tusk announced that the 1,600-member Polish force in Afghanistan would be reinforced by 400 troops (despite the Government's intention to implement defence expenditure reductions in that year).

Government

Under the Constitution, which came into force in October 1997, legislative power is vested in the bicameral Zgromadzenie Narodowe (National Assembly), which is elected for a four-year term and comprises the 100-member Senat (Senate, upper chamber) and the 460-member Sejm (Assembly, lower chamber). The Senat reviews the laws adopted by the Sejm and may propose their rejection. Senators and deputies are elected by universal, direct suffrage. In the Sejm, deputies are elected under a system of proportional representation. Executive power is vested in the President of the Republic, who is directly elected (a second ballot being held if necessary) for a five-year term and may be re-elected only once, and in the appointed Council of Ministers, led by the Prime Minister. The Council of Ministers is responsible to the Sejm for its activities. On 1 January 1999 new legislation on local government came into effect, as a result of which Poland is divided into 16 voivodships (provinces) and 308 powiats (districts).

Defence

As assessed at November 2008, the strength of Poland's active armed forces (including conscripts) was estimated to be 121,808 (including an estimated 24,855 joint staff): army 62,762, air force 23,327 and navy 10,864. Paramilitary forces of some 21,400 comprised border guards (14,100) and interior ministry units (7,300). Reserves totalled 222,003. In 1988 legislation was enacted permitting conscientious objectors to perform an alternative community service, and from January 2005 compulsory military service was reduced from one year to nine months. The state budget for 2008 allocated 22,550m. new złotys to defence. In 1994 Poland joined the North Atlantic Treaty Organization's (NATO, see p. 351) 'Partnership for Peace' programme of military co-operation, and it became a full member of the Alliance in March 1999.

Economic Affairs

In 2007, according to the World Bank, Poland's gross national income (GNI), measured at average 2005–07 prices, was US $374,633m., equivalent to $9,840 per head (or $15,330 per head on an international purchasing-power parity basis). During 2000–07 the population decreased by 0.1%, while gross domestic product (GDP) per head increased, in real terms, at an average annual rate of 4.2%. Overall GDP increased, in real terms, at an average annual rate of 4.0% in 2000–07; growth was 6.5% in 2007.

Agriculture contributed 4.3% of GDP and engaged 14.7% of the employed labour force in 2007. The principal crops are potatoes, sugar beet, wheat, rye and barley. Livestock production is important to the domestic food supply. During 2000–07 the average annual GDP of the agricultural sector increased, in real terms, by 3.6%; real agricultural GDP increased by 6.7% in 2006 and by 3.0% in 2007.

Industry (including mining, manufacturing, power and construction) accounted for 31.1% of GDP and engaged 30.7% of the employed labour force in 2007. During 2000–07 industrial GDP increased, in real terms, by an average of 4.1% per year; real industrial GDP increased by 4.4% in 2007.

Mining and quarrying contributed 2.3% of GDP and engaged 1.6% of the employed labour force in 2007. Poland is a significant producer of copper, silver and sulphur, and there are also considerable reserves of natural gas. During 1992–96 mining GDP declined at an average annual rate of 1.5%; the sector's GDP declined by an estimated 4.6% in 1998.

The manufacturing sector contributed 17.6% of GDP and engaged 20.8% of the employed labour force in 2007. In 2000–07 manufacturing GDP increased, in real terms, at an average annual rate of 6.3%. Manufacturing GDP increased by 5.2% in 2007.

Energy is derived principally from coal, which satisfied 93.4% of the country's total energy requirements in 2005. In 1998 the Government announced plans to reduce Poland's dependence on coal: it was projected that by 2010 some 15% of power generation would be fuelled by imported natural gas. Mineral fuels and lubricants accounted for 9.9% of the value of merchandise imports in 2007; some 6.5% of electricity generated was exported in 2000.

The services sector contributed 64.6% of GDP and engaged 54.5% of the employed labour force in 2007. Services expanded rapidly from the early 1990s, with considerable growth in financial services, retailing, tourism and leisure. The GDP of the services sector increased, in real terms, by an average of 3.8% per year in 2000–07. Real services GDP increased by 7.1% in 2007.

In 2007 Poland recorded a visible trade deficit of US $15,553m., and there was a deficit of $18,595m. on the current account of the balance of payments. In 2007 the principal source of imports was Germany (accounting for 24.0%); other major suppliers were Russia, the People's Republic of China, Italy and France. Germany was also the principal market for exports (25.9%); other significant purchasers were Italy, France, the United Kingdom and the Czech Republic. The principal exports in 2007 were machinery and transport equipment (accounting for 40.8% of all exports), basic manufactures, miscellaneous manufactured articles, food and live animals, and chemicals and related products. The principal imports in that year were machinery and transport equipment (which accounted for 35.3% of total imports), basic manufactures, chemicals and related products, mineral fuels and lubricants, miscellaneous manufactured articles, and food and live animals.

According to government figures, Poland's overall budgetary deficit for 2006 was 22,420m. new złotys (equivalent to some 2.1% of GDP). Poland's external debt totalled US $125,831m. at the end of 2006, of which $39,248m. was long-term public debt. In that year the cost of debt-servicing was equivalent to 24.7% of the value of exports of goods and services. The average annual rate of inflation was 2.5% in 2000–07. Consumer prices increased by 2.4% in 2007. In 2007 9.6% of the labour force were registered as unemployed.

Poland is a member, as a 'Country of Operations', of the European Bank for Reconstruction and Development (EBRD, see p. 251). Poland joined the WTO in 1995 and the OECD in 1996. In May 2004 Poland became a full member of the European Union (EU, see p. 255).

In the 1990s Poland undertook an ambitious, market-orientated programme of economic reform. Poland's economic performance was adversely affected by the Russian financial crisis in August 1998. However, economic recovery was evident by 2002, and was further sustained by Poland's accession to the EU in 2004, with a concomitant increase in exports to other member nations. Following Poland's assumption of EU membership, unemployment declined, as a result of increasing numbers of Poles moving abroad to find work, notably to the United Kingdom and Ireland. It was estimated that some 1.95m. Poles, equating to over 10% of the work-force, had emigrated by the end of 2006. Meanwhile, in March 2006 the EU initiated legal proceedings against Poland, which it accused of protectionism, after the Government continued to obstruct attempts by an Italian company to merge two majority foreign-owned banks in Poland, thereby challenging the influence of the leading state-owned Polish bank. According to the central bank, foreign direct investment in Poland declined by 14.8% in 2007, totalling US $12,834m. in that year. The Government of Prime Minister Donald Tusk that took office in late 2007 favoured a strategy of liberalizing the labour market in order to improve productivity, privatizing state enterprises and reducing bureaucracy. The need to reduce the budgetary deficit to less than 3% of GDP remained the most challenging element of the EU's financial criteria for the adoption of the common European currency, the euro. Though the new central bank Governor, appointed in January 2007, advocated far greater caution towards the adoption of the currency than had his predecessor, in late 2008 the Government outlined a series of moves aimed at the adoption of the euro by 2012. The decision came in the wake of the global financial crisis, which led to a significant weakening of the national currency, the złoty. Furthermore, by early 2009 the Government announced its application for $20,500m. of credit from the IMF, which would support the economy in the event of further financial turmoil. The złoty strengthened on the news, reaching a three month high against the euro by April 2009. GDP growth was 4.9% in 2008, according to official sources. The IMF anticipated that the rate of inflation would fall to 3.3% during 2009. Meanwhile, the central bank estimated that GDP growth could slow to just 1.1% in 2009.

Education

Education is free and compulsory for eight years, between the ages of seven and 14 years. Before the age of seven, children may attend crèches (złobki) and kindergartens (przedszkola). A reform of primary and secondary education was undertaken in 1999–2004. Basic schooling begins at seven years of age with primary school (szkoła podstawowa), for which there is a common curriculum throughout the country. Primary education lasts for six years, divided into two equal cycles. Lower secondary education (at the gimnazjum) is compulsory for three years. In 2003/04 net enrolment at primary schools included 97.3% of children in the relevant age-group and enrolment in lower secondary schools included 90.0% of children in the relevant age-group. Three years of education at general secondary schools (liceum ogólnokształcące) commence at the age of 16 years, for pupils who successfully complete the entrance examination; in 2000/01 enrolment at secondary schools was equivalent to 90.1% of children in the appropriate age-group. At this level, there are general secondary schools (accounting for 34%), vocational technical schools (technika zawodowe—56%) and basic vocational schools (zasadnicze szkoły—20%). The last provide courses consisting of three days' theoretical and three days' practical training per week, and in addition some general education is given. New post-secondary schools (szkoła policealna) were introduced in 1999 to prepare students from technical and vocational schools for skilled jobs. Curricula are standardized throughout Poland. In 2004/05 there were 400 higher education establishments in Poland, including 17 universities and 22 technical universities, attended by about 2,146 students. In 2006 state budgetary expense on education amounted to 58,500m. new złotys (12.9% of total expenditure).

Public Holidays

2009: 1 January (New Year's Day), 13 April (Easter Monday), 1 May (State Holiday), 3 May (Polish National Day, Proclamation of 1791 Constitution), 11 June (Corpus Christi), 15 August (Assumption), 1 November (All Saints' Day), 11 November (Independence Day), 25–26 December (Christmas).

2010: 1 January (New Year's Day), 5 April (Easter Monday), 1 May (State Holiday), 3 May (Polish National Day, Proclamation of 1791 Constitution), 3 June (Corpus Christi), 15 August (Assumption), 1 November (All Saints' Day), 11 November (Independence Day), 25–26 December (Christmas).

Weights and Measures

The metric system is in force.

POLAND

Statistical Survey

Source (unless otherwise indicated): Główny Urząd Statystyczny (Central Statistical Office), 00-925 Warsaw, Al. Niepodległości 208; tel. (22) 6083161; fax (22) 6083869; internet www.stat.gov.pl.

Area and Population

AREA, POPULATION AND DENSITY

Area (sq km)	
Land	304,465
Inland water	8,220
Total	312,685*
Population (census results)†	
7 December 1988	37,879,105
20 May 2002	
Males	18,516,403
Females	19,713,677
Total	38,230,080
Population (official estimates at 31 December)†	
2005	38,157,055
2006	38,125,479
2007	38,115,641
Density (per sq km) at 31 December 2007	121.9

* 120,728 sq miles.
† Figures exclude civilian aliens within the country and include civilian nationals temporarily outside the country.

VOIVODSHIPS
(official estimates at 31 December 2007)

	Area (sq km)	Population ('000)	Density*	Principal city
Dolnośląskie	19,948	2,878.4	144.3	Wrocław
Kujawsko-Pomorskie	17,970	2,066.1	115.0	Bydgoszcz
Lubelskie	25,114	2,166.2	86.3	Lublin
Lubuskie	13,984	1,008.5	72.1	Gorzów Wlkp†
Łódzkie	18,219	2,555.9	140.3	Łódź
Małopolskie	15,144	3,279.0	216.5	Kraków
Mazowieckie	35,597	5,188.5	145.8	Warsaw
Opolskie	9,412	1,037.1	110.2	Opole
Podkarpackie	17,926	2,097.3	117.0	Rzeszów
Podlaskie	20,180	1,192.6	59.1	Białystok
Pomorskie	18,293	2,210.9	120.9	Gdańsk
Śląskie	12,294	4,654.1	378.6	Katowice
Świętokrzyskie	11,672	1,275.6	109.3	Kielce
Warmińsko-Mazurskie	24,203	1,426.2	58.9	Olsztyn
Wielkopolskie	29,826	3,386.9	113.6	Poznań
Zachodniopomorskie	22,902	1,692.3	73.9	Szczecin
Total	312,685	38,115.6	121.9	—

* Per sq km.
† Gorzów Wielkopolski.

PRINCIPAL TOWNS
(official estimates at 31 December 2005)

Warszawa (Warsaw, the capital)	1,697,596	Bielsko-Biała	176,684
Łódź	767,628	Olsztyn	174,473
Kraków	756,629	Rzeszów	158,539
Wrocław	635,932	Ruda Śląska	146,582
Poznań	567,882	Rybnik	141,580
Gdańsk	458,053	Tychy	131,153
Szczecin	411,119	Dąbrowa Górnicza	130,128
Bydgoszcz	366,074	Opole	128,268
Lublin	354,967	Płock	127,461
Katowice	317,220	Elbląg	127,275
Białystok	291,823	Wałbrzych	126,465
Gdynia	252,791	Gorzów Wielkopolski	125,467
Częstochowa	246,890	Włocławek	119,939
Radom	227,018	Zielona Góra	118,221
Sosnowiec	226,034	Tarnów	117,560
Kielce	208,193	Chorzów	114,686
Toruń	208,007	Kalisz	108,841
Gliwice	199,451	Koszalin	107,886
Zabrze	191,247	Legnica	105,750
Bytom	187,943		

BIRTHS, MARRIAGES AND DEATHS

	Registered live births Number	Rate (per 1,000)	Registered marriages Number	Rate (per 1,000)	Registered deaths Number	Rate (per 1,000)
2000	378,348	9.8	211,150	5.5	368,028	9.5
2001	368,205	9.5	195,122	5.0	363,220	9.4
2002	353,765	9.3	191,935	5.0	359,486	9.4
2003	351,072	9.2	195,446	5.1	365,230	9.6
2004	356,131	9.3	191,824	5.0	363,522	9.5
2005	366,095	9.6	206,916	5.4	368,285	9.7
2006	376,035	9.8	226,181	5.9	369,686	9.7
2007	389,713	n.a.	248,702	n.a.	377,226	n.a.

Life expectancy (years at birth, WHO estimates): 75.2 (males 70.9; females 79.5) in 2006 (Source: WHO, *World Health Statistics*).

IMMIGRATION AND EMIGRATION
('000)*

	2005	2006	2007
Immigrants	9.3	10.8	15.0
Emigrants	22.2	46.9	35.5

* Figures refer to immigrants arriving for permanent residence in Poland and emigrants leaving for permanent residence abroad.

ECONOMICALLY ACTIVE POPULATION*
('000 persons aged 15 years and over)

	2005	2006	2007
Agriculture, hunting and forestry	2,439	2,294	2,239
Fishing	13	10	8
Mining and quarrying	225	237	248
Manufacturing	2,831	2,988	3,162
Electricity, gas and water supply	228	223	218
Construction	843	925	1,054
Wholesale and retail trade; repair of motor vehicles, motorcycles, and personal and household goods	2,020	2,060	2,264
Hotels and restaurants	247	272	291
Transport, storage and communications	862	942	973
Financial intermediation	294	329	363
Real estate, renting and business activities	822	836	953
Public administration and defence; compulsory social security	892	917	937

POLAND

—continued	2005	2006	2007
Education	1,103	1,140	1,128
Health and social work	820	871	871
Other community, social and personal service activities	459	534	511
Private households with employed persons	12	11	16
Activities not adequately defined and unallocated	5	5	5
Total employed	14,116	14,594	15,241
Unemployed	3,045	2,344	1,619
Total labour force	17,161	16,938	16,860
Males	9,362	9,283	9,234
Females	7,800	7,653	7,626

* Excluding regular military personnel living in barracks, and conscripts.

Note: Totals may not be equal to the sum of component parts, owing to rounding.

Source: ILO.

Health and Welfare

KEY INDICATORS

Total fertility rate (children per woman, 2006)	1.2
Under-5 mortality rate (per 1,000 live births, 2006)	7
HIV/AIDS (% of persons aged 15–49, 2007)	0.1
Physicians (per 1,000 head, 2005)	2.0
Hospital beds (per 1,000 head, 2005)	5.2
Health expenditure (2006): US $ per head (PPP)	910
Health expenditure (2006): % of GDP	6.2
Health expenditure (2006): public (% of total)	69.9
Human Development Index (2006): ranking	39
Human Development Index (2006): value	0.875

For sources and definitions, see explanatory note on p. vi.

Agriculture

PRINCIPAL CROPS
('000 metric tons)

	2005	2006	2007
Wheat	8,771.0	7,059.7	8,378.6
Barley	3,582.0	3,161.0	4,065.8
Maize	1,945.4	1,260.7	1,639.7
Rye	3,404.0	2,621.6	3,194.1
Oats	1,324.1	1,034.7	1,486.5
Triticale (wheat-rye hybrid)	3,903.0	3,197.0	4,201.6
Mixed grain	3,916.4	3,379.0	4,298.9
Potatoes	10,369.3	8,982.0	11,221.1
Sugar beet	11,912.4	11,474.8	11,057.8
Rapeseed	1,449.8	1,651.5	2,112.6
Cabbages and other brassicas	1,381.6	1,249.1	1,375.9
Tomatoes	600.7	651.6	652.0*
Cauliflowers and broccoli	238.8	250.4	277.2
Cucumbers and gherkins	468.5	491.9	492.0*
Onions, dry	714.1	590.2	653.3
Carrots and turnips	929.0	833.2	902.1
Mushrooms and truffles*	160.0	137.0	138.0
Apples	2,075.0	2,304.9	1,039.1
Pears	59.3	59.3	28.7
Sour (Morello) cherries	139.9	194.9	195.0*
Plums and sloes	91.4	93.6	53.4
Strawberries	184.6	193.7	168.2
Currants	186.8	194.5	139.9

* FAO estimate(s).

Aggregate production ('000 metric tons, may include official, semi-official or estimated data): Total cereals 26,928 in 2005, 21,776 in 2006, 27,365 in 2007; Total roots and tubers 10,369 in 2005, 8,982 in 2006, 11,221 in 2007; Total vegetables (incl. melons) 5,618 in 2005, 5,257 in 2006, 5,567 in 2007; Total fruits (excl. melons) 2,898 in 2005, 3,104 in 2006, 1,682 in 2007.

Source: FAO.

LIVESTOCK
('000 head year ending September)

	2005	2006	2007
Horses	312	307	310*
Cattle	5,483	5,606	5,696
Pigs	18,112	18,881	18,129
Sheep	316	301	332
Chickens	134,424	124,870	125,000*
Geese and guinea fowls	4,418	3,943	4,000*
Turkeys	7,658	8,099	8,100*
Ducks	6,299	4,895	5,000*

* FAO estimate.

Source: FAO.

LIVESTOCK PRODUCTS
('000 metric tons)

	2005	2006	2007*
Cattle meat	309.5	355.3	355.0
Pig meat	1,955.5	2,071.4	2,100.0
Horse meat	10.7	9.6	10.0
Game meat*	10.0	6.2	6.2
Chicken meat*	795.8	824.4	825.0
Duck meat*	18.2	16.0	17.0
Turkey meat*	25.0	26.0	27.0
Cows' milk	11,922.3	11,982.4	11,800.0
Hen eggs	536.0	537.2	537.5
Honey	10.0	13.5	13.6

* FAO estimates.

Source: FAO.

Forestry

ROUNDWOOD REMOVALS
('000 cubic metres, excl. bark)

	2005	2006	2007
Sawlogs, veneer logs and logs for sleepers	12,715	13,142	15,772
Pulpwood	13,640	13,570	14,800
Other industrial wood	2,176	2,055	1,889
Fuel wood	3,413	3,617	3,474
Total	31,944	32,384	35,935

Source: FAO.

SAWNWOOD PRODUCTION
('000 cubic metres, incl. railway sleepers)

	2005	2006	2007
Coniferous (softwood)	2,813	3,018	2,844
Broadleaved (hardwood)	547	589	461
Total	3,360	3,607	3,304

Source: FAO.

POLAND

Fishing

('000 metric tons, live weight)

	2004	2005	2006
Capture	192.1	155.2	144.4
Freshwater fishes	23.5	22.1	21.4
European flounder	8.7	11.1	9.4
Atlantic cod	16.5	13.8	15.9
Atlantic herring	27.9	22.9	22.1
European sprat	95.8	74.3	55.9
Antarctic krill	9.0	4.3	5.3
Aquaculture	35.1	37.9	35.9
Common carp	18.3	19.0	15.6
Rainbow trout	14.6	17.1	17.0
Total catch	227.2	193.2	180.3

Source: FAO.

Mining

('000 metric tons, unless otherwise indicated)

	2004	2005	2006
Hard coal	101,230	97,903	95,220
Brown coal (incl. lignite)	61,197	61,136	60,844
Crude petroleum	886	849	797
Salt (unrefined)	5,142	4,885	4,955
Native sulphur	821	802	800
Copper ore (metric tons)*	590,000	614,800	670,000
Lead ore (metric tons)*	51,000	78,000	63,300
Magnesite ore—crude	52,000	50,000	50,000
Silver (metric tons)*	1,344	1,306	1,300
Zinc ore (metric tons)*	170,000†	150,000	160,000
Natural gas (million cu metres)	5,630	5,742	5,650

* Figures refer to the metal content of ores.
† Estimate.
Source: US Geological Survey.

Industry

SELECTED PRODUCTS
('000 metric tons, unless otherwise indicated)

	2005	2006	2007
Sausages and smoked meat	756	826	845
Refined sugar	2,258	1,749	2,062
Margarine	348	345	345
Beer ('000 hl)	31,572	33,953	36,896
Wine, mead and other fermented beverages ('000 hl)	2,765	2,680	2,456
Cigarettes (million)	102,355	110,976	123,960
Leather footwear ('000 pairs)	14,904	14,642	15,154
Mechanical wood pulp*	86,200	64,500	65,354
Chemical wood pulp*	802,000	824,600	813,758
Newsprint*	221	191	204
Rubber tyres ('000)[1]	47,056	43,003	43,701
Sulphuric acid—100%	1,807	1,907	2,010
Caustic soda—96%	84	90	101
Soda ash—98%	1,136	1,119	1,132
Nitrogenous fertilizers (a)[2]	4,908	4,850	5,087
Phosphate fertilizers (b)[2]	410	359	n.a.
Motor spirit—Petrol[3]	4,185	4,263	4,035
Diesel oils	6,144	7,460	7,573
Residual fuel oils	3,362	n.a.	n.a.
Coke-oven coke	5,610	7,458	7,906
Cement	12,646	14,688	16,964
Pig-iron[4]	4,477	5,333	5,804
Crude steel	8,336	9,992	10,631
Rolled steel products	6,207	7,682	8,011
Aluminium—unwrought[5]	42.7	38.7	37.2
Refined copper—unwrought	556	556	518

—continued	2005	2006	2007
Refined lead—unwrought	75.1	58.5	59.9
Zinc—unwrought[5]	114	110	65
Radio receivers ('000)	15	18	33
Television receivers ('000)	6,733	9,427	20,240
Merchant ships launched (gross reg. tons)	722	692	517
Passenger motor cars ('000)	540	632	695
Lorries and tractors (number)	67,683	76,412	88,528
Domestic washing machines ('000)	1,481	1,637	1,938
Domestic refrigerators and freezers ('000)	1,674	1,976	2,305
Electric energy (million kWh)	156,936	161,489	158,670

* Source: FAO.
[1] Tyres for passenger motor cars and commercial vehicles, including inner tubes and tyres for animal-drawn road vehicles, and tyres for non-agricultural machines and equipment.
[2] Fertilizer production is measured in terms of (a) nitrogen or (b) phosphoric acid. Phosphate fertilizers include ground rock phosphate.
[3] Including synthetic products.
[4] Including blast furnace ferro-alloys.
[5] Figures refer to both primary and secondary metal. Zinc production includes zinc dust and remelted zinc.

Finance

CURRENCY AND EXCHANGE RATES

Monetary Units
100 groszy (singular: grosz) = 1 new złoty.

Sterling, Dollar and Euro Equivalents (31 December 2008)
£1 sterling = 4.318 new złotys;
US $1 = 2.962 new złotys;
€1 = 4.122 new złotys;
100 new złotys = £23.16 = $33.76 = €24.26.

Average Exchange Rate (new złotys per US dollar)
2006 3.1032
2007 2.7680
2008 2.4089

GOVERNMENT FINANCE
(general government transactions, non-cash basis, '000 million new zlotys)

Summary of Balances

	2004	2005	2006
Revenue	347.17	379.39	413.27
Less Expense	389.88	409.24	435.69
Net operating balance	−42.71	−29.85	−22.42
Less Net acquisition of non-financial assets	8.95	12.49	17.09
Net lending/borrowing	−51.67	−42.34	−39.51

Revenue

	2004	2005	2006
Taxes	181.68	203.67	228.04
Taxes on income, profits and capital gains	54.24	63.10	74.04
Taxes on goods and services	109.73	122.57	134.49
Social contributions	113.75	120.84	128.89
Grants	5.57	6.83	6.85
Other revenue	46.18	48.05	49.49
Total	347.17	379.39	413.27

POLAND

Statistical Survey

Expense/Outlays

Expense by economic type	2004	2005	2006
Compensation of employees	94.21	98.87	104.35
Use of goods and services	53.40	55.61	60.86
Consumption of fixed capital	18.83	19.71	20.76
Interest	25.74	27.52	25.89
Subsidies	5.26	5.09	7.33
Grants	2.37	10.12	10.06
Social benefits	169.52	170.95	183.47
Other expense	20.55	21.38	22.99
Total	389.88	409.24	435.69

Outlays by functions of government*	2004	2005	2006
General public services	53.99	60.40	60.03
Defence	11.75	12.31	14.61
Public order and safety	17.14	19.04	20.23
Economic affairs	29.46	35.37	43.68
Environmental protection	6.04	6.05	6.20
Housing and community amenities	12.37	10.74	10.23
Health	40.63	41.36	46.63
Recreation, culture and religion	7.61	8.05	9.65
Education	50.85	54.75	58.48
Social protection	168.99	173.67	183.04
Total	398.84	421.73	452.78

* Including net acquisition of non-financial assets.

Source: IMF, *Government Finance Statistics Yearbook*.

INTERNATIONAL RESERVES
(US $ million at 31 December)

	2006	2007	2008
Gold (national valuation)	2,103.1	2,767.4	2,862.1
IMF special drawing rights	89.1	100.7	108.7
Reserve position in IMF	174.9	145.8	265.9
Foreign exchange	46,107.0	62,720.3	58,931.0
Total	48,474.1	65,734.2	62,167.7

Source: IMF, *International Financial Statistics*.

MONEY SUPPLY
(million new złotys at 31 December)

	2006	2007	2008
Currency outside banks	68,768	77,160	90,741
Demand deposits at commercial banks	204,987	254,254	252,467
Total money (incl. others)	275,831	335,266	349,717

Source: IMF, *International Financial Statistics*.

COST OF LIVING
(Consumer Price Index; base: 2000 = 100)

	2005	2006	2007
Food (incl. alcoholic beverages)	110.6	110.6	115.9
Electricity, gas and other fuels	129.5	138.1	143.2
Clothing (incl. footwear)	89.5	83.3	77.1
Rent	138.2	142.0	147.6
All items (incl. others)	114.6	115.8	118.6

Source: ILO.

NATIONAL ACCOUNTS
(million new złotys at current prices)

Expenditure on the Gross Domestic Product

	2005	2006	2007
Final consumption expenditure	801,145	856,020	921,472
Households			
Non-profit institutions serving households	623,360	662,313	711,403
General government	177,785	193,707	210,069
Gross capital formation	189,445	223,162	277,910
Gross fixed capital formation	179,180	208,308	253,792
Changes in inventories			
Acquisitions, less disposals, of valuables	10,265	14,854	24,118
Total domestic expenditure	990,590	1,079,182	1,199,382
Exports of goods and services	364,658	427,776	477,294
Less Imports of goods and services	371,946	446,927	508,881
GDP in purchasers' values	983,302	1,060,031	1,167,795

Source: IMF, *International Financial Statistics*.

Gross Domestic Product by Economic Activity

	2005	2006	2007
Agriculture, hunting, forestry and fishing	39,051	39,712	43,948
Construction	52,207	59,777	80,985
Other industry	213,836	231,402	236,983
Mining and quarrying	21,960	22,484	23,418
Manufacturing	160,374	176,406	179,339
Electricity, gas and water	31,502	32,512	34,226
Trade and repair	164,154	176,559	200,646
Other services	397,081	426,405	459,304
Gross value added in basic prices *	866,329	933,855	1,021,866
Taxes, *less* subsidies, on products	116,973	126,176	145,930
GDP in market prices	983,302	1,060,031	1,167,795

* Financial intermediation services indirectly measured (FISIM) is distributed to uses.

BALANCE OF PAYMENTS
(US $ million)

	2005	2006	2007
Exports of goods f.o.b.	96,395	117,468	144,609
Imports of goods f.o.b.	−99,161	−124,474	−160,162
Trade balance	−2,766	−7,006	−15,553
Exports of services	16,258	20,592	28,790
Imports of services	−15,520	−19,856	−24,072
Balance on goods and services	−2,028	−6,270	−10,835
Other income received	6,998	9,040	10,039
Other income paid	−13,695	−18,768	−26,292
Balance on goods, services and income	−8,725	−15,998	−27,088
Current transfers received	9,766	11,955	15,241
Current transfers paid	−4,757	−5,351	−6,748
Current balance	−3,716	−9,394	−18,595
Capital account (net)	995	2,105	4,771
Direct investment abroad	−3,358	−9,149	−4,983
Direct investment from abroad	10,309	19,876	22,959
Portfolio investment assets	−2,509	−4,649	−5,962
Portfolio investment liabilities	15,109	1,527	930
Financial derivatives liabilities	193	−689	−2,010
Other investment assets	−2,782	−3,919	−1,443
Other investment liabilities	−1,732	10,104	30,341
Net errors and omissions	−4,361	−3,323	−12,964
Overall balance	8,146	2,489	13,044

Source: IMF, *International Financial Statistics*.

External Trade

PRINCIPAL COMMODITIES
(distribution by SITC, US $ million)

Imports c.i.f.	2005	2006	2007
Food and live animals	5,268.2	6,197.2	8,589.0
Crude materials (inedible) except fuels	2,999.4	3,764.6	4,836.6
Mineral fuels, lubricants, etc.	11,547.0	13,017.7	16,319.0
Chemicals and related products	14,196.1	16,690.9	20,980.7
Basic manufactures	20,465.4	25,676.9	34,093.6
Machinery and transport equipment	35,628.4	44,678.7	57,887.9
Miscellaneous manufactured articles	8,304.2	9,768.8	13,817.2
Total (incl. others)	101,538.8	125,645.3	164,172.5

Exports f.o.b.	2005	2006	2007
Food and live animals	7,700.2	9,130.0	11,519.1
Crude materials (inedible) except fuels	1,922.1	2,428.7	3,120.7
Mineral fuels, lubricants, etc.	4,575.1	4,909.9	5,222.4
Chemicals and related products	5,981.3	7,767	10,045.3
Basic manufactures	19,775.4	24,904.1	31,627.9
Machinery and transport equipment	34,472.8	43,870.3	56,661.0
Miscellaneous manufactured articles	12,412.4	14,254.0	17,460.3
Total (incl. others)	89,378.1	109,584.1	138,785.0

Source: UN, *International Trade Statistics Yearbook*.

PRINCIPAL TRADING PARTNERS
(US $ million)*

Imports c.i.f.	2005	2006	2007
Austria	1,738.4	2,146.3	2,733.6
Belgium	2,670.4	3,156.4	4,152.6
China, People's Republic	5,496.6	7,711.7	11,753.4
Czech Republic	3,633.3	4,380.8	5,673.8
Denmark	1,372.1	1,634.8	2,113.3
Finland	1,313.0	1,618.5	2,150.2
France (incl. Monaco)	6,094.7	6,883.6	8,380.5
Germany	25,053.4	30,144.5	39,399.7
Hungary	1,838.0	2,699.9	3,449.8
Italy	7,181.2	8,535.9	11,235.9
Japan	1,992.2	2,076.8	3,171.2
Korea, Republic	1,583.0	2,895.3	3,856.1
Netherlands	3,474.0	3,953.8	5,602.4
Norway	1,597.7	1,663.3	1,773.9
Russia	8,985.5	12,142.0	14,352.8
Slovakia	1,872.2	2,219.1	2,986.9
Spain	2,193.7	2,473.3	3,503.7
Sweden	2,327.2	2,770.0	3,622.3
Switzerland (incl. Liechtenstein)	1,114.1	1,282.1	1,628.6
Turkey	1,314.4	1,576.0	2,137.6
Ukraine	1,021.0	1,319.4	1,693.5
United Kingdom	3,143.4	3,600.4	5,107.0
USA	2,415.8	2,772.0	3,463.5
Total (incl. others)	101,538.8	125,645.3	164,172.5

Exports f.o.b.	2005	2006	2007
Austria	1,863.3	2,008.2	2,609.3
Belgium	2,663.2	3,025.8	3,721.6
Czech Republic	4,076.9	6,066.9	7,683.8
Denmark	1,878.8	2,155.9	2,659.1
France (incl. Monaco)	5,558.5	6,823.1	8,443.1
Germany	25,222.7	29,701.3	35,901.2
Hungary	2,538.2	3,330.7	4,033.8
Italy	5,482.8	7,174.7	9,151.6
Lithuania	1,232.4	1,627.5	2,266.9
Netherlands	3,721.4	4,209.0	5,302.1
Norway	1,888.9	2,122.4	2,493.4

Exports f.o.b.—continued	2005	2006	2007
Romania	1,018.9	1,292.9	2,153.9
Russia	3,960.5	4,711.1	6,432.3
Slovakia	1,709.1	2,292.9	3,026.3
Spain	2,221.4	2,721.7	4,006.5
Sweden	2,749.8	3,512.8	4,464.6
Turkey	1,197.2	1,304.5	1,508.2
Ukraine	2,588.2	3,967.8	5,511.3
United Kingdom	4,995.6	6,254.0	8,238.0
USA	1,849.7	2,103.7	2,057.5
Total (incl. others)	89,378.1	109,584.1	138,785.0

* Imports by country of purchase; exports by country of sale.

Source: UN, *International Trade Statistics Yearbook*.

Transport

POLISH STATE RAILWAYS
(traffic)

	2002	2003	2004
Paying passengers ('000 journeys)	304,144	283,390	272,162
Passenger-kilometres (million)	20,809	19,653	18,690*
Freight carried ('000 metric tons)	222,908	241,629	282,919
Freight ton-kilometres (million)	47,756	49,584	52,332*

* Source: UN, *Statistical Yearbook*.

ROAD TRAFFIC
('000 motor vehicles registered at 31 December)

	2001	2002	2003
Passenger cars	10,503	11,029	11,244
Lorries and vans (incl. road tractors)	1,979	2,163	2,313
Buses and coaches	82	83	83
Motorcycles*	803	869	845

* Figures for 2001 and 2002 also include scooters.

INLAND WATERWAYS
(traffic, including coastal transport)

	2001	2002	2003
Passengers carried ('000)	1,637	1,648	1,795
Passenger-kilometres (million)	42	37	34
Freight carried ('000 metric tons)	10,255	7,729	7,976
Freight ton-kilometres (million)	1,264	1,126	872

2004: Freight carried 8,748,000 metric tons.

SHIPPING

Merchant Fleet
(registered at 31 December)

	2005	2006	2007
Number of vessels	359	355	351
Displacement ('000 gross registered tons)	190.1	193.4	193.3

Source: Lloyd's Register-Fairplay, *World Fleet Statistics*.

Sea Transport
(by owned or leased ships)

	2001	2002	2003
Passengers carried ('000)	582	559	526
Passenger-kilometres (million)	154	150	137
Freight carried ('000 metric tons)	22,426	25,222	25,435
Freight ton-kilometres (million)	108,517	104,190	100,455

International Sea-borne Shipping at Polish Ports

	2001	2002	2003
Vessels entered ('000 net reg. tons)	39,594	41,563	50,794
Vessels entered (number)	32,299	30,212	29,771
Passengers ('000): arrivals	2,220	1,718	1,617
Passengers ('000): departures	2,197	1,587	1,572
Cargo ('000 metric tons): loaded*	31,526	33,168	35,848
Cargo ('000 metric tons): unloaded*	14,684	14,943	15,171

* Including ships' bunkers and transshipments.

Source: Centre of Maritime Statistics.

CIVIL AVIATION
(traffic on scheduled services)

	2002	2003	2004
Kilometres flown (million)	66	68	73
Passengers carried ('000)	2,846	3,252	3,493
Passenger-kilometres (million)	5,111	5,434	5,861
Total ton-kilometres (million)	581	608	654

Source: UN, *Statistical Yearbook*.

Tourism

FOREIGN TOURIST ARRIVALS
('000, including visitors in transit)

Country of residence	2005	2006	2007
Belarus	3,651	3,992	3,861
Czech Republic	7,855	7,102	7,292
Germany	37,436	37,192	38,103
Lithuania	1,344	1,459	1,392
Russia	1,599	1,722	1,626
Slovakia	3,378	3,422	3,210
Ukraine	5,279	5,642	5,444
Total (incl. others)	64,606	65,115	66,208

Receipts from tourism (US $ million): 6,230 in 2005; 7,187 in 2006; 10,573 in 2007.

Source: Institute of Tourism.

Communications Media

	2001	2002	2003
Radio subscribers ('000)*	9,219	n.a.	n.a.
Television subscribers ('000)*	8,969	n.a.	n.a.
Telephones ('000 main lines in use)†	11,400.0	11,859.5	12,292.5
Mobile cellular telephones ('000 subscribers)†	10,004.7	13,898.5	17,401.2
Personal computers ('000 in use)†	3,300	4,079	5,480
Internet users ('000)†	3,800	8,880	8,970
Book production: titles‡	19,189	19,246	20,686
Book production: copies (million)‡	74.4	67.6	81.5
Daily and non-daily newspapers: number	66	67	54
average circulation ('000 copies)	4,438	4,191	4,335
Other periodicals: number	5,771	6,122	5,627
Other periodicals: average circulation ('000 copies)	74,043	71,903	69,409

* At 31 December.
† Source: International Telecommunication Union.
‡ Including pamphlets.

2004: Telephones ('000 main lines in use) 12,292.5; Mobile cellular telephones ('000 subscribers) 23,096.1; Personal computers ('000 in use) 7,362; Internet users ('000) 9,000 (Source: International Telecommunication Union).

2005: Telephones ('000 main lines in use) 11,836.2; Mobile cellular telephones ('000 subscribers) 29,166.4; Internet users ('000) 12,553.8; Broadband subscribers ('000) 945.2 (Source: International Telecommunication Union).

2006: Telephones ('000 main lines in use) 11,475.6; Mobile cellular telephones ('000 subscribers) 36,745.5; Internet users ('000) 14,084.6; Broadband subscribers ('000) 2,911.2 (Source: International Telecommunication Union).

2007: Telephones ('000 main lines in use) 10,336.3; Mobile cellular telephones ('000 subscribers) 41,388.8; Internet users ('000) 16,000 (Source: International Telecommunication Union).

Facsimile machines (estimate, 1995): 55,000 in use (Source: UN, *Statistical Yearbook*).

Education

(2005/06, unless otherwise indicated)

	Institutions	Teachers*	Males	Females	Total
Pre-primary	17,337†	48,882	429.8	410.2	840.0
Primary	15,344‡	231,609	1,338.0	1,264.0	2,602.0
Secondary	17,825‡	261,050	1,710.4	1,606.5	3,316.9
Tertiary	400‡	98,223	914.1	1,231.6	2,145.7

Students ('000)*

* Data from UNESCO Institute for Statistics.
† 2001/02 figure.
‡ 2004/05 figure.

Adult literacy rate (UNESCO estimates): 99.3% (males 99.7%; females 99.0%) in 2007 (Source: UNESCO Institute for Statistics).

Directory

The Constitution

The Constitution of the Republic of Poland was adopted by the National Assembly on 2 April 1997 and endorsed by popular referendum on 25 May of that year. The following is a summary of the main provisions of the Constitution, which came into force on 17 October 1997:

THE REPUBLIC

The Republic of Poland shall be a unitary, democratic state, ruled by law, and implementing the principles of social justice. The Republic shall safeguard the independence and integrity of its territory, ensure the freedom and rights of persons and citizens, and safeguard the national heritage. The Constitution shall be the supreme law of the Republic, which shall respect international law binding upon it. Legislative power shall be vested in the Sejm (Assembly) and the Senat (Senate), executive power shall be vested in the President and the Council of Ministers, and judicial power shall be vested in the courts and tribunals.

The Republic shall ensure freedom for the creation and functioning of political parties, trade unions and other voluntary associations. The financing of political parties shall be open to public inspection. Political parties and other organizations whose programmes are based upon totalitarian methods and the modes of activity of nazism, fascism and communism, as well as those whose programmes or activities sanction racial or national hatred, or the application of violence for the purpose of obtaining power or to influence the State's policy, or provide for the secrecy of their own structure or membership, shall be forbidden. The Republic shall ensure freedom of the press and other means of social communication.

A social market economy, based on the freedom of economic activity, private ownership, and solidarity, dialogue and co-operation between social partners, shall be the basis of the economic system of Poland.

Churches and other religious organizations shall have equal rights. Public authorities shall be impartial in matters of personal conviction, and shall ensure their freedom of expression within public life. The Armed Forces shall observe neutrality regarding political matters and shall be subject to civil and democratic control.

THE FREEDOMS, RIGHTS AND OBLIGATIONS OF PERSONS AND CITIZENS

All persons shall be equal before the law. Polish citizens belonging to national or ethnic minorities shall be guaranteed the freedom to maintain and develop their own language, to maintain customs and traditions, and to develop their own culture.

The Republic shall ensure the legal protection of the life of every human being; the inviolability of the person and of the home; freedom of movement; freedom of faith and religion; and the freedom to express opinions. The freedom of peaceful assembly and association shall be guaranteed. At the age of 18 every citizen shall have the right to participate in referendums, and to vote in presidential, legislative and local elections. Everyone shall have the right to own property; the freedom to choose and pursue his occupation; the right to health protection; and the right to education.

THE SEJM AND THE SENAT

The Sejm shall be composed of 460 Deputies. Elections to the Sejm shall be universal, equal, direct, proportional and conducted by secret ballot. The Senat shall be composed of 100 Senators. Elections to the Senat shall be universal, direct and conducted by secret ballot. The Sejm and the Senat shall be elected for a four-year term of office. At the ages of 21 and 30, respectively, every citizen having the right to vote shall be eligible for election to the Sejm and the Senat.

The Sejm shall elect from among its members a Marshal and Vice-Marshals. The Sejm adopts laws; may adopt a resolution on a state of war; may order a nation-wide referendum; and may appoint investigative committees to examine particular matters.

The Senat reviews laws adopted by the Sejm; it may adopt amendments or resolve upon complete rejection. A decision of the Senat can be overridden by the Sejm by an absolute majority vote in the presence of at least one-half of the statutory number of Deputies.

In instances specified in the Constitution, the Sejm and the Senat, sitting in joint session, shall act as the National Assembly (Zgromadzenie Narodowe). The right to introduce legislation shall belong to Deputies, to the Senat, to the President of the Republic, to the Council of Ministers, and to a group of at least 100,000 citizens having the right to vote in elections to the Sejm.

THE PRESIDENT OF THE REPUBLIC

The President of the Republic of Poland shall be the supreme representative of the Polish State and the guarantor of the continuity of state authority. The President shall ensure observance of the Constitution, safeguard the sovereignty and security of the State, as well as the inviolability and integrity of its territory. The President shall be elected in universal, equal and direct elections by secret ballot. The President shall be elected for a five-year term, and may be re-elected only once. Only a Polish citizen aged over 35 years, with full electoral rights in elections to the Sejm, may be elected President. Any such candidature shall be supported by the signatures of at least 100,000 citizens having the right to vote in elections to the Sejm. If the President of the Republic is unable to discharge the duties of his office, the Marshal of the Sejm shall temporarily assume presidential duties.

The President's duties include the calling of elections to the Sejm and the Senat; heading the Armed Forces; nominating and appointing the Prime Minister; appointing senior public officials; and representing the State in foreign affairs.

Bringing an indictment against the President shall be done by resolution of the National Assembly, passed by a majority of at least two-thirds of the statutory number of members, on the motion of at least 140 members.

THE COUNCIL OF MINISTERS AND GOVERNMENT ADMINISTRATION

The Council of Ministers shall conduct the internal affairs and foreign policy of the Republic, and shall manage the government administration. The President shall nominate a Prime Minister who shall propose the composition of a Council of Ministers. The Prime Minister shall, within 14 days following his appointment, submit a programme of activity of the Council of Ministers to the Sejm, together with a motion requiring a vote of confidence.

The members of the Council of Ministers shall be responsible to the Sejm, both collectively and individually. The Sejm may pass a vote of no confidence in the Council of Ministers by a majority of votes of the statutory number of Deputies, on a motion of at least 46 Deputies, specifying the name of a candidate for Prime Minister.

LOCAL SELF-GOVERNMENT

The commune (*gmina*) shall be the basic unit of local self-government. Other units of regional and/or local self-government shall be specified by statute. Public duties aimed at satisfying the needs of a self-governing community shall be the direct responsibility of such units. Units of local self-government shall perform their duties through constitutive and executive organs. Units of local self-government shall be assured public funds for the performance of the duties assigned to them.

COURTS AND TRIBUNALS

The courts and tribunals shall constitute a separate and independent power. The administration of justice in Poland shall be implemented by the Supreme Court, the common courts, administrative courts and military courts. Judges, within the exercise of their office, shall be independent and subject only to the Constitution and statutes. The Supreme Court shall exercise supervision over common and military courts.

The Constitutional Tribunal

The Constitutional Tribunal shall adjudicate on the conformity of statutes and other normative acts issued by central state organs to the Constitution. Its judgments shall be universally binding and final. Judges of the Tribunal shall be independent and subject only to the Constitution.

The Tribunal of State

Persons holding high state positions (as specified in the Constitution) shall be accountable to the Tribunal of State for violations of the Constitution or statutes. The First President of the Supreme Court shall be Chairman of the Tribunal. Its members shall be independent and subject only to the Constitution and statutes.

ORGANS OF STATE CONTROL FOR THE DEFENCE OF RIGHTS

The Supreme Chamber of Control shall be the chief organ of state order, and shall be subordinate to the Sejm. It shall audit the activity of the organs of government administration, the National Bank of Poland, state legal persons and other state organizational units. The Commissioner for Citizens' Rights shall safeguard the freedoms and rights of persons and citizens as specified in the Constitution and other normative acts. The National Council of Radio and Television Broadcasting shall safeguard freedom of speech and the right to information, as well as the public interest regarding radio and television broadcasting.

EXTRAORDINARY MEASURES

In situations of particular danger, if ordinary constitutional measures are inadequate, any of the following appropriate extraordinary measures may be introduced in a part or upon the whole territory of the State: martial law, a state of emergency or a state of natural disaster.

The Government

HEAD OF STATE

President: LECH KACZYŃSKI (inaugurated 23 December 2005).

COUNCIL OF MINISTERS
(April 2009)

A coalition comprising the Civic Platform (PO) and the Polish People's Party (PSL).

Prime Minister: DONALD TUSK (PO).

Deputy Prime Minister and Minister of the Economy: WALDEMAR PAWLAK (PSL).

Deputy Prime Minister and Minister of Internal Affairs and Administration: GRZEGORZ SCHETYNA (PO).

Minister of Foreign Affairs: RADOSŁAW SIKORSKI (PO).

Minister of National Defence: BOGDAN KLICH (PO).

Minister of the State Treasury: ALEKSANDER GRAD (PO).

Minister of Justice: ANDRZEJ CZUMA (PO).

POLAND

Minister of Science and Higher Education: BARBARA KUDRYCKA (PO).
Minister of Labour and Social Policy: JOLANTA FEDAK (PSL).
Minister of National Education: KATARZYNA HALL (PO).
Minister of Agriculture and Rural Development: MAREK SAWICKI (PSL).
Minister of Regional Development: ELŻBIETA BIEŃKOWSKA (Independent).
Minister of Culture and National Heritage: BOGDAN ZDROJEWSKI (PO).
Minister of Health: EWA KOPACZ (PO).
Minister of the Environment: MACIEJ NOWICKI (PO).
Minister of Finance: JACEK VINCENT-ROSTOWSKI (Independent).
Minister of Sport and Tourism: MIROSŁAW DRZEWIECKI.
Minister of Infrastructure: CEZARY GRABARCZYK (PO).
Minister, Member of the Council of Ministers: MICHAŁ BONI (Independent).

MINISTRIES

Chancellery of the President: 00-902 Warsaw, ul. Wiejska 10; tel. (22) 6952900; fax (22) 6952238; e-mail listy@prezydent.pl; internet www.prezydent.pl.

Chancellery of the Prime Minister: 00-583 Warsaw, Al. Ujazdowskie 1/3; tel. (22) 8413832; fax (22) 6284821; e-mail cirinfo@kprm.gov.pl; internet www.kprm.gov.pl.

Ministry of Agriculture and Rural Development: 00-930 Warsaw, ul. Wspólna 30; tel. (22) 6231000; fax (22) 6231782; e-mail kanceleria@minrol.gov.pl; internet www.minrol.gov.pl.

Ministry of Culture and National Heritage: 00-071 Warsaw, ul. Krakowskie Przedmieście 15/17; tel. (22) 4210100; fax (22) 8260726; e-mail rzecznik@mkidn.gov.pl; internet www.mkidn.gov.pl.

Ministry of the Economy: 00-507 Warsaw, pl. Trzech Krzyży 3/5; tel. (22) 6935000; fax (22) 6934048; e-mail bpi@mg.gov.pl; internet www.mg.gov.pl.

Ministry of the Environment: 00-922 Warsaw, ul. Wawelska 52/54; tel. (22) 5792900; fax (22) 5792511; e-mail info@mos.gov.pl; internet www.mos.gov.pl.

Ministry of Finance: 00-916 Warsaw, ul. Świętokrzyska 12; tel. (22) 6945555; fax (22) 8272722; e-mail kancelaria@mf.gov.pl; internet www.mf.gov.pl.

Ministry of Foreign Affairs: 00-580 Warsaw, Al. Szucha 23; tel. (22) 5239000; fax (22) 6290287; e-mail dsi@msz.gov.pl; internet www.msz.gov.pl.

Ministry of Health: 00-952 Warsaw, ul. Miodowa 15; tel. (22) 6349600; fax (22) 6349213; e-mail kancelaria@mz.gov.pl; internet www.mz.gov.pl.

Ministry of Infrastructure: 00-928 Warszawa, ul. Chałubińskiego 4/6; tel. (22) 6301000; fax (22) 6301116; e-mail info@mi.gov.pl; internet www.mi.gov.pl.

Ministry of Internal Affairs and Administration: 02-591 Warsaw, ul. Stefana Batorego 5; tel. (22) 6014427; fax (22) 6227973; e-mail wp@mswia.gov.pl; internet www.mswia.gov.pl.

Ministry of Justice: 00-950 Warsaw, Al. Ujazdowskie 11; tel. (22) 5212888; fax (22) 6215540; e-mail nagorska@ms.gov.pl; internet www.ms.gov.pl.

Ministry of Labour and Social Policy: 00-513 Warsaw, ul. Nowogrodzka 1/3/5; tel. (22) 6610100; fax (22) 6610709; internet www.mps.gov.pl.

Ministry of National Defence: 00-909 Warsaw, ul. Klonowa 1; tel. (22) 6280031; fax (22) 8455378; e-mail bpimon@wp.mil.pl; internet www.wp.mil.pl.

Ministry of National Education: 00-918 Warsaw, Al. Szucha 25; tel. (22) 3474100; fax (22) 5224100; e-mail informacja@men.gov.pl; internet www.men.gov.pl.

Ministry of Regional Development: 00-926 Warsaw, ul. Wspólna 2/4; tel. (22) 4613000; fax (22) 4613000; internet www.mrr.gov.pl.

Ministry of Science and Higher Education: 00-529 Warsaw, ul. Wspólna 1/3; tel. (22) 5292718; fax (22) 6280922; e-mail sekretariat.minister@mnisw.gov.pl; internet www.nauka.gov.pl.

Ministry of Sport and Tourism: 00-921 Warsaw, ul. Senatorska 14; tel. (22) 2443142; fax (22) 2443255; e-mail rzecznik@msport.gov.pl; internet www.msport.gov.pl.

Ministry of the State Treasury: 00-522 Warsaw, ul. Krucza 36; tel. (22) 6958000; fax (22) 6280872; e-mail minister@msp.gov.pl; internet www.msp.gov.pl.

Directory

President

Presidential Election, First Ballot, 9 October 2005

Candidates	Votes	%
Donald Tusk	5,429,666	36.33
Lech Kaczyński	4,947,927	33.10
Andrzej Lepper	2,259,094	15.11
Marek Borowski	1,544,642	10.33
Others	765,360	5.12
Total	**14,946,689**	**100.00**

Second Ballot, 23 October 2005

Candidates	Votes	%
Lech Kaczyński	8,257,468	54.04
Donald Tusk	7,022,319	45.96
Total	**15,279,787**	**100.00**

Legislature

The Zgromadzenie Narodowe (National Assembly) is bicameral, comprising the Sejm (Assembly), the lower chamber, and the Senat (Senate), the upper chamber.

Sejm
(Assembly)

00-902 Warsaw, ul. Wiejska 4/6; tel. (22) 6285927; e-mail zjablon@sejm.gov.pl; internet www.sejm.gov.pl.

Marshal: BRONISŁAW KOMOROWSKI.

Election, 21 October 2007

Parties and alliances	Votes	% of votes	Seats
Civic Platform (PO)	6,701,010	41.51	209
Law and Justice (PiS)	5,183,477	32.11	166
Left and Democrats (LiD)*	2,122,981	13.15	53
Polish People's Party (PSL)	1,437,638	8.91	31
German Minority (MN)	32,462	0.20	1
Self-Defence Party of the Republic of Poland (SRP)	247,335	1.53	—
League of Polish Families (LPR)	209,171	1.30	—
Others	208,128	1.29	—
Total	**16,142,202**	**100.00**	**460**

*A coalition of the Democratic Left Alliance (SLD), Polish Social Democracy (SDPL), the Democratic Party and the Union of Labour (UP).

Senat
(Senate)

00-902 Warsaw, ul. Wiejska 6; tel. (22) 6949265; fax (22) 6949428; internet www.senat.gov.pl.

Marshal: BOGDAN BORUSEWICZ.

Election, 21 October 2007

Parties and alliances	Seats
Civic Platform	60
Law and Justice	39
Independent	1
Total	**100**

Election Commission

Państwowa Komisja Wyborcza (PKW) (State Election Commission): 00-902 Warsaw, ul. Wiejska 10; tel. (22) 6250617; fax (22) 6293959; internet www.pkw.gov.pl; Pres. FERDYNAND RYMARZ.

Political Organizations

Civic Platform (PO) (Platforma Obywatelska): 00-159 Warsaw, ul. Andersa 21; tel. (22) 6357879; fax (22) 6357641; e-mail poczta@platforma.org; internet www.platforma.org; f. 2001 by independent presidential candidate and factions of the Freedom Union (UW) and

Solidarity Electoral Action (AWS); conservative-liberal; Leader DONALD TUSK.

Democratic Left Alliance (SLD) (Sojusz Lewicy Demokratycznej): 00-419 Warsaw, ul. Rozbrat 44 A; tel. (22) 6210341; fax (22) 6216069; e-mail rk@sld.org.pl; internet www.sld.org.pl; f. 1999; contested 2007 legislative elections as mem. of Left and Democrats coalition; Chair. GRZEGORZ NAPIERALSKI.

Democratic Party (PD) (Partia Demokratyczna): 00-683 Warsaw, ul. Marszałkowska 77/79; tel. (22) 3355800; fax (22) 3355817; e-mail sekretariat@demokraci.pl; internet www.demokraci.pl; f. 2005 to replace Freedom Union (UW); contested 2007 legislative elections as mem. of Left and Democrats coalition; Leader BRYGIDA KUŹNIAK.

German Minority (Mniejszość Niemiecka—MN): 45-004 Opole, ul. M. Konopnickiej 6; tel. (77) 4021070; fax (77) 4230262; internet www.mniejszoscniemiecka.pl; Leader HENRYK KRÓL.

Law and Justice (PiS) (Prawo i Sprawiedliwość): 02-018 Warsaw, ul. Nowogrodzka 84/86; tel. (22) 6215035; fax (22) 6216767; e-mail biuro@pis.org.pl; internet www.pis.org.pl; f. 2001; conservative; Leader JAROSŁAW KACZYŃSKI.

League of Polish Families (LPR) (Liga Polskich Rodzin): 00-528 Warsaw, ul. Hoża 9; tel. (22) 6223648; fax (22) 6223138; e-mail biuro@lpr.pl; internet www.lpr.pl; f. 2001 as alliance comprising the National Party, All-Poland Youth, the Polish Accord Party, the Catholic National movement and the Peasant National Bloc; Roman Catholic, nationalist, anti-EU; Leader MIROSŁAW ORZECHOWSKI.

Polish Labour Party (Polska Partia Pracy—PPP): 00-570 Warsaw, ul. Wyzwolenia 18; tel. (22) 6293095; e-mail sekretariat@partiapracy.pl; internet www.partiapracy.pl; f. 2001; Chair. BOGUSŁAW ZIĘTEK.

Polish People's Party (PSL) (Polskie Stronnictwo Ludowe): 00-902 Warsaw, ul. Wiejska 4/6/8; tel. (22) 6942321; fax (22) 6941773; e-mail kp-psl@sejm.pl; internet www.psl.pl; f. 1990 on basis of United Peasant Party (f. 1949) and Polish Peasant Party—Rebirth (f. 1989); centrist, advocates devt of agriculture and social market economy; Chair. WALDEMAR PAWLAK.

Polish Social Democracy (SDPL) (Socjaldemokracja Polski): 00-560 Warsaw, ul. Mokotowska 29A; tel. (22) 6213640; fax (22) 6215342; e-mail sdpl@sdpl.pl; internet www.sdpl.pl; f. 2004; contested 2007 legislative elections as mem. of Left and Democrats coalition; Leader WOJCIECH FILEMONOWICZ.

Right of the Republic (PR) (Prawica Rzeczypospolitej): 00-687 Warsaw, ul. Wspólna 61; tel. (22) 4247722; e-mail biuro@prawicarzeczypospolitej.org; internet www.prawicarzeczypospolitej.org; f. 2007; opposed to abortion, euthanasia, and supportive of traditional Roman Catholic values; Leader MAREK JUREK.

Self-Defence Party of the Republic of Poland (SRP) (Partia Samoobrona Rzeczypospolitej Polskiej): 00-024 Warsaw, Al. Jerozolimskie 30; tel. (22) 6250472; fax (22) 6250477; e-mail samoobrona@samoobrona.org.pl; internet www.samoobrona.pl; agrarian, populist, anti-EU; Leader ANDRZEJ LEPPER.

Union of Labour (UP) (Unia Pracy): 00-513 Warsaw, ul. Nowogrodzka 4; tel. (22) 6285859; fax (22) 6256776; e-mail biuro@uniapracy.pl; internet www.uniapracy.org.pl; f. 1992; contested 2007 legislative elections as mem. of Left and Democrats coalition; Chair. WALDEMAR WITKOWSKI.

Women's Party (Partia Kobiet—PK): Warsaw; tel. (22) 4440022; e-mail info@polskajestkobieta.org; internet www.polskajestkobieta.org; f. 2007; Chair. ANNA KORNACKA.

Diplomatic Representation

EMBASSIES IN POLAND

Afghanistan: 02-954 Warsaw, ul. Goplańska 1; tel. (22) 8855410; fax (22) 8856500; e-mail warsaw@afghanembassy.com.pl; internet www.afghanembassy.com.pl; Ambassador ZIAUDDIN MOJADEDI.

Albania: 02-386 Warsaw, ul. Altowa 1; tel. (22) 8241427; fax (22) 8241426; e-mail ambasada@albania.waw.pl; Ambassador FLORENT ÇELIKU.

Algeria: 03-932 Warsaw, ul. Dąbrowiecka 21; tel. (22) 6175855; fax (22) 6160081; e-mail ambalggovdz@zigzag.pl; Ambassador ABDELAZIZ LAHIOUEL.

Angola: 02-635 Warsaw, ul. Balonowa 20; tel. (22) 6463529; fax (22) 8447452; e-mail embaixada@emb-angola.pl; Ambassador LIZETH NAWANGA SATUMBO PENA.

Argentina: 03-973 Warsaw, ul. Brukselska 9; tel. (22) 6176028; fax (22) 6177162; e-mail epolo@home.pl; Ambassador CARLOS ALBERTO PASSALACQUA.

Armenia: 02-803 Warsaw, ul. Bekasów 50; tel. (22) 8990940; fax (22) 8990935; e-mail secretariat@armenia.internetdsl.pl; Ambassador ASHOT GALOYAN.

Australia: 00-513 Warsaw, ul. Nowogrodzka 11; tel. (22) 5213444; fax (22) 6273500; e-mail ambasada.australia@dfat.gov.au; internet www.australia.pl; Ambassador RUTH LORRAINE PEARCE.

Austria: 00-748 Warsaw, ul. Gagarina 34; tel. (22) 8410081; fax (22) 8410085; e-mail warschau-ob@bmaa.gv.at; internet www.ambasadaaustrii.pl; Ambassador ALFRED LÄNGLE.

Azerbaijan: 03-941 Warsaw, ul. Zwycięców 12; tel. (22) 6162188; fax (22) 6161949; e-mail info@azer-embassy.pl; internet www.azer-embassy.pl; Ambassador VILAYAT M. GULIYEV.

Belarus: 02-952 Warsaw, ul. Wiertnicza 58; tel. (22) 7420990; fax (22) 7420980; e-mail poland@belembassy.org; internet www.belembassy.org/poland; Ambassador WIKTAR GAISENAK.

Belgium: 00-095 Warsaw, ul. Senatorska 34; tel. (22) 5512800; fax (22) 5512888; e-mail warsaw@diplobel.fed.be; internet www.diplomatie.be/warsawfr; Ambassador JAN LUYKX.

Bosnia and Herzegovina: 00-789 Warsaw, ul. Humańska 10; tel. (22) 8569935; fax (22) 8481521; e-mail amb-bih.pl@poczta.internetdsl.pl; Ambassador ZORAN SKENDERIJA.

Brazil: 03-931 Warsaw, ul. Poselska 11; tel. (22) 6174800; fax (22) 6178689; e-mail brasil@brasil.org.pl; internet www.brasil.org.pl; Ambassador CARLOS ALBERTO SIMAS MAGALHÃES.

Bulgaria: 00-540 Warsaw, Al. Ujazdowskie 33/35; tel. (22) 6294071; fax (22) 6282271; e-mail office@bgemb.com.pl; Ambassador IVAN A. NAYDENOV.

Canada: 00-481 Warsaw, ul. Matejki 1/5; tel. (22) 5843100; fax (22) 5843100; e-mail wsaw@international.gc.ca; internet www.canada.pl; Ambassador DAVID PRESTON.

Chile: 02-925 Warsaw, ul. Okrężna 62; tel. (22) 8582330; fax (22) 8582329; e-mail embachile@onet.pl; internet www.embachile.pl; Ambassador JOSÉ MANUEL SILVA VIDAURRE.

China, People's Republic: 00-203 Warsaw, ul. Bonifraterska 1; tel. (22) 8313836; fax (22) 6354211; e-mail ambchina@pol.pl; internet www.chinaembassy.org.pl; Ambassador SUN RONGMIN.

Colombia: 03-936 Warsaw, ul. Zwycięzców 29; tel. (22) 6170973; fax (22) 6176684; e-mail embcol@medianet.pl; Ambassador JORGE ALBERTO BARRANTES ULLOA.

Congo, Democratic Republic: 02-637 Warsaw, ul. Starościńska 1/22; tel. and fax (22) 6460860; e-mail ambardcvarsovie@yahoo.fr; Chargé d'affaires a.i. PHILIPPE ELIFA ABOMBO.

Croatia: 02-611 Warsaw, ul. Ignacego Krasickiego 25; tel. (22) 8442393; fax (22) 8444808; e-mail croemb.warszawa@mvpei.hr; internet pl.mvp.hr; Ambassador IVAN DEL VECHIO.

Cuba: 02-516 Warsaw, ul. Rejtana 15/8; tel. (22) 8481715; fax (22) 8482231; e-mail embacuba@medianet.pl; internet emba.cubaminrex.cu/polonia; Ambassador ROSARIO CRISTINA NAVAS MORATA.

Cyprus: 02-629 Warsaw, ul. Pilicka 4; tel. (22) 8444577; fax (22) 8442558; e-mail ambasada@ambcypr.pl; Ambassador KALLIOPI AVRAAM.

Czech Republic: 00-555 Warsaw, ul. Koszykowa 18; tel. (22) 5251850; fax (22) 5251898; e-mail warsaw@embassy.mzv.cz; internet www.mfa.cz/warsaw; Ambassador JAN SECHTER.

Denmark: 02-517 Warsaw, ul. Rakowiecka 19; tel. (22) 5652900; fax (22) 5652970; e-mail wawamb@um.dk; internet www.ambwarszawa.um.dk; Ambassador HANS MICHAEL KOFOED-HANSEN.

Ecuador: 02-516 Warsaw, ul. Rejtana 15/15; tel. (22) 8487230; fax (22) 8488196; e-mail eccupolonia@mmrree.gov.ec; Ambassador FERNANDO FLORES MACÍAS.

Egypt: 03-972 Warsaw, ul. Alzacka 18; tel. (22) 6176973; fax (22) 6179058; e-mail embassyofegypt@neostrada.pl; Ambassador FAHMY AHMED FAYED SALAMA.

Estonia: 02-639 Warsaw, ul. Karwińska 1; tel. (22) 8811810; fax (22) 8811812; e-mail embassy@estemb.pl; internet www.estemb.pl; Ambassador ANTS FROSCH.

Finland: 00-559 Warsaw, ul. Chopina 4/8; tel. (22) 5989500; fax (22) 6213442; e-mail sanomat.var@formin.fi; internet www.finland.pl; Ambassador VESA TAPANI HIMANEN.

France: 00-477 Warsaw, ul. Piękna 1; tel. (22) 5293000; fax (22) 5293001; e-mail presse@ambafrance-pl.org; internet www.ambafrance-pl.org; Ambassador FRANÇOIS BARRY MARTIN-DELONGCHAMPS.

Georgia: 03-976 Warsaw, ul. Berneńska 6; tel. (22) 6166221; fax (22) 6166226; e-mail warsaw.emb@mfa.gov.ge; internet www.poland.mfa.gov.ge; Ambassador KONSTANTIN KAVTARADZE.

Germany: 00-467 Warsaw, ul. Jazdów 12; tel. (22) 5841700; fax (22) 5841739; e-mail warszawa@wars.diplo.de; internet www.ambasadaniemiec.pl; Ambassador Dr MICHAEL H. GERDTS.

Greece: 00-432 Warsaw, ul. Górnośląska 35; tel. (22) 6229460; fax (22) 6229464; e-mail gremb.war@mfa.gr; internet www.greece.pl; Ambassador GABRIEL COPTSIDIS.

POLAND

Holy See: 00-582 Warsaw, Al. J. Ch. Szucha 12, POB 163; tel. (22) 6288488; fax (22) 6284556; e-mail nuncjatura@episkopat.pl; Apostolic Nuncio Most Rev. JÓZEF KOWALCZYK (Titular Archbishop of Heraclea).

Hungary: 00-559 Warsaw, ul. Chopina 2; tel. (22) 6284451; fax (22) 6218561; e-mail mission.vao@kum.hu; internet www.mfa.gov.hu/emb/warsaw; Ambassador RÓBERT KISS.

India: 02-516 Warsaw, ul. Rejtana 15/2–7; tel. (22) 8495800; fax (22) 8496705; e-mail hoc.warsaw@mea.gov.in; internet www.indianembassy.pl; Ambassador CHANDRA MOHAN BHANDARI.

Indonesia: 03-903 Warsaw, ul. Estońska 3–5; tel. (22) 6175179; fax (22) 6178451; e-mail info@indonesianembassy.pl; internet www.indonesianembassy.pl; Ambassador HAZAIRIN POHAN.

Iran: 03-928 Warsaw, ul. Królowej Aldony 22; tel. (22) 6171585; fax (22) 6178452; e-mail iranemb@iranemb.warsaw.pl; internet www.iranemb.warsaw.pl; Ambassador HADI FARAJVAND.

Iraq: 03-932 Warsaw, ul. Dąbrowiecka 9A; tel. (22) 6175773; fax (22) 6177065; e-mail iraqembassy@ambasadairaku.pl; Ambassador Dr WALID HAMID SHILTAGH.

Ireland: 00-496 Warsaw, ul. Mysia 5; tel. (22) 8496633; fax (22) 8498431; e-mail warsawembassy@dfa.ie; internet www.embassyofireland.pl; Ambassador DECLAN O'DONOVAN.

Israel: 02-078 Warsaw, ul. Krzywickiego 24; tel. (22) 5970500; fax (22) 8251607; e-mail publicaffairs@warsaw.mfa.gov.il; internet www.israel.pl; Ambassador DAVID ABRAHAM AKIVA PELEG.

Italy: 00-055 Warsaw, pl. Dąbrowskiego 6; tel. (22) 8263471; fax (22) 8278507; e-mail ambasciata.varsavia@esteri.it; internet www.ambvarsavia.esteri.it; Ambassador ALDO MANTOVANI.

Japan: 00-464 Warsaw, ul. Szwoleżerów 8; tel. (22) 6965000; fax (22) 6965001; e-mail info-cul@emb-japan.pl; internet www.pl.emb-japan.go.jp; Ambassador RYUICHI TANABE.

Kazakhstan: 02-954 Warsaw, ul. Królowej Marysieńki 14; tel. (22) 6425388; fax (22) 6423427; e-mail kazdipmis@hot.pl; internet www.kazakhstan.pl; Ambassador ALEKSEI VOLKOV.

Korea, Democratic People's Republic: 00-728 Warsaw, ul. Bobrowiecka 1A; tel. (22) 8405813; fax (22) 8405710; e-mail korembpl@yahoo.com; Ambassador KIM PYONG IL.

Korea, Republic: 00-464 Warsaw, ul. Szwoleżerów 6; tel. (22) 5592900; fax (22) 5592905; e-mail koremb_waw@mofat.go.kr; Chargé d'affaires a.i. KYONG-YUL LEE.

Kuwait: 00-486 Warsaw, ul. Franciszka Nullo 13; tel. (22) 6222860; fax (22) 6274314; e-mail embassy@kue.com.pl; Ambassador KHALED MOHAMMED ASH-SHAIBANI.

Laos: 02-386 Warsaw, ul. Usypiskowa 8; tel. (22) 6686699; fax (22) 6686690; e-mail sotholaw@yahoo.com; Chargé d'affaires a.i. SENGPHET HOUNGBOUNGNUANG.

Latvia: 03-928 Warsaw, ul. Królowej Aldony 19; tel. (22) 6174389; fax (22) 6174289; e-mail embassy.poland@mfa.gov.lv; internet www.latvia.pl; Ambassador ALBERTS SARKANIS.

Lebanon: 02-516 Warsaw, ul. Starościńska 1B/10–11; tel. (22) 8445065; fax (22) 6460030; e-mail embassy@lebanon.com.pl; internet www.lebanon.com.pl; Ambassador HIKMAT AOUAD.

Lithuania: 00-478 Warsaw, Al. Ujazdowskie 14; tel. (22) 6253368; fax (22) 6253440; e-mail ambasada@lietuva.pl; internet www.lietuva.pl; Ambassador EGIDIJUS MEILŪNAS.

Luxembourg: 00-789 Warsaw, ul. Słoneczna 15; tel. (22) 5078650; fax (22) 5078661; e-mail varsovie.amb@mae.etat.lu; Ambassador RONALD DOFING.

Macedonia, former Yugoslav republic: 02-954 Warsaw, ul. Królowej Marysieńki 40; tel. (22) 6517291; fax (22) 6517292; e-mail ambrmwar@zigzag.pl; internet www.ambasadarm.zigzag.pl; Ambassador DIMKO KOKAROVSKI.

Malaysia: 03-902 Warsaw, ul. Gruzińska 3; tel. (22) 6174413; fax (22) 6176256; e-mail mwwarsaw@poczta.neostrada.pl; Ambassador ROSMIDAH BINTE ZAHID.

Malta: 02-956 Warsaw, ul. Królewicza Jakuba 50; tel. (22) 6428694; fax (22) 6428698; e-mail maltaembassy.warsaw@gov.mt; Ambassador GAETAN NAUDI ACIS.

Mexico: 02-017 Warsaw, Al. Jerozolimskie 123, 20th floor; tel. (22) 6468800; fax (22) 6464222; e-mail embamex@embamex.pl; internet www.sre.gob.mx/polonia; Ambassador RAPHAEL STEGER CATAÑO.

Moldova: 02-710 Warsaw, ul. Imielińska 1; tel. and fax (22) 6462099; e-mail embassy@moldova.pl; internet www.moldova.pl; Ambassador BORIS GAMURARI.

Mongolia: 02-516 Warsaw, ul. Rejtana 15/16; tel. and fax (22) 8499391; e-mail mongamb@ikp.atm.com.pl; internet www.ambmong.net7.pl; Ambassador OTGON DAMBIINYAM.

Morocco: 02-516 Warsaw, ul. Starościńska 1/11–12; tel. (22) 8496341; fax (22) 8481840; e-mail info@moroccoembassy.org.pl; Ambassador MOHA OUALI TAGMA.

Directory

Netherlands: 00-468 Warsaw, ul. Kawalerii 10; tel. (22) 5591200; fax (22) 8402638; e-mail war@minbuza.nl; internet www.nlembassy.pl; Ambassador MARNIX KROP.

New Zealand: 00-536 Warsaw, Al. Ujazdowskie 51; tel. (22) 5210500; fax (22) 5210510; e-mail nzwsw@nzembassy.pl; Ambassador PENELOPE JANE RIDINGS.

Nigeria: 02-516 Warsaw, ul. Starościńska 1B/17; tel. (22) 5424117; fax (22) 5424113; e-mail info@nigeriaembassy.pl; Ambassador ASALINA RAYMOND MAMUNO.

Norway: 00-559 Warsaw, ul. Chopina 2A; tel. (22) 6964030; fax (22) 6280938; e-mail emb.warsaw@mfa.no; internet www.amb-norwegia.pl; Ambassador ENOK NYGAARD.

Pakistan: 02-516 Warsaw, ul. Starościńska 1/1–2; tel. (22) 8494808; fax (22) 8491160; e-mail parepwarsaw@wp.pl; Ambassador SEEMA ILAHI BALOCH.

Panama: 02-946 Warsaw, ul. Biedronki 13A; tel. (22) 6422143; fax (22) 6517616; e-mail panamaembassy@neostrada.pl; Ambassador ROKO IVÁN SETKA SAGEL.

Peru: 02-516 Warsaw, ul. Starościńska 1/3; tel. (22) 6468806; fax (22) 6468617; e-mail embperpl@atomnet.pl; internet www.perupol.pl; Ambassador JORGE DANTE FEDERICO CHÁVEZ SOTO.

Portugal: 03-905 Warsaw, ul. Francuska 37; tel. (22) 5111010; fax (22) 5111013; e-mail embaixada@embport.internetdsl.pl; internet www.ambasadaportugalii.pl; Ambassador JOSÉ DUARTE SEQUEIRA E SERPA.

Qatar: 00-493 Warsaw, ul. Prusa 2/271; tel. (22) 6222288; fax (22) 6225566; e-mail qtrembassypl@yahoo.com; Chargé d'affaires a.i. YOUSEF MOHAMED BILAL.

Romania: 00-559 Warsaw, ul. Chopina 10; tel. (22) 6283156; fax (22) 6285264; e-mail embassy@roembassy.com.pl; internet varsovia.mae.ro; Ambassador GHEORGHE PREDESCU.

Russia: 00-761 Warsaw, ul. Belwederska 49; tel. (22) 6213453; fax (22) 6253016; e-mail rusemb_poland@mail.ru; internet www.poland.mid.ru; Ambassador VLADIMIR M. GRININ.

Saudi Arabia: 00-739 Warsaw, ul. Stępińska 55; tel. (22) 8400000; fax (22) 8405636; e-mail info@saudiembassy.pl; internet www.saudiembassy.pl; Ambassador NASSER BIN AHMED AL-BRAIK.

Serbia: 00-729 Warsaw, Al. Rolna 175A–B; tel. (22) 6285161; fax (22) 6297173; e-mail embassy.warsaw@mfa.rs; Chargé d'affaires a.i. NIKOLA ŽUROVAC.

Slovakia: 00-581 Warsaw, ul. Litewska 6; tel. (22) 5258110; fax (22) 5258122; e-mail emb.warsaw@mzv.sk; internet www.ambasada-slowacji.pl; Ambassador FRANTIŠEK RUŽIČKA.

Slovenia: 02-516 Warsaw, ul. Starościńska 1/23–24; tel. (22) 8498282; fax (22) 8484090; e-mail vvr@gov.si; Ambassador JOŽEF DROFENIK.

South Africa: 00-675 Warsaw, ul. Koszykowa 54, 6th floor; tel. (22) 6256228; fax (22) 6256270; e-mail warsaw.political@foreign.gov.za; Ambassador FÉBÉ CHARLENE POTGIETER-GQUBULE.

Spain: 00-459 Warsaw, ul. Myśliwiecka 4; tel. (22) 5834000; fax (22) 6225408; e-mail embesppl@mail.mae.es; Ambassador FRANCISCO FERNÁNDEZ FÁBREGAS.

Sri Lanka: 02-665 Warsaw, Al. Wilanowska 313A; tel. (22) 8535648; fax (22) 8435348; e-mail lankaemb@medianet.pl; Ambassador (vacant).

Sweden: 00-585 Warsaw, ul. Bagatela 3; tel. (22) 6408900; fax (22) 6408983; e-mail ambassaden.warszawa@foreign.ministry.se; internet www.swedenabroad.com/warsaw; Ambassador DAG FILIP HARTELIUS.

Switzerland: 00-540 Warsaw, Al. Ujazdowskie 27; tel. (22) 6280481; fax (22) 6210548; e-mail var.vertretung@eda.admin.ch; internet www.eda.admin.ch/warsaw; Ambassador HANS BÉNÉDICT DE CERJAT.

Syria: 02-610 Warsaw, ul. Goszczyńskiego 30; tel. (22) 8484809; fax (22) 8489178; e-mail embsyria@palmyra.neostrada.pl; internet www.syrian-embassy.com; Chargé d'affaires a.i. WISSAL ISSA.

Thailand: 00-790 Warsaw, ul. Willowa 7; tel. (22) 8496414; fax (22) 8492630; e-mail thaiemb@thaiemb.internetdsl.pl; Ambassador THAKUR PHANIT.

Tunisia: 00-459 Warsaw, ul. Myśliwiecka 14; tel. (22) 6286330; fax (22) 6216295; e-mail at.varsovie@it.com.pl; Ambassador BÉCHIR CHEBAANE.

Turkey: 02-622 Warsaw, ul. Malczewskiego 32; tel. (22) 6464321; fax (22) 6463757; e-mail turkemb@zigzag.pl; Ambassador REŞIT UMAN.

Ukraine: 00-580 Warsaw, Al. J. Ch. Szucha 7; tel. (22) 6293446; fax (22) 6298103; e-mail emb_pl@mfa.gov.ua; internet www.mfa.gov.ua/poland; Ambassador OLEKSANDR F. MOTSYK.

United Kingdom: 00-556 Warsaw, Al. Róż 1; tel. (22) 3110000; fax (22) 3110311; e-mail info@britishembassy.pl; internet ukinpoland.fco.gov.uk; Ambassador DAMIAN RODERIC (RIC) TODD.

POLAND

USA: 00-540 Warsaw, Al. Ujazdowskie 29/31; tel. (22) 5042000; fax (22) 5042688; e-mail publicwrw@state.gov; internet poland.usembassy.gov; Ambassador VICTOR HENDERSON ASHE.

Uruguay: 02-516 Warsaw, ul. Rejtana 15/12; tel. (22) 8495040; fax (22) 6466887; e-mail urupol@urupol.ikp.pl; Ambassador JULIO GIAMBRUNO VIANA.

Uzbekistan: 02-804 Warsaw, ul. Kraski 21; tel. (22) 8946230; fax (22) 8946231; e-mail info@uzbekistan.pl; internet www.uzbekistan.pl; Chargé d'affaires a.i. UKTUR TURAEV.

Venezuela: 02-516 Warsaw, ul. Rejtana 15/20–21; tel. (22) 6468760; fax (22) 6468761; e-mail embajada@embavenez.pl; Chargé d'affaires a.i. ERICK MIGUEL MÁRQUEZ RODRÍGUEZ.

Viet Nam: 02-956 Warsaw, ul. Resorowa 36; tel. (22) 6516098; fax (22) 6516095; e-mail vnemb.pl@mofa.gov.vn; internet www.vietnamembassy-poland.org; Ambassador NGUYEN VAN XUONG.

Yemen: 02-956 Warsaw, ul. Królewicza Jakuba 54; tel. (22) 6176025; fax (22) 6176022; e-mail biuro@ambasada-jemenu.pl; Ambassador ALI ALI ABDULAZIZ AQLAN.

Judicial System

Supreme Court (Sąd Najwyższy Rzeczpospolitej Polskiej): 00-951 Warsaw, pl. Krasińskich 2/4/6; tel. (22) 5308000; fax (22) 5309100; e-mail pp@sn.pl; internet www.sn.pl; the highest judicial organ; exercises supervision over the decision-making of all other courts; justices are appointed by the President of the Republic on motions of the National Council of Judiciary and serve until the age of retirement. The First President of the Supreme Court is appointed from among the Supreme Court Justices by the President of the Republic, and serves a six-year term. The First President is also the Chairman of the Tribunal of State (Trybunał Stanu), before which certain, constitutionally determined, high state positions are accountable for violations of the Constitution or statutes; First Pres. Prof. LECH GARDOCKI.

Supreme Administrative Court (Naczelny Sąd Administracyjny): 00-013 Warsaw, ul. Jasna 6; tel. (22) 5516000; fax (22) 8267531; e-mail informacje@nsa.gov.pl; internet www.nsa.gov.pl; f. 1980; examines complaints concerning the legality of administrative decisions; 11 regional brs; Pres. JANUSZ TRZCIŃSKI.

Constitutional Tribunal (Trybunał Konstytucyjny): 00-918 Warsaw, Al. J. Ch. Szucha 12A; tel. and fax (22) 6295526; e-mail prasainfo@trybunal.gov.pl; internet www.trybunal.gov.pl; comprises 15 judges, each appointed by the Sejm for a nine-year term; supervises compliance of legislation with the Constitution; Pres. JERZY STĘPIEŃ.

Religion

CHRISTIANITY

The Roman Catholic Church

The Roman Catholic Church was granted full legal status in May 1989, when legislation guaranteeing freedom of worship was approved. The Church was also permitted to administer its own affairs, and to operate schools, hospitals and other charitable organizations. A Concordat, agreed by the Polish Government and the Holy See in 1993, was ratified in January 1998.

For ecclesiastical purposes, Poland comprises 15 archdioceses (including one for the Catholics of the Byzantine-Ukrainian rite) and 28 dioceses (including one for the Catholics of the Byzantine-Ukrainian rite), an Ordinariate for the faithful of the Oriental rite, and a Military Ordinariate. At 31 December 2006 there were some 34.3m. adherents in Poland (96.2% of the population).

Bishops' Conference: 01-015 Warsaw, Skwer Kardynała Stefana Wyszyńskiego 6; tel. (22) 5304800; fax (22) 8380967; Pres. Most Rev. JÓZEF MICHALIK (Latin Rite Archbishop of Przemyśl).

Primate of Poland: Cardinal JÓZEF GLEMP (Archbishop Emeritus of Warsaw).

Latin Rite

Archbishop of Białystok: Most Rev. EDWARD OZOROWSKI, 15-087 Białystok, Pl. Jana Pawła II 1; tel. (85) 7416473; fax (85) 7322213; e-mail sekretariat@bialystok.opoka.org.pl.

Archbishop of Częstochowa: Most Rev. STANISŁAW NOWAK, 42-200 Częstochowa, Al. Najśw. Maryi Panny 54; tel. (34) 3241044; fax (34) 3651182; e-mail kuria@czestochowa.opoka.org.pl.

Archbishop of Gdańsk: Most Rev. SŁAWOJ LESZEK GŁÓDŹ, 80-330 Gdańsk-Oliwa, ul. Biskupa Edmunda Nowickiego 1; tel. (58) 5520051; fax (58) 5522775; e-mail kuria@diecezja.gda.pl.

Archbishop of Gniezno: Most Rev. HENRYK MUSZYŃSKI, 62-200 Gniezno, ul. Kanclerza Jana Łaskiego 7; tel. (61) 4262102; fax (61) 4262105; e-mail kuriagni@gniezno.opoka.org.pl.

Archbishop of Katowice: Most Rev. DAMIAN ZIMOŃ, 40-043 Katowice, ul. Jordana 39; tel. (32) 2512160; fax (32) 2514830; e-mail kancelaria@kuria.katowice.pl.

Archbishop of Kraków: Cardinal STANISŁAW DZIWISZ, 31-004 Kraków, ul. Franciszkańska 3; tel. (12) 6288100; fax (12) 4294617; e-mail kuria@diecezja.krakow.pl.

Archbishop of Łódź: Most Rev. WŁADYSŁAW ZIÓŁEK, 90-458 Łódź, ul. Ks Ignacego Skorupki 1; tel. (42) 6648700; fax (42) 6648796; e-mail kuria@archidiecezja.lodz.pl.

Archbishop of Lublin: Most Rev. JÓZEF MIROSŁAW ŻYCIŃSKI, 20-950 Lublin, ul. Ks Prymasa Stefana Wyszyńskiego 2; tel. (81) 5321058; fax (81) 5346141; e-mail kanclerz@kuria.lublin.pl.

Archbishop of Poznań: Most Rev. STANISŁAW GĄDECKI, 61-109 Poznań, ul. Ostrów Tumski 2; tel. (61) 8512800; fax (61) 8512814; e-mail kuria@archpoznan.org.pl.

Archbishop of Przemyśl (Latin Rite): Most Rev. JÓZEF MICHALIK, 37-700 Przemyśl, pl. Katedralny 4A; tel. (16) 6786694; fax (16) 6782674; e-mail kuria@przemysl.opoka.org.pl.

Archbishop of Szczecin-Kamień: Most Rev. ANDRZEJ DZIĘGA, 71-459 Szczecin, ul. Papieża Pawła VI 4; tel. (91) 4542292; fax (91) 4536908; e-mail kuria@szczecin.opoka.org.pl.

Archbishop of Warmia: Most Rev. WOJCIECH ZIEMBA, 10-006 Olsztyn, ul. Pieniężnego 22; tel. (89) 5272280; fax (89) 5355172; e-mail kuria@olsztyn.opoka.org.pl.

Archbishop of Warsaw: Most Rev KAZIMIERZ NYCZ, 00-246 Warsaw, ul. Miodowa 17/19; tel. (22) 5317200; fax (22) 6354324; e-mail kanclerz@mkw.pl; internet www.spp.episkopat.pl.

Archbishop of Wrocław: Most Rev. MARIAN GOŁĘBIEWSKI, 50-328 Wrocław, ul. Katedralna 13; tel. (71) 3271111; fax (71) 3228269; e-mail kuria@archidiecezja.wroc.pl.

Byzantine-Ukrainian Rite

Archbishop of Przemyśl-Warsaw: Most Rev. IVAN MARTYNIAK, 37-700 Przemyśl, ul. Basztowa 13; tel. and fax (16) 6787868; e-mail kuria@przemyslgr.opoka.pl.

The Orthodox Church

Polish Autocephalous Orthodox Church (Polski Autokefaliczny Kościół Prawosławny): 03-402 Warsaw, Al. Solidarności 52; tel. (22) 6190886; fax (22) 6192996; e-mail kancelaria@orthodox.pl; internet www.orthodox.pl; comprises six dioceses, seven archbishoprics and three bishoprics; 509,500 mems (2001); Archbishop of Warsaw and Metropolitan of All Poland Sawa (MICHAŁ HRYCUNIAK).

Protestant Churches

In 1999 there were an estimated 148,738 Protestants in Poland.

Evangelical Augsburg (Lutheran) Church in Poland (Kościół Ewangelicko-Augsburski czyli Luterański w Polsce): 00-246 Warsaw, ul. Miodowa 21; tel. (22) 8870200; fax (22) 8870218; e-mail luteranie@luteranie.pl; internet www.luteranie.pl; 75,000 mems, 134 parishes (2007); Bishop and Pres. of Consistory JANUSZ JAGUCKI.

Pentecostal Church in Poland (Kościół Zielonoświątkowy w Polsce): 00-825 Warsaw, ul. Sienna 68/70; tel. and fax (22) 5951820; e-mail sekretariat@kz.pl; internet www.kz.pl; f. 1910; 20,000 mems (2000); Chief Presbyter Bishop MIECZYSŁAW CZAJKO.

There are also several other small Protestant churches, including the Church of Christ, the Church of Evangelical Christians, the Evangelical Christian Church, the Jehovah's Witnesses, the Pentecostal Church, the Seventh-day Adventist Church and the United Methodist Church.

ISLAM

In 1999 there were about 5,125 Muslims, principally of Tatar origin, in Białystok Voivodship (Prefecture), in eastern Poland, and smaller communities in Warsaw, Gdańsk and elsewhere.

Religious Union of Muslims in Poland (Muzułmański Związek Religijny): 15-426 Białystok, Rynek Kosciuszki 26/2; tel. (85) 414970; Chair. STEFAN MUCHARSKI.

JUDAISM

The overwhelming majority of the Jewish population of Poland were killed during the occupation by Nazi Germany in the Second World War (1939–45). In the mid-2000s there were believed to be between 10,000 and 20,000 Jews in Poland.

Union of Jewish Communities in Poland (Związek Gmin Wyznaniowych Żydowskich w Rzeczypospolitej Polskiej): 00-950 Warsaw, ul. Twarda 6; tel. (22) 6204324; fax (22) 6201037; e-mail union@

POLAND

jewish.org.pl; 14 synagogues and about 2,500 registered mems; Pres. Piotr Kadlčik.

The Press

In 2003 there were 54 newspapers in Poland, with a total circulation of 4,335,000. In that year there were 5,627 periodicals, with a combined circulation of 69.4m. copies.

Axel Springer Polska Sp. z o.o.: 02-672 Warsaw, ul. Domaniewska 52; tel. (22) 2320000; e-mail asp@axelspringer.pl; internet axelspringer.pl; subsidiary of Axel Springer AG (Germany); publishes two major dailies, *Dziennik* and *Fakt*, and is the country's second largest magazine publisher, printing women's, fiction, computer, food, economics, news and motoring magazines; Chair. of Management Bd Florian Fels.

WARSAW DAILIES

Dziennik (Daily): 02-672 Warsaw, ul. Domaniewska 52; fax (22) 2325550; internet www.dziennik.pl; f. 2006; Mon.–Sat; publ. by Axel Springer Polska; Editor-in-Chief Robert Krasowski; circ. 259,039 (2006).

Fakt (Fact): 02-672 Warsaw, ul. Domaniewska 52; tel. (22) 6085554; fax (22) 6085508; e-mail redakcja@efakt.pl; internet www.efakt.pl; f. 2003; owned by Axel Springer Polska Sp. z o.o.; Editor Katarzyna Sielicka; circ. 520,000.

Gazeta Wyborcza: 00-732 Warsaw, ul. Czerska 8/10; tel. (22) 5556000; fax (22) 5554780; e-mail listy@agora.pl; internet wyborcza.gazeta.pl; f. 1989; non-party; national edn and 20 local edns; weekend edn: *Gazeta Świateczna* ; special supplements; Editor-in-Chief Adam Michnik; circ. 516,000 (weekdays), 86,000 (weekends).

Nasz Dziennik (Our Daily): 04-476 Warsaw, ul. Żeligowskiego 16/20; tel. (22) 5157777; fax (22) 5157778; e-mail redakcja@naszdziennik.pl; internet www.naszdziennik.pl; national; Editor Ewa Sołowiej; circ. 250,000.

Polska Zbrojna (Military Poland): 00-909 Warsaw, Al. Jerozolimskie 97; tel. (22) 6845365; fax (22) 6845503; e-mail sekretariat@redakcjawojskowa.pl; internet www.polska-zbrojna.pl; f. 1943; Editor Jerzy Śląski; circ. 50,000.

Przegląd Sportowy (Sports Review): 02-672 Warsaw, Al. Domaniewska 52; tel. (22) 2320000; fax (22) 218697; e-mail asp@axelspringer.pl; internet www.sports.pl; f. 1921; Editor Maciej Polkowski; circ. 110,000.

Rzeczpospolita (The Republic): 02-015 Warsaw, pl. Starynkiewicza 7; tel. (22) 6283401; fax (22) 6280588; e-mail p.aleksandrowicz@rzeczpospolita.pl; internet www.rp.pl; f. 1982; 51% owned by Orkla (Norway); Editor-in-Chief Grzegorz Gauden; circ. 275,000.

Super Express: 00-939 Warsaw, ul. Jubilerska 10; tel. (22) 5159000; fax (22) 5159100; e-mail listy@superexpress.com.pl; internet www.se.com.pl; f. 1991; popular; Editor-in-Chief Sławomir Jastrzębowski; circ. 371,106.

Trybuna (Tribune): 00-835 Warsaw, ul. Miedziana 11; tel. (22) 3898831; fax (22) 6204100; e-mail redakcja@trybuna.com.pl; f. 1990; organ of Polish Social Democracy; Editor-in-Chief Wiesław Dębski; circ. 110,000 (weekdays), 150,000 (weekends).

Wprost (To The Point): 02-017 Warsaw, Al. Jerozolimskie 123, Reform Plaza; tel. (22) 5291100; fax (22) 8529016; e-mail redakcja@wprost.pl; internet www.wprost.pl; f. 1982; news and comment; Publr Marek Król; Editor-in-Chief Stanisław Janecki.

Życie Warszawy (Warsaw Life): 00-175 Warsaw, Al. Jana Pawła II 80; tel. (22) 3348855; fax (22) 3348863; e-mail zycie@zw.com.pl; internet www.zw.com.pl; f. 1944; independent; Editor-in-Chief Andrzej Załucki; circ. 250,000 (weekdays), 460,000 (weekends).

REGIONAL DAILIES

Dziennik Bałtycki (Baltic Newspaper): 80-894 Gdańsk, Targ Drzewny 9/11; tel. (58) 3003180; fax (58) 3003303; e-mail opinie@prasabalt.gda.pl; internet www.dziennikbaltycki.pl; f. 1945; non-party; Chief Editor Maciej Wośko; circ. 180,000.

Dziennik Łódzki (Łódź Daily): 90-532 Łódź, ul. Ks. Skorupki 17/19; tel. (42) 6303565; fax (42) 6377364; e-mail dziennik@dziennik.lodz.pl; internet www.dziennik.lodz.pl; f. 1945; non-party; Editor Julian Beck; circ. 50,000 (weekdays), 110,000 (weekends).

Dziennik Polski (Polish Daily): 31-072 Kraków, ul. Wielopole 1; tel. (12) 6199200; fax (12) 6199276; e-mail redakcja@dziennik.krakow.pl; internet www.dziennik.krakow.pl; Editor Piotr Aleksandrowicz.

Dziennik Wschodni (Eastern Daily): 20-081 Lublin, ul. Staszica 20; tel. (81) 4626800; fax (81) 4626801; e-mail redakcja@dziennikwschodni.pl; internet www.dziennikwschodni.pl; Chief Editor Krzysztof Wiejak.

Dziennik Zachodni (Western Daily): 40-954 Katowice, ul. Młyńska 1; tel. (32) 3582100; fax (32) 1538196; e-mail redakcja@dz.com.pl; internet www.dz.com.pl; f. 1945; non-party; Chief Editor Marek Chyliński; circ. 510,000.

Echo Dnia (Echo of the Day): 25-520 Kielce, ul. Targowa 18; tel. (41) 3495353; fax (41) 3682218; e-mail redakcja@echodnia.eu; internet www.echondnia.eu; f. 1971; Chief Editor Stanisław Wróbel.

Gazeta Krakowska (Kraków Gazette): 31-548 Kraków, Al. Pokoju 3; tel. (12) 6888000; fax (12) 6888109; e-mail sekretariat@gk.pl; internet www.gk.pl; f. 1949; Editor-in-Chief Marek Zalejski; circ. 60,000 (weekdays), 150,000 (weekends).

Gazeta Lubuska: 65-042 Zielona Góra, Al. Niepodległości 25, POB 120; tel. (68) 3248811; fax (68) 3248815; e-mail redakcja@gazetalubuska.pl; internet www.gazetalubuska.pl; f. 1952; independent; Chief Editor Iwona Zielińska; circ. 60,000 (weekdays), 150,000 (weekends).

Gazeta Olsztyńska (Olsztyn Gazette): 10-364 Olsztyn, ul. Tracka 5; tel. (89) 5397520; e-mail internet@gazetaolsztynska.pl; internet gazetaolsztynska.wm.pl; f. 1886; Editor-in-Chief Tomasz Srutkowski; circ. 45,000 (weekdays), 90,000 (weekends).

Gazeta Pomorska: 85-063 Bydgoszcz, ul. Zamoyskiego 2; tel. (52) 3263100; fax (52) 3221542; internet www.pomorska.pl; f. 1948; independent; Editor Maciej Kamiński; circ. 100,000 (weekdays), 300,000 (weekends).

Gazeta Robotnicza (Workers' Gazette): 50-010 Wrocław, ul. Podwale 62; tel. and fax (71) 335756; f. 1948; Editor Andrzej Bułat; circ. 30,000 (weekdays), 315,000 (weekends).

Gazeta Wrocławska (Wrocław Gazette): 53-611 Wrocław, ul. Strzegomska 42a; tel. (71) 3748151; fax (71) 3748175; e-mail redakcja@gazeta.wroc.pl; internet gazeta.naszemiasto.pl; Editor-in-Chief Marek Twaróg.

Gazeta Współczesna: 15-419 Białystok, POB 193, ul. Św. Mikołaja 1; tel. (85) 7487474; fax (85) 7487473; e-mail online@wspolczesna.pl; internet www.wspolczesna.pl; f. 1951; Editor Konrad Kruszewski; circ. 35,000.

Głos Pomorza (Voice of Pomerania): 76-200 Słupsk, ul. Pobożnego 19; tel. (59) 8488100; fax (59) 8488104; e-mail online@gp24.pl; internet www.gp24.pl; f. 1952; Chief Editor Krzysztof Nałęcz; circ. 60,000 (weekdays), 130,000 (weekends).

Głos Szczeciński (Szczecin Voice): 70-550 Szczecin, ul. Nowy Rynek 3; tel. (91) 4813300; fax (91) 4334864; e-mail online@gs24.pl; internet www.gs24.pl; f. 1947; Chief Editor Krzysztof Nałęcz; circ. 30,000 (weekdays), 100,000 (weekends).

Głos Wielkopolski (Voice of Wielkopolska): 60-782 Poznań, ul. Grunwaldzka 19; tel. (61) 8694100; fax (61) 8659672; e-mail glosmar@sylaba.poznan.pl; internet www.glos.com; f. 1945; independent; Editor-in-Chief Marek Przybylski; circ. 110,000 (weekdays), 160,000 (weekends).

Kurier Lubelski (Lublin Courier): 20-950 Lublin, POB 176; tel. (81) 5326634; fax (81) 5326835; e-mail redakcja@kurierlubelski.pl; internet www.kurier.lublin.pl; f. 1830; independent; evening; Editor Małgorzata Ilka; circ. 40,000 (weekdays), 100,000 (weekends).

Kurier Szczeciński (Szczecin Courier): 70-550 Szczecin, pl. Hołdu Pruskiego 8; tel. and fax (91) 4345741; e-mail redakcja@kurier.szczecin.pl; internet www.kurier.szczecin.pl; Editor Andrzej Łapciewicz.

Noviny (News): 35-016 Rzeszów, ul. Kraszewskiego 2; tel. (17) 8672200; fax (17) 8672201; e-mail nowiny@gcnowiny.pl; internet www.gcnowiny.pl; f. 1949; evening; Editor-in-Chief Janusz Pawlak; circ. 100,000.

Nowa Trybuna Opolska (New Opole Tribune): 45-086 Opole, ul. Powstańców Śląskich 9; tel. (77) 4432500; fax (77) 4432515; e-mail nto@nto.pl; internet www.nto.pl; f. 1952; independent; Editor Wojciech Potocki; circ. 80,000.

Trybuna Śląska (Silesian Tribune): 40-092 Katowice, ul. Młyńska 1; tel. (32) 2537822; fax (32) 2537997; f. 1945; independent; Editor Romuald Orzet; circ. 180,000 (weekdays), 800,000 (weekends).

PERIODICALS

Computerworld Polska: 04-204 Warsaw, ul. Jordanowska 12, POB 73; tel. (22) 3217810; fax (22) 3217888; e-mail Krzysztof_Frydrychowicz@idg.com.pl; internet www.computerworld.pl; weekly; Editor-in-Chief Krzysztof Frydrychowicz.

Dobre Rady (Good Advice): 54-238 Wrocław, ul. Ostrowkiego 7; tel. (71) 3517758; fax (71) 3737288; e-mail a.sokolowska@burda.pl; internet burdamedia.pl/gazeta1.php?g=dr; f. 2002; publ. by Burda Polska; Chief Editor Beata Dzięgielewska.

Dom i Wnętrze (Home and Interior): 00-480 Warsaw, ul. Wiejska 19; tel. (22) 5842200; fax (22) 5842318; internet www.domiwnetrze.pl; f. 1991; illustrated monthly; Editor-in-Chief EWA MIERZEJEWSKA.

Dziecko (Child): 00-732 Warsaw, ul. Czerska 8/10; tel. (22) 5556882; fax (22) 5556669; e-mail dziecko@agora.pl; internet www.edziecko.pl; f. 1995; monthly; women's magazine concerning children's affairs; Editor JUSTYNA DĄBROWSKA; circ. 150,000 (2008).

Dziewczyna (Girl): 02-222 Warsaw, Al. Jerozolimskie 181, Axel Springer Polska; tel. (22) 6363681; fax (22) 6365281; e-mail redakcja@dziewczyna.pl; internet www.dziewczyna.pl; f. 1990; monthly; lifestyle magazine for young women; Editor DONATA CIEŚLIK; circ. 420,000.

Les Echos de Pologne: 02-536 Warsaw, ul. Narbutta 15A/6; tel. (22) 6464212; fax (22) 6462369; e-mail echos@echos.pl; internet www.echos.pl; f. 2003; fortnightly; in French; Editor-in-Chief SYLWIA KAMIŃSKA.

Gazeta Bankowa (Banking Gazette): 00-140 Warsaw, Al. Solidarności 117; tel. (22) 6525914; fax (22) 6525910; e-mail redakcja@wtrendy.pl; internet www.gazetabankowa.pl; f. 1988; weekly; business and finance; Editor-in-Chief ANDRZEJ S. NARTOWSKI.

Głos Nauczycielski (Teachers' Voice): 00-389 Warsaw, ul. J. Smulikowskiego 6/8; tel. (22) 8263420; fax (22) 8281355; e-mail glos@glos.pl; internet www.glos.pl; f. 1917; weekly; organ of the Polish Teachers' Union; Chief Editor JAKUB RZEKANOWKSI (acting); circ. 40,000.

Lubię Gotować (I Love Cooking): 00-732 Warsaw, ul. Czerska 8/10; tel. (22) 5556606; fax (22) 5556668; e-mail czasopisma@agora.pl; internet www.lubiegotowac.pl; f. 1997; monthly; cookery; Editor-in-Chief JOANNA NOWICKA.

Nie (No): 00-789 Warsaw, ul. Słoneczna 25; tel. (22) 6286794; fax (22) 6220731; e-mail nie@redakija.nie.com.pl; internet www.nie.com.pl; f. 1990; satirical; weekly; Editor JERZY URBAN; circ. 500,000.

Nowa Fantastyka (New Fantasy): 02-651 Warsaw, ul. Garażowa 7; tel. (22) 6077790; fax (22) 8482266; e-mail nowafantastyka@fantastyka.pl; internet www.fantastyka.pl; f. 1982; monthly; science fiction and fantasy; Editor-in-Chief PAWEŁ MATUSZEK; circ. 57,000.

Nowe Życie Gospodarcze (New Economic Life): 00-549 Warsaw, ul. Piękna 24/26; tel. (22) 6280628; fax (22) 6288392; e-mail nzg@nzg.pl; internet www.nzg.pl; f. 1945 as Życie Gospodarcze (Economic Life); weekly; economic; Chair. and Editor-in-Chief ADAM CYMER; circ. 35,700.

Państwo i Prawo (State and Law): 00-330 Warsaw, ul. Nowy Świat 72; tel. (22) 6288296; e-mail panstwoiprawo@pwp.pl; internet www.panstwoiprawo.pl; f. 1946; monthly organ of the Polish Academy of Sciences; publ. by Wolters Kluwer Polska; Chief Editor Dr LESZEK KUBICKI; circ. 3,000.

Polityka (Politics): 02-309 Warsaw, ul. Słupecka 6, POB 13; tel. (22) 4516133; fax (22) 4516135; e-mail polityka@polityka.com.pl; internet polityka.onet.pl; f. 1957; weekly; political, economic, cultural; Editor JERZY BACZYŃSKI; circ. 340,000.

Poradnik Gospodarski (Farmers' Guide): 60-163 Poznań, ul. Sieradzka 29; tel. and fax (61) 8685492; e-mail poradnik.gospodarsk@wodr.poznan.pl; internet www.poradnik.wodr.poznan.pl; f. 1889; monthly; agriculture; Editor-in-Chief TADEUSZ SZALCZYK; circ. 10,000.

Przekrój (Review): 00-480 Warsaw, ul. Wiejska 19; tel. (22) 2842533; fax (22) 5842521; e-mail redakcja@przekroj.pl; internet www.przekroj.pl; f. 1945; weekly; illustrated; cultural; Chief Editor JACEK KOWALCZYK; circ. 77,500.

Przyjaciółka (Girlfriend): 00-480 Warsaw, ul. Wiejska 19; tel. (22) 5842438; fax (22) 5842436; e-mail info@przyjaciolka.pl; internet www.przyjaciolka.pl; f. 1948; weekly; women's magazine; Editor-in-Chief AGNIESZKA SWIECKA-PILASZEK; circ. 720,000.

Res Publica Nowa (The New Republic): 02-309 Warsaw 1, ul. Słupecka 6, POB 856; tel. (22) 4516180; fax (22) 4516109; e-mail respublica@pro.onet.pl; internet respublica.onet.pl; f. 1987; monthly; political and cultural; Editor MARCIN KRÓL; circ. 5,000.

Sprawy Międzynarodowe (International Affairs): 02-630 Warsaw, ul. Tyniecka 15/17; tel. (22) 5239086; fax (22) 5239027; e-mail sprawy@pism.pl; internet www.sprawymiedzynarodowe.pl; f. 1948; quarterly; publ. by Polish Institute of International Affairs; Editor HENRYK SZLAJFER; circ. 800.

Swiat Nauki (World of Science): 02-651 Warsaw, ul. Garażowa 7; tel. (22) 6077815; fax (22) 8482266; e-mail swiatnauki@proszynskimedia.pl; internet www.swiatnauki.pl; f. 1991; monthly; Polish edn of Scientific American; Editor-in-Chief JOANNA ZIMAKOWSKA; circ. 45,000.

Szpilki (Needles): Warsaw; tel. (22) 6280429; f. 1935; weekly; illustrated; satirical; Editor JACEK JANCZARSKI; circ. 100,000.

Tygodnik Solidarność (Solidarity Weekly): 02-390 Warsaw, ul. Grójecka 186, POB 613; tel. and fax (22) 8822796; e-mail redakcja@tygodniksolidarnosc.com; internet www.tygodniksolidarnosc.com; f. 1981; reactivated 1989; weekly; Editor-in-Chief JERZY KŁOSIŃSKI; circ. 60,000.

The Warsaw Voice: 01-452 Warsaw, ul. Księcia Janusza 64; tel. (22) 3359700; fax (22) 3359720; e-mail voice@warsawvoice.pl; internet www.warsawvoice.pl; f. 1988; weekly; political, social, cultural and economic; in English; Editor ANDRZEJ JONAS; circ. 10,500.

Wiedza i Życie (Knowledge and Life): 02-651 Warsaw, ul. Garażowa 7; tel. (22) 6077630; fax (22) 6077645; e-mail wiedza@proszynski.com.pl; internet www.proszynski.com.pl/wiedzaizycie; f. 1926; monthly; popular science; Editor ANDRZEJ GORZYM; circ. 112,000.

NEWS AGENCY

Polska Agencja Prasowa (PAP) (Polish Press Agency): 00-502 Warsaw, ul. Bracka 6/8; tel. (22) 6280001; fax (22) 6286407; e-mail webmaster@pap.com.pl; internet www.pap.com.pl; f. 1944; brs in 28 Polish towns and 22 foreign capitals; 274 journalist and photojournalist mems; Pres. PIOTR SKWIECINSKI.

PRESS ASSOCIATION

Stowarzyszenie Dziennikarzy Polskich (SDP) (Polish Journalists' Association): 00-366 Warsaw, ul. Foksal 3/5; tel. and fax (22) 8278720; e-mail sdp@sdp.pl; internet www.sdp.pl; f. 1951; dissolved 1982, legal status restored 1989; 2,320 mems; Pres. KRYSTYNA MOKROSIŃSKA; Gen. Sec. STEFAN TRUSZCZYŃSKI.

Publishers

Bertelsmann Media Sp. z o.o.: 02-786 Warsaw, ul. Rosoła 10; tel. (22) 6458200; fax (22) 6484732; e-mail poczta@swiatksiazki.com.pl; internet www.swiatksiazki.com.pl; f. 1994 as Bertelsmann Publishing Świat Książki Sp. z o.o.; belles lettres, science fiction, popular science, albums, books for children and teenagers; Pres. ANDRZEJ KOSTARCZYK; Editor-in-Chief BOGUSŁAW DĄBROWSKI.

Dom Wydawniczy ABC Sp. z o.o.: 01-231 Warsaw, ul. Płocka 5A; tel. (22) 5358000; fax (22) 5358001; e-mail info@abc.com.pl; internet www.abc.com.pl; f. 1989; legal, business and financial books; part of Polskie Wydawnictwa Profesjonalne Sp. z o.o; owned by Wolters Kluwer (Netherlands); Owners WŁODZIMIERZ ALBIN, KRZYSZTOF BRZESKI.

Dom Wydawniczy Bellona: 00-844 Warsaw, ul. Grzybowska 77; tel. (22) 6204291; fax (22) 6522695; e-mail bellona@bellona.pl; internet www.bellona.pl; f. 1947; fiction, history and military; Pres. Col JÓZEF SKRZYPIEC; Dir ZBIGNIEW CZERWIŃSKI.

Dom Wydawniczy Rebis Sp. z o.o.: 60-171 Poznań, ul. Żmigrodzka 41/49; tel. (61) 8678140; fax (61) 8673774; e-mail rebis@rebis.com.pl; internet www.rebis.com.pl; f. 1990; historical fiction, history of art; Pres. and Man. Dir TOMASZ SZPONDER.

Drukarnia i Księgarnia św. Wojciecha (St Adalbert—Wojciech Printing and Publishing Co): 60-967 Poznań, pl. Wolności 1; tel. (61) 8529186; fax (61) 8523746; e-mail wydawnictwo@ksw.com.pl; internet www.ksw.com.pl; f. 1895; textbooks and Catholic publications; Dir Rev. BOGDAN REFORMAT; Editor-in-Chief BOŻYSŁAW WALCZAK.

Egmont Sp. z o.o.: 01-029 Warsaw, ul. Dzielna 60; tel. (22) 8384100; fax (22) 8384200; e-mail kluby@egmont.pl; internet www.egmont.pl; f. 1990; books and comics for children and teenagers; Man. Dir JACEK BEŁDOWSKI; Editor-in-Chief HANNA BALTYN.

Instytut Wydawniczy Pax (Pax Publishing Institute): 00-390 Warsaw, ul. Wybrzeże Kościuszkowskie 21A; tel. (22) 6253398; fax (22) 6251378; e-mail iwpax@iwpax.com.pl; internet sklep.iwpax.com.pl; f. 1949; theology, philosophy, religion, history, literature; Dir KRZYSZTOF PRZESTRZELSKI; Editor-in-Chief ZBIGNIEW BOROWIK.

Muza SA: 00-590 Warsaw, ul. Marszałkowska 8; tel. (22) 6211776; fax (22) 6292349; e-mail muza@muza.com.pl; internet www.muza.com.pl; f. 1991; albums, encyclopedias, lexicons, handbooks, dictionaries, belles lettres, books for children and youth; Man. Dir MARCIN GARLINSKI.

Oficyna Wydawnicza Volumen: 00-354 Warsaw, ul. Dynasy 2A; tel. and fax (22) 8260501; f. 1984 (working clandestinely as WERS), 1989 officially; science, popular history, anthropology and sociopolitical sciences; Dir MIROSLAWA LATKOWSKA.

Pallottinum—Wydawnictwo Stowarzyszenia Apostolstwa Katolickiego: 60-959 Poznań, Al. Przybyszewskiego 30, POB 23; tel. (61) 8675233; fax (61) 8675238; e-mail pallottinum@pallottinum.pl; internet www.pallottinum.pl; f. 1947; religious and philosophical books; Dir STEFAN DUSZA.

Państwowe Wydawnictwo Rolnicze i Leśne (State Agricultural and Forestry Publishers): 02-272 Warsaw, ul. Malownicza 14; tel. and fax (22) 8684529; e-mail pwril@pwril.com; internet www.pwril.com; f. 1947; professional publications on agriculture, forestry,

POLAND
Directory

health and veterinary science; Dir and Editor-in-Chief JOLANTA KUCZYŃSKA.

Państwowy Instytut Wydawniczy (State Publishing Institute): 00-372 Warsaw, ul. Foksal 17; tel. (22) 8260201; fax (22) 8261536; e-mail piw@piw.pl; internet www.piw.pl; f. 1946; Polish and foreign classical and contemporary literature, fiction, literary criticism, biographies, performing arts, culture, history, popular science, and fine arts; Dir and Editor-in-Chief RAFAŁ SKĄPSKI.

Pierwszy wybór profesjonalisty: 01-231 Warsaw, ul. Płocka 5A; tel. (22) 5358000; fax (22) 5358001; e-mail obsluga.klienta@wolterskluwer.pl; internet www.pwp.pl; country's largest legal publisher; Pres. ALBIN WŁODZIMIERZ.

Polskie Przedsiębiorstwo Wydawnictw Kartograficznych im. E. Romera (E. Romer Polish Cartographical Publishing House): 02-389 Warsaw, Al. Bohaterów Września 9; tel. (22) 5851800; fax (22) 5851801; e-mail ppwk@ppwk.com.pl; internet www.ppwk.com.pl; f. 1951; maps, atlases, travel guides, books on geodesy and cartography; Man. Dir JACEK BŁASCZYŃSKI.

Polskie Wydawnictwo Muzyczne (Polish Publishing House for Music): 31-111 Kraków, Al. Krasińskiego 11 A; tel. (12) 4227044; fax (12) 4220174; e-mail pwm@pwm.com.pl; internet www.pwm.com.pl; f. 1945; music and books on music; Chair. and Man. Dir Dr SŁAWOMIR J. TABKOWSKI; Editor-in-Chief ANDRZEJ KOSOWSKI.

Prószyński i S-ka Publishing House: 02-651 Warsaw, ul. Garazowa 7; tel. (22) 6077700; fax (22) 6077704; e-mail wydawnictwo@proszynski.pl; internet www.proszynski.pl; f. 1990; poetry, fiction, non-fiction, educational text and reference books, popular science, etc.; Pres. MIECZYSŁAW PRÓSZYŃSKI; 110 employees.

Spółdzielnia Wydawnicza Czytelnik ('Reader' Co-operative Publishing House): 00-490 Warsaw, ul. Wiejska 12A; tel. (22) 5831407; fax (22) 6283178; e-mail sekretariat@czytelnik.pl; internet www.czytelnik.pl; f. 1944; general, especially fiction and contemporary Polish literature; Pres. MAREK ŻAKOWSKI; Editor-in-Chief JANUSZ DRZEWUCKI.

Spółdzielnia Wydawniczo-Handlowa 'Książka i Wiedza' ('Books and Knowledge' Trade Co-operative Publishing House): 00-375 Warsaw, ul. Smolna 13; tel. (22) 8275401; fax (22) 8279423; e-mail publisher@kiw.com.pl; internet www.kiw.com.pl; f. 1948; philosophy, religion, linguistics, literature and history; Chair. WŁODZIMIERZ GAŁĄSKA; Editor-in-Chief ELŻBIETA KONECKA.

Wydawnictwa Naukowo-Techniczne (Scientific-Technical Publishers): 00-048 Warsaw, ul. Mazowiecka 2/4, POB 359; tel. (22) 8267271; fax (22) 8268293; e-mail wnt@pol.pl; internet www.wnt.com.pl; f. 1949; scientific and technical; Man. Dir and Editor Dr ANIELA TOPULOS.

Wydawnictwa Szkolne i Pedagogiczne (WSiP) (School and Pedagogical Publishers): 00-965 Warsaw, Al. Jerozolimskie 136, p. 9; tel. (22) 5762510; fax (22) 5762509; e-mail wsip@wsip.com.pl; internet www.wsip.pl; f. 1945; school textbooks and popular science books, scientific literature for teachers, visual teaching aids, periodicals for teachers and youth; Chair. (vacant).

Wydawnictwo Arkady: 00-344 Warsaw, ul. Dobra 28, POB 137; tel. (22) 8269316; fax (22) 8274194; e-mail arkady@arkady.com.pl; internet www.arkady.com.pl; f. 1957; publications on building, town planning, architecture and art; Dir and Pres. JANINA KRYSIAK.

Wydawnictwo C. H. Beck.: 01-518 Warsaw, ul. Gen. Zajączka 9; tel. (22) 3377600; fax (22) 3377601; e-mail redakcja@beck.pl; internet www.beck.pl; f. 1993; law and economics; Man. Dir PAWEŁ ESSE.

Wydawnictwo Dolnośląskie Sp. z o.o.: 50-010 Wrocław, ul. Podwale 62; tel. (71) 7859040; fax (71) 7859066; e-mail sekretariat@wd.wroc.pl; internet www.wd.wroc.pl; f. 1986; *belles lettres*, essays, memoirs, translations, general non-fiction; Pres. of Bd ANDRZEJ ADAMUS.

Wydawnictwo Iskry (Sparks Publishing House Ltd): 00-375 Warsaw, ul. Smolna 11; tel. and fax (22) 8279415; e-mail iskry@iskry.com.pl; internet www.iskry.com.pl; f. 1952; travel, Polish and foreign fiction, science fiction, essays, popular science, history, memoirs; Chair. Dr WIESŁAW UCHAŃSKI; Editor-in-Chief MAGDALENA SŁYSZ.

Wydawnictwo Kurpisz: 01-341 Poznań, ul. Przemysława 46; tel. (61) 8331517; fax (61) 8351294; e-mail kurpisz@kurpisz.pl; internet www.kurpisz.pl; f. 1991; *belles lettres*, reprints, dictionaries, encyclopedias, periodicals; Dir KAZIMIERZ GRZESIAK.

Wydawnictwo Lekarskie PZWL (PZWL Medical Publishers): 00-251 Warsaw, ul. Miodowa 10; tel. and fax (22) 6954497; e-mail promocja@pzwl.pl; internet www.pzwl.pl; f. 1945; medical literature and manuals, lexicons, encyclopedias; Pres. KRYSTYNA REGULSKA.

Wydawnictwo Literackie (Literary Publishing House): 31-147 Kraków, ul. Długa 1; tel. (12) 4232254; fax (12) 4225423; e-mail redakcja@wl.net.pl; internet www.wl.net.pl; f. 1953; works of literature and *belles lettres*; Dir BARBARA DRWOTA; Editor-in-Chief MAŁGORZATA NYCZ.

Wydawnictwo Nasza Księgarnia (Our Booksellers' Publishing House): 02-868 Warsaw, ul. Sarabandy 24C; tel. (22) 6439389; fax (22) 6437028; e-mail naszaksiegarnia@nk.com.pl; internet www.nk.com.pl/nasza; f. 1921; books and periodicals for children and young readers; educational publications; Pres. AGNIESZKA TOKARCZYK; Editor JOLANTA SZTUCZYŃSKA.

Wydawnictwo Naukowe PWN (PWN Scientific Publishers): 02-676 Warsaw, ul. Postepu 18; tel. (22) 6954180; fax (22) 6954288; e-mail international@pwn.com.pl; internet www.pwn.pl; f. 1951; reference, academic, incl. multimedia; Pres. BARBARA JOZWIAK.

Wydawnictwo Nowa Era: 02-305 Warsaw, Al. Jerozolimskie 146D; tel. (22) 5702580; fax (22) 5702581; e-mail nowaera@nowaera.com.pl; internet www.nowaera.com.pl; school textbooks; Chair. MARIUSZ KOPER.

Wydawnictwo Ossolineum (Ossolineum Publishing House): 50-062 Wrocław, pl. Solny 14A; tel. (71) 3436961; fax (71) 3448103; e-mail wydawnictwo@ossolineum.pl; internet www.ossolineum.pl; f. 1817; publishing house of the Polish Academy of Sciences; academic publications in humanities and sciences; Man. Dir WOJCIECH KARWACKI; Editor-in-Chief STANISŁAW ROŚCICKI.

Wydawnictwo Prawnicze LexisNexis—LexPolonia (LexPolonia—LexisNexis Legal Publishing House): Warsaw; tel. (22) 5729500; fax (22) 5729508; e-mail biuro@lexisnexis.pl; internet www.lexisnexis.pl; f. 1952; present name adopted 2003; Exec. Dir OLGA DYMKOWSKA-PULCHNY.

Wydawnictwo Publicat: 61-003 Poznań, ul. Chlebowa 24; tel. (61) 8679546; fax (61) 6529200; internet www.najlepszyprezent.pl; f. 1990 as Wydawnictwo Podsiedlik-Raniowski Sp. z o.o.; popular and children's literature, poetry, prose, classical works, educational books; Pres. MICHAŁ KAIK.

Wydawnictwo Śląsk Sp. z o.o. (Silesia Publishing House Ltd): 40-161 Katowice, Al. W. Korfantego 51; tel. (32) 580756; fax (32) 583229; e-mail biuro@slaskwn.com.pl; internet www.slaskwn.com.pl; f. 1952; social, popular science, technical, and regional literature; Chair. and Editor-in-Chief Dr TADEUSZ SIERNY.

Wydawnictwo W.A.B. (WAB Publishers): 02-502 Warsaw, ul. Łowicka 31; tel. (22) 6460510; fax (22) 6460511; e-mail wab@wab.com.pl; internet www.wab.com.pl; f. 1991; contemporary Polish fiction, historical and cultural essays, and literature for children.

Wydawnictwo Wam (For You Publishers): 31-501 Kraków, ul. Kopernika 26; tel. (12) 6293200; fax (12) 4295003; e-mail wam@wydawnictwowam.pl; internet www.wydawnictwowam.pl; f. 1872; Roman Catholic textbooks, encyclopedias, non-fiction, fiction and children's books; Dir HENRYK PIETRAS.

Wydawnictwo Wiedza Powszechna (General Knowledge Publishers): 00-054 Warsaw, ul. Jasna 26; tel. and fax (22) 8270799; e-mail info@wiedza.pl; internet www.wiedza.pl; f. 1952; popular science books, Polish and foreign language dictionaries, foreign language textbooks, encyclopedias and lexicons; Dir TERESA KORSAK.

Wydawnictwo Zysk i S-ka (Zysk Publishers): 61-744 Poznań, ul. Wielka 10; tel. (61) 8532767; fax (61) 8526326; e-mail sekretariat@zysk.com.pl; internet www.zysk.com.pl; f. 1994; *belles lettres*, popular, scientific and religious literature; Pres. TADEUSZ ZYSK.

Znak Społeczny Instytut Wydawniczy (Znak Social Publishing Institute): 30-105 Kraków, ul. Kościuszki 37; tel. (12) 6199500; fax (12) 6199502; internet www.znak.com.pl; f. 1959; religion, philosophy, *belles lettres*, essays, history; Chief Exec. HENRYK WOŹNIAKOWSKI; Editor-in-Chief JERZY ILLG.

Broadcasting and Communications

TELECOMMUNICATIONS

Regulatory Authority

Office of Electronic Communications (Urząd Komunikacji Elektronicznej—UKE): 01-211 Warsaw, ul. Kasprzaka 18/20; tel. (22) 5349190; fax (22) 5349162; e-mail uke@uke.gov.pl; internet www.uke.gov.pl; f. 2001; formerly the Office of Telecommunications and Post Regulation (URTIP); reorganized Jan. 2006; Chair. ANNA STREŻYŃSKA.

Service Providers

Polkomtel: 02-676 Warsaw, ul. Postępu 3; tel. (22) 6071000; fax (22) 4260103; internet www.polkomtel.com.pl; f. 1996; provides mobile cellular telecommunications services under the brand names Plus GSM, SimplusTeam and mixPlus; 3G network commenced operations Sept. 2004; Pres. WŁADYSŁAW BARTOSZEWICZ.

Polska Telefonia Cyfrowa (PTC) (Polish Digital Telephone): 02-222 Al. Jerozolimskie 181, Warsaw; tel. (22) 4136000; fax (22) 4134949; e-mail biznes@era.pl; internet www.era.pl; f. 1996; provides mobile cellular telecommunications under the brand names

Era, Heyah and Blue Connect; 70.5% owned by T-Mobile Deutschland GmbH; 22.5% owned by T-Mobile Poland Holding B.V.; Chair. Dr KLAUS HARTMANN.

PTK Centertel (Polish Cellular Telecommunications Co 'Centertel'): 01-230 Warsaw, ul. Skierniewicka 10A; tel. (22) 6342882; fax (22) 5887883; e-mail info@idea.pl; internet www.orange.pl; f. 1998; provides mobile cellular telecommunications services under the brand name Orange; 66% owned by TP, 34% by France Telecom (France).

TP—Telekomunikacja Polska (Polish Telecommunications): 00-105 Warsaw, ul. Twarda 18; tel. (22) 5270000; internet www.tp.pl; f. 1992; mem. of France Telecom group (France); Chair. MACIEJ WITUCKI.

BROADCASTING

Regulatory Authority

National Broadcasting Council (Krajowa Rada Radiofonii i Telewizji—KRRiTV): 00-015 Warsaw, Skwer Kardinala Wyszyńskiego, Prymasa Polski 9; tel. (22) 5973001; fax (22) 5973054; internet www.krrit.gov.pl; f. 1993; Chair. ELŻBIETA KRUK.

Radio

Polskie Radio (Polish Radio): 00-977 Warsaw, Al. Niepodległości 77/85; tel. (22) 6459259; fax (22) 6455924; internet www.polskieradio.pl; home Service comprises four national channels, broadcasting 24 hours a day; foreign service broadcasts in Polish, English, German, Russian, Belarusian, Ukrainian and Hebrew; Pres. KRZYSZTOF CZABAŃSKI.

Radio Maryja: 87-100 Toruń, ul. Żwirki i Wigury 80; tel. (56) 6552361; fax (56) 6552362; e-mail radio@radiomaryja.pl; internet www.radiomaryja.pl; traditionalist Catholic; Dir TADEUSZ RYDZYK.

Radio Musyka Fakty (RMF FM): 30-204 Kraków, Al. Waszyngtona 1, Kopiec Kosciuszki; tel. (12) 4219696; fax (12) 4217895; e-mail redakcja@rmf.pl; internet www.rmf.pl; Pres. STANISŁAW TYCZYNSKI; Dir JOLANTA WIŚNIEWSKA.

Radio Zet: 00-503 Warsaw, ul. Żurawia 8; tel. (22) 5833382; fax (22) 5833356; e-mail radiozet@radiozet.com.pl; internet www.radiozet.com.pl; f. 1990; independent; 24 hours; national broadcasts commenced 1994; wholly owned by the Eurozet media group; Pres. and Editor-in-Chief ROBERT KOZYRA.

Television

Telewizja Polska (Polish Television): 00-999 Warsaw, ul. J. P. Woronicza 17, POB 211; tel. (22) 5474450; fax (22) 5477719; e-mail pr@tvp.pl; internet www.tvp.pl; f. 1952; Chair. BRONISŁAW WILDSTEIN.

PolSat: 04-028 Warsaw, Al. Stanów Zjednoczonyck 53; tel. (22) 5104001; fax (22) 5134295; internet www.polsat.com.pl; f. 1992; satellite broadcasts; Propr ZYGMUNT SOLORZ.

TVN: 02-952 Warsaw, ul. Wiertnicza 166; tel. (22) 8566060; fax (22) 8566666; e-mail widzowie@tvn.pl; internet www.tvn.pl; f. 1997; Pres. PIOTR WALTER.

Finance

(cap. = capital; res = reserves; dep. = deposits; m. = million; amounts in new złotys unless otherwise indicated; brs = branches)

BANKING

Foreign banks were permitted to operate freely in the country from 1997. In early 2009 there were 53 domestic commercial banks and 20 branches of credit institutions operating in Poland.

Supervisory Authority

Polish Financial Supervision Authority (PFSA) (Komisja Nadzoru Finansowego): 00-950 Warsaw, Plac Powstańców Warszawy 1; tel. (22) 3326600; fax (22) 3326602; internet www.knf.gov.pl; f. 2008 to succeed Financial Supervision Commission; Chair. STANISŁAW KLUZA.

National Bank

Narodowy Bank Polski—NBP (National Bank of Poland): 00-919 Warsaw, ul. Świętokrzyska 11/21, POB 1011; tel. (22) 6531000; fax (22) 6208518; e-mail nbp@nbp.pl; internet www.nbp.pl; f. 1945; state central bank; cap. 1,500.0m., res 943.0m., dep. 63,704.8m. (Dec. 2006); Pres. SŁAWOMIR SKRZYPEK; 16 brs.

Other Banks

Bank BPH SA: 31-548 Kraków, Al. Pokoju 1; tel. (12) 6186888; fax (12) 6186863; e-mail bank@bphpbk.pl; internet www.bph.pl; f. 1989; fmrly Bank Przemysłowo-Handlowy PBK SA; present name adopted 2004; 52.1% owned by Bank Austria Creditanstalt AG (HVB Group, Austria); total assets 13,027.4m., dep. 9,698.7m. (Dec. 2007); Pres. JÓZEF WANCER; 201 brs.

Bank Gospodarki Żywnościowej—BGZ (BGZ) (Bank of Food Economy): 01-211 Warsaw, ul. Kasprzaka 10/16; tel. (22) 8604000; fax (22) 8605000; e-mail info@bgz.pl; internet www.bgz.pl; f. 1919; present name adopted 1994; universal commercial bank; finances agriculture, forestry and food-processing; 37.3% state-owned; 44.5% owned by Rabobank (Netherlands); cap. 37.0m., res 1,386.1m., dep. 16,038.7m. (Dec. 2006); Exec. Pres. JACEK BARTKIEWICZ; 256 brs.

Bank Gospodarstwa Krajowego—BGK (National Economy Bank): 00-955 Warsaw, Al. Jerozolimskie 7, POB 41; tel. (22) 5229127; fax (22) 6270378; e-mail bgk@bgk.com.pl; internet www.bgk.com.pl; f. 1924; 100% state-owned; cap. 964.2m., res 5,124.7m., dep. 17,154.3m. (Dec. 2006); Pres. of Bd IRENEUSZ FAFARA; 20 brs.

Bank Millennium: 02-593 Warsaw, Stanisława Żaryna 2A; tel. (22) 5981565; fax (22) 5981563; e-mail wojciech.kaczorowski@bankmillennium.pl; internet www.bankmillennium.pl; f. 1989 as Bank Inicjatyw Gospodarczych (BIG); present name adopted 2003; 65.0% owned by Banco Comercial Português SA (Portugal); cap. 849.2m., res 469.0m., dep. 26,533.8m. (Dec. 2007); Chair. of Bd BOGUSŁAW KOTT; 410 brs.

Bank Ochrony Środowiska—BOS (Environmental Protection Bank): 00-950 Warsaw 1, Al. Jana Pawła II 12, POB 150; tel. (22) 8508735; fax (22) 8508891; e-mail bos@bosbank.pl; internet www.bosbank.pl; f. 1991; 77.2% by Polish National Fund for the Protection of the Environment and Water; cap. 525.9m., res –12.5m., dep. 8,051.4m. (Dec. 2007); Pres. of Exec. Bd MARIUSZ KLIMCZAK; 48 brs.

Bank Polska Kasa Opieki—Bank Pekao: 00-950 Warsaw, ul. Grzybowska 53/57; tel. (22) 6560000; fax (22) 6560004; e-mail info@pekao.com.pl; internet www.pekao.com.pl; f. 1929; universal bank; 52.9% owned by UniCredito Italiano SpA (Italy); cap. 261.9m., res 12,393.6m., dep. 105,839.9m. (Dec. 2007); Pres. JAN KRZYSZTOF BIELECKI; Chair. JERZY WOZNICKI; 720 brs and sub-brs.

Bank Polskiej Spółdzielczości: 01-231 Warsaw, ul. Plocka 9/11B; tel. (22) 5396224; fax (22) 5395133; e-mail sekretariat.bps@bankbps.pl; internet www.bankbps.pl; f. 1992; present name adopted 2002; cap. 133.2m., res 170.4m., dep. 8,730.5m. (Dec. 2007); Pres. MIROSŁAW POTULSKI.

Bank Zachodni WBK (Western Bank): 50-950 Wrocław, Dolnośląskie Rynek 9/11; tel. (71) 3701000; fax (71) 3702771; e-mail dorota.bernatowicz@bzwbk.pl; internet www.bzwbk.pl; f. 1989; present name adopted 2001; 70.5% owned by AIB European Investments Ltd (Ireland); cap. 729.6m., res 2,311.7m., dep. 34,517.9m. (Dec. 2007); Pres. JACEK KSEŃ; 433 brs.

BRE Bank: 00-950 Warsaw, ul. Senatorska 18, POB 728; tel. (22) 8290000; fax (22) 8290033; e-mail info@brebank.pl; internet www.brebank.com.pl; f. 1987 as Bank Rozwoju Eksportu; 70.3% owned by Commerzbank AG (Germany); present name adopted 1999; specializes in corporate banking; cap. 118.6m., res 2,324.3m., dep. 42,925.4m. (Dec. 2007); Pres. and CEO SŁAWOMIR LACHOWSKI; 172 brs.

Citibank Handlowy: 00-923 Warsaw, ul. Senatorska 16; tel. (22) 6904000; fax (22) 6925023; e-mail listybh@citicorp.com; internet www.citibankhandlowy.pl; f. 1870; trade and finance bank; specializes in corporate and investment banking; fmrly Bank Handlowy w Warszawie (Trade Bank in Warsaw); 89.3% owned by Citibank Overseas Investment Corpn (USA); cap. 522.6m., res 4,144.4m., dep. 31,816.4m. (Dec. 2007); Pres. SŁAWOMIR SIKORA; Chair. STANISŁAW SOŁTYSIŃSKI; 149 brs.

Deutsche Bank PBC: 00-609 Warsaw, Al. Armii Ludowej 26; tel. (22) 5799800; fax (22) 5799801; e-mail info@db-pbc.pl; internet www.deutsche-bank-pbc.pl; f. 1991; fmrly Bank Wspolpracy Regionalnej SA w Krakowie; present name adopted 2003; 99.7% owned by Deutsche Bank Privat- und Geschäftskunden Aktiengesellschaft (Germany); cap. 581.7m., res 224.5m., dep. 7,119.8m. (Dec. 2007); Chair. of Supervisory Bd ULRICH KISSING; Pres. MAREK KULCZYCKI.

Deutsche Bank Polska: 00-609 Warsaw, Al. Armii Ludowej 26; tel. (22) 5799000; fax (22) 5799001; e-mail public.relations@db.com; internet www.db-polska.pl; f. 1995; 100% owned by Deutsche Bank AG (Germany); corporate banking; cap. 230.0m., res 194.5m., dep. 5,513.0m. (Dec. 2007); Pres. KRZYSZTOF KALICKI; Chair. TESSEN VON HEYDEBRECK.

Fortis Bank Polska: 02-676 Warsaw, ul. Suwak 3; tel. (22) 5669000; fax (22) 5669010; e-mail info@fortisbank.com.pl; internet www.fortisbank.com.pl; f. 1990; present name adopted 2000; 99.1% owned by Fortis Bank (Belgium); cap. 503.1m., res 473.2m., dep. 12,404.4m. (Dec. 2007); Pres. JAN BUJAK; Chair. JOS CLIJSTERS.

Getin Bank: 40-479 Katowice, ul. Pszczyńska 10, POB 593; tel. (32) 2008500; fax (32) 2008685; e-mail marketing@getinbank.pl; internet www.getinbank.pl; f. 1990; fmrly Górnośląski Bank Gospodarczy; present name adopted 2004; cap. 295.9m., res 807.4m., dep.

POLAND

13,228.0m. (Dec. 2007); Pres. Michał Handzlik; Chair. Krzysztof Rosiński; 146 brs.

ING Bank Śląski: 40-086 Katowice, ul. Sokolska 34; tel. (32) 3577000; e-mail info@ing.pl; internet www.ing.pl; f. 1989; 75% owned by ING Bank NV (Netherlands); cap. 130.1m., res 881.3m., dep. 47,529.5m. (Dec. 2007); Chair. Anna Fornalczyk; Pres. Brunon Bartkiewicz; 350 brs and sub-brs.

Kredyt Bank: 01-211 Warsaw, ul. Kasprzaka 2/8, POB 93; tel. (22) 6345400; fax (22) 6345335; internet www.kredytbank.com.pl; f. 1997; 80% owned by KBC Bank NV (Belgium); cap. 1,358.3m., res 475.0m., dep. 24,078.3m. (Dec. 2007); Chair. Andrzej Witkowski; Pres. Maciej Bardan; 75 brs.

Nordea Bank Polska: 81-303 Gdynia, ul. Kielecka 2, POB 11; tel. (58) 6691111; fax (58) 6691110; e-mail nordea@nordea.com; internet www.nordea.pl; f. 1991; 98.9% owned by Nordea Bank AB (Sweden); cap. 227.1m., res 623.2m., dep. 9,031.9m. (Dec. 2007); Pres. Włodzimierz Kicinski; Chair. Wojciech Rybowski.

PKO Bank Polski—Powszechna Kasa Oszczędności Bank Państwowy—PKO (State Savings Bank): 00-975 Warsaw, ul. Pulawska 15, POB 183; tel. (22) 5356565; fax (22) 5218862; internet www.pkobp.pl; f. 1919; 51.5% state-owned; cap. 1,000.0m., res 8,009.6m., dep. 90,152.5m. (Dec. 2007); Pres. of Management Bd Jerzy Pruski; Chair. of Supervisory Bd Marzena Piszczek; 1,153 brs and sub-brs.

Raiffeisen Bank Polska: 00-549 Warsaw, ul. Piekna 20, POB 53; tel. (22) 5852000; fax (22) 5852585; internet www.raiffeisen.pl; f. 1991; present name adopted 2000; 100% owned by Raiffeisen International Bank Holding AG (Austria); cap. 573.0m., res 710.6m., dep. 18,832.9m. (Dec. 2007); Pres. Piotr Czarnecki; Chair. Herbert Stepic; 37 brs.

WestLB Bank Polska: 02-781 Warsaw, ul. Pileckiego 65; tel. (22) 6530500; fax (22) 6530501; e-mail westlb@westlb.pl; internet www.westlb.pl; f. 1995; present name adopted 2003; 100% owned by WestLB AG (Germany); cap. 183.6m., res 60.9m., dep. 2,197.2m. (Dec. 2007); Chair. and Gen. Man. Maciej Stanczuk.

STOCK EXCHANGE

The Warsaw Stock Exchange was re-established in April 1991. In January 1998 a derivatives market was launched. At the end of 2008 the Stock Exchange's shareholders included 35 entities, comprising banks, brokerage firms, an Exchange company and the State Treasury (which held a share of 98.8%).

Warsaw Stock Exchange: 00-498 Warsaw, ul. Książęca 4; tel. (22) 6283232; fax (22) 6281754; e-mail wse@wse.com.pl; internet www.wse.com.pl; opened for trading in 1991; Pres. and Chief Exec. Dr Ludwik Sobolewski.

INSURANCE

In early 2005 there were 32 insurance companies operating in Poland. The largest companies were Polish National Insurance (Powszechny Zakład Ubezpieczeń—PZU), which dominated the property insurance market, and Warta Insurance and Reinsurance, which specialized in vehicle insurance and foreign business. PZU's subsidiary, PZU Life, was the largest life insurance company.

Commercial Union Polska—Towarzystwo Ubezpieczeń na Życie: 00-838 Warsaw, ul, Prosta 70; tel. (22) 5574050; fax (22) 5574075; e-mail bok@cu.com.pl; internet www.cu.com.pl; f. 1991; owned by Aviva Group (United Kingdom); pensions, life insurance; Pres. Zbigniew Andrzejewski.

Grupa Powszechny Zakład Ubezpieczeń (PZU) (Polish National Insurance Group): 00-133 Warsaw, Al. Jana Pawła II 24; tel. (22) 5823400; fax (22) 5823401; internet www.pzu.pl; f. 1803; insurance group comprising two principal companies dealing in various areas of insurance (PZU SA—property insurance, and PZU Życie SA—life insurance), and six support companies; 55% state-owned; further privatization scheduled; Pres. Cezary Stypułkowski; 400 brs; 14,000 employees.

Warta—Towarzystwo Ubezpieczeń i Reasekuracji Warta (Warta Insurance and Reinsurance Co): 00-805 Warsaw, ul. Chmielna 85/87; tel. (22) 5810100; fax (22) 5811374; e-mail info@warta.pl; internet www.warta.pl; f. 1920; marine, air, motor, fire, luggage and credit; Pres. Agenor Jan Gawrzyal; 25 brs.

Trade and Industry

GOVERNMENT AGENCIES

Agency for the Restructuring and Modernization of Agriculture (Agencja Restrukturyzacji i Modernizacji Rolnictwa): 00-175 Warsaw, Al. Jana Pawła II 70; fax (22) 3185330; e-mail info@arimr.gov.pl; internet www.arimr.gov.pl; f. 1994; Pres. Prof. Grzegorz Spychalski.

Agricultural Market Agency (Agencja Rynku Rolnego): 00-400 Warsaw, ul. Nowy Świat 6/12; tel. (22) 6617272; fax (22) 6289353; e-mail tpi@arr.gov.pl; internet www.eng.arr.gov.pl; f. 1991; implements selected schemes under the Common Agricultural Policy (CAP) of the European Union; Pres. Stanisław Grzegorz Kamiński.

Polish Agency for Enterprise Development (PARP) (Polska Agencja Rozwoju Przedsiębiorczości): 00-834 Warsaw, ul. Pańska 81/83; tel. (22) 4328080; fax (22) 4328620; e-mail biuro@parp.gov.pl; internet www.parp.gov.pl; f. 2000; manages funds assigned from the state budget and the European Union for the support of entrepreneurship and devt of human resources, particularly concerning small and medium-sized enterprises; Chief Exec. Danuta Jabłońska.

Polish Information and Foreign Investment Agency (Polska Agencja Informacji i Inwestycji Zagranicznych): 00-585 Warsaw, ul. Bagatela 12; tel. (22) 3349800; fax (22) 3349999; e-mail post@paiz.gov.pl; internet www.paiz.gov.pl; f. 2003; Pres. Andrzej Kanthak.

DEVELOPMENT AGENCY

Industrial Development Agency (Agencja Rozwoju Przemysłu): 02-675 Warsaw, ul. Woloska 7, Budynek Mars, Klatka A; tel. (22) 4603636; fax (22) 4603637; e-mail lucyna.stepien@arp.com.pl; internet www.arp.com.pl; Pres. Paweł Brzezicki.

CHAMBERS OF COMMERCE

Polish Chamber of Commerce (National Economic Chamber—Krajowa Izba Gospodarcza): 00-074 Warsaw, ul. Trębacka 4, POB 361; tel. (22) 6309600; fax (22) 8274673; e-mail kig@kig.pl; internet www.kig.pl; f. 1990; Pres. Andrzej Arendarski; Chair. Wojciech Kruk; 145 mems.

Foreign Investors' Chamber of Industry and Trade in Poland (Izba Przemysłowo-Handlowa Inwestorów Zagranicznych—IPHIZ): 00-834 Warsaw, ul. Pańska 73; tel. (22) 3147575; fax (22) 3147576; e-mail biuro@iphiz.com.pl; internet www.iphiz.com.pl; f. 1989; Pres. Zdzisław Jagodziński.

UTILITIES

Energy Regulatory Authority (Urząd Regulacji Energetyki): 00-872 Warsaw, ul. Chłodna 64; tel. (22) 6616107; fax (22) 6616152; e-mail ure@ure.gov.pl; internet www.ure.gov.pl; Pres. Dr Leszek Juchniewicz.

Electricity

The electricity sector has been reorganized into separate generation, transmission and distribution entities.

Koncern Energetyczny ENERGA: 80-557 Gdańsk, ul. Marynarki Polskiej 130; tel. (58) 3473013; fax (58) 3010152; internet www.energa.pl; f. 2004; renamed as above 2005; group of eight regional electricity distributors in central and northern Poland, known as G8; partial privatization suspended in 2004; Chief Exec. Waldemar Bartelik; 7,500 employees.

PGE Polska Grupa Energetyczna: 00-496 Warsaw, ul. Mysia 2; tel. (22) 6931580; fax (22) 6285964; internet www.pgesa.pl; national transmission-system operator; fmrly Polskie Sieci Elektroenergetyczne (PSE); Chair. of Bd Tomasz Zadroga.

National Atomic Energy Agency (Państwowa Agencja Atomistyki): 00-522 Warsaw, ul. Krucza 36; tel. (22) 6282722; fax (22) 6290164; e-mail niewodniczanski@paa.gov.pl; internet www.paa.gov.pl; f. 1982; central govt organ concerned with issues of nuclear safety and radiological protection; Pres. Prof. Jerzy Niewodniczański.

STOEN Stołeczny Zakład Energetyczny (STOEN Capital-City Power Distribution Co): 00-347 Warsaw, Wybrzeże Kopciuszkowskie 41; tel. (22) 8214646; fax (22) 8214647; e-mail stoen@stoen.pl; internet www.stoen.pl; f. 1993; transmits and distributes electric energy; privatized in 2002; 85% owned by RWE Energie AG (Germany); 15% state-owned; Chief Exec. Harry Schur; Chair. of Supervisory Bd Dr Andreas Radmacher.

Gas

EuRoPol GAZ: 04-028 Warsaw, Al. Stanów Zjednoczonych 61; tel. (22) 5174000; fax (22) 5174040; e-mail konto@europolgaz.com.pl; internet www.europolgaz.com.pl; f. 1993; jt venture between PGNiG and Gazprom (Russia); Pres. Kazimierz Adamczyk.

Polish Oil and Gas Co (Polskie Górnictwo Naftowe i Gazownictwo—PGNiG): 00-537 Warsaw, ul. Krucza 6/14; tel. (22) 5835000; fax (22) 5835856; e-mail pr@pgnig.pl; internet www.pgnig.pl; f. 1982; divided into six regional distribution subsidiaries in 2003; state-owned natural gas producer and supplier; scheduled for partial privatization; Pres. of Bd Krzysztof Głogowski; 47,300 employees.

TRADE UNIONS

All Poland Trade Unions' Alliance (Ogólnopolskie Porozumienie Związków Zawodowych—OPZZ): 00-924 Warsaw, ul. Kopernika 36/40; tel. (22) 8267106; fax (22) 8265102; e-mail opzz@opzz.org.pl; internet www.opzz.org.pl; f. 1984; Chair. JAN GUZ.

Independent Self-governing Trade Union—Solidarity (NSZZ Solidarność): 80-855 Gdańsk, ul. Wały Piastowskie 24; tel. (58) 3016737; fax (58) 3010143; e-mail zagr@solidarnosc.org.pl; internet www.solidarnosc.org.pl; f. 1980; outlawed 1981–89; Chair. JANUSZ SNIADEK.

Transport

RAILWAYS

At the end of 2002 there were 21,073 km of railway lines making up the state network, of which 12,207 km were electrified.

Office for Railway Transport (Urząd Transportu Kolejowego): 00-928 Warsaw, ul. Chałubinskiego 4/6; tel. (22) 6301950; fax (22) 6301892; e-mail utk@utk.gov.pl; internet www.utk.gov.pl; reorganized in July 2003; fmrly the General Railway Inspectorate; Pres. WIESŁAW JAROSIEWICZ; Dir-Gen. LIDIA OSTROWSKA.

Polish State Railways (Polskie Koleje Państwowe—PKP): 00-973 Warsaw, ul. Szczęśliwicka 62; tel. (22) 4749000; fax (22) 4749102; e-mail biuro.zarzadu@pkp.pl; internet www.pkp.pl; f. 1926; freight and passenger transport; PKP Group comprises 12 cos; from 2004 Regional Services (WKD), a principal subsidiary, has been operated by local govts; Polskie Koleje Państwowe Polskie Linie Kolejowe (PKP PLK) operates the railway network; Pres. ANDRZEJ WACH; Gen. Dir MACIEJ MECLEWSKI; 125,000 employees.

ROADS

In 2003 there were 423,997 km of roads, of which 484 km were motorways; 69.7% of the road network was paved. Poland launched a road construction scheme in mid-2002, partly funded by the European Union (EU), which aimed to enhance the country's position as a major transit route between western and eastern Europe. The EU was, additionally, to provide funding of €19,000m. for road construction in Poland in 2007–13.

General Directorate of Public Roads and Motorways (Generalna Dyrekcja Dróg Krajowych i Autostrad): 00-848 Warsaw, ul. Żelazna 59; tel. (22) 3758888; fax (22) 3758763; e-mail kancelaria@gddkia.gov.pl; internet www.gddkia.gov.pl; Dir ZBIGNIEW KOTLAREK.

INLAND WATERWAYS

Poland has 6,850 km of waterways, of which 3,640 km were navigable in 2002. The main rivers are the Wisła (Vistula), Odra (Oder), Bug, Warta and San. There are some 5,000 lakes. In addition, there is a network of canals.

SHIPPING

Poland has three large harbours on the Baltic Sea: Gdynia, Gdańsk and Szczecin. At 31 December 2007 the Polish merchant fleet comprised 351 vessels, with a total displacement of 193,289 grt.

Authority of Szczecin and Świnoujście Authority Co: 70-603 Szczecin, ul. Bytomska 7; tel. (91) 4308240; fax (91) 4624842; e-mail info@port.szczecin.pl; internet www.port.szczecin.pl; f. 1950; Pres. and Man. Dir JANUSZ CATEWICZ.

Port of Gdańsk Authority Co: 80-955 Gdańsk, ul. Zamknięta 18; tel. (58) 7379100; fax (58) 7379485; e-mail info@portgdansk.pl; internet www.portgdansk.pl; f. 1997; management of land and port infrastructure; Pres. of Bd STANISLAW CORA.

Port of Gdynia Authority Co: 81-337 Gdynia, ul. Rotterdamska 9; tel. (58) 6274002; fax (58) 6203191; e-mail marketing@port.gdynia.pl; internet www.port.gdynia.pl; f. 1922; Pres. PRZEMYSLAW MARCHLEWICZ.

Principal Shipping Companies

Polska Żegluga Bałtycka—Polferries (Polish Baltic Shipping Co—POLFERRIES): 78-100 Kołobrzeg, ul. Portowa 41; tel. (94) 3552102; fax (94) 3552208; internet www.polferries.pl; f. 1976; operates three ferries on four routes between Denmark and Sweden; also serves as travel agency and tour operator.

Polska Żegluga Morska (PZM) (Polish Steamship Co—Polsteam): 70-419 Szczecin, Pl. Rodła 8; tel. (91) 3594333; fax (91) 3594288; e-mail pzmmanagement@polsteam.com.pl; internet www.polsteam.com.pl; f. 1951; state-owned; world-wide tramping; operates 75 vessels totalling 2m. dwt, incl. four liquid sulphur carriers; largest dry bulk carrier in Europe; operates ferry service between Poland and Sweden (Unity Line); Gen. Dir PAWEŁ SZYNKARUK; 2,800 employees.

Polskie Linie Oceaniczne (PLO) (Polish Ocean Lines): 81-364 Gdynia, ul. 10 Lutego 24; tel. (58) 6900670; fax (58) 6900672; e-mail pol@pol.com.pl; internet www.pol.com.pl; f. 1951; holding co for six shipping cos operating within PLO group; tonnage operated by the POL-Levant Shipping Lines; Pres. of Bd ANDRZEJ OSIECIMSKI.

CIVIL AVIATION

Fryderyka Chopin—Okęcie international airport is situated near Warsaw. In addition, international flights serve a number of other airports, including those at Bydgoszcz, Gdańsk, Katowice, Kraków, Łódź, Poznań, Rzeszów, Szczecin, and Wrocław.

Civil Aviation Office (Urząd Lotnictwa Cywilnego): 00-848 Warsaw, ul. Żelazna 59; tel. (22) 5207200; fax (22) 5207300; e-mail kancelaria@ulc.gov.pl; internet www.ulc.gov.pl; Pres. GRZEGORZ KRUSZYŃSKI.

Centralwings: Łódź; e-mail comments@centralwings.com; internet www.centralwings.com; f. 2004; 'low-cost' subsidiary of LOT (q.v.), in association with Germanwings, a subsidiary of Lufthansa (Germany); operates flights to 11 European destinations from Warsaw, Katowice and Kraków; Pres. PIOTR KOCIOŁEK.

LOT—Polskie Linie Lotnicze (Polish Airlines): 00-906 Warsaw, ul. 17 Stycznia 39; tel. (22) 6066111; fax (22) 8460909; e-mail lot@lot.com; internet www.lot.com; f. 1929; 67.97% state-owned; domestic and international services; operates low-cost subsidiary Eurolot (f. 1996); Pres. SEBASTIAN MIKOSZ (acting).

Tourism

Poland is rich in historic cities, such as Gdańsk, Wrocław, Kraków, Poznań and Warsaw. There are numerous health and climatic resorts, while the mountains, forests and rivers provide splendid scenery and excellent facilities for touring and sporting holidays. In 2007 Poland was visited by some 66.2m. foreign tourists, 57.6% of whom were from Germany. Receipts from tourism amounted to US $10,573m. in that year.

Polish Tourist Organization (Polska Organizacja Turystyczna—POT): 00-613 Warsaw, ul. Chałubskińego 8, XIX piętro; tel. (22) 5367070; fax (22) 5367004; e-mail pot@pot.gov.pl; internet www.pot.gov.pl; Pres. TOMASZ WILCZAK.

PORTUGAL

Introductory Survey

Location, Climate, Language, Religion, Flag, Capital

The mainland portion of the Portuguese Republic lies in western Europe, on the Atlantic side of the Iberian peninsula, bordered by Spain to the north and east. The country also includes two archipelagos in the Atlantic Ocean, the Azores and the Madeira Islands. The climate is mild and temperate, with an annual average temperature of 16°C (61°F). In the interior the weather is drier and hotter. Almost all of the inhabitants speak Portuguese and are adherents of the Roman Catholic Church. The national flag (proportions 2 by 3) has two vertical stripes, of green and red, the green occupying two-fifths of the total area; superimposed on the stripes (half on the green, half on the red) is the state coat of arms: a white shield, containing five small blue shields (each bearing five white roundels) in the form of an upright cross, with a red border containing seven yellow castles, all superimposed on a yellow armillary sphere. The capital is Lisbon (Lisboa).

Recent History

The monarchy that had ruled Portugal from the 11th century was overthrown in 1910, when the King was deposed in a bloodless revolution, and a republic was proclaimed. A period of great instability ensued until a military coup installed the regime of the Estado Novo (New State) in 1926. Dr António de Oliveira Salazar became Minister of Finance in 1928 and Prime Minister in 1932, establishing a right-wing dictatorial regime, influenced by Italian Fascism. A new Constitution, establishing a corporate state, was adopted in 1933. Only one political party was authorized, and suffrage was limited. Portugal remained neutral during the Second World War. The Government strove to achieve international acceptance, but Portugal was not admitted to the UN until 1955. Unlike the other European colonial powers, Portugal insisted on maintaining its overseas possessions, regarding them as 'inalienable'. In 1961 Portuguese enclaves in India were successfully invaded by Indian forces, and in the same year a rebellion against Portuguese rule began in Angola. Similar rebellions followed, in Portuguese Guinea (1963) and Mozambique (1964), and protracted guerrilla warfare ensued in the three African provinces. Salazar remained in power until illness forced his retirement in September 1968. He was succeeded by Dr Marcello Caetano, who had been Deputy Prime Minister in 1955–58. Caetano pursued slightly more liberal policies. Opposition parties were legalized for elections to the Assembléia Nacional in October 1969, but the União Nacional, the government party, won all 130 seats. Immediately after the elections, the opposition groups were outlawed again. The government party, renamed Acção Nacional Popular in February 1970, also won every seat at the next elections to the Assembléia, in October 1973, following the withdrawal of all opposition candidates.

The drain on Portugal's economy by the long wars against nationalist forces in the overseas provinces contributed to the overthrow of Caetano in a bloodless coup on 25 April 1974, initiated by the Movimento das Forças Armadas (MFA), a group of young army officers. Gen. António Ribeiro de Spínola, head of the Junta da Salvação Nacional (Junta of National Salvation) that assumed power, became President in May and promised liberal reforms. The new Government recognized the right of Portugal's overseas territories to self-determination. The independence of Guinea-Bissau (formerly Portuguese Guinea), proclaimed in September 1973, was recognized by Portugal in September 1974. The remaining African territories were all granted independence in 1975. Portugal also withdrew from Portuguese Timor (Timor-Leste) in that year.

Following a split between the Junta's right and left wings, President Spínola resigned in September 1974 and was replaced by Gen. Francisco da Costa Gomes. An abortive counter-coup by senior officers in March 1975 resulted in a move to the left. All existing organs of the MFA were dissolved, a Supreme Revolutionary Council (SRC) was created, and six of the country's political parties agreed that the SRC would stay in power for five years. On 25 April a general election was held for a Constituent Assembly. Of the 12 parties contesting the election, the Partido Socialista (PS) obtained the largest share of the votes cast and won 116 of the Assembly's 250 seats. However, disputes between Socialists and Communists provoked withdrawals from the new coalition Government, and the Prime Minister, Gen. Vasco Gonçalves, was dismissed. Adm. José Pinheiro de Azevedo became Prime Minister in August. In September a new Government of 'united action' was formed, including members of the armed forces, the PS, the Partido Popular Democrático (PPD) and the Partido Comunista Português (PCP). In November the Government suspended its activities, owing to a lack of support from the armed forces. An abortive leftist military coup resulted from the political turmoil. Changes took place within the SRC, and in December the armed forces announced a plan to reduce their political power.

A new Constitution, committing Portugal to make a transition to socialism, took effect on 25 April 1976. The SRC was renamed the Council of the Revolution, becoming a consultative body, headed by the President, with powers to delay legislation and the right of veto in military matters. At the general election for the new Assembléia da República (Assembly of the Republic), the PS won 107 of the Assembléia's 263 seats. In June the Army Chief of Staff, Gen. António Ramalho Eanes, a non-party candidate supported by the PS, the PPD and the Centro Democrático Social (CDS), was elected President. He took office in July, when a minority Socialist Government was formed under Dr Mário Lopes Soares, who had been Minister of Foreign Affairs in 1974–75. The Government resigned in December 1977, but the President again invited Soares to take office as Prime Minister. A new PS-CDS coalition was established in January 1978, but it collapsed after only six months. A new Government was formed in November under Prof. Carlos Mota Pinto, but he resigned in July 1979.

President Eanes appointed Dr Maria de Lourdes Pintasilgo to head a provisional Government. The centre-right alliance, Aliança Democrática (AD), which included the Partido Social Democrata (PSD, formerly the PPD) and the CDS, won 128 of the 250 seats in the Assembléia da República in an early general election held in December 1979. Dr Francisco Sá Carneiro, the leader of the PSD, was appointed Prime Minister. At the general election held in October 1980, the AD increased its parliamentary majority. In December Sá Carneiro and his Minister of Defence, Adelino Amaro da Costa, were killed in an apparent air accident. (In 2004 tests revealed that a bomb had exploded on board the aircraft, and the eighth commission of inquiry into the crash cited Amaro da Costa's attempt to stop the illegal sale of arms to Iran as a possible motive for the bombing.) The presidential election took place as planned, however, and Eanes was re-elected. Dr Francisco Pinto Balsemão, co-founder of the PSD, was appointed Prime Minister. In March 1981 the offices of the President of the Republic and the Chief of Staff of the Armed Forces were formally separated.

In August 1982 the Assembléia da República approved the final draft of the new Constitution, which completed the transition to full civilian government. Following divisions within the PSD, and losses at local elections in December, Balsemão resigned as Prime Minister. In addition, the Deputy Prime Minister and leader of the CDS, Prof. Diogo Freitas do Amaral, resigned from all party and political posts. In February 1983 Mota Pinto became leader of the PSD. At an early general election, held in April, the PS won 101 seats. Soares formed a coalition Government with the PSD (the AD having been dissolved).

In February 1985 Mota Pinto resigned as leader of the PSD, and subsequently as Deputy Prime Minister and Minister of Defence, and was replaced by Rui Machete, the Minister of Justice. In May Machete was replaced as party leader by Prof. Aníbal Cavaco Silva, a former Minister of Finance. In June, on the day after Portugal signed its treaty of accession to the European Community (EC, now European Union—EU, see p. 255), the PS-PSD coalition disintegrated. Eanes called a general election for October, at which the PSD won 88 seats, while the PS won 57 seats and the Partido Renovador Democrático (PRD, a new party founded in early 1985 by supporters of

President Eanes) won 45 seats. Cavaco Silva was able to form a minority PSD-led Government.

During the mid-1980s a number of terrorist attacks were perpetrated by the radical left-wing group Forças Populares 25 de Abril (FP-25) and other groups. Targets including both Portuguese and foreign business interests, installations of the North Atlantic Treaty Organization (NATO) and the US embassy in Lisbon. In July 1985 the trial opened of more than 70 alleged members of FP-25—including Lt-Col Otelo Saraiva de Carvalho, the former revolutionary commander—but was adjourned owing to the fatal shooting of a key prosecution witness. The trial later resumed and, in May 1987, Saraiva de Carvalho was found guilty of subversion and sentenced to 15 years' imprisonment (subsequently increased to 18 years). In March 1996, following a personal initiative by President Soares, the Assembléia da República approved a pardon for Saraiva de Carvalho and other members of FP-25.

Four candidates contested the January 1986 presidential election. As no candidate achieved the requisite 50% majority, a second round of voting was held in February: Mário Soares narrowly defeated Freitas do Amaral, former leader of the CDS, to become Portugal's first civilian President for 60 years, taking office in March.

Cavaco Silva's minority Government encountered difficulties in securing the adoption of reformist legislation. In April 1987 Cavaco Silva resigned, following his defeat in a motion of censure. President Soares dissolved the Assembléia da República, prior to the holding of an early general election in July. The PSD secured 148 of the 250 seats in the Assembléia, becoming the first party since 1974 to win an absolute majority. The PS won 60 seats, and the Coligação Democrático Unitária (CDU, a new left-wing coalition comprising mainly the PCP) won 31 seats.

Cavaco Silva was reappointed as Prime Minister and announced a programme of radical economic reform, which included the partial privatization of state-owned companies. Fundamental changes in the sectors of agriculture, education and the media were also proposed. The most controversial aspect of the programme, however, was the Government's renewed attempt to reform the restrictive labour laws. In March 1988 an estimated 1.5m. workers took part in a 24-hour general strike to protest against the Government's proposed legislation. Nevertheless, in April the labour laws were approved by the Assembléia da República; the following month, however, the Constitutional Court ruled that the new legislation violated the Constitution. The legislation was approved by President Soares in February 1989, although labour unrest persisted. Having gained the approval of both the Assembléia and the President, amendments removing Marxist elements from the Constitution entered into force in August.

Supported by both the PS and the PSD, Soares was re-elected President at an election held in January 1991, defeating three other candidates to secure an outright victory with more than 70% of the votes cast. At legislative elections held in October the PSD renewed its absolute majority, winning 135 of the 230 seats (reduced from 250) in the Assembléia da República. The PS secured 72 seats, the CDU 17 and the CDS five. A new Government was appointed in late October. In February 1992 Jorge Sampaio was replaced as Secretary-General of the PS by António Guterres. During 1992 tension between President Soares and Cavaco Silva became more evident, owing to the President's increasingly frequent use of his power of veto in order to obstruct the passage of legislation.

In February 1995 Cavaco Silva was replaced as PSD leader by the Minister of Defence, Joaquim Fernando Nogueira. Nogueira resigned as Minister of Defence in March, following the President's veto of his proposed appointment as Deputy Prime Minister. At legislative elections held in October the PS won 112 of the 230 seats in the Assembléia da República. The PSD won 88 seats, the Centro Democrático Social-Partido Popular (CDS-PP—formerly the CDS) 15 and the CDU also 15. The Secretary-General of the PS, Guterres, was appointed Prime Minister, leading a minority administration that incorporated several non-party ministers.

In November 1995 Sampaio resigned as Mayor of Lisbon, a post he had held since 1999, and declared his candidacy for the forthcoming presidential election. At the election, held in January 1996, Sampaio secured 53.9% of the votes cast, defeating Cavaco Silva. President Sampaio took office in March. Following the presidential election, Fernando Nogueira resigned from the leadership of the PSD and was replaced by Marcelo Rebelo de Sousa.

In August 1996 the Prime Minister announced proposals for radical reform of the country's political system. The opening of electoral lists to independent citizens (thus ending the monopoly of the major parties) and provision for the holding of referendums on issues of national interest were among the changes envisaged. In early 1997 the ruling PS and the opposition PSD reached a broad consensus on these proposals, also agreeing upon the gradual establishment of a professional army and a reduction in compulsory military service. In September the Assembléia da República gave its approval to the various constitutional reforms.

In February 1997, in a free vote, the Assembléia da República narrowly rejected proposals to liberalize the country's abortion law. The issue aroused bitter controversy, and created a deep division within the PS. The Prime Minister expressed his strong opposition, while certain PS veterans supported the proposed change in the legislation. In February 1998 the legislature voted by a narrow margin to relax the law on abortion. A referendum on the issue was held in June. Although 51% of those casting a vote favoured the liberalization of the law, the result was declared null and void, owing to the low rate of participation.

In October 1998 the Prime Minister announced the establishment of an anti-corruption unit and various other measures, in response to repeated accusations that political parties and public officials had been in receipt of illicit payments in return for the awarding of public works contracts.

Guterres suffered a setback in November 1998 when a referendum on the question of regional devolution resulted in an overwhelming rejection (by 63.6% of participants) of the Government's proposals to divide mainland Portugal into eight administrative regions, each with a proposed elected local assembly and regional president. However, owing to the high abstention rate, the referendum result was declared invalid.

In March 1999 Rebelo de Sousa announced his resignation as leader of the PSD and the termination of the party's recently established electoral alliance with the CDS-PP, citing disloyalty on the part of that party's leader, Paulo Portas.

The general election conducted on 10 October 1999 was partially overshadowed by the crisis in the former Portuguese colony of Timor-Leste (see below). Nevertheless, the PS secured 115 of the 230 seats in the Assembléia da República, while the PSD won 81 seats and the left-wing CDU 17 seats (including two seats allocated to the ecologist Partido Ecologista 'Os Verdes'—PEV). The recently established Bloco de Esquerda (BE), a militant left-wing grouping, unexpectedly obtained two seats. Thus, one seat short of an absolute majority, Guterres was returned to office and a new Council of Ministers was appointed. In November the incoming Government announced a programme of reforms aimed at narrowing the disparity between Portugal and the more developed member states of the EU.

At a presidential election held on 14 January 2001 Sampaio was re-elected for a second term, obtaining 55.8% of the votes cast and defeating four other candidates. His nearest rival, the PSD candidate Joaquim Ferreira do Amaral, secured 34.5% of the votes. In October 2001 the Assembléia da República ratified the Treaty of Nice, which aimed to reform the institutions of the EU in anticipation of its forthcoming enlargement. The PS, the PSD and the CDS-PP voted in favour of the ratification, while the BE and the PCP rejected the Treaty.

Following municipal elections held in December 2001, at which the PS suffered significant losses, Guterres resigned both as Prime Minister and as leader of the PS. The poor electoral results were widely attributed to a decline in the economy, as well as to discontent with public services, which had been adversely affected by reductions in government expenditure. President Sampaio announced that legislative elections would be held in early 2002. Guterres was replaced as Secretary-General of the PS in January by Eduardo Ferro Rodrigues. At the elections, held on 17 March, the PSD, whose campaign had featured reductions in corporate taxation and public expenditure and the privatization of state services, emerged victorious, winning 105 seats in the Assembléia da República, although without an overall majority. The PS secured 96 seats, the CDS-PP 14 seats, the PCP-PEV alliance 12 seats and the BE three seats. The leader of the PSD, José Manuel Durão Barroso, was appointed Prime Minister and formed a centre-right coalition Government with the CDS-PP.

Durão Barroso's Government announced its intention to introduce austerity measures to counter the large public deficit, which contravened the country's obligations under the regulations for the European single currency. In July 2002 the Government proposed a new labour code designed to combat low productivity by increasing the ease of recruitment and dismissal of staff and limiting the power of the unions. In November and December two public sector one-day general strikes, involving up to 500,000 workers, were organized to protest against the introduction of the labour legislation and other recent austerity measures. In November many public sector workers observed a one-day strike to demand higher wages and in protest at government proposals to reform the public sector. Following the extension for a second consecutive year of a freeze on certain public sector salaries, in January 2004 the public sector unions organized a further one-day strike.

In May 2003 Paolo Pedroso, the deputy leader and parliamentary spokesman of the PS, was arrested in connection with a child abuse scandal surrounding the Casa Pia children's home in Lisbon. Several other establishment figures had been arrested earlier that year. Throughout his custody Pedroso maintained that the allegations against him were part of a PSD plot to discredit him and requested that his parliamentary immunity be lifted to enable him to be questioned. Pedroso was released in October and permitted to resume his former role. However, he was charged in December (with nine other prominent figures) on 23 counts of sexual abuse, although the charges against him were later dropped. (In September 2008 Pedroso was awarded damages of around €100,000, following a civil court case in which the judge ruled that his arrest and subsequent imprisonment constituted a 'grave error'.) The investigation was concluded in May 2004, and seven people went on trial in late November; the proceedings were finally concluded in December 2008, although the presiding judges were not expected to reach a verdict until early 2009. Meanwhile, the Government established a tribunal to consider compensation claims brought by victims of abuse at Casa Pia, which in March 2006 awarded a total of more than €50m. to 44 claimants.

At elections to the European Parliament on 13 June 2004 the ruling coalition performed poorly, winning only 33.3% of the votes cast, compared with the 48.9% it had achieved in the 2002 legislative elections. The PS made significant gains, winning 44.5% of the votes cast, compared with 37.8% in the previous legislative elections. Unexpectedly, Durão Barroso was invited in late June to take over the role of President of the European Commission in October. In order to accept this appointment, Durão Barroso resigned as leader of the PSD, and subsequently as Prime Minister on 5 July; the populist Mayor of Lisbon and Secretary-General of the PSD, Pedro Santana Lopes, was elected as his successor. President Sampaio invited Santana Lopes to form a new Government, which was inaugurated on 17 July. Ferro Rodrigues subsequently resigned as Secretary-General of the PS, claiming that Sampaio had betrayed the party's interests by not holding early legislative elections. José Sócrates, a moderate and a former Minister of the Environment, was elected Secretary-General of the PS in September.

Santana Lopes's Government was beset by problems, including claims that it was trying to control the media. In November 2004 directors and a prominent newscaster resigned from the state broadcasting company, Radiotelevisão Portuguesa (RTP), in protest at perceived pressure from the Government, and the state media authority criticized the Government for attempting to limit RTP's freedom. A series of cabinet reorganizations took place, culminating in the resignation of Henrique Chaves, formerly a close associate of the Prime Minister, as Minister for Youth and Sport. Chaves, who had been moved from the position of Minister in Assistance to the Prime Minister days earlier, cited Santana Lopes's disloyalty. At the end of November President Sampaio informed Santana Lopes of his decision to dissolve parliament and call legislative elections. Prior to the dissolution, the President permitted time for the adoption of the 2005 budget. However, the expansionary budget, which was approved by the Assembléia da República in early December, proved controversial as it contained tax reductions and increases in the state pension that were likely to cause Portugal to breach the budget deficit limit (equivalent to 3% of gross domestic product—GDP) specified in the EU's Stability and Growth Pact. Sampaio formally dissolved the legislature on 10 December, citing a loss of confidence in the Government, and announced that legislative elections would be held on 20 February 2005.

At the elections, which took place as scheduled on 20 February 2005, the PS, which during the campaign had advocated institutional reform and policies to increase economic growth, achieved an overwhelming victory, winning an outright majority; voter participation was 64.3%. The PS won 121 of the 230 seats in the Assembléia da República, with 45.0% of the votes cast; the PCP-PEV coalition and the BE also performed well at the expense of the right. The PSD won 75 seats, with 28.8% of the votes cast, while its junior partner in the previous Government, the CDS-PP, won 12 seats (7.2%). Santana Lopes and Portas resigned as leader of the PSD and the CDS-PP, respectively. In April Luís Marques Mendes was elected leader of the PSD, while José Ribeiro e Castro became President of the CDS-PP.

A new 16-member Council of Ministers, headed by Sócrates, took office in March 2005. It included an equal number of members of the PS and independents, most notably former CDS leader Diogo Freitas do Amaral, who had been an outspoken critic of the US-led invasion of Iraq in 2003, as Minister of Foreign Affairs. Another independent, and former deputy governor of the Banco de Portugal, Luís Campos e Cunha, was allocated the finance portfolio.

On taking office the new Government adopted a policy of strict economic austerity in an effort to reduce the budget deficit, which was forecast to be considerably higher than the EU limit of 3% of GDP. Disagreements arose between Campos e Cunha and Sócrates, however, and the Minister of Finance resigned in July 2005; he was replaced by Fernando Teixeira dos Santos of the PS. Plans to increase value-added tax and reduce government expenditure, notably on social security, led to a series of protests and strikes by public sector employees. A one-day general strike in July, observed by an estimated 500,000 workers, was followed, in September and October, by protests and industrial action staged by employees in various sectors. The ruling PS performed poorly in local elections in October, with the PSD retaining control over a majority of municipalities. In November, and again in February 2006, public sector workers participated in large-scale protests against the reduction in social welfare benefits, a wage freeze and the raising of the retirement age.

In November 2005 President Sampaio announced that a presidential election would take place on 22 January 2006. Six candidates contested the election, including former President Soares and former Prime Minister Cavaco Silva. (Sampaio was not eligible to stand for a third term.) Cavaco Silva was the only candidate representing the centre-right parties, while the centre-left vote was largely split between Soares and Manuel Alegre, also a member of the PS, who was standing as an independent. Cavaco Silva narrowly won an overall majority (with 50.5% of the valid votes cast), thereby avoiding the need for a second round of voting. Alegre won 20.7% of the vote, while Soares took 14.3%. Some 62.6% of the electorate participated in the ballot. Cavaco Silva, the first centre-right President since the coup of 1974, took office on 9 March. In June Freitas do Amaral resigned as Minister of Foreign Affairs, for health reasons, and was replaced by Luís Amado, hitherto Minister of National Defence; Amado's portfolio was taken by Nuno Severiano Teixeira.

In November 2006 the draft budget for 2007 was approved in the Assembléia da República with the sole support of the PS. All other parties opposed the budget, which included significant reductions in public expenditure, to be largely financed by a reform of public administration. The public sector trade unions organized a two-day strike to coincide with the passage of the legislation, in protest against cuts in wages and pensions for public sector workers. General discontent with government policies had also been manifested in a demonstration organized by one of the principal trade union federations, the Confederação Geral dos Trabalhadores Portugueses-Intersindical Nacional (CGTP—General Confederation of Portuguese Workers) in October and by industrial action by the teaching unions in the same month. In January 2007 the Government began negotiations with trade unions over the reform of labour legislation, which was to be implemented in 2008. The trade unions expressed vehement opposition to the proposals, which were likely to entail significant reductions in the number of civil servants. In March 2007 the CGTP organized a further demonstration to protest against government employment and fiscal policy, which was attended by 120,000 protesters.

In a referendum held in February 2007, 59.2% of those voting approved plans to legalize abortion for all women up to the 10th week of pregnancy; however, only 43.6% of the electorate voted, below the 50% needed to make the result legally binding. None the less, Sócrates declared that the result represented a mandate for reform. Legislation providing for decriminalization was adopted by the Assembléia da República in March and, after receiving presidential approval in April, entered into force in

July. Abortion had hitherto only been permitted in restricted circumstances, including those where the pregnancy was as a result of rape or posed a danger to the mother's health.

In March 2007 the former President of the CDS-PP, Portas, challenged Ribeiro e Castro for the leadership of the party. An election was held in April at which Portas was re-elected President by 74.6% of party members. In May António Costa, the Minister of Internal Administration, resigned from his post to stand as the PS candidate for Mayor of Lisbon, where a city council election had been precipitated by a corruption scandal. He was replaced by Rui Pereira, hitherto a judge of the Constitutional Court. Costa was duly elected as Mayor of Lisbon in July.

The Government's reform programme continued to provoke labour unrest in mid-2007, with a one-day general strike called by the CGTP causing significant disruption to public services in late May. In June the Government approved a new system of remuneration and career progression for civil servants, despite ongoing opposition from the CGTP. (However, elements of the new legislation, under which judges would be considered as civil servants rather than separately, as they were under the current system, were declared unconstitutional by the Constitutional Court in December.) In November the three principal public sector unions organized a one-day strike in protest against a 2.1% pay increase for civil servants for 2008. The unions had demanded rises of between 3.5% and 5.8%. None the less, the Government appeared to be succeeding in its efforts to reduce the budget deficit, despite the unpopularity of its reforms, and it was expected to achieve its target of reducing the deficit to below 3% of GDP by 2008.

In late September 2007 Luís Filipe Menezes, the Mayor of Vila Nova de Gaia, was narrowly elected leader of the PSD, defeating the incumbent, Marques Mendes, with 54.1% of the votes cast. The resignation of two ministers in late January 2008 prompted Sócrates to effect a minor government reorganization. Ana Jorge was appointed as Minister of Health, replacing António Correia de Campos, whose plans to restructure hospital emergency services had prompted a series of protests, while José António Pinto Ribeiro became Minister of Culture, succeeding Isabel Pires de Lima, who had also been criticized in recent months over her ministry's policies.

After only seven months as leader of the PSD, in April 2008 Menezes resigned from the post, citing criticism of his performance by a number of senior party members and ongoing disagreements within the PSD. Manuela Ferreira Leite, the Minister of State and of Finance in 2002–04, was elected to succeed him as party leader at a special conference held on 31 May 2008.

Relations between the two main parties deteriorated in early 2009 as the PS and the PSD began preparations for the forthcoming general election. Opinion polls indicated a decline in support for the governing PS, partly owing to the economic recession and an apparent fall in public support for Sócrates. In January the Prime Minister accused his opponents of conducting a smear campaign against him, following media reports linking him with an ongoing investigation into alleged financial improprieties related to the redesignation, in 2002, of land in an environmental protection zone in Alcochete, near Lisbon, for the construction of a shopping centre; Sócrates, who was Minister of the Environment and Territorial Planning at the time of the redesignation, denied any impropriety. None the less, in February 2009 he was re-elected unopposed as Secretary-General of the PS, with 96.4% of the votes cast. In March negotiations between the PS and the PSD over the nomination of a new state ombudsman collapsed after a disagreement over the process of selection. The PSD leadership refused to support the Government's chosen candidate, insisting that, in keeping with prior convention, the leading opposition party should assume responsibility for the nomination.

The EU Treaty establishing a Constitution for Europe was signed by the EU heads of state and of government in October 2004. In March 2005 the new PS administration announced its intention to hold a referendum on the EU constitutional treaty in October, after seeking the necessary constitutional amendment. However, following the rejection of the treaty in referendums in France and the Netherlands, in June 2005 the Portuguese Government postponed its own national referendum. The constitutional treaty was subsequently abandoned and, shortly after Portugal assumed the six-month rotating Presidency of the Council of the European Union, an Intergovernmental Conference was convened in Lisbon in July 2007 to draft a replacement. The resulting Treaty of Lisbon amending the Treaty on European Union and the Treaty establishing the European Community, which retained many of the provisions of the constitutional treaty (although it amended existing treaties rather than replacing them), was signed by EU leaders in December. In January 2008 Sócrates announced that the treaty was to be ratified by parliamentary vote in Portugal, rather than by a national referendum, as had been promised for the constitutional treaty. It was speculated that the Prime Minister had come under pressure from other European leaders who feared that a referendum in Portugal might jeopardize the ratification process in their own countries. The treaty was ratified by the Assembléia da República on 23 April and received presidential approval on 9 May. However, by mid-2008 the future of the treaty was uncertain, following its rejection by the Irish electorate at a referendum in June.

Support for the proposed US-led military campaign to remove the regime of Saddam Hussein in Iraq by the Prime Minister, Durão Barroso, provoked strong opposition from rival politicians, including President Sampaio, and public disapproval in early 2003. In January the Government authorized the USA to use the Lajes airbase in the Azores in the event of war. In March Durão Barroso affirmed his Government's support for the proposed military action in Iraq, with or without a UN mandate, and later that month he hosted an emergency summit between the leaders of the USA, the United Kingdom and Spain. However, following the rejection by the UN Security Council of a resolution endorsing military action against Iraq, a compromise on Portugal's stance was announced by President Sampaio: Portuguese troops would not participate in the conflict, although transit facilities would be made available for use by coalition forces. The Government defeated motions of censure submitted to the Assembléia da República in March by the four left-wing opposition parties and, in April, the Prime Minister indicated Portugal's willingness to deploy troops in Iraq for humanitarian and peace-keeping purposes. The proposed deployment gained the conditional support of opposition parties, who insisted that any such mission should take place under UN auspices. In November some 120 members of the paramilitary National Republican Guard were sent to Iraq. The contingent returned to Portugal in February 2005, following democratic elections in Iraq, although six troops remained in Iraq. Following an agreement between the Portuguese and Iraqi Governments, the contingent of six troops completed its mission and returned to Portugal in January 2009.

In mid-2005 Portuguese troops were deployed in Afghanistan as part of the NATO-led International Security Assistance Force (ISAF). In February 2008 some 132 Portuguese troops, who had been stationed in the Afghan capital, Kabul, returned to Portugal following the completion of their mission, although some 162 Portuguese troops continued to participate in ISAF. The gradual reduction of Portuguese forces in Afghanistan continued during 2008: in August some 60 troops returned to Portugal following the completion of their mission; in April 2009 a contingent of 30 Portuguese troops remained in Afghanistan as part of ISAF.

Relations with Spain improved in the late 1970s and 1980s following the restoration of democracy in both countries, and in May 1989 the Spanish monarch, King Juan Carlos I, addressed the Portuguese Assembléia da República. By the mid-1990s the principal bilateral issue had become that of the division of water supply, and in November 1998 Portugal and Spain signed an historic accord relating to the sharing of river resources. In December 2003 the two Governments reached a reciprocal agreement, to last 10 years, defining access to fishing waters.

Negotiations with the People's Republic of China on the question of the Portuguese overseas territory of Macao commenced in June 1986, and in April 1987 Portugal and China signed an agreement whereby Portugal would transfer the administration of Macao to China in December 1999. At midnight on 19 December 1999 the sovereignty of Macao was duly transferred (see chapter on Macao).

The former Portuguese territory of Timor-Leste (East Timor) was unilaterally annexed by Indonesia in 1976. UN-sponsored negotiations between Portugal and Indonesia began in 1983, but proved inconclusive. Under UN auspices, talks between Portugal and Indonesia on the Timor-Leste issue were resumed in December 1992, but again ended without agreement. In January 1995 Portugal and Indonesia agreed to the holding of discussions, under UN auspices, between the factions of Timor-Leste. In August 1998, following President Suharto's replacement in May and the subsequent implementation of a series of Indonesian troop withdrawals from the disputed region, the UN Secretary-

General announced that Portugal and Indonesia had agreed to hold discussions on the possibility of autonomy for Timor-Leste. In March 1999 it was announced that Portugal and Indonesia had reached an accord providing for the holding of a referendum in the territory on the question of either autonomy or independence. The referendum finally proceeded in August, and resulted in an overwhelming endorsement of proposals for full independence for Timor-Leste. The announcement of the result, however, precipitated a rapid decline in the security situation, leading to the declaration of martial law in the territory. In mid-September a multinational peace-keeping force, led by Australia, was deployed in the territory. Following the restoration of order in Timor-Leste and the Indonesian Government's acceptance of the result of the referendum, in December 1999 Portugal and Indonesia resumed full diplomatic relations, which had been severed in 1975, and in January 2001 a new Indonesian ambassador to Portugal was appointed. Meanwhile, Portugal committed an initial 700 troops to the UN peace-keeping force that replaced the Australian-led multinational force in early 2000. The Portuguese Government also pledged an annual sum of US $75m. towards the reconstruction of Timor-Leste. Official diplomatic relations with Timor-Leste were established with the creation of an embassy in Lisbon in 2002. In June 2006 120 members of the National Republican Guard were dispatched to Timor-Leste, following an upsurge in violence in that country. Portugal also contributed police and military liaison officers to the UN Integrated Mission in Timor-Leste, which was established in August.

Portugal played a significant role in the peace process in Angola, a former Portuguese overseas possession. Several meetings between representatives of the Angolan Government and the União Nacional para a Independência Total de Angola (UNITA) rebel group were held in Lisbon, culminating in the signing of a peace accord in 1991. In June 1993, following the resumption of hostilities in January, UNITA rejected Portugal's status as an observer in the new peace process; however, in May 1994 a UNITA spokesman welcomed the possibility of further Portuguese mediation. A new peace agreement was signed in November of that year. In early 1995, however, the neutrality of the Portuguese Government was impugned by allegations that it had given technical assistance to the Angolan Government. In July 1998, following renewed hostilities in Angola, Portugal requested the intervention of the UN Secretary-General. In August UNITA severed its links with Portugal and the other observers in the peace process, accusing them of bias towards the Angolan Government. In March 2000 tensions between Angola and Portugal increased, following comments by the Angolan Minister of Social Communication, accusing the former Portuguese President, Mario Soares, and his son, João, of benefiting from UNITA's illegal trade in diamonds. The allegations were strongly denied by UNITA. However, in May it was announced that military co-operation between Portugal and the government forces was to be increased. Following the cessation of hostilities in Angola in April 2002, Portugal was one of three states with representatives observing the peace process according to the Lusaka Protocol. Portugal was to continue with military support, including overseeing the integration of UNITA soldiers into new armed forces and the establishment of a military academy.

Portugal was also involved in attempts to reach a peace settlement in Mozambique. Relations with Mozambique deteriorated in March 1989, however, when a Mozambican diplomat was expelled from Portugal, following his implication in the assassination, in April 1988, of a Mozambican resistance leader. Nevertheless, in January 1992 Portugal received a formal invitation to attend the peace talks as an observer, and in October a peace treaty was signed in Italy.

In July 1996 Portugal hosted the inaugural meeting of the Comunidade dos Países de Língua Portuguesa (CPLP, see p. 438), a grouping of lusophone countries (including Angola, Brazil, Mozambique and Guinea-Bissau), which aimed to promote closer political and economic co-operation. In late 1998, as part of a CPLP initiative, Portugal played a major role in the implementation of a peace agreement in Guinea-Bissau, ending several months of conflict between government and rebel forces in the former colony. In the aftermath of a coup in May 1999, the deposed President of Guinea-Bissau, João Vieira, was granted asylum in Portugal. Following the bloodless coup in Guinea-Bissau in September 2003, the Portuguese Government provided US $1.5m. in aid to the new Government. New Portuguese legislation on immigration, which entered into force in August 2007, was aimed, *inter alia*, at integrating foreign workers by facilitating the granting of residence permits to undocumented migrants, the majority of whom came from Brazil and lusophone African countries.

Government

A new Constitution, envisaging the construction of a socialist society in Portugal, was promulgated in 1976 and revised in 1982. Subsequent revisions included the provision in 1997 for the holding of referendums on issues of national interest. The organs of sovereignty are the President, the Assembléia da República and the Government. The President, elected by popular vote for a five-year term, appoints the Prime Minister and, on the latter's proposal, other members of the Government, principally the Council of Ministers. The Council of State (Conselho de Estado) is a consultative body. Following the election of October 1991, the unicameral Assembléia had 230 members, including four representing Portuguese citizens abroad, elected by universal adult suffrage for four years (subject to dissolution). The mainland comprises 18 administrative districts. The Azores and Madeira (integral parts of the Portuguese Republic) were granted autonomy in 1976. The overseas territory of Macao was governed by special statute until December 1999, when it reverted to Chinese sovereignty.

Defence

Compulsory military service was abolished in 2004. Portugal is a member of the North Atlantic Treaty Organization (NATO, see p. 351) and of Western European Union (see p. 442). As assessed at November 2008, the total strength of the armed forces was 43,920, comprising: army 26,700, navy 10,120 (including 1,430 marines) and air force 7,100. There were reserves of 210,900. The paramilitary National Republican Guard and the Public Security Police totalled 26,100 and 21,600, respectively. A total of 792 US troops were stationed in Portugal, mainly at the air force base at Lajes in the Azores. In November 2004 Portugal confirmed its participation (with Italy, Spain and Greece) in one of a number of European Union (EU, see p. 255) 'battlegroups', each comprising about 1,500 troops. The battlegroups, two of which were to be ready for deployment at any one time, following a rotational schedule, reached full operational capacity from 1 January 2007. Portugal subsequently agreed to participate in a second EU battlegroup, led by Spain and also involving Germany and France. The 2008 state budget allocated €1,960m. to defence.

Economic Affairs

In 2007, according to estimates by the World Bank, Portugal's overall gross national income (GNI), measured at average 2005–07 prices, was US $201,079m., equivalent to $18,950 per head (or $20,890 on an international purchasing-power parity basis). During 2000–07, it was estimated, the population increased at an average rate of 0.5% per year, while gross domestic product (GDP) per head increased, in real terms, by an average of 0.5% per year. Overall GDP expanded, in real terms, at an average annual rate of 1.0% in 2000–07; GDP increased by 1.9% in 2007.

Agriculture (including forestry and fishing) contributed an estimated 2.7% of GDP in 2007, while engaging 11.6% of the employed labour force. The principal crops are grapes, tomatoes, potatoes, maize, sugar beets, olives, wheat, apples and oranges. The production of wine, particularly port, is significant. The fishing industry is important, the sardine catch, at 74,100 metric tons in 2006, being by far the largest. Agricultural GDP decreased, in real terms, by 0.5% per year during 2000–06, although agricultural GDP increased by 8.2% in 2006, owing largely to the recovery following a severe drought in 2005.

Industry (comprising mining, manufacturing, construction and power) contributed an estimated 24.5% of GDP and engaged 30.5% of the employed labour force in 2007. The GDP of the industrial sector declined, in real terms, by an estimated 0.5% per year during 2000–07; however, industrial GDP increased by 0.2% in 2006. The mining and quarrying industry makes a minimal contribution to GDP, engaging just 0.4% of the employed labour force in 2007. Limestone, granite, marble, copper pyrites, gold and uranium are the most significant products.

Manufacturing provided 15.8% of GDP in 2005, and engaged 18.5% of the employed labour force in 2007. Manufacturing GDP grew by a negligible amount annually in 2000–03. The textile industry is the most important branch of manufacturing. Basic manufactures accounted for 21.6% of total export earnings in 2007. Other significant manufactured products include cork items, chemicals, electrical appliances, ceramics and paper pulp.

In 2005 33.0% of electricity production was derived from coal, 29.5% from natural gas, 19.0% from petroleum and 10.2% from hydroelectric power. In 2007 imports of mineral fuels accounted for 13.9% of total import costs. Portugal's heavy dependence on petroleum was reduced in 1997 when a pipeline carrying natural gas from Algeria (via Morocco and Spain) was inaugurated. Investment in renewable energy sources has increased significantly during recent years, in accordance with the Government's aim to produce some 60% of Portugal's energy from renewable sources by 2020. (In 2007 40.7% of energy production was from renewable sources.) In January 2007 the construction of an 11-MW solar power plant was completed in Serpa, some 200 km south-east of Lisbon; a 62-MW plant under construction at Moura, in the southern region of Alentejo, which was to be the largest in the world, was scheduled for completion in 2010. The use of wind power has expanded in recent years: by March 2007 wind farms with a total generating capacity of 1,874.0 MW had been connected to the national electricity grid, while additional farms with a capacity of 908.5 MW were under construction. In addition, a commercial wave-energy project was under way off the coast of northern Portugal. In February 2009 an agreement was signed between Energias de Portugal and the US-based Principle Power to generate electricity from wind turbines off the Portuguese coast.

Services provided 72.9% of GDP and engaged 57.8% of the employed labour force in 2007. The tourism industry remained a significant source of foreign exchange earnings in 2006, when receipts totalled an estimated US $10,036m. In 2006 there were 7.0m. tourist arrivals in Portugal. Emigrants' remittances are also important to the Portuguese economy, reaching €1,277m. in 2005. The GDP of the services sector increased, in real terms, by an estimated average of 1.5% per year during 2000–06; services GDP increased by 1.2% in 2006.

In 2007 Portugal recorded a visible trade deficit of US $24,108m., and there was a deficit of $21,418m. on the current account of the balance of payments. Most of Portugal's trade is with other members of the European Union (EU, see p. 255). In 2007 Spain, Germany and France (including Monaco) supplied 29.5%, 12.8% and 8.3%, respectively, of total imports. The principal export markets were also Spain (which purchased 26.7% of the total), Germany (12.5%) and France-Monaco (12.0%). The main exports in 2007 were machinery and transport equipment (31.2%), basic manufactures (21.6%), miscellaneous manufactured articles (15.9%), and chemicals and related products (7.0%). The principal imports were machinery and transport equipment, basic manufactures, mineral fuels, and food and live animals.

The central government budget deficit for 2007 was estimated at €4,325m., equivalent to 2.7% of GDP, compared with 3.9% in 2006 and 6.1% in 2005. In 2007 Portugal's general government debt was estimated at €103,552.0m., equivalent to 63.6% of GDP. In 2000–07 the annual rate of inflation averaged 3.0%. The average rate of inflation was 2.5% in 2007. The unemployment rate averaged 8.0% in 2007.

Portugal became a member of the European Community (EC, now EU) in January 1986, and participated in the introduction of the European single currency, the euro, on 1 January 1999. Portugal is also a member of the Organisation for Economic Co-operation and Development (OECD, see p. 358) and of the Comunidade dos Países de Língua Portuguesa (CPLP, see p. 438), which was established in Lisbon in 1996.

Following a period of strong growth during the late 1990s, the economy slowed considerably in the early 2000s. There was a modest recovery in 2004, when growth of 1.5% was achieved, but it slowed again in 2005 to just 0.5% before rising to 1.4% in 2006, making Portugal the slowest growing economy in the EU. By 2005 the budget deficit had increased to the equivalent of 6.1% of GDP, exceeding the 3% stipulated in the EU's Stability and Growth Pact. The Government that took office in early 2005 announced a four-year economic programme including the promotion of private investment in infrastructure and the reversal of the previous administration's policy of tax cuts. The Government achieved some progress in its programme of fiscal and administrative reforms during 2005–07, most notably reducing benefit payments and raising the minimum age of retirement for public sector workers from 60 to 65 years, and the budget deficit decreased to 2.6% in 2007 and an estimated 2.2% in 2008. However, the Portuguese economy officially entered recession at the end of 2008, owing to the effects of the global economic crisis. As a small, open economy Portugal was vulnerable to external conditions, which had an adverse effect on exports and investment. In addition, the country's high levels of household debt contributed to low levels of consumer confidence, which was likely to slow recovery. In October the Government announced that it would provide up to €20,000m. in loan guarantees to banks based in Portugal, in an attempt to encourage inter-bank lending. However, the following month the Government was forced to nationalize the Banco Português de Negócios, after it was revealed that the bank had suffered losses of some €700m. The budget deficit was expected to increase significantly in 2009, owing to the effects of the economic downturn and the impact of a fiscal stimulus package to encourage growth. Real GDP growth was negligible in 2008. GDP was forecast to contract by 3.5% in 2009.

Education

Formal education at all levels is provided at both public and private institutions. Pre-school education, for three- to six-year olds, is not compulsory, and is available free of charge. Basic education is compulsory for nine years, between the ages of six and 15, and is provided free of charge in public schools. It is divided into three cycles: the first lasts for four years, the second for two years and the third for three years. Secondary education, which is not compulsory, lasts for three years, and comprises a single three-year cycle, with two types: general and vocational. In April 2009 the Prime Minister announced a government proposal to introduce legislation that would compel pupils to remain in compulsory education until the age of 18 years, which was to enter into effect by 2014. In 2005/06 98% of children in the relevant age-group were enrolled in primary schools, while 82% of children in the relevant age-group were enrolled in secondary schools (males 78%; females 86%).

Higher education comprises two systems. Universities award the following academic degrees: the *licenciatura*, after four to six years of study, the *mestrado*, after one or two years of study and research work, and the *doutoramento*. Regional polytechnic institutes, grouping technical, management, educational and fine arts schools, offer three-year courses leading to the *bacharel* and specialized studies leading to a diploma after one to two years. New curricula were introduced in 2003/04 and 2004/05. In 2007/08 a total of 376,917 students were enrolled in higher education. Expenditure on education in 2004 was €7,132m. (representing 15.9% of general government expenditure).

Public Holidays

2009: 1 January (New Year's Day), 24 February (Carnival Day), 10 April (Good Friday), 25 April (Liberty Day), 1 May (Labour Day), 10 June (Portugal Day), 11 June (Corpus Christi), 13 June (St Anthony—Lisbon only), 24 June (St John the Baptist—Oporto only), 15 August (Assumption), 5 October (Proclamation of the Republic), 1 November (All Saints' Day), 1 December (Restoration of Independence), 8 December (Immaculate Conception), 25 December (Christmas Day).

2010: 1 January (New Year's Day), 16 February (Carnival Day)*, 2 April (Good Friday), 25 April (Liberty Day), 1 May (Labour Day), 3 June (Corpus Christi), 10 June (Portugal Day), 13 June (St Anthony—Lisbon only)*, 24 June (St John the Baptist—Oporto only)*, 15 August (Assumption), 5 October (Proclamation of the Republic), 1 November (All Saints' Day), 1 December (Restoration of Independence), 8 December (Immaculate Conception), 25 December (Christmas Day).

* Optional.

Weights and Measures

The metric system is in force.

PORTUGAL

Statistical Survey

Source (unless otherwise stated): Instituto Nacional de Estatística (INE), Av. António José de Almeida 2, 1000-043 Lisbon; tel. (21) 8426100; fax (21) 8426380; e-mail ine@ine.pt; internet www.ine.pt.

Area and Population

AREA, POPULATION AND DENSITY

Area (sq km)	
Land	91,906
Inland water	439
Total	92,345*
Population (census results)	
15 April 1991	9,862,540
1 March 2001	
Males	5,000,141
Females	5,355,976
Total	10,356,117
Population (official estimates at 31 December)	
2005	10,569,592
2006	10,599,095
2007	10,617,575
Density (per sq km) at 31 December 2007	115.5

*35,655 sq miles.

REGIONS
(official estimates at 31 December 2007)

	Area (sq km)*	Population	Density (per sq km)
Continental Portugal	88,796	10,126,880	114.0
Norte	21,278	3,745,236	176.0
Centro	23,668	2,385,911	100.8
Lisboa e Vale do Tejo	11,931	2,808,414	235.4
Alentejo	26,931	760,933	28.3
Algarve	4,988	426,386	85.5
Autonomous Regions	3,109	490,695	157.8
Os Açores (Azores)	2,330	244,006	104.7
Madeira	779	246,689	316.7
Total	91,905	10,617,575	115.5

*Excluding river estuaries (439 sq km).

PRINCIPAL TOWNS
(population at 2001 census)

Lisboa (Lisbon, the capital)	564,657	Vila Nova de Gaia	69,698
Porto (Oporto)	263,131	Guimarães	63,058
		Algueirão-Mem Martins	62,557
Amadora	151,486	Parede	61,821
Braga	112,039	Odivelas	53,449
Coimbra	104,489	Amora	50,991
Funchal	103,961	Leiria	50,167
Setúbal	96,776		
Agualva-Cacém	81,845		

Source: Thomas Brinkhoff, *City Population* (internet www.citypopulation.de).

Mid-2006: (UN estimates) Lisboa (Lisbon) 514,773; Porto (Oporto) 230,628; Amadora 175,000 (Source: UN, *Demographic Yearbook*).

BIRTHS, MARRIAGES AND DEATHS

	Registered live births		Registered marriages		Registered deaths	
	Number	Rate (per 1,000)	Number	Rate (per 1,000)	Number	Rate (per 1,000)
2000	120,008	11.7	63,752	6.2	105,813	10.3
2001	112,774	11.0	58,390	5.7	105,092	10.2
2002	114,456	11.0	56,457	5.4	106,690	10.2
2003	112,589	10.8	53,735	5.1	109,148	10.4
2004	109,356	10.4	49,178	4.7	102,371	9.7
2005	109,399	10.4	48,671	4.6	107,462	10.2
2006	105,449	10.0	47,857	4.5	101,990	9.6
2007	102,567	9.7	46,329	4.4	103,888	9.8

Life expectancy (years at birth, WHO estimates): 78.9 (males 75.5; females 82.3) in 2006. (Source: WHO, *World Health Statistics*).

ECONOMICALLY ACTIVE POPULATION
(ISIC major divisions, '000 persons aged 15 years and over)

	2005	2006	2007
Agriculture, hunting and forestry	587.5	587.7	584.3
Fishing	18.7	16.2	17.1
Mining and quarrying	19.1	17.6	19.3
Electricity, gas and water supply	24.9	26.1	33.7
Manufacturing	968.6	980.5	954.0
Construction	554.1	553.0	570.8
Wholesale and retail trade; repair of motor vehicles, motorcycles and personal and household goods	773.0	751.2	750.2
Hotels and restaurants	275.8	280.0	288.8
Transport, storage and communications	220.8	239.6	223.7
Financial intermediation	95.2	90.1	95.7
Real estate, renting and business activities	283.7	294.5	325.4
Public administration and defence; compulsory social security	347.5	354.3	327.0
Education	314.9	318.7	306.7
Health and social work	326.8	329.8	340.2
Other community, social and personal service activities*	158.6	164.9	162.4
Private households with employed persons	150.9	152.4	167.5
Unallocated	2.6	2.9	2.8
Total employed*	5,122.6	5,159.5	5,169.7
Unemployed	422.3	427.8	448.6
Total labour force	5,544.9	5,587.3	5,618.3
Males	2,963.5	2,984.5	n.a.
Females	2,581.3	2,602.9	n.a.

*Including regular members of the armed forces, but excluding persons on compulsory military service.

Source: ILO.

PORTUGAL

Health and Welfare

KEY INDICATORS

Total fertility rate (children per woman, 2005)	1.5
Under-5 mortality rate (per 1,000 live births, 2006)	4
HIV/AIDS (% of persons aged 15–49, 2006)	0.5
Physicians (per 1,000 head, 2005)	3.4
Hospital beds (per 1,000 head, 2005)	3.7
Health expenditure (2006): US $ per head (PPP)	2,080
Health expenditure (2006): % of GDP	10.0
Health expenditure (2006): public (% of total)	71.8
Human Development Index (2006): ranking	33
Human Development Index (2006): value	0.900

For sources and definitions, see explanatory note on p. vi.

Agriculture

PRINCIPAL CROPS
('000 metric tons)

	2005	2006	2007
Wheat	82	250	136
Rice, paddy	121	147	155
Barley	20	106	74
Maize	513	514	647
Rye	19	24	24
Oats	25	87	48
Triticale (wheat-rye hybrid)	8	40	20
Potatoes	576	611	639
Sweet potatoes*	22	25	26
Sugar beets	605	319	320
Olives	212	373	375*
Sunflower seeds	2	4	17
Cabbages and other brassicas*	200	145	150
Lettuce and chicory*	95	100	105
Tomatoes	1,085	983	1,000
Cauliflower and broccoli*	35	38	44
Onions, dry*	115	115	117
Broad beans, horse beans, dry*	17	18	18
Beans, green*	15	16	17
Carrots and turnips*	150	160	170
Carobs*	20	22	23
Chestnuts	22	31	32*
Bananas*	30	32	34
Oranges	219	235	201
Tangerines, mandarins, clementines and satsumas	58	59	59
Apples	249	247	198
Pears	130	175	170
Peaches and nectarines	52	50	45
Grapes	989	1,029	1,050*
Cantaloupes and other melons*	20	22	22

* FAO estimate(s).

Aggregate production ('000 metric tons, may include official, semi-official or estimated data): Total cereals 790 in 2005, 1,167 in 2006, 1,103 in 2007; Total roots and tubers 600 in 2005, 639 in 2006, 668 in 2007; Total vegetables (incl. melons) 2,379 in 2005, 2,269 in 2006, 2,342 in 2007; Total fruits (excl. melons) 1,853 in 2005, 1,964 in 2006, 1,893 in 2007.

Source: FAO.

LIVESTOCK
('000 head, year ending September)

	2005	2006	2007
Horses*	17	18	19
Asses*	125	n.a.	n.a.
Cattle	1,443	1,441	1,407
Pigs	2,348	2,344	2,295
Sheep	3,541	3,583	3,549
Goats	547	551	547
Chickens*	35,000	36,000	37,000
Turkeys*	7,000	7,200	7,500

* FAO estimates.
Source: FAO.

LIVESTOCK PRODUCTS
('000 metric tons)

	2005	2006	2007
Cattle meat	118	105	106
Sheep meat	22*	24†	23†
Pig meat	327	339	332†
Chicken meat	198	193	206†
Cows' milk	1,991	1,851	1,925
Sheep's milk	100	96	96
Goats' milk	29	29	28
Hen eggs	120	121	119

* Unofficial figure.
† FAO estimate.
Source: FAO.

Forestry

ROUNDWOOD REMOVALS
('000 cubic metres, excluding bark)

	2004	2005	2006
Sawlogs, veneer logs and logs for sleepers	2,246	2,483	2,510
Pulpwood	7,843	7,483	7,514
Other industrial wood*	180	180	180
Fuel wood*	600	600	600
Total	10,869	10,746	10,805

* FAO estimates.

2007: Production assumed to be unchanged from 2006 (FAO estimates).
Source: FAO.

SAWNWOOD PRODUCTION
('000 cubic metres, including railway sleepers)

	2003	2004	2005
Coniferous (softwood)	910	954	909
Broadleaved (hardwood)	473	106	101
Total	1,383	1,060	1,010

2006–07: Production assumed to be unchanged from 2005 (FAO estimates).
Source: FAO.

Fishing

('000 metric tons, live weight)

	2004	2005	2006
Capture	221.3	211.8	229.1
Atlantic horse mackerel	16.7	15.9	17.3
European pilchard (sardine)	75.9	67.4	74.1
Black scabbardfish	7.1	6.8	5.4
Atlantic redfishes	10.7	12.1	12.8
Chub mackerel	15.2	15.6	17.8
Blue shark	5.2	8.4	9.4
Octopuses	7.8	7.9	3.6
Aquaculture	6.7	6.7	6.8
Total catch	228.0	218.5	235.9

Note: Figures exclude aquatic plants ('000 metric tons): 0.3 in 2004; 0.6 in 2005; 0.8 in 2006.
Source: FAO.

PORTUGAL

Mining

('000 metric tons, estimated production, unless otherwise indicated)

	2004	2005	2006
Iron ore: gross weight	14.0	14.0	14.0
Iron ore: metal content	10.0	10.0	10.0
Copper ore*	95.7†	89.5†	78.6
Tungsten ore (metric tons)*	746†	816†	780
Silver ore (metric tons)*	24.4†	23.8†	20.1
Marble	749†	752†	n.a.
Granite (crushed and ornamental)	30.3†	30.7	n.a.
Kaolin	152.1†	164.1†	n.a.
Salt (rock)	661.7†	597.9†	586.2
Gypsum and anhydrite	461.2†	289.2†	n.a.
Talc (metric tons)	6,231†	5,362†	5,517

* Figures refer to the metal content of ores.
† Official figure.

Source: US Geological Survey.

Industry

SELECTED PRODUCTS
('000 metric tons, unless otherwise indicated)

	2002	2003	2004
Frozen fish	39.8	37.6	42.7
Tinned fish	43.3	43.3	48.9
Wheat flour	689	692	650
Refined sugar	400	370	n.a.
Prepared animal feeds	3,747	3,942	4,315
Distilled alcoholic beverages ('000 hectolitres)	284	297	266
Wine ('000 hectolitres)	6,449	7,149	7,257
Beer ('000 hectolitres)	6,689	7,110	7,712
Cigarettes (million units)	25,581	24,950	26,415
Wool yarn (pure and mixed)	5.3	3.6	n.a.
Cotton yarn (pure and mixed)	95.9	82.9	n.a.
Woven cotton fabrics (million sq metres)	350	305	n.a.
Woven woollen fabrics (million sq metres)	9.0	5.4	n.a.
Knitted fabrics	51.6	59.4	58.6
Footwear, excl. rubber ('000 pairs)	73,191	67,272	n.a.
Wood pulp (sulphate and soda)	714	677	647
Caustic soda (Sodium hydroxide)	87	88	81
Soda ash (Sodium carbonate)*	150	150	150
Nitrogenous fertilizers	123	n.a.	n.a.
Jet fuels	511	703	779
Motor spirit (petrol)	2,518	2,732	2,551
Naphthas	1,084	1,130	1,175
Distillate fuel oils	4,827	4,955	4,703
Residual fuel oils	2,358	2,388	2,969
Liquefied petroleum gas	341	379	365
Household ware of porcelain or china (metric tons)	29,223	26,939	n.a.
Household ware of other ceramic materials (metric tons)	95,712	115,241	n.a.
Cement	9,728	8,598	8,839
Pig-iron*	100	100	100
Crude steel (ingots)*	894	722	720
Refrigerators for household use ('000)	440	452	399
Radio receivers ('000)	8,470	7,310	7,805
Electric energy (million kWh)	46,107	46,852	45,105

* Figures from US Geological Survey.

2005 ('000 metric tons, unless otherwise indicated): Wine ('000 hectolitres) 7,051.3; Soda ash (sodium carbonate) 150; Pig-iron 100 (estimate); Crude steel (ingots) 725.

2006 ('000 metric tons, estimates): Soda ash (sodium carbonate) 150; Pig-iron 100; Crude steel (ingots) 725.

Source: mainly UN, *Industrial Commodity Statistics Yearbook*.

Statistical Survey

Finance

CURRENCY AND EXCHANGE RATES

Monetary Units
100 cent = 1 euro (€).

Sterling and Dollar Equivalents (31 December 2008)
£1 sterling = 1.0475 euros;
US $1 = 0.7185 euros;
€10 = £9.55 = $13.92.

Average Exchange Rate (euros per US dollar)
2006 0.7971
2007 0.7306
2008 0.6827

Note: The national currency was formerly the Portuguese escudo. From the introduction of the euro, with Portuguese participation, on 1 January 1999, a fixed exchange rate of €1 = 200.482 escudos was in operation. Euro notes and coins were introduced on 1 January 2002. The euro and local currency circulated alongside each other until 28 February, after which the euro became the sole legal tender.

BUDGET
(€ million)*

Revenue	2005	2006	2007
Current revenue	59,838	64,162	68,753
Taxes on income and wealth	12,574	13,662	15,892
Taxes on production and imports	22,384	23,995	24,541
Social contributions	18,697	19,360	20,702
Sale of goods and services	3,569	3,868	4,097
Other current revenue	2,614	3,277	3,521
Capital revenue	2,148	1,750	1,460
Total	61,986	65,912	70,213

Expenditure	2005	2006	2007
Current expenditure	64,613	66,684	68,911
Wages and salaries	21,541	21,165	21,006
Social transfers	27,516	29,221	31,308
Intermediate consumption	6,316	6,428	6,670
Interest payments	3,827	4,318	4,676
Subsidies	2,339	2,155	1,901
Other current expenditure	3,075	3,397	3,350
Capital expenditure	6,396	5,263	5,627
Gross capital formation	4,380	3,617	3,926
Other	2,016	1,647	1,701
Total	71,009	71,947	74,538

* Figures refer to the consolidated accounts of the central Government, excluding assets and liabilities.

Source: Direcção-Geral do Orçamento, Ministério das Finanças.

INTERNATIONAL RESERVES
(US $ million at 31 December)*

	2006	2007	2008
Gold†	7,819	10,288	10,639
IMF special drawing rights	113	123	123
Reserve position in IMF	115	90	165
Foreign exchange	1,835	1,044	1,022
Total	9,882	11,545	11,949

* Reserves are defined in accordance with the Eurosystem's statistical definition.
† Valued at $635.7 per troy ounce in 2006, $836.4 in 2007 and $865.04 in 2008.

Source: IMF, *International Financial Statistics*.

PORTUGAL

MONEY SUPPLY
(€ million at 31 December)

	2006	2007	2008
Currency in circulation*	1,472	1,583	1,775
Demand deposits at banking institutions	57,830	56,150	53,990

* Currency put into circulation by the Banco de Portugal was €4,970m. in 2006, €3,520m. in 2007 and €2,070m. in 2008.

Source: IMF, *International Financial Statistics*.

COST OF LIVING
(Consumer Price Index; base: 2000 = 100)

	2005	2006	2007
Food	111.3	114.2	117.0
Clothing	103.1	103.9	106.3
Electricity, gas and other fuels	119.4	124.3	128.7
Rent	119.5	123.4	123.7
All items (incl. others)*	116.7	120.3	123.3

* Excluding rent.

Source: ILO.

NATIONAL ACCOUNTS
(€ million at current prices, preliminary)

Composition of the Gross National Income

	2005	2006	2007
Gross domestic product at market prices	149,123.5	155,322.6	162,756.1
Primary incomes received from abroad	8,731.8	11,714.1	13,590.1
Less Primary incomes paid abroad	11,631.5	17,529.3	20,565.9
Gross national income	146,223.8	149,507.4	155,780.3
Less Consumption of fixed capital*	24,753.4	25,836.7	26,997.3
Net national income*	121,470.4	123,670.7	128,783.0
Current transfers from abroad	4,603.1	5,103.9	5,115.8
Less Current transfers paid abroad	3,120.8	2,998.1	3,002.7
Net national disposable income	122,952.7	125,776.5	130,896.1

* Figures obtained as a residual.

Expenditure on the Gross Domestic Product

	2005	2006	2007
Final consumption expenditure	128,680.9	133,223.1	138,231.5
Households and non-profit institutions serving households	96,706.7	101,015.2	105,260.3
General government	31,974.2	32,207.9	32,971.2
Gross capital formation	33,649.5	34,574.2	36,184.6
Total domestic expenditure	162,330.4	167,797.3	174,416.1
Exports of goods and services	42,567.1	48,531.5	53,606.7
Less Imports of goods and services	55,774.0	61,006.2	65,266.7
GDP in market prices	149,123.5	155,322.6	162,756.1
GDP at constant 2000 prices	127,711.2	129,345.7	131,610.6

Gross Domestic Product by Economic Activity

	2005	2006	2007
Agriculture, hunting, forestry and fishing	3,641.8	3,895.7	3,709.1
Electricity, gas and water	3,336.1	3,599.2	3,796.6
Industry	19,358.6	20,139.8	21,526.6
Construction	8,794.8	8,641.9	8,863.4
Trade, restaurants and hotels	22,393.6	23,355.3	24,686.6
Transport, storage and communications	8,849.6	9,031.5	9,202.8
Finance, insurance and real estate	18,476.8	19,918.7	21,336.6
Other services	43,511.5	44,556.9	46,471.9
Gross value added in basic prices	128,362.8	133,139.0	139,593.0
Taxes on products (net)	20,760.5	22,181.9	22,997.5
Statistical discrepancy	0.2	1.7	165.6
GDP in market prices	149,123.5	155,322.6	162,756.1

BALANCE OF PAYMENTS
(US $ million)

	2005	2006	2007
Exports of goods f.o.b.	38,577	43,592	51,746
Imports of goods f.o.b.	−58,916	−64,510	−75,853
Trade balance	−20,339	−20,918	−24,108
Exports of services	15,193	17,839	23,156
Imports of services	−10,456	−11,758	−13,950
Balance on goods and services	−15,603	−14,836	−14,901
Other income received	9,307	13,518	17,332
Other income paid	−14,151	−21,492	−27,467
Balance on goods, services and income	−20,446	−22,810	−25,036
Current transfers received	7,226	8,054	8,709
Current transfers paid	−4,398	−4,884	−5,090
Current balance	−17,619	−19,640	−21,418
Capital account (net)	2,115	1,527	2,837
Direct investment abroad	−2,252	−7,003	−6,205
Direct investment from abroad	4,059	11,344	5,534
Portfolio investment assets	−19,659	−9,580	−12,104
Portfolio investment liabilities	18,141	13,514	25,117
Financial derivatives assets	4,865	6,790	11,513
Financial derivatives liabilities	−5,076	−7,053	−10,583
Other investment assets	−1,246	−17,051	−15,881
Other investment liabilities	15,797	23,366	21,779
Net errors and omissions	−866	1,430	−1,552
Overall balance	−1,741	−2,357	−962

Source: IMF, *International Financial Statistics*.

External Trade

PRINCIPAL COMMODITIES
(US $ million)

Imports c.i.f.	2005	2006	2007
Food and live animals	5,645.3	6,216.9	7,890.0
Fish, crustaceans and molluscs	1,321.8	1,504.3	1,840.1
Cereal and cereal preparations	939.0	959.1	1,312.0
Mineral fuels, lubricants and related materials	8,969.6	10,078.9	10,924.3
Petroleum and petroleum products	6,887.1	7,932.1	8,471.0
Chemicals and related products	6,459.8	7,246.5	8,415.9
Medicinal and pharmaceutical products	2,045.6	2,301.1	2,579.3
Basic manufactures	9,700.4	10,958.6	13,069.2
Paper, paperboard and articles thereof	1,113.2	1,158.2	1,424.3
Textile yarn, fabrics and related products	1,735.4	1,784.1	2,007.7
Machinery and transport equipment	18,794.9	19,763.2	23,633.3
General industrial machinery and equipment	1,930.7	2,006.4	2,468.2
Office machines and data processing machines	1,378.6	1,531.9	1,726.4
Telecommunications and sound recording equipment	1,981.7	2,028.8	2,533.1
Miscellaneous manufactured articles	6,166.3	6,515.5	7,850.9
Articles of clothing and clothing accessories	1,603.9	1,699.0	2,110.5
Total (incl. others)	61,167.1	66,693.8	78,325.6

Exports f.o.b.	2005	2006	2007
Food and live animals	1,695.9	1,960.1	2,574.4
Vegetables and fruit	479.1	531.3	679.5
Beverages and tobacco	1,106.0	1,285.8	1,625.6
Wine	657.3	672.4	827.2
Crude materials (inedible), except fuels	1,321.5	1,752.7	2,076.0
Metalliferous ore and metal scrap	521.1	835.1	977.1
Mineral fuels, lubricants and related materials	1,625.0	2,368.1	2,280.9
Petroleum and petroleum products	1,445.6	2,085.0	2,072.4
Chemicals and related products	2,480.3	2,837.2	3,611.0
Organic chemicals	622.1	671.6	843.0
Basic manufactures	7,952.4	9,083.2	11,109.9
Cork and wood manufactures	1,319.7	1,385.7	1,640.0
Cork manufacture	917.4	931.4	1,039.2
Textile yarn, fabrics and related products	1,632.3	1,696.2	1,949.5
Non-metallic mineral manufactures	1,350.0	1,461.2	1,885.0
Iron and steel	832.8	1,083.8	1,390.9
Manufactures of metal	1,246.3	1,481.4	1,872.6
Machinery and transport equipment	11,791.2	13,662.5	16,074.8
General industrial machinery and equipment	1,294.6	1,644.8	1,996.0
Telecommunications and sound recording equipment	1,296.5	1,397.8	1,592.8
Electrical machinery and appliances	2,393.9	3,422.3	4,250.3
Road vehicles	4,799.4	5,414.7	6,058.6
Miscellaneous manufactured articles	6,608.9	6,854.8	8,186.0
Total (incl. others)	38,085.7	43,358.4	51,517.0

Source: UN, *International Trade Statistics Yearbook*.

PRINCIPAL TRADING PARTNERS
(US $ million)

Imports c.i.f.	2005	2006	2007
Algeria	1,362.7	1,124.6	789.1
Belgium	1,730.3	1,763.4	2,184.7
Brazil	1,215.3	1,543.5	1,872.7
China, People's Repub.	703.3	966.1	1,437.8
France (incl. Monaco)	5,176.6	5,398.1	6,534.5
Germany	8,207.0	8,739.2	10,034.0
Ireland	571.7	594.0	629.1
Italy	3,176.8	3,713.7	4,096.1
Japan	723.5	687.1	774.8
Libya	375.5	579.2	1,085.0
Netherlands	2,613.4	2,933.9	3,521.0
Norway	638.8	846.0	933.1
Russia	463.5	806.4	752.5
Spain	17,694.7	19,306.8	23,100.1
Sweden	668.9	600.8	826.1
United Kingdom	2,573.1	2,651.5	2,692.8
USA	1,327.2	977.9	1,288.8
Total (incl. others)	61,167.1	66,693.8	78,325.6

Exports f.o.b.	2005	2006	2007
Angola	996.0	1,518.5	2,302.1
Belgium	1,402.1	1,338.6	1,250.3
Brazil	220.4	319.3	351.6
Denmark	295.2	291.3	340.5
Finland	269.3	290.9	284.5
France (incl. Monaco)	4,949.8	5,176.0	6,160.3
Germany	4,438.7	5,532.6	6,446.7
Italy	1,609.7	1,679.6	1,978.3
Netherlands	1,230.6	1,282.8	1,402.5
Poland	197.0	259.2	326.5
Singapore	472.8	879.5	969.4
Spain	9,833.6	11,486.9	13,774.1
Sweden	409.0	461.8	573.5
Switzerland (incl. Liechtenstein)	310.4	335.6	340.8
Turkey	255.8	258.1	253.2
United Kingdom	3,006.3	2,859.1	2,974.9
USA	2,047.9	2,642.4	2,318.9
Total (incl. others)	38,085.7	43,358.4	51,517.0

Source: UN, *International Trade Statistics Yearbook*.

Transport

RAILWAYS
(traffic)

	2002	2003	2004
Passenger journeys (million)	161	151	153
Passenger-km (million)	3,926	3,585	3,693
Freight ('000 metric tons)	10,739	8,718	11,151
Freight ton-km (million)	2,583	2,073	2,589

ROAD TRAFFIC
(motor vehicles registered at 31 December)

	2001	2002	2003
Light and heavy vehicles	7,361,572	7,690,019	7,910,572
Motorcycles	371,114	390,209	402,759
Tractors	309,775	322,283	329,761
Trailers and semi-trailers	363,722	376,719	377,552

SHIPPING

Merchant Fleet
(registered at 31 December)

	2005	2006	2007
Number of vessels	451	460	469
Total displacement (grt)	1,239,618	1,223,616	1,070,055

Source: Lloyd's Register-Fairplay, *World Fleet Statistics*.

PORTUGAL

International Sea-borne Freight Traffic
(Figures exclude the Azores)

	2005	2006	2007
Vessels entered ('000 gross registered tons)	136,225	148,826	151,816
Goods loaded ('000 metric tons)	17,828	19,975	21,174
Goods unloaded ('000 metric tons)	47,473	46,886	47,055

CIVIL AVIATION
(million)

	2001	2002	2003
Passenger-km	12,857	14,244	16,421
Freight ton-km	218	206	217
Mail ton-km	20	20	21

2004: 18,591m. passenger-km.

Tourism

FOREIGN TOURIST ARRIVALS BY COUNTRY OF RESIDENCE*

Country of origin	2004	2005	2006
Belgium	124,122	129,653	158,005
Brazil	150,492	174,650	211,789
France	510,097	490,603	561,701
Germany	678,813	679,570	825,556
Ireland	124,573	126,756	175,222
Italy	326,552	315,226	416,905
Japan	119,223	99,686	80,667
Netherlands	289,716	296,951	374,224
Spain	1,066,889	1,168,246	1,404,404
Sweden	117,834	106,486	117,557
United Kingdom	1,084,392	1,135,065	1,357,334
USA	223,785	229,695	261,917
Total (incl. others)	5,654,081	5,769,293	6,976,978

* Arrivals at all accommodation establishments.

Receipts from tourism (US $ million, incl. passenger transport): 8,863 in 2004; 9,009 in 2005, 10,036 in 2006.

Source: World Tourism Organization.

Communications Media

	2005	2006	2007
Telephones ('000 main lines in use)	4,233.7	4,234.0	4,138.9
Mobile cellular telephones ('000 subscribers)	11,447.3	12,226.4	13,413.0
Internet users ('000)	2,856.1	3,190.0	3,549.0
Broadband subscribers ('000)	1,165.4	1,425.6	1,607.5

Personal computers ('000 in use): 1,402 in 2004.

Source: International Telecommunication Union.

Facsimile machines ('000 in use): 70 in 1997.

Radio receivers ('000 in use): 3,020 in 1997.

Television receivers ('000 in use): 6,319 in 2000.

Books published (titles): 2,186 in 1998.

Daily newspapers (number of titles): 28 (total distribution 1,026,000) in 2000; 27 in 2004.

Non-daily newspapers: 242 (average circulation 1,152,000) in 1999; 596 in 2004.

Sources: mainly UN, *Statistical Yearbook*; UNESCO Institute for Statistics; UNESCO, *Statistical Yearbook*.

Education

(public and private, 2006/07, unless otherwise indicated)

	Institutions	Teachers	Students
Pre-school	6,856	18,352	263,887
Basic: 1st cycle	6,815	34,499	500,823
Basic: 2nd cycle	1,146	32,871	255,766
Basic: 3rd cycle	1,521	88,280	398,592
Secondary	920		356,711
Higher*	305	35,178	376,917

* 2007/08.

Adult literacy rate (UNESCO estimates): 94.9% (males 96.68%; females 93.3%) in 2007. (Source: UNESCO Institute for Statistics).

Directory

The Constitution

The Constitution of the Portuguese Republic was promulgated on 2 April 1976, and came into force on 25 April. It was revised in 1982, when ideological elements were diminished and the Council of the Revolution was abolished; in 1989, to permit economic reforms and a greater role for the private sector; in 1992, prior to the ratification of the Treaty on European Union (the Maastricht Treaty); in 1997 when changes included provision for the holding of referendums on questions of national interest; in 2001 to incorporate reciprocal political rights for citizens of lusophone countries, to impose a ban on strike action by police trade unions and officially to recognize the UN International Criminal Court; in 2004 to enable the creation of an independent regulatory authority for the media; and in 2005 to allow for the holding of referendums on questions regarding reform of, and increased co-operation within, the European Union. The following is a summary of the Constitution's main provisions:

FUNDAMENTAL PRINCIPLES

Portugal is a sovereign Republic based on the dignity of the individual and the will of the people, which strives to create a just, caring and free society and to realize economic, social and cultural democracy. It comprises the territory defined by history on the European continent and the archipelagos of the Azores and Madeira. The Azores and Madeira shall constitute autonomous regions.

The fundamental duties of the State include the following: to safeguard national independence; to guarantee fundamental rights and freedoms; to defend political democracy and to encourage citizens' participation in the solving of national problems; and to promote the welfare, quality of life and equality of the people.

FUNDAMENTAL RIGHTS AND DUTIES

All citizens are equal before the law. Rights, freedoms and safeguards are upheld by the State and include the following: the right to life; of habeas corpus; to the inviolability of the home and of correspondence; to freedom of expression and of conscience; to freedom of movement, emigration and of assembly. Freedom of the press is guaranteed.

Rights and duties of citizens include the following: the right and the duty to work; the right to vote (at 18 years of age); the right to form and participate in political associations and parties; the freedom to form trade unions and the right to strike; the right to set up co-operatives; the right to private property; the right to social security and medical services; the duty of the State and of society to protect the family and the disabled; the right to education, culture and sport; consumer rights.

ECONOMIC ORGANIZATION

The economic and social organization of Portugal shall be based on the subordination of economic power to political power, the co-existence of the public, private, co-operative and social sectors of ownership, and the public ownership of the means of production and land, in accordance with the public interest, as well as natural resources; and on the democratic planning of the economy, and democratic intervention by the workers. Enterprises nationalized after 25 April 1974 may be reprivatized. The aims of economic and social development plans include the promotion of economic growth, the harmonious development of sectors and regions, the fair individual and regional distribution of the national product and the defence of the environment and of the quality of life of the Portuguese people. The consultative Economic and Social Council participates in the formulation of development plans. It comprises representatives of the Government, workers' organizations, economic enterprises and representatives of autonomous regions and local organizations.

The aims of agrarian policy are to improve the situation of farm workers and to increase agricultural production and productivity. *Latifúndios* (large estates) will be adjusted in size, and property which has been expropriated, with compensation, shall be handed over to small farmers or co-operatives for exploitation. *Minifúndios* (small estates) will be adjusted in size, through the granting of incentives to integrate or divide. The aims of commercial policy include the development and diversification of foreign economic relations. The aims of industrial policy include an increase in production in the context of modernization and adjustment, greater competition, the support of small and medium—sized enterprises and the support of industrial and technological innovation. The financial and fiscal system aims at encouraging savings and achieving the equal distribution of wealth and incomes. The State Budget shall be supervised by the Accounts Court and by parliament. Economic policy includes the stimulation of competition, the protection of consumers and the combating of speculative activities and restrictive trade practices.

POLITICAL ORGANIZATION

Political power shall lie with the people. The organs of sovereignty shall be: the President of the Republic, the Assembly of the Republic, the Government and the Courts. Direct, secret and regular elections shall be held. No-one shall hold political office for life.

PRESIDENT OF THE REPUBLIC

The President of the Republic shall represent the Republic. The President guarantees national independence, the unity of the State, and the proper working of democratic institutions. The President shall be elected by direct and secret universal adult suffrage. The candidate who obtains more than one-half of the valid votes will be elected President. The President shall hold office for five years. The President may not be re-elected for a third consecutive term of office.

The duties of the President include the following: to preside over the Council of State; to set dates for elections; to convene extraordinary sessions of the Assembly of the Republic; to dissolve the Assembly; to appoint and dismiss the Prime Minister; to appoint and dismiss the members of the Government at the proposal of the Prime Minister; to promulgate laws; to veto laws; to apply to the Constitutional Court; to nominate ambassadors, upon the proposal of the Government; to accredit diplomatic representatives; to ratify international treaties, after they have been duly approved; to dismiss the Government if and when the normal functioning of institutions is at stake.

COUNCIL OF STATE

The Council of State (Conselho de Estado) is the political consultative organ of the President of the Republic. It is presided over by the President of the Republic and comprises the President of the Assembly of the Republic, the Prime Minister, the President of the Constitutional Court, the Superintendent of Justice, the Presidents of the Regional Governments, certain former Presidents of the Republic, five citizens nominated by the President of the Republic and five citizens elected by the Assembly.

ASSEMBLY OF THE REPUBLIC

The Assembly of the Republic (Assembléia da República) represents all Portuguese citizens, and shall have a minimum of 180 and a maximum of 230 members, elected under a system of proportional representation by the electoral constituencies. The duties of the Assembly include the following: to present and approve amendments to the Constitution and to approve the political and administrative statutes of the Autonomous Regions; to enact legislation; to confer legislative authority on the Government; to approve plans and the Budget; to approve international conventions and treaties; to propose to the President of the Republic that questions of national interest be submitted to referendum; to supervise the fulfilment of the Constitution and laws. The Assembly supports the participation of Portugal in the process of building the European Union. Each legislative period shall last four years. The legislative session shall run from 15 September to 15 June each year.

GOVERNMENT

The Government formulates the general policy of the country and is the highest organ of public administration. It shall comprise the Prime Minister, Ministers, Secretaries and Under-Secretaries of State and may include one or more Deputy Prime Ministers. The Prime Minister is appointed and dismissed by the President. Other members of the Government are appointed by the President at the proposal of the Prime Minister. The Government shall be responsible to the President and the Assembly. The Government's programme shall be presented to the Assembly of the Republic for scrutiny within 10 days of the appointment of the Prime Minister.

JUDICIARY

The courts are independent organs of sovereignty with competence to administer justice. There shall be Courts of First Instance (District Courts), Courts of Second Instance (Courts of Appeal), the Supreme Administrative Court and the Supreme Court of Justice, in addition to the Constitutional Court. There shall also be military courts (when the State is at war) and an Accounts Court. There may be maritime courts and courts of arbitration.

The jury shall comprise the judges of the plenary court and the jurors. People's judges may be created. It is the duty of the Ministério Público to represent the State. Its highest organ is the Procuradoria-Geral, which is presided over by the Procurador-Geral, who is appointed and dismissed by the President of the Republic.

AUTONOMOUS REGIONS

The special political and administrative arrangements for the archipelagos of the Azores and Madeira shall be based on their geographical, economic and social conditions and on the historic aspirations of the people to autonomy. The State is represented in each of the Autonomous Regions by a Minister of the Republic, who is appointed by the President of the Republic on the recommendation of the Government.

The organs of government in the Autonomous Regions (which are subject to dissolution by the President of the Republic if a major breach of the Constitution occurs) are: the Regional Legislative Assembly, elected by direct and secret universal adult suffrage, and the Regional Government which shall be politically responsible to the Regional Legislative Assembly. Its Chairman is appointed by the Minister of the Republic. The Minister shall appoint or dismiss members of the Regional Government on the proposal of its Chairman.

LOCAL GOVERNMENT

The local authorities shall be territorial bodies corporate with representative organs serving the particular interests of the local population. The local authorities on the mainland shall be the parishes, municipal authorities and administrative regions. The Autonomous Regions of the Azores and Madeira shall comprise parishes and municipal authorities.

PUBLIC ADMINISTRATIVE AUTHORITIES

The public administrative authorities shall seek to promote the public interest whilst respecting the legal interests and rights of all citizens. Citizens shall have the right to be informed of, and to have redress against, the public administrative authorities when the matter directly concerns them.

ARMED FORCES

The President of the Republic is Supreme Commander-in-Chief of the Armed Forces, and appoints and dismisses the Chiefs of Staff. The defence forces shall safeguard national independence and territorial integrity. Military service shall be regulated by law, which shall decide the form (compulsory, or otherwise), duration and content of that service. The right to conscientious objection is recognized.

SAFEGUARDS AND REVISION OF THE CONSTITUTION

Changes in the Constitution must be approved by a majority of two-thirds of the members of the Assembly of the Republic. Constitutional revisions must comply with the independence, unity and secularism of the State; the rights, freedoms and safeguards of citizens; universal, direct and secret suffrage and the system of proportional representation, etc.

The Government

HEAD OF STATE

President: ANÍBAL CAVACO SILVA (took office 9 March 2006).

COUNCIL OF MINISTERS
(April 2009)

The Government comprises the Partido Socialista (PS) and independents (Ind.).

Prime Minister: JOSÉ SÓCRATES CARVALHO PINTO DE SOUSA (PS).
Minister of State and of Foreign Affairs: LUÍS FILIPE MARQUES AMADO (PS).

PORTUGAL

Minister of State and of Finance: FERNANDO TEIXEIRA DOS SANTOS (PS).
Minister of the Presidency: MANUEL PEDRO CUNHA DA SILVA PEREIRA (PS).
Minister of National Defence: NUNO SEVERIANO TEIXEIRA (PS).
Minister of Internal Administration: RUI CARLOS PEREIRA (Ind.).
Minister of Justice: ALBERTO BERNARDES COSTA (PS).
Minister of the Environment, Territorial Planning and Regional Development: FRANCISCO CARLOS DA GRAÇA NUNES CORREIA (Ind.).
Minister of the Economy and Innovation: MANUEL ANTÓNIO GOMES DE ALMEIDA DE PINHO (Ind.).
Minister of Agriculture, Rural Development and Fisheries: JAIME DE JESUS LOPES SILVA (Ind.).
Minister of Public Works, Transport and Communications: MÁRIO LINO SOARES CORREIA (PS).
Minister of Labour and Social Solidarity: JOSÉ ANTÓNIO FONSECA VIEIRA DA SILVA (PS).
Minister of Health: ANA MARIA TEODORO JORGE (PS).
Minister of Education: MARIA DE LURDES REIS RODRIGUES (Ind.).
Minister of Science, Technology and Higher Education: JOSÉ MARIANO REBELO PIRES GAGO (Ind.).
Minister of Culture: JOSÉ ANTÓNIO DE MELO PINTO RIBEIRO (Ind.).
Minister of Parliamentary Affairs: AUGUSTO SANTOS SILVA (PS).

There are also 26 secretaries of state.

MINISTRIES

Office of the President: Presidência da República, Palácio de Belém, Calçada da Ajuda 11, 1349-022 Lisbon; tel. (21) 3614600; fax (21) 3614611; e-mail belem@presidencia.pt; internet www.presidencia.pt.

Office of the Prime Minister, Presidency of the Council of Ministers: Rua da Imprensa à Estrela 4, 1200-888 Lisbon; tel. (21) 3923500; fax (21) 3951616; e-mail pm@pm.gov.pt; internet www.portugal.gov.pt.

Ministry of Agriculture, Rural Development and Fisheries: Praça do Comércio, 1149-010 Lisbon; tel. (21) 3234600; fax (21) 3234601; e-mail geral@min-agricultura.pt; internet www.min-agricultura.pt.

Ministry of Culture: Palácio Nacional da Ajuda, 1349-021 Lisbon; tel. (21) 3614500; fax (21) 3649872; e-mail infocultura@min-cultura.pt; internet www.portaldacultura.gov.pt.

Ministry of the Economy and Innovation: Rua da Horta Seca 15, 1200-221 Lisbon; tel. (21) 3245400; fax (21) 3245440; e-mail gmei@mei.gov.pt; internet www.min-economia.pt.

Ministry of Education: Av. 5 de Outubro 107, 1069-018 Lisbon; tel. (21) 7811800; fax (21) 7811835; e-mail gme@me.gov.pt; internet www.min-edu.pt.

Ministry of the Environment, Territorial Planning and Regional Development: Rua de O Século 51, 1200-433 Lisbon; tel. (21) 3232500; fax (21) 3232531; e-mail imprensa@maotdr.gov.pt; internet www.maotdr.gov.pt.

Ministry of Finance and Public Administration: Av. Infante D. Henrique 1, 1149-009 Lisbon; tel. (21) 8816800; fax (21) 8816819; e-mail gab.mf@mf.gov.pt; internet www.min-financas.pt.

Ministry of Foreign Affairs: Palácio das Necessidades, Largo do Rilvas, 1399-030 Lisbon; tel. (21) 3946000; fax (21) 3946070; e-mail ministro@mne.gov.pt; internet www.mne.gov.pt.

Ministry of Health: Av. João Crisóstomo 9, 1049-062 Lisbon; tel. (21) 7984200; fax (21) 7984220; e-mail info_portal@sg.min-saude.pt; internet www.portaldasaude.pt.

Ministry of Internal Administration: Praça do Comércio, 1149-015 Lisbon; tel. (21) 3233000; fax (21) 3468031; e-mail dirp@sg.mai.gov.pt; internet www.mai.gov.pt.

Ministry of Justice: Praça do Comércio, 1149-019 Lisbon; tel. (21) 3222300; fax (21) 3479208; e-mail gmj@mj.gov.pt; internet www.mj.gov.pt.

Ministry of Labour and Social Solidarity: Praça de Londres 2, 1049-056 Lisbon; tel. (21) 8441100; fax (21) 8441322; e-mail secretaria.geral@sg.mtss.gov.pt; internet www.mtss.gov.pt.

Ministry of National Defence: Av. Ilha da Madeira 1, 1400-204 Lisbon; tel. (21) 3038528; fax (21) 3020284; e-mail gcrp@sg.mdn.gov.pt; internet www.mdn.gov.pt.

Ministry of Parliamentary Affairs: Palácio de São Bento, 1249-068 Lisbon; tel. (21) 3920500; fax (21) 3920515; e-mail map@map.gov.pt.

Ministry of the Presidency: Rua Prof. Gomes Teixeira, 1399-265 Lisbon; tel. (21) 3923600; fax (21) 3927860; e-mail gab.mp@mp.gov.pt; internet www.mp.gov.pt.

Ministry of Public Works, Transport and Communications: Palácio do Conde de Penafiel, Rua de São Mamede (ao Caldas) 21, 1149-050 Lisbon; tel. (21) 8815100; fax (21) 8867622; e-mail gmoptc@moptc.gov.pt; internet www.moptc.pt.

Ministry of Science, Technology and Higher Education: Palácio das Laranjeiras, Estrada das Laranjeiras 197–205, 1649-018 Lisbon; tel. (21) 7231000; fax (21) 7271457; e-mail mctes@mctes.gov.pt; internet www.mctes.pt.

COUNCIL OF STATE

The Council of State (Conselho de Estado) is a consultative body, presided over by the President of the Republic (see The Constitution).

President

Election, 22 January 2006

Candidate	Votes	% of votes
Aníbal Cavaco Silva (PSD)	2,773,431	50.54
Manuel Alegre de Melo Duarte (Ind.)	1,138,297	20.74
Mário Lopes Soares (PS)	785,355	14.31
Jerónimo Carvalho de Sousa (PCP)	474,083	8.64
Francisco Anacleto Louçã (BE)	292,198	5.32
António Pestana Garcia Pereira (PCTP/MRPP)	23,983	0.44
Total	**5,487,347***	**100.00**

* Excluding 59,636 blank and 43,149 spoiled votes.

Legislature

Assembléia da República
(Assembly of the Republic)

Palácio de São Bento, 1249-068 Lisbon; tel. (21) 3919000; fax (21) 3917440; e-mail correio.geral@ar.parlamento.pt; internet www.parlamento.pt.

President: JAIME JOSÉ MATOS DA GAMA.

General Election, 20 February 2005

Party	Votes	% of votes	Seats
Partido Socialista (PS)	2,588,312	45.03	121
Partido Social Democrata (PSD)	1,653,425	28.77	75
Partido Comunista Português (PCP)-Partido Ecologista 'Os Verdes' (PEV)	433,369	7.54	14
Centro Democrático Social-Partido Popular (CDS-PP)	416,415	7.24	12
Bloco de Esquerda (BE)	364,971	6.35	8
Total (incl. others)	**5,747,834**	**100.00**	**230**

Autonomous Regions

Following the promulgation of a new Constitution in 1976, the mid-Atlantic archipelagos of the Azores and Madeira were officially designated as Autonomous Regions of the Portuguese Republic. Each region is afforded a degree of political and administrative autonomy, as well as the power to raise funds through taxation. Members of the Legislative Assemblies are elected by universal suffrage for a term of four years, according to a system of proportional representation. Executive functions are vested in a Regional Government. The state is represented in each region by a Minister of the Republic, who appoints both the President of the Regional Government and its members.

OS AÇORES
(The Azores)

President of the Regional Government: CARLOS MANUEL MARTINS DO VALE CÉSAR (PS).

Assembléia Legislativa da Região Autónoma dos Açores
Rua Marcelino Lima, 9901 858 Horta, Azores; tel. (292) 207600; fax (292) 293798; e-mail secgeral@alra.pt; internet www.alra.pt.

President of the Assembly: FRANCISCO COELHO.

PORTUGAL

Election, 19 October 2008

Party	Seats
Partido Socialista (PS)	30
Partido Social Democrata (PSD)	18
Centro Democrático Social-Partido Popular (CDS-PP)	5
Bloco de Esquerda (BE)	2
Coligação Democrática Unitária (PCP/PEV)	1
Partido Popular Monárquico (PPM)	1
Total	57

MADEIRA

President of the Regional Government: Dr ALBERTO JOÃO JARDIM (PSD).

Assembléia Legislativa da Região Autónoma da Madeira
Av. do Mar e das Comunidades Madeirenses, 9004 506 Funchal, Madeira; tel. (291) 210500; fax (291) 232977; e-mail info@alram.pt; internet www.alram.pt.

President of the Assembly: JOSÉ MIGUEL JARDIM D'OLIVAL DE MENDONÇA.

Election, 6 May 2007

Party	Seats
Partido Social Democrata (PSD)	33
Partido Socialista (PS)	7
Coligação Democrática Unitária (PCP/PEV)	2
Centro Democrático Social-Partido Popular (CDS-PP)	2
Bloco de Esquerda (BE)	1
Partido da Terra (MPT)	1
Nova Democrácia (PND)	1
Total	47

Election Commission

Comissão Nacional de Eleições (CNE): Av. D. Carlos I 128, 7°, 1249-065 Lisbon; tel. (21) 3923800; fax (21) 3953543; e-mail cne@cne.pt; internet www.cne.pt; Pres. appointed by the judiciary, other mems by the Assembléia da República and the Govt; Pres. Dr JOÃO CARLOS DE BARROS CALDEIRA.

Political Organizations

Bloco de Esquerda (BE) (Left Bloc): Av. Almirante Reis 131, 2°, 1150-015 Lisbon; tel. (21) 3510510; fax (21) 3510519; e-mail bloco.esquerda@bloco.org; internet www.bloco.org; f. 1999 by several left-wing groups.

Centro Democrático Social-Partido Popular (CDS-PP) (Social Democratic Centre-Popular Party): Largo Adelino Amaro da Costa 5, 1149-063 Lisbon; tel. (21) 8814700; fax (21) 8860454; e-mail cds-pp@cds.pt; internet www.cds.pt; f. 1974 as Centro Democrático Social; present name adopted 1993; centre-right; mem. of International Democrat Union; supports social market economy and reduction of public sector intervention in the economy; defended revision of 1976 Constitution; Pres. PAULO SACADURA CABRAL PORTAS.

Coligação Democrática Unitária (CDU): coalition of left-wing parties, led by PCP:

Partido Comunista Português (PCP) (Portuguese Communist Party): Rua Soeiro Pereira Gomes 3, 1600-196 Lisbon; tel. (21) 7813800; fax (21) 7969126; e-mail pcp@pcp.pt; internet www.pcp.pt; f. 1921; legalized 1974; theoretical foundation is Marxism-Leninism; aims are the defence and consolidation of the democratic regime and the revolutionary achievements, and ultimately the building of a socialist society in Portugal; Sec.-Gen. JERÓNIMO DE SOUSA.

Partido Ecologista 'Os Verdes' (PEV) (The Greens): Rua da Boavista 83, 3° dto, 1200-066 Lisbon; tel. (21) 3960291; fax (21) 3960424; e-mail osverdes@mail.telepac.pt; internet www.osverdes.pt; f. 1982; ecological party.

Movimento Esperança Portugal (MEP) (Movement for Hope): Travessa das Pedras Negras 1, r/c, 1100-404 Lisbon; tel. (21) 8880116; e-mail secretariado@mep.pt; internet www.mep.pt; f. 2008; centrist; Leader RUI MARQUES.

Nova Democracia (PND): Rua da Trinidade 36, 1200-302 Lisbon; tel. (21) 3247020; fax (21) 3247029; e-mail partidonovademocracia@gmail.com; internet www.pnd.pt; f. 2003 by disaffected mems of the CDS-PP; right-wing, nationalist and Eurosceptic; Pres. MANUEL MONTEIRO.

Partido Comunista dos Trabalhadores Portugueses/Movimento Revolucionário Português do Proletariado (PCTP/MRPP) (Communist Workers' Party/Proletarian Portuguese Revolutionary Movement): Rua da Palma 159, 2° dto, 1100-391 Lisbon; tel. (21) 8880780; fax (21) 8884036; e-mail pctp@pctpmrpp.org; internet www.pctpmrpp.org; f. 1970 as Movimento Reorganizativo do Partido do Proletariado; present name adopted 1976; Leader LUÍS FRANCO.

Partido Nacional Renovador (PNR) (National Renewal Party): Apartado 2130, 1103-001 Lisbon; tel. 964378225; internet www.pnr.pt; extreme nationalist; f. 2000 by fmr mems of Movimento de Acção Nacional and Partido Renovador Democrático; Leader JOSÉ PINTO-COELHO.

Partido Popular Monárquico (PPM) (Popular Monarchist Party): Travessa da Pimenteira 2, r/c esq., 1300-460 Lisbon; tel. and fax (213) 622153; e-mail ppm.geral@sapo.pt; internet www.ppm.pt; f. 1974; advocates a system of constitutional monarchy; Pres. NUNO MARIA DE FIGUEIREDO CABRAL DA CAMARA PEREIRA.

Partido Social Democrata (PSD) (Social Democratic Party): Rua de São Caetano 9, 1249-087 Lisbon; tel. (21) 3918500; fax (21) 3976967; e-mail psd@psd.pt; internet www.psd.pt; f. 1974 as Partido Popular Democrático; present name adopted 1976; centre-right; aims to promote market economy, taking into account the welfare of the community; encourages European integration; Leader MANUELA FERREIRA LEITE; Sec.-Gen. LUÍS MARQUES GUEDES.

Partido Socialista (PS) (Socialist Party): Largo do Rato 2, 1269-143 Lisbon; tel. (21) 3822000; fax (21) 3822049; e-mail portal@ps.pt; internet www.ps.pt; f. 1973 from fmr Acção Socialista Portuguesa (Portuguese Socialist Action); affiliate of the Socialist International and Party of European Socialists; advocates a society of greater social justice and co-operation between public, private and co-operative sectors, while respecting public liberties and the will of the majority attained through free elections; Pres. ANTÓNIO DE ALMEIDA SANTOS; Sec.-Gen. JOSÉ SÓCRATES CARVALHO PINTO DE SOUSA.

Partido da Terra (MPT) (The Earth Party): Rua da Beneficência 111, 1°, Apartado 43050, 1601-301 Lisbon; tel. (96) 9640021; fax (21) 8438029; e-mail mpt@mpt.pt; internet www.mpt.pt; f. 1993; contested 2005 election in coalition with PSD; Pres. PAULO NORONHA TRANCOSO.

Diplomatic Representation

EMBASSIES IN PORTUGAL

Algeria: Rua Duarte Pacheco Pereira 58, 1400-140 Lisbon; tel. (21) 3041520; fax (21) 3010393; e-mail embaixada-argelia@clix.pt; internet www.emb-argelia.pt; Ambassador SABRI BOUKADOUM.

Andorra: Rua do Possolo 76, 2°, 2350-251 Lisbon; tel. (21) 3913740; fax (21) 3913749; Ambassador JAUME GAYTÁN.

Angola: Av. da República 68, 1069-213 Lisbon; tel. (21) 7961830; fax (21) 7971238; e-mail embaixadadeangola@mail.telepac.pt; internet www.embaixadadeangola.org; Ambassador ASSUNÇÃO AFONSO SOUSA DOS ANJOS.

Argentina: Av. João Crisóstomo 8, r/c esq., 1000-178 Lisbon; tel. (21) 7977311; fax (21) 7959225; e-mail eport@mrecic.gov.ar; Ambassador JORGE MARCELO FAURIE.

Australia: Av. da Liberdade 200, 2°, 1250-147 Lisbon; tel. (21) 33101500; fax (21) 3101555; e-mail austemb.lisbon@dfat.gov.au; internet www.portugal.embassy.gov.au; Ambassador LUKE WILLIAMS.

Austria: Av. Infante Santo 43, 4°, 1399-046 Lisbon; tel. (21) 3943900; fax (21) 3958224; e-mail lissabon-ob@bmeia.gv.at; Ambassador EWALD JÄGER.

Belgium: Praça Marquês de Pombal 14, 6°, 1269-024 Lisbon; tel. (21) 3170510; fax (21) 3561556; e-mail lisbon@diplobel.fed.be; internet www.diplomatie.be/lisbon; Ambassador RUDY HUYGELEN.

Brazil: Quinta de Mil Flores, Estrada das Laranjeiras 144, 1649-021 Lisbon; tel. (21) 7248510; fax (21) 7267623; e-mail geral@embaixadadobrasil.pt; internet www.embaixadadobrasil.pt; Ambassador CELSO MARCOS VIEIRA DE SOUZA.

Bulgaria: Rua do Sacramento à Lapa 31, 1200-792 Lisbon; tel. (21) 3976364; fax (21) 3979272; e-mail ebul@mail.telepac.pt; Ambassador MAKSIM GEORGIEV GAYTANDZHIEV.

Canada: Av. da Liberdade 196–200, 3°, 1269-121 Lisbon; tel. (21) 3164600; fax (21) 3164691; e-mail lsbon@international.gc.ca; internet international.gc.ca/lisbon; Ambassador ANNE-MARIE BOURCIER.

Cape Verde: Av. do Restelo 33, 1449-025 Lisbon; tel. (21) 3041440; fax (21) 3041466; e-mail info@embcv.pt; internet www.embcv.pt; Ambassador ARNALDO ANDRADE RAMOS.

PORTUGAL

Chile: Av. Miguel Bombarda 5, 1°, 1000-207 Lisbon; tel. (21) 3148054; fax (21) 3150909; e-mail embachile@net.novis.pt; internet www.emb-chile.pt; Ambassador Francisco Pérez Walker.

China, People's Republic: Rua do Pau de Bandeira 11–13, 1200-756 Lisbon; tel. (21) 3928430; fax (21) 3928431; e-mail chinaemb_pt@mfa.gov.cn; internet pt.china-embassy.org/pot; Ambassador Gao Kexiang.

Colombia: Palácio Sottomayor, 6°, Av. Fontes Pereira de Melo 16, 1050-021 Lisbon; tel. (21) 3188480; fax (21) 3188499; e-mail elisboa@cancilleria.gov.co; Ambassador Fuad Ricardo Char Abdala.

Congo, Democratic Republic: Av. Fontes Pereira de Melo 31, 7°, 1050-117 Lisbon; tel. (21) 0101622; fax (21) 3174733; e-mail ambalisbonne@minaffecirde.cd; Chargé d'affaires a.i. Lokosu N'Kulufa.

Croatia: Rua D. Lourenço de Almeida 24, 1400-126 Lisbon; tel. (21) 3021033; fax (21) 3021251; e-mail lisabon@mvpei.hr; Ambassador Željko Vukosav.

Cuba: Rua Pero da Covilhã 14 (Restelo), 1400-297 Lisbon; tel. (21) 3041860; fax (21) 3011895; e-mail embaixada.cuba@netcabo.pt; internet pwp.netcabo.pt/embaixada.cuba; Ambassador Jorge Castro Benítez.

Cyprus: Av. da Liberdade 229, 1°, 1250-142 Lisbon; tel. (21) 3194180; fax (21) 3194189; e-mail chipre@netcabo.pt; internet www.mfa.gov.cy/embassylisbon; Ambassador George Zodiates.

Czech Republic: Rua Pêro de Alenquer 14, 1400-294 Lisbon; tel. (21) 3010487; fax (21) 3010629; e-mail lisbon@embassy.mzv.cz; internet www.mfa.cz/lisbon; Ambassador Ladislav Skeřík.

Denmark: Rua Castilho 14c, 3°, 1269-077 Lisbon; tel. (21) 3512960; fax (21) 3554615; e-mail lisamb@um.dk; internet www.amblissabon.um.dk; Ambassador Dr Lars Vissing.

Dominican Republic: Av. Campo Grande 35, 12° a, 1700-087 Lisbon; tel. (21) 7811120; fax (21) 7811129; e-mail embajadom@mail.ptprime.pt; Ambassador Ana Silvia Reynoso de Abud.

Egypt: Av. D. Vasco da Gama 8, 1400-128 Lisbon; tel. (21) 3018301; fax (21) 3017909; e-mail egyptianembassyportugal@net.novis.pt; Ambassador Amgad Maher Abdel Ghaffar.

Estonia: Rua Filipe Folque 10j, 2° esq., 1050-113 Lisbon; tel. (21) 3194150; fax (21) 3194155; e-mail embest@embest.pt; internet www.embest.pt; Ambassador Mart Tarmak.

Finland: Rua do Possolo 76, 1°, 1350-251 Lisbon; tel. (21) 3933040; fax (21) 3904758; e-mail sanomat.lis@formin.fi; internet www.finlandia.org.pt; Ambassador Sauli Erik Feodorow.

France: Rua de Santos-o-Velho 5, 1249-079 Lisbon; tel. (21) 3939100; fax (21) 3939151; e-mail ambafrance@hotmail.com; internet www.ambafrance-pt.org; Ambassador Denis Delbourg.

Germany: Campo dos Mártires da Pátria 38, 1169-043 Lisbon; tel. (21) 8810210; fax (21) 8810261; e-mail info@lissabon.diplo.de; internet www.lissabon.diplo.de; Ambassador Joachim Broudré-Gröger.

Greece: Rua do Alto do Duque 13, 1449-026 Lisbon; tel. (21) 3031260; fax (21) 3011205; e-mail gremb.lis@mfa.gr; Ambassador Spyridon Theocharopoulos.

Guinea-Bissau: Rua de Alcolena 17, 1400-004 Lisbon; tel. (21) 3009080; fax (21) 3009081; Ambassador Constantino Lopes da Costa.

Holy See: Av. Luís Bivar 18, 1069-147 Lisbon; tel. (21) 3171130; fax (21) 3171149; e-mail nunciatura@netcabo.pt; Apostolic Nuncio Most Rev. Rino Passigato (Titular Archbishop of Nova Caesaris).

Hungary: Calçada de Santo Amaro 85, 1349-042 Lisbon; tel. (21) 3630395; fax (21) 3632314; e-mail mission.lis@kum.hu; internet www.mfa.gov.hu/emb/lisbon; Ambassador Attila Gecse.

India: Rua Pêro da Covilhã 16, 1400-297 Lisbon; tel. (21) 3041090; fax (21) 3016576; e-mail main@indembassy-lisbon.org; internet www.indembassy-lisbon.org; Ambassador Nilima Mitra.

Indonesia: Rua Miguel Lupi 12, 1°, 1249-080 Lisbon; tel. (21) 3932070; fax (21) 3932079; e-mail info@embaixada-indonesia.pt; Ambassador Francisco Xavier Lopes da Cruz.

Iran: Rua do Alto do Duque 49, 1400-009 Lisbon; tel. (21) 3010871; fax (21) 3010777; e-mail iranembassy@emb-irao.pt; internet www.emb-irao.pt; Ambassador Sayed Rasul.

Iraq: Rua do Arriaga à Lapa 9, 1200-608 Lisbon; tel. (21) 3933310; fax (21) 3977052; e-mail lisemb@iraqmofa.net; Chargé d'affaires a.i. Mowafak Y. Maroki.

Ireland: Rua da Imprensa à Estrela 1, 4°, 1200-684 Lisbon; tel. (21) 3929440; fax (21) 3977363; e-mail lisbon@dfa.ie; internet www.embassyofireland.pt; Ambassador James Brennan.

Israel: Rua António Enes 16, 4°, 1050-025 Lisbon; tel. (21) 3553640; fax (21) 3553658; e-mail israemb@lisboa.mfa.gov.il; internet lisbon.mfa.gov.il; Ambassador Aharon Ram.

Italy: Largo Conde de Pombeiro 6, 1150-100 Lisbon; tel. (21) 3515320; fax (21) 3521516; e-mail ambasciata.lisbona@esteri.it; internet www.amblisbona.esteri.it; Ambassador Luca del Balzo di Presenzano.

Japan: Av. da Liberdade 245–6, 1269-033 Lisbon; tel. (21) 3110560; fax (21) 3534802; e-mail ryoji@embjapao.pt; internet www.pt.emb-japan.go.jp; Ambassador Akira Miwa.

Korea, Republic: Edif. Presidente 7°, Av. Miguel Bombarda 36, 1051-802 Lisbon; tel. (21) 7937200; fax (21) 7977176; e-mail embpt@mofat.go.kr; internet prt.mofat.go.kr; Ambassador Chung Eui-Min.

Latvia: Rua Sacramento à Lapa 50, 1200-794, Lisbon; tel. (21) 3407170; fax (21) 3469045; e-mail embassy.portugal@mfa.gov.lv; Ambassador Artis Bertulis.

Libya: Av. das Descobertas 24, 1400-092 Lisbon; tel. (21) 3016301; fax (21) 302921; e-mail bureau.popular.libia@clix.pt; Chargé d'affaires Ali Emdored.

Lithuania: Av. 5 de Outubro 81, 1°, 1050-050 Lisbon; tel. (21) 7990110; fax (21) 7996363; e-mail ambasadorius@mail.telepac.pt; internet pt.mfa.lt; Ambassador Algimantas Rimkūnas.

Luxembourg: Rua das Janelas Verdes 43, 1200-690 Lisbon; tel. (21) 3931940; fax (21) 3901410; e-mail lisbonne.amb@mae.etat.lu; Ambassador Alain de Muyser.

Malta: Av. da Liberdade 49, 5°, 1250-139 Lisbon; tel. (21) 3405470; fax (21) 3405479; e-mail maltaembassy.lisbon@gov.mt; Ambassador Dr Joseph Cassar (designate).

Mexico: Estrada de Monsanto 78, 1500-462 Lisbon; tel. (21) 7621290; fax (21) 7620045; e-mail embamex.port@mail.telepac.pt; internet www.sre.gob.mx/portugal; Ambassador Mauricio Toussaint Ribot.

Moldova: Rua Gonçalo Velho Cabral 31a, 1400-188 Lisbon; tel. (21) 3009064; fax (21) 3009067; e-mail lisabona@mfa.md; internet www.embaixada-moldova.pt; Ambassador Mihail Camarzan.

Morocco: Rua Alto do Duque 21, 1400-099 Lisbon; tel. (21) 3020842; fax (21) 3020935; e-mail sifmar@emb-marrocos.pt; internet www.emb-marrocos.pt; Ambassador Karima Benyaich.

Mozambique: Av. de Berna 7, 1050-036 Lisbon; tel. (21) 7971994; fax (21) 7932720; e-mail embamoc.portugal@minec.gov.mz; Ambassador Miguel da Costa Mkaima.

Netherlands: Av. Infante Santo 43, 5°, 1399-011 Lisbon; tel. (21) 3914900; fax (21) 3966436; e-mail nlgovlis@netcabo.pt; internet www.emb-paisesbaixos.pt; Ambassador Robert Jan van Houtum.

Nigeria: Av. D. Vasco da Gama 3, 1400-127 Lisbon; tel. (21) 3016189; fax (21) 3018152; e-mail nigerieemblisbon@portugal.pt; Ambassador Emmanuel Mbanefo Obiako.

Norway: Av. D. Vasco da Gama 1, 1400-127 Lisbon; tel. (21) 3015344; fax (21) 3016158; e-mail emb.lisboa@mfa.no; internet www.noruega.org.pt; Ambassador Inga Magistad.

Pakistan: Rua António Saldanha 46, 1400-021 Lisbon; tel. (21) 3009070; fax (21) 3013514; e-mail parep.lisbon.1@mail.telepac.pt; Ambassador Fausia M. Sana.

Panama: Av. Helen Keller 15, Lote C, 4° esq., 1400-197 Lisbon; tel. (21) 3642899; fax (21) 3644589; e-mail panemblisboa@netcabo.pt; Ambassador Minerva Lara Batista.

Paraguay: Av. Campo Grande 4, 7° dto, 1700-092 Lisbon; tel. (21) 7965907; fax (21) 7965905; e-mail embaparlisboa@mail.telepac.pt; Chargé d'affaires a.i. José María González Avila.

Peru: Rua Castilho 50, 4° dto, 1250-071 Lisbon; tel. (21) 3827470; fax (21) 3827479; e-mail info@embaixadaperu.pt; Ambassador Luzmila Zanabria Ishikawa.

Poland: Av. das Descobertas 2, 1400-092 Lisbon; tel. (21) 3012350; fax (21) 3041429; e-mail emb.polonia@mail.telepac.pt; internet www.lizbona.polemb.net; Ambassador Katarzyna Skórzyńska.

Romania: Rua de São Caetano à Lapa 5, 1200-828 Lisbon; tel. (21) 3968812; fax (21) 3960984; e-mail ambrom@mail.telepac.pt; internet lisabona.mae.ro; Ambassador Gabriel Gafița.

Russia: Rua Visconde de Santarém 57, 1000-286 Lisbon; tel. (21) 8462423; fax (21) 8463008; e-mail mail@embaixadarussia.pt; internet www.portugal.mid.ru; Ambassador Pavel F. Petrovskii.

São Tomé and Príncipe: Edif. EPAC 6°, Av. Gago Coutinho 26, 1000-017 Lisbon; tel. (21) 8461917; fax (21) 8461895; e-mail embstp@mail.telepac.pt; Ambassador Alda Alves de Melo dos Santos.

Saudi Arabia: Av. do Restelo 40, 1400-315 Lisbon; tel. (21) 3041750; fax (21) 3014209; e-mail saudiembassy@netcabo.pt; Ambassador Hisham bin Sultan az-Zafer al-Qahtani.

Senegal: Rua António Pedro 46, 2º, 1000-039 Lisbon; tel. (21) 3160180; fax (21) 3162530; e-mail senconsul@hotmail.com; Ambassador Gen. Pathé Seck.

Serbia: Av. das Descobertas 12, 1400-092 Lisbon; tel. (21) 3015311; fax (21) 3015313; e-mail serviaemba@netcabo.pt; Ambassador Duško Lopandić.

PORTUGAL

Slovakia: Av. Fontes Pereira de Melo 19, 7° dto, 1050-116 Lisbon; tel. (21) 3583300; fax (21) 3583309; e-mail emb.lisbon@mzv.sk; Ambassador JAROSLAV JARÚNEK.

Slovenia: Av. da Liberdade 49, 6° esq., 1250-139 Lisbon; tel. (21) 3423301; fax (21) 3423305; e-mail vli@gov.si; Ambassador PETER ANDREJ BEKEŠ.

South Africa: Av. Luís Bivar 10, 1069-024 Lisbon; tel. (21) 3192200; fax (21) 3535713; e-mail embsa@embaixada-africadosul.pt; internet www.embaixada-africadosul.pt; Ambassador THANDIWE PROFIT-MCLEAN.

Spain: Rua do Salitre 1, 1296-052 Lisbon; tel. (21) 3472381; fax (21) 3472384; e-mail emb.lisboa@mae.es; internet www.maec.es/embajadas/lisboa; Ambassador ALBERTO JOSÉ NAVARRO GONZÁLEZ.

Sweden: Rua Miguel Lupi 12, 2°, 1249-077 Lisbon; tel. (21) 3942260; fax (21) 3942261; e-mail ambassaden.lissabon@foreign.ministry.se; internet www.swedenabroad.com/lissabon; Ambassador BENGT LUNDBORG.

Switzerland: Travessa do Jardim 17, 1350-185 Lisbon; tel. (21) 3944090; fax (21) 3955945; e-mail lis.vertretung@eda.admin.ch; internet www.eda.admin.ch/lisbon; Ambassador RUDOLF SCHALLER.

Thailand: Rua de Alcolena 12, 1400-005 Lisbon; tel. (21) 3014848; fax (21) 3018181; e-mail thai.lis@mail.telepac.pt; internet www.thaiembassy.org/lisbon; Ambassador KASIVAT PARUGGAMANONT.

Timor-Leste: Av. Infante Santo 17, 6°, 1350-175 Lisbon; tel. (21) 3933730; fax (21) 3933739; e-mail embaixada.rdtl@mail.telepac.pt; Ambassador MANUEL SOARES ABRANTES.

Tunisia: Rua Rodrigo Rebelo 16, 1400-318 Lisbon; tel. (21) 3010330; fax (21) 3016817; e-mail at.lisbonne@netcabo.pt; Ambassador MUHAMMAD RIDHA FARHAT.

Turkey: Av. das Descobertas 22, 1400-092 Lisbon; tel. (21) 3003110; fax (21) 3017934; e-mail info-turk@mail.telepac.pt; Ambassador ÖMER KAYA TÜRKMEN.

Ukraine: Av. das Descobertas 18, 1400-092 Lisbon; tel. (21) 3010043; fax (21) 3010059; e-mail emb_pt@mfaa.gov.ua; internet www.mfa.gov.ua/portugal; Ambassador ROSTYSLAV V. TRONENKO.

United Kingdom: Rua de São Bernardo 33, 1249-082 Lisbon; tel. (21) 3924000; fax (21) 3924178; e-mail ppa.lisbon@fco.gov.uk; internet ukinportugal.fco.gov.uk; Ambassador ALEXANDER ELLIS.

USA: Av. das Forças Armadas (Sete Rios), 1600-081 Lisbon; Apdo 43033, 1601-301 Lisbon; tel. (21) 7273300; fax (21) 7269109; e-mail reflisbon@state.gov; internet portugal.usembassy.gov; Ambassador THOMAS F. STEPHENSON.

Uruguay: Rua Sampaio Pina 16, 2°, 1070-249 Lisbon; tel. (21) 3889265; fax (21) 3889245; e-mail urulusi@sapo.pt; Ambassador GASTÓN LASARTE.

Venezuela: Av. Duque de Loulé 47, 4°, 1050-086 Lisbon; tel. (21) 3573803; fax (21) 3527421; e-mail embavenez@mail.telepac.pt; internet www.embavenezuela.pt; Ambassador LUCAS ENRIQUE RINCÓN ROMERO.

Judicial System

The judicial system of the Portuguese Republic comprises several categories of courts which, according to the Constitution, are sovereign bodies. The country is divided into four judicial districts, which are, in turn, divided into 37 judicial circuits. The principle of habeas corpus is recognized. Citizens who have been unjustly convicted are entitled to a review of their sentence and to compensation. The death penalty is prohibited by the Constitution. The jury system, reintroduced for certain types of crime in 1976, operates only at the request of the Public Prosecutor or defendant.

Judges are appointed for life and are irremovable. Practising judges may not hold any other office, whether public or private, except a non-remunerated position in teaching or research in the legal field. The Conselho Superior da Magistratura controls their appointment, transfer and promotion and the exercise of disciplinary action.

PUBLIC PROSECUTION

The State is represented in the courts by the Public Prosecution, whose highest organ is the Procuradoria-Geral da República (Attorney-General's Office).

Procuradoria-Geral da República: Rua da Escola Politécnica 140, 1269-269 Lisbon; tel. (21) 3921900; fax (21) 3975255; e-mail mailpgr@pgr.pt; internet www.pgr.pt; Attorney-General Dr FERNANDO JOSÉ MATOS PINTO MONTEIRO.

SUPREME COURT

Supremo Tribunal de Justiça
Praça do Comércio, 1149-012 Lisbon; tel. (21) 3218900; fax (21) 3474919; e-mail correio@lisboa.stj.pt; internet www.stj.pt.

The highest organ of the judicial system; consists of 60 judges, incl. the President.

President: LUÍS ANTÓNIO NORONHA DO NASCIMENTO.

COURTS OF SECOND INSTANCE

There are five Courts of Second Instance (or Courts of Appeal):

Tribunal da Relação de Coímbra: Palácio da Justiça, Rua da Sofia, 3004-501 Coimbra; tel. (239) 852950; fax (239) 838985; e-mail coimbra.tr@tribunais.org.pt; internet www.trc.pt; 46 judges, incl. the President; Pres. ANTÓNIO JOAQUIM PIÇARRA.

Tribunal da Relação de Évora: Palácio Barahona, Rua da República 141–143, 7004-501 Évora; tel. (266) 758800; fax (266) 701529; e-mail evora.tr@tribunais.org.pt; internet www.tre.pt; 39 judges, incl. the President; Pres. MANUEL CIPRIANO NABAIS.

Tribunal da Relação de Guimarães: Largo João Franco 248, 4810-269 Guimarães; tel. (253) 439900; fax (253) 439999; e-mail guimaraes.tr@tibunais.org.pt; internet www.trg.mj.pt; 31 judges, incl. the President; Pres. Dr ANTÓNIO DA SILVA GONÇALVES.

Tribunal da Relação de Lisboa: Rua Arsenal, Letra G, 1100-038 Lisbon; tel. (21) 3222900; fax (21) 3479844; e-mail lisboa.tr@tribunais.org.pt; internet www.trl.pt; 108 judges, incl. the President; Pres. Dr LUÍS MARIA VAZ DAS NEVES.

Tribunal da Relação do Porto: Campo Mártires de Pátria, 4099-012 Porto; tel. (22) 2008531; fax (22) 2000715; e-mail porto.tr@tribunais.org.pt; internet www.trp.pt; 91 judges, incl. the President; Pres. Dr GONÇALO XAVIER SILVANO.

COURTS OF FIRST INSTANCE

There are 258 Courts of First Instance within Portuguese territory: 195 *comarca* courts hear cases of a general nature, while 46 labour courts hear specific matters. There are five family courts and two courts for the enforcement of sentences. Circuit Courts total 33.

CONSTITUTIONAL COURT

Tribunal Constitucional
Palácio Ratton, Rua de O Século 111, 1249-117 Lisbon; tel. (21) 3233600; fax (21) 3233649; e-mail tribunal@tribconstitucional.pt; internet www.tribunalconstitucional.pt.

Rules on matters of constitutionality according to the terms of the Constitution of the Portuguese Republic; exercises jurisdiction over all Portuguese territory; consists of 13 judges, incl. the President.

President: RUI MANUEL GENS DE MOURA RAMOS.

SUPREME ADMINISTRATIVE COURT

Supremo Tribunal Administrativo
Rua de S. Pedro de Alcântara 73–79, 1269-137 Lisbon; tel. (21) 3216200; fax (21) 3466129; e-mail correio@lisboa.sta.mj.pt; internet www.stadministrativo.pt.

The highest organ of the administrative system; has jurisdiction over metropolitan Portugal, the Azores and Madeira; there is also a Supremo Tribunal Administrativo Norte and Sul; consists of 37 judges, incl. the President.

President: MANUEL FERNANDO DOS SANTOS SERRA.

Religion

There is freedom of religion in Portugal. The dominant Christian denomination is Roman Catholicism. In the 2001 census, of the 8,699,515 respondents to the question regarding religion, 7,353,548 identified themselves as Roman Catholic, 17,443 as Orthodox Christian, 48,301 as Protestant and 122,745 as other Christian. A further 1,773 were Jewish, 12,014 were Muslim and 13,882 followed another religion.

CHRISTIANITY

The Roman Catholic Church

For ecclesiastical purposes, Portugal comprises 17 dioceses, grouped into three metropolitan sees (the patriarchate of Lisbon and the archdioceses of Braga and Évora). At 31 December 2006 some 9,058,788 Portuguese were adherents of the Roman Catholic Church, representing 86.4% of the population.

Bishops' Conference

Conferência Episcopal Portuguesa, Quinta do Cabeço, Porta D, 1885-076 Moscavide, Lisbon; tel. (21) 8855460; fax (21) 8855461; e-mail webmaster@ecclesia.pt; internet www.ecclesia.pt.

PORTUGAL

f. 1932; Pres. Most Rev. JORGE FERREIRA DA COSTA ORTIGA (Archbishop of Braga); Sec. Fr MANUEL MORUJÃO.

Patriarch of Lisbon: Cardinal JOSÉ DA CRUZ POLICARPO, Casa Patriarcal, Quinta do Cabeço, 1800-076, Moscavide, Lisbon; tel. (21) 9457310; fax (21) 9457329; e-mail gab.patriarca@patriarcado-lisboa.pt; internet www.patriarcado-lisboa.pt.

Archbishop of Braga: Most Rev. JORGE FERREIRA DA COSTA ORTIGA, Paço Arquiepiscopal, Rua de Santa Margarida 181, 4710-306 Braga; tel. (253) 203189; fax (253) 203191; e-mail csociais@diocese-braga.pt; internet www.diocese-braga.pt.

Archbishop of Évora: Most Rev. JOSÉ FRANCISCO SANCHES ALVES, Cúria Arquidiocesana, Largo Marquês de Marialva, 7000-809 Évora; tel. (266) 748850; fax (266) 748851; e-mail diocese@diocese-evora.pt; internet www.diocese-evora.pt.

Other Christian Churches and Organizations

Associação de Igrejas Baptistas Portuguesas (Asscn of Portuguese Baptist Churches): Rua da Escola 18, Maceira, 2715 Pero Pinheiro; tel. (21) 9271150; f. 1955; Pres. Rev. JOÃO S. REGUEIRAS.

Conselho Português de Igrejas Cristãs (COPIC) (Portuguese Council of Christian Churches): Apto 392, 4430-003 Vila Nova de Gaia; tel. (22) 3754018; fax (22) 3752016; e-mail igreja@lusitana.org; f. 1971; mems include the Igreja Lusitana Católica Apostólica Evangélica, the Igreja Evangélica Metodista Portuguesa and the Igreja Evangélica Presbiteriana de Portugal; Pres. Rt Rev. FERNANDO LUZ SOARES.

Convenção Baptista Portuguesa (Portuguese Baptist Convention): Rua Luís Simões 7, 1°, Apdo 3085, 2745 Queluz; tel. (21) 4343370; fax (21) 4343379; e-mail geral@acampamentobaptista.com.pt; f. 1920; Pres. Pastor ANTÓNIO PIRES; Sec. MARIA HERCÍLIA MELO; 4,338 mems (2003).

Igreja Evangélica Metodista Portuguesa (Portuguese Evangelical Methodist Church): Praça Coronel Pacheco 23, 4050-453 Porto; tel. (22) 2007410; fax (22) 2086961; e-mail sede-geral@igreja-metodista.pt; internet www.igreja-metodista.pt; Bishop SIFREDO TEIXEIRA.

Igreja Evangélica Presbiteriana de Portugal (Presbyterian Church of Portugal): Rua Tomás da Anunciação, 56, 1° dto, 1350-328 Lisbon; tel. (21) 3974959; fax (21) 3956326; e-mail office@iepp.org; internet www.iepp.org; f. 1952; Pres. JOSÉ SALVADOR; Gen. Sec. DAVID VALENTE.

Igreja Lusitana Católica Apostólica Evangélica—Comunhão Anglicana (Lusitanian Catholic Apostolic Evangelical Church—Anglican Communion): Rua de Afonso Albuquerque 86, Apdo 392, 4431-905 Vila Nova de Gaia; tel. (22) 3754018; fax (22) 3752016; e-mail comunicacao@igreja-lusitana.org; internet www.igreja-lusitana.org; f. 1880; extraprovincial diocese of the Anglican Communion under the metropolitan authority of the Archbishop of Canterbury (United Kingdom) since 1980; Bishop Rt Rev. FERNANDO LUZ SOARES.

ISLAM

Comunidade Islamica de Lisboa: Mesquita Central de Lisboa, Rua da Mesquita 1, 1070 Lisbon; tel. (21) 3874142; fax (21) 3872230; e-mail info@comunidadeislamica.pt; internet www.comunidadeislamica.pt; f. 1968; Pres. ABDUL MAJID KARIM VAKIL.

JUDAISM

There are Jewish communities in Lisbon, Oporto, Belmonte and Portimão.

Comunidade Israelita de Lisboa: Rua do Monte Olivete 16, r/c, 1200-280 Lisbon; tel. (21) 3931130; fax (21) 3931139; e-mail administrativo@cilisboa.org; internet www.cilisboa.org; Pres. Dr JOSÉ OULMAN CARP.

Comunidade Israelita do Porto: Rua Guerra Junqueiro 340, 4150-186 Oporto; tel. (93) 3192747; e-mail direccao@comunidade-israelita-porto.org; internet comunidade-israelita-porto.org; f. 1923.

The Press

PRINCIPAL DAILIES
(circulation figures refer to Oct.–Dec. 2007, unless otherwise indicated)

Aveiro

Diário de Aveiro: Av. Dr Lourenço Peixinho 15, 5°, 3800-801 Aveiro; tel. (234) 000030; fax (234) 000033; e-mail diarioaveiro@diarioaveiro.pt; internet www.diarioaveiro.pt; f. 1985; morning; Dir ADRIANO CALLÉ LUCAS; circ. 4,073.

Braga

Diário do Minho: Rua de Santa Margarida 4, 4710-306 Braga; tel. (253) 609460; fax (253) 609465; e-mail redaccao@diariodominho.pt; internet www.diariodominho.pt; f. 1919; morning; Dir JOSÉ MIGUEL PEREIRA; circ. 5,033.

Coímbra

Diário as Beiras: Rua 25 de Abril, Apdo 44, 3040-935 Taveiro, Coímbra; tel. (239) 980280; fax (239) 983574; e-mail beirastexto@asbeiras.pt; internet www.asbeiras.pt; Dir ANTÓNIO ABRANTES; circ. 7,959.

Diário de Coímbra: Rua Adriano Lucas, 3020-264 Coímbra; tel. (239) 492133; fax (239) 492128; e-mail redac@diariocoimbra.pt; internet www.diariocoimbra.pt; f. 1930; morning; *Domingo* publ. on Sun. (f. 1974; circ. 8,000); Dir ADRIANO MÁRIO DA CUNHA LUCAS; circ. 10,079.

Évora

Diário do Sul: Estrada de Arraiolos, Évora; tel. (266) 730410; fax (266) 730411; internet www.diariodosul.com.pt; f. 1969; morning; Dir MANUEL MADEIRA PIÇARRA; circ. 5,520.

Leiria

Diário de Leiria: Edif. Maringá, Rua S. Franciso 7, 4° esq., 2400-232 Leiria; tel. (244) 000031; fax (244) 000032; e-mail diarioleiria@diarioleiria.pt; internet www.diarioleiria.pt; f. 1987; morning; Dir ADRIANO CALLÉ LUCAS; circ. 2,267.

Lisboa
(Lisbon)

A Bola: Travessa da Queimada 23, 2°D r/c esq., 1294 Lisbon; tel. (21) 3463981; fax (21) 3432275; internet www.abola.pt; f. 1945; sport; Dir VICTOR SERPA.

Correio da Manhã: Av. João Crisóstomo 72, 1069-043 Lisbon; tel. (21) 3185200; fax (21) 3156146; e-mail geral@correiomanha.pt; internet www.correiomanha.pt; f. 1979; morning; independent; Dir OCTÁVIO RIBEIRO; circ. 112,116.

Diário Económico: Rua de Oliveira ao Carmo 8, 1249-111 Lisbon; tel. (21) 3236800; fax (21) 3236775; e-mail deconomico@economicasgps.com; internet diarioeconomico.sapo.pt; Dir ANDRÉ MACEDO; circ. 14,639.

Diário de Notícias: Av. da Liberdade 266, 1250-149 Lisbon; tel. (21) 3187500; fax (21) 3187515; e-mail webmaster@dn.pt; internet dn.sapo.pt; f. 1864; morning; Dir JOÃO MARCELINO; circ. 35,932.

Público: Rua Viriato 13, 1069-315 Lisbon; tel. (21) 0111000; fax (21) 0111006; internet www.publico.pt; f. 1990; morning; Dir JOSÉ MANUEL FERNANDES; circ. 40,913.

Record: Av. Conde Valbom 30, 4-5°, 1050-068 Lisbon; tel. (21) 0124900; fax (21) 3476279; e-mail record@record.pt; internet www.record.pt; f. 1949; sport; Dir ALEXANDRE PAIS; circ. 70,436.

24Horas: Av. da Liberdade 266, 5°, 1250-149 Lisbon; tel. (21) 3187500; e-mail pedro.tadeu@24horas.com.pt; internet www.24horasnewspaper.com; also publishes edn in USA; Editor PEDRO TADEU; circ. 37,903.

Porto
(Oporto)

O Jogo: Rua de Gil Vicente 129, 1°, 4000-814 Porto; tel. (22) 5071900; fax (22) 5504550; e-mail ojogo@mail.telepac.pt; internet www.ojogo.pt; sporting news; Dir MANUEL TAVARES; circ. 32,741.

Jornal de Notícias: Rua Gonçalo Cristóvão 195–219, 4049-011 Porto; tel. (22) 2096111; fax (22) 2096140; e-mail noticias@jn.pt; internet www.jn.pt; f. 1888; morning; Dir JOSÉ LEITE PEREIRA; circ. 89,480.

O Primeiro de Janeiro: Rua Coelho Neto 65, 4000 Porto; tel. (22) 0109100; fax (22) 5103291; e-mail geral@oprimeirodejaneiro.pt; internet www.oprimeirodejaneiro.pt; f. 1868; independent; morning; Dir NASSALETE MIRANDA; circ. 20,200.

Setúbal

Correio de Setúbal: Rua Camilo Castelo Branco 163 F–H, Apdo 549, 2900-450 Setúbal; tel. (265) 538810; fax (265) 538813; e-mail correiodesetubal@sado2000.pt; internet www.cs.publ.pt.

Viseu

Diário Regional de Viseu: Rua Alexandre Herculano 198, 1° esq., 3510-033 Viseu; tel. (232) 000031; fax (232) 000032; e-mail diarioviseu@diarioregional.pt; internet www.diarioregional.pt; Dir ADRIANO CALLÉ LUCAS; circ. 1,839.

PORTUGAL

Notícias de Viseu: Av. do Convento 1, Apdo 3115, 3511-689 Viseu; tel. (232) 410410; fax (232) 410418; e-mail geral@noticiasdeviseu.com; internet www.noticiasdeviseu.com; f. 1974; Dir FERNANDO ABREU.

Os Açores
(The Azores)

Açoriano Oriental: Rua Dr Bruno Tavares Carreiro 36, 9500-055 Ponta Delgada; tel. (296) 202800; fax (296) 202826; e-mail pub.ao@acorianooriental.pt; internet www.acorianooriental.pt; f. 1835; morning; Dir PAOLO SIMÕES; circ. 4,226.

Correio dos Açores: Rua Dr João Francisco de Sousa 14, 9500 Ponta Delgada; tel. (296) 201060; fax (296) 286119; f. 1920; morning; Dir AMÉRICO NATALINO VIVEIROS.

Diário dos Açores: Rua Dr João Francisco de Sousa 16, 9500-187 Ponta Delgada; tel. (296) 284355; fax (296) 284840; e-mail diario@da.online.pt; internet www.da.online.pt; f. 1870; morning; Dir PAULO HUGO VIVEIROS.

Diário Insular: Av. Infante D. Henrique 1, 9700-098 Angra do Heroísmo, Terceira; tel. (295) 401050; fax (295) 214246; e-mail diarioins@mail.telepac.pt; internet www.diarioinsular.com; f. 1946; morning; Dir JOSÉ LOURENÇO.

O Telégrafo: Rua Conselheiro Medeiros 30, 9902 Horta; tel. and fax (292) 22245; f. 1893; morning; Dir RUBEN RODRIGUES.

Madeira

Diário de Notícias: Rua Dr Fernão de Ornelas 56, 3°, 9054-514 Funchal; tel. (291) 202300; fax (291) 202306; e-mail dnmad@dnoticias.pt; internet www.dnoticias.pt; f. 1876; morning; independent; Dir JOSÉ BETTENCOURT DA CÂMARA; circ. 13,677.

Jornal da Madeira: Rua Dr Fernão de Ornelas 35, 4°, 9001-905 Funchal; tel. (291) 210400; fax (291) 210401; e-mail editorial@jornaldamadeira.pt; internet www.jornaldamadeira.pt; f. 1927; morning; Catholic; Dir JOÃO AFONSO DE ALMEIDA.

PRINCIPAL PERIODICALS

Activa: Rua Calvet de Magalhães 242, Laveiras, 2770-022 Paço de Arcos; tel. (21) 4143078; fax (21) 4107050; internet pub.edimpresa.pt; f. 1991; monthly; for women; Editor ROSÁRIA BARRETO; circ. 80,279 (2006).

Africa Hoje: Rua Joaquim António de Aguiar 45, 5° esq., 1070 Lisbon; tel. (21) 557175; fax (21) 3557667; e-mail geral@lucidus.pt; f. 1985; monthly; African affairs; Dir ALBÉRICO CARDOSO; circ. 30,000.

Anglo-Portuguese News: Apdo 113, 2766-902 Estoril, Lisbon; tel. (21) 4661471; fax (21) 4660358; e-mail apn@mail.telepac.pt; f. 1937; Thurs.; English language newspaper; Publr and Editor NIGEL BATLEY; circ. 30,000.

Autosport: Edif. São Francisco de Sales, Rua Calvet de Magalhães 242, 2770-022 Paço de Arcos; tel. (21) 4698197; fax (21) 4698552; e-mail autosport@autosport.pt; internet www.autosport.pt; weekly; motoring; Dir RUI FREIRE; circ. 10,880 (2006).

Avante: Av. Almirante Gago Coutinho 121, 1700-029 Lisbon; tel. (21) 7817190; fax (21) 7817193; e-mail avante.pcp@mail.telepac.pt; internet www.avante.pt; weekly; organ of the Portuguese Communist Party; Dir JOSÉ CASANOVA.

Brotéria—Revista de Cultura: Rua Maestro António Taborda 14, 1249-094 Lisbon; tel. (21) 3961660; fax (21) 3956629; e-mail broteria@netcabo.pt; internet www.broteria.pt; f. 1902; monthly; review of culture; Dir HERMÍNIO RICO; circ. 1,400.

Casa e Decoração: Av. Duque d'Avila 26, 3°, 1049-042 Lisbon; tel. (21) 3168500; fax (21) 3168535; f. 1981; 12 a year; home and interior decoration; Dir URSULA BASTOS; circ. 35,000.

Casa & Jardim: Rua da Misericórdia 137, s/loja, 1249-037 Lisbon; tel. (21) 3472127; fax (21) 3421490; e-mail direccao@casajardim.pt; internet www.casajardim.net; f. 1978; monthly; home, interior and exterior design, fine arts, exhibitions and antique fairs; Dir EDUARDO FORTUNATO DE ALMEIDA; circ. 14,486 (2006).

Colecções Moda & Beleza: Rua Dona Filipa de Vilhena 4, 5° esq., 1000-135 Lisbon; tel. (21) 3105300; fax (21) 3105309; e-mail bdesenhada@meriberica.pt; internet www.meriberica.pt; 5 a year; fashion and beauty; Editor CRISTINA COSTA; circ. 240,000.

Colóquio/Letras: Av. de Berna 45A, 1067-001 Lisbon; tel. (21) 7823000; fax (21) 7823021; e-mail coloquioletras@gulbenkian.pt; internet www.gulbenkian.pt/educacao/revista.asp; f. 1971; 4 a year; literary; Dir Dra JOANA VARELA; circ. 3,600.

Correio da Madeira: Rua do Carmo 19, 3° dto, 9000 Funchal; tel. (291) 20738; f. 1987; weekly newspaper; Dir JOSÉ CAMPOS; circ. 5,000.

Cosmopolitan: Rua Calvet de Magalhães 242, Laveiras, 2770-022 Paço de Arcos; tel. (21) 4698861; internet pub.edimpresa.pt; f. 1992; monthly; women's magazine; Editor MARIA SERINA; circ. 53,787 (2006).

Eles e Elas: Praça Luiz de Camões 36, 2°D, 1200-243 Lisbon; tel. (21) 3224660; fax (21) 3224679; e-mail gabinete1@gabinete1.pt; internet www.gabinete1.pt; f. 1983; monthly; fashion, culture, social events; Dir MARIA DA LUZ DE BRAGANÇA.

Elle: Rua Filipe Folque 40, 4°, 1050 Lisbon; tel. (21) 3156907; fax (21) 3164205; e-mail elle@hachette.pt; f. 1988; monthly; women's magazine; Dir FÁTIMA COTTA; circ. 54,697 (2006).

Expresso: Edif. S. Francisco de Sales, Rua Calvet de Magalhães 242, 2770-022 Paço de Arcos; tel. (21) 4554000; fax (21) 4435349; e-mail director@expresso.pt; internet www.expresso.pt; weekly newspaper; Dir HENRIQUE MONTEIRO; circ. 123,115 (Oct.–Dec. 2007).

Gente e Viagens: Rua Joaquim António de Aguiar 45, 1099-058 Lisbon; tel. (21) 3839810; fax (21) 862746; e-mail lucidus@mail.telepac.pt; internet genteviagens.sapo.pt; f. 1980; monthly; tourism; Dir ALBÉRICO CARDOSO; circ. 30,000.

Guia—Revista Prática: Av. Almirante Gago Coutinho 113, 1749-087 Lisbon; tel. (21) 8474410; fax (21) 8474396; e-mail mpcorreia@tvguia.pt; weekly women's magazine; fashion and housekeeping; Dir MARGARIDA PINTO CORREIA; Editor-in-Chief PALMIRA SIMÕES; circ. 40,000.

JL (Jornal de Letras, Artes e Ideias): Rua Calvet de Magalhães 242, Laveiras, 2770-022 Paço de Arcos; tel. (21) 574520; e-mail jcvasconcelos@edimpresa.pt; internet pub.edimpresa.pt; fortnightly; Dir JOSÉ CARLOS DE VASCONCELOS; circ. 8,358 (2006).

Manchete: Rua das Flores 105, 1° esq., 1200-194 Lisbon; tel. (21) 3224660; fax (21) 3224679; e-mail gabinete1@gabinete1.pt; f. 1992; monthly; national and international events; Dir MARIA DA LUZ DE BRAGANÇA.

Maria: Av. Miguel Bombarda 33, 2745 Queluz; tel. 4364401; fax 4365001; internet www.impala.pt; f. 1977; weekly; women's magazine; Dir JACQUES RODRIGUES; Editor-in-Chief PAULA RODRIGUES; circ. 251,404 (2006).

Máxima: Av. João Crisóstomo 72, 3°, 1069-043 Lisbon; tel. (21) 3309400; fax (21) 3540410; e-mail lauratorres@maxima.cofina.pt; internet www.maxima.pt; f. 1989; women's magazine; Dir LAURA LUZES TORRES; circ. 68,459 (2006).

Moda & Moda: Rua Braamcamp 12, r/c esq., 1250-050 Lisbon; tel. (21) 3886068; fax (21) 3862426; e-mail modaemoda@netcabo.pt; f. 1984; 5 a year; fashion, beauty and art; Dir MARIONELA GUSMÃO; circ. 20,000.

Mulher Moderna: Av. Miguel Bombarda 33, 2745 Queluz; tel. 4364401; fax 4365001; internet www.impala.pt; f. 1988; weekly; women's magazine; Dir JACQUES RODRIGUES; Editor-in-Chief PAULA RODRIGUES; circ. 16,512 (2006).

Nova Gente: Av. Miguel Bombarda 33, 2745 Queluz; tel. 4364388; fax 4365001; internet www.impala.pt; f. 1979; weekly; popular; Dir JACQUES RODRIGUES; Editor-in-Chief ANTÓNIO SIMÕES; circ. 200,000.

Portugal Socialista: Largo do Rato 2, 1269-143 Lisbon; tel. (21) 3822000; f. 1967; quarterly; organ of the Socialist Party; Dir AUGUSTO SANTOS SILVA; circ. 5,000.

Povo Livre: Rua S. Caetano 9, 1249-087 Lisbon; tel. (21) 3952140; fax (21) 3976967; e-mail povolivre@psd.pt; weekly; organ of the Social Democratic Party; Dir JORGE MANUEL FERRAZ DE FREITAS NETO.

Revista ACP: Rua Rosa Araújo 24, 1250-195 Lisbon; tel. (21) 3180100; fax (21) 3180170; e-mail apoio.socio@acp.pt; internet www.acp.pt; f. 1908; monthly; motoring and tourism; Propr Automóvel Club de Portugal; Editor ANTÓNIO RAPOSO DE MAGALHÃES; circ. 177,765 (2006).

Revista Exame: Rua Calvet de Magalhães 242, Laveiras, 2770-022 Paço de Arcos; tel. (21) 4698000; fax (21) 4698500; e-mail icanha@edimpresa.pt; internet www.exame.pt; monthly; finance; Dir ISABEL CANHA; circ. 24,468 (2006).

Segredos de Cozinha: Edif. do Grupo Impala, Ranholas, 2710-460 Sintra; tel. (21) 92398033; fax (21) 9238044; e-mail gracamorais@impala.pt; internet www.impala.pt; f. 1985; weekly; cookery; Dir GRAÇA MORAIS; Editor-in-Chief PAULA RODRIGUES; circ. 20,736 (2006).

Selecções do Reader's Digest: Rua Joaquim António de Aguiar 43, 1092-001 Lisbon; tel. (21) 3810000; fax (21) 3859203; internet www.rd.com/international/shared/index.jhtml?countryid=pt; monthly magazine; Dir ISABEL BIVAR; circ. 103,690 (Oct.–Dec. 2007).

Semanário: Av. Almirante Reis 73, 5°, 1150-012 Lisbon; tel. (21) 0994844; fax (21) 3504799; e-mail jornal@semanario.pt; internet www.semanario.pt; weekly newspaper; Dir PAULO GAIÃO; circ. 20,291 (Oct.–Dec. 2007).

Semanário Económico: Rua da Oliveira ao Carmo 8, 5°, 1249-111 Lisbon; tel. (21) 3236900; fax (21) 3236901; e-mail seconomico@economicasgps.com; internet www.semanarioeconomico.com; weekly; economy, business and finance; Dir INÊS SERRA LOPES; circ. 10,616 (Oct.–Dec. 2007).

Sol: Rua de São Nicolau 120, 1100-550 Lisbon; tel. (21) 3246500; fax (21) 3246540; e-mail geral@sol.pt; internet sol.sapo.pt; f. 2006;

PORTUGAL   *Directory*

weekly newspaper; Sat.; publ. by O Sol é Essencial; Dir José António Saraiva; circ. 49,046 (Oct.–Dec. 2007).

TV Guia: Av. Almirante Gago Coutinho 113, 1749-087 Lisbon; tel. (21) 8474410; fax (21) 8474395; e-mail jgobern@tvguia.pt; weekly; TV programmes and general features; Dir João Gobern; circ. 73,065 (2006).

TV 7 Dias: Av. Miguel Bombarda 33, 2745 Queluz; tel. 4364401; fax 4365001; internet www.impala.pt; f. 1985; weekly; television magazine; Dir Ventura Martins; Editor-in-Chief Frederico Valarinho; circ. 174,789 (2006).

Vida Económica: Rua Gonçalo Cristovão 111, 5°–7°, 4049-037 Porto; tel. (22) 3399400; fax (22) 2058098; e-mail redaccao@vidaeconomica.pt; internet www.vidaeconomica.pt; weekly; financial; Dir João Peixoto de Sousa; Editor-in-Chief João Luís de Sousa; circ. 13,733 (Oct.–Dec. 2007).

Visão: Rua Calvet de Magalhães 242, Laveiras, 2770-022 Paço de Arcos; tel. (22) 4698000; fax (22) 8347557; e-mail visao@ajc.pt; internet www.visaoonline.pt; f. 1993; weekly magazine; Dir-Gen. Pedro Camaho; circ. 100,334 (Oct.–Dec. 2007).

NEWS AGENCY

Lusa (Agência de Notícias de Portugal, SA): Rua Dr João Couto, Lote C, 1500 Lisbon; tel. (21) 7116500; fax (21) 7116531; e-mail agencialusa@lusa.pt; internet www.lusa.pt; f. 1987; Pres. José Manuel dos Reis Barroso; News Editor Luís Miguel Viana.

PRESS ASSOCIATIONS

Associação Portuguesa da Imprensa (APIMPRENSA) (Portuguese Press Association): Rua Gomes Freire 183, 4° esq., 1169-041 Lisbon; tel. (21) 3555092; fax (21) 3142191; e-mail geral@apimprensa.pt; internet www.apimprensa.pt; f. 1961; represents 600 publications, both local and national; Pres. João Palmeiro; Sec.-Gen. Joana Ramada Curto.

Associação da Imprensa Diária (Association of the Daily Press): Rua de Artilharia Um 69, 2°, 1250-138 Lisbon; tel. (21) 3857584; fax (21) 3873541; e-mail associacao.imprensa.diaria@gmail.com; f. 1976; 7 mems; Pres. José Miguel Piçarra; Sec. Fernando Alves Monteiro.

Associação da Imprensa Estrangeira em Portugal (AIEP): Sala da Imprensa, Palácio Foz, Praça dos Restauradores, 1250-187 Lisbon; fax (21) 3464145; e-mail belenchurg@yahoo.com; internet www.aiep.eu; f. 1976; Pres. Belén Rodrigo; Exec. Sec. Anne Governo.

Publishers

Âncora Editora: Av. Infante Santo 52, 3° esq., 1350-179 Lisbon; tel. (21) 3951223; fax (21) 3951222; e-mail ancora.editora@ancora-editora.pt; internet www.ancora-editora.pt; f. 1998; Portuguese literature and culture, factual and educational works.

Areal Editores: Rua da Torrinha 228h, 3°, 4050-610 Porto; tel. (22) 3393900; fax (22) 2005708; e-mail areal@arealeditores.pt; internet www.arealeditores.pt; educational.

Assírio & Alvim: Rua Passos Manuel 67b, 1150-258 Lisbon; tel. (21) 3583030; fax (21) 3583039; e-mail assirio@assirio.com; internet www.assirio.pt; f. 1972; poetry, fiction, essays, gastronomy, photography, art, children's literature, history, social science; Man. Vasco David.

Bertrand Editora, SA: Rua Anchieta 15, 1249-060 Lisbon; tel. (21) 3476122; fax (21) 3479728; e-mail info@bertrand.pt; internet www.bertrand.pt; literature, arts, humanities, educational; Man. Mario Correia.

Campo das Letras: Edif. Mota-Galiza, Rua Júlio Dinis 247, 6°, 4050-324 Porto; tel. (22) 6080870; fax (22) 6080880; e-mail campo.letras@mail.telepac.pt; internet www.campo-letras.pt; f. 1994; literature, juvenile, current affairs.

Casa das Letras: Rua Bento de Jesus Caraça 17, 1495-686 Cruz Quebrada; tel. (21) 0052350; fax (21) 0052340; e-mail info@casadasletras.pt; fiction, politics, religion, history, economics, management, biographies, dictionaries, memoirs.

Circulo de Leitores: Rua Prof. Jorge da Silva Horta 1, 1500-499 Lisbon; tel. (21) 7626100; fax (21) 7607149; e-mail correio@circuloleitores.pt; internet www.circuloleitores.pt; fiction and non-fiction.

Coímbra Editora, Lda: Rua do Armado, Apdo 101, 3001-951 Coímbra; tel. (239) 8526540; fax (239) 852651; e-mail info@coimbraeditora.pt; internet www.coimbraeditora.pt; f. 1920; law, education, linguistics; Man. Dr João Carlos A. Oliveira Salgado.

Edições Afrontamento, Lda: Rua de Costa Cabral 859, 4200-225 Porto; tel. (22) 5074220; fax (22) 5074229; e-mail editorial@edicoesafrontamento.pt; internet www.edicoesafrontamento.pt; f. 1963; fiction, poetry, cinema, children's books, history, sociology, philosophy, economics, politics, etc.; Dirs J. Sousa Ribeiro, A. Sousa Luís.

Edições Almedina, SA: Av. Fernão de Magalhães 584, 5°, 3000-174 Coimbra; tel. (239) 851903; e-mail editora@almedina.net; internet www.almedina.net; law, education; Dir Joaquim Machado.

Edições Asa: Estrada de Paço de Arcos 66–66a, 2735-336 Cacém; tel. (22) 6166030; fax (22) 5322831; e-mail edicoes@asa.pt; internet www.asa.pt; f. 1951; literature, arts, schoolbooks, children's books, educational equipment; Gen. Man. Américo A. Areal.

Edições Caixotim: Rua dos Clérigos 23, 4050-205 Porto; tel. (22) 3390831; fax (22) 3390833; e-mail edicoescaixotim@mail.telepac.pt; internet www.caixotim.pt; f. 2001; literature, history, criticism, essays, art, etc.; Publr and Editorial Dir Paulo Samuel.

Edições 70, Lda: Rua Luciano Cordeiro 123, 1° esq., 1069-157 Lisbon; tel. (21) 3190240; fax (21) 3190249; e-mail geral@edicoes70.pt; internet www.edicoes70.pt; f. 1970; history, linguistics, anthropology, philosophy, psychology, education, art, architecture, science, reference books; Dir Carlos Pinto.

Editora Educação Nacional, Lda: Rua do Almada 125, 4050 Porto; tel. (22) 2005351; fax (22) 2080742; e-mail contacto@editoraeducnacional.pt; internet www.editoraeducnacional.pt; school textbooks and review, *Educação Nacional*.

Editora Livros do Brasil, SA: Estrada da Outurela 121, 2794-051 Carnaxide; tel. (21) 3462621; fax (21) 3428487; e-mail geral@livrosdobrasil.com; internet www.livrosdobrasil.com; f. 1944; literature, history, politics, science, management, health, children's books; Dir António Luis de Souza Pinto.

Editora Pergaminho, Lda: Rua de Alegria 486a, Amoreira, 2645-167 Cascais; tel. (21) 4646110; fax (21) 4674008; e-mail info@editorapergaminho.pt; internet www.editorapergaminho.pt; f. 1991; cinema, music, humour, fiction; Dir Mário Mendes de Moura.

Editora Portugalmundo, Lda: Rua Gonçalves Crespo 47, r/c, 1150-184 Lisbon; tel. (21) 3304685; fax (21) 3590420; e-mail editoraportugalmundo@gmail.com; internet www.editoraportugalmundo.com; f. 1976; children's books, poetry, biographies, law, music, fiction, theatre; Dir Maria Alexandra Santos.

Editora Replicação, Lda: Av. Infante Santo 343, r/c, 1350-277 Lisbon; fax (21) 3969808; e-mail replic@mail.telepac.pt; f. 1982; textbooks, children's books, dictionaries, language materials; Dir José Carlos Anaia Cristo.

Editorial Bizancia, Lda: Largo Luis Chaves 11–11a, 1600-487 Lisbon; tel. (21) 7550228; fax (21) 7520072; e-mail bizancio@editorial-bizancio.pt; internet www.editorial-bizancio.pt; f. 1998; general fiction and non-fiction.

Editorial Confluência: Calçada do Combro 99, 1200-112 Lisbon; tel. and fax (21) 3466917; e-mail livroshorizonte@mail.telepac.pt; f. 1945; dictionaries; Man. Rogério Mendes de Moura.

Editorial Estampa, Lda: Rua da Escola do Exército 9, r/c dto, 1169-090 Lisbon; tel. (21) 3555663; fax (21) 3141911; e-mail estampa@estampa.pt; internet www.estampa.pt; sociology, economics, occult, fiction, sport, history, art, alternative medicine, children's; Dir António Carlos Manso Pinheiro.

Editorial Futura: Rua General Morais Sarmento 9, c/v esq., 1500-310 Lisbon; tel. and fax (21) 7155848; e-mail editorialfutura@netcabo.pt; literature, comics.

Editorial Minerva: Rua da Alegria 30, 1250-007 Lisbon; tel. (21) 3224950; fax (21) 3224952; e-mail minerva_dna@netcabo.pt; internet www.editorialminerva.com; f. 1927; literature, politics, children's; Man. Narcisa Fernandes.

Editorial Nova Ática, SA: Calçado Nova de S. Francisco, 10, 1° esq., 1200-300 Lisbon; tel. (21) 3420557; fax (21) 3420305; e-mail editorialnovaatica@sapo.pt; f. 1935; poetry, literature, essays, theatre, history, philosophy; Chief Execs Vasco Silva, José Rodrigues.

Editorial Presença, Lda: Estrada das Palmeiras 59, Queluz de Baixo, 2730-132 Barcarena; tel. (21) 4347000; fax (21) 4346502; e-mail info@presenca.pt; internet www.presenca.pt; f. 1960; social sciences, fiction, textbooks, computer books, business, leisure, health, children's books, etc.; Dir Francisco Espadinha.

Editorial Verbo SA: Av. António Augusto de Aguiar 148, 2b, 1069-019 Lisbon; tel. (21) 3801100; fax (21) 3865397; e-mail comerciais@editorialverbo.pt; internet www.editorialverbo.pt; f. 1958; imprints include Editora Ulisseia; encyclopaedias, dictionaries, reference, history, general science, textbooks, education and children's books; Dir Fernando Guedes.

Europress—Editores e Distribuidores de Publicações, Lda: Praceta da República, Loja A, 2620-162 Póvoa de Santo Adrião; tel. (21) 9381450; fax (21) 9381452; e-mail europress@mail.telepac.pt; internet www.europress.pt; f. 1982; academic, children's, law, poetry, health, novels, history, social sciences, medicine, etc.; Man. António Bento Vintém.

PORTUGAL

FCA (Editora de Informática, Lda): Rua D. Estefânia 183, 1° esq., 1000-154 Lisbon; tel. (21) 3532735; fax (21) 3577827; e-mail fca@fca.pt; internet www.fca.pt; f. 1991; computer science.

Gradiva—Publicações, Lda: Rua Almeida e Sousa 21, r/c esq., 1399-041 Lisbon; tel. (21) 3933760; fax (21) 3953471; e-mail geral@gradiva.mail.pt; internet www.gradiva.pt; f. 1981; philosophy, education, history, fiction, science, social science, children's books, cartoons; Man. Dir GUILHERME VALENTE.

Guimarães Editores Lda: Rua da Misericórdia 68–70, 1200-273 Lisbon; tel. (21) 3243120; fax (21) 3243129; e-mail geral@guimaraes-ed.pt; internet www.guimaraes-ed.pt; f. 1899; literature, philosophy, history, etc.

Imprensa Nacional—Casa da Moeda, SA (INCM): Edif. Casa da Moeda, Av. António de José de Almeida, 1000-042 Lisbon; tel. (21) 7810700; e-mail comercial@incm.pt; internet www.incm.pt; f. 1972 as Imprensa Nacional—Casa da Moeda, EP; changed status as above in 1999; Portuguese literature, arts, philosophy, history, geography, sociology, economics, encyclopaedias, dictionaries, and the *Diário da República*; Dir Dr ALCIDES GAMA.

Lello Editores, Lda: Rua Dom João de Castro 539, 4435-674 Baguim do Monte; tel. (22) 3326084; fax (22) 3326086; e-mail joselello@lelloeditores.com; internet www.lelloeditores.com; fiction, poetry, history, reference, biography, religion; Dir-Gen. JOSÉ MANUEL BERNARDES PEREIRA LELLO.

Lidel Edições Técnicas, Lda: Rua D. Estefânia 183, r/c dto, 1049-057 Lisbon; tel. (21) 3511440; fax (21) 3577827; e-mail lidel@lidel.pt; internet www.lidel.pt; f. 1963; Portuguese as a foreign language, management, technology, computer science; Man. Dir FREDERICO CARLOS DA SILVA ANNES.

Lisboa Editora, Lda: Av. dos Estados Unidos da América 1B, 1700-163 Lisbon; tel. (21) 8430910; fax (21) 8430911; e-mail geral@lisboaeditora.pt; internet www.lisboaeditora.pt; textbooks; Editorial Dirs MARIA DE LOURDES PAIXÃO, BRIGITTE THUDICHUM.

Livraria Civilização Editora: Rua Alberto Aires de Gouveia 27, 4050-023 Porto; tel. (22) 6050917; fax (22) 6050999; e-mail info@civilizacao.pt; internet www.civilizacao.pt; f. 1920; social sciences, politics, economics, history, art, medicine, fiction, children's; Man. Dir MOURA BESSA.

Livraria Editora Figueirinhas, Lda: Rua do Freixo 643, 4300-217 Porto; tel. (22) 5309026; fax (22) 5309027; e-mail correio@liv-figueirinhas.pt; f. 1898; literature, school textbooks; Dir FRANCISCO GOMES PIMENTA.

Livraria Multinova: Av. Santa Joana Princesa 12E, 1700-357 Lisbon; tel. (21) 8421820; fax (21) 8483436; e-mail geral@multinova.pt; internet www.multinova.pt; f. 1970; schoolbooks, general, religion, Brazilian works; Dir CARLOS SANTOS.

Livraria Romano Torres: Rua João de Paiva 9A e B, 1400-225 Lisbon; tel. (21) 3014914; fax (21) 3015625; e-mail info@estudodidactico.pt; f. 1885; fiction; Dir FRANCISCO NORONHA DE ANDRADE.

Livros Cotovia: Rua Nova da Trindade 24, 1200-303 Lisbon; tel. (21) 3471447; fax (21) 3470467; e-mail geral@livroscotovia.pt; internet www.livroscotovia.pt; f. 1988; literature, drama, poetry, etc.

Livros Horizonte, Lda: Rua das Chagas 17, 1° dto, 1200-106 Lisbon; tel. (21) 3466917; fax (21) 3159259; e-mail info@livroshorizonte.pt; internet www.livroshorizonte.pt; f. 1953; art, education, history, social sciences; Dir MANUELA DUARTE.

Lusodidacta (Sociedade Portuguesa de Materia Didáctico, Lda): Rua Darío Cannas 5A, 2670-427 Loures; tel. (21) 9839840; fax (21) 9839847; e-mail loures1@lusodidacta.pt; internet www.lusodidacta.pt; f. 1976; textbooks, dictionaries, medicine.

McGraw-Hill de Portugal: Edif. Castilho 5, r/c A, Rua Barata Salgueiro, 51A, 1250-043 Lisbon; tel. (21) 3553180; fax (21) 3553189; e-mail servico_clientes@mcgraw-hill.com; internet www.mcgraw-hill.pt; scientific, technical and medical; Gen. Man. ANTÓNIO DE MARCO.

PAULUS Editora: Rua Dom Pedro de Cristo 10, 1749-092 Lisbon; tel. (21) 8437620; fax (21) 8437629; e-mail editor@paulus.pt; internet www.paulus.pt; religion, theology, psychology, etc.; Dir DARLEI ZANON.

Plátano Editora, SARL: Av. de Berna 31, 2° esq., 1069-054 Lisbon; tel. (21) 7979278; fax (21) 7954019; e-mail geral@platanoeditora.pt; internet www.platanoeditora.pt; f. 1972; literature, educational, science, technical, dictionaries, etc.; Dir FRANCISCO PRATA GINJA.

Porto Editora, Lda: Rua da Restauração 365, 4099-023 Porto; tel. (22) 6088300; fax (22) 6088301; e-mail secretariado@portoeditora.pt; internet www.portoeditora.pt; f. 1944; general literature, school books, dictionaries, children's books, multimedia; Dirs VASCO TEIXEIRA, JOSÉ ANTÓNIO TEIXEIRA, ROSÁLIA TEIXEIRA.

Publicações Dom Quixote: Edif. Anas, 2°, Rua Ivan Silva 6, 1050-124 Lisbon; tel. (21) 1203010; fax (21) 1209030; e-mail editorial@dquixote.pt; internet www.dquixote.pt; f. 1965; general fiction, poetry, history, philosophy, psychology, politics, didactics and sociology; university textbooks; children's books.

Publicações Europa-América, Lda: Estrada Nacional 249 (Lisboa–Sintra), Km 14, Apdo 8, 2725-397 Mem Martins; tel. (21) 9267700; fax (21) 9267771; e-mail secretariado@europa-america.pt; internet www.europa-america.pt; f. 1945; imprints include Edições CETOP, Editorial Inquerito, Livros de Vida Editores, Lyon Edições and Publicações Alfa; fiction, current affairs, economics, reference, history, technical, children's; Dir TITO LYON DE CASTRO.

Quimera Editores Lda: Rua do Vale Formoso 37, 1949-013 Lisbon; tel. (21) 8455950; fax (21) 8455951; e-mail quimera@quimera-editores.com; internet www.quimera-editores.com; f. 1987; literature, art, history, photography, etc.; Dirs JOSÉ ALFARO, LUÍS VEIGA.

Rés—Editora, Lda: Praça Marquês de Pombal 78, 4000-390 Porto; tel. (22) 5024174; fax (22) 5026098; e-mail res-editora@res-editora.pt; internet www.res-editora.pt; f. 1975; economics, philosophy, law, sociology; Dir REINALDO DE CARVALHO.

Texto Editora, Lda: Estrada de Paço de Arcos 66 e 66A, 2735-336 Cacém; tel. (21) 4272200; fax (21) 4272201; e-mail info@textoeditores.com; internet pt.textoeditores.com; f. 1977; school textbooks, management, pedagogy, health, beauty, cooking, children's books, multimedia; Man. Dir MANUEL JOSÉ DO ESPÍRITO SANTO FERRÃO.

PUBLISHERS' ASSOCIATION

Associação Portuguesa de Editores e Livreiros (Portuguese Association of Publishers and Booksellers): Av. dos Estados Unidos da América 97, 6°, 1700-167 Lisbon; tel. (21) 8435180; fax (21) 8489377; e-mail apel@apel.pt; internet www.apel.pt; f. 1927; Pres. ANTÓNIO BAPTISTA LOPES; Sec.-Gen. AUGUSTO SILVA.

Broadcasting and Communications

REGULATORY AUTHORITY

Autoridade Nacional de Comunicações (ANACOM): Av. José Malhoa 12, 1009-017 Lisbon; tel. (21) 7211000; fax (21) 7211001; e-mail info@anacom.pt; internet www.anacom.pt; formerly known as the Instituto das Comunicações de Portugal (ICP); Pres. JOSÉ MANUEL AMADO DA SILVA.

TELECOMMUNICATIONS

Portugal Telecom, SA (PT): Av. Fontes Pereira de Melo 40, 6°, 1069-300 Lisbon; tel. (21) 5002000; fax (21) 3562624; e-mail geral@telecom.pt; internet www.telecom.pt; f. 1994; by merger of three regional telecommunications operators; state holding reduced to 25% in 1997; relinquished monopoly on fixed-line operations in Jan. 2000; Chair. HENRIQUE GRANADEIRO; CEO ZEINAL BAVA.

AR Telecom, SA: Edif. Diogo Cão, Doca de Alcântara Norte, 1350-352 Lisbon; tel. (21) 0301030; fax (21) 0301300; e-mail contacto@artelecom.pt; internet www.artelecom.pt; f. 2000 as Jazztel Portugal, SA; renamed as above in 2005; subsidiary of Grupo SGC; fixed-line operator.

Novis Telecom, SA: Edif. Sonaecom, Av. D. João II, Lote 1.06.24, 1990-095 Lisbon; tel. (21) 0100000; fax (21) 0129210; e-mail info@novis.pt; internet www.novis.pt; fixed-line operator.

Oni Communications, SA: Edif. Qualidade A1 e A2, Tagus Park, Av. Prof. Dr Cavaco Silva, 2740-269 Porto Salvo; tel. (21) 0005300; fax (21) 0007175; e-mail geral@oni.pt; internet www.oni.pt; f. 2000; fixed-line operator; CEO XAVIER RODRÍGUEZ-MARTÍN.

Optimus Telecomunicações, SA: Edif. Green Park, 13° e 14°A, Av. do Combatentes 43, 1600 Lisbon; tel. (21) 7233600; fax (21) 7546275; e-mail contacto@optimus.pt; internet www.optimus.pt; f. 1998; provides mobile telephone services.

TMN (Telecomunicações Móveis Nacionais), SA: Av. Álvaro Pais 2, 1649-041 Lisbon; tel. (21) 7914400; fax (21) 7914500; e-mail tmn.comunica@tmn.pt; internet www.tmn.pt; commenced mobile telephone services in 1989; part of Portugal Telecom; CEO ZEINAL ABEDIN MAHOMED BAVA.

UZO: Av. Álvaro Pais 2, 1649-041 Lisbon; e-mail info@uzo.pt; internet www.uzo.com.pt; f. 2005; part of Portugal Telecom; mobile operator; Exec. Dir JOÃO MENDES.

Vodafone Portugal—Comunicações Pessoais, SA: Parque das Nações, Av. D. João II, Lote 1.04.01, 1998-017 Lisbon; tel. (21) 0915000; fax (21) 0915953; e-mail press.pt@vodafone.com; internet www.vodafone.pt; f. 1991; fmrly Telecel-Comunicações Pessoais; subsidiary of Vodafone Group PLC (United Kingdom); provides mobile and fixed-line telephone services; Chief Exec. ANTÓNIO CARRAPATOSO.

Other fixed-line operators include Cabovisão, Coltel, Refer Telecom, Telemilénio, TV Cabo and TVTEL.

PORTUGAL

BROADCASTING

In 2006 there were around 350 radio stations in operation.

Radio

State-controlled Radio

Radiodifusão Portuguesa, SA (RDP): Av. Marechal Gomes da Costa 37, Lisbon; tel. (21) 7947000; fax (21) 7947669; internet tv.rtp.pt/EPG/radio; f. 1975; part of Radio e Televisão de Portugal SA (see below); Dir of Programmes RUI FERNANDES PÊGO.

Domestic Services:

Antena 1: tel. (21) 7947000; fax (21) 3873972; e-mail rdp.antena1@rtp.pt; internet www.rtp.pt/antena1; broadcasts 24 hours daily on medium-wave and FM; news, sport, music, etc.; Dir JOÃO COELHO.

Antena 2: tel. (21) 7947000; fax (21) 3820199; e-mail rdp.antena2@rtp.pt; internet tv1.rtp.pt/antena2; broadcasts classical music 24 hours daily on FM; Dir JOÃO PEREIRA BASTOS.

Antena 3: tel. (21) 7947000; fax (21) 3820017; e-mail antena3@programas.rdp.pt; internet tv1.rtp.pt/antena3; broadcasts 24 hours daily on FM; music and entertainment for young people; Dir JORGE ALEXANDRE LOPES.

Commercial and Private Radio

Cidade FM: Rua Sampaio e Pina 24, 1099-044 Lisbon; tel. (21) 3821500; fax (21) 3821589; internet cidadefm.clix.pt; one FM transmitter; broadcasts 24 hours a day; Dir-Gen. JORDI JORDÀ; Dir of Programmes NUNO GONÇALVES.

Orbital FM: Travessa do Olival 6, 2685 Sacavém; tel. (21) 9401019; fax (21) 9427757; e-mail orbital@orbital.pt; internet www.orbital.pt; one FM transmitter; broadcasts 24 hours a day in Lisbon region.

Rádio Capital: Rua Viriato 25, 4° dto, 1050-234 Lisbon; tel. (21) 0105760; fax (21) 2740781; e-mail net@radiocapital.fm; internet www.radiocapital.fm; one FM transmitter; broadcasts 24 hours a day in Lisbon and Oporto; Dir-Gen. JOSÉ AUGUSTO MADALENO.

Rádio Clube: Rua Sampaio e Pina 26, 1099-044 Lisbon; tel. (21) 3821500; fax (21) 3821559; e-mail internet@radiocomercial.pt; f. 1992; fmrly Radio Nostalgia; broadcasts music 24 hours daily on FM; Head LUÍS MONTEZ; Dir of Programmes MIGUEL CRUZ.

Rádio Comercial, SA: Rua Sampaio e Pina 24/26, 1000 Lisbon; tel. (21) 3821500; fax (21) 3821559; e-mail geral@radiocomercial.pt; internet www.radiocomercial.pt; f. 1979 as RDP-3; transferred to private ownership in 1993; broadcasts music, news and sport 24 hours daily on Rádio Comercial: (FM); and since March 1998 on Rádio Nacional on MW to central and southern Portugal, also music, news and sport; Head LUÍS MONTEZ; Dir of Programmes MIGUEL CRUZ.

Rádio Europa Lisboa: Rua Latino Coelho 50, 1°, 1050-137 Lisbon; tel. (21) 3510580; fax (21) 3510598; e-mail programas@radioeuropa.fm; internet www.radioeuropa.fm; fmrly Rádio Paris Lisboa; present name adopted 2006; one FM transmitter; broadcasts 24 hours a day; Dir ANTONIETA LOPES DA COSTA.

Rádio Juventude: Edif. Plátano, Loja A, Rua Prof. Hugo Correia Pardal, 6000-267 Castelo Branco; tel. (272) 341758; fax (272) 347660; e-mail radiojuventude@netvisao.pt; internet www.radiojuventude.com; one FM transmitter; broadcasts 24 hours a day.

Rádio Viriato: Complexo Conventurispress, Orgens, Apdo 3115, 3511-689 Viseu; tel. (232) 410416; fax (232) 410417; e-mail inforadio@viriato.fm.com; internet www.viriatofm.com; f. 1987; one FM transmitter; broadcasts 24 hours a day; Dir ANABELA ABREU.

RR (Rádio Renascença): Rua Capelo 5, 1294-108 Lisbon; tel. (21) 3239200; fax (21) 3239220; e-mail info@rr.pt; f. 1937; Roman Catholic station; broadcasts 24 hours a day on Rádio Renascença (FM, medium-wave and satellite; internet www.rr.pt), on RFM (FM and satellite; internet www.rfm.pt; Dir ANTÓNIO MENDES) and on MEGA FM (FM and satellite; internet www.mega.fm.pt; Dir NELSON RIBEIRO); Chair. FERNANDO MAGALHÃES CRESPO.

TSF—Rádio Jornal: Edif. Altejo, Sala 301, Rua 3 da Matinha, 1900-823 Lisbon; tel. (21) 8612500; fax (21) 8612510; e-mail tsf@tsf.pt; internet www.tsf.pt; broadcasts news and sport 24 hours daily on FM; Pres. JOAQUIM OLIVEIRA.

Television

State-controlled Television

Radio e Televisão de Portugal, SA (RTP): Av. Marechal Gomes da Costa 37, 1849-030 Lisbon; tel. (21) 7947000; fax (21) 7947570; e-mail rtp@rtp.pt; internet www.rtp.pt; f. 1956; nationalized in 1975; became jt-stock co (with 100% public capital) in 1992; 12 studios incl. Lisbon, Porto, Ponta Delgada and Funchal; Pres. GUILHERME COSTA; Dir of Programmes JOSÉ MANUEL FRAGOSO.

Regional Centres:

RTP/Porto: Rua Conceição Fernandes, Apdo 174, 4402 Vila Nova de Gaia; tel. (22) 7156000; fax (22) 7110963; Dir DJALME NEVES.

RTP/Açores: Rua Ernesto Canto 40, 9500 Ponta Delgada, São Miguel; tel. (296) 202700; fax (296) 202771; e-mail rtpa@rtp.pt; internet www.rtp.pt; Dir PEDRO BICUDO.

RTP/Madeira: Caminho Santo António 145, 9020-002 Funchal; tel. (291) 709100; fax (291) 741859; e-mail rjmadeira@rtp.pt; Dir J. LEONEL FREITAS.

RTP/Internacional (RTPi): e-mail rtpi@rtp.pt; internet rtpi.rtp.pt; commenced satellite transmissions in June 1992; broadcasts in Portuguese 24 hours a day; Dir FERNANDO BALSINHA.

RTP/Africa: commenced transmissions to lusophone countries of Africa in 1997; broadcasts 24 hours a day; Dir AFONSO RATO.

Cable, Commercial and Private Television

Bragatel—Companhia de Televisão por Cabo de Braga, SA: Av. 31 de Janeiro 177, Apdo 17, 4715-052 Braga; tel. (253) 616600; fax (253) 616998; e-mail mail@bragatel.pt; internet www.bragatel.pt; f. 1993; authorized to operate in Braga, Barceios and Espsende.

Cabo TV Açoreana: Av. Antero de Quental 9c, 1°, 9500-160 Ponta Delgada; tel. (296) 302401; fax (296) 302405; internet www.cabotva.net.

Cabo TV Madeirense: Av. Estados Unidos da América, Nazaré, 9000-090 Funchal; tel. (291) 700800; fax (291) 766132; e-mail tvcabo@cabotvm.pt; internet www.cabotvm.pt; 71% owned by TV Cabo.

Cabovisão—Sociedade de Televisão por Cabo, SA: Lugar de Poços, Vale de Touros, 2950-425 Palmela; tel. (21) 0801080; fax (21) 0801000; e-mail info@cabovisao.pt; internet www.cabovisao.pt; authorized to operate in 156 municipalities (4.5m. homes).

Pluricanal Leiria: Av. General Humberto Delgado 2, 2400 Leiria; tel. (244) 824925; fax (244) 824943.

Pluricanal Santarém: Edif. Ribatel, Estrada Nacional 3, S. Pedro, 2000 Santarém; tel. (244) 824925; fax (244) 824943.

SIC (Sociedade Independente de Comunicação, SA): Estrada da Outurela, Carnaxide, 2795 Linda-a-Velha; tel. 4173111; fax 4173118; e-mail atendimento@sic.pt; internet www.sic.pt; commenced transmissions in 1992; news and entertainment; Head FRANCISCO PINTO BALSEMÃO; Dir of Programmes EMÍDIO RANGEL.

TV Cabo: Rua Adelina Abranches Ferrão 10, 1600 Lisbon; tel. 808 200400; e-mail cliente@netcabo.pt; internet www.tvcabo.pt; offers subscription-based television services, also broadband internet access and fixed-line telecommunications; operates 17 regional companies.

TVI (Televisão Independente, SA): Rua Mário Castelhano 40, 2740-502 Barcarena; tel. (21) 4347500; fax (21) 4347654; internet www.tvi.pt; commenced transmissions in 1993; Pres. MANUEL POLANCO; Gen. Man. JOSÉ EDUARDO MONIZ.

TVTEL Comunicações, SA: Rua Delfim Ferreira 383, 4100-201 Porto; tel. (22) 0325800; fax (22) 6154949; e-mail info@tvtel.pt; internet www.tvtel.pt.

Zon Multimédia—Serviços de Telecomunicações e Multimédia, SGPS, SA: Av. 5 de Outubro 208, 1069-203, Lisbon; tel. (21) 7824725; fax (21) 7824735; e-mail ir@pt-multimedia.pt; internet www.pt-multimedia.pt; fmrly PT Multimédia; renamed as above in 2008; Chair. RODRIGO JORGE LUÍS DE ARAÚJO COSTA; 1.7m. customers.

Finance

(cap. = capital; res = reserves; dep. = deposits; m. = million; brs = branches; amounts in euros)

BANKING

Central Bank

Banco de Portugal: Rua do Ouro 27, 1100-150 Lisbon; tel. (21) 3213200; fax (21) 3464843; e-mail info@bportugal.pt; internet www.bportugal.pt; f. 1846; reorganized 1931 with the sole right to issue notes; nationalized in 1974; cap. 1m., res 4,034m., dep. 5,149m. (Dec. 2006); Gov. VÍTOR MANUEL RIBEIRO CONSTÂNCIO; also maintains br. in Oporto.

Principal Banks

Banco Activobank (Portugal), SA (ActivoBank7): Rua Augusta 84, 1149-023 Lisbon; tel. (21) 4232673; fax (21) 0066883; e-mail ab7_dop@activobank7.pt; internet www.activobank7.pt; f. 1969 as Sociedade Financeira Portuguesa; nationalized 1975; privatized 1991 and name changed to Banco Mello, SA; name changed to above in 2001; 100% owned by Banco Comercial Português, SA; Chair. PAULO TEIXEIRA PINTO.

PORTUGAL

Banco Bilbao Vizcaya Argentaria (Portugal), SA: Av. da Liberdade 222, 1250-148 Lisbon; tel. (21) 3117200; fax (21) 3117500; e-mail helpdesk@bbva.pt; internet www.bbva.pt; f. 1991 as Banco Bilbao Vizcaya; name changed 2000; cap. 160m., res 42m., dep. 4,382m. (Dec. 2005); Man. Dir ALBERTO CHARRO; 100 brs.

Banco BPI, SA: Rua Tenente Valadim 284, 4100-476 Porto; tel. (22) 2075000; fax (22) 6002954; e-mail dirint@bpi.pt; internet www.bancobpi.pt; f. 1998 following the absorption of Banco Fonsecas e Burnay and Banco Borges e Irmão by Banco de Fomento e Exterior; cap. 760m., res 520m., dep. 33,783m. (Dec. 2007); Chair. FERNANDO ULRICH; 700 brs.

Banco Comercial Português (Millennium BCP): Praça D. João I 28, 4000-295 Porto; tel. (22) 7502424; fax (22) 2064139; internet www.millenniumbcp.pt; f. 1985; cap. 3,611m., res 451m., dep. 69,591m. (Dec. 2006); Chair., Exec. Bd CARLOS JORGE RAMALHO DOS SANTOS FERREIRA; 867 brs.

Banco Efisa, SA: Av. António Augusto de Aguiar 134, 4°, 1050-020 Lisbon; tel. (21) 3117800; fax (21) 3117915; e-mail dcb@bancoefisa.pt; internet www.bancoefisa.pt; f. 1994 by merger; nationalized in Nov. 2008; cap. 22m., res 3m., dep. 308m. (Dec. 2006); Man. Dir JOSÉ AUGUSTO OLIVEIRA COSTA.

Banco Espírito Santo, SA: Av. da Liberdade 195, 1250-142 Lisbon; tel. (21) 3501000; fax (21) 8557491; e-mail info@bes.pt; internet www.bes.pt; f. 1884; nationalized 1975; transfer to private sector completed 1992; 40% owned by BESPAR SGPS Lisbon, 10.8% owned by Crédit Agricole SA (France); cap. 2,500m., res 2,166m., dep. 58,617m. (Dec. 2007); Pres. and CEO RICARDO ESPÍRITO SANTO SILVA SALGADO; 457 brs.

Banco Finantia, SA: Rua General Firmino Miguel 5, 1600-100 Lisbon; tel. (21) 7202000; fax (21) 7202030; e-mail finantia@finantia.com; internet www.finantia.com; f. 1987; investment bank; 50% owned by Finantipar SGPS, SA; cap. 115m., res 232m., dep. 3,528m. (Dec. 2007); Pres. ANTÓNIO MANUEL AFONSO GUERREIRO; also br. in Oporto.

Banco Itaú Europa, SA: Centro Comercial Amoreiras, Torre 3, 11°, Rua Tierno Galvan, 1099-048 Lisbon; tel. (21) 3811000; fax (21) 3887219; e-mail bie.global@itaueuropa.pt; internet www.itaueuropa.pt; f. 1994; owned by Itaúsa Portugal SGPS, Lisbon; cap. 318m., res 39m., dep. 2,540m. (Dec. 2006); Pres. and Chair. ROBERTO EGYDIO SETÚBAL; CEO ALMIR VIGNOTO.

Banco Popular Portugal, SA: Rua Ramalho Ortigão 51, 1099-090 Lisbon; tel. (21) 0071000; fax (21) 0071187; e-mail s.mercados@bancopopular.pt; internet www.bancopopular.pt; f. 1991 as Banco Nacional de Crédito; present name adopted 2005; cap. 376m., res 145m., dep. 6,206m. (Dec. 2006); owned by Banco Popular Español (Spain); CEO RUI MANUEL MORGANHO SEMEDO; 174 brs.

Banco Privado Português, SA: Rua Mouzinho da Silveira 12, 1250-167 Lisbon; tel. (21) 3137000; fax (21) 3137092; internet www.bpp.pt; f. 1996; cap. 125m., res 14m., dep. 649m. (Dec. 2006); CEO FERNANDO ADÃO DA FONSECA.

Banco Santander Totta: Rua do Ouro 88, 1100-063 Lisbon; tel. (21) 3262000; fax (21) 3262271; e-mail santandertotta@santandertotta.pt; internet www.santandertotta.pt; f. 2004 by merger of Banco Totta & Açores, Banco Santander Portugal and Crédito Predial Português; owned by Banco Santander (Spain); cap. 590m., res 749m., dep. 34,717m. (Dec. 2007); CEO NUNO MANUEL DA SILVA AMADO; 640 brs.

Banif—Banco Internacional do Funchal SA: Rua de João Tavira 30, 9000-509 Funchal, Madeira; tel. (291) 207731; fax (291) 230221; e-mail info@banif.pt; internet www.banif.pt; f. 1988; cap. 240m., res 22m., dep. 6,057m. (Dec. 2006); absorbed Banco Banif e Comercial dos Açores in 2008; Chair. HORÁCIO DA SILVA ROQUE; CEO Dr JOAQUIM FILIPE MARQUES DOS SANTOS.

BPN (Banco Português de Negócios, SA): Edif. Fronteira, Av. António Augusto de Aguiar 132, 1050-020 Lisbon; tel. (21) 3598000; fax (21) 3598669; e-mail marketing@banco.bpn.pt; internet www.bpn.pt; f. 1993; nationalized in Nov. 2008; cap. 360m., res 15m., dep. 5,509m. (Dec. 2006); Chair. FRANCISCO MANUEL MARQUES BANDEIRA; 213 brs.

Caixa-Banco de Investimento, SA (CaixaBI): Rua Barata Salgueiro 33, 1269-057 Lisbon; tel. (21) 3137300; fax (21) 3526327; e-mail caixabi@caixabi.pt; internet www.caixabi.pt; f. 1984 as Manufacturers Hanover Trust Co; present name adopted 2000; 99.7% owned by Caixa Geral de Depósitos, SA; cap. 81m., res 75m., dep. 1,291m. (Dec. 2006); Pres. and Chair. Dr JOSÉ LOURENÇO SOARES; CEO JORGE HUMBERTO CORREIA TOMÉ; 3 brs.

Caixa Central de Crédito Agrícola Mútuo, CRL (Crédito Agrícola): Rua Castilho 233–233A, 1099-004 Lisbon; tel. (21) 3860006; fax (21) 3805546; e-mail dint.cccam@creditoagricola.pt; internet www.creditoagricola.pt; f. 1984; co-operative bank; cap. 678.2m., res 54.5m., dep. 8,790.3m. (Dec. 2006); Chair. and Pres. CARLOS COURELAS; CEO JOÃO ANTÓNIO MORAIS DA COSTA PINTO; 670 brs.

Caixa Económica Montepio Geral (Montepio Geral): Rua Áurea 219–241, POB 2882, 1100-062 Lisbon; tel. (21) 3248220; fax (21) 3248228; internet www.montepio.pt; f. 1844 as Caixa Económica de Lisboa; present name adopted 1991; cap. 585m., res 177m., dep. 13,885m. (Dec. 2006); Chair. ANTÓNIO TOMÁS CORREIA; 55 brs.

Caixa Geral de Depósitos, SA (CGD): Av. João XXI 63, 1000-300 Lisbon; tel. (21) 7953000; fax (21) 7905050; e-mail cgd@cgd.pt; internet www.cgd.pt; f. 1876; state-owned; grants credit for agriculture, industry, building, housing, energy, trade and tourism; dep. 80,302m., total assets 104,976m. (Dec. 2007); Pres. and Chair. FERNANDO MANUEL BARBOSA FARIA DE OLIVEIRA; 768 brs.

Deutsche Bank (Portugal), SA: Rua Castilho 20, 1250-069 Lisbon; tel. (21) 3111200; fax (21) 3535241; e-mail dbonline.dbp@db.com; internet www.deutsche-bank.pt; f. 1990 as Deutsche Bank de Investimento; name changed 1999; owned by Deutsche Bank AG (Germany); cap. 80m., res 28m., dep. 4,100m. (Dec. 2006); Pres., Exec. Cttee FILIPE SILVA; 49 brs.

Finibanco, SA: Av. de Berna 10, 5°, 1050-040 Lisbon; tel. (21) 7902800; fax (21) 7902801; e-mail comunicacao@finibanco.pt; internet www.finibanco.pt; f. 1993; cap. 104m., res 8m., dep. 2,022m. (Dec. 2006); Pres. ÁLVARO DA COSTA LEITE; CEO HUMBERTO DA COSTA LEITE; 158 brs.

Banking Association

Associação Portuguesa de Bancos (APB): Av. da República 35, 5°, 1050-186 Lisbon; tel. (21) 3510070; fax (21) 3579533; e-mail apbancos@apb.pt; internet www.apb.pt; f. 1984; Pres. Dr JOÃO SALGUEIRO; Sec.-Gen. Dr JOÃO MENDES RODRIGUES; 29 mems.

STOCK EXCHANGE

Euronext Lisbon: Av. da Liberdade 196, 1250-147 Lisbon; tel. (21) 7900000; fax (21) 7952021; internet www.euronext.com; f. 1769 as Bolsa de Valores de Lisboa e Porto; merged with Euronext in 2002 and adopted current name; merged with New York Stock Exchange in 2007 to form NYSE Euronext; Chair. MIGUEL ATHAYDE MARQUES.

Regulatory Authority

Comissão do Mercado de Valores Mobiliários (CMVM): Av. da Liberdade 252, 1056-801 Lisbon; tel. (21) 3177000; fax (21) 3537077; e-mail cmvm@cmvm.pt; internet www.cmvm.pt; f. 1991; independent securities exchange commission; Pres. Dr CARLOS TAVARES.

INSURANCE

The Portuguese insurance market is developing in accordance with EU regulations and practices. At the end of 2007 there were 46 insurance companies based in Portugal, of which 15 specialized in life insurance. In that year 37 foreign-owned comapnies were operating in Portugal.

Principal Companies

Axa-Portugal—Companhia de Seguros, SA: Rua Gonçalo Sampaio 39, 4002-001 Porto; tel. (22) 6081100; fax (22) 6081136; e-mail contacto@axa-seguros.pt; internet www.axa.pt; non-life; net profits 27.3m. (2005); Pres. Dr JOÃO LEANDRO.

Axa-Portugal—Companhia de Seguros de Vida, SA: Praça Marquês de Pombal 14, Apdo 1953, 1250-162 Lisbon; tel. (21) 3506100; fax (21) 3506136; e-mail contacto@axa-seguros.pt; internet www.axa.pt; life and pension funds; Pres. Dr CARLOS PEDRO BRANDÃO DE MELO DE SOUSA E BRITO.

BPI Vida—Companhia de Seguros de Vida, SA: Rua Braamcamp 11, 8°, 1250-049 Lisbon; tel. (21) 3111020; fax (21) 3111082; internet www.bpiinvestimentos.pt; life and pension funds; net profits 23.7m. (2006); Pres. Dr FERNANDO MARIA COSTA DUARTE ULRICH.

Companhia de Seguros Açoreana, SA: Largo da Matriz 45–52, 9500-094 Ponta Delgada, S. Miguel, Azores; tel. (296) 201400; fax (296) 201483; e-mail info@csanet.pt; internet www.acornet.pt; f. 1892; life and non-life; net profits 17.7m. (2006); Pres. Dr HORÁCIO DA SILVA ROQUE.

Companhia de Seguros Allianz Portugal, SA: Rua Andrade Corvo 32, 1069-014 Lisbon; tel. (21) 3165300; fax (21) 3193125; e-mail info@allianz.pt; internet www.allianz.pt; f. 1907; fmrly Allianz Portugal; life, non-life and pension funds; net profits 21.4m. (2004); CEO IVÁN JOSÉ DE LA SOTA DUÑABEITIA.

Companhia de Seguros Fidelidade–Mundial, SA: Largo do Calhariz 30, 1249-001 Lisbon; tel. (21) 3238000; fax (21) 3238001; e-mail csc@fidelidademundial.pt; internet www.fidelidademundial.pt; f. 1980 from merger of four cos; life, non-life and pension funds; net profits 95.4m. (2005); Pres. Dr VITOR MANUEL LOPES FERNANDES.

Companhia de Seguros Tranquilidade, SA: Av. da Liberdade 242, 1250-149 Lisbon; tel. (21) 3503500; fax (21) 8553051; e-mail infogeral@tranquilidade.pt; internet www.tranquilidade.pt; f. 1871;

non-life; net profits 32.5m. (2006); 100% privatized in 1990; Pres. PEDRO DE BRITO E CUNHA.

Companhia de Seguros Tranquilidade Vida, SA (T-Vida): Av. da Liberdade 230, 1250-148 Lisbon; tel. (21) 3167500; fax (21) 3153194; e-mail correio@tranquilidade-vida.pt; internet www.tranquilidade.pt; life and pension funds; net profits 34.2m. (2005); Pres. Dr LUÍS FREDERICO REDONDO LOPES.

Cosec (Companhia de Seguro de Créditos, SA): Av. da República 58, 1069-057 Lisbon; tel. and fax (21) 7913700; e-mail cosec@cosec.pt; internet www.cosec.pt; f. 1969; domestic and export credit insurance; bond insurance; net profits 5.5m. (2007); Chair. JOSÉ MIGUEL GOMES DA COSTA.

Crédito Agrícola Vida, SA: Rua Castilho 233A, 1050-185 Lisbon; tel. (21) 3805660; fax (21) 3859695; e-mail linhadirecta@creditoagricola.pt; internet www.credito-agricola.pt; life; net profits 3.4m. (2004); Pres. JOAQUIM DA SILVA BERNARDO.

Eurovida, SA: Rua Castilho 39, 14°, 1250-068 Lisbon; tel. (21) 7924700; fax (21) 7924701; e-mail seguros@eurovida.pt; internet www.eurovida.pt; net profits 1.9m. (2004); Pres. Dr LUÍS BARBOSA.

Global—Companhia de Seguros, SA: Av. Duque de Avila 171, 1069-031 Lisbon; tel. (21) 3137500; fax (21) 3554021; e-mail globalseguros@global-seguros.pt; internet www.global-seguros.pt; non-life; net profits 12.1m. (2006); Exec. Pres. ALBERTINO SILVA.

GroupAMA Seguros: Av. de Berna 24D, 1069-170 Lisbon; tel. (21) 7923187; fax (21) 7923232; e-mail groupama@groupama.pt; internet www.groupama.pt; life and non-life; cap. 31.0m. (2004).

Império Bonança—Companhia de Seguros, SA: Rua Alexandre Herculano 53, 1269-152 Lisbon; tel. (21) 3702000; fax (21) 3702835; internet www.imperiobonanca.pt; f. by merger of Companhia de Seguros Bonança, SA and Companhia de Seguros Império, SA; net income 29.0m. (2006); Chair. Dr JORGE MANUEL BAPTISTA MAGALHÃES CORREIA.

Liberty Seguros, SA: Av. Fontes Pereira de Melo 6, 1069-001 Lisbon; tel. (21) 3124300; fax (21) 3183800; e-mail producao@libertyseguros.pt; internet www.libertyseguros.pt; f. 1922; life and non-life; fmrly Companhia Europeia de Seguros, SA; net profits 9.6m. (2006); CEO JOSÉ ANTÓNIO SOUSA.

Lusitânia—Companhia de Seguros, SA: Rua São Domingos à Lapa 35–41, 1249-130 Lisbon; tel. (21) 3926900; fax (21) 3973090; e-mail sede@lusitania-cs.pt; internet www.lusitania-cs.pt; non-life; net profits 2.3m. (2006); Pres. Dr JOSÉ DA SILVA LOPES.

MAPFRE Seguros Gerais, SA: Rua Castilho 52, 1250-071 Lisbon; tel. (21) 3819700; fax (21) 3819799; e-mail marketing@mapfre.pt; internet www.mapfre.pt; f. 1998; non-life; net profits 5.5m., cap. 33.1m. (2007); CEO ANTÓNIO MANUEL CARDOSO BELO (acting).

Real Seguros, SA: Edif. Capitólio, Av. de França 316, 4050-276 Porto; tel. (22) 8330100; fax (22) 8330149; e-mail info@realseguros.pt; internet www.realseguros.pt; f. 1988; non-life; net profits 7.3m. (2006); Pres. FERNANDO SOARES FERREIRA.

Totta Seguros—Companhia de Seguros de Vida, SA: Rua da Mesquita 6, Torre A, S. S. Pedreira, Lisbon; internet www.totta.pt; life; net profits 10.9m. (2006); Pres. PEDRO AIRES CORUCHE DE CASTRO E ALMEIDA.

Victoria—Seguros de Vida, SA/Victoria—Seguros, SA: Edif. Victoria, Av. da Liberdade 200, 1250-147 Lisbon; tel. (21) 3134450; fax (21) 334451; e-mail victoria@victoria-seguros.pt; internet www.victoria-seguros.pt; f. 1930/1981; transferred to private sector in 1993; life and pensions; non-life; total net profits 7.0m. (2006); Pres. MICHAEL ROSENBERG.

Zurich—Companhia de Seguros, SA/Zurich—Companhia de Seguros Vida, SA: Rua Barata Salgueiro 41, 1269-058 Lisbon; tel. (21) 3133100; fax (21) 3133111; internet www.zurichportugal.com; f. 1918; fmrly Companhia de Seguros Metrópole; net profits (non-life) 25.7m., (life) 5.8m. (2006); Pres. Dr NUNO MARIA SERRA SOARES DA FONSECA; Chief Exec. JOSÉ M. COELHO.

Mutual Companies

Mútua dos Armadores da Pesca do Arrasto: Av. António Augusto de Aguiar 7, 1°, 1069-145 Lisbon; tel. (21) 3561051; fax (21) 3561058; f. 1942; marine and workers' compensation, personal accident, sickness, fire, etc.; Pres. Dr ANTÓNIO ALBERTO CARVALHO DA CUNHA.

Mútua dos Pescadores—Mútua dos Seguros, C.R.L.: Av. Santos Dumont 57, 6°, 1050-202 Lisbon; tel. (21) 3936300; fax (21) 3936310; e-mail geral@mutuapescadores.pt; internet www.mutuapescadores.pt; f. 1942; co-operative; personal accident, marine, fire, workers' compensation, etc.; net profits 0.5m. (2007); Dir-Gen. JERÓNIMO TEIXEIRA.

Supervisory Authority

Instituto de Seguros de Portugal (ISP): Av. da República 76, 1600-205 Lisbon; tel. (21) 7903100; fax (21) 7938568; e-mail isp@isp.pt; internet www.isp.pt; f. 1982; office in Oporto; Pres. FERNANDO DIAS NOGUEIRA.

Insurance Association

Associação Portuguesa de Seguradores (APS): Rua Rodrigo da Fonseca 41, 1250-190 Lisbon; tel. (21) 3848100; fax (21) 3831422; e-mail aps@apseguradores.pt; internet www.apseguradores.pt; f. 1982; Pres. PEDRO ROGÉRIO DE AZEVEDO SEIXAS VALE.

Trade and Industry

GOVERNMENT AGENCIES

AICEP Portugal Global: Av. 5 de Outubro 101, 1050-051 Lisbon; tel. (21) 7909500; fax (21) 7935028; e-mail aicep@portugalglobal.pt; internet www.portugalglobal.pt; fmrly Agência para o Investimento e Comércio Externo de Portugal; promotes internationalization of the Portuguese economy; Chair. and Chief Exec. BASÍLIO HORTA.

Autoridade de Segurança Alimentar e Económica (ASAE): Av. Conde de Valbom 98, 1050-070 Lisbon; tel. (21) 7983600; fax (21) 7983654; e-mail correio.asae@asae.pt; internet www.asae.pt; f. 2005; regulatory authority for food safety and economic activities (Ministry of the Economy and Innovation); Inspector-Gen. Dr ANTÓNIO NUNES.

Gabinete de Estratégia e Estudos (GEE): Av. da República 79, 1050-243 Lisbon; tel. (21) 7998150; fax (21) 7998154; e-mail gee@gee.min-economia.pt; internet www.gee.min-economia.pt; advises on economic policy and strategy (Ministry of the Economy and Innovation); Dir MIGUEL LEBRE DE FREITAS.

Instituto de Apoio às Pequenas e Médias Empresas e a Inovação (IAPMEI): Rua Rodrigo da Fonseca 73, 1269-158 Lisbon; tel. (21) 3836000; fax (21) 3836283; internet www.iapmei.pt; financial and technical support to small and medium-sized enterprises (Ministry of the Economy and Innovation); Pres. JAIME SERRÃO ANDREZ.

Instituto de Financiamento da Agricultura e Pescas (IFAP): Rua Castilho 45–51, 1269-163 Lisbon; tel. (21) 3846000; fax (21) 3846170; e-mail ifap@ifap.min-agricultura.pt; internet www.ifap.min-agricultura.pt; f. 2007; provides loans for agriculture and fisheries, acts as intermediary with the European Agricultural Guarantee Fund (EAGF), the European Agricultural Fund for Rural Development (EAFRD) and the European Fisheries Fund (EFF); Pres. Dr JOAQUIM MESTRE.

Instituto Nacional de Engenharia Tecnologia e Inovação (INETI): Estrada do Paço do Lumiar, 1649-038 Lisbon; tel. (21) 0924602; fax (21) 71619211; e-mail teresa.leao@ineti.pt; internet www.ineti.pt; f. 1977; industrial and technological research (Ministry of the Economy and Innovation); Pres. Prof. MARIA TERESA COSTA PEREIRA DA SILVA PONCE DE LEÃO.

Instituto Português de Apoio ao Desenvolvimento (IPAD): Av. da Liberdade 192, 2°, 1250-147 Lisbon; tel. (21) 3176700; fax (21) 3147897; e-mail cooperacao.portuguesa@ipad.mne.gov.pt; internet www.ipad.mne.gov.pt; f. 2003; part of Ministry of Foreign Affairs; supports international devt; Pres. AUGUSTO MANUEL CORREIA.

Instituto Português da Qualidade (IPQ): Rua António Gião 2, 2829-513 Caparica; tel. (21) 2948100; fax (21) 2948101; e-mail ipq@mail.ipq.pt; internet www.ipq.pt; manages and develops the Portuguese Quality System (Ministry of the Economy and Innovation); Pres. JOSÉ MANUEL DIOGO MARQUES DOS SANTOS.

DEVELOPMENT ORGANIZATIONS

Centro para o Desenvolvimento e Inovação Tecnológicos (CEDINTEC): Rua de São Domingos à Lapa 117, 2° dto, 1200-834 Lisbon; tel. (21) 3955302; fax (21) 3961203; e-mail geral@cedintec.pt; internet www.cedintec.pt; f. 1982; supports the creation of technological infrastructures; Pres. Eng. JOÃO PEDRO DE SALDANHA VERSCHNEIDER GONÇALVES.

Cotec Portugal: Rua de Salazares 842, 4149-002 Porto; tel. (22) 6192910; fax (22) 6192919; e-mail secretariado@cotec.pt; internet www.cotec.pt; f. 2003; co-ordinates research and innovation between public and private bodies; Pres. Dr ARTUR SANTOS SILVA; Dir-Gen. Prof. RUI CAMPOS GUIMARÃES.

Instituto do Vinho do Douro e do Porto (IVDP): Rua dos Camilos 90, 5050–272 Peso da Régua; tel. (25) 4320130; fax (25) 4320149; e-mail ivdp@ivdp.pt; internet www.ivdp.pt; an official body dealing with quality control and the promotion of port and Douro wines; also gives technical advice to exporters; Pres. Eng. JORGE NICOLAU DA COSTA MONTEIRO.

Sociedade de Desenvolvimento da Madeira (SDM): Rua da Mouraria 9, 1°, 9000-047 Funchal, Madeira; tel. (291) 201333; fax (291) 201399; e-mail sdm@sdm.pt; internet www.sdm.pt; concessionaire of Madeira's International Business Centre; Chair. Dr FRANCISCO COSTA.

PORTUGAL

Sociedade Nacional de Empreendimentos e Desenvolvimento Económico, SA (SNEDE): Av. Fontes Pereira de Melo 35, 19A, 1050-118 Lisbon; tel. and fax (21) 3139889; e-mail snede@mail.telepac.pt; internet www.snede.pt; f. 1976; private consultancy co in economy and management; Pres. Dr ALFREDO GONZALEZ ESTEVES BELO.

CHAMBERS OF COMMERCE AND TRADE ASSOCIATIONS

Associação Comercial e Industrial do Funchal/Câmara de Comércio e Indústria da Madeira (ACIF/CCIM): Rua dos Aranhas 24–26, 9000-044 Funchal; tel. (291) 206800; fax (291) 206868; e-mail geral@acif-ccim.pt; internet www.acif-ccim.pt; f. 1836; Pres. FRANCISCO MIGUEL AZINHAIS ABREU DOS SANTOS.

Associação Comercial de Lisboa/Câmara de Comércio e Indústria Portuguesa (ACL/CCIP): Palácio do Comércio, Rua das Portas de Santo Antão 89, 1169-022 Lisbon; tel. (21) 3224050; fax (21) 3224051; e-mail geral@port-chambers.com; internet www.port-chambers.com; f. 1834; Pres. BRUNO BOBONE; Sec.-Gen. Dr PEDRO MADEIRA RODRIGUES; 2,100 mems.

Associação Comercial do Porto/Câmara de Comércio e Indústria do Porto (ACP/CCIP): Palácio da Bolsa, Rua Ferreira Borges, 4050-253 Porto; tel. (22) 3399000; fax (22) 3399090; e-mail cciporto@mail.telepac.pt; internet www.cciporto.com; f. 1834; Pres. Dr RUI MOREIRA; 800 mems.

Associação Industrial Portuguesa—Confederação Empresarial (AIP-CE): Praça das Indústrias, Apdo 3200, 1300-965 Lisbon; tel. (21) 3601000; fax (21) 3641301; e-mail info@aip.pt; internet www.aip.pt; f. 1837; Chief Exec. ANTÓNIO MANUEL VINAGRE ALFAIATE; 4,500 mems (2008).

Câmara de Comércio e Indústria de Ponta Delgada/Associação Empresarial das Ilhas de São Miguel e Santa Maria (CCIPD): Rua Ernesto do Canto 13–15, 9504-531 Ponta Delgada, Azores; tel. (296) 305000; fax (296) 305050; e-mail ccipd@ccipd.pt; internet www.ccipd.pt; f. 1979; Dir CARLOS ALBERTO DA COSTA MARTINS; 800 mems.

OTHER INDUSTRIAL AND TRADE ASSOCIATIONS

Associação dos Comerciantes e Industriais de Bebidas Espirituosas e Vinhos (ACIBEV): Largo do Carmo 15, 1°, 1200-095 Lisbon; tel. (21) 3462318; fax (21) 3427517; e-mail acibevmail@acibev.pt; internet www.acibev.pt; f. 1975; spirit and wine traders and manufacturers; Chair. Eng. JOÃO CALLEYA SERRA; Pres. Dr ANTÓNIO SOARES FRANCO.

Associação Empresarial de Portugal: Av. da Boavista 2671, 4100-135 Porto; tel. (22) 6158500; fax (22) 6176840; e-mail aep@aeportugal.com; internet www.aeportugal.pt; f. 1849; represents industry in northern Portugal in all sectors; organizes trade fairs, exhibitions, congress, etc.; Pres. Eng. ANGELO LUDGERO MARQUES; 2,500 mems.

Associação dos Industriais e Exportadores de Cortiça (AIEC): Av. Duque de Avila 169, 2° esq., 1050-081 Lisbon; tel. (21) 3158506; fax (21) 3570878; e-mail geral@aiec.pt; internet www.aiec.pt; f. 1993; national asscn of cork manufacturers and exporters; Pres. EDMUNDO PEREIRA.

Associação Nacional de Comerciantes e Industriais de Produtos Alimentares (ANCIPA): Largo de São Sebastião da Pedreira 31, 1050-205 Lisbon; tel. (21) 3528803; fax (21) 3154665; e-mail ancipa@netcabo.pt; internet www.ancipa.pt; f. 1975; national asscn of food products manufacturers and traders; Pres. MANUEL FULGÉNCIO TARRÉ FERNANDES; Gen. Sec. DOMITÍLIA LOPES DE ALMEIDA.

Associação Nacional das Indústrias de Vestuário e Confecção (ANIVEC/APIV): Av. da Boavista 3523, 7°, 4100-139 Porto; tel. (22) 6165470; fax (22) 6100049; e-mail geral@anivec.com; internet www.anivec.com; clothing manufacturers' asscn; Pres. ORLANDO LOPES DA CUNHA.

Associação Portuguesa da Indústria de Cerâmica (APICER): Edif. C, Rua Col Veiga Simão, 3020-053 Coimbra; tel. (239) 497600; fax (239) 497601; e-mail info@apicer.pt; internet www.apicer.pt; ceramics asscn; Pres. DUARTE MANUEL PALMA LEAL GARCIA.

Associação Portuguesa de Cortiça (APCOR) (Portuguese Cork Association): Av. Comendador Henrique Amorim 580, 4536-904 Sta Maria de Lamas; tel. (22) 7474040; fax (22) 7474049; e-mail realcork@apcor.pt; internet www.corkmasters.com; www.apcor.pt; f. 1956; asscn of cork manufacturers and exporters; Pres. ANTÓNIO RIOS DE AMORIM.

Associação Portuguesa dos Industriais de Calçado, Componentes, e Artigos de Pele e seus Sucedâneos (APICCAPS): Rua Alves Redol 372, 4011-001 Porto; tel. (22) 5074150; fax (22) 5074179; e-mail apiccaps@mail.telepac.pt; internet www.apiccaps.pt; f. 1975; footwear and leather goods manufacturers' asscn; Pres. FORTUNATO FREDERICO.

Associação Têxtil e Vestuário de Portugal (ATP): Edif. do Citeve, Rua Fernando Mesquita 2785, 4760-034 Vila Nova de Famalicão; tel. (22) 5074250; fax (22) 5074259; e-mail atp@atp.pt; internet www.atp.pt; knitwear and ready-to-wear clothing industries; Pres. Dr PAULO NUNES DE ALMEIDA.

Confederação dos Agricultores de Portugal (CAP): Av. do Colégio Militar, Lote 1786, 1549-012 Lisbon; tel. (21) 7100000; fax (21) 7166122; e-mail cap@cap.pt; internet www.cap.pt; farmers' confederation; Pres. JOÃO PEDRO GORJÃO CYRILLO MACHADO.

Confederação do Comércio e Serviços de Portugal (CCP): Av. D. Vasco da Gama 29, 1449-032 Lisbon; tel. (21) 3031380; fax (21) 3031401; e-mail ccp@ccp.pt; internet www.ccp.pt; f. 1976; Pres. Dr JOSÉ ANTÓNIO DA SILVA; c. 100 mem. trade asscns.

Confederação da Indústria Portuguesa (CIP): Av. 5 de Outubro 35, 1°, 1069-193 Lisbon; tel. (21) 3164700; fax (21) 3579986; e-mail geral@cip.org.pt; internet www.cip.org.pt; f. 1974; represents employers; Pres. FRANCISCO VAN ZELLER; over 35,000 mems.

UTILITIES

In 2006 Spain and Portugal began operating an integrated electricity market, the Mercado Ibérico de Electricidade (MIBEL). One of the world's largest solar power plants, an 11-MW station near Serpa in Alentejo, opened in 2007.

Regulatory Authority

Entidade Reguladora dos Serviços Energéticos (ERSE): Rua Dom Cristovão da Gama 1, 1400-113 Lisbon; tel. (21) 3033200; fax (21) 3033201; e-mail erse@erse.pt; internet www.erse.pt; regulator of electricity and natural gas in Portugal; Pres. Prof. VÍTOR MANUEL DA SILVA SANTOS.

Electricity

Rede Eléctrica Nacional, SA (REN): Av. Estados Unidos da América 55, 1749-061 Lisbon; tel. (21) 0013500; fax (21) 0013950; e-mail secretariaren@ren.pt; internet www.ren.pt; f. 1994; subsidiary of Redes Energéticas Nacionais, SGPS, SA; concessionaire of the Portuguese transmission grid and transmission system operator in mainland Portugal; Pres. JOSÉ RODRIGUES PEREIRA DOS PENEDOS.

Energias de Portugal—EDP, SA: Praça Marquês de Pombal 12, 1250-162 Lisbon; tel. (21) 0012500; fax (21) 0021403; internet www.edp.pt; fmrly Electricidade de Portugal; production, purchase, transport, distribution and sale of electrical energy in Portugal and Spain (via Hidrocantábrico); partially privatized in 2004; Pres. ANTÓNIO MEXIA.

EDP Comercial—Comercialização de Energia, SA: Rua Camilo Castelo Branco 46, 5°, 1050-045 Lisbon; tel. (21) 0015318; fax (21) 0015491; internet www.corporate.edp.pt; Pres. Eng. JORGE CRUZ MORAIS.

EDP Distribuição—Energia, SA: Rua Camilo Castelo Branco 43, 1050-044 Lisbon; tel. (21) 0021000; fax (21) 0021610; internet www.edp.pt; electricity distribution.

EDP Produção—Gestãoda Produção de Energia, SA: Av. José Malhoa, Lote A-13, 1070-157 Lisbon; tel. (21) 0012300; fax (21) 0012490; e-mail edpproducao.edp.pt; internet www.edp.pt; production and sale of electrical energy; in 2005 the Govt reduced its stake from 30% to 10%; Pres. Eng. JOÃO TALONE; Vice-Pres. Eng. JORGE RIBEIRINHO MACHADO.

Gas

REN Gasodutos, SA: Av. Estados Unidos da América 55, 1749-061 Lisbon; tel. (21) 0013500; fax (21) 0013950; e-mail secretariaren@ren.pt; internet www.ren.pt; f. 2006; subsidiary of Redes Energéticas Nacionais, SGPS, SA; concessionaire of the national gas transmission network; Pres. JOSÉ RODRIGUES PEREIRA DOS PENEDOS.

Galp Energia, SGPS, SA: Edif. Galp Energia, Rua Tomás de Fonseca, 1600-209 Lisbon; tel. (21) 7242500; fax (21) 7242965; e-mail comunicacao@galpenergia.com; internet www.galpenergia.com; partially privatized in 2000; also comprises Petróleos de Portugal (Petrogal), SA, a petroleum refining co, and Gás de Portugal (GDP), SA, a gas distribution co; Chair. FRANCISCO LUÍS MURTEIRA NABO; CEO MANUEL FERREIRA DE OLIVEIRA.

Lisboagás GDL—Sociedade Distribuidora de Gás Natural de Lisboa, SA: Rua Tomás da Fonseca, Torre C, 4°, 1600-209 Lisbon; tel. (21) 7242500; fax (21) 8686743; e-mail lisboagas@galpenergia.com; f. 1995; regional natural gas distribution; there are 8 other regional distributors operating in Portugal: Beiragás, Dianagás, Duriensegás, Lusitaniagás, Medigás, Paxgás, Setgás and Tagusgás; Pres. Dr JOÃO CARLOS FEVEREIRO FERREIRA DE LIMA; Man. Dir CARLOS AUGUSTO.

Water

Aguas de Portugal, SGPS, SA (AdP): Rua Visconde de Seabra 3, 1700-421 Lisbon; tel. (21) 2469500; fax (21) 2469501; e-mail info@adp.pt; internet www.adp.pt; f. 1993; Pres. PEDRO CUNHA SERRA.

TRADE UNIONS

National Confederations

Confederação Geral dos Trabalhadores Portugueses-Intersindical Nacional (CGTP-IN) (General Confederation of Portuguese Workers): Rua Victor Cordon 1, 2°, 1249-102 Lisbon; tel. (21) 3236500; fax (21) 3236695; e-mail cgtp@cgtp.pt; internet www.cgtp.pt; f. 1970; reorganized 1974; 107 affiliated unions; Sec.-Gen. MANUEL CARVALHO DA SILVA.

União Geral dos Trabalhadores de Portugal (UGT) (General Union of Portuguese Workers): Av. Almirante Gago Coutinho 132, 1700-033 Lisbon; tel. (21) 3931200; fax (21) 3974612; e-mail ugt@mail.telepac.pt; internet www.ugt.pt; f. 1978; pro-socialist; comprises 58 unions and two feds; Pres. JOÃO DIAS DA SILVA; Sec.-Gen. JOÃO PROENÇA.

Principal Federations and Unions

Federação Intersindical das Indústrias Metalúrgica, Química, Farmacêutica, Eléctrica, Energia e Minas (FIEQUIMETAL) (Metal, Chemical, Pharmaceutical, Electrical, Energy and Mining): Rua dos Douradores 160, 1100-207 Lisbon; tel. (21) 8818500; fax (21) 8818555; e-mail mail@fiequimetal.pt; internet www.fiequimetal.pt; f. 2007 by merger of Fequimetal and Federação das Indústrias Eléctricas; affiliated to CGTP-IN.

Federação Nacional dos Médicos (FNAM) (Doctors): Praça da República 28, 2°, 3000 Coimbra; tel. (239) 827737; e-mail fnam@fnam.pt; internet www.fnam.pt; f. 1988; non-affiliated; Pres. MÁRIO JORGE NEVES.

Federação Nacional de Professores (FENPROF) (Teachers): Rua Fialho de Almeida 3, 1070-128 Lisbon; tel. (21) 3819190; fax (21) 3819198; e-mail fenprof@fenprof.pt; internet www.fenprof.pt; non-affiliated; Sec.-Gen. MÁRIO NOGUEIRA.

Federação Nacional dos Sindicatos da Educação (FNE): Rua Costa Cabral 1035, 4200-226 Oporto; tel. (22) 5073880; fax (22) 5092906; e-mail secretariado@fne.pt; internet www.fne.pt; f. 1982; affiliated to UGT; Sec.-Gen. Prof. JOÃO DIAS DA SILVA.

Federação Nacional dos Sindicatos da Função Pública (FNSFP): Rua Rodrigues Sampaio 138, 3°, 1150-282 Lisbon; tel. (21) 3172480; fax (21) 3172489; e-mail fnsfp@fnsfp.pt; internet www.fnsfp.pt; represents public sector workers; affiliated to CGTP-IN.

Federação Portuguesa dos Sindicatos da Construção, Ceramica e Vidro (FEVICCOM): Rua dos Douradores 160, 1100–207 Lisbon; tel. (21) 8818585; fax (21) 8818599; e-mail feviccom@mail.sitepac.pt; affiliated to CGTP-IN.

Federação dos Sindicatos da Agricultura, Alimentação, Bebidas, Hotelaria e Turismo de Portugal (FESAHT): Páteo do Salema 4, 3°, 1150-062 Lisbon; tel. (21) 8873844; fax (21) 8870510; e-mail fesaht@fesaht.pt; internet www.fesaht.pt; affiliated to CGTP-IN.

Federação dos Sindicatos do Sector da Pesca (Fisheries): Av. Elias Garcia 123, 2° dto, 1050-098 Lisbon; tel. (21) 7802250; fax (21) 7802259; e-mail fpescas@mail.telepac.pt; affiliated to CGTP-IN; Pres. FREDERICO PEREIRA.

Federação dos Sindicatos dos Trabalhadores Têxteis, Lanifícios, Vestuário, Calçado e Peles de Portugal (FESETE) (Textiles, Wool, Clothing, Shoes, Leather): Av. da Boavista 583, 4100–127 Oporto; tel. (22) 6002377; fax (22) 6002164; e-mail fesete@netcabo.pt; internet www.fesete.pt; f. 1976; affiliated to CGTP-IN; Sec.-Gen. MANUEL FREITAS.

Federação dos Sindicatos dos Transportes e Comunicações (FECTRANS) (Transport and Communications): Av. António José de Almeida 22, 1049–009 Lisbon; tel. (21) 8453466; fax (21) 8453469; e-mail fectrans@fectrans.pt; affiliated to CGTP-IN; Sec.-Gen. VÍTOR PEREIRA.

Federação dos Trabalhadores do Comércio, Escritórios e Serviços de Portugal (CESP): Rua Almirante Barroso 3, 1049-023 Lisbon; tel. (21) 3583330; fax (21) 3583339; e-mail cesplisboa@mail.telepac.pt; internet www.cesp.pt; f. 1998; represents workers in commercial, administrative and service sectors; affiliated to CGTP-IN; 51,998 mems (2006).

Sindicato Democrático da Energia, Química, Têxtil e Indústrias Diversas (SINDEQ) (Energy, Chemicals, Textiles and Industry): Rua Padre Luís Aparicio 9, 1° esq, 1150-248 Lisbon; tel. (21) 3300920; fax (21) 3300929; e-mail reglisboa@sindeq.pt; internet www.sindeq.pt; affiliated to UGT; Sec.-Gen. FRANCISCO AFONSO NEGRÕES.

Sindicato Democrático dos Trabalhadores das Comunicações e dos Média (SINDETELCO) (Communications and Media): Rua Bernardim Ribeiro 52, 1° and 2°, 1150-073 Lisbon; tel. (21) 3148620; fax (21) 3145826; e-mail sindetelco@netcabo.pt; internet www.sindetelco.pt; f. 1981; affiliated to UGT; Sec.-Gen. MANUEL DA SILVA.

Transport

RAILWAYS

In 2006 the total length of the rail track totalled 3,614.8 km, of which 1,436.2 km was electrified. In 2005 the Government announced plans to develop high-speed rail links connecting Lisbon and Oporto with the Spanish capital, Madrid, and Vigo in north-west Spain. Construction was expected to begin in 2010, with the Lisbon–Madrid link scheduled to open in 2013, followed by the link between Lisbon and Oporto in 2015. The link between Oporto and Vigo was scheduled to open in 2013.

Rede Ferroviária Nacional—REFER, E.P.: Estação de Santa Apolónia, Largo dos Caminhos de Ferro, 1100-105 Lisbon; tel. (21) 1022000; fax (21) 1022439; internet www.refer.pt; f. 1997; assumed responsibility for rail infrastructure in 1999; Pres. LUÍS FILIPE MELO E SOUSA PARDAL.

Comboios de Portugal (CP): Calçada do Duque 20, 1249-109 Lisbon; tel. (21) 1023000; fax (21) 3474468; e-mail webmaster@mail.cp.pt; internet www.cp.pt; f. 1856; nationalized in 1975 as Caminhos de Ferro Portugueses; incorporated Sociedade Estoril Caminhos de Ferro from Cais do Sodré to Cascais in 1977; renamed as above in 2004; Pres. FRANCISCO JOSÉ CARDOSO DOS REIS.

Metropolitano de Lisboa, EP (ML): Av. Fontes Pereira de Melo 28, 1069-095 Lisbon; tel. (21) 7980600; fax (21) 7980605; e-mail relacoes.publicas@metrolisboa.pt; internet www.metrolisboa.pt; opened 1959; operates the underground system, consisting of 46 stations and four lines covering 37.7 km (2007); Pres. JOAQUIM JOSÉ DE OLIVEIRA REIS.

ROADS

In 2006 there were 12,890 km of roads in continental Portugal, of which 2,545 km were motorway.

Brisa (Auto-Estradas de Portugal, SA): Edif. Brisa, Quinta da Torre da Aguilha, 2785-599 São Domingos de Rana; tel. (21) 4448500; fax (21) 4448672; e-mail ir@brisa.pt; internet www.brisa.pt; f. 1972; responsible for construction, maintenance and operation of motorways; Pres. VASCO MARIA GUIMARÃES JOSÉ DE MELLO.

Estradas de Portugal (EP): Praça da Portagem, 2809-013 Almada; tel. (21) 2879000; fax (21) 2951997; e-mail ep@estradasdeportugal.pt; internet www.estradasdeportugal.pt; f. 1999 as Instituto de Estradas de Portugal; merged with Instituto para a Conservação e Exploração da Rede Rodoviária (ICERR) and Instituto para a Construção Rodoviária (ICOR) in 2002; present name adopted 2004; road infrastructure policy, construction and maintenance of the road network; Pres. ALMERINDO DA SILVA MARQUES.

SHIPPING

The principal Portuguese ports are Aveiro, Lisbon, Leixões (Oporto), Setúbal, Sines, and Funchal (Madeira). The ports of Portimão (Algarve) and the Azores regularly receive international cruise liners. At December 2007 Portugal's registered merchant fleet comprised 469 vessels, totalling 1,070,055 grt.

Principal Shipping Companies

Portline (Transportes Marítimos Internacionais, SA): Av. Infante D. Henrique 332, 3°, 1849-025 Lisbon; tel. (21) 8391800; fax (21) 8376680; e-mail mail@portline.pt; internet www.portline.pt; f. 1984; marine transport; Gen. Man. MANUEL PINTO DE MAGALHÃES.

Sacor Marítima, SA: Rua do Açúcar 86, 1950-010 Lisbon; tel. (21) 3585100; fax (21) 3585195; e-mail sacor.maritima@petrogal.pt; tanker transport; owned by Petrogal SA, subsidiary of Galp Energia; Chair. LUÍS MARTINS CARNEIRO.

CIVIL AVIATION

There are international airports at Lisbon, Oporto, Faro, Funchal (Madeira), Santa Maria and São Miguel (both Azores). Construction of a second international airport serving Lisbon was expected to be completed by 2017.

TAP Portugal: Aeroporto de Lisboa, CP 50194, 1704-801 Lisbon; tel. (21) 8415000; fax (21) 8415881; e-mail gcrp.com@tap.pt; internet www.flytap.com; f. 1945; state-owned; national airline serving destinations in Europe, Africa, North, Central and South America; scheduled, international, domestic, passenger and cargo services; joined Star Alliance in 2005; Chair., Supervisory Bd MANUEL PINTO BARBOSA; CEO FERNANDO PINTO.

Portugália Airlines (PGA): Edif. 70, Aeroporto de Lisboa, Rua C, 1749-078 Lisbon; tel. (21) 8938070; fax (21) 8938049; f. 1988; subsidiary of TAP Portugal; regional airline operating scheduled and charter, international and domestic flights from Lisbon.

SATA (Air Açores—Serviço Açoreano de Transportes Aéreos—EP): Av. Infante D. Henrique 55, 9505-528 Ponta Delgada, São Miguel, 9500 Azores; tel. (296) 209727; fax (296) 209722; e-mail pdlsd@sata.pt; internet www.sata.pt; f. 1941; owned by the regional

PORTUGAL

govt of the Azores; inter-island services in the Azores archipelago; Pres. and Chief Exec. ANTÓNIO GOMES DE MENEZES.

Tourism

Portugal is popular with visitors because of its mild and clement weather. Apart from Lisbon and the Algarve on the mainland, Madeira and the Azores are much favoured as winter resorts. In 2006 the number of tourist arrivals at accommodation establishments totalled 7.0m.; revenue from tourism (including passenger transport) totalled US $10,036m. in that year.

Turismo de Portugal: Rua Ivone Silva 6, 1050-124 Lisbon; tel. (21) 7808800; fax (21) 7937537; e-mail info@turismodeportugal.pt; internet www.turismodeportugal.pt; f. 2007 to replace the Direcção-Geral do Turismo, the Instituto de Formação Turística and the Instituto de Turismo de Portugal; an agency of the Ministry of the Economy and Innovation; Pres. LUÍS MANUEL DOS SANTOS SILVA PATRÃO.

QATAR

Introductory Survey

Location, Climate, Language, Religion, Flag, Capital

The State of Qatar occupies a peninsula, projecting northwards from the Arabian mainland, on the west coast of the Persian (Arabian) Gulf. It is bordered, to the south, by Saudi Arabia and the United Arab Emirates. The archipelago of Bahrain lies to the north-west. On the opposite side of the Gulf lies Iran. The climate is exceptionally hot in the summer, when temperatures may reach 49°C (120°F), with high humidity on the coast; conditions are relatively mild in the winter. Rainfall is negligible. The official language is Arabic. Almost all of the inhabitants are adherents of Islam, although an influx of guest workers in recent years has precipitated official recognition of Christian denominations. Native Qataris, who comprise less than one-quarter of the total population, belong mainly to the strictly orthodox Wahhabi sect of Sunni Muslims. The national flag (proportions 11 by 28) is maroon, with a broad vertical white stripe at the hoist, the two colours being separated by a serrated line. The capital is Doha.

Recent History

Qatar was formerly dominated by the al-Khalifa family of Bahrain. The peninsula became part of Turkey's Ottoman Empire in 1872, but Turkish forces evacuated Qatar at the beginning of the First World War (1914–18). The United Kingdom recognized Sheikh Abdullah ath-Thani as Ruler of Qatar, and in 1916 made a treaty with him, providing British protection against aggression in return for supervision of Qatar's external affairs. A 1934 treaty extended fuller British protection to Qatar.

In October 1960 Sheikh Ali ath-Thani, Ruler of Qatar since 1949, abdicated in favour of his son, Sheikh Ahmad. In 1968 the British Government announced its intention to withdraw British forces from the Persian (Arabian) Gulf area by 1971. Qatar thus attempted to associate itself with Bahrain and Trucial Oman (now the United Arab Emirates—UAE) in a proposed federation. In April 1970 Sheikh Ahmad announced a provisional Constitution, providing for a partially elected Consultative Assembly, although he retained effective power. In May the Deputy Ruler, Sheikh Khalifa ath-Thani (a cousin of Sheikh Ahmad), was appointed Prime Minister. After the failure of attempts to agree terms for union with neighbouring Gulf countries, Qatar became fully independent on 1 September 1971, whereupon the Ruler took the title of Amir. The 1916 treaty was replaced by a new treaty of friendship with the United Kingdom.

In February 1972 the Amir was deposed in a bloodless coup. Claiming support from the royal family and the armed forces, Sheikh Khalifa proclaimed himself Amir. Sheikh Khalifa, who retained the premiership, adopted a policy of wide-ranging social and economic reform, and the previous extravagance and privileges of the royal family were curbed. In accordance with the 1970 Constitution, the Amir appointed an Advisory Council in April 1972 to complement the ministerial Government. The Council was expanded from 20 to 30 members in 1975 and to 35 members in 1988. Its term has been extended at regular intervals since its establishment, most recently, for a period of two years, in July 2008.

On 27 June 1995 the Deputy Amir, Heir Apparent, Minister of Defence and Commander-in-Chief of the Armed Forces, Maj.-Gen. Sheikh Hamad bin Khalifa ath-Thani, deposed his father in a bloodless coup. Sheikh Hamad proclaimed himself Amir, claiming the support of the royal family and the Qatari people. Sheikh Khalifa, who was in Switzerland at the time of the coup, immediately denounced his son's actions, and vowed to return to Qatar. Although Sheikh Khalifa had effectively granted Sheikh Hamad control of the emirate's affairs (with the exception of the treasury) in 1992, a power struggle was reported to have emerged between the two in the months prior to the coup: Sheikh Khalifa was particularly opposed to his son's independent foreign policy (notably the strengthening of relations with both Iran and Iraq, and with Israel), and had attempted to regain influence in policy-making. Sheikh Hamad, however, reputedly enjoyed widespread support both nationally and internationally, and his domestic reforms were perceived as having contributed to Qatar's stability at a time when social unrest and Islamist extremism were emerging in the region. The United Kingdom, the USA and Saudi Arabia swiftly recognized the new Amir. In July 1995 Sheikh Hamad reorganized the Council of Ministers and appointed himself Prime Minister, while retaining the posts of Minister of Defence and Commander-in-Chief of the Armed Forces.

Meanwhile, the deposed Amir took residence in the UAE, and visited several other countries of the region in an apparent attempt to assert his legitimacy as ruler of Qatar. In January 1996 it was confirmed that Sheikh Khalifa had gained control of a substantial part of Qatar's financial reserves. In the following month security forces in Qatar were reported to have foiled an attempted coup. As many as 100 people were arrested, and a warrant was issued for the arrest of Sheikh Hamad bin Jasim bin Hamad ath-Thani, a former government minister and a cousin of the Amir. Sheikh Khalifa denied any involvement, although he was quick to imply that the alleged plot indicated popular support for his return. In July legal proceedings were initiated in Qatar, Europe and the USA in an attempt to recover some US $3,000m.–$8,000m. in overseas assets that were asserted by the new Amir to have been amassed by his father from state oil and investment revenues. In October, however, it was reported that Sheikh Hamad and Sheikh Khalifa had been reconciled and had reached an out-of-court settlement regarding the return of state funds. By early 1997 all lawsuits issued against the former Amir had been withdrawn. In November 1997 the trial began of 110 people (40 of whom were charged *in absentia*) accused of involvement in the attempted coup of February 1996. Hearings were immediately adjourned. A number of those being tried *in absentia* were apprehended during 1998, including Qatar's former deputy head of intelligence, who was extradited from Yemen.

In October 1996 Sheikh Hamad named the third of his four sons, Sheikh Jasim bin Hamad bin Khalifa ath-Thani, as Heir Apparent. The Amir subsequently appointed his younger brother, Sheikh Abdullah bin Khalifa ath-Thani (the Minister of the Interior), as Prime Minister. Further to the ending of media censorship earlier in the year, the post of Minister of Information and Culture was abolished. (The relevant ministry was dissolved in March 1998.) In November 1996 Sheikh Hamad announced the creation of a new Defence Council, over which he would preside. The Council, to be comprised of senior ministers and armed forces and security personnel, was expected to function in an advisory and consultative capacity. It was also reported that the Amir had appointed the Gulf region's first female member of government (as Under-Secretary of State for Education and Culture).

Elections to Qatar's new 29-member Central Municipal Council (CMC), held by universal suffrage on 8 March 1999, were the first in the country's history. Announced by Sheikh Hamad in November 1997 and provided for by law in July 1998, the CMC was to have a consultative role in the operations of the Ministry of Municipal Affairs and Agriculture. The rate of participation by voters reportedly exceeded 90% in Doha, and was estimated at 60%–70% of the registered electorate in rural areas. However, only about 22,000 voters of an eligible 40,000 actually participated in the elections.

In July 1999 a 32-member constitutional committee was established to draft a permanent constitution; this was to include provision for the creation of a new National Assembly. The committee produced a draft constitution in July 2002, which provided for a separation of the executive, the judiciary and the legislature, but which would retain executive power in the hands of the Amir and the Council of Ministers. The draft constitution also guaranteed freedom of expression, religion and association, and provided for the establishment of an independent judiciary and of a new 45-member Consultative Council (to replace the Advisory Council), comprising 30 elected and 15 appointed members. Under the proposed constitution, the Amir would be obliged to provide reasons for rejecting draft laws adopted by the Council. The Amir would be required to approve such legislation sent to him a second time by the Council with two-thirds' majority support, although he would have a discretionary right to halt implementation of laws in question on a temporary basis if he deemed this to be in the greater interests of the country. The parliament was to have a four-year mandate, and suffrage was to be extended to all citizens, including women, aged 18 years and above. In a referendum held in April 2003, an overwhelming majority (96.6%) of the 71,406 voters approved the new Constitution, and it was expected that the affirmative vote would lead to legislative elections being conducted in 2004. These were delayed, however, and in March 2005 the Amir announced that the elections would take place between June 2005 and June 2006. In December 2005 the First Deputy Prime Minister and Minister of Foreign Affairs, Sheikh Hamad bin Jasim bin Jaber ath-Thani, stated that preparations were now directed at holding the elections in early 2007. The delay was apparently related partly to the controversy over the legal status of the Murra tribe, whose Qatari citizenship had been revoked after it had been discovered that some members of the tribe also held Saudi citizenship. Dual nationality is not recognized under Qatari law and some members of the tribe were expelled to Saudi Arabia over the issue; in addition, it was alleged that severe punishments were extended to individuals who expressed sympathy for the victims. It was reported in February 2006, however, that the tribe members were expected to have their Qatari citizenship returned. In October it was announced that only 'original' Qatari nationals above the age of 30 would be eligible to register as candidates in the elections. The projected deadline of early 2007 for the staging of elections lapsed, and it was announced in February 2008 that further delays—while an appropriate legal framework was finalized and implemented—were expected.

Meanwhile, Sheikh Hamad bin Jasim bin Hamad ath-Thani was arrested in July 1999 for his alleged role in the coup plot of 1996. The trial of those accused of involvement in the coup ended in February 2000, with the former minister and 32 co-defendants sentenced to life imprisonment; 85 others were acquitted. Appeal proceedings were subsequently lodged by all 33 who had been convicted. In May 2001 the Court of Appeal overruled the previous sentences of life imprisonment, sentencing to death 19 of the defendants (including Sheikh Hamad bin Jasim bin Hamad); the court was also reported to have sentenced 26 defendants to terms of life imprisonment, and acquitted two others.

In January 2002 it was reported that a group styling itself the General Congress of the Qatari Opposition had emerged to demand that the Amir stand down in favour of his son, Crown Prince Jasim. The group, which claimed to include former members of the armed forces, tribal chiefs, businessmen, students and officials who had served under the previous regime, accused the Amir of pursuing 'reckless' policies, of corruption and of alienating Qatar's Gulf neighbours. This last charge was interpreted as possibly referring not only to Qatar's pursuit of an increasingly independent foreign policy but also to the activities of Al-Jazeera, a satellite television station linked to the ath-Thani family with a wide audience throughout the region. Al-Jazeera's reporting style and scope of coverage had on occasions caused several governments to threaten to restrict its freedom to operate in their country: notably, in May 2002 authorities in Bahrain announced that the station was to be banned from reporting there, apparently in response to its recent unauthorized coverage of anti-US demonstrations in Bahrain, and in June the Jordanian Government ordered the closure of Al-Jazeera's Amman office after the station broadcast programmes considered unfavourable to Jordan. In January 2005 it was announced that Al-Jazeera was to be privatized; the proposed sale was regarded as a means of distancing the Qatari Government from Al-Jazeera's more controversial broadcasts and was a further indication of the closeness of the relationship between Qatar and the US Administration, which had allegedly considered launching a military attack on the station. However, by early 2009 privatization was being described as a long-term goal for the channel, unlikely to occur before 2010. An English-language sister channel, Al-Jazeera English, was launched in November 2006, meanwhile, together with a complementary website, which served to raise the organization's international profile by securing the participation of respected media personalities and by establishing broadcast centres in Malaysia, the United Kingdom and the USA.

The second elections to the CMC were held on 7 April 2003. A turn-out of about 35% was estimated for the country as a whole, but the rate of participation was reportedly as low as 25% of the registered electorate at several polling stations, including in the largest constituency, al-Kharitaat. A female candidate, Sheikha al-Jufairi, was elected unopposed after the competing candidates stood aside, and thus became the first woman in the Gulf region to hold elected office, but none of the five other women who contested the elections was successful. Three further candidates were also elected unopposed, and the remaining 25 seats were contested by 85 candidates, including 18 incumbents. In May the Amir appointed Sheikha bint Ahmad al-Mahmoud as Minister of Education; she replaced Dr Ahmad bin Khalifa Busherbak al-Mansouri and became the first woman to join the Council of Ministers. Further government changes were effected in December, when Sheikh Muhammad bin Ahmad bin Jasim ath-Thani replaced Sheikh Hamad bin Faisal ath-Thani as Minister of Economy and Commerce, and in March 2004, when the Amir appointed Sultan bin Hassan adh-Dhabit ad-Dousary as Minister of Municipal Affairs and Agriculture in place of Ali bin Saad al-Kawari.

Meanwhile, in February 2004 the Government approved an anti-terrorism law, which included the provision of the death penalty for anyone who killed 'through a terror act' and for anyone 'founding, organizing or managing a group or organization to commit a terror act'. In addition, the crime of assisting a terrorist group was to be punishable by a life sentence. In May a law permitting the formation of trade unions was approved. In addition, the legislation granted workers the right to strike, banned children aged under 16 years from employment and set a maximum eight-hour working day.

In April 2005 the Amir removed from their posts his Chief of Staff, Abdullah bin Muhammad bin Sa'ud ath-Thani, and two recently appointed ministers—Muhammad bin Abd al-Latif bin Abd ar-Rahman al-Mana, the Minister of Awqaf (Religious Endowments) and Islamic Affairs, and Muhammad bin Isa Hamad al-Mehannadi, the Minister of State for Council of Ministers' Affairs—amid allegations that three cabinet members and several businessmen had been questioned by officials over their connections to fraudulent activities relating to the sale of the state-owned Qatar Gas Transport Co (Nakilat) in early 2005. Faisal bin Abdullah al-Mahmud was awarded the religious affairs portfolio, ad-Dousary, the Minister of Municipal Affairs and Agriculture, received the position of Minister of State for Council of Ministers' Affairs in addition to his existing responsibilities and Sheikh Abd ar-Rahman bin Sa'ud ath-Thani was appointed as the new Chief of Staff.

A bomb exploded outside a theatre frequented by Western expatriates in Doha in March 2005. One British citizen was killed in the suicide attack and 12 people were injured. The bomber was reported to be an Egyptian citizen, Omar Ahmad Abdullah Ali, and Jund ash-Sham (the Army of the Levant), a previously little-known militant grouping, claimed responsibility for the attack. Although the bombing was the first of its kind in Qatar, Western embassies had previously issued warnings to expatriates that the threat from terrorism in the emirate was high.

In March 2006 the Minister of Economy and Commerce, Sheikh Muhammad, was unexpectedly dismissed from the Council of Ministers. No official explanation was given for his removal; however, the decision was widely believed to have been prompted by a recent crash on the Doha Securities Market. The ministerial portfolio was added to the responsibilities of the Minister of Finance, Yousuf bin Hussain Kamal. In December Qatar hosted the Asian Games, becoming the first Arab nation to do so since the Games' inception in 1951; it was hoped that the publicity garnered by staging the event would have boosted Qatar's profile on the international stage, as well as significantly increasing tourism revenues in that year.

The third elections to the CMC, contested by 118 candidates, took place on 1 April 2007. Turn-out, although relatively low, exceeded expectations, at 51.1% of the electorate, compared with an estimated 35% in the 2003 polls. Of the three female candidates standing for election, only one was successful: Sheikha al-Jufairi was re-elected, securing 800 of the 879 votes cast in the Old Airport constituency—the highest proportion of votes achieved by any candidate. A few days later it was announced that the Prime Minister, Sheikh Abdullah, had resigned, but no explanation was offered for his decision. Sheikh Hamad, hitherto First Deputy Prime Minister and Minister of Foreign Affairs, was sworn in as his replacement; he retained the foreign affairs portfolio.

A new electoral law was adopted by the Advisory Council in May 2008 and was awaiting ratification by the Amir in early 2009. It was hoped that the new legislation would facilitate the organization of long-awaited elections to the Consultative Council provided for in the Constitution. Meanwhile, the extension of the Advisory Council's term for a further two years in July 2008 indicated the possibility that legislative elections would not take place before mid-2010.

In July 2008 the Amir effected a major reorganization of the Council of Ministers. Seven new ministerial portfolios were created—including those of culture, arts and heritage, business and trade, environment, and international co-operation—bringing the number of members of the Council of Ministers to 20, in addition to the Amir himself. A new Minister of Public Health, Sheikha Ghalia bint Muhammad bin Hamad ath-Thani, was appointed, increasing the number of female ministers to two. However, the two serving female ministers, Sheika Ghalia and the Minister of Education and Higher Education, Sheikha bint Ahmad al-Mahmoud, were replaced in April 2009, following a minor reallocation of cabinet portfolios.

Launched in October 2008, meanwhile, under the supervision of the General Secretariat for Development Planning, Qatar's National Vision 2030 outlined the country's long-term development strategy. The Vision aims to promote and manage Qatar's ambitious economic and social development programme, while protecting its culture, traditions and environment. A new Museum of Islamic Art opened in Doha in November. Designed by renowned Chinese-born US architect I. M. Pei, the museum, which became the world's largest dedicated Islamic art museum, was the first in a series of planned cultural projects in the Qatari capital.

In July 1991 Qatar instituted proceedings at the International Court of Justice (ICJ) regarding sovereignty of the Hawar islands (in 1939 a British judgment had awarded sovereignty of the islands to Bahrain), the shoals of Fasht ad-Dibal and Qit'at Jaradah (over which the British had recognized Bahrain's 'sovereign rights' in 1947), together with the delimitation of the maritime border between Qatar and Bahrain. Bahrain's insistence that the two countries seek joint recourse to the ICJ was rejected by Qatar. The matter was further confused in April 1992, when the Government of Qatar issued a decree redefining its maritime borders to include territorial waters claimed by Bahrain. Furthermore, Bahrain attempted to widen the issue to include its long-standing claim to the area around Zubarah, in mainland Qatar. In February 1994 a hearing of the ICJ opened in The Hague, Netherlands, in order to determine whether the court was competent to rule on the dispute. In July the ICJ requested that Qatar and Bahrain resubmit their dispute by 30 November, either jointly or separately. The two states failed to reach agreement on joint presentation to the court, and in November Qatar submitted a unilateral request to pursue its case through the ICJ. In February 1995, while the ICJ declared that it would have authority to adjudicate in the dispute (despite Bahrain's refusal to accept the principle of an ICJ ruling), Saudi Arabia also proposed to act as mediator between the two countries. Qatar subsequently indicated its willingness to withdraw the case from the ICJ if Saudi arbitration proved successful.

Relations with Bahrain subsequently deteriorated, and in December 1996 Bahrain boycotted the annual summit meeting of the Co-operation Council for the Arab States of the Gulf (Gulf Co-operation Council—GCC, see p. 229), which took place in Doha. The meeting none the less decided to establish a quadripartite committee, comprising those GCC countries not involved in the dispute, to mediate between Qatar and Bahrain. The committee's efforts achieved a degree of success, and meetings between senior Qatari and Bahraini representatives in London, United Kingdom, and Manama, Bahrain, in early 1997 resulted in the announcement that diplomatic relations at ambassadorial level were to be established. In September, however, Bahrain challenged the authenticity of documents presented to the ICJ by Qatar in support of its territorial claim; the ICJ subsequently directed Qatar to produce a report on the authenticity of the documents by September 1998. Following the submission of the report, in which four experts differed in their opinion of the documents, Qatar announced its decision to disregard them, to enable the case to proceed.

In December 1999 the Amir made his first official visit to Manama, during which it was agreed that a joint committee, headed by the Crown Princes of Bahrain and Qatar, would be established to encourage bilateral co-operation. Qatar also agreed to withdraw its petition from the ICJ in the event of the joint committee reaching a solution to the territorial disputes. A second senior-level meeting was held in January 2000, when the new Amir of Bahrain made his first visit to Qatar. The two countries agreed to expedite the opening of embassies in Manama and Doha. In February, following the first meeting of the Bahrain-Qatar Supreme Joint Committee, it was announced that the possibility of constructing a causeway to link the two states was to be investigated. In May Bahrain announced its decision to suspend the activities of the Supreme Joint Committee pending the ICJ ruling on the dispute. Hearings at the ICJ, which began later that month, ended in June. The final verdict, issued in March 2001, was virtually identical to the British judgment of 1939. Bahrain was found to have sovereignty over the Hawar islands and Qit'at Jaradah, while Qatar held sovereignty over Zubarah, Janan island and the low-tide elevation of Fasht ad-Dibal; the Court drew a single maritime boundary between the two states. Both Qatar and Bahrain accepted the ICJ ruling, and declared that their territorial dispute was ended. Later in March 2001 it was announced that meetings of the Supreme Joint Committee would resume.

In August 2002 a Danish consortium completed a feasibility study for the construction of the planned causeway linking Qatar to Bahrain (the Friendship Bridge). Both Governments had approved the project by May 2004, and international companies were invited to present bids for the contract in late 2004. By this time Bahrain and Qatar were reportedly also discussing co-operation on gas projects and other economic issues. Following extensive negotiations, a US $3,000m. contract to design and build the causeway was signed in May 2008 by a consortium led by VINCI Construction, a French company, and the Qatar-Bahrain Causeway Foundation. Construction was expected to commence in mid-2009, with completion scheduled for 2013–14. However, substantial revisions to the design were required after a decision, in late 2008, to incorporate a railway line into the project. The rail link was expected to add up to $1,000m. to the cost of constructing the causeway.

Following the multinational military operation to liberate Kuwait from Iraqi occupation in early 1991, Qatar resumed tentative contact with Iraq in 1993. In March 1995, during the first official visit to the country by a senior Iraqi official since the Gulf War, Iraq's Minister of Foreign Affairs met with his Qatari counterpart to discuss the furtherance of bilateral relations; the Qatari Minister subsequently indicated Qatar's determination to pursue a foreign policy independent from that of its GCC neighbours when he announced his country's support for the ending of UN sanctions against Iraq. In early 1998, as the crisis deepened regarding UN weapons inspections in Iraq (see the chapter on Iraq), Qatar urged a diplomatic solution, and appealed to Iraq to comply with all pertinent UN Security Council resolutions. With Qatar continuing to advocate an end to sanctions against Iraq, in December 2001 a meeting took place in Doha between the new Iraqi Minister of Foreign Affairs, Naji Sabri, and Qatari and Omani officials. In June 2003, after the removal of Saddam Hussain's regime by the US-led coalition, Qatar Airways became the first airline for 12 years to operate commercial air services to Iraq, after the scheduling of a bi-weekly service to Basra. Meanwhile, in September the US-appointed interim Cabinet in Iraq voted to expel Al-Jazeera reporters for one month, pending a review of their broadcasts, after the station was accused of inciting violence against US and Iraqi authorities. Despite official announcements in 2004 that the Government planned to cancel most of the estimated US $4,000m. worth of debt owed to Qatar by Iraq, by late 2008 significant Iraqi debt relief had yet to be authorized.

In September 1992 tension arose with Saudi Arabia (with which Qatar had previously enjoyed close ties) when Qatar accused Saudi forces of attacking a Qatari border post, killing two border guards and capturing a third in the process. In protest, in October Qatar suspended a 1965 border agreement with Saudi Arabia (which had never been fully ratified) and temporarily withdrew its 200-strong contingent from the Saudi-based GCC 'Peninsula Shield' force (at the time stationed in Kuwait). The Saudi Government denied the involvement of its armed forces, claiming that the incident had been caused by fighting between rival Bedouin tribes within Saudi territory. Relations between the two countries reportedly improved as a result of Kuwaiti mediation, and the Qatari hostage was released later in October 1992; Qatar nevertheless registered its disaffection by not attending meetings of GCC ministers held in Abu Dhabi (the UAE) and Kuwait in November. In December, after mediation by Egypt, Sheikh Khalifa and King Fahd of Saudi Arabia signed an agreement whereby a committee was to be established formally to demarcate the border between the two states. In November 1994, however, Qatar boycotted a GCC ministerial meeting in Saudi Arabia, in protest at what it alleged to have been armed incidents on the border with Saudi Arabia in March and October. Bilateral relations appeared to improve in August 1995, when the new Amir held talks with King Fahd in Saudi Arabia. In December, nevertheless, Qatar boycotted the closing session of the annual GCC summit, following the appointment of a Saudi national as the next GCC Secretary-General (in preference to a Qatari candidate). In March 1996 the dispute was reported to have been settled, after mediation by Oman, and in April Qatar and Saudi Arabia agreed to establish a joint committee to complete the demarcation of their mutual border. Officials from both countries met in Saudi Arabia in June 1999 to sign the border demarcation maps. In March 2001, at a ceremony in Doha, Saudi and Qatari officials signed an apparently final agreement concerning the land and maritime demarcation of their joint border; the accord included provision for a joint Saudi-Qatari committee, whose task was to ensure that all provisions of the 1965 accord were implemented.

In October 2002 relations between Saudi Arabia and Qatar worsened, however, when the Saudi ambassador to Qatar was recalled following the airing of a television programme via the Al-Jazeera network that was deemed to be critical of the Saudi regime. Relations had already been strained by the expansion of US military facilities in Qatar and by the relocation, in April, of the main US air operations in the Gulf region from Saudi Arabia to Doha (see the chapter on Saudi Arabia). Furthermore, Saudi Arabia subsequently reopened the border dispute, despite the 2001 agreement, threatening in July 2007 to block a US $3,500m. gas pipeline between Qatar and the UAE on the grounds that sections of the undersea pipeline ran through what it claimed to be Saudi territory. A visit to Jeddah, Saudi Arabia, undertaken by Sheikh Hamad in September 2007 engendered optimism for an improvement in bilateral ties, however, with the announcement of a number of agreements arising from the Amir's dialogue with King Abdullah: Sheikh Hamad gave an assurance that Al-Jazeera would not broadcast material that could be regarded as defamatory in respect of Saudi Arabia, in return for which Al-Jazeera would be permitted to establish a presence in the kingdom. Saudi Arabia also confirmed the return of its diplomatic envoy to Qatar, and King Abdullah agreed to attend the forthcoming GCC summit in Doha (an invitation he had refused in 2002, when Qatar had last hosted a meeting of the organization). Saudi objections to the Qatar–UAE gas pipeline were also resolved. Qatar's Amir subsequently attended a summit of the Organization of the Petroleum Exporting Countries (OPEC, see p. 386) in Saudi Arabia in November. The new Saudi ambassador to Qatar acceded to his position in March 2008, and relations were further bolstered in that month by an official visit to the emirate by Saudi Crown Prince Sultan ibn Abd al-Aziz as-Sa'ud for talks with the Amir on the countries' bilateral relations and other international issues. In July the Qatari and Saudi Governments agreed to resolve the issue of border demarcation and to establish a Joint Co-ordination Council to encourage co-operation in military, industrial, agricultural and energy affairs. A definitive Land and Maritime Border Delimitation Agreement was signed in December, together with various other agreements on bilateral co-operation, at the first meeting of the Saudi-Qatari Joint Co-ordination Council, and was registered with the UN in March 2009.

In January 1994 Qatar was reported to have commenced discussions with Israel regarding the supply of natural gas to that country, in apparent disregard for the Arab economic boycott of Israel. Following pressure from its GCC allies, Qatar subsequently announced that the proposed sale would depend on Israel's withdrawal from all Arab territories occupied in 1967. In September 1994, however, Qatar, along with the other GCC states, revoked aspects of the economic boycott of Israel. In November 1995 Israel signed a memorandum of intent to purchase Qatari liquefied natural gas (LNG). Relations between the two countries were consolidated further in April 1996, when Shimon Peres made the first official visit to Qatar by an Israeli Prime Minister. However, in late 1996 Israel declared that the memorandum of intent had expired, although negotiations would continue, and in November Qatar stated that any deal would be dependent on progress in the peace process. The fourth Middle East and North Africa economic summit was scheduled to take place in Doha in November 1997. However, in protest at the intended presence of representatives of Israel, which was regarded by the Arab states as failing to comply with its obligations with regard to the Middle East peace process, most of Qatar's fellow members of the League of Arab States (the Arab League, see p. 344) and the GCC refused to attend. As a result of the boycott, the summit was downgraded to a conference, and was attended by representatives of only seven Arab states; a low-level Israeli delegation attended, as did the US Secretary of State, Madeleine Albright.

In March 1998 the Qatari Government stated that it was reviewing its relations with Israel, given the severe difficulties in the Middle East peace process. Nevertheless, Qatar was criticized by other Arab states in September 2000 following a meeting in New York, USA, at the UN Millennium Summit between the Amir and the Israeli Prime Minister, Ehud Barak. Prior to the ninth conference of the Organization of the Islamic Conference (OIC, see p. 382), held in Doha in November, several Islamic states (notably Saudi Arabia and Iran) threatened to boycott the summit unless Qatar agreed to sever its low-level diplomatic relations with Israel. (Arab and Islamic states were keen to demonstrate support for the Palestinians in their renewed uprising against Israeli occupation from late September.) The Qatari leadership apparently bowed to regional pressure when, in November, it announced that the Israeli trade office in Doha was to be closed, although there were subsequent reports that the office was still functioning. An emergency session of the OIC was convened in Doha in December 2001 to demonstrate solidarity with the Palestinians as the crisis deepened still further; Sheikh Hamad proposed the establishment of a panel comprising prominent representatives of the Islamic community to lobby Western governments to support an independent Palestinian state. In March 2002 Qatar's Minister of Foreign Affairs travelled to the Palestinian territories for talks with the leader of the Palestinian (National) Authority (PA), Yasser Arafat, who at that time remained under Israeli siege in Ramallah. In late 2002 it was again reported that the Israeli trade office in Doha was still functioning; Qatar's continuing refusal to close the establishment exacerbated tensions with Saudi Arabia in particular. In October 2006 the Secretary-General of the GCC, Abd ar-Rahman al-Attiya, praised Qatar's mediation efforts between the two rival Palestinian movements, the Islamic Resistance Movement (Hamas) and Fatah, singling out in particular the endeavours of Sheikh Hamad. In the same month the Israeli Vice-Prime Minister and Minister of Foreign Affairs, Tzipi Livni, cancelled a scheduled visit to Doha to attend an international conference upon learning that the PA was to be represented by members of Hamas, which refuses to recognize the State of Israel.

Delegations from both Israel and Qatar attended the 62nd UN General Assembly in New York in September 2007. At a meeting with Livni initiated by Sheikh Hamad, the Israeli Minister of Foreign Affairs reiterated the importance of the involvement of 'moderate' Arab states in regional discussions towards promoting political negotiations with the Palestinians, and appealed for greater solidarity with Israel against the emergence of extremist elements in the region. Despite Qatar's unprecedented, and isolated, invitation to Iran to attend the GCC's annual summit meeting, held in Doha in early December (see below), Livni maintained Israeli dialogue with Qatar and subsequently embarked on a series of diplomatic visits to the country in early 2008, including attendance at the Doha Forum on Democracy, Development and Free Trade in April. While Qatar, together with other GCC members, strongly condemned Israel's renewed military offensive in the Gaza Strip in January 2008 (see the chapters on Israel and the Palestinian Autonomous Areas), in February the country pledged its willingness to facilitate a cease-fire agreement between Israel and Hamas. Qatar's accommodation of the Israeli Minister of Foreign Affairs, however, precipitated the withdrawal from the conference of several other participants, notably members of the Hezbollah-led opposition in Lebanon.

In response to the military offensive launched by Israel against Hamas targets in the Gaza Strip in late December 2008 (see the chapters on Israel and the Palestinian Autonomous Areas), Sheikh Hamad sought to convene an emergency Arab League summit in Doha to formulate a unified Arab response to the crisis. By mid-January 2009 more than 1,300 Palestinians were reported to have been killed and some 5,400 wounded in the Israeli offensive. However, the proposed Doha summit on Gaza was resisted by several countries, notably Saudi Arabia and Egypt, which were strongly opposed to any measures that would offer support to Hamas. Thirteen Arab states agreed to attend the summit, including Algeria, Lebanon, Syria and the UAE; however, this was two fewer than the quorum of 15 required to grant the meeting official status. Delegates at the summit, which was convened on 16 January, including the President of Iran,

Mahmoud Ahmadinejad, proposed the suspension of the Arab League peace initiative originally conceived in 2002 and an end to all relations with Israel, and denounced Israel's actions as war crimes. The presence of Khalid Meshaal, the Syria-based head of Hamas's political bureau, and the absence of Mahmud Abbas, the Executive President of the PA, underlined the partisan nature of the gathering. During the summit the Qatari Government announced the closure of Israel's trade office in Doha and the suspension of diplomatic ties. The Doha summit failed in its stated aim of developing a united Arab response to the Israeli aggresion in Gaza. Instead, it highlighted regional divisions on the subject of Israel and Palestine, exemplified by the emergence of two opposing blocs: one broadly supportive of Hamas and open to Iranian influence, the other supportive of the Fatah-led PA and generally aligned with the USA. Meanwhile, Sheikh Hamad attended an emergency GCC summit on Gaza in the Saudi capital, Riyadh, on 15 January 2009, which focused on seeking an end to the hostilities and on the provision of aid. The Amir also attended the Arab Economic, Social and Development Summit in Kuwait on 19–20 January and argued strongly for Arab reconciliation. On the sidelines of the summit King Abdullah of Saudi Arabia hosted a private meeting with the leaders of Qatar, Egypt, Kuwait and Syria, which was heralded as achieving substantial progress towards Arab unity. However, despite the plethora of high-level meetings during January, a unified Arab political response to the Gaza crisis failed to be agreed.

An emergency summit meeting of the OIC was convened in Doha in October 2001, in response to the previous month's suicide attacks against New York and Washington, DC, and the subsequent commencement of US-led military action against targets in Afghanistan linked to the Taliban regime and to the al-Qa'ida (Base) organization of Osama bin Laden, the Saudi-born fundamentalist Islamist held principally responsible for the attacks in the USA.

Despite Qatar's active support for an end to UN sanctions against Iraq, and its pursuit of contacts with the incumbent regime of Saddam Hussain (see above), by the time US Vice-President Dick Cheney visited Qatar in March 2002—as part of a tour of the Gulf aimed at garnering support for a potential extension of the US-led 'war on terror' to target the Iraqi regime—Qatar was apparently alone among the Gulf states in indicating that it would allow the use of its territory as a base for action against Saddam Hussain. During the decade after the Gulf War the Government had signed a number of defence agreements with the USA and there was reported to have been a significant increase in the amount of US military personnel and equipment positioned in Qatar since September 2001. Furthermore, the construction of a major air facility at the Al-Udaid military base enhanced its strategic importance within the US military network in the region; in December 2002 the US Department of Defense dispatched more than 600 personnel from the US military command centre to the base, which was to act as the main US command post in the Gulf. None the less, Qatar, concerned about the popular reaction to a US-led war in Iraq and the regional implications such a conflict might have, continued to advocate a diplomatic solution to the crisis. By the time of the commencement of hostilities in March 2003, the USA had stationed some 3,000 air force personnel and 36 tactical jets at Al-Udaid. In April, following the removal of Saddam Hussain's regime by the US-led coalition, Qatar's Minister of Foreign Affairs, Sheikh Hamad, urged the USA to reject the possibility of pursuing its 'war on terror' to target the Syrian regime of President Bashar al-Assad. The announcement in December 2006 that Qatar was to pay the salaries of teachers in the Palestinian territories prompted concern among some US officials that the funds might be misappropriated by Hamas militants. However, following a meeting between US Secretary of State Condoleezza Rice and Sheikh Hamad, the US Administration appeared content not to impose any change of policy towards Qatar, which remained one of its closest allies in the Gulf region. In January 2007 US Secretary of Defense Robert Gates visited Doha as part of a tour of the Middle East, the focus of which was the situation in Iraq. During his stay he met with the Amir to discuss the further improvement of bilateral relations. In March the Qatari Government announced that it would not allow from its soil the launch by the USA of any military action against Iran, and strongly advocated a peaceful resolution to the ongoing impasse between the US and Iranian Governments.

In October 2005 Qatar was elected to a non-permanent seat on the UN Security Council. The two-year term commenced on 1 January 2006, expiring on 31 December 2007. Qatar's decision to endorse the candidacy of Ban Ki-Moon, rather than that of the Jordanian candidate, Prince Zeid bin Hussein, for the position of UN Secretary-General prompted Jordan to recall its ambassador from Doha in October 2006. Jordanian officials insisted that the decision had been based not on specific grievances, but rather on Qatar's persistent 'negative attitude' towards Jordan. Doha hosted the annual summit of the GCC in December 2007, when, *inter alia*, consensus was reached upon the establishment of a common market, to become effective on 1 January 2008, which would permit the free movement of both capital and citizens of GCC member countries for the purposes of travel, residency and employment, and serve to enhance regional integration and co-operation.

Relations with Jordan improved significantly during 2008, and in early November the Jordanian Prime Minister, Nader ad-Dahabi, led a high-ranking delegation to Doha to discuss economic and commercial co-operation. During the visit ad-Dahabi confirmed the appointment of Jordan's first ambassador to Qatar since the recall of its envoy in 2006. This was followed, later in November, by a two-day state visit to Qatar by Jordan's King Abdullah, during which the King and the Amir reaffirmed their commitment to strengthening bilateral ties and economic co-operation. In January 2009 a reconvened joint Qatari-Jordanian economic committee held its first meeting; plans for a Qatari investment fund in Jordan, worth up to US $1,000m., were announced.

In June 2007, and again in February 2008, Qatari negotiators played a leading role in brokering peace agreements between the Government of Yemen and rebels loyal to the late Shi'a cleric Hussain al-Houthi, who had been engaged in a sporadic civil war in Saada province since 2004. Although the Qatari-brokered accords ultimately failed to end the hostilities, they demonstrated the gulf state's willingness and capability to act as an independent mediator in regional conflicts. In May 2008 Qatari diplomats brokered a deal in Doha to resolve an 18-month-long political stalemate between rival factions in Lebanon (see the chapter on Lebanon). The agreement, which provided for the formation of a power-sharing government, the election of a President and the drafting of a new electoral law, was widely believed to have averted the threat of civil war. Qatar's success in brokering the Lebanese accord was attributed to its independent foreign policy and lack of vested interests in the region, and significantly bolstered its reputation as a regional mediator. Further confirmation of Qatar's growing stature in regional affairs was provided by the emirate's presence at a four-nation summit, also involving Syria, France and Turkey, in Damascus, Syria, in September. Qatari mediators were also involved in efforts during 2008 to conclude a peace agreement between participants in the conflict in Darfur, Sudan. Talks between Darfur-based rebel group the Sudan Justice and Equality Movement and the Government of Sudan, which were sponsored by the African Union and the Arab League, were held in Doha in February 2009 and resulted in the signing of a confidence-building agreement intended to lead to broader peace negotiations.

Qatar hosted the 21st regular Arab League summit in Doha in late March 2009. The summit's agenda was overshadowed by the attendance of the Sudanese President, Lt-Gen. Omar al-Bashir, who was invited in defiance of a warrant for his arrest for alleged war crimes in Darfur, issued by the International Criminal Court (ICC) earlier that month. Qatar is not a signatory to the 2002 Rome Statute establishing the ICC and rejected the Court's request for co-operation with the warrant. Immediately after the Arab League summit, Doha hosted the second summit of Arab-South American countries, which was attended by almost all the relevant heads of state and aimed to promote political and economic co-operation between the two regions.

The Ethiopian authorities accused Qatar of promoting instability in the Horn of Africa in April 2008, alleging that Qatar's relationship with Eritrea was a threat to Ethiopia's national security. Ethiopia broke off diplomatic relations, while Qatar strongly denied the allegations.

Qatar and Singapore were engaged in discussions on a free trade agreement (FTA) during 2006–07, and Singapore established an embassy in Doha for the first time in December 2006. A joint economic committee and a Qatar-Singapore Business Forum were created in 2007, leading to increased co-operation in business, technology and training. However, in accordance with the GCC's policy that its members should pursue FTAs at GCC-level, the Qatar-Singapore FTA became the template for a

GCC-Singapore FTA, which was signed in Doha in December 2008. The agreement, which covered trade in goods and services, investment, e-commerce and government procurement, was expected to boost trading opportunities not only between the Gulf states and Singapore, but also with fast-growing Asian markets in general.

During a state visit to the People's Republic of China by the Qatari Prime Minister and Minister of Foreign Affairs, Sheikh Hamad, in April 2008, economic relations were augmented through an agreement for Qatar, as the largest producer of LNG globally, to supply annual shipments of 2m. metric tons of LNG to China's largest offshore oil producer, the China National Offshore Oil Corporation. A separate contract, incorporating the purchase of 3m. tons of LNG per year from Qatargas by Petro-China over a period of 25 years, was also signed between the two companies and Shell of the United Kingdom during Sheikh Hamad's discussions with Chinese President Hu Jintao as part of enhanced Qatari-Chinese investment and co-operative initiatives.

Relations between Qatar and India have strengthened considerably in recent years. Sheikh Hamad visited India in 2005, followed by Prime Minister ath-Thani in 2006. Between 2004 and 2007 the volume of trade between the two countries increased three-fold; by 2008 Qatar was the largest supplier of LNG to India, exporting around 5m. metric tons annually, while there were an estimated 300,000 Indians living and working in Qatar. During an official visit to Doha by Indian Prime Minister Manmohan Singh in November 2008, two security co-operation agreements were signed, covering matters such as maritime security, intelligence sharing and law enforcement.

Government

According to the provisional Constitution that took effect in 1970, Qatar is an absolute monarchy, with full powers vested in the Amir as Head of State. Executive power is exercised by the Council of Ministers, appointed by the Head of State. An Advisory Council was formed in April 1972, with 20 nominated members (expanded to 30 in 1975 and to 35 in 1988). The Advisory Council's constitutional entitlements include the power to debate legislation drafted by the Council of Ministers before ratification and promulgation. It also has the power to request ministerial statements on matters of general and specific policy, including the draft budget. In March 1999 elections took place, by universal adult suffrage, for a 29-member Central Municipal Council, which was to have a consultative role in the operations of the Ministry of Municipal Affairs and Agriculture; further elections were held in April 2003 and April 2007. The Amir formally adopted a new Constitution following its approval at a referendum held on 29 April 2003. Under the Constitution, the Amir is to remain head of the executive, while a 45-member unicameral parliament, of which two-thirds are to be directly elected (the remainder being appointed by the Amir), is to have the powers, *inter alia*, to legislate, review the state budget and monitor government policy. However, elections to the new legislature, after which the Advisory Council was to be abolished, were repeatedly postponed, most recently owing to the need to introduce an appropriate legal framework. A new electoral law was duly adopted by the Advisory Council in May 2008 and was awaiting ratification by the Amir in early 2009.

Defence

As assessed at November 2008, the armed forces comprised 11,800 men: army 8,500; navy 1,800 (including Marine Police); air force 1,500. In September 2006 Qatar became the first Arab nation to contribute personnel to the UN Interim Force in Lebanon (UNIFIL); Qatar's 200-strong contingent was largely withdrawn in February 2008, leaving only three Qatari officers deployed in Lebanon. Government expenditure on defence was budgeted at an estimated QR 4,000m. in 2007.

Economic Affairs

In 1997, according to estimates by the World Bank, Qatar's gross national income (GNI), measured at average 1995–97 prices, was US $11,627m., equivalent to $22,147 per head. According to unofficial sources, GNI totalled $17,150m. in 2001 and $17,490m. in 2002 (equivalent to some $28,300 per head). During 2000–07, it was estimated, the population increased at an average annual rate of 4.4%, while gross domestic product (GDP) per head increased, in real terms, by an average of 2.9% per year. Non-Qataris accounted for some 80% of the total population by the beginning of the 21st century. Overall GDP was estimated to have increased, in real terms, at an average rate of 10.4% per year in 2000–07; according to official figures, real GDP growth was 6.1% in 2005 and 12.2% in 2006.

Agriculture (including fishing) contributed an estimated 0.1% of GDP in 2008, and the sector engaged some 2.3% of the employed population in October 2007. All agricultural land is owned by the Government, and most farm managers are immigrants employing a largely expatriate work-force. The main crops are cereals (principally barley), vegetables and dates. Qatar is self-sufficient in winter vegetables and nearly self-sufficient in summer vegetables. Some vegetables are exported to other Gulf countries. The Government has prioritized education in agricultural techniques and experimentation with unconventional methods of cultivation (including the use of sea water and solar energy to produce sand-based crops). Livestock-rearing and fishing are also practised. The GDP of the agricultural sector was estimated to have declined at an average annual rate of 4.5% during 1993–2002, but increased by an average annual rate of 2.9% during 2002–06. Real agricultural GDP increased by an estimated 11.2% in 2003 and by 1.0% in 2004. The sector's contribution to GDP, in real terms, remained constant in 2005 and 2006.

Industry (including mining, manufacturing, construction and power) contributed 73.7% of GDP in 2008, and the sector engaged 51.8% of the employed population in October 2007. Industrial GDP was estimated to have increased by an average of 9.8% per year during 1993–2002, and by an average of 8.1% per year in 2002–06. According to official figures, growth in the sector's real GDP was 16.1% in 2004, 5.2% in 2005 and 7.2% in 2006.

The mining and quarrying sector (comprising principally the extraction and processing of petroleum and natural gas) provided 60.7% of GDP in 2008, and engaged just 5.3% of the employed population in October 2007. Petroleum is currently the major mineral export. Proven recoverable petroleum reserves at the end of 2007 were 27,400m. barrels, sufficient to maintain production for almost 63 years at 2007 levels—averaging some 1,197,000 barrels per day (b/d). As a member of the Organization of the Petroleum Exporting Countries (OPEC, see p. 386), Qatar is subject to production quotas agreed by the Organization's Conference. Proven gas reserves were 25,600,000m. cu m at the end of 2007 (representing 14.4% of known world reserves at that date—behind only Russia and Iran), primarily located in the North Field, the world's largest gas reserve not associated with petroleum. The real GDP of the mining and quarrying sector was estimated to have increased at an average annual rate of 11.7% in 1993–2002, and of 6.0% in 2002–06. According to official figures, growth in the sector was 18.0% in 2004, 0.6% in 2005 and 5.4% in 2006.

Manufacturing contributed 6.7% of GDP in 2008 (excluding activities related to petroleum and natural gas), and the sector engaged 8.7% of the employed population in October 2007. The principal manufacturing activities are linked to the country's oil and gas resources—petroleum refining and the production of liquefied natural gas (LNG—developed as part of the North Field project), together with industrial chemicals (particularly fertilizers) and steel production. Manufacturing GDP (excluding hydrocarbons) was estimated to have increased by an average of 4.5% per year in 1993–2002, and by an average of 7.7% per year in 2002–06. According to official figures, the sector's real GDP increased by 6.5% in 2004, by 12.6% in 2005 and by 4.8% in 2006.

Electrical energy is derived almost exclusively from Qatar's natural gas resource. Solar energy is being developed in conjunction with desalination.

The services sector contributed 26.2% of GDP in 2008, and engaged 45.8% of the employed population in October 2007. The establishment in March 2005 of the Qatar Financial Centre, which was to provide a hub for the emirate's financial services sector, had reportedly proved popular with investors by early 2006 and was expected to stimulate further activity in the sector. The GDP of the services sector was estimated to have increased by an average of 6.1% per year in 1993–2002, and by an average of 13.6% per year in 2002–06. According to official figures, services GDP increased by 27.2% in 2004, by 8.6% in 2005 and by 20.4% in 2006.

According to preliminary official figures for 2007, Qatar recorded a visible trade surplus of QR 80,793m., while there was a surplus of QR 38,022m. on the current account of the balance of payments. In 2007 the principal source of imports (11.4% of the total value) was the USA; other important suppliers in that year were Italy (10.2%), Japan, Germany and the United Arab Emirates (UAE). In the same year Japan took 40.6% of Qatar's exports by value (excluding re-exports); the Republic of

Korea and Singapore were also significant markets for exports in 2007. The principal exports are petroleum and gas and their derivatives (mineral fuels and oils provided 90.7% of domestic export revenues in 2007). The principal imports in 2007 were machinery and electrical equipment (39.5% of the total value of imports), iron and steel products (15.4%) and road vehicles.

In the financial year ending 31 March 2008 Qatar recorded an estimated budget surplus of QR 38,055m. According to the IMF, the annual rate of inflation averaged 6.3% in 2000–07; consumer prices increased by an average of 13.8% in 2007. The Qatari economy is heavily dependent on immigrant workers, owing to a shortage of indigenous labour; 88.5% of the employed population were non-Qataris at the census of March 2004.

Other than its membership of OPEC, Qatar is a member of the Organization of Arab Petroleum Exporting Countries (OAPEC, see p. 379), the Co-operation Council for the Arab States of the Gulf (GCC, see p. 229), the Arab Fund for Economic and Social Development (AFESD, see p. 183), the Arab Monetary Fund (see p. 184) and the Islamic Development Bank (see p. 340). GCC member states created a unified regional customs tariff in January 2003, and have undertaken to establish a single market and currency no later than January 2010. The economic convergence criteria for the proposed monetary union were agreed at a heads of state meeting in Abu Dhabi, the UAE, in December 2005, and in January 2008 the GCC launched its common market.

Although petroleum remains Qatar's principal export, the generation of income through sales of LNG since 1997 must be considered the emirate's most notable achievement in recent years. Qatar has become the largest exporter of LNG, with exports in 2007 valued at US $10,524m., and production set to increase from some 30m. metric tons per year (t/y) in 2008 to 77m. t/y by 2012. Efforts have also been made to expand petroleum production capacity (which was expected to reach 1m. b/d by the end of 2009—considerably in excess of Qatar's recent OPEC production quotas). Although extensive investment in oil and gas projects from the mid-1990s led to a succession of budgetary deficits and the accumulation of an external debt equivalent to some 90% of GDP by the end of 2002, revenue from the gas industry (particularly LNG) ensured the prompt dispatch of debt; since the 2000/01 financial year successive fiscal surpluses have been recorded, and by late 2006 external debt was equivalent to less than 40% of GDP. Major infrastructure projects were undertaken in Doha prior to the holding of the 2006 Asian Games tournament, while there was significant investment in multipurpose complexes such as Entertainment City (due for completion in 2015–16), comprising residential, commercial and leisure facilities, covering an area of more than 1m. sq m. In response to an anticipated increase in tourism arrivals and migrant labour following the establishment of the GCC common market, investment was directed at the construction of a new airport and at boosting hotel capacity. The nation's greater wealth, however, has been accompanied by higher inflation. Consumer prices rose by an annual average of 15% in 2008, the highest in the region, and Qatar's chances of joining the GCC single currency appeared bleak. The Government announced in mid-2008 that it would neither devalue its currency nor remove the dollar peg to curb inflation; however, a series of measures were adopted, including subsidies for diesel and a three-year price freeze on raw materials such as cement and steel. Strong GDP growth was anticipated for 2009.

Education

A state education system was introduced in 1956. Education is free at all levels, although not compulsory. In the 2006/07 academic year, at the primary, preparatory and general secondary levels, there was a combined total of 49,717 students in government schools, 57,921 students in private schools, 27,677 students in independent schools and 1,362 students at the Qatar Foundation for Education, Science and Community Development and the Academy for Sports Excellence. Primary education begins at six years of age and lasts for six years. The next level of education, beginning at the age of 12, is divided into two cycles of three years (preparatory and secondary). In 2006/07 94.3% of children in the relevant age-group were enrolled at primary schools, while the comparable ratio for secondary enrolment was 92.6%. In late 2004 12 government-funded schools were leased to private operators in an attempt to improve educational standards. There are specialized religious, industrial, commercial and technical secondary schools for boys; the technical school admitted its first students in 1999/2000, as did two scientific secondary schools (one for girls). In 2006/07 there were 8,088 undergraduate students, 96 postgraduate students and a teaching staff of 504 (excluding teaching assistants) at the University of Qatar. The Qatar Foundation for Education, Science and Community Development, established in 1995, is involved in various programmes to develop educational and research facilities, including through partnerships with international institutions. Education City Qatar, the foundation's flagship project, which opened in October 2003, hosts branch campuses of five US universities and numerous other educational and research institutions. A Science and Technology Park, designed to establish Qatar as a regional hub for research and development, was officially opened at Education City in February 2009, following investment of some US $800m. Government expenditure on education in 2007/08 amounted to an estimated QR 4,362m. (equivalent to 5.1% of total expenditure).

Public Holidays

2009: 27 June (Anniversary of the Amir's Accession), 19 July* (Leilat al-Meiraj, Ascension of the Prophet), 22 August* (Ramadan begins), 20 September* (Id al-Fitr, end of Ramadan), 27 November* (Id al-Adha, Feast of the Sacrifice), 18 December* (Islamic New Year and National Day).

2010: 27 June (Anniversary of the Amir's Accession), 8 July* (Leilat al-Meiraj, Ascension of the Prophet), 11 August* (Ramadan begins), 10 September* (Id al-Fitr, end of Ramadan), 16 November* (Id al-Adha, Feast of the Sacrifice), 7 December* (Islamic New Year), 18 December* (National Day).

*These holidays are dependent on the Islamic lunar calendar and may differ by one or two days from the dates given.

Weights and Measures

The metric system has been adopted legally, but imperial measures are still used.

QATAR

Statistical Survey

Source (unless otherwise stated): Dept of Economic Policies, Qatar Central Bank, POB 1234, Doha; tel. 4456456; fax 4413650; e-mail elzainys@qcb.gov.qa; internet www.qcb.gov.qa; Qatar Statistics Authority, POB 7283, Doha; tel. 4958888; fax 4839999; e-mail customer_services@planning.gov.qa; internet www.qsa.gov.qa.

Area and Population

AREA, POPULATION AND DENSITY

Area (sq km)	11,493*
Population (census results)	
1 March 1997	522,023
1 March 2004	
Males	496,382
Females	247,647
Total	744,029
Population (official estimate at mid-year)†	
2007	1,226,210
2008	1,448,449
Density (per sq km) at mid-2008	126.0

* 4,437 sq miles.
† Including resident workers from abroad.

PRINCIPAL TOWNS
(estimated population of municipalities at March 2006)

Ar-Rayyan	347,349	Umm Said (Mesaieed)		14,922
Ad-Dawhah (Doha, the capital)	310,683	Jaryan al-Batna		12,831
Al-Khawr (Al-Khor)	50,917	Al-Jemailiya		11,308
Al-Wakrah	43,958	Ash-Shamal		4,873
Umm Salal	34,568	Al-Ghuwiairiya		3,345

BIRTHS, MARRIAGES AND DEATHS

	Registered live births Number	Rate (per 1,000)	Registered marriages Number	Rate (per 1,000)	Registered deaths Number	Rate (per 1,000)
2000	11,250	18.2	2,096	3.4	1,173	1.9
2001	12,118	18.7	2,194	3.4	1,210	1.9
2002	12,200	17.9	2,351	3.4	1,220	1.8
2003	12,856	17.9	2,550	3.6	1,311	1.8
2004	13,190	17.5	2,649	3.5	1,341	1.8
2005	13,401	16.8	2,734	3.4	1,545	1.9
2006	14,120	16.8	3,019	3.6	1,750	2.1
2007	15,681	12.8	3,206	2.6	1,776	1.5

Life expectancy (years at birth, WHO estimates): 77.0 (males 77.0; females 77.0) in 2006 (Source: WHO, *World Health Statistics*).

ECONOMICALLY ACTIVE POPULATION
(population aged 15 years and over, labour force sample survey, October 2007)

	Qatari	Non-Qatari	Total
Agriculture, hunting and forestry	0	15,854	15,854
Fishing	10	3,571	3,581
Mining and quarrying	5,225	38,609	43,834
Manufacturing	942	70,996	71,938
Electricity, gas and water	1,421	4,085	5,506
Construction	407	307,373	307,780
Wholesale and retail trade; repair of motor vehicles, motorcycles and personal and household goods	941	100,730	101,671
Hotels and restaurants	42	16,179	16,221
Transport, storage and communications	1,469	34,629	36,098
Financial intermediation	1,540	7,484	9,024
Real estate, renting and business activities	341	28,131	28,472
Public administration	32,087	20,862	52,949

—continued	Qatari	Non-Qatari	Total
Education	11,285	15,067	26,352
Health and social work	3,968	17,174	21,142
Other community, social and personal service activities	1,979	10,857	12,836
Private households with employed persons	15	72,765	72,780
Extra-territorial organizations and bodies	35	1,729	1,764
Total employed	61,707	766,095	827,802
Unemployed	2,049	2,254	4,303
Total labour force	63,756	768,349	832,105
Males	41,119	687,322	728,441
Females	22,637	81,027	103,664

Health and Welfare

KEY INDICATORS

Total fertility rate (children per woman, 2006)	2.7
Under-5 mortality rate (per 1,000 live births, 2006)	11
Physicians (per 1,000 head, 2005)	2.6
Hospital beds (per 1,000 head, 2006)	2.5
Health expenditure (2006): US $ per head (PPP)	1,426
Health expenditure (2006): % of GDP	4.3
Health expenditure (2006): public (% of total)	78.1
Human Development Index (2006): ranking	34
Human Development Index (2006): value	0.899

For sources and definitions, see explanatory note on p. vi.

Agriculture

PRINCIPAL CROPS
('000 metric tons)

	2005	2006	2007
Barley	4.9	4.9*	5.0*
Cauliflowers and broccoli	1.1	1.2*	1.2*
Pumpkins, squash and gourds	1.3	1.3*	1.4*
Aubergines (Eggplants)	3.1	3.2*	3.2*
Chillies and peppers, green*	0.3	0.3	0.3
Onions, dry	3.0	3.0*	3.0*
Tomatoes	5.3	5.4*	5.4*
Cantaloupes and other melons*	4.3	4.3	4.3
Dates	19.8	20.0*	21.0*

* FAO estimate(s).

Aggregate production ('000 metric tons, may include official, semi-official or estimated data): Total cereals 7.1 in 2005, 7.1 in 2006, 7.2 in 2007; Total fruits (excl. melons) 20.9 in 2005, 21.0 in 2006, 22.0 in 2007; Total vegetables (incl. melons) 22.8 in 2005, 25.1 in 2006, 25.4 in 2007.

Source: FAO.

QATAR

LIVESTOCK
('000 head, year ending September)

	2005	2006	2007
Horses	2.0	2.0*	2.1*
Cattle	6.6	7.5*	8.0*
Camels	13.8	14.0*	14.0*
Sheep	111.6	115.0*	120.0*
Goats	152.7	155.0*	160.0*
Chickens*	4,500	4,500	4,500

* FAO estimate(s).
Source: FAO.

LIVESTOCK PRODUCTS
('000 metric tons)

	2005	2006	2007
Camel meat*	1.1	1.1	1.1
Sheep meat*	4.0	4.1	4.2
Chicken meat*	4.9	5.0	5.0
Cows' milk*	4.5	4.8	5.1
Camels' milk*	4.5	4.6	4.6
Goats' milk*	5.7	5.7	6.0
Hen eggs	4.1	4.2*	4.2*

* FAO estimate(s).
Source: FAO.

Fishing
('000 metric tons, live weight)

	2004	2005	2006
Capture	11.1	13.9	16.4
Groupers	1.3	2.1	1.7
Grunts and sweetlips	0.8	0.8	1.0
Emperors (Scavengers)	3.7	4.2	5.5
Narrow-barred Spanish mackerel	1.5	1.9	2.0
Aquaculture	—	—	0.0
Total catch	11.1	13.9	16.4

Source: FAO.

Mining

	2004	2005	2006
Crude petroleum ('000 barrels)*	270,000	280,000	295,000
Natural gas (million cu ft)	718,300	612,100	546,400

* Source: US Geological Survey.

2007: Crude petroleum 299m. barrels (Source: US Geological Survey).

Industry

SELECTED PRODUCTS
('000 metric tons unless otherwise indicated)

	2004	2005	2006
Ammonia (for fertilizer)	1,737.2	2,133.8	2,170.2
Urea (for fertilizer)	2,238.7	2,978.8	2,908.9
Organic fertilizers	24	42	57
Cement	1,202	1,182	2,169
'Super' petrol (motor spirit—gasoline)	801.0	754.6	889.4
'Premium' petrol (motor spirit—gasoline)	857.9	901.7	1,004.7
Jet fuel (incl. kerosene)	957.7	905.5	1,087.1
Gas diesel (distillate fuel) oils	995.1	925.6	997.9
Residual fuel oils	250.7	418.3	614.6
Liquefied petroleum gas	127.6	131.0	217.0
Natural gas condensate	1,545.1	1,556.1	1,667.9
Butane	963.0	1,075.4	1,151.8
Propane	1,242.6	1,403.1	1,576.2
Electric energy (million kWh)	12,992.6	14,395.9	14,983.2

Finance

CURRENCY AND EXCHANGE RATES

Monetary Units
100 dirhams = 1 Qatar riyal (QR).

Sterling, Dollar and Euro Equivalents (31 December 2008)
£1 sterling = 5.306 riyals;
US $1 = 3.640 riyals;
€1 = 5.066 riyals;
100 Qatar riyals = £18.85 = $27.47 = €19.74.

Average Exchange Rate

Note: Since June 1980 the official mid-point rate has been fixed at US $1 = QR 3.64.

BUDGET
(QR million, year ending 31 March)

Revenue	2005/06	2006/07*	2007/08*
Petroleum and natural gas	43,616	54,919	70,120
Investments	14,233	20,644	30,370
Other	7,135	9,435	14,970
Total	64,984	84,998	115,460

Expenditure	2005/06	2006/07*	2007/08*
Current expenditure	32,761	49,444	48,357
Wages and salaries	6,657	12,971	13,613
Interest payments	1,922	1,938	1,550
Supplies and services	1,008	1,076	6,166
Other	23,174	33,459	27,028
Development expenditure	18,072	16,912	29,048
Total	50,833	66,356	77,405

* Preliminary.
Source: Ministry of Economy and Finance, Doha.

INTERNATIONAL RESERVES
(US $ million at 31 December)

	2006	2007	2008
Gold (national valuation)	12.2	335.2	348.1
IMF special drawing rights	40.4	44.4	45.2
Reserve position in IMF	35.2	27.0	51.3
Foreign exchange	5,307.1	9,345.0	9,553.0
Total	5,394.9	9,751.6	9,997.6

Source: IMF, *International Financial Statistics*.

QATAR

MONEY SUPPLY
(QR million at 31 December)

	2006	2007	2008
Currency outside banks	3,959	4,487	5,368
Demand deposits at commercial banks	23,924	30,887	38,061
Total money	27,883	35,374	43,429

Source: IMF, *International Financial Statistics*.

COST OF LIVING
(Consumer Price Index; base: 2001 = 100)

	2005	2006	2007
Food, beverages and tobacco	107.5	115.4	123.9
Clothing and footwear	101.8	114.5	128.9
Rent, fuel and energy	176.2	221.9	287.0
Transport and communication	99.7	101.6	103.5
All items (incl. others)	119.1	133.2	151.6

NATIONAL ACCOUNTS
(QR million at current prices)

Expenditure on the Gross Domestic Product

	2004	2005	2006
Government final consumption expenditure	15,094	17,769	29,923
Private final consumption expenditure	20,166	28,165	41,988
Increase in stocks	3,756	2,953	4,012
Gross fixed capital formation	34,810	51,887	70,745
Total domestic expenditure	73,826	100,774	146,668
Exports of goods and services	74,122	105,497	139,208
Less Imports of goods and services	32,434	51,706	79,233
GDP in purchasers' values	115,512	154,564	206,644
GDP at constant 2001 prices	85,524	90,726	101,822

Gross Domestic Product by Economic Activity

	2006	2007	2008
Agriculture and fishing	233	250	268
Mining and quarrying*	118,443	146,476	229,729
Manufacturing	15,875	19,179	25,390
Electricity, gas and water	3,513	4,329	5,456
Construction	11,991	14,634	18,166
Trade, restaurants and hotels	9,452	12,002	13,311
Transport and communications	7,159	9,803	12,274
Finance, insurance, real estate and business services	21,392	31,865	37,019
Government services	19,271	20,828	32,755
Social services	1,719	2,264	2,409
Other services	1,143	1,237	1,378
Sub-total	210,191	262,866	378,155
Import duties	2,462	2,703	3,316
Less Imputed bank service charge	6,009	6,978	9,087
GDP in purchasers' values	206,644	258,591	372,384

* Including services incidental to mining of petroleum and natural gas.

BALANCE OF PAYMENTS
(QR million)

	2005	2006	2007*
Exports of goods f.o.b.	93,773	123,945	152,951
Crude petroleum	46,749	58,171	69,820
Natural gas liquids	28,899	43,121	53,859
Imports of goods f.o.b.	−32,992	−53,911	−72,158
Trade balance	60,781	70,034	80,793
Exports of services	11,723	15,263	13,075
Imports of services	−15,085	−25,322	−26,637
Balance on goods and services	57,419	59,975	67,231
Other income received	5,139	7,207	4,978
Other income paid	−25,944	−19,148	−20,408
Balance on goods, services and income	36,614	48,034	51,801
Current transfers (net)	−9,380	−13,604	−13,779
Expatriates' remittances	−10,945	−14,252	−16,264
Current balance	27,234	34,430	38,022
Capital account (net)	−2,742	−3,608	−4,118
Financial account (net)	−1,579	−16,731	6,098
Net errors and omissions	−6,594	5,709	6,090
Overall balance	16,319	19,800	46,092

*Preliminary.

Source: Qatar Central Bank.

External Trade

PRINCIPAL COMMODITIES
(distribution by HS, QR million, preliminary)

Imports	2005	2006	2007
Live animals; animal products	953.8	1,080.5	1,367.6
Mineral products	1,222.2	1,720.5	2,572.7
Chemical products, etc.	2,053.7	2,517.6	3,255.1
Base metals and articles of base metal	6,160.5	11,764.1	16,158.7
Articles of iron and steel	4,871.9	9,001.8	12,343.7
Machinery and electrical equipment	12,176.0	21,593.5	31,599.9
Boilers, machinery and mechanical appliances and other apparatus (such as nuclear reactors)	8,175.4	14,121.8	21,232.1
Electrical machinery and equipment; sound and television recorders and reproducers	4,000.7	7,471.7	10,367.8
Vehicles, vessels, aircraft and other transport equipment	5,808.6	9,448.7	11,027.0
Vehicles other than trains, vessels and air and spacecraft	5,184.2	8,825.9	9,580.4
Total (incl. others)	36,621.0	59,841.4	80,097.0

Exports*	2005	2006	2007
Mineral products	83,330.5	111,292.1	137,080.9
Mineral fuels and oils, and products thereof	83,222.6	111,206.4	136,916.4
Chemical products, etc.	4,873.6	5,530.6	7,247.9
Plastics, rubber and articles thereof	2,308.2	4,101.6	4,974.8
Plastics and articles thereof	2,307.8	4,101.4	4,974.6
Total (incl. others)	92,233.6	122,401.7	151,025.2

*Excluding re-exports (QR million): 1,540.2 in 2005; 1,546.7 in 2006; 1,927.5 in 2007.

QATAR

PRINCIPAL TRADING PARTNERS
(QR million)

Imports	2005	2006	2007
Australia	450.9	757.8	857.2
Belgium	437.1	881.0	784.0
Brazil	431.9	543.9	270.9
China, People's Republic	1,892.3	3,482.8	4,660.2
France	1,547.3	2,311.6	2,881.9
Germany	3,361.9	5,581.0	6,209.5
India	1,411.7	1,642.0	2,276.1
Indonesia	381.6	475.2	779.4
Italy	2,364.7	5,543.3	8,229.2
Japan	4,263.0	7,182.8	7,982.5
Korea, Republic	1,657.8	3,278.4	4,862.8
Malaysia	434.9	857.6	1,135.0
Saudi Arabia	2,093.1	3,054.9	3,924.6
Singapore	410.1	583.8	1,191.8
Spain	417.3	580.9	879.4
Switzerland	510.0	883.2	1,113.0
Thailand	522.6	935.7	1,077.9
Turkey	253.9	1,217.0	1,716.4
United Arab Emirates	2,355.9	3,606.5	5,632.3
United Kingdom	2,096.3	2,985.0	3,769.4
USA	4,232.4	5,899.6	9,120.5
Total (incl. others)	36,621.0	59,841.1	80,097.0

Exports*	2005	2006	2007
Belgium	56.5	345.4	2,194.5
China, People's Republic	1,369.1	1,449.6	1,219.2
India	3,203.4	6,035.6	9,720.2
Japan	37,502.3	51,387.5	62,072.2
Korea, Republic	14,770.9	17,198.5	26,698.2
Pakistan	752.9	1,363.9	1,714.4
Philippines	1,092.2	600.6	1,377.7
Singapore	7,657.9	11,715.4	17,293.7
Spain	892.2	3,050.9	3,410.0
Taiwan	2,381.6	1,943.6	1,849.8
Thailand	1,893.8	3,389.5	7,003.1
United Arab Emirates	3,822.4	5,355.0	5,693.1
USA	1,133.4	529.5	1,065.1
Total (incl. others)	92,233.6	123,945.0	152,951.0

* Excluding re-exports (QR million, preliminary): 1,540.2 in 2005; 1,546.7 in 2006; 1,927.5 in 2007.

Transport

ROAD TRAFFIC
(registered vehicles)

	2004	2005	2006
Private cars	265,609	293,355	337,056
Other private transport	114,115	126,541	148,436
Heavy equipment	11,162	13,262	17,438
Motorcycles and mopeds	4,420	4,698	5,048
Total (incl. others)	406,626	451,388	525,795

SHIPPING

Merchant Fleet
(vessels registered at 31 December)

	2005	2006	2007
Number of vessels	80	86	84
Total displacement ('000 grt)	570.1	652.3	619.5

Source: Lloyd's Register-Fairplay, *World Fleet Statistics*.

INTERNATIONAL SEA-BORNE FREIGHT TRAFFIC
(2003)

	Traffic
Doha Port	
Vessels entered and cleared	751
Containers	272
Capacity ('000 grt)	1,258
Umm Said (Mesaieed) Port	
Vessels entered and cleared	1,557
Tankers	633
Containers	604
Capacity ('000 grt)	53,189
Halul Port	
Vessels entered and cleared	109
Tankers	109
Capacity ('000 grt)	15,881
Ras Laffan Port	
Vessels entered and cleared	617
Tankers	342
Capacity ('000 grt)	36,675
Total	
Vessels entered and cleared	3,034
Tankers	1,084
Containers	876
Capacity ('000 grt)	118,324

CIVIL AVIATION
(Doha International Airport)

	2004	2005	2006
Aircraft arrivals	49,614	60,828	67,472
Passenger arrivals ('000)*	2,790	3,654	4,424
Passengers in transit ('000)	1,589	2,185	4,573
Cargo and mail received (metric tons)	102,455	127,042	161,759
Cargo and mail dispatched (metric tons)	61,047	83,554	105,760

* Excluding private aircraft.

Tourism

TOURIST ARRIVALS
(arrivals of non-resident tourists in hotels and similar establishments)

Region of residence	2004	2005	2006
Asia	145,974	159,279	180,543
Europe	195,732	233,315	201,187
Middle East	295,335	364,977	413,523
Total (incl. others)	732,454	912,997	945,970

Tourism receipts (US $ million, excl. passenger transport): 498 in 2004; 760 in 2005; 374 in 2006.

Source: World Tourism Organization.

Communications Media

	2005	2006	2007
Telephones ('000 main lines in use)	205.4	228.3	237.4
Mobile cellular telephones ('000 in use)	716.8	919.8	1,264.4
Internet users ('000)	219.0	289.9	351.0
Broadband subscribers ('000)	25.1	46.8	70.3

Personal computers: 133,000 in use in 2004.

Source: International Telecommunication Union.

Newspapers: *Daily:* 5 titles in 2004; total circulation 90,000 in 1996. *Weekly:* 2 titles in 2001; total circulation 7,000 in 1995 (Source: UNESCO).

Book Production: 209 titles in 1996 (Source: UNESCO).

Education

(2006/07)

	Teachers	Males	Females	Total
Government schools	6,360	21,821	27,987	49,808
Pre-primary	12	40	51	91
Primary	3,224	11,417	12,322	23,739
Preparatory	1,505	4,623	7,543	12,166
General secondary	1,619	5,741	8,071	13,812
Private schools	5,602	40,160	33,137	73,297
Pre-primary	364	7,982	7,394	15,376
Primary	717	20,592	16,414	37,006
Preparatory	612	6,552	5,334	11,886
General secondary	3,909	5,034	3,995	9,029
Independent schools	2,333	15,541	13,795	29,336
Pre-primary	—*	737	922	1,659
Primary	1,177	6,335	7,719	14,054
Preparatory	718	5,339	3,193	8,532
General secondary	438	3,130	1,961	5,091
Qatar Foundation and Aspire†	223	970	681	1,651
Pre-primary	16	152	137	289
Primary	71	330	322	652
Preparatory	78	261	105	366
General secondary	58	227	117	344
Total	14,518	78,492	75,600	154,092
Pre-primary	392	8,911	8,504	17,415
Primary	5,189	38,674	36,777	75,451
Preparatory	2,913	16,775	16,175	32,950
General secondary	6,024	14,132	14,144	28,276
University of Qatar	504‡	2,198	5,986	8,184

* Included in primary.
† Comprising the Qatar Foundation for Education, Science and Community Development (including the Qatar Academy and the Qatar Leadership Academy and Learning Centre) and the Academy for Sports Excellence (Aspire).
‡ Excluding teaching assistants and administrators.

Note: General secondary includes specialized secondary education.

Institutions (2006/07): Government 164; Private 291; Independent 65.

Directory

The Constitution

According to the provisional Constitution adopted on 2 April 1970, executive power was vested in the Amir, as Head of State, and exercised by the Council of Ministers, appointed by the Head of State. The Amir was assisted by the appointed Advisory Council of 20 members (increased to 30 in 1975 and to 35 in 1988), whose term was extended for six years in 1975, for a further four years in 1978, and for further four-year terms in 1982, 1986, 1990, 1994 and 1998. Most recently, the Council's term was renewed for a further two years in July 2008. All fundamental democratic rights were guaranteed. In 1975 the Advisory Council was granted the power to summon individual ministers to answer questions on legislation before promulgation. In March 1999 elections took place, by universal adult suffrage, for a 29-member Central Municipal Council, which was to have a consultative role in the operations of the Ministry of Municipal Affairs and Agriculture. The Amir formally adopted a new Constitution following a referendum held on 29 April 2003. Under this Constitution, the Amir was to remain head of the executive, while a 45-member unicameral parliament, of which two-thirds was to be directly elected (the remainder being appointed by the Amir), was to have the powers to legislate, review the state budget, monitor government policy and hold ministers accountable for their actions. The parliament was to have a four-year mandate. Suffrage was to be extended to all citizens, including women, aged 18 years and above. Elections to the new legislature, after which the Advisory Council was to be abolished, were initially expected to be conducted in 2004; however, owing to alleged difficulties pertaining to the electoral roll, they were subsequently deferred, pending the introduction of a new electoral law. Such a law was adopted by the Advisory Council in May 2008 and was awaiting ratification by the Amir in early 2009. The Constitution guarantees freedom of association, expression and religious affiliation, and provides for the establishment of an independent judiciary; however, it does not authorize political parties.

The Government

HEAD OF STATE

Amir: Maj.-Gen. Sheikh Hamad bin Khalifa ath-Thani (assumed power 27 June 1995).

Crown Prince and Commander-in-Chief of the Armed Forces: Sheikh Tamim bin Hamad bin Khalifa ath-Thani.

COUNCIL OF MINISTERS
(April 2009)

Amir and Minister of Defence: Maj.-Gen. Sheikh Hamad bin Khalifa ath-Thani.

Prime Minister and Minister of Foreign Affairs: Sheikh Hamad bin Jasim bin Jaber ath-Thani.

Deputy Prime Minister and Minister of Energy and Industry: Abdullah bin Hamad al-Attiya.

Minister of Economy and Finance: Yousuf Hussain Kamal.

Minister of Business and Trade: (vacant).

Minister of the Interior: Sheikh Abdullah bin Khalid ath-Thani.

Minister of Awqaf (Religious Endowments) and Islamic Affairs: Ahmad bin Abdullah al-Marri.

Minister of Municipal Affairs and Urban Planning: Sheikh Abd ar-Rahman bin Khalifa bin Abd al-Aziz ath-Thani.

Minister of the Environment: Abdullah bin Mubarak bin Aboud al-Midhadhi.

QATAR

Minister of Justice: HASSAN BIN ABDULLAH AL-GHANEM.

Minister of Education and Higher Education: SAAD BIN IBRAHIM AL-MAHMOUD.

Minister of Labour: Dr SULTAN BIN HASSAN ADH-DHABIT AD-DOUSARY.

Minister of Social Affairs: NASSER BIN ABDULLAH AL-HEMAIDI.

Minister of Public Health: ABDULLAH BIN KHALID AL-QAHTANI.

Minister of Culture, Arts and Heritage: Dr HAMAD BIN ABD AL-AZIZ AL-KAWARI.

Minister of State for Foreign Affairs: AHMAD BIN ABDULLAH AL-MAHMOUD.

Minister of State for the Interior: Sheikh ABDULLAH BIN NASSER BIN KHALIFA ATH-THANI.

Minister of State for Energy and Industrial Affairs: Dr MUHAMMAD SALEH AS-SADA.

Minister of State for International Co-operation: Dr KHALID BIN MUHAMMAD AL-ATTIYA.

Minister of State for Cabinet Affairs: Sheikh NASSER BIN MUHAMMAD ABD AL-AZIZ ATH-THANI.

Minister of State without Portfolio: Sheikh MUHAMMAD BIN KHALID ATH-THANI.

MINISTRIES

Ministry of Awqaf (Religious Endowments) and Islamic Affairs: POB 422, Doha; tel. 4470777; fax 4470700; e-mail minister@islam.gov.qa; internet www.islam.gov.qa.

Ministry of Business and Trade: POB 1968, Doha; tel. 4945555; fax 4932111; e-mail webmaster@mec.gov.qa; internet www.mbt.gov.qa.

Ministry of Culture, Arts and Heritage: POB 23700, Doha; tel. 4243110; fax 4314914; e-mail info@nccah.com; internet www.nccah.com.

Ministry of Economy and Finance: POB 83, Doha; tel. 4461444; fax 4431177; e-mail qatfin@mof.gov.qa; internet www.mof.gov.qa.

Ministry of Education and Higher Education: POB 80, Al-Waqf Tower, Dafna, Doha; tel. and fax 4941111; fax 4941445; e-mail e.alhorr@moe.edu.qa; internet www.moe.edu.qa.

Ministry of Energy and Industry: POB 2599, Doha; tel. 4846444; fax 4832024; e-mail did@mei.gov.qa; internet www.mei.gov.qa.

Ministry of the Environment: tel. 4207777; fax 4415246; e-mail moe@qatarenv.org.qa; internet www.moe.gov.qa.

Ministry of Foreign Affairs: POB 250, Doha; tel. 4334334; fax 4324131; e-mail webmaster@mofa.gov.qa; internet www.mofa.gov.qa.

Ministry of the Interior: POB 115, Doha; tel. 4330000; fax 4449228; e-mail info@moi.gov.qa; internet www.moi.gov.qa.

Ministry of Justice: POB 917 (Dept of Legal Affairs), Doha; tel. 4842222; fax 4832875; e-mail info@moj.gov.qa; internet www.moj.gov.qa.

Ministry of Labour: POB 36, Doha; tel. 4841111; fax 4841441; e-mail customerservice@mlsa.gov.qa; internet www.mlsa.gov.qa.

Ministry of Municipal Affairs and Urban Planning: POB 22332, Main Bldg, Corniche St, Doha; tel. 4413331; fax 4430239; e-mail info@baladiya.gov.qa; internet www.baladiya.gov.qa.

Ministry of Public Health: POB 42, Doha; tel. 4437111; fax 4446294; e-mail info@nha.org.qa; internet www.nha.org.qa.

Ministry of Social Affairs: POB 36, Doha; tel. 4841137; fax 4841472; e-mail mosa@mol.gov.qa; internet www.mosa.gov.qa.

ADVISORY COUNCIL

The Advisory or *Shura* Council was established in 1972, with 20 nominated members. It was expanded to 30 members in 1975, and to 35 members in 1988. Under the terms of the new Constitution, promulgated in 2003, the Advisory Council was to be replaced by a 45-member unicameral parliament, of which two thirds of the members were to be directly elected.

Speaker: MUHAMMAD BIN MUBARAK AL-KHOLAIFI.

Political Organizations

There are no political organizations in Qatar.

Diplomatic Representation

EMBASSIES IN QATAR

Afghanistan: POB 22104, Isteolal St, West Bay, Doha; tel. 4930821; fax 4930819; e-mail afgembqatar@hotmail.com; Ambassador WALI MONAWAR.

Algeria: POB 2494, Doha; tel. 4831186; fax 4836452; Ambassador ISSA BIKRAR.

Azerbaijan: Doha; tel. 4932450; fax 4931755; e-mail azembassy@qatar.com.qa; Ambassador ELDAR N. SALIMOV.

Bahrain: POB 24888, Doha; tel. 4839360; fax 4831018; e-mail doha.mission@mofa.gov.bh; Ambassador KHALID MUHAMMAD JABER AL-MUSALEM.

Bangladesh: POB 2080, Doha; tel. 4671927; fax 4671190; e-mail bdootqat@qatar.net.qa; internet www.bdembassydoha.com; Ambassador MUHAMMAD SHAHADAT HUSSAIN.

Belgium: POB 24418, As-Sanaaa St, District 64, Doha; tel. 4931542; fax 4930151; e-mail doha@diplobel.fed.be; internet www.diplomatie.be/doha; Ambassador LUC DEVOLDER.

Bosnia and Herzegovina: POB 876, Doha; tel. 4113828; fax 4113234; e-mail ambasada@qatar.net.qa; internet www.bhembassyqatar.org; Ambassador AZRA KALAJDŽISALIHOVIĆ.

Brunei: POB 22772, Doha; tel. 4831956; fax 4836798; e-mail bruemb@qatar.net.qa; Chargé d'affaires Haji ALI HASSAN Haji MUHAMMAD SALLEH.

China, People's Republic: POB 17200, Doha; tel. 4934203; fax 4934201; e-mail chinashi@qatar.net.qa; internet qa.china-embassy.org; Ambassador YUE XIAOYONG.

Cuba: POB 12017, Saha 76, New Dafna, West Bay Lagoon, Doha; tel. 4110713; fax 4110387; e-mail embacuba@qatar.net.qa; internet www.embacubaqatar.com; Ambassador ARMANDO VERGARA BUENO.

Cyprus: POB 24482, 3 Saba Saba 12 St, District 63, West Bay, Doha; tel. 4934390; fax 4933087; e-mail kyprosdoha@qatar.net.qa; internet www.mfa.gov.cy/embassydoha; Ambassador PANICOS KYRIACOU.

Egypt: POB 2899, Doha; tel. 4832555; fax 4832196; e-mail info@egyptembqatar.com; Ambassador ABD AL-AZIZ DAWOUD.

Eritrea: POB 4309, D-Ring Rd 14, Doha; tel. 4667934; fax 4664139; Ambassador ALI IBRAHIM AHMED.

France: POB 2669, Doha; tel. 4832283; fax 4832254; e-mail ambadoha@qatar.net.qa; internet www.ambafrance-qa.org; Ambassador GILLES BONNAUD.

Gambia: POB 22377, Doha; tel. 4651429; fax 4651705; Ambassador ANTOUMAN SAHO.

Germany: POB 3064, 6 Al-Jazeera al-Arabiya St, Doha; tel. 4876959; fax 4876949; e-mail germany@qatar.net.qa; internet www.doha.diplo.de; Ambassador Dr DIRK BAUMGARTNER.

Hungary: POB 23525, Doha; tel. 4932531; fax 4932537; e-mail mission.doh@kum.hu; internet www.mfa.gov.hu/kulkepviselet/qu; Ambassador LÁSZLÓ SZABÓ.

India: POB 2788, Doha; tel. 4255777; fax 4670488; e-mail indembdh@qatar.net.qa; internet www.indianembassy.gov.qa; Ambassador DEEPA GOPALAN WADHWA.

Indonesia: POB 22375, Al-Maheed St, Doha; tel. 4657945; fax 4657610; e-mail inemb@qatar.net.qa; internet www.kbridoha.com; Ambassador ROZY MUNIR.

Iran: POB 1633, Doha; tel. 4835300; fax 4831665; e-mail irembsdoha@yahoo.com; internet www.iranembassy.org.qa; Ambassador MUHAMMAD TAHER RABBANI.

Iraq: POB 1526, Doha; tel. 4672237; fax 4673347; e-mail dohemb@iraqmofamail.net; Ambassador Dr JAWAD AL-HINDAWI.

Italy: POB 4188, Doha; tel. 4831828; fax 4831909; e-mail ambasciata.doha@esteri.it; internet sedi.esteri.it/doha; Ambassador ANDREA FERRARI.

Japan: POB 2208, Diplomatic Area, West Bay, Doha; tel. 4840888; fax 4832178; e-mail eojqatar@eoj.com.qa; internet www.qa.emb-japan.go.jp; Ambassador YUKIO KITAZUME.

Jordan: POB 2366, Doha; tel. 4832202; fax 4832173; e-mail jordand@qatar.net.qa; internet www.jordanembassy.com.qa; Ambassador AHMAD AL-MEFLEH.

Kazakhstan: POB 25513, Doha; tel. and fax 4128015; e-mail kazembassyqatar@mail.ru; Ambassador AZAMAT R. BERDYBAI.

Korea, Democratic People's Republic: POB 799, Doha; tel. 4417614; fax 4424735; Ambassador HO JONG.

Korea, Republic: POB 3727, Diplomatic Area, West Bay, Doha; tel. 4832238; fax 4833264; e-mail koemb_ga@mofa.go.kr; Ambassador KIM JONG-YONG.

Kuwait: POB 1177, Doha; tel. 4832111; fax 4832042; e-mail kuwaitembassy@qatar.net.qa; Ambassador SULEIMAN IBRAHIM AL-MARJAN.

QATAR

Lebanon: POB 2411, 63 United Nations St, Al-Haditha Area, Doha; tel. 4933330; fax 4933331; e-mail embleb@qatar.net.qa; Ambassador HASSAN SAAD.

Libya: POB 574, Doha; tel. 4429546; fax 4429548; Ambassador HASSONA AL-LAFI ASH-SHAWISH.

Malaysia: POB 23760, Doha; tel. 4836463; fax 4836453; e-mail maldoha@kln.gov.my; internet www.kln.gov.my/perwakilan/doha; Ambassador Dato' MUHAMMAD SHAHRUL IKRAM YAAKOB.

Mauritania: POB 3132, Doha; tel. 4836003; fax 4836015; Ambassador MUHAMMAD FAL OULD BILAL.

Morocco: POB 3242, Doha; tel. 4831885; fax 4833416; e-mail moroccoe@qatar.net.qa; Ambassador ABDELADIM TABIR.

Nepal: POB 23002, Doha; tel. 4675681; fax 4675680; e-mail nembdoha@qatar.net.qa; internet www.nembdoha.org.qa; Ambassador Dr SURYA NATH MISHRA.

Netherlands: POB 23675, 6th floor, Al-Mirqab Tower, Al-Dafna, Corniche, Doha; tel. 4954700; fax 4836340; e-mail doh@minbuza.nl; internet qatar.nlembassy.org; Ambassador J. G. VAN VLOTEN DISSEVELT.

Oman: POB 1525, 41 Ibn al-Qassim St, Villa 7, Doha; tel. 4931514; fax 4932278; e-mail oman_e126@hotmail.com; Ambassador RASHED BIN MUBARAK BIN RASHED AL-GHELANY.

Pakistan: POB 334, Diplomatic Area, Plot 30, West Bay, Doha; tel. 4832525; fax 4832227; e-mail parepqat@qatar.net.qa; internet www.pakmissiondoha.com; Ambassador MUHAMMAD ASGHAR AFRIDI.

Philippines: POB 24900, Doha; tel. 4831585; fax 4831595; e-mail dohape@qatar.net.qa; Ambassador ISAIAS FLORENDO BEGONIA.

Poland: POB 23380, Al-Qutaifiya 66, West Bay, Doha; tel. 4113230; fax 4110307; e-mail doha@ct.futuro.pl; internet www.doha.polemb.net; Ambassador ROBERT ROSTEK.

Romania: POB 22511, Doha; tel. 4934848; fax 4934747; e-mail romamb@qatar.net.qa; Ambassador ADRIAN MĂCELARU.

Russia: POB 15404, Doha; tel. 4836231; fax 4836243; e-mail rusemb@qatar.net.qa; internet www.qatar.mid.ru; Ambassador ANDREW V. ANDREEV.

Saudi Arabia: POB 1255, Doha; tel. 4832030; fax 4832720; Ambassador AHMAD BIN ALI AL-QAHTANI.

Senegal: Ibn Almoutas St, House 65, Dafna, Doha; tel. 4837644; fax 4838872; Ambassador ADAMA SARR.

Singapore: POB 24497, Doha; tel. 4128082; fax 4128180; e-mail singemb_doh@sgmfa.gov.sg; internet www.mfa.gov.sg/doha; Chargé d'affaires a.i. UMEJ SINGH BHATIA.

Somalia: POB 1948, Doha; tel. 4832771; fax 4834568; Ambassador ISMA'IL QASIM NAJI.

South Africa: POB 24744, Doha; tel. 4857111; fax 4835961; e-mail doha.admin@foreign.gov.za; Ambassador Dr VINCENT TINIZA ZULU.

Spain: POB 24616, Lusail Street, West Bay, Doha; tel. 4835886; fax 4835887; e-mail emb.doha@mae.es; Ambassador JUAN JOSÉ SANTOS AGUADO.

Sri Lanka: 4 Al-Kharja St, POB 19705, Doha; tel. 4677627; fax 4674788; e-mail lankaemb@qatar.net.qa; Ambassador VIJAYASIRI PADUKKAGE.

Sudan: POB 2999, Doha; tel. 4831474; fax 4833031; e-mail suemdoha@yahoo.com; Ambassador IBRAHIM ABDULLAH FAKIRI.

Syria: POB 1257, Doha; tel. 4831844; fax 4832139; Ambassador DEEB ABU LATIF.

Thailand: POB 22474, Doha; tel. 4550715; fax 4550835; e-mail thaidoh@qatar.net.qa; internet www.thaiembqatar.com; Ambassador SUVAT CHIRAPANT.

Tunisia: POB 2707, Doha; tel. 4832645; fax 4832649; e-mail at .doha@qatar.net.qa; Ambassador MUHAMMAD AL-QARWI.

Turkey: POB 1977, Doha; tel. 4951300; fax 4951320; e-mail tcdohabe@qatar.net.qa; Ambassador MITHAT RENDE.

United Arab Emirates: POB 3099, 22 al-Markhiyah St, Khalifa Northern Town, Doha; tel. 4838880; fax 4836186; e-mail emarat@qatar.net.qa; Ambassador ABD AR-REDHA ABDULLAH KHOURI.

United Kingdom: POB 3, Doha; tel. 4962000; fax 4962086; e-mail embassy.qatar@fco.gov.uk; internet ukinqatar.fco.gov.uk; Ambassador JOHN HAWKINS.

USA: 22nd February St, Al-Luqta district, POB 2399, Doha; tel. 4884101; fax 4884298; e-mail pasdoha@state.gov; internet qatar.usembassy.gov; Ambassador JOSEPH LEBARON.

Yemen: POB 3318, Doha; tel. 4432555; fax 4429400; Ambassador ABD AL-MALIK SAID.

Judicial System

The independence of the judiciary was guaranteed by the provisional Constitution and further augmented in the Constitution formally adopted by the Amir in April 2003. All aspects pertaining to the civil judiciary are supervised by the Ministry of Justice, which organizes courts of law through its affiliated departments. The *Shari'a* judiciary hears all cases of personal status relating to Muslims, other claim cases, doctrinal provision and crimes under its jurisdiction. Legislation adopted in 1999 unified all civil and *Shari'a* courts in one judicial body, and determined the jurisdictions of each type of court. The law also provided for the establishment of a court of cassation; this was to be competent to decide on appeals relating to issues of contravention, misapplication and misinterpretation of the law, and on disputes between courts regarding areas of jurisdiction. In addition, the law provided for the establishment of a supreme judiciary council, to be presided over by the head of the court of cassation and comprising, *inter alia*, the heads of the *Shari'a* and civil courts of appeal. The legislation came into effect in 2003. An Amiri decree published in June 2002 provided for the establishment of an independent public prosecution system. A Supreme Constitutional Court was established in 2008 to adjudicate on the constitutionality of laws and to arbitrate in disputes between different branches of the judiciary.

Presidency of Shari'a Courts: POB 232, Doha; tel. 4452222; Pres. Sheikh ABD AR-RAHMAN BIN ABDULLAH AL-MAHMOUD.

Public Prosecution Office: POB 705, Doha; tel. 4843333; fax 4839941; e-mail info@pp.gov.qa; internet www.pp.gov.qa; Prosecutor-Gen. Dr ALI BIN FITAISE AL-MERRI.

Supreme Judiciary Council: POB 9673, Doha; tel. 4859111; fax 4249955; e-mail sjc@sjc.gov.qa; internet www.sjc.gov.qa; f. 2003; Pres. MUBARAK BIN KHALIFA AL-ASARI.

Religion

The indigenous population are Muslims of the Sunni sect, most being of the strict Wahhabi persuasion. In March 2008 the first official Christian church (of the Roman Catholic branch) was consecrated in Doha; open worship among adherents of Christianity had previously been prohibited.

CHRISTIANITY

The Anglican Communion

Within the Episcopal Church in Jerusalem and the Middle East, Qatar forms part of the diocese of Cyprus and the Gulf. The Anglican congregation in Qatar is entirely expatriate. The Bishop in Cyprus and the Gulf is resident in Cyprus, while the Archdeacon in the Gulf is resident in Bahrain.

The Roman Catholic Church

An estimated 100,000 adherents in Qatar, mainly expatriates, form part of the Apostolic Vicariate of Arabia. The Vicar Apostolic is resident in the United Arab Emirates.

The Press

NEWSPAPERS

Al-'Arab (The Arabs): POB 22612, Doha; tel. 4997333; fax 4677879; e-mail alarab@alarab.com.qa; internet www.alarab.com.qa; f. 1972; ceased publication in 1996, but recommenced following relaunch in Nov. 2007; daily; Arabic; publ. by Dar al-Ouroba Printing and Publishing; Editor-in-Chief Prof. ABD AL-AZIZ IBRAHIM AL-MAHMOUD.

Gulf Times: POB 2888, Doha; tel. 4350478; fax 4350474; e-mail edit@gulf-times.com; internet www.gulf-times.com; f. 1978; daily and weekly edns; English; political; publ. by Gulf Publishing and Printing Co; Man. Editor NEIL COOK; circ. 20,000 (daily).

The Peninsula: POB 3488, Doha; tel. 4557777; fax 4557746; e-mail editor@thepeninsulaqatar.com; internet www.thepeninsulaqatar.com; f. 1995; daily; English; political; publ. by Dar ash-Sharq Printing, Publishing and Distribution; Chair. Sheikh THANI BIN ABDULLAH ATH-THANI; Man. Editor RACHEL MORRIS; circ. 8,000.

Qatar Tribune: POB 23493, Doha; tel. 4422077; fax 4416790; e-mail editor-in-chief@qatar-tribune.com; internet www.qatar-tribune.com; f. 2006; daily; English; Editor-in-Chief Dr HASSAN MUHAMMAD AL-ANSARI; circ. 10,000.

Ar-Rayah (The Banner): POB 3464, Doha; tel. 4466636; fax 4320080; e-mail edit@raya.com; internet www.raya.com; f. 1979; daily and weekly edns; Arabic; political; publ. by Gulf Publishing and Printing Co; Editor NASSER AL-OTHMAN; circ. 25,000.

QATAR

Ash-Sharq (The Orient): POB 3488, Doha; tel. 4662444; fax 4662450; e-mail jaber.alharmi@gmail.com; internet www.al-sharq.com; f. 1985; daily; Arabic; political; publ. by Dar ash-Sharq Printing, Publishing and Distribution; Editor-in-Chief ABDULLATIF AL-MAHMOUD; Dep. Editor JABER AL-HARMI; circ. 45,018.

Al-Watan: POB 22345, Doha; tel. 4652244; fax 4654482; e-mail alwatan@qatar.net.qa; internet www.al-watan.com; f. 1995; daily; Arabic; political; publ. by Dar al-Watan Printing, Publishing and Distribution; Editor-in-Chief AHMAD ALI AL-ABDULLAH; circ. 25,000.

PERIODICALS

Al-Jawhara (The Jewel): POB 2531, Doha; tel. 4414575; fax 4671388; f. 1977; monthly; Arabic; magazine covering watches and jewellery; publ. by al-Ahd Establishment for Journalism, Printing and Publications Ltd; Editor-in-Chief ABDULLAH YOUSUF AL-HUSSAINI; circ. 8,000.

Al-Ouroba (Arabism): POB 663, Doha; tel. 4325874; fax 4429424; f. 1970; weekly; Arabic; political; publ. by Dar al-Ouroba Printing and Publishing; Editor-in-Chief YOUSUF NAAMA; circ. 12,000.

Qatar Al-Yom: POB 3272, Doha; tel. 4550983; e-mail qtoday@omsqatar.com; internet www.omsqatar.com/qt_arabic.htm; f. 2005; Arabic; news, business and lifestyle; publ. by Oryx Advertising Co; Editor-in-Chief YOUSUF JASSEM AD-DARWISH; circ. 22,000.

Qatar Today: 18 Al-Khalejia Bldg, 930 Al-Wafa St, Doha; tel. 4672139; fax 4550982; e-mail qtoday@omsqatar.com; internet www.omsqatar.com; f. 1978; monthly; English; news, business and lifestyle; publ. by Oryx Publishing and Advertising Co; Editor-in-Chief YOUSUF JASSEM AD-DARWISH; circ. 27,000.

QT Dossier: POB 3272, Doha; tel. 4550983; e-mail qtoday@omsqatar.com; internet www.omsqatar.com/dossier.htm; quarterly; Arabic and English; business and finance; publ. by Oryx Advertising Co.

At-Tarbiya (Education): POB 9865, Doha; tel. 4941709; fax 4838890; e-mail netcom@qatar.net.qa; f. 1971; quarterly; publ. by Qatar National Commission for Education, Culture and Science; Editor-in-Chief MUHAMMAD SIDDIQ; circ. 2,000.

At-Tijara Wal A'amal: POB 272, Doha; tel. 4478042; fax 4478063; e-mail info@mashaheermedia.com; internet www.mashaheermedia.com; English; business and industry; publ. by Mashaheer Media Qatar.

Al-Ufuq: POB 3488, Doha; tel. 4602844; fax 4601294; e-mail alsharqpp@qatar.net.qa; f. 2002; monthly; Arabic; business; publ. by Dar ash-Sharq Printing, Publishing and Distribution.

Al-Ummah: POB 893, Doha; tel. 4447300; fax 4447022; e-mail m_dirasat@islam.gov.qa; f. 1982; bi-monthly; Islamic thought and affairs, current cultural issues, book serializations.

NEWS AGENCY

Qatar News Agency (QNA): POB 3299, Doha; tel. 4450321; fax 4438316; e-mail info@qnaol.com; internet www.qnaol.net; f. 1975; affiliated to Ministry of Foreign Affairs; Dir and Editor-in-Chief AHMAD JASSIM AL-HUMAR.

Publishers

Ali bin Ali Printing and Publishing: POB 75, Doha; tel. 4423481; fax 4432045; e-mail publishing@alibinali.com; internet www.alibinali.com; part of Ali bin Ali Group; publrs of Qatar Telephone Directory and Yellow Pages; Chair. and Pres. ADEL ALI BIN ALI; Gen. Man. MUHAMMAD MUSTAFA.

Dar ash-Sharq Printing, Publishing and Distribution: POB 3488, Doha; tel. 4557866; fax 4557871; e-mail alsharqpp@qatar.net.qa; internet www.al-sharq.com/DarAlSharq.aspx; publrs of Ash-Sharq and The Peninsula newspapers, and Al-Ufuq magazine; distributor for various foreign newspapers; Gen. Man. ABDULLATIF AL-MAHMOUD.

Gulf Publishing and Printing Co: POB 533, Doha; tel. 4350475; fax 4350474; e-mail gm@gulftimes.com; internet www.gulf-times.com; f. 1978; publrs of Gulf Times and Arrayah; Chair. ABDULLAH BIN KHALIFA AL-ATTIYA.

Oryx Advertising Co WLL: POB 405, Doha; tel. 4672139; fax 4550982; e-mail qtoday@omsqatar.com; internet www.omsqatar.com; publrs of Qatar Today, Woman Today and QT Dossier among others; Publr and Editor-in-Chief YOUSUF JASSEM AD-DARWISH.

Qatar National Printing Press: POB 355, Doha; tel. 4448452; fax 4449550; e-mail qnppgm@gmail.com; Man. ABD AL-KARIM DEEB.

Broadcasting and Communications

TELECOMMUNICATIONS

Supreme Council for Communications and Information Technology (ictQATAR): POB 23264, Al-Mirqab Tower, Al-Corniche St, Doha; tel. 4995333; fax 4935913; e-mail info@ict.gov.qa; internet www.ict.gov.qa; f. 2004 to oversee the deregulation of the telecommunications sector; Chair. Crown Prince Sheikh TAMIM BIN HAMAD BIN KHALIFA ATH-THANI; Exec. Dir WILLIAM FAGAN; Sec.-Gen. Dr HESSA SULTAN AL-JABER.

Qatar Telecommunications Corpn—Qatar Telecom (Q-Tel): POB 217, Doha; tel. 4830000; fax 4476231; e-mail customer.service@qtel.com.qa; internet www.qtel.com.qa; f. 1987; majority state-owned; provides telecommunications services within Qatar; Chair. Sheikh ABDULLAH BIN MUHAMMAD ATH-THANI; CEO Dr NASSER MARAFIH.

Vodafone Qatar QSC: POB 74057, Doha; e-mail lana.khachan@vodafone.com.qa; internet www.vodafone.com.qa; f. 2008; majority shareholders Vodafone Group PLC (United Kingdom) and Qatar Foundation for Education, Science and Community Development; initial public offering for Qatari nationals of 40% of shares conducted in April 2009; awarded Qatar's second mobile telephone operating licence in June 2008; CEO GRAHAME MAHER.

BROADCASTING

Regulatory Authority

Qatar Radio and Television Corpn (QRTC): POB 1414, Doha; tel. 4894444; fax 4882888; e-mail ksaid@rtc.gov.qa; internet www.qrtc.com; f. 1997; autonomous authority reporting direct to the Council of Ministers; Dir-Gen. ABD AR-RAHMAN OBEIDAN.

Radio

Qatar Broadcasting Service (QBS): POB 3939, Doha; tel. 4894444; fax 4882888; f. 1968; govt service transmitting in Arabic, English, French and Urdu; programmes include Holy Quran Radio and Doha Music Radio; Dir ALI NASSER AL-KUBAISI.

Sout al-Khaleej: POB 1414, Doha; tel. 4888334; fax 4879999; e-mail info@soutalkhaleej.fm; internet www.soutalkhaleej.fm; f. 2002; Arabic arts broadcasting.

Television

Al-Jazeera Satellite Network: POB 23123, Doha; tel. 4896044; fax 4873577; e-mail imr@aljazeera.net; internet www.aljazeera.net; f. 1996; 24-hr broadcasting of news and current affairs in Arabic; English-language service launched Nov. 2006; documentary channel launched Jan. 2007; Dir-Gen. WADAH KHANFAR; Chief Editor AHMED SHEIKH.

Qatar Television Service (QTV): POB 1944, Doha; tel. 4894444; fax 4874170; f. 1970; operates two channels (of which one broadcasts in English); 24-hr broadcasting; Dir MUHAMMAD AL-KUWARI; Asst Dir ABD AL-WAHAB MUHAMMAD AL-MUTAWA'A.

Finance

(cap. = capital; res = reserves; dep. = deposits; m. = million; brs = branches; amounts in Qatar riyals, unless otherwise indicated)

STATE FINANCIAL AUTHORITIES

In March 2005 the Government established the Qatar Financial Centre (QFC), which was intended to attract international financial institutions and multinational corporations to Qatar, 'to establish business operations in a best-in-class international environment'. The QFC comprised the QFC Authority and the QFC Regulatory Authority (QFCRA—see below), as well as two legal bodies—the QFC Regulatory Tribunal and the QFC Civil and Commercial Court—which were charged with upholding the rule of law and ensuring the transparency of QFC transactions. In July 2007 plans were announced for the creation of a single, integrated, fully independent financial regulatory authority, which would merge the regulatory activities of the QFCRA, the Qatar Financial Markets Authority and the Qatar Central Bank and oversee all banking, insurance, securities, asset management and other financial services. The new body was not expected to become operational before 2010.

Qatar Financial Centre Authority (QFCA): POB 23245, Doha; tel. 4967777; fax 4967676; e-mail info@qfc.com.qa; internet www.qfc.com.qa; f. 2005; charged with promoting Qatar as an attractive location for international banking, insurance and financial services; Chair. YOUSUF HUSSAIN KAMAL (Minister of Economy and Finance); CEO and Dir-Gen. STUART PEARCE.

Qatar Financial Centre Regulatory Authority (QFCRA): POB 22989, Level 14, Qatar Financial Centre Tower, Doha; tel. 4956888;

QATAR
Directory

fax 4835031; e-mail info@qfcra.com; internet www.qfcra.com; f. 2005; charged with the regulation and supervision of a wide range of financial activities, incl. banking, insurance, asset management and financial advisory services; Chair. and CEO PHILLIP THORPE.

Qatar Financial Markets Authority: POB 25552, Doha; tel. 4289999; fax 4441221; e-mail info@qfma.org.qa; internet www.visionwmg.com/qfma/website; f. 2007 to supervise the Stock Exchange and securities industry; Chair. YOUSUF HUSSAIN KAMAL (Minister of Economy and Finance); CEO NASSER AHMAD ASH-SHAIBI (acting).

BANKING
Central Bank

Qatar Central Bank: POB 1234, Doha; tel. 4456456; fax 4414190; e-mail webmaster@qcb.gov.qa; internet www.qcb.gov.qa; f. 1966 as Qatar and Dubai Currency Board; became Qatar Monetary Agency in 1973; renamed Qatar Central Bank in 1993; state-owned; cap. and res 7,751.2m., total assets 20,206.6m., currency in circulation 5,069.8m. (Dec. 2006); Gov. ABDULLAH SAUD ATH-THANI.

Commercial Banks

Ahli Bank QSC: POB 2309, Suhmin bin Hamad St, As-Sadd Area, Doha; tel. 4232222; fax 4232323; e-mail info@ahlibank.com.qa; internet www.ahlibank.com.qa; f. 1984 as Al-Ahli Bank of Qatar QSC; name changed as above in 2004; cap. 406.3m., res 759.6m., dep. 8,174.7m. (Dec. 2006); Chair. AHMED ABD AR-RAHMAN ABD AL-LATIF AL-MANA; CEO SALAH JASSIM MURAD; 9 brs.

Commercial Bank of Qatar QSC (CBQ): POB 3232, Grand Hamad Ave, Doha; tel. 4900000; fax 4490072; e-mail info@cbq.com.qa; internet www.cbq.com.qa; f. 1975; cap. 1,401.6m., res 4,629.8m., dep. 30,704.1m. (Dec. 2007); Chair. ABDULLAH BIN KHALIFA AL-ATTIYA; Group CEO ANDREW C. STEVENS; 21 brs.

Doha Bank: POB 3818, Grand Hamad Ave, Doha; tel. 4456600; fax 4410625; e-mail international@dohabank.com.qa; internet www.dohabank.com.qa; f. 1979; cap. 1,248.2m., res 2,330.3m., dep. 24,414.3m. (Dec. 2007); Chair. Sheikh FAHAD BIN MUHAMMAD BIN JABER ATH-THANI; CEO R. SEETHARAMAN; 28 brs in Qatar, 2 abroad.

International Bank of Qatar QSC (IBQ): POB 2001, Suhaim bin Hamad St, Doha; tel. 4473700; fax 4473710; e-mail qatarenq@ibq.com.qa; internet www.ibq.com.qa; f. 2000 as Grindlays Qatar Bank QSC; previously a branch of ANZ Grindlays Bank, f. 1956; name changed as above in 2004, after National Bank of Kuwait SAK assumed management of the bank; cap. 281.3m., res 909.5m., dep. 5,262.8m. (Dec. 2006); Chair. HAMAD BIN JASIM BIN JABER ATH-THANI; Man. Dir GEORGE NASRA.

Al-Khalij Commercial Bank (QSC) (al-khaliji): POB 28000, Doha; tel. 4996000; fax 4996020; e-mail info@alkhaliji.com; internet www.alkhaliji.com; f. 2007; cap. 3,600m., res 886.9m. (Dec. 2007); Chair. TARIQ AL-MALIKI; CEO DAVID PROCTOR.

Qatar Development Bank (QDB): POB 22789, Doha; tel. 4421600; fax 4350433; e-mail contact@qdb.org.qa; internet www.qidb.com.qa; f. 1996 as the Qatar Industrial Development Bank; inaugurated Oct. 1997; relaunched under above name in April 2007 with expanded capital provision to facilitate private sector involvement in national economic devt; state-owned; provides long-term low-interest industrial loans; finances wide range of industrial and social projects; broadened consultancy services following relaunch; cap. 200m., total assets 392.0m. (Dec. 2006); Chair. Sheikh ABDULLAH BIN SA'UD ATH-THANI; Gen. Man. Sheikh HAMAD NASSER ATH-THANI.

Qatar International Islamic Bank QSC (QIIB): POB 664, Grand Hamad St, Doha; tel. 4385555; fax 4444101; e-mail qiibit@qiib.com.qa; internet www.qiib.com.qa; f. 1990; cap. 700.8m., res 1,638.9m., dep. 7,272.4m. (Dec. 2007); Chair. and Man. Dir KHALID BIN THANI BIN ABDULLAH ATH-THANI; CEO ABD AL-BASIT ASH-SHAIBEI; 5 brs.

Qatar Islamic Bank SAQ (QIB): POB 559, Grand Hamad St, Doha; tel. 4409409; fax 4412700; e-mail qib@qib.com.qa; internet www.qib.com.qa; f. 1982; cap. 1,193.4m., res 2,912.0m., dep. 15,805.2m. (Dec. 2007); Chair. Sheikh JASSIM BIN HAMAD BIN JASIM BIN JABER ATH-THANI; CEO SALAH JAIDAH; 23 brs.

Qatar National Bank SAQ: POB 1000, Doha; tel. 4407777; fax 4413753; e-mail ccsupport@qnb.com.qa; internet www.qnb.com.qa; f. 1964; owned 50% by Govt of Qatar and 50% by Qatari nationals; cap. 1,824.9m., res 10,579.3m., dep. 91,787.4m. (Dec. 2007); Chair. YOUSUF HUSSAIN KAMAL (Minister of Economy and Finance); Chair. of Exec. Cttee Sheikh HAMAD BIN FAISAL ATH-THANI; CEO ALI SHARIF AL-EMADI; 32 brs in Qatar, 3 abroad.

STOCK EXCHANGE

Doha Securities Market (DSM): POB 22114, Grand Hamad St, Doha; tel. 4333666; fax 4319233; e-mail dsm@dsm.com.qa; internet www.dsm.com.qa; f. 1997; 43 cos listed in March 2009; Gen. Man. SAIF KHALIFA AL-MANSORI.

INSURANCE

Doha Insurance Co: POB 7171, Doha; tel. 4335077; fax 4657777; e-mail gm@dicqatar.com; internet www.dicqatar.com; f. 1999 as public shareholding co; cap. 127.2m., total assets 518.3m. (Dec. 2007); Chair. Sheikh NAWAF BIN NASSER BIN KHALID ATH-THANI; Gen. Man. BASSAM HUSSAIN.

Al-Khaleej Insurance and Reinsurance Co QSC (SAQ): POB 4555, Doha; tel. 4414151; fax 4430530; e-mail alkhalej@qatar.net.qa; internet www.alkhaleej.com; f. 1978; cap. and res 568.4m. (2007); all classes except life; Chair. ABDULLAH BIN MUHAMMAD JABER ATH-THANI; Gen. Man. KARAM AHMAD MAHMOUD.

Qatar General Insurance and Reinsurance Co SAQ: POB 4500, A Ring Road, Al-Asmakh Area, Doha; tel. 4282222; fax 4437302; e-mail qgirc-tec@qatar.net.qa; internet www.qgirco.com; f. 1979; total assets 1,729.7m. (2007); all classes; Chair. and Man. Dir Sheikh NASSER BIN ALI ATH-THANI; Gen. Man. GHAZI ABU NAHL.

Qatar Insurance Co SAQ: POB 666, Tamin St, West Bay, Doha; tel. 4962222; fax 4831569; e-mail qatarins@qic.com.qa; internet www.qatarinsurance.com; f. 1964; cap. 424.7m., total assets 5,860.7m. (Dec. 2007); all classes; the Govt has a majority share; Chair. and Man. Dir Sheikh KHALID BIN MUHAMMAD ALI ATH-THANI; Pres. and CEO KHALIFA A. AS-SUBAYI; brs in Doha and Khalifa Town, Dubai and Abu Dhabi (UAE), Saudi Arabia, Kuwait, Oman and Malta.

Qatar Islamic Insurance Co: POB 22676, Doha; tel. 4658888; fax 4550111; e-mail qiic@qatar.net.qa; internet www.qiic.net.qa; f. 1993; cap. 150.0m., res 137.0m. (Dec. 2007); Chair. Sheikh THANI BIN ABDULLAH ATH-THANI; Gen. Man. IZZAT M. AR-RASHID.

Trade and Industry
DEVELOPMENT ORGANIZATIONS

Department of Industrial Development: POB 2599, Doha; tel. 4846444; fax 4832024; e-mail did@mei.gov.qa; a div. of the Ministry of Energy and Industry; conducts research, licensing, devt and supervision of new industrial projects; Dir-Gen. SAID MUBARAK AL-KUWAIRI.

General Secretariat for Development Planning: POB 1588, Doha; tel. 4958888; e-mail webmaster@planning.gov.qa; internet www.gsdp.gov.qa; f. 2006; responsible for co-ordination of the emirate's long-term devt strategy; monitors progress of Qatar's National Vision 2030 and National Strategy; Sec.-Gen. Dr IBRAHIM AL-IBRAHIM; Dir-Gen. Sheikh HAMAD BIN JABER BIN JASIM ATH-THANI.

Public Works Authority (Ashghal): POB 22188, Doha; tel. 4950000; fax 4950999; e-mail info@ashghal.gov.qa; internet www.ashghal.com; f. 2004; responsible for the management and devt of public infrastructure projects; Chair. Sheikh ABD AR-RAHMAN BIN KHALIFA BIN ABD AL-AZIZ ATH-THANI (Minister of Municipal Affairs and Urban Planning); Man. Dir NASSER ALI ABDULLAH AL-MAWLAWI (acting).

Urban Planning and Development Authority: POB 22423, Doha; tel. 4955549; fax 4955594; e-mail general@up.org.qa; internet www.up.org.qa; f. 2005; planning, co-ordination and management of urban devt projects; oversees devt of the Master Plan for the State of Qatar; Dir-Gen. ALI ABDULLAH AL-ABDULLAH.

CHAMBER OF COMMERCE

Qatar Chamber of Commerce and Industry: POB 402, Doha; tel. 4559111; fax 4661693; e-mail info@qcci.org; internet www.qcci.org; f. 1963; 17 elected mems; Chair. Sheikh KHALIFA BIN JASIM BIN MUHAMMAD ATH-THANI; Gen. Man. KHALID AL-HAJRI.

STATE HYDROCARBONS COMPANIES

Qatar International Petroleum Marketing Co (Tasweeq): POB 24183, Doha; tel. 4976111; fax 4976276; e-mail info@tasweeq.com.qa; internet www.tasweeq.com.qa; f. 2007 to take sole responsibility for all exports of natural gas and oil products; 100% govt-owned; CEO ALI AL-HAMADI.

Qatar Petrochemical Co SAQ (QAPCO): POB 756, Doha; tel. 4242444; fax 4324700; e-mail information@qapco.com.qa; internet www.qapco.com; f. 1974; 80% owned by Industries Qatar (IQ), 20% by Total Petrochemicals (France); total assets QR 5,090.7m. (2006); operation of petrochemical plant at Mesaieed; produced 549,928 metric tons of ethylene, 359,460 tons of low-density polyethylene, and 32,297 tons of solid sulphur in 2007; Chair. ABDULLAH BIN HAMAD AL-ATTIYA (Minister of Energy and Industry); Gen. Man. MUHAMMAD YOUSEF AL-MULLA; 879 employees (2004).

Qatar Petroleum (QP): POB 3212, Doha; tel. 4402000; fax 4831125; e-mail webmaster@qp.com.qa; internet www.qp.com.qa; f. 1974 as Qatar General Petroleum Corpn (QGPC), name changed 2001; total assets QR 137,851m. (2006); sales QR 2,243m. (2006); oil production 850,000 b/d (2006); the State of Qatar's interest in companies active in petroleum and related industries has passed to QP; has responsibility for all phases of oil and gas industry both on shore and off shore, including exploration, drilling, production, refining, transport and storage, distribution, sale and export of oil, natural gas and other hydrocarbons; Oryx gas to liquids (GTL) plant became operational in 2006, with capacity for 34,000 b/d of GTL products; Chair. and Man. Dir ABDULLAH BIN HAMAD AL-ATTIYA (Minister of Energy and Industry); Gen. Man. MUHAMMAD AL-MULLA; 5,500 employees.

Qatar Liquefied Gas Co (QATARGAS): POB 22666, Doha; tel. 4736000; fax 4736666; e-mail infos@qatargas.com.qa; internet www.qatargas.com; f. 1984 to develop the North Field of unassociated gas; cap. QR 500m.; 65% owned by Qatar Petroleum, 10% each by ExxonMobil and Total, and 7.5% each by Marubeni Corpn and Mitsui & Co of Japan; expansion plans to supply 42m. metric tons of LNG to European, Asian and North American markets scheduled for completion by 2010; Chair. ABDULLAH BIN HAMAD AL-ATTIYA (Minister of Energy and Industry); Vice-Chair. and CEO FAISAL MUHAMMAD AS-SUWAIDI.

Ras Laffan LNG Co Ltd (RasGas): POB 24200, Doha; tel. 4738000; fax 4738480; e-mail site-admin@rasgas.com.qa; internet www.rasgas.com; f. 1993; 70% owned by Qatar Petroleum, 30% by ExxonMobil; operates five LNG trains, which had a production capacity of 20.7m. metric tons per year in 2007; CEO HAMAD RASHID AL-MOHANNADI.

Qatar Petroleum also wholly or partly owns: Industries Qatar (IQ) and its subsidiaries, Qatar Gas Transport Co (Nakilat), Gulf Helicopters Co Ltd (GHC), Qatar Vinyl Co (QVC), Qatar Chemical Co (Q-Chem), Qatar Clean Energy Co (QACENCO), Qatar Electricity and Water Co (QEWC), Qatar Shipping Co (Q-Ship), Arab Maritime Petroleum Transport Co (AMPTC), Arab Petroleum Pipelines Co (SUMED), Arab Shipbuilding and Repair Yard Co (ASRY), Arab Petroleum Services Co (APSC) and Arab Petroleum Investments Corpn (APICORP).

UTILITIES

Qatar General Electricity and Water Corpn (Kahramaa): POB 41, Doha; tel. 4845555; fax 4845496; e-mail kmcontact@km.com.qa; internet www.kahramaa.com.qa; f. 2000; state authority for planning, implementation, operation and maintenance of electricity and water sectors; Chair. ABDULLAH BIN HAMAD AL-ATTIYA (Minister of Energy and Industry).

Qatar Electricity and Water Co (QEWC): POB 22046, Doha; tel. 4858585; fax 4831116; e-mail welcome@qewc.com; internet www.qewc.com; f. 1990; 57% privately owned; development and operation of power generation and water desalination facilities; total assets 9,189m. (Dec. 2007); Chair. ABDULLAH BIN HAMAD AL-ATTIYA (Minister of Energy and Industry); Gen. Man. FAHAD HAMAD AL-MOHANNADI.

Transport

A Transportation Master Plan for Qatar, intended to provide a comprehensive framework for the development of the transport infrastructure over a 20-year period, was implemented in late 2007. Projected government expenditure on infrastructure projects, particularly roads, amounted to US $8,400m. for the 2008/09 fiscal year, equivalent to 31.3% of total budgeted expenditure.

RAILWAYS

There are no railways in Qatar, although plans for a regional rail network, connecting Qatar with member countries of the Co-operation Council for the Arab States of the Gulf (Gulf Co-operation Council—GCC), were under discussion in 2009.

ROADS

In 1991 there were some 1,191 km of surfaced road linking Doha and the petroleum centres of Dukhan and Umm Said with the northern end of the peninsula. The total road network in 1999 was estimated to be 1,230 km, 90% of which was paved. By 2006, according to the Qatar Statistics Authority, the network comprised 6,210 km of single-lane and 1,580 km of dual-lane roads. A 105-km road from Doha to Salwa was completed in 1970, and joins one leading from Al-Hufuf in Saudi Arabia, giving Qatar land access to the Mediterranean. A 418-km highway, built in conjunction with Abu Dhabi, links both states with the Gulf network. A major upgrading of the national road network was planned for the first years of the 21st century. A project to construct a causeway (the Friendship Bridge) linking Qatar with Bahrain was approved by both Governments in 2004. After protracted discussions and numerous delays, in May 2008 the contract to design and build the causeway, at a cost of some US $3,000m., was awarded to a France-based consortium. Construction was expected to commence in mid-2009, with completion scheduled for 2013–14. However, the decision, in late 2008, to incorporate a railway line into the project necessitated substantial design revisions that were expected to add up to $1,000m. to the cost of the causeway. In addition, contracts for the construction of a 327-km Mafraq–Ghoueifat highway, linking Qatar with Saudi Arabia and the United Arab Emirates, and a 19-km Doha ring-road, linking New Doha International Airport and New Doha Port, were expected to be awarded in mid-2009.

SHIPPING

Doha Port has nine general cargo berths of 7.5 m–9.0 m depth. The total length of the berths is 1,699 m. In addition, there is a flour mill berth, and a container terminal (with a depth of 12.0 m and a length of 600 m) with a roll-on roll-off (ro-ro) berth at the north end currently under construction. Cold storage facilities exist for cargo of up to 500 metric tons. At Umm Said Harbour the Northern Deep Water Wharves consist of a deep-water quay 730-m long with a dredged depth alongside of 15.5 m, and a quay 570-m long with a dredged depth alongside of 13.0 m. The General Cargo Wharves consist of a quay 400-m long with a dredged depth alongside of 10.0 m. The Southern Deep Water Wharves consist of a deep water quay 508-m long with a dredged depth alongside of 13.0 m. The North Field gas project has increased the demand for shipping facilities. A major new industrial port was completed at Ras Laffan in 1995, providing facilities for LNG and condensate carriers and ro-ro vessels. Qatar Petroleum initiated a US $1,000m. expansion of Ras Laffan port in mid-2005; work was scheduled for completion by the end of 2008. Further expansion plans at Ras Laffan, to accommodate the shipping requirements of the burgeoning LNG and associated industries, were finalized early in 2008; completion of the project would render Ras Laffan the largest man-made harbour in the world, bounded by 26 km of breakwaters. In October 2007 Sheikh Hamad issued a decree announcing that the new Doha port development would be located at Mesaieed industrial city. On completion of its first phase (scheduled for 2014), which was estimated to cost some $5,500m., the port was expected to have annual handling capacity of 2m. 20-ft equivalent units (TEUs), with capacity projected to increase to 6m. TEUs by 2025. Capacity at Doha's existing port, which was to be decommissioned on completion of the new port, was some 400,000 TEUs, with 340,000 TEUs handled in 2007.

Customs and Ports General Authority (CPGA): POB 81, Doha; tel. 4414187; fax 4414959; e-mail admin@customs.gov.qa; internet www.customs.gov.qa; Dir-Gen. Sheikh ABDULLAH BIN JASSIM ATH-THANI.

Qatar Gas Transport Co Ltd (Nakilat): POB 22271, Doha; tel. 4998111; fax 4326788; e-mail info@qgtc.com.qa; internet www.nakilat.com.qa; f. 2004; 50% owned by private Qatari investors, 15% by Qatar Shipping Co, 15% by Qatar Navigation, 5% by Qatar Petroleum and 15% by other Qatari companies; specializes in the shipment of LNG, LPG and petroleum products; wholly owns 27 vessels and jointly owns 33 vessels; wholly owned fleet set to rise to 54 by 2010; Chair. ABDULLAH BIN HAMAD AL-ATTIYA (Minister of Energy and Industry); Man. Dir MUHAMMAD AL-GHANIM.

Qatar Navigation QSC: POB 153, 60 Al-Tameen St, West Bay, Doha; tel. 4468666; fax 4468777; e-mail info@qatarnavigation.com; internet www.qatarnav.com; f. 1957 as Qatar National Navigation and Transport Co Ltd; 100% owned by Qatari nationals; shipping agents, stevedoring, chandlers, forwarding, shipowning, repair, construction, etc.; Chair. Sheikh HAMAD BIN SUHAIM ATH-THANI; CEO KHALIFA BIN ALI AL-HITMI.

Qatar Shipping Co QSC (Q-Ship): POB 22180, Al-Muntazah St, Doha; tel. and fax 4191760; e-mail rahul@qship.com; internet www.qship.com; f. 1992; oil and bulk cargo shipping; Chair. and Man. Dir SALEM BIN BUTTI AN-NAIMI; CEO K. K. KOTHARI.

CIVIL AVIATION

Doha International Airport is equipped to receive all types of aircraft. In 2001 some 2.7m. passengers used the airport. In 2004 Bechtel, a US engineering company, won the contract to manage the redevelopment of the airport (to be known upon completion of the project as New Doha International Airport), 4 km to the east of the existing site. Phase one of the project, which was expected to cost some QR 9,500m., involved the construction of two runways and a new terminal building and was set to increase annual passenger-handling capacity to around 12m.; phase two was expected to double passenger capacity to 24m. After delays to the original schedule, phases one and two were expected to be completed in 2011. Upon completion of phase three of the expansion, scheduled for 2015, passenger-handling capacity was to reach 50m.

Civil Aviation Authority: POB 3000, Doha; tel. 4557333; fax 4557105; e-mail info@caa.gov.qa; internet www.caa.gov.qa; Chair. and Man. Dir ABD AL-AZIZ MUHAMMAD AN-NOAIMI.

Doha International Airport: POB 22550, Doha; tel. 4622999; fax 4622044; e-mail diainfo@qatarairways.com.qa; internet www.dohaairport.com; CEO AKBAR AL-BAKER.

Gulf Helicopters Co Ltd (GHC): POB 811, Doha; tel. 4333888; fax 4411004; e-mail enquiries@gulfhelicopters.com; internet www.gulfhelicopters.com; f. 1974; owned by Qatar Petroleum; Chair. ABDULLAH BIN HAMAD AL-ATTIYA (Minister of Energy and Industry); CEO MUHAMMAD AL-MOHANNADI.

Qatar Airways: POB 22550, Qatar Airways Tower, Airport Rd, Doha; tel. 4496666; fax 4621792; e-mail infodesk@qatarairways.com; internet www.qatarairways.com; f. 1993; state-owned; services to 83 international destinations; operated a fleet of 64 aircraft in Oct. 2008; planned fleet expansion to 110 aircraft by 2013; CEO AKBAR AL-BAKER.

Tourism

Since 2000 the tourism industry has been undergoing a programme of expansion and development, and Qatar's reputation as a venue for international conferences and sporting events has grown. The 15th Asian Games, held in Doha in December 2006, provided a substantial impetus for increased hotel construction from 2004. Doha's status as an applicant city to host the 2016 Olympic Games promoted further extensive construction of accommodation facilities; there were expected to be 45 hotels operating in the capital by 2010, almost double the number in 2002. (The fact that Doha was unsuccessful in its bid to host the Games was not expected to curtail ongoing plans to increase hotel capacity.) A new Museum of Islamic Art opened in Doha in late 2008, and several other new museums and cultural establishments were planned. Notable tourist attractions outside the capital include the historic forts and archaeological sites at Az-Zubarah, and the natural beauty of the Khor al-Adaid, or Inland Sea, region. There were 945,970 tourist arrivals in 2006, in which year receipts from tourism totalled US $374m.

Qatar National Hotels Co: POB 2977, Doha; tel. 4237777; fax 4270707; internet www.qnhc.com; f. 1993; develops and manages hotels and other tourist facilities; govt-owned; Chair. Sheikh NAWAF BIN JASIM BIN JABER ATH-THANI; CEO JAN POUL N. DE BOER.

Qatar Tourism and Exhibitions Authority (QTEA): POB 24624, Doha; tel. 4997499; fax 4991919; e-mail soha@qatartourism.gov.qa; internet www.qatartourism.gov.qa; f. 2000; affiliated with Council of Ministers; Chair. AHMED ABDULLAH AN-NUAIMI; Head of Promotions SOHA MOUSSA.

ROMANIA

Introductory Survey

Location, Climate, Language, Religion, Flag, Capital

Romania lies in south-eastern Europe, bounded to the north and east by Ukraine, to the north-east by Moldova, to the north-west by Hungary, to the south-west by Serbia and to the south by Bulgaria. The south-east coast is washed by the Black Sea. Romania has hot summers and cold winters, with moderate rainfall. The average summer temperature is 23°C (73°F) and the winter average is −3°C (27°F). The official language is Romanian, although minority groups speak Hungarian (Magyar), German and other languages. Most of the inhabitants profess Christianity, and about 87% of believers are adherents of the Romanian Orthodox Church. The national flag (proportions 3 by 5) consists of three equal vertical stripes, of blue, yellow and red. The capital is Bucharest (București).

Recent History

Formerly part of Turkey's Ottoman Empire, Romania became an independent kingdom in 1881. During the dictatorship of the Fascist 'Iron Guard' movement, Romania entered the Second World War as an ally of Nazi Germany. However, Soviet forces entered Romania in 1944, when the pro-Nazi regime was overthrown. Under Soviet pressure, King Michael (Mihail) I accepted the appointment of a communist-led coalition Government in March 1945. At elections in November 1946 a communist-dominated bloc claimed 89% of the votes cast, but the results were widely believed to have been fraudulent. In 1947 the small Romanian Communist Party (RCP) merged with the Social Democratic Party to become the Romanian Workers' Party (RWP). King Michael was forced to abdicate on 30 December 1947, when the Romanian People's Republic was proclaimed. The republic's first Constitution was adopted in 1948, and in the same year the nationalization of the main industrial and financial institutions was begun. In 1949 private landholdings were expropriated and amalgamated into state and collective farms. The implementation of Soviet-style economic policies was accompanied by the establishment of full political control by the RWP.

In 1952, following a purge of the RWP membership, a new Constitution, closer to the Soviet model, was adopted. Gheorghe Gheorghiu-Dej, the First Secretary of the RWP, became Romania's unchallenged leader and proceeded to implement large-scale plans for industrialization. Gheorghiu-Dej died in 1965; he was succeeded as First Secretary of the RWP by Nicolae Ceaușescu, a Secretary of the RWP Central Committee since 1954. In June 1965 the RWP again became the RCP, and Ceaușescu's post of First Secretary was restyled General Secretary. A new Constitution, adopted in August, changed the country's name to the Socialist Republic of Romania.

Ceaușescu continued his predecessor's relatively independent foreign policy, criticizing the invasion of Czechoslovakia by troops of the Warsaw Pact (the defence grouping of the Soviet bloc) in 1968, and establishing links with Western states and institutions. However, the use of foreign loans for investment led to severe economic problems by the early 1980s. In order to strengthen his position, Ceaușescu (who had become President of the Republic in 1974) implemented frequent changes in the RCP leadership and the Government. In March 1980 his wife, Elena, became a First Deputy Chairman of the Council of Ministers, and numerous other family members held government and party posts.

In late 1985 an energy crisis resulted in a declaration of a state of emergency in the electric power industry and the dismissal of ministers and senior officials. Shortages led to strict energy rationing in 1987, and strikes were organized in provincial factories. In November thousands of people marched through the city of Brașov and stormed the local RCP headquarters, protesting against the decline in living standards and in working conditions. Hundreds of arrests were made, and similar protests followed in other cities. In March 1988 Ceaușescu announced details of a rural urbanization programme, to entail the demolition of some 8,000 villages, and the resettlement of their residents (mostly ethnic Hungarians) in new 'agro-industrial centres'. The plan attracted much domestic and international criticism, but Ceaușescu maintained that the programme would raise living standards and ensure social equality.

In December 1989 there was unrest in the western city of Timișoara as supporters of László Tökés, a Protestant clergyman (an ethnic Hungarian who had repeatedly criticized the Government's policies), demonstrated their opposition to his eviction from his church. A further protest was attended by thousands of local residents. Security forces opened fire on the crowd, reportedly killing several hundred people. There were reports of protests in other towns, and the country's borders were closed.

On 21 December 1989 President Ceaușescu attended a mass rally in Bucharest, intended to demonstrate popular support. Instead, his address was interrupted by hostile chanting, and anti-Government demonstrations followed later in the day, leading to clashes between protesters and members of the Securitate (the secret police force), during which many civilians were killed. The disturbances quickly spread to other parts of the country, and on the following day Ceaușescu declared a state of emergency; however, soldiers of the regular army declared their support for the protesters. Nicolae and Elena Ceaușescu escaped from the RCP Central Committee headquarters by helicopter as demonstrators stormed the building. The Ceaușescus were captured near Târgoviște and, on 25 December, after a summary trial, were executed by firing squad. Fighting continued for several days, mainly between Securitate forces and regular soldiers.

Meanwhile, a 145-member National Salvation Front (NSF) was formed, and a provisional Government was established. Ion Iliescu, a former Secretary of the RCP Central Committee, became interim President, and Petre Roman, an academic, was appointed Prime Minister. The new Government immediately decreed an end to the RCP's constitutional monopoly of power, and cancelled the rural urbanization programme. The RCP was banned, it was announced that free elections would be held in 1990, and the designation of Socialist Republic was abandoned. By early January 1990 the army had restored order, and the Securitate was abolished. According to official figures, 689 people were killed during the revolution.

Special military tribunals were established to try Ceaușescu's former associates. In February 1990 four senior RCP officials were found guilty of responsibility for the shootings in Timișoara and Bucharest and were sentenced to life imprisonment. Numerous other former government and RCP members were similarly charged. In September Ceaușescu's son, Nicu, who was found to have ordered security forces to open fire on demonstrators in Sibiu in December 1989, received a 20-year prison sentence. (He was released in 1992 on the grounds of ill health, and died in 1996.) Gen. Iulian Vlad, the former head of the Securitate, was sentenced to 12 years' imprisonment in 1991; in January 1994, however, he was released as part of a general amnesty. In December 1991 eight associates of the former President were sentenced to prison terms of up to 25 years for their part in the shootings in Timișoara.

Despite the widespread jubilation that followed the downfall of Ceaușescu, the NSF did not enjoy total public support. Many citizens believed that the Front's leadership was too closely linked with the Ceaușescu regime, and were particularly critical of the NSF's control of the media. Furthermore, the NSF's announcement, in January 1990, that it was to contest the forthcoming elections, and its reversal of the prohibition of the RCP, increased fears that members of the disgraced regime were attempting to regain power. In January the offices of two opposition parties, the National Liberal Party (NLP) and the National Peasants' Party, were attacked by NSF supporters. In February, after negotiations among representatives of 29 political parties, the NSF agreed to share power with the opposition, pending the elections, in a 180-member Provisional National Unity Council (PNUC). Each of the political parties represented in the talks was allocated three seats on the Council, and the PNUC was subsequently expanded to 253 members to permit representation by other political parties; nevertheless, NSF members and supporters occupied 111 seats in the Council. The PNUC elected an Executive Bureau, with Iliescu as its President. Opposition to the NSF persisted, particularly in the armed forces. The Minister of National Defence was replaced in compliance with demands from within the military, but shortly afterwards thousands of anti-Government demonstrators demanded the resignation of Iliescu, and some 250 protesters forcibly entered the NSF headquarters.

As the elections approached, there were mass anti-communist demonstrations in Bucharest. The election campaign was acrimonious, and there were widespread accusations of systematic intimidation and harassment of the NSF's opponents. At the presidential and legislative elections, held on 20 May 1990, the NSF achieved an overwhelming victory. Allegations of irregularities were, however, confirmed by international observers. According to official figures, Iliescu won 85.1% of the valid votes cast in the presidential poll. In the elections to the bicameral legislature, the NSF won 65% of the votes cast, securing 263 of the 387 seats in the Camera Deputaţilor (Chamber of Deputies) and 91 of the 119 seats in Senatul (the Senate).

Unrest continued, and in June 1990 a protest in Bucharest was forcibly broken up by the police. The brutal treatment of the demonstrators provoked renewed clashes, in which the armed forces opened fire on rioters. Following an appeal for support by Iliescu, some 7,000 miners and other workers were transported to the capital, where they swiftly seized control of the streets. The disturbances resulted in several deaths and hundreds of injuries. Following President Iliescu's inauguration in late June, Roman was reappointed Prime Minister, and a new Council of Ministers was formed, in which nearly all the members of the interim administration were replaced. In the following months, as popular discontent at the deteriorating economic situation intensified, there was widespread strike action. In October Roman announced extensive economic reforms. In the following month price increases led to demonstrations in Bucharest, including a protest march by some 100,000 people, organized by a new opposition grouping, the Civic Alliance. Nevertheless, the Government proceeded with its (slightly modified) reform programme, resulting in further large price rises in April 1991. At the end of that month Roman allocated three government portfolios to opposition politicians.

In September 1991 miners, by this time opposed to President Iliescu, began a strike in support of demands for pay increases and the resignation of the Government. Thousands of miners travelled to Bucharest, where they attacked government offices and ransacked the parliament building. Four people were killed and hundreds injured during violent clashes with the security forces, as a result of which the Council of Ministers was obliged to resign. Theodor Stolojan, a former Minister of Finance, was appointed as Prime Minister, leading a coalition Government formed in October, comprising members of the NSF, the NLP, the Agrarian Democratic Party of Romania (ADPR) and the Romanian Ecological Movement.

A new Constitution, enshrining a multi-party system, a free-market economy and guarantees of the respect of human rights, was approved by the legislature in November 1991 and was endorsed by some 77.3% of voters in a referendum in December. The results of local elections, which took place between February and April 1992, confirmed the decline in support for the NSF. Many seats were won by the centre-right Democratic Convention of Romania (DCR), an alliance of 18 parties and organizations, including the Christian-Democratic National Peasants' Party (CDNPP) and the Party of the Civic Alliance. The NSF divided into two factions, and in April the faction loyal to Iliescu, which favoured only limited reforms, was registered as the Democratic National Salvation Front (DNSF).

Against a background of renewed labour unrest, legislative and presidential elections took place on 27 September 1992. The DNSF won 117 of the 328 elective seats in the Camera Deputaţilor and 49 of the 143 seats in Senatul, making it the largest party in the new Parlamentul (Parliament). Its closest rival was the DCR, with 82 seats in the Camera Deputaţilor and 34 in Senatul. The NSF secured only 43 and 18 seats, respectively. In the presidential election, the two leading candidates, Iliescu and Emil Constantinescu, representing the DCR, proceeded to a second round of voting on 11 October, at which Iliescu won 61.4% of the votes cast. In November Nicolae Văcăroiu, an economist with no professed political party affiliation, formed a Government comprising equal numbers of DNSF members and independents.

The abolition of price subsidies for many basic commodities and services, from May 1993, precipitated renewed labour unrest. The Government's position was also undermined by successive confidence motions. Meanwhile, the DNSF had changed its name to the Party of Social Democracy of Romania (PSDR) in July and absorbed three other parties. In May, in an apparently similar attempt to distance itself from the events of 1989–90, Roman's NSF renamed itself the Democratic Party—National Salvation Front (DP—NSF). By late 1993 Văcăroiu's administration appeared increasingly unstable. In November a protest march in Bucharest, demanding rapid economic reforms, was the largest public demonstration in the country since the overthrow of the Ceauşescu regime. In February 1994 renewed industrial unrest led to a general strike. A government reorganization in March continued the pattern of single-party (PSDR) rule supplemented by independent 'technocrats' (although later in the year two members of the Romanian National Unity Party—RNUP—were appointed to the Council of Ministers). In November 1995 Iliescu approved legislation providing for the restitution of property confiscated by the communist regime in the late 1940s and 1950s.

In May 1996 the PSDR terminated its parliamentary co-operation with the RNUP. Although the PSDR secured the largest number of mayoral and council seats at the local elections in June, the results indicated a decline in support for the party. The DCR and the Social Democratic Union (SDU), formed by the DP—NSF and the Romanian Social Democratic Party (RSDP) in January, won control of many major cities, including Bucharest. In September the RNUP ministers were dismissed from the Government: the breakdown in relations with the PSDR had been exacerbated by the RNUP's opposition to the signing of a treaty with Hungary (see below).

Legislative and presidential elections took place on 3 November 1996. The DCR won the largest number of parliamentary seats, with 122 of the 328 seats in the Camera Deputaţilor and 53 of the 143 seats in Senatul. The PSDR took 91 and 41 seats in the respective chambers, and the SDU 53 and 23. The DCR and the SDU subsequently reached agreement on political co-operation. In the first round of the presidential election, which was contested by 16 candidates, Iliescu won 32.3% of the valid votes cast, and Constantinescu took 28.2%. With the support of nearly all the opposition parties, Constantinescu was duly elected in a second round on 17 November, with 54.4% of the votes cast. Constantinescu pledged to combat corruption and accelerate economic reform, and had asserted his commitment to the integration of Romania into Western political, economic and defence institutions. At the end of November Victor Ciorbea of the DCR, who had been elected as Mayor of Bucharest earlier in the year, was nominated as Prime Minister, and in mid-December a new coalition Government, comprising the DCR, the SDU and the Democratic Alliance of Hungarians in Romania (DAHR), was officially sworn in.

Despite protests from opposition parties, the Government restored citizenship to former King Michael, who visited Romania in February 1997. Meanwhile, in January a National Council for Action against Corruption and Organized Crime, headed by Constantinescu, was established; a number of leading bankers were subsequently arrested, principally on charges of fraud, and several senior members of the security forces were dismissed. The arrest, in February, of Miron Cozma, the leader of the miners' demonstrations in Bucharest in June 1990 and September 1991, prompted protests from miners and their trade union leaders. In November 1997 an estimated 40,000 people attended a rally in Bucharest to protest against increasing poverty.

Meanwhile, several prominent members of the PSDR resigned from the party in June 1997, and formed a new party, the Alliance for Romania (AFR). A government reorganization in December, which included the appointment of a number of technocrats to principal portfolios, failed to ease mounting tensions within the coalition, and the DAHR temporarily suspended its participation in the Government.

Adrian Severin, Minister of State and Minister of Foreign Affairs, and a member of the DP (as the DP—NSF had been renamed), resigned in December 1997, after a judicial investigation failed to confirm his allegations that certain political leaders and newspaper editors were working with foreign intelligence services. In January 1998 the resignation of the Minister of Transport, Traian Băsescu of the DP, owing to his criticism of Ciorbea's Government, led the DP to demand his reinstatement, and DP ministers eventually withdrew from the Government.

In March 1998, in response to increasing pressure within the coalition, Ciorbea and his Government resigned. Radu Vasile, the Secretary-General of the CDNPP and a Deputy Chairman of Senatul, was designated Prime Minister in April. A new Council of Ministers was appointed, which was endorsed by Parlamentul in mid-April. A new coalition protocol was designed to strengthen the authority of the Prime Minister and improve co-operation between government members. In June the approval of legislation by Senatul that debarred former secret police agents from holding public office led to the resignation of the Minister of Health, Francis Baranyi.

As Romania's economic situation worsened, the Minister of Finance, Daniel Dăianu, was dismissed in September 1998; he was replaced by Decebal Trăian Remes. In October Sorin Dimitriu resigned as Minister of Privatization and head of the State Ownership Fund. Meanwhile, in early September the DAHR threatened to leave the ruling coalition unless Parlamentul adopted legislation providing for the establishment of a minority-language university. At the end of the month the Government duly agreed to create an independent university in Cluj-Napoca for Hungarian and German minorities.

Protests against austerity measures, which had begun the previous month, intensified in December 1998. In January 1999 a strike by miners escalated when Vasile refused to negotiate with Cozma, who had been released from prison in mid-1998, after serving an 18-month sentence for the possession of firearms and ammunition. Encouraged by nationalist politicians (notably from the Greater Romania Party—GRP), 10,000–20,000 miners marched towards Bucharest, and in Costeşti, some 190 km north-west of Bucharest, violent clashes broke out with the security forces. Following emergency talks between the Prime Minister and miners' leaders, a temporary agreement was reached. The Minister of the Interior, Gavril Dejeu, resigned, amid severe criticism of the security forces' failure to halt the march; he was replaced by Constantin Dudu Ionescu. In February the Supreme Court of Justice sentenced Cozma, *in absentia*, to 18 years' imprisonment for undermining state authority. In protest, some 2,000–4,000 miners, led by Cozma, again marched towards Bucharest. The miners were stopped by the security forces some 160 km west of Bucharest, where more than 100 people were injured and one miner died during the violence that ensued; Cozma and several hundred miners were arrested. Labour unrest continued throughout the first half of 1999. (In June 2002 Cozma was sentenced to an additional 12 years' imprisonment—to be served concurrently—for his involvement in the 1999 violence; in January 2007, however, it was reported that he had been granted early release.)

In early June 1999 the Camera Deputaţilor approved amendments to the electoral law, increasing the threshold for parliamentary representation from 3% to 5%, with alliances required to secure a further 3% for each member party. Later that month the Camera Deputaţilor voted in favour of providing public access to the files of the Securitate (although many documents were believed to have been destroyed); the President promulgated the legislation in December. Also in June legislation was approved by Parlamentul, providing for minority-language education at every level of the education system. In July Gen. Victor Stănculescu and Gen. Mihai Chiţac were sentenced to 15 years' imprisonment, having been found guilty of the murders of 72 people, by ordering the security forces to open fire on protesters during the Timişoara uprising in December 1989. The ruling was severely criticized by Victor Babiuc, the Minister of National Defence, whose ministry was ordered to pay damages to those wounded in the shootings and the relatives of the dead. (Babiuc resigned from the Government and from his party several months later.)

In November 1999 students undertook strike action, and some 10,000 trade union members participated in protest rallies to demand the resignation of the Government. In mid-December, as labour unrest continued, Constantinescu dismissed Vasile, after all seven CDNPP government ministers, followed by the three NLP ministers, resigned from the Government. Constantinescu nominated Mugur Isărescu, hitherto Governor of the National Bank of Romania (and without affiliation to any political party), as Prime Minister. The legislature subsequently approved the appointment of Isărescu and his Council of Ministers, which remained largely unchanged, although Roman joined the new Government as Minister of State and Minister of Foreign Affairs. Vasile was expelled from the CDNPP later that month.

In local elections, held on 4 June 2000, the PSDR won the largest proportion of the votes cast (36.7%). Băsescu left the Government, after being elected as Mayor of Bucharest. In July President Constantinescu unexpectedly announced that he would not stand for re-election at the forthcoming presidential election. In September the RSDP withdrew from the governing coalition, announcing that it was to merge with the main opposition party, the PSDR.

Legislative and presidential elections took place concurrently on 26 November 2000. The PSDR secured 155 seats in the Camera Deputaţilor and 65 in Senatul, while the GRP obtained 84 and 37 seats, respectively. The rate of voter participation was the lowest recorded since the collapse of communism, at 57.5%. Representatives of the PSDR and the GRP were also the principal candidates in the presidential election, in which the former President, Iliescu, obtained 36.4% of the votes cast and Corneliu Vadim Tudor of the GRP won 28.3%. As neither candidate secured an overall majority, a 'run-off' election was held on 10 December, in which Iliescu won 66.8% of the votes cast. The increased support for the extreme nationalists was thought to reflect popular disillusionment with economic hardship and high unemployment.

In December 2000 President Iliescu nominated Adrian Năstase of the PSDR as Prime Minister. Năstase subsequently signed a joint statement on priorities for the development of Romania with the leaders of the DAHR, the NLP and the DP. Although Năstase insisted that the declaration did not represent a coalition agreement, the support of those parties enabled the PSDR to form a minority Government, and ensured the isolation of the GRP. The new, expanded Council of Ministers was sworn in on 28 December. Despite their shared objective of implementing reform with a view to attaining membership of the European Union (EU, see p. 255), the new President and Prime Minister came from different ideological backgrounds.

In February 2001 President Iliescu endorsed a law, which provided for the return of some 300,000 properties nationalized during the communist era to their original owners; it superseded legislation on the restitution of property that had been approved in 1995. In mid-June the PSDR and the RSDP formally merged, creating the Social Democratic Party (SDP), under the leadership of Prime Minister Năstase. In November some 15,000 people took part in a demonstration in Bucharest against poverty and the Government's austerity programme. A further large-scale protest took place in December.

In March 2002 attempts to tackle corruption led the Government to announce the establishment, with effect from September, of a new National Anti-corruption Prosecution office. Also in March the Government sought to moderate the power of labour organizations through the signature of a 'social pact' with three of the five largest trade unions, which provided for an increased minimum wage and the creation of 10,000 jobs. In September Senatul approved a new law on political parties, which required all parties to re-register by 31 December, and to be composed of a minimum of 10,000 members from at least 21 of Romania's 41 administrative sub-divisions. On 10 November local elections took place in 21 counties, in which the SDP was the most successful party. In early 2003 a number of prominent CDNPP members were expelled from the party after participating in the foundation of the new Popular Action civic movement, led by former President Constantinescu; in February it was confirmed that the movement was to become a political party.

In June 2003 Năstase reorganized the Council of Ministers, reducing the number of portfolios from 23 to 14. In a referendum held on 18–19 October, some 90% of votes cast by 55.7% of the electorate approved 79 proposed amendments to the Constitution, which aimed to bring it into conformity with EU requirements (by, *inter alia*, guaranteeing the right to private property, strengthening legal rights for ethnic minorities and limiting the powers of the executive branch of government). The revised Constitution entered into force on 29 October.

In March 2004 Năstase announced the appointment of three new Ministers of State (effectively deputy prime ministers). Three existing ministers also assumed the additional positions of Ministers of State. In August charges of abuse of office and embezzlement were brought against 79 people, including Băsescu (in his former capacity as Minister of Transport in 1991–92 and 1997–2000), relating to the alleged illegal sale of 16 ships from the national maritime fleet in 1991–2000. Some commentators suggested that the charge was an attempt to discredit the opposition prior to national legislative and presidential elections; Băsescu had been re-elected as Mayor of Bucharest two months earlier. In local elections held on 6 and 20 June 2004 the SDP received the greatest number of mayoral mandates, closely followed by the NLP.

In September 2004 the SDP and the Humanist Party of Romania (HPR) formed an electoral alliance, the National Union. Meanwhile, the NLP and the DP announced their intention to contest the forthcoming legislative elections as the Justice and Truth Alliance. On 28 November presidential and legislative elections were held, as scheduled. The National Union emerged as the largest bloc in both legislative chambers, with 132 seats (of a total of 332) in the Camera Deputaţilor and 57 (of a total of 137) in Senatul. The Justice and Truth Alliance received 112 seats in the Camera Deputaţilor, and 49 in Senatul. The representation of the GRP was markedly reduced in both chambers, to 48 deputies in the lower chamber, and 21 senators. In the presidential ballot, no candidate secured an absolute majority of votes cast, and Năstase (with 40.9%) and Traian Băsescu (with 33.9%) proceeded to a second round of voting on 12 December. In the 'runoff' election, Băsescu achieved a narrow victory, with 51.2% of the votes cast. (As President, Băsescu was immune from prosecution.) On 18 December Băsescu resigned from the DP, in compliance with constitutional requirements, and he was inaugurated as President two days later. Năstase was elected as Chairman of the Camera Deputaţilor, and Văcăroiu, a Deputy Chairman of the SDP, was elected as Chairman of Senatul in a vote that was boycotted by senators of the Justice and Truth Alliance and the DAHR.

Băsescu nominated Călin Popescu-Tăriceanu to form a government, but the approval of a cabinet was dependent upon its ability to achieve a majority in Parlamentul; ultimately, the grouping that would hold the majority in the legislature was to be determined by the allegiance of the HPR (as the DAHR did not possess a sufficient number of mandates to decide the issue). The HPR was persuaded to abandon its electoral partner, the SDP, but even collectively, the NLP, the DP, the DAHR and the HPR only amounted to one more than the requisite quorum in the bicameral legislature. On 28 December 2004 the new coalition Council of Ministers was approved by both chambers of the legislature. In February 2005 Popescu-Tăriceanu was elected as Chairman of the NLP.

The HPR was renamed the Conservative Party (CP) in May 2005. In June Iliescu reportedly became the subject of an investigation into the deaths of six people during the demonstrations by miners in 1990 (see above); however, as a member of Senatul and a former Head of State, Iliescu was immune from prosecution. In late June 2005 Emil Boc was elected President of the DP. In early July the Constitutional Court rejected a programme for judicial reform that had been proposed by the Government in order to satisfy requirements for membership of the EU, prompting Popescu-Tăriceanu to announce that he intended to submit the resignation of his administration, in an attempt to precipitate early elections. However, on 13 July an extraordinary session of Parlamentul approved amendments to the legislation on judicial reform, in conformity with the Court's objections. Meanwhile, central and eastern parts of the country were affected by severe flooding, which resulted in more than 20 deaths, and on 19 July Popescu-Tăriceanu announced that his Government would remain in place in order to respond to the emergency. In August Popescu-Tăriceanu reorganized the Council of Ministers.

In October 2005 the EU Commissioner responsible for Enlargement, Olli Rehn, warned Romania that its planned accession to the EU in 2007 could be subject to delay if measures were not taken to combat corruption and accelerate the pace of judicial reform. In early 2006 a number of political figures duly came under investigation as a result of allegations of fraud, and in January Năstase resigned from the leadership of the SDP, following concerns about the legitimacy of an inheritance received by his wife. In early February Năstase was indicted on charges of bribery, pertaining to the acquisition of land in 1998. However, Senatul rejected legislation that would have permitted officials from the National Anti-corruption Prosecution office increased powers to facilitate the investigation of senior politicians and members of the judiciary (and subsequently restricted prosecutors from searching Năstase's property). Năstase resigned as Chairman of the Camera Deputaţilor in mid-March, following a vote of no confidence by the SDP; he was succeeded by Bogdan Olteanu of the NLP.

In September 2006 the Minister of National Defence, Teodor Atanasiu of the NLP, was removed from his post by President Băsescu, following allegations of abuse of military intelligence; he was replaced in late October by Sorin Frunzăverde of the DP, who had previously held that position in 2000. In December 2006 the CP announced its withdrawal from the coalition Government, prompting the resignation of two ministers and ending the parliamentary majority commanded by Popescu-Tăriceanu.

In January 2007 Băsescu publicly accused Popescu-Tăriceanu of attempting to influence a criminal investigation against a close associate accused of financial misconduct, while the Prime Minister issued counter-accusations that Băsescu was undermining government stability. In February Mihai Ungureanu tendered his resignation as Minister of Foreign Affairs at the request of Popescu-Tăriceanu, after he had failed to inform the Government about the detention of two Romanian nationals by US forces in Iraq; Băsescu subsequently refused to endorse the Prime Minister's nomination of an NLP representative, Adrian Cioroianu, to the post. The intra-administrative tensions were further exacerbated in March, when Popescu-Tăriceanu repeated demands for the withdrawal of Romania's military contingent in Iraq, and for the replacement of three DP ministers, notably the Minister of Justice, Monica Luisa Macovei (whose efforts to reform the legal system had helped to ensure Romania's admission to the EU on 1 January). At the beginning of April Popescu-Tăriceanu accused Băsescu of provoking dissension within the Government and ended his party's coalition with the DP, thereby removing eight DP ministers. He formed a new minority Government, comprising 13 representatives of the NLP and four of the DAHR, which was approved by Parlamentul, with the support of the SDP, on 3 April (and endorsed by Băsescu on the following day). Cioroianu became Minister of Foreign Affairs, while Tudor Chiuariu of the NLP, who had hitherto headed the anti-corruption department in the Office of the Prime Minister, was appointed Minister of Justice; Teodor Meleşcanu of the NLP was appointed Minister of Defence. On 19 April a motion initiated by the SDP to suspend Băsescu from office on grounds of unconstitutional conduct (by creating political instability, pressurizing the judiciary and interfering in government affairs) was approved by Parlamentul, after receiving the support of the ruling coalition deputies. Văcăroiu, as Chairman of Senatul, was to act as interim President, and a national referendum on Băsescu's impeachment was scheduled to take place one month later, in accordance with the Constitution. A Constitutional Court ruling earlier in April on the charges against Băsescu had been in his favour, and it was widely believed that his efforts to combat corruption had antagonized former communists. At a rally of his supporters in early May, Băsescu demanded the resignation of Chiuariu, who had reportedly proposed the dismissal of a prominent anti-corruption prosecutor. On 9 May, in accordance with EU requirements, Senatul approved legislation providing for the creation of a national agency to monitor the activities of civil servants, including parliamentary deputies, in an effort to prevent corruption. At the national referendum, held on 19 May, Băsescu's removal from office was opposed by about 74.5% of those who voted. Băsescu was officially reinstated as President on 23 May. In the same month he was obliged to issue an apology, following the disclosure of remarks he had made about a journalist that referred to the Roma ethnic group in a racially offensive manner.

In early October 2007 a motion of no confidence against Popescu-Tăriceanu's Government was narrowly defeated in a joint session of both parliamentary chambers. The continuation of the minority administration, and of the hostility between Popescu-Tăriceanu and Băsescu, subsequently proved an impediment to the adoption of reforms required by the EU. In the same month Decebal Traian Remeş, the Minister of Agriculture and Rural Development, resigned, after an investigation into allegations of corruption against him was initiated.

On 25 November 2007 elections (postponed since May) to 35 seats in the European Parliament (see below) were conducted. The DP won 13 seats and the SDP 10 seats, while the NLP secured six seats and its coalition partner, the DAHR, two seats; the Liberal Democratic Party (formed in late 2006 by breakaway members of the NLP, and led by Theodor Stolojan) won three seats, and the remaining seat was obtained by an independent. A referendum on changing the electoral system to single-mandate voting was organized on the same day; although more than 80% of voters supported the proposed amendment, the referendum was ruled to be invalid, owing to a rate of participation of only 26% of the electorate. In January 2008 the DP merged with the Liberal Democratic Party to form the Democratic Liberal Party (DLP), under the continued leadership of Boc.

In early December 2007 Chiuariu resigned from his post as Minister of Justice, following the initiation of a criminal investigation into his alleged abuse of office. In January 2008 Băsescu refused to endorse Popescu-Tăriceanu's selected candidate, demanding that the new minister be a representative of a party other than the NLP. After the Constitutional Court ruled in

ROMANIA

Introductory Survey

support of Băsescu, in March Cătălin Marian Predoiu, a lawyer with no political affiliation, was appointed as the new Minister of Justice. Following the failure of the November 2007 referendum on the adoption of a single-mandate voting system, in March 2008 Senatul adopted legislation providing for the introduction of compromise electoral reforms: rather than the existing party list system, candidates were to be directly elected by an absolute majority of votes in single-member constituencies, while the overall distribution of seats in each chamber was to be determined by proportional representation among parties securing a minimum of 5% of votes cast nationally. Prior to local elections, Constantinescu's Popular Action party merged with the NLP, which also conducted co-operation discussions with the CDNPP. Local, county and municipal elections were conducted throughout Romania on 1 June, with a second round of voting held in mayoral elections, where required, on 15 June. Notably, following two rounds of voting, Sorin Oprescu, an independent candidate who, none the less, was closely affiliated with the SDP (and had represented the party in Senatul in 2000–08), was elected as Mayor of Bucharest. In August the Camera Deputaților voted against the official prosecution of Năstase on charges of bribery. However, later that month Senatul voted in favour of investigating Paul Păcuraru, the Minister of Labour, the Family and Equal Opportunities, who was alleged to have accepted bribes, and also a former Minister of the Economy suspected of having connections with organized crime.

Elections to the bicameral legislature were conducted under the new mixed-member proportional representation system on 30 November 2008. The DLP marginally secured the greatest representation in both chambers, with 115 of the total 334 seats in the Camera Deputaților (with 32.4% of the votes cast), and 51 of 137 seats in Senatul (and 33.6% of the votes cast); the SDP, allied with the CP, won 114 seats (33.1% of votes) in the Camera Deputaților and 49 seats (34.2%) in Senatul, and the NLP 65 seats (18.6%) in the Camera Deputaților and 28 seats (18.7%) in Senatul. In early December Băsescu invited former Prime Minister Stolojan, of the DLP, to establish a new administration; however, Stolojan unexpectedly ceded the nomination to Boc. Following a coalition agreement between the DLP and the SDP, a new Government comprising members of both parties was approved by the legislature on 22 December. The Vice-President of the SDP, Dan Nica, became Deputy Prime Minister; the DLP and the SDP were each allocated nine ministries, while Predoiu retained the justice portfolio. In January 2009 the first SDP representative appointed as Minister of the Interior and Administrative Reform resigned, after attracting censure from the party for his nomination of a former associate of Băsescu as head of the intelligence service. In early February the candidate appointed to succeed him, Liviu Dragnea, also tendered his resignation after only 12 days in the post (reportedly after nominations he made were also rejected), citing an inadequate budget and tensions within the governing coalition. Nica subsequently received the post of Minister of the Interior and Administrative Reform (while remaining deputy premier). Also in February the Presidential Commission for the Analysis of the Political and Constitutional Regime in Romania published a number of proposals for extensive changes to the political system, including a substantial increase in the powers of the President (who would, notably, be empowered to dissolve the legislature). Meanwhile, the European Commission issued a report urging the Romanian authorities to make progress with anti-corruption and judicial reforms, in particular criticizing the legislature for preventing high-level investigations of corruption from proceeding.

Romania experienced frequent occurrences of ethnic unrest after the fall of Ceaușescu. In 1991 there were organized attacks on Roma (Gypsy) communities throughout Romania, resulting in the emigration of many Roma to Germany. In September 1992 Germany repatriated 43,000 Romanian refugees, more than one-half of whom were Roma, having agreed to provide financial assistance for their resettlement in Romania. The migration of Roma to the member countries of the EU strained relations with Romania throughout the remainder of the 1990s. However, in January 2002 the Council of Europe (see p. 236) published a report condemning police brutality and widespread discrimination against Roma communities in Romania, and the EU made the improvement of the treatment of the Roma minority a requirement for Romania to be declared eligible to accede to the Union. In February 2005 Romania was one of eight countries in the region to announce its adherence to a World Bank-financed 10-year plan to assist the Roma community.

Following the overthrow of Ceaușescu, ethnic Hungarians (a sizeable minority, numbering more than 7% of the total population at the 1992 census) sought to increase their cultural and linguistic autonomy in Transylvania. In March 1990 demonstrations by ethnic Hungarians demanding such rights were attacked by Romanian nationalists in Târgu Mureș. Tanks and troops were deployed to quell the unrest, in which several people were killed, and a state of emergency was declared in the town. In mid-1992 there was renewed tension when the Mayor of Cluj-Napoca, Gheorghe Funar (later head of the right-wing RNUP), ordered the removal of Hungarian-language street signs in the city, and ethnic Hungarian prefects in Covasna and Harghita were replaced by ethnic Romanians. The Government attempted to calm the situation by appointing 'parallel' prefects of ethnic Hungarian background, but further controversy was caused by the removal, in September, of the only ethnic Hungarian State Secretary in the Government. An agreement on Hungarian minority rights was signed in July 1993, which included guarantees for the training of Hungarian-speaking schoolteachers and bilingual street signs in areas with Hungarian populations of at least 30%. In August Béla Markó, the President of the DAHR, insisted that any Hungarian-Romanian state treaty should enshrine a 'special status' for ethnic Hungarians in Romania. Markó's proposals included the equal status of the Hungarian and Romanian languages in predominantly Hungarian-populated areas and greater control for the minority over educational and cultural affairs. In May Romania ratified the Framework Convention of the Council of Europe on the general protection of national minorities. In September 1996 Romania and Hungary signed a treaty of friendship, as a result of which Romania agreed to safeguard the rights of ethnic Hungarians, and Hungary relinquished any claim to territory in Transylvania. In December two DAHR leaders were appointed to the new Government. Relations between Romania and Hungary improved further in February 1997 with the signature of a defence co-operation agreement. Proposals to amend legislation on education, in favour of ethnic minorities, provoked controversy in Romania in 1997 and 1998, although the amendments were finally approved in June 1999.

In January 2001 the Camera Deputaților approved a new public administration law, which made compulsory bilingual place names and signs, and the use of a given minority's language in local administration, in towns where that minority formed at least 20% of the population. In June the Government condemned Hungary's intention to introduce a new 'status law', which was to grant education, employment and medical rights to ethnic Hungarians living in neighbouring countries (including Romania) from January 2002. In December 2001 the Prime Ministers of the two countries signed a memorandum of understanding, which extended the short-term employment rights offered to ethnic Hungarians under the terms of the status law to all Romanian citizens. Finally, in September 2003 Prime Minister Năstase and his Hungarian counterpart, Péter Medgyessy, signed a bilateral agreement on the implementation of the status law in Romania. Hungary proved to be a staunch supporter of Romania's candidacy for EU membership. In October 2005 the first joint Romanian-Hungarian inter-governmental meeting was held in Bucharest, at which a treaty was concluded on the border regime, co-operation and mutual assistance.

Diplomatic relations with the former Soviet republic of Moldova (much of which formed part of Romania in 1918–40, and where a majority of the population are ethnic Romanians) were established in August 1991, and some political groups began to advocate the unification of the two states. The Romanian leadership opposed unification, but encouraged the development of closer cultural and economic ties with Moldova. The support of the Russian military in Moldova for the secessionist movement in the self-proclaimed 'Transdnestrian Moldovan Soviet Socialist Republic' damaged relations between Romania and Russia. In March 1994 a plebiscite was held in Moldova on the question of reunification with Romania; more than 95% of those who took part in the referendum voted for an independent state, effectively signalling the demise of the pro-unification movement. In 2000, as formal negotiations on Romania's accession to the EU commenced, hundreds of Moldovans applied for Romanian citizenship, in anticipation of the eventual tightening of border regulations. Relations with Moldova deteriorated from late 2001.

In October Năstase cancelled a planned visit to Moldova, after President Vladimir Voronin of Moldova accused Romania of 'expansionism'. Relations had improved by 2003, following a meeting between the respective Presidents at a conference in Beirut, Lebanon, in September 2002, and inter-ministerial co-operation was restored in April 2003; Romania confirmed that it would not require Moldovan citizens to possess entry visas until its accession to the EU. Relations improved further over the course of 2004, with the apparent reorientation of Moldovan foreign policy towards the West. Moldova was the first country to which newly elected President Traian Băsescu made a state visit in January 2005, and Romania offered support for Moldova's objective of securing eventual membership of the EU. After Romania's official accession to the EU on 1 January 2007 necessitated the possession of entry visas for Moldovan citizens wishing to visit Romania, the Moldovan Government strongly criticized Romania for granting Romanian citizenship to large numbers of Moldovan nationals, and in March reversed a decision to allow Romania to open two new consulates in the country. In December Moldova expelled two Romanian diplomats, who had allegedly supplied funds to opposition newspapers, for activities 'incompatible with their status'. In January 2009 the Ministers of Foreign Affairs of Romania and Moldova jointly announced plans to resolve remaining border issues during that year, including the signature of a border treaty, and also declared that the two new Romanian consulates would be opened in Moldova. However, violent protests in Moldova, which erupted in early April following legislative elections, precipitated a breach in relations with Romania. Voronin accused the Romanian Government of organizing a coup attempt (since many of the protesters had exhibited pro-Romanian sentiments) and immediately expelled the Romanian ambassador, recalled the Moldovan envoy in Bucharest, and introduced visa requirements for Romanians (thereby refusing a number of Romanian journalists entry to the country). Romania denied the allegations of involvement and demanded an EU investigation into alleged abuses by the Moldovan authorities. Băsescu subsequently pledged that the Romanian Government would expedite the process of granting Romanian citizenship to Moldovans, claiming that some 1m. applications had been received.

A basic treaty between Romania and Ukraine, signed in early June 1997, guaranteed the inviolability of their joint border, and provided for separate treaties to be established regarding the administration of the frontier and the disputed ownership of the Black Sea continental shelf. In June 2003 President Iliescu and President Leonid Kuchma of Ukraine signed an accord confirming the mutual land border of the two countries, as it was delineated in 1961, with the exception of the continental shelf. No further progress was made in resolving the disagreement over the disputed maritime area (comprising an islet, known as Serpents' Island, and surrounding waters, which were believed to have significant petroleum and gas reserves). In 2004 both states agreed to refer the issue to the International Court of Justice (ICJ, see p. 22). In February 2009 the ICJ finally issued a ruling awarding some 79% of the maritime area under dispute to Romania.

Following the overthrow of President Ceauşescu in 1989, President François Mitterrand of France visited Romania in April 1991, and in April 1992 Romania and Germany signed a treaty of friendship and co-operation. An association agreement with the European Community (now EU) was signed in February 1993; in June 1995 Romania formally applied for full membership of the EU. Romania applied for membership of the Council of Europe in May 1993, but was initially rejected, owing to its poor record on civil liberties. In October, however, Romania was admitted to the organization. In December 1999 Romania was one of six countries invited to begin negotiations on possible entry to the EU, and formal accession talks finally commenced in February 2000. In December the EU decided to impose conditions on Romania before granting its citizens the right to visa-free travel in Europe, partly in response to Romania's failure to combat illegal immigration. In December 2004 Romania concluded accession negotiations, but with a cautionary clause whereby the country's accession could be delayed by one year if it failed to meet its reform commitments. In April 2005 members of the European Parliament voted to approve 2007 as the anticipated accession date for Romania (despite the concerns remaining among some existing members). Formal accession agreements were signed by both Bulgaria and Romania on 25 April 2005. In mid-May both chambers of the legislature unanimously ratified the EU accession treaty.

In May 2006 the European Commission announced that a final decision on Romania's scheduled date of accession to the EU was to be postponed until October, and emphasized the need to implement further reform measures. In a report issued at the end of September, the European Commission confirmed that Romania was sufficiently prepared to meet the accession criteria by 1 January 2007, but also identified issues requiring further attention; a mechanism was to be established for co-operation and verification of progress in the areas of judicial reform and measures against corruption, money-laundering, and organized crime. In October a principal negotiator with the EU, Leonard Orban, was appointed to represent Romania in the European Commission. Romania's accession to the EU on 1 January 2007 was welcomed with mass celebrations in Bucharest.

In June 1992 Romania, together with 10 other countries (including six of the former Soviet republics), established what became known as the Organization of the Black Sea Economic Co-operation (see p. 380), which aimed to encourage regional trade and co-operation in developing transport and infrastructure.

In early 1997 Romania appealed directly to member countries of the North Atlantic Treaty Organization (NATO, see p. 351) to support its candidacy for admittance to the Alliance. Following the large-scale suicide attacks against the USA on 11 September 2001, attributed by the USA to the Saudi-born Islamist fundamentalist Osama bin Laden (see the chapter on the USA), Romania immediately pledged full co-operation with US efforts to assemble a coalition of allied countries to combat global terrorism, and opened its airspace to US military flights to and from Afghanistan, the Taliban regime of which was harbouring militants of bin Laden's al-Qa'ida (Base) organization. The strategic importance of the Black Sea increased, and Romania made available basing facilities in the port city of Constanţa, and offered the USA the use of its air bases. None the less, concerns remained about the presence in the Romanian intelligence services of former members of the communist-era Securitate, and there were doubts about Romania's economic preparedness for NATO membership. However, the intelligence services were restructured in January 2002, and Romania secured an invitation to join NATO at a summit meeting held in Prague, Czech Republic, in November, after which US President George W. Bush paid a visit to the country. Romania supported US-led military action in Iraq in early 2003 (despite some criticism from within the EU, notably France), opening its airspace and offering other resources to the coalition. Romania was officially admitted to NATO on 29 March 2004, together with six other countries. In 2005 a parliamentary commission was established to investigate allegations that Romania had permitted US aircraft (transporting possible terrorist suspects) to use one of its airbases, without due attention to international law; the Council of Europe also launched an investigation. In December 2005 the US Secretary of State signed an agreement with the Romanian Minister of Foreign Affairs, granting US troops access to military bases under the command of the Romanian army. Romania hosted a NATO summit meeting, which was convened in Bucharest on 2–4 April 2008. President Bush subsequently met President Băsescu in Constanţa for consultations. Meeting outgoing NATO Secretary-General Jaap de Hoop Scheffer in Bucharest in April 2009, Băsescu pledged to reinforce the 1,000-member Romanian contingent deployed in Afghanistan by a further 150 troops.

Government

Under the Constitution of 1991 (and as subsequently modified, most substantially in 2003), legislative power is vested in the bicameral Palamentul (Parliament), comprising the Camera Deputaţilor (Chamber of Deputies, lower house) and Senatul (the Senate, upper house). Parlamentul is elected by universal adult suffrage for a term of four years. Executive power is vested in the President of the Republic, who may serve a maximum of two five-year terms and who is directly elected by universal adult suffrage. The President appoints the Prime Minister, who in turn appoints the Council of Ministers.

For administrative purposes, Romania comprises 40 administrative divisions (counties) and the municipality of Bucharest.

Defence

As assessed at November 2008, active forces totalled 73,200: army 43,000, navy 6,500, air force 10,200 and a joint force of 13,500. Reserves totalled 45,000. There were also 22,900 border guards and a gendarmerie of an estimated 57,000 (under the control of the Ministry of the Interior and Administrative Reform). Conscription was officially abolished in October 2006. The defence budget for 2008 was an estimated 7,520,000m. lei. In January 1994 Romania became the first former Warsaw Pact state to join the North Atlantic Treaty Organization's (NATO) 'Partnership for Peace' (see p. 353) programme. Romania became a full member of NATO on 29 March 2004.

Economic Affairs

In 2007, according to the World Bank, Romania's gross national income (GNI), measured at average 2005–07 prices, totalled US $132,502m., equivalent to $6,150 per head (or $10,980 per head on an international purchasing-power parity basis). During 2000–07, it was estimated, the population decreased at an average annual rate of 0.6%, while gross domestic product (GDP) per head increased, in real terms, at an average annual rate of 6.7%. Overall GDP increased, in real terms, by an average of 6.0% annually during 2000–07. Real GDP increased by 6.2% in 2007.

Agriculture (including hunting, forestry and fishing) contributed 8.8% of GDP in 2006, and the sector employed 29.5% of the employed labour force in 2007. The principal crops are maize, wheat, potatoes, sugar beet, barley, apples and grapes. Wine production plays a significant role. Forestry, the cropping of reeds (used as a raw material in the paper and cellulose industry) and the breeding of fish are also important. By 1999, according to the IMF, some 97.2% of agricultural land was privately owned. During 2000–07, according to the World Bank, agricultural GDP increased, in real terms, by an average of 7.2% per year. Real agricultural GDP decreased by 1.0% in 2007.

Industry (including mining, manufacturing, construction, power and water) accounted for 35.9% of GDP in 2006, and employed 31.4% of the working population in 2007. According to the World Bank, industrial GDP increased, in real terms, by an average of 5.8% annually in 2000–07. Real industrial GDP increased by 6.0% in 2007.

The mining sector employed 1.2% of the employed labour force in 2007. Lignite (brown coal), hard coal, salt, iron ore, bauxite, copper, lead and zinc are mined. Onshore production of crude petroleum began to increase in the early 1990s. At the end of 2007 Romania had proven reserves of 500m. barrels of petroleum, remaining the largest producer in central and eastern Europe, despite a dramatic decline in production. At the beginning of the 1990s seven offshore platforms were operating in the Romanian sector of the Black Sea, accounting for more than 10% of annual hydrocarbons production. Methane gas is also extracted. In April 1996 Romania launched an international invitation to tender for exploration and production rights on 15 new blocks in the Black Sea. IMF figures indicated that mining output declined by 0.3% in 2005.

Manufacturing accounted for 19.1% of GDP in 2007, according to the World Bank, when it engaged 21.1% of the employed labour force in The sector is based mainly on the metallurgical, mechanical engineering, chemical and timber-processing industries. However, many industries (particularly iron and steel) have been hampered by shortages of electricity and raw materials. According to the World Bank, manufacturing GDP increased, in real terms, by an average of 0.1% annually in 1994–2001. Real sectoral GDP increased by some 8.0% in 2001.

According to the World Bank, in 2005 some 37.3% of gross electricity production was derived from coal, 34.0% from hydro-electric power and 16.2% from natural gas. The initial unit of Romania's first nuclear power station, at Cernavoda, became operational in December 1996; the second (700 MW) unit entered into operation in 2008. A further two units at the site were expected to commence operations by 2016. In 2006 an agreement was reached with the Turkish power grid operator TEIAŞ on the construction of a 400-km undersea transmission cable, which was to be completed by 2009. A natural gas pipeline to connect the country with Hungary, and ultimately with a 'corridor' between Austria and Turkey (the Nabucco project), was also under construction. In April 2008 Romania signed an agreement with Croatia and Serbia on a project that envisaged the construction of a pipeline linking the Romanian port city of Constanţa with Trieste, Italy, via Croatia, Serbia and Slovenia. According to official data, 36.1% of energy resources were imported in 2005. In that year mineral fuels accounted for 14.0% of total imports.

According to official figures, in 2006 the services sector contributed 55.2% of GDP and engaged 39.1% of the labour force in 2007. According to the World Bank, the GDP of the services sector increased, in real terms, by an average of 4.8% per year in 2000–07; the real GDP of the sector increased by 2.2% in 2007.

In 2007 Romania recorded a visible trade deficit of US $24,566m., and there was a deficit of $23,032m. on the current account of the balance of payments. In 2007 the principal source of imports was Germany, which provided 17.2% of the total. Other major suppliers were Italy, Hungary, Russia and France. The main market for exports in that year was Italy (accounting for 17.2% of the total); other important purchasers were Germany, France, Turkey and the Hungary. In 2007 the principal imports were machinery and transport equipment, basic manufactures, mineral fuels and lubricants, chemical products, and miscellaneous manufactured articles. The major exports in that year were machinery and transport equipment, miscellaneous manufactured articles, basic manufactures, mineral fuels, and chemical products.

The overall budget deficit for 2005 was an estimated 79,300m. new lei (equivalent to 2.9% of GDP). The budgetary deficit for 2006 was forecast at 45,100m. new lei (1.3% of GDP). Romania's total external debt at the end of 2006 was US $55,114m., of which $14,204m. was long-term public debt. In that year the cost of debt-servicing was equivalent to 18.4% of revenue from exports of goods and services. The annual rate of inflation averaged 14.5% in 2000–07; the rate of inflation was 4.8% in 2007. In 2007 some 6.4% of the labour force were unemployed.

Romania is a member (as a 'Country of Operations') of the European Bank for Reconstruction and Development (EBRD, see p. 251). In January 2007 Romania acceded to full membership of the EU.

During the 1990s Romania's progress towards the development of a market economic system was considerably slower than that of many other post-communist states of central and eastern Europe. In October 2003 the EU stated that Romania could be considered to have achieved the status of a functioning market economy, provided it continued to consolidate the progress that it had made. Uncomfortable reforms remained to be implemented in preparation for EU membership and in conformity with a two-year IMF stand-by agreement (finalized in July 2004); the Government committed to making some 7,000 redundancies in the mining sector in 2005, as part of a national restructuring plan that also encompassed the iron, steel and railway industries. The Romanian currency (the leu) was redenominated in July 2005, but was subject to strong appreciation pressures thereafter. None the less, the Romanian economy demonstrated considerable growth prior to EU accession on 1 January 2007. High-level corruption remained endemic in 2007, despite the establishment in May of a national agency to monitor the activities of civil servants. Legislative elections in November 2008 contributed to pressure on the Government to increase public sector expenditure (in October a 50% wage increase was offered to teachers). However, the increasing severity of the global economic crisis challenged the implementation of the Government's economic plans. The leu decreased in value by 2% after Standard & Poors, the credit rating agency, downgraded the country's sovereign debt rating in October 2008. Foreign direct investment and demand for Romanian exports contracted sharply, and in March 2009 multilateral financial assistance amounting to €20,000m. was approved for Romania to support an IMF-supervised programme of reforms, which were to include large reductions in government spending and the strengthening of supervisory powers over the financial sector. The Government aimed to limit the budget deficit to 3% of GDP by 2011.

Education

Children under the age of six years may attend crèches (creşe), and kindergartens (grădiniţe de copii). In 2002/03 76.5% of pre-school age children were attending kindergarten. Between the ages of six and 16 years, children are obliged to attend the general education school (şcoală de cultură generală de zece ani). The general secondary school (liceul), for which there is an entrance examination, provides a specialized education suitable for entering college or university. There are also specialized secondary schools, where the emphasis is on industrial, agricultural and teacher training, and art schools, which correspond to secondary schools, but cover several years of general education. Vocational secondary schools (şcoli profesionale de ucenici) train pupils for a particular career. Tuition in minority languages, particularly Hungarian and German, is available. In 2003/04 primary enrolment included 91.9% of children in the relevant age-group, while the comparable ratio for secondary education was 80.8%. Enrolment in tertiary education was equivalent to 40.7% in 2002/03. Expenditure on education by the state budget

ROMANIA

in 2003 amounted to 15,561m. lei (representing 5.5% of total expenditure).

Public Holidays

2009: 1–2 January (New Year), 6 January (Epiphany), 19–20 April (Orthodox Easter), 1 May (Labour Day), 8 June (Pentecost Monday), 15 August (Dormition of the Virgin Mary), 1 December (National Day), 25–26 December (Christmas).

2008: 1–2 January (New Year), 6 January (Epiphany), 4–5 April (Orthodox Easter), 1 May (Labour Day), 24 May (Pentecost Monday), 15 August (Dormition of the Virgin Mary), 1 December (National Day), 25–26 December (Christmas).

Weights and Measures

The metric system is in force.

Statistical Survey

Source (unless otherwise indicated): Institutul National de Statistică (National Institute of Statistics), 050706 Bucharest, Bd. Libertății 16; tel. (21) 3124875; fax (21) 3124873; e-mail romstat@insse.ro; internet www.insse.ro/cms/rw/pages/index.ro.do.

Area and Population

AREA, POPULATION AND DENSITY

Area (sq km)	238,391*
Population (census results)	
7 January 1992	22,810,035
18–27 March 2002	
Males	10,568,741
Females	11,112,233
Total	21,680,974
Population (official estimates at 1 January)	
2006	21,610,213
2007	21,565,119
2008	21,528,627
Density (per sq km) at 1 January	90.3

*92,043 sq miles.

POPULATION BY ETHNIC GROUP
(2002 census)

	Number	% of total
Romanian	19,399,597	89.5
Hungarian	1,431,807	6.6
Gypsy (Roma)	535,140	2.5
Others and unknown	314,430	1.5
Total	21,680,974	100.0

ADMINISTRATIVE DIVISIONS
(estimates at 1 January 2008)

	Area (sq km)	Population	Density (per sq km)	Administrative capital
Counties				
Alba	6,242	374,727	60.0	Alba Iulia
Arad	7,754	457,318	59.0	Arad
Argeş	6,826	644,487	94.4	Piteşti
Bacău	6,621	719,655	108.7	Bacău
Bihor	7,544	593,897	78.7	Oradea
Bistriţa-Năsăud	5,355	316,869	59.2	Bistriţa
Botoşani	4,986	453,958	91.0	Botoşani
Brăila	4,766	363,979	76.4	Brăila
Braşov	5,363	596,467	111.2	Braşov
Buzău	6,103	486,445	79.7	Buzău
Călăraşi	5,088	314,081	61.7	Călăraşi
Caraş-Severin	8,520	326,067	38.3	Reşiţa
Cluj	6,674	692,021	103.7	Cluj-Napoca
Constanţa	7,071	719,727	101.8	Constanţa
Covasna	3,710	223,208	60.2	Sfântu Gheorghe
Dâmboviţa	4,054	531,441	131.1	Târgovişte
Dolj	7,414	710,669	95.9	Craiova
Galaţi	4,466	613,509	137.4	Galaţi
Giurgiu	3,526	282,638	80.2	Giurgiu
Gorj	5,602	380,061	67.8	Târgu Jiu
Harghita	6,639	325,682	49.1	Miercurea-Ciuc
Hunedoara	7,063	470,103	66.6	Deva
Ialomiţa	4,453	289,501	65.0	Slobozia
Iaşi	5,476	818,929	149.5	Iaşi
Ilfov*	1,593	298,021	187.1	Bucharest
Maramureş	6,304	512,560	81.3	Baia Mare

—continued	Area (sq km)	Population	Density (per sq km)	Administrative capital
Mehedinţi	4,933	296,609	60.1	Drobeta-Turnu Severin
Mureş	6,714	581,400	86.6	Târgu Mureş
Neamţ	5,896	566,740	96.1	Piatra Neamţ
Olt	5,498	473,128	86.1	Slatina
Prahova	4,716	819,600	173.8	Ploieşti
Sălaj	3,864	242,854	62.9	Zalău
Satu Mare	4,418	365,975	82.8	Satu Mare
Sibiu	5,432	423,144	77.9	Sibiu
Suceava	8,553	707,251	82.7	Suceava
Teleorman	5,790	410,288	48.0	Alexandria
Timiş	8,697	673,212	77.4	Timişoara
Tulcea	8,499	249,779	29.4	Tulcea
Vâlcea	5,765	410,309	71.2	Râmnicu Vâlcea
Vaslui	5,318	456,020	85.8	Vaslui
Vrancea	4,857	392,317	80.8	Focşani
Capital City				
Bucharest*	228	1,943,981	8,526.2	Bucharest
Total	238,391	21,528,627	90.3	

* Although Bucharest is a separate administrative division, the city is also the capital of the surrounding Ilfov County. The area and population given for Ilfov County do not include data for Bucharest.

PRINCIPAL TOWNS
(at mid-2006)

Bucureşti (Bucharest, the capital)	1,931,236	Arad	167,980
Iaşi	316,716	Sibiu	154,452
Cluj-Napoca	305,620	Târgu Mureş	146,448
Constanţa	305,550	Baia Mare	140,581
Timişoara	303,796	Buzău	135,861
Craiova	300,587	Botoşani	116,286
Galaţi	296,697	Satu Mare	114,678
Braşov	281,375	Râmnicu Vâlcea	111,658
Ploieşti	231,620	Drobeta-Turnu Severin	109,134
Brăila	216,814	Piatra Neamţ	108,940
Oradea	205,956	Suceava	106,508
Bacău	179,507	Focşani	100,782
Piteşti	170,217		

ROMANIA

BIRTHS, MARRIAGES AND DEATHS

	Registered live births Number	Rate (per 1,000)	Registered marriages Number	Rate (per 1,000)	Registered deaths Number	Rate (per 1,000)
2000	234,521	10.5	135,808	6.1	255,820	11.4
2001	220,368	9.8	129,930	5.8	259,603	11.6
2002	210,529	9.7	129,018	5.9	269,666	12.4
2003	212,459	9.8	133,953	6.2	266,575	12.3
2004	216,261	10.0	143,304	6.6	258,890	11.9
2005	221,020	10.2	141,832	6.6	262,101	12.1
2006	219,483	10.2	146,637	6.8	258,094	12.0
2007	214,728	10.0	189,240	8.8	251,965	11.7

Life expectancy (years at birth, WHO estimates): 72.6 (males 69.2; females 76.1) in 2006 (Source: WHO, *World Health Statistics*).

ECONOMICALLY ACTIVE POPULATION
(labour force surveys, '000 persons aged 15 years and over)

	2005	2006	2007
Agriculture, hunting and forestry	2,939.3	2,840.3	2,756.7
Fishing*	4.1	3.1	5.3
Mining and quarrying	119.2	119.7	109.2
Manufacturing	1,959.7	1,978.5	1,973.8
Electricity, gas and water	190.3	197.5	175.9
Construction	506.6	557.6	678.6
Wholesale and retail trade; repair of motor vehicles, motorcycles, and personal and household goods	967.7	1,049.3	1,151.4
Hotels and restaurants	150.7	143.0	136.6
Transport, storage and communications	450.0	491.8	488.7
Financial intermediation	85.5	92.0	97.2
Real estate, renting and business services	231.7	281.6	282.0
Public administration	520.1	507.5	468.4
Education	412.7	410.6	400.2
Health and social assistance	353.5	378.3	375.4
Other services	255.5	262.5	253.9
Total employed	9,146.6	9,313.3	9,353.3
Unemployed	704.5	728.4	641.0
Total labour force	9,851.0	10,041.7	9,994.3
Males	5,431.5	5,526.4	5,515.0
Females	4,419.5	4,515.3	4,479.3

* Figures obtained as residuals.
Source: ILO.

Health and Welfare

KEY INDICATORS

Total fertility rate (children per woman, 2006)	1.3
Under-5 mortality rate (per 1,000 live births, 2006)	16
HIV/AIDS (% of persons aged 15–49, 2007)	0.1
Physicians (per 1,000 head, 2006)	1.9
Hospital beds (per 1,000 head, 2006)	6.5
Health expenditure (2006): US $ per head (PPP)	610
Health expenditure (2006): % of GDP	5.7
Health expenditure (2006): public (% of total)	71.0
Access to water (% of persons, 2006)	88
Access to sanitation (% of persons, 2006)	72
Human Development Index (2006): ranking	62
Human Development Index (2006): value	0.825

For sources and definitions, see explanatory note on p. vi.

Agriculture

PRINCIPAL CROPS
('000 metric tons)

	2005	2006	2007
Wheat	7,340.7	5,526.2	2,866.2
Barley	1,079.1	772.9	503.7
Maize	10,388.5	8,984.7	3,686.5
Rye	49.0	35.7	30.9
Oats	377.5	346.9	240.0
Potatoes	3,738.6	4,015.9	3,498.4
Sugar beet	729.7	1,152.2	698.6
Beans, dry	41.7	34.9	9.9
Peas, dry	38.8	35.7	16.6
Walnuts, with shell	47.8	38.5	38.5*
Soybeans (Soya beans)	312.8	344.9	123.3
Sunflower seed	1,340.9	1,526.2	521.5
Rapeseed	147.6	175.1	348.2
Cabbages and other brassicas	1,011.6	1,112.7	1,120.0*
Lettuce and chicory	1.8	4.4	4.4*
Tomatoes	627.0	835.0	555.4
Pumpkins, squash and gourds	49.2	69.2	70.0*
Cucumbers and gherkins	142.9	156.4	157.0*
Chillies and peppers, green	203.8	279.1	280.0*
Onions, dry	363.6	390.7	312.2
Garlic	68.4	64.2	65.0*
Beans, green	54.3	64.2	41.9
Peas, green	23.3	26.1	7.3
Watermelons	628.3	587.8	640.0*
Cantaloupes and other melons	63.4	54.0	63.0*
Apples	638.0	590.4	374.8
Pears	88.9	62.4	48.6
Cherries	117.9	104.8	24.3
Apricots	52.4	38.8	5.9
Plums and sloes	622.4	598.8	203.6
Grapes	505.8	912.4	821.3
Tobacco, unmanufactured	3.7	1.7	1.7*

* FAO estimate.

Aggregate production ('000 metric tons, may include official, semi-official or estimated data): Total cereals 19,350.5 in 2005, 15,759.3 in 2006, 7,461.4 in 2007; Total roots and tubers 3,738.6 in 2005, 4,015.9 in 2006, 3,498.4 in 2007; Total vegetables (incl. melons) 3,963.0 in 2005, 4,141.1 in 2006, 3,812.7 in 2007; Total fruits (excl. melons) 2,155.3 in 2005, 2,354.7 in 2006, 1,509.8 in 2007.

Source: FAO.

LIVESTOCK
('000 head, year ending September)

	2005	2006	2007
Horses	840	834	805
Cattle	2,808	2,862	2,934
Pigs	6,495	6,622	6,815
Sheep	7,425	7,611	7,678
Goats	661	687	727
Chickens	87,014	86,552	84,991

Source: FAO.

LIVESTOCK PRODUCTS
('000 metric tons)

	2005	2006	2007
Cattle meat	190.2	159.3	186.0
Sheep meat	48.7	42.0	56.8
Goat meat	3.1	3.3	3.9
Pig meat	436.4	451.8	525.6
Horse meat*	9.0	10.0	9.4
Chicken meat	308.6	273.3	317.6
Cows' milk	5,007.8	6,011.5	5,441.1
Sheep's milk	544.4	650.8	484.6
Hen eggs	355.4	356.7	320.9
Other poultry eggs	10.2	14.8	13.4
Honey	19.2	18.2	15.0
Wool, greasy	17.6	17.6*	17.7*

* FAO estimate(s).
Source: FAO.

ROMANIA — Statistical Survey

Forestry

ROUNDWOOD REMOVALS
('000 cubic metres, excluding bark)

	2005	2006	2007
Sawlogs, veneer logs and logs for sleepers	7,847	6,387	9,777
Pulpwood	1,878	822	1,248
Other industrial wood	1,817	2,245	547
Fuel wood	2,959	4,516	3,769
Total	14,501	13,970	15,341

Source: FAO.

SAWNWOOD PRODUCTION
('000 cubic metres, including railway sleepers)

	2005	2006	2007
Coniferous (softwood)	2,584	1,832	2,159
Broadleaved (hardwood)	1,737	1,644	1,984
Total	4,321	3,476	4,143

Source: FAO.

Fishing

(metric tons, live weight)

	2004	2005	2006
Capture	5,095	6,068	6,664
Freshwater bream	615	581	1,278
Goldfish	1,447	1,917	2,507
Pontic shad	403	518	220
European sprat	1,350	1,487	491
Aquaculture	8,137	7,284	8,088
Common carp	1,726	2,256	3,136
Goldfish	1,249	1,139	1,268
Silver carp	1,588	1,562	2,091
Bighead carp	867	921	894
Rainbow trout	964	815	111
Total catch	13,232	13,352	14,752

Source: FAO.

Mining

('000 metric tons, unless otherwise indicated)

	2004	2005	2006
Brown coal (incl. lignite)	31,592	31,122	30,050
Crude petroleum	5,465	5,212	5,200
Iron ore*	275	265	300
Copper concentrates†	20.4	14.9	12.2
Lead concentrates†	18.3	11.6	7.5
Zinc concentrates†	23.6	13.8	9.6
Salt (unrefined)	2,400	2,420	2,420
Natural gas (million cu metres)	13,290	12,472	12,700

* Figures refer to gross weight.
† Figures refer to the metal content of concentrates.
Source: US Geological Survey.

Industry

SELECTED PRODUCTS
('000 metric tons, unless otherwise indicated)

	2004	2005	2006
Meat and meat products	464	555	652
Refined sugar	523	514	605
Margarine	60.9	65.8	61.3
Wine ('000 hectolitres)	7,071	2,602	5,014
Beer ('000 hectolitres)	14,406	15,295	17,484
Tobacco products	35	33	30
Cotton yarn—pure and mixed	32	28	29
Cotton fabrics—pure and mixed (million sq metres)	201	112	114
Woollen yarn—pure and mixed	24	22	24
Woollen fabrics—pure and mixed (million sq metres)	12	15	18
Silk fabrics—pure and mixed (million sq metres)*	31	23	21
Flax and hemp yarn—pure and mixed	4	2	2
Linen, hemp and jute fabrics—pure and mixed (million sq metres)	2	1	1
Chemical filaments and fibres	21	16	13
Footwear (million pairs)	75	72	69
Chemical wood pulp	237	134	108
Paper and paperboard	521	411	434
Synthetic rubber	12	12	2
Rubber tyres ('000)	12,408	14,208	15,330
Sulphuric acid	28	11	0
Caustic soda (sodium hydroxide)	414	443	477
Soda ash (sodium carbonate)	398	346	453
Nitrogenous fertilizers (a)†	1,104	1,580	1,061
Phosphatic fertilizers (b)†	86	76	61
Pesticides	3	3	2
Motor spirit (petrol)	4,292	4,956	4,888
Kerosene and white spirit	429	455	461
Distillate fuel oils	3,947	4,542	4,484
Residual fuel oils	1,560	1,707	1,303
Petroleum bitumen (asphalt)	203	157	242
Liquefied petroleum gas	366	658	677
Coke	1,675	1,891	1,790
Cement	6,239	7,043	8,253
Pig-iron	4,244	4,098	3,946
Crude steel	6,076	6,280	6,266
Aluminium—unwrought	229	258	277
Television receivers ('000)	76	32	43
Merchant ships launched ('000 deadweight tons)	222	103	155
Passenger motor cars ('000)	99	175	202
Motor tractors, lorries and dump trucks (number)	277	171	530
Buses ('000)	2	—	5
Domestic refrigerators ('000)	700	826	1,169
Domestic washing and drying machines ('000)	42	25	23
Domestic vacuum cleaners ('000)	112	318	393
Domestic cookers ('000)	737	855	825
Electric energy (million kWh)	56,482	59,413	62,696

* Including fabrics of artificial silk.
† Production in terms of (a) nitrogen or (b) phosphoric acid.

ROMANIA   *Statistical Survey*

Finance

CURRENCY AND EXCHANGE RATES

Monetary Units
100 bani (singular: ban) = 1 Romanian leu (plural: lei).

Sterling, Dollar and Euro Equivalents (31 December 2008)
£1 sterling = 4.132 lei;
US $1 = 2.834 lei;
€1 = 3.944 lei;
100 Romanian lei = £24.20 = $35.28 = €25.35.

Average Exchange Rate (lei per US $)
2006   2.8090
2007   2.4383
2008   2.5189

Note: On 1 July 2005 the leu was revalued at a rate of 10,000 old lei = 1 new leu. Some figures given in the survey are in terms of the former valuation.

STATE BUDGET
(hundred million new lei)

Revenue	2004*	2005*	2006†
Tax revenue	610.6	698.3	782.3
Value-added tax	138.1	151.0	160.2
Social security taxes	228.2	257.7	276.6
Profits tax	48.8	55.5	59.3
Income tax	73.2	86.1	98.4
Excise taxes	62.0	83.2	118.7
Customs duties	9.0	9.4	10.1
Other indirect taxes	51.3	55.4	59.0
Non-tax revenue	32.5	27.0	26.5
Capital revenue (incl. grants)	0.9	0.9	1.0
Total	**644.0**	**726.2**	**809.8**

Expenditure	2004*	2005*	2006†
Public authorities	36.8	38.6	40.9
Defence	41.5	47.7	52.9
Public order and safety	40.4	42.2	43.9
Education	86.7	98.8	108.8
Health	78.4	82.6	83.9
Social security and welfare	216.2	235.5	249.9
Community services, public development and housing	47.5	50.3	52.6
Recreational, cultural and religious affairs	11.3	12.1	12.7
Agriculture and forestry	24.9	28.9	31.4
Industry	16.5	18.4	19.1
Transport and communications	77.1	81.9	85.2
Other economic affairs and services	14.4	16.1	18.1
National debt expenditure	48.0	40.9	42.4
Other	8.4	9.8	11.4
Loans	1.6	1.7	1.7
Total	**749.7**	**805.5**	**854.9**

* Estimates.
† Forecasts.
Source: Ministry of Public Finance, Bucharest.

INTERNATIONAL RESERVES
(US $ million at 31 December)

	2006	2007	2008
Gold (national valuation)	2,140	2,762	2,882
IMF special drawing rights	—	—	79
Foreign exchange	28,066	37,194	36,747
Total	**30,206**	**39,957**	**39,708**

Source: IMF, *International Financial Statistics*.

MONEY SUPPLY
('000 million lei at 31 December)

	2006	2007	2008
Currency outside banks	15.13	21.32	25.32
Demand deposits at deposit money banks	22.91	40.61	46.29
Total money	**38.04**	**61.92**	**71.61**

Source: IMF, *International Financial Statistics*.

COST OF LIVING
(Consumer Price Index; base: 2000 = 100)

	2005	2006	2007
Food	213.8	222.0	230.6
Fuel and light	350.9	388.2	417.1
Clothing	183.2	188.7	194.9
Rent	204.6	216.7	372.2
All items (incl. others)	**231.7**	**246.9**	**258.8**

Source: ILO.

NATIONAL ACCOUNTS

Expenditure on the Gross Domestic Product
(million new lei at current prices)

	2004	2005	2006
Government final consumption expenditure	19,104.9	25,335.4	26,166.4
Private final consumption expenditure	191,050.3	226,947.0	268,586.3
Changes in inventories	4,792.8	–1,240.0	3,013.6
Gross fixed capital formation	53,850.3	66,503.8	88,272.0
Total domestic expenditure	**268,798.3**	**317,546.2**	**386,038.3**
Exports of goods and services (net)	–22,329.5	–29,370.1	–41,502.8
GDP in purchasers' values	**246,468.8**	**288,176.1**	**344,535.5**

Gross Domestic Product by Economic Activity
('000 million new lei at current prices)

	2004	2005	2006
Agriculture, hunting and forestry	31,030.1	24,277.9	26,898.2
Fishing	13.8	13.8	15.8
Construction	14,648.7	18,468.4	25,607.1
Other industry*	60,794.9	71,009.8	83,612.3
Trade	22,349.8	28,132.6	36,510.2
Hotels and restaurants	4,469.0	6,028.4	7,325.7
Transport, storage and communications	24,205.0	28,116.9	33,455.5
Financial intermediation	5,578.4	5,826.4	6,396.6
Real estate transactions, renting and service activities	30,036.1	38,745.8	47,168.3
Public administration and defence	12,610.7	16,282.6	16,393.5
Education	8,138.4	9,739.3	11,717.3
Health and social assistance	6,101.0	7,860.9	9,054.2
Gross value added in basic prices	**219,975.9**	**254,502.8**	**304,154.7**
Taxes on products	26,278.2	33,715.4	39,506.9
Import duties	1,632.5	2,047.8	2,443.4
Less Subsidies on products	1,417.8	2,089.9	1,569.5
GDP in market prices	**246,468.8**	**288,176.1**	**344,535.5**

*Comprising mining and quarrying, manufacturing, electricity, gas and water.

ROMANIA

BALANCE OF PAYMENTS
(US $ million)

	2005	2006	2007
Exports of goods f.o.b.	27,730	32,336	40,555
Imports of goods f.o.b.	−37,348	−47,172	−65,121
Trade balance	**−9,618**	**−14,836**	**−24,566**
Exports of services	5,083	7,032	9,502
Imports of services	−5,518	−7,027	−8,879
Balance on goods and services	**−10,053**	**−14,831**	**−23,943**
Other income received	1,533	2,176	3,287
Other income paid	−4,432	−6,255	−8,987
Balance on goods, services and income	**−12,952**	**−18,910**	**−29,643**
Current transfers received	4,939	6,995	9,871
Current transfers paid	−607	−870	−3,260
Current balance	**−8,621**	**−12,785**	**−23,032**
Capital account (net)	731	−34	1,142
Direct investment abroad	30	−422	−279
Direct investment from abroad	6,482	11,393	9,924
Portfolio investment assets	−140	−828	141
Portfolio investment liabilities	1,089	589	481
Financial derivatives assets	36	48	337
Financial derivatives liabilities	−62	−156	−753
Other investment assets	−1,078	−1,323	−1,459
Other investment liabilities	7,731	9,598	20,875
Net errors and omissions	612	521	−1,098
Overall balance	**6,811**	**6,602**	**6,279**

Source: IMF, *International Financial Statistics*.

External Trade

PRINCIPAL COMMODITIES
(distribution by SITC, US $ million)

Imports c.i.f.	2005	2006	2007
Food and live animals	1,897.1	2,296.4	3,567.1
Crude materials (inedible) except fuels	1,126.9	1,268.5	1,786.0
Mineral fuels, lubricants, etc.	5,644.3	6,909.6	7,523.6
Petroleum, petroleum products, etc.	3,735.4	4,612.2	5,251.7
Gas, natural and manufactured	1,164.3	1,761.0	1,492.6
Chemicals and related products	4,109.3	5,413.8	6,997.6
Medicinal and pharmaceutical products	1,118.8	1,576.5	2,005.6
Basic manufactures	9,859.2	11,929.9	15,821.6
Textiles and textile articles	3,309.6	3,328.9	3,685.8
Iron and steel	1,618.0	2,187.8	3,554.1
Manufactures of metals	1,438.2	1,979.5	2,773.1
Machinery and transport equipment	13,427.6	18,099.3	26,093.3
Machinery specialized for particular industries	1,278.8	1,952.8	2,637.7
General industrial machinery and parts	1,866.9	2,559.1	3,614.9
Telecommunications, sound recording and reproducing equipment	1,352.8	1,552.4	2,273.0
Electric machinery, apparatus, etc.	3,007.5	3,851.0	4,941.8
Road vehicles	3,796.3	5,417.3	8,832.1
Miscellaneous manufactured articles	3,762.9	4,618.4	5,927.8
Total (incl. others)	**40,462.9**	**51,106.0**	**69,946.2**

Exports f.o.b.	2005	2006	2007
Crude materials (inedible) except fuels	1,337.5	1,840.3	2,097.8
Cork and wood	561.7	617.3	689.0
Mineral fuels, lubricants, etc.	2,961.0	3,238.0	3,044.4
Petroleum, petroleum products, etc.	2,698.8	2,917.9	2,740.3
Chemicals and related products	1,590.6	1,834.5	2,283.7
Basic manufactures	5,776.1	6,548.6	8,667.2
Iron and steel	2,521.1	2,471.6	3,267.0
Non-ferrous metals	567.0	833.0	1,068.2
Machinery and transport equipment	7,035.4	9,684.4	13,460.0
Telecommunications, sound recording and reproducing equipment	389.1	357.3	405.7
Electrical machinery, apparatus, etc.	2,442.8	3,279.3	4,300.6
Road vehicles	1,313.3	1,998.7	3,243.6
Miscellaneous manufactured articles	8,130.7	8,333.7	8,771.6
Furniture and parts	1,125.6	1,217.3	1,525.4
Clothing and accessories (excl. footwear)	4,627.0	4,423.0	4,315.2
Footwear	1,589.0	1,703.2	1,782.5
Total (incl. others)	**27,729.6**	**32,336.0**	**40,264.7**

Source: UN, *International Trade Statistics Yearbook*.

PRINCIPAL TRADING PARTNERS
(US $ million)*

Imports c.i.f.	2005	2006	2007
Austria	1,499.7	1,923.2	3,395.8
Belgium	580.2	786.6	1,376.4
China, People's Republic	1,633.0	2,186.6	2,284.5
Czech Republic	928.7	1,263.6	1,703.8
France (incl. Monaco)	2,729.9	3,342.2	4,375.4
Germany	5,652.1	7,756.0	12,029.4
Greece	464.3	603.8	1,072.3
Hungary	1,337.7	1,670.1	4,856.7
Italy	6,262.7	7,471.6	8,944.6
Japan	583.9	659.9	425.3
Kazakhstan	1,316.0	1,626.2	1,357.7
Korea, Republic	550.0	759.6	820.7
Netherlands	715.1	928.2	2,536.8
Poland	1,172.7	1,416.0	2,380.6
Russia	3,338.2	4,022.0	4,417.2
Slovakia	441.2	578.1	895.7
Spain	902.3	1,195.4	1,421.4
Turkey	1,966.2	2,534.8	3,763.8
Ukraine	524.6	707.6	785.0
United Kingdom	1,159.9	1,267.6	1,351.9
USA	1,114.8	1,243.0	936.3
Total (incl. others)	**40,462.9**	**51,106.0**	**69,946.2**

Exports f.o.b.	2005	2006	2007
Austria	861.3	853.8	1,033.8
Belgium	484.5	533.6	942.6
Bulgaria	735.1	911.2	1,032.6
Czech Republic	264.9	368.0	557.1
France (incl. Monaco)	2,063.1	2,424.8	3,117.1
Germany	3,890.6	5,078.7	6,827.6
Greece	591.2	633.7	687.7
Hungary	1,147.3	1,596.1	2,248.3
India	272.3	240.9	449.1
Italy	5,383.7	5,846.6	6,922.5
Moldova	326.0	427.0	632.5
Netherlands	746.7	798.4	831.8
Poland	404.3	585.9	870.1
Russia	230.7	374.1	582.8
Serbia	n.a.	493.9	434.8
Spain	670.5	756.3	933.1
Turkey	2,197.2	2,498.5	2,819.1
Ukraine	167.5	424.3	741.5
United Arab Emirates	255.4	483.4	452.8
United Kingdom	1,512.1	1,520.9	1,660.7
USA	1,126.7	827.5	808.3
Total (incl. others)	27,729.6	32,336.0	40,264.7

* Imports by country of production; exports by country of last consignment.

Source: UN, *International Trade Statistics Yearbook*.

Transport

RAILWAYS
(traffic)

	2004	2005	2006
Passenger journeys (million)	99	92	94
Passenger-km (million)	8,638	7,985	8,093
Freight transported (million metric tons)	73	69	68
Freight ton-km (million)	17,022	16,582	15,791

ROAD TRAFFIC
('000 motor vehicles in use at 31 December)

	2004	2005	2006
Passenger cars	3,225	3,364	3,603
Buses and coaches	43	39	40
Lorries and vans	482	494	545
Motorcycles and mopeds	235	197	194

INLAND WATERWAYS
(traffic)

	2004	2005	2006
Passenger journeys ('000)	214	218	190
Passenger-km (million)	19	24	13
Freight transported (million metric tons)	15	17	15
Freight ton-km ('000 million)	4	5	5

SHIPPING
Merchant Fleet
(registered at 31 December)

	2005	2006	2007
Number of vessels	209	193	192
Total displacement ('000 grt)	336.5	272.1	269.5

Source: Lloyd's Register-Fairplay, *World Fleet Statistics*.

International Sea-borne Freight Traffic
('000 metric tons)

	2004	2005	2006
Goods loaded	18,225	24,534	34,727
Goods unloaded	22,306	28,444	41,286

CIVIL AVIATION
(traffic)

	2004	2005	2006
Passengers carried ('000)	1,337	1,750	2,109
Passenger-km (million)	1,613	2,093	2,618
Freight transported ('000 metric tons)	5	6	6
Freight ton-km (million)	7	7	7

Tourism

FOREIGN VISITOR ARRIVALS
('000)*

Country of origin	2004	2005	2006
Austria	90.3	129.2	151.5
Bulgaria	375.4	389.5	399.3
France	93.0	110.0	129.5
Germany	296.1	353.6	342.7
Hungary	2,603.5	1,522.2	1,366.7
Italy	230.6	270.9	277.9
Moldova	1,212.8	1,435.2	1,489.7
Poland	132.9	62.0	74.6
Serbia and Montenegro	220.3	148.0	166.8
Turkey	195.3	200.9	219.1
Ukraine	309.8	328.4	433.4
USA	110.6	119.9	130.2
Total (incl. others)	6,600.1	5,839.4	6,037.0

* Figures refer to arrivals at frontiers of visitors from abroad, including same day visitors (excursionists).

Tourism receipts (US $ million, incl. passenger transport): 607 in 2004; 1,325 in 2005; 1,676 in 2006.

Source: World Tourism Organization.

Communications Media

	2004	2005	2006
Radio users ('000 subscribers)	5,369	5,313	5,095
Television users ('000 subscribers)	5,822	5,618	5,478
Telephones ('000 main lines in use)	4,389.0	4,383.0	4,197.0
Mobile cellular telephones ('000 subscribers)	10,215.4	13,354.1	17,400.0
Personal computers ('000 in use)	2,450	2,450	n.a.
Internet users ('000)	4,500	6,800	11,300
Broadband subscribers ('000)	382.8	376.4	1,087.9
Book production (incl. pamphlets):			
titles	13,288	14,115	14,373
copies ('000)	9,288	11,746	9,720
Daily newspapers	84	80	81
Other periodicals	2,036	2,044	2,180

2007: Telephones ('000 main lines in use) 4,300.0; Mobile cellular telephones ('000 subscribers) 22,875.1; Internet users ('000) 12,000; Broadband subscribers ('000) 2,132.3.

Source: partly International Telecommunication Union.

Education

(2006/07)

	Institutions	Pupils	Teachers
Kindergartens	1,720	648,862	36,555
Primary and gymnasium schools	5,045	1,842,208	141,601
Secondary schools	1,421	780,925	62,048
Vocational schools	115	250,383	5,643
Specialized technical schools	79	37,697	888
Higher education	104	785,506	30,583

Adult literacy rate (UNESCO estimates): 97.6% (males 98.3%; females 96.9%) in 2007 (Source: UNESCO Institute for Statistics).

Directory

The Constitution

Following its assumption of power in December 1989, the National Salvation Front decreed radical changes to the Constitution of 1965. The name of the country was changed from the Socialist Republic of Romania to Romania. The leading role of a single political party was abolished, a democratic and pluralist system of government being established.

The combined chambers of the legislature elected in May 1990, working as a constituent assembly, drafted a new Constitution (based on the Constitution of France's Fifth Republic), which was approved in a national referendum on 8 December 1991. A plebiscite held on 18–19 October 2003 approved 79 amendments to the Constitution, bringing it into conformity with EU legislation. The amendments entered into force on 29 October.

Under the amended Constitution, political power in Romania belongs to the people and is exercised according to the principles of democracy, freedom, human dignity, and the inviolability and inalienability of basic human rights. Romania is governed on the basis of a multi-party democratic system and of the separation of the legal, executive and judicial powers. Romania's legislature, comprising the Camera Deputaţilor (Chamber of Deputies—the lower house) and Senatul (the Senate—the upper house), is elected by universal, free, direct and secret vote for a term of four years. The President is directly elected for a term of five years, and may serve a maximum of two terms. Citizens have the right to vote at the age of 18, and may be elected at the age of 21 to the Camera Deputaţilor and at the age of 30 to Senatul, with no upper age limit in either case. Those ineligible for election include former members of the Securitate (the secret police of President Ceauşescu) and other former officials guilty of repression and abuses. Once elected, the President may not remain a member of any political party. The President appoints the Prime Minister, who in turn appoints the Council of Ministers.

The Government

HEAD OF STATE

President: Traian Băsescu (elected 12 December 2004; inaugurated 14 December 2004).

COUNCIL OF MINISTERS
(April 2009)

A coalition, comprising members of the Democratic Liberal Party (DLP) and the Social Democratic Party (SDP).

Prime Minister: Emil Boc (DLP).
Deputy Prime Minister and Minister of the Interior and Administrative Reform: Dan Nica (SDP).
Minister of Public Finance: Gheorghe Pogea (DLP).
Minister of Foreign Affairs: Cristin Diaconescu (SDP).
Minister of the Economy: Adriean Videanu (DLP).
Minister of Justice and Citizens' Freedoms: Cătălin Marian Predoiu (Independent).
Minister of Defence: Mihai Stănişoară (DLP).
Minister of Transport and Infrastructure: Radu Berceanu (DLP).
Minister of Education, Research and Innovation: Ecaterina Andronescu (SDP).
Minister of Labour, the Family and Equal Opportunities: Marian Sârbu (SDP).
Minister of Small and Medium-Sized Enterprises, Trade and the Business Environment: Constantin Niţă (SDP).
Minister of Agriculture and Rural Development: Ilie Sârbu (SDP).
Minister of Tourism: Elena Udrea (DLP).
Minister of Public Health: Ion Bazac (SDP).
Minister of Regional Development and Housing: Vasile Blaga (DLP).
Minister of the Environment: Nicolae Nemirschi (SDP).
Minister of Culture, Religious Affairs and National Cultural Heritage: Theodor Paleologu (DLP).
Minister of Communications and Information Technology: Gabriel Sandu (DLP).
Minister of Youth and Sports: Monica Iacob Ridzi (DLP).
Minister-delegate for Relations with Parliament: Victor Ponta (SDP).

MINISTRIES

Office of the President: 060116 Bucharest 5, Palatul Cotroceni, Str. Geniuliu 1–3; tel. (21) 4100581; fax (21) 4103858; e-mail presedinte@presidency.ro; internet www.presidency.ro.

Office of the Prime Minister: 011791 Bucharest 1, Piaţa Victoriei 1; tel. (21) 3131450; fax (21) 3139846; e-mail drp@guv.ro; internet www.guv.ro.

Ministry of Agriculture and Rural Development: 020921 Bucharest 3, Bd. Carol I 24, POB 37; tel. (21) 3078500; fax (21) 3078554; e-mail comunicare@madr.ro; internet www.madr.ro.

Ministry of Communications and Information Technology: 050706 Bucharest 5, Bd. Libertăţii 14; tel. (21) 4001190; fax (21) 3365887; e-mail office@mcti.ro; internet www.mcti.ro.

Ministry of Culture, Religious Affairs and National Cultural Heritage: 011374 Bucharest 1, Şos. Kiseleff 30; tel. (21) 2242510; fax (21) 2234951; e-mail cabinet.ministru@cultura.ro; internet www.cultura.ro.

Ministry of Defence: 050561 Bucharest 5, Str. Izvor 3–5; tel. (21) 4023400; fax (21) 3195698; e-mail drp@mapn.ro; internet www.mapn.ro.

Ministry of the Economy: 010096 Bucharest 1, Calea Victoriei 152; tel. (21) 2025106; fax (21) 2025108; e-mail dezbateri_publice@minind.ro; internet www.minind.ro.

ROMANIA

Ministry of Education, Research and Innovation: 010168 Bucharest 1, Str. Gen. Berthelot 28–30; tel. (21) 4056200; fax (21) 3124719; internet www.edu.ro.

Ministry of the Environment: 040129 Bucharest 5, Bd. Libertății 12; tel. (21) 3160215; fax (21) 3124227; e-mail mmediu@mmediu.ro; internet www.mmediu.ro.

Ministry of Foreign Affairs: 011822 Bucharest, Al. Alexandru 31; tel. (21) 3192108; fax (21) 3196862; e-mail mae@mae.ro; internet www.mae.ro.

Ministry of the Interior and Administrative Reform: 010086 Bucharest 1, Piața Revoluției 1A; tel. (21) 3037080; fax (21) 3103072; e-mail drp@mai.gov.ro; internet www.mai.gov.ro.

Ministry of Justice and Citizens' Freedoms: 050741 Bucharest 5, Str. Apolodor 17; tel. (37) 2041005; fax (37) 2041226; e-mail relatiipublice@just.ro; internet www.just.ro.

Ministry of Labour, the Family and Equal Opportunities: 010026 Bucharest 1, Str. Demetru I. Dobrescu 2–4; tel. (21) 3156563; fax (21) 3122768; e-mail relatiicupublicul@mmssf.ro; internet www.mmssf.ro.

Ministry of Public Finance: 050741 Bucharest 5, Str. Apolodor 17; tel. (21) 3199759; fax (21) 3199752; e-mail presamfp@mfinante.gv.ro; internet www.mfinante.ro.

Ministry of Public Health: 010024 Bucharest 1, Str. Cristian Popișteanu 1–3; tel. (21) 3072500; fax (21) 3141526; e-mail presa@ms.ro; internet www.ms.ro.

Ministry of Regional Development and Housing: 050741 Bucharest 5, Str. Apolodor 17; tel. (37) 2111502; fax (37) 2111600; e-mail info@mdlpl.ro; internet www.mdlpl.ro.

Ministry of Small and Medium-sized Enterprises, Trade and the Business Environment: 010096 Bucharest 1, Calea Victoriei 152; tel. (21) 2025109; e-mail comunicare@minind.ro; internet www.mimmctpl.ro.

Ministry of Tourism: 010873 Bucharest 1, Bd. Dinicu Golescu 38; tel. (21) 3118967; fax (21) 3134952; e-mail secretariat.turism@gov.ro; internet www.turism.gov.ro.

Ministry of Transport and Infrastructure: 010873 Bucharest 1, Bd. Dinicu Golescu 38; tel. (21) 3196124; fax (21) 3138869; e-mail relpub5@mt.ro; internet www.mt.ro.

Ministry of Youth and Sports: Bucharest 2, Strada Vasile Conta 16; tel. (21) 3189032; fax (21) 3076418; internet www.mts.ro.

President

Presidential Election, First Ballot, 28 November 2004

Candidates	Votes	%
Adrian Năstase (National Union*)	4,278,864	40.94
Traian Băsescu (Justice and Truth Alliance†)	3,545,236	33.92
Corneliu Vadim Tudor (Greater Romania Party)	1,313,714	12.57
Béla Markó (Democratic Alliance of Hungarians in Romania)	533,446	5.10
Others	780,945	7.47
Total	**10,452,205**	**100.00**

Second Ballot, 12 December 2004

Candidates	Votes	%
Traian Băsescu (Justice and Truth Alliance†)	5,126,794	51.23
Adrian Năstase (National Union*)	4,881,520	48.77
Total	**10,008,314**	**100.00**

* An alliance of the Social Democratic Party and the Humanist Party of Romania (renamed the Conservative Party in 2005).
† An alliance of the National Liberal Party and the Democratic Party (renamed the Democratic Liberal Party in 2008).

Legislature

PARLAMENTUL ROMÂNIEI
(The Romanian Parliament)

The bicameral Parlamentul României comprises the 334-member lower chamber, the Camera Deputaților (Chamber of Deputies), and the 137-member upper chamber, Senatul (the Senate). Members of both chambers are directly elected, for a term of four years.

Camera Deputaților
(Chamber of Deputies)

050563 Bucharest, Palatul Parlamentului, Str. Izvor 2–4, Sector 5; tel. (21) 3160300; fax (21) 4022149; e-mail secretar.general@cdep.ro; internet www.cdep.ro.

Chairman: ROBERTA ALMA ANASTASE.

General Election, 30 November 2008

Parties	Votes	% of votes	Seats
Democratic Liberal Party	2,228,860	32.36	115
Social Democratic Party–Conservative Party alliance	2,279,449	33.10	114
National Liberal Party	1,279,063	18.57	65
Democratic Alliance of Hungarians in Romania	425,008	6.17	22
Minority parties	199,871	2.90	18
Greater Romania Party	217,595	3.16	—
New Generation—Christian Democratic Party	156,901	2.28	—
Others	100,047	1.45	—
Total	**6,886,794**	**100.00**	**334**

Senatul
(The Senate)

050711 Bucharest 5, Calea 13 Septembrie 1–3; tel. (21) 4021111; fax (21) 3121184; e-mail csava@senat.ro; internet www.senat.ro.

Chairman: MIRCEA DAN GEOANĂ.

General Election, 30 November 2008

Parties	Votes	% of votes	Seats
Democratic Liberal Party	2,312,358	33.57	51
Social Democratic Party–Conservative Party alliance	2,352,968	34.16	49
National Liberal Party	1,291,029	18.74	28
Democratic Alliance of Hungarians in Romania	440,449	6.39	9
Greater Romania Party	245,930	3.57	—
New Generation—Christian Democratic Party	174,519	2.53	—
Others	70,802	1.03	—
Total	**6,888,055**	**100.00**	**137**

Election Commission

Central Electoral Office (Biroul Electoral Central): Bucharest 1, Str. Ion Câmpineanu 28; tel. (21) 3188641; fax (21) 3188642; e-mail secretariat@becparlamentare2008.ro; internet www.becparlamentare2008.ro; Pres. OCTAVIAN OPRIȘ.

Political Organizations

Christian-Democratic National Peasants' Party (CDNPP) (Partidul Național Țărănesc Creștin Democrat): 020922 Bucharest 2, Bd. Carol I 24; tel. (21) 2641460; fax (21) 2641490; internet www.pntcd.ro; f. 1989 by merger of centre-right Christian Democratic Party and traditional National Peasant Party, as revival of party originally founded in 1869 and banned in 1947; absorbed the Union for the Reconstruction of Romania in March 2005; supports pluralist democracy and the restoration of peasant property; Pres. RADU SÂRBU.

Conservative Party (CP) (Partidul Conservator): 010093 Bucharest 1, Calea Victoriei 118, etaj 5, Sector 1; tel. (21) 3170614; fax (21) 3170613; e-mail secretariat@partidulconservator.ro; internet www.partidulconservator.ro; f. 1991 as the Humanist Party of Romania; contested legislative and presidential elections in 2004 in alliance with the SDP, as the National Union; renamed in May 2005; absorbed the Romanian National Unity Party in Feb. 2006; Pres. DANIELA POPA.

Democratic Alliance of Hungarians in Romania (DAHR) (Uniunea Democrată Maghiară din România/Romániai Magyar Demokrata Szövetség—UDMR/RMDSZ): 024015 Bucharest, Str. Avram Iancu 8; tel. (21) 3144356; fax (21) 3144583; e-mail elhivbuk@rmdsz.ro; internet www.rmdsz.ro; f. 1990; supports the rights of ethnic Hungarians in Romania; Pres. BÉLA MARKÓ; Exec. Pres. HUNOR KELEMEN.

ROMANIA

Democratic Liberal Party (DLP) (Partidul Democrat Liberal—PDL): 011825 Bucharest, Al. Modrogan 1; tel. and fax (21) 2301332; e-mail office@pd.ro; internet www.pd-l.ro; f. 1993; fmrly Democratic Party—National Salvation Front, then Democratic Party; present name adopted 2008, following merger with Liberal Democratic Party; contested legislative and presidential elections in 2004 in alliance with the NLP, as the Justice and Truth Alliance; Pres. EMIL BOC; Sec.-Gen. VASILE BLAGA.

Greater Romania Party (GRP) (Partidul România Mare—PRM): 010296 Bucharest, Str. G. Clemenceau 8–10; tel. (21) 3130967; fax (21) 3126182; e-mail prm@prm.org.ro; internet www.prm.org.ro; f. 1991; known as the Popular Greater Romania Party (under the chairmanship of Corneliu Ciontu) in March–June 2005; nationalist; splinter group formed under Ciontu in mid-2005 (People's Party), which subsequently merged with the New Generation—Christian Democratic Party; Chair. CORNELIU VADIM TUDOR.

National Liberal Party (NLP) (Partidul Național Liberal—PNL): 011866 Bucharest, Bd. Aviatorilor 86; tel. (21) 2310795; fax (21) 2310796; e-mail dre@pnl.ro; internet www.pnl.ro; f. 1990 as revival of party originally founded in 1869 and banned in 1947; merged with Liberal Party in 1993, and with Party of the Civic Alliance and Liberal Party of Romania in 1998, absorbed Alliance for Romania in 2002 and the Union of Rightist Forces in 2003; supports the integration of Romania into the European Union and the North Atlantic Treaty Organization, advocates freedom of expression and religion, a market economy and the decentralization of state powers; contested legislative and presidential elections in 2004 in alliance with the Democratic Party, as the Justice and Truth Alliance; Pres. CRIN ANTONESCU; Sec.-Gen. DAN STEFAN MOTREANU.

New Generation—Christian Democratic Party (Partidul Noua Generatie—Crestin Democrat—PNG): 030061 Bucharest 3, Str. Blănari 21–23; tel. (21) 3149360; fax (21) 3149361; e-mail contact@png.ro; internet www.png.ro; f. 2003; Chair. GHEORGHE BECALI.

Social Democratic Party (SDP) (Partidul Social Democrat—PSD): 011346 Bucharest 1, Şos. Kiseleff 10; tel. (21) 2222953; fax (21) 2223272; internet www.psd.ro; f. 2001 by the merger of the Romanian Social Democratic Party and the Party of Social Democracy of Romania; contested legislative and presidential elections in 2004 in alliance with the Humanist Party of Romania, as the National Union; Pres. MIRCEA DAN GEOANĂ; Sec.-Gen. TITUS CORLATEAN.

Diplomatic Representation

EMBASSIES IN ROMANIA

Albania: 011811 Bucharest, Str. Duiliu Zamfirescu 7, Sector 1; tel. (21) 2118743; fax (21) 2108039; e-mail embassy.bucharest@mfa.gov.al; Ambassador DASHNOR DERVISHI.

Algeria: 010663 Bucharest, Bd. Lascăr Catargiu 29, Sector 1; tel. (21) 2124185; fax (21) 2115695; e-mail ambalgerie@roumanie.eunet.ro; Ambassador ABDEL HAMID SENOUCI BEREKSI.

Argentina: 010031 Bucharest, Union International Centre, Str. Ion Campineanu 11, 3rd Floor, Rm 101; tel. (21) 3122626; fax (21) 3120116; e-mail eruma@mrecic.gov.ar; Chargé d'affaires a.i. GABRIEL EDUARDO PUENTE.

Armenia: 014136 Bucharest, Str. Poiana 27, Sector 1; tel. (21) 2332452; fax (21) 2332725; e-mail armembro@cinor.ro; Ambassador YEGHISHE SARKISSIAN.

Austria: 020461 Bucharest, Str. Dumbrava Roşie 7, Sector 2; tel. (21) 2015612; fax (21) 2100885; e-mail bukarest-ob@bmeia.gv.at; Ambassador MARTIN EICHTINGER.

Azerbaijan: 014132 Bucharest 1, Str. Grigore Gafencu 10, Sector 1; tel. (21) 2332484; fax (21) 2332465; e-mail azsefroman@azembassy.ro; internet www.azembassy.ro; Ambassador ELDAR HASANOV.

Belarus: 011411 Bucharest, Str. Tuberozelor 6, Sector 1; tel. (21) 2231776; fax (21) 2231763; e-mail romania@belembassy.org; Chargé d'affaires a.i. DMITRIY SHEMETOV.

Belgium: 020061 Bucharest, Bd. Dacia 58, Sector 2; tel. (21) 2102970; fax (21) 2102803; e-mail bucharest@diplobel.fed.be; internet www.diplobel.org/bucharest; Ambassador LEO D'AES.

Bosnia and Herzegovina: 011786 Bucharest 1, Str. Stockholm 12; tel. (21) 4092601; fax (21) 4092603; e-mail amb.bukurest@mvp.gov.ba; Ambassador BRANKO T. NEŠKOVIĆ.

Brazil: 011863 Bucharest, Bd. Aviatorilor 40, Sector 1; tel. (21) 2301130; fax (21) 2301599; e-mail braembuc@starnets.ro; Ambassador VITOR CANDIDO PAIM GOBATO.

Bulgaria: 011835 Bucharest, Str. Rabat 5; tel. (21) 2302150; fax (21) 2307654; e-mail bulembassy@rdsmail.ro; internet www.bgembassy-romania.org; Ambassador VALENTIN RADOMIRSKI.

Canada: 011411 Bucharest, Str. Tuberozelor 1–3, Sector 1; tel. (21) 3075000; fax (21) 3075010; e-mail bucst@international.gc.ca; internet geo.international.gc.ca/canada-europa/romania; Ambassador MARTA MOSZCZENSKA.

Chile: 010732 Bucharest, Calea Griviței 24; tel. (21) 3127239; fax (21) 3127246; e-mail info@chile.ro; Ambassador CARLOS PARKER.

China, People's Republic: 014103 Bucharest, Şos. Nordului 2, Sector 1; tel. (21) 2321732; fax (21) 2330684; e-mail chinaemb_ro@mfa.gov.cn; internet www.chinaembassy.org.ro; Ambassador LIU ZENGWEN.

Congo, Democratic Republic: 010517 Bucharest, Str. Mihai Eminescu 50–54/15, Sector 1; tel. (21) 2105498; e-mail ambardcbuc@yahoo.fr; Chargé d'affaires a.i. PHOBA KI KUMBU.

Croatia: 024031 Bucharest, Str. Dr Burghelea 1, Sector 2; tel. (21) 3130457; fax (21) 3130384; e-mail croemb.bucharest@mvp.hr; Ambassador IVICA MAŠTRUKO.

Cuba: 010516 Bucharest, Str. Mihai Eminescu 44–48, 2nd Floor, Rm 5; tel. and fax (21) 2118916; e-mail embacuba@embacuba.ro; Ambassador MANUEL ISMAEL HERMIDA MEDINA.

Cyprus: 050726 Bucharest, J. W. Marriot Grand Hotel, Calea 13 Septembrie 90, Sector 5; tel. (21) 4034900; fax (21) 4034901; Ambassador SPYROS ATTAS.

Czech Republic: 011406 Bucharest, Str. Petofi Sandor 2, Sector 1; tel. (21) 2230455; fax (21) 2230456; e-mail bucharest@embassy.mzv.cz; internet www.mzv.cz/bucharest; Ambassador SPYROS ATTAS.

Denmark: 024031 Bucharest, Str. Dr Burghelea 3, Sector 2; tel. (21) 3000800; fax (21) 3120358; e-mail buhamb@um.dk; internet www.ambbukarest.um.dk; Ambassador ULRIK HELWEG-LARSEN.

Egypt: 010407 Bucharest 1, Bd. Dacia 67, Sector 1; tel. (21) 2110938; fax (21) 2100337; e-mail embassy.bucharest@mfa.gov.eg; Ambassador DNA SANAA ESMAIL ATALLAH ESMAIL.

Finland: 011832 Bucharest, Str. Atena 2 bis; tel. (21) 2307525; fax (21) 2307505; e-mail sanomat.buk@formin.fi; internet www.finland.ro; Ambassador IRMELI MUSTONEN.

France: 010392 Bucharest, Str. Biserica Amzei 13–15, Sector 1; tel. (21) 3031000; fax (21) 3031090; e-mail chancellerie.bucarest-amba@diplomatie.gouv.fr; internet www.ambafrance-ro.org; Ambassador HENRI PAUL.

Georgia: 010516 Bucharest 1, Str. Mihai Eminescu 44–48/8, Sector 1; tel. (21) 2100602; fax (21) 2113999; e-mail embgeoromania@yahoo.com; internet www.romania.mfa.gov.ge; Ambassador LEVAN METREVELI.

Germany: 011849 Bucharest, Str. Capt. Aviator Gh. Demetriade 6–8, Sector 1; tel. (21) 2029830; fax (21) 2305846; e-mail info@bukarest.diplo.de; internet www.bukarest.diplo.de; Ambassador ROLAND LOHKAMP.

Greece: 021403 Bucharest, Bd. Pache Protopopescu 1–3, Sector 2; tel. (21) 2094170; fax (21) 2094175; e-mail gremb.buc@mfa.gr; internet www.grembassy.ro; Ambassador GEORGIOS POUKAMISSAS.

Holy See: 010187 Bucharest, Str. Pictor Stahi 5–7; tel. (21) 3123883; fax (21) 3120316; e-mail nuntius@clicknet.ro; Apostolic Nuncio Monsignor FRANCISCO-JAVIER LOZANO (Titular Archbishop of Penafiel).

Hungary: 020027 Bucharest, Str. Dimitrie Gerotă 63–65; tel. (21) 3120073; fax (21) 3120467; e-mail hunembro@ines.ro; internet www.mfa.gov.hu/kulkepviselet/RO; Ambassador OSZKÁR LÁSZLÓ FÜZES.

India: 020078 Bucharest, Str. Mihai Eminescu 183, Sector 2; tel. and fax (21) 2115451; e-mail office@embassyofindia.ro; internet www.embassyofindia.ro; Ambassador DEBASHISH CHAKRAVARTI.

Indonesia: 010488 Bucharest 1, Str. Orlando 10, Sector 1; tel. (21) 3120742; fax (21) 3120214; e-mail indobuch@indonezia.ro; Chargé d'affaires a.i. ISHLAH R. ABDULLAH.

Iran: 010633 Bucharest, Bd. Lascăr Catargiu 39, Sector 1; tel. (21) 3120495; fax (21) 3120496; e-mail iranembassyro@gmail.ro; internet www.iranembassy.ro; Ambassador HAMID REZA ARSHADI.

Iraq: 011834 Bucharest 1, Str. Venezuela 6–8, Sector 1; tel. (21) 2339008; fax (21) 2339007; e-mail iraqbuchrest@yahoo.com; Ambassador ADEL MURAD.

Ireland: 011015 Bucharest 1, Str. Buzeşti 50–52, 3rd Floor; tel. (21) 3102131; fax (21) 3112285; e-mail bucharestembassy@dfa.ie; internet www.embassyofireland.ro; Ambassador JOHN MORAHAN.

Israel: 040231 Bucharest 4, Bd. Dimitrie Cantemir 1, tronson 2 & 3, B2, 5th Floor; tel. (21) 3189416; fax (21) 3189402; e-mail israel.embassy@algoritma.ro; internet bucharest.mfa.gov.il; Ambassador OREN DAVID.

Italy: 010667 Bucharest, Str. Henri Coandă 7–9, Sector 1; tel. (21) 3052100; fax (21) 3120422; e-mail ambasciata.bucharest@esteri.it; internet www.ambbucarest.esteri.it; Ambassador MARIO COSPITO.

Japan: 011141 Bucharest 1, Şos. Nicolae Titulescu 4–8, Sector 1; tel. (21) 3191890; fax (21) 3191895; e-mail embjpn@b.astral.ro; internet www.ro.emb-japan.go.jp; Ambassador YOSHINOBU HIGASHI.

Jordan: 020461 Bucharest 2, Str. Dumbrava Roşie 1; tel. (21) 2104705; fax (21) 2100320; e-mail jordan.embassy@pcnet.ro; Ambassador RASSEM YAQOUB HASHEM.

Kazakhstan: 020225 Bucharest, Str. Giuseppe Garibaldi 26 bis, Sector 2; tel. (21) 1071083; fax (21) 1071548; e-mail dipmissionkz@zappmobile.ro; Chargé d'affaires a.i. KAIRAT AMAN.

Korea, Democratic People's Republic: 014103 Bucharest, Şos. Nordului 6, Sector 1; tel. and fax (21) 2321994; e-mail ambasadarpdc@yahoo.com; Chargé d'affaires a.i. HA PYONG GUK.

Korea, Republic: 012013 Bucharest, Bd. Mircea Eliade 14; tel. (21) 2307198; fax (21) 2307629; e-mail koerom@mofat.go.kr; Ambassador IHL-SONG CHOI.

Kuwait: 011751 Bucharest 1, Str. Louis Blanc 19A-B; tel. (21) 3154444; fax (21) 3159992; e-mail kuwaitstampa@tiscalinet.it; internet www.kuwaitembassy.ro; Ambassador YAQOUB YOUSEF AL-ATEEQI.

Lebanon: 011817 Bucharest 1, Str. Paris 46, Sector 1; tel. (21) 2309205; fax (21) 2307534; e-mail ambasada.liban@gmail.com; Ambassador MUHAMMAD EL-DIB.

Lithuania: 011973 Bucharest 1, Bd. Primăverii 51/2, Sector 1; tel. (21) 3115997; fax (21) 3115919; e-mail amb.ro@urm.lt; internet www.ro.mfa.lt; Ambassador VLADIMIR JARMOLENKO.

Macedonia, former Yugoslav Republic: 020083 Bucharest, Str. Mihai Eminescu 144, Sector 2; tel. (21) 2100880; fax (21) 2117295; e-mail ammakbuk@rdsmail.ro; Ambassador LJUPČO ARSOVSKI.

Malaysia: 020521 Bucharest, Str. Drobeta 11, Sector 2; tel. (21) 2113801; fax (21) 2100270; e-mail mwbucrst@itcnet.ro; Ambassador DATIN PADUKA HALIMAH ABDULLAH.

Mexico: 020082 Bucharest, Str. Mihai Eminescu 124c/13–14, Sector 2; tel. (21) 2104577; fax (21) 2104713; e-mail embamex@xnet.ro; internet www.embamex.ro; Chargé d'affaires a.i. MARIA PATRICIA DELUERA CANCHOLA.

Moldova: 011824 Bucharest 1, Al. Alexandru 40, Sector 1; tel. (21) 2300474; fax (21) 2307790; e-mail bucuresti@mfa.md; internet www.romania.mfa.gov.md; Ambassador LIDIA GUŢU.

Morocco: 010459 Bucharest 1, Str. Dionisie Lupu 78, Sector 1; tel. (21) 3174124; fax (21) 3174144; e-mail ambamarbuc@ambasadamaroc.ro; internet www.ambasadamaroc.ro; Chargé d'affaires a.i. AHMED SENDAGUE.

Netherlands: 011832 Bucharest, Al. Alexandru 20; tel. (21) 2086030; fax (21) 2307620; e-mail bkr@minbuza.nl; internet www.olanda.ro; Ambassador JAAP L. WERNER.

Nigeria: 010449 Bucharest, Str. Orlando 9, POB 1-305, Sector 1; tel. (21) 3128685; fax (21) 3120622; e-mail nigerembrinro@yahoo.com; Ambassador MBA AMA MBA.

Norway: 020463 Bucharest, Str. Dumbrava Roşie 4; tel. (21) 2100274; fax (21) 2100275; e-mail emb.bucharest@mfa.no; internet www.norvegia.ro; Ambassador ØYSTEIN HOVDKINN.

Pakistan: 011352 Bucharest 1, Str. Barbu Delavrancea 22, Sector 1; tel. (21) 3187873; fax (21) 3187874; e-mail parepbucharest@live.com; Ambassador D. SANAULLAH.

Peru: 020372 Bucharest, Bd. Lacul Tei 29/4, Sector 2; tel. (21) 2111816; fax (21) 2111818; e-mail embajadaperu.bk_ro@yahoo.com; Ambassador ELARD ALBERTO ESCALA.

Philippines: 050453 Bucharest 5, Str. Carol Davila 105–107, 5th Floor, Rm 10–11; tel. (21) 3198252; fax (21) 3198253; e-mail bucharestpe@rdsmail.ro; Chargé d'affaires a.i. TERESITA C. DAZA.

Poland: 011821 Bucharest 1, Al. Alexandru 23, Sector 1; tel. (21) 3082200; fax (21) 2307832; e-mail ambasada@bukareszt.ro; internet www.bukareszt.polemb.net; Ambassador WOJCIECH ZAJĄCZKOWSKI.

Portugal: 011815 Bucharest 1, Str. Paris 55, POB 63-91; tel. (21) 2304136; fax (21) 2304117; e-mail secretariat@embportugal.ro; internet www.embportugal.ro; Ambassador ALEXANDRE VASSALO.

Qatar: 011834 Bucharest, Str. Venezuela 10A, Sector 1; tel. (21) 2304741; fax (21) 2305446; e-mail qtr_embassy@b.astral.ro; Ambassador SALEM ABDULLAH SULTAN AL-JABER.

Russia: 011341 Bucharest 1, Şos. Kiseleff 6, Sector 1; tel. (21) 2223170; fax (21) 2229450; e-mail rab@mb.roknet.ro; internet www.romania.mid.ru; Ambassador ALEKSANDR A. CHURILIN.

Saudi Arabia: 010501 Bucharest 1, Str. Polonă 6, Sector 1; tel. (21) 2109109; fax (21) 2107093; e-mail ksa_embassy@yahoo.com; Ambassador AHMAD M. AL-ZUGHAIBI.

Serbia: 010573 Bucharest 1, Calea Dorobanţilor 34, Sector 1; tel. (21) 2119871; fax (21) 2100175; e-mail mail@ambserbia.ro; internet www.ambserbia.ro; Ambassador DUŠAN CRNOGORČEVIĆ.

Slovakia: 020977 Bucharest 2, Str. Oţetari 3, Sector 2; tel. (21) 3006100; fax (21) 3006101; e-mail emb.bucharest@mzv.sk; internet www.bucharest.mfa.sk; Ambassador DAGMAR REPCEKOVÁ.

Slovenia: 011995 Bucharest, Str. Puşkin 10, Sector 1; tel. (21) 3002780; fax (21) 3150927; e-mail vbk@gov.si; internet www.bukaresta.veleposlanistvo.si; Chargé d'affaires a.i. MARCEL KOPROL.

South Africa: 010113 Bucharest, Str. Ştirbei Vodă 26–28, Sector 1; tel. (21) 3133725; fax (21) 3133795; e-mail saembassy.bucharest@yahoo.com; Chargé d'affaires a.i. JOHANNES HENDRIK KOTZE.

Spain: 011822 Bucharest, Str. Aleea Alexandru 43, Sector 1; tel. (21) 3181080; fax (21) 3181072; e-mail emb.bucarest@maec.es; internet www.maec.es/Embajadas/Bucarest; Ambassador JUAN PABLO GARCÍA-BERDOY Y CEREZO.

Sudan: 011941 Bucharest 1, Str. Pictor Negulici 3, Sector 1; tel. (21) 2339189; fax (21) 2339188; e-mail sudanbuc@sudanembassy.ro; Ambassador AJING ADIANG MARIK.

Sweden: 011343 Bucharest, Şos. Kiseleff 43, Sector 1; tel. (21) 4067100; fax (21) 4067124; e-mail ambassaden.bukarest@foreign.ministry.se; internet www.swedenabroad.com/bukarest; Ambassador MATS O. ABERG.

Switzerland: 010626 Bucharest, Str. Grigore Alexandrescu 16–20, Sector 1; tel. (21) 2061600; fax (21) 2061620; e-mail buc.vertretung@eda.admin.ch; internet www.eda.admin.ch/bucarest; Ambassador LIVIO HÜRZELER.

Syria: 010673 Bucharest, Bd. Lascăr Catargiu 50, Sector 1; tel. (21) 3192467; fax (21) 3129554; e-mail syrambro@yahoo.com; Ambassador Dr WALID ALI OSMAN.

Thailand: 020953 Bucharest, Str. Vasile Conta 12, Sector 2; tel. (21) 3110031; fax (21) 3110044; e-mail thaibuh@speedmail.ro; Ambassador RUSHDA THAVARAVEJ.

Tunisia: 010517 Bucharest 1, Str. Mihai Eminescu 50–54/10; tel. (21) 2101197; fax (21) 2101114; e-mail at.bucarest@b.astral.ro; Ambassador SALOUA BAHRI.

Turkey: 010575 Bucharest, Calea Dorobanţilor 72, Sector 1; tel. (21) 2063700; fax (21) 2063737; e-mail bukres.be@mfa.gov.tr; Ambassador AYŞE SINIRLIOGLU.

Ukraine: 010572 Bucharest, Bd. Aviatorilor 24, Sector 1; tel. (21) 2303660; fax (21) 2303661; e-mail emb_ukr@itcnet.ro; internet www.ucraina.ro; Ambassador MARKIYAN Z. KUPYK.

United Arab Emirates: 011825 Aleea Modrogan 4; tel. (21) 2317676; fax (21) 2315588; e-mail uae@zappmobile.ro; Ambassador YA'QUB YUSUF AL-HOUSNI.

United Kingdom: 010463 Bucharest, Str. Jules Michelet 24, Sector 1; tel. (21) 2017200; fax (21) 2017299; e-mail press@bucharest.mail.fco.gov.uk; internet ukinromania.fco.gov.uk; Ambassador ROBIN BARNETT.

USA: 020942 Bucharest, Str. Tudor Arghezi 7–9; tel. (21) 2003300; fax (21) 2003442; internet www.usembassy.ro; Chargé d'affaires a.i. JERI GUTHRIE-CORN.

Uruguay: 011952 Bucharest, Str. Maxim Gorki 22/1, Sector 1; tel. and fax (21) 3138129; Ambassador PEDRO MO AMARO.

Venezuela: 011396 Bucharest 1, Str. Pictor Mirea 18, Sector 1; tel. (21) 2225874; fax (21) 2225073; e-mail embavero@clicknet.ro; Chargé d'affaires a.i. MARGOT JULY MÁRQUEZ GARCÍA.

Viet Nam: 020011 Bucharest, Str. C. A. Rosetti 35; tel. (21) 3111604; fax (21) 3121626; e-mail viethuru@b.astral.ro; internet www.vietnamembassy-romania.org; Ambassador NGUYEN QUANG CHIEN.

Judicial System

In preparation for its entry into the European Union on 1 January 2007, Romania implemented a programme of judicial reform, with a particular emphasis on guaranteeing the independence of the judiciary.

High Court of Cassation and Justice
(Înalte Curte de Casaţie şi Justiţie a României)

020936 Bucharest 2, Str. Batişte 2; tel. (21) 3137656; fax (21) 3137655; internet www.scj.ro.

The High Court of Cassation and Justice, which was reorganized in June 2004, exercises control over the judicial activity of all courts. It ensures the correct and uniform application of the law. The Court includes sections dealing with: civil and intellectual property law; criminal law; commercial law; and administrative and fiscal regulations.

President: NICOLAE POPA.

Constitutional Court of Romania (Curtea Constituţională a României): 050725 Bucharest, Palatul Parlamentului, Calea 13 Septembrie 2, Sector 5; tel. (21) 4022121; fax (21) 3124359; e-mail ccr@ccr.ro; internet www.ccr.ro; f. 1992; Pres. IOAN VIDA.

Office of the Prosecutor-General: 050706 Bucharest 5, Bd. Libertăţii 14; tel. (21) 4102727; fax (21) 3113939; e-mail pg@kappa.ro; Prosecutor-General LAURA CODRUTA KOVESI.

COUNTY COURTS AND LOCAL COURTS

The judicial organization of courts at the county and local levels was established by Law 92 of 4 August 1992. In each of the 40 counties, there is a county court and between three and six local courts. The county courts also form 15 circuits of appeal courts, where appeals against sentences passed by local courts are heard, which are generally considered courts of first instance. There is also a right of appeal from the appeal courts to the Supreme Court. In both county courts and local courts, the judges are professional magistrates.

Religion

In Romania there are 15 religious denominations and more than 400 religious associations recognized by the state. According to census figures, about 87% of the population belonged to the Romanian Orthodox Church in January 1992.

State Secretariat for Religious Affairs: 020962 Bucharest, Str. Nicolae Filipescu 40; tel. (21) 2118116; fax (21) 2109471; e-mail ssc@mediasat.ro; f. 1990; State Sec. LAURENȚIU TĂNASE.

CHRISTIANITY

The Romanian Orthodox Church

The Romanian Orthodox Church is the major religious organization in Romania (with more than 19m. believers) and is organized as an autocephalous patriarchate, led by the Holy Synod and headed by a patriarch. The Patriarchate comprises five metropolitanates, 10 archdioceses and 13 dioceses.

Romanian Patriarchate
(Patriarhia Română)

040163 Bucharest, Al. Dealul Mitropoliei 25; tel. (21) 3374035; fax (21) 3370097; e-mail externe@patriarhia.ro; internet www.patriarhia.ro.

Patriarch, Metropolitan of Muntênia and Dobrogea and Archbishop of Bucharest: DANIEL (CIOBOTEA), 040161 Bucharest, Str. Patriarhiei 21; tel. (21) 3372776.

Metropolitan of Banat and Archbishop of Timișoara and Caransebeș: Dr NICOLAE (CORNEANU), 300021 jud. Timiș, Timișoara, Bd. Constantin Diaconovici Loga 7; tel. (256) 190960; internet www.mitropolia-banatului.home.ro.

Metropolitan of Cluj, Alba, Crișana and Maramureș and Archbishop of Vad, Feleac and Cluj: BARTOLOMEU (ANANIA), 400117 jud. Cluj, Cluj-Napoca, Piața Avram Iancu 18; tel. (264) 593944; fax (264) 595184; e-mail bartolomeu@arhiepiscopia-ort-cluj.org; internet www.arhiepiscopia-ort-cluj.org.

Metropolitan of Moldova and Bucovina and Archbishop of Iași: TEOFAN (SAVU), 700064 jud. Iași, Iași, Bd. Ștefan cel Mare și Sfânt 16; tel. (232) 214771; fax (232) 212656; e-mail iecum@mail.dntis.ro; internet www.mmb.ro.

Metropolitan of Oltenia and Archbishop of Craiova: (vacant), 200381 jud. Dolj, Craiova, Str. Mitropolit Firmilian 3; tel. (251) 415054; fax (251) 418369; internet www.m-ol.ro.

Metropolitan of Transylvania and Archbishop of Sibiu: LAURENȚIU , 550179 jud. Sibiu, Sibiu, Str. Mitropoliei 24; tel. (269) 412867.

The Roman Catholic Church

Roman Catholics in Romania include adherents of the Armenian, Latin and Romanian (Byzantine) Rites.

Bishops' Conference: 010804 Bucharest, via Popa Tatu 68; tel. (21) 3111289; fax (21) 3111591; e-mail b_cazmir@pcnet.ro; internet www.catholica.ro; f. 1990; Pres. Most Rev. IOAN ROBU (Archbishop of Bucharest).

Latin Rite

There are two archdioceses (including one directly subordinate to the Holy See) and four dioceses. At 31 December 2006 there were 1,114,879 adherents of the Latin Rite (about 5.1% of the total population).

Archbishop of Alba Iulia: Most Rev. GYÖRGY-MIKLÓS JAKUBÍNYI, 510010 jud. Alba, Alba Iulia, Str. Mihai Viteazul 21; tel. (258) 811689; fax (258) 811454; e-mail albapress@gyrke.uab.ro.

Archbishop of Bucharest: Most Rev. IOAN ROBU, 010164 Bucharest, Str. Gen. Berthelot 19; tel. (21) 3158349; fax (21) 3121208; e-mail secretariat@arcb.ro.

Romanian Rite

There is one archbishopric-major and four dioceses. At 31 December 2006 there were 769,729 adherents of the Romanian Rite (about 3.5% of the total population).

Archbishop-Major of Făgăraș and Alba Iulia: Most Rev. LUCIAN MUREȘAN, 515400 jud. Alba, Blaj, Str. Petru Pavel Aron 2; tel. (258) 712057; fax (258) 713602; e-mail mitropolia@bru.ro.

Armenian Rite

There were 806 adherents of the Armenian Rite in Romania at 31 December 2006, represented by an Ordinariate.

Reformed (Calvinist) Church

The Reformed (Calvinist) Church has some 700,000 mems. There are two bishoprics.

Bishop of Oradea: 410210 jud. Bihor, Oradea, Str. J. Calvin 1; tel. (259) 431710; e-mail krekpht@partium.ro; internet www.kiralyhagomellek.ro; Bishop LÁSZLÓ TŐKÉS.

Bishop of the Transylvanian Reformed Church District: 400079 jud. Cluj, Cluj-Napoca, Str. I. C. Brătianu 51; tel. (264) 597472; fax (264) 595104; e-mail office@reformatus.ro; internet portal.reformatus.ro; Bishop Rev. Dr GÉZA PAP.

Other Protestant Churches

Evangelical-Lutheran Church in Romania: 400105 jud. Cluj, Cluj-Napoca, Bd. 21 Decembrie 1989 1; tel. (264) 596614; fax (264) 593897; internet www.lutheran.ro; comprises about 27,100 Hungarians, 4,600 Slovaks and 340 Romanians; Superintendent Bishop ZOLTÁN ADORJANI DEZSŐ.

Romanian Evangelical Church (Biserica Evanghelica România): 050454 Bucharest, Str. Carol Davila 48; tel. (21) 4119622; fax (21) 4103652; e-mail ber@rdsmail.ro; internet www.ber.ro.

Unitarian Church in Transylvania: 400105 jud. Cluj, Cluj-Napoca, Str. 21 Decembrie 1989 9; tel. (264) 593236; fax (264) 595927; e-mail ekt@unitarius.com; internet www.unitarius.com; f. 1568; comprises about 75,000 mems, principally of Hungarian ethnicity; 125 churches and 30 fellowships; Bishop ÁRPÁD SZABÓ.

Other Christian Churches

Belaya Krinitsa Old Believers' Orthodox Church: 810140 jud. Brăila, Brăila, Str. Zidari 5; tel. (239) 647023; Metropolitan LEONTY IZOTOV.

Pentecostal Church: 050453 Bucharest, Str. Carol Davila 81; tel. (21) 2126419; fax (21) 2204303; e-mail cuvadev@fx.ro; f. 1922; 2,455 churches, 525 pastors (Dec. 2001); 450,000 mems; Pres. Rev. RIVIS TIPEI PAVEL; Gen. Sec. Rev. IOAN GURĂU.

Seventh-day Adventist Church: 077190 jud. Ilfov, Voluntari, Str. Erou Iancu Nicolae 38; tel. (21) 4908590; fax (21) 4908570; e-mail communicatii@adventist.ro; internet www.adventist.ro; f. 1920; 67,000 mems; Pres. of the Union Rev. ADRIAN BOCANEANU; Sec.-Gen. TEODOR HUTANU.

ISLAM

There are an estimated 55,000 Muslims in Romania, mostly of Turkish or Tatar origin.

Muftiatul Cultului Musulman din Romania: Grand Mufti OSMAN NEGEAT, 900742 jud. Constanța, Constanța, Bd. Tomis 41; tel. (241) 611390.

JUDAISM

In 1999 there were about 14,000 Jews, organized in some 70 communities, in Romania.

Federation of Jewish Communities (Federatia Comunitatilor Evreiesti din Romania): 030202 Bucharest 3, Str. Sf. Vineri 9–11; tel. (21) 3132538; fax (21) 3120869; e-mail vainer@jewish.ro; internet www.jewish.ro; Pres. AUREL VAINER; Chief Rabbi MENACHEM HACOHEN.

The Press

The Romanian press is highly regionalized. In 2005 there were 80 daily newspapers and 2,044 periodicals in circulation. In 2002 some 10 newspapers and 207 periodicals were published in the languages of minority ethnic groups in Romania, including Hungarian, German, Serbian, Ukrainian, Armenian and Yiddish.

The publications listed below are in Romanian, unless otherwise indicated.

PRINCIPAL DAILY NEWSPAPERS

Adevărul (The Truth): 013701 Bucharest, Piața Presei Libere 1; tel. (21) 2240067; fax (21) 2243612; e-mail redactia@adevarul.kappa.ro; internet www.adevarulonline.ro; f. 1888; daily except Sun.; independent; Dir CHRISTIAN TUDOR POPESCU; circ. 200,000.

ROMANIA   *Directory*

Azi (Today): 010062 Bucharest, Calea Victoriei 39A, CP 45–49; tel. (21) 3144215; fax (21) 3120128; e-mail redactie@azi.ro; internet www.azi.ro; f. 1990; independent; Editor-in-Chief ANA MOD.

Cotidianul (The Daily): 020922 Bucharest 2, Bd. Carol I 34–36; tel. (21) 3173192; fax (21) 3173124; e-mail rhpress@cotidianul.ro; internet www.cotidianul.ro; f. 1991; daily except Sun.; Editorial Dir DORU BUSCU; Editor-in-Chief CAROL SEBASTIAN; circ. 120,000.

Cronica Română: 013701 Bucharest 1, POB 33, Piața Presei Libere 1, corp. C, etaj 1, camera 31; tel. (21) 3179165; fax (21) 3179169; internet www.cronicaromana.ro; f. 1992; daily; Dir HORIA ALEXANDRESCU; Editor-in-Chief DAN OLTEANU; circ. 29,000.

Curierul Național (The National Courier): 010024 Bucharest, Str. Cristian Popișteanu 2–4; tel. (21) 3159512; fax (21) 3121300; internet www.curierulnational.ro; f. 1991; Editor-in-Chief CRISTINA OROVEANU; circ. 55,000.

Evenimentul Zilei (The Event of the Day): 020337 Bucharest 2, Bd. Dimitrie Pompeiu 6; tel. (21) 2226381; fax (21) 2226382; internet www.evz.ro; f. 1991; owned by Ringier (Switzerland); tabloid; Bucharest, Transylvania and western regional editions; Editor-in-Chief RAZVAN IONESCU; circ. 200,000.

Gândul: 013701 Bucharest 1, Piața Presei Libere 1, Corp. A3–A4; tel. (21) 2053125; fax (21) 2053188; e-mail redactia@gandul.info; internet www.gandul.info; f. 2005; independent; Editor-in-Chief ADRIAN URSU.

Gazeta Sporturilor (Sports Gazette): 051431 Bucharest 1, Șos. Bucuresti–Ploiești 17; tel. (21) 2087460; fax (21) 2087484; e-mail gazeta@gsp.ro; internet www.gazetasporturilor.ro; f. 1924; daily except Sun.; independent; Editor-in-Chief CATALIN TOLONTAN; circ. 50,000.

Jurnalul National (The National Journal): 013701 Bucharest 1, Piața Presei Libere 1, Corp. D, etaj 8; tel. (21) 2243701; fax (21) 2243351; e-mail off@jurnalul.ro; internet www.jurnalul.ro; f. 1993; Editor-in-Chief MARIUS TUCĂ; circ. 70,000.

Libertatea (Freedom): 020337 Bucharest, Bd. Dimitrie Pompeiu 6, Sector 2; tel. (21) 2030940; fax (21) 2030832; internet www.libertatea.ro; f. 1989; owned by Ringier (Switzerland); daily; Sunday edition, *Libertatea de Duminica*, launched in 2002; tabloid; morning paper; Editor-in-Chief ADRIAN HALPERT; circ. 140,000.

ProSport: 020337 Bucharest 2, Bd. Dimitrie Pompeiu 6, Novo Parc; internet www.prosport.ro; f. 1997; owned by Ringier (Switzerland); sports news.

România Libera (Free Romania): 013701 Bucharest, Piața Presei Libere 1, Corp. C, etaj 4; tel. (21) 2224770; fax (21) 2232071; e-mail redactia@romanialibera.ro; internet www.romanialibera.ro; f. 1877; daily except Sun.; independent; Editor-in-Chief BOGDAN FICEAC; circ. 100,000.

Ziarul Financiar: 030195 Bucharest, Str. Bărăției 31; tel. (31) 8256235; fax (31) 8256285; e-mail zf@zf.ro; internet www.zf.ro.

Ziua (The Day): 010036 Bucharest, Str. Ion Câmpineanu 4; tel. and fax (21) 3113155; e-mail ziua@ziua.ro; internet www.ziua.net; f. 1930; Dir SORIN ROSCA STANESCU.

DISTRICT NEWSPAPERS

Adevărul (The Truth): 310130 jud. Arad, Arad, Bd. Revoluției 81; tel. (257) 281802; fax (257) 280904; e-mail adevarul@arad.ro; internet www.adevarul.arad.ro; f. 1989; independent; daily; Dir DOREL ZAVOIANU; circ. 25,900.

Adevărul Harghitei (Harghita Truth): 530190 jud. Harghita, Miercurea-Ciuc, Str. Leliceni 45; tel. (266) 171805; fax (266) 172065; f. 1990; independent; daily; Editor-in-Chief MIHAI GROZA.

Argeșul Liber (Free Argeș): 110177 jud. Argeș, Pitești, Str. Republicii 88; tel. (276) 30490; e-mail argesul@rdspt.ro; internet www.cotidianul-argesul.ro; f. 1990; independent; daily; Editor-in-Chief MARIN MANOLACHE.

Bună Ziua Brașov (Good Afternoon Brașov): 500090 jud. Brașov, Brașov, Str. Mihai Kogalniceanu 19, etaj 7; tel. (268) 411073; fax (268) 314692; e-mail bzb@bzb.ro; internet www.bzb.ro; f. 1995; Dir OVIDIU FODOR; circ. 30,000.

Ceahlăul: 610263 jud. Neamț, Piatra-Neamț, Al. Tiparului 14; tel. and fax (233) 625282; f. 1989; daily; Editor-in-Chief VIOREL TUDOSE; circ. 20,000.

Crai nou: 720059 jud. Suceava, Suceava, Str. Mihai Viteazul 32; tel. and fax (230) 214723; e-mail redactie@crainou.ro; internet www.crainou.ro; f. 1990; daily; Editor-in-Chief DUMITRU TEODORESCU.

Cuget Liber (Free Thinking): 900711 jud. Constanța, Constanța, Șos. I. C. Brătianu 5; tel. (241) 582120; fax (241) 619524; internet www.cugetliber.ro; f. 1989; independent; daily; Editor-in-Chief ION TIȚA CĂLIN.

Curierul de Vâlcea (Courier of Vâlcea): 240165 jud. Vâlcea, Râmnicu Vâlcea, Calea lui Traian 127; tel. (250) 702942; fax (250) 702941; e-mail office@curierul.ro; internet www.curierul.ro; f. 1990; independent; daily except Mon.; commerce; Dir IOAN BARBU.

Cuvântul Liber (The Free Word): 540015 jud. Mureș, Târgu Mureș, Str. Gh. Doja 9; tel. and fax (265) 266629; internet www.cuvantul-liber.ro; f. 1989; independent; daily; Editor-in-Chief LAZĂR LADARIU; circ. 10,000 (2009).

Cuvântul Libertății (The Word of Liberty): 200020 jud. Dolj, Craiova, Str. Lyon 8; tel. (251) 2457; fax (251) 4141; f. 1989; daily except Sun.; Editor-in-Chief DAN LUPESCU; circ. 40,000.

Cuvântul nou (The New Word): 520064 jud. Covasna, Sfântu Gheorghe, Str. Pieței 8; tel. (240) 2311388; f. 1968; new series 1990; daily except Mon.; Editor-in-Chief DUMITRU MÂNOLĂCHESCU.

Dâmbovița: 130082 jud. Dâmbovița, Târgoviște, Bul. Unirii 32; f. 1990; independent; daily; Editor-in-Chief ALEXANDRU ILIE.

Datina (Tradition): 220134 jud. Mehedinți, Drobeta-Turnu Severin, Str. Trâian 89; tel. (2978) 119950; f. 1990; independent; daily; Editor-in-Chief GHEORGHE BUREȚEA.

Delta (The Delta): 820180 jud. Tulcea, Tulcea, Str. Spitalului 4; tel. (2405) 124061; fax (2405) 16616; f. 1885; new series 1990; daily except Mon.; Editor-in-Chief NECULAI AMIHULESEI.

Deșteptarea (The Awakening): 600010 jud. Bacău, Bacău, Str. Vasile Alecsandri 41; tel. (234) 511272; fax (234) 524927; e-mail dsa@desteptarea.ro; internet www.desteptarea.ro; f. 1989; Editor-in-Chief DORIAN POCOVNICU; circ. 50,000.

Erdélyi Napló: 400750 jud. Bihor, Oradea, POB 1320; tel. (264) 420773; fax (259) 417126; e-mail erdelyinaplo@cluj.astral.ro; internet www.hhrf.org/erdelyinaplo; in Hungarian; weekly; Editor-in-Chief LÁSZLÓ DÉNES.

Evenimentul: 700497 jud. Iași, Iași, Stradelă Ștefan cel Mare și Sfânt 4; tel. (232) 112023; fax (232) 112025; internet www.evenimentul.ro/sectiune/iasi.html; f. 1991; daily; Editor-in-Chief CONSTANTIN PALADUTA.

Făclia de Cluj (Cluj Torch): 401050 jud. Cluj, Cluj-Napoca, Str. Napoca 16; tel. and fax (264) 597418; e-mail redactia@ziarulfaclia.ro; internet www.ziarulfaclia.ro; f. 1989; daily; fmrly Adevărul de Cluj (Cluj Truth); present name adopted 2007; independent; Editor-in-Chief ILIE CĂLIAN; circ. 200,000.

Gazeta de Transilvania (Transylvanian Gazette): 550030 jud. Brașov, Brașov, Str. M. Sadoveanu 3; tel. (268) 8142029; fax (268) 8152927; f. 1838; ceased publication 1946, re-established 1989; daily except Mon.; independent; Editor-in-Chief EDUARD HUIDAN.

Gorjanul: 210192 jud. Gorj, Târgu Jiu, Str. Constantin Brâncuși 15; tel. (2929) 17464; f. 1990; daily; Editor-in-Chief NICOLAE BRÎNZAN.

Graiul Maramureșului (The Voice of Maramureș): 430051 jud. Maramureș, Baia Mare, Bd. București 25; tel. (262) 221017; fax (262) 224871; e-mail graiul@graiul.ro; internet www.graiul.ro; f. 1989; independent; daily except Sun.; Editor-in-Chief AUGUSTIN COZMUȚA; circ. 10,000.

Graiul Sălajului (Voice of Sălaj): 450042 jud. Sălaj, Zalău, Piața Unirii 7; tel. (299) 614120; f. 1990; daily; Editor-in-Chief IOAN LUPA.

Hargita Népe: 530190 jud. Harghita, Miercurea-Ciuc, Str. Leliceni 45; tel. and fax (266) 171322; e-mail hargitanepe@topnet.to; internet www.topnet.ro/hargitanepe; daily; in Hungarian; Dir LÁSZLÓ BORBELY.

Háromszék (Three Chairs): 520064 jud. Covasna, Sfântu Gheorghe, Str. Presei 8A; tel. (240) 67351504; fax (240) 67351253; e-mail hpress@3szek.ro; internet www.3szek.ro; f. 1989; socio-political; daily; in Hungarian; Editor-in-Chief FARKAS ÁRPÁD.

Mesagerul de Bistrița-Năsăud: 420074 jud. Bistrița-Năsăud, Bistrița, Str. Ursului 14; tel. (402) 63234688; fax (402) 63234689; e-mail mesagerul@mesagerul.ro; internet www.mesagerul.ro; daily.

Milcovul Liber (Free Milcov): 620095 jud. Vrancea, Focșani, Bd. Unirii 18; tel. (237) 614579; fax (237) 613588; f. 1989; weekly; Dir OVIDIU BUTUC.

Monitorul de Botoșani: 710210 jud. Botoșani, Botoșani, Str. Mihail Kogălniceanu 4; tel. (231) 515053; fax (231) 515130; e-mail monitorul@monitorulbt.ro; internet www.monitorulbt.ro; Editor-in-Chief CATALIN MORARU.

Monitorul de Iași (Iași Monitor): 700237 jud. Iași, Iași, Șos. Națională 45; tel. (332) 430806; fax (332) 430807; e-mail redactia@monitorul.com.ro; internet www.monitorul.com.ro; f. 1991; daily; Editor-in-Chief CĂTĂLINA TERCHEA.

Népújság (People's Journal): 540015 jud. Mureș, Târgu Mureș, Str. Gh. Doja 9; tel. (265) 266780; fax (265) 266270; e-mail nepujsag@e-nepujsag.ro; internet www.hhrf.org/nepujsag; f. 1990; daily; in Hungarian; Editor-in-Chief JÁNOS MAKKAI.

Opinia (Opinion): 120189 jud. Buzău, Buzău, Str. Unirii, bloc PTTR, magazin 39 Lumea Copiilor; tel. (238) 711063; fax (238) 412764; e-mail opinia@buzau.ro; internet ziarul.opiniabuzau.ro; f. 1990; independent; daily; Editor-in-Chief GABRIEL COSTIANU.

ROMANIA

in Arabic, Bulgarian, Chinese, English, German, Greek, Hungarian, Italian, Portuguese, Romanian, Russian, Serbian, Spanish, Turkish and Ukrainian; Pres. MARIA TOGHINA.

Kiss FM: 060022 Bucharest 6, Spl. Independenței 202A; tel. (21) 3188000; fax (21) 3125346; e-mail kissfm@kissfm.ro; internet www.kissfm.ro; owned by SBS Broadcasting Sa.r.l.

Pro FM: 021409 Bucharest 2, Bd. Protopopescu Pache 109, etaj 6; tel. (21) 2501430; internet www.profm.ro; f. 1993; owned by Central European Media Enterprises Ltd (Bermuda); Gen. Dir ADRIAN SARBU.

Radio Europa FM: 010541 Bucharest 1, Intr. Camil Petrescu 5; tel. (21) 2010500; fax (21) 2010519; e-mail europafm@europafm.ro; internet www.europafm.ro; Gen. Dir ILIE NĂSTASE.

Radio Nord-Est: 700479 jud. Iași, Iași, Str. Codrescu 1; tel. and fax (232) 211570; e-mail rneiasi@dntis.ro; f. 1992; independent; Man. MIHAI GRETY.

Societatea Națională de Radiocommunicații, SA (National Radiocommunications Co): 050706 Bucharest 5, Bd. Libertății 14; tel. (21) 3073007; fax (21) 3149798; e-mail info@snr.ro; internet www.snr.ro; f. 1991 through the reorganization of Rom Post Telecom; state-owned; radio and television broadcasting (including digital), high-speed internet and broadband services, satellite communications; 2,445 employees.

Television

Televiziunea Română (TVR) (Romanian Television): 015089 Bucharest, Calea Dorobanților 191, POB 63-1200; tel. (21) 2312704; fax (21) 2307514; e-mail tvr@tvr.ro; internet www.tvr.ro; f. 1956; state-owned; public broadcasting service; four channels broadcasting 24 hours; Pres. and Dir-Gen. GIURGIU TUDOR.

Antena 1: 013682 Bucharest, Șos. București-Ploiești 25–27; tel. (21) 2121844; internet www.antena1.ro; f. 1993; independent commercial television station.

Prima TV: 040204 Bucharest 4, Calea Serban Voda 95–101; tel. (21) 3359341; e-mail focus@primatv.ro; internet www.primatv.ro; f. 1997; owned by SBS Broadcasting SA.

Pro TV: 021409 Bucharest 2, Bd. Pache Protopopescu 109, etaj 6; tel. (21) 2505063; fax (21) 2501951; e-mail info@protv.ro; internet www.protv.ro; f. 1995; owned by Central European Media Enterprises Ltd (CME), Bermuda; commercial station; Gen. Dir ADRIAN SARBU.

Finance

(cap. = capital; res = reserves; dep. = deposits; m. = million; brs = branches; amounts in new lei, unless otherwise indicated)

BANKING

Central Bank

National Bank of Romania (Banca Națională a României): 030031 Bucharest 3, Str. Lipscani 25; tel. (21) 3130410; fax (21) 3123831; e-mail info@bnro.ro; internet www.bnro.ro; f. 1880; central bank and bank of issue; manages monetary policy; supervises commercial banks and credit business; cap. 30.0m., res 670.8m., dep. 36,496.0m. (Dec. 2007); Gov. MUGUR CONSTANTIN ISĂRESCU; 22 brs.

Other Banks

Alpha Bank Romania SA: 010566 Bucharest 1, Calea Dorobanților 237B; tel. (21) 2092100; fax (21) 2316570; e-mail bbr@alphabank.ro; internet www.alphabank.ro; f. 1994; present name adopted 2000; 99.9% owned by Alpha Bank AE (Greece); cap. 618.0m., res 223.6m., dep. 11,571.0m. (Dec. 2007); Pres. SERGIU BOGDAN OPRESCU.

Banca Comercială Carpatica SA (BCC): 550135 jud. Sibiu, Sibiu, Str. Autogarii 1; tel. (269) 233815; fax (269) 233371; e-mail extern@carpatica.ro; internet www.carpatica.ro; f. 1999; cap. 116.0m., res 37.2m., dep. 1,223.9m. (Dec. 2006); Pres. and Chair. NICOLAIE HOANTA.

Banca Comercială Română SA—BCR (Romanian Commercial Bank): 030016 Bucharest 3, Bd. Regina Elisabeta 5; tel. (21) 3126185; fax (21) 3122096; internet www.bcr.ro; f. 1990; 69.2% owned by Erste Bank (Austria); cap. 2,119.7m., res 1,101.8m., dep. 56,509.4m. (Dec. 2007); Pres. ANDREAS TREICHL; 372 brs and sub-brs.

Banca de Export-Import a României (Eximbank Romania): 050092 Bucharest 5, Str. Splaiul Independenței 15; tel. (21) 3192971; fax (21) 3192999; e-mail pr@eximbank.ro; internet www.eximbank.ro; f. 1992; 93.4% state-owned; cap. 758.8m., res 115.5m., dep. 195.8m. (Dec. 2007); Chair. and Chief Exec. CARMEN RADU; 7 brs.

Banca Românească SA (Romanian Bank): 030822 Bucharest 3, Bd. Unirii 35, Bloc A3; tel. (21) 3059300; fax (21) 3059550; e-mail office@brom.ro; internet www.brom.ro; f. 1993; 88.7% owned by National Bank of Greece SA (NBG); cap. 479.9m., res 87.0m., dep. 2,819.3m. (Dec. 2006); Gen. Man. ANDREAS MARAGKOUDAKIS.

Banca Transilvania SA (Transylvanian Bank): 400027 jud. Cluj, Cluj-Napoca, Str. G. Baritiu 8; tel. (264) 407150; fax (264) 407179; e-mail bancatransilvania@bancatransilvania.ro; internet www.bancatransilvania.ro; f. 1994; cap. 701.0m., res 295.6m., dep. 12,396.0m. (Dec. 2007); Chair. HORIA CIORCILA; Chief Exec. ROBERT C. REKKERS; 55 brs, 341 agencies.

Bancpost SA: 031296 Bucharest 3, Calea Vitan 6–6A; tel. (21) 3080901; fax (21) 3268520; e-mail bpt@bancpost.ro; internet www.bancpost.ro; f. 1991; 77.6% owned by EFG Eurobank Ergasias SA (Greece); cap. 619.6m., res 197.6m., dep. 6,405.8m. (Dec. 2006); Chair. MIHAI BOGZA; Gen. Man. MANUELA PLAPCIANU.

BRD-Groupe Société Générale SA (Romanian Bank for Development): 011171 Bucharest 1, Bd. Ion Mihalache 1–7; tel. (21) 3016100; fax (21) 3016636; e-mail communication@brd.ro; internet www.brd.ro; f. 1990 to replace Investment Bank of Romania (f. 1923); present name adopted 2004; financial and banking services and operations to individuals and private and small cos; 58.3% owned by Société Générale (France); cap. 2,515.6m., res 0.7m., dep. 28,608.3m. (Dec. 2007); Chair. and Chief Exec. PATRICK GELIN; 191 brs.

CEC Bank SA: 030022 Bucharest 3, Calea Victoriei 11–13; tel. (21) 3111119; fax (21) 3143970; e-mail office@cec.ro; internet www.cec.ro; f. 1864; fmrly Casa de Economii și Consemnațiuni; present name adopted 2008; state-owned; scheduled for privatization; handles private savings, loans for the inter-banking market and mortgages; cap. 649.7m., res 195.4m., dep. 5,877.3m. (Dec. 2006); Chair. and Chief Exec. RADU GRATIAN GHETEA; 42 brs.

Citibank Romania SA: 011742 Bucharest 1, Bd. Iancu de Hunedoara 8, POB 63-5; tel. (21) 2035550; fax (21) 2035565; internet www.citibank.ro; f. 1996; 99.6% owned by Citigroup Overseas Investment Corpn (USA); cap. 70.5m., res 248.1m., dep. 3,253.5m. (Dec. 2007); Country Officer SHAHMIR KHALIQ; 40 brs.

Credit Europe Bank (Romania) SA: 040034 Bucharest 4, Str. Splaiul Unirii 12, Bloc B6; tel. (21) 3017100; fax (21) 3310970; e-mail office@crediteurope.ro; internet www.crediteurope.ro; f. 1993; fmrly Finansbank (Romania) in 2000; present name adopted 2007; 89.8% owned by Fiba International Holding (Netherlands); cap. 249.4m., res 23.8m., dep. 1,607.2m. (Dec. 2006); Pres. TAMER OZATAKUL; 85 brs.

Marfin Bank (Romania) SA: 010775 Bucharest 1, Str. Emanoil Porumbaru 90-92, BP 22-155; tel. (21) 2064200; fax (21) 2064281; e-mail office@egnatiabank-rom.ro; internet www.egnatiabank-rom.ro; f. 1998; fmrly Egnatia Bank (Romania); present name adopted 2008; 98.98% owned by Marfin Egnatia Bank SA (Greece); total assets €427.6m. (Dec. 2007); Gen. Man. STYLIANOS SOFIANOS.

MKB Romexterra Bank SA: 540447 jud. Mureș, Târgu Mureș, Bd. 1 Decembrie 1918 93; tel. (265) 266640; fax (265) 266047; e-mail info@romexterra.ro; internet www.romexterra.ro; f. 1993; 75.49% owned by MKB Bank Nyrt (Hungary); present name adopted 2007; cap. 200.0m., res 29.3m., dep. 1,057.2m. (Dec. 2006); CEO ADRIAN RADU; 68 brs.

OTP Bank Romania SA: 011017 Bucharest 3, Str. Buzesti 66–68; tel. (21) 3075700; fax (21) 3075736; e-mail office@otpbank.ro; internet www.otpbank.ro; f. 1995; present name adopted 2005; 99.99% owned by OTP Bank Ltd (Hungary); cap. 432.9m., res 42.8m., dep. 2,246.9m. (Dec. 2007); Chair. of Bd Dr ANTAL PONGRACZ.

Piraeus Bank Romania SA: 020922 Bucharest 2, Bd. Carol I 34–36, International Business Centre, 3rd Floor; tel. (21) 3036900; fax (21) 2501799; e-mail office@piraeusbank.ro; internet www.piraeusbank.ro; f. 1995; present name adopted 2000; 88.0% owned by Piraeus Bank (Greece); cap. 204.7m., res 24.5m., dep. 1,666.9m. (Dec. 2006); Pres. EMANUEL ODOBESCU; 3 brs.

Raiffeisen Bank SA: 011857 Bucharest 1, Piața Charles de Gaulle 15; tel. (21) 3061000; fax (21) 2300700; e-mail centrala@rzb.ro; internet www.raiffeisen.ro; f. 1968; present name adopted 2002; 99.5% owned by Raiffeisen International Beteiligungs AG (Austria); cap. 1,196.3m., res 22.0m., dep. 13,954.1m. (Dec. 2007); Pres. STEVEN VAN GRONIGEN; 329 brs.

UniCredit Tiriac Bank SA: 014106 Bucharest, Str. Ghetarilor 23–25, Sector 1; tel. (21) 2002000; fax (21) 2002002; e-mail office@unicredittiriac.ro; internet www.unicredit-tiriac.ro; f. 1991; present name adopted 2007; cap. 1,101.7m., res 204.5m., dep. 10,528.7m. (Dec. 2007); Chair. DAN PASCARIU; Chief Exec. RADU RASVAN; 50 brs.

Volksbank România SA: 021323 Bucharest 2, Șos. Mihai Bravu 171; tel. (21) 2094000; fax (21) 2094490; e-mail marketing@volksbank.com.ro; internet www.volksbank.com.ro; f. 2000; 97.9% owned by Volksbank International AG (Austria); cap. 229.1m., res 320.1m., dep. 3,778.5m. (Dec. 2006); Pres. GERALD SCHREINER.

BANKING ASSOCIATION

Romanian Banking Association (Asociația Română a Băncilor): 030205 Bucharest 3, Str. Sfanta Vineri 34, Bloc A6; tel. (21) 3212078; fax (21) 3212095; e-mail arb@arb.ro; internet www.arb.ro; f. 1991; 39 mems; Chair. RADU GRAȚIAN GHEȚEA; Sec.-Gen. RADU NEGREA.

ROMANIA   *Directory*

STOCK EXCHANGE

Bucharest Stock Exchange (Bursa de Valori Bucureşti): 020922 Bucharest 2, Bd. Carol I 34–36, 14th Floor; tel. (21) 3079500; fax (21) 3079519; e-mail bvb@bvb.ro; internet www.bvb.ro; f. 1882; reopened 1995 (ceased operations 1948); 128 listed cos; Pres. SERGIU OPRESCU; Gen. Man. STERE FARMACHE.

COMMODITIES EXCHANGE

Romanian Commodities Exchange (Bursa Română de Mărfuri): 013701 Bucharest 1, Piaţa Presei Libere 1; tel. (21) 2244560; fax (21) 2242878; e-mail bursa@brm.ro; internet www.brm.ro; Pres. MIRCEA FILIPOIU.

INSURANCE

In 2003 there were 46 insurance companies.

Allianz-Tiriac Asigurări: 010616 Bucharest, Str. Căderea Bastiliei 80–84; tel. (21) 2082222; fax (21) 2082211; e-mail office@allianztiriac.ro; internet www.allianztiriac.ro.

Asigurarea Românească SA (ASIROM) (Romanian Insurance): 020912 Bucharest 2, Bd. Carol I 31–33; tel. (21) 2504271; fax (21) 2504145; internet www.asirom.com.ro; f. 1991; life and non-life; Dir-Gen. ION GHEORGHE BRATULESCU; 41 brs.

Astra SA: 011996 Bucharest 1, Str. Puşkin 10–12; tel. (21) 2318080; fax (21) 2305248; e-mail info@astrasig.ro; internet www.astrasig.ro; f. 1991; Gen. Man. DAN ADAMESCU.

ING Asigurări de Viaţa SA: 050552 Bucharest 3, Str. Costache Negri 1–5, Opera Centre; tel. (21) 4028580; fax (21) 4028581; e-mail client@ingasigurari.ro; internet www.ingasigurari.ro; f. 1997; life; Gen. Man. BRAM BOON.

Omniasig SA: 011862 Bucharest 1, Bd. Aviatorilor 28; tel. (21) 2315040; fax (21) 2315029; e-mail secretary@omniasig.ro; internet www.omniasig.ro; f. 1994; insurance and reinsurance co; 98.9% owned by Vienna Insurance Group (Austria); Chair. CONSTANTIN TOMA.

Unita: 010413 Bucharest 1, Bd. Dacia 30; tel. (21) 2120852; fax (21) 2120843; e-mail unita@unita.ro; internet www.unita.ro; f. 1990; mem. of Uniqa Group (Austria); Dir DAN ODOBESCU.

Insurance Association

Uniunea Naţională a Societăţilor de Asigurare şi Reasigurare din România (National Association of Insurance and Re-insurance Companies of Romania): 040129 Bucharest 4, Bd. Libertăţii 12, Bloc 114, sc. 3, 4th Floor, ap. 68; tel. (21) 3351269; fax (21) 3372243; e-mail unsar@dnt.ro; internet www.unsar.ro; f. 1994; 22 mems; Pres. CRISTIAN CONSTANTINESCU; Gen. Sec. FLORENTINA ALMAJANU.

Trade and Industry

GOVERNMENT AGENCIES

Agency for Small and Medium Enterprises and Co-operatives (Agenţia Naţionala pentru Întreprinderi Mici şi Mijlocii şi Cooperaţie): 040263 Bucharest 4, Str. Poteraşi 11; tel. (21) 3352620; fax (21) 3361683; e-mail mariana.spranceana@mimmc.ro; internet www.mimmc.ro; Pres. (vacant).

Authority for the Recovery of State Assets (Autoritatea pentru Valorificarea Activelor Statului—AVAS): 715151 Bucharest 1, Str. Capt. A. Şerbănescu 50; tel. (21) 3036122; fax (21) 3036680; e-mail infopublic@avas.gov.ro; internet www.avas.gov.ro; created by merger of the Banking Assets Resolution Agency (AVAB) and the Authority for Privatization and Management of State Ownership (APAPS); successor org. to the State Ownership Fund; Pres. TEODOR ATANASIU.

Romanian Agency for Foreign Investment: 011974 Bucharest 1, Bd. Primaverii 22; tel. (21) 2339103; fax (21) 2339104; e-mail aris@arisinvest.ro; internet www.arisinvest.ro; f. 2002; Sec.-Gen. FLORIN VASILACHE.

Romanian Trade Promotion Centre (Centrul Român pentru Promovarea Comertului—CRPC): 050741 Bucharest 5, Str. Apolodor 17, POB 1/756; tel. (21) 3185050; fax (21) 3111491; e-mail office@traderom.ro; internet www.traderom.ro; f. 1995; Dir-Gen. SANDOR NEMES.

CHAMBER OF COMMERCE

Chamber of Commerce and Industry of Romania: 030982 Bucharest 3, Bd. Octavian Goga 2; tel. (21) 3229536; fax (21) 3229542; e-mail ccir@ccir.ro; internet www.ccir.ro; f. 1868; Pres. GHEORGHE COJOCARU.

EMPLOYERS' ASSOCIATIONS

Alliance of Employers' Confederations of Romania (ACPR) (Alianţa Confederaţiilor Patronale din România): 030982 Bucharest 3, Str. Octavian Goga 2, floor 10; tel. (21) 3211381; fax (21) 3211443; internet www.acpr.ro; f. 2004; includes the National Confederation of Romanian Employers (CNPR), the Employer Confederation of Romanian Industry (CONPIROM) and four others; Pres. GHEORGHE COPOS.

National Confederation of Romanian Employers (Confederaţia Naţională a Patronatului Român—CNPR): 020982 Bucharest 3, Bd. Octavian Goga 2; tel. (21) 3212074; fax (21) 3212075; e-mail cnpr@untrr.ro; internet www.cnpr.org.ro; Pres. DINU PATRICIU; Dir-Gen. CRISTIAN PARVAN.

Romanian Private Farmers' Federation (Federaţia agricultorilor privatizaţi din România): 010043 Bucharest 1, Bd. Nicolae Bălcescu 17–19; tel. (21) 6131869; fax (21) 6133043; f. 1991; represents 4,000 farming co-operatives and 41 district unions; Pres. GHEORGHE PREDILA.

Union of Romanian Employers (Uniunea Patronatelor din România—UPR): 020361 Bucharest 2, Str. Luigi Galvani 17–19, c/o Romanian Employers' Organization (PR); tel. (21) 2111246; fax (21) 2103075; e-mail office@patronatulroman.ro; internet www.patronatulroman.ro; f. 2004; consists of 6 nationally representative employers' organizations; Pres. OVIDIU TENDER.

UTILITIES

Regulatory Authorities

National Energy Regulatory Authority (Autoritatea Nationala de Reglementare in domeniul Energiei—ANRE): 020995 Bucharest 2, Str. Constantin Nacu 3; tel. (21) 3112244; fax (21) 3124365; internet www.anre.ro; f. 1999; Pres. NICOLAE OPRIS.

National Regulatory Authority for the Natural Gas Sector (Autoritatea Nationala de Reglementare in domeniul Gazelor Naturala—ANRGN): 060114 Bucharest 6, Şos. Cotroceni 4; tel. (21) 3033800; fax (21) 3033808; e-mail anrgn@anrgn.ro; internet www.anrgn.ro; f. 2000; Pres. STEFAN COSMEANU.

Electricity

Electrica SA: 010621 Bucharest, Str. Grigore Alexandrescu 9, Sector 1; tel. (21) 2085999; fax (21) 2085998; internet www.electrica.ro; f. 2002; electricity distributor and supplier; 3 regional generating and 4 regional distribution branches, based in Cluj-Napoca (Transilvania Nord), Transilvania Sud (Braşov), Muntenia Nord (Ploieşti) and Muntenia (Bucharest), 1 national servicing branch; Chair. CRISTIAN ISTODORESCU.

Hidroelectrica SA: 020995 Bucharest, Str. Constantin Nacu 3, Sector 2; tel. (21) 3112231; fax (21) 3111174; e-mail generala@hidroelectrica.ro; internet www.hidroelectrica.ro; state-owned; administers 120 hydropower plants and 4 pumping stations through 10 regional subsidiaries; Gen. Man. EUGEN PENA.

Nuclearelectrica SA: 010494 Bucharest 1, POB 22–102, Str. Polonă 65; tel. (21) 2038200; fax (21) 3169400; e-mail office@nuclearelectrica.ro; internet www.nuclearelectrica.ro; f. 1998; electrical and thermal power generation; production of nuclear fuel; Gen. Dir Dr TEODOR MINODOR CHIRICA; 2,308 employees (2003).

Transelectrica SA: 021012 Bucharest 2, Str. Armand Calinescu 2–4; tel. (21) 3035611; fax (21) 3035820; e-mail office@transelectrica.ro; internet www.transelectrica.ro; f. 2000; 73.7% state-owned; transmission system operator; includes 9 brs and 6 subsidiaries; Chair. and Gen. Dir ADRIAN BAICUSI; 2,188 employees.

Gas

DistriGaz Sud SA: 040254 Bucharest 4, Bd. Mărăşeşti 4–6; tel. (21) 9366; fax (21) 3012116; e-mail contact@distrigazsud.ro; internet www.distrigazsud.ro; privatized 2004/05; 51% owned by GDF Suez (France); natural gas distributor.

E.ON Gaz România: 540069 jud. Mureş, Tîrgu Mureş, Justiţiei 12; tel. (365) 403836; fax (365) 403807; e-mail office@eon-gaz-romania.ro; internet www.eon-gaz-romania.ro; f. 1975; fmrly DistriGaz Nord SA; 51% owned by E.ON Ruhrgas (Germany); natural gas distributor; Dir-Gen. VIRGIL METEA; 500 employees.

SNTGN Transgaz SA (Societăţii Naţionale de transport Gaze Naturale Transgaz SA): 551130 jud. Sibiu, Mediaş, Piaţa Constantin I. Moţas 1; tel. (269) 803333; fax (269) 839031; e-mail cabinet@transgaz.ro; internet www.transgaz.ro; 75.5% state-owned; exploration, transmission and distribution of natural gas; Gen. Dir IOAN RUSU.

TRADE UNIONS

Cartel Alfa National Trade Union Confederation (Confederaţia Naţionala Sindicală Cartel Alfa—CNS Cartel Alfa): 060041 Buchar-

ROMANIA

est 6, Spl. Independenţei 202A, 2nd Floor; tel. (21) 3171045; fax (21) 3123481; e-mail alfa@cartel-alfa.ro; internet www.cartel-alfa.ro; f. 1990; 750,000 mems (2008); 46 professional affiliations; Pres. BOGDAN IULIU HOSSU.

Confederation of Democratic Trade Unions of Romania (Confederaţia Sindicatelor Democratice din România—CSDR): 010155 Bucharest 1, Piaţa Walter Maracineanu 1–3; tel. (21) 3156542; e-mail csdr@b.astral.ro; f. 1994; 20 professional federations; 101,000 mems (2007); Pres. IACOB BACIU.

Frăţia (Brotherhood) National Confederation of Free Trade Unions of Romania (Confederaţia Naţională a Sindicatelor Libere din România Frăţia—CNSLR Frăţia): 010024 Bucharest 1, Str. Cristian Popisteanu 1–3; tel. and fax (21) 3151632; e-mail biroupresa@cnslr-fratia.ro; internet www.cnslr-fratia.ro; merged with the National Trade Union Bloc (Blocul Naţional Sindical—f. 1991) in 2004; 520,000 mems (2007); 44 professional federations; Pres. MARIUS PETCU.

Meridian National Trade Union Confederation (MNTUC) (Confederaţia Sindicala Nationala Meridian): 010366 Bucharest 1, Str. D. I. Mendeleev 36–38; tel. (21) 3168017; fax (21) 3168018; e-mail csnmeridian@csnmeridian.ro; internet www.csnmeridian.ro; f. 1994; 27 br. federations; Gen. Sec. ION ALBU.

Transport

RAILWAYS

In 2003 there were 11,077 km of track in operation (of which 3,965 km were electrified).

Romanian Railway Authority (Autoritatea Feroviara Româna—AFER): 010719 Bucharest 1, Calea Grivitei 393; tel. (21) 3077900; fax (21) 2241832; e-mail secretariat@afer.ro; internet www.afer.ro; f. 1998; under the jurisdiction of the Ministry of Transport and Infrastructure; Gen. Dir VASILE BELIBOU.

National Freight Railway Transport Co (Societatea Naţională de Transport Feroviar de Marfă) (CFR Marfă SA): 010873 Bucharest, Bd. Dinicu Golescu 38; tel. (21) 2249336; fax (21) 3124700; e-mail vtulbure@marfa.cfr.ro; internet www.cfrmarfa.cfr.ro; f. 1998 after the reorganization of the SNCFR; main railway freight transport operator in Romania; Gen. Man. LIVIU BOBAR.

National Passenger Railway Transport Co (Societatea Naţională de Transport Feroviar de Călători—CFR Călători SA): 010873 Bucharest, Bd. Dinicu Golescu 38; tel. (21) 3190322; fax (21) 4112054; e-mail marketing.calatori@cfr.ro; internet www.cfr.ro/calatori; f. 1998; divided into eight regional administrations since 1999; reorganized in Feb. 2001 and merged with eight regional companies; operates all local, regional, long-distance and international passenger rail services; Chair. and Chief Exec. ALEXANDRU NOAPTES.

National Railways Company (CFR SA): 010873 Bucharest, Bd. Dinicu Golescu 38; tel. (21) 3192400; fax (21) 3123200; e-mail virgil.daschievici@cfr.ro; internet www.cfr.ro; management of railway infrastructure; Gen. Dir CONSTANTIN AXINIA; 28,936 employees.

City Underground Railway

The Bucharest underground railway network totals 63.5 km in length.

Metrorex SA—Societatea Comercială de Transport cu Metroul Bucureşti: 010873 Bucharest 1, Bd. Dinicu Golescu 38; tel. (21) 2248975; fax (21) 3125149; e-mail contact@metrorex.ro; internet www.metrorex.ro; f. 1977; Gen. Man. MARIUS IONEL LĂPĂDAT.

ROADS

In 2004 the total length of the national road network was 198,817 km, of which only 30.2% was paved; there were 14,809 km of highways and 36,010 km of secondary roads.

National Administration of Roads (Administraţia Naţională a Drumurilor RA—AND): Ministerul Transporturilor, 010873 Bucharest 1, Bd. Dinicu Golescu 38; tel. (21) 2232606; fax (21) 3120984; e-mail and@andnet.ro; internet www.andnet.ro; Gen. Dir MIHAI GRECU.

INLAND AND OCEAN SHIPPING

The Danube–Black Sea Canal was officially opened to traffic in 1984, and has an annual handling capacity of 80m. metric tons. Romania's principal ports are at Constanţa, on the Black Sea; and Tulcea, Galaţi, Brăila and Giurgiu, on the Danube. In 2007 Romania's merchant fleet had 192 vessels, with a combined aggregate displacement of 269,500 grt.

Administration of Navigable Canals SH (Administraţia Canalelor Navigabile SA): 907015 jud. Constanţa, Constanţa, Str. Ecluzei Agigea 1; tel. (241) 738505; fax (241) 702705; e-mail compania@acn.ro; internet www.acn.ro; fmrly Constanţa Corpn for Navigable Channels; Gen. Man. SEVASTIAN STEFAN.

Maritime Port Administration of Constanţa SA (NC MPA SA): 900900 jud. Constanţa, Constanţa, Portului Incinta, Gara Maritima; tel. (241) 611540; fax (241) 619512; internet www.portofconstantza.com; f. 1991; also administrates Midia and Mangalia ports, and Tomis marina; Gen. Man. IOAN BALAN.

National Co for the Administration of Maritime Ports on the Danube (CN APDM SA) (CN Administraţia Porturilor Dunării Maritime SA—Galaţi): 800025 jud. Galaţi, Galaţi, Str. Portului 34; tel. (236) 460660; fax (236) 460140; e-mail apdm@apdm.galati.ro; internet apdm.galati.ro; f. 1998; manages ports at Galaţi, Brăila, Tulcea, Chilia, Sulina and Sf. Gheorghe; Gen. Man. CARMEN COSTACHE.

National Co for the Administration of River Ports on the Danube (Compania Naţională Administraţia Porturilor Dunării Fluviale SA—APDF SA): 080011 jud. Giurgiu, Giurgiu, Şos. Portului 1; tel. (246) 213003; fax (21) 3110521; internet www.apdf.ro; f. 1998; Gen. Man. CRISTIAN NEMTESCU.

NAVROM—Romanian River Navigation Co (Compania de Navigatie Fluviala Romana SA—NAVROM): 800025 jud. Galaţi, Galaţi, Str. Portului 34; tel. (236) 460706; fax (236) 460190; e-mail navrom@rls.roknet.ro; fleet of over 400 barges and tugs on the Danube River.

Petromin Shipping Co (CNM Petromin SA): 900125 jud. Constanţa, Constanţa, Portului Incinta, Poarta 2; tel. (241) 617802; fax (241) 619690; e-mail office@petromin.cunet.ro; undergoing privatization; merchant fleet of 30 ships and tankers; Chair. ANDREI CARAIANI.

River Administration of the Lower Danube–Galaţi (Administraţia Fluvială a Dunării de Jos RA–Galaţi): 800025 jud. Galaţi, Galaţi, Str. Portului 28–30; tel. (236) 460812; fax (236) 460847; e-mail secretariat@afdj.ro; internet www.afdj.ro; 2 brs and 3 agencies; Gen. Man. MIHAI OCHIALBESCU.

CIVIL AVIATION

There are two international airports at Bucharest: Aurel Vlaicu International (Băneasa) and the larger, Henri Coandă International (Otopeni). There are other international airports at Constanţa (M. Kogălniceanu), Timişoara, Sibiu and Cluj-Napoca. Domestic airports include those at Arad, Bacău, Iaşi and Oradea.

Romanian Civil Aeronautic Authority (Regia Autonomă Autoritatea Aeronautică Civilă Română): 715621 Bucharest, District 1, Şos. Bucureşti-Ploieşti 38–40; tel. (21) 2081508; fax (21) 2081572; e-mail dir.gen@caa.ro; internet www.caa.ro; f. 1993; Dir-Gen. ADRIAN VASILACHE.

Blue Air Transport Aerian: 013695 Bucharest, Şos. Bucureşti-Ploieşti 40, Aeroport Bucureşti-Băneasa-Aurel Vlaicu International; tel. (21) 2088686; e-mail info@blue-air.ro; internet www.blueair-web.com; f. 2004; low-cost charter-flight co; Gen. Dir GHEORGHE RACARU.

Carpatair: 307201 jud. Timiş, Timişoara, Timişoara International Airport; tel. (256) 306933; fax (256) 306962; e-mail timisoara@carpatair.com; internet www.carpatair.ro; f. 1999 as Veg Air; assumed present name in 1999; scheduled domestic and international flights; Pres. NICOLAE PETROV.

Tarom—Compania Nationala de Transporturi Aeriene Române SA (TAROM): 013697 Bucharest, Şos. Bucureşti–Ploieşti, km 16.5, Henri Coandă International (Otopeni) Airport; tel. (21) 2322494; fax (21) 3125686; e-mail secrgen@tarom.ro; internet www.tarom.ro; f. 1954; joint-stock co; services throughout Europe, the Middle East, Asia, the USA and domestically; Pres. GHEORGHE RACARU.

Tourism

The Carpathian Mountains, with their numerous painted monasteries, the Danube delta and the Black Sea resorts (Mamaia, Eforie, Mangalia and others) are the principal attractions. In 2006 there were 6.0m. foreign tourist arrivals, in which year receipts from tourism (including passenger transport) totalled US $1,676m.

National Tourism Authority: 010873 Bucharest 1, Bd. Dinicu Golescu 38; tel. (21) 3149957; fax (21) 3149960; e-mail promovare@mturism.ro; internet www.romaniatravel.com; govt org.; Pres. IULIU MARIAN OVIDIU.

THE RUSSIAN FEDERATION

Introductory Survey

Location, Climate, Language, Religion, Flag, Capital

The Russian Federation, or Russia, constituted the major part of the USSR, providing some 76% of its area and approximately 51% of its population in 1989. It is bounded by Norway, Finland, Estonia and Latvia to the north-west and by Belarus and Ukraine to the west. The southern borders of European Russia are with the Black Sea, Georgia, Azerbaijan, the Caspian Sea and Kazakhstan. The Siberian and Far Eastern regions have southern frontiers with the People's Republic of China, Mongolia and the Democratic People's Republic of Korea. The eastern coastline is on the Sea of Japan, the Sea of Okhotsk, the Pacific Ocean and the Barents Sea, and the northern coastline is on the Arctic Ocean. The region around Kaliningrad (formerly Königsberg in East Prussia), on the Baltic Sea, became part of the Russian Federation in 1945. Separated from the rest of Russia by Lithuania and Belarus, it borders Poland to the south, Lithuania to the north and east and has a coastline on the Baltic Sea. The climate of Russia is extremely varied, ranging from extreme Arctic conditions in northern areas and much of Siberia to generally temperate weather in the south. The average temperature in Moscow in July is 19°C (66°F); the average for January is −9°C (15°F). Average annual rainfall in Moscow is 575 mm (23 ins). The official language is Russian, but many other languages are also used. Christianity is the major religion, with the Russian Orthodox Church (Moscow Patriarchate) the largest denomination. The main concentrations of adherents of Islam are among the Tatar, Bashkir and Chuvash peoples of the middle Volga, and the peoples of the northern Caucasus, including the Chechen, Ingush, Kabardins and the peoples of Dagestan. Buddhism is the main religion of the Buryats, the Tyvans and the Kalmyks. The large pre-1917 Jewish population has been depleted by war and emigration, but some 230,000 Jews remained in the Russian Federation in 2002, according to census results. The national flag (proportions 2 by 3) consists of three equal horizontal stripes of (from top to bottom) white, blue and red. The capital is Moscow (Moskva).

Recent History

By the late 19th century the Russian Empire extended throughout vast territories in eastern Europe, and included much of northern and central Asia, a result of the territorial expansionism of the Romanov dynasty, which had ruled Russia as an autocracy since 1613. Growing dissatisfaction with economic conditions in urban areas, combined with the adverse effect of defeats in the Russo–Japanese War (1904–05), led Tsar Nicholas (Nikolai) II (1894–1917) to issue a manifesto in October 1905, which promised respect for civil liberties and the introduction of some constitutional order, although the ensuing attempt at reforms failed to placate the increasingly restive workers and peasants. In 1917 there were strikes and demonstrations in the capital, Petrograd (as St Petersburg had been renamed in 1914). In March 1917 the Tsar was forced to abdicate and a liberal Provisional Government, composed mainly of landowners, took power. However, most real authority lay with the soviets (councils), composed largely of workers and soldiers, which were attracted to socialist ideas.

The inability of the Provisional Government, led first by Prince Georgii Lvov and then by the moderate socialist Aleksandr Kerenskii, to implement land reforms, or to effect a withdrawal from the First World War, allowed more extreme groups, such as the Bolshevik faction of the Russian Social Democratic Labour Party (RSDLP) led by Vladimir Ulyanov (Lenin), to attain prominence. On 7 November 1917 (25 October in the Old Style calendar, which remained in use until February 1918) the Bolsheviks, who had come to dominate the Petrograd Soviet, seized power in the capital, with minimal use of force, and proclaimed the Russian Soviet Federative Socialist Republic (RSFSR or Russian Federation). The Bolsheviks subsequently adopted the name All-Russian Communist Party (Bolsheviks).

The Bolsheviks asserted that they would respect the self-determination of the former Empire's many nations. Poland, Finland and the Baltic states of Estonia, Latvia and Lithuania achieved independence, but other independent states established in 1917–18 were forced, militarily, to declare themselves Soviet Republics. These were proclaimed as independent republics, in alliance with the RSFSR, but the laws, Constitution and Government of the Federation were supreme in all of them. However, in 1922 the RSFSR joined the Belarusian, Ukrainian and Transcaucasian republics as constitutionally equal partners in a Union of Soviet Socialist Republics (USSR, or Soviet Union), and institutions of the RSFSR were re-formed as institutions of the new Union. The USSR eventually numbered 15 constituent Soviet Socialist Republics (SSRs). Moscow, the RSFSR's seat of government since 1918, became the capital of the USSR.

The RSFSR, in common with the other republics, experienced hardship as a result of the collectivization campaign of the early 1930s and the widespread repression under Iosif Dzhugashvili (Stalin), who established a brutal dictatorship after the death of Lenin in 1924. The Five-Year Plans, introduced in the late 1920s, effected rapid industrialization, a process that was reinforced by the removal of strategic industries from the west of the republic to the Ural regions during the Second World War (or 'Great Patriotic War'), which the USSR was drawn into in 1941. Under the Nazi German-Soviet Treaty of Non-Aggression (the 'Molotov-Ribbentrop Pact') of August 1939, the USSR annexed the Baltic states as well as other territories. Victory in the war in 1945 led to further territorial gains for the Russian Federation. In the west it gained part of East Prussia around Königsberg (now Kaliningrad) from Germany, a small amount of territory from Estonia and Latvia and those parts of Finland annexed during the Soviet–Finnish War (1939–40). In the east it acquired the Kurile Islands from Japan. The nominally independent People's Republic of Tuva (Tyva), situated between the USSR and Mongolia, was annexed in 1944. In 1954 the peninsula of Crimea was ceded by the Russian Federation to the Ukrainian SSR.

Shortly after the death of Stalin in 1953, Nikita Khrushchev became First Secretary of the Communist Party of the Soviet Union (CPSU—as the Communist Party had been renamed in 1952), and gradually assumed predominance over his rivals. The most brutal aspects of the regime were ended, and in 1956 Khrushchev admitted the existence of large-scale repression under Stalin. Khrushchev was dismissed in 1964. He was replaced as First Secretary (later General Secretary) of the CPSU by Leonid Brezhnev. During the 1970s relations with the West, which had, since the late 1940s, been generally characterized by the intense mutual hostility of the 'Cold War', experienced a considerable *détente*; however, this was ended by the Soviet invasion of Afghanistan in 1979. Brezhnev's successor as CPSU General Secretary, following his death in 1982, was Yurii Andropov. He was succeeded upon his death, in February 1984, by Konstantin Chernenko, who, in turn, died in March 1985.

Chernenko's successor as General Secretary was Mikhail Gorbachev. A policy of glasnost (openness) provided a greater degree of freedom for the mass media. In November 1987, however, supporters of perestroika (restructuring), as Gorbachev's reform programme was known, seemed to suffer a reverse, with the dismissal from the Politburo (the executive committee of the CPSU) of Boris Yeltsin. In June 1988 Gorbachev announced plans for the introduction of a two-tier legislature, elected largely by competitive elections. In elections to the new USSR Congress of People's Deputies, held in March 1989, many reformist politicians, including Yeltsin, were successful in achieving election. In May the Congress elected Gorbachev to the new post of executive President of the USSR.

Within the USSR the RSFSR was clearly pre-eminent, both economically and politically, and ethnic Russians dominated the Soviet élite. However, this prominence meant that Russia developed few autonomous institutions. The initial stage in the process of instituting Russian sovereignty was the election of the RSFSR Congress of People's Deputies in March 1990 by largely free and competitive elections. In May the Congress elected Yeltsin to the highest state post in the RSFSR, the Chairman of the Supreme Soviet (the permanent working body of the Congress). On 12 June the Congress adopted a declaration asserting the sovereignty of the RSFSR in which the federation laws had primacy over all-Union legislation. In March 1991, when a referendum was held in nine republics to determine whether a restructured USSR should be retained, voters in the RSFSR also approved an additional question on the introduction of a Russian presidency. A direct presidential election, held in June, was won by Yeltsin and his Vice-President, Aleksandr Rutskoi, with 57.3% of the votes cast.

On 19 August 1991, one day before the new union treaty was due to be signed, the conservative communist 'State Committee for the State of Emergency' (SCSE), led by the Soviet Vice-President, Gennadii Yanayev, seized power in Moscow, taking advantage of Gorbachev's absence from the city. The attempted coup collapsed within three days, and Yeltsin asserted control over all-Union bodies, appointing RSFSR ministers to head central institutions.

In October 1991 Yeltsin announced a programme of radical economic reforms. In November a new Government was announced, with Yeltsin as Chairman (Prime Minister). The CPSU was banned. In November 1991 the Congress granted Yeltsin special powers for one year, including the right to issue decrees with legislative force and to appoint government ministers without parliamentary approval, and elected Ruslan Khasbulatov, hitherto First Deputy Chairman of the Supreme Soviet, to succeed Yeltsin as Chairman.

On 8 December 1991 the leaders of Belarus, Ukraine and Russia announced the annulment of the 1922 Union Treaty creating the USSR; the Commonwealth of Independent States (CIS, see p. 225), defined as a co-ordinating organization, was created in its place. The CIS was formally established by the Alma-Ata (Almaty) Declaration, signed on 21 December 1991. Of the former Soviet republics, only Georgia, Estonia, Latvia and Lithuania remained outside the new body. (Georgia acceded to the CIS in December 1993.) On 25 December 1991 Gorbachev resigned as President of the USSR, and the Russian Supreme Soviet formally changed the name of the RSFSR to the Russian Federation.

In June 1992 Yeltsin appointed Yegor Gaidar, an advocate of radical economic reform, as acting Chairman, and in the same month the Supreme Soviet adopted legislation permitting large-scale privatization. In December the Congress of People's Deputies refused to endorse Gaidar's nomination, and Yeltsin was forced to appoint a new, substantially less reformist, premier, Viktor Chernomyrdin. Following the annulment, in March 1993, of an agreement on constitutional reform by the Congress, Yeltsin announced that he would rule by decree prior to the holding of a referendum on a draft constitution, which was held on 25 April 1993. A question on confidence in Yeltsin as President received a positive response from 57.4% of voters, while 53.7% of voters expressed support for Yeltsin's socio-economic policies. Support for early presidential elections was only 49.1%, but 70.6% of voters favoured early elections to the Congress of People's Deputies.

In July 1993 the Constitutional Conference approved a draft that provided for a presidential system with a bicameral parliament—the Federalnoye Sobraniye (Federal Assembly)—comprising a lower chamber (Gosudarstvennaya Duma—State Duma) and an upper chamber (Sovet Federatsii—Federation Council); however, the Congress of People's Deputies rejected this draft. The long-standing impasse between the presidential administration and the legislature eventually resulted in violent confrontation. On 21 September Yeltsin suspended the Congress of People's Deputies and the Supreme Soviet, and scheduled elections to the Federalnoye Sobraniye for December. The Supreme Soviet consequently voted to dismiss Yeltsin as President, announcing the appointment of Rutskoi in his place; an emergency session of the Congress of People's Deputies confirmed this appointment, and voted to impeach Yeltsin. On 27 September government troops surrounded the parliament building: some 180 deputies remained inside, with armed supporters. Conflict erupted in early October, as supporters of the rebel deputies attempted to seize control of strategic buildings in Moscow, and Yeltsin declared a state of emergency in the capital. On 4 October army tanks bombarded the parliament building, forcing the surrender of the rebels. The leaders of the rebellion were imprisoned and charged with inciting mass disorder. According to official figures, 160 people were killed in the fighting.

The new draft constitution, which strengthened the powers of the President, was submitted to a referendum on 12 December 1993, held concurrently with elections to the Federalnoye Sobraniye. Of the 54.8% of the registered electorate that participated in the plebiscite, 58.4% endorsed the draft. In the elections to the Gosudarstvennaya Duma, Vladimir Zhirinovskii's nationalist Liberal Democratic Party of Russia (LDPR) secured a total of 64 seats, the largest number obtained by any single party or alliance. (Of the 450 members of the lower chamber, 225 were elected by proportional representation on the basis of party lists, and 225 within single-member constituencies.) Russia's Choice, an alliance of pro-reform groups, led by Gaidar, secured 58 seats. The Communist Party of the Russian Federation (CPRF), which had been founded earlier in the year, took 48 seats, while the Agrarian Party of Russia (APR) won 33 seats. With the ensuing alignment of parties and the 130 independents into parliamentary factions, Russia's Choice emerged as the largest group in the Duma, although no coherent pro-Government majority was established. The Sovet Federatsii was to comprise two representatives from each of Russia's 89 federal subjects (as the constituent territories of the Federation were known), although in December representatives were not elected in the separatist republics of Tatarstan and Chechnya, owing to a voter boycott. The majority of the Council's members were non-partisan republican or regional leaders. A new Government was appointed in January 1994. In February the Duma voted in favour of granting amnesties to Rutskoi, Khasbulatov and other leaders of the 1993 rebellion, as well as to the SCSE.

In October 1994 a sudden decline in the value of the rouble prompted the resignation or dismissal of government members and the Chairman of the Central Bank, Viktor Gerashchenko. In November the reformist Anatolii Chubais, who had hitherto been responsible for the privatization programme, was promoted to the post of First Deputy Chairman, although other government appointments appeared to advance those opposed to further economic liberalization.

In late 1994 Russia commenced military intervention in the separatist Chechen Republic (Chechnya); an apparent lack of progress there, together with the continued deterioration of the economy, were instrumental in the approval by the Duma, in June 1995, of a motion expressing no confidence in the Government. Yeltsin subsequently dismissed a number of ministers, and in July a second vote of no confidence (as required by the Constitution) failed to secure the necessary majority.

Elections to the Duma took place on 17 December 1995. In accordance with a new electoral law, which introduced a minimum requirement of 5% of the votes cast for seats allocated on the basis of party lists, only four parties—the CPRF, the LDPR, Chernomyrdin's Our Home is Russia (OHR) and the liberal Yabloko—secured representation on this basis, while an additional 10 parties and 77 independent candidates obtained seats through voting in single-member constituencies. The CPRF emerged as the largest single party in the Duma, with 157 of the 450 deputies. OHR won 55 seats, the LDPR 51 and Yabloko 45.

In January 1996 Yeltsin dismissed Chubais as First Deputy Chairman. In the same month the Duma elected Gennadii Seleznev, a CPRF deputy, as its Chairman. In the first round of presidential voting, held on 16 June, and contested by 10 candidates, Yeltsin, with 35.8% of the votes cast, narrowly defeated Gennadii Zyuganov (of the CPRF), with 32.5%. Gen. Aleksandr Lebed, who had until recently commanded Russian forces in the separatist Transnistria (Pridnistrovie) region of Moldova, was placed third, with 14.7%. Since neither had received the 50% of the votes required for outright victory, Yeltsin and Zyuganov proceeded to a second round of voting. Yeltsin subsequently appointed Lebed as Secretary of the Security Council and National Security Adviser, and granted him particular responsibility for resolving the crisis in Chechnya. Despite increasingly infrequent public appearances, apparently a result of poor health, Yeltsin was re-elected as President in the second ballot, on 3 July, with 54% of the total votes cast. Chernomyrdin was subsequently re-appointed as premier, and Chubais was promoted to head the Presidential Administration. Despite the successful negotiation of a cease-fire agreement in Chechnya in August, in October Yeltsin dismissed Lebed. In November Yeltsin underwent heart surgery, reassuming full presidential duties in December, although he was again hospitalized shortly afterwards, and there was growing pressure for his resignation.

Although Yeltsin delivered a vehement criticism of the Government in his annual address to the Federalnoye Sobraniye in March 1997, in a subsequent government reorganization Chernomyrdin retained his post, thereby avoiding the need to seek parliamentary approval of the new, broadly reformist, cabinet.

Chubais was appointed First Deputy Chairman and Minister of Finance, and Boris Nemtsov was appointed as First Deputy Chairman, with responsibility for dismantling state monopolies, particularly in the areas of fuel and energy. In November Nemtsov lost the fuel and energy portfolio, and Chubais was dismissed as Minister of Finance, although both retained their posts as First Deputy Chairmen.

In March 1998 Yeltsin removed Chernomyrdin from office. The Duma confirmed the appointment of Sergei Kiriyenko, hitherto Minister of Fuel and Energy, as Chairman in mid-April. Several ministers, including Nemtsov, retained their portfolios in the new Government formed during April–May. Chubais, meanwhile, was appointed Chairman of the electricity monopoly, Unified Energy System of Russia. An attempt by the CPRF to initiate impeachment charges against Yeltsin was ruled unconstitutional by a parliamentary commission in late July. In mid-August, however, the Duma succeeded in approving a resolution demanding the voluntary resignation of Yeltsin.

In August 1998 mounting political instability was exacerbated by severe economic difficulties. Yeltsin dismissed Kiriyenko and his Government, reappointing Chernomyrdin as Chairman. However, Chernomyrdin's candidacy to the premiership was twice rejected by the Duma. In mid-September Yeltsin (aware that should his candidate be rejected for a third time he would be constitutionally obliged to dissolve the Duma) nominated Yevgenii Primakov (Minister of Foreign Affairs since 1996, and a former Director of the Foreign Intelligence Service) as Chairman, a candidacy that was endorsed by a large majority.

In May 1999 Yeltsin dismissed Primakov. Sergei Stepashin, hitherto First Deputy Chairman and Minister of Internal Affairs, was appointed as Chairman, and a new Government was formed later in the month. However, Yeltsin dismissed Stepashin in August. Later in the month the Duma endorsed his replacement by Vladimir Putin, a former colonel in the Soviet Committee for State Security (KGB), First Deputy Chairman of St Petersburg City Government in 1994–96, and hitherto head of the Federal Security Service (FSB) and Secretary of the Security Council.

Following a number of incursions by Chechen militants into the neighbouring Republic of Dagestan in August 1999, tensions resurfaced relating to the unresolved status of Chechnya and the emergence there, from the mid-1990s, of militant Islamist groups. Moreover, Putin attributed to Chechen militant groups a series of bomb explosions in Moscow, in Dagestan and in Rostov Oblast, which took place in August–September, killing more than 300 people. Citing the threat posed by militants in the separatist republic, Putin announced that military action was to recommence, and, prior to the large-scale deployment of ground troops, the aerial bombardment of Chechnya began on 23 September.

In the months preceding Duma elections in December 1999 several new political alliances were formed; in August Fatherland-All Russia (FAR) was formed by the merger of the centrist party of the Mayor of Moscow, Yurii Luzhkov, with a grouping of regional governors. In September a pro-Government bloc, Unity, was formed under the leadership of Sergei Shoigu, the civil defence and emergencies minister, while Kiriyenko and Nemtsov were among the leaders of a new pro-market bloc, the Union of Rightist Forces (URF).

Some 29 parties and blocs contested the elections to the Gosudarstvennaya Duma on 19 December 1999, in which 62% of the electorate participated. Six parties obtained representation on the basis of party lists; a further eight parties and blocs, and 106 independent candidates, secured representation from single-member constituency ballots. The CPRF, with 24.3% of the votes, again won the largest number of seats, with 113. Unity, which received 23.3% of the votes cast, was the second largest party in the Duma, with 72 seats; FAR won 67, the URF 29, Yabloko 21 and the Zhirinovskii bloc (chiefly comprising the LDPR) 17.

On 31 December 1999 Boris Yeltsin unexpectedly resigned as President. Putin assumed the presidency in an acting capacity. He granted Yeltsin immunity from prosecution, and removed from office principal members of Yeltsin's administration. When the new Duma convened in mid-January 2000, the CPRF and Unity factions formed an alliance; thus, for the first time since the dissolution of the USSR, pro-Government forces held a majority in the legislature.

Putin received 52.9% of the votes cast in the presidential election held on 26 March 2000, having received the support of FAR, as well as Unity. His closest rival was Zyuganov, of the CPRF, with 29.2%. Putin was inaugurated as President on 7 May. In mid-May Mikhail Kasyanov, hitherto First Deputy Chairman and Minister of Finance, was approved as Chairman of the Council of Ministers. A new Government was appointed shortly afterwards.

Concerns regarding the freedom of the media in Russia were heightened following the presidential approval in September 2000 of a new information doctrine and by the severe restrictions imposed over coverage of the conflict in Chechnya. Meanwhile, Vladimir Gusinskii, the owner of the Mediya-Most holding company (which included Russia's only wholly independent national television broadcaster, NTV), was arrested in June and charged with fraud. Although all charges were withdrawn in July, Gusinskii fled to Spain. In September the state-controlled gas monopoly, Gazprom (to which Mediya-Most was heavily indebted), brought charges of criminal embezzlement against Mediya-Most's management. Gusinskii lost control of the company in November, and the deal reached with Alfred Kokh, the head of the Gazprom subsidiary, Gazprom-Mediya, effectively gave the state a controlling stake in all Mediya-Most enterprises, with the exception of NTV. In December the Moscow fiscal authorities demanded that Mediya-Most be closed, on grounds of insolvency, and Gusinskii was detained in Spain in the same month. Following the refusal of the Spanish authorities to extradite Gusinskii to Russia, in April 2001 he took up residence in Israel (where he held dual citizenship). None the less, Russia issued a fresh warrant for Gusinskii's arrest, on charges of money-laundering. In October 2003, following Gusinskii's arrest in Greece, a Greek court ruled against his extradition to Russia.

Meanwhile, other prominent businessmen were subjected to examinations of their business affairs, in what was interpreted as an attempt by the Government to reduce the powers of the 'oligarchs', as a number of wealthy businessmen, who in many cases had acquired control of formerly nationalized industries in the 1990s, were widely known. In July 2000 Boris Berezovskii, a prominent business executive and former Deputy of the Security Council and Executive Secretary of the CIS (who had played a major role in promoting Putin's candidacy as President), relinquished his seat in the Duma and, therefore, his immunity from prosecution, accusing Putin of having adopted an increasingly authoritarian style of governance. In September Berezovskii announced his intention to relinquish his 49% of shares in the state-controlled television station, ORT, claiming that he had received an ultimatum that he should surrender his holding to the state or risk imprisonment; the sale finally took place in February 2001. None the less, a warrant for Berezovskii's arrest was issued in November 2000, after he failed to return to Russia from France to answer questions relating to charges of money-laundering and illegal entrepreneurship in a case that had recently been reopened.

Putin introduced significant changes to regional governance during 2000. In May, as part of measures intended to promote structures of 'vertical power', seven Federal Okrugs (Districts) were created, each of which was headed by a presidential appointee, to whom regional governments and governors were to be answerable. A new consultative body, the State Council, comprising the heads of the federal subjects, was created by presidential decree in September.

In March 2001 Putin implemented a minor ministerial reorganization, appointing Boris Gryzlov, the head of the Unity faction in the Duma, as Minister of Internal Affairs, and Sergei Ivanov (hitherto Secretary of the Security Council and a former deputy head of the FSB) as Minister of Defence. In April it was announced that the Unity faction in the Duma was, henceforth, to form an alliance with FAR, in preference to the CPRF.

NTV was acquired by Gazprom-Mediya in April 2001. Following the dismissal of NTV's management, Yevgenii Kiselyev, the company's former Director-General and Editor-in-Chief, was appointed to head a small television channel owned by Berezovskii, TV6, to which the majority of the former NTV journalists transferred. Later in the year Berezovskii, who remained outside Russia, formed a political party, Liberal Russia. Meanwhile, in July the legislature approved a law banning foreign citizens, as well as Russians holding dual citizenship, from acquiring a majority stake in Russian television channels.

In July 2001 Putin signed a law imposing new conditions on political parties; henceforth, parties would be required to have a minimum of 10,000 members, including no fewer than 100 members in at least 50 of the 89 federal subjects, in order to be permitted to participate in elections. At the beginning of December the first congress of Unity and Fatherland-United

Russia (subsequently known simply as United Russia—UR), formed by the merger of FAR and Unity, marked the formal establishment of the party, which held a majority of seats in both parliamentary houses. Although not a member of that party or of any other, Putin attended the founding congress.

In January 2002 TV6 ceased transmissions, following a court case brought by a minority shareholder, a subsidiary of the state-controlled petroleum company LUKoil, which had demanded the television company's liquidation on the grounds of unprofitability. In March it was announced that a new, non-profit organization, Mediya-Sotsium, associated with Primakov, had been awarded the contract to broadcast formerly held by TV6; Kiselyev and many TV6 journalists transferred to the new channel, which commenced operations as TVS. Meanwhile, Berezovskii presented a video-recording in London, United Kingdom, which purported to demonstrate the FSB's involvement, and Putin's acquiescence, in the bombings of mid-1999.

A new session of the Sovet Federatsii, chaired by Sergei Mironov, an ally of Putin, opened in January 2002, with a reformed composition. In place of regional leaders and chairmen of regional legislative assemblies, the Council comprised their full-time appointees; the formation of political factions and groups in the Council was to be prohibited.

In October 2002 Berezovskii was charged, *in absentia*, with defrauding the state. (Berezovskii was arrested in the United Kingdom, where he was resident, in March 2003 in response to an extradition request from the Russian authorities, but was granted political asylum in September, and the extradition proceedings were dismissed.) Meanwhile, in mid-October 2002, following the publication of an interview in a nationalist journal in which Berezovskii appeared to support the formation of a united opposition front by liberal and left-wing forces, he was suspended from Liberal Russia; one week later the Ministry of Justice agreed to register the party, which had hitherto been denied registration on several occasions, and which had obtained only negligible public support.

In late October 2002, following the deaths of at least 129 people as the result of an armed siege at a Moscow theatre by heavily armed militants, linked to Chechen extremists (see below), the Government implemented a number of personnel changes in Chechnya, and in mid-November Stanislav Ilyasov, hitherto the Prime Minister of Chechnya, was appointed to the federal Government as Minister without Portfolio, responsible for the Social and Economic Development of the Chechen Republic.

In March 2003 presidential decrees provided for the transfer of powers from various other organs of state to the FSB and to the Ministry of Internal Affairs. In April one of the co-chairmen of Liberal Russia, Sergei Yushenkov, was assassinated in Moscow (another deputy of the party, Vladimir Golovlev, had been murdered in August 2002); in June 2003 a party member, Mikhail Kodanev, was arrested on suspicion of involvement in the killing of Yushenkov, along with three others. (In March 2004 Kodanev was sentenced to 20 years' imprisonment for organizing the assassination; the three other suspects each received custodial sentences of between 11 and 20 years.) In June the Ministry of the Press, Broadcasting and Mass Media ordered the closure of TVS, purportedly as a result of financial difficulties experienced by the station, the broadcasts of which were replaced by a newly established, state-controlled sports channel.

On 18 June 2003 the Duma failed to approve a motion of no confidence in the Government that had been presented by the CPRF and Yabloko factions. Meanwhile, attacks against civilian targets by militants associated with Chechen separatist, or Islamist, rebels continued to occur, particularly in regions of southern Russia near Chechnya and in Moscow. In July at least 18 people were killed following two suicide bombings at a music festival near Moscow. A suicide bombing, in early December, on a train in southern Russia killed at least 42 people, and injured some 200 others. On 9 December, two days after the legislative elections (see below), a suicide bombing in central Moscow resulted in at least six deaths. In early February 2004 at least 39 people were killed and more than 100 injured in a further bomb attack on a train on the Moscow Metro.

During the latter half of 2003 several court cases and judicial investigations were instigated against senior officials of the prominent privately owned petroleum company Yukos, and its subsidiary companies. The chief executive of the company, Mikhail Khodorkovskii (who was reported to be the wealthiest person in Russia), had recently announced that he was providing financial support to Yabloko and the URF. On 25 October Khodorkovskii was arrested by FSB officers; he was subsequently charged with tax evasion and fraud, and imprisoned pending further investigations. At the end of the month it was announced that a significant stake in the company had been 'frozen' by the authorities. (In early November Khodorkovskii resigned as head of Yukos, and at the end of the month it was announced that the proposed merger of Yukos with another prominent petroleum company, Sibneft, had been suspended.) In December charges of tax evasion worth US $3,300m. were brought against Yukos.

Elections to the Duma, held on 7 December 2003, were contested by 32 parties and blocs. Only four of these groupings received the minimum 5% share of votes cast required to obtain representation on the basis of federal party lists: UR won an absolute majority of seats in the new legislature, with 226 seats, while the representation of the CPRF was substantially reduced, to 53 seats. The LDPR secured 38 seats, while a recently formed electoral bloc, Motherland—People's Patriotic Union (Motherland), which comprised several communist and nationalist groups, received 37 seats. Nine other groups and 57 independent deputies achieved representation in the new Duma on the basis of constituency voting. The failure of the URF and Yabloko to obtain representation on the basis of proportional representation (the two parties received around 8% of the votes between them, and a total of seven seats) was regarded as a serious reverse for pro-Western reformists. The URF, Yabloko and the CPRF alleged that electoral fraud had been perpetrated, and electoral observers of the Organization for Security and Co-operation in Europe (OSCE, see p. 366) expressed concern that UR, which had become increasingly identified with the presidential administration, had benefited from the use of state administrative resources in support of the party. Moreover, several government members held senior positions in UR, in apparent defiance of a constitutional clause prohibiting ministers from holding membership of political parties, and the party had effectively received the endorsement of Putin on several occasions. Gryzlov, the Chairman of the Supreme Council of UR, was elected as the Chairman of the Duma on 24 December. (He was replaced as Minister of Internal Affairs by Col-Gen. Rashid Nurgaliyev.)

Campaigning for the presidential election held on 14 March 2004 was characterized by an absence of prominent or credible challengers to Putin, who contested the election as an independent candidate, and refused to participate in televised debates with other candidates. In place of their leaders, who had contested the presidential elections in 1996 and 2000, the CPRF and LDPR nominated relatively obscure figures, Nikolai Kharitonov and Oleg Malyshkin, respectively, as their candidates. The URF's refusal to endorse the candidacy of one of its leading members, Irina Khakamada, obliged her to campaign as an independent candidate; Khakamada and Nemtsov both subsequently resigned from the URF. Meanwhile, the candidacy of Sergei Glazyev, an economist who had been regarded as the principal instigator of the Motherland electoral bloc, failed to obtain the support of any of its constituent parties, and he therefore contested the election as an independent candidate. Mironov contested the election, as the candidate of his party, the Russian Party of Life (RPL), but none the less expressed support for Putin. (A further candidate, Ivan Rybkin, an ally of Berezovskii, withdrew his candidacy in early March, after he had apparently been taken hostage in Ukraine for several days.) Meanwhile, the leader of Yabloko, Grigorii Yavlinskii, announced that his party was to boycott the presidential election. On 24 February Putin dismissed the Government, and on 1 March Putin announced the nomination of Mikhail Fradkov, hitherto the permanent representative of Russia to the European Communities, as the new Chairman of the Government. The appointment of Fradkov, widely regarded as a 'technocrat', without significant political support of his own, was subsequently approved by the Duma, and on 9 March the formation of a new Government was announced; the number of ministers was significantly reduced to 17, compared with 31 in the outgoing administration. Although most of the principal positions within the Government remained unchanged, a new Minister of Foreign Affairs, Sergei Lavrov, hitherto ambassador to the UN, was appointed.

On 14 March 2004 Putin was re-elected, as had been widely anticipated, for a second, and, in accordance with the Constitution, final, term of office, receiving 71.3% of the votes cast. His nearest rival, Kharitonov, took 13.7%. The rate of participation was 64.4%. Putin's inauguration took place on 7 May.

Violent attacks on Russian civilians, attributed to extremist Chechen separatists, culminated in a series of incidents in mid-

2004, which intensified following the assassination of the President of the Republic in May (see below). On 24 August two passenger planes, both flying from Moscow's Domodedovo airport, crashed, killing all 89 people on board. Both crashes were subsequently attributed to Chechen suicide bombers. On 1 September, the first day of the school year, armed militants occupied a school in Beslan, in the Republic of North Osetiya—Alaniya, taking at least 1,100 children, parents and teachers hostage. On 3 September troops stormed the building, reportedly in reaction to a series of explosions. Some 350 hostages, including 186 children, died in the ensuing battle, according to official figures. The militant Chechen leader, Shamil Basayev, subsequently claimed responsibility for the hostage-taking operation.

Apparently in reaction to this event, President Putin proposed a series of political reforms, chief among which was the introduction of a system whereby all regional governors would be appointed by the federal President, subject to the approval of the appropriate regional legislature. (Directly elected governors had become almost universal across the subjects of the Russian Federation in the second half of the 1990s.) Putin signed legislation to this end on 12 December 2004, following its approval by both chambers of the Federalnoye Sobraniye. The final scheduled gubernatorial election in the Federation took place on 6 February 2005, and henceforth all regional governors were appointed in accordance with the new system. Putin also announced proposals that all 450 members of the Duma be elected on the basis of proportional representation and party lists. Moreover, the minimum membership required of a political party for it to be eligible for registration was to be increased from 10,000 to 50,000, with effect from January 2006. The quota for representation in the Duma on the basis of federal party lists was also to be increased from 5% of the total votes cast to 7%.

Meanwhile, in June 2004 the trial of Khodorkovskii and his business associate, Platon Lebedev, the Chairman of the Menatep financial group, began in Moscow, on seven charges, including tax evasion, forgery and fraud. While the trial was in progress, the state authorities presented Yukos with a series of demands for unpaid taxes for 2000–03, totalling some US $27,500m. In order that this sum be paid, the authorities demanded that the principal production subsidiary of Yukos, Yuganskneftegaz, be brought to auction. In December Yuganskneftegaz was sold for $9,350m. to a previously unknown company, Baikalfinansgrup, which was acquired by the state-owned petroleum company Rosneft shortly after the auction. In May 2005 Khodorkovskii and Lebedev were each sentenced to nine years' imprisonment. (In February 2007 state prosecutors brought further charges of money-laundering and embezzlement against Khodorkovskii.) In July 2005 a criminal investigation, on charges of corruption related to the illicit acquisition of a state property, was opened against former premier Kasyanov, amid widespread speculation that the charges were politically motivated; in September Kasyanov announced that he intended to contest the presidential election scheduled for early 2008. Meanwhile, liberal-democratic and pro-Western opposition to the Putin administration was increasingly expressed by a grouping known as the United Civil Front, led by the former international chess champion, Garri Kasparov.

On 14 November 2005 President Putin announced a government reorganization. Dmitrii Medvedev, the Chairman of the Board of Directors of Gazprom and hitherto Chief of the Presidential Staff, was appointed to the newly created post of First Deputy Chairman (Medvedev was, additionally, to retain his position at Gazprom). Sergei Ivanov, while retaining his responsibilities as Minister of Defence, was also to serve as one of two Deputy Chairmen of the Government.

A major focus of parliamentary activity during the second half of 2005 was the development of measures intended to result in greater government supervision and regulation of civil society and non-governmental organizations (NGOs); at least in part, demands for increased control in these areas had evolved in response to apparent concern that the so-called 'colour revolutions' that had taken place in Georgia in 2003, Ukraine in 2004 and Kyrgyzstan earlier in 2005 had been, to a certain extent, facilitated by externally financed NGOs. After several months of discussions, new legislation that, *inter alia*, permitted the authorities to close NGOs deemed to infringe Russia's sovereignty, unity or cultural heritage was signed into law by President Putin in January 2006. On 12 March, after the restrictions on party registration entered into effect on 1 January, the first 'unified election day' (for elections to various levels of government, or to certain local and regional assemblies in the Federation) took place. (Henceforth, the overwhelming majority of such elections were to take place in March and October each year.) UR won control of the overwhelming majority of regional assemblies to which elections were conducted, a pattern that was repeated at the following two unified election days, although the rate of voter participation was relatively low. In June Putin nominated the Minister of Justice, Yurii Chaika, to serve as Prosecutor-General; Chaika was succeeded as Minister of Justice by Vladimir Ustinov, who had been dismissed as Prosecutor-General at his own request earlier in the month. In October Motherland, the RPL and the Russian Pensioners' Party united to form a new political party, A Just Russia (AJR). Mironov was elected as Chairman of AJR (which absorbed another small party, the People's Party, in April 2007).

In October 2006 a journalist of the independent newspaper *Novaya Gazeta*, Anna Politkovskaya, a leading critic of the Russian military campaigns in Chechnya and the official Chechen leadership, was shot dead at her apartment building in Moscow. Her death attracted international attention, amid widespread speculation that the Chechen authorities may have been implicated in her killing. (According to independent estimates, at least 13 journalists had been murdered in Russia since 2000; a substantially greater number of journalists had been killed in suspicious circumstances during the 1990s.) In November 2006 Aleksandr Litvinenko, a former officer in the FSB and exile to the United Kingdom, died in a London hospital as a result of radiation poisoning, having publicly accused Putin of responsibility for his sickness. Medical tests concluded that Litvinenko had been exposed to the radioactive substance Polonium-210. Police investigations into the killing of Litvinenko, who had been a close associate of Berezovskii, and had published a book accusing elements within the FSB of committing the apartment bombings of September 1999 (see below), commenced in both the United Kingdom and Russia. The Russian authorities subsequently refused to accede to a request by the British Government for the extradition of the principal suspect, Andrei Lugovoi, who had met with Litvinenko in London around the time of his poisoning, on the grounds that it convened the Constitution. (In December 2007 Lugovoi was elected to the Gosudarstvennaya Duma, thereby securing immunity from prosecution within Russia.)

In early December 2006 Putin signed into law further amendments to electoral legislation, including the abolition of the minimum voter turn-out requirement for elections at every level. At the end of that month the Chairman of the Central Electoral Commission (CEC), Aleksandr Veshnyakov, announced that the forthcoming presidential election would take place on 9 March 2008, on the expiry of Putin's second four-year term. On 15 February 2007 Putin reorganized the Government, appointing Sergei Ivanov to the office of First Deputy Chairman (thereby granting him equal status to Medvedev). Anatolii Serdyukov, hitherto the head of the Federal Tax Service, replaced Ivanov as Minister of Defence, becoming the first appointee to that position not to have a background in the military or security services. Putin also appointed the President of the Chechen Republic, Maj.-Gen. Alu Alkhanov, to the post of deputy justice minister in the federal Government, enabling the controversial Prime Minister of that territory, Ramzan Kadyrov, to become acting President of the Republic (see below). In early March a mass opposition rally was organized in St Petersburg by Another Russia, a coalition of both left- and right-wing groups opposing Putin; leaders of Another Russia included Kasparov, Kasyanov and the leader of the extremist and prohibited National Bolshevik Party, Eduard Limonov. The subsequent removal of Veshnyakov from the post of Chairman of the CEC was attributed in the Russian media to his public criticism of the pro-Government parties and the amendments to the electoral legislation. Later in March, following continued speculation (repeatedly denied by the President) that Putin would contrive to serve a third presidential term, Mironov proposed to the Sovet Federatsii that the constitutional restriction to two consecutive four-year terms be abolished.

In April 2007, after Berezovskii declared to the British newspaper *The Guardian* that he planned the forcible ousting of the Putin administration, Minister of Foreign Affairs Lavrov reiterated demands for his extradition from the United Kingdom and announced further criminal proceedings against him. The insistence of the British authorities that Berezovskii was immune from extradition, owing to his political asylum status, further exacerbated tensions between the two countries (relations having been particularly strained by the death of Litvinenko). (In

November Berezovskii was sentenced *in absentia* by a Moscow district court to six years' imprisonment for embezzlement; a number of criminal cases against him were pending.) In mid-April Another Russia organized anti-Government demonstrations in Moscow and St Petersburg, which were violently suppressed by troops associated with the Ministry of the Interior (OMON). Some 350 protesters, including Kasparov and Kasyanov, were briefly detained in Moscow.

On 14 September 2007, following the resignation of Fradkov and his Government, the Gosudarstvennaya Duma approved Putin's nomination of Viktor Zubkov, hitherto head of the Federal Financial Monitoring Service, as Chairman. Later that month Putin announced a government reorganization; three new ministers were appointed, including Elvira Nabiullina, who received the economic development and trade portfolio, while the Minister of Finance, Aleksei Kudrin, also became a Deputy Chairman. In October Putin announced, in a statement made at UR's party congress, that he would head the party's list of candidates in the forthcoming legislative elections on 2 December and that he viewed favourably a proposal by delegates that he, eventually, become Chairman of the Government. Popular support for Putin's continued leadership increased during campaigning, and a number of regional organizations that had staged rallies in favour of a third presidential term for him grouped in November to form a 'For Putin' movement. In the same month Another Russia organized demonstrations in Moscow and St Petersburg, which resulted in the temporary detention of opposition leaders, including Kasparov. In November the Office for Democratic Institutions and Human Rights (ODIHR) of the OSCE announced the abandonment of plans to monitor the elections, after Russia imposed restrictions on the number of observers who would be invited; however, the Parliamentary Assemblies of the OSCE and Council of Europe (see p. 236) dispatched small monitoring missions. At the elections to the Gosudarstvennaya Duma on 2 December, UR won a substantial majority, securing 64.3% of the votes cast, according to official results, and 315 seats; the CPRF received 11.6% of votes and 57 seats, the LDPR 8.1% and 40 seats, and AJR 7.7% and 38 seats. Voter turn-out was 63.7% of the electorate. Reports emerged that students and public sector workers had been placed under considerable pressure by the authorities to vote for UR. The Russian Government dismissed a subsequent joint statement by the OSCE and the Council of Europe that the conduct of the elections had failed to meet international standards for democracy, following widespread allegations of media bias in favour of UR and voting irregularities. (A report by CIS observers upheld the organization of the elections.) On 10 December Putin announced his support for the nomination by UR and three other parties of Medvedev as a candidate in the forthcoming presidential election on 2 March 2008. Putin subsequently indicated approval of a proposal made by Medvedev that he serve as premier in the event that Medvedev be elected to the presidency.

In December 2007, amid continuing strained relations with the United Kingdom, Russia ordered the closure of two regional offices of a British state cultural and educational organization, the British Council, from January 2008, on the grounds that it was operating illegally. After the British Government insisted that the offices remain open, a number of the British Council's Russian employees were questioned by the FSB, and the head of the Council in St Petersburg was briefly detained on an alleged traffic offence. On 17 January the British Council suspended operations at the two offices. In February Medvedev reiterated allegations that the British Council was involved in espionage. In March the Council confirmed its intention to continue its operations in Moscow. In June the Council announced that it had received a disproportionately large tax bill in May from the Russian authorities for the period 2004–06, which it was disputing. In October a Moscow arbitration court ruled that much of the bill was invalid; however, in December an appeals court was reported to have overturned the lower court's ruling, reinstating a demand for an estimated 100m. roubles.

In January 2008 the CEC rejected the presidential candidacy of Kasyanov, ruling that a number of the signatures collected in his support were invalid; he subsequently urged a boycott of the poll. In February the ODIHR again announced that it would not dispatch a monitoring mission to Russia, on the grounds that a stipulation by the Russian authorities that 70 observers be invited only three days before the poll would prevent adequate monitoring of the elections. On 2 March, as widely anticipated, Medvedev (following his endorsement by Putin) was elected to the presidency, with some 70.3% of the votes cast, according to final official results; Zyuganov of the CPRF received 17.7% of the votes, and Zhirinovskii of the LDPR about 9.4%. The official rate of participation by the electorate was estimated at 69.8%. Observers from the Parliamentary Assembly of the Council of Europe acknowledged popular support for Medvedev, but reported that aspects of the electoral campaign had failed to meet democratic principles. At a UR congress in April Putin formally accepted an invitation to assume the new post of Chairman of the party, although it was confirmed that he would not become a member of the party. Medvedev was inaugurated as President on 7 May (when Putin, on relinquishing the presidency, officially became Chairman of UR). Shortly afterwards Medvedev nominated Putin as Chairman of the Government; on 8 May the Gosudarstvennaya Duma approved his nomination to the office by an overwhelming majority (with only CPRF deputies opposing it). On 12 May Putin announced a government reorganization, in which an additional three ministries were created. Zubkov became First Deputy Chairman, and was to assume particular responsibility for the agricultural sector, while a senior presidential aide, Igor Shuvalov, was also accorded the post of First Deputy Chairman. Igor Sechin, the Chairman of Rosneft and hitherto deputy head of the presidential administration, was appointed to the Government as a Deputy Chairman and was to supervise industrial development programmes. Ivanov remained in the new administration as a Deputy Chairman; other principal ministers, including Kudrin, Lavrov and Serdyukov, retained their posts.

At the end of July 2008 President Medvedev announced a new, extensive programme to suppress corruption by state officials. In October Dmitrii Kozak, hitherto Minister of Regional Development, was appointed as a Deputy Chairman of the Government. On 12 October a 'unified election day', which included polls to five regional legislatures, took place. In his first annual address on 5 November, Medvedev announced proposed amendments to the Constitution that principally extended the term of office of the President from four to six years and that of the deputies of the Gosudarstvennaya Duma from four to five years. The constitutional amendments were adopted by both parliamentary chambers later in November. On 12 December opposition leaders from many organizations, including Nemtsov and Kasparov, officially established an opposition movement, to be known as Solidarity. Marches of dissent were organized by Another Russia in Moscow and St Petersburg, in protest at the Government's failure to address the economic crisis (see below) and at the extension of the presidential and legislative mandates. Demonstrations were also staged in Vladivostok, the administrative centre of the far-eastern Maritime (Primorskii) Krai, and some 30 other cities later in December, in protest at government plans to increase tariffs on imported cars; the rally in Vladivostok was violently suppressed by OMON forces. With the incidence of racially motivated attacks increasing, in December seven extreme nationalist 'skinheads', who had killed at least 20 people in a series of racist attacks in Moscow, were sentenced to terms of between six and 20 years' imprisonment. The constitutional amendments (which had been approved by all 83 regional legislatures) were signed into law by Medvedev on 30 December.

In January 2009 a prominent human rights lawyer, Sergei Markelov, who had represented the relatives of a Chechen woman murdered by a Russian officer in 2000, was shot and killed in Moscow. In February four suspects charged with involvement in the killing of Anna Politkovskaya in 2006 (of whom two were Chechen nationals, one was a former police officer, and one was an FSB officer) were acquitted by a Moscow court; human rights groups criticized the investigation into the case. Also in February the Minister of Agriculture, Aleksei Gordeyev (who had been appointed to the Government in 1999), was transferred to the post of Governor of Voronezh Oblast; he was replaced by the head of a state agro-industrial company, Yelena Skrynnik, in early March. Elections to nine regional legislatures, as well as to municipal authorities in 77 territories, were conducted on 1 March; UR won an absolute majority of seats in eight of the contested legislatures. A mayoral election in the Russian Black Sea town of Sochi (where the 2014 Winter Olympics were to take place) was scheduled for 26 April, after the regional Governor removed the incumbent in the post. After many of the original 26 registered candidates were disqualified on technical grounds, six contested the poll (which attracted international attention); the acting mayor, Anatolii Pakhomov of UR, secured some 77% of the votes cast, while Nemtsov was placed second, with about 13.5% of the votes. In

April Medvedev dismissed the head of the Main Intelligence Directorate, Gen. Valentin Korabelnikov (who had been appointed to the post in 1997), on grounds of old age, and also removed a further two senior defence officials.

In the early 1990s the Russian Federation encountered difficulties in attempting to satisfy the aspirations of its many minority ethnic groups for self-determination. In March 1992 some 18 of Russia's 20 nominally autonomous republics signed a federation treaty. The two dissenters, both predominately Islamic and petroleum-producing regions, were Tatarstan, which had voted for self-rule earlier in the month, and the Checheno-Ingush Republic, which had declared independence from Russia in November 1991 (as the Chechen Republic—Chechnya). The new treaty granted the republics greater authority, including control of natural resources and formal borders, and allowed them to conduct their own foreign trade. An agreement signed with the Russian Government in February 1994 accorded Tatarstan a considerable measure of sovereignty. Other power-sharing agreements, granting varying degrees of sovereignty, were eventually signed by some 42 of the 89 federal subjects during Yeltsin's presidency, although from 2000 Putin implemented a number of measures intended to curtail the power of regional governors, which led to the rescission of the vast majority of the power-sharing treaties by mid-2002. In May 2000 the Gosudarstvennaya Duma approved legislation according the President the right to dismiss regional governors, a prerogative that was extended to governors with regard to those elected officials subordinate to them; however, by 2004 these powers had been seldom used, although, as a result of legislation approved in December (see above), the appointment of regional governors (the election of whom had become almost universal across the Federation by the late 1990s) by the federal President, subject to the approval of regional legislatures, became the norm from early 2005.

In March 1992, in response to the unilateral declaration of independence by Chechnya, the Ingush inhabitants of the former Checheno-Ingush Republic demanded the establishment of a separate republic. The formation of the new republic, Ingushetiya, was approved by the federal Supreme Council in June. Additionally, Ingush activists claimed territories in neighbouring North Osetiya, which had formed part of the Ingush Republic prior to the Second World War, when the Ingush (and Chechens, in common with several other nationalities of the USSR) were deported *en masse* to Central Asia. In October 1992 violent conflict broke out in the disputed Prigorodnyi district in North Osetiya. By November more than 300 people had died in the conflict and some 50,000 Ingush had fled the region. In September 1997, following mediation by Yeltsin, a treaty on normalizing relations was signed by the republican Governments of North Osetiya and Ingushetiya.

In late 1993 armed hostilities commenced in Chechnya between forces loyal to the republican authorities and those of the separatist leader, Gen. Dzhokhar Dudayev (who had been elected President of the Republic in October 1991, following a coup against the republic's communist Government, led by Doku Zavgayev). Chechnya boycotted the Russian general election and referendum of December 1993; in August 1994 an unsuccessful attempt to overthrow the Dudayev regime was reputedly aided by the federal security services. Following the defeat of a further offensive in November, federal troops entered Chechnya in December. The troops rapidly gained control of the lowland area of northern Chechnya. Dudayev's forces, estimated to number some 15,000 irregular troops, were concentrated in the Chechen capital, Groznyi, a city upon which federal troops launched an assault in late December, following heavy bombardment from the air. Despite sustaining significant casualties, federal troops gradually took control of the city and seized the presidential palace (the headquarters of Dudayev's forces) in January 1995. Groznyi suffered great devastation during the assault, and there were reported to be thousands of civilian casualties. In June 1995 Chechen gunmen engaged local security forces in Budennovsk, some 200 km from the border with Chechnya, and took hostage more than 1,000 people in the city hospital. The rebels demanded that the Russian Government initiate talks with Dudayev on the immediate withdrawal of troops from Chechnya. Following the failure of attempts by federal army units to free the hostages, telephone negotiations were conducted between the rebel leader, Shamil Basayev, and federal premier Chernomyrdin, by which time some 100 people had reportedly been killed. Subsequently, as a cease-fire took effect in Chechnya, the rebels began gradually to release hostages. Peace talks between a delegation from the federal Government and the Chechen leadership commenced in Groznyi in late June, and a cease-fire agreement was formalized in July.

In October 1995, following an assassination attempt on the commander of the federal forces in Chechnya, the federal Government announced a temporary suspension of the July agreement. In response, the Chechen leadership announced its complete rejection of the accord. In December elections took place in Chechnya, to both the republican Duma and presidency. Zavgayev was elected republican President, reportedly receiving some 93% of the votes cast in elections that Dudayev rejected as invalid.

In January 1996 Chechen militants seized about 2,000 civilians in Kizlyar, Dagestan, and held them hostage in a hospital. Following negotiations, most were released, and the rebels departed, accompanied by some 150 hostages, for Chechnya. Federal troops halted the rebels in the border village of Pervomaiskoye and demanded the release of the remaining hostages. After further negotiations failed, federal forces attacked and captured the village. Although the rebels' leader, Salman Raduyev, escaped to Chechnya with some of his forces and around 40 hostages, some 150 rebels, and a number of their captives, were reportedly killed in the assault. In April Dudayev was killed in a missile attack. He was succeeded as leader of the separatists by Zemlikhan Yandarbiyev, who subsequently developed an association with the Islamist Taliban regime in Afghanistan. Sporadic fighting persisted, but a new cease-fire agreement between the federal authorities and Yandarbiyev was reached in May. A formal military agreement, concluded in June, envisaged a withdrawal of the federal troops by the end of August and the disarmament of the separatist fighters. In August separatist forces, led by Basayev, launched a sustained offensive against Groznyi, routing many of the federal troops stationed in the city and trapping thousands of civilians. Yeltsin granted Gen. Lebed, the recently appointed Secretary of the Security Council, extensive powers to co-ordinate federal operations in the republic and to conduct a negotiated settlement. Following discussions involving Yandarbiyev and the Chechen military leader, Gen. Khalid ('Aslan') Maskhadov, a fresh cease-fire was brokered in mid-August. Following further negotiations, the withdrawal of troops commenced, and on 31 August Lebed and Maskhadov signed a conclusive peace agreement (the Khasavyurt Accords) in Dagestan, according to which any decision regarding Chechnya's future political status was to be deferred until December 2001. The withdrawal of federal troops and the exchange of prisoners of war began, and the cease-fire was largely respected. In September 1996 a Chechen Government was created, with Maskhadov as Prime Minister, and Yandarbiyev as Chairman of the cabinet. Nevertheless, sporadic violence continued: by early 1997 it was estimated that the conflict had caused some 80,000 deaths, and resulted in the displacement of 415,000 civilians.

All federal troops were withdrawn before the republican presidential and legislative elections, held on 27 January 1997. Maskhadov was elected President, with some 59.3% of the total votes cast. Of the 12 remaining candidates, Basayev won 23.5% of the votes, and Yandarbiyev 10.1%. The rate of voter participation was reported to be 79.4%, and international observers reported no serious discrepancies in the electoral process. Maskhadov declined his seat in the Sovet Federatsii, and affirmed his support for Chechen independence. Elections to the Chechen legislature were inconclusive, and, after a second round of voting, only 45 of the 63 seats had been filled; further rounds were held in May and June. On 12 May Yeltsin and Maskhadov signed a formal peace treaty, defining the principles of future relations between Chechnya and the Russian Federation, and renouncing the use of violence as a means of resolving differences. The treaty, however, did not address the issue of Chechnya's constitutional status and, moreover, was refused ratification by the Gosudarstvennaya Duma.

Attacks and, in particular, hostage-taking continued to be perpetrated by rebels opposed to the peace agreement. Meanwhile, Chechnya's introduction of elements of *Shari'a* (Islamic religious) law in 1997, in particular the holding of public executions, was strongly opposed by the federal authorities. In January 1998 Maskhadov dismissed his cabinet and entrusted Basayev (who had been indicted by the federal authorities on charges of terrorism), hitherto Chechen First Deputy Prime Minister, but now acting Prime Minister, with the formation of a new government. In late March the republican parliament announced that the territory was henceforth to be known as the

'Chechen Republic of Ichkeriya'. Increasing lawlessness and militancy was reported in the republic. In May Chechen rebels kidnapped Yeltsin's special representative to Chechnya, Vladimir Vlasov; he was freed in November by interior ministry troops. Four employees of a British telecommunications company were kidnapped in Chechnya in October; their decapitated bodies were found several weeks later. As disorder increased, Maskhadov dismissed the entire Chechen administration in October, and declared a further state of emergency in December. It became apparent that militant Islamist groups, including a faction led in Chechnya by Omar ibn al-Khattab (believed to be of Saudi or Jordanian origin), were increasingly implicated in the violence in Chechnya.

In August–September 1999 Islamist factions associated with Basayev launched a series of attacks on Dagestan from Chechnya, with the aim of protecting and extending the jurisdiction of a 'separate Islamic territory' in Dagestan, over which rebels had obtained control in the previous year. (The territory was returned to federal rule in mid-September.) Federal troops were dispatched to the area, and after two weeks of fighting and aerial bombardment the rebels withdrew. However, there were renewed incursions and fighting in September. Meanwhile, in mid-August Maskhadov declared a one-month state of emergency in Chechnya, following threats by the federal authorities to bomb alleged terrorist bases in the republic. A series of bomb explosions in August and September in Moscow, Dagestan and Volgodonsk (Rostov Oblast), including two that destroyed entire apartment blocks, officially attributed by the Government to Chechen separatists, killed almost 300 people, prompting the redeployment of federal armed forces in the republic from late September; the recently inaugurated premier, Putin, described the deployment as an 'anti-terrorist operation'. Allegations persisted that sources associated with the FSB had ordered the attacks, in order to justify a renewed military campaign in Chechnya; notably, the discovery of an apparent attempt to initiate a further bombing in an apartment block in Ryazan heightened concerns of FSB involvement, although the authorities insisted that the incident was simply an exercise designed to ensure a heightened state of public vigilance. (In January 2004 two men were sentenced to life imprisonment for their part in the attacks.) Following air and ground offensives, federal troops had advanced to within 10 km of Groznyi by late October 1999, and both sides claimed to have inflicted heavy losses on the other. In December many republican and federal administrative bodies were relocated to Gudermes, Chechnya's second city. In February 2000 federal forces obtained control of Groznyi and proceeded to destroy much of the city.

In May 2000 President Putin decreed that, henceforth, Chechnya would be governed federally. Mufti Akhmad haji Kadyrov was inaugurated as administrative leader (Governor) of the republic in June. Kadyrov, a former ally of Maskhadov, was to be directly responsible to the federal authorities. In January 2001 Putin signed a decree transferring control of operations in Chechnya from the Ministry of Defence to the FSB, and announced the intention of withdrawing the majority of the 80,000-strong federal forces from the region, in order to leave a 15,000-strong infantry division and 7,000 interior ministry troops. The local administration in Chechnya was restructured, and Stanislav Ilyasov, a former Governor of Stavropol Krai, was appointed as the Chechen premier. Despite claims that federal military operations had effectively ended, guerrilla attacks showed no sign of abating, and concern escalated among international human rights organizations about the conduct of 'cleansing' operations by federal troops, in which entire towns or areas were searched for rebels; in 2001–02 the discovery of a number of mass graves, containing severely mutilated corpses, prompted outrage internationally.

In early 2001 a number of violent incidents outside Chechnya were staged by rebels, with the intention of drawing attention to the ongoing conflict. In mid-March three armed Chechen rebels hijacked a passenger aeroplane en route from Istanbul, Turkey, to Moscow, causing it to be diverted to Medina, Saudi Arabia. The rebels demanded that federal forces withdraw from Chechnya. Following the intervention of Saudi security forces, three hijackers were detained; three people, including one of the hijackers, were killed in the struggle. Later in the month 23 people were killed and more than 140 were injured in three simultaneous bomb attacks in southern Russia, which were attributed to associates of Khattab. In May the continuing disorder in Chechnya was demonstrated by the announcement that the planned withdrawal of troops from the province had been halted.

In November 2001 the first direct negotiations between the warring factions since the renewal of hostilities in 1999, held in Moscow between the presidential representative to the Southern Federal Okrug, Col-Gen. Viktor Kazantsev, and Maskhadov's deputy, Akhmed Zakayev, reached no substantive agreement, and no further high-level meetings took place. In December Raduyev, the only prominent Chechen rebel leader to have been captured by federal forces, was sentenced to life imprisonment, having been found guilty of 10 charges, including murder, terrorism and hostage-taking. (Raduyev died in prison in December 2002.)

In April 2002 Khattab was killed by federal forces. Rebel activity increased markedly in the months that followed; although the political authority of Maskhadov had dwindled, his military leadership of what was known as the State Defence Committee became increasingly prominent as a focus for resistance to the federal troops. In July it was reported that Basayev had been appointed to a senior position on the Committee. Meanwhile, on 9 May, during celebrations in Kaspiisk, Dagestan, to mark 'Victory Day', some 45 people were killed and more than 130 injured in an explosion, which the federal authorities attributed to Chechen rebels. In mid-August federal forces experienced their single largest loss of life since the recommencement of operations in 1999, when a military helicopter was shot down by rebels in Groznyi, killing some 118 troops; at the end of the month a second federal helicopter was attacked, killing its two crew members, and two further helicopters had been shot down by early November. Meanwhile, in late September rebels staged incursions into Ingushetiya; at least 17 deaths were reported in fighting. Moreover, an explosion outside a police station in Groznyi in mid-October resulted in the deaths of at least 24 people.

On 23–26 October 2002 over 40 heavily armed rebels, led by Movsar Barayev, the cousin of a Chechen rebel leader who had been killed by federal troops in 2001, held captive more than 800 people in a Moscow theatre, and demanded the withdrawal of federal troops from the republic. The rebels described themselves as members of a 'suicide battalion'. The siege ended when élite federal forces stormed the theatre, having initially filled the building with an unidentified incapacitating gas. The rebels were killed, and it subsequently emerged that at least 129 hostages had also died, in almost all cases owing to the toxic effects of the gas. Maskhadov issued a statement condemning the rebels' use of terrorist methods, but, despite denials by the rebel Chechen leadership of their involvement in the incident, Zakayev was arrested in late October, reportedly on the orders of the federal Government, in Denmark. In December the Danish authorities refused to extradite Zakayev to Russia, citing a lack of credible evidence of his involvement in terrorist activities. Zakayev's presence in Denmark resulted in the relocation to Brussels, Belgium, of the European Union (EU, see p. 255)-Russia summit that had been scheduled to take place in Copenhagen, Denmark, in November. Zakayev subsequently fled to the United Kingdom, where, in November 2003, he was granted political asylum, following the dismissal of a Russian request for his extradition.

In mid-November 2002 Ilyasov was removed from his position as Prime Minister of Chechnya and, in what was widely perceived as a promotion, appointed as a minister in the federal Government, in which capacity he was to be responsible for the social and economic development of Chechnya; Ilyasov was succeeded as the premier of Chechnya by Capt. (retd) Mikhail Babich, who had previously held senior positions in two regional administrations elsewhere in Russia. In late November Ilyasov announced that a referendum on a new draft Chechen constitution, which would, *inter alia*, determine the status of the republic within the Russian Federation, was to be held in March 2003. At the end of December 2002 at least 83 people died, and more than 150 others were injured, when suicide bombers detonated bombs in two vehicles stationed outside the headquarters of the republican Government in Groznyi; no senior officials were killed. (Basayev subsequently claimed responsibility for the attack.) By late December 2002 federal losses during the campaign, according to official figures, were put at 4,572 dead and 15,549 wounded, with 29 missing, although Chechen estimates were considerably higher. (It was also estimated that more than 14,000 rebel fighters had been killed since September 1999.) In late January 2003 Babich resigned as premier. On 10 February Anatolii Popov, the hitherto deputy chairman of the state commission for the reconstruction of Chechnya, was appointed as the new republican premier.

THE RUSSIAN FEDERATION

The referendum on the draft constitution for Chechnya, describing the republic (which was to be renamed the Chechen—Nokchi Republic) as both a sovereign entity, with its own citizenship, and as an integral part of the Russian Federation, proceeded, as scheduled, on 23 March 2003, despite concerns that the instability of the republic would prevent the poll from being free and fair. The draft constitution also provided for the holding of fresh elections to a strengthened republican presidency and legislature. According to the official results, some 88.4% of the electorate participated in the plebiscite, of whom 96.0% supported the draft constitution. Two further questions, on the method of electing the President and the Parliament of Chechnya, were supported by 95.4% and 96.1% of participants, respectively. However, independent observers challenged the results, reporting that the rate of participation by the electorate had been much lower than officially reported.

Political violence continued to dominate Chechen affairs after the referendum; in early April 2003 at least 22 people were killed in two separate incidents when their vehicles detonated landmines. In early May at least 59 people were killed when suicide bombers attacked government offices in the north of Chechnya. Two days later another suicide bombing at a religious festival attended by Kadyrov resulted in at least 14 deaths, although Kadyrov escaped unhurt; Basayev claimed responsibility for the organization of both attacks. On 21 June Kadyrov inaugurated an interim legislative body, the State Council, comprising the head of, and an appointed representative of, each administrative district. In July Putin announced that presidential elections in Chechnya would be held in October. None the less, clashes continued, and in August at least 50 people were killed in an attack on a military hospital in neighbouring North Osetiya.

From 1 September 2003 control of military operations in Chechnya was transferred from the FSB to the federal Ministry of Internal Affairs; such operations were no longer regarded as having an 'anti-terrorist' character but were, rather, to form part of an 'operation to protect law and constitutional order'. Meanwhile, campaigning for the presidential election commenced, and by mid-August 11 valid applications for candidacies had been made. However, the subsequent withdrawal of Aslanbek Aslakhanov, a representative of Chechnya in the Gosudarstvennaya Duma, and the debarring of a business executive, Malik Saidullayev, effectively removed any major challenges to Kadyrov's candidacy. As had been widely anticipated, on 5 October Kadyrov was elected as President, receiving 87.7% of the votes cast, according to official figures. The rate of participation by the electorate was stated to be 82.6%. In mid-December at least 12 people were killed in clashes that followed incursions by heavily armed Chechen rebels into Dagestan, resulting in the imposition of a state of emergency in the region. An explosion in a Moscow Metro train on 6 February 2004, which resulted in the deaths of at least 39 people, was attributed to Chechen militants. In mid-February Yandarbiyev was killed by a car bomb in Doha, Qatar. (Two Russian intelligence agents were subsequently sentenced to life imprisonment for Yandarbiyev's murder by a Qatari court; however, they were returned to Russia to serve out their sentences in December, and in early 2005 it was reported that they were no longer being held in detention.) In early March 2004 another influential rebel leader, Ruslan Gelayev, was reported to have been killed in clashes with federal troops in Dagestan. In mid-March Popov was formally dismissed as premier of Chechnya, following a period of ill health; he was replaced by Sergei Abramov, who had previously worked in the republican Ministry of Finance. In accordance with the provisions of the constitutional referendum held in the previous year, his appointment required, and duly obtained, the endorsement of the republican State Council.

An explosion in Groznyi on 9 May 2004, at a celebration to mark 'Victory Day', resulted in the deaths of several senior officials, including Kadyrov and Khusain Isayev, the head of the republican legislature. (Basayev subsequently claimed responsibility for the attack.) Abramov assumed presidential responsibilities in an acting capacity, pending elections, while Ramzan Kadyrov, the son of the assassinated President and the leader of the presidential security service (often known as the *Kadyrovtsi* and which was widely believed to have been implicated in several unexplained 'disappearances'), was appointed as First Deputy Prime Minister. Chechen militants were suspected of involvement in a series of raids on interior ministry targets in the neighbouring republic of Ingushetiya, which took place in June. In the presidential election held on 29 August, Maj.-Gen. Alu Alkhanov, an officer in the interior ministry troops, and generally acknowledged to be the candidate favoured by the federal Government, was elected President, receiving 73.7% of the votes cast, according to official figures, which evaluated the rate of participation at 85.3%. The Council of Europe described the elections as undemocratic. Alkhanov retained Abramov as Prime Minister, while Ramzan Kadyrov was retained both as First Deputy Prime Minister and as head of the presidential security service. In the period immediately before and after the election, attacks on Russian civilians, attributed to extremist Chechen separatists, intensified, with the destruction, apparently by suicide bombers, of two passenger planes, the explosion of a bomb outside a Moscow Metro station, and the occupation of a school in Beslan, in the Republic of North Osetiya—Alaniya, on 1–3 September (see above). Basayev subsequently released a statement claiming that the attacks had occurred under his orchestration, and describing the demands of the Beslan hostage-takers as the complete withdrawal of federal troops from Chechnya and the resignation of President Putin.

In February 2005 Maskhadov announced that he had ordered separatist fighters to observe a unilateral one-month cease-fire, in what he described as a 'goodwill gesture' towards the Russian authorities. On 8 March Russian media reported that Maskhadov had been killed during a special operation by FSB forces north of Groznyi. Footage of what appeared to be Maskhadov's corpse was broadcast on national television later that day. Maskhadov was replaced as leader of the State Defence Committee by his chosen successor, Abdul-Khalim Sadulayev. Sadulayev, like Maskhadov before him, announced his willingness to enter into negotiations with the federal authorities, but maintained that the use of force was legitimate in the absence of such negotiations. In June Sadulayev issued a decree appointing Doku Umarov, a radical Islamist believed to be a close associate of Basayev (who had, earlier in the year, stated that Chechen militants would launch large-scale operations in other regions of Russia as part of a so-called 'Caucasus Front'), as vice-president of the rebel leadership; he also issued a statement to the effect that the expulsion of Russian forces from Chechnya would not constitute an end to the conflict, as the Chechens would be obligated to take vengeance against 'unbelievers' (i.e. non-Muslims) for their actions in Chechnya. In mid-July at least 15 people were killed following the detonation of a car bomb in Znamenskoye. In mid-August Sadulayev dismissed the rebel Chechen 'parliament-in-exile' and a network of 'ambassadors', which he collectively accused of financial malpractice and incompetence; he also appointed a new rebel 'Government' at the end of the month, to which, notably, Basayev was appointed as 'First Deputy Prime Minister', while Zakayev was appointed to represent the rebel authorities internationally. In September Basayev was interviewed by a US television station, and stated that he accepted his designation as a 'terrorist', but that he regarded his use of violence as justified. In early October a coordinated series of attacks by some 100 militants against law-enforcement bodies in Nalchik, the capital of the Kabardino-Balkar Republic, in the western North Caucasus, resulted in the deaths of at least 130 people; Basayev claimed responsibility for the organization of the attack. An Islamist group active in the Kabardino-Balkar Republic, the Yarmuk Dzhamaat, also claimed to have participated in the attacks, as part of the 'Caucasus Front'. Meanwhile, tensions between Chechens and the most numerous ethnic group in neighbouring Dagestan, the Avars, were also heightened on several occasions from the first half of 2005, as a result of security forces associated with the Chechen authorities (most notably members of the *Kadyrovtsi*) making incursions into Dagestan, apparently in response to Chechen rebels taking refuge there. Clashes were also reported between those troops loyal to Ramzan Kadyrov and those loyal to the federal authorities.

On 27 November 2005 elections were held in Chechnya to a new, bicameral legislature, comprising the 18-seat Council of the Republic (the upper chamber) and the 40-seat People's Assembly (the lower chamber). The federal Government cited the ballot as evidence that normality was returning to Chechnya, although no candidates advocating Chechen independence were allowed to stand. The rate of participation by the electorate was estimated as some 60%, well above the 25% required to validate the election; however, international observers expressed doubt that the vote was free and fair. As predicted, the majority of deputies in the new parliament (33 out of 58) were from UR. Thus, the position of Kadyrov, a member of UR and for a long time perceived as de facto leader of the Chechen Government, was consolidated; furthermore, Kadyrov at this time held the position of acting premier, after Abramov sustained injuries in an automobile accident earlier in the month.

On 28 February 2006 Abramov resigned as Prime Minister of Chechnya. On 4 March the republican legislature unanimously approved the appointment of Kadyrov as his successor. Although this appointment effectively confirmed the distribution of power that had been in place in the Republic for several months, it was not without controversy. As acting Prime Minister, Kadyrov had spoken in favour of permitting men to marry up to four women, although this would be in clear breach of the family code; moreover, before being overruled by Alkhanov, Kadyrov had prohibited a Danish humanitarian relief organization from operating in Chechnya, as part of international protests by Muslims that followed the publication of cartoons depicting the Islamic Prophet Muhammad, initially in a Danish newspaper (and their circulation, by a group of imams, alongside several more inflammatory images, in various countries of the Middle East), which were deemed to be offensive towards Islam. In June Sadulayev was killed in an operation by special forces in Chechnya. He was succeeded as leader of the separatist Chechen rebels by Umarov. In July Basayev was killed, in an explosion in Ingushetiya (for which the FSB claimed responsibility). In October Kadyrov reached 30 years of age (the minimum age for eligibility to serve as Chechen President). On 15 February 2007 Putin's transferral of Alkhanov to the federal Government (see above) allowed Kadyrov, as Chairman of the republican Government, to assume the duties of President, in an acting capacity. Later in the month it was confirmed that he was the federal authorities' preferred nominee to become President; his appointment was endorsed by the republican legislature on 2 March. On 21 June the Chechen Constitutional Assembly approved amendments to the republican Constitution, proposed by Kadyrov, which included the replacement of the bicameral legislature with a 41-member unicameral Parliament, the abolition of direct elections to the republican presidency, the extension of the presidential term from four to five years, and the adoption of Chechen as a state language, in addition to Russian; the changes were endorsed by 96.9% of the votes cast in a referendum in December. Meanwhile, in October Umarov issued a statement proclaiming himself emir of a 'North Caucasus Islamic state', thereby precipitating a split in the separatist movement between Islamist and nationalist elements. In November the rebel Chechen 'parliament-in-exile' announced that Umarov's powers as 'President' of the 'Chechen Republic of Ichkeriya' had been formally removed. The rebel 'Minister of Foreign Affairs' based in London, United Kingdom, Zakayev, condemned Umarov's statement, and subsequently received the support of senior rebel commanders. The chairman of the 'parliament-in-exile' issued a decree appointing Zakayev as 'Prime Minister', although this appointment was not recognized by supporters of Umarov.

Legislative elections were conducted in Chechnya on 12 October 2008; according to official results, UR secured some 88.4% of the votes cast and 37 of the 41 seats in the reconstituted unicameral Parliament. Following the completion of the post-conflict reconstruction of much of Groznyi, on 16 April 2009 Medvedev issued a decree formally ending the counter-terrorism operation in Chechnya and providing for the withdrawal of some 20,000 of the 50,000 Russian troops deployed in the republic at that time. However, the federal military authorities rapidly reinstated special security measures in five southern districts of Chechnya, in response to renewed rebel activity; later in April it was reported that further bomb attacks had been staged and Russian soldiers had been killed in ambush shootings.

Following the dissolution of the USSR in December 1991, Russia's most immediate foreign policy concerns were with the other former Soviet republics, generally referred to in Russia as the 'near abroad'. Relations with Ukraine were, initially, dominated by a dispute over the division of the former Soviet Black Sea Fleet, based mainly in Sevastopol, on the Crimean peninsula (Ukraine). Russia and Ukraine signed an agreement on the division of the Fleet in June 1995, but Russia subsequently refused to implement the accord, owing to continued disagreement concerning the status of Sevastopol. In May 1997 an agreement was concluded with Ukraine, whereby Russia was to lease part of the city's naval base for 20 years, and was to provide financial compensation for ships and equipment received from Ukraine. (Upon expiry, the treaty could be renewed for five years, should both parties agree, but would then be subject to renegotiation.) A Treaty on Friendship, Co-operation and Partnership was signed by the two countries in that month. In January 2003 a treaty delineating the land boundary between Russia and Ukraine (which remained largely unmarked and unregulated) was signed by Putin and President Leonid Kuchma of Ukraine, although discussions on the status of the Sea of Azov, which lies between the two countries, remained unresolved. Work on the construction of a dam in the Sea, which commenced, apparently at the instigation of the regional authorities in Krasnodar Krai, in September, precipitated considerable controversy, and raised concerns that the territorial integrity of Ukraine was being violated. In December the Presidents of the two countries signed an agreement on the use of the Sea of Azov, the entirety of which was defined as comprising the internal waters of both countries. Agreement was also reached on the maritime state boundary of Russia and Ukraine in the region.

Relations with Ukraine were damaged by the circumstances of the disputed 2004 presidential election in that country (see the chapter on Ukraine), as Putin openly supported the candidacy of the incumbent Prime Minister, Viktor Yanukovych, whose reported victory in the second round was subsequently overturned following large public protests over the conduct of the poll. Notably, Putin visited Ukraine twice during the campaign, appearing publicly with Yanukovych on both occasions, and telephoned Yanukovych to congratulate him on his victory before the official (and later discredited) results had been announced. Putin also described the protests that led to the election being repeated, and which became known as the 'orange revolution', as a violation of constitutional order. In a move widely interpreted as acknowledging the necessity of continued co-operation between the two countries (and reflecting the substantial ethnic Russian and Russian-speaking population of Ukraine), the newly elected President, Viktor Yushchenko, visited Moscow the day after his inauguration in January 2005. However, relations between the two countries were again strained later in 2005, following the announcement by the Russian state-controlled company Gazprom that it intended to charge Ukraine market prices for the supply of natural gas, which had hitherto been supplied at a subsidized rate. After failing to negotiate new terms, on 1 January 2006 Gazprom halted supplies to Ukraine, a measure that resulted in a reduced output of gas in several countries in central and western Europe supplied by pipelines crossing Ukraine. Supplies were restored on 4 January, following agreement on new terms of supply less favourable to Ukraine. In October 2007 Gazprom threatened again to suspend natural gas supplies to Ukraine, stating that it was owed US $1,300m.; a few days later it was announced that a compromise agreement had been reached, whereby Ukraine was to repay $1,200m. by transferring gas from underground storage facilities in Ukraine to Gazprom for further export. In February 2008 Gazprom warned that it would reduce supplies to Ukraine, in response to debts incurred during the previous month; it was subsequently announced that Ukraine and Russia had reached a debt settlement, and also agreed to discontinue use of the intermediary trading company in gas supplies to Ukraine, the Swiss-registered RosUkrEnergo. Later in February, however, Gazprom claimed that Ukraine had failed to sign the negotiated agreements. After further discussions, in April the Ukrainian Government announced that agreement had been reached on a new payment scheme; at the insistence of the Russian authorities, RosUkrEnergo was to remain the intermediary company, operating within Russia.

A further acrimonious dispute over the price Ukraine would pay for Russian gas and the level of transit fees to be paid by Gazprom during 2009 resulted in Russia's suspension of gas supplies to Ukraine on 1 January. After accusing Ukraine of abstracting gas flowing through its pipelines intended for export to Europe, Russia also halted supplies to Europe via Ukraine on 7 January (during a period of extremely cold weather). Following intensive EU mediation and emergency discussions between Gazprom and Ukrainian state utility Naftogaz, on 19 January Putin and the Ukrainian Prime Minister, Yuliya Tymoshenko, signed an agreement in Moscow, whereby Ukraine would pay an average price for Russian gas in 2009 that would be 20% lower than the European price, while the transit price would remain unchanged; Ukraine was obliged to purchase 40,000m. cu m of Russian gas in that year. Gas supplies to Europe were finally restored on 21 January. Gazprom was reported to have lost US $1,500m. in revenue by the end of January as a result of the dispute, and European energy officials urged measures to address the EU's over-dependence on Russian gas. Following further discussions between Putin and Tymoshenko in Moscow at the end of April, it was agreed that Gazprom would not penalize Ukraine for failure to accept the contracted amount of gas in 2009 and would assist in payment of the transit fee to ensure supply, while Russia was invited to participate in an EU-supported programme to modernize Ukraine's gas transportation system (which had been announced in March).

In April 1996 Russia and Belarus signed an agreement creating a 'Community of Russia and Belarus', according to which the two countries would pursue economic integration and close co-ordination of foreign and defence policies. In May 1997 a 'Charter of the Union of Belarus and Russia' was concluded, which, while promoting greater co-operation between the two countries, moved away from advocating full union, although in June the first official session of the Union's joint Parliamentary Assembly was convened. During 1998 the Union was strengthened by the decision to grant joint citizenship to residents, and the establishment of a joint legislative and representative body to deal with union issues. A treaty on unification, which came into force on 26 January 2000, when the President of Belarus, Alyaksandr Lukashenka, was appointed Chairman of the High State Council of the Union, did not satisfy the Belarusian President's wishes for the formation of a single state. A union budget was approved at a session of the Parliamentary Assembly (established under the 1996 Treaty, and comprising 36 members from the legislature of each country) in May. Although agreement was reached in March 2002 on the harmonization of the two countries' customs and tax laws, and on the removal of trade barriers, Putin was increasingly dismissive of Lukashenka's proposals for a closer union of the two states. In early February 2009 it was announced that Belarus and Russia had signed an official treaty providing for the creation of a joint air defence system; in the same month Medvedev declared that the two countries would increase efforts to establish a customs union in that year.

Concern at the treatment and status of ethnic Russians in Estonia and Latvia remained a particular source of tension, and the demarcation of mutual frontiers also created difficulties. In the early 2000s Russia expressed particular concern for its citizens in the Russian exclave of Kaliningrad, which is separated from the remainder of the Russian Federation by Belarus and Lithuania. Russian premier Kasyanov attempted to ensure that residents of the exclave would be exempted from visa requirements that were to be imposed by Lithuania and Poland prior to the two countries' accession to the EU (which took effect from 1 May 2004). In November 2002, at an EU-Russia summit meeting, held in Brussels, Russia finally agreed to an EU proposal for simplified visa arrangements. According to the compromise accord, multiple-transit travel documentation would be made available to residents of the exclave travelling by motor vehicle; the new regulations came into effect on 1 July 2003. In 2006 President Putin inaugurated a railway ferry service, initially servicing only cargo, connecting the exclave to metropolitan Russia.

Following the dissolution of the USSR, Russia maintained significant political and military influence in many former Soviet republics, especially in those areas involved in civil or ethnic conflicts. Russian troops were deployed in Tajikistan to support the Tajikistani Government against rebel forces during the civil war of 1992–97, and remained thereafter to ensure the security of the Tajikistani–Afghan border. In 2004 it was announced that Russian troops were to transfer responsibility for border security to the Tajikistani military; in October, meanwhile, it was announced that Russia had been formally granted a permanent military base in Tajikistan. In October 2003 a Russian military base commenced operations in Kyrgyzstan, the first to be established outside Russia subsequent to the dissolution of the USSR; the base was intended to meet the requirements of the Collective Security Treaty Organization (CSTO, see p. 438), inaugurated in April to succeed the CIS Collective Security Treaty. In November 2005 Putin and President Islam Karimov of Uzbekistan signed a defence pact, which provided for mutual support in the event that one of the countries came under attack; this measure followed the departure of US troops from a base in Uzbekistan, on the orders of Karimov, following US (and widespread international) criticism of the use of violence by Uzbekistani troops against demonstrators in the city of Andijon in May of that year (see the chapter on Uzbekistan). Russia, together with Belarus, Kazakhstan, Kyrgyzstan and Tajikistan, was a founding member of the Eurasian Economic Community (EURASEC, see p. 426), which was formally established in 2001. In October 2007 EURASEC leaders approved the legal basis for the establishment of a new customs union that was initially to comprise Belarus, Kazakhstan and Russia, with Kyrgyzstan, Tajikistan and Uzbekistan expected to join by 2011.

Considerable controversy arose from the 1990s because of the Russian Government's provision of support for separatist factions in Moldova and Georgia. In 1999 it was announced that all Russian troops in the separatist Transnistria region of Moldova were to be withdrawn by the end of 2002; however, this was subsequently postponed, and in February 2004 the Russian Minister of Defence, Sergei Ivanov, indicated that Russia intended to maintain a military presence in the region. Meanwhile, in December 1998 Russia and Georgia signed an agreement that provided for the incremented transfer of the control of their mutual frontiers, from Russian to Georgian guards. (Control of the frontier was, however, complicated by the existence of separatist and rebel-controlled regions on both sides of the border—Chechnya within Russia, and Abkhazia and South Ossetia within Georgia). In November 1999 it was agreed that two of the four Russian bases on Georgian territory would be closed by mid-2001. Russian troops had left the two bases in Georgia by November 2001. (An agreement signed between Russia and Georgia in March 2006 provided for a Russian withdrawal from the military base that it maintained at Akhalkalaki and headquarters at Tbilisi by the end of 2007, and from the second base at Batumi in 2008; in the event, the withdrawal of Russian forces from the military bases was completed in November 2007, earlier than scheduled.) In September 2002 the Russian authorities accused Georgia of permitting Chechen rebels to operate from bases within its territory, and declared that Russia reserved the right to instigate 'pre-emptive' military action, in self-defence, should the situation persist. However, in early October tensions abated somewhat, when Russia and Georgia agreed to commence joint patrols of their common border. Putin attended talks in Moscow with the newly inaugurated President of Georgia, Mikheil Saakashvili, in February 2004.

In October 2006 Russia temporarily withdrew its ambassador and closed all transport, postal and banking communications with Georgia, following the detention, in late September, of four Russian military officers in Georgia, on charges of espionage. In subsequent weeks large numbers of Georgian citizens residing illegally in Russia were deported. In August 2007 the Georgian authorities protested at an alleged incident, in which two military jets had entered Georgia's airspace from Russia and launched a missile on its territory, near South Ossetia. The Russian Government strongly denied the allegations; however, international experts subsequently confirmed that at least one aircraft had violated Georgian airspace from Russia. Shortly after the declaration of independence of Kosovo from Serbia in February 2008 (see below), prompting international concern regarding other secessionist regions, Russia stated that it upheld the territorial integrity of Georgia and Moldova. In April, however, a Russian presidential decree providing for increased co-operation in trade and culture with Abkhazia and South Ossetia, and protection to Russian citizens living in those regions, was strongly criticized by the international community. Also in April, following the resumption of direct air links with Georgia in March, the Russian authorities announced the restoration of postal services between the two countries and envisaged the removal of other sanctions. Tension between the two countries increased later in April, after a Georgian reconnaissance aeroplane was shot down over Abkhazia, allegedly by a Russian military aircraft; although Russia denied involvement in the incident, the Georgian Government condemned it as an act of aggression and announced that it was to demand an emergency meeting of the UN Security Council in response. Meanwhile, at a summit meeting of the North Atlantic Treaty Organization (NATO, see p. 351), which was convened in Bucharest, Romania, on 2 April, leaders indicated that Ukraine and Georgia would be offered Membership Action Plans in the future; Russia's permanent representative at NATO had criticized US support for the aspirations towards NATO accession of those countries.

On 8 August 2008, following an offensive by Georgia against the Russian-supported separatist region of South Ossetia (see the chapter on Georgia), Russia launched an intensive counter-attack, dispatching large numbers of troops through the Roki tunnel to South Ossetia, where they engaged in hostilities with Georgian forces at Tskhinvali; the Russian Government stated that it sought to protect its citizens and peace-keeping troops present in the region, and alleged that Georgia sought to commit 'genocide' against the South Ossetian population. (Many South Ossetians had been issued with Russian passports by the separatist authorities since the mid-2000s.) Russian aircraft commenced bombardment of Georgian targets beyond the separatist territory, including the port of Poti and the military base at

Senaki. Russian forces rapidly gained control of Tskhinvali, expelling the Georgian troops, and also advanced into the other separatist region of Abkhazia. On 12 August President Medvedev ordered an end to Russia's military operation in Georgia, claiming that its aims had been achieved. Georgia and Russia agreed to a peace plan, mediated by French President Nicolas Sarkozy (on behalf of the EU), providing for an immediate cease-fire, humanitarian assistance, and the withdrawal of Russian troops to pre-conflict positions. On 19 August, after Russia failed to implement fully the withdrawal of troops as stipulated, NATO foreign ministers decided to suspend meetings of the NATO-Russia Council until Russia was considered to have observed the terms of the peace plan. Two days later Russia announced its suspension of military co-operation with NATO. On 26 August President Medvedev endorsed a resolution, which had been approved in both chambers of the Russian legislature, officially recognizing South Ossetia and Abkhazia as independent, sovereign states. Georgia, the USA and the EU condemned the decision. (Nicaragua was the only other country to have recognized the two regions as independent states.) On 29 August Georgia formally suspended diplomatic relations with Russia, in protest at the continued Russian occupation of South Ossetia and Abkhazia, and at security zones around the two regions. In early September, following further negotiations with an EU delegation led by President Sarkozy in Moscow, Russia agreed on additional measures for the implementation of the August cease-fire plan, principally the withdrawal of all remaining forces from Georgian territory (apart from South Ossetia and Abkhazia) within 10 days of the deployment of EU monitors (scheduled for 1 October). On 17 September Russia signed friendship and co-operation treaties with the leaders of South Ossetia and Abkhazia, pledging to support the two regions militarily; the treaties also formalized economic co-operation between Russia and the regions. EU monitors were deployed in Georgia, and the withdrawal of the remaining Russian troops from areas adjacent to South Ossetia and Abkhazia was verified by 10 October, as scheduled. However, the Georgian Government claimed that Russia continued to be in violation of the cease-fire agreement until it reduced the number of troops it deployed within South Ossetia and Abkhazia to pre-conflict levels and also withdrew from areas previously held by Georgian forces. (Russia had confirmed its intention to maintain a total of at least 7,600 troops within the two separatist regions, and to establish military bases there.) Direct negotiations between Russia and Georgia, convened in Geneva, Switzerland, in mid-October under the aegis of the UN, the EU and the OSCE, were abandoned, after the Georgian delegation rejected Russia's demand that the representatives of South Ossetia and Abkhazia be allowed to participate. In November discussions between Russian, US and Georgian representatives, which were also attended by South Ossetian and Abkhazian officials, were reconvened in Geneva, again under the aegis of the UN, the EU and the OSCE.

On 5 March 2009 NATO decided to restore diplomatic relations with Russia, despite Russia's unchanged policy regarding South Ossetia and Abkhazia. On 29 April Medvedev signed agreements with the leaders of the separatist authorities of South Ossetia and Abkhazia, under which Russia was to assist in securing and patrolling the borders of the two regions with Georgia for an initial period of five years, pending the establishment of their own border services. (The deployment of Russian guards in the border region of South Ossetia began immediately.) A co-operation agreement between the FSB, the State Security Committee of South Ossetia and the State Security Service of Abkhazia was also signed. The Russian Government accused Georgia of intensifying the military and security presence at the border with the separatist regions, and also strongly denounced NATO plans to conduct military exercises in Georgia in the following week. The Parliamentary Assembly of the Council of Europe adopted a resolution urging the Russian and South Ossetian authorities to allow the return of displaced civilians to the territory in accordance with international law. Also on 29 April NATO resumed formal discussions with Russia at ambassadorial level (prior to meetings of the NATO-Russia Council planned for May); however, later that day NATO ordered the expulsion of two Russian diplomats (one of whom was the son of Russia's ambassador to the EU) attached to the Russian mission at NATO headquarters on suspicion of espionage. NATO's action followed the imprisonment in February of the head of the security department at the Estonian Ministry of Defence during 2000–06, Herman Simm, who had been convicted of having passed classified Estonian, and later NATO, military documents to the Russian Foreign Intelligence Service over a period of more than 10 years. The Russian Government refuted the accusations of espionage against the two diplomats, and protested vehemently at their expulsion; Lavrov subsequently announced that he would not attend a planned ministerial meeting of the NATO-Russia Council. (Russia had previously announced its withdrawal from a NATO-Russia Council meeting of chiefs of staff, in protest at the forthcoming military manoeuvres in Georgia.) In early May NATO expelled two Canadian diplomats based at NATO's office in Moscow, reportedly over allegations of espionage. NATO strongly criticized the agreements signed by Russia with South Ossetia and Abkhazia as being in contravention of the Russian Government's commitments under the EU-mediated peace agreements. On 5 May, after an uprising in Georgia by disaffected military officials was suppressed, the Georgian Government accused Russia of orchestrating a coup attempt to overthrow President Saakashvili. On the following day NATO commenced military exercises in Georgia, involving more than 1,000 troops.

After December 1991 the Russian Federation was recognized as the successor to the USSR. It was granted the USSR's permanent seat on the UN Security Council and, additionally, was to be responsible for the receipt and destruction of all nuclear weapons of the former USSR located in other newly independent republics (Belarus, Kazakhstan and Ukraine), a process that was successfully completed by the mid-1990s. In January 1993 Russia and the USA signed the second Strategic Arms Reduction Treaty (START II), which envisaged a reduction in the strategic nuclear weapons of both powers. The Russian legislature ratified START II in April 2000. Following the first meeting of President Putin and President George W. Bush of the USA, in Ljubljana, Slovenia, in June 2001, relations appeared to improve markedly. Putin assumed a notably measured approach towards the proposed abrogation by the USA of the Anti-Ballistic Missile (ABM) treaty (signed with the USSR in 1972), which formed a principal part of the Bush Administration's foreign defence policy.

Russia offered assistance and gave support to the USA in its attempts to form a global coalition against militant Islamist terrorism, after the suicide air attacks against the USA of 11 September 2001 (see the chapter on the USA). Although Russia refused to commit troops to participate in the military campaign against targets of the Taliban regime in Afghanistan, which commenced in October, it provided military intelligence, and allowed access to its airspace. Russia also increased logistical and military support to the anti-Taliban forces of the United Islamic Front for the Salvation of Afghanistan.

In mid-November 2001, at a meeting in Texas, USA, Bush and Putin announced that significant reductions would be made to their countries' nuclear arsenals over the following decade; Putin did not specify how many weapons would be destroyed, and emphasized his desire to formalize the agreement by means of a treaty, together with clear verification procedures, in contrast to the more informal measures envisaged by Bush. In mid-December, following the USA's announcement that it was to withdraw unilaterally from the ABM treaty, with effect from June 2002, Putin reiterated earlier claims that, while he did not support the abrogation of the treaty, its abandonment did not pose a security threat to Russia. In mid-May 2002 Russia and the USA announced that agreement had been reached on the reduction of their nuclear arsenals by approximately two-thirds, and a nuclear accord and a declaration on strategic partnership were duly signed by Presidents Putin and Bush on 24 May. The USA withdrew from the ABM treaty on 13 June, and the following day Russia withdrew from START II, which had been superseded by the treaty signed with the USA in the previous month.

The Russian Government consistently condemned intermittent US-led missile attacks on Iraq during the 1990s and early 2000s; additionally, in 1996, in contravention of a UN embargo, Russia concluded an agreement with Iraq on the development of oilfields in that country. In late 1997, following Iraq's refusal to permit weapons inspectors of the UN Special Commission (UNSCOM) access to contentious sites, the Russian Government intervened in an attempt to avert a renewal of hostilities, and the conclusion of an agreement between the UN and Iraq in late February 1998 was regarded by Russia as a significant diplomatic success. Russia resumed scheduled flights to Iraq in late 2000, in contravention of UN sanctions. In mid-2001 Russia, which supported Iraq in its demands that the sanctions regime in force since 1990 should be revoked, effectively obstructed a British-drafted proposal before the Security Council for the introduction of a new, US-advocated, programme of 'smart' sanctions. As the US Administration of George W. Bush, from the second half of 2002, utilized increasingly bellicose rhetoric against Iraq, Russia urged the USA to avoid the use of unilateral force, and encouraged Iraq's compliance with UN demands regarding weapons inspections, so as to facilitate the lifting of sanctions. Although Russia voted to support UN Security Council Resolution 1441, approved in November 2002, which provided for the expedited return of weapons inspectors to Iraq under the auspices of the UN Monitoring, Verification and Inspection Commission (UNMOVIC), it was a leading opponent of attempts, led by the USA and the United Kingdom in February–March 2003, to approve a further Security Council resolution explicitly to endorse military action in Iraq, and President Putin described the conflict, which commenced in mid-March, as a 'political mistake'. Although senior members of the US Government criticized various aspects of Russian policy (including, notably, progress towards establishing democratic governance and the rule of law in Russia) during 2003, Putin, in particular, emphasized the importance of maintaining co-operative relations with the USA. Observers speculated that Russia's commitment to renew exports of nuclear fuel to Iran in early 2005 (see below), and seeming pursuit of closer ties with Syria (with reports in 2005 suggesting that Russia was to sell missiles to Syria), could be harmful to relations with the USA, the foreign policy of which was notably hostile towards those countries.

In early 2007 the Russian Government declared emphatically its opposition to the establishment of a radar installation in the Czech Republic and missile interceptors in Poland by 2011–12 as part of the USA's proposed National Missile Defence programme, despite repeated US assurances that the plan was not intended to threaten Russian interests. Russia warned that it would take retaliatory measures against the US programme, including withdrawal from the Conventional Forces in Europe (CFE) Treaty, prompting the Czech and Polish Governments to demand security and legal guarantees from the USA and further exacerbating strained relations with the West. At a conference on security policy, held in Munich, Germany, in February 2007, President Putin strongly criticized the US Administration for its stance on defence, which he described as being against the fundamental principles of international law. Legislation providing for Russia's suspension of the CFE Treaty was formally adopted by both parliamentary chambers in November, and, after its endorsement by Putin, entered into effect in December. At the NATO summit meeting in April 2008 (see above), member states endorsed US plans to position missile defence bases in the Czech Republic and Poland (a previous suggestion by Putin that bases in Azerbaijan be used having been rejected by the USA). A formal treaty signed between Poland and the USA in August, providing for the installation of 10 US anti-missile interceptors, and guaranteeing the permanent stationing of missiles on Polish territory, prompted strenuous protests by the Russian Government. (A provisional accord providing for the installation of a US anti-missile radar system in the Czech Republic had also been signed in July.) However, following the election of US President Barack Obama in November, the new US Administration indicated in early 2009 that it would review security policy, including the planned missile defence system. In January 2009 the Russian authorities announced that plans to deploy missiles in Kaliningrad (bordering Poland), in response to the US deployment in Poland and the Czech Republic, had been suspended. Lavrov and US Secretary of State Hillary Clinton, meeting in Geneva, Switzerland, in early March, affirmed commitment to the revision of US-Russian relations. Lavrov declared the adoption of a successor agreement to the START I nuclear treaty (which had been signed in 1991 and was due to expire at the end of 2009) to be a priority, and urged the US Administration to consider Russian concerns in the review of its planned missile defence system. Medvedev and Obama met for the first time at a summit of the heads of state and of government of the Group of 20 (G20) leading economies, which took place in London, United Kingdom, on 2 April. Lavrov was to visit Washington, DC, in early May for the initiation of US-Russian consultations on a new treaty, prior to a bilateral summit meeting, to be attended by Medvedev and Obama, which was scheduled for July.

In June 1994 Russia joined NATO's 'Partnership for Peace' (see p. 353) programme of military co-operation with former Eastern bloc states. A 'Founding Act on Mutual Relations, Co-operation and Security between NATO and the Russian Federation' was signed in May 1997. The Act provided for enhanced Russian participation in all NATO decision-making activities, equal status in peace-keeping operations and representation at the Alliance headquarters at ambassadorial level. A NATO-Russian Permanent Joint Council was established. Russia's relations with NATO became increasingly strained in 1999, in particular after the situation in the province of Kosovo, in the Republic of Serbia, then Yugoslavia, precipitated the aerial bombardment of Yugoslav targets by NATO forces in late March (see chapter on Serbia). Russia condemned the air offensive, and suspended its relations with the Alliance. Following the capitulation of Yugoslav forces in mid-June, and their withdrawal from Kosovo, Russian troops were the first to enter the province, before NATO forces. Contacts were resumed between Russia and NATO in February 2000. In July 2001 Putin called for a pan-European security pact to be established in place of NATO, to incorporate Russia. On 28 May 2002 Putin and the heads of state and of government of the 19 NATO member states, meeting in Italy, signed the Rome Declaration, inaugurating a new NATO-Russia Council to replace the Permanent Joint Council. The new Council would enable Russia to enter into negotiations with its members on a range of issues, including terrorism, non-proliferation, defence and peace-keeping. Although Russia had expressed concern at the expansion of NATO to include seven eastern European countries, including the three Baltic states, from early 2004, Putin emphasized that the expansion would not have negative consequences for the Alliance's relations with Russia. The Russian Government expressed support for Serbia in opposing a proposal, presented to the UN Security Council by UN special envoy Martii Ahtisaari at the end of March 2007, to grant internationally supervised independence to Kosovo. In July UN Security Council draft resolutions on the future status of Kosovo were abandoned, owing to Russia's insistence that it would veto any resolution that was not acceptable to the Serbian Government. A further series of negotiations between Serbian and Kosovo delegations, beginning in August, were mediated by US, EU and Russian envoys, but again ended in failure. Following Kosovo's unilateral declaration of independence on 17 February 2008, Russia, in continued strong support of Serbia, opposed Kosovo's sovereignty among the permanent members of the Council, and subsequently obstructed the deployment of an EU mission (see the chapter on Kosovo). Meanwhile, in late January relations between Russia and Serbia were consolidated with the signature of an agreement whereby Serbia was to join Russia's 'South Stream' pipeline project (see below), and Gazprom acquired a 51% share in the Serbian state-owned petroleum enterprise, Naftna Industrija Srbije. (The sale of the majority share in Naftna Industrija Srbije was completed in February 2009; contractual agreements on the 'South Stream' project were signed with Italy, Bulgaria, Serbia and Greece in Sochi on 15 May.)

In January 1996 Russia was admitted as a member of the Council of Europe. As a condition of membership, Russia was to abolish the death penalty by the end of February 1999. However, the Duma has yet to approve its abolition, although capital punishment has been subject to a moratorium since Russia's admission to the organization. Russia's voting rights were suspended between April 2000 and January 2001, as a result of allegations of human rights abuses committed during Russia's renewed military campaign in Chechnya. In April 2003 the Parliamentary Assembly of the Council of Europe voted, by a large majority, in favour of the establishment of an international tribunal to try those suspected of war crimes in the republic. In February 2005 the European Court of Human Rights, a subsidiary institution of the Council of Europe, in ruling on cases brought by six Chechen citizens, concluded that serious human rights abuses had been committed by the Russian military in Chechnya and ordered the Russian Government to pay compensation to the victims' relatives. In 2006 Russia became the rotating chairman of the Group of Eight leading industrialized nations (G8), to which it had been admitted in 2000.

In November 2004, following approval by both chambers of the legislature, President Putin signed a bill ratifying the Kyoto Protocol to the United Nations Framework Convention on Climate Change, thereby bringing the Protocol into force for its signatories. Observers suggested that the decision to approve the protocol may have been motivated by the Russian Government's ongoing pursuit of membership of the World Trade Organization (WTO, see p. 410). In May 2007, following a deterioration in relations with Estonia (see above), the EU announced that it would not support Russia's application to join the WTO unless the Government demonstrated commitment to resolving political issues.

Russia's relations with Iran in the late 1990s and early 2000s were a cause of concern for the USA. In mid-1997 Iran and Russia held discussions on nuclear co-operation, primarily focusing on the development of a nuclear power plant in Bushehr, Iran. In December 2000 Igor Sergeyev, the Russian Minister of Defence, paid the first official visit to Iran by a Russian official since the Islamic Revolution in that country of 1979, with a view to increasing military and technical co-operation. In March 2001, during a visit to Moscow by the Iranian President, Muhammad Khatami, Russia agreed to resume the sale of conventional weapons to Iran and to assist with the construction of the Bushehr power plant; an agreement for arms sales worth some US $300m., the first such agreement between the two countries since 1995, was signed in October. Although in December 2002 it was announced that Russia was to increase its nuclear co-operation with Iran, the Russian Minister of Foreign Affairs, Igor Ivanov, reiterated that this co-operation was of a civilian nature and that Russia remained opposed to Iran's potential development of nuclear weapons. In mid-2003 Russia announced that it was to suspend exports of nuclear fuel to Iran; however, in February 2005 a new agreement was reached between the two countries on the provision of nuclear fuel (which would, however, be returned to Russia, once it was spent). In February 2006 Russia was one of 27 countries represented on the 35-member Board of Governors of the International Atomic Energy Agency (IAEA) to vote in favour of Iran's referral to the UN Security Council, after it was discovered not to have complied with the conditions of an agreement reached with the IAEA; none the less, Russia remained opposed to the use of military force against Iran to bring it into compliance. In October 2007 Putin visited the Iranian capital, Tehran, to attend a summit meeting of the five Caspian state leaders. The declaration adopted by the parties at the end of the summit postponed settlement of territorial issues, but asserted that each country would not allow its territory to be used by other states for the purposes of a military attack against another state.

Relations with Japan were complicated by a continuing dispute over the status of the Kurile Islands (in Sakhalin Oblast, and known in Japan as the Northern Territories), which became part of the USSR at the end of the Second World War; Japan maintained its long-standing demand that four of the islands be returned to Japanese sovereignty. Discussions on the territorial dispute between the leaderships of Russia and Japan were ongoing from the late 1990s, but resulted in little progress. Despite Russian President Vladimir Putin's repudiation of Japan's claim to any of the islands during his first official visit to Tokyo in September 2000, Russia subsequently offered to abide by a 1956 declaration that it would relinquish two of the islands after the signature of a peace treaty, but Japan rejected this partial solution. In August 2006 Russian security troops killed one Japanese fisherman and detained three others who had allegedly been fishing illegally in Russian waters; the captain of the Japanese vessel subsequently received a fine for intrusion into Russian waters and poaching. The revocation, in the following month, of an environmental permit associated with the Sakhalin-2 natural gas project, and the subsequent enforced reduction of the share held in the project by Japanese companies (see Economy Affairs), was a further cause of heightened tensions between Russia and Japan. In April 2008, during an official visit by Japanese Prime Minister Yasuo Fukuda to Russia, he and President Putin agreed that further discussions would be conducted, in an effort to resolve the territorial dispute; pledges for increased bilateral co-operation were also made.

Relations with the People's Republic of China improved significantly during the 1990s. In 1999 several agreements on bilateral economic and trade co-operation, and a final accord on the demarcation of a common border between the two countries, were signed. Meanwhile, negotiations in the mid-1990s that initially focused on defining the mutual borders of China, Kazakhstan, Kyrgyzstan, Russia and Tajikistan appeared to be instrumental in bringing about closer co-operation between these countries, which in 1996 formed the so-called Shanghai Five group. The group subsequently broadened its areas of activity to include trade, cultural, military and security co-operation; in June 2001 Uzbekistan joined the grouping, which was renamed the Shanghai Co-operation Organization (see p. 440). In September 2003 the Organization announced its intention to establish a joint anti-terrorism centre, to be located in Tashkent, Uzbekistan, and a secretariat, in the Chinese capital, Beijing. Kasyanov visited Beijing in August 2002, to discuss strategic issues, and Putin visited China in December, when he met President Jiang Zemin and his appointed successor, Hu Jintao. The two countries issued a joint declaration on a number of global strategic issues, particularly urging a peaceful resolution to the USA's diplomatic crisis with Iraq. Russia also participated in multilateral negotiations in China in mid-2003, attended by representatives of the Governments of China, the Democratic People's Republic of Korea (DPRK—North Korea), Japan, the Republic of Korea (South Korea) and the USA, which were intended to encourage the DPRK to abandon its nuclear weapons programme. In October 2004 a treaty was signed by Presidents Putin and Hu settling a long-running dispute over the course of the border between the two states. In 2005 Russia and China conducted joint military manoeuvres for the first time. In March 2009 the Russian Ministry of Defence announced that further joint military exercises were to be conducted in north-eastern China later that year.

Government

Under the Constitution of December 1993, the Russian Federation is a democratic, federative, multi-ethnic republic, in which state power is divided between the legislature, executive and judiciary, which are independent of one another. The President of the Russian Federation is Head of State and Commander-in-Chief of the Armed Forces, and also holds broad executive powers. The President, who is elected for a term of six years, renewable once, by universal direct suffrage, appoints the Chairman of the Government (Prime Minister). Supreme legislative power is vested in the bicameral Federalnoye Sobraniye (Federal Assembly). The upper chamber is the Sovet Federatsii (Federation Council), which comprises two representatives from each of the country's federal territorial units (appointed by the legislature and the executive in each region); its lower chamber is the 450-member Gosudarstvennaya Duma (State Duma), which is elected by direct universal suffrage for a period of five years.

For much of the 1990s and the first half of the 2000s the Russian Federation comprised 89 federal territorial units (federal subjects). From the mid-2000s a number of territorial mergers took place, comprising the absorption of nominally Autonomous Okrugs into the territories of which they had hitherto formed part, while remaining as federal subjects in their own right. By March 2008 the number of territorial subjects had been reduced to 83, comprising 21 republics, nine krais (provinces), 46 oblasts (regions), two cities of federal status, one autonomous oblast and four autonomous okrugs (districts). The republics and the autonomous oblast and okrugs are nominally representative of ethnic groups, and the administrative oblasts and krais of geographic regions. In May 2000 the federal subjects were grouped into seven federal okrugs, each headed by a presidential appointee. In December 2004 the federal legislature approved proposals, initially presented by President Putin, in accordance with which governors of all federal subjects were henceforth to be appointed by the federal authorities, subject to approval by regional legislatures.

Defence

In May 1992 the Russian Federation established its own armed forces, on the basis of former Soviet forces on the territory of the Russian Federation, and former Soviet forces outside its territory not subordinate to other former republics of the USSR. As assessed at November 2008, the total Russian active armed forces numbered an estimated 1,027,000, with an estimated 20,000,000 reserves. These included an estimated 80,000 permanent members of the Strategic Deterrent Forces, an estimated 395,000 in the army (including some 190,000 conscripts), 142,000 in the navy, and an estimated 160,000 in the air force, following its merger with the air defence troops. There were a further estimated 449,000 paramilitary troops. A presidential decree in March 2007 reduced the length of compulsory military service (for males over the age of 18 years) from two years to one, with effect from January 2008. The defence budget for 2008 allocated 956,000m. roubles to defence.

Economic Affairs

In 2007, according to estimates by the World Bank, Russia's gross national income (GNI), measured at average 2005–07 prices, was US $1,070,999m., equivalent to $7,560 per head (or $14,400 per head on an international purchasing-power parity basis). In 2000–07, it was estimated, the population declined by an annual average of 0.5%, while gross domestic product (GDP) per head increased, in real terms, at an average annual rate of 6.6%. According to the World Bank, overall GDP increased, in real terms, at an average annual rate of 4.9% in

1996–2006. Real GDP increased by 7.4% in 2006 and by 8.1% in 2007.

Agriculture (including forestry and fishing) contributed 4.9% of GDP in 2008. In 2006, according to the ILO, 10.0% of the employed labour force were engaged in the agricultural sector. The principal agricultural products are grain, potatoes and livestock. In 1990 the Russian Government began a programme to encourage the development of private farming, to replace the state and collective farms. Legislation to permit the sale and purchase of agricultural land from 2003 was approved by the Gosudarstvennaya Duma in June 2002. According to World Bank estimates, real agricultural GDP increased at an average annual rate of 4.3% in 2000–07; the GDP of the sector increased by 3.6% in 2006 and by 3.1% in 2007.

Industry contributed 36.1% of GDP in 2008. In 2006 the industrial sector (including mining, manufacturing, construction and utilities) provided 29.3% of employment. According to estimates by the World Bank, industrial GDP increased, in real terms, by an annual average of 5.7% in 2000–07. Industrial GDP increased by 3.9% in 2006 and by 6.5% in 2007.

Mining and quarrying contributed 9.2% of GDP in 2008 and employed 1.7% of the employed labour force in 2006. Russia has considerable reserves of energy-bearing minerals, including one-third of the world's natural gas reserves and substantial deposits of petroleum, coal and peat. It also has large supplies of palladium, platinum and rhodium. Other minerals exploited include bauxite, cobalt, copper, diamonds, gold, iron ore, mica, nickel and tin.

The manufacturing sector contributed 17.5% of GDP in 2008, and the sector provided 18.1% of employment in 2006.

Electric energy is derived from petroleum-, gas- and coal-fired power stations, nuclear power stations and hydroelectric installations. In 2005 nuclear reactors supplied some 15.7% of total electricity generation, while coal accounted for some 17.4% of Russia's generating capacity; hydroelectric power accounted for 18.2% of electricity production, and 46.2% of the country's generating capacity originated from natural gas. Russia is a major exporter of natural gas and crude petroleum, and Russia's largest company, Gazprom, is also the world's largest producer of natural gas. Countries of the CIS remain highly dependent on Russia for imports of these fuels. From the late 1990s Russia sought to increase its exports of mineral fuels to other countries, particularly in central and western Europe. The construction of the 'Blue Stream' pipeline, which was to carry natural gas from Novorossiisk, Krasnodar Krai, in southern Russia, to Ankara, Turkey, was completed in October 2002, and was expected to facilitate further growth in Russia's energy exports (see below). In early 2005 it was announced that a pipeline would be constructed from eastern Siberia to the port of Nakhodka on the Pacific Coast, enabling exports to Japan and the wider Pacific region; this route was chosen in favour of a long-discussed alternative route to the People's Republic of China (see above). In November 2007 Gazprom and Italian energy company Eni signed an agreement creating the 'South Stream' joint venture for the construction of a pipeline to transport Russian natural gas to Italy; Bulgaria, Hungary, Serbia and Greece subsequently agreed to participate in the project. Following the successful completion of feasibility studies, contractual procedure relating to the 'South Stream' project was concluded on 15 May 2009. Work on the pipeline was scheduled to be completed by 2015. Imports of fuel comprised just 2.4% of the value of Russia's total merchandise imports in 2007.

The services sector contributed 59.0% of GDP in 2008, and provided 60.7% of employment in 2006. According to estimates by the World Bank, the GDP of the services sector increased, in real terms, at an average annual rate of 7.1% in 2000–07. The GDP of the sector increased by 9.8% in 2006 and 9.1% in 2007.

In 2007 Russia recorded a visible trade surplus of US $130,915m., and there was a surplus of $76,241m. on the current account of the balance of payments. In 2007 the most significant source of imports was Germany (accounting for 13.3% of the total), followed by the People's Republic of China (12.2%), Ukraine and Japan. The largest market for Russian exports in 2007 was the Netherlands (accounting for 12.1% of total exports), followed by Italy, Germany and Turkey. The principal exports in 2007 were mineral fuels (accounting for 64.7% of total exports), followed by metals, precious stones, and articles thereof (16.1%), chemical products and rubber and machinery, vehicles and transport equipment (5.8%). The principal imports in that year were machinery and transport equipment (accounting for 51.1% of total imports), followed by foodstuffs and agricultural raw materials, excluding textiles (13.8%), chemical products and rubber (13.8%), and metals, precious stones, and articles thereof.

In 2005 Russia recorded a surplus on the federal budget of 278,111.8m. roubles, equivalent to 1.3% of GDP. At the end of 2006 the country's total external debt was US $251,067m., of which $50,254m. was long-term public debt. In that year the cost of debt-servicing was equivalent to 13.8% of the value of exports of goods and services. In 1995–2005 the average annual rate of inflation was 25.5%. Following the collapse of the rouble in 1998, the rate of inflation was 85.7% in 1999, but it declined thereafter. The rate of inflation was 11.9% in 2007 and 13.3% in 2008. In November 2007 some 4.2m. people (5.6% of the labour force) were unemployed.

Russia became a member of the World Bank and the IMF in 1992. Russia is also a member (as a 'Country of Operations') of the European Bank for Reconstruction and Development (EBRD, see p. 251). In 1994 Russia signed an agreement of partnership and co-operation with the EU. Russia is also pursuing membership of the World Trade Organization (WTO, see p. 410). Russia joined the Asia-Pacific Economic Co-operation forum (APEC, see p. 185) in 1998.

After the dissolution of the USSR, a programme of economic reforms was initiated to effect the transition to a market-orientated system. Following a financial crisis in mid-1998, Russia recorded sustained growth, largely attributable to high international prices for petroleum, natural gas and metals, Russia's principal exports. The dismantling, in late 2004, of the privately owned petroleum company Yukos, and the effective renationalization of its most productive subsidiary, Yugansknefregaz, through its effective acquisition by the state-owned petroleum company Rosneft (see Recent History), and the approval in 2005 of legislation that limited the degree of involvement permitted to foreign companies in the exploitation of natural resources in certain designated regions and projects, demonstrated a reverse from the free market principles and raised concerns that Russia was becoming less hospitable to foreign investors. Meanwhile, Russia has moved to expand its network of international pipelines to East Asia and Eastern, Northern and Southern Europe. Concerns persisted that the successes of the fossil fuel sector were obscuring the relative lack of progress in the wider economy. This view was compounded when prices for crude oil began to fall sharply amid the US banking crisis in September 2008, while the situation was exacerbated by a sharp downturn (equivalent to around three-quarters of their total value) in the value of equities traded on the principal index of the RTS Stock Exchange in Moscow during mid-2008, although there had been a partial recovery by mid-2009. The federal budget, which had, hitherto, benefited from the revenues generated from oil prices, was projected to realise substantial deficits during 2008–10, as a result of the deterioration of this income source. Industrial output declined sharply in late 2008, while unemployment rose every month following September, to reach 10% in March 2009. In April 2009 a fiscal stimulus, worth around US $50,000m., was announced by the presidential administration; which reduced taxation on income and consumption and increased welfare provisions to poor households. In the same month, the authorities revealed that external financing would be sought to help fund the budget deficit, which was projected to reach 8.0% of GDP in 2009. (International reserves, which had previously bridged shortfalls in fiscal revenue, were depleted by around 40% between November 2008 and January 2009, owing largely to exchange rate interventions managed by the central bank.) Real GDP was forecast to decline by 6% in 2009, according to IMF estimates.

Education

Education is compulsory for nine years, to be undertaken between the ages of six and 15 years. State education is generally provided free of charge, although in 1992 some higher education establishments began charging tuition fees. Students of selected courses in higher education receive a small stipend from the state. Primary education usually begins at six years of age and lasts for four years. Secondary education lasts for seven years, comprising a first cycle of five years and a second of two years. In 2006 enrolment at primary schools included 91% of pupils in the relevant age-group. Secondary enrolment in that year was equivalent to 84% of children in the appropriate age-group. In 2007/08 7.5m. students were enrolled at institutes of higher education. Budgetary expenditure on education (excluding scientific research and technology) in 2005 was an estimated 155,338.0m. roubles (representing 5.1% of total federal government expenditure).

THE RUSSIAN FEDERATION

All educational institutions were state-owned under Soviet rule, but a wide range of independent schools and colleges commenced operations in the early 1990s. In 2007/08 there were 697 independent primary and general secondary schools, 233 independent vocational secondary schools and 450 independent higher education institutions. Although Russian is the principal language used in educational establishments, a number of local languages are also in use.

Public Holidays

2009: 1–6 January (New Year), 7–8 January (Orthodox Christmas), 23 February (Defenders of the Fatherland Day), 9 March (for International Women's Day), 1 May (Spring Holiday and Labour Day), 8 May (for Victory Day), 12 June (Russia Day), 4 November (National Unity Day).

2010: 1–6 January (New Year), 7–8 January (Orthodox Christmas), 23 February (Defenders of the Fatherland Day), 8 March (International Women's Day), 3 May (for Spring Holiday and Labour Day), 9 May (Victory Day), 11 June (Russia Day), 4 November (National Unity Day).

Weights and Measures

The metric system is in force.

Statistical Survey

Source (unless otherwise indicated): Federal Service of State Statistics 103450 Moscow, ul. Myasnitskaya 39; tel. (495) 207-49-02; fax (495) 207-40-87; e-mail stat@gks.ru; internet www.gks.ru.

Area and Population

AREA, POPULATION AND DENSITY

Area (sq km)	17,075,400*
Population (census results)	
12 January 1989	147,021,869
9–16 October 2002	
Males	67,605,133
Females	77,561,598
Total	145,166,731
Population (official estimates at 1 January)	
2007	142,220,968
2008	142,008,838
2009	141,903,979
Density (per sq km) at 1 January 2009	8.3

*6,592,850 sq miles.

POPULATION BY ETHNIC GROUP
(census of 9–16 October 2002)

	'000	%
Russian[1]	115,889.1	79.83
Tatar[2]	5,554.6	3.83
Ukrainian	2,943.0	2.03
Bashkir	1,673.4	1.15
Chuvash	1,637.1	1.13
Chechen[3]	1,360.2	0.94
Armenian	1,130.5	0.78
Mordovian[4]	843.4	0.58
Avar[5]	814.5	0.56
Belarusian	808.0	0.56
—continued	'000	%
Kazakh	654.0	0.45
Udmurt	636.9	0.44
Azeri	621.8	0.43
Mari[6]	604.3	0.42
German	597.2	0.41
Kabardin	520.1	0.36
Osetiyan[7]	514.9	0.35
Dargin[8]	510.2	0.35
Others[9]	7,853.5	5.41
Total	**145,166.7**	**100.00**

[1] Including Cossacks (140,028) and Pomors (6,571).
[2] Including Astrakhan Tatars (2,003), Kryashens (Christian Tatars, 24,668) and Siberian Tatars (9,611), but excluding Crimean Tatars (4,131).
[3] Including Chechen-akkintsy (218).
[4] Including Erzya-Mordovians (84,407) and Moksha-Mordovians (49,624).
[5] Including Akhvakhtsy (6,376), Andiitsy (21,808), Archintsy (89), Bagulaly (40), Bezhtintsy (6,198), Botlikhtsy (16), Chamalaly (12), Didoitsy (15,256), Ginukhtsy (531), Godoberintsy (39), Gunzibtsy (998), Karatintsy (6,052), Khvarshiny (128) and Tindaly (44).
[6] Including Lugovo-Vostochnye Mari (56,119) and Mountain Mari (18,515).
[7] Including Digor-Osetiyans (607) and Irontsy-Osetiyans (97).
[8] Including Kaitagtsy (5) and Kubachintsy (88).
[9] Including 1,460,751 respondents (1.01% of the total) who did not state their nationality or ethnic group.

ADMINISTRATIVE DIVISIONS
(1 January 2009, official estimates, except where otherwise stated)

Federal territory	Area ('000 sq km)	Population	Density (per sq km)	Capital (with population, '000)[1]
Central Federal Okrug	650.7	37,121,812	57.0	Moscow
Moscow City	1.0	10,508,971	10,509.0	Moscow (10,442.7)
Belgorod Oblast	27.1	1,525,083	56.3	Belgorod (348.2)
Bryansk Oblast	34.9	1,299,690	37.2	Bryansk (416.2)
Ivanovo Oblast	21.8	1,073,071	49.2	Ivanovo (409.0)
Kaluga Oblast	29.9	1,002,859	33.5	Kaluga (327.5)
Kostroma Oblast	60.1	692,315	11.5	Kostroma (273.4)
Kursk Oblast	29.8	1,155,417	38.8	Kursk (405.9)
Lipetsk Oblast	24.1	1,163,348	48.3	Lipetsk (502.6)
Moscow Oblast	46.0	6,712,582	145.9	Moscow[2]
Orel Oblast	24.7	816,895	33.1	Orel (323.0)
Ryazan Oblast	39.6	1,157,740	29.2	Ryazan (512.2)
Smolensk Oblast	49.8	974,139	19.6	Smolensk (317.7)
Tambov Oblast	34.3	1,096,879	32.0	Tambov (281.8)
Tula Oblast	25.7	1,553,145	60.4	Tula (504.0)
Tver Oblast	84.1	1,369,413	16.3	Tver (405.5)
Vladimir Oblast	29.0	1,439,761	49.6	Vladimir (339.8)
Voronezh Oblast	52.4	2,270,031	43.3	Voronezh (840.7)
Yaroslavl Oblast	36.4	1,310,473	36.0	Yaroslavl (604.0)

THE RUSSIAN FEDERATION

Federal territory—continued	Area ('000 sq km)	Population	Density (per sq km)	Capital (with population, '000)[1]
North-Western Federal Okrug	1,677.9	13,462,259	8.0	St Petersburg
St Petersburg City	0.6	4,581,854	7,613.4	St Petersburg (4,571.2)
Republic of Kareliya	172.4	687,500	4.0	Petrozavodsk (266.3)
Republic of Komi	415.9	958,544	2.3	Syktyvkar (229.2)
Archangel Oblast	587.4	1,262,036	2.1	Archangel (348.6)
Nenets Autonomous Okrug	176.7	42,023	0.2	Naryn-Mar (19.2)
Kaliningrad Oblast	15.1	937,360	62.1	Kaliningrad (422.3)
Leningrad Oblast	85.3	1,631,894	19.1	St Petersburg[2]
Murmansk Oblast	144.9	842,452	5.8	Murmansk (317.5)
Novgorod Oblast	55.3	645,986	11.7	Velikii Novgorod (216.7)
Pskov Oblast	55.3	696,392	12.6	Pskov (194.9)
Vologda Oblast	145.7	1,218,241	8.4	Vologda (286.3)
Southern Federal Okrug	589.2	22,901,524	38.9	Rostov-on-Don
Republic of Adygeya	7.6	442,775	58.3	Maikop (156.7)
Chechen (Nokchi) Republic	19.5[3]	1,238,452	89.6[3]	Groznyi (222.0)
Republic of Dagestan	50.3	2,711,679	53.9	Makhachkala (466.9)
Republic of Ingushetiya	19.5[3]	508,090	89.6[3]	Magas (0.3)
Kabardino-Balkar Republic	12.5	892,389	71.4	Nalchik (270.4)
Republic of Kalmykiya	75.9	284,001	3.7	Elista (102.7)
Karachai-Cherkess Republic	14.1	427,194	30.3	Cherkessk (116.3)
Republic of North Osetiya—Alaniya	8.0	701,807	87.7	Vladikavkaz (313.8)
Krasnodar Krai	76.0	5,141,852	67.7	Krasnodar (709.0)
Stavropol Krai	66.5	2,707,290	40.7	Stavropol (359.7)
Astrakhan Oblast	44.1	1,005,241	22.8	Astrakhan (500.2)
Rostov Oblast	100.8	4,241,821	42.1	Rostov-on-Don (1,051.6)
Volgograd Oblast	113.9	2,598,933	22.8	Volgograd (986.3)
Volga Federal Okrug	1,038.0	30,157,844	29.1	Nizhnii Novgorod
Republic of Bashkortostan	143.6	4,057,292	28.3	Ufa (1,022.6)
Chuvash Republic	18.3	1,279,359	69.9	Cheboksary (441.3)
Republic of Marii-El	23.2	700,118	30.2	Yoshkar-Ola (249.8)
Republic of Mordoviya	26.2	833,031	31.8	Saransk (295.4)
Republic of Tatarstan	68.0	3,768,580	55.4	Kazan (1,116.0)
Udmurt Republic	42.1	1,528,488	36.3	Izhevsk (615.7)
Perm Krai	160.6	2,708,419	16.9	Perm (990.2)
Kirov Oblast	120.8	1,401,201	11.6	Kirov (466.3)
Nizhnii Novgorod Oblast	76.9	3,340,684	43.4	Nizhnii Novgorod (1,278.3)
Orenburg Oblast	124.0	2,111,531	17.0	Orenburg (529.6)
Penza Oblast	43.2	1,379,839	31.9	Penza (509.2)
Samara Oblast	53.6	3,171,446	59.2	Samara (1,139.0)
Saratov Oblast	100.2	2,572,866	25.7	Saratov (841.4)
Ulyanovsk Oblast	37.3	1,304,990	35.0	Ulyanovsk (611.7)
Urals Federal Okrug	1,788.9	12,254,976	6.9	Yekaterinburg
Chelyabinsk Oblast	87.9	3,508,733	39.9	Chelyabinsk (1,091.5)
Kurgan Oblast	71.0	952,673	13.4	Kurgan (326.4)
Sverdlovsk Oblast	194.8	4,394,649	22.6	Yekaterinburg (1,315.1)
Tyumen Oblast	1,435.2	3,398,921	2.4	Tyumen (549.9)
Khanty-Mansii Autonomous Okrug—Yugra	523.1	1,519,962	2.9	Khanty-Mansiisk (63.2)
Yamalo-Nenets Autonomous Okrug	750.3	543,651	0.7	Salekhard (40.3)
Siberian Federal Okrug	5,114.8	19,545,470	3.8	Novosibirsk
Altai Republic	92.6	209,207	2.3	Gorno-Altaisk (53.7)
Republic of Buryatiya	351.3	960,742	2.7	Ulan-Ude (343.0)
Republic of Khakasiya	61.9	538,054	8.7	Abakan (163.1)
Republic of Tyva	170.5	313,940	1.8	Kyzyl (108.3)
Altai Krai	169.1	2,496,776	14.8	Barnaul (600.1)
Krasnoyarsk Krai	2,339.7	2,889,785	1.2	Krasnoyarsk (927.2)
Transbaikal Krai	431.5	1,117,030	2.6	Chita (305.8)
Irkutsk Oblast	767.9	2,505,577	3.3	Irkutsk (575.9)
Kemerovo Oblast	95.5	2,821,859	29.5	Kemerovo (519.8)
Novosibirsk Oblast	178.2	2,639,857	14.8	Novosibirsk (1,391.4)
Omsk Oblast	139.7	2,014,135	14.4	Omsk (1,134.7)
Tomsk Oblast	316.9	1,038,508	3.3	Tomsk (493.0)

THE RUSSIAN FEDERATION

Statistical Survey

Federal territory—*continued*	Area ('000 sq km)	Population	Density (per sq km)	Capital (with population, '000)[1]
Far Eastern Federal Okrug	6,215.9	6,460,094	1.0	Khabarovsk
Republic of Sakha (Yakutiya)	3,103.2	949,753	0.3	Yakutsk (245.6)
Kamchatka Krai	472.3	343,539	0.7	Petropavlovsk-Kamchatskii (195.1)
Khabarovsk Krai	788.6	1,401,915	1.8	Khabarovsk (577.4)
Maritime (Primorskii) Krai	165.9	1,988,008	12.0	Vladivostok (580.8)
Amur Oblast	363.7	864,458	2.4	Blagoveshchensk (209.1)
Magadan Oblast	461.4	162,969	0.4	Magadan (100.2)
Sakhalin Oblast	87.1	514,520	5.9	Yuzhno-Sakhalinsk (173.2)
Jewish Autonomous Oblast	36.0	185,412	5.2	Birobidzhan (74.7)
Chukot Autonomous Okrug	737.7	49,520	0.1	Anadyr (11.5)
Russian Federation	17,075.4	141,903,979	8.3	Moscow

[1] Official estimates at 1 January 2007.
[2] Although Moscow and St Petersburg are the administrative centres of Moscow and Leningrad Oblasts, respectively, the cities themselves do not form part of the oblasts.
[3] Data on area and density for the Chechen (Nokchi) Republic and the Republic of Ingushetiya are duplicated and refer to the former Checheno-Ingush Autonomous Republic.

PRINCIPAL TOWNS
(1 January 2007, official estimates)

Town	Population	Town	Population
Moskva (Moscow, the capital)	10,442,700	Naberezhnye Chelnyi	506,400
Sankt-Peterburg (St Petersburg)	4,571,200	Tula	504,000
Novosibirsk	1,391,400	Lipetsk	502,600
Yekaterinburg	1,315,100	Astrakhan	500,200
Nizhnii Novgorod	1,278,300	Tomsk	493,000
Samara	1,139,000	Makhachkala	466,900
Omsk	1,134,700	Kirov	466,300
Kazan	1,116,000	Cheboksary	441,300
Chelyabinsk	1,091,500	Kaliningrad	422,300
Rostov-na-Donu (Rostov-on-Don)	1,051,600	Bryansk	416,200
Ufa	1,022,600	Magnitogorsk	410,500
Perm	990,200	Ivanovo	409,000
Volgograd	986,300	Kursk	405,900
Krasnoyarsk	927,200	Tver	405,500
Saratov	841,400	Nizhnii Tagil	377,500
Voronezh	840,700	Stavropol	359,700
Krasnodar	709,000	Arkhangelsk (Archangel)	348,600
Tolyatti	705,300	Belgorod	348,200
Izhevsk	615,700	Ulan-Ude	343,000
Ulyanovsk	611,700	Vladimir	339,800
Yaroslavl	604,000	Sochi	331,100
Barnaul	600,100	Kaluga	327,500
Vladivostok	580,800	Kurgan	326,400
Khabarovsk	577,400	Orel	323,000
Irkutsk	575,900	Smolensk	317,700
Novokuznetsk	560,900	Murmansk	317,500
Tyumen	549,900	Vladikavkaz	313,800
Orenburg	529,600	Cherepovets	307,800
Kemerovo	519,800	Volzhskii	307,300
Ryazan	512,200	Chita	305,800
Penza	509,200		

Note: Figures are rounded.

BIRTHS, MARRIAGES AND DEATHS

	Registered live births Number	Rate (per 1,000)	Registered marriages Number	Rate (per 1,000)	Registered deaths Number	Rate (per 1,000)
2000	1,266,800	8.7	897,327	6.2	2,225,332	15.3
2001	1,311,604	9.0	1,001,589	6.9	2,254,856	15.6
2002	1,396,967	9.7	1,019,762	7.1	2,332,272	16.2
2003	1,477,301	10.2	1,091,778	7.6	2,365,826	16.4
2004	1,502,477	10.4	979,667	6.8	2,295,402	16.0
2005	1,457,376	10.2	1,066,366	7.5	2,303,935	16.1
2006	1,476,937	10.4	1,113,562	7.8	2,166,703	15.2
2007	1,610,122	11.3	1,262,500	8.9	2,080,445	14.7

Life expectancy (years at birth, WHO estimates): 66.4 (males 60.0; females 73.2) in 2006 (Source: WHO, *World Health Statistics*).

IMMIGRATION AND EMIGRATION

	2005	2006	2007
Immigrants	177,230	186,380	286,956
Emigrants	69,798	54,061	47,013

ECONOMICALLY ACTIVE POPULATION
(sample surveys, '000 persons aged 15 to 72 years, at November, excl. Chechen Republic)

	2004	2005	2006
Agriculture, hunting and forestry	6,627	6,769	6,685
Fishing	205	166	176
Mining and quarrying	1,212	1,236	1,196
Manufacturing	12,674	12,534	12,470
Electricity, gas and water supply	2,001	1,959	2,063
Construction	4,127	4,575	4,460
Wholesale and retail trade; repair of motor vehicles and motorcycles and personal and household goods	10,131	10,383	10,594
Restaurants and hotels	1,223	1,297	1,392
Transport, storage and communications	6,261	6,249	6,212
Financial intermediation	918	962	1,060
Real estate, renting and business activities	4,119	4,039	4,146
Public administration and defence; compulsory social security	4,702	4,815	4,875
Education	6,142	6,204	6,196
Health and social work	4,833	4,701	4,894
Other community, social and personal service activities	2,100	2,247	2,389
Private households with employed persons	—	26	21
Extra-territorial organizations and bodies	1	4	4
Total employed	67,275	68,169	68,834
Males	34,181	34,549	34,685
Females	33,094	33,620	34,149
Unemployed	5,675	5,263	5,312
Total labour force	72,950	73,432	74,146

Source: ILO.

2004 (sample survey, '000 persons aged 15 to 72 years, at November, excl. Chechen Republic, revised figures): Total employed 67,134 (males 34,177, females 32,958); Unemployed 5,775; Total labour force 72,909.

2005 (sample survey, '000 persons aged 15 to 72 years, at November, excl. Chechen Republic, revised figures): Total employed 68,603 (males 34,710, females 33,893); Unemployed 5,208; Total labour force 73,811.

2006 (sample survey, '000 persons aged 15 to 72 years, at November, incl. Chechen Republic, revised figures): Total employed 69,157 (males 34,996, females 34,161); Unemployed 4,999; Total labour force 74,156.

2007 (sample survey, '000 persons aged 15 to 72 years, at November, incl. Chechen Republic): Total employed 70,813 (males 35,702, females 35,111); Unemployed 4,232; Total labour force 75,046.

THE RUSSIAN FEDERATION

Statistical Survey

Health and Welfare

KEY INDICATORS

Total fertility rate (children per woman, 2006)	1.3
Under-5 mortality rate (per 1,000 live births, 2006)	13
HIV/AIDS (% of persons aged 15–49, 2007)	1.1
Physicians (per 1,000 head, 2006)	4.3
Hospital beds (per 1,000 head, 2006)	9.7
Health expenditure (2006): US $ per head (PPP)	638
Health expenditure (2006): % of GDP	5.3
Health expenditure (2006): public (% of total)	63.2
Access to water (% of persons, 2006)	97
Access to sanitation (% of persons, 2006)	87
Human Development Index (2006): ranking	73
Human Development Index (2006): value	0.806

For sources and definitions, see explanatory note on p. vi.

Agriculture

PRINCIPAL CROPS
('000 metric tons)

	2005	2006	2007
Wheat	47,697.5	45,006.3	49,389.9
Rice, paddy	574.6	686.4	708.6
Barley	15,791.4	18,153.6	15,663.1
Maize	3,210.8	3,668.6	3,953.2
Rye	3,628.4	2,965.1	3,910.3
Oats	4,564.5	4,880.3	5,407.0
Millet	455.9	600.4	420.9
Buckwheat	605.6	865.5	1,004.9
Potatoes	37,279.8	38,572.6	36,784.2
Sugar beet	21,420.1	30,861.2	29,000.0
Peas, dry	1,126.8	1,157.6	871.0
Soybeans (Soya beans)	688.7	806.6	651.8
Sunflower seed	6,440.9	6,752.9	5,656.5
Rapeseed	302.7	522.2	600.0
Cabbages and other brassicas	4,051.1	4,073.2	4,054.0*
Tomatoes	2,295.9	2,414.9	2,393.0*
Cucumbers and gherkins	1,414.0	1,423.2	1,410.0*
Onions, dry	1,758.7	1,788.8	1,770.0*
Garlic	257.3	255.9	254.0*
Carrots and turnips	1,793.3	1,918.4	1,900.0*
Watermelons	964.6	985.5	1,000.0*
Apples	1,800†	1,609*	2,211*
Sweet cherries	93†	47*	65*
Sour (Morello) cherries	230*	111*	153*
Plums and sloes	169†	98*	135*
Strawberries	221†	235*	324*
Currants	432†	435*	600*
Grapes	333.3	243.5	326.8

* FAO estimate.
† Unofficial figure.

Aggregate production ('000 metric tons, may include official, semi-official or estimated data): Total cereals 76,563.6 in 2005, 76,866.1 in 2006, 80,495.5 in 2007; Total roots and tubers 37,279.8 in 2005, 38,572.6 in 2006, 36,784.2 in 2007; Total primary oilcrops 2,923.4 in 2005, 3,148.3 in 2006, 2,685.4 in 2007; Total pulses 1,645.1 in 2005, 1,763.5 in 2006, 1,300.9 in 2007; Total vegetables (incl. melons) 16,126.1 in 2005, 16,629.2 in 2006, 16,516.2 in 2007; Total fruits (excl. melons) 3,731.1 in 2005, 2,978.8 in 2006, 4,090.6 in 2007.

Source: FAO.

LIVESTOCK
('000 head at 1 January)

	2005	2006	2007
Horses	1,409	1,319	1,304
Cattle	22,988	21,474	21,466
Pigs	13,413	13,455	15,793
Sheep	15,494	16,074	17,508
Goats	2,277	2,138	2,167
Chickens	328,707	342,866	358,249
Turkeys	8,518	9,429	9,107

Source: FAO.

LIVESTOCK PRODUCTS
('000 metric tons)

	2005	2006	2007
Cattle meat	1,793.4	1,704.9	1,828.0*
Sheep meat	134.4	135.4	140.0*
Pig meat	1,520.1	1,641.5	1,788.0
Chicken meat	1,345.7	1,580.2	1,722.0
Cows' milk	30,892.6	31,186.2	31,950.0*
Goats' milk	253.7	249.1	255.0*
Hen eggs	2,049.9	2,100.0	2,093.1*
Honey	52.1	55.3	56.0*
Wool, greasy	48.0	49.3	52.0*

* FAO estimate.
Source: FAO.

Forestry

ROUNDWOOD REMOVALS
('000 cubic metres, excl. bark; figures are rounded)

	2005	2006	2007
Sawlogs, veneer logs and logs for sleepers	70,400	73,800	82,700
Pulpwood	53,500	56,000	60,600
Other industrial wood	14,100	14,800	18,700
Fuel wood	47,000	46,000	45,000
Total	185,000	190,600	207,000

Source: FAO.

SAWNWOOD PRODUCTION
('000 cubic metres, incl. railway sleepers)

	2005	2006	2007
Coniferous (softwood)	19,385	19,470	20,415
Broadleaved (hardwood)	2,648	2,657	2,785
Total	22,033	22,127	23,200

Source: FAO.

Fishing

('000 metric tons, live weight)

	2004	2005	2006
Capture	2,941.5	3,197.6	3,284.1
Pink (humpback) salmon	114.8	202.3	202.3
Atlantic cod	205.0	203.7	207.5
Alaska (Walleye) pollock	849.6	961.7	1,021.7
Blue whiting (Poutassou)	346.8	332.2	329.4
Atlantic herring	123.3	140.1	131.1
Pacific herring	194.4	205.4	222.3
Aquaculture	109.8	114.8	105.5
Total catch	3,051.3	3,312.3	3,389.7

Note: Figures exclude seaweeds and other aquatic plants ('000 metric tons): 58.2 (capture 58.0, aquaculture 0.2) in 2004; 50.5 (capture 50.3, aquaculture 0.2) in 2005; 61.4 (capture 60.6, aquaculture 0.8) in 2006. Also excluded are aquatic mammals, recorded by number rather than weight. The number of whales caught was: 139 in 2004; 131 in 2005; 139 in 2006. The number of seals (incl. walrus) caught was: 14,855 in 2004; 28,379 in 2005; 23,176 in 2006.

Source: FAO.

THE RUSSIAN FEDERATION

Mining

('000 metric tons, unless otherwise indicated)

	2003	2004	2005
Iron ore: gross weight	91,760	96,980	96,764
Copper ore*†	675	675	700
Nickel ore*†	260	261	266
Bauxite	5,442	6,000*	6,400*
Lead ore*†	24.0	23.0	36.0
Zinc ore*†	159	179	180
Tin (metric tons)*†	2,000	2,500	3,000
Manganese ore*†	23	23	23
Chromium ore	116.5	320.2	772.0
Tungsten concentrates (metric tons)*†	5,450	5,500	600
Molybdenum (metric tons)*	2,900	2,900	2,900
Cobalt ore (metric tons)*†	4,800	4,700	5,000
Mercury (metric tons)*	50	50	50
Silver (metric tons)*†	700	1,277	1,350
Uranium concentrate (metric tons)*†	3,150	3,200	3,430
Gold (metric tons)*†	170.1	163.1	169.3
Platinum (metric tons)*	28	28	30
Palladium (metric tons)*	97	97	97
Kaolin (concentrate)*	45	45	45
Magnesite*	1,200	1,200	1,200
Phosphate rock (Apatite)*‡	4,121	4,120	4,200
Potash*§	4,740	5,000	5,000
Native sulphur*	50	50	50
Fluorspar (concentrate)	170	226	246
Barite (Barytes)*	78	63	63
Salt (unrefined)*	2,800	2,800	2,800
Diamonds: gems ('000 metric carats):			
gem*	20,000	21,400	23,000
industrial*	13,000	14,200	15,000
Gypsum (crude)*	1,750	2,077	2,200
Asbestos	878	923	925*
Mica*	100	100	100
Talc*	100	100	100
Feldspar*	45	45	45
Peat (horticulture and fuel use)	1,000	1,500	1,500

* Estimated production.
† Figures refer to the metal content of ores.
‡ Figures refer to the phosphoric acid content. The data exclude sedimentary rock (estimates, '000 metric tons): 300 per year in 2002–05.
§ Figures refer to the potassium oxide content.

Source: US Geological Survey.

Crude petroleum (million metric tons): 379.6 in 2002; 421.4 in 2003; 458.8 in 2004; 470.0 in 2005; 480.5 in 2006; 491.3 in 2007 (Source: BP, *Statistical Review of World Energy*).

Natural gas (excl. flared or recycled, '000 million cu m): 555.4 in 2002; 578.6 in 2003; 591.0 in 2004; 598.0 in 2005; 612.1 in 2006; 607.4 in 2007 (Source: BP, *Statistical Review of World Energy*).

Coal (commercial solid fuels only, million metric tons): 255.8 in 2002; 276.7 in 2003; 281.7 in 2004; 298.3 in 2005; 309.9 in 2006; 314.2 in 2007 (Source: BP, *Statistical Review of World Energy*).

Industry

SELECTED PRODUCTS

('000 metric tons, unless otherwise indicated)

	2005	2006	2007
Flour	10,356	10,364	10,095
Granulated sugar	5,600	5,833	6,069
Cotton fabrics (million sq metres)	2,225	2,222	2,143
Woollen fabrics (million sq metres)	30.3	29.0	28.5
Linen fabrics (million sq metres)	122	124	101
Footwear, excl. rubber footwear ('000 pairs)	47,200	57,300	50,800
Plywood ('000 cubic metres)	2,556	2,615	2,763
Particle board ('000 cubic metres)	3,750	3,880	4,020
Newsprint	1,753	1,716	2,087
Cardboard	3,125	3,396	3,496
Paper	4,001	4,038	4,063
Sulphuric acid	9,452	9,379	9,652

—continued	2005	2006	2007
Soda ash (sodium carbonate)	2,582	2,938	2,940
Mineral fertilizers	16,625	16,207	17,655
Synthetic ammonia	12,473	12,954	13,005
Gasoline	32.0	34.4	35.1
Rubber tyres ('000)	41,436	40,413	43,214
Rubber footwear ('000 pairs)	16,100	17,400	22,100
Cement	48,500	54,700	59,900
Pig-iron	49,175	52,362	51,523
Steel	66,262	70,816	72,389
Steel pipes	6,695	7,898	8,706
Rolled metal products	54,661	58,215	59,635
Tractors (number)	8,600	10,900	13,500
Refrigerators and freezers ('000)	2,777	2,995	3,573
Domestic washing machines ('000)	1,582	2,016	2,708
Televisions ('000)	6,278	4,601	6,154
Electric vacuum cleaners ('000)	890	584	626
Passenger motor cars ('000)	1,069	1,178	1,290
Electric energy (million kWh)	953,000	996,000	1,016,000

Finance

CURRENCY AND EXCHANGE RATES

Monetary Units
100 kopeks = 1 Russian rubl (ruble or rouble).

Sterling, Dollar and Euro Equivalents (31 December 2008)
£1 sterling = 42.831 roubles;
US $1 = 29.380 roubles;
€1 = 40.889 roubles;
1,000 roubles = £23.35 = $34.04 = €24.46.

Average Exchange Rate (roubles per US dollar)
2006   27.1910
2007   25.5808
2008   24.8529

Note: On 1 January 1998 a new rouble, equivalent to 1,000 of the former units, was introduced. Figures in this Survey are expressed in terms of new roubles, unless otherwise indicated.

FEDERAL BUDGET

(million roubles)

Revenue	2003	2004	2005
Tax revenue	1,892,363.7	2,071,384.5	3,151,745.6
Taxes on corporate profit and capital gains	179,550.5	164,587.4	259,003.3
Taxes on goods and services	1,178,971.2	1,088,389.6	791,822.6
Value-added tax	946,218.5	988,389.6	713,226.9
Excise duties	227,708.8	94,357.7	78,595.7
Natural gas	133,112.1	20,000.0	—
Taxes on the use of natural resources	183,129.5	279,381.1	483,035.6
Taxes on international trade and transactions	335,975.5	532,538.2	919,093.8
Customs duties on imports	150,355.9	180,613.5	249,762.0
Customs duties on exports	185,619.6	351,924.7	618,207.0
Non-tax revenue	145,721.8	219,194.4	174,295.5
Income from state property and activities	83,158.8	165,612.1	73,004.0
Special budgetary funds	14,066.3	14,061.5	—
Contribution of unified social tax to federal budget	365,640.0	438,210.0	—
Total	2,417,791.8	2,742,850.4	3,326,041.1

THE RUSSIAN FEDERATION

Expenditure	2003	2004	2005
State administration	66,506.9	76,967.2	123,353.1
Judicial system	25,481.9	33,250.8	36,769.0
National defence	219,884.6	255,390.2	531,139.2
Public order and state security	190,080.1	250,025.3	398,889.5
Education	97,672.0	117,791.9	155,338.0
Health and sport	39,344.8	47,097.8	85,672.2
Social security and welfare	150,685.0	161,193.5	167,360.9
Servicing of government debt	277,510.1	287,570.6	244,150.4
Federal transfers	714,600.2	813,969.8	954,545.2
Total (incl. others)	2,123,424.9	2,400,751.2	3,047,929.3

2005 ('000 million roubles, budget execution excl. deficit financing): *Revenue:* Tax revenue 3,188.2 (Value-added tax 1,472.2, Profit tax 377.6, Excise taxes 107.2, Social Tax (ST) revenues 267.5, Other 963.6); Non-tax revenue 1,936.9 (Customs duties 1,622.8, Other non-tax revenues 314.1); Total 5,125.1. *Expenditure:* Debt service 208.4 (Domestic 53.4, Foreign 154.9); Non-interest expenditure 3,303.8 (State administration 290.9, Defence, law and order 1,031.2, Social and cultural sphere 475.9, National economy 260.1, Financial aid to regions 486.7, Transfers to extrabudgetary accounts 758.9); Total 3,512.2.

2006 ('000 million roubles, budget execution excl. deficit financing): *Revenue:* Tax revenue 3,569.7 (Value-added tax 1,510.9, Profit tax 509.9, Excise taxes 110.5, Social Tax (ST) revenues 315.8, Other 1,122.6); Non-tax revenue 2,532.2 (Customs duties 2,306.3, Other non-tax revenues 225.9); Total (incl. others) 6,278.9. *Expenditure:* General government 533.1 (Debt service 172.8); National defence and national security and militia 1,232.0; National economy 345.0 (Fuel and electric power 7.5, Agriculture and fishing 26.1, Transport 132.2, Communication and informatics 6.1); Housing and communal utilities 52.7; Social and cultural activities 616.4; Transfers to non-budget funds 914.3; Total (incl. others) 4,284.8.

2007 ('000 million roubles, budget execution excl. deficit financing, provisional): *Revenue:* Tax revenue 4,604.1 (Value-added tax 2,261.5, Profit tax 641.3, Excise taxes 135.0, Social Tax (ST) revenues 405.0, Other 1,161.3); Non-tax revenue 2,735.0 (Customs duties 2,408.3, Other non-tax revenues 326.7); Total (incl. others) 7,779.1. *Expenditure:* General government 812.1 (Debt service 143.1); National defence and national security and militia 1,498.9; National economy 692.6 (Fuel and electric power 8.3, Agriculture and fishing 27.8, Transport 172.6, Communication and informatics 14.1, Other 409.0); Housing and communal utilities 294.9; Social and cultural activities 776.1; Transfers to non-budget funds 1,043.9; Total (incl. others) 5,983.0.

Source: Ministry of Finance, Moscow.

INTERNATIONAL RESERVES
(US $ million at 31 December)

	2006	2007	2008
Gold (national valuation)	8,164.4	12,011.9	14,533.4
IMF special drawing rights	7.1	0.8	0.8
Reserve position in IMF	283.3	373.9	1,053.4
Foreign exchange	295,277.1	466,375.7	411,494.1
Total	303,731.9	478,762.3	427,081.7

Source: IMF, *International Financial Statistics*.

MONEY SUPPLY
('000 million roubles at 31 December)

	2006	2007	2008
Currency outside banks	2,785.2	3,702.3	3,794.8
Transferable deposits	2,747.2	4,200.3	3,796.7
Other deposits	4,616.9	6,734.2	9,183.3
Total money	10,149.3	14,636.8	16,774.8

Source: IMF, *International Financial Statistics*.

COST OF LIVING
(Consumer Price Index; base: previous year = 100)

	2006	2007	2008
Food and beverages	108.7	115.6	116.5
Other consumer goods	106.0	106.5	108.0
Services	113.9	113.3	115.9
All items	109.0	111.9	113.3

NATIONAL ACCOUNTS
('000 million roubles at current prices)

Expenditure on the Gross Domestic Product

	2006	2007	2008
Final consumption expenditure	17,629.7	21,785.8	27,237.4
Households	12,887.9	15,900.9	20,054.2
Non-profit institutions serving households	152.6	182.3	207.5
General government	4,589.2	5,702.6	6,975.7
Gross capital formation	5,748.8	8,031.7	10,642.5
Gross fixed capital formation. Acquisitions, less disposals, of valuables	4,980.6	6,982.5	9,136.4
Changes in inventories	768.2	1,049.2	1,506.1
Total domestic expenditure	23,378.5	29,817.5	37,879.9
Exports of goods and services	9,079.3	10,032.4	12,926.7
Less Imports of goods and services	5,656.8	7,185.3	9,135.5
Sub-total	26,801.0	32,664.6	41,671.1
Statistical discrepancy*	102.5	446.8	−3.1
GDP in market prices	26,903.5	33,111.4	41,668.0

* Referring to the difference between the sum of the expenditure components and official estimates of GDP, compiled from the production approach.

Gross Domestic Product by Economic Activity

	2006	2007	2008
Agriculture, hunting and forestry	1,102.9	1,349.7	1,696.3
Fishing	69.1	71.4	80.2
Mining and quarrying	2,528.6	2,890.5	3,362.2
Manufacturing	4,272.8	5,265.3	6,366.7
Electricity, gas and water supply	755.2	900.5	1,087.8
Construction	1,231.8	1,680.9	2,356.7
Wholesale and retail trade; repair of motor vehicles, motorcycles and personal and household goods	4,726.1	5,848.8	7,535.1
Hotels and restaurants	211.2	279.2	362.2
Transport, storage and communications	2,283.8	2,733.2	3,413.0
Financial intermediation	1,050.1	1,386.1	1,696.9
Real estate, renting and business activities	2,311.1	3,141.2	3,999.4
Public administration and defence; compulsory social security	1,189.2	1,456.6	1,797.9
Education	620.5	766.1	941.8
Health and social work	767.6	964.7	1,135.3
Other community, social and personal services	422.2	524.9	637.6
Sub-total	23,542.2	29,259.1	36,469.1
Less Financial intermediation services indirectly measured	578.6	783.1	1,084.3
Gross value added in basic prices	22,963.6	28,476.0	35,384.8
Taxes, *less* subsidies, on products	3,939.9	4,635.4	6,283.2
GDP in market prices	26,903.5	33,111.4	41,668.0

BALANCE OF PAYMENTS
(US $ million)

	2005	2006	2007
Exports of goods f.o.b.	243,798	303,550	354,401
Imports of goods f.o.b.	−125,434	−164,281	−223,486
Trade balance	118,364	139,269	130,915
Exports of services	24,970	31,102	39,416
Imports of services	−38,865	−44,839	−59,187
Balance on goods and services	104,470	125,533	111,144
Other income received	17,382	29,504	46,784
Other income paid	−36,405	−59,160	−78,170
Balance on goods, services and income	85,446	95,877	79,748
Current transfers received	4,490	6,403	8,423
Current transfers paid	−5,528	−7,940	−11,929
Current balance	84,409	94,340	76,241
Capital account (net)	−12,764	191	−10,224

THE RUSSIAN FEDERATION

Statistical Survey

—continued	2005	2006	2007
Direct investment abroad	−12,767	−23,151	−45,916
Direct investment from abroad	12,886	29,701	55,073
Portfolio investment assets	−10,666	6,248	−9,986
Portfolio investment liabilities	−713	9,455	16,854
Financial derivatives assets	858	1,242	2,762
Financial derivatives liabilities	−1,091	−1,342	−2,430
Other investment assets	−33,208	−49,299	−59,637
Other investment liabilities	45,846	30,340	139,398
Net errors and omissions	−7,821	9,741	−13,208
Overall balance	**64,968**	**107,466**	**148,928**

Source: IMF, *International Financial Statistics*.

External Trade

PRINCIPAL COMMODITIES
(US $ '000 million)

Imports	2005	2006	2007
Foodstuffs and agricultural raw materials (excl. textiles)	17.4	21.6	27.6
Mineral products	3.0	3.3	4.7
Chemical products and rubber	16.3	21.8	27.5
Leather, fur, and articles thereof	0.3	0.4	0.7
Wood, pulp and paper products	3.3	4.0	5.3
Textiles, textile articles and footwear	3.6	5.5	8.6
Metals, precious stones, and articles thereof	7.6	10.6	16.4
Machinery, vehicles and transport equipment	43.4	65.7	102.0
Other	3.7	4.8	7.1
Total	**98.7**	**137.5**	**199.7**

Exports	2005	2006	2007
Foodstuffs and agricultural raw materials (excl. textiles)	4.5	5.5	9.1
Mineral products	156.0	199.0	228.0
Chemical products and rubber	14.4	16.8	20.8
Leather, fur, and articles thereof	0.3	0.4	0.3
Wood, pulp and paper products	8.3	9.5	12.3
Textiles, textile articles and footwear	1.0	1.0	0.9
Metals, precious stones, and articles thereof	40.6	48.9	56.9
Machinery, vehicles and transport equipment	13.5	17.4	19.7
Other	2.5	3.1	4.4
Total	**241.5**	**301.2**	**352.5**

PRINCIPAL TRADING PARTNERS
(US $ million)

Imports	2005	2006	2007
Austria	1,211	1,845	2,458
Belarus	5,716	6,845	8,887
Belgium	1,476	2,178	3,185
Brazil	2,346	2,987	4,108
China, People's Republic	7,265	12,910	24,401
Czech Republic	989	1,530	2,451
Denmark	921	1,347	1,595
Finland	3,100	4,003	5,023
France	3,673	5,863	7,759
Germany	13,272	18,464	26,572
Hungary	1,100	1,868	2,602
India	784	968	1,310
Italy	4,416	5,726	8,535
Japan	5,834	7,787	12,712
Kazakhstan	3,225	3,840	4,613
Korea, Republic	4,005	6,781	8,836

Imports—continued	2005	2006	2007
Netherlands	1,941	2,685	3,853
Poland	2,747	3,410	4,629
Spain	1,227	1,952	3,197
Sweden	1,861	2,145	3,123
Turkey	1,738	2,753	4,180
Ukraine	7,819	9,238	13,323
United Kingdom	2,776	3,674	5,642
USA	4,563	6,405	9,425
Uzbekistan	904	1,292	1,451
Total (incl. others)	**98,707**	**137,807**	**199,708**

Exports	2005	2006	2007
Austria	2,353	3,353	2,737
Belarus	10,118	13,099	17,187
Belgium	2,464	2,694	2,810
China, People's Republic	13,048	15,758	15,893
Cyprus	5,095	4,515	4,838
Czech Republic	3,817	4,665	4,655
Finland	7,651	9,192	10,722
France	6,111	7,675	8,674
Germany	19,736	24,498	26,290
Greece	1,930	2,752	2,613
Hungary	5,004	6,245	6,092
India	2,314	2,925	4,012
Israel	1,538	1,544	2,031
Italy	19,053	25,090	27,518
Japan	3,740	4,457	7,383
Kazakhstan	6,524	8,967	11,963
Korea, Republic	2,359	2,735	6,150
Netherlands	24,614	35,884	42,786
Poland	8,623	11,481	13,298
Romania	3,041	3,272	3,211
Slovakia	3,190	4,587	5,151
Spain	2,823	3,343	4,318
Sweden	2,320	2,198	3,001
Switzerland	10,774	12,167	14,201
Taiwan	1,438	930	895
Turkey	10,841	14,290	18,332
Ukraine	12,402	14,983	16,323
United Kingdom	8,280	10,396	11,024
USA	6,323	8,638	8,048
Total (incl. others)	**241,473**	**301,244**	**352,473**

Transport

RAILWAYS
(traffic)

	2005	2006	2007
Paying passengers ('000 journeys)	1,339,000	1,347,000	1,278,000
Freight carried ('000 metric tons)	1,273,000	1,312,000	1,344,000
Passenger-km (million)	172,200	177,800	174,100
Freight ton-km (million)	1,858,000	1,951,000	2,090,000

ROAD TRAFFIC
(motor vehicles in use)

	1998	1999	2000
Passenger cars	18,819,600	19,717,800	20,353,000
Buses and coaches	627,500	633,200	640,100
Lorries and vans	4,260,000	4,387,800	4,400,600
Motorcycles and mopeds	7,165,900	6,328,600	n.a.

Source: IRF, *World Road Statistics*.

THE RUSSIAN FEDERATION

SHIPPING

Merchant Fleet
(registered at 31 December)

	2005	2006	2007
Number of vessels	3,722	3,656	3,481
Total displacement ('000 grt)	8,334.5	8,046.0	7,587.3

Source: Lloyd's Register-Fairplay, *World Fleet Statistics*.

International Sea-borne Freight Traffic
('000 metric tons, rounded data)

	2004	2005	2006
Goods loaded	8,200	9,100	7,700
Goods unloaded	1,100	700	400

Note: Annual data extrapolated from monthly averages.

Source: UN, *Monthly Bulletin of Statistics*.

CIVIL AVIATION
(traffic on scheduled services)

	2005	2006	2007
Passengers carried ('000)	37,000	40,000	47,000
Freight carried (million metric tons)	0.8	0.9	1.0
Passenger-km (million)	85,800	93,900	111,000
Freight ton-km (million)	2.8	2.9	3.4

Kilometres flown (million): 694 in 2004. (Source: *UN, Statistical Yearbook*).

Tourism

FOREIGN VISITOR ARRIVALS
('000, incl. excursionists)

Country of origin	2004	2005	2006
Azerbaijan	823.5	824.6	935.5
China, People's Republic	813.1	798.7	765.3
Estonia	521.1	510.3	438.2
Finland	1,092.3	1,115.5	1,078.2
Germany	567.2	550.8	553.7
Kazakhstan	2,761.5	2,453.2	2,598.6
Latvia	371.1	709.3	380.7
Lithuania	949.6	1,251.5	980.5
Moldova	804.9	837.1	925.9
Poland	1,128.5	1,195.9	1,149.0
Tajikistan	456.4	466.5	600.8
Ukraine	6,683.2	6,416.9	6,447.0
Uzbekistan	677.0	660.6	958.9
Total (incl. others)	22,064.2	22,200.6	22,486.0

Receipts from tourism (US $ million, incl. passenger transport): 7,262 in 2004; 7,806 in 2005; 9,720 in 2006.

Source: World Tourism Organization.

Communications Media

	2005	2006	2007
Telephones ('000 main lines in use)	40,100	43,900	n.a.
Mobile cellular telephones ('000 subscribers)	120,000	150,674	170,000
Internet users ('000)	21,800	25,688.6	30,000.0
Broadband subscribers ('000)	1,589	2,900	n.a.

Source: International Telecommunication Union.

Television receivers ('000 in use): 79,000 in 2000.

Radio receivers ('000 in use): 61,500 in 1997.

Facsimile machines (number in use): 52,900 in 1998.

Book production (including pamphlets): 36,237 titles in 1996 (421,387,000 copies).

Daily newspapers: 285 in 1996 (average circulation 15,517,000 copies); 333 in 2000.

Non-daily newspapers: 4,596 in 1996 (average circulation 98,558,000 copies); 10,188 in 2000.

Other periodicals: 2,751 in 1996 (average circulation 387,832,000 copies).

Personal computers: 17.4m. in use in 2005.

Sources: UNESCO, *Statistical Yearbook*; and UN, *Statistical Yearbook*.

Education

(2007/08, except where otherwise specified)

	Institutions	Students*	Teachers
Pre-primary	45,730	4,713,000†	610,828‡
Primary and general secondary	56,407	13,766,100	1,537,000*
Vocational secondary	2,799	2,408,000	137,200*
Higher	1,108	7,461,300	419,200*

* Rounded figure(s).
† 2006/07.
‡ 2004/05.

Adult literacy rate (UNESCO estimates): 99.5% (males 99.7%; females 99.4%) in 2007 (Source: UNESCO Institute for Statistics).

Directory

The Constitution

The current Constitution of the Russian Federation came into force on 12 December 1993, following its approval by a majority of participants in a nation-wide plebiscite. It replaced the Constitution originally adopted on 12 April 1978, but amended many times after 1990. Amendments to the Constitution, extending the terms of the President and the Gosudarstvennaya Duma, were enacted on 30 December 2008.

THE PRINCIPLES OF THE CONSTITUTIONAL SYSTEM

The Russian Federation (Russia) is a democratic, federative, law-based state with a republican form of government. Its multi-ethnic people bear its sovereignty and are the sole source of authority. State power is divided between the legislative, executive and judicial branches, which are independent of one another. Ideological pluralism and a multi-party political system are recognized. The state is secular.

HUMAN AND CIVIL RIGHTS AND FREEDOMS

Basic human rights and freedoms of the Russian citizen are guaranteed regardless of sex, race, ethnicity or religion. The rights to life and to freedom and personal inviolability are guaranteed. The principles of freedom of movement, freedom of expression and freedom of conscience are upheld. Censorship is prohibited. Citizens are guaranteed the right to vote in and to contest state and local elections and to participate in referendums. Individuals shall have equal access to state employment, and may establish trade unions and public associations. The State is committed to the protection of motherhood and childhood, and the granting of social security, state pensions and social benefits. Each person has the right to housing. Health care and education are free of charge. Basic general education is compulsory. Citizens are guaranteed the right to receive qualified legal assistance. Payment of statutory taxes and levies is obligatory, as is military service.

THE ORGANIZATION OF THE FEDERATION

The federal subjects (territorial units) of the Federation are named. Russian is declared the state language, but all peoples of the Federation are guaranteed the right to preserve their native tongue. The state flag, emblem and anthem of the Federation are established by constitutional law. The separate roles of the authority of the Federation, as distinct from that of the joint authority of the Federation and the federal subjects, are defined. The powers of the federal executive bodies and the executive bodies of the members of the Federation are defined.

THE PRESIDENT OF THE RUSSIAN FEDERATION

The powers and responsibilities of the Head of State, the President of the Russian Federation, are defined. The President, who must be aged at least 35 years, and have been resident in Russia for at least 10 years, is elected to office for a term of six years by universal, direct suffrage, for no more than two consecutive terms. The President appoints the Chairman of the Government (Prime Minister) of the Russian Federation, with the approval of the Gosudarstvennaya Duma (State Duma), and may dismiss the Government. The President is entitled to chair sessions of the Government. The President's responsibilities include scheduling referendums and elections to the Gosudarstvennaya Duma, dissolving the Gosudarstvennaya Duma, submitting legislative proposals to the Gosudarstvennaya Duma, promulgating federal laws, and nominating candidates, subject to approval by the Federalnoye Sobraniye, to the posts of Chairman of the Central Bank, judges of the Constitutional Court, the Supreme Court and the Supreme Arbitration Court, and of Prosecutor-General. The President forms and heads the Security Council, the status of which is determined by federal law. The President is responsible for the foreign policy of the Russian Federation. The President is Commander-in-Chief of the Armed Forces and may introduce martial law or a state of emergency under certain conditions.

If the President is unable to carry out the presidential duties, these will be assumed by the Chairman of the Government. The acting President, however, will not possess the full powers of the President, such as the right to dissolve the Gosudarstvennaya Duma or to order a referendum. The President may only be removed from office by the Sovet Federatsii (Federation Council) on the grounds of a serious accusation by the Gosudarstvennaya Duma.

THE FEDERALNOYE SOBRANIYE

The Federalnoye Sobraniye (Federal Assembly) is the highest representative and legislative body in the Russian Federation. It comprises two chambers: the Sovet Federatsii (upper chamber) and the Gosudarstvennaya Duma (lower chamber). The Sovet Federatsii comprises two representatives from each member of the Russian Federation, one appointed by its legislative and one by its executive body. The Gosudarstvennaya Duma is composed of 450 deputies, elected for a term of five years. The deputies of the Russian Federation must be over 21 years of age and may not hold government office or any other paid job.

Both chambers of the Federalnoye Sobraniye elect their Chairman and Deputy Chairmen. The powers of the Sovet Federatsii include the approval of the President's decrees on martial law and a state of emergency, the scheduling of presidential elections and the impeachment of the President. The Gosudarstvennaya Duma has the power to approve the President's nominee to the office of Chairman of the Government. Both chambers of the Federalnoye Sobraniye adopt resolutions by a majority vote of the total number of members. All federal and federal constitutional laws are adopted by the Gosudarstvennaya Duma and submitted for approval first to the Sovet Federatsii and then to the President. If the Sovet Federatsii or the President reject proposed legislation if it is submitted for repeat consideration to one or both chambers of the Federalnoye Sobraniye.

The Gosudarstvennaya Duma may be dissolved by the President if it adopts two successive votes of 'no confidence' in the Government. If the Gosudarstvennaya Duma rejects three candidates to the office of Chairman, the President will appoint the Chairman, dissolve the Gosudarstvennaya Duma and order new elections. However, it may not be dissolved during a period of martial law or a state of emergency or in the case of charges being lodged against the President. A newly elected Gosudarstvennaya Duma should be convened no later than four months after dissolution of the previous parliament.

THE GOVERNMENT OF THE RUSSIAN FEDERATION

The executive authority of the Russian Federation is vested in the Government, which comprises the Chairman, the Deputy Chairmen and federal ministers. The Chairman is appointed by the President and his nomination approved by the Gosudarstvennaya Duma. The Government submits the federal budget to the Gosudarstvennaya Duma and supervises its execution, guarantees the implementation of a uniform state policy, conducts foreign policy, and ensures the country's defence and security.

Regulations for the activity of the Government are determined by a federal constitutional law. The Government adopts resolutions and directives, which may be vetoed by the President. The Government must submit its resignation to a newly elected President of the Russian Federation, which the President may accept or reject. A vote of 'no confidence' in the Government may be adopted by the Gosudarstvennaya Duma. The President can reject this decision or demand the Government's resignation. If the Gosudarstvennaya Duma adopts a second vote of 'no confidence' within three months, the President will announce the Government's resignation or dissolve the Gosudarstvennaya Duma.

JUDICIAL POWER

Justice is administered by means of constitutional, civil, administrative and criminal judicial proceedings. Judges in the Russian Federation must be aged 25 or over, have a higher legal education and have a record of work in the legal profession of no less than five years. Judges are independent, irremovable and inviolable. Proceedings in judicial courts are open. No criminal case shall be considered in the absence of a defendant. Judicial proceedings may be conducted with the participation of a jury.

The Constitutional Court comprises 19 judges. The Court decides cases regarding the compliance of federal laws and enactments, the constitutions, statutes, laws and other enactments of the federal subjects, state treaties and international treaties that have not yet come into force. The Constitutional Court settles disputes about competence among state bodies. Enactments or provisions thereof that have been judged unconstitutional by the Court are invalid. At the request of the Sovet Federatsii, the Court will pronounce its judgment on bringing an accusation against the President of the Russian Federation.

The Supreme Court is the highest judicial authority on civil, criminal, administrative and other cases within the jurisdiction of the common plea courts. The Supreme Arbitration Court is the highest authority in settling economic and other disputes within the jurisdiction of the courts of arbitration.

The judges of the three higher courts are appointed by the Federation Council on the recommendation of the President. Judges of other federal courts are appointed by the President.

The Prosecutor's Office is a single centralized system. The Prosecutor-General is appointed and dismissed by the Sovet Federatsii on the recommendation of the President. All other prosecutors are appointed by the Prosecutor-General.

LOCAL SELF-GOVERNMENT

The exercise of local self-government is provided for through referendums, elections and elected and other bodies. The responsibilities of local self-government bodies include: independently managing municipal property; forming, approving and executing the local budget; establishing local taxes and levies; and maintaining law and order.

CONSTITUTIONAL AMENDMENTS AND REVISION OF THE CONSTITUTION

No provision contained in Chapters One (on The Principles of the Constitutional System), Two (on Human and Civil Rights and Freedoms) and Nine (on Constitutional Amendments and Revision of the Constitution) may be reviewed by the Federalnoye Sobraniye, while amendments to the remaining Chapters may be adopted in accordance with the procedure for a federal constitutional law. If a proposal for a review of the provisions of Chapters One, Two and Nine wins a three-fifths' majority in both chambers, a Constitutional Assembly will be convened.

CONCLUDING AND TRANSITIONAL PROVISIONS

Should the provisions of a federal treaty contravene those of the Constitution, the constitutional provisions will apply. All laws and other legal acts enforced before the Constitution came into effect will remain valid unless they fail to comply with the Constitution.

The Government

HEAD OF STATE

President of the Russian Federation: DMITRII A. MEDVEDEV (elected 2 March 2008; inaugurated 7 May).

THE RUSSIAN FEDERATION

THE GOVERNMENT
(April 2009)

Chairman: VLADIMIR V. PUTIN.
First Deputy Chairman: VIKTOR A. ZUBKOV.
First Deputy Chairman: IGOR I. SHUVALOV.
Deputy Chairman: ALEKSANDR D. ZHUKOV.
Deputy Chairman: SERGEI B. IVANOV.
Deputy Chairman: DMITRII N. KOZAK.
Deputy Chairman, Minister of Finance: ALEKSEI L. KUDRIN.
Deputy Chairman: IGOR I. SECHIN.
Deputy Chairman, Head of the Government Staff: SERGEI S. SOBYANIN.
Minister of Agriculture: YELENA B. SKRYNNIK.
Minister of Civil Defence, Emergencies and Clean-up Operations: Col.-Gen. SERGEI K. SHOIGU.
Minister of Communications and the Mass Media: IGOR O. SHCHEGOLEV.
Minister of Culture: ALEKSANDR A. AVDEYEV.
Minister of Defence: ANATOLII E. SERDYUKOV.
Minister of Economic Development: ELVIRA S. NABIULLINA.
Minister of Education and Science: ANDREI A. FURSENKO.
Minister of Energy: SERGEI I. SHMATKO.
Minister of Foreign Affairs: SERGEI V. LAVROV.
Minister of Health and Social Development: TATYANA A. GOLIKOVA.
Minister of Industry and Trade: VIKTOR B. KHRISTENKO.
Minister of Internal Affairs: Col.-Gen. RASHID G. NURGALIYEV.
Minister of Justice: ALEKSANDR V. KONOVALOV.
Minister of Natural Resources and Ecology: YURII P. TRUTNEV.
Minister of Regional Development: VIKTOR F. BASAGRIN.
Minister of Sport, Tourism and Youth Policy: VITALII L. MUTKO.
Minister of Transport: IGOR YE. LEVITIN.

MINISTRIES

Office of the President: 103132 Moscow, Staraya pl. 4; tel. (495) 925-35-81; fax (495) 206-07-66; e-mail president@gov.ru; internet www.kremlin.ru.

Office of the Government: 103274 Moscow, Krasnopresnenskaya nab. 2; tel. (495) 205-57-35; fax (495) 205-42-19; internet www.government.ru.

Ministry of Agriculture: 107139 Moscow, Orlikov per. 1/11; tel. (495) 607-83-62; fax (495) 607-80-80; e-mail info@mcx.ru; internet www.mcx.ru.

Ministry of Civil Defence, Emergencies and Clean-up Operations: 109012 Moscow, Teatralnyi proyezd 3; tel. (495) 626-35-00; fax (495) 623-57-45; e-mail info@mchs.gov.ru; internet www.mchs.gov.ru.

Ministry of Communications and the Mass Media: 125375 Moscow, ul. Tverskaya 7; tel. (495) 771-81-00; fax (495) 771-87-10; e-mail office@minsvyaz.ru; internet www.minsvyaz.ru.

Ministry of Culture: 125009 Moscow, M. Gnezdnikovskii per. 7/6; tel. (495) 629-20-08; fax (495) 629-72-69; e-mail info@mkrf.ru; internet www.mkrf.ru.

Ministry of Defence: 105175 Moscow, ul. Myasnitskaya 37; tel. and fax (495) 696-71-71; internet www.mil.ru.

Ministry of Economic Development: 125993 Moscow, ul. 1-ya Tverskaya-Yamskaya 1/3; tel. (495) 694-03-53; fax (495) 251-69-65; e-mail presscenter@economy.gov.ru; internet www.economy.gov.ru.

Ministry of Education and Science: 125993 Moscow, ul. Tverskaya 11; tel. (495) 629-70-62; fax (495) 629-08-91; internet www.mon.gov.ru.

Ministry of Energy: 107996 Moscow, ul. Shepkina 42; tel. (495) 631-98-58; fax (495) 631-83-64; internet minenergo.com.

Ministry of Finance: 109097 Moscow, ul. Ilinka 9; tel. (495) 987-91-01; fax (495) 925-08-89; internet www.minfin.ru.

Ministry of Foreign Affairs: 119200 Moscow, Smolenskaya-Sennaya pl. 32/34; tel. (495) 244-16-06; fax (495) 230-21-30; e-mail ministry@mid.ru; internet www.mid.ru.

Ministry of Health and Social Development: 127994 Moscow, Rakhmanovskii per. 3; tel. (495) 628-44-53; fax (495) 627-28-40; internet www.minzdravsoc.ru.

Ministry of Industry and Trade: 109074 Moscow, Kitaigorodskii proyezd 7; tel. (495) 710-55-00; fax (495) 710-57-22; e-mail okt@minprom.gov.ru; internet www.minprom.gov.ru.

Ministry of Internal Affairs: 119049 Moscow, ul. Zhitnaya 16; tel. (495) 239-05-54; fax (495) 293-59-98; e-mail mvd12@mvdrf.ru; internet www.mvd.ru.

Ministry of Justice: 119991 Moscow, ul. Zhitnaya 14; tel. (495) 955-59-99; fax (495) 955-57-79; e-mail pst@minjust.ru; internet www.minjust.ru.

Ministry of Natural Resources and Ecology: 123995 Moscow, ul. B. Gruzinskaya 4/6; tel. (495) 254-48-00; fax (495) 254-43-10; e-mail admin@mnr.gov.ru; internet www.mnr.gov.ru.

Ministry of Regional Development: 127994 Moscow, ul. Sadovaya-Samotechnaya 10/23/1; tel. (495) 980-25-47; fax (495) 699-38-41; e-mail info@minregion.ru; internet www.minregion.ru.

Ministry of Sport, Tourism and Youth Policy: 105064 Moscow, ul. Kazakova 18; tel. (495) 601-91-20; fax (495) 617-11-20; e-mail minsportturism@mail.ru; internet www.minstm.gov.ru.

Ministry of Transport: 109012 Moscow, ul. Rozhdestvenka 1/1; tel. (495) 626-10-00; e-mail info@mintrans.ru; internet www.mintrans.ru.

President

Presidential Election, 2 March 2008

Candidates	Votes	%
Dmitrii A. Medvedev (United Russia)	52,530,712	70.28
Gennadii A. Zyuganov (Communist Party of the Russian Federation)	13,243,550	17.72
Vladimir V. Zhirinovskii (Liberal Democratic Party of Russia)	6,988,510	9.36
Andrei V. Bogdanov (Independent)	968,344	1.30
Total*	74,746,649	100.00

* Including 1,005,533 invalid votes, equivalent to 1.34% of the total.

Legislature

The Federalnoye Sobraniye (Federal Assembly) is a bicameral legislative body, comprising the Sovet Federatsii (Federation Council) and the Gosudarstvennaya Duma (State Duma).

Sovet Federatsii (Federation Council)

103426 Moscow, ul. B. Dmitrovka 26; tel. (495) 692-11-50; fax (495) 692-43-05; e-mail post_sf@gov.ru; internet www.council.gov.ru.

The Sovet Federatsii is the upper chamber of the Federalnoye Sobraniye. It comprises two deputies appointed from each of the constituent members (federal territorial units) of the Russian Federation, representing the legislative and executive branches of power in each republic and region.

Chairman: SERGEI M. MIRONOV.

Gosudarstvennaya Duma (State Duma)

103265 Moscow, Okhotnyi ryad 1; tel. (495) 692-80-00; fax (495) 203-42-58; e-mail stateduma@duma.ru; internet www.duma.ru.

Chairman: BORIS V. GRYZLOV.

General Election, 2 December 2007

Parties and blocs	Votes	%	Seats
United Russia	44,714,241	64.30	315
Communist Party of the Russian Federation	8,046,886	11.57	57
Liberal Democratic Party of Russia	5,660,823	8.14	40
A Just Russia: Motherland/Pensioners/Life	5,383,639	7.74	38
Others	4,971,547	7.15	—
Invalid votes	759,929	1.09	
Total	69,537,065	100.00	450

Election Commission

Central Electoral Commission of the Russian Federation (Tsentralnaya izbiratelnaya komissiya Rossiiskoi Federatsii): 109012 Moscow, B. Cherkasii per. 9; tel. (495) 606-79-57; e-mail info@cikrf.ru; internet www.cikrf.ru; Chair. VLADIMIR CHUROV.

Political Organizations

Legislation approved in 2004 required each political party to have at least 50,000 members, including no fewer than 500 members resident in at least one-half of the subjects (territorial units) of the Federation, with at least 250 members in each of the remaining regions, in order to register and to function legally. Based on the requirements of the amended legislation, only 11 parties were officially registered to contest elections to the Gosudarstvennaya Duma in December 2007. The following were the principal parties to be officially registered in mid-2009.

Communist Party of the Russian Federation (CPRF) (Kommunisticheskaya partiya Rossiiskoi Federatsii—KPRF): 103051 Moscow, per. M. Sukharevskii 3/1; tel. (495) 628-04-90; fax (495) 292-90-50; e-mail kprf2005@yandex.ru; internet www.kprf.ru; f. 1993; claims succession to the Russian Communist Party, which was banned in 1991; Chair. of Central Committee GENNADII A. ZYUGANOV; 184,181 mems (2006).

A Just Russia (AJR) (Spravedlivaya Rossiya): 107031 Moscow, ul. B. Dmitrovka 32/1; tel. (495) 650-38-80; e-mail nfo@spravedlivo.ru; internet www.spravedlivo.ru; f. 2006 by merger of Motherland, Russian Party of Life and Russian Pensioners' Party; absorbed People's Party of the Russian Federation in Apr. 2007; statist, patriotic party; Chair. SERGEI M. MIRONOV.

Liberal Democratic Party of Russia (LDPR) (Liberalno-demokraticheskaya partiya Rossii): 103045 Moscow, Lukov per. 9; tel. (495) 692-11-95; fax (495) 692-92-42; e-mail pressldpr@rambler.ru; internet www.ldpr.ru; f. 1988; nationalist; Chair. VLADIMIR V. ZHIRINOVSKII; 168,000 mems (2008).

Patriots of Russia (Patrioty Rossii): 119121 Moscow, Smolenskii bulv. 11/2; tel. (495) 692-15-50; fax (495) 692-15-50; e-mail partia-korn@rambler.ru; internet www.patriot-rus.ru; f. 2002; fmrly Russian Party of Labour; Leader GENNADII YU. SEMIGIN.

The Right Cause (Pravoye Delo): 101000 Moscow, ul. Myasnitskaya 16; tel. (495) 620-96-81; fax (495) 229-32-11; e-mail pressa@pravoedelo.ru; internet www.pravoedelo.ru; f. 2008, registered 2009 by fmr mems of Union of Rightist Forces, Civic Force and the Democratic Party of Russia; economically liberal; Co-Chair. of Federal Political Council GEORGII BOVT, LEONID YA. GOZMAN, BORIS TITOV; 56,000 mems (2009).

United Russia (UR) (Yedinaya Rossiya): 129110 Moscow, Pereyaslavskii per. 4; tel. (495) 786-82-89; fax (495) 975-30-78; e-mail centrpr@edinros.ru; internet www.er.ru; f. 2001 as Unity and Fatherland—United Russia, on the basis of Unity (f. 1999, incorporating Our Home is Russia), Fatherland (f. 1999, and led by Mayor of Moscow YURII LUZHKOV) and the All Russia grouping of regional governors; pragmatic centrist grouping that promotes moderate economic reforms and a strong state; absorbed Agrarian Party of Russia in Oct. 2008; Chair. VLADIMIR V. PUTIN; Chair. of Supreme Council BORIS V. GRYZLOV; 659,654 mems (2006).

Yabloko Russian United Democratic Party (Rossiiskaya obyedinennaya demokraticheskaya partiya 'Yabloko'): 119034 Moscow, per. M. Levshinskii 7/3; tel. (495) 201-43-79; fax (495) 292-34-50; e-mail admin@yabloko.ru; internet www.yabloko.ru; f. 1993 on the basis of the Yavlinskii-Boldyrev-Lukin electoral bloc; present name adopted 2008; democratic, politically and socially liberal; Chair. SERGEI S. MITROKHIN; 60,440 mems (2006).

Diplomatic Representation

EMBASSIES IN RUSSIA

Afghanistan: 121069 Moscow, ul. Povarskaya 42; tel. and fax (495) 290-01-46; e-mail safarat_moscow@yahoo.com; Ambassador ZALMAI AZIZ.

Albania: 119049 Moscow, ul. Mytnaya 3/8; tel. (495) 982-38-52; fax (495) 982-38-54; e-mail alebmassy@gtmail.ru; Chargé d'affaires a.i. ARBEN DOÇI.

Algeria: 103051 Moscow, Krapivinskii per. 1A; tel. (495) 937-46-00; fax (495) 937-46-25; e-mail algamb@ntl.ru; internet www.algerianembassy.ru; Ambassador SMAIL CHERGUI.

Angola: 119590 Moscow, ul. U. Palme 6; tel. (499) 143-63-24; fax (495) 956-18-80; e-mail angomosc@col.ru; Ambassador SAMUEL TITO ARMANDO.

Argentina: 119017 Moscow, ul. B. Ordynka 72; tel. (495) 502-10-20; fax (495) 502-10-21; e-mail efrus@co.ru; Ambassador LEOPOLDO ALFREDO BRAVO.

Armenia: 101990 Moscow, Armyanskii per. 2; tel. (495) 624-12-69; fax (495) 624-45-35; e-mail incom@armen.ru; internet www.armenianembassy.ru; Ambassador ARMEN B. SMBATIAN.

Australia: 109028 Moscow, Podkolokolnyi per. 10A/2; tel. (495) 956-60-70; fax (495) 956-61-70; e-mail austembmos@dfat.gov.au; internet www.russia.embassy.gov.au; Ambassador MARGARET EILEEN TWOMEY.

Austria: 119034 Moscow, Starokonyushennyi per. 1; tel. (495) 780-60-66; fax (495) 937-42-69; e-mail moskau-ob@bmeia.gv.at; internet www.aussenministerium.at/moskau; Ambassador Dr MARTIN VUKOVICH.

Azerbaijan: 125009 Moscow, Leontyevskii per. 16; tel. (495) 629-43-32; fax (495) 202-50-72; e-mail ismail@azerirus.cnt.ru; internet www.azembassy.ru; Ambassador POLAD BÜLBÜL OĞLU.

Bahrain: 109017 Moscow, ul. B. Ordynka 18/1; tel. (495) 953-00-22; fax (495) 953-74-74; e-mail moscowbah@yahoo.com; Ambassador ABDULHAMEED ALI HASAN ALI.

Bangladesh: 119121 Moscow, Zemledelcheskii per. 6; tel. (499) 246-78-04; fax (499) 248-31-85; e-mail bdoot.moscow@mail.ru; internet www.bangladeshembassy.ru; Ambassador MOHAMED MIJARUL QUAYES.

Belarus: 101990 Moscow, ul. Maroseika 17/6; tel. (495) 777-66-44; fax (495) 777-66-33; e-mail mail@embassybel.ru; internet www.embassybel.ru; Ambassador VASIL DALHALYOV.

Belgium: 121069 Moscow, ul. M. Molchanovka 7; tel. (495) 780-03-31; fax (495) 780-03-32; e-mail moscow@diplobel.org; internet www.diplomatie.be/moscow; Ambassador BERTRAND DE CROMBRUGGE DE PICQUENDAELE.

Benin: 127006 Moscow, Uspenskii per. 7; tel. (495) 699-23-60; fax (495) 694-02-26; e-mail amba_beninmos@yahoo.fr; Ambassador VISSINTO AYI D'ALMEIDA.

Bolivia: 115191 Moscow, ul. Serpukhovskii val 8/135–137; tel. (495) 954-06-30; fax (495) 958-07-55; e-mail embolrus@online.ru; internet www.emborus.com; Ambassador SERGIO HUGO SÁNCHEZ BALLIVIÁN.

Bosnia and Herzegovina: 119590 Moscow, ul. Mosfilmovskaya 50, korp. 1; tel. (495) 147-64-88; fax (495) 147-64-89; e-mail embassybih@mail.ru; Ambassador ŽELJKO JANJETOVIĆ.

Brazil: 121069 Moscow, ul. B. Nikitskaya 54; tel. (495) 363-03-66; fax (495) 363-03-67; e-mail brasrus@brasemb.ru; internet www.brasemb.ru; Ambassador CARLOS ANTONIO DA ROCHA PARANHOS.

Brunei: 121059 Moscow, Berezhkovskaya nab. 2, Radisson-Slavyanskaya Hotel, kom. 413, 440–441; tel. (495) 941-82-15; fax (495) 941-82-14; e-mail moscow.russia@mfa.gov.bn; Ambassador (vacant).

Bulgaria: 119590 Moscow, ul. Mosfilmovskaya 66; tel. (495) 143-90-22; fax (495) 232-33-02; e-mail bulemrus@bolgaria.ru; internet www.bolgaria.ru; Ambassador PLAMEN I. GROZDANOV.

Burundi: 119049 Moscow, Kaluzhskaya pl. 1/226–227; tel. (495) 230-25-64; fax (495) 230-20-09; e-mail bdiamb@yahoo.fr; Ambassador RENOVAT NDAYIRUKIYE.

Cambodia: 121002 Moscow, Starokonyushennyi per. 16; tel. (495) 637-47-36; fax (495) 956-65-73; e-mail cambemoscow@stream.ru; Ambassador THAVIKA KHIEU.

Cameroon: 121069 Moscow, ul. Povarskaya 40; tel. (495) 690-65-49; fax (495) 690-61-16; e-mail ambacamos@yahoo.fr; Ambassador MAHAMAT PABA SALE.

Canada: 119002 Moscow, Starokonyushennyi per. 23; tel. (495) 105-60-00; fax (495) 105-60-25; e-mail mosco@international.gc.ca; internet www.dfait-maeci.gc.ca/missions/russia-russie/menu.asp; Ambassador RALPH JAMES LYSYSHYN.

Central African Republic: 117571 Moscow, ul. 26-i Bakinskikh Kommissarov 9/124–125; tel. (495) 434-45-20; fax (495) 933-28-99; Ambassador (vacant).

Chad: 117393 Moscow, ul. Akademika Pilyugina 14, korp. 3/895–896; tel. (495) 936-17-63; fax (495) 936-11-01; Ambassador DJIBRINE ABDOUL.

Chile: 119002 Moscow, Denezhnii per. 7, str. 1; tel. (499) 241-01-45; fax (499) 241-68-67; e-mail echile@col.ru; internet www.embachilerusia.ru; Ambassador CESAR AUGUSTO PARRA MUÑOZ.

China, People's Republic: 117330 Moscow, ul. Druzhby 6; tel. (495) 938-20-06; fax (495) 956-11-69; e-mail chiemb@microdin.ru; internet ru.china-embassy.org; Ambassador LIU GUCHANG.

Colombia: 119121 Moscow, ul. Burdenko 20/2; tel. (495) 248-30-73; fax (495) 248-30-25; e-mail emrusia@colombia.ru; Ambassador DIEGO JOSÉ TÓBON ECHEVERRI.

Congo, Democratic Republic: 117556 Moscow, Simferopolskii bulv. 7A/49-50; tel. and fax (499) 613-83-48; e-mail amba_rdc_moscow@yahoo.fr; Ambassador MOÏSE KABAKU MUTSHALL.

Congo, Republic: 119049 Moscow, ul. Korovii val 7/1/10–12; tel. (495) 236-33-68; fax (495) 236-41-16; e-mail ambacoru@yahoo.gv; Ambassador JEAN-PIERRE LOUYÉBO.

Costa Rica: 121615 Moscow, Rublevskoye shosse 26/1/23; tel. (495) 415-40-14; fax (495) 415-40-42; e-mail conscr@rol.ru; internet www.geocities.com/posolstvo.kosta_rika; Chargé d'affaires a.i. PAUL CHRISTIAN CHEN WENDORF.

THE RUSSIAN FEDERATION

Côte d'Ivoire: 119034 Moscow, Korobeinikov per. 14/9; tel. (495) 637-24-00; fax (495) 637-21-57; e-mail ambacimow@hotmail.com; internet ambaci-russie.org; Ambassador GNAGNO PHILIBERT FAGNIDI.

Croatia: 119034 Moscow, Korobeinikov per. 16/10; tel. (495) 637-38-68; fax (495) 637-46-24; e-mail admin@croemba.msk.ru; internet ru.mvp.hr; Ambassador NEBOJSA KOHAROVIĆ.

Cuba: 119017 Moscow, ul. B. Ordynka 66; tel. and fax (495) 933-79-57; e-mail embsecret@ecurusia.ru; Ambassador JUAN VALDES FIGUEROA.

Cyprus: 121069 Moscow, ul. Povarskaya 9; tel. (495) 744-29-44; fax (495) 744-29-45; e-mail moscowembassy@mfa.gov.cy; internet www.mfa.gov.cy/embassymoscow; Ambassador PETROS KESTORAS.

Czech Republic: 123056 Moscow, ul. Yu. Fuchika 12/14; tel. (495) 251-05-44; fax (045) 250-15-23; e-mail moscow@embassy.mzv.cz; internet www.mfa.cz/moscow; Ambassador MIROSLAV KOSTELKA.

Denmark: 119034 Moscow, Prechistenskii per. 9; tel. (495) 642-68-00; fax (495) 775-01-91; e-mail mowamb@um.dk; internet www.ambmoskva.um.dk; Ambassador PER CARLSEN.

Dominican Republic: 121615 Moscow, Rublevskoye shosse 26, korp. 1, podyezd 4, of. 211; tel. (495) 415-25-96; fax (495) 415-36-01; Ambassador JORGE LUIS PÉREZ ALVARADO.

Ecuador: 103064 Moscow, Gorokhovskii per. 12; tel. (499) 261-55-27; fax (499) 267-70-79; e-mail embajada@embajada-ecuador.ru; internet www.embajada-ecuador.ru; Ambassador PATRICIO ALBERTO CHÁVEZ ZAVALA.

Egypt: 119034 Moscow, Kropotkinskii per. 12; tel. (495) 246-02-34; fax (495) 246-10-64; e-mail egyemb_moscow@yahoo.com; Ambassador EZZAT SAAD AS-SAYED AL-BURAEY.

Equatorial Guinea: 119017 Moscow, Pogorelskii per. 7/1; tel. (495) 953-27-66; fax (495) 953-35-63; e-mail embajada1968@mail.ru; Ambassador FAUSTO ABESO FUMA.

Eritrea: 119049 Moscow, ul. Kirovii val 7/31; tel. (499) 238-30-25; fax (499) 238-18-68; e-mail erembassy@yandex.ru; Ambassador TEKLAY MINASSIE ASGEDOM.

Estonia: 125009 Moscow, M. Kislovskii per. 5; tel. (495) 737-36-40; fax (495) 737-36-46; e-mail embassy.moskva@estemb.ru; internet www.estemb.ru; Ambassador SIIMU TIIK.

Ethiopia: 129041 Moscow, Orlovo-Davydovskii per. 6; tel. (495) 680-16-16; fax (495) 680-66-08; e-mail eth-emb@col.ru; Ambassador Dr TEKETEL FORSIDO WAMISHO.

Finland: 119034 Moscow, Kropotkinskii per. 15/17; tel. (495) 787-41-74; fax (495) 247-33-80; e-mail sanomat.mos@formin.fi; internet www.finland.org.ru; Ambassador MATTI KALERVO ANTTONEN.

France: 119049 Moscow, ul. B. Yakimanka 45; tel. (495) 937-15-00; fax (495) 937-14-46; e-mail amba@ambafrance.ru; internet www.ambafrance.ru; Ambassador JEAN DE GLINIASTY (designate).

Gabon: 119002 Moscow, Denezhnyi per. 16; tel. (499) 241-00-80; fax (499) 241-15-85; e-mail ambgab_ru@mail.ru; Ambassador PAUL BIÉ-EYENÉ.

The Gambia: 115035 Moscow, Kadashevskaya nab. 32/2/3; tel. and fax 258-36-82.

Germany: 119285 Moscow, ul. Mosfilmovskaya 56; tel. (495) 937-95-00; fax (495) 938-23-54; e-mail germanmo@aha.ru; internet www.moskau.diplo.de; Ambassador Dr WALTER SCHMID.

Ghana: 121069 Moscow, Skatertnyi per. 14; tel. (495) 690-19-61; fax (495) 690-21-98; e-mail embghmos@astelit.ru; Ambassador Air Vice-Marshall EDWARD APAU MANTEY.

Greece: 103009 Moscow, Leontiyevskii per. 4; tel. (495) 290-14-46; fax (495) 771-65-10; e-mail gremb.mow@mfa.gr; internet www.hellas.ru; Ambassador MIHALIS SPINELLIS.

Guatemala: 119049 Moscow, ul. Korovii val 7/98; tel. (499) 238-22-14; fax (499) 238-14-46; e-mail embrusia@minex.gob.gt; Ambassador ARTURO ROMEO DUARTE ORTIZ.

Guinea: 119049 Moscow, ul. Korovii val 7/1/101–102; tel. (499) 238-10-85; fax (499) 238-97-68; Ambassador Lt-Col AMARA BANGOURA.

Guinea-Bissau: 117556 Moscow, Simferopolskii bulv. 7A/180; tel. and fax (495) 317-95-82; Ambassador ROGERIO ARAUJO ADOLPHO HERBERT.

Holy See: 127055 Moscow, Vadkovskii per. 7/37; tel. (495) 726-59-30; fax (495) 726-59-32; e-mail nuntius@inbox.ru; Apostolic Nuncio Most Rev. ANTONIO MENNINI (Titular Archbishop of Ferentium).

Hungary: 119590 Moscow, ul. Mosfilmovskaya 62; tel. (495) 796-93-70; fax (495) 796-93-80; e-mail mission.mow@kum.hu; internet www.mfa.gov.hu/emb/moscow; Ambassador GYÖRGY GILYÁN.

Iceland: 121069 Moscow, Khlebnyi per. 28; tel. (495) 956-76-04; fax (495) 956-76-12; e-mail icemb.moscow@utn.sthr.is; internet www.iceland.org/ru; Ambassador BENEDIKT ASGEIRSSON.

India: 101000 Moscow, ul. Vorontsovo Pole 6–8; tel. (495) 783-75-35; fax (495) 917-22-85; e-mail indambru@com2com.ru; internet www.indianembassy.ru; Ambassador PRABHAT PRAKASH SHUKLA.

Indonesia: 109017 Moscow, ul. Novokuznetskaya 12; tel. (495) 951-95-50; fax (495) 230-64-31; e-mail kbrimos@online.ru; internet www.kbrimoskow.org; Ambassador HAMID AWALUDDIN.

Iran: 117292 Moscow, Pokrovskii bulv. 7; tel. (495) 917-72-82; fax (495) 230-96-83; internet www.iranembassy.ru; Ambassador SEYED MAHMOUD REZA SAJJADI.

Iraq: 119121 Moscow, ul. Pogodinskaya 12; tel. (499) 246-55-07; fax (499) 246-27-34; e-mail mosemb@iraqmofamail.net; Ambassador Dr ABDUL-KARIM HASHIM MOSTAFA.

Ireland: 129010 Moscow, Grokholskii per. 5; tel. (495) 937-59-11; fax (495) 680-06-23; e-mail moscowembassy@dfa.ie; internet www.embassyofireland.ru; Ambassador JUSTIN HARMAN.

Israel: 115095 Moscow, ul. B. Ordynka 56; tel. (495) 230-67-00; fax (495) 230-23-38; e-mail info@moscow.mfa.gov.il; internet moscow.mfa.gov.il; Ambassador ANNA AZARI.

Italy: 121002 Moscow, Denezhnyi per. 5; tel. (495) 796-96-91; fax (495) 253-92-89; e-mail embitaly.mosca@esteri.it; internet www.ambmosca.esteri.it; Ambassador VITTORIO CLAUDIO SURDO.

Japan: 129090 Moscow, Grokholskii per. 27; tel. (495) 229-25-50; fax (495) 229-25-55; e-mail embjapan@mail.cnt.ru; internet www.ru.emb-japan.go.jp; Ambassador YASUO SAITO.

Jordan: 123001 Moscow, Mamonovskii per. 3; tel. (495) 699-12-42; fax (495) 699-43-54; e-mail emjordan@umail.ru; Ambassador (vacant).

Kazakhstan: 101000 Moscow, Chistoprudnyi bulv. 3A; tel. (495) 627-17-01; fax (495) 608-26-50; e-mail kazembassy@kazembassy.ru; internet www.kazembassy.ru; Ambassador ADILBEK JAKSYBEKOV.

Kenya: 119034 Moscow, Lopukhinskii per. 5; tel. (495) 637-21-86; fax (495) 637-54-63; e-mail kenemb@kenemb.ru; internet www.kenemb.ru; Ambassador Dr SOSPETER MAGITA MACHAGE.

Korea, Democratic People's Republic: 107140 Moscow, ul. Mosfilmovskaya 72; tel. (499) 143-62-31; fax (499) 143-63-12; Ambassador KIM YONG JAE.

Korea, Republic: 131000 Moscow, ul. Plyushchikha 56/1; tel. (495) 783-27-27; fax (495) 783-27-77; e-mail info@koreaemb.ru; internet rus-moscow.mofat.go.kr; Ambassador LEE KYU-HYUNG.

Kuwait: 119285 Moscow, ul. Mosfilmovskaya 44A; tel. (495) 147-00-40; fax (495) 956-60-32; e-mail kuwaitmoscow@yahoo.com; internet kuwaitembassy-russia.com; Ambassador NASSER HAJI EBRAHEEM AL-MUZAYYAN.

Kyrgyzstan: 119017 Moscow, ul. B. Ordynka 64; tel. (495) 237-48-82; fax (495) 951-60-62; e-mail embassy@embas-kyrg.msk.ru; Ambassador RAIMKUL A. ATTAKUROV.

Laos: 101000 Moscow, ul. M. Nikitskaya 18; tel. (495) 201-01-58; fax (495) 203-49-24; e-mail post@laoembassy.ru; internet www.laoembassy.ru; Ambassador THONGSAVANH PHOMVIHANE.

Latvia: 105062 Moscow, ul. Chaplygina 3; tel. (495) 232-97-60; fax (495) 232-97-50; e-mail embassy.russia@am.gov.lv; internet www.am.gov.lv/lv/moscow; Ambassador EDGARS SKUJA (designate).

Lebanon: 115127 Moscow, ul. Sadovaya-Samotechnaya 14; tel. (495) 694-13-20; fax (495) 694-32-22; e-mail leb.emb.moscow@mtu-net.ru; Ambassador Dr ASSEM JABER.

Libya: 131940 Moscow, ul. Mosfilmovskaya 38; tel. (495) 143-03-54; fax (495) 938-21-62; e-mail libyanbureau@mail.ru; Ambassador MUSTAFA M. T. TAJOURI.

Lithuania: 121069 Moscow, Borisoglebskii per. 10; tel. (495) 785-86-05; fax (495) 785-86-00; internet ru.mfa.lt; Ambassador ANTANAS VINKUS.

Luxembourg: 119034 Moscow, Khrushchevskii per. 3; tel. (495) 786-66-63; e-mail moscou.amb@mae.etat.lu; Ambassador GASTON PIERRE JEAN STRONCK.

Macedonia, former Yugoslav republic: 117292 Moscow, ul. D. Ulyanova 16, korp. 2/509–510; tel. (495) 124-33-57; fax (495) 982-36-34; e-mail mkambmos@mail.tascom.ru; Ambassador ZLATKO LEČEVSKI.

Madagascar: 119034 Moscow, Kursovoi per. 5; tel. (495) 695-28-92; fax (495) 695-28-54; e-mail info@ambamadagascar.ru; internet www.ambamadagascar.ru; Ambassador ELOI ALPHONSE MAXIME DOVO.

Malaysia: 119192 Moscow, ul. Mosfilmovskaya 50; tel. (499) 147-15-14; fax (495) 937-96-02; e-mail malmoscow@kln.gov.my; Ambassador Dato' MUHAMMAD KHALIS ALI HASSAN.

Mali: 113184 Moscow, ul. Novokuznetskaya 11; tel. (495) 951-06-55; fax (495) 951-58-04; e-mail amaliru@mail.ru; Ambassador Gen. BRAHIMA COULIBALY.

Malta: 119049 Moscow, ul. Korovii val 7/219; tel. (495) 237-19-39; fax (495) 237-21-58; e-mail maltaembassy.moscow@gov.mt; Ambassador Dr MARIO COSTA.

Mauritania: 119121 Moscow, B. Sabbinskii per. 21; tel. (495) 245-11-76; fax (495) 246-25-19; e-mail mauritanie@redline.ru; Ambassador BOULAH OULD MOGUEYE.

Mauritius: 109240 Moscow, ul. Nikolo-Yamskaya 8; tel. (495) 915-76-17; fax (495) 915-76-65; Ambassador Mahendr Dosieah.

Mexico: 119034 Moscow, B. Levshinskii per. 4; tel. (495) 969-28-79; fax (495) 969-28-77; e-mail info@embamex.ru; internet portal.sre.gob.mx/rusia; Ambassador Alfredo Rogerio Pérez Bravo.

Moldova: 107031 Moscow, ul. Kuznetskii most 18; tel. (495) 624-53-53; fax (495) 624-95-90; e-mail info@moldembassy.ru; internet www.moldembassy.ru; Ambassador Andrei Neguța (designate).

Mongolia: 121069 Moscow, Borisoglebskii per. 11; tel. (495) 290-67-92; fax (495) 291-46-36; e-mail mongolia@online.ru; internet www.mongoliaembassy.ru; Ambassador Luvsandandaryn Khangai.

Montenegro: 119049 Moscow, ul. Mytnaya 3/23–25; tel. (499) 230-18-65; fax (499) 230-18-86; e-mail ambasadacg@ya.ru; Ambassador Slobodan Backović.

Morocco: 121069 Moscow, ul. B. Nikitskaya 51; tel. (495) 291-17-62; fax (495) 609-94-93; e-mail sifmamos@xrus.ru; Ambassador Abdelkader Lecheheb.

Mozambique: 129090 Moscow, ul. Gilyarovskogo 8/45–48; tel. (495) 684-40-07; fax (495) 684-36-54; e-mail embamocru@hotmail.com; Ambassador Bernardo Marcelino Cherinda.

Myanmar: 121069 Moscow, ul. B Nikitskaya 41; tel. (495) 291-56-14; fax (495) 956-18-78; e-mail mofa.aung@mptmail.net.mm; Ambassador Min Thein.

Namibia: 113096 Moscow, 2-i Kazachii per. 7; tel. (495) 230-32-75; fax (495) 230-22-74; e-mail namembrf@online.ru; Ambassador Dr Samuel Kaveto Mbambo.

Nepal: 119121 Moscow, 2-i Neopalimovskii per. 14/7; tel. (495) 244-02-15; fax (495) 244-00-00; e-mail nepalemb@mtu-net.ru; internet www.nepalembassyrus.org; Ambassador Surya Kiran Gurung.

Netherlands: 125009 Moscow, Kalashnyi per. 6; tel. (495) 797-29-00; fax (495) 797-29-04; e-mail mos@minbuza.nl; internet www.netherlands-embassy.ru; Ambassador Jan-Paul Dirkse.

New Zealand: 121069 Moscow, ul. Povarskaya 44; tel. (495) 956-35-79; fax (495) 956-35-83; e-mail nzembmos@umail.ru; internet www.nzembassy.com/russia; Ambassador Christopher J. Elder.

Nicaragua: 117330 Moscow, ul. Mosfilmovskaya 50, korp. 1; tel. and fax (495) 938-20-09; e-mail embajada@rol.ru.

Nigeria: 121069 Moscow, ul. M. Nikitskaya 13; tel. (495) 690-37-83; fax (495) 956-28-25; e-mail info@nigerianembassy.ru; internet www.nigerianembassy.ru; Ambassador Maj.-Gen. (retd) Timothy Mai Shelpidi.

Norway: 131940 Moscow, ul. Povarskaya 7; tel. (495) 933-14-10; fax (495) 933-14-11; e-mail emb.moscow@mfa.no; internet www.norvegia.ru; Ambassador Knut Hauge.

Oman: 109180 Moscow, Staromonetnyi per. 14, str. 1; tel. (495) 230-15-87; fax (495) 230-15-44; e-mail embomn-mos@rambler.ru; Ambassador Abdullah bin Zaher al-Hussni.

Pakistan: 123001 Moscow, ul. Sadovaya-Kudrinskaya 17; tel. (495) 254-97-91; fax (495) 956-90-97; e-mail parepmoscow@yahoo.com; internet www.pakistanembassy.ru; Ambassador Mohammad Khalid Khattak.

Panama: 119590 Moscow, ul. Mosfilmovskaya 50, korp. 1; tel. (495) 956-07-29; fax (495) 956-07-30; e-mail empanrus@aha.ru; Ambassador Augusto Aurelio Fabrego Donado.

Paraguay: 119049 Moscow, ul. Korovii val 7/142; tel. (499) 230-18-10; e-mail embajada@embapar.ru; Ambassador Marcial Bobadilla Guillen.

Peru: 121002 Moscow, Smolenskii bulv. 22/14, off. 15; tel. (499) 248-77-38; fax (499) 248-00-72; e-mail leprumoscu@mtu-net.ru; Ambassador Dr Humberto Umeres Alvarez.

Philippines: 121099 Moscow, Karmanitskii per. 6; tel. (499) 241-05-63; fax (499) 241-26-30; e-mail moscowpe@stream.ru; internet www.phil-embassy.ru; Ambassador Victor G. Garcia, III.

Poland: 123557 Moscow, ul. Klimashkina 4; tel. (495) 231-15-00; fax (495) 231-15-15; e-mail embassy@polandemb.ru; internet www.moskwa.polemb.net; Ambassador Jerzy Bahr.

Portugal: 129010 Moscow, Botanicheskii per. 1; tel. (495) 981-34-10; fax (495) 981-34-16; e-mail embptrus@moscovo.dgaccp.pt; Ambassador Manuel Marcelo Montiero Curto.

Qatar: 117049 Moscow, ul. Korovii Val 7/196–198; tel. (495) 980-69-18; fax (495) 980-69-17; e-mail moscow@mofa.gov.qa; Ambassador Ahmad Saif Khalaf al-Meathady.

Romania: 119590 Moscow, ul. Mosfilmovskaya 64; tel. (499) 143-04-24; fax (499) 143-04-49; e-mail ambasada@orc.ru; internet moscova.mae.ro; Ambassador Constantin Mihail Grigorie.

Saudi Arabia: 119121 Moscow, 3-i Neopalimovskii per. 3; tel. (495) 245-23-10; fax (495) 246-94-71; e-mail saudiemb@msk.org.ru; internet www.mofa.gov.sa/detail.asp?InServiceID=238; Ambassador Ali Hassan Jaafar.

Senegal: 119049 Moscow, ul. Korovii val 7/1/193–195; tel. (499) 230-20-72; fax (499) 230-20-63; Ambassador Mountaga Diallo.

Serbia: 119285 Moscow, ul. Mosfilmovskaya 46; tel. (499) 147-41-06; fax (499) 147-41-04; e-mail ambasada@co.ru; Ambassador Jelica Kurjak (designate).

Sierra Leone: 121615 Moscow, Rublevskoye shosse 26, korp. 1/58–59; tel. (495) 415-41-24; fax (495) 415-29-85; Chargé d'affaires Ibrahim Vandi Kondoh.

Singapore: 121099 Moscow, per. Kamennoi Slobody 5; tel. (495) 241-39-13; fax (495) 241-78-95; e-mail sinembmow@co.ru; Ambassador Simon Tensing de Cruz.

Slovakia: 123056 Moscow, ul. Yu. Fuchika 17/19; tel. (495) 250-10-70; fax (495) 250-15-91; e-mail embassy@moskva.mfa.sk; internet www.moscow.mfa.sk; Ambassador Dr Augustín Cisár.

Slovenia: 127006 Moscow, ul. M. Dmitrovka 14/1; tel. (495) 737-63-55; fax (495) 694-15-68; e-mail vmo@gov.si; internet moscow.embassy.si; Ambassador Andrej Benedejčič.

Somalia: 117556 Moscow, Simferopolskii bulv. 7A /145; tel. and fax (499) 317-06-22; e-mail somembassy@nabad.org; Ambassador Mohamed Mohamoud Handulle.

South Africa: 123001 Moscow, Granatnyi per. 1, str. 9; tel. (495) 926-11-77; fax (495) 926-11-78; e-mail moscow.ambassador@foreign.gov.za; internet saembassy.ru; Ambassador Dr Bheki Winston Joshua Langa.

Spain: 121069 Moscow, ul. B. Nikitskaya 50/8; tel. (495) 202-21-61; fax (495) 291-91-71; e-mail embespru@mail.mae.es; internet www.maec.es/embajadas/moscu; Ambassador Juan Antonio March Pujol.

Sri Lanka: 129090 Moscow, ul. Shchepkina 24; tel. (495) 688-16-20; fax (495) 688-17-57; e-mail lankaemb@com2com.ru; Ambassador Udayanga Weeratunga.

Sudan: 127006 Moscow, Uspenskii per. 4A; tel. (495) 699-54-61; fax (495) 699-33-42; e-mail sudmos@cityline.ru; Ambassador Sirajuddin Hamid Yousuf.

Sweden: 119590 Moscow, ul. Mosfilmovskaya 60; tel. (495) 937-92-00; fax (495) 937-92-02; e-mail moscow.sweinfo@foreign.ministry.se; internet www.swedenabroad.com/moscow; Ambassador Lars Peter Tomas Bertelman.

Switzerland: 101000 Moscow, per. Ogorodnoi slobody 2/5; tel. (495) 258-38-30; fax (495) 200-17-28; e-mail mos.vertretung@eda.admin.ch; internet www.eda.admin.ch/moscow; Ambassador Walter Bruno Gyger (designate).

Syria: 119034 Moscow, Mansurovskii per. 4; tel. (499) 766-95-28; fax (495) 956-31-91; Ambassador Hassan Risheh.

Tajikistan: 103001 Moscow, Granatnyi per. 13; tel. (495) 290-38-46; fax (495) 291-89-98; e-mail embassy_moscow@tajikistan.ru; internet www.tajikistan.ru; Ambassador Abdulmajid S. Dostiyev.

Tanzania: 109017 Moscow, ul. Pyatnitskaya 33; tel. (495) 953-82-21; fax (495) 953-07-85; e-mail tzmos@wm.west.call.com; internet www.tanzania.ru; Ambassador Jaka Mgwabi Mwambi.

Thailand: 129090 Moscow, ul. B. Spasskaya 9; tel. (495) 608-08-17; fax (495) 290-96-59; e-mail thaiemb@nnt.ru; internet www.thaiembassymoscow.com; Ambassador Suphot Dhirakaosal.

Tunisia: 113105 Moscow, ul. M. Nikitskaya 28/1; tel. (495) 691-28-58; fax (495) 691-75-88; e-mail atmos@post.ru; Ambassador Khemaies Jhinaoui.

Turkey: 119121 Moscow, 7-i Rostovskii per. 12; tel. (495) 956-55-95; fax (495) 956-55-97; e-mail turemb@co.ru; Ambassador Halil Akinci.

Turkmenistan: 119019 Moscow, Filippovskii per. 22; tel. (495) 291-66-36; fax (495) 291-09-35; Ambassador Khalnazar A. Agakhanov.

Uganda: 119049 Moscow, ul. Korovii val 7, str. 1/3; tel. (499) 230-22-76; fax (499) 230-21-31; e-mail info@uganda.ru; internet www.uganda.ru; Ambassador Dr Moses Ebuku.

Ukraine: 103009 Moscow, Leontiyevskii per. 18; tel. (495) 629-35-42; fax (495) 629-46-81; e-mail emb_ru@mfa.gov.ua; internet www.mfa.gov.ua/russia; Ambassador Kostyantyn I. Hryshchenko.

United Arab Emirates: 101000 Moscow, ul. U. Palme 4; tel. (499) 234-40-60; fax (495) 234-40-70; e-mail uaemirates@mtu-net.ru; Ambassador Omar Saif Ghobash.

United Kingdom: 121099 Moscow, Smolenskaya nab. 10; tel. (495) 956-72-00; fax (495) 956-72-01; e-mail moscow@britishembassy.ru; internet www.britaininrussia.ru; Ambassador Anne Pringle.

USA: 121099 Moscow, B. Devyatinskii per. 8; tel. (495) 728-50-00; fax (495) 728-50-90; e-mail pamoscow@pd.state.gov; internet moscow.usembassy.gov; Ambassador John Ross Beyrle.

Uruguay: 119049 Moscow, ul. Mytnaya 3/16; tel. (495) 230-77-65; fax (495) 938-20-45; e-mail urururu@uruguay.org.ru; internet www.uruguay.org.ru; Ambassador Jorge Alberto Meyer Long.

Uzbekistan: 109017 Moscow, Pogorelskii per. 12; tel. (495) 230-00-76; fax (495) 238-89-18; e-mail info@uzembassy.ru; internet www.uzembassy.ru; Ambassador ILHOMJON NEMATOV.

Venezuela: 115127 Moscow, B. Karetnyi per. 13/15; tel. (495) 699-40-42; fax (495) 956-61-08; e-mail info@embaven.ru; internet www.embaven.ru; Ambassador HUGO JOSÉ GARCIA HERNÁNDEZ.

Viet Nam: 119021 Moscow, ul. B. Pirogovskaya 13; tel. (495) 245-09-25; fax (495) 246-31-21; e-mail dsqvn@com2com.ru; Ambassador BUI DINH DINH.

Yemen: 119121 Moscow, 2-i Neopalimovskii per. 6; tel. (499) 246-15-40; fax (495) 230-23-05; Ambassador MUHAMMAD SALEH AHMED AL-HELALI.

Zambia: 129041 Moscow, pr. Mira 52A; tel. (495) 688-50-01; fax (495) 975-20-56; Ambassador Rev. Dr PETER LUSAKA CHINTALA.

Zimbabwe: 119121 Moscow, per. Serpov 6; tel. (499) 248-43-67; fax (499) 230-24-97; e-mail zimbabwe@rinet.ru; Ambassador PHELEKEZELA MPHOKO.

Judicial System

In January 1995 the first section of a new code of civil law came into effect. It included new rules on commercial and financial operations, and on ownership issues. The second part of the code was published in January 1996. The Constitutional Court rules on the conformity of government policies, federal laws, international treaties and presidential enactments with the Constitution. The Supreme Arbitration Court rules on disputes between commercial bodies. The Supreme Court oversees all criminal and civil law, and is the final court of appeal from lower courts. A system of Justices of the Peace, to deal with certain civil cases, and with criminal cases punishable by a maximum of two years' imprisonment, was established in 1998. The majority of Russia's regions introduced jury trials, in many cases only for the most serious crimes, during 2003.

Constitutional Court of the Russian Federation (Konstitutsionnyi Sud Rossiiskoi Federatsii): 190000 St Petersburg, pl. Dekabristov 1; tel. (812) 404-33-11; e-mail ksrf@krsf.ru; internet www.ksrf.ru; f. 1991; Chair. VALERII D. ZORKIN; Sec.-Gen. YELENA V. KRAVCHENKO.

Office of the Prosecutor-General: 125993 Moscow, ul. B. Dmitrovka 15A; tel. (495) 692-26-82; fax (495) 292-88-48; internet www.genproc.gov.ru; Prosecutor-General YURII YA. CHAIKA.

Supreme Arbitration Court of the Russian Federation (Vysshii Arbitrazhnyi Sud Rossiiskoi Federatsii): 101000 Moscow, M. Kharitonevskii per. 12; tel. (495) 208-11-19; fax (495) 208-11-62; internet www.arbitr.ru; f. 1993; Chair. ANTON A. IVANOV.

Supreme Court of the Russian Federation (Verkhovnyi Sud Rossiiskoi Federatsii): 103289 Moscow, ul. Ilinka 7/3; tel. (495) 924-23-47; fax (495) 202-71-18; e-mail gastello@ilinka.supcourt.ru; internet www.supcourt.ru; Chair. VYACHESLAV M. LEBEDEV.

Religion

The majority of the population of the Russian Federation are adherents of Christianity, but there are significant Islamic, Buddhist and Jewish minorities.

In 1997 legislation restricted the operation of religious groups to those that were to prove that they had been established in Russia for a minimum of 15 years. Russian Orthodoxy, Islam, Buddhism and Judaism, together with some other Christian denominations, were deemed to comply with the legislation. Religious organizations failing to satisfy this requirement were, henceforth, obliged to register annually for 15 years, before being permitted to publish literature, hold public services or invite foreign preachers into Russia. Moreover, foreign religious groups were additionally obliged to affiliate themselves to Russian organizations.

CHRISTIANITY

The Russian Orthodox Church (Moscow Patriarchate)

The Russian Orthodox Church (Moscow Patriarchate) is the dominant religious organization in the Russian Federation, with an estimated 75m. adherents. In 2004 there were 12,638 parishes operating under the auspices of the Patriarchate in Russia.

Moscow Patriarchate: 115191 Moscow, Danilov Monastery, ul. Danilovskii Val 22; tel. (495) 954-04-54; fax (495) 633-72-81; e-mail cs@mospatr.ru; internet www.mospat.ru; Patriarch of Moscow and all Rus KIRILL (GUNDYAYEV).

The Roman Catholic Church

At 31 December 2006 there were an estimated 774,900 Roman Catholics in the Russian Federation. In 1991 administrative structures of the Roman Catholic Church in Russia were restored. The organization of the Church in Russian comprises one archdiocese, three dioceses, one apostolic prefecture, and an apostolic exarchate for adherents of the Byzantine Rite.

Conference of Catholic Bishops of the Russian Federation 101031 Moscow, ul. Petrovka 19/5/35; tel. and fax (495) 923-16-97; e-mail ostastop@glasnet.ru; internet www.catholic.ru.
f. 1999; Pres. Most. Rev. JOSEPH WERTH (Bishop of the Diocese of the Transfiguration at Novosibirsk).

Archbishop of the Archdiocese of the Mother of God at Moscow: Most Rev. PAOLO PEZZI, 107078 Moscow, POB 116, ul. N. Basmannaya 16/31; tel. and fax (499) 261-67-14; e-mail cathmos@dol.ru.

Protestant Churches

Russian Church of Christians of the Evangelical Faith: 123363 Moscow, ul. Fabritsiusa 31A; tel. (495) 493-57-88; internet hve.ru; f. 1907, re-established 1990; fmrly known as Union of Christians of the Evangelical Faith-Pentecostalists in Russia; 1,600 parishes and more than 300,000 adherents in 2005; Elder NAZAR P. RESHCHIKOVETS.

Russian Union of Evangelical Christians-Baptists: 117015 Moscow, Varshavskoye shosse 29/2; tel. (495) 958-13-36; fax (495) 975-23-67; e-mail bapt.un@g23.relcom.ru; internet baptist.org.ru; affiliated to the Euro-Asiatic Federation of Evangelical Christians-Baptists; Exec. Sec. YURII APATOV.

Other Christian Churches

Armenian Apostolic Church: 123022 Moscow, ul. S. Makeyeva 10; tel. (495) 255-50-19.

Russian Autonomous Orthodox Church: 125212 Moscow, Church of the New Martyrs and Confessors of Russia, Golovinskoye shosse 13 A; tel. (495) 152-50-76; formally established in 1990 as the Free Russian Orthodox Church; re-registered in 1998 under above name following opposition by local, 'catacomb' priests to moves of reconciliation between the Russian Orthodox Church Abroad and the Moscow Patriarchate; 100 parishes in 2001; First Hierarch Metropolitan of Suzdal and Vladimir VALENTIN (RUSANTSOV).

Russian Orthodox Old Belief (Old Ritual) Church (Russkaya Pravoslavnaya Staroobryadcheskaya Tserkov): 109052 Moscow, ul. Rogozhskii pos. 1B/3; tel. (495) 361-51-92; e-mail expers2rpsc.ru; internet www.rpsc.ru; f. 1666 by separation from the Moscow Patriarchate; some 300 groups registered in 2005; divided into two main branches: the *popovtsi* (which have priests) and the *bespopovtsi* (which reject the notion of ordained priests and the use of all sacraments, other than that of baptism). Both branches are further divided into various groupings. The largest group of *popovtsi* are those of the Belokrinitskii Concord, under the Archbishop of Novozybkov, Moscow and All Rus, KORNILII (TITOV); c. 250 parishes, seven bishops in Russia, Ukraine and Moldova; a further significant group of *popovtsi* Old Believers are those of the Beglopopovtsyi Concord.

ISLAM

Most Muslims in the Russian Federation are adherents of the Sunni sect. Islam is the predominant religion among many peoples of the North Caucasus, such as the Chechens, the Ingush and many smaller groups, and also in the Central Volga region, among them the Tatars, Chuvash and Bashkirs.

Central Muslim Spiritual Board for Russia and European Countries of the CIS: 450057 Bashkortostan, Ufa, ul. Tukaya 50; tel. (3472) 50-80-86; f. 1789; 27 regional branches in the Russian Federation, and one branch in Ukraine; Chair. (vacant).

Council of Muftis of Russia: 129090 Moscow, per. Vypolzov 7; tel. and fax (495) 681-49-04; e-mail mufty@muslim.ru; internet www.muslim.ru; Chair. Mufti Sheikh RAVIL KHAZRAT GAINUTDIN.

JUDAISM

At the beginning of the 20th century approximately one-half of the world's Jews lived in the Russian Empire. Although many Jews emigrated from the USSR in the 1970s and 1980s, there is still a significant Jewish population (230,000 in late 2002, according to the official results of the census, although some estimates were considerably higher) in the Russian Federation.

Congress of Jewish Religious Communities and Organizations of Russia: 101000 Moscow, B. Spasoglinishevskii per. 10, Moscow Choral Synagogue; tel. (495) 917-95-92; fax (495) 740-12-18; e-mail keroor@mail.ru; f. 1996; co-ordinates activities of 120 Jewish communities throughout Russia; Chief Rabbi ADOLF SHAYEVICH; Dir ZINOVY KOGAN.

Federation of the Jewish Communities of Russia: 121099 Moscow, ul. Novyi Arbat 36/9/2; tel. (495) 290-75-18; fax (495) 290-

86-49; e-mail office@fjc.ru; internet www.fjc.ru; unites 179 communities in Russia; affiliated to Federation of the Jewish Communities of the CIS and the Baltic States; Chief Rabbi of Russia, Chair. of Rabbinical Alliance of Russia and the CIS BEREL LAZAR.

Russian Jewish Congress: 101000 Moscow, B. Spasoglinishchevskii per. 9/1/936; tel. (495) 780-61-00; fax (495) 780-60-90; e-mail rjc@rjc.ru; internet www.rjc.ru; Pres. VYACHESLAV KANTOR.

BUDDHISM

Buddhism (established as an official religion in Russia in 1741) is most widespread in the Republic of Buryatiya, where the Traditional Buddhist Sangkha of Russia has its seat, in the Republics of Kalmykiya and Tyva, in Transbaikal Krai (formerly Chita Oblast) and in Irkutsk Oblast.

Buddhist Traditional Sangkha of Russia (Buddiiskaya Traditsionnaya Sangkha Rossii): 670000 Buryatiya, Ulan-Ude, Ivolginskii datsan; e-mail buddhism@buryatia.ru; internet buddhism.buryatia.ru; Head Pandito Khambo Lama DAMBA AYUSHEYEV.

The Press

In 2004 there were 46,000 officially registered printed media, including some 26,000 newspapers. However, the number of titles in circulation was only around one-half of the total. The total print run of Russian newspapers in that year was 8,500m. copies, and that of magazines was around 600m. copies. At that time *Moskovskii Komsomolets*, with a circulation of 2.2m., was the best-selling daily, while the weekly, *Argumenty i Fakty*, which had a circulation of 2.9m. in 2007, was the best-selling newspaper overall.

Federal Agency for the Press and the Mass Media (Federalnoye Agentstvo po pechati i massovym kommunikatsiyam): 127994 Moscow, Strastnoi bulv. 5; tel. (495) 650-39-86; e-mail sekretarr@fapmc.ru; internet www.fapmc.ru; f. 2004; Chair. MIKHAIL V. SESLAVINSKII.

PRINCIPAL NEWSPAPERS

Moscow

Argumenty i Fakty (Arguments and Facts): 101000 Moscow, ul. Myasnitskaya 42; tel. (495) 923-35-41; fax (495) 925-61-82; e-mail n-boris@aif.ru; internet www.aif.ru; f. 1978; weekly; Editor-in-Chief NIKOLAI ZYATKOV; circ. 2.9m. (2007).

Gazeta (Newspaper): 123242 Moscow, ul. Zoologicheskaya 4; tel. (495) 787-39-99; fax (495) 787-39-98; e-mail info@gzt.ru; internet www.gzt.ru; f. 2001; Editor-in-Chief PETR YE. FADEYEV; circ. 726,000 (2005).

Gazeta.ru: 117152 Moscow, Zagorodnoye shosse 1/1; tel. (495) 785-09-76; internet www.gazeta.ru; online only; has no asscn with the newspaper *Gazeta*; Editor-in-Chief ALEKSANDR PISAREV.

Grani.ru: Moscow; tel. (495) 363-36-08; e-mail info@grani.ru; internet grani.ru; f. 2000; online only; Dir-Gen. YULIYA BEREZOVSKAYA; Editor-in-Chief VLADIMIR KORSUNSKII.

Gudok (The Horn): 105066 Moscow, ul. Staraya Basmannaya 38/2/3; tel. (495) 262-26-53; fax (495) 262-45-74; e-mail welcome@gudok.ru; internet www.gudok.ru; f. 1917 as newspaper of railway workers; daily; Editor-in-Chief IGOR T. YANIN; circ. 214,000 (2007).

Izvestiya (News): 127994 Moscow, ul. Tverskaya 18/1, POB 4; tel. (495) 209-05-81; fax (495) 933-64-62; e-mail info1@izvestia.ru; internet www.izvestia.ru; f. 1917; 50.19% owned by Gazprom Mediya, 49.81% by Prof-Mediya; Editor-in-Chief VLADIMIR MAMONTOV; circ. 130,000 (2007).

Kommersant (Businessman): 125080 Moscow, ul. Vrubelya 4/1; tel. (499) 943-97-71; fax (499) 943-97-28; e-mail kommersant@kommersant.ru; internet www.kommersant.com; f. 1989; daily; Editor ANDREI VASILYEV; circ. 119,322 (2007).

Komsomolskaya Pravda (Young Communist League Truth): 103287 Moscow, Staryi Petrovsko-Razumovskii proyezd 1/23/1; tel. (495) 257-51-39; fax (495) 200-22-93; e-mail kp@kp.ru; internet www.kp.ru; f. 1925; fmrly organ of the Lenin Young Communist League (Komsomol); independent; weekly supplements *KP-Tolstushka* (KP-Fat volume), *KP-Ponedelnik* (KP-Monday); managed by Prof-Mediya; Chair. OLEG RUDNOV; Editor VLADIMIR SUNGORKIN; circ. 700,000.

Krasnaya Zvezda (Red Star): 123007 Moscow, Khoroshevskoye shosse 38; tel. (495) 941-21-58; fax (495) 941-40-66; e-mail redstar@mail.cnt.ru; internet www.redstar.ru; f. 1924; organ of the Ministry of Defence; Editor N. N. YEFIMOV; circ. 80,000 (2000).

The Moscow News: 119021 Moscow, Zubovskii bulv. 4; tel. (495) 645-65-65; e-mail info@mnweekly.ru; internet www.mnweekly.ru; f. 1930; weekly; in English; democratic, liberal; Editor-in-Chief TIM WALL; circ. c. 79,500 (2009).

Moscow Times: 127018 Moscow, ul. Polkovaya 3/1; tel. (495) 234-32-23; fax (495) 232-65-29; e-mail moscowtimes.editors@imedia.ru; internet www.themoscowtimes.com; f. 1992; daily; in English; Publr MAXINE MATERS; Editor ANDREW MCCHESNEY.

Moskovskaya Pravda (The Moscow Truth): 123846 Moscow, ul. 1905 Goda 7, POB D-22; tel. (495) 259-82-33; fax (495) 259-63-60; e-mail newspaper@mospravda.ru; internet www.mospravda.ru; f. 1918; fmrly organ of the Moscow city committee of the CPSU and the Moscow City Council; 5 a week; independent; Editor SHOD S. MULADZHANOV; circ. 400,000 (2007).

Moskovskii Komsomolets (MK): 123995 Moscow, ul. 1905 Goda 7; tel. (495) 259-50-36; fax (495) 259-46-39; e-mail letters@mk.ru; internet www.mk.ru; f. 1919 as *Moskovskii Komsomolets* (The Moscow Young Communist); 6 a week; independent; Editor-in-Chief PAVEL GUSEV; circ. 800,000 in Moscow, 2.2m. nation-wide (2004).

Nezavisimaya Gazeta (NG) (Independent Newspaper): 101000 Moscow, ul. Myasnitskaya 13; tel. (495) 645-61-54; e-mail info@ng.ru; internet www.ng.ru; f. 1990; 5 a week; regular supplements include *NG-Nauka* (NG-Science), *NG-Regiony* (NG-Regions), *NG-Politekonomiya* (NG-Political Economy), *NG-Dipkuryer* (NG-Diplomatic Courier); Gen. Man. and Editor-in-Chief KONSTANTIN REMCHUKOV; circ. 53,000 (2005).

Novaya Gazeta (New Newspaper): 101000 Moscow, Potapovskii per. 3; tel. and fax (495) 623-68-88; e-mail pr@novayagazeta.ru; internet www.novayagazeta.ru; f. 1993; weekly; Editor DMITRII A. MURATOV.

Novye Izvestiya (New News): 107076 Moscow, ul. Elektrozavodskaya 33; tel. (495) 783-06-36; fax (495) 783-06-37; e-mail webmaster@newizv.ru; internet www.newizv.ru; f. 2003 following the closure of the fmr *Novye Izvestiya* (f. 1997); daily; Editor-in-Chief VALERII YAKOV.

Parlamentskaya Gazeta (Parliamentary Newspaper): 125993 Moscow, ul. 1–ya Yamskogo Polya 28; tel. (495) 257-50-90; fax (495) 257-50-82; e-mail pg@pnp.ru; internet www.pnp.ru; f. 1998; 5 a week; organ of the Federalnoye Sobraniye; Editor-in-Chief PETR A. KOTOV; circ. 50,000 (2005).

Polit.ru: 101000 Moscow, Krivokolennyi per. 10/6A; tel. (495) 624-80-09; e-mail edit@polit.ru; internet www.polit.ru; f. 1998; independent; online only; Editor-in-Chief ANDREI LEVKIN.

Pravda (Truth): 125867 Moscow, ul. Pravdy 24; tel. (499) 257-52-13; e-mail pravda2@cnt.ru; internet www.gazeta-pravda.ru; f. 1912; fmrly organ of the Cen. Cttee of the CPSU; independent; communist; Editor-in-Chief VALENTIN S. SHURCHANOV; circ. 100,300 (2007).

Pravda.ru: Moscow, ul. Staraya Basmannaya 16/2; tel. and fax (499) 261-48-85; e-mail home@pravda.ru; internet pravda.ru; f. 1999; online only, in Russian, English and Portuguese; has no asscn with the newspaper *Pravda*; Editor-in-Chief INNA S. NOVIKOVA.

Rossiiskaya Gazeta (Russian Newspaper): 125993 Moscow, ul. Pravdy 24, POB 40; tel. (495) 257-52-52; fax (495) 973-22-56; e-mail sekretar@rg.ru; internet www.rg.ru; f. 1990; organ of the Russian Govt; 6 a week; Gen. Man. ALEKSANDR N. GORBENKO; Editor-in-Chief VLADISLAV A. FRONIN; circ. 373,820 (2004).

Rossiiskiye Vesti (Russian News): 119034 Moscow, ul. Prechistenka 28; tel. (495) 933-06-47; fax (495) 201-51-02; e-mail mail@rosvesty.ru; internet www.rosvesty.ru; f. 1991; weekly; Editor-in-Chief ALEKSEI TITKOV.

Russkii Zhurnal (Russian Journal): 125009 Moscow, per. M. Gnezdnikovskii 9/8/3A; tel. and fax (495) 745-52-25; e-mail russ@russ.ru; internet www.russ.ru; f. 1997; online only; culture, politics, society; Editor-in-Chief and Publr GLEB PAVLOVSKII.

Selskaya Zhizn (Country Life): 125869 Moscow, ul. Pravdy 24, POB 137; tel. (495) 257-51-51; fax (495) 257-58-39; e-mail sg@sgazeta.ru; internet www.sgazeta.ru; f. 1918 as *Bednota* (Poverty), present name adopted in 1960; 2 a week; fmrly organ of the Cen. Cttee of the CPSU; independent; Editor-in-Chief and Gen. Man. SHAMUN M. KAGERMANOV; circ. 94,500.

Tribuna (Tribune): 125993 Moscow, ul. Pravdy 24, POB A-40; tel. (495) 257-59-13; fax (495) 973-20-02; e-mail tribuna@tribuna.ru; internet www.tribuna.ru; f. 1969; national industrial daily; Editor-in-Chief OLEG KUZIN.

Trud (Labour): 125993 Moscow, ul. Pravdy 24/5; tel. (495) 580-66-93; e-mail letter@trud.ru; internet www.trud.ru; f. 1921; 5 a week; Editor ALEKSANDR S. POTAPOV.

Vechernyaya Moskva (Evening Moscow): 123995 Moscow, ul. 1905 Goda 7, POB 5/22; tel. (495) 259-81-87; fax (495) 253-95-75; e-mail post@vm.ru; internet www.vm.ru; f. 1923; Chair. VLADIMIR V. ZUBKOV.

Vedomosti (Gazette): 125212 Moscow, ul. Vyborgskaya 16; tel. (495) 232-32-00; fax (495) 956-07-16; e-mail vedomosti@media.ru; internet www.vedomosti.ru; f. 1999; independent business newspaper, publ. jointly with the *Financial Times* (United Kingdom) and the *Wall Street Journal* (USA); Editor-in-Chief YELIZABETA OSETINSKAYA.

Vremya Novosti (News Time): 115326 Moscow, ul. Pyatnitskaya 25; tel. (495) 231-18-77; e-mail nter@vremya.ru; internet www.vremya.ru; f. 2000; Editor-in-Chief VLADIMIR S. GUREVICH.

Zhizn (Life): 125212 Moscow, ul. Vyborgskaya 16/1; tel. (495) 510-29-84; fax (495) 510-29-81; e-mail info@zhizn.ru; internet www.zhizn.ru; weekly; Editor-in-Chief RUSLAN SAGAYEV; circ. 2.2.m. within Russia (2007).

St Petersburg

Novosti Peterburga (Petersburg News): 191084 St Petersburg, Mitrofanyevskoye shosse 29T; tel. (812) 334-27-20; e-mail idop@bk.ru; internet www.novostispb.ru; f. 1997; independent; Editor-in-Chief KIRILL METELEV.

Peterburgskii Chas Pik (Petersburg Rush Hour): 191040 St Petersburg, Nevskii pr. 81; tel. (812) 579-25-65; fax (812) 579-19-12; e-mail nabor@chaspik.spb.ru; internet www.chaspik.spb.ru; f. 1990; weekly; owned by Gazprom-Mediya; Editor-in-Chief LARISA AFONINA; circ. 30,000 (2005).

Sankt-Peterburgskiye Vedomosti (St Petersburg Gazette): 191025 St Petersburg, ul. Marata 25; tel. (812) 325-31-00; fax (812) 764-48-40; e-mail post@spbvedomosti.ru; internet www.spbvedomosti.ru; f. 1991 as revival of 1728–1917 title; re-established 1991; Editor-in-Chief and Gen. Man. SERGEI A. SLOBODSKOI.

Smena (The Rising Generation): 191119 St Petersburg, ul. Marata 69; tel. (812) 315-04-76; fax (812) 315-03-53; e-mail info@smena.ru; internet www.smena.ru; f. 1919; 6 a week, controlled by Sistema Mass-Mediya; Editor-in-Chief LEONID DAVYDOV; circ. 80,000 (2002).

The St Petersburg Times: 190000 St Petersburg, Isaakevskaya pl. 4; tel. and fax (812) 325-60-80; e-mail letters@sptimesrussia.com; internet www.sptimes.ru; f. 1993; 2 a week; in English; independent; Editor TOBIN AUBER.

Vechernii Peterburg (Evening Petersburg): 191023 St Petersburg, ul. Fontanka 59; tel. (812) 311-88-75; fax (812) 314-31-05; e-mail gazeta@vspb.spb.ru; internet vppress.ru; f. 1917; Editor VLADIMIR G. GRONSKII.

PRINCIPAL PERIODICALS

Agriculture, Forestry, etc.

Ekologiya i Promlyshlennost Rossii (The Ecology and Industry of Russia): 119049 Moscow, Leninskii pr. 4; tel. (495) 913-80-94; fax (495) 647-23-08; e-mail ecip@online.ru; internet ecip.newmail.ru; f. 1996; monthly; environmental protection; Editor-in-Chief Prof. Dr V. D. KALNER.

Lesnaya Promyshlennost (Forest Industry): 141400 Moscow Obl., Khimki, ul. Moskovskaya 21; tel. and fax (495) 777-26-74; f. 1921; monthly; publ. by the state forest industrial company, Roslesprom; Editor V. G. ZAYEDINOV.

Zashchita i Karantin Rastenii (Plant Protection and Quarantine): 107996 Moscow, ul. Sadovaya-Spasskaya 18, GSB-6, B-78; tel. (495) 607-21-30; fax (495) 607-10-15; e-mail fitopress@ropnet.ru; internet www.z-i-k-r.ru; f. 1932; monthly; Editor YURII N. NEIPERT; circ. 5,000 (2009).

Zemledeliye (Farming): 127434 Moscow, POB 9; tel. and fax (495) 976-11-93; e-mail zemledelie@mtu-net.ru; internet www.jurzemledelie.ru; f. 1939; 8 a year; publ. by Ministry of Agriculture, Russian Academy of Agricultural Sciences, Russian Scientific Research Institute of Farming; Editor MARIANNA G. LOGVINOVA; circ. 2,500 (2005).

For Children

Koster (Campfire): 193024 St Petersburg, ul. Mytninskaya 1/20; tel. (812) 274-15-72; fax (812) 274-46-26; e-mail root@kostyor.spb.org; internet www.kostyor.ru; f. 1936; monthly; journal of the International Union of Children's Organizations (UPO-FCO); fiction, poetry, sport, reports and popular science; for ages 10–14 years; Editor-in-Chief N. B. KHARLAMPIYEV; circ. 7,500 (2000).

Murzilka: 127015 Moscow, ul. Novodmitrovskaya 5A; tel. and fax (495) 685-18-81; e-mail murzilka@dateline.ru; internet www.murzilka.org; f. 1924; monthly; illustrated; for first grades of school; Editor TATYANA ANDROSENKO; circ. 75,000 (2007).

Pionerskaya Pravda (Pioneers' Truth): 127994 Moscow, ul. Sushchevskaya 21; tel. and fax (495) 787-62-43; e-mail info@pionerka.ru; internet www.pionerka.ru; f. 1925; 4 a week; Editor MIKHAIL N. BARANNIKOV.

Veselye Kartinki (Merry Pictures): 109147 Moscow, ul. Taganskaya 34; tel. (495) 632-71-26; e-mail info@merrypictures.ru; internet www.merrypictures.ru; f. 1956; monthly; humorous, illustrated; for pre-school and first grades; Editor MARINA DRUZHININAYA.

Yunyi Naturalist (Young Naturalist): 125015 Moscow, ul. Novodmitrovskaya 5A; tel. (495) 685-39-31; e-mail post@unnaturalist.ru; internet www.unnaturalist.ru; f. 1928; monthly; popular science for children of fourth–10th grades, who are interested in biology; Editor L. M. SAMSONOVA.

Yunyi Tekhnik (Young Technician): 125015 Moscow, ul. Novodmitrovskaya 5A; tel. (495) 685-44-80; e-mail yut.magazine@gmail.com; internet www.utechnik.org; f. 1956; monthly; popular science for children and youth; Chief Editor ALEKSANDR A. FIN.

Culture and Arts

Iskusstvo Kino (The Art of the Cinema): 125319 Moscow, ul. Usiyevicha 9; tel. (495) 151-56-51; fax (495) 151-02-72; e-mail filmfilm@yandex.ru; internet www.kinoart.ru; f. 1931; monthly; journal of the Russian Film-makers' Union; Editor DANIIL B. DONDUREI; circ. 5,000 (2004).

Knizhnoye Obozreniye (The Book Review): 129272 Moscow, ul. Sushchevskii Val 64; tel. (495) 681-62-66; fax (495) 681-51-45; internet www.knigoboz.ru; f. 1966; weekly; summaries of newly published books; Editor-in-Chief ALEKSANDR F. GAVRILOV; circ. 10,500 (2003).

Kultura (Culture): 127055 Moscow, ul. Novoslobodskaya 73; tel. (495) 685-06-40; fax (496) 685-31-50; e-mail kultura@dol.ru; internet www.kulturagz.ru; f. 1929; controlled by Sistema Mass-Mediya; weekly; Editor-in-Chief YURII I. BELYAVSKII; circ. 30,000 (2008).

Literaturnaya Gazeta (Literary Newspaper): 109028 Moscow, Khokhlovskii per. 10/6; tel. and fax (499) 788-02-10; e-mail litgazeta@lgz.ru; internet www.lgz.ru; f. 1831; publ. restored 1929; weekly; literature, politics, society; controlled by Sistema Mass-Mediya; Editor-in-Chief YU. M. POLYAKOV.

Literaturnaya Rossiya (Literary Russia): 103051 Moscow, Tsvetnoi bulv. 32/3; tel. and fax (495) 694-50-10; e-mail litrossia@litrossia.ru; internet www.litrossia.ru; f. 1958; weekly; essays, verse, literary criticism; Editor VYACHESLAV OGRYZKO; circ. 19,650 (2007).

Oktyabr (October): 125040 Moscow, ul. Pravdy 11/13; tel. (495) 214-62-05; fax (495) 214-50-29; internet magazines.russ.ru/october; f. 1924; monthly; independent literary journal; new fiction and essays by Russian and foreign writers; Editor-in-Chief IRINA N. BARMETOVA.

Sem Dnei (Seven Days): 125871 Moscow, Leningradskoye shosse 5A; tel. (495) 195-92-76; fax (495) 753-41-32; e-mail 7days@7days.ru; internet www.7days.ru; f. 1967; celebrity news and television listings magazine; Editor V. V. ORLOVA; circ. 937,000 (2000).

Znamya (Banner): 103001 Moscow, ul. B. Sadovaya 2/46; tel. (495) 299-52-38; e-mail admin@znamlit.ru; internet magazines.russ.ru/znamia; f. 1931; monthly; independent; novels, poetry, essays; Editor-in-Chief SERGEI I. CHUPRININ; circ. 5,300 (2004).

Economics and Finance

Chelovek i Trud (Man and Labour): 105064 Moscow, Yakovoapostolski per. 6/3; tel. and fax (495) 917-76-36; e-mail chelt@yandex.ru; internet www.chelt.ru; monthly; f. 1956 as *Sotsialisticheskii trud* (Socialist Labour); present name adopted 1992; employment issues, unemployment, social policy, pensions, personnel management etc.; Editor-in-Chief M. A. BARINOVA; circ. 10,000 (2005).

D': 125866 Moscow, Bumazhnyi proyezd 14/1; tel. (495) 609-64-98; fax (495) 228-00-78; e-mail shu@expert.ru; internet www.expert.ru/printissues/d; f. 2005; personal finance; Chief Editor TATYANA GUROVA; circ. 50,500 (2008).

Delovye Lyudi (Business People): 123995 Moscow, ul. 1905 goda 7; tel. (495) 781-47-37; fax (495) 781-47-44; e-mail dl@mk.ru; f. 1990; monthly; business, management and economics; Editor-in-Chief SERGEI I. ROGOZHKIN; circ. 50,000 (2007).

Dengi (Money): 125080 Moscow, ul. Vrubelya 4/1; tel. (499) 943-97-71; fax (499) 943-97-28; e-mail dengi@kommersant.ru; internet www.kommersant.ru/k-money; weekly; publ. by the Kommersant Publishing House; Chief Editor SERGEI YAKOVLEV.

Dengi i Kredit (Money and Credit): 107016 Moscow, ul. Neglinnaya 12; tel. (495) 771-99-87; fax (495) 771-99-93; e-mail una@cbr.ru; internet www.cbr.ru/publ/main.asp?Prtid=MoneyAndCredit; f. 1927; monthly; publ. by the Central Bank; all aspects of banking and money circulation; Chief Editor VLADIMIR S. PALEVICH; circ. 3,500 (2009).

Ekonomika i Zhizn (Economics and Life): 125319 Moscow, ul. Chernyakhovskogo 16; tel. and fax (495) 152-51-38; e-mail eg@ekonomika.ru; internet www.ekonomika.ru; f. 1918; weekly; fmrly *Ekonomicheskaya gazeta*; news and information about the economy and business; Editor TATYANA A. IVANOVA; circ. 150,000 (2005).

Ekspert (Expert): 125866 Moscow, ul. Pravdy 24, Novyi Gazetnyi kor., POB 33; tel. (495) 789-44-65; fax (495) 228-00-78; e-mail ask@expert.ru; internet www.expert.ru; f. 1995; weekly; business and economics; financial and share markets; policy and culture; regional edns: *Ekspert Severo-Zapad* (St Petersburg and North-Western Russia), *Ekspert Sibir* (Siberia), *Ekspert Ural* (Urals), *Ekspert Volga*

(The Volga region), *Ekspert Yug* (Southern Russia), and edns for Kazakhstan and Ukraine; Editor-in-Chief VALERII FADEYEV.

Finans (Finance): 127238 Moscow, Lokomotivnyi proyezd 21A; tel. and fax (495) 788-53-10; e-mail inform@finansmag.ru; internet www.fr.ru; f. 2003; weekly; economics, business, finance, society; Editor-in-Chief OLEG ANISIMOV; circ. 48,700 (2007).

Finansy (Finances): 125009 Moscow, ul. Tverskaya 22B; tel. (495) 699-44-27; fax (495) 699-96-16; e-mail finance-journal@mail.ru; internet www.finance-journal.ru; f. 1926; monthly; theory and information on finances; compilation and execution of the state budget, insurance, lending, taxation, etc.; Editor YU. M. ARTEMOV; circ. 10,000 (2004).

Kompaniya (The Firm): 109544 Moscow, ul. B. Andronyevskaya 17; tel. (495) 745-84-10; e-mail ko@idr.ru; internet www.ko.ru; f. 1997; weekly; politics, economics, finance; Editor-in-Chief ANDREI GRIGORYEV; circ. 78,000 (2007).

Mirovaya Ekonomika i Mezhdunarodniye Otnosheniya (World Economy and International Relations): 117859 Moscow, ul. Profsoyuznaya 23; tel. (495) 128-08-83; fax (495) 310-70-27; e-mail memojour@imemo.ru; internet www.imemo.ru; f. 1957; monthly; journal of the Institute of the World Economy and International Relations of the Russian Academy of Sciences; theory and practice of socio-economic development, international policies, economic cooperation; Editor A. V. RYABOV.

Rossiiskii Ekonomicheskii Zhurnal (Russian Economic Journal): 109542 Moscow, Ryazanskii pr. 99; tel. and fax (495) 377-25-56; internet www.e-rej.ru; f. 1958; monthly; economics; Editor A. YU. MELENTEV; circ. 6,100 (2004).

Voprosy Ekonomiki (Questions of Economics): 117218 Moscow, Nakhimovskii pr. 32; tel. and fax (499) 124-52-28; e-mail mail@vopreco.ru; internet www.vopreco.ru; f. 1929; monthly; journal of the Institute of Economics of the Russian Academy of Sciences; theoretical problems of economic development, market relations, social aspects of transition to a market economy, international economics, etc.; Editor LEONID ABALKIN; circ. 5,300 (2009).

Education

Semya (The Family): 107996 Moscow, Orlikov per. 5; tel. (495) 975-05-29; fax (495) 975-00-76; e-mail mail@semya.ru; internet www.semya.ru; f. 1988; weekly; Editor-in-Chief SERGEI A. ABRAMOV; circ. 50,000 (2004).

Uchitelskaya Gazeta (Teachers' Gazette): 107045 Moscow, Ananyevskii per. 4/2/1; tel. (495) 928-82-53; fax (495) 928-82-53; e-mail ug@ug.ru; internet www.ug.ru; f. 1924; weekly; independent; Editor PETR POLOZHEVETS; circ. 95,000 (2007).

International Affairs

Ekho Planety (Echo of the Planet): 103860 Moscow, Tverskoi bulv. 10/12; tel. (495) 202-67-48; fax (495) 290-59-11; e-mail echotex@itar-tass.com; internet www.explan.ru; f. 1988; weekly; publ. by ITAR—TASS; international affairs, economic, social and cultural; Editor-in-Chief VALENTIN VASILETS.

Mezhdunarodnaya Zhizn (International Life): 105064 Moscow, Gorokhovskii per. 14; tel. (495) 265-37-81; fax (495) 265-37-71; e-mail inter_affairs@mid.ru; f. 1954; monthly; Russian and English; publ. by the Pressa Publishing House; foreign policy and diplomacy; Editor-in-Chief B. D. PYADYSHEV; circ. 70,000.

Novoye Vremya—The New Times: 125009 Moscow, Tverskoi bulv. 14/1; tel. (495) 648-07-60; fax (495) 648-07-61; e-mail info@newtimes.ru; internet www.newtimes.ru; f. 1943; weekly; foreign and Russian affairs; Editor-in-Chief IRENA LESNEVSKAYA.

Russkii Reporter (Russian Reporter): 125866 Moscow, Bumazhnyi proyezd 14/1; tel. (495) 609-66-74; e-mail reporter@expert.ru; internet www.expert.ru/printissues/russian_reporter; f. 2007; monthly; domestic and international affairs and culture; Chief Editor VITALII LEIBIN.

Language and Literature

Ex Libris-NG: 113935 Moscow, ul. Myasnitskaya 13; tel. (495) 928-48-50; fax (495) 975-23-46; e-mail info@ng.ru; internet exlibris.ng.ru; weekly; literature; Editor-in-Chief IGOR ZOTOV.

Voprosy Literatury (Questions of Literature): 125009 Moscow, B. Gnezdnikovskii per. 10; tel. (495) 629-49-77; fax (495) 629-64-71; e-mail vopli@arion.ru; internet magazines.russ.ru/voplit; f. 1957; 6 a year; publ. by Foundation for Literary Criticism; theory and history of modern literature and aesthetics; Editor L. I. LAZAREV; circ. 2,500 (2007).

Leisure and Sport

Afisha (Poster): 103009 Moscow, per. B. Gnezdnikovskii 7/28/1; tel. (495) 785-17-00; fax (495) 785-17-01; e-mail info@afisha.net; internet www.afisha.ru; f. 1999; every 2 weeks; listings and reviews of events; 3 edns, for Moscow, St Petersburg, and the rest of Russia; Chief Editor YURII SAPRYKIN.

Avtopilot (Autopilot): 123308 Moscow, Khoroshevskoye shosse 41; tel. (495) 493-91-44; fax (495) 493-91-64; e-mail autopilot@kommersant.ru; internet autopilot.kommersant.ru; cars; publ. by the Kommersant Publishing House; Editor-in-Chief ALEKSANDR FEDOROV.

Bolshoi Gorod (Big City): 125009 Moscow, B. Gnezdnikovskii per. 7/28/1; tel. (495) 785-17-00; fax (495) 785-17-01; e-mail info@bg.ru; internet www.bg.ru; f. 2001; every two weeks; Moscow and St Petersburg edns; culture, travel, technology; Chief Editors FILIPP DZYADKO (Moscow edn), YULIYA TARNAVSKAYA (St Petersburg edn).

FiS—Fizkultura i Sport (Exercise and Sport): 125130 Moscow, per. 6-i Novopodmoskovnii 3, POB 198; tel. (495) 786-60-62; fax (495) 786-61-39; e-mail fisemail@mtu-net.ru; internet www.fismag.ru; f. 1922; monthly; activities and development of Russian sports, health; Editor I. SOSNOVSKII.

Rossiiskaya Okhotnichya Gazeta (Russian Hunters' Magazine): 123995 Moscow, ul. 1905 Goda 7; tel. (495) 250-72-72; e-mail rog@mk.ru; internet www.gusevhunting.ru/numbers.php?tip=1; weekly; hunting, shooting, fishing; Editor-in-Chief PAVEL GUSEV.

Sovetskii Sport (Soviet Sport): 103287 Moscow, Staryi Petrovsko-Razumovskii proyezd 1/23/1; tel. (495) 637-64-33; fax (495) 637-64-24; e-mail sport@sovsport.ru; internet www.sovsport.ru; f. 1924; weekly; Editor-in-Chief IGOR KOTS.

Sport Ekspress (Sport Express): 123056 Moscow, ul. Krasina 27/2; tel. (495) 254-47-87; fax (495) 733-93-08; e-mail sport@sport-express.ru; internet www.sport-express.ru; f. 1991; daily; sport; Editor-in-Chief VLADIMIR KUCHMII; circ. in Moscow and St Petersburg 190,000 (2004).

Za Rulem (Behind The Wheel): 103045 Moscow, per. Selivyerstov 10; tel. (495) 607-23-82; fax (495) 737-43-07; e-mail stas@zr.ru; internet www.zr.ru; f. 1928; monthly; cars and motorsport; Editor-in-Chief PETR S. MENSHIKH.

Politics and Military Affairs

Nezavisimoye Voyennoye Obozreniye (Independent Military Review): 101000 Moscow, ul. Myasnitskaya 13; tel. and fax (495) 925-88-29; internet nvo.ng.ru; f. 1995; Editor VADIM SOLOVYEV; circ. 20,140 (2004).

Put Domoi (The Road Home): 191123 St Petersburg, POB 43; tel. (812) 272-16-02; fax (812) 310-52-09; e-mail putdomoi@yandex.ru; internet www.putdomoi.ru; f. 1994; fmrly *Na Dne* (The Lower Depths); current affairs; social issues; 2 a month; also regional Siberian edn; Editor ARKADII TYURIN.

Rossiiskaya Federatsiya Segodnya (The Russian Federation Today): 103800 Moscow, ul. M. Dmitrovka 3/10; tel. (495) 933-54-79; fax (495) 933-54-74; e-mail rfs@russia-today.ru; internet www.russia-today.ru; f. 1994; journal of the Gosudarstvennaya Duma; Editor YURII A. KHRENOV.

Rossiya v Globalnoi Politike/ Russia in Global Affairs: 125009 Moscow, ul. Mokhovaya 11/3v; tel. (495) 980-73-53; fax (495) 937-76-11; e-mail info@globalaffairs.ru; internet www.globalaffairs.ru; f. 2002; co-founded by the Russian Union of Industrialists and Entrepreneurs, the Council for Foreign and Defence Politics and the newspaper *Izvestiya*, in collaboration with the US journal, *Foreign Affairs*; 6 a year (Russian); 4 a year (English); online edns in Czech and Polish; Chair. of Editorial Bd SERGEI A. KARAGANOV; Editor-in-Chief FEDOR A. LUKYANOV.

Russia Profile: 119021 Moscow, Zubovskii bulv. 4; tel. (495) 981-64-86; fax (495) 201-30-71; e-mail info@russiaprofile.org; internet www.russiaprofile.org; f. 1966; monthly; in English; publ. by Independent Media for RIA-Novosti in association with the International Relations and Security Network (Zurich, Switzerland) and the Center for Defense Information (Washington, DC, USA); Editor ANDREI ZOLOTOV, Jr.

Shchit i Mech (Shield and Sword): 127434 Moscow, Ivanovskii pr. 18; tel. (495) 976-66-44; fax (495) 619-80-90; e-mail gazeta@simech.ru; internet www.simech.ru; f. 1989; weekly; military, security, geopolitical concerns; publ. by the Ministry of Internal Affairs; Editor-in-Chief VALERII KULIK; circ. 50,000 (2004).

Sovershenno Sekretno (Top Secret): 121099 Moscow, Smolenskaya pl. 13/21, POB 255; tel. (495) 241-68-73; fax (495) 241-75-55; e-mail velekhov@topsecret.cnt.ru; internet sovsekretno.ru; f. 1989; monthly; Editor-in-Chief GALINA SIDOROVA.

Vlast (Power): 123308 Moscow, Khoroshevskoye shosse 41; tel. (499) 943-97-71; fax (499) 234-16-60; e-mail vlast@kommersant.ru; internet www.kommersant.ru/k-vlast; f. 1997; weekly; Chief Editor MAKSIM KOVALSKII.

Yezhenedelnyi Zhurnal (Weekly Magazine): 129110 Moscow, Pereyaslavskii per. 4; tel. (495) 785-82-50; fax (495) 785-82-51;

e-mail info@ej.ru; internet www.ej.ru; f. 2001; Editor-in-Chief SERGEI PARKHOMENKO.

Zavtra (Tomorrow): 119146 Moscow, Frunzenskaya nab. 18/60; tel. (495) 726-54-83; e-mail zavtra@zavtra.ru; internet www.zavtra.ru; extreme left, nationalist; Editor-in-Chief ALEKSANDR A. PROGANOV.

Popular, Fiction and General

Inostrannaya Literatura (Foreign Literature): 109017 Moscow, ul. Pyatnitskaya 41; tel. (495) 953-51-47; fax (495) 953-50-61; e-mail inolit@rinet.ru; internet magazines.russ.ru/inostran; f. 1891; monthly; independent; Russian translations of modern foreign authors and literary criticism; Editor-in-Chief ALEKSEI SLOVESNII.

Krokodil (Crocodile): 129090 Moscow, Potapovskii per. 3, POB 94; tel. (495) 625-64-46; e-mail info@krakadil.ru; internet www.krakadil.ru; f. 1922, re-established 2006; monthly; satirical; Editor SERGEI MOSTOVSHCHIKOV.

Nash Sovremennik (Our Contemporary): 127994 Moscow, Tsvetnoi bulv. 32/2; tel. (495) 200-24-24; fax (495) 200-24-12; e-mail mail@nash-sovremennik.ru; internet www.nash-sovremennik.ru; f. 1956; monthly; publ. by the Union of Writers of Russia; contemporary prose and 'patriotic polemics'; Editor STANISLAV KUNAYEV.

Novyi Mir (New World): 103806 Moscow, M. Putinkovskii per. 1/2; tel. and fax (495) 200-08-29; e-mail nmir@aha.ru; internet magazines.russ.ru/novyi_mi; f. 1925; monthly; publ. by the Izvestiya (News) Publishing House; new fiction and essays; Editor ANDREI V. VASILEVSKII; circ. c. 8,000 (2005).

Ogonek (Beacon): 127055 Moscow, ul. Lesnaya 55/1–2; tel. (495) 660-94-47; fax (499) 973-14-30; e-mail ogoniok@ogoniokpress.ru; internet www.ogoniok.com; f. 1899; weekly; politics, popular science, economics, literature; Editor VIKTOR LOSHAK; circ. 69,000 (2007).

Rodina (Motherland): 127025 Moscow, ul. Novyi Arbat 19; tel. (495) 203-75-98; fax (495) 203-47-45; e-mail istrodina@mail.ru; internet www.istrodina.com; f. 1989 as revival of 1879–1917 publication; monthly; publ. by Administration of the President of the Russian Federation and Government of the Russian Federation; popular historical; supplement Istochnik (Source), every two months, documents state archives; Chief Editor YURII BORISENOK; circ. 20,000 (2003).

Rodnaya Gazeta (Native Gazette): 119121 Moscow, Smolenskii bulv. 11/2; tel. (499) 241-58-26; e-mail mail@rodgaz.ru; internet www.rodgaz.ru; f. 2003; weekly; politics, culture, nationalist, left-wing; Dir-Gen. and Chief Editor KONSTANTIN PATRIN.

Sobesednik (Interlocutor): 127055 Moscow, ul. Novoslobodskaya 73; tel. (495) 685-56-65; fax (495) 973-20-54; e-mail info@sobesednik.ru; internet www.sobesednik.ru; f. 1984; weekly; Editor-in-Chief YURII PILIPENKO.

Speed-Info: 125284 Moscow, POB 42; tel. (495) 255-02-99; fax (495) 252-09-20; e-mail mail@si.ru; internet www.s-info.ru; f. 1991; two a month; popular; Editor-in-Chief OLGA BELAN; Gen. Dir IGOR SAZONOV; circ. 850,000 (2008).

Vokrug Sveta (Around the World): 125015 Moscow, ul. Argunovskaya 12/1/6A; tel. (495) 491-96-45; fax (495) 490-57-25; e-mail editor@vokrugsveta.ru; internet www.vokrugsveta.ru; f. 1861; monthly; geographical, travel and adventure; illustrated; Chief Editor YELENA KNYAZEVA (acting).

Zvezda (Star): 191028 St Petersburg, ul. Mokhovaya 20; tel. (812) 272-71-38; fax (812) 273-52-56; e-mail mail@zvezdaspb.ru; internet zvezdaspb.ru; f. 1923; monthly; publ. by the Zvezda Publishing House; novels, short stories, poetry and literary criticism; Editors A. YU. ARYEV, YA. A. GORDIN.

Popular Scientific

Meditsinskaya Gazeta (Medical Gazette): 129090 Moscow, B. Sukharevskaya pl. 1/2; tel. (495) 608-86-95; fax (495) 208-69-80; e-mail inform@mgzt.ru; internet www.mgzt.ru; f. 1938; 2 a week; professional international periodical; Editor ANDREI POLTORAK.

Nauka i Zhizn (Science and Life): 101990 Moscow, ul. Myasnitskaya 24; tel. (495) 624-18-35; fax (495) 625-05-90; e-mail mail@nkj.ru; internet www.nkj.ru; f. 1890, resumed 1934; monthly; recent developments in all branches of science and technology; Editor-in-Chief YELENA LOZOVSKAYA; circ. 47,000 (2008).

PC Week: 109047 Moscow, ul. Marksistskaya 34/10; tel. (495) 974-22-60; fax (495) 974-22-63; e-mail editorial@pcweek.ru; internet www.pcweek.ru; f. 1995; 48 a year; Editor-in-Chief EDUARD PROYDAKOV.

Priroda (Nature): 117810 Moscow, Maronovskii per. 26; tel. (495) 238-24-56; fax (495) 238-26-33; f. 1912; monthly; publ. by the Nauka (Science) Publishing House; journal of the Presidium of the Academy of Sciences; natural sciences; Editor A. F. ANDREYEV.

Radio: 107045 Moscow, per. Seliverstov 10/1; tel. (495) 207-31-18; fax (495) 208-77-13; internet www.radio.ru; f. 1924; monthly; audio, video, communications, practical electronics, computers; Editor Y. I. KRYLOV.

Tekhnika-Molodezhi (Engineering Is For Youth): 127051 Moscow, ul. Petrovka 26/3, POB 94; tel. (495) 625-17-41; fax (495) 628-34-79; e-mail post@tm-magazin.ru; internet www.tm-magazin.ru; f. 1933; monthly; engineering and science; Editor A. N. PEREVOZCHIKOV.

Vrach (Physician): 119991 Moscow, ul. Trubetskaya 8; tel. (495) 248-33-69; fax (499) 766-07-58; e-mail rvrach@mmascience.ru; internet www.rusvrach.ru; f. 1990; monthly; medical, scientific and sociopolitical; illustrated; Editor-in-Chief I. N. DENISOV; circ. 3,700 (2004).

Zdorovye (Health): 127994 Moscow, Bumazhnyi proyezd 14/1; tel. (495) 250-58-28; fax (495) 257-32-51; e-mail zdorovie@zdr.ru; internet www.zdr.ru; f. 1955; monthly; Editor TATYANA YEFIMOVA; circ. 170,000 (2006).

The Press, Printing and Bibliography

Bibliografiya (Bibliography): 119019 Moscow, Kremlevskaya nab. 1/9; tel. (499) 766-00-85; e-mail bibliogr@bookchamber.ru; internet www.bookchamber.ru/content/bibliomag/bibliomag.html; f. 1929; 6 a year; theoretical, practical and historical aspects of bibliography, publishing and book trade; Editor K. M. SUKHORUKOV; circ. 65,000 (2009).

Poligrafist i Izdatel (Printer and Publisher): 119313 Moscow, Leninskii pr. 87/392-395; tel. (499) 134-78-43; fax (495) 288-94-44; e-mail mediarama@mediarama.ru; internet www.mediarama.ru/pp/pp.html; f. 1994; monthly; Editor A. I. OVSYANNIKOV; circ. 3,000 (2008).

Zhurnalist (Journalist): 125190 Moscow, Chezniyahovskogo ul. 16; tel. (495) 152-88-71; e-mail jour-nal@yandex.ru; internet www.journalist-virt.ru; f. 1920; monthly; publ. by Ekonomicheskaya Gazeta Publishing House; Editor G. P. MALTSEV; circ. 10,150 (2007).

Religion

Bratskii Vestnik (Herald of the Brethren): 109028 Moscow, M. Trexsvyatitelskii per. 3; tel. (495) 917-96-26; fax (495) 917-33-63; e-mail july.kulikov@gmail.com; internet mbchurch.ru/content/category/5/38/100; f. 1945; 4 a year; organ of the Russian Union of Evangelical Christians-Baptists; Chief Editor YULII KULIKOV.

Foma (Thomas): 123242 Moscow, ul. Druzhinnikovskaya 15; e-mail info@foma.ru; internet www.foma.ru; f. 1998; Orthodox; monthly; Chief Editor VLADIMIR R. LEGOIDA; circ. 30,000.

Istina i Zhizn (Truth and Life): 105264 Moscow, ul. 7-aya Parkovaya 26/1/303; tel. and fax (495) 786-35-89; e-mail istina@aha.ru; internet istina.religare.ru; f. 1990; inter-confessional magazine of Christian culture; monthly; Editor Fr ALEKSANDR KHMELNITSKII.

Mezhdunarodnaya Yevreyskaya Gazeta (International Jewish Newspaper): 107005 Moscow, Pleteshkovskii per. 3A; tel. and fax (495) 225-44-84; e-mail meg@spacenet.ru; internet www.jig.ru; f. 1989; weekly; Dir-Gen. YAKOV POLISCHUK; circ. 15,000 (2002).

NG-Religii (The Independent-Religions): 101000 Moscow, ul. Myasnitskaya 13; tel. (495) 923-42-40; fax (495) 921-58-47; e-mail ngr@ng.ru; internet religion.ng.ru; f. 1997; analysis of religious affairs and their domestic and global social and political implications; 2 a month; Editor-in-Chief MAKSIM SHEVCHENKO.

Tserkovnyi Vestnik (Church Herald): 119435 Moscow, ul. Pogodinskaya 20/2; tel. and fax (495) 246-01-65; e-mail info03@rop.ru; internet www.e-vestnik.ru; f. 1989; 24 a year; organ of the Russian Orthodox Church (Moscow Patriarchate); Editor-in-Chief Protohierarch VLADIMIR SILOVYEV; circ. 20,000 (2007).

Yevreiskoye Slovo (The Jewish Word): 127018 Moscow, 2-i Vysheslavtsev per. 5A; tel. (495) 792-31-13; e-mail redaktor@e-slovo.ru; internet www.e-slovo.ru; f. 2000; Editor-in-Chief VLADIMIR DYNKIN.

Zhurnal Moskovskoi Patriarkhii (Journal of the Moscow Patriarchate): 119435 Moscow, ul. Pogodinskaya 20/2; tel. (495) 246-98-48; fax (495) 246-21-41; e-mail eugpol@rop.ru; internet www.jmp.ru; f. 1934; monthly; official publication of the Russian Orthodox Church (Moscow Patriarchate); Editor Archpriest VLADIMIR (SILOVYEV).

Transport and Communication

Grazhdanskaya Aviatsiya (Civil Aviation): 125167 Moscow, Leningradskii pr. 37; tel. (495) 950-22-68; e-mail anatoly.40@bk.ru; internet civilavia.info; f. 1931; monthly; journal of the Union of Civil Aviation Workers; development of air transport; utilization of aviation in construction, agriculture and forestry; Editor ANATOLII M. TROSHIN; circ. 7,000 (2009).

Radiotekhnika (Radio Engineering): 103031 Moscow, Kuznetskii most 20/6/31; tel. (495) 921-48-37; fax (495) 925-92-41; e-mail iprzhr@online.ru; internet www.radiotec.ru/catalog.php?cat=jr1; f. 1937; monthly; publ. by the Svyaz (Communication) Publishing House; journal of the A. S. Popov Scientific and Technical Society of Radio Engineering, Electronics and Electrical Communication; theoretical and technical problems of radio engineering; other publications include Advances in Radio Science, Radio Systems and Antennae; Editor Yu. V. GULYAYEV.

Vestnik Svyazi (Herald of Communication): 101000 Moscow, Krivokolennyi per. 14/1; tel. (495) 625-42-57; fax (495) 621-27-97; e-mail vs@vestnik-sviazy.ru; internet www.vestnik-sviazy.ru; f. 1917; monthly; telecommunications; Editor E. B. KONSTANTINOV.

Women's Interest

Domovoi (House-Sprite): 109544 Moscow, ul. B. Andronyevskaya 17; tel. (495) 745-84-43; fax (495) 956-22-09; e-mail domovoy@idr.ru; internet www.domovoy.ru; monthly; Chief Editor VALERIYA KUDRYAVTSEVA.

Elle: 115162 Moscow, ul. Shabolovka 31B; tel. (495) 891-39-10; e-mail achukovskaya@hfs.ru; internet www.elle.ru; f. 1996; monthly; fashion; Editor-in-Chief YELENA SOTNIKOVA.

Krestyanka (Peasant Woman): 109544 Moscow, ul. B. Andronyevskaya 17; tel. (495) 745-84-12; fax (495) 956-22-09; e-mail krestyanka@idr.ru; internet www.krestyanka.ru; f. 1922; monthly; popular; Chief Editor TAMARA VIRKUNEN; circ. 85,000 (2004).

Mir Zhenshchiny (Woman's World): 101999 Moscow, Glinishchevskii per. 6; tel. and fax (495) 209-95-33; f. 1945; monthly; fmrly *Zhenshchina* (Woman); in Russian, Chinese, English, French, German and Spanish; fmrly publ. by the Soviet Women's Committee and the General Confederation of Trade Unions; popular; illustrated; Editor-in-Chief V. I. FEDOTOVA.

Youth

Rovesnik (Contemporary): 125015 Moscow, ul. Novodmitrovskaya 5A; tel. (495) 285-89-20; fax (495) 285-06-27; e-mail rovesnik@rovesnik.ru; internet www.rovesnik.ru/dom/rovesnik.asp; f. 1962; popular illustrated monthly of fiction, music, cinema, sport for 10–19 year olds; Editor I. A. CHERNYSHKOV; circ. 70,000 (2007).

Smena (The Rising Generation): 127994 Moscow, Bumazhnyi proyezd 19/2; tel. (495) 612-15-07; fax (495) 250-59-28; e-mail jurnal@smena-id.ru; internet www.smena-id.ru; f. 1924; monthly; popular illustrated, short stories, essays and problems of youth; Editor-in-Chief M. G. KIZILOV.

Yunost (Youth): 125047 Moscow, ul. Tverskaya-Yamskaya 8/1, POB 182; tel. and fax (495) 250-40-74; e-mail unost-contact@mail.ru; internet www.unost.org; f. 1955; monthly; novels, short stories, essays and poems by beginners; Editor TAMARA ANDREYEVA.

NEWS AGENCIES

ANP—Agentstvo novostei i prognozy (News and Forecasting Agency): 103009 Moscow, Kalashnyi per. 10/2; tel. (495) 782-33-71; fax (495) 153-57-45; e-mail aninons@online.ru; f. 2001 on basis of ANI News and Information Agency (f. 1991); Editor-in-Chief ALEKSEI SHCHAVELEV.

Interfax: 127006 Moscow, ul. 1-aya Tverskaya-Yamskaya 2; tel. (495) 250-98-40; fax (495) 250-97-27; e-mail info@interfax.ru; internet www.interfax.ru; f. 1989; independent information agency; Chief Exec. MIKHAIL KOMISSAR.

ITAR—TASS (Information Telegraphic Agency of Russia—Telegraphic Agency of the Sovereign Countries): 125993 Moscow, Tverskoi bulv. 10/12; tel. (495) 202-29-81; fax (495) 202-54-74; e-mail worldmarket@itar-tass.com; internet www.itar-tass.com; f. 1904 as St Petersburg Telegraph Agency, renamed as TASS (Telegraph Agency of the Soviet Union) in 1925; present name adopted 1992; state information agency; 74 bureaux in Russia and the states of the former USSR, 65 foreign bureaux outside the former USSR; Dir-Gen. VITALII N. IGNATENKO.

Prima Human Rights News Agency: 111399 Moscow, POB 5; tel. and fax (495) 455-30-11; e-mail prima@prima-news.ru; internet www.prima-news.ru; f. 2000; Editor-in-Chief ALEKSANDR PODRABINEK.

RIA—Novosti (Russian Information Agency—News): 103786 Moscow, Zubovskii bulv. 4; tel. (495) 201-82-09; fax (495) 201-45-45; e-mail marketing@rian.ru; internet www.rian.ru; f. 1961 as Agentsvo Pechati 'Novosti' (APN); present name adopted 1991; collaborates by arrangement with foreign press and publishing organizations in 110 countries; provider of Russian news features and photographs; Chair. SVETLANA MIRONYUK.

RosBalt Information Agency: 190000 St Petersburg, Konnogvardeiskii bulv. 7; tel. (812) 320-50-30; fax (812) 320-50-31; e-mail rosbalt@rosbalt.ru; internet www.rosbalt.ru; news coverage of European Russia and other countries in northern Europe; Chair. NATALIYA CHERKESOVA.

Rossiiskoye Informatsionnoye Agentstvo 'Oreanda' (RIA 'Oreanda'): 117342 Moscow, POB 21; tel. (495) 330-98-50; fax (495) 23-04-39; e-mail info@oreanda.ru; internet www.oreanda.ru; f. 1994.

Strana.Ru (Country-Russia): 119021 Moscow, Zubovskii bulv. 4, podyezd 8; tel. (495) 981-62-52; fax (495) 981-62-53; e-mail mail@strana.ru; internet www.strana.ru; f. 2000; news agency; central bureau in Moscow, regional bureaux in Groznyi (Chechen—Nokchi Republic) and in Kyiv, Ukraine; controlled by the All-Russian State Television and Radio Broadcasting Company (VGTRK); Editor-in-Chief YULIYA PANFILOVA.

PRESS ASSOCIATIONS

Russian Guild of Publishers of Periodical Press: 125047 Moscow, ul. Lesnaya 20/6-211; tel. and fax (495) 978-41-89.

Union of Journalists of Russia: 119021 Moscow, Zubovskii bulv. 4; tel. (495) 201-51-01; fax (495) 201-35-47; f. 1991; Sec.-Gen. IGOR YAKOVENKO.

Publishers

Ad Marginem-Ad Patres: 105082 Moscow, Perevedenovskii per. 18; tel. and fax (495) 988-15-32; e-mail info@admarginem.ru; internet admarginem.ru; f. 1993; fiction, philosophy, artistic and literary criticism; Dir ALEKSANDR IVANOV.

AST: 129085 Moscow, Zvezdnyi bulv. 21; tel. (495) 215-01-01; fax (495) 215-51-10; e-mail astpub@aha.ru; internet www.ast.ru; original and translated fiction and non-fiction, children's and schoolbooks.

Avrora (Aurora): 191065 St Petersburg, Nevskii pr. 7/9; tel. (812) 312-37-53; fax (812) 312-54-60; e-mail aurora@mail.nevalink.ru; f. 1969; fine arts; Dir ZENOBIUS SPETCHINSKII.

Azbuka (Alphabet): 191014 St Petersburg, ul. Chekhova 9, POB 192; tel. (812) 327-04-55; fax (812) 327-01-60; e-mail assistant@azbooka.spb.ru; internet www.azbooka.ru; f. 1995; literary fiction, including translations; Dir-Gen. GENNADII MOLCHANOV.

Bolshaya Rossiiskaya Entsiklopediya (The Great Russian Encyclopedia): 109028 Moscow, Pokrovskii bulv. 8; tel. (495) 917-90-00; fax (495) 916-01-22; e-mail secretar@greatbook.ru; internet www.greatbook.ru; f. 1925; encyclopedias and reference; Dir-Gen. NIKOLAI S. ARTEMOV.

Drofa: 127018 Moscow, ul. Sushchevskii Val 49; tel. (495) 795-05-50; fax (495) 795-05-44; e-mail info@drofa.ru; internet www.drofa.ru; f. 1991; school textbooks, children's fiction; Dir-Gen. ALEKSANDR F. KISELEV.

Ekonomika (Economy): 123955 Moscow, Berezhkovskaya nab. 6; tel. (499) 240-58-18; fax (499) 240-48-178; e-mail info@economizdat.ru; internet www.economizdat.ru; f. 1963; various aspects of economics, management and marketing; Dir YELIZABETA V. POLIYEVKTOVA.

Eksmo: 127299 Moscow, ul. K. Tsetkina 18/5; tel. and fax (495) 411-68-86; e-mail info@eksmo.ru; internet www.eksmo.ru; f. 1991; fiction; Gen. Dir OLEG YE. NOVIKOV.

Energoatomizdat (Atomic Energy Press): 107031 Moscow, ul. Rozhdestvenka 5/7; tel. (495) 624-22-28; e-mail atompublish@mail.ru; internet www.energoatomizdat.ru; f. 1981; energy, nuclear science and technology; Dir-Gen. NIKOLAI A. KOSOLAPOV.

Finansy i Statistika (Finance and Statistics): 101000 Moscow, ul. Pokrovka 7; tel. (495) 625-47-08; fax (495) 625-09-57; e-mail mail@finstat.ru; internet www.finstat.ru; f. 1924; education, economics, tourism, finance, statistics, banking, insurance, accounting, computer science; Dir Dr ALEVTINA N. ZVONOVA.

Forum: 101000 Moscow, Kolpachnyi per. 9A; tel. and fax (495) 625-52-43; e-mail mail@forum-books.ru; internet www.forum-books.ru; f. 2001; general and professional educational textbooks; Gen. Man. SVETLANA P. SILVANOVICH.

Galart: 125319 Moscow, ul. Chernyakhovskogo 4; tel. and fax (495) 151-25-02; e-mail galart@m9com.ru; internet www.galart-moscow.ru; f. 1969; fmrly Sovetskii Khudozhnik (Soviet Artist); art reproduction, art history and criticism; Gen. Dir A. D. SARABYANOV.

Gorodets: 109386 Moscow, ul. Krasnodonskaya 20/2; tel. and fax (495) 351-55-80; e-mail info@gorodets.com; internet www.gorodets.com; f. 1996; law, politics, international relations, economics.

INFRA-M: 127282 Moscow, ul. Polyarnaya 31B; tel. and fax (495) 363-42-60; e-mail books@infra-m.ru; internet www.infra-m.ru; f. 1992; economics, law, computing, history, reference works, encyclopedias; Man. Dir VADIM D. SINYANSKII.

Izobrazitelnoye Iskusstvo (Fine Art): 129272 Moscow, ul. Sushchevskii Val 64; tel. (495) 681-65-48; fax (495) 681-41-11; e-mail iskusstvo@id.ru; reproductions of pictures, pictorial art, books on art, albums, calendars, postcards; Dir G. SH. YERITSYAN.

Khimiya (Chemistry): 107976 Moscow, ul. Strominka 21/2; tel. (495) 268-29-76; f. 1963; chemistry and the chemical industry; Dir BORIS S. KRASNOPEVTSEV.

Khudozhestvennaya Literatura (Fiction): 107078 Moscow, ul. Novobasmannaya 19; tel. (499) 261-88-65; fax (499) 261-83-00; fiction

THE RUSSIAN FEDERATION

and works of literary criticism, history of literature, etc.; Dir A. N. PETROV; Editor-in-Chief V. S. MODESTOV.

Kolos (Ear of Corn): 107996 Moscow, ul. Sadovaya-Spasskaya 18/1; tel. (495) 207-19-45; fax (495) 207-28-70; internet www.koloc.ru; f. 1999; all agricultural production; Dir ANATOLII M. ULYANOV.

Kompozitor (Composer): 119034 Moscow, M. Levshinskii per. 7/2; tel. (495) 955-19-66; fax (495) 209-54-98; e-mail komp@kompubl.com; internet www.idk.su; f. 1957; music and music criticism; Dir GRIGORII A. VORONOV.

Meditsina (Medicine): 101838 Moscow, Petroverigskii per. 6/8; tel. (495) 924-87-85; fax (495) 928-60-03; e-mail meditsina@iname.com; internet www.medlit.ru; f. 1918; state-owned; imprint of Association for Medical Literature; books and journals on medicine and health; Dir A. M. STOCHIK.

Mezhdunarodnye Otnosheniya (International Relations): 107078 Moscow, ul. Sadovaya-Spasskaya 18/709; tel. (495) 207-67-93; fax (495) 200-22-04; e-mail info@inter-rel.ru; internet www.inter-rel.ru; f. 1957; international relations, economics and politics of foreign countries, foreign trade, international law, foreign language textbooks and dictionaries, translations and publications for the UN and other international organizations; Dir B. P. LIKHACHEV.

Molodaya Gvardiya (The Young Guard): 127994 Moscow, ul. Sushchevskaya 21; tel. (495) 972-05-46; fax (495) 972-05-82; e-mail dsel@gvardiya.ru; f. 1922; books, magazines; Gen. Dir V. F. YURKIN.

Moscow M. V. Lomonosov State University Press: 119899 Moscow, ul. Khokhlova 11; tel. (495) 939-33-23; fax (495) 203-66-71; e-mail kd_mgu@rambler.ru; internet www.msu.ru/depts/MSUPubl2005/; f. 1756; scientific, educational and reference, books and journals; Dir YURIY YU. PETRUNIN.

Muzyka (Music): 127051 Moscow, ul. Petrovka 26; tel. (495) 921-51-70; fax (495) 928-33-04; e-mail muz-sekretar@yandex.ru; f. 1861; sheet music, music scores and related literature; Dir MARK ZILBERQUIT.

Mysl (Thought): 117071 Moscow, Leninskii pr. 15; tel. (495) 955-04-58; f. 1963; science, popular science, philosophy, history, political science, geography; Dir YEVGENYI A. TIMOFEYEV.

Nauka (Science): 117997 Moscow, ul. Profsoyuznaya 90; tel. (495) 334-71-51; fax (495) 420-22-20; e-mail secret@naukaran.ru; internet www.naukaran.ru; f. 1923; publishing house of the Academy of Sciences; general and social science, mathematics, physics, chemistry, biology, earth sciences, oriental studies, books in foreign languages, university textbooks, scientific journals, translation, export, distribution, typesetting and printing services; Dir-Gen. V. VASILIYEV.

Nauka i Tekhnologiya (Science and Technology): 107076 Moscow, Stromynskii per. 4; tel. (495) 164-47-74; fax (495) 164-47-74; e-mail admin@nait.ru; internet www.nait.ru; f. 2000; journals on chemistry, electronics and telecommunications; Gen. Dir MAKSIM A. KOVALEVSKII.

Nedra Biznestsentr (Natural Resources Business Centre): 125047 Moscow, pl. Tverskoi Zastavy 3; tel. (495) 251-31-77; fax (495) 250-27-72; e-mail business@nedrainform.ru; internet www.nedrainform.ru; f. 1964; geology, natural resources, mining and coal industry, petroleum and gas industry; Dir V. D. MENSHIKOV.

Nezavisimaya Gazeta ('Independent Newspaper' Publishing House): 101000 Moscow, ul. Myasnitskaya 13/10; tel. and fax (495) 981-61-53; e-mail ngbooks@ng.ru; internet www.ng.ru/izdatelstvo; f. 1991; books on history, literary essays, poetry, history of literature and of art, biography, dictionaries, encyclopaedias; Dir VIKTOR A. OBUKHOV.

Pedagogika Press (Pedagogy Press): 119034 Moscow, Smolenskii bulv. 4; tel. and fax (495) 246-59-69; f. 1969; scientific and popular books on pedagogics, didactics, psychology, developmental physiology; young people's encyclopaedia, dictionaries; Dir I. KOLESNIKOVA.

Pressa (The Press): 127137 Moscow, ul. Pravdy 24; tel. (499) 257-46-22; fax (499) 257-09-38; e-mail adm@media-pressa.ru; internet www.media-pressa.ru; f. 1934 as Pravda (Truth) Publishing House; booklets, newspapers and periodicals; Dir I. V. POLTAVTSEV.

Profizdat (Professional Publishers): 101000 Moscow, ul. Myasnitskaya 13/18; tel. (495) 924-57-40; fax (495) 975-23-29; e-mail profizdat@profizdat.ru; f. 1930; books and magazines; Gen. Dir VLADIMIR SOLOVYEV.

Progress (Progress): 119992 Moscow, Zubovskii bulv. 17; tel. (495) 246-90-32; fax (495) 230-24-03; e-mail progress@mcn.ru; f. 1931; translations of Russian language books into foreign languages and of foreign language books into Russian; political and scientific, fiction, literature for children and youth; encyclopedias; Dir-Gen. SARKIS V. OGANIAN.

Prosveshcheniye (Enlightenment): 127521 Moscow, 3-i proyezd Maryinoi roshchi 41; tel. (495) 789-30-40; fax (495) 789-30-41; e-mail prosv@prosv.ru; internet www.prosv.ru; f. 1930; school textbooks, dictionaries, atlases, reference and scientific books, educational materials; Dir ALEKSANDR M. KONDAKOV.

Raduga (Rainbow): 129090 Moscow, Grokholskii per. 32/2; tel. and fax (495) 680-12-39; e-mail radugarel@sumail.ru; internet www.raduga-publ.ru; f. 1982; translations of Russian fiction into foreign languages and of foreign authors into Russian; Gen. Dir KSENIYA ATAROVA.

Respublika (Republic): 125811 Moscow, Miusskaya pl. 7; tel. and fax (495) 656-09-70; e-mail respublik@dataforce.net; internet www.republik.ru; f. 1918; fmrly Politizdat (Political Publishing House); dictionaries, books on politics, human rights, philosophy, history, economics, religion, fiction, arts, reference; Dir VLADIMIR V. AKIMOV.

Rosmen (Rosman): 127018 Moscow, ul. Oktyabrskaya 4/2; tel. (495) 933-70-70; fax (495) 933-71-36; e-mail rosman@rosman.ru; internet www.rosman.ru; children's literature, general, popular science; Dir-Gen. OLEG V. ZHIVYKH.

Rosspen Publishing House—Russian Political Encyclopedia: 117393 Moscow, ul. Profsoyuznaya 82; tel. and fax (495) 334-81-62; e-mail rosspen@rosspen.com; internet www.rosspen.com; f. 1992; politics, history, other academic and reference publishing; Dir-Gen. A. K. SOROKIN.

Russkii Yazyk (Russian Language): 117303 Moscow, ul. M. Yushunski 1; tel. (495) 319-83-13; fax (495) 319-83-16; e-mail rlm@tpost.net; f. 2001; textbooks, reference, dictionaries; Dir ELIZABET BRATERSKAYA.

Shkola-Press (School-Press): 127254 Moscow, ul. Sh. Rustaveli 10/3; tel. and fax (495) 219-83-80; e-mail marketing@schoolpress.ru; internet www.schoolpress.ru; books on psychology, pedagogy, magazines.

Slovo (Word): 109147 Moscow, ul. Vorontsovskaya 41; tel. and fax (495) 911-61-33; internet www.slovo-online.ru; f. 1989; illustrated books on art, world literature in translation; Dir-Gen. NATALIYA AVETISYAN.

Stroyizdat (Construction Publishing House): 101442 Moscow, ul. Kalyayevskaya 23A; tel. (495) 251-69-67; f. 1932; building, architecture, environmental protection, fire protection and building materials; Dir V. A. KASATKIN.

Tekst (Text): 127299 Moscow, ul. Kosmonavta Volkova 7; tel. and fax (495) 150-0472; e-mail textpubl@yandex.ru; internet www.textpubl.ru; f. 1988; foreign poetry and prose fiction in translation, Russian poetry and prose, children's literature, social sciences, history, law; Dir OLGET M. LIBKIN.

Vagrius: 125993 Moscow, ul. Nikoloyamskaya 1; tel. (495) 221-61-80; fax (495) 510-56-10; e-mail vagrius@vagrius.com; internet www.vagrius.com; f. 1992; fiction, politics, history; Pres. and Dir-Gen. GLEB USPENSKII.

Ves Mir (The Whole World): 101000 Moscow, Kolpachnyi per. 9A; tel. (495) 623-68-39; fax (495) 625-42-69; e-mail info@vesmirbooks.ru; internet www.vesmirbooks.ru; f. 1994; university textbooks, scholarly works in social sciences and humanities; Dir Dr OLEG A. ZIMARIN.

Vysshaya Shkola (Higher School): 127994 Moscow, ul. Neglinnaya 29/14; tel. (495) 200-04-56; fax (495) 200-34-86; e-mail info_vshkola@mail.ru; internet www.vshkola.ru; f. 1939; textbooks for higher-education institutions; Dir MIKHAIL L. ZORIN.

Yuridicheskaya Literatura (Legal Literature): 121069 Moscow, ul. M. Nikitskaya 14; tel. (495) 203-83-84; fax (495) 291-98-83; internet www.jurizdat.ru; f. 1917; legal; official publishers of enactments of the Russian President and Govt; Dir IVAN A. BUNIN.

Znaniye (Knowledge): 101835 Moscow, proyezd Serova 4; tel. (495) 928-15-31; f. 1951; popular books and brochures on politics and science; Dir V. K. BELYAKOV.

Broadcasting and Communications

TELECOMMUNICATIONS

Golden Telecom: 115114 Moscow, Kozhevnicheskii proyezd 1; tel. (495) 797-93-00; fax (495) 797-93-32; e-mail publicrelations@gldn.net; internet www.goldentelecom.ru; f. 1994; operates mobile cellular telecommunications network in cities across the Russian Federation, and in Almaty (Kazakhstan) and Kyiv (Ukraine); Chief Exec. JEAN-PIERRE VANDROMME.

Megafon: 119435 Moscow, Savvinskaya nab. 15; tel. (495) 504-50-20; fax (495) 504-50-21; e-mail aklimov@megafon.ru; internet www.megafon.ru; f. 2002; operates mobile cellular communications networks across Russia; 6 regional cos; 15.6m. subscribers (March 2005); Gen. Dir SERGEI SOLDATENKOV.

Mobilnye TeleSistemi/Mobile TeleSystems (MTS): 109147 Moscow, ul. Marksistskaya 4; tel. (495) 766-01-77; e-mail info@mts.ru; internet www.mts.ru; f. 1993; provides mobile cellular telecommunications in 82 regions of Russia; majority-owned by Sistema Telecom; 35.1% owned by Deutsche Telekom (Germany); Pres. LEONID A. MELAMED; over 85m. subscribers (incl. subsidiary cos in Armenia, Belarus, Turkmenistan, Ukraine and Uzbekistan) (2008).

Moscow City Telephone Network (MGTS—Moskovskaya Gorodskaya Telefonnaya Set): 103051 Moscow, Petrovskii bulv. 12/3; tel. (495) 950-00-00; fax (495) 950-06-18; e-mail mgts@mgts.ru; internet www.mgts.ru; f. 1882; provides telecommunications services in Moscow City; Gen. Man. NIKOLAI A. MAKSIMENKA.

Petersburg Telephone Network (PTS—Peterburgsskaya Telefonnaya Set): 119186 St Petersburg, ul. B. Morskaya 24; tel. (812) 314-15-50; fax (812) 110-68-34; e-mail office@ptn.ru; internet www.ptn.ru; f. 1993; Dir IGOR N. SAMYLIN.

Rostelekom (Rostelecom): 125047 Moscow, ul. 1-aya Tverskaya-Yamskaya 14; tel. (495) 787-28-49; fax (495) 972-82-83; e-mail info@rostelecom.ru; internet www.rt.ru; 50.7% owned by Svyazinvest; dominant long-distance and international telecommunications service provider; 7 regional cos based in St Petersburg, Samara, Novosibirsk, Yekaterinburg, Khabarovsk, Moscow and Rostov-on-Don; Dir DMITRII YEROKHIN.

Svyazinvest: 119121 Moscow, ul. Plyushchikha 55/2; tel. (495) 248-24-71; fax (495) 248-24-53; e-mail dms@svyazinvest.ru; internet www.sinvest.ru; f. 1995; 75% state-owned; holds controlling stakes in 7 'mega-regional' telecommunications operators, 1 international and domestic long–distance operator, and 2 local telecommunications cos, and non-controlling stakes in 2 city telecommunications cos; Chair. LEONID D. REIMAN.

VympelKom-Bilain (Vympelcom-Beeline): 127006 Moscow, ul. Krasnoproletarskaya 4; tel. (495) 725-07-00; fax (495) 991-79-03; e-mail info@beeline.ru; internet www.beeline.ru; operates mobile cellular telecommunications in 78 regions of Russia, and in Armenia, Georgia, Kazakhstan, Tajikistan, Ukraine and Uzbekistan; 26.6% owned by Telenor (Norway); Chief Exec. ALEKSANDR V. IZOSIMOV.

BROADCASTING

Pervyi Kanal (First Channel), operated by Public Russian Television (ORT), is received throughout Russia and many parts of the CIS. The All-Russian State Television Company (VGTRK) broadcasts Telekanal 'Rossiya', which reaches some 92% of the Russian population, and Telekanal 'Kultura' and Telekanal 'Sport'. In addition to the nation-wide television channels, there are local channels, and the NTV (Independent Television) channel (65% owned by the gas utility Gazprom, in which the Government holds a majority stake) is broadcast in most of Russia. In the regions, part of Rossiya's programming is devoted to local affairs, with broadcasts in minority languages. A state-supported, international, English-language TV station, Russia Today, commenced broadcasts in 2006. In mid-2005 there were four nation-wide radio stations, as well as 11 urban radio networks and more than 200 regional stations. At that time Radio Rossiya had more listeners than any other state-run channel, but the commercial music station Russkoye Radio, established in 1995, was the most popular station overall.

Association of Regional State Television and Radio Broadcasters: 113326 Moscow, ul. Pyatnitskaya 25/226; tel. and fax (495) 950-60-28; e-mail fstratyv@rzn.rosmail.com; Chair. of Bd ALEKSANDR N. LEVCHENKO.

Regulatory Authority

Russian Television and Radio Broadcasting Network: 113326 Moscow, ul. Pyatnitskaya 25; tel. (495) 233-66-03; fax (495) 233-28-93; f. 2001; Gen. Man. GENNADII I. SKLYAR.

Radio

All-Russian State Television and Radio Broadcasting Company (VGTRK): 125040 Moscow, ul. 5-aya Yamskogo Polya 19/21; tel. (495) 745-39-78; fax (495) 975-26-11; e-mail rtrinterdep@rfn.ru; internet www.tvradio.ru; f. 1991; broadcasts 'Rossiya' 'Kultura', 'Sport' and 'Planeta' television channels, 89 regional television and radio cos, and national radio stations 'Radio Rossiya', 'Radio Mayak' and 'Radio Nostalzhi'; Chair. OLEG DOBRODEYEV.

Radio Mayak (Radio Beacon): 113326 Moscow, ul. Pyatnitskaya 25; tel. (495) 950-67-67; fax (495) 959-42-04; e-mail inform@radiomayak.ru; internet www.radiomayak.ru; f. 1964; state-owned; Chair. IRINA A. GERASIMOVA.

Radio Nostalzhi (Radio Nostalgia): 113162 Moscow, ul. Shabolovka 37; tel. (495) 955-84-00; e-mail nostalgie@vimain.vitpc.com; f. 1993; Gen. Man. IRINA A. GERASIMOVA.

Radio Rossiya (Radio Russia): 125040 Moscow, ul. 5-aya Yamskogo Polya 19/21; tel. (495) 234-85-94; fax (495) 730-42-77; e-mail direction@radiorus.ru; internet www.radiorus.ru; f. 1990; broadcasts information, social, political, musical, literary and investigative programming; Dir-Gen. ALEKSEI V. ABAKUMOV.

Ekho Moskvy (Moscow Echo): 119992 Moscow, ul. Novyi Arbat 11; tel. (495) 202-92-29; e-mail info@echo.msk.ru; internet www.echo.msk.ru; f. 1990; stations in Moscow, St Petersburg, Rostov-on-Don and Vologda; also broadcasts from Moscow to Chelyabinsk, Krasnoyarsk, Novosibirsk, Omsk, Perm, Saratov and Yekaterinburg; 66% owned by Gazprom-Mediya, 34% staff-owned; Gen. Man. YURII FEDUTINKOV.

Golos Rossii (The Voice of Russia): 115326 Moscow, ul. Pyatnitskaya 25; tel. (495) 950-63-31; fax (495) 951-20-17; e-mail voiceofrussia@ruvr.ru; internet www.vor.ru; fmrly Radio Moscow International; international broadcasts in 34 languages; Man. Dir ARMEN G. OGANESIAN.

Russkoye Radio (Russian Radio): 105064 Moscow, ul. Kazakova 16; tel. (495) 232-16-36; fax (495) 956-13-60; internet www.rusradio.ru; f. 1995; owned by Russkaya Mediyagruppa (Russian Media Group); nation-wide commercial music station; broadcasts to more than 700 towns in Russia, Ukraine, Kazakhstan, Moldova, Kyrgyzstan, the Baltic Republics and the USA; also *Russkoye Radio 2*, principally news and talk programming, broadcast to Moscow; Dir-Gen. SERGEI KOZHEVNIKOV.

Serebryanyi Dozhd (Silver Rain): 127083 Moscow, Petrovsko-Razumovskaya alleya 12A; tel. (495) 925-10-01; internet www.silver.ru; f. 1995; commercial station broadcasting information and entertainment programming; broadcasts to 98 cities in Russia and the 'near abroad'; Dir-Gen. DMITRII SAVITSKII.

Yevropa Plyus (Europa Plus): 127427 Moscow, ul. Akademika Koroleva 19; tel. (495) 217-82-57; fax (495) 956-35-08; e-mail main@europaplus.ru; internet www.europaplus.ru; FM station, broadcasting music, entertainment and information programmes to 500 cities; Pres. ZHORZH POLINSKI.

Television

All-Russian State Television and Radio Broadcasting Company (VGTRK): 125040 Moscow, ul. 5-aya Yamskogo Polya 19/21; tel. (495) 745-39-78; fax (495) 975-26-11; e-mail rtrinterdep@rfn.ru; internet www.tvradio.ru; f. 1991; broadcasts 'Rossiya' 'Kultura', 'Sport' and 'Planeta' television channels, 89 regional television and radio cos, and national radio stations 'Radio Rossiya', 'Radio Mayak' and 'Radio Nostalzhi'; Chair. OLEG DOBRODEYEV.

Telekanal 'Kultura' (Television Channel 'Culture'): 123995 Moscow, ul. M. Nikitskaya 24; e-mail kultura@tvkultura.ru; internet www.tvkultura.ru; f. 1997; Gen. Dir ALEKSANDR S. PONOMAREV.

Telekanal 'Rossiya' (Television Channel 'Russia'): 115162 Moscow, ul. Shabolovka 37; tel. (495) 924-63-74; fax (495) 234-87-71; e-mail info@rutv.ru; internet www.rutv.ru; fmrly RTR-TV; name changed as above in 2002; Dir-Gen. ALEKSANDR S. PONAMAREV.

Telekanal 'Sport' (Television Channel 'Sport'): 115162 Moscow, ul. Shabolovka 37; e-mail reception@sport.vgtek.com; internet sportbox.ru; f. 2003; Dir-Gen. VASILII KIKNADZE.

Telekanal 'Zvezda' (Television Channel 'Star'): 129110 Moscow, Suvorovskaya pl. 2; tel. (495) 631-58-83; internet www.tvzvezda.ru; f. 2005; Gen. Dir SERGEI V. SABUSHKIN.

NTV—Independent Television: 127427 Moscow, ul. Akademika Koroleva 12; tel. (495) 725-54-03; fax (495) 725-54-01; e-mail info@ntv.ru; internet www.ntv.ru; f. 1993; 65% owned by Gazprom-Mediya; also NTV World (NTV Mir), broadcasting to Russian communities in Israel, Europe and the USA; Dir-Gen. NIKOLAI YU. SENKEVICH.

Pervyi Kanal—First Channel (Channel One): 127427 Moscow, ul. Akademika Koroleva 12; tel. (495) 617-73-87; fax (495) 215-82-47; e-mail ort_int@ortv.ru; internet www.1tv.ru; f. 1995; fmrly ORT—Public Russian Television; name changed as above in 2002; 51% state-owned; 49% owned by private shareholders; Chair. MIKHAIL PYATKOVSKII; Dir-Gen. KONSTANTIN ERNST.

Ren-TV Network: 119843 Moscow, Zubovskii bulv. 17/510; tel. (495) 246-25-06; fax (495) 245-09-98; e-mail site@rentv.dol.ru; internet www.ren-tv.com; f. 1991; network of more than 100 television stations in the Russian Federation and 60 stations in republics of the CIS; Chair. LYUBOV SOVERSHAYEVA; Gen. Man. DMITRII A. LESNEVSKII.

STS—Network of Television Stations: 123298 Moscow, ul. 3-aya Khoroshevskaya 12; tel. (495) 797-41-73; fax (495) 797-41-01; e-mail www@ctc-tv.ru; internet www.ctc-tv.ru; f. 1996; owned by StoryFirst Communications (USA); broadcasts programmes of popular entertainment to 350 cities in Russia; Dir-Gen. ALEKSANDR YE. RODNYANSKII.

TNT—Territory of Our Viewers—TV Network: 127427 Moscow, ul. Akademika Koroleva 19; tel. (495) 217-81-88; fax (495) 748-14-90; e-mail info@tnt-tv.ru; internet www.tnt-tv.ru; f. 1997; cable television network broadcasting to 582 cities in Russia; Chief Exec. ALEKSANDR DYBAL; Dir-Gen. ROMAN PETRENKO.

TV-Tsentr (TVTs—TV-Centre): 113184 Moscow, ul. B. Tatarskaya 33/1; tel. (495) 959-39-87; fax (495) 959-39-66; e-mail info@tvc.ru; internet www.tvc.ru; f. 1997; broadcasting consortium for terrestrial cable and satellite television; receives funding from Govt of Moscow City; Pres. OLEG M. POPTSOV; Dir PAVEL V. KASPAROV.

Finance

(cap. = capital; res = reserves; dep. = deposits; m. = million; brs = branches; amounts in new roubles, unless otherwise stated)

BANKING
Central Bank

Bank Rossii—Central Bank of the Russian Federation: 107016 Moscow, ul. Neglinnaya 12; tel. (495) 771-91-00; fax (495) 621-64-65; e-mail webmaster@www.cbr.ru; internet www.cbr.ru; f. 1990; cap. 3,000m., res 303,732m., dep. 9,700,000m. (Jan. 2007); Chair. SERGEI M. IGNATIYEV; 79 brs.

Major Banks

Absolut Bank (Absolyut Bank): 127051 Moscow, Tsvetnoi bulv. 18; tel. (495) 995-10-01; fax (495) 995-10-22; e-mail info@absolutbank.ru; internet www.absolutbank.ru; 95% owned by KBC Bank NV (Belgium); f. 1993; cap. 1,954.6m., res 3,393.7m., dep. 104,671.2m. (Dec. 2007); Chair. of Management Bd NIKOLAI SIDOROV.

AK BARS Bank: 420066 Tatarstan, Kazan, ul. Dekabristov 1; tel. (843) 519-38-02; fax (843) 519-39-75; e-mail mail@akbars.ru; internet www.akbars.ru; f. 1993; cap. 25,244.0m., res 349.6m., dep. 109,497.3m. (Dec. 2007); Chair. of Bd ROBERT MINNEGALIYEV; 22 brs.

Alfa-Bank: 107078 Moscow, ul. Kalanchevskaya 27; tel. (495) 974-25-15; fax (495) 745-57-84; e-mail mail@alfabank.ru; internet www.alfabank.ru; f. 1990; cap. US $694.8m., res $56.8m., dep. $15,819.0m. (Dec. 2007); Chair. of Exec. Bd RUSHAN KHVESYUK; Pres. PETR AVEN.

Bank of Moscow (Bank Moskvy): 107996 Moscow, ul. Rozhdestvenka 8/15/3; tel. (495) 925-80-00; fax (495) 795-26-00; e-mail info@mmbank.ru; internet www.mmbank.ru; f. 1995; present name adopted 2004; 60% owned by Govt of Moscow City; cap. 15,476.8m., res 31,689.1m., dep. 476,381.2m. (Dec. 2007); Pres. and Chief Exec. ANDREI BORODIN.

Bank Petrocommerce (Bank Petrokommertz): 127051 Moscow, ul. Petrovka 24; tel. (495) 625-95-65; fax (495) 623-36-07; e-mail welcome@pkb.ru; internet www.pkb.ru; f. 1992; cap. 6,752.6m., res −23.3m., dep. 145,234.0m. (Dec. 2007); Pres. and Chair. of Bd VLADIMIR N. NIKITENKO.

Bank Sankt-Peterburg: 191167 St Petersburg, Nevskii pr. 178; tel. (812) 329-50-34; fax (812) 329-50-70; e-mail corel@bspb.ru; internet www.bspb.ru; f. 1990; cap. 3,564.3m., res 10,867.4m., dep. 103,418.6m. (Dec. 2007); Chair. ALEKSANDR SAVELIYEV.

Bank Soyuz: 127006 Moscow, ul. Dolgorukovskaya 34/1; tel. (495) 729-55-00; fax (495) 729-55-05; e-mail info@banksoyuz.ru; internet www.banksoyuz.ru; f. 1993; cap. 5,389m., res 158m., dep. 75,177m. (Dec. 2007); Chair. VLADIMIR V. IZUTIN.

Bank Uralsib: 119048 Moscow, ul. Yefremova 8; tel. (495) 705-90-39; fax (495) 745-70-10; e-mail pr@nikoil.ru; internet www.uralsib.ru; f. 1993; cap. 32,607m., res 10,156m., dep. 316,496m. (Dec. 2007); Chair. NIKOLAI TSVETKOV.

Bank VTB 24: 101000 Moscow, ul. Myasnitskaya 35; tel. (495) 771-78-78; fax (495) 980-46-66; e-mail info@vtb24.ru; internet www.vtb24.ru; f. 1991; present name adopted 2006; cap. 34,964.0m., res 12,081.8m., dep. 256,825.7m. (Dec. 2007); Chief Exec. MIKHAIL M. ZADORNOV; 44 brs.

Bank VTB Severo-Zapad (Bank VTB North-West): 191014 St Petersburg, ul. Kovenskii 17/18; tel. (812) 329-84-51; fax (812) 310-61-73; e-mail lider@icbank.ru; internet www.vtb-sz.ru; f. 1870 as Volga-Kama Bank; fmrly Industry and Construction Bank; present name adopted 2007; cap. 1,932.5m., res 3,298.8m., dep. 171,714.5m. (Dec. 2007); Chair. VLADIMIR SKATIN; 54 brs.

Bank Zenit: 129110 Moscow, Bannyi per. 9; tel. (495) 937-07-37; fax (495) 777-57-06; e-mail info@zenit.ru; internet www.zenit.ru; f. 1994; 26% owned by Tatneft; cap. US $392.9m., res $60.8m., dep. $3,216.3m. (Dec. 2006); Chair. of Bd ALEKSEI A. SOKOLOV; 4 brs.

Gazprombank: 117420 Moscow, ul. Nametkina 16/1; tel. (495) 719-17-63; fax (495) 913-73-19; e-mail mailbox@gazprombank.ru; internet www.gazprombank.ru; f. 1990; 87.5% owned by Gazprom; cap. US $1,160.9m., res $2,222.3m., dep. $27,289.4m. (Dec. 2007); Chair. of Management Bd ANDREI I. AKIMOV; 32 brs.

ING Bank (Eurasia): 127473 Moscow, ul. Krasnoproletarskaya 36; tel. (495) 755-54-00; fax (495) 755-54-99; e-mail russia@ingbank.com; internet www.ing.ru; f. 1993; 99% owned by ING Bank NV (Netherlands); cap. 2,024.7m., res 2,788.1m., dep. 73,830.5m. (Dec. 2007); Dir-Gen. HENDRIK WILLEM TEN BOSCH.

Khanty-Mansiiskii Bank: 628012 Tyumen obl., Khanty-Mansii AOk—Yugra, Khanty-Mansiisk, ul. Mira 38; tel. (34671) 302-10; fax (34671) 302-19; e-mail hmbank@khmb.ru; internet www.khmb.ru; f. 1992; cap. 5,787.3m., res 1,455.3m., dep. 60,521.5m. (Dec. 2006); Pres. DMITRII MIZGULIN; 16 brs.

MDM Bank (Moskovskiy Delovoy Mir—Moscow Business World): 115172 Moscow, Kotelnicheskaya nab. 33/1; tel. (495) 797-95-00; fax (495) 797-95-01; e-mail info@mdmbank.com; internet www.mdmbank.ru; f. 1993; cap. 1,794m., res 17,229m., dep. 273,999m. (Dec. 2007); Chief Exec. MICHEL PERKHIRIN; 98 brs and sub-brs.

Mezhdunarodnyi Promyshlennyi Bank (International Industrial Bank): 125009 Moscow, ul. B. Dmitrovka 23/1; tel. (495) 626-44-46; fax (495) 692-82-84; e-mail mail@iib.ru; internet www.iib.ru; f. 1992; cap. 25,000m., res 179.0m., dep. 89,911.9m. (Dec. 2007); Chair. ALEKSANDR V. GNUSAREV; 5 brs.

Moscow Bank for Reconstruction and Development (Moskovskii Bank Rekonstruktsii i Razvitiya): 119034 Moscow, Yeropkinskii per. 5; tel. and fax (495) 101-28-00; e-mail mbrd@mbrd.ru; internet www.mbrd.ru; 58.44% owned by Sistema; cap. 1,023.4m., res 5,405.3m., dep. 110,806.6m. (Dec. 2007); Chair. of Bd SERGEI YE. CHEREMIN.

Nomos-Bank: 109240 Moscow, ul. Verkhnyaya Radishchevskaya 3/1; tel. (495) 737-73-55; fax (495) 797-32-50; e-mail nmosmail@online.ru; internet www.nomos.ru; f. 1992; cap. 5,656.0m., res 9,011.2m., dep. 168,327.4m. (Dec. 2007); Pres. DMITRII SOKOLOV.

Orgresbank: 125040 Moscow, ul. 3-aya Yamskogo Polya 19/1; tel. (495) 777-34-77; fax (495) 777-34-75; e-mail all@orgres.ru; internet www.orgresbank.ru; f. 1994; cap. 944.9m., res 2,617.4m., dep. 65,013.3m. (Dec. 2007); Chair. IGOR KOGAN.

Promsvyazbank: 109052 Moscow, ul. Smirnovskaya 10/22; tel. (495) 727-10-20; fax (495) 727-10-21; e-mail postmaster@psbank.ru; internet www.psbank.ru; f. 1995; cap. 7,468.8m., res 10,001.7m., dep. 239,038.8m. (Dec. 2007); Chair. of Council DMITRII N. ANANIYEV; Pres. ALEKSANDR A. LEVKOVSKII; 11 brs.

Raiffeisenbank ZAO: 129090 Moscow, ul. Troitskaya 17/1; tel. (495) 721-99-00; fax (495) 721-99-01; e-mail info@raiffeisen.ru; internet www.raiffeisen.ru; f. 1996; owned by Raiffeisenbank (Austria); absorbed Impexbank in 2007; cap. 13,439.3m., res 1,368.1m., dep. 166,355.6m. (Dec. 2006); Chair. of Man. Bd JOHANN JONACH; 7 brs and sub-brs.

Rosbank: 107078 Moscow, ul. M. Poryvayevoi 11, POB 208; tel. (495) 921-01-01; fax (495) 725-05-11; e-mail mailbox@rosbank.ru; internet www.rosbank.ru; f. 1993; 50% owned by Société Générale (France); cap. 9,270.9m., res 21,773.6m., dep. 356,105.8m. (Dec. 2007); Pres. and Chair. of Bd of Dirs ANDREI KLISHAS; Chief Exec. ALEKSANDR POPOV; 68 brs.

Russ-Bank: 107078 Moscow, ul. Myasnitskaya 43/2; tel. (495) 925-80-82; fax (495) 925-80-81; e-mail office@russbank.ru; internet www.russbank.ru; f. 1994; present name adopted 2006; cap. 1,907.7m., res 3,445.6m., dep. 61,081.5m. (Dec. 2007); Chair. VLADIMIR BALABANOV.

Russkii Standart Bank: 105066 Moscow, ul. Spartakovskaya 2/1/6; tel. (495) 748-15-19; fax (495) 797-84-04; e-mail nignatova@rs.ru; internet www.rs.ru; f. 1993; cap. 1,739m., res 801m., dep. 157,376m. (Dec. 2007); Chair. RUSTAM V. TARIKO; Chief Exec. DMITRII O. LEVIN.

Sberbank—Savings Bank of the Russian Federation: 117997 Moscow, ul. Vavilova 19; tel. (495) 957-58-62; fax (495) 957-57-31; e-mail sbrf@sbrf.ru; internet www.sbrf.ru; f. 1841 as a deposit-taking institution, reorganized as a joint-stock commercial bank in 1991; 60.6% owned by Bank Rossii—Central Bank of the Russian Federation; cap. 87,742m., res 25,064m., dep. 4,121,768m. (Dec. 2007); Chair. of Bd and Chief Exec. GERMAN O. GREF; 17 regional head offices, 823 brs and 19,307 sub-brs.

Svyaz-Bank (Interregional Bank for Settlements of the Telecommunications and Postal Services): 125375 Moscow, ul. Tverskaya 7; tel. (495) 771-32-60; fax (495) 771-32-76; e-mail MAV@sviaz-bank.ru; internet www.sviaz-bank.ru; f. 1991; absorbed Russian Industrial Bank in 2008; cap. 5,745.8m., res −13.3m., dep. 127,605.8m. (Dec. 2007); Chair. of Bd of Dirs ANDREI KONOVAL.

TransKreditBank (TransCreditBank): 105066 Moscow, ul. N. Basmannaya 37A/1; tel. (495) 788-08-80; fax (495) 788-08-79; e-mail info@bnk.ru; internet www.tcb.ru; f. 1992; 55.1% owned by Russian Railways; cap. 3,373.6m., res 56.3m., dep. 124,485.9m. (Dec. 2007); Pres. SERGEI N. PUSHKIN.

Trust National Bank (Natsionalnyi Bank 'Trast'): 107045 Moscow, Ulanskii per. 24/1; tel. (800) 200-11-44; e-mail secretar@trust.ru; internet bank.trust.ru; f. 1995; fmrly Bank MENATEP St Petersburg; present name adopted 2005; cap. 2,896.4m., res 4,850.5m., dep. 57,783.1m. (Dec. 2007); Chair. ILYA YUROV.

UniCredit Bank: 119034 Moscow, Prechistenskaya nab. 9; tel. (495) 258-72-00; fax (495) 258-72-72; e-mail unicredit@

unicreditgroup.ru; internet wwww.unicreditbank.ru; f. 1989; fmrly International Moscow Bank; present name adopted 2007; 100% owned by Bank Austria Creditanstalt AG (Austria); cap. 16,787.7m., res 437.3m., dep. 316,685.5m. (Dec. 2007); Pres. HELMUT BERNKOPR (acting); 22 brs.

URSA Bank: 630102 Novosibirsk, ul. Inskaya 54; tel. (3832) 27-75-99; fax (3832) 34-00-25; e-mail secret@ursabank.ru; internet www.ursabank.ru; f. 1990; present name adopted 2006; cap. 1,629.1m., res 21,439.8m., dep. 131,317.9m. (Dec. 2007); Chair. of Bd of Dirs IGOR KIM.

Vneshekonombank (State Corporation Bank for Development and Foreign Economic Affairs): 107996 Moscow, pr. Sakharova 9; tel. (495) 604-66-90; fax (495) 975-21-43; e-mail info@veb.ru; internet www.veb.ru; f. 1924; state-owned; dep. US $11,042m., total assets $12,429m. (Dec. 2006); Chair. VLADIMIR A. DMITRIYEV.

Vozrozhdeniye—V-Bank: 101999 Moscow, per. Luchnikov 7/4/1, POB 9; tel. (495) 777-08-88; fax (495) 620-19-99; e-mail vbank@co.voz.ru; internet www.vbank.ru; f. 1991; cap. 250m., res 7,306m., dep. 93,560m. (Dec. 2007); Chair. of Managing Bd DMITRII L. ORLOV; 170 brs.

VTB Bank: 190000 St Petersburg, ul. B. Morskaya 29; tel. (812) 314-60-59; fax (812) 312-78-18; e-mail info@vtb.ru; internet www.vtb.ru; f. 1990; fmrly Bank for Foreign Trade; present name adopted 2007; 77.5% owned by Govt of Russian Federation; cap. US $3,084m., res $10,130m., dep. $68,381m. (Dec. 2007); Chair. of Bd and Chief Exec. ANDREI L. KOSLIN.

Yevrofinans Mosnarbank (Evrofinance Mosnarbank): 121099 Moscow, ul. Novyi Arbat 29; tel. (495) 967-81-82; fax (495) 967-81-33; e-mail info@evrofinance.ru; internet www.evrofinance.ru; f. 1990; present name adopted 2003; cap. 3,510.3m., res 7,765.9m., dep. 44,321.2m. (Dec. 2006); Pres. and Chair. of Bd VLADIMIR STOLYARENKO.

Bankers' Association

Association of Russian Banks (Assostiatsiya Rossiiskikh Bankov): 121069 Moscow, Skatertnyi per. 20/1; tel. (495) 291-66-30; fax (495) 291-66-66; e-mail arb@arb.ru; internet www.arb.ru; f. 1991; 755 mem. orgs, incl. 576 credit orgs (2007); Pres. GAREGIN A. TOSUNYAN.

INSURANCE

Agroinvest Insurance Co: 127422 Moscow, ul. Timiryazevskaya 26; tel. (495) 976-94-56; fax (495) 977-05-88; health, life and general insurance services; Pres. YURII I. MORDVINTSEV.

AIG Russia: 103009 Moscow, ul. Tverskaya 16/2; tel. (495) 935-89-50; fax (495) 935-89-52; e-mail aig.russia@aig.com; internet www.aigrussia.ru; f. 1994; mem. of the American International Group Inc; personal and business property insurance, also marine, life, financial, etc.; Pres. GARY COLEMAN.

Allianz Insurance Co: 127473 Moscow, 3-i Samotechnii per. 3; tel. (495) 937-69-96; fax (495) 937-69-80; e-mail allianz@allianz.ru; internet www.allianz.ru; engineering, professional liability, life, medical, property, marine and private; Man. Dir MICHAEL HERGESELL.

Ingosstrakh Insurance Co: 115998 Moscow, ul. Pyatnitskaya 12/2; tel. (495) 232-32-11; fax (495) 959-45-18; e-mail ingos@ingos.ru; internet www.ingos.ru; f. 1947; undertakes all kinds of insurance and reinsurance; Chair. NATALIYA A. RAYEVSKAYA; Gen. Dir YEVGENII TUMANOV.

Medstrakh—Medical Insurance Fund of the Russian Federation: 107076 Moscow, pl. Preobrazhenskaya 7A/1; tel. (495) 964-84-27; fax (495) 964-84-21; e-mail mz@mcramn.ru; internet www.medstrah.ru; f. 1991; health, life, property, travel, liability; also provides compulsory medical insurance; Pres. PETR KUZNETSOV.

RESO-Garantiya Insurance Co: 125047 Moscow, ul. Gasheka 12/1; tel. (495) 730-30-00; fax (495) 956-25-85; e-mail reso@orc.ru; internet www.reso.ru; f. 1991; Dir-Gen. DMITRII G. RAKOVSHCHIK.

Rosgosstrakh—Russian State Insurance: 127994 Moscow, ul. Novoslobodskaya 23; tel. (495) 781-24-00; fax (495) 978-27-64; e-mail admin@rgs.ru; internet www.gosstrah.ru; majority state-owned; 49% stake transferred to private ownership in 2001; undertakes domestic insurance; subsidiary cos in 80 federal subjects (territorial units) of the Russian Federation; Chair. VLADISLAV REZNIK; Gen. Dir RUBEN VARDANIAN.

ROSNO—Russian National Society Insurance Co: 115184 Moscow, Ozerkovskaya nab. 30; tel. (495) 232-33-33; fax (495) 232-00-14; e-mail info@rosno.ru; internet www.rosno.ru; f. 1992; 100 brs and 186 agencies; 47% owned by AFK Sistema; 45.3% owned by Allianz AG (Germany); CEO LEONID MELAMED.

Russkiye Strakhovye Traditsii (Russian Traditions Insurance Co): 129366 Moscow, Raketnyi bulv. 13/2; tel. (495) 283-88-03; fax (495) 283-88-05; e-mail info@rustrad.ru; internet www.rustrad.ru; f. 1992; Pres. IVAN I. DAVYDOV.

SOGAZ—Insurance Co of the Gas Industry: 117997 Moscow, ul. Nametkina 16; tel. (495) 782-09-17; fax (495) 432-90-05; e-mail sogaz@sogaz.ru; internet www.sogaz.ru; f. 1993; owned by gas industry interests; Chair. of Bd of Dirs SERGEI A. LUKASH.

Soglasiye (Agreement) Insurance Co: 109017 Moscow, M. Tolmachevskii per. 8–11/3; tel. and fax (495) 959-46-32; e-mail official@soglasie.ru; internet www.soglasie.ru; f. 1993 as Interros-Soglasiye; owned by Interros; Gen. Man. IGOR ZHUK.

STOCK EXCHANGES

Moscow Stock Exchange (MSE) (Moskovskaya Fondovaya Birzha): 127422 Moscow, ul. Vsevoloda Vishnevskogo 4; tel. (495) 771-35-80; fax (495) 250-17-34; e-mail mse@mse.ru; internet www.mse.ru; f. 1997; Pres. ALEKSEI RYZHKOV.

RTS—Russian Trading System: 127006 Moscow, ul. Dolgorukovskaya 1/38; tel. (495) 705-90-31; fax (495) 733-95-15; e-mail info@rts.ru; internet www.rts.ru; f. 1995; Chief Exec. ROMAN YU. GORYUNOV.

Siberian Stock Exchange: 630104 Novosibirsk, ul. Frunze 5, POB 233; tel. (3832) 21-60-67; fax (3832) 21-06-90; e-mail sibex@sibex.nsk.su; f. 1991; Pres. ALEKSANDR V. NOVIKOV.

COMMODITY EXCHANGES

Asiatic Commodity Exchange: 670000 Buryatiya, Ulan-Ude, ul. Sovetskaya 23/37; tel. and fax (3012) 22-26-81; f. 1991; Chair. ANDREI FIRSOV.

European-Asian Exchange (EAE): 101000 Moscow, ul. Myasnitskaya 26; tel. and fax (495) 787-58-93; e-mail info@eae.ru; internet www.eae.ru; f. 2000; Chair. of Council TATYANA S. SOKOLOVA; Gen. Man. ALEKSANDR B. YEREMIN.

Khabarovsk Commodity Exchange (KhCE): 680000 Khabarovsk; tel. and fax (4212) 33-65-60; f. 1991; Pres. YEVGENII V. PANASENKO.

Komi Commodity Exchange (KoCE): 167610 Komi, Syktyvkar, Oktyabrskii pr. 16; tel. (8212) 22-32-86; fax (8212) 23-84-43; f. 1991; Pres. PETR S. LUCHENKOV.

Kuzbass Commodity and Raw Materials Exchange (KECME): 650090 Kemerovo, ul. Novgorodskaya 19; tel. (3842) 23-45-40; fax (3842) 23-49-56; f. 1991; Gen. Man. FEDOR MASENKOV.

Moscow Commodity Exchange (MCE): 129223 Moscow, pr. Mira, Russian Exhibition Centre, Pavilion 69 (4); tel. (495) 187-86-14; fax (495) 187-88-76; f. 1990; organization of exchange trading (cash, stock and futures market); Pres. and Chair. of Bd YURII MILYUKOV.

Petrozavodsk Commodity Exchange (PCE): 185028 Kareliya, Petrozavodsk, ul. Krasnaya 31; tel. and fax (8142) 7-80-57; f. 1991; Gen. Man. VALERII SAKHAROV.

Russian Commodity Exchange of the Agro-Industrial Complex (RosAgroBirzha): 125080 Moscow, Volokolamskoye shosse 11; tel. (495) 209-52-25; f. 1990; Chair. of Exchange Cttee ALEKSANDR VASILIYEV.

Russian Exchange (RE): 101000 Moscow, ul. Myasnitskaya 26; tel. (495) 787-84-34; fax (495) 262-57-57; e-mail ic@ci.re.ru; internet www.re.ru; f. 1990; Pres. PAVEL PANOV.

St Petersburg Exchange: 199026 St Petersburg, Vasilyevskii Ostrov, 26-aya liniya 15; tel. (812) 322-44-11; fax (812) 322-73-90; e-mail spbex@spbex.ru; internet www.spbex.ru; f. 1991; Pres. and Chief Exec. VIKTOR V. NIKOLAYEV.

Udmurt Commodity Universal Exchange (UCUE): 426075 Udmurt Rep., Izhevsk, ul. Soyuznaya 107; tel. (3412) 37-08-88; fax (3412) 37-16-57; e-mail iger@udmnet.ru; f. 1991; Pres. N. F. LAZAREV.

Yekaterinburg Commodity Exchange (UCE): 620012 Sverdlovsk obl., Yekaterinburg, pr. Kosmonavtov 23; tel. (343) 234-43-01; fax (343) 251-53-64; f. 1991; Chair. of Exchange Cttee KONSTANTIN ZHUZHLOV.

Trade and Industry

GOVERNMENT AGENCY

Russian Federal Property Fund (Rossiiskii Fond Federalnogo Imushchestva): 119049 Moscow, Leninskii pr. 9; tel. (495) 236-71-15; fax (495) 956-27-80; e-mail rffi@dol.ru; internet www.fpf.ru; f. 1992 to ensure consistency in the privatization process and to implement privatization legislation; Chair. YURII A. PETROV.

THE RUSSIAN FEDERATION

NATIONAL CHAMBER OF COMMERCE

Chamber of Commerce and Industry of the Russian Federation (Torgovo-Promyshlennaya Palata RF): 109012 Moscow, ul. Ilinka 6; tel. (495) 929-00-09; fax (495) 929-03-60; e-mail dios-inform@tpprf.ru; internet www.tpprf.ru; f. 1991; Pres. YEVGENII M. PRIMAKOV.

REGIONAL CHAMBERS OF COMMERCE

In early 2002 there were a total of 148 regional chambers of commerce in the Russian Federation. The following are among the most important.

Astrakhan Chamber of Commerce: 414040 Astrakhan, ul. Zhelyabova 50; tel. (8512) 25-58-44; fax (8512) 28-14-42; e-mail cci@mail.astrakhan.ru; internet astrcci.astrakhan.ru; f. 1992; Pres. ALEKSEI D. KANTEMIROV.

Bashkortostan Chamber of Commerce: 450007 Bashkortostan, Ufa, ul. Vorovskogo 22; tel. (3472) 23-23-80; fax (3472) 51-70-79; e-mail office@tpprb.ru; internet www.tpprb.ru; f. 1990; Chair. BORIS A. BONDARENKO.

Central Siberian Chamber of Commerce: 660049 Krasnoyarsk, ul. Kirova 26; tel. (3912) 23-96-13; fax (3912) 23-96-83; e-mail cstp@mail.ru; internet www.cstpp.ru; f. 1985; Chair. VALERII A. KOSTIN.

East Siberian Chamber of Commerce: 664003 Irkutsk, ul. Sukhe-Batora 16; tel. (3952) 33-50-60; fax (3952) 33-50-66; e-mail info@ccies.ru; internet www.ccies.ru; f. 1974; Pres. KONSTANTIN S. SHAVRIN.

Far East Chamber of Commerce: 680670 Khabarovsk, ul. Sheronova 113; tel. (4210) 30-47-70; fax (4210) 30-54-58; e-mail dvtpp@fecci.khv.ru; f. 1970; Pres. MIKHAIL V. KRUGLIKOV.

Kaliningrad Chamber of Commerce and Industry: 236010 Kaliningrad, ul. Vatutina 20; tel. (4012) 95-68-01; fax (4012) 95-47-88; e-mail kaliningrad_cci@baltnet.ru; internet www.kaliningrad-cci.ru; f. 1990; Pres. IGOR V. TSARKOV.

Kamchatka Chamber of Commerce: 683000 Kamchatka Krai, Petropavlovsk-Kamchatskii, ul. Leninskaya 38/208; tel. and fax (4152) 12-35-10; e-mail kamtpp@iks.ru; Pres. ALLA V. PARKHOMCHUK.

Krasnodar Chamber of Commerce: 350063 Krasnodar, ul. Kommunarov 8; tel. and fax (861) 268-22-13; e-mail tppkk@tppkuban.ru; internet www.tppkuban.ru; f. 1969; Chair. YURII N. TKACHENKO.

Kuzbass Chamber of Commerce: 650099 Kemerovo, pr. Sovetskii 63/407; tel. and fax (3842) 58-77-64; e-mail ktpp@mail.kuzbass.net; internet city.info.kuzbass.net/ktpp; f. 1991; Pres. TATYANA O. IVLEVA.

Maritime (Primorskii) Krai Chamber of Commerce: 690600 Maritime Krai, Vladivostok, Okeanskii pr. 13A; tel. (4232) 26-96-30; fax (4232) 22-72-26; e-mail palata@online.vladivostok.ru; internet www.ptpp.ru; f. 1964; Pres. VLADIMIR B. BREZHNEV.

Moscow Chamber of Commerce: 117393 Moscow, ul. Akademika Pilyugina 22; tel. (495) 132-07-33; fax (495) 132-75-03; e-mail extern@mtpp.org; internet www.mtpp.org; f. 1991; Chair. YURII I. KOTOV; Pres. LEONID V. GOVOROV.

Nizhnii Novgorod Chamber of Commerce: 603005 Nizhnii Novgorod, pl. Oktyabrskaya 1; tel. (8312) 19-42-10; fax (8312) 19-40-09; e-mail tpp@rda.nnov.ru; internet www.tpp.nnov.ru; f. 1990; Pres. GENNADII M. KHODYRYEV.

Northern Chamber of Commerce and Industry: 183766 Murmansk, per. Rusanova 10; tel. (8152) 47-29-99; fax (8152) 47-39-78; e-mail ncci@online.ru; internet www.ncci.ru; f. 1990; Pres. ANATOLII M. GLUSHKOV.

Novosibirsk Chamber of Commerce: 630064 Novosibirsk, pr. K. Marksa 1; tel. and fax (383) 346-41-50; e-mail org@ntpp.ru; internet www.ntpp.ru; f. 1991; Chair. BORIS V. BRUSILOVSKII; 315 mems (2002).

Omsk Chamber of Commerce: 644007 Omsk, ul. Gertsena 51/53; tel. (3812) 25-43-50; fax (3812) 23-45-80; e-mail omtpp@omsknet.ru; internet www.omsktpp.ru; f. 1992; Pres. TATYANA A. KHOROSHAVINA.

Rostov Chamber of Commerce: 344022 Rostov-on-Don, ul. Pushkinskaya 176; tel. and fax (836) 264-45-47; e-mail tpp@rost.ru; internet www.tpp.tis.ru; f. 1992; Pres. NIKOLAI I. PRISYAZHNYUK.

Sakha (Yakutiya) Chamber of Commerce: 677000 Sakha (Yakutiya), Yakutsk, ul. Lenina 22/214; tel. (4112) 26-64-96; e-mail palata91@mail.ru; f. 1991; Chair. SERGEI G. BAKULIN.

Samara Chamber of Commerce: 443099 Samara, ul. A. Tolstogo 6; tel. (8462) 32-11-59; fax (8462) 70-48-96; e-mail ccisr@samara.ru; internet www.cci.samara.ru; f. 1988; Pres. BORIS V. ARDALIN.

Saratov Regional Chamber of Commerce and Industry: 410600 Saratov, ul. B. Kazachya 30; tel. (8452) 27-70-78; fax (8452) 27-70-82; e-mail srcci@sgtpp.ru; internet www.sgtpp.ru; f. 1986; Pres. MAKSIM A. FATEYEV.

Smolensk Chamber of Commerce: 214000 Smolensk, ul. Bakunina 10A; tel. and fax (481) 238-74-50; e-mail smolenskcci@keytown.com; internet www.smolcci.keytown.com; f. 1993; Pres. VLADIMIR P. ARKHIPENKOV.

South Urals Chamber of Commerce: 454080 Chelyabinsk, ul. S. Krivoi 56; tel. (351) 266-18-16; fax (351) 265-41-53; e-mail mail@uralreg.ru; internet www.uralreg.ru; f. 1992; Pres. FEDOR L. DEGTYAREV; 550 mems (2007).

St Petersburg Chamber of Commerce: 191123 St Petersburg, ul. Chaikovskogo 46–48; tel. (812) 273-48-96; fax (812) 273-48-96; e-mail spbcci@spbcci.ru; internet www.spbcci.ru; f. 1921; Pres. VLADIMIR I. KATENEV.

Stavropol Chamber of Commerce and Industry: 355003 Stavropol, ul. Lenina 384; tel. (8652) 94-53-34; fax (8652) 34-05-10; e-mail stcci@statel.stavropol.ru; f. 1991; Pres. VITALII S. NABATNIKOV.

Tatarstan Republic Chamber of Commerce and Industry: 420111 Tatarstan, Kazan, ul. Pushkina 18; tel. (843) 264-62-07; fax (843) 236-09-66; e-mail tpprt@tpprt.ru; internet www.tpprt.ru; f. 1992; Gen. Dir SHAMIL R. AGEYEV; 1,200 mems (2007).

Ulyanovsk Chamber of Commerce: 432063 Ulyanovsk, ul. Engelsa 19; tel. (8422) 41-03-61; fax (8422) 41-02-31; e-mail info@ultpp.ru; f. 1992; Pres. YEVGENII S. BALANDIN.

Urals Chamber of Commerce and Industry: 620027 Sverdlovsk obl., Yekaterinburg, ul. Vostochnaya 6; tel. (343) 353-04-49; fax (343) 353-58-63; e-mail ucci@ucci.ur.ru; internet ucci.ur.ru; f. 1959; Pres. YURII P. MATUSHKIN.

Volgograd Chamber of Commerce: 400005 Volgograd, ul. 7-aya Gvardeiskaya 2; tel. (8442) 93-61-35; fax (8442) 34-22-02; e-mail cci@volgogradcci.ru; internet www.volgogradcci.ru; f. 1990; Pres. ALEKSANDR D. BELITSKII.

Vologda Chamber of Commerce and Industry: 160000 Vologda, ul. Lermontova 15; tel. and fax (8172) 72-46-87; e-mail grant@vologda.ru; internet www.vologdatpp.ru; f. 1992; Pres. GALINA D. TELEGINA.

Voronezh Chamber of Commerce: 394030 Voronezh, 'Voronezhvnesh-servis', POB 63; tel. and fax (473) 252-49-38; e-mail mail@oootpp.vm.ru; f. 1991; fmrly Central-Black Earth Chamber of Commerce and Industry; Pres. VYACHESLAV A. KONDRATYEV.

EMPLOYERS' ORGANIZATIONS

Co-ordinating Council of Employers' Unions of Russia (Koordinatsionnyi Sovet Obyedinenii Rabotodatelei Rossii—KSORR): 109017 Moscow, per. M. Tolmachevskii 8–11; tel. (495) 232-55-77; fax (495) 959-46-06; e-mail official@ksorr.ru; internet www.ksorr.ru; f. 1994; co-ordinates and represents employers in relations with government bodies and trade unions, and represents Russian employers in the ILO and the International Organization of Employers (IOE); Chair. OLEG V. YEREMEYEV; Gen. Dir SERGEI V. LUKONIN; unites 35 major employers' unions, including the following:

Agro-Industrial Union of Russia: 107139 Moscow, POB 139; tel. (495) 204-41-04; fax (495) 207-83-62; e-mail sva@gvs.aris.ru; Pres. VASILII A. STARODUBTSEV.

All-Russian Social Organization of Small and Medium-sized Businesses (OPORA Rossii) (Obshcherossiiskaya Obshchestvennaya Organizatsiya Malogo i Srednego Predprinimatelstva): 125047 Moscow, ul. 4-ya Tverskaya-Yamskaya 21/22/3; tel. (495) 775-81-11; fax (495) 775-81-91; internet www.opora.ru; f. 2002; Pres. SERGEI BORISOV.

Russian Union of Industrialists and Entrepreneurs (Employers) (RSPPR) (Rossiiskii Soyuz Promyshlennikov i Predprinimatelei): 103070 Moscow, Staraya pl. 10/4; tel. (495) 748-42-37; fax (495) 206-11-29; e-mail pr_dep@rspp.net; internet www.rspp.ru; f. 1991; Pres. ALEKSANDR SHOKHIN; Exec. Sec. NIKOLAI TONKOV.

UTILITIES

Electricity

Federal Energy Commission: 103074 Moscow, Kitaigorodskii proyezd 7; tel. (495) 220-40-15; fax (495) 206-81-08; e-mail fecrf@orc.ru; regulatory authority for natural energy monopolies; sole responsibility for establishing tariff rates for energy, transportation, shipping, postal and telecommunications industries in the Russian Federation from Sept. 2001; Chair. ANDREI ZADERNYUK.

Irkutskenergo (Irkutsk Energy Co): 664000 Irkutsk, ul. Sukhe-Batora 1; tel. (3952) 21-73-00; fax (3952) 21-78-99; e-mail idkan@irkutskenergo.ru; internet www.irkutskenergo.ru; f. 1954; generation and transmission of electrical and thermal energy; Dir-Gen. VLADIMIR V. KOLMOGOROV.

Mosenergo (Moscow Energy Co): 113035 Moscow, Raushskaya nab. 8; tel. (495) 957-35-30; fax (495) 957-34-70; e-mail press-centre@mosenergo.ru; internet www.mosenergo.ru; f. 1887; 49% owned by Unified Energy System of Russia; power generator and distributor; Chair. YURII A. UDALTSOV.

THE RUSSIAN FEDERATION											Directory

Rosenergoatom (Russian Atomic Energy Concern): 119017 Moscow, ul. B. Ordynka 24/26; tel. (495) 239-24-22; fax (495) 239-46-03; e-mail npp@rosatom.ru; internet www.rosenergoatom.ru; f. 1992; electricity-generating co, manages Russia's 10 nuclear reactors; Dir-Gen. SERGEI OBOZOV.

Sverdlovenergo (Sverdlovsk Energy Co): 620219 Sverdlovsk obl., Yekaterinburg, pr. Lenina 38; tel. (343) 259-13-99; fax (343) 259-12-22; e-mail post@energo.pssr.ru; internet www.po.pssr.ru; f. 1942; Chair. of Bd ALEKSANDR V. CHIKUNOV; Gen. Man. VLADIMIR V. KALSIN.

Uralenergo (Ural Energy): 454006 Chelyabinsk, ul. Rossiiskaya 17; tel. (3512) 67-59-54; fax (3512) 67-59-48; e-mail info@uralenergo.com; internet www.uralenergo.com; manages 22 joint-stock cos; oversees 55 thermal power stations and 6 hydroelectric stations; total installed capacity of over 28,500m. kW; Dir ALEKSANDR S. NEMTSEV.

Gas

Gazprom: 117997 Moscow, ul. Nametkina 16; tel. (495) 719-30-01; fax (495) 719-83-33; e-mail gazprom@gazprom.ru; internet www.gazprom.ru; f. 1989 from assets of Soviet Ministry of Oil and Gas; became independent joint-stock co in 1992, privatized in 1994; 51% state-owned; Chair. of Bd of Dirs VIKTOR A. ZUBKOV; Chair. of Management Bd and Deputy Chair. of Bd of Dirs ALEKSEI B. MILLER.

Mezhregiongaz (Inter-Regional Gas Co): 142770 Moscow obl., Leninskii raion, p/o Kommunarkap. Gazoprovod; tel. (495) 719-53-36; fax (495) 719-52-67; e-mail pr@mrg.gazprom.ru; internet www.mrg.ru; f. 1997; gas marketing co; subsidiary of Gazprom; brs in more than 60 federal subjects; Dir-Gen. KIRILL SELEZNEV.

Water

MosVodoKanal: 105005 Moscow, per. Pleteshkovskii 2; tel. (495) 763-34-9634; fax (495) 265-22-01; e-mail post@mosvodokanal.ru; internet www.mosvodokanal.ru; f. 1937; state-owned; provides water and sewerage services to Moscow and the surrounding region; Dir-Gen. STANISLAV KHRAMENKOV.

Vodokanal: 191015 St Petersburg, ul. Kavalergardskaya 42; tel. (812) 274-16-79; fax (812) 274-13-61; e-mail office@vodokanal.spb.ru; internet www.vodokanal.spb.ru; water and sewerage utility; Gen. Man. FELIKS V. KARMAZINOV.

TRADE UNIONS

In 1990 several branch unions of the All-Union Central Council of Trade Unions (ACCTU) established the Federation of Independent Trade Unions of the Russian Federation (FITUR), which took control of part of the property and other assets of the ACCTU. The ACCTU was re-formed as the General Confederation of Trade Unions of the USSR, which was, in turn, renamed the General Confederation of Trade Unions—International Organization in 1992.

Principal Trade Union Coalitions

All-Russian Labour Confederation: 103031 Moscow, ul. Rozhdestvenka 5/7; tel. (495) 785-21-30; fax (495) 915-83-67; e-mail vktrussia@online.ru; internet www.trud.org/guide/VKT.htm; f. 1995; unites five national trade unions and 40 regional orgs with 1,270,900 mems; Pres. ALEKSANDR N. BUGAYEV.

Federation of Independent Trade Unions of Russia (FITUR) (Federatsiya Nezavisimykh Profsoyuzov Rossii—FNPR): 119119 Moscow, Leninskii pr. 42; tel. (495) 938-73-12; fax (495) 137-06-94; e-mail korneev@fnpr.ru; internet www.fnpr.ru; f. 1990; unites 48 national trade unions and 78 regional orgs (with c. 40m. mems); affiliated to General Confederation of Trade Unions (q.v.); Pres. MIKHAIL V. SHMAKOV.

General Confederation of Trade Unions (VKP): 119119 Moscow, Leninskii pr. 42; tel. (495) 938-01-12; fax (495) 938-21-55; e-mail inter@vkp.ru; internet www.vkp.ru; f. 1992 to replace General Confederation of Trade Unions of the USSR; co-ordinating body for trade unions in CIS member states; unites 10 national and 32 regional industrial orgs with 52m. mems; publishes *Profsoyuzy* (Trade Unions), weekly, *Vestnik profsoyuzov* (Herald of the Trade Unions), every two weeks, and *Inform-Contact*, in English and French, quarterly; Pres. MIKHAIL SHMAKOV; Sec.-Gen. VLADIMIR SCHERBAKOV.

Moscow Trade Unions Federation: 121205 Moscow, ul. Novyi Arbat 36/9; tel. (495) 290-82-62; fax (495) 202-92-70; e-mail main@mtuf.ru; f. 1990; largest regional branch of FITUR (q.v.); Chair. MIKHAIL D. NAGAITSEV; 2.2m. mems.

Transport

RAILWAYS

At the end of 2006 the total length of railway track in use was 84,821 km, around one-half of which was electrified.

Russian Railways OAO (RZhD) (Rossiiskiye zheleznyye dorogi): 107174 Moscow, ul. Novobasmannaya 2; tel. (495) 262-16-28; fax (495) 975-24-11; e-mail info@rzd.ru; internet www.rzd.ru; f. 2003; Pres. VLADIMIR YAKUNIN.

City Underground Railways

Moscow Metro: 129110 Moscow, pr. Mira 41/2; tel. (495) 622-10-01; fax (495) 631-37-44; e-mail info@mosmetro.ru; f. 1935; 12 lines (294 km) with 176 stations in 2007; Gen. Man. DMITRII V. GAYEV.

Nizhnii Novgorod Metro: 603002 Nizhnii Novgorod, pl. Revolutsii 7; tel. (8312) 44-17-60; fax (8312) 44-20-86; e-mail metro@sandy.ru; f. 1985; 15 km with 13 stations; Gen. Man. A. KUZMIN.

Novosibirsk Metro: 630099 Novosibirsk, ul. Serebrennikovskaya 34; tel. (3832) 90-81-10; fax (3832) 46-56-82; e-mail nsk@metro.snt.su; internet www.nsk.su/~metro; f. 1986; 2 lines (13.2 km) with 11 stations, and a further 6 km under construction; Gen. Man. V. I. DEMIN.

St Petersburg Metro: 190013 St Petersburg, Moskovskii pr. 28; tel. (812) 251-66-68; fax (812) 316-14-41; e-mail np@metro.spb.ru; internet www.metro.spb.ru; f. 1955; 4 lines (106 km) with 60 stations; Gen. Man. VLADIMIR A. GARYUGIN.

Short underground railways began to operate in Samara, Yekaterinburg and Kazan in 1987, 1991 and 2005, respectively. In 2008 the construction of underground railways was under way in Chelyabinsk, Krasnoyarsk and Omsk, and a light railway was scheduled to open in Sochi, prior to the holding of the Winter Olympics there in 2014.

ROADS

At the end of 2006 the total length of roads was 597,421 km, and 85.2% of roads were paved. In Siberia and the Far East there are few roads, and they are often impassable in winter, while the *rasputitsa*, or spring thaw, notoriously impedes rural road traffic, even in European Russia.

SHIPPING

The seaports of the Russian Federation provide access to the Pacific Ocean, in the east, the Baltic Sea and the Atlantic Ocean, in the west, and the Black Sea, in the south. Major eastern ports are at Vladivostok, Nakhodka, Vostochnyi, Magadan and Petropavlovsk. In the west, St Petersburg and Kaliningrad provide access to the Baltic Sea, and the northern ports of Murmansk and Archangel (Arkhangelsk) have access to the Atlantic Ocean, via the Barents Sea. Novorossiisk and Sochi are the principal Russian ports on the Black Sea.

Principal Ship-owning Companies

Baltic Shipping Co: 198035 St Petersburg, Mezhevoi kanal 5; tel. (812) 251-33-97; fax (812) 186-85-44; freight and passenger services; Chair. MIKHAIL A. ROMANOVSKII.

Baltic Transport Systems: 199106 St Petersburg, pl. Morskoi Slavy 1; tel. (812) 303-99-14; fax (812) 380-34-76; e-mail bts@baltics.ru; internet www.baltics.ru; f. 1994; freight and passenger services; Gen. Dir ALEKSEI E. SHUKLETSOV.

Far Eastern Shipping Co: 690019 Maritime (Primorskii) Krai, Vladivostok, ul. Aleutskaya 15; tel. (4232) 41-14-32; fax (4232) 52-15-51; e-mail 41401@41.fesco.ru; internet www.fesco.ru; f. 1880; Gen. Man. YEVGENII N. AMBROSOV.

Kamchatka Shipping Co: 683600 Kamchatka Krai, Petropavlovsk-Kamchatskii, ul. Radiosvyazi 65; tel. (41522) 2-82-21; fax (41522) 2-19-60; f. 1949; freight services; Pres. NIKOLAI M. ZABLOTSKII.

Murmansk Shipping Co: 183038 Murmansk, ul. Kominterna 15; tel. (8152) 48-10-48; fax (8152) 48-11-48; e-mail postmaster@msco.ru; f. 1939; shipping and ice-breaking services; Gen. Dir VYACHESLAV RUKSHA.

Northern Shipping Co (NSC Arkhangelsk) (Severnoye morskoye parokhodstvo OAO—SMP): 163000 Archangel, nab. Severnoi Dviny 30; tel. (8182) 63-72-03; fax (8182) 63-71-95; e-mail nsosnina@ansc.ru; internet www.ansc.ru; f. 1870; dry cargo shipping, liner services; Gen. Dir VIKTOR A. IZBITSKII.

Novorossiisk Shipping Co: 353900 Krasnodar Krai, Novorossiisk, ul. Svobody 1; tel. (8617) 25-31-26; fax (8617) 25-11-43; e-mail novoship@novoship.ru; internet www.novoship.ru; f. 1992; Chair. V. I. YAKUNIN.

Primorsk Shipping Corpn: 692900 Maritime (Primorskii) Krai, Nakhodka-4, Administrativnyi Gorodok; tel. (4236) 69-45-05; fax (4236) 69-45-75; e-mail psc@prisco.ru; internet www.prisco.ru; f. 1972; tanker shipowner; Dir-Gen. ALEKSANDR MIGUNOV.

Sakhalin Shipping Co: 694620 Sakhalin obl., Kholmsk, ul. Pobedy 16; tel. (42433) 6-62-07; fax (42433) 6-60-20; e-mail chief@sasco.sakhalin.ru; internet www.sasco.org; f. 1945; ship-owners and

THE RUSSIAN FEDERATION

managers, carriage of cargo and passengers; Pres. YAKUB ZH. ALEGEDPINOV.

Sovfrakht: 127944 Moscow, Rakhmanovskii per. 4, Morskoi Dom; tel. (495) 258-27-41; fax (495) 230-26-40; e-mail general@sovfracht.ru; internet www.sovfracht.ru; f. 1929; jt-stock co; chartering and broking of tanker, cargo and other ships; forwarding, booking and insurance agency; ship management; Dir-Gen. D. YU. PURIM; 120 employees (2003).

White Sea and Onega Shipping Co (Belomorsko-Onezhskoye parokhodstvo): 185005 Kareliya, Petrozavodsk, ul. Rigachina 7; tel. (8142) 71-12-01; fax (8142) 71-12-67; e-mail dir@bop.onego.ru; internet bop.onego.ru; f. 1940; cargo-shipping, cargo-ship construction and repair; Gen. Dir STANISLAV ROZOLINSKII; Pres. ALEKSANDR LYALLYA.

CIVIL AVIATION

Until 1991 Aeroflot—Soviet Airlines was the only airline operating on domestic routes in the former USSR. In 1992–94 some 300 different independent airlines emerged on the basis of Aeroflot's former regional directorates. Several small private airlines were also established. In 2003 there were 451 airports in Russia.

Aeroflot-Don: 344009 Rostov-on-Don, pr. Sholokhova 272; tel. (863) 276-78-11; fax (863) 252-11-78; e-mail avia1@aeroflot-don.ru; internet www.aeroflot-don.ru; f. 1925; present name adopted 2000; 100% owned by Aeroflot—Russian Airlines; operates scheduled and chartered passenger and cargo flights to various domestic and international destinations (incl. Armenia, Austria, Egypt, Germany, Israel, Turkey, Ukraine, United Arab Emirates) from Rostov-on-Don, Moscow and Sochi, and betwen Moscow and Groznyi; Dir-Gen. MIKHAIL S. KRITSKII.

Aeroflot—Russian Airlines: 125167 Moscow, Leningradskii pr. 37/9; tel. and fax (495) 223-55-55; e-mail presscentr@aeroflot.ru; internet www.aeroflot.ru; f. 1923; 51% state-owned; operates flights to 94 destinations in 49 countries; Chair. IGOR YE. LEVITIN; Gen. Dir VALERII M. OKULOV.

Gazpromavia: 117997 Moscow, ul. Novocheremushkinskaya 71/32; tel. (495) 719-18-32; fax (495) 719-11-85; e-mail gazpromavia@gazprom.ru; internet www.gazpromavia.ru; f. 1995; Dir-Gen. ANDREI S. OVCHARENKO.

KD Avia: 238315 Kaliningrad obl., Guryevskii raion, Khrabrovo, Aeroport; tel. (401) 235-51-75; e-mail info@kdavia.ru; internet www.kdavia.ru; f. 1945; present name adopted 2005; international and domestic flights from Kaliningrad; Dir-Gen. VALERII MIKHAILOV.

Kuban Airlines (Kubanskiye Avialinii): 350026 Krasnodar, Krasnodar—Pashkovskaya Airport; tel. (861) 237-06-00; fax (861) 237-38-11; e-mail info@kuban-airlines.com; internet www.kuban-airlines.de; f. 1932; regional and international flights.

Rossiya—Russian Airlines: 191025 St Petersburg, Nevskii pr. 61; tel. (812) 333-22-22; fax (812) 333-22-44; internet www.rossiya-airlines.ru; f. 1992; merged with Pulkovo Airlines in 2006; state-owned; operates scheduled and charter passenger flights from St Petersburg and Moscow to domestic and international destinations; Gen. Dir SERGEI MIKHALIENKO.

S7 Airlines (Siberia Airlines): 633115 Novosibirsk obl., gorod Ob-4; tel. (3832) 59-90-11; fax (3832) 59-90-64; e-mail pr@s7.ru; internet www.s7.ru; fmrly Sibir Airlines; scheduled and charter flights to domestic, CIS, Asian, European and Middle Eastern destinations; Gen. Dir VLADISLAV FILEV.

SkyExpress: 119027 Moscow, Vnukovo, ul. Tsentralnaya 2/2; tel. (495) 648-93-60; fax (495) 980-74-61; e-mail info@skyexpress.ru; internet www.skyexpress.ru; f. 2006; 'low cost' airline operating passenger flights between Moscow (Vnukovo) and Murmansk, Rostov-on-Don and Sochi (Krasnodar Krai), also international charter flights; Chief Exec. MARINA BUKALOVA.

Transaero Airlines: 127083 Moscow, Mishina 56/3; tel. (495) 788-80-80; fax (495) 937-84-64; e-mail info@transaero.ru; internet www.transaero.ru; f. 1991; Russia's largest privately owned airline; operates scheduled and charter passenger services to the CIS, Europe, Asia and Central America; CEO OLGA PLESHAKOVA.

Ural Airlines (Uralskiye Aviyalinii): 620910 Sverdlovsk obl., Yekaterinburg, ul. Sputnikov 6; tel. (343) 226-81-26; fax (343) 226-82-49; e-mail margarita@uralairlines.ru; internet www.uralairlines.ru; f. 1993; flights from Yekaterinburg to domestic and international destinations; Gen. Dir SERGEI SKURATOV.

Vladivostok Avia: 692756 Maritime (Primorskii) Krai, Artem, ul. Portovaya 41, Vladivostok Airport; tel. (4232) 30-73-33; fax (4232) 30-73-43; e-mail office@vladavia.ru; internet www.vladavia.ru; f. 1994; freight and scheduled passenger services from Vladivostok and Moscow to domestic and international destinations; Gen. Dir VLADIMIR SAIBEL.

Tourism

In 2006 there were 22,486,043 tourist arrivals in Russia, and receipts from tourism totalled US $9,720m.

Intourist: 129366 Moscow, pr. Mira 150; tel. (495) 730-19-19; fax (495) 956-42-02; e-mail info@intourist.ru; internet www.intourist.ru; f. 1929; brs throughout Russia and abroad; Chair. VYACHESLAV KOPIEV.

RWANDA

Introductory Survey

Location, Climate, Language, Religion, Flag, Capital

The Rwandan Republic is a land-locked country in eastern central Africa, just south of the Equator, bounded by the Democratic Republic of the Congo to the west, by Uganda to the north, by Tanzania to the east and by Burundi to the south. The climate is tropical, although tempered by altitude. It is hot and humid in the lowlands, but cooler in the highlands. The average annual rainfall is 785 mm (31 ins). The main rainy season is from February to May. The population is composed of three ethnic groups: Hutu (85%), Tutsi (14%) and Twa (1%). French, English and Kinyarwanda, the native language, are all in official use, and Kiswahili is widely spoken. About one-half of the population adhere to animist beliefs. Most of the remainder are Christians, mainly Roman Catholics. There are Protestant and Muslim minorities. The national flag (proportions 1 by 2) has three unequal horizontal stripes, of blue, yellow and green, with a blue-ringed yellow disc (framed by 24 yellow rays) depicted near the fly end of the top stripe. The capital is Kigali.

Recent History

Rwanda, with the neighbouring state of Burundi, became part of German East Africa in 1899. In 1916, during the First World War, it was occupied by Belgian forces from the Congo. From 1920 Rwanda was part of Ruanda-Urundi, administered by Belgium under a League of Nations mandate and later as a UN Trust Territory. Long-standing dissension between the majority Hutu tribe and their former overlords, the Tutsi, caused a rebellion and the proclamation of a state of emergency in 1959. In September 1961 it was decided by referendum to abolish the monarchy and to establish a republic. Full independence followed on 1 July 1962. Serious tribal conflict erupted in December 1963, and massacres (of an estimated 20,000) were perpetrated by the Hutu against the Tutsi. During 1964–65 large numbers of displaced Rwandans were resettled in neighbouring countries. In 1969 Grégoire Kayibanda, the new Republic's first President, was re-elected, and all 47 seats in the legislature were retained by the governing party, the Mouvement démocratique républicain (MDR).

Tension between Hutu and Tutsi escalated again at the end of 1972 and continued throughout February 1973. In July the Minister of Defence and head of the National Guard, Maj.-Gen. Juvénal Habyarimana, led a bloodless coup against President Kayibanda, proclaimed a Second Republic and established a military administration. In August a new Council of Ministers, with Habyarimana as President, was formed. All political activity was banned until July 1975, when a new ruling party, the Mouvement révolutionnaire national pour le développement (MRND), was formed.

A national referendum in December 1978 approved a new Constitution, which was intended to return the country to democratically elected government (in accordance with an undertaking made by Habyarimana in 1973 to end the military regime within five years). Elections to the legislature, the Conseil national de développement (CND), took place in December 1981 and in December 1983; also in December 1983 Habyarimana was re-elected President. In December 1988 Habyarimana was again elected (unopposed) to the presidency, securing 99.98% of the votes cast. Elections to the CND were conducted in the same month.

In September 1990 a Commission was appointed to compile recommendations for a draft national charter, which was to provide for the establishment of a multi-party system. In April 1991, following the CND's revision of the Commission's proposals, a draft constitution was presented to an extraordinary congress of the MRND, at which the party was renamed the Mouvement républicain national pour la démocratie et le développement (MRNDD). On 10 June the reforms were promulgated by Habyarimana, and legislation regulating the formation of political parties was adopted; parties were to be non-tribal and independent, while members of the security forces and the judiciary were to be banned from political activity. (By June 1992 15 parties, among them the MRNDD and a revived MDR, had officially registered.) In October 1991 Sylvestre Nsanzimana, hitherto Minister of Justice, was appointed to the new post of Prime Minister, and in December he formed a transitional Government, in which all but two portfolios (assigned to the Parti démocratique chrétien—PDC) were allocated to members of the MRNDD. Opposition parties, which had been excluded from participation in the transitional Government for their rejection of a MRNDD Prime Minister, organized anti-Government demonstrations in late 1991 and early 1992, demanding the removal of Nsanzimana and the convening of a national conference. A series of negotiations between the Government and the major opposition parties was initiated in February 1992, and in April a protocol agreement was signed, providing for the establishment of a new transitional administration, with Dismas Nsengiyaremye of the MDR as Prime Minister. Habyarimana announced that multi-party elections would be conducted within one year of the installation of the new Government.

Relations with neighbouring Uganda were frequently strained, owing mainly to the presence of some 250,000 Rwandan refugees in Uganda (mainly members of Rwanda's Tutsi minority), who had fled their homeland following successive outbreaks of persecution by the Hutu regime in 1959, 1963 and 1973. In October 1990 rebel forces, based in Uganda, invaded northern Rwanda, occupying several towns. The 4,000-strong rebel army, known as the Front patriotique rwandais (FPR), which mainly comprised Rwandan Tutsi refugees, aimed to overthrow the Habyarimana regime and secure the repatriation of all Rwandan refugees. The Rwandan Government accused the Ugandan leadership of supporting the rebel forces (many of whom had served in the Ugandan armed forces), although this accusation was strenuously denied. With the assistance of French, Belgian and Zairean troops, the Rwandan army succeeded in repelling the FPR before it could reach Kigali. In late October the Government declared a cease-fire, although hostilities continued in northern Rwanda.

Unsuccessful negotiations took place during 1991 and early 1992, but further talks held in Arusha, Tanzania, in July resulted in an agreement on the implementation of a new cease-fire, effective from the end of that month, and the creation of a military observer group (GOM), sponsored by the Organization of African Unity (OAU—now the African Union, see p. 172, AU), to comprise representatives from both sides, together with officers from the armed forces of Nigeria, Senegal, Zimbabwe and Mali. However, subsequent negotiations failed to resolve outstanding problems concerning the creation of a proposed 'neutral zone' between the Rwandan armed forces and the FPR, the incorporation of the FPR in a future combined Rwandan national force, the repatriation of refugees, and FPR demands for full participation in a transitional government and legislature.

A resurgence in violence followed the breakdown of negotiations in February 1993. An estimated 1m. civilians fled the advancing FPR forces into neighbouring Uganda and Tanzania. France dispatched reinforcements to join a small military contingent that had been stationed in Kigali since October 1990 to protect French nationals. Meanwhile, the commander of the 50-member GOM declared that the group had inadequate manpower and resources to contain the FPR, and requested the deployment of an additional 400 troops from the OAU. In late February 1993 the Government accepted FPR terms for a cease-fire, in return for an end to attacks against FPR positions and Tutsi communities, and the withdrawal of foreign troops. Although fighting continued with varying intensity, fresh peace negotiations were convened in Arusha in March, and France subsequently began to withdraw its troops. Negotiations conducted during April failed to produce a solution to the crucial issue of the structure of a future single armed Rwandan force. In the same month the five participating parties in the ruling coalition agreed to a three-month extension of the Government's mandate, in order to facilitate the successful conclusion of a peace accord. Significant progress was made during renewed talks between the Government and the FPR during May, when a timetable for the demobilization of the 19,000-strong security forces was agreed. In June the UN Security Council approved the creation of the UN Observer Mission Uganda-Rwanda (UNOMUR), to be deployed on the Ugandan side of the border, for an initial period of six months, in order to prevent the maintenance of a military supply line for the FPR.

In July 1993 President Habyarimana met with delegates from those political parties represented in the Government to seek a further extension of the coalition's mandate. However, the Prime Minister's insistence that the FPR should be represented in any new government exacerbated existing divisions within the MDR, prompting Habyarimana to conclude the agreement with a conciliatory group of MDR dissidents, including the Minister of Education, Agathe Uwilingiyimana, who was elected to the premiership.

In August 1993 a peace accord was formally signed in Arusha by Habyarimana and Col Alex Kanyarengwe of the FPR. A new transitional government, to be headed by a mutually approved Prime Minister, would be installed, and multi-party elections would be conducted after a 22-month period. In October the UN Security Council adopted Resolution 872, providing for the establishment of the UN Assistance Mission to Rwanda (UNAMIR), to be deployed in Rwanda for an initial period of six months, with a mandate to monitor observance of the cease-fire, to contribute to the security of the capital and to facilitate the repatriation of refugees. UNAMIR, which was to incorporate UNOMUR and GOM and to comprise some 2,500 personnel, was formally inaugurated on 1 November. In December the UN expressed the opinion that conditions had been sufficiently fulfilled to allow the inauguration of the transitional institutions.

On 5 January 1994 Habyarimana was invested as President of a transitional administration, for a 22-month period, under the terms of the Arusha accord. The inauguration of the transitional government and legislature was, however, repeatedly delayed, owing to political opposition to the proposed Council of Ministers, and to the insistence of Habyarimana that the list of proposed legislative deputies, presented in March, should be modified to include representatives of additional political parties, including the reactionary Coalition pour la défense de la République (CDR). Meanwhile, political frustration had erupted into violence in February, with the murder of the Minister of Public Works and Energy, Félicien Gatabazi of the Parti social-démocrate (PSD), who had been a prominent supporter of the Arusha accord and of the transitional administration. Within hours the CDR leader, Martin Bucyana, was killed in a retaliatory attack by PSD supporters, and a series of violent confrontations ensued.

On 6 April 1994 the presidential aircraft was fired on, above Kigali airport, and exploded, killing all 10 passengers, including Habyarimana. (The President of Burundi, Cyprien Ntaryamira, two Burundian cabinet ministers and the Chief of Staff of the Rwandan armed forces were among the other victims.) In Kigali the presidential guard immediately initiated a campaign of retributive violence against Habyarimana's political opponents, although it remained unclear who had been responsible for the attack on the aircraft. As politicians and civilians fled the capital, the brutality of the political assassinations was compounded by attacks on the clergy, UNAMIR personnel and members of the Tutsi tribe. Many Hutu civilians were reportedly forced to murder their Tutsi neighbours, and the mobilization of the Interahamwe unofficial militias (allegedly affiliated to the MRNDD and the CDR), committed to the massacre of Tutsi civilians and opponents of the Government, was encouraged by the presidential guard (with support from some factions of the armed forces) and by inflammatory radio broadcasts. The Prime Minister, the President of the Constitutional Court and the Ministers of Labour and Social Affairs and of Information were among the prominent politicians murdered (or declared missing and presumed dead) within hours of Habyarimana's death. On 8 April the Speaker of the CND, Dr Théodore Sindikubwabo, announced that he had assumed the office of interim President of the Republic, in accordance with the provisions of the 1991 Constitution. The five remaining participating political parties and factions of the Government selected a new Prime Minister, Jean Kambanda, and a new Council of Ministers (drawn largely from the MRNDD) from among their ranks. The legality of the new administration was immediately challenged by the FPR, which claimed that the terms of the Constitution regarding succession had been superseded by the terms of the Arusha accord. The legitimacy of the Government was subsequently rejected by several political parties and factions.

In mid-April 1994 the FPR resumed operations from its northern stronghold, with the stated aim of relieving its beleaguered battalion in Kigali, restoring order there and halting the massacre of civilians. Belgium's UNAMIR contingent of more than 400 troops was also withdrawn, having encountered increasing hostility as a result of persistent rumours of Belgian complicity in the attack on President Habyarimana's aircraft, and accusations that Belgian troops were providing logistical support to the FPR. The FPR's refusal to enter into dialogue with the 'illegal' administration proved a major obstacle to attempts, undertaken by the UN and the Presidents of Tanzania and of Zaire, to sponsor a new cease-fire agreement in late April and early May.

As the violent campaign initiated by the presidential guard and the estimated 30,000 Interahamwe gathered national momentum, the militia's identification of all Tutsi as political opponents of the State provoked tribal polarization and an effective pogrom. Reports of mass Tutsi graves and of unprovoked attacks on fleeing Tutsi refugees and those sheltering in schools, hospitals and churches provoked unqualified international outrage, and promises were made of financial and logistical aid for an estimated 2m. displaced Rwandans. By late May 1994 attempts to assess the full scale of the humanitarian catastrophe in Rwanda were complicated by reports that the FPR (who claimed to control more than one-half of the territory) was perpetrating retaliatory atrocities against Hutu civilians.

In view of the deteriorating security situation, in late April 1994 the UN Security Council approved a resolution to reduce UNAMIR to just 270 personnel. This was condemned by the Rwandan authorities, and in mid-May, following intense international pressure and the disclosure of the vast scale of the humanitarian crisis in the region, the Security Council approved Resolution 917, providing for the eventual deployment of some 5,500 UN troops with a revised mandate, including the protection of refugees in designated 'safe areas'. In early June the UN Security Council extended the mandate of what was designated UNAMIR II until December. However, the UN Secretary-General continued to encounter considerable difficulty in securing equipment and armaments requested by those countries that had agreed to participate.

By mid-June 1994 the emergence of confirmed reports of retributive murders committed by FPR members and the collapse of an OAU-brokered truce prompted the French Government to announce its willingness to lead an armed police action, endorsed by the UN, in Rwanda. Despite French insistence that its force (expected to total 2,000 troops) would maintain strict political neutrality, and operate in a purely humanitarian capacity pending the arrival of a multinational UN force, the FPR was vehemently opposed to its deployment, citing political bias. The UN Secretary-General welcomed the French initiative; however, the OAU expressed serious reservations as to the appropriateness of the action. In late June a first contingent of 150 French marine commandos launched 'Operation Turquoise', entering the western town of Cyangugu, in preparation for a large-scale operation to protect refugees in the area. An estimated 1m. Rwandans sought refuge in the Zairean border town of Goma, while a similar number attempted to cross the border elsewhere in the south-west. The FPR, meanwhile, swiftly secured all major cities and strategic territorial positions, but halted its advance several kilometres from the boundaries of the French-controlled neutral zone, requesting the apprehension and return for trial of those responsible for the recent atrocities. (In early July the UN announced the creation of a commission of inquiry to investigate allegations of genocide, following an initial report that as many as 500,000 Rwandans had been killed since April.)

On 19 July 1994 Pasteur Bizimungu, a Hutu, was inaugurated as President for a five-year term. On the same day the FPR announced the composition of a new Government of National Unity, with the leader of the MDR moderate faction, Faustin Twagiramungu, as Prime Minister. The majority of cabinet posts were assigned to FPR members (including the FPR military chief, Maj.-Gen. Paul Kagame, who became Minister of Defence and also assumed the newly created post of Vice-President), while the remainder were divided among the MDR, the PSD, the Parti libéral (PL) and the Parti démocrate chrétien (PDC). The new administration urged all refugees to return to Rwanda, and issued assurances that civilian Hutus could return safely to their homes. The new Government declared its intention to honour the terms of the Arusha accord within the context of an extended period of transition. The claims to legitimacy of the exiled former administration were seriously undermined by recognition by the European Union (EU, see p. 255) of the new Government of National Unity in September.

Amid persistent rumours that the Rwandan armed forces were attempting to regroup and rearm in Zaire, in preparation for a counter-offensive against the FPR, in late August 1994 the UN initiated the deployment of some 2,500 UNAMIR II forces in the security zone (redesignated 'zone four'). French troops began to withdraw from the area (the final contingent departed in late September), prompting hundreds of thousands of internally displaced Hutu refugees within the zone to move to Zairean border areas. An estimated 500,000 refugees remained at camps in the former security zone at the end of August. The UNAMIR II mandate was extended for a further six months. (In June 1995, at the request of the Rwandan Government, the six-month mandate of the force, which was reduced from 5,586 to 2,330 personnel, was again renewed.)

In November 1994 a number of amendments to the terms of the August 1993 Arusha accord were adopted under a multi-party protocol of understanding. The most notable of the new provisions was the exclusion from the legislative process of those parties implicated in alleged acts of genocide during 1994. A 70-member National Transitional Assembly was formally inaugurated in December, with a composition including five representatives of the armed forces and one member of the national police force. On 5 May 1995 this legislature adopted a new Constitution, which was based on selected articles of the 1991 Constitution, the terms of the Arusha accord, the FPR's victory declaration of July 1994 and the November multi-party protocol.

In late 1994 Hutu refugees within Rwanda and in neighbouring countries were continuing to resist the exhortations of the UN and the new Rwandan administration to return to their homes, despite the deteriorating security situation in many camps (which had, moreover, forced the withdrawal of a number of relief agencies). Hutu militias were reported to have assumed control of several camps, notably Katale in Zaire and Benaco in Tanzania. Reports also emerged that Hutu civilians intending to return to their homes had been subjected to violent intimidation by the Interahamwe. The reluctance of many refugees to return to their homes was also attributed to persistent allegations that the Tutsi-dominated FPR armed forces (the Armée patriotique rwandaise—APR) were conducting a systematic campaign of reprisal attacks against returning Hutus.

International scepticism regarding the Government's programme of refugee resettlement increased in early 1995, following a series of uncompromising initiatives to encourage the return of internally displaced Rwandans (including the interruption of food supplies to refugee camps), culminating in the forcible closure of the camps through military intervention. An attempt in April to dismantle the Kibeho camp in southern Rwanda provoked widespread international condemnation, after APR troops opened fire on refugees; independent sources estimated as many as 5,000 fatalities.

A political crisis emerged in August 1995, after the Prime Minister expressed dissatisfaction with the Government's lack of adherence to the provisions of the Arusha accord regarding power-sharing, and with the security forces' repeated recourse to violence in their management of the refugee crisis. Twagiramungu and four other disaffected ministers were subsequently replaced. Pierre Célestin Rwigyema of the MDR, also Hutu and the former Minister of Primary and Secondary Education, was named as the new Prime Minister at the end of the month. The new Council of Ministers included representatives of both major ethnic groups and four political parties.

Also in August 1995, in response to requests made by the Rwandan Government, the UN Security Council voted to suspend the arms embargo to Rwanda (imposed in May 1994) for one year, in order to allow the Government to safeguard against the threat of a military offensive by Hutu extremists encamped in neighbouring countries. Meanwhile, the security situation in refugee camps along the Zairean border had deteriorated to such an extent that the Zairean Government initiated a programme of forcible repatriation, attracting widespread international concern. Despite a formal agreement between the office of the UN High Commissioner for Refugees (UNHCR) and the Zairean Government for a more regulated approach to the refugee crisis, APR attacks near the border with Zaire further deterred refugees. At a conference of the Great Lakes countries, convened in Cairo, Egypt, in late November President Mobutu of Zaire indicated that the forcible return of remaining refugees in early 1996 was no longer a realistic objective. The conference also accepted the Rwandan President's assertion that the participation of UNAMIR forces in peace-keeping operations in Rwanda was no longer necessary, but urged the Rwandan Government to accept the extension of a revised, three-month mandate for the forces to provide assistance in the refugee repatriation process. (A three-month mandate for a 1,200-strong force was thus renewed in December 1995, and the mission was formally terminated in April 1996.)

Meanwhile, in February 1995 the UN Security Council adopted Resolution 977, whereby Arusha was designated the seat for the International Criminal Tribunal for Rwanda (ICTR), which was to investigate allegations made against some 400 individuals of direct involvement in the planning and execution of crimes against humanity perpetrated in Rwanda during 1994. The six-member Tribunal, to be headed by a Senegalese lawyer, Laïty Kama, was inaugurated in June for a four-year term.

The ICTR began formal proceedings in November 1995. The first court session of the ICTR was convened in September 1996, but hearings concerning the first two (of 21) individuals indicted on charges of crimes against humanity were almost immediately postponed. Tribunal officials attributed the virtual collapse of proceedings to the escalating conflict in eastern Zaire, but widespread concern was expressed at the high number of administrative errors committed. In contrast, in January 1997 regional courts within Rwanda passed death sentences on five individuals accused of acts of genocide. (Whereas capital punishment would not be invoked by the ICTR, legislation published by the Rwandan authorities in September 1996 regarding penalties for crimes committed during 1994 made provision for the application of the death penalty.) In July 1997 former Prime Minister Jean Kambanda, two senior armed forces officers and a former government minister were arrested in Kenya and transferred for trial to Arusha. Later in July a Belgian journalist, who had worked for the extremist Radio Télévision Libre des Mille Collines at the time of the massacres, was arrested by the Kenyan authorities and similarly transferred for trial (becoming the first foreign national to be indicted by the ICTR).

Some 300 genocide suspects were tried by Rwandan courts during 1997, and an estimated 125,000 defendants were in detention awaiting trial; arrests reportedly continued at a rate of 1,000 per month. In late 1997, in an attempt to address the problem of severe overcrowding in prisons, the release was authorized of elderly, infirm or juvenile detainees. (This policy was denounced by organizations representing survivors of the 1994 massacres, and there were reports of attacks on freed genocide suspects.) The announcement that 23 people convicted of acts of genocide were to be publicly executed provoked international condemnation. Amnesty International and other human rights organizations expressed serious concerns that those convicted had been denied adequate opportunity to prepare a defence. The Rwandan authorities refuted such claims, and dismissed pleas for clemency. The public executions proceeded in April 1998.

Meanwhile, in August 1996, during a visit to Kigali by the Zairean Prime Minister, a bilateral agreement for the organized and unconditional repatriation of all Rwandan refugees in Zaire was concluded (without the participation of UNHCR officials). During September, however, relations between the two countries were placed under renewed strain, when the attempts of the Interahamwe and the Zairean armed forces to displace large numbers of Zairean Banyamulenge (ethnic Tutsis) from eastern Zaire encountered large-scale armed resistance from the Banyamulenge, resulting in Zairean accusations of Rwandan support for the Banyamulenge, and culminating in a cross-border exchange of fire later that month. Throughout October, as the rebels made significant gains in the region, the Rwandan Government continued to deny Zairean allegations of its involvement in the Banyamulenge insurrection, and at the end of the month admitted that Rwandan troops had been deployed in eastern Zaire in response to an artillery attack on the Rwandan town of Cyangugu, allegedly made by the Zairean armed forces.

There was renewed international concern for the estimated 1m. refugees previously encamped in eastern Zaire, following reports that the regional conflict had resulted in the sudden exodus of some 250,000 refugees, and the interruption of food aid distribution. The rebel army in Zaire (known as the Alliance des forces démocratiques pour la libération du Congo-Zaïre—AFDL) declared a cease-fire for returning refugees, and later in the month announced the creation of a humanitarian corridor to the Rwandan border. The large-scale return of refugees was finally prompted by an AFDL attack on Interahamwe units operating from the camp. In April 1997 the AFDL leader, Laurent-Désiré Kabila, demanded that the UN complete full repatriation of the refugees within 60 days, after which time their return would be undertaken unilaterally by the rebels. The Rwandan authorities, meanwhile, expressed concern that the UN was delaying the rapid repatriation of refugees from eastern Zaire. (By the end of May the AFDL had gained control of most of Zaire, which was renamed the Democratic Republic of Congo—DRC, and Kabila assumed power as Head of State.) Continuing ethnic unrest and violence, particularly in north-west Rwanda, throughout 1997 were exacerbated by the return from the DRC of large numbers of Hutus (see also the chapter on the DRC). An extensive demobilization programme was undertaken from September, with the aim of reintegrating former combatants into civil society; some 57,500 personnel were to be demobilized over a three-year period.

The trial of genocide suspects continued in 1998, both in Rwanda and at the ICTR, and in early September the ICTR reached its first verdict. A former mayor of Taba, Jean-Paul Akayesu, was convicted and sentenced to life imprisonment; Kambanda, who had pleaded guilty to six charges of genocide and crimes against humanity, was also given a life sentence. Rwandan courts convicted and sentenced some 1,000 genocide suspects during 1998 (the authorities had aimed to hear 5,000 cases during the year). By June about 5,000 suspects in Rwandan prisons had pleaded guilty to acts of genocide in order to lessen their sentences, apparently in response to the public executions in April. In June Maj. Augustine Cyiza, the Vice-President of the Supreme Court and President of the Court of Cassation, resigned (he had been suspended for misconduct in March), and in October some controversy was caused by the decision to release at least 10,000 genocide suspects owing to lack of evidence against them. It was announced in November that 34,000 suspects had been freed since 1994.

Voting in local elections (the first elections to be held since 1988) were conducted on a non-party basis on 29–31 March 1999. Voter participation was estimated to have been 95%, and at the end of the month the EU special envoy to the Great Lakes region commended the manner in which the elections were conducted. In June the Transitional National Assembly approved draft legislation establishing a commission that was to prepare a new constitution and the period of political transition, originally set at five years in 1994, was extended by a further four years. Legislation establishing a national police force (which was to unify the existing national gendarmerie, and the communal and judicial police) was adopted in August.

During 1999 a number of prominent Hutu, including three former government ministers, were arrested on suspicion of involvement in the 1994 genocide and extradited to the ICTR. In May a former Rwandan mayor (the first Rwandan to be tried abroad for genocide) was convicted by a Swiss court on charges of inciting the killing of Tutsi civilians, and sentenced to life imprisonment. In June Navanethem Pillay succeeded Kama as President of the ICTR, and in September Carla del Ponte became UN Chief Prosecutor.

In February 2000 the National Assembly voted in favour of investigating alleged abuses of power by Rwigyema. On 28 February he resigned from the office of Prime Minister, citing differences with the legislature. Bernard Makuza, hitherto the Rwandan ambassador in Germany, was appointed Prime Minister in March, and subsequently announced a government reorganization, in which six ministers were replaced. The new Government was the first since 1994 in which the parties were not represented in accordance with the 1993 Arusha peace accords. At its inauguration, Kagame (who remained Vice-President and Minister of Defence and National Security) failed to swear allegiance to the President. On 23 March Bizimungu resigned from office, owing to disagreement over the composition of the new Government, and Kagame was subsequently appointed interim President by the Supreme Court. On 17 April he was formally elected President of Rwanda by members of the Transitional National Assembly and the Government, securing 81 of 86 votes cast. He was inaugurated on 22 April (becoming the first Tutsi Head of State since 1959).

In July 2000 Rwigyema was removed from the leadership of the MDR by the party's political bureau, which accused him of acting contrary to its interests. In April 2001 an international warrant was issued for the arrest of Rwigyema, who had taken refuge in the USA, on suspicion of participating in the genocide of 1994. The trial of four Hutus (including two nuns), on charges of complicity in massacres in the southern Butare prefecture, commenced in Belgium later that month (under Belgian legislation permitting foreign nationals to be arraigned there for war crimes). In early June all four were sentenced to terms of imprisonment. Also in early June a former mayor became the first defendant to be acquitted by the ICTR (which at this time had convicted eight people on charges of involvement in the genocide). In July four Hutus, including a close associate of former President Habyarimana, Protais Zigiranyirazo, were arrested in western Europe and subsequently transferred to the ICTR (increasing the number of suspects held in detention there to more than 50). In the same month a Tribunal of First Instance officially banned the MRNDD and CDR for inciting violence in 1994. In December 2001 a new national flag, emblem and anthem officially replaced those adopted at independence in 1962.

In February 2000 legislation introducing a traditional system of justice, known as *gacaca* (on the grass), was adopted; on 4 October 2001 some 250,000 judges for the *gacaca* courts were elected in a national ballot. With the number of prisoners awaiting trial having increased to some 115,000, those suspected of lesser crimes relating to the genocide were henceforth to be tried by the *gacaca* system. In April 2002 the trial of Col Theoneste Bagosora, who was considered to be the principal organizer of the genocide, commenced at the ICTR. Bagosora, who had been in custody since his arrest in Cameroon in 1996, had allegedly planned the massacre of Tutsi civilians by the militia and had personally ordered the assassination of prominent politicians. He, and a further three former senior army officers on trial, refused to attend the initial session of the ICTR, on the grounds that their right to defence had been violated. Later in April security forces arrested former President Bizimungu (who had attempted to form an opposition political party in May 2001), and searched his residence. The authorities subsequently announced that Bizimungu had continued to engage in illegal political activity, and would be charged with endangering state security.

In early August 2002 Gen. Augustin Bizimungu, the army Chief of Staff in 1994, who had been indicted by the ICTR jointly with four other former military commanders, was arrested in Angola and transferred to the Tribunal. Later that month he pleaded not guilty to 10 charges, including that of genocide. In November trials by the *gacaca* court system officially commenced in large parts of the country. In the same month several principal ministers, including those responsible for the portfolios of foreign affairs and defence, were replaced in a government reorganization.

In January 2003, in an effort to reduce numbers in prisons, Kagame issued a decree providing for the provisional release of some 40,000 of those held in detention, including many who had pleaded guilty to charges related to the 1994 genocide. Although the Ministry of Justice maintained that legal proceedings against the released prisoners would continue, organizations representing survivors of the genocide criticized the measure. Most of the prisoners due for release were to be dispatched to 'solidarity camps', where they were to be prepared for reintegration into society. (By the end of 2003 some 25,000 suspects had been released.)

On 23 April 2003 the Transitional National Assembly adopted a new Constitution, which was to be submitted for approval at a national referendum. The draft Constitution provided for the establishment of a bicameral legislature (comprising an 80-member Chamber of Deputies and a 26-member Senate) and a President, who was to be elected by universal suffrage. At the national referendum, which took place on 26 May, the draft Constitution was endorsed by 93.4% of the electorate. The new Constitution entered into effect on 4 June; under its provisions, political associations formed on the basis of ethnicity, tribal or regional affiliation, religion or any other grounds for discrimination were prohibited. (Some existing political organizations were restructured to end such affiliations.) The presidential election was subsequently scheduled for 25 August, and was to be followed by legislative elections in late September. Kagame announced his intention to seek re-election, while former Prime Minister Twagiramungu returned to Rwanda from exile in Belgium in order to contest the presidency.

The first presidential election to take place in Rwanda since the single candidate poll of 1988 was conducted on 25 August 2003 (thereby marking the end of the nine-year transitional period). Kagame was returned to power, with 95.1% of votes cast, while Twagiramungu won 3.6%, and Nayinzira 1.3% of the votes.

However, Twagiramungu accused the authorities of electoral malpractice, and submitted a challenge against the official results at the Supreme Court. EU monitors confirmed that irregularities had been noted, although a South African observer mission declared that the poll had been 'free and fair'. In early September the Supreme Court rejected Twagiramungu's appeal, and he announced that he would not pursue the claim further. Kagame was officially inaugurated on 12 September. Four political parties subsequently agreed to contest the forthcoming legislative elections in alliance with the FPR. Following the dissolution of the MDR, many of its former members joined the newly emerged Parti du progrès et de la concorde. In addition to the FPR-led coalition, the PSD, the PL and a number of independent candidates registered to contest the legislative elections. Elections to the Chamber of Deputies commenced on 29 September, with voting for seats allocated to one disabled and two youth representatives. The poll for the 53 seats contested by political parties and independent candidates followed on 30 September; the FPR-led coalition, with 73.8% of votes cast, secured 40 seats, while the PSD (12.3% of votes) won seven seats, and the PL (10.6%) six seats. The remaining 24 female representatives were selected at provincial level on 2 October. Kagame formed a new Council of Ministers on 19 October; Makuza was reappointed to the office of Prime Minister and most principal ministers retained their portfolios. Twagiramungu left the country in early November, after claiming that he faced detention owing to his opposition to Kagame's Government.

In August 2003, following a two-day mass trial, a *gacaca* court in the prefecture of Butare convicted 105 people of participation in the 1994 genocide, of whom 11 were sentenced to death. In early September a Gambian judge, Hassan Bubacar Jallow, was appointed Chief Prosecutor of the ICTR, replacing del Ponte. In early December the owners of Radio Télévision Libre des Mille Collines and the Hutu extremist newspaper *Kangura* were sentenced to life imprisonment at the ICTR, on charges relating to public incitement to commit genocide. By February 2004 the ICTR had convicted 18 and acquitted three defendants and in that month the Rwandan authorities urged those prisoners awaiting trial in connection with the genocide to qualify for a general amnesty by confessing to the charges against them. Meanwhile, at the ongoing trial of Bagosora at the ICTR, the testimony of a principal witness, a former Canadian UN commander, Gen. (retd) Romeo Dallaire, implicated French forces in failing to prevent the genocide.

In June 2004 former President Bizimungu (who had remained in detention since April 2002) was sentenced to a term of 15 years' imprisonment, after being convicted of corruption, inciting civil disobedience and criminal association; he was, however, acquitted of the principal charge of endangering state security through anti-Government activities. In July the Minister of Finance of the 1994 Government, Emmanuel Ndindabahizi, who had been arrested in Belgium in July 2001, received a sentence of life imprisonment at the ICTR on charges of genocide and two counts of crimes against humanity for his participation in the massacre of Tutsi refugees during that period. Proceedings for some of the large number of cases to be transferred from the ICTR to the *gacaca* courts commenced in early 2005. In February the Minister of Family and Women's Affairs of the 1994 Government became the first woman to be charged with genocide in connection with organized killings in the Butare prefecture. At the end of March the serving Minister of Defence, Gen. Marcel Gatsinzi, appeared before a *gacaca* court, where he pleaded not guilty to charges of failing to prevent troops under his command from perpetrating massacres in Butare.

In early October 2005 the trial began of Zigiranyirazo (who had been extradited to the ICTR in October 2001); he pleaded not guilty to all charges relating to the genocide. (By late 2005 it was reported that some 4,162 cases, including those of several former officials, had been tried by the *gacaca* system.) In July 2006 phase two of the *gacaca* system began. While those charged with crimes related to the genocide were in prison in Rwanda, many of those suspected of issuing the orders had fled and were living in exile. However, an announcement was made in October 2006 that France, Belgium and the Netherlands had agreed to seek those who had taken up residence in those countries and bring them to trial. Frustrated at the slow progress being made by the ICTR—since 1997 only 29 of those responsible for the genocide had been convicted—the Rwandan Government wanted suspects transferred to face trial in Rwanda. Since the country maintained the death penalty suspects could not be extradited, but in July 2007 legislation to abolish this was officially promulgated; it was reported that those who had been sentenced to death would instead be subjected to terms of life imprisonment. Proceedings began in August to seek extradition orders.

Meanwhile, in October 2005 both legislative chambers approved a number of constitutional amendments, which principally provided for the reorganization of local government structures (reducing the number of provinces, formerly prefectures, from 12 to five) to allow greater decentralization; the territorial reforms entered into effect at the beginning of 2006. In February the Supreme Court upheld the 15-year sentence imposed on Bizimungu (who had submitted an appeal against the charges in October 2005). Also in February 2006 the Rwandan Government denied a request by Jallow for the transfer of the trial of a suspected Interahamwe military leader to Norway. In March a new Minister of Finance was appointed in a government reorganization, which was designed to assist efforts to reconstruct the economy; a new portfolio of science, information technology and research was also created. In April 2007 Bizimungu received a presidential pardon and was released from prison.

In 2003 the UN Security Council had mandated the ICTR to complete the first instance trials of genocide suspects by December 2008, and all appeals proceedings were to be completed by 2010. However, there were concerns that the trials would not be completed before the expiry of the ICTR's mandate and that too few of the suspected key perpetrators of the genocide had been prosecuted. In May the USA announced that it was to re-establish a programme offering large financial rewards for information leading to the arrest of 13 genocide suspects still at large before the ICTR ceased operations, while in June 2008 legislation was approved granting *gacaca* courts the jurisdiction to try up to 90% of those suspects who would otherwise be required to be brought before the ICTR. In November the ICTR concluded the trial of several high-profile suspects: Bagosora received a life sentence for genocide, war crimes and crimes against humanity and Zigiranyirazo was sentenced to 20 years in prison. By late 2008 31 suspects had been convicted and five acquitted since trials began. However, the ICTR received criticism for failing to prosecute members of the FPR for their crimes committed during the conflict.

Meanwhile, in a major governmental reorganization in March 2008, the number of full cabinet positions was increased to 22 from 19, while the number of ministers of state was reduced from 11 to six. Charles Murigande, hitherto Minister of Foreign Affairs and Co-operation, became Minister of Cabinet Affairs at the newly created ministry; Rosemary Museminari replaced Murigande, one of four women to enter the cabinet.

On 15 September 2008, in only the second legislative election to be held since the genocide of 1994, the FPR secured a resounding victory with 78.76% of the votes cast and winning 42 of the 53 directly elected seats; the PSD took seven seats and the PL four. It was the first time that women outnumbered men in the legislature, occupying some 56% of the seats. Turn-out for the elections was estimated at over 98%. The following month Rose Mukantantabana was nominated as Speaker of the Chamber of Deputies, the first woman to hold that position in the country's history. A minor cabinet reshuffle was effected, although no new ministers were introduced, following the election of Jean-Damascène Ntawukuriryayo, hitherto Minister of Health, to the Chamber of Deputies; he was replaced by Richard Sezibera.

At the end of July 1998 Laurent-Désiré Kabila (the President of the DRC since 31 May 1997) announced that military co-operation with both Rwanda and Uganda was to end, and demanded that all foreign forces leave the DRC. Relations between Rwanda and the DRC subsequently deteriorated. Kabila claimed that a rebellion, which commenced in the east of the DRC in August, constituted a Rwandan invasion; the Rwandan Government denied any involvement, but in late 1998 conceded that Rwandan troops were present in the DRC to provide logistical support to the rebel-led action. The Rwandan Government participated in a series of regional peace negotiations, at which Kabila refused to negotiate directly with the rebels. Rwanda later denied reports that it was maintaining a joint military command with Uganda in the DRC (see also the chapter on the DRC).

Rwandan action in the DRC continued in 1999, although Rwanda's alliance with Uganda became increasingly unstable during that year. At the end of April Uganda temporarily recalled its ambassador to Rwanda, following an incident in the DRC, in which Rwandan troops killed a number of members of the Ugandan armed forces. A split within the rebel movement in the DRC, the Rassemblement congolais pour la démocratie (RCD), resulted in the creation of two factions, one supported by Rwanda and one by Uganda. Following further clashes in the DRC between Rwandan and Ugandan troops in Kisangani in August, both armies agreed to leave the city. In June the DRC instituted proceedings against Burundi, Rwanda and Uganda at the International Court of Justice (ICJ) in The Hague, Netherlands, accusing these countries of acts of armed aggression. (In early February 2001, however, the DRC abandoned proceedings against Burundi and Rwanda.)

In May 2000 Rwandan and Ugandan forces again clashed in the town of Kisangani (despite a cease-fire agreement, which had been reached by all forces involved in the conflict in April). After meeting a UN Security Council delegation, the Rwandan and Ugandan contingents agreed to the demilitarization of the town, and its transfer to the control of the UN Mission in the Democratic Republic of the Congo (MONUC, see p. 88) deployed in the country. Despite further fighting, it was confirmed at the end of June that all Rwandan and Ugandan forces had withdrawn from Kisangani. In December, however, the principal RCD faction, supported by Rwandan troops, succeeded in gaining control of the south-eastern town of Pweto. The Rwandan Government denied any involvement in the assassination of Kabila in January 2001 (see the chapter on the DRC). In February Kagame met the new DRC President, Joseph Kabila (the son of Laurent-Désiré), in Washington, DC, USA, to discuss the ongoing conflict. Later that month the groups involved in the conflict, under the aegis of the UN Security Council, agreed to a disengagement of their forces by mid-March, followed by a complete withdrawal of foreign troops from the DRC by mid-May. Although some military disengagement of forces took place accordingly in March, factions subsequently refused to continue until MONUC guaranteed security in the region. In April the Governments of Burundi, Rwanda and Uganda rejected the claims of a UN report that the forces of these countries had exploited the natural resources of the DRC. In June it was reported that Interahamwe militia, led by former members of the Rwandan army, had intensified incursions into north-western Rwanda from the DRC. Despite continued pressure from the UN Security Council, in August Kagame insisted that Kabila fulfil pledges to demobilize the Interahamwe (who were supporting DRC government forces), as a precondition to the withdrawal of Rwandan forces from the DRC.

At the end of July 2002, after further discussions mediated by the South African Government, a peace agreement was signed by Kabila and Kagame in Pretoria. Under the accord, Kabila pledged to arrest and disarm the Interahamwe militia in the DRC, while the Rwandan Government agreed to withdraw all troops from the country. In October it was announced that all 23,400 Rwandan troops had been withdrawn from the DRC. The Rwandan authorities denied reports that they planned to redeploy forces in the DRC, in response to the continued Ugandan involvement in hostilities there. In September 2003 the Governments of Rwanda and the DRC agreed to re-establish diplomatic links, and the improvement in relations between the two countries was further demonstrated by the visit to Rwanda of the DRC Minister of Foreign Affairs in October. In July 2004, however, a report by a UN commission contained accusations, which were denied by the Rwandan Government, of Rwandan support for an insurrection by dissident members of the armed forces in eastern DRC (see chapter on the DRC). Following a massacre of Banyamulenge refugees from the DRC at a border camp in Burundi in August, the Governments of Rwanda and Burundi claimed that the Interahamwe militia operating within the DRC were implicated and threatened to resume military engagement in the country. Repeated reports (confirmed by MONUC) that Rwandan troops had re-entered DRC territory ensued.

In November 2001 Kagame and the Ugandan Head of State, Lt-Gen. Yoweri Kaguta Museveni, met in London, United Kingdom, in an effort to resolve the increasing tension between the two nations, following the repeated clashes in the DRC. The Ugandan Government had accused Rwanda of supporting dissidents who intended to overthrow Museveni's administration, while Kagame claimed that Ugandan troops were amassing on the joint border between the two countries. In February 2002 further discussions between Kagame and Museveni, with mediation by the British Secretary of State for International Development, were conducted in Uganda. It was agreed that both Governments would urge the dissidents based in their respective countries to take refuge elsewhere, and the adoption of a mutual extradition treaty was envisaged. In July 2003 the Rwandan Government signed a tripartite agreement with the Ugandan authorities and UNHCR, providing for the voluntary repatriation of some 26,000 Rwandans resident in refugee camps in western Uganda. (Similar accords were signed between Rwanda and the Governments of Malawi, Togo, Zambia and Tanzania.) In February 2004 an improvement in diplomatic relations between Rwanda and Uganda (following progress in the situation in the DRC) was demonstrated by a bilateral agreement to strengthen co-operation in several fields. In October 2008 the DRC accused Rwanda of military incursions into Nord-Kivu to support Laurent Nkunda's Tutsi rebels; UN peace-keepers intervened to investigate the claims and relations between Rwanda and the DRC deteriorated. However, an unexpected accord was concluded between Presidents Kagame and Kabila in January 2009, and on 22 January Rwandan forces detained Nkunda as he attempted to cross the border into Rwandan territory. Although it had appeared that Nkunda and Rwanda shared the common goal of overpowering the Hutu militia, responsible for the genocide, intense diplomacy was believed to have been behind the tentative allegiance between Rwanda and the DRC. The joint operation aimed at suppressing rebel groups and restoring order to the region was nevertheless viewed with apprehension and suspicion by some observers.

Since 1994 the role of the international community in failing to avert the genocide has come under frequent scrutiny. In late 1997 the report of a Belgian Senate investigation concluded that the international community, and more specifically the UN and the Belgian authorities, was directly or indirectly responsible for certain aspects of the developments arising from the political violence from April 1994. Testifying before the ICTR in February 1998, the former UNAMIR commander stated that he had warned the UN in early 1994 of the impending ethnic catastrophe in Rwanda, but that the international community had lacked the will to intervene adequately. Suggestions that Kofi Annan, the head of UN peace-keeping operations at the time of the conflict, had failed to respond to such warnings prompted tensions between the UN Secretary-General (as Annan had subsequently become) and the Rwandan authorities in May 1998, as government officials refused to receive the Secretary-General in the course of a visit to Rwanda. Meanwhile, in February the OAU announced the establishment of a committee to investigate the genocide; the committee held its first meeting in October. In December a French parliamentary committee, established in March, presented its report on French involvement in events prior to and at the time of the genocide. (Despite evidence to the contrary, the French authorities have persistently denied allegations that France continued to supply military equipment and support to Rwanda after the imposition of the UN arms embargo in May 1994.) The report cleared France of any direct complicity in the genocide, although it conceded that 'Operation Turquoise' both delayed the accession to power of the FPR, and facilitated the escape of Hutu extremist forces into the DRC. The report attributed responsibility for the genocide to the international community as a whole, particularly to the USA (which had failed to support UN peace-keeping operations in Rwanda).

In March 1999 the UN Security Council approved a proposal for the establishment of a commission of inquiry into the actions of the UN prior to and during the genocide. The three-member commission of inquiry presented its report in December after a six-month investigation. The report criticized the UN for failing in its mission to prevent the genocide and for ignoring the warnings of the head of the peace-keeping mission. It also cited the UN Security Council's failure to deploy a sufficient peace-keeping force at the end of 1993. Following the report, Kofi Annan issued a personal apology for UN inaction at the time. In January 2000 it was announced that two Rwandan genocide survivors were to sue the UN for its 'complicity' in the genocide. In March a Canadian newspaper published a UN memorandum, stating that the FPR was responsible for the attack on the aircraft on 6 April 1994, which killed President Juvénal Habyarimana, and that Kagame had been in overall command of the force that carried out the attack. Kagame subsequently dismissed the allegations, claiming that the report was part of a UN attempt to absolve itself of blame for the genocide of 1994.

In August 2001 the French Minister of Foreign Affairs made an official visit to Rwanda (the first by a senior French official since 1994), in an effort to normalize bilateral relations. (Diplomatic links were restored in 2002.) In March 2002 the French Government (which, within the UN Security Council, had placed increasing pressure on Rwanda to withdraw forces from the DRC) protested that Rwandan troops had launched a major offensive in the east of that country. In March 2004 the results of an official French investigation into the destruction of President Habyarimana's aircraft alleged that Kagame, as leader of the FPR, had ordered the missile attack. Kagame again denied any responsibility, and claimed that French forces had, by training and arming the Hutu militia, supported the mass killings. In early April the French Secretary of State for Foreign Affairs curtailed his visit to Rwanda, after Kagame repeated these accusations at an official ceremony in Kigali commemorating the 10th anniversary of the genocide. On the following anniversary in April 2005 the Rwandan Government reiterated demands that the UN instigate legal proceedings against French officials for complicity in the genocide. In December a French military tribunal began to investigate claims by survivors of the genocide that French forces had facilitated attacks against Tutsi in 1994 (by failing to prevent massacres and then by allowing the perpetrators of the genocide to evade capture). In November 2006 Rwanda severed diplomatic relations with France, recalling the ambassador to that country and closing the French embassy. The move followed the order by the French judiciary to issue international arrest warrants against President Kagame and nine high-ranking Rwandan officials. In September 2007, for the first time since the severance of diplomatic ties, a delegation of French officials visited Kigali with the aim of making progress towards the restoration of normal relations. Despite the abolition of the death penalty in Rwanda in July 2007, the French Government had refused to extradite genocide suspects; however, in November a French court approved the extradition of one of the suspects currently resident in France. In January 2008 French Minister of Foreign and European Affairs Bernard Kouchner met briefly with President Kagame to resume dialogue with Rwanda, and in a press conference Kouchner admitted that France had made a political mistake in its response to the 1994 genocide; nevertheless, he denied any military responsibility. Relations between the two countries had been improving since a meeting between the two Heads of State at a summit in Lisbon in December 2007. However, in August 2008 a Rwandan commission of inquiry issued a report accusing high-ranking French officials of involvement in the genocide; among those mentioned were former President François Mitterrand and former Prime Minister Dominique de Villepin. Rwanda demanded that the French officials named be brought to trial and submitted the findings of the report as the basis for issuing arrest warrants. France denied all accusations made by Rwanda but reiterated its commitment to rebuilding a relationship with the African country. In November Rose Kabuye, a senior presidential aide and former guerrilla fighter with the now ruling FPR, was detained in Frankfurt, Germany, and extradited to France on charges of involvement in the attack on President Habyarimana's aircraft. Kabuye denied the accusations against her and was subsequently released from custody under a supervision order. A popular figure in Rwanda, her arrest prompted demonstrations in Kigali. Kabuye was one of nine officials implicated in Habyarimana's assassination. Relations between Rwanda and Germany were severed as a result of the arrest, although diplomatic ties were restored in January 2009.

Government

Under the terms of the Constitution, which entered into force on 4 June 2003, legislative power is vested in a bicameral Parliament, comprising a Chamber of Deputies and a Senate. The Chamber of Deputies has 80 deputies, who are elected for a five-year term. In addition to 53 directly elected deputies, 27 seats are allocated, respectively, to two youth representatives, one disabilities representative, and 24 female representatives, who are indirectly elected. The Senate comprises 26 members, of whom 12 are elected by local government councils in the 12 provinces, and two by academic institutions, while the remaining 12 are nominated (eight by the President and four by a regulatory body, the Parties' Forum). Members of the Senate serve for eight years. Executive power is exercised by the President (Head of State), assisted by an appointed Council of Ministers. The President is elected by universal suffrage for a seven-year term, and is restricted to two mandates.

Following territorial reforms, which entered into effect at the beginning of 2006, the country is divided into five provinces and subdivided into 30 districts, each administered by an elected mayor. Local government elections took place on a non-party basis in April 2001.

Defence

As assessed at November 2008, the total strength of the armed forces was estimated at 33,000: army 32,000, air force 1,000. In addition, there were local defence forces of about 2,000. Defence expenditure for 2007 was budgeted at 33,900m. Rwanda francs. A programme to restructure the army, which was expected to be reduced in size to number about 25,000, was planned and a Rwanda Demobilization and Reintegration Commission was mandated to facilitate the reintegration of discharged military personnel into civilian life.

Economic Affairs

In 2007, according to estimates by the World Bank, Rwanda's gross national income (GNI), measured at average 2005–07 prices, was US $3,072m., equivalent to $320 per head (or $860 per head on an international purchasing-power parity basis). During 2000–07, it was estimated, the population increased at an average annual rate of 2.5%, while gross domestic product (GDP) per head rose, in real terms, by an average of 3.6% per year. Overall GDP increased, in real terms, at an average annual rate of 6.2% in 2000–07; growth of 6.0% was recorded in 2007.

Agriculture (including forestry and fishing) contributed 35.6% of GDP in 2007. According to FAO estimates, 89.8% of the employed labour force were engaged in the sector (mainly at subsistence level) at mid-2005. The principal food crops are plantains, sweet potatoes, cassava, dry beans and sorghum. The principal cash crops are coffee (which contributed 17.7% of total export earnings in 2007) and tea (16.5%). Pyrethrum and quinquina are also cultivated for export. Goats and cattle are traditionally the principal livestock raised. According to the World Bank, agricultural GDP increased by an average of 4.4% per year during 2000–07; sectoral GDP declined by 2.9% in 2007, following an increase of 11.0% in 2006.

Industry (including mining, manufacturing, power and construction) accounted for 14.1% of GDP in 2007, and the industrial sector engaged 2.8% of the employed labour force in 2002. According to the World Bank, industrial GDP increased at an average annual rate of 8.8% during 2000–07; the GDP of the industrial sector increased by 13.4% in 2007.

Mining and quarrying contributed just 0.6% of GDP in 2003. Cassiterite (a tin-bearing ore) is Rwanda's principal mineral resource. Exports of tin ores and concentrates contributed 21.5% of the value of total merchandise exports in 2007. There are also reserves of wolframite (a tungsten-bearing ore), columbo-tantalite, gold and beryl, and work is under way to exploit natural methane gas reserves, estimated to total at least 55,000m. cu m, beneath Lake Kivu. Mining GDP declined at an estimated average annual rate of 0.4% in 1990–2002, according to the Banque Nationale du Rwanda. Mining GDP increased by 16.6% in 2001, but declined by an estimated 5.7% in 2002.

Manufacturing accounted for 13.3% of GDP in 2006, while production activities engaged 1.3% of the employed labour force in 2002. The principal branches of manufacturing are beverages and tobacco, food products and basic consumer goods, including soap, textiles and plastic products. According to the World Bank, manufacturing GDP increased by an average of 7.5% per year during 2000–07; the GDP of the sector increased by 9.8% in 2007.

Output of electricity is insufficient to meet domestic needs, and the rate of connection is low. In 1999 Rwanda imported 35.5% of its electricity, but subsequently benefited from the completion of the Ruzizi-II plant (a joint venture with Burundi and the Democratic Republic of the Congo—DRC). In March 2009 the Government of Rwanda signed an agreement with a US-based company for the development of an integrated extraction and generation facility to supply methane gas-fired electricity from the Lake Kivu resource to Rwanda and the East Africa region. (Rwanda's first pilot methane gas plant was inaugurated in late 2008, and subsequently began supplying the national grid.) Projects such as the Nyabarongo hydroelectric dam, construction of which was under way in the late 2000s, and other planned 'micro-dams', are expected to reduce Rwanda's reliance on thermal energy sources. Imports of fuels and lubricants comprised 8.7% of the total value of merchandise imports in 2007.

The services sector contributed 50.0% of GDP in 2007, and engaged 8.6% of the employed labour force in 2002. According to the World Bank, the GDP of the services sector increased at an average annual rate of 6.9% during 2000–07; growth in the services sector was 12.0% in 2007.

In 2006 Rwanda recorded a visible trade deficit of US $343m., and there was a deficit of $180m. on the current account of the balance of payments. In 2007 the principal source of imports was

RWANDA

Kenya, which supplied 17.8% of merchandise imports in that year; other major suppliers were Uganda, the United Arab Emirates, Tanzania, Belgium, the People's Republic of China and France. In the same year the principal markets for exports were the United Kingdom and Kenya, each of which took 18.7% of Rwanda's exports; other significant purchasers were Belgium, Hong Kong, Switzerland-Liechtenstein and the USA. The principal exports in 2007 were tin ores and concentrates, coffee and tea. The main imports in that year were road vehicles, petroleum and petroleum products, medicinal and pharmaceutical products, and iron and steel.

An overall budgetary deficit of 27.7m. Rwanda francs was recorded in 2007 (equivalent to 1.5% of GDP). At the end of 2006 Rwanda's external debt totalled US $419m., of which $390m. was long-term public debt. The cost of debt-servicing in that year was equivalent to 9.6% of the value of exports of goods and services. In 2000–07 the average annual rate of inflation was 7.3%. Consumer prices increased by 9.1% in 2007.

Rwanda is a member of the Organization for the Management and Development of the Kagera River Basin (see p. 428), and, with Burundi and the DRC, is a founding member of the Economic Community of the Great Lakes Countries (see p. 426) and of the Common Market for Eastern and Southern Africa (see p. 215). Rwanda joined the East African Community (EAC, see p. 425) in 2007. The country is also a member of the International Coffee Organization (see p. 422).

By the late 2000s, through a sustained programme of donor-funded assistance, the Government of Rwanda had achieved considerable success in its efforts towards economic recovery and restructuring. Strong annual growth rates (growth of 8.5% was forecast for 2008) were based principally on expansion in the services, manufacturing and construction sectors. As a result of relief under the heavily indebted poor countries and multilateral debt relief initiatives (for which Rwanda qualified in 2005 and 2006, respectively), Rwanda's external debt fell from the equivalent of 71.6% of GNI at the end of 2005 to 16.9% in 2006—a level that was expected to have been broadly maintained in 2007. The Government's Economic Development and Poverty Reduction Strategy, inaugurated in late 2007, aimed to address inadequacies in key areas of infrastructure, such as education, health, energy, roads, the financial sector, and information and communications technology; to enhance agricultural development and trade; and to promote business development and private sector activity. It was planned to increase the country's revenue-to-GDP ratio by 0.2% annually over the medium term by means of fiscal reform. The budget for the first six months of 2009 (thereafter, Rwanda was to adopt the EAC's July–June fiscal year) envisaged a revenue-to-GDP ratio of 7.1%, while an increase in investment expenditure of a budgeted 1% of GDP was to be financed largely by foreign grants and concessionary loans. Monetary policy would be targeted to bring inflation, which had exceeded 20% in the latter part of 2008 (reflecting high international prices for food and fuels, in conjunction with increased domestic demand), below 10% in the second half of 2009. Rwanda's external current account deficit, projected at about 18.4% of GDP in 2008 (from 15.5% in 2007) was expected to remain at a similar level in 2009, despite lower international commodity prices: higher volumes were anticipated of sales of Rwanda's traditional exports, while revenue from tourism was expected to increase; meanwhile, the public investment programme was to be a major factor influencing a higher volume of imports. Rwanda's membership of the EAC was expected to allow easier access to regional trading routes and business development, to provide access to skilled labour, and to facilitate the supply of energy to supplement generating capacity pending the completion of new domestic projects. Provisions for entry to the EAC customs union were expected to have been completed by mid-2009. In a review of the economy published in early 2009, the IMF emphasized that, despite some progress towards the achievement of universal primary education, gender equality, women's promotion and reduction in child mortality, poverty in Rwanda remained 'pervasive'. The IMF, which was lending assistance under a three-year Poverty Reduction and Growth Facility to June 2009, noted progress made in structural reforms and economic liberalization, but emphasized the need to diversify and improve productive capacity and to increase public investment while preserving macroeconomic stability and the sustainability of debt. Rwanda's narrow export base, founded on an overwhelming reliance on the agricultural sector, was considered vulnerable to external shocks that might compromise the country's ability to meet its debt obligations. The IMF considered that the deterioration in the global economy would have some dampening effect on Rwanda's rate of growth in 2009, with the principal impact being on the services and construction sectors. There was, in addition, some evidence that donor countries' levels of budgetary assistance and foreign direct investment would be significantly reduced in the current economic climate.

Education

Primary education, beginning at seven years of age and lasting for six years, is officially compulsory. Secondary education, which is not compulsory, begins at the age of 14 and lasts for a further six years. In 2003, however, the Government announced plans to introduce a nine-year system of basic education, including three years of attendance at lower secondary schools. Schools are administered by the state and by Christian missions. In 2006/07 93.6% of children in the relevant age-group (males 92.3%, females 94.9%) were enrolled in primary schools, according to UNESCO estimates, while secondary enrolment was equivalent to only 13.4% of children in the appropriate age-group (males 14.2%, females 12.7%) in 2005/05. The Ministry of Education established 94 new secondary schools in 2003, and a further 58 in 2005. Rwanda has a university, with campuses at Butare and Ruhengeri, while some students attend universities abroad, particularly in Belgium, France or Germany. In 2004/05 the number of students in tertiary education (there are six public higher education institutions and seven private higher institutions) was 26,378. In 2008 the Government decreed that English would henceforth be the language of instruction in all Rwandan educational establishments. In 2005 spending on education represented 12.2% of total budgetary expenditure.

Public Holidays

2009: 1 January (New Year), 28 January (Democracy Day), 7 April (National Mourning Day), 13 April (Easter Monday), 1 May (Labour Day), 21 May (Ascension Day), 1 July (Independence Day), 1 August (Harvest Festival), 15 August (Assumption), 8 September (Culture Day), 25 September (Kamarampaka Day, anniversary of 1961 referendum), 1 October (Armed Forces Day), 1 November (All Saints' Day), 25 December (Christmas).

2010: 1 January (New Year), 28 January (Democracy Day), 5 April (Easter Monday), 7 April (National Mourning Day), 1 May (Labour Day), 13 May (Ascension Day), 1 July (Independence Day), 1 August (Harvest Festival), 15 August (Assumption), 8 September (Culture Day), 25 September (Kamarampaka Day, anniversary of 1961 referendum), 1 October (Armed Forces Day), 1 November (All Saints' Day), 25 December (Christmas).

Weights and Measures

The metric system is in force.

RWANDA

Statistical Survey

Source (unless otherwise stated): Office rwandais d'information, BP 83, Kigali; tel. 75724.

Area and Population

AREA, POPULATION AND DENSITY

Area (sq km)	26,338*
Population (census results)	
15 August 1991	7,142,755
16 August 2002†	
Males	3,879,448
Females	4,249,105
Total	8,128,553
Population (UN estimate at mid-year)‡	
2006	9,210,000
2007	9,455,000
2008	9,721,000
Density (per sq km) at mid-2008	369.1

* 10,169 sq miles.
† Provisional results.
‡ Source: UN, *World Population Prospects: The 2008 Revision.*

PREFECTURES
(1991 census)

	Area (sq km)	Population*	Density (per sq km)
Butare	1,830	765,910	418.5
Byumba	4,987	779,365	159.2
Cyangugu	2,226	517,550	232.5
Gikongoro	2,192	462,635	211.1
Gisenyi	2,395	728,365	304.1
Gitarama	2,241	849,285	379.0
Kibungo	4,134	647,175	156.5
Kibuye	1,320	472,525	358.0
Kigali	3,251	921,050	355.2
Kigali-Ville		233,640	
Ruhengeri	1,762	765,255	434.3
Total	26,338	7,142,755	271.2

* Source: UN, *Demographic Yearbook.*

PRINCIPAL TOWNS
(population at 1978 census)

Kigali (capital)	117,749	Ruhengeri	16,025
Butare	21,691	Gisenyi	12,436

Mid-2007 (incl. suburbs, UN estimate): Kigali 860,000 (Source: UN, *World Urbanization Prospects: The 2007 Revision*).

BIRTHS AND DEATHS
(annual averages, UN estimates)

	1990–95	1995–2000	2000–05
Birth rate (per 1,000)	40.7	40.3	41.0
Death rate (per 1,000)	41.6	22.2	16.8

Source: UN, *World Population Prospects: The 2008 Revision.*

Life expectancy (years at birth, WHO estimates): 51.7 (males 50.7; females 52.6) in 2006 (Source: WHO, *World Health Statistics*).

ECONOMICALLY ACTIVE POPULATION
(persons aged 14 years and over, at census of August 2002)

	Males	Females	Total
Agriculture	1,218,181	1,731,411	2,949,592
Fishing	3,374	94	3,468
Industrial activities	3,692	1,636	5,328
Production activities	32,994	10,649	43,643
Electricity and water	2,390	277	2,667
Construction	41,641	1,244	42,885
Trade reconstruction	56,869	32,830	89,699
Restaurants and hotels	4,525	2,311	6,836
Transport and communications	29,574	1,988	31,562
Financial intermediaries	1,560	840	2,400
Administration and defence	22,479	5,585	28,064
Education	22,688	17,046	39,734
Health and social services	7,521	7,054	14,575
Activities not adequately defined	69,042	39,458	108,500
Total employed	1,516,530	1,852,423	3,368,953

Source: IMF, *Rwanda: Selected Issues and Statistical Appendix* (December 2004).

Mid-2005 (estimates in '000): Agriculture, etc. 4,376; Total labour force 4,873 (Source: FAO).

Health and Welfare

KEY INDICATORS

Total fertility rate (children per woman, 2006)	6.0
Under-5 mortality rate (per 1,000 live births, 2006)	160
HIV/AIDS (% of persons aged 15–49, 2007)	2.8
Physicians (per 1,000 head, 2004)	0.05
Hospital beds (per 1,000 head, 2007)	1.6
Health expenditure (2006): US $ per head (PPP)	210
Health expenditure (2006): % of GDP	10.4
Health expenditure (2006): public (% of total)	63.7
Access to water (% of persons, 2006)	65
Access to sanitation (% of persons, 2006)	23
Human Development Index (2006): ranking	165
Human Development Index (2006): value	0.435

For sources and definitions, see explanatory note on p. vi.

Agriculture

PRINCIPAL CROPS
('000 metric tons)

	2005	2006	2007*
Maize	97.3	91.8	90.0
Sorghum	227.9	187.4	187.0
Potatoes	1,314.1	128.5	120.0
Sweet potatoes	885.6	777.0	940.0
Cassava (Manioc)	781.6	588.2	830.0
Taro (Cocoyam)	136.9	125.4	130.0
Sugar cane*	70.0	68.0	70.0
Beans, dry	199.6	283.4	230.0
Peas, dry	18.9	14.2	17.0
Groundnuts, with shell	10.1	9.0	10.0
Pumpkins, squash and gourds*	210.0	210.0	210.0
Plantains	2,593.1	2,653.3	2,580.0
Coffee, green	18.6	21.0	18.9
Tea	16.5	16.0	19.0

* FAO estimates.

Aggregate production ('000 metric tons, may include official, semi-official or estimated data): Total cereals 413 in 2005, 366 in 2006, 341 in 2007; Total roots and tubers 3,122 in 2005, 2,780 in 2006, 3,104 in 2007; Total pulses 219 in 2005, 298 in 2006, 247 in 2007; Total vegetables (incl. melons) 268 in 2005, 267 in 2006, 267 in 2007; Total fruits (excl. melons) 2,671 in 2005, 2,653 in 2006, 2,580 in 2007.

Source: FAO.

RWANDA

LIVESTOCK
('000 head, year ending September)

	2005	2006*	2007*
Cattle	1,004.1	926.0	950.0
Pigs	346.9	256.0	270.0
Sheep	464.3	470.0	470.0
Goats	1,339.7	1,300.0	1,300.0
Chickens*	2,000	1,800	1,800

* FAO estimates.
Source: FAO.

LIVESTOCK PRODUCTS
('000 metric tons, FAO estimates)

	2005	2006	2007
Cattle meat	23.1	22.0	22.0
Goat meat	4.7	3.7	3.9
Pig meat	6.4	4.7	5.0
Chicken meat	2.3	2.0	2.0
Game meat	12.0	11.0	11.0
Cows' milk	120.0	120.0	120.0
Sheep's milk	1.9	2.0	2.0
Goats' milk	25.2	22.0	22.0
Hen eggs	2.3	2.3	2.3

Source: FAO.

Forestry

ROUNDWOOD REMOVALS
('000 cubic metres, excluding bark, FAO estimates)

	2005	2006	2007
Sawlogs, veneer logs and logs for sleepers	245	245	245
Other industrial wood	250	250	250
Fuel wood	5,000	9,416	9,503
Total	**5,495**	**9,911**	**9,998**

Source: FAO.

SAWNWOOD PRODUCTION
('000 cubic metres, including railway sleepers)

	1997	1998	1999
Coniferous (softwood)	20	21	22
Non-coniferous (hardwood)	54	55	57
Total	**74**	**76**	**79**

2000–07: Figures assumed to be unchanged from 1999 (FAO estimates).
Source: FAO.

Fishing
(metric tons, live weight)

	2004	2005*	2006*
Capture	7,826	7,800	7,800
Nile tilapia	3,120	3,100	3,100
Aquaculture	386	386	400
Nile tilapia	340	340	340
Total catch	**8,212**	**8,186**	**8,200**

* FAO estimates.
Source: FAO.

Mining
(metric tons, unless otherwise indicated)

	2004	2005	2006*
Tin concentrates†*	550	700	700
Tungsten concentrates†	113	401	400
Columbo-tantalite‡	220	276	280
Natural gas (million cubic metres)§	140	170	170

* Estimates.
† Figures refer to the metal content of ores and concentrates.
‡ Figures refer to the estimated production of mineral concentrates. The metal content (estimates, metric tons) was: Niobium (Columbium) 69 in 2004, 86 in 2005, 88 in 2006; Tantalum 49 in 2004, 61 in 2005, 62 in 2006.
§ Figures refer to gross output.
Source: US Geological Survey.

Industry

SELECTED PRODUCTS

	2001	2002	2003
Beer ('000 hectolitres)	479	539	412
Soft drinks ('000 hectolitres)	228	n.a.	n.a.
Cigarettes (million)	278	391	402
Soap (metric tons)	7,056	5,571	4,456
Cement (metric tons)	83,024	100,568	105,105

Source: IMF, *Rwanda: Statistical Annex* (August 2002) and IMF, *Rwanda: Selected Issues and Statistical Appendix* (December 2004).

Cement ('000 metric tons): 104.3 in 2004; 101.1 in 2005; 100.0 in 2006 (estimate) (Source: US Geological Survey).

Electric energy (million kWh): 122 in 2003; 130 in 2004; 135 in 2005 (Source: UN, *Industrial Commodity Statistics Yearbook*).

Finance

CURRENCY AND EXCHANGE RATES

Monetary Units
100 centimes = 1 franc rwandais (Rwanda franc).

Sterling, Dollar and Euro Equivalents (31 October 2008)
£1 sterling = 893.114 Rwanda francs;
US $1 = 552.191 Rwanda francs;
€1 = 704.430 Rwanda francs;
10,000 Rwanda francs = £11.20 = $18.11 = €14.20.

Average Exchange Rate (Rwanda francs per US $)
2005   557.823
2006   551.710
2007   546.955

Note: Since September 1983 the currency has been linked to the IMF special drawing right (SDR). Until November 1990 the mid-point exchange rate was SDR 1 = 102.71 Rwanda francs. In November 1990 a new rate of SDR 1 = 171.18 Rwanda francs was established. This remained in effect until June 1992, when the rate was adjusted to SDR 1 = 201.39 Rwanda francs. The latter parity was maintained until February 1994, since when the rate has been frequently adjusted. In March 1995 the Government introduced a market-determined exchange rate system.

RWANDA

Statistical Survey

BUDGET
('000 million Rwanda francs)

Revenue*	1999	2000	2001†
Tax revenue	60.4	65.3	79.5
Taxes on income and profits	15.2	17.9	23.9
Company profits tax	7.4	10.0	14.4
Individual income tax	6.1	7.5	9.0
Domestic taxes on goods and services	33.6	35.2	41.0
Excise taxes	17.9	18.8	14.2
Turnover tax	12.9	13.8	24.2
Road fund	2.7	2.5	2.6
Taxes on international trade	11.0	11.6	14.0
Import taxes	8.4	9.3	11.1
Non-tax revenue	3.2	3.3	6.7
Total	**63.6**	**68.7**	**86.2**

Expenditure‡	1999	2000	2001†
Current expenditure	86.0	89.2	107.4
General public services	31.5	35.7	53.7
Defence	27.0	25.8	28.6
Social services	21.9	30.5	36.2
Education	17.2	24.0	29.8
Health	3.3	3.8	5.1
Economic services	2.6	2.1	4.9
Energy and public works	0.7	0.4	2.3
Interest on public debt	4.0	1.8	2.8
Adjustment	−1.1	−6.7	−18.8
Capital expenditure	40.8	42.0	50.0
Sub-total	**126.8**	**131.2**	**157.5**
Adjustment for payment arrears§	2.0	−1.2	31.7
Total	**128.8**	**130.0**	**189.2**

* Excluding grants received ('000 million Rwanda francs): 38.5 in 1999; 63.7 in 2000; 63.3† in 2001.
† Estimates.
‡ Excluding lending minus repayments ('000 million Rwanda francs): −0.4 in 1999; 0.5 in 2000; 0.6 in 2001†.
§ Minus sign indicates increase in arrears.

Source: IMF, *Rwanda: Statistical Annex* (August 2002).

2002 (estimates, '000 million Rwanda francs): *Revenue:* Tax revenue 94.6; Non-tax revenue 6.6; Total 101.2, excl. grants received 70.8. *Expenditure:* Current 123.7; Capital 56.4; Total 180.1, excl. net lending 11.5 (Source: IMF, *Rwanda: First Review Under the Three-Year Arrangement Under the Poverty Reduction and Growth Facility and Request for Waiver of Nonobservance of Performance Criteria—Staff Report; Staff Statement; Press Release on the Executive Board Discussion; and Statement by the Executive Director for Rwanda*—June 2003).

2005 ('000 million Rwanda francs): *Revenue:* Tax revenue 162.6; Non-tax revenue 17.7; Total 180.3, excl. grants received 169.1. *Expenditure:* Current 214.9; Capital 121.4; Total 336.3, excl. net lending 4.4 (Source: IMF, *Rwanda: Third Review Under the Three-Year Arrangement Under the Poverty Reduction and Growth Facility and Request for Waiver of Nonobservance of Performance Criterion—Staff Report; Staff Supplement; Press Release on the Executive Board Discussion; and Statement by the Executive Director for Rwanda*—March 2008).

2006 ('000 million Rwanda francs): *Revenue:* Tax revenue 193.6; Non-tax revenue 14.6; Total 208.2, excl. grants received 167.8. *Expenditure:* Current 254.1; Capital 118.7; Total 372.9, excl. net lending 9.6 (Source: IMF, *Rwanda: Third Review Under the Three-Year Arrangement Under the Poverty Reduction and Growth Facility and Request for Waiver of Nonobservance of Performance Criterion—Staff Report; Staff Supplement; Press Release on the Executive Board Discussion; and Statement by the Executive Director for Rwanda*—March 2008).

2007 ('000 million Rwanda francs): *Revenue:* Tax revenue 237.8; Non-tax revenue 15.1; Total 252.9, excl. grants received 183.8. *Expenditure:* Current 312.6; Capital 159.9; Total 472.5, excl. net lending -8.1 (Source: IMF, *Rwanda: 2008 Article IV Consultation, Fifth Review Under the Three-Year Arrangement Under the Poverty Reduction and Growth Facility, and Request for Waiver of Nonobservance of Performance Criterion - Staff Report; Staff Supplement and Statement; Public Information Notice and Press Release on the Executive Board Discussion; and Statement by the Executive Director for Rwanda*—February 2009).

INTERNATIONAL BANK RESERVES
(US $ million at 31 December)

	2006	2007	2008
IMF special drawing rights	22.85	24.06	31.42
Foreign exchange	416.82	528.73	564.86
Total	**439.67**	**552.79**	**596.28**

Source: IMF, *International Financial Statistics*.

MONEY SUPPLY
(million Rwanda francs at 31 December)

	2003	2004	2005
Currency outside banks	29,246	36,512	46,277
Demand deposits at deposit money banks	52,220	62,604	82,524
Total money (incl. others)	**82,305**	**99,941**	**129,326**

2006: Currency outside banks 52,620.

Source: IMF, *International Financial Statistics*.

COST OF LIVING
(Consumer Price Index for Kigali; base: 2000 = 100)

	2005	2006	2007
All items	138.1	150.3	164.0

Source: IMF, *International Financial Statistics*.

NATIONAL ACCOUNTS
Expenditure on the Gross Domestic Product
(US $ million)

	2005	2006	2007
Government final consumption expenditure	287.24	335.95	369.74
Private final consumption expenditure	1,817.78	2,108.55	2,413.33
Gross capital formation	487.67	533.56	658.43
Total domestic expenditure	**2,592.69**	**2,978.06**	**3,441.50**
Exports of goods and services	227.91	296.09	320.23
Less Imports of goods and services	666.74	784.43	939.82
GDP in purchasers' values	**2,153.86**	**2,489.72**	**2,821.91**

Source: African Development Bank.

Gross Domestic Product by Economic Activity
('000 million Rwanda francs at current prices)

	2001	2002	2003
Agriculture, hunting, forestry and fishing	305.2	341.6	373.9
Mining and quarrying	14.5	9.1	5.7
Manufacturing	73.9	80.5	80.3
Electricity, gas and water	3.4	3.4	3.6
Construction	71.2	82.9	103.1
Trade, restaurants and hotels	75.2	82.0	91.7
Transport, storage and communications	55.1	60.7	61.7
Public administration	54.2	55.8	64.8
Other services	101.6	109.0	120.4
GDP at market prices	**754.3**	**825.0**	**905.3**

Source: IMF, *Rwanda: Selected Issues and Statistical Appendix* (December 2004).

RWANDA

BALANCE OF PAYMENTS
(US $ million)

	2004	2005	2006
Exports of goods f.o.b.	98	128	145
Imports of goods f.o.b.	–276	–355	–488
Trade balance	**–178**	**–227**	**–343**
Exports of services	103	129	131
Imports of services	–240	–304	–243
Balance on goods and services	**–315**	**–402**	**–455**
Other income received	6	27	27
Other income paid	–39	–44	–48
Balance on goods, services and income	**–349**	**–418**	**–476**
Current transfers received	169	352	319
Current transfers paid	–18	–18	–23
Current balance	**–198**	**–84**	**–180**
Capital account (net)	61	93	1,323
Direct investment abroad	—	—	14
Direct investment from abroad	8	8	11
Other investment assets	8	–14	–30
Other investment liabilities	–37	–52	–1,199
Net errors and omissions	23	26	87
Overall balance	**–168**	**–23**	**26**

Source: IMF, *International Financial Statistics*.

2007 (US $ million, estimated figures): Exports of goods 176.8; Imports of goods –581.2; *Trade balance* –404.4; Services (net) –207.6; Income (net) –17.2; Current transfers (net) 461.3; *Current balance* –167.9; Capital account 92.3; Financial account 183.4; *Overall balance* 107.9. (Source: IMF, *Rwanda: Fourth Review Under the Three-Year Arrangement Under the Poverty Reduction and Growth Facility and Request for Waiver of Nonobservance of Performance Criterion and Modification of Performance Criteria—Staff Report; Staff Statement; Press Release on the Executive Board Discussion; and Statement by the Executive Director for Rwanda—July 2008*).

External Trade

PRINCIPAL COMMODITIES
(US $ million)

Imports c.i.f.	2005	2006	2007
Food and live animals	34.6	51.9	67.0
Cereals and cereal preparations	19.7	29.4	33.6
Rice	3.6	6.2	7.5
Vegetables and fruit	3.3	1.8	2.2
Sugar, sugar preparations and honey	6.1	12.2	17.9
Crude materials, inedible, except fuels	16.7	22.3	30.6
Textile fibres and their wastes	8.3	10.0	11.5
Mineral fuels, lubricants and related materials	55.7	93.0	60.3
Petroleum, petroleum products and related materials	55.4	92.5	59.8
Animal and vegetable oils, fats and waxes	13.0	17.6	21.5
Chemicals and related products	61.0	69.6	105.5
Medicinal and pharmaceutical products	32.3	34.2	57.1
Basic manufactures	73.9	110.0	133.5
Iron and steel	18.7	32.7	40.7
Machinery and transport equipment	115.5	143.3	213.8
Telecommunications, sound recording and reproducing equipment	15.7	22.1	28.4
Electric machinery, apparatus and appliances, and parts	10.0	13.3	12.5
Road vehicles	42.9	53.5	89.7
Miscellaneous manufactured articles	41.0	44.7	58.3
Total (incl. others)	**415.0**	**557.0**	**696.9**

Exports f.o.b.	2005	2006	2007
Food and live animals	61.3	75.2	67.9
Coffee	37.0	48.0	32.4
Tea	23.3	25.3	30.3
Crude materials, inedible, except fuels	64.6	51.8	90.5
Metalliferous ores and metal scrap	59.3	46.2	83.1
Tin ores and concentrates	43.0	22.4	39.5
Ores and concentrates of other non-ferrous base metals	12.6	11.4	22.1
Ores of molybdenum, niobium and titanium	2.2	12.1	20.8
Total (incl. others)	**146.8**	**137.7**	**183.5**

Source: UN, *International Trade Statistics Yearbook*.

PRINCIPAL TRADING PARTNERS
(US $ million)

Imports	2005	2006	2007
Belgium	42.5	38.2	43.9
China	12.5	20.3	43.2
Denmark	4.9	10.6	4.6
Egypt	5.1	9.2	11.9
France (incl. Monaco)	12.3	11.8	38.8
Germany	17.2	18.4	28.5
India	15.0	20.8	24.8
Italy	3.2	5.3	8.4
Japan	18.2	11.4	14.6
Kenya	74.7	145.2	123.8
Netherlands	7.6	10.4	12.5
Saudi Arabia	22.0	7.3	1.3
South Africa	17.9	15.2	25.4
Switzerland-Liechtenstein	2.3	8.8	10.2
Tanzania	21.5	32.9	47.1
Uganda	48.2	74.0	97.3
UAE	33.0	38.7	54.6
United Kingdom	9.5	9.1	12.1
USA	9.4	14.8	24.9
Total (incl. others)	**415.0**	**557.0**	**696.9**

Exports	2005	2006	2007
Belgium	37.4	22.3	25.6
Burundi	2.1	3.3	7.3
China	2.2	2.7	0.9
France (incl. Monaco)	0.6	0.7	1.2
Germany	2.9	1.0	1.3
Hong Kong	13.7	14.7	23.0
Italy	0.5	0.6	1.3
Kenya	32.5	29.3	34.3
Netherlands	1.0	0.5	0.8
Pakistan	1.0	0.1	0.0
South Africa	0.5	0.2	4.3
Swaziland	0.6	3.6	5.9
Switzerland-Liechtenstein	10.7	12.4	13.3
Tanzania	0.2	0.8	0.5
Uganda	1.7	1.7	3.2
United Kingdom	27.8	29.5	34.4
USA	2.5	5.1	9.5
Total (incl. others)	**146.8**	**137.7**	**183.5**

Source: UN, *International Trade Statistics Yearbook*.

Transport

ROAD TRAFFIC
(estimates, motor vehicles in use at 31 December)

	1995	1996
Passenger cars	12,000	13,000
Lorries and vans	16,000	17,100

Source: IRF, *World Road Statistics*.

RWANDA

CIVIL AVIATION
(traffic on scheduled services)

	1992	1993	1994
Passengers carried ('000)	9	9	9
Passenger-km (million)	2	2	2

Source: UN, *Statistical Yearbook*.

Tourism

(by country of residence)

	2000	2001*
Africa	93,058	99,928
Burundi	20,972	9,455
Congo, Democratic Republic	10,450	28,514
Kenya	2,050	2,243
Tanzania	18,320	18,697
Uganda	38,897	38,472
Americas	2,250	2,785
Europe	6,412	8,395
Belgium	1,866	2,057
Total (incl. others)	104,216	113,185

* January–November.

Tourism receipts (US $ million, excl. passenger transport): 23 in 2000; 25 in 2001; 31 in 2002; 30 in 2003; 44 in 2004.

Source: World Tourism Organization.

Communications Media

	2005	2006	2007
Telephones ('000 main lines in use)	23.6	16.5	23.1
Mobile cellular telephones ('000 subscribers)	219.7	314.2	635.1
Internet users ('000)	50	100	n.a.
Broadband subscribers ('000)	1.2	1.7	2.2

Radio receivers ('000 in use): 601 in 1997.

Facsimile machines (number in use): 900 in 1998.

Daily newspapers: 1 in 1998.

Sources: International Telecommunication Union; UN, *Statistical Yearbook*; UNESCO, *Statistical Yearbook*.

Education

(2004/05, unless otherwise indicated)

	Teachers	Males	Females	Total
Primary*	31,037	1,058,597	1,091,833	2,150,430
Secondary: general	} 7,764 {	68,695	62,444	131,139
technical and vocational		38,048	34,635	72,683
Tertiary	1,817	16,083	10,295	26,378

* 2006/07.

Source: UNESCO Institute for Statistics.

Adult literacy rate (UNESCO estimates): 64.9% (males 71.4%; females 59.8%) in 2000 (Source: UNESCO Institute for Statistics).

Directory

The Constitution

A new Constitution was approved at a national referendum on 26 May 2003 and entered into effect on 4 June. The main provisions are summarized below:

PREAMBLE

The state of Rwanda is an independent sovereign Republic. Fundamental principles are: the struggle against the ideology of genocide and all its manifestations; the eradication of all ethnic and regional divisions; the promotion of national unity; and the equal sharing of power. Human rights and personal liberties are protected. All forms of discrimination are prohibited and punishable by law. The state recognizes a multi-party political system. Political associations are established in accordance with legal requirements, and may operate freely, providing that they comply with democratic and constitutional principles, without harm to national unity, territorial integrity and state security. The formation of political associations on the basis of race, ethnicity, tribal or regional affiliation, sex, religion or any other grounds for discrimination is prohibited.

LEGISLATURE

Legislative power is vested in a bicameral Parliament, comprising a Chamber of Deputies and a Senate. The Chamber of Deputies has 80 deputies, who are elected for a five-year term. In addition to 53 directly elected deputies, 27 seats are allocated, respectively, to two youth representatives, one disabilities representative, and 24 female representatives, who are indirectly elected. The Senate comprises 26 members, of whom 12 are elected by local government councils in the 12 provinces, and two by academic institutions, while the remaining 12 are nominated (eight by the President and four by a regulatory body, the Parties' Forum). Members of the Senate serve for eight years.

PRESIDENT

The President of the Republic is the Head of State, protector of the Constitution, and guarantor of national unity. He is the Commander-in-Chief of the armed forces. Presidential candidates are required to be of Rwandan nationality and aged a minimum of 35 years. The President is elected by universal suffrage for a seven-year term, and is restricted to two mandates. He signs into law presidential decrees in consultation with the Council of Ministers.

GOVERNMENT

The President nominates the Prime Minister, who heads the Council of Ministers. Ministers are proposed by the Prime Minister and appointed by the President.

JUDICIARY

The judiciary is independent and separate from the legislative and executive organs of government. The judicial system is composed of the Supreme Court, the High Court of the Republic, and provincial, district and municipal Tribunals. In addition, there are specialized judicial organs, comprising *gacaca* and military courts. The *gacaca* courts try cases of genocide or other crimes against humanity committed between 1 October 1990 and 31 December 1994. Military courts (the Military Tribunal and the High Military Court) have jurisdiction in military cases. The President and Vice-President of the Supreme Court and the Prosecutor-General are elected by the Senate two months after its installation.

The Government

HEAD OF STATE

President: Maj.-Gen. PAUL KAGAME (took office 22 April 2000; re-elected 25 August 2003).

COUNCIL OF MINISTERS
(April 2009)

Prime Minister: BERNARD MAKUZA.
Minister of Defence: Gen. MARCEL GATSINZI.
Minister of Local Government, Good Governance, Community Development and Social Affairs: PROTAIS MUSONI.
Minister of Internal Security: MUSA FAZIL HERERIMANA.
Minister of Foreign Affairs and Co-operation: ROSEMARY MUSEMINARI.
Minister of Finance and Economic Planning: JAMES MUSONI.
Minister of Agriculture and Animal Resources: CHRISTOPHER BAZIVAMO.
Minister of Education: Dr DAPHROSE GAHAKWA.
Minister of Infrastructure: LINDA BIHIRE.
Minister of Trade and Industry: MONIQUE NSANZABAGANWA.
Minister of Natural Resources: STANISLAS KAMANZI.
Minister of Justice and Attorney-General: THARCISSE KARUGARAMA.
Minister of Public Service and Labour: MUREKEZI ANASTSE.
Minister of Health: Dr RICHARD SEZIBERA.
Minister of Sports and Culture: JOSEPH HABINEZA.
Minister of Youth: PROTAIS MITALI KABANDA.
Minister in the Office of the President: SOLINA NYIRAHABIMANA.
Minister of Cabinet Affairs: CHARLES MURIGANDE.
Minister in the Office of the President, in charge of Science and Technology: Prof. ROMAIN MURENZI.
Minister in the Office of the Prime Minister, in charge of Family and Gender Promotion: Dr JEANNE D'ARC MUJAWAMARIYA.
Minister in the Office of the Prime Minister, in charge of Information: LOUISE MUSHIKIWABO.
Minister of the East African Community: MONIQUE MUKARULIZA.
Minister of State at the Ministry of Local Government, Good Governance, Community Development and Social Affairs, in charge of Community Development and Social Affairs: CHRISTINE NYATANYI.
Minister of State at the Ministry of Education, in charge of Primary and Secondary Education: THEONESTE MUTSINDASHYAKA.
Minister of State at the Ministry of Natural Resources, in charge of the Environment, Water and Mines: VINCENT KAREGA.
Minister of State at the Ministry of Infrastructure, in charge of Energy: ALBERT BUTARE.
Minister of State at the Ministry of Agriculture and Animal Resources, in charge of Agriculture: AGNES KALIBATA.
Minister of State at the Ministry of Trade and Industry, in charge of Industry and Investment Promotion: VINCENT KAREGA.

MINISTRIES

Office of the President: BP 15, Kigali; tel. 59062000; fax 572431; e-mail info@presidency.gov.rw; internet www.presidency.gov.rw.
Office of the Prime Minister: Kigali; tel. 585444; fax 583714; e-mail primature@gov.rw; internet www.primature.gov.rw.
Ministry of Agriculture and Animal Resources: BP 621, Kigali; tel. 585008; fax 585057; internet www.minagri.gov.rw.
Ministry of Defence: Kigali; tel. 577942; fax 576969; internet www.minadef.gov.rw.
Ministry of Education: BP 622, Kigali; tel. 583051; fax 582161; e-mail info@mineduc.gov.rw; internet www.mineduc.gov.rw.
Ministry of Finance and Economic Planning: BP 158, Kigali; tel. 575756; fax 577581; e-mail mfin@rwanda1.com; internet www.minecofin.gov.rw.
Ministry of Foreign Affairs and Co-operation: blvd de la Révolution, BP 179, Kigali; tel. 574522; fax 572904; internet www.minaffet.gov.rw.
Ministry of Gender and the Promotion of Women: Kigali; tel. 577626; fax 577543.
Ministry of Health: BP 84, Kigali; tel. 577458; fax 576853; e-mail info@moh.gov.rw; internet www.moh.gov.rw.
Ministry of Infrastructure: tel. 585503; fax 585755; e-mail webmaster@mininfra.gov.rw; internet www.mininfra.gov.rw.
Ministry of Internal Security: BP 446, Kigali; tel. 586708; e-mail sec_cent@mininter.gov.rw; internet www.mininter.gov.rw.
Ministry of Justice: BP 160, Kigali; tel. 586561; fax 586509; e-mail mjust@minijust.gov.rw; internet www.minijust.gov.rw.
Ministry of Lands, Environment, Forestry, Water and Natural Resources: Kigali; tel. 582628; fax 582629; internet www.minitere.gov.rw.
Ministry of Local Government, Good Governance, Rural Development and Social Affairs: BP 790, Kigali; tel. 585406; fax 582228; e-mail webmaster@minaloc.gov.rw; internet www.minaloc.gov.rw.
Ministry of Public Service and Labour: BP 403, Kigali; tel. 585714; fax 583621; e-mail mifotra@mifotra.gov.rw; internet www.mifotra.gov.rw.
Ministry of Trade and Industry: BP 2378, Kigali; tel. 574725; fax 575465; internet www.minicom.gov.rw.
Ministry of Youth, Sports and Culture: BP 1044, Kigali; tel. 583527; fax 583518; e-mail minicult@rwanda1.com; internet www.mijespoc.gov.rw.

President and Legislature

PRESIDENT

Presidential Election, 25 August 2003

Candidate	Votes	% of votes
Paul Kagame	3,544,777	95.05
Faustin Twagiramungu	134,865	3.62
Jean-Népomuscène Nayinzira	49,634	1.33
Total*	3,729,274	100.00

* Excluding 49,634 invalid votes.

CHAMBER OF DEPUTIES

Speaker: ROSE MUKANTANTABANA.

General Election, 15 September 2008, provisional results

Party	Votes	% of votes	Seats
Front patriotique rwandais*	3,655,956	78.76	42
Parti social-démocrate	609,327	13.12	7
Parti libéral	348,186	7.5	4
Independent	27,848	0.6	—
Total	4,641,317	100.00	80†

* Contested the elections in alliance with the Parti démocrate chrétien, the Parti démocratique islamique, the Union démocratique du peuple rwandais, the Parti de prospérité et de solidarité and the Parti socialiste rwandais.

† In addition to the 53 directly elected deputies, 27 seats are allocated, respectively, to two youth representatives, one disabilities representative and 24 female representatives, who are indirectly elected.

SENATE

Speaker: Dr VINCENT BIRUTA.

The Senate comprises 26 members, of whom 12 are elected by local government councils in the 12 provinces and two by academic institutions, while the remaining 12 are nominated (eight by the President and four by a regulatory body, the Parties' Forum).

Election Commission

Commission électorale nationale du Rwanda: BP 6449, Kigali; tel. 597800; fax 597851; e-mail comelena@rwanda1.com; internet www.comelena.gov.rw; f. 2000; independent; Chair. Prof. CHRYSOLOGUE KARANGWA.

Political Organizations

Under legislation adopted in June 2003, the formation of any political organization based on ethnic groups, religion or sex was prohibited.

Front patriotique rwandais (FPR): internet www.rpfinkotanyi.org; f. 1990; also known as Inkotanyi; comprises mainly Tutsi exiles, but claims multi-ethnic support; commenced armed invasion of Rwanda from Uganda in Oct. 1990; took control of Rwanda in July 1994; Chair. Maj.-Gen. PAUL KAGAME; Vice-Chair. CHRISTOPHE BAZIVAMO; Sec.-Gen. CHARLES MURIGANDE.

Parti démocrate chrétien (PDC): BP 2348, Kigali; tel. 576542; fax 572237; f. 1990; Leader ALFRED MUKEZAMFURA.

Parti démocratique islamique (PDI): Kigali; f. 1991; Leader ANDRÉ BUMAYA HABIB.

RWANDA

Directory

Parti démocratique rwandais (Pader): Kigali; f. 1992; Sec. JEAN NTAGUNGIRA.

Parti libéral (PL): BP 1304, Kigali; tel. 577916; fax 577838; f. 1991; restructured 2003; Chair. PROSPER HIGORO; Sec.-Gen. Dr ODETTE NYIRAMIRIMO.

Parti du progrès et de la concorde (PPC): f. 2003; incl. fmr mems of Mouvement démocratique républicain; Leader Dr CHRISTIAN MARARA.

Parti progressiste de la jeunesse rwandaise (PPJR): Kigali; f. 1991; Leader ANDRÉ HAKIZIMANA.

Parti de prospérité et de solidarité (PSP): Kigali.

Parti républicain rwandais (Parerwa): Kigali; f. 1992; Leader AUGUSTIN MUTAMBA.

Parti social-démocrate (PSD): Kigali; f. 1991 by a breakaway faction of fmr Mouvement révolutionnaire national pour le développement; Leader Dr VINCENT BIRUTA.

Parti socialiste rwandais (PSR): BP 827, Kigali; tel. 576658; fax 83975; f. 1991; workers' rights; Leader Dr MEDARD RUTIJANWA.

Rassemblement travailliste pour la démocratie (RTD): BP 1894, Kigali; tel. 575622; fax 576574; f. 1991; Leader EMMANUEL NIZEYIMANA.

Union démocratique du peuple rwandais (UDPR): Kigali; f. 1992; Leader ADRIEN RANGIRA.

Other political organizations have been formed by exiled Rwandans and operate principally from abroad; these include:

Rassemblement républicain pour la démocratie au Rwanda (RDR): Postbus 3124, 2280 GC, Rijswijk, Netherlands; tel. (31) 623075674; fax (31) 847450374; e-mail info@rdrwanda.org; internet www.rdrwanda.org; f. 1995; prin. opposition party presenting Hutu refugees in exile; Pres. VICTOIRE UMUHOZA INGABIRE.

Union du peuple rwandais (UPR): Brussels, Belgium; f. 1990; Hutu-led; Pres. SILAS MAJYAMBERE; Sec.-Gen. EMMANUEL TWAGILIMANA.

Diplomatic Representation

EMBASSIES IN RWANDA

Belgium: rue Nyarugenge, BP 81, Kigali; tel. 575551; fax 573995; e-mail kigali@diplobel.fed.be; internet www.diplomatie.be/kigali; Ambassador FRANÇOIS ROUX.

Burundi: rue de Ntaruka, BP 714, Kigali; tel. 575010; Ambassador (vacant).

Egypt: BP 1069, Kigali; tel. and fax 82686; e-mail egypt@rwanda1.com; Ambassador AHMED RAMI AWWAD EL HOSENI.

Germany: 8 rue de Bugarama, BP 355, Kigali; tel. 575141; fax 502087; internet www.kigali.diplo.de; Ambassador Dr CHRISTIAN CLAGES.

Holy See: 49 ave Paul VI, BP 261, Kigali (Apostolic Nunciature); tel. 575293; fax 575181; e-mail nuntrw@rwanda1.com; Apostolic Nuncio Most Rev. IVO SCAPOLO (Titular Archbishop of Tagaste).

Kenya: BP 1215, Kigali; tel. 583332; fax 510919; e-mail kigali@mfa.go.ke; Ambassador ALEX KETTER.

Korea, Democratic People's Republic: Kigali; Ambassador KIM PONG GI.

Libya: BP 1152, Kigali; tel. 576470; Secretary of the People's Bureau MOUSTAPHA MASAND EL-GHAILUSHI.

Russia: 19 ave de l'Armée, BP 40, Kigali; tel. 575286; fax 574818; e-mail ambruss@rwandatel1.rwanda1.com; Ambassador MIRGAYAS M. SHIRINSKII.

South Africa: 1370 blvd de l'Umuganda, POB 6563, Kacyiru-Sud, Kigali; tel. 583185; fax 583191; e-mail saemkgl@rwanda1.com; internet www.saembassy-kigali.org.rw; Ambassador EZRA M. SIGWELA.

Uganda: 31 ave de la Paix, BP 656, Kigali; tel. and fax 503537; e-mail embassy@ugandaembassy.rw; internet www.ugandaembassy.rw; Ambassador RICHARD KABONERO.

United Kingdom: Parcelle 1131, Blvd de l'Umuganda, Kacyiru, BP 576, Kigali; tel. 584098; fax 582044; e-mail embassy.kigali@fco.gov.uk; internet ukinrwanda.fco.gov.uk/en; Ambassador NICHOLAS CANNON.

USA: blvd de la Révolution, BP 28, Kigali; tel. 505601; fax 507143; e-mail irckigali@state.gov; internet kigali.usembassy.gov; Ambassador W. STUART SYMINGTON.

Judicial System

The judicial system is composed of the Supreme Court, the High Court of the Republic, and provincial, district and municipal Tribunals. In addition, there are specialized judicial organs, comprising *gacaca* and military courts. The *gacaca* courts were established to try cases of genocide or other crimes against humanity committed between 1 October 1990 and 31 December 1994. Trials for categories of lesser genocide crimes were to be conducted by councils in the communities in which they were committed, with the aim of alleviating pressure on the existing judicial system. Trials under the *gacaca* court system formally commenced on 25 November 2002. Military courts (the Military Tribunal and the High Military Court) have jurisdiction in military cases. The President and Vice-President of the Supreme Court and the Prosecutor-General are elected by the Senate.

Supreme Court

Kigali; tel. 587407.

The Supreme Court comprises five sections: the Department of Courts and Tribunals; the Court of Appeals; the Constitutional Court; the Council of State; and the Revenue Court.

President of the Supreme Court: ALOYSIA CYANZAIRE.

Vice-President: Prof. SAM RUGEGE.

Prosecutor-General: MARTIN NGOGAEU.

Religion

AFRICAN RELIGIONS

About one-half of the population hold traditional beliefs.

CHRISTIANITY

Union des Eglises Rwandaises: BP 79, Kigali; tel. 85825; fax 83554; f. 1963; fmrly Conseil Protestant du Rwanda.

The Roman Catholic Church

Rwanda comprises one archdiocese and eight dioceses. At 31 December 2006 the estimated number of adherents represented about 48.6% of the total population.

Bishops' Conference
Conférence Episcopale du Rwanda, BP 357, Kigali; tel. 575439; fax 578080; e-mail cerwanda@rwanda1.com.

f. 1980; Pres. Rt Rev. ALEXIS HABIYAMBERE (Bishop of Nyundo).

Archbishop of Kigali: Most Rev. THADDÉE NTIHINYURWA, Archevêché, BP 715, Kigali; tel. 575769; fax 572274; e-mail kigarchi@yahoo.fr.

The Anglican Communion

The Church of the Province of Rwanda, established in 1992, has nine dioceses.

Archbishop of the Province and Bishop of Kigali: Most Rev. EMMANUEL MUSABA KOLINI, BP 61, Kigali; tel. and fax 576340; fax 573213; e-mail ek@rwanda1.com.

Provincial Secretary: Rev. EMMANUEL GATERA, BP 61, Kigali; tel. and fax 576340; e-mail egapeer@yahoo.com.

Protestant Churches

Eglise Baptiste: Nyantanga, BP 59, Butare; Pres. Rev. DAVID BAZIGA; Gen. Sec. ELEAZAR ZIHERAMBERE.

Eglise Luthérienne du Rwanda: BP 3099, Kigali; tel. 55110035; fax 519734; e-mail luthchurchlcr@yahoo.com; Bishop GEORGE W. KALIISA; 40,000 mems (2009).

There are about 250,000 other Protestants, including a substantial minority of Seventh-day Adventists.

BAHÁ'Í FAITH

National Spiritual Assembly: BP 652, Kigali; tel. 572550.

ISLAM

There is a small Islamic community.

The Press

REGULATORY AUTHORITY

Haut Conseil de la Presse (HCP): Revolution Ave, POB 6929, Kigali; tel. 570333; fax 570334; e-mail hcp@terramail.rw; internet

RWANDA *Directory*

www.hcp.gov.rw; f. 2002; Pres. DOMINIQUE KAREKEZI PADIRI; Exec. Sec. PATRICE MULAMA.

PERIODICALS

Bulletin Agricole du Rwanda: OCIR—Café, BP 104, Kigali-Gikondo; f. 1968; quarterly; French; Pres. of Editorial Bd Dr AUGUSTIN NZINDUKIYIMANA; circ. 800.

L'Ere de Liberté: BP 1755, Kigali; fortnightly.

Etudes Rwandaises: Université Nationale du Rwanda, Rectorat, BP 56, Butare; tel. 30302; f. 1977; quarterly; pure and applied science, literature, human sciences; French; Pres. of Editorial Bd CHARLES NTAKIRUTINKA; circ. 1,000.

Hobe: BP 761, Kigali; f. 1955; monthly; children's interest; circ. 95,000.

Inkingi: BP 969, Kigali; tel. 577626; fax 577543; monthly.

Inkoramutima: Union des Eglises Rwandaises, BP 79, Kigali; tel. 85825; fax 83554; quarterly; religious; circ. 5,000.

Kinyamateka: 5 blvd de l'OUA, BP 761, Kigali; tel. 576164; e-mail km@rwanda1.com; internet www.kinyamateka.org.rw; f. 1933; fortnightly; economics; circ. 11,000; Dir Fr PIERRE CLAVER NKUSI.

The New Times: BP 4953, Kigali; tel. 08301166; fax 574166; e-mail editorial@newtimes.co.rw; internet www.newtimes.co.rw; f. 1995; daily; English; CEO and Editor-in-Chief JOSEPH BIDERI.

Nouvelles du Rwanda: Université Nationale du Rwanda, BP 117, Butare; every 2 months.

Nyabarongo—Le Canard Déchaîné: BP 1585, Kigali; tel. 576674; monthly.

Le Partisan: BP 1805, Kigali; tel. 573923; fortnightly.

La Patrie—Urwatubyaye: BP 3125, Kigali; tel. 572552; monthly.

La Relève: Office Rwandais d'Information, BP 83, Kigali; tel. 575665; f. 1976; monthly; politics, economics, culture; French; Dir CHRISTOPHE MFIZI; circ. 1,700.

Revue Dialogue: BP 572, Kigali; tel. 574178; f. 1967; bi-monthly; Christian issues; Belgian-owned; circ. 2,500.

Revue Médicale Rwandaise: Ministry of Health, BP 84, Kigali; tel. 576681; f. 1968; quarterly; French.

Revue Pédagogique: Ministry of Education, Science, Technology and Research, BP 622, Kigali; tel. 85697; quarterly; French.

Rwanda Herald: Kigali; f. Oct. 2000; owned by Rwanda Independent Media Group.

Rwanda Libération: BP 398, Kigali; tel. 577710; monthly; Dir and Editor-in-Chief ANTOINE KAPITENI.

Rwanda Renaître: BP 426, Butare; fortnightly.

Rwanda Rushya: BP 83, Kigali; tel. 572276; fortnightly.

Le Tribun du Peuple: BP 1960, Kigali; tel. 82035; bi-monthly; Owner JEAN-PIERRE MUGABE.

Ukuli Gacaca: BP 3170, Kigali; tel. 585239; monthly; Dir CHARLES GAKUMBA.

Umucunguzi: Gisenyi; f. 1998; organ of Palir; Kinyarwanda and French; Chief Editor EMILE NKUMBUYE.

Umuhinzi-Mworozi: OCIR—Thé, BP 1334, Kigali; tel. 514797; fax 514796; f. 1975; monthly; circ. 1,500.

Umusemburo—Le Levain: BP 117, Butare; monthly.

Umuseso: Kigali; independent Kinyarwanda language weekly newspaper; Editor CHARLES KABONERO.

Urunana: Grand Séminaire de Nyakibanda, BP 85, Butare; tel. 530793; e-mail wellamahoro@yahoo.fr; f. 1967; 3 a year; religious; Pres. WELLAS UWAMAHORO; Editor-in-Chief DAMIEN NIYOYIREMERA.

NEWS AGENCIES

Agence Rwandaise d'information (ARP): BP 453, Kigali; tel. 587215; fax 587216; internet www.ari-rna.co.rw; f. 1975.

Office Rwandais d'Information (Orinfor): BP 83, Kigali; tel. 575735; fax 576539; internet www.orinfor.gov.rw; f. 1973; Dir JOSEPH BIDERI.

Publishers

Editions Rwandaises: Caritas Rwanda, BP 124, Kigali; tel. 575786; fax 574254; e-mail caritas1@rwanda1.com; Man. Dir Abbé CYRIAQUE MUNYANSANGA; Editorial Dir ALBERT NAMBAJE.

Implico: BP 721, Kigali; tel. 573771.

Imprimerie de Kabgayi: BP 66, Gitarama; tel. 562252; fax 562345; e-mail imprikabgayi@yahoo.fr; f. 1932; Dir Abbé CYRILLE UWIZEYE.

Imprimerie de Kigali, SARL: 1 blvd de l'Umuganda, BP 956, Kigali; tel. 582032; fax 584047; e-mail impkig@rwandatel1.rwanda1.com; f. 1980; Dir LÉONCE NSENGIMANA.

Imprimerie URWEGO: BP 762, Kigali; tel. 86027; Dir JEAN NSENGIYUNVA.

Pallotti-Presse: BP 863, Kigali; tel. 574084.

GOVERNMENT PUBLISHING HOUSES

Imprimerie Nationale du Rwanda: BP 351, Kigali; tel. 576214; fax 575820; f. 1967; Dir JUVÉNAL NDISANZE.

Régie de l'Imprimerie Scolaire (IMPRISCO): BP 1347, Kigali; tel. 85818; fax 85695; e-mail imprisco@rwandatel1.rwanda1.com; f. 1985; Dir JEAN DE DIEU GAKWANDI.

Broadcasting and Communications

TELECOMMUNICATIONS

MTN Rwandacell: BP 264, MTN Centre, Nyarutarama, Kigali; tel. 586863; fax 586865; internet www.mtn.co.rw; f. 1998; provides mobile cellular telephone services; CEO THEMBA KHUMALO.

Rwanda Utilities Regulatory Agency: POB 7289 Kigali, Rwanda; tel. 584562; fax 584563; e-mail arms@rwanda1.com; internet www.rura.gov.rw; f. 2001; regulatory authority; also responsible for regulation of electricity, water, sanitation, gas and transportation sectors; Dir-Gen DIOGNE MUDENGE.

Rwandatel: ECOBANK Bldg, 7th Floor, ave de La Paix, BP 1332, Kigali; tel. 50326; e-mail info@rwandatel.rw; internet www.rwandatel.rw; national telecommunications service; privatized 2007.

BROADCASTING

Radio

Radio Rwanda: BP 83, Kigali; tel. 575665; fax 576185; f. 1961; state-controlled; daily broadcasts in Kinyarwanda, Swahili, French and English; Dir of Programmes DAVID KABUYE.

Deutsche Welle Relay Station Africa: Kigali; daily broadcasts in German, English, French, Hausa, Swahili, Portuguese and Amharic.

Television

Télévision rwandaise (TVR): Kigali; fax 575024; f. 1992; transmissions reach more than 60% of national territory; broadcasts for 10 hours daily in Kinyarwanda, French and English.

Finance

(cap. = capital; res = reserves; dep. = deposits; m. = million; brs = branches; amounts in Rwanda francs)

BANKING

Central Bank

Banque Nationale du Rwanda: ave Paul VI, BP 531, Kigali; tel. 575282; fax 572551; e-mail info@bnr.rw; internet www.bnr.rw; f. 1964; bank of issue; cap. 2,000m., res 15,600.6m., dep. 183,317.7m. (Dec. 2006); Gov. FRANÇOIS KANIMBA.

Commercial Banks

Following the privatization of two commercial banks, government control of the banking section was reduced from 45% in 2003 to 22% in 2005, although the three largest banks continued to control two-thirds of the system's assets, valued at US $365m. (equivalent to 34% of GDP).

Access Bank (Rwanda) Ltd: 3rd Floor, UTC Bldg, 1232 ave de la Paix, BP 2059, Kigali; tel. 500091; fax 575761; e-mail bancor@rwanda1.com; internet www.bancor.co.rw; f. 1995 as Banque à la Confiance d'Or; fmrly Bancor SA; name changed as above in 2009 when acquired by private investors; 75% owned by Access Bank (Nigeria); cap. and res 3,417.1m., total assets 34,549.3m. (Dec. 2005); Chair. NICHOLAS WATSON.

Banque de Commerce, de Développement et d'Industrie (BCDI): ave de la Paix, BP 3268, Kigali; tel. 574437; fax 573790; e-mail info@bcdi.co.rw; internet www.bcdi.co.rw; cap. and res 3,158.4m., total assets 45,950.9m. (Dec. 2003); Pres. and Dir-Gen. ALFRED KALISA.

Banque Commerciale du Rwanda, SA: BP 354, 11 blvd de la Revolution, Kigali; tel. 595200; fax 573395; e-mail bcr@rwanda1.com; internet www.bcr.co.rw; f. 1963; privatized Sept. 2004; cap. 3,478.8m., res 673,350.0m., dep. 42,040.3m. (Dec. 2005); Chair. Dr NKOSANA MOYO; Man. Dir DAVID KUWANA; 6 brs.

RWANDA

Banque de l'Habitat du Rwanda (CHR): BP 1034, Kigali; tel. 576382; fax 572799; internet bhr@rwanda1.com; internet www.bhr.co.rw; f. 1975 as Caisse Hypothécaire du Rwanda; name changed as above in 2005; 56% state-owned; cap. 778.2m., total assets 6,966.8m. (Dec. 2003); Pres. FRANÇOIS RUTISHASHA; Dir-Gen. GERVAIS NTAGANDA.

Banque de Kigali, SA: 63 ave du Commerce, BP 175, Kigali; tel. 576931; fax 573461; e-mail bkig10@rwanda1.com; internet www.bk.co.rw; f. 1966; cap. 1,500.0m., res 4,330.1m., dep. 59,378.6m. (Dec. 2005); Chair. FRANÇOIS NKURIKIYIMFURA; Gen. Man. THIBAUT DE MAISIÈRES; 7 brs.

Compagnie Générale de Banque: blvd de l'Umuganda, BP 5230, Kigali; tel. 597500; fax 503336; e-mail cogebank@cogebank.com; internet www.cogebank.com; f. 1999; cap. and res 1,210.8m., total assets 7,297.4m. (Dec. 2003); Pres. ANDRÉ KATABARWA; 13 brs.

Fina Bank SA: 20 blvd de la Révolution, BP 331, Kigali; tel. 598600; fax 573486; e-mail info@finabank.co.rw; internet www.finabank.com; f. 1983 as Banque Continentale Africaine (Rwanda); name changed 2005; cap. 1,650m., res 1,028.7m., dep. 22,730m. (Dec. 2006); privatized; Chair. ROBERT BINYOU; Man. Dir STEPHEN CALEY; 5 brs.

Development Banks

Banque Rwandaise de Développement, SA (BRD): blvd de la Révolution, BP 1341, Kigali; tel. 575079; fax 573569; e-mail brd@brd.com.rw; internet www.brd.com.rw; f. 1967; 56% state-owned; cap. and res 4,104.6m., total assets 13,920.7m. (Dec. 2003); Man. Dir JACK NKUSI KAYONGA (acting).

Union des Banques Populaires du Rwanda (Banki z'Abaturage mu Rwanda): BP 1348, Kigali; tel. 573559; fax 573579; e-mail ubpr@rwandatel1.rwanda1.com; internet www.ubpr.co.rw; f. 1975; cap. and res 1,180.5m., total assets 20,433.8m. (Dec. 2002); Pres. INNOCENT KAYITARE; 145 brs.

INSURANCE

Compagnie Générale d'Assurances et de Réassurances au Rwanda (COGEAR): ave de l'Armée, BP 2753, Kigali; tel. 576041; fax 576082; Dir-Gen. ANASTASE MUNYANDAMUTSA.

Société Nationale d'Assurances du Rwanda (SONARWA): BP 1035, Kigali; tel. 572101; fax 572052; e-mail sonarwa@rwandatel1.rwanda1.com; internet www.sonarwa.co.rw; f. 1975; 35% owned by Industrial and General Insurance Co Ltd (Nigeria); cap. 500m.; Pres. FRANÇOIS NGARAMBE; Dir-Gen. HOPE MURERA.

Société Rwandaise d'Assurances, SA (SORAS): BP 924, Kigali; tel. 573716; fax 573362; e-mail sorasinf@rwanda1.com; f. 1984; cap. 1,002m. (2007); Pres. CHARLES MHORANYI; Dir-Gen. MARC RUGENERA.

Trade and Industry

GOVERNMENT AGENCIES

Rwanda Investment and Export Promotion Agency: Kimihurura, ave du Lac Muhazi, POB 6239, Kigali; tel. 510248; fax 510249; e-mail info@rwandainvest.com; internet www.rwandainvest.com; f. 1998 as Rwanda Investment Promotion Agency; Dir-Gen. FRANCIS GATARE.

Rwanda Public Procurement Authority: ave de la Paix, POB 4276, Kigali; tel. 501403; fax 501402; e-mail rppa1@rwanda1.com; internet www.rppa.gov.rw; f. 2008 to replace the Nat. Tender Bd (f. 1998); organizes and monitors general public procurement; Dir AUGUSTUS SEMINEGA.

Rwanda Revenue Authority (RRA): ave du Lac Muhazi, POB 3987, Kimihurura, Kigali; tel. 595520; fax 578488; e-mail cg@rra.gov.rw; internet www.rra.gov.rw; f. 1998 to maximize revenue collection; Commissioner-Gen. MARY BAINE.

DEVELOPMENT ORGANIZATIONS

Coopérative de Promotion de l'Industrie Minière et Artisanale au Rwanda (COOPIMAR): BP 1139, Kigali; tel. 82127; fax 572128; Dir DANY NZARAMBA.

Institut de Recherches Scientifiques et Technologiques (IRST): BP 227, Butare; tel. 530395; fax 530939; e-mail irst@irst.ac.rw; internet www.irst.ac.rw; Dir-Gen. Dr JEAN BAPTISTE NDUWAYEZU.

Institut des Sciences Agronomiques du Rwanda (ISAR): BP 138, Butare; tel. 530642; fax 530644; for the devt of subsistence and export agriculture; Dir MUNYANGANIZI BIKORO; 12 centres.

Office des Cultures Industrielles du Rwanda—Café (OCIR—Café): BP 104, Kigali; tel. 575600; fax 573992; e-mail ocircafe@rwanda1.com; internet ocir.vrsrv.com; f. 1978; devt of coffee and other new agronomic industries; operates a coffee stabilization fund; Dir-Gen. EPHREM NIYONSABA.

Office des Cultures Industrielles du Rwanda—Thé (OCIR—Thé): BP 1344, Kigali; tel. 514797; fax 514796; e-mail ocirthe@rwanda1.com; internet www.ocir-the.co.rw; devt and marketing of tea; Dir CÉLESTIN KAYITARE.

Office National pour le Développement de la Commercialisation des Produits Vivriers et des Produits Animaux (OPROVIA): BP 953, Kigali; tel. 82946; fax 82945; privatization pending; Dir DISMAS SEZIBERA.

Régie d'Exploitation et de Développement des Mines (REDEMI): BP 2195, Kigali; tel. 573632; fax 573625; e-mail ruzredem@yahoo.fr; f. 1988 as Régie des Mines du Rwanda; privatized in 2000; state org. for mining tin, columbo-tantalite and wolfram; Man. Dir JEAN-RUZINDANA MUNANA.

Société de Pyrèthre au Rwanda (SOPYRWA): BP 79, Ruhengeri; tel. and fax 546364; e-mail info@sopyrwa.com; internet www.sopyrwa.com; f. 1978; cultivation and processing of pyrethrum; post-war activities resumed in Oct. 1994; current production estimated at 80% pre-war capacity; Dir SYLVAIN NZABAGAMBA.

INDUSTRIAL ASSOCIATIONS

Association des Industriels du Rwanda: BP 39, Kigali; tel. and fax 575430; Pres. YVES LAFAGE; Exec. Sec. MUGUNGA NDOBA.

Private Sector Federation (PSF): Gikonda Magerwa, POB 319, Kigali; tel. 583541; fax 583574; e-mail info@rpsf.org.rw; internet psf.org.rw; f. 1999 to replace the Chambre de Commerce et d'Industrie de Rwanda; promotes and represents the interests of the Rwandan business community; Dir JEAN BOSCO KABAGEMBE; Sec.-Gen. EMMANUEL HATEGEKA.

UTILITIES

Rwanda Utilities Regulatory Agency: see Telecommunications.

Electrogaz: POB 537, Kigali; tel. 572392; fax 573802; e-mail fgatanazi@electrogaz.co.rw; internet www.electrogaz.co.rw; state-owned water, electricity and gas supplier; Dir JOSEPH MUJENGA.

TRADE UNIONS

Centrale d'Education et de Coopération des Travailleurs pour le Développement/Alliance Coopérative au Rwanda (CECOTRAD/ACORWA): BP 295, Kigali; f. 1984; Pres. ELIE KATABARWA.

Centrale Syndicale des Travailleurs du Rwanda: BP 1645, Kigali; tel. 85658; fax 84012; e-mail cestrav@rwandatel1.rwanda1.com; Sec.-Gen. FRANÇOIS MURANGIRA.

Transport

RAILWAYS

There are no railways in Rwanda, although plans exist for the eventual construction of a line passing through Uganda, Rwanda and Burundi, to connect with the Kigoma–Dar es Salaam line in Tanzania. Rwanda has access by road to the Tanzanian railways system.

ROADS

In 2004 there were an estimated 14,008 km of roads, of which 2,662 km were paved. There are road links with Uganda, Tanzania, Burundi and the Democratic Republic of the Congo. Internal conflict during 1994 caused considerable damage to the road system and the destruction of several important bridges.

Office National des Transports en Commun (ONATRACOM): BP 619, Kigali; tel. 575411; fax 576126; e-mail onatraco@rwanda1.com; internet www.onatracom.rw; f. 1978; Dir-Gen. ESDRAS NKUNDUMUKIZA.

INLAND WATERWAYS

There are services on Lake Kivu between Cyangugu, Gisenyi and Kibuye, including two vessels operated by ONATRACOM.

CIVIL AVIATION

The Kanombe international airport at Kigali can process up to 500,000 passengers annually. There is a second international airport at Kamembe, near the border with the Democratic Republic of the Congo. There are airfields at Butare, Gabiro, Ruhengeri and Gisenyi, servicing internal flights.

Rwandair Express: Centenary House, 2nd Floor, ave de la Paix, BP 7275, Kigali; tel. 503687; fax 503686; e-mail info@rwandair.com; internet www.rwandair.com; f. 1998; privately owned; operates two

RWANDA

passenger aircraft; regional services; CEO Pierre Claver Kabera (acting).

Tourism

Attractions for tourists include the wildlife of the national parks (notably mountain gorillas), Lake Kivu and fine mountain scenery. Since the end of the transitional period in late 2003, the Government has increased efforts to develop the tourism industry. In 1998 there were only an estimated 2,000 foreign visitors to Rwanda, but by 2001 the number of tourist arrivals had increased to 113,185. Total receipts from tourism were estimated at US $44m. in 2004.

Office Rwandais du Tourisme et des Parcs Nationaux (ORTPN): blvd de la Révolution 1, BP 905, Kigali; tel. 576514; fax 576515; e-mail info@rwandatourism.com; internet www.rwandatourism.com; f. 1973; govt agency; Dir-Gen. Rosette Rugamba.

SAINT CHRISTOPHER* AND NEVIS

Introductory Survey

Location, Climate, Language, Religion, Flag, Capital

The Federation of Saint Christopher and Nevis is situated at the northern end of the Leeward Islands chain of the West Indies, with Saba and St Eustatius (both in the Netherlands Antilles) to the north-west, Barbuda to the north-east and Antigua to the south-east. Nevis lies about 3 km (2 miles) to the south-east of Saint Christopher, separated by a narrow strait. The tropical heat, varying between 17°C (62°F) and 33°C (92°F), is tempered by constant sea winds, and annual rainfall averages 1,400 mm (55 ins) on Saint Christopher and 1,220 mm (48 ins) on Nevis. English is the official language. The majority of the population are Christians of the Anglican Communion, and other Christian denominations are represented. The national flag (proportions 2 by 3) comprises two triangles, one of green (with its base at the hoist and its apex in the upper fly) and the other of red (with its base in the fly and its apex in the lower hoist), separated by a broad, yellow-edged black diagonal stripe (from the lower hoist to the upper fly) bearing two five-pointed white stars. The capital is Basseterre, on Saint Christopher.

Recent History

Saint Christopher, settled in 1623, was Britain's first colony in the West Indies. The French settled part of the island a year later, and conflict over possession continued until 1783, when Saint Christopher was eventually ceded to Britain under the Treaty of Versailles. Nevis was settled by the British in 1628, and remained one of the most prosperous of the Antilles until the middle of the 19th century. The island of Anguilla was first joined to the territory in 1816. The St Kitts-Nevis-Anguilla Labour Party, formed in 1932, campaigned for independence for the islands. In 1958 Saint Christopher-Nevis-Anguilla became a member of the West Indies Federation, remaining so until the Federation's dissolution in 1962. A new Constitution, granted to each of the British territories in the Leeward Islands in 1960, provided for government through an Administrator and an enlarged Legislative Council. After an abortive attempt to form a smaller East Caribbean Federation, Saint Christopher-Nevis-Anguilla attained Associated Statehood in February 1967, as part of an arrangement that gave five of the colonies full internal autonomy, while the United Kingdom retained responsibility for defence and foreign relations. The House of Assembly replaced the Legislative Council, the Administrator became Governor, and the Chief Minister, Robert Bradshaw, leader of the Labour Party, became the state's first Premier. Three months later Anguilla rebelled against government from Saint Christopher, and in 1971 reverted to being a de facto British dependency. Anguilla was formally separated from the other islands in 1980.

A general election in 1971 returned Robert Bradshaw to the premiership. In the 1975 election the Labour Party again won the largest number of seats, while the Nevis Reformation Party (NRP) once more took both the Nevis seats. Bradshaw died in May 1978 and was succeeded as Premier by Paul Southwell, hitherto Deputy Premier (and a former Chief Minister). Southwell died in May 1979, and was replaced by the party's leader, Lee L. Moore (hitherto the Attorney-General).

In February 1980 the Labour Party was removed from government for the first time in nearly 30 years: the Labour Party secured four seats in the legislative election, while the People's Action Movement (PAM) took three and the NRP retained the two Nevis seats. Although the Labour Party had won 58% of the popular vote, a PAM-NRP coalition Government was formed under PAM leader Dr Kennedy A. Simmonds. The change of government led to the suspension of a timetable for independence, which had been scheduled for June 1980. In 1982 proposals for a greater degree of autonomy for Nevis and for independence for the whole state were approved by the House of Assembly, although the Labour Party opposed the plans, arguing that the coalition Government did not have a mandate for its independence policy. Disagreements concerning the content of the proposed independence constitution led to civil disturbances in 1982 and 1983. Nevertheless, Saint Christopher and Nevis became an independent state, under a federal Constitution, on 19 September 1983. The Labour Party denounced the special provisions for Nevis in the Constitution (see below) as giving the island a powerful role in government that was disproportionate to its size and population. Elections to the Nevis Island Assembly were held in August, at which the NRP, led by Simeon Daniel, won all five elective seats. Upon independence, Saint Christopher and Nevis became a full member of the Commonwealth (see p. 217).

Early elections to an enlarged National Assembly (now with 11 elective seats) took place in June 1984, at which the ruling PAM-NRP coalition was returned to power. The PAM, which won a clear majority of the popular vote on Saint Christopher, secured six seats, while the NRP no longer held the balance of power in the National Assembly. The three Nevis seats were won by the NRP.

At an election to the Nevis Island Assembly in December 1987, the NRP retained four seats and the Concerned Citizens' Movement (CCM) secured one. At the general election of March 1989, however, the CCM took one of the three Nevis seats from the NRP. The PAM retained its six seats, and the Labour Party its two. Moore resigned as leader of the Labour Party and was succeeded by Denzil Douglas. The electoral success of the coalition Government under the leadership of Simmonds was attributed to its economic policies, and was achieved despite persistent rumours of official connivance in drugs-trafficking activities on the islands.

The CCM secured a majority in the Nevis Island Assembly at an election in June 1992. The CCM leader, Vance Amory, became Premier of the Nevis Island Administration.

At a general election in November 1993 neither the PAM nor the Labour Party managed to secure a majority in the National Assembly. Following the refusal of Amory to form a coalition government with either the PAM or the Labour Party, the Governor-General, Sir Clement Arrindell, invited Simmonds to form a minority government with the support of the NRP. Douglas protested against the decision and appealed for a general strike to support his demands for a further general election. Serious disturbances ensued, and in early December the Governor-General declared a 21-day state of emergency. Meanwhile, Simmonds withdrew from negotiations with Douglas, although an initial agreement to hold a further general election had been reached, in protest at Douglas's premature public revelation of the agreement.

In October 1994 six people were charged in connection with the murder, in Basseterre, of the head of the Saint Christopher special investigations police unit, Jude Matthew, who had been conducting an investigation into the recent disappearances of William Herbert, the country's Permanent Representative to the UN, and Vincent Morris, a son of the Deputy Prime Minister Sidney Morris. Preliminary investigations suggested that these events were connected to the discovery, at the same time as Morris's disappearance, of a large consignment of cocaine in Saint Christopher. In November Sidney Morris resigned, following the arrest of two other sons on charges related to drugs and firearms offences.

A 'forum for national unity' was convened in November 1994, at which representatives of all political parties, church organizations, and tourism, trade, labour and law associations agreed to seek closer political co-operation in the months preceding an early general election, in order to halt the advance of drugs-related crime and the attendant erosion of investor confidence in the islands. None the less, fierce electoral campaigning culminated, in June 1995, in a violent clash between rival PAM and Labour Party supporters, which resulted in a number of serious injuries. The general election, conducted on 3 July, was won decisively by the Labour Party, and Denzil Douglas became Prime Minister. Simmonds was among prominent PAM politicians who lost their seats. Douglas resolved to address promptly the problems of increasingly violent crime and of deteriorating prison conditions. The Prime Minister also announced plans to draft proposals for constitutional reform that would provide for the establishment of separate governments for the two islands.

---

*While this island is officially called Saint Christopher as part of the state, the name is usually abbreviated to St Kitts.

On 1 January 1996 Sir Cuthbert Montroville Sebastian succeeded Sir Clement Arrindell as Governor-General.

In June 1996 Amory announced that the Nevis Island Assembly was initiating proceedings (as detailed in the Constitution—see below) for the secession of Nevis from the federation with Saint Christopher. The announcement was made as plans proceeded for the establishment of a federal government office on Nevis (which Amory considered to be unconstitutional) and as the National Assembly considered a financial services bill that proposed referring all potential investors in Nevis to the federal administration for approval. The Nevis Island Assembly was reported to have interpreted both measures as serious infringements of its administrative rights. Despite the prompt intervention of a number of regional diplomatic initiatives to preserve the federation, a secession bill for Nevis received its preliminary reading in the National Assembly in July. In October the NRP, while supportive of the right to secede, expressed concern at the precipitant nature of Amory's secession timetable, and in November the NRP representative in the National Assembly boycotted a second reading of the bill, forcing a postponement of the debate.

At elections to the Nevis Island Assembly in February 1997 Amory's CCM retained three of the five elective seats, while the NRP retained the remaining two. In October the Nevis Assembly voted unanimously in favour of secession; a referendum on the issue was held in August 1998, in which 61.7%, less than the two-thirds' majority required by the Constitution, voted for autonomy. The leaders of the two islands immediately announced that they would work to improve relations, and Douglas pledged to implement the principal recommendations of a constitutional review commission intended to augment inter-island affairs.

In July 1997 the National Assembly approved legislation to restore a full-time defence force, to include the coastguard, with the principal aim of strengthening the islands' anti-drugs operations. (The Simmonds administration had disbanded the army in 1981.) The Nevis administration and the PAM accused the Labour Government of seeking to enhance its authority by recruiting party loyalists to the force. In July 1998 a convicted murderer was executed—the first implementation of the death penalty in the country since 1985. The Attorney-General, Delano Bart, defended the reintroduction of capital punishment, against criticism from the Roman Catholic Church and the human rights organization Amnesty International, as part of the Government's strategy to reduce crime rates.

In March 1999 a Constitutional Task Force, chaired by former Governor Sir Fred Phillips, began work on the drafting of a new constitution. In August the Task Force submitted its report to the Prime Minister, who appointed a seven-member select committee, comprising representatives of all the major parties, to review its recommendations and to draft proposals for constitutional change.

At a general election in March 2000 the Labour Party won all eight seats available on Saint Christopher (with 65% of the votes cast), gaining the seat previously held by the PAM, which won 36% of the votes. There was no change in the position on Nevis, where the CCM retained its two seats and the NRP its one. In October Lindsay Grant, a lawyer, was elected the new leader of the PAM, replacing Simmonds.

In elections to the Nevis Island Assembly in September 2001 the CCM, led by Amory, strengthened its control of the legislature, gaining a total of four elective seats. The NRP, under the leadership of Joseph Parry, took the remaining one seat.

In October 2002 Douglas, pronouncing on the recurring issue of greater autonomy for Nevis, said that, while he supported the constitutional right of Nevis to secede from the federation, the federal Government was willing to discuss ways to increase the autonomy of the Nevis Island Administration and Assembly. Amory, however, remained convinced that full autonomy and separate membership of the Organisation of Eastern Caribbean States (OECS, see p. 440) would be a better option for Nevis. In January 2004 an OECS Heads of Government meeting urged the Nevis administration to review its intention to campaign for independence in favour of preserving the status quo. The Caribbean Community and Common Market (CARICOM, see p. 206), in 2003, and the US Government, earlier in January 2004, also indicated their support for the existing federation.

The Government sought to address the increasing crime rate on the islands, which was affecting the tourism industry. In February 2001 a curfew for all children under 15 was introduced in an effort to reduce youth crime, and in June the Government sought to persuade the US Navy to relocate one of its bases to Saint Christopher. Douglas stated his hope that the country would derive 'economic, social and financial' benefits from the US presence. The per-head murder rate in 2004 (22 murders per 100,000 people) was the third highest of the CARICOM countries, behind Jamaica and Belize. Although still alarmingly high by international standards, this rate declined to 17 murders per 100,000 people by 2005 before increasing again, to 33 murders per 100,000 people in 2007. On 19 December 2008 a convicted murderer was hanged in Basseterre, the first execution to be carried out in the territory for 10 years. In January 2009 the Government engaged the services of former US Federal Bureau of Investigation chief Mark Mershon to devise a crime reduction strategy.

The Labour Party was returned to office for a third consecutive term at a general election held on 25 October 2004. The incumbent administration, which campaigned on its social development record, won seven of the eight seats on Saint Christopher (with 60.4% of the votes cast—slightly fewer than in 2000); the PAM, whose leader, Lindsay Grant, narrowly failed to get elected, secured the other seat and attracted 37.8% of Saint Christopher's votes. The balance of power remained the same on Nevis, where the CCM secured two seats (with 54% of the votes cast on Nevis) and the NRP secured one seat (and the remaining 46% of the island's votes). Turn-out on Saint Christopher was 62.2%, but was less than 50% overall, reflecting the dissatisfaction of many Nevisians with the current system. Although the voter-registration process was regarded as imperfect, the team of CARICOM observers monitoring the election reported the contest to be generally free and fair.

The NRP emerged from 15 years in opposition to secure a legislative majority at an election to the Nevis Island Assembly, on 10 July 2006. The party captured three of the five elective seats, while the CCM won the remaining two seats. The NRP's leader, Joseph Parry, took office as Nevis Island Premier later in the same month. The issue of secession was again foregrounded, with the participating parties presenting opposing stances on a move towards greater autonomy; the outgoing CCM had campaigned for independence from Saint Christopher, while the NRP indicated a preference for constitutional reform. In January 2007 Prime Minister Douglas encouraged the pursuit of greater collaboration between the two islands; by this time the possibility of an imminent referendum on Nevis, promulgated by the former CCM Government, seemed, once again, to have receded.

Remarks made by Commonwealth and CARICOM observers of the 2004 general election precipitated governmental discussions from that year towards electoral reform in an effort to achieve a more comprehensive and democratic system of voting and greater regulation of campaign practices. Amendments proposed under the 'Road Map for Electoral Reform', submitted to the National Assembly in August 2006, included: the supervision of campaign spending; the consideration of constitutional revisions to provide for more inclusive consultations, particularly with political organizations without parliamentary representation; and a review and possible redefinition of constituency boundaries to achieve more proportional representation of the electorate. It was also suggested that a national registration scheme be conducted to ensure that records of eligible voters were current and accurate, and proposals for a voter identification card initiative, first advanced by the St Kitts-Nevis Labour Party in 2000, were also resurrected. The Electoral Reform Consultative Committee (ERCC) was to conduct a public consultation and submit a report of its findings to the National Advisory Electoral Reform and Boundaries Commission (NAERBC) by 17 November 2006, following which the NAERBC would present its recommendations to a parliamentary committee. However, the initial ERCC report was only received on 1 February 2007, inciting opposition party consternation and public concern about the transparency and effectiveness of the reform process. Nevertheless, the Government began to implement new legislation in early 2008 when the National Identification Card was introduced for registered voters, who were to receive the card on re-registering at an electoral office. The opposition again expressed dissatisfaction, claiming there were a number of discrepancies with the process, including the opportunity for voters to confirm their addresses in multiple constituencies.

Saint Christopher and Nevis is a member of CARICOM and of the OECS. In the late 1980s regional discussions were held on the issue of political unity in the East Caribbean. Saint Christopher and Nevis expressed interest in political unity only if the proposed merger included its Leeward Island neighbours and the Virgin Islands, where an estimated 10,000 Kittitians and Nevisians reside. From January 1990 the OECS agreed to relax restrictions on travel between member states. Moreover, in February 2002 it was agreed, with effect from March, to allow nationals of member states to travel freely within the OECS area and to remain in the territory of any other member state for up to six months. A CARICOM passport, designed to enhance a sense of community and facilitate intra- and extra-regional travel for citizens of participating nations, was launched in January 2005 and implemented by Saint Christopher and Nevis in October of that year. In early 2006 the Prime Minister indicated that Saint Christopher and Nevis would join CARICOM's Caribbean Single Market and Economy (CSME), which was established by six founding member states on 1 January, later in that year. The CSME was intended to enshrine the free movement of goods, services and labour throughout the CARICOM region, although no OECS countries were signatories to the new project from its inauguration. Subsequently, at the 27th CARICOM Heads of Government Conference held in Saint Christopher and Nevis on 6 July, the Government—together with those of five other Caribbean states—signed a declaration of participation in the CSME. The country acceded to the Non-aligned Movement in September 2006, and, in the same month, became the 102nd state delegation to join the International Criminal Court (instituted in The Hague, Netherlands, in July 2002).

In September 2005 Douglas reiterated the Government's commitment to its lucrative diplomatic relationship with Taiwan. Saint Christopher and Nevis, along with Saint Vincent and the Grenadines, remained the only Caribbean countries still to recognize the statehood of Taiwan, which was losing a contest of so-called 'dollar diplomacy' in the region with the People's Republic of China. In January 2008 Saint Christopher and Nevis opened an embassy in Taiwan, the first embassy of a Caribbean country to be located in Asia. However, relations were briefly strained in April when the Government of Saint Christopher and Nevis failed to send a congratulatory message to the winner of Taiwan's presidential election, Ma Ying-jeou, until some two weeks after the ballot. Vice-President Annette Lu Hsu-lien claimed that diplomatic relations were fragile, but the Chargé d'affaires of Saint Christopher and Nevis in Taiwan, Jasmine Huggins, denied the pronouncement and claimed that her message had not been sent earlier owing to personal problems.

Government

Saint Christopher and Nevis is a constitutional monarchy. Executive power is vested in the British monarch, as Head of State, and is exercised locally by the monarch's personal representative, the Governor-General, who acts in accordance with the advice of the Cabinet. Legislative power is vested in Parliament, comprising the monarch and the National Assembly. The National Assembly is composed of the Speaker, three (or, if a nominated member is Attorney-General, four) nominated members, known as Senators (two appointed on the advice of the Premier and one appointed on the advice of the Leader of the Opposition), and 11 elected members (Representatives), who are chosen from single-member constituencies for up to five years by universal adult suffrage. The Cabinet comprises the Prime Minister, who must be able to command the support of the majority of the members of the National Assembly, the Attorney-General (ex officio) and four other ministers. The Prime Minister and the Cabinet are responsible to Parliament.

The Nevis Island legislature comprises the Nevis Island Assembly and the Nevis Island Administration, headed by the British monarch (who is represented on the island by the Deputy Governor-General). It operates similarly to the Saint Christopher and Nevis legislature but has power to secede from the federation, subject to certain restrictions (see Constitution, below).

Defence

The small army was disbanded by the Government in 1981, and its duties were absorbed by the Volunteer Defence Force and a special tactical unit of the police. In July 1997 the National Assembly approved legislation to re-establish a full-time defence force. Coastguard operations were to be brought under military command; the defence force was also to include cadet and reserve forces. Saint Christopher and Nevis participates in the US-sponsored Regional Security System, comprising police, coastguards and army units, which was established by independent East Caribbean states in 1982. Budgetary expenditure on national security in 1998 was approximately EC $23.8m.

Economic Affairs

In 2007, according to estimates by the World Bank, Saint Christopher and Nevis's gross national income (GNI), measured at average 2005–07 prices, was US $470m., equivalent to $9,630 per head (or $13,320 per head on an international purchasing-power parity basis). During 2000–08 the population increased by an average of 1.9% per year, while over the same period, it was estimated, gross domestic product (GDP) per head increased, in real terms, at an average annual rate of 2.5%. Overall GDP increased, in real terms, by an average of 4.4% annually in 2000–08; according to the Eastern Caribbean Central Bank (ECCB, see p. 430), growth was 9.7% in 2008.

Agriculture (including forestry and fishing) contributed 2.2% of GDP in 2008. According to FAO estimates, some 19.0% of the working population were employed in the agriculture sector (including sugar-manufacturing) in 2005. Major crops include coconuts and sea-island cotton, although some vegetables are also exported. Sugar and sugar products had dominated the economy since the 1960s, but the industry, which had accumulated a debt of US $141.5m. (mainly with the St Kitts-Nevis-Anguilla National Bank and the Development Bank of St Kitts and Nevis), closed after the 2005 harvest, and workers at the St Kitts Sugar Manufacturing Corporation received their final payments in March 2006. In spite of a guaranteed European Union (EU, see p. 255) sugar price, which was well above world market levels, the sugar industry had survived only as a result of government subsidies, which were equivalent to 3.5% of GDP in 2001. Large areas formerly used for sugar have been redesignated for tourism, and the Government was expected to make provision for the retraining of sugar industry employees. Other important crops include yams, sweet potatoes, groundnuts, onions, sweet peppers, cabbages, carrots and bananas. In 2004 the Government entered into a partnership with a Canadian corporation to cultivate Stevia—a herb used as a sweetener or dietary supplement. In addition, fishing is an increasingly important commercial activity. According to ECCB estimates, agricultural GDP increased at an average annual rate of 0.2% in 2000–08. The real value of agricultural GDP increased by 8.3% in 2007, but decreased by 2.8% in 2008.

Industry (including mining, manufacturing, construction and public utilities) provided 24.0% of GDP in 2008. Excluding sugar-manufacturing, the sector employed 21.0% of the working population in 1994. The 2007 Cricket World Cup increased the demand for construction services, with much of the public sector work concentrated on the Warner Park sports complex. According to ECCB estimates, the construction sector expanded by 9.0% in 2006. Real industrial GDP increased at an average annual rate of 1.0% in 2000–08. In 2008 the GDP of the sector expanded by an estimated 3.9%.

Manufacturing provided 7.9% of GDP in 2008, and the sector (excluding sugar-manufacturing) employed 7.8% of the working population in 1994. Apart from the sugar industry (the production of raw sugar and ethyl alcohol), the principal manufactured products are garments, electrical components, food products, beer and other beverages. The sector recorded average annual growth of 0.9% during 2000–08. In 2008, according to the ECCB, real manufacturing GDP increased by 3.5%.

The islands are dependent upon imports of fuel and energy (6.8% of total imports in 2007) for their energy requirements. In September 2005 the Government became one of 13 Caribbean administrations to sign the PetroCaribe accord, under which Saint Christopher and Nevis would be allowed to purchase petroleum from Venezuela at reduced prices. In the 2008 budget address the Government signalled its intention to explore alternative energy sources and thereby decrease its dependency on costly fuel imports.

The services sector contributed 73.8% of GDP in 2008, and employed 64.4% of the working population in 1994. Tourism is a major contributor to the economy. In 2002, mainly as a result of a contraction in the US tourism market and hurricane damage to the hotel stock, the number of stop-over arrivals fell by 10.1% and the number of cruise-ship passengers decreased by 34.0%. However, the sector stabilized in 2003, and in 2004 the sector built strongly on its recovery when the total number of visitors increased by 54.9%. Thereafter, however, visitor arrivals declined: by 8.3% in 2005 to 350,737, and by 2.4% in the following year, to 342,165. Nevertheless, during this period the number of stop-over tourists (who traditionally spend more money) increased. The real GDP of the services sector increased at an average annual rate of 4.3% in 2000–08; growth was an estimated 5.9% in 2008.

SAINT CHRISTOPHER AND NEVIS

In 2008 Saint Christopher and Nevis recorded a visible trade deficit of EC $537.98m. and there was a deficit of some $349.70m. on the current account of the balance of payments. The USA was the islands' principal trading partner in 2007, supplying 58.8% of imports and purchasing 86.5% of exports. Trade with the United Kingdom and with other Caribbean states is also important. In 2007 electrical machinery was the country's leading export (accounting for 41.9% of total export revenues in 2007), and the principal imports were machinery and transport equipment, basic manufactures, and food and live animals.

In 2007 the central Government of Saint Christopher and Nevis recorded an estimated budgetary deficit of EC $49.7m., equivalent to 3.6% of GDP. The country's total external debt was estimated to be US $293.1m. at the end of 2006, of which US $290.7m. was long-term public debt. In 2005 the cost of debt-servicing was equivalent to 21.6% of the value of exports of goods and services. Total public sector debt reached an estimated 107% of GDP in December 2007, although since 2005 the Government has negotiated no further loans from external financiers, preferring instead to borrow from an existing overdraft facility. The annual rate of inflation averaged 3.6% in 2000–07; consumer prices increased by 4.5% in 2007. The rate of unemployment, reported to be around 10% in early 2003, is mitigated by mass emigration, particularly from Nevis; remittances from abroad provide an important source of revenue.

Saint Christopher and Nevis is a member of the Caribbean Community and Common Market (CARICOM, see p. 206), and of the Organisation of Eastern Caribbean States (OECS, see p. 440). The ECCB is based in Basseterre. In 2001 a regional stock exchange, the Eastern Caribbean Securities Exchange, opened in Basseterre. Saint Christopher and Nevis is a party to the Cotonou Agreement (see p. 311), the successor agreement to the Lomé Convention, signed in June 2000 between the EU and a group of developing countries.

Successive governments attempted to reduce economic dependence on the cultivation and processing of sugar cane, the traditional industry of the islands, and in 2005 the state-run industry was finally closed and its assets dismantled and recycled. The EU provided grants worth US $14.6m. to Saint Christopher and Nevis to assist with structural adjustment and economic diversification. A further €165m. was pledged in 2007. The total cost of the transition to a non-sugar-producing economy was estimated at some $50m. The most rapidly developing industry has been tourism, which was estimated by the World Travel and Tourism Council (WTTC) to provide some 31.7% of the country's GDP and 32.2% of employment in 2009. In more recent years greater focus has been placed on 'up-market' tourism, with a number of luxury resorts and a marina village scheduled for construction during 2007–09. However, the WTTC estimated that tourism would decline by 10.5% in 2009, and that employment in the sector would contract by 9.6%. The decline was mainly owing to the global economic downturn, but the rising crime rate also acted as a deterrent to any further expansion in tourism. It was hoped that domestic security improvements introduced by the Government in 2009 would restore confidence in the sector. The development of light manufacturing, particularly of electronic components and textiles, has also helped to broaden the islands' economic base. In addition, a small 'offshore' financial sector on Nevis, which, by 2004, had registered 15,000 International Business Companies and 950 trusts, has been developed; the banking and insurance sector was estimated to have grown by 7.5% in 2005. In 2002 the Government committed to sharing tax information with other countries in a bid to improve transparency in the financial sector; however, in 2009 the Organisation for Economic Co-operation and Development included Saint Christopher on its so-called 'grey list' of territories that had failed thus far to implement any substantive change in this area. The Labour Government, campaigning for a fourth term in office in 2009, oversaw five consecutive years of economic growth; nevertheless, GDP was forecast to contract by 1.5% in 2009 as the world-wide recession took hold.

Education

Education is compulsory for 12 years between five and 17 years of age. Primary education begins at the age of five, and lasts for seven years. Secondary education, from the age of 12, generally comprises a first cycle of four years, followed by a second cycle of two years. In 2004/05 enrolment at primary schools included 93.4% of children in the relevant age-group, while comparable enrolment at secondary schools included 86.1% of pupils. There are 30 state, eight private and five denominational schools. There is also a technical college. In September 2000 a privately financed 'offshore' medical college, the Medical University of the Americas, opened in Nevis with 40 students registered. The Ross University School of Veterinary Medicine and the International University of Nursing also operated on Saint Christopher. A Basic Education Project, funded by the Caribbean Development Bank, was in 2003 complemented by a Secondary Education Project, which was to include the construction of a new secondary school and Multi-Purpose Learning Complex in Saddlers. Public expenditure on education was equivalent to 12.7% of total government expenditure in 2003.

Public Holidays

2009: 1 January (New Year's Day), 2 January (Carnival Last Lap), 10 April (Good Friday), 13 April (Easter Monday), 4 May (May Day), 1 June (Whit Monday), 4 August (August Monday), 4 August (Nevis only: Culturama Last Lap), 17 September (Heroes Day), 19 September (Independence Day), 25–26 December (Christmas).

2010: 1 January (New Year's Day), 2 January (Carnival Last Lap), 4 April (Good Friday), 5 April (Easter Monday), 3 May (May Day), 24 May (Whit Monday), 3 August (August Monday), 5 August (Nevis only: Culturama Last Lap), 16 September (Heroes Day), 19 September (Independence Day), 25–26 December (Christmas).

Weights and Measures

The imperial system is used.

Statistical Survey

Source (unless otherwise stated): St Kitts and Nevis Information Service, Government Headquarters, Church St, POB 186, Basseterre; tel. 465-2521; fax 466-4504; e-mail skninfo@caribsurf.com; internet www.stkittsnevis.net.

AREA AND POPULATION

Area (sq km): 269.4 (Saint Christopher 176.1, Nevis 93.3).

Population: 40,618 (males 19,933, females 20,685) at census of 12 May 1991; 45,841 (males 22,784, females 23,057) at census of 14 May 2001. *2008:* 51,298 (mid-year estimate). Sources: UN, *Population and Vital Statistics Report* and Eastern Caribbean Central Bank.

Density (mid-2008): 190.4 per sq km.

Principal Town (estimated population incl. suburbs, mid-2003): Basseterre (capital) 13,262. Source: UN, *World Urbanization Prospects: The 2003 Revision*.

Births and Deaths (2001): Registered live births 803 (birth rate 17.4 per 1,000); Registered deaths 352 (death rate 7.6 per 1,000). *2003:* Crude birth rate 15.6 per 1,000; Crude death rate 7.6 per 1,000 (Source: Caribbean Development Bank, *Social and Economic Indicators*).

Life Expectancy (years at birth, WHO estimates): 71.2 (males 69.5; females 72.9) in 2006. Source: WHO, *World Health Statistics*.

Employment (labour force survey, 1994): Sugar cane production/manufacturing 1,525; Non-sugar agriculture 914; Mining and quarrying 29; Manufacturing (excl. sugar) 1,290; Electricity, gas and water 416; Construction 1,745; Trade (except tourism) 1,249; Tourism 2,118; Transport and communications 534; Business and general services 3,708; Government services 2,738; Other statutory bodies 342; *Total* 16,608 (Saint Christopher 12,516, Nevis 4,092). Source: IMF, *St Kitts and Nevis: Recent Economic Developments* (August 1997).

SAINT CHRISTOPHER AND NEVIS

HEALTH AND WELFARE
Key Indicators

Total Fertility Rate (children per woman, 2006): 2.3.

Under-5 Mortality Rate (per 1,000 live births, 2006): 19.

Physicians (per 1,000 head, 1997): 1.19.

Hospital Beds (per 1,000 head, 2005): 5.5.

Health Expenditure (2006): US $ per head (PPP): 654.

Health Expenditure (2006): % of GDP: 5.8.

Health Expenditure (2006): public (% of total): 61.5.

Access to Water (% of persons, 2006): 99.

Access to Sanitation (% of persons, 2006): 96.

Human Development Index (2006): ranking: 60.

Human Development Index (2006): value: 0.831.

For sources and definitions, see explanatory note on p. vi.

AGRICULTURE, ETC.

Principal Crops ('000 metric tons, 2007, FAO estimates): Sugar cane 105.0; Coconuts 1.0. *Aggregate Production* ('000 metric tons, may include official, semi-official or estimated data): Roots and tubers 1.1; Vegetables (incl. melons) 0.8; Fruits (excl. melons) 1.3.

Livestock ('000 head, 2007, FAO estimates): Cattle 4.9; Sheep 12.6; Goats 16.0; Pigs 4.0.

Livestock Products ('000 metric tons, 2007, FAO estimates): Pig meat 0.1; Chicken meat 0.2; Hen eggs 0.2.

Fishing (metric tons, live weight, 2006, FAO estimates): Groupers 25; Snappers 70; Grunts, sweetlips 15; Goatfishes, red mullets 80; Parrotfishes 45; Surgeonfishes 40; Triggerfishes, durgons 20; Caribbean spiny lobster 40; Stromboid conchs 90; *Total catch* (incl. others) 450.

Source: FAO.

INDUSTRY

Production: Raw sugar 10,700 metric tons in 2005; Electric energy 226.0 million kWh in 2008. Sources: IMF, *St Kitts and Nevis: Statistical Appendix* (April 2008) and Eastern Caribbean Central Bank.

FINANCE

Currency and Exchange Rates: 100 cents = 1 Eastern Caribbean dollar (EC $). *Sterling, US Dollar and Euro Equivalents* (31 December 2008): £1 sterling = EC $3.936; US $1 = EC $2.700; €1 = EC $3.758; EC $100 = £25.41 = US $26.61 = €23.88. *Exchange Rate:* Fixed at US $1 = EC $2.70 since July 1976.

Budget (EC $ million, 2007, estimates): *Revenue:* Revenue from taxation 319.9 (Taxes on income 96.1, Taxes on property 7.6, Taxes on domestic goods and services 50.0, Taxes on international trade and transactions 166.2); Other current revenue 91.3; Capital revenue 4.1; Foreign grants 20.0; Total 435.3. *Expenditure:* Current expenditure 385.7 (Personal emoluments and wages 148.1, Goods and services 94.5, Interest payments 83.7, Transfers and subsidies 59.3); Capital expenditure and net lending 99.3; Total 485.0. *2008* (EC $ million): Total recurrent revenue 543.17; Total recurrent expenditure 542.02.

International Reserves (US $ million at 31 December 2007): Reserve position in IMF 0.13; Foreign exchange 95.66; Total 95.79. Source: IMF, *International Financial Statistics*.

Money Supply (EC $ million at 31 December 2007): Currency outside banks 56.19; Demand deposits at deposit money banks 206.53; Total money 262.72. Source: IMF, *International Financial Statistics*.

Cost of Living (Consumer Price Index; base: 2000 = 100): All items 112.7 in 2005; 122.3 in 2006; 127.8 in 2007. Source: IMF, *International Financial Statistics*.

Gross Domestic Product (EC $ million at constant 1990 prices): 799.01 in 2006; 830.58 in 2007; 911.28 in 2008. Source: Eastern Caribbean Central Bank.

Expenditure on the Gross Domestic Product (EC $ million at current prices, 2008): Government final consumption expenditure 279.52; Private final consumption expenditure 1,048.00; Gross capital formation 609.84; *Total domestic expenditure* 1,937.36; Exports of goods and services 600.59; *Less* Imports of goods and services 1,047.57; *GDP at market prices* 1,490.35. Source: Eastern Caribbean Central Bank.

Gross Domestic Product by Economic Activity (EC $ million at current prices, 2008): Agriculture, hunting, forestry and fishing 30.73; Mining and quarrying 3.46; Manufacturing 108.83; Electricity and water 31.75; Construction 185.61; Wholesale and retail trade 156.80; Restaurants and hotels 95.43; Transport 136.35; Communications 63.80; Finance and insurance 253.09; Real estate and housing 29.15; Government services 227.69; Other community, social and personal services 52.50; *Sub-total* 1,375.19; *Less* Financial intermediation services indirectly measured 143.27; *Total in basic prices* 1,231.92; Taxes, less subsidies, on products 258.43; *GDP at market prices* 1,490.35. Source: Eastern Caribbean Central Bank.

Balance of Payments (EC $ million, 2008): *Trade balance* −537.98; Services (net) 188.75; *Balance on goods and services* −349.23; Other income received (net) −89.46; *Balance on goods, services and income* −438.69; Current transfers received (net) 88.99; *Current balance* −349.70; Capital account (net) 24.46; Direct investment (net) 236.68; Portfolio investment (net) 42.22; Other investment (net) 10.32; Net errors and omissions 22.05; *Overall balance* −13.97. Source: Eastern Caribbean Central Bank.

EXTERNAL TRADE

Principal Commodities (US $ million, 2007): *Imports c.i.f.:* Food and live animals 42.7; Mineral fuels, lubricants, etc. 18.6 (Refined petroleum products 16.3); Chemicals 19.0; Basic manufactures 49.3 (Iron and steel manufactures 8.3); Machinery and transport equipment 84.6 (Road vehicles 18.3); Total (incl. others) 271.7. *Exports f.o.b.:* Food and live animals 0.7; Beverages and tobacco 2.6; Basic manufactures 0.8 (Metal manufactures 0.6); Machinery and transport equipment 28.5 (Electrical machinery 14.3); Miscellaneous manufactures 1.3 (Printed matter 0.4); Total (incl. others) 34.1. Source: UN, *International Trade Statistics Yearbook*.

Principal Trading Partners (US $ million, 2007): *Imports:* Antigua and Barbuda 2.1; Barbados 4.4; Canada 8.2; China, People's Rep. 3.5; Denmark 4.2; Dominican Republic 4.6; France 2.0; Germany 4.7; Grenada 1.5; Jamaica 2.0; Japan 10.1; Netherlands Antilles 3.2; Trinidad and Tobago 29.3; United Kingdom 9.7; USA 159.8; Total (incl. others) 271.7. *Exports* (excl. re-exports): Antigua and Barbuda 0.6; Dominica 0.4; Netherlands Antilles 0.5; Trinidad and Tobago 0.2; United Kingdom 0.8; USA 29.5; Total (incl. others) 34.1. Source: UN, *International Trade Statistics Yearbook*.

TRANSPORT

Road Traffic (registered motor vehicles): 11,352 in 1998; 12,432 in 1999; 12,917 in 2000.

Shipping: *Arrivals* (2000): 1,981 vessels. *International Sea-borne Freight Traffic* ('000 metric tons, 2000): Goods loaded 24.7; Goods unloaded 234.2. *Merchant Fleet* (vessels registered at 31 December 2007): Number 217; Total displacement 662,032 grt (Source: Lloyd's Register-Fairplay, *World Fleet Statistics*).

Civil Aviation (aircraft arrivals): 24,800 in 1998; 23,500 in 1999; 19,400 in 2000.

TOURISM

Visitor Arrivals: 382,290 (117,638 stop-over visitors, 3,045 excursionists, 7,072 yacht passengers, 254,535 cruise ship passengers) in 2004; 350,737 (127,025 stop-over visitors, 3,471 excursionists, 6,023 yacht passengers, 214,218 cruise ship passengers) in 2005 (estimate); 342,165 (132,321 stop-over visitors, 3,893 excursionists, 2,876 yacht passengers, 203,075 cruise ship passengers) in 2006 (estimate). *2008:* Cruise ship passengers 276,490; Stop-over visitors 120,280.

Tourism Receipts (EC $ million): 327.1 in 2005; 329.7 in 2006; 286.9 in 2007 (provisional).

Source: Eastern Caribbean Central Bank.

COMMUNICATIONS MEDIA

Radio Receivers ('000 in use, 1997): 28.

Television Receivers ('000 in use, 1999): 10.

Telephones ('000 main lines in use, 2005): 25.

Facsimile Machines (1996): 450.

Mobile Cellular Telephones (subscribers, 2004): 10,000.

Personal Computers (2004): 11,000.

Internet Users (2004): 10,000.

Broadband Subscribers (2004): 500.

Non-daily Newspapers (2000): Titles 4; Circulation 34,000 (1996).

Sources: mainly UNESCO, *Statistical Yearbook*; UN, *Statistical Yearbook*; International Telecommunication Union.

SAINT CHRISTOPHER AND NEVIS

EDUCATION

Pre-primary (2003/04 unless otherwise indicated): 77 schools; 315 teachers (2004/05); 1,910 pupils.

Primary (2004/05 unless otherwise indicated): 23 schools (2003/04); 360 teachers; 6,350 pupils.

Secondary (2004/05 unless otherwise indicated): 7 schools (2003/04); 397 teachers; 3,939 pupils.

Tertiary (2003/04): 1 institution; 79 teachers; 751 students.

Adult Literacy Rate: 97.8% in 2004 (Source: UN Development Programme, *Human Development Report*).

Source: mostly UNESCO Institute for Statistics.

Directory

The Constitution

The Constitution of the Federation of Saint Christopher and Nevis took effect from 19 September 1983, when the territory achieved independence. Its main provisions are summarized below:

FUNDAMENTAL RIGHTS AND FREEDOMS

Regardless of race, place of origin, political opinion, colour, creed or sex, but subject to respect for the rights and freedoms of others and for the public interest, every person in Saint Christopher and Nevis is entitled to the rights of life, liberty, security of person, equality before the law and the protection of the law. Freedom of conscience, of expression, of assembly and of association is guaranteed, and the inviolability of personal privacy, family life and property is maintained. Protection is afforded from slavery, forced labour, torture and inhuman treatment.

THE GOVERNOR-GENERAL

The Governor-General is appointed by the British monarch, whom the Governor-General represents locally. The Governor-General must be a citizen of Saint Christopher and Nevis, and must appoint a Deputy Governor-General, in accordance with the wishes of the Premier of Nevis, to represent the Governor-General on that island.

PARLIAMENT

Parliament consists of the British monarch, represented by the Governor-General, and the National Assembly, which includes a Speaker, three (or, if a nominated member is Attorney-General, four) nominated members (Senators) and 11 elected members (Representatives). Senators are appointed by the Governor-General: one on the advice of the Leader of the Opposition, and the other two in accordance with the wishes of the Prime Minister. The Representatives are elected by universal suffrage, one from each of the 11 single-member constituencies.

Every citizen over the age of 18 years is eligible to vote. Parliament may alter any of the provisions of the Constitution.

THE EXECUTIVE

Executive authority is vested in the British monarch, as Head of State, and is exercised on the monarch's behalf by the Governor-General, either directly or through subordinate officers. The Governor-General appoints as Prime Minister that Representative who, in the Governor-General's opinion, appears to be best able to command the support of the majority of the Representatives. Other ministerial appointments are made by the Governor-General, in consultation with the Prime Minister, from among the members of the National Assembly. The Governor-General may remove the Prime Minister from office if a resolution of 'no confidence' in the Government is passed by the National Assembly and if the Prime Minister does not resign within three days or advise the Governor-General to dissolve Parliament.

The Cabinet consists of the Prime Minister and other Ministers. When the office of Attorney-General is a public office, the Attorney-General shall, by virtue of holding that office, be a member of the Cabinet in addition to the other Ministers. The Governor-General appoints as Leader of the Opposition in the National Assembly that Representative who, in the Governor-General's opinion, appears to be best able to command the support of the majority of the Representatives who do not support the Government.

CITIZENSHIP

All persons born in Saint Christopher and Nevis before independence who, immediately before independence, were citizens of the United Kingdom and Colonies automatically become citizens of Saint Christopher and Nevis. All persons born in Saint Christopher and Nevis after independence automatically acquire citizenship, as do those born outside Saint Christopher and Nevis after independence to a parent possessing citizenship. There are provisions for the acquisition of citizenship by those to whom it is not automatically granted.

THE ISLAND OF NEVIS

There is a Legislature for the island of Nevis, which consists of the British monarch, represented by the Governor-General, and the Nevis Island Assembly. The Assembly consists of three nominated members (one appointed by the Governor-General in accordance with the advice of the Leader of the Opposition in the Assembly, and two appointed by the Governor-General in accordance with the advice of the Premier) and such number of elected members as corresponds directly with the number of electoral districts on the island.

There is a Nevis Island Administration, consisting of a premier and two other members who are appointed by the Governor-General. The Governor-General appoints the Premier as the person who, in the Governor-General's opinion, is best able to command the support of the majority of the elected members of the Assembly. The other members of the Administration are appointed by the Governor-General, acting in accordance with the wishes of the Premier. The Administration has exclusive responsibility for administration within the island of Nevis, in accordance with the provisions of any relevant laws.

The Nevis Island Legislature may provide that the island of Nevis is to cease to belong to the Federation of Saint Christopher and Nevis, in which case this Constitution would cease to have effect in the island of Nevis. Provisions for the possible secession of the island contain the following requirements: that the island must give full and detailed proposals for the future Constitution of the island of Nevis, which must be laid before the Assembly for a period of at least six months prior to the proposed date of secession; and that a two-thirds' majority has been gained in a referendum, which is to be held after the Assembly has approved the motion.

The Government

HEAD OF STATE

Monarch: HM Queen Elizabeth II.

Governor-General: Sir Cuthbert Montroville Sebastian (took office 1 January 1996).

CABINET
(April 2009)

Prime Minister and Minister of Foreign Affairs, National Security, Immigration, Sustainable Development, Tourism, Culture and Sport: Dr Denzil Llewellyn Douglas.

Deputy Prime Minister and Minister of Education, Youth Affairs, Labour, Social Security, and Information and Technology: Sam Terrence Condor.

Minister of Public Works, Utilities, Transport and Postal Services: Dr Earl Asim Martin.

Minister of Health, Gender Affairs, and Social and Community Development: Rupert Emmanuel Herbert.

Minister of Finance, International Trade, Industry, Commerce and Consumer Affairs: Timothy Sylvester Harris.

Minister of Housing, Agriculture and Fisheries: Cedric Roy Liburd.

Attorney-General and Minister of Justice and of Legal Affairs: Dennis Merchant.

Minister of State in the Ministry of Education, Youth Affairs, Labour, Social Security, and Information and Technology: Nigel Alexis Carty.

Minister of State in the Ministry of Tourism, Culture and Sport: Richard Oliver Skerritt.

MINISTRIES

Office of the Governor-General: Government House, Basseterre; tel. 465-2315.

SAINT CHRISTOPHER AND NEVIS

Government Headquarters: Church St, POB 186, Basseterre; tel. 465-2521; fax 466-4505; e-mail infocom@sisterisles.kn; internet www.gov.kn.

Prime Minister's Office: Government Headquarters, Church St, POB 186, Basseterre; tel. 465-9698; fax 465-9997; e-mail sknpmpressec@cuopm.com; internet www.cuopm.org.

Attorney-General's Office and Ministry of Legal Affairs: Church St, POB 164, Basseterre; tel. 465-2521; fax 465-5040; e-mail attorneygeneral@gov.kn.

Ministry of Education and Youth Affairs: Church St, POB 333, Basseterre; tel. 465-2521.

Ministry of Finance, International Trade, Industry, Commerce and Consumer Affairs: Church St, POB 186, Basseterre; tel. 465-2521; fax 465-0198; e-mail adminskbmof@caribsurf.com; internet gip.gov.kn/mp.asp?mp=7.

Ministry of Foreign Affairs: Church St, POB 186, Basseterre; tel. 465-2521; fax 465-5202; e-mail foreigna@sisterisles.kn; internet gip.gov.kn/mp.asp?mp=6.

Ministry of Health, Gender Affairs, and Social and Community Development: Church St, POB 186, Basseterre; tel. 465-2521.

Ministry of Housing, Agriculture and Fisheries: East Park Range, Basseterre; tel. 466-4701; fax 466-4702; e-mail nhcorp@hotmail.com.

Ministry of Justice and Legal Affairs: Church St, Basetere; tel. 465-2521; fax 466-1896.

Ministry of Labour, Social Security, and Information and Technology: Church St, POB 186, Basseterre.

Ministry of National Security and Immigration: Pelican Mall, Basseterre; tel. 465-2521; fax 466-1896; e-mail natsec@caribsurf.com.

Ministry of Public Works, Utilities, Transport and Postal Services: Needsmust, Basseterre; tel. 465-2521; fax 465-5501.

Ministry of Sustainable Development, Tourism, Culture and Sport: POB 878, Port Zante, Basseterre; tel. 465-2521; fax 465-7075; e-mail culture@sisterisles.kn.

NEVIS ISLAND ADMINISTRATION

Premier: JOSEPH W. PARRY.

There are also two appointed members.

Administrative Centre: Main St, POB 689, Charlestown, Nevis; tel. 469-1469; fax 469-0039; e-mail nevfin@caribsurf.com; internet www.gisnevis.com.

Legislature

NATIONAL ASSEMBLY

Speaker: CURTIS MARTIN.

Elected members: 11. Nominated members: 3. Ex officio members: 1.

Election, 25 October 2004

Party	% of votes	Seats
St Kitts-Nevis Labour Party	50.6	7
Concerned Citizens' Movement	8.8	2
People's Action Movement	31.7	1
Nevis Reformation Party	7.5	1
Total (incl. others)	100.0	11

NEVIS ISLAND ASSEMBLY

Elected members: 5. Nominated members: 3.

Elections to the Nevis Island Assembly took place in July 2006. The Nevis Reformation Party took three seats and the Concerned Citizens' Movement secured the remaining two seats.

Political Organizations

Concerned Citizens' Movement (CCM): Charlestown, Nevis; tel. 469-3519; e-mail renaissance_trust@yahoo.com; internet myccmparty.com; Leader VANCE W. AMORY.

Nevis Reformation Party (NRP): Government Rd, POB 480, Charlestown, Nevis; tel. 469-0630; e-mail JosephParry@VoteNRP.com; internet www.votenrp.com; f. 1970; Leader JOSEPH W. PARRY; Sec. DWIGHT COZIER.

People's Action Movement (PAM): POB 1294, Basseterre; tel. 466-2726; fax 466-3854; e-mail pamdemocrat@pamdemocrat.org; internet www.pamdemocrat.org/party; f. 1965; Political Leader LINDSAY GRANT; Deputy Leaders SHAWN RICHARDS, EUGENE HAMILTON.

St Kitts-Nevis Labour Party (SKNLP): Masses House, Church St, POB 239, Basseterre; tel. 465-5347; fax 465-8328; e-mail wanda.connor@sknlabourparty.com; internet www.sknlabourparty.org; f. 1932; socialist party; Chair. Dr TIMOTHY HARRIS; Leader Dr DENZIL LLEWELLYN DOUGLAS.

Diplomatic Representation

EMBASSIES IN SAINT CHRISTOPHER AND NEVIS

China (Taiwan): Taylor's Range, POB 119, Basseterre; tel. 465-2421; fax 465-7921; e-mail rocemb@caribsurf.com; Ambassador RONG-CHUEN WU.

Cuba: 34 Bladen Housing Devt, POB 600, Basseterre; tel. 466-3374; fax 465-8072; e-mail cubask@caribsurf.com; Ambassador ANA MARÍA GONZÁLEZ SUÁREZ.

Venezuela: Delisle St, POB 435, Basseterre; tel. 465-1078; fax 465-5452; e-mail frontado@caribsurf.com; Chargé d'affaires a.i. NELSON MANUEL CAMACHO ROSALES.

Diplomatic relations with other countries are maintained at consular level, or with ambassadors and high commissioners resident in other countries of the region, or directly with the other country.

Judicial System

Justice is administered by the Eastern Caribbean Supreme Court (ECSC), based in Saint Lucia and consisting of a Court of Appeal and a High Court. Two of the 16 puisne judges of the High Court are responsible for Saint Christopher and Nevis and preside over the Court of Summary Jurisdiction. One of two ECSC Masters, chiefly responsible for procedural and interlocutory matters, is also resident in the territory. The Magistrates' Courts deal with summary offences and civil offences involving sums of not more than EC $5,000. Saint Christopher and Nevis acceded to the International Criminal Court, administered in The Hague, Netherlands, in September 2006. In 2008 the death penalty was employed in Saint Christopher and Nevis for the first time since 2000.

Puisne Judges: FRANCIS BELLE, IANTHEA LEIGERTWOOD-OCTAVE (acting).

Master: PEARLETTA LANNS.

Registrar: CLAUDETTE JENKINS.

Magistrates' Office: Losack Rd, Basseterre; tel. 465-2170.

Religion

CHRISTIANITY

St Kitts Christian Council: Victoria Rd, POB 48, Basseterre; tel. 465-2167; e-mail stgeorgessk@hotmail.com; Chair. Archdeacon VALENTINE HODGE.

The Anglican Communion

Anglicans in Saint Christopher and Nevis are adherents of the Church in the Province of the West Indies. The islands form part of the diocese of the North Eastern Caribbean and Aruba. The Bishop is resident in The Valley, Anguilla.

The Roman Catholic Church

The diocese of Saint John's-Basseterre, suffragan to the archdiocese of Castries (Saint Lucia), includes Anguilla, Antigua and Barbuda, the British Virgin Islands, Montserrat and Saint Christopher and Nevis. At 31 December 2006 the diocese contained an estimated 15,677 adherents. The Bishop participates in the Antilles Episcopal Conference (currently based in Port of Spain, Trinidad and Tobago).

Bishop of Saint John's-Basseterre: (vacant), POB 836, St John's, Antigua; e-mail djr@candw.ag.

Other Churches

There are also communities of Methodists, Moravians, Seventh-day Adventists, Baptists, Pilgrim Holiness, the Church of God, Apostolic Faith and Plymouth Brethren.

The Press

The Democrat: Cayon St, POB 30, Basseterre; tel. 466-2091; fax 465-0857; e-mail thedemocrat@caribsurf.com; internet www

.pamdemocrat.org/Newspaper; f. 1948; weekly (Saturdays); organ of PAM; Man. Editor DENIECE ALLEYNE; circ. 3,000.

The Labour Spokesman: Masses House, Church St, POB 239, Basseterre; tel. 465-2229; fax 466-9866; e-mail sknunion@sisterisles.kn; internet www.labourspokesman.com; f. 1957; Wednesdays and Saturdays; organ of St Kitts-Nevis Trades and Labour Union; Editor DAWUD ST LLOYD BYRON; Man. WALFORD GUMBS; circ. 6,000.

The Leewards Times: Pinneys Industrial Site, POB 146, Nevis; tel. 469-1049; fax 469-0662; e-mail hbramble@caribsurf.com; internet www.leewardstimes.net; weekly (Fridays); Editor HOWELL BRAMBLE.

The St Kitts and Nevis Observer: Cayon St, POB 657, Basseterre; tel. 466-4994; fax 466-4995; e-mail observsk@caribsurf.com; internet www.stkittsnevisobserver.com; weekly (Fridays); independent; Publr and Editor-in-Chief KENNETH WILLIAMS.

Publishers

Caribbean Publishing Co (St Kitts-Nevis) Ltd: Dr William Herbert Complex, Frigate Bay Rd, POB 745, Basseterre; tel. 465-5178; fax 466-0307; e-mail sbrisban@caribpub.com; internet www.caribpub.com.

MacPennies Publishing Co: 10A Cayon St East, POB 318, Basseterre; tel. 465-2274; fax 465-8668; e-mail mcpenltd@macpennies.com; internet www.macpennies.com; f. 1969.

St Kitts-Nevis Publishing Association Ltd: 1 Observer Plaza, Observer Dr., POB 510, Charlestown, Nevis; tel. 469-5907; fax 469-5891; e-mail observnv@sisterisles.kn; internet www.thestkittsnevisobserver.com; f. 1994; Publr and Editor-in-Chief KENNETH A. WILLIAMS.

Broadcasting and Communications

TELECOMMUNICATIONS

Regulatory Authority

Eastern Caribbean Telecommunications Authority: e-mail ectel@ectel.int; internet www.ectel.int; f. 2000; based in Castries, Saint Lucia; regulates telecommunications in Saint Christopher and Nevis, Dominica, Grenada, Saint Lucia and Saint Vincent and the Grenadines; Dir (Saint Christopher and Nevis) BARCHELLE CROOKE.

Service Providers

Digicel St Kitts and Nevis: Wireless Ventures (Saint Kitts and Nevis) Ltd, The Cable Bldg, cnr Cayon and New Sts, POB 1033, Basseterre; tel. 466-4000; fax 465-4193; e-mail customercarestkittsandnevis@digicelgroup.com; internet www.digicelstkittsandnevis.com; acquired Cingular Wireless' Caribbean operations and licences in 2005; owned by an Irish consortium; Chair. DENIS O'BRIEN; Eastern Caribbean CEO KEVIN WHITE.

LIME (St Kitts and Nevis): Cayon St, POB 86, Basseterre; tel. 465-1000; fax 465-1106; internet www.time4lime.com; f. 1985 as St Kitts and Nevis Telecommunications Co Ltd (SKANTEL); fmrly Cable & Wireless St Kitts and Nevis; name changed as above 2008; CEO RICHARD DODD.

BROADCASTING

Radio

Radio One (SKNBC): Bakers Corner, POB 1773, Basseterre; tel. 466-0941; fax 465-0406; e-mail radio1941fm@yahoo.com; internet www.radioone941fm.com; owned by St Kitts & Nevis Broadcasting Corpn; music and commentary; Man. Dir GUS WILLIAMS.

Radio Paradise: Bath Plains, POB 508, Nevis; tel. 469-1994; fax 469-1642; e-mail info@radioparadiseonline.com; internet www.radioparadiseonline.com; owned by Trinity Broadcasting Network (USA); Christian; Man. ANDRE GILBERT.

Sugar City Rock FM: Greenlands, Basseterre; tel. 466-1113; e-mail sugarcityrock@hotmail.com; internet www.sugarcityrock.com; Gen. Man. VAL THOMAS.

Voice of Nevis (VON) Radio 895 AM: Bath Plain, Bath Village, POB 195, Charlestown, Nevis; tel. 469-1616; fax 469-5329; e-mail gmanager@vonradio.com; internet www.vonradio.com; f. 1988; owned by Nevis Broadcasting Co Ltd; Gen. Man. EVERED (WEBBO) HERBERT.

WINN FM: Unit C24, The Sands, Newtown Bay Rd, Basseterre; tel. 466-9586; fax 466-7904; e-mail info@winnfm.com; internet www.winnfm.com; owned by Federation Media Group; Chair. MICHAEL KING.

ZIZ Radio and Television: Springfield, POB 331, Basseterre; tel. 465-2622; fax 465-5624; e-mail info@zizonline.com; internet www.zizonline.com; f. 1961; television from 1972; commercial; govt-owned; Gen. Man. WINSTON MCMAHON.

Television

ZIZ Radio and Television: see Radio.

Finance

(cap. = capital; res = reserves; dep. = deposits; brs = branches)

BANKING

Central Bank

Eastern Caribbean Central Bank (ECCB): Headquarters Bldg, Bird Rock, POB 89, Basseterre; tel. 465-2537; fax 465-9562; e-mail info@eccb-centralbank.org; internet www.eccb-centralbank.org; f. 1965 as East Caribbean Currency Authority; expanded responsibilities and changed name 1983; responsible for issue of currency in Anguilla, Antigua and Barbuda, Dominica, Grenada, Montserrat, Saint Christopher and Nevis, Saint Lucia and Saint Vincent and the Grenadines; res EC $181.3m., dep. EC $1,132.8m., total assets EC $2,080.8m. (March 2007); Gov. and Chair. Sir K. DWIGHT VENNER; Country Dir WENDELL LAWRENCE.

Other Banks

Bank of Nevis Ltd: Main St, POB 450, Charlestown, Nevis; tel. 469-5564; fax 469-5798; e-mail bon@caribsurf.com; internet www.thebankofnevis.com; dep. EC $0.3m., total assets EC $0.4m. (Dec. 2006); Chair. IVAN BROWNE.

FirstCaribbean International Bank (Barbados) Ltd: The Circus, POB 42, Basseterre; tel. 465-2449; fax 465-1041; internet www.firstcaribbeanbank.com; f. 2002 following merger of Caribbean operations of Barclays Bank PLC and CIBC; Barclays relinquished its stake to CIBC in 2006; res EC $0.8m. (March 2006); Exec. Chair. MICHAEL MANSOOR; CEO JOHN D. ORR.

RBTT Bank (SKN) Ltd: Main and Chappel Sts, POB 673, Charlestown, Nevis; tel. 469-5277; fax 469-1493; internet www.rbtt.com; f. 1955 as Nevis Co-operative Banking Co Ltd; acquired by Royal Bank of Trinidad and Tobago (later known as RBTT) in 1996; Group Chair. PETER J. JULY.

St Kitts-Nevis-Anguilla National Bank Ltd: Central St, POB 343, Basseterre; tel. 465-2204; fax 466-1050; e-mail webmaster@sknanb.com; internet www.sknanb.com; f. 1971; Govt of St Kitts and Nevis owns 51%; cap. EC $81.0m., res EC $154.8m., dep. EC $1,336.3m. (June 2007); Chair. WALFORD GUMBS; Man. Dir EDMUND LAURENCE; 5 brs.

Development Bank

Development Bank of St Kitts and Nevis: Church St, POB 249, Basseterre; tel. 465-2288; fax 465-4016; e-mail info@skndb.com; internet www.skndb.com; f. 1981; cap. EC $10.8m., res EC $4.3m., dep. EC $26.4m. (Dec. 2005); Chair. ELVIS NEWTON; Gen. Man. LENWORTH HARRIS.

STOCK EXCHANGE

Eastern Caribbean Securities Exchange: Bird Rock, POB 94, Basseterre; tel. 466-7192; fax 465-3798; e-mail info@ecseonline.com; internet www.ecseonline.com; f. 2001; regional securities market designed to facilitate the buying and selling of financial products for the eight member territories—Anguilla, Antigua and Barbuda, Dominica, Grenada, Montserrat, Saint Christopher and Nevis, Saint Lucia and Saint Vincent and the Grenadines; Chair. Sir K. DWIGHT VENNER; Gen. Man. and CEO TREVOR E. BLAKE.

INSURANCE

National Caribbean Insurance Co Ltd: Central St, POB 374, Basseterre; tel. 465-2694; fax 465-3659; internet www.nci-biz.com; f. 1973; subsidiary of St Kitts-Nevis-Anguilla National Bank Ltd; Gen. Man. JUDITH ATTONG.

St Kitts-Nevis Insurance Co Ltd (SNIC): Central St, POB 142, Basseterre; tel. 465-2845; fax 465-5410; internet www.tdclimited.com/snic; subsidiary of St Kitts Nevis Anguilla Trading & Devt Co Ltd (TDC).

Several foreign companies also have offices in Saint Christopher and Nevis.

Trade and Industry

GOVERNMENT AGENCIES

Central Marketing Corpn (CEMACO): Pond's Pasture, POB 375, Basseterre; tel. 465-2628; fax 465-7823; Man. VERNA HERBERT.

Frigate Bay Development Corporation (FBDC): Frigate Bay, POB 315, Basseterre; tel. 465-8339; fax 465-4463; promotes tourist and residential devts; Chair. JANET HARRIS; Man. Dir RANDOLPH MORTON.

Nevis Investment Promotion Agency (NIPA): Charlestown, Nevis; f. 2008.

St Kitts Investment Promotion Agency: Pelican Mall, Bay Rd, POB 132, Basseterre; tel. 465-4040; fax 465-6968; f. 1987.

Social Security Board: Robert Llewellyn Bradshaw Bldg, Bay Rd, POB 79, Basseterre; tel. 465-2535; fax 465-5051; e-mail pubinfo@socialsecurity.kn; internet www.socialsecurity.kn; f. 1977; Dir SEPHLIN LAWRENCE.

CHAMBER OF COMMERCE

St Kitts-Nevis Chamber of Industry and Commerce: Horsford Rd, Fortlands, POB 332, Basseterre; tel. 465-2980; fax 465-4490; e-mail sknchamber@sisterisles.kn; internet www.stkittsnevischamber.org; incorporated 1949; 137 mems (2006); Pres. FRANKLIN BRAND; Exec. Dir WENDY PHIPPS.

EMPLOYERS' ORGANIZATIONS

Building Contractors' Association: Anthony Evelyn Business Complex, Paul Southwell Industrial Park, POB 1046, Basseterre; tel. 465-6897; fax 465-5623; e-mail sknbca@caribsurf.com; Pres. ANTHONY E. EVELYN.

Nevis Cotton Growers' Association Ltd: Charlestown, Nevis; Pres. IVOR STEVENS.

Small Business Association: Anthony Evelyn Business Complex, Paul Southwell Industrial Park, POB 367, Basseterre; tel. 465-8630; fax 465-6661; e-mail sb-association@caribsurf.com; Pres. EUSTACE WARNER.

UTILITIES

Nevis Electricity Company Ltd (Nevlec): POB 852, Charlestown, Nevis; tel. 469-7245; fax 469-7249; e-mail info@nevlec.com; internet www.nevlec.com; Gen. Man. CARTWRIGHT FARRELL.

TRADE UNIONS

Nevis Teachers' Union: POB 559, Charlestown, Nevis; tel. 469-8465; fax 469-5663; e-mail nevteach@caribsurf.com; Pres. WAKELY DANIEL; Gen. Sec. BERNELLA CAINES HAMILTON.

St Kitts-Nevis Trades and Labour Union (SKTLU): Masses House, Church St, POB 239, Basseterre; tel. 465-2229; fax 466-9866; e-mail sknunion@caribsurf.com; f. 1940; affiliated to Caribbean Maritime and Aviation Council, Caribbean Congress of Labour, International Federation of Plantation, Agricultural and Allied Workers, and International Trade Union Confederation; associated with St Kitts-Nevis Labour Party; Pres. CLIFFORD THOMAS; Gen. Sec. BATUMBA TAK; c. 3,000 mems.

St Kitts Teachers' Union: Green Tree Housing Devt, POB 545, Basseterre; tel. 465-1921; e-mail stkittsteachersunion@hotmail.com; Pres. CLYDE CHRISTOPHER; Gen. Sec. CARLENE HENRY-MORTON.

Transport

RAILWAYS

There are 58 km (36 miles) of narrow-gauge light railway on Saint Christopher, serving the sugar plantations. The railway, complete with new trains and carriages, was restored and developed for tourist excursions and opened in late 2002.

St Kitts Scenic Railway: Sands Unit A6, Bay Rd, POB 191, Basseterre; tel. 465-7263; e-mail scenicreservations@sisterisles.kn; internet www.stkittsscenicrailway.com; f. 2002; Gen. Man. THOMAS A. WILLIAMS.

St Kitts Sugar Railway: St Kitts Sugar Manufacturing Corpn, POB 96, Basseterre; tel. 465-8099; fax 465-1059; e-mail agronomy@caribsurf.com; Gen. Man. J. E. S. ALFRED.

ROADS

In 1999 there were 320 km (199 miles) of road in Saint Christopher and Nevis, of which approximately 136 km (84 miles) are paved. In July 2001 the Caribbean Development Bank loaned US $3.75m. to the Nevis Government for a road improvement scheme. Further improvements were to be undertaken in 2006 in preparation for the Cricket World Cup, principally the construction of the West Basseterre Bypass Road, at an estimated cost of EC $20m. However, only certain sections had been completed as the cricket tournament commenced. The collapse of a bridge in May 2008 delayed construction, and by the following December the project was reported to be only 47% complete.

SHIPPING

The Government maintains a commercial motor-boat service between the islands, and numerous regional and international shipping lines call at the islands. A deep-water port, Port Zante, was opened at Basseterre in 1981. In June 2003 the Government of Kuwait agreed to provide a loan of EC $15m. to help fund the development of the cruise ship facilities at Port Zante.

St Christopher Air and Sea Ports Authority: Bird Rock, POB 963, Basseterre; tel. 465-8121; fax 465-8124; e-mail info@scaspa.com; internet www.scaspa.com; f. 1993 to combine St Kitts Port Authority and Airports Authority; Chair. LINKON MAYNARD; CEO and Gen. Man. ERROL DOUGLAS; Airport Man. DENZIL JONES; Sea Port Man. ROSEVELT TROTMAN.

Shipping Companies

Delisle Walwyn and Co Ltd: Liverpool Row, POB 44, Basseterre; tel. 465-2631; fax 465-1125; e-mail info@delislewalwyn.com; internet www.delislewalwyn.com; f. 1951; Chair. KISHU CHANDIRAMANI; Man. Dir DENZIL V. CROOKE.

Tony's Ltd: Main St, POB 564, Charlestown, Nevis; tel. 469-5413.

CIVIL AVIATION

Robert Llewellyn Bradshaw (formerly Golden Rock) International Airport, 4 km (2.5 miles) from Basseterre, is equipped to handle jet aircraft and is served by scheduled links with most Caribbean destinations, the United Kingdom, the USA and Canada. In 2005 Taiwan and the St Kitts-Nevis-Anguilla National Bank Ltd financed a US $17m. expansion and development project at the airport, completed in December 2006. Saint Christopher and Nevis is a shareholder in the regional airline, LIAT (see chapter on Antigua and Barbuda), which began operating a joint flight schedule with its troubled rival, Caribbean Star Airlines (also headquartered in Antigua and Barbuda) in February 2007; LIAT's full acquisition of Caribbean Star was completed in October 2007. Vance W. Amory International Airport (formerly Newcastle Airfield), 11 km (7 miles) from Charlestown, Nevis, has regular scheduled services to St Kitts and other islands in the region. A new airport, Castle Airport, was opened on Nevis in 1998. In September 2002 a US $5.9m. project to construct a new passenger terminal at Vance W. Amory Airport was completed.

St Kitts Air and Sea Ports Authority: see Shipping.

Private Airlines

Air St Kitts-Nevis: Vance W. Amory International Airport, Newcastle, Nevis; tel. 465-8571.

LIAT (1974) Ltd: Robert Llewellyn Bradshaw International Airport; tel. 465-2098; fax 465-3168; e-mail customerrelations@liatairline.com; internet www.liatairline.com; f. 1956 as Leeward Islands Air Transport Services, jtly owned by 11 regional Govts; privatized in 1995; shares are held by the Govts of Antigua and Barbuda, Montserrat, Grenada, Barbados, Trinidad and Tobago, Jamaica, Guyana, Dominica, Saint Lucia, Saint Vincent and the Grenadines and Saint Christopher and Nevis (30.8%), Caribbean Airlines (29.2%), LIAT employees (13.3%) and private investors (26.7%); merger negotiations with Caribbean Star Airlines were finalized in March 2007; deal was abandoned in July in favour of a buyout arrangement in which LIAT would acquire all remaining shares in Caribbean Star; scheduled passenger and cargo services to 19 destinations in the Caribbean; charter flights are also undertaken; Chair. JEAN STEWART HOLDER; CEO MARK DARBY.

Tourism

The introduction of regular air services to the US cities of Miami and New York has opened up the islands as a tourist destination. Visitors are attracted by the excellent beaches and the historical Brimstone Hill Fortress National Park on Saint Christopher, the spectacular mountain scenery of Nevis and the islands' associations with Lord Nelson and Alexander Hamilton. In 2008 there were an estimated 276,490 cruise ship passengers and 120,280 stop-over visitors. Receipts from tourism were a provisional EC $286.9m. in 2007. From 2005 many hotels and other tourist accommodation were constructed or refurbished in preparation for the 2007 Cricket World Cup, hosted by several Caribbean nations, including Saint Christopher and Nevis.

SAINT CHRISTOPHER AND NEVIS

Nevis Tourism Authority: Main St, POB 917, Charlestown, Nevis; tel. 469-7550; fax 469-7551; e-mail info@nevisisland.com; internet www.nevisisland.com; Chair. CHRIS MARTIN; Dir TIMOTHY HOFFMAN.

Nevis Tourism Bureau: Main St, Charlestown, Nevis; tel. 469-1042; fax 469-1066; e-mail nevtour@caribsurf.com; Dir ELMEADER BROOKES.

St Kitts Tourism Authority: Pelican Mall, Bay Rd, POB 132, Basseterre; tel. 465-4040; fax 465-8794; e-mail ceo@stkittstourism.kn; internet www.stkittstourism.kn; CEO ROSECITA JEFFERS.

St Kitts-Nevis Hotel and Tourism Association: Liverpool Row, POB 438, Basseterre; tel. 465-5304; fax 465-7746; e-mail stkitnevhta@caribsurf.com; f. 1972; Pres. KISHU CHANDIRAMANI; Man. MICHAEL HEAD.

SAINT LUCIA

Introductory Survey

Location, Climate, Language, Religion, Flag, Capital

Saint Lucia is the second largest of the Windward Islands group of the West Indies, lying 40 km (25 miles) to the south of Martinique and 32 km (20 miles) to the north-east of Saint Vincent, in the Caribbean Sea. The island is volcanic, with spectacular mountain scenery; the Pitons, the island's twin, jungle-clad volcanic mountains, were designated a UNESCO (see p. 144) World Heritage Site in June 2004. The average annual temperature is 26°C (79°F), with a dry season from January to April, followed by a rainy season from May to August. The average annual rainfall is 1,500 mm (60 ins) in the low-lying areas, and 3,500 mm (138 ins) in the mountains. The official language is English, although a large proportion of the population speak a French-based patois. Almost all of the island's inhabitants profess Christianity, and 64% are adherents of the Roman Catholic Church. The national flag (proportions 1 by 2) is blue, bearing in its centre a white-edged black triangle partly covered by a gold triangle rising from a common base. The capital is Castries.

Recent History

British settlers made an unsuccessful attempt to colonize the island (originally inhabited by a Carib people) in 1605. A further British party arrived in 1638 but were killed by the indigenous Carib population. France claimed sovereignty in 1642, and fighting between French and Caribs continued until 1660, when a peace treaty was signed. Control of Saint Lucia was transferred 14 times before it was ceded by the French and became a British colony in 1814. It remained under British rule for the next 165 years.

Representative government was introduced in 1924. The colony was a member of the Windward Islands, under a federal system, until December 1959. It joined the newly formed West Indies Federation in January 1958, and remained a member until the Federation's dissolution in May 1962. From January 1960 Saint Lucia, in common with other British territories in the Windward Islands, was given a new Constitution, with its own Administrator and an enlarged Legislative Council.

In 1951 the first elections under adult suffrage were won by the Saint Lucia Labour Party (SLP), which retained power until 1964, when John (later Sir John) Compton, of the newly formed conservative United Workers' Party (UWP), became Chief Minister. In March 1967 Saint Lucia became one of the West Indies Associated States, gaining full autonomy in internal affairs, with the United Kingdom retaining responsibility for defence and foreign relations only. The Legislative Council was replaced by a House of Assembly, the Administrator was designated Governor, and the Chief Minister became Premier.

In 1975 the Associated States agreed that they would seek independence individually. After three years of negotiations, Saint Lucia became independent on 22 February 1979, remaining within the Commonwealth. Compton became the country's first Prime Minister.

A general election in July 1979 returned the SLP to government with a clear majority, and its leader, Allan Louisy, succeeded Compton as Prime Minister. In February 1980 a new Governor-General, Boswell Williams, was appointed. This led to disputes within the Government and contributed to a split in the SLP. Louisy's resignation was demanded by 12 SLP members of the House of Assembly, who favoured his replacement by George Odlum, the Deputy Prime Minister. The controversy continued until April 1981, when Louisy was forced to resign after Odlum and three other SLP members of the House voted with the opposition against the Government's budget. In May Winston Cenac, the Attorney-General in the Louisy Government, took office as Prime Minister. In September the Cenac administration defeated by one vote a motion of no confidence, introduced jointly by UWP and Progressive Labour Party (PLP—formed by Odlum) members of the House, who accused the Government of political and economic mismanagement. In January 1982 a government proposal to alter legislation regarding the expenses of members of Parliament produced widespread accusations of corruption and provoked a series of strikes. Demands for the Government's resignation increased from all sectors of the community, culminating in a general strike. Cenac resigned, and an all-party interim administration was formed, under the deputy leader of the PLP, Michael Pilgrim, pending a general election. At the election in May the UWP was returned to power, and John Compton was re-elected Prime Minister. In December Sir Allen Lewis was reappointed Governor-General, following the dismissal of Boswell Williams because of his previous close association with the SLP.

In 1984 the opposition parties began to reorganize in order to present a more effective opposition to the UWP Government. At a general election to the 17-member House of Assembly in early April 1987, the UWP secured nine seats and the SLP eight. A further election took place at the end of the month, in the hope of a more decisive result, but the distribution of seats remained unchanged. In June the UWP's majority in the House was increased to three seats, when Cenac defected from the SLP. He was subsequently appointed Minister of Foreign Affairs.

In October 1988 the Government introduced legislation whereby it assumed control of the banana industry for one year. Subsequently, the 1988 annual convention of the Saint Lucia Banana Growers' Association (SLBGA) was cancelled, and the Government dismissed the association's board of directors. The opposition parties alleged that these actions had been motivated by the fact that prominent supporters of the ruling UWP were the SLBGA's principal debtors. Despite continued protests, particularly by banana producers and the SLP, Government control was extended until July 1990.

The UWP won a further term in office at a general election in April 1992. The SLP attributed its defeat largely to a redefinition of constituency boundaries by the Government prior to the election. In October 1993 a three-day strike was organized by a new pressure group, the Banana Salvation Committee (BSC), in support of demands for an increase in the minimum price paid to local producers for bananas and for the dismissal of the board of directors of the SLBGA. Following recommendations made by a government-appointed committee, the Government implemented price increases and dismissed the board of directors of the SLBGA, who were replaced by an interim board including representatives of the BSC. An announcement by the Government, in January 1994, that the SLBGA was to be placed into receivership provoked a strike by the BSC in March. The BSC organized further strikes by banana farmers in December and in February and July 1995, in support of demands for an extraordinary meeting of the SLBGA, and for an inquiry into the deaths of two demonstrators during the October 1993 strike. Further industrial action was undertaken by the BSC in February 1996, in protest at the monopoly on banana exports exercised by the state-run Windward Islands Banana Development and Exporting Co (Wibdeco), in the context of higher prices for produce being offered to banana growers by a US distributor. In September the House of Assembly approved a bill to revise the selection procedure for members of the SLBGA and the responsibilities of its general manager. The new legislation effectively transferred control of the association from the Government to the banana growers, who would henceforth elect six members of the board of directors (while the Government would continue to nominate the remaining five). In October the BSC co-ordinated industrial action by banana growers in support of renewed demands for an end to the Wibdeco monopoly, and for reform of the industry's management and payment systems. Attempts by a number of farmers who opposed the strike to transport produce to ports resulted in violent clashes. Subsequent negotiations with a parliamentary review committee and with the Government (which promised to transfer some responsibility for the industry to the private sector) failed to appease the farmers.

In August 1995 the report of a commission of inquiry into allegations of the Government's involvement in the misappropriation, for electoral purposes, of some US $100,000 in UN contributions concluded that the former Permanent Representative to the UN, Charles Flemming, had been the sole perpetrator of the fraud. Flemming, who insisted that he had acted with the knowledge and endorsement of senior members of the UWP (including the Prime Minister), failed to return from a visit to the USA undertaken during the commission's hearings. The Minister of State with Responsibility for Financial Services and the National Development Corporation, Rufus Bousquet (who claimed to have been an unwitting recipient of the funds), had been dismissed in May, after he publicly questioned whether it was appropriate that the Government remain in office pending investigation of the affair.

A UWP party conference, convened in January 1996, endorsed the appointment of Vaughan Lewis, the former Director-General of the Organisation of Eastern Caribbean States (OECS, see p. 440), to the vacancy created by the Prime Minister's retirement from the party leadership. Lewis contested and won the Central Castries parliamentary by-election in February, and was subsequently appointed Minister without Portfolio. SLP leader Julian Hunte resigned later in the month, following criticism of the party's poor performance at the by-election; Kenny Anthony, a former SLP education and culture minister, replaced him. In late March Compton resigned the premiership, and was succeeded in early April by Lewis.

A general election in May 1997 was won decisively by the SLP, which was returned to power after 15 years, securing 16 of the 17 seats in the House of Assembly. Kenny Anthony was sworn in as the new Prime Minister. Among the nine ministers in his first Cabinet was George Odlum, who had rejoined the SLP in July 1996. Following his electoral defeat Lewis announced his intention to resign the leadership of the UWP; Sir John Compton (as he had become), the former UWP leader and former Prime Minister, replaced him in June 1998.

In August 1997 the Governor-General, Sir George Mallet, resigned. His appointment, in June 1996, had been opposed by the SLP, on the grounds that the post's tradition of neutrality would be compromised: Mallet had previously been Deputy Prime Minister, and his portfolio had included several influential ministries. Saint Lucia's first female Governor-General, Dr Pearlette Louisy, was appointed in September 1997.

In September 1997 the inquiry into allegations of corruption under the UWP, which had been promised by the SLP Government after its election, began. However, legal challenges to the impartiality of the sole commissioner, Monica Joseph, effectively stalled proceedings and she withdrew from the inquiry in March 1998. Sir Louis Blom-Cooper, a prominent British jurist, was appointed in her place. In August 1999 Blom-Cooper submitted his report to the Government. The report cleared Compton and Lewis of corruption, but noted instances of impropriety and a 'high degree of maladministration' in their Governments.

In September 1997 the directors of the SLBGA resigned, at Anthony's request: the Government was reportedly concerned that divisions at boardroom level were damaging the association's operations. Such divisions became increasingly pronounced as plans proceeded for the privatization of the SLBGA, one of the stated aims of the SLP Government. The Concerned Farmers Group (CFG), formed in December and led by the ousted Chairman, Rupert Gajadhar, which grouped larger farmers, expressed concern that the more numerous smaller producers in the BSC (whose secretary, Patrick Joseph, was also a government senator) would unduly dominate the new company, since decision-making was to be on the basis of 'one member, one vote'. Members of the CFG threatened to establish their own company unless their concerns were addressed.

In July 1998 the SLBGA was privatized and the Saint Lucia Banana Corpn (SLBC) was created in its place. The Government agreed to assume the debts incurred by the dissolved SLBGA, equivalent to EC $44m. The CFG, which had refused to participate in the process, subsequently established a rival company, the Tropical Quality Fruit Co (TQF). In October a court judgment ruled that the SLBC did not enjoy monopoly rights in the banana trade. This ruling followed complaints from the TQF that Wibdeco had been refusing to accept its fruit for shipment. The TQF alleged that this refusal was owing to pressure exerted by the SLBC Chairman, Patrick Joseph, in his capacity as a member of the Wibdeco board.

In January 1999 the SLBC announced that it had incurred losses of EC $6m. in 1998 and would therefore be forced to reduce the price paid to farmers. The SLBC blamed its operating deficit primarily on the fact that, because banana production had been underestimated, Wibdeco had failed to obtain sufficient European Union (EU, see p. 255) licences, meaning that much of the fruit produced did not reach high-paying markets. The TQF also announced a deficit, but claimed that its lower operating costs had reduced its losses. The TQF further suggested that the SLBC had damaged its own profitability by keeping prices deliberately high in an attempt to force the TQF out of business.

In July 1999 the Government founded a Banana Industry Trust, which was to oversee the improvement of farming practices in the banana sector and manage the financial resources available to the industry, including EC $21m. in funds provided by the EU. In the same month the Government announced that it was to make official loans of $7m. to the SLBC and $1.9m. to the TQF. However, falling prices and the ongoing lack of confidence among growers led the Government to announce that it was to hold talks with representatives of Wibdeco and Geest Bananas in order to discuss future pricing arrangements, while the Chairman of the SLBC urged Wibdeco and Geest to release money from their emergency funds to farmers threatened with bankruptcy. In August Wibdeco agreed to finance a temporary subsidy on prices in order to alleviate hardship among growers. In late 1999, however, the company encountered increasing pressure from the SLBC and from the Government to deliver increased returns to farmers, and in January 2000, following the expiry of its agreement to sell through Wibdeco, the SLBC announced plans to sell direct to Geest, despite criticism from its other regional partners in Wibdeco. In March Wibdeco announced that it would not contest the SLBC's decision, although it suggested that it might itself bypass the SLBC by buying direct from farmers.

In January 2001, following an increase in tourist cancellations, Prime Minister Anthony announced a series of measures intended to reduce the crime rate in Saint Lucia. These included the establishment of a National Anti-Crime Commission, the creation of a 10-member police 'rapid response unit', a review of the penal code, and reforms to the police service. In June Anthony announced the creation of four more rapid response units, a special task force to target known criminals, plans for more severe penalties for gun crimes, an increase in police patrols and an amnesty for holders of illegal firearms. A special joint session of Parliament convened in the following month to debate the increase in violent crime.

In March 2001 the Minister of Foreign Affairs and International Trade, George Odlum, left the Government and the SLP to join a new opposition grouping, the National Alliance (NA). The former premier, Sir John Compton, and the UWP leader, Morella Joseph, had founded the NA in advance of legislative elections due in 2002 but widely expected to be held in late 2001. Prime Minister Anthony stated that he had dismissed Odlum from his ministerial post, although Odlum himself claimed that he had resigned from the Government. Julian Hunte, a former Permanent Representative to the UN, replaced Odlum as foreign minister.

In October 2001 the NA's assembly elected Compton to head the party. However, Odlum rejected the decision and claimed the voting process was flawed. Later the same month the UWP withdrew from the Alliance and announced it would contest the elections as a single party. Odlum chose to retain the National Alliance name for his group.

As expected, the ruling SLP achieved another convincing victory at the 3 December 2001 general election, winning 14 of the 17 parliamentary seats (and 54% of the valid votes cast). The remaining seats were taken by the UWP. Joseph and Odlum, leaders of the UWP and the NA, respectively, both lost their seats. The voter turn-out rate was 53%. Joseph resigned as UWP leader and was replaced by Vaughan Lewis. Meanwhile, in the same month, Prime Minister Anthony announced a new 15-member Cabinet.

In July 2003 Parliament approved a constitutional amendment abolishing the oath of allegiance to the British monarch; instead, elected members were to pledge loyalty to the Saint Lucian people. In November the Government announced the establishment of a Constitutional Review Commission. The development, which was supported by the opposition, was designed to expand public participation in Saint Lucia's democracy. Meanwhile, also in November the Government adopted a new Criminal Code, which included two particularly controversial clauses. The first, Section 361, provided for a two-year prison sentence for anyone convicted of spreading 'false news'. The clause provoked consternation among local media representatives and the UWP, whose parliamentary members absented themselves from the vote. The second controversial element of the Code, Section 166, allowed for the legalization of abortion, previously illegal in all circumstances, in cases of rape, incest and medical danger to the mother. The law prompted trenchant criticism from anti-abortion and religious groups, and in January 2004 led to the dismissal of Sarah Flood-Beaubrun from her post as Minister of Home Affairs and Gender Relations, following a vehement disagreement with her fellow ministers over the new legislation; she resigned from the SLP in March and later established a new political party, the Organization for National Empowerment.

Flood-Beaubrun's dismissal from the Government was part of a wider cabinet realignment in early 2004, which included the appointment of the erstwhile Minister of Agriculture, Forestry and Fisheries, Calixte George, as head of a new Ministry of Home Affairs and Internal Security. The new department was to oversee the police service, previously the responsibility of the Attorney-General's Office, and was charged with finding a solution to the island's spiralling crime rate. Nevertheless, in 2004 the number of murders reached a record level, 37, a rate maintained in 2005. In November 2005 an Interception of Communication bill, which granted extra powers to law enforcement authorities and attracted emphatic criticism from opposition parties, received senate approval. In the first 10 months of that year 154 illegal guns were recovered through police raids and under a new 'amnesty' scheme, compared with 48 in the whole of 2004. Despite the recruitment of 10 British police officers in November 2006 and renewed pledges by the Government for more rigorous anti-crime initiatives and deterrents, the murder rate escalated to 39 by the end of that year. In January 2006 Anthony pledged to make greater use of the death penalty as a weapon against the increasing problem of crime, a promise reiterated by his successor, Sir John Compton (see below), in early 2007.

In November 2003 the High Court ruled that the Government's approval of the refinancing of the construction of the Hyatt Hotel in 1997 was 'void and illegal'. The opposition criticized the Government for not having sought parliamentary approval for the authorization of the loan and demanded the resignation of the Attorney-General, Petrus Compton, whose actions, it claimed, were particularly implicated by the judgment. In October 2004 the much-criticized Compton was moved to the Ministry of Foreign Affairs, International Trade and Civil Aviation. His predecessor, Julian Hunte, had been reappointed ambassador of Saint Lucia to the UN. Victor La Corbiniere was given the vacant role of Attorney-General and Minister of Justice. Meanwhile, in December 2004 Prime Minister Anthony announced his intention to stand for a third term in office at the forthcoming elections, constitutionally due in 2006.

In April 2004 Marcus Nicholas, a UWP deputy, withdrew his support for Arsene James, Leader of the Opposition since January 2003, whose popularity had fallen in recent months. Nicholas became the new leader of a four-member opposition, leading the UWP hierarchy to cancel his party membership. In addition to James being the party's sole loyal supporter in the House of Assembly, the UWP remained unable to develop a strong party executive and in March 2005 elected veteran politician Sir John Compton to lead the party into the next general election, in preference to the incumbent candidate, Vaughan Lewis. In September 2006 Lewis resigned from the UWP and joined the SLP.

The election of Compton as party leader proved highly perspicacious, as the UWP celebrated an unprecedented and decisive victory in the 11 December 2006 general election: the party secured 11 of the 17 parliamentary seats contested (equivalent to 51.4% of votes cast), while the incumbent SLP secured the remaining six seats (with 48.2% of the vote). Turn-out of the estimated 139,958 eligible electorate was preliminarily put at approximately 60%, and election monitors from the Organization of American States (see p. 373) declared the ballot free and fair. Compton, an octogenarian politician who had presided over the Saint Lucia Government twice before, including for a 29-year term spanning the country's transition to independence, was sworn in as premier on 15 December.

Mindful of the significant public debt burden requiring the new Government's urgent attention, Prime Minister Compton announced in January 2007 that an audit commission was to be established to investigate considerable ministerial overspending on public sector projects. The inquiry followed reports of widespread financial irregularities and unexplained delays in implementation. Furthermore, proposals for policy reform of election campaign financing, both within Saint Lucia and the wider Caribbean community, were promulgated for consideration at the state opening of Parliament on 15 January; the motion was prompted by the high levels of spending in the months preceding the December 2006 election and fears that a continuing lack of regulation in campaign practice could expose the electoral process to corrupting influences.

The newly elected UWP administration also confirmed in January 2007 that proposals by the previous Government to grant an amnesty to Caribbean Community and Common Market (CARICOM, see p. 206) nationals residing in Saint Lucia illegally would be sustained, offering those concerned the opportunity to 'regularize' their citizenship status upon payment of a stipulated fee. It was estimated that approximately 1,000 Guyanese, in addition to Jamaican, Trinidadian and other CARICOM nationals would benefit from the agreement.

Compton suffered a series of minor strokes in late April 2007. Stephenson King, the Minister of Health and UWP Chairman, was appointed acting Prime Minister in his absence. Compton died on 7 September after experiencing a further stroke. The remaining 10 elected members of the UWP designated King as Compton's permanent successor, and he was duly sworn in as Prime Minister. The new premier announced his Cabinet on 12 September, in which he assumed the portfolios for finance, external affairs, home affairs and national security. Former health minister Edmund Estephane acquired the newly created post of Minister of Labour, Information and Broadcasting, and Keith Mondesir became Minister of Health Wellness, Family Affairs, National Mobilisation, Human Services and Gender Relations.

In May 2008 Minister of Economic Affairs, Economic Planning, National Development and Public Service Ausbert d'Auvergne tendered his resignation following criticism from UWP colleagues over an alleged business relationship with convicted criminals. His departure prompted Prime Minister King to execute a reallocation of cabinet portfolios. Notable in the reshuffle was the reappointment of Rufus Bousquet to the Government, as trade and industry minister. Bousquet had been dismissed from the Cabinet in the previous June, reportedly after he re-established diplomatic relations with Taiwan (see below) without the knowledge of Compton. At the end of the year Bousquet was allocated the external affairs portfolio, in addition to his existing duties.

The SLBC entered into a dispute with Wibdeco in early 2008 when, in February, the latter announced plans to terminate its contract with the SLBC as it had not been certified by the Fairtrade Labelling Organization of the United Kingdom. The Chairman of the SLBC, Eustace Monrose, claimed that the company had not been given adequate notice to achieve fair trade status and instructed Wibdeco to withdraw its notice of termination. However, in late March Wibdeco signed a sales and purchase agreement with two other companies, one of which was the Windward Islands Farmers' Association, in order to bring the supply chain of the island's bananas into line with fair trade regulations. The SLBC, now faced with the threat of closure, was subsequently granted a court injunction preventing Wibdeco from effecting its termination notice. Instability within the SLBC continued into May after Monrose stepped down as Chairman following criticism of his handling of the Corporation's funds.

Fears over rising crime rates prompted the Government in early 2009 to announce its intention to resume capital punishment of convicted murderers. In 2008 there were 38 murders in Saint Lucia, compared with 25 unlawful killings in 2007. Although the law allowed for capital punishment, the last execution in Saint Lucia occurred in 1995.

Saint Lucia's most important export market is the United Kingdom, which receives most of the banana crop under the terms of the Cotonou Agreement (see p. 311). In July 1993 new regulations came into effect governing the level of imports of bananas by the European Community (now EU, of which the United Kingdom is a member). The regulations were introduced to protect traditional producers from competition from the expanding Latin American producers. At the instigation of the Latin American producers, consecutive dispute panels were appointed by the General Agreement on Tariffs and Trade (GATT, which was succeeded by the World Trade Organization—WTO, see p. 410) to rule on whether the EU's actions contravened GATT rules. Although the dispute panels ruled in favour of the Latin American producers, the rulings were not enforceable. In February 1996, with support from Ecuador, Guatemala, Mexico and Honduras, the USA renewed consultations, begun in September 1995, with the WTO concerning the EU's banana import quota regime. A WTO interim report in 1997 appeared to uphold many of the charges of unfair discrimination brought by the plaintiffs. The WTO Appellate Body rejected representations by the EU against the ruling in September, and the EU was informed that it must formulate a new system for banana imports by early 1998; new arrangements were duly proposed by the EU, under which it would apply a system of quotas and tariffs to both groups of producers, while retaining an import-licensing system.

The EU's new banana import regime was implemented on 1 January 1999 in compliance with the WTO ruling, though the USA criticized the reforms as negligible. Further discussions on the issue broke down in late January 1999 when Saint Lucia, backed by other countries, objected to any discussion of US demands for sanctions on EU goods. On 1 February the USA introduced punitive import duties on various EU goods, and in March the WTO disputes panel was asked to consider whether the EU had done enough to amend its import regime and whether the USA could legally impose retaliatory import tariffs. In retaliation, the banana-exporting countries threatened to withdraw their co-operation with the US campaign against drugs-trafficking, while banana producers warned that they might switch to growing marijuana if they were forced out of business. On 6 April WTO arbitrators awarded damages against the EU, although at a lower level than the USA had been claiming, and a week later delivered a ruling criticizing aspects of the EU banana-importing regime, which gave the USA permission to impose retaliatory tariffs on certain European goods. In April 2001 the USA agreed to suspend these sanctions from July, after the dispute was resolved: following a transition period, a new, tariff-only regime was introduced from January 2006. Despite substantial government and EU assistance, augmented by the efforts of a Banana Emergency Recovery Unit and the Banana Industry Trust, the Saint Lucian banana industry continued to exhibit decline.

Saint Lucia is a member of the OECS, and, since May 1987, has been a prominent advocate of the creation of a unitary East Caribbean state. In 1988, however, Antigua and Barbuda expressed opposition to political union, thereby discouraging any participation by Montserrat or Saint Christopher and Nevis. The four English-speaking Windward Islands countries (Saint Lucia, Dominica, Grenada, and Saint Vincent and the Grenadines) thus announced plans to proceed independently towards a more limited union. In 1990 the leaders of the four countries established a Regional Constituent Assembly. Following a series of discussions, the Assembly issued its final report in late 1992, in which it stated that the four countries were committed to the establishment of economic and political union under a federal system. Saint Lucia has also been a full participating member of the CARICOM regional community since May 1974. In February 2006 the House of Assembly approved legislation allowing Saint Lucia to join the Caribbean Single Market and Economy, and, together with five other Caribbean nations (Antigua and Barbuda, Dominica, Grenada, Saint Christopher and Nevis, and Saint Vincent and the Grenadines), the country was formally admitted to the initiative in July (see Economic Affairs). An intra-regional common passport initiative, regarded as an integral component in the advance towards economic union and designed to facilitate travel for citizens of participating nations, was implemented in Saint Lucia on 16 January 2007.

In August 1997 the new SLP Government effected a significant reorientation of foreign policy when it was announced that diplomatic relations were to be established with the People's Republic of China; it was reported that China was to provide educational materials valued at US $1m. immediately, and was to finance the construction of a new national sports stadium, a cultural centre, a new highway and a free trade zone. Taiwan subsequently severed relations with Saint Lucia. By 2004 it was estimated that China had provided Saint Lucia with funds worth US $100m. throughout the seven years of their association. In late 2005 Prime Minister Anthony accused the UWP of jeopardizing Saint Lucia's profitable relationship with China after allegations emerged that Sir John Compton had secretly met the President of Taiwan and sought to develop a relationship between the UWP and Taiwan. Such fears were partly allayed with the signing of a technical co-operation agreement between the premier and the Chinese Minister of Foreign Affairs, Li Zhaoxing, in September 2006, although the UWP's victory in the December general election precipitated renewed uncertainties about the future of bilateral relations. In February 2007 the new foreign affairs minister, Rufus Bousquet, reiterated his Government's intention to maintain links with China, but in April he announced that the country would resume diplomatic relations with Taiwan; China subsequently suspended ambassadorial relations with Saint Lucia. During an official state visit to the island in January 2008, Taiwan's President Chen Shui-bian stated his commitment to provide aid and investment, including US $100,000 for repairs to an earthquake-damaged school and funds for the redevelopment of a hospital. The opposition SLP accused the Taiwanese ambassador on the island of interfering in political affairs in March 2009 after it emerged that Taiwan was funding the establishment of a computer-literacy centre in the constituency headquarters of a prominent UWP politician (the centre was subsequently moved to a more neutral location).

Together with 12 other Caribbean administrations, in September 2005 the Government signed the PetroCaribe accord, under which Saint Lucia would be allowed to purchase petroleum from Venezuela at reduced prices. However, owing to very limited storage facilities in the region, many of the signatories—including Saint Lucia—were unable to proceed further in accepting fuel shipments. In September 2006 Hess Oil (St Lucia) Ltd announced an arrangement with Venezuelan state-owned oil company PDVSA whereby its plant at Cul de Sac would be employed as a repository, enabling receipt of the 1,700 barrels per day of oil products under the terms of the initiative. However, following his accession to the premiership in December, Sir John Compton indicated that implementation of the PetroCaribe initiative would not be a priority of his Government and the enterprise was abandoned indefinitely.

In November 2003 Parliament approved legislation enabling the Government to pledge US $2.5m. towards the establishment of the Caribbean Court of Justice (CCJ), to be headquartered in Trinidad. The CCJ, which replaced the Privy Council in the United Kingdom as the region's highest court, was inaugurated in April 2005.

Government

Saint Lucia is a constitutional monarchy. Executive power is vested in the British monarch, as Head of State, and is exercisable by the Governor-General, who represents the monarchy and is appointed on the advice of the Prime Minister. Legislative power is vested in Parliament, comprising the monarch, the 17-member House of Assembly, elected from single-member constituencies for up to five years by universal adult suffrage, and the Senate, composed of 11 members appointed by the Governor-General, including six appointed on the advice of the Prime Minister and three on the advice of the Leader of the Opposition. Government is effectively by the Cabinet. The Governor-General appoints the Prime Minister and, on the latter's recommendation, the other Ministers. The Prime Minister must have majority support in the House, to which the Cabinet is responsible.

Defence

The Royal Saint Lucia Police Force, which numbers about 300 men, includes a Special Service Unit for purposes of defence. Saint Lucia participates in the US-sponsored Regional Security System, comprising police, coastguards and army units, which was established by independent East Caribbean states in 1982. There are also two patrol vessels for coastguard duties.

Economic Affairs

In 2007, according to estimates by the World Bank, Saint Lucia's gross national income (GNI), measured at average 2005–07 prices, was US $929m., equivalent to $5,530 per head (or $9,430 per head on an international purchasing-power parity basis). During 2000–07, it was estimated, the population increased at an average annual rate of 1.1%, while gross domestic product (GDP) per head rose by 1.7% per year during the same period. Overall GDP increased, in real terms, at an average annual rate of 2.8% in 2000–07; according to the Eastern Caribbean Central Bank (ECCB, see p. 430), real GDP increased by 2.3% in 2008.

Agriculture (including hunting, forestry and fishing) accounted for 3.8% of GDP in 2008. The sector employed some 12.7% of the active working population in 2006. Despite the decline in the banana industry, the fruit remains Saint Lucia's principal cash crop, although in 2007 it accounted for 19.0% of the total value of merchandise exports, compared with 49.9% in 2002. Other important crops include coconuts, mangoes, citrus fruit, cocoa and spices. Commercial fishing was being developed, and in August 2001 Japan granted US $10.6m. towards the rehabilitation and improvement of fishery facilities in the Choiseul and Soufrière districts. During 2000–08 real agricultural GDP decreased at an average annual rate of 6.7%, largely as a result of an average annual decline of 9.5% in the banana sector over the same period. The agriculture sector's GDP grew by 7.2% in 2008.

Industry (including mining, manufacturing, public utilities and construction) accounted for 18.0% of GDP in 2008, and the sector engaged an estimated 22.3% of the active working population in 2006. During 2000–08 industrial GDP increased at an average annual rate of 1.0%. However, in 2008 the sector's real GDP declined by 0.7%. Construction contributed 7.3% to GDP in 2008, and the sector's GDP increased at an average annual rate of 0.2% in 2000–08.

Manufacturing accounted for 5.6% of GDP in 2008, and employed 5.5% of the employed population in 2006. The principal manufacturing industries, which have been encouraged by the establishment of 'free zones', include the processing of agricultural products, the assembly of electronic components and the production of garments, plastics, paper and packaging (associated with banana production), and beer, rum and other beverages. During 2000–08 the sector's real GDP increased at an average annual rate of 3.1%. Real manufacturing GDP increased by 1.0% in 2008.

Energy is traditionally derived from imported hydrocarbon fuels (mineral fuels and lubricants comprised an estimated 21.2% of total imports in 2007). There is a petroleum storage and transshipment terminal on the island. Saint Lucia was a signatory to the PetroCaribe accord, introduced in 2005, under which the country was allowed to purchase petroleum from Venezuela at reduced prices, although implementation of the initiative was postponed after the United Workers' Party was returned to power in December 2006.

The services sector contributed 78.2% of GDP in 2008, and engaged an estimated 65.0% of those employed in 2006. Tourism is the most important of the service industries, and in 2007 tourist receipts totalled EC $798.0m. The number of tourist arrivals declined by 8.2% in 2005 and by a further 7.0% in 2006, owing largely to a drop in the number of excursionists and cruise-ship passengers visiting the island. However, total visitor arrivals increased by 33.9% in 2007, largely as a result of a 69.7% increase in cruise-ship passengers in that year. The real GDP of the hotels and restaurants sector decreased by 7.4% in the same year. However, the sector recovered in 2008, growing by 6.0%. During 2000–08 the real GDP of the services sector increased at an average annual rate of 7.8%. The sector's GDP increased by 4.2% in 2008.

In 2008 Saint Lucia recorded an estimated visible trade deficit of EC $1,174.15m., and a deficit of some EC $816.82m. on the current account of the balance of payments. The principal source of imports in 2007 was the USA (41.6% of the total); other important markets in that year were Trinidad and Tobago (19.9%) and Japan (6.3%). The principal market for exports in 2006 was Trinidad and Tobago (30.1% of the total); other major export markets were the United Kingdom (20.7%) and the USA (20.6%). The Caribbean states accounted for 27.6% of imports in 2007 and 52.6% of exports in 2006. Refined petroleum was the principal export commodity in 2006, ahead of food and live animals (comprising mainly bananas sent to the United Kingdom), machinery and transport equipment, and beverages and tobacco (mainly beer). The principal imports in that year were machinery and transport equipment, and food and live animals.

In 2007 there was an overall budgetary deficit of EC $64.8m., equivalent to 2.5% of GDP. Saint Lucia's total external debt at the end of 2006 was US $373.5m., of which US $256.5m. was long-term public debt. In 2005 the cost of debt-servicing was equivalent to 6.6% of the value of exports of goods and services. The annual rate of inflation averaged 2.4% in 2000–07; inflation averaged 1.9% in 2007. In 2006 the average rate of unemployment was 14%.

Saint Lucia is a member of the Caribbean Community and Common Market (CARICOM, see p. 206), the ECCB (see p. 430), and the Organisation of Eastern Caribbean States (OECS, see p. 440). Saint Lucia is also a member of the regional stock exchange, the Eastern Caribbean Securities Exchange (based in Saint Christopher and Nevis), established in 2001. Saint Lucia has been a strong advocate of closer political and economic integration within the Caribbean region and became a signatory to CARICOM's Caribbean Single Market and Economy (CSME) on 3 July 2006. The CSME, which was established by six founding member states on 1 January 2006, was to enshrine the free movement of goods, services and labour throughout most of the CARICOM region. Saint Lucia is party to the Caribbean Basin Initiative (CBI) and to the Cotonou Agreement (see p. 311), the successor accord to the Lomé Convention.

The Saint Lucian economy, which traditionally relied on the production of bananas for export, underwent considerable structural change at the end of the 20th century, with the emergence of service industries as the most important sectors of the economy, while investment in the island's infrastructure also benefited the tourism industry, which became the principal source of foreign exchange. In 2009 the World Travel and Tourism Council estimated that the tourism sector accounted for about 37% of Saint Lucia's GDP and employment. The tourism sector performed well in 2008, when cruise-ship passengers increased by more than one-half compared with the previous year. The sector also benefited from lower global fuel prices in the latter half of the year. None the less, receipts were expected to decline in 2009, owing to the global downturn. In an attempt to alleviate this expected contraction, in December 2008 the Government announced the formation of a task force to examine measures to bolster the tourism sector, including tax reductions. The agricultural sector, nevertheless, remained a significant source of employment, and the loss of Saint Lucia's preferential access to European markets was of considerable concern. Banana production declined dramatically from the 1990s as a result of poor climatic conditions and the retrenchments in the industry caused by increased international competition and lower market prices. This sector encountered more difficulties during 2007–08: 'Hurricane Dean', which swept across the island in August 2007, wreaked severe damage to that year's banana crop. The industry was further threatened by the actions of the banana-exporting company Wibdeco in early 2008 (see Recent History). The 2009 budget introduced several economic stimulus measures, including tax concessions for those on a minimum wage, a decrease in fuel prices and several public sector projects, to be financed by European Union and Taiwanese loans and grants. GDP per head was expected to decline in 2009, while real GDP growth of just 2.5% was forecast for the year.

Education

Education is compulsory for 10 years between five and 15 years of age. Primary education begins at the age of five and lasts for seven years. Secondary education, beginning at 12 years of age, lasts for five years, comprising a first cycle of three years and a second cycle of two years. Enrolment at primary schools in 2006/07 included 98.8% of children in the relevant age-group, while in 2005/06 enrolment in secondary level education included 76.3% of pupils in the relevant age category. Free education is provided in more than 90 government-assisted schools. Facilities for industrial, technical and teacher-training are available at the Sir Arthur Lewis Community College at Morne Fortune, which also houses an extra-mural branch of the University of the West Indies. Some EC $162.7m. was allocated to the Ministry of Education and Culture in the 2007/08 budget (equivalent to 18.3% of total planned budgetary expenditure).

Public Holidays

2009: 1–2 January (New Year), 22 February (Independence Day), 10 April (Good Friday), 13 April (Easter Monday), 1 May (Labour Day), 1 June (Whit Monday), 11 June (Corpus Christi), 1 August (Emancipation Day), 5 October (Thanksgiving Day), 1 November (All Saints' Day), 2 November (All Souls' Day), 22 November (Feast of St Cecilia), 13 December (Saint Lucia Day), 25–26 December (Christmas).

2010: 1–2 January (New Year), 22 February (Independence Day), 2 April (Good Friday), 5 April (Easter Monday), 1 May (Labour Day), 24 May (Whit Monday), 2 June (Corpus Christi), 1 August (Emancipation Day), 4 October (Thanksgiving Day), 1 November (All Saints' Day), 2 November (All Souls' Day), 22 November (Feast of St Cecilia), 13 December (Saint Lucia Day), 25–26 December (Christmas).

Weights and Measures

The imperial system is in use, although conversion to the metric system was under way.

SAINT LUCIA

Statistical Survey

Source (unless otherwise indicated): St Lucian Government Statistics Department, Block A, Government Bldgs, Waterfront, Castries; tel. 452-7670; fax 451-8254; e-mail statsdept@candw.lc; internet www.stats.gov.lc.

AREA AND POPULATION

Area: 616.3 sq km (238 sq miles).

Population: 135,685 (males 65,988, females 69,697) at census of 12 May 1991; 162,982 (males 79,877, females 83,105) at census of 22 May 2001 (including estimate for underenumeration). *2006:* 166,838 (mid-year estimate). *By District* (estimates at mid-2006): Castries 68,209; Anse La Raye 6,468; Canaries 1,920; Soufrière 8,037; Choiseul 6,376; Laborie 7,705; Vieux-Fort 15,942; Micoud 16,794; Dennery 13,458; Gros Islet 21,929. *2008:* 175,678 (mid-year estimate). Source: Eastern Caribbean Central Bank.

Density (mid-2008): 285.1 per sq km.

Principal Town (population incl. suburbs, mid-2006): Castries (capital) 14,509.

Births, Marriages and Deaths (2005, provisional): Registered live births 2,215 (birth rate 13.5 per 1,000); Registered marriages 591; Registered deaths 1,107 (death rate 6.7 per 1,000).

Life Expectancy (years at birth, WHO estimates): 75.2 (males 72.2; females 78.3) in 2006. Source: WHO, *World Health Statistics*.

Economically Active Population (persons aged 15 years and over, labour survey for October–December 2006): Agriculture, hunting and forestry 7,830; Fishing 930; Manufacturing 3,820; Electricity, gas and water 1,230; Construction 10,300; Wholesale and retail trade, repair of motor vehicles, motorcycles and personal and household goods 12,530; Hotels and restaurants 8,980; Transport, storage and communications 3,960; Financial intermediation 1,550; Real estate, renting and business activities 2,210; Public administration and compulsory social security 10,630; Education 1,230; Health and social work 370; Other community, social and personal service activities 1,190; Private households with employed persons 2,190; Activities not adequately defined 320; Not reported 6,750; *Total employed* 76,020; Unemployed 12,090; *Total labour force* 88,110 (males 54,540, females 33,570).

HEALTH AND WELFARE
Key Indicators

Total Fertility Rate (children per woman, 2006): 2.2.

Under-5 Mortality Rate (per 1,000 live births, 2006): 14.

Physicians (per 1,000 head, 1999): 5.2.

Hospital Beds (per 1,000 head, 2005): 3.

Health Expenditure (2006): US $ per head (PPP): 421.

Health Expenditure (2006): % of GDP: 5.9.

Health Expenditure (2006): public (% of total): 56.4.

Access to Water (% of persons, 2006): 98.

Access to Sanitation (% of persons, 2004): 89.

Human Development Index (2006): ranking: 66.

Human Development Index (2006): value: 0.821.

For sources and definitions, see explanatory note on p. vi.

AGRICULTURE, ETC.

Principal Crops ('000 metric tons, 2007, FAO estimates): Cassava 1.1; Yams 0.5; Coconuts 14.0; Bananas 34.0; Plantains 0.8; Citrus fruits 2.2. *Aggregate Production* ('000 metric tons, may include official, semi-official or estimated data): Roots and tubers 7.2; Vegetables (incl. melons) 1.2; Fruits (excl. melons) 37.8.

Livestock ('000 head, 2007, FAO estimates): Cattle 12.5; Sheep 12.5; Goats 9.9; Pigs 15.0; Horses 1.1; Poultry 280.

Livestock Products ('000 metric tons, 2007, FAO estimates): Pig meat 1.1; Chicken meat 1.0; Cows' milk 1.1; Hen eggs 1.1.

Fishing (metric tons, live weight, 2006): Capture 1,496 (Wahoo 187; Skipjack tuna 120; Blackfin tuna 182; Yellowfin tuna 103; Common dolphinfish 382; Stromboid conchs 35); Aquaculture 0; Total catch 1,496. Figures exclude aquatic plants.

Source: FAO.

INDUSTRY

Production (2006, unless otherwise indicated): Electric energy 330.8 million kWh; Copra 1,094 metric tons (2004); Coconut oil (unrefined) 1.2m. litres; Coconut oil (refined) 88,700 litres; Coconut meal 499,300 kg; Rum 191,900 proof gallons.

FINANCE

Currency and Exchange Rates: 100 cents = 1 Eastern Caribbean dollar (EC $). *Sterling, US Dollar and Euro Equivalents* (31 December 2008): £1 sterling = EC $3.936; US $1 = EC $2.700; €1 = EC $3.758; EC $100 = £25.41 = US $37.04 = €26.61. *Exchange Rate:* Fixed at US $1 = EC $2.70 since July 1976.

Budget (EC $ million, 2007): *Revenue:* Tax revenue 658.6 (Taxes on income and profits 176.6; Taxes on property 4.9; Taxes on domestic goods and services 119.3; Taxes on international trade and transactions 357.9); Other current revenue 39.3; Capital revenue 0.1; Total 698.0 (excl. grants 9.3). *Expenditure:* Current expenditure 549.2 (Personal emoluments 249.9; Goods and services 103.4; Interest payments 84.0; Transfers and subsidies 111.9); Capital expenditure and net lending 213.6; Total 762.8. Source: Eastern Caribbean Central Bank.

International Reserves (US $ million at 31 December 2007): IMF special drawing rights 2.51; Reserve position in IMF 0.01; Foreign exchange 151.20; Total 153.72. Source: IMF, *International Financial Statistics*.

Money Supply (EC $ million at 31 December 2007): Currency outside banks 128.05; Demand deposits at deposit money banks 583.07; Total money 711.12. Source: IMF, *International Financial Statistics*.

Cost of Living (Consumer Price Index; base: 2000 = 100): 112.0 in 2005; 114.6 in 2006; 117.5 in 2007. Source: IMF, *International Financial Statistics*.

Gross Domestic Product (EC $ million at constant 1990 prices): 1,723.61 in 2006; 1,742.85 in 2007; 1,783.23 in 2008.

Expenditure on the Gross Domestic Product (EC $ million at current prices, 2006, preliminary): Government final consumption expenditure 414.43; Private final consumption expenditure 1,534.35; Gross capital formation 736.21; *Total domestic expenditure* 2,684.99; Exports of goods and services 1,150.92; *Less* Imports of goods and services 1,337.50; *GDP at market prices* 2,498.41.

Gross Domestic Product by Economic Activity (EC $ million in current prices, 2008): Agriculture, hunting, forestry and fishing 92.58; Mining and quarrying 8.09; Manufacturing 137.92; Electricity and water 118.53; Construction 178.07; Wholesale and retail trade 278.18; Restaurants and hotels 293.55; Transport 241.33; Communications 180.58; Banking and insurance 246.46; Real estate and housing 221.95; Government services 352.78; Other services 102.31; *Sub-total* 2,452.33; *Less* Imputed bank service charge 193.59; *Total in basic prices* 2,258.74; Taxes, less subsidies, on products 492.34; *GDP at market prices* 2,751.08. Source: Eastern Caribbean Central Bank.

Balance of Payments (EC $ million, 2008): *Trade balance* −1,174.15; Services (net) 521.60; *Balance on goods and services* −652.55; Other income received (net) −198.83; *Balance on goods, services and income* −851.38; Current transfers received (net) 34.56; *Current balance* −816.82; Capital account (net) 23.41; Direct investment (net) 485.56; Portfolio investment (net) −23.27; Other investment 318.19; Net errors and omissions 4.16; *Overall balance* −8.77. Source: Eastern Caribbean Central Bank.

EXTERNAL TRADE

Principal Commodities (US $ million): *Imports c.i.f.* (2007): Food and live animals 97.2 (Meat and preparations thereof 23.0; Cereals and preparations thereof 19.3); Beverages and tobacco 26.5 (Beverages 22.8); Mineral fuels, lubricants, etc. 130.4 (Refined petroleum products 122.5); Chemicals 36.6; Basic manufactures 77.1 (Metal manufactures 15.6); Machinery and transport equipment 152.7 (Telecommunications equipment 8.8; Road vehicles 72.4); Miscellaneous manufactured articles 81.2; Total (incl. others) 616.0. *Exports f.o.b.* (incl. re-exports, 2006): Food and live animals 19.3 (Bananas 17.8); Beverages and tobacco 15.2 (Beer 13.1); Mineral fuels, lubricants, etc. 20.3 (Refined petroleum products 20.3); Basic manufactures 6.5 (Paper products 4.8); Machinery and transport equipment 17.1 (Telecommunications equipment 3.1; Electric machinery, etc. 3.7; Road vehicles 1.5); Miscellaneous manufactured articles 10.9; Total (incl. others) 93.7. Source: UN, *International Trade Statistics Yearbook*.

Principal Trading Partners (US $ million): *Imports c.i.f.* (2007): Barbados 25.7; Canada 11.4; China, People's Repub. 6.0; Finland 7.4; France (incl. Monaco) 7.3; Germany 6.9; Japan 39.0; Netherlands 5.8; Panama 7.2; Saint Vincent and the Grenadines 4.7; Thailand 13.7; Trinidad and Tobago 122.4; United Kingdom 28.0; USA 256.0; Total (incl. others) 616.0. *Exports f.o.b.* (excl. re-exports,

2006): Antigua and Barbuda 2.0; Barbados 6.2; Dominica 5.1; France (incl. Monaco) 2.2; Grenada 2.2; Saint Vincent and the Grenadines 2.7; Trinidad and Tobago 28.2; United Kingdom 19.4; USA 19.3; Total (incl. others) 93.7.

TRANSPORT

Road Traffic (registered motor vehicles, 2002): Goods vehicles 9,554; Taxis and hired vehicles 1,880; Motorcycles 797; Private vehicles 21,421; Passenger vans 3,439; Total (incl. others) 38,572.

Shipping: *Arrivals* (2006): 1,557 vessels. *International Sea-borne Freight Traffic* (metric tons, 2006): Goods loaded 15,957; Goods unloaded 622,976.

Civil Aviation (traffic at George F. L. Charles and Hewanorra airports, 2006, Jan.–Oct.): Aircraft movements 26,756; Passenger departures 312,047; Passenger arrivals 325,532; Cargo loaded (metric tons) 1,203.8; Cargo unloaded (metric tons) 1,315.5. Source: Saint Lucia Air and Sea Ports Authority.

TOURISM

Visitor Arrivals: 747,308 (317,939 stop-over visitors, 7,541 excursionists, 27,464 yacht passengers, 394,364 cruise-ship passengers) in 2005; 695,279 (302,510 stop-over visitors, 7,051 excursionists, 26,145 yacht passengers, 359,573 cruise-ship passengers) in 2006; 931,111 (287,518 stop-over visitors, 7,841 excursionists, 25,587 yacht passengers, 610,165 cruise-ship passengers) in 2007. *Stop-over visitors by country* (2007): USA 113,516; Canada 18,640; United Kingdom 79,180; Caribbean 59,049; Other countries 17,133.

Tourism Receipts (EC $ million): 961.1 in 2005; 768.4 in 2006; 798.0 in 2007.

Source: Eastern Caribbean Central Bank.

COMMUNICATIONS MEDIA

Radio Receivers ('000 in use, 1997): 111.

Television Receivers ('000 in use, 1999): 56.

Telephones ('000 main lines in use, 2006): 39.4.

Mobile Cellular Telephones ('000 subscribers, 2005): 105.7.

Personal Computers ('000 in use, 2004): 26.

Internet Users ('000 subscribers, 2007): 110.0.

Non-daily Newspapers (1996): Titles 5; Circulation 34,000.

Sources: UN, *Statistical Yearbook*; UNESCO, *Statistical Yearbook*; International Telecommunication Union; Eastern Caribbean Telecommunications Authority, *Annual Telecommunications Sector Review 2006*.

EDUCATION

Pre-primary (state institutions only, 2005/06): 148 schools; 480 teachers; 5,062 pupils.

Primary (state institutions only, 2006/07): 75 schools; 919 teachers; 21,329 pupils.

General Secondary (state institutions only, 2006/07): 23 schools; 855 teachers; 14,699 pupils.

Special Education (state institutions only, 2000/01): 5 schools; 39 teachers; 227 students.

Adult Education (state institutions only, 2000/01): 19 centres; 80 facilitators; 729 learners.

Tertiary (state institutions, including part-time, 2000/01): 127 teachers; 1,403 students.

Source: partly Caribbean Development Bank, *Social and Economic Indicators*.

Adult Literacy Rate (UNESCO estimate): 94.8% in 2004. Source: UN Development Programme, *Human Development Report*.

Directory

The Constitution

The Constitution came into force at the independence of Saint Lucia on 22 February 1979. Its main provisions are summarized below:

FUNDAMENTAL RIGHTS AND FREEDOMS

Regardless of race, place of origin, political opinion, colour, creed or sex but subject to respect for the rights and freedoms of others and for the public interest, every person in Saint Lucia is entitled to the rights of life, liberty, security of the person, equality before the law and the protection of the law. Freedom of conscience, of expression, of assembly and of association is guaranteed, and the inviolability of personal privacy, family life and property is maintained. Protection is afforded from slavery, forced labour, torture and inhuman treatment.

THE GOVERNOR-GENERAL

The British monarch, as Head of State, is represented in Saint Lucia by the Governor-General.

PARLIAMENT

Parliament consists of the British monarch, represented by the Governor-General, the 11-member Senate and the House of Assembly, composed of 17 elected Representatives. Senators are appointed by the Governor-General: six on the advice of the Prime Minister, three on the advice of the Leader of the Opposition and two acting on his own deliberate judgement. The life of Parliament is five years.

Each constituency returns one Representative to the House who is directly elected in accordance with the Constitution.

At a time when the office of Attorney-General is a public office, the Attorney-General is an ex officio member of the House.

Every citizen over the age of 21 is eligible to vote.

Parliament may alter any of the provisions of the Constitution.

THE EXECUTIVE

Executive authority is vested in the British monarch and exercisable by the Governor-General. The Governor-General appoints as Prime Minister that member of the House who, in the Governor-General's view, is best able to command the support of the majority of the members of the House, and other Ministers on the advice of the Prime Minister. The Governor-General may remove the Prime Minister from office if the House approves a resolution expressing 'no confidence' in the Government, and if the Prime Minister does not resign within three days or advise the Governor-General to dissolve Parliament.

The Cabinet consists of the Prime Minister and other Ministers, and the Attorney-General as an ex officio member at a time when the office of Attorney-General is a public office.

The Leader of the Opposition is appointed by the Governor-General as that member of the House who, in the Governor-General's view, is best able to command the support of a majority of members of the house who do not support the Government.

CITIZENSHIP

All persons born in Saint Lucia before independence who immediately prior to independence were citizens of the United Kingdom and Colonies automatically become citizens of Saint Lucia. All persons born in Saint Lucia after independence automatically acquire Saint Lucian citizenship, as do those born outside Saint Lucia after independence to a parent possessing Saint Lucian citizenship. Provision is made for the acquisition of citizenship by those to whom it is not automatically granted.

The Government

HEAD OF STATE

Monarch: HM Queen ELIZABETH II.

Governor-General: Dame PEARLETTE LOUISY (took office 17 September 1997).

CABINET
(April 2009)

Prime Minister and Minister for Finance (International Financial Services), and for Economic Affairs, Economic Planning and National Development: STEPHENSON KING.

Minister for Social Transformation, Public Service, Human Resource Development, Youth and Sports: LENARD SPIDER MONTOUTE.

SAINT LUCIA

Minister for Health Wellness, Family Affairs, National Mobilisation, Human Services and Gender Relations: Dr KEITH MONDESIR.

Minister for Physical Planning, Housing, Urban Renewal, Local Government and the Environment: RICHARD FREDRICK.

Minister for Education and Culture: ARSENE VIGIL JAMES.

Minister for Agriculture, Lands, Fisheries, and Forestry: EZECHIEL JOSEPH.

Minister for Home Affairs and National Security: GEORGE GUY MAYERS.

Minister for External Affairs and for International Trade and Investment: RUFUS GEORGE BOUSQUET.

Minister for Communications, Works, Transport and Public Utilities: GUY EARDLEY JOSEPH.

Minister for Tourism and Civil Aviation: ALLEN M. CHASTANET.

Minister for Labour, Information and Broadcasting: EDMUND ESTEPHANE.

Minister of Commerce, Industry and Consumer Affairs: CHARLOTTE ELIZABETH THERESA TESSA MANGAL.

Attorney-General and Minister for Justice: Dr NICHOLAS FREDERICK.

Minister in the Ministry of Education and Culture: GASPARD PETER DAVID CHARLEMAGNE.

MINISTRIES

Office of the Prime Minister: Greaham Louisy Administrative Bldg, 5th Floor, Waterfront, Castries; tel. 468-2111; fax 453-7352; e-mail admin@pm.gov.lc; internet www.pm.gov.lc.

Attorney-General's Office and Ministry of Justice: Old Education Bldg, Cnr Micoud and Laborie Sts, Castries; tel. 452-3772; fax 453-6315; e-mail atgen@gosl.gov.lc.

Ministry of Agriculture, Lands, Fisheries and Forestry: Stanislaus James Bldg, 5th Floor, Waterfront, Castries; tel. 468-4210; fax 453-6314; e-mail admin@candw.lc; internet www.slumaffe.org.

Ministry of Commerce, Industry and Consumer Affairs: Ives Heraldine Rock Bldg, 4th Floor, Block B, Waterfront, Castries; tel. 468-4202; fax 452-2728.

Ministry of Communications, Works, Transport and Public Utilities: Williams Bldg, Bridge St, Castries; tel. 468-4300; fax 453-2769.

Ministry of Economic Affairs, Economic Planning and National Development: Greaham Louisy Administrative Bldg, 2nd Floor, Waterfront, Castries; tel. 468-2202; fax 453-1305.

Ministry of Education and Culture: Francis Compton Bldg, Waterfront, Castries; tel. 468-5203; fax 453-2299; e-mail mineduc@candw.lc; internet www.education.gov.lc.

Ministry of External Affairs: Conway Business Centre, Waterfront, Castries; tel. 468-4501; fax 452-7427; e-mail foreign@candw.lc.

Ministry of Finance (International Financial Services): Financial Centre, 2nd Floor, Bridge St, Castries; tel. 468-5520; fax 451-9231; e-mail minfin@gosl.gov.lc.

Ministry of Health Wellness, Family Affairs, National Mobilisation, Human Services and Gender Relations: Chaussee Rd, Castries; tel. 452-2859; fax 452-5655; e-mail health@candw.lc.

Ministry of Home Affairs and National Security: Erdiston's Pl., Manoel St, Castries; tel. 468-3600; fax 453-6315.

Ministry of International Trade and Investment: Heraldine Rock Bldg, 4th Floor, Waterfront, Castries; tel. 468-4202; fax 451-6986.

Ministry of Labour, Information and Broadcasting: Conway Business Centre, 5th Floor, Waterfront, Castries; tel. 468-2701; fax 456-0490; e-mail agencyadmin@gosl.gov.lc.

Ministry of Physical Planning, Housing, Urban Renewal, Local Government and the Environment: Castries; internet www.planning.gov.lc.

Ministry of Social Transformation, Public Service, Human Resource Development, Youth and Sports: Greaham Louisy Administrative Bldg, 4th Floor, Waterfront, Castries; tel. 468-5101; fax 453-7921.

Ministry of Tourism and Civil Aviation: Sir Stanislaus James Bldg, 3rd Floor, Waterfront, Castries; tel. 468-4629; fax 451-6986; e-mail mitandt@candw.lc.

Legislature

PARLIAMENT

Senate

The Senate has nine nominated members and two independent members.

President: EVERISTUS JEAN-MARIE.

House of Assembly

Speaker: ROSEMARY HUSBANDS-MATHURIN.
Clerk: KURT THOMAS.
Election, 11 December 2006

Party	Seats
United Workers' Party	11
Saint Lucia Labour Party	6
Total	**17**

Election Commission

Election Commission: St Lucia Electoral Dept, 23 High St, POB 1074, Castries; tel. 452-3725; fax 451-6513; e-mail info@electoral.gov.lc; internet www.electoral.gov.lc; Election Commr CARSON RAGGIE.

Political Organizations

Organization for National Empowerment (ONE): POB 1496, Castries; f. 2004; Leader PETER ALEXANDER; Chair. ROSEMUND CLERY.

Saint Lucia Freedom Party: Castries; f. 1999; campaigns against the political establishment; Spokesman MARTINUS FRANÇOIS.

Saint Lucia Labour Party (SLP): Tom Walcott Bldg, 2nd Floor, Jeremie St, POB 427, Castries; tel. 451-8446; fax 451-9389; e-mail slp@candw.lc; f. 1946; socialist party; Leader Dr KENNY DAVIS ANTHONY; Chair. JULIAN HUNTE.

United Workers' Party (UWP): 9 Coral St, POB 1550, Castries; tel. 451-9103; fax 451-9207; e-mail unitworkers@netscape.net; f. 1964; right-wing; Chair. and Leader STEPHENSON KING.

Diplomatic Representation

EMBASSIES AND HIGH COMMISSION IN SAINT LUCIA

Brazil: Choc Estate, Gros Islet, POB 6136, Castries; Ambassador JOÃO BATISTA CRUZ.

China (Taiwan): Reduit Beach Ave, Rodney Bay; tel. 452-8105; fax 458-0441; Ambassador TOM CHOU.

Cuba: Rodney Heights, Gros Islet, POB 2150, Castries; tel. 458-4665; fax 458-4666; e-mail embacubasantalucia@candw.lc; Ambassador HUGO RUIZ CABRERA.

France: French Embassy to the OECS, GPO Private Box 937, Vigie, Castries; tel. 455-6060; fax 455-6056; e-mail frenchembassy@candw.lc; internet www.ambafrance-lc.org; Ambassador MICHÈLE SAUTERAUD.

Mexico: Nelson Mandela Dr., POB 6096, Vigie, Castries; tel. 453-1250; fax 451-4252; e-mail mexicanembassy@candw.lc; internet www.sre.gob.mx/santalucia; Ambassador GERARDO LOZANO ARREDONDO.

United Kingdom: Francis Compton Bldg, Waterfront, POB 227, Castries; tel. 452-2484; fax 453-1543; e-mail britishhc@candw.lc; High Commissioner DUNCAN JOHN RUSHWORTH TAYLOR (resident in Barbados).

Venezuela: Vigie House, POB 494, Castries; tel. 452-4033; fax 453-6747; e-mail vembassy@candw.lc; Ambassador EDUARDO ALFONZO BARRANCO HERNÁNDEZ.

Judicial System

SUPREME COURT

Eastern Caribbean Supreme Court: Heraldine Rock Bldg, Block B, Waterfront, POB 1093, Castries; tel. 452-7998; fax 452-5475; e-mail appeal@candw.lc; the West Indies Associated States Supreme Court was established in 1967 and was known as the Supreme Court of Grenada and the West Indies Associated States from 1974 until

SAINT LUCIA

1979, when it became the Eastern Caribbean Supreme Court. Its jurisdiction extends to Anguilla, Antigua and Barbuda, the British Virgin Islands, Dominica, Grenada (which rejoined in 1991), Montserrat, Saint Christopher and Nevis, Saint Lucia and Saint Vincent and the Grenadines. It is composed of the High Court of Justice and the Court of Appeal. The High Court is composed of the Chief Justice, who is head of the judiciary, and 16 High Court Judges, three of whom are resident in Saint Lucia. The Court of Appeal is itinerant and presided over by the Chief Justice and three other Justices of Appeal. Additionally, there are two Masters whose principal responsibilities extend to procedural and interlocutory matters. Jurisdiction of the High Court includes fundamental rights and freedoms, membership of the parliaments, and matters concerning the interpretation of constitutions. Following the inauguration of the Caribbean Court of Justice in April 2005, appeals from the Court of Appeal would no longer be made to the Judicial Committee of the Privy Council, based in the United Kingdom, but to the new regional court.

Chief Justice: HUGH ANTHONY RAWLINS (acting).
Justices of Appeal: DENYS ARTHUR BARROW, OLA MAE EDWARDS.
Managing Judge: ESBON ANTHONY ROSS.
Chief Registrar: KIMBERLY CENAC PHULGENCE.
Puisne Judges: KENNETH ANDREW CHARLES BENJAMIN, SANDRA PRUNELLA MASON, BRIAN COTTLE.
Registrar: AISHA BAPTISTE.

Religion

CHRISTIANITY

The Roman Catholic Church

Saint Lucia forms a single archdiocese. The Archbishop participates in the Antilles Episcopal Conference (currently based in Port of Spain, Trinidad and Tobago). At 31 December 2006 there were an estimated 105,755 adherents, equivalent to some 66.9% of the population.

Archbishop of Castries: ROBERT RIVAS, Archbishop's House, Nelson Mandela Dr., POB 267, Castries; tel. 452-2416; fax 452-3697; e-mail secretaries@archdioceseofcastries.org; internet www.archdioceseofcastries.org.

The Anglican Communion

Anglicans in Saint Lucia are adherents of the Church in the Province of the West Indies, comprising eight dioceses. The Archbishop of the West Indies is the Bishop of Nassau and the Bahamas. Saint Lucia forms part of the diocese of the Windward Islands (the Bishop is resident in Kingstown, Saint Vincent).

Other Christian Churches

Seventh-day Adventist Church: St Louis St, POB 117, Castries; tel. 452-4408; e-mail khansamuel@hotmail.com; internet www.tagnet.org/cacoasda; Pastor THEODORE JARIA.

Trinity Evangelical Lutheran Church: Gablewoods Mall, POB 858, Castries; tel. 458-4638; e-mail spiegelbergs@candw.lc; Pastor Rev. TOM SPIEGELBERG.

Baptist, Christian Science, Methodist, Pentecostal and other churches are also represented in Saint Lucia.

The Press

The Catholic Chronicle: POB 778, Castries; f. 1957; monthly; Editor Rev. PATRICK A. B. ANTHONY; circ. 3,000.

The Crusader: 19 St Louis St, Castries; tel. 452-2203; fax 452-1986; f. 1934; weekly (Saturday); circ. 4,000.

The Mirror: Bisee Industrial Estate, POB 1782, Castries; tel. 451-6181; fax 451-6197; e-mail webmaster@stluciamirror.com; internet www.stluciamirroronline.com; f. 1994; weekly (Friday); Man. Editor GUY ELLIS; circ. 3,900.

One Caribbean: POB 852, Castries; e-mail dabread@candw.lc; weekly; Editor D. SINCLAIR DABREO.

She Caribbean: Rodney Bay Industrial Estate, Massade, Gros Islet, POB 1146, Castries; tel. 450-7827; fax 450-8694; e-mail shanna.h@stluciastar.com; internet www.shecaribbean.com; quarterly; Publr and Editor-in-Chief MAE WAYNE.

The Star: Rodney Bay Industrial Estate, Gros Islet, POB 1146, Castries; tel. 450-7827; fax 450-8694; e-mail shanna.h@stluciastar.com; internet www.stluciastar.com; f. 1987; 3 a week (Monday, Wednesday and weekend edns); circ. 8,000; Propr RICK WAYNE; Man. Editor NICOLE MCDONALD.

Tropical Traveller: Rodney Bay Industrial Estate, Massade, Gros Islet, POB 1146, Castries; tel. 450-7827; fax 450-8694; e-mail infostar@stluciastar.com; internet www.tropicaltraveller.com; f. 1989; monthly; Editorial Dir MAE WAYNE; Man. Editor NANCY ATKINSON.

Visions of St Lucia Island Guide: 7 Maurice Mason Ave, Sans Souci, POB 947, Castries; tel. 453-0427; fax 452-1522; e-mail visions@candw.lc; internet www.visionsofstlucia.com; f. 1989; official tourist guide; publ. by Island Visions Ltd; annual; Chair. and Man. Dir ANTHONY NEIL AUSTIN; circ. 120,000.

The Weekend Voice: Odessa Bldg, Darling Rd, POB 104, Castries; tel. 452-2590; fax 453-1453; weekly (Saturdays); circ. 8,000.

PRESS ORGANIZATION

Eastern Caribbean Press Council (ECPC): Castries; f. 2003; independent, self-regulating body designed to foster and maintain standards in regional journalism, formed by 14 newspapers in the Eastern Caribbean and Barbados; Chair. Lady MARIE SIMMONS.

NEWS AGENCY

Caribbean Media Corporation: Bisee Rd, Castries; tel. 453-7162; e-mail admin@cmccaribbean.com; internet www.cananews.com; f. 2000 by merger of Caribbean News Agency and Caribbean Broadcasting Union.

Publishers

Caribbean Publishing Co Ltd: American Drywall Bldg, Vide Boutielle Highway, POB 104, Castries; tel. 452-3188; fax 452-3181; e-mail publish@candw.lc; f. 1978; publr of telephone directories and magazines.

Crusader Publishing Co Ltd: 19 St Louis St, Castries; tel. 452-2203; fax 452-1986.

Island Visions Ltd: 7 Maurice Mason Ave, Sans Soucis, POB 947, Castries; tel. 453-0472; fax 452-1522; e-mail visions@candw.lc; internet www.visionsofstlucia.com; f. 1989; Chair. and Man. Dir ANTHONY NEIL AUSTIN.

Mirror Publishing Co Ltd: Bisee Industrial Estate, POB 1782, Castries; tel. 451-6181; fax 451-6503; e-mail mirror@candw.lc; f. 1994; Man. Editor GUY ELLIS.

Star Publishing Co: Rodney Bay Industrial Estate, Massade, Gros Islet, POB 1146, Castries; tel. 450-7827; fax 450-8694; e-mail infostar@stluciastar.com; internet www.stluciastar.com; Propr RICK WAYNE.

Voice Publishing Co Ltd: Odessa Bldg, Darling Rd, POB 104, Castries; tel. 452-2590; fax 453-1453.

Broadcasting and Communications

TELECOMMUNICATIONS

Regulatory Authorities

Eastern Caribbean Telecommunications Authority (ECTEL): Vide Boutielle, POB 1886, Castries; tel. 458-1701; fax 458-1698; e-mail ectel@ectel.int; internet www.ectel.int; f. 2000 to regulate telecommunications in Saint Lucia, Dominica, Grenada, Saint Christopher and Nevis and Saint Vincent and the Grenadines; Chair. ISAAC SOLOMON; Man. Dir EMBERT CHARLES.

National Telecommunications Regulatory Commission (NTRC): S & S Bldg, Suite 1, 35 Chisel St, POB GM 690, Castries; tel. 458-2035; fax 453-2558; e-mail slufeedback@ectel.int; internet www.ntrc.org.lc; f. 2000; regulates the sector in conjunction with ECTEL; Chair. ELMA GENE ISAAC.

Major Service Providers

Digicel St Lucia: Rodney Bay, Gros Islet, POB GM 791, Castries; tel. 456-3400; fax 450-3872; e-mail customercare.stlucia@digicelgroup.com; internet www.digicelstlucia.com; f. 2003; owned by an Irish consortium; acquired operations of Cingular Wireless in Saint Lucia in 2006; Chair. DENIS O'BRIEN; Eastern Caribbean CEO KEVIN WHITE.

LIME: Bridge St, POB 111, Castries; tel. 453-9720; fax 453-9700; e-mail talk2us@candw.lc; internet www.time4lime.com; fmrly Cable & Wireless St Lucia; name changed as above 2008; provides fixed-line, mobile, internet and cable-television services; CEO RICHARD DODD.

Saint Lucia Boatphone Ltd: Gros Islet, POB 2136, Castries; tel. 452-0361; fax 452-0394; e-mail boatphone@candw.lc; wholly owned subsidiary of Cable & Wireless Caribbean Cellular.

SAINT LUCIA

BROADCASTING

Radio

Radio Caribbean International: 11 Mongiraud St, POB 121, Castries; tel. 452-2636; fax 452-2637; e-mail rci@candw.lc; internet www.rcistlucia.com; operates Radio Caraïbes; English and Creole services; broadcasts 24 hrs; Station Mans PETER EPHRAIM, PET GIBSON.

Saint Lucia Broadcasting Corporation: Morne Fortune, POB 660, Castries; tel. 452-2337; fax 453-1568; govt-owned; Man. KEITH WEEKES.

Radio 100-Helen FM: Morne Fortune, POB 621, Castries; tel. 451-7260; fax 453-1737; e-mail radio@htsstlucia.com; internet www.htsstlucia.com; Gen. Man. STEPHENSON ANIUS.

Radio Saint Lucia Co Ltd (RSL): Morne Fortune, POB 660, Castries; tel. 452-2337; fax 453-1568; e-mail info@rslonline.com; internet www.rslonline.com; f. 1972; English and Creole services; Chair. LINDELL GUSTAVE; Man. Dir MARY POLIUS.

Television

Cablevision: George Gordon Bldg, Bridge St, POB 111, Castries; tel. 453-9311; fax 453-9740.

Catholic Broadcasting TV Network (CBTN): Micoud St, Castries; tel. 452-7050.

Daher Broadcasting Service Ltd (DBS): Vigie, POB 1623, Castries; tel. 453-2705; fax 452-3544; e-mail dbstv@candw.lc; internet dbstelevision.com; Man. Dir LINDA DAHER.

Helen Television System (HTS): National Television Service of St Lucia, POB 621, The Morne, Castries; tel. 452-2693; fax 454-1737; e-mail hts@candw.lc; internet www.htsstlucia.com; f. 1967; commercial station; Gen. Man. STEPHENSON ANIUS.

National Television Network (NTN): Castries; f. 2001; operated by the Government Information Service; provides information on the operations of the public sector.

Finance

(cap. = capital; dep. = deposits; m. = million; brs = branches)

BANKING

The Eastern Caribbean Central Bank, based in Saint Christopher, is the central issuing and monetary authority for Saint Lucia.

Eastern Caribbean Central Bank—Saint Lucia Office: Financial Centre, 3rd Floor, Bridge St, POB 295, Castries; tel. 452-7449; fax 453-6022; e-mail eccbslu@candw.lc; Country Dir TREVOR BRATHWAITE; Rep. GREGOR FRANKLIN.

Local Banks

Bank of Saint Lucia Ltd: Financial Centre, 5th Floor, 1 Bridge St, POB 1862, Castries; tel. 456-6000; fax 456-6702; e-mail bankofstlucia@candw.lc; internet www.bankofsaintlucia.com; f. 2001 by merger of National Commercial Bank of St Lucia Ltd and Saint Lucia Devt Bank; total assets EC $1,600m. (Dec. 2007); 35% state-owned; parent co is East Caribbean Financial Holding Co Ltd; Chair. VICTOR A. EUDOXIE; Gen. Man. RYAN DEVEAUX; 7 brs.

1st National Bank Saint Lucia Ltd: 21 Bridge St, POB 168, Castries; tel. 455-7000; fax 453-1630; e-mail manager@1stnationalbankslu.com; inc. 1937 as Saint Lucia Co-operative Bank Ltd; name changed as above Jan. 2005; commercial bank; share cap. EC $5m., asset base EC $221.4m. (Dec. 2004); Man. Dir C. CARLTON GLASGOW; 4 brs.

FirstCaribbean International Bank (Barbados) Ltd: Bridge St, POB 335, Castries; tel. 456-2422; fax 452-3735; internet www.firstcaribbeanbank.com; f. 2002 following merger of Caribbean operations of Barclays Bank PLC and CIBC; CIBC acquired Barclays' 43.7% stake in 2006; Exec. Chair. MICHAEL MANSOOR; CEO JOHN D. ORR.

RBTT Bank Caribbean Ltd: 22 Micoud St, POB 1531, Castries; tel. 452-2265; fax 452-1668; e-mail rbttslu.isd@candw.lc; internet www.rbtt.com; f. 1985 as Caribbean Banking Corpn Ltd, name changed as above in March 2002; owned by R and M Holdings Ltd; Chair. PETER JULY; Country Man. EARL P. CRICHTON; 4 brs.

STOCK EXCHANGE

Eastern Caribbean Securities Exchange: based in Basseterre, Saint Christopher and Nevis; e-mail info@ecseonline.com; internet www.ecseonline.com; f. 2001; regional securities market designed to facilitate the buying and selling of financial products for the eight member territories—Anguilla, Antigua and Barbuda, Dominica, Grenada, Montserrat, Saint Christopher and Nevis, Saint Lucia and Saint Vincent and the Grenadines; Chair. Sir K. DWIGHT VENNER; Gen. Man. and CEO TREVOR E. BLAKE.

INSURANCE

Local companies include the following:

Caribbean General Insurance Ltd: Laborie St, POB 290, Castries; tel. 452-2410; fax 452-3649.

Eastern Caribbean Insurance Ltd: Laborie St, POB 290, Castries; tel. 452-2410; fax 452-3393; e-mail cgi.ltd@candw.lc.

Saint Lucia Insurances Ltd: 48 Micoud St, POB 1084, Castries; tel. 452-3240; fax 452-2240; e-mail sl.ins@candw.lc; principal agents of Alliance Insurance Co Ltd.

Saint Lucia Motor and General Insurance Co Ltd: 38 Micoud St, POB 767, Castries; tel. 452-3323; fax 452-6072.

Trade and Industry

DEVELOPMENT ORGANIZATION

National Development Corporation (NDC): 1st Floor, Heraldine Rock Bldg, The Waterfront, POB 495, Castries; tel. 452-3614; fax 452-1841; e-mail devcorp@candw.lc; internet www.investstlucia.com; f. 1971 to stimulate, facilitate and promote investment opportunities for foreign and local investors and to promote the economic devt of Saint Lucia; owns and manages seven industrial estates; br. in New York, USA; Exec. Chair. NICHOLAS JOHN; CEO WAYNE VITALIS.

CHAMBER OF COMMERCE

Saint Lucia Chamber of Commerce, Industry and Agriculture: Vide Bouteille, POB 482, Castries; tel. 452-3165; fax 453-6907; e-mail info@stluciachamber.org; internet www.stluciachamber.org; f. 1884; 150 mems; Pres. CHRISTIAN HUSBANDS; Exec. Dir BRIAN LOUISY.

INDUSTRIAL AND TRADE ASSOCIATIONS

Saint Lucia Banana Corporation (SLBC): 7 Manoel St, POB 197, Castries; tel. 452-2251; f. 1998 following privatization of Saint Lucia Banana Growers' Asscn (f. 1967); Chair. (vacant); Sec. FREEMONT LAWRENCE.

Saint Lucia Industrial and Small Business Association: POB 585, Castries; tel. 452-7616; fax 453-1023; e-mail info@slisbastlucia.com; internet www.slisbastlucia.com; Pres. HILTON BAPTISTE.

Small Enterprise Development Unit (SEDU): Ministry of Commerce, Industry and Consumer Affairs, Heraldine Rock Bldg, 4th Floor, Waterfront, Castries; tel. 468-4220; fax 453-2891; f. 2000; Dir PETER LORDE.

EMPLOYERS' ASSOCIATIONS

Saint Lucia Agriculturists' Association Ltd: Mongiraud St, POB 153, Castries; tel. 452-2494; fax 453-2693; distributor and supplier of agricultural, industrial and organic products; exporter of cocoa; Chair. CUTHBERT PHILLIPS; CEO KERDE M. SEVERIN.

Saint Lucia Coconut Growers' Association Ltd: Palmiste Rd, POB 269, Castries; tel. 459-7227; fax 459-7216; e-mail slcga1@candw.lc; f. 1939; Chair. RAPHAEL ST MARK; Gen. Man. GERALD MORRIS.

Saint Lucia Employers' Federation: c/o The Morgan Bldg, L'Anse Rd, POB 160, Castries; tel. 452-2190; fax 452-7335; e-mail slefslu@candw.lc; Pres. CALLISTUS VERN GILL.

Saint Lucia Fish Marketing Corpn: POB 891, Castries; tel. 452-1341; fax 451-7073; e-mail slfmc@candw.lc.

Saint Lucia Marketing Board (SLMB): Conway, POB 441, Castries; tel. 452-3214; fax 453-1424; e-mail slmb@candw.lc; Gen. Man. THERESA DESIR (acting).

Windward Islands Banana Development and Exporting Co (Wibdeco): Manoel St, POB 115, Castries; tel. 452-2411; fax 453-1638; e-mail wibdeco@candw.lc; internet www.wibdeco.com; f. 1994 in succession to the Windward Islands Banana Growers' Asscn (WINBAN); regional org. dealing with banana devt and marketing; jtly owned by the Windward govts and island banana asscns; CEO BERNARD CORNIBERT.

UTILITIES

Electricity

Caribbean Electric Utility Services Corpn (CARILEC): Desir Ave, Sans Soucis, POB CP 5907, Castries; tel. 452-0140; fax 452-0142; e-mail admin@carilec.org; internet www.carilec.com; f. 1989; Chair. TREVOR LOUISY.

SAINT LUCIA

St Lucia Electricity Services Ltd (LUCELEC): St Lucia Electricity Services Ltd, Sans Soucis, POB 230, Castries; tel. 457-4400; fax 457-4409; e-mail lucelec@candw.lc; internet www.lucelec.com; f. 1964; Canadian energy co Emera acquired a 19% share in LUCELEC in Jan. 2007; Chair. MARIUS ST ROSE; Man. Dir TREVOR LOUISY.

Water

Water and Sewerage Company (WASCO): L'Anse Rd, POB 1481, Castries; tel. 452-5344; fax 452-6844; e-mail wasco@candw.lc; f. 1999 as the Water and Sewerage Authority (WASA); planned privatization under review in 2009; Chair. GORDON CHARLES; Man. Dir JOHN C. JOSEPH.

TRADE UNIONS

National Workers' Union (NWU): Bour Bon St, POB 713, Castries; tel. 452-3664; fax 453-2896; e-mail natwork3@hotmail.com; f. 1973; represents daily-paid workers; affiliated to World Federation of Trade Unions; Pres.-Gen. TYRONE MAYNARD; Sec.-Gen. GEORGE GODDARD, Jr; 3,200 mems (2005).

Saint Lucia Civil Service Association: Sans Soucis, POB 244, Castries; tel. 452-3903; fax 453-6061; e-mail csa@candw.lc; internet www.csastlucia.org; f. 1951; Pres. JOSEPH DOSSERIE; Gen. Sec. DAVID J. DEMACQUE; 2,381 mems.

Saint Lucia Medical and Dental Association: POB 691, Castries; tel. 451-8441; fax 458-1147; e-mail slmdaoffice@gmail.com; internet www.slmda.org; f. 1969; Pres. Dr TANYA DESTANG-BEAUBRUN; Gen. Sec. Dr KIMBERLEY JOHNNY.

Saint Lucia Nurses' Association: POB 819, Castries; tel. 452-1403; fax 453-0121; e-mail slna1947@gmail.com; f. 1947; Pres. LUCY LOUIS JOSEPH; Gen. Sec. FRANCES LESMOND.

Saint Lucia Seamen, Waterfront and General Workers' Trade Union: L'Anse Rd, POB 166, Castries; tel. 452-1669; fax 452-5452; e-mail seamen@candw.lc; f. 1945; affiliated to Int. Trade Union Confed., Int. Transport Fed. and Caribbean Congress of Labour; Pres. ESTHER ST MARIE (acting); Sec. CECILIA W. ADOLPH; 1,000 mems.

Saint Lucia Teachers' Union: La Clery, POB 821, Castries; tel. 452-4469; fax 453-6668; e-mail sltu@candw.lc; f. 1934; Pres. JULIAN MONROSE; Gen. Sec. WAYNE CUMBERBATCH.

Saint Lucia Trade Union Federation: c/o Saint Lucia Teachers' Union, La Clery, POB 821, Castries; tel. 452-4469; fax 453-6668; e-mail cumbatch42@gmail.com; f. 2005; comprises nine trade unions of Saint Lucia, including the Saint Lucia Civil Service Asscn, Saint Lucia Teachers' Union, Saint Lucia Medical and Dental Asscn, Saint Lucia Nurses' Asscn, Saint Lucia Seamen and Waterfront General Workers' Union, National Farmers' Asscn, Police Welfare Asscn, Saint Lucia Fire Service Asscn and Vieux Fort General and Dock Workers' Union; Pres. JOSEPH DOSSERIRE; Gen. Sec. WAYNE CUMBERBATCH.

Saint Lucia Workers' Union: Reclamation Grounds, Conway, Castries; tel. 452-2620; f. 1939; affiliated to International Trade Union Confederation; Pres. GEORGE LOUIS; Sec. TITUS FRANCIS; 1,000 mems.

Vieux Fort General and Dock Workers' Union: New Dock Rd, POB 224, Vieux Fort; tel. 454-5128; e-mail dockworkersunion@hotmail.com; f. 1954; Pres. ATHANATIUS DOLOR; Gen. Sec. CLAUDIA AUGUSTE (acting); 846 mems (1996).

Transport

RAILWAYS

There are no railways in Saint Lucia.

ROADS

In 2000 there was an estimated total road network of 910 km, of which 150 km were main roads and 127 km were secondary roads. In that year only 5.2% of roads were paved. The main highway passes through every town and village on the island. The construction of a coastal highway, to link Castries with Cul de Sac Bay, was completed in February 2000. Improvements to the road infrastructure outlined in the 2008/09 budget address included the construction of 20.2 km of tunnels under the Barre de l'Isle and the rehabilitation of 28.1 km of community and agricultural feeder roads, at a cost of EC $12.9m. The total allocation for the Ministry of Communications, Works, Transport and Public Utilities was EC $72.9m. in that financial year. Internal transport is handled by private concerns and controlled by the Government.

SHIPPING

The ports at Castries and Vieux Fort have been fully mechanized. Castries has six berths with a total length of 2,470 ft (753 m). The two dolphin berths at the Pointe Seraphine cruise ship terminal have been upgraded to a solid berth of 1,000 ft (305 m) and one of 850 ft (259 m). The port of Soufrière has a deep-water anchorage, but no alongside berth for ocean-going vessels. There is a petroleum trans-shipment terminal at Cul de Sac Bay. In 2007 610,169 cruise ship passengers called at Saint Lucia. Regular services are provided by a number of shipping lines, including ferry services to neighbouring islands. In January 2007 Island Global Yachting Facilities Ltd (New York, USA) acquired the marina at Rodney Bay, and plans for substantial upgrade work to enhance facilities and operations were announced. There were plans to develop and expand the waterfront area at Castries in order for it to become a dedicated cruise ship port; the port at Vieux Fort was also to be expanded in order to handle all commercial cargo.

Saint Lucia Air and Sea Ports Authority (SLASPA): Manoel St, POB 651, Castries; tel. 452-2893; fax 452-2062; e-mail info@slaspa.com; internet www.slaspa.com; f. 1983; Chair. ISAAC ANTHONY; Gen. Man. SEAN MATTHEW; Dir of Airports PETER F. JEAN.

Saint Lucia Marine Terminals Ltd: POB VF 355, Vieux Fort; tel. 454-8742; fax 454-8745; e-mail slumarterm@candw.lc; f. 1995; private port management co.

CIVIL AVIATION

There are two airports in use: Hewanorra International (formerly Beane Field near Vieux Fort), 64 km (40 miles) from Castries, which is equipped to handle large jet aircraft and underwent expansion works in 2006 in preparation for the anticipated increase in traffic ahead of the Cricket World Cup in 2007; and George F. L. Charles Airport, which is at Vigie, in Castries, and which is capable of handling medium-range jets. Saint Lucia is served by scheduled flights to the USA, Canada, Europe and most destinations in the Caribbean. The country is a shareholder in the regional airline LIAT (see chapter on Antigua and Barbuda), which in late 2006 announced that it was to merge with its troubled rival Caribbean Star Airlines (headquartered in Antigua and Barbuda); the two airlines began operating a joint flight schedule from February 2007 under LIAT's airline designation code. The planned merger was subsequently abandoned in favour of negotiations towards LIAT's full acquisition of Caribbean Star, which were completed in October 2007.

Saint Lucia Air and Sea Ports Authority: see Shipping.

Air Antilles: Laborie St, POB 1065, Castries; f. 1985; designated as national carrier of Grenada in 1987; flights to destinations in the Caribbean, the United Kingdom and North America; charter co.

Caribbean Air Transport: POB 253, Castries; f. 1975 as Saint Lucia Airways; local shuttle service, charter flights.

Eagle Air Services Ltd: George F. L. Charles Airport, POB 838, Castries; tel. and fax 452-9683; e-mail eagleairslu@candw.lc; charter flights; Man. Dir Capt. EWART F. HINKSON.

Tourism

Saint Lucia possesses spectacular mountain scenery, a tropical climate and sandy beaches. Historical sites, rich birdlife and the sulphur baths at Soufrière are other attractions. Visitor arrivals totalled 931,111 in 2007, representing a 33.9% increase on the previous year. Tourism receipts in that year were an estimated EC $798.0m. The USA is the principal market (39.5% of total stop-over visitors in 2007), followed by the United Kingdom (with 27.5%).

Saint Lucia Hotel and Tourism Association (SLHTA): John Compton Hwy, POB 545, Castries; tel. 452-5978; fax 452-7967; e-mail slhta@candw.lc; internet www.slhta.org; f. 1963; Pres. ANTHONY BOWEN; Exec. Gen. Man. SILVANIUS FONTENARD.

Saint Lucia Tourist Board: Sureline Bldg, Top Floor, Vide Bouteille, POB 221, Castries; tel. 452-4094; fax 453-1121; e-mail slutour@candw.lc; internet www.stlucia.org; f. 1981; 2 brs overseas; Chair. LAURIE BARNAD; Dir LOUIS LEWIS.

SAINT VINCENT AND THE GRENADINES

Introductory Survey

Location, Climate, Language, Religion, Flag, Capital

Saint Vincent and the Grenadines is situated in the Windward Islands group, approximately 160 km (100 miles) west of Barbados, in the West Indies. The nearest neighbouring countries are Saint Lucia, some 34 km (21 miles) to the northeast, and Grenada, to the south. As well as the main volcanic island of Saint Vincent, the state includes the 32 smaller islands and cayes known as the Saint Vincent Grenadines, the northerly part of an island chain stretching between Saint Vincent and Grenada. The principal islands in that part of the group are Bequia, Canouan, Mustique, Mayreau, Isle D'Quatre and Union Island. The climate is tropical, with average temperatures of between 18°C and 32°C (64°F–90°F). Annual rainfall ranges from 1,500 mm (60 ins) in the extreme south, to 3,750 mm (150 ins) in the mountainous interior of the main island. English is the official language. Most of the inhabitants profess Christianity and are adherents of the Anglican, Methodist or Roman Catholic Churches. The national flag (proportions 2 by 3) has three unequal vertical stripes, of blue (at the hoist), yellow and green (at the fly), with three lozenges in green, in a 'V' formation, superimposed on the broad central yellow stripe. The capital is Kingstown, on the island of Saint Vincent.

Recent History

The islands were first settled by an Arawak people, who were subsequently conquered by the Caribs. The arrival of shipwrecked and escaped African slaves resulted in the increase of a so-called 'Black Carib' population, some of whose descendants still remain. Under the collective name of Saint Vincent, and despite the opposition of the French and the indigenous population, the islands finally became a British possession during the 18th century. With other nearby British territories, the Governor of the Windward Islands administered Saint Vincent, under a federal system, until December 1959. The first elections under universal adult suffrage took place in 1951. The islands participated in the West Indies Federation from its foundation in January 1958 until its dissolution in May 1962. From January 1960, Saint Vincent, in common with the other Windward Islands, had a new Constitution, with its own Administrator and an enlarged Legislative Council.

After the failure of negotiations to form a smaller East Caribbean Federation, most of the British colonies in the Leeward and Windward Islands became Associated States, with full internal self-government, in 1967. This change of status was delayed in Saint Vincent because of local political differences. At controversial elections to the Legislative Council in 1966, the ruling People's Political Party (PPP) was returned with a majority of only one seat. Further elections took place in May 1967, when the Saint Vincent Labour Party (SVLP) secured six of the nine seats in the Council. Milton Cato, leader of the SVLP, became Chief Minister, in succession to Ebenezer Joshua of the PPP. On 27 October 1969, despite objections from the PPP, Saint Vincent became an Associated State, with the United Kingdom retaining responsibility for defence and foreign relations only. The Legislative Council was renamed the House of Assembly, the Administrator was designated Governor, and the Chief Minister became Premier.

Elections were held in April 1972 for an enlarged, 13-seat House of Assembly. The PPP and the SVLP each obtained six seats, while James Mitchell, formerly a minister in the SVLP Government and standing as an independent, secured the remaining one. The PPP agreed to form a Government with Mitchell as Premier and Joshua as Deputy Premier and Minister of Finance. In September 1974 Joshua resigned after policy disagreements with the Premier. A motion expressing no confidence in Mitchell's Government was approved, and the House was dissolved. In the ensuing election, which took place in December, the PPP and SVLP campaigned in a 'unity agreement'. The SVLP secured 10 of the 13 seats, and the PPP two. (Mitchell was again elected as an independent.) Cato became Premier again, at the head of a coalition with the PPP, and committed his Government to attaining full independence from the United Kingdom.

After a constitutional conference in September 1978, the colony became fully independent, within the Commonwealth, as Saint Vincent and the Grenadines, on 27 October 1979. The Governor became Governor-General, while Cato took office as the country's first Prime Minister.

Cato's position was reinforced in the general election of December 1979, when the SVLP obtained 11 of the 13 elective seats in the 19-member House of Assembly. In 1982 the leader of the opposition United People's Movement (UPM), Dr Ralph Gonsalves, resigned, accusing the UPM of harbouring Marxist tendencies, and founded a new party, the Movement for National Unity (MNU). In June 1984 Cato announced an early general election, hoping to take advantage of divisions within the opposition. However, the repercussions of scandals surrounding the Cato Government, and the economic and taxation policies of the SVLP, contributed to an unexpected victory for the centrist New Democratic Party (NDP) at the election in July. The NDP's leader, James Mitchell, became Prime Minister. Cato subsequently retired from politics and in the ensuing by-election the NDP gained another seat. Hudson Tannis replaced Cato as leader of the SVLP in January 1985; Vincent Beache succeeded him as party leader in August 1986.

At a general election conducted in May 1989 the NDP won all 15 elective seats in the newly enlarged House of Assembly. Mitchell remained as Prime Minister and formed a new Cabinet.

The NDP secured its third consecutive term of office at a general election in February 1994, obtaining 12 seats in the House of Assembly. An electoral alliance formed by the SVLP and the MNU and headed by Vincent Beache won the three remaining elective seats. In September 1994 the MNU and the SVLP announced their formal merger as the Unity Labour Party (ULP).

Opposition charges that the Government had failed to address problems presented by a marked decline in banana production, a crisis in the health and education sectors and persistent allegations that drugs-related activities were being conducted on the islands culminated in the defeat, by 10 votes to three, of a motion of no confidence in the Government, brought by the opposition in August 1994. The execution, by hanging, of three convicted murderers in February 1995 provoked outrage from international human rights organizations, which expressed concern at the alacrity and secrecy with which the sentences had been implemented.

At a general election in June 1998 the NDP lost four seats, retaining eight, while the ULP obtained the remaining seven. The reverse sustained by the NDP was attributed to voter dissatisfaction with the state of the economy. Although the ULP had obtained around 55% of the vote, Mitchell claimed that the result was a mandate for his Government to undertake a record fourth term of office. The ULP leader, Vincent Beache, called on the NDP to hold fresh elections within nine months, and not to govern on the basis of a minority vote. The ULP also claimed to have obtained evidence of irregularities during the elections, particularly in the four seats won by the NDP with margins of between 27 and 109 votes. In early July, at the opening of the first session of the House of Assembly, several hundred protesters demonstrated against the new Government and two ministers were attacked as they tried to drive through the crowd.

In November 1998 members of the public and of the opposition demonstrated outside government offices to demand the resignation of Mitchell and Arnhim Eustace, the Minister of Finance and Public Services. The protests followed the announcement of the details of an agreement reached by the Government with the Government of Italy and a consortium of European financial institutions on the repayment of US $67m., incurred because the Government had guaranteed a loan of $50m. made to a company of Italian developers that subsequently went into liquidation. The loan had been made to finance the failed Ottley Hall marina and shipyard project, valued at only $5m. The new agreement stipulated that the shipyard should be sold and that repayments of $32m. of debt should begin immediately, with the remaining $30m. to be set aside.

In late November 1998 marijuana growers demonstrated outside the Prime Minister's office against plans to use regional and US troops to destroy the marijuana crop in the highlands of Saint Vincent. Mitchell refused to meet representatives of the protesters, telling them to take advantage of government schemes to promote economic diversification. In December US marines and troops provided by the Regional Security System destroyed crops during a two-week operation, despite opposition from growers. Mitchell subsequently warned the USA that, if Saint Vincent's banana producers were bankrupted by the US initiative to challenge the preferential treatment accorded by the European Union (EU, see p. 255) to banana exports from Caribbean and African states, it was likely that producers would turn instead to the cultivation of marijuana. In March 1999 Saint Vincent and the Grenadines was one of a number of Caribbean states to warn that, if the USA continued to threaten their economic stability by pursuing its case against the EU banana import regime at the World Trade Organization (see p. 410), they would withdraw co-operation with US-sponsored anti-drugs initiatives. (See the Recent History of Saint Lucia for further details of the trade dispute over bananas between the USA and the EU.) In December, however, a large-scale marijuana eradication exercise took place in Saint Vincent with backing from US marines.

In December 1999 a committee chaired by Dwight Venner, the Governor of the Eastern Caribbean Central Bank (see p. 430), recommended that members of the House of Assembly should receive increased salaries. The committee, however, suggested that the increases should not be awarded until legislation on political integrity had been implemented, and reforms of the public sector had been effected. The proposed increases were opposed by the ULP, which in late January 2000 threatened to introduce a motion of no confidence in the Government, accusing it of corruption, excessive expenditure on development projects, a failure to reduce crime levels and of neglecting education. The Government's subsequent introduction in April of legislation increasing the salaries and benefits of members of the House of Assembly provoked protests throughout the islands, which were directed by the ULP and by public sector trade unions, which accused the Government of 'disregard and contempt' for ordinary workers. Members of the Saint Vincent Union of Teachers undertook industrial action in protest, while there were several days of public demonstrations at the end of April, culminating in a mass rally in Kingstown. In early May the Government and the workers reached an agreement, known as the Grand Beach accord, whereby fresh legislative elections were to be called before March 2001; the accord also allowed for a national dialogue on constitutional reform.

In August 2000 Mitchell relinquished the post of NDP President in favour of the Minister of Finance and Public Services, Arnhim Eustace. On 27 October Eustace also succeeded Mitchell as Prime Minister, following the latter's retirement as head of government. Mitchell remained in the Cabinet as Senior Minister.

A general election was held on 28 March 2001. The ULP secured an overwhelming victory, winning 12 of the 15 parliamentary seats and 57% of the votes cast. The NDP, which had been in power since 1984, secured 41% of the votes cast and the remaining three House of Assembly seats. The new Government took office in mid-April, led by Dr Ralph Gonsalves, leader of the ULP since 1998. In December 2002 Gonsalves established a 25-member Constitutional Review Commission, the first report of which was presented in late March 2004. Among the issues to be addressed were local government organization and finance, civil service reform and the electoral system.

In June 2002 the Governor-General, Sir Charles Antrobus, died. Sir Frederick Ballantyne was appointed as his successor in September.

In March 2004 the parliamentary opposition boycotted the House of Assembly and established an 'alternative parliament' at the NDP's headquarters; Eustace claimed that the parliamentary Speaker, Hendrick Alexander, had consistently demonstrated a pro-Government bias. In late February Eustace had led NDP members out of Parliament after the Prime Minister was allowed to present an amendment to a motion on a day when opposition business should have taken precedence. The opposition again boycotted the House of Assembly and re-established its 'alternative parliament' in March 2005. On this occasion, the NDP was particularly unhappy about constituency boundaries and the registration of voters before the next elections, which were due by March 2006.

Despite the concerns of the opposition, Gonsalves' Government maintained its popularity; however, in 2004–05 the issue of violent crime was increasingly prominent and it was widely held that the Government had devoted insufficient funds to attempting to resolve the problem. Moreover, Saint Vincent remained one of the largest cultivators of marijuana in the region, and in 2003 the Government reported that 40% of prison inmates had been gaoled for drugs-related offences. In November 2004 Gonsalves, who had previously expressed severe reservations about capital punishment, claimed that the use of the death penalty was necessary to reduce the influence of criminal gangs in the country. The comments were made in the House of Assembly, during the passage of the Firearm Amendment Act, which was to introduce stricter penalties for illegal possession of weapons.

At legislative elections, held on 7 December 2005, the ULP again secured 12 of the 15 seats in the House of Assembly and 55% of the popular vote. The NDP secured the remaining three legislative seats, although the party increased its share of the vote to 45%, compared with 41% in 2001. A third party, the newly formed Saint Vincent and the Grenadines Green Party, garnered just 34 votes from the four constituencies in which it competed. Registered votes were cast by 63.7% of the electorate. Monitoring teams from various international organizations described the contest as free and fair.

Following the ULP's re-election Gonsalves reorganized and expanded the Cabinet: Louis Straker, the Deputy Prime Minister, was given his former portfolio of foreign affairs, commerce and trade. The previous holder of that post, Michael Browne, meanwhile, was placed in charge of a wide-ranging new Ministry of National Mobilization, Social Development, NGO Relations, Family, Gender Affairs and Persons with Disabilities, and Julian Francis was appointed Minister of Housing, Informal Human Settlements, Physical Planning, Lands and Surveys. The Prime Minister also pledged to use the Government's new mandate to introduce constitutional reform, after popular consultation via referendums. In addition, Gonsalves announced his intention to ask the House of Assembly to approve legislation making the Caribbean Court of Justice (which had been inaugurated in Trinidad and Tobago in April 2005) the country's senior court of appeal, in place of the Privy Council in the United Kingdom. (The Privy Council remained the country's highest appellate body in April 2009.)

Prime Minister Gonsalves and his ULP Government suffered a significant threat in February 2007 when the NDP marshalled a demonstration in Kingstown demanding the removal of the premier from office and requisitioning a general election. Public and opposition unrest had escalated during the preceding months following increased public concerns over crime, despite an announcement by the Criminal Investigation Department of Saint Vincent and the Grenadines in September 2006 that the overall crime rate had declined during that year and that a sustained decline had been recorded from 2001. The early release of a convicted drugs offender caused particular disquiet. The NDP contested that Gonsalves' endorsement of the decision and failure to provide an explanation had severely compromised the Government's integrity and had undermined public confidence. Gonsalves asserted that the decision to release the convict had been justified in the interests of national security. Eustace further suggested that the increasing prevalence of drugs-related and violent crime in the country was directly attributable to Gonsalves' inadequate enforcement of penal law, and that the Government was implicated in the alleged engagement of drugs magnates in the financing of political campaigns.

Tensions between the Government and opposition parties intensified during 2007 and early 2008. An inquiry into the failed Ottley Hall marina and shipyard development project remained ongoing in April 2008; the losses incurred under the scheme, according to some reports, accounted for more than one-quarter of Saint Vincent's total external debt. The NDP attempted to increase its popularity by challenging government plans to introduce a value-added tax, and in January 2008 it accused Gonsalves of misleading teachers in a 'reclassification' exercise of the public sector pay grade structure. The NDP claimed that the remuneration benefits were not, in reality, as generous as Gonsalves had initially suggested, and, on 9 and

10 January, more than 1,000 teachers went on strike in protest at the changes, supported by the Saint Vincent and the Grenadines Teachers' Union.

Saint Vincent and the Grenadines is a member of the Caribbean Community and Common Market (CARICOM, see p. 206) and of the Organisation of Eastern Caribbean States (OECS, see p. 440), and is a signatory of the Cotonou Agreement (see p. 311), the successor agreement to the Lomé Convention. In February 2004 Parliament approved legislation allowing nationals of OECS member states to travel freely within the OECS area and to remain in a foreign territory within the area for up to six months. Saint Vincent and the Grenadines implemented CARICOM's intra-regional common passport initiative, regarded as an integral component in the advance towards economic union, in April 2006. Saint Vincent and the Grenadines, together with five other Caribbean states, became a signatory to CARICOM's Caribbean Single Market and Economy (CSME) on 3 July, which had been established by six founding member states on 1 January of that year. The CSME was intended to enshrine the free movement of goods, services and labour throughout the CARICOM region. Following an Inter-Sessional Conference of CARICOM heads of government in Saint Vincent and the Grenadines in February 2007, it was announced that the single economy component of the initiative was advancing in accordance with the scheduled completion dates. Two phases of implementation were to ensue: the first would be consolidation of the single market and initiation of the single economy by 1 January 2009; while the second phase, spanning 2010–15, would define and institute the single economy and regional monetary union. The Inter-American Development Bank pledged financial assistance to facilitate the regional integration process between 2007 and 2010.

In 1992 the islands established diplomatic relations with Cuba. The two countries signed accords pledging further co-operation in a number of areas, including health and education, in 2001 and 2002. Taiwan and Saint Vincent and the Grenadines celebrated 25 years of diplomatic relations in August 2006; in the same month the Taiwanese Government announced the donation of US $15m. and extension of a $10m. loan towards the construction of an international airport on the islands, while reiterating its commitment to assisting in the infrastructural and human resource development of the Caribbean nation. Following a visit to the Taiwanese capital, Taipei, in mid-2008, Gonsalves announced that the Taiwanese Government had agreed to increase funding for development projects in Saint Vincent and the Grenadines.

In 2001 Libya granted the islands, in common with other eastern Caribbean countries, access to a US $2,000m. development fund. It was also reported in September that Libya had agreed to provide Saint Vincent and the Grenadines with a grant of $4.5m. (including an immediate disbursement of $1.5m.), following Gonsalves' controversial visit to the Libyan capital, Tripoli, earlier in the month. Further controversy arose after Japan pledged to provide $6m. for the construction of a fish market. It was claimed that, in return for Japanese financial aid, Saint Vincent and the Grenadines would support the pro-whaling bloc at meetings of the International Whaling Commission (IWC); Gonsalves refuted the allegation, pointing out that the Government had abstained on crucial votes relating to the provision of whale sanctuaries in the South Atlantic and the Pacific. However, the controversy re-emerged at the IWC meeting in June 2006 when Saint Vincent and the Grenadines endorsed Japan's proposal to end a 20-year moratorium on commercial whaling, invoking the vehement criticism of prominent international trading partners and creating a potential threat to the region's crucial tourist industry. Moreover, the subsequent announcement of a new EC $33m. fisheries complex to be financed by the Japanese Government provoked allegations of diplomacy motivated by economic incentive.

There was some public unease over Saint Vincent and the Grenadines' burgeoning economic relations with Venezuela. Specific protest was made against a memorandum of understanding, signed by Gonsalves in February 2007, subscribing to the principles of President Hugo Chávez's Bolivarian Alternative for the Americas (Alternativa Bolivariana para las Américas—ALBA), an economic integration initiative to rival the stagnant Free Trade Areas of the Americas proposed by the USA. Eustace cautioned that the accord conspicuously aligned the country with Venezuela at the possible expense of its diplomatic relationship with the USA. Gonsalves maintained that relations with these respective nations were not mutually exclusive and emphasized the importance of Venezuela's influence upon the progress of national development, citing the benefits of the recently implemented PetroCaribe initiative (under which the country could purchase petroleum from Venezuela at discounted prices) and the Venezuelan Government's contribution to the construction of an international airport. In April 2009 Chávez announced that Saint Vincent and the Grenadines had been accepted as a member of ALBA; Eustace criticized the Government's failure to explain to the public what membership of the bloc would involve.

It was announced in August 2008 that Saint Vincent and the Grenadines was to establish diplomatic relations with Iran, with Iran providing US $7m. in development loans and grants for the airport construction project. The US Ambassador to the Eastern Caribbean expressed concern at the decision at a time when there were US anxieties at Iran's nuclear activities.

In February 2003 Saint Vincent and the Grenadines was admitted to the Non-Aligned Movement (see p. 439).

Government

Saint Vincent and the Grenadines is a constitutional monarchy. Executive power is vested in the British monarch, as Head of State, and is exercisable by the Governor-General, who represents the British monarch locally and who is appointed on the advice of the Prime Minister. Legislative power is vested in Parliament, comprising the Governor-General and the House of Assembly (composed of 21 members: six nominated Senators and 15 Representatives, elected for up to five years by universal adult suffrage). Senators are appointed by the Governor-General: four on the advice of the Prime Minister and two on the advice of the Leader of the Opposition. Government is effectively by the Cabinet. The Governor-General appoints the Prime Minister and, on the latter's recommendation, selects the other Ministers. The Prime Minister must be able to command the support of the majority of the House, to which the Cabinet is responsible.

Defence

Saint Vincent and the Grenadines participates in the US-sponsored Regional Security System, comprising police, coastguards and army units, which was established by independent East Caribbean states in 1982. Since 1984, however, the paramilitary Special Service Unit has had strictly limited deployment. In the 2008 budget, EC $17.9m. of capital funding (equivalent to 7.5% of total capital expenditure) was allocated for national security. The recurrent budget for 2008 allocated some 10.3% of total expenditure (projected at EC $517.5m.) for defence purposes.

Economic Affairs

In 2007, according to estimates by the World Bank, Saint Vincent and the Grenadines' gross national income (GNI), measured at average 2005–07 prices, was US $507m., equivalent to $4,210 per head (or $7,170 per head on an international purchasing-power parity basis). During 2000–08, it was estimated, the population declined at an average annual rate of 0.7%, while gross domestic product (GDP) per head increased, in real terms, by an average of 5.2% per year. Overall GDP increased, in real terms, at an average annual rate of 4.5% in 2000–08; according to the Eastern Caribbean Central Bank (ECCB, see p. 430), real GDP increased by 1.0% in 2008.

Agriculture (including forestry and fishing) contributed 6.4% of GDP in 2008. The sector employed an estimated 22.2% of the working population in 2005, according to FAO, and agricultural products account for the largest share of export revenue. The principal cash crop is bananas, which contributed an estimated 29.4% of the value of total exports in 2006. Other important crops are arrowroot, sweet potatoes, tannias, taro, plantains and coconuts. According to the ECCB, during 2000–2008 real agricultural GDP (growth of which is heavily reliant on weather conditions and banana production) decreased at an annual average rate of 4.3%. Although an increase of 9.3% was recorded in 2007, sectoral GDP declined by 7.3% in 2008.

Industry (including mining, manufacturing, electricity, water and construction) employed 21.1% of the working population in 1991, and contributed 23.3% of GDP in 2008. During 2000–08 real industrial GDP increased at an average annual rate of 5.1%, according to the ECCB; the sector's GDP expanded by 2.5% in 2008. In September 2005 the Prime Minister announced that a Canadian company was conducting preliminary petroleum-exploration work in Saint Vincent and the Grenadines' territorial waters.

The manufacturing sector contributed 3.6% of GDP in 2008, and engaged 8.5% of the employed labour force in 1991. Apart from a garment industry and the assembling of electrical components, the most important activities involve the processing of agricultural products, including flour- and rice-milling, brewing, rum distillation, and processing dairy products. During 2000–08 real manufacturing GDP increased by an average annual rate of 0.2%, according to ECCB figures. The sector's real GDP expanded by 1.1% in 2007 before declining by 7.0% in 2008.

Energy is derived principally from the use of hydrocarbon fuels (mineral fuels and lubricants accounted for around 14.6% of total imports in 2006). The islands imported most of their energy requirements. There is, however, an important hydroelectric plant in Cumberland. In September 2005 the Government became one of 13 Caribbean administrations to sign the Petro-Caribe accord, under which Saint Vincent and the Grenadines would be allowed to purchase petroleum from Venezuela at reduced prices.

The services sector contributed an estimated 70.3% of GDP in 2008 and engaged 53.8% of the employed population at the time of the 1991 census. Tourism is the most important activity within the sector, but is smaller in scale than in most other Caribbean islands; the World Travel and Tourism Council forecast that the sector would account for 29% of GDP in 2009. Tourist activity remains concentrated in the Grenadines and caters for the luxury market. Visitors aboard yachts have traditionally been the most important sector, although the numbers of stop-over and cruise-ship visitors have increased in recent years. In 2005 visitor arrivals decreased by 3.2%, although the number of stop-over tourists continued to climb, by an estimated 9.5%. The sector recovered in 2006; arrivals increased by an estimated 19.7% in that year, owing largely to the greater number of yacht and cruise-ship passengers visiting the islands (which rose by 14.3% and 52.6%, respectively). Although total arrivals increased in 2007 by 14.8%, this was primarily owing to 35.7% growth in the number of cruise-ship passengers. Total visitor arrivals declined by 1.6% in 2008. Aside from tourism, a small 'offshore' financial sector also contributes to the services sector. During 2000–08 the real GDP of the services sector as a whole increased by an average annual rate of 4.7%, according to the ECCB; an estimated increase of 4.1% was recorded in 2008.

In 2008 Saint Vincent and the Grenadines recorded an estimated visible trade deficit of EC $679.82m., while there was a deficit of $585.24m. on the current account of the balance of payments. The principal source of imports is the USA (accounting for an estimated 32.7% of the total in 2006). Other important suppliers in that year were Trinidad and Tobago and the United Kingdom. The United Kingdom is the principal market for exports (accounting for an estimated 25.5% of total exports in 2006). Other important markets in that year were the USA, Barbados, Trinidad and Tobago and Saint Lucia. The principal exports in 2006 were bananas (29.4%) and rice (10.0%), while the principal imports were machinery and transport equipment (23.0%), basic manufactures and food and live animals.

In 2006 there was an estimated overall budget deficit of EC $57.4m., equivalent to 4.2% of GDP. Saint Vincent and the Grenadines' total external debt was US $300.1m. at the end of 2006, of which US $242.1m. was long-term public debt. The cost of debt-servicing was equivalent to 11.5% of the value of exports of goods and services in 2005. The average annual rate of inflation was 2.6% in 2000–07, and consumer prices increased by an average of 7.0% in 2007. At the 1991 census 20.0% of the labour force were unemployed. In February 2002 the IMF estimated that the rate of unemployment remained at a similar level.

In May 2000 the Financial Stability Forum categorized Saint Vincent and the Grenadines' banking supervision in the lowest group. In June the Organisation for Economic Co-operation and Development (OECD) included Saint Vincent and the Grenadines in a report on countries with harmful tax policies, and in the same month it was also included on a list of 'non-co-operative' governments in the fight against money-laundering, by the Financial Action Task Force (FATF—based at the Secretariat of OECD). In July the International Financial Services Authority revoked the licences of six 'offshore' banks in an immediate response to an advisory by the US Department of the Treasury. Following further government commitments to improving the transparency of its tax and regulatory systems, Saint Vincent and the Grenadines was removed from OECD's harmful tax policy list in February 2002. In May of that year the Government established a Financial Intelligence Unit to counter money-laundering, and in June 2003 Saint Vincent and the Grenadines was finally removed from the FATF's blacklist. Only four licensed 'offshore' banks remained in 2009, compared with a peak of 30 in 2002. Some 8,855 International Business Companies were also registered in 2009. Nevertheless, in April 2009 Saint Vincent and the Grenadines was included in OECD's so-called 'grey list' of territories that had committed to improving financial transparency, but had yet substantially to implement reform.

Saint Vincent and the Grenadines is a member of the ECCB, of the Caribbean Community and Common Market (CARICOM, see p. 206), which seeks to encourage regional development, particularly by increasing trade between member states, and of the Organisation of Eastern Caribbean States (OECS, see p. 440). The country is also a member of the regional stock exchange, the Eastern Caribbean Securities Exchange (based in Saint Christopher and Nevis), established in 2001. Saint Vincent and the Grenadines joined CARICOM's Caribbean Single Market and Economy (CSME) in July 2006.

Traditionally the dominant sector of the economy, agriculture declined in importance in the 1990s. The introduction of other crops reduced dependence on the vulnerable banana harvest, although performance is significantly affected by weather conditions. The erosion of the islands' preferential access to European markets, together with lower prices and poor climatic conditions (not least the passage of 'Hurricane Ivan' in September 2004), proved disastrous for the sector. In 2006 exports of bananas represented just 29.4% of the total value of merchandise exports (compared with 52.2% in 1990). The decline of the industry, and a related increase in unemployment and poverty, appeared inevitable. Therefore, the prospects for long-term growth were dependent on economic diversification and a prolonged stabilization of the increasingly important tourism sector. This sector had previously been disadvantaged (relative to neighbouring countries) by the absence of an international airport; consequently, efforts had been made to increase cruise-ship traffic and visiting yacht passengers. The 2008 budget increased tourism-related expenditure and allocated a substantial portion of its capital outlay to the International Airport Project at Argyle, construction of which began in August 2008. Preliminary estimates valued the project at EC $589m.— which was to be partially financed by the Governments of Venezuela, Cuba and Taiwan—and it was hoped that the new facility would increase overall capacity and attract a greater number of stop-over arrivals (a more lucrative market than cruise-ship passengers). The airport was scheduled for completion in 2011. In 2009 the IMF commended the Government's progress in reducing the fiscal deficit and achieving poverty reduction goals, but warned that falling tourism receipts and lower foreign investment in light of the global economic downturn in 2009 would have to be addressed.

Education

Free primary education, beginning at five years of age and lasting for seven years, is available to all children in government schools, although it is not compulsory. There are 61 government and five private primary schools. Secondary education, beginning at 12 years of age, comprises a first cycle of five years and a second, two-year cycle. The Goverment announced in 2005 that it had succeeded in instituting universal secondary education. There are also a number of junior secondary schools. There is a teacher-training college and a technical college. In 2006/07 enrolment at primary schools included an estimated 91.0% of children in the relevant age-group, while in 2004/05 enrolment in secondary schools included an estimated 63.9% of pupils. Expenditure on education by the central Government was projected at EC $127m. in 2009 (equivalent to some 23% of the total expenditure).

Public Holidays

2009: 1 January (New Year's Day), 10 April (Good Friday), 13 April (Easter Monday), 7 May (Labour Day/Fisherman's Day), 1 June (Whit Monday), 6 July (CARICOM Day), 7 July (Carnival Tuesday), 1 August (Emancipation Day), 27 October (Independence Day), 25–26 December (Christmas).

2010: 1 January (New Year's Day), 2 April (Good Friday), 5 April (Easter Monday), 7 May (Labour Day/Fisherman's Day), 24 May (Whit Monday), 5 July (CARICOM Day), 6 July (Carnival Tuesday), 1 August (Emancipation Day), 27 October (Independence Day), 25–26 December (Christmas).

Weights and Measures

The imperial system is used.

SAINT VINCENT AND THE GRENADINES

Statistical Survey

Source (unless otherwise stated): Statistical Office, Ministry of Finance and Economic Planning, Administrative Centre, Bay St, Kingstown; tel. 456-1111; e-mail statssvg@vincysurf.com.

AREA AND POPULATION

Area: 389.3 sq km (150.3 sq miles). The island of Saint Vincent covers 344 sq km (133 sq miles).

Population: 97,914 at census of 12 May 1980; 106,499 (males 53,165, females 53,334) at census of 12 May 1991; 109,202 at preliminary census count of May 2001. *2008:* 106,141 (mid-year estimate). Source: Eastern Caribbean Central Bank.

Density (mid-2008): 272.6 per sq km.

Principal Town: Kingstown (capital) population 13,526 at preliminary census count of May 2001. *Mid-2007* (population incl. suburbs, UN estimate): Kingstown 26,000. Source: UN, *World Urbanization Prospects: The 2007 Revision.*

Births, Marriages and Deaths (registrations, 2005): Live births 1,779 (birth rate 17.1 per 1,000); Marriages 576 (marriage rate 5.6 per 1,000); Deaths 813 (death rate 7.8 per 1,000). Source: UN, *Demographic Yearbook.*

Life Expectancy (years at birth, WHO estimates): 70.0 (males 66; females 74) in 2006. Source: WHO, *World Health Statistics.*

Economically Active Population (persons aged 15 years and over, 1991 census): Agriculture, hunting, forestry and fishing 8,377; Mining and quarrying 98; Manufacturing 2,822; Electricity, gas and water 586; Construction 3,535; Trade, restaurants and hotels 6,544; Transport, storage and communications 2,279; Financing, insurance, real estate and business services 1,418; Community, social and personal services 7,696; *Total employed* 33,355 (males 21,656, females 11,699); Unemployed 8,327 (males 5,078, females 3,249); *Total labour force* 41,682 (males 26,734, females 14,948). Source: ILO, *Yearbook of Labour Statistics.*

HEALTH AND WELFARE
Key Indicators

Total Fertility Rate (children per woman, 2006): 2.2.

Under-5 Mortality Rate (per 1,000 live births, 2006): 20.

Physicians (per 1,000 head, 2000): 0.8.

Hospital Beds (per 1,000 head, 2005): 3.

Health Expenditure (2006): US $ per head (PPP): 464.

Health Expenditure (2006): % of GDP: 6.0.

Health Expenditure (2006): public (% of total): 62.8.

Access to Water (% of persons, 2000): 93.

Access to Sanitation (% of persons, 2000): 96.

Human Development Index (2006): ranking: 92.

Human Development Index (2006): value: 0.766.

For sources and definitions, see explanatory note on p. vi.

AGRICULTURE, ETC.

Principal Crops ('000 metric tons, 2007, FAO estimates): Maize 0.7; Cassava 0.8; Sweet potatoes 1.3; Yams 2.3; Sugar cane 20.0; Coconuts 2.7; Bananas 51.0; Plaintains 3.6; Oranges 1.7; Lemons and limes 1.2; Apples 1.3; Mangoes 1.6. *Aggregate Production* ('000 metric tons, may include official, semi-official or estimated data): Roots and tubers 14.3; Vegetables (incl. melons) 4.5; Fruits (excl. melons) 61.2.

Livestock ('000 head, year ending September 2007, FAO estimates): Cattle 5.1; Sheep 12.0; Goats 7.3; Pigs 9.2; Chickens 130.

Livestock Products ('000 metric tons, 2007, FAO estimates): Pig meat 0.6; Chicken meat 0.3; Cows' milk 1.3; Hen eggs 0.7.

Fishing (capture production, metric tons, live weight, 2006): Albacore 141; Skipjack tuna 356; Wahoo 241; Yellowfin tuna 2,781; Other tuna-like fishes 613; Other marine fishes 603; *Total catch* (incl. others) 4,739.

Source: FAO.

INDUSTRY

Selected Products ('000 metric tons, 2005, unless otherwise stated): Copra 2 (FAO estimate); Raw sugar 2 (FAO estimate); Rum 9,000 hectolitres (2003); Electric energy 136.4 million kWh. Sources: FAO, Eastern Caribbean Central Bank and UN, *International Commodity Statistics Yearbook.*

FINANCE

Currency and Exchange Rates: 100 cents = 1 Eastern Caribbean dollar (EC $). *Sterling, US Dollar and Euro Equivalents* (31 December 2008): £1 sterling = EC $3.939; US $1 = EC $2.700; €1 = EC $3.758; EC $100 = £25.41 = US $37.04 = €26.61. *Exchange Rate:* Fixed at US $1 = EC $2.70 since July 1976.

Budget (EC $ million, 2006): *Revenue:* Revenue from taxation 361.7 (Taxes on income 98.8; Taxes on goods and services 98.2; Taxes on property 2.6; Taxes on international trade and transactions 162.1); Other current revenue 31.6; Capital revenue 6.0; Foreign grants 5.5; Total 404.8. *Expenditure:* Current expenditure 355.4 (Personal emoluments 171.3; Other goods and services 75.8; Interest payments 43.2; Transfers and subsidies 65.2); Capital expenditure and net lending 101.3; Total 456.7. *2008* (EC $ million): Total recurrent revenue 477.74; Total recurrent expenditure 422.97. Source: Eastern Caribbean Central Bank.

International Reserves (US $ million at 31 December 2007): Reserve position in IMF 0.79; Foreign exchange 86.18; Total 86.97. Source: IMF, *International Financial Statistics.*

Money Supply (EC $ million at 31 December 2007): Currency outside banks 96.94; Demand deposits 333.45; Total money (incl. others) 430.53. Source: IMF, *International Financial Statistics.*

Cost of Living (Consumer Price Index; base: 2000 = 100): 108.8 in 2005; 112.1 in 2006; 119.9 in 2007. Source: IMF, *International Financial Statistics.*

Gross Domestic Product (EC $ million at constant 1990 prices): 948.89 in 2006; 1,021.89 in 2007; 1,032.30 in 2008. Source: Eastern Caribbean Central Bank.

Expenditure on the Gross Domestic Product (EC $ million at current prices, 2008): Government final consumption expenditure 314.30; Private final consumption expenditure 1,068.32; Gross capital formation 612.24; *Total domestic expenditure* 1,994.86; Exports of goods and services 694.41; *Less* Imports of goods and services 1,074.84; *GDP at market prices* 1,614.44. Source: Eastern Caribbean Central Bank.

Gross Domestic Product by Economic Activity (EC $ million at current prices, 2008): Agriculture, hunting, forestry and fishing 90.34; Mining and quarrying 3.38; Manufacturing 51.03; Electricity and water 59.91; Construction 216.60; Wholesale and retail trade 268.49; Restaurants and hotels 22.88; Transport 186.32; Communications 69.99; Banking and insurance 142.71; Real estate and housing 24.85; Government services 255.90; Other services 26.86; *Subtotal* 1,419.26; *Less* Financial intermediation services indirectly measured 110.68; *Total in basic prices* 1,308.58; Taxes, less subsidies, on products 305.86; *GDP at market prices* 1,614.44. Source: Eastern Caribbean Central Bank.

Balance of Payments (EC $ million, 2008): *Trade balance* −679.82; Services (net) 109.28; *Balance on goods and services* −570.54; Other income received (net) −67.17; *Balance on goods, services and income* −637.71; Current transfers (net) 52.48; *Current balance* −585.24; Capital account (net) 109.88; Direct investment (net) 258.41; Portfolio investment (net) −1.62; Other investment (net) 175.87; Net errors and omissions 33.90; *Overall balance* −8.81. Source: Eastern Caribbean Central Bank.

EXTERNAL TRADE

Principal Commodities (US $ million, 2006): *Imports c.i.f.:* Food and live animals 46.3; Beverages and tobacco 7.3; Crude materials 7.3; Mineral fuels, lubricants, etc. 39.5; Chemicals and related products 21.6; Basic manufactures 55.8; Machinery and transport equipment 62.5; Total (incl. others) 271.3. *Exports f.o.b.:* Food and live animals 27.6 (Rice 3.8, Vegetables and fruit 16.0); Beverages and tobacco 1.7; Basic manufactures 3.4 (Iron and steel 1.3); Machinery and transport equipment 3.5; Miscellaneous manufactured articles 1.5; Total (incl. others) 38.1. Source: UN, *International Trade Statistics Yearbook.*

Principal Trading Partners (US $ million, 2006): *Imports c.i.f.:* Barbados 9.4; Brazil 4.9; Canada 9.9; China, People's Rep. 8.4; France (incl. Monaco) 3.0; Germany 5.2; Guyana 2.9; Italy 4.4; Japan 10.5; Trinidad and Tobago 70.4; United Kingdom 19.2; USA 88.6; Total (incl. others) 271.3. *Exports f.o.b.:* Antigua and Barbuda 3.0; Barbados 5.3; Dominica 1.8; Jamaica 0.9; Saint Lucia 4.6; Trinidad and Tobago 5.6; United Kingdom 9.7; USA 1.9; Total (incl. others) 38.1. Source: UN, *International Trade Statistics Yearbook.*

SAINT VINCENT AND THE GRENADINES

TRANSPORT

Road Traffic (motor vehicles in use, 2003): Private cars 11,679; Buses and coaches 1,247; Lorries and vans 3,340; Motorcycles 685.
Source: International Road Federation, *World Road Statistics*.

Shipping: *Arrivals* (2000): Vessels 1,007. *International Sea-borne Freight Traffic* ('000 metric tons, 2000): Goods loaded 54; Goods unloaded 156. *Merchant Fleet* (vessels registered at 31 December 2007): Number 1,048; Total displacement 5,927,619 grt (Source: Lloyd's Register-Fairplay, *World Fleet Statistics*).

Civil Aviation (visitor arrivals): 89,631 in 2003; 99,657 in 2004; 104,221 in 2005 (estimate). Source: IMF, *St Vincent and the Grenadines: Statistical Appendix* (November 2007).

TOURISM

Visitor Arrivals: 256,075 (95,504 stop-over visitors, 8,928 excursionists, 81,890 yacht passengers, 69,753 cruise-ship passengers) in 2005; 306,578 (97,432 stop-over visitors, 9,034 excursionists, 93,638 yacht passengers, 106,474 cruise-ship passengers) in 2006; 378,191 (100,560 stop-over visitors, 7,766 excursionists, 107,389 yacht passengers, 162,476 cruise-ship passengers) in 2007 (preliminary). *2008:* Stop-over visitors 88,640; Cruise-ship passengers 141,570. *Stop-over visitors by country* (2007): USA 29,368; Canada 7,064; United Kingdom 18,008; Caribbean 35,643; Other countries 10,477.

Tourism Receipts (EC $ million): 280.5 in 2005; 305.8 in 2006; 322.3 in 2007 (preliminary).

Source: Eastern Caribbean Central Bank.

COMMUNICATIONS MEDIA

Radio Receivers ('000 in use, 2000): 100.

Television Receivers ('000 in use, 2000): 50.

Telephones ('000 main lines in use, 2007): 22.8.

Facsimile Machines (1996): 1,500.

Mobile Cellular Telephones (subscribers, 2007): 104,000.

Personal Computers ('000 in use, 2004): 16.

Internet Users ('000, 2007): 57.

Broadband Subscribers ('000, 2007): 6.9.

Non-daily Newspapers (2000): Titles 8; Circulation 50,000.

Sources: mainly UNESCO, *Statistical Yearbook*; UN, *Statistical Yearbook*; and International Telecommunication Union.

EDUCATION

Pre-primary (2004/05 unless otherwise indicated): 97 schools (1993/94); 340 teachers; 3,894 pupils.

Primary (2004/05 unless otherwise indicated): 60 schools (2000); 1,020 teachers; 17,858 pupils.

Secondary (2004/05 unless otherwise indicated): 21 schools (2000); 547 teachers; 9,780 pupils.

Teacher Training (2000): 1 institution; 10 teachers; 107 students.

Technical College (2000): 1 institution; 19 teachers; 187 students.

Community College (2000): 1 institution; 13 teachers; 550 students.

Nursing College (2000): 1 institution; 6 teachers; 60 students.

Sources: partly Caribbean Development Bank, *Social and Economic Indicators*, and UNESCO Institute for Statistics.

Adult Literacy Rate: 88.1% in 2004. Source: UN Development Programme, *Human Development Report*.

Directory

The Constitution

The Constitution came into force at the independence of Saint Vincent and the Grenadines on 27 October 1979. The following is a summary of its main provisions.

FUNDAMENTAL RIGHTS AND FREEDOMS

Regardless of race, place of origin, political opinion, colour, creed or sex, but subject to respect for the rights and freedoms of others and for the public interest, every person in Saint Vincent and the Grenadines is entitled to the rights of life, liberty, security of the person and the protection of the law. Freedom of conscience, of expression, of assembly of and association is guaranteed, and the inviolability of a person's home and other property is maintained. Protection is afforded from slavery, forced labour, torture and inhuman treatment.

THE GOVERNOR-GENERAL

The British Monarch is represented in Saint Vincent and the Grenadines by the Governor-General.

PARLIAMENT

Parliament consists of the British monarch, represented by the Governor-General, and the House of Assembly, comprising 15 elected Representatives (increased from 13 under the provisions of an amendment approved in 1986) and six Senators. Senators are appointed by the Governor-General—four on the advice of the Prime Minister and two on the advice of the Leader of the Opposition. The life of Parliament is five years. Each constituency returns one Representative to the House who is directly elected in accordance with the Constitution. The Attorney-General is an ex officio member of the House. Every citizen over the age of 18 is eligible to vote. Parliament may alter any of the provisions of the Constitution.

THE EXECUTIVE

Executive authority is vested in the British monarch and is exercisable by the Governor-General. The Governor-General appoints as Prime Minister that member of the House who, in the Governor-General's view, is the best able to command the support of the majority of the members of the House, and selects other Ministers on the advice of the Prime Minister. The Governor-General may remove the Prime Minister from office if a resolution of 'no confidence' in the Government is adopted by the House and the Prime Minister does not either resign within three days or advise the Governor-General to dissolve Parliament.

The Cabinet consists of the Prime Minister and other Ministers and the Attorney-General as an ex-officio member. The Leader of the Opposition is appointed by the Governor-General as that member of the House who, in the Governor-General's view, is best able to command the support of a majority of members of the House who do not support the Government.

CITIZENSHIP

All persons born in Saint Vincent and the Grenadines before independence who, immediately prior to independence, were citizens of the United Kingdom and Colonies automatically become citizens of Saint Vincent and the Grenadines. All persons born outside the country after independence to a parent possessing citizenship of Saint Vincent and the Grenadines automatically acquire citizenship, as do those born in the country after independence. Citizenship can be acquired by those to whom it would not automatically be granted.

The Government

HEAD OF STATE

Monarch: HM Queen ELIZABETH II.

Governor-General: Sir FREDERICK BALLANTYNE (took office 2 September 2002).

CABINET
(April 2009)

Prime Minister and Minister of Finance and Economic Planning, National Security, Legal Affairs, Grenadines Affairs and Energy: Dr RALPH E. GONSALVES.

Deputy Prime Minister and Minister of Foreign Affairs, Commerce and Trade: LOUIS STRAKER.

Minister of Tourism, Youth and Sports: GLEN BEACHE.

Minister of National Mobilization, Social Development, Non-Governmental Organization (NGO) Relations, Family, Gender Affairs and Persons with Disabilities: MICHAEL BROWNE.

Minister of Education: GIRLYN MIGUEL.

Minister of Rural Transformation, Information, Postal Services and Ecclesiastical Affairs: SELMON WALTERS.

SAINT VINCENT AND THE GRENADINES

Minister of Health and the Environment: Dr DOUGLAS SLATER.
Minister of Telecommunications, Science, Technology and Industry: Dr JERROL THOMPSON.
Minister of Urban Development, Labour, Culture and Electoral Matters: RENEÉ MERCEDES BAPTISTE.
Minister of Transportation and Works: CLAYTON BURGIN.
Minister of Agriculture, Forestry and Fisheries: MONTGOMERY DANIEL.
Minister of Housing, Informal Human Settlements, Physical Planning, and Lands and Surveys: JULIAN EVERARD FRANCIS.
Minister of State in the Office of the Prime Minister: CONRAD SAYERS.
Attorney-General: JUDITH S. JONES-MORGAN.

MINISTRIES

Office of the Governor-General: Government House, Kingstown; tel. 456-1401; fax 457-9701.
Office of the Prime Minister: Administrative Bldg, 4th Floor, Bay St, Kingstown; tel. 451-2939; fax 457-2152; e-mail pmosvg@caribsurf.com.
Office of the Attorney-General and Ministry of Legal Affairs: Methodist Bldg, Granby St, Kingstown; tel. 456-1111; fax 457-2898; e-mail office.ageneral@mail.gv.vc.
Ministry of Agriculture, Forestry and Fisheries: Richmond Hill, Kingstown; tel. 456-1410; fax 457-1688; e-mail office.agriculture@mail.gov.vc.
Ministry of Education: Halifax St, Kingstown; tel. 456-1877; fax 457-1114.
Ministry of Finance and Economic Planning: Administrative Bldg, Bay St, Kingstown; tel. 456-1111; fax 457-2152.
Ministry of Foreign Affairs, Commerce and Trade: Administrative Bldg, 3rd Floor, Bay St, Kingstown; tel. 456-2060; fax 456-2610; e-mail office.foreignaffairs@mail.gov.vc.
Ministry of Health and the Environment: Ministerial Bldg, 1st Floor, Bay St, Kingstown; tel. 456-1111; fax 457-2684; e-mail office.health@mail.gov.vc.
Ministry of Housing, Informal Human Settlements, Physical Planning, and Lands and Surveys: Methodist Church Bldg, Granby St, Kingstown; tel. 451-2479; fax 457-2898; e-mail office.housing@mail.gov.vc.
Ministry of National Mobilization, Social Development, Non-Governmental Organization (NGO) Relations, Family, Gender Affairs and Persons with Disabilities: Egmont St, Kingstown; tel. 456-1111; fax 457-2476; e-mail office.socialdevelopment@mail.gov.vc.
Ministry of National Security: Ministerial Bldg, 3rd Floor, Halifax St, Kingstown; tel. 451-2707; fax 451-2820; e-mail office.natsec@mail.gov.vc.
Ministry of Rural Transformation, Information, Postal Services and Ecclesiastical Affairs: Ministerial Bldg, 2nd Floor, Halifax St, Kingstown; tel. 451-2707; fax 451-2820; e-mail office.rutrans@mail.gov.vc; internet www.gov.vc/Govt/api1.
Ministry of Telecommunications, Science, Technology and Industry: Egmont St, Kingstown; tel. 456-1223; fax 457-2880; e-mail webunit.telecom@mail.gov.vc.
Ministry of Tourism, Youth and Sports: c/o Ministry of Tourism and Culture, Cruise Ship Terminal, Harbour Quay, POB 834, Kingstown; tel. 457-1502; fax 451-2425; e-mail tourism@caribsurf.com.
Ministry of Transportation and Works: Grenville St, Kingstown; tel. 457-2039; fax 456-2168; e-mail office.transport@mail.gov.vc.
Ministry of Urban Development, Labour, Culture and Electoral Matters: Marion House Bldg, Ground Floor, Murray's Rd, Kingstown; tel. 457-1789; fax 485-6737; e-mail office.elections@mail.gov.vc.

Legislature

HOUSE OF ASSEMBLY

Senators: 6.
Elected Members: 15.
Speaker: HENDRICK ALEXANDER.
Clerk: NICOLE HERBERT, House of Assembly, Kingstown; tel. 457-1872; fax 457-1825.

Election, 7 December 2005

Party	Votes	% of votes	Seats
Unity Labour Party	31,848	55.26	12
New Democratic Party	25,748	44.68	3
Saint Vincent and the Grenadines Green Party	34	0.06	—
Total	57,630	100.00	15

Election Commission

Electoral Office: Administrative Centre, Bay St, Kingstown; tel. 457-1762; fax 485-6844; e-mail electoraloffice@gov.vc; Supervisor of Elections RODNEY ADAMS.

Political Organizations

New Democratic Party (NDP): Democrat House, Murray Rd, POB 1300, Kingstown; tel. 456-2114; fax 457-2647; e-mail ndp@caribsurf.com; internet www.ndpsvg.com; f. 1975; democratic party supporting political unity in the Caribbean, social devt and free enterprise; Leader ARNHIM ULRIC EUSTACE; Gen. Sec. DANIEL E. CUMMINGS; 7,000 mems.
Saint Vincent and the Grenadines Green Party: POB 1707, Kingstown; tel. and fax 456-9579; e-mail mail@svggreenparty.org; internet www.svggreenparty.org; f. 2005; Leader IVAN O'NEAL; Gen. Sec. ORDAN O. GRAHAM.
Unity Labour Party (ULP): Beachmont, Kingstown; tel. 457-2761; fax 456-2811; e-mail ulpweb@aol.com; f. 1994 by merger of Movement for National Unity and the Saint Vincent Labour Party; moderate, social-democratic party; Leader Dr RALPH E. GONSALVES.

Diplomatic Representation

EMBASSIES IN SAINT VINCENT AND THE GRENADINES

China (Taiwan): Murray Rd, POB 878, Kingstown; tel. 456-2431; fax 456-2913; e-mail rocemsvg@caribsurf.com; Ambassador LEO LEE.
Cuba: Ratho Mill, Kingstown; tel. 458-5844; fax 456-9344; e-mail embacubasvg@gmail.com; internet www.embacu.cubaminrex.cu/sanvicenteing; Ambassador OLGA CHAMERO TRÍAS.
Venezuela: Baynes Bros Bldg, Granby St, POB 852, Kingstown; tel. 456-1374; fax 457-1934; e-mail embavenezsanvicente@vincysurf.com; Ambassador MARÍA TIBISAY URDANETA TROCONIS.

Judicial System

Justice is administered by the Eastern Caribbean Supreme Court, based in Saint Lucia and consisting of a Court of Appeal and a High Court. Two Puisne Judges are resident in Saint Vincent and the Grenadines. There are five Magistrates, including the Registrar of the Supreme Court, who acts as an additional Magistrate.
Puisne Judges: FREDERICK BRUCE-LYLE, GERTEL THOM, MONICA JOSEPH.

Office of the Registrar of the Supreme Court

Registry Dept, Court House, Kingstown; tel. 457-1220; fax 457-1888; e-mail svgregistry@caribsurf.com; Registrar TAMARA GIBSON-MARKS.
Chief Magistrate: SIMONE CHURAMAN.
Magistrates: DONALD BROWNE, ZOILA ELLIS-BROWNE, LESTER CAESAR.
Director of Public Prosecutions: COLIN WILLIAMS.

Religion

CHRISTIANITY

Saint Vincent Christian Council: Melville St, POB 445, Kingstown; tel. 456-1408; f. 1969; four mem. churches; Chair. Mgr RENISON HOWELL.

The Anglican Communion

Anglicans in Saint Vincent and the Grenadines are adherents of the Church in the Province of the West Indies, comprising eight dioceses. The Archbishop of the West Indies is the Bishop of Nassau and the

SAINT VINCENT AND THE GRENADINES

Bahamas, and is resident in Nassau. The diocese of the Windward Islands includes Grenada, Saint Lucia and Saint Vincent and the Grenadines.

Bishop of the Windward Islands: Rt Rev. CALVERT LEOPOLD FRIDAY, Bishop's Court, POB 502, Kingstown; tel. 456-1895; fax 456-2591; e-mail diocesewi@vincysurf.com.

The Roman Catholic Church

Saint Vincent and the Grenadines comprises a single diocese (formed when the diocese of Bridgetown-Kingstown was divided in October 1989), which is suffragan to the archdiocese of Castries (Saint Lucia). The Bishop participates in the Antilles Episcopal Conference, currently based in Port of Spain, Trinidad and Tobago. At 31 December 2006 there were an estimated 15,359 adherents in the diocese, comprising about 13% of the population.

Bishop of Kingstown: Rt Rev. ROBERT RIVAS, Bishop's Office, POB 862, Edinboro, Kingstown; tel. 457-2363; fax 457-1903; e-mail rcdok@caribsurf.com.

Other Christian Churches

The Methodists, Seventh-day Adventists, Baptists and other denominations also have places of worship.

BAHÁ'Í FAITH

National Spiritual Assembly: POB 1043, Kingstown; tel. 456-4717.

The Press

DAILY

The Herald: Blue Caribbean Bldg, Kingstown; tel. 456-1242; fax 456-1046; e-mail info@heraldsvg.com; daily; internationally distributed.

SELECTED WEEKLIES

The News: Frenches Gate, POB 1078, Kingstown; tel. 456-2942; fax 456-2941; e-mail thenews@caribsurf.com; weekly; Man. Dir SHELLEY CLARKE.

Searchlight: Interactive Media Ltd, POB 152, Kingstown; tel. 456-1558; fax 457-2250; e-mail search@caribsurf.com; internet www.searchlight.vc; weekly on Fridays; Chair. CORLITA OLLIVERRE; CEO and Acting Man. Editor CLAIRE KEIZER.

The Vincentian: St George's Pl., Kingstown; tel. 456-1123; fax 457-2821; e-mail info@thevincentian.com; internet www.thevincentian.com; f. 1919; weekly; owned by the Vincentian Publishing Co; Man. Dir EGERTON M. RICHARDS; Editor-in-Chief TERRANCE PARRIS; circ. 6,000.

The Westindian Crusader: Kingstown; tel. 458-0073; fax 456-9315; e-mail crusader@caribsurf.com; weekly; Editor ELSEE CARBERRY; Man. Editor LINA CLARKE.

SELECTED PERIODICALS

Caribbean Compass: POB 175, Bequia; tel. 457-3409; fax 457-3410; e-mail tom@caribbeancompass.com; internet www.caribbeancompass.com; marine news; monthly; free distribution in Caribbean from Puerto Rico to Panama; circ. 11,000; Editor SALLY ERDLE.

Government Gazette: POB 12, Kingstown; tel. 457-1840; f. 1868; Govt Printer OTHNIEL WHITE; circ. 492.

Unity: Middle and Melville St, POB 854, Kingstown; tel. 456-1049; fortnightly; organ of the Unity Labour Party.

Publishers

CJW Communications: POB 1078, Frenches Gate, Kingstown; tel. 456-2942; fax 456-2941.

Great Works Depot: Commission A Bldg, Granby St, POB 1849, Kingstown; tel. 456-2057; fax 457-2055; e-mail gwd@caribsurf.com.

The Vincentian Publishing Co Ltd: St George's Pl., Kingstown; tel. 456-1123; fax 457-2821; e-mail info@thevincentian.com; internet www.thevincentian.com; Man. Dir EGERTON M. RICHARDS.

Broadcasting and Communications

TELECOMMUNICATIONS

Regulatory Authorities

Eastern Caribbean Telecommunications Authority (ECTEL): based in Castries, Saint Lucia; f. 2000 to regulate telecommunications in Saint Vincent and the Grenadines, Dominica, Grenada, Saint Christopher and Nevis and Saint Lucia.

National Telecom Regulatory Commission (NTRC): KCCU Financial Centre, Granby St, Kingstown; tel. 457-2279; fax 457-2834; e-mail info@ntrc.vc; internet www.ntrc.vc; f. 2001 by the Telecommunications Act to regulate the sector in collaboration with ECTEL (q.v.); Chair K. DOUGLAS.

Major Service Providers

Digicel: Suite KO59, cnr Granby and Sharpe Sts, Kingstown; tel. 453-3000; fax 453-3010; e-mail customercaresvg@digicelgroup.com; internet www.digicelsvg.com; f. 2003; mobile cellular phone operator; owned by an Irish consortium; Chair. DENIS O'BRIEN; Eastern Caribbean CEO KEVIN WHITE.

LIME: Halifax St, POB 103, Kingstown; tel. 457-1901; fax 457-2777; e-mail support@vincysurf.com; internet www.time4lime.com; fmrly Cable & Wireless (St Vincent and the Grenadines) Ltd; name changed as above 2008; CEO RICHARD DODD.

BROADCASTING

National Broadcasting Corporation of Saint Vincent and the Grenadines (NBC): Richmond Hill, POB 705, Kingstown; tel. 457-1111; fax 456-2749; e-mail nbcsvgadmin@nbcsvg.com; internet www.nbcsvg.com; govt-owned; Chair. KENNETH BROWNE; Gen. Man. CORLITA OLLIVERRE.

Radio

NBC Radio: National Broadcasting Corpn, Richmond Hill, POB 705, Kingstown; tel. 457-1111; fax 456-2749; e-mail nbcsvgadmin@nbcsvg.com; internet www.nbcsvg.com; commercial; broadcasts BBC World Service (United Kingdom) and local programmes.

Nice Radio FM: Kingstown; internet www.niceradio.org; Man. Dir DOUGLAS DE FREITAS.

Television

National Broadcasting Corporation of Saint Vincent and the Grenadines: see above.

SVG Television (SGVTV): Dorsetshire Hill, POB 617, Kingstown; tel. 456-1078; fax 456-1015; e-mail svgbc@vincysurf.com; internet www.svgbc.com/svgtv.htm; f. 1980; broadcasts local, regional and international programmes; Man. Dir R. PAUL MACLEISH.

Television services from Barbados can be received in parts of the islands.

Finance

(cap. = capital; res = reserves; dep. = deposits; m. = million; br. = branch)

BANKING

The Eastern Caribbean Central Bank, based in Saint Christopher, is the central issuing and monetary authority for Saint Vincent and the Grenadines.

Eastern Caribbean Central Bank—Saint Vincent and the Grenadines Office: Frenches House, POB 839, Frenches; tel. 456-1413; fax 456-1412; e-mail eccbsvg@vincysurf.com; Country Dir ELRITHA DICK.

Regulatory Authority

International Financial Services Authority (IFSA): Upper Bay St, POB 356, Kingstown; tel. 456-2577; fax 457-2568; e-mail info@svgifsa.com; internet www.svgifsa.com; f. 1996; Chair. CLAUDE SAMUEL; Exec. Dir SHARDA SINANAN-BOLLERS.

Financial Intelligence Unit (FIU): POB 1826, Kingstown; tel. 451-2070; fax 457-2014; e-mail svgfiu@vincysurf.com; internet www.svgifsa.com/fin_intl_unit.htm; f. 2002; Dir GRENVILLE WILLIAMS.

Local Banks

Bank of Nova Scotia Ltd (Canada): 76 Halifax St, POB 237, Kingstown; tel. 457-1601; fax 457-2623; e-mail bruce.sali@scotiabank.com; Man. BRUCE SALI.

SAINT VINCENT AND THE GRENADINES

FirstCaribbean International Bank (Barbados) Ltd: Lower Halifax St, POB 212, Kingstown; tel. 457-1587; e-mail Earl.Crichton@firstcaribbeanbank.com; internet www.firstcaribbeanbank.com; f. 2002 following merger of Caribbean operations of Barclays Bank PLC and CIBC; CIBC acquired Barclays' 43.7% stake in 2006; Exec. Chair. MICHAEL MANSOOR; CEO JOHN D. ORR; Man. EARL CRICHTON.

National Commercial Bank (SVG) Ltd: Cnr Halifax and Egmont Sts, POB 880, Kingstown; tel. 457-1844; fax 456-2612; e-mail natbank@caribsurf.com; internet www.svgncb.com; f. 1977; govt-owned; share cap. EC $14.0m., res EC $19.1m., dep. EC $520.7m. (June 2006); CEO PHILIP H. HERNANDEZ; Chair. DESMOND MORGAN.

RBTT Bank Caribbean Ltd: 81 South River Rd, POB 81, Kingstown; tel. 456-1501; fax 456-2141; internet www.rbtt.com; f. 1985 as Caribbean Banking Corpn Ltd, name changed as above in 2002; Chair. PETER J. JULY.

'OFFSHORE' FINANCIAL SECTOR

Legislation permitting the development of an 'offshore' financial sector was introduced in 1976 and revised in 1996 and 1998. International banks are required to have a place of business on the islands and to designate a licensed registered agent. International Business Companies registered in Saint Vincent and the Grenadines are exempt from taxation for 25 years. Legislation also guarantees total confidentiality. In 2009 the 'offshore' financial sector comprised 8,855 International Business Companies, 149 trusts and four banks.

Saint Vincent Trust Service: Trust House, 112 Bonadie St, POB 613, Kingstown; tel. 457-1027; fax 457-1961; e-mail info@st-vincent-trust.com; internet www.jeeves-group.com; br. in Liechtenstein; Pres. BRYAN JEEVES.

'Offshore' Banks

European Commerce Bank: The Financial Services Centre, Paul's Ave, POB 1822, Kingstown; tel. 456-1460; fax 456-1455; e-mail info@eurocombank.com; internet www.eurocombank.com.

Loyal Bank Ltd: Cedar Hill Crest, POB 1825, Kingstown; tel. 485-6705; fax 451-2757; e-mail ceo@loyalbank.com; internet www.loyalbank.com; f. 1997; owned by Ost West Stiftung; CEO ADRIAN BARON.

Safe Harbor Bank Ltd: Nanton's Bldg, Egmont St, POB 2630, Kingstown; tel. 451-2030; fax 451-2031; e-mail iofo@safeharborbank.com; internet www.safeharborbank.com; f. 2000; Contact GRAHAME BOLLERS.

Trend Bank Ltd: The Financial Services Centre, Paul's Ave, POB 1823, Kingstown; tel. 457-0548; fax 451-2672; internet www.trendb.com; Pres. ADOLPHO J. SILVA MELLO NETO.

STOCK EXCHANGE

Eastern Caribbean Securities Exchange: based in Basseterre, Saint Christopher and Nevis; tel. (869) 466-7192; fax (869) 465-3798; e-mail info@ecseonline.com; internet www.ecseonline.com; f. 2001; regional securities market designed to facilitate the buying and selling of financial products for the eight mem. territories—Anguilla, Antigua and Barbuda, Dominica, Grenada, Montserrat, Saint Christopher and Nevis, Saint Lucia, and Saint Vincent and the Grenadines; Chair. Sir K. DWIGHT VENNER; Gen. Man. and CEO TREVOR E. BLAKE.

INSURANCE

A number of foreign insurance companies have offices in Kingstown. Local companies include the following:

Abbott's Insurance Co: Cnr Sharpe and Bay St, POB 124, Kingstown; tel. 456-1511; fax 456-2462.

BMC Agencies Ltd: Sharpe St, POB 1436, Kingstown; tel. 457-2041; fax 457-2103.

Durrant Insurance Services: South River Rd, Kingstown; tel. 457-2426.

Haydock Insurances Ltd: Granby St, POB 1179, Kingstown; tel. 457-2903; fax 456-2952.

Metrocint General Insurance Co Ltd: St George's Pl., POB 692, Kingstown; tel. 456-1821.

Saint Hill Insurance Co Ltd: Bay St, POB 1741, Kingstown; tel. 457-1227; fax 456-2374.

Saint Vincent Insurances Ltd: Lot 69, Grenville St, POB 210, Kingstown; tel. 456-1733; fax 456-2225; e-mail vinsure@caribsurf.com.

Trade and Industry

DEVELOPMENT ORGANIZATIONS

Invest SVG: POB 608, Kingstown; tel. 457-2159; fax 457-2688; e-mail info@investsvg.com; internet www.svg-nipi.com; f. 2003 as National Investment Promotions Inc; assumed DEVCO's (q.v.) responsibilities for investment promotion and foreign direct investment; reports to the Office of the Prime Minister; board mems appointed from both public and private sectors by the Cabinet; Exec. Dir CLEO HUGGINS; Chair. EDMOND A. JACKSON.

Saint Vincent Development Corporation (DEVCO): Grenville St, POB 841, Kingstown; tel. 457-1358; fax 457-2838; e-mail devco@caribsurf.com; f. 1970; finances industry, agriculture, fisheries, tourism; Chair. SAMUEL GOODLUCK; Man. CLAUDE M. LEACH.

CHAMBER OF COMMERCE

Saint Vincent and the Grenadines Chamber of Industry and Commerce (Inc): Corea's Bldg, Hillsborough St, POB 134, Kingstown; tel. 457-1464; fax 456-2944; e-mail info@svg-cic.com; f. 1925; Pres. MARTIN BOLLERS; Exec. Dir JOYLYN DENNIS.

INDUSTRIAL AND TRADE ASSOCIATION

Saint Vincent Marketing Corporation: Upper Bay St, POB 873, Kingstown; tel. 457-1603; fax 456-2673; e-mail svmc@caribsurf.com; f. 1959; CEO SONNY WILLIAMS.

EMPLOYERS' ORGANIZATIONS

Saint Vincent Arrowroot Industry Association: Upper Bay St, POB 70, Kingstown; tel. 457-1511; fax 457-2151; e-mail info@svgarrowroot.com; f. 1930; producers, manufacturers and sellers; 186 mems; Chair. GEORGE O. WALKER.

Saint Vincent Banana Growers' Association: Sharpe St, POB 10, Kingstown; tel. 457-1605; fax 456-2585; f. 1955; over 7,000 mems; Chair. LESLINE BEST; Gen. Man. HENRY KEIZER.

Saint Vincent Employers' Federation: Corea's Bldg, 3rd Floor, Middle St, POB 348, Kingstown; tel. 456-1269; fax 457-2777; e-mail svef@caribsurf.com; Pres. NOEL DICKSON; Exec. Dir (vacant).

Windward Islands Farmers' Association (WINFA): POB 817, Kingstown; tel. 456-2704; fax 456-1383; e-mail winfa@winfa.org; f. 1982; Co-ordinator RENWICK ROSE.

UTILITIES

Electricity

Saint Vincent Electricity Services Ltd (VINLEC): Paul's Ave, POB 865, Kingstown; tel. 456-1701; fax 456-2436; e-mail vinlec@vinlec.com; internet www.vinlec.com; 100% state-owned; country's sole electricity supplier; Chair. DOUGLAS COLE; CEO THORNLEY O. A. O. MYERS; 275 employees.

Water

Central Water and Sewerage Authority (CWSA): New Montrose, POB 363, Kingstown; tel. 456-2946; fax 456-2552; e-mail cwsa@vincysurf.com; internet www.cwsasvg.com; f. 1961; Chair. SIMMS MARTIN; Gen. Man. GARTH SAUNDERS.

CO-OPERATIVES

There are 26 Agricultural Credit Societies, which receive loans from the Government, and five Registered Co-operative Societies.

TRADE UNIONS

Commercial, Technical and Allied Workers' Union (CTAWU): Lower Middle St, POB 245, Kingstown; tel. 456-1525; fax 457-1676; e-mail ctawu@vincysurf.com; f. 1962; affiliated to CCL, ICFTU and other international workers' orgs; Pres. ALICE MANDEVILLE; Gen. Sec. LLOYD SMALL; 2,500 mems.

National Labour Congress: POB 875, Kingstown; tel. 457-1801; fax 457-1705; five affiliated unions; Pres. CECIL JACK.

National Workers' Movement: Burkes Bldg, Grenville St, POB 1290, Kingstown; tel. 457-1950; fax 456-2858; e-mail natwok@karicable.com; Gen. Sec. NOEL C. JACKSON.

Public Services Union of Saint Vincent and the Grenadines: McKie's Hill, POB 875, Kingstown; tel. 457-1950; fax 456-2858; e-mail psuofsvg@caribsurf.com; f. 1943; Pres. AUBREY BURGIN; Gen. Sec. ELROY BOUCHER; 738 mems.

Saint Vincent and the Grenadines Teachers' Union: POB 304, Kingstown; tel. 457-1062; fax 456-1098; e-mail svgtu@caribsurf.com; f. 1952; Pres. OSWALD ROBINSON; Gen. Sec. JOY MATTHEWS; 1,250 mems.

SAINT VINCENT AND THE GRENADINES

Transport

RAILWAYS
There are no railways in the islands.

ROADS
In 2003 there was an estimated total road network of 829 km (515 miles), of which 580 km (360 miles) were paved. A government plan to extend and rehabilitate the Windward Highway was well advanced by mid-2008, while the first stage of a three-phase project to link Troumaca with Fergusson Gap was completed in 2007, at a cost of EC $2.5m.

SHIPPING
The deep-water harbour at Kingstown can accommodate two ocean-going vessels and about five motor vessels. There are regular motor-vessel services between the Grenadines and Saint Vincent. Geest Industries, formerly the major banana purchaser, operated a weekly service to the United Kingdom. Numerous shipping lines also call at Kingstown harbour. Some exports are flown to Barbados to link up with international shipping lines. A new marina and shipyard complex at Ottley Hall, Kingstown, was completed in 1995. A new container port at Campden Park, near Kingstown, was opened in the same year. A new dedicated Cruise Terminal opened in 1999, permitting two cruise ships to berth at the same time.

Saint Vincent and the Grenadines Port Authority: POB 1237, Kingstown; tel. 456-1830; fax 456-2732; e-mail pkirby@svgpa.com; internet www.svgpa.com; Port Dir PAUL KIRBY.

CIVIL AVIATION
There is a civilian airport, E. T. Joshua Airport, at Arnos Vale, situated about 3 km (2 miles) south-east of Kingstown, that does not accommodate long-haul jet aircraft. The island of Canouan has a small airport with a recently upgraded runway and passenger terminal; construction of a jet airport began in October 2006 and was completed, at a reported cost of US $21.5m., in May 2008 when it commenced operations. In March 2009 LIAT began scheduled flights from Grenada and Barbados to Canouan. Mustique island has a landing strip for light aircraft only. In August 2005 Prime Minister Gonsalves pledged to build an international airport on Saint Vincent. Construction of the facility—located at Argyle, 13 miles east of Kingstown, at an estimated cost of EC $589m.—began in August 2008 and was due to be completed in 2011. Cuba, Taiwan, Iran and Venezuela were committed to providing funding for the project, and several other countries had been approached for assistance.

American Eagle: POB 1232, E. T. Joshua Airport, Arnos Vale; tel. 456-5555; fax 456-5616.

Leeward Islands Air Transport (LIAT): tel. 456-6333; fax 456-6111; e-mail pattersond@liatairline.com; internet www.liatairline.com; f. 2009; Station Man. DOMINIQUE PATTERSON; CEO MARK DARBY.

Mustique Airways: POB 1232, E. T. Joshua Airport, Arnos Vale; tel. 458-4380; fax 456-4586; e-mail info@mustique.com; internet www.mustique.com; f. 1979; charter and scheduled flights; Chair. JONATHAN PALMER.

Saint Vincent and the Grenadines Air Ltd (SVG Air): POB 39, Arnos Vale; tel. 457-5124; fax 457-5077; e-mail info@svgair.com; internet www.svgair.com; f. 1990; charter and scheduled flights; CEO MARTIN BARNARD.

Tourism

The island chain of the Grenadines is the country's main tourism asset. There are superior yachting facilities, but the lack of major air links with countries outside the region has resulted in a relatively slow development for tourism. In 2008 Saint Vincent and the Grenadines received an estimated 141,570 cruise-ship passengers and 88,640 stop-over tourists. Tourism receipts were estimated to total EC $322.3m. in 2007. In early 2008 the Government announced it would invest €5m. in a Tourism Development Project. The plan would involve an upgrade of tourism and airport facilities.

Department of Tourism: Cruise Ship Terminal, Upper Bay St, POB 834, Kingstown; tel. 457-1502; fax 451-2425; e-mail tourism@caribsurf.com; internet www.svgtourism.com; CEO YVONNE ARMOUR-SHILLINGFORD.

Saint Vincent and the Grenadines Hotel and Tourism Association (SVGHTA): E. T. Joshua International Airport, Arnos Vale; tel. 458-4379; fax 456-4456; e-mail office@svghotels.com; internet www.svghotels.com; f. 1968 as Saint Vincent Hotel Asscn; renamed as above in 1999; non-profit org.; mem. of the Caribbean Hotels Asscn; Pres. LEROY LEWIS; Exec. Dir DAWN SMITH; 71 mems.

SAMOA

Introductory Survey

Location, Climate, Language, Religion, Flag, Capital

The Independent State of Samoa (formerly Western Samoa) lies in the southern Pacific Ocean, about 2,400 km (1,500 miles) north of New Zealand. Its nearest neighbour is American Samoa, to the east. The country comprises two large and seven small islands, of which five are uninhabited. The climate is tropical, with temperatures generally between 23°C (73°F) and 30°C (86°F). The rainy season is from November to April. The languages spoken are Samoan (a Polynesian language) and English. Almost all of the inhabitants profess Christianity, and the major denominations are the Congregational, Roman Catholic and Methodist Churches. The national flag (proportions 1 by 2) is red, with a rectangular dark blue canton, containing five differently sized white five-pointed stars in the form of the Southern Cross constellation, in the upper hoist. The capital is Apia.

Recent History

The islands became a German protectorate in 1899. During the First World War (1914–18) they were occupied by New Zealand forces, who overthrew the German administration. In 1919 New Zealand was granted a League of Nations mandate to govern the islands. In 1946 Western Samoa (as it was known until July 1997) was made a UN Trust Territory, with New Zealand continuing as the administering power. From 1954 measures of internal self-government were gradually introduced, culminating in the adoption of an independence Constitution in October 1960. This was approved by a UN-supervised plebiscite in May 1961, and the islands became independent on 1 January 1962. The office of Head of State was held jointly by two traditional rulers but, upon the death of his colleague in April 1963, Malietoa Tanumafili II became sole Head of State for life, performing the duties of a constitutional monarch.

Fiame Mata'afa Mulinu'u, Prime Minister since 1959, lost the general election in 1970, and a new Cabinet, led by Tupua Tamasese Lealofi, was formed. Mata'afa regained power in 1973, following another general election, and remained in office until his death in May 1975. He was again succeeded by Tamasese, who, in turn, lost the general election in March 1976 to his cousin, Tupuola Taisi Efi. The previously unorganized opposition members formed the Human Rights Protection Party (HRPP) in 1979, and won the elections in February 1982, with 24 of the 47 seats in the Fono (Legislative Assembly). Va'ai Kolone was appointed Prime Minister, but in September he was removed from office as a result of past electoral malpractice. His successor, Tupuola Efi, with much popular support, sought to nullify an earlier agreement between Kolone and the New Zealand Government which, in defiance of a ruling by the British Privy Council, denied automatic New Zealand citizenship to all Western Samoans except those already living in New Zealand. However, Tupuola Efi resigned in December 1982, after the Fono had rejected his budget, and was replaced by the new HRPP leader, Tofilau Eti Alesana. At elections in February 1985 the HRPP won 31 of the 47 seats, increasing its majority in the Fono from one to 15 seats; the newly formed Christian Democratic Party (CDP), led by Tupuola Efi, obtained the remaining 16 seats. In December Tofilau Eti resigned, following the rejection of the proposed budget by the Fono and the Head of State's refusal to call another general election. Va'ai Kolone, with the support of a number of CDP members and HRPP defectors, was appointed Prime Minister of a coalition Government in January 1986.

At the February 1988 general election the HRPP and an alliance composed of independents and the CDP (later known as the Samoa National Development Party—SNDP) both initially gained 23 seats, with votes in the remaining constituency being tied. After two recounts proved inconclusive, a judge from New Zealand presided over a third and declared the CDP candidate the winner. However, before a new government could be formed, a newly elected member of the Legislative Assembly defected from the SNDP alliance to the HRPP. In April Tofilau Eti was re-elected Prime Minister, and a new Government, composed of HRPP members, was appointed.

In early 1990 proposed legislation to permit local village councils to fine, or to impose forced labour or exile on, individuals accused of offending communal rules was widely perceived as an attempt by the Government to ensure the support of the Matai (elected clan chiefs) at the next general election. Of the 47 seats in the Fono, 45 were traditionally elected by holders of Matai titles. However, the political importance of the Matai had been increasingly diminished by the procurement of Matai titles by those seeking to be elected to the Fono. This practice was believed to have undermined the system of chief leadership to such an extent that universal suffrage would have to be introduced to decide all of the seats in the Fono. A referendum was conducted in October 1990, at which voters narrowly accepted government proposals for the introduction of universal suffrage. A second proposal, to create an upper legislative chamber composed of the Matai, was rejected. A bill to implement universal adult suffrage was approved by the Fono in December 1990, despite strong opposition from the SNDP.

A general election was held in April 1991 (the election had been postponed from February, owing to the need to register an estimated 80,000 newly enfranchised voters). In the following weeks petitions were filed with the Supreme Court against 11 newly elected members of the Fono who were accused of corrupt or illegal electoral practices. Moreover, subsequent political manoeuvring resulted in the HRPP increasing its parliamentary representation from an initial 26 to 30 seats, while the SNDP ultimately secured only 16 seats in the Fono, and the remaining seat was retained by an independent. At the first meeting of the new Fono, convened in early May, Tofilau Eti was re-elected for what, he later announced, would be his final term of office as Prime Minister. In November the Fono approved legislation to increase the parliamentary term from three to five years and to create an additional two seats in the Fono. These seats were contested in early 1992 and won by the HRPP.

The introduction of a value-added tax on goods and services in January 1994 (which greatly increased the price of food and fuel in the country) provoked a series of demonstrations and protest rallies, as well as demands for the resignation of the Prime Minister. As a result of overwhelming opposition to the new regulations, the Government agreed, in March, to amend the most controversial aspects of the tax. Meanwhile, four members of the Fono (including three recently expelled HRPP members), who had opposed the financial reforms, established a new political organization, the Samoa Liberal Party, under the leadership of the former Speaker, Nonumalo Leulumoega Sofara.

In May 1994 treasury officials warned the Government that a financial crisis at Polynesian Airlines, the national carrier, was threatening the country's economic stability. It was estimated that the company's debts totalled more than 45m. tala. A report by the Chief Auditor, Tom Overhoff, accused the Government of serious financial mismanagement relating to a series of decisions to commit public funds to the airline, and charged seven cabinet ministers with fraud and negligence in their handling of government resources. An inquiry into the allegations conducted in late 1994 cleared the ministers in question of all the charges, although its findings were harshly criticized by Overhoff, who claimed that the inquiry had been neither independent nor impartial. (In 2005 Polynesian Airlines established a joint venture with Australia's Virgin Blue to form Polynesian Blue, resulting in many job losses among the employees of the Samoan carrier.)

Protests against the value-added tax on goods and services continued in early 1995, following the Government's decision to charge two prominent members of the Tumua ma Pule group of traditional leaders and former members of the Fono with sedition, for organizing demonstrations against the tax during 1994. In March 1995 3,000 people delivered a petition to the Prime Minister, bearing the signatures of 120,000 people (some 75% of the population), that demanded that the tax be revoked. The Prime Minister questioned the authenticity of the signatures and appointed a 14-member committee to investigate the matter. In late June the case against the two members of Tumua ma Pule, which had attracted attention from several international non-governmental organizations (including the World Council of

Churches and Amnesty International) was dismissed on the grounds of insufficient evidence.

In December 1995 the HRPP unanimously re-elected Tofilau Eti as the leader of the party, despite concern over the Prime Minister's deteriorating health, as well as a previous declaration that he would retire from politics upon completion of his current term in office. In March 1996 one of the two female members of the Fono, Matatumua Naimoaga, left the HRPP in order to form the Samoa All-People's Party. The formation of the new party, in preparation for the forthcoming general election, was reportedly a result of dissatisfaction with the Government's alleged mismanagement of public assets together with concern over corruption. Legislation introduced in April attempted to distinguish between the traditional Samoan practice of exchanging gifts and acts of bribery, amid numerous reports that voters were demanding gifts and favours from electoral candidates in return for their support.

A general election took place on 26 April 1996. The opposition was highly critical of the delay in the counting of votes (which took some three weeks in total), claiming that the length of time involved allowed the HRPP to recruit successful independent candidates in an attempt to gain a majority of seats in the Fono. It was eventually announced in mid-May that the HRPP had secured a total of 28 seats (with the recruitment of several independent members to their ranks), the SNDP had won 14 seats and independent candidates had secured seven. Tofilau Eti was subsequently re-elected as Prime Minister, defeating the Leader of the Opposition, Tuiatua Tupua Tamasese, with 34 votes to 14.

In May 1997 the Prime Minister proposed a constitutional amendment in the Fono to change the country's name to Samoa. (The country has been known simply as Samoa at the UN since its admission to the organization in 1976.) In July the Fono voted by 41 votes to one to approve the change, which took effect on the next day. However, the neighbouring US territory of American Samoa expressed dissatisfaction with the change (which was believed to undermine the Samoan identity of its islands and inhabitants), and in September introduced legislation to prohibit recognition of the new name within the territory. In March 1998 the House of Representatives in American Samoa voted against legislation that proposed not to recognize Samoan passports (thereby preventing Samoans from travelling to the territory), but decided to continue to refer to the country as Western Samoa and to its inhabitants as Western Samoans. Nevertheless, in January 2000 Samoa and American Samoa signed a memorandum of understanding, increasing co-operation in areas including health, trade and education.

A series of reports in *The Samoa Observer* in mid-1997 alleged that a serious financial scandal involving the disappearance of some 500 blank passports, and their subsequent sale to Hong Kong Chinese purchasers for up to US $26,000 each, had occurred. The Government refused to comment on the newspaper's allegations, stating only that several senior immigration officials had been suspended pending the outcome of an investigation into the affair. Moreover, the Government subsequently brought charges of defamatory libel against the editor, Savea Sano Malifa, for publishing a letter criticizing the Prime Minister (who was reported to have told the Fono of his intention to change legislation governing business licences, such that publications could have their licences withdrawn for publishing dissenting material). The regional Pacific Islands News Association also condemned the Prime Minister's comments as an attack on freedom of information and expression. The continued existence of the newspaper was placed in jeopardy when Savea Sano Malifa was found guilty of defaming the Prime Minister in two libel cases in July and September 1998, and was ordered to pay a total of some $17,000 in costs. The newspaper had alleged that public funds had been used to construct a hotel owned by the Prime Minister and had criticized the allocation of $0.25m. in the 1998 budget to Tofilau Eti's legal costs. The Government's increasingly autocratic style, its apparent intolerance of dissent and the perceived lack of accountability of its members, coupled with its poor economic record, resulted in frequent expressions of popular discontent during 1997. These culminated in a series of protest marches in late 1997 and early 1998, organized by the Tumua ma Pule group of chiefs and attended by several thousand people, which aimed to increase pressure on the Prime Minister to resign.

A long-standing dispute over land rights near Faleolo airport appeared to be the cause of violent activity in June 1998, when villagers shot a government official, burnt buildings and slaughtered or stole hundreds of cattle on a government estate. However, it was subsequently revealed that the incidents had been perpetrated by members of a gang styling themselves as Japanese Ninja warriors, who were believed to be involved in the cultivation of marijuana and cattle theft. Some 38 men, thought to be members of the gang, were later arrested. The dispute, which originated in a land survey carried out in 1871, re-emerged in January 2003 when villagers presented the Government with a petition and a list of demands relating to land rights and revenue from the airport. In July 2005 the Government stated that it wanted all families living on the disputed land to vacate the area (covering about 22 acres) and move to a nearby and larger plot of government land. One of the official reasons given for the request was in order to comply with health and safety regulations. However, the villagers resolved to resist the Government's request, restating their original demand for the return of 6,000 acres close to the airport, which they claimed had been wrongfully taken from them at the end of the 19th century. They were led in their resistance by senior Matai and former Minister of Civil Aviation, Toalepaiali'i Toeolesulusulu Suafaiga Siueva Pose Salesa III, who claimed that during his tenure in the Cabinet the Government had revealed its desire to remove the villagers' coconut trees in order to create a clearer flight path for aircraft and that this remained their motivation for moving the families.

In November 1998 Tofilau Eti Alesana resigned as Prime Minister, owing to ill health. He was replaced by the Deputy Prime Minister, Tuila'epa Sailele Malielegaoi, and, at the same time, the Cabinet was reorganized. Tofilau Eti Alesana died in March 1999.

In July 1999 the Minister of Public Works, Luagalau Levaula Kamu, was shot dead while attending an event commemorating the 20th anniversary of the foundation of the ruling HRPP. Speculation followed that the killer's intended target had been the Prime Minister, but this was denied both by Tuila'epa Sailele and by the New Zealand police officers sent to the island to assist in the investigation. The son of the Minister of Women's Affairs, Leafa Vitale, was later convicted of the murder and sentenced to death (subsequently commuted to a life sentence). Leafa Vitale was subsequently charged with the murder of Luagalau, together with the former Minister for Telecommunications, Toi Akuso, who faced additional charges of inciting others to murder Luagalau and Prime Minister Tuila'epa Sailele. In mid-April 2000 the two former ministers were found guilty of murdering Luagalau and were sentenced to death, which was similarly commuted to life imprisonment. It later emerged that Luagalau had been killed in an attempt to prevent him from uncovering cases of corruption and bribery in which the two ministers had become involved.

Meanwhile, in November 1999 the ruling HRPP increased its number of seats in the Fono to 34 (out of a possible 49) following the defection of an independent candidate to the HRPP. By-elections for the two imprisoned former ministers' seats were held in June 2000, and HRPP candidates were successful in both constituencies.

In August 2000 a supreme court ruling ordered the Government to allow opposition politicians access to the state-controlled media. For several years the opposition had been denied free access to the media.

At a general election on 2 March 2001 the HRPP won 22 seats, the SNDP secured 13 seats and independent candidates took 14 seats. On 16 March Tuila'epa Sailele won 28 votes in the Fono, after securing the support of six independents, to be re-elected Prime Minister. However, the opposition mounted a number of legal challenges to his election. In August eight elected members of Parliament, including the Deputy Prime Minister, the Minister of Health and the Minister of Internal Affairs, Women's Affairs and Broadcasting, faced charges of electoral malpractice in the Supreme Court. None of the cabinet ministers was found guilty, and by-elections for the vacant parliamentary seats were held in October and November. The HRPP won all four contested seats.

An Electoral Commission, established shortly after the March elections, published its recommendations in October 2001, urging the replacement of the two Individual Voters Roll seats with two Urban Seats and that government employees who wished to stand for Parliament should first be obliged to resign from their offices.

In mid-2003 members of the medical profession expressed alarm at the increasing numbers of qualified medical staff choosing to emigrate or to leave the profession. It was estimated that one-third of Samoa's nurses had left the profession between 2002 and 2003, while half of all doctors' positions remained vacant. The situation was attributed to relatively low levels of pay. In September 2005 Samoan doctors went on strike in protest against entry-level rates of pay and working conditions. When doctors refused to return to work, the Government was forced to recruit temporary staff from overseas. In late November some 1,500 people marched through the streets of Apia in support of 23 doctors who had resigned earlier that month as part of the continuing protest. A petition was presented to the Prime Minister's Department, whereupon two cabinet ministers stated that the issue would be addressed. A commission of inquiry made recommendations for changes, to which the Government then agreed, but no increase in doctors' starting salaries, as demanded by protesters, was forthcoming. By January 2006 four of the doctors involved in the protests had relocated overseas; 11 others returned to government employment.

Concern was expressed in early 2005 that the proliferation of Matai titles was leading to the making of hasty and undesirable decisions by village councils. A senior village chief and member of the Fono, Leva'a Sauaso, claimed that many of the new title-holders were lacking in knowledge and experience of village affairs and that these clan leaders were consequently making decisions that were detrimental to Samoan society.

The general election held on 31 March 2006 was contested by a total of 211 candidates, including 18 women. The ruling HRPP regained power, securing 33 of the 49 parliamentary seats, thus decisively defeating the Samoa Democratic United Party (SDUP, formed upon the merger of the SNDP and the Samoa Independent Party), which won 10 seats. The remaining seats were taken by independent candidates. However, violence ensued when it was declared that the Minister for Public Works, Faumui Liuga, had defeated Letagaloa Pita, a senior-ranking Matai, in the constituency of Savai'i. In late August 2006 the opposition SDUP announced the appointment of a new leader, Asiata Sale'imoa Va'ai. The party's long-standing leader, Lemamea Mualia, initially disputed his replacement but formally resigned in late September, subsequently sitting as an independent member of the Fono.

The Samoan Head of State, Malietoa Tanumafili II, died in May 2007 at the age of 95. He had served as sole Head of State, for life, since 1963. His funeral was attended by regional leaders, including the King of Tonga and the New Zealand Prime Minister. In June 2007 the Fono unanimously elected former Prime Minister Tuiatua Tupua Tamasese Efi as Head of State, for a term of five years.

Concerns with regard to the issue of press freedom re-emerged in October 2008, when Savea Sano Malifa, the editor and publisher of the independent *Samoa Observer*, criticized the imposition of 'guidelines' in relation to the reporting of the proceedings of a public commission of inquiry into the conduct of the islands' Commissioner of Police. Malifa claimed that such restrictions were tantamount to a 'nebulous gag on the media'.

Despite independence, Samoa maintains strong links with New Zealand, where many Samoans live and many more receive secondary and tertiary education. In June 2002 New Zealand formally apologized for injustices it had committed against its former colony during its administration between 1914 and 1962. These included carelessness in allowing the 1918 influenza pandemic to kill 22% of Samoa's population (the virus having been brought in on a ship from New Zealand); the murder of a Samoan paramount chief and independence leader, Tupua Tamasese Lealofi III, and the killing of nine other supporters of the pacifist Mau movement during a non-violent protest in 1929; and the banishment of native leaders, who were also stripped of their chiefly titles. The apology, while accepted, attracted mixed reactions from Samoans, many of whom were more concerned with the issue of the restoration of their rights to New Zealand citizenship (which had been severely curtailed by the Citizenship Western Samoa Act of 1982). Moreover, in March 2003 large protest marches took place in Samoa and New Zealand demanding the repeal of the 1982 law. In May 2004 a parliamentary select committee rejected a 100,000-signature petition seeking a repeal of the law and upheld the principles of the 1982 ruling. In 2004 the number of Samoans applying for New Zealand citizenship under a quota scheme increased by more than 50% to some 8,600. Bilateral ministerial consultations continued on a regular basis. In February 2009 the recently appointed Minister of Foreign Affairs of New Zealand, Murray McCully, embarked upon his first official visit to Samoa, where he had meetings with the King of Tonga, the Prime Minister and other senior government officials. In a reflection of New Zealand's fresh approach to its provision of foreign aid, renewed emphasis was to be placed on sustainable development. As part of plans to promote the private sector (see Economic Affairs), McCully also had discussions with local business leaders.

In September 2004 the Samoan Government announced that it was seeking to formalize its maritime boundary with American Samoa, owing to a number of recent, unspecified incidents. Discussions began in Apia in March 2005. In January 2006 the Samoan Government announced that it was to open a consulate in the American Samoan capital of Pago Pago. In February it was announced that Samoa had established diplomatic relations with Brunei, and in October 2007 diplomatic relations were established with Cuba. In May 2007 Samoa hosted a regional meeting attended by ministers from countries including New Zealand, Solomon Islands and Tonga, in order to discuss maritime issues.

Samoa hosted the 13th South Pacific Games in August–September 2007, in which 22 Pacific island nations participated. The Government of the People's Republic of China financed much of the cost of Samoa's preparations, including a US $12.7m. aquatic centre and the reconstruction of Apia Park Stadium, at a cost of $6.9m. However, the total cost was estimated at approximately $92m., and in September Deputy Prime Minister Misa Telefoni acknowledged that preparations for the event had left Samoa in debt. The Chinese Government was also financing the construction of buildings for the legislature and the judiciary in 2007.

Following her visit to New Zealand in July 2008, the US Secretary of State, Condoleezza Rice, travelled on to Samoa, for a brief meeting with the country's Prime Minister. She also had discussions with her regional counterparts, meeting the ministers responsible for foreign affairs of the member countries of the Pacific Islands Forum (see p. 393).

Government

The Constitution provides for the Head of State to be elected by the Legislative Assembly for a term of five years. Until 2007 the Head of State held office for life. The Legislative Assembly is composed of 49 members, all of whom are elected by universal suffrage. A total of 47 members are elected from among holders of Matai titles (elected clan chiefs), and two are selected from non-Samoan candidates. Members hold office for five years. Executive power is held by the Cabinet, comprising the Prime Minister and other selected members of the Assembly. The Prime Minister is appointed by the Head of State with the necessary approval of the Assembly.

Defence

In August 1962 Western Samoa and New Zealand signed a Treaty of Friendship, whereby the New Zealand Government, on request, acts as the sole agent of the Samoan Government in its dealings with other countries and international organizations.

Economic Affairs

In 2007, according to estimates by the World Bank, Samoa's gross national income (GNI), measured at average 2005–07 prices, was US $454m., equivalent to $2,430 per head (or $3,930 per head on an international purchasing-power parity basis). During 2000–07, it was estimated, the population increased at an average annual rate of 0.7%, while during the same period gross domestic product (GDP) per head increased, in real terms, by an average of 3.0% per year. Overall GDP increased, in real terms, at an average annual rate of 3.6% in 2000–07. According to the Asian Development Bank (ADB), growth reached 5.5% in 2007 and 0.3% in 2008.

Agriculture (including hunting, forestry and fishing), measured in 2002 constant prices, accounted for 10.5% of GDP in 2008 and engaged some 40.6% of the employed labour force in 2001. About 30% of the economically active population were engaged in agriculture at mid-2005, according to FAO. The principal cash crops are coconuts and taro (also the country's primary staple food). Breadfruit, yams, maize, passion fruit and mangoes are cultivated as food crops. Exports of breadfruit and papaya to New Zealand increased significantly following the installation in early 2003 of a treatment facility to eradicate fruit fly from the produce. Plans to expand fresh fruit exports to include pineapples, mangoes and limes were announced in early 2005. Pigs, cattle, poultry and goats are raised, mainly for local consumption. The country's commercial fishing industry expanded considerably from the late 1990s; revenue from exports of fresh fish totalled 20.0m. tala in 2007. Exports of food and live animals earned 28.2m. tala (78.0% of total export receipts) in 2007. Between 2000 and 2007, according to figures from the ADB, the GDP of the entire agricultural sector decreased, in real terms, at an average annual rate of 1.4%. In real terms, compared with the previous year, agricultural GDP increased by 6.9% in 2007, but decreased by 9.0% in 2008, according to official figures.

Industry (comprising manufacturing, mining, construction and power) employed 20.0% of the employed labour force in 2001 and provided 28.0% of GDP (measured in constant 2002 prices) in 2008. According to ADB figures, between 2000 and 2007 industrial GDP increased, in real terms, at an average annual rate of 4.4%. The GDP of the industrial sector grew by 13.8% in 2007, before contracting by 10.3% in 2008, according to official figures.

Manufacturing (including handicrafts), measured in constant 2002 prices, provided 11.5% of GDP in 2008 and employed 12.8% of the employed labour force in 2001. The manufacturing sector expanded considerably in the early 1990s with the establishment of a Japanese-owned factory producing electrical components for road vehicles. By 1996 the Yazaki EDS Samoa factory, which assembled wire harnessing systems for export to car-manufacturing plants, engaged about 2,500 workers, making it the largest private sector employer in the country. However, by 2005 reductions in the factory's operations were being recorded, and it was reported that the plant's labour force had been reduced by one-third during 2008. Other products of the manufacturing sector include beverages. Beer accounted for 8.6% of exports in 2007. Soft drinks are also manufactured, mainly for local consumption. A major water-bottling plant, which hoped to sell its product to the US market, opened in 2008. Coconut-based products and cigarettes are also produced. Between 2000 and 2007, according to figures from the ADB, manufacturing GDP increased, in real terms, at an average annual rate of 1.5%. However, the GDP of the manufacturing sector grew by 17.5% in 2007 before contracting by 19.0% in 2008, according to official figures.

Energy is derived principally from hydroelectric power and thermal power stations. A programme for the generation of electricity from coconut oil commenced in early 2009. The construction of a 5MW solar power station, with assistance from the Chinese Government, was also under consideration. Imports of mineral fuels accounted for 18.6% of the value of total imports in 2007. In 2005 a US company announced plans to begin conducting exploration activity in Samoan waters, hoping to find new sources of petroleum and natural gas.

The services sector provided 61.5% of GDP in 2008 (measured in constant 2002 prices) and engaged 39.4% of the employed labour force in 2001. Between 2000 and 2007, according to ADB figures, the sector's GDP increased at an average annual rate of 4.7%. Compared with the previous year, the GDP of the services sector expanded by 3.1% in 2007 and by 6.0% in 2008, according to official figures. Tourism makes a significant contribution to the economy, with revenue from this source (including passenger transport) rising to 288.4m. tala in 2008. Tourist arrivals decreased from 122,352 in 2007 to 122,163 in 2008. In April 2009 Samoa and six neighbouring Pacific countries formed the South Pacific Cruise Group, the priority of which was to attract higher levels of cruise-ship visitors to the countries. 'Offshore' banking was introduced to the islands in 1989, and by July of that year more than 30 companies had registered in Apia. A large proportion of the islands' revenue is provided by remittances from nationals working abroad, which reached the equivalent of 24.8% of GDP in 2008.

In 2007 the country recorded a visible trade deficit of US $213.2m., and a deficit of $37.5m. on the current account of the balance of payments. In 2007, when imports totalled 694.2m. tala and exports reached 253.8m. tala, New Zealand was Samoa's principal supplier of imports, providing 30.7% of the total. Australia was the dominant buyer of Samoan goods, accounting for 81.4% of exports. The USA was also an important trading partner in that year, accounting for 12.8% of imports and purchasing 2.5% of total exports. The principal exports, excluding re-exports to Australia, are fish, garments, coconut cream, copra and beer. The main imports are food and beverages, industrial supplies and fuels.

The large budget deficits of the early 2000s reflected an increase in development spending financed by external borrowing and a decrease in lending to the domestic banking system. Deficits were financed by means of concessional loans, with the remainder being provided through the issuance of government securities. In the year ending 30 June 2009 an overall budget surplus, including external funding, of 84.0m. tala was projected, the surplus being estimated at the equivalent of 5.8% of GDP. Aid from Australia and New Zealand is a major source of revenue. An estimated $A28.3m. was to be provided by Australia in 2008/09, with $NZ10.5m. to be supplied by New Zealand in that year. In September 2008 the European Union (EU) agreed to provide aid of US $65m. for the purposes of various development projects, which included the improvement of health and education facilities. At the end of 2008 the country's total external debt was estimated by the ADB at US $179m. The cost of debt-servicing in that year was equivalent to 3.5% of the value of exports of goods and services. In 2000–08 the annual rate of inflation (excluding rents) averaged 6.3%. According to the ADB, consumer prices increased by 5.5% in 2007 and by 11.5% in 2008. The rate of unemployment was estimated at 4.0% of the labour force in 2006.

Samoa is a member of the Pacific Islands Forum (see p. 393), the Pacific Community (see p. 391), the Asian Development Bank (ADB, see p. 191) and the UN Economic and Social Commission for Asia and the Pacific (ESCAP, see p. 36), and is a signatory to the Lomé Conventions and the successor Cotonou Agreement (see p. 311) with the EU.

The Samoan economy was adversely affected by Cyclone Heta, which struck in January 2004, causing severe damage to infrastructure and the agricultural sector. Subsequent economic growth was largely due to increased activity in the construction industry. In addition to rehabilitation projects in the aftermath of the cyclone, private sector hotel development continued; the construction sector was also sustained by the building of facilities for the South Pacific Games, which Samoa hosted in mid-2007. The economy remained vulnerable to external factors, notably fluctuations in world commodity prices and variations in global demand for Samoa's export items. In December 2008 the weakening of the market for new vehicles, notably in Australia, led the Yazaki automotive parts plant to seek financial assistance from the Samoan Government. The decline in the number of orders placed at the Samoan plant resulted in further redundancies and a reduction in the working hours of the remaining employees. Also owing to the contraction in global economic activity, in comparison with the previous year receipts from tourism were reported to have decreased by 7.6% in 2008. Remittances from Samoan workers employed overseas were estimated to have declined by 4.6%, with a further decrease forecast in 2009 in view of the reduction in job opportunities for Samoans in the USA. Largely as a result of the higher costs of imported fuel and foodstuffs, combined with a reduction in supplies of locally produced food, the rate of inflation reached a high point of 18.7% in November 2008; however, inflationary pressures were expected to ease during 2009. In February 2009 the Central Bank of Samoa reduced its lending rate for commercial banks from 7.85% to 5.0%. The ADB forecast that GDP would contract by 1.0% in 2009. The Strategy for the Development of Samoa (2008–12), supported by Australia and New Zealand, placed particular emphasis on the development of the private sector; initiatives included the creation of the Private Sector Support Fund (co-financed by the UN Development Programme) and the establishment of the Small Business Enterprise Centre. The 2008–12 plan also envisaged the expansion of the agricultural sector and the development of tourism, along with the improvement of health and education facilities.

Education

The education system is based on that of New Zealand. About 97% of the adult population are literate in Samoan. In 2006/07 enrolment at primary schools included an estimated 95.4% of children in the relevant age-group, while in 2005/06 enrolment at secondary level included an estimated 83.1% of pupils of the relevant age. In 1988 a national university was established, with an initial intake of 328 students. Faculties of arts and commerce, science, nursing and education exist. A project to upgrade the university campus was completed in early 1997. In 1992 the Government decided to reintroduce bonds for students awarded government scholarships for overseas study. Expenditure on education by the central Government in 2005/06 was an estimated 55.3m. tala (15.0% of total budgetary expenditure).

Public Holidays

2009: 1 January (New Year's Day), 2 January (Holiday for New Year), 10–13 April (Easter), 11 May (Mother's Day), 1–3 June (Independence Celebrations), 10 August (Father's Day), 12 Octo-

SAMOA

ber (Monday after Lotu a Tamaiti, Children's Day), 6 November (Arbor Day), 19 November (National Women's Day), 25 December (Christmas Day), 26 December (Boxing Day).
2010: 1 January (New Year's Day), 2 January (Holiday for New Year), 2–5 April (Easter), 3 May (Mother's Day), June (Independence Celebrations), 9 August (Father's Day), 11 October (Monday after Lotu a Tamaiti, Children's Day), November (National Women's Day), 5 November (Arbor Day), 25 December (Christmas Day), 26 December (Boxing Day).

Weights and Measures
The metric system of weights and measures is now the primary system in force, although the imperial system is still used in some areas.

Statistical Survey

Source (unless otherwise indicated): Statistical Service Division, Ministry of Finance, Government Building (MFMII), POB 1151, Apia; tel. (685) 24384; fax (685) 24675; e-mail info.stats@mof.gov.ws; internet www.spc.int/prism/country/ws/stats.

AREA AND POPULATION

Area: Savai'i and adjacent small islands 1,708 sq km, Upolu and adjacent small islands 1,123 sq km; Total 2,831 sq km (1,093 sq miles).

Population: 176,710 at census of 5 November 2001; 179,186 (males 92,961, females 86,225) at census of 5 November 2006 (provisional results). *By Island* (2006 census, provisional): Savai'i 43,103; Upolu 136,083.

Density (2006 census): 63.3 per sq km.

Principal Towns (population at 2006 census): Apia (capital) 37,237 (urban area); Vaitele 6,294; Faleasi'u 3,548; Vailele 3,174; Le'auva'a 3,015.

Births, Marriages and Deaths (registrations, 2001): Live births 3,516; Marriages 821; Deaths 339. *2004:* Live births 1,679; Deaths 547. Note: Registration is incomplete. *2000–05* (annual averages, UN estimates): Birth rate 29.4 per 1,000; Death rate 5.7 per 1,000 (Source: UN, *World Population Prospects: The 2006 Revision*).

Life Expectancy (years at birth, WHO estimates): 67.9 (males 65.7; females 70.3) in 2006. Source: WHO, *World Health Statistics*.

Economically Active Population (persons aged 15 years and over, 2001 census): Agriculture, hunting and forestry 17,514; Fishing 2,562; Manufacturing and handicrafts 7,327; Electricity, gas and water supply 905; Construction 1,669; Wholesale and retail trade, repair of motor vehicles, motorcycles and personal and household goods 2,753; Hotels and restaurants 1,522; Transport, storage and communications 1,928; Financial intermediation 1,080; Real estate, renting and business activities 268; Public administration and defence, compulsory social security 3,321; Education 2,341; Health and social work 842; Other community, social and personal service activities 2,090; Private households with employed persons 2,877; Extra-territorial organizations and bodies 472; Activities not adequately defined 853; Total employed 50,325 (males 35,118, females 15,207); Unemployed 2,620 (males 1,621, females 999); *Total labour force* 52,945 (males 36,739, females 16,206). *Mid-2005* (estimates): Agriculture, etc. 20,000; Total labour force 67,000 (Source: FAO).

HEALTH AND WELFARE
Key Indicators

Total Fertility Rate (children per woman, 2006): 4.1.

Under-5 Mortality Rate (per 1,000 live births, 2006): 28.

Physicians (per 1,000 head, 2003): 0.3.

Hospital Beds (per 1,000 head, 2005): 1.0.

Health Expenditure (2006): US $ per head (PPP): 232.

Health Expenditure (2006): % of GDP: 4.9.

Health Expenditure (2006): public (% of total): 81.0.

Human Development Index (2006): ranking 96.

Human Development Index (2006): value 0.760.

For sources and definitions, see explanatory note on p. vi.

AGRICULTURE, ETC.

Principal Crops ('000 metric tons, 2007, FAO estimates): Taro 18; Yams 2.7; Other roots and tubers 3.0; Coconuts 146; Bananas 23.0; Papayas 3.8; Pineapples 4.6; Guavas, mangoes and mangosteens 4.0; Avocados 1.2; Other fruits 1.8; Vegetables 1.0; Cocoa beans 0.5.

Livestock ('000 head, year ending September 2007, FAO estimates): Pigs 202; Cattle 29; Horses 1.9; Chickens 450.

Livestock Products (metric tons, 2007, FAO estimates): Cattle meat 1,000; Pig meat 4,000; Chicken meat 340; Cows' milk 1,500; Hen eggs 260; Honey 400.

Forestry ('000 cubic metres, 1979): *Roundwood Removals* (excl. bark): Sawlogs and veneer logs 58; Other industrial roundwood 3; Fuel wood 70; Total 131. *Sawnwood Production* (incl. sleepers): 21. *1980–2007* (FAO estimates): Annual output as in 1979.

Fishing (metric tons, live weight, 2006): Albacore 2,113; Sharks, rays, skates, etc. 33; Other marine fishes 77; Marine crustaceans 203 (FAO estimate); Marine molluscs 300 (FAO estimate); Sea-urchins and other echinoderms 104 (FAO estimate); Total catch (incl. others) 3,340 (FAO estimate).

Source: FAO.

INDUSTRY

Electric Energy (million kWh): 123.3 in 2004; 128.9 in 2005; 113.5 in 2006. Note: Figures relate only to government-owned power schemes. Source: Treasury Department of Samoa.

FINANCE

Currency and Exchange Rates: 100 sene (cents) = 1 tala (Samoan dollar). *Sterling, US Dollar and Euro Equivalents* (31 December 2008): £1 sterling = 4.2341 tala; US $1 = 2.9044 tala; €1 = 4.0421 tala; 100 tala = £23.62 = US $34.43 = €24.74. *Average Exchange Rate* (tala per US $): 2.7793 in 2006; 2.6166 in 2007; 2.6442 in 2008.

Budget (million tala, year ending 30 June 2006): *Revenue:* Tax revenue 273.1 (Income tax 47.2; Excise tax 69.0; Taxes on international trade 40.9; Value-added gross receipts and services tax 108.6); Other revenue 42.2; Total 315.4, excl. external grants received (71.8). *Expenditure:* Current expenditure 281.9 (General administration 69.5, Law and order 20.2, Education 55.3, Health 47.3, Social security and pensions 14.0, Agriculture 11.7, Public works 29.6, Natural resources 12.4, Other economic services 2.6, Interest on public debt 4.3, Other purposes 29.7, Less Value-added gross receipts and services tax payable by government 14.7); Development expenditure 86.1; Total 368.0, excl. net lending (23.7) (Source: IMF, *Samoa: Selected Issues and Statistical Appendix*—June 2007). *2008/09* (million tala, budget forecast): Total revenue 510.8 (Domestic receipts 400.1, External grants 110.7); Total expenditure 594.8 (Domestically financed 378.4) (Source: Ministry of Finance, *Quarterly Economic Review*—October–December 2008).

International Reserves (US $ million at 31 December 2008): IMF special drawing rights 4.07; Reserve position in IMF 1.07; Foreign exchange 82.37; Total 87.51. Source: IMF, *International Financial Statistics*.

Money Supply (million tala at 31 December 2008): Currency outside banks 52.24; Demand deposits at banks 122.13; Total money 174.37. Source: IMF, *International Financial Statistics*.

Cost of Living (Consumer Price Index, excluding rent; base: 2000 = 100): 138.0 in 2006; 146.7 in 2007; 162.5 in 2008. Source: IMF, *International Financial Statistics*.

Gross Domestic Product (million tala at constant 2002 prices): 1,041.4 in 2006; 1,108.4 in 2007; 1,070.4 in 2008.

Gross Domestic Product by Economic Activity (million tala at constant 2002 prices, 2008): Agriculture and fishing 113.6; Manufacturing 125.1; Electricity, gas and water 49.5; Construction 129.1; Trade 190.5; Hotels and restaurants 38.5; Transport and communications 156.3; Finance and business services 103.8; Public administration 87.1; Other services 91.2; *Sub-total* 1,084.7; *Less* Financial intermediation services indirectly measured 13.3; Total 1,070.4. Note: Totals may not be equal to the sum of components, owing to rounding.

SAMOA

Balance of Payments (US $ million, 2007): Exports of goods f.o.b. 13.9; Imports of goods f.o.b. −227.1; *Trade balance* −213.2; Exports of services 138.7; Imports of services −55.5; *Balance on goods and services* −130.0; Other income received 7.0; Other income paid −23.7; *Balance on goods, services and income* −146.7; Current transfers received 119.0; Current transfers paid −9.8; *Current balance* −37.5; Capital account (net) 28.8; Direct investment from abroad 2.5; Portfolio investment assets −0.1; Portfolio investment liabilities 0.9; Other investments assets −5.5; Other investment liabilities 7.8; Net errors and omissions 12.0; *Overall balance* 8.8. Source: IMF, *International Financial Statistics*.

EXTERNAL TRADE

Principal Commodities (million tala, 2007): *Imports c.i.f.:* Food and live animals 133.1; Crude materials (excl. fuels) 20.3; Mineral fuels, etc. 129.2; Chemicals 45.3; Basic manufactures 148.2; Machinery and transport equipment 132.7 Miscellaneous manufactured articles 63.9; Total (incl. others) 694.2. *Exports (incl. re-exports) f.o.b.:* Food and live animals 28.2; Beverages and tobacco 5.3; Basic manufactures 8.5; Machinery and transport equipment 202.1; Total (incl. others) 253.8. *2008* (million tala): Total imports 659.2 (Public sector goods 24.4, Petroleum 171.0, Other private sector goods 463.8); Total exports (excluding re-exports) 25.9 (Fish 12.3; Beer 2.8; Nonu juice 2.8; Coconut cream 2.1).

Principal Trading Partners (million tala, 2007): *Imports:* Australia 108.7; China, People's Republic 20.7; Japan 33.8; New Zealand 213.1; USA 88.7; Total (incl. others) 694.2. *Exports (incl. re-exports):* Australia 206.5; New Zealand 22.7; USA 6.4; Total (incl. others) 253.8.

TRANSPORT

Road Traffic (motor vehicles registered, 2005): Private cars 4,638; Pick-ups 3,724; Taxis 1,286; Trucks 872; Buses 298; Motorcycles 93; Tractors 32; Total (incl. others) 14,238.

International Shipping (freight traffic, '000 metric tons, 2006): Goods loaded 211.1; Goods unloaded 52.6. *Merchant Fleet* (at 31 December 2007): Vessels 10; Total displacement ('000 grt) 10.5 (Source: Lloyd's Register-Fairplay, *World Fleet Statistics*).

Civil Aviation (traffic on scheduled services, 2004): Kilometres flown 5 million; Passengers carried 247,000; Passenger-kilometres 343 million; Total ton-kilometres 32 million. Source: UN, *Statistical Yearbook*.

TOURISM

Visitor Arrivals: 115,882 in 2006; 122,352 in 2007; 122,163 in 2008.

Visitor Arrivals by Country (2006): American Samoa 26,183; Australia 23,603; Fiji 2,740; New Zealand 42,966; USA 8,682; Total (incl. others) 115,882.

Tourism Receipts (million tala, incl. passenger transport): 236.4 in 2006; 262.5 in 2007; 288.4 in 2008.

COMMUNICATIONS MEDIA

Telephones (2006): 19,500 main lines in use*.

Facsimile Machines (1999): 500 in use*.

Personal Computers (2002): 1,000*.

Internet Users (2006): 8,000*.

Broadband Subscribers (2006): 100*.

Mobile Cellular Telephones (2007): 86,000 subscribers*.

Radio Receivers (1997): 410,000 in use†.

Television Receivers (2001): 26,000 in use*.

Non-daily Newspapers (1988): 5 (estimated circulation 23,000)†.

* Source: International Telecommunication Union.

† Source: UNESCO, *Statistical Yearbook*.

EDUCATION

Primary (2005): 167 schools; 1,392 teachers; 40,074 pupils.

Secondary (2001): 1,064 teachers; 22,185 pupils.

Universities and other Higher (2001): 140 teachers; 1,179 students.

Source: mainly UN, *Statistical Yearbook for Asia and the Pacific*.

Adult Literacy Rate (UNESCO estimates): 98.7% (males 98.9%; females 98.4%) in 2007. Source: UNESCO Institute for Statistics.

Directory

The Constitution

A new Constitution was adopted by a constitutional convention on 28 October 1960. After being approved by a UN-supervised plebiscite in May 1961, the Constitution came into force on 1 January 1962, when Western Samoa became independent. A constitutional amendment adopted in July 1997 shortened the country's name to Samoa. The main provisions of the Constitution are summarized below:

HEAD OF STATE

The office of Head of State was occupied (from 5 April 1963, when his co-ruler died) by HH Malietoa Tanumafili II, who held this post until his death in May 2007. After that the Head of State was to be elected by the Fono (Legislative Assembly) for a term of five years.

EXECUTIVE

Executive power lies with the Cabinet, consisting of the Prime Minister, supported by the majority in the Fono, and ministers selected by the Prime Minister. Cabinet decisions are subject to review by the Executive Council, which is made up of the Head of State and the Cabinet.

LEGISLATURE

The Fono consists of 49 members. It has a five-year term and the Speaker is elected from among the members. Beginning at the election of 5 April 1991, members are elected by universal adult suffrage: 47 members of the Assembly are elected from among the Matai (elected clan leaders) while the remaining two are selected from non-Samoan candidates.

The Government

HEAD OF STATE

O le Ao o le Malo: TUIATUA TUPUA TAMASESE EFI (elected by the Fono 15 June 2007).

CABINET
(April 2009)

Prime Minister and Minister of Foreign Affairs and Trade: TUILA'EPA SAILELE MALIELEGAOI.

Deputy Prime Minister and Minister of Commerce, Tourism, Industry and Labour: MISA TELEFONI RETZLAFF.

Minister of Women, Community and Social Development: FIAME NAOMI MATA'AFA.

Minister of Police, Prisons and Fire Services: TOLEAFOA APULU FAAFISI.

Minister of Works, Transport and Infrastructure: TUISUGALETAUA SOFARA AVEAU.

Minister of Natural Resources and Environment: FAUMUINA TIATIA LIUGA.

Minister of Finance: NIKO LEE HANG.

Minister of Revenue: TUU'U ANASI'I LEOTA.

Minister of Health: GATOLOAIFAANA AMATAGA ALESANA GIDLOW.

Minister of Communications and Information Technology: SAFUNEITUUGA PA'AGA NERI.

Minister of Education, Sports and Culture: TOOMATA ALAPATI POESE TOOMATA.

Minister for Justice and Courts Administration: UNASA MESI GALO.

Minister of Agriculture: TAUA TAVAGA KITIONA SEUALA.

MINISTRIES AND MINISTERIAL DEPARTMENTS

Prime Minister's Department: POB L 1861, Apia; tel. 63222; fax 21339; e-mail pmdept@ipasifika.net.

Ministry of Agriculture, Forestry, Fisheries and Meteorology: POB 1874, Apia; tel. 22561; fax 21865; e-mail maffm@lesamoa.net.

Broadcasting Department: POB 200, Apia; tel. 21420.

Ministry of Commerce, Industry and Labour: Apia; tel. 20441; fax 20443; e-mail mpal@mcil.gov.ws; internet www.mcil.gov.ws.

Ministry of Communications and Information Technology: Private Bag, Apia; tel. 26117; fax 24671; e-mail mcit@mcit.gov.ws; internet www.mcit.gov.ws.

Customs Department: POB 44, Apia; tel. 21561.

Economic Affairs Department: POB 862, Apia; tel. 20471.

Ministry of Education, Sports and Culture: POB 1869, Apia; tel. 21911; fax 21917; e-mail samoamesc@lesamoa.net; internet www.mesc.gov.ws.

Ministry of Finance: Private Bag, Apia; tel. 34333; fax 21312; e-mail information@mof.gov.ws; internet www.mof.gov.ws.

Ministry of Foreign Affairs and Trade: POB L 1859, Apia; tel. 211171; fax 21504; e-mail mfat@mfat.gov.ws; internet www.mfat.gov.ws.

Ministry of Health: Private Bag, Apia; tel. 68100; fax 24496; e-mail MOH@health.gov.ws; internet www.health.gov.ws.

Inland Revenue Department: POB 209, Apia; tel. 20411.

Ministry of Justice and Courts Administration: POB 49, Apia; tel. 22671; fax 21050.

Lands, Survey and Environment Department: Private Bag, Apia; tel. 22481; fax 23176.

Ministry of Natural Resources and Environment: PMB, Apia; tel. 23800; fax 23176; e-mail info@mnre.gov.ws; internet www.mnre.gov.ws.

Ministry of Police: Apia; tel. 28055; fax 21319.

Public Works Department: Private Bag, Apia; tel. 20865; fax 21927; e-mail pwdir@lesamoa.net.

Ministry for Revenue: Apia; tel. 22244; fax 23876; internet www.revenue.gov.ws.

Statistics Department: POB 1151, Apia; tel. 21371; fax 24675.

Ministry of Women, Community and Social Development: PMB, Apia; tel. 63410; fax 23639; internet www.mwcsd.gov.ws.

Ministry of Works, Transport and Infrastructure: Apia; tel. 24031; fax 20964.

Legislature

FONO
(Legislative Assembly)

The Assembly has 47 Matai members, representing 41 territorial constituencies, and two individual members. Elections are held every five years. At a general election on 31 March 2006, the Human Rights Protection Party (HRPP) won 33 seats, the Samoa Democratic United Party (SDUP) won 10 seats and independent candidates secured six seats.

Speaker: TOLOFUAIVALELEI FALEMOE LEIATAUA.

Political Organizations

Human Rights Protection Party (HRPP): c/o The Fono, Apia; f. 1979; Western Samoa's first formal political party; Leader TUILA'EPA SAILELE MALIELEGAOI; Gen. Sec. LAULU DAN STANLEY.

Samoa Democratic United Party (SDUP): POB 1233, Apia; tel. 23543; fax 20536; f. 1988; est. as Samoa National Development Party (SNDP); coalition party comprising the Christian Democratic Party (CDP) and several independents; assumed present name after the 2001 election following merger of the SNDP and the Samoa Independent Party; Leader Hon. ASIATA SALE'IMOA VA'AI; Sec. VALASI TAFITO.

Diplomatic Representation

EMBASSIES AND HIGH COMMISSIONS IN SAMOA

Australia: Beach Rd, POB 704, Apia; tel. 23411; fax 23159; internet www.samoa.embassy.gov.au; High Commissioner MATT ANDERSON.

China, People's Republic: Private Bag, Vailima, Apia; tel. 22474; fax 21115; e-mail tce@samoa.ws; Ambassador SHI LONGZHUANG.

New Zealand: Beach Rd, POB 1876, Apia; tel. 21711; fax 20086; e-mail nzhcapia@samoa.ws; High Commissioner CAROLINE BILKEY.

USA: POB 3430, Apia; tel. 21631; fax 22030; e-mail usembassy@samoa.net; internet samoa.usembassy.gov; Chargé d'affaires ROBIN L. YEAGER (resident in New Zealand).

Judicial System

Attorney-General: MING LEUNG WAI.

The Supreme Court
Presided over by the Chief Justice. It has full jurisdiction for both criminal and civil cases. Appeals lie with the Court of Appeal.

Chief Justice: PATU TIAVA'ASU'E FALEFATU SAPOLU.
Secretary for Justice: FAAITAMAI P. F. MEREDITH.

The Court of Appeal: consists of the President (the Chief Justice of the Supreme Court), and of such persons possessing qualifications prescribed by statute as may be appointed by the Head of State. Any three judges of the Court of Appeal may exercise all the powers of the Court.

The District Courts
Replaced the Magistrates' Court in 1998.
Judges: LESATELE RAPI VAAI, TAGALOA ENOKA FERETI PUNI.

The Land and Titles Court
Has jurisdiction in respect of disputes over Samoan titles. It consists of the President (who is also a judge of the Supreme Court) and three Deputy Presidents, assisted by Samoan judges and Assessors.

President of the Land and Titles Court: PATU TIAVA'ASU'E FALEFATU SAPOLU.

Religion

Almost all of Samoa's inhabitants profess Christianity.

CHRISTIANITY

Fono a Ekalesia i Samoa (Samoa Council of Churches): POB 574, Apia; f. 1967; four mem. churches; Sec. Rev. EFEPAI KOLIA.

The Anglican Communion
Samoa lies within the diocese of Polynesia, part of the Church of the Province of New Zealand. The Bishop of Polynesia is resident in Fiji, while the Archdeacon of Tonga and Samoa is resident in Tonga.

Anglican Church: POB 16, Apia; tel. 20500; fax 24663; Rev. PETER E. BENTLEY.

The Roman Catholic Church
The islands of Samoa constitute the archdiocese of Samoa-Apia. At 31 December 2006 there were an estimated 40,179 adherents in the country. The Archbishop participates in the Catholic Bishops' Conference of the Pacific, based in Fiji.

Archbishop of Samoa-Apia: Cardinal ALAPATI L. MATA'ELIGA, Archbishop's House, Fetuolemoana, POB 532, Apia; tel. 20400; fax 20402; e-mail archdiocese@samoa.ws.

Other Churches

Church of Jesus Christ of Latter-day Saints (Mormon): Samoa Apia Mission, POB 1865, Apia; tel. 64210; fax 64222; f. 1888; Pres. RENDAL V. BROOMHEAD; f. 1888; 65,000 mems.

Congregational Christian Church in Samoa: Tamaligi, POB 468, Apia; tel. 22279; fax 20429; e-mail cccsgsec@lesamoa.net; f. 1830; 100,000 mems; Gen. Sec. Rev. MAONE F. LEAUSA.

Congregational Church of Jesus in Samoa: 505 Borie St, Honolulu, HI 96818, USA; Rev. NAITULI MALEPEAI.

Methodist Church in Samoa (Ekalesia Metotisi i Samoa): POB 1867, Apia; tel. 22283; e-mail afereti@samoa.ws; f. 1828; 37,000 mems; Pres. Rev. AFRETI SAMUELU; Gen. Sec. Rev. TUPU FOLASA.

Seventh-day Adventist Church: POB 600, Apia; tel. 20451; f. 1895; covers Samoa and American Samoa; 5,000 mems; Pres. Pastor SAMUELU AFAMASAGA; Sec. UILI SOLOFA.

BAHÁ'Í FAITH

National Spiritual Assembly: POB 1117, Apia; tel. 23348; fax 21363.

SAMOA

The Press

Newsline: POB 2441, Apia; tel. 24216; fax 23623; twice a week; Editor Pio Sioa.

Samoa News: POB 1160, Apia; daily; merged with the weekly *Samoa Times* (f. 1967) in Sept. 1994; Publr Rhona Annesley.

The Samoa Observer: POB 1572, Apia; tel. 21099; fax 21195; e-mail sanomalifa@yahoo.com; internet www.samoaobserver.ws; f. 1979; five times a week; independent; English and Samoan; also publ. in New Zealand twice a week; Editor Savea Sano Malifa; Devt Editor Russel Hunter; circ. 4,500.

Samoa Weekly: Saleufi, Apia; f. 1977; weekly; independent; bilingual; Editor Lance Polu; circ. 4,000.

Savali: POB L 1861, Apia; publ. of Lands and Titles Court; monthly; govt-owned; Samoan edn f. 1904; Editor Faleseu L. Fua; circ. 6,000; English edn f. 1977; circ. 500; bilingual commercial edn f. 1993; circ. 1,500; Editor Tupuola Terry Tavita.

South Seas Star: POB 800, Apia; tel. 23684; weekly.

PRESS ASSOCIATION

Journalists' Association of Samoa (JAWS): Apia; tel. 7773776; e-mail jawsexec@yahoo.com; internet jawsamoa.blogspot.com; f. 1980; Pres. Uale Papalii Taimalelagi.

Broadcasting and Communications

TELECOMMUNICATIONS

Digicel Samoa Ltd: Vaimea, Apia; fax 28005; e-mail customercaresamoa@digicelgroup.com; internet www.digicelsamoa.com; f. 2006 following the acquisition of Telecom Samoa by the Digicel Group; 90% owned by the Digicel Group, 10% govt-owned; Gen. Man. Alex Abraham.

SamoaTel: Maluafou, Private Bag, Apia; tel. 60000; fax 61000; internet www.samoatel.ws; corporatized in July 1999; telecommunications and postal services provider; CEO Mike Johnstone.

BROADCASTING

Radio and Television

Samoa Broadcasting Corpn: Apia; tel. 21420; fax 21072; f. 1948; govt-controlled with commercial sponsorship; operates SBC Radio 1 and SBC Television 1; CEO Faiasea Lei Sam Matafeo.

Magik 98 FM: POB 762, Apia; tel. 25149; fax 25147; e-mail magic98fm@samoa.net; f. 1989; privately-owned; operates on FM wavelengths 98.1 and 99.9 MHz; Man. Corey Keil.

Graceland Broadcasting Network: POB 3444, Apia; tel. 20197; fax 25487; e-mail gbn@lesamoa.net; internet www.welcome.to/gbn; f. 1992; telecommunications, television and radio.

Star Television: Apia; f. 2009; Man. Dir Apulu Lance Polu.

Finance

(cap. = capital; res = reserves; dep. = deposits; m. = million; brs = branches; amounts in tala, unless otherwise indicated)

BANKING

Central Bank

Central Bank of Samoa: Private Bag, Apia; tel. 34100; fax 20293; e-mail centralbank@cbs.gov.ws; internet www.cbs.gov.ws; f. 1984; cap. 10.0m., res 14.8m., dep. 84.3m. (Dec. 2006); Gov. Papali'i Tommy Scanlan.

Commercial Banks

ANZ Bank (Samoa) Ltd: Beach Rd, POB L 1885, Apia; tel. 69999; fax 24595; e-mail samoa@anz.com; internet www.anz.com/samoa; f. 1959; est. as Bank of Western Samoa, name changed 1997; 100% owned by ANZ Funds Pty Ltd; cap. 1.5m., res 28.4m., dep. 246.1m. (Sept. 2001); Dir R. G. Lyon; Man. Dir Mandy R. Simpson; 1 br.

Industrial Bank Inc: POB 3271, Lotemau Centre, Vaea St, Apia; tel. 21878; fax 21869; f. 1995; owned by Industrial Pacific Investments Ltd; Chair. and Pres. Ian Bystrov.

National Bank of Samoa: Beach Rd, Apia 00685; tel. 26766; fax 23477; e-mail info@nationalbanksamoa.com; internet www.nationalbanksamoa.com; f. 1995; owned by consortium of private interests in Samoa, American Samoa and the USA; Chair. Sala Epa Tuioti; CEO Douglas M. Crombie; 15 agencies; 5 brs.

Samoa Commercial Bank: POB L602, Matafele; tel. 31233; fax 30250; e-mail info@scbl.ws; internet www.scbl.ws; f. 2003; CEO Ray Ah Liki.

Westpac Bank Samoa Ltd: Beach Rd, POB 1860, Apia; tel. 20000; fax 22848; e-mail westpac@samoa.com.ws; internet www.westpac.com.ws; f. 1977; est. as Pacific Commercial Bank Ltd, current name adopted 2001; first independent bank; 93.5% owned by Westpac Banking Corpn (Australia); cap. 1.2m., res 5.5m., dep. 99.8m. (Sept. 2004); Chair. Alan Walter; Gen. Man. Jason Green; 3 brs.

Development Bank

Development Bank of Samoa: POB 1232, Apia; tel. 22861; fax 23888; e-mail dbs@dbsamoa.ws; internet www.dbsamoa.ws; f. 1974; est. by Govt to foster economic and social development; Chair. Hinauri Petana; Gen. Man. Falefa Lima.

INSURANCE

National Pacific Insurance Ltd: DBS Bldg, Level 5, Private Bag, Apia; tel. 20481; fax 23374; f. 1977; Gen. Man. Darryl Williamson.

Progressive Insurance Company: POB 620, Lotemau Centre, Apia; tel. 26110; fax 26112; e-mail progins@samoa.ws; f. 1993; Gen. Man. I. O. Filemu.

Western Samoa Life Assurance Corporation: POB 494, Apia; tel. 23360; fax 23024; f. 1977; Gen. Man. A. S. Chan Ting.

Trade and Industry

CHAMBER OF COMMERCE

Chamber of Commerce and Industry: Level 1, Lotemau Centre, Convent St, POB 2014, Apia; tel. 31090; fax 31089; f. 1938; Pres. Sina Retzlaff-Lima; Vice-Pres. Daryl Clarke.

INDUSTRIAL AND TRADE ASSOCIATIONS

Samoa Coconut Products: Apia.

Samoa Forest Corporation: Apia.

UTILITIES

Electricity

Electric Power Corporation: POB 2011, Apia; tel. 65246; fax 23748; e-mail fepuleait@epc.ws; internet www.epc.ws; f. 1972; autonomous govt-owned corpn; part of Public Works Dept, known as Electric Power Scheme, until 1972; Gen. Man. Muaausa Joseph Walter.

Water

Samoa Water Authority: POB 245, Apia; tel. 20409; fax 21298; e-mail taputoa@swa.gov.ws; internet www.swa.gov.ws; Man. Dir Mafaa'uo Taputoa Titimaea.

TRADE UNIONS

Samoa Association of Manufacturers and Exporters (SAME): POB 3428, Apia; tel. 23377; fax 26895; e-mail info@same.org.ws; f. 1981; Pres. Eddie Wilson.

Samoa Nurses' Association (SNA): POB 3491, Apia; Pres. Faamanatu Nielsen; 252 mems.

Samoa Trade Union Congress (STUC): POB 1515, Apia; tel. 24134; fax 20014; f. 1981; affiliate of ITUC; Pres. Falefata Tuaniu Petaia; Dir Matafeo R. Matafeo; 5,000 mems.

Transport

Public Works Department: see under The Government; Dir of Works Isikuki Punivalu.

ROADS

In 1999 there were 790 km of roads on the islands, of which some 42% were paved. In 2004 the Government announced a programme of road-building, including new roads from Apia to the airport and to the inter-island wharves.

SHIPPING

There are deep-water wharves at Apia and Asau. Regular cargo services link Samoa with Australia, New Zealand, American Samoa, Fiji, New Caledonia, Solomon Islands, Tonga, US Pacific coast ports and various ports in Europe.

Samoa Ports Authority: POB 2279, Apia; tel. 64400; fax 25870; e-mail spa@spasamoa.ws; internet www.spasamoa.ws; f. 1999; Gen. Man. TOLEAFOA ELON BETHAM.

Samoa Shipping Services Ltd: POB 1884, Apia; tel. 20790; fax 20026; e-mail sss@lesamoa.net; internet www.sssl.ws.

Samoa Shipping Corporation Ltd: Private Bag, Shipping House Matautu-tai, Apia; tel. 20935; fax 22352; e-mail info@samoashipping.com; internet www.samoashipping.com; Gen. Man. OLOIALII KOKI TUALA.

CIVIL AVIATION

There is an international airport at Faleolo, about 35 km from Apia and an airstrip at Fagali'i, 4 km east of Apia Wharf, which receives light aircraft from American Samoa.

Polynesian Blue: internet www.polynesianblue.com; f. 2005; 49% owned by the Samoan Govt, 49% owned by Virgin Blue, 2% owned by independent Samoan shareholder; flies between Samoa, Australia and New Zealand; replaced the services of Polynesian Airlines upon that carrier's cessation of international operations in 2005; CEO JOHN BARTLETT.

Polynesian Ltd: 2nd Floor, SNPF Bldg, Beach Rd, POB 599, Apia; tel. 21261; fax 20023; e-mail enquiries@polynesianairlines.com; internet www.polynesianairlines.com; f. 1959; 100% govt-owned; operates service to American Samoa and offers charter services between the islands of Upolu and Savai'i; Chair. TUILA'EPA SAILELE MALIELEGAOI; CEO TAUA FATU TIELU.

Tourism

The principal attractions are the scenery and the pleasant climate. Samoa has traditionally maintained a cautious attitude towards tourism, fearing that the Samoan way of life might be disrupted by an influx of foreign visitors. A major project to construct a 400-room resort on Taumeasina island, off Apia, began in September 2004. Tourist arrivals were reported to have decreased from 122,250 in 2007 to 121,578 in 2008. Most visitors come from New Zealand, American Samoa, Australia and the USA. Tourist receipts (including passenger transport) totalled 288.4m. tala in 2008.

Samoa Tourism Authority: POB 2272, Apia; tel. 63500; fax 20886; e-mail info@visitsamoa.ws; internet www.visitsamoa.ws; CEO MATATAMALI'I SONJA HUNTER.

Samoa Hotel Association: POB 3973, Apia; tel. 30160; fax 30161; e-mail info@samoa-hotels.ws; internet www.samoa-hotels.ws; f. 1999; owned by Asscn of Accommodation Providers; Pres. STEVE YOUNG.

SAN MARINO

Introductory Survey

Location, Climate, Language, Religion, Flag, Capital

The Republic of San Marino lies in southern Europe. The country is situated on the slopes of Mount Titano, in the Apennines, bordered by the central Italian region of Emilia-Romagna to the north, and the Marches region to the south. San Marino has cool winters and warm summers, with temperatures generally between −2°C (28°F) and 30°C (86°F). Average annual rainfall totals 880 mm (35 ins). The language is Italian. Almost all of the inhabitants profess Christianity, and the state religion is Roman Catholicism. The civil flag (proportions 3 by 4) has two equal horizontal stripes, of white and light blue. The state flag has, in addition, the national coat of arms (a shield, framed by a yellow cartouche, bearing three green mountains—each with a white tower, surmounted by a stylized ostrich feather, at the summit— the shield being surmounted by a bejewelled crown and framed by branches of laurel and oak, and surmounting a white ribbon bearing, in black, the word 'libertas') in the centre. The capital is San Marino.

Recent History

San Marino evolved as a city-state in the early Middle Ages and is the sole survivor of the numerous independent states that existed in Italy prior to its unification in the 19th century. A treaty of friendship and co-operation with Italy was signed in 1862, renewed in March 1939 and revised in September 1971.

From 1945 to 1957 San Marino was ruled by a left-wing coalition of the Partito Comunista Sammarinese (PCS) and the Partito Socialista Sammarinese (PSS). Defections from the PCS in 1957 led to a bloodless revolution, after which a coalition of the Partito Democratico Cristiano Sammarinese (PDCS) and the Partito di Democrazia Socialista came to power. In early 1973 an internal dispute over economic policy led to the resignation of the Government, and a new Government was formed by an alliance between the PDCS and the PSS. The PSS withdrew from the coalition in November 1975, resulting in the collapse of the Government. The Captains-Regent took over the administration until March 1976, when a new coalition between the PDCS and the PSS was formed. This Government collapsed in late 1977 but continued in an interim capacity until a new administration was formed. Attempts by the PCS to form a government were frustrated by the lack of a clear majority in the unicameral legislature, the Great and General Council (Consiglio Grande e Generale). Eventually the Council agreed to a dissolution and elections were held in May 1978, when the PDCS secured 26 of the 60 seats. However, they were still unable to form an administration and the three left-wing parties, the PCS, PSS and the Partito Socialista Unitario, which together held 31 seats, agreed to form a coalition Government led by the PCS. San Marino thus became the only Western European country with a communist-led government. A left-wing coalition again formed the administration following the May 1983 elections.

In 1986 a political crisis, resulting from a financial scandal which allegedly involved several prominent PSS members, led to the formation of a new coalition Government, the first to be composed of the PDCS and the PCS. The coalition was renewed in June 1988, following a general election in May. In 1990 the PCS was renamed the Partito Progressista Democratico Sammarinese (PPDS). In 1992 the PDCS negotiated the formation of a coalition Government with the PSS.

At the general election of May 1993 the PDCS and the PSS obtained 26 and 14 seats, respectively. The election was regarded as a defeat for the PPDS, which secured only 11 seats, and was also notable for the success of three recently formed parties, the Alleanza Popolare dei Democratici Sammarinese (known as the Alleanza Popolare—AP), the Movimento Democratico and the Rifondazione Comunista Sammarinese (RCS). In June the PDCS and the PSS agreed to form a coalition Government. The PDCS and the PSS were again dominant at the general election of 31 May 1998, winning 25 and 14 seats, respectively. The PPDS won 11 seats, the AP six, and the RCS two. The remaining two seats were secured by a new grouping, Socialisti per le Riforme, which had been founded in 1997. A coalition Government was formed by the PDCS and the PSS in July 1998. In February 2000 the PSS left the Government, and in March a new coalition Government was formed, with six members of the PDCS, three members of the PPDS and one member of the Socialisti per le Riforme; it also had parliamentary support from Idee in Movimento (as the Movimento Democratico had been renamed in 1998). In March 2001 the Partito dei Democratici Sammarinese (PdD) was formed, following an alliance between Idee in Movimento, the PPDS and the Socialisti per le Riforme; the PPDS Secretary-General, Claudio Felici, was appointed as the PdD's Secretary-General.

At legislative elections held on 10 June 2001, the PDCS won 25 seats, and the PSS obtained 15. The two parties subsequently formed a coalition Government. The PdD won 12 seats, while the AP secured five, the RCS two and the Alleanza Nazionale Sammarinese one.

In June 2002 the PDCS-PSS coalition Government collapsed after the PSS withdrew its support, ending the long-term domination of Sammarinese politics by the PDCS. A new coalition Government was formed on 25 June, incorporating five members of the PSS, three of the PdD and two members of the AP. By December, however, the alliance between the PSS and the PDCS had been renewed, and a new coalition Government was instituted on 17 December, with five members from each party. In January 2003 a new political party, Sammarinesi per la Libertà, was formed. In December the coalition Government collapsed owing to disagreements between the two ruling parties, and a new coalition comprising four PDCS members and two each from the PSS and the PdD was installed. In early 2005 the PSS and the PdD merged to form the Partito dei Socialisti e dei Democratici (PSD). Former members of the PSS founded a new party, the Nuovo Partito Socialista, in November.

On 4 June 2006 a general election took place, at which the PDCS won 32.9% of the valid votes cast (21 of the 60 seats in the Great and General Council). However, the PSD, which secured 31.8% of the votes (20 seats), subsequently formed a coalition Government with the AP and the Sinistra Unita (SU, an alliance of the RCS and Zona Franca), which received 12.1% (seven seats) and 8.7% (five seats), respectively. The abstention rate was 28.2%. The new Government, comprising six members of the PSD and two each from the AP and the SU, took office on 29 July. In March 2007 a new political party, the Democratici di Centro (DdC), was formed by disaffected former members of the PDCS.

In late October 2007 the coalition collapsed after a government bill regarding judicial reform was narrowly rejected by the Great and General Council. In November a new four-party coalition, comprising the PSD (five members), the AP, the SU (each two) and the DdC (one), was formed. However, by June 2008 this coalition had also collapsed due to disagreements between the AP and the other ruling parties; an early general election was subsequently held on 9 November. Under the terms of new regulations approved earlier in the year, which had aligned the country's electoral system more closely to that of the Italian model, the parties contested the elections in two major coalitions: the Patto per San Marino (a right-wing coalition that included the PDCS, the AP, the Lista della Libertà, Europopolari per San Marino, Arengo e Libertà and the Unione Sammarinesi dei Moderati); and Riforme e Libertà (a left-wing coalition including the PSD, Sammarinesi per la Libertà, the SU and the DdC). The Patto per San Marino won 54.2% of the valid votes cast and 35 seats, while Riforme e Libertà won 45.8% of the votes and 25 seats. The rate of participation by eligible voters was 68.48%. A new coalition Government was sworn in at the beginning of December, comprising three members of the PDCS, two each from the AP and the Lista della Libertà, and a sole representative each from the Unione Sammarinesi dei Moderati and Arengo e Libertà.

San Marino became a member of the UN in 1992. In early 2006 San Marino was represented at a conference of small European states, held in Monaco.

Government

San Marino is divided into nine 'Castles' (Castelli) corresponding to the original parishes of the Republic. Each 'Castle' is governed by a Castle-Captain (Capitano di Castello), who holds office for two years, and a Castle Board (Giunta di Castello), which holds office for five years.

Legislative power is vested in the unicameral Great and General Council (Consiglio Grande e Generale), with 60 members elected by universal adult suffrage, under a system of proportional representation, for five years (subject to dissolution). The Council elects two of its members to act jointly as Captains-Regent (Capitani Reggenti), with the functions of Head of State and Government, for six months at a time (ending in March and September). Executive power is held by the Congress of State (Congresso di Stato), with 10 members elected by the Council for the duration of its term. The Congress is presided over by the Captains-Regent.

Defence

There are combined Voluntary Military Forces. There is no obligatory military service but citizens between 16 and 55 years may be enlisted, in certain circumstances, to defend the state.

Economic Affairs

San Marino's gross national product (GNP) was €978m. in 2007, equivalent to €30,510 per head. Annual GDP growth averaged 2.8% in 2003–2007; GDP increased by 3.5% in 2007.

Agriculture contributed only 0.1% of GDP in 2007 and engaged 0.2% of the employed population (excluding the self-employed) in 2008. The principal crops are wheat, barley, maize, olives and grapes. Livestock-rearing and dairy farming are also significant. Olive oil and wine are produced for export.

Industry (including manufacturing and construction) contributed 44.5% of GDP in 2007 and engaged 38.6% of the employed population (excluding the self-employed) in 2008. Stone-quarrying is the only mining activity in San Marino, and is an important export industry. Manufacturing contributed 38.0% of GDP in 2007 and engaged 31.2% of the employed population (excluding the self-employed) in 2008. The most important branches of manufacturing are the production of cement, synthetic rubber, leather, textiles and ceramics. The sector is largely export orientated, owing to integration with firms in Italy.

Energy is derived principally from gas (more than 75%). San Marino is dependent on the Italian state energy companies for much of its energy requirements.

The services sector contributed 55.4% of GDP in 2007 and engaged 61.2% of the employed population (excluding the self-employed) in 2008. Tourism is a significant source of government revenue. In 2004 the number of visitor arrivals was 2,127,573; however, of that number, only 41,546 stayed at least one night. Total visitor arrivals numbered 2,111,736 in 2008. Tourism receipts totalled an estimated €27,620m. in 2003. The sale of coins and postage stamps, mainly to foreign collectors, is also a significant source of foreign exchange. San Marino, along with the Vatican and Monaco, was granted special dispensation to mint its own euro coins in 2002, with a view to providing for this specialist market. The sale of uncirculated minted coins to collectors plays a significant role in San Marino's economy and it was permitted to continue to mint gold scudi as a legal tender for San Marino only. The financial sector is increasingly important, with the credit and insurance sectors contributing 18.6% of GDP in 2007.

In 2002, according to official figures, San Marino recorded a trade deficit of €96.2m. In the same year, according to the IMF, there was a deficit of €302.5m. on the current account of the balance of payments. Data concerning imports and exports are included in those of Italy, with which San Marino maintains a customs union. A customs union is also maintained with the European Union (EU, see p. 255). The principal source of imports (estimated at 87%) is Italy, upon which the country is dependent for its supply of raw materials. The major exports are wine, woollen goods, furniture, ceramics, building stone and artisan- and hand-made goods.

San Marino receives a subsidy from the Italian Government, under the *Canone Doganale*, amounting to about €11m. annually, in exchange for the Republic's acceptance of Italian rules concerning exchange controls and the renunciation of customs duties. In January 1999 San Marino adopted the European single currency, the euro, which became the sole currency in circulation at the start of 2002.

No consolidated general government accounts are published by San Marino, and separate accounts and budgets are prepared by the central administration, the Social Security Institute, and each of the public enterprises, on an accrual basis. Figures published by the IMF, on a cash basis, for the budget of the central administration indicated a surplus of €71.7m. for 2005 (equivalent to some 6.5% of GDP). The annual rate of inflation averaged 1.8% in 2002–06; consumer prices increased by 2.1% in 2006. In 2008 501 people were unemployed—equivalent to 2.4% of the total labour force (excluding the self-employed). An increasingly large proportion of the work-force (31.0% of the employed labour force, excluding the self-employed, in 2005, compared with 10.8% in 1991) are cross-border workers, mainly Italians from the surrounding regions.

San Marino's economy is linked to that of its neighbour, Italy, with which it shares a monetary and customs union. Owing to its size, it is extremely vulnerable to economic developments in Italy and the wider EU. Although traditionally manufacturing was the principal sector of the economy, its contribution to GDP has been in decline and the financial sector, which benefited from alternative taxation and regulation structures, is becoming increasingly significant. Tourism and commerce were also increasing in importance. Growth in the financial sector was stimulated by advantageous banking confidentiality, which aroused some concern from the Organisation for Economic Co-operation and Development (OECD) that this would encourage money-laundering. However, commitment was expressed in 2000 to adherence to OECD guidelines on 'harmful tax competition'. In November 2004 the EU reached an agreement with San Marino on the adoption by the latter of measures equivalent to those contained in the EU's savings tax directive, which aimed to prevent EU citizens from avoiding taxes on savings by keeping their money in foreign bank accounts. Under the agreement, which took effect in July 2005, the Sammarinese authorities were to levy a withholding tax on interest payments made to residents of the EU, part of which was to be transferred to investors' states of residence. As an alternative, tax-payers could opt to permit the disclosure of the income to their member states of residence for tax purposes. Supervisory structures in the financial sector were being strengthened in the mid-2000s, following the transfer of supervisory responsibility from the Government to the central bank, which was also implementing reforms to modernize the sector. San Marino adopted new legislation in 2008 in relation to combating money-laundering and the financing of terrorism, in accordance with EU directives. GDP growth, which slowed in the early 2000s following a rapid rate of growth in the 1990s, improved later in the decade, owing to higher growth rates in Italy and the euro area and the continued success of the financial sector. Successive budget surpluses were achieved from 2003–07, reversing years of budget deficits, as a result of spending restraint, notably on public sector wages and health care. Pension reforms were introduced in 2006 to address the fiscal problems associated with an ageing population. Labour market reforms and tax cuts exerted a positive effect on competitiveness and encouraged higher levels of growth, with real GDP growth of 3.5% in 2007. Despite the global economic downturn, San Marino's real GDP increased by an estimated 2% in 2008 and the budget remained in surplus. However, in early 2009 the economy was adversely affected by the international economic crisis, with unemployment increasing to 5% in February. The Government allocated significant funds in the 2009 budget to mitigate the effects of the downturn, including increased investment in infrastructure projects and renewable energy sources.

Education

Education is compulsory for 10 years between the ages of six and 16 years. Primary education begins at six years of age and lasts for five years. Secondary education begins at the age of 11 years and may last for up to eight years: a first cycle of three years, a second of two years and a third, non-compulsory, cycle of three years. A state-administered university was inaugurated in 1987. Government expenditure on education was €38.5m. in 2004, equivalent to 8.1% of public spending.

Public Holidays

2009: 1 January (New Year's Day), 6 January (Epiphany), 5 February (Liberation Day), 19 March (St Joseph's Day), 25 March (Anniversary of the Arengo), 1 April (Investiture of the new Captains-Regent), 13 April (Easter Monday), 1 May (Labour Day), 11 June (Corpus Christi), 28 July (Fall of Fascism), 15 August (Assumption), 3 September (San Marino Day and Republic Day), 1 October (Investiture of the new Captains-Regent), 1 November (All Saints' Day), 2 November (Commemoration of the Dead), 8 December (Immaculate Conception), 25 December (Christmas Day), 26 December (St Stephen's Day).

SAN MARINO

2010: 1 January (New Year's Day), 6 January (Epiphany), 5 February (Liberation Day), 19 March (St Joseph's Day), 25 March (Anniversary of the Arengo), 1 April (Investiture of the new Captains-Regent), 5 April (Easter Monday), 1 May (Labour Day), 3 June (Corpus Christi), 28 July (Fall of Fascism), 15 August (Assumption), 3 September (San Marino Day and Republic Day), 1 October (Investiture of the new Captains-Regent), 1 November (All Saints' Day), 2 November (Commemoration of the Dead), 8 December (Immaculate Conception), 25 December (Christmas Day), 26 December (St Stephen's Day).

Weights and Measures
The metric system is in force.

Statistical Survey

Source (unless otherwise stated): Ufficio Programmazione Economica e Centro Elaborazione Dati e Statistica, Viale Antonio Onofri 109, 47890 San Marino; tel. 0549 885150; fax 0549 885154; e-mail statistica.upeceds@pa.sm; internet www.upeceds.sm.

AREA AND POPULATION

Area: 61.2 sq km (23.6 sq miles).

Population: 30,792 (males 15,122, females 15,670) at 31 December 2007 (*of which* Sammarinese 26,555, Others 4,237); 31,328 (males 15,381, females 15,947) at 28 February 2009.

Density (at 28 February 2009): 511.9 per sq km.

Principal Towns (population at 28 February 2009): Serravalle 10,180; Borgo Maggiore 6,286; San Marino (capital) 4,367.

Births, Marriages and Deaths (registrations, 2006 unless otherwise indicated): Live births 284 in 2005 (birth rate 10.0 per 1,000, 2003–07); Marriages 216 (marriage rate 7.1 per 1,000, 2003–07); Deaths 225 (death rate 7.2 per 1,000, 2003–07).

Life Expectancy (years at birth, official estimates): Males 79.6, females 85.3 in 2007.

Economically Active Population (2008): Agriculture 31; Manufacturing 6,281; Construction 1,478; Trade and hospitality 3,113; Communication and transport 538; Finance 993; Real estate, information technology and business services 2,413; Health 138; Education 39; Public sector 4,130; Other services 946; Activities not adequately defined 7; *Total employed* 20,108 (males 11,555, females 8,553); Unemployed 501 (males 148, females 353); *Total labour force* 20,609 (males 11,703, females 8,906). Note: Figures exclude self-employed (2,050).

HEALTH AND WELFARE
Key Indicators

Total Fertility Rate (children per woman, 2006): 1.3.

Under-5 Mortality Rate (per 1,000 live births, 2006): 3.

Physicians (per 1,000 head, 1990): 47.35.

Hospital Beds (per 1,000 head, 1990): 7.2.

Health Expenditure (2006): US $ per head (PPP): 3,297.

Health Expenditure (2006): % of GDP: 7.1.

Health Expenditure (2006): public (% of total): 83.9.

For sources and definitions, see explanatory note on p. vi.

FINANCE

Currency and Exchange Rates: Italian currency: 100 cent = 1 euro (€). *Sterling and Dollar Equivalents* (31 December 2008): £1 sterling = 1.04750 euros; US $1 = 0.7185 euros; €10 = £9.55 = $13.92. *Average Exchange Rates* (euros per US $): 0.7971 in 2006; 0.7306 in 2007; 0.6827 in 2008. Note: The local currency was formerly the Italian lira (plural = lire). From the introduction of the euro, with Italian participation, on 1 January 1999, a fixed exchange rate of €1 = 1,936.27 lire was in operation. Euro notes and coins were introduced on 1 January 2002. The euro and local currency circulated alongside each other until 28 February, after which the euro became the sole legal tender.

General Budget (€ million, 2005, provisional): *Revenue:* Tax revenue 243.2 (Taxation on individuals 101.8; Taxes on goods and services 118.9); Social contributions 107.6; Grants 4.6; Other revenue 149.3; Total revenue 504.8. *Expenditure:* Compensation of employees 153.3; Use of goods and services 98.3; Consumption of fixed capital 14.5; Interest 2.8; Subsidies 16.9; Social benefits 132.2; Other expense 15.1; Total expenditure 433.1. Source: IMF, *Government Finance Statistics Yearbook*.

International Reserves (US $ million at 31 December 2007): IMF special drawing rights 1.54; Reserve position in IMF 6.48; Foreign exchange 639.79; *Total* 647.81. Source: IMF, *International Financial Statistics*.

Money Supply (€ '000 at 31 December 2007): Demand deposits at banks 1,015,105. Source: IMF, *International Financial Statistics*.

Cost of Living (Consumer Price Index for the families of workers and employees; base: December 2002 = 100): All items 105.1 in 2005; 107.3 in 2006.

Gross Domestic Product (€ million at constant 1995 prices): 882.0 in 2005; 916.0 in 2006; 948.0 in 2007.

Expenditure on the Gross Domestic Product (€ million at current prices, 2007): Final consumption expenditure 571; Increase in stocks 57; Gross fixed capital formation 575; *Total domestic expenditure* 1,203; Exports of goods and services 2,491; *Less* Imports of goods and services 2,461; *GDP in purchasers' values* 1,233.

Gross Domestic Product by Economic Activity (€ million at current prices, 2004): Agriculture 1.2; Manufacturing 438.5; Construction 78.8; Services 542.9 (Trade 107.8, Transport and communications 15.5, Finance and insurance 174.8, Public sector 145.2, Other services 99.6); Total 1,061.4.

Balance of Payments (US $ million, 1996, estimates): Merchandise exports f.o.b. 1,741,9; Merchandise imports c.i.f. −1,719.3; *Trade balance* 22.6; Exports of services 120.4; Imports of services −102.2; *Balance on goods and services* 40.9; Interest payments 63.5; Net labour income −57.9; Other capital income −45.5; *Balance on goods, services and income* 1.0; Net transfers 9.7; *Current balance* 10.7; Capital account (net) 218.5; Errors and omissions −219.8; *Overall balance* 9.4. Source: IMF, *San Marino: Recent Economic Developments* (April 1999).

EXTERNAL TRADE

Data concerning imports and exports are included in those of Italy, with which San Marino maintains a customs union.

TRANSPORT

Road Traffic (registered motor vehicles, 2005): Motorcycles 10,268; Passenger cars 31,747; Buses and coaches 3,421; Agricultural vehicles 1,015; Total (incl. others) 47,876.

TOURISM

Visitor Arrivals (incl. excursionists): 2,135,589 in 2006; 2,163,858 in 2007; 2,111,736 in 2008.

Tourist Arrivals (staying at least one night): 45,508 in 2002; 40,686 in 2003; 41,546 in 2004.

COMMUNICATIONS MEDIA

Radio Receivers (1998): 35,100 in use.

Television Receivers (1999): 23,000 in use.

Telephones (2006): 21,000 main lines in use.

Facsimile Machines (1998): 5,800 in use.

Mobile Cellular Telephones (subscribers, 2006): 17,400.

Internet Users (2005): 15,200.

Broadband Subscribers (2006): 1,500.

Daily Newspapers (1998): 3 titles; 2,000 copies circulated.

Non-Daily Newspapers (1998): 8 titles; 12,000 copies circulated.

Periodicals (1998): 17 titles; 10,000 copies circulated.

Sources: Direzione Generale Poste e Telecomunicazioni; International Telecommunication Union.

EDUCATION

Pre-primary (2008/09): 14 schools; 142 teachers; 1,048 pupils.

Primary (2008/09): 14 schools; 252 teachers; 1,568 pupils.

SAN MARINO

Secondary (Scuola Media) (2008/09): 3 schools; 167 teachers; 895 pupils.

Secondary and Vocational (Scuola Secondaria Superiore e Formazione Professionale): 4 schools (2004/05); 86 teachers (2008/09); 635 pupils (2008/09—a further 756 pupils were studying outside San Marino).

University (2008/09): 1 university, 42 students (a further 832 students were attending courses outside San Marino).

Directory

The Constitution

San Marino, founded in 301 AD, is reputed to be the world's oldest surviving republic. In 1243 the first two Capitani Reggenti (Captains-Regent) were elected to serve as Heads of State by the Consiglio Grande e Generale (Great and General Council). The *Leges Statutae Sancti Marini* date back to 1600 and outline the main administrative posts and legal basis of the state. Electoral legislation dates from 1926.

San Marino is divided into nine Castelli ('Castles') corresponding to the original parishes of the Republic. Each Castello is governed by a Capitano di Castello (Castle-Captain), who holds office for two years, and a Giunta di Castello (Castle Board), which holds office for five years. Legislative power is vested in the unicameral Consiglio Grande e Generale, with 60 members elected by universal adult suffrage, under a system of proportional representation, for five years (subject to dissolution). The Consiglio elects two of its members to act jointly as Capitani Reggenti, with the functions of Head of State and Government, for six months at a time (ending in March and September). Executive power is held by the Congresso di Stato (Congress of State), with 10 members elected by the Consiglio for the duration of its term. The Congresso is presided over by the Capitani Reggenti.

The Government

HEADS OF STATE

Capitani Reggenti (Captains-Regent): MASSIMO CENCI (NPS), OSCAR MINA (PDCS) (1 April 2009–1 October 2009).

CONGRESSO DI STATO
(Congress of State)
(April 2009)

A coalition of the Partito Democratico Cristiano Sammarinese (PDCS), the Alleanza Popolare (AP), the Lista della Libertà (LdL), Arengo e Libertà, the Europopolari per San Marino (EPS) and the Unione Sammarinese dei Moderati (USM).

Secretary of State for Foreign and Political Affairs, Telecommunications and Transport: ANTONELLA MULARONI (AP).

Secretary of State for Internal Affairs and Civil Protection: VALERIA CIAVATTA (AP).

Secretary of State for Finance, the Budget and Relations with the Azienda Autonoma di Stato Filatelica e Numismatica (AASFN): GABRIELE GATTI (PDCS).

Secretary of State for Education, Culture and the University: ROMEO MORRI (USM).

Secretary of State for Health, Social Security, Welfare, Family and Social Affairs and Equal Opportunities: CLAUDIO PODESCHI (PDCS).

Secretary of State for Territory, Environment, Agriculture and Relations with the Azienda Autonoma di Stato di Produzione (AASP): GIANCARLO VENTURINI (PDCS).

Secretary of State for Labour, Co-operation and the Postal Service: GIANMARCO MARCUCCI (EPS).

Secretary of State for Industry, Handicrafts and Trade: MARCO ARZILLI (LdL).

Secretary of State for Justice, Information, Research and Relations with the Castle Boards: AUGUSTO CASALI (LdL).

Secretary of State for Tourism, Sport, Economic Planning and Relations with the Azienda Autonoma di Stato per i Servizi Pubblici (AASS): FABIO BERARDI (Arengo e Libertà).

MINISTRIES

Secretariat of State for Education, Culture and the University: Contrada Omerelli, 47890 San Marino; tel. 0549 882548; fax 0549 882301; e-mail segreteria.ic@gov.sm; internet www.educazione.sm.

Secretariat of State for Finance, the Budget and Relations with the Azienda Autonoma di Stato Filatelica e Numismatica (AASFN): Palazzo Begni, Contrada Omerelli, 47890 San Marino; tel. 0549 882661; fax 0549 882244; e-mail lbeccari@finanze.sm; internet www.finanze.sm.

Secretariat of State for Foreign and Political Affairs: Palazzo Begni, Contrada Omerelli, 47890 San Marino; tel. 0549 882312; fax 0549 882814; e-mail info.affariesteri@gov.sm; internet www.esteri.sm.

Secretariat of State for Health, Social Security and Equal Opportunities: Via V. Scialoia, 47895 Cailungo; tel. 0549 883040; fax 0549 883041; e-mail dic.sanita@omniway.sm; internet www.sanita.segreteria.sm.

Secretariat of State for Industry, Handicrafts and Trade: Palazzo Mercuri, Contrada del Collegio, 47890 San Marino; tel. 0549 882528; fax 0549 882529.

Secretariat of State for Internal Affairs: Parva Domus, Piazza della Libertà, 47890 San Marino; tel. 0549 882425; fax 0549 885080; e-mail segreteria.interni@gov.sm; internet www.interni.segreteria.sm.

Secretariat of State for Justice, Information, Research and Relations with the Castle Boards: Via A. di Superchio 16, 47893 Borgo Maggiore; tel. 0549 883777; fax 0549 883766; e-mail info.giustizia@gov.sm; internet www.giustizia.sm.

Secretariat of State for Labour and Co-operation: Palazzo Mercuri, Contrada del Collegio 38, 47890 San Marino; tel. 0549 882532; fax 0549 882535; e-mail segr.lavoro@omniway.sm.

Secretariat of State for Territory, Environment, Agriculture and Relations with the Azienda Autonoma di Stato di Produzione (AASP): Contrada Omerelli, 47890 San Marino; tel. 0549 882470; fax 0549 882473; e-mail segr.territorio@omniway.sm.

Secretariat of State for Tourism, Sport, Telecommunications, Transport and Economic Co-operation: Palazzo del Turismo, Contrada Omagnano, 47890 San Marino; tel. 0549 883158; fax 0549 885399; e-mail segreteria.turismo@gov.sm; internet www.visitsanmarino.com.

Legislature

Consiglio Grande e Generale
(Great and General Council)

Palazzo Pubblico, Piazza della Libertà, 47890 San Marino; tel. 0549 882259; fax 0549 882389; e-mail info.segristituzionale@pa.sm; internet www.consigliograndeegenerale.sm.

Election, 9 November 2008

Party	Votes	% of votes	Seats
Patto per San Marino	11,371	54.22	35
Partito Democratico Cristiano Sammarinese (PDCS)/ Europopolari per San Marino (EPS)/Arengo e Libertà	6,692	31.91	22
Alleanza Popolare (AP)	2,415	11.52	7
Lista della Libertà (LdL)	1,317	6.28	4
Unione Sammarinesi dei Moderati (USM)	874	4.17	2
Riforme e Libertà	9,601	45.78	25
Partito dei Socialisti e dei Democratici (PSD)/Sammarinesi per la Libertà	6,702	31.91	18
Sinistra Unita (SU)	1,797	8.57	5
Democratici di Centro (DdC)	1,037	4.94	2
Total	**20,972**	**100.00**	**60**

Political Organizations

Alleanza Nazionale Sammarinese (ANS) (San Marino National Alliance): Via Ventotto Luglio 187, 47893 Borgo Maggiore; tel. 0549

907815; fax 0549 875203; e-mail anrsm@omniway.sm; internet www.alleanzanazionalersm.sm; right-wing; formed a coalition, the Unione Sammarinese dei Moderati, with the Popolari Sammarinesi in early 2008 in order to contest the Nov. 2008 general election; Pres. ENNIO VITTORIO PELLANDRA; Political Sec. GLAUCO SANSOVINI.

Alleanza Popolare (AP) (Popular Alliance): Via Luigi Cibrario 25, 47893 Cailungo; tel. 0549 907080; fax 0549 907082; e-mail ap@alleanzapopolare.net; internet www.alleanzapopolare.net; f. 1993 as Alleanza Popolare Democratici Sammarinesi; advocates a constitution and institutional reform; Pres. CARLO FRANCIOSI; Co-ordinator MARIO VENTURINI.

Arengo e Libertà (Arengo and Freedom): Via del Serrone e Via Trasmundo da Fano, 47890 Murata; tel. 0549 878087; e-mail info@arengoeliberta.sm; internet www.arengoeliberta.sm; f. 2008 by fmr mems of the Partito dei Socialisti e dei Democratici; social democratic.

Democratici di Centro (DdC) (Democrats of the Centre): Via Cà Franceschino 3, 47893 Borgo Maggiore; tel. 0549 909884; fax 0549 972855; e-mail gruppo.dc@omniway.sm; internet www.democraticidicentro.sm; f. 2007 by fmr mems of the Partito Democratico Cristiano Sammarinese; Pres. ORAZIO MAZZA; Co-ordinator GIOVANNI LONFERNINI.

Europopolari per San Marino (EPS) (European People for San Marino): Via dei Pini 1, 47895 Domagnano; tel. 0549 906622; fax 0549 902431; e-mail europopolari@omniway.sm; internet www.europopolari.sm; f. 2007 by fmr mems of the Partito Democratico Cristiano Sammarinese; Pres. GIAN MARCO MARCUCCI; Political Sec. LORENZO LONFERNINI.

Lista della Libertà (LdL) (Freedom List): e-mail info@listadellaliberta.com; internet listadellaliberta.com; f. Aug. 2008 to contest the Nov. 2008 general election; comprising Noi Sammarinesi and Nuovo Partito Socialista.

Noi Sammarinesi (We Sammarinese): Via XXVIII Luglio 160, 47893 Borgo Maggiore; tel. and fax 0549 902591; e-mail info@noisammarinesi.com; internet www.noisammarinesi.com; f. 2006; contested Nov. 2008 general election as part of Lista della Libertà; Spokesman MARCO ARZILLI.

Nuovo Partito Socialista (NPS) (New Socialist Party): Via XXV Marzo 36, 47895 Domagnano; tel. 0549 980093; fax 0549 902212; e-mail nuovopartitosocialista@omniway.sm; internet www.nuovopartitosocialista.sm; f. 2005 by fmr mems of the Partito Socialista Sammarinese; contested Nov. 2008 general election as part of Lista della Libertà; Pres. ANTONIO VOLPINARI; Political Sec. AUGUSTO CASALI.

Partito Democratico Cristiano Sammarinese (PDCS) (San Marino Christian Democrat Party): Via delle Scalette 6, 47890 San Marino; tel. 0549 991193; fax 0549 992694; e-mail pdcs@omniway.sm; internet www.pdcs.sm; f. 1948; in 2007 four representatives to the Consiglio Grande e Generale left the party to form the Democratici di Centro; Political Sec. PASQUALE VALENTINI; 2,400 mems.

Partito dei Socialisti e dei Democratici (PSD) (Party of Socialists and Democrats): Via Ordelaffi 46, 47893 Borgo Maggiore; tel. 0549 903806; fax 0549 906438; e-mail info@democratici.sm; internet www.socialistiedemocratici.sm; f. 2005 by merger of the Partito dei Democratici and the Partito Socialista Sammarinese; Pres. PATRIZIA BUSIGNANI; Sec.-Gen. PARIDE ANDREOLI.

Patto per San Marino (Pact for San Marino): f. mid-2008 to contest the Nov. 2008 general election; centre-right coalition, comprising the Partito Democratico Cristiano Sammarinese, Europopolari per San Marino, Arengo e Libertà, Alleanza Popolare, Noi Sammarinesi, Nuovo Partito Socialista, and Unione Sammarinese dei Moderati (comprising Alleanza Nazionale Sammarinese and the Popolari Sammarinesi).

Popolari Sammarinesi (PS) (Sammarinese People): Via XXV Marzo 19B, 47895 Domagnano; tel. 0549 907776; fax 0549 944431; e-mail infosegreteria@popolarisammarinesi.sm; internet www.popolarisammarinesi.sm; formed a coalition, the Unione Sammarinese dei Moderati, with the Alleanza Nazionale Sammarinese in early 2008 in order to contest the Nov. 2008 general election; Pres. ANTONIO PUTTI; Political Sec. ANGELA VENTURINI.

Riforme e Libertà (Reform and Freedom): coalition formed to contest the Nov. 2008 general election; comprising Democratici di Centro, Partito dei Socialisti e dei Democratici, Sammarinesi per la Libertà and Sinistra Unita.

Sammarinesi per la Libertà (Sammarinese for Liberty): Via Ranco Mauro 16, 47891 Dogana; tel. 0549 908400; fax 0549 905970; e-mail info@sammarinesiperlaliberta.sm; internet www.sammarinesiperlaliberta.sm; f. 2002; Pres. GIUSEPPE ROSSI.

Sinistra Unita (SU) (United Left): Via delle Tamerici 1A, 47893 Domagnano; tel. 0549 907656; fax 0549 944397; e-mail sinistraunita@omniway.sm; internet www.sxun.org; f. 2006; left-wing coalition, comprising Rifondazione Comunista Sammarinese and Zona Franca, formed to contest 2006 general election.

Rifondazione Comunista Sammarinese (RCS) (San Marino Communist Refoundation): Via Ca' dei Lunghi 70A, 47893 Borgo Maggiore; tel. and fax 0549 906682; e-mail rcs@omniway.sm; internet www.rifondazionecomunista-rsm.org; f. 1992; communist; Political Sec. ANGELO DELLA VALLE.

Unione Sammarinese dei Moderati (USM) (Sammarinese Union of Moderates): coalition formed in early 2008 by the Alleanza Nazionale Sammarinese and Popolari Sammarinesi in order to obtain the requisite 3.5% threshold to contest the Nov. 2008 general election.

Diplomatic Representation

By June 2008 San Marino had established full diplomatic relations with 97 countries, five of which maintained a consular office in San Marino.

EMBASSIES IN SAN MARINO

Holy See: Domus Plebis 1, 47890 San Marino; tel. 0549 992448; Apostolic Nuncio Most Rev. GIUSEPPE BERTELLO (Titular Archbishop of Urbs Salvia) (resident in Rome, Italy).

Italy: Viale Antonio Onofri 117, 47890 San Marino; tel. 0549 991146; fax 0549 992229; e-mail ambasciata.sanmarino@esteri.it; internet www.ambsanmarino.esteri.it; Ambassador FABRIZIO SANTURRO.

Judicial System

The administration of justice is entrusted to foreign judges, with the exception of the Justice of the Peace, who must be of San Marino nationality, and who judges minor civil suits. The major judicial institutions are as follows:

Tribunale Commissariale Civile e Penale (Civil and Criminal Commissionary Tribunal): Via Luglio 28, 47893 Borgo Maggiore; tel. 0549 882626; fax 0549 8825980; e-mail tribunale@omniway.sm.

Commissario della Legge (Law Commissioner): deals with civil and criminal cases where the maximum sentence does not exceed three years' imprisonment.

Giudice Penale di Primo Grado (Criminal Judge of the Primary Court of Claims): deals with criminal cases that are above the competence of the Law Commissioner.

Giudice Amministrativo di Appello (Court of Appeal): two judges, who deal with civil and criminal proceedings.

Consiglio dei XII (Council of Twelve): has authority as a Supreme Court of Appeal, for civil proceedings only.

Religion

CHRISTIANITY

The Roman Catholic Church

Roman Catholicism is the official state religion of San Marino. The Republic forms part of the diocese of San Marino-Montefeltro (comprising mainly Italian territory), suffragan to the archdiocese of Ravenna-Cervia.

Bishop of San Marino-Montefeltro: Rt Rev. LUIGI NEGRI, Curia Vescovile, Piazza Giovanni Paolo II 1, 61016 Pennabilli, Pesaro, Italy; tel. (0541) 913721; fax (0541) 928832; e-mail vescovo.negri@diocesi-sanmarino-montefeltro.it; internet www.diocesi-sanmarino-montefeltro.it.

The Press

Argomenti: c/o CSdL, Via V Febbraio 17, Fiorina C-3, 47895 Domagnano; tel. 0549 962060; fax 0549 962075; organ of the Confederazione Sammarinese del Lavoro (CSdL); periodical; Dir ANDREA LEARDINI; circ. 5,000.

Corriere di Informazione Sammarinese: Via Piana, 47890 San Marino; tel. 0549 995147; fax 0549 879021; e-mail corriere@rimini.com; daily.

Fixing: Via G. Giacomini 37, 47890 San Marino; tel. 0549 991117; e-mail fixing@omniway.sm; periodical.

Il San Marino: Via delle Scalette 6, 47890 San Marino; tel. 0549 991193; fax 0549 992694; e-mail pdcs@omniway.sm; internet www.pdcs.sm; periodical; organ of the PDCS; quarterly; Dir JEROME CELLAROSI.

San Marino Oggi: Via dei Boschetti 53, 47893 Borgo Maggiore; tel. 0549 906607; fax 0549 906556; e-mail redazione@sanmarinooggi.sm; f. 1997; daily; circ. 750; Dir. RENATO CORNACCHIA.

La Tribuna Sammarinese: Via Gino Giacomini 86A, 47890 San Marino; tel. 0549 990420; fax 0549 990398; e-mail redazione@latribunasammarinese.net; internet www.latribunasammarinese.net; daily; Dir DAVIDE GRAZIOSI.

Publishers

AIEP Editore: Via III Settembre 72, 47891 Dogana; tel. 0549 941457; fax 0549 973164; e-mail info@aiepeditore.net; internet www.aiepeditore.net; f. 1980; general book publishing; Man. GIUSEPPE MARIA MORGANTI.

Guardigli Editore: Via Istriani 94, 47890 San Marino; tel. 0549 995144; fax 0549 990454; e-mail guardiglieditore@omniway.sm; f. 1991; book publishing; Man. Dir PIER PAOLO GUARDIGLI.

Broadcasting and Communications

TELECOMMUNICATIONS

Direzione Generale Poste e Telecomunicazioni: Contrada Omerelli 17, 47890 San Marino; tel. 0549 882555; fax 0549 992760; e-mail federico.valentini.telecomunicazioni@pa.sm; state body responsible for telecommunications; Dir-Gen. Dott. ROSA ZAFFERANI.

Telecom Italia San Marino, SpA: Strada degli Angariari 3, 47891 Falciano; tel. 0549 886111; fax 0549 886188; e-mail secretary@telecomitalia.sm; internet www.telecomitalia.sm; f. 1992; provides international telecommunications services; Pres. and Man. Dir ANDREA CENDALI PIGNATELLI.

Telefonia Mobile Sammarinese, SpA (TMS): Via XXVIII Luglio 148, 47893 Borgo Maggiore; tel. 0549 980222; fax 0549 980044; e-mail info@tms.sm; internet www.tms.sm; f. 1999; mobile services.

BROADCASTING

In 1987 a co-operation agreement with Italy, preventing San Marino from operating its own broadcasting services, was abrogated, and a joint venture between San Marino and the Italian state-owned radio and television corporation, Radiotelevisione Italiana (Rai), was established in order to operate an independent broadcasting station for 15 years. Rai (see the chapter on Italy) broadcasts a daily information bulletin about the Republic under the title 'Notizie di San Marino'. San Marino RTV began broadcasting in mid-1993.

Radio

San Marino RTV (Radiotelevisione della Repubblica de San Marino): Viale Kennedy 13, 47890 San Marino; tel. 0549 882000; fax 0549 882855; e-mail redazione@sanmarinortv.sm; internet www.sanmarinortv.sm; f. 1991; Pres. STEFANO VALENTINO PIVA; Dir-Gen. Dott. CARMEN LASORELLA.

Radio San Marino: San Marino; tel. 0549 995013; e-mail redazione@radiosanmarino.sm; internet www.radiosanmarino.sm.

Radio Titano: Via delle Carrare 35, Frazione Murata, 47890 San Marino; tel. 0549 997251; Dir P. FAETANINI.

Television

San Marino RTV (Radiotelevisione della Repubblica de San Marino): (see Radio).

Finance

(cap. = capital; res = reserves; dep. = deposits; m. = million; brs = branches; amounts in euros)

In September 2005 there were 12 banks and 42 other financial institutions operating in San Marino.

BANKING

Central Bank

Banca Centrale della Repubblica di San Marino: Via del Voltone 120, 47890 San Marino; tel. 0549 882325; fax 0549 882328; e-mail info@bcsm.sm; internet www.bcsm.sm; f. 2003; formed by a merger between the Istituto di Credito Sammarinese and the Ispettorato per il Credito e le Valute; manages both state and public-sector deposits; cap. 12.9m., res 10.4m., dep. 321.4m. (Dec. 2006); Chair. BIAGIO BOSSONE; Dir-Gen. LUCA PAPI.

Commercial Banks

Banca Agricola Commerciale della Repubblica di San Marino SpA: Piazza Marino Tini 26, 47891 Dogana; tel. 0549 871111; fax 0549 871222; internet www.bac.sm; f. 1920; cap. 16.8m., res 84.3m., dep. 1,543.3m (Dec. 2007); Pres. LUIGI LONFERNINI; Dir PIER PAOLO FABBRI; 8 brs.

Banca di San Marino, SpA: Strada della Croce 39, 47896 Faetano; tel. 0549 873411; fax 0549 873401; e-mail info@bsm.sm; internet www.bsm.sm; f. 1920 as Cassa Rurale Depositi e Prestiti di Faetano, Scrl; changed name as above in 2001; cap. 114.6m., res 31.0m., dep. 1,300.5m. (Dec. 2006); Chair. FAUSTO MULARONI; Gen. Man. Prof. VINCENZO TAGLIAFERRO; 9 brs.

Cassa di Risparmio della Repubblica di San Marino: Piazzetta del Titano 2, 47890 San Marino; tel. 0549 872311; fax 0549 872700; e-mail info@carisp.sm; internet www.carisp.sm; f. 1882; cap. 350m., res 59.5m., dep. 2,611.7m. (Dec. 2005); Pres. Dott. GILBERTO GHIOTTI; CEO MARIO FANTINI; 16 brs.

Credito Industriale Sammarinese: Piazza Bertoldi 8, 47899 Serravalle; tel. 0549 8740; fax 0549 874116; e-mail info@cis.sm; internet www.cis.sm; f. 1933; owned by Banca Carim (Italy); cap. 35.0m., res 44.2m., dep. 584.1m. (Dec. 2008); Chair. FRANCO CAPICCHIONI; CEO ARNALDO ANTONINI; 4 brs.

Euro Commercial Bank SpA: Strada dei Censiti 21, 47891 Rovereta; tel. 0549 943711; fax 0549 943737; e-mail info@ecb.sm; internet www.ecb.sm; f. 2000; cap. and res 26.9m., total assets 242.1m. (2006); Dir-Gen. GIUSEPPE GUIDI; 2 brs.

Istituto Bancario Sammarinese SpA: Via III Settembre 99, 47891 Dogana; tel. 0549 872011; fax 0549 872050; e-mail direzione@ibs.sm; internet www.ibs.sm; f. 2000 as Merchant Bank di San Marino SpA; changed name in 2001 following expansion into commercial banking; Pres. and Man. Dir Dott. GIOVANNI MERCADINI; 7 brs.

INSURANCE

Several major Italian insurance companies have agencies in San Marino.

Trade and Industry

GOVERNMENT AGENCIES

Azienda Autonoma di Stato Filatelica e Numismatica (AASFN): Piazza Garibaldi 5, 47890 San Marino; tel. 0549 882365; fax 0549 885179; e-mail aasfn@omniway.sm; internet www.aasfn.sm; autonomous public enterprise; responsible for production and distribution of postage stamps and coins; Pres. PIGNATTA ORAZIO; Dir-Gen. Dott. OTTAVIANO ROSSI.

Azienda Autonoma di Stato di Produzione (AASP): Via Ventotto Luglio 50, 47031 Borgo Maggiore; tel. 0549 883600; fax 0549 883600; e-mail aasp@omniway.sm; civil engineering works, road works, land reclamation; Pres. PAOLO RONDELLI; Dir FABIO BERARDI.

Azienda Autonoma di Stato per la gestione della Centrale del Latte: Strada Genghe di Atto 71, 47031 Acquaviva; tel. 0549 999207; fax 0549 999606; operates state monopoly in production and distribution of dairy products; Pres. TIZIANO CANINI; Dir PAOLO MUSCI.

CHAMBER OF COMMERCE

Camera di Commercio, Industria, Artigianato e Agricoltura di San Marino (CCIAA): Piazza Mercatale 29, 47893 Borgo Maggiore; tel. 0549 980380; fax 0549 944554; e-mail info@cc.sm; internet www.cc.sm; f. 2004; Dir Dott. MASSIMO GHIOTTI.

INDUSTRIAL AND TRADE ASSOCIATIONS

Associazione Nazionale dell'Industria Sammarinese (ANIS) (National Association for Industry): Via Gino Giacomini 39, 47890 San Marino; tel. 0549 873911; fax 0549 992832; e-mail anis@omniway.sm; internet www.anis.sm; Pres. PIER GIOVANNI TERENZI; Sec.-Gen. CARLO GIORGI.

Associazione Sammarinese Coltivatori Diretti, Affittuari e Mezzadri (ASCDAM): San Marino; tel. 0549 998222; farmers' association.

Associazione Sammarinese Produttori Agricoli (ASPA): Serrabolino 42, 47893 Borgo Maggiore; tel. 0549 902617; agricultural producers' association.

Consorzio San Marino 2000 srl: Via Piana 103, 47890 San Marino; tel. 0549 995031; fax 0549 990573; e-mail info@sanmarino2000.sm; internet www.sanmarino2000.sm; f. 1998; fmrly Unione Sammarinese Operatori Turistici (USOT); hotels and restaurants association.

Organizzazione Sammarinese degli Imprenditori (OSLA): Via N. Bonaparte 75, 47890 San Marino; tel. 0549 992885; fax 0549 992620; e-mail osla@omniway.sm; internet www.osla.sm;

f. 1985; organization for the self-employed; Pres. MARIA TERESA VENTURINI.

Unione Nazionale Artigiani di San Marino (UNAS): Piazzale M. Giangi 2, San Marino; tel. 0549 992148; e-mail info@unas.sm; artisans' association; Pres. GIANFRANCO TERENZI.

Unione Sammarinese Commercianti (USC): Via Piana 111, 47890 San Marino; tel. 0549 992892; shopkeepers' association; Pres. MARCO ARZILLI.

UTILITIES

All utilities are imported from Italy.

Azienda Autonoma di Stato per i Servizi Pubblici (AASS): Via Andrea di Superchio 16, 47031 Cailungo; tel. 0549 883782; fax 0549 883720; e-mail info@aass.sm; internet www.aass.sm; f. 1981; autonomous state service company; distributes electricity, gas and water within San Marino; Pres. Dott. MARCO PODESCHI; Dir-Gen. EMANUELE VALLI.

TRADE UNIONS

Centrale Sindacale Unitaria (CSU): Via V Febbraio 17, 47895 Domagnano; tel. 0549 962011; fax 0549 962055; e-mail csu@omniway.sm; internet www.csu.sm; f. 1976; Pres. LUCIANO NICOLINI.

Confederazione Democratica dei Lavoratori Sammarinesi (CDLS): Via V Febbraio 17, 47895 Domagnano; tel. 0549 962080; fax 0549 962095; e-mail info@cdls.sm; internet www.cdls.sm; f. 1957; affiliated to ITUC and ETUC; Sec.-Gen. MARCO BECCARI; 4,960 mems.

Confederazione Sammarinese del Lavoro (CSdL): Via V Febbraio 17, 47895 Domagnano; tel. 0549 962060; fax 0549 962075; e-mail info@csdl.sm; internet www.csdl.sm; f. 1943; Sec.-Gen. GIOVANNI GHIOTTI; 5 mem. feds; 4,500 individual mems.

Transport

The capital, San Marino, is connected with Borgo Maggiore, about 1.5 km away, by funicular. There is also a bus service, and a highway down to the Italian coast at Rimini, about 24 km away. San Marino has an estimated 220 km of roads. The nearest airport to the Republic is at Rimini. There are no frontier or customs formalities.

Azienda Autonoma di Stato per i Servizi Pubblici (AASS): (see Utilities); numerous responsibilities include public transport and funicular railway.

Tourism

The mild climate attracts many visitors to San Marino each year, as do the contrasting scenery and well-preserved medieval architecture. In 2008 San Marino received approximately 2.1m. visitors (including excursionists). Tourism receipts totalled an estimated €27,620m. in 2003.

Ufficio di Stato per il Turismo (State Tourist Board): Contrada Omagnano 20, 47890 San Marino; tel. 0549 882914; fax 0549 882575; e-mail info@visitsanmarino.com; internet www.visitsanmarino.com; Dir ANTONIO MACINA.

SÃO TOMÉ AND PRÍNCIPE

Introductory Survey

Location, Climate, Language, Religion, Flag, Capital

The Democratic Republic of São Tomé and Príncipe lies in the Gulf of Guinea, off the west coast of Africa. There are two main islands, São Tomé and Príncipe, and the country also includes the rocky islets of Caroço, Pedras and Tinhosas, off Príncipe, and Rôlas, off São Tomé. The climate is warm and humid, with average temperatures ranging between 22°C (72°F) and 30°C (86°F). The rainy season extends from October to May, and average annual rainfall varies from 500 mm (20 ins) in the southern highlands to 1,000 mm (39 ins) in the northern lowlands. Portuguese is the official language and native dialects are widely spoken. Almost all of the inhabitants profess Christianity, and the overwhelming majority (some 83%) are adherents of the Roman Catholic Church. The national flag (proportions 1 by 2) has three horizontal stripes, of green, yellow (one-half of the depth) and green, with a red triangle at the hoist and two five-pointed black stars on the yellow stripe. The capital is the town of São Tomé, on São Tomé island.

Recent History

A former Portuguese colony, São Tomé and Príncipe became an overseas province of Portugal in 1951 and received local autonomy in 1973. A nationalist group, the Comissão de Libertação de São Tomé e Príncipe, was formed in 1960 and became the Movimento de Libertação de São Tomé e Príncipe (MLSTP) in 1972, under the leadership of Dr Manuel Pinto da Costa. Based in Libreville, Gabon, the MLSTP was recognized by the Organization of African Unity (now the African Union—AU, see p. 172) in 1973.

Following the military coup in Portugal in April 1974, the Portuguese Government recognized the right of the islands to independence. Negotiations began in November, at which Portugal recognized the MLSTP as the sole representative of the people. On 12 July 1975 independence was achieved, with da Costa as the country's first President and Miguel dos Anjos da Cunha Lisboa Trovoada as Prime Minister. In December a legislative Assembleia Popular Nacional (National People's Assembly) was elected.

In March 1978 the Prime Minister stated that an attempted coup by foreign mercenaries, orchestrated from Gabon by Carlos Alberto Monteiro Dias da Graça, an exiled former Minister of Health, had been suppressed. Angolan troops were called in to support the Government, and in March 1979 the alleged conspirators were sentenced to terms of imprisonment. President da Costa took over the post of Prime Minister, and Trovoada was arrested in September and charged with complicity in the coup attempt. He was released and allowed to go into exile in 1981.

Worsening economic conditions, following a severe drought in 1982, prompted the Government to review the country's close ties with communist regimes and its consequent isolation from major Western aid sources. In late 1984 da Costa declared São Tomé and Príncipe to be politically non-aligned.

In October 1987 the Central Committee of the MLSTP announced major constitutional reforms, including the election by universal adult suffrage of the President of the Republic and of members of the Assembleia Popular Nacional. The amended Constitution also allowed 'independent' candidates to contest legislative elections, although the President of the MLSTP, chosen by the MLSTP Congress from two candidates proposed by the Central Committee, would continue to be the sole candidate for the presidency of the Republic. In January 1988 the premiership was restored, and Celestino Rochas da Costa, hitherto Minister of Education, Labour and Social Security, was appointed as Prime Minister.

In March 1990 a joint meeting of the Assembleia Popular Nacional and the MLSTP Central Committee approved a new draft Constitution, which provided for the establishment of a multi-party system, limited the President's tenure of office to two five-year terms, and permitted independent candidates to participate in legislative elections. In May 1990 Trovoada returned from exile to contest the forthcoming presidential election. On 22 August, in a national referendum, 72% of the electorate endorsed the new Constitution. In the following month new legislation on the formation of political parties came into effect. Delegates to the MLSTP Congress in October voted to replace da Costa as party President, appointing da Graça to the new post of Secretary-General. The party's name was amended to the Movimento de Libertação de São Tomé e Príncipe—Partido Social Democrata (MLSTP—PSD).

In January 1991 elections to the new Assembleia Nacional resulted in defeat for the MLSTP—PSD, which secured only 21 seats in the 55-member legislature, while the Partido de Convergência Democrática—Grupo de Reflexão (PCD—GR) won 33 seats. The Partido Democrático de São Tomé e Príncipe—Coligação Democrático da Oposição (PDSTP—CODO) took the remaining seat. In February a transitional Government, headed by the Secretary-General of the PCD—GR, Daniel Lima dos Santos Daio, was installed. In the same month President da Costa announced that he would not be contesting the presidential election, to be held in March. The MLSTP—PSD did not present an alternative candidate. In late February two of the three remaining presidential candidates withdrew from the election. Miguel Trovoada, who stood as an independent candidate (with the support of the PCD—GR), was thus the sole contender, and on 3 March he was elected President with the support of 81% of those who voted. He took office on 3 April. The transitional Government resigned in mid-April and was reappointed shortly afterwards.

In April 1992, following demonstrations demanding the resignation of the Daio Government due to the unpopular imposition of stringent austerity measures, Trovoada dismissed the Daio administration. The PCD—GR was invited to designate a new Prime Minister, and in May Norberto Costa Alegre (hitherto Minister of Economy and Finance) was chosen as Prime Minister. A new Government was named shortly afterwards.

In April 1994 the Assembleia Nacional adopted legislation, drafted by the MLSTP—PSD, reinforcing the rights of the parliamentary opposition. All opposition parties represented in the legislature were to be consulted on major political issues, including defence, foreign policy and the budget. In the same month deputies began discussion of a draft bill providing for a degree of autonomy for the island of Príncipe, to include the creation of a regional council. The proposed legislation was prompted by concern among inhabitants of Príncipe that the island had been neglected by the central administration.

Meanwhile, relations between the Government and the presidency deteriorated, and in April 1994 Trovoada publicly dissociated himself from government policy. Political tension increased in June, when the PCD—GR accused Trovoada of systematic obstruction of the government programme. In that month opposition parties petitioned the President to dismiss the Government, conduct early legislative elections and appoint foreign auditors to investigate the management of public finances under the PCD—GR administration. In July Trovoada dismissed the Alegre Government and appointed Évaristo do Espírito Santo de Carvalho (the Minister of Defence and Security in the outgoing administration) as Prime Minister. The PCD—GR, refusing to participate in an administration formed on presidential initiative, subsequently expelled Carvalho from the party. An interim Government, comprising principally technocrats and senior civil servants, was appointed. Shortly afterwards Trovoada dissolved the Assembleia Nacional, thus preventing the PCD—GR from using its parliamentary majority to declare the new Government unconstitutional.

Legislative elections were held on 2 October 1994, at which the MLSTP—PSD secured 27 seats, one short of an absolute majority. The PCD—GR and Acção Democrática Independente (ADI) each obtained 14 seats; da Graça was subsequently appointed Prime Minister. Despite initial efforts to involve opposition parties in a government of national unity, his Council of Ministers was dominated by members of the MLSTP—PSD.

In March 1995 the first elections to a new seven-member regional assembly and five-member regional government were conducted on Príncipe, which had been granted local autonomy by the Assembleia Nacional in 1994. The elections resulted in an absolute majority for the MLSTP—PSD; the ADI and the PCD—

GR did not present candidates, supporting instead a local opposition group. The new regional Government began functioning in April 1995.

In mid-August 1995 a group of some 30 soldiers, led by five junior officers, seized control of the presidential palace in a bloodless coup. Trovoada was detained at the headquarters of the armed forces and da Graça was placed under house arrest. The legislature was disbanded, the Constitution suspended and a curfew imposed. Following talks mediated by an Angolan delegation, the insurgents and the Government signed a 'memorandum of understanding', providing for the reinstatement of Trovoada and the restoration of constitutional order. In return, the Government gave an undertaking to restructure the armed forces, and the Assembleia Nacional granted a general amnesty to all those involved in the coup.

In late December 1995 Armindo Vaz d'Almeida was appointed Prime Minister, by presidential decree, to head a Government of National Unity. The new administration included six members of the MLSTP—PSD, four members of the ADI and one of the PDSTP—CODO. The three parties had signed a political pact, with the aim of ensuring political stability. In February 1996, at the request of the Comissão Eleitoral Nacional (National Electoral Commission), the forthcoming presidential election, which had been set for March, was postponed, pending the satisfactory completion of the electoral rolls. The date of the election was subsequently rescheduled for 30 June. In March Pinto da Costa was selected as the presidential candidate of the MLSTP—PSD, while Francisco Fortunato Pires was appointed Secretary-General of the party, replacing the more moderate da Graça. In April Trovoada declared his candidacy for the presidential election, supported by the ADI and the PDSTP—CODO.

At the presidential election of 30 June 1996 no candidate secured an absolute majority. The two leading candidates thus proceeded to a second round of voting on 21 July, at which Trovoada won 52.7% of the votes, defeating Pinto da Costa. In late July da Costa, who had initially acknowledged Trovoada's victory, claimed that irregularities had occurred in the registration process; however, on 20 August Trovoada was confirmed as President. Although he did not command majority support in the Assembleia Nacional, Trovoada dismissed the possibility of new legislative elections, announcing instead his intention to seek a broadly based government of national consensus. In September the Vaz d'Almeida administration was dissolved, following its defeat in a confidence motion in the Assembleia Nacional. The motion had been proposed by Vaz d'Almeida's own party, the MLSTP—PSD, which accused the Government of inefficiency and corruption, and had received the support of the PCD—GR. Vaz d'Almeida remained as Prime Minister in an interim capacity until November, when Raul Wagner da Conceição Bragança Neto, Assistant Secretary-General of the MLSTP—PSD, was appointed Prime Minister. A new coalition Government, including five members of the MLSTP—PSD, three members of the PCD—GR and one independent, was inaugurated later that month.

At an extraordinary congress of the MLSTP—PSD in May 1998, Pinto da Costa was elected unopposed as President of the party. (The ruling party of Angola, the Movimento Popular de Libertação de Angola (MPLA), had made the resumption of financial support for the MLSTP—PSD conditional on da Costa's election; following his defeat in the 1996 presidential election, the MPLA had ceased payments, creating serious problems for the MLSTP—PSD.) New party statutes were approved, creating the position of party President, together with three vice-presidential posts.

At legislative elections held on 8 November 1998 the MLSTP—PSD secured a majority, with 31 seats, while the ADI won 16 seats and the PCD—GR obtained the remaining eight seats. In December Guilherme Pósser da Costa (a Vice-President of the MLSTP—PSD and former Minister of Foreign Affairs and Co-operation) was appointed Prime Minister. However, the MLSTP—PSD accused Trovoada of interfering in areas outside his jurisdiction when, later that month, he vetoed Pósser da Costa's initial nominations for the Council of Ministers. A revised Council of Ministers was finally installed on 5 January 1999.

A presidential election took place on 29 July 2001. Among the five candidates to succeed Trovoada were former President Manuel Pinto da Costa, the leader of the MLSTP—PSD, and Fradique de Menezes, a businessman standing for the ADI. In the event, de Menezes was elected to the presidency, winning 56.3% of the votes cast, while da Costa secured 38.7%. De Menezes was inaugurated as President on 3 September. Following the dissolution by de Menezes of Pósser da Costa's administration (owing to disagreements over the distribution of ministerial positions), a new Government of 'presidential initiative', which did not include any members of the MLSTP—PSD, was appointed in late September. The new Council of Ministers, led by Evaristo de Carvalho as Prime Minister, was composed of members of the ADI, the PCD (which had voted to remove the suffix Grupo de Reflexão from its official name at a recent congress) and one independent. In early December de Menezes dissolved the Assembleia Nacional and announced that legislative elections would be held in March 2002, after which a new, more broadly based Government would be formed, according to an agreement reportedly signed by the President and representatives of political parties. In January 2002 the PCD formed an electoral alliance with the Movimento Democrático Força da Mudança (MDFM), which had been created in December by supporters of de Menezes.

At legislative elections, held on 3 March 2002, no party obtained an absolute majority in the Assembleia Nacional. Provisional results indicated that the MLSTP—PSD and the MDFM-PCD alliance had each secured 23 of the 55 seats, while the remaining nine seats had been won by Uê Kédadji (UK), an alliance of the ADI and four minor parties. However, following a re-run of voting in one district, the MLSTP—PSD secured an extra seat, to the cost of the UK alliance, and was proclaimed victorious. Gabriel da Costa, the former ambassador to Portugal, was subsequently appointed as the nominally independent Prime Minister, and in April a new coalition Government of National Unity, which included representatives of the MLSTP—PSD, the MDFM-PCD and UK, as well as a number of independents, was installed.

In late September 2002 da Costa's Government was dismissed by de Menezes, who appointed Maria das Neves de Souza, of the MLSTP—PSD, hitherto Minister of Trade, Industry and Tourism, as Prime Minister in early October. A new Government of National Unity, with six representatives from the MLSTP—PSD, five from the MDFM-PCD alliance, two from the UK alliance and one independent, was formed. In December the first MDFM congress elected Tomé Vera Cruz as Secretary-General of the party.

Meanwhile, in November 2002 the Assembleia Nacional approved a resolution for constitutional reform, altering the structure of the semi-presidential system to reduce presidential power. However, the draft revisions caused a political crisis over President de Menezes' delays in their promulgation and his repeated threats to veto them, according to powers vested in him by the Constitution of 1990. An apparent consensus was reached in December 2002, but the situation deteriorated further in early 2003, and in mid-January the President vetoed the new draft Constitution on the grounds that it should be endorsed by public referendum before coming into force. De Menezes dissolved the Assembleia Nacional by presidential decree later that month and called early elections for 13 April. However, Prime Minister das Neves vowed to continue working and transferred the Government of National Unity to the island of Príncipe. Following negotiations between the Government and the President, de Menezes reversed his decree, reinstating the Government, and a 'memorandum of understanding' was signed by de Menezes and the Assembleia Nacional, which provided for the immediate promulgation of the new Constitution.

The new Constitution, which took effect in March 2003, provided for the establishment of an advisory Council of State and a Constitutional Tribunal, with jurisdiction over issues of constitutionality. The President's right to veto constitutional amendments was removed. The changes were regarded as significantly reducing the executive power of the President, although maintaining a semi-presidential system pending the referendum.

On 16 July 2003, while de Menezes was in Nigeria, Maj. Fernando Pereira 'Cobo', together with Sabino dos Santos and Alércio Costa, the leaders of a small political party, the Frente Democrata Cristã (FDC), took power in a bloodless coup d'état. They formed a Junta Militar de Salvação Nacional and detained government ministers. The coup was condemned by the international community, which demanded a return to civilian rule. Following successful regional mediation efforts, co-ordinated by Rodolphe Adada, the Republic of the Congo's Minister of Foreign Affairs, Co-operation and Francophone Affairs, on 22 July de Menezes returned to São Tomé. On the same day de Menezes, Pereira and Adada signed a 'memorandum of understanding', which provided for the restoration of de Menezes to the presidency, an amnesty for the coup leaders, a more transparent system of government finance, and the formation of a new government. In accordance with the conditions of the memorandum, Prime Minister das Neves resigned. She was subsequently reappointed by de Menezes to head a new Government of National Unity, comprising representatives of the MLSTP—PSD, the MDFM and the ADI. Vera Cruz was appointed to the increasingly significant post of Minister of Natural Resources and the Environment, and Lt-Col Óscar Sousa, an independent reportedly with close ties to de Menezes, became Minister of Defence and Internal Affairs.

In March 2004 tension increased between das Neves and de Menezes. Das Neves had repeatedly requested the dismissal of Vera Cruz and of Mateus Rita, the Minister of Foreign Affairs and Co-operation, claiming that she had not been appropriately consulted by either minister on government decisions. The subsequent resignations of Rita and Vera Cruz—both members of the MDFM—prompted the remaining two MDFM ministers, responsible for health and justice, to resign in protest. Agreements that Vera Cruz had signed with Canadian and South African mining companies were subsequently annulled. Later that month members of the ADI were appointed to head the ministries of health and of natural resources and the environment, while Elsa Pinto of the MLSTP—PSD became Minister of Justice, State Reform and Public Administration, and an independent, Ovídio Manuel Barbossa Pequeno, was appointed Minister of Foreign Affairs and Co-operation. In April 2004 Leonel Mário d'Alva was elected President of the PCD, while later that month Vera Cruz was re-elected as Secretary-General of the MDFM, which was renamed the MDFM—Partido Liberal, although it subsequently reverted to its original name.

In early September 2004 a report issued by the Auditor-General, Adelino Pereira, accused the das Neves Government of the embezzlement of funds provided by foreign donors and also revealed a series of financial irregularities during 2001–04, including illicit transfers of funds to the Ministry of Finance. Following requests by the MDFM and UK (the latter resigned from the Government in mid-September) for the removal of the das Neves Government, President de Menezes held a series of meetings with the main political parties in an attempt to establish a consensus. Das Neves and her Council of Ministers were dismissed in September, and Damião Vaz de Almeida, hitherto Minister of Labour, Employment and Security and Vice-President of the MLSTP—PSD, was asked to form a new administration. The new 14-member Government was a coalition of the MLSTP—PSD, the ADI and independents and comprised six members of the previous administration.

In late September 2004 Diógenes Moniz, the former Director of the Gabinete de Gestão das Ajudas (GGA—a department attached to the Ministry of Trade, Industry and Tourism responsible for the administration of food aid counterpart funds) was arrested on charges of embezzlement. In October das Neves was among a number of former ministers questioned by the Public Prosecutor about their involvement with the GGA.

In January 2005 an attempt by de Menezes to sue das Neves for libel was rejected by the Assembleia Nacional, on the grounds that das Neves enjoyed parliamentary immunity. (In September 2004, following her dismissal from the premiership, she had accused de Menezes and other members of the Government of corruption.) However, in February 2005 the Assembleia voted to remove parliamentary immunity from the former Prime Minister, Guilherme Pósser da Costa, in order that he be questioned regarding an alleged assault on Pereira in November 2004. (Pósser da Costa received a suspended sentence in March 2005.) A further four members of the Assembleia, including das Neves, also had their immunity lifted, thus providing for the possibility of them being tried in connection with the GGA case. In May das Neves and Arzemiro dos Prazeres, a former Minister of Trade, Industry and Tourism, were charged with embezzlement. Meanwhile, in late February Pósser da Costa was elected President of the MLSTP—PSD.

In April 2005 trade unions representing public sector workers demanded a significant increase in the minimum salaries of their members. The Government, however, citing budgetary constraints, was unable to accede to the unions' demands and in late May the unions commenced a five-day general strike. Following declarations by de Menezes that the Government was responsible for the action, Prime Minister Vaz de Almeida abruptly resigned, accusing the President of a lack of institutional solidarity with the Government. On 9 June a new MLSTP—PSD Council of Ministers, led by Maria do Carmo Silveira, hitherto the Governor of the central bank, took office, and in late July the Assembleia Nacional approved the new Government's budget and a preliminary agreement on a pay rise for public sector workers was reached. Relations between de Menezes and the Government remained strained, however.

Voting in the legislative elections began as scheduled on 26 March 2006; however, owing to boycotts and protests against continuing poor living conditions, voting at 26 polling stations was rescheduled for 2 April when it proceeded without incident. According to results released by the Constitutional Court on 18 April, the renewed MDFM-PCD alliance won 23 seats in the Assembleia Nacional, the MLSTP—PSD took 20 and the ADI 11, while a newly formed party, the Novo Rumo, secured the remaining seat. The Secretary-General of the MDFM, Tomé Vera Cruz, was subsequently appointed Prime Minister (also assuming the media and regional integration portfolios) while Maria dos Santos Tebús Torres of the PCD became Deputy Prime Minister, with responsibility for finance and planning. The new 12-member Government took office on 21 April.

In April 2006 President de Menezes announced that a presidential election would be held on 30 July. De Menezes was re-elected to the presidency on that date after securing 60.58% of the votes cast. His nearest rival, Patrice Emery Trovoada, of the ADI, received 38.83%. International observers deemed the election, at which voter turn-out was 64.9%, to have been transparent and fair. In late August, at the first local elections to be held on the islands since 1992, the MDFM-PCD alliance won six of the seven constituencies on São Tomé and secured an absolute majority in five of the six local assemblies. Supported by the ruling MDFM-PCD, the União para a Mudança e Progresso do Príncipe won all seven seats in the Assembleia Regional on Príncipe.

At an extraordinary party congress in February 2007, the MLSTP—PSD elected Joaquim Rafael Branco as party President; he defeated António Quintas by 675 votes to 221. Prime Minister Vera Cruz was re-elected Secretary-General of the MDFM at a convention in May; at the same time President de Menezes was elected Chairman of that party, despite a provision in the Constitution preventing the Head of State from accepting other public roles. De Menezes stated that he would not assume the role publicly while he remained President. In November a ministerial reorganization was effected in which Ovídio Barbosa Pequeno assumed responsibility for the foreign affairs, co-operation and communities portfolio, while Arlindo Carvalho was named as the new Minister of Planning and Finance. Valdimira Tavares was appointed Minister of the Economy.

Vera Cruz announced his resignation as Prime Minister on 7 February 2008 after the Assembleia Nacional failed to approve his Government's budget for 2008. He was replaced by Patrice Emery Trovoada, who was sworn in on 14 February. Trovoada's ADI had agreed to form a coalition government with the MDFM-PCD on the condition that his party was awarded, inter alia, the premiership and the natural resources and environment portfolio. Trovoada named a Council of Ministers, which included Rául Cravid as Minister of Planning and Finance, while both Pequeno and Carvalho retained the portfolios assigned to them in November 2007.

Although a revised national budget for 2008 was eventually approved by the Assembleia Nacional, in May 2008 the MLSTP—PSD presented a motion of no confidence against Trovoada's administration. Members of the PCD, which accused Trovoada of lacking transparency in government affairs, supported the motion which was adopted and the Government was dissolved. The MDFM denounced the coalition agreement with the PCD; therefore the MLSTP—PSD again became the largest party in the legislature. Following several weeks of tense negotiations, in late June Branco was sworn in as Prime Minister at the head of a new Council of Ministers (comprising members of the MLSTP—PSD, the PCD and the MDFM), in which Carlos Tiny assumed responsibility for the foreign affairs, co-operation and communities portfolio, Elsa Pinta became the country's first female Minister of National Defence, and Cravid was appointed Minister of the Interior, Territorial Administration and Civil Protection. Minister of Natural Resources, Energy and the Environment Agostinho Rita was dismissed in October and was replaced by Carlos Fernandes Marques. A series of electricity outages were reported during late 2008, believed to be the result of a power generating deficit, and Marques resigned in November, although he cited health concerns as his reason for stepping down. Marques was succeeded by Cristina Dias, hitherto a senior official at the Agência Nacional do Petróleo de São Tomé e Príncipe.

São Tomé and Príncipe maintains cordial relations with the other former Portuguese African colonies and with Portugal. In July 1996 São Tomé and Príncipe was among the five lusophone African countries that, together with Portugal and Brazil, formed the Comunidade dos Países de Língua Portuguesa (CPLP, see p. 438), a Portuguese-speaking commonwealth seeking to achieve collective benefits from co-operation in technical, cultural and social matters. In February 2004 Angola and São Tomé and Príncipe signed an agreement on the creation of a permanent joint commission on parliamentary co-operation.

São Tomé and Príncipe has important trade links with the nearby mainland states of Gabon, Cameroon and Equatorial Guinea. In November 1999 São Tomé and Príncipe was a founder of the seven-member Gulf of Guinea Commission to assist in solving inter-state conflicts within the region.

In 2000 São Tomé and Príncipe and Nigeria agreed to establish a joint development zone (JDZ) for the exploitation of petroleum resources. A further accord, on the joint exploitation of a variety of mineral resources, was signed in February 2001; Nigeria was to receive 60% of revenues and São Tomé and Príncipe 40%. In January 2002 the Presidents of both countries inaugurated a development authority to oversee the affairs of the JDZ. Disagreements developed during 2002, however, over Nigeria's commitment to provide São Tomé and Príncipe with 60,000 barrels of petroleum per day (reduced to 40,000 in September, and to 10,000 in October) and the relative lack of Santomean representation in the development authority. In November de Menezes refused to continue with the proposed sale of oil blocs until the issue was resolved; he was supported in this by a report from the World Bank, which suggested that the division of profits was unfair to São Tomé and Príncipe. By 2003, however, issues had been resolved sufficiently for bids for exploration rights in the first nine of the 25 blocs in the JDZ to open in October.

Government

Under the 2003 Constitution, legislative power is vested in the Assembleia Nacional, which comprises 55 members, elected by universal adult suffrage for a term of four years. No limit is placed on the number of political parties permitted to operate. Executive power is vested in the President of the Republic, who is Head of State, and who governs with the assistance of an appointed Council of Ministers, led by the Prime Minister. The Council of State acts as an advisory body to the President, who is elected by universal suffrage for a term of five years. The President's tenure of office is limited to two successive terms. The Prime Minister, who is appointed by the President, is, in theory, nominated by the deputies of the Assembleia Nacional.

In 1994 the Assembleia Nacional granted political and administrative autonomy to the island of Príncipe. Legislation was adopted establishing a seven-member Assembleia Regional and a five-member regional government; both are accountable to the Government of São Tomé and Príncipe.

Defence

In early 2005 the armed forces were estimated to number some 300. Military service, which is compulsory, lasts for 30 months. There is also a presidential guard numbering some 160. In the budget for 2000 expenditure on defence amounted to 1,100m. dobras.

Economic Affairs

In 2007, according to estimates by the World Bank, São Tomé and Príncipe's gross national product (GNI), measured at average 2005–07 prices, was US $138m., equivalent to $870 per head (or $1,630 per head on an international purchasing-power parity basis). During 2000–07, it was estimated, the population increased at an average annual rate of 1.7%, while gross domestic product (GDP) per head, in real terms, increased at an average annual rate of 0.8% in 1995–2005. Overall GDP increased, in real terms, at an average annual rate of 3.5% in 1998–2005; growth of 6.0% was recorded in 2007.

Agriculture (including fishing) contributed an estimated 17.9% of GDP in 2006, and accounted for an estimated 61.6% of the labour force in mid-2005, according to FAO. The principal cash crop is cocoa, which accounted for 89.7% of export earnings in 2007. Secondary cash crops include coconuts and coffee. Staple crops for local consumption include bananas, taro and cassava. Agricultural production is principally concentrated on export commodities, although smallholder agriculture has become increasingly important. An agricultural policy charter, the Carta de Política e Desenvolvimento Rural, which was introduced in 2000, aimed to emphasize private sector involvement and diversification into areas such as ylang ylang, pepper, vanilla, fruits, vegetables and flowers. Fishing is also a significant activity. The sale of fishing licences to foreign fleets is an important source of income. According to the World Bank, agricultural GDP increased at an average annual rate of 3.6% in 1995–2005; growth in 2005 was 3.8%.

Industry (including mining, manufacturing, construction and power) contributed an estimated 19.9% of GDP in 2006, and employed 17.0% of the employed population in 2001. According to the World Bank, industrial GDP increased by an average of 2.8% per year in 1995–2003; growth in 2003 was 4.6%.

In 2006 mining contributed an estimated 0.4% of GDP. There are no mineral resources on the islands, but offshore prospecting for hydrocarbons resulted in the discovery of significant quantities of petroleum in 1998, including an estimated 4,000m. barrels in the joint development zone (JDZ) with Nigeria (see Recent History), as well as higher-risk resources in São Tomé's exclusive economic zone (EEZ). More than 20 companies lodged bids for exploration rights in the first nine of the 25 blocks in the JDZ in October 2003. In February 2005 a consortium led by ChevronTexaco was awarded a concession to exploit the first section of the JDZ. That company signed a production sharing agreement with the Joint Development Authority responsible for overseeing activities in the JDZ in 2005 and began drilling activities in January 2006. Inquiries into the subsequent award of a further five blocks to the Environmental Remedial Holding Corp (ERHC), resulted in the Attorney-General concluding that the procedures used in selecting petroleum companies was flawed. He recommended a restructuring of the procedures for future bidding rounds that would conform to international standards. The Attorney-General's report also demanded the re-examination of ERHC's preferential rights for Blocks 2–6 within the JDZ.

The manufacturing sector consists solely of small processing factories, producing soap, soft drinks, textiles and beer. Manufacturing contributed an estimated 9.5% of GDP in 2007, according to the World Bank, and manufacturing GDP increased at an average annual rate of 2.4% in 1995–2003. Growth in 2003 was 4.5%.

In 2000 some 74% of electricity generation was derived from thermal sources and 26% from hydroelectric sources. Imports of petroleum products comprised 20.5% of the value of merchandise imports in 2007. In late 2004 the national utility company was privatized. In early 2006 it was announced that a thermal power plant, which would increase São Tomé's energy production by 70%, was to be built by a Nigerian company.

The services sector contributed an estimated 62.2% of GDP in 2006, and engaged 51.5% of the employed population in 2001. According to the World Bank, the GDP of the services sector increased by an average of 2.3% per year in 1995–2003; growth in 2003 was 4.4%.

In 2007 São Tomé and Príncipe recorded a trade deficit of US $58.1m. and a deficit of $66.9m. on the current account of the balance of payments. In 2007 the principal source of imports (66.1%) was Portugal; the other major supplier was Angola. The principal market for exports in that year were Portugal (46.2%), Belgium, France, the Netherlands, and Gabon. The principal export in 2007 was cocoa. The principal imports in that year were petroleum and petroleum products, foodstuffs, beverages, construction materials and transport equipment.

In 2007 there was a budgetary surplus of 244,800m. dobras. São Tomé's total external debt was US $355.3m. at the end of 2006, of which $336.4m. was long-term public debt. In 2003 the cost of debt-servicing was equivalent to 31.4% of the total value of exports of goods and services. Annual inflation averaged 18.9% in 2003–07. Consumer prices increased by an average of 24.6% in 2006 and by 27.6% in 2007. According to official figures, 14.2% of the labour force were unemployed in 2006.

São Tomé and Príncipe is a member of the International Cocoa Organization (see p. 422) and of the Communauté économique des états de l'Afrique centrale (see p. 425).

São Tomé and Príncipe's economy has traditionally been dominated by cocoa production and is therefore vulnerable to adverse weather conditions and to fluctuations in international prices for that commodity. While the discovery of petroleum in Santomean waters, and the anticipated increase in government revenues the sale of that commodity would provide, was a welcome development, concerns were raised by international institutions regarding the lack of transparency and accountability in the petroleum sector. Thus, in mid-2004 the Government agreed to establish a National Petroleum Fund into which all petroleum earnings were to be deposited, and which was to be subject to annual independent audits; it was also announced that 65% of the total revenue from petroleum was to be allocated to the upgrading of infrastructure and to improvements in the health care and education sectors. Despite ongoing investigations into the misappropriation of donor funds, São Tomé and Príncipe continued to be a major recipient of external assistance. Following a series of missions since the suspension of the Poverty Reduction and Growth Facility (PRGF) arrangement in 2000, the IMF announced a new three-year PRGF, worth US $4.3m., which the country successfully completed in June 2008. In early 2009 the Fund approved a further three-year $3.8m. arrangement under the PRGF to support the authorities' economic programme. The Fund's work in the country in 2008 had focused, *inter alia*, on proposing measures to improve São Tomé and Príncipe's poor domestic revenue performance which saw tax contributing only 17.5% of GDP compared to an average of 21% in other sub-Saharan African countries. The authorities aimed to combat these problems with new legislation to simplify and modernize the tax system and encourage tax compliance. GDP growth in 2007 and 2008 averaged 6.0%, sustained by oil exploration in the JDZ and continued buoyant construction activity, and was forecast to decline slightly, to 5.5%, in 2009. The country struggled with high levels of inflation in 2008, which reached 37.0% in June of that year, owing to higher international import prices for fuel and food, before falling to 24.5% in December, and reducing this figure to single digits represented a key challenge for the country in 2009.

Education

Primary education is officially compulsory between six and 14 years of age. Secondary education lasts for a further seven years, comprising a first cycle of four years and a second cycle of three years. According to UNESCO estimates, in 2007/08 enrolment at primary schools included 97.1% of children in the relevant age-group (males 97.8%; females 96.5%), while the comparable ratio for secondary enrolment in 2004/05 was 32.6% (males 30.9%; females 34.3%). The country's first university, Universidade Lusíada, was inaugurated in October 2006. In 2000 public investment in education (including culture and sport) amounted to US $1.3m., equivalent to 6.7% of total public investment. The budget for 2005 allocated 13.4% of total government expenditure to education.

Public Holidays

2009: 1 January (New Year), 4 January (King Amador Day), 3 February (Martyrs' Day), 1 May (Labour Day), 12 July (Independence Day), 6 September (Armed Forces Day), 30 September (Agricultural Reform Day), 21 December (São Tomé Day), 25 December (Christmas Day).
2010: 1 January (New Year), 4 January (King Amador Day), 3 February (Martyrs' Day), 1 May (Labour Day), 12 July (Independence Day), 6 September (Armed Forces Day), 30 September (Agricultural Reform Day), 21 December (São Tomé Day), 25 December (Christmas Day).

Weights and Measures

The metric system is in force.

Statistical Survey

Source (unless otherwise stated): Instituto Nacional de Estatística, CP 256, São Tomé; tel. 221982.

AREA AND POPULATION

Area: 1,001 sq km (386.5 sq miles); São Tomé 859 sq km (331.7 sq miles), Príncipe 142 sq km (54.8 sq miles).

Population: 117,504 at census of 4 August 1991; 137,599 (males 68,236, females 69,363) at census of September 2001; 157,847 (males 77,641, females 80,206) at mid-2008 (official estimate).

Density (mid-2008): 157.7 per sq km.

Population by District (2006): Água-Grande 56,492, Mé-Zochi 38,668, Cantagolo 14,681, Caué 6,324, Lembá 11,759, Lobata 17,251, Pagué (Príncipe) 6,737; Total 151,912.

Principal Towns (population at census of 1991): São Tomé (capital) 42,300; Trindade 11,400; Santana 6,200; Santo Amaro 5,900; Neves 5,900. Source: Stefan Helders, *World Gazetteer* (internet www.world-gazetteer.com). *Mid-2007* (incl. suburbs): São Tomé (capital) 58,000 (Source: UN, *World Urbanization Prospects: The 2007 Revision*).

Births, Marriages and Deaths (2006): Registered live births 5,072 (birth rate 33.40 per 1,000); Registered marriages 171 (marriage rate 1.2 per 1,000) (2003); Registered deaths 1,111 (death rate 7.3 per 1,000). *2007:* Birth rate 32.4 per 1,000; Death rate 7.5 per 1,000 (Source: African Development Bank).

Life Expectancy (years at birth, WHO estimates): 61.4 (males 59.7; females 63.1) in 2006. (Source: WHO, *World Health Statistics*).

Economically Active Population (census of 2001): Agriculture and fishing 13,518; Industry, electricity, gas and water 2,893; Public works and civil construction 4,403; Trade, restaurants and hotels 8,787; Transport, storage and communications 792; Public administration 3,307; Health 776; Education 1,373; Other activities 7,088; *Total employed* 42,937. *2006:* Total employed 53,725 (males 28,729, females 24,996); Unemployed 8,894 (males 4,276, females 4,618); Total labour force 62,619 (males 33,005, females 29,614).

HEALTH AND WELFARE
Key Indicators

Total Fertility Rate (children per woman, 2006): 4.0.

Under-5 Mortality Rate (per 1,000 live births, 2006): 96.

Physicians (per 1,000 head, 2004): 0.5.

Hospital Beds (per 1,000 head, 2003): 3.2.

Health Expenditure (2006): US $ per head (PPP): 120.

Health Expenditure (2006): % of GDP: 10.5.

Health Expenditure (2006): public (% of total): 85.4.

Access to Water (% of persons, 2006): 86.

Access to Sanitation (% of persons, 2006): 24.

Human Development Index (2006): ranking: 128.

Human Development Index (2006): value: 0.643.

For sources and definitions, see explanatory note on p. vi.

AGRICULTURE, ETC.

Principal Crops (metric tons, 2007, FAO estimates, unless otherwise indicated): Bananas 27,000; Maize 3,000; Cassava (Manioc) 5,800; Taro 27,000; Yams 1,500; Cocoa beans 3,500 (unofficial figure); Coconuts 28,000; Oil palm fruit 40,000; Coffee, green 20; Cinnamon 30.

Livestock (head, 2007, FAO estimates): Cattle 4,600; Sheep 2,800; Goats 5,000; Pigs 2,500; Chickens 350,000.

Livestock Products (metric tons, 2007, FAO estimates): Cattle meat 122; Pig meat 92; Sheep meat 6; Goat meat 19; Chicken meat 600; Hen eggs 385; Cows' milk 145.

Forestry ('000 cubic metres, 1988): Roundwood removals 9; Sawnwood production 5. *1989–2007:* Annual output assumed to be unchanged since 1988.

Fishing (metric tons, live weight, 2006): Total catch 4,000 (FAO estimate) (Croakers and drums 145–FAO estimate; Pandoras 175–FAO estimate; Threadfins and tasselfishes 120–FAO estimate; Wahoo 76; Little tunny 179; Atlantic sailfish 292; Flyingfishes 750–FAO estimate; Jacks and crevalles 155–FAO estimate; Sharks, rays and skates 132).

Source: FAO.

INDUSTRY

Production (metric tons, unless otherwise indicated): Bread and biscuits 3,768 (1995); Soap 261.1 (1995); Beer (litres) 529,400 (1995); Palm oil 2,000 (2007, FAO estimate); Electric energy (million kWh) 41.5 (2005). Sources: IMF, *Democratic Republic of São Tomé and Príncipe: Selected Issues and Statistical Appendix* (September 1998, February 2002, April 2004 and September 2006); FAO.

SÃO TOMÉ AND PRÍNCIPE

FINANCE

Currency and Exchange Rates: 100 cêntimos = 1 dobra (Db). *Sterling, Dollar and Euro Equivalents* (30 June 2008): £1 sterling = 29,135.4 dobras; US $1 = 14,628.4 dobras; €1 = 23,060.2 dobras; 100,000 dobras = £3.43 = $6.84 = €4.34. *Average Exchange Rate* (dobras per US $): 10,558.0 in 2005; 12,445.4 in 2006; 13,536.8 in 2007.

Budget ('000 million dobras, 2007, estimates): *Revenue:* Taxation 296; Non-tax revenue 55; Grants 2,450; Oil signature bonuses 413; Total 3,214. *Expenditure:* Current expenditure 431 (Personnel costs 177, Goods and services 74, Interest on external debt 30, Transfers 117, Other current expenditure 33); Capital expenditure 277; HIPC-related social expenditure 58; Total 766. Source: IMF, *Democratic Republic of São Tomé and Príncipe: 2008 Article IV Consultation and Sixth Review Under the Three-Year Arrangement Under the Poverty Reduction and Growth Facility, and Request for Waivers of Performance Criteria—Staff Report; Staff Supplement; Public Information Notice and Press Release on the Executive Board Discussion; and Statement by the Executive Director for the Democratic Republic of São Tomé and Príncipe* (September 2008).

International Reserves (US $ million at 31 December 2007): IMF special drawing rights 0.01; Foreign exchange 39.32; Total 39.33. Source: IMF, *International Financial Statistics*.

Money Supply ('000 million dobras at 31 December 2007): Currency outside banks 109.3; Demand deposits at commercial banks 177.8; Total money 287.1. Source: IMF, *International Financial Statistics*.

Cost of Living (Consumer Price Index; base: 1996 = 100): 590.5 in 2005; 735.5 in 2006; 938.2 in 2007. Source: Banco Central de São Tomé e Príncipe.

Expenditure on the Gross Domestic Product (US $ million at current prices, 2007): Government final consumption expenditure 36.86; Private final consumption expenditure 64.12; Gross capital formation 67.07; *Total domestic expenditure* 168.05; Exports of goods and services 24.87; *Less* Imports of goods and services 102.87; *GDP in purchasers' values* 90.04. Source: African Development Bank.

Gross Domestic Product by Economic Activity ('000 million dobras at current prices, 2006): Agriculture 159.1; Fishing 80.2; Mining 5.7; Manufacturing, electricity, gas and water 102.6; Construction 157.9; Trade and transport 573.7; Hotels and restaurants 25.1; Public administration 72.2; Financial institutions 93.2; Other services 66.5; *Sub-total* 1,336.4; Taxes, less subsidies, on products 92.1; *GDP at market prices* 1,428.5.

Balance of Payments (US $ million, 2007): Exports of goods f.o.b. 6.81; Imports of goods f.o.b. −64.87; *Trade balance* −58.06; Exports of services 4.20; Imports of services −18.67; *Balance on goods and services* −72.52; Other income received 6.76; Other income paid −2.29; *Balance of goods, services and income* −68.05; Current transfers received 6.47; Current transfers paid −5.27; *Current balance* −66.85; Capital account (net) 62.42; Direct investment abroad −3.10; Direct investment from abroad 35.31; Other investment assets 5.24; Other investment liabilities −181.11; Net errors and omissions 1.68; *Overall balance* −146.40. Source: IMF, *International Financial Statistics*.

EXTERNAL TRADE

Principal Commodities (US $ million, 2007): *Imports f.o.b.:* Foodstuffs 14.9; Beverages 7.1; Petroleum and petroleum products 16.2; Equipment 13.8; Transport equipment 6.1; Construction materials 6.8; Total (incl. others) 79.1. *Exports f.o.b.:* Cocoa 3.5; Coconuts 0.2; Total (incl. others) 3.9.

Principal Trading Partners (US $ million, 2007): *Imports c.i.f.:* Angola 15.9; Belgium 1.8; Gabon 1.7; Japan 0.2; Netherlands 1.1; Portugal 52.3; Total (incl. others) 79.1. *Exports f.o.b.:* Belgium 0.7; France 0.6; Gabon 0.07; Netherlands 0.5; Portugal 1.8; Total (incl. others) 3.9. Source: Banco Central de São Tomé e Príncipe.

TRANSPORT

Road Traffic (registered vehicles, 1996, estimates): Passenger cars 4,000; Lorries and vans 1,540. Source: International Road Federation, *World Road Statistics*.

Shipping: *International Freight Traffic* (estimates, metric tons, 1992): Goods loaded 16,000; Goods unloaded 45,000. *Merchant Fleet* (registered at 31 December 2007): Number of vessels 30; Total displacement 29,588 grt (Source: Lloyd's Register-Fairplay, *World Fleet Statistics*).

Civil Aviation (traffic on scheduled services, 2004): Kilometres flown (million) 0.5; Passengers carried ('000) 40.1; Passenger-km (million) 17.0; Total ton-km (million) 1.6. Source: UN, *Statistical Yearbook*.

TOURISM

Foreign Tourist Arrivals: 10,576 in 2004; 15,746 in 2005; 12,266 in 2006.

Arrivals by Country of Residence (2006): Angola 999; Brazil 248; Cape Verde 432; France 1,186; Gabon 351; Germany 467; Nigeria 468; Portugal 5,138; Spain 395; USA 277; Total (incl. others) 12,266.

Tourism Receipts (US $ million, excl. passenger transport): 10.6 in 2003; 12.8 in 2004; 13.6 in 2005.

Source: World Tourism Organization.

COMMUNICATIONS MEDIA

Radio Receivers (1998): 45,000 in use. Source: UNESCO, *Statistical Yearbook*.

Television Receivers (1999): 33,000 in use. Source: UNESCO, *Statistical Yearbook*.

Newspapers and Periodicals (2000 unless otherwise indicated): Titles 14 (1997); Average circulation 18,500 copies.

Telephones ('000 main lines, 2007): 7.7 in use. Source: International Telecommunication Union.

Mobile Cellular Telephones ('000 subscribers, 2007): 30.1. Source: International Telecommunication Union.

Facsimile Machines (2000): 372 in use.

Internet Users (2007): 25,000. Source: International Telecommunication Union.

Broadband Subscribers (2007): 3,000. Source: International Telecommunication Union.

EDUCATION

Pre-primary (2007/08, unless otherwise indicated): 6,382 pupils (males 3,134, females 3,248); 240 teachers (males 125, females 115) (2005/06).

Primary (2007/08, unless otherwise indicated): 32,616 pupils (males 16,645, females 15,971); 1,009 teachers (males 450, females 559)(2005/06).

Secondary (2007/08): 8,518 pupils (males 4,162, females 4,356); 375 teachers (males 328, females 47).

Tertiary (2000/01): 1 polytechnic; 29 teachers; 117 pupils.

Source: UNESCO Institute for Statistics; *Carta Escolar de São Tomé e Príncipe,* Ministério de Educação de Portugal.

Adult Literacy Rate (UNESCO estimates): 87.9% (males 93.4; females 82.9) in 2007. Source: UNESCO Institute for Statistics.

Directory

The Constitution

A new Constitution came into force on 4 March 2003, after the promulgation by the President of a draft approved by the Assembleia Nacional (National Assembly) in December 2002. A 'memorandum of understanding', which was signed in January 2003 by the President and the Assembleia Nacional, provided for the scheduling of a referendum on the system of governance in early 2006. However, the referendum did not take place. The following is a summary of the main provisions of the Constitution:

The Democratic Republic of São Tomé and Príncipe is a sovereign, independent, unitary and democratic state. Sovereignty resides in the people, who exercise it through universal, equal, direct and secret vote, according to the terms of the Constitution. There shall be complete separation between Church and State. There shall be freedom of thought, expression and information and a free and independent press, within the terms of the law.

Executive power is vested in the President of the Republic, who is elected for a period of five years by universal adult suffrage. The President's tenure of office is limited to two successive terms. He is

SÃO TOMÉ AND PRÍNCIPE

the Supreme Commander of the Armed Forces and is accountable to the Assembleia Nacional. In the event of the President's death, permanent incapacity or resignation, his functions shall be assumed by the President of the Assembleia Nacional until a new President is elected.

The Council of State acts as an advisory body to the President and comprises the President of the Assembleia Nacional, the Prime Minister, the President of the Constitutional Tribunal, the Attorney-General, the President of the Regional Government of Príncipe, former Presidents of the Republic who have not been dismissed from their positions, three citizens of merit nominated by the President and three elected by the Assembleia Nacional. Its meetings are closed and do not serve a legislative function.

Legislative power is vested in the Assembleia Nacional, which comprises 55 members elected by universal adult suffrage. The Assembleia Nacional is elected for four years and meets in ordinary session twice a year. It may meet in extraordinary session on the proposal of the President, the Council of Ministers or of two-thirds of its members. The Assembleia Nacional elects its own President. In the period between ordinary sessions of the Assembleia Nacional its functions are assumed by a permanent commission elected from among its members.

The Government is the executive and administrative organ of State. The Prime Minister is the Head of Government and is appointed by the President. Other ministers are appointed by the President on the proposal of the Prime Minister. The Government is responsible to the President and the Assembleia Nacional.

Judicial power is exercised by the Supreme Court and all other competent tribunals and courts. The Supreme Court is the supreme judicial authority and is accountable only to the Assembleia Nacional. Its members are appointed by the Assembleia Nacional. The right to a defence is guaranteed.

The Constitutional Tribunal, comprising five judges with a mandate of five years, is responsible for jurisdiction on matters of constitutionality. During periods prior to, or between, the installation of the Constitutional Tribunal, its function is assumed by the Supreme Court. The Constitution may be revised only by the Assembleia Nacional on the proposal of at least three-quarters of its members. Any amendment must be approved by a two-thirds' majority of the Assembleia Nacional. The President does not have right of veto over constitutional changes.

Note: In 1994 the Assembleia Nacional granted political and administrative autonomy to the island of Príncipe. Legislation was adopted establishing a seven-member Assembleia Regional and a five-member Regional Government; both are accountable to the Government of São Tomé and Príncipe.

The Government

HEAD OF STATE

President and Commander-in-Chief of the Armed Forces: FRADIQUE DE MENEZES (took office 3 September 2001; re-elected 30 July 2006).

COUNCIL OF MINISTERS
(April 2009)

The Government comprises members of the Movimento de Libertação de São Tomé e Príncipe—Partido Social Democrata (MLSTP—PSD), the Partido de Convergência Democrática (PCD) and the Movimento Democrática Força da Mundança (MDFM).

Prime Minister: JOAQUIM RAFAEL BRANCO (MLSTP—PSD).
Minister of Defence and Internal Order: ELSA PINTO (MLSTP—PSD).
Minister of Foreign Affairs, Co-operation and Communities: CARLOS TINY (MLSTP—PSD).
Minister of Education and Culture: JORGE BOM JESUS (MLSTP—PSD).
Minister of Trade, Industry and Tourism: CELESTINO ANDRADE (MLSTP—PSD).
Minister of Planning and Finance: ÂNGELA VIEGAS (MLSTP—PSD).
Minister of Public Works, Infrastructure, Transport and Communications: BENJAMIN VERA CRUZ (PCD).
Minister of Health: ARLINDO DE CARVALHO (PCD).
Minister of Media, Youth and Sports: MARIA DE CHRISTO DE CARVALHO (PCD).
Minister of Agriculture, Rural Development and Fishing: XAVIER MENDES (PCD).
Minister of Labour, Solidarity and Family: MARIA TOMÉ (MDFM).
Minister of the Interior, Territorial Administration and Civil Protection: RÁUL CRAVID (MDFM).
Minister of Natural Resources, Energy and the Environment: CRISTINA DIAS (MDFM).
Minister of Justice, State Reform, Public Administration and Parliamentary Affairs: JUSTINO VEIGA (MDFM).

Provisional Government of the Autonomous Region of Príncipe
(March 2009)

President: JOSÉ CARDOSO CASSANDRA.
Secretary for Social and Cultural Affairs: FELÍCIA FONSECA DE OLIVEIRA E SILVA.
Secretary for Economic and Financial Affairs: HÉLIO LAVRES.
Secretary for Infrastructure and the Environment: TIAGO ROSAMONTE.
Secretary for Political, Organizational and Institutional Affairs: CARLOS GOMES.

MINISTRIES

Office of the President: Palácio Presidêncial, São Tomé; internet www.presidencia.st.
Office of the Prime Minister: Rua do Município, CP 302, São Tomé; tel. 223913; fax 224679; e-mail gpm@cstome.net.
Ministry of Agriculture, Rural Development and Fishing: Av. Marginal 12 de Julho, Edif. Ministério da Agricultura, 1° andar, CP 47, São Tomé; tel. 222714; fax 222347.
Ministry of Commerce, Industry and Tourism: São Tomé.
Ministry of Education and Culture: Rua Misericórdia, CP 41, São Tomé; tel. 222861; fax 221466; e-mail mineducal@cstome.net.
Ministry of Foreign Affairs, Co-operation and Communities: Av. 12 de Julho, CP 111, São Tomé; tel. 221017; fax 222597; e-mail minecoop@cstome.net; internet www.mnecc.gov.st.
Ministry of Health: Av. Patrice Lumumba, CP 23, São Tomé; tel. 241200; fax 221306; e-mail msaude@cstome.net.
Ministry of Justice, State Reform, Public Administration and Parliamentary Affairs: Av. 12 de Julho, CP 4, São Tomé; tel. 222318; fax 222256; e-mail emilioma@cstome.net.
Ministry of Labour, Solidarity and Family: Rua Município, Edif. Ministério do Trabalho, São Tomé; tel. 221466.
Ministry of Media, Youth and Sports: Rua Misericórdia, CP 41, São Tomé; tel. 222861; fax 221466.
Ministry of National Defence: Av. 12 de Julho, CP 427, São Tomé; tel. 222041; e-mail midefesa@cstome.net.
Ministry of Natural Resources, Energy and the Environment: CP 1093, São Tomé; tel. 225272; fax 226262; e-mail mirecurna@cstome.net.
Ministry of Planning and Finance: Largo Alfândega, CP 168, São Tomé; tel. 224173; fax 222683; e-mail mpfc@cstome.net.
Ministry of the Interior, Territorial Administration and Civil Protection: Av. Kwame Nkrumah, CP 136, São Tomé; tel. 224750; fax 222824.
Ministry of Public Works, Infrastructure Transport, and Communications: São Tomé.

President and Legislature

PRESIDENT

Presidential Election, 30 July 2006

Candidate	Votes	% of votes
Fradique de Menezes	34,859	60.58
Patrice Emery Trovoada	22,339	38.82
Nilo de Oliveira Guimarães	340	0.59
Total	**57,538**	**100.00**

There were, in addition, 1,640 blank and other invalid votes

ASSEMBLEIA NACIONAL

Assembleia Nacional: Palácio dos Congressos, CP 181, São Tomé; tel. 222986; fax 222835; e-mail romao.couto@parlamento.st; internet www.parlamento.st.
President: FRANCISCO DA SILVA.

SÃO TOMÉ AND PRÍNCIPE

General Election, 26 March and 2 April 2006

Party	% of valid votes	Seats
Movimento Democrático Força da Mudança-Partido de Convergência Democrática	36.79	23
Movimento de Libertação de São Tomé e Príncipe—Partido Social Democrata	29.47	20
Acção Democrática Independente (ADI)	20.00	11
Novo Rumo (NR)	4.71	1
Others	9.03	—
Total	100.00	55

Election Commission

Comissão Eleitoral Nacional (CEN): Av. Amílcar Cabral, São Tomé; tel. 225497; fax 224116; e-mail censtome@cstome.net; Pres. JOSÉ CARLOS BARREIROS.

Political Organizations

Acção Democrática Independente (ADI): Av. Marginal 12 de Julho, Edif. C. Cassandra, São Tomé; tel. 222201; f. 1992; Sec.-Gen. EVARISTO CARVALHO.

Frente Democrata Cristã—Partido Social da Unidade (FDC—PSU): São Tomé; f. 1990; Pres. ARLÉCIO COSTA; Vice-Pres. SABINO DOS SANTOS.

Geração Esperança (GE): São Tomé; f. 2005; Leader EDMILZA BRAGANÇA.

Movimento Democrático Força da Mudança (MDFM): São Tomé; f. 2001; Chair. FRADIQUE DE MENEZES; Sec.-Gen. AGOSTINHO RITA.

Movimento de Libertação de São Tomé e Príncipe—Partido Social Democrata (MLSTP—PSD): Estrada Riboque, Edif. Sede do MLSTP, São Tomé; tel. 222253; f. 1972 as MLSTP; adopted present name in 1990; sole legal party 1972–90; Pres. JOAQUIM RAFAEL BRANCO; Sec.-Gen. JOSÉ VIEGAS.

Novo Rumo: São Tomé; f. 2006 by citizens disaffected by current political parties; Leader JOÃO GOMES.

Partido de Convergência Democrática (PCD): Av. Marginal 12 de Julho, CP 519, São Tomé; tel. and fax 223257; f. 1990 as Partido de Convergência—Grupo de Reflexão; formed alliance with MDFM to contest legislative elections in 2006; Pres. ALBERTINO BRAGANÇA; Sec.-Gen. DELFIM SANTIAGO DAS NEVES.

Partido de Coligação Democrática (CÓDÓ): São Tomé; f. 1990 as Partido Democrático de São Tomé e Príncipe—Coligação Democrática da Oposição; renamed as above June 1998; Leader MANUEL NEVES E SILVA.

Partido Social e Liberal (PSL): São Tomé; f. 2005; promotes devt and anti-corruption; Leader AGOSTINHO RITA.

Partido Popular do Progresso (PPP): São Tomé; f. 1998; Leader FRANCISCO SILVA.

Partido de Renovação Democrática (PRD): São Tomé; tel. 903109; e-mail prd100@hotmail.com; f. 2001; Pres. ARMINDO GRAÇA.

Partido Social Renovado (PSR): São Tomé; f. 2004; Leader HAMILTON VAZ.

Partido Trabalhista Santomense (PTS): CP 254, São Tomé; tel. 223338; fax 223255; e-mail pascoal@cstome.net; f. 1993 as Aliança Popular; Leader ANACLETO ROLIN.

União para a Democracia e Desenvolvimento (UDD): São Tomé; f. 2005; Leader MANUEL DIOGO.

União Nacional para Democracia e Progresso (UNDP): São Tomé; f. 1998; Leader PAIXÃO LIMA.

The União para a Mudança e Progresso do Príncipe (UMPP) led by JOSÉ CARDOSO CASSANDRA operates on the island of Príncipe and there is also a local civic group, O Renascimento de Água Grande, in the district of Agua Grande, which includes the city of São Tomé.

Diplomatic Representation

EMBASSIES IN SÃO TOMÉ AND PRÍNCIPE

Angola: Av. Kwame Nkrumah 45, CP 133, São Tomé; tel. 222400; fax 221362; e-mail embrang@cstome.net; Ambassador (vacant).

Brazil: Av. Marginal de 12 de Julho 20, São Tomé; tel. 226060; fax 226895; e-mail brasembsaotome@cstome.net; Ambassador MANUEL INNOCENCIO DE LACERDA SANTOS, Jr.

China (Taiwan): Av. Marginal de 12 de Julho, CP 839, São Tomé; tel. 223529; fax 221376; e-mail rocstp@cstome.net; Ambassador JOHN-C. CHEN.

Equatorial Guinea: Av. Kwame Nkrumah, São Tomé; tel. 225427.

Gabon: Rua Damão, CP 394, São Tomé; tel. 224434; fax 223531; e-mail ambagabon@cstome.net; Ambassador BEKALÉ MICHEL.

Nigeria: Av. Kwame Nkrumah, CP 1000, São Tomé; tel. 225404; fax 225406; e-mail nigeria@cstome.net; Ambassador SUNDAY DOGONYARO OON.

Portugal: Av. Marginal de 12 de Julho, CP 173, São Tomé; tel. 221130; fax 221190; e-mail eporstp@cstome.net; Ambassador FERNANDO JOSÉ RODRIGUES RAMOS MACHADO.

South Africa: Av. da Independencia, No. 7 Representanção da República da Africa de Sul, São Tomé; tel. 227568; e-mail consuafricasul@cstome.net; Chargé d'affaires a.i. T. E. MAMUREMI.

Judicial System

Judicial power is exercised by the Supreme Court of Justice and the Courts of Primary Instance. The Supreme Court is the ultimate judicial authority. There is also a Constitutional Court, which rules on election matters.

Supremo Tribunal de Justiça: Av. Marginal de 12 de Julho, CP 04, São Tomé; tel. 222615; fax 222329; e-mail info@stj.st; internet www.stj.st; Pres. MARIA ALICE VERA CRUZ CARVALHO.

Religion

According to the 2001 census more than 80% of the population are Christians, almost all of whom are Roman Catholics.

CHRISTIANITY

The Roman Catholic Church

São Tomé and Príncipe comprises a single diocese, directly responsible to the Holy See. At 31 December 2006 an estimated 73.5% of the population were adherents. The bishop participates in the Episcopal Conference of Angola and São Tomé (based in Luanda, Angola).

Bishop of São Tomé and Príncipe: Rt Rev. MANUEL ANTÓNIO MENDES DOS SANTOS, Centro Diocesano, CP 104, Rua P. Pinto da Rocha 1, São Tomé; tel. 223455; fax 227348; e-mail diocese@cstome.net.

Other Churches

Igreja Adventista do 7° Dia (Seventh-Day Adventist Church): Rua Barão de Agua Izé, São Tomé; tel. 223349.

Igreja Evangélica: Rua 3 de Fevereiro, São Tomé; tel. 221350.

Igreja Evangélica Assembleia de Deus: Rua 3 de Fevereiro, São Tomé; tel. and fax 222442; e-mail iead@cstome.net.

Igreja Maná: Av. Amílcar Cabral, São Tomé; tel. and fax 224654; e-mail imana@cstome.net.

Igreja do Nazareno: Vila Dolores, São Tomé; tel. 223943; e-mail nszst@cstome.net.

Igreja Nova Apostólica: CP 220, Vila Maria, São Tomé; tel. and fax 222797; e-mail j.cunha@ina-stp.org; internet ina-stp.org.

Igreja Universal do Reino de Deus: Travessa Imprensa, São Tomé; tel. 224047.

The Press

Correio da Semana: Av. Amílcar Cabral 382, São Tomé; tel. 225299; e-mail correiodasemana@cstome.net; internet www.correiodasemana.info; f. 2005; weekly; Dir JUVENAL RODRIGUES; circ. 3,000.

Diário da República: Cooperativa de Artes Gráficas, Rua João Devs, CP 28, São Tomé; tel. 222661; internet dre.pt/stp; f. 1836; official gazette; Dir OSCAR FERREIRA.

Jornal Maravilha: São Tomé; tel. 911690; f. 2006; Dir NELSON SIGNO.

Jornal Tropical: Rua Padre Martinho Pinto da Rocha, São Tomé; tel. 923140; e-mail jornaltropical06@hotmail.com; internet www.jornaltropical.st; Dir OCTÁVIO SOARES.

O Parvo: CP 535, São Tomé; tel. 221031; f. 1994; weekly; Publr AMBRÓSIO QUARESMA; Editor ARMINDO CARDOSO.

SÃO TOMÉ AND PRÍNCIPE

Téla Nón: Largo Água Grande, Edif. Complexo Técnico da CST, São Tomé; tel. 225099; e-mail diario_digital@cstome.net; internet www.cstome.net/diario; f. 2000; provides online daily news service; Chief Editor ABEL VEIGA.

Online newspapers include the Jornal de São Tomé e Príncipe (www.jornal.st) and Jornal Horizonte (www.cstome.net/jhorizonte) and Vitrina (www.vitrina.st).

PRESS ASSOCIATION

Associação Nacional de Imprensa (ANI): São Tomé; Pres. MANUEL BARRETO.

NEWS AGENCY

STP-Press: Av. Marginal de 12 de Julho, CP 112, São Tomé; tel. 223431; fax 221973; e-mail stp_press@cstome.net; internet www.cstome.net/stp-press; f. 1985; operated by the radio station in asscn with the Angolan news agency ANGOP; Dir MANUEL DÊNDE.

Broadcasting and Communications

TELECOMMUNICATIONS

Companhia Santomense de Telecomunicações, SARL (CST): Av. Marginal 12 de Julho, CP 141, São Tomé; tel. 222226; fax 222500; e-mail webmaster@cstome.net; internet www.cstome.net; f. 1989 by Govt of São Tomé (49%) and Grupo Portugal Telecom (Portugal, 51%) to facilitate increased telecommunications links and television reception via satellite; in March 1997 CST introduced internet services; Rádio Marconi's shares subsequently assumed by Portugal Telecom SA; introduced mobile cellular telephone service in 2001; Pres. FELISBERTO AFONSO L. NETO; Sec. JORGE LIMA D'ALVA TORRES.

BROADCASTING

Portuguese technical and financial assistance in the establishment of a television service was announced in May 1989. Transmissions commenced in 1992 and the service currently broadcasts seven days a week. In 1995 Radio France Internationale and Rádio Televisão Portuguesa Internacional began relaying radio and television broadcasts, respectively, to the archipelago. In 1997 Voice of America, which had been broadcasting throughout Africa since 1993 from a relay station installed on São Tomé, began local transmissions on FM. In 2004 there were plans for Televisão Pública de Angola to begin transmitting by the end of the year. The liberalization of the sector was approved by the Government in early 2005 and Rádio Jubilar, Rádio Tropicana (operated by the Roman Catholic Church) and Rádio Viva FM subsequently began broadcasting. The French television channel TV5 began broadcasting in December 2007.

Radio

Rádio Nacional de São Tomé e Príncipe: Av. Marginal de 12 de Julho, CP 44, São Tomé; tel. 223293; fax 221973; e-mail rnstp@cstome.net; f. 1958; state-controlled; home service in Portuguese and Creole; Dir MÁXIMO CARLOS.

Rádio Jubilar: Av. Kwam Kruman-Edifício da Catequese, CP 104, São Tomé; tel. 223868; f. 2005; operated by the Roman Catholic Church; Dir FERNANDO CORREIA.

Rádio Tropicana: Travessa João de Deus, CP 709, São Tomé; tel. 226856; f. 2005; Dir AGUINALDO SALVATERRA.

Television

Televisão Santomense (TVS): Bairro Quinta de Santo António, CP 393, São Tomé; tel. 221041; fax 221942; state-controlled; Dir MATEUS FERREIRA.

Finance

(cap. = capital; res = reserves; dep. = deposits; m. = million; br(s). = branch(es); amounts in dobras, unless otherwise indicated)

BANKING

Central Bank

Banco Central de São Tomé e Príncipe (BCSTP): Praça da Independência, CP 13, São Tomé; tel. 221300; fax 222777; e-mail bcstp@bcstp.st; internet www.bcstp.st; f. 1992 to succeed fmr Banco Nacional de São Tomé e Príncipe; bank of issue; cap. 100m., res 109,091.1m., dep. 484,521.2m. (Dec. 2005); Gov. LUÍS FERNANDO MOREIRA DE SOUSA.

Commercial Banks

Afriland First Bank/STP: Praça da Independência, CP 202, São Tomé; tel. 226749; fax 226747; e-mail stp@afrilandfirstbank.com; internet www.afrilandfirstbank.com; f. 2003; private bank; owned by Afriland First Bank, SA, Cameroon; cap. US $1.8m.; Gen. Man. AUGUSTIN DIAYO; Administrator-Delegate JOSEPH TINDJOU.

Banco Equador SARL: Rua Moçambique 3B, CP 361, São Tomé; tel. 226150; fax 226149; e-mail be@bancoequador.st; internet www.bancoequador.st; f. 1995 as Banco Comercial do Equador; restructured and name changed to above in 2003; owned by Monbaka, Angola (40%) and Grupo António Mbakassi (40%); cap. US $3m.; Pres. DIONÍSIO MENDONÇA; Gen. Man. RUI MENDONÇA; 1 br.

Banco Internacional de São Tomé e Príncipe (BISTP) (International Bank of São Tomé and Príncipe): Praça da Independência, CP 536, São Tomé; tel. 243100; fax 222427; e-mail bistp@cstome.net; internet www.bistp.st; f. 1993; 48% govt-owned, 27% by Caixa Geral de Depósitos (Portugal), 25% by Banco Africano de Investimentos SARL (Angola); cap. US $3.0m., res $3.1m., dep. $22.2m. (2004); CEO JOÃO CARLOS AGUIAR CRISTÓVÃO; 3 brs.

Commercial Bank—São Tomé e Príncipe: Av. Marginal 12 de Julho, CP 1109, São Tomé; tel. 227678; fax 227676; e-mail cobstp@cstome.net; internet www.cbc-bank.com; f. 2005; 42% owned by Groupe FOTSO (Cameroon); cap. US $3m. (2005); Chair. YVES MICHEL FOTSO; Gen. Man. JAQUES PAUL WOUENDJI.

Ecobank São Tomé: Edifício HB, Traversa de Pelorinho, CP 316, São Tomé; tel. 222141; fax 222672; e-mail ecobankstp@cstome.net; f. 2007; cap. US $1.5m.

Island Bank, SA: Rua de Guiné, CP 1044, São Tomé; tel. 222521; f. 2005; cap. US $1.8m. (2005); Pres. MARC WABARA; Dir CHRIS U. MMEJE.

INSURANCE

Instituto de Segurança Social: Rua Soldado Paulo Ferreira, São Tomé; tel. 221382; e-mail inss@cstome.net; f. as Caixa de Previdência dos Funcionários Públicos, adopted present name 1994; insurance fund for civil servants; Pres. of Admin. Bd ALBINO GRAÇA DA FONSECA; Dir JUVENAL DO ESPÍRITO SANTO.

SAT INSURANCE: Av. Amilcar Cabral, CP 293, São Tomé; tel. 226161; fax 226160; e-mail satinsuran@cstome.net; f. 2001; general insurance; cap. US $1.0m.; Dir MICHEL SOBGUI.

Trade and Industry

GOVERNMENT AGENCIES

Agência Nacional do Petróleo de São Tomé e Príncipe (ANP—STP): Av. Nações Unidas, CP 1048, São Tomé; tel. 226940; fax 226937; e-mail anp_geral@cstome.net; internet www.anp-stp.gov.st; f. 2004; manages and implements govt policies relating to the petroleum sector; Exec. Dir LUÍS PRAZERES.

Nigeria-São Tomé and Príncipe Joint Development Authority (JDA): Plot 1101, Aminu Kano Cres., Wuse II, Abuja, Nigeria; Praça da UCCLA, São Tomé; tel. (234) 95241069; fax (234) 95241061; e-mail enquiries@nigeriasaotomejda.com; internet www.nigeriasaotomejda.com; f. 2002; manages devt of petroleum and gas resources in Joint Development Zone; Exec. Dir Dr JORGE PEREIRA DOS SANTOS.

DEVELOPMENT ORGANIZATION

Instituto para o Desenvolvimento Económico e Social (INDES): Travessa do Pelourinho, CP 408, São Tomé; tel. 222491; fax 221931; e-mail indes@cstome.net; f. 1989 as Fundo Social e de Infrastructuras; adopted present name 1994; channels foreign funds to local economy; Dir HOMERO JERÓNIMO SALVATERRA.

CHAMBER OF COMMERCE

Câmara do Comércio, Indústria, Agricultura e Serviços (CCIAS): Av. Marginal de 12 de Julho, CP 527, São Tomé; tel. 222723; fax 221409; e-mail ccias@cstome.net; Pres. ABÍLIO AFONSO HENRIQUES.

UTILITIES

Electricity and Water

Empresa de Água e Electricidade (EMAE): Av. Água Grande, CP 46, São Tomé; tel. 222096; fax 222488; e-mail emae@cstome.net; f. 1979; Synergie Investments (UK); state electricity and water co; privatized in 2004; Dir Lt-Col OSCAR SACRAMENTO E SOUSA.

TRADE UNIONS

Federação Nacional dos Pequenos Agricoltores (FENAPA): Rua Barão de Agua Izé, São Tomé; tel. 224741; Pres. TEODORICO CAMPOS.

Organização Nacional de Trabalhadores de São Tomé e Príncipe (ONTSTP): Rua Cabo Verde, São Tomé; tel. 222431; e-mail ontstpdis@cstome.net; Sec.-Gen. JOÃO TAVARES.

Sindicato de Jornalistas de São Tomé e Príncipe (SJS): São Tomé; Pres. AMBRÓSIO QUARESMA.

Sindicato dos Trabalhadores do Estado (STE): São Tomé; Sec.-Gen. AURÉLIO SILVA.

União Geral dos Trabalhadores de São Tomé e Príncipe (UGSTP): Av. Kwame Nkrumah, São Tomé; tel. 222443; e-mail ugtdis@cstome.net; Sec.-Gen. COSTA CARLOS.

Transport

RAILWAYS
There are no railways in São Tomé and Príncipe.

ROADS
In 1999 there were an estimated 320 km of roads, of which 218 km were asphalted. In 2005 the European Union granted €930,000 towards upgrading the road network.

SHIPPING
The principal ports are at São Tomé city and at Neves on São Tomé island. At December 2007 São Tomé and Príncipe's registered merchant fleet comprised 30 vessels, totalling 29,588 grt.

Companhia Santomense de Navegação, SA (CSN): CP 49, São Tomé; tel. 222657; fax 221311; e-mail csn@setgrcop.com; shipping and freight forwarding.

Empresa Nacional de Administração dos Portos (ENAPORT): Largo Alfândega, CP 437, São Tomé; tel. 221841; fax 224949; e-mail enaport@cstome.net; internet www.enaport.st; Dir-Gen. DEODATO GOMES RODRIGUES.

Navetur-Navegação e Turismo, Lda: CP 147, Rua Viriato da Cruz, São Tomé; tel. 223781; fax 222122; e-mail navequatur@cstome.net; internet www.navetur-equatour.st.

Transportes e Serviços, Lda (TURIMAR): Rua Patrice Lumumba, CP 48, São Tomé; tel. 221869; fax 222162; e-mail turimar@cstome.net; internet www.turimar-stp.com; Man. ALBERTO PEREIRA.

CIVIL AVIATION
The international airport is at São Tomé.

Empresa Nacional de Aeroportos e Segurança Aérea (ENASA): Aeroporto, CP 703, São Tomé; tel. 221878; fax 221154; e-mail enasa@cstome.net; Dir JORGE COELHO.

Linhas Aéreas São-tomenses (LAS): Rua Santo António do Príncipe, São Tomé; tel. 227282; fax 227281; e-mail hba.saotome@gmail.com; f. 2002; owned by Aerocontractors, Nigeria; Dir ANTÓNIO AGUIAR.

STP-Airways: Av. Marginal 12 de Julho, São Tomé; tel. 221160; fax 223449; e-mail stp-airways@cstome.net; internet www.stpairways.st; f. 2006; 35% govt-owned; Dir FELISBERTO NETO.

Tourism

The islands benefit from spectacular mountain scenery, unspoilt beaches and unique species of flora and wildlife. Although still largely undeveloped, tourism is currently the sector of the islands' economy attracting the highest level of foreign investment. However, the high level of rainfall during most of the year limits the duration of the tourist season, and the expense of reaching the islands by air is also an inhibiting factor. There were 12,266 tourist arrivals in 2006, and receipts totalled some US $13.6m. in 2005.

SAUDI ARABIA

Introductory Survey

Location, Climate, Language, Religion, Flag, Capital

The Kingdom of Saudi Arabia occupies about four-fifths of the Arabian peninsula, in south-western Asia. It is bordered by Jordan, Iraq and Kuwait to the north, by Yemen to the south, by Oman to the south and east, and by Qatar and the United Arab Emirates to the north-east. Saudi Arabia has a long western coastline on the Red Sea, facing Egypt, Sudan and Eritrea, and a shorter coastline (between Kuwait and Qatar) on the Persian (Arabian) Gulf, with the Bahrain archipelago just off shore and Iran on the opposite coast. Much of the country is arid desert, and some places are without rain for years. In summer average temperatures in coastal regions range from 38°C to 49°C, and humidity is high. Temperatures sometimes reach 54°C in the interior. Winters are mild, except in the mountains. Annual rainfall averages between 100 mm and 200 mm in the north, and is even lower in the south. The official language is Arabic, which is spoken by almost all of the population. Except for the expatriate community (estimated to represent some 27% of the total population in 2007), virtually all of the inhabitants are adherents of Islam, the official religion. About 85% of the population are Sunni Muslims, and most of the indigenous inhabitants belong to the strictly orthodox Wahhabi sect. About 15% of the population are Shi'a Muslims, principally in the east of the country. The national flag (proportions 2 by 3) is green and bears, in white, an Arabic inscription ('There is no God but Allah and Muhammad is the Prophet of Allah') above a white sabre. The capital is Riyadh.

Recent History

The whole of the Arabian peninsula became part of Turkey's Ottoman Empire in the 16th century. Under the suzerainty of the Ottoman Sultan, the local tribal rulers enjoyed varying degrees of autonomy. The Wahhabi movement, dedicated to the reform of Islam, was launched in the Najd (Nejd) region of central Arabia in the 18th century. A Wahhabi kingdom, ruled by the House of Sa'ud from its capital at Riyadh, quickly expanded into the Hedjaz region on the west coast of Arabia. In 1890 the rival Rashidi family seized control of Riyadh, but in 1902 a member of the deposed Sa'udi family, Abd al-Aziz ibn Abd ar-Rahman, expelled the Rashidi dynasty and proclaimed himself ruler of Najd. In subsequent years he recovered and consolidated the outlying provinces of the kingdom, defeating Turkish attempts to subjugate him. Having restored the House of Sa'ud as a ruling dynasty, Abd al-Aziz became known as Ibn Sa'ud. In order to strengthen his position, he instituted the formation of Wahhabi colonies, known as Ikhwan ('Brethren'), throughout the territory under his control.

During the First World War, in which Turkey was allied with Germany, the Arabs under Ottoman rule rebelled. In 1915 the United Kingdom signed a treaty of friendship with Ibn Sa'ud, who was then master of central Arabia, securing his co-operation against Turkey. Relations subsequently deteriorated as a result of the British Government's decision to support Hussein ibn Ali, who proclaimed himself King of the Hedjaz in 1916, as its principal ally in Arabia. Hussein was also Sharif of Mecca (the holiest city of Islam), which had been governed since the 11th century by his Hashimi (Hashemite) family, rivals of the House of Sa'ud. At the end of the war, following Turkey's defeat, the Ottoman Empire was dissolved. Continuing his conquests, Ibn Sa'ud successfully campaigned against the rulers of four Arabian states (the Hedjaz, Asir, Hayil and Jauf) between 1919 and 1925. In September 1924 his forces captured Mecca, forcing Hussein to abdicate, and in 1925 they overran the whole of the Hedjaz. In January 1926 Ibn Sa'ud was proclaimed King of the Hedjaz and Sultan of Najd. On 23 September 1932 the dual monarchy ended when the two areas were merged as the unified Kingdom of Saudi Arabia.

Commercially exploitable deposits of petroleum (the basis of Saudi Arabia's modern prosperity) were discovered in the Eastern Province in 1938, and large-scale exploitation of the kingdom's huge reserves of petroleum began after the Second World War. Petroleum royalties were used to develop and modernize the country's infrastructure and services.

Ibn Sa'ud remained in power until his death in November 1953; all subsequent rulers of Saudi Arabia have been sons of his. The kingdom has remained an absolute monarchy and a traditional Islamic society. The King is the supreme religious leader as well as the Head of State, and governs by royal decree. In foreign affairs, Saudi Arabia has historically allied itself with the USA and other Western countries.

Ibn Sa'ud was succeeded by the Crown Prince, Sa'ud ibn Abd al-Aziz. Another of the late King's sons, Faisal ibn Abd al-Aziz, replaced Sa'ud as Crown Prince and Prime Minister. In 1958, bowing to pressure from the royal family, King Sa'ud conferred on Crown Prince Faisal full powers over foreign, internal and economic affairs. In March 1964 King Sa'ud relinquished power to Crown Prince Faisal, and in November was forced by the royal family to abdicate in his favour. The new King Faisal retained the post of Prime Minister, and appointed his half-brother, Khalid ibn Abd al-Aziz, to be Crown Prince in 1965. In the Six-Day War of June 1967 Saudi Arabian forces collaborated with Iraqi and Jordanian troops in action against Israel. As a result of the Arab–Israeli War of October 1973, Saudi Arabia led a movement by Arab petroleum producers to exert pressure on Western countries by reducing supplies of crude oil.

In March 1975 King Faisal was assassinated by one of his nephews, and was immediately succeeded by Crown Prince Khalid. The new King also became Prime Minister, and appointed his brother, Fahd ibn Abd al-Aziz (Minister of the Interior since 1962), as Crown Prince and First Deputy Prime Minister.

The religious fervour that the Middle East experienced in the wake of the Iranian Revolution also arose in Saudi Arabia in late 1979, when an armed group of about 250 Sunni Muslim extremists attacked and occupied the Grand Mosque in Mecca, the most important centre of pilgrimage for Muslims. There was also a riot by Shi'a Muslims in the Eastern Province. In response to the unrest, Crown Prince Fahd announced in early 1980 that a consultative assembly would be formed to act as an advisory body, although the assembly was not inaugurated until December 1993 (see below).

King Khalid died in June 1982 and was succeeded by Crown Prince Fahd, who, following precedent, became Prime Minister and appointed a half-brother, Abdullah ibn Abd al-Aziz (Commander of the National Guard since 1962), to be Crown Prince and First Deputy Prime Minister.

As a result of its position as the world's leading exporter of petroleum, Saudi Arabia is a dominant member of the Organization of the Petroleum Exporting Countries (OPEC, see p. 386) and one of the most influential countries in the Arab world. In May 1981 the kingdom joined five neighbouring states in establishing the Co-operation Council for the Arab States of the Gulf (the Gulf Co-operation Council—GCC, see p. 229). In August Crown Prince (subsequently King) Fahd announced an eight-point plan for the settlement of the Arab–Israeli conflict. His proposals, by implication, recognized Israel as a legitimate state. At a summit conference of Arab states in September 1982, the so-called 'Fahd Plan' formed the basis of an agreed proposal for the achievement of peace in the Middle East, and during 1983 Saudi Arabia sponsored repeated diplomatic initiatives within the region. In November 1987 Saudi Arabia resumed full diplomatic relations with Egypt. Relations had been severed in 1979, following the signing of the peace treaty between Egypt and Israel.

Relations with Iran, already strained as a result of Saudi Arabia's support for Iraq in the Iran–Iraq War, deteriorated further in July 1987 following fierce clashes between Iranian pilgrims and Saudi security forces during the *Hajj*, in which 402 people, including 275 Iranians, were killed. Mass demonstrations took place in Tehran, where the Saudi Arabian embassy was sacked, and Iranian leaders vowed to avenge the pilgrims' deaths by overthrowing the Saudi ruling family. In March 1988 the Government announced its intention to limit the number of foreign pilgrims during the *Hajj* season by allocating national quotas. Saudi Arabia severed diplomatic relations with Iran, which subsequently refused to send pilgrims on that year's *Hajj*.

In July 1988, after the US Congress had refused to sanction an agreement to supply military equipment to Saudi Arabia (following the delivery of an unspecified number of medium-range missiles from the People's Republic of China to Saudi Arabia earlier that year), the Government signed a large-scale defence procurement agreement with the United Kingdom, which as a result superseded the USA as Saudi Arabia's main supplier of military equipment.

Widely held misgivings regarding national defence capabilities, and fears of Iraqi expansionist policy (a pact of non-aggression was signed with Iraq in March 1989), were exacerbated in August 1990, when Iraq invaded and annexed Kuwait and proceeded to deploy armed forces along the Kuwaiti–Saudi Arabian border. King Fahd requested that US forces be deployed in Saudi Arabia, as part of a multinational force, in order to deter a possible attack by Iraq. The dispatch of US combat troops and aircraft to Saudi Arabia signified the beginning of 'Operation Desert Shield' for the defence of Saudi Arabia, in accordance with Article 51 of the UN Charter. By the beginning of 1991 some 30 countries had contributed ground troops, aircraft and warships to the US-led multinational force based in Saudi Arabia and the Gulf region. The entire Saudi Arabian armed forces (numbering about 67,500 men) were mobilized. In January, following the failure of international diplomatic efforts to secure Iraq's withdrawal from Kuwait, the multinational force launched a military campaign ('Operation Desert Storm') to liberate Kuwait. As part of its response to the initial aerial bombardment, Iraq launched *Scud* missiles against targets in Saudi Arabia. However, fighting on Saudi Arabian territory was confined to a few minor incidents. In February Iraq formally severed diplomatic relations with Saudi Arabia.

Following the liberation of Kuwait in February 1991, the ministers responsible for foreign affairs of the GCC met their Syrian and Egyptian counterparts in Damascus, Syria, in March in order to discuss regional security issues. The formation of an Arab peace-keeping force, comprising mainly Egyptian and Syrian troops, was subsequently announced. In May, however, following the endorsement by the GCC member states of US proposals for an increased Western military presence in the Gulf region, Egypt announced its decision to withdraw all of its forces from the region, casting doubt on the future of joint Arab regional security arrangements. Diplomatic relations between Saudi Arabia and Iran were re-established in March, and Iranian pilgrims resumed attendance of the *Hajj*, their numbers regulated in accordance with the quota system.

In March 1992 King Fahd announced by royal decree the imminent creation of an advisory Consultative Council (Majlis ash-Shoura), with 60 members to be selected by the King every four years. Two further decrees provided for the establishment of regional authorities, and a 'basic law of government', equivalent to a written constitution. In September Sheikh Muhammad al-Jubair, hitherto Minister of Justice, was appointed Chairman of the Majlis. The Majlis was inaugurated by King Fahd at the end of 1993. (Its membership was increased to 90 in July 1997, to 120 in May 2001 and to 150 in April 2005—see below.)

In May 1993 the Saudi authorities disbanded the Committee for the Defence of Legitimate Rights (CDLR), recently established by a group of six prominent Islamist scholars and lawyers. The organization's founders were also dismissed from their positions, and their spokesman, Muhammad al-Masari, was arrested. In April 1994 members of the CDLR, including al-Masari (who had recently been released from custody), relocated their organization to the United Kingdom. In January 1996 the British authorities ordered the deportation of al-Masari to Dominica: prominent British defence and aerospace companies were believed to have exerted pressure on their Government to concede to Saudi Arabia's demands that al-Masari be expelled in order to secure the continuation of lucrative trade agreements with Saudi Arabia. However, in April al-Masari was granted exceptional leave to remain in the United Kingdom for a period of at least four years, although he was not granted asylum.

In September 1994 more than 1,000 people, including clerics and academics, were reportedly detained, after most of them had attended a demonstration in Buraidah, north-west of Riyadh, to protest at the arrest of two religious leaders who had allegedly been agitating for the stricter enforcement of *Shari'a* (Islamic) law. The Government announced in October that only 157 people had been arrested in September, 130 of whom had since been released. Also in October the King approved the creation of a Higher Council for Islamic Affairs, in a measure apparently aimed at limiting the influence of militant clerics and at diminishing the authority of the powerful 18-member Council of Ulema (Saudi Arabia's most senior Islamic authority). In mid-1995 King Fahd replaced six of the seven University chancellors and more than one-half of the members of the Council of Ulema, in an attempt to counter the perceived spread of Islamist fundamentalism.

In June 1995 an opposition activist, Abdullah Abd ar-Rahman al-Hudaif, was sentenced to 20 years' imprisonment for his part in an attack on a security officer and for maintaining links with the CDLR in the United Kingdom. In August al-Hudaif was reported to have been executed. A further nine opposition activists reportedly received prison sentences ranging from three to 18 years; according to prominent human rights organization Amnesty International, as many as 200 'political suspects' remained in detention in Saudi Arabia.

In August 1995 the King announced the most far-reaching reorganization of the Council of Ministers for two decades, although no changes were made to the portfolios held by members of the royal family. The strategic portfolios of finance and national economy and of petroleum and mineral resources were allocated to younger, though highly experienced, officials.

A Supreme Economic Council, established by royal decree, convened for the first time in October 1997 under the chairmanship of the Crown Prince. A Supreme Petroleum and Minerals Council was established by royal decree in January 2000. The Government declared in May that ministers were to lose their right to hold company posts while in office, with the exception of employees of the state-owned Saudi Aramco petroleum corporation. In June the inaugural session was held of the newly formed Royal Family Council, an officially apolitical body to be chaired by Crown Prince Abdullah.

Saudi Arabia's human rights record has for many years been the focus of international scrutiny, particularly regarding the use of public beheading in the Saudi judicial system. A report issued by Amnesty International in March 2000 alleged that Saudi Arabia was guilty of widespread human rights abuses, including use of torture and refusal to allow prisoners access to family members and lawyers. In another document, published in September, Amnesty accused the Saudi authorities of widespread discrimination against women and cited serious abuses of their human rights, including arbitrary detention and torture. The organization also reiterated its criticism of the Saudi judiciary for failing to conduct trials in compliance with internationally recognized standards. However, it was reported in late 2000 that Saudi Arabia had agreed to sign the UN Convention on the Elimination of All Forms of Discrimination against Women, although it stated that it would lodge reservations regarding any section deemed to contravene *Shari'a* law.

King Fahd announced a restructured 27-member Council of Ministers in April 2003; this was only the third reorganization of the Government in almost 30 years. Reformists were disappointed that most of the key positions were unchanged, and that all the senior ministers belonging to the ruling as-Sa'ud family remained in post.

Following reports in the early part of 2003 that the Saudi Government intended to follow the example of Bahrain and hold elections to the Majlis ash-Shoura in 2005, in October 2003, at a human rights conference in Riyadh, the Government disclosed plans to create municipal councils and hold local elections by October 2004. The news was received with some scepticism among Saudi reformists, who noted that one-half of the councillors would be centrally appointed and that there had been no suggestion in the official announcement that suffrage would be extended to women. The decision by the authorities to introduce a degree of democracy to the kingdom came amid huge pressure both from inside and outside the country to implement social, economic, political and constitutional reforms. The human rights conference was Saudia Arabia's first such meeting, although Western human rights bodies were not invited to attend. Several hundred protesters took part in an illegal demonstration, organized by the British-based Movement for Islamic Reform, outside the conference, demanding widespread reforms including the removal of the House of Sa'ud. Reports indicated that around 150 people were arrested the following day in connection with the demonstration. In November 2003 King Fahd issued a decree widening the legislative power of the Majlis. Under the new regulations, the Majlis was to be allowed to propose new laws and amendments to existing legislation without first asking permission from the King. In addition, the Council of Ministers was to be obliged to return laws to the Majlis for amendment should there be disagreement on an issue. (Under the previous system,

SAUDI ARABIA

Introductory Survey

whereby the Majlis was a purely advisory body, the matter would be resolved by the King.) In April 2005 a royal decree increased the membership of the Majlis to 150; the expansion prompted renewed demands for the introduction of a partially elected membership.

In February 2004 a reported 251 *Hajj* pilgrims died and some 244 others were injured in a stampede close to the Jamarat Bridge in Mina, near Mecca. Some 345 pilgrims were killed and a further 289 were injured in another stampede near the foot of the bridge in January 2006. Amid growing concerns among the Saudi authorities about safety during the *Hajj*, it was subsequently announced that the Jamarat Bridge area was to be restructured at a cost of some US $1,400m.; the project was expected to be completed in late 2009.

In January 2005 15 people were sentenced to short prison sentences and 150–200 lashes each for taking part in an anti-monarchy demonstration in December 2004. Three Saudi reformists were sentenced to terms of imprisonment ranging from six to nine years in May 2005 for having appealed for the establishment of a constitutional monarchy, but were pardoned in October. In the same month the Government announced the establishment of a human rights watchdog headed by Turki ibn Khalid as-Sudairi, who would be given the equivalent rank to that of a government minister. Nevertheless, pressure for real liberalization, from both inside and outside the administration, was limited.

The first stage of the elections for 178 municipal authorities in all 13 of the kingdom's provinces took place on 10 February 2005 in Riyadh, having been postponed from September 2004; disappointingly for reformists, suffrage was not extended to women. In excess of 1,800 candidates stood for the 592 contested seats in the 178 councils; however, reportedly only about one-quarter of eligible voters in the capital had registered for the elections. Some analysts attributed this apathy to public dissatisfaction with the magnitude of the legislative reforms, which were widely seen merely as token measures. The second phase of the elections took place in the Eastern, Aseer, Jazan, Najran and al-Baha provinces on 3 March. According to the local chamber of commerce, only around 12% of the local male population in the Eastern province had registered to vote. The final phase, in the northern border provinces, was held on 21 April. Nationally, Islamist candidates secured a comfortable majority of the council seats. Later in the year women were allowed to campaign openly for elected positions on the 18-member board of the Jeddah Chamber of Commerce and Industry; two women secured seats on the board. In December a female candidate secured an elected position on the 10-member board of the Saudi Engineers' Council.

In May 2005 the increasingly frail King Fahd was declared to have been admitted to hospital in Riyadh suffering from pneumonia. The King died on 1 August and was succeeded by his half-brother, Crown Prince Abdullah, also aged 84, who had been the de facto ruler of the kingdom since King Fahd suffered a stroke in 1995. The Second Deputy Prime Minister, Minister of Defence and Civil Aviation and Inspector General, Prince Sultan ibn Abd al-Aziz, a full brother of King Fahd and also in his eighties, was named as the new Crown Prince. The Council of Ministers remained essentially unchanged; in accordance with the Constitution, King Abdullah assumed the role of Prime Minister and the Crown Prince was appointed Deputy Prime Minister. No replacement was named for the position of Second Deputy Prime Minister (until March 2009—see below), which increased the speculation surrounding the succession to the throne after Crown Prince Sultan. In October 2005 it was announced that a National Security Council (NSC), chaired by King Abdullah, was to be established. Among its extensive powers, the NSC was to: have the power to declare states of emergency and war; be given control over diplomatic relations; and be tasked with combating public corruption and mismanagement. In December the Crown Prince announced that popular elections to the Majlis were not necessary on the basis that its existing members were highly capable; he claimed, however, not to be opposed to legislative elections in principle.

In May 2006 the Ministry of the Interior announced that the authority of the national religious police force (the *mutawwa'in*)—under the control of the Commission for the Promotion of Virtue and the Prevention of Vice—was to be reduced: those arrested on suspicion of moral offences were henceforth to be tried by a public prosecutor. On 20 October a constitutional amendment—first proposed by King Abdullah while he was still Crown Prince—was adopted that removed the monarch's power to choose his successor. Following the forthcoming accession to the throne of Crown Prince Sultan, subsequent heirs were to be elected by the Bay'ah Council (comprising senior members of the royal family). In May 2007 the Crown Prince stated that in the future it was intended that one-third of Saudi government posts would be allocated to women. Following Saudi Arabia's accession to the World Trade Organization (WTO, see p. 410) in December 2005, in October 2007 King Abdullah issued a royal decree allowing for the creation of a supreme court in Riyadh and special tribunals intended to settle commercial and labour grievances, as well as the introduction of appeal courts in each of the country's 13 regions, which were to be granted the legal authority to overrule the judgments of lower courts. The new Judiciary Law also included provision for the modernization of the judicial system. In March 2008 the Minister of Commerce and Industry, Dr Hashem ibn Abdullah Yamani, resigned; he was replaced by Abdullah ibn Ahmad Zainal Alireza shortly afterwards.

In February 2007 nine political activists, who were believed to be preparing to launch a reformist political party, were arrested and subsequently held without trial; they remained in custody in late 2008. One of the reformists pardoned in October 2005 (see above), Abdullah al-Hamed, received a six-month prison sentence in November 2007, having been convicted of encouraging women to demonstrate against the arrest of their relatives in 2004, as part of a large security operation by the authorities against alleged Islamist militants in the kingdom. In May 2008 Matruk al-Faleh, another of the pardoned reformists, was arrested on unknown charges, while acting as legal representative for al-Hamed. After almost eight months in custody without being charged, al-Faleh was released in January 2009. An author of a popular pro-reform website, Fouad al-Farhan, who had written about the issue of political prisoners, was released without charge in April 2008 after five months' imprisonment. These cases provoked persistent protests from domestic and foreign human rights activists throughout 2008. Meanwhile, in April 2008 a report by US-based Human Rights Watch urged the Saudi authorities to reform their policies of sex segregation and male guardianship over women, which, it claimed, resulted in serious infringements of Saudi women's human rights, noting that Saudi women require the consent of a male guardian in order to work, travel, receive health care or avail of public services.

Evidence of King Abdullah's commitment to gradual social and political reform was seen in his patronage of several inter-faith and inter-cultural forums in 2008. In June the King inaugurated the International Islamic Conference for Dialogue in Mecca. The conference, organized by the Muslim World League and attended by some 600 senior Muslim clerics and world leaders, was established to foster co-operation and understanding between Muslims world-wide, including between Sunnis and Shi'as. In a conciliatory gesture, King Abdullah (a Sunni Muslim) entered the opening ceremony hand-in-hand with the former Iranian President, Ali Akbar Rafsanjani (a Shi'a Muslim). Then, in July, the King hosted a three-day inter-faith conference in Madrid, Spain, attended by almost 300 religious, political and cultural leaders from 50 countries, including Jews, Muslims, Christians, Hindus and Buddhists. King Abdullah also sponsored a UN 'Culture of Peace' conference in November, in New York, USA, which was attended by numerous world leaders. The stated aim of the conference was to promote understanding and communication between different cultures and religions and, in doing so, to facilitate the resolution of political conflicts. In one of the meeting's more significant speeches, Israeli President Shimon Peres addressed King Abdullah directly and praised his contribution to the Middle East peace process.

In September 2008 Human Rights Watch published a report criticizing the 'systematic discrimination' experienced by the Shi'a minority in Saudi Arabia (which constitutes an estimated 10% of the population), particularly in the areas of government employment, the judicial system, education and religious freedom. Evidence of sectarian tensions within the kingdom surfaced in February 2009, when violence broke out between Shi'a pilgrims from the Eastern Province and members of the *mutawwa'in* near the tomb of the Prophet Muhammad in Medina. Sporadic clashes occurred over several days, leading to numerous injuries and the arrests of several pilgrims. Following the incidents, each side accused the other of provoking the violence. Two rallies protesting against the treatment of the pilgrims were held near Al-Qatif in the Eastern Province. In early March, after receiving a delegation of Shi'a leaders, King Abdullah announced the release from custody of 38 Shi'a detainees.

King Abdullah implemented an extensive government reorganization in February 2009—his first since acceding to the throne in 2005—effecting wide-ranging changes at senior level throughout the kingdom's administrative, legal and education systems. Dr Abdullah ibn Muhammad ibn Ibrahim ash-Sheikh, hitherto Minister of Justice, was appointed Chairman of the Majlis ash-Shoura, while Dr Muhammad ibn Abd al-Karim ibn Abd al-Aziz al-Eissa, an official at the Grievances Court, was accorded the justice portfolio. Prince Faisal ibn Abdullah ibn Muhammad as-Sa'ud became Minister of Education, replacing Dr Abdullah ibn Salih ibn Ubayd; Dr Hamad ibn Abdullah al-Mane was succeeded as Minister of Health by renowned surgeon Dr Abdullah ibn Abd al-Aziz ar-Rabea; and Dr Abd al-Aziz ibn Mohi ed-Din Khoja, hitherto ambassador to Lebanon, replaced Dr Iyad ibn Amin Madani as Minister of Culture and Information. In a move that gained widespread international media coverage, Nora bint Abdullah al-Fayez, hitherto an official at the Institute of Public Administration, was appointed Deputy Minister for Girls' Education, the first ever ministerial-rank appointment for a woman in the kingdom. The outgoing Chairman of the Majlis, Dr Salih ibn Humayd, was installed as the new Chairman of the Supreme Council of Justice, the most senior post in the judiciary, replacing Sheikh Salih bin Muhammad al-Luhaidan, who had held the post since the mid-1980s. Sheikh al-Luhaidan, a staunchly conservative religious cleric who was extremely influential in Saudi society, had provoked domestic and international dismay when he issued a *fatwa* (edict) in September 2008 that described as lawful the killing of the owners of satellite television channels that broadcast 'depraved' programmes, such as soap operas and game shows, during Ramadan; channels targeted by his disapproval included those owned by members of the Saudi royal family. In another notable change to the conservative establishment, Sheikh Ibrahim al-Ghaith, President of the Commission for the Promotion of Virtue and the Prevention of Vice, was replaced by a more moderate scholar, Sheikh Abd al-Aziz al-Humayun. Several clerics were appointed to a restructured Council of Ulema, which, for the first time, included representatives of all four schools of Sunni religious thought; however, Shi'ite clerics were still excluded. Further changes included a new Governor at the Saudi Arabian Monetary Agency; a new Commander of Land Forces; several new advisers at the Royal Court; and appointments to several prominent judicial posts. Most of the new appointments were expected to facilitate the King's programme of gradual reform and modernization, and several analysts suggested that the reorganization constituted the most progressive development in the kingdom's recent political history. In late March the King appointed his half-brother Prince Nayef ibn Abd al-Aziz as-Sa'ud, Minister of the Interior since 1975, as Second Deputy Prime Minister; vacant since King Abdullah's accession in 2005, the position had previously been held by the heir to the throne, Crown Prince Sultan, now First Deputy Prime Minister.

From the mid-1990s numerous bombings and terrorist attacks, often targeted against foreign civilians, took place in Saudi Arabia. In November 1995 a car bomb exploded outside the offices of the Saudi Arabian National Guard in Riyadh, which was being used by US civilian contractors to train Saudi personnel. Seven foreign nationals (including five US citizens) were killed in the explosion, responsibility for which was claimed by several organizations, including the Islamic Movement for Change, which earlier in the year had warned that it would initiate attacks if non-Muslim Western forces did not withdraw from the Gulf region. In May 1996 four Saudi nationals were executed, having been convicted of involvement in the attack.

In June 1996 19 US military personnel were killed, and as many as 400 others (including 147 Saudi, 118 Bangladeshi and 109 US citizens) were injured, when an explosive device attached to a petroleum tanker was detonated outside a military housing complex in al-Khobar, near Dhahran. By late 1996 there was speculation that the investigating authorities were holding Saudi Shi'a groups with possible links to Iran responsible for the atrocity, rather than the Sunni extremist factions that were widely blamed for the November 1995 bombing. The Iranian Government, however, repeatedly denied any involvement in the incident. In March 1997 the Canadian intelligence service announced the detention of Hani Abd ar-Rahim as-Sayegh, a Saudi Shi'a Muslim implicated in the al-Khobar attack, who was alleged to have links with the militant Hezbollah. As-Sayegh was extradited from Canada to stand trial in the USA, but in September US officials announced that there was insufficient evidence to secure a conviction. In May 1998 Saudi Arabia's Minister of the Interior stated that there was no indication of a foreign role in the bombing, despite continuing US assertions of Iranian involvement. In October 1999 as-Sayegh was extradited from the USA to Saudi Arabia, shortly after the Saudi Minister of the Interior stated that the country's security services possessed information regarding his involvement in the attack. Several Saudi nationals were arrested in January 2001 in connection with the bombing. In June US investigators indicted 14 individuals on charges relating to the explosion, although three of them remained at large in June 2002 when the Saudi authorities announced that sentences had been imposed on a number of the detainees. Meanwhile, as-Sayegh remained in custody in Saudi Arabia.

In October 2000 a Saudi Arabian Airlines passenger flight, en route from Jeddah to the United Kingdom, was hijacked by two armed Saudi nationals. The aircraft finally landed in the Iraqi capital, Baghdad, where the hijackers (who were reportedly protesting against human rights abuses in Saudi Arabia and the presence of US and British troops on Saudi territory) were detained by the Iraqi authorities. One British national died and three were injured in November, as a result of two separate car bomb attacks in Riyadh. No group claimed responsibility for the blasts, although they were initially believed to have been perpetrated by militant Islamists in protest at the role of Western states in the Israeli–Palestinian crisis. In December it was reported that a US citizen was among several foreign nationals arrested for questioning in relation to the bombings; Saudi officials suggested that the attacks may not have been politically motivated. A third bomb was detonated in al-Khobar in that month, and was followed by several more attacks in 2001. In February four expatriates (three British nationals and a Belgian) were detained by the Saudi authorities. Saudi television subsequently broadcast alleged confessions by the three British men relating to their involvement in the November bomb explosions, an admission punishable by the death penalty. By August three more Britons had been detained and their alleged confessions broadcast on Saudi television. The confessions, however, were later withdrawn amid allegations that the accused had been tortured.

In December 2002 one of four British nationals who had in December 2000 been sentenced to 12 years' imprisonment for the al-Khobar bombing admitted responsibility for the attack as part of a wider bombing campaign, which was said to be related to gang warfare over illegal trade in alcohol. (The man's family claimed that his confession had been extracted under torture and that Islamist dissidents were responsible for the bombings.) Meanwhile, another Briton was detained (but not charged) in November 2002 for the alleged murder of a German national in a car bomb attack in September. A total of six Britons were convicted in connection with the bombing campaign (two were sentenced to death; the remainder were given prison terms), although in February 2003 a report by the Special Rapporteur of the UN Commission on Human Rights on the independence of judges and lawyers, which cited 'substantial procedural irregularities' and noted that the men's descriptions of torture were 'consistent', cast considerable doubt on the validity of their trials. (In May one of the men was released from prison.) In August the six Britons, the Belgian and the British expatriate arrested in November 2002 for the killing of the German national were released, having been granted a royal pardon; the decision was seen as a tacit admission by the authorities that militant Islamists were the more likely perpetrators of the recent wave of bombings. Following the murders of a British defence contractor in February 2003 and of two North Americans in March, fears of intensified attacks against Westerners proved well-founded when a series of co-ordinated suicide attacks devastated an expatriate housing compound in Riyadh on 12 May (see below).

Saudi Arabia severed diplomatic relations with the Taliban regime in Afghanistan in September 2001, in response to the suicide attacks on the mainland USA. Saudi Arabia was one of only three countries (along with Pakistan and the United Arab Emirates—UAE) to have recognized the Taliban administration in Afghanistan. Although the USA's principal suspect in the attacks, Osama bin Laden (who was at that time based in Afghanistan), was born to a wealthy Saudi Arabian family, the Saudi authorities emphasized that bin Laden had been exiled since 1991 and his nationality revoked because of his subversive activities against the royal family. It was later revealed that 15 of the 19 hijackers were also of Saudi descent (although many of the identities were forged or stolen). Visiting

Washington, DC, shortly after the attacks, Saudi Arabia's Minister of Foreign Affairs stated that he had conveyed to the US Secretary of State, Colin Powell, the support of the Saudi people for efforts to eliminate terrorism. Saudi Arabia also agreed to investigate alleged Saudi funding of bin Laden's al-Qa'ida (Base) network, said to be raised through certain charitable organizations and individual donations. However, the Saudi regime, under pressure from internal Islamist groups implacably opposed to the US military presence on Saudi territory and to any military action against another Islamic state, subsequently refused permission for the use of its airbases for military action against Afghanistan (although an air 'command and control' base in the kingdom was made available to support the military operation).

Following the launch of military attacks against Afghanistan by the US-led 'coalition against terror' in October 2001, the USA briefly closed its embassy in Saudi Arabia because of fear of reprisals. Later that month Crown Prince Abdullah accused the US media of conspiring to damage Saudi Arabia's reputation following the publication of articles highly critical of Saudi Arabia's perceived lack of co-operation after the September attacks. Although official statements by the US Administration continued to praise the Saudi regime, rumours of a deterioration in their relationship persisted. In January 2002 the Saudi authorities asked for the return of all Saudi citizens (reported to number more than 100 detainees), captured in Afghanistan while apparently fighting for the Taliban, who were imprisoned at Camp X-Ray, Guantánamo Bay, Cuba. This request was denied by the US authorities, but in June a delegation of Saudi government officials was reported to have been allowed access to the Saudi prisoners.

Relations between Saudi Arabia and the USA were placed under renewed strain in August 2002, after a group representing 900 relatives of victims of the September 2001 attacks filed a civil suit in Washington, DC, against senior Saudi ministers and institutions (and the Government of Sudan) seeking compensation amounting to US $1,000,000m. for their alleged funding of al-Qa'ida activities. Saudi investors reacted angrily to the suit, threatening to withdraw from the USA some $750,000m. in Saudi investments. In late 2002 Saudi Arabia was criticized by the USA for ignoring the funding of alleged terrorist organizations by Saudi nationals, and in November US media reports claimed that a charitable donation from the Saudi royal family had assisted two hijackers responsible for the suicide attacks on the USA. The allegations were strenuously denied by the Saudi authorities, and the US Administration was swift to defend the role Saudi Arabia had played in President George W. Bush's 'war on terror'. Nevertheless, it emerged that the US authorities were investigating the affairs of a number of wealthy Saudis in connection with alleged sponsorship of Islamist extremists, including al-Qa'ida. Saudi Arabia countered that it was being unfairly maligned, reiterating that it had begun auditing all charitable organizations operating in the country and that it had frozen three bank accounts allegedly linked to radical Islamist groups. Also in November the Saudi authorities, hitherto reluctant to admit to an al-Qa'ida presence in the country, conceded that some 100 Saudis had been detained under suspicion of involvement with the organization and that a further 700 people had been questioned. The Minister of the Interior, Prince Nayef ibn Abd al-Aziz as-Sa'ud, subsequently confirmed that 90 suspects were referred for trial in February 2003, while 250 people remained under investigation.

Despite the Saudi–US tensions, in September 2002, following intense pressure from the USA and the United Kingdom, the Saudi Minister of Foreign Affairs indicated that Saudi Arabia might be prepared to approve the use of military bases in Saudi Arabia for a future US-led attack on the regime of Saddam Hussain in Iraq. However, he emphasized that Saudi co-operation would only be forthcoming if the Iraqi authorities continued to reject UN resolutions demanding the unconditional return of weapons inspectors to Iraq and if such a military undertaking was to be conducted under UN auspices. It was established in December that the highly equipped Prince Sultan airbase would be made available to the US military, and that, although combat aircraft would not be allowed to fly offensive missions from the base with the primary aim of bombing Iraqi targets, aircraft launched from Iraqi soil would be permitted to open fire or release bombs in self-defence. In January 2003 Saudi Arabia attempted to secure support for a plan to persuade Saddam Hussain to relinquish power and go into exile in order to avert a US-led war to oust his regime. In the following month, however, as conflict appeared increasingly inevitable, the Saudi authorities deployed warships, troops and military helicopters to Kuwait, in order to strengthen the emirate's defences. In late April, after most of the USA's principal military objectives in Iraq had been achieved, it was announced that all but 400 of the 5,000 US military personnel in the country were to be withdrawn from Saudi Arabia by the end of August. Those troops that remained were to assist in training the Saudi armed forces. (Saudi Arabia had also advocated a diplomatic solution to the 1997–98 crisis regarding access to Iraqi sites by UN weapons inspectors. However, although Saudi officials had stated in February 1998 that they would not allow the USA to use Saudi territory as a base for air-strikes against Iraq, it was later claimed that discreet support had been given, including the use of Saudi bases.)

On 12 May 2003 suicide bomb attacks on three expatriate residential compounds in Riyadh killed 34 people. The Minister of Foreign Affairs indicated that 19 people, including 17 Saudis, were believed to have been responsible for the attacks. The bombings, widely held to be the work of al-Qa'ida, provoked further US criticism of Saudi security measures, and led to the withdrawal of most of the US diplomats stationed in the kingdom. It emerged after the attacks that the Saudi authorities had made an unsuccessful attempt to apprehend the perpetrators in the week prior to 12 May. The Saudi leadership responded to the bombings by acknowledging more openly that the threat presented by al-Qa'ida was indeed serious and pledged to take effective action against the terrorist network, including those fundamentalist Islamic figures suspected of converting Saudis to al-Qa'ida's cause. In August the Crown Prince announced that the kingdom was engaged in a 'decisive battle' against terrorism, and throughout mid-2003 security forces intensified their campaign against militants, in particular against those linked to the recent suicide bombings.

In total, between 12 May 2003 and late October, at least 600 suspected militant Islamists were arrested, 70–90 of whom were charged, and more than 2,000 people were interrogated. In addition, in June some 1,000 Muslim clergy were suspended and ordered to undergo retraining aimed at eliminating Islamist militancy from the profession. Despite these measures, the terrorist violence reached new levels of intensity from late 2003. On 8 November al-Qa'ida apparently struck again when 17 people were killed and more than 120 others were injured in a suicide attack on a housing complex, mostly populated by Arab expatriates, in Riyadh. In December the Government stated that, according to DNA evidence, two Saudi nationals had carried out the 8 November suicide bombing.

On 21 April 2004 a car bomb exploded close to one of the headquarters of Riyadh's security services, killing five people and wounding up to 150. A militant Islamist group called the al-Haramain Brigades (alleged to have links to al-Qa'ida) claimed responsibility for the attack, which was regarded as the first direct assault on the Saudi regime. On 1 May gunmen in the Red Sea port of Yanbu killed at least one Saudi and five Western petroleum industry workers. On 29 May an attack by a minimum of four militants against a compound housing oil workers at al-Khobar resulted in the deaths of three Saudis and 19 expatriate workers. The compound was eventually surrounded by Saudi police, which resulted in a 25-hour siege. Despite an attempt by security forces to storm the compound, three of the attackers managed to escape. It was alleged that the militants had agreed a deal with police officers sympathetic to al-Qa'ida, an accusation that was angrily denied by the Saudi ambassador to the United Kingdom, Prince Turki al-Faisal. On 2 June two of those responsible for the atrocity were reported to have been killed by Saudi forces near Mecca. One of the men was believed to be Abd ar-Rahman Muhammad Yazji, one of the kingdom's most wanted militants. On 23 June, during a public address broadcast on Saudi television, the Crown Prince announced that a dozen named individuals with alleged ties to al-Qa'ida would not face the death penalty should they surrender to the security forces within one month. The Saudi authorities were particularly keen to obtain the surrender of Saleh Muhammad al-Oufi, regarded as the overall leader of al-Qa'ida in the kingdom following the death of Abd al-Aziz al-Muqrin in a police raid in June. It was, however, reported on 1 November that al-Qa'ida had appointed Saud bin Hamoud al-Otaibi as the new leader of its Saudi network; some commentators presumed that this confirmed suspicions that al-Oufi had been killed by security forces in July. In February 2005 the Government launched a national awareness campaign to mobilize people against militant activity.

SAUDI ARABIA

Although relations remained cool, Saudi Arabia was keen to improve its ties with the USA. On 28 July 2004, during a visit to Jeddah by Secretary of State Powell, Crown Prince Abdullah raised the possibility of Saudi Arabia taking a leading role in the formation of a Muslim security force for Iraq. Meanwhile, Saudi Arabia and Iraq announced that their embassies in Baghdad and Riyadh, respectively, would be reopened for the first time since 1990. In mid-2004 the deteriorating domestic security situation reportedly led some US companies to scale back their operations in the kingdom. In December seven expatriates and five Saudis died when gunmen attacked the US consulate in Jeddah. Significant militant activity and regular reprisals from security forces continued into early 2006, including an attempted suicide bombing on 24 February at the strategically important Abqaiq oil facility, which produces some 4% of the kingdom's petroleum output. Four suspected al-Qa'ida operatives were killed in government reprisals three days later.

In February 2006, following the victory of the Islamic Resistance Movement (Hamas) in the Palestinian legislative elections of the previous month, the Saudi Government incurred US displeasure when it refused to support a US-led plan to deny regional aid to the new Hamas-led administration. During 2007 and early 2008 Saudi Arabia continued to play a mediatory role in both the dispute between the rival Palestinian factions Fatah and Hamas—particularly following Hamas's takeover of the Gaza Strip in June 2007—and the negotiations between the various feuding parties in Lebanon following that country's failure to elect a successor to President Emile Lahoud. Meanwhile, during a visit to Riyadh in November 2006, US Vice-President Dick Cheney was reportedly warned by King Abdullah that the Saudi Government would lend its support to the Sunni Muslims in the event of a US military withdrawal from Iraq; however, the comments were dismissed by the Bush Administration. In the following month Prince Turki al-Faisal, who had been transferred from the United Kingdom to the post of Saudi ambassador to the USA just 15 months previously, abruptly announced his resignation, providing a stark contrast to his immediate predecessor, who had remained in the post for over two decades; the reason behind al-Faisal's decision was uncertain. During a wider tour of the Middle East in January 2008, US President Bush visited Riyadh, where he reiterated his intention to pursue a controversial arms agreement with the Saudi Government, at an estimated cost of US $20,000m.; the deal formed part of a broader package of US military aid to its allies in the Gulf region aimed at countering any increased Iranian military strength. Bush's visit to Riyadh was, however, marred by Saudi demands that the US Administration hand over to the kingdom 13 of its citizens currently being held in the US detention camp at Guantánamo Bay.

Meanwhile, in June 2006 Saudi security forces killed six suspected members of al-Qa'ida when they raided a property in Riyadh. In the same month the Saudi authorities announced that 42 people had been detained on suspicion of involvement in militant Islamism during the previous few months. In August it was announced that more than 700 alleged al-Qa'ida sympathizers had been released after undergoing a 'correction' programme intended to uproot their belief in Islamist fundamentalism. In October the Deputy Minister of the Interior announced that trials of suspected Islamist militants in Islamic courts had commenced and that many defendants had already been sentenced and 'finished with'; no confirmation or denial was offered as to whether this meant that some had been executed. In what was described by the Saudi authorities as a terrorist attack, and the first attack resulting in foreign fatalities since 2004, three French nationals were shot dead near the town of Tabuk reportedly while travelling on a pilgrimage to Mecca in February 2007; a fourth died later in hospital from injuries sustained in the ambush. In the same month Saudi security forces detained several people on suspicion of fund-raising on behalf of foreign terrorist organizations, and in April it was reported that a further 172 people had been arrested for allegedly plotting attacks against public figures, oil refineries and military targets in Saudi Arabia and other neighbouring countries. In an effort to ensure that Saudi oil installations were protected from the threat of terrorist attacks, it was revealed in August that the Government had begun to establish an Industrial Security Force of some 35,000 personnel specifically charged with providing security at the country's petroleum facilities; by mid-November an estimated 9,000 members had been deployed, and a further 8,000 were expected to be deployed each year. In late November the Ministry of the Interior declared that 208 suspected al-Qa'ida-affiliated militants (including a number of other Arab nationals) had been detained in recent months, again for allegedly planning attacks against various Saudi targets. A reported 28 people, most of whom were Saudi citizens, were arrested in late December, on suspicion of preparing terrorist actions in the holy cities of Mecca and Medina during the *Hajj*. The detainees were alleged members of an organization taking its instructions from Ayman az-Zawahiri, believed to be the deputy leader of al-Qa'ida; by March 2008 Saudi security forces had reportedly dismantled the unit. The Ministry of the Interior announced in June that 701 suspected militants had been arrested thus far that year (although 181 had later been released owing to lack of evidence against them), and in October that 991 detainees had been charged with involvement in more than 30 terrorist attacks in the kingdom over the preceding five years, in which 164 had been killed and more than 1,000 injured. Nevertheless, throughout 2007 and 2008 the frequency of violent attacks was clearly declining and the kingdom's policies, which included stronger security and intelligence measures, as well as the retraining of clerics and the re-education, and hopefully deradicalization, of convicted militants, appeared to be having some success.

Despite the apparent effectiveness of domestic counter-terrorism measures, the activities of Saudi militants outside the kingdom remained a source of considerable concern in early 2009. In late January two Saudi nationals appeared in an al-Qa'ida video posted on a jihadist website. Both men were former detainees at Guantánamo Bay who had been released in 2007 and, despite undergoing the Saudi rehabilitation programme, had absconded to Yemen and allegedly resumed their jihadist activities. Saeed ash-Shihri, who was suspected by US investigators of involvement in the bombing of the US embassy in the Yemeni capital, San'a, in September 2008 (see the chapter on Yemen), was described in the video as deputy leader of al-Qa'ida in Yemen; Muhammad al-Oufi was described as a field commander. In early February 2009 the Saudi authorities released a list of 85 wanted alleged militants living abroad; 83 were Saudi nationals, two were Yemeni, and all were suspected of illegal activities with various al-Qa'ida-affiliated groups abroad and of plotting attacks against targets within Saudi Arabia. The list, which was subsequently distributed by the International Criminal Police Organization (INTERPOL), included several former Guantánamo detainees. Later that month al-Oufi reportedly surrendered to the security forces in Yemen and was handed over to the Saudi authorities.

In October 2008 the Saudi Minister of Foreign Affairs, Prince Sa'ud al-Faisal as-Sa'ud, confirmed reports that the kingdom had hosted talks, in Mecca during the previous month, between representatives of the Afghan Government and Taliban insurgents. However, spokespersons for all sides denied that the discussions, apparently initiated at the request of the President of Afghanistan, Hamid Karzai, amounted to peace negotiations.

In September 2000, meanwhile, Iraq accused Saudi Arabia and Kuwait of inflicting (through the maintenance of the sanctions regime) suffering on the Iraqi population, and alleged that Saudi Arabia was appropriating Iraqi petroleum transported under the oil-for-food programme. Saudi Arabia, encouraged by the mediation of the League of Arab States (the Arab League, see p. 344), indicated at the beginning of 2002 that it was ready for a cautious rapprochement with Iraq. In October the border crossing from Saudi Arabia to Iraq was reopened, providing a fifth land route for Iraqi trade under the UN oil-for-food arrangement. Following the US-led military campaign to remove Saddam Hussain's regime in Iraq in 2003 (see above), Saudi Arabia announced its intention to reopen its embassy in Baghdad. (Diplomatic relations between Iraq and Saudi Arabia had been severed in 1991, following Iraq's invasion of Kuwait.) In March 2007 King Abdullah publicly emphasized Saudi opposition to foreign intervention in Iraqi domestic affairs, insisting that Iraq's sovereignty and independence must be safeguarded. However, by early 2009 a Saudi embassy had yet to be opened in Baghdad, with the kingdom's authorities citing security concerns as the reason for the continuing delay. Meanwhile, a contract to construct a 900-km 'security fence' along Saudi Arabia's border with Iraq, at a cost of some US $900m., was awarded to a joint Saudi-European consortium in June 2008. The fence, which would incorporate sophisticated surveillance equipment, represented the first phase of a planned 6,500-km barrier along all the kingdom's borders. The contract for the second phase of the project, which would complete the barrier, was awarded to the same Saudi-European consortium in February 2009 and was estimated to be worth $2,600m.

Relations between Saudi Arabia and Iran, which were particularly strained by suspicions of Iranian involvement in the 1996 al-Khobar bombing (see above), improved considerably following the election of Muhammad Khatami to the Iranian presidency in 1997. Co-operation was notably strengthened following the September 2001 attacks on New York and Washington, DC, as Saudi Arabia and Iran sought to counter the emergence of anti-Islamic sentiment in the West. The election of Mahmoud Ahmadinejad to the Iranian presidency in June 2005 proved somewhat damaging to bilateral relations, however, with the Saudi Government becoming increasingly concerned by what it perceived to be Ahmadinejad's destabilizing effect on the region. Nevertheless, in January 2007 the two states were reported to be conducting negotiations to seek an end to the political impasse in Lebanon (q.v.). Furthermore, President Ahmadinejad was unexpectedly granted an audience with King Abdullah in Riyadh in March, which was widely seen as an implicit snub by the Saudi monarch of the US policy of exclusion towards Iran. The two leaders concurred that the greatest danger facing Muslims world-wide was the deliberate exacerbation by unnamed aggressors of divisions between the Sunni and Shi'ite factions. However, despite an exchange of public expressions of goodwill between King Abdullah and Ahmadinejad, the visit did not appear to have resulted in the establishment of any joint initiatives. Ahmadinejad returned to Saudi Arabia in December to participate, at the King's invitation, in the *Hajj* pilgrimage to Mecca, becoming the first President of the Islamic Republic of Iran to do so. Notwithstanding public displays of harmony, bilateral relations remained somewhat adversarial throughout 2008 and early 2009. In May 2008 Saudi Minister of Foreign Affairs Prince Sa'ud al-Faisal, referring to Iran's support for Hezbollah's recent military clashes with government forces in Lebanon, accused Iran of inciting sectarian conflict and interfering in the affairs of an independent state. In March 2009, at a meeting of Arab foreign ministers, Prince al-Faisal appealed for a unified Arab strategy in dealing with what he described as the 'Iranian challenge'. Meanwhile, President Ahmadinejad, in January 2009, appeared to accuse Saudi Arabia of complicity in the killing of Palestinians in the Israeli military operation in Gaza in late December 2008 and early January 2009 (see below), alleging that the kingdom was silent in the face of Israel's aggression and urging Saudi Arabia to end its trade ties with the Jewish state. None the less, Iranian Minister of Foreign Affairs Manouchehr Mottaki made an unannounced visit to Riyadh in March and held talks on bilateral relations with King Abdullah and Prince al-Faisal.

In February 2002 Crown Prince Abdullah put forward a proposal, based on the 1981 'Fahd Plan', to end the escalating conflict between Israel and the Palestinians based on the principle of 'land-for-peace'. In return for a collective Arab recognition of the State of Israel, the plan insisted on Israel's complete withdrawal from Arab territories occupied since 1967. The Crown Prince also urged the US Administration to exert pressure on Israel to withdraw its forces from the West Bank. The Saudi peace initiative was unanimously endorsed at a summit conference of the Arab League Council held in March 2002 in Beirut, Lebanon, but was rejected by Israel. During a summit meeting with US President George W. Bush in Crawford, Texas, in April, Crown Prince Abdullah reiterated his call for the USA to restrain Israel's actions against the Palestinians. In March 2007 Riyadh hosted the annual summit meeting of the Arab League Council, at which negotiations were dominated by the Israeli–Palestinian conflict, as well as by the situations in Iraq and Lebanon. The Council reaffirmed its endorsement of the 'land-for-peace' proposal, which had been amassing increasing levels of support, and which Israeli Prime Minister Ehud Olmert had conceded might provide an initial basis for the renewal of formal peace discussions with Arab leaders. A proposed military pact to assist the 22 member states to resolve regional conflicts without the need for external intervention was also discussed. Saudi Arabia participated in the US-sponsored international peace meeting held at Annapolis, Maryland, in November, at which negotiations towards a resolution of the Israeli–Palestinian conflict were officially relaunched.

In response to the military offensive launched by Israel against Hamas targets in the Gaza Strip in late December 2008 (see the chapters on Israel and the Palestinian Autonomous Areas), King Abdullah hosted an emergency GCC summit in Riyadh on 15 January 2009, which focused on seeking an end to the hostilities and on the provision of aid. Meanwhile, Sheikh Hamad bin Khalifa ath-Thani, the Amir of Qatar, planned to convene an emergency Arab League summit in the Qatari capital, Doha, to formulate a unified Arab response to the conflict in Gaza, which by mid-January had reportedly resulted in more than 1,300 Palestinians deaths, with some 5,400 wounded. However, the Saudi King did not send a delegation to the Doha meeting, which was held on 16 January, stating his preference for the forthcoming Arab Economic, Social and Development Summit in Kuwait as a forum for pan-Arab discussions. As a result of the absence of Saudi Arabia, Egypt and others, the Doha summit failed to attain the quorum required to grant the meeting official status. The disagreement over Doha highlighted regional divisions on the subject of Israel and Palestine, with Saudi Arabia and Egypt committed to the principles of the existing peace process and broadly aligned with the USA, while Iran, Qatar and Syria offered support to Hamas and appealed for the severing of ties with Israel. During the scheduled summit in Kuwait, on 19–20 January, King Abdullah hosted a private meeting with the leaders of Egypt, Kuwait, Qatar and Syria, which was heralded as achieving substantial progress towards greater Arab unity. None the less, many commentators noted the lack of a unified Arab political response to events in Gaza.

In December 1994, meanwhile, Yemen accused Saudi Arabia of erecting monitoring posts and constructing roads on Yemeni territory. In January 1995 the two countries failed to renew the 1934 Ta'if agreement (renewable every 20 years), delineating their de facto frontier. Following military clashes between Saudi and Yemeni forces, and intense mediation by Syria, the two sides undertook to halt all military activity in the disputed border area. In February the Saudi and Yemeni Governments signed a memorandum of understanding that reaffirmed their commitment to the legitimacy of the Ta'if agreement and provided for the establishment of six joint committees to delineate the land and sea borders and to develop economic and commercial ties. The two countries signed a border security agreement in July 1996. In May 1998, however, Saudi Arabia invaded the disputed island of Huraym in the Red Sea and was reported to have sent a memorandum to the UN stating that it did not recognize the 1992 border agreement between Yemen and Oman, claiming that parts of the area involved were Saudi Arabian territory. The Saudi objection to the accord was widely believed to be related to its attempts to gain land access to the Arabian Sea, via a corridor between Yemen and Oman, which it had thus far been denied in its negotiations with Yemen.

Yemen submitted a memorandum to the Arab League in July 1998, refuting the Saudi claim to the land and stating that the Saudi protests contravened the Ta'if agreement signed by that country. Further clashes were reported close to the land and sea border between Yemen and Saudi Arabia in June, and in July three Yemeni troops were killed during fighting with a Saudi border patrol on the disputed island of Duwaima in the Red Sea; Saudi Arabia claimed its actions there were in self-defence and that, under the Ta'if agreement, three-quarters of the island was Saudi territory. In January 2000 both countries denied further reports of armed confrontations in the border area, and a meeting of a joint military committee began in San'a in February. In June, during a visit to Saudi Arabia by Yemeni President Ali Abdullah Saleh, a final agreement delineating land and sea borders was signed. As part of the accord, which incorporated the 1934 Ta'if agreement and much of the 1995 memorandum of understanding, both sides agreed to promote economic, commercial and cultural relations, and each undertook not to permit on its territory activities against the other by opposition groups. The agreement did not demarcate sections of the eastern border, and in August 2000 three Saudi border guards and one Yemeni soldier were reportedly killed in border clashes. Nevertheless, the first meeting of the Saudi-Yemen Co-operation Council for more than a decade took place in December; a further meeting followed in June 2001. Meanwhile, it was reported that the withdrawal from the border region of troops of both countries, in accordance with the border agreement, was almost complete. However, relations deteriorated again in early 2004 after the Saudi Government began construction of a 'security fence' along the border that risked violating the border demarcation treaty signed in June 2000. The construction of the barrier reflected a profound lack of trust on the part of the Saudi authorities in Yemen's ability to prevent weapons smugglers from infiltrating Saudi territory. In June 2006 the Saudi and Yemeni ministers responsible for internal affairs signed an agreement on the final demarcation of their shared border.

In September 1992 Qatar accused a Saudi force of attacking a Qatari border post, killing two border guards and capturing a third. As a result, Qatar suspended a 1965 border agreement with Saudi Arabia, which had never been fully ratified. In December 1992, following mediation by President Hosni Mubarak of Egypt, the Qatari Amir, Sheikh Khalifa ath-Thani, signed an agreement in Medina with King Fahd to establish a committee to demarcate the disputed border. In June 1999 officials of the two countries met in Riyadh to sign maps defining their joint border, and an apparently final land and maritime demarcation agreement was signed in Doha in March 2001. The border agreement provided for a joint Saudi-Qatari committee, charged with ensuring full implementation of the 1965 accord. In October 2002 the Saudi ambassador to Qatar was recalled, apparently following broadcasts by the Qatari television news channel Al-Jazeera that were deemed to be critical of the Saudi regime. Despite the 2001 agreement, the border dispute was revived in July 2007, when Saudi Arabia threatened to block a US $3,500m. gas pipeline between Qatar and the UAE, claiming that sections of the undersea pipeline ran through Saudi territory. The Qatari Amir, Sheikh Hamad, visited Jeddah in September for talks on bilateral relations. Sheikh Hamad gave an assurance that Al-Jazeera would not broadcast material that could be regarded as defamatory in respect of Saudi Arabia, in return for which Al-Jazeera would be permitted to establish a presence in the kingdom. Saudi Arabia confirmed the return of its diplomatic envoy to Qatar, and King Abdullah agreed to attend the forthcoming GCC summit in Doha (an invitation he had refused in 2002, when Qatar had last hosted a meeting of the organization). Saudi objections to the Qatar–UAE gas pipeline were also resolved. The new Saudi ambassador to Qatar acceded to his position in March 2008, and relations were further bolstered in that month by an official visit to Qatar by Crown Prince Sultan for talks with the Amir on bilateral ties and other international issues. In July the Qatari and Saudi Governments agreed to resolve the issue of border demarcation and to establish a Joint Co-ordination Council to encourage co-operation in military, industrial, agricultural and energy affairs. A definitive Land and Maritime Border Delimitation Agreement was signed in December, together with various other agreements on bilateral co-operation, at the first meeting of the Saudi-Qatari Joint Co-ordination Council, and was registered with the UN in March 2009.

In July 1995 officials from Saudi Arabia and Oman signed documents to demarcate their joint border. In March 1999 Saudi Arabia held talks with Iran in an effort to mediate in its dispute with the UAE over the Tunb islands. Following a statement by the GCC condemning both Iran's recent military exercises near the islands and its claim to them and emphasizing UAE sovereignty of the islands, the Iranian President cancelled a planned visit to Saudi Arabia (the visit proceeded in May). Saudi Arabia's rapprochement with Iran had resulted in a deterioration in its relations with the UAE, and in March the UAE boycotted a meeting of GCC ministers responsible for petroleum production in protest at Saudi exploration of an oilfield in disputed territory prior to an agreement being reached. In September 2000 the Saudi Government approved an agreement, signed in July, which ended the long-standing dispute with Kuwait regarding their mutual sea border. Final maps delineating that border were signed by officials from both sides in January 2001.

At a summit meeting of the Arab League Council in March 2003, Libya was strongly critical of Saudi Arabia for hosting US forces on its territory. Relations deteriorated further when, in July 2004, allegations were made in the Saudi-owned pan-Arab daily *al-Sharq al-Aswat* concerning a Libyan plot to assassinate Crown Prince Abdullah. In December Saudi Arabia recalled its ambassador to Tripoli over the alleged conspiracy and expelled the Libyan ambassador to Riyadh from the kingdom. However, the respective embassies remained open during the dispute, and relations were normalized in late 2005.

In 2005 relations deteriorated between Saudi Arabia and three of its Gulf neighbours: Bahrain, Oman and the UAE. Bahrain and Oman had signed free trade agreements with the USA in September 2004 and October 2005, respectively, and in April 2006 the UAE was involved in negotiations with a view to signing a similar accord. Saudi Arabia, which argued that the GCC should negotiate a trade deal as a single body, claimed that the agreements contravened the GCC's external tariff treaty. In December relations with the UAE were further strained by a border dispute relating to the Shaybah oilfield in the Rub al-Khali desert region, which dated back to the 1970s and which formed the focal point of discussions between the UAE President, Sheikh Khalifa bin Zayed an-Nahyan, and the Saudi Minister of the Interior, Prince Nayef ibn Abd al-Aziz as-Sa'ud, in June 2006.

Following the transfer of its ambassador in Damascus to Doha in early 2008, Saudi Arabia declined to appoint a new ambassador to Syria, demonstrating its disapproval at Syria's role in the ongoing political crisis in Lebanon. Saudi relations with Syria remained strained throughout 2008, and the two countries' conflicting interests in the region were highlighted by their divergent responses to the Israeli military offensive in Gaza launched in late December 2008 (see above). However, there were hopes of a rapprochement after Syria and other Arab states held private talks with King Abdullah during the Arab Economic, Social and Development Summit in Kuwait in January 2009. By February unofficial reports suggested that Saudi Arabia might be preparing to appoint a new ambassador to Syria. In early March Minister of Foreign Affairs Prince Sa'ud al-Faisal held talks with Syrian President Bashar al-Assad in Damascus on Arab reconciliation and other regional issues; both sides described the discussions as positive and constructive. On 11 March the King hosted a one-day summit on regional affairs, which was attended by Assad (on his first visit to Saudi Arabia for four years), President Mubarak of Egypt and the Kuwaiti Amir, Sheikh Sabah al-Ahmad al-Jaber as-Sabah. Foremost among the objectives of the summit were the promotion of Arab unity and support for Egyptian-brokered reconciliation talks between the rival Palestinian factions, Fatah and Hamas.

King Abdullah visited China in January 2006—the first such visit by a Saudi monarch since the formal establishment of diplomatic relations in 1990—whereupon he signed a bilateral agreement to co-operate in the petroleum and natural gas sectors. With the deterioration in Saudi-US relations, the kingdom was keen to diversify its international trade, and China, as the world's second largest petroleum consumer, was an ideal candidate for partnership. In the same month Abdullah also became the first Saudi monarch to visit India since 1955. In February 2006 a visit to Pakistan further bolstered traditionally strong bilateral relations, with the signing of five agreements aimed at increasing co-operation on the economy, education, investment, science and technology. In April Crown Prince Sultan embarked upon a tour of the Far East, visiting Japan, Singapore and China. This 'look-east' policy was adopted principally for economic gain, but it also served as a demonstration of Saudi independence from the USA.

In August 2006 Saudi Arabia reached agreement with the United Kingdom regarding the purchase of 72 *Eurofighter Typhoon* military aircraft as part of efforts to establish 'a greater partnership to modernize the Saudi Arabian armed forces'; the deal was confirmed by the Saudi authorities in September 2007. King Abdullah, accompanied by a large delegation of senior Saudi officials, began a high-profile state visit to the United Kingdom in late October, during which protests were held by those angered at what they deemed to be Saudi Arabia's poor record on human rights and curbing Islamist extremism. Early in the following month King Abdullah undertook a landmark visit to the Vatican City, where he became the first Saudi monarch to hold discussions with a Supreme Pontiff of the Roman Catholic Church; the talks with Pope Benedict XVI were reported to have focused on how to promote peace between Christians, Muslims and Jews world-wide and to achieve a just solution to the Israeli–Palestinian conflict. In March 2008 discussions were said to be ongoing between Saudi and Vatican officials concerning the possibility of the first Catholic church being built in the kingdom; however, no agreement had been reached on the issue by early 2009.

Government

Saudi Arabia is an absolute monarchy, with no legislature or political parties. Constitutionally, the King rules in accordance with the *Shari'a*, the sacred law of Islam. He appoints and leads a Council of Ministers, which serves as the instrument of royal authority in both legislative and executive matters. Decisions of the Council are reached by majority vote, but require royal sanction. A Consultative Council (Majlis ash-Shoura) was officially inaugurated in December 1993. Members of the Majlis are chosen by the King. Membership of the Majlis was increased from 60 to 90 in July 1997, to 120 in May 2001 and to 150 in April 2005.

The organs of local government are the General Municipal Councils and the tribal and village councils. A General Municipal Council is established in the towns of Mecca, Medina and Jeddah.

Its members are proposed by the inhabitants and must be approved by the King. Functioning concurrently with each General Municipal Council is a General Administration Committee, which investigates ways and means of executing resolutions passed by the Council. Every village and tribe has a council with the power to enforce regulations; it is composed of the presiding sheikh, his legal advisers and two other prominent personages. A system of provincial government was announced in late 1993 by royal decree: this defined the nature of government for 13 newly created regions, as well as the rights and responsibilities of their governors, and appointed councils of prominent citizens for each region to monitor development and advise the government. Each council was to meet four times a year under the chairmanship of a governor, who would be an emir with ministerial rank. A royal decree, issued in April 1994, further divided the 13 regions into 103 governorates. In October 2003 it was announced that new municipal councils, of which one-half of the membership would be elected by universal suffrage and one-half appointed by the central Government, would be introduced. Municipal elections took place in early 2005 (for further details, see Recent History).

Defence

As assessed at November 2008, the active armed forces totalled an estimated 112,500 men: army 75,000, air force 20,000, navy 13,500 (including 3,000 marines); air defence forces 4,000. There were also paramilitary forces totalling more than 15,500 men, which included a frontier force of 10,500 and a 4,500-strong coastguard. There was a National Guard, comprising 75,000 active personnel and 25,000 tribal levies, and an Industrial Security Force, numbering 9,000, which was established in 2007 to protect petroleum and other important installations; the force was to expand by an additional 8,000 personnel each year, until reaching its maximum intended capacity of 35,000. The Peninsula Shield Force of the Co-operation Council for the Arab States of the Gulf (the Gulf Co-operation Council—GCC), based in Saudi Arabia, comprised some 9,000 troops in 2006; however, plans by the GCC to expand the force to comprise some 22,000 personnel based in the various member states were discussed in 2008. Military service is voluntary. The allocation for defence and security in the budget for 2008 was SR 143,000m.

Economic Affairs

In 2007, according to estimates by the World Bank, Saudi Arabia's gross national income (GNI), measured at average 2005–07 prices, was US $373,491m., equivalent to $15,440 per head (or $22,910 per head on an international purchasing-power parity basis). During 2000–07, it was estimated, the population increased at an average annual rate of 2.3%, while gross domestic product (GDP) per head increased, in real terms, by an average of 1.3% per year. Overall GDP increased, in real terms, at an average annual rate of 3.6% in 2000–07; according to official figures, real GDP increased by 3.4% in 2007 and by a preliminary 4.2% in 2008.

Agriculture (including forestry and fishing) contributed 2.8% of GDP in 2007, according to preliminary figures, and employed 4.7% of the economically active population in that year, according to the International Labour Organization (ILO). The principal crop is wheat, the production of which depends almost entirely on irrigation. Saudi Arabia has exported a large wheat surplus since the late 1980s; however, the kingdom planned gradually to reduce output of the crop (with production scheduled to cease entirely by 2016), owing to the increasing scarcity of water resources. Sorghum, barley, potatoes, tomatoes, watermelons and dates are also significant crops. Saudi Arabia is self-sufficient in many dairy products, and in eggs and broiler chickens. Agricultural GDP increased by an average of 1.3% per year in 2000–07; the sector's GDP increased by an estimated 1.0% in 2007.

Industry (including mining, manufacturing, construction and power) provided 65.1% of GDP in 2007, according to preliminary figures, and employed 19.8% of the active labour force in that year, according to ILO. During 2000–07, it was estimated, industrial GDP increased at an average annual rate of 3.6%; the sector expanded by an estimated 2.9% in 2007.

Mining and quarrying contributed 50.3% of GDP in 2007, according to preliminary figures, but engaged only 1.3% of the employed population in that year, according to ILO. The sector is dominated by petroleum and natural gas, which provided a preliminary 50.0% of GDP in that year. Saudi Arabia remained the world's largest petroleum producer in 2007, and mineral products provided 88.1% of total export revenue in 2007. At the end of 2007 Saudi Arabia's proven recoverable reserves of petroleum were 264,200m. barrels, equivalent to 21.3% of the world's proven oil reserves. Crude petroleum production averaged 10.4m. barrels per day (b/d) in 2007. As a member of the Organization of the Petroleum Exporting Countries (OPEC, see p. 386), Saudi Arabia is subject to production quotas agreed by the Organization's Conference. The Ministry of Petroleum and Mineral Resources announced in early 2007 that it planned to increase oil production capacity from 11.3m. b/d to 12.5m. b/d by the end of 2009. It was reported in April 2008 that the Government had no plans significantly to increase capacity beyond this target. Observers conjectured that Saudi Arabia was not providing accurate information pertaining to its recoverable reserves and, moreover, that the country might not possess sufficient petroleum to meet demand in the long term. Gas reserves, mostly associated with petroleum, totalled 7,170,000m. cu m at the end of 2007. In 2002 the world's largest natural gas plant was opened at Hawiya; the plant, which was the first Saudi project to produce gas not associated with petroleum, was expected to increase the country's production of gas by more than 30%. Further non-associated gas reserves are yet to be fully exploited. Other minerals produced include limestone, gypsum, marble, clay and salt, while there are substantial deposits of phosphates, bauxite, gold and other metals. The GDP of the mining sector increased at an average annual rate of 2.2% in 2000–07; the rate of growth was an estimated 0.2% in 2007.

Manufacturing contributed 9.5% of GDP in 2007, according to preliminary figures, and provided 7.3% of employment in that year, according to ILO. The most important activity is the refining of petroleum, which contributed a preliminary 3.2% of GDP in 2007. The production of petrochemicals, fertilizers, construction materials (particularly steel and cement), and food- and drink-processing are also important activities. Manufacturing GDP increased by an average of 5.9% per year in 2000–07; the GDP of the sector increased by an estimated 6.5% in 2007.

Electrical energy is generated by thermal power stations, using Saudi Arabia's own petroleum resources, although an increasing amount of electricity is now produced in association with sea-water desalination. Electricity expansion projects were planned in the early part of the 21st century to satisfy increased demand.

The services sector contributed 32.1% of GDP in 2007, according to preliminary figures, and engaged 75.5% of the employed labour force in that year, according to ILO. The GDP of the services sector increased by an average of 5.1% per year in 2000–07; the rate of growth was an estimated 5.6% in 2007.

In 2007 Saudi Arabia recorded a visible trade surplus of US $151,547m., and a surplus of $95,080m. on the current account of the balance of payments. In 2007 the principal source of imports (13.6%) was the USA; other important suppliers were the People's Republic of China, Germany and Japan. Japan was the principal market for exports (16.5%) in 2006; other major markets in that year were the USA, the Republic of Korea (South Korea), China and India. (Export data for 2007 appeared to be distorted by the exclusion of petroleum sales to many countries.) In 2007 the dominant exports were mineral products (particularly crude petroleum) and chemical products. The principal imports in that year were machinery and transport equipment, basic manufactures, and food and live animals.

A budgetary surplus of SR 20,000m. was forecast for 2007; however, revised figures indicated a surplus of SR 176,552m. A budget surplus of SR 40,000m. was forecast for 2008. Consumer prices increased by an annual average of 0.9% in 2000–07, and by 4.1% in 2007. The overall unemployment rate was 5.6% in 2007, although for Saudi nationals the rate was higher, at 11.0%. In 2007 non-Saudi nationals comprised an estimated 51.0% of the total labour force, according to official figures. The Government approved legislation in 2005 to reduce the number of foreign workers to 20% of the population by 2015; the new law was also to provide maternity leave rights and childcare facilities, in order to encourage greater female participation in the work-force. Women, including non-Saudi nationals, comprised an estimated 15.4% of the total labour force in 2007, with Saudi women comprising only 8.1% of the total.

In addition to its membership of OPEC, Saudi Arabia is a member of the Islamic Development Bank (see p. 340), and the Organization of Arab Petroleum Exporting Countries (OAPEC, see p. 379). Saudi Arabia is the major aid donor in the region, disbursing loans to developing countries through the Arab Fund for Economic and Social Development (AFESD, see p. 183), the

Arab Bank for Economic Development in Africa (BADEA, see p. 345) and other organizations. The kingdom acceded to the World Trade Organization (WTO, see p. 410) in December 2005. Saudi Arabia is also a member of the Co-operation Council for the Arab States of the Gulf (GCC, see p. 229), which created a unified regional customs tariff in January 2003 and agreed to establish a single market and currency no later than January 2010. The economic convergence criteria for the proposed monetary union were agreed at a heads of state meeting in Abu Dhabi, the United Arab Emirates, in December 2005, and in January 2008 the GCC launched its common market.

Saudi Arabia's prosperity is based on exploitation of its petroleum reserves. Although the country remained the world's largest oil producer at the beginning of the 21st century, and continued to play a crucial role in determining OPEC production levels and thus world prices, the decline in the price of petroleum in the early 1990s caused the Government to seek alternative sources of revenue. Since 2000 the Saudi authorities have aimed to increase private investment and growth in the private and non-oil sectors, and sought to expand employment opportunities for the rapidly expanding Saudi population, most of whom (some 88% in 2008) reside in urban areas. The Manpower Development Fund was launched in April 2002 to promote the 'Saudiization' of the work-force, and the Eighth Five-Year Development Plan (for the period 2005–09) aimed to increase the participation of Saudi women in the labour force. Tourism, regarded as hugely underdeveloped in the kingdom, was one sector that the authorities sought to stimulate. To this end, a Supreme Commission for Tourism was established in 2001 with the primary aim of increasing the number of visitors to the kingdom to 21m. by 2020. The construction of the new King Abdullah Economic City, situated on the west coast between Jeddah and Rabigh, commenced in 2006 and was projected to be fully completed by 2025. A further five 'economic cities' were planned for other regions of the kingdom, as its huge petroleum revenues were utilized to increase private sector growth, establish new industries and create jobs. However, economic diversification was likely significantly to increase domestic energy demand, which—given the growing reliance on petroleum for generating electricity—would diminish resources available for export. The US Energy Information Administration projected in 2007 that one-third of oil produced in Saudi Arabia would be used domestically by 2020. In December 2008 the Ministry of Finance announced the 2009 budget, projecting revenue of SR 410,000m. and expenditure of SR 475,000m., leaving a deficit of SR 65,000m. (around 1.2% of GDP). The kingdom's first forecast fiscal shortfall since 2002 (following a record surplus of SR 590,000m. in 2008, according to revised figures) was explained by anticipated lower petroleum revenues and high public expenditure. The budget assumed a GDP growth rate of around 4.2% in 2009, in spite of the global economic downturn. However, given that much of Europe and the USA had moved into recession by early 2009, demand for Saudi exports was expected to decline. From the end of 2008 and into 2009 the international price of petroleum fell sharply, resulting in significantly lower revenues compared with recent years. Meanwhile, the Government was planning a number of social development projects in 2009, specifically in the education and health sectors, including the second phase of the King Khaled University Medical Complex. The construction sector was also set to benefit indirectly from measures included in the budget. The inflation rate was estimated at an average of 9.9% in 2008 (increasing substantially from 4.1% in 2007), although inflationary pressures began to ease in late 2008, a trend that was expected to continue in 2009. Real GDP grew by 4.2% in 2008, according to provisional official figures.

Education

Elementary, secondary and higher education are available free of charge, but education is not compulsory. Primary education begins at six years of age and lasts for six years. From the age of 12 there are three years of intermediate education, followed by three years of secondary schooling. According to UNESCO estimates, primary enrolment was equivalent to 90.7% of pupils in the relevant age-group in 2004/05; the comparable ratio at the secondary level was 87.6%. The proportion of females enrolled in Saudi Arabian schools increased from 25% of the total number of pupils in 1970 to 47.8% in 2005. In 2006 636,445 students were enrolled in higher education (including postgraduate studies), of whom 217,781 were newly admitted that year. Saudi Arabia had 16 universities in 2006, comprising 362 colleges. The kingdom's first private university, Alfaisal University, developed in partnership with a US technology institute, began operating in October 2008. In 2007 74,462 students were enrolled at the 117 colleges and institutes of the Technical and Vocational Training Corporation. Education was reportedly allocated 24.5% of total expenditure in the 2006 budget, equivalent to SR 87,300m.

Public Holidays

2009: 15–24 September* (Id al-Fitr, end of Ramadan), 23 September (National Day), 22–30 November* (Id al-Adha, Feast of the Sacrifice).

2010: 4–14 September* (Id al-Fitr, end of Ramadan), 23 September (National Day), 11–19 November* (Id al-Adha, Feast of the Sacrifice).

* These holidays are dependent on the Islamic lunar calendar and may vary by one or two days from the dates given.

Weights and Measures

The metric system is in force.

Statistical Survey

Sources (unless otherwise indicated): Central Department of Statistics, Ministry of Economy and Planning, POB 358, University St, Riyadh 11182; tel. (1) 401-3333; fax (1) 401-9300; e-mail info@cds.gov.sa; internet www.cdsi.gov.sa; Saudi Arabian Monetary Agency, *Annual Report* and *Statistical Summary*.

Area and Population

AREA, POPULATION AND DENSITY

Area (sq km)	2,240,000*
Population (census results)	
27 September 1992	16,948,388†
15 September 2004	
Males	12,557,240
Females	10,121,022
Total	22,678,262
Population (official estimates at mid-year)	
2005	23,118,994
2006	23,678,849
2007	24,242,578‡
Density (per sq km) at mid-2007	10.6

* 864,869 sq miles.
† Of the total population at the 1992 census, 12,310,053 (males 6,215,793, females 6,094,260) were nationals of Saudi Arabia, while 4,638,335 (males 3,264,180, females 1,374,155) were foreign nationals.
‡ Comprising an estimated 17,691,336 Saudi nationals and 6,551,242 foreign nationals.

Saudi Arabia-Iraq Neutral Zone: The Najdi (Saudi Arabian) frontier with Iraq was defined in the Treaty of Mohammara in May 1922. Later a Neutral Zone of 7,044 sq km was established adjacent to the western tip of the Kuwait frontier. No military or permanent buildings were to be erected in the zone and the nomads of both countries were to have unimpeded access to its pastures and wells. A further agreement concerning the administration of this zone was signed between Iraq and Saudi Arabia in May 1938. In July 1975 Iraq and Saudi Arabia signed an agreement providing for an equal division of the diamond-shaped zone between the two countries, with the border following a straight line through the zone.

Saudi Arabia-Kuwait Neutral Zone: A Convention signed at Uqair in December 1922 fixed the Najdi (Saudi Arabian) boundary with Kuwait. The Convention also established a Neutral Zone of 5,770 sq km immediately to the south of Kuwait in which Saudi Arabia and Kuwait held equal rights. The final agreement on this matter was signed in 1963. Since 1966 the Neutral Zone, or Partitioned Zone as it is sometimes known, has been divided between the two countries and each administers its own half, in practice as an integral part of the State. However, the petroleum deposits in the Zone remain undivided and production from the onshore oil concessions in the Zone is shared equally between the two states' concessionaires.

ADMINISTRATIVE REGIONS
(demographic survey for 2007)*

Riyadh	5,835,613	Ha'il	551,523
Makkah	6,097,077	Northern Borders	294,896
Al-Madinah	1,614,644	Jazan	1,253,089
Qassim	1,077,068	Najran	449,186
Eastern	3,545,644	Al-Baha	387,717
Aseer	1,756,625	Al-Jouf	382,070
Tabouk	735,682	**Total**	**23,980,834**

* Islamic year AH 1428, which corresponds to the period 20 January 2007 to 9 January 2008 in the Gregorian calendar.

PRINCIPAL TOWNS
(population at 2004 census)

Riyadh (royal capital)	4,087,152	Al-Mobarraz	285,067
Jeddah (administrative capital)	2,801,481	Ha'il (Hayil)	267,005
Makkah (Mecca)	1,294,168	Najran	246,880
Al-Madinah (Medina)	918,889	Hafar al-Batin	231,978
Dammam	744,321	Jubail	222,544
At-Ta'if	521,273	Abha	201,912
Tabouk	441,351	Al-Kharj	200,958
Buraidah	378,422	Ath-Thuqbah	191,826
Khamis-Mushait	372,695	Yanbu	188,430
Hufuf	287,841	Al-Khubar	165,799

Source: UN, *Demographic Yearbook*.

Mid-2007 ('000, incl. suburbs, UN estimates): Riyadh 4,465; Jeddah 3,012; Mecca 1,385; Medina 1,010; Dammam 822 (Source: UN, *World Urbanization Prospects: The 2007 Revision*).

BIRTHS AND DEATHS
(UN estimates, annual averages)

	1990–95	1995–2000	2000–05
Birth rate (per 1,000)	33.5	29.5	26.5
Death rate (per 1,000)	4.6	4.0	3.8

Source: UN, *World Population Prospects: The 2006 Revision*.

Life expectancy (years at birth, WHO estimates): 70.0 (males 68.0; females 72.7) in 2006 (Source: WHO, *World Health Statistics*).

ECONOMICALLY ACTIVE POPULATION
(persons aged 15 years and over at April 2007)

	Males	Females	Total
Agriculture, hunting, forestry and fishing	359,754	4,430	364,184
Mining and quarrying	101,610	1,197	102,807
Manufacturing	557,442	8,332	565,774
Electricity, gas and water	74,381	—	74,381
Construction	790,726	2,860	793,586
Wholesale and retail trade	1,242,461	7,809	1,250,270
Restaurants and hotels	246,024	2,673	248,697
Transport and communications	331,813	11,739	343,552
Financial intermediation	79,305	4,482	83,787
Real estate, renting and business activities	245,826	4,421	250,247
Public administration and defence	1,367,622	32,470	1,400,092
Education	512,983	416,216	929,199
Health and social work	248,937	86,984	335,921
Other community and personal services	168,188	7,689	175,877
Private households with employed persons	327,092	511,034	838,126
Extra-territorial organizations	9,850	—	9,850
Total employed	6,664,014	1,102,336	7,766,350
Unemployed	295,474	167,841	463,315
Total labour force	6,959,488	1,270,177	8,229,665

Source: ILO.

SAUDI ARABIA

Health and Welfare

KEY INDICATORS

Total fertility rate (children per woman, 2006)	3.5
Under-5 mortality rate (per 1,000 live births, 2006)	26
Physicians (per 1,000 head, 2004)	1.4
Hospital beds (per 1,000 head, 2005)	2.3
Health expenditure (2006): US $ per head (PPP)	607
Health expenditure (2006): % of GDP	3.4
Health expenditure (2006): public (% of total)	77.2
Access to water (% of persons, 2002)	90
Human Development Index (2006): ranking	55
Human Development Index (2006): value	0.835

For sources and definitions, see explanatory note on p. vi.

Agriculture

PRINCIPAL CROPS
('000 metric tons)

	2005	2006*	2007*
Wheat	2,648	2,400	2,700
Barley	47	47	47
Maize	91	91	91
Millet	7	8	8
Sorghum	205	244	243
Potatoes	441	502	570
Tomatoes	496	500	500
Pumpkins, squash and gourds	135	135	135
Cucumbers and gherkins	212	212	212
Aubergines (Eggplants)	74	72	72
Onions, dry	73	73	73
Carrots and turnips	56	52	50
Okra	46	46	46
Watermelons	364	365	365
Cantaloupes and other melons	243	250	250
Grapes	132	132	132
Dates	970	970	970

* FAO estimates.

Aggregate production ('000 metric tons, may include official, semi-official or estimated data): Total cereals 2,999 in 2005, 2,790 in 2006, 3,089 in 2007; Total roots and tubers 441 in 2005, 502 in 2006, 570 in 2007; Total vegetables (incl. melons) 2,097 in 2005, 2,105 in 2006, 2,103 in 2007; Total fruits (excl. melons) 1,646 in 2005, 1,277 in 2006, 1,277 in 2007.

Source: FAO.

LIVESTOCK
('000 head, year ending September)

	2005	2006*	2007*
Asses	100*	n.a.	n.a.
Camels	268†	260	260
Cattle	352	362	372
Sheep	8,230†	7,000	7,000
Goats	2,230†	2,200	2,200
Chickens	141,000*	142,000	145,000

* FAO estimate(s).
† Unofficial figure.

Source: FAO.

LIVESTOCK PRODUCTS
('000 metric tons)

	2005	2006	2007
Cattle meat	22.4	23.0*	24.0*
Sheep meat*	81.4	76.0	76.0
Goat meat*	22.5	22.5	22.5
Chicken meat†	537.0	548.0	559.0
Camel meat*	90.0	90.0	90.0
Cows' milk*	940.0	967.0	993.0
Sheep's milk*	96.0	82.5	82.5
Goats' milk*	70.0	76.5	76.5
Camels' milk*	90.0	90.0	90.0
Hen eggs	169.5	170.5*	174.0*
Wool, greasy*	12.5	10.8	10.8

* FAO estimate(s).
† Unofficial figures.

Source: FAO.

Fishing

(metric tons, live weight)

	2004	2005	2006
Capture	55,418	60,407	65,471
Groupers and seabasses	1,936	1,650	1,556
Pink ear emperors	2,238	2,443	2,574
Emperors (Scavengers)	4,459	4,396	3,987
Spinefeet (Rabbitfishes)	2,276	2,402	2,393
Narrow-barred Spanish mackerel	5,365	5,547	5,385
Indian mackerel	3,111	3,003	3,225
Green tiger prawns	6,568	7,399	7,488
Aquaculture	11,172	14,375	15,586
Nile tilapia	2,276	2,902	3,402
Indian white prawn	8,705	11,259	11,615
Total catch	66,590	74,782	81,057

Source: FAO.

Mining

('000 metric tons, unless otherwise indicated)

	2004	2005	2006
Crude petroleum (million barrels)*	3,256	3,414	3,361
Natural gas (million cu metres)*†	68,000	68,547	70,878‡
Silver (kilograms)§	14,494	13,501	9,100
Gold (kilograms)§	8,268	7,456	5,180‡
Salt (unrefined)	1,530	1,738	1,752‡
Gypsum (crude)	641	713	2,200‡
Pozzolan	320	372	400‡

* Including 50% of the total output of the Neutral or Partitioned Zone, shared with Kuwait (Source: Saudi Arabian Monetary Agency).
† On a dry basis.
‡ Preliminary.
§ Figures refer to the metal content of concentrate and bullion.

2007: Crude petroleum 3,218m. barrels (Source: Saudi Arabian Monetary Agency).

Source: mainly US Geological Survey.

SAUDI ARABIA

Industry

SELECTED PRODUCTS
(including 50% of the total output of the Neutral Zone; estimates, '000 barrels, unless otherwise indicated)

	2005	2006	2007
Phosphatic fertilizers ('000 metric tons)*†	300	300	n.a.
Motor spirit (petrol) and naphtha	198,872	186,414	188,644
Jet fuel and kerosene	80,908	77,334	67,282
Gas-diesel (distillate fuel) oils	236,371	241,785	238,496
Residual fuel oils	177,971	181,000	174,385
Petroleum bitumen (asphalt)	13,781	14,156	15,041
Liquefied petroleum gas	12,739	14,732	11,521
Cement ('000 metric tons)	26,536	27,913†	31,058
Crude steel ('000 metric tons)	4,185	4,000†	n.a.
Electric energy (million kWh sold)	153,283	163,151	169,303

* Production in terms of phosphoric acid.
† Estimate(s).

Sources: Saudi Arabian Monetary Agency; US Geological Survey.

Finance

CURRENCY AND EXCHANGE RATES

Monetary Units
100 halalah = 20 qurush = 1 Saudi riyal (SR).

Sterling, Dollar and Euro Equivalents (31 December 2008)
£1 sterling = 5.467 riyals;
US $1 = 3.750 riyals;
€1 = 5.219 riyals;
100 Saudi riyals = £18.29 = $26.67 = €19.16.

Exchange Rate: Since June 1986 the official mid-point rate has been fixed at US $1 = 3.75 riyals.

BUDGET ESTIMATES
(million riyals)

Revenue	2006	2007	2008
Petroleum revenues	320,000	330,000	370,000
Other revenues	70,000	70,000	80,000
Total	390,000	400,000	450,000

Expenditure	2006	2007	2008
Human resource development	87,164	96,483	104,600
Transport and communications	9,804	11,329	12,143
Economic resource development	12,454	13,902	16,317
Health and social development	26,798	31,010	34,426
Infrastructure development	4,555	5,188	6,384
Municipal services	11,588	13,576	14,954
Defence and security	110,779	132,922	143,336
Public administration and other government spending	62,814	61,756	63,031
Government lending institutions*	575	1,026	479
Local subsidies	8,469	12,808	14,329
Total	335,000	380,000	410,000

* Including transfers to the Saudi Fund for Development (SFD).

2005 (revised figures, million riyals): Total revenue 564,335 (Petroleum revenue 504,540, Other revenue 59,795); Total expenditure 346,474.

2006 (revised figures, million riyals): Total revenue 673,682 (Petroleum revenue 604,470, Other revenue 69,212); Total expenditure 393,322.

2007 (revised figures, million riyals): Total revenue 642,800 (Petroleum revenue 562,186, Other revenue 80,614); Total expenditure 466,248.

INTERNATIONAL RESERVES
(US $ million in December)

	2005	2006	2007
Gold*	230	242	254
IMF special drawing rights	550	640	721
Reserve position in IMF	1,906	912	731
Foreign exchange	24,074	25,971	32,308
Total	26,760	27,765	34,014

* Valued at US $50 per troy ounce at 31 December 2007.

Source: IMF, *International Financial Statistics*.

MONEY SUPPLY
('000 million riyals in December)

	2005	2006	2007
Currency outside banks	64.29	69.32	72.19
Demand deposits at commercial banks	220.28	243.62	311.92
Total money	284.57	312.94	384.11

Source: IMF, *International Financial Statistics*.

COST OF LIVING
(Consumer Price Index for all cities; base: 1999 = 100)

	2005	2006	2007
Food and beverages	106.5	112.2	120.1
Housing, fuel and water	100.0	101.0	109.2
Textiles and clothing (incl. footwear)	88.3	87.7	85.6
House furnishing	94.9	95.2	96.4
Medical care	101.4	102.7	107.0
Transport and communications	91.8	89.9	88.1
Entertainment and education	98.4	98.7	98.9
All items (incl. others)	99.6	101.8	106.0

NATIONAL ACCOUNTS

Expenditure on the Gross Domestic Product
(million riyals at current prices)

	2005	2006	2007*
Government final consumption expenditure	262,650	311,082	322,086
Private final consumption expenditure	312,957	354,913	404,574
Increase in stocks	20,055	26,437	25,711
Gross fixed capital formation	195,632	233,065	286,244
Total domestic expenditure	791,294	925,497	1,038,615
Exports of goods and services	719,898	835,122	936,811
Less Imports of goods and services	328,678	425,038	544,879
GDP in purchasers' values	1,182,514	1,335,581	1,430,547
GDP at constant 1999 prices	762,277	786,348	813,005

Gross Domestic Product by Economic Activity
(million riyals at current prices)

	2005	2006	2007*
Agriculture, forestry and fishing	38,280	39,373	40,154
Mining and quarrying:			
crude petroleum and natural gas	567,992	665,278	719,170
other	3,016	3,145	3,292
Manufacturing:			
petroleum refining	39,453	43,710	46,418
other	71,253	80,202	89,818
Electricity, gas and water	11,020	11,664	12,419
Construction	54,946	59,139	65,017
Trade, restaurants and hotels	62,759	67,868	73,990

SAUDI ARABIA

Statistical Survey

—continued	2005	2006	2007*
Transport, storage and communications	38,429	41,367	45,087
Finance, insurance, real estate and business services:			
ownership of dwellings	50,012	52,223	54,778
other	47,772	52,575	55,948
Government services	176,350	196,386	200,306
Other community, social and personal services	27,855	29,203	30,631
Sub-total	1,189,137	1,342,133	1,437,028
Import duties	10,115	11,025	11,801
Less Imputed bank service charge	16,739	17,575	18,280
GDP in purchasers' values	1,182,514	1,335,581	1,430,547

* Preliminary figures.

BALANCE OF PAYMENTS
(US $ million)

	2005	2006	2007
Exports of goods f.o.b.	180,712	211,305	234,145
Imports of goods f.o.b.	−54,595	−63,914	−82,597
Trade balance	126,117	147,391	151,547
Exports of services	6,677	7,297	7,901
Imports of services	−14,520	−19,390	−30,798
Balance on goods and services	118,274	135,298	128,650
Other income received	4,964	10,376	15,014
Other income paid	−4,963	−9,734	−14,776
Balance on goods, services and income	118,275	135,940	128,888
Current transfers paid	−28,215	−36,874	−33,808
Current balance	90,060	99,066	95,080
Direct investment from abroad	464	660	−8,069
Portfolio investment assets	−67,420	−78,567	−81,727
Other investment assets	−28,717	−17,664	−11,391
Other investment liabilities	5,149	−2,601	12,275
Overall balance	−465	894	6,168

Source: IMF, *International Financial Statistics*.

External Trade

PRINCIPAL COMMODITIES
(distribution by SITC, US $ million)

Imports c.i.f.	2005	2006	2007
Food and live animals	7,751.4	8,367.4	10,604.9
Cereals and cereal preparations	2,092.5	2,273.9	3,620.9
Chemicals and related products	5,779.8	6,604.2	8,022.0
Medicinal and pharmaceutical products	1,729.5	1,940.7	2,230.3
Basic manufactures	10,601.7	14,684.8	18,508.1
Iron and steel	3,352.1	5,720.4	7,612.1
Machinery and transport equipment	26,925.0	31,431.7	42,376.1
General industrial machinery equipment and parts	3,923.8	5,374.2	9,009.5
Electrical machinery, apparatus, etc.	2,460.2	2,807.4	4,677.0
Road vehicles and parts	9,786.1	10,401.7	12,017.6
Passenger motor cars (excl. buses)	6,630.7	7,466.3	7,761.9
Miscellaneous manufactured articles	5,346.5	5,857.4	7,076.5
Total (incl. others)	59,510.3	69,800.2	90,214.0

Exports f.o.b.	2005	2006	2007
Mineral fuels, lubricants, etc.	161,703.8	188,399.3	206,996.9
Petroleum, petroleum products and related materials	155,816.0	180,520.0	198,157.3
Crude petroleum (bituminous)	137,175.9	162,218.8	180,030.4
Natural gas, manufactured	5,887.6	7,877.8	8,839.0
Chemicals and related products	11,073.6	12,019.5	14,258.9
Organic chemicals	4,767.1	5,004.0	5,662.2
Basic manufactures	2,673.4	3,314.3	4,231.7
Machinery and transport equipment	2,935.4	4,150.5	5,643.8
Total (incl. others)	180,737.2	211,305.8	234,950.8

Source: UN, *International Trade Statistics Yearbook*.

PRINCIPAL TRADING PARTNERS
(US $ million)

Imports c.i.f.	2005	2006	2007
Australia	1,673.3	2,065.2	1,946.8
Belgium	870.2	901.3	1,096.3
Brazil	1,313.5	1,466.0	1,751.4
Canada	517.8	684.4	956.5
China, People's Republic	4,409.2	5,978.9	8,716.0
Finland	1,032.7	1,174.0	1,285.5
France (incl. Monaco)	2,051.5	2,692.1	3,068.8
Germany	4,867.2	5,667.1	8,010.9
India	1,837.3	2,633.8	3,076.3
Indonesia	541.6	628.5	938.1
Italy	2,260.0	2,817.9	4,104.3
Japan	5,362.5	5,646.4	7,888.5
Korea, Republic	2,171.8	2,645.7	4,045.7
Netherlands	988.4	1,031.9	1,214.5
Spain	670.0	769.1	1,181.9
Sweden	966.5	1,069.3	1,272.4
Switzerland (incl. Liechtenstein)	1,284.0	1,117.5	1,420.4
Thailand	1,018.6	1,320.7	1,489.4
Turkey	837.8	850.0	1,253.8
United Arab Emirates	1,564.4	1,913.9	2,251.2
United Kingdom	2,787.0	2,755.2	3,514.1
USA	8,803.2	10,114.8	12,253.1
Total (incl. others)	59,510.3	69,800.2	90,214.0

Exports (incl. re-exports)	2005	2006	2007*
Bahrain	4,974.4	6,065.9	1,205.7
Belgium	2,276.3	2,869.5	905.4
China, People's Republic	10,814.9	13,232.7	2,667.3
Egypt	2,046.2	2,755.7	2,818.7
France (incl. Monaco)	4,297.7	4,117.7	2,922.1
India	10,739.7	12,956.1	3,387.4
Indonesia	2,447.6	3,066.6	683.6
Italy	5,377.0	5,169.3	3,376.6
Japan	28,180.5	34,811.5	62,970.9
Korea, Republic	15,312.1	19,377.8	1,624.2
Netherlands	6,488.1	6,497.0	3,855.1
Singapore	9,472.2	9,988.1	2,889.0
South Africa	3,065.9	3,220.3	694.1
Spain	2,971.9	3,582.7	2,826.0
Thailand	3,207.2	3,541.8	604.7
United Arab Emirates	4,811.7	6,805.9	8,404.7
USA	27,958.5	31,842.2	41,033.0
Total (incl. others)	180,737.2	211,305.8	234,950.8

* Data for many countries assumed to exclude petroleum exports.

Source: UN, *International Trade Statistics Yearbook*.

SAUDI ARABIA — *Statistical Survey*

Transport

RAILWAYS
(traffic)

	1999	2000	2001
Passenger journeys ('000)	770.4	853.8	790.4
Freight carried ('000 metric tons)	1,800	1,600	1,500

ROAD TRAFFIC
(motor vehicles in use at 31 December)

	1989	1990	1991
Passenger cars	2,550,465	2,664,028	2,762,132
Buses and coaches	50,856	52,136	54,089
Goods vehicles	2,153,297	2,220,658	2,286,541
Total	4,754,618	4,936,822	5,103,205

1996 (estimates): Passenger cars 1,744,000; Buses and coaches 23,040; Goods vehicles 1,169,000; Total 2,935,000.

Source: IRF, *World Road Statistics*.

SHIPPING
Merchant Fleet
(vessels registered at 31 December)

	2005	2006	2007
Oil tankers:			
vessels	26	25	21
displacement ('000 grt)	231	153	88
Others:			
vessels	274	279	290
displacement ('000 grt)	797	869	854
Total vessels	300	304	311
Total displacement ('000 grt)	1,028	1,022	942

Source: Lloyd's Register-Fairplay, *World Fleet Statistics*.

International Sea-borne Freight Traffic
('000 metric tons)*

	1988	1989	1990
Goods loaded	161,666	165,989	214,070
Goods unloaded	42,546	42,470	46,437

* Including Saudi Arabia's share of traffic in the Neutral or Partitioned Zone.

Source: UN, *Monthly Bulletin of Statistics*.

2001 ('000 metric tons, excluding crude oil): Goods loaded 68,894; Goods unloaded 31,668.

CIVIL AVIATION
(traffic on scheduled services)

	2002	2003	2004
Kilometres flown (million)	124	125	135
Passengers carried ('000)	13,564	13,822	14,943
Passenger-kilometres (million)	20,804	20,801	22,557
Total ton-km (million)	2,748	2,739	3,000

Source: UN, *Statistical Yearbook*.

2005 (Saudi Arabian airlines): Passengers carried ('000) 16,900; Number of flights 130,942; Cargo carried ('000 metric tons) 295.

2006 (Saudi Arabian airlines): Passengers carried ('000) 17,800; Number of flights 141,964; Cargo carried ('000 metric tons) 296.

Tourism

Country of nationality	2004	2005	2006
Bahrain	277,618	356,163	389,513
Bangladesh	255,402	52,633	92,088
Egypt	976,931	799,665	609,831
India	474,467	117,101	345,431
Indonesia	486,869	226,037	373,027
Iran	386,507	519,865	387,556
Jordan	306,495	279,288	322,548
Kuwait	1,238,382	1,462,879	1,681,843
Pakistan	654,059	351,672	510,449
Qatar	434,944	511,143	501,157
Sudan	157,548	130,098	111,961
Syria	726,752	576,950	605,150
Turkey	236,267	100,167	266,072
United Arab Emirates	238,536	1,043,076	800,059
Yemen	220,759	261,520	200,260
Total (incl. others)	8,599,430	8,036,13	8,620,485

Tourism receipts (US $ million, incl. passenger transport): 6,916 in 2004; 5,626 in 2005; 5,391 in 2006.

Source: World Tourism Organization.

PILGRIMS TO MECCA FROM ABROAD*

	2003/04	2004/05	2005/06
Total	1,419,706	1,534,769	1,557,447

* Figures relate to Islamic lunar years. The equivalent dates in the Gregorian calendar are: 5 March 2003 to 21 February 2004; 22 February 2004 to 9 February 2005; 10 February 2005 to 30 January 2006.

Communications Media

	2005	2006	2007
Telephones ('000 main lines in use)	3,844.0	3,951.0	3,996.0
Mobile cellular telephones ('000 subscribers)	14,164.2	19,662.6	28,381.0
Personal computers ('000 in use)	8,476	n.a.	n.a.
Internet users ('000)	3,000.0	4,700.0	6,200.0
Broadband subscribers ('000)	67.8	218.2	600.0

1995 (estimate): 150,000 facsimile machines in use.

1996: 13 daily newspapers; 185 non-daily newspapers.

1997: 6,250,000 radio receivers in use; Book titles published 3,780.

Sources: UNESCO, *Statistical Yearbook*; International Telecommunication Union.

Education

(2007/08, projections)

	Institutions	Teachers	Students
Pre-primary	1,650	11,125	125,433
Primary	13,993	215,625	2,694,161
Intermediate	7,175	106,856	1,175,409
Secondary (general)	3,861	73,509	916,872
Special	673	6,658	22,834
Adult education	4,446	11,570	84,298

Source: Ministry of Education, Riyadh.

Adult literacy rate (UNESCO estimates): 85.0% (males 89.1%; females 79.4%) in 2007 (Source: UNESCO Institute for Statistics).

Directory

The Constitution

The Basic Law of Government was introduced by royal decree in 1992.

Chapter 1 defines Saudi Arabia as a sovereign Arab, Islamic state. Article 1 defines God's Book and the Sunnah of his prophet as the constitution of Saudi Arabia. The official language is Arabic. The official holidays are Id al-Fitr and Id al-Adha. The calendar is the Hegira calendar.

Chapter 2 concerns the system of government, which is defined as a monarchy, hereditary in the male descendants of Abd al-Aziz ibn Abd ar-Rahman al-Faisal as-Sa'ud. It outlines the duties of the Heir Apparent. The principles of government are justice, consultation and equality in accordance with Islamic law (*Shari'a*).

Chapter 3 concerns the family. The State is to aspire to strengthen family ties and to maintain its Arab and Islamic values. Article 11 states that 'Saudi society will be based on the principle of adherence to God's command, on mutual co-operation in good deeds and piety and mutual support and inseparability'. Education aims to instil the Islamic faith.

Chapter 4 defines the economic principles of the State. All natural resources are the property of the State. The State protects public money and freedom of property. Taxation is only to be imposed on a just basis.

Chapter 5 concerns rights and duties. The State is to protect Islam and to implement the *Shari'a* law. The State protects human rights in accordance with the *Shari'a*. The State is to provide public services and security for all citizens. Punishment is to be in accordance with the *Shari'a*. The Royal Courts are open to all citizens.

Chapter 6 defines the authorities of the State as the judiciary, the executive and the regulatory authority. The judiciary is independent, and acts in accordance with *Shari'a* law. The King is head of the Council of Ministers and Commander-in-Chief of the Armed Forces. The Prime Minister and other ministers are appointed by the King. It provides for the establishment of a Consultative Council (Majlis ash-Shoura).

Chapter 7 concerns financial affairs. It provides for the annual presentation of a state budget. Corporate budgets are subject to the same provisions.

Chapter 8 concerns control bodies. Control bodies will be established to ensure good financial and administrative management of state assets.

Chapter 9 defines the general provisions pertaining to the application of the Basic Law of Government.

The Government

HEAD OF STATE

King: HM King ABDULLAH IBN ABD AL-AZIZ AS-SA'UD (acceded to the throne 1 August 2005).
Crown Prince: SULTAN IBN ABD AL-AZIZ AS-SA'UD.

COUNCIL OF MINISTERS
(April 2009)

Prime Minister and Commander of the National Guard: King ABDULLAH IBN ABD AL-AZIZ AS-SA'UD.

First Deputy Prime Minister, Minister of Defence and Civil Aviation and Inspector General: Crown Prince SULTAN IBN ABD AL-AZIZ AS-SA'UD.

Second Deputy Prime Minister and Minister of the Interior: Prince NAYEF IBN ABD AL-AZIZ AS-SA'UD.

Minister of Municipal and Rural Affairs: Prince MUTAIB IBN ABD AL-AZIZ AS-SA'UD.

Minister of Foreign Affairs: Prince SA'UD AL-FAISAL AS-SA'UD.

Minister of Petroleum and Mineral Resources: Eng. ALI IBN IBRAHIM AN-NUAIMI.

Minister of Labour: GHAZI AL-GOSAIBI.

Minister of Social Affairs: Dr YOUSUF BIN AHMAD AL-OTHMAN.

Minister of Agriculture: Dr FAHD IBN ABD AR-RAHMAN IBN SULAIMAN BALGHUNAIM.

Minister of Water and Electricity: ABDULLAH AL-HUSSEIN.

Minister of Education: Prince FAISAL IBN ABDULLAH IBN MUHAMMAD AS-SA'UD.

Minister of Higher Education: Dr KHALID IBN MUHAMMAD AL-ANGARI.

Minister of Communications and Information Technology: MUHAMMAD IBN JABIL IBN AHMAD MULLA.

Minister of Finance: Dr IBRAHIM IBN ABD AL-AZIZ AL-ASSAF.

Minister of Economy and Planning: KHALED IBN MUHAMMAD AL-QUSAIBI.

Minister of Culture and Information: Dr ABD AL-AZIZ IBN MOHI ED-DIN KHOJA.

Minister of Commerce and Industry: ABDULLAH IBN AHMAD ZAINAL ALIREZA.

Minister of Justice: Dr MUHAMMAD IBN ABD AL-KARIM IBN ABD AL-AZIZ AL-EISSA.

Minister of Pilgrimage (Hajj) Affairs: FOUAD IBN ABD AS-SALAM IBN MUHAMMAD FARSI.

Minister of Awqaf (Religious Endowments), Dawa, Mosques and Guidance Affairs: SALEH IBN ABD AL-AZIZ MUHAMMAD IBN IBRAHIM ASH-SHEIKH.

Minister of Health: Dr ABDULLAH IBN ABD AL-AZIZ AR-RABEA.

Minister of the Civil Service: Dr MUHAMMAD IBN ALI AL-FAYEZ.

Minister of Transport: Dr JUBARAH IBN EID AS-SURAISERI.

Minister of State for Foreign Affairs: NIZAR IBN UBAYD MADANI.

Minister of State for Consultative Council Affairs: Dr SAUD IBN SAEED IBN ABD AL-AZIZ AL-MATHAMI.

Ministers of State: Dr MUTLIB IBN ABDULLAH AN-NAFISA, Dr MUSAID IBN MUHAMMAD AL-AYBAN, Dr ABD AL-AZIZ AL-ABDULLAH AL-KHUWAITER, Prince ABD AL-AZIZ IBN FAHD AS-SA'UD.

MINISTRIES

Most ministries have regional offices in Jeddah.

Council of Ministers: Murabba, Riyadh 11121; tel. (1) 488-2444.

Ministry of Agriculture: Airport Rd, Riyadh 11195; tel. (1) 403-1317; fax (1) 404-4565; e-mail pubrel@moa.gov.sa; internet www.moa.gov.sa.

Ministry of Awqaf (Religious Endowments), Dawa, Mosques and Guidance Affairs: Riyadh 11232; tel. (1) 473-0401; internet hajj.al-islam.com.

Ministry of the Civil Service: POB 18367, Riyadh 11114; tel. (1) 402-6666; fax (1) 403-5665; e-mail mcswebmaster@mcs.gov.sa; internet www.mcs.gov.sa.

Ministry of Commerce and Industry: POB 1774, Airport Rd, Riyadh 11162; tel. (1) 401-2222; fax (1) 403-8421; e-mail info@commerce.gov.sa; internet www.commerce.gov.sa.

Ministry of Communications and Information Technology: Intercontinental Rd, Riyadh 11112; tel. (1) 452-2222; fax (1) 452-2220; e-mail info@mcit.gov.sa; internet www.mcit.gov.sa.

Ministry of Culture and Information: POB 570, Nasseriya St, Riyadh 11161; tel. (1) 401-4440; fax (1) 402-3570; internet www.moci.gov.sa.

Ministry of Defence and Civil Aviation: POB 26731, Airport Rd, Riyadh 11165; tel. (1) 478-5900; fax (1) 401-1336; internet www.moda.gov.sa.

Ministry of Economy and Planning: POB 358, 44 University St, Riyadh 11182; tel. (1) 404-9212; fax (1) 405-2051; e-mail minister@planning.gov.sa; internet www.mep.gov.sa.

Ministry of Education: POB 3734, Airport Rd, Riyadh 11148; tel. (1) 404-2888; fax (1) 401-2365; e-mail webmaster@moe.gov.sa; internet www.moe.gov.sa.

Ministry of Finance: Airport Rd, Riyadh 11177; tel. (1) 405-0000; fax (1) 405-9202; e-mail info@mof.gov.sa; internet www.mof.gov.sa.

Ministry of Foreign Affairs: POB 55937, Riyadh 11544; tel. (1) 405-5000; fax (1) 403-0645; e-mail admin.dep@mofa.gov.sa; internet www.mofa.gov.sa.

Ministry of Health: Airport Rd, Riyadh 11176; tel. (1) 401-2220; fax (1) 402-9876; e-mail f_otaibi@moh.gov.sa; internet www.moh.gov.sa.

Ministry of Higher Education: King Faisal Hospital St, Riyadh 11153; tel. (1) 464-4444; fax (1) 441-9004; e-mail contact@mohe.gov.sa; internet www.mohe.gov.sa.

Ministry of the Interior: POB 2933, Airport Rd, Riyadh 11134; tel. (1) 401-1111; fax (1) 403-1185; internet www.moi.gov.sa.

Ministry of Justice: University St, Riyadh 11137; tel. (1) 405-7777; internet www.moj.gov.sa.

Ministry of Labour: Omar bin al-Khatab St, Riyadh 11157; tel. (1) 477-1480; fax (1) 477-7336; e-mail webmaster@mol.gov.sa; internet www.mol.gov.sa.

Ministry of Municipal and Rural Affairs: POB 955, Nasseriya St, Riyadh 11136; tel. (1) 456-9999; fax (1) 456-3196; e-mail info@momra.gov.sa; internet www.momra.gov.sa.

SAUDI ARABIA

Ministry of Petroleum and Mineral Resources: POB 247, Al Ma'ather St, Riyadh 11191; tel. (1) 478-7777; fax (1) 476-0270; e-mail pr@mopm.gov.sa; internet www.mopm.gov.sa.

Ministry of Pilgrimage (Hajj) Affairs: Al-Maazar St, Riyadh 11183; tel. (1) 404-3003; fax (1) 402-2555; internet www.hajinformation.com.

Ministry of Social Affairs: Omar bin al-Khatab St, Riyadh 11157; tel. (1) 477-1480; fax (1) 477-7336; internet www.mosa.gov.sa.

Ministry of Transport: Airport Rd, Riyadh 11178; tel. (1) 404-9975; fax (1) 403-5743; e-mail info@mot.gov.sa; internet www.mot.gov.sa.

Ministry of Water and Electricity: King Fahd Rd, Riyadh 11233; tel. (1) 205-6666; fax (1) 205-2749; e-mail info@mowe.gov.sa; internet www.mowe.gov.sa.

MAJLIS ASH-SHOURA
(Consultative Council)

In March 1992 King Fahd issued a decree to establish a Consultative Council of 60 members, whose powers include the right to summon and question ministers. The composition of the Council was announced by King Fahd in August 1993, and it was officially inaugurated in December. Each member serves a term of four years. The Council's membership was increased to 90 when its second term began in July 1997; it was increased further, to 120, in May 2001, and to 150 in April 2005. King Fahd issued a decree extending the legislative powers of the Council in November 2003, including the right to propose new legislation.

Chairman: Dr ABDULLAH IBN MUHAMMAD IBN IBRAHIM ASH-SHEIKH.
Vice-Chairman: Dr BANDAR IBN MUHAMMAD HAMZAH HAJJAR.
Secretary-General: Dr MUHAMMAD IBN ABDULLAH AL-GHAMDI.

Political Organizations

There are no political organizations in Saudi Arabia.

Diplomatic Representation

EMBASSIES IN SAUDI ARABIA

Afghanistan: POB 93337, Riyadh 11673; tel. (1) 480-3459; fax (1) 480-3451; e-mail afgembriyad@hotmail.com; Ambassador AZIZ KARZAI.

Albania: POB 94004, Riyadh 11693; tel. (1) 470-4217; fax (1) 470-4214; e-mail embassy.riyadh@mfa.gov.al; Ambassador ADMIRIM BANAJ.

Algeria: POB 94388, Riyadh 11693; tel. (1) 488-7171; fax (1) 482-1703; Ambassador Dr HABIB ADAMI.

Argentina: POB 94369, Riyadh 11693; tel. (1) 465-2600; fax (1) 465-3057; e-mail earab@nesma.net.sa; Ambassador ENRIQUE ANTONIO PAREJA.

Australia: POB 94400, Riyadh 11693; tel. (1) 488-7788; fax (1) 488-7973; internet www.saudiarabia.embassy.gov.au; Ambassador KEVIN MAGEE.

Austria: POB 94373, Riyadh 11693; tel. (1) 480-1217; fax (1) 480-1526; e-mail riyadh-ob@bmeia.gv.at; internet www.bmeia.gv.at/riyadh; Ambassador Dr JOHANNES WIMMER.

Azerbaijan: 59 Al-Worood Quarter St, off Amir Failsal bin Sa'ud Abd ar-Rahman, Aloroba Rd, Riyadh; tel. (1) 419-2382; fax (1) 419-2260; e-mail info@azembriyadh.org; internet www.azembriyadh.org; Ambassador TOFIQ ABDULLAYEV.

Bahrain: POB 94371, Riyadh 11693; tel. (1) 488-0044; fax (1) 488-0208; e-mail riyadh.mission@mofa.gov.bh; Ambassador MUHAMMAD SALEH ASH-SHEIKH.

Bangladesh: POB 94395, Riyadh 11693; tel. (1) 419-5300; fax (1) 419-3555; e-mail bangladootriyadh04@hotmail.com; internet www.mofa.gov.bd/lbra/saudi.htm; Ambassador MUHAMMAD FAZLUL KARIM.

Belgium: POB 94396, Riyadh 11693; tel. (1) 488-2888; fax (1) 488-2033; e-mail riyadh@diplobel.fed.be; internet www.diplomatie.be/riyadh; Ambassador MICHEL LASTSCHENKO.

Bosnia and Herzegovina: POB 94301, Riyadh 11693; tel. (1) 456-7914; fax (1) 454-4360; e-mail baembsaruh@awalnet.net.sa; Ambassador RAZIM ĆOLIĆ.

Brazil: POB 94348, Riyadh 11693; tel. (1) 488-0018; fax (1) 488-1073; e-mail arabras@shabakah.net.sa; Ambassador ISNARD PENHA BRASIL JÚNIOR.

Brunei: POB 94314, Al-Warood, Area 29, al-Fujairah St, Riyadh 11693; tel. (1) 456-0814; fax (1) 456-1594; e-mail riyadh.arabsaudi@mfa.gov.bn; Ambassador Pengiran Haji JABARUDDIN BIN Pengiran Haji MUHAMMAD SALLEH.

Burkina Faso: POB 94330, Riyadh 11693; tel. (1) 465-2244; fax (1) 465-3397; e-mail burkinafaso.ksa@arab.net.sa; Ambassador OUMAR DIAWARA.

Cameroon: POB 94336, Riyadh 11693; tel. (1) 488-0022; fax (1) 488-1463; e-mail ambacamriyad@ifrance.com; internet www.ambacamriyad.org.sa; Ambassador Dr MOHAMADOU LABARANG.

Canada: POB 94321, Riyadh 11693; tel. (1) 488-2288; fax (1) 488-1997; e-mail ryadh@international.gc.ca; internet www.saudiarabia.gc.ca; Ambassador RODERICK BELL.

Chad: POB 94374, Riyadh 11693; tel. and fax (1) 465-7702; Ambassador SAQR YOUSUF ANTO.

China, People's Republic: POB 75231, Riyadh 11578; tel. (1) 483-2126; fax (1) 281-2070; e-mail chinaemb_sa@mfa.com.cn; internet www.chinaembassy.org.sa; Ambassador YANG HONGLIN.

Comoros: Riyadh; tel. (1) 293-4697; fax (1) 293-4797; Ambassador ASSIANDI ABDOU RAHMANE AMIR.

Côte d'Ivoire: POB 94303, Riyadh 11693; tel. (1) 482-5582; fax (1) 482-9629; e-mail acisa@ambaci-riyadh.org; Ambassador LANCINA DOSSO.

Denmark: POB 94398, Riyadh 11693; tel. (1) 488-0101; fax (1) 488-1366; e-mail ruhamb@um.dk; internet www.ambriyadh.um.dk; Ambassador HANS KLINGENBERG.

Djibouti: POB 94340, Riyadh 11693; tel. (1) 454-3182; fax (1) 456-9168; e-mail dya_bamakhrama@hotmail.com; Ambassador DYA-EDDINE SAID BAMAKHRAMA.

Egypt: POB 94333, Riyadh 11693; tel. (1) 481-0464; fax (1) 481-0463; internet www.mfa.gov.eg/Missions/ksa/riyadh/embassy/en-gb/; Ambassador MAHMOUD MUHAMMAD OUF.

Eritrea: POB 94002, Riyadh; tel. (1) 480-1726; fax (1) 482-7537; Ambassador MOHAMMED OMAR MAHMOUD.

Ethiopia: POB 94341, Riyadh 11693; tel. (1) 482-3919; fax (1) 483-3281; e-mail ethiopian@awalnet.net.sa; Ambassador YUSUF ABDULLAH SUKAR.

Finland: POB 94363, Riyadh 11693; tel. (1) 488-1515; fax (1) 488-2520; e-mail sanomat.ria@formin.fi; internet www.finland.org.sa; Ambassador MARTTI ISOARO.

France: POB 94367, Riyadh 11693; tel. (1) 488-1255; fax (1) 488-2882; e-mail diplomatie@ambafrance.org.sa; internet www.ambafrance.org.sa; Ambassador BERTRAND BESANCENOT.

Gabon: POB 94325, Riyadh 11693; tel. (1) 456-7171; fax (1) 453-6121; e-mail ambagabonriyad@yahoo.com; Ambassador ONUNJA YUBIGI.

Gambia: POB 94322, Riyadh 11693; tel. (1) 205-2158; fax (1) 456-2024; e-mail gamextriyadh@yahoo.com; Ambassador LAMIN KITI JABANG.

Germany: POB 94001, Riyadh 11693; tel. (1) 488-0700; fax (1) 488-0660; e-mail info@riad.diplo.de; internet www.riad.diplo.de; Ambassador VOLKMAR WENZEL.

Ghana: POB 94339, Riyadh 11693; tel. (1) 454-5122; fax (1) 450-9819; e-mail ghanaemb@naseej.com; Ambassador Alhaji RASHID BAWA.

Greece: POB 94375, Riyadh 11693; tel. (1) 480-1975; fax (1) 480-1969; e-mail gremb.ria@mfa.gr; Ambassador DIMITRIOS LETSIOS (designate).

Guinea: POB 94326, Riyadh 11693; tel. (1) 488-1101; fax (1) 482-6757; e-mail riydambagunee@yahoo.fr; Ambassador el-Hadj CANDIDO RIVAS.

Hungary: POB 94014, al-Waha District, Ahmad Tonsy St 23, Riyadh 11693; tel. (1) 454-6707; fax (1) 456-0834; e-mail mission.ryd@kum.hu; e-mail www.mfa.gov.hu/emb/riyadh; Ambassador LÁSZLÓ FODOR.

India: POB 94387, Riyadh 11693; tel. (1) 488-4144; fax (1) 488-4189; e-mail info@indianembassy.org.sa; internet www.indianembassy.org.sa; Ambassador M. O. H. FAROUK.

Indonesia: POB 94343, Riyadh 11693; tel. (1) 488-2800; fax (1) 488-2966; e-mail contact@kbri-riyadh.org.sa; internet www.kbri-riyadh.org.sa; Ambassador Dr SALIM SEGAF AL-JUFRIE.

Iran: POB 94394, Riyadh 11693; tel. (1) 488-1916; fax (1) 488-1890; Ambassador SAYED MUHAMMAD HOSSEINI.

Iraq: Riyadh; Ambassador Dr GHANIM ALWAN JAWAD AL-JUMAILI (designate).

Ireland: POB 94349, Riyadh 11693; tel. (1) 488-2300; fax (1) 488-0927; e-mail riyadhembassy@dfa.ie; internet www.embassyofireland.org.sa; Ambassador TOM RUSSELL.

Italy: POB 94389, Riyadh 11693; tel. (1) 488-1212; fax (1) 480-6964; e-mail segreteria1.riad@esteri.it; internet www.ambriad.esteri.it; Ambassador EUGENIO D'AURIA.

Japan: POB 4095, Riyadh 11491; tel. (1) 488-1100; fax (1) 488-0189; e-mail info@jpn-emb-sa.com; internet www.ksa.emb-japan.go.jp; Ambassador SHIGERU NAKAMURA.

SAUDI ARABIA

Jordan: POB 94316, Riyadh 11693; tel. (1) 488-0051; fax (1) 488-0072; e-mail jordan.embassy@nesma.net.sa; Ambassador QAFTAN MAJALI.

Kazakhstan: POB 94012, Riyadh 11693; tel. (1) 480-6406; fax (1) 480-9106; e-mail office@kazembgulf.net; internet www.kazembgulf.net; Ambassador KAIRAT LAMA-SHARIF.

Kenya: POB 94358, Riyadh 11693; tel. (1) 488-1238; fax (1) 488-2629; e-mail riyaadh@mfa.gov.ke; Ambassador ABOUBAKAR ABDI.

Korea, Republic: POB 94399, Riyadh 11693; tel. (1) 488-2211; fax (1) 488-1317; e-mail emsaudi@yahoo.co.kr; internet sau.mofat.go.kr/eng/index.jsp; Ambassador HONG JONG-KI.

Kuwait: POB 94304, Riyadh 11693; tel. (1) 488-3401; fax (1) 488-3682; Ambassador Sheikh HAMAD JABER AL-ALI AS-SABAH.

Kyrgyzstan: POB 75871, 32 Muhammad Khamid al-Fikki St, Riyadh; tel. (1) 229-3272; fax (1) 229-3274; Ambassador YOUSEF SHARIF.

Lebanon: POB 94350, Riyadh 11693; tel. (1) 480-4060; fax (1) 480-4703; e-mail marozein@gmail.com; internet www.lebanon.org.sa; Ambassador MARWAN ZEIN.

Libya: POB 94365, Riyadh 11693; tel. (1) 488-9757; fax (1) 488-3252; Ambassador MUHAMMAD SA'ID AL-QASHAT.

Malaysia: POB 94335, Riyadh 11693; tel. (1) 488-7100; fax (1) 482-4177; e-mail malriyadh@kln.gov.my; internet www.kln.gov.my/perwakilan/riyadh; Ambassador OMAR SYED AS-SAQQAF.

Maldives: 8 Abu El Izzu El Kharasaani Lane, al-Jauf St, as-Sulaimaniya District, Riyadh; tel. (1) 462-6787; fax (1) 464-3725; e-mail adhanu@gmail.com; Ambassador HUSSAIN SHIHAB.

Mali: POB 94331, Riyadh 11693; tel. (1) 464-5640; fax (1) 419-5016; e-mail consulat@sbm.net.sa; Ambassador MUHAMMAD MAHMOUD BEN LABAT.

Malta: POB 94361, Riyadh 11693; tel. (1) 463-2345; fax (1) 463-3993; e-mail maltaemb@shabakah.net.sa; Ambassador GODWIN MONTANARO.

Mauritania: POB 94354, Riyadh 11693; tel. (1) 464-6749; fax (1) 465-8355; Ambassador MUHAMMAD MAHMOUD WALD ABDULLAH.

Mexico: POB 94391, Riyadh 11693; tel. (1) 480-8822; fax (1) 480-8833; Ambassador JOSÉ ARTURO TREJO NAVA.

Morocco: POB 94392, Riyadh 11693; tel. (1) 481-1858; fax (1) 482-7016; e-mail ambassaderiyad@maec.gov.ma; Ambassador ABD AL-KRIM SEMMAR.

Myanmar: Villa No 5, Al-Kadi St, King Fahd Area, Riyadh; tel. (1) 229-3523; fax (1) 229-3306; e-mail meriyadh@awalnet.net.sa; Ambassador KHIN ZAW WIN.

Nepal: POB 94384, Riyadh 11693; tel. (1) 461-1108; fax (1) 464-0690; e-mail neksa@zajil.net; internet www.neksa.org; Ambassador HAMID ANSARI.

Netherlands: POB 94307, Riyadh 11693; tel. (1) 488-0011; fax (1) 488-0544; e-mail riy@minbuza.nl; internet www.mfa.nl/riy-en; Ambassador RONALD G. STRIKKER.

New Zealand: POB 94397, Riyadh 11693; tel. (1) 488-7988; fax (1) 488-7912; e-mail info@nzembassy.org.sa; Ambassador TREVOR MATHESON.

Niger: POB 94334, Riyadh 11693; tel. and fax (1) 464-2931; Ambassador HACHIMI AL-KAIDI TOURÉ.

Nigeria: POB 94386, Riyadh 11693; tel. (1) 482-3024; fax (1) 482-4134; e-mail nigeria@nigeriariyadh.com; internet www.nigeriariyadh.com; Ambassador ALHAJI A. GARBA AMINCI.

Norway: POB 94380, Riyadh 11693; tel. (1) 488-1904; fax (1) 488-0854; e-mail emb.riyadh@mfa.no; internet www.al-norwige.org.sa; Ambassador JAN BUGGE-MAHRT.

Oman: POB 94381, Riyadh 11693; tel. (1) 482-3120; fax (1) 482-3738; e-mail riyadh@mofa.gov.om; Ambassador SAEED AL-KALABANY.

Pakistan: POB 94007, Riyadh 11693; tel. (1) 488-7272; fax (1) 488-7953; e-mail webmaster@pakembassy.org.sa; Ambassador Adm. (retd) SHAHID KARIMULLAH.

Philippines: POB 94366, Riyadh 11693; tel. (1) 482-0507; fax (1) 488-3945; e-mail filembry@sbm.net.sa; Ambassador ANTONIO P. VILLAMOR.

Poland: POB 94016, Riyadh 11693; tel. (1) 454-9274; fax (1) 454-9089; e-mail rijadamb@shabakah.net.sa; internet www.rijad.polemb.net; Ambassador ADAM KUŁACH.

Portugal: POB 94328, Riyadh 11693; tel. (1) 462-2115; fax (1) 462-2105; e-mail portriade@nesma.net.sa; Ambassador Dr HENRIQUE M. V. DE SILVEIRA BORGES.

Qatar: POB 94353, Riyadh 11461; tel. (1) 482-5544; fax (1) 482-5394; e-mail riyadh@mofa.gov.qa; Ambassador ALI ABDULLAH AL-MAHMOUD.

Romania: POB 94319, Riyadh 11693; tel. (1) 456-6205; fax (1) 456-9985; e-mail office@embrom.org.sa; internet www.embrom.org.sa; Ambassador ION DOBRECI.

Russia: POB 94308, Riyadh 11693; e-mail rusposolksa@zajil.net; tel. (1) 481-1875; fax (1) 481-1890; Ambassador VIKTOR S. KUDRYAVTSEV.

Rwanda: POB 94383, Riyadh 11693; tel. (1) 454-0808; fax (1) 456-1769; Ambassador SIMON INSONERE.

Senegal: POB 94352, Riyadh 11693; tel. (1) 488-0146; fax (1) 488-3804; Ambassador MOUHAMADOU DOUDOU LO.

Sierra Leone: POB 94329, Riyadh 11693; tel. (1) 464-3982; fax (1) 464-3662; e-mail slembrdh@zajil.net; Ambassador Alhaji WUSU MUNU.

Singapore: POB 94378, Riyadh 11693; tel. (1) 480-3855; fax (1) 483-0632; e-mail singemb_ruh@sgmfa.gov.sg; internet www.mfa.gov.sg/riyadh; Ambassador V. P. HIRUBALAN.

Somalia: POB 94372, Riyadh 11693; tel. (1) 464-3456; fax (1) 464-9705.

South Africa: POB 94006, Riyadh 11693; tel. (1) 442-9716; fax (1) 442-9708; e-mail riyadh.info@foreign.gov.za; Ambassador JOHN A. DAVIES.

Spain: POB 94347, Riyadh 11693; tel. (1) 488-0606; fax (1) 488-0420; e-mail embespas@nesma.net.sa; Ambassador MANUEL ALBERT FERNÁNDEZ CAVADA.

Sri Lanka: POB 94360, Riyadh 11693; tel. (1) 460-8689; fax (1) 460-8846; e-mail contact@lankaemb-riyadh.org; internet www.lankaemb-riyadh.org; Ambassador MUHAMMAD MARLEEN ABD AL-MAJID.

Sudan: POB 94337, Riyadh 11693; tel. (1) 488-7979; fax (1) 488-7729; Ambassador ABD AL-HAFEZ IBRAHIM MUHAMMAD.

Sweden: POB 94382, Riyadh 11693; tel. (1) 488-3100; fax (1) 488-0604; e-mail ambassaden.riyadh@foreign.ministry.se; internet www.swedenabroad.se/riyadh; Ambassador JAN THESLEFF.

Switzerland: POB 94311, Riyadh 11693; tel. (1) 488-1291; fax (1) 488-0632; e-mail rya.vertretung@eda.admin.ch; internet www.eda.admin.ch/riad; Ambassador MAURICE DARIER.

Syria: POB 94323, Riyadh 11693; tel. (1) 482-6191; fax (1) 482-6196; Chargé d'affaires AMMAR AS-SABBAGH.

Tanzania: POB 94320, Riyadh 11693; tel. (1) 454-2839; fax (1) 454-9660; e-mail tzriyad@deltasa.com; Ambassador KHALID AMIR MOSWAMI.

Thailand: POB 94359, Riyadh 11693; tel. (1) 488-1174; fax (1) 488-1179; e-mail thaiemryadsl@awalnet.net.sa; internet www.thaiembassy.org/riyadh; Chargé d'affaires a.i. CHARN JULLAMON.

Tunisia: POB 94368, Riyadh 11693; tel. (1) 488-7900; fax (1) 488-7641; Ambassador NAJIB AL-MUNIF.

Turkey: POB 94390, Riyadh 11693; tel. (1) 482-0101; fax (1) 488-7823; e-mail vtn.riyad.be@mfa.gov.tr; Ambassador NACI KORU.

Turkmenistan: POB 94019, Riyadh 11693; tel. (1) 205-4898; fax (1) 205-2990; e-mail info@turkmenemb-sa.org; internet www.turkmenemb-sa.org; Ambassador MUKHAMED ABALAKOV.

Uganda: POB 94344, Riyadh 11693; tel. (1) 454-4910; fax (1) 454-9264; e-mail ugariyadh@hotmail.com; Ambassador AZIZ KALUNGI KASUJJA.

Ukraine: 6 Hassan al-Badr St, Salah ad-Din, Riyadh; tel. (1) 450-8536; fax (1) 450-8534; e-mail uaembassy@awalnet.net.sa; internet www.ukremb.org.sa; f. 1996; Ambassador LEONID HURIANOV.

United Arab Emirates: POB 94385, Riyadh 11693; tel. (1) 488-1227; fax (1) 482-7504; e-mail uaer@cyberia.net.sa; Ambassador ASRI SAEED AHMAD ADH-DHAHIRI.

United Kingdom: POB 94351, Riyadh 11693; tel. (1) 488-0077; fax (1) 488-1209; e-mail PressOffice.Riyadh@fco.gov.uk; internet www.ukinsaudiarabia.fco.gov.uk; Ambassador WILLIAM PATEY.

USA: POB 94309, Riyadh 11693; tel. (1) 488-3800; fax (1) 488-7360; e-mail usembriyadhwebsite@state.gov; internet riyadh.usembassy.gov; Chargé d'affaires a.i. DAVID H. RUNDELL.

Uruguay: POB 94346, Riyadh 11693; tel. (1) 462-0739; fax (1) 462-0648; e-mail ururia@nesma.net.sa; Ambassador RODOLFO INVERNIZZI ARENA.

Uzbekistan: POB 94008, Riyadh 11693; tel. (1) 263-5223; fax (1) 263-5105; Ambassador ALISHER QADIROV.

Venezuela: POB 94364, Riyadh 11693; tel. (1) 480-7141; fax (1) 480-0901; e-mail embvenar@embvenar.org.sa; Ambassador RAMÓN HERRERA NAVARRO.

Yemen: POB 94356, Riyadh 11693; tel. (1) 488-1769; fax (1) 488-1562; Ambassador MUHAMMAD ALI MOHSEN AL-AHWAL.

Judicial System

Judges are independent and governed by the rules of Islamic *Shari'a*. Although a new Judicial Law introduced in October 2007 provided

SAUDI ARABIA

for a number of significant changes to the courts system (see Recent History), the following courts currently operate:

Supreme Council of Justice: consists of 11 members and supervises work of the courts; reviews legal questions referred to it by the Minister of Justice and expresses opinions on judicial questions; reviews sentences of death, cutting and stoning; Chair. Dr SALIH IBN HUMAYD.

Court of Cassation: consists of Chief Justice and an adequate number of judges; includes department for penal suits, department for personal status and department for other suits.

General (Public) Courts: consist of one or more judges; sentences are issued by a single judge, with the exception of death, stoning and cutting, which require the decision of three judges.

Summary Courts: consist of one or more judges; sentences are issued by a single judge.

Specialized Courts: Article 26 of the judicial system stipulates that the setting up of specialized courts is permissible by Royal Decree on a proposal from the Supreme Council of Justice.

Religion

ISLAM

Arabia is the centre of the Islamic faith, and Saudi Arabia includes the holy cities of Mecca and Medina. Except in the Eastern Province, where a large number of people follow Shi'a rites, the majority of the population are Sunni Muslims, and most of the indigenous inhabitants belong to the strictly orthodox Wahhabi sect. The Wahhabis originated in the 18th century, but first became unified and influential under Abd al-Aziz (Ibn Sa'ud), who became the first King of Saudi Arabia. They are now the keepers of the holy places and control the pilgrimage to Mecca. In 1986 King Fahd adopted the title of Custodian of the Two Holy Mosques; the title passed to King Abdullah upon his accession to the throne in August 2005. The country's most senior Islamic authority is the Council of Ulema.

Mecca: Birthplace of the Prophet Muhammad, seat of the Grand Mosque and Shrine of Ka'ba, visited by 1,557,447 Muslims in the Islamic year 1424 (2005/06).

Medina: Burial place of Muhammad, second sacred city of Islam.

Grand Mufti and Chairman of Council of Ulema: Sheikh ABD AL-AZIZ IBN ABDULLAH ASH-SHEIKH.

CHRISTIANITY

The Roman Catholic Church

A small number of adherents, mainly expatriates, form part of the Apostolic Vicariate of Arabia. The Vicar Apostolic is resident in the United Arab Emirates.

The Anglican Communion

Within the Episcopal Church in Jerusalem and the Middle East, Saudi Arabia forms part of the diocese of Cyprus and the Gulf. The Anglican congregations in the country are entirely expatriate. The Bishop in Cyprus and the Gulf is resident in Cyprus, while the Archdeacon in the Gulf is resident in Bahrain.

Other Denominations

The Greek Orthodox Church is also represented.

The Press

Since 1964 most newspapers and periodicals have been published by press organizations, administered by boards of directors with full autonomous powers, in accordance with the provisions of the Press Law. These organizations, which took over from small private firms, are privately owned by groups of individuals experienced in newspaper publishing and administration (see Publishers).

There are also a number of popular periodicals published by the Government and by the Saudi Arabian Oil Co, and distributed free of charge. The press is subject to no legal restriction affecting freedom of expression or the coverage of news.

DAILIES

Arab News: POB 10452, SRP Bldg, Madinah Rd, Jeddah 21433; tel. (2) 639-1888; fax (2) 639-3223; e-mail arabnews@arabnews.com; internet www.arabnews.com; f. 1975; English; publ. by Saudi Research and Publishing Co; Editor-in-Chief KHALED AL-MAEENA; circ. 110,000.

Al-Bilad (The Country): POB 6340, Jeddah 21442; tel. (2) 672-3000; fax (2) 671-2545; internet www.albilad-daily.com; f. 1934; Arabic; publ. by Al-Bilad Publishing Organization; Editor-in-Chief QUINAN AL-GHOMDI; circ. 66,210.

Al-Eqtisadiah: POB 10452, Jeddah 21433; tel. (2) 651-1333; fax (2) 667-6212; internet www.aleqt.com; f. 1992; business and finance; publ. by Saudi Research and Publishing Co; Editor-in-Chief ABD AL-WAHAB FAYEZ; circ. 81,000.

Al-Jazirah (The Peninsula): POB 354, Riyadh 11411; tel. (1) 487-0911; fax (1) 487-1063; e-mail ccs@al-jazirah.com.sa; internet www.al-jazirah.com; f. 1972; Arabic; publ. by Al-Jazirah Corpn for Press, Printing and Publishing; Dir-Gen. BIN SAAD ABD AL-LATIF; Editor-in-Chief KHALID BIN HAMAD AL-MALIK; circ. 110,000.

Al-Madina al-Munawara (Medina—The Enlightened City): POB 807, Makkah Rd, Jeddah 21421; tel. (2) 671-2100; fax (2) 671-1877; e-mail webmaster@al-madina.com; internet al-madina.com; f. 1937; Arabic; publ. by Al-Madina Press Establishment; Chief Editor FAHD HASSAN AL-AQRAN; circ. 46,370.

An-Nadwah (The Council): POB 5803, Jarwal Sheikh Sayed Halabi Bldg, Mecca; tel. (2) 520-0111; fax (2) 520-3055; e-mail info@al-nadwah.com; internet www.alnadwah.com.sa; f. 1958; Arabic; publ. by Makkah Printing and Information Establishment; Editor AHMAD BIN SALEH BAYUSUF; circ. 35,000.

Okaz: POB 1508, Seaport Rd, Jeddah 21441; tel. (2) 672-7621; fax (2) 672-4297; e-mail 104127.266@compuserve.com; internet www.okaz.com.sa; f. 1948; Arabic; publ. by Okaz Organization for Press and Publication; Editor-in-Chief MUHAMMAD AT-TUNISI; circ. 110,000.

Ar-Riyadh: POB 2943, Riyadh 11476; tel. (1) 487-1000; fax (1) 441-7417; internet www.alriyadh.com; f. 1965; Arabic; publ. by Al-Yamama Press Establishment; Editor TURKI A. AS-SUDARI; circ. 150,000 (Sat.–Thur.), 90,000 (Fri.).

Saudi Gazette: POB 5576, Jeddah 21432; tel. (2) 676-0000; fax (2) 672-7621; e-mail news@saudigazette.com.sa; internet www.saudigazette.com.sa; f. 1976; English; publ. by Okaz Organization for Press and Publication; Editor-in-Chief MUHAMMAD NASIR SHOUKANI; circ. 15,000.

Al-Watan: POB 15156, Airport Road, Abha; tel. (7) 227-3333; fax (7) 227-3756; e-mail editor@alwatan.com.sa; internet www.alwatan.com.sa; f. 1998; publ. by Assir Establishment for Press and Publishing; Dir-Gen. HATEM HAMID; Editor-in-Chief JAMAL AHMAD KHASHOGGI; circ. 150,000.

Al-Yaum (Today): POB 565, Dammam 31421; tel. (3) 858-0800; fax (3) 858-8777; e-mail mail@alyaum.com; internet www.alyaum.com; f. 1965; publ. by Dar al-Yaum Press, Printing and Publishing Ltd; Dir-Gen. SALEH ALI HAMID; Editor-in-Chief MUHAMMAD ABDULLAH AL-WAEEL; circ. 40,000.

WEEKLIES

BusinessWeek Arabic Edition: POB 478, Riyadh 11411; tel. (1) 441-9933; fax (1) 442-9555; f. 2005; Arabic edn of US business publ; publ. by Saudi Research & Publishing Co.

Al-Muslimoon (The Muslims): POB 13195, Jeddah 21493; tel. (2) 669-1888; fax (2) 669-5549; f. 1985; Arabic; cultural and religious affairs; publ. by Saudi Research and Publishing Co; Editor-in-Chief Dr ABDULLAH AR-RIFA'E; circ. 68,665.

Saudi Economic Survey: POB 1989, Jeddah 21441; tel. (2) 657-8551; fax (2) 657-8553; e-mail info@saudieconomicsurvey.com; internet www.saudieconomicsurvey.com; f. 1967; English; review of Saudi Arabian economic and business activity; Publr SAIFUDDIN A. ASHOOR; Gen. Man. WALID S. ASHOOR.

Sayidaty (My Lady): POB 4556, Madina Rd, Jeddah 21412; tel. (2) 639-1888; fax (2) 669-5549; internet www.sayidaty.net; f. 1981; publ. in Arabic and English edns; women's magazine; publ. by Saudi Research and Publishing Co; Editor-in-Chief MUHAMMAD FAHAD AL-HARTHI.

Ash-Shams (The Sun): Riyadh; internet shms.pressera.com; f. 2005; tabloid format; sports, culture, entertainment; publishing licence revoked by the Govt in Feb. 2006, but restored after some six weeks; Editor-in-Chief KHALAF AL-HARBI.

Al-Yamama: POB 851, Riyadh 11421; tel. (1) 442-0000; fax (1) 441-7114; f. 1952; literary magazine; Editor-in-Chief ABDULLAH AL-JAHLAN; circ. 35,000.

OTHER PERIODICALS

Ahlan Wasahlan (Welcome): POB 8013, Jeddah 21482; tel. (2) 686-2349; fax (2) 686-2006; internet pr.sv.net/aw; monthly; flight journal of Saudi Arabian Airlines; Gen. Man. and Editor-in-Chief YARUB A. BALKHAIR; circ. 150,000.

Ad-Daragh: POB 2945, Riyadh 11461; tel. (1) 401-1999; fax (1) 401-3597; e-mail info@aldarahmagazine.com; internet aldarahmagazine.com; history journal; publ. by King Abdulaziz Foundation for Research and Archives.

Al-Faysal: POB 3, Riyadh 11411; tel. (1) 465-3027; fax (1) 464-7851; monthly; f. 1976; Arabic; culture, education, health, interviews; Man. Editor ABDULLAH Y. AL-KOWAILEET.

Majallat al-Iqtisad wal-Idara (Journal of Economics and Administration): King Abd al-Aziz University, POB 9031, Jeddah 21413; twice a year; Chief Editor Prof. ABD AL-AZIZ A. DIYAB.

Al-Manhal (The Spring): POB 2925, Jeddah; tel. (2) 643-2124; fax (2) 642-8853; e-mail info@manhalmagazine.com; f. 1937; monthly; Arabic; cultural, literary, political and scientific; Editor ZUHAIR N. AL-ANSARI.

The MWL Journal: Press and Publications Department, Rabitat al-Alam al-Islami, POB 537, Mecca; fax (2) 544-1622; e-mail info@themwl.org; internet www.themwl.org; monthly; English; Dir MURAD SULAIMAN IRQISOUS.

Ar-Rabita: POB 537, Mecca; tel. (2) 560-0919; fax (2) 543-1488; e-mail info@themwl.org; internet www.themwl.org; Arabic; Chief Editor Dr OSMAN ABUZAID.

Saudi Review: POB 4288, Jeddah 21491; tel. (2) 651-7442; fax (2) 653-0693; f. 1966; English; monthly; newsletter from Saudi newspapers and broadcasting service; publ. by International Communications Co; Chief Editor SAAD AL-MABROUK; circ. 5,000.

Ash-Sharkiah-Elle (Oriental Elle): POB 6, Riyadh; monthly; Arabic; women's magazine; Editor SAMIRA M. KHASHAGGI.

As-Soqoor (Falcons): POB 2973, Riyadh 11461; tel. (1) 476-6566; f. 1978; 2 a year; air-force journal; cultural activities; Editor HAMAD A. AS-SALEH.

At-Tadhamon al-Islami (Islamic Solidarity): Ministry of Pilgrimage (Hajj) Affairs, Omar bin al-Khatab St, Riyadh 11183; monthly; Editor Dr MUSTAFA ABD AL-WAHID.

At-Tijarah (Commerce): POB 1264, Jeddah 21431; tel. (2) 651-5111; fax (2) 651-7373; e-mail jcci@mail.gcc.com.bh; f. 1960; monthly; publ. by Jeddah Chamber of Commerce and Industry; Chair. Sheikh ISMAIL ABU DAUD; circ. 8,000.

NEWS AGENCIES

International Islamic News Agency (IINA): POB 5054, Jeddah 21422; tel. (2) 665-2056; fax (2) 665-9358; e-mail iina@islamicnews.org.sa; internet www.islamicnews.org.sa; f. 1972; operates under the auspices of the Organization of the Islamic Conference; Dir-Gen. ABD AL-WAHAB KASHIF.

Saudi Press Agency (SPA): POB 7186, King Fahd Rd, Riyadh 11171; tel. (1) 419-5485; fax (1) 419-5685; e-mail wass@spa.gov.sa; internet www.spa.gov.sa; f. 1970; the Govt planned to transform the SPA into a public corpn; Dir-Gen. ABDULLAH BIN FAHD AL-HUSSAIN.

Publishers

Assir Establishment for Press and Publishing: POB 15156, Abha; tel. (7) 227-3333; fax (7) 227-3590; f. 1998; publishes Al-Watan; cap. SR 200m.; Chair. FAHD AL-HARITHI.

Al-Bilad Publishing Organization: POB 6340, As-Sahafa St, Jeddah 21442; tel. (2) 672-3000; fax (2) 671-2545; publishes Al-Bilad and Iqra'a; Dir-Gen. AMIN ABDULLAH AL-QARQOURI.

Dar al-Maiman Publishers and Distributors: POB 90020, Riyadh 11613; tel. and fax (1) 4880806.

Dar ash-Shareff for Publishing and Distribution: POB 58287, Riyadh 11594; tel. (1) 403-4931; fax (1) 405-2234; f. 1992; fiction, religion, science and social sciences; Pres. IBRAHIM AL-HAZEMI.

Dar al-Yaum Press, Printing and Publishing Ltd: POB 565, Dammam 31421; tel. (3) 858-0800; fax (3) 858-8777; e-mail mail@alyaum.com; internet www.alyaum.com; f. 1964; publishes Al-Yaum; Chair. ABD AL-AZIZ MUHAMMAD AL-HUGAIL; Gen. Man. SALIH ALI AL-HUMAIDAN.

International Publications Agency (IPA): POB 70, Dhahran 31942; tel. and fax (3) 895-4925; publishes material of local interest; Man. SAID SALAH.

Al-Jazirah Corpn for Press, Printing and Publishing: POB 354, Riyadh 11411; tel. (1) 441-9999; fax (1) 441-2536; e-mail ccs@al-jazirah.com; internet www.al-jazirah.com.sa; f. 1964; 42 mems; publishes Al-Jazirah daily newspaper; Chair. MUTLAQ BIN ABDULLAH AL-MUTLAQ; Editor-in-Chief KHALID EL-MALEK.

Al-Madina Press Establishment: POB 807, Jeddah 21421; tel. (2) 671-2100; fax (2) 671-1877; f. 1937; publishes Al-Madina al-Munawara; Gen. Man. AHMAD SALAH JAMJOUM.

Makkah Printing and Information Establishment: POB 5803, Jarwal Sheikh Sayed Halabi Bldg, Mecca; tel. (2) 542-7868; publishes An-Nadwah daily newspaper; Chair. MUHAMMAD ABDOU YAMANI.

Okaz Organization for Press and Publication: POB 1508, Jeddah 21441; tel. (2) 672-2630; fax (2) 672-8150; publishes Okaz and Saudi Gazette; Chair. SAEED AL-HARTHI.

Al Rushed Publishers: POB 17522, Riyadh 11494; tel. (1) 459-3451; fax (1) 457-3381; e-mail alrushd@alrushdryh.com; internet www.rushd.com; scientific and academic publs.

Saudi Publishing and Distributing House: Umm Aslam District, nr Muslaq, POB 2043, Jeddah 21451; tel. (2) 629-4278; fax (2) 629-4290; e-mail info@spdh-sa.com; internet www.spdh-sa.com; f. 1966; publishers, importers and distributors of English and Arabic books; Chair. MUHAMMAD SALAHUDDIN.

Saudi Research and Publishing Co: POB 478, Riyadh 11411; tel. (1) 441-9933; fax (1) 442-9555; internet www.srpc.com; publs incl. Arab News, Asharq al-Awsat, Al-Majalla, Al-Muslimoon and Sayidati; Chair. Prince FAISAL BIN SALMAN BIN ABD AL-AZIZ; Gen. Man. AZZAM AD-DAKHIL.

Al-Yamama Press Establishment: POB 2943, Riyadh 11476; tel. (1) 442-0000; fax (1) 441-7116; publishes Ar-Riyadh and Al-Yamama; Dir-Gen. SAKHAL MAIDAN.

Broadcasting and Communications

TELECOMMUNICATIONS

Regulatory Authority

Communications and Information Technology Commission (CITC): POB 75606, Riyadh; tel. (1) 461-8000; fax (1) 461-8002; internet www.citc.gov.sa; f. 2001 under the name Saudi Communications Commission; present name adopted in 2003; ind. regulatory authority; Gov. ABD AR-RAHMAN BIN AHMAD AL-JAAFARI.

Principal Operators

Ettihad Etisalat: POB 9979, Riyadh 11423; tel. (1) 211-8015; fax (1) 211-8029; e-mail info@mobily.com.sa; internet www.mobily.com.sa; f. 2004; owned by a consortium led by Emirates Telecommunications Corpn (United Arab Emirates); awarded the second licence to provide mobile telephone services in 2004; operates under the brand name Mobily (launched 2005); 14.8m. subscribers (Dec. 2008); Chair. ABD AL-AZIZ BIN SALEH AS-SUGHAYIR; CEO KHALID AL-KAF.

Saudi Telecommunications Co—Saudi Telecom (STC): POB 87912, Riyadh 11652; tel. (1) 215-3030; fax (1) 215-2734; e-mail contactus@stc.com.sa; internet www.stc.com.sa; f. 1998; partially privatized in 2002; provides telecommunications services in Saudi Arabia; cap. SR 12,000m.; Chair. Dr MUHAMMAD BIN SULIMAN AL-JASER; Pres. Eng. SA'UD BIN MAJID AD-DAWEESH.

Zain Saudi Arabia: POB 295814, Riyadh 11351; tel. (1) 216-1800; e-mail corporate.communications@sa.zain.com; internet www.sa.zain.com; f. 2007; wholly owned by Mobile Telecommunications Co KSC (Zain Kuwait); awarded the third licence to provide mobile telephone services in 2007; Chair. Prince HUSSAM IBN SA'UD IBN ABD AL-AZIZ AS-SA'UD; CEO SAAD AL-BARRAK.

In February 2008 three further fixed-line licences were awarded to Etihad Atheeb Telecom, Al-Mutakamilah Consortioum and Optical Communications Co.

BROADCASTING

Radio

Saudi Arabian Broadcasting Service: c/o Ministry of Information and Culture, POB 60059, Riyadh 11545; tel. (1) 401-4440; fax (1) 403-8177; e-mail saudi-radio@saudiradio.net.sa; internet www.saudiradio.net; 24 medium- and short-wave stations, incl. Jeddah, Riyadh, Dammam and Abha, broadcast programmes in Arabic and English; 23 FM stations; overseas service in Bengali, English, Farsi, French, Hausa, Indonesian, Somali, Swahili, Turkestani, Turkish and Urdu; Dir-Gen. MUHAMMAD AL-MANSOOR.

Saudi Aramco FM Radio: Bldg 3030 LIP, Dhahran 31311; tel. (3) 876-1845; fax (3) 876-1608; f. 1948; English; private; for employees of Saudi Aramco; Man. ESSAM Z. TAWFIQ.

Television

Saudi Arabian Government Television Service: POB 7971, Riyadh 11472; tel. (1) 401-4440; fax (1) 404-4192; e-mail satepjeng@moci.gov.sa; began transmission 1965; 112 stations, incl. six main stations at Riyadh, Jeddah, Medina, Dammam, Qassim and Abha, transmit programmes in Arabic and English; operates four channels: Channel 1 (Arabic), Channel 2 (English and French); Channel 3 (sport); Al-Ekhbariya (news); Dir-Gen. ABD AL-AZIZ AL-HASSAN (Channel 1).

SAUDI ARABIA

Finance

(cap. = capital; res = reserves; dep. = deposits; m. = million; brs = branches; amounts in Saudi riyals unless otherwise stated)

BANKING

In 2007 the Saudi Arabian banking system consisted of: the Saudi Arabian Monetary Agency, as central note-issuing and regulatory body; 11 local commercial banks; 13 foreign banks; and six specialist banks. There is a policy of 'Saudiization' of the foreign banks.

Central Bank

Saudi Arabian Monetary Agency (SAMA): POB 2992, Riyadh 11169; tel. (1) 463-3000; fax (1) 466-2966; e-mail info@sama.gov.sa; internet www.sama.gov.sa; f. 1952; functions include stabilization of currency, administration of monetary reserves, regulation of banking and insurance sectors, and issue of notes and coins; dep. 414,323.6m., total assets 878,963.6m. (June 2007); Gov. Dr MUHAMMAD IBN SULAYMAN AL-JASSER; 10 brs.

National Banks

Alinma Bank: POB 66674, Al-Anoud Tower, King Fahad Rd, Riyadh 11586; internet www.alinma.com; f. 2006; cap. 15,000m., total assets 15,556m. (Dec. 2008); Chair. ABD AL-AZIZ ABDULLAH AZ-ZAMIL; CEO ABD AL-MOSHEN AL-FARES.

National Commercial Bank (NCB): POB 3555, King Abd al-Aziz St, Jeddah 21481; tel. (2) 649-3333; fax (2) 644-6468; e-mail contact@alahli.com; internet www.alahli.com; f. 1950; 69.3% govt-owned; cap. 15,000.0m., res 12,408.2m., dep. 78,560.0m. (Dec. 2007); Chair. and Man. Dir Sheikh ABDULLAH SALIM BAHAMDAN; CEO ABD AL-KAREEM ABU AN-NASR; 275 brs (2008).

Ar-Rajhi Banking and Investment Corpn (Ar-Rajhi Bank): POB 28, Al-Akariya Bldg, Oleya St, Riyadh 11411; tel. (1) 211-6000; fax (1) 460-0922; e-mail contactus@alrajhibank.com.sa; internet www.alrajhibank.com.sa; f. 1988; operates according to Islamic financial principles; cap. 13,500.0m., res 8,517.8m., dep. 97,224.2m. (Dec. 2007); Chair. and Man. Dir Sheikh SULAYMAN BIN ABD AL-AZIZ AR-RAJHI; CEO ABDULLAH SULAIMAN AR-RAJHI; 425 brs (2008).

Riyad Bank Ltd: POB 22601, King Abd al-Aziz St, Riyadh 11416; tel. (1) 401-3030; fax (1) 404-1255; internet www.riyadbank.com.sa; f. 1957; cap. 6,250.0m., res 6,459.7m., dep. 104,001.5m. (Dec. 2007); Chair. RASHED A. AR-RASHED; Pres. and CEO TALAL I. AL-QUDAIBI; 201 brs (2008).

Specialist Bank

Arab Investment Co SAA (TAIC): POB 4009, King Abd al-Aziz St, Riyadh 11491; tel. (1) 476-0601; fax (1) 476-0514; e-mail taic@taic.com; internet www.taic.com; f. 1974 by 17 Arab countries for investment and banking; cap. US $500.0m., res $193.0m., dep. $2,625,429m. (Dec. 2006); Chair. Dr MUHAMMAD SULAYMAN AL-JASSER; Dir-Gen. Dr SALIH AL-HUMAIDAN; 1 br.

Banks with Foreign Interests

Arab National Bank (ANB): POB 56921, King Faisal St, North Murabba, Riyadh 11564; tel. (1) 402-9000; fax (1) 402-7747; e-mail info@anb.com.sa; internet www.anb.com.sa; f. 1980; ownership: Arab Bank PLC, Jordan, 40%, Saudi shareholders 60%; cap. 4,550.0m., res 5,887.6m., dep. 76,308.2m. (Dec. 2007); Chair. ABDULLATIF HAMAD AL-JABR; Man. Dir and CEO Dr ROBERT EID; 131 brs (2008).

Bank al-Jazira: POB 6277, Khalid bin al-Waleed St, Jeddah 21442; tel. (2) 651-8070; fax (2) 653-2478; e-mail info@baj.com.sa; internet www.baj.com.sa; 94.17% Saudi-owned; cap. 2,250.0m., res 1,537.5m., dep. 15,647.1m. (Dec. 2007); Chair. TAHA ABDULLAH AL-KUWAIZ; CEO KHALID OUDGHIRI; 24 brs (2008).

Banque Saudi Fransi (Saudi French Bank): POB 56006, Ma'ather Rd, Riyadh 11554; tel. (1) 404-2222; fax (1) 404-2311; e-mail communications@alfransi.com.sa; internet www.alfransi.com.sa; f. 1977; name changed as above in 2002; Saudi shareholders 68.9%, Calyon, Paris La Défense 31.1%; cap. 5,625.0m., res 5,547.3m., dep. 82,130.0m. (Dec. 2007); Chair. IBRAHIM A. AT-TOUQ; Man. Dir JEAN MARION; 75 brs (2008).

SAMBA Financial Group: POB 833, Riyadh 11421; tel. and fax (1) 477-4770; e-mail sambacare@samba.com; internet www.samba.com.sa; f. 1980; 96.4% owned by Saudi nationals; merged with United Saudi Bank in 1999; cap. 6,000.0m., res 6,305.8m., dep. 102,666.3m. (Dec. 2006); Chair. SAUD A. AL-GOSAIBI; Man. Dir and CEO EISA AL-EISA; 65 brs (2008).

Saudi British Bank (SABB): POB 9084, Prince Abdulaziz bin Mossaid bin Jalawi St, Riyadh 11413; tel. (1) 405-0677; fax (1) 405-0660; e-mail sabb@sabb.com; internet www.sabb.com.sa; f. 1978; 60% owned by Saudi nationals, 40% by HSBC Holdings BV; cap. 3,750.0m., res 4,624.4m., dep. 84,118.8m. (Dec. 2007); Chair. KHALED SULIMAN OLAYAN; Man. Dir RICHARD GROVES; 68 brs (2008).

Saudi Hollandi Bank (Saudi Dutch Bank): POB 1467, Head Office Bldg, adh-Dhabab St, Riyadh 11431; tel. (1) 406-7888; fax (1) 403-1104; e-mail csc@shb.com.sa; internet www.shb.com.sa; f. 1977 to assume activities of Algemene Bank Nederland NV in Saudi Arabia; a jt-stock co; ownership: ABN AMRO Bank (Netherlands) 40%, Saudi citizens 60%; cap. 2,646.0m., res 1,759.7m., dep. 43,762.6m. (Dec. 2007); Chair. Sheikh MUBARAK ABDULLAH AL-KHAFRAH; Man. Dir GEOFFREY CALVERT; 43 brs (2008).

Saudi Investment Bank (SAIB): POB 3533, Riyadh 11481; tel. (1) 478-6000; fax (1) 477-6781; e-mail info@saib.com.sa; internet www.saib.com.sa; f. 1976; provides a comprehensive range of traditional and specialized banking services; cap. 2,406.3m., res 2,089.3m., dep. 32,378.0m. (Dec. 2006); Chair. Dr ABD AL-AZIZ O'HALI; Pres. and Gen. Man. SA'UD AS-SALEH; 33 brs (2008).

Government Specialized Credit Institutions

Real Estate Development Fund (REDF): POB 5591, Riyadh 11139; tel. (1) 479-2222; fax (1) 479-0148; f. 1974; provides interest-free loans to Saudi individuals and cos for private or commercial housing projects; loans granted amounted to 5,264m. in 2002; Gen. Dir AHMAD AL-AKEIL; 25 brs.

Saudi Arabian Agricultural Bank (SAAB): POB 1811, Riyadh 11126; tel. (1) 402-3911; fax (1) 402-2359; f. 1963; provides loans to farmers for industry-specific use; loans disbursed amounted to 1,320.0m. in 2002; Controller-Gen. ABDULLAH SAAD AL-MENGASH; Gen. Man. ABD AL-AZIZ MUHAMMAD AL-MANQUR; 70 brs.

Saudi Credit Bank: POB 3401, Riyadh 11471; tel. (1) 402-9128; f. 1973; provides interest-free loans for specific purposes to Saudi citizens of moderate means; loans disbursed amounted to 348.0m. in 2002; Chair. SAID IBN SAIED; Dir-Gen. MUHAMMAD AD-DRIES; 24 brs.

STOCK EXCHANGE

The Electronic Securities Information System (ESIS) was formed in 1990 and operated by the Saudi Arabian Monetary Agency (see Central Bank). The ESIS was superseded by a new market system, Tadawul, in 2001. Since 2003 Tadawul has been supervised by the Capital Market Authority. A total of 59,680m. shares were traded in 2008, amounting to SR 1,962,950m.

Saudi Stock Exchange (Tadawul): POB 60612, Riyadh 11555; tel. (1) 218-9999; e-mail webinfo@tadawul.com.sa; internet www.tadawul.com.sa; f. 2001; restructured as a jt stock co in 2007; 115 cos listed in April 2008; Chair. FAHAD AL-MUBARAK.

Regulatory Authority

Capital Market Authority: POB 220022, Riyadh 11311; fax (1) 279-7770; e-mail info@cma.org.sa; internet www.cma.org.sa; f. 2003 to regulate and develop the Saudi Arabian capital market; Chair. Dr ABD AR-RAHMAN A. AT-TUWAIJRI.

INSURANCE

A new Co-operative Insurance Law, promulgated in 2004, required all companies operating in the kingdom to be locally registered and brought the sector under the supervision of the Saudi Arabian Monetary Agency (see Central Bank). In 2007 42 insurance companies were operating in Saudi Arabia.

Allied Cooperative Insurance Group: POB 7076, Jeddah 21462; tel. (2) 657-4999; fax (2) 657-6643; e-mail webmaster@acig.com.sa; internet www.acig.com.sa; Chair. MUHAMMAD HANI ABD AL-KADER AL-BAKRI; CEO Dr OMAR Z. HAFIZ.

Arabia Ace Insurance Co Ltd (E.C.): POB 276, Dammam 31411; tel. (3) 832-4441; fax (3) 834-9389; e-mail ace@ace-arabia.com; internet www.ace-arabia.com; cap. US $1m.; Chair. Sheikh ABD AL-KARIM AL-KHEREIJI; Man. Dir TAJUDDIN HASSAN.

Bank Al-Jazira Takaful Ta'awuni: POB 6277, Jeddah 21442; tel. and fax (2) 651-8070; e-mail infotakaful@baj.com.sa; internet www.takaful.com.sa; Islamic life insurance; Gen. Man. DAWOOD Y. TAYLOR.

Mediterranean and Gulf Cooperative Insurance and Reinsurance Co (MEDGULF): POB 2302, Riyadh 11451; tel. (1) 477-9229; fax (1) 478-9219; e-mail riyadh@medgulf.com; internet www.medgulf.com.

Ar-Rajhi Co for Co-operative Insurance: POB 67791, Riyadh 11517; tel. (1) 475-2211; fax (1) 475-5017; e-mail alrajhi@alrajhiinsurance.com.sa; internet www.alrajhiinsurance.com.sa; f. 1990 as Ar-Rajhi Insurance Co; renamed as above 2006; cap. 200m.; Chair. ABDULLAH SULAIMAN AR-RAJHI.

Red Sea Insurance Group of Cos: POB 5627, Jeddah 21432; tel. (2) 660-3538; fax (2) 665-5418; e-mail redsea@anet.net.sa; internet www.redseains.com; f. 1974; insurance, devt and reinsurance; Chair. KHALDOUN B. BARAKAT.

SAUDI ARABIA

RSA Saudi Arabia—Al-Alamiya: POB 2374, Jeddah 21451; tel. (2) 692-7085; fax (2) 692-7125; e-mail alamiya.insurance@sa.rsagroup.com; internet www.alamiyainsurance.com.sa; part of the Royal & Sun Alliance (RSA) Group; total assets US $73.0m. (2002); Chair. WAHIB S. BINZAGR; Man. Dir P. W. HEAD; Country Man. W. J. DAVIES.

SABB Takaful Co: POB 9086, Riyadh 11413; tel. (1) 403-0087; fax (1) 402-5832; internet www.sabbtakaful.com; f. 2007; 32.5% owned by Saudi British Bank (SABB), 32.5% by HSBC, 35% by private investors; cap. 100m.; Man. Dir DAVID HUNT.

Sanad Cooperative Insurance and Reinsurance Co: Third Floor, Dareen Centre, Alahsa St, Riyadh 27477; tel. (1) 292-7111; fax (1) 292-7888; e-mail info@sanad.com.sa; internet www.sanad.com.sa; Chair. AHMAD AL-ABDULLAH AL-AKEIL; CEO AZMIN F. DAYA.

Saudi IAIC Cooperative Insurance Co (SALAMA): POB 122392, Jeddah 21332; tel. (2) 664-7877; fax (2) 664-7387; e-mail customers.relation@salama.com.sa; internet www.salama.com.sa; Chair. SALEH J. MALAIKAH; Gen. Man. KHALID BARBOUD.

Saudi National Insurance Co (E.C.): POB 5832, Jeddah 21432; tel. (2) 660-6200; fax (2) 667-4530; e-mail snic@eajb.com.sa; internet www.snic.com.sa; f. 1974; Gen. Man. OMAR S. BILANI.

Tawuniya (NCCI): POB 86959, Riyadh 11632; tel. (1) 218-0100; fax (1) 218-0102; e-mail info@ncci.com.sa; internet tawuniya.com.sa; f. 1985 by royal decree as National Co for Co-operative Insurance; name changed as above 2007; owned by three govt agencies; proposed privatization approved by the Supreme Economic Council in May 2004; initial public offering of shares in Dec. 2004; auth. cap. 500m.; Chair. SULAYMAN AL-HUMMAYYD; Man. Dir and Gen. Man. ALI A. AS-SUBAIHIN; 13 brs.

United Cooperative Assurance Co (UCA): POB 5019, Medina Rd, Jeddah 21422; tel. (2) 653-0068; fax (2) 651-1936; e-mail jeddah@uca.com.sa; internet www.uca.com.sa; f. 1974 as United Commercial Agencies Ltd; name changed as above 2007; all classes of insurance; cap. 200m.; Chair. HASSAN M. MAHASSINI; CEO MACHAAL A. KARAM.

Wala'a Insurance: POB 31616, Al-Khobar 31952; tel. (3) 865-2200; fax (3) 865-2255; e-mail walaa@walaa.com; internet www.walaa.com; f. 1976; operated by Saudi United Cooperative Insurance Co; provides all classes of insurance for businesses and govt agencies; majority shareholding held by Ahmad Hamad al-Gosaibi & Bros; cap. US $5m.; Chair. and Man. Dir Sheikh ABD AL-AZIZ HAMAD AL-GOSAIBI; CEO ABDULLAH M. AL-OTHMAN (acting); 6 brs.

Trade and Industry

DEVELOPMENT ORGANIZATIONS

Arab Petroleum Investments Corpn: POB 9599, Dammam 31423; tel. (3) 847-0444; fax (3) 847-0011; e-mail apicorp@apicorp-arabia.com; internet www.apicorp-arabia.com; f. 1975; affiliated to the Organization of Arab Petroleum Exporting Countries; specializes in financing petroleum and petrochemical projects and related industries in the Arab world and in other developing countries; shareholders: Kuwait, Saudi Arabia and the United Arab Emirates (17% each), Libya (15%), Iraq and Qatar (10% each), Algeria (5%), Bahrain, Egypt and Syria (3% each); auth. cap. US $1,200m.; cap. $550m. (Dec. 2006); Chair. ABDULLAH A. AZ-ZAID; Gen. Man. and CEO AHMAD BIN HAMAD AN-NUAIMI.

National Agricultural Development Co (NADEC): POB 2557, Riyadh 11461; tel. (1) 404-0000; fax (1) 405-5522; e-mail info@nadec.com.sa; internet www.nadec.com.sa; f. 1981; interests include four dairy farms, 40,000 ha for cultivation of wheat, barley, forage and vegetables and processing of dates; the Govt has a 20% share; chief agency for agricultural devt; cap. SR 400m.; Chair. SULAYMAN ABD AL-AZIZ AR-RAJHI; CEO ABD AL-AZIZ AL-BABTAIN.

Public Investment Fund: POB 6847, Riyadh 11452; tel. (1) 477-4488; fax (1) 474-2693; e-mail info@mof.gov.sa; internet www.mof.gov.sa/en/docs/ests/sub_invbox.htm; f. 1971 to facilitate devt of the nat. economy; under the control of the Ministry of Finance; provides the Govt's share of capital to mixed capital cos; has managed Sanabil al-Saudia, a sovereign wealth fund with cap. of US $5,300m., since 2008; 100% state-owned; Chair. Dr IBRAHIM IBN ABD AL-AZIZ AL-ASSAF (Minister of Finance); Sec.-Gen. MANSOUR AL-MAIMAN.

Saudi Arabian General Investment Authority (SAGIA): POB 5927, Riyadh 11432; tel. (1) 203-5555; fax (1) 263-2894; e-mail marketing_dept@sagia.gov.sa; internet www.sagia.gov.sa; f. 2000 to promote foreign investment; Gov. AMIR BIN ABDULLAH AD-DABBAGH.

Saudi Fund for Development (SFD): POB 50483, Riyadh 11523; tel. (1) 464-0292; fax (1) 464-7450; e-mail info@sfd.gov.sa; internet www.sfd.gov.sa; f. 1974 to help finance projects in developing countries; owned by Saudi Govt; had financed 417 projects by 2007; total commitments amounted to SR 27,728.36m.; Chair. Dr IBRAHIM IBN ABD AL-AZIZ AL-ASSAF (Minister of Finance); Vice-Chair. and Man. Dir E. YOUSUF I. AL-BASSAM.

Directory

Saudi Industrial Development Fund (SIDF): POB 4143, Riyadh 11149; tel. (1) 477-4002; fax (1) 479-0165; e-mail sidf@sidf.gov.sa; internet www.sidf.gov.sa; f. 1974; supports and promotes local industrial devt, providing medium-term interest-free loans; also offers marketing, technical, financial and administrative advice; loans disbursed amounted to SR 8,544m. in 2007; cap. SR 20,000m. (2007); Chair. YOUSUF BIN IBRAHIM AL-BASSAM; Dir-Gen. ABDULLAH MUHAMMAD AL-OBOUDI.

TASNEE: POB 26707, Riyadh 11496; tel. (1) 476-7166; fax (1) 477-0898; e-mail general@tasnee.com; internet www.tasnee.com; f. 1985 as the National Industrialization Co to promote and establish industrial projects in Saudi Arabia; cap. SR 785m.; 100% owned by Saudi nationals; Chair. MUBARAK BIN ABDULLAH AL-KHAFRAH; CEO MOAYYED BIN ISSA AL-QURTAS.

CHAMBERS OF COMMERCE

Council of Saudi Chambers of Commerce and Industry: POB 16683, Riyadh 11474; tel. (1) 218-2222; fax (1) 218-2111; e-mail council@saudichambers.org.sa; internet www.saudichambers.org.sa; comprises one delegate from each of the chambers of commerce in the kingdom; Chair. MUHAMMAD ABD AL-QADER AL-FADEL; Sec.-Gen. Dr FAHD AS-SULTAN.

Abha Chamber of Commerce and Industry: POB 722, Abha; tel. (7) 227-1818; fax (7) 227-1919; e-mail info@abhacci.org.sa; internet www.abhacci.org.sa; Pres. ABDULLAH SAID AL-MOBTY; Sec.-Gen. Dr HAMDI ALI AL-MALIKI.

Al-Ahsa Chamber of Commerce and Industry: POB 1519, al-Ahsa 31982; tel. (3) 582-0458; fax (3) 587-5274; internet www.hcci.org.sa; Pres. SULAYMAN A. AL-HAMAAD.

Ar'ar Chamber of Commerce and Industry: POB 440, Ar'ar; tel. (4) 662-6544; fax (4) 662-4581; Sec.-Gen. THANI B. AL-ANEZI.

Al-Baha Chamber of Commerce and Industry: POB 311, al-Baha; tel. (7) 727-0291; fax (7) 828-0146; Pres. ABDULLAH M. AL-MOAGEB; Sec.-Gen. YAHYA AZ-ZAHRANI.

Eastern Province Chamber of Commerce and Industry (Asharqia Chamber): POB 719, Dammam 31421; tel. (3) 857-1111; fax (3) 857-0607; e-mail info@chamber.org.sa; internet www.chamber.org.sa; f. 1952; Pres. ABD AR-RAHMAN RASHID AR-RASHID; Sec.-Gen. IBRAHIM ABDULLAH AL-OLAYAN.

Federation of Gulf Co-operation Council Chambers (FGCCC): POB 2198, Dammam 31451; tel. (3) 826-5943; fax (3) 826-6794; e-mail fgccc@zajil.net; internet www.fgccc.org; Pres. SALIM H. ALKHALILI; Sec.-Gen. MUHAMMAD A. AL-MULLA.

Ha'il Chamber of Commerce and Industry: POB 1291, Ha'il; tel. (6) 532-1060; fax (6) 533-1366; e-mail info@hail_chamber.org.sa; internet www.hail-chamber.org.sa; Pres. KHALID A. AS-SAIF.

Jeddah Chamber of Commerce and Industry: POB 1264, Jeddah 21431; tel. (2) 651-5111; fax (2) 651-7373; e-mail customerservice@jcci.org.sa; internet www.jcci.org.sa; f. 1946; 26,000 mems; Pres. MUHAMMAD ABD AL-QADER AL-FADEL; Sec.-Gen. Dr MUSTAFA K. SABRI.

Jizan Chamber of Commerce and Industry: POB 201, Jizan; tel. (7) 322-5155; fax (7) 322-3635; Pres. Eng. FAHD A. QALM.

Al-Jouf Chamber of Commerce and Industry: POB 585, al-Jouf; tel. (4) 624-9060; fax (4) 624-0108; Pres. MARZOUK S. AL-RASHID; Sec.-Gen. AHMAD KHALIFA AL-MUSALLAM.

Al-Majma' Chamber of Commerce and Industry: POB 165, al-Majma' 11952; tel. (6) 432-0268; fax (6) 432-2655; Pres. FAHD MUHAMMAD AR-RABIAH; Sec.-Gen. ABDULLAH IBRAHIM AL-JAAWAN.

Mecca Chamber of Commerce and Industry: POB 1086, Mecca; tel. (2) 534-3838; fax (2) 534-2904; f. 1947; Pres. ADEL ABDULLAH KA'AKI; Sec.-Gen. YASSER ABDULLAH AWAN.

Medina Chamber of Commerce and Industry: POB 443, King Abd al-Aziz Rd, Medina; tel. (4) 838-8909; fax (4) 838-8905; e-mail info@mcci.org.sa; internet www.mcci.org.sa; Pres. SALEH R. AS-SOHIME; Sec.-Gen. Dr LOUI BAKUR AT-TAYAR.

Najran Chamber of Commerce and Industry: POB 1138, Najran; tel. (7) 522-2216; fax (7) 522-3926; e-mail ywadidi@najcci.org.sa; internet www.najcci.org.sa; Pres. ALI BIN HAMAD HAMROUR AL-ABAAS; Sec.-Gen. ALI BIN SALEH AL-QUMAISH.

Al-Qassim Chamber of Commerce and Industry: POB 444, Buraydah, Qassim; tel. (6) 381-4000; fax (6) 381-2231; e-mail info@qcc.org.sa; internet www.qcc.org.sa; Pres. ABDULLAH S. AL-OTHIM.

Al-Qurayat Chamber of Commerce and Industry: POB 416, al-Qurayat; tel. (4) 642-6200; fax (4) 642-3172; Pres. OTHMAN ABDULLAH AL-YOUSUF; Sec.-Gen. JAMAL ALI AL-GHAMDI.

Riyadh Chamber of Commerce and Industry: POB 596, Riyadh 11421; tel. (1) 404-0044; fax (1) 402-1103; internet www.riyadhchamber.com; f. 1961; acts as arbitrator in business disputes, information centre; Pres. ABD AR-RAHMAN ALI AL-JERAISY; Sec.-Gen. HUSSEIN ABD AR-RAHMAN AL-AZAL; 23,000 mems.

SAUDI ARABIA
Directory

Tabouk Chamber of Commerce and Industry: POB 567, Tabouk; tel. (4) 422-2736; fax (4) 422-7387; internet www.tcci.org.sa; Pres. MUHAMMAD H. AL-WABSI; Sec.-Gen. AWADH AL-BALAWI.

Ta'if Chamber of Commerce and Industry: POB 1005, Ta'if; tel. (2) 736-6800; fax (2) 738-0040; e-mail info@taifchamber.org.sa; internet www.taifcci.com; Pres. NAIF A. AL-ADWANI; Sec.-Gen. Eng. YOUSUF MUHAMMAD ASH-SHAFI.

Yanbu Chamber of Commerce and Industry: POB 58, Yanbu; tel. (4) 322-7878; fax (4) 322-6800; f. 1979; publishes quarterly magazine; 5,000 members; Pres. Dr MANSOUR M. AL-ANSARI; Sec.-Gen. KHALED SALMAN AS-SAHALI.

STATE HYDROCARBONS COMPANIES

Saudi Arabian Oil Co (Saudi Aramco): POB 5000, Dhahran 31311; tel. (3) 872-0115; fax (3) 873-8190; e-mail webmaster@aramco.com.sa; internet www.saudiaramco.com; f. 1933; previously known as Arabian-American Oil Co (Aramco); in 1993 incorporated the Saudi Arabian Marketing and Refining Co (SAMAREC, f. 1988) by merger of operations; holds the principal working concessions in Saudi Arabia; operates five wholly owned refineries (at Jeddah, Rabigh, Ras Tanura, Riyadh and Yanbu) with total capacity of more than 1m. barrels per day; Pres. and CEO KHALID A. AL-FALIH; Sr Vice-Pres. (Engineering and Project Management) SALIM S. AL-AYDH.

Aramco Gulf Operations Co (AGOC): POB 688, Khafji City 31971; tel. (3) 766-4024; fax (3) 767-5514; e-mail alsultanbf@kjo.com.sa; internet www.agoc.com.sa; f. 2000; wholly owned by Saudi Aramco; holds concession for offshore exploitation of Saudi Arabia's half-interest in the Saudi Arabia-Kuwait Neutral Zone; Pres. and CEO MUHAMMAD A. ASH-SHAMMARY.

Rabigh Refining and Petrochemical Co (Petro Rabigh): POB 666, Rabigh 21911; tel. (2) 425-1855; fax (2) 425-2732; internet www.petrorabigh.com; f. 2005; jt venture between Saudi Aramco and Sumitomo Chemical (Japan); operation of integrated oil-refining and petrochemical production facilities at Rabigh; initial public offering of 20% of shares announced in Jan. 2008; Chair. ABD AL-AZIZ F. AL-KHAYYAL; Pres. and CEO SAAD FAHAD AD-DOSARI.

Saudi Arabian Lubricating Oil Co (Petromin Oils): POB 1432, Jeddah 21431; tel. (2) 661-3333; fax (2) 661-3322; e-mail info@petrominoils.com; internet www.petrominoils.com; f. 1968; 71% owned by Saudi Aramco, 29% by Mobil; manufacture and marketing of lubricating oils and other related products; production 140m. litres (2002); cap. 110m. riyals; Chair. Eng. ALI A. AL-MUHAREB; Pres. and CEO Eng. SALEM H. SHAHEEN.

Saudi Aramco Lubricating Oil Refining Co (LUBEREF): POB 5518, Jeddah 21432; tel. (2) 427-5497; fax (2) 636-6933; e-mail webmaster@luberef.com; internet www.luberef.com; f. 1975; owned 70% by Saudi Aramco and 30% by Jadwa Industrial Investment Co; Pres. and CEO ABDULLAH O. AL-BAIZ.

Saudi Aramco Mobil Refinery Co Ltd (SAMREF): POB 30078, Yanbu; tel. (4) 396-4443; fax (4) 396-0942; e-mail amrihh@samref.com.sa; internet www.samref.com.sa; f. 1981; operation of oil-refining facilities at Yanbu; operated by Saudi Aramco and Mobil, capacity 360,000 b/d; Pres. and CEO FAWWAZ I. NAWWAB.

Saudi Aramco Shell Refinery Co (SASREF): POB 10088, Madinat al-Jubail, as-Sinaiyah 31961; tel. (3) 357-2000; fax (3) 357-2525; e-mail info@sasref.com.sa; internet www.sasref.com.sa; operation of oil-refining facilities at Jubail; operated by Saudi Aramco and Shell; capacity 300,000 b/d; exports began in 1985; Chair. HAMID T. AS-SAUDOON.

Saudi Basic Industries Corpn (SABIC): POB 5101, Riyadh 11422; tel. (1) 225-8000; fax (1) 225-9000; internet www.sabic.com; f. 1976 to foster the petrochemical industry and other hydrocarbon-based industries through jt ventures with foreign partners, and to market their products; 70% state-owned; production 55m. tons (2007); Chair. Prince SA'UD BIN THUNAYAN AS-SA'UD; Vice-Chair. and CEO MUHAMMAD AL-MADY.

Projects include:

Al-Jubail Petrochemical Co (Kemya): POB 10084, Jubail 31961; tel. (3) 357-6000; fax (3) 358-7858; f. 1980; began production of linear low-density polyethylene in 1984, of high-density polyethylene in 1985, and of high alfa olefins in 1986, capacity of 330,000 tons per year of polyethylene; jt venture with Exxon Corpn (USA) and SABIC; Pres. ABD AL-AZIZ SULAYMAN AL-HAMAAD.

Arabian Petrochemical Co (Petrokemya): POB 10002, Jubail 31961; tel. (3) 358-7000; fax (3) 358-4480; e-mail otaibifr@petrokemya.sabic.com; produced 2.4m. tons of ethylene, 135,000 tons of polystyrene, 100,000 tons of butene-1; 570,000 tons of propylene, 100,000 tons of butadiene and 150,000 tons of benzene in 2001; wholly owned subsidiary of SABIC; owns 50% interest in ethylene glycol plant producing 610,000 tons per year of monoethylene glycol, 65,000 tons per year of diethylene glycol and 3,900 tons per year of triethylene glycol; Gen. Man. ABD AL-AZIZ AL-MAJID.

Eastern Petrochemical Co (Sharq): POB 10035, Jubail 31961; tel. (3) 357-5000; fax (3) 358-0383; f. 1981 to produce linear low-density polyethylene, ethylene glycol; total capacity 660,000 tons of ethylene glycol and 280,000 tons of polyethylene per year; a SABIC jt venture with Japanese companies led by Mitsubishi Corpn; Chair. ABD AL-AZIZ AL-JARBOOA.

National Industrial Gases Co (Gas): POB 10110, Jubail 31961; tel. (3) 357-5700; fax (3) 358-5542; total capacity of 876,000 tons of oxygen and 492,750 tons of nitrogen per year; 70% SABIC-owned jt venture with Saudi private sector; Pres. ALI AL-GHAMDI.

National Plastic Co (Ibn Hayyan): POB 10002, Jubail 31961; tel. (3) 358-7000; fax (3) 358-4736; f. 1984; produces 390,000 tons per year of vinylchloride monomer and 324,000 tons per year of polyvinylchloride; 86.5% owned by SABIC; Pres. KHALED AR-RAWAF.

Saudi-European Petrochemical Co (Ibn Zahr): POB 10330, Jubail 31961; tel. (3) 341-5060; fax (3) 341-2966; f. 1985; annual capacity 1.4m. tons of methyl-tertiary-butyl ether (MTBE), 0.3m. tons of propylene; SABIC has an 80% share, Ecofuel and APICORP each have 10%; Chair. Dr ABD AR-RAHMAN S. AL-UBAID.

Saudi Methanol Co (ar-Razi): POB 10065, Jubail Industrial City 31961; tel. (3) 357-7820; fax (3) 358-0838; e-mail emt@arrazi.com; f. 1979; capacity of 3,158,000 tons per year of chemical-grade methanol; total methanol exports in 2001 were 3,248,000 tons; jt venture with a consortium of Japanese cos; Pres. NABIL A. MANSOURI; Exec. Vice-Pres. H. MIZUNO.

Saudi Petrochemical Co (Sadaf): POB 10025, Jubail 31961; tel. (3) 357-3000; fax (3) 357-3142; e-mail thierry.capelle@shell.com; f. 1980 to produce ethylene, ethylene dichloride, styrene, crude industrial ethanol, caustic soda and methyl-tertiary-butyl-ether (MTBE); total capacity of 4,330,000 tons per year; Shell (Pecten) has a 50% share; Pres. MOSAED S. AL-OHALI.

Saudi Yanbu Petrochemical Co (Yanpet): POB 30139, Yanbu; tel. (4) 396-5000; fax (4) 396-5006; f. 1980 to produce 820,000 tons per year of ethylene, 600,000 tons per year of high-density polyethylene and 340,000 tons per year of ethylene glycol; total capacity 1,692,200 tons per year by 1990; ExxonMobil and SABIC each have a 50% share; Pres. SULAYMAN AL-HUSSAIN.

Foreign Concessionaire

Saudi Arabian Chevron: POB 363, Riyadh; tel. (1) 462-7274; fax (1) 464-1992; internet www.sachevron.com; also office in Kuwait; f. 1928; fmrly Getty Oil Co; renamed Saudi Arabian Texaco Inc. 1993, renamed as above 2007; holds concession (5,200 sq km at Dec. 1987) for exploitation of Saudi Arabia's half-interest in the Saudi Arabia-Kuwait Neutral Zone; Pres. AHMAD AL-OMAR.

UTILITIES

Power and Water Utility Company for Jubail and Yanbu (MARAFIQ): POB 11133, Jubail 31961; tel. (3) 340-1111; fax (3) 340-1168; e-mail marafiqworld@marafiq.com.sa; internet www.marafiq.com.sa; f. 2003; equal ownership held by the Royal Comm. for Jubail and Yanbu, Saudi Aramco, Saudi Basic Industries Corpn and the Public Investment Fund; operation and devt of utility services; Chair. Prince SA'UD IBN ABDULLAH IBN THUNAYAN AS-SA'UD; CEO THAMIR S. ASH-SHARHAN.

Water and Electricity Co: POB 300091, Riyadh 11372; tel. (1) 211-3362; fax (1) 211-3313; e-mail info@wec.com.sa; internet www.wec.com.sa; f. 2003; jointly owned by Saline Water Conversion Corpn and Saudi Electricity Co; responsible for managing supply and demand of electricity and water; Chair. FAHID ASH-SHARIF.

Electricity

Electricity and Co-generation Regulatory Authority (ECRA): PO Box 4540, Riyadh 11412; tel. (1) 201-9045; e-mail public@ecra.gov.sa; internet www.ecra.gov.sa; f. 2001 to regulate the power industry and to recommend tariffs for the sector; Gov. Dr FAREED M. ZEDAN.

Saudi Electricity Co (SEC): POB 57, Riyadh 11411; tel. (1) 403-2222; fax (1) 405-1191; internet www.se.com.sa; f. 1999 following merger of 10 regional cos, to organize the generation, transmission and distribution of electricity into separate operating cos; jt-stock co; cap. 33,758m.; Chair. (vacant); CEO ALI SALEH AL-BARRAK.

Water

National Water Co: POB 676, Riyadh 11421; tel. (1) 211-3014; fax (1) 211-3016; e-mail info@nwc.com.sa; internet www.nwc.com.sa; f. 2008 to consolidate all government-run water and wastewater management services and to facilitate the gradual privatization of the sector; Chair. ABDULLAH AL-HUSSEIN (Minister of Water and Electricity); CEO LOAY A. AL-MUSALLAM.

SAUDI ARABIA

Saline Water Conversion Corpn (SWCC): POB 4931, 21412 Jeddah; tel. (2) 682-1240; fax (2) 682-0415; e-mail computerdirector@swcc.gov.sa; internet www.swcc.gov.sa; f. 1974; undergoing privatization in early 2009; provides desalinated water; 24 plants; Gov. FAHID ASH-SHARIF; Dir-Gen. ABD AL-AZIZ OMAR NASSIEF.

TRADE UNIONS

Trade unions are illegal in Saudi Arabia.

Transport

RAILWAYS

Saudi Arabia has the only rail system in the Arabian peninsula. The Saudi Government Railroad comprises 719 km of single and 157 km of double track. In addition, the total length of spur lines and sidings is 348 km. The main line, which was opened in 1951, is 578 km in length; it connects Dammam port, on the Gulf coast, with Riyadh, and passes Dhahran, Abqaiq, Hufuf, Harad and al-Kharj. A 310-km line, linking Hufuf and Riyadh, was inaugurated in May 1985. New 950-km and 115-km lines, connecting Riyadh with Jeddah and Dammam with Jubail, respectively, known as the Saudi Landbridge Project, were planned. The revamped network was to connect the Red Sea with the Persian (Arabian) Gulf and was to be closely linked with Jeddah Islamic Port and King Abd al-Aziz Port (at Dammam); Tarabot consortium was named as the preferred bidder for the US $5,000m. project in March 2008, but bidding was reopened in December owing to subsequent developments in the global economic climate. Concessions to build a 450-km Western Region line, connecting the west-coast centres of Mecca, Medina and Jeddah, and to operate a passenger service for millions of *Umrah* and *Hajj* pilgrims every year, were tendered in 2006. The project, renamed the Haramain High-Speed Rail Project, was restructured and retendered in mid-2008. The SR 6,900m. contract to implement the first phase of the project was awarded in March 2009, with completion of the entire project anticipated by the end of 2012. The concession for a 2,400-km North–South line, connecting Riyadh, Qassim, Ha'il, az-Zubayrah and al-Jalamid, to be mainly utilized for transporting minerals, was tendered, in several stages, from September 2007. Some contracts were retendered in 2008, with work scheduled to commence by July 2009. A $400m. project to construct two light urban lines in Riyadh was also planned; tenders were expected to be issued in early 2009. The $1,800m. contract to build a high-speed monorail linking the holy sites in Mecca was awarded to the China Railway Co in February 2009. A total of 1.1m. passengers travelled by rail in the kingdom in 2007.

Saudi Railways Organization (SRO): POB 36, Dammam 31241; tel. (3) 871-3000; fax (3) 827-1130; e-mail sro@sro.org.sa; internet www.saudirailways.org; Pres. ABD AL-AZIZ BIN MUHAMMAD AL-HOQAIL.

ROADS

Asphalted roads link Jeddah to Mecca, Jeddah to Medina, Medina to Yanbu, at-Ta'if to Mecca, Riyadh to al-Kharj, and Dammam to Hufuf, as well as the principal communities and certain outlying points in Saudi Aramco's area of operations. The trans-Arabian highway links Dammam, Riyadh, at-Ta'if, Mecca and Jeddah. The construction of an 810-km road connecting Qassim, Medina, Yanbu, Rabigh and Thuwal, at a cost of some SR 5,350m., was under way, and in February 2006 the long-considered project to build a causeway between Saudi Arabia and Egypt across the Straits of Tiran was revived. The contract to construct a 327–km Mafraq-Ghoueifat highway, which would link Saudi Arabia with Qatar and the United Arab Emirates, was expected to be awarded in mid-2009. In 2006 there were 174,429 km of roads, of which 15,548 km were main roads (including motorways), 9,098 km were secondary roads and 25,845 km were asphalted agricultural roads. Metalled roads link all the main population centres.

Saudi Public Transport Co (SAPTCO): POB 10667, Riyadh 11443; tel. (1) 454-5000; fax (1) 454-2100; e-mail info@saptco.com.sa; internet www.saptco.com.sa; f. 1979; operates a public bus service throughout Saudi Arabia and to neighbouring countries; the Govt holds a 30% share; Chair. ABDULLAH AL-MUGHBIL; CEO Dr ABD AL-AZIZ AL-OHALY.

SHIPPING

Responsibility for the management, operation and maintenance of the commercial ports of Jeddah, Dammam, Jubail, Yanbu, Dhiba and Jizan, the King Fahd Industrial Ports of Jubail and Yanbu, and the oil port of Ras Tanura, as well as a number of minor ports, began to be transferred to the private sector after 1997, but all ports remain subject to regulation and scrutiny by the Ports Authority. On average over 95% of Saudi Arabia's imports and exports pass through the country's sea ports. In 2007 the eight major sea ports received 11,821 vessels at their 183 mechanized and organized berths. In 2008 the total cargo handled by Saudi Arabian ports, excluding crude petroleum, was 154.9m. metric tons, compared with 68.2m. tons in 1990/91. Some 1.3m. passengers were also embarked and disembarked in that year.

Jeddah is the principal commercial port and the main point of entry for pilgrims bound for Mecca. It has a total of 58 berths for general cargo, container traffic, roll-on roll-off (ro-ro) traffic, livestock and bulk grain shipments, with draughts ranging from 8 m to 16 m. The port also has a 200-ton floating crane, cold storage facilities and a fully equipped ship-repair yard. In 2007 a total of 4,850 vessels called at Jeddah Islamic Port. In 2008 some 45.7m. tons of cargo, excluding crude petroleum, were handled and 0.4m. passengers were processed. A new deep-water terminal, the Red Sea Gateway, with draughts of up to 18 m and a handling capacity of 1.5m. 20-ft equivalent units, was expected to be completed by late 2009 at a cost of US $443m.

Dammam is the second largest commercial port and has general cargo, container, ro-ro, dangerous cargo and bulk grain berths. Draughts at this port range from 8 m to 13.5 m. It has a 200-ton floating crane and a fully equipped ship-repair yard. In 2007 a total of 2,502 vessels called at King Abd al-Aziz Port in Dammam. In 2008 some 23.6m. tons of cargo, excluding crude petroleum, were handled.

Jubail has one commercial and one industrial port. The commercial port has general cargo, bulk grain and container berths with ro-ro facilities, and a floating crane. Draughts at this port range from 12 m to 14 m. In 2007 a total of 445 vessels called at Jubail Commercial Port. In 2008 4.1m. tons of goods, excluding crude petroleum, were handled. The industrial port has bulk cargo, refined and petrochemical and ro-ro berths, and an open sea tanker terminal suitable for vessels up to 300,000 dwt. Draughts range from 6 m to 30 m. In 2007 a total of 1,483 vessels called at King Fahd Industrial Port in Jubail In 2008 42.5m. tons of cargo, excluding crude petroleum, were handled.

Yanbu, which comprises one commercial and one industrial port, is Saudi Arabia's nearest major port to Europe and North America, and is the focal point of the most rapidly growing area, in the west of Saudi Arabia. The commercial port has general cargo, ro-ro and bulk grain berths, with draughts ranging from 10 m to 12 m. It also has a floating crane, and is equipped to handle minor ship repairs. A total of 206 vessels called at Yanbu Commercial Port in 2007. In 2008 1.7m. tons of cargo, excluding crude petroleum, were handled. The industrial port has berths for general cargo, containers, ro-ro traffic, bulk cargo, crude petroleum, refined and petrochemical products and natural gas liquids, and a tanker terminal on the open sea. In 2007 a total of 1,396 vessels called at King Fahd Industrial Port in Yanbu. The port handled 35.9m. tons of cargo, excluding crude petroleum, in 2008. The third phase of a project to increase the port's handling capacity was announced in November 2008.

Jizan is the main port for the southern part of the country. It has general cargo, ro-ro, bulk grain and container berths, with draughts ranging from 8 m to 11 m. It also has a 200-ton floating crane. In 2007 a total of 71 vessels called at Jizan Port. In 2008 0.9m. tons of cargo, excluding crude petroleum, were handled.

Dhiba port, on the northern Red Sea coast, serves the Tabouk region. It has three general cargo berths with a ro-ro ramp, and passenger-handling facilities. Maximum draught is 10.5 m. In 2007 a total of 868 vessels called at Dhiba. In 2008 some 0.4m. tons of cargo, excluding crude petroleum, were handled, and 0.8m. passengers were processed.

In addition to these major ports, there are a number of minor ports suitable only for small craft, including Khuraiba, Haql, al-Wajh, Umlujj, Rabigh, al-Lith, Qunfoudah, Farasan and al-Qahma on the Red Sea coast and al-Khobar, al-Qatif, Uqair, Darin and Ras al-Khafji on the Gulf coast. Ras Mishab, on the Gulf coast, is operated by the Ministry of Defence and Civil Aviation.

In January 2008 the Ports Authority announced the signing of a US $586m. contract with the China Harbour Engineering Company Ltd to build a new port at Ras Azzawr.

Saudi Ports Authority: POB 5162, Riyadh 11422; tel. (1) 405-0005; fax (1) 405-3508; e-mail info@ports.gov.sa; internet www.ports.gov.sa; f. 1976; regulatory authority; Pres. Dr KHALED AHMAD ABD AR-RAHMAN BUBSHAIT; Chair. Dr JUBARAH IBN EID AS-SURAISERI (Minister of Transport).

Dammam: POB 28062, Dammam 31188; tel. (3) 858-3199; fax (3) 857-1727; Dir-Gen. NAEEM IBRAHIM AN-NAEEM.

Dhiba: POB 190, Dhiba; tel. (4) 432-1060; fax (4) 432-2679; Dir-Gen. MAHMOUD AL-HARBI.

Jeddah: POB 9285, Jeddah 21188; tel. (2) 647-1200; fax (2) 647-7411; Dir-Gen. SAHIR M. TAHLAWI.

Jizan: POB 16, Jizan; tel. (7) 317-1000; fax (7) 317-0777; Dir-Gen. ALI HAMOUD BAKRI.

Jubail Commercial Port: POB 276, Jubail; tel. (3) 362-0600; fax (3) 361-3337; Dir-Gen. FAHD A. AL-AMER.

SAUDI ARABIA   *Directory*

Jubail Industrial Port: POB 547, Jubail 31951; tel. (3) 357-8000; fax (3) 357-8011; Dir-Gen. ABDULLAH NASIR AT-TWAIJRI.

Yanbu Commerial Port: POB 1019, Yanbu; tel. (4) 322-2100; fax (4) 322-7643; Dir-Gen. ABDULLAH BIN AWAD AZ-ZAIMI.

Yanbu Industrial Port: POB 30325, Yanbu; tel. (4) 396-7000; fax (4) 396-7037; Dir-Gen. Dr HUMOOD SAADI.

Arabian Petroleum Supply Co Ltd: POB 1408, Al-Qurayat St, Jeddah 21431; tel. (2) 637-1120; fax (2) 636-2366; e-mail marine@apsco-ksa.com; internet www.apsco.com.sa; f. 1961; Chair. Sheikh MUHAMMAD YOUSSUF ALI AR-REZA; Gen. Man. E. D. CONNOLLY.

Baaboud Trading and Shipping Agencies: POB 7262, Jeddah 21462; tel. (2) 627-0000; fax (2) 627-1111; e-mail info@baaboud.net; internet www.baaboud.net; Chair. AHMED M. BAABOUD; Man. Dir AHMED ABOUD BAABOUD.

Bakri Navigation Co Ltd: POB 3757, Jeddah 21481; tel. (2) 651-9995; fax (2) 651-2908; e-mail info@bakrinavigation.com; internet www.bakrinavigation.com; f. 1973; owns and operates a fleet of oil tankers, tug boats and utility vessels; Chair. Sheikh A. K. AL-BAKRY; Man. Dir G. A. K. AL-BAKRY.

National Shipping Co of Saudi Arabia (NSCSA): POB 8931, Riyadh 11492; tel. (1) 478-5454; fax (1) 477-8036; e-mail info@nscsa.com.sa; internet www.nscsa.com; f. 1979; transportation of crude petroleum and petrochemical products; routes through Red Sea and Mediterranean to USA and Canada; operates a fleet of 37 ships; Chair. ABDULLAH SULAIMAN AR-RUBAIAN; CEO HUMOUD AL-AJLAN.

Saudi Shipping and Maritime Services Co Ltd (TRANSHIP): POB 7522, Jeddah 21472; tel. (2) 642-4255; fax (2) 643-2821; e-mail saudishipping@transhipsa.com; Chair. Prince SA'UD IBN NAYEF IBN ABD AL-AZIZ; Man. Dir Capt. MUSTAFA T. AWARA.

Shipping Corpn of Saudi Arabia Ltd: POB 1691, Arab Maritime Center, Malik Khalid St, Jeddah 21441; tel. (2) 647-1137; fax (2) 647-8222; e-mail arablines@arabjeddah.com; Pres. and Man. Dir ABD AL-AZIZ AHMAD ARAB.

CIVIL AVIATION

King Abd al-Aziz International Airport (KAIA), in Jeddah, which was opened in 1981, has three terminals, one of which is specifically designed to cope with the needs of the many thousands of pilgrims who visit Mecca and Medina each year. Plans to expand the aiport have been under discussion since 2003. The contract to design a new passenger terminal was awarded to French company Aéroports de Paris in mid-2008; revised and extended plans were finalized in early 2009, with construction expected to commence by 2010. The new terminal, which was not expected to be completed before 2013, was designed to accommodate up to 30m. passengers per year. A further two expansion phases, which could increase annual passenger-handling capacity to 80m. by 2035, were also planned. King Khalid International Airport, in Riyadh, opened in 1983 with four terminals. It handled an estimated 11m. passengers in 2007. A third major airport, King Fahd International Airport (with an initial handling capacity of 5.2m. passengers per year), opened in the Eastern Province, near Dammam, in 1994. Some 3.8m. passengers used the airport in 2007. Plans to expand capacity and develop new commercial zones in the vicinities of the airports at Riyadh and Dammam were under discussion in early 2009. Prince Muhammad Bin Abd al-Aziz Airport in Medina, which opened in 1972, began handling international flights in 2006. Plans to build two new terminals and increase capacity to around 12m. passengers per year by 2019 were announced in 2008. Overall, the country's airports were used by some 40m. passengers in 2007. There are 27 commercial airports in the kingdom. Plans to privatize the kingdom's airports, which were first announced in 2003, had yet to be realized by early 2009. However, concessions to manage the kingdom's three main airports were awarded to two foreign companies in 2008.

General Authority of Civil Aviation (GACA): POB 887, Jeddah 21165; tel. (2) 640-5000; fax (2) 640-2444; e-mail feedback@pca.gov.sa; internet www.gaca.gov.sa; fmrly the Presidency of Civil Aviation; regulatory authority; Pres. Dr ABDULLAH MUHAMMAD NOOR REHAIMY.

National Air Services (NAS): POB 18118, 2nd Floor, Al-Jirasi Bldg, Madinah Rd, Jeddah 21415; tel. (2) 6910122; fax (2) 6520394; e-mail info@nasaviation.com; internet www.nasaviation.com; f. 1998; privately owned; cap. 60m. riyals; also operates low-cost air carrier, Nas Air; CEO SULAIMAN AL-HAMDAN.

Sama Airlines: POB 361662, Riyadh 11313; tel. (1) 263-9500; fax (1) 454-8720; e-mail contact@flysama.com; internet www.flysama.com; f. 2006; low-cost airline providing domestic and regional services; Chair. Prince BANDAR BIN KHALID AL FAISAL; CEO BRUCE ASHBY.

Saudi Arabian Airlines: POB 620, Jeddah 21231; tel. (2) 686-4588; fax (2) 686-4587; e-mail webmaster@saudiairlines.com.sa; internet www.saudiairlines.com; f. 1945; began operations in 1947; carried 15.4m. passengers in 2004; regular services to 25 domestic and 52 international destinations; catering and cargo divisions part-privatized in 2008, with further divestment of shares in technical services and training divisions expected during 2009; Chair. Prince SULTAN IBN ABD AL-AZIZ; Dir-Gen. KHALID ABDULLAH AL-MULHIM; Exec. Vice-Pres. (Operations) ADNAN AD-DABBAGH.

Tourism

All devout Muslims try to make at least one visit to the holy cities of Medina, the burial place of Muhammad, and Mecca, his birthplace. In 2000 the Government decided to issue tourist visas for the first time. A Supreme Commission for Tourism (SCT—now known as the Saudi Commission for Tourism and Antiquities—SCTA) was subsequently established to develop the tourism industry in Saudi Arabia. In 2005 the SCT announced plans to increase the kingdom's supply of hotel rooms to 150,000 by 2013 (from 95,000). It was reported in 2008 that the SCTA planned to invest almost US $40,000m. to develop 19 tourism resorts on the Red Sea coast. Tourist numbers increased to 8.6m. in 2004 (compared with 7.3m. in 2003), but declined to 8.0m. in 2005. Tourist numbers increased again, to over 8.6m., in 2006. Receipts from tourism amounted to $5,391m. in that year. An estimated 2m. foreign pilgrims visited Mecca and Medina in 2008, accounting for 51% of foreign visitors to the kingdom.

Saudi Commission for Tourism and Antiquities (SCTA): POB 66680, Riyadh 11586; tel. (1) 880-8855; fax (1) 880-8844; internet www.scta.gov.sa; f. 2001 as the Supreme Commission for Tourism, renamed as above 2008; Pres. Prince SULTAN IBN SALMAN IBN ABD AL-AZIZ AS-SA'UD.

Saudi Hotels and Resort Areas Co (SHARACO): POB 5500, Riyadh 11422; tel. (1) 481-6666; fax (1) 480-1666; e-mail info@saudi-hotels.com.sa; internet www.saudi-hotels.com.sa; f. 1975; construction and management of hotels, resorts and other tourism facilities; Saudi Govt has a 40% interest; Chair. MUSAAD AS-SENANY; Dir-Gen. ABD AL-AZIZ AL-AMBAR.

SENEGAL

Introductory Survey

Location, Climate, Language, Religion, Flag, Capital

The Republic of Senegal lies on the west coast of Africa, bordered to the north by Mauritania, to the east by Mali, and to the south by Guinea and Guinea-Bissau. In the southern part of the country The Gambia forms a narrow enclave extending some 320 km (200 miles) inland. The climate is tropical, with a long dry season followed by a short wet season—from June to September in the north, and from June to October in the south. Average annual temperatures range from 22°C (72°F) to 28°C (82°F). French is the official language; the most widely spoken national languages at the time of the 1988 census were Wolof (spoken by 49.2% of the population), Peul (22.2%), Serer (12.8%) and Diola (5.1%). At the 1988 census almost 94% of the population were Muslims, and some 4% Christians, mostly Roman Catholics; a small number followed traditional beliefs. The national flag (proportions 2 by 3) has three equal vertical stripes, of green, yellow and red, with a five-pointed green star in the centre of the yellow stripe. The capital is Dakar. In July 2005 the Assemblée nationale approved legislation providing for the creation of a new administrative capital, near Kébèmer, on the Atlantic littoral.

Recent History

After 300 years as a French colony, Senegal became a self-governing member of the French Community in November 1958. The Mali Federation, linking Senegal with Soudan (later the Republic of Mali), had only two months of independence before being dissolved when Senegal seceded, to become a separate independent state, on 20 August 1960. The Republic of Senegal was proclaimed on 5 September, with Léopold Sédar Senghor, leader of the Union progressiste sénégalaise (UPS), as the country's first President.

In late 1962, following the discovery of a coup attempt led by the Prime Minister, Mamadou Dia, Senghor assumed the premiership; other political parties were gradually absorbed into the UPS or outlawed, effectively creating a one-party state by 1966. In 1970 the office of Prime Minister was restored and assigned to a provincial administrator, Abdou Diouf, who in 1976 was made Senghor's constitutional successor. In 1973 Senghor, the sole candidate, was re-elected President. Senghor amended the Constitution in March 1976 to allow three parties to contest elections—the UPS, renamed the Parti socialiste (PS), the Parti démocratique sénégalais (PDS) and the Parti africain de l'indépendance (PAI). The first national elections under the three-party system took place in February 1978; the PS won 83 of the 100 seats in the Assemblée nationale, the remainder being won by the PDS. In the concurrent presidential election, Senghor overwhelmingly defeated the leader of the PDS, Abdoulaye Wade.

Senghor was succeeded as President by Diouf in January 1981. An amnesty was declared for political dissidents, and the Constitution was amended to allow the existence of an unlimited number of political parties. At elections in February 1983 Diouf received 83.5% of the presidential vote (compared with 14.8% for his nearest rival, Wade), while in legislative elections the PS won 111 of the 120 seats. In April Diouf abolished the post of Prime Minister, which had latterly been held by Habib Thiam.

When preliminary results of the February 1988 presidential and legislative elections indicated clear victories for both Diouf and the PS, opposition parties alleged fraud on the part of the ruling party, and, following the outbreak of rioting in Dakar, a state of emergency was imposed. According to the official results of the presidential election, contested by four candidates, Diouf obtained 73.2% of the votes cast, and Wade 25.8%. In the legislative elections, the PS won 103 seats, and the PDS the remaining 17.

In March 1991 the legislature approved several amendments to the Constitution, notably the restoration of the post of Prime Minister, to which post Thiam was again named in the following month. Thiam's Government included four representatives of the PDS (including Wade, as Minister of State, effectively the most senior post in the Government other than the Prime Minister). In September the Assemblée nationale adopted amendments to the electoral code. Presidential elections would henceforth take place, in two rounds if necessary (to ensure that the President would be elected by an absolute majority of votes cast), every seven years, with a mandate that would be renewable only once. Legislative voting would, however, continue to take place at five-yearly intervals.

In October 1992 Wade and his three PDS colleagues resigned from the Council of Ministers, protesting that they had been excluded from the governmental process. Eight candidates contested the presidential election, which took place in February 1993. Despite some irregularities, voting was reported to be orderly in most areas, outwith Casamance (see below). The opposition denounced the preliminary results, which indicated that Diouf had won a clear majority. In March the Constitutional Council announced that Diouf had been re-elected with 58.4% of the votes cast (51.6% of the electorate had voted); Wade secured 32.0% of the votes.

Elections to the Assemblée nationale took place in May 1993, in which the PS won 84 of the 120 elective seats; the PDS took 27 seats. The rate of participation by voters was 40.7%. Shortly after the announcement of the results the Vice-President of the Constitutional Council, Babacar Sèye, was assassinated. Wade and three other PDS leaders were detained for three days in connection with the killing and in October Wade was charged with complicity in the assassination of Sèye; Wade's wife and a PDS deputy were also charged in connection with the killing. In November Ousmane Ngom, the PDS parliamentary leader, and Landing Savané, the leader of And Jëf—Parti africain pour la démocratie et le socialisme (AJ—PADS), were among those detained following a protest in Dakar to demand the cancellation of austerity measures. Ngom, Savané and some 87 others were convicted of participating in an unauthorized demonstration, and received suspended prison sentences.

Following the devaluation of the CFA franc, in January 1994, emergency measures were adopted to offset the immediate adverse economic effects and consequent hardship. In February a demonstration in Dakar to denounce the devaluation degenerated into serious rioting, as a result of which eight people were killed. Wade and Savané were among those subsequently charged in association with the unrest. Charges against Wade and his opposition associates in connection with the murder of Sèye were dismissed in May 1994, although Wade and Savané remained in custody until July, in connection with the post-devaluation violence. In October three of Sèye's alleged assassins were convicted and sentenced to 18–20 years' imprisonment.

Five members of the PDS, including Wade, as Minister of State at the Presidency, were appointed to a new Council of Ministers in March 1995. Djibo Kâ, a long-serving government member who, as Minister of the Interior, had been associated with the legal proceedings against Wade and other opposition leaders, left the Government. In January 1996 Diouf announced that a second legislative chamber, the Sénat, was to be established.

In February 1998 Wade appealed to the Constitutional Council to reject an amendment to the electoral code whereby the number of deputies in the Assemblée nationale was to be increased to 140; later in the month the Council annulled the proposed increase, the first occasion on which the Council had ruled against a decision of the legislature. In March, however, the Assemblée nationale again voted to increase the number of deputies. In April Kâ resigned from the PS to present his own list of candidates, as the Union pour le renouveau démocratique (URD).

Some 18 parties and coalitions contested the legislative elections on 24 May 1998. Outwith Casamance, voting was reported to have taken place generally in an atmosphere of calm. The PS obtained 93 seats in the enlarged assembly, with 50.2% of the valid votes cast, while the number of PDS deputies was reduced to 23; Kâ's URD, in alliance with the Alliance pour le progrès et la justice—Jëf-Jël (APJ—JJ), secured 11 seats. The rate of participation by voters was 39% of the registered electorate. In July Thiam resigned as Prime Minister, and was replaced by Mamadou Lamine Loum. A new Council of Ministers was named shortly afterwards, in which Serigne Diop, the leader of the

Parti démocratique sénégalais—Rénovation, (which had broken away from the PDS in 1997) was the only non-PS member.

In August 1998 the Assemblée nationale voted to revise the Constitution to remove the clause restricting the Head of State to a maximum of two terms of office, thus permitting Diouf to contest the next presidential election, in 2000. A requirement that the President be elected by more than 25% of all registered voters was also abandoned. The opposition parties, condemning the amendments, boycotted the vote.

The PS won all 45 elective seats in the first, indirect, elections to the Sénat in January 1999; these 45 members were chosen by an electoral college of deputies, local, municipal and regional councillors. Only the PS, the Parti libéral du Sénégal (formed in 1998 by Ngom, leading a breakaway movement from the PDS), and a coalition of the Parti de l'indépendance et du travail (PIT) and AJ—PADS contested the elections; the PDS and other opposition parties were opposed to the introduction of an additional parliamentary chamber. A further 12 senators were appointed by the President of the Republic, including two opposition figures, and three were elected by Senegalese resident abroad. One of the 12 senators nominated by Diouf, Abdoulaye Diack, a prominent member of the PS, was elected President of the new body.

In March 1999 an alliance of AJ—PADS, the PIT, the PDS and the Ligue démocratique—Mouvement pour le parti du travail (LD—MPT) agreed to nominate Wade, who had resigned from the Assemblée nationale in mid-1998, as their joint candidate in the presidential election scheduled for 2000. In June Niasse announced his intention of contesting the presidential election, and published a document accusing Diouf and the PS of corruption; Niasse was consequently expelled from the PS and subsequently formed the Alliance des forces de progrès (AFP).

Although Diouf won the largest proportion of votes cast (41.3%) at the election, held on 27 February 2000, his failure to secure an absolute majority of votes cast necessitated a second round of voting, between Diouf and Wade (who had secured 31.0% of votes cast). Of the remaining candidates, Niasse received 16.8% of votes cast, while Kâ took 7.1%. Prior to the second round of voting, Wade received the endorsement of Niasse, and of the majority of the candidates defeated in the first round, with the notable exception of Kâ, who defied the wishes of his party and gave public support to Diouf. At the second round, on 19 March, Wade won 58.5% of the total votes cast, thus taking the presidency from the PS for the first time. Turn-out in the second round was estimated at 60.1%, marginally lower than in the first round.

Wade was sworn in as President on 1 April 2000 and named Niasse as Prime Minister. The 29-member Council of Ministers appointed later in the month included several other opposition leaders, including Savané of AJ—PADS and Bathily of the LD—MPT. Wade announced that he did not envisage governing alongside an Assemblée nationale dominated by the PS, and that he therefore intended to hold fresh legislative elections, following a constitutional referendum initially scheduled for 27 November 2000. Among the proposed changes, the President would gain the power to dissolve the Assemblée nationale, while other presidential powers would be transferred to the Prime Minister, and the presidential mandate would again be reduced from seven to five years, renewable only once. Furthermore, the Sénat was to be abolished.

The constitutional referendum was held, following several postponements, on 7 January 2001. Some 94.0% of votes cast in the plebiscite supported the new Constitution; 65.8% of the registered electorate voted. Most provisions of the Constitution, including the abolition of the Sénat and the Economic and Social Council, took immediate effect, following its promulgation by the President, with only those sections relating to the legislature necessitating new elections before their implementation. Future presidential mandates would be reduced from seven to five years, and the number of deputies in the Assemblée nationale was reduced from 140 to 120.

The President dissolved the Assemblée nationale in mid-February 2001 and announced that the new legislature, which was to be elected in April, would consist of 65 seats elected by majority voting in departments, and 55 by proportional representation using national lists. In March Wade appointed Mame Madior Boye, a politically unaffiliated magistrate, and hitherto Minister of Justice, as Prime Minister. In the ensuing reshuffle Niasse and other members of the AFP were removed from office, in what was regarded as an attempt by Wade to create a more unified Government, which incorporated greater representation for the PDS and its allies, prior to the legislative elections.

Legislative elections duly took place on 29 April 2001, in conditions that were widely praised for their democracy and transparency; outbreaks of violence in Casamance were none the less reported. Apart from the pro-Wade Sopi (Change) coalition (comprising 40 parties, led by the PDS), a further 24 parties contested the polls. The Sopi coalition won 49.6% of votes cast, and 89 of the 120 seats in the Assemblée nationale. The AFP obtained 11 seats, with 16.1% of the vote. The PS, despite receiving a slightly larger share of the vote than the AFP (17.4%), secured only 10 seats. The rate of electoral participation was 67.5%. Boye was reappointed as Prime Minister on 10 May. The new 24-member Government comprised 11 members of the PDS (who obtained most principal posts), nine representatives of civil society, and two members each of AJ—PADS and the LD—MPT.

Following the elections, nine parties, including the AFP, the APJ—JJ and the URD, announced that they were to join the PS in an informal opposition alliance. In August 2001 some 25 parties, led by the PDS, formed a pro-presidential electoral alliance, the Convergence des actions autour du Président en perspective du 21ième siècle (CAP-21), in advance of local and municipal elections (initially scheduled for November, but subsequently postponed); meanwhile, opposition groups also formed an electoral alliance, the Cadre permanent de concertation. In February 2002 the three men convicted of the assassination of Babacar Sèye in 1993 were granted presidential pardons and subsequently released from prison, provoking renewed controversy about the case. In the delayed local and municipal elections, which were eventually held on 12 May 2002, CAP-21 won control of nine of the 11 regional governments, as well as a majority of municipal and communal seats.

The sinking of a state-owned passenger ferry, the MV *Joola*, in late September 2002, en route from Ziguinchor, the principal city of Casamance, to Dakar led to a national political crisis, even before the final death toll of the accident, subsequently enumerated at more than 1,800 people, became apparent. In early October the Minister of Equipment and Transport, Youssouph Sakho, and the Minister of the Armed Forces, Yoba Sambou, resigned in response to the tragedy, as it became clear that the vessel had been severely overloaded; only 64 survivors were reported. Later in the month the head of the navy was dismissed, and Wade announced that the Government accepted responsibility for the disaster. In early November Wade dismissed Boye and her Government; although no official reason for the dismissal was given, it was widely believed to have been prompted by the Government's response to the disaster. Shortly after Boye's dismissal, an inquiry into the incident found that safety regulations had been widely violated on the *Joola*, and that the dispatch of rescue equipment and staff to the ship by the armed forces had been inexplicably delayed. Idrissa Seck, the Mayor of Thiès, a close ally of Wade and previously a senior official in the PDS, was appointed as the new Prime Minister; several principal posts in the new Government remained unchanged. In August 2003 the Chief of Staff of the Armed Forces and the Chief of Staff of the Air Force were dismissed as a result of disciplinary action related to the response to the sinking of the *Joola*.

Political tensions intensified in early 2004 as several parties that had supported Wade's candidacy in the presidential election of 2000 and had ministerial representation in the Government, including the LD—MPT and AJ—PADS, declined to participate in celebrations organized to mark the fourth anniversary of Wade's accession to power. Moreover, while the President continued to announce his intention of forming a broadly based Government, most opposition parties reiterated their reluctance to participate in any such administration. In late April Wade dismissed Seck's Government, appointing Macky Sall, hitherto Minister of State, Minister of the Interior and Local Communities, Government Spokesperson, as premier. Although the allocation of most strategic portfolios in the new Council of Ministers remained largely unchanged, Cheikh Sadibou Fall was accorded the post of Minister of the Interior. In November Wade reorganized the Government, dismissing Fall from his position as Minister of the Interior and replacing him with Ngom (who had been appointed as Minister of Trade in July).

In March 2005 Wade effected a further government reorganization, replacing two members of the LD—MPT with affiliates of the PDS, leaving AJ—PADS as the only party (other than the PDS) to retain ministerial representation from the alliance that supported Wade's presidential candidacy in 2000. The dismissals followed several months of discord between the PDS and the LD—MPT over the latter's criticism of Wade's presidency and its opposition to the amnesty legislation. Amid ongoing tensions within the PDS, a further reorganization of the Government in May was interpreted as an attempt to strengthen support for the President.

In May 2005 opposition leaders condemned the detention of Abdourahim Agne, the Secretary-General of a minor opposition party, the Parti de la réforme, who was charged with threatening state security after he called for street demonstrations against the President. Wade appointed members to a new Commission électorale nationale autonome in early June; however, the opposition expressed concern at the composition of the body. Further minor reorganizations of the Government took place in June, July and August.

Seck was questioned by police in mid-July 2005, after he was accused by President Wade of overspending on work to upgrade roads in Thiès, where he served as mayor. The former Prime Minister, whose house had been attacked in May, refuted any suggestion that he had embezzled government funds from the project. Later that month Seck was formally charged with endangering national security; there was no immediate explanation of the charges, which Seck's defence lawyers claimed to be politically motivated. In early September the Assemblée nationale ruled that Seck should be brought to trial on charges of embezzlement at the High Court of Justice, which was reserved for cases concerning crimes committed by members of the Government in the exercise of their duties. Meanwhile, the Assemblée nationale adopted legislation providing for the eventual creation of a new administrative and political capital some 150 km north-east of Dakar, near Kébèmer (rather than at Mékhé-Pékesse, which had been the location proposed in December 2002).

In mid-December 2005 the Assemblée nationale approved legislation, supported by President Wade, that delayed the legislative elections, which had been scheduled for mid-2006, until 2007, when they were to be held concurrently with presidential voting. Wade justified this postponement (which was condemned by the parliamentary opposition) on financial grounds, stating that the Government had recently been obliged to make unplanned spending on mitigating the effects of flooding. (The legislative elections were later postponed further until June 2007.) Further minor governmental reorganizations took place in early February and mid-March 2006.

Meanwhile, in early February 2006 Seck was released from detention, following the partial dismissal of the charges of corruption and embezzlement against him (some minor charges remained against him, however); the charges of endangering state security had been dropped in the previous month.

In November 2006 President Wade effected changes to the composition of the Council of Ministers; five new ministers from the opposition were appointed, including Abdourahim Agne, who became Minister of Micro-finance and Decentralized Co-operation. In mid-November, prior to the forthcoming presidential election, the Assemblée nationale adopted new legislation ending the obligation for a candidate to receive votes from one-quarter of the total registered electorate to be elected in the first round. Under the new law it became possible for a candidate to secure victory in the first round by obtaining a majority of more than 50% of recorded votes.

The presidential election took place on 25 February 2007. President Wade secured a second five-year mandate in the first round, winning 55.90% of votes cast; his closest rival, with 14.92% of the votes, was Seck. Two days after the elections five ministers resigned and a government reorganization was implemented. Those who left the Government were members of AJ—PADS, hitherto an ally of the ruling PDS, and cited changes in the relationship with the ruling party as reasons for their resignations.

Legislative elections were held on 3 June 2007, at which President Wade's Sopi Coalition (comprising some 40 parties and movements, led by the PDS) secured 131 of the 150 available seats. However, many of the principal opposition parties chose to boycott the ballot when their demands for the establishment of an independent electoral commission were not met, and voter turn-out was estimated at just 34.7%. Later that month Prime Minister Sall resigned and was replaced by Cheikh Hadjibou Soumaré, hitherto Minister-delegate at the Office of the Minister of State of the Economy and Finance, responsible for the Budget. Soumaré subsequently named a new Government, which included 13 new appointments, eight of whom were women; the key portfolios remained unaltered.

Meanwhile, in May 2007 the Assemblée nationale voted to reinstate the Sénat, which had been dissolved in 2001 by President Wade owing to financial constraints. Opposition members who had contested the inauguration of the second chamber in 1999 accused President Wade of proposing contradictory policies. On 19 August 2007 parliamentarians and local officials elected 35 of the 100 senators; 34 of those seats were secured by PDS members. President Wade appointed the remaining 65 members, prompting concern that balance in the newly restored chamber would weigh in favour of the ruling party. The Sénat was officially installed in September; Pape Diop was elected President of that body and was replaced as President of the Assemblée nationale by former Prime Minister Sall.

A governmental reorganization was carried out in April 2008 in which Madické Niang was named Minister of State, Keeper of the Seals, Minister of Justice, replacing Cheikh Tidjane Sy, who in turn moved to the Ministry of the Interior. Ousmane Ngom, hitherto responsible for that portfolio, was appointed Minister of State, Minister of Mines, Industry and Small and Medium-sized Enterprises. A number of former ministers were returned to cabinet positions, including Abdou Aziz Sow as Minister of Information, Telecommunications, ICT, NEPAD and Relations with the Institutions, Spokesperson for the Government. Further minor government changes were implemented in August.

In May 2008 President Wade proposed an amendment to the Constitution, approved by the Council of Ministers, that would result in the extension of the presidential term of office from five to seven years. Wade suggested that the current mandate did not allow sufficient time to develop long-term policies, although it was stated that the new legislation would not be applicable to the current presidency, and would only enter into force after the next presidential election, which was due to be held in 2012. It was not immediately known whether the issue would be put to a public referendum. In October 2008 the Sénat approved the amendment of the mandate of the President of the Assemblée nationale, from five years to a renewable term of one year. The move was regarded as preparation for removing Sall from office and the following month he was dismissed; Mamadou Seck, a former finance minister, was appointed in Sall's place. Sall subsequently announced that he had left the PDS to establish his own party, the Alliance pour la République (APR—Yaakaar). In March 2009 it was announced that Senegal's first Prime Minister, Mamadou Dia, had died.

In late April 2009 Prime Minister Soumaré tendered his resignation and that of the Government. The announcement followed local elections, held the previous month, in which opposition parties had secured the majority of the seats available for the first time since 2000. In early May President Wade nominated Souleymane Ndéné Ndiaye, hitherto Minister of State, Minister of the Maritime Economy, Maritime Transport, Fisheries and Fishbreeding, as Prime Minister and a new Council of Ministers was announced. Although the key portfolios remained unchanged, Karim Wade, son of the President, entered the administration as Minister of State, Minister of International Co-operation, Land Settlement, Air Transport and Infrastructure.

Long-standing resentment against the Government of Senegal in the southern province of Casamance (which is virtually cut off from the rest of the country by the enclave of The Gambia) was embodied from the early 1980s by the separatist Mouvement des forces démocratiques de la Casamance (MFDC). The announcement in May 1991 of the imminent release of more than 340 detainees (including the Secretary-General and executive leader of the MFDC, Fr Augustin Diamacouné Senghor) who had been arrested in connection with unrest in Casamance facilitated the conclusion, shortly afterwards in Guinea-Bissau, of a cease-fire agreement by representatives of the Senegalese Government and of the MFDC. An amnesty was approved by the Assemblée nationale later in June, and some 400 detainees were released. A period of relative calm ensued.

In January 1992 a peace commission, comprising government representatives and members of the MFDC, was established, with mediation by Guinea-Bissau. A resurgence of violence in Casamance from July prompted the Government to redeploy armed forces in the region, giving rise to MFDC protests that the 'remilitarization' of Casamance contravened the truce. Contradictory statements made by MFDC leaders regarding their commitment to the peace accord evidenced a split within the movement. The 'Front nord' and the MFDC Vice-President, Sidi

Badji, appealed to the rebels to lay down their arms; meanwhile, the 'Front sud', led by Diamacouné Senghor (who was now based in Guinea-Bissau), appeared determined to continue the armed struggle. After an escalation of the conflict in late 1992 and early 1993 a new round of negotiations resulted in the signing, in July 1993, of a cease-fire agreement, known as the Ziguinchor Accord, between the Government and Diamacouné Senghor (who had returned to Ziguinchor in March). Guinea-Bissau was to act as a guarantor of the agreement, and the Government of France was to be asked to submit an historical arbitration regarding the Casamance issue. In December France issued its judgment that Casamance had not existed as an autonomous territory prior to the colonial period, and that independence for the region had been neither demanded nor considered at the time of decolonization.

From early 1995, renewed violence indicated a re-emergence of divisions between the two factions of the MFDC. Rebels in the south accused the Senegalese armed forces of violating the provisions of the 1993 cease-fire accord. In June MFDC rebels announced an end to the cease-fire, again accusing government forces of having violated the 1993 accord. Although Diamacouné Senghor appealed to the rebels not to break the truce, renewed violence in the south-west resulted in some 60 deaths.

In September 1995 a Commission nationale de paix (CNP) was established and members of the commission reportedly sought a dialogue with Diamacouné Senghor and the MFDC's four other political leaders (all of whom remained under house arrest). During October, renewed rebel attacks on government forces were accompanied by a major army offensive in the south-west. By the end of November it was reported that about 150 separatists and 15 members of the armed forces had been killed in clashes. In December Diamacouné Senghor made a televised appeal to the rebels to lay down their arms. He proposed that preliminary talks between the MFDC and the CNP take place in January 1996, to be followed by peace negotiations, in a neutral country, three months later. The members of the MFDC 'political bureau' were released from house arrest at the end of December 1995. Peace talks, scheduled to begin in Ziguinchor in April, were postponed indefinitely, following the refusal of Diamacouné Senghor and other MFDC leaders to attend, citing the failure of the Government to meet a number of their conditions, and renewed violence was reported in the region.

There was renewed optimism regarding the possible resumption of negotiations between a united MFDC and the authorities, following discussions in July 1996 between Diamacouné Senghor and Diouf's personal Chief of Staff in Ziguinchor. However, in March 1997 more than 40 rebels and two members of the armed forces were killed in clashes near the border with Guinea-Bissau. The MFDC denied that it had ended its cease-fire, stating that it would investigate these incidents.

While both the Senegalese authorities and the MFDC leadership appeared committed to reviving the peace process, the deaths of 25 soldiers in August 1997 near Ziguinchor prompted fears of a revival of the conflict. In September the armed forces launched a new offensive, in which rebel forces were reported to have sustained heavy losses. A further armed forces offensive in October, the largest such operation in Casamance since the 1995 cease-fire, involved as many as 3,000 soldiers and resulted in the deaths of 12 soldiers and 80 rebels in clashes near the border with Guinea-Bissau, according to Senegalese military sources. Salif Sadio, the MFDC's military leader, stated that the organization remained committed to the peace process, but maintained that its forces were justified in defending themselves against armed attack.

In January 1998 Diamacouné Senghor appealed for a cease-fire, indicating that his organization would be prepared to abandon its demand for independence, subject to the Government instituting measures to ensure greater economic and social development in Casamance. Nevertheless, rebel violence continued intermittently throughout the second half of 1998.

In June 1999 talks between several MFDC factions began in Banjul, The Gambia, although several leaders of military and exiled factions of the MFDC did not attend, claiming that Diamacouné Senghor was effectively a hostage of the Senegalese Government. At the meeting, Léopold Sagna was confirmed as the head of the armed forces of the MFDC, replacing Sadio, who was reportedly less prepared to compromise with government demands. The Senegalese authorities subsequently acceded to the MFDC's demand that Diamacouné Senghor be released from house arrest; his movements were, however, to remain restricted.

In November 1999 Diamacouné Senghor agreed to recommence negotiations with the Senegalese Government, demanding, however, that the safety of MFDC negotiators be guaranteed, and that representatives of Casamançais civil society be included in the negotiations. At the meeting, held in Banjul in late December, the Senegalese Government and the MFDC agreed to an immediate cease-fire and to create the conditions necessary to bring about lasting peace; the Governments of The Gambia and of Guinea-Bissau were to monitor the situation in the region. A further meeting between the two parties took place in January 2000.

In early February 2000 a joint mission of the Senegalese Government and the MFDC was established to oversee the cease-fire. Following his election as President in early March, Abdoulaye Wade announced that he was to continue the process of negotiations, but that his preference was to conduct direct dialogue with the MFDC. Wade further announced that Diamacouné Senghor would be permitted total freedom of movement. In August Senegal and Guinea-Bissau announced that they would undertake joint military border patrols in order to restrict rebel activities in the region.

In November 2000 members of a peace commission, headed by the Minister of the Interior, Maj.-Gen. Mamadou Niang, and by Diamacouné Senghor, signed a joint statement that envisaged a series of official meetings between the Senegalese Government and the MFDC, the first of which would convene on 16 December. The Government simultaneously warned that full legal action would be taken against any person promoting or distributing speeches in favour of separatism. The discussions in mid-December were boycotted by representatives of the Front sud of the MFDC, led by Ali Badji. However, a senior MFDC official present at the onset of negotiations, Alexandre Djiba (who had long been resident outside Senegal), subsequently reportedly met Ali Badji's representatives in Guinea-Bissau. The Senegalese Minister of the Armed Forces, Yoba Sambou, himself a native of Casamance, meanwhile stated that the Government preferred the rebels to unite into a single faction, so that more militant factions within the MFDC would not dispute the peace talks. As a result of renewed unrest, however, the MFDC postponed a proposed meeting in Banjul, to be held in January 2001, which had been intended to establish a common position between its various factions.

The overwhelming support in Casamance for the new Constitution, which was endorsed by 96% of voters in the region at the referendum in January 2001, prompted Wade to announce that Casamance had definitively voted to remain part of Senegal. In mid-January the Guinea-Bissau armed forces reportedly destroyed all the Casamance rebel bases in that country, in response to clashes between rival MFDC factions there. Continued unrest in the region south-west of Ziguinchor further delayed the signature of a cease-fire agreement, originally intended to take place at the meeting of mid-December, which had been rescheduled to occur in Dakar in early February.

In February 2001 Diamacouné Senghor announced that, in order to accelerate the peace process in Casamance, several senior members of the MFDC, including Sidi Badji and Djiba, had been removed from their positions. However, Sidi Badji, who had served as Military Affairs Adviser to Diamacouné Senghor, rejected the legitimacy of his dismissal. Also in mid-February, in what was reportedly the most serious attack on civilian targets in Casamance for several years, separatist rebels killed some 13 civilians in an ambush. Both Sidi Badji and Diamacouné Senghor denied any knowledge of their supporters' involvement and condemned the attack, into which Wade announced the opening of a judicial inquiry.

In mid-March 2001 Niang and Diamacouné Senghor signed a cease-fire agreement at a meeting in Ziguinchor, which provided for the release of detainees, the return of refugees, the removal of landmines (which had been utilized in the region since 1998) and for economic aid to reintegrate rebels and to ameliorate the infrastructure of Casamance. Some 16 prisoners were released several days after the accord was signed. The Gambian Government issued a communiqué in mid-March, in which it promised to prevent armed rebel groups from operating on Gambian territory; it was suspected that the renewed violence had been co-ordinated by groups based in The Gambia. Later in March Niang and Diamacouné Senghor signed a further agreement, which provided for the disarmament of rebel groups and the confinement to barracks of military forces in Casamance. In April Wade and Sambou participated in negotiations with

Diamacouné Senghor, at which other MFDC leaders, including Sidi Badji, were also present.

As a result of the renewed conflict, Diamacouné Senghor announced, in late May 2001, that a proposed reconciliation forum, intended to unite the various factions of the MFDC, had been postponed indefinitely, and a number of members of the movement, including Djiba, were reportedly expelled. None the less, Diamacouné Senghor and Sidi Badji attended a meeting convened by the Gambian Government in Banjul in early June, in an attempt to overcome the impasse. As tensions between factions within the MFDC intensified, with further clashes reported in June and July, Diamacouné Senghor was removed from the position of Secretary-General of the MFDC in August, at the much-delayed reconciliation forum, and appointed as honorary President. Jean-Marie François Biagui, who had previously been involved in the French-based section of the MFDC, became Secretary-General and de facto leader. Sidi Badji, who continued to question the tactics of Diamacouné Senghor, was appointed as the organization's head of military affairs. Biagui not only demonstrated considerable reluctance to play a leadership role, but was also apparently unable to prevent Sadi Badji, who was reputed to have support from the authorities in The Gambia, from becoming the dominant force in the movement.

Despite these personnel changes within the MFDC, President Wade met Diamacouné Senghor at the presidential palace in Dakar in September 2001; both leaders reiterated the importance of implementing the cease-fire agreement. In response to this meeting, it was reported that the new leadership of the MFDC had suspended all further negotiations with the Government. Following further attacks by rebels, Biagui resigned as Secretary-General in early November. Sidi Badji was announced as Biagui's successor, in an acting capacity, although Diamacouné Senghor rejected this appointment, and reappointed Biagui as Secretary-General. In November MFDC rebels launched numerous attacks on civilians in Casamance and the following month violence in the province intensified. In an attempt to quell the rebellion, Diamacouné Senghor appointed an envoy, his nephew, Laurent Diamacouné, to seek negotiations with Sidi Badji, but with only limited success. In mid-December Diamacouné Senghor's position was further undermined, when an episcopal conference declared that his leadership of a movement that was using armed struggle to attain its ends was incompatible with his role as a Roman Catholic priest.

In August 2002, following a joint declaration signed by Diamacouné Senghor and Sidi Badji urging the resumption of peace talks between the rebels and the Government, Wade appointed an official delegation, chaired by the Second Vice-President of the Assemblée nationale and President of Ziguinchor Regional Council, Abdoulaye Faye, and including among its membership Niang and Sambou, to undertake negotiations with the MFDC. Meanwhile, the holding of an intra-Casamance conference, in early September, appeared to indicate a decline in support for separatist aspirations, as the conference produced a declaration, signed by representatives of 10 ethnic groups resident in the region, in favour of a 'definitive peace in Casamance', and which referred to the region as 'belonging to the great and single territory of Senegal'. Moreover, the absence from the meeting of the MFDC faction loyal to Sidi Badji appeared to refute reports that the various wings of the MFDC had effectively reunited. In late September five civilians, including the brother of Sambou, were killed in an attack attributed to separatist rebels north of Ziguinchor. The internal disunity of the MFDC was emphasized in mid-October, when Biagui, announcing that the conflict had definitively ended, publicly demanded forgiveness from the people of Casamance and Senegal for the actions of the organization and acknowledged that the MFDC was responsible for causing suffering to the populace; this statement was emphatically rejected by Sidi Badji. In spite of further discussions between the government commission and Diamacouné Senghor and Sidi Badji in January 2003, intermittent conflict and banditry continued to be reported in Casamance in early 2003, although by the end of April all members of the MFDC who had been imprisoned on charges other than murder had been released on bail.

In early May 2003 President Wade announced that several substantive measures towards the normalization of the political and economic situation in Casamance were to be implemented, notably major infrastructural projects and the rehabilitation of damaged villages. The Assemblée nationale was to consider an amnesty for all those implicated in crimes related to the conflict, following a convention of the MFDC, to be held, at an unspecified date, in Guinea-Bissau, prior to the conclusion of final peace talks between the MFDC and the Government. Wade also announced that the Government intended to accede to a further MFDC demand, by dismissing those implicated in the failed attempt to rescue the passengers of the stricken *Joola* ferry in September 2002 (see above), and arranging the provision of a replacement for the vessel, which had provided a key transport link between the Casamance region and Dakar. Mine-clearing operations, to involve both regular members of the army and former rebel fighters, were also to commence. Meanwhile, Diamacouné Senghor reiterated on several occasions that the Casamance conflict had concluded; reports suggested that the apparent death of Sadio, regarded as a leading opponent of compromise within the MFDC, had been a major factor in facilitating the improved relationship between the organization and the Government. (However, no clear proof of Sadio's death was presented.)

In late May 2003 Diamacouné Senghor announced that the MFDC convention, comprising 460 participants from the various factions of the organization, was to be held in Guinea-Bissau in early June, although it was reported that factions opposed to the proposed peace agreement would refuse to attend the gathering. Following the death of Sidi Badji, from natural causes, in late May, the convention was postponed, initially to late July. However, the Guinea-Bissau authorities announced that they would be unable to provide sufficient guarantees of security for participants, and the meeting was again postponed, until early October, when the gathering was held in Ziguinchor. On this occasion, which was not attended by hardline factions of the MFDC loyal to Djiba, both Diamacouné Senghor and Biagui issued statements confirming that the conflict had ended, and announced that what was termed the emancipation of Casamance did not, as a matter of course, necessarily entail its independence from Senegal. Following the restoration of peace in Casamance, it was anticipated that some 15,000 displaced persons would return to their home villages in the Ziguinchor administrative region, while demining operations commenced in July.

In mid-March 2004 unconfirmed reports suggested that Diamacouné Senghor had removed Biagui from the post of Secretary-General of the MFDC. The organization held a convention in Ziguinchor in early May, at which it proposed the cantonment of its combatants while observing a unilateral one-month cease-fire, in return for the withdrawal of government troops deployed in Casamance since 1982. In July the Assemblée nationale adopted legislation providing for an amnesty for all MFDC combatants; however, MFDC leaders claimed that their members had done nothing from which they required amnesty and urged the Government to engage in negotiations with the organization.

In September 2004 it was reported that an extraordinary general assembly of the MFDC had dismissed Diamacouné Senghor as the organization's leader and, as in 2001, appointed him Honorary President, while Biagui was reappointed Secretary-General and de facto leader. Biagui subsequently announced that the MFDC intended to transform itself into a legitimate political party and contest national elections; however, his status as leader was rejected by the MFDC's military wing, which issued a statement declaring its continuing recognition of Diamacouné Senghor as the movement's leader, while also reaffirming its commitment to full independence for Casamance. (The Senegalese Government was also reported to regard Diamacouné Senghor as remaining the MFDC's legitimate leader for the purposes of negotiations.) Following talks in Paris, France, between representatives of the Government and the external wing of the MFDC, plans were announced for the signing of a cease-fire between the two parties in late December 2004, to be followed by detailed negotiations towards a peaceful political settlement, although the Government's representatives insisted that there would be no concessions offered on the issue of independence for the region. Concerns persisted, however, over internal divisions within the MFDC: Diamacouné Senghor's appeal for a general assembly of the movement in late November, intended to reconcile the various factions in advance of the signing of the cease-fire, was reportedly rejected by his rivals in the movement's political wing, while Abdoulaye Diedhiou, leader of the military wing Atika ('arrow'), insisted that independence remained the MFDC's primary aim and criticized Diamacouné Senghor for making excessive concessions to the Senegalese Government.

On 30 December 2004 a 'General Peace Accord' was signed in Ziguinchor by the Minister of the Interior, on behalf of the Government, and Diamacouné Senghor, representing the MFDC. President Wade also signed the accord, which was, however, rejected by several factions of the MFDC, including Atika, the Front nord and elements of the movement's international wing. Negotiations aimed at achieving a definitive resolution of the conflict in Casamance were opened by Prime Minister Sall on 1 February 2005 in the town of Foundiougne, some 160 km south-east of Dakar, but were boycotted by Biagui and Diédhiou, who reportedly favoured further dialogue within the MFDC before engaging in talks with the Government. Both sides agreed to establish joint technical commissions to address reconstruction, economic and social development, and disarmament, demobilization and demining. Meanwhile, Diamacouné Senghor appointed Ansoumana Badji, formerly the MFDC's representative in Portugal, as Secretary-General of the movement; Badji stated that he aimed to persuade as many MFDC members as possible to join the peace process. Biagui rejected the legitimacy of Badji's appointment.

Since the signing of the 2004 peace agreement, outbreaks of violence had been sporadic. However, in August 2006 violent incidents between the Senegalese armed forces and the MFDC in Casamance began to escalate and by mid-August fighting resumed. Although the fighting spread north towards The Gambia, there were no reports of the conflict crossing the border. Nevertheless, many civilians fled to that country, seeking refuge and medical treatment. By October the violence began to subside as the army took control of the rebels' base. However, many civilians refused to return to the region until the security forces had departed. In 2007 small-scale operations were conducted to clear the region of landmines and the people of Casamance slowly began to return to their homes. However, having been empty for over a decade, many of the villages were uninhabitable with no water supplies and there was severe infrastructural damage. Tensions persisted between the MFDC and the Government and a rebel faction of the MFDC had been blamed for sabotaging demining efforts. Consequently, reconstruction work in villages across Casamance was yet to begin, leaving little to which the Casamançais could return. Small-scale conflicts continued and in December the presidential envoy to the region was killed, threatening to destabilize the reconstruction process.

From 1989 Senegal's regional relations underwent a period of considerable strain. A long-standing border dispute with Mauritania, which also involved ethnic and economic rivalries, was exacerbated by the deaths, in April of that year, of two Senegalese farmers, who had been involved in a dispute regarding grazing rights with Mauritanian livestock-breeders. Mauritanian nationals residing in Senegal were attacked, and their businesses looted, while Senegalese nationals in Mauritania suffered similar aggression. By early May it was believed that several hundred people, mostly Senegalese, had been killed. Operations to repatriate nationals of both countries commenced, with international assistance. Diplomatic relations, which had been suspended in August 1989, were fully restored in April 1992, and the process of reopening the border began in May, although the contentious issues that had hitherto impeded the normalization of relations remained largely unresolved. In December 1994, however, the Governments of Senegal and Mauritania agreed new co-operation measures, including efforts to facilitate the free movement of goods and people between the two countries.

In January 1995 the Governments of Senegal, Mauritania and Mali undertook to co-operate in resolving joint border issues and in combating extremism, arms-smuggling and drugs-trafficking. In July the office of the UN High Commissioner for Refugees (UNHCR) began a census of Mauritanian refugees in Senegal, estimated to number some 66,000, as part of initiatives for their eventual repatriation. In May 1998 the Ministers of the Interior of Mauritania, Mali and Senegal met to discuss border security, following reports of increased cross-border banditry, particularly in eastern Senegal. The unrest in the region was blamed by the Senegalese press on the continued presence there of Mauritanian refugees; in September it was reported that the Senegalese authorities had ceased to issue the refugees with travel documents. In May 1999 the two countries signed a further agreement on the joint exploitation of fisheries. In mid-2000, however, a dispute over water rights resulted in a period of substantial tension between Senegal and Mauritania. Following renewed negotiations, the visit of President Taya of Mauritania to Dakar in April, as the guest of honour at a ceremony to commemorate the 41st anniversary of the independence of Senegal, was widely regarded as indicating an improvement in relations between the countries. Presidents Taya and Wade met again in July 2003, when negotiations were conducted on a range of bilateral and international issues; Wade reiterated his support for Taya's administration, following an attempted *coup d'état* in Mauritania in the previous month. The extradition of one of the suspected coup plotters from Senegal to Mauritania was also interpreted as an indication of improved relations between the countries, as was the Mauritanian Government's decision to accord 270 temporary fishing licences to Senegalese fishermen in June 2004. According to provisional figures, 19,503 UNHCR-assisted Mauritanian refugees remained in Senegal at the end of 2007.

In October 1993 Senegal and Guinea-Bissau signed an agreement regarding the joint exploitation and management of fishing and petroleum resources in their maritime zones. This treaty was ratified in December 1995, to the effect that fishing resources were to be shared equally between the two countries, while Senegal was to benefit from an 85% share of revenue obtained from petroleum deposits. During bilateral contacts in 1995–97 Senegal and Guinea-Bissau pledged co-operation in matters of joint defence and security. It was hoped that the movement of refugees from the conflict in Casamance to Guinea-Bissau, which began, under the auspices of UNHCR, in February 1996, would expedite efforts to restore security in the border region between the countries. In January 1998 it was announced that the authorities in Guinea-Bissau had intercepted a consignment of armaments destined for MFDC rebels, and that some 15 officers of the Guinea-Bissau armed forces had been arrested and suspended from duty, including the head of the armed forces, Brig. (later Gen.) Ansumane Mané. In June, however, troops loyal to Mané rebelled against President Commdr João Vieira of Guinea-Bissau, and civil war broke out in that country. Senegalese troops intervened in support of the armed forces loyal to Vieira. By the end of the month refugees from the conflict were crossing into Casamance, exacerbating security concerns in the province, while it was also reported that members of the MFDC were fighting alongside the rebels against the Government of Guinea-Bissau and Senegalese forces. From December, as a result of a peace-keeping agreement brokered by the Economic Community of West African States (ECOWAS, see p. 243), Senegalese troops began to depart from Guinea-Bissau, but strengthened their presence in the border area, while the ECOWAS peace-keeping force, ECOMOG (see p. 246), assumed positions on the Guinea-Bissau side of the frontier with Casamance.

In May 1999 fighting again broke out in Guinea-Bissau, and Vieira was overthrown. Tensions between the two countries resurfaced in April 2000, when an armed group, reportedly composed of members of the MFDC operating from within Guinea-Bissau, attacked a Senegalese border post, killing three soldiers, and later that month the border between the two countries was temporarily closed. In August the terms of the agreement concerning the joint exploitation of maritime resources by the two countries was revised; henceforth, Guinea-Bissau was to receive 20% rather than 15% of the revenue generated from petroleum deposits. In early September, following clashes near the border in Guinea-Bissau, attributed to an armed faction of the MFDC, the Senegalese Government closed all border posts between the two countries. Following the killing of Mané in November 2000, during an attempted *coup d'état*, relations between Senegal and Guinea-Bissau improved significantly.

In August 1989 Diouf announced the withdrawal of Senegalese troops from The Gambia, in protest at a request by President Jawara of that country that The Gambia be accorded more power within the confederal agreement of Senegambia that had been formed by the two countries in 1982. Diouf subsequently stated that, in view of The Gambia's reluctance to proceed towards full political and economic integration with Senegal, the functions of the Confederation would be suspended. The Confederation was dissolved in September. In January 1991 the two countries signed a bilateral treaty of friendship and co-operation. Senegal's abrupt decision to close the Senegalese–Gambian border in September 1993, apparently to reduce smuggling between the two countries, again strained relations, although subsequent negotiations sought to minimize the adverse effects of the closure on The Gambia's regional trading links. Since the *coup d'état* in The Gambia in July 1994 Senegal has fostered cordial relations with the Government of President Jammeh and in June 1996 the two countries agreed to take joint measures to combat insecurity, illegal immigration, arms-trafficking and drugs-smuggling. In early 1998 Jammeh offered to act as a mediator between the Senegalese Government and the MFDC, and subsequently held regular meetings with MFDC representatives. None the less, intermittent disputes relating to transportation issues between the two countries have occurred, and tensions between the two countries again heightened in mid-2005, following a 100% increase in transportation fees on the ferry across the Gambia river by the Gambian port authorities. Senegalese trade unionists blockaded border crossings between Senegal and The Gambia to protest at the increase, and the Senegalese Government granted fuel subsidies to drivers who used a longer, alternative route between the southern and northern parts of Senegal, avoiding The Gambia. Although tensions lessened later in the year, when the port authority reduced the ferry charges by 15%, in what was described as a gesture of goodwill, there was increasing speculation that the Senegalese authorities were considering the construction of a tunnel to link the southern and northern parts of Senegal. Bilateral relations were again strained in March 2006, however, following allegations of Senegalese complicity in an abortive coup in The Gambia. One of those arrested in connection with the plot reportedly claimed to have been instructed by the alleged leader of the coup (who was believed to have fled to Senegal) to liaise with the Senegalese embassy in The Gambia. The Senegalese Government denied any involvement in the plot, which it condemned, and recalled its ambassador to The Gambia for consultations; a new ambassador was appointed in June.

Since his election in March 2000, President Wade has on several occasions promoted greater democratization in other West African countries and encouraged an expansion in the international political engagement of African countries. Notably, Wade's well-publicized condemnation, at an international conference on racism and xenophobia held under the auspices of the office of the UN High Commissioner for Human Rights in Dakar in January 2001, of the increasing importance of ethnically based politics in Côte d'Ivoire prompted violent demonstrations across Côte d'Ivoire. At the UN World Conference against Racism, Racial Discrimination, Xenophobia and Related Intolerance, held in Durban, South Africa, in August–September, Wade, notably among African leaders, condemned the notion that reparations should be paid by Western nations to the descendants of slaves.

President Wade was one of the four African leaders most closely involved in the initial development of the New Partnership for Africa's Development (NEPAD, see p. 178), a long-term plan for socio-economic recovery in Africa that was launched in October 2001 in accordance with a decision of the Organization of African Unity (OAU, now the African Union—AU, see p. 172) summit of heads of state and government held in Lusaka, Zambia, in July of that year.

Relations with France have remained particularly strong since independence, and the existing defence arrangements between France and Senegal remained substantially unaltered following the major restructuring of the French armed forces undertaken by the administration of Jacques Chirac in the late 1990s and early 2000s. Relations between Senegal and France were strengthened in September 2006 when the two countries signed an agreement, which provided for, *inter alia*, a relaxation of visa regulations between the two countries and the provision of €2.5m. to fund development projects.

In late 2005 Senegal announced that it was to terminate its diplomatic relations with Taiwan in order to resume relations with the People's Republic of China. The respective embassies in Dakar and Beijing were re-opened, and ambassadors were exchanged between the two countries in early 2006.

Senegal is an active participant in regional and international peace-keeping operations. In February 1998 Senegal, with Mali and Mauritania, was among the principal participants in multinational military exercises conducted in eastern Senegal under the auspices of the UN and the OAU, as part of efforts to establish a regional crisis-intervention force. The exercise was organized by France and involved almost 3,500 troops from eight West African countries, as well as units from the USA, the United Kingdom and Belgium. Senegal is a member of the Accord de Non-agression et d'assistance en matière de défense, which in April 1999 adopted a draft protocol on the setting up of a peace-keeping force in the region. In September 1999 a Senegalese contingent joined the international peace-keeping operation in the Kosovo and Metohija province of Yugoslavia (now Serbia and Montenegro). In April 2001 more than 500 Senegalese soldiers joined UN observer missions in the Democratic Republic of the Congo. In early 2003 it was announced that Senegal was to contribute some 650 troops to the ECOWAS military mission in Côte d'Ivoire (ECOMICI); Senegalese troops were also expected to play a prominent role in the UN Operation in Côte d'Ivoire (UNOCI, see p. 91) that assumed the responsibilities of ECOMICI from April 2004. Meanwhile, in August 2003 some 260 Senegalese troops were dispatched to serve in the ECOWAS Mission in Liberia (ECOMIL), which was replaced by the UN Mission in Liberia (UNMIL, see p. 86) in October. More recently, in 2007 Senegal agreed to contribute 1,600 peace-keeping troops to the AU/UN Hybrid Operation in Darfur, which was deployed in Sudan.

Government

Under the terms of the Constitution, approved by popular referendum in January 2001, executive power is held by the President, who is directly elected for a mandate of five years, which is renewable only once. (President Wade will, however, complete the seven-year mandate to which he was elected in March 2000 by the terms of the former Constitution). Legislative power rests with the Assemblée nationale, with 120 members elected for five years by universal adult suffrage. (In late 2005 the existing legislature voted to extend its mandate, exceptionally, by one further year.) The formation of parties on an ethnic, religious or geographical basis is prohibited. The President appoints the Prime Minister, who, in consultation with the President, appoints the Council of Ministers. Senegal comprises 11 regions, each with an appointed governor, an elected local assembly and a separate budget.

Defence

As assessed at November 2008, Senegal's active armed forces totalled 13,620 men: army 11,900, navy 950, air force 770. There was also a 5,000-strong paramilitary gendarmerie. Military service is by selective conscription and lasts for two years. France and the USA provide technical and material aid, and in November 2008 there were 610 French troops stationed in Senegal. The defence budget for 2007 was 92,500m. francs CFA.

Economic Affairs

In 2007, according to estimates by the World Bank, Senegal's gross national income (GNI), measured at average 2005–07 prices, was US $10,170m., equivalent to $820 per head (or $1,640 on an international purchasing-power parity basis). During 2000–07, it was estimated, the population increased at an average annual rate of 2.7%, while gross domestic product (GDP) per head increased by an average of 1.6% per year. Overall GDP increased, in real terms, at an average annual rate of 4.3% per year in 2000–07; growth in 2007 was 4.8%.

Agriculture (including forestry and fishing) contributed 14.4% of GDP in 2007. The sector engaged 39.8% of the employed labour force in 2006. The principal cash crops are groundnuts and cotton. Senegal also exports fruit and vegetables to European markets. Groundnuts, millet, sorghum, rice, maize and vegetables are produced for domestic consumption, although Senegal has yet to achieve self-sufficiency in basic foodstuffs. The fishing sector makes an important contribution to both the domestic food supply and export revenue: fish and fish products are in most years Senegal's principal export commodity, contributing 20.9% of export earnings in 2007. The sale of fishing licences to the European Union (EU, see p. 255) has been an important source of revenue. However, despite the inclusion of safeguards intended to preserve stocks, the Senegalese Government and the domestic fishing industry have expressed concerns regarding the impact of fishing by EU vessels on supplies in easily attainable waters, and negotiations for a new agreement with the EU, following the expiry of the 2002–06 accord, remained suspended in early 2009. According to the World Bank, during 2000–07 agricultural GDP increased by an average of 1.0% per year; agricultural GDP increased by 3.1% in 2007.

Industry (including mining, manufacturing, construction and power) contributed 24.0% of GDP in 2007. Some 17.5% of the employed labour force were engaged in the sector in 2006. During 2000–07, according to the World Bank, industrial GDP increased at an average annual rate of 3.8%. Industrial GDP increased by 5.7% in 2007.

Mining contributed just 1.2% of GDP in 2007, and the sector engaged only 0.5% of the employed labour force in 2006. The principal mining activity is the extraction of calcium phosphates (aluminium phosphates are also mined in smaller quantities).

Deposits of salt, fuller's earth (attapulgite), clinker and natural gas are also exploited, and investigations are under way into the feasibility of mining copper, alluvial diamonds, uranium and iron ore. Explorations at Sabodala, in the south-east, have revealed gold reserves estimated at 30 metric tons; the first gold pour was made in March 2009. Offshore deposits of petroleum are also to be developed, in co-operation with Guinea-Bissau.

Manufacturing contributed 13.8% of GDP in 2007. The sector engaged 9.2% of the employed labour force in 2006. The most important manufacturing activities are food-processing (notably fish, groundnuts and sugar), chemicals, textiles and petroleum-refining (using imported crude petroleum). Exports of petroleum products contributed 20.3% of the value of total exports in 2007. According to the World Bank, manufacturing GDP increased at an average annual rate of 1.8% in 2000–07; growth in 2007 was 4.2%.

In 2005 Senegal derived 79.4% of its electrical energy from petroleum sources. Senegal also receives supplies from the Manantali hydroelectric power installation (constructed under the auspices of the Organisation pour la mise en valeur du fleuve Sénégal—OMVS): 10.5% of Senegal's electricity was derived from hydropower. Imports of fuels (including petroleum for refining) accounted for 21.7% of the value of merchandise imports in 2007.

The services sector contributed 61.5% of GDP in 2007. Some 42.6% of the employed labour force were engaged in the sector in 2006. Tourism is a major source of foreign exchange, with receipts totalling US $334m. in 2005. Dakar's port is of considerable importance as a centre for regional trade. According to the World Bank, the GDP of the services sector increased by an average of 5.7% per year in 2000–07. The GDP of the sector increased by 8.4% in 2007.

In 2007 Senegal's visible trade deficit was estimated at 1,078,000m. francs CFA, and the deficit on the current account of the balance of payments at 571,000m. francs CFA. In 2007 the principal source of imports was France, which supplied 23.5% of total imports; other major suppliers were Nigeria, the People's Republic of China and Thailand. Mali was the principal market for exports in that year, taking 22.8% of the total; France, India, Italy, Spain and The Gambia were also important purchasers. The principal exports in 2007 were fish and fish products, petroleum products, phosphoric acid and cement. The principal imports in that year were petroleum and petroleum products, agricultural and industrial machinery, and rice.

Senegal's overall fiscal deficit was estimated at 198,000m. francs CFA in 2007 (equivalent to 3.7% of GDP). Total external debt was US $1,984m. at the end of 2006, of which $1,712m. was long-term public debt. In 2004, when external debt totalled $3,940m., the cost of debt-servicing was equivalent to 11.8% of the value of exports of goods and services. The average annual rate of inflation in 2000–07 was 2.2%. Consumer prices increased by an average of 5.8% in 2007 and 2008. Some 10% of the economically active population were unemployed in 2006.

Senegal is a member of the Economic Community of West African States (ECOWAS, see p. 243), of the West African organs of the Franc Zone (see p. 316), of the African Groundnut Council (see p. 421), of the West Africa Rice Development Association (see p. 423), of the Gambia River Basin Development Organization (see p. 426) and of the OMVS (see p. 428).

The attainment of sustained economic growth has been impeded by Senegal's dependence on revenue from a narrow export base, and by its consequent vulnerability to fluctuations in international prices for its principal commodities. A slowing in the overall rate of economic growth 2008, to an estimated 3.9%, despite a strong performance in the agricultural sector, reflected the impact of high international prices for food and fuels, which kept inflation significantly higher than the recent annual average, and which was forecast to result in a widening of the external current account to 12.3% of GDP, from 10.7% in 2007; ongoing disruption to the phosphates industry arising from the insolvency, declared in 2006, of Industries Chimiques du Sénégal (ICS); and delays in government payments to the private sector, which slowed activity especially in the construction sector. Pressure had been exerted on the budget by the Government's efforts, through subsidies on food and energy, to ease social tensions and minimize the impact of high prices on vulnerable groups. The phased elimination of budget subsidies for food and fuels, and the introduction (from August 2008) of a new pricing structure for electricity, were to be accompanied by measures intended to protect the poorest members of the population. Meanwhile, the Government undertook to preserve spending allocations to social sectors such as health, education and sanitation. Continued commitment to the programme of infrastructural development through public investment was considered essential to the maintenance of economic activity and promotion of employment. In November 2008 the IMF approved a one-year Exogenous Shocks Facility of SDR 48.54m., in support of Senegal's efforts to offset the impact on the balance of payments of high food and energy prices. (The IMF had in November 2007 approved a three-year Policy Support Instrument whereby Senegal would receive the advice, monitoring and endorsement of its economic reform programme by the IMF, but no financial assistance.) Reviewing the economy in late 2008, the IMF emphasized the necessity of addressing delayed payments: the Government aimed to eliminate arrears by mid-2009. The Fund also noted that the resumption of activities by ICS, following its rehabilitation under an Indian majority owner in early 2008, would help offset pressure on the balance of payments from 2009. External debt obligations, following relief from the mid-2000s under the heavily indebted poor countries and multilateral debt relief initiatives, were considered to be sustainable. However, in view of possible depressed international demand, there was perceived risk to key sectors such as tourism, and to export markets for fish and groundnut products. Furthermore, remittances from abroad by Senegalese nationals, which contribute some 8% of annual GDP and which have in recent years notably contributed to the expansion of the construction sector through demand for housing, were likely to be vulnerable to economic downturn in host countries.

Education

Primary education, which usually begins at seven years of age, lasts for six years and is officially compulsory. In 2006/07 primary enrolment included 71.9% of children in the relevant age-group (males 72.0%; females 71.9%), according to UNESCO estimates. Secondary education usually begins at the age of 13, and comprises a first cycle of four years (also referred to as 'middle school') and a further cycle of three years. According to UNESCO estimates, in 2005/06 secondary enrolment was equivalent to only 20.4% of children in the relevant age-group (males 23.1%; females 17.6%). There are three universities in Senegal, the Université Cheikh Anta Diop and the Université du Sahel in Dakar and the Université Gaston Berger in Saint-Louis. Since 1981 the reading and writing of national languages has been actively promoted, and is expressly encouraged in the 2001 Constitution. In 2005 spending on education represented 18.9% of total budgetary expenditure.

Public Holidays

2009: 1 January (New Year's Day), 7 January*† (Ashoura), 9 March* (Mouloud, Birth of the Prophet), 4 April (National Day), 10 April (Good Friday), 13 April (Easter Monday), 1 May (Labour Day), 21 May (Ascension Day), 1 June (Whit Monday), 14 July (Day of Association), 15 August (Assumption), 20 September* (Korité, end of Ramadan), 1 November (All Saints' Day), 27 November* (Tabaski, Feast of the Sacrifice), 25 December (Christmas), 27 December† (Ashoura).

2010: 1 January (New Year's Day), 26 February* (Mouloud, Birth of the Prophet), 2 April (Good Friday), 4 April (National Day), 5 April (Easter Monday), 1 May (Labour Day), 13 May (Ascension Day), 24 May (Whit Monday), 14 July (Day of Association), 15 August (Assumption), 10 September* (Korité, end of Ramadan), 1 November (All Saints' Day), 16 November* (Tabaski, Feast of the Sacrifice), 16 December* (Ashoura), 25 December (Christmas).

* These holidays are determined by the Islamic lunar calendar and may vary by one or two days from the dates given.

† This festival occurs twice (in the Islamic years AH 1430 and 1431) within the same Gregorian year.

Weights and Measures

The metric system is in force.

Statistical Survey

Source (unless otherwise stated): Agence nationale de la Statistique et de la Démographie, blvd de l'Est, Point E, BP 116, Dakar; tel. 33-824-0301; fax 33-824-9004; e-mail statsenegal@yahoo.fr; internet www.ansd.org.

Area and Population

AREA, POPULATION AND DENSITY

Area (sq km)	197,021*
Population (census results)†	
27 May 1988	6,896,808
8 December 2002	
Males	4,846,126
Females	5,009,212
Total	9,855,338
Population (UN estimates at mid-year)‡	
2006	11,583,000
2007	11,893,000
2008	12,211,000
Density (per sq km) at mid-2008	62.0

* 76,070 sq miles.
† Figures for 1988 and 2002 refer to the *de jure* population. The de facto population at the 1988 census was 6,773,417, and at the 2002 census was 9,552,442.
‡ Source: UN, *World Population Prospects: The 2008 Revision*.

POPULATION BY ETHNIC GROUP
(at 1988 census)

Ethnic group	Number	%
Wolof	2,890,402	42.67
Serere	1,009,921	14.91
Peul	978,366	14.44
Toucouleur	631,892	9.33
Diola	357,672	5.28
Mandingue	245,651	3.63
Rural-Rurale	113,184	1.67
Bambara	91,071	1.34
Maure	67,726	1.00
Manjaag	66,605	0.98
Others	320,927	4.74
Total	**6,773,417**	**100.00**

Source: UN, *Demographic Yearbook*.

REGIONS
(2002 census)

	Area (sq km)	Population	Density (per sq km)
Dakar	547	2,167,793	3,963.1
Diourbel	4,903	1,053,856	214.9
Fatick	7,910	609,853	77.1
Kaolack	15,449	1,069,880	69.3
Kolda	21,112	817,714	38.7
Louga	25,254	677,750	26.8
Matam	29,041	424,106	14.6
Saint-Louis	19,241	695,498	36.1
Tambacounda	59,542	612,288	10.3
Thiès	6,670	1,317,067	197.5
Ziguinchor	7,352	409,533	55.7
Total	**197,021**	**9,855,338**	**50.0**

PRINCIPAL TOWNS
(2002 census, provisional results)

Dakar (capital)	955,897	Mbour	153,503
Pikine	768,826	Diourbel	95,984
Rufisque	284,263	Louga	73,662
Guediawaye	258,370	Tambacounda	67,543
Thiès	237,849	Kolda	53,921
Kaolack	172,305	Mbacké	51,124
Saint-Louis	154,555		

Note: Data given pertain to communes, except for Dakar, Pikine, Rufisque and Guediawaye, where the population figure given is that of the département.

Mid-2007 ('000, incl. suburbs, UN estimate): Dakar 2,604 (Source: UN, *World Urbanization Prospects: The 2007 Revision*).

BIRTHS AND DEATHS
(annual averages, UN estimates)

	1990–95	1995–2000	2000–05
Birth rate (per 1,000)	43.5	41.4	39.6
Death rate (per 1,000)	13.3	12.4	11.6

Source: UN, *World Population Prospects: The 2008 Revision*.

2006: Birth rate 35.7 per 1,000; Death rate 9.2 per 1,000 (Source: African Development Bank).

2007: Birth rate 35.2 per 1,000; Death rate 9.0 per 1,000 (Source: African Development Bank).

Life expectancy (years at birth, WHO estimates): 58.8 (males 56.9; females 60.7) in 2006 (Source: WHO, *World Health Statistics*).

ECONOMICALLY ACTIVE POPULATION
('000 persons, 2006)

	Males	Females	Total
Agriculture, hunting and forestry	631.9	354.6	986.5
Fishing	66.5	10.4	76.9
Mining and quarrying	11.5	2.6	14.1
Manufacturing	203.7	41.7	245.4
Electricity, gas and water supply	18.5	3.3	21.8
Construction	179.7	6.9	186.6
Wholesale and retail trade; repair of motor vehicles, motorcycles and personal household goods	388.0	397.9	785.9
Hotels and restaurants	12.2	16.4	28.6
Transport, storage and communication	135.9	5.8	141.7
Financial intermediation	11.8	4.9	16.7
Public administration and defence; compulsory social security; education; health and social work	118.7	39.0	157.7
Extra-territorial organizations and bodies	3.3	3.7	7.0
Not classified by economic activity	266.5	217.5	484.0
Total	**2,048.1**	**1,104.8**	**3,152.9**
Unemployed	174.5	176.8	351.4
Total labour force	**2,222.6**	**1,281.6**	**3,504.3**

Source: ILO.

Health and Welfare

KEY INDICATORS

Total fertility rate (children per woman, 2006)	4.9
Under-5 mortality rate (per 1,000 live births, 2006)	116
HIV/AIDS (% of persons aged 15–49, 2007)	1.0
Physicians (per 1,000 head, 2004)	0.06
Hospital beds (per 1,000 head, 2007)	0.1
Health expenditure (2006): US $ per head (PPP)	72
Health expenditure (2006): % of GDP	5.4
Health expenditure (2006): public (% of total)	31.5
Access to water (% of persons, 2006)	77
Access to sanitation (% of persons, 2006)	28
Human Development Index (2006): ranking	153
Human Development Index (2006): value	0.502

For sources and definitions, see explanatory note on p. vi.

Agriculture

PRINCIPAL CROPS
('000 metric tons)

	2005	2006	2007
Rice, paddy	279.1	190.5	215.2
Maize	400.0	181.6	185.2
Millet	608.6	494.3	362.9
Sorghum	144.0	121.0	120.3
Cassava (Manioc)	281.5	120.8	178.2
Sugar cane*	829.0	829.5	836.0
Cashew nuts*	4.5	4.5	5.0
Groundnuts, with shell	703.4	460.5	427.1
Oil palm fruit*	70	70	71
Tomatoes	114.1	104.8	105.0
Onions, dry	45.0	60.0	65.0
Watermelons	241.4	225.9	117.6
Oranges	35.5	38.6	40.0
Guavas, mangoes and mangosteens	61.6	82.2	84.0

* FAO estimates.

Aggregate production ('000 metric tons, may include official, semi-official or estimated data): Total cereals 1,432.8 in 2005, 988.3 in 2006, 884.7 in 2007; Total pulses 93.2 in 2005, 53.2 in 2006, 60.1 in 2007; Total roots and tubers 314.5 in 2005, 165.1 in 2006, 228.2 in 2007; Total vegetables (incl. melons) 532.4 in 2005, 595.3 in 2006, 507.6 in 2007; Total fruits (excl. melons) 146.0 in 2005, 150.8 in 2006, 158.0 in 2007.

Source: FAO.

LIVESTOCK
('000 head, year ending September)

	2005	2006	2007*
Cattle	3,091	3,137	3,181
Sheep	4,863	4,996	5,131
Goats	4,144	4,263	4,383
Pigs	309	318	327
Horses	514	518	521
Asses	413	n.a.	n.a.
Camels	4	4	4
Chickens	26,959	29,243	31,700

* FAO estimates.
Source: FAO.

LIVESTOCK PRODUCTS
('000 metric tons)

	2005	2006	2007*
Cattle meat	47.2	48.3	49.0
Sheep meat	17.1	17.1	17.6
Goat meat	11.2	11.5	11.9
Pig meat	9.8	10.3	10.6
Horse meat*	7.0	7.1	7.2
Chicken meat	29.0	28.9	31.1
Cows' milk	97.3	98.8	101.1
Sheep's milk	8.3	8.7	8.8
Goats' milk	10.6	10.7	11.0
Hen eggs*	27	28	32

* FAO estimates.
Source: FAO.

Forestry

ROUNDWOOD REMOVALS
('000 cubic metres, excl. bark, FAO estimates)

	2005	2006	2007
Sawlogs, veneer logs and logs for sleepers*	40	40	40
Other industrial wood†	754	754	754
Fuel wood	5,276	5,306	5,336
Total	6,070	6,100	6,130

* Annual output assumed to be unchanged since 1986 (FAO estimates).
† Annual output assumed to be unchanged since 1999 (FAO estimates).
Source: FAO.

SAWNWOOD PRODUCTION
('000 cubic metres, incl. railway sleepers)

	1989	1990	1991
Total (all broadleaved)	15	22	23

1992–2007: Annual production assumed to be unchanged from 1991 (FAO estimates).
Source: FAO.

Fishing

('000 metric tons, live weight)

	2004	2005	2006
Capture*	445.3	412.1	377.7
Freshwater fishes*	51.8	53.3	51.8
Sea catfishes	18.8	18.8	11.7
Round sardinella	137.6	114.0	101.9
Madeiran sardinella	115.3	118.4	95.6
Bonga shad	21.8	19.2	18.9
Octopuses	5.0	1.8	3.0
Aquaculture	0.2	0.2*	0.2*
Total catch*	445.5	412.3	377.9

* FAO estimate(s).
Source: FAO.

Mining

('000 metric tons, unless otherwise stated, estimates)

	2004	2005	2006
Cement, hydraulic	2,391	2,623	2,884
Gold (kg)*	600	600	600
Calcium phosphates	1,576	1,451	584
Aluminium phosphates	4	4	4
Fuller's earth (attapulgite)	200	127	140
Salt (unrefined)	168	134	199

* Government estimate of unreported production of artisanal gold.

Source: US Geological Survey.

Industry

PETROLEUM PRODUCTS
('000 metric tons)

	2003	2004	2005
Jet fuels	126	132	88
Motor gasoline (petrol)	151	148	118
Kerosene	26	19	19
Gas-diesel (distillate fuel) oils	463	471	356
Residual fuel (Mazout) oils	316	327	279
Lubricating oils	5	5	5
Liquefied petroleum gas	12	10	3

Source: UN, *Industrial Commodity Statistics Yearbook*.

SELECTED OTHER PRODUCTS
('000 metric tons, unless otherwise indicated)

	2001	2002	2003
Raw sugar	95.0*	95.0†	95.0†
Sugar cubes	27.2	19.8	23.2
Tobacco products (tons)	2,132	2,245	2,218
Groundnut oil—crude	125.3	98.1	39.2
Vegetable oil—refined	70.6	78.5	75.7
Canned tuna	12.1	10.7	6.9
Footwear (million pairs)	0.6	n.a.	n.a.
Cotton yarn (tons)	411	n.a.	n.a.
Soap	38.6	34.8	33.4
Paints and varnishes	4.6	4.3	4.6
Cement	1,539.0	1,653.2	1,693.9
Metal cans (million)	113.2	185.2	182.2
Electricity (million kWh)	1,651.2	1,557.3	1,855.5

* Unofficial figure.
† FAO estimate.

Source: mainly IMF, *Senegal: Selected Issues and Statistical Appendix* (May 2005).

Nitrogenous fertilizers (nitrogen content, '000 metric tons, unofficial figures): 38.8 in 1998; 24.5 in 1999; 19.4 in 2000 (Source: FAO).

Phosphate fertilizers (phosphoric acid content, '000 metric tons, unofficial figures): 67.5 in 1998; 45.0 in 1999; 32.4 in 2000 (Source: FAO).

Cement ('000 metric tons, estimates): 1,700 annually in 2004–06 (Source: US Geological Survey).

Electric energy (million kWh): 2,171.9 in 2005; 2,159.5 in 2006; 2,296.0 in 2007.

Finance

CURRENCY AND EXCHANGE RATES

Monetary Units
100 centimes = 1 franc de la Communauté financière africaine (CFA).

Sterling, Dollar and Euro Equivalents (31 December 2008)
£1 sterling = 687.112 francs CFA;
US $1 = 471.335 francs CFA;
€1 = 655.957 francs CFA;
10,000 francs CFA = £14.55 = $21.22 = €15.24.

Average Exchange Rate (francs CFA per US $)
2006 522.89
2007 479.27
2008 447.81

Note: An exchange rate of 1 French franc = 50 francs CFA, established in 1948, remained in force until January 1994, when the CFA franc was devalued by 50%, with the exchange rate adjusted to 1 French franc = 100 francs CFA. This relationship to French currency remained in effect with the introduction of the euro on 1 January 1999. From that date, accordingly, a fixed exchange rate of €1 = 655.957 francs CFA has been in operation.

BUDGET
('000 million francs CFA)

Revenue*	2006	2007†	2008‡
Tax revenue	922	1,088	1,161
Taxes on goods and services (excl. petroleum)	533	628	645
Taxes on petroleum products	170	215	242
Non-tax revenue	41	51	48
Total	**963**	**1,139**	**1,209**

Expenditure§	2006	2007†	2008‡
Current expenditure	829	881	994
Wages and salaries	286	327	358
Other operational expenses	500	519	601
Transfers and subsidies	308	287	359
Goods and services	186	217	229
Capital expenditure	475	605	550
Domestically financed	337	392	324
Externally financed	138	213	231
Total	**1,304**	**1,486**	**1,544**

* Excluding grants received ('000 million francs CFA): 73 in 2006; 138 in 2007 (estimate); 132 in 2008 (projection).
† Estimates.
‡ Projections.
§ Excluding net lending ('000 million francs CFA): 27 in 2006; 5 in 2007 (estimate); −3 in 2008 (projection).

Source: IMF, *Senegal: Second Review Under the Policy Support Instrument, Request for a Twelve-Month Arrangement Under the Exogenous Shocks Facility, and Request for Waivers and Modification of Assessment Criteria-Staff Report; Staff Statement; Press Release on the Executive Board Discussion; and Statement by the Executive Director for Senegal* (January 2009).

INTERNATIONAL RESERVES
(excluding gold, US $ million at 31 December)

	2005	2006	2007
IMF special drawing rights	1.4	0.1	0.1
Reserve position in IMF	2.2	2.4	2.6
Foreign exchange	1,187.4	1,331.8	1,657.3
Total	**1,191.0**	**1,334.2**	**1,660.0**

Source: IMF, *International Financial Statistics*.

SENEGAL

Statistical Survey

MONEY SUPPLY
('000 million francs CFA at 31 December)

	2005	2006	2007
Currency outside banks	378.6	451.9	483.6
Demand deposits at deposit money banks	576.0	633.8	759.7
Checking deposits at post office	7.6	12.5	22.7
Total money (incl. others)	962.7	1,098.7	1,266.6

Source: IMF, *International Financial Statistics*.

COST OF LIVING
(Consumer Price Index; base: 2000 = 100)

	2005	2006	2007
Food (incl. tobacco)	114.5	116.0	124.5
Clothing	87.3	85.9	88.4
Electricity, gas and other fuels	113.7	112.0	123.2
Rent	104.6	108.2	119.1
All items (incl. others)	107.7	110.0	116.4

Source: ILO.

2008: All items 123.1 (Source: IMF, *International Finacial Statistics*).

NATIONAL ACCOUNTS
('000 million francs CFA at current prices)

Expenditure on the Gross Domestic Product

	2005	2006	2007
Final consumption expenditure	3,936.3	4,303.5	4,731.5
Private final consumption expenditure	3,341.4	3,435.6	3,872.8
Government final consumption expenditure	594.9	867.9	858.7
Gross fixed capital formation	1,251.0	1,284.8	1,570.7
Changes in inventories	102.6	113.0	124.0
Total domestic expenditure	5,289.9	5,701.3	6,426.2
Exports of goods and services	1,240.8	1,254.0	1,255.7
Less Imports of goods and services	1,948.4	2,109.0	2,337.6
GDP in purchasers' values	4,582.3	4,846.3	5,344.3
GDP in constant 1999 prices*	4,086.5	4,235.5	n.a.

* Source: IMF, *International Financial Statistics*.

Gross Domestic Product by Economic Activity

	2005	2006	2007
Agriculture, hunting, forestry and fishing	671.0	631.4	668.8
Mining and quarrying	43.6	38.3	53.3
Manufacturing	604.8	605.8	639.0
Electricity, gas and water	100.2	112.9	137.3
Construction	195.5	238.3	281.6
Trade	737.7	772.2	849.4
Transport, storage and communications	452.4	524.2	587.9
Other services	1,176.4	1,261.8	1,411.6
Sub-total	3,981.6	4,184.9	4,628.9
Import taxes and duties	600.7	661.6	715.5
GDP in purchasers' values	4,582.3	4,846.3	5,344.3

Source: Banque Centrale des Etats de l'Afrique de l'Ouest.

BALANCE OF PAYMENTS
('000 million francs CFA)

	2005	2006	2007*
Exports of goods f.o.b.	832	833	801
Imports of goods f.o.b.	−1,524	−1,661	−1,879
Trade balance	−691	−828	−1,078
Exports of services and incomes received	518	512	530
Imports of services and incomes paid	−587	−577	−592
Balance on goods, services and income	−761	−893	−1,140
Current transfers (net)	405	437	570
Current balance	−355	−455	−571
Capital account (net)	69	1,234	182
Direct investment (net)	28	110	171
Portfolio investment (net)	14	−11	26
Other investment (net)	117	−845	314
Net errors and omissions	6	24	−71
Overall balance	−122	57	51

* Estimates.

Source: IMF, *Senegal: Second Review Under the Policy Support Instrument, Request for a Twelve-Month Arrangement Under the Exogenous Shocks Facility, and Request for Waivers and Modification of Assessment Criteria-Staff Report; Staff Statement; Press Release on the Executive Board Discussion; and Statement by the Executive Director for Senegal* (January 2009).

External Trade

PRINCIPAL COMMODITIES
('000 million francs CFA)

Imports c.i.f.	2005	2006	2007
Rice	132.9	122.5	174.8
Animal and vegetable oils and fats	58.3	61.7	77.2
Crude petroleum	203.4	85.8	193.2
Other petroleum products	123.2	298.0	267.0
Pharmaceutical products	53.2	58.7	62.0
Artificial plastic materials	56.9	62.8	76.1
Common metals	86.1	68.3	89.3
Agricultural and industrial machinery	197.1	238.8	269.0
Vehicles	60.8	54.0	64.5
Total (incl. others)	1,696.7	1,790.9	2,123.6

Exports f.o.b.	2005	2006	2007
Fresh fish	82.1	83.5	86.5
Crustaceans, molluscs and other shellfish	64.6	57.3	54.4
Frozen fish	15.7	8.0	6.1
Peanut oil	15.7	27.8	32.4
Hydraulic cement	27.1	41.3	43.5
Petroleum products	122.3	193.3	142.5
Phosphoric acid	98.0	40.3	47.0
Total (incl. others)	686.6	715.7	702.5

SENEGAL

PRINCIPAL TRADING PARTNERS
('000 million francs CFA)

Imports c.i.f.	2005	2006	2007
Argentina	20.1	41.8	42.6
Belgium-Luxembourg	48.7	45.6	57.2
Brazil	76.6	43.3	91.8
China, People's Republic	64.5	80.2	128.2
Côte d'Ivoire	49.0	56.7	54.9
France (incl. Monaco)	387.2	448.9	498.9
Germany	42.5	44.3	62.5
India	45.3	46.3	77.7
Ireland	25.3	26.1	29.4
Italy	48.1	60.7	53.0
Japan	30.3	49.8	38.1
Morocco	17.3	30.7	25.4
Netherlands	35.7	56.5	87.5
Nigeria	193.1	62.8	196.6
South Africa	23.5	28.8	35.3
Spain	62.6	72.1	68.3
Thailand	72.5	85.3	113.4
Turkey	13.2	13.7	28.8
Ukraine	29.5	30.9	37.2
United Kingdom	68.4	93.9	50.3
USA	70.9	56.6	48.7
Viet Nam	19.6	20.1	10.5
Total (incl. others)	1,696.7	1,790.9	2,123.6

Exports f.o.b.	2005	2006	2007
Benin	7.5	6.9	8.6
Burkina Faso	7.9	9.0	11.1
Cameroon	4.4	5.3	15.8
Côte d'Ivoire	18.0	20.1	20.2
France (incl. Monaco)	69.4	60.9	70.9
The Gambia	33.7	38.0	36.9
Greece	17.1	12.6	13.4
Guinea	20.6	19.4	20.6
Guinea-Bissau	17.2	15.5	19.3
India	99.9	41.4	49.7
Italy	41.5	37.0	37.6
Japan	5.9	7.5	5.7
Mali	117.3	137.1	160.0
Mauritania	19.0	18.2	19.2
Netherlands	6.3	8.3	10.4
Spain	46.3	39.0	37.1
Switzerland	2.2	24.2	21.3
Togo	6.4	8.2	9.8
United Arab Emirates	2.3	10.5	8.3
Total (incl. others)	686.6	715.7	702.5

Transport

RAILWAYS
(traffic)

	2002	2003	2004
Passenger-km (million)	105	129	122
Net ton-km (million)	345	375	358

Passengers ('000): 4,789 in 1999.

Freight carried ('000 metric tons): 2,017 in 1999.

Statistical Survey

ROAD TRAFFIC
(motor vehicles in use)

	1997	1998	1999
Passenger cars	76,971	85,805	98,260
Buses and coaches	9,236	9,974	10,477
Lorries and vans	21,693	23,851	25,276
Road tractors	2,110	2,278	2,458
Motorcycles and mopeds	3,624	4,155	4,515

Source: IRF, *World Road Statistics*.

SHIPPING

Merchant Fleet
(vessels registered at 31 December)

	2005	2006	2007
Number of vessels	181	183	186
Total displacement ('000 grt)	41.6	42.5	46.4

Source: Lloyd's Register-Fairplay, *World Fleet Statistics*.

International Sea-borne Freight Traffic
('000 metric tons)

	2003	2004	2005
Goods loaded	3,028	2,875	2,911
Goods unloaded	7,521	7,144	8,026

Source: Port Autonome de Dakar.

CIVIL AVIATION
(traffic on scheduled services)*

	2002	2003	2004
Kilometres flown (million)	7	6	8
Passengers carried ('000)	231	130	416
Passenger-km (million)	572	388	767
Total ton-km (million)	20	35	69

* Including an apportionment of the traffic of Air Afrique.

Source: UN, *Statistical Yearbook*.

Tourism

FOREIGN TOURIST ARRIVALS BY NATIONALITY*

	2004	2005	2006
African states	89,660	87,565	106,396
Belgium, Luxembourg and the Netherlands	16,160	21,712	23,896
East Asian and Pacific states	3,705	3,837	3,846
France	172,878	191,580	184,376
Germany	8,374	9,615	8,708
Italy	9,413	11,493	13,705
Spain	13,415	15,353	17,021
United Kingdom	4,092	4,380	5,582
USA	10,422	11,080	12,404
Total (incl. others)	363,490	386,565	405,827

* Figures refer to arrivals at hotels and similar establishments.

Receipts from tourism (US $ million, excl. passenger transport): 287 in 2004; 334 in 2005.

Source: World Tourism Organization.

Communications Media

	2005	2006	2007
Telephones ('000 main lines in use)	266.6	282.6	269.1
Mobile cellular telephones ('000 subscribers)	1,730.1	2,982.6	4,123.0
Internet users ('000)	540	650	820
Broadband subscribers ('000)	18.0	28.9	38.1

Personal computers ('000 in use): 242 in 2004.

Television receivers ('000 in use): 380 in 2000.

Radio receivers ('000 in use): 1,240 in 1997.

Daily newspapers: 1 (average circulation 45,000 copies) in 1996; 13 in 2004.

Non-daily newspapers: 6 (average circulation 37,000 copies) in 1995.

Sources: mainly International Telecommunication Union; UNESCO, *Statistical Yearbook*, UNESCO Institute for Statistics.

Education

(2006/07, unless otherwise indicated)

	Institutions*	Teachers	Males	Females	Total
Pre-primary	460	5,670	47.1	51.9	99.0
Primary	5,670	45,957	792.0	780.2	1,572.2
Secondary	591	15,394†	255.8‡	191.6‡	447.4‡
Tertiary	n.a.	n.a.	n.a.	n.a.	59.1†

Students ('000)

* 2002/03 (Source: Ministry of Education, Dakar).
† 2004/05.
‡ 2005/06.

Source: UNESCO Institute for Statistics.

Adult literacy rate (UNESCO estimates): 42.6% (males 53.1%; females 32.3%) in 2007 (Source: UNESCO Institute for Statistics).

Directory

The Constitution

The Constitution of the Republic of Senegal was promulgated following its approval by popular referendum on 7 January 2001, and entered into force thereafter, with the exception of those sections relating to the Assemblée nationale and the relations between the executive and legislative powers (articles 59–87), which took effect following legislative elections on 29 April 2001. The main provisions (including subsequent amendments) are summarized below:

PREAMBLE

The people of Senegal, recognizing their common destiny, and aware of the need to consolidate the fundaments of the Nation and the State, and supporting the ideals of African unity and human rights, proclaim the principle of national territorial integrity and a national unity respecting the diverse cultures of the Nation, reject all forms of injustice, inequality and discrimination, and proclaim the will of Senegal to be a modern democratic State.

THE STATE AND SOVEREIGNTY

Articles 1–6: Senegal is a secular, democratic Republic, in which all people are equal before the law, without distinction of origin, race, sex or religion. The official language of the Republic is French; the national languages are Diola, Malinké, Pular, Sérère, Soninké, Wolof and any other national language that may be so defined. The principle of the Republic is 'government of the people, by the people and for the people'. National sovereignty belongs to the people who exercise it, through their representatives or in referenda. Suffrage may be direct or indirect, and is always universal, equal and secret. Political parties and coalitions of political parties are obliged to observe the Constitution and the principles of national sovereignty and democracy, and are forbidden from identifying with one race, one ethnic group, one sex, one religion, one sect, one language or one region. All acts of racial, ethnic or religious discrimination, including regionalist propaganda liable to undermine the security or territorial integrity of the State are punishable by law. The institutions of the Republic are: the President of the Republic; the Parlement (comprising the Assemblée nationale and the Sénat); the Government and the Constitutional Council; the Council of State; the Final Court of Appeal (Cour de Cassation); the Revenue Court (Cour de Comptes); and Courts and Tribunals.

PUBLIC LIBERTIES AND THE HUMAN PERSON; ECONOMIC AND SOCIAL RIGHTS AND COLLECTIVE RIGHTS

Articles 7–25: The inviolable and inalienable rights of man are recognized as the base of all human communities, of peace and justice in the world, and are protected by the State. All humans are equal before the law. The Republic protects, within the rule of law, the right to free opinion, free expression, a free press, freedom of association and of movement, cultural, religious and philosophical freedoms, the right to organize trade unions and businesses, the right to education and literacy, the right to own property, to work, to health, to a clean environment, and to diverse sources of information. No prior authorization is required for the formation of an organ of the press. Men and women are guaranteed equal rights to possess property.

Marriage and the family constitute the natural and moral base of the human community, and are protected by the State. The State is obliged to protect the physical and moral health of the family, in particular of the elderly and the handicapped, and guarantees to alleviate the conditions of life of women, particularly in rural areas. Forced marriages are forbidden as a violation of individual liberty. The State protects youth from exploitation, from drugs, and from delinquency.

All children in the Republic have the right to receive schooling, from public schools, or from institutions of religious or non-religious communities. All national educational institutions, public or private, are obliged to participate in the growth of literacy in one of the national languages. Private schools may be opened with the authorization of, and under the control of, the State.

Freedom of conscience is guaranteed. Religious communities and institutions are separate from the State.

All discrimination against workers on grounds of origins, sex, political opinions or beliefs are forbidden. All workers have the right to join or form trade or professional associations. The right to strike is recognized, under legal conditions, as long as the freedom to work is not impeded, and the enterprise is not placed in peril. The State guarantees sanitary and human conditions in places of work.

THE PRESIDENT OF THE REPUBLIC

Articles 26–52: The President of the Republic is elected, for a term of five years, by universal direct suffrage. The mandate may be renewed once. Candidates for the presidency must be of solely Senegalese nationality, enjoy full civil and political rights, be aged 35 years or more on the day of elections, and must be able to write, read and speak the official language fluently. All candidates must be presented by a political party or a legally constituted coalition of political parties, or be accompanied by a petition signed by at least 10,000 electors, including at least 500 electors in each of six administrative regions. Candidates may not campaign predominately on ethnic or regional grounds. Each political party or coalition of political parties may present only one candidate. If no candidate receives an absolute majority of votes cast in the first round, representing the support of at least one-quarter of the electorate, a second round of elections is held between the two highest-placed candidates in the first round. In the case of incapacity, death or resignation, the President's position is assumed by the President of the Sénat, and in the case of his or her incapacity, by the President of the Assemblée nationale, in all cases subject to the same terms of eligibility that apply to the President. The President presides over the Council of Ministers, the Higher Council of National Defence, and the National Security Council, and is the Supreme Chief of the Armed Forces. The President appoints a Prime Minister, and appoints ministers on the recommendation of the Prime Minister.

THE GOVERNMENT

Articles 53–57: The head of the Government is the Prime Minister. In the event of the resignation or removal from office of a Prime Minister, the entire Government is obliged to resign.

SENEGAL

THE OPPOSITION
Article 58: The Constitution guarantees the right to oppose political parties that are opposed to Government policy, and recognizes the existence of a parliamentary opposition.

THE PARLEMENT
Article 59–66: Deputies of the Assemblée nationale are elected by universal direct suffrage, for a five-year mandate, subject only to the dissolution of the Assemblée nationale. Any serving deputy who resigns from his or her party shall have his or her mandate removed. Deputies enjoy immunity from criminal proceedings, except with the authorization of the bureau of the Assemblée nationale. The Assemblée nationale votes on the budget. Deputies vote as individuals and must not be obligated to vote in a certain way. Except in exceptional and limited circumstances, sessions of the Assemblée nationale are public.

The members of the Sénat are elected by universal direct suffrage, for a five-year mandate. Two-fifths of the members of the Sénat must be women.

RELATIONS BETWEEN THE EXECUTIVE AND LEGISLATIVE POWERS
Articles 67–87: The Parlement is the sole holder of legislative power. The Assemblée nationale votes on the budget and authorizes a declaration of war. The President of the Republic may, having received the opinion of the Prime Minister and the President of the Assemblée nationale, pronounce by decree the dissolution of the Assemblée nationale, except during the first two years of any Assemblée.

INTERNATIONAL TREATIES
Articles: 88–91: The President of the Republic negotiates international engagements, and ratifies or approves them with the authorization of the Parlement. The Republic of Senegal may conclude agreements with any African State that would comprise a partial or total abandonment of national sovereignty in order to achieve African unity.

JUDICIAL POWER
Articles 92–98: The judiciary is independent of the legislature and the executive power. The judiciary consists of the Constitutional Council, the Council of State, the Court of Final Appeal, the Revenue Court and Courts and Tribunals. The Constitutional Council comprises five members, including a President, a Vice-President and three judges. Each member serves for a mandate of six years (which may not be renewed) with partial renewals occurring every two years. The President of the Republic appoints members of the Constitutional Council, whose decisions are irreversible.

THE HIGH COURT OF JUSTICE
Articles 99–101: A High Court of Justice, presided over by a magistrate and comprising members elected by the Assemblée nationale and the Sénat, is instituted. The President of the Republic can only be brought to trial for acts accomplished in the exercise of his duties in the case of high treason. The High Court of Justice tries the Prime Minister and other members of the Government for crimes committed in the exercise of their duties.

LOCAL GOVERNMENT
Article 102: Local government bodies operate independently, by means of elective assemblies, in accordance with the law.

ON REVISION
Article 103: The Prime Minister proposes any amendments to the Constitution to the President of the Republic after they have been approved by both the Assemblée nationale and the Sénat. Amendments may be approved by referendum or, at the initiative of the President of the Republic, solely by approval by the Parlement, in which case a three-fifths' majority must be in favour.

The Government

HEAD OF STATE
President: ABDOULAYE WADE (took office 1 April 2000, re-elected 25 February 2007).

COUNCIL OF MINISTERS
(May 2009)

Prime Minister: SOULEYMANE NDÉNÉ NDIAYE.
Secretary-General of the Government: PAPE OUSMANE GUÈYE.
Minister of State, Minister of the Interior, Local Communities and Decentralization: CHEIKH TIDJANE SY.
Minister of State, Minister of Foreign Affairs: CHEIKH TIDIANE GADIO.
Minister of State, Minister of the Armed Forces: BÉCAYE DIOP.
Minister of State, Keeper of the Seals, Minister of Justice: MADICKÉ NIANG.
Minister of State, Minister of the Economy and Finance: ABDOULAYE DIOP.
Minister of State, Minister of Town Planning, Housing, Hydraulics and Sanitation: OUMAR SARR.
Minister of State, Minister of the Environment, Conservation, Retention Basins and Man-made Lakes: DJIBO LEYTI KÂ.
Minister of State, Minister of the Civil Service, Employment and Professional Organizations: HABIB SY.
Minister of State, Minister of International Co-operation, Land Settlement, Air Transport and Infrastructure: KARIM WADE.
Minister of State, Minister of the Family, National Solidarity, Food Security, Female Entrepreneurship, Microfinance and Early Childhood: NDÈYE KHADY DIOP.
Minister of State, Minister of Mines, Industry and Small and Medium-sized Enterprises: OUSMANE NGOM.
Minister of Telecommunications, ICT and Land and Rail Transport: ABDOURAHIM AGNE.
Minister of Higher Education, Universities and University Centres: Prof. MOUSTAPHA SOURANG.
Minister of Nursery, Primary and Middle School Education: KALIDOU DIALLO.
Minister of Energy and Biofuels: SAMUEL AMET SARR.
Minister of the Maritime Economy, Fisheries and Maritime Transport: KHOUREYSSY THIAM.
Minister of Health, Preventive Medicine and Public Hygiene: THÉRÈSE COUMBA DIOP.
Minister of Agriculture and Fishbreeding: FATOU GAYE SARR.
Minister of Livestock-rearing: OUMOU KHAIRY GUÈYE SECK.
Minister of the Agri-food Industry and Agricultural Products: AÏDA MBODJ.
Minister of Culture, Francophone Affairs and National Languages: SERIGNE MODOU BOUSSO LÈYE.
Minister of Scientific Research: Prof. AMADOU TIDIANE BÂ.
Minister of Technical and Professional Training: MOUSSA SAKHO.
Minister of Youth, Sports and Leisure: MAMADOU LAMINE KEITA.
Minister of NEPAD and Relations with Parliament: FAUSTIN DIATTA.
Minister of Senegalese Nationals Abroad: SADA NDIAYE.
Minister of Communication, Government Spokesperson: MOUSTAPHA GUIRASSY.
Minister of Handicrafts, Tourism and Relations with the Private and Informal Sectors: THIERNO LÔ.
Minister of Trade: AMADOU NIANG.
Minister-delegate to the Minister of State, Minister of the Economy and Finance, responsible for the Budget: MAMADOU ABDOULAYE SOW.
Minister-delegate to the Minister of the Interior, Local Communities and Decentralization, responsible for Local Communities and Decentralization: ALIOU SOW.
Minister-delegate to the Minister of Agriculture and Fishbreeding, responsible for Rural Organizations and the Unionization of Farmers: KHADIM GUÈYE.

MINISTRIES

Office of the President: ave Léopold Sédar Senghor, BP 168, Dakar; tel. 33-823-1088; internet www.gouv.sn/institutions/president.html.
Office of the Prime Minister: Bldg Administratif, ave Léopold Sédar Senghor, BP 4029, Dakar; tel. 33-889-6969; fax 33-823-4479; internet www.gouv.sn.
Ministry of Agriculture and Fishbreeding: Bldg Administratif, BP 4005, Dakar; tel. 33-849-7000; fax 33-823-3268; internet www.agriculture.gouv.sn.
Ministry of the Agri-food Industry and Agricultural Products: Bldg Administratif, Dakar.
Ministry of the Armed Forces: Bldg Administratif, ave Léopold Sédar Senghor, BP 4041, Dakar; tel. 33-849-7612; fax 33-823-6338; internet www.forcesarmees.gouv.sn.

SENEGAL

Ministry of the Civil Service, Employment and Professional Organizations: Bldg Administratif, BP 4007, Dakar; tel. 33-849-7000; fax 33-823-7429; e-mail mineladiallo@yahoo.fr; internet www.fonctionpublique.gouv.sn.

Ministry of Communication: Bldg Administratif, Dakar.

Ministry of Culture, Francophone Affairs and National Languages: Bldg Administratif, ave Léopold Sédar Senghor, BP 4001, Dakar; tel. 33-822-4303; fax 33-822-1638; internet www.culture.gouv.sn.

Ministry of the Economy and Finance: ave Carde, Bâtiment CEPOD, Dakar; tel. 33-823-3427; fax 33-821-8312; e-mail i_diouf@minfinances.sn; internet www.finances.gouv.sn.

Ministry of Energy and Biofuels: 15 blvd Djily Mbaye, Immeuble Ascoma, Dakar; tel. 33-889-5200.

Ministry of the Environment, Conservation, Man-made Lakes and Retention Basins: Bldg Administratif, BP 4055, Dakar; tel. 33-889-0234; fax 33-822-2180; e-mail mepn@environnement.gouv.sn; internet www.environnement.gouv.sn.

Ministry of the Family, National Solidarity, Female Entrepreneurship, Microfinance and Early Childhood: Bldg Administratif, BP: 4050, Dakar; tel. 33-889-1700; fax 33-822-9490; e-mail communication@famille.gouv.sn; internet www.famille.gouv.sn.

Ministry of Foreign Affairs: pl. de l'Indépendance, BP 4044, Dakar; tel. 33-889-1300; fax 33-823-5496; e-mail maeuase@senegal.diplomatie.sn; internet www.diplomatie.gouv.sn.

Ministry of Handicrafts, Tourism and Relations with the Private Sector: Bldg Administratif, Dakar.

Ministry of Health, Preventive Medicine and Public Hygiene: Fann Résidence, rue Aimé Césaire, BP 4024, Dakar; tel. 33-869-4242; fax 33-869-4269; e-mail mdseck@minsante.sn; internet www.sante.gouv.sn.

Ministry of Higher Education, Universities and University Centres: 23 rue Calmette, angle René Ndiaye, Dakar; tel. 33-849-5454; fax 33-822-1463; internet www.education.gouv.sn.

Ministry of Industry, Mining and Small and Medium-sized Enterprises: 122 bis ave André Peytavin, BP 4037, Dakar; tel. 33-822-9994; fax 33-822-5594.

Ministry of the Interior, Local Communities and Decentralization: pl. Washington, BP 4002, Dakar; tel. 33-889-9100; fax 33-821-0542; e-mail mint@primature.sn; internet www.interieur.gouv.sn.

Ministry of International Co-operation, Land Settlement, Air Transport and Infrastructure: Bldg Administratif, Dakar.

Ministry of Justice: Bldg Administratif, ave Léopold Sédar Senghor, BP 4030, Dakar; tel. 33-849-7000; fax 33-823-2727; e-mail justice@justice.gouv.sn; internet www.justice.gouv.sn.

Ministry of Livestock-rearing: Dakar; tel. 33-859-0630.

Ministry of the Maritime Economy, Fisheries and Maritime Transport: Bldg Administratif, BP 4050, Dakar; tel. 33-823-3426; fax 33-823-8720; e-mail abdoumbodj@yahoo.fr; internet www.ecomaritime.gouv.sn.

Ministry of NEPAD and Relations with Parliament: Bldg Administratif, Dakar.

Ministry of Nursery, Primary and Middle School Education: rue Docteur Calmette, BP 4025, Dakar; tel. 33-849-5454; fax 33-822-1463; internet www.education.gouv.sn.

Ministry of Higher Education, Universities and University Centres: 23 rue Calmette, angle René Ndiaye, Dakar; tel. 33-849-5454; fax 33-822-1463; internet www.education.gouv.sn.

Ministry of Senegalese Nationals Abroad: VDN, rue 50 X 23, Villa 23 bis, BP 45510, Dakar; tel. 33-867-0171; fax 33-867-0183; internet www.senex.gouv.sn.

Ministry of Scientific Research: Bldg Administratif, Dakar.

Ministry of Technical and Professional Education: Dakar.

Ministry of Telecommunications, ICT and Land and Rail Transport: 58 blvd de la République, BP 4027, Dakar; tel. 33-823-1065; fax 33-821-4504.

Ministry of Town Planning, Housing, Urban Hydraulics and Sanitation: BP 15363, Dakar; tel. 33-869-1526; fax 33-864-5932; internet www.habitat.gouv.sn.

Ministry of Trade: Bldg Administratif, Dakar; tel. 33-822-9542.

Ministry of Youth, Sports and Leisure: rue Carnot 58, BP 4019, Dakar; tel. 33-825-2982; fax 33-829-2428; internet www.sports.gouv.sn.

President and Legislature

PRESIDENT

Presidential Election, 25 February 2007

Candidate	Votes	% of valid votes
Abdoulaye Wade	1,914,403	55.90
Idrissa Seck	510,922	14.92
Ousmane Tanor Dieng	464,287	13.56
Moustapha Niasse	203,129	5.93
Robert Sagna	88,446	2.58
Abdoulaye Bathily	75,797	2.21
Landing Savané	70,780	2.07
Others	97,162	2.84
Total	**3,424,926**	**100.00**

LEGISLATURE

Assemblée nationale

pl. Soweto, BP 86, Dakar; tel. 33-823-1099; fax 33-823-6708; e-mail assnat@assemblee-nationale.sn; internet www.assemblee-nationale.sn.

President: MAMADOU SECK.

General Election, 3 June 2007

Party	Votes	% of votes	Seats
Sopi Coalition*	1,190,609	69.21	131
Takku Defaraat Sénégal Coalition	86,621	5.04	3
And Defar Sénégal Coalition	84,998	4.94	3
Waar Wi Coalition	74,919	4.35	3
Rassemblement pour le peuple (RP)	73,083	4.25	2
Front pour le socialisme et la démocratie—Benno Jubël (FSD—BJ)	37,427	2.18	1
Alliance Jëf-Jël	33,297	1.94	1
Convergence pour le renouveau et la citoyenneté (CRC)	30,658	1.78	1
Parti socialiste authentique (PSA)	26,320	1.53	1
Union nationale patriotique (UNP)	22,271	1.29	1
Mouvement de la réforme pour le développement social (MRDS)	20,041	1.16	1
Rassemblement des écologistes du Sénégal (RES)	17,267	1.00	1
Parti social-démocrate—Jant Bi (PSD—JB)	15,968	0.93	1
Rassemblement patriotique sénégalais—Jammi Rewmi (RPS—JR)	6,847	0.40	—
Total	**1,720,326**	**100.00**	**150**

* A coalition of some 40 parties and movements, led by the PDS.

Sénat

President: PAPE DIOP.

Election, 19 August 2007

Party	Seats
Parti démocratique sénégalais (PPS)	34
And Jëf—Parti africain pour la démocratie et le socialisme (AJ—PADS)	1
Total	**100***

* The remaining 65 members are appointed by the President.

Election Commission

Commission électorale nationale autonome (CENA): BP 28900, Dakar; internet www.cena.sn; f. 2005; Pres. MAMADOU MOUSTAPHA TOURÉ.

SENEGAL

Political Organizations

In mid-2008 there were 77 political parties registered in Senegal, of which the following were among the most important:

Alliance des forces de progrès (AFP): rue 1, angle rue A, point E, BP 5825, Dakar; tel. 33-825-4021; fax 33-825-7770; e-mail admin@afp-senegal.org; internet www.afp-senegal.org; f. 1999; mem. of opposition Cadre permanent de concertation (f. 2001); Sec.-Gen. MOUSTAPHA NIASSE.

Alliance Jëf Jël: Villa 5, rue 1, Castors Front de Terre, Dakar; tel. 77-652-2232; e-mail tallasylla@hotmail.com; f. 1997; mem. of opposition; Pres. TALLA SYLLA.

Alliance pour la République (APR—Yaakaar): Dakar; f. 2008; Leader MACKY SALL.

And Defar Sénégal Coalition: Kolda; Leader LANDING SAVANÉ.

And Jëf—Parti africain pour la démocratie et le socialisme (AJ—PADS): Villa 1, Zone B, BP 12136, Dakar; tel. 33-825-7667; fax 33-823-5860; e-mail webmaster@ajpads.org; internet x.ajpads.org; f. 1992; Sec.-Gen. LANDING SAVANÉ.

Bloc des centristes Gaïndé (BCG): Villa 734, Sicap Baobabs, Dakar; tel. 33-825-3764; e-mail issa_dias@sentoo.sn; f. 1996; Pres. and First Sec. JEAN-PAUL DIAS.

Convergence pour le renouveau et la citoyenneté (CRC): Leader ALIOU DIA.

Front pour le socialisme et la démocratie—Benno Jubël (FSD—BJ): contested 2001 election as mem. of Sopi Coalition; Leader ABDOULAYE DIÈYE.

Ligue démocratique—Mouvement pour le parti du travail (LD—MPT): ave Bourguiba, Dieuppeul 2, Villa 2566, BP 10172, Dakar Liberté; tel. 33-825-6706; fax 33-827-4300; regd 1981; social-democrat; Sec.-Gen. ABDOULAYE BATHILY.

Mouvement pour la démocratie et le socialisme—Naxx Jarinu (MDS—NJ): Unité 20, Parcelles Assainies, Villa 528, Dakar; tel. 33-869-5049; f. 2000; Leader OUMAR KHASSIMOU DAI.

Mouvement de la réforme pour le développement social (MRDS): HLM 4, Villa 858, Dakar; tel. 77-644-3170; e-mail sgmrds@mrds.sn; internet www.mrds.sn; f. 2000; Pres. IBRAHIMA DIENG; Sec.-Gen. Imam BABACAR NIANG.

Mouvement pour le socialisme et l'unité (MSU): HLM 1, Villa 86, Dakar; tel. 33-825-8544; f. 1981 as Mouvement démocratique populaire; mem. of opposition Cadre permanent de concertation (f. 2001); National Co-ordinator-Gen. MOUHAMADOU BAMBA N'DIAYE.

Mouvement républicain sénégalais (MRS): Résidence du Cap-Vert, 10e étage, 5 pl. de l'Indépendance, BP 4193, Dakar; tel. 33-822-0319; fax 33-822-0700; e-mail agaz@omnet.sn; Sec.-Gen. DEMBA BA.

Parti africain de l'indépendance (PAI): Maison du Peuple, Guediewaye, BP 820, Dakar; tel. 33-837-0136; f. 1957; reorg. 1976; Marxist; Sec.-Gen. MAJMOUT DIOP.

Parti démocratique sénégalais (PDS): blvd Dial Diop, Immeuble Serigne Mourtada Mbacké, Dakar; tel. 33-823-5027; fax 33-823-1702; e-mail cedobe@aol.com; internet www.sopionline.com; f. 1974; liberal democratic; Sec.-Gen. Me ABDOULAYE WADE.

Parti de l'indépendance et du travail (PIT): route front de terre, BP 10470, Dakar; tel. 33-827-2907; fax 33-820-9000; regd 1981; Marxist-Leninist; mem. of opposition Cadre permanent de concertation (f. 2001); Sec.-Gen. AMATH DANSOKHO.

Parti libéral sénégalais (PLS): 13 ave Malick Sy, BP 28277, Dakar; tel. and fax 33-823-1560; f. 1998 by breakaway faction of PDS; Leader Me OUSMANE NGOM.

Parti populaire sénégalais (PPS): Quartier Escale, BP 212, Diourbel; tel. 33-971-1171; regd 1981; populist; mem. of opposition Cadre permanent de concertation (f. 2001); Sec.-Gen. Dr OUMAR WANE.

Parti pour le progrès et la citoyenneté (PPC): Quartier Merina, Rufique; tel. 33-836-1868; absorbed Rassemblement pour le progrès, la justice et le socialisme in 2000; Sec.-Gen. Me MBAYE JACQUES DIOP.

Parti pour la renaissance africaine—Sénégal (PARENA): Sicap Dieuppeul, Villa 2685/B, Dakar; tel. 77-636-8788; fax 33-823-5721; e-mail mariamwane@yahoo.fr; f. 2000; Sec.-Gen. MARIAM MAMADOU WANE LY.

Parti de la renaissance et de la citoyenneté: Liberté 6, Villa 7909, Dakar; tel. 33-827-8568; f. 2000; supports Pres. Wade; Sec.-Gen. SAMBA DIOULDÉ THIAM.

Parti social-démocrate—Jant Bi (PSD—JB): Leader MAMOUR CISSE.

Parti socialiste authentique (PSA): internet psa-senegal.org; Leader SOUTY TOURÉ.

Parti socialiste du Sénégal (PS): Maison du Parti Socialiste Léopold Sédar Senghor, Colobane, BP 12010, Dakar; tel. and fax 33-824-7744; e-mail senegalpartisocialiste@gmail.com; internet www.partisocialiste.sn; f. 1958 as Union progressiste sénégalaise; reorg. 1978; democratic socialist; First Sec. OUSMANE TANOR DIENG.

Rassemblement des écologistes du Sénégal—Les verts (RES): rue 67, angle rue 52, Gueule Tapée, BP 25226, Dakar-Fann; tel. and fax 33-842-3442; f. 1999; Sec.-Gen. OUSMANE SOW HUCHARD.

Rassemblement national démocratique (RND): Sacré-Coeur III, Villa no 972, Dakar; tel. 33-827-5072; f. 1976; legalized 1981; mem. of opposition Cadre permanent de concertation (f. 2001); Sec.-Gen. MADIOR DIOUF.

Rassemblement patriotique sénégalais—Jammi Rewmi (RPS—JR): Leader ELY MADIODO FALL FALL.

Rassemblement des travailleurs africains—Sénégal (RTA—S): Villa 999, HLM Grand Yoff, BP 13725, Dakar; tel. 33-827-1579; e-mail sambmomar@hotmail.com; f. 1997; Co-ordinator El Hadj MOMAR SAMBE.

Takku Defaraat Sénégal Coalition: VDN à côté de la Poste; tel. 33-860-5019; fax 33-860-5020; internet www.robertsagna.com; f. 2000; Leader ROBERT SAGNA.

Union nationale patriotique (UNP): Leader NDÈYE FATOU TOURÉ.

Union pour le renouveau démocratique (URD): Bopp Villa 234, rue 7, Dakar; tel. 33-864-7431; fax 33-820-7317; e-mail urd@urdsenegal.sn; internet www.urdsenegal.sn; f. 1998 by breakaway faction of PS; mem. of opposition Cadre permanent de concertation (f. 2001); Sec.-Gen. DJIBO LEÏTY KÂ.

Waar Wi Coalition: Leader MOUDOU DIAGNE FADA.

In August 2001 some 25 pro-Government parties, which were formerly members of the Sopi (Change) Coalition that contested the legislative elections in April 2001, formed an electoral alliance, the **Convergence des actions autour du Président en perspective du 21ième siècle (CAP-21)**, to contest municipal and local elections in May 2002. In May 2001 several opposition parties (numbering eight in February 2004 and led by the AFP) formed an opposition consultative framework, the **Cadre permanent de concertation (CPC)**, which was also to operate as an electoral alliance in the municipal and local elections.

The **Mouvement des forces démocratiques de la Casamance (MFDC)** was founded in 1947; it had paramilitary and political wings and formerly sought the independence of the Casamance region of southern Senegal. The MFDC is not officially recognized as a political party (the Constitution of 2001 forbids the formation of parties on a geographic basis) and waged a campaign of guerrilla warfare in the region from the early 1980s. Representatives of the MFDC have participated in extensive negotiations with the Senegalese Government on the restoration of peace and the granting of greater autonomy to Casamance, and in December 2004 a cease-fire agreement was signed between the two sides, pending further peace negotiations. The Honorary President of the MFDC, Fr AUGUSTIN DIAMACOUNÉ SENGHOR, died in January 2007; the post of Secretary-General was disputed between JEAN-MARIE FRANÇOIS BIAGUI and ANSOUMANA BADJI.

Diplomatic Representation

EMBASSIES IN SENEGAL

Algeria: 5 rue Mermoz, Plateau, Dakar; tel. 33-849-5700; fax 33-849-5701; e-mail ambalgdak@orange.sn; f. 1963; Ambassador ABDELHAMID CHEBCHOUB.

Austria: 18 rue Emile Zola, BP 3247, Dakar; tel. 33-849-4000; fax 33-849-4370; e-mail dakar-ob@bmaa.gv.at; Ambassador GERHARD DOUJAK.

Belgium: ave des Jambaars, BP 524, Dakar; tel. 33-889-4390; fax 33-889-4398; e-mail ambeldak@orange.sn; internet www.diplomatie.be/dakar; Ambassador GEORGES S. GODART.

Brazil: Immeuble Fondation Fahd, 4e étage, blvd Djily Mbaye, angle rue Macodou Ndiaye, BP 136, Dakar; tel. 33-823-1492; fax 33-823-7181; e-mail embdakar@sentoo.sn; Ambassador KÁTIA GODINHO GILABERTE DO NASCIMENTO BORGES.

Burkina Faso: Sicap Sacré Coeur III, Extension VDN No. 10628B, BP 11601, Dakar; tel. 33-864-5824; fax 33-864-5823; e-mail ambabf@sentoo.sn; Ambassador SALAMATA SAWADOGO.

Cameroon: 157–9 rue Joseph Gomis, BP 4165, Dakar; tel. 33-849-0292; fax 33-823-3396; Ambassador EMMANUEL MBONJO-EJANGUE.

Canada: rue Galliéni angle rue Amadou Cissé Dia, BP 3373, Dakar; tel. 33-889-4700; fax 33-889-4720; e-mail dakar@international.gc.ca; internet www.dakar.gc.ca; Ambassador JEAN-PIERRE BOLDUC.

Cape Verde: 3 blvd El-Hadji Djilly M'Baye, BP 11269, Dakar; tel. 33-822-4285; fax 33-821-0697; e-mail acvc.sen@metissacana.sn; Ambassador RAÚL JORGE VERA CRUZ BARBOSA.

SENEGAL

China, People's Republic: rue 18 prolongée, BP 342, Dakar-Fann; tel. 33-864-7775; fax 33-864-7780; Ambassador Lu Shaye.
Congo, Democratic Republic: Fenêtre Mermoz, Dakar; tel. 33-825-1280; Chargé d'affaires a.i. Fataki Nicolas Lunguele Musambya.
Congo, Republic: Statut Mermoz, BP 5242, Dakar; tel. 77-634-5022; fax 33-825-7856; Ambassador Valentin Ollessongo.
Côte d'Ivoire: ave Birago Diop, BP 359, Dakar; tel. 33-869-0270; fax 33-825-2115; e-mail cmrci@ambaci-dakar.org; internet www.ambaci-dakar.org; Ambassador Fatimata Tanoe Touré.
Cuba: 43 rue Aimé Césaire, BP 4510, Dakar-Fann Résidence; tel. 33-869-0240; fax 33-864-1063; e-mail embacuba@orange.sn; Ambassador Llusif Sadín Tassé.
Egypt: 22 ave Brière de l'Isle, Plateau, BP 474, Dakar; tel. 33-889-2474; fax 33-821-8993; e-mail ambegydk@telecomplus.sn; Ambassador Sanaa Ismail Atta Allah.
Ethiopia: 18 blvd de la République, BP 379, Dakar; tel. 33-821-9896; fax 33-821-9895; e-mail ethembas@sentoo.sn; Ambassador Ato Hassen Abdulkadik.
France: 1 rue El Hadj Amadou Assane Ndoye, BP 4035, Dakar; tel. 33-839-5100; fax 33-839-5181; e-mail webmestre.dakar-amba@diplomatie.gouv.fr; internet www.ambafrance-sn.org; Ambassador Jean-Christophe Rufin.
Gabon: ave Cheikh Anta Diop, cnr Fann Résidence, BP 436, Dakar; tel. 33-865-2234; fax 33-864-3145; Ambassador Vincent Boule.
The Gambia: 11 rue Elhadji Ismaïla Guèye (Thiong), BP 3248, Dakar; tel. 33-821-4416; fax 33-821-6279; Ambassador Gibril Seman Joof.
Germany: 20 ave Pasteur, angle rue Mermoz, BP 2100, Dakar; tel. 33-889-4884; fax 33-822-5299; e-mail reg1@daka.auswaertiges-amt.de; internet www.dakar.diplo.de; Ambassador Doretta Loschelder.
Ghana: Lot 27, Parcelle B, Almadies, BP 25370, Dakar; tel. 33-869-1990; fax 33-820-1950; Ambassador Frederick Daniel Laryea.
Guinea: rue 7, angle B&D, point E, BP 7123, Dakar; tel. 33-824-8606; fax 33-825-5946; Ambassador Hadja Koumba Diakité.
Guinea-Bissau: rue 6, angle B, point E, BP 2319, Dakar; tel. 33-823-0059; fax 33-825-2946; Ambassador Lansana Touré.
Holy See: rue Aimé Césaire, angle Corniche-Ouest, Fann Résidence, BP 5076, Dakar; tel. 33-824-2674; fax 33-824-1931; e-mail vatemb@orange.sn; Apostolic Nuncio Most Rev. Luis Mariano Montemayor (Titular Archbishop of Illici).
India: 5 rue Carde, BP 398, Dakar; tel. 33-822-5875; fax 33-822-3585; e-mail indiacom@sentoo.sn; internet www.ambassadeinde.sn; Ambassador N. Parthasarathi.
Indonesia: ave Cheikh Anta Diop, BP 5859, Dakar; tel. 33-825-7316; fax 33-825-5896; e-mail kbri@sentoo.sn; internet www.indonesia-senegal.org; Ambassador Sukarni Sikar.
Iran: rue AX8, point E, BP 735, Dakar; tel. 33-825-2528; fax 33-824-2314; e-mail ambiiran@telecomplus.sn; Ambassador Mohammad Hoseini.
Israel: Immeuble SDIH, 3 pl. de l'Indépendance, BP 2096, Dakar; tel. 33-823-7965; fax 33-823-6490; e-mail info@dakar.mfa.gov.il; internet dakar.mfa.gov.il; Ambassador Gideon Béhar.
Italy: rue Alpha Achamiyou Tall, BP 348, Dakar; tel. 33-822-0578; fax 33-821-7580; e-mail ambasciata.dakar@esteri.it; internet sedi.esteri.it/dakar; Ambassador Giuseppe Calvetta.
Japan: blvd Martin Luther King, Corniche-Ouest, BP 3140, Dakar; tel. 33-849-5500; fax 33-849-5555; Ambassador Akira Nakajima.
Korea, Republic: 4e étage, Immeuble Fayçal, 3 rue Parchappe, BP 3338, Dakar; tel. 33-822-5822; fax 33-821-6600; e-mail senegal@mofat.go.kr; internet www.mofat.go.kr/senegal; Ambassador Jae Chol Hahn.
Kuwait: blvd Martin Luther King, Dakar; tel. 33-824-1723; fax 33-825-0899; Ambassador Muhammad az-Zuwaikh.
Lebanon: 56 ave Jean XXIII, BP 6700 Dakar-Etoile, Dakar; tel. 33-822-0255; fax 33-823-5899; e-mail ambaliban@orange.sn; internet www.ambaliban.org; Ambassador Michel Haddad.
Libya: route de Ouakam, Dakar; tel. 33-824-5710; fax 33-824-5722; Ambassador Al Hady Salem Hammad.
Madagascar: Immeuble rue 2, angle Ellipse, Point E, BP 25395, Dakar; tel. 33-825-2666; fax 33-864-4086; e-mail ambadak@yahoo.fr; internet www.ambamad.sn; Ambassador Lila Hanitra Ratsifandrihamanana.
Malaysia: 7 Extension VDN, Fann Mermoz, BP 15057, Dakar; tel. 33-825-8935; fax 33-825-4719; e-mail mwdakar@orange.sn; Ambassador Dato' Jamaiyah Mohamed Yusof.
Mali: Fann Résidence, Corniche-Ouest, rue 23, BP 478, Dakar; tel. 33-824-6252; fax 33-825-9471; e-mail ambamali@sentoo.sn; Ambassador N'Tji Laïco Traoré.

Mauritania: 37 blvd Charles de Gaulle, Dakar; tel. 33-823-5344; fax 33-823-5311; Ambassador Mohammed Vall Ould Bellal.
Morocco: 73 ave Cheikh Anta Diop, BP 490, Dakar; tel. 33-824-6927; fax 33-825-7021; e-mail ambmadk@sentoo.sn; Ambassador Taleb Berrada.
Netherlands: 37 rue Jaques Bugnicourt, BP 3262, Dakar; tel. 33-849-0360; fax 33-821-7084; e-mail dak@minbuza.nl; internet www.nlambassadedakar.org; Ambassador Dr J. W. G. Jansing.
Nigeria: 8 ave Cheikh Anta Diop, BP 3129, Dakar; tel. 869-86-00; tel. 33-869-8600; fax 33-825-8136; e-mail info@nigeriandakar.sn; Ambassador Azuka Cecilia Uzoka-Emejulu.
Pakistan: Stèle Mermoz, Villa 7602, BP 2635, Dakar; tel. 33-824-6135; fax 33-824-6136; e-mail parepdakar@yahoo.com; Ambassador Abdul Malik Abdullah.
Portugal: 5 ave Carde, BP 281, Dakar; tel. 33-864-0317; fax 33-864-0322; e-mail ambportdakar@sentoo.sn; Ambassador António Augusto Montenegro Vieira Cardoso.
Qatar: 25 blvd Martin Luther King, BP 5150, Dakar; tel. 33-820-9559; fax 33-869-1012; Ambassador Ali Abdul Latif Ahmed al-Masalamani.
Romania: rue A prolongée, point E, BP 3171, Dakar; tel. 33-825-2068; fax 33-824-9190; e-mail romania@sentoo.sn; Ambassador Simona Corlan-Ioan.
Russia: ave Jean Jaurès, angle rue Carnot, BP 3180, Dakar; tel. 33-822-4821; fax 33-821-1372; e-mail ambrus@sentoo.sn; Ambassador Aleksandr A. Romanov.
Saudi Arabia: route Corniche-Ouest, face Olympique Club, BP 3109, Dakar; tel. 33-864-0141; fax 33-864-0130; e-mail snemb@mofa.gov.sa; Chargé d'affaires a.i. Fahd Nasser Al-Bihairan.
South Africa: Memoz SUD, Lotissement Ecole de Police, BP 21010, Dakar-Ponty; tel. 33-865-1959; fax 33-864-2359; e-mail ambafsud@orange.sn; internet www.saesenegal.info; Chargé d'affaires a.i. M. A. Cassimjee.
Spain: 18–20 ave Nelson Mandela, BP 2091, Dakar; tel. 33-821-1178; fax 33-821-6845; e-mail ambespsn@mail.mae.es; Ambassador Dr Jorge Toledo Albiñana.
Sudan: 31 route de la Pyrotechnie, Mermoz, BP 15033, Dakar-Fann; tel. 33-824-9853; fax 33-824-9852; e-mail sudembse@sentoo.sn; Ambassador Mahmoud Hassan el-Amin.
Sweden: 18 rue Emile Zola, BP 6087, Dakar; tel. 33-849-0333; fax 33-849-0340; e-mail ambassaden.dakar@foreign.ministry.se; internet www.swedenabroad.com/dakar; Ambassador Agneta Bohman.
Switzerland: rue René N'Diaye, angle rue Seydou, BP 1772, Dakar; tel. 33-823-0590; fax 33-822-3657; e-mail dak.vertretung@eda.admin.ch; internet www.eda.admin.ch/dakar; Ambassador Jean-François Paroz.
Syria: rue 1, point E, angle blvd de l'Est, BP 498, Dakar; tel. 33-824-6277; fax 33-825-1755; Ambassador Hamzeh Dawalibi.
Thailand: 10 rue Léon Gontran Damas, BP 3721, Dakar-Fann; tel. 33-869-3290; fax 33-824-8458; e-mail thaidkr@sentoo.sn; internet www.mfa.go.th/web/2366.php; Ambassador Itti Ditbanjong.
Tunisia: rue Alpha Hachamiyou Tall, BP 3127, Dakar; tel. 33-823-4747; fax 33-823-7204; Ambassador Jalel Lakhdar.
Turkey: ave des Ambassadeurs, Fann Résidence, BP 6060, Etoile, Dakar; tel. 33-869-2542; fax 33-825-6977; e-mail trambdkr@sentoo.sn; Ambassador Ali Savut.
United Kingdom: 20 rue du Dr Guillet, BP 6025, Dakar; tel. 33-823-7392; fax 33-823-2766; e-mail britembe@orange.sn; internet www.britishembassy.gov.uk/senegal; Ambassador Chris Trott.
USA: ave Jean XXIII, angle rue Kleber, BP 49, Dakar; tel. 33-823-4296; fax 33-823-5163; e-mail usadakar@state.gov; internet dakar.usembassy.gov; Ambassador Marcia Stephens Bloom Bernicat.

Judicial System

In 1992 the Supreme Court was replaced by three judicial bodies. The Constitutional Council verifies that legislation and international agreements are in accordance with the Constitution. It decides disputes between the Executive and the Legislature, and determines the relative jurisdictions of the Council of State and the Court of Cassation. The Council of State judges complaints brought against the Executive. It also resolves electoral disputes. The Court of Cassation is the highest court of appeal, and regulates the activities of subordinate courts and tribunals. The Revenue Court supervises the public accounts.

Constitutional Council: BP 45732, Dakar; tel. 33-822-5252; fax 33-822-8187; e-mail magou_51@hotmail.com; internet www.gouv.sn/institutions/conseil_const.html; 5 mems; Pres. Mireille Ndiaye.

SENEGAL

Council of State: rue Béranger Ferraut, Dakar; tel. 33-822-4786; internet www.gouv.sn/institutions/conseil_etat.html; Pres. ABDOU AZIZ BA.

Court of Cassation: blvd Martin Luther King, BP 15184, Dakar-Fann; tel. 33-889-1010; fax 33-821-1890; e-mail pasakho@yahoo.fr; internet www.gouv.sn/institutions/cour_cassation.html; First Pres. PAPA OUMAR SAKHO; Procurator-Gen. ABDOULAYE CRAYE; Sec.-Gen. MAMADOU BADIO CAMARA.

Revenue Court (Cour des Comptes): 15 ave Franklin Roosevelt, BP 9097, Peytavin, Dakar; tel. 33-849-4001; fax 33-849-4362; e-mail askonte@courdescomptes.sn; internet www.courdescomptes.sn; Pres. ABDOU BAME GUEYE; Sec.-Gen. El Hadji MALICK KONTE; Pres. of Chambers ABBA GOUDIABY, MOUSTAPHA GUEYE, MAMADOU HADY SARR; Chief Administrator ABDOURAHMANE DIOUKNANE.

High Court of Justice: Dakar; competent to try the Prime Minister and other members of the Government for crimes committed in the exercise of their duties; The President of the Republic may only be brought to trial in the case of high treason; mems elected by the Assemblée nationale.

Religion

At the time of the 1988 census almost 94% of the population were Muslims, while some 4% professed Christianity (the dominant faith being Roman Catholicism); a small number, mostly in the south, followed traditional beliefs.

ISLAM

There are four main Islamic brotherhoods active in Senegal: the Tidjanes, the Mourides, the Layennes and the Qadiriyas.

Association pour la coopération islamique (ACIS): Dakar; f. 1988; Pres. Dr THIERNAO KÂ.

Grande Mosquée de Dakar: Dakar; tel. 33-822-5648; Grand Imam El Hadj BAYE DAME DIÈNE.

CHRISTIANITY

The Roman Catholic Church

Senegal comprises one archdiocese and six dioceses. At 31 December 2006 there were an estimated 551,343 adherents of the Roman Catholic Church, representing about 5.1% of the total population.

Bishops' Conference
Conférence des Evêques du Sénégal, de la Mauritanie, du Cap-Vert et de Guinée-Bissau, BP 941, Dakar; tel. 33-836-3309; fax 33-836-1617; e-mail archevchedkr@sentoo.sn.
f. 1973; Pres. Most Rev. JEAN-NOËL DIOUF (Bishop of Tambacounda).

Archbishop of Dakar: Cardinal THÉODORE-ADRIEN SARR, Archevêché, ave Jean XXIII, BP 1908, Dakar; tel. 33-889-0600; fax 33-823-4875; e-mail archevechedkr@sentoo.sn.

The Anglican Communion

The Anglican diocese of The Gambia, part of the Church of the Province of West Africa, includes Senegal and Cape Verde. The Bishop is resident in Banjul, The Gambia.

Protestant Church

Eglise Protestante du Sénégal: 65 rue Wagane Diouf, BP 22390, Dakar; tel. 33-821-5564; fax 33-821-7132; f. 1862; Pastor ETITI YOMO DJERIWO.

BAHÁ'Í FAITH

National Spiritual Assembly: Point E, rue des Ecrivains, 2è impasse à droite après la Direction de la statistique, BP 1662, Dakar; tel. 33-824-2359; e-mail bahai@sentoo.sn; internet www.sn.bahai.org; regd 1975; Sec. ABOUBAKRINE BA.

The Press

DAILY NEWSPAPERS

L'Actuel: route du Front de Terre, angle ave Bourguiba, Immeuble Dramé, BP 11874, Dakar; tel. 33-864-2601; fax 33-864-2602; e-mail lactuel@sentoo.sn.

Dakar Soir: Dakar; tel. and fax 33-832-1093; f. 2000.

Dekeu Bi: Quartier Casier, Thiès; tel. 77-557-2915.

L'Evénement du Soir: Fann Résidence, rue A, angle rue 4, point E, BP 16060, Dakar; tel. 33-864-3430; fax 33-864-3600; evenings.

Frasques Quotidiennes: 51 rue du Docteur Thèze, BP 879, Dakar; tel. 33-842-4226; fax 33-842-4277; e-mail frasques@arc.sm.

L'Info 7: Sicap rue 10, BP 11357, Dakar; tel. and fax 33-864-2658; e-mail comsept@sentoo.sn; f. 1999.

Le Matin: route de l'Aéroport Léopold Sédar Senghor, BP 6472, Dakar; tel. 33-825-7359; fax 33-825-7358; e-mail lematin@metissacana.sn; internet www.lematindusenegal.info; daily; independent; Dir MAME LESS CAMARA; Editor-in-Chief ALIOUNE FALL.

La Pointe: Dakar; tel. 33-820-5035; fax 33-820-5043.

Le Populaire: 114 ave Peytavin, Immeuble Serigne Massamba Mbacké, Dakar; tel. 33-822-7977; fax 33-822-7927; f. 2000; Editor-in-Chief MAMADOU THIERNO TALLA.

Le Quotidien: 12 Cité Adama Diop, Yoff Routes de Cimétieres, BP 25221, Dakar; tel. 33-869-8484; fax 33-820-7297; e-mail lequotidien@lequotidien.sn; internet www.lequotidien.sn; f. 2003; Dir MAMADOU BIAYE.

Scoop: route du Service Géographique, BP 92, Dakar; tel. 33-859-5959; fax 33-859-6050.

Le Soleil: Société sénégalaise de presse et de publications, route du Service géographique, Hann, BP 92, Dakar; tel. 33-859-5940; fax 33-859-6050; e-mail lesoleil@lesoleil.sn; internet www.lesoleil.sn; f. 1970; Dir-Gen. and Dir of Publication MAMADOU SEYE; Editors-in-Chief HABIB DEMBA FALL, IBRAHIMA MBODJ; circ. 25,000 (2005).

Sud Quotidien: Immeuble Fahd, BP 4130, Dakar; tel. 33-824-3306; fax 33-824-3322; e-mail info@sudonline.sn; internet www.sudonline.sn; independent; Dir ABDOULAYE NDIAGA SYLLA; circ. 30,000.

Tract: 13 rue de Thann, BP 3683, Dakar; tel. and fax 33-823-4725; e-mail tract.sn@laposte.net; f. 2000.

Le Volcan: Dakar; tel. 33-820-5035; fax 33-820-5043.

Wal Fadjri/L'Aurore (The Dawn): Sicap Sacré-Coeur no 8542, BP 576, Dakar; tel. 33-824-2343; fax 33-824-2346; e-mail walf@walf.sn; internet www.walf.sn; f. 1984; Exec. Dir MBAYE SIDY MBAYE; circ. 15,000.

24 Heures Chrono: Sacré coeur 3, Villa 10595; tel. 77-576-0358; internet www.24sn.com; Editor-in-Chief SÉCKOU DIANKO DIATTA; Editor EL MALICK SECK.

PERIODICALS

Afrique Médicale: 10 rue Abdou Karim Bourgi, BP 1826, Dakar; tel. 33-823-4880; fax 33-822-5630; f. 1960; 11 a year; review of tropical medicine; Editor P. CORREA; circ. 7,000.

Afrique Nouvelle: 9 rue Paul Holle, BP 283, Dakar; tel. 33-822-5122; f. 1947; weekly; devt issues; Roman Catholic; Dir RENÉ ODOUN; circ. 15,000.

Afrique Tribune: Dakar; tel. and fax 33-821-1592; monthly.

Amina: BP 2120, Dakar; e-mail amina@calva.net; monthly; women's magazine.

Le Cafard Libéré: 10 rue Tolbiac, angle Autoroute, Soumédioune, BP 7292, Dakar; tel. 33-822-8443; fax 33-822-0891; f. 1987; weekly; satirical; Editor PAPE SAMBA KANE; circ. 12,000.

Construire l'Afrique: Dakar; tel. 33-823-0790; fax 33-824-1961; f. 1985; six a year; African business; Dir and Chief Editor CHEIKH OUSMANE DIALLO.

Le Courrier du Sud: BP 190, Ziguinchor; tel. 33-991-1166; weekly.

Démocratie: Liberté V, 5375 M, 71 rue du rond-point Liberté V et VI; tel. 33-824-8669; fax 33-825-1879.

Eco Hebdo: 22 x 19 rue Médina, BP 11451, Dakar; tel. and fax 33-837-1414; weekly.

L'Equipe Sénégal: Dakar; tel. 33-824-0013; e-mail lequipesenegal@yahoo.fr; weekly; sports.

Ethiopiques: BP 2035, Dakar; tel. and fax 33-821-5355; f. 1974; literary and philosophical review; publ. by Fondation Léopold Sédar Senghor.

Le Journal de l'Economie: 15 rue Jules Ferry, BP 2851, Dakar; tel. 33-823-8733; fax 33-823-6007; weekly.

Journal Officiel de la République du Sénégal: Rufisque; f. 1856; weekly; govt journal.

Momsareew: BP 820, Dakar; f. 1958; monthly; publ. by PAI; Editor-in-Chief MALAMINE BADJI; circ. 2,000.

Nord Ouest: Immeuble Lonase, BP 459, Louga; tel. 76-680-7943; e-mail lenordouest@yahoo.fr; f. 2000; regional monthly; Dir of Publication PAPE MOMAR CISSÉ.

Nouvel Horizon: Dakar; tel. and fax 33-822-7414; weekly.

Nuit et Jour: Dakar; tel. 33-832-1570; weekly.

Le Politicien: Dakar; tel. and fax 33-827-6396; f. 1977; weekly; satirical.

Promotion: BP 1676, Dakar; tel. 33-825-6969; fax 33-825-6950; e-mail giepromo@telecomplus.sn; f. 1972; fortnightly; Dir BOUBACAR DIOP; circ. 5,000.

République: BP 21740, Dakar; tel. 33-822-7373; fax 33-822-5039; e-mail republike@yahoo.fr; f. 1994.

Sénégal d'Aujourd'hui: Dakar; monthly; publ. by Ministry of Culture; circ. 5,000.

Sopi (Change): 5 blvd Dial Diop, Dakar; tel. 33-824-4950; fax 33-824-4700; f. 1988; weekly; publ. by PDS; Dir of Publishing JOSEPH NDONG; Editor CHEIKH KOUREYSSI BA.

Le Témoin: Gibraltar II, Villa no 310, Dakar; tel. 33-822-3269; fax 33-821-7838; f. 1990; weekly; Editor-in-Chief MAMADOU OUMAR NDIAYE; circ. 5,000.

Unir Cinéma: 1 rue Neuville, BP 160, Saint Louis; tel. 33-861-1027; fax 33-861-2408; f. 1973; quarterly African cinema review; Editor PIERRE SAGNA.

Vive La République: Sicap Amitié III, Villa no. 4057, Dakar; tel. 33-864-0631; weekly.

Xareli (Struggle): BP 12136, Dakar; tel. 33-822-5463; fortnightly; publ. by AJ—PADS; circ. 7,000.

NEWS AGENCIES

Agence Panafricaine d'Information—PANA-Presse SA: ave Bourjuiba, BP 4056, Dakar; tel. 33-824-1395; fax 33-824-1390; e-mail marketing@panapress.com; internet www.panapress.com; f. 1979 as Pan-African News Agency (under the auspices of the Organization of African Unity), restructured as 75% privately owned co in 1997; Co-ordinator-Gen. BABACAR FALL.

Agence de Presse Sénégalaise: 58 blvd de la République, BP 117, Dakar; tel. 33-823-1667; fax 33-822-0767; e-mail aps@aps.sn; internet www.aps.sn; f. 1959; govt-controlled; Dir AMADOU DIENG.

PRESS ORGANIZATION

Syndicat des Professionnels de l'Information et de la Communication du Sénégal (SYNPICS): BP 21722, Dakar; tel. 33-842-4256; fax 33-842-0269; e-mail synpics@yahoo.fr; Sec.-Gen. DIATA CISSÉ.

Publishers

Africa Editions: BP 1826, Dakar; tel. 33-823-4880; fax 33-822-5630; f. 1958; general, reference; Man. Dir JOËL DECUPPER.

Agence de Distribution de Presse: km 2.5, blvd du Centenaire de la Commune de Dakar, BP 374, Dakar; tel. 33-832-0278; fax 33-832-4915; e-mail adpresse@telecomplus.sn; f. 1943; general, reference; Man. Dir PHILIPPE SCHORP.

Centre Africain d'Animation et d'Echanges Culturels Editions Khoudia: BP 5332, Dakar-Fann; tel. 33-821-1023; fax 33-821-5109; f. 1989; fiction, education, anthropology; Dir AISSATOU DIA.

Editions Clairafrique: 2 rue El Hadji Mbaye Guèye, BP 2005, Dakar; tel. 33-822-2169; fax 33-821-8409; f. 1951; politics, law, sociology, anthropology, literature, economics, devt, religion, school books.

Editions des Ecoles Nouvelles Africaines: ave Cheikh Anta Diop, angle rue Pyrotechnie, Stèle Mermoz, BP 581, Dakar; tel. 33-864-0544; fax 33-864-1352; e-mail eenas@sentoo.sn; youth and adult education, in French.

Editions Juridiques Africaines (EDJA): 18 rue Raffenel, BP 22420, Dakar-Ponty; tel. 33 821-6689; fax 33 823-2753; e-mail edja.ed@orange.sn; internet www.edja.sn; f. 1986; law; Dir NDÉYE NGONÉ GUÈYE.

Editions des Trois Fleuves: blvd de l'Est, angle Cheikh Anta Diop, BP 123, Dakar; tel. 33-825-7923; fax 33-825-5937; f. 1972; general non-fiction; luxury edns; Dir GÉRARD RAZIMOWSKY; Gen. Man. BERTRAND DE BOISTEL.

Enda—Tiers Monde Editions (Environmental Development Action in the Third World): 54 rue Carnot, BP 3370, Dakar; tel. 33-822-9890; fax 33-823-5157; e-mail editions@enda.sn; internet www.enda.sn; f. 1972; third-world environment and devt; Dir RAPHAËL NDIAYE; Exec. Sec. JOSÉPHINE OUÉDRAOGO.

Grande imprimerie africaine (GIA): 9 rue Amadou Assane Ndoye, Dakar; tel. 33-822-1408; fax 33-822-3927; f. 1917; law, administration; Man. Dir CHEIKH ALIMA TOURÉ.

Institut fondamental d'Afrique noire (IFAN)—Cheikh Anta Diop: BP 206, Campus universitaire, Dakar; tel. 33-825-9890; fax 33-824-4918; internet www.afrique-ouest.auf.org; f. 1936; scientific and humanistic studies of Black Africa, for specialist and general public.

Nouvelles éditions africaines du Sénégal (NEAS): 10 rue Amadou Assane Ndoye, BP 260, Dakar; tel. 33-822-1580; fax 33-822-3604; e-mail neas@telecomplus.sn; f. 1972; literary fiction, schoolbooks; Dir-Gen. SAYDOU SOW.

Per Ankh: BP 2, Popenguine; e-mail perankheditions@arc.sn; internet www.perankhbooks.com; history.

Société africaine d'édition: 16 bis rue de Thiong, BP 1877, Dakar; tel. 33-821-7977; f. 1961; African politics and economics; Man. Dir PIERRE BIARNES.

Société d'édition 'Afrique Nouvelle': 9 rue Paul Holle, BP 283, Dakar; tel. 33-822-3825; f. 1947; information, statistics and analyses of African affairs; Man. Dir ATHANASE NDONG.

Société nationale de Presse, d'édition et de publicité (SONAPRESS): Dakar; f. 1972; Pres. OBEYE DIOP.

Sud-Communication: BP 4100, Dakar; operated by a journalists' co-operative; periodicals.

Xamal, SA: BP 380, Saint-Louis; tel. 33-961-1722; fax 33-961-1519; general literature, social sciences, in national languages and in French; Dir ABOUBAKAR DIOP.

GOVERNMENT PUBLISHING HOUSE

Société sénégalaise de presse et de publications—Imprimerie nationale (SSPP): route du Service géographique, BP 92, Dakar; tel. 33-832-4692; fax 33-832-0381; f. 1970; 62% govt-owned; Dir SALIOU DIAGNE.

Broadcasting and Communications

TELECOMMUNICATIONS

Regulatory Authority

Agence de Régulation des Télécommunications et des Postes (ARTP): route des Almadies Angle Dioulikayes, BP 14130, Dakar-Peytavin; tel. 33-869-0369; fax 33-869-0370; e-mail contact@artp.sn; internet www.artp.sn; f. 2001; Pres. Prof. ABDOULAYE SAKHO; Dir-Gen. DANIEL G. GOUMALO SECK.

Service Providers

Excaf Telecom: Domaine Industriel SODIDA, rue 14 Prolongée, BP 1656, Dakar; tel. 33-824-2424; fax 33-824-2191; e-mail dunyaa@excaf.com; internet www.excaf.com; f. 1972 as L'Agence Africaine de Commercialisation Artistique; name changed as above in 1992; Pres. and Dir-Gen. IBRAHIMA DIAGNE.

Sentel Sénégal GSM: ave Nelson Mandela, angle ave Moussé Diop. BP 146, Dakar; tel. 76-675-4202; fax 33-823-1873; internet www.sentel.sn; mobile cellular telephone operator in Dakar, most western regions, and in selected localities nation-wide; 75% owned by Millicom International Cellular (Luxembourg), 25% by Senegalese private investors; Gen. Man. YOUVAL ROSH; 250,000 subscribers (2003).

Société Nationale des Télécommunications du Sénégal (SONATEL): 46 blvd de la République, BP 69, Dakar; tel. 33-839-1118; fax 33-823-6037; internet www.sonatel.sn; f. 1985; 42.3% owned by France Câbles et Radio (France Télécom, France), 27.67% owned by Govt; Pres. MICHEL HIRSCH; Man. Dir CHEIKH TIDIANE MBAYE; 2,340 employees (2007).

Alizé: 46 blvd de la République, BP 2352, Dakar; tel. 33-839-1700; fax 33-839-1754; e-mail webmaster@alize.sn; internet www.alize.sn; f. 1996 as Sonatel Mobiles.

Télécom Plus SARL: 20 rue Amadou Assane Ndoye, BP 21100, Dakar; tel. 33-839-9700; fax 33-823-4632; telecommunications products and services.

BROADCASTING

Regulatory Authority

Haut Conseil de l'Audiovisuel: Immeuble Fahd, Dakar; tel. and fax 33-823-4784; f. 1991; Pres. AMINATA CISSÉ NIANG.

Radio

Société nationale de la Radiodiffusion-Télévision Sénégalaise (RTS): Triangle sud, angle ave Malick Sy, BP 1765, Dakar; tel. 33-849-1212; fax 33-822-3490; e-mail rts@rts.sn; internet www.rts.sn; f. 1992; state broadcasting co; broadcasts two national and eight regional stations; Dir-Gen. DAOUDA NDIAYE.

Radio Sénégal Internationale: Triangle sud, angle ave El Hadj Malick Sy, BP 1765, Dakar; tel. 33-849-1212; fax 33-822-3490; f. 2001; broadcasts news and information programmes in French, English, Arabic, Portuguese, Spanish, Italian, Soninké, Pulaar and Wolof from 14 transmitters across Senegal and on cable; Dir CHÉRIF THIAM.

RST1: Triangle sud, angle ave El Hadj Malick Sy, BP 1765, Dakar; tel. 33-849-1212; fax 33-822-3490; f. 1992; broadcasts in French, Arabic and six vernacular languages from 16 transmitters across Senegal; Dir MANSOUR SOW.

JDP FM (Jeunesse, Développement, Paix): Dakar; tel. 33-991-4813; e-mail abdousarr@orange.sn; Dir ABDOU SARR.

Radio Nostalgie Dakar: BP 21021, Dakar; tel. 33-821-2121; fax 33-822-2222; e-mail nostafric@globeaccess.net; f. 1995; music; broadcasts in French and Wolof; Gen. Man. SAUL SAVÏOTE.

Oxy-Jeunes: Fojes BP 18303, Pikine, Dakar; tel. 33-834-4919; fax 33-827-3215; e-mail cheikh_seck@eudoramail.com; f. 1999; youth and community radio station supported by the World Asscn of Community Radio Stations and the Catholic Organization for Development and Peace.

Radio PENC-MI: BP 51, Khombole; tel. 33-957-9103; fax 33-824-5898; e-mail rdoucoure@oxfam.org.uk.

Radio Rurale FM Awagna de Bignona: BP 72, Bignona; tel. 33-994-1021; fax 33-994-1909; e-mail mksonko2000@yahoo.fr.

Sud FM: Immeuble Fahd, 5e étage, BP 4130, Dakar; tel. 33-822-5393; fax 33-822-5290; e-mail info@sudonline.sn; f. 1994; operated by Sud-Communication; regional stations in Saint-Louis, Kaolack, Louga, Thiès, Ziguinchor and Diourbel; Man. Dir CHERIF EL-WAHIB SEYE.

Wal Fadjri FM: Sicap Sacré-Coeur no 8542, BP 576, Dakar; tel. 33-824-2343; fax 33-824-2346; internet www.walf.sn/radio; f. 1997; Islamic broadcaster; Exec. Dir MBAYE SIDY MBAYE.

Television

Radiodiffusion-Télévision Sénégálaise (RTS): see Radio; Dir of Television DAOUDA NDIAYE.

Canal Horizons Sénégal: 31 ave Albert Sarrault, BP 1390, Dakar; tel. 33-889-5050; fax 33-823-3030; e-mail infos@canalhorizons.sn; internet www.canalhorizons.com; f. 1990; private encrypted channel; 18.8% owned by RTS and Société Nationale des Télécommunications du Sénégal, 15% by Canal Horizons (France); Man. Dir JACQUES BARBIER DE CROZES.

Réseau MMDS-EXCAF Télécom: rue 14 prolongée, HLM 1, Domaine Industriel SODIDA, BP 1656, Dakar; tel. 33-824-2424; fax 33-824-2191; broadcasts selection of African, US, European and Saudi Arabian channels.

The French television stations, France-2, TV5 and Arte France, are also broadcast to Senegal.

Finance

(cap. = capital; res = reserves; dep. = deposits; m. = million; br(s). = branch(es); amounts in francs CFA)

BANKING

Central Bank

Banque centrale des états de l'Afrique de l'ouest (BCEAO): blvd du Général de Gaulle, angle rue 11, BP 3159, Dakar; tel. 33-889-4545; fax 33-823-5757; e-mail akangni@bceao.int; internet www.bceao.int; f. 1962; bank of issue for mem. states of the Union économique et monétaire ouest africaine (UEMOA, comprising Benin, Burkina Faso, Côte d'Ivoire, Guinea-Bissau, Mali, Niger, Senegal and Togo); cap. and res 1,148,589m., total assets 5,099,908m. (Dec. 2005); Gov. PHILIPPE-HENRI DACOURY-TABLEY; Dir in Senegal SEYNI NDIAYE; brs at Kaolack and Ziguinchor.

Commercial Banks

Attijari Bank Sénégal—CBAO: 97 ave André Peytavin, POB 4111, Dakar; tel. 33-889-9898; fax 33-823-4857; e-mail bst@bst.sn; internet www.attijaribanksenegal.com; f. 2007 by merger of Banque Sénégalo-Tunisienne and Attijariwafa Bank Sénégal; name changed as above in 2008 following merger with Compagnie Bancaire de l'Afrique Occidentale (CBAO); 100% owned by Attijariwafa Bank Group (Morocco); Dirs-Gen. ABDELKRIM RAGHNI (CBAO), BOUBKER JAÏ (Attijari Bank Sénégal).

Bank of Africa—Sénégal: Résidence Excellence, 4 ave Léopold Sédar Senghor, BP 1992, Dakar; tel. 33-849-6240; fax 33-842-1667; e-mail information@boasenegal.com; internet www.boasenegal.com; f. 2001; cap. 2,750m., res 82,011m., dep. 48,703m. (Dec. 2007); Pres. PAUL DERREUMAUX; Dir-Gen. FAUSTIN AMOUSSOU; 8 brs.

Banque Internationale pour le Commerce et l'Industrie du Sénégal (BICIS): 2 ave Léopold Sédar Senghor, BP 392, Dakar; tel. 33-839-0390; fax 33-823-0737; e-mail bicis@africa.bnpparibas.com; internet www.bicis.sn; f. 1962; 54.11% owned by Groupe BNP Paribas (France); cap. and res 15,638m., total assets 227,702m. (Dec. 2003); Chair. SERIGNE LOMINO DIOP; Dir-Gen. AMADOU KANE; 17 brs.

Citibank Senegal SA: Immeuble SDIH, 4e étage, 2 pl. de l'Indépendance, BP 3391, Dakar; tel. 33-849-1104; fax 33-823-8817; e-mail thioro.ba@citicorp.com; f. 1975; wholly owned subsidiary of Citibank NA (USA); cap. 1,626m., total assets 84,864m. (Dec. 2001); Pres. JOHN REED; Man. KEVIN A. MURRAY; 1 br.

Compagnie Ouest Africaine de Crédit Bail (LOCAFRIQUE): Immeuble Coumaba Castel, 11 rue Galandou Diouf, BP 292, Dakar; tel. 33-849-8100; fax 33-822-0894; e-mail locafrique@arc.sn; f. 1977; cap. 579m., total assets 1,241m. (Dec. 2003); Dir-Gen. AMADOU SY.

Crédit National du Sénégal (CNS): 7 ave Léopold Sédar Senghor, BP 319, Dakar; tel. 33-823-3486; fax 33-823-7292; f. 1990 by merger; 87% state-owned; cap. 1,900m., total assets 2,032m. (Dec. 1996); Pres. ABDOU NDIAYE.

Crédit du Sénégal (CLS): blvd El Hadji Djily Mbaye, angle rue Huart, BP 56, Dakar; tel. 33-849-0000; fax 33-823-8430; e-mail cl_senegal@creditdusenegal.com; internet www.creditdusenegal.com; f. 1989 by acquisition of USB by Crédit Lyonnais (France); name changed as above in 2007 following merger with Crédit Agricole (France); 95% owned by Attijariwafa Bank Group (Morocco); cap. 2,000m., res 8,018m., dep. 100,817m. (Dec. 2004); Pres. and Chair. BAUDOUIN MERLET; Dir-Gen. JEAN PAUL VERU; 5 brs.

Ecobank Sénégal: 8 ave Léopold Sédar Senghor, BP 9095, Dakar; tel. 33-849-2000; fax 33-823-4707; internet www.ecobank.com; 41.45% owned by Ecobank Transnational Inc (Togo, operating under the auspices of the Economic Community of West African States), 17.0% by Ecobank Bénin, 12.43% by Ecobank Côte d'Ivoire, 4.56% by Ecobank Niger, 4.56% by Ecobank Togo; cap. and res 3,181m., total assets 48,591m. (Dec. 2003); Pres. MAHENTA BIRIMA FALL; Dir-Gen. EVELYNE TALL.

International Commercial Bank (Senegal) SA: 18 ave Léopold Sédar Senghor, Dakar; tel. 33-823-5647; fax 33-842-2585; e-mail info@icbank-senegal.com; f. 2006; Sec. KANTOME NIANG; 1 br.

Société Générale de Banques au Sénégal (SGBS): 19 ave Léopold Sédar Senghor, BP 323, Dakar; tel. 33-839-5500; fax 33-823-9036; e-mail sgbs@sentoo.sn; internet www.sgbs.sn; f. 1962; 57.72% owned by Société Générale (France), 35.23% owned by private Senegalese investors; cap. 4,528m., res 22,026m., dep. 325,030m. (Dec. 2004); Pres. PAPA-DEMBA DIALLO; Dir-Gen. SANDY GILLIOT; 30 brs and sub-brs.

Development Banks

Banque de l'Habitat du Sénégal (BHS): 69 blvd du Général de Gaulle, BP 229, Dakar; tel. 33-839-3333; fax 33-823-8043; e-mail bdld10@calva.com; internet www.bhs.sn; f. 1979; cap. and res 19,661.0m., total assets 12,554.6m. (Dec. 2003); Pres. AHMED YÉRO DIALLO; Dir-Gen. SOULEYMANE LY; 2 brs.

Caisse Nationale de Crédit Agricole du Sénégal (CNCAS): pl. de l'Indépendance, Immeuble ex-Air Afrique, 31–33 rue El Hadji Asmadou Assane Ndoye, angle ave Colbert, Dakar; tel. 33-839-3636; fax 33-821-2606; e-mail cncas@cncas.sn; internet www.cncas.sn; f. 1984; 23.8% state-owned; cap. 2,300m., res 3,952m., dep. 59,196m. (Dec. 2003); Pres. ABDOULAYE DIACK; Dir-Gen. ARFANG BOUBACAR DAFFE; 13 brs.

Société Financière d'Equipement (SFE): 2e étage, Immeuble Sokhna Anta, rue Dr Thèze, BP 252, Dakar; tel. 33-823-6626; fax 33-823-4337; 59% owned by Compagnie Bancaire de l'Afrique Occidentale; cap. and res 388m., total assets 6,653m. (Dec. 1999); Pres. ARISTIDE ORSET ALCANTARA; Dir-Gen. MOHAMED A. WILSON.

Islamic Bank

Banque Islamique du Sénégal (BIS): Immeuble Abdallah Fayçal, rue Huart, angle rue Amadou Ndoye, BP 3381, 18524 Dakar; tel. 33-849-6262; fax 33-822-4948; e-mail contact@bis-bank.com; internet www.bis-bank.com; f. 1983; 44.5% owned by Dar al-Maal al-Islami (Switzerland), 33.3% by Islamic Development Bank (Saudi Arabia), 22.2% state-owned; cap. 2,706m., res 4,120m., dep. 38,845m. (Dec. 2006); Pres. of Bd of Administration BADER EDDINE NOUIOUA; Dir-Gen. AZHAR S. KHAN; 4 brs.

Banking Association

Association Professionnelle des Banques et des Etablissements Financiers du Sénégal (APBEF): 5 rue Calmette, angle A. Assane Ndoye, BP 6403, Dakar; tel. 33-823-6093; fax 33-823-8596; e-mail apbef@orange.sn; Pres. ABDOUL MBAYE.

STOCK EXCHANGE

Bourse Régionale des Valeurs Mobilières (BRVM): BP 22500, Dakar; tel. 33-821-1518; fax 33-821-1506; e-mail nksy@brvm.org; internet www.brvm.org; f. 1998; national branch of BRVM (regional stock exchange based in Abidjan, Côte d'Ivoire, serving the member states of UEMOA); Man. KHADY SY.

INSURANCE

AGF Sénégal Assurances: rue de Thann, angle ave Abdoulaye Fadiga, Dakar; tel. 33-849-4400; fax 33-823-1078; e-mail agf.senegal@agf-sn.com; Dir-Gen. BERNARD GIRARDIN.

Les Assurances Conseils Dakarois A. Gueye et cie: 20 rue Mohamed V, BP 2345, Dakar; tel. 33-822-6997; fax 33-822-8680.

SENEGAL

Assurances Générales Sénégalaises (AGS): 43 ave Albert Sarraut, BP 225, Dakar; tel. 33-839-3600; fax 33-823-3701; e-mail ags@metissacana.sn; f. 1977; cap. 2,990m.; Dir-Gen. IBRAHIM GUEYE.

Assurances La Sécurité Sénégalaise (ASS): BP 2623, Dakar; tel. 33-849-0599; fax 33-821-2581; e-mail ass.dk@orange.sn; internet ass-assurances.com; f. 1984; cap. 1,000m. (2007); Pres. MOUSSA SOW; Man. Dir MBACKE SENE.

AXA Assurances Sénégal: 5 pl. de l'Indépendance, BP 182, Dakar; tel. 33-849-1010; fax 33-823-4672; e-mail info@axa.sn; f. 1977; fmrly Csar Assurances; 51.5% owned by AXA (France); cap. 1,058m. (Mar. 2004); Pres. MOUSTAPHA CISSÉ; Dir-Gen. ALIOUNE NDOUR DIOUF.

V. Capillon Assurances: BP 425, Dakar; tel. 33-821-1377; fax 33-822-2435; f. 1951; cap. 10m.; Pres. and Man. Dir GILLES DE MONTALEMBERT.

Compagnie d'Assurances-Vie et de Capitalisation (La Nationale d'Assurances-Vie): 7 blvd de la République, BP 3853, Dakar; tel. 33-822-1181; fax 33-821-2820; f. 1982; cap. 80m.; Pres. MOUSSA DIOUF; Man. Dir BASSIROU DIOP.

Compagnie Sénégalaise d'Assurances et de Réassurances (CSAR): 5 pl. de l'Indépendance, BP 182, Dakar; tel. 33-823-2776; fax 33-823-4672; f. 1972; cap. 945m.; 49.8% state-owned; Pres. MOUSTAPHA CISSÉ; Man. Dir MAMADOU ABBAS BA.

Gras Savoye Sénégal: 15 blvd de la République, BP 9, Dakar; tel. 33-823-0100; fax 33-821-5462; e-mail olivier.destriau@grassavoye.sn; affiliated to Gras Savoye (France); Man. OLIVIER DESTRIAU.

Intercontinental Life Insurance Co (ILICO): BP 1359, Dakar; tel. 33-821-7520; fax 33-822-0449; f. 1993; life insurance; fmrly American Life Insurance Co; Pres. and Dir-Gen. MAGATTE DIOP.

Mutuelles Sénégalaises d'Assurance et de Transport (MSAT): Dakar; tel. 33-822-2938; fax 33-823-4247; f. 1981; all branches; Dir MOR ATJ.

La Nationale d'Assurances: 5 ave Albert Sarrault, BP 3328, Dakar; tel. 33-822-1027; fax 33-821-2820; f. 1976; fire, marine, travel and accident insurance; privately owned; Pres. AMSATA DIOUF; also La Nationale d'Assurances—Vie; life insurance.

Société Africaine d'Assurances: Dakar; tel. 33-823-6475; fax 33-823-4472; f. 1945; cap. 9m.; Dir CLAUDE GERMAIN.

Société Nationale d'Assurances Mutuelles (SONAM): 6 ave Léopold Sédar Senghor, BP 210, Dakar; tel. 33-823-1003; fax 33-820-7025; f. 1973; cap. 1,464m.; Pres. ABDOULAYE FOFANA; Man. Dir DIOULDÉ NIANE.

Société Nouvelle d'Assurances du Sénégal (SNAS): rue de Thann, BP 2610, Dakar; tel. 33-823-4176; fax 33-823-1078; e-mail snas@telecomplus.sn; Dir-Gen. FRANÇOIS BURGUIERRE.

Société Sénégalaise de Courtage et d'Assurances (SOSECODA): 16 ave Léopold Sédar Senghor, BP 9, Dakar; tel. 33-823-5481; fax 33-821-5462; f. 1963; cap. 10m.; 55% owned by SONAM; Man. Dir A. AZIZ NDAW.

Société Sénégalaise de Réassurances SA (SENRE): 6 ave Léopold Sédar Senghor, angle Carnot, BP 386, Dakar; tel. 33-822-8089; fax 33-821-5652; cap. 600m.

Insurance Association

Syndicat Professionnel des Agents Généraux d'Assurances du Sénégal: 43 ave Albert Sarraut, BP 1766, Dakar; Pres. URBAIN ALEXANDRE DIAGNE; Sec. JEAN-PIERRE CAIRO.

Trade and Industry

GOVERNMENT AGENCIES

Agence de Développement et d'Encadrement des Petites et Moyennes Entreprises (ADEPME): 9 Fenêtre Mermoz, ave Cheikh Anta Diop, BP 333, Dakar-Fann; tel. 33-863-7071; fax 33-860-1363; e-mail adepme@sentoo.sn; internet www.adepme.sn; f. 2001; assists in the formation and operation of small and medium-sized enterprises; Dir MARIE THÉRÈSE DIEDHIOU.

Agence nationale pour la promotion des investissements et des grands travaux (APIX): 52–54 rue Mohamed V, BP 430, 18524 Dakar; tel. 33-849-0555; fax 33-823-9489; e-mail contact@apix.sn; internet www.investinsenegal.com; f. 2000; promotes investment and major projects; Dir-Gen. AMINATA NIANE.

Agence Sénégalaise de Promotion des Exportations (ASEPEX): Route du Meridien Président Almadies, BP 14709, Dakar; tel. 33-869-2021; fax 33-869-2022; e-mail asepex@asepex.sn; internet www.asepex.sn; f. 2005; promotes exports; Dir-Gen. MAIMOUNA SAVANÉ.

Société de Développement Agricole et Industriel (SODAGRI): blvd Djily Mbaye, angle rue Macodou Ndiaye, BP 222, Dakar; tel. 33-821-0426; fax 33-822-5406; internet www.sodagri.net; f. 1974; cap. 120m. francs CFA; agricultural and industrial projects; Pres. and Dir-Gen. AMADOU TIDIANE WANE.

Société de Gestion des Abattoirs du Sénégal (SOGAS): BP 14, Dakar; tel. 33-854-0740; fax 33-834-2365; e-mail sogas@sentoo.sn; f. 1962; cap. 619.2m. francs CFA; 28% state-owned; livestock farming; Dir-Gen. SOW SADIO.

Société Nationale d'Aménagement et d'Exploitation des Terres du Delta du Fleuve Sénégal et des Vallées du Fleuve Sénégal et de la Falémé (SAED): 200 ave Insa Coulibaly-Sor, BP 74, Saint-Louis; tel. 33-961-1533; fax 33-961-1463; e-mail saed@orange.sn; internet www.saed.sn; f. 1965; cap. 2,500m. francs CFA; 100% state-owned; controls the agricultural devt of more than 40,000 ha around the Senegal river delta; Dir-Gen. MAMOUDOU DEME.

Société Nationale d'Etudes et de Promotion Industrielle (SONEPI): Dakar; tel. 33-825-2130; fax 33-824-65465; f. 1969; cap. 150m. francs CFA; 28% state-owned; promotion of small and medium-sized enterprises; Chair. and Man. Dir HADY MAMADOU LY.

Société Nouvelle des Etudes de Développement en Afrique (SONED—AFRIQUE): 22 rue Moussé Diop, BP 2084, Dakar; tel. 33-823-9457; fax 33-823-4231; e-mail sonedaf@telecomplus.sn; f. 1974; cap. 150m. francs CFA; Pres. ABDOU WAHAB TALLA; Man. Dir El Hadj AMADOU WONE.

DEVELOPMENT ORGANIZATIONS

Agence Française de Développement (AFD): 15 ave Mandela, BP 475, Dakar; tel. 33-849-1999; fax 33-823-4010; e-mail afddakar@groupe-afd.org; Country Dir JEAN-MARC GRAVELLINI.

Association Française des Volontaires du Progrès (AFVP): BP 1010, route de la VDN, Sacré coeur 3, Villa no 9364, Dakar; tel. 33-827-4075; fax 33-827-4074; e-mail afvp@telecomplus.sn; internet www.afvp.org; f. 1972; Regional Delegate for Senegal, Cape Verde, Guinea, Guinea-Bissau, Mali and Mauritania JEAN-LOUP CAPDEVILLE; Nat. Delegate KARIM DOUMBIA.

Centre International du Commerce Extérieur du Sénégal: route de l'Aéroport, BP 8166, Dakar-Yoff, Dakar; tel. 33-827-5466; fax 33-827-5275; e-mail cices@metissacana.sn; Sec.-Gen. AMADOU SY.

Service de Coopération et d'Action Culturelle: BP 2014, Dakar; tel. 33-839-5305; administers bilateral aid from France; fmrly Mission Française de Coopération et d'Action Culturelle; Dir XAVIN ROZE.

CHAMBERS OF COMMERCE

Union Nationale des Chambres de Commerce, d'Industrie et d'Agriculture du Sénégal: 1 pl. de l'Indépendance, BP 118, Dakar; tel. 33-823-7169; fax 33-823-9363; f. 1888; restructured 2002; Pres. MAMADOU LAMINE NIANG.

Chambre de Commerce, d'Industrie et d'Agriculture de Dakar: 1 pl. de l'Indépendance, BP 118, Dakar; tel. 33-823-7189; fax 33-823-9363; e-mail cciad@orange.sn; internet www.cciad.sn; f. 1888; Pres. MAMADOU LAMINE NIANG; Sec.-Gen. ALY MBOUP (acting).

Chambre de Commerce, d'Industrie et d'Agriculture de Diourbel: 744 ave Léopold Sédar Senghor, BP 7, Diourbel; tel. 33-971-1203; fax 33-971-3849; e-mail mamandiaye@hotmail.com; f. 1969; Pres. MOUSTAPHA CISSÉ LO; Sec.-Gen. MAMADOU NDIAYE.

Chambre de Commerce de Fatick: BP 66, Fatick; tel. and fax 33-949-1425; e-mail ccfatick@cosec.sn; Pres. BABOUCAR BOP; Sec.-Gen. SEYDOU NOUROU LY.

Chambre de Commerce et d'Industrie de Kaolack: BP 203, Kaolack; tel. 33-941-2052; fax 33-941-2291; e-mail cciak@netcourrier.com; internet www.cciak.fr.st; Pres. IDRISSA GUÈYE; Sec.-Gen. SALIMATA S. DIAKHATE.

Chambre de Commerce d'Industrie et d'Agriculture de Kolda: BP 23, Quartier Escale, Kolda; tel. 33-996-1230; fax 33-996-1068; Pres. AMADOU MOUNIROU DIALLO; Sec.-Gen. YAYA CAMARA.

Chambre de Commerce, d'Industrie et d'Agriculture de Louga: 2 rue Glozel, BP 26, Louga; tel. 33-967-1114; fax 33-967-0825; e-mail ccial@orange.sn; Pres. CHEIKH MACKÉ FAYE; Sec.-Gen. DOUDOU NIANG.

Chambre de Commerce, d'Industrie et d'Agriculture de Matam: BP 95, Matam; tel. and fax 33-966-6591; Pres. MAMADOU NDIADE; Sec.-Gen. MOUSSA NDIAYE.

Chambre de Commerce, d'Industrie et d'Agriculture de Saint-Louis: 10 rue Blanchot, BP 19, Saint-Louis; tel. 33-961-1088; fax 33-961-2980; f. 1879; Pres. El Hadj ABIBOU DIEYE; Sec.-Gen. MOUSSA NDIAYE.

Chambre de Commerce, d'Industrie et d'Agriculture de Tambacounda: 120 blvd Diogoye, BP 127, Tambacounda; tel. 33-981-1014; fax 33-981-2995; Pres. DJIBY CISSÉ; Sec.-Gen. TENGUELLA BA.

SENEGAL

Chambre de Commerce, d'Industrie et d'Agriculture de Thiès: 96 ave Lamine Guèye, BP 3020, Thiès; tel. 33-951-1002; fax 33-952-1397; e-mail ccthies@cosec.sn; f. 1883; 38 mems; Pres. ATTOU NDIAYE; Sec.-Gen. ABDOULKHADRE CAMARA.

Chambre de Commerce, d'Industrie et d'Artisanat de Ziguinchor: rue du Gen. de Gaulle, BP 26, Ziguinchor; tel. 33-991-1310; fax 33-991-5238; f. 1908; Pres. MAMADOU DIALLO; Sec.-Gen. ALASSANE NDIAYE.

EMPLOYERS' ASSOCIATIONS

Chambre des Métiers de Dakar: route de la Corniche-Ouest, Soumbedioune, Dakar; tel. 33-821-7908; e-mail dakarmetiers@orange.sn; Sec.-Gen. MBAYE GAYE.

Confédération Nationale des Employeurs du Sénégal: Dakar; tel. 33-821-7662; fax 33-822-9658; e-mail cnes@sentoo.sn; Pres. MANSOUR CAMA.

Conseil National du Patronat du Sénégal (CNP): 70 rue Jean Mermoz, BP 3537, Dakar; tel. 33-821-5803; fax 33-822-2842; e-mail cnp@sentoo.sn; internet www.cnp.sn; Pres. YOUSSOUPHA WADE; Sec.-Gen. MABOUSSO THIAM.

Groupement Professionnel de l'Industrie du Pétrole au Sénégal (GPP): rue 6, km 4.5, blvd du Centenaire de la Commune de Dakar, BP 479, Dakar; tel. and fax 33-849-3115; fax 33-832-5212; e-mail noeljp@orange.sn; Pres. BRUNO VINCENT; Sec.-Gen. JEAN-PIERRE NOËL.

Organisation des Commerçants, Agriculteurs, Artisans et Industriels: 52 rue Paul Holl, angle rue Tolbiac, Dakar; tel. 33-823-6794; fax 33-823-6550; Pres. ALASSANE SECK.

Rassemblement des Opérateurs Economiques du Sénégal (ROES): BP 5001/2, Dakar; tel. 33-825-5717; fax 33-825-5713; Pres. KHADIM BOUSSO.

Syndicat des Commerçants Importateurs, Prestataires de Services et Exportateurs de la République du Sénégal (SCIMPEX): 2 rue Parent, angle ave Abdoulaye Fadiga, BP 806, Dakar; tel. 33-821-3662; fax 33-842-9648; e-mail scimpex@orange.sn; f. 1943; Pres. PAPA ALSASSANE DIENG.

Syndicat Patronal de l'Ouest Africain des Petites et Moyennes Entreprises et des Petites et Moyennes Industries: BP 3255, 41 blvd Djily M'Baye, Dakar; tel. 33-821-3510; fax 33-823-3732; e-mail mactarniang@yahoo.fr; f. 1937; Pres. BABACAR SEYE; Sec.-Gen. MACTAR NIANG.

Syndicat Professionnel des Entrepreneurs de Bâtiments et de Travaux Publics du Sénégal: ave Abdoulaye Fadiga, BP 593, Dakar; tel. 33-823-4373; f. 1930; 130 mems; Pres. CHRISTIAN VIRMAUD.

Syndicat Professionnel des Industries du Sénégal (SPIDS): BP 593, Dakar; tel. 33-823-4324; fax 33-822-0884; e-mail spids@spids.sn; internet www.spids.sn; f. 1944; 110 mems; Pres. CHRISTIAN BASSE.

Union des Entreprises du Domaine Industriel de Dakar: BP 10288, Dakar-Liberté; tel. 33-825-0786; fax 33-825-0870; e-mail snisa@orange.sn; Pres. ARISTIDE TINO ADEDIRAN.

Union Nationale des Chambres de Métiers: Domaine Industriel SODIDA, ave Bourguiba, BP 30040, Dakar; tel. 33-825-0588; fax 33-824-5432; e-mail uncm@orange.sn; internet www.artisanat-senegal.org; f. 1981; Pres. El Hadj SEYNI SECK; Sec.-Gen. BABOUCAR DIOUF.

Union Nationale des Commerçants et Industriels du Sénégal (UNACOIS): ave Cheikh Ahmadou Bamba 3780, BP 3698, Dakar; tel. 33-821-6080; fax 33-822-0185; e-mail unacois.as@orange.sn; internet www.unacois.sn; Exec. Sec. MAME BOU DIOP.

UTILITIES

Electricity

Société Nationale d'Electricité (SENELEC): 28 rue Vincent, BP 93, Dakar; tel. 33-839-3030; fax 33-823-1267; e-mail webmaster@senelec.sn; internet www.senelec.sn; f. 1983; 100% state-owned; Pres. ABDOURAHMANE SOW.

Gas

Société Sénégalaise des Gaz: Dakar; tel. 33-832-8212; fax 33-823-5974.

Water

Société Nationale des Eaux du Sénégal (SONES): route de Front de Terre, BP 400, Dakar; tel. 33-839-7800; fax 33-832-2038; e-mail sones@sones.sn; internet www.sones.sn; f. 1995; water works and supply; state-owned; Pres. ABDOUL ALY KANE; Dir-Gen. AMADOU NDIAYE.

Sénégalaise des Eaux (SDE): Centre de Hann-Route du Front de Terre, BP 224, Dakar; tel. 33-839-3737; fax 33-839-3705; e-mail eau@sde.sn; internet www.sde.sn; f. 1996; subsidiary of Groupe Saur International (France); water distribution services; Pres. ABDOULAYE BOUNA FALL; Dir-Gen. BERNARD DEBENEST.

TRADE UNIONS

Confédération Nationale des Travailleurs du Sénégal (CNTS): 7 ave du Président Laminé Gueye, BP 937, Dakar; tel. 33-821-0491; fax 33-821-7771; e-mail cnts@orange.sn; internet cnts-senegal.net; f. 1969; affiliated to PS; Sec.-Gen. MODY GUIRO.

Confédération Nationale des Travailleurs du Sénégal—Forces de Changement (CNTS—FC): Dakar; f. 2002 following split from CNTS; Sec.-Gen CHEIKH DIOP; 31 affiliated asscns.

Confédération des Syndicats Autonomes (CSA): BP 10224, Dakar; tel. 33-835-0951; fax 33-893-5299; e-mail csasenegal@yahoo.com; organization of independent trade unions; Sec.-Gen. MAMADOU DIOUF.

Union Démocratique des Travailleurs du Sénégal (UDTS): BP 7124, Médina, Dakar; tel. 33-835-3897; fax 33-854-1070; 18 affiliated unions; Sec.-Gen. ALIOUNE SOW.

Union Nationale des Syndicats Autonomes du Sénégal (UNSAS): BP 10841, HLM, Dakar; fax 33-824-8013; Sec.-Gen. MADEMBA SOCK.

Transport

RAILWAYS

There are 922 km of main line including 70 km of double track. One line runs from Dakar north to Saint-Louis (262 km), and the main line runs to Bamako (Mali). All the locomotives are diesel-driven.

Société Nationale des Chemins de Fer du Sénégal (SNCS): BP 175A, Thiès; tel. 33-939-5300; fax 33-951-1393; f. 1905; state-owned; operates passenger and freight services on Dakar–Thiès and Djourbel–Kaoulack lines, following transfer of principal Dakar–Bamako (Mali) line to private management in 2003; suburban trains operate on Dakar–Thiès route as 'Le Petit Train Bleu', pending their proposed transfer to private management by 2006; Pres. DRAME ALIA DIENE; Man. Dir DIOUF MBAYE.

ROADS

In 2003 there were 13,576 km of roads, of which 4,216 km were main roads. Some 3,972 km of the network were paved. A 162.5 km road between Dialakoto and Kédougou, the construction of which (at a cost of some 23,000m. francs CFA) was largely financed by regional donor organizations, was inaugurated in March 1996. The road is to form part of an eventual transcontinental highway linking Cairo (Egypt) with the Atlantic coast, via N'Djamena (Chad), Bamako (Mali) and Dakar. In 1999 new highways were completed in the east of Senegal, linking Tambacounda, Kidira and Bakel.

Comité Executif des Transports Urbains de Dakar (CETUD): Résidence Fann, route du Front de Terre Hann, BP 17265 Dakar; tel. 33-859-4720; fax 33-832-4744; e-mail cetud@orange.sn; f. 1997; regulates the provision of urban transport in Dakar; Pres. OUSMANE THIAM.

Dakar-Bus: Dakar; f. 1999; operates public transport services within the city of Dakar; owned by RATP (France), Transdev (France), Eurafric-Equipment (Senegal), Mboup Travel (Senegal) and Senegal Tours (Senegal).

INLAND WATERWAYS

Senegal has three navigable rivers: the Senegal, navigable for three months of the year as far as Kayes (Mali), for six months as far as Kaédi (Mauritania) and all year as far as Rosso and Podor, and the Saloun and the Casamance. Senegal is a member of the Organisation de mise en valeur du fleuve Gambie and of the Organisation pour la mise en valeur du fleuve Sénégal, both based in Dakar. These organizations aim to develop navigational facilities, irrigation and hydroelectric power in the basins of the Gambia and Senegal rivers, respectively.

SHIPPING

The port of Dakar is the second largest in West Africa, after Abidjan (Côte d'Ivoire), and the largest deep sea port in the region, serving Senegal, Mauritania, The Gambia and Mali. It handled more than 7m. metric tons of international freight in 1999. The port's facilities include 40 berths, 10 km of quays, and also 53,000 sq m of warehousing and 65,000 sq m of open stocking areas. There is also a container terminal with facilities for vessels with a draught of up to 11 m. In March 2005 the Governments of Mauritania, Morocco and Senegal agreed that a shipping line linking the three countries and to transport merchandise was to commence operations, following the completion of a tendering process.

Compagnie Sénégalaise de Navigation Maritime (COSE-NAM): Dakar; tel. 33-821-5766; fax 33-821-0895; f. 1979; 26.1% state-owned, 65.9% owned by private Senegalese interests, 8.0% by private French, German and Belgian interests; river and ocean freight transport; Pres. ABDOURAHIM AGNE; Man. Dir SIMON BOISSY.

Conseil Sénégalais des Chargeurs (COSEC): BP 1423, Dakar; tel. 33-849-0707; fax 33-823-1144; e-mail cosec@cyg.sn; Dir-Gen. AMADOU KANE DIALLO.

Dakarnave: blvd du Centenaire de la Commune, 2POB 438, Dakar; tel. 33-849-1001; fax 33-823-8399; e-mail commercial@dakarnave.sn; internet dakarnaveshipyard.com; responsible for Senegalese shipyards; owned by Chantier Navals de Dakar, SA (Dakarnave), a subsidiary of Lisnave International, Portugal; CEO FREDERICO J. SPRANGER.

Maersk Sénégal: route de Rufisque, BP 3836, Dakar; tel. 33-859-1111; fax 33-832-1331; e-mail senmkt@maersk.com; internet www.maersksealand.com/senegal; f. 1986.

SDV Sénégal: 47 ave Albert Sarrault, BP 233, Dakar; tel. 33-839-0000; fax 33-839-0069; e-mail sdv.shipping@sn.dti.bollore.com; f. 1936; 51.6% owned by Groupe Bolloré (France); shipping agents, warehousing; Pres. ANDRÉ GUILLABERT; Dir-Gen. BERNARD FRAUD.

Société pour le Développement de l'Infrastructure de Chantiers Maritimes du Port de Dakar (Dakar-Marine): Dakar; tel. 33-823-3688; fax 33-823-8399; f. 1981; privately controlled; operates facilities for the repair and maintenance of supertankers and other large vessels; Man. YORO KANTE.

Société Maritime de l'Atlantique (SOMAT): c/o Port Autonome de Dakar, BP 3195, Dakar; internet www.somat.sn; f. 2005; 51% owned by Compagnie Marocaine de Navigation, COMANAV (Morocco), 24.5% by Conseil Sénégalais des Chargeurs, COSEC, 24.5% by Société Nationale de Port Autonome de Dakar, PAD; operates foot passenger and freight ferry service between Dakar and Ziguinchor (Casamance).

Société Nationale de Port Autonome de Dakar (PAD): 21 blvd de la Libération, BP 3195, Dakar; tel. 33-823-4545; fax 33-823-3606; e-mail pad@portdakar.sn; internet www.portdakar.sn; f. 1865; state-owned port authority; Pres. and Dir-Gen. BARA SADY.

SOCOPAO-Sénégal: BP 233, Dakar; tel. 33-823-1001; fax 33-823-5614; e-mail socopao@sn.dti.bollore.com; f. 1926; warehousing, shipping agents, sea and air freight transport; Man. Dir GILLES CUCHE.

TransSene: 1 blvd de l'Arsenal, face à la gare ferroviaire, Dakar; tel. 33-821-8181; e-mail transsen@telecomplus.sn; internet www.transsene.com.

Yenco Shipping: Fondation Fahd, blvd Djily Mbaye, Dakar; tel. 33-821-2726; fax 33-822-0781; e-mail yencoshi@sentoo.sn; f. 1988; Dir of Finance M. DIANKA; Dir of Shipping M. DIOKHANE.

CIVIL AVIATION

The international airport is Dakar-Léopold Sédar Senghor. There are other major airports at Saint-Louis, Ziguinchor and Tambacounda, in addition to about 15 smaller airfields. Facilities at Ziguinchor and Cap-Skirring were upgraded during the mid-1990s, with the aim of improving direct access to the Casamance region. In 1998 the Islamic Development Bank agreed to fund a new international airport at Tobor, Casamance. In 2000 work began to extend the runway at Saint-Louis in order to accommodate larger aircraft. The construction of a new international airport, at Ndiass, commenced in 2003.

Agence nationale de l'aviation civile du Sénégal (ANACS): BP 8184, Dakar; fax 33-820-0403; internet www.anacs.sn; civil aviation authority; Dir-Gen. MATHIACO BESSANE.

Aeroservices: Dakar; f. 1996; charter flights; Sec.-Gen. El Hadj OMAR BA.

African West Air: Dakar; tel. 33-822-4538; fax 33-822-4610; f. 1993; services to western Europe and Brazil; Man. Dir J. P. PIEDADE.

Air Sénégal International (ASI): 45 ave Albert Serraut, Dakar; tel. 33-842-4100; e-mail resadkr@airsenegalinternational.sn; internet www.air-senegal-international.com; f. 2000; 51% owned by Royal Air Maroc, 43% state-owned; domestic, regional and international services; Dir-Gen. MOHAMED FATTAHI.

Tourism

Senegal's attractions for tourists include six national parks (one of which, Djoudj, is listed by UNESCO as a World Heritage Site) and its fine beaches. The island of Gorée, near Dakar, is of considerable historic interest as a former centre for the slave-trade. In 1993 the number of foreign tourist arrivals declined dramatically, largely as a result of the suspension of tourist activity in the Casamance region in that year. The sector recovered strongly from 1995 onwards, and in 2006 visitor arrivals of 405,827 were recorded; receipts from tourism in 2005 were US $334m.

Ministry of Tourism and Air Transport: rue Calmette, BP 4049, Dakar; tel. 33-821-1126; fax 33-822-9413; internet www.tourisme.gouv.sn.

SERBIA

Introductory Survey

Location, Climate, Language, Religion, Flag, Capital

The Republic of Serbia (formerly part of the State Union of Serbia and Montenegro, and prior to that the Federal Republic of Yugoslavia—FRY) is situated in the central Balkan Peninsula, in south-eastern Europe, and is landlocked. There are western borders (from south to north) with Montenegro, Bosnia and Herzegovina and Croatia, a border with Hungary to the north, with Romania and Bulgaria to the east, and with the former Yugoslav republic of Macedonia to the south. Kosovo (a former Serbian province, which made a declaration of independence in February 2008) also lies to the South. Serbia includes the province of Vojvodina. The climate is continental, with steady rainfall throughout the year. The average summer temperature in Belgrade is 22°C (71°F), the winter average being 0°C (32°F). The official language is Serbian, which is officially written in the Cyrillic script. Orthodox Christianity is predominant, the Serbian Orthodox Church being the largest denomination. Roman Catholicism is especially strong in Vojvodina. There is a small Jewish community. The national flag (proportions 1 by 2) has three equal horizontal stripes, of blue, white and red. The capital is Belgrade (Beograd).

Recent History

A movement for the union of the South Slav peoples, despite long-standing ethnic rivalries and cultural diversity, began in the early 19th century. However, it was not until the end of the First World War, and the collapse of the Austro-Hungarian empire (which ruled Croatia, Slovenia and Bosnia and Herzegovina), that the project for a Yugoslav (south Slav) state could be realized. A pact between Serbia (which was under Ottoman Turkish rule until the 19th century) and the other South Slavs was signed in July 1917, declaring the intention to merge all the territories in a united state under the Serbian monarchy. Accordingly, when the First World War ended and Austria-Hungary was dissolved, the Kingdom of Serbs, Croats and Slovenes was proclaimed on 4 December 1918.

Prince Aleksandar, Regent of Serbia since 1914, accepted the regency of the new state, becoming King in August 1921. Following bitter disputes between Serbs and Croats, King Aleksandar assumed dictatorial powers in January 1929. He formally changed the country's name to Yugoslavia in October. Aleksandar's regime was Serb-dominated, and in October 1934 he was assassinated in France by Croat extremists. His brother, Prince Pavle, assumed power as Regent on behalf of King Petar II. Pavle's regime retained power with the support of the armed forces, despite internal unrest, particularly in Croatia. Among the anti-Government groups was the Communist Party of Yugoslavia (CPY), which had been officially banned in 1921, but continued to operate clandestinely. In 1937 the CPY appointed a new General Secretary, Josip Broz (Tito).

In March 1941 the increasingly pro-German regime of Prince Pavle was overthrown in a coup, and a Government that supported the Allied Powers was installed, with King Peter as Head of State. In April, however, German and Italian forces invaded, forcing the royal family and Government into exile. Resistance to the occupation forces was initially divided between two rival groups. The Yugoslav Army of the Fatherland (Četniks) operated mainly in Serbia and represented the exiled Government, while the National Liberation Army (Partisans), led by the CPY, under Gen. (later Marshal) Tito, recruited supporters from Bosnia, Croatia, Montenegro and Slovenia. Rivalry between the two groups led to civil war, eventually won by the communist Partisans. On 29 November 1943 the Partisans proclaimed their own government in liberated areas. Attempts to reconcile the Tito regime with the exiled Government proved unsuccessful, and King Petar II was deposed in 1944.

After the war ended, elections were held, under communist supervision, for a Provisional Assembly. The Federative People's Republic of Yugoslavia was proclaimed on 29 November 1945, with Tito as Prime Minister. A Soviet-style Constitution, establishing a federation of six republics (Serbia, Montenegro, Croatia, Slovenia, Macedonia, and Bosnia and Herzegovina) and two autonomous provinces (Kosovo—with a substantial Albanian population, but also the location of the seat of the Serbian Orthodox Patriarchate, and Vojvodina—with a large Hungarian population, both within Serbia), was adopted in January 1946.

In 1948 Yugoslavia was expelled from the Soviet-dominated Cominform. The CPY was renamed the League of Communists of Yugoslavia (LCY) in November 1952, by which time it had established exclusive political control. A new Constitution was adopted in January 1953, with Tito becoming President of the Republic. Another Constitution, promulgated in April 1963, changed the country's name to the Socialist Federal Republic of Yugoslavia (SFRY). Links with the USSR were resumed in 1955, but Yugoslavia largely pursued a policy of non-alignment, the first conference of the Non-aligned Movement (see p. 439) being held in the Serbian and federal capital, Belgrade, in 1961.

In July 1971 President Tito introduced a system of collective leadership and regular rotation of personnel between posts, in an attempt to unify the various nationalities. A collective State Presidency, headed by Tito, was established. The two autonomous provinces within Serbia obtained substantially the same powers, with regard to representation at federal level, as the six republics, as a result of which three of the eight members of the rotating collective presidency represented Serbia and its provinces. A new Constitution, introduced in February 1974, granted Tito the presidency for an unlimited term of office, and in May he became Life President of the LCY. Tito died in 1980, and his responsibilities were transferred to the collective State Presidency and to the Presidium of the LCY.

Inter-ethnic tensions, largely suppressed during Tito's period in power, became increasingly evident in various regions of Yugoslavia. The most serious tensions were experienced in Kosovo, where a state of emergency was declared in 1981, following widespread demonstrations by ethnic Albanian nationalists, who supported the province being granted the status of a republic within the SFRY. Tensions were exacerbated in April 1987, when thousands of Serbs and Montenegrins protesting at Kosovo Polje (the site of a famous battle between Serbian forces and Osmanlı—Ottoman Turkish troops in 1389) against alleged harassment by the Albanian majority population clashed violently with the security forces. The perceived failure of the Serbian and federal leadership to curb Albanian nationalism led to the dismissal in September of the First Secretary of the League of Communists of Serbia (LCS—the Serbian branch of the LCY), Ivan Stambolić. His replacement, Slobodan Milošević, had denounced the Serbian leadership's policy on Kosovo (which was regarded as being too sympathetic to the demands of ethnic Albanians) and promised to reverse the emigration of Serbs from the area and halt the activities of Albanian nationalists.

During 1988 and 1989 ethnic unrest increased. Proposals to amend the Serbian Constitution to reduce the level of autonomy of the two provinces were supported by regular demonstrations by Serbs. Demonstrations against the local party leadership were organized by Milošević and his supporters in Vojvodina. In October 1988 protests by some 100,000 demonstrators in Novi Sad, the administrative centre of Vojvodina, forced the resignation of the Presidium of the League of Communists of Vojvodina, which had opposed some of the proposed constitutional amendments. Tension between the respective party leaderships of Kosovo and Serbia increased, and in November, following the resignation of several members of the Kosovo leadership, some 100,000 ethnic Albanians demonstrated in Prishtina (Prishtinë—Priština—the administrative capital of Kosovo) to demand their reinstatement. In Belgrade a further mass rally was staged by Serbs in protest at alleged discrimination against them by the ethnic Albanian population in Kosovo. Public demonstrations in Kosovo were banned in late November. In Montenegro continuing unrest resulted in the resignations of the members of the Montenegrin Presidency and of the republican party leadership in January 1989, and their replacement by leaders more sympathetic to Milošević. In May 1989 Milošević, who had become increasingly associated with the cause of Serbian nationalism, particularly with regard to Kosovo, was elected President of the State Presidency of Serbia.

Meanwhile, in May 1988 an emergency conference of the LCY took place. Radical economic and political reforms, including the separation of the powers of the LCY and the state, and greater democracy within the LCY, were proposed. In January 1989 Ante Marković, a member of the Croatian Presidency, was appointed to head a new Federal Government. In September the Slovenian Assembly voted to adopt radical amendments to the Constitution of Slovenia, affirming its sovereignty and its right to secede from the SFRY. In early December Serbia imposed economic sanctions on Slovenia. In January 1990 the abolition of the LCY's constitutional monopoly of power and the introduction of a multi-party system were formally approved, but a proposal by Slovenia to award greater autonomy to the republican branches of the LCY was defeated. As a result, the Slovenian delegation left the Congress, which was then adjourned. The Congress resumed its work in May, but was not attended by delegations from Croatia, Slovenia or Macedonia, where the local communist parties had effectively seceded from the LCY.

Multi-party elections took place in Slovenia and Croatia in April and May 1990, respectively; in both cases opponents of Serbian nationalism and the regime of Milošević were elected to senior positions. In May, under the system of rotating leadership, Dr Borisav Jović of Serbia replaced Janez Drnovšek of Slovenia as President of the Federal Presidency. Jović promised to uphold Yugoslav territorial integrity and advocated the introduction of a stronger federal constitution. In Serbia a new Constitution, which entered into effect in September, included provisions removing the autonomous status of the provinces of Kosovo (which was officially renamed Kosovo and Metohija, the name the territory had held in 1946–74) and Vojvodina. The Kosovo Provincial Assembly and Government were dissolved by the Serbian authorities. In response, a group of 114 ethnic Albanian deputies to the Assembly attempted to declare Kosovo's independence from Serbia. Unrest continued, and in September a general strike was organized to protest against the mass dismissals of ethnic Albanian officials by the Serbian authorities. Criminal charges were brought against more than 100 members of the Provincial Assembly who attempted to re-establish the body, and several former ministers in the Government of Kosovo were charged with establishing an illegal separatist organization.

During November and December 1990 multi-party elections were held in four republics. In Bosnia and Herzegovina (in which republic no ethnic group represented a majority of the population) and in Macedonia nationalist parties were successful. In Montenegro the League of Communists (subsequently renamed the Democratic Party of Montenegrin Socialists—DPMS) was able to secure the Presidency and a majority of seats in the Skupština Republike Crne Gore (Assembly of the Republic of Montenegro). In Serbia, amid allegations of widespread irregularities, Milošević was re-elected President, overcoming a challenge by Vuk Drašković of the nationalist and anti-communist Serbian Renewal Movement (SRM). In the Narodna skupština Republike Srbije (National Assembly of the Republic of Serbia—as the republican legislature had been renamed) 194 of the 250 seats were won by the Socialist Party of Serbia (SPS—led by Milošević), which had been formed in July 1990 by the LCS and a smaller left-wing faction.

In October 1990 Croatia and Slovenia had proposed the transformation of the Yugoslav federation into a looser confederation, in which constituent republics would have the right to maintain armed forces and enter into diplomatic relations with other states. Serbia and Montenegro, however, advocated a centralized federal system, while Macedonia and Bosnia and Herzegovina supported the concept of a federation of sovereign states. Tension increased in December, when Croatia adopted a new Constitution, giving the republic the right to secede from Yugoslavia, while in Slovenia a majority voted in favour of secession at a referendum. In January 1991 Macedonia declared its sovereignty and right to secede from the SFRY.

In March 1991 mass demonstrations, led by Drašković's SRM, demanding the resignation of Milošević, were violently suppressed by the security forces. Jović resigned as President of the Federal Presidency, following his failure to secure approval from other members of the Presidency for emergency measures; his resignation was withdrawn following an appeal from the Narodna skupština Republike Srbije.

Meanwhile, in February 1991 Slovenia formally initiated its process of 'dissociation' from Yugoslavia, and Croatia asserted the primacy of its Constitution and laws over those of the federation. Later that month the self-proclaimed 'Serb Autonomous Region (SAR) of Krajina' (which subsequently formed part of a self-styled 'Republic of the Serb Krajina'—RSK) declared its separation from Croatia and the intention to unite with Serbia. In Croatia, in May the population voted in favour of independence at a referendum that was largely boycotted by the Serb minority, and armed clashes between Serbs and Croats ensued. Relations between Serbia and Croatia deteriorated further in that month, when Serbian representatives in the Federal Presidency refused to sanction the scheduled transfer of the Presidency to Stipe Mesić of Croatia. On 25 June Slovenia and Croatia declared independence. In response, federal troops (largely Serb-dominated) attacked a number of targets in Slovenia, including Ljubljana airport, resulting in 79 deaths, according to official figures. A cease-fire agreement, mediated by the European Community (EC—now European Union—EU, see p. 255), resulted in Serbia's acceptance of Mesić as President of the Federal Presidency. In early July agreement was reached on the immediate cessation of hostilities and on a three-month suspension in the implementation of dissociation by Croatia and Slovenia. The withdrawal of federal troops from Slovenia (which had a negligible Serb population) began almost immediately, but fighting intensified in Croatia, where federal troops increasingly identified openly with local Serb forces. By September Serb forces controlled almost one-third of Croatia's territory, and successive cease-fire agreements failed to end the conflict. In the same month, at a referendum in Macedonia, voters approved the establishment of an independent republic.

In late September 1991 the UN Security Council adopted Resolution 713, which imposed an armaments embargo on all governments within the territories that had formed part of the SFRY and urged that all hostilities end immediately. However, sporadic fighting continued in Croatia. In October Croatia and Slovenia formally ended their association with Yugoslavia, the moratoriums on independence (agreed in July) having expired. In the same month the Assembly of Bosnia and Herzegovina declared the republic's sovereignty, despite the objections of ethnic Serb deputies. The Federal Prime Minister, Ante Marković, resigned, having been defeated in a vote of no confidence in the bicameral Savezna skupština (Federal Assembly, comprising the directly elected Veće građana—Chamber of Citizens—and the indirectly elected Veće Republika—Chamber of Republics). In December, declaring that Yugoslavia had ceased to exist, Stipe Mesić resigned as President of the Federal Presidency. In January 1992 Slovenia and Croatia were recognized as independent states by the EC; numerous other countries followed. The deployment in Croatia of a UN contingent of 14,000 peacekeeping troops, the UN Protection Force UNPROFOR (agreed by the Federal Presidency in December 1991), commenced in February 1992.

Following the international recognition of the independence of Croatia and Slovenia, Serbia and Montenegro agreed to uphold the Yugoslav state. Macedonia's representative to the Federal Presidency had resigned in January, but EC recognition of Macedonian independence was delayed, owing to opposition from Greece (see the chapter on the former Yugoslav republic of Macedonia). In March Bosnia and Herzegovina declared its independence from the SFRY, the decision having been approved in a referendum that had been largely boycotted by the large ethnic Serb population, some of whom had established several SARs during 1991. Later that month the 'Serb Republic (Republika Srpska) of Bosnia and Herzegovina' (renamed Republika Srpska in August 1992) was proclaimed, and a severe escalation in the Bosnian conflict ensued, as troops from Republika Srpska launched military action against Bosniaks and besieged several cities, including the capital of Bosnia and Herzegovina, Sarajevo.

In April 1992 the Savezna skupština adopted a new Constitution, formally establishing the Federal Republic of Yugoslavia (FRY), which comprised Serbia (including the provinces of Kosovo and Metohija and Vojvodina) and Montenegro, thereby effectively acknowledging the secession of the other four republics. (The Constitution was formally promulgated on 28 September.) In May elections to the Savezna skupština were held, the SPS enjoying considerable success as a result of an opposition boycott. In June Dobrica Ćosić became President of the FRY, and the collective Federal Presidency ceased to exist. In that month an alliance of opposition parties formed the Democratic Movement of Serbia (Depos), led by Drašković.

In May 1992 elections, declared to be illegal by the Serbian authorities, were held in Kosovo to establish a provincial 'Assembly', which described itself as the legislature of the self-proclaimed 'Republic of Kosovo'. In July Milan Panić was elected Federal Prime Minister by the Savezna skupština. At a conference on the former Yugoslavia, which took place in London, United Kingdom, in August 1992, Panić condemned the policy of 'ethnic cleansing', following the discovery of Serb-run concentration camps in Bosnia and Herzegovina, and reiterated the claim that there was no federal military involvement in the republic. In an attempt to force Milošević's removal from office, presidential and legislative elections were scheduled for December. In October Milošević retaliated by using Serbian police forces to seize control of the federal police headquarters in Belgrade, blockading the building for several weeks. In November Panić narrowly survived a second vote of no confidence in the Savezna skupština. The Federal Minister of Foreign Affairs resigned in September, in protest at Panić's policies; in November three more federal ministers resigned.

Presidential and parliamentary elections, at both federal and republican levels, took place on 20 December 1992. Ćosić was re-elected Federal President, with some 85% of the votes cast. Milošević was re-elected President of Serbia, receiving 57.5% of the votes cast, and the SPS secured 47 of the 138 seats in the Veće građana. Panić, who contested the Serbian presidency, winning some 35% of the votes, subsequently demanded that new elections be held, alleging malpractice on the part of the SPS. However, he was removed from the office of Federal Prime Minister on 29 December, after losing a third vote of no confidence. The SPS won 101 seats in the 250-member Narodna skupština Republike Srbije, while the extreme nationalist Serbian Radical Party (SRP) secured 73. In February 1993 a new Federal Government, comprising the SPS and the DPMS, was established, with Radoje Kontić as Federal Prime Minister. In the same month the SPS formed a new Serbian Government, headed by Nikola Šainović. Depos, which had obtained 49 seats in the Narodna skupština, commenced a legislative boycott, claiming that the elections had been fraudulent.

On 1 June 1993 Ćosić (who was accused of conspiring with army generals to overthrow Milošević) was removed from office by a vote of no confidence in the Savezna skupština; the motion had been initiated by deputies of the SPS and the SRP, in what was widely regarded as an attempt by Milošević to consolidate his power. Ćosić's dismissal was followed by a large anti-Government demonstration in Belgrade. In late June the Savezna skupština appointed Zoran Lilić of the SPS, regarded as sympathetic to Milošević, as Federal President, and a reorganization of the Serbian Government followed in July. In August it was announced that the Supreme Defence Council was to assume responsibility for all military and defence duties, and that the republican defence ministries were to be abolished (a measure that was opposed by the Montenegrin Government).

By the second half of 1993 it appeared that the co-operation between Milošević and the SRP had ended; in October an attempt by the SRP to force a parliamentary vote expressing no confidence in the Šainović Government prompted Milošević to dissolve the Narodna skupština Republike Srbije. In response to SRP allegations that the Serbian leadership was betraying national interests by its involvement in attempts to end the conflict in Bosnia and Herzegovina, the party's leader, Dr Vojislav Šešelj, and his associates were accused of involvement in atrocities, and prominent members connected with its paramilitary wing were arrested.

In the elections to the Narodna skupština Republike Srbije, which took place on 19 December 1993, the SPS increased its representation to 123 deputies, winning 36.7% of the votes cast. Depos secured 45 seats, and the SRP took 39. In February 1994 a new Serbian Government was formed, with the support of the six members of the New Democracy (ND) party, which had campaigned in the elections as a member of the Depos coalition. Mirko Marjanović, a pro-Milošević business executive, was appointed Prime Minister, replacing Šainović, who became a Deputy Prime Minister in the Federal Government. In September a new Federal Government, in which Kontić remained Prime Minister, was appointed. The results of the elections in Serbia and the defection of the ND to the Government permitted Milošević to distance himself further from his erstwhile allies in the nationalist opposition, notably the SRP, and to consolidate his political control in the FRY. Šešelj's personal position was further discredited when he was sentenced to a short term of imprisonment in September for assaulting the parliamentary Speaker.

In August 1995, in a military offensive, Croatian troops took control of the RSK, prompting a mass exodus of ethnic Serbs from the region. The Yugoslav leadership protested strongly against the Croatian action, demanding UN intervention and a withdrawal of Croatian troops from the area. However, President Milošević also blamed the leadership of the RSK, criticizing its reluctance to comply with international peace proposals. The Croatian offensive against the RSK resulted in the exodus of some 150,000 Serb refugees to Yugoslavia and Serb-controlled areas of Bosnia and Herzegovina. Many were settled in Vojvodina, prompting protests from ethnic Hungarians in that region.

In early November 1995 peace negotiations were convened in Dayton, Ohio, USA, with the aim of resolving the conflict in the former Yugoslavia. The conference, at which Milošević represented not only Yugoslavia, but also the Bosnian Serbs, resulted in an agreement on the future territorial and constitutional structure of Bosnia and Herzegovina, including the recognition of Republika Srpska as one of two constituent entities within Bosnia and Herzegovina. In response to Yugoslav acceptance of the plan, all UN sanctions against the FRY were suspended in late November. The SRP denounced the Dayton agreement, which was also criticized by the Democratic Party (DP), the Democratic Party of Serbia (DPS—founded in 1992 by former members of the DP) and the increasingly nationalist leadership of the Serbian Orthodox Church. However, the SRM supported the agreement. In late November Milošević dismissed several leading members of the SPS, who were known to be critical of the Dayton accord and supportive of militant factions within Republika Srpska. In June 1996 the Serbian Government was reorganized. All the new ministers appointed were members of the increasingly influential Yugoslav United Left (YUL), led by Milošević's wife, Mirjana Marković.

A number of new coalitions were formed in advance of elections held in late 1996, notably a grouping known as Together (Zajedno), which comprised the SRM, the DP, the DPS and the Civic Alliance of Serbia. The SPS established an alliance with the YUL and the ND, which became known as the United List. On 3 November municipal elections, and elections to the Veće građana and the Skupština Republike Crne Gore were held. At the elections to the Veće građana (which were boycotted by many Kosovo Albanians), the United List secured 64 seats, Together took 22, the DPMS 20 and the SRP 16; of the 138 elected deputies, 108 were from Serbia and 30 from Montenegro. Following a second round of voting in the Serbian municipal elections, provisional results indicated that Together had obtained control of 14 principal towns, including Belgrade. After the SPS challenged the results, however, most of the opposition victories were annulled by (SPS-dominated) municipal courts and electoral commissions, precipitating mass demonstrations.

In December 1996 daily demonstrations (which had developed into general protests against the Milošević Government) continued in Belgrade and other towns. The Serbian Minister of Information resigned in protest at the Government's temporary closure of two independent radio stations, which had reported the demonstrations. Milošević denied government involvement in electoral malpractice and condemned the protests. In late December the demonstrations degenerated into violent clashes with members of the security forces in Belgrade; it was reported that two people had been killed and 58 injured. The Ministry of Internal Affairs subsequently ordered a ban on demonstrations, which the security forces attempted to enforce; nevertheless, anti-Government rallies continued. At the end of December a delegation from the Organization for Security and Co-operation in Europe (OSCE, see p. 366), which had been invited by the Federal Minister of Foreign Affairs to visit Serbia, issued a report upholding the results of the municipal elections that had been invalidated. The international community exerted pressure on Milošević to comply with the OSCE ruling. In early February 1997 the violent suppression of anti-Government demonstrations attracted further international criticism. Shortly afterwards Milošević publicly instructed Marjanović to prepare emergency legislation providing for the official recognition of the results of the municipal elections, in accordance with the OSCE ruling. However, the leader of the DP, Zoran Đinđić, urged his supporters to continue protests until the election results were officially verified, further demanding that the electoral code and legislation governing the media be reformed and that members of the security forces involved in the violence earlier that month be charged. On 11 February the Narodna skupština Republike Srbije voted in favour of reinstating the annulled results (with deputies from the opposition and extreme nationalist parties boycotting the session); Together consequently obtained control of the municipal assemblies in Belgrade and 13 other towns. At the same time seven ministers were replaced in a reorganization of the Serbian Government. Later in February Đinđić was elected Mayor of Belgrade by Together members, who controlled 69 of the 110 seats in the city's municipal council.

In June 1997 it was announced that the SRM had withdrawn from the Together coalition. The SPS nominated Milošević as a candidate for the federal presidency and proposed constitutional amendments for the direct election of the President. Later that month a DPMS committee declared its support for Milošević's candidature (which was, however, strongly opposed by elements within the party, including Milo Đukanović, Prime Minister of Montenegro since 1991), but rejected the proposed amendments. On 25 June Lilić relinquished office; the Speaker of the Veće Republika, Srđan Božović, was to act as interim President, pending an election. In July supporters of Đukanović within the DPMS voted to remove Momir Bulatović, President of Montenegro since 1990 (who continued to demonstrate support for Milošević), from the party leadership. In mid-July Milošević was elected to the federal presidency by the Savezna skupština. Opposition deputies boycotted the vote in the Veće građana, which they subsequently declared to be invalid. On 23 July Milošević formally resigned from the office of President of Serbia and was inaugurated as Federal President.

In September 1997 students demonstrated in Belgrade in support of Đinđić, who, following the dissolution of Together, urged a boycott of the forthcoming Serbian presidential and legislative elections, on the grounds that they would be biased in favour of the incumbent administration. At the elections to the Narodna skupština Republike Srbije, held on 21 September, the United List coalition won 110 seats (failing to secure an outright majority); the SRP increased its representation to 82 seats and the SRM obtained 45 seats. In the concurrent presidential election, Lilić (the candidate of the United List) received 35.7% of the votes cast, while Šešelj, who contested the poll on behalf of the SRP, won 27.3% of the votes and Drašković 20.6%. Some 62% of the electorate participated in the poll. Since none of the candidates had secured the requisite majority of more than one-half of the votes cast, a second round was to take place. In early October SPS and SRP councillors in the Belgrade municipal assembly voted in support of an SRM initiative to remove Đinđić from the office of Mayor of Belgrade. Security forces subsequently suppressed protests in Belgrade by supporters of the DP, who demanded that further legislative and municipal elections be conducted. In the second round of voting in the presidential election on 5 October, Šešelj won 49.1% and Lilić 47.9% of the votes cast. However, owing, in part, to the boycott organized by Đinđić, less than 50% of the electorate participated in the poll, which was consequently declared to be invalid. The Serbian authorities announced that a new presidential election would take place on 7 December.

Following his appointment as a Federal Deputy Prime Minister in November 1997, Lilić withdrew his candidacy to the Serbian presidency. In the Serbian presidential election, which was contested by seven candidates on 7 December, the United List coalition was represented by the Federal Minister of Foreign Affairs, Milan Milutinović, who secured 43.7% of the votes cast; Šešelj received 32.2% of the votes. In the second round, which took place on 21 December, Milutinović won 59.2% of the votes cast, defeating Šešelj. The Serbian Electoral Commission announced that about 50.1% of the electorate had participated in the poll, which was consequently pronounced to be valid. However, Šešelj claimed that the Serbian authorities had perpetrated electoral malpractice, particularly in Kosovo, where ethnic Albanians had again boycotted the polls. OSCE observers reported that severe irregularities had taken place. On 29 December Milutinović was inaugurated as President of Serbia.

In February 1998 Milutinović reappointed Marjanović as Serbian Prime Minister. The SPS formed an alliance with the SRP in March. Marjanović subsequently formed a new coalition Government, comprising 15 representatives of the SRP (including Šešelj, who became a Deputy Prime Minister), 13 representatives of the SPS, and four of the YUL. In May the Savezna skupština adopted a motion expressing no confidence in the Federal Prime Minister, Kontić, which had apparently been initiated by DPMS deputies. Milošević's subsequent nomination of Bulatović to the office was approved by the Savezna skupština, and a new Federal Government was established. Đukanović, however, declared Bulatović's Government to be illegitimate. In June the Montenegrin legislature (in which supporters of Đukanović had obtained a majority in elections the previous month) withdrew the 20 deputies representing the Republic from the Veće Republika and replaced them with members of Đukanović's coalition, to ensure that Milošević would not command the requisite two-thirds' majority for constitutional amendments. (Milošević, however, refused to allow deputies from Đukanović's coalition to assume seats in the Veće Republika.) In August a new Montenegrin Government, headed by Filip Vujanović of the DPMS, announced that it had suspended links with the Federal Government until Bulatović agreed to resign from the office of Prime Minister in favour of a supporter of Đukanović.

During 1998 and early 1999 inter-ethnic hostilities in Kosovo further intensified, frequently resulting in violence, and, following the failure of internationally sponsored negotiations, culminated in the aerial bombardment of military, and subsequently certain civilian, targets in Serbia and Montenegro in March–June 1999 by North Atlantic Treaty Organization (NATO, see p. 351) forces, which sought to defend Kosovo Albanians from the Serbian security forces (see below). In late April Drašković was dismissed as Deputy Prime Minister of the FRY, after he publicly opposed Milošević's refusal to comply with NATO demands.

In May 1999 the International Criminal Tribunal for the former Yugoslavia (ICTY, see p. 19) indicted Milošević, together with Milutinović, Šainović, the former Serbian Minister of the Interior, Vlajko Stojiljković, and the Yugoslav Army Chief of Staff, Gen. (retd) Dragoljub Ojdanić, for crimes against humanity. In June SRP ministers and legislative deputies temporarily suspended participation in the Serbian Government, in protest at Milošević's acceptance of the peace plan for Kosovo, whereby NATO peace-keeping forces were to be deployed in the province (see below). From July a series of demonstrations was conducted by a loose grouping of opposition associations, known as Alliance for Change, in support of Milošević's resignation. In August Milošević reorganized the Federal Government. Also in August the Montenegrin Government presented proposals for the dissolution of the FRY, and its replacement with an 'Association of States of Serbia and Montenegro', and announced that a referendum on independence for the republic would be conducted if Milošević failed to agree to the demands. In September the Alliance for Change initiated a campaign against Milošević; however, Drašković refused to endorse the protests. In January 2000, following inter-party discussions, leaders of the Alliance for Change presented unified demands for elections to be conducted in Serbia by the end of April.

In mid-January 2000 a notorious Serbian paramilitary leader and war crimes suspect, Željko Ražnatović ('Arkan'), was shot and killed in Belgrade. Speculation regarding his killing included the suggestion that, following his indictment by the ICTY in 1997, he had been prepared to implicate Milošević in war crimes. In February 2000 the Federal Minister of Defence, Pavle Bulatović, was also killed. Milošević subsequently appointed Ojdanić to the post. In July the Savezna skupština approved constitutional amendments removing limits on the President's tenure of office, providing for direct election to the presidency and the Veće Republika, and reducing Montenegro's status within the FRY. The amendments attracted immediate criticism from Serbian opposition parties and the international community. The Skupština Republike Crne Gore subsequently voted to reject the amendments, which Vujanović condemned as an attempt by Milošević to retain power. At the end of July Milošević announced that federal presidential and legislative elections were to take place on 24 September. The Montenegrin Government announced that the republic would not participate in the forthcoming elections, in protest at the amendments. In early August an alliance of 18 opposition parties, known as the Democratic Opposition of Serbia (DOS), presented the leader of the DPS, Dr Vojislav Koštunica, as their joint candidate to oppose Milošević in the presidential election.

Numerous allegations of electoral malpractice and intimidation emerged, both prior to and following the elections to the federal presidency and legislature on 24 September 2000. Preliminary results, released by the Federal Election Commission, indicated that Koštunica had won about 48% of the votes cast, compared with the 40% of the votes received by Milošević, and thereby failed to obtain the 50% majority required to secure the presidency. Milošević subsequently insisted that a second round of voting be conducted on 8 October, while Koštunica rejected the results of the Commission, claiming to have won the election outright. The international community declared its support for Koštunica and urged Milošević to accept defeat. The Yugoslav

Army announced that it would not intervene on Milošević's behalf, while the SRP and Serbian parties in Montenegro also acknowledged Koštunica's victory. Opposition supporters commenced a campaign of peaceful protest in Serbia (including a widely observed general strike), in an effort to compel Milošević to resign. On 5 October protesters, who had gathered to stage a mass rally in Belgrade, overpowered security forces and seized control of the parliament building, the state television station and the official news agency, declaring Koštunica to be the elected President. On the following day, amid increasing international pressure, Milošević finally relinquished the presidency. Koštunica was officially inaugurated as President on 7 October. According to the final official results, Koštunica received 51.7% of the votes cast and Milošević 38.2%; in the concurrent legislative elections, the DOS secured 58 seats in the 138-member Veće građana, and the SPS 44. After the DOS negotiated an agreement with the SPS in mid-October, the Narodna skupština Republike Srbije was dissolved, and a transitional Government, in which the SPS retained the premiership, was installed, pending legislative elections, which were brought forward to December. Since only about 30% of the Montenegrin electorate had participated in the voting, as a result of Đukanović's boycott, Koštunica was obliged to form an administration with the Socialist People's Party of Montenegro (SNP, led by Predrag Bulatović—the only Montenegrin party to be represented in the legislature). A member of that party, Zoran Žižić, was nominated to the post of Prime Minister, and a new Federal Government, comprising representatives of the DOS and the SNP, was established in early November. The normalization of relations between the FRY and the international community proceeded rapidly thereafter, and the country was formally admitted to the UN (from which it had been absent since the dissolution of the SFRY) on 1 November. In December Koštunica reorganized the armed forces, removing officers loyal to Milošević.

In the elections to the 250-member Narodna skupština Republike Srbije, held on 23 December 2000, the DOS secured a substantial majority, with 176 seats, while the SPS won 37 seats and the SRP 23. Later that month Đukanović announced proposals that the FRY become a loose union of two separate, internationally recognized states. At the end of December the People's Party of Montenegro, which supported a continued federation, withdrew from the governing coalition. Đukanović subsequently announced that elections to the Skupština Republike Crne Gore would take place in April 2001. In January Đinđić was elected to the Serbian premiership, and a new Government, comprising members of the DOS, was installed later that month.

In early 2001 the Federal Government came under increasing pressure from the EU and USA to arrest Milošević and other war crimes suspects; Koštunica maintained that their extradition would contravene the Constitution. Following a warning by the USA that it would end financial aid to the FRY unless the new administration fully co-operated with the ICTY by the end of March 2001, Milošević was taken into custody on 1 April. The federal Public Prosecutor issued a series of charges against Milošević for abuses of power during his term of office (principally extensive embezzlement from state funds, and involvement in political assassinations, electoral malpractice and organized crime). Later that month Milošević, who was in detention in Belgrade, received the ICTY indictment. At the end of April Serbian courts authorized the extension of Milošević's period of detention for a further two months, despite an appeal that he be released on grounds of ill health. Koštunica, however, refused to comply with international demands that Milošević be dispatched for trial at the ICTY (apparently owing to concern that his extradition might prompt political unrest). Meanwhile, at the elections to the expanded 78-member Skupština Republike Crne Gore, which were conducted on 22 April, the pro-independence alliance, led by the DPMS, won 36 seats. Despite having failed to secure a decisive majority in the legislature, Đukanović announced that he would continue to pursue his aim of organizing a referendum on Montenegrin independence.

In June 2001, following continued international pressure for the authorities to co-operate with the ICTY, the Serbian Government approved a decree, providing for the extradition of Milošević and other indicted war criminals to the ICTY. Supporters of Milošević subsequently staged a large demonstration in Belgrade. The Serbian Government refused to comply with a ruling by the federal Constitutional Court that the decree was invalid, and on 29 June (shortly before an important international donor conference was to take place) Milošević was extradited to the ICTY. On the following day Žižić resigned from the office of Federal Prime Minister, in protest at Milošević's extradition (which had been strongly opposed by the SNP). In July Koštunica appointed Dragiša Pešić, also a member of the SNP and hitherto Federal Minister of Finance, to the post. Later that month a reorganized Federal Government, proposed by Pešić, was approved in the legislature. In August the division between Koštunica and Đinđić resulting from the Serbian Government's decision to extradite Milošević was further exacerbated by the killing in Belgrade of a security agent, who had reportedly been investigating alleged connections of prominent state officials to organized crime. Koštunica accused Đinđić's administration of failing to address widespread crime, and withdrew the DPS ministers from the Government.

In October 2001 the initial indictment against Milošević relating to Kosovo was amended, henceforth alleging that he had organized security-force operations against Kosovo Albanians, which had resulted in the expulsion of 80,000 civilians from the province. Also in October Milošević was further indicted in connection with war crimes perpetrated in Croatia in 1991–92; he was accused of ordering the forcible removal of the majority of the non-Serb population from one-third of the territory of Croatia, with the aim of incorporating the region into a Serb-dominated state. Four former naval officers were indicted for participation in an offensive against Dubrovnik, in Croatia, in late 1991. The former Commander of the Yugoslav Navy, Pavle Strugar, surrendered to the ICTY later in October 2001. (He was sentenced to eight years' imprisonment in January 2005, but was released early owing to ill health in February 2009.) In November Milošević (hitherto indicted for crimes against humanity, breaches of the 1949 Geneva Convention, and violations of the laws or customs of war) was charged with genocide, in connection with the atrocities perpetrated by Serb forces in Bosnia and Herzegovina in 1992–95. He continued to refuse to recognize the authority of the ICTY, and 'not guilty' pleas were submitted on his behalf for all three indictments. The trial of Milošević, who had decided to conduct his own defence, officially commenced on 12 February 2002.

In December 2001 the Speaker of the Narodna skupština Republike Srbije, Dragan Maršićanin, who was the deputy leader of the DPS and a close associate of Koštunica, resigned, having accused parties belonging to the DOS coalition of electoral malpractice. In January 2002 the Federal Minister of Finance also tendered his resignation. In that month the Narodna skupština Republike Srbije voted in favour of partially restoring the autonomous status of Vojvodina. In March one of the Serbian deputy prime ministers, Momčilo Perišić, was arrested, and subsequently resigned, after military intelligence sources claimed to have evidence that he had given classified information to a US diplomat. Đinđić rejected demands by Koštunica that he submit his resignation over the issue, and requested the dismissal of the head of the military security service responsible for Perišić's arrest. Perišić claimed that the charges had been fabricated, in an attempt to cause the dissolution of Đinđić's Government. In June the DPS withdrew from the Narodna skupština Republike Srbije, in protest at the expulsion of 21 DPS deputies. (The party was formally expelled from the ruling DOS coalition in the following month.) The Serbian Government was reorganized in the same month.

Following protracted negotiations on the issue of Montenegro's independence (which were mediated by the EU from November 2001), the government leaders of the FRY and the two republics signed a framework agreement on 14 March 2002, providing for the establishment of a State Union of Serbia and Montenegro. Under the accord, the two republics were to maintain separate economies, but have joint foreign and defence ministries, and elect a new, joint presidency and legislature. Montenegro was to retain the right to refer the issue of independence to a referendum after a period of three years. It was envisaged that, following endorsement of the agreement by the Savezna skupština and the legislatures of the two republics, a new constitution would be adopted, and elections to the new joint parliament would take place later that year. Later in March the Liberal Alliance of Montenegro (LAM) withdrew from Đukanović's coalition (thereby ending its narrow majority in the Skupština Republike Crne Gore), in protest at the agreement, which prompted widespread criticism from pro-independence supporters.

Meanwhile, the USA renewed pressure on the Federal Government to demonstrate co-operation with the ICTY. Following the expiry of a deadline for Yugoslav compliance with these demands, economic aid to the FRY was suspended at the end of

March 2002. In April the Savezna skupština finally approved legislation providing for the extradition of indicted war crimes suspects, and the issue of arrest warrants for those who did not surrender to the ICTY. Shortly afterwards Stojiljković (the former Serbian Minister of the Interior who had been indicted in May 1999) committed suicide. Of 10 former Yugoslav state officials indicted, six (including Ojdanić and Sainović) agreed to surrender to the Tribunal. In early May 2002 Sainović was voluntarily transferred to the ICTY.

In late May 2002 the Savezna skupština officially approved the agreement on the creation of a State Union (which had been ratified by the legislatures of both republics in April). In July Lilić was arrested and extradited to the ICTY, having been subpoenaed as a prosecution witness in the trial of Milošević. He refused to testify unless he was guaranteed immunity from prosecution. It was announced that the presidential election in Serbia would be brought forward to 29 September, to allow the extradition of Milutinović to the ICTY.

At the Serbian presidential election, held on 29 September 2002, Koštunica won some 30.9% of the votes cast, while Miroljub Labus (the incumbent federal Deputy Prime Minister and Minister of Foreign Trade, who was supported by Đinđić) received 27.4% and Sešelj 23.2%; some 55.5% of the registered electorate voted. A second round of voting took place on 13 October between Koštunica and Labus, at which Koštunica secured some 68.4% of the votes cast. However, the election was declared invalid, owing to the participation of only 44.0% of the electorate, lower than the required minimum level of 50%. (Sešelj had urged his supporters not to participate in the poll, and it was reported that Đinđić had also unofficially supported a boycott).

On 6 December 2002 a 27-member commission on constitutional reform, comprising representatives of the principal parties of the two republics, submitted a draft of the new Constitutional Charter for the proposed State Union. A third presidential poll in Serbia on 8 December (in which Koštunica won just 57.7% of the votes) was again annulled, owing to a rate of participation of just 45.0%. On 30 December Milutinović was replaced, on an interim basis, by the President of the Narodna skupština Republike Srbije, Nataša Mićić. (Đukanović's pro-independence coalition, by now known as Democratic List for a European Montenegro, had obtained an overall majority in the republican legislature at elections held in Montenegro in late October, although presidential elections in the republic, held on 22 December were invalidated as a result of an insufficient level of participation by the electorate; a further vote was similarly declared invalid in mid-February 2003.)

In January 2003 Milutinović was voluntarily transferred to the ICTY, where he subsequently pleaded not guilty to charges relating to crimes perpetrated during the 1999 conflict in Kosovo. In February Sešelj surrendered to the ICTY, where he was charged in connection with the forcible removal of the non-Serb population from various regions of Bosnia and Herzegovina, Croatia and Serbia (Vojvodina) in 1991–95. Meanwhile, the new Constitutional Charter, which provided for the creation of the State Union of Serbia and Montenegro, was approved by the Narodna skupština Republike Srbije on 27 January 2003 and by the Skupština Republike Crne Gore on 29 January. On 4 February both chambers of the Savezna skupština approved the Constitutional Charter, thereby officially replacing the FRY with the State Union of Serbia and Montenegro. On 25 February, in accordance with the Charter, the existing federal and republican legislatures elected a 126-member Skupština Srbije i Crne Gore (Assembly of Serbia and Montenegro), comprising 91 Serbian and 35 Montenegrin deputies. On 7 March a former Speaker of the Montenegrin legislature, Svetozar Marović, was elected unopposed as President of Serbia and Montenegro by the Skupština Srbije i Crne Gore. The President was also to chair a five-member Council of Ministers (with portfolios that included foreign affairs, defence, and human and minority rights), which was approved by the Skupština Srbije i Crne Gore on 18 March.

On 12 March 2003 Đinđić, having survived an apparent assassination attempt in February, was shot dead outside government buildings in Belgrade. Mićić immediately imposed a state of emergency in Serbia, and some 1,200 suspects, including a former Serbian Minister of Security, were arrested in connection with the assassination. The DP's nomination of former Federal Minister of Internal Affairs Zoran Živković to replace Đinđić as Serbian Prime Minister was approved by the Narodna skupština Republike Srbije on 18 March. At the end of March security forces discovered the remains of Ivan Stambolić, who had been abducted in August 2000. The Serbian authorities issued an international arrest warrant for Mirjana Marković and her son (who were in hiding in Russia), in connection with the killing of Stambolić; Milošević was subsequently also charged. In mid-April the Skupština Srbije i Crne Gore voted in favour of extending the state's co-operation with the ICTY, ending a stipulation that all war crimes suspects indicted by the Tribunal from that month be tried by domestic courts. Later that month the state of emergency in Serbia was ended and some 45 suspects, including Sešelj, were charged with alleged involvement in the assassination of Đinđić. Two former senior security advisers of Koštunica were also charged with conspiring to overthrow the Government in a coup, which, according to the Serbian authorities, was to have followed Đinđić's killing, with the aim of reinstating an administration opposed to co-operation with the ICTY. In May two former heads of the Serbian security services and close associates of Milošević, already in detention in Belgrade in connection with Đinđić's assassination, were also indicted by the ICTY for war crimes.

In May 2003 Vujanović was elected as President of Montenegro, following the abolition of the requirement that 50% of the electorate participate in polling; he subsequently pledged to hold a referendum on Montenegrin independence within three years. In August the Serbian Government issued arrest warrants for 44 people suspected of involvement in Đinđić's assassination, principally Milorad 'Legija' Luković, the leader of an organized criminal group and a prominent member of a paramilitary unit of Milošević's regime. In September the Serbian Government announced that Milošević would be arraigned at a special court on charges of ordering the killing of Stambolić. In October the ICTY issued indictments against four senior Serbian military and security officials, including the former Chief of General Staff of the Yugoslav Army, Col-Gen. (retd) Nebojsa Pavković (who had been removed from his post by Koštunica in June 2002), for war crimes perpetrated against the civilian population of Kosovo in 1998–99. Serbian leaders, including Živković, condemned the measure, claiming that they had been implicitly assured of indemnity from prosecution.

In November 2003, following long-standing dissension within the DOS, two small parties withdrew from the coalition, thereby ending its parliamentary majority. The DOS subsequently dissolved, and Živković scheduled fresh elections to the Narodna skupština Republike Srbije. Meanwhile, on 16 November a further presidential poll in Serbia (at which the acting leader of the SRP, Tomislav Nikolić, was placed first, securing 47.9% of the votes cast) was declared invalid, owing to a rate of electoral participation of only 38.8%. In December the trial began of 36 suspects charged in connection with Đinđić's assassination (15 of them, including Luković, in absentia). At the elections to the Narodna skupština Republike Srbije, held on 28 December, the SRP, with 28.0% of the votes cast, secured 82 seats, the DPS (18.0%) 53 seats, the DP (12.8%) 37 seats, a newly emerged reformist grouping known as G17 Plus (11.6%) 34 seats, an alliance of the SRM and New Serbia (NS—7.8%) 22 seats, and the SPS (7.7%) 22 seats. Candidates contesting parliamentary seats notably included four indicted war crimes suspects, two of whom (Milošević and Sešelj) were in detention at the ICTY. Following lengthy inter-party discussions, the DPS formed a minority coalition with G17 Plus and the SRM-NS alliance, which was also, to the concern of the international community, reliant on the support of the SPS. On 4 February 2004 the DPS Vice-President, Maršićanin, was elected President of the Narodna skupština Republike Srbije (from which position he had resigned in December 2001), thereby replacing Mićić as the Republic's acting President. In that month the Narodna skupština voted to abolish the minimum rate of participation for elections to the republican presidency, as a means of ending the protracted political impasse. A new Council of Ministers, headed by Koštunica, was formed in March; owing to Maršićanin's inclusion in the administration as Minister of the Economy, he was replaced as President of the Narodna skupština Republike Srbije (and therefore acting President of Serbia) by the hitherto deputy speaker, Predrag Marković. In mid-April the Skupština Srbije i Crne Gore approved a reorganization of the State Union's Council of Ministers; Drašković received the foreign affairs portfolio, Prvoslav Davinić of G17 Plus replaced Boris Tadić as Minister of Defence, and Predrag Ivanović of the DPMS became Minister of Foreign Economic Relations. The principal suspect in the assassination of Đinđić, Luković, surrendered to the Serbian authorities in early May, subsequently denying all charges.

Some 15 candidates contested the elections to the presidency of Serbia, held on 13 June 2004. Nikolić secured 30.1% of the votes cast, and Tadić, the candidate (and leader) of the DP, won 27.7% of the votes. Bogoljub Karić, who was considered to be one of the most wealthy businessmen in Serbia, won 18.5% of the votes, and Maršićanin (having resigned his ministerial post, and contesting the election for a coalition of parties led by the DPS) 13.5%. Nikolić's narrow victory in the first round was attributed to the failure of the reformist parties to agree on a common candidate. A second round between Nikolić and Tadić was conducted on 27 June; Tadić, who benefited from the transferred support of the governing coalition parties, was elected to the presidency, receiving 54.0% of the votes. At his inauguration on 17 July, Tadić pledged commitment to the continuation of economic reforms and for the eventual integration of Serbia into the EU.

In December 2004 a former Yugoslav Army officer, Gen. (retd) Dragoljub Milošević, surrendered to the Serbian authorities and was extradited to the ICTY, where he was charged with crimes relating to the blockade and bombardment of Sarajevo in 1994. In January 2005, however, the USA expressed dissatisfaction with the failure of Serbia and Montenegro to co-operate with the ICTY, and announced a reduction in financial aid and the withdrawal of US technical advisers from Serbian ministries. Representatives of the international community repeatedly accused the Serbian authorities of aiding the continuing evasion from the Tribunal of former Bosnian Serb military commander Gen. (retd) Ratko Mladić (who had originally been indicted in 1995 on a number of counts, including two of genocide), and cited his extradition as essential for Serbia and Montenegro's accession to NATO's 'Partnership for Peace' (PfP, see p. 353) programme. In February 2005 one of those indicted, a former military commander in Prishtina, Gen. (retd) Vladimir Lazarević, agreed to surrender to the ICTY after meeting with Koštunica, and was subsequently extradited.

Amid increasing concern over the future of the State Union, in February 2005 Koštunica and Đukanović met for discussions on the scheduling of elections to the Skupština Srbije i Crne Gore. On 7 April, following mediation by the EU High Representative for Common Foreign and Security Policy, Javier Solana Madriaga, the Presidents agreed that the election of representatives to the Skupština Srbije i Crne Gore would take place concurrently with elections to the two republican legislatures; the Constitutional Charter was to be amended to allow the extension of the mandates of the incumbent deputies. The Montenegrin Government favoured the organization of a referendum on independence prior to elections, while supporters of the continuation of the State Union insisted that such a measure would require adherence to EU conditions and arbitration. Solana welcomed the agreement and commended Serbia's improved co-operation with the ICTY (following the transfer, between late 2004 and mid-2005, of 13 Serbian and Bosnian Serb war crime suspects, in surrenders reportedly mediated by the Koštunica Government, including that of Pavković in April 2005). Shortly afterwards the European Commission indicated that sufficient progress had been made for Serbia and Montenegro to commence negotiations on a Stabilization and Association Agreement (SAA) with the EU.

At the end of June 2005 the head of Milošević's secret service, Radomir Marković, together with Milorad Luković and three other former paramilitary members, were sentenced to terms of imprisonment for involvement in an assassination attempt against Drašković in 1999. In July 2005 Luković was sentenced to 40 years' and Marković to 15 years' imprisonment for the killing of Stambolić in August 2000; six former secret service officers also received custodial terms. In September 2005 a further international arrest warrant was issued for Mirjana Marković, who had failed to fulfil pledges to return from exile in Russia. On 10 October negotiations on the SAA officially commenced between the Government of Serbia and Montenegro and the EU. In early October five members of a former Serb paramilitary unit were charged in Serbia with the killing of six Muslims at Srebrenica, Bosnia and Herzegovina, following the release of video evidence of the killings; their trial commenced in December. Also in December some 14 members of a former Serb militia were sentenced by a Serbian court to terms of between five and 20 years for killing 200 Croat prisoners near the Croatian town of Vukovar in November 1991.

On 27 February 2006 a case submitted by Bosnia and Herzegovina against Serbia in 1993, demanding reparations for the alleged genocide of the Bosnian Muslim population in 1992–95, finally commenced at the International Court of Justice (ICJ, see p. 22) at The Hague, Netherlands. At the end of February 2006 the Montenegrin Government and opposition agreed that the planned referendum on Montenegrin's secession from the State Union would take place on 21 May.

On 11 March 2006 Milošević (whose trial had repeatedly been adjourned on grounds of ill health) died while in custody at the ICTY. Preliminary autopsy results concluded that the cause of death was a heart attack, but supporters of Milošević immediately criticized the medical treatment that he had received in detention and the Tribunal's refusal in late February to grant a request for his transfer to hospital in Russia. (It emerged that shortly before his death Milošević had written to the Russian Minister of Foreign Affairs, claiming that he was being poisoned in detention.) The Serbian authorities refused to organize a state funeral, and members of Milošević's family, including Mirjana Marković (despite the temporary suspension of the international arrest warrant against her), failed to attend the ceremony, which took place at his family residence in the Serbian town of Pozarevac; although there were scenes of public mourning, former nationalist supporters at the funeral were reported to number only a few hundred. In April an independent investigation by Dutch pathologists confirmed that Milošević's death was the result of a heart attack.

In early 2006 the Serbian authorities came under increasing pressure from the EU to effect Mladić's extradition to the ICTY. In March the ICTY Prosecutor, Carla Del Ponte, visited Belgrade, with the aim of securing assurances that Mladić would be apprehended, and the EU issued an ultimatum that failure to arrest Mladić by 5 April would result in the suspension of the negotiations on the SAA. Discussions continued during that month, but were, however, suspended, after the Serbian Government failed to meet a further deadline, of 30 April, for Mladić's extradition. In early May Labus resigned from the post of Deputy Prime Minister of Serbia in protest at the failure of the authorities to apprehend Mladić. Labus subsequently resigned from the leadership of G17 Plus, after the party refused to withdraw other representatives from the Government. Ivana Dulić-Marković (hitherto Minister of Agriculture) was appointed Deputy Prime Minister in June.

At the referendum held in Montenegro on 21 May 2006, some 55.5% of votes were cast in favour of independence, narrowly exceeding the minimum requirement of 55% stipulated by the EU. Following Montenegro's subsequent declaration of independence on 3 June, the Narodna skupština Republike Srbije officially declared Serbia to be the successor state to the State Union of Serbia and Montenegro on 5 June. The Serbian Government announced that the central administration and other organs of the former State Union had ceased to exist. (Drašković and the hitherto Minister of Defence of Serbia and Montenegro, Zoran Stanković, retained their portfolios in an acting capacity, becoming ministers of the Republic of Serbia, without being officially appointed to its Government.) In mid-June the Serbian Government adopted a decision recognizing Montenegro's independence, and the Ministers of Foreign Affairs of the two countries signed a protocol on the establishment of diplomatic relations on 22 June. At the end of that month Tadić became the first Head of State to make an official visit to independent Montenegro.

In July 2006 the trial of six senior Serbian officials who had served under Milošević began at the ICTY: Milutinović, Šainović, Ojdanić, Pavković, Lazarević, and Gen. (retd) Sreten Lukić (the former head of police in Kosovo) were charged with crimes relating to human rights violations committed against ethnic Albanians in Kosovo during 1998–99. On 30 September 2006 the Narodna skupština Republike Srbije adopted a new draft Constitution by a unanimous vote (with 242 deputies attending). The new Constitution, which included increased provisions for the guarantee of human and minority rights, and notably referred to Kosovo and Metohija as an integral part of the Republic of Serbia, was approved by 53.0% of votes cast at a national referendum on 29 October and entered into effect on 8 November. At the end of November NATO invited Serbia (together with Bosnia and Herzegovina and Montenegro) to join the PfP programme; Del Ponte strongly criticized Serbia's admission to the programme (which officially took place on 14 December), in view of the authorities' continued failure to extradite Mladić to the ICTY. In early December Šešelj (who had refused to attend the opening of his trial at the ICTY in November) ended a four-week hunger strike, after an appeals chamber at the Tribunal restored his right to defend himself. Also in December an SPS congress elected a former presidential candidate, Ivica Dačić, to replace Milošević as party leader. Two ethnic Albanian parties from the Preševo region established an alliance to contest the legislative elections, ending a boycott after the new Constitution no longer required minority parties to secure a minimum of 5% of the votes in order to obtain parliamentary representation.

At the elections to the Narodna skupština Republike Srbije, contested by 20 political parties and alliances on 21 January 2007, the SRP, with 29.1% of votes cast, obtained the largest number of seats (81), while the DP secured 23.1% of the votes (64 seats), and an alliance led by the DPS 16.8% of the votes (47 seats). The representation of G17 Plus, which received 6.9% of votes cast, declined to 19 seats, and that of the SPS, with 5.7% of the votes, to 16 seats, while a new reformist alliance led by the Liberal Democratic Party won 5.4% of the votes and 15 seats. (The SRM, having undergone internal dissension, failed to secure any parliamentary representation.) After smaller parliamentary parties declared reluctance to enter into a minority administration with the SRP, Tadić engaged in consultations with party leaders regarding the establishment of a new coalition government. EU officials urged the establishment of a new administration in favour of democratic reforms, indicating that this would allow negotiations on an SAA to proceed (thereby abandoning the previous stipulation for the prior extradition of Mladić). However, the expected formation of a coalition between the DP and DPS was impeded by ideological differences between the two parties, compounded by resistance to a UN proposal for supervised independence for Kosovo (see below). It was reported that Koštunica insisted on remaining as Prime Minister, while Tadić favoured the nomination of Božidar Đelić to the office. Under the terms of the Constitution, following the inauguration of the Narodna skupština on 14 February, failure to form a new government by mid-May would require further elections to be held.

On 26 February 2007 the ICJ issued a decision on the case submitted by Bosnia and Herzegovina against Serbia, claiming reparations for the genocide of Bosnian Muslims in 1992–95. The ICJ ruled that the Serbian state was not directly responsible for genocide or complicity in genocide in Bosnia and Herzegovina in 1992–95; however, the Court declared that Serbia was in violation of its obligation under international law by having failed to prevent the 1995 massacre of more than 7,000 Bosnian Muslims in the east Bosnian town of Srebrenica and to act against its perpetrators. In April four members of a Serb paramilitary unit were sentenced to terms of imprisonment by a Belgrade court for the killing of six Muslims in south-eastern Bosnia and Herzegovina in 1995, after the emergence of video footage of the executions (which had been broadcast on Serbian television in 2005, prompting national outrage).

On 8 May 2007 Nikolić was elected President of the Narodna skupština Republike Srbije, after Koštunica instructed DPS deputies to support his nomination. However, Nikolić's appointment prompted international consternation (which coincided with Serbia's assumption of the rotational chairmanship of the Council of Europe), and EU officials offered Serbia strong incentives to form a pro-democracy Government. On 11 May Tadić announced that a coalition agreement had been reached between the DP, the DPS and New Serbia alliance, and G17 Plus, and that he had nominated Koštunica for a second term as Prime Minister. On 13 May Nikolić tendered his resignation from his new post. On 15 May, shortly before the expiry of the constitutional deadline, a coalition Government was approved by 133 votes in the Narodna skupština Republike Srbije; notably, the Government included the new position of a Minister of Kosovo and Metohija.

On 7 June 2007 the President of the European Commission invited Serbia to resume negotiations on an SAA, citing improved co-operation with the ICTY, following the arrest in Republika Srpska of a former Bosnian Serb army officer, Zdravko Tolimir, believed to be a close associate of Mladić and to be assisting his evasion of capture. Negotiations officially recommenced on 13 June; the EU (at the particular insistence of the Netherlands and Belgium) emphasized that conclusion of the Agreement continued to be conditional on full co-operation with the ICTY, resulting in the arrest and transfer of all ICTY indictees, including Mladić.

In early December 2007 several laws, including legislation on the election of the President in accordance with the new Constitution, were adopted in the Narodna skupština Republike Srbije, allowing a pre-term presidential election to be scheduled for early 2008. At the first round of the election, which was contested by nine candidates on 20 January, Nikolić won about 40.0% of the votes cast and Tadić 35.4%. Later that month, in the absence of a finalized SAA, EU foreign ministers offered Serbia an interim political agreement, which provided for increased co-operation in trade and education, and relaxed visa requirements for Serbian nationals. Koštunica failed to transfer support to Tadić in the second round of the presidential election, after Tadić rejected his demand to pledge not to sign an SAA with the EU if the EU deployed a mission in Kosovo without UN authorization. Nevertheless, at the second round, which was conducted on 3 February, Tadić was re-elected to the presidency, narrowly defeating Nikolić with about 50.3% of the votes cast, according to official figures. The rate of participation by the electorate was estimated at some 67%. EU officials welcomed the election results, which were widely viewed as an endorsement of Tadić's policy of favouring rapid EU integration. Tadić was inaugurated on 15 February. However, the ideological division between Tadić and Koštunica continued to impede effective governance; in early February Koštunica rejected the proposed political agreement with the EU (which had been supported by Tadić), owing to his strenuous opposition to the EU's decision to establish EULEX Kosovo, a police and justice mission for Kosovo.

Kosovo's declaration of independence on 17 February 2008, which was rapidly recognized by a number of EU nations (see below), presented a further obstacle to prospects for EU integration, since the United Kingdom, France and Germany (principal supporters of Kosovo's independence) indicated that Serbia would be required to relinquish its territorial claim on Kosovo for accession. In early March Koštunica declared support for a draft resolution, proposed in the Narodna skupština Republike Srbije by the SRP, which made further progress towards EU accession conditional on the rejection of Kosovo's independence by the Union. However, on 8 March Koštunica resigned from the premiership, citing irreconcilable differences within the ruling coalition over Kosovo and EU integration. On 13 March Tadić dissolved the Narodna skupština, at the request of the Government, and scheduled legislative elections for 11 May (when local elections and elections to the Vojvodina Assembly were also due to be conducted). In April EU foreign ministers reached a decision to sign the SAA with Serbia, an offer that was widely perceived as an effort to strengthen popular support for reformist parties contesting the forthcoming elections and to prevent nationalist groups from gaining ascendancy. On 29 April the EU signed the SAA, together with a provisional document whereby Serbia would be granted access to benefits based on the SAA before all EU members had ratified the Agreement; however, its implementation was to be suspended until EU member states agreed unanimously on Serbia's full co-operation with the ICTY. Koštunica had continued to oppose signature of the SAA, maintaining that it implied Serbian acquiescence to the recognition of Kosovo by most EU member states.

At the legislative elections on 11 May 2008, an electoral coalition of parties supporting EU integration promoted by Tadić, known as For a European Serbia—Boris Tadić, won 38.4% of the votes cast, according to official results, increasing the DP and its allied parties' strength in the Narodna skupština Republike Srbije to 102 seats. The SRP secured 29.4% of the votes and 78 seats, and the alliance between the DPS and New Serbia 11.6% of votes and 30 seats; a coalition comprising the SPS, the Party of United Pensioners of Serbia and United Serbia increased its joint representation in the chamber to 20 seats, with 7.6% of the votes cast. The participation rate (including Serbs voting in Kosovo) was recorded at 60.1%. (Following a number of complaints submitted by the SRP, voting was repeated in three constituencies on 18 May, owing to irregularities.) At the concurrent poll in Vojvodina on 11 May (which was followed by a second round on 25 May), For a European Vojvodina secured 64 seats and the SRP 24 seats in the 120-member Assembly. Neighbouring states, the EU and the USA welcomed the election results (which had followed predictions of success for the SRP) and urged the rapid formation of a new administration. On 23 June, following lengthy discussions, SPS leader Dačić announced that the party's council had overwhelmingly decided to enter into a coalition agreement with For a European Serbia—Boris Tadić. On 7 July a new Government, comprising representatives of For a European Serbia—Boris Tadić and the SPS-led alliance, narrowly secured approval in the Narodna skupština Republike Srbije. A former Minister of Finance, Mirko Cvetković (a member of Tadić's DP), became Prime Minister, while Dačić became First Deputy Prime Minister and Minister of Internal Affairs. Later that month the new Minister of Foreign Affairs, Vuk Jeremić, announced that ambassadors that had been recalled from EU states that had recognized Kosovo would be allowed to return to their posts. On 21 July Tadić released a statement announcing that the former Bosnian Serb leader Radovan Karadžić, the most senior war crimes suspect indicted by the ICTY, had been located and apprehended in an operation by Serbian security officers. The unexpected arrest of Karadžić (who was transferred to the War Crimes Panel of the Belgrade District Court and subsequently extradited to the ICTY) was strongly welcomed by the international community.

In September 2008 the Narodna skupština Republike Srbije ratified the SAA; its implementation remained conditional on full co-operation with the ICTY, specifically the arrest of Mladić and the other remaining major war crimes suspect, Croatian Serb Goran Hadžić ('President' of the RSK in 1992–94), who had been indicted by the ICTY in 2004. Nikolić, who had accepted ratification of the SAA, was obliged to resign from the post of acting leader of the SRP, owing to opposition to the Agreement from Šešelj, who was supported by more traditionalist elements of the party; it was reported that Nikolić had formed a breakaway faction. In October 2008 the trial began at the ICTY of Momčilo Perišić, the Chief of the General Staff of the Yugoslav Army in 1993–98, who had surrendered to the Tribunal in March 2005 after being indicted on 13 counts relating to crimes committed in Sarajevo, Zagreb and Srebrenica in 1993–95. The trial of six senior Serbian officials, which had begun in July 2006, was concluded in February 2009. Sainović, Pavković and Lukić were each sentenced to 22 years' imprisonment, while Lazarević and Ojdanić each received a term of 15 years, on five counts relating to the killing and forced deportation of Kosovo Albanian civilians; Milutinović was acquitted (on the grounds that he had not been directly responsible for the command of forces). In the same month the ongoing trial of Šešelj was suspended, owing to prosecution claims of witness intimidation. Meanwhile, at the end of January Serbia began to implement unilaterally an interim trade agreement with the EU, which had been signed as part of the SAA but remained officially suspended. Of the EU member states, the Netherlands had vetoed implementation of the trade agreement, continuing to insist on the arrest of Mladić as a precondition. In May the ICTY Chief Prosecutor announced that Serbia had made considerable progress in procedural co-operation with the Tribunal.

In early 1996 an ethnic Albanian paramilitary movement, the Kosovo Liberation Army (KLA), emerged and began to launch attacks against Serbian special forces operating in the province. In early 1998 the USA and EU issued statements condemning the violent measures taken by the Serbian security forces in Kosovo to suppress the activities of the KLA, while also criticizing the violence employed by the movement, which had announced its intention to achieve independence for the province through armed resistance. The US Government announced that it was to withdraw the concessions that it had granted to the FRY in February, and threatened possible military intervention in Kosovo. The 'Contact Group', comprising the United Kingdom, France, Germany, Italy, Russia and the USA, which had been established in response to the conflict in Bosnia and Herzegovina, was convened in London; member nations envisaged the imposition of further sanctions against the FRY, including an embargo on armaments, unless the Serbian authorities acceded to a number of demands, including the withdrawal of security forces from Kosovo and the initiation of negotiations regarding the future status of the province. The British Government subsequently submitted a draft resolution to the UN Security Council for the imposition of an embargo on armaments against the FRY. Following a further meeting of the Contact Group, which took place in Bonn, Germany, later in March 1998, a statement was issued demanding that the Serbian authorities engage in negotiations regarding the future status of Kosovo. At the end of March the UN Security Council officially imposed an embargo on armaments against the FRY; of the member nations of the Council, only the People's Republic of China failed to endorse the resolution. The members of the Contact Group (apart from Russia) announced in April that Yugoslav assets abroad were to be 'frozen' and in May imposed a ban on foreign investment in Serbia.

In July 1998 Milošević agreed that diplomatic observers from the EU, the USA and Russia would be allowed access to all regions of Kosovo to report on the activities of Serbian security forces. The Contact Group, which met in Bonn to discuss a peace settlement for Kosovo, recognized for the first time that it would be necessary to include KLA representatives in future negotiations on the province. Meanwhile, Serbian security forces continued to initiate attacks against the KLA. Violence in the province continued during August, with further Serbian offensives against the KLA and killings of ethnic Albanian civilians.

In September 1998 the UN Security Council adopted Resolution 1199 (with the People's Republic of China abstaining), which demanded the immediate cessation of hostilities in Kosovo, the withdrawal of Serbian forces from the province, unrestricted access for humanitarian aid organizations, and the continuation of negotiations to determine the status of the province. NATO subsequently authorized its Supreme Allied Commander, Gen. Wesley Clark, to request member states to provide forces for possible military intervention. Despite an announcement by Serbian Prime Minister Marjanović at the end of September that hostilities against the KLA had been suspended, intensive fighting south of Prishtina (Prishtinë—Priština) was reported. NATO officially approved air bombardments against the FRY, and issued an ultimatum to Milošević that attacks would commence unless he complied with UN demands by a stipulated date later that month. (Russia continued to oppose military intervention against the FRY and had indicated that it would veto a further Security Council resolution authorizing such action.) Following intensive discussions with the US special envoy, Richard Holbrooke, Milošević agreed to the presence in Kosovo of a 2,000-member Organization for Security and Co-operation in Europe (OSCE) 'verification force' (to be known as the Kosovo Diplomatic Observer Mission), and to NATO surveillance flights in FRY airspace, to monitor the implementation of the Security Council's demands. Serbian leaders in Kosovo criticized Milošević's acceptance of the peace settlement, while the KLA considered the deployment of the OSCE monitors to be inadequate and continued to urge NATO military intervention. It was subsequently reported that the majority of federal army units had been withdrawn from Kosovo, but that some 11,600 members of the special Serbian security forces remained in the province. NATO urged further progress in the withdrawal of Serbian forces from Kosovo, but at the end of October suspended indefinitely the implementation of military action against the FRY.

In November 1998 the deployment of OSCE observers in Kosovo commenced; however, intermittent violations of the cease-fire were reported. Following the outbreak of heavy fighting between the KLA and Serbian forces in northern Kosovo in December, it became evident that the OSCE monitoring force was inadequate (and had no mandate) for peace-keeping operations. A 2,300-member NATO 'extraction force' was deployed in the former Yugoslav republic of Macedonia (FYRM), near the border with Kosovo, to effect the evacuation of the OSCE monitors in the event of attacks against them. In early January 1999 further clashes between Serbian and KLA forces were reported. In mid-January the discovery that some 45 ethnic Albanian civilians had been killed at the village of Reçak (Račak) prompted international condemnation of the Serbian authorities. OSCE observers dismissed claims by the Federal Government that those killed had been members of the KLA. At the end of January the 'Contact Group', meeting in London, decided that a peace conference should be convened at the French town of Rambouillet in early February. The British Secretary of State for Foreign and Commonwealth Affairs, Robin Cook, visited Belgrade to present the demands of the Contact Group (which he chaired) that Serbian, DAK and KLA leaders attend the negotiations on a draft peace agreement. Following international pressure, the KLA agreed to attend the conference, while in early February the Serbian legislature approved participation.

In early February 1999 the peace conference was convened in Rambouillet, as scheduled. Under the Contact Group's proposed peace plan, the Serbian authorities would be required to withdraw most of the 14,000 armed and security forces from Kosovo, while the KLA would be required to disarm within a period of three months. It was envisaged that NATO troops would be deployed in Kosovo to enforce the peace agreement. Negotiations at Rambouillet were extended, owing to the opposition of the Serbian delegation to the proposed deployment of the NATO force, and to the reluctance of elements of the KLA to accept the provisions in the agreement for disarmament. At the end of February, however, the ethnic Albanian delegation, including the KLA representatives, agreed, in principle, to accept the peace plan. Meanwhile, in early March it was reported that Serbian troops had forced several thousand ethnic Albanian civilians to flee from southern Kosovo, amid continued heavy fighting in the province. The peace conference was reconvened at Rambouillet in mid-March. The ethnic Albanian representatives signed the agreement; however, the Serbian delegation continued to present objections and proposed amendments to the peace plan, which were rejected by the Contact Group. It was subsequently reported that the Federal Government had deployed a further 30,000 Serbian forces in, or near, Kosovo. NATO reiterated threats of imminent air bombardments, despite continued opposition from the Russian Government, which attempted unsuccessfully to persuade Milošević to accept the peace plan. In the absence of a negotiated settlement to the conflict, the NATO Secretary-General ordered the commencement of air attacks against the FRY, in a campaign, codenamed Operation Allied Force, which was designed to force Milošević's capitulation to the demands of the Contact Group.

On 24 March 1999 NATO forces commenced an aerial bombardment of air defences and military installations across Serbia and Montenegro, notably in Belgrade, Novi Sad, Prishtina and Podgorica. The Federal Government declared a state of war (which, however, the Montenegrin administration refused to recognize), suspended diplomatic relations with the USA, France, Germany and the United Kingdom (the countries directly involved in the attacks), and ordered foreign journalists to leave the country. The People's Republic of China and Russia immediately condemned the air offensive (which NATO justified on humanitarian grounds, despite the lack of endorsement by a UN Security Council resolution). Serbian security forces in Kosovo subsequently intensified the campaign of mass expulsions and large-scale massacres of the ethnic Albanian civilian population, precipitating a continued exodus of refugees from the province. By early April some 140,000 ethnic Albanians had fled to the FYRM, 300,000 to Albania, and 32,000 to Montenegro. Some 12,000 NATO troops were stationed at the FYRM border with Kosovo, after the reinforcement of the extraction force.

During April 1999 the NATO air offensive intensified, with the extension of targets to include those of political and economic significance, including the Serbian state television station. The increasing number of civilian casualties was condemned by opponents of the air offensive; notably, NATO aircraft bombarded a convoy of ethnic Albanian refugees in Kosovo in mid-April, killing about 64, apparently owing to confusion over Serbian military targets. The Russian special envoy to the Balkans (and former premier), Viktor Chernomyrdin, became engaged in intensive mediation efforts with the Federal Government, while urging a suspension of the NATO air offensive. NATO, however, continued to demand the full withdrawal of Serbian forces from Kosovo, and the return of refugees with an international military presence, as a precondition to the suspension of air attacks. In early May the Group of Eight (G8—comprising seven Western industrialized nations and Russia), meeting in Bonn, agreed on general principles for a political solution to the conflict (which was referred to the UN Security Council), although differences over the composition of the international military force for Kosovo remained. Shortly afterwards, apparently owing to faulty military information, NATO forces bombarded the embassy of the People's Republic of China in Belgrade. Violent anti-NATO protests ensued in the Chinese capital, Beijing, and the Chinese Government, supported by Russia, demanded a cessation of the air offensive as a precondition to the discussion of the settlement at the UN Security Council. The Federal Government protested to the ICJ that the NATO air offensive was an illegal act of aggression, on the grounds that it had not received UN authorization. (The ICJ subsequently rejected the legal appeal.) At mid-May it was estimated that the NATO air campaign had resulted in the deaths of 1,200 civilians; about 600,000 ethnic Albanian refugees from Kosovo had fled to neighbouring countries.

In early 1999 the Federal Government announced that it had accepted the G8 principles for a solution to the conflict. On 3 June, following mediation by the President of Finland, Martti Ahtisaari, the Narodna skupština Republike Srbije formally approved a peace plan presented to the Federal Government by EU and Russian envoys. The peace agreement provided for the withdrawal of Serbian forces from Kosovo, and the deployment of a joint NATO-Russian peace-keeping force of about 50,000 personnel. Ethnic Albanian refugees were to be allowed to return to Kosovo, and the province was to be granted some autonomy under an interim administration. On 9 June, following discussions between NATO and Yugoslav military commanders in the FYRM, a Military Technical Agreement, providing for the complete withdrawal of Serbian forces within 11 days, was signed. On the following day the UN Security Council adopted Resolution 1244 (with the People's Republic of China abstaining) approving the peace plan for Kosovo, and NATO announced the suspension of the air offensive, after it had been verified that the withdrawal of Serbian forces had commenced. NATO formally approved the establishment of a Kosovo Force (KFOR), and divided the province into five sectors (which were to be under the respective control of the United Kingdom, Germany, France, the USA and Italy). Shortly before NATO troops commenced deployment in Kosovo, however, about 200 Russian forces unexpectedly entered the province, and assumed control of the airport at Prishtina. Following discussions between the US Secretary of Defense, William Cohen, and his Russian counterpart, Igor Sergeyev, an agreement was reached whereby a Russian contingent, numbering about 3,600, would participate in KFOR (without controlling a separate sector as the Russian Government had previously demanded). Under the terms of the UN Resolution, the UN Interim Administration Mission in Kosovo (UNMIK, see p. 83) was established as the supreme legal and executive authority in Kosovo, with responsibility for civil administration, and for facilitating the reconstruction of the province as an autonomous region. A 3,100-member international police unit (which constituted part of UNMIK) was to supervise the creation of a new security force in Kosovo. The OSCE was allocated primary responsibility for installing democratic institutions, organizing elections in 2000 and monitoring human rights in the province. On 20 June 1999 NATO announced that the air campaign had officially ended, following the completion of the withdrawal of Serbian forces from Kosovo. The KLA subsequently signed an agreement with NATO, whereby the paramilitary organization was to disarm within a period of 90 days. On 24 June the Narodna skupština Republike Srbije formally ended the state of war in Serbia. Meanwhile, following the deployment of KFOR troops, nearly one-half of the ethnic Albanian refugees in neighbouring countries had returned to Kosovo by the end of the month, while an estimated 70,000 Serbian civilians had fled from the province, after reprisal attacks from KLA forces and members of the returning Albanian community. Investigators from the ICTY discovered increasing forensic evidence of large-scale massacres perpetrated by the Serbian forces against ethnic Albanian civilians during the conflict. Under a programme to establish partial provisional self-government in the province, elections to a Kosovo Assembly (Kuvendi i Kosovës/Skupština Kosova) were conducted in 2001 (see the chapter on Kosovo).

After the European Commission released a favourable report on Serbia and Montenegro in early April 2005, the resolution of Kosovo's future status became an increasingly pressing issue. The European Commission pledged to continue support for the eventual integration of Kosovo into European institutions, provided that the Kosovo Government demonstrated progress in meeting UN-endorsed standards of reform and democratic principles in eight areas. The process towards an agreement on a future status for Kosovo was expected to be problematic, since the authorities of Serbia and Montenegro strongly favoured conditions of increased autonomy, but less than total independence, while the Kosovo Albanian population insisted on unconditional independence; any final settlement was also to exclude any partition or border changes. In early June UN Secretary-General Kofi Annan appointed the Norwegian ambassador to NATO, Kai Eide, as the special envoy responsible for assessing standards in Kosovo, who was to undertake a comprehensive review of the provincial Government's commitment to democracy, good governance and human rights. A positive review would allow negotiations on the final status of the province to proceed; following their conclusion, a draft settlement would, together with a draft constitution prepared by the Kosovo Assembly, be submitted for endorsement by a UN-sponsored international conference. Later that month Eide conducted further discussions with leading members of the Serbian Government, including Tadić, to urge Serb participation in Kosovo's provisional institutions of government.

In September 2005 delegations from the Governments of Serbia and Kosovo met in Vienna, Austria, for preliminary discussions on decentralization and other technical issues. On 4 October Eide officially submitted the review on Kosovo to Annan; the report stated that the Government of Kosovo had made significant progress in establishing executive, legislative and judicial institutions, although efforts to maintain the rule of law and reduce the incidence of inter-ethnic attacks, violence and organized crime remained limited. On 24 October the UN Security Council endorsed the initiation of final status negotiations on Kosovo. In November the Serbian Government adopted a unanimous resolution rejecting any eventual proclamation of independence by Kosovo, while the Kosovo Assembly approved a motion stating that it would accept only independence as the final status of the territory. Later that month a former Finnish President, Martti Ahtisaari, who had been appointed by Annan as the Special Envoy for the negotiations of Kosovo's future status, commenced separate discussions with Serbian and Kosovo leaders. Also in November the ICTY imposed a sentence (the first relating to crimes committed in Kosovo) of 13 years' imprisonment on a former KLA commander who had been convicted of human rights abuses.

The first round of final status negotiations on Kosovo, which was conducted in Vienna on 20–21 February 2006, focused on issues related to decentralization, particularly the financing of ethnic Serb-majority municipalities. Serbia submitted a formal objection to the participation in the negotiations of the former KLA leader, Hashim Thaçi, accusing him of having committed crimes during the conflict in Kosovo. A third round of negotiations between the Kosovo Albanian and Serbian delegations again ended without agreement in April. After Montenegro's secession from the State Union of Serbia and Montenegro on 3 June (see above), the Serbian Government continued to resist strongly full independence for Kosovo, while agreeing to 'essential autonomy' for the province. At the instigation of Ahtisaari, direct high-level discussions, the first to involve the Presidents and Prime Ministers of Serbia and Kosovo since 1999, were conducted in Vienna in July 2006; the Kosovo delegation reiterated demands for full independence for the province by the end of that year, while the Serbian Prime Minister maintained that Serbia would not accept a loss of territory. The Kosovo delegation remained opposed to increased decentralization (including a Serbian proposal that a number of new Serb municipalities with autonomous powers be created), owing to concern that an effectively autonomous Serb polity would be established within the province. By the end of 2006 the two delegations had failed to reach any agreement on Kosovo's future status.

A new Serbian Constitution, which entered into effect in early November 2006, reaffirmed that Kosovo (again referred to as Kosovo and Metohija) was an integral part of the territory of Serbia, but one that was entitled to substantial autonomy. Following a subsequent announcement by the Serbian authorities that early legislative elections would take place on 21 January 2007, Ahtisaari declared that a proposed resolution for Kosovo's status (previously expected by the end of 2006) would be postponed until after the poll. Protests were subsequently staged in Kosovo, notably by supporters of an extreme ethnic Albanian movement, Self-Determination (Vetevendosje), who attacked official buildings, including the Assembly and UNMIK headquarters. The province's authorities indicated that they would envisage a unilateral declaration of independence in the absence of a diplomatic resolution. On 2 February 2007 Ahtisaari presented his proposal for the future status of Kosovo to the Serbian and Kosovo authorities and invited the delegations to engage in consultations on the draft in Vienna. The discussions, which commenced on 21 February, ended on 10 March, with a meeting of the Serbian and Kosovo government leaders; Ahtisaari concluded that, in view of the failure of the delegations to compromise on previously stated positions, there was no further prospect of achieving a negotiated agreement. On 26 March Ahtisaari submitted to the UN Security Council the finalized Comprehensive Proposal for the Kosovo Status Settlement, which recommended independence, to be supervised and supported for an initial period by an international military and civilian presence. On 3 April, at the beginning of a debate in the UN Security Council, Prime Minister Koštunica declared that Serbia rejected the Proposal (following a vote in the Serbian legislature in February), and requested that a new mediator be appointed. On 5 April Ahtisaari's plan was approved by 100 of 101 votes cast in the Kosovo Assembly.

In August 2007, after Russia obstructed the adoption of a resolution based on Ahtisaari's plan at the UN Security Council, a further series of negotiations began between Serbian and Kosovo delegations, with mediation by the USA, the EU and Russia. On 7 December, shortly before the deadline stipulated by the UN, it was announced that the negotiations had failed to result in an agreement. On 26 December the Serbian legislature approved a resolution urging the Serbian Government to 'reconsider' diplomatic relations with any Western country that recognized Kosovo as independent. Relations between Russia and Serbia were consolidated in early 2008, with the signature of an agreement (approved by the Narodna skupština Republike Srbije in September) whereby Serbia was to join Russia's 'South Stream' pipeline project and Russian state-controlled energy producer Gazprom acquired a 51% share in the Serbian state-owned petroleum enterprise, Naftna Industrija Srbije. (The sale of the majority share in Naftna Industrija Srbije was completed in February 2009; agreements with Serbia, together with Italy, Bulgaria and Greece, were signed in Sochi, Russia, on 15 May.)

In January 2008 Thaçi, who had recently become Prime Minister of Kosovo after elections, announced his intention to achieve independence for the territory. On 17 February 2008 the Kosovo Assembly adopted a declaration establishing the province as the Republic of Kosovo (Kosova), a sovereign state independent from Serbia, the resolution being based on Ahtisaari's Comprehensive Proposal for the Kosovo Status Settlement and in accordance with UN Security Council Resolution 1244 of 1999. Serbia, with the continued support of Russia, immediately protested that the declaration of independence contravened international law and demanded that it be annulled. On the following day the Serbian Ministry of the Interior issued arrest warrants against Thaçi and other Kosovo government officials for treason. KFOR reinforced the border between Kosovo and Serbia, after the destruction of two border posts by Serb protesters and reports that Serbian security forces had entered northern Kosovo. On 21 February Serb protesters rioted in Belgrade, attacking several embassies, including that of the United Kingdom and the USA. Several nations, including Albania, France, the USA and the United Kingdom, extended recognition to Kosovo on 18 February, followed by many others; Serbia immediately recalled its ambassadors based in those countries. In March the Serbian Government announced that it intended to submit a legal challenge against Kosovo's declaration of independence at the ICJ and would also apply for international support at the UN General Assembly. After elections were conducted in predominantly Serb municipalities in Kosovo on 11 May, a parallel 'Assembly of the Community of Municipalities of the Autonomous Province of Kosovo and Metohija', including representatives of four Serb parties, was established in June.

A new Constitution entered into effect in Kosovo on 15 June 2008, when UNMIK was scheduled to be replaced by an EU Rule of Law Mission in Kosovo (EULEX). However, the deployment of EULEX failed to proceed as envisaged, owing to the refusal of Kosovo Serbs and the Serbian Government (which was supported by Russia) to accept an EU mission. In July the Serbian Government announced its decision to return its ambassadors to the EU nations that had recognized Kosovo, in order to further the country's EU integration aspirations following the arrest of Radovan Karadžić (see above). In early October the Serbian Ministry of Foreign Affairs announced that it was to return the remaining ambassadors to the countries from where they had been withdrawn (notably including the USA). The decision of the FYRM and Montenegro in the same month to extend recognition to Kosovo prompted strong protests from the Serbian Government, which expelled the ambassadors of both countries (but in November invited the appointment of new envoys). On 8 October the UN General Assembly adopted a Serbian resolution requesting that the ICJ arbitrate on the validity under international law of Kosovo's unilateral declaration of independence from Serbia. Representatives of 77 countries (including the five of the 27 EU nations that had not recognized Kosovo) voted in favour of the Serbian resolution, while six opposed it and 74 abstained. Following the continued refusal of Kosovo Serbs to accept the deployment of EULEX, in early November the UN Secretary-General presented an amended six-point plan on the reconfiguration of the international presence in Kosovo, under which officials in the Serb-majority areas would receive directives from UNMIK, while those in Albanian-majority areas would be the responsibility of EULEX. The Serbian Government insisted, as a precondition of its acceptance of EULEX, that the plan be officially approved by the UN Security Council, that it be neutral with regard to Kosovo's status and that it would not be mandated to implement Ahtisaari's Comprehensive Proposal. On 26 November the UN Security Council unanimously endorsed the six-point plan under the stipulated terms; full deployment of EULEX throughout Kosovo began on 9 December. In April 2009 Serbia and Kosovo both officially submitted motions regarding the legality of Kosovo's independence to the ICJ; it was envisaged that the Court would issue a non-binding ruling in 2010.

Government

On 5 June 2006 the Serbian legislature officially declared the Republic of Serbia to be the successor state to the State Union of Serbia and Montenegro (following Montenegro's declaration of

SERBIA

independence on 3 June). Under the terms of a new Constitution, which officially entered into effect on 8 November, legislative power continued to be vested in the 250-member Narodna skupština Republike Srbije (National Assembly of the Republic of Serbia), which is directly elected for a period of four years. The President of the Republic, who is directly elected for a term of five years, nominates the Prime Minister for approval by the Narodna skupština. Executive power is vested in the Government, which is proposed to the Narodna skupština by the designated Prime Minister. The Narodna skupština is to be dissolved if it fails to appoint a new Government within 90 days of its inaugural session. The 11-member High Judicial Council ensures the independence of courts and judges, and is empowered to nominate or remove judges. Serbia formally comprises 24 administrative regions, including the seven regions of the province of Vojvodina, in the north of Serbia, which are divided into 170 municipalities; the territory of the former autonomous province of Kosovo, which declared independence from Serbia on 17 February 2008, comprised seven regions.

Defence

Military service is compulsory for men, and lasts for six months. Voluntary military service for women was introduced in 1983. As assessed at November 2008, the estimated total strength of the armed forces was 24,257, of which the army accounted for 11,180 (including 1,724 conscripts) and the air force 4,155. Reserves totalled 54,249 personnel. In December Serbia was admitted to the 'Partnership for Peace' programme of the North Atlantic Treaty Organization (NATO) (see p. 353). The budget for 2008 allocated 57,500m. dinars to defence.

Economic Affairs

In 2007, according to estimates by the World Bank, the gross national income (GNI) of Serbia, measured at 2005–07 prices, was US $34,969m., equivalent to $4,730 per head (or $10,220 per head on an international purchasing-power parity basis). During 2000–07, it was estimated, the population declined at an average annual rate of 0.2%, while gross domestic product (GDP) per head increased, in real terms, by an average of 5.7% per year. Overall GDP increased, in real terms, at an average annual rate of 5.5% in 2000–07; according to revised official figures, growth was 7.1% in 2007 and an estimated 6.1% in 2008.

Agriculture (including hunting, forestry and fishing) contributed 10.2% of GDP in 2007. In that year 20.8% of the employed labour force were engaged in the sector. Serbia's principal crops are maize, wheat, sugar beet and potatoes. The cultivation of fruit and vegetables is also important. Agricultural GDP increased at an average annual rate of 1.0% in 2003–07, according to official figures; sectoral GDP but decreased by 7.8% in 2007.

Industry (including mining, manufacturing, construction and power) contributed 28.8% of GDP and engaged 29.5% of the employed labour force in 2007. Industrial GDP increased at an average annual rate of 4.3% in 2003–07; growth of 4.7% was estimated in 2007.

The mining and quarrying sector contributed 1.5% of GDP and engaged 1.6% of the employed labour force in 2007. The principal minerals extracted are coal (mainly brown coal), copper ore and bauxite. Iron ore, crude petroleum, lead and zinc ore and natural gas are also produced. The GDP of the mining and quarrying sector increased at an average annual rate of 2.3% in 2003–07; mining GDP increased by 4.9% in 2007, but declined by an estimated 0.2% in 2007.

The manufacturing sector contributed 18.2% of GDP and engaged 19.6% of the employed labour force in 2007. Manufacturing GDP increased at an average annual rate of 4.7% in 2003–07; growth of 4.8% was estimated in 2007.

Energy in Serbia (including Montenegro) is derived principally from coal (which provided about 69.9% of total electricity generated in 2003) and hydroelectric power (27.9%). Imports of mineral fuels accounted for 19.7% of the value of total imports to Serbia in 2006.

Services contributed 60.9% of GDP in 2007. Some 49.7% of the employed labour force were engaged in the sector in that year. Total foreign tourist arrivals in Serbia increased from 339,000 in 2003 to 469,000 in 2006. Services GDP increased at an average annual rate of 12.3% in 2003–07; sectoral GDP increased by an estimated 10.5% in 2007.

In 2007 Serbia recorded a trade deficit of an estimated US $9,139.6m., and there was a deficit of an estimated $6,346.2m. on the current account of the balance of payments. In 2006 the principal source of imports to Serbia was Russia (accounting for 16.3% of the total); other major sources were Germany, Italy and the People's Republic of China. The principal market for exports in that year was Italy (taking 14.4% of all exports); other important purchasers were Bosnia and Herzegovina and Germany. (These figures excluded trade to or from Kosovo.) The main exports in 2006 were basic manufactures, food and live animals, miscellaneous manufactured articles, machinery and transport equipment, and chemicals. The principal imports in that year were machinery and transport equipment, basic manufactures, mineral fuels and lubricants, chemicals, and miscellaneous manufactured articles.

In 2007 Serbia recorded an overall budgetary deficit of 44,000m. dinars (equivalent to 1.9% of GDP). At the end of 2006 the total external debt of Serbia and Montenegro was $13,831m., of which $7,686m. was long-term public debt. In 2003 the cost of debt-servicing was equivalent to 7.8% of the value of exports of goods and services. In 2000–07, according to the International Labour Organization (ILO), the annual rate of inflation in Serbia averaged 21.6%. Consumer prices increased by an annual average of 6.5% in 2007. The rate of unemployment in Serbia was estimated at 18.1% in 2007 and at 14.0% in October 2008.

Following the dissolution of the State Union of Serbia and Montenegro in 2006, Serbia was admitted to the Organization for Security and Co-operation in Europe (OSCE, see p. 366) the IMF, the World Bank and the Council of Europe (see p. 236) in its own right.

In February 2006 the IMF approved the completion of its extended three-year stand-by credit arrangement with Serbia and Montenegro, allowing the country to secure a final cancellation of outstanding debt, under the terms of an agreement made with the 'Paris Club' of international creditors in 2001. In May 2006, however, the European Union (EU, see p. 255) suspended negotiations on a Stabilization and Association Agreement (SAA) with Serbia and Montenegro after Serbia failed to comply with an ultimatum for the extradition of former Bosnian Serb military commander Gen. (retd) Ratko Mladić to the International Criminal Tribunal for the former Yugoslavia (ICTY, see p. 19). On 5 June, after Montenegro officially proclaimed independence, Serbia officially declared itself the successor state to the State Union (thereby inheriting membership of international organizations). In July an agreement was reached on the division of the financial rights and obligations of the two states. Serbia resumed negotiations with the EU on an SAA in June 2007 and, despite the failure of the Government to arrest and extradite Mladić and other suspected war criminals, an Agreement was signed in April 2008. However, implementation of the SAA was to be suspended until EU member states agreed unanimously that Serbia was co-operating fully with the ICTY. In January 2009 the Serbian Government began to implement unilaterally an interim trade agreement that had been signed as part of the SAA (which remained suspended); the agreement provided for a substantial reduction in customs duties on industrial and agricultural products imported from the EU. The adverse effects of the international financial crisis, which was expected to lead to a downturn in GDP growth in 2009, resulted in trade union action at the beginning of that year, after the Government withdrew a pledge to increase public sector salaries. In May the Government announced a number of stimulus measures (at a cost of some 40,000m. dinars) to counteract the economic downturn, including provisions for lower rates for business loans in order to prevent insolvencies. In the same month the IMF confirmed that it was to increase its support to Serbia in a stand-by credit arrangement (initially approved in January) to some €2,900m. over a period of 27 months, of which immediately available funds of €788m. were to be used to strengthen state currency reserves. Meanwhile, the involvement of Serbia in Russia's 'South Stream' gas pipeline project (that was to supply natural gas from Russia to various countries in southern and eastern Europe) was expected to provide economic advantages to Serbia; an agreement on Serbia's association with the project, agreed in early 2008, also provided for a 51% stake in the Serbian state-owned petroleum enterprise, Naftna Industrija Srbije, to be sold to the Russian state-controlled energy producer Gazprom; this sale was effected in February 2009.

Education

Elementary education is free and compulsory for all children between the ages of seven and 15, when children attend the 'eight-year school'. Various types of secondary education are available to all who qualify, but the vocational and technical schools are the most popular. Alternatively, children may attend

SERBIA

a general secondary school (gymnasium) where they follow a four-year course, prior to university entrance. At the secondary level there are also a number of art schools, apprentice schools and teacher-training schools. In 2006/07 an estimated 95% of children in the appropriate age-group were enrolled in primary schools, while enrolment at secondary schools was equivalent to an estimated 88% of students in the relevant age-group. In 2006/07 238,710 students were enrolled in higher education faculties. Serbia has seven state universities, including the University of Belgrade, which was established in 1863, and seven private universities.

Public Holidays

2009: 1–2 January (New Year), 7–8 January (Christmas), 15 February (National Day), 17–20 April (Orthodox Easter), 1–2 May (Labour Day).

2010: 1–2 January (New Year), 7–8 January (Christmas), 15 February (National Day), 2–5 April (Orthodox Easter), 1–2 May (Labour Day).

Weights and Measures

The metric system is in force.

Statistical Survey

Source (unless otherwise indicated): Statistical Office of the Republic of Serbia, 11000 Belgrade, Milana Rakića 5; tel. (11) 2412922; fax (11) 2411260; internet webrzs.statserb.sr.gov.yu/axd/en/index.php.

Note: Except where otherwise stated, figures in this survey exclude data for Kosovo, which declared independence from Serbia on 17 February 2008. Certain figures pertain to the former Federal Republic of Yugoslavia, comprising Serbia and Montenegro, or to the State Union of those two republics that succeeded it from 2003 to 2006, when Montenegro achieved independence.

Area and Population

AREA, POPULATION AND DENSITY

Area (sq km)	77,498*
Population (census results)	
31 March 1991	7,576,837
31 March 2002	
Males	3,645,930
Females	3,852,071
Total	7,498,001
Population (official estimates at mid-year)	
2005	7,440,769
2006	7,411,569
2007	7,381,579
Density (per sq km) at mid-2007	95.2

* 29,922 sq miles, according to 2002 census.

POPULATION BY ETHNIC GROUP

(2002 census)

Ethnic group	Population ('000)	%
Serbs	6,213	82.9
Hungarians	293	3.9
Bosniaks	136	1.8
Roma	108	1.4
Yugoslavs	81	1.1
Croats	71	0.9
Montenegrins	69	0.9
Others	527	7.0
Total	**7,498**	**100.0**

ADMINISTRATIVE DIVISIONS

(2002 census)

	Area (sq km)	Population ('000)	Density (per sq km)	Principal city
Capital				
Belgrade	3,224	1,576,124	488.9	—
Okruzi (Districts)				
Bor	3,507	146,551	41.8	Bor
Braničevo	3,865	200,503	51.9	Požarevac
Jablanica	2,769	240,923	87.0	Leskovac
Kolubara	2,474	192,204	77.7	Valjevo
Mačva	3,268	329,625	100.9	Šabac
Moravica	3,016	224,772	74.5	Čačak
Nišava	2,729	381,757	139.9	Niš
Pčinja	3,520	227,690	64.7	Vranje
Pirot	2,761	105,654	38.3	Pirot
Podunavlje	1,248	210,290	168.5	Smederevo
Pomoravlje	2,614	227,435	87.0	Jagodina
Rasina	2,668	259,441	97.2	Kruševac
—continued	Area (sq km)	Population ('000)	Density (per sq km)	Principal city
Raška	3,918	291,230	74.3	Kraljevo
Šumadija	2,387	298,778	125.2	Kragujevac
Toplica	2,231	102,075	45.8	Prokuplje
Zaječar	3,623	137,561	38.0	Zaječar
Zlatibor	6,140	313,396	51.0	Užice
Province				
Vojvodina	21,536	2,031,992	94.4	Novi Sad
Okruzi (Districts) within the Province of Vojvodina				
Central Banat	3,256	208,456	64.0	Zrenjanin
North Bačka	1,784	200,140	112.2	Subotica
North Banat	2,329	165,881	71.2	Kikinda
South Bačka	4,016	593,666	147.8	Novi Sad
South Banat	4,245	313,937	74.0	Pančevo
Srem	3,486	335,901	96.4	Sremska Mitrovica
West Bačka	2,420	214,011	88.4	Sombor
Total	**77,498**	**7,498,001**	**96.8**	—

PRINCIPAL TOWNS

(population at 2002 census unless otherwise indicated)

Beograd (Belgrade, the capital)	1,576,124	Kraljevo	121,707
Novi Sad	299,294	Čačak	117,072
Niš	250,518	Smederevo	109,809
Kragujevac	175,802	Sombor	97,263
Leskovac	156,252	Valjevo	96,761
Subotica	148,401	Vranje	87,288
Zrenjanin	132,051	Loznica	86,413
Kruševac	131,368	Novi Pazar	85,996
Pančevo	127,162	Sremska Mitrovica	85,902
Šabac	122,893	Užice	83,022

SERBIA

BIRTHS, MARRIAGES AND DEATHS

	Registered live births Number	Rate (per 1,000)	Registered marriages Number	Rate (per 1,000)	Registered deaths Number	Rate (per 1,000)
2000	73,764	9.6	42,586	5.7	104,042	13.6
2001	78,435	10.1	41,406	5.5	99,008	12.8
2002	78,101	10.4	41,947	5.6	102,785	13.7
2003	79,025	10.6	41,914	5.6	103,946	13.9
2004	78,186	10.5	42,030	5.6	104,320	14.0
2005	72,180	9.7	n.a.	n.a.	106,771	14.3
2006	70,997	9.6	39,756	5.4	102,884	13.9
2007	68,102	9.2	41,083	5.6	102,805	13.9

ECONOMICALLY ACTIVE POPULATION
(labour force survey, persons aged 15 years and over, October 2007)

	Males	Females	Total
Agriculture, forestry, fishing and water works	336,066	216,527	552,592
Mining and quarrying	31,566	9,695	41,261
Manufacturing	347,016	174,728	521,744
Electricity, gas and water	41,729	16,232	57,961
Construction	144,403	16,848	161,251
Wholesale and retail trade	186,511	211,958	398,470
Hotels and restaurants	34,882	37,435	72,317
Transport, storage and communications	135,584	34,185	169,769
Financial intermediation	17,358	25,687	43,044
Real estate and property	51,685	37,169	88,855
Public administration and social security	80,340	61,598	141,938
Education	38,337	79,727	118,064
Health and social work	38,202	128,203	166,405
Other community, social and personal services	61,207	52,914	114,121
Households with employed persons	389	6,046	6,435
Extra-territorial organizations and bodies	483	1,026	1,509
Total employed	1,545,758	1,109,979	2,655,736
Unemployed	289,803	295,669	585,472
Total labour force	1,835,561	1,405,648	3,241,208

Health and Welfare

KEY INDICATORS
(data for Serbia only, unless otherwise indicated)

Total fertility rate (children per woman, 2006)	1.8
Under-5 mortality rate (per 1,000 live births, 2006)	8
HIV/AIDS (% of persons aged 15–49, 2007, Serbia and Montenegro)	0.1
Physicians (per 1,000 head, 2006)	2.0
Hospital beds (per 1,000 head, 2006)	5.4
Health expenditure (2006): US $ per head (PPP)	525
Health expenditure (2006): % of GDP	7.6
Health expenditure (2006): public (% of total)	71.0
Access to water (% of persons, 2006, Serbia and Montenegro)	99
Access to sanitation (% of persons, 2006, Serbia and Montenegro)	87

For sources and definitions, see explanatory note on p. vi.

Agriculture

PRINCIPAL CROPS
('000 metric tons)

	2005*	2006†	2007†
Wheat	2,009.7	1,875.3	1,863.8
Barley	311.1	275.6	259.0
Maize	7,095.0	6,016.8	3,904.8
Oats	91.0	84.4	76.9
Potatoes	1,102.4	930.3	743.3
Sugar beet	3,101.2	3,188.9	3,206.4
Beans, dry	58.7	54.6	54.5‡
Soybeans (Soya beans)	368.0	429.6	304.0
Sunflower seed	350.8	384.9	294.5
Cabbages and other brassicas	297.2	324.7	280.2
Tomatoes	189.9	189.2	11.1
Chillies and peppers, green	167.5	177.3	150.3
Onions, dry	133.1	140.3	116.0
Carrots and turnips	63.7	68.1	56.7
Watermelons	313.5	251.1	205.4
Apples	202.1	240.3	245.2
Pears	48.8	57.7	60.5
Sour (Morello) cherries	63.9	80.5	28.5
Peaches and nectarines	55.5	59.1	65.6
Plums and sloes	311.8	556.2	680.6
Raspberries and other berries	112.0	79.7	n.a.
Grapes	277.6	359.5	353.3
Tobacco, unmanufactured	11.8	10.8	11.1

* Data for Serbia and Montenegro (incl. Kosovo).
† Data for Serbia only (incl. Kosovo).
‡ FAO estimate.

Aggregate production (data for Serbia and Montenegro, incl. Kosovo, unless otherwise indicated, '000 metric tons, may include official, semi-official or estimated data): Total cereals 9,533.9 in 2005, 8,277.4 in 2006 (Serbia only, incl. Kosovo), 6,125.2 in 2007 (Serbia only, incl. Kosovo); Total roots and tubers 1,102.4 in 2005, 930.3 in 2006 (Serbia only, incl. Kosovo), 743.3 in 2007 (Serbia only, incl. Kosovo); Total vegetables (incl. melons) 1,251.8 in 2005, 1,337.4 in 2006 (Serbia only, incl. Kosovo), 1,123.9 in 2007 (Serbia only, incl. Kosovo); Total fruits (excl. melons) 1,162.5 in 2005, 1,444.4 in 2006 (Serbia only, incl. Kosovo), 1,603.2 in 2007 (Serbia only, incl. Kosovo).

Source: FAO.

LIVESTOCK
('000 head, year ending 30 September)

	2005*	2006†	2007†
Horses	42	19	20
Cattle	1,213	1,096	1,106
Pigs	3,224	3,212	3,999
Sheep	1,866	1,609	1,556
Goats	139	139	162
Chickens	15,683‡	17,905	16,595

* Data for Serbia and Montenegro.
† Data for Serbia only (incl. Kosovo).
‡ FAO estimate.

Source: FAO.

LIVESTOCK PRODUCTS
('000 metric tons)

	2005*	2006†	2007†‡
Cattle meat	156	83	80
Sheep meat	21	20	20
Pig meat	562	563†	560
Chicken meat	67	75	75
Cows' milk	1,833	1,725	1,700
Sheep's milk	24	16	16
Hen eggs	77	73	73
Honey	4	4	4

* Data refer to Serbia and Montenegro (incl. Kosovo).
† Data refer to Serbia (incl. Kosovo).
‡ FAO estimate(s).

Source: FAO.

SERBIA

Forestry

(data for Serbia and Montenegro, incl. Kosovo)

ROUNDWOOD REMOVALS

('000 cubic metres, excl. bark)

	2005*	2006†	2007†
Sawlogs, veneer logs and logs for sleepers	1,096	1,058	1,292
Pulpwood	168	132	91
Other industrial roundwood	52	60	44
Fuel wood	1,854	1,626	1,554
Total	3,170	2,876	2,981

* Data refer to Serbia and Montenegro (incl. Kosovo).
† Data refer to Serbia (incl. Kosovo).

Source: FAO.

SAWNWOOD PRODUCTION

('000 cubic metres, including railway sleepers)

	2005*	2006†	2007†
Coniferous (softwood)	154	131	146
Non-coniferous (hardwood)	343	362	456
Total	497	493	602

* Data refer to Serbia and Montenegro (incl. Kosovo).
† Data refer to Serbia (incl. Kosovo).

Source: FAO.

Fishing

(data for Serbia and Montenegro, incl. Kosovo)

('000 metric tons, live weight)

	2003	2004	2005
Capture	1.8	2.4	2.5*
Freshwater fishes	1.0	1.6	1.7
Common carp	0.1	0.2	0.1*
Aquaculture	3.2	4.6	4.6*
Rainbow trout	2.6	4.0	n.a.
Total catch	5.0	7.0	7.0*

* FAO estimate.

Note: Figures exclude marine shells (metric tons): 3.1 in 2002; 3.1 in 2003; 3.0 in 2004; n.a. in 2005.

Source: FAO.

Mining

('000 metric tons unless otherwise indicated)

	2004	2005	2006
Coal	34,786	35,635	37,327
Lignite	33,753	34,565	n.a.
Crude petroleum	653	648	654
Natural gas (million cubic metres)	317	282	283
Lead and zinc ore	111	162	n.a.
Copper ore	5,495	6,005	n.a.
Clay and kaolin	108	135	215

Industry

SELECTED PRODUCTS

('000 metric tons, unless otherwise indicated)

	2004	2005	2006
Refined vegetable oils	101.6	102.7	110.4
Fruit and vegetable juices	126.0	167.9	181.2
Beer ('000 hectolitres)	5,328	5,206	6,568
Cigarettes (million)	15,107	17,324	27,581
Cotton yarn (metric tons)	1,048	765	1,239
Wool yarn (metric tons)	762	535	36
Hosiery ('000 pairs)	73,505	76,934	68,984
Underwear ('000 units)	9,463	7,398	7,270
Leather footwear ('000 pairs)	2,775	3,143	5,678
Parquet wooden flooring ('000 sq metres)	441.5	331.5	363.3
Paper and cardboard	106.6	102.6	92.3
Newsprint	42.2	37.7	45.9
Cement	2,240	2,276	2,565
Motor spirit (gasoline)	808	728	n.a.
Gas-diesel (distillate fuel) oil	1,005	876	n.a.
Residual fuel oil	714	900	n.a.
Nitrogenous fertilizers	630.1	596.4	679.6
Rubber tyres for vehicles ('000)	7,839	8,114	13,230
Pig-iron	959.0	1,115.2	n.a.
Flat-rolled steel products	1,543.5	1,890.3	n.a.
Electric light bulbs ('000)	3,241	4,441	n.a.
Alternating current motors (units)	114,438	72,916	n.a.
Tractors (number)	5,392	4,356	2,387
Motor cars (number)	14,549	15,666	11,762
Kitchen wooden furniture ('000 units)	44.5	44.8	n.a.
Electric energy (million kWh)	33,874	36,474	36,495

Finance

CURRENCY AND EXCHANGE RATES

Monetary Units
100 para = 1 Serbian dinar.

Sterling, Dollar and Euro Equivalents (31 November 2008)
£1 sterling = 105.850 dinars;
US $1 = 69.021 dinars;
€1 = 87.843 dinars;
1,000 Serbian dinars = 9.45 = $14.49 = €11.38.

Average Exchange Rate (dinars per US $)
2005   66.71
2006   67.15
2007   58.45

CONSOLIDATED BUDGET

('000 million dinars; incl. Kosovo)

Revenue*	2005	2006	2007†
Current revenue	715.6	855.3	988.5
Personal income tax	94.3	118.6	115.0
Social security contributions	185.3	231.4	268.7
Corporate income tax	10.3	18.3	29.3
Retail sales tax; value added tax	216.0	225.2	270.0
Excises	71.3	86.9	99.8
Taxes on international trade and operations	39.0	45.3	58.9
Other taxes and non-tax revenue	99.5	129.6	146.9
Capital revenue	7.9	10.3	12.1
Total	723.5	865.6	1,000.6

SERBIA

Statistical Survey

Expenditure	2005	2006	2007†
Current expenditure	660.3	807.3	913.3
Wages and salaries	171.3	204.4	244.1
Expenditure on goods and services	125.5	156.6	183.1
Interest payments	24.9	30.2	21.7
Subsidies and other current transfers	338.5	416.1	464.3
Capital expenditure	45.0	80.4	101.4
Lending minus repayments	5.4	10.7	11.0
Total	710.7	898.4	1,025.7

* Excluding grants received ('000 million dinars): 1.1 in 2005; 1.9 in 2006; 0.5 in 2007 (projected).
† Projected figures.

Source: IMF, *Republic of Serbia: 2007 Article IV Consultation—Staff Report; Staff Statement; Public Information Notice on the Executive Board Discussion; and Statement by the Executive Director for the Republic of Serbia* (February 2008).

INTERNATIONAL RESERVES
(US $ million at 31 December; incl. Kosovo)

	2006	2007	2008
Gold	235.9	323.2	354.1
IMF special drawing rights	8.8	0.8	2.2
Foreign exchange	11,638.9	13,891.8	11,120.7
Total	11,883.6	14,215.8	11,477.0

Source: IMF, *International Financial Statistics*.

MONEY SUPPLY
(million dinars at 31 December; incl. Kosovo)

	2005	2006	2007
Currency outside banks	53,649.9	68,460.8	76,948.5
Demand deposits	85,310.5	122,143.7	161,945.9
Total money (incl. others)	144,948.9	200,089.7	248,873.2

2008 (million dinars at 31 December; incl. Kosovo): Total money 240,969.8.

Source: IMF, *International Financial Statistics*.

COST OF LIVING
(Consumer Price Index at January; base: 2004 = 100; incl. Kosovo)

	2007	2008	2009
Food	111.2	132.1	146.4
Tobacco and beverages	128.4	140.4	169.6
Clothing (incl. footwear)	115.4	120.6	128.3
Rent	115.2	123.7	139.7
All items (incl. others)	114.0	128.0	140.4

NATIONAL ACCOUNTS
('000 million dinars at current prices)

Expenditure on the Gross Domestic Product

	2005	2006	2007
Final consumption expenditure	1,613.9	1,883.4	2,205.9
Households	1,281.0	1,492.7	1,714.0
Non-profit institutions serving households	16.7	19.4	24.2
General government	194.8	232.3	289.9
Collective consumption expenditure	121.3	139.0	177.8
Gross fixed capital formation	319.9	412.8	552.3
Changes in inventories	79.8	56.9	123.1
Statistical discrepancy	24.3	36.8	44.9
Total domestic expenditure	2,037.9	2,389.9	2,926.2
Exports of goods and services	484.2	627.0	722.2
Less Imports of goods and services	834.5	1,036.9	1,285.9
Gross domestic product at market prices	1,687.8	1,980.2	2,362.8

Gross Domestic Product by Economic Activity

	2005	2006	2007
Agriculture, hunting, forestry and water works	173.6	191.0	206.1
Fishing	0.5	0.6	0.5
Mining and quarrying	25.7	28.4	29.5
Manufacturing	252.2	310.7	368.4
Electricity, gas and water	59.6	74.2	80.3
Construction	65.3	81.4	103.9
Wholesale and retail trade; and repairs	177.1	218.3	274.0
Restaurants and hotels	17.7	22.6	25.2
Transport, storage and communications	125.5	138.4	166.1
Financial intermediation	41.3	48.9	61.6
Real estate, renting and business activities	229.3	278.7	325.2
Public administration and defence; compulsory social security	69.8	68.0	91.9
Education	64.5	79.0	96.5
Health and social work	83.5	98.8	124.9
Other community, social and personal services	41.5	51.6	64.0
Private households with employed persons	1.5	1.5	1.5
Sub-total	1,428.6	1,691.9	2,019.8
Less Financial intermediation services indirectly measured	30.9	38.1	43.6
Gross value added in basic prices	1,397.7	1,653.8	1,976.2
Taxes on products	329.5	361.6	426.9
Less Subsidies on products	39.4	35.2	40.3
GDP in market prices	1,687.8	1,980.2	2,362.8

BALANCE OF PAYMENTS
(US $ million, incl. Kosovo)

	2007
Exports of goods f.o.b.	8,776.5
Imports of goods c.i.f.	−17,916.1
Trade balance	−9,139.6
Exports of services	3,168.3
Imports of services	−3,516.1
Balance on goods and services	−9,487.5
Other income received	710.0
Other income paid	−1,539.0
Balance on goods, services and income	−10,316.5
Current transfers received	4,285.4
Current transfers paid	−315.0
Current balance	−6,346.2

SERBIA —continued

	2007
Capital account (net)	–407.6
Direct investment abroad	–943.2
Direct investment from abroad	3,447.8
Portfolio investment assets	–4.7
Portfolio investment liabilities	920.5
Financial derivatives liabilities	1.6
Other investment assets	–2,300.8
Other investment liabilities	6,572.0
Net errors and omissions	323.1
Overall balance	**1,262.6**

Source: IMF, *International Financial Statistics*.

External Trade

PRINCIPAL COMMODITY GROUPS
(US $ million, distribution by SITC)

Imports c.i.f.	2004	2005	2006
Food and live animals	625	591	649
Beverages and tobacco	162	115	160
Crude materials (inedible) except fuels	333	467	627
Mineral fuels, lubricants, etc.	1,634	2,029	2,595
Chemicals and related products	1,411	1,467	1,867
Basic manufactures	2,116	2,168	2,743
Machinery and transport equipment	3,388	2,693	3,376
Miscellaneous manufactured articles	1,023	879	1,098
Total (incl. others)	**10,753**	**10,461**	**13,172**

Exports f.o.b.	2004	2005	2006
Food and live animals	641	776	1,065
Crude materials (inedible) except fuels	196	198	278
Mineral fuels, lubricants, etc.	91	164	225
Chemicals and related products	385	494	650
Basic manufactures	1,184	1,595	2,418
Machinery and transport equipment	378	443	711
Miscellaneous manufactured articles	507	703	914
Total (incl. others)	**3,523**	**4,482**	**6,428**

2007 (US $ million): Total imports 18,554; Total exports 8,825.

PRINCIPAL TRADING PARTNERS
(US $ million)

Imports c.i.f.	2004	2005	2006
Austria	289	254	227
Bosnia and Herzegovina	235	292	343
Bulgaria	221	203	421
China, People's Republic	521	509	782
Croatia	205	258	334
Czech Republic	213	194	214
France	347	290	342
Germany	1,446	1,091	1,251
Greece	200	157	200
Hungary	311	267	306
Italy	1,039	909	1,100
Romania	202	274	437
Russia	1,396	1,669	2,142
Slovenia	332	285	308
Sweden	219	129	166
Turkey	198	211	256
Ukraine	275	284	289
USA	355	279	240
Total (incl. others)	**10,753**	**10,461**	**13,170**

Exports f.o.b.	2004	2005	2006
Bosnia and Herzegovina	626	744	749
Croatia	149	196	251
France	135	162	235
Germany	352	435	637
Greece	119	122	153
Hungary	120	131	188
Italy	448	652	926
Macedonia, former Yugoslav republic	257	261	300
Romania	123	130	177
Russia	153	225	311
Slovenia	155	189	253
Total (incl. others)	**3,523**	**4,482**	**6,427**

Transport

(data include Kosovo)

RAILWAYS
(traffic)

	2004	2005	2006
Passengers carried ('000)	7,569	6,492	6,445
Passenger-kilometres (million)	821	713	684
Freight carried ('000 metric tons)	12,293	12,568	14,139
Freight ton-kilometres (million)	3,164	3,482	4,232

ROAD TRAFFIC
(motor vehicles in use)

	2004	2005	2006
Passenger cars	1,449,843	1,481,498	1,511,837
Buses and coaches	9,125	9,696	9,312
Goods vehicles	109,292	116,440	126,045
Special purpose vehicles			
Passenger	16,462	15,920	15,109
Cargo	109,292	116,440	n.a.
Articulated vehicles	91,546	101,465	103,859
Tractors	132,711	126,816	128,017
Motorcycles and mopeds	14,771	16,042	20,380

INLAND WATERWAYS

Traffic
('000 metric tons, national and international traffic at river ports, excl. transit)

	2004	2005	2006
Goods loaded	2,876	6,338	6,045
Goods unloaded	5,841	8,708	7,979

CIVIL AVIATION
(scheduled and non-scheduled services)

	2004	2005	2006
Kilometres flown (million)	19	17	18
Passengers carried ('000)	1,289	1,122	1,216
Passenger-kilometres (million)	1,387	1,219	1,252
Cargo carried (metric tons)	6,058	4,945	4,678
Total ton-kilometres (million)	8	6	5

Tourism

FOREIGN TOURIST ARRIVALS
('000 at accommodation establishments)

Country of origin	2004	2005	2006
Bosnia and Herzegovina	45	49	54
Bulgaria	16	16	18
Croatia	25	29	34
Germany	25	29	28
Greece	19	25	27
Italy	24	28	28
Macedonia, former Yugoslav republic	29	30	26
Slovenia	42	56	54
Total (incl. others)	392	453	469

Tourism receipts (Serbia and Montenegro, US $ million, excl. passenger transport): 220 in 2004; 308 in 2005; 398 in 2006 (Source: World Tourism Organization).

Communications Media

(data includes Kosovo)

	2005	2006	2007
Telephones (fixed network, '000 subscribers)	2,687.1	2,760.3	2,993.4
Mobile cellular telephones ('000 subscribers)	5,222.1	6,643.7	8,452.6

Education

(2005/06, unless otherwise indicated)

	Institutions	Teachers	Students
Pre-primary	2,062	19,738	173,203
Regular primary	3,572	46,353	639,293
Special primary	245	1,606	7,707
Primary education of adults	19	235	2,653
Regular secondary	478	27,565	287,397
Special secondary	41		1,465
Accessory	100	n.a.	20,965
Higher*	272	6,304	238,710

* 2006/07, preliminary.

Adult literacy rate (Serbia and Montenegro): 96.4% (males 98.9%; females 94.1%) in 2002 (Source: UNESCO Institute for Statistics).

Directory

The Constitution

Serbia officially declared itself to be the successor state to the State Union of Serbia and Montenegro on 5 June 2006. A new Constitution of the Republic of Serbia was endorsed by national referendum on 28–29 October and entered into force on 8 November. Under the Constitution, the Province of Kosovo and Metohija (which declared its independence from Serbia, as the Republic of Kosovo, on 17 February 2008) is an integral part of Serbia and has substantial autonomy within Serbia. The Constitutions's main provisions are summarized below.

PRINCIPLES

The Republic of Serbia is a state of the Serb people and of all citizens who live in the Republic, based on the rule of law and social justice, principles of human rights and freedoms, and commitment to European principles and values. Sovereignty is vested in all citizens, who exercise it through referendums, people's initiatives, and by way of their freely elected representatives. Judicial power is independent. The territory of the Republic of Serbia is indivisible. The Republic of Serbia is a secular state. The right of citizens to provincial autonomy and local self-government is subject only to the terms of constitutionality and legality. The Constitution provides guarantees for human and minority rights and freedoms. There is no death penalty in the Republic of Serbia. Criminal prosecution or punishment for war crimes, genocide, or crimes against humanity is not subject to a statute of limitations. The economic system in the Republic of Serbia is based on the principles of the market economy. The official language is Serbian and the official script is Cyrillic. The official use of other languages and scripts shall be regulated by law.

ORGANIZATION OF GOVERNMENT

The Narodna skupština Republike Srbije (National Assembly of the Republic of Serbia) is the supreme representative body in the Republic of Serbia. The Narodna skupština comprises 250 deputies, who are directly elected for a term of four years. The Narodna skupština adopts decisions by a majority vote. The President of the Republic may dissolve the Narodna skupština, in response to a request by the Government. The Government may not propose the dissolution of the Narodna skupština if a proposal has been submitted for a vote of 'no confidence' in the Government. The Narodna skupština shall be dissolved if it fails to elect the Government within 90 days from the day of its inauguration.

The President of the Republic, who is directly elected for a term of five years, nominates the Prime Minister for approval by the Narodna skupština. In accordance with the law, the President commands the army, and appoints and dismisses army officers. Executive power is vested in the Government, which is proposed to the Narodna skupština by the nominee for Prime Minister.

Certain affairs of public administration may be delegated to the bodies of the autonomous provinces or to of local self-government. The Civic Defender, who shall be elected by the Narodna skupština, is empowered to protect citizens' rights and monitor the work of public administrative bodies.

The Supreme Court of Cassation, which is the Supreme Court of Serbia, is the highest court in the Republic; its President is elected for a five-year term by the Narodna skupština. The 11-member High Judicial Council is an independent body, which provides for and guarantees the independence and autonomy of courts and judges. The Narodna skupština elects judges on the proposal of the High Judicial Council, while the High Judicial Council elects permanent judges. The 15-member Constitutional Court protects constitutionality and legality, as well as human and minority rights and freedoms.

TERRITORIAL ORGANIZATION

Citizens have the right to provincial autonomy and local self-government. Autonomous provinces and local self-government units have the status of legal entities. The Skupština (Assembly) is the supreme body of the autonomous provinces and units of local self-government. In those autonomous provinces and local self-government units with an ethnically diverse population, the representation of national minorities in the relevant Skupština is assured. New autonomous provinces may be established, and existing ones may be revoked or merged, following the proceedings envisaged for amending the Constitution and subject to approval in a referendum. An autonomous province shall have direct revenue for financing its competencies.

AMENDING THE CONSTITUTION

Proposals to amend the Constitution may be submitted by at least one-third of the total number of parliamentary deputies, by the President of the Republic, by the Government or by at least 150,000 voters. Any amendment to the Constitution requires the approval of at two-thirds of the total number of deputies in the Narodna skupština. Additionally, at the request of the Narodna skupština, amendments may be subject to approval by a national referendum.

SERBIA
Directory

The Government

HEAD OF STATE

President of the Republic: BORIS TADIĆ (elected 27 June 2004; re-elected 3 February 2008; inaugurated 15 February 2008).

COUNCIL OF MINISTERS
(April 2009)

A coalition Government, comprising representatives of an alliance led by the Democratic Party, For a European Serbia—Boris Tadić, and an alliance of the Socialist Party of Serbia, the Party of United Pensioners of Serbia and United Serbia.

Prime Minister: MIRKO CVETKOVIĆ.
First Deputy Prime Minister and Minister of Internal Affairs: IVICA DAČIĆ.
Deputy Prime Minister, in charge of European Integration, and Minister of Science and Technological Development: BOŽIDAR ĐELIĆ.
Deputy Prime Minister and Minister of the Economy and Regional Development: MLAĐAN DINKIĆ.
Deputy Prime Minister: JOVAN KRKOBABIĆ.
Minister of Defence: DRAGAN ŠUTANOVAC.
Minister of Foreign Affairs: VUK JEREMIĆ.
Minister of Finance: DIANA DRAGUTINOVIĆ.
Minister of Justice: SNEŽANA MALOVIĆ.
Minister of Public Administration and Local Self-Government: MILAN MARKOVIĆ.
Minister of Agriculture, Forestry and Water Management: SAŠA DRAGIN.
Minister of Infrastructure: MILUTIN MRKONJIĆ.
Minister of Telecommunications and Information Technology: JASNA MATIĆ.
Minister of Trade and Services: SLOBODAN MILOSAVLJEVIĆ.
Minister of Labour and Social Affairs: RASIM LJAJIĆ.
Minister of Mining and Energy: PETAR ŠKUNDRIĆ.
Minister of the Environment and Spatial Planning: OLIVER DULIĆ.
Minister of Education: ŽARKO OBRADOVIĆ.
Minister of Youth and Sports: SNEŽANA SAMARDŽIĆ-MARKOVIĆ.
Minister of Culture: NEBOJŠA BRADIĆ.
Minister of the National Investment Plan: VERICA KALANOVIĆ.
Minister of Health: TOMICA MILOSAVLJEVIĆ.
Minister of Faith: BOGOLJUB ŠIJAKOVIĆ.
Minister of the Diaspora: SRĐAN SREĆKOVIĆ.
Minister of Kosovo and Metohija: GORAN BOGDANOVIĆ.
Minister of Human and Minority Rights: SVETOZAR ČIPLIĆ.
Minister without Portfolio: SULEJMAN UGLJANIN (DP).
Secretary-General of the Government: TAMARA STOJČEVIĆ.

MINISTRIES

Office of the President: 11000 Belgrade, Andrićev venac 1; tel. (11) 3231033; fax (11) 3030868; e-mail kontakt.predsednik@predsednik.rs; internet www.predsednik.rs.
Office of the Prime Minister: 11000 Belgrade, Nemanjina 11; tel. (11) 3617719; fax (11) 3617609; e-mail predsednikvladesrbije@srbija.sr.gov.yu; internet www.srbija.gov.rs.
Ministry of Agriculture, Forestry and Water Management: 11000 Belgrade, Nemanjina 22–26; tel. (11) 3065038; fax (11) 3616272; e-mail office@minpolj.sr.gov.yu; internet www.minpolj.sr.gov.yu.
Ministry of Culture: 11000 Belgrade, Vlajkovićeva 3; tel. (11) 3398172; fax (11) 3398936; e-mail kabinet@min-cul.sr.gov.yu; internet www.kultura.sr.gov.yu.
Ministry of Defence: 11000 Belgrade, Birčaninova 5; tel. (11) 3006323; fax (11) 3117809; e-mail info@mod.gov.rs; internet www.mod.gov.rs.
Ministry of the Diaspora: 11000 Belgrade, Vase Čarapića 20; tel. (11) 3202900; fax (11) 2636815; e-mail info@mzd.gov.rs; internet www.mzd.gov.rs.
Ministry of the Economy and Regional Development: 11000 Belgrade, bul. Kralja Aleksandra 15; tel. (11) 2855000; fax (11) 2855097; e-mail press@merr.gov.rs; internet www.merr.gov.rs.
Ministry of Education: 11000 Belgrade, Nemanjina 22–26; tel. (11) 3616489; fax (11) 3616491; e-mail webmaster@mps.sr.gov.yu; internet www.mp.gov.rs.
Ministry of the Environment and Spatial Planning: 11000 Belgrade, Nemanjina 11; tel. (11) 3617717; fax (11) 3617722; e-mail info@ekoplan.gov.rs; internet www.ekoplan.gov.rs.
Ministry of Faith: 11000 Belgrade, bul. Mihaila Pupina 2; tel. and fax (11) 3112811; fax (11) 3113527; e-mail kabinet.mv@mv.sr.gov.yu; internet www.mv.gov.rs.
Ministry of Finance: 11000 Belgrade, Kneza Miloša 20; tel. (11) 3619900; fax (11) 3618914; e-mail informacije@mfin.gov.rs; internet www.mfin.gov.rs.
Ministry of Foreign Affairs: 11000 Belgrade, Kneza Miloša 24–26; tel. (11) 3068351; fax (11) 3618052; e-mail mfa@mfa.rs; internet www.mfa.gov.rs.
Ministry of Health: 11000 Belgrade, Nemanjina 22–26; tel. (11) 3616251; fax (11) 3616596; e-mail kabinet.zdravlje@zdravlje.sr.gov.yu; internet www.zdravlje.gov.rs.
Ministry of Human and Minority Rights: 11000 Belgrade, bul. Mihaila Pupina 2; tel. (11) 3112410; e-mail kabinet@ljudskaprava.gov.rs; internet www.ljudskaprava.gov.rs.
Ministry of Infrastructure: 11000 Belgrade, Nemanjina 22–26; tel. (11) 3616431; fax (11) 3617486; internet www.mi.gov.rs.
Ministry of Internal Affairs: 11000 Belgrade, bul. Mihaila Pupina 2; tel. (11) 3062000; fax (11) 3617814; e-mail muprs@mup.sr.gov.yu; internet www.mup.gov.rs.
Ministry of Justice: 11000 Belgrade, Nemanjina 22–26; tel. (11) 3616548; fax (11) 3616419; e-mail kabinet@mpravde.sr.gov.yu; internet www.mpravde.gov.rs.
Ministry of Kosovo and Metohija: 11000 Belgrade, bul. Mihaila Pupina 2; tel. (11) 3111019; fax (11) 3617693; internet www.kim.sr.gov.yu.
Ministry of Labour and Social Affairs: 11000 Belgrade, bul. Mihaila Pupina 2; tel. (11) 3112916; fax (11) 3114650; e-mail ministar@minrzs.gov.rs; internet www.minrzs.gov.rs.
Ministry of Mining and Energy: 11000 Belgrade, Kralja Milana 36; tel. (11) 3346755; fax (11) 3616603; e-mail kabinet.mem@mem.sr.gov.yu; internet www.mem.gov.rs.
Ministry of the National Investment Plan: 11000 Belgrade, Vlajkovićeva 10; tel. (11) 3617583; internet www.mnip.gov.rs.
Ministry of Public Administration and Local Self-Government: 11000 Belgrade, Birčaninova 6; tel. (11) 3613654; fax (11) 2685396; e-mail info@mduls.gov.rs; internet www.drzavnauprava.gov.rs.
Ministry of Science and Technological Development: 11000 Belgrade, Nemanjina 22–26; tel. and fax (11) 3616516; e-mail info@nauka.gov.rs; internet www.nauka.gov.rs.
Ministry of Telecommunications and Information Technology: 11000 Belgrade, Nemanjina 22–26; tel. and fax (11) 2020057; e-mail kabinet@mtid.gov.rs; internet www.mtid.gov.rs.
Ministry of Trade and Services: 11000 Belgrade, Nemanjina 22–26; tel. (11) 3618852; fax (11) 3610285; e-mail trgovina@mtu.gov.rs; internet www.mtu.gov.rs.
Ministry of Youth and Sports: 11000 Belgrade, bul. Mihaila Pupina 2; tel. (11) 3130912; fax (11) 3130915; e-mail sport@mos.sr.gov.yu; internet www.mos.gov.rs.

President

Presidential Election, First Ballot, 20 January 2008

Candidate	Votes	% of votes
Tomislav Nikolić (Serbian Radical Party)	1,646,172	39.99
Boris Tadić (Democratic Party)	1,457,030	35.39
Velimir Ilić (New Serbia)	305,828	7.43
Milutin Mrkonjić (Socialist Party of Serbia)	245,889	5.97
Čedomir Jovanović (Liberal Democratic Party)	219,689	5.34
Others	163,765	3.69
Total*	4,116,844	100.00

* Including invalid votes.

Second Ballot, 3 February 2008

Candidate	Votes	% of votes
Boris Tadić (Democratic Party)	2,304,467	50.31
Tomislav Nikolić (Serbian Radical Party)	2,197,155	47.97
Total*	4,580,428	100.00

* Including invalid votes.

SERBIA

Legislature

Narodna skupština Republike Srbije
(National Assembly of the Republic of Serbia)
11000 Belgrade, Kralja Milana 14; tel. (11) 3222001; e-mail webmaster@parlament.sr.gov.yu; internet www.parlament.sr.gov.yu.

President: Prof. SLAVICA ĐUKIĆ-DEJANOVIĆ.

Election, 11 May 2008

Parties	% of votes	Seats
For a European Serbia—Boris Tadić*	38.44	102
Serbian Radical Party	29.36	78
Democratic Party of Serbia-New Serbia	11.59	30
Socialist Party of Serbia-Party of United Pensioners of Serbia-United Serbia	7.60	20
Liberal Democratic Party	5.24	13
Hungarian Coalition—István Pastor†	1.83	4
Bosniak List for a European Sandžak—Dr Sulejman Ugljanin‡	0.92	2
Albanian Coalition from the Preševo Valley	0.39	1
Strength of Serbia Movement	0.54	—
Others	1.86	—
Total§	**100.00**	**250**

* Coalition, principally comprising the Democratic Party, G17 Plus, the Serbian Renewal Movement, the League of Social-Democrats of Vojvodina and the Sandžak Democratic Party.
† Coalition of the Alliance of Vojvodina Hungarians, the Democratic Fellowship of Vojvodina Hungarians and the Democratic Party of Vojvodina Hungarians.
‡ Coalition of five parties from the Sandžak region.
§ Including invalid votes.

Election Commission

Electoral Commission of the Republic of Serbia: 11000 Belgrade, Kralja Milana 14; tel. (11) 3222001; fax (11) 3617839; e-mail rik@parlament.sr.gov.yu; internet www.rik.parlament.sr.gov.yu; Chair. SONJA BRKIĆ.

Political Organizations

A total of 342 political parties were registered in 2008.

Alliance of Vojvodina Hungarians (Vajdasági Magyar Szövetség/Savez Vojvođanskih Mađara): 24000 Subotica, Age Mamužića 11/I; tel. and fax (24) 553801; e-mail office@vmsz.org.rs; internet www.vmsz.org.rs; f. 1994; supports autonomous status for Vojvodina; contested legislative elections in May 2008 as part of the Hungarian Coalition—Istvan Pásztor; Chair. IŠTVAN PÁSZTOR.

Democratic Party (DP) (Demokratska Stranka—DS): 11000 Belgrade, Krunska 69; tel. (11) 3443003; fax (11) 2444864; e-mail info@ds.org.rs; internet www.ds.org.rs; f. 1990; led For a European Serbia—Boris Tadić coalition in legislative elections in May 2008; Pres. BORIS TADIĆ.

Democratic Party of Serbia (DPS) (Demokratska stranka Srbije—DSS): 11000 Belgrade, Pariska 13; tel. (11) 3204719; fax (11) 3204743; e-mail info@dss.rs; internet www.dss.rs; f. 1992 following split from Democratic Party; Leader Dr VOJISLAV KOŠTUNICA.

G17 Plus: 11000 Belgrade, trg Republike 5; tel. and fax (11) 3210355; fax (11) 3284054; e-mail office@g17plus.rs; internet www.g17plus.rs; f. 2003; contested legislative elections in May 2008 as part of the For a European Serbia—Boris Tadić coalition; Pres. MLAĐAN DINKIĆ.

League of Social-Democrats of Vojvodina (LSV) (Liga Socijaldemokrata Vojvodine): 21000 Novi Sad, trg Mladenaca 10; tel. (21) 529139; fax (21) 420628; e-mail infolsv@eunet.rs; internet www.lsv.org.rs; Pres. NENAD ČANAK.

Liberal Democratic Party (LDP) (Liberalno-demokratska Stranka—LDS): 11000 Belgrade, Simina 41; tel. (11) 3208300; fax (11) 3208301; e-mail predsednik@ldp.rs; internet www.ldp.rs; f. 2005 by fmr mems of the Democratic Party; Pres. ČEDOMIR JOVANOVIĆ.

New Serbia (Nova Srbija): 11000 Belgrade, Obilićev venac 4/1; tel. and fax (11) 3284766; fax (11) 2631748; e-mail nscentrala@gmail.com; internet www.nova-srbija.org; Pres. VELIMIR ILIĆ.

Party of United Pensioners of Serbia (PUPS) (Partija Ujedinjenih Penzionera Srbije): 11000 Belgrade, Svetozara Markovića 32; tel. (11) 2131487; e-mail office@pups.org.yu; internet www.pups.org.rs; Leader JOVAN KRKOBABIĆ.

Roma Party (Romska Partija): represents Roma ethnic minority; Leader ŠAJN SRĐAN.

Roma Union of Serbia (Unija Roma Srbije): 11000 Belgrade, Sarajevska 11; tel. (11) 2681693; e-mail unijaromasrbije@hotmail.com; internet www.unijaromasrbije.org.rs; f. 2004; represents Roma ethnic minority; Pres. Dr RAJKO ĐURIĆ.

Serbian Radical Party (SRP) (Srpska Radikalna Stranka—SRS): 11080 Belgrade, Zemun, Magistratski trg 3; tel. (11) 3164621; e-mail info@srs.org.yu; internet www.srpskaradikalnastranka.org.rs; f. 1991; extreme nationalist; advocates a 'Greater Serbian' state of territories inhabited by Serbs within and outside Serbia; leader Dr Vojislav Šešelj in detention at the International Criminal Tribunal for the former Yugoslavia; Leader Dr VOJISLAV ŠEŠELJ; Vice-Pres. DRAGAN TODOROVIĆ.

Serbian Renewal Movement (SRM) (Srpski pokret obnove—SPO): 11000 Belgrade, Kneza Mihailova 48; tel. (11) 3283620; fax (11) 2628170; e-mail vuk@spo.rs; internet www.spo.rs; f. 1990; nationalist; Pres. VUK DRAŠKOVIĆ.

Social Democratic Party (SDP) (Socijaldemokratska Partija): 11000 Belgrade, Ruzveltova 45; tel. (11) 3290820; fax (11) 3294507; e-mail ncovic@sdp.org.yu; internet www.sdp.org.rs; f. 1997; Pres. Dr NEBOJŠA ČOVIĆ.

Social Democratic Union (Socijaldemokratska Unija): 11000 Belgrade, Kralja Milana 34/1; tel. and fax (11) 3613649; fax (11) 3620862; e-mail info@sdu.org.yu; internet www.sdu.org.rs; f. 1996; Pres. ŽARKO KORAĆ.

Socialist Party of Serbia (SPS) (Socijalistička partija Srbije): 11000 Belgrade, Studentski trg 15; tel. (11) 3282713; fax (11) 2627170; e-mail glavniodbor@sps.org.rs; internet www.sps.org.rs; f. 1990 by merger of League of Communists of Serbia and Socialist Alliance of Working People of Serbia; Pres. IVICA DAČIĆ.

Strength of Serbia Movement (Pokret snaga Srbije): 11040 Belgrade, bul. Kneza Aleksandra Karađorđevića 49; tel. (11) 3692183; fax (11) 2651976; e-mail info@snagasrbije.com; internet www.snagasrbije.com; f. 2004; Leader BOGOLJUB KARIĆ.

United Serbia: 35000 Jagodina, Lole Ribara br. 14; tel. (81) 35233104; fax (81) 35852443; e-mail info@jedinstvenasrbija.org.rs; internet www.jedinstvenasrbija.org.rs; Leader DRAGAN MARKOVIĆ.

Diplomatic Representation

EMBASSIES IN SERBIA

Albania: 11000 Belgrade, bul. Kneza Aleksandra Karađorđevića 25A; tel. (11) 3066642; fax (11) 2665439; e-mail embassy.belgrade@mfa.gov.al; Chargé d'affaires a.i. ANTON KOLIQI.

Algeria: 11000 Belgrade, Maglajska 26 B; tel. (11) 3671211; fax (11) 2668200; e-mail ambalg@eunet.yu; Ambassador ABDELKADER MESDOUA.

Angola: 11000 Belgrade, Vase Pelagića 32; tel. (11) 3690241; fax (11) 3690191; e-mail ambasada.angole@sbb.rs; Chargé d'affaires a.i. VINCENTE MUANDA.

Argentina: 11000 Belgrade, Kneza Mihajlova 24/I; tel. (11) 2623569; fax (11) 2622630; e-mail argentinabg@nadlanu.com; Ambassador MARIO EDUARDO BOSSI DE EZCURRA.

Australia: 11070 Novi Belgrade, Vladimira Popovića 38–40, 8th floor; tel. (11) 3303400; fax (11) 3303409; e-mail belgrade.embassy@dfat.gov.au; internet www.serbia.embassy.gov.au; Ambassador CLARE BIRGIN.

Austria: 11000 Belgrade, Kneza Sime Markovića 2; tel. (11) 3336500; fax (11) 2635606; e-mail belgrade-ob@bmeia.gv.at; internet www.aussenministerium.at/belgrad; Ambassador CLEMENS KOJA.

Belarus: 11000 Belgrade, Deligradska 13; tel. (11) 3616938; fax (11) 3616836; e-mail sam@belembassy.org; Chargé d'affaires a.i. SIARHEI CHICHUK.

Belgium: 11000 Belgrade, Krunska 18; tel. (11) 3230018; fax (11) 3244394; e-mail belgrade@diplobel.fed.be; Ambassador DENISE DE HAUWERE.

Bosnia and Herzegovina: 11000 Belgrade, Krunska 9; tel. (11) 3241170; fax (11) 3241057; Chargé d'affaires a.i. AMIRA ARIFOVIĆ-HARMS.

Brazil: 11000 Belgrade, Krunska 14; tel. (11) 3239781; fax (11) 3230653; e-mail brasbelg@eunet.rs; internet www.ambasadabrazila.org.rs; Ambassador DANTE COELHO DE LIMA.

Bulgaria: 11000 Belgrade, Birčaninova 26; tel. (11) 3613980; fax 3611136; e-mail bulgamb@eunet.yu; internet www.mfa.bg/belgrade; Ambassador GEORGI DIMITROV.

Canada: 11000 Belgrade, Kneza Miloša 75; tel. (11) 3063000; fax (11) 3063042; e-mail bgrad@international.gc.ca; internet www.canada.org.rs; Ambassador JOHN ARTHUR MORRISON.

SERBIA

China, People's Republic: 11000 Belgrade, Augusta Cesarca 2v; tel. (11) 3695057; fax (11) 3066001; e-mail chinaemb_yu@mail.mfa.gov.cn; Ambassador WEI JINGHUA.

Congo, Democratic Republic: 11000 Belgrade, Moravska 5; tel. and fax (11) 3446431; e-mail ambardcbelgrade@yahoo.fr; Chargé d'affaires a.i. PAUL-EMILE TSHINGA AHUKA.

Croatia: 11000 Belgrade, Kneza Miloša 62; tel. (11) 3610535; fax (11) 3610032; e-mail crobg@mvpei.hr; internet rs.mvp.hr; Ambassador ŽELJKO KUPREŠAK.

Cuba: 11000 Belgrade, Vukovarska 3; tel. (11) 3692441; fax (11) 3692442; e-mail ambasada@ambasadakube.org.rs; internet www.ambasadakube.org.rs; Ambassador JULIO CÉSAR CANCIO FERRER.

Cyprus: 11000 Belgrade, Generala Save Grujića 18; tel. (11) 3620002; fax (11) 3621122; e-mail belgradeembassy@mfa.gov.cy; Ambassador HOMER MAVROMMATIS.

Czech Republic: 11000 Belgrade, bul. Kralja Aleksandra 22; tel. (11) 3230133; fax (11) 3236448; e-mail belgrade@embassy.mzv.cz; internet www.mzv.cz/belgrade; Ambassador HANA HUBÁČKOVÁ.

Denmark: 11040 Belgrade, Neznanog Junaka 9A; tel. (11) 3679500; fax (11) 3679502; e-mail begamb@um.dk; internet www.ambbeograd.um.dk; Ambassador METTE KJUEL NIELSEN.

Egypt: 11000 Belgrade, Andre Nikolića 12; tel. (11) 2650585; fax (11) 2652036; e-mail embassy.belgrade@mfa.gov.eg; Ambassador ADEL AHMED MUHAMMAD NAGUIB.

Finland: 11001 Belgrade, Birčaninova 29, POB 926; tel. (11) 3065400; fax (11) 3065375; e-mail sanomat.beo@formin.fi; Ambassador KARI JOHANNES VEIJALAINEN.

France: 11000 Belgrade, Pariska 11, POB 283; tel. (11) 3023500; fax (11) 3023510; e-mail amba_fr1@eunet.yu; internet www.ambafrance-srb.org; Ambassador JEAN-FRANÇOIS TERRAL.

Germany: 11000 Belgrade, Kneza Miloša 76; tel. (11) 3064300; fax (11) 3064303; e-mail germany@sbb.rs; internet www.belgrad.diplo.de; Ambassador WOLFRAM JOSEF MAAS.

Ghana: 11000 Belgrade, Đorđa Vajferta 50; tel. (11) 3440856; fax (11) 3440071; e-mail ghana@eunet.yu; internet www.ghanaembelgrade.com; Chargé d'affaires a.i. DORIS ADZO DENYO BRESE.

Greece: 11000 Belgrade, Francuska 33; tel. (11) 3226523; fax 3344746; e-mail office@greekemb.co.yu; internet www.greekemb.co.yu; Ambassador DIMOSTHENIS STOIDIS.

Guinea: 11000 Belgrade, Ohridska 4; tel. (11) 2451391; fax (11) 3444870; e-mail ambaguineebelgrade@eunet.yu; Ambassador El Hadj MUHAMMAD ISSIAGA KOUROUMA.

Holy See: 11000 Belgrade, Svetog Save 24; tel. (11) 3085356; fax (11) 3085216; e-mail nunbel@eunet.yu; Apostolic Nuncio Most Rev. EUGENIO SBARBARO (Titular Archbishop of Tiddi).

Hungary: 11000 Belgrade, Krunska 72; tel. (11) 2440472; fax (11) 3441876; e-mail mission.blg@kum.hu; internet www.hunemblg.hu; Ambassador SÁNDOR PAPP.

India: 11040 Belgrade, Ljutice Bogdana 8; tel. (11) 2661029; fax (11) 3674209; e-mail ssindemb@eunet.yu; internet www.embassyofindiabelgrade.org; Ambassador AJAY SWARUP.

Indonesia: 11000 Belgrade, bul. Kneza Aleksandra Karađorđevića 18; tel. (11) 3674062; fax (11) 3672984; e-mail kombeojo@eunet.yu; internet www.indonesia-bgd.org; Ambassador MUHAMMAD ABDUH DALIMUNTHE.

Iran: 11000 Belgrade, Ljutice Bogdana 40; tel. (11) 3674360; fax (11) 3674363; e-mail iran-emb@bitsyu.net; Ambassador (vacant).

Iraq: 11000 Belgrade, Neznanog Junaka 27A; tel. (11) 2662681; fax (11) 2668068; e-mail bgremb@iraqmofamail.net; Chargé d'affaires a.i. YAHYA SALIH MAHDI AL-GORANI.

Israel: 11000 Belgrade, bul. Kneza Aleksandra Karađorđevića 47; tel. (11) 3643500; fax (11) 3643555; e-mail info@belgrade.mfa.gov.il; internet belgrade.mfa.gov.il; Ambassador ARTHUR KOLL.

Italy: 11000 Belgrade, ul. Birčaninova 11; tel. (11) 3066100; fax (11) 3249413; e-mail segreteria.belgrado@esteri.it; internet www.ambbelgrado.esteri.it; Ambassador ALESSANDRO MEROLA.

Japan: 11070 Novi Belgrade, Vladimira Popovića 6; tel. (11) 3012800; fax (11) 3118258; e-mail protocol@jpemb.org.yu; internet www.yu.emb-japan.go.jp; Ambassador TOSHIO TSUNOZAKI.

Korea, Republic: 11070 Belgrade, Užička 32; tel. (11) 3674225; fax (11) 3674229; e-mail mail@koreanemb.org.yu; Ambassador Dr KIM JONG-HEE.

Lebanon: 11000 Belgrade, Diplomatska kolonija 5; tel. (11) 3675153; fax (11) 3675156; e-mail ambaleb@sbb.co.yu; Ambassador CHÉHADÉ MOUALLEM.

Libya: 11000 Belgrade, Sime Lozanića 6; tel. (11) 2663445; fax (11) 3670805; e-mail libyaamb@eunet.yu; Chargé d'affaires a.i. HANAN KHALED ZOGHBIA.

Macedonia, former Yugoslav republic: 11000 Belgrade, Gospodar Jevremova 34; tel. (11) 3284924; fax (11) 3285076; e-mail belgrade@mfa.gov.mk; Chargé d'affaires a.i. VLADIMIR KRSTEVSKI.

Malaysia: 11040 Belgrade, Krajiška 2; tel. (11) 2662736; fax (11) 3679080; e-mail malbelgrade@sbb.co.yu; Chargé d'affaires a.i. AMIZAL FADZLI BIN RAJALI.

Mexico: 11040 Belgrade, Ljutice Bogdana 5; tel. (11) 3674170; fax (11) 3675013; e-mail embamex@net.yu; internet www.mexican-embassy.org.yu; Chargé d'affaires a.i. EDUARDO HÉCTOR MOGUEL FLORES.

Montenegro: Belgrade, Užička 1; tel. and fax (11) 2668975; e-mail ambasadacg@gmail.com; Chargé d'affaires a.i. IGOR GRAĐEVIĆ.

Morocco: 11000 Belgrade, Sanje Živanović 4; tel. (11) 3691866; fax (11) 3690499; e-mail midi@sifamabe.org.yu; Ambassador KAMAL FAQIR BENAISSA.

Myanmar: 11000 Belgrade, Kneza Miloša 72; tel. (11) 3617165; fax (11) 3614968; e-mail myanbel@sezampro.yu; Ambassador SOE NWE.

Netherlands: 11000 Belgrade, Simina 29; tel. (11) 2023900; fax (11) 2023999; e-mail bel@minbuza.nl; internet www.nlembassy.org.yu; Ambassador RONALD JACOBUS PETRUS MARIE VAN DARTEL.

Norway: 11000 Belgrade, Užička 43; tel. (11) 3670404; fax (11) 3690158; internet emb.belgrade@mfa.no; Ambassador HÅKON BLANKENBORG.

Pakistan: 11000 Belgrade, bul. Kneza Aleksandra Karađorđevića 62; tel. (11) 2661676; fax (11) 2661667; e-mail ambpakistana@sbb.co.yu; internet www.pakistanembassy.org.yu; Ambassador MUHAMMAD NAWAZ CHAUDHRY.

Poland: 11000 Belgrade, Kneza Miloša 38; tel. (11) 2065318; fax (11) 3616939; e-mail ambrpfrj@eunet.yu; Ambassador MACIEJ SZYMAŃSKI.

Portugal: 11040 Belgrade, Vladimira Gaćinovića 4; tel. (11) 2662895; fax (11) 2662892; e-mail portugalambs@sbb.co.yu; Ambassador CAETANO LUÍS PEQUITO DE ALMEIDA SAMPAIO.

Romania: 11000 Belgrade, Užička 10; tel. (11) 3675772; fax (11) 3675771; e-mail ambelgro@infosky.net; Ambassador ION MACOVEI.

Russia: 11000 Belgrade, ul. Deligradska 32; tel. (11) 3610192; fax (11) 3611900; e-mail ambarusk@eunet.rs; internet www.ambasadarusije.org.rs; Ambassador ALEKSANDR V. KONUZIN.

San Marino: 11000 Belgrade, Makedonska 24/25; tel. (11) 3223509; fax (11) 3374144; e-mail sanmarino@sezampro.yu; Ambassador UBALDO LIVOLSI.

Slovakia: 11070 Belgrade, bul. Umetnosti 18; tel. (11) 2223800; fax (11) 2223820; e-mail embassy@belehrad.mfa.sk; internet www.belehrad.mfa.sk; Ambassador IGOR FURDÍK.

Slovenia: Belgrade, Pariska 15; tel. (11) 3038477; fax (11) 3288657; e-mail vbg@gov.si; internet beograd.veleposlanistvo.si; Ambassador MIROSLAV LUCI.

Spain: 11000 Belgrade, Prote Mateje 45; tel. (11) 3440231; fax (11) 3444203; e-mail emb.belgrado@mae.es; Ambassador IGNACIO DE PALACIO ESPAÑA.

Sweden: 11040 Belgrade, Ledi Pedzet 2; tel. (11) 2069200; fax (11) 2069250; e-mail ambassaden.belgrad@foreign.ministry.se; internet www.swedenabroad.se/belgrad; Ambassador NILS KRISTER BRINGÉUS.

Switzerland: 11000 Belgrade, Birčaninova 27; tel. (11) 3065820; fax (11) 2657253; e-mail bel.vertretung@eda.admin.ch; Ambassador ERWIN HELMUT HOFER.

Syria: 11000 Belgrade, Aleksandra Stamboliskog 13; tel. (11) 2666124; fax (11) 2660221; e-mail syremb@net.yu; Ambassador Dr MAJED SHADOUD.

Tunisia: 11000 Belgrade, Vase Pelagića 19; tel. (11) 3691961; fax (11) 3690642; e-mail at.belgr@eunet.yu; Ambassador HOURIA FERCHICHI.

Turkey: 11000 Belgrade, Krunska 1; tel. (11) 3232400; fax (11) 3332433; e-mail turem@eunet.yu; Ambassador AHMET SÜHA UMAR.

Ukraine: 11000 Belgrade, bul. Oslobođenja 87; tel. (11) 3978987; fax (11) 3978998; e-mail emb_sm@mfa.gov.ua; internet www.mfa.gov.ua/serbia; Ambassador ANATOLIY T. OLIYNYK.

United Kingdom: 11000 Belgrade, Resavska 46; tel. (11) 3060900; fax (11) 3061077; e-mail belgrade.ppd@fco.gov.uk; internet ukinserbia.fco.gov.uk; Ambassador STEPHEN JOHN WORDSWORTH.

USA: 11000 Belgrade, Kneza Miloša 50; tel. (11) 3619344; fax (11) 3615489; internet belgrade.usembassy.gov; Ambassador CAMERON PHELPS MUNTER.

Judicial System

The judicial system in the Republic of Serbia comprises the courts of regular competence (138 municipal courts, 30 district courts and the

SERBIA

Supreme Court of Serbia) and courts of the special competence (17 commercial courts, High Commercial Court). A new Constitution, which entered into effect on 8 November 2006, provided for an 11-member independent High Judicial Council, which was to guarantee the independence and autonomy of courts and judges. The legislature was to elect judges on the proposal of the High Judicial Council, while the High Judicial Council was to elect permanent judges. The Constitutional Court, which was to comprise 15 judges, protects constitutionality and legality, as well as human and minority rights and freedoms.

Constitutional Court (Ustavni Sud Srbije): 11000 Belgrade, Nemanjina 26; tel. (11) 3616372; fax (11) 2658970; e-mail informacija@ustavni.sud.sr.gov.yu; internet www.ustavni.sud.sr.gov.yu; f. 1963; Pres. BOSA NENADIĆ.

Supreme Court (Vrhovni Sud Srbije): 11000 Belgrade, Resavska 42; tel. (11) 3634207; fax (11) 3619376; e-mail vss@vrh.sud.rs; internet www.vrh.sud.rs; Pres. NATA NATA MESAROVIĆ.

Office of the Public Prosecutor of Serbia: 11000 Belgrade; tel. (11) 658755; Public Prosecutor SLOBODAN RADOVANOVIĆ.

Religion

Most of the inhabitants of Serbia are, at least nominally, Christian, but there is a significant Muslim minority. The main Christian denomination is Eastern Orthodox, but there is a strong Roman Catholic presence. There are also small minorities of Old Catholics, Protestants and Jews.

CHRISTIANITY

The Eastern Orthodox Church

Serbian Orthodox Church (Srpska Pravoslavna Crkva): 11001 Belgrade, Kralja Petra 5, POB 182; tel. (11) 3025112; e-mail info@spc.rs; internet www.spc.rs; 11m. adherents; Patriarch of Serbia, Archbishop of Peć and Metropolitan of Belgrade-Karlovci PAVLE.

The Roman Catholic Church

Serbia comprises one archdiocese and three dioceses. There is also an apostolic exarchate of Serbia and Montenegro for Catholics of the Byzantine rite. At 31 December 2006 adherents of the Roman Catholic Church represented about 5.7% of the total population of Serbia (including those adherents of the Byzantine rite resident within Montenegro).

International Bishops' Conference of SS Cyril and Methodius: 11000 Belgrade, Višegradska 23; tel. (11) 3032246; fax (11) 3032248; f. 2006; Pres. Most Rev. STANISLAV HOČEVAR (Archbishop of Belgrade).

Archbishop of Belgrade: Most Rev. STANISLAV HOČEVAR, 11000 Belgrade, Svetozara Markovića 20; tel. (11) 3032246; fax (11) 3032248; e-mail nadbisbg@eunet.yu; internet www.kc.org.rs.

Apostolic Exarch to Serbia and Montenegro for Catholics of the Byzantine Rite: ĐURA DŽUDŽAR (Titular Archbishop of Acrasso), 21000 Novi Sad, D. Magaraševića 18; tel. (21) 6371609; fax (21) 6371613; 22,653 adherents (2006).

Protestant Churches

Christian Reformed Church: 24323 Feketić, Bratsva 26; tel. and fax (24) 738070; f. 1919; 22,000 mems; Bishop ISTVAN CSETE-SZEMESI.

Evangelical Christian Church of the Augsburg (Lutheran) Confession in Serbia-Vojvodina: 24000 Subotica, Braće Radića 17; tel. and fax (24) 527778; e-mail lutheran@stcable.net; internet www.lutheran.org.rs; Superintendent DOLINSZKY ÁRPÁD.

Slovak Evangelical Church of the Augsburg (Lutheran) Confession: 21000 Novi Sad, Karadžićeva 2; tel. (21) 6611882; e-mail secav@eunet.yu; 50,000 mems (2002); Bishop Dr SAMUEL VRBOVSKY.

Union of Baptist Churches in Serbia: 11000 Belgrade, Slobodanke D. Savić 33; tel. and fax (11) 410964; f. 1992; Gen. Sec. Rev. AVRAM DEGA.

ISLAM

There are ethnic Slav Muslims (Bosniaks) in the part of Sandžak located in south-west Serbia, in particular in and around the town of Novi Pazar. Most Muslims in the country are Sunni.

Islamic Community of Serbia: Belgrade, G. Jevremova 11; tel. (11) 2622428; e-mail reis@rijaset.rs; internet www.rijaset.rs; Reis-ul-ulema ADEM EF. ZILKIĆ.

Islamic Community of Vojvodina: 21000 Novi Sad, Futoška 61; tel. and fax (21) 6619444; internet www.islamvojvodina.com; Chair. ZIJA ZEKIR.

JUDAISM

Federation of Jewish Communities in Serbia: 11000 Belgrade, Kralja Petra 71 A/III, POB 512; tel. (11) 2624359; fax (11) 2621837; e-mail office@savezscg.net; f. 1919, revived 1944; Pres. ALEKSANDAR NEĆAK.

The Press

PRINCIPAL DAILIES
(In Serbian, except where otherwise stated)

Belgrade

Blic: 11000 Belgrade, Masarikova 5; tel. (11) 3619471; fax (11) 3619326; e-mail redakcija@blic.rs; internet www.blic.rs; f. 1996; Editor-in-Chief VESLIN SIMONOVIĆ; circ. 230,000.

Borba: 11000 Belgrade, trg Nikole Pašića 7; tel. (11) 3398137; fax (11) 344913; e-mail office@borba.rs; internet www.borba.rs; f. 1922; morning; Editor-in-Chief OLIVERA ZEKIĆ.

Glas Javnosti (Voice of the Public): 11000 Belgrade, Vlajkovićeva 8; tel. (11) 3249125; fax (11) 3225095; e-mail webmaster@glas-javnosti.co.yu; internet www.glas-javnosti.rs; f. 1874; Editor-in-Chief LJILJANA STALETOVIĆ.

Politika: 11000 Belgrade, Makedonska 29; tel. (11) 3301681; fax (11) 3373164; e-mail redakcija@politika.rs; internet www.politika.rs; f. 1904; Dir-Gen. SRĐANO JANIĆIJEVIĆ; Editor-in-Chief LJILJANA SMAJLOVIĆ; circ. 110,000.

Politika Ekspres: 11000 Belgrade, Makedonska 29; tel. (11) 325630; evening; Editor-in-Chief MILE KORDIĆ; circ. 76,000.

Pregled: 11000 Belgrade, Jasenova 5; tel. and fax (11) 3282405; e-mail info@pregled.com; internet www.pregled.com; f. 1950; business and economics; Dir and Chief Editor ALEKSANDAR JOVANOVIĆ.

Večernje novosti (Evening News): 11000 Belgrade, trg Nikole Pašića 7; tel. (11) 3028000; e-mail redakcija@novosti.rs; internet www.novosti.rs; f. 1953; Gen. Dir and Editor-in-Chief MANOJLO MANJO VUKOTIĆ; circ. 270,000.

Niš

Narodne Novine (The People's News): 18000 Niš, Vojvode Gojka 14; internet www.narodne.com; morning.

Novi Sad

Dnevnik (Daily News): 21000 Novi Sad, bul. Oslobođenja 81; tel. (21) 421493; e-mail redakcija@dnevnik.rs; internet www.dnevnik.rs; f. 1942 as *Slobodna Vojvodina* (Free Vojvodina); morning; Editor-in-Chief PETAR PETROVIĆ.

PERIODICALS

Belgrade

Ekonomist: Belgrade, Kosovska 1/IV; tel. (11) 3284034; internet www.emportal.rs; f. 1948; quarterly; journal of the Yugoslav Association of Economists; Editor Dr HASAN HADŽIOMEROVIĆ.

Ekonomska Politika (Economic Policy): 11000 Belgrade, trg Nikole Pašića 7; tel. (11) 3398298; fax (11) 3398300; e-mail office@ekopol.co.yu; f. 1952; weekly; Dir ČEDOMIR ŠOŠKIĆ; Editor-in-Chief SLAVKA KOVAČ.

Ilustrovana Politika: 11000 Belgrade, 29 Novembra 24; tel. (11) 3301442; fax (11) 3373346; f. 1958; weekly illustrated review; Gen. Dir DARKO RIBNIKAR; Editor-in-Chief GORDANA KNEŽEVIĆ; circ. 90,000.

Jisa Info: 11000 Belgrade, Zmaj Jovina 4; tel. (11) 2620374; fax (11) 2626576; e-mail jisa@jisa.rs; internet www.jisa.rs; f. 1993; publ. by Jisa (Jedinstveni informatički savez Srbije—Union of ICT Societies of Serbia); computing, technology; Pres. ĐORĐE DUKIĆ.

Međunarodni Problemi/International Problems: 11000 Belgrade, Institute of International Politics and Economics, Makedonska 25; tel. (11) 3373633; fax (11) 3373835; e-mail iipe@diplomacy.bg.ac.yu; internet www.diplomacy.bg.ac.yu/mpro.htm; f. 1949; quarterly; in Serbian and English; Editor BRANA MARKOVIĆ; circ. 1,000.

Mikro/PC World: 11030 Belgrade, Požeška 81A; tel. (11) 3055010; fax (11) 3058034; internet www.mikro.rs; f. 1997; 11 a year; computing; Editorial Dir ALEKSANDAR SPASIĆ; circ. 23,000 (2007).

Nezavisna Svetlost: 34000 Kragujevac, Branka Radičevića 9; tel. (34) 336176; fax (34) 335218; e-mail office@svetlost.rs; internet www.svetlost.rs; f. 1995; weekly news; Editor-in-Chief MIROSLAV MILOSAVLJEVIĆ.

NIN—Nedeljne informativne novine (Weekly Informative News): 11000 Belgrade, Cetinjska 1, POB 208; tel. (11) 3373111; fax (11) 3373171; e-mail redakcija@nin.co.yu; internet www.nin.co

SERBIA

.rs; f. 1935; politics, economics, culture; Dir DRAŠKO TANKOSIĆ; Editor-in-Chief SLOBODAN RELJIĆ; circ. 35,000.

Odbrana (Defence): 11002 Belgrade, Brace Jugovića 19; internet www.odbrana.mod.gov.rs; tel. (11) 3241258; fax (11) 3241363; f. 2005 to replace *Vojska* (Soldier); two a month; publ. by Ministry of Defence; Editor-in-Chief Lt-Col SLAVOLJUB M. MARKOVIĆ.

Ošišani Jež (Trimmed Hedgehog): 11000 Belgrade, Resavska 28; tel. (11) 3232211; fax (11) 3232423; f. 1935 as *Jež* (Hedgehog); fortnightly; satirical; Editor RADIVOJE BOJIČIĆ; circ. 50,000.

Politikin Zabavnik: Belgrade 11001, Cetinska 1; tel. (11) 3301452; fax (11) 3373319; e-mail editors@politika-ad.com; internet www.politikin-zabavnik.rs; f. 1939; weekly; comic; Editor-in-Chief ZEFIRINO GRASI; circ. 41,000.

Pravoslavlje (Orthodoxy): 11000 Belgrade, Kralja Petra 5; tel. (11) 3282596; fax (11) 630865; e-mail pravoslavlje@spc.yu; internet www.pravoslavlje.com; f. 1967; fortnightly; Orthodox Christian.

Pregled Republika Srbija/Survey—Republic of Serbia: 11000 Belgrade, Dečanska 8, POB 677; tel. (11) 3233610; fax (11) 3240291; e-mail info@pregled-rs.rs; internet www.pregled-rs.rs; f. 1957 as *Jugoslovenski pregled/Yugoslav Survey*, renamed *Pregled SCG/Survey Serbia & Montenegro* in 2003, present name adopted 2006; quarterly; general reference publication of basic documentary information about Serbia; Serbian and English edns; Editor-in-Chief ILE KOVAČEVIĆ.

Viva: 11000 Belgrade, Cetinjska 1v; tel. (11) 3220132; fax (11) 3220552; e-mail viva@politika.co.uk; monthly; health; Editor DRAGUTIN GREGORIĆ; circ. 25,000.

Vreme (Time): Belgrade, Mišarska 12–14; tel. (11) 3234774; fax (11) 3238662; internet www.vreme.com; Editor-in-Chief DRAGOLJUB ŽARKOVIĆ.

Novi Sad

Letopis Matice Srpske: 21000 Novi Sad, Matice srpske 1; tel. (21) 527622; fax (21) 528901; e-mail ms@maticasrpska.org.yu; internet www.maticasrpska.org.yu/pages/izdanja/letopis.htm; f. 1824; monthly; literary review; Editors Dr DRAGAN STANIĆ, IVAN NEGRISORAC.

NEWS AGENCIES

Beta News Agency: 11000 Belgrade, Kraljana Milana 4; tel. (11) 3602400; fax (11) 2642551; e-mail marketing@beta.co.yu; internet www.beta.co.yu; f. 1992; regional independent news service; Dir LJUBICA MARKOVIĆ; Editor-in-Chief IVAN CVEJIĆ.

Tanjug News Agency (Novinska Agencija Tanjug): 11001 Belgrade, Obilićev Venac 2, POB 439; tel. (11) 3281608; fax (11) 3282766; e-mail direkcija@tanjug.rs; internet www.tanjug.rs; f. 1943; press and information agency; in Serbian, English, French and Spanish.

PRESS ASSOCIATION

Independent Association of Journalists of Serbia: 11000 Belgrade, Resavska 28/II; tel. (11) 3343255; fax (11) 3343136; e-mail nuns@nuns.org.yu; internet www.nuns.org.yu; Pres. NADEŽDA GAĆE.

Publishers

Alfa-Narodna knjiga (Alfa-People's Books): 11000 Belgrade, Višegradska 1A; tel. and fax (11) 3660349; internet www.narodnaknjigaskola.com; f. 1955; fiction, non-fiction, children's books and dictionaries; Gen. Man. MILIČKO MIJOVIĆ.

BIGZ (Beogradski izdavačko-grafički zavod) Publishing a.d. (Belgrade Publishing and Graphics Cp): 11000 Belgrade, bul. Vojvode Mišića 17/III; tel. (11) 3691259; fax (11) 3690519; internet www.bigz-publishing.co.yu; f. 1831; privately owned; literature and criticism, children's books, pocket books, popular science, philosophy, politics; Dir MIRJANA MILORADOVIĆ.

Dečje novine: 32300 Gornji Milanovac, T. Matijevića 4; tel. (32) 711195; fax (32) 711248; general literature, children's books, science, science fiction, textbooks; Gen. Dir MIROSLAV PETROVIĆ.

Forum Publishing House: 21000 Novi Sad, Vojvode Mišića 1, POB 200; tel. (21) 611300; f. 1957; newspapers, periodicals and books in Hungarian; Dir GYULA GOBBY.

Građevinska Knjiga (Citizens' Books) **Publishing House:** 11000 Belgrade, trg Nikole Pašića 8/II; tel. (11) 3233565; fax (11) 3233563; f. 1948; technical, scientific and educational textbooks; Dir LJUBINKO ANĐELIĆ.

Jugoslovenska knjiga (Yugoslav Books) **Publishing House:** 11000 Belgrade, trg Republike 5, POB 36; tel. (11) 621992; fax (11) 625970; art, economics and culture; Dir ZORAN NIKODIJEVIĆ.

Vuk Karadžič Publishing House: 11000 Belgrade, Kraljevića Marka 9, POB 762; tel. (11) 628066; fax (11) 623150; scientific and academic literature, popular science, children's books, general; Gen. Man. VOJIN ANČIĆ.

Matice srpske Publishing House: 21000 Novi Sad, Matice Srpske 1; tel. (21) 527622; fax (21) 528901; e-mail ms@maticasrpska.org.yu; internet www.maticasrpska.org.yu; f. 1826; domestic and foreign fiction and humanities; Man. Dir MILORAD GRUJIĆ.

Medicinska knjiga (Medical Books) Publishing House: 11001 Belgrade, Mata Vidakovića 24–26; tel. (11) 458165; f. 1947; medicine, pharmacology, stomatology, veterinary; Dir MILE MEDIĆ.

Minerva Publishing House: 24000 Subotica, trg 29 Novembra 3; tel. (24) 25712; fax (24) 23208; novels and general; Dir LADISLAV ŠEBEK.

Naučna knjiga (Scientific Books) Publishing House: 11000 Belgrade, Uzun Mirkova 5; tel. (11) 637220; f. 1947; school, college and university textbooks, publications of scientific bodies; Dir Dr BLAŽO PEROVIĆ.

Nolit: 11000 Belgrade, Terazije 27; tel. (11) 3245017; fax (11) 627285; f. 1928; belles-lettres, philosophy and fine art; scientific and popular literature; Dir-Gen. RADIVOJE NEŠIĆ; Editor-in-Chief RADIVOJE MIKIĆ.

Prosveta (Education) Publishing House: 11000 Belgrade, Čika Ljubina 1; tel. (11) 2629843; fax (11) 2627465; e-mail prosveta@prosveta.co.yu; f. 1944; general literature, art books, dictionaries, encyclopaedias, science, music; Dir ZOVICA MIŠIĆ.

Rad (Labour) Publishing House: 11000 Belgrade, Dečanska 12; tel. (11) 3239998; fax (11) 3230923; f. 1949; politics, economics, sociology, psychology, literature, biographies; Man. Dir SIMON SIMONOVIĆ; Editor-in-Chief NOVICA TADIĆ.

Savremena administracija (Contemporary Administration) Publishing House: 11000 Belgrade, Crnotravska 7–9; tel. (11) 667633; fax (11) 667277; e-mail m.jovic@savremena-ad.com; internet www.savremena-ad.com; f. 1954; economy, law, science university textbooks, encyclopedias and dictionaries; Dir MILUTIN PEJČIĆ.

Srpska književna zadruga (Serb Publishing Collective): 11000 Belgrade, Srpskih Vladara 19/I; tel. (11) 330305; fax (11) 626224; f. 1892; works of classical and modern Serb writers, and translations of works of foreign writers; Pres. RADOVAN SAMARDŽIĆ; Editor RADOMIR RADOVANAČ.

Tehnička Knjiga (Technical Books) Publishing House: 11000 Belgrade, Vojvode Stepe 89; tel. (11) 468596; fax (11) 473442; f. 1948; technical works, popular science, reference books, hobbies; Dir RADIVOJE GRBOVIĆ.

Zavod za udžbenike i nastavna sredstva (Institute for School Books and Teaching Aids): 11000 Belgrade, Obilićev Venac 5; tel. (11) 2637433; fax (11) 2637426; internet www.zavod.co.rs; f. 1957; textbooks and teaching aids; Dir and Editor-in-Chief MILOLJUB ALBIJANIĆ.

PUBLISHERS' ASSOCIATIONS

Asscn of Publishers and Booksellers of Serbia (Udruženje izdavača i knjižara Srbije): 11000 Belgrade, Kneza Miloša 25, POB 570; tel. (11) 642533; fax (11) 646339; e-mail ognjenl@eunet.yu; f. 1954; organizes Belgrade International Book Fair; Dir OGNJEN LAKIĆEVIĆ; 116 mem. organizations.

Asscn of Publishers and Booksellers of Vojvodina (Poslovno udruženje izdavača i knjižara Vojvodine): 21000 Novi Sad; tel. and fax (21) 4720452; e-mail info@knjigavoj.co.rs; internet www.knjigavoj.co.rs; f. 2001; Dir ROMAN VEHOVEĆ; Chair. of Council ĐEZE BORDAS.

Broadcasting and Communications

TELECOMMUNICATIONS

Telekom Srbija (Telecom Serbia): 11000 Belgrade, Takovska 7; tel. (11) 3229991; internet www.telekomsrbija.com; 20% owned by OTE (Greece); provides fixed line and mobile cellular telecommunications services in Serbia; Dir-Gen. BRANKO RADUJKO.

Telenor d.o.o.: 11070 Belgrade, Omladinskih Brigada 90; e-mail pr@telenor.rs; internet www.telenor.co.rs; f. 1994 as Mobtel Srbija; present name adopted 2006, following acquisition by Telenor Group (Norway); provides mobile cellular telecommunications in Serbia; CEO KJELL-MORTEN JOHNSEN.

BROADCASTING

Association of Independent Electronic Media: 11000 Belgrade, Maršala Birjuzova 13A; tel. and fax (11) 2622467; e-mail anem@anem

.org.rs; internet www.anem.org.rs; f. 1993; comprises 16 television and 28 radio stations, and 60 affiliated orgs; Chair. SAŠA MIRKOVIĆ.

Radiotelevizija Srbije (RTS) (Radio-Television of Serbia): 11000 Belgrade, Takovska 10; tel. (11) 3212200; fax (11) 3212211; internet www.rts.rs; f. 1929; 5 radio programmes; comprises Radiotelevizija Beograd (Radio-Television of Belgrade), Radiotelevizija Novi Sad (Radio-Television of Novi Sad, Vojvodina) and Radiotelevizija Priština (Radio-Television of Priština, Kosovo); Dir-Gen. ALEKSANDAR TIJANIĆ.

Radio

Međunarodni Radio Srbija (International Radio Serbia): 11000 Belgrade, Hilandarska 2, POB 200; tel. (11) 3244455; fax (11) 3232014; e-mail radioyu@bitsyu.net; internet www.glassrbije.org; f. 1951; fmrly Radio Jugoslavija (Radio Yugoslavia); state-owned short-wave station; broadcasts daily in Serbian, English, French, German, Russian, Spanish, Hungarian, Chinese, Albanian, Greek, Italian and Arabic; Dir MILENA JOKIĆ.

Radio B92: 11000 Belgrade, bul. Avnoja 64; tel. (11) 3012000; fax (11) 3012001; internet www.b92.net; f. 1989; independent; Dir VERAN MATIĆ; Dir of Radio Programming GORICA NEŠOVIĆ.

Radio JAT: 11000 Belgrade, Svetog Save 1/XVI; tel. (11) 2440142; e-mail radio_jat@jat.com.

Radiotelevizija Košava: 11000 Belgrade, Aleksandra Dubčeka 14; tel. (11) 3061491; fax (11) 3612135; internet www.kosava.co.rs; f. 1994; radio station broadcasting popular music and talk programmes to most regions of Serbia; Editor-in-Chief MILOMIR MARIĆ.

Radio TV Bajina Basta: 31250 Bajina Basta, Svetosavska 34; tel. (31) 851688; fax (31) 853162; e-mail office@bajinabasta.org; internet www.bajinabasta.org; f. 1986; independent radio and television station; Dir BOBAN TOMIĆ.

Television

B92 Televizija: 11000 Belgrade, bul. Avnoja 64; tel. (11) 3012000; fax (11) 3012001; internet www.b92.net; f. 2000; independent; Dir VERAN MATIĆ; Dir of Programming IVA IVANIŠEVIĆ.

BK Telecom (BK): 11070 Belgrade, Nikole Tesle 42A; tel. (11) 3013555; fax (11) 3013526; internet www.bktv.com; f. 1994; independent television station; Dir-Gen. Dr TIMOHIR SIMIĆ; Editor-in-Chief MILOMIR MARIĆ.

RTV Pink: 11000 Belgrade, Neznanog Junaka 1; tel. (11) 3063400; fax (11) 3063500; internet www.rtvpink.com; f. 1993; Pres. and CEO ŽELJKO MITROVIĆ.

Finance

(cap. = capital; res = reserves; dep. = deposits; m. = million; amounts in Serbian dinars, unless otherwise stated; br. = branch)

BANKING

Central Banking System

In 2003, following the reconstitution of the Federal Republic of Yugoslavia as the State Union of Serbia and Montenegro, the National Bank of Yugoslavia became Serbia's central bank, and was renamed the National Bank of Serbia. In 2008 there were 34 banks in Serbia, 19 of which were in majority foreign ownership, seven in majority domestic private ownership and eight in majority state ownership.

National Bank of Serbia (Narodna banka Srbije): 11000 Belgrade, Kralja Petra 12, POB 1010; tel. (11) 3027100; fax (11) 3027394; e-mail kabinet@nbs.rs; internet www.nbs.rs; f. 1884; present name adopted 2003; cap. 14,751m., res 7,692m., dep. 705,635m. (Dec. 2007); Gov. RADOVAN JELAŠIĆ; 6 brs.

Other Banks

Alpha Bank Srbija a.d.: 11000 Belgrade, Kralja Milana 11; tel. (11) 3234931; fax (11) 3246840; e-mail alphabankserbia@alphabankserbia.com; internet www.alphabankserbia.com; f. 1956; 100% owned by Alpha Bank AE (Greece); present name adopted 2006; cap. 12,589.1m., res −2,947.3m., dep. 32,872.1m. (Dec. 2007); Chair. SPYROS N. FILARETOS; 23 brs.

Banca Intesa a.d. Beograd: 11070 Belgrade, Milentija Popovića 7B; tel. (11) 2011213; fax (11) 2011207; e-mail bi@bancaintesabeograd.com; internet www.bancaintesabeograd.com; f. 1991; present name adopted 2005; 90% owned by Intesa Holding International SA (Luxembourg); absorbed Panonska Banka a.d. in Jan. 2008; cap. 18,753.8m., res 7,106.5m., dep. 153,151.5m. (Dec. 2007); Chief Exec. DRAGINJA ĐURIĆ; 150 brs.

Erste Bank a.d. Novi Sad: 21000 Novi Sad, bul. Oslobođenja 5; tel. (21) 4809402; fax (21) 4890651; e-mail info@erstebank.rs; internet www.erstebank.rs; f. 1864 as Novosadska Banka a.d.; present name adopted 2005; 99.9% owned by Erste Bank Group AG (Austria); cap. 12,279.3m., res 23.4m., dep. 25,777.0m. (Dec. 2007); Pres. SAVA DALBOKOV.

Hypo Alpe-Adria-Bank a.d. Beograd: 11070 Novi Beograd, bul. Mihaila Pupina 6; tel. (11) 2226000; fax (11) 2226555; e-mail office@hypo-alpe-adria.rs; internet www.hypo-alpe-adria.rs; f. 1991 as Depositno-Kreditna Banka; merged with Hypo Alpe-Adria-Bank 2002; cap. 11,683.8m., res 2,159.9m., dep. 79,838.9m. (Dec. 2006); Chair. VLADIMIR ČUPIĆ.

Komercijalna Banka a.d. Beograd: 11000 Belgrade, Svetog Save 14; tel. (11) 3080100; fax (11) 3441335; e-mail posta@kombank.com; internet www.kombank.com; f. 1970; 40.3% state-owned, 25.0% owned by European Bank for Reconstruction and Development (United Kingdom); cap. 13,187.6m., res 2,802.3m., dep. 124,610.4m. (Dec. 2007); Pres. IVICA SMOLIĆ.

NLB Continental Banka a.d. Novi Sad: 21000 Novi Sad, trg Mladenaca 1–3; tel. (21) 6615500; fax (21) 6616560; e-mail podrska@nlb.rs; internet www.nlb.rs; f. 1991; 99.5% owned by Nova Ljubljanska banka d.d. (Slovenia); present name adopted 2006; cap. 3,795.6m., res 779.0m., dep. 19,171.3m. (Dec. 2006); Chair. ANDREJ HAZABENT.

OTP Banka a.d. Novi Sad: 21000 Novi Sad, bul. Oslobođenja 80; tel. (21) 4800000; fax (21) 4800032; e-mail office@otpbanka.co.yu; internet www.otpbanka.rs; f. 2007 by merger of Niška Banka a.d. Niš, Kulska Banka a.d. Novi Sad and Zepter banka a.d. Beograd; 91.4% owned by OTP Bank (Hungary); cap. 6,950.3m., res 3,766.8m., dep. 22,873.6m. (Dec. 2007); Pres. of Exec. Bd SZÁSZ KÁROLY.

ProCredit Bank a.d. Beograd: 11000 Belgrade, bul. Despota Stefana 68C; tel. (11) 2077906; fax (11) 2077905; e-mail info@procreditbank.rs; internet www.procreditbank.rs; f. 2001; 66.7% owned by ProCredit Holding AG (Germany); cap. 2,363.3m., res 1,989.0m., dep. 31,438.7m. (Dec. 2007); Chair. of Exec. Bd DOERTE WEIDIG.

Raiffeisenbank a.d. Beograd: 11000 Belgrade, bul. Zorana Đinđića 64A; tel. (11) 3202100; fax (11) 2207080; e-mail info@raiffeisenbank.rs; internet www.raiffeisenbank.rs; f. 2001; 100% owned by Raiffeisenbank International Bank-Holding AG (Austria); cap. 24,702.7m., dep. 112,754.4m., total assets 157,173.1m. (Dec. 2007); Chair. and Gen. Man. OLIVER ROEGL.

UniCredit Bank Srbija a.d.: 11000 Belgrade, Rajićeva 27–29; tel. (11) 3344100; fax (11) 3204639; e-mail office@unicreditbank.co.yu; internet www.unicreditbank.co.yu; f. 2001; present name adopted 2007; 99.5% owned by Bank Austria Creditanstalt AG (Austria); cap. 10,219.8m., res 2,512.9m., dep. 54,972.3m. (Dec. 2007); Chair. of Management Bd KLAUS PRIVERSCHEK.

Vojvodjanska Banka, a.d. Novi Sad: 21000 Novi Sad, POB 391, trg Slobode 7; tel. (21) 4886600; fax (21) 6624859; e-mail office@voban.co.yu; internet www.voban.co.rs; f. 1962; 100% owned by National Bank of Greece SA (Greece); cap. 8,946.7m., res 1,665.9m., dep. 41,229.9m. (Dec. 2007); Pres. MARINIS STRATOPOULOS.

Banking Association

Association of Serbian Banks (Udruženje banaka Srbije): 11001 Belgrade, bul. Kralja Aleksandra 86; tel. (11) 3020760; fax (11) 3370179; e-mail ubs@ubs-asb.com; internet www.ubs-asb.com; f. 1955; association of business banks; works on improving inter-bank co-operation, organizes agreements of mutual interest for banks, gives expert assistance, establishes co-operation with foreign banks, other financial institutions and their associations, represents banks in relations with the Government and the National Bank of Serbia; Sec.-Gen. VEROLJUB DUGALIĆ.

STOCK EXCHANGE

Belgrade Stock Exchange (Beogradska Berza): 11070 Belgrade, Omladinskih brigada 1, POB 50; tel. (11) 3117297; fax (11) 138242; e-mail info@belex.co.yu; internet www.belex.co.rs; Chair. of Bd GORDANA DOSTANIĆ.

INSURANCE

AMS Osiguranje (AMS Insurance): 11000 Belgrade, Ruzveltova 16; tel. (11) 3084900; e-mail info@ams.co.rs; internet www.ams.co.yu; non-life; Gen. Dir DRAGOLJUB RADOJEVIĆ.

DDOR Novi Sad: 21000 Novi Sad, Železnička 5; tel. (21) 4871000; internet www.ddor.co.yu; f. 1990; life and non-life insurance and reinsurance; Gen. Dir DARKO BOTIĆ.

Delta Generali Osiguranje: 11070 Novi Beograd, Milentija Popovića 7B; tel. (11) 2011720; fax (11) 2011727; e-mail kontakt@deltagenerali.rs; internet www.deltagenerali.rs; life and non-life insurance and reinsurance.

Dunav Osiguranje (Danube Insurance): 11000 Belgrade, Makedonska 4, POB 624; tel. (11) 3224001; fax (11) 2624652; e-mail info@

dunav.com; internet www.dunav.com; f. 1974; life and non-life insurance and reinsurance; Gen. Man. MIRKO PETROVIĆ.

SIM Osiguranje (SIM Insurance): 11000 Belgrade, Oblakovska 28; tel. and fax (11) 3690110; e-mail simosg@eunet.yu.

Uniqa Osiguranje: 11000 Belgrade, Milutina Milankovića 134G; tel. (11) 2024100; e-mail info@uniqa.rs; internet www.uniqa.co.yu/uniqa_rs; fmrly Zepter Osiguranje; present name adopted 2006, following acquisition by Uniqa (Austria); life and non-life insurance; KONSTANTIN KLIJEN.

Trade and Industry

GOVERNMENT AGENCIES

Foreign Trade Institute (Institut za Spoljnu Trgovinu): 11000 Belgrade, Moše Pijade 8; tel. (11) 3235391; fax (11) 3235306; e-mail radovank@eunet.yu; Dir Dr SLOBODAN MRKŠA.

Investment and Export Promotion Agency of the Republic of Serbia (Agencija za strana ulaganja i promociju izvoza Republike Srbije—SIEPA): 11000 Belgrade, Vlajkovićeva 3; tel. (11) 3398550; fax (11) 3398814; e-mail office@siepa.gov.rs; internet www.siepa.gov.rs; f. 2001; Dir VESNA PERIĆ.

CHAMBER OF COMMERCE

Chamber of Commerce of Serbia (Privredna Komora Srbije): 11000 Belgrade, Resavska 13–15; tel. (11) 3300900; fax (11) 3230949; internet pks.komora.net; Pres. MILOŠ BUGARIN.

UTILITIES
Electricity

Elektroprivreda Srbije (EPS) (Serbia Electricity Corpn): 11000 Belgrade, Balkanska 13; tel. (11) 3610580; fax (11) 3611908; e-mail dragomir.markovic@eps.rs; internet www.eps.rs; state-owned; production, transmission and distribution of electric power in Serbia (incl. Kosovo); Chair. PETAR KNEŽEVIĆ; Gen. Man. DRAGOMIR MARKOVIĆ.

Gas

Naftna Industrija Srbije—NIS a.d. Novi Sad (Oil Industry of Serbia): 21000 Novi Sad, Narodnog fronta 12; tel. (21) 4811111; fax (21) 4814321; e-mail office@nis.yu; internet www.nis.rs; four principal subsidiaries: NIS-Naftagas (NIS Oil and Gas); NIS-Petrol Jugpetrol (NIS Petrol); NIS-TNG (liquid petroleum gas); NIS-Ogostiteljstvo i turizam (Hospitality and Tourism); owns oil refineries at Pančevo and Novi Sad; 51% owned by Gazprom (Russia); Pres. Dr PETAR ŠKUNDRIĆ; Gen. Dir. KIRIL KRAVČENKO; 13,900 employees (2009).

Srbijagas: 21000 Novi Sad, Narodnog fronta 12; tel. (11) 4812703; fax (11) 4814305; internet www.srbijagas.com; f. 2005 following restructuring of divisions of Naftna Industrija Srbije; transportation and distribution of natural gas and liquid petrol gas, civil engineering; Dir-Gen. DUŠAN BAJATOVIĆ.

TRADE UNIONS

Association of Free and Independent Trade Unions: 11000 Belgrade, Karađorđeva 71; tel. and fax (11) 2623671; e-mail asns@asns.org.yu; internet www.asns.org.yu; Pres. RANKA SAVIĆ.

Confederation of Autonomous Trade Unions of Serbia (Savez Samostalnih Sindikata Srbije): 11000 Belgrade, trg Nikole Pašić 5; tel. (11) 3230922; fax (11) 3241911; 600,000 mems.

Transport

RAILWAYS

In 2009 there were 3,809 km of railway track in use in Serbia, excluding Kosovo, of which 1,196 km were electrified. A major infrastructure project for the relocation of the central railway station in Belgrade has been repeatedly delayed, with completion not expected before 2010; the rehabilitation of the capital's rail system was also under way.

Železnice Srbije (Serbian Railways): 11000 Belgrade, Nemanjina 6; tel. (11) 3614811; fax (11) 3616722; internet www.zeleznicesrbije.com; Pres. ZORAN ANĐELKOVIĆ; Dir-Gen. MILOVAN MARKOVIĆ.

ROADS

In 2001 there were an estimated 44,993 km of roads in Serbia and Montenegro, of which 28,031 km were paved.

INLAND WATERWAYS

About 5.4m. metric tons of freight were carried on inland water transport in Serbia and Montenegro in 2007.

SHIPPING

Jugoagent Pomorska-rečna Agencija (Yugo Maritime and Rivers Shipping Agency): 11070 Belgrade, bul. Mihaila Pupina 165A, POB 210; tel. (11) 2018700; fax (11) 3112070; e-mail office@jugoagent.net; internet www.jugoagent.net; f. 1947; fmrly Jugoslovenska Pomorska Agencija (Yugoslav Maritime Agency); charter services, liner and container transport, port agency, passenger service, air cargo service; Gen. Man. ZORAN NETKOVIĆ.

CIVIL AVIATION

There is an international airport at Belgrade, and several domestic airports.

Jat Airways: 11070 Belgrade, bul. Umetnosti 16; tel. (11) 3114222; fax (11) 3112853; e-mail pr@jat.com; internet www.jat.com; f. 1927 as Aeroput; fmrly Jugoslovenski Aerotransport (JAT—Yugoslav Airlines); 51% owned by Govt; flights between Serbia and destinations in Central, Western, Eastern and Southern Europe and the Middle East; Chair. of Management Bd and Acting Dir-Gen. SAŠA VLAISAVLJEVIĆ.

Tourism

Serbia's tourism industry is considered to have considerable potential for development, with notable attractions including the mountain scenery, traditional thermal spas, historical cultural cities, and heritage of monuments and monasteries. In 2006 tourist arrivals (excluding Kosovo) totalled some 469,000. Receipts from tourism to Serbia and Montenegro amounted to US $398m. in that year.

National Tourism Organization of Serbia (Turistička Organizacija Srbije): 11000 Belgrade, POB 433, Dečanska 8; tel. (11) 3232586; fax (11) 3221068; e-mail office@serbia.travel; internet www.serbia.travel; f. 1994; produces information and conducts market research and promotion in the field of tourism; Dir GORDANA PLAMENAC.

SEYCHELLES

Introductory Survey

Location, Climate, Language, Religion, Flag, Capital

The Republic of Seychelles comprises about 115 islands, widely scattered over the western Indian Ocean. Apart from the Seychelles archipelago, the country includes several other island groups, the southernmost being about 210 km (130 miles) north of Madagascar. The climate is tropical, with small seasonal variations in temperature and rainfall. The average temperature in Victoria is nearly 27°C (80°F) and average annual rainfall 236 cm (93 ins). In 1981 Seselwa, a creole spoken by virtually all Seychellois, replaced English and French as the official language. Almost all of the inhabitants are Christians, of whom more than 90% belong to the Roman Catholic Church. The national flag (proportions 1 by 2) has five rays, extending from the lower hoist corner, of blue, yellow, red, white and green. The capital is Victoria, on the island of Mahé.

Recent History

Seychelles was uninhabited until colonized by France in 1770. It was ceded to the United Kingdom in 1814 and administered as a dependency of Mauritius until 1903, when it became a Crown Colony. A ministerial system of government was introduced in 1970, and Seychelles proceeded to full independence, as a sovereign republic within the Commonwealth, on 29 June 1976, under a coalition Government with James (later Sir James) Mancham as President and Albert René, the leader of the Seychelles People's United Party (SPUP), as Prime Minister. Under the independence agreement, the United Kingdom returned to Seychelles the islands of Aldabra, Farquhar and Desroches, detached in 1965 to form part of the British Indian Ocean Territory (q.v.) and subsequently leased to the USA

In June 1977 the SPUP staged an armed coup while Mancham was absent from the islands. René was declared President, the National Assembly was dissolved and the Constitution suspended. In May 1978 the SPUP was renamed the Seychelles People's Progressive Front (SPPF). A new Constitution, proclaimed in March 1979, established a one-party state. In June elections for a new National Assembly were held. René was the sole candidate in the concurrent presidential election and was re-elected in June 1984 and again in 1989 as sole candidate, for a third term of office, the maximum period permitted under the 1979 Constitution. During this period opponents of René's socialist Government made a number of attempts to overthrow the regime. The most serious assault took place in November 1981, when about 50 mercenaries, mainly South Africans posing as tourists, flew to join insurgents already on the islands. When the rebellion collapsed, most of the mercenaries escaped to South Africa, where several of their number were later tried and imprisoned. Further plots, discovered in October 1982 and November 1983, were ascribed to the same Seychellois exiles who had planned the 1981 coup attempt.

Until the early 1990s exiled opposition to René remained split among a number of small groups based principally in London, United Kingdom. In July 1991 five of these parties formed a coalition, the United Democratic Movement (UDM), under the leadership of Dr Maxime Ferrari, a former political associate of René, while ex-President Mancham established a 'Crusade for Democracy'. René, meanwhile, came under increasing pressure from France and the United Kingdom, the islands' principal aid donors, to restore a democratic political system. Internally, open opposition to the SPPF was fostered by the newly formed Parti Seselwa, or Parti Seychellois (PS), led by an Anglican clergyman, Wavel Ramkalawan. In August 1991 Ferrari returned from exile to organize support for the UDM, and in November the Government invited all political dissidents to return to the islands.

In December 1991 the SPPF agreed to surrender the party's monopoly of power. It was announced that, from January 1992, political groups numbering at least 100 members would be granted official registration, and that multi-party elections would take place in July for a constituent assembly, whose proposals for constitutional reform would be submitted to a national referendum, with a view to holding multi-party parliamentary elections before the end of 1992. In April Mancham returned from exile to lead the New Democratic Party (NDP). At the July elections for the 20-seat constitutional commission, the SPPF secured 11 representatives, while the NDP took eight. The PS was the only other political party to gain representation on the commission, obtaining the remaining seat.

The commission completed its work in October 1992; however, following publication of the draft Constitution, the Democratic Party (DP, as the NDP had been restyled) challenged the proposed voting arrangements for a new National Assembly, whose members were to be elected on a basis of one-half by direct vote and one-half by proportional representation. The latter formula was to reflect the percentage of votes obtained by the successful candidate in presidential election, and was intended to ensure a legislative majority for the President's party. Other sections of the proposed Constitution, relating to social issues, were strongly opposed by the Roman Catholic Church, to which more than 90% of the islanders at that time belonged.

The draft Constitution, which required the approval of at least 60% of voters, was endorsed by only 53.7% at a referendum held in November 1992. A second constitutional commission, whose meetings were opened to the public, began work in January 1993 on proposals for submission to a further referendum, unanimously agreeing on a new draft Constitution, in which a compromise plan was reached on the electoral formula for a new National Assembly. With the joint endorsement of René and Mancham, the draft document was submitted to a national referendum in June, approved by 73.9% of voters. Opponents of the new constitutional arrangements comprised the PS, the Seychelles National Movement (SNM) and the National Alliance Party (NAP). At the presidential and legislative elections that followed in July, René received 59.5% of the vote, against 36.7% for Mancham and 3.8% for Philippe Boullé, the candidate representing an electoral alliance of the PS, the Seychelles Christian Democrat Party (SCDP), the SNM and the NAP. In the legislative elections, the SPPF secured 21 of the 22 seats elected by direct vote, and the DP one seat. Of the 11 additional seats allocated on a proportional basis, the SPPF received a further seven seats, the DP three seats and the PS one seat.

Following the 1993 elections the Government began to promote a gradual transition from socialism to free-market policies, aimed at maximizing the country's potential as an 'offshore' financial and business centre. State-owned port facilities were transferred to private ownership in 1994, when plans were also announced for the creation of a duty-free International Trade Zone to provide transshipment facilities. Measures were introduced to implement the privatization of government activities in tourism, agriculture and tuna-processing.

In early 1995 tensions developed within the opposition DP, whose only directly elected MP, Christopher Gill, sought to remove Mancham from the party leadership on the grounds that the former President was insufficiently vigorous in opposing the policies of the René Government. Gill was suspended from the DP in June, and subsequently formed a breakaway 'New Democratic Party' with the aim of restructuring the DP under a new leader. The official registration of active political organizations, affording them corporate status, led to the formal amalgamation of the PS, the SNM, the SCDP and the NAP as a single party, the United Opposition (UO), under the leadership of Ramkalawan.

In continued efforts to promote Seychelles as an international 'offshore' financial centre, the Government introduced, in November 1995, an Economic Development Act (EDA), under whose provisions investors of a minimum US $10m. would receive immunity in Seychelles from extradition or seizure of assets. It was feared in international financial circles, however, that the operation of the EDA would make Seychelles a refuge for the proceeds of drugs-trafficking and other crimes. Protest was led by the United Kingdom, France and the USA, and in February 1996 the EDA was described by the Financial Action Task Force on Money Laundering (see p. 430) as a 'serious threat to world financial systems'. The Government, while refusing to rescind the EDA, established an Economic Development Board under the chairmanship of René, to vet potential EDA investors. In April 1996 the Government introduced legislation aimed at preventing the use of the EDA for 'laundering' illicit funds. Following reports critical of Seychelles' financial sector from two international organizations, the EDA was finally repealed in July 2000.

In July 1996 the SPPF introduced a series of constitutional amendments, creating the post of Vice-President, to which James Michel, the Minister of Finance, Communications and Defence and a long-standing political associate of René, was appointed in the following month. The constitutional changes also provided for revisions in constituency boundaries, which were generally interpreted as favouring SPPF candidates in future parliamentary elections. Measures were also implemented whereby the number of seats in the National Assembly was to be increased (see Government).

In January 1998 René announced that the elections would be held in March, and that he was to seek the second of a maximum of three consecutive five-year terms as president permitted under the 1993 Constitution. The outcome of the elections provided the SPPF with a decisive victory. René obtained 66.7% of the presidential ballot, while his party secured 30 of the 34 seats in the enlarged National Assembly. Ramkalawan, with 19.5% of the presidential vote, substantially exceeded support for Mancham, who received 13.8%. In the National Assembly the UO increased its representation from one to three seats, with the DP losing three of the four seats previously held. Since the 1993 elections, effective opposition to the Government had increasingly been led by Ramkalawan's UO, as the DP opted to pursue a policy of 'reconciliation' with the SPPF. In mid-1998 the UO changed its name to the Seychelles National Party (SNP).

In July 2001 René declared a presidential election almost two years early, claiming that this was in order to reassure investors about the long-term stability of the country. On 31 August–2 September René was re-elected as President, but with the smallest mandate of his career, securing 54.2% of the valid votes cast. Ramkalawan, the SNP candidate, won 45.0% of the votes, but refused to accept the result, claiming serious irregularities in the electoral process, and subsequently filed a formal complaint with the Constitutional Court. Legislative elections, which were due in 2003, took place early, on 4–6 December 2002. The SPPF retained its majority in the National Assembly, but with a reduced margin, securing 23 of the 34 seats, while the SNP won the remaining 11 seats. In March 2003 René indicated during the congress of the SPPF that he would progressively relinquish control of certain presidential duties to Vice-President Michel, who was also designated as the party's candidate for the next presidential election.

On 14 April 2004 President René formally retired, having spent almost 27 years in office. He was succeeded by Vice-President Michel, who was inaugurated as President on the same day. René retained his position as President of the SPPF. Joseph Belmont was subsequently appointed Vice-President, retaining responsibility for tourism and transport.

In the weeks prior to the 2006 presidential election, tensions increased between supporters of the leading political parties contesting the vote, and there were reports of numerous violent incidents. Nevertheless, the election proceeded as scheduled on 28–30 July at which Michel secured victory with 53.73% of the valid votes cast; Ramkalawan received 45.71%. A voter turn-out of 88.7% was recorded. In mid-August a new Government was sworn in, including three new appointments to the 10-member administration. In October several high-ranking SNP officials, including Ramkalawan, were the victims of a violent attack by the paramilitary police. The incident occurred after Ramkalawan made a speech at the National Assembly denouncing a proposal to ban all political parties from establishing private radio stations. Ramkalawan was among three members of the SNP who were subsequently charged with attending an illegal demonstration. They were brought to trial that month; however, President Michel later suspended the charges in an attempt to quell rising violence among the political parties and their supporters. An independent inquiry into the incident was launched in March 2007, and in February 2008 the Government accepted responsibility for injuries caused during the protests. Attempts were made to settle the issue of compensation out of court; however, the Government's legal representatives insisted that an initial claim for some SR 1m. was inappropriate.

Meanwhile, the SNP threatened to boycott the parliamentary elections, scheduled to be held by the end of 2007, unless certain demands were met and in January Ramkalawan held talks with the Electoral Commissioner, Hendrick Gappy, and requested that the electoral register remain open up to two months prior to the ballot. President Michel announced in March that he would dissolve the National Assembly and called an early election, which was held on 10–12 May 2007. According to official results released later that month, the SPPF retained 23 seats and its majority in the National Assembly, securing 56.2% of the votes cast. Prior to the election the SNP and the DP announced that, for the first time since the re-emergence of multi-party politics in 1992, they would form an alliance and nominate common candidates to contest the ballot. The SNP-DP alliance received 43.8% of the votes, and secured the 11 remaining seats. International observers praised the country for the conduct of the elections, at which 85.9% of the registered electorate turned out to vote. In July 2007 President Michel reduced the number of government ministries from 10 to eight. Although the key ministers retained their positions, the Ministry of Finance was to encompass three separate departments for finance and commerce, the Treasury and the Revenue Authority, while the Ministry of Health became the Ministry of Social Development and Health.

In April 2008 President Michel established a committee, chaired by former Attorney-General Francis Chang-Sam, to review the Constitution; the committee held its first meeting in June and was expected to present its recommendations within one year.

Seychelles has traditionally pursued a policy of non-alignment in international affairs, and supports movements for the creation of a 'zone of peace' in the Indian Ocean area. Until 1983 all naval warships wishing to dock at Seychelles had to provide a guarantee that they were not carrying nuclear weapons. The British and US Governments refused to agree to this condition, and their respective naval fleets were therefore effectively banned from using Seychelles port facilities. This requirement was withdrawn in September 1983, although Seychelles continued, in theory, to refuse entry to ships carrying nuclear weapons.

Since the late 1980s Seychelles has expanded the scope of its formal diplomatic contacts. Relations have been established with the Comoros and with Mauritius, and agreements have been made with the latter for co-operation in health and economic development matters. In 1989 diplomatic relations were established with Morocco, Madagascar and Côte d'Ivoire, and in 1990 with Kenya. During 1992 formal relations were established with Israel and South Africa, and in 1998 Seychelles proposed to establish a diplomatic mission in Malaysia to expand its relations in Asia and Oceania. Libya opened a diplomatic mission in Seychelles in January 2000, and diplomatic ties were established with Sudan in October. Following years of minimal interaction between France and Seychelles, owing to Seychelles' accumulated debt to the Agence Française de Développement, the French Minister for Co-operation was the first minister in over four years to visit Seychelles in February 2001. It was hoped that a resolution to the situation could be found and a new schedule for repayments negotiated. In 2001 relations were restored with Japan, which granted a subsidy for fishery development to Seychelles; this was said to be a consequence of the reversal of Seychelles' whaling policy. President Michel paid a state visit to Mauritius in March 2005, as guest of honour at that country's annual celebration of independence; various economic and co-operative agreements between the two countries were also signed. In December 2005, as a result of the seventh session of the Seychelles-Mauritius Commission on Bilateral Co-operation, a further agreement was signed on the sharing of expertise in a wide range of fields. The Government also strengthened relations with the People's Republic of China, following a state visit to that country by Michel in November 2006.

Government

Under the 1993 Constitution, executive power is vested in the President, who is Head of State and Commander-in-Chief of the Armed Forces. The President, who is elected by direct popular vote, appoints and leads the Council of Ministers, which acts in an advisory capacity to him. The President also appoints the holders of certain public offices and the judiciary. The President may hold office for a maximum period of three five-year terms. The legislature is the unicameral National Assembly, presently comprising 34 members, of whom 25 are directly elected for five years and nine allocated on a proportional basis. Constitutional changes, introduced in July 1996, provide for an enlargement to 35 members: 25 directly elected and a maximum of 10 allocated on a proportional basis.

Defence

As assessed at November 2008, the army numbered 200 men, including a coastguard of 200. Paramilitary forces comprised a 250-strong national guard. The defence budget for 2007 allocated SR 77m. to defence. Seychelles was to contribute servicemen to the East African Stand-by Brigade, part of the African Union (see p. 172) stand-by peace-keeping force; the unit was intended to be ready for rapid response by 2010.

Economic Affairs

In 2007, according to estimates by the World Bank, Seychelles' gross national income (GNI), measured at average 2005–07 prices, was US $762m., equivalent to $8,960 per head (or $15,450 per head on an international purchasing-power parity basis). During 2000–07, it was estimated, the population increased at an average annual rate of 0.7%, while gross domestic product (GDP) per head decreased, in real terms, by an average of 0.3% per year. Overall GDP increased, in real terms, at an average annual rate of 11.7% in 2000–07. Real GDP increased by 6.3% in 2007.

Agriculture (including forestry and fishing) contributed 2.3% of GDP in 2007, according to preliminary estimates, and accounted for 2.6% of total employment (excluding self-employed) in that year. Much of Seychelles' production of coconuts has traditionally been exported in the form of copra, but exports dwindled in the late 1990s. Other cash crops include cinnamon bark (although production declined from 205 metric tons in 2004 to just nine tons in 2005, before recovering to 315 tons in 2007), tea, patchouli, vanilla and limes. Tea, sweet potatoes, cassava, yams, sugar cane, bananas, eggs and poultry meat are produced for local consumption. However, imports of food and live animals constituted an estimated 20.1% of the value of total imports in 2007. Fishing has become increasingly important since the 1980s, and exports of canned tuna alone contributed an estimated 50.6% of the value of total exports in 2007. Licence fees from foreign fishing vessels, allowed to operate in Seychelles' waters, contribute significantly to foreign exchange. A three-year fishing protocol, worth €3.48m., was signed with the European Union in 2001; a further six-year protocol was agreed in October 2004, and in December 2005 an agreement, valid until 2011, increased the payment for fishing rights to €4.12m. a year as well as raising the value of some licences, meaning that the Government could expect payments of some €6.0m. a year. Agricultural GDP increased at an average annual rate of 0.4% during 2000–07, according to the World Bank; it increased by 6.2% in 2007.

Industry (including mining, manufacturing, construction and power) contributed an estimated 19.3% of GDP in 2007 and accounted for 24.8% of total employment (excluding self-employed) in 2007. Industrial GDP increased at an average annual rate of 4.6% during 2000–07, according to the World Bank; the sector contracted by 2.0% in both 2005 and 2006, but grew by 48.4% in 2007.

The mining sector is small (it accounted for less than 1.0% of total employment in 2007) and mineral production consists mainly of quantities of construction materials, such as clay, coral, stone and sand. There are deposits of natural gas, and during the 1980s concessions were sold to several foreign companies, allowing exploration for petroleum. Exploratory drilling has so far proved unsuccessful; however, an agreement to renew exploration was made in 2005. A survey of offshore areas, initiated in 1980, revealed the presence of nodules, containing deposits of various metals, on the sea-bed. The renewed commercial exploitation of Seychelles' granite reserves is under investigation and the future development of offshore petroleum reserves is a possibility.

Manufacturing contributed an estimated 10.2% of GDP in 2007 and accounted for 11.3% of total employment in 2007. Apart from a tuna-canning plant (opened in 1987), the manufacturing sector consists mainly of small-scale activities, including boat-building, printing and furniture-making. According to the World Bank, manufacturing GDP decreased at an average annual rate of 3.4% during 2000–07. Manufacturing GDP contracted by 2.0% in both 2005 and 2006, but increased by 1.5% in 2007.

Energy is derived principally from oil-fired power stations. In 2007 mineral fuels and lubricants accounted for an estimated 25.1% of the total value of imports. The vast majority of fuel imports are re-exported, mainly as bunker sales to visiting ships and aircraft—exports of refined petroleum products contributed 30.0% of total export earnings in 2004, and re-exports accounted for an estimated 44.7% of the value of total exports in 2007. It is envisaged that the proceeds from re-exports eventually will fund fully fuel imports.

Services provided an estimated 78.4% of GDP in 2007 and accounted for 72.6% of total employment (excluding self-employed) in 2007. In that year tourist arrivals totalled some 161,300 and income from tourism amounted to SR $1,194m., according to central bank estimates. The majority of visitors were from western Europe, notably from France, Germany, Italy and the United Kingdom. The GDP of the services sector decreased at an average annual rate of 1.8% during 2000–07, according to the World Bank. Services GDP increased by 8.5% in 2006, but declined by 10.6% in 2007.

In 2007 Seychelles recorded a visible trade deficit of US $412.3m., and there was a deficit of $274.8m. on the current account of the balance of payments. The principal source of imports (24.8%) in 2007 was Saudi Arabia; other important suppliers were Germany, Singapore, France, Spain and South Africa. The principal market for domestic exports (excluding re-exports) in 2005 was the United Kingdom (45.4%); other significant purchasers were France, Italy and Germany. The principal export is canned tuna (following the expansion of the Indian Ocean Tuna Co in 1995 and increasing production thereafter); in 2007 canned tuna represented 91.4% of domestic exports. The main imports in 2007 were machinery and transport equipment, mineral fuels and lubricants, food and live animals, and basic manufactures.

In 2007 Seychelles recorded a budgetary surplus of SR 66.8m. (equivalent to 1.1% of GDP). Seychelles' total external debt was US $905.2m. at the end of 2006, of which $299.4m. was long-term public debt. In that year the cost of debt-servicing was equivalent to 20.6% of the value of exports of goods and services. According to the IMF, the annual rate of inflation averaged 6.5% in 2000–08; consumer prices increased by 5.3% in 2007, but rose by 37.0% in 2008. Some 8.3% of the labour force were registered as unemployed in 1993.

Seychelles is a member of the African Development Bank (see p. 170), of the Common Market for Eastern and Southern Africa (see p. 215) and of the Indian Ocean Commission (see p. 426), which aims to promote co-operation in the region. It was announced in December 1996 that Seychelles was to provide the headquarters of the Indian Ocean Tuna Commission.

Since the early 1970s tourism has been the mainstay of the Seychelles economy, and despite measures introduced in 1995 to develop Seychelles as an 'offshore' financial services centre (see Recent History), and to establish the islands as a centre for transshipment and air freight in the Indian Ocean area, the continuing dependence of the economy on tourism leaves the country highly vulnerable to outside economic influences, while the cost of servicing the external debt remains a major impediment to balanced growth. The new Government of President James Michel (who was also the Minister of Finance) from 2004, and his avowed commitment to the programme of economic reform gave rise to a degree of economic optimism, particularly with regard to privatization. However, a primary obstacle to relations with international donor institutions such as the IMF was the country's refusal to devalue the national currency, owing to its fears of incurring inflation (related to the country's dependence on imported items). It was argued, though, that the over-valuation of the rupee was a contributing factor to the ongoing shortage of foreign-exchange. In October 2007 the currency was eventually devalued from 7.5 rupees per US dollar to 8.0 rupees and in November 2008 the rupee was allowed to float freely on foreign exchange markets, resulting in a depreciation in its value of some 48%. Inflation subsequently rose rapidly, reaching 63.3% by December, although this was projected to decline steadily during 2009 due to weaker international prices and slower domestic demand. Furthermore, a comprehensive economic reform programme introduced in November 2008 with the assistance of the IMF was adversely affected by the worsening global fiscal environment. In particular Seychelles' tourism and manufacturing sectors were expected to experience severe contractions, and overall GDP was projected to decline by 9.6% in 2009. As part of the programme, the IMF also agreed a two-year Stand-By Arrangement valued at US $26.1m. to enable Seychelles to service its external debt (estimated to amount to some $800m., equivalent to 175% of GDP). Nevertheless, the ongoing balance of payments and public debt crisis threatened seriously to jeopardize the living standards of the Seychellois and the country's future economic development.

SEYCHELLES

Education

In 1979 free and compulsory primary education was introduced for children between six and 16 years of age. A programme of educational reform, based on the British comprehensive schools system, was introduced in 1980. The language of instruction in primary schools is English. The duration of primary education is six years, while that of general secondary education is five years (of which the first four years are compulsory), beginning at 12 years of age. Pre-primary and special education facilities are also available. According to UNESCO estimates, in 2003/04 enrolment at primary schools included 99.4% of children in the relevant age-group (males 98.9%; females 100.0%), while the comparable ratio for secondary enrolment in 2006/07 was 94.3%. There were 2,130 students in post-secondary (non-tertiary) education in 2008. A number of students study abroad, principally in the United Kingdom. Government expenditure on education in 2007 was SR 190.1m., or about 7.4% of total expenditure.

Public Holidays

2009: 1–2 January (New Year), 10–13 April (Easter), 1 May (Labour Day), 5 June (Liberation Day, anniversary of 1977 coup), 11 June (Corpus Christi), 18 June (National Day), 29 June (Independence Day), 15 August (Assumption), 1 November (All Saints' Day), 8 December (Immaculate Conception), 25 December (Christmas Day).

2010: 1–2 January (New Year), 2–5 April (Easter), 1 May (Labour Day), 3 June (Corpus Christi), 5 June (Liberation Day, anniversary of 1977 coup), 18 June (National Day), 29 June (Independence Day), 15 August (Assumption), 1 November (All Saints' Day), 8 December (Immaculate Conception), 25 December (Christmas Day).

Weights and Measures

The imperial system is being replaced by the metric system.

Statistical Survey

Source (unless otherwise stated): Statistics and Database Administration Section, Management and Information Systems Division, POB 206, Victoria; e-mail misdstat@seychelles.net; internet www.nsb.gov.sc.

AREA AND POPULATION

Area: 455.3 sq km (175.8 sq miles), incl. Aldabra lagoon (145 sq km).

Population: 74,331 at census of 26 August 1994; 75,876 (males 37,589, females 38,287) at census of 29 August 1997. *Mid-2008* (official estimate): 86,956 (males 44,999, females 41,957).

Density (mid-2008): 191.0 per sq km.

Principal Town: Victoria (capital), estimated population 60,000 (incl. suburbs) in 1994. *Mid-2003* (incl. suburbs, UN estimate): Victoria 20,050. (Source: UN, *World Urbanization Prospects: The 2003 Revision*).

Births, Marriages and Deaths (registrations, 2007): Live births 1,499 (birth rate 17.6 per 1,000); Marriages (of residents) 405 (marriage rate 4.8 per 1,000); Deaths 630 (death rate 7.4 per 1,000).

Life Expectancy (years at birth, official estimates): 72.2 (males 68.9; females 75.7) in 2006.

Employment (2007, averages): Agriculture, forestry and fishing 1,046; Mining and quarrying 18; Manufacturing 4,455; Electricity and water 1,087; Construction 4,255; Trade, restaurants and hotels 8,579; Transport, storage and communications 3,917; Financial intermediation 781; Real estate, renting and business activities 1,897; Public administration 6,095; Education 2,643; Health and social work 1,705; Other services 3,094; *Total* 39,572.

HEALTH AND WELFARE

Key Indicators

Total Fertility Rate (children per woman, 2007): 2.2.

Under-5 Mortality Rate (per 1,000 live births, 2006): 13.

Physicians (per 1,000 head, 2004): 1.51.

Hospital Beds (per 1,000 head, government establishments only, 2007): 4.7.

Health Expenditure (2006): US $ per head (PPP): 812.

Health Expenditure (2006): % of GDP: 6.8.

Health Expenditure (2006): public (% of total): 74.2.

Access to Water (% of persons, 2004): 88.

Human Development Index (2006): ranking: 54.

Human Development Index (2006): value: 0.836.

For sources and definitions, see explanatory note on p. vi.

AGRICULTURE, ETC.

Principal Crops (metric tons, 2007, FAO estimates): Coconuts 3,200; Vegetables (incl. melons) 1,940; Bananas 2,000; Other fruit 265; Tea 190; Cinnamon 315.

Livestock (head, 2007, FAO estimates): Cattle 1,420; Pigs 18,700; Goats 5,200.

Livestock Products (metric tons, 2007, FAO estimates): Pig meat 1,100; Chicken meat 820; Hen eggs 2,200.

Fishing ('000 metric tons, live weight, 2006): Capture 92.6 (Skipjack tuna 47.5; Yellowfin tuna 30.9; Bigeye tuna 7.4); Aquaculture 0.7 (Giant tiger prawn 0.7); *Total catch* 93.3.

Source: FAO.

INDUSTRY

Industrial Production (2007): Canned tuna 31,569 metric tons; Beer ('000 litres) 7,506; Soft drinks ('000 litres) 8,515; Cigarettes 33 million; Electric energy 271m. kWh.

FINANCE

Currency and Exchange Rates: 100 cents = 1 Seychelles rupee (SR). *Sterling, Dollar and Euro Equivalents* (28 November 2008): £1 sterling = 25.253 rupees; US $1 = 16.467 rupees; €1 = 20.957 rupees; 100 Seychelles rupees = £3.96 = $6.07 = €4.77. *Average Exchange Rate* (Seychelles rupees per US $): 5.5000 in 2005; 5.5197 in 2006; 6.7011 in 2007. Note: In November 1979 the value of the Seychelles rupee was linked to the IMF's special drawing right (SDR). In March 1981 the mid-point exchange rate was set at SDR 1 = 7.2345 rupees. This remained in effect until February 1997, when the fixed link with the SDR was ended.

Budget (SR million, 2007): *Revenue:* Taxation 1,511.1 (Taxes on income, etc. 360.8, Domestic taxes on goods and services 885.1, Import duties 265.2); Other current revenue 1,028.3; Total 2,539.4, excl. grants received (17.1). *Expenditure:* General government services 290.6; Community and social services 269.6; Education 190.1; Health 200.2; Economic services 9.8; Agriculture, environment and fishing 83.4; Transport and communications 20.9; Other purposes 691.8; Interest payments 422.1; Capital 373.7; Total 2,552.2, excl. lending minus repayments (–62.5). Note: Figures represent the consolidated accounts of the central Government, covering the operations of the Recurrent and Capital Budgets and of the Social Security Fund.

International Reserves (US $ million at 30 December 2008): Reserve position in IMF 0.01; Foreign exchange 73.71; Total 73.72. Source: IMF, *International Financial Statistics*.

Money Supply (SR million at 30 December 2007): Currency outside banks 407.8; Demand deposits at commercial banks 1,899.8; Total money (incl. others) 2,646.3. Source: IMF, *International Financial Statistics*.

Cost of Living (Consumer Price Index; base: 2000 = 100): All items 114.5 in 2006; 120.6 in 2007; 165.2 in 2008. Source: IMF, *International Financial Statistics*.

Expenditure on the Gross Domestic Product (SR million at current prices, 2007, preliminary estimates): Government final consumption expenditure 2,148.0; Private final consumption expenditure 3,534.6; Gross fixed capital formation 1,984.0; *Total domestic expenditure* 7,666.5; Exports, less imports, of goods and services –1,701.7; Statistical discrepancy 148.4; *GDP in purchasers' values* 6,113.2.

Gross Domestic Product by Economic Activity (SR million at current prices, 2007, preliminary estimates): Agriculture, forestry and fishing 137.7; Manufacturing 608.7; Electricity and water 126.1;

Construction 424.3; Trade, restaurants and hotels 1,180.0; Transport, storage and communications 1,174.2; Finance, insurance, real estate and business services 1,089.9; Education 229.8; Public administration and defence, and social security 545.5; Other services 476.8 Sub-total 5,993.0; Import duties, less subsidies 498.3; Less Imputed bank service charge 377.9; GDP in purchasers' values 6,113.2.

Balance of Payments (US $ million, 2007): Exports of goods f.o.b. 391.7; Imports of goods f.o.b. –804.0; Trade balance –412.3; Exports of services 472.2; Imports of services –302.5; Balance on goods and services –242.6; Other income received 9.6; Other income paid –80.7; Balance on goods, services and income –313.7; Current transfers received 49.5; Current transfers paid –10.6; Current balance –274.8; Capital account (net) 4.6; Direct investment abroad –8.5; Direct investment from abroad 249.3; Portfolio investment assets –0.0; Portfolio investment liabilities 31.3; Other investment assets –59.0; Other investment liabilities 81.7; Net errors and omissions 2.0; Overall balance 26.6. Source: IMF, International Financial Statistics.

EXTERNAL TRADE

Principal Commodities (distribution by SITC, SR million, 2007, provisional): Imports c.i.f.: Food and live animals 1,154.1; Mineral fuels 1,439.0; Basic manufactures 763.2; Machinery and transport 1,460.4; Total (incl. others) 5,728.4. Exports f.o.b.: Canned tuna 1,231.2; Fish (fresh/frozen) 13.9; Crustaceans 17.2; Fish meal 29.6; Medicaments, etc. 29.0; Total (incl. others) 2,435.3 (of which domestic exports SR 1,346.5m. and re-exports SR 1,088.7m).

Principal Trading Partners (SR million, 2007, provisional): Imports c.i.f.: France 445.2; Germany 545.1; Saudi Arabia 1,418.9; Singapore 486.4; South Africa 337.9; Spain 378.3; Total (incl. others) 5,728.4. Exports f.o.b.: Total 2,435.3 (of which domestic exports SR 1,346.5m. and re-exports SR 1,088.7m).

TRANSPORT

Road Traffic (registered motor vehicles, 2007,): Private 7,375; Commercial 2,524; Taxis 287; Self-drive 1,442; Motor cycles 34; Omnibuses 191; Total 11,853.

Shipping: Merchant Fleet (registered at 31 December 2007): Vessels 54; Total displacement 182,643 grt (Source: Lloyd's Register-Fairplay, World Fleet Statistics); International Sea-borne Freight Traffic (2007): Freight ('000 metric tons): Imports 526; Exports 3,814; Trans-shipment (of fish) 222.

Civil Aviation (traffic on scheduled services, 2004): Kilometres flown 13.7 million; Passengers carried 461,900; Passenger-km 1,134 million; Total ton-km 310.7 million (Source: UN, Statistical Yearbook). 2007: Aircraft movements 3,532; Passengers embarked 222,000; Passengers disembarked 215,000; Freight embarked 2,200 metric tons; Freight disembarked 6,100 metric tons.

TOURISM

Foreign Tourist Arrivals ('000): 128.7 in 2005; 140.6 in 2006; 161.3 in 2007.

Arrivals by Country of Residence (2006): CIS 5,408; France 27,350; Germany 19,256; Italy 23,217; South Africa 6,277; Switzerland 4,953; United Kingdom 15,529; Total (incl. others) 140,627. Source: World Tourism Organization.

Tourism Receipts (SR million, central bank estimates): 824 in 2005; 885 in 2006; 1,194 in 2007.

COMMUNICATIONS MEDIA

Radio Receivers (1997): 42,000 in use. Source: UNESCO, Statistical Yearbook.

Television Receivers (2000): 16,500 in use. Source: International Telecommunication Union.

Telephones (2007): 21,559 main lines in use.

Facsimile Machines (2002): 590 in use.

Mobile Cellular Telephones (2007): 83,293 subscribers.

Personal Computers (2005): 16,000 in use. Source: International Telecommunication Union.

Internet Users (2007): 5,780 accounts.

Broadband Subscribers (2007): 3,000. Source: International Telecommunication Union.

Book Production (1980): 33 titles (2 books, 31 pamphlets).

Daily Newspapers (2006): 1.

Non-daily Newspapers (2006): 3.

EDUCATION

Pre-primary (2008): 32 schools; 206 teachers; 2,923 pupils.

Primary (2008): 25 schools; 616 teachers (males 94, females 522); 8,744 pupils (males 4,416, females 4,328).

Secondary (2008): 13 schools; 502 teachers (males 218, females 284); 7,542 pupils (males 3,731, females 3,811).

Post-secondary (2008): 9 schools; 216 teachers; 2,130 pupils.

Vocational (2004): 7 institutions; 82 teachers; 1,099 pupils.

Adult Literacy Rate (official estimate): 96% (males 96%; females 96%) in 2008.

Directory

The Constitution

The independence Constitution of 1976 was suspended after the coup in June 1977 but reintroduced in July with substantial modifications. A successor Constitution, which entered into force in March 1979, was superseded by a new Constitution, approved by national referendum on 18 June 1993.

The President is elected by popular vote simultaneously with elections for the National Assembly. The President fulfils the functions of Head of State and Commander-in-Chief of the armed forces and may hold office for a maximum period of three consecutive five-year terms. The Assembly, elected for a term of five years, consists of 34 seats, of which 25 are filled by direct election and nine are allocated on a proportional basis. Constitutional amendments, introduced in July 1996, provided for an Assembly of 25 directly elected seats and a maximum of 10 proportionally allocated seats. There is provision for an appointed Vice-President. The Council of Ministers is appointed by the President and acts in an advisory capacity to him. The President also appoints the holders of certain public offices and the judiciary.

The Government

HEAD OF STATE

President: JAMES MICHEL (took office 14 April 2004, elected 28–30 July 2006).

Vice-President: JOSEPH BELMONT.

COUNCIL OF MINISTERS
(April 2009)

President, with additional responsibility for Defence, the Police, Information and Public Relations, Legal Affairs and Risk and Disaster Management: JAMES MICHEL.

Vice-President, Minister of Tourism, and Minister of Public Administration and Internal Affairs: JOSEPH BELMONT.

Minister of Finance: DANNY FAURE.

Minister of Foreign Affairs: PATRICK PILLAY.

Minister of National Development: JACQUELIN DUGASSE.

Minister of the Environment, Natural Resources and Transport: JOEL MORGAN.

Minister of Community Development, Youth, Sports and Culture: VINCENT MERITON.

Minister of Education: BERNARD SHAMLAYE.

Minister of Employment and Human Resources Development: MACSUZY MONDON.

Minister of Social Development and Health: MARIE-PIERRE LLOYD.

MINISTRIES

Office of the President: State House, POB 55, Victoria; tel. 224155; fax 224985; internet www.statehouse.gov.sc.

Office of the Vice-President: State House, POB 1303, Victoria; tel. 225509; fax 225152; e-mail jbelmont@statehouse.gov.sc.

SEYCHELLES

Ministry of Community Development, Youth, Sports and Culture: Oceangate House, POB 731, Victoria; tel. 225477; fax 225770; e-mail frevet@seychelles.net.

Ministry of Education: POB 48, Mont Fleuri; tel. 283283; fax 224859; e-mail ps@eduhq.edu.sc; internet www.education.gov.sc.

Ministry of Employment and Human Resources Development: Independence House, POB 1097, Victoria; tel. 676250; fax 610795; e-mail department@employment.gov.sc; internet www.employment.gov.sc.

Ministry of the Environment, Natural Resources and Transport: Independence House, POB 166, Victoria; tel. 611120; fax 225438; internet www.env.gov.sc.

Ministry of Finance: Liberty House, POB 113, Victoria; tel. 382004; fax 225265; e-mail psf@finance.gov.sc.

Ministry of Foreign Affairs: Maison Queau de Quincy, POB 656, Mont Fleuri; tel. 283500; fax 225398; e-mail jnourice@mfa.gov.sc; internet www.mfa.gov.sc.

Ministry of National Development: International Conference Centre, POB 648, Victoria; tel. 611200; fax 225374.

Ministry of Social Development and Health: POB 52, Mont Fleuri; tel. 388000; fax 226042; internet www.moh.gov.sc/.

President and Legislature

PRESIDENT

Election, 28–30 July 2006

Candidate	Votes	% of votes
James Michel (SPPF)	30,119	53.73
Wavel Ramkalawan (SNP)	25,626	45.71
Philippe Boullé (Independent)	314	0.56
Total	**56,059**	**100.00**

NATIONAL ASSEMBLY

Speaker: PATRICK HERMINIE.
Election, 10–12 May 2007

Party	Votes	% of votes	Seats*
Seychelles People's Progressive Front (SPPF)	30,571	56.2	23
Seychelles National Party (SNP)-Democratic Party (DP)	23,869	43.8	11
Total	**54,440**	**100.0**	**34**

* Of the Assembly's 34 seats, 25 were filled by direct election and nine by allocation on a proportional basis.

Election Commission

Electoral Commission: Suite 203, Aarti Bldg, Mont Fleuri, POB 741, Victoria; tel. 295555; fax 225474; e-mail hendrick@seychelles.net; f. 1993; Electoral Commissioner HENDRICK PAUL GAPPY.

Political Organizations

Democratic Party (DP): POB 169, Mont Fleuri; tel. 224916; fax 224302; e-mail management@dpseychelles.com; internet www.dpseychelles.com; f. 1992; successor to the Seychelles Democratic Party (governing party 1970–77); Leader RALPH VOLCERE (acting); Sec.-Gen. (vacant).

Mouvement Seychellois pour la Démocratie: Mont Fleuri; tel. 224322; fax 224460; f. 1992; Leader JACQUES HODOUL.

Seychelles National Party (SNP): Arpent Vert, Mont Fleuri, POB 81, Victoria; tel. 224124; fax 225151; e-mail secretariat@snpseychelles.sc; internet www.snpseychelles.sc; f. 1995 as the United Opposition, comprising the fmr mem. parties of a coalition formed to contest the 1993 elections; adopted present name in 1998; Leader Rev. WAVEL RAMKALAWAN; Sec.-Gen. ROGER MANCIENNE.

Seychelles People's Progressive Front (SPPF): POB 1242, Victoria; tel. 324622; fax 225070; e-mail admin@sppf.sc; internet www.sppf.sc; fmrly the Seychelles People's United Party (f. 1964), which assumed power in 1977; renamed in 1978; sole legal party 1978–91; Pres. FRANCE ALBERT RENÉ; Sec.-Gen. JAMES MICHEL.

Diplomatic Representation

EMBASSIES AND HIGH COMMISSIONS IN SEYCHELLES

China, People's Republic: POB 680, St Louis; tel. 266588; fax 266866; e-mail china@seychelles.net; internet sc.china-embassy.org/eng/; Ambassador WANG WEIGUO.

Cuba: Bel Eau, POB 730, Victoria; tel. 224094; fax 224376; e-mail cubasey@seychelles.net; internet emba.cubaminrex.cu/seychellesing; Ambassador MARIA AIDA NOGALES JIMÉNEZ.

France: La Ciotat Bldg, Mont Fleuri, POB 478, Victoria; tel. 382500; fax 382510; e-mail ambafrance@intelvision.net; internet www.ambafrance-sc.org; Ambassador PHILLIPE DELACROIX (designate).

India: Le Chantier, POB 488, Francis Rachel St, Victoria; tel. 610301; fax 610308; e-mail hicomind@seychelles.net; internet www.seychelles.net/hicomind; High Commissioner MALAY MISHRA.

Russia: Le Niol, POB 632, St Louis; tel. 266590; fax 266653; e-mail rfembsey@seychelles.net; Ambassador (vacant).

United Kingdom: 3rd Floor, Oliaji Trade Centre, Francis Rachel St, POB 161, Victoria; tel. 283666; fax 283657; e-mail bhcvictoria@fco.gov.uk; internet ukinseychelles.fco.gov.uk/en; High Commissioner FERGUS COCHRANE-DYET.

Judicial System

The legal system is derived from English Common Law and the French Code Napoléon. There are three Courts, the Court of Appeal, the Supreme Court and the Magistrates' Courts. The Court of Appeal hears appeals from the Supreme Court in both civil and criminal cases. The Supreme Court is also a Court of Appeal from the Magistrates' Courts as well as having jurisdiction at first instance. The Constitutional Court, a division of the Supreme Court, determines matters of a constitutional nature, and considers cases bearing on civil liberties. There is also an industrial court and a rent tribunal.

Supreme Court: POB 157, Victoria; tel. 224071; fax 224197; Chief Justice ANDREW RANJAN PERERA.

President of the Court of Appeal: STEPHEN BWANA (acting).

Justices of Appeal: ANNEL SILUNGWE, A. PILLAY, G. P. S. DE SILVA, K. P. MATADEEN.

Puisne Judges: RANJAN PERERA, D. KARUNAKARAN, N. JUDDOO.

Attorney-General: RONNY GOVINDEN.

Religion

The majority of the inhabitants are Christians, of whom more than 85% are Roman Catholics and about 8% Anglicans. Hinduism, Islam, and the Bahá'í Faith are also practised, however.

CHRISTIANITY

The Anglican Communion

The Church of the Province of the Indian Ocean comprises six dioceses: four in Madagascar, one in Mauritius and one in Seychelles. The Archbishop of the Province is the Bishop of Antananarivo, Madagascar.

Bishop of Seychelles: Rt Rev. SANTOSH MARRAY, POB 44, Victoria; tel. 321977; fax 323879; e-mail angdio@seychelles.net.

The Roman Catholic Church

Seychelles comprises a single diocese, directly responsible to the Holy See. At 31 December 2006 there were an estimated 71,350 adherents in the country, representing 85.0% of the total population.

Bishop of Port Victoria: Rt Rev. DENIS WIEHE, Bishop's House-Evêché, Olivier Maradan St, POB 43, Victoria; tel. 322152; fax 324045; e-mail rcchurch@seychelles.net.

Other Christian Churches

Pentecostal Assemblies of Seychelles: Victoria; tel. 224598; e-mail paos@seychelles.net; Pastor HERMITTE FREMINOT.

The Press

L'Echo des Iles: POB 12, Victoria; tel. 322262; fax 321464; monthly; French, Creole and English; Roman Catholic; Editor Fr EDWIN MATHIOT; circ. 2,800.

The People: Maison du Peuple, Revolution Ave, Victoria; tel. 224455; internet www.thepeople.sc; owned by the SPPF; monthly; Creole, French and English; circ. 1,000.

SEYCHELLES

Seychelles Nation: Information Technology and Communication Division, POB 800, Victoria; tel. 225775; fax 321006; e-mail seynat@seychelles.net; internet www.nation.sc; f. 1976; govt-owned; Mon.–Sat.; English, French and Creole; the country's only daily newspaper; Dir DENIS ROSE; circ. 3,500.

Seychelles Review: POB 29, Victoria; tel. 241881; fax 241545; e-mail surmer@seychelles.net; internet www.seychellesreview.com; f. 1994; monthly; business, politics, real estate and tourism; Editor ROLAND HOARAU.

Seychelles Weekly: POB 269, Victoria; e-mail editor@seychellesweekly.com; internet www.seychellesweekly.com; supports the Democratic Party; Editor RALPH VOLCERE.

Seychellois: POB 32, Victoria; f. 1928; publ. by Seychelles Farmers Asscn; quarterly; circ. 1,800.

Vizyon: Arpent Vert, Mont Fleuri, Victoria; tel. 224507; fax 224987; internet www.snpseychelles.sc/vizyon.htm; f. 2007; political fortnightly magazine of the opposition SNP; successor to weekly Regar; Creole, English and French; Editor ROGER MANCIENNE.

Broadcasting and Communications

TELECOMMUNICATIONS

Cable and Wireless (Seychelles) Ltd: Mercury House, Francis Rachel St, POB 4, Victoria; tel. 284000; fax 322777; e-mail cws@seychelles.net; internet www.cwseychelles.com; f. 1990; Chief Exec. CHARLES HAMMOND.

Atlas Seychelles Ltd (XNET): POB 903, Victoria; tel. 304060; fax 324565; e-mail atlas@seychelles.net; internet www.seychelles.net; f. 1996 by a consortium of Space95, VCS and MBM; acquired by Cable and Wireless (Seychelles) Ltd in 2005; internet service provider; Gen. Man. ANTHONY DELORIE.

Telecom Seychelles Ltd (AirTel): POB 1358, Providence; tel. 345505; fax 345499; internet www.airtel.sc; f. 1998; 80% owned by private investors, 10% by Govt of Seychelles; provides fixed-line, mobile and satellite telephone and internet services; Chief Exec. RAJAN SWAROOP.

BROADCASTING

Radio

Seychelles Broadcasting Corpn (SBC): Hermitage, POB 321, Victoria; tel. 289600; fax 225641; e-mail sbcradtv@seychelles.sc; internet www.sbc.sc; f. 1983; reorg. as independent corpn in 1992; programmes in Creole, English and French; Man. Dir IBRAHIM AFIF.

SBC Radio: Union Vale, POB 321, Victoria; tel. 289600; fax 289720; e-mail sbcradtv@seychelles.sc; internet www.sbc.sc; f. 1941; programmes in Creole, English and French; Man. Dir IBRAHIM AFIF.

Television

Seychelles Broadcasting Corpn (SBC): see Radio.

SBC TV: Hermitage, POB 321, Victoria; tel. 224161; fax 225641; e-mail sbcradtv@seychelles.sc; f. 1983; programmes in Creole, English and French; Head of TV Production JUDE LOUANGE.

Finance

(cap. = capital; res = reserves; dep. = deposits; m. = million; brs = branches; amounts in Seychelles rupees)

BANKING

Central Bank

Central Bank of Seychelles (CBS): Independence Ave, POB 701, Victoria; tel. 282000; fax 224958; e-mail enquiries@cbs.sc; internet www.cbs.sc; f. 1983; bank of issue; cap. 1.0m., res 88.0m., dep. 1,256.3m. (Dec. 2006); Gov. PIERRE LAPORTE.

National Banks

Development Bank of Seychelles: Independence Ave, POB 217, Victoria; tel. 294400; fax 224274; e-mail devbank@dbs.sc; internet www.dbs.sc; f. 1977; 55.5% state-owned; cap. 39.2m., res 43.9m. (Dec. 2006); Chair. ANTONIO LUCAS; Man. Dir ROGER TOUSSAINT.

Seychelles International Mercantile Banking Corporation Ltd (Nouvobanq) (SIMBC): Victoria House, State House Ave, POB 241, Victoria; tel. 293000; fax 224670; e-mail nvb@nouvobanq.sc; f. 1991; 78% state-owned, 22% by Standard Chartered Bank (UK); cap. 50.0m., res 49.7m., dep. 1,773.0m. (Dec. 2006); Chair. VISWANATHAN SHANKAR; Pres. AHMED SAEED; 2 brs.

Seychelles Savings Bank Ltd (SSB): Kingsgate House, POB 531, Victoria; tel. 294000; fax 224713; e-mail ssb@savingsbank.sc; f. 1902; state-owned; term deposits, savings and current accounts; cap. and res 7.8m. (Dec. 1992), dep. 356.4m. (1999); Chair. JOSEPH NOURRICE; 4 brs.

Foreign Banks

Bank of Baroda (India): Trinity House, Albert St, POB 124, Victoria; tel. 610333; fax 324057; e-mail ce.seychelles@bankofbaroda.com; internet www.bankofbaroda.com/seychelles.asp; f. 1978; Man. M. S. PHOGAT.

Barclays Bank (Seychelles) Ltd (United Kingdom): Independence Ave, POB 167, Victoria; tel. 383838; fax 324054; e-mail barclays@seychelles.sc; f. 1959; Seychelles Dir LOGANADEN SIDAMBARAM; 3 brs and 4 agencies.

Habib Bank Ltd (Pakistan): Frances Rachel St, POB 702, Victoria; tel. 224371; fax 225614; e-mail habibsez@seychelles.net; f. 1976; Vice-Pres. and Chief Man. SOHAIL ANWAR.

Mauritius Commercial Bank (Seychelles) Ltd (MCB Seychelles): POB 122, Manglier St, Victoria; tel. 284555; fax 322676; e-mail contact@mcbseychelles.com; internet www.mcbseychelles.com; f. 1978 as Banque Française Commerciale (BFCOI); changed name in 2003; cap. 14.0m., res 14.0m., dep. 958.4m. (Dec. 2003); Man. Dir JOCELYN AH-YU; 5 brs.

INSURANCE

H. Savy Insurance Co Ltd (HSI): Maison de la Rosière, 2nd Floor, POB 887; Victoria; tel. 322272; fax 321666; e-mail insurance@mail.seychelles.net; f. 1995; all classes; majority-owned by Corvina Investments; Gen. Dir JEAN WEELING-LEE.

Seychelles Assurance Company Ltd (SACL): Pirate's Arms Bldg, POB 636, Victoria; tel. 225000; fax 224495; e-mail sacos@sacos.sc; internet www.sacos.sc; f. 1980; state-owned; scheduled for privatization (excluding the Life Insurance Fund); all classes of insurance; subsidiaries include SUN Investments (Seychelles) Ltd, property-development company; fmrly State Assurance Corporation of Seychelles—SACOS; current name adopted 2006; Chair. and Man. Dir ANTONIO A. LUCAS.

Trade and Industry

GOVERNMENT AGENCIES

Seychelles Fishing Authority (SFA): POB 449, Fishing Port, Victoria; tel. 670300; fax 224508; e-mail management@sfa.sc; internet www.sfa.sc; f. 1984; assessment and management of fisheries resources; Chair. VÉRONIQUE HERMINIE; Man. Dir RONDOLPH PAYET.

Seychelles Trading Co Ltd (STC): Latanier Rd, POB 634, Victoria; tel. 285000; fax 224735; e-mail mail@stcl.sc; internet stcl.sc; f. 1984; replaced import and distribution arm of the fmr Seychelles Marketing Board (SMB) in 2008; manufacturing and marketing of products, retailing, trade; Chair. COLIN JEAN-LOUIS; CEO PATRICK VEL.

DEVELOPMENT ORGANIZATIONS

Indian Ocean Tuna Commission (IOTC) (Commission de Thons de l'Océan Indien): Le Chantier Mall, 2nd Floor, POB 1011, Victoria; tel. 225494; fax 224364; e-mail secretariat@iotc.org; internet www.iotc.org; f. 1996; an inter-governmental organization mandated to manage tuna and tuna-like species in the Indian Ocean and adjacent seas; to promote co-operation among its members with a view to ensuring, through appropriate management, the conservation and optimum utilization of stocks and encouraging sustainable development of fisheries based on such stocks; Exec. Sec. ALEJANDRO ANGANUZZI.

Seychelles International Business Authority (SIBA): Industrial Trade Zone, POB 991, Victoria; Bois de Rose Ave, Roche Caiman; tel. 380800; fax 380888; e-mail siba@seychelles.net; internet www.siba.net; f. 1995 to supervise registration of companies, transshipment and 'offshore' financial services in an international free-trade zone covering an area of 23 ha near Mahé International Airport; Chief Exec. and Man. Dir STEVE FANNY.

Seychelles Investment Bureau (SIB): POB 1167, Caravelle House, 2nd floor, Manglier St, Victoria; tel. 295500; fax 225125; e-mail sib@seychelles.sc; internet www.sib.gov.sc; f. 2004; Chief Exec. JOSEPH NOURRICE.

Small Enterprises Promotion Agency (SEnPA): Camion Hall Bldg, Victoria; tel. 323151; fax 324121; e-mail senpa@senpa.sc; internet www.senpa.sc; f. 2004; fmrly the Seychelles Industrial Development Corpn, f. 1988; promotes and develops small enterprises, crafts and cottage industries; CEO SYLVIANE VALMONT.

CHAMBER OF COMMERCE

Seychelles Chamber of Commerce and Industry: Ebrahim Bldg, 2nd Floor, POB 1399, Victoria; tel. 323812; fax 321422; e-mail scci@seychelles.int; Chair. VAITHUNASAMY RAMADOSS; Sec.-Gen. NICHOLE TIRANT-GHÉRARDI.

EMPLOYERS' ORGANIZATION

Federation of Employers' Associations of Seychelles (FEAS): POB 214, Victoria; tel. 324969; fax 324996; Chair. BASIL SOUNDY.

UTILITIES

Electricity

Public Utilities Corporation (Electricity Division): Electricity House, POB 174, Roche Caiman; tel. 678000; fax 321020; e-mail pmorin@puc.sc; Man. Dir PHILIPPE MORIN.

Water

Public Utilities Corporation (Water and Sewerage Division): Unity House, POB 34, Victoria; tel. 322444; fax 325612; e-mail pucwater@seychelles.net; Man. Dir STEPHEN ROUSSEAU.

TRADE UNION

Seychelles Federation of Workers' Unions (SFWU): Maison du Peuple, Latanier Rd, POB 154, Victoria; tel. 224455; fax 225351; e-mail sfwu@seychelles.net; f. 1978 to amalgamate all existing trade unions; affiliated to the Seychelles People's Progressive Front; 25,200 mems; Pres. OLIVIER CHARLES; Gen. Sec. ANTOINE ROBINSON.

Transport

RAILWAYS

There are no railways in Seychelles.

ROADS

In 2004 there were 498 km of roads, of which 478 km were surfaced. Most surfaced roads are on Mahé and Praslin.

SHIPPING

Privately owned ferry services connect Victoria, on Mahé, with the islands of Praslin and La Digue. At 31 December 2007 Seychelles' merchant fleet numbered 54 vessels, totalling 182,643 grt.

Seychelles Ports Authority (SPA): POB 47, Mahé Quay, Victoria; tel. 224701; fax 224004; e-mail enquiries@seychellesports.sc; internet www.spa.sc; Dir-Gen. (Port of Victoria) Capt. W. ERNESTA.

Aquarius Shipping Agency Ltd: POB 865, Victoria; tel. 225050; fax 225043; e-mail aqua@seychelles.net; Gen. Man. ANTHONY SAVY.

Hunt, Deltel and Co Ltd: Trinity House, Albert St, POB 14, Victoria; tel. 380300; fax 225367; e-mail hundel@seychelles.net; internet www.hundel.sc; f. 1937; Man. Dir E. HOUAREAU.

Mahé Shipping Co Ltd: Maritime House, POB 336, Victoria; tel. 380500; fax 380538; e-mail mail@maheship.sc; internet www.maheship.sc; f. 1969; shipping agents; Chair. Capt. G. C. C. ADAM.

Harry Savy & Co Ltd: POB 20, Victoria; tel. 322120; fax 321421; e-mail hsavyco@seychelles.net; shipping agents; Man. Dir GUY SAVY.

Seychelles Shipping Line Ltd: POB 977, Providence, Victoria; tel. 373737; fax 373647; e-mail ssl@gondwana.sc; f. 1994; operates freight services between Seychelles and Durban, South Africa; Chair. SELWYN GENDRON; Man. Dir HASSAN OMAR.

CIVIL AVIATION

Seychelles International Airport is located at Pointe Larue, 10 km from Victoria. A new international passenger terminal and aircraft parking apron were constructed in the mid-2000s on land reclaimed in 1990; the existing terminal (which underwent SR 3m. in renovations in 2002) was to be converted into a cargo terminal. The airport also serves as a refuelling point for aircraft traversing the Indian Ocean. There are airstrips on several outlying islands.

Seychelles Civil Aviation Authority (SCAA): POB 181, Victoria; tel. 384000; fax 384009; e-mail secretariat@scaa.sc; internet www.scaa.sc; formerly Directorate of Civil Aviation; offers ground and cargo handling and refuelling services, as well as holding responsibility for the Flight Information Region of 2.6m. sq km of Indian Ocean airspace; Chair. MAURICE LOUSTAU LALANNE; CEO GILBERT FAURE.

Air Seychelles: The Creole Spirit Bldg, Quincy St, POB 386, Victoria; tel. 381002; fax 224305; e-mail airseymd@seychelles.net; internet www.airseychelles.net; f. 1979; operates scheduled internal flights from Mahé to Praslin; also charter services to Bird, Desroches and Denis Islands and to outlying islands of the Amirantes group; international services to Europe, Far East, East and South Africa; CEO Dr RAJIV BISSESSUR.

Emirates Airlines: 5th June Ave and Manglier St, Victoria; tel. 292700; f. 2005; Dir ABDULRAHMAN AL BALOOSHI.

Tourism

Seychelles enjoys an equable climate, and is renowned for its fine beaches and attractive scenery. There are more than 500 varieties of flora and many rare species of birds. Most tourist activity is concentrated on the islands of Mahé, Praslin and La Digue, although the potential for ecological tourism of the outlying islands received increased attention in the late 1990s. It is government policy that the development of tourism should not blight the environment, and strict laws govern the location and construction of hotels. In 1998 the Government indicated that up to 200,000 visitors (although not more than 4,000 at any one time) could be accommodated annually without detriment to environmental quality. However, several new luxury resorts were constructed in the early 2000s, and the yachting sector was also under development. Receipts from tourism totalled an estimated SR 1,194m. in 2007. In that year there were 161,300 tourist arrivals; most visitors (approximately 65.2% in 2005) are from Europe.

Compagnie Seychelloise de Promotion Hotelière Ltd: POB 683, Victoria; tel. 224694; fax 225291; e-mail cosproh@seychelles.net; promotes govt-owned hotels.

Seychelles Tourism Board (STB): POB 1262, Victoria; tel. 671300; fax 620620; e-mail info@seychelles.com; internet www.seychelles.travel; f. 1998 as Seychelles Tourism Marketing Authority; merged with Seychelles Tourism Office in 2005; Chair. MAURICE LOUSTAU-LALANNE.

SIERRA LEONE

Introductory Survey

Location, Climate, Language, Religion, Flag, Capital

The Republic of Sierra Leone lies on the west coast of Africa, with Guinea to the north and east, and Liberia to the south. The climate is hot and humid, with an average annual temperature of 27°C (80°F). The rainy season lasts from May to October. The average annual rainfall is about 3,436 mm (13.5 ins). English is the official language, while Krio (Creole), Mende, Limba and Temne are also widely spoken. The majority of the population follow animist beliefs, but there are significant numbers of Islamic and Christian adherents. The national flag (proportions 2 by 3) has three equal horizontal stripes, of green, white and blue. The capital is Freetown.

Recent History

Sierra Leone was formerly a British colony and protectorate. A new Constitution, which provided for universal adult suffrage, was introduced in 1951. In that year the Sierra Leone People's Party (SLPP) won the majority of votes in elections. The leader of the SLPP, Dr (later Sir) Milton Margai, became Chief Minister in 1953 and Prime Minister in 1958. On 27 April 1961 Sierra Leone achieved independence as a constitutional monarchy within the Commonwealth. Margai died in April 1964 and was succeeded as Prime Minister by his half-brother, Dr (later Sir) Albert Margai, previously the Minister of Finance.

In March 1967 the army assumed control and established a ruling body, the National Reformation Council. In April 1968 a further coup was staged by army officers, and power was subsequently transferred to a civilian Government; Dr Siaka Stevens, the leader of the All-People's Congress (APC), was elected as Prime Minister. In April 1971 a republican Constitution was introduced and Stevens became executive President.

The general election in May 1973 was not contested by the SLPP, and in 1976 Stevens, the sole candidate, was unanimously re-elected to the presidency for a second five-year term of office. A new Constitution, which provided for a one-party system, was adopted by the House of Representatives in June. The APC thus became the sole legitimate political organization. Stevens was inaugurated as President for a seven-year term on 14 June 1978. He subsequently released political detainees and allocated ministerial posts to several former SLPP members (who had joined the APC).

During the 1980s civil unrest, prompted by economic hardship, increased and in April 1985 Stevens announced that (contrary to earlier indications) he would not seek re-election to the presidency upon the expiry, in June, of his existing mandate. Stevens' term of office was subsequently extended for six months, to allow time for registration of voters and the nomination of a presidential candidate. At a conference of the APC in August, Maj.-Gen. Joseph Momoh, a cabinet minister and the Commander of the Army, was the sole candidate for the leadership of the party and for the presidential nomination. Momoh was elected to the national presidency in October, with 99% of the votes cast, and was inaugurated on 28 November. Although retaining his military status, Momoh appointed a civilian Cabinet, which included several members of the previous administration. Elections to the House of Representatives took place in May 1986.

Despite a campaign against financial malpractice in the public sector, Momoh's administration failed to improve the serious economic situation, and popular discontent continued. In March 1987 the Government announced that it had suppressed an attempted coup; more than 60 people were subsequently arrested, including the First Vice-President, Francis Minah. In October Minah and 15 other defendants were sentenced to death for plotting to assassinate Momoh and to overthrow the Government, and two defendants received custodial sentences on charges of treason. In October 1989 Minah and five others were executed, despite international appeals for clemency.

Following the outbreak of civil conflict in Liberia in December 1989, an estimated 125,000 Liberians took refuge in Sierra Leone. The Sierra Leonean Government contributed troops to the cease-fire monitoring group (ECOMOG) of the Economic Community of West African States (ECOWAS, see p. 243), which was dispatched to Liberia in August 1990. In November of that year Charles Taylor, the leader of the principal Liberian rebel faction, the National Patriotic Front of Liberia (NPFL), threatened to attack Freetown International Airport (alleged to be a base for ECOMOG offensives against rebel strongholds). In early April 1991, following repeated border incursions by members of the NPFL, government forces entered Liberian territory and launched a retaliatory attack against NPFL bases. By the end of that month, however, NPFL forces had advanced 150 km within Sierra Leone. The Momoh Government alleged that the rebel offensive had been instigated by Taylor, in an attempt to force Sierra Leone's withdrawal from ECOMOG, and also accused the Government of Burkina Faso of actively assisting the rebels. It was reported, however, that members of a Sierra Leonean resistance movement, known as the Revolutionary United Front (RUF), had joined the NPFL in attacks against government forces. In mid-1991 government troops, with the assistance of military units from Nigeria and Guinea, initiated a counter-offensive against the rebels, and succeeded in recapturing several towns in the east and south of the country.

In early August 1991 the House of Representatives formally approved a new Constitution (which provided for the adoption of a multi-party system and stipulated that the President, who was to appoint the Cabinet, was to be elected by a majority of votes cast nationally and by at least 25% of the votes cast in more than one-half of the electoral districts), and at a national referendum, which was conducted later in August, it was endorsed by 60% of voters, with 75% of the electorate participating. In the same month six newly created political associations formed an alliance, known as the United Front of Political Movements, which subsequently demanded that the forthcoming elections be monitored by international observers, and that the incumbent Government be dissolved and an interim administration established. In June the parliamentary term, which was due to end that month, had been extended until May 1992 to allow time for the transition to a multi-party system. On 23 September 1991, following the resignation of the First Vice-President and Second Vice-President from both the APC and the Government, Momoh announced the formation of a new 18-member Cabinet, which retained only seven members of the previous Government. Later that month legislation that formally permitted the formation of political associations was introduced; several organizations were subsequently granted legal recognition.

On 29 April 1992 members of the armed forces, led by a five-member military junta, seized a radio station in Freetown and broadcast demands for improvements in conditions in the armed forces. The rebel troops later occupied the presidential offices, and the leader of the military junta, Capt. Valentine E. M. Strasser, announced that the Government had been overthrown. On the following day Momoh fled to Guinea, and Strasser announced the establishment of a governing council, to be known as the National Provisional Ruling Council (NPRC). Strasser affirmed the NPRC's commitment to the introduction of a multi-party system, and pledged to end the conflict in the country. On the same day the Constitution was suspended, the House of Representatives was dissolved and a state of emergency was imposed. On 1 May the NPRC (which principally comprised military officers), chaired by Strasser, was formed. Shortly afterwards a new 19-member Cabinet, which included a number of members of the NPRC, was appointed, and the Commander of the Armed Forces and the head of the security forces were replaced. On 6 May Strasser was inaugurated as Head of State.

In July 1992 Strasser replaced the three members of the NPRC in the Cabinet with civilians, and removed all civilian cabinet ministers from the NPRC. Later that month he announced extensive structural changes, which were designed to reduce the direct involvement of the NPRC in government administration: the NPRC was officially designated the Supreme Council of State, while the Cabinet was reconstituted as the Council of Secretaries (headed by the Chief Secretary of State), which was to be responsible for government administration, subject to the authority of the NPRC. In December Strasser announced a reorganization of the Council of Secretaries, in which the two remaining members of the Momoh administration were replaced. In the same month the Deputy Chairman of the NPRC, Capt. Solomon A. J. Musa, became Chief Secretary of State. Later in December, in an apparent attempt to regain public support, the Government established a 19-member National Advisory Council, comprising representatives of various non-governmental organizations, which was to draft a programme for transition to civilian rule.

At the end of December 1992 the Government announced that the security forces had suppressed a coup attempt. Shortly afterwards nine of those accused of involvement in the attempted coup were convicted by a special military tribunal, and, together with 17 prisoners who had been convicted in November on charges of treason, were summarily executed. Human rights organizations subsequently contested the Government's statement that a coup attempt had been staged, and condemned the trial by special military tribunal. In January 1993 the United Kingdom announced the suspension of economic aid to Sierra Leone in protest at the executions.

In April 1993 Strasser announced that a programme providing for a transition to civilian rule within a period of three years was to be adopted; in addition, all political prisoners were to be released, press restrictions would be relaxed, and the function of special military tribunals was to be reviewed. In July Musa was replaced as Deputy Chairman of the NPRC and Chief Secretary of State by Capt. Julius Maada Bio. Musa (who was widely believed to be responsible for the repressive measures undertaken by the Government) took refuge in the Nigerian high commission in Freetown, amid widespread speculation regarding his dismissal, and subsequently emigrated to the United Kingdom.

At the end of November 1993 Strasser announced the details of a two-year transitional programme, which provided for the installation of a civilian government by January 1996. The registration of political parties was to take place in June 1995, prior to a presidential election in November and legislative elections in December of that year. In December a five-member Interim National Electoral Commission was established to organize the registration of voters and the demarcation of constituency boundaries, in preparation for forthcoming local government elections. In the same month the National Advisory Council submitted constitutional proposals (which included a number of similar provisions to the 1991 Constitution), stipulating that: executive power was to be vested in the President, who was to be required to consult with the Cabinet, and was to be restricted to a tenure of two four-year terms of office; only Sierra Leonean nationals of more than 40 years of age were to qualify to contest a presidential election (thereby precluding Strasser and the majority of NPRC members, on grounds of age); the legislature was to comprise a House of Representatives, which was to be elected by universal adult suffrage for a term of five years, and a 30-member upper chamber, the Senate. A draft Constitution was submitted to the NPRC in October 1994.

In January 1995 the RUF, which had been joined by disaffected members of the armed forces, gained control of the mining installations owned by the Sierra Leone Ore and Metal Company (SIEROMCO) and Sierra Rutile Ltd, and seized a number of employees of the two enterprises, including eight foreign nationals. In the same month the RUF threatened to kill the British hostages if the Sierra Leonean authorities executed an officer, who had been convicted by military tribunal of collaborating with the rebels. In February the RUF rejected appeals by the UN and the Organization of African Unity (now the African Union, see p. 172) that peace negotiations be initiated, and demanded that all troops that had been dispatched by foreign Governments to assist the Strasser administration be withdrawn as a precondition to discussions. In mid-February government forces (which had succeeded in recapturing the mining installations owned by Sierra Rutile) launched an offensive against a principal rebel base in the Kangari region, east of Freetown. Meanwhile, continued atrocities perpetrated against civilians were increasingly attributed to disaffected members of the armed forces.

In February 1995 the military administration engaged 58 Gurkha mercenaries, who had previously served in the British army, prompting further concern regarding the safety of the British hostages in Sierra Leone. In March government forces regained control of the mining installations owned by SIEROMCO and the principal town of Moyamba, 100 km south-east of Freetown (which had been captured by the RUF earlier that month). Despite the successful counter-offensives by government forces, by April the RUF had advanced towards Freetown and had initiated a series of attacks against towns in the vicinity (including Songo, which was situated only 35 km east of Freetown), apparently prior to besieging the capital. Later in April the remaining foreign nationals who had been seized by the RUF were released.

In March 1995 the Council of Secretaries was reorganized to allow principal military officials in the Government to assume active functions within the armed forces (following the advance of RUF forces towards Freetown); Lt-Col Akim Gibril became Chief Secretary of State, replacing Bio, who was appointed Chief of Defence Staff. At the end of April, on the anniversary of the NPRC's assumption of power, Strasser formally announced that the ban on political activity was to be rescinded, and that a National Consultative Conference was to be convened to discuss the transitional process; he further indicated that elections were to take place by the end of that year, prior to the installation of a civilian government in January 1996, in accordance with the transitional programme. The ban on political activity was formally ended on 21 June; some 15 parties were subsequently granted registration (although the RUF failed to respond to government efforts to include the movement in the electoral process).

In May 1995 government forces initiated a number of counter-attacks against the RUF, and succeeded in recapturing Songo. By the end of June government forces had regained control of significant diamond-mining regions in the eastern Kono District, and part of Bo District, in a successful counter-offensive, which was generally attributed to the assistance of South African mercenaries. In September, however, the RUF launched further offensives in Bo District, while increasing reports of massacres and other violations of human rights perpetrated by the rebels against the civilian population emerged.

In December 1995 it was announced that the presidential and legislative elections were to take place concurrently on 26 February 1996. In January 1996, however, Strasser was deposed by military officers, led by Bio, in a bloodless coup. Bio, who assumed the office of Head of State, announced that the coup had been instigated in response to efforts by Strasser to remain in power. (It was reported that Strasser had intended to amend restrictions on the age of prospective candidates to enable himself to contest the elections.) Strasser (who had been expelled to Guinea) claimed, however, that the new military administration planned to delay the transition to civilian government. A reconstituted Supreme Council of State and Council of Secretaries were formed and it was announced that the elections were to take place as scheduled. The RUF indicated that it was prepared to enter into negotiations with the new Government, and declared a temporary cease-fire to allow voter registration to proceed throughout the country, but urged a postponement of the elections, pending a peace settlement that would allow the movement to participate in the democratic process. However, delegates at the National Consultative Conference, which was convened in early February, voted in favour of adherence to the scheduled date. The RUF subsequently abandoned the cease-fire and launched a series of attacks in various parts of the country, in an apparent attempt to undermine the electoral process.

On 26 February 1996 presidential and legislative elections took place as scheduled. However, some 27 people were killed in attacks by armed groups, particularly in Bo and parts of Freetown, which were generally attributed to the RUF; voting was consequently extended for a further day. The reconstituted SLPP secured 36.1% of votes cast in the legislative elections, while its presidential candidate, Ahmed Tejan Kabbah, also received most support, with 35.8% of votes. A second round of the presidential election, which took place on 15 March, was contested by Kabbah and the candidate of the United National People's Party (UNPP), John Karefa-Smart (who had obtained 22.6% of votes cast in the first round): Kabbah was elected President by 59.5% of the votes. Later in March seats in the new 80-member Parliament were allocated on a basis of proportional representation, with the SLPP securing 27, the UNPP 17, the People's Democratic Party 12 and the reconstituted APC only five seats; the 12 provincial districts were represented in the legislature by Paramount Chiefs. Kabbah was inaugurated on 29 March, when the military Government officially relinquished power to the new civilian administration. In April Kabbah appointed a Cabinet, which was subsequently approved by the new Parliament.

Following the elections, the Government announced in March 1996 that the RUF had agreed to a cease-fire; at a meeting between RUF Leader Foday Sankoh and Bio in Yamoussoukro,

Côte d'Ivoire, later that month, the RUF undertook to observe the cease-fire for a period of two months and to continue negotiations with the newly elected civilian Government. Following discussions between Sankoh and Kabbah in April, the Government and RUF reaffirmed their commitment to a permanent cessation of hostilities, and announced the establishment of three joint committees, which would consider issues regarding the demobilization of rebel forces. However, Sankoh continued to refuse to recognize the legitimacy of the new Government, and demanded that a transitional administration be installed pending further elections. Despite the official cease-fire, sporadic attacks by the RUF were subsequently reported and further clashes occurred later that year between government forces and the Kamajors (traditional fighters reconstituted as an auxiliary defence force).

In July 1996 the Parliament adopted legislation that formally reinstated the Constitution of 1991. In September 1996 Kabbah ordered the compulsory retirement of some 20 officers, including Strasser and Bio, from the armed forces. Shortly afterwards it was reported that a conspiracy to overthrow the Government had been thwarted by senior military officers. About 17 members of the armed forces were arrested, of whom nine were subsequently charged with involvement in the conspiracy. Following reports of a further conspiracy to overthrow the Government in January 1997, Kabbah announced that an investigative mission from Nigeria had concluded that former members of the NPRC administration had instigated the coup attempt of September 1996.

In November 1996 Kabbah demanded that the RUF relinquish armaments within a period of two weeks, threatening that government forces would resume military operations. At the end of that month Kabbah and Sankoh signed a peace agreement in Abidjan, Côte d'Ivoire, whereby RUF forces were to be demobilized and the movement was to be reconstituted as a political organization, while all foreign troops were to be withdrawn from the country and replaced with foreign observers. A National Commission for the Consolidation of Peace was subsequently established to monitor the peace settlement. By February 1997 all foreign mercenaries had left Sierra Leone in accordance with the agreement, while the repatriation of Sierra Leonean refugees from Liberia had commenced. However, at the end of that month (when the implementation of the peace agreement was scheduled for completion) it was reported that members of the RUF had repeatedly violated the peace agreement and had failed to report to designated centres for disarmament. In March members of the political wing of the RUF issued a declaration that Sankoh had been removed as leader of the organization, owing to his failure to implement the peace accord. Later that month, however, RUF forces loyal to Sankoh kidnapped members of the movement who had supported his replacement, together with the Sierra Leonean ambassador to Guinea; the faction issued demands for the release of Sankoh, who had been detained in Nigeria earlier that month (being reportedly in possession of armaments).

On 25 May 1997 dissident members of the armed forces, led by Maj. Johnny Paul Koroma, seized power, deposing Kabbah, who fled to Guinea. The new authorities imposed a curfew in Freetown, following widespread violent looting by armed factions, and most foreign nationals were evacuated. In early June Nigerian forces initiated a naval bombardment of Freetown in an effort to force the new military leaders to resign. However, forces loyal to the coup leaders, assisted by RUF members, succeeded in repelling Nigerian attacks. Koroma announced the establishment of a 20-member Armed Forces Revolutionary Council (AFRC), with himself as Chairman and Sankoh (who remained in detention in Nigeria) as Vice-Chairman; the AFRC (which was not internationally recognized as the legitimate Government) included a further three members of the RUF and several civilians. All political activity, the existing Constitution and government bodies were suspended, although Koroma pledged that democratic rule would be restored. Nigeria reiterated that it intended to reinstate the ousted Government with the support of ECOWAS, and a further two Nigerian warships were dispatched to the region; further clashes between Nigerian troops, who had been serving under the mandate of ECOMOG in neighbouring Liberia (q.v.), and supporters of the new military leaders occurred at the international airport at Lungi. In mid-June the AFRC announced that it had suppressed a coup attempt, following the arrest of 15 people, including several senior military officers. In the same month it was reported that troops supporting the junta had repulsed an attack by Kamajors (who remained loyal to Kabbah) at the town of Zimmi, 250 km south-east of Freetown. On 17 June Koroma was formally inaugurated as the self-proclaimed Head of State. However, despite appeals from Koroma, a campaign of civil disobedience, organized by the labour congress in protest at the coup, continued.

By early July 1997 the new military Government had been completely isolated by the international community. The Commonwealth Ministerial Action Group on the Harare Declaration (CMAG—which had been established to ensure adherence to the principles of democracy by member states) suspended Sierra Leone from meetings of the Commonwealth, pending the restoration of constitutional order and the reinstatement of a democratically elected government. The UN Security Council also condemned the coup, and expressed support for ECOWAS efforts to resolve the situation. Meanwhile, a four-member ministerial committee, comprising representatives of Nigeria, Côte d'Ivoire, Guinea and Ghana, which had been established by ECOWAS, urged the Government to relinquish power during a series of negotiations with an AFRC delegation.

In mid-July 1997 Koroma formed a cabinet, known as the Council of Secretaries, comprising representatives of the RUF and the army, together with a number of civilians. Later that month, following further reports of clashes between Kamajors and forces loyal to the junta in the south of the country, AFRC representatives and the ECOWAS committee, meeting in Abidjan, agreed to an immediate cease-fire; negotiations were to continue, with the aim of restoring constitutional order. At the end of July continuing discussions between the ECOWAS committee and AFRC representatives in Abidjan were abandoned, after Koroma insisted that he retain power for a tenure of four years, and refused to restore the Constitution and to end the ban on political activity. Consequently, in late August an ECOWAS conference, which was convened at Abuja, Nigeria, officially endorsed the imposition of sanctions against Sierra Leone, with the aim of obliging the AFRC to relinquish power. ECOMOG was granted a mandate to monitor the cease-fire and to enforce the economic embargo; it was also agreed that the ECOWAS monitoring committee would henceforth include Liberia (following the election of a democratic Government in that country).

In September 1997 CMAG voted in support of the decision of the ECOWAS committee to effect the reinstatement of the Kabbah administration. In early October the UN Security Council imposed sanctions on the import of armaments and petroleum products to Sierra Leone. Following aerial bombardments of Freetown by ECOMOG troops a mass demonstration was held in the capital to demand that the Nigerian Government withdraw its troops from Sierra Leone. Negotiations between the AFRC and the five-member committee continued, however, and later in October an agreement, which was signed in Conakry, Guinea, provided for an immediate cease-fire, and the reinstatement of Kabbah's Government by April 1998, together with immunity from prosecution for AFRC members; all troops loyal to the incumbent military administration and RUF members were to be demobilized, under the supervision of a disarmament committee, comprising representatives of the AFRC, ECOMOG and local forces loyal to Kabbah. In January 1998 ECOMOG forces again bombarded the port at Freetown (for the first time since the peace agreement in October), apparently with the aim of preventing merchant vessels from contravening the sanctions.

In early February 1998 further clashes erupted near Freetown between ECOMOG troops and supporters of the military junta. Nigerian troops belonging to ECOMOG subsequently launched an intensive bombardment against Freetown and succeeded in gaining control of the capital, after senior members of the AFRC, including Koroma, fled into hiding, or surrendered to the ECOMOG forces. About 50 members of the military junta were arrested in Monrovia, Liberia, prompting protests from the Liberian Government regarding the Nigerian military intervention. It was announced that the Government that had been ousted on 25 May 1997 was to be reinstated, and that all subsequent appointments were to be considered invalid. ECOMOG forces were to remain in the country to assist in the restructuring of the armed forces. Meanwhile, following reports that troops loyal to the former military junta, with the assistance of the RUF, had taken control of Bo, ECOMOG forces were deployed in the region to support the Kamajors, and rapidly succeeded in regaining control of most of the region (prompting speculation that the Nigerian military initiative had been undertaken with the aim of gaining access to Sierra Leone's mineral resources).

On 10 March 1998 Kabbah returned from exile and was officially reinstated as President; he subsequently appointed a Cabinet (which included a number of members of his previous administration). The new Government declared a state of emergency under which members of the former military junta could be detained for a maximum of 30 days without being formally charged. It was announced that some 1,500 civilians and members of the armed forces (including Momoh) had been placed in detention and were to be charged for their alleged connections with the former military junta. Also in March the UN Security Council voted to end its embargo on imports of petroleum products to Sierra Leone (which had resulted in severe fuel shortages), although an embargo on the supply of armaments was maintained. It was reported that ECOMOG forces had launched an offensive in the east of the country, in an effort to eradicate the remaining forces loyal to the former military junta and members of the RUF. In July the UN Security Council adopted a resolution establishing a UN Observer Mission in Sierra Leone (UNOMSIL), comprising 70 military observers, with an initial six-month mandate to monitor the security situation, supervise the disarmament of former combatants, and advise the authorities on the restructuring of the security forces. In the same month it was announced that the national army had been dissolved.

In late July 1998 the Nigerian Government returned Sankoh (who had been in detention in Nigeria since early 1997) to Sierra Leone, where he was charged with treason following his support for the military coup of May 1997. In August 16 civilians, including five journalists, were sentenced to death, after being convicted of supporting the former military junta. In October 24 army officers were publicly executed, following their conviction for involvement with the military junta, provoking condemnation from many foreign Governments and human rights organizations, which had appealed for clemency. Death penalties imposed against a further 10 officers were commuted to terms of life imprisonment. In November a further 15 civilians, including several ministers who had served in the AFRC Government, were sentenced to death for their part in the May 1997 coup; Momoh received a custodial term of 10 years for colluding with the military junta.

Meanwhile, ECOMOG continued efforts to suppress rebel activity, particularly in the north and east of the country, and in October 1998 transferred its operational headquarters from the Liberian capital, Monrovia, to Freetown. In that month the RUF intensified hostilities, after it was announced that Sankoh had been sentenced to death by the High Court on charges of treason. In November ECOMOG forces commenced aerial bombardments of rebel bases. By late December, however, RUF forces, together with supporters of the former military junta, had advanced towards Freetown, and had seized control of the principal town of Makeni, 140 km north-east of Freetown. The Governments of Nigeria and Ghana dispatched additional troops to reinforce the ECOMOG contingent (which henceforth numbered about 15,000). At the end of December the acting Commander of the RUF, Sam Bockarie, rejected a government invitation to enter into peace negotiations, and ECOMOG forces, supported by Kamajors, attempted to repulse rebel attacks in the outskirts of Freetown.

On 6 January 1999 rebel forces attacked Freetown (where thousands of civilians from the surrounding area had taken refuge), releasing a number of supporters of the former junta from the capital's prison and seizing the Nigerian High Commission and government offices; Kabbah and a number of cabinet ministers were obliged to flee to ECOMOG headquarters. (It was subsequently discovered that two ministers had been killed by the rebels.) Bockarie announced that Freetown was under the control of the RUF, and demanded that Sankoh be released from detention. ECOMOG troops initiated a counter-offensive, with an aerial bombardment of Freetown, forcing the rebels to retreat to the outskirts of the capital. By late January ECOMOG forces claimed to have regained control of Freetown, and a cease-fire was agreed, pending peace negotiations, which were convened in Conakry, with mediation by the Governments of Guinea, Côte d'Ivoire and Togo. It was reported that Sankoh (who had been allowed by the Sierra Leonean authorities to attend the peace discussions) demanded his release and the official recognition of the RUF as a political movement as preconditions for the cessation of hostilities. Some 100 members of ECOMOG were arrested, following claims by a UN report (which were denied by ECOMOG) that suspected rebels had been summarily executed; the Kamajors were also implicated in summary killings.

Following the rebel offensive in January 1999, a number of West African Governments, particularly those of Nigeria and Ghana, reiterated claims that the Liberian Government was supporting the RUF with mercenaries and illicit exports of armaments in exchange for diamonds. ECOMOG also accused Burkina Faso and Libya of assisting rebel operations. Charles Taylor (now the Liberian President) denied any connections with the RUF, dismissing the allegations as an attempt to destabilize his administration. In April the Nigerian President-elect, Olusegun Obasanjo, agreed that the Nigerian contingent (then numbering nearly 15,000) would remain in Sierra Leone until peace was restored, apparently in response to the influence of the international community; however, a gradual withdrawal of ECOMOG troops, to be completed by early 2000, was envisaged. Meanwhile, Kabbah authorized discussions between Sankoh and active RUF leaders to clarify RUF demands, and, following pressure from the Nigerian, US and British Governments, agreed to conduct formal peace negotiations with the rebels. In late April, following discussions between RUF leaders, formal negotiations between the RUF and a government delegation commenced in the Togolese capital, Lomé, with mediation by President Gnassingbé Eyadéma of Togo. In early May the Government and the RUF signed a cease-fire agreement, which came into effect later that month. In early July the Government and the RUF reached a power-sharing agreement, after government negotiators acceded to rebel demands that Sankoh be granted vice-presidential powers, with responsibility for the mineral resources industry, and the RUF be allocated a number of cabinet posts. The accord provided for the release of civilians who had been abducted by the rebels, and the disarmament and reintegration into the armed forces of former combatants; the RUF was to be reconstituted as a political organization. Following the completion of disarmament, legislative and presidential elections were to take place by February 2001.

In early October 1999 Sankoh (who had been conducting discussions with Taylor) and Koroma returned to Freetown from Monrovia, and pledged to co-operate with Kabbah in the implementation of the Lomé peace accord. Later that month the UN Security Council adopted Resolution 1270, establishing a 6,000-member force, the UN Mission in Sierra Leone (UNAMSIL), which was granted a six-month mandate to supervise the implementation of the peace agreement, and to assist in a programme for the disarmament and reintegration of the former rebel factions; at the same time the mandate of UNOMSIL was terminated. The withdrawal of the ECOMOG contingent was to be completed following the deployment of UNAMSIL, although, in effect, the new peace-keeping force (which was to comprise 4,000 Nigerian troops and 2,000 principally Kenyan and Indian troops) would incorporate a number of the Nigerian forces belonging to ECOMOG. On 2 November a new coalition Cabinet was officially installed; four former members of the RUF and the AFRC junta were allocated ministerial posts. Sankoh became Chairman of a commission overseeing the reconstruction of the mineral resources industry, with vice-presidential status, while Koroma was nominated Chairman of the Commission for the Consolidation of Peace. In the same month the Government announced the establishment of a Truth and Reconciliation Commission (TRC), which was to make recommendations regarding compensation for victims of human rights violations. However, reports of atrocities perpetrated against the civilian population by rebels continued, and in November division between the AFRC and RUF leadership emerged, apparently as a result of the former junta's dissatisfaction with its cabinet posts. The arrival of UNAMSIL troops in Sierra Leone commenced at the end of November.

In early 2000 reports emerged of RUF forces in the Kailahun District of eastern Sierra Leone (where illegal diamond-mining continued) resisting disarmament and the deployment of UNAMSIL troops. In February the UN Security Council adopted a resolution in favour of expanding UNAMSIL to number 11,100, and extended its mandate for six months. In March Kabbah established a commission to supervise the elections, which, under the terms of the peace agreement, were to take place following the disarmament of the former rebel factions. By the end of that month, however, only about 17,000 of the 45,000 former combatants had been disarmed.

In April 2000 UNAMSIL troops stationed in the eastern town of Kenema repulsed attacks from rebel forces. In early May, following a further dispute over disarmament, RUF forces attacked UNAMSIL troops in Makeni and the neighbouring town of Magburaka, killing at least four Kenyan members of the contingent, and seizing a number of UN personnel as hostages. Six civilian UN observers were subsequently released, following intervention by Taylor. However, rebel forces continued to hold about 300 members of UNAMSIL (principally Zambians) hostage, while a further Zambian contingent of the peace-keeping force, numbering about 200, was reported missing. The British Government dispatched a military task force to the region (stationing troops at the airport at Lungi, and in Senegal), which evacuated most European nationals. RUF supporters guarding Sankoh's residence in Freetown fired on civilian demonstrators, who were demanding that Sankoh comply with the peace agreement; some 20 protesters were killed. (UN officials were subsequently unable to contact Sankoh, who had fled from Freetown.) Sierra Leonean government forces, led by Koroma (who continued to support the Kabbah administration), were deployed to halt rebel advances, and claimed to have recaptured territory from the RUF. At an ECOWAS summit meeting in Abuja, Taylor was authorized to negotiate with the RUF regarding their release of the hostages; the redeployment of Nigerian troops under an ECOMOG mandate was considered. In late May Sankoh was arrested in Freetown by troops loyal to Kabbah. By the end of that month, following mediation by Taylor, the hostages held by the RUF were released. In early June, however, 21 Indian members of UNAMSIL were seized by the RUF at the eastern town of Pendembu, while a further 233 peace-keeping troops were surrounded by rebels at nearby Kailahun. By mid-June most of the British forces had withdrawn (with about 250 troops remaining in the country to train new members of the Sierra Leone armed forces, and to assist in establishing the operations of a British military advisory team).

In early July 2000 the UN Security Council adopted a resolution, proposed by the British Government, imposing an international embargo on the purchase of unauthenticated diamonds (in an effort to prevent illicit trade from RUF-held regions, thereby ending the rebels' principal source of funding for armaments); the Sierra Leonean Government was to implement a system whereby officially mined diamonds would be granted certification. In the same month government forces clashed with one of the most notorious militia groups, the West Side Boys (WSB), which had hitherto supported the former AFRC junta. In mid-July the battalion of (principally Indian) peace-keeping personnel, who had been besieged by the RUF at Kailahun, were rescued in a military operation by UNAMSIL; one member of the contingent was killed during the offensive. In early August the UN Security Council approved the establishment of an international tribunal, where Sankoh and others responsible for atrocities committed during the civil conflict would be placed on trial. The RUF leadership announced the nomination of Gen. Issa Sesay (who was reported to be a more moderate commander) to replace Sankoh. Later in August the WSB abducted 11 British military personnel and one member of the Sierra Leonean armed forces, subsequently issuing a number of demands as a precondition to releasing the hostages. Five of the British personnel were freed after negotiations, but additional British troops were dispatched to Sierra Leone, following the failure of government officials to secure an agreement on the remaining hostages. In early September about 150 British troops attacked the main WSB base, 48 km east of Freetown, and succeeded in rescuing the other seven hostages. One member of the British armed forces died during the military operation, while 25 members of the WSB were killed, and a further 18 (including the movement's leader, Foday Kallay) were captured.

In September 2000 the Indian Government announced that it was to withdraw its contingent (then numbering 3,073 troops) from UNAMSIL, despite a proposal by the UN Secretary-General that the maximum strength of the peace-keeping force be increased. In October several nations, notably Bangladesh, Ghana and Kenya, pledged to dispatch additional troops to replace those of India. The number of British troops in the country had been increased to 400, while a 500-member naval task force was deployed off Freetown to provide additional support to the UN peace-keeping operations. On 10 November, following further negotiations mediated by ECOWAS, the Government and the RUF signed a cease-fire agreement in Abuja, providing for the demobilization and disarmament of all militia forces, and the deployment of UNAMSIL throughout the country.

Meanwhile, civilians continued to flee from the country, and by August 2000 some 331,000 Sierra Leonean refugees were registered in Guinea. In September the Guinean President, Gen. Lansana Conté, claimed that Liberian and Sierra Leonean refugees were supporting the activity of rebels attempting to overthrow his Government (see the chapter on Guinea), and ordered them to leave the country. Following clashes on Guinea's border with Liberia, tripartite discussions between Guinea, Liberia and Sierra Leone commenced in October. In March 2001, however, Taylor expelled the ambassadors of Guinea and Sierra Leone from Liberia, on the stated grounds that they had been engaged in activity incompatible with their office. Kabbah retaliated by ordering the Liberian chargé d'affaires to leave the country, and announced the closure of the joint border with Liberia. As a result of the continued violence and the hostility of the Guinean authorities, large numbers of the refugees in Guinea began to return to Sierra Leone. (Diplomatic links between Liberia and Sierra Leone and Guinea were normalized in August, following a request to Taylor by ECOWAS Heads of State.)

In February 2001 the National Assembly unanimously approved a proposal by Kabbah that presidential and legislative elections, scheduled to take place in February and March, respectively, be postponed for six months, owing to the continued civil unrest in the country. At the end of March the UN Security Council adopted a resolution increasing the strength of UNAMSIL (which then numbered 9,500) to 17,500 troops. In April UNAMSIL began to deploy troops in northern regions of the country, including the towns of Lunsar and Makeni, formerly held by the RUF. In early May, however, it was reported that the pro-Government Kamajor militia, now known as the Civil Defence Forces (CDF), had attacked RUF positions in eastern towns. UNAMSIL accused the CDF, which had advanced within RUF-held territory, of instigating the hostilities. In mid-May the RUF and CDF signed an agreement, providing for the immediate cessation of hostilities and resumption of disarmament for both forces. In June UNAMSIL and (British-trained) government forces regained control of part of the significant diamond-mining regions and the eastern border with Guinea and Sierra Leone (thereby forestalling renewed rebel activity originating from the neighbouring countries). Further clashes between the RUF and CDF continued to impede the disarmament process, and in mid-July discussions regarding the implementation of the peace agreement were conducted at Bo; the Government, the RUF and UNAMSIL agreed to a ban on diamond-mining in eastern regions still controlled by the rebels, in order to facilitate the demobilization of combatants.

In early September 2001 the Government announced that presidential and legislative elections would take place, under the aegis of the UN, on 14 May 2002 (after a further postponement, owing to the continued uncertainty of the security situation). The RUF, however, protested at the delay and threatened to withdraw from the peace process unless an interim coalition administration replaced the incumbent Government. In November representatives of the Government, the RUF and civil society agreed that parliamentary deputies in the forthcoming elections were to be elected by district (rather than under the previous system of proportional representation). In December the UN Security Council extended its ban on trade in uncertified diamonds for a further 11 months (effective from 5 January 2002).

In January 2002 the UN and the Government reached agreement on the establishment of a war crimes tribunal, to be known as the Special Court, which was to be based in Sierra Leone; the Special Court had a three-year mandate to prosecute crimes perpetrated from the end of November 1996. Meanwhile, the continuing rebel insurgency in northern Liberia, which had advanced rapidly towards Monrovia by early 2002, prompted concern that the resumption of civil conflict there would cause further instability in Sierra Leone. Despite UN pressure on the Liberian Government to end assistance for the RUF, it was reported that Bockarie, supported by 4,000 rebel forces, continued to be based in Liberia.

Following the completion of the disarmament of an estimated 45,000 former combatants in January 2002, the RUF announced its reconstitution as a political organization, the Revolutionary United Front Party (RUFP), with the aim of contesting the elections. In early March, however, Sankoh (who remained titular leader of the RUFP) was formally charged with murder, in connection with the killing of some 20 civilian protesters by his supporters in May 2000. (The trial of Sankoh, together with a further 49 former RUF members, commenced later in March.) In mid-March Kabbah was elected unopposed as the presidential candidate of the SLPP. A total of 24 political parties had officially registered by this time, notably the Peace and Liberation Party (PLP), led by Koroma. However, after the collapse of an opposition alliance, which had been established in late 2001, no serious challenge to the SLPP had emerged. In early April, after the authorities announced that Sankoh would not be permitted to contest the elections on behalf of the RUFP, the party's Secretary-General, Pallo Bangura, was nominated as its presidential candidate. By the end of that month an estimated 60,000 of the 150,000 Sierra Leonean refugees in Guinea and Liberia had returned voluntarily in order to participate in the elections.

Presidential and legislative elections took place peacefully on 14 May 2002. Kabbah was elected to a second term in office by 70.1% of the votes cast, while Ernest Bai Koroma of the APC received 22.4% of the votes. The SLPP also secured an outright majority in the expanded 124-member Parliament, with 83 seats, while the APC won 27 seats and the PLP two. Later that month Solomon Berewa (hitherto Minister of Justice) became the new Vice-President, and a reorganized Cabinet was installed.

In July 2002 the authorities announced that a seven-member TRC had been established. In August Pallo Bangura resigned his RUFP office, having secured less than 2% of votes cast in the presidential election. In September the UN Security Council adopted a resolution extending the mandate of UNAMSIL for a further six months, but also advocating that the contingent be reduced in size, while in December the UN embargo on illicit trade in diamonds was renewed for a further six months. In February 2003 a further 300 British troops were deployed in Sierra Leone, owing to concern that the intensification of hostilities between government and rebel Liberians United for Reconciliation and Democracy (LURD) forces in Liberia might destabilize the situation in Sierra Leone. (The British military presence in Sierra Leone had been reduced to number some 100 officers in July 2002.)

After the appointment of a British lawyer, Geoffrey Robertson, as President of the Special Court and a US lawyer, David Crane, as Chief Prosecutor, trial activities commenced at the end of 2002. In March 2003 the Special Court approved indictments for war crimes against seven former faction leaders, notably Sankoh, Koroma, the former RUF Commanders, Bockarie and Sesay, and the incumbent Minister of the Interior (and Kamajor leader), Sam Hinga Norman. Five of those indicted, including Hinga Norman, were taken into custody. Koroma went into hiding, following an attempt by the authorities to arrest him, while it was reported that Bockarie was supporting Liberian government forces against the LURD. In April Hinga Norman pleaded not guilty at the Special Court to charges relating to atrocities perpetrated during the civil war. Public hearings before the TRC commenced in mid-April. In early May the Liberian authorities announced that Bockarie had been killed near the border with Côte d'Ivoire, after clashing with Liberian troops attempting to arrest him, and ordered an investigation. Officials at the Special Court claimed that Bockarie and his immediate family had been captured and murdered by Liberian security forces, in an effort to prevent him from testifying against prominent regional figures. In June it was reported that Koroma had also been killed while at large in Liberia.

On 4 June 2003 the Special Court officially indicted Taylor for crimes against humanity, owing to his alleged long-standing support for the RUF, and an international warrant was issued for his arrest. The indictment against Taylor immediately precipitated a major offensive against the Liberian capital by rebels demanding his resignation (see the chapter on Liberia). The renewed humanitarian crisis in Liberia during June resulted in further large numbers of Liberian refugees fleeing to southern Sierra Leone. Having accepted an offer of asylum from the Nigerian Head of State, Olusegun Obasanjo, Taylor formally resigned his office and left for exile in Nigeria on 11 August, thereby evading arrest for the charges brought against him by the Special Court. Meanwhile, progress in the case against Sankoh was hindered by the deterioration of his state of health, and, after receiving medical treatment in hospital under UN custody from March, he died at the end of July. Also in July the UN Security Council adopted a resolution recommending the gradual withdrawal of UNAMSIL by the end of 2004, in view of improved security conditions.

In early February 2004 the five-year programme for 'disarmament, demobilization and reintegration' (in which 72,490 former combatants, including 6,845 children, had been disarmed) officially ended. In March Robertson was removed from the office of President of the Special Court, after being accused of demonstrating bias against the RUF in a book he had written concerning the atrocities committed during the civil conflict. At the end of that month, owing to renewed concern that the Sierra Leonean authorities would be unable to maintain stability, particularly in view of the security situations in Guinea and Côte d'Ivoire, the UN Security Council approved a resolution in favour of maintaining a reduced UNAMSIL contingent in the country until the end of September, with further extensions possible.

On 23 September 2004 UNAMSIL officially transferred primary responsibility for security in the remaining parts of the country where it was deployed, including Freetown, to government forces. The UN Security Council approved a further resolution in the same month, authorizing the contingent's continued presence in the country until the end of June 2005.

At the end of June 2005 the UN Security Council extended the mandate of UNAMSIL for a final six months, until the end of that year. In August a further resolution provided for the creation of United Nations Integrated Office in Sierra Leone (UNIOSIL). Following the complete withdrawal of UNAMSIL as scheduled, UNIOSIL was established on 1 January 2006, for an initial period of one year; the mission was authorized to support the consolidation of peace and assist the Government in strengthening state institutions, the rule of law, human rights, and the security sector, and the organization of presidential and legislative elections, scheduled for July 2007. In December 2006 UNIOSIL's mandate was extended until 31 December 2007. In mid-December the UN Secretary-General recommended that UNIOSIL's mandate be extended for a further nine months, to assist the Government in conducting the forthcoming elections. A new, smaller office was to replace UNIOSIL after that time, which would continue to aid the Sierra Leonean authorities in consolidating peace in the country. At the end of December the UN Security Council approved the final, nine-month extension (until September 2008) of UNIOSIL's mandate. In October 2008 the United Nations Integrated Peacebuilding Office in Sierra Leone (UNIPSIL) became operational, replacing UNIOSIL; UNIPSIL was granted an initial mandate of one year.

Meanwhile, in early September 2005 Kabbah reorganized the Cabinet. Most notably, John Oponjo Benjamin replaced Joseph Dauda as Minister of Finance, while Pascal Egbenda assumed the internal affairs portfolio and Lloyd During was appointed Minister of Energy and Power.

In February 2006 the trial of Hinga Norman officially commenced at the Special Court; proceedings against him were expected to be highly controversial, owing to the popular support retained by the Kamajors. In early February 2007 Hinga Norman was taken to a hospital in Dakar, Senegal, for what was termed a routine procedure. On 22 February it was reported that he had collapsed and died in his hospital room. An autopsy report released the following month concluded that he died of natural causes, although Hinga Norman's family voiced their suspicions at the verdict and were believed to be considering initiating a private investigation into the circumstances surrounding his death.

In March 2006 Nigeria announced that it had received a formal request from the new Liberian Government (see chapter on Liberia) to extradite Taylor to the Special Court. Later that month Taylor fled from his residence in Nigeria in an attempt to evade custody, but was apprehended two days later, near the border with Cameroon, and dispatched to Liberia, from where he was immediately extradited by peace-keeping forces to the Special Court. In early April Taylor (who initially refused to accept the authority of the Court) pleaded not guilty to 11 charges relating to his involvement in the civil conflict in Sierra Leone. Tribunal officials subsequently requested that his trial be transferred to the International Criminal Court (see p. 324) at The Hague (while remaining under the jurisdiction of the Special Court), in the interests of regional stability. The Dutch authorities acceded to that request on the condition that any sentence handed down to Taylor was served in another country. The United Kingdom subsequently agreed to host Taylor should he be imprisoned and, following the unanimous approval of the UN Security Council, on 20 June Taylor was transferred to The Hague. Taylor's trial commenced in early April 2007. Taylor remained absent from the trial until July, at which time he offered no explanation for his decision to attend and spoke only to plead 'not guilty' to the charges against him. Proceedings were, however, subsequently delayed while his legal representatives prepared his case; the trial resumed in January 2008. In August it was reported that the Special Court, intended only to function until 2005, was to cease operations by the end of 2009. In June 2007 the Special Court had handed down its first verdicts, finding three former AFRC members guilty of war crimes and crimes against humanity. The following month two of those convicted were sentenced to 50 years' imprisonment, while the third defendant received a prison term of 45 years. All three appealed against their convictions; however, in February 2008 those sentences were upheld by the Special Court. In February 2009 the last trials (of three former RUF members) to be held at the Special Court in Sierra Leone concluded. The men were found guilty of war crimes and crimes against humanity, and in April were sentenced to terms of imprisonment ranging from 25 to 52 years.

Legislative and presidential elections, initially due to be held in July 2007, were postponed until August to allow more time for campaigning and logistical preparations; voting eventually took place on 11 August. Official results indicated that the opposition APC had secured the largest representation in Parliament, taking 59 of the 124 available seats. The SLPP returned 43 deputies and the People's Movement for Democratic Change, led by Charles Margai, the son of Sir Abert Margai, took 10 seats. In the presidential election Koroma, contesting the election on behalf of the APC, secured 44.34% of the vote, while Berewa, of the SLPP, received 38.28% and Margai 13.89%. As no candidate secured more than 50% of the vote, Koroma and Berewa contested a second round on 8 September, at which Koroma won 60.22% of the vote. The elections were conducted in a largely peaceful manner, despite a small number of disturbances and opposition claims of procedural irregularities. In October President Koroma, who stated the tackling of corruption as one of his priorities, named a partial cabinet list, which included Zainab Hawa Bangura as Minister of Foreign Affairs and David Carew as Minister of Finance and Development. Further appointments were announced later that month, including Abdul Serry Kamal, who assumed the position of Minister of Justice and Attorney-General, and Paolo Conteh, who was awarded the defence portfolio.

In December 2008 a court repealed the sentences of 11 former armed rebels convicted of treason, the first time death sentences had been overturned in Sierra Leone. This was believed by many analysts as marking the beginning of a process to abolish the death penalty in the country. Meanwhile, in September Brig. Alfred Nelson Williams replaced Maj.-Gen. Sam Mboma as Chief of Staff of the Armed Forces.

Government

Under the terms of the Constitution of 1991, executive power is vested in the President, who is directly elected by universal adult suffrage. The President appoints the Cabinet (subject to approval by the legislature). The maximum duration of the President's tenure of office is limited to two five-year terms. Legislative power is vested in a unicameral Parliament, which is elected for a five-year term and comprises 112 members elected by a system of proportional representation, in 14 constituencies, and 12 Paramount Chiefs, who represent the provincial districts.

The country is divided into four regions: the Northern, Eastern and Southern Provinces, and the Western Area, which comprise 12 districts. There are 147 chiefdoms, each controlled by a Paramount Chief and a Council of Elders, known as the Tribal Authority.

Defence

As assessed at November 2008, active members of the armed forces of the Republic of Sierra Leone numbered about 10,500, with a navy of 200. In October 1999 the UN Security Council adopted a resolution establishing the UN Mission in Sierra Leone (UNAMSIL), which was to supervise the implementation of a peace agreement between the Government and rebel forces, signed in July of that year. Following the completion of disarmament in January 2002, a new army, restructured with British military assistance, was established. Some 100 British troops remained in the country to support peace-keeping operations and to continue reorganization of the Sierra Leone armed forces. Following the completion of UNAMSIL's mandate, the United Nations Integrated Office in Sierra Leone (UNIOSIL) was established on 1 January 2006 for an initial period of one year (in accordance with a Security Council resolution of 31 August 2005), extended in December of that year until the end of 2007. In December 2007 UNIOSIL's mandate was extended until September 2008. In October the United Nations Integrated Peacebuilding Office in Sierra Leone (UNIPSIL) officially replaced UNIOSIL with an initial mandate of one year. Preparations were under way in early 2009 to reduce the size of the armed forces and focus on improving efficiency. Expenditure on defence in 2007 was budgeted at Le 88,000m.

Economic Affairs

In 2007, according to the World Bank, Sierra Leone's gross national income (GNI), measured at average 2005–07 prices, was US $1,537m., equivalent to $260 per head (or $660 per head on an international purchasing-power parity basis). During 2000–07, it was estimated, the population increased at an average annual rate of 3.7%, while gross domestic product (GDP) per head rose, in real terms, by an average of 7.7% per year. Overall GDP increased, in real terms, at an average annual rate of 5.3% in 2000–07; growth was 6.5% in 2007.

Agriculture (including forestry and fishing) contributed 51.0% of GDP in 2007, according to UN estimates. About 59.4% of the labour force were employed in the sector in 2005. The principal cash crops are cocoa beans and coffee. Staple food crops include rice, cassava, and citrus fruit. Chickens, cattle and goats are the principal livestock. According to the African Development Bank (AfDB), during 2000–07 the GDP of the agricultural sector increased at an average annual rate of 5.1%; growth in agricultural GDP was 10.8% in 2007.

According to the UN, industry (including mining, manufacturing, construction and power) contributed an estimated 10.6% of GDP in 2007. This sector employed 6.5% of the working population in 2004. According to the AfDB, the GDP of the industrial sector increased by an average of 11.9% per year in 2000–07; industrial GDP increased by 10.4% in 2007.

Mining and quarrying contributed 17.5% of GDP in 1994/95, and employed 3.6% of the working population in 2004. The principal mineral exports are diamonds (which, according to official figures, accounted for 58.6% of total export earnings in 2007), rutile (titanium dioxide), bauxite and gold. The production of iron ore, previously an important mineral export, was suspended in 1985. In 1995 increased rebel activity effectively suspended official mining operations (although illicit exports of diamonds by rebel forces continued). In October 2000 official exports of diamonds were resumed under a certification scheme. Following reinvestment in a major kimberlite diamond field at Koidu, production commenced at the end of 2003. The Sierra Rutile mines (the largest source of private-sector employment and foreign-exchange earnings prior to 1995) resumed full mining operations in early 2006, while rehabilitation of the country's bauxite mine was completed in 2005, also allowing production to recommence in early 2006.

Manufacturing contributed an estimated 2.7% of GDP in 2007 and engaged 0.5% of the employed population in 2004. The manufacturing sector consists mainly of the production of palm oil and other agro-based industries, textiles and furniture-making. During 2000–07 the GDP of the manufacturing sector increased at an average annual rate of 6.5%, according to the AfDB. Manufacturing GDP increased by 10.4% in 2007.

Energy is derived principally from oil-fired thermal power stations. With the electricity sector continuing to deteriorate, the Government planned to bring a delayed hydroelectric project at Bumbuna, in the north of the country, into operation by 2006. Imports of mineral fuels comprised 37.7% of the value of total imports in 2007.

The services sector contributed 38.4% of GDP in 2007, according to UN estimates, and employed 26.4% of the engaged population in 2004. According to the AfDB, the GDP of the services sector increased by an average of 21.5% per year in 2000–07; it grew by 3.7% in 2007.

In 2007 Sierra Leone recorded an estimated trade deficit of US $102.6m., and there was a deficit of $237.9m. on the current account of the balance of payments. In 2003, according to official estimates, the principal source of imports (42.8%) was Germany; other major suppliers were the United Kingdom and France. Belgium was the principal market for exports (taking 57.0% of the total); the other significant purchaser was Germany. The principal export in 2007 was diamonds. The principal imports in that year were mineral fuels, machinery and transport equipment, and food and live animals.

In 2008 an overall budget deficit of Le 144,400m. was projected. Sierra Leone's external debt totalled US $1,428m. at the end of 2006, of which $1,323m. was long-term public debt. In that year the cost of debt-servicing was equivalent to 9.6% of the value of exports of goods and services. The annual rate of inflation averaged 7.5% in 2000–07. Consumer prices increased by 9.6% in 2006 and by 11.7% in 2007. An estimated 68,252 people were unemployed, according to the 2004 census.

Sierra Leone is a member of the Economic Community of West African States (see p. 243) and of the Mano River Union (see

p. 427), which aims to promote economic co-operation with Guinea and Liberia.

Civil conflict, which commenced in 1991, resulted in the progressive destruction of Sierra Leone's infrastructure, and severe disruption, or complete suspension, of traditional economic activities. However, since the end of the civil war in January 2002 the country has experienced substantial real economic growth and falling inflation. Additionally, improvements in fiscal control and considerable support from international financial institutions have resulted in some progress in reconstruction. Sierra Leone's economic prospects improved further with the post-war resumption of the production and export of rutile and bauxite in early 2006, resulting in an increase in exports of 28% in that year and a further 11% in 2007. The restoration of peace was also expected to aid the promotion of Sierra Leone as a tourist destination in the long term. In May 2006 the IMF approved a three-year US $46.3m. arrangement for Sierra Leone under the existing Poverty Reduction and Growth Facility (PRGF) for low income countries. The Fund praised the country's performance under the previous PRGF-supported programme and commended the Government's 2006–2008 economic programme, which aimed, inter alia, to target poverty reduction and improve revenue administration. Despite obvious economic progress and improved business confidence, Sierra Leone remained heavily dependent on international aid, and private sector investment projects were problematic. In late 2006, however, the IMF announced that Sierra Leone had made sufficient macroeconomic progress to reach completion point of the initiative for heavily indebted poor countries, granting the country debt relief totalling $675.2m., thus reducing the country's external debt to $483m. at the end of that year. Nevertheless, Sierra Leone's population continues to suffer from extremely high levels of poverty (the country has one of the lowest per-head gross national incomes in the world, at just $260). The agricultural and service sector experienced strong growth in 2008 and together facilitated an estimated 5.5% expansion in real GDP. President Koroma has indicated his intention to reduce the dependence of the economy on the mining sector, which was expected to yield lower export revenues during 2009, owing to weakened external demand for diamonds and other minerals.

Education

Primary education begins at five years of age and lasts for seven years. Secondary education, beginning at the age of 12, also lasts for a further seven years, comprising a first cycle of five years and a second cycle of two years. In 1987 tuition fees for government-funded primary and secondary schools were abolished. In 2000/01 primary enrolment was equivalent to 92.8% of children in the relevant age-group (males 106.0%; females 79.8%), while about 22.8% of children of the relevant age-group were enrolled at secondary schools (males 26.7%; females 19.0%) in 2006/07. In 2003/04 85% of the total school-age population was enrolled at primary and secondary schools. There is one university, which comprises six colleges. A total of 9,041 students were enrolled in tertiary education in 2001/02. Budgetary expenditure on education by the central Government in 2001 was estimated at Le 30,700m., increasing to a projected Le 36,400m. in 2002.

Public Holidays

2009: 1 January (New Year's Day), 9 March (Mouloud, Birth of the Prophet)*, 10–13 April (Easter), 27 April (Independence Day), 20 September (Id al-Fitr, end of Ramadan)*, 27 November (Id al-Adha, Feast of the Sacrifice)*, 25–26 December (Christmas and Boxing Day).

2010: 1 January (New Year's Day), 26 February (Mouloud, Birth of the Prophet)*, 2–5 April (Easter), 27 April (Independence Day), 10 September (Id al-Fitr, end of Ramadan)*, 16 November* (Id al-Adha, Feast of the Sacrifice), 25–26 December (Christmas and Boxing Day).

* These holidays are dependent on the Islamic lunar calendar and may vary by one or two days from the dates given.

Weights and Measures

The metric system is in force.

Statistical Survey

Source (unless otherwise stated): Central Statistics Office, PMB 595, Tower Hill, Freetown; tel. (22) 223287; fax (22) 223897; internet www.sierra-leone.org/cso.html and www.statistics-sierra-leone.org.

Area and Population

AREA, POPULATION AND DENSITY

Area (sq km)	71,740*
Population (census results)†	
14 December 1985	3,515,812
4 December 2004	
Males	2,420,218
Females	2,556,653
Total	4,976,871
Population (UN estimates at mid-year)‡	
2006	5,271,000
2007	5,420,000
2008	5,560,000
Density (per sq km) at mid-2008	77.5

* 27,699 sq miles.
† Excluding adjustment for underenumeration, estimated to have been 9% in 1985.
‡ Source: UN, *World Population Prospects: The 2008 Revision*.

ADMINISTRATIVE DISTRICTS
(population at 2004 census)

	Population
Bo	463,668
Bombali	408,390
Bonthe	129,947
Kailahun	358,190
Kambia	270,462
Kenema	497,948
Koinadugu	265,758
Kono	335,401
Moyamba	260,910
Port Loko	453,746
Pujehun	228,392
Sherbo	9,740
Tonkolili	347,197
Western Area Rural District	174,2489
Western Area Urban District	772,873
Total	**4,976,871**

PRINCIPAL TOWNS
(population at 2004 census)

Freetown (capital)	772,873*	Makeni	82,840
Bo	149,957	Koindu	80,025
Kenema	128,402		

* Western Area Urban District.

Mid-2007 (incl. suburbs, UN estimate): Freetown 827,000 (Source: UN, *World Urbanization Prospects: The 2007 Revision*).

SIERRA LEONE

BIRTHS AND DEATHS
(annual averages, UN estimates)

	1990–95	1995–2000	2000–05
Birth rate (per 1,000)	42.4	42.7	41.9
Death rate (per 1,000)	24.9	23.7	18.7

Source: UN, *World Population Prospects: The 2008 Revision*.

Life expectancy (years at birth, WHO estimates): 40 (males 39; females 42) in 2006 (Source: WHO, *World Health Report*).

EMPLOYMENT
(persons aged 10 years and over, 2004 census)

	Male	Female	Total
Agriculture, hunting and forestry	618,335	654,507	1,272,842
Fishing	33,337	17,828	51,165
Mining and quarrying	59,403	9,674	69,077
Manufacturing	7,411	2,016	9,427
Electricity, gas and water supply	7,128	1,247	8,375
Construction	28,296	10,836	39,132
Wholesale and retail trade; Repair of motor vehicles, motorcycles and personal and household goods	102,425	167,463	269,888
Hotels and restaurants	2,626	2,318	4,944
Transport, communications and storage	14,476	1,262	15,738
Financial intermediation	4,001	2,948	6,949
Real estate, renting and business activities	5,479	5,312	10,791
Public administration and defence; compulsory social security	21,146	4,864	26,010
Education	23,318	11,345	34,663
Health and social work	9,878	9,997	19,875
Other community, social and personnel service activities	44,541	39,130	83,671
Households with employed persons	4,001	4,318	8,319
Extra-territorial organizations and bodies	2,516	1,341	3,857
Total employed	**988,317**	**946,406**	**1,934,723**

Source: ILO.

Unemployed: 68,252 at census of 2004 (males 45,936, females 22,316).

Mid-2005 (estimates in '000): Agriculture, etc. 1,249; Total labour force 2,103 (Source: FAO).

Health and Welfare

KEY INDICATORS

Total fertility rate (children per woman, 2006)	6.5
Under-5 mortality rate (per 1,000 live births, 2006)	269
HIV/AIDS (% of persons aged 15–49, 2007)	1.7
Physicians (per 1,000 head, 2004)	0.03
Hospital beds (per 1,000 head, 2006)	0.4
Health expenditure (2006): US $ per head (PPP)	41
Health expenditure (2006): % of GDP	3.5
Health expenditure (2006): public (% of total)	49.0
Access to water (% of persons, 2006)	53
Access to sanitation (% of persons, 2006)	11
Human Development Index (2006): ranking	179
Human Development Index (2006): value	0.329

For sources and definitions, see explanatory note on p. vi.

Statistical Survey

Agriculture

PRINCIPAL CROPS
('000 metric tons)

	2005	2006	2007
Rice, paddy	738.0	1,062.0	650.0*
Maize	39.1	48.8	50.0*
Millet	20†	25†	16*
Sorghum*	23.0	18.0	20.0
Sweet potatoes*	27.0	25.0	25.0
Cassava (Manioc)*	320.0	350.0	370.0
Sugar cane*	70	70	70
Groundnuts, with shell	104.7	115.2	90.0*
Oil palm fruit*	210.0	195.0	195.0
Tomatoes*	17.8	15.1	15.0
Plantains*	35.0	33.0	33.0
Citrus fruit*	90.0	85.0	85.0
Coffee, green*	18.0	18.0	18.0
Cocoa beans*	8.7	13.9	12.0

* FAO estimate(s).
† Unofficial figure.

Aggregate production ('000 metric tons, may include official, semi-official or estimated data): Total cereals 823.3 in 2005, 1,157.4 in 2006, 739.3 in 2007; Total roots and tubers 349.8 in 2005, 377.6 in 2006, 397.6 in 2007; Total vegetables (incl. melons) 235.1 in 2005, 235.1 in 2006, 235.0 in 2007; Total fruits (excl. melons) 197.8 in 2005, 124.5 in 2006, 125.0 in 2007.

Source: FAO.

LIVESTOCK
('000 head, year ending September)

	2005	2006	2007*
Cattle	250.0	350.0	300.0
Pigs*	52	52	52
Sheep	375	470	470
Goats	438	540	500
Chickens*	7,500	7,500	7,500
Ducks*	70	70	70

* FAO estimates.

Source: FAO.

LIVESTOCK PRODUCTS
('000 metric tons, FAO estimates)

	2005	2006	2007
Chicken meat	10.8	11.3	11.3
Pig meat	2.3	2.3	2.3
Game meat	2.5	2.5	2.5
Cows' milk	13.3	20.0	17.0
Hen eggs	8.3	8.3	8.3

Source: FAO.

Forestry

ROUNDWOOD REMOVALS
('000 cubic metres, excl. bark, FAO estimates)

	2005	2006	2007
Sawlogs, veneer logs and logs for sleepers*	3.6	3.6	3.6
Other industrial wood†	120.0	120.0	120.0
Fuel wood	5,422.8	5,448.3	5,477.0
Total	**5,546.4**	**5,571.9**	**5,600.6**

* Annual output assumed to be unchanged since 1993.
† Annual output assumed to be unchanged since 1980.

Source: FAO.

SIERRA LEONE

SAWNWOOD PRODUCTION
('000 cubic metres, incl. railway sleepers)

	1991	1992	1993
Total (all broadleaved)	9.0	9.0*	5.3

* FAO estimate.

1994–2007: Annual production as in 1993 (FAO estimates).
Source: FAO.

Fishing
('000 metric tons, live weight of capture)

	2004	2005	2006
West African ilisha	3.1	3.5	3.3
Tonguefishes	1.0	1.1	1.0
Bobo croaker	7.3	7.9	11.1
Sardinellas	18.2	22.1	15.2
Bonga shad	51.0	52.7	60.1
Tuna-like fishes	2.5	2.0	1.2
Marine molluscs	1.3	1.9	1.1
Total catch (incl. others)	134.4	146.0	148.1

Source: FAO.

Mining
(metric tons, unless otherwise indicated)

	2003	2004	2005
Gypsum	4,000	—	—
Diamonds ('000 carats)	507	693	669
Salt	1,005	827	—

2006: Diamonds ('000 carats) 604.
Source: US Geological Survey.

Industry

PETROLEUM PRODUCTS
('000 metric tons, estimates)

	2003	2004	2005
Jet fuels	20	21	21
Motor spirit (petrol)	31	32	32
Kerosene	10	10	10
Distillate fuel oils	74	60	60
Residual fuel oils	55	45	35

Source: UN, *Industrial Commodity Statistics Yearbook*.

SELECTED OTHER PRODUCTS
('000 metric tons, unless otherwise indicated)

	2005	2006	2007
Beer and stout ('000 crates)	1,012	832	780
Soft drinks ('000 crates)	1,908	2,089	2,432
Confectionery ('000 kg)	2,074.3	2,329.9	3,141.0
Soap (metric tons)	417	n.a.	n.a.
Paint ('000 litres)	135	649	714
Cement*	172.1	234.4	n.a.

* Source: US Geological Survey.

Source: mainly IMF, *Sierra Leone: Selected Issues and Statistical Appendix* (January 2009).

Finance

CURRENCY AND EXCHANGE RATES

Monetary Units
100 cents = 1 leone (Le).

Sterling, Dollar and Euro Equivalents (31 October 2008)
£1 sterling = 4,853.399 leones;
US $1 = 3,000.740 leones;
€1 = 3,828.046 leones;
10,000 leones = £2.06 = $3.33 = €2.61.

Average Exchange Rate (leones per US $)
2005 2,889.59
2006 2,961.91
2007 2,985.19

CENTRAL GOVERNMENT BUDGET
(Le '000 million)

Revenue*	2006	2007	2008†
Income tax department	137.9	146.2	196.5
Customs and excise department	278.8	308.4	370.9
Mines department	14.7	18.6	26.2
Other departments	24.5	29.4	45.3
Road user charges	39.7	34.4	53.8
Total	495.6	536.9	692.7

Expenditure	2006	2007	2008†
Current expenditure	741.3	660.9	887.0
Wages and salaries	271.5	296.5	356.2
Goods and services	205.5	157.3	278.9
Transfers to local councils	26.9	19.3	41.5
Grants to educational institutions	29.6	27.4	27.2
Transfers to road fund	39.7	34.4	53.8
Elections	6.1	13.8	7.5
Interest payments	162.0	112.1	121.0
Capital expenditure and net lending	216.3	176.7	331.4
Contingency spending	—	39.0	—
Total	957.5	876.6	1,218.4

* Excluding grants received (Le '000 million): 855.5 in 2006; 1,592.5 in 2007; 381.3 in 2008 (projected).
† Projected.

Source: IMF, *Sierra Leone: Second Review Under the Three-Year Arrangement Under the Poverty Reduction and Growth Facility, Financing Assurances Review, and Request for Waivers of Nonobservance of Performance Criterion, Extension of the Arrangement, and Rephasing of Disbursements-Staff Report; Staff Supplement and Statement; Press Release on the Executive Board Discussion; and Statement by the Executive Director for Sierra Leone* (July 2008).

INTERNATIONAL RESERVES
(US $ million at 31 December)

	2005	2006	2007
IMF special drawing rights	32.8	29.2	30.7
Foreign exchange	137.7	154.7	185.8
Total	170.5	183.9	216.5

Source: IMF, *International Financial Statistics*.

MONEY SUPPLY
(Le million at 31 December)

	2005	2006	2007
Currency outside banks	231,274	275,405	309,837
Demand deposits at commercial banks	176,649	195,870	218,503
Total money (incl. others)	424,173	489,298	550,291

Source: IMF, *International Financial Statistics*.

SIERRA LEONE

COST OF LIVING
(Consumer Price Index for Freetown; base: 2000 = 100)

	2001	2002	2003
Food	105.2	104.4	112.2
All items (incl. others)	102.2	98.8	106.3

All items: 135.9 in 2005; 148.9 in 2006; 166.3 in 2007.

Source: IMF, *International Financial Statistics*.

NATIONAL ACCOUNTS
(US $ million at current prices, UN estimates)

Expenditure on the Gross Domestic Product

	2005	2006	2007
Government final consumption expenditure	1,391	1,405	1,731
Private final consumption expenditure	226	220	205
Gross fixed capital formation	129	84	85
Changes in inventories	117	221	224
Statistical discrepancy	—	—	−21
Total domestic expenditure	1,863	1,930	2,224
Exports of goods and services	229	264	259
Less Imports of goods and services	595	539	548
GDP in purchasers' values	1,497	1,655	1,935
GDP at constant 1990 prices	783	843	898

Gross Domestic Product by Economic Activity

	2005	2006	2007
Agriculture, hunting, forestry and fishing	740	856	944
Industry	151	146	197
Manufacturing	39	42	50
Construction	116	30	36
Trade, restaurants and hotels	143	136	184
Transport, storage and communications	104	118	134
Other services	307	329	393
Gross value added in basic prices	1,445	1,585	1,852
Taxes, less subsidies, on products*	51	70	83
GDP in purchasers' values	1,496	1,655	1,935

* Figures calculated as residual.

Source: UN Statistics Division, National Accounts Main Aggregates Database.

BALANCE OF PAYMENTS
(US $ million)

	2005	2006	2007
Exports of goods f.o.b.	183.6	261.9	292.9
Imports of goods f.o.b.	−361.7	−351.2	−395.4
Trade balance	−178.0	−89.3	−102.6
Exports of services	78.2	42.5	42.1
Imports of services	−91.4	−85.9	−94.2
Balance on goods and services	−191.3	−132.7	−154.6
Other income received	5.4	12.2	43.3
Other income paid	−56.3	−52.0	−147.6
Balance on goods, services and income	−242.2	−172.5	−259.0
Current transfers received	73.6	73.5	155.9
Current transfers paid	−2.0	−36.5	−134.8
Current balance	−170.6	−135.5	−237.9
Capital account (net)	36.8	224.1	239.5
Direct investment (net)	90.7	58.6	94.5
Other investment (net)	−28.0	−23.1	13.7
Net errors and omissions	−58.5	−63.8	−139.8
Overall balance	−129.6	60.4	−29.9

Source: IMF, *International Financial Statistics*.

External Trade

PRINCIPAL COMMODITIES
(US $'000)

Imports c.i.f.	2005	2006	2007
Food and live animals	53,115.3	56,139.9	67,948.6
Beverages and tobacco	9,920.2	9,295.3	12,074.4
Crude materials (inedible) except fuels	8,754.2	21,702.7	14,654.6
Mineral fuels, lubricants, etc.	115,597.0	147,080.4	168,576.5
Animal and vegetable oils and fats	1,306.8	3,327.0	6,205.7
Chemicals	22,746.8	23,999.9	31,008.7
Basic manufactures	40,674.5	48,601.3	51,900.0
Machinery and transport equipment	71,824.1	69,111.0	75,112.8
Miscellaneous manufactured articles	17,125.1	15,571.3	19,119.9
Total	341,063.9	394,828.8	446,601.2

Exports f.o.b.	2005	2006	2007
Coffee	873.8	1,093.4	1,854.7
Cocoa beans	5,236.7	11,570.7	11,368.1
Diamonds	142,202.3	125,041.2	142,048.6
Total (incl. others)*	159,010.6	231,037.4	242,517.8

* Including re-exports: 7,189.5 in 2005; 28,399.8 in 2006; 2,720.2 in 2007.

Source: Bank of Sierra Leone.

PRINCIPAL TRADING PARTNERS

Imports c.i.f. (US $ million)	2002
Canada	23.0
China, People's Repub.	11.8
Côte d'Ivoire	129.1
Germany	9.1
India	13.2
Japan	14.9
Netherlands	19.4
United Kingdom	11.9
USA	17.4
Total (incl. others)	352.0

Source: UN, *International Trade Statistics Yearbook*.

Exports (Le million)	1992	1993	1994
Belgium	25,770	54	11,412
Germany	1,060	2,486	1,328
Guinea	1,315	817	1,331
Netherlands	5,307	1,201	2,815
Switzerland	7,546	486	215
United Kingdom	5,567	5,988	11,767
USA	13,832	17,564	30,431
Total (incl. others)	75,034	67,077	67,930

Source: Central Statistics Office, Freetown.

Transport

ROAD TRAFFIC
(motor vehicles in use at 31 December)

	2000	2001	2002
Passenger cars	2,045	2,263	11,353
Buses and coaches	2,597	3,516	4,050
Goods vehicles	2,309	2,898	3,565
Motorcycles	1,398	1,532	1,657

Source: IRF, *World Road Statistics*.

SHIPPING

Merchant Fleet
(registered at 31 December)

	2005	2006	2007
Number of vessels	69	194	302
Displacement (gross registered tons)	77,244	293,872	486,843

Source: Lloyd's Register-Fairplay, *World Fleet Statistics*.

International Sea-borne Freight Traffic
(estimates, '000 metric tons)

	1991	1992	1993
Goods loaded	1,930	2,190	2,310
Goods unloaded	562	579	589

Source: UN Economic Commission for Africa, *African Statistical Yearbook*.

CIVIL AVIATION
(traffic on scheduled services)

	2000	2001	2002
Kilometres flown (million)	1	1	1
Passengers carried ('000)	19	14	14
Passenger-km (million)	93	73	74
Total ton-km (million)	18	13	13

2003: Figures assumed to be unchanged from 2002.

Source: UN, *Statistical Yearbook*.

Tourism

	2004	2005	2006
Tourist arrivals	43,560	40,023	33,704
Tourism receipts (US $ million, excl. passenger transport)	58	64	23

Source: World Tourism Organization.

Communications Media

	2000	2001	2002
Television receivers ('000 in use)	64	65	n.a.
Telephones ('000 main lines in use)	19.0	22.7	24.0
Mobile cellular telephones ('000 subscribers)	11.9	26.9	67.0
Internet users ('000)	5	7	8

2003 ('000): Mobile cellular telephones (subscribers) 113.2; Internet users 9.

2004–05 ('000): Mobile cellular telephones (subscribers) 113.2 (estimates); Internet users 11.

2006 ('000): Mobile cellular telephones (subscribers) 776.0; Internet users 12.

Radio receivers ('000 in use): 1,120 in 1997.

Facsimile machines (number in use, year beginning 1 April): 2,500 in 1998.

Daily newspapers: 1 (average circulation 20,000) in 1996.

Sources: UNESCO, *Statistical Yearbook*; UN, *Statistical Yearbook*; and International Telecommunication Union.

Education

(2006/07, unless otherwise indicated)

	Schools*	Teachers	Males	Females	Total
Pre-primary	n.a.	1,224	11,989	12,818	24,807
Primary	2,704	30,239	693,710	628,495	1,322,205
Secondary	246	10,024	141,418	98,161	239,579
Tertiary*	n.a.	1,198	6,439	2,602	9,041

*2001/02.

Source: mainly UNESCO Institute for Statistics.

Adult literacy rate (UNESCO estimates): 38.1% (males 50.0%; females 26.8%) in 2007 (Source: UNESCO Institute for Statistics).

Directory

The Constitution

Following the transfer of power to a democratically elected civilian administration on 29 March 1996, the Constitution of 1991 (which had been suspended since April 1992) was reinstated. The Constitution provided for the establishment of a multi-party system, and vested executive power in the President, who was to be elected by the majority of votes cast nationally and by at least 25% of the votes cast in each of the four provinces. The maximum duration of the President's tenure of office was limited to two five-year terms. The President was to appoint the Cabinet, subject to approval by the Parliament. The Parliament was elected for a five-year term and comprised 124 members, 112 of whom were elected by a system of proportional representation, in 14 constituencies, while 12 Paramount Chiefs also represented the provincial districts in the legislature. Members of the Parliament were not permitted concurrently to hold office in the Cabinet.

The Government

HEAD OF STATE

President and Commander-in-Chief of the Armed Forces: ERNEST BAI KOROMA (elected 8 September 2007; inaugurated 15 November 2007).

Vice-President: SAHR SAM-SUMANA.

CABINET
(April 2009)

Minister of Finance and Economic Development: Dr SAMURA KAMARA.

Minister of Foreign Affairs and International Co-operation: ZAINAB HAWA BANGURA.

Minister of Justice and Attorney-General: ABDUL SERRY-KAMAL.

Minister of Information and Communications: Alhaji IBRAHIM BEN KARGBO.

Minister of Mineral Resources: Alhaji ALPHA SAAHID BAKARR KANU.

Minister of Health and Sanitation: Dr SHEKU TEJAN KOROMA.

Minister of Agriculture, Food Security and Forestry: Dr SAM SESAY.

Minister of Presidential and Public Affairs: JOSEPH KOROMA.

Minister of Works, Housing and Infrastructure: ALIMAMY P. KOROMA.

Minister of Lands, Country Planning and the Environment: Dr DENNIS SANDI.

Minister of Defence: Maj. (retd) ALFRED PALO CONTEH.

Minister of Internal Affairs, Local Government and Rural Development: DAUDA SULAIMAN KAMARA.

Minister of Marine Resources and Fisheries: HAJA AFSATU KABBA.

Minister of Energy and Water Resources: Prof. OGUNLADE DAVIDSON.

Minister of Tourism and Cultural Affairs: HINDOLO TRYE.

Minister of Social Welfare, Gender and Children's Affairs: Dr SOCCOH KABIA.

Minister of Education, Youths and Sports: Dr MINKAILU BAH.

Minister of Employment and Social Security: MINKAILU MANSARAY.

Minister of Trade and Industry: DAVID CAREW.

SIERRA LEONE

Minister of Transport and Aviation: Capt. ALLIEU PAT SOWE.
Minister of State, Office of the Vice-President: LEONARD BALOGUN KOROMA.
Resident Minister, East: WILLIAM JUANA SMITH.
Resident Minister, South: MUSA TARAWALI.
Resident Minister, North: ALIE KAMARA.
There were also 21 Deputy Ministers.

MINISTRIES

Office of the President: Freetown; tel. (22) 232101; fax (22) 231404; e-mail info@statehouse-sl.org; internet www.statehouse-sl.org/president.html.
Ministry of Agriculture, Food Security and Forestry: Youyi Bldg, 3rd Floor, Brookfields, Freetown; tel. (22) 222242; fax (22) 241613.
Ministry of Defence: State Ave, Freetown; tel. (22) 227369; fax (22) 229380.
Ministry of Education, Youths and Sports: New England, Freetown; tel. (22) 240881; fax (22) 240137.
Ministry of Employment and Social Security: New England, Freetown; tel. (22) 241947.
Ministry of Energy and Water Resources: Electricity House, Siaka Stevens St, Freetown; tel. (22) 226566; fax (22) 228199.
Ministry of Finance and Economic Development: Secretariat Bldg, George St, Freetown; tel. (22) 225612; fax (22) 228472.
Ministry of Foreign Affairs and International Co-operation: Gloucester St, Freetown; tel. (22) 223260; fax (22) 225615; e-mail mfaicsl@yahoo.com.
Ministry of Health and Sanitation: Youyi Bldg, 4th Floor, Brookfields, Freetown; tel. (22) 240187; fax (22) 241613; e-mail info@health.sl; internet www.health.sl.
Ministry of Information and Communications: Youyi Bldg, 8th Floor, Brookfields, Freetown; tel. (22) 240339; fax (22) 241757.
Ministry of Internal Affairs, Local Government and Rural Development: Liverpool St, Freetown; tel. (22) 226979; fax (22) 227727.
Ministry of Justice: Guma Bldg, Lamina Sankoh St, Freetown; tel. (22) 227444; fax (22) 229366.
Ministry of Lands, Country Planning and the Environment: Youyi Bldg, 4th Floor, Brookfields, Freetown; tel. (22) 242013.
Ministry of Marine Resources and Fisheries: Marine House, 11 Old Railway Line, Brookfields, Freetown; tel. (22) 242117.
Ministry of Mineral Resources: Youyi Bldg, 5th Floor, Brookfields, Freetown; tel. and fax (22) 240467; e-mail contact@mmr-sl.org; internet www.mmr-sl.org.
Ministry of Presidential and Public Affairs: State House, State Ave, Freetown; tel. (22) 229728; fax (22) 229799.
Ministry of Social Welfare, Gender and Children's Affairs: New England, Freetown; tel. (22) 241256; fax (22) 242076.
Ministry of Trade and Industry: 6th Floor, Youyi Bldg, Brookfields, Freetown; tel. (22) 225211; e-mail info@mtisl.org; internet www.mtisl.org.
Ministry of Transport and Aviation: Ministerial Bldg, George St, Freetown; tel. (22) 221245; fax (22) 227337.
Ministry of Tourism and Cultural Affairs: Ministerial Bldg, George St, Freetown; tel. (22) 222588.
Ministry of Works, Housing and Infrastructure: New England, Freetown; tel. (22) 240937; fax (22) 240018.

President and Legislature

PRESIDENT

Presidential Election, First Round, 11 August 2007

Candidate	Votes	% of votes
Ernest Bai Koroma (APC)	815,523	44.34
Solomon Berewa (SLPP)	704,012	38.28
Charles Margai (PMDC)	255,499	13.89
Andrew Turay (CPP)	28,610	1.56
Amadu Jalloh (NDA)	17,748	0.96
Kandeh Baba Conteh (PLP)	10,556	0.57
Abdul Kady Karim (UNPP)	7,260	0.39
Total	**1,839,208**	**100.00**

Presidential Election, Second Round, 8 September 2007

Candidate	Votes	% of votes
Ernest Bai Koroma (APC)	859,144	60.22
Solomon Berewa (SLPP)	567,449	39.78
Total	**1,426,593**	**100.00**

PARLIAMENT

Speaker: Justice E. K. COWAN.

General Election, 11 August 2007

Party	Seats
All-People's Congress (APC)	59
Sierra Leone People's Party (SLPP)	43
People's Movement for Democratic Change (PMDC)	10
Total	**112***

*A further 12 seats were allocated to Paramount Chiefs, who represented the 12 provincial districts.

Election Commission

National Electoral Commission (NEC): NEC Bldg, 15 Industrial Estate, Wellington, Freetown; tel. 76547299; internet www.nec-sierraleone.org; f. 2000; Chair. CHRISTIANA AYOKA MARY THORPE.

Political Organizations

A ban on political activity was rescinded in June 1995. Numerous political parties were officially granted registration, prior to elections in May 2002.

All-People's Congress (APC): 137H Fourah Bay Rd, Freetown; e-mail info@new-apc.org; internet apcparty.org; f. 1960; sole authorized political party 1978–91; merged with the Democratic People's Party in 1992; reconstituted in 1995; Leader ERNEST BAI KOROMA.
Citizens United for Peace and Progress (CUPP): e-mail info@cupp.org; internet www.cupp.org; f. 2002; Chair. ABUBAKARR YANSSANEH.
National Unity Party (NUP): e-mail johnben@nupsl.org; internet www.nupsl.org; Leader JOHN OPONJO BENJAMIN (acting).
Peace and Liberation Party (PLP): Freetown; f. 2002; Leader (vacant).
People's Democratic Party (PDP): Freetown; supported Sierra Leone People's Party in May 2002 elections; Leader OSMAN KAMARA.
People's Movement for Democratic Change (PMDC): 9A Hannah Benka-Coker St, Freetown; e-mail karamohslylhorg@aol.com; internet www.pmdcsl.net; f. April 2006 by fmr mems of Sierra Leone People's Party; Leader CHARLES F. MARGAI; Sec.-Gen. ANSU B. LANSANA.
People's National Convention (PNC): Leader EDWARD JOHN KARGBO.
Sierra Leone People's Party (SLPP): 15 Wallace Johnson St, Freetown; tel. and fax (22) 2256341; e-mail info@slpp.ws; internet www.slpp.ws; f. 1951; Nat. Chair. Alhaji U. N. S. JAH; Leader SOLOMAN BEREWA.
United National People's Party (UNPP): Leader Dr JOHN KAREFA-SMART.
Young People's Party (YPP): 19 Lewis St, Freetown; tel. (22) 232907; e-mail info@yppsl.org; internet www.yppsl.org; f. 2002; Leader SYLVIA BLYDEN; Sec.-Gen. ABDUL RAHMAN YILLA.

Diplomatic Representation

EMBASSIES AND HIGH COMMISSIONS IN SIERRA LEONE

China, People's Republic: 29 Wilberforce Loop, POB 778, Freetown; tel. and fax (22) 231797; e-mail chinaemb_sl@mfa.gov.cn; internet sl.china-embassy.org; Ambassador QIU SHAOFANG.
Egypt: 174c Wilkinson Rd, POB 652, Freetown; tel. (22) 231245; fax (22) 234297; Ambassador MAHMOUD YEHIA M. EZZAT.
The Gambia: 6 Wilberforce St, Freetown; tel. (22) 225191; fax (22) 226846; High Commissioner DEMBO BADJIE.

SIERRA LEONE

Ghana: 13 Walpole St, Freetown; tel. (22) 223461; fax (22) 227043; High Commissioner KABRAL BLAY-AMIHERE.

Guinea: 6 Wilkinson Rd, Freetown; tel. (22) 232584; fax (22) 232496; Ambassador MOHAMED LAMIN SOMPARE.

Lebanon: 22A Spur Rd, Wilberforce, Freetown; tel. (22) 222513; fax (22) 234665; Ambassador GHASSAN ABDEL SATER.

Liberia: 10 Motor Rd, Brookfields, POB 276, Freetown; tel. (22) 230991; Chargé d'affaires a.i. THOMAS BRIMA.

Libya: 1A and 1B P. Z. Compound, Wilberforce, Freetown; tel. (22) 235231; fax (22) 234514; Ambassador Dr MOHAMED AL-HARARI ABDUL SALAAM.

Nigeria: 37 Siaka Stevens St, Freetown; tel. (22) 224224; fax (22) 2242474; High Commissioner GODSON O. ECHEGILE.

United Kingdom: 6 Spur Rd, Wilberforce, Freetown; tel. (22) 232565; fax (22) 232070; e-mail freetown.consular.enquiries@fco.gov.uk; internet ukinsierraleone.fco.gov.uk; High Commissioner IAN HUGHES.

USA: Leicester, Freetown; tel. (22) 515000; fax (22) 515355; e-mail TaylorJB2@state.gov; internet freetown.usembassy.gov; Ambassador JUNE CARTER PERRY.

Judicial System

The Supreme Court
The ultimate court of appeal in both civil and criminal cases. In addition to its appellate jurisdiction, the Court has supervisory jurisdiction over all other courts and over any adjudicating authority in Sierra Leone, and also original jurisdiction in constitutional issues.

Chief Justice: UMU HAWA TEJAN JALLOH.

Supreme Court Justices: C. A. HARDING, AGNES AWUNOR-RENNER, PATRICK HAMILTON.

The Court of Appeal
The Court of Appeal has jurisdiction to hear and determine appeals from decisions of the High Court in both criminal and civil matters, and also from certain statutory tribunals. Appeals against its decisions may be made to the Supreme Court.

Justices of Appeal: S. C. E. WARNE, C. S. DAVIES, S. T. NAVO, M. S. TURAY, E. C. THOMPSON-DAVIS, M. O. TAJU-DEEN, M. O. ADOPHY, GEORGE GELAGA KING, Dr A. B. Y. TIMBO, VIRGINIA A. WRIGHT.

High Court
The High Court has unlimited original jurisdiction in all criminal and civil matters. It also has appellate jurisdiction against decisions of Magistrates' Courts.

Judges: FRANCIS C. GBOW, EBUN THOMAS, D. E. M. WILLIAMS, LAURA MARCUS-JONES, L. B. O. NYLANDER, A. M. B. TARAWALLIE, O. H. ALGHALLI, W. A. O. JOHNSON, N. D. ALHADI, R. J. BANKOLE THOMPSON, M. E. T. THOMPSON, C. J. W. ATERE-ROBERTS (acting).

Magistrates' Courts: In criminal cases the jurisdiction of the Magistrates' Courts is limited to summary cases and to preliminary investigations to determine whether a person charged with an offence should be committed for trial.

Local Courts have jurisdiction, according to native law and custom, in matters that are outside the jurisdiction of other courts.

Religion

A large proportion of the population holds animist beliefs, although there are significant numbers of Islamic and Christian adherents.

ISLAM

In 1990 Islamic adherents represented an estimated 30% of the total population.

Ahmadiyya Muslim Mission: 15 Bath St, Brookfields, POB 353, Freetown; Emir and Chief Missionary KHALIL A. MOBASHIR.

Kankaylay (Sierra Leone Muslim Men and Women's Association): 15 Blackhall Rd, Kissy, POB 1168, Freetown; tel. 33635205; fax (22) 224439; e-mail kankaylay@yahoo.com; internet www.kankaylay.com; f. 1972; 500,000 mems; Pres. Alhaji IBRAHIM ALPHA TURAY; Lady Pres. Haja MARIAM TURAY.

Sierra Leone Muslim Congress: POB 875, Freetown; f. 1928; Pres. Alhaji MUHAMMAD SANUSI MUSTAPHA.

CHRISTIANITY

Council of Churches in Sierra Leone: 4A King Harman Rd, Brookfields, POB 404, Freetown; tel. (22) 240569; fax (22) 421109;

Directory

f. 1924; 17 mem. churches; Pres. Rev. MOSES B. KHANU; Gen. Sec. ALIMAMY P. KOROMA.

The Anglican Communion
Anglicans in Sierra Leone are adherents of the Church of the Province of West Africa, comprising 12 dioceses, of which two are in Sierra Leone. The Archbishop of the Province is the Bishop of Koforidua, Ghana.

Bishop of Bo: Rt Rev. SAMUEL SAO GBONDA, MacRobert St, POB 21, Bo, Southern Province; e-mail bishop@sierratel.sl.

Bishop of Freetown: Rt Rev. JULIUS O. PRINCE LYNCH, Bishopscourt, Fourah Bay Rd, POB 537, Freetown; tel. (22) 251307; fax (22) 251306; e-mail bishop@sierratel.sl.

Baptist Churches
Sierra Leone Baptist Convention: POB 64, Lunsar; 119 mem. churches; 994 mems; Pres. Rev. JOSEPH S. MANS; Sec. Rev. N. T. DIXON.

The Nigerian Baptist Convention is also active.

Methodist Churches
Methodist Church Sierra Leone: Wesley House, George St, POB 64, Freetown; tel. (22) 222216; fax (22) 227539; e-mail methodistchurchsierraleone@yahoo.com; autonomous since 1967; Pres. of Conf. Rt Rev. FRANCIS S. NABIEU; Sec. Rev. ARNOLD C. TEMPLE; 26,421 mems.

United Methodist Church: Freetown; Presiding Bishop T. S. BANGURA; 36,857 mems.

Other active Methodist bodies include the African Methodist Episcopal Church, the Wesleyan Church of Sierra Leone, the Countess of Huntingdon's Connexion and the West African Methodist Church.

The Roman Catholic Church
Sierra Leone comprises one archdiocese and two dioceses. At 31 December 2006 there were an estimated 263,600 adherents in the country, representing about 4.1% of the total population.

Inter-territorial Catholic Bishops' Conference of The Gambia and Sierra Leone
Santanno House, POB 893, Freetown; tel. (22) 228240; fax (22) 228252.

f. 1971; Pres. Rt Rev. GEORGE BIGUZZI (Bishop of Makeni).

Archbishop of Freetown and Bo: Most Rev. EDWARD TAMBA CHARLES, Santanno House, 10 Howe St, POB 893, Freetown; tel. (22) 224590; fax (22) 224075; e-mail jhg3271@sierratel.sl.

Other Christian Churches
The following are represented: the Christ Apostolic Church, the Church of the Lord (Aladura), the Evangelical Church, the Evangelical Lutheran Church in Sierra Leone, the Missionary Church of Africa, the Sierra Leone Church and the United Brethren in Christ.

AFRICAN RELIGIONS

There is a diverse range of beliefs, rites and practices, varying between ethnic and kinship groups.

The Press

DAILIES

Daily Mail: 29–31 Rawdon St, POB 53, Freetown; tel. (22) 223191; f. 1931; state-owned; Editor AIAH MARTIN MONDEH; circ. 10,000.

For di People: Freetown; independent; Editor PAUL KAMARA.

PERIODICALS

African Crescent: 15 Bath St, POB 353, Brookfields, Freetown; Editor MAULANA-KHALIL A. MOBASHIR.

The Catalyst: Christian Literature Crusade Bookshop, 92 Circular Rd, POB 1465, Freetown; tel. (22) 224382; Editor JUSU-WAI SAWI.

Concord Times: 51 Krootown Rd, Freetown; tel. (22) 229199; e-mail info@concordtimessl.com; internet www.concordtimessl.com; 3 a week; Editor DOROTHY GORDON.

Leonean Sun: 49 Main Rd, Wellington, Freetown; tel. (22) 223363; f. 1974; monthly; Editor ROWLAND MARTYN.

Liberty Voice: 139 Pademba Rd, Freetown; tel. (22) 242100; Editor A. MAHDIEU SAVAGE.

New Breed: Freetown; weekly; independent; Man. Editor (vacant).

The New Citizen: 7 Wellington St, Freetown; tel. (22) 228693; e-mail info@thenewcitizen-sl.com; internet www.thenewcitizen-sl.com; f. 1982; Man. Editor SAMUEL B. CONTEH.

SIERRA LEONE

The New Globe: 49 Bathurst St, Freetown; tel. (22) 228245; weekly; Man. Editor SAM TUMOE; circ. 4,000.

The New Shaft: 60 Old Railway Line, Brookfields, Freetown; tel. (22) 241093; 2 a week; independent; Editor FRANKLIN BUNTING-DAVIES; circ. 10,000.

The Pool Newspaper: 1 Short St, 5th Floor, Freetown; tel. and fax (22) 220102; e-mail pool@justice.com; internet www.poolnewspaper.tripod.com; f. 1992; 3 a week; independent; Man. Dir CHERNOR OJUKU SESAY; circ. 3,000.

Progress: 1 Short St, Freetown; tel. (22) 223588; weekly; independent; Editor FODE KANDEH; circ. 7,000.

Sierra Leone Chamber of Commerce Journal: Sierra Leone Chamber of Commerce, Industry and Agriculture, Guma Bldg, 5th Floor, Lamina Sankoh St, POB 502, Freetown; tel. (22) 226305; fax (22) 228005; monthly.

Unity Now: 82 Pademba Rd, Freetown; tel. (22) 227466; Editor FRANK KPOSOWA.

The Vision: 60 Old Railway Line, Brookfields; tel. (22) 241273; Editor SIAKA MASSAQUOI.

Weekend Spark: 7 Lamina Sankoh St, Freetown; tel. (22) 223397; f. 1983; weekly; independent; Editor ROWLAND MARTYN; circ. 20,000.

Weekly Democrat: Freetown; Editor JON FORAY.

NEWS AGENCY

Sierra Leone News Agency (SLENA): 15 Wallace Johnson St, PMB 445, Freetown; tel. (22) 224921; fax (22) 224439; f. 1980; Man. Dir ABDUL KARIM JALLOH (acting).

Publishers

Njala University Publishing Centre: Njala University College, PMB, Freetown; science and technology, university textbooks.

Sierra Leone University Press: Fourah Bay College, POB 87, Freetown; tel. (22) 22491; fax (22) 224439; f. 1965; biography, history, Africana, religion, social science, university textbooks; Chair. Prof. ERNEST H. WRIGHT.

United Christian Council Literature Bureau: Bunumbu Press, POB 28, Bo; tel. (32) 462; books in Mende, Temne, Susu; Man. Dir ROBERT SAM-KPAKRA.

Broadcasting and Communications

TELECOMMUNICATIONS

Comium (SL) Ltd: Comium Bldg, 30D Wilkinson Rd, Freetown; tel. 33333030; fax 33333060; e-mail info@comium.com.sl; internet www.comium.com.sl; f. 2005; mobile cellular telephone and broadband internet provider; Gen. Man. PAUL HYDE.

Millicom SL Ltd: 117 Wilkinson Rd, Freetown; tel. 30157000; e-mail info@tigo.sl; internet www.tigo.sl; f. 2001; subsidiary of Millicom International Cellular; operates mobile cellular telephone network under brand name Tigo; Gen. Man. PABLO GUARDIA.

Sierra Leone Telecommunications Co (SIERRATEL): 7 Wallace Johnson St, POB 80, Freetown; tel. (22) 222801; fax (22) 224439; internet www.sierratel.sl; state-owned telecommunications operator; Chair. Dr TOM OBALEH KARGBO; Man. Dir ALPHA SESAY.

Zain Sierra Leone: Zain House, 42 Main Motor Rd, Wilberforce, Freetown; tel. (22) 233222; internet www.sl.zain.com; f. 2000; Man. Dir TED SAUTI-PHIRI.

Mobile cellular telephone services are also operated by Africell (www.africell.sl) and Datatel GSM.

BROADCASTING

Sierra Leone Broadcasting Service: New England, Freetown; tel. (22) 240403; f. 1934; state-controlled; programmes mainly in English and the four main Sierra Leonean vernaculars, Mende, Limba, Temne and Krio; weekly broadcast in French; television service established 1963; Dir-Gen. JEANA BANDATOMO.

Finance

(cap. = capital; res = reserves; dep. = deposits; m. = million; br(s). = branch(es); amounts in leones)

BANKING

Central Bank

Bank of Sierra Leone: Siaka Stevens St, POB 30, Freetown; tel. (22) 226501; fax (22) 224764; e-mail info@bankofsierraleone-centralbank.org; internet www.bankofsierraleone-centralbank.org; f. 1964; cap. 24,001.5m., res −5,873.7m., dep. 758,193.1m. (Dec. 2006); Gov. Dr JAMES D. ROGERS; Dep. Gov. ANDRINA ROSA COKER; 1 br.

Other Banks

Guaranty Trust Bank: Sparta Bldg, 12 Wilberforce St, POB 1168, Freetown; tel. (22) 228493; fax (22) 228318; internet www.gtb.sl; f. Feb. 2002 through the acquisition of 90% of shareholding of First Merchant Bank of Sierra Leone by Guaranty Trust Bank of Nigeria; cap. 2,261.0m., total assets 17,769.0m. (Dec. 2003); Chair. TAYO ADERINOKUN; 3 brs.

International Commercial Bank (Sierra Leone) Ltd: 22 Rawdon St, POB 515, Freetown; tel. (22) 222877; fax (22) 290002; e-mail icb@icbank-sl.com; f. 2004; 1 br.

National Development Bank Ltd: Leone House, 6th Floor, 21–23 Siaka Stevens St, Freetown; tel. (22) 226792; fax (22) 224468; f. 1968; 99% state-owned; provides medium- and long-term finance and tech. assistance to devt-orientated enterprises; cap. 1,604.3m., total assets 2,200m. (Dec. 2003); Chair. MURRAY E. S. LAMIN; Man. Dir MOHAMED M. TURAY; 3 brs.

Rokel Commercial Bank (Sierra Leone) Ltd: 25–27 Siaka Stevens St, POB 12, Freetown; tel. (22) 222501; fax (22) 222563; e-mail rokelsl@sierratel.sl; internet www.rokelsl.com; f. 1971; cap. 6,718.5m., res 4,611.7m., dep. 167,903.6m. (Dec. 2006); 51% govt-owned; Chair. YAYAH TOBIAS SESAY; Man. Dir HENRY AKIN MACAULEY; 11 brs.

Sierra Leone Commercial Bank Ltd: Christian Smith Bldg, 29–31 Siaka Stevens St, Freetown; tel. (22) 225264; fax (22) 225292; e-mail slcb@slcb.biz; internet www.slcb.biz; f. 1973; state-owned; cap. 6,000.0m., res 22,891.9m., dep. 189,170.8m. (Dec. 2006); Chair. SHEIKI G. BANGURA; Man. Dir CHRISPIN BISHOP DEIGH; 8 brs.

Standard Chartered Bank Sierra Leone Ltd: 9–11 Lightfoot-Boston St, POB 1155, Freetown; tel. (22) 225021; fax (22) 225760; e-mail scbsl@sierratel.sl; internet www.standardchartered.com/sl; f. 1894; cap. 813.6m., res 7,023.2m., dep 132,467.0m. (Dec. 2005); Chair. ALEX B. KAMARA; CEO and Man. Dir ALBERTO R. SALTSON; 3 brs.

Union Trust Bank Ltd: Lightfoot-Boston St, PMB 1237, Freetown; tel. (22) 226954; fax (22) 226214; e-mail info@utrustbank.com; internet www.utrustbank.com; fmrly Meridien BIAO Bank Sierra Leone Ltd; adopted present name in 1995; cap. 7,477.9m., res 8,275.1m., total assets 60,720.1m. (Dec. 2007); Chair. Alhaji Dr SHEKU TEJAN KAMARA; Man. Dir and CEO JAMES SANPHA KOROMA; 7 brs.

INSURANCE

Aureol Insurance Co Ltd: Kissy House, 54 Siaka Stevens St, POB 647, Freetown; tel. (22) 223435; fax (22) 229336; e-mail info@aureolinsurance.com; internet aureolinsurance.com; f. 1986; Man. Dir SOLOMON J. SAMBA.

National Insurance Co Ltd: 18–20 Walpole St, PMB 84, Freetown; tel. (22) 222535; fax (22) 226097; e-mail nic@sierratel.sl; f. 1972; state-owned; Chair. P. J. KUYEMBEH; CEO ARTHUR NATHANIEL YASKEY.

New India Assurance Co Ltd: 18 Wilberforce St, POB 340, Freetown; tel. (22) 226453; fax (22) 222494; e-mail niasl@sierratel.sl; Man. Dir A. CHOPRA.

Reliance Insurance Trust Corpn Ltd: 24 Siaka Stevens St, Freetown; tel. (22) 225115; fax (22) 228051; e-mail oonomake@yahoo.com; f. 1985; Chair. MOHAMED B. COLE; Man. Dir ALICE M. ONOMAKE.

Sierra Leone Insurance Co Ltd: 31 Lightfoot Boston St, POB 836, Freetown; tel. (22) 224920; fax (22) 222115; Man. Dir IDRISSE YILLE.

Trade and Industry

GOVERNMENT AGENCY

Government Gold and Diamond Office (GGDO): c/o Bank of Sierra Leone, Siaka Stevens St, Freetown; tel. (22) 222600; fax (22) 229064; f. 1985; govt regulatory agency for diamonds and gold; combats illicit trade; Chair. Alhaji M. S. DEEN.

SIERRA LEONE

CHAMBER OF COMMERCE

Sierra Leone Chamber of Commerce, Industry and Agriculture: Guma Bldg, 5th Floor, Lamina Sankoh St, POB 502, Freetown; tel. (22) 226305; fax (22) 220696; e-mail info@cocsl.com; internet www.cocsl.com; f. 1961; 215 mems; Pres. AMADU B. NDOEKA.

TRADE AND INDUSTRIAL ASSOCIATIONS

Sierra Leone Investment and Export Promotion Agency (SLIEPA): Standard Chartered Bank Bldg, 3rd Floor, Lightfoot-Boston St, Freetown; tel. (22) 220788; e-mail info@sliepa.org; f. 2007; fmrly Sierra Leone Export Development and Investment Corporation; Man. Dir CHRIS JASABE.

Small-Medium Scale Businesses Association (Sierra Leone): O.A.U. Dr., Tower Hill, PMB 575, Freetown; tel. (22) 222617; fax (22) 224439; Dir ABU CONTEH.

EMPLOYERS' ORGANIZATIONS

Sierra Leone Employers' Federation: POB 562, Freetown; Chair. AMADU B. NDOEKA; Exec. Officer L. E. JOHNSON.

Sierra Leone Chamber of Mines: POB 456, Freetown; tel. (22) 226082; f. 1965; mems comprise the principal mining concerns; Pres. JOHN SISAY; Exec. Officer N. H. T. BOSTON.

UTILITIES

Electricity

National Power Authority: Electricity House, 36 Siaka Stevens St, Freetown; tel. (22) 229868; fax (22) 227584; e-mail Sierra_Leone@iaeste.org; supplies all electricity in Sierra Leone.

Water

Guma Valley Water Co: Guma Bldg, 13/14 Lamina Sankoh St, POB 700, Freetown; tel. (22) 25887; e-mail gumasl@yahoo.co.uk; f. 1961; responsible for all existing water supplies in Freetown and surrounding villages, including the Guma dam and associated works.

TRADE UNIONS

Artisans', Ministry of Works Employees' and General Workers' Union: 4 Pultney St, Freetown; f. 1946; 14,500 mems; Pres. IBRAHIM LANGLEY; Gen. Sec. TEJAN A. KASSIM.

Sierra Leone Labour Congress: 35 Wallace Johnson St, POB 1333, Freetown; tel. (22) 226869; f. 1966; 51,000 mems in 19 affiliated unions; Pres. H. M. BARRIE; Sec.-Gen. KANDEH YILLA; 25,000 mems (2007).

Principal affiliated unions:

Clerical, Mercantile and General Workers' Union: 35 Wallace Johnson St, Freetown; f. 1945; 3,600 mems; Pres. M. D. BENJAMIN; Gen. Sec. M. B. WILLIAMS.

Sierra Leone Association of Journalists: 31 Garrisson Street, Freetown; tel. 76605811; e-mail slajalone@hotmail.com; Pres. PHILIP NEVILLE.

Sierra Leone Dockworkers' Union: 165 Fourah Bay Rd, Freetown; f. 1962; 2,650 mems; Pres. ABDUL KANISURE; Gen. Sec. A. C. CONTEH.

Sierra Leone Motor Drivers' Union: 10 Charlotte St, Freetown; f. 1960; 1,900 mems; Pres. A. W. HASSAN; Gen. Sec. ALPHA KAMARA.

Sierra Leone Teachers' Union: Regaland House, Lowcost Step—Kissy, POB 477, Freetown; f. 1951; 18,500 mems; Pres. ABDULAI KOROMA; Sec.-Gen. DAVIDSON KUYATEH.

Sierra Leone Transport, Agricultural and General Workers' Union: 4 Pultney St, Freetown; f. 1946; 1,600 mems; Pres. S. O. SAWYERR-MANLEY; Gen. Sec. S. D. KARGBO.

United Mineworkers' Union: 35 Wallace Johnson St, Freetown; f. 1944; 6,500 mems; Gen. Sec. EZEKIEL DYKE.

Also affiliated to the Sierra Leone Labour Congress: the **General Construction Workers' Union**, the **Municipal and Local Government Employees' Union** and the **Sierra Leone National Seamen's Union**.

Transport

RAILWAYS

There are no passenger railways in Sierra Leone.

Marampa Mineral Railway: Delco House, POB 735, Freetown; tel. (22) 222556; 84 km of track linking iron ore mines at Marampa (inactive since 1985) with Pepel port; Gen. Man. SYL KHANU.

ROADS

In 2002 there were an estimated 11,300 km of classified roads, including 2,138 km of main roads and 1,950 km of secondary roads; about 904 km of the total network was paved.

Sierra Leone Road Transport Corpn: Blackhall Rd, POB 1008, Freetown; tel. (22) 250442; fax (22) 250000; f. 1965; state-owned; operates transport services throughout the country; Gen. Man. DANIEL R. W. FAUX.

INLAND WATERWAYS

Established routes for launches, which include the coastal routes from Freetown northward to the Great and Little Scarcies rivers and southward to Bonthe, total almost 800 km. Although some of the upper reaches of the rivers are navigable only between July and September, there is a considerable volume of river traffic.

SHIPPING

Freetown, the principal port, has full facilities for ocean-going vessels.

Sierra Leone National Shipping Co Ltd: 45 Cline St, POB 935, Freetown; tel. (22) 229883; fax (22) 229513; f. 1972; state-owned; shipping, clearing and forwarding agency; representatives for foreign lines; Chair. Alhaji B. M. KOROMA; Man. Dir SYLVESTER B. FOMBA.

Sierra Leone Ports Authority: Queen Elizabeth II Quay, PMB 386, Cline Town, Freetown; tel. (22) 226480; fax (22) 226443; f. 1965; parastatal body, supervised by the Ministry of Transport and Communications; operates the port of Freetown.

Sierra Leone Shipping Agencies Ltd: Deep Water Quay, Clinetown, POB 74, Freetown; tel. (22) 221709; fax (22) 293111; e-mail fna.otal@bollore.com; f. 1949; Man. Dir MICHEL MEYNARD.

CIVIL AVIATION

There is an international airport at Lungi.

Directorate of Civil Aviation: Ministry of Transport and Communications, Ministerial Bldg, George St, Freetown; tel. (22) 222106; fax (22) 228488; Dir GEORGE GBONGBOR.

Sierra National Airlines: Leone House, 25 Pultney St, POB 285, Freetown; tel. (22) 222075; fax (22) 222026; internet www.flysna.com; f. 1982; state-owned; operates domestic and regional services, and a weekly flight to Paris, France; operations resumed, following civil conflict, in Nov. 2000; Chair. TAMBA MATTURI; Man. Dir ADAM CORMACK.

Tourism

The main attractions for tourists are the coastline, the mountains and the game reserves. Civil conflict throughout most of the 1990s effectively suspended tourist activity. By 2005, however, according to the World Tourism Organization, tourist arrivals had increased to 40,023, compared with 10,615 in 1999. Arrivals decreased to 33,704 in 2006. Receipts from tourism totalled an estimated US $23m. in that year.

Sierra Leone National Tourist Board: Cape Sierra Hotel, Room 100, Aberdeen, POB 1435, Freetown; tel. (22) 236620; fax (22) 236621; e-mail info@welcometosierraleone.org; internet www.welcometosierraleone.org; f. 1990; Gen. Man. CECIL J. WILLIAMS.

SINGAPORE

Introductory Survey

Location, Climate, Language, Religion, Flag, Capital

The Republic of Singapore lies in South-East Asia. The country comprises one main island and some 64 offshore islands, situated approximately 137 km (85 miles) north of the Equator, off the southernmost tip of the Malay Peninsula, to which it is linked by a causeway. The climate is equatorial, with a uniformly high daily and annual temperature varying between 24°C and 27°C (75°F–80°F). Relative humidity is high (often exceeding 90%), and the average annual rainfall is 235 cm (93 ins). There are four official languages—Malay (the national language), Chinese (Mandarin), Tamil and English. The language of administration is English. Chinese dialects were spoken as a first language by 24% of the population in 2000. The principal religions are Daoism, Buddhism, Islam, Christianity and Hinduism. The national flag (proportions 2 by 3) has two equal horizontal stripes of red and white, with a white crescent moon and five white stars, arranged in a pentagram, in the upper hoist. The capital is Singapore City.

Recent History

In 1826 the East India Company formed the Straits Settlements by the union of Singapore and the dependencies of Penang and Malacca on the Malay Peninsula. They came under British rule in 1867 as a crown colony. Singapore was occupied by Japan for three years during the Second World War. At the end of the war, following Japan's defeat, Singapore was governed by a British military administration. When civil rule was restored in 1946, Singapore was detached from the other Straits Settlements and became a separate crown colony. A new Constitution, adopted in February 1955, introduced some measure of self-government, and in June 1959 the state achieved complete internal self-government, with Lee Kuan Yew as Prime Minister. The Federation of Malaysia came into being in September 1963, with Singapore as a constituent state. On 9 August 1965, following irreconcilable differences with the central Government in Malaysia, Singapore seceded from the federation and became an independent country. Singapore joined the UN in September and became a member of the Commonwealth in October. In December Singapore was proclaimed a republic, with a President as constitutional Head of State. In May 1973 the last major links with Malaysia, concerning currency and finance, were renounced. In September 1972 Lee Kuan Yew's ruling People's Action Party (PAP) won all 65 parliamentary seats in a general election.

After independence the Government supported a strong US military presence in South-East Asia. However, with the collapse of US influence in the area during 1974–75, at the end of the war in Viet Nam, Singapore adopted a conciliatory attitude towards the People's Republic of China and its communist neighbours. The Government urged the removal of foreign bases from member states of the Association of South East Asian Nations (ASEAN, see p. 194), and advocated a policy of neutrality. Singapore sought to consolidate its trade links with China, although diplomatic relations were not established until 1982.

At general elections in December 1976 and again in December 1980, the PAP won all 69 seats in the enlarged Parliament. However, the PAP's monopoly ended in October 1981, when the Secretary-General of the opposition Workers' Party, J. B. Jeyaretnam, won a by-election. This posed no direct threat, but, in order to reassert its authority, the Government increased its control over trade unions and restructured the ownership of major newspapers. The PAP was again returned to power in December 1984 with a large majority in Parliament (now expanded to 79 seats), but the party lost two seats to opposition parties, and its share of the total votes was reduced to 62.9% from 75% in 1980. A constitutional amendment approved in July 1984 provided for up to three 'non-constituency' parliamentary seats for the opposition (with restricted voting rights) if none was won in the election. One extra seat was subsequently offered to the losing opposition candidate with the highest percentage of votes. However, this seat was refused by the Workers' Party in January 1985. In March the state President, Devan Nair, resigned. A new President, Wee Kim Wee (hitherto the Chairman of the Singapore Broadcasting Corporation), was elected by Parliament in August.

During 1986 the Government exhibited signs of increasing intolerance towards its critics. In August amendments to the Parliament (Privileges, Immunities and Powers) Act were hurriedly adopted, enabling Parliament to fine, expel or imprison members who were deemed to have abused their parliamentary privileges. In the same month Parliament also approved a Newspaper and Printing Presses (Amendment) Act, which empowered the Government to restrict the distribution of foreign publications deemed to be interfering in domestic political affairs; the circulation of several foreign periodicals was subsequently restricted.

In November 1986 Jeyaretnam (one of the two opposition members of Parliament) was sentenced to one month's imprisonment and fined S $5,000 (enough, according to the Constitution, to deprive him of his parliamentary seat and prevent him from standing for election for five years), when the Supreme Court upheld a conviction for perjury in connection with bankruptcy proceedings brought against the Workers' Party four years previously. In February 1987 Jeyaretnam was also fined by a parliamentary committee for abuse of privilege, having made allegations of government interference in the judiciary; further fines were imposed on him for publishing 'distorted' accounts of an earlier hearing of the committee, and (in May) for alleged contempt of Parliament and abuse of parliamentary privilege. In October Jeyaretnam's removal from the Law Society register was ordered by a three-judge court. An appeal to the Judicial Committee of the Privy Council in the United Kingdom (then the highest court of appeal for Singapore) resulted, in October 1988, in his reinstatement as a practising lawyer. During the course of the appeal, investigations into Jeyaretnam's previous convictions found that they had been 'fatally flawed'. However, since the criminal case had been considered in the District Court, where there was no right of appeal to the Privy Council, the original convictions prevented Jeyaretnam from re-entering Parliament without a presidential pardon. This was refused by Wee Kim Wee in May 1989.

In May and June 1987 the Government detained a total of 22 people (including 10 Roman Catholic church workers and four members of the Workers' Party) without trial, under the Internal Security Act, for their alleged involvement in a 'Marxist conspiracy' to subvert state organizations. The arrests were denounced by Jeyaretnam, who claimed that the Government wished to intimidate Singaporeans so that they would not support opposition parties. In November the Government was also criticized by international human rights groups, including Amnesty International, for its refusal to present evidence of such a conspiracy in court. By December most of the alleged conspirators had been released, but eight of them were re-arrested in April 1988, after complaining that they had been tortured while in detention. Four prisoners were released by June, and in December a further four detainees were released in accordance with a ruling by the Court of Appeal, based on a fault in their detention orders. They were immediately rearrested. However, the trial had established a precedent for the judicial review of cases brought under the Internal Security Act, including the acceptability to the courts of evidence used in warrants for the arrest of suspects. In January 1989 Parliament approved legislation ensuring that the judiciary could examine such detentions only on technical grounds, and abolishing the right of appeal to the Privy Council in cases brought under the Internal Security Act. In March three detainees were released. The two remaining prisoners (of the original 22) remained in detention until June 1990.

A general election was held in September 1988. The electoral system was altered so that 39 of the existing 79 constituencies were replaced by 13 'group representation constituencies', to be contested by teams of three representatives for each party, at least one of whom was to be a member of an ethnic minority (i.e. non-Chinese). The declared aim was to ensure the presence of racial minorities in Parliament; however, in practice opposition parties with few resources were restricted by the difficulty of presenting three candidates. The PAP won 80 of the elective seats (which now totalled 81); one was taken by the leader of the Singapore Democratic Party (SDP), Chiam See Tong. Two 'non-constituency' seats were offered to Francis Seow (Workers' Party) and Lee Siew Choh (Socialist Front). In December, however, while Seow (who had already been detained in May under the Internal Security Act for organizing a meeting between a US diplomat and lawyers critical of the Government) was undergoing medical treatment in the USA, he was convicted *in absentia* for tax evasion and fined S $19,000: he was thus debarred from taking his seat in Parliament.

In January 1989 Lee began his eighth term as Prime Minister, and announced that he would retire from the premiership before the expiry of the term. This announcement was followed by a statement from the First Deputy Prime Minister, Goh Chok Tong (Lee's chosen successor), that Lee was adopting a secondary and more advisory role in the government of the country. In August Parliament unanimously re-elected Wee Kim Wee for a further four-year term as President. In early 1990 Parliament approved legislation enabling the Government to nominate as many as six unelected MPs. The politically neutral nominated MPs would be appointed for two years, and would be able to vote on all legislative proposals except those concerning financial and constitutional affairs.

On 28 November 1990 Lee was duly replaced as Prime Minister by Goh Chok Tong. Lee remained in the Cabinet as Senior Minister in the Prime Minister's Office, and retained the position of Secretary-General of the PAP, while Lee's son, Brig.-Gen. Lee Hsien Loong, was appointed as a Deputy Prime Minister.

In January 1991 the Constitution was amended to provide for a popularly elected presidency with extensive powers of veto on proposed financial legislation, a role as final arbiter in cases of detention for reasons of national security, and influence in civil and military appointments. The changes to the (hitherto highly ceremonial) functions of the President were initially proposed by Lee in 1984, and were criticized by members of opposition parties as being intended to accommodate the former Prime Minister. Under the amendment, Wee Kim Wee was to continue in office until October 1993. Legislation empowering him with the authority of an elected president took effect from 30 November 1991. Candidates for the presidency were limited to those who had held the post of a minister, chief justice or senior civil servant or were at the head of a large company. The candidates were to be scrutinized by a new presidential election committee, which was to comprise the head of the Society of Accountants, the Chairman of the Public Service Commission and a member of the Presidential Council of Human Rights. The last two officials were appointed by the Government, prompting fears that the selected candidates would be those favoured by the PAP. The constitutional amendment also included a clause increasing the number of candidates required to contest a 'group representation constituency' in a general election to a minimum of three and a maximum of four, one of whom was to be a member of an ethnic minority.

In early 1991 the Government promoted the acceptance of five 'shared values', based on Confucian philosophy, as the basis of a national ideology. Critics alleged that the ideology would be used to reinforce support for the PAP and to obviate opposition challenges. Goh attempted, in principle, to introduce a more 'open', consultative form of government. He instituted an extensive programme of community visits to assess popular opinion, showing solicitude for the views of the minority Malay and Indian communities. Although film censorship was relaxed, the Internal Security Act and restrictions on the foreign press remained in force. In early August, seeking a popular mandate for his style of government, Goh announced that there would be a general election at the end of the month. Under a plan conceived by Chiam, the opposition parties contested only 40 of the 81 seats, thus guaranteeing an absolute majority for the incumbent PAP. Chiam issued an appeal to the electorate to take the opportunity to elect a strong opposition. Goh indicated that a failure to receive a popular endorsement would result in a return to a more authoritarian and paternalistic form of government. At the election, held on 31 August, the PAP's share of the vote was 61.0% (compared with 63.2% in 1988), and the party won 77 seats (compared with 80 in 1988). Chiam's SDP secured three seats, and the Workers' Party one seat. Jeyaretnam was unable to contest the election, as his disqualification remained in force until November. In response to Jeyaretnam's accusations that he had been deliberately excluded from the election, and also because the election schedule had prevented the PAP from presenting enough new candidates, Goh had announced, prior to the polls, that he would organize by-elections within 12–18 months of the general election.

In October 1991 Seow, who had remained in exile in the USA since 1988, was convicted *in absentia* of a further 60 offences involving tax evasion, rendering him ineligible to contest any potential by-election. Later that month Jeyaretnam paid S $392,838 in legal costs to Lee, thus avoiding bankruptcy, which would have prevented his candidacy. Lee had instituted a successful defamation suit against Jeyaretnam in 1990, over remarks made by Jeyaretnam at a 1988 election rally.

Following the general election, Lee, who had temporarily withdrawn from public attention after Goh's accession to the premiership, resumed a prominent role in domestic politics. He attributed the decline in PAP support to neglect of the Mandarin-educated ethnic Chinese majority, and advocated a greater emphasis on Chinese culture and language. In April 1991 Goh announced that the level of electoral support among residents would be one of the criteria used to determine the order in which refurbishments would be undertaken in public housing estates. Since about 86% of Singaporeans lived in public housing, this was widely interpreted as a warning against voting for the opposition in the forthcoming by-elections.

Prior to the convening of Parliament in September 1992 the Government appointed the maximum of six nominated MPs. This too was generally regarded as an attempt to discourage support for opposition candidates in the impending by-elections. In October the implementation of legislation prohibiting MPs from using the ground floors of public housing blocks as office space adversely affected all four opposition MPs, who, because of a shortage of party funds, were unable to afford commercial rents.

In November 1992 Goh announced to the Central Executive Committee of the PAP that the renewal of national leadership was the party's most urgent consideration. This statement was followed two days later by the public disclosure that both Deputy Prime Ministers, Lee Hsien Loong and Ong Teng Cheong, had been diagnosed as suffering from cancer. The revelation strengthened Goh's position as Prime Minister, since many had previously regarded his incumbency as an interim arrangement prior to Lee Hsien Loong's assumption of the premiership. In December Goh was unanimously elected to replace Lee Kuan Yew (who proposed his candidacy) as Secretary-General of the PAP.

In December 1992 Goh relinquished his parliamentary seat (which formed part of a four-member 'group representation constituency') in order to contest a by-election. Jeyaretnam was unable to contest the by-election as only three candidates from the Workers' Party registered with the authorities. The results of the by-election were regarded as an endorsement of Goh's leadership, as the four PAP candidates received 72.9% of the votes cast, while the opposition SDP secured 24.5%.

In March 1993 Chee Soon Juan, who contested the December by-election as a candidate for the SDP, was dismissed from his post as a lecturer at the National University of Singapore for 'dishonest conduct'. The Government denied that the dismissal was politically motivated, and defamation proceedings were initiated by university officials against Chee. In June, following a rejection by the SDP Central Committee of a motion of censure proposed by Chiam against Chee for bringing the party into disrepute, Chiam resigned as Secretary-General of the party. Chee replaced him as acting Secretary-General, pending party elections in early 1995. In August 1993 the SDP expelled Chiam for alleged indiscipline; however, a High Court ruling in December declared the expulsion 'illegal and invalid'. (This enabled Chiam to retain his seat in Parliament: under the Constitution a member of the legislature is obliged to relinquish his seat if he resigns or is expelled from the party he has been elected to represent.) The following month, under a judicial ruling, a 'breakaway' central executive committee, formed in 1993 by a faction of the SDP that remained loyal to Chiam, was declared void. Chee subsequently published a book entitled *Dare to Change*, which demanded greater democracy and was adopted as official party policy by the SDP in June 1994. Chee was formally elected Secretary-General of the SDP in January 1995.

Meanwhile, in August 1993 Ong Teng Cheong was elected President with 58.7% of the votes cast. However, contrary to expectation the only other candidate, Chua Kim Yeow, a former government official, who adopted an apolitical position, secured a substantial proportion (41.3%) of the vote. The candidacies of both Jeyaretnam and Tan Soo Phuan, another member of the

Workers' Party, were rejected by the Presidential Election Committee on the grounds that they were unsuitable 'in regard to integrity, good character and reputation'.

In October 1996 Parliament approved amendments to the Constitution that redefined the role of the President and partially reformed the voting system. The President's powers were restricted by new provisions empowering the Government to call a referendum if the President vetoed certain constitutional amendments, and also enabling Parliament to overrule (by a two-thirds' majority) a presidential veto on senior civil service appointments. A further amendment expanded the number of 'group representation constituencies' and increased the maximum number of group candidates from four to six. The electoral reforms were opposed by the opposition parties on the grounds that the amendments favoured large, well-established parties such as the PAP, while smaller parties would have difficulty in finding and funding large numbers of candidates.

Prior to the general election, which took place on 2 January 1997, the success of the PAP was predetermined by the opposition parties' decision to contest only 36 of the 83 seats. Nevertheless, the PAP conducted a rigorous campaign in an effort to ensure that the party received two-thirds of the total votes cast, a margin regarded as sufficient endorsement of Goh and his administration. During the campaign, it was again announced that public housing improvements would be prioritized according to levels of electoral support for the PAP. The party secured a resounding victory, winning 65% of the votes and 81 seats (including all nine single-member constituencies). The remaining two elective seats were won by Chiam See Tong of the Singapore People's Party (for the fourth time, although previously he had been elected as a representative of the SDP) and Low Thia Khiang of the Workers' Party (for a second time). The Workers' Party, as the opposition party with the most votes but less than three seats, was also allocated a non-constituency seat; this was accepted by Jeyaretnam. The SDP lost the three seats it had previously held.

Seemingly a particular focus for attack by the PAP during the election campaign was Tang Liang Hong, a candidate of the Workers' Party. The PAP accused Tang of being anti-Christian, of promoting Chinese interests over those of Singapore's ethnic minorities and of attempting to foment discontent among the ethnic Chinese community. Tang, standing in the same 'group representation constituency' as Jeyaretnam, failed to secure election. (Goh, unopposed in a single-member constituency, personally campaigned against Tang in the group constituency.) Tang's public rebuttal of the accusations of the PAP leaders prompted them to issue writs against him for defamation. Tang fled to Malaysia in January 1997, claiming to have received anonymous death threats. Tang was found guilty of defamation by the High Court in March, as he failed to attend the trial and provide a defence, and was ordered in May to pay a record sum of S $8m. in libel damages to Goh and 10 senior PAP leaders. Tang appealed against the judgment in September on the grounds that it contained legal errors and that the cases had been brought for political motives. The Court of Appeal ruled in November that the damages awarded against Tang were disproportionate to the injury caused, and reduced the sum to S $4.53m. In February 1998, despite this concession, Tang, against whom a warrant for arrest had been issued on 33 counts of tax evasion, was declared bankrupt.

Goh and 10 senior PAP members also sued Jeyaretnam for alleged defamation following remarks made at an election rally concerning two police reports submitted by Tang accusing the PAP leadership of criminal conspiracy and lying. In September 1997 Jeyaretnam was ordered to pay damages of S $20,000; however, the award represented only 10% of the amount sought by the PAP leadership, and the judge, who criticized Goh's lawyers for their handling of the case, ordered that Jeyaretnam pay only 60% of the legal costs. During the trial Goh admitted under cross-examination that he had authorized the unofficial disclosure of the police reports to the press, and it was put to him that the legal suits were an attempt to bankrupt Jeyaretnam and thus disqualify him from Parliament. However, the Court of Appeal dismissed an appeal by Jeyaretnam in July 1998, increasing the damages to S $100,000, and awarding full costs against him. However, it was subsequently agreed that Jeyaretnam would be permitted to pay the damages in five instalments, thereby enabling him to avoid bankruptcy proceedings and to continue as a legislator.

In November 1998 the Government revoked the remaining restrictions on the activities of the political activist Chia Thye Poh. Chia had been arrested in 1966, imprisoned for more than 22 years without trial under the Internal Security Act, confined to a fortress on an island off the coast of Singapore for a further three years, then permitted to reside in Singapore from 1992, although prohibited from taking part in any political activity. Despite this concession to Chia, government suppression of expressions of opposition continued. In January 1999 Chee was charged twice under the Public Entertainment Act for making unlicensed public speeches. Chee had deliberately refused to apply for licences to make the two public speeches, in which he criticized government policy, on the grounds that freedom of expression was guaranteed under the Constitution. During the first trial Chee was represented by Jeyaretnam, who attempted to expose the alleged use of the above Act to restrict political opposition. However, Chee was found guilty at the beginning of February, and was sentenced to seven days' imprisonment, owing to his refusal to pay a fine of S $1,400. Following his release, Chee appeared in court for a second time in February, and was sentenced, with the Assistant Secretary-General of the SDP, Wong Hong Toy, who had reportedly assisted Chee at the speech, to 12 days' imprisonment after Chee and Wong refused to pay respective fines of S $2,500 and S $2,400. The level of the fines automatically disqualified both men from seeking political office for five years; however, following an appeal, the two had their fines reduced to S $1,900 each, below the level that would have rendered them ineligible to stand for election. For its part, the Government maintained that opposition politicians had adequate opportunity to expound their views in Parliament or in the media (although in February 1998 the Government had banned political parties from producing videos and from promoting their opinions on television). In April 1999 it was reported that, subsequent to his release from prison after serving his second term of imprisonment, Chee had been fined S $600 for illegal sales of a book he had produced on Asian opposition leaders. In March members of the PAP filed a petition to close the Workers' Party, owing to its inability to pay more than S $280,000 in damages and costs awarded against it in a defamation case. The party's closure would force the resignation of its two parliamentary representatives. It was subsequently reported that the party had lost a judicial appeal against the award.

In May 2000 Jeyaretnam was declared bankrupt by the High Court after he failed to make payments of S $30,000 in libel damages arising from a lawsuit concerning an article that appeared in the Workers' Party newspaper, *The Hammer*, in 1995. The bankruptcy ruling would have disqualified Jeyaretnam from serving in Parliament, but the orders were set aside after the outstanding debt was paid, and he was authorized to retain his non-constituency seat. In January 2001, however, Jeyaretnam was once again declared bankrupt by the High Court, with a S $235,000 debt as a result of a defamation claim against a Workers' Party newsletter. The appeal against the bankruptcy ruling was dismissed in February. In May Jeyaretnam was replaced as Secretary-General of the Workers' Party by Low Thia Khiang. In July he finally lost his seat in Parliament when the Court of Appeals confirmed that it would not rescind the bankruptcy ruling against him.

Meanwhile, legislation introduced in May 1997 increased the number of nominated MPs from six to nine; the Constitution was amended accordingly in September. During the year nine Community Development Councils (CDCs) were formed. The CDCs encompassed all constituencies, including the two opposition wards, although opposition representatives would not be permitted to serve as council leaders and would have no power to disburse funds.

During 1999 Lee Hsien Loong, who had been appointed Chairman of the Monetary Authority of Singapore (MAS) in December 1997, began to assume a more prominent political role. George Yeo, hitherto the Minister for Information and the Arts, also gained prominence following his promotion to the trade and industry portfolio in a minor cabinet reorganization in June 1999. Singapore's second presidential election was scheduled to take place in August. President Ong, despite his PAP affiliation, had proved an independent President, whose determination to exercise the full powers of the elected presidency had resulted in strained relations with his former government colleagues. His allegations of government obstruction of his efforts to establish the details of the Republic's financial reserves (in order to fulfil his role of guardian of those reserves as specified in the constitutional amendments of 1991) had led to a rare display of disunity among senior PAP officials, involving public disputes with both Goh and Lee. Despite a medical report confirming that Ong was in complete remission from a cancer diagnosed in 1992, the PAP announced that, on the grounds of health, it would not support his candidacy should he choose to seek a second term of office. Ong, who was widely believed to command sufficient popular support to secure the presidency without a government endorsement, finally announced his decision not to contest the election in July, but unexpectedly proceeded to enumerate his political difficulties while in office. Despite Goh's expressed support for a more consultative style of governance, in mid-August a government-appointed committee declared that only one of three potential presidential candidates, S. R. Nathan (a former Singaporean ambassador to the USA whose presidential candidature was supported by the Cabinet), had fulfilled the criteria set by the committee; Nathan was subsequently nominated as the new President of Singapore on 18 August, and was formally appointed to the position on 1 September, prompting criticism of the Government's autocratic approach.

In September 2000 the Government appeared to have relaxed its strict control over public speaking, with the opening of a 'Speakers' Corner', theoretically allowing a forum for any citizen to air issues of concern. However, in practice speakers were obliged to register with the police beforehand, and to refrain from speaking on certain racial issues. The opportunity to speak was taken up by members of two Singaporean policy centres, after they were refused a permit to organize a marathon run to protest against the Internal Security Act in December. The gathering of around 50 people was not dispersed, but a report on the event broadcast by the Radio Corporation of Singapore was later edited at the request of the management, and the presenter who publicized the re-editing was dismissed. In April 2001 the Government permitted a rare opposition political rally. It was the first authorized protest to be openly critical of the Government since independence. The rally, intended as a pro-democracy fund-raising event for Jeyaretnam, was attended by over 1,000 people.

In July 2001 four opposition parties—the Singapore People's Party, the Singapore Malay National Organization, the National Solidarity Party and the Singapore Justice Party—formed the Singapore Democratic Alliance (SDA). The new coalition was chaired by Chiam See Tong, and it was hoped that its formation would strengthen the fragmented political opposition to the PAP. In October President Nathan unexpectedly announced that a general election was to be held in early November 2001, significantly in advance of the August 2002 deadline. During the campaign the Government declared that the allocation of priority to public housing improvements would again be affected by levels of electoral support. Electoral boundaries were also redrawn, leading to the enlargement of 14 multi-member constituencies and to an increase in the number of parliamentary seats to 84, in order to accommodate a rise in the number of registered voters. The opposition protested that it had been disadvantaged by the rearrangements. When nominations closed in late October PAP candidates were unopposed for 55 of the 84 seats. The Government thus secured victory by default before the polls opened. However, the Prime Minister urged voters to turn out on election day to decide the outcome of the contests for the remaining 29 seats, warning that Singapore confronted its 'gravest challenge since independence'. He also officially announced that he would leave office upon the conclusion of his next term.

The elections were held on 3 November 2001. The level of voter participation was low, owing to the large number of uncontested seats. Despite speculation that the PAP would lose some ground in the election because of the deterioration in the economy, it succeeded in winning 82 seats and increasing its share of the votes cast to 75.3%. The remaining two seats went to Chiam See Tong, Chairman of the SDA, and Low Thia Khiang of the Workers' Party. Steve Chia of the SDA was awarded a non-constituency seat.

Shortly after the election it was reported that Lee and Goh were suing Chee Soon Juan of the SDP for defamation. Chee had alleged that the Government had lent more than S $17,000m. of public money to the Suharto administration in Indonesia during the 1997–98 financial crisis. He had issued a public apology for the comments soon afterwards and admitted fabricating the accusation, but had later retracted his statement, claiming that it had been made under duress. Goh claimed that, while the loan had been offered to the Suharto administration, it had never been disbursed. In February 2002 Chee was the focus of further legal action after he contravened the rule banning the discussion of racial and religious issues in 'Speakers' Corner'. He had criticized the Government's policy of banning Muslim girls from wearing headscarves in public schools and urged the promotion of cultural diversity. His comments followed the suspension of three Muslim girls from school for their wearing of headscarves.

In April 2002 Jeyaretnam made a public apology in the High Court in an attempt to bring to an end the series of defamation suits that had been brought against him by the Government; seven outstanding lawsuits were subsequently abandoned. In the same month Chee stated that he intended to defend the lawsuits against him. In May Chee and the Vice-Chairman of the SDP, Gandhi Ambalam, led an unauthorized rally outside the presidential palace demanding workers' rights. Following the rally, Chee and Ambalan were both sentenced to brief prison terms, having chosen not to pay the fines imposed upon them. However, Ambalan's family subsequently paid his fine, in order to enable his release from prison on the grounds of ill health. In August the High Court ordered Chee to pay damages of S $500,000 to Lee and Goh, after his request for a trial was rejected; the verdict was confirmed in January 2005. Meanwhile, a constitutional amendment was approved stipulating that any member of Parliament declared bankrupt or found guilty of a crime would be banned from speaking or voting in Parliament for the duration of any appeal. In February 2003 Ambalam's appeal against his fine (which was sufficient to prohibit him from standing for political office for five years) was rejected by the Chief Justice. In October 2004 the Jeyaretnam affair resumed when he again appealed for early discharge from bankruptcy in order to secure re-entry into the political arena. However, the Court of Appeal deemed him to have been dishonest about his assets, ruling that he had failed to declare property in Johor Baru worth more than S $350,000. Consequently, the Court's original decision was upheld and Jeyaretnam's application for clemency was denied. Jeyaretnam was discharged from bankruptcy in May 2007 after paying the damages he owed.

In April 2003, meanwhile, Prime Minister Goh announced a cabinet reorganization. The acting Minister for Information, Communications and the Arts, David Lim Tik En, resigned and was replaced by Dr Lee Boon Yang, the former Minister for Manpower, who was succeeded by Dr Ng Eng Hen. Khaw Boon Wan was appointed to be acting Minister for Health, replacing Lim Hng Kiang, who became a Minister in the Prime Minister's Office. Meanwhile, Deputy Prime Minister and former Minister for Defence Dr Tony Tan Keng Yam was appointed to the newly created position of Co-ordinating Minister for Security and Defence in the Prime Minister's Office (effective from August 2003). The defence portfolio was allocated to the former Minister for Education, Teo Chee Hean, who was to be succeeded in an acting capacity by Tharman Shanmugaratnam.

In August 2003 Prime Minister Goh announced that he intended to resign from his post at least two years prior to the country's next general election, scheduled to be held in 2007. He designated his deputy, Lee Hsien Loong, as his successor. In early 2004 Lee indicated that, following his accession to power, he would implement measures to reduce the control of the Government over Singaporean citizens and to promote a culture of political 'openness' in the country.

On 12 August 2004 Lee was formally sworn in as Prime Minister, amid claims that a dynastic succession had been contrived. Both former Prime Ministers were included within the new Cabinet: Goh was retained as Senior Minister, while Lee Kuan Yew was redesignated as Minister Mentor. Shanmugam Jayakumar became Singapore's first Deputy Minister of Indian origin, and Dr Tony Tan Keng Yam was also reappointed to this position. Lee retained the finance portfolio but, in an unexpected development, relinquished the chairmanship of the MAS to Goh. Wong Kan Seng remained the Minister for Home Affairs but was also designated as successor to Dr Tan as Deputy Prime Minister upon the latter's retirement, scheduled for June 2005. Brig.-Gen. George Yeo was named the new Minister for Foreign Affairs and Rear-Adm. Teo Chee Hean retained the defence portfolio, while Tharman Shanmugaratnam was confirmed in the permanent position of Minister for Education. Two women were appointed as Ministers of State: Lim Hwee Hua was named Minister of State for Finance and Transport, and Yu-Foo Yee Shoon became Minister for State for Community Development and Sports.

The reversal of the decline in Singapore's birth rate was immediately rendered a major government priority following Lee's inauguration. In late August 2004 Lee added responsibility for the revival of the country's population growth to the brief of

Wong Kan Seng and implemented an array of measures aimed at increasing the birth rate, which since the 1960s had decreased sharply. Government bonuses were offered to parents producing a third or fourth child, maternity leave was lengthened and tax rebates were introduced for working mothers.

In April 2005 Prime Minister Lee announced that the Government was no longer opposed to the construction of two major casino resorts in Singapore, to be built at an estimated cost of US $3,000m. In the same month the Government approved a draft bill to legalize gambling on the island, thereby proposing to remove a ban that had been in place for 40 years. It was hoped that the resorts, which were expected to become operational by 2009, would significantly boost the country's tourism industry and contribute to the Government's campaign to double the number of tourist arrivals by 2015, as well as allowing Singapore to retain the money of its nationals who had hitherto been obliged to travel abroad in order to engage in gambling activities. However, the decision encountered widespread disapproval, particularly from religious groups, which accused the Government of prioritizing profit over the country's moral standing. The Minister for Trade and Industry, Lim Hng Kiang, suggested that the project itself would create as many as 30,000 new jobs.

Following a series of bomb attacks targeting commuters on the public transport network of the British capital city of London, in July 2005, and a series of attacks in neighbouring Indonesia by the Islamist militant organization Jemaah Islamiah (JI), Minister for Transport Yeo Cheow Tong announced the creation of the Singaporean Police Mass Rapid Transport (MRT) Unit, intended to protect the island's transport system from terrorist attack. The unit commenced random patrols in the following month.

Presidential elections were scheduled to be held in August 2005. However, of the four candidates who had applied for inclusion in the contest only the incumbent, S. R. Nathan, was granted a Certificate of Eligibility, the other three candidates being deemed to be lacking in political experience. Consequently, Nathan was returned unopposed for a second term in office; he was formally sworn in on 1 September. In October the Deputy Prime Minister, Co-ordinating Minister for National Security and Minister of Law, Shanmugam Jayakumar, announced the development of the Risk Assessment and Horizon Scanning programme, an early warning system intended to identify and monitor the activities of newly emerging threats to national and regional security. In April 2006, following months of speculation that Prime Minister Lee Hsien Loong was to call an early legislative election in order to take advantage of Singapore's strong economic position, it was announced that the poll (which had not been due until June 2007) would be held on 6 May. At the election, opposition parties contested 47 of the 84 parliamentary seats. The PAP won 82 seats, as it had done at the 2001 election, while the SDA and the Workers' Party secured one seat each. However, the PAP's share of the votes cast decreased to 66.6%, compared with 75.4% at the 2001 election.

In February 2006, meanwhile, Chee Soon Juan was declared bankrupt by the High Court, having failed to pay the stipulated damages of S $500,000 to Lee Kuan Yew and Goh Chok Tong for the comments he had made during the 2001 elections (see above). Under the bankruptcy order, Chee was forbidden from contesting legislative elections for five years and was required to seek official permission to travel overseas. In the following month Chee was convicted of contempt of court for his criticism of Singapore's judiciary during the February court hearing, and was ordered to pay a fine of S $6,000. Upon his refusal to pay the fine, Chee was imprisoned for seven days, after which he refused to pay and his imprisonment was subsequently extended for a further seven days. In April Chee and several other SDP officials were sued for defamation by Lee Kuan Yew and Lee Hsien Loong in connection with articles published in February in the party's newsletter, *The New Democrat*, which had compared the PAP Government's running of the country to the management of the National Kidney Foundation (NKF), which was embroiled in a corruption scandal. (The controversy at the NKF had emerged in July 2005; amid allegations of misuse of funds, the entire executive board of the charitable organization tendered its resignation and the wife of Senior Minister Gok Chok Tong, hitherto the patron of NKF, also relinquished her position.) Chee Soon Juan and his sister, Chee Siok Chin, were found guilty of defamation in September 2006 in a summary judgment by the High Court, their request for a trial having been rejected, and in October 2008 the High Court ordered Chee to pay S $610,000 in defamation damages to Prime Minister Lee and his father. In November 2006 Chee was sentenced to five weeks' imprisonment for not paying a fine for speaking in public without a government permit during the 2006 election period.

Human rights issues were brought to the fore in 2006/07 as the Government sought to curb freedom of expression, attempting to restrict public gatherings, political demonstrations and views portrayed over the internet. At the annual meeting of the IMF and the World Bank in September 2006 the Government prevented five activists from attending, although it had originally yielded to international pressure by allowing access to 22 others. Despite criticism from the President of the World Bank, the Government claimed that the activists posed a security threat and could endanger the attending delegates. In February 2007 the *Far Eastern Economic Review*, a Hong Kong-based journal, failed in its second attempt to have a defamation action dismissed after the publication in July 2006 of an article entitled 'Singapore's 'Martyr' Chee Soon Juan'. The *Review* vowed to defend itself vigorously against the suit filed by Prime Minister Lee Hsien Loong and Minister Mentor Lee Kuan Yew, over alleged negative comments made about them and the Government by Chee. In its defence, the journal argued that, as it was published in Hong Kong and employed no Singaporean journalists, it was not bound by Singaporean law. Distribution of the journal in Singapore had been banned by the Government in September 2006 on the grounds that it had failed to comply with media regulations. In September 2008 the High Court of Singapore ruled that the *Review* had defamed the country's leaders.

The application of the death penalty also continued to be a contentious issue after the execution of two convicted drugs-smugglers, one from Nigeria and the other from South Africa, in January 2007. The case drew international condemnation from various governments and human rights organizations, while Philip Alston, the UN Special Rapporteur on extra-judicial, summary or arbitrary executions, described it as failing to meet international legal standards for criminal prosecution.

In April 2007 it was revealed that cabinet ministers were to receive a salary increase of 60%, to be implemented by 2008. While the decision prompted large-scale public opposition, Prime Minister Lee argued that the increase was well deserved and a necessary precaution against corruption. (Lee himself was to donate his extra salary to various good causes.) Chee Soon Juan criticized the pay rises at an unauthorized forum on democracy in Asia and Europe organized by the SDP. Several members of the European Parliament, as well as two legislators from Cambodia and the Philippines, were denied permission to address the forum by the Singaporean authorities on the grounds that their contributions would constitute interference in Singaporean domestic politics and would not be in the public interest. In September the bankrupt Chee served a three-week prison sentence after failing to pay a fine for attempting to leave Singapore without permission in April 2006. Chee was arrested again in October 2007, together with three other members of the SDP, as they attempted to stage a protest outside the presidential palace in support of their demands for the full disclosure of investments by Singaporean state-controlled companies in Myanmar, following the recent violent suppression of anti-Government marches in that country. In March 2008 Chee was among 18 activists arrested and charged with unlawful assembly, after taking part in an unauthorized demonstration in protest over the rising cost of living in Singapore. His trial, one of seven Chee awaited over the coming months, began in late October. In January 2009 Chee posted a recorded plea to the new US President, Barack Obama, on the video sharing website YouTube, in which he expressed the hope that Obama would 'pay more attention to the human rights abuses of the Singapore Government' and of governments elsewhere in Asia.

In December 2007 the Minister for Education, Tharman Shanmugaratnam, a former Managing Director of the MAS, assumed additional responsibility for the finance portfolio, which had hitherto been held by Prime Minister Lee. In a cabinet reorganization announced in late March 2008, Tharman was retained as Minister for Finance, but relinquished the education portfolio to Ng Eng Hen, who was replaced as Minister of Manpower in an acting capacity by Gan Kim Yong. From May K. Shanmugam, a senior lawyer, was to succeed Shanmugam Jayakumar as Minister of Law, while also being appointed Second Minister for Home Affairs. Jayakumar remained as Deputy Prime Minister and Co-ordinating Minister for National Security.

In April 2008 veteran opposition leader J. B. Jeyaretnam established the Reform Party, urging a restructuring of the electoral system and stating his intention to bring an end to the 'enslavement' of Singapore after nearly 50 years of rule by the PAP. Shortly after the formation of his party, however, at the end of September Jeyaretnam died of heart failure. The activist's son, Kenneth Jeyaretnam, subsequently assumed the leadership of the Reform Party.

In March 2009 Prime Minister Lee announced several changes to the Cabinet. Shanmugan Jayakumar relinquished his role as Deputy Prime Minister, while retaining his position as Co-ordinating Minister for National Security. Gan Kim Yong, who had served as acting Minister of Manpower, was confirmed in that post. Lui Tuck Yew was appointed as Minister for Information, Communications and the Arts in an acting capacity, replacing Dr Lee Boon Yang who retired from the Government. The Minister for Defence, Tee Chee Hean, was promoted to the rank of Deputy Prime Minister, retaining the defence portfolio.

In April 2009 Parliament approved a new Public Order Act, imposing further restrictions on the right to peaceful assembly and enhancing the powers of the police. The Government claimed that the increasing threat from international terrorist activity had necessitated the enactment of the new legislation, particularly in view of the forthcoming summit meeting of Asia-Pacific Economic Co-operation (APEC, see p. 185), which was scheduled to be convened in Singapore in November. Amnesty International urged the Singaporean Government to amend the law in order to meet global standards of human rights and to comply with Article 14 of the Singaporean Constitution, which provided for freedom of speech and expression.

Singapore's foreign policy has been dominated by its membership of the regional grouping, ASEAN (which comprised all 10 South-East Asian nations by mid-1999), although it has also maintained strong political and military links with more distant allies, including the USA. In November 2000 the fourth informal summit meeting of the ASEAN + 3 group of leaders was convened in Singapore. The summit comprised the leaders of all 10 ASEAN members, as well as those of the People's Republic of China, Japan and the Republic of Korea. An outcome of the meeting was the commissioning of an East Asia Study Group to report on the feasibility of a larger East Asia political and economic grouping and free trade area. However, despite ASEAN's ongoing attempts to curb alleged human rights abuses by the Myanma Government, Singapore continued its support of the military regime in April 2007 when Minister for Foreign Affairs, George Yeo, visited the new administrative capital, Pyinmana (Nay Pyi Taw). This followed the revelation that several Singaporean firms had recently signed contracts to search for natural gas in Myanma waters, a decision seen as greatly reducing the impact of Western sanctions. Singapore hosted the 13th ASEAN summit and related meetings in November, having assumed the chairmanship of the Association for one year in August. The summit meeting was overshadowed to some extent by concerns regarding the violence used to quell anti-Government protests in Myanmar in September. Singapore had invited the UN envoy to Myanmar, Ibrahim Gambari, to address the meeting, but the Myanma Government, with the support of several other member states, succeeded in forcing the cancellation of his briefing. Achievements of the summit meeting included the adoption of a Declaration on Environmental Sustainability, which contained commitments related to environmental protection and management, climate change, and the conservation of natural resources; the approval of plans for the establishment of an Asian Economic Community by 2015; and the signature of an ASEAN Charter codifying the principles and purposes of the Association. In December Singapore became the first country to ratify the new Charter.

Singapore's relations with Indonesia improved in the late 1980s: the process of establishing joint military training facilities with Indonesia, which had begun in 1986, was accomplished in February and March 1989 by the signing of two agreements. In January 1995 the two countries launched a bilateral Defence Forum and signed a Defence Co-operation Pact. In June 1996 Singapore and Indonesia jointly opened the Bintan tourist resort in the Riau Islands. Following the resignation of President Suharto in May 1998, relations deteriorated, in part owing to Lee's criticism of the new President, Prof. Dr Ir B. J. Habibie. In February 1999 Habibie accused Singapore of racism for allegedly discriminating against its Malay minority. However, the principal issue was Singapore's refusal to meet Indonesia's high expectations of aid in response to the regional economic crisis. In March the Singaporean Minister for Foreign Affairs, Shanmugam Jayakumar, eased tensions in relations between Singapore and Indonesia by declaring in Parliament that Singapore had a vested interest in the economic and political stability of the Indonesian archipelago and pledging the Singaporean Government's intention to co-operate with the Indonesian administration. Relations improved temporarily following Habibie's replacement as President by Abdurrahman Wahid in October 1999. In November 2000, however, Wahid jeopardized the relationship by accusing Singapore of discriminating against Malays, after Singapore rejected certain motions proposed by its neighbour at the ASEAN summit. Nevertheless, Singapore subsequently concluded an agreement with Indonesia to supply the city-state with natural gas for the next 22 years. In February 2002 bilateral relations deteriorated once more following the publication of an article in *The Straits Times* in which Lee Kwan Yew remarked that Singapore's national security was being compromised by the fact that terrorists remained at large in Indonesia. In response, the Indonesian Government summoned the Singaporean envoy to Jakarta and lodged an objection to the accusations, claiming that they were provocative and unsubstantiated. Meanwhile, Indonesian Islamic groups held protests outside Singapore's embassy in Jakarta. In March 2002 Abu Bakar Bashir, an Indonesian cleric accused of being linked to the international terrorist al-Qa'ida (Base) network, issued a writ of defamation against Lee in relation to his comments. In February 2006 the Indonesian authorities agreed to the deportation to Singapore of Mas Selamat Kastari, the alleged leader of the Singaporean branch of JI, following his rearrest in Indonesia on suspicion of immigration offences. Kastari, first arrested in Indonesia in 2003, also on charges of suspected illegal immigration, had been the subject of several previous extradition requests from Singapore, which accused Kastari of a central role in an alleged plot, thwarted in late 2001, to crash a hijacked aeroplane into Changi International Airport. The Indonesian Government had rejected those requests, on the grounds that Indonesia and Singapore had no formal extradition treaty; it was unclear why Indonesia subsequently chose to reverse its decision. In February 2008 Kastari escaped from a detention centre in Singapore, where he was being held under the Internal Security Act. Of considerable embarrassment to the Singaporean authorities, Kastari's escape prompted an increase in border security, amid fears that he would attempt to enter Indonesia or Malaysia. In May 2009 Kastari was reportedly reapprehended in Malaysia. Earlier in that year the Singapore Government announced that it had released two suspected JI members, stating that they no longer posed a security threat.

Meanwhile, fires resulting from uncontrolled 'slash and burn' land-clearing practices in Indonesia caused a prolonged haze in late 2006, affecting Singapore and other countries in the region. Singapore was reported to have suffered US $50m. in economic losses. Relations between the two nations came under further pressure in February 2007 after Indonesia imposed an outright ban on all sand exports to Singapore. Owing to the latter's land reclamation projects, as well as its burgeoning construction industry, large amounts of sand from Indonesia had been exported in deals worth millions of dollars. The Indonesian Government took the decision after independent environmental experts highlighted the extensive damage caused to the environment by sand exports. (Singapore had been importing sand from Indonesia after Malaysia banned all exports in 1997.) Myanmar later offered to be Singapore's long-term supplier of sand, cement, granite and other construction materials. It was hoped that relations between Singapore and Indonesia would improve following the signature of an extradition treaty and a new agreement on defence co-operation in April 2007. There had been speculation that Indonesia's recent ban on sand exports to Singapore had been introduced in protest at delays in the conclusion of the extradition treaty. However, differences emerged in May, when Indonesia sought amendments to the defence accord regarding arrangements for Singaporean troops to use Indonesian military training facilities. With Singapore refusing to consider any revisions, the ratification of both the defence and extradition agreements remained indefinitely suspended in early 2008. After nearly four years of negotiations, in February 2009 the Governments of Singapore and Indonesia signed a maritime boundary agreement that redrew the border between the Singaporean island of Sultan Shoal and Pulau Nipah in Indonesia. Both Governments expressed their belief that the new, more clearly defined boundary would assist the economic development of border islands and increase Singapore's border security.

In September 1994 Singapore and Malaysia agreed to settle their long-standing dispute over the ownership of Pedra Branca Island (Batu Putih) by referring the case to the International Court of Justice (ICJ) in The Hague, the Netherlands. An agreement on the referral was finally signed in early 2003. The ICJ began deliberating its judgment in November 2007, following the conclusion of public hearings on the case. In May 2008 the ICJ ruled in favour of Singapore, by 12 votes to four. In August 1995 Singapore and Malaysia agreed on the permanent boundary of their territorial waters following 15 years of negotiations. In March 1997 Lee Kuan Yew provoked tension between the two countries by making disparaging comments about security in the Malaysian state of Johor. Lee subsequently made an apology to Malaysia, which was accepted. In April 1999 Singapore and Malaysia undertook joint defence exercises within the context of the regional Five-Power Defence Arrangements; Malaysia had withdrawn from similar exercises in 1998, citing tensions between the two countries as well as economic difficulties.

In February 1998 Goh made an official visit to Malaysia. In the latter half of 1998, however, relations between the two countries deteriorated as a result of conflict over a number of issues. In early August the Malaysian Prime Minister condemned Singapore for requesting that Malaysia transfer its customs, immigration and quarantine facilities from Tanjung Pagar, a railway station in central Singapore situated on land owned by the Malaysian Government; Malaysia subsequently decided to continue using its facilities at Tanjung Pagar, while Singapore moved its customs office to a new location. In September Malaysia announced its decision to insist on prior clearance for Singaporean military aircraft wishing to enter its airspace; combined operations and exercises between the two countries' air forces were also terminated. In the same month the publication of the memoirs of Lee Kuan Yew, which referred to the events surrounding the secession of Singapore from the Federation of Malaysia, exacerbated tensions in bilateral relations. An improvement in relations between the two countries was perceived in November, when Goh visited Malaysia at the invitation of Malaysian Prime Minister Mahathir. However, Lee Kuan Yew further angered Malaysian politicians in August 2000, when he publicly criticized Mahathir over his handling of the dismissal and detention of Malaysia's former Deputy Prime Minister, Anwar Ibrahim.

In September 2001 Lee Kuan Yew visited Malaysia and held talks with Mahathir to address the outstanding issues affecting the relationship between the two countries. A framework agreement was subsequently signed under which Malaysia agreed to relocate its facilities at Tanjung Pagar in return for Singapore's agreement to construct a railway tunnel under the strait. Lee also reported that the two countries would work together to construct a suspension bridge, which would enable the demolition of the causeway linking the two countries. However, in January 2002 the Malaysian Government denied the existence of such an agreement and proposed that Malaysia should build a suspension bridge and a railway swing bridge to replace its half of the road link, enabling the Malaysian half of the causeway to be demolished without Singapore's co-operation. Tension was also promoted by the ongoing renegotiation of the terms upon which Malaysia would continue to supply water to Singapore (based upon an agreement originally concluded in 1961 and due to expire in 2061). While an agreement had provisionally been reached in September 2001, the Malaysian Government was dissatisfied with its terms and continued to increase its demands. In March 2002 relations were further strained when Malaysia claimed that reclamation work being carried out by Singapore in the Tebrau Straits was too close to its border and was obstructing ships sailing into ports in Johor. Malaysia later applied to the International Tribunal for the Law of the Sea (see p. 336) for a suspension of the reclamation work. The issue was among those discussed when Deputy Prime Minister Lee Hsien Loong visited Malaysia in the same month. In July the two countries held talks in an attempt to find a solution to the ongoing water supply problem; further negotiations over the issue also took place in September and October of that year. While the Government wished to link resolution of the matter to other issues it considered to be a cause of tension in the bilateral relationship, Malaysia threatened to take Singapore to an international court of arbitration to seek a solution. In February 2003 Mahathir pledged that his country would continue to supply water to Singapore indefinitely. However, he stated that Malaysia would cease its provision of untreated water to the city-state upon the termination of an existing agreement in 2011 and provide filtered water instead, at what it considered to be a reasonable price. Singapore continued to insist that any proposed price was too high and that it received too little for the treated water that it supplied to Malaysia in return.

In October 2003 the International Tribunal for the Law of the Sea ruled that the land reclamation work being carried out by Singapore in the Tebrau Straits was in accordance with international law and could, therefore, proceed. The long-running dispute was ostensibly resolved in January 2005 when the respective Governments of Singapore and Malaysia issued a joint statement declaring their agreement that the Tebrau Straits constituted a shared body of water and that the two countries had 'a common interest in co-operating to protect the environment, including the monitoring of water quality'.

Meanwhile, following the accession of Abdullah Ahmad Badawi to the Malaysian premiership in October 2003, it was hoped that Singapore's relations with Malaysia would improve. In January 2004 Abdullah Badawi visited Singapore and held talks with Prime Minister Goh in an attempt to ease the tensions between the two countries. Moreover, the transfer of the premiership to Lee augured well for bilateral relations; in his first National Day Rally speech, in August 2004, the incoming Prime Minister stressed his deep commitment to working in close unison with Abdullah Badawi, whom he had known for many years, in order to consolidate Singapore's links with Malaysia. Discussions aimed at strengthening relations between the two countries were resumed in March 2005. In mid-2005 Abdullah announced the abandonment of his predecessor's plans for the construction of a replacement causeway linking Singapore and Malaysia. It was hoped that this decision would dissipate bilateral tensions. Further negotiations were held in September. However, in January 2006 Malaysia unexpectedly announced that it was to commence construction of its section of the new bridge, also referred to as the 'scenic bridge', in the hope that Singapore would agree in due course to the construction of its part. Construction of the Malaysian section of the bridge began in March, but was halted by Abdullah in the following month; the Malaysian Prime Minister announced that all negotiations with Singapore pertaining to the bridge were also to be abandoned. Prime Minister Lee Hsien Loong visited Malaysia in May 2007 for two days of informal talks with Abdullah Badawi. The main outcome of the discussions was a decision to form a joint ministerial committee to oversee collaboration on Malaysia's plan to establish a 2,217-sq-km economic development zone in its southern state of Johor, to be known as the Iskandar Development Region, with both leaders agreeing that outstanding issues of dispute, such as water sales to Singapore and the suspended construction of the bridge, should not be allowed to impede bilateral co-operation in other areas.

In November 1990 representatives of the Governments of the USA and Singapore signed an agreement providing the US navy and air force with increased access to existing bases in Singapore following the planned US withdrawal from military installations in the Philippines. In January 1992 the two countries reached an agreement, in principle, on the relocation of a naval logistic command headquarters from Subic Bay, in the Philippines. However, relations with the USA were occasionally strained by attacks on the authoritarian style of government in Singapore by the liberal US media. Following the attacks on the USA in September 2001 (see the chapter on the USA), Singapore affirmed its support for the US-led alliance against terrorism.

Following the 2001 terrorist attacks in the USA, a number of suspects with alleged links to al-Qa'ida and its regional affiliates Abu Sayyaf and JI were arrested in Singapore under the Internal Security Act; among those detained were two Singaporean nationals in 2003. Alleged members of the Moro Islamic Liberation Front (MILF) were also detained in November 2005 under the Internal Security Act. In the same month the Government announced that it had detained for a two-year period Mohammad Sharif Rahmat, an alleged member of JI. While JI's network seemed to have been severely damaged by the arrests, leading members of both groups remained at large in the region. In order to address the ensuing national security concerns, the Government announced the establishment of a national security secretariat, within the Ministry of Defence, intended to strengthen co-ordination between the security services of Singapore and the USA. In October 2007 Singapore's Parliament approved counter-terrorism legislation designed to give effect to the International Convention for the Suppression of Terrorist Bombings (adopted by the UN General Assembly in 1997). The new law provided for the extradition of those suspected of perpetrating terrorist bombings, even in the absence of an extradition treaty between Singapore and the other country, and gave Singapore the power to prosecute foreign nationals accused of committing terrorist offences within its territory.

In March 2003 the Government announced its support for the US-led military campaign to oust the regime of Saddam Hussain in Iraq. Security measures within Singapore were strengthened subsequently, as the conflict was perceived to have raised the level of the terrorist threat to the country. In an apparent display of approval for Singapore's firm stance on terrorism, the US Government dispatched Secretary of Homeland Security Tom Ridge to Singapore's National Day reception held in Washington, DC, in August 2004. It was the first time that a US official of cabinet rank had attended this annual event during the nine-year tenure of Singapore's ambassador to the USA, Chan Heng Chee.

In October 2004 officials from Bahrain, Bangladesh, Egypt, Jordan, Kuwait, Malaysia, Singapore and Thailand convened in Singapore and agreed to hold the inaugural Asia-Middle East Dialogue (AMED) in mid-2005. This diplomatic initiative had been instigated by former Prime Minister Goh owing to concern that terrorism was being equated with Islam and also out of respect for Middle Eastern states' general suspicion of dialogues initiated by the USA or Europe. It was to focus on improving political, economic and business links between the two regions, as well as on promoting a greater level of mutual cultural understanding. The meeting was held in Singapore in June and was attended by representatives of approximately 50 Asian and Middle Eastern states. It was agreed that AMED would convene on a biennial basis, at venues alternating between Asia and the Middle East. In January 2008 Singapore concluded negotiations with the Gulf Co-operation Council (comprising Bahrain, Kuwait, Oman, Qatar, Saudi Arabia and the United Arab Emirates) on its second free trade agreement in the Middle East, the first having been signed with Jordan in May 2004.

Despite the establishment of important economic links during the 1980s, Singapore's relations with the People's Republic of China were adversely affected by the perceived threat of Chinese domination, owing to the preponderance of ethnic Chinese in Singapore (76.8% in 2000). Relations were also strained by Singapore's close military and economic links with Taiwan. In October 1990, however, Singapore and the People's Republic of China established diplomatic relations at ambassadorial level. This development was prompted mainly by the resumption of diplomatic relations between the People's Republic of China and Indonesia, and followed a visit by the Chinese Premier, Li Peng, to Singapore in August. Nevertheless, Prime Minister Goh made his first official visit to Taiwan in October 1993. In October 1996 Singapore and Australia issued a joint communiqué urging the integration of the People's Republic of China into the Asian regional security structure, and reaffirming their commitment to a co-operative dialogue with the People's Republic. However, a private visit to Singapore in January 1998 by the Taiwanese Vice-President, Lien Chan, during which he met with Goh and with Singaporean cabinet ministers, provoked the disapproval of the People's Republic. Relations improved in November 1998 when Goh made an official visit to the People's Republic, and in November 1999 the Chinese Premier, Zhu Rongji, made a reciprocal visit to Singapore. However, further visits to Taiwan, by Lee Kuan Yew in September 2000 and September 2002, and by Lee Hsien Loong in July 2004 shortly before he assumed the premiership, caused further damage to bilateral relations. The diplomatic furore caused by Lee's visit in 2004 served to delay the start of negotiations concerning a free trade pact between the People's Republic and Singapore, which had been due to commence in November 2004, despite Lee's insistence that his visit in no way weakened his country's commitment to the 'One China' policy that denied recognition of Taiwan. The Chinese Prime Minister, Wen Jiabao, and Lee consequently agreed to commence free trade talks as planned, but they withheld from offering any indication as to when negotiations might begin. In October 2005, at a meeting in Beijing of Singaporean and Chinese delegates, led by Lee Hsien Loong and Wen Jiabao, both countries affirmed their commitment to accelerating the holding of free trade negotiations. The two countries also agreed to work together to address the regional threats of terrorism and piracy in the Straits of Melaka (Malacca). China and Singapore held their first round of free trade talks in October 2006; several further sessions took place in 2007, and final negotiations in October 2008 resulted in the signing of a free trade agreement that entered into force in January 2009.

Government

Legislative power is vested in the unicameral Parliament, with 84 members who are elected by universal adult suffrage for five years (subject to dissolution—within three months of which a general election must be held) in single-member and multi-member constituencies. As many as three additional 'non-constituency' seats may be offered to opposition parties, and up to nine non-elected, neutral MPs may be nominated: all have restricted voting rights. The President is directly elected by universal adult suffrage for a six-year term as a constitutional Head of State, vested with limited powers of veto in financial matters, public appointments and detentions for reasons of national security. Effective executive authority rests with the Cabinet, led by the Prime Minister, which is appointed by the President and responsible to Parliament.

Defence

As assessed at November 2008, the Singapore armed forces had an estimated total active strength of 72,500 troops (including 35,000 conscripts): 50,000 in the army, an estimated 9,000 in the navy and 13,500 in the air force. The length of compulsory military service was 24 months. Paramilitary forces comprised a civil defence force (numbering an estimated 81,800) and a police force (numbering an estimated 8,500). Singapore is a participant in the Five-Power Defence Arrangements (with Australia, Malaysia, New Zealand and the United Kingdom). In 2008 the Government budgeted S $10,800m. for defence.

Economic Affairs

In 2007, according to estimates by the World Bank, Singapore's gross national income (GNI), measured at average 2005–07 prices, was US $148,992m., equivalent to US $32,470 per head (or US $48,520 per head on an international purchasing-power parity basis). During 2000–07, it was estimated, the population increased at an average annual rate of 1.9%, while gross domestic product (GDP) per head increased, in real terms, at an average rate of 3.3% per year. Overall GDP increased, in real terms, at an average annual rate of 6.2% in 2000–07. According to official figures, GDP expanded by 7.8% in 2007 and by an estimated 1.1% in 2008.

Agriculture (including fishing and quarrying—mainly of granite) contributed was estimated to have contributed less than 0.1% of GDP in 2008 and, including utilities, engaged only 0.7% of the employed labour force in 2007. Vegetables, plants and orchid flowers are the principal crops. According to figures from the World Bank, agricultural GDP (again including fishing and quarrying) declined at an average annual rate of 2.0% during 2000–07. According to official figures, agricultural GDP (including fishing and quarrying) contracted by 3.0% in 2007 and by an estimated 4.0% in 2008.

Industry (including manufacturing, construction and utilities) contributed an estimated 26.0% of GDP in 2008, and, excluding utilities, engaged 31.2% of the employed labour force in 2007. During 2000–07, according to figures from the World Bank, industrial GDP increased at an average annual rate of 4.5%. According to official figures, the GDP of the sector expanded by 7.2% in 2007 but declined by an estimated 1.0% in 2008.

Manufacturing contributed an estimated 19.4% of GDP in 2008 and engaged 20.8% of the employed labour force in 2007. The principal branches of manufacturing in 2008 (measured in terms of the value of output) were electronic products and components (which accounted for an estimated 26.3% of total manufacturing production), biomedical and pharmaceutical products, transport engineering (especially ship-building), chemicals and chemical products, and precision engineering. According to figures from the World Bank, manufacturing GDP increased at an average annual rate of 5.5% in 2000–07. According to official figures, manufacturing GDP increased by 5.9% in 2007. However, a sharp decline in foreign demand for Singaporean goods (notably electronics and pharmaceuticals), concomitant with the onset of global recession, resulted in 2008 in a contraction of manufacturing GDP, which was provisionally estimated at 4.1% in real terms.

Singapore relies on imports of hydrocarbons to fuel its three thermal power stations. In 2005 natural gas accounted for 74.4% of the total amount of electrical energy produced; petroleum accounted for 25.6%. In 2008 imports of crude petroleum accounted for 11.4% of merchandise imports.

The services sector contributed an estimated 74.0% of GDP in 2008, and engaged 68.1% of the employed labour force in 2007. Financial and business services provided an estimated 27.1% of GDP in 2008, and in 2007 engaged 12.8% of the employed labour force. The GDP of the financial services sector increased by 15.7% in 2007 and by an estimated 5.5% in 2008. Singapore is a major regional foreign-exchange dealing centre. Banking is an important sector, with a total of 113 commercial banks (of which 107 were foreign) and 44 representative offices in operation in May 2008. Tourism is a significant source of foreign exchange, and receipts from tourism amounted to approximately US $7,069m. in 2006. However, the number of tourist arrivals declined from 10.3m. in 2007 to 10.1m. in 2008. Singapore is the world's busiest port in tonnage terms and has one of the largest merchant shipping registers in the world. According to figures from the World Bank, the GDP of the services sector increased at an average annual rate of 5.7% in 2000–07. According to official figures, the sector expanded by 7.7% in 2007 and by an estimated 4.5% in 2008.

In 2008 Singapore recorded a visible trade surplus of an estimated US $43,470m., and there was a surplus of US $38,177m. on the current account of the balance of payments. In 2008 the principal sources of imports were Malaysia (11.9%), the USA (11.7%) and the People's Republic of China (10.6%); other major suppliers were Japan and the Republic of Korea. Malaysia (12.1%), Hong Kong (10.4%) and China (9.2%) were the principal markets for exports in that year; other major purchasers were the USA and Japan. Principal imports in 2008 included machinery and equipment (notably electronic components and parts), mineral fuels, basic manufactures, miscellaneous manufactured articles and chemicals. Principal exports included machinery and equipment (notably electronic components and parts), mineral fuels (notably petroleum products), chemicals and miscellaneous manufactured articles. Singapore is an important entrepôt, and re-exports accounted for 48.1% of total exports in 2008.

The 2008/09 budget recorded an operating surplus of S $3,907m., equivalent to around 1.5% of GDP. A significant deficit (projected at 3.5% of GDP) was forecast for 2009/10, owing to the increased expenditure required to implement a counter-recessionary programme of fiscal stimulus (see below). According to the ADB, at the end of 2008 Singapore's external debt totalled US $427,715m. The annual rate of inflation averaged 0.9% in 2000–07; consumer prices increased by 6.6% in 2008. The rate of unemployment reached 2.8% of the labour force in 2008.

Singapore is a member of the World Trade Organization (WTO, see p. 410), the UN Economic and Social Commission for Asia and the Pacific (ESCAP, see p. 36), the Asian Development Bank (ADB, see p. 191), the Association of South East Asian Nations (ASEAN, see p. 194), Asia-Pacific Economic Co-operation (APEC, see p. 185) and the Colombo Plan (see p. 425). As a member of ASEAN, Singapore signed an accord in January 1992 pledging the creation of a free trade zone to be known as the ASEAN Free Trade Area (AFTA). A reduction of tariffs to between 0% and 5% was originally envisaged to be completed by 2008 but this was subsequently advanced to 2002, when AFTA was formally implemented. However, Malaysia applied for an extension of this date for its automotive industry, fearing direct competition. Target dates for the removal of all tariffs were brought forward from 2015 to 2010 in November 1999.

Singapore's post-independence economic success was based largely on its efficient planning, advanced infrastructure and highly skilled work-force. The country consolidated its position as a financial and trading centre through various reforms. However, by the early 21st century there was some concern with regard to the increasing disparities in income levels, as the real wages of less-skilled Singaporeans were failing to keep pace with those of the better-educated. While efforts to diversify economic activities have provided for strong growth in areas such as biomedical manufacturing and financial services, these initiatives have increased dependency on foreign demand. Despite the negotiation of various free trade agreements (including an accord with China—see Recent History), Singapore's high degree of vulnerability to variations in export demand was highlighted from mid-2008 when adverse conditions emanating from the international banking crisis in September precipitated a sharp deterioration in Singapore's economic performance. The economy entered recession in the third quarter of 2008, when the second consecutive quarterly contraction in GDP was recorded. Non-oil domestic exports declined for the 11th consecutive month in March 2009, by 11%. In March 2009 the Prime Minister warned that Singapore confronted its worst economic crisis since the Second World War. In comparison with the corresponding quarter of the previous year, GDP contracted by 11.5% in the first three months of 2009. The revelation of this unprecedented contraction obliged the Government substantially to revise its forecast for the coming year: official sources projected that the economy would contract by between 6% and 9% in 2009 as a whole. In early 2009 the Government announced a fiscal stimulus plan, which envisaged expenditure of about S $20,500m. The programme provided incentives for businesses and allowed for working capital grants of up to S $5m. to small and medium-sized firms. In an effort to bolster exports, the Monetary Authority of Singapore (MAS) effected a currency devaluation in April, although some analysts feared that this measure would further discourage inflows of foreign investment. Foreign direct investment was reported to have decreased from US $31,550m. in 2007 to US $22,726m. in 2008.

Education

Primary and secondary education is available in the four official languages of Malay, Chinese, Tamil and English. In 1978, as part of a policy of bilingualism, examinations in English and Mandarin Chinese became compulsory for pupils seeking to enter secondary education. In 1987 English became the medium of instruction in all schools. In 2003 the Government introduced a six-year period of compulsory education, covering the whole duration of primary education, which begins at six years of age. In 2004/05 enrolment at primary education was equivalent to 78% of children in the relevant age-group (males 78%; females 78%). Secondary education lasts for four or five years from the age of 12. In 2004/05 enrolment at secondary education was equivalent to 63% of children in the relevant age-group (males 62%, females 64%). Post-secondary education lasts for two or three years and provides pre-university instruction. Outside the school system there are several higher education centres and vocational institutes, providing craft and industrial training, and technical institutes providing advanced craft training. In 2004 57.8% of resident non-students aged 15 years and over held secondary or higher qualifications. According to UNESCO, in 1996 total enrolment in tertiary-level education was equivalent to 38.5% of those in the relevant age-group (males 41.5%; females 35.3%). At June 2007 a total of 65,746 students were enrolled at Singapore's four universities. A total of 72,379 students were enrolled at the country's five polytechnics in June 2007. Adult education courses are conducted by a statutory board. Operating expenditure on education by the central Government in 2008 was budgeted at S $7.298m. (19.5% of total spending).

Public Holidays

2009: 1 January (New Year's Day), 26–27 January (Chinese New Year), 10 April (Good Friday), 1 May (Labour Day), 2 May (Vesak Day), 9 August (National Day), 20 September* (Hari Raya Puasa, end of Ramadan), 17 October (Deepavali), 27 November* (Hari Raya Haji, Feast of the Sacrifice), 25 December (Christmas Day).

2010: 1 January (New Year's Day), 14–16 February (Chinese New Year), 2 April (Good Friday), 28 April (Vesak Day), 1 May (Labour Day), 9 August (National Day), 10 September* (Hari Raya Puasa, end of Ramadan), 5 November (Deepavali), 16 November* (Hari Raya Haji, Feast of the Sacrifice), 25 December (Christmas Day).

* These holidays are dependent on the Islamic lunar calendar and may vary by one or two days from the dates given.

Weights and Measures

The metric system is in force, but local units are also used.

SINGAPORE

Statistical Survey

Source (unless otherwise stated): Department of Statistics, 100 High St, 05-01 The Treasury, Singapore 179434; tel. 63327686; fax 63327689; e-mail info@singstat.gov.sg; internet www.singstat.gov.sg.

Area and Population

AREA, POPULATION AND DENSITY

Area (sq km)	707.1*
Population (census results)†	
30 June 1990	3,047,132‡
30 June 2000	
Males	2,061,800§
Females	1,955,900§
Total	4,017,733
Population (official estimates at mid-year)§	
2006	4,401,400
2007	4,588,600
2008	4,839,400
Density (per sq km) at mid-2008	6,844.0

* 273.0 sq miles.
† Includes non-residents, totalling 311,264 in 1990 and 754,524 in 2000.
‡ Includes resident population temporarily residing overseas.
§ Rounded figure(s).

ETHNIC GROUPS
(at 30 June 2008, '000 persons)*

	Males	Females	Total
Chinese	1,339.6	1,382.2	2,721.8
Malays	247.0	248.1	495.1
Indians	167.1	156.3	323.4
Others	49.2	53.1	102.3
Total	1,803.0	1,839.7	3,642.7

* Figures refer to the resident population of Singapore only.

BIRTHS, MARRIAGES AND DEATHS*

	Registered live births		Registered marriages		Registered deaths	
	Number	Rate (per 1,000)	Number	Rate (per 1,000)	Number	Rate (per 1,000)
2002	40,760	11.4	23,198	5.6	15,820	4.4
2003	37,485	10.5	21,962	5.2	16,036	4.5
2004	37,174	10.3	22,189	5.2	15,860	4.4
2005	37,492	10.2	22,992	5.3	16,215	4.4
2006	38,317	10.3	23,706	n.a.	16,393	4.4
2007	39,490	10.3	23,966	n.a.	17,140	4.5
2008	39,935	n.a.	24,596	n.a.	17,127	n.a.

* Data are tabulated by year of registration, rather than by year of occurrence.

Life expectancy (years at birth, WHO estimates): 80.5 (males 78.1; females 82.9) in 2006 (Source: WHO, *World Health Statistics*).

Employment
('000 persons aged 15 years and over, at June of each year)

	2005	2006	2007
Agriculture, fishing, mining and quarrying, utilities, sewage and waste management	19.8	15.7	17.3
Manufacturing	485.1	495.3	543.5
Construction	184.4	244.2	271.9
Wholesale and retail trade; repair of motor vehicles, motorcycles and personal and household goods	350.6	353.0	373.7
Hotels and restaurants	124.2	135.8	152.2
Transport and storage	185.8	176.2	181.7
Information and communications	74.3	69.6	76.4
Financial intermediation	111.2	121.3	136.8
Real estate, renting and business activities	246.4	171.6	196.9
Public administration and defence; compulsory social security		107.3	119.3
Community, social and personal service activities; private households with employed persons and extra-territorial organizations and bodies	485.1	511.3	540.0
Total employed	2,266.7	2,401.4	2,609.7

Health and Welfare

KEY INDICATORS

Total fertility rate (children per woman, 2006)	1.3
Under-5 mortality rate (per 1,000 live births, 2006)	3
HIV/AIDS (% of persons aged 15–49, 2007)	0.2
Physicians (per 1,000 head, 2004)	1.5
Hospital beds (per 1,000 head, 2006)	3.2
Health expenditure (2006): US $ per head (PPP)	1,228
Health expenditure (2006): % of GDP	3.4
Health expenditure (2006): public (% of total)	33.6
Human Development Index (2006): ranking	28
Human Development Index (2006): value	0.918

For sources and definitions, see explanatory note on p. vi.

Agriculture

PRINCIPAL CROPS
('000 metric tons)

	2005	2006	2007
Groundnut oil*	1,122	3,700	3,700
Sesame oil*	2,418	2,300	2,300
Soybean oil*	3,425	3,600	3,600
Cabbages and other brassicas	465	533	610*
Spinach	1,722	1,704	1,700*

* FAO estimate(s).

Total vegetables (incl. melons, '000 metric tons, may include official, semi-official or estimated data): 8.4 in 2005, 20.7 in 2006, 20.8 in 2007.

Source: FAO.

SINGAPORE

LIVESTOCK
('000 head, year ending September, FAO estimates)

	2004	2005	2006
Pigs	250	250	260
Chickens	2,900	2,600	2,700
Ducks	600	600	600

2007: Production assumed to be unchanged from 2006 (FAO estimates).
Source: FAO.

LIVESTOCK PRODUCTS
('000 metric tons)

	2005	2006	2007
Pig meat	20.2	15.9	19.0*
Chicken meat*	75.7	76.0	76.3
Hen eggs	20.6	21.3	21.3*

* FAO estimate(s).
Source: FAO.

Forestry

SAWNWOOD PRODUCTION
('000 cubic metres, incl. railway sleepers, FAO estimates)

	1990	1991	1992
Coniferous (softwood)	5	10	5
Broadleaved (hardwood)	50	20	20
Total	55	30	25

1993–2007: Annual production assumed to be unchanged since 1992 (FAO estimates).
Source: FAO.

Fishing

(metric tons, live weight)

	2004	2005	2006
Capture	2,173	1,920	3,103
Prawns and shrimps	245	251	460
Aquaculture	5,406	5,917	8,573
Indonesian snakehead	428	416	303
Milkfish	1,839	1,500	1,183
Green mussel	2,391	2,958	5,891
Total catch	7,579	7,837	11,676

Note: Figures exclude crocodiles, recorded by number rather than by weight. The number of estuarine crocodiles caught was: 1,136 in 2004; 1,330 in 2005; 1,712 in 2006.
Source: FAO.

Industry

PETROLEUM PRODUCTS
('000 metric tons)

	2003	2004	2005
Liquefied petroleum gas	870	872	848
Naphtha	3,284	3,870	4,783
Motor spirit (petrol)	3,350	3,948	4,879
Kerosene	426	501	619
Jet fuel	6,322	6,481	7,610
Gas-diesel (distillate fuel) oils	9,938	11,711	14,474
Residual fuel oil	6,400	7,523	9,798
Lubricating oils	1,575	1,951	2,183
Petroleum bitumen (asphalt)	1,644	1,974	1,975

Source: UN, *Industrial Commodity Statistics Yearbook*.

SELECTED OTHER PRODUCTS

	1988	1989	1990
Paints ('000 litres)	48,103.6	52,746.9	58,245.9
Broken granite ('000 metric tons)	6,914.0	7,007.5	6,371.7
Bricks ('000 units)	103,136	116,906	128,386
Soft drinks ('000 litres)	269,689.4	252,977.6	243,175.1
Plywood, plain and printed ('000 sq m)	31,307.0	28,871.3	26,106.9
Vegetable cooking oil (metric tons)	75,022	103,003	102,854
Animal fodder (metric tons)	110,106	115,341	104,541
Electricity (million kWh)	13,017.5	14,039.0	15,617.6
Gas (million kWh)	681.1	722.4	807.1
Cassette tape recorders ('000 sets)	15,450	14,006	18,059

Source: UN, *Industrial Commodity Statistics Yearbook*.

Plywood ('000 cu m, estimates): 280 per year in 1991–2006 (Source: FAO).

Electric energy (million kWh): 38,213 in 2005; 39,442 in 2006; 41,138 in 2007 (Source: mainly Asian Development Bank, *Key Indicators of Developing Asian and Pacific Countries*).

Finance

CURRENCY AND EXCHANGE RATES

Monetary Units
100 cents = 1 Singapore dollar (S $).

Sterling, US Dollar and Euro Equivalents (31 December 2008)
£1 sterling = S $2.0981;
US $1 = S $1.4392;
€1 = S $2.0029;
S $100 = £47.66 = US $69.48 = €49.93.

Average Exchange Rate (Singapore dollars per US $)
2006   1.5890
2007   1.5071
2008   1.4149

BUDGET
(S $ million)

Revenue*	2006	2007	2008
Tax revenue	28,718	36,061	37,519
Income tax	14,948	16,410	18,559
Corporate and personal income tax	12,925	14,616	16,403
Contributions by statutory board	2,022	1,794	2,156
Assets taxes	2,052	2,432	2,891
Taxes on motor vehicles	1,723	2,101	2,003
Customs and excise duties	1,943	2,034	2,083
Betting taxes	1,548	1,665	1,777
Stamp duty	1,312	4,078	1,838
Goods and services tax	3,960	5,612	6,632
Others	1,232	1,729	1,736
Fees and charges	2,120	3,232	3,726
Total (incl. others)	31,072	39,516	41,377

Expenditure	2006	2007	2008
Operating expenditure	23,463	24,352	28,590
Security and external relations	11,973	11,309	13,588
Social development	9,685	10,996	12,568
Education	5,685	6,567	7,298
Health	1,764	2,016	2,295
Community development and sports	898	833	1,173
Environment and water resources	418	436	560
Economic development	954	1,117	1,436
Trade and industry	459	579	624
Transport	284	284	374
Government administration	852	931	998
Development expenditure	6,412	6,983	8,880
Total	29,875	31,335	37,470

* Figures refer to operating revenue only; the data exclude investment income and capital revenue.

SINGAPORE

Statistical Survey

INTERNATIONAL RESERVES
(US $ million at 31 December)

	2006	2007	2008
Gold and foreign exchange	136,259	162,957	173,649
IMF special drawing rights	316	350	370
Reserve position in the IMF	130	90	174
Total	136,706	163,397	174,193

Source: IMF, *International Financial Statistics*.

MONEY SUPPLY
(S $ million at 31 December)

	2006	2007	2008
Currency outside banks	15,285	16,669	18,997
Demand deposits at commercial banks	36,958	47,270	56,706
Total money	52,243	63,939	75,703

Source: IMF, *International Financial Statistics*.

COST OF LIVING
(Consumer Price Index; base: 2004 = 100)

	2006	2007	2008
Food	102.8	105.9	114.1
Transport and communication	96.4	98.3	101.6
Clothing and footwear	100.6	101.3	102.8
Housing	103.5	103.9	117.1
Education	104.0	105.3	108.9
Health	101.3	105.5	111.5
All items (incl. others)	101.4	103.5	110.3

NATIONAL ACCOUNTS
(S $ million at current prices)

National Income and Product

	2006	2007	2008*
Compensation of employees	91,420.4	103,209.4	115,505.0
Gross operating surplus	113,895.5	125,481.9	119,403.5
Gross domestic product (GDP) at factor cost	205,315.9	228,691.3	234,908.5
Taxes, less subsidies, on production and imports	15,149.7	21,294.8	20,654.0
Statistical discrepancy	677.2	1,624.0	1,856.0
GDP in market prices	221,142.8	251,610.1	257,418.5
Net primary incomes received from abroad	−7,959.7	−17,363.9	−7,030.6
Gross national income (GNI)	213,183.1	234,246.2	250,387.9

* Preliminary figures.

Expenditure on the Gross Domestic Product

	2006	2007	2008*
Government final consumption expenditure	23,449.9	24,450.0	27,525.2
Private final consumption expenditure	87,264.6	97,003.6	105,548.2
Change in inventories	−4,350.7	−8,220.1	6,176.7
Gross fixed capital formation	48,770.5	60,415.2	73,343.0
Statistical discrepancy	−834.5	−1,732.7	−4,271.4
Total domestic expenditure	154,299.8	171,916.0	208,321.7
Trade in goods and services (net)	66,843.0	79,694.1	49,096.8
GDP in market prices	221,142.8	251,610.1	257,418.5
GDP at constant 2000 prices	214,233.5	230,871.4	233,524.5

* Preliminary figures.

Gross Domestic Product by Economic Activity

	2006	2007	2008*
Agriculture, fishing and quarrying	184.6	180.5	177.9
Manufacturing	56,549.3	58,564.3	50,275.2
Electricity, gas and water	3,695.2	3,925.1	3,729.2
Construction	7,595.8	9,242.9	13,255.8
Wholesale and retail trade	39,537.3	43,444.0	44,347.7
Hotels and restaurants	4,316.7	4,900.8	5,433.5
Transport and storage	20,172.9	22,844.8	23,317.5
Information and communications	8,478.4	9,121.2	9,612.7
Financial services	24,796.3	31,117.5	33,789.4
Business services	25,171.6	30,600.1	36,295.6
Owner-occupied dwellings	8,628.7	11,067.6	13,373.7
Other services	21,578.1	23,158.6	25,278.4
Sub-total	220,704.9	248,167.3	258,886.6
Less Financial intermediation services indirectly measured	10,811.8	13,068.0	16,730.1
Gross value added at basic prices	209,893.1	235,099.4	242,156.1
Taxes on products	11,249.7	16,510.7	15,262.4
GDP in market prices	221,142.8	251,610.1	257,418.5

* Preliminary figures.

BALANCE OF PAYMENTS
(US $ million)

	2006	2007	2008*
Exports of goods	436,506.3	457,639.2	485,690.1
Imports of goods	−368,560.2	−386,575.6	−442,219.7
Trade balance	67,946.1	71,063.6	43,470.4
Exports of services	101,835.6	121,484.3	117,546.6
Imports of services	−102,938.7	−112,853.8	−111,920.2
Balance on goods and services	66,843.0	79,694.1	49,096.8
Income (net)	−7,959.7	−17,363.9	−7,030.6
Balance on goods, services and income	58,883.3	62,330.2	42,066.2
Current transfers (net)	−2,661.8	−3,238.2	−3,889.4
Current balance	56,221.5	59,092.0	38,176.8
Capital account (net)	−367.0	−390.5	−435.6
Direct investment (net)	22,852.7	10,688.7	19,520.0
Portfolio investment (net)	−8,297.9	−14,359.7	−32,784.3
Other investments (net)	−49,320.1	−29,855.6	−2,559.5
Net errors and omissions	5,906.5	4,122.7	−3,386.3
Overall balance	26,995.7	29,297.6	18,531.1

* Preliminary figures.

External Trade

PRINCIPAL COMMODITIES
(S $ million)

Imports c.i.f.	2006	2007	2008
Mineral fuels, lubricants, etc.	74,645	83,367	128,792
Chemicals and related products	22,695	23,919	23,723
Basic manufactures	27,933	30,715	35,020
Machinery and equipment	207,372	208,407	210,232
Electronic components and parts	80,812	79,814	75,151
Miscellaneous manufactured articles	27,693	29,239	29,074
Total (incl. others)	378,924	395,980	450,893

SINGAPORE

Exports f.o.b.*	2006	2007	2008
Mineral fuels, lubricants, etc.	70,553	79,724	115,479
Petroleum products	55,736	61,376	87,339
Chemicals and related products	49,070	55,615	48,514
Basic manufactures	18,496	21,890	22,331
Machinery and equipment	249,241	247,655	242,702
Electronic components and parts	109,988	108,153	104,273
Miscellaneous manufactured articles	28,273	29,159	29,885
Total (incl. others)	431,559	450,628	476,762

*Including re-exports (S $ million); 204,181 in 2006; 215,725 in 2007; 229,144 in 2008.

PRINCIPAL TRADING PARTNERS
(S $ million)

Imports c.i.f.	2006	2007	2008
Australia	5,934	4,764	6,459
China, People's Republic	43,194	48,013	47,595
France	8,523	9,300	11,118
Germany	10,794	12,241	13,023
Hong Kong	6,507	5,805	4,909
India	7,755	8,814	11,922
Italy	4,160	4,708	4,873
Japan	31,640	32,423	36,580
Korea, Republic	16,636	19,254	25,335
Kuwait	7,163	7,635	9,222
Malaysia	49,481	51,809	53,814
Netherlands	3,266	4,422	5,819
Philippines	8,967	8,756	6,929
Saudi Arabia	14,767	13,241	20,692
Switzerland	2,920	3,440	3,643
Taiwan	24,207	23,306	23,195
Thailand	13,856	12,797	15,923
United Arab Emirates	6,636	6,910	8,908
United Kingdom	6,819	7,235	6,606
USA	47,474	48,656	52,847
Total (incl. others)	378,924	395,980	450,893

Exports f.o.b.*	2006	2007	2008
Australia	16,182	16,832	19,537
China, People's Republic	42,061	43,549	43,818
France	5,030	6,738	5,846
Germany	10,418	8,951	9,378
Hong Kong	43,335	47,155	49,526
India	12,166	15,046	16,835
Japan	23,590	21,663	23,487
Korea, Republic	13,877	15,960	17,318
Malaysia	56,372	58,100	57,639
Netherlands	8,635	8,626	10,217
Philippines	8,067	9,224	10,265
Taiwan	15,065	13,771	13,411
Thailand	17,945	18,653	18,612
United Arab Emirates	5,048	5,256	5,858
United Kingdom	11,540	12,259	9,284
USA	42,829	39,493	33,452
Viet Nam	8,665	9,803	12,280
Total (incl. others)	431,559	450,628	476,762

*Including re-exports (S $ million); 204,181 in 2006; 215,725 in 2007; 229,144 in 2008.

Transport

ROAD TRAFFIC
(registered vehicles)

	2006	2007	2008
Cars*	474,717	517,041	552,846
Motorcycles and scooters	142,736	144,340	146,120
Motor buses	14,120	14,530	15,327
Taxis	23,334	24,446	24,300
Goods and other vehicles (incl. private)	144,466	150,979	156,089
Total	799,373	851,336	894,682

*Including private, company, tuition and private hire cars.

SHIPPING

Merchant Fleet
(at 31 December)

	2005	2006	2007
Number of vessels	1,977	2,079	2,257
Displacement ('000 grt)	30,989.8	32,173.9	36,251.7

Source: Lloyd's Register-Fairplay, *World Fleet Statistics*.

International Sea-borne Shipping

	2006	2007	2008
Vessels entered	128,922	128,568	131,695
Total cargo ('000 metric tons)	448,504	483,616	515,415

Source: Maritime and Ports Authority of Singapore.

CIVIL AVIATION

	2006	2007	2008
Passengers:			
arrived	16,677,822	17,639,556	18,185,230
departed	16,690,277	17,581,646	18,102,820
in transit	1,664,984	1,480,353	1,406,774
Mail (metric tons):			
landed	8,921	10,801	12,721
dispatched	11,746	12,592	14,234
Freight (metric tons):			
discharged	952,876	963,873	951,939
loaded	958,341	930,896	905,002

Source: partly Civil Aviation Authority of Singapore.

Tourism

FOREIGN VISITOR ARRIVALS
('000, incl. excursionists)

Country of nationality	2006	2007	2008
Australia	691,632	768,490	833,146
China, People's Republic	1,037,201	1,113,956	1,078,637
Germany	161,125	164,900	175,277
Hong Kong	291,474	302,110	278,106
India	658,902	748,728	778,299
Indonesia	1,922,217	1,962,055	1,765,404
Japan	594,406	594,514	571,020
Korea, Republic	454,722	464,292	423,011
Malaysia	634,303	645,774	647,339
Philippines	386,119	418,775	418,920
Taiwan	219,463	208,156	175,920
Thailand	356,367	353,416	333,892
United Kingdom	488,166	495,693	492,928
USA	399,782	408,885	396,618
Total (incl. others)	9,750,952	10,284,550	10,115,640

Tourism receipts (US $ million, excl. passenger transport): 5,226 in 2004; 5,903 in 2005; 7,069 in 2006 (Source: World Tourism Organization).

SINGAPORE

Communications Media

(at 31 December)

	2005	2006	2007
Telephones ('000 main lines in use)	1,844.4	1,853.5	1,859.3
Mobile cellular telephones ('000 subscribers)	4,384.6	4,788.6	5,619.2
Internet users ('000)	2,654.4	2,610.7	3,104.9
Broadband subscribers ('000)	665.6	799.7	881.3

Personal computers ('000 in use): 2,590 in 2004.

Radio receivers ('000 in use): 2,550 in 1997.

Television receivers ('000 in use): 1,200 in 2000.

Facsimile machines ('000 in use, estimate): 100 in 1998.

Daily newspapers: 11 (with average circulation of 1,542,000 copies) in 2004.

Non-daily newspapers: 9 (with average circulation of 1,134,000 copies) in 2004.

Sources: mainly International Telecommunication Union; UNESCO, *Statistical Yearbook*; UNESCO Institute for Statistics; UN, *Statistical Yearbook*.

Education

(June 2007)

	Institutions	Students	Teachers
Primary	170	277,772	12,472
Secondary	154	202,858	10,850
Centralized institutes	13	30,224	2,225
Junior colleges			
Institute of Technical Education	3	23,465	1,408
Polytechnics	5	72,379	4,303
National Institute of Education	1	4,447	536
Universities*	3	65,746	3,582

*Student and teacher numbers are not available for Singapore's fourth university (SIM University) which opened in 2005.

Adult literacy rate (official estimate): 96.0% in 2008.

Directory

The Constitution

A new Constitution came into force on 3 June 1959, with the establishment of the self-governing State of Singapore. This was subsequently amended as a consequence of Singapore's affiliation to Malaysia (September 1963 to August 1965) and as a result of its adoption of republican status on 22 December 1965. The Constitution was also amended in January 1991 to provide for the election of a President by universal adult suffrage, and to extend the responsibilities of the presidency, which had previously been a largely ceremonial office. A constitutional amendment in October 1996 placed restrictions on the presidential right of veto. The main provisions of the Constitution are summarized below:

HEAD OF STATE

The Head of State is the President, elected by universal adult suffrage for a six-year term. He normally acts on the advice of the Cabinet, but is vested with certain functions and powers for the purpose of safeguarding the financial reserves of Singapore and the integrity of the Public Services.

THE CABINET

The Cabinet, headed by the Prime Minister, is appointed by the President and is responsible to Parliament.

THE LEGISLATURE

The Legislature consists of a Parliament of 84 elected members, presided over by a Speaker who may be elected from the members of Parliament themselves or appointed by Parliament although he may not be a member of Parliament. Members of Parliament are elected by universal adult suffrage for five years (subject to dissolution) in single-member and multi-member constituencies.* Additionally, up to three 'non-constituency' seats may be offered to opposition parties, in accordance with a constitutional amendment approved in 1984, while legislation approved in 1990, and amended in 1997, enables the Government to nominate up to nine additional, politically neutral members for a term of two years; these members have restricted voting rights.

A 21-member Presidential Council, chaired by the Chief Justice, examines material of racial or religious significance, including legislation, to see whether it differentiates between racial or religious communities or contains provisions inconsistent with the fundamental liberties of Singapore citizens.

CITIZENSHIP

Under the Constitution, Singapore citizenship may be acquired either by birth, descent or registration. Persons born when Singapore was a constituent State of Malaysia could also acquire Singapore citizenship by enrolment or naturalization under the Constitution of Malaysia.

*A constitutional amendment was introduced in May 1988, whereby 39 constituencies were merged to form 13 'group representation constituencies', which would return 'teams' of three Members of Parliament. At least one member of each team was to be of minority (non-Chinese) racial origin. In January 1991 the Constitution was further amended, stipulating that the number of candidates contesting 'group representation constituencies' should be a minimum of three and a maximum of four. The maximum was increased to six by constitutional amendment in October 1996.

The Government

HEAD OF STATE

President: SELLAPAN RAMANATHAN (S. R.) NATHAN (took office 1 September 1999).

CABINET
(April 2009)

Prime Minister: Brig.-Gen. (retd) LEE HSIEN LOONG.

Senior Minister in the Prime Minister's Office: GOH CHOK TONG.

Minister Mentor: LEE KUAN YEW.

Deputy Prime Minister and Minister for Home Affairs: WONG KAN SENG.

Deputy Prime Minister and Minister for Defence: Rear-Adm. (retd) TEO CHEE HEAN.

Senior Minister and Co-ordinating Minister for National Security: Prof. SHANMUGAM JAYAKUMAR.

Minister for Foreign Affairs: Brig.-Gen. (retd) GEORGE YONG-BOON YEO.

Minister for Finance: THARMAN SHANMUGARATNAM.

Minister for Trade and Industry: LIM HNG KIANG.

Minister for Information, Communications and the Arts: LUI TUCK YEW (acting).

Minister for Education and Second Minister for Defence: Dr NG ENG HEN.

Minister for Manpower: GAN KIM YONG.

Minister for Health: KHAW BOON WAN.

Minister for Transport and Second Minister for Foreign Affairs: RAYMOND LIM SIANG KEAT.

Minister in the Prime Minister's Office, Second Minister for Finance and Transport: LIM HWEE HUA.

Ministers in the Prime Minister's Office: LIM SWEE SAY, LIM BOON HENG.

Minister for National Development: MAH BOW TAN.

Minister for Community Development, Youth and Sports: Dr VIVIAN BALAKRISHNAN.

Minister for the Environment and Water Resources and Minister-in-charge of Muslim Affairs: Dr YAACOB IBRAHIM.

SINGAPORE

Minister for Law and Second Minister for Home Affairs: K. SHANMUGAM.

MINISTRIES

Office of the President: The Istana, Orchard Rd, Singapore 238823; e-mail istana_general_office@istana.gov.sg; internet www.istana.gov.sg.

Office of the Prime Minister: The Istana, Orchard Rd, Singapore 238823; tel. 63327200; fax 63328983; e-mail lee_hsien_loong@pmo.gov.sg; internet www.pmo.gov.sg.

Ministry of Community Development, Youth and Sports: 512 Thomson Rd, MCYS Bldg, Singapore 298136; tel. 62589595; fax 63536695; e-mail mcys_email@mcys.gov.sg; internet www.mcys.gov.sg.

Ministry of Defence: Gombak Dr., off Upper Bukit Timah Rd, Mindef Bldg, Singapore 669645; tel. 67608844; fax 67646119; internet www.mindef.gov.sg.

Ministry of Education: 1 North Buona Vista Dr., MOE Bldg, Singapore 138675; tel. 68722220; fax 67755826; e-mail contact@moe.edu.sg; internet www.moe.gov.sg.

Ministry of the Environment and Water Resources: 40 Scotts Rd, Environment Bldg, 24-00, Singapore 228231; tel. 67327733; fax 67319456; e-mail mewr_feedback@mewr.gov.sg; internet www.mewr.gov.sg.

Ministry of Finance: 100 High St, 10-01 The Treasury, Singapore 179434; tel. 62259911; fax 63327435; e-mail mof_qsm@mof.gov.sg; internet www.mof.gov.sg.

Ministry of Foreign Affairs: MFA Bldg, Tanglin, off Napier Rd, Singapore 248163; tel. 63798000; fax 64747885; e-mail mfa@mfa.gov.sg; internet www.mfa.gov.sg.

Ministry of Health: 16 College Rd, College of Medicine Bldg, Singapore 169854; tel. 63259220; fax 62241677; e-mail moh_info@moh.gov.sg; internet www.moh.gov.sg.

Ministry of Home Affairs: New Phoenix Park, 28 Irrawaddy Rd, Singapore 329560; tel. 64787010; fax 62546250; e-mail mha_feedback@mha.gov.sg; internet www.mha.gov.sg.

Ministry of Information, Communications and the Arts: 140 Hill St, 02-02 MICA Bldg, Singapore 179369; tel. 62707988; fax 68379837; e-mail mica@mica.gov.sg; internet www.mica.gov.sg.

Ministry of Law: 100 High St, 08-02 The Treasury, Singapore 179434; tel. 63328840; fax 63328842; e-mail contact@mlaw.gov.sg; internet www.minlaw.gov.sg.

Ministry of Manpower: 18 Havelock Rd, 07-01, Singapore 059764; tel. 64385122; fax 65344840; e-mail mom_hq@mom.gov.sg; internet www.mom.gov.sg.

Ministry of National Development: 5 Maxwell Rd, 21/22-00 Tower Block, MND Complex, Singapore 069110; tel. 62221211; fax 63257254; e-mail mnd_hq@mnd.gov.sg; internet www.mnd.gov.sg.

Ministry of Trade and Industry: 100 High St, 09-01 The Treasury, Singapore 179434; tel. 62259911; fax 63327260; e-mail mti_email@mti.gov.sg; internet www.mti.gov.sg.

Ministry of Transport: 460 Alexandra Rd, 39-00 PSA Bldg, Singapore 119963; tel. 62707988; fax 63757734; e-mail mot@mot.gov.sg; internet www.mot.gov.sg.

President and Legislature

PRESIDENT

On 13 August 2005, at the end of his six-year term, the incumbent SELLAPAN RAMANATHAN (S. R.) NATHAN was again nominated as President by a state-appointed committee. S. R. Nathan was the sole candidate for the Presidency, following the rejection by the committee of three other potential candidates on the grounds of their insufficient experience. He was officially reappointed to the post on 1 September.

PARLIAMENT

Parliament House

1 Parliament Place, Singapore 178880; tel. 63326666; fax 63325526; e-mail parl@parl.gov.sg; internet www.parliament.gov.sg.

Speaker: ABDULLAH TARMUGI.

General Election, 6 May 2006

	Seats
People's Action Party	82*
Workers' Party	1
Singapore Democratic Alliance	1
Total	**84**

* 37 seats were unopposed.

Election Commission

Elections Department of Singapore (ELD): Prime Minister's Office, 11 Prinsep Link, Singapore 187949; fax 63323428; internet www.elections.gov.sg; govt body; Chair. LEE SENG LUP.

Political Organizations

National Solidarity Party: 397 Jalan Besar, 02-01A, Singapore 209007; tel. and fax 83823961; fax 63968645; e-mail nsp-cec@yahoogroups.com; internet www.nsp.sg; f. 1987; joined Singapore Democratic Alliance (SDA) in July 2001; Pres. SEBASTIAN TEO; Sec.-Gen. KEN SUN.

People's Action Party (PAP): Blk 57B, PCF Bldg, 01-1402 New Upper Changi Rd, Singapore 463057; tel. 62444600; fax 62430114; e-mail paphq@pap.org.sg; internet www.pap.org.sg; f. 1954; governing party since 1959; 18-member Cen. Exec. Cttee; Chair. LIM BOON HENG; Sec.-Gen. LEE HSIEN LOONG.

Pertubuhan Kebangsaan Melayu Singapura (PKMS) (Singapore Malay National Organization): 218F Changi Rd, 4th Floor, PKM Bldg, Singapore 1441; tel. 64470468; fax 63458724; e-mail pkms_melayu@pacific.net.sg; internet www.geocities.com/pkms218; f. 1950 as the United Malay National Organization (UMNO) of Malaysia; renamed as UMNO Singapore in 1954 and as PKMS in 1967; seeks to advance the implementation of the special rights of Malays in Singapore, as stated in the Constitution, to safeguard and promote the advancement of Islam and to encourage racial harmony and goodwill in Singapore; joined Singapore Democratic Alliance (SDA) in July 2001; Pres. Haji BORHAN ARIFFIN.

Reform Party: 18A Smith St, Singapore 058932; tel. 65349641; fax 65349640; f. 2008; Sec.-Gen. KENNETH JEYARETNAM.

Singapore Democratic Alliance (SDA): Singapore; f. 2001; est. to contest 2001 general election; coalition of Pertubuhan Kebangsaan Melayu Singapura (PKMS), Singapore People's Party (SPP), National Solidarity Party and the Singapore Justice Party; Chair. CHIAM SEE TONG.

Singapore Democratic Party (SDP): 1357A Serangoon Rd, Singapore 328240; tel. and fax 63981675; e-mail speakup@yoursdp.org; internet www.singaporedemocrat.org; f. 1980; 12-mem. Cen. Cttee; Chair. GANDHI AMBALAM; Sec.-Gen. CHEE SOON JUAN.

Singapore Justice Party: Singapore; f. 1972; joined Singapore Democratic Alliance (SDA) in July 2001; Pres. A. R. SUIB; Sec.-Gen. AMINUDDIN BIN AMI.

Singapore People's Party (SPP): Singapore; tel. 68585771; fax 62970138; e-mail feedback@spp.org.sg; internet www.spp.org.sg; f. 1993; a breakaway faction of the SDP, espousing more moderate policies; joined Singapore Democratic Alliance (SDA) in July 2001; 12-mem. Cen. Exec. Cttee; Chair. SIN KEK TONG; Sec.-Gen. CHIAM SEE TONG.

Workers' Party: 216G Syed Alwi Rd 02-03, Singapore 207799; tel. 62984765; fax 64544404; e-mail wp@wp.org.sg; internet www.wp.org.sg; f. 1961; active as opposition party in Singapore since 1957, merged with Barisan Sosialis (Socialist Front) in 1988; seeks to establish a democratic socialist govt with a constitution guaranteeing fundamental citizens' rights; Chair. SYLVIA LIM SWEE LIAN; Sec.-Gen. LOW THIA KHIANG.

Other parties are the Alliance Party Singapura, the Democratic People's Party, the Democratic Progressive Party, the National Party of Singapore, the Partai Rakyat, the Parti Kesatuan Ra'ayat (United Democratic Party), the People's Front, the People's Republican Party, the Persatuan Melayu Singapura, the Singapore Chinese Party, the Singapore Indian Congress, the Singapore National Front, the United National Front, the United People's Front and the United People's Party.

SINGAPORE

Diplomatic Representation

EMBASSIES AND HIGH COMMISSIONS IN SINGAPORE

Angola: 9 Temasek Blvd, 44-03 Suntec Tower Two, Singapore 038989; tel. 63419360; fax 63419367; e-mail embangola@pacific.net.sg; Ambassador FLÁVIO SARAIVA DE CARVALHO FONSECA.

Australia: 25 Napier Rd, Singapore 258507; tel. 68364100; fax 67375481; e-mail public-affairs-sing@dfat.gov.au; internet www.australia.org.sg; High Commissioner DOUG CHESTER.

Bangladesh: 91 Bencoolen St, 6 Sunshine Plaza, Singapore 189652; tel. 62550075; fax 62551824; e-mail bdoot@singnet.com.sg; internet www.bangladesh.org.sg; High Commissioner KAMRUL AHSAN.

Belgium: 8 Shenton Way, 14-01 Temasek Tower, Singapore 068811; tel. 62207677; fax 62226976; e-mail singapore@diplobel.org; internet www.diplomatie.be/singapore; Ambassador MARC A. M. CALCOEN.

Brazil: 101 Thomson Rd, 10-05 United Sq., Singapore 307591; tel. 62566001; fax 62564565; e-mail cinbrem@brazil.org.sg; internet www.brazil.org.sg; Ambassador PAULO ALBERTO DE SILVEIRA SOARES.

Brunei: 325 Tanglin Rd, Singapore 247955; tel. 67339055; fax 67375275; High Commissioner ABDUL GHAFAR BIN ISMAIL.

Cambodia: 400 Orchard Rd, 10-03/04 Orchard Towers, Singapore 238875; tel. 63419785; fax 63419201; e-mail cambodiaembassy@pacific.net.sg; internet www.recambodia.net; Ambassador SEREY SIN.

Canada: 1 George St 11-01, Singapore 049145; tel. 68545900; fax 68545930; e-mail echiesg@pacific.net.sg; internet www.dfait-maeci.gc.ca/singapore; High Commissioner DAVID SEVIGNY.

Chile: 105 Cecil St, 25-00 The Octagon, Singapore 069534; tel. 62238577; fax 62250677; e-mail echilesg@pacific.net.sg; Ambassador GRACIELA MERCEDES FERNÁNDEZ SOBARZO.

China, People's Republic: 150 Tanglin Rd, Singapore 247969; tel. 64712117; fax 64795345; e-mail chinaemb_sg@fmprc.gov.cn; internet www.chinaembassy.org.sg; Ambassador ZHANG XIAOKANG.

Costa Rica: 271 Bukit Timah Rd, 04-08 Balmoral Plaza, Singapore 259708; tel. 67380566; fax 67380567; e-mail embassycostarica@singnet.com.sg; Ambassador JUAN FERNANDO CORDERO ARIAS.

Denmark: 101 Thomson Rd, 13-01/02 United Sq., Singapore 307591; tel. 63555010; fax 62533764; e-mail sinamb@um.dk; internet www.denmark.com.sg; Ambassador VIBEKE ROVSING LAURITZEN.

Egypt: 75 Grange Rd, Singapore 249579; tel. 67371811; fax 67323422; e-mail admin@egyptemb-sin.org; Ambassador NASSER HAMDY.

Finland: 101 Thomson Rd, 21-03 United Sq., Singapore 307591; tel. 62544042; fax 62534101; e-mail sanomat.sin@formin.fi; internet www.finland.org.sg; Ambassador SATU MATTILA.

France: 101–103 Cluny Park Rd, Singapore 259595; tel. 68807800; fax 68807801; e-mail ambassadeur@france.org.sg; internet www.france.org.sg; Ambassador PIERRE BUHLER.

Germany: 12-00 Singapore Land Tower, 50 Raffles Place, Singapore 048623; tel. 65336002; fax 65331132; e-mail germany@singnet.com.sg; internet www.sing.diplo.de; Ambassador JÖRG RANAU.

Hungary: 250 North Bridge Rd, 29-01 Raffles City Tower, Singapore 179101; tel. 68830882; fax 68830177; e-mail mission.sin@kum.hu; internet www.mfa.gov.hu/emb/singapore; Ambassador TAMAS MAGDA.

India: 31 Grange Rd, India House, Singapore 239702; tel. 67376777; fax 67326909; e-mail indiahc@pacific.net.sg; internet www.embassyofindia.com; High Commissioner SUBRAHMANYAM JAISHANKAR.

Indonesia: 7 Chatsworth Rd, Singapore 249761; tel. 67377422; fax 67375037; e-mail info@kbrisingapura.com; internet www.kbrisingapura.com; Ambassador WARDANA.

Ireland: Ireland House, 541 Orchard Rd, 8th Floor, Liat Towers, Singapore 238881; tel. 62387616; fax 62387615; e-mail singaporeembassy@dfa.ie; internet www.embassyofireland.sg; Ambassador RICHARD O'BRIEN.

Israel: 24 Stevens Close, Singapore 257964; tel. 68349200; fax 67337008; e-mail press@singapore.mfa.gov.il; internet singapore.mfa.gov.il; Ambassador ILAN BEN-DOV.

Italy: 101 Thomson Rd, 27-02/03 United Sq., Singapore 307591; tel. 62506022; fax 62533301; e-mail ambitaly@italyemb.org.sg; internet www.italian-embassy.org.ae/Ambasciata_Singapore; Ambassador FOLCO DE LUCA GABRIELLI.

Japan: 16 Nassim Rd, Singapore 258390; tel. 62358855; fax 67331039; e-mail eojsingfv@vsystem.com.sg; internet www.sg.emb-japan.go.jp; Ambassador MAKOTO YAMANAKA.

Kazakhstan: 20 Raffles Place, 14-06 Ocean Towers, Singapore 048620; tel. 65366100; fax 64388990; e-mail office@kazakhstan.org.sg; internet www.kazakhstan.org.sg; Ambassador YERLAN BAUDARBEK-KOZHATAYEV.

Korea, Democratic People's Republic: 7500 Beach Rd, 09-320 The Plaza, Singapore 199591; tel. 64403498; fax 63482026; e-mail embdprk@singnet.com.sg; Ambassador JONG SONG IL.

Korea, Republic: 47 Scotts Rd, 08-00 Goldbell Towers, Singapore 228233; tel. 62561188; fax 62543191; e-mail info@koreaembassy.org.sg; internet www.koreaembassy.org.sg; Ambassador KIM JOONG-KEUN.

Kuwait: c/o The Ritz-Carlton Millenia Singapore, 7 Raffles Ave, Suite 3108, Singapore 039799; tel. 64345388; fax 64345387; Ambassador ABDULAZIZ AHMED S. AL-ADWANI.

Laos: 51 Newton Rd, 13-04/05 Goldhill Plaza, Singapore 308900; tel. 62506044; fax 62506014; e-mail laoemb.sg@singnet.com.sg; Ambassador THOUANE VORASARN.

Malaysia: 30 Hill St, 02-01, Singapore 179360; tel. 62350111; fax 67336135; e-mail mwspore@singnet.com.sg; High Commissioner Dato' NAGALINGAM PARAMESWARAN.

Maldives: 101 Thomson Rd, 30-01A, United Sq., Singapore 307591; tel. 67209012; fax 67209014; e-mail info@maldiveshighcommission.sg; High Commissioner HASSAN SOBIR.

Mexico: 152 Beach Rd, 06-07/08, 6th Floor, Gateway East Tower, Singapore 189721; tel. 62982678; fax 62933484; e-mail embamexsing@embamexsing.org.sg; internet www.embamexsing.org.sg; Ambassador JUAN JOSÉ GOMEZ CAMACHO.

Mongolia: 600 North Bridge Rd, 24-08 Parkview Sq., Singapore 188778; tel. 63480745; fax 63481753; e-mail consulmn@singnet.com.sg; Ambassador PÜREVJAVYN GANSÜKH (designate).

Myanmar: 15 St Martin's Drive, Singapore 257996; tel. 7969858; fax 7965570; e-mail ambassador@mesingapore.org.sg; internet www.mesingapore.org.sg; Ambassador WIN MYINT.

Netherlands: 541 Orchard Rd, 13-01 Liat Towers, Singapore 238881; tel. 67371155; fax 67371940; e-mail nlgovsin@singnet.com.sg; internet www.mfa.nl/sin; Ambassador CHRISTIAAN CORNELIS SANDERS.

New Zealand: 391A Orchard Rd, Tower A, 15-06/10 Ngee Ann City, Singapore 238873; tel. 62359966; fax 67339924; e-mail enquiries@nz-high-com.org.sg; internet www.nzembassy.com/singapore; High Commissioner MARTIN WILFRED HARVEY.

Nigeria: 08-02 Anson House, 72 Anson Rd, Singapore 079911; tel. 67321743; fax 67321742; e-mail highcommission@nigeriahc.org.sg; internet www.nigeriahc.org.sg; High Commissioner Dr OZICHI J. ALIMOLE (acting).

Norway: 16 Raffles Quay, 44-01 Hong Leong Bldg, Singapore 048581; tel. 62207122; fax 62202191; e-mail emb.singapore@mfa.no; internet www.norway.sg; Ambassador JANNE JULSRUD.

Pakistan: 1 Scotts Rd, 24-02/04 Shaw Centre, Singapore 228208; tel. 67376988; fax 67374096; e-mail parep@singnet.com.sg; internet www.parep.org.sg; High Commissioner SAJJAD ASHRAF.

Panama: 16 Raffles Quay, 41-06 Hong Leong Bldg, Singapore 048581; tel. 62218677; fax 62240892; e-mail general@panamaemb.org.sg; Ambassador EDUARDO A. REAL.

Peru: 390 Orchard Rd, 12-03 Palais Renaissance, Singapore 238871; tel. 67388595; fax 67388601; e-mail embperu@pacific.net.sg; internet www.embassyperu.org.sg; Ambassador J. ARTURO MONTOYA.

Philippines: 20 Nassim Rd, Singapore 258395; tel. 67373977; fax 67339544; e-mail php@pacific.net.sg; internet www.philippine-embassy.org.sg; Ambassador MINDA CRUZ.

Poland: 435 Orchard Rd, 10-01/02 Wisma Atria, Singapore 238877; tel. 62359478; fax 62359479; e-mail secretary@pacific.net.sg; internet www.singapore.polemb.net; Ambassador WOLDEMAR DUBANIOWSKI.

Qatar: c/o Shangri-La Hotel, 22 Orange Grove Rd, Rms 1832 & 1833, Singapore 258350; tel. 67373644; fax 62134021; Ambassador RASHID BIN ALI HASSAN AL-KHATER.

Romania: 48 Jalan Harom Setangkai, Singapore 258827; tel. 64683424; fax 64683425; e-mail comofrom@starhub.net.sg; Chargé d'affaires a.i. SILVIU IONESCU.

Russia: 51 Nassim Rd, Singapore 258439; tel. 62351834; fax 67334780; e-mail rosposol@pacific.net.sg; internet www.singapore.mid.ru; Ambassador ANDREY N. ROZHKOV.

Saudi Arabia: 40 Nassim Rd, Singapore 258449; tel. 67345878; fax 67385291; e-mail enquiries@saudiembassy.org.sg; internet www.saudiembassy.org.sg; Ambassador Dr JAMEEL MAHMOUD MERDAD.

South Africa: 331 North Bridge Rd, 15/01-06 Odeon Towers, Singapore 188720; tel. 63393319; fax 63396658; e-mail singhc@foreign.gov.za; internet www.southafrichac.org.sg; High Commissioner SIMEON SELBY RIPINGA.

Spain: 7 Temasek Blvd, 39-00 Suntec Tower 1, Singapore 038987; tel. 67259220; fax 63333025; Ambassador ANTONIO SÁNCHEZ JARA.

Sri Lanka: 13-07/12 Goldhill Plaza, 51 Newton Rd, Singapore 308900; tel. 62544595; fax 62507201; e-mail slhcs@lanka.com.sg;

SINGAPORE

internet www.lanka.com.sg; High Commissioner RANJANI SAMARAKOON.

Sweden: 111 Somerset Rd, 05-01 Singapore Power Bldg, Singapore 238164; tel. 64159720; fax 64159747; e-mail ambassaden.singapore@foreign.ministry.se; internet www.swedenabroad.com/singapore; Ambassador PÄR AHLBERGER.

Switzerland: 1 Swiss Club Link, Singapore 288162; tel. 64685788; fax 64668245; e-mail sin.vertretung@eda.admin.ch; internet www.eda.admin.ch/singapore; Ambassador JORG REDING.

Thailand: 370 Orchard Rd, Singapore 238870; tel. 67372158; fax 67320778; e-mail thaisgp@singnet.com.sg; internet www.thaiembassy.sg; Ambassador NOPADOL GUNAVIBOOL.

Turkey: 2 Shenton Way 10-03, SGX Centre 1, Singapore 068804; tel. 65333390; fax 65333380; e-mail turksin@singnet.com.sg; internet www.turkishembassy.org.sg; Ambassador BÜLENT MERIÇ.

Ukraine: 50 Raffles Place, 16-05 Singapore Land Tower, Singapore 048623; tel. 65356550; fax 65352116; e-mail emb_sg@mfa.gov.ua; internet www.embassy-ukraine.com; Ambassador Dr VIKTOR MASHTABEI.

United Arab Emirates: 600 North Bridge Road, 09-01/05 Parkview Sq., Singapore 188778; tel. 62388206; fax 62380081; e-mail emarat@singnet.com.sg; internet www.uaeembassy-sg.com; Chargé d'affaires a.i. ASIM MIRZA ALRAHMAH.

United Kingdom: 100 Tanglin Rd, Singapore 247919; tel. 64244200; fax 64244218; e-mail commercial.singapore@fco.gov.uk; internet www.ukinsingapore.fco.gov.uk; High Commissioner PAUL MADDEN.

USA: 27 Napier Rd, Singapore 258508; tel. 64769100; fax 64769340; e-mail singaporeusembassy@state.gov; internet singapore.usembassy.gov; Ambassador (vacant).

Uzbekistan: 5 Shenton Way 37-02, Rms 34 & 35, UIC Bldg, Singapore 068808; tel. 63251843; fax 63251844; e-mail uz-emb.sg@hotmail.com; Ambassador ALISHER A. KURMANOV.

Venezuela: 3 Killiney Rd, 07–03 Winsland House I, Singapore 239519; tel. 64911172; fax 62353167; e-mail embassy@embavenez.org.sg; Chargé d'affaires a.i. GEOMAR CATTAFI-ANDRADE.

Viet Nam: 10 Leedon Park, Singapore 267887; tel. 64625938; fax 64625936; e-mail vnemb@singnet.com.sg; Ambassador NGUYEN TRUNG THANH.

Judicial System

Supreme Court: 1 Supreme Court Lane, Singapore 178879; tel. 63360644; fax 63379450; e-mail supcourt_qsm@supcourt.gov.sg; internet www.supcourt.gov.sg.

The judicial power of Singapore is vested in the Supreme Court and in the Subordinate Courts. The Judiciary administers the law with complete independence from the executive and legislative branches of the Government; this independence is safeguarded by the Constitution. The Supreme Court consists of the High Court and the Court of Appeal. The Chief Justice is appointed by the President if the latter, acting at his discretion, concurs with the advice of the Prime Minister. The other judges of the Supreme Court are appointed in the same way, in consultation with the Chief Justice. Under a 1979 constitutional amendment, the position of judicial commissioner of the Supreme Court was created 'to facilitate the disposal of business in the Supreme Court'. A judicial commissioner has the powers and functions of a judge, and is appointed for such period as the President thinks fit.

The Subordinate Courts consist of District Courts and Magistrates' Courts. In addition, there are also specialized courts such as the Coroner's Court, Family Court, Juvenile Court, Mentions Court, Night Court, Sentencing Courts and Filter Courts. The Primary Dispute Resolution Centre and the Small Claims Tribunals are also managed by the Subordinate Courts. The Subordinate Courts have also established the Multi-Door Courthouse, which serves as a one-stop centre for the screening and channelling of any cases to the most appropriate forum for dispute resolution.

District Courts and Magistrates' Courts have original criminal and civil jurisdiction. District Courts try offences for which the maximum penalty does not exceed 10 years of imprisonment and in civil cases where the amount claimed does not exceed S $250,000. Magistrates' Courts try offences for which the maximum term of imprisonment does not exceed three years. The jurisdiction of Magistrates' Courts in civil cases is limited to claims not exceeding S $60,000. The Coroners' Court conducts inquests. The Small Claims Tribunal has jurisdiction over claims relating to a dispute arising from any contract for the sale of goods or the provision of services and any claim in tort in respect of damage caused to any property involving an amount that does not exceed S $10,000. The Juvenile Court deals with offences committed by young persons aged under 16 years.

The High Court has unlimited original jurisdiction in criminal and civil cases. In its appellate jurisdiction it hears criminal and civil appeals from the District Courts and Magistrates' Courts. The Court of Appeal hears appeals against the decisions of the High Court in both criminal and civil matters. In criminal matters, the Court of Appeal hears appeals against decisions made by the High Court in the exercise of its original criminal jurisdiction. In civil matters, the Court of Appeal hears appeals against decisions made by the High Court in the exercise of both its original and appellate jurisdiction. With the enactment of the Judicial Committee (Repeal) Act 1994 in April of that year, the right of appeal from the Court of Appeal to the Judicial Committee of the Privy Council in the United Kingdom was abolished. The Court of Appeal is now the final appellate court in the Singapore legal system.

Attorney-General: Prof. WALTER WOONG CHEONG MING.

Chief Justice: CHAN SEK KEONG.

Judges of Appeal: V. K. RAJAH, ANDREW PHANG BOON LEONG, CHAO HICK TIN.

Judges of the High Court: KAN TING CHIU, LAI SIU CHIU, JUDITH PRAKASH, TAN LEE MENG, CHOO HAN TECK, BELINDA ANG, WOO BIH LI, TAY YONG KWANG, ANDREW ANG, LEE SEIU KIN, CHAN SENG ONN.

Religion

According to the 2000 census, 64.4% of ethnic Chinese, who constituted 76.8% of the population, professed either Buddhism or Daoism (including followers of Confucius, Mencius and Lao Zi) and 16.5% of Chinese adhered to Christianity. Malays, who made up 13.9% of the population, were 99.6% Muslim. Among Indians, who constituted 7.9% of the population, 55.4% were Hindus, 25.6% Muslims, 12.1% Christians and 6.3% Sikhs, Jains or adherents of other faiths. There are small communities of Zoroastrians and Jews. Freedom of worship is guaranteed by the Constitution.

BAHÁ'Í FAITH

The Spiritual Assembly of the Bahá'ís of Singapore: 110D Wishart Rd, Singapore 098733; tel. 62226200; fax 62229166; e-mail secretariat@bahai.org.sg; internet www.bahai.org.sg.

BUDDHISM

Buddhist Union: 28 Jalan Senyum, Singapore 418152; tel. 62419419; fax 64443280; e-mail thebu@singnet.com.sg.

Singapore Buddhist Federation: 12 Ubi Ave 1, Singapore 408932; tel. 67444635; fax 67473618; e-mail buddhist@singnet.com.sg; internet www.buddhist.org.sg; f. 1948.

Singapore Buddhist Sangha Organization: 88 Bright Hill Drive, Singapore 579644.

CHRISTIANITY

National Council of Churches: 1 Coleman St, B1-27 The Adelphi, Singapore 179803; tel. 63368177; fax 63368178; e-mail admin@nccs.org.sg; internet www.nccs.org.sg; f. 1948; six mem. churches, six assoc. mems; Pres. Dr JOHN CHEW; Gen. Sec. LIM K. TAN.

Singapore Council of Christian Churches (SCCC): Singapore; f. 1956.

The Anglican Communion

The Anglican diocese of Singapore (also including Indonesia, Laos, Thailand, Viet Nam and Cambodia) is part of the Province of the Anglican Church in South-East Asia.

Bishop of Singapore: The Rt Rev. Dr JOHN HIANG CHEA CHEW, 4 Bishopsgate, Singapore 249970; tel. 64741661; fax 64791054; e-mail bpoffice@anglican.org.sg.

Orthodox Churches

The Orthodox Syrian Church and the Mar Thoma Syrian Church are both active in Singapore.

The Roman Catholic Church

Singapore comprises a single archdiocese, directly responsible to the Holy See. In December 2006 there were an estimated 174,109 adherents in the country, representing 3.9% of the total population.

Archbishop of Singapore: Most Rev. NICHOLAS CHIA, Archbishop's House, 31 Victoria St, Singapore 187997; tel. 63378818; fax 63334735; e-mail nc@veritas.org.sg.

Other Christian Churches

Brethren Assemblies: Bethesda Hall (Ang Mo Kio), 601 Ang Mo Kio Ave 4, Singapore 569898; tel. 64587474; fax 64566771; e-mail

SINGAPORE

bethesdahall@gmail.com; internet www.bethesdahall.com; f. 1864; Hon. Sec. WONG TUCK KEONG.

Evangelical Fellowship of Singapore (EFOS): Singapore; f. 1980.

Methodist Church in Singapore: 70 Barker Rd, Singapore 309936; tel. 64784784; fax 64784794; e-mail episcopacy@methodist.org.sg; internet www.methodist.org.sg; f. 1885; 34,232 mems (Dec. 2006); Leader Bishop Dr ROBERT SOLOMON.

Presbyterian Church: 3 Orchard Rd, cnr Penang Rd, Singapore 238825; tel. 63376681; fax 63391979; e-mail orpcenglish@orpc.org.sg; internet www.orpc.org.sg; f. 1856; services in English, Chinese (Mandarin), Indonesian and German; 2,000 mems; Chair. Rev. DAVID BURKE.

Singapore Baptist Convention: 01 Goldhill Plaza, 03-19 Podium Blk, Singapore 308899; tel. 62538004; fax 62538214; e-mail info@baptistconvention.org.sg; internet www.baptistconvention.org.sg; f. 1974; Chair. Rev. EDWIN LAM HON MUN; Exec. Dir PETER TANG.

Other denominations active in Singapore include the Lutheran Church and the Evangelical Lutheran Church.

HINDUISM

Hindu Advisory Board: c/o 397 Serangoon Rd, Singapore 218123; tel. 62963469; fax 62929766; e-mail heb@pacific.net.sg; f. 1985; Chair. R. BAJAWEE; Sec. M. MADHUBALA.

Hindu Endowments Board: 397 Serangoon Rd, Singapore 218123; tel. 62963469; fax 62929766; e-mail heb@pacific.net.sg; internet www.heb.gov.sg; f. 1968; Chair. S. RAJENDRAN; Sec. P. AVADIAR.

ISLAM

Majlis Ugama Islam Singapura (MUIS) (Islamic Religious Council of Singapore): 1 Lorong 6 Toa Payoh, Singapore 319376; tel. 62568188; fax 62537572; e-mail info@muis.gov.sg; internet www.muis.gov.sg; f. 1968; Pres. Haji MOHD ALAMI MUSA; Sec. ABDUL RAZAK MARICAR.

Muslim Missionary Society Singapore (JAMIYAH): 31 Lorong, 12 Geylang Rd, Singapore 399006; tel. 62568188; fax 62537272; e-mail info@jamiyah.org.sg; internet www.jamiyah.org.sg; Pres. Haji ABU BAKAR MAIDIN; Sec.-Gen. ISMAIL ROZIZ.

SIKHISM

Central Sikh Gurdwara Board (CSGB): c/o 2 Towner Rd, 03-01, Singapore 327804; tel. 62993855; e-mail csgb@sikhs.org.sg; internet www.sikhs.org.sg; Pres. KARPAL SINGH MEHLI.

The Press

Compulsory government scrutiny of newspaper management has been in operation since 1974. All newspaper enterprises must be public companies. The Newspaper and Printing Presses (Amendment) Act 1986 empowers the Government to restrict the circulation of foreign periodicals that are deemed to exert influence over readers on domestic political issues. An amendment to the Newspaper and Printing Presses Act was promulgated in October 1990. Under this amendment, all publications of which the 'contents and editorial policy were determined outside Singapore' and which dealt with politics and current events in South-East Asia would be required to obtain a ministerial licence, renewable annually. The permit would limit the number of copies sold and require a deposit in case of legal proceedings involving the publication. Permits could be refused or revoked without any reason being given. In November, however, a statement was issued exempting 14 of the 17 foreign publications affected by the amendment, which came into effect in December.

DAILIES

English Language

Business Times: 1000 Toa Payoh North, Podium Blk, Level 3, Singapore 318994; tel. 63196319; fax 63198277; e-mail btnews@sph.com.sg; internet business-times.asiaone.com; f. 1976; morning; Editor ALVIN TAY; circ. 30,400 in 2006 (Singapore only).

The New Paper: 1000 Toa Payoh North, Annexe Blk, Level 6, Singapore 318994; tel. 63196319; fax 63198266; e-mail tnp@asia1.com.sg; internet newpaper.asia1.com.sg; f. 1988; afternoon tabloid; Editor IVAN FERNANDEZ; circ. 111,400 in 2006 (Singapore only).

The Straits Times: 1000 Toa Payoh North, Singapore 318994; tel. 63196319; fax 63198282; e-mail sti@sph.com.sg; internet straitstimes.asiaone.com; f. 1845; morning; Editor-in-Chief PATRICK DANIEL; circ. 388,500 in 2006 (Singapore only).

Today: Caldecott Broadcast Centre, Andrew Road, Singapore 299939; tel. 62364889; fax 64812098; e-mail news@newstoday.com.sg; internet www.todayonline.com; f. 2000; merged with Streats newspaper, a rival free morning tabloid, in 2004; Editor WALTER FERNANDEZ; circ. 550,000.

Chinese Language

Lianhe Wanbao: 1000 Toa Payoh North, Podium Blk, Level 4, Singapore 318994; tel. 63196319; fax 63198133; e-mail wanbao@sph.com.sg; f. 1983; evening; Editor KOH LIN HOE; circ. 178,400 (week), 94,640 (Sun.) in 2006.

Lianhe Zaobao: 1000 Toa Payoh North, Podium Blk, Level 4, Singapore 318994; tel. 63196319; fax 63198119; e-mail cnzbmgt@sph.com.sg; internet www.zaobao.com; f. 1923; Editor LIM JIM KOON; circ. 183,000 (week), 191,300 (weekend) in 2006.

My Paper: Singapore; tel. 63192222; fax 63198115; e-mail mypaper@sph.com.sg; internet mypaper.sg; f. 2006; free tabloid aimed at bilingual working adults aged between 20 and 40 years old; Tues.-Sat; Editor APRIL PUNG KOON KING; circ. 120,000 (2006).

Shin Min Daily News (S) Ltd: 1000 Toa Payoh North, Podium Blk, Level 4, Singapore 318994; tel. 63196319; fax 63198166; e-mail shinmin@sph.com.sg; f. 1967; evening; Editor TOH LAM HHAT; circ. 120,800 (week), 122,600 (weekend) in 2006.

Malay Language

Berita Harian: 1000 Toa Payoh North, Singapore 318994; tel. 63195137; fax 63198255; e-mail aadeska@sph.com.sg; internet cyberita.asia1.com.sg; f. 1957; morning; Editor MOHD GUNTOR SADALI; circ. 62,500 in 2006.

Tamil Language

Tamil Murasu: 82 Genting Lane 06-07, Singapore 349567; tel. 63196319; fax 63194001; e-mail murasu4@cyberway.co.sg; internet tamilmurasu.asia1.com.sg; f. 1935; Editor CHITRA RAJARAM; circ. 10,200 (week), 17,600 (Sunday) in 2006.

WEEKLIES

English Language

The New Paper on Sunday: 1000 Toa Payoh North, Annexe Blk, Level 6, Singapore 318994; tel. 63196319; fax 63198266; e-mail tnp@asia1.com.sg; internet newpaper.asia1.com.sg; f. 1999; tabloid; Editor IVAN FERNANDEZ; circ. 145,300 in 2006.

The Sunday Times: 1000 Toa Payoh North, Singapore 318994; tel. 63195397; fax 67320131; e-mail sti@sph.com.sg; internet straitstimes.asiaone.com; f. 1931; Editor-in-Chief CHEONG YIP SENG; circ. 402,600 in 2006 (Singapore only).

Weekend Today: 24 Raffles Place, 28–01/06 Clifford Centre, Singapore 048621; tel. 62364889; fax 64812098; e-mail sales_enquiry@newstoday.com.sg; internet www.todayonline.com; f. 2002; Editor P. N. BALJI; circ. 300,000.

Malay Language

Berita Minggu: 1000 Toa Payoh North, Singapore 318994; tel. 63195665; fax 63198255; e-mail aadeska@sph.com.sg; internet cyberita.asia1.com.sg; f. 1960; Sunday; Editor MOHD GUNTOR SADALI; circ. 72,100 in 2006 (Singapore only).

SELECTED PERIODICALS

English Language

Accent: Accent Communications, 215 Intrepid Warehouse Complex, 4 Ubi Ave, Singapore 1440; tel. 67478088; fax 67472811; f. 1983; monthly; lifestyle; Senior Editor DORA TAY; circ. 65,000.

Cherie Magazine: 12 Everton Rd, Singapore 0208; tel. 62229733; fax 62843859; f. 1983; bi-monthly; women's; Editor JOSEPHINE NG; circ. 20,000.

8 Days: 10 Ang Mo Kio St 65, 01-06/08 Techpoint, Singapore 569059; tel. 62789822; fax 62724800; e-mail feedback@8daysonline.com; internet www.8days.sg; f. 1990; weekly; Editor-in-Chief TAN LEE SUN; circ. 113,258.

Her World: SPH Magazines Pte Ltd, 82 Genting Lane, Singapore 349567; tel. 63196319; fax 63196345; e-mail nguislc@sph.com.sg; internet www.herworld.com; f. 1960; monthly; women's; Editor CAROLINE NGUI; circ. 62,529.

Her World Brides: SPH Magazines Pte Ltd, 82 Genting Lane, Singapore 349567; tel. 63196319; fax 63196345; e-mail sphmag@sph.com.sg; f. 1998; quarterly; circ. 13,193.

Home and Decor: 82 Genting Lane, SPH Media Centre, 5th Floor, Singapore 349567; tel. 63196319; fax 63196345; e-mail hdecor@sph.com.sg; internet www.homeanddecor.com.sg; f. 1981; 6 a year; home-owners; Editor SOPHIE KHO; circ. 27,000.

SINGAPORE

LIME: 10 Ang Mo Kio St 65, 01-06/08 Techpoint, Singapore 569059; tel. 64837118; fax 64837286; f. 1996; Editor PAMELA QUEK; circ. 34,947.

Mondial Collections: Singapore; f. 1990; bimonthly; arts; Chair. CHRIS CHENEY; circ. 100,000.

NSman: SAFRA National Service Association, 5200 Jalan Bukit Merah, Singapore 159468; tel. 62786011; fax 63779898; e-mail hq@safra.org.sg; internet www.safra.sg; f. 1972; bi-monthly; publication of the SAF National Service; Gen. Man. TAN KEE BOO; circ. 130,000.

Republic of Singapore Government Gazette: SNP Corpn Ltd, 1 Kim Seng Promenade, 18-01 Great World City East Tower, Singapore 237994; tel. 68269600; fax 68203341; e-mail egazinfo@snpcorp.com; internet www.egazette.com; weekly; Friday.

Reservist: 5200 Jalan Bukit Merah, Singapore 0315; tel. 62786011; fax 6273441; f. 1973; bi-monthly; men's; Editor SAMUEL EE; circ. 130,000.

Singapore Medical Journal: Singapore Medical Association, Level 2, Alumni Medical Centre, 2 College Rd, Singapore 169850; tel. 62231264; fax 62247827; e-mail smj@sma.org.sg; internet www.sma.org.sg/smj; monthly; Editor Prof. W. C. G. PEH; circ. 5,000.

Times Guide to Computers: 1 New Industrial Rd, Times Centre, Singapore 536196; tel. 62139300; fax 62139398; e-mail ttd@corp.tpl.com.sg; internet www.tpl.com.sg; f. 1986; annually; computing and communications; Vice-Pres. LESLIE LIM; circ. 30,000.

Visage: Ubi Ave 1, 02-169 Blk 305, Singapore 1440; tel. 67478088; fax 67472811; f. 1984; monthly; Editor-in-Chief TENG JUAT LENG; circ. 63,000.

WEEKENDeast: 82 Genting Lane, News Centre, Singapore 349567; tel. 67401200; fax 67451022; e-mail focuspub@cyberway.com.sg; f. 1986; Editor VICTOR SOH; circ. 75,000.

Woman's Affair: 140 Paya Lebar Rd, 04-10 A-Z Bldg, Singapore 1440; tel. 67478088; fax 67479119; f. 1988; 2 a month; Editor DORA TAY; circ. 38,000.

Young Parents: SPH Magazines Pte Ltd, 82 Genting Lane, Singapore 349567; tel. 63196319; fax 63196345; e-mail magyoungparents@sph.com.sg; internet www.youngparents.com.sg; f. 1986; quarterly; family; Editor STEPHANIE YEO; circ. 15,000.

Chinese Language

Characters: 1 Kallang Sector, 04-04/04-05 Kolam Ayer Industrial Park, Singapore 349276; tel. 67458733; fax 67458213; f. 1987; monthly; television and entertainment; Editor SAM NG; circ. 45,000.

The Citizen: People's Association, 9 Stadium Link, Singapore 397750; tel. 63405138; fax 63468657; monthly; English, Chinese, Tamil and Malay; Man. Editor OOI HUI MEI.

Icon: 82 Genting Lane, SPH Media Centre, Singapore 349567; tel. 63196319; f. 2005; Chinese language; lifestyle magazine.

i-weekly: 10 Ang Mo Kio St 65, 01-06/08 Techpoint, Singapore 569059; tel. 62789822; fax 62724811; e-mail feedback@i-weeklyonline.com; internet i-weekly.mediacorppublishing.com; f. 1981; weekly; radio and television; Editor-in-Chief LOKE TAI TAY; circ. 113,000.

Punters' Way: 4 Ubi View (off Ubi Rd 3), Pioneers and Leaders Centre, Singapore 408557; tel. 67458733; fax 67458213; e-mail pnlhldg@pnl-group.com; f. 1977; bi-weekly; English and Chinese; sport; Editor T. S. PHAN; circ. 90,000.

Racing Guide: 1 New Industrial Rd, Times Centre, Singapore 1953; tel. 62848844; fax 62881186; f. 1987; 2 a week; English and Chinese; sport; Editorial Consultant BENNY ORTEGA; Chinese Editor KUEK CHIEW TEONG; circ. 20,000.

Singapore Literature: Singapore Literature Society, 122B Sims Ave, Singapore 1438; quarterly; Pres. YAP KOON CHAN; Editor LUO MING.

Tune Monthly Magazine: Henderson Rd 06-04, Blk 203A, Henderson Industrial Park, Singapore 0315; tel. 62733000; fax 62749538; f. 1988; monthly; women's and fashion; Editor CHAN ENG; circ. 25,000.

You Weekly: SPH Magazines Pte Ltd, 82 Genting Lane, Singapore 349567; tel. 63196319; fax 63196345; e-mail sphmag@sph.com.sg; f. 2001; weekly; entertainment; circ. 80,000.

Young Generation: SNP Panpac Pte Ltd, 97 Ubi Avenue 4, Singapore 408754; tel. 67412500; fax 67454129; e-mail yg@snpcorp.com; internet www.snpcorp.com; monthly; children's; Editor EVELYN TANG; circ. 80,000.

Malay Language

Manja: 10 Ang Mo Kio St 65, 01-06/08 Techpoint, Singapore 569059; tel. 64837118; fax 64812098; e-mail hello@manja.sg; internet www.manja.sg; monthly; entertainment and lifestyle; Editor AIDLI MOSBIT.

NEWS AGENCIES

Foreign Bureaux

Sixteen foreign bureaux operate in Singapore.

Publishers

ENGLISH LANGUAGE

Butterworths Asia: 1 Temasek Ave, 17-01 Millenia Tower, Singapore 039192; tel. 63369661; fax 63369662; e-mail sales@butterworths.com.sg; internet www.lexisnexis.com.sg/butterworths-online; f. 1932; law texts and journals; Gen. Man. DEAN CORKERY.

Caldecott Publishing Pte Ltd: 10 Ang Mo Kio St 65, 01-06/08 Techpoint, Singapore 569059; tel. 64837118; fax 64837286; f. 1990; Editorial Dir MICHAEL CHIANG; Group Editor TAN LEE SUN.

EPB Publishers Pte Ltd: Blk 162, 04-3545 Bukit Merah Central, Singapore 150162; tel. 62780881; fax 62782456; e-mail epb@sbg.com.sg; fmrly Educational Publications Bureau Pte Ltd; textbooks and supplementary materials, general, reference and magazines; English and Chinese; Gen. Man. ROGER PHUA.

FEP International Pte Ltd: 11 Arnsal Chetty Rd, 03-02, Singapore 239949; tel. 67331178; fax 67375561; f. 1960; textbooks, reference, children's and dictionaries; Gen. Man. RICHARD TOH.

Flame of the Forest Publishing Pte Ltd: Blk 5, Ang Mo Kio Industrial Park 2A, 07-22/23, AMK Tech II, Singapore 567760; tel. 64848887; fax 64842208; e-mail mail@flameoftheforest.com; internet www.flameoftheforest.com; Man. Dir ALEX CHACKO.

Graham Brash Pte Ltd: 45 Kian Teck Drive, Blk 1, Level 2, Singapore 628859; tel. 62624843; fax 62621519; e-mail graham_brash@giro.com.sg; internet www.grahambrash.com.sg; f. 1947; general, academic, educational; English, Chinese and Malay; CEO CHUAN I. CAMPBELL; Dir HELENE CAMPBELL.

HarperCollins, Asia Pte Ltd: 970 Toa Payoh North, 04-24/26, Singapore 1231; tel. 62501985; fax 62501360; f. 1983; educational, trade, reference and general; Man. Dir FRANK FOLEY.

Institute of Southeast Asian Studies: 30 Heng Mui Keng Terrace, Pasir Panjang Rd, Singapore 119614; tel. 67780955; fax 67781735; e-mail admin@iseas.edu.sg; internet www.iseas.edu.sg; f. 1968; scholarly works on contemporary South-East Asia and the Asia-Pacific region; Chair. Prof. WANG GUNGWU; Dir K. KESAVAPANY.

Intellectual Publishing Co: 113 Eunos Ave 3, 04-08 Gordon Industrial Bldg, Singapore 1440; tel. 67466025; fax 67489108; f. 1971; Man. POH BE LECK.

Marshall Cavendish International (Singapore) Pte Ltd: Times Centre, 1 New Industrial Rd, Singapore 536196; tel. 62139300; fax 62854871; e-mail duriyaaziz@sg.marshallcavendish.com; internet www.marshallcavendish.com/education; f. 1957; fmrly Times Media Pte Ltd; academic texts; Group Publr SHANE ARMSTRONG; Publr DURIYA AZIZ.

NUS Press (Pte) Ltd: National University of Singapore, 3 Arts Link, AS3–01–02, Singapore 117569; tel. 67761148; fax 67740652; e-mail nusbooks@nus.edu.sg; internet www.nus.edu.sg/npu; f. 1971; scholarly; Man. Dir PAUL KRATOSKA.

Pearson Education South Asia Pte Ltd: 23/25 First Lok Yang Rd, Jurong Town, Singapore 629733; tel. 63199388; fax 63199175; e-mail asia.product@pearson.com; educational; Dir, Business Support, South Asia RASMIATI HARTANTO.

Simon & Schuster Asia Pte Ltd: 317 Alexandra Rd, 04-01 Ikea Bldg, Singapore 159965; tel. 64764688; fax 63780370; e-mail prenhall@signet.com.sg; f. 1975; educational; Man. Dir GUNAWAN HADI.

Stamford College Publishers: Colombo Court 05-11A, Singapore 0617; tel. 63343378; fax 63343080; f. 1970; general, educational and journals; Man. LAWRENCE THOMAS.

Times Editions Pte Ltd: Times Centre, 1 New Industrial Rd, Singapore 536196; tel. 62139288; fax 62844733; e-mail tpl@tpl.com.sg; internet www.tpl.com.sg; f. 1978; political, social and cultural books, general works on Asia; Chair. LIM KIM SAN; Pres. and CEO LAI SECK KHUI.

World Scientific Publishing Co Pte Ltd: 5 Toh Tuck Link, Singapore 596224; tel. 64665775; fax 64677667; e-mail wspc@wspc.com.sg; internet www.worldscientific.com; f. 1981; academic and research texts and science journals; Chair. and Editor-in-Chief Prof. K. K. PHUA; Man. Dir DOREEN LIU.

MALAY LANGUAGE

Malaysia Press Sdn Bhd (Pustaka Melayu): Singapore; tel. 62933454; fax 62911858; f. 1962; textbooks and educational; Man. Dir ABU TALIB BIN ALLY.

SINGAPORE

Pustaka Nasional Pte Ltd: 548 Changi Rd, Singapore 419931; tel. 67454321; fax 67452417; e-mail enquiry@pustaka.com.sg; internet www.pustaka.com.sg; f. 1963; Arabic, English, Malay and Islamic religious books and CD-Roms; Dir SYED ALI SEMAIT.

CHINESE LANGUAGE

Shanghai Book Co (Pte) Ltd: 231 Bain St, 02-73 Bras Basah Complex, Singapore 180231; tel. 63360144; fax 63360490; e-mail shanghaibook@pacific.net.sg; f. 1925; educational and general; Man. Dir MA JI LIN.

Shing Lee Publishers Pte Ltd: 120 Hillview Ave, 05-06/07 Kewalram Hillview, Singapore 2366; tel. 67601388; fax 67625684; e-mail shingleebook@sbg.com.sg; f. 1935; educational and general; Man. PEH CHIN HUA.

Union Book Co (Pte) Ltd: 231 Bain St, 03-01, Bras Basah Complex, Singapore 180231; tel. 63380696; fax 63386306; general and reference; Gen. Man. CHOW LI-LIANG.

TAMIL LANGUAGE

EVS Enterprises: Singapore; tel. 62830002; f. 1967; children's books, religion and general; Man. E. V. SINGHAN.

GOVERNMENT PUBLISHING HOUSE

SNP Corpn Ltd: 1 Kim Seng Promenade, 18-01 Great World City East Tower, Singapore 237994; tel. 68269600; fax 68203341; e-mail enquiries@snpcorp.com; internet www.snpcorp.com; f. 1973; printers and publishers; Pres. and CEO YEO CHEE TONG.

PUBLISHERS' ORGANIZATIONS

National Book Development Council of Singapore (NBDCS): 50 Geylang East Ave 1, Singapore 389777; tel. 68488290; fax 67429466; e-mail info@bookcouncil.sg; internet www.bookcouncil.sg; f. 1969; independent non-profit org.; promotes reading, writing and publishing and organizes the annual Asian Congress of Storytellers and Asian Children's Writers and Illustrators' Conference; offers professional training programmes through Centre for Literary Arts and Publishing; Chair. Prof. SERENE WEE.

Singapore Book Publishers' Association: 86 Marine Parade Central 03-213, Singapore 440086; tel. 63447801; fax 64470897; e-mail twcsbpa@singnet.com.sg; internet www.publishers-sbpa.org.sg; Pres. TRIENA WONG.

Broadcasting and Communications

TELECOMMUNICATIONS

Infocomm Development Authority of Singapore (IDA): 8 Temasek Blvd, 14-00 Suntec Tower Three, Singapore 038988; tel. 62110888; fax 62112222; e-mail info@ida.gov.sg; internet www.ida.gov.sg; f. 1999; formed as result of merger of National Computer Board and Telecommunication Authority of Singapore; the national policy maker; regulator of telecommunications and promoter of infocommunications in Singapore; CEO RONNIE TAY.

MobileOne (M1): 10 International Business Park, Singapore 609928; tel. 68951111; fax 68993929; e-mail ir@m1.com.sg; internet www.m1.com.sg; f. 1997; Chair. TEO SOON HOE; CEO KAREN KOOI.

Netrust Pte Ltd: 70 Bendemeer Rd, 05-03, Luzerne, Singapore 339940; tel. 62121388; fax 62121366; e-mail infoline@netrust.net; internet www.netrust.net; f. 1997; the only licensed Certification Authority (CA) in Singapore, jtly formed by the National Computer Board and the Network for Electronic Transfers; the authority verifies the identity of parties doing business or communicating in cyberspace through the issuing of electronic identification certificates, in order to enable government organizations and private enterprises to conduct electronic transactions in a secure manner; CEO FOO JONG AI.

Singapore Technologies Telemedia: 51 Cuppage Rd, 10-11/17, Starhub Centre, Singapore 229469; tel. 67238777; fax 67207277; e-mail contactus@stt.st.com.sg; internet www.sttelemedia.com; Pres. and CEO LEE THENG KIAT.

Singapore Telecommunications Ltd (SingTel): 19-00 Comcentre, 31 Exeter Rd, Singapore 239732; tel. 68383388; fax 67383769; e-mail contact@singtel.com; internet www.singtel.com; f. 1992; a postal and telecommunications service operator and a holding company for a number of subsidiaries, serving both the corporate and consumer markets; 61.79%-owned by Temasek Holdings (Private) Ltd (a government holding company), 38.21% transferred to the private sector; Chair. CHUMPOL NALAMLIENG; Group CEO CHUA SOCK KOONG.

StarHub Pte Ltd: Head Office, 51 Cuppage Rd, 07-00 StarHub Centre, Singapore 229469; tel. 68255000; fax 67215000; e-mail corpcomms@starhub.com; internet www.starhub.com.sg; f. 2000; telecommunications service provider; consortium includes Singapore Technologies Telemedia Pte Ltd, Singapore Power Ltd, Nippon Telegraph and Telephone Corpn (NTT) and British Telecom (BT); Pres. and CEO TERRY CLONTZ.

BROADCASTING

Regulatory Authority

Media Development Authority (MDA): MITA Bldg 04-01, 140 Hill St, Singapore 179369; tel. 68379973; fax 63368023; internet www.mda.gov.sg; f. 1994; fmrly Singapore Broadcasting Authority, name changed as above in Jan. 2003; licenses and regulates the media industry in Singapore; encourages, promotes and facilitates the development of media industries in Singapore, ensures the provision of an adequate range of media services to serve the interests of the general public, maintains fair and efficient market conduct and effective competition in the media industry, ensures the maintenance of a high standard of media services, regulates public service broadcasting; Chair. Dr TAN CHIN NAM; CEO Dr CHRISTOPHER CHIA.

Radio

Far East Broadcasting Associates (FEBA Ltd): 30 Lorong Ampas, 07-01 Skywaves Industrial Bldg, Singapore 328783; tel. 62508577; fax 62508422; e-mail febadmin@febaltd.com; f. 1960; Chair. GOH EWE KHENG; Exec. Dir LEE CHI KWAN (acting).

Media Corporation of Singapore: Caldecott Broadcast Centre, Andrew Rd, Singapore 299939; tel. 63333888; fax 62515628; e-mail cherfern@mediacorpradio.com; internet www.mediacorp.com.sg; f. 1994; est. as Singapore International Media (SIM), following the corporatization of the Singapore Broadcasting Corpn; holding co for seven operating cos—Television Corpn of Singapore (TCS), Singapore Television Twelve (STV12), Radio Corpn of Singapore (RCS), MediaCorp Studios, MediaCorp News, MediaCorp Interactive and MediaCorp Publishing; Chair. HO KWON PING; CEO LUCAS CHOW.

Radio Corpn of Singapore Pte Ltd (RCS): Caldecott Broadcast Centre, Radio Bldg, Andrew Rd, Singapore 299939; tel. 62518622; fax 62569533; e-mail feedback@rcs.com.sg; internet www.mediacorpradio.com; f. 1936; operates 12 domestic services—incl. in English (five), Chinese (Mandarin) (three), Malay (two) and Tamil (one)—and three international radio stations (manages Radio Singapore International (RSI)—services in English, Mandarin and Malay for three hours daily and service in Bahasa Indonesia for one hour daily); COO CHUA FOO YONG.

Rediffusion (Singapore) Pte Ltd: 6 Harper Rd, 04-01/08 Leong Huat Bldg, Singapore 369674; tel. 63832633; fax 62850421; e-mail md@rediffusion.com.sg; internet www.rediffusion.com.sg; f. 1949; commercial audio wired broadcasting service and wireless digital audio broadcasting service; broadcasts two programmes in Mandarin (18 hours daily) and English (24 hours daily); Man. Dir WONG BAN KUAN.

SAFRA Radio: Bukit Merah Central, POB 1315, Singapore 911599; tel. 63731924; fax 62783039; e-mail power98@pacific.net.sg; internet www.power98.com.sg; f. 1994; broadcasts in Chinese (Mandarin) and English.

Union Works Pte Ltd: Singapore; internet www.wrkz913.com; f. 1991; fmrly Radio Heart; name changed as above in 2000; first private radio station; broadcasts in English; 2 channels broadcasting a total of 336 hours weekly.

Television

CNBC Asia Business News (S) Pte Ltd: 10 Anson Rd, 06-01 International Plaza, Singapore 079903; tel. 63230488; fax 63230788; e-mail talk2us@cnbcasia.com; internet www.cnbcasia.com.sg; f. 1998; cable and satellite broadcaster of global business and financial news; US controlled; broadcasts in English (24 hours daily) and Mandarin; Pres. PAUL FRANCE.

Media Corporation of Singapore: see Radio.

Singapore Television Twelve Pte Ltd (STV12): 12 Prince Edward Rd, 05-00 Bestway Bldg, Singapore 079212; tel. 62258133; fax 62203881; internet www.stv12.com.sg; f. 1994; terrestrial television station; 2 channels—Suria (Malay, 58 hours weekly) and Central (110.5 hours weekly); COO WOON TAI HO.

SPH MediaWorks Ltd: 82 Genting Lane, Singapore 349567; tel. 63197988; fax 67443318; e-mail mwcc@sphmediaworks.com; f. 2000; subsidiary of Singapore Press Holdings Ltd (SPH); two channels—Channel U (Mandarin) and Channel i (English); also owns two radio stations; Exec. Dir WEE LEONG HOW.

Starhub CableVision Ltd: 51 Cuppage Rd 07-00, Singapore 229469; tel. 68255000; fax 67215000; internet www.starhub.com;

SINGAPORE

Directory

f. 1992; fmrly Singapore CableVision Ltd; name changed as above in 2002 following acquisition by Starhub Ltd; broadcasting and communications co, subscription television service; launched cable service in June 1995; offers 83 digital channels (March 2005); offers broadband access services; CEO TERRY CLOONTZ.

Television Corpn of Singapore (TCS): Caldecott Broadcast Centre, Andrew Rd, Singapore 299939; tel. 62560401; fax 62538119; e-mail webmaster@mediacorptv.com; internet www.mediacorptv.com; f. 1994; est. following the corporatization of Singapore Broadcasting Corpn; four channels—TCS 5 (English), TCS 8 (Mandarin), Suria (Malay) and Central; teletext service on two channels; also owns TVMobile, Singapore's first digital television channel, and Digital TV; Chair. HO KWON PING; CEO LIM HUP SENG.

Finance

(cap. = capital; res = reserves; dep. = deposits; m. = million; brs = branches; amounts in Singapore dollars)

BANKING

The Singapore monetary system is regulated by the Monetary Authority of Singapore (MAS) and the Ministry of Finance. The MAS performs all the functions of a central bank and also assumed responsibility for the issuing of currency following its merger with the Board of Commissioners of Currency in October 2002. In May 2008 there were 113 commercial banks (six local, 107 foreign) and 44 representative offices in Singapore. Of the foreign banks, 25 had full licences, 42 had wholesale licences and 40 had 'offshore' banking licences.

Government Financial Institution

Monetary Authority of Singapore (MAS): 10 Shenton Way, MAS Bldg, Singapore 079117; tel. 62255577; fax 62299491; e-mail webmaster@mas.gov.sg; internet www.mas.gov.sg; merged with Board of Commissioners of Currency Oct. 2002; cap. 100m., res 17,463m., dep. 8,441m. (March 2006); Chair. GOH CHOK TONG; Man. Dir HENG SWEE KEAT.

Domestic Full Commercial Banks

Bank of Singapore Ltd: 18 Church St, 01-00 OCBC Centre South, Singapore 049479; tel. 65863200; fax 64383718; e-mail clientservice@finatiq.com; internet www.finatiq.com; f. 1954; subsidiary of Oversea-Chinese Banking Corpn Ltd; Chair. DAVID PHILBRICK CONNER; CEO TAN NGIAP JOO.

DBS Bank (Development Bank of Singapore Ltd): 6 Shenton Way, DBS Bldg, Tower One, Singapore 068809; tel. 68788888; fax 64451267; e-mail dbs@dbs.com; internet www.dbs.com/sg; f. 1968; 29% govt-owned; merged with Post Office Savings Bank in 1998; cap. 12,096m., res 7,110m., dep. 121,662m. (Dec. 2006); Chair. and CEO KOH BOON HWEE; 107 local brs, 9 overseas brs.

Far Eastern Bank Ltd: 156 Cecil St, 01-00 FEB Bldg, Singapore 069544; tel. 62219055; fax 62242263; internet www.uobgroup.com; f. 1959; subsidiary of United Overseas Bank Ltd; cap. 100m., res 69.8m., dep. 645.7m. (Dec. 2006); CEO WEE EE CHEONG; 3 brs.

Oversea-Chinese Banking Corpn (OCBC) Ltd: 65 Chulia St, 08-00 OCBC Centre, Singapore 049513; tel. 65357222; fax 65337955; e-mail info@ocbc.com.sg; internet www.ocbc.com.sg; f. 1932; merged with Keppel TatLee Bank Ltd in Aug. 2001; cap. 5,480.9m., res 7,923.3m., dep. 89,639.5m. (Dec. 2006); Chair. Dr CHEONG CHOONG KONG; CEO DAVID PHILBRICK CONNER; 63 local brs, 52 overseas brs.

United Overseas Bank Ltd: 80 Raffles Place, UOB Plaza, Singapore 048624; tel. 65394439; fax 65342334; internet www.uobgroup.com; f. 1935; merged with Overseas Union Bank Ltd in Jan. 2002 and Industrial and Commercial Bank Ltd in Aug. 2002; cap. 2.013.7m., res 8,080.1m., dep. 118,501.6m. (Dec. 2007); Chair. and CEO WEE CHO YAW; Pres. WEE EE CHEONG; 61 local brs, 21 overseas brs.

Foreign Banks

Full Commercial Banks

ABN AMRO Asia Merchant Bank (Singapore) Ltd (Netherlands): 63 Chulia St, Singapore 049514; tel. 62318888; fax 65323108; Chair. DAVID WONG SEE HONG; Man. Dir ROBERT R. DAVIS.

American Express Bank Ltd (USA): 16 Collyer Quay, Hitachi Tower, Singapore 049318; tel. 65384833; fax 65343022; Sr Country Exec. S. LACHLAN HOUGH.

Bangkok Bank Public Co Ltd (Thailand): 180 Cecil St, Bangkok Bank Bldg, Singapore 069546; tel. 62219400; fax 62255852; e-mail torpong.cha@bbl.co.th; Sr Vice-Pres. and Gen. Man. TORPHONG CHARUNGCHAREONVEJI.

Bank of America NA (USA): 9 Raffles Place, 18-00 Republic Plaza Tower 1, Singapore 048619; tel. 62393888; fax 62393068; CEO ALAN KOH; Man. Dir GOETZ EGGELHOEFER.

Bank of China (People's Republic of China): 4 Battery Rd, Bank of China Bldg, Singapore 049908; tel. 65352411; fax 65343401; Gen. Man. ZHU HUA.

Bank of East Asia Ltd (Hong Kong): 137 Market St, Bank of East Asia Bldg, Singapore 048943; tel. 62241334; fax 62251805; e-mail info@hkbea.com.sg; Gen. Man. KHOO KEE CHEOK.

Bank of India (India): 01-01 to 03-01, Hong Leong Centre, 138 Robinson Rd, Singapore 068906; tel. 62220011; fax 62254407; Chief Exec. VIJAY MEHTA; Gen. Man. B. RAMASUBRAMANIAM.

PT Bank Negara Indonesia (Persero) Tbk (Indonesia): 158 Cecil St, 01-00 to 04-00 Dapenso Bldg, Singapore 069545; tel. 62257755; fax 62254757; Gen. Man. MUHAMMAD YAZEED.

Bank of Tokyo-Mitsubishi UFJ Ltd (Japan): 9 Raffles Place, 01-01 Republic Plaza, Singapore 048619; tel. 65383388; fax 65388083; Gen. Man. HAKOTO NAKAGAWA; Dep. Gen. Man. HIDEMITSU OTSUKA.

BNP Paribas (France): 20 Collyer Quay, 18-01 Tung Centre, Singapore 049319; tel. 62101288; fax 62243459; internet www.bnpparibas.com.sg; Regional Man. JEAN-PIERRE BERNARD.

Calyon (France): 168 Robinson Rd, 22-01, Capital Tower, Singapore 068912; tel. 65354988; fax 65322422; internet www.calyon.com; formed through merger of Crédit Agricole Indosuez and Crédit Lyonnais.

Citibank NA (USA): Capital Square, 23 Church St, 01-01, Singapore 049481; tel. 62255225; fax 6325880; internet www.citibank.com.sg; Country Corporate Officer SANJIV MISRA.

HL Bank (Malaysia): 20 Collyer Quay, 01-02 and 02-02 Tung Centre, Singapore 049319; tel. 65352466; fax 65339340; Country Head GAN HUI TIN.

Hongkong and Shanghai Banking Corpn Ltd (Hong Kong): 01-00 HSBC Bldg, 21 Collyer Quay, Singapore 049320; tel. 65305000; fax 62214676; e-mail direct@hsbc.com.sg; internet www.hsbc.com.sg; CEO (Singapore) PAUL LAWRENCE.

Indian Bank (India): 3 Raffles Place, Bharat Bldg, Singapore 048617; tel. 65343511; fax 65331651; e-mail ceibsing@mbox3.singnet.com.sg; Chief Exec. V. SRINIVASAN.

Indian Overseas Bank (India): 94 Serangoon Rd, Singapore 217999; tel. 62941385; fax 62970701; e-mail iobrem@iob.com.sg; Chief Exec. KONIDALA PERUMAL MUNIRATHNAM.

JP Morgan Chase Bank (USA): 168 Robinson Rd, 15th Floor, 14-01 Capital Tower, Singapore 068912; tel. 68822888; fax 68821756; Sr Country Officer RAYMOND CHANG.

Maybank (Malaysia): Maybank Tower, 2 Battery Rd 01-00, Singapore 049907; tel. 65507000; fax 65333071; e-mail cs@maybank.com.sg; internet www.maybank2u.com.sg; Country Head POLLIE SIM; 22 brs.

RHB Bank Bhd (Malaysia): 5th Floor, 90 Cecil St 05-00, Singapore 069531; tel. 62202736; fax 62216646; internet www.rhbbank.com.my/cbob/singapore.shtm; Country Head ANTHONY YEO.

Southern Bank Bhd (Malaysia): 39 Robinson Rd, 01-02 Robinson Point, Singapore 068911; tel. 65321318; fax 65355366; Dir YEAP LAM YANG.

Standard Chartered Bank (UK): 6 Battery Rd, Singapore 049909; tel. 62258888; fax 67893756; internet www.standardchartered.com.sg; Group Chair. BRYAN SANDERSON; Chief Exec. (Singapore) EULEEN GOH.

Sumitomo Mitsui Banking Corpn (Japan): 3 Temasek Ave, 06-01 Centennial Tower, Singapore 039190; tel. 68820001; fax 68870330; Gen. Man. MASAMI TASHIRO.

UCO Bank (India): 3 Raffles Place, 01-01 Bharat Bldg, Singapore 048617; tel. 65325944; fax 65325044; e-mail general@ucobank.com.sg; Chief Exec. P. K. TAGORE.

Wholesale Banks

Australia and New Zealand Banking Group Ltd (Australia): 10 Collyer Quay, 17-01/07 Ocean Bldg, Singapore 049315; tel. 65358355; fax 65396111; Gen. Man. BILL FOO.

Bank of Nova Scotia (Canada): 10 Collyer Quay, 15-01/09 Ocean Bldg, Singapore 049315; tel. 65358688; fax 65363325; Country Head, Vice-Pres. and Man. SEONG KOON WAH SUN.

Barclays Bank PLC (UK): 23 Church St, 13-08 Capital Sq., Singapore 049481; tel. 63953000; fax 63953139; Regional Head JAMES LOH; Country Man. QUEK SUAN KIAT.

Bayerische Hypo- und Vereinsbank AG (Germany): 30 Cecil St, 26-01 Prudential Tower, Singapore 049712; tel. 64133688; fax 65368591; Gen. Man. RICHARD LEE.

Bayerische Landesbank Girozentrale (Germany): 300 Beach Rd, 37-01 The Concourse, Singapore 199555; tel. 62983322; fax 62932151; e-mail sgblb@blb.de; Gen. Man. and Sr Vice-Pres. MANFRED WOLF; Exec. Vice-Pres. HEINZ HOFFMANN.

SINGAPORE

Directory

BNP Paribas Private Bank (France): 20 Collyer Quay, 18-01 Tung Centre, Singapore 049319; tel. 62101037; fax 62103671; internet www.bnpparibas.com.sg; CEO SERGE FORTI.

Commerzbank AG (Germany): 8 Shenton Way, 41-01 Temasek Tower, Singapore 068811; tel. 63110000; fax 62253943; Gen. Man. MICHAEL OLIVER.

Crédit Lyonnais (France): 3 Temasek Ave, 11-01 Centennial Tower, Singapore 039190; tel. 63336331; fax 63336332; Gen. Man. PIERRE EYMERY.

Crédit Suisse (Switzerland): 1 Raffles Link, 05-02, Singapore 039393; tel. 62126000; fax 62126200; e-mail ask.us@credit-suisse.com; internet www.cspb.com.sg; Br. Man. DIDIER VON DAENIKEN.

Crédit Suisse First Boston (Switzerland): 1 Raffles Link, 03/04-01 South Lobby, Singapore 039393; tel. 62122000; fax 62123100; Br. Man. ERIC M. VARVEL.

Deutsche Bank AG (Germany): 6 Shenton Way, 15-08 DBS Bldg, Tower Two, Singapore 068809; tel. 64238001; fax 62259442; Gen. Man. RONNY TAN CHONG TEE.

Dresdner Bank AG (Germany): 20 Collyer Quay, 22-00 Tung Centre, Singapore 049319; tel. 62228080; fax 62244008; Man. Dirs ANDREAS RUSCHKOWSKI, RAYMOND B. T. KOH, PIERS WILLIS; CEO BAUDOUIN GROONENBERGHS.

First Commercial Bank (Taiwan): 76 Shenton Way, 01-02 ONG Bldg, Singapore 079119; tel. 62215755; fax 62251905; e-mail fcbsin@singnet.com.sg; Gen. Man. TSENG CHI-LUNG.

Fortis Bank SA/NV (Belgium/Netherlands): 63 Market St, 21-01, Singapore 048942; tel. 65394988; fax 65394933; Gen. Man. PETER FOO.

Habib Bank Ltd (Pakistan): 3 Phillip St, 01-03 Commerce Pt, Singapore 048693; tel. 64380055; fax 64380644; e-mail gmhbl@singnet.com.sg; Regional Gen. Man. ASHRAF MAHMOOD WATHRA.

HSBC Republic Bank (Suisse) SA (Switzerland): 21 Collyer Quay, 21-01 HSBC Bldg, Singapore 049320; tel. 62248080; fax 62237146; CEO KENNETH SIT YIU SUN.

Industrial and Commercial Bank of China (People's Republic of China): 6 Raffles Quay, 12-01 John Hancock Tower, Singapore 048580; tel. 65381066; fax 65381370; e-mail icbcsg@icbc.com.sg; Chair. and Pres. JIANG JIANQING.

ING Bank NV (Netherlands): 9 Raffles Place, 19-02 Republic Plaza, Singapore 048619; tel. 65353688; fax 65338329; Country Head J. KESTEMONT.

Intesa Sanpaolo SpA (Italy): 6 Temasek Blvd, 42/04-05 Suntec Tower Four, Singapore 038986; tel. 63338270; fax 63338252; e-mail singapore.sg@intesasanpaolo.com; internet www.intesasanpaolo.com; fmrly San Paolo IMI SpA; Gen. Man. GIOVANNI FIORENDI.

KBC Bank NV (Belgium): 30 Cecil St, 12-01/08 Prudential Tower, Singapore 049712; tel. 63952828; fax 65342929; Gen. Man. THIERRY MEZERET.

Korea Exchange Bank (Republic of Korea): 30 Cecil St, 24-03/08 Prudential Tower, Singapore 049712; tel. 65361633; fax 65382522; e-mail kebspore@singnet.com.sg; Gen. Man. HO SUN YUN.

Landesbank Baden-Württemberg (Germany): 25 International Business Park, 01-72 German Centre, Singapore 609916; tel. 65627722; fax 65627729; Man. Dr WOLFHART AUER VAN HERRENKIRCHEN.

Mega International Commercial Bank Co Ltd (Taiwan): 80 Raffles Place, 23-20 UOB Plaza II, Singapore 048624; tel. 65366311; fax 65360680; Gen. Man. HSIANG YEN-PING.

Mizuho Corporate Bank Ltd (Japan): 168 Robinson Rd, 13-00 Capital Tower, Singapore 068912; tel. 64230330; fax 64230012; Gen. Man. TADAO OGOSHI.

Moscow Narodny Bank Ltd (UK): 50 Robinson Rd, MNB Bldg, Singapore 068882; tel. 62209422; fax 62250140; Man. Dir EVGENY MIKHAILOVICH GREVTSEV.

National Australia Bank Ltd (Australia): 5 Temasek Blvd, 15-01 Suntec City Tower Five, Singapore 038985; tel. 63380038; fax 63380039; Gen. Man. FRANK OLSSON.

National Bank of Kuwait SAK (Kuwait): 9 Raffles Place, 51-01/02 Republic Plaza, Singapore 048619; tel. 62225348; fax 62245438; Gen. Man. RICHARD MCKEGNEY.

Norddeutsche Landesbank Girozentrale (Germany): 6 Shenton Way, 16-08 DBS Bldg Tower Two, Singapore 068809; tel. 63231223; fax 63230223; e-mail nordlb.singapore@nordlb.com; Gen. Man. and Regional Head Asia/Pacific HEINZ WERNER FRINGS.

Northern Trust Company (USA): 1 George St, 12-06, Singapore 049145; tel. 64376666; fax 64376609; e-mail LA16@ntrs.com; internet www.northerntrust.com; f. 1889; Sr Vice-Pres. LAWRENCE AU.

Rabobank International (Netherlands): 77 Robinson Rd, 09-00 SIA Bldg, Singapore 068896; tel. 65363363; fax 65363236; Regional Man. (Asia) ROB VAN ZADELHOFF.

Royal Bank of Scotland PLC (UK): 50 Raffles Place, 08-00 Singapore Land Tower, Singapore 048623; tel. 64168600; fax 62259827; Gen. Man. ALAN ROY GOODYEAR.

Société Générale (France): 80 Robinson Rd, 25-00, Singapore 068898; tel. 62227122; fax 62252609; Chief Country Officer ERIC WORMSER.

State Street Bank and Trust Co (USA): 8 Shenton Way, 33-03 Temasek Tower, Singapore 068811; tel. 63299600; fax 62259377; Br. Man. LEE YOW FEE.

UBS AG (Switzerland): 5 Temasek Blvd, 18-00 Suntec City Tower, Singapore 038985; tel. 64318000; fax 64318188; e-mail rolf-w.gerber@wdr.com; Man. Dir and Head of Br. (Singapore) BRAD ORGILL.

UniCredito Italiano SpA (Italy): 80 Raffles Place, 51-01 UOB Plaza 1, Singapore 048624; tel. 62325728; fax 65344300; e-mail singaporebranch@gruppocredit.it; Gen. Man. MAURIZIO BRENTEGANI.

WestLB AG (Germany): 3 Temasek Ave, 33-00 Centennial Tower, Singapore 039190; tel. 63332388; fax 63332399; Gen. Man. TEO EE-NGOH.

'Offshore Banks'

ABSA Bank Ltd (South Africa): 9 Temasek Blvd, 40-01 Suntec Tower Two, Singapore 038989; tel. 63331033; fax 63331066; Gen. Man. DAVID MEADOWS.

Agricultural Bank of China (People's Republic of China): 80 Raffles Place, 27-20 UOB Plaza 2, Singapore 048624; tel. 65355255; fax 65387960; e-mail aboc@abchina.com.sg; Gen. Man. SUN MEIYU.

Arab Bank PLC (Jordan): 80 Raffles Place, 32-20 UOB Plaza 2, Singapore 048624; tel. 65330055; fax 65322150; e-mail abplc@pacific.net.com.sg; Exec. Vice-Pres. and Area Exec. Asia Pacific KIM EUN-YOUNG.

Banca Monte dei Paschi di Siena SpA (Italy): 10 Collyer Quay, 13-01 Ocean Bldg, Singapore 0104; tel. 65352533; fax 65327996; Gen. Man. GIUSEPPE DE GIOSA.

Banca di Roma (Italy): 9 Raffles Place, 20-20 Republic Plaza II, Singapore 048619; tel. 64387509; fax 65352267; e-mail bdrsi@singnet.com.sg; Gen. Man. MARIO FATTORUSSO.

Bank of Communications (People's Republic of China): 50 Raffles Place, 26-04 Singapore Land Tower, Singapore 048623; tel. 65320335; fax 65320339; Gen. Man. NIU KE RONG.

PT Bank Mandiri (Persero) (Indonesia): 16 Collyer Quay, 28-00 Hitachi Tower, Singapore 049318; tel. 65320200; fax 65320206; Gen. Man. MUHADJIR SANGIDU.

Bank of New York Mellon (USA): 1 Temasek Ave, 02-01 Millenia Tower, Singapore 039192; tel. 64320222; fax 63374302; formed through merger of Bank of New York with Mellon Financial Corpn in 2007; Sr Vice-Pres. and Man. Dir JAI ARYA.

Bank of New Zealand (New Zealand): 5 Temasek Blvd, 15-01 Suntec City Tower, Singapore 038985; tel. 63322990; fax 63322991; Gen. Man. VIVIEN KOH.

Bank of Taiwan (Taiwan): 80 Raffles Place, 28-20 UOB Plaza 2, Singapore 048624; tel. 65365536; fax 65368203; Gen. Man. CHIOU YE-CHIN.

Bumiputra Commerce Bank Bhd (Malaysia): 7 Temasek Blvd, 37-01/02/03 Suntec Tower One, Singapore 038987; tel. 63375115; fax 63371335; e-mail bpsp3700@pacific.net.sg; Gen. Man. DHANA SEGARAM.

Canadian Imperial Bank of Commerce (Canada): 16 Collyer Quay, 04-02 Hitachi Tower, Singapore 049318; tel. 65352323; fax 65357565; Br. Man. NORMAN SIM CHEE BENG.

Chang Hwa Commercial Bank Ltd (China): 1 Finlayson Green, 08-00, Singapore 049246; tel. 65320820; fax 65320374; Gen. Man. YANG JIH-CHENG.

China Construction Bank Corpn (People's Republic of China): 9 Raffles Place, 33-01/02 Republic Plaza, Singapore 048619; tel. 65358133; fax 65356533; e-mail enquiry@ccb.com.sg; internet www.ccb.com.sg; Gen. Man. JIN YU.

Commonwealth Bank of Australia (Australia): 22-04 Singapore Land Tower, 50 Raffles Place, Singapore 048623; tel. 62243877; fax 62245812; Gen. Man. ROBERT LEWIS BUCHAN.

Crédit Industriel et Commercial (France): 63 Market St, 15-01, Singapore 048942; tel. 65366008; fax 65367008; internet www.cic.com.sg; Gen. Man. JEAN-LUC ANGLADA.

Crédit Lyonnais (Suisse) SA (Switzerland): 3 Temasek Ave 11-01, Centennial Tower, Singapore 039190; tel. 68320900; fax 63338590; e-mail singaporebranch@creditlyonnais.ch; Man. Dir ANTOINE CANDIOTTI.

Deutsche Zentral Genossenschaftsbank (DZ Bank AG) (Germany): 50 Raffles Place, 40-01 Singapore Land Tower, Singapore

SINGAPORE

048623; tel. 64380082; fax 62230082; Gen. Man. KLAUS GERHARD BORIG.

Dexia Banque Internationale à Luxembourg (Luxembourg): 9 Raffles Place, 42-01 Republic Plaza, Singapore 048619; tel. 62227622; fax 65360201; Gen. Man. ALEXANDRE JOSSET.

DnB NOR (Norway): 8 Shenton Way, 48-02 Temasek Tower, Singapore 068811; tel. 62206144; e-mail dnb.singapore@dnb.no; internet www.dnbnor.no.

Hana Bank (Republic of Korea): 8 Cross St, 23-06 PWC Bldg, Singapore 048424; tel. 64384100; fax 64384200; Gen. Man. CHO YOUNG-SEOK.

Hang Seng Bank Ltd (Hong Kong): 21 Collyer Quay, 14-01 HSBC Bldg, Singapore 049320; tel. 65363118; fax 65363148; e-mail sgp@hangseng.com; Country Man. ANTHONY KAM PING LEUNG.

HSH Nordbank AG (Germany): 3 Temasek Ave, 32-03 Centennial Tower, Singapore 039190; tel. 65509000; fax 65509003; e-mail info@hsh-nordbank.com.sg; Gen. Man. and Regional Head KLAUS HEINER BORITZKA.

Hua Nan Commercial Bank Ltd (Taiwan): 80 Robinson Rd, 14-03, Singapore 068898; tel. 63242566; fax 63242155; Gen. Man. HUANG YUN-LUNG.

ICICI Bank Ltd (India): 9 Raffles Place, 50-01 Republic Plaza, Singapore 048619; tel. 67239288; fax 67239268; e-mail globalinvest@icicibank.com; internet www.icicibank.com.sg; Chief. Exec. SUVEK NAMBIAR.

Korea Development Bank (Republic of Korea): 8 Shenton Way, 07-01 Temasek Tower, Singapore 068811; tel. 62248188; fax 62256540; Gen. Man. KIM BYOUNG SOO.

Krung Thai Bank Public Co Ltd (Thailand): 65 Chulia St, 32-05/08 OCBC Centre, Singapore 049513; tel. 65336691; fax 65330930; e-mail br.singapore@ktb.co.th; Gen. Man. PUMIN LEELAYOOVA.

Land Bank of Taiwan: UOB Plaza 1, 34-01 Raffles Place, Singapore 048624; tel. 63494555; fax 63494545; Gen. Man. WILSON W. B. LIN.

Lloyds TSB Bank PLC (UK): 1 Temasek Ave 18-01, Millenia Tower, Singapore 039192; tel. 65341191; fax 65322493; e-mail mktg@lloydstsb.com.sg; internet www.lloydstsb.com.sg; Country Head WALLACE WONG.

Mitsubishi Trust and Banking Corpn (Japan): 50 Raffles Place, 42-01/06 Singapore Land Tower, Singapore 048623; tel. 62259155; fax 62241857; Gen. Man. MIKIO KOBAYASHI.

Natexis Banques Populaires (France): 50 Raffles Place, 41-01, Singapore Land Tower, Singapore 048623; tel. 62241455; fax 62248651; Gen. Man. PHILIPPE PETITGAS.

Nedcor Bank Ltd (South Africa): 30 Cecil St, 10-05 Prudential Tower, Singapore 049712; tel. 64169438; fax 64388350; e-mail nedsing@nedcor.com; Gen. Man. BRIAN SHEGAR.

Nordea Bank Finland Plc (Finland): 3 Anson Rd, 22–01 Springleaf Tower, Singapore 079909; tel. 63176500; fax 63275616; e-mail singapore@nordea.com; Gen. Man. THOR ERLING KYLSTAD.

Norinchukin Bank (Japan): 80 Raffles Place, 53-01 UOB Plaza 1, Singapore 048624; tel. 65351011; fax 65352883; Gen. Man. AKITA KURIHARA.

Philippine National Bank (Philippines): 96 Somerset Rd, 04-01/04 UOL Bldg, Singapore 238183; tel. 67374646; fax 67374224; e-mail singapore@pnb.com.ph; Vice-Pres. and Gen. Man. RODELO G. FRANCO.

Raiffeisen Zentralbank Österreich Aktiengesellschaft (Austria): 50 Raffles Place, 45-01 Singapore Land Tower, Singapore 048623; tel. 62259578; fax 62253973; Gen. Man. RAINER SILHAVY.

Royal Bank of Canada (Canada): 20 Raffles Place, 27-03/08 Ocean Towers, Singapore 048620; tel. 65369206; fax 65322804; Gen. Man. TREVOR DAVID WYNN.

Shinhan Bank (Republic of Korea): 50 Raffles Place, 04-02/03 Singapore Land Tower, Singapore 048623; tel. 65361144; fax 65331244; merged with Chohun Bank 2006; Gen. Man. CHOI HEUNG MIN.

Siam Commercial Bank Public Company Ltd (Thailand): 16 Collyer Quay, 25-01 Hitachi Tower, Singapore 049318; tel. 65364338; fax 65364728; Gen. Man. BANDIT ROJANAVONGSE.

Skandinaviska Enskilda Banken AB Publ (Sweden): 50 Raffles Place, 36-01 Singapore Land Tower, Singapore 048623; tel. 62235644; fax 62253047; Gen. Man. SVEN BJÖRKMAN.

State Bank of India (India): 6 Shenton Way, 22-08 DBS Bldg Tower Two, Singapore 068809; tel. 62222033; fax 62253348; e-mail sbinsgsg@pacific.net.sg; CEO PADMA RAMASUBBAN.

Sumitomo Trust & Banking Co Ltd (Japan): 8 Shenton Way, 45-01 Temasek Tower, Singapore 068811; tel. 62249055; fax 62242873; Gen. Man. MASAYUKI IMANAKA.

Svenska Handelsbanken AB (publ) (Sweden): 65 Chulia St, 21-01/04 OCBC Centre, Singapore 049513; tel. 65323800; fax 65344909; Gen. Man. JAN BIRGER DJERF.

Toronto-Dominion (South East Asia) Ltd (Canada): 15-02 Millenia Tower, 1 Temasek Ave, Singapore 039192; tel. 64346000; fax 63369500; Br. Dir AKHILESHWAR LAMBA.

Union de Banques Arabes et Françaises (UBAF) (France): 6 Temasek Blvd, 25-04-05 Suntec Tower Four, Singapore 038986; tel. 63336188; fax 63336789; e-mail ubafsg@singnet.com.sg; Gen. Man. ERIC REINHART.

Westpac Banking Corpn (Australia): 77 Robinson Rd, 19-00 SIA Bldg, Singapore 068896; tel. 65309898; fax 65326781; e-mail yhlee@westpac.wm.au; Gen. Man. CHRISTOPHER DAVID RAND.

Woori Bank (Republic of Korea): 5 Shenton Way, 17-03 UIC Bldg, Singapore 068808; tel. 62235855; fax 62259530; e-mail combksp@singnet.com.sg; Gen. Man. PARK DONG YOUNG.

Bankers' Association

The Association of Banks in Singapore: 10 Shenton Way, 12-08 MAS Bldg, Singapore 079117; tel. 62244300; fax 62241785; e-mail banks@abs.org.sg; internet www.abs.org.sg; f. 1973; Chair. DAVID P. CONNOR.

STOCK EXCHANGE

Singapore Exchange Limited (SGX): 2 Shenton Way, 19-00 SGX Centre One, Singapore 068804; tel. 62368888; fax 65356994; e-mail webmaster@sgx.com; internet www.sgx.com; f. 1999; demutualized and integrated securities and derivatives exchange; Chair. J. Y. PILLAY; CEO HSIEH FU HUA; Chief Finance Officer SECK WAI KWONG.

INSURANCE

The insurance industry is supervised by the Monetary Authority of Singapore (see Banking). In May 2008 there were 147 insurance companies, comprising 59 direct insurers (12 life insurance, 42 general insurance, five composite insurers), 25 professional reinsurers (three life reinsurers, 13 general reinsurers, nine composite reinsurers), five authorized reinsurers (one life reinsurer, three general reinsurers, one composite reinsurer) and 60 captive insurers.

Domestic Companies

Life Insurance

Aviva Ltd: 4 Shenton Way, 01-01, SGX Centre 2, Singapore 068807; tel. 68277988; fax 68277900; internet www.aviva-singapore.com.sg; f. 2002; Prin. Officer KEITH PERKINS.

Axa Life Insurance Singapore Pte Ltd: 143 Cecil St, 03-01/10 GB Bldg, Singapore 069542; tel. 68805500; fax 68805501; e-mail comsvc@axa-life.com.sg; internet www.axa-life.com.sg; Prin. Officer RICHARD MARC SHERMON.

China Life Insurance Co Ltd: 105 Cecil St, 18-00 and 19-00 The Octagon, Singapore 069534; tel. 62222366; fax 62221033; Prin. Officer SHEN NAN NING.

Friends Provident International Ltd (Singapore): 63 Market St, 06-05, Singapore 048942; tel. 63274019; fax 63274020; e-mail singapore.enquiries@fpiom.com; Prin. Officer CHRISTOPHER GAVIN GILL.

International Medical Insurers Pte Ltd: 585 North Bridge Rd, 13-00, Raffles Hospital, Singapore 188770; tel. 62982266; fax 63112396; e-mail enquiries@imi.sg; internet www.imi.sg; f. 1996; Prin. Officer VICTOR LYE.

Manulife (Singapore) Pte Ltd: 491B River Valley Rd, 07-00 Valley Pt, Singapore 248373; tel. 67371221; fax 68362374; e-mail service@manulife.com; internet www.manulife.com.sg; acquired John Hancock Life Assurance Co Ltd in Dec. 2004; Pres. and CEO DARREN THOMSON.

TM Asia Life Singapore Ltd: 80 Anson Rd, 14-00 Fuji Xerox Towers, Singapore 079907; tel. 62243181; fax 62239120; e-mail asialife@asialife.com.sg; internet www.tmasialife.com; f. 1948; fmrly The Asia Life Assurance Society Ltd; Man. Dir ARTHUR LEE KING CHI.

Transamerica Life (Singapore) Ltd: 1 Finlayson Green, 13-00, Singapore 049246; tel. 62120620; fax 62120621; internet www.transamerica.com.sg; wholly owned subsidiary of Transamerica Occidental Life Insurance Co; Prin. Officer LAURENCE WONG YUEN TIN.

Transamerica Occidental Life Insurance Co: 9 Raffles Place, 53-02, Republic Plaza, Singapore 048619; tel. 62362366; fax 62362123; internet www.transamerica.com.sg; Prin. Officer LAURENCE WONG YUEN TIN.

UOB Life Assurance Ltd: 156 Cecil St, 10-01 Far Eastern Bank Bldg, Singapore 069544; tel. 62278477; fax 62243012; e-mail uoblife@uobgroup.com; internet www.uoblife.com.sg; Man. Dir TOI SEE JONG.

SINGAPORE

Zurich International Life (Singapore) Ltd: 50 Raffles Place, 23-02, Singapore Land Tower, Singapore 048623; tel. 68766750; fax 68766751; Regional Dir CARLOS SABUGUEIRO.

General Insurance

Allianz Insurance Company of Singapore Pte Ltd: 3 Temasek Ave, 09-01 Centennial Tower, Singapore 039190; tel. 62972529; fax 62971956; e-mail askme@allianz.com.sg; internet www.allianz.com.sg; formed by merger between Allianz Insurance (Singapore) Pte Ltd and AGF Insurance (Singapore) Pte Ltd; Man. Dir ROWAN D'ARCY.

Asia Insurance Co Ltd: 2 Finlayson Green, 03-00 Asia Insurance Bldg, Singapore 049247; tel. 62243181; fax 62214355; e-mail asiains@asiainsurance.com.sg; internet www.asiainsurance.com.sg; f. 1923; Prin. Officer and Exec. Dir LARRY CHAN; Gen. Man. TAN KAH HO.

Asian Securitization and Infrastructure Assurance (Pte) Ltd: 9 Temasek Blvd, 38-01 Suntec Tower 2, Singapore 038989; tel. 63342555; fax 63342777; e-mail general@asialtd.com; Dir ELEANOR L. LIPSEY.

Aviva General Insurance Ltd: 4 Shenton Way, 21-01, SGX Centre 2, Singapore 068807; tel. 68277888; fax 68277800; e-mail service@aviva-gi.com; internet www.aviva-gi.com.sg; subsidiary of Mitsui Sumitomo Insurance Co Ltd following acquisition in 2004.

Axa Insurance Singapore Pte Ltd: 143 Cecil St, 01-01 GB Bldg, Singapore 069542; tel. 68804741; fax 68804740; e-mail customer.service@axa.com.sg; internet www.axa.com.sg; CEO BERNARD MARSEILLE.

Cosmic Insurance Corpn Ltd: 410 North Bridge Rd, 04-01 Cosmic Insurance Bldg, Singapore 188726; tel. 63387633; fax 63397805; e-mail query@cosmic.com.sg; internet www.cosmic.com.sg; f. 1971; Gen. Man. SWEE LEE CHUN.

ECICS-COFACE Guarantee Co (Singapore) Ltd: 7 Temasek Blvd, 10-03 Suntec City Tower 1, Singapore 038987; tel. 63374779; fax 63389267; e-mail ecics@ecics.com.sg; internet www.ecics.com.sg; Chair. KWAH THIAM HOCK; Asst Vice-Pres. KIM LIN MIN.

First Capital Insurance Ltd: 6 Raffles Quay 21-00, Singapore 048580; tel. 62222311; fax 62223547; e-mail enquiry@first-insurance.com.sg; internet www.first-insurance.com.sg; CEO RAMASWAMY ATHAPPAN.

India International Insurance Pte Ltd: 64 Cecil St, 04-00/05-00 IOB Bldg, Singapore 049711; tel. 63476100; fax 62244174; e-mail insure@iii.com.sg; internet www.iii.com.sg; f. 1987; all non-life insurance; CEO B. SUNDARRAMAN.

Kemper International Insurance Co (Pte) Ltd: 3 Shenton Way, 22-09 Shenton House, Singapore 068805; tel. 68369120; fax 68369121; e-mail vchia@kemper.com.sg; internet www.kemper.com.sg; Gen. Man. VIOLET CHIA.

Liberty Insurance Pte Ltd: 51 Club St, 03-00 Singapore 069428; tel. 62218611; fax 62263360; e-mail feedback@libertycitystate.com.sg; internet www.libertyinsurance.com.sg; division of Liberty Mutual Group (USA); fmrly Citystate Insurance Pte Ltd; Man. Dir A. K. CHER.

Mitsui Sumitomo Insurance (Singapore) Pte Ltd: 16 Raffles Quay, 24-01 Hong Leong Bldg, Singapore 048581; tel. 62209644; fax 62256371; internet www.ms-ins.com.sg; fmrly Mitsui Marine and Fire Insurance (Asia) Private Ltd; merged with The Sumitomo Marine and Fire Insurance Co Ltd and name changed as above in 2001; Man. Dir TAKAAKI NAKAMURA.

Royal & Sun Alliance Insurance (Singapore) Ltd: 77 Robinson Rd, 17-00 SIA Bldg, Singapore 068896; tel. 64230888; fax 64230798; e-mail customer.service@sg.royalsun.com; internet www.royalsunalliance.com.sg; Man. Dir and CEO EDMUND LIM.

SHC Capital Ltd: 302 Orchard Rd, 09-01 Tong Bldg, Singapore 238862; tel. 68299199; fax 68299249; e-mail shccapital@shcsb.com.sg; internet www.shccapital.com.sg; f. 1956; fmrly The Nanyang Insurance Co Ltd; name changed as above following takeover in June 2004; Dir and Prin. Officer QUEK SUN HUI.

Singapore Aviation and General Insurance Co (Pte) Ltd: 25 Airline Rd, 06-A Airline House, Singapore 819829; tel. 65423333; fax 65450221; f. 1976; Man. AMARJIT KAUR SIDHU.

Standard Steamship Owners' Protection and Indemnity Association (Asia) Ltd: 140 Cecil St, 10-02 PIL Bldg, Singapore 069540; tel. 65062896; fax 62211082; e-mail p&i.singapore@ctcplc.com; internet www.standard-club.com; Prin. Officer ROBERT DRUMMOND.

Tenet Insurance Co Ltd: 10 Collyer Quay, 04-01 Ocean Bldg, Singapore 049315; tel. 65326022; fax 65333871; Chair. ONG CHOO ENG.

The Tokio Marine & Fire Insurance Co (Singapore) Pte Ltd: 6 Shenton Way, 23-08 DBS Bldg Tower Two, Singapore 068809; tel. 62216111; fax 62240895; Man. Dir KYOZO HANAJIMA.

United Overseas Insurance Ltd: 156 Cecil St, 09-01 Far Eastern Bank Bldg, Singapore 069544; tel. 62227733; fax 63273870; e-mail contactus@uoi.com.sg; internet www.uoi.com.sg; f. 1971; Man. Dir DAVID CHAN MUN WAI.

Zürich Insurance (Singapore) Pte Ltd: 78 Shenton Way, 06-01, Singapore 079120; tel. 62202466; fax 62255749; Prin. Officer and Man. Dir RONALD CHENG JUE SENG.

Composite Insurance

American International Assurance Co Ltd: 1 Robinson Rd, AIA Tower, Singapore 048542; tel. 62918000; fax 65385802; internet www.aia.com.sg; Prin. Officer MARK O'DELL.

Great Eastern Life Assurance Co Ltd: 1 Pickering St, 13-01 Great Eastern Centre, Singapore 048659; tel. 62482000; fax 65322214; e-mail wecare@lifeisgreat.com.sg; internet www.lifeisgreat.com.sg; f. 1908; Dir and CEO TAN BENG LEE.

HSBC Insurance (Singapore) Pte Ltd: 3 Killiney Rd, 10-01/09, Winsland House 1, Singapore 239519; tel. 62256111; fax 62212188; internet www.insurance.hsbc.com.sg; Prin. Officer JASON DOMINIC SADLER.

NTUC Income Insurance Co-operative Ltd: 75 Bras Basah Rd, NTUC Income Centre, Singapore 189557; tel. 63363322; fax 63381500; e-mail inbox@income.wm.sg; internet www.income.com.sg; CEO TAN SUEE CHIEH; Gen. Man. ALOYSIUS TEO SENG LEE.

Overseas Assurance Corpn Ltd: 1 Pickering St, 13-01 Great Eastern Centre, Singapore 048659; tel. 62482000; fax 65322214; e-mail general@oac.com.sg; internet www.oac.com.sg; f. 1920; fully-owned subsidiary of Great Eastern Holdings; Chair. MICHAEL WONG PAKSHONG.

Prudential Assurance Co Singapore (Pte) Ltd: 30 Cecil St, 30-01 Prudential Tower, Singapore 049712; tel. 65358988; fax 65354043; e-mail customer.service@prudential.com.sg; internet www.prudential.com.sg; CEO TAN SUEE CHIEH.

Associations

General Insurance Association of Singapore: 112 Robinson Rd, 05-03 HB Robinson, Singapore 068902; tel. 62218788; fax 62272051; e-mail feedback@gia.org.sg; internet www.gia.org.sg; f. 1965; Pres. DEREK TEO; Exec. Dir MARK LIM.

Life Insurance Association, Singapore: 20 Cross St, 02-07/08 China Court, China Sq. Central, Singapore 048422; tel. 64388900; fax 64386989; e-mail lia@lia.org.sg; internet www.lia.org.sg; f. 1967; Pres. DARREN THOMPSON.

Reinsurance Brokers' Association: 69 Amoy St, Singapore 069888; tel. 63723189; fax 62241091; e-mail secretariat@rbas.org.sg; internet www.rbas.org.sg; f. 1995; Chair. RICHARD AUSTEN.

Singapore Insurance Brokers' Association: 138 Cecil St, 15-00 Cecil Court, Singapore 069538; tel. 62227777; fax 62220022; e-mail siba@stcsamasmgt.com.sg; Pres. ANTHONY LIM; Vice-Pres. DAVID LUM.

Singapore Reinsurers' Association: 85 Amoy St, Singapore 069904; tel. 63247388; fax 62248910; e-mail secretariat@sraweb.org.sg; internet www.sraweb.org.sg; f. 1979; Chair. CHRISTOPHER HO SIOW SOONG.

Trade and Industry

GOVERNMENT AGENCIES

Housing and Development Board: 480 Lorong 6, Toa Payoh, Singapore 310480; tel. 64901111; fax 63972070; e-mail hdbmailbox@hdb.gov.sg; internet www.hdb.gov.sg; f. 1960; public housing authority; Chair. JAMES KOH CHER SIANG.

Singapore Land Authority (SLA): 8 Shenton Way, 26-01 Temasek Tower, Singapore 068811; tel. 63239829; fax 63239937; e-mail SLA_enquiry@sla.gov.sg; internet www.sla.gov.sg; responsible for management and development of state land resources; Chair. GREG SEOW.

Urban Redevelopment Authority (URA): 45 Maxwell Rd, URA Centre, Singapore 069118; tel. 62216666; fax 62275069; e-mail ura_email@ura.gov.sg; internet www.ura.gov.sg; statutory board; responsible for national planning; Chair. BOBBY CHIN; CEO CHEONG-CHUA KOON HEAN.

DEVELOPMENT ORGANIZATIONS

Agency for Science, Technology and Research (A*STAR): 20 Biopolis Way 01-03, Singapore 138668; tel. 68266111; fax 67771711; e-mail astar_contact@a-star.gov.sg; internet www.a-star.gov.sg; f. 1990; fmrly National Science and Technology Board; statutory board; responsible for the development of science and technology; Chair. LIM CHUAN POH; Man. Dir YENA LIM.

Applied Research Corpn (ARC): independent non-profit-making research and consultancy org. aiming to facilitate and enhance the use of technology and expertise from the tertiary institutions to benefit industry, businesses and joint institutions.

Asian Infrastructure Fund (AIF): Singapore; f. 1994; promotes and directs investment into regional projects; Chair. MOEEN QURESHI.

Economic Development Board (EDB): 250 North Bridge Rd, 24-00 Raffles City Tower, Singapore 179101; tel. 68326832; fax 68326565; e-mail webmaster@edb.gov.sg; internet www.edb.gov.sg; f. 1961; statutory body for industrial planning, development and promotion of investments in manufacturing, services and local business; Chair. LIM SIONG GUAN; Man. Dir BEH SWAN GIN.

Government of Singapore Investment Corpn Pte Ltd (GIC): 168 Robinson Rd, 37-01 Capital Tower, Singapore 068912; tel. 68898888; fax 68898722; e-mail contactus@gic.com.sg; internet www.gic.com.sg; f. 1981; Exec. Dir Dr TONY TAN KENG YAM.

Infocomm Development Authority of Singapore (IDA): see under Telecommunications.

International Enterprise Singapore: 230 Victoria St, 07-00 Bugis Junction Office Tower, Singapore 188024; tel. 63376628; fax 63376898; e-mail enquiry@iesingapore.gov.sg; internet www.iesingapore.gov.sg; f. 1983; formed to develop and expand international trade; fmrly Trade Development Board; statutory body; Chair. EULEEN GOH; CEO LIT CHEONG CHONG.

Jurong Town Corpn (JTC): The JTC Summit, 8 Jurong Town Hall Rd, Singapore 609434; tel. 65600056; fax 65655301; e-mail askjtc@jtc.gov.sg; internet www.jtc.gov.sg; f. 1968; statutory body responsible for planning, promoting and developing industrial space; Chair. CEDRIC FOO; CEO OW FOONG PHENG.

Standards, Productivity and Innovation Board Singapore (SPRING): 2 Bukit Merah Central, Singapore 159835; tel. 62786666; fax 62786667; e-mail queries@spring.gov.sg; internet www.spring.gov.sg; f. 1996; est. as Singapore Productivity and Standards Board (PSB), following merger of Singapore Institute of Standards and Industrial Research and the National Productivity Board; name changed as above in 2001; workforce devt, training, productivity and innovation promotion, standards devt, etc; assistance for small and medium-sized enterprises; Chair. PHILIP YEO; Chief Exec. PNG CHEONG BOON.

CHAMBERS OF COMMERCE

Singapore Business Federation (SBF): 10 Hoe Chiang Rd, 22-01 Keppel Towers, 089315 Singapore; tel. 68276828; fax 68276807; internet www.sbf.org.sg; f. 2002; est. following restructuring of Singapore Fed. of Chambers of Commerce and Industry; Chair. TONY CHEW LEONG CHEE; mems include the following:

Singapore Chinese Chamber of Commerce and Industry: 47 Hill St, 09-00 Singapore 179365; tel. 63378381; fax 63390605; e-mail corporate@sccci.org.sg; internet www.sccci.org.sg; f. 1906; promotes trade and industry and economic development of Singapore; Pres. CHUA THIAN POH; Sec.-Gen. LIM SAH SOON.

Singapore Indian Chamber of Commerce and Industry: 101 Cecil St, 23-01/04 Tong Eng Bldg, Singapore 069533; tel. 62222855; fax 62231707; e-mail sicci@sicci.com; internet www.sicci.com; Chair. VIJAY IYENGAR; Exec. Dir PREDEEP KUMAR MENON.

Singapore International Chamber of Commerce: 6 Raffles Quay, 10-01 John Hancock Tower, Singapore 048580; tel. 65000988; fax 62242785; e-mail general@sicc.com; internet www.sicc.com.sg; f. 1837; Chair. LEE TZU YANG.

Singapore Malay Chamber of Commerce: 72A Bussorah St, Singapore 199485; tel. 62979296; fax 63924527; e-mail smcci@smcci.org.sg; internet www.smcci.org.sg; Pres. Dato' MOHAMAD ZAIN ABDULLAH.

Singapore Manufacturers' Federation (SMa): The Enterprise 02-02, 1 Science Centre Rd, Singapore 609077; tel. 68263000; fax 68228828; e-mail hq@smafederation.org.sg; internet www.smafederation.org.sg; f. 1932 as Singapore Manufacturers' Association; renamed Singapore Confederation of Industries in 1996; name changed as above in 2002; Pres. RENNY YEO; Sec.-Gen. Dr ROGER LOW.

INDUSTRIAL AND TRADE ASSOCIATIONS

Association of Singapore Marine Industries (ASMI): 20 Science Park Rd, 02-04/05 TeleTech Park, Singapore Science Park II, Singapore 117674; tel. 68720030; fax 68725747; e-mail asmi@pacific.net.sg; internet www.asmi.com; f. 1968; 12 hon. mems, 70 assoc. mems, 51 ord. mems (Oct. 2003); Pres. MICHAEL CHEA; Exec. Dir WINNIE LOW.

Singapore Commodity Exchange (SICOM): 111 North Bridge Rd, 23-04/05 Peninsula Plaza, Singapore 179098; tel. 65788080; fax 63389116; e-mail marketing@sicom.com.sg; internet www.sicom.com.sg; f. 1968; est. as Rubber Asscn of Singapore; adopted present name in 1994; regulates, promotes, develops and supervises commodity futures trading in Singapore, including the establishment and dissemination of official prices for various grades and types of rubber; provides clearing facilities; endorses certificates of origin and licences for packers, shippers and mfrs; Chair. LIM HOW TECK; Pres. JEFFREY TAN.

EMPLOYERS' ORGANIZATION

Singapore National Employers' Federation: Keppel Towers 22-00, 10 Hoe Chiang Rd, Singapore; tel. 68276827; fax 68276800; e-mail webmaster@snef.org.sg; internet www.sgemployers.com; f. 1948; Pres. STEPHEN LEE CHING YEN; Vice-Pres ALEX MELCHERS, BOB BENG HAI TAN, LANDIS W. HICKS.

UTILITIES

Electricity and Gas

Singapore Power Ltd: 111 Somerset Rd 10-01, Singapore Power Bldg, Singapore 238164; tel. 68238888; fax 68238188; e-mail corpcomms@singaporepower.com.sg; internet www.singaporepower.com.sg; incorporated in 1995 to take over the piped gas and electricity utility operations of the Public Utilities Board (see Water), which now acts as a regulatory authority for the privately owned cos; 100% owned by government holding co, Temasek Holdings Pte Ltd; f. 1995; subsidiaries incl. PowerGrid, PowerGas, SP Services, Singapore Power International, Power Automation, Singapore District Cooling and SP Telecommunications; Chair. KEE CHOE NG; CEO POH HUAT QUEK.

Water

Public Utilities Board: 40 Scotts Rd, 22-01, Singapore 228231; tel. 62358888; fax 67313020; e-mail pub_pr@pub.gov.sg; internet www.pub.gov.sg; statutory board responsible for water supply; manages Singapore's water system to optimize use of water resources, develops additional water sources; Chair. TAN GEE PAW.

TRADE UNIONS

At the end of 2003 there were 68 employees' trade unions and associations, with 417,166 members, and three employer unions, with 2,052 members.

National Trades Union Congress (NTUC): NTUC Centre, 1 Marina Blvd B1-01, Singapore 018989; tel. 62138000; fax 63278800; e-mail membership@ntuc.org.sg; internet www.ntuc.org.sg; f. 1961; 60 affiliated unions, 6 affiliated associates and approx. 500,000 mems (2008); Pres. JOHN DE PAYVA; Sec.-Gen. LIM SWEE SAY.

Transport

RAILWAYS

Singapore is linked to the Malaysian railway system via the Johor causeway. Branch lines provide a link to the industrial estate at Jurong.

The Mass Rapid Transit (MRT) system opened in 1990. In 2002 the extension of the East–West line to Changi Airport was completed. A 33.3-km orbital line was to link all the radial lines into the city, with the last phase of construction scheduled for completion in 2010.

Singapore's first Light Rapid Transit (LRT) system, the Bukit Panjang LRT opened in 1998. Construction of the 2.1-km Sentosa Express monorail system was completed in June 2006, and operations commenced in January 2007.

Land Transport Authority: 1 Hampshire Rd, Singapore 219428; tel. 63757100; fax 63757200; internet www.lta.gov.sg; Chair. MICHAEL LIM CHOO SAN; Chief Exec. YAM AH MEE.

ROADS

In 2006 Singapore had a total of 3,262 km of roads, of which 150 km were motorway; in that year 100% of the road network was paved. In 1990 the Government introduced a quota system to control the number of vehicles using the roads. This was replaced by a system of Electronic Road Pricing (ERP) in 1998, whereby each vehicle was charged according to road use in congested areas. In 2001 construction of the 12-km Kallang–Paya Lebar expressway began; an estimated 9 km of the expressway was to be under ground, which would render it the longest underground expressway in South-East Asia. It was scheduled for completion in 2008.

SHIPPING

Singapore is one of the world's busiest ports. The Port of Singapore Authority operates six cargo terminals: Tanjong Pagar Terminal, Keppel Terminal, Brani Terminal, Pasir Panjang Terminal, Semba-

SINGAPORE

wang Terminal and Jurong Port. Tanjong Pagar Terminal and Keppel Terminal have the capacity to handle 10.7m. 20-foot equivalent units (TEUs). The third container terminal, Brani, built on an offshore island connected to the mainland by a causeway, has a capacity of 5.5m. TEUs. Pasir Panjang Terminal, Singapore's main gateway for conventional cargo has five deep-water berths, eight coastal berths and 17 lighter berths. Sembawang Terminal has three deep-water berths and one coastal berth. This terminal is the main point of entry for car carriers, and it also handles steel and timber products. Jurong Port (which handles general and dry-bulk cargo, is situated in south-western Singapore, and serves the Jurong Industrial Estate) has 20 deep-water berths and one coastal berth. A new container terminal, at Pasir Panjang, was officially opened in 2000, following the completion of the second of four planned phases of building work. Upon completion, scheduled for 2009, the terminal was to have 49 berths and a handling capacity of 35m. TEUs.

Maritime and Port Authority of Singapore: 460 Alexandra Rd, 18-00 PSA Bldg, Singapore 119963; tel. 63751600; fax 62759247; e-mail media_enquiries@mpa.gov.sg; internet www.mpa.gov.sg; f. 1996; regulatory body responsible for promotion and development of the port, overseeing all port and maritime matters in Singapore; Chair. LUCIEN WONG; Chief Exec. TAY LIM HENG.

PSA International Pte Ltd: 460 Alexandra Rd, 36-00 PSA Bldg, Singapore 119963; tel. 62747111; fax 62794113; e-mail gca@psa.com.sg; internet www.internationalpsa.com; f. 1964 as a statutory board under the Ministry of Communications; est. as Port of Singapore Authority; changed name to above in 2003; made a corporate entity in 1997 in preparation for privatization; responsible for the provision and maintenance of port facilities and services; Chair. FOCK SIEW WAH; CEO EDDIE TEH.

Major Shipping Companies

American President Lines Ltd (APL): 456 Alexandra Rd, 08-00 NOL Bldg, Singapore 119962; tel. 62789000; fax 62742113; e-mail hung-song-goh@apl.com; internet www.apl.com; container services to North and South Asia, the USA and the Middle East; COO ED ALDRIDGE.

Glory Ship Management Private Ltd: 24 Raffles Place, 17-01/02, Clifford Centre, Singapore 048621; tel. 65361986; fax 65361987; e-mail gene@gloryship.com.sg.

Guan Guan Shipping Pte Ltd: 2 Finlayson Green, 13-05 Asia Insurance Bldg, Singapore 049247; tel. 65343988; fax 62276776; e-mail golden@golden.com.sg; f. 1955; shipowners and agents; cargo services to East and West Malaysia, Indonesia, Pakistan, Sri Lanka, Bengal Bay ports, Persian (Arabian) Gulf ports, Hong Kong and China; Man. Dir RICHARD THIO.

IMC Shipping Co Pte Ltd: 5 Temasek Blvd, 12-01 Suntec City Tower, Singapore 038985; tel. 63362233; fax 63379715; e-mail biz@imcpaa.com; internet www.imcshipping.com; Chair. FRANK TSAO WEN KING.

Nedlloyd Lines Singapore Pte Ltd: 138 Robinson Rd, 01-00 Hong Leong Centre, Singapore 068906; tel. 62218989; fax 62255267; f. 1963; Gen. Man. F. C. SCHUCHARD.

Neptune Orient Lines Ltd: 456 Alexandra Rd, 05-00 NOL Bldg, Singapore 119962; tel. 62789000; fax 62784900; e-mail nol_group_corp_comms@nol.com.sg; internet www.nol.com.sg; f. 1968; liner containerized services on the Far East/Europe, Far East/North America, Straits/Australia, South Asia/Europe and South-East Asia, Far East/Mediterranean routes; logistics services and terminals; Chair. CHENG WAI KEUNG; Group Pres. and CEO RON WIDDOWS.

New Straits Shipping Co Pte Ltd: 51 Anson Rd, 09-53 Anson Centre, Singapore 0207; tel. 62201007; fax 62240785.

Ocean Tankers (Pte) Ltd: 37 Tuas Rd, Singapore 638503; tel. 68632202; fax 68639480; e-mail admin@oceantankers.com.sg; internet www.oceantankers.com.sg; Marine Supt V. LIM.

Osprey Maritime Ltd: 8 Cross St, 24-02/03 PWC Bldg, Singapore 048424; tel. 62129722; fax 65570450; CEO PETER GEORGE COSTALAS.

Pacific International Lines (Pte) Ltd: 140 Cecil St, 03-00 PIL Bldg, POB 3206, Singapore 069540; tel. 62218133; fax 62273933; e-mail sherry.chua@sgp.pilship.com; internet www.pilship.com; shipowners, agents and managers; liner services to South-East Asia, the Far East, India, the Red Sea, the Persian (Arabian) Gulf, West and East Africa; container services to South-East Asia; worldwide chartering, freight forwarding, container manufacturing, depot operators, container freight station operator; Exec. Chair. Y. C. CHANG; Man. Dir S. S. TEO.

Petroships Private Ltd: 460 Alexandra Rd, 25-04 PSA Bldg, Singapore 119963; tel. 62731122; fax 62732200; e-mail gen@petroships.com.sg; Man. Dir KENNETH KEE.

Singa Ship Agencies Ltd: 78 Shenton Way 16-02, Singapore 079120; tel. 62244308; fax 62235848; e-mail agency@singaship.com.sg; Chair. OLE HEGLAND; Man. Dir EILEEN LEONG.

Syabas Tankers Pte Ltd: 10 Anson Rd, 34-10 International Plaza, Singapore 0207; tel. 62259522.

Tanker Pacific Management (Singapore) Private Ltd: 1 Temasek Ave, 38-01 Millenia Tower, Singapore; tel. 63365211; fax 63375570; internet www.tanker.com.sg; Chair. and CEO ALASTAIR MCGREGOR.

CIVIL AVIATION

Singapore's international airport at Changi was opened in 1981. Construction of a terminal solely for the use of budget carriers was completed in January 2006, and became operational in March of that year, thereby increasing the airport's total capacity to 64m. passengers a year. Separate facilities for premium air travellers were opened in September 2006. Construction of a third main terminal was completed in January 2008. A second airport at Seletar operates as a base for charter and training flights.

Civil Aviation Authority of Singapore: Singapore Changi Airport, POB 1, Singapore 918141; tel. 65421122; fax 65421231; e-mail thennarasee_R@caas.gov.sg; internet www.caas.gov.sg; responsible for regulatory and advisory services, air services development, airport management and development and airspace management and organization; Chair. LIEW MUN LEONG; Dir-Gen. LIM KIM CHOON.

Jetstar Asia Airways: Singapore Changi Airport; internet www.jetstar.com; f. 2004; 49% owned by Qantas (Australia); service to regional destinations; merged with ValuAir in 2005; continues to operate under the Jetstar name; CEO CHONG PHIT LIAN.

SilkAir: 77 Robinson Rd, 25-01 SIA Bldg, Singapore 068896; tel. 65428111; fax 65426286; internet www.silkair.com; f. 1975; fmrly Tradewinds Private; wholly owned subsidiary of Singapore Airlines Ltd; began scheduled services in 1989; Chair. SOO KHIANG BEY; CEO YAU SENG CHIN.

Singapore Airlines Ltd (SIA): 7D Airline House, 25 Airline Rd, Singapore 819829; tel. 65415880; fax 65423002; e-mail investor_relations@singaporeair.com.sg; internet www.singaporeair.com; f. 1972; passenger services to over 90 destinations in about 40 countries; Chair. STEPHEN LEE CHING YEN; CEO CHEW CHOON SENG.

Tiger Airways: Singapore Changi Airport, POB 82, Singapore 918143; tel. 65384437; fax 65807564; internet www.tigerairways.com; f. 2003; 49% owned by Singapore Airlines, 24% owned by US co Indigo Partners, 11% owned by Temasek Holdings Pte Ltd; services to 10 regional destinations; Chair. WILLIAM FRANKE; CEO TONY DAVIS.

ValuAir: POB 323, Singapore 918144; tel. 68222288; e-mail feedback@valuair.com.sg; internet www.valuair.com.sg; f. 2003; regional destinations; merged with Jetstar Asia in 2005; continues to operate under the ValuAir name; Chair. LIM CHIN BENG.

Tourism

Singapore's tourist attractions include its blend of cultures and excellent shopping facilities. In April 2005 the Government approved draft legislation to permit gambling on the island for the first time in 40 years. The new law opened the way for the construction of two major casino resorts, at Marina Bay and on Sentosa Island. The resorts were scheduled to become operational by 2009 and were expected significantly to increase the number of visitors to Singapore. Tourist arrivals totalled 10.1m. in 2008. Receipts from tourism (excluding passenger transport) totalled US $7,069m. in 2006.

Singapore Tourism Board: Tourism Court, 1 Orchard Spring Lane, Singapore 247729; tel. 67366622; fax 67369423; e-mail feedback@stb.com.sg; internet www.stb.com.sg; f. 1964; Chair. SIMON ISRAEL; Chief Exec. AW KAH PENG.

SLOVAKIA

Introductory Survey

Location, Climate, Language, Religion, Flag, Capital

The Slovak Republic (formerly a constituent republic of the Czech and Slovak Federative Republic, or Czechoslovakia) is a landlocked state located in central Europe, bordered to the north by Poland, to the east by Ukraine, to the south by Hungary, to the west by Austria and to the north-west by the Czech Republic. The climate is typically continental, with cold, dry winters and hot, humid summers. Average temperatures in Bratislava range from −0.7°C (30.7°F) in January to 21.1°C (70.0°F) in July. Average annual rainfall in the capital is 649 mm (26 ins). The official language is Slovak, although Hungarian, Czech and other languages are also spoken. The major religion is Christianity, the Roman Catholic Church being the largest denomination, followed by the Evangelical Church of the Augsburg (Lutheran) Confession. The national flag (proportions 2 by 3) consists of three equal horizontal stripes, of white, blue and red; in the centre hoist there is a white-rimmed red shield containing a silver archiepiscopal (double-barred) cross surmounted on the central (and highest) of three blue hillocks. The capital is Bratislava.

Recent History

Slovaks and Czechs (who are closely related members of the western Slavic peoples) were first united in the ninth century AD, in the Great Moravian Empire, but were divided following the Empire's dissolution in 907. While the Slovaks came under Hungarian rule (which was to last, in different forms, until the early 20th century), the Czechs established a kingdom that remained an important political force until the incorporation of the Czech Lands into the Habsburg Empire in the 16th and 17th centuries.

A movement of nationalist revival, closely linked with a similar movement in the Czech Lands, evolved in Slovakia in the late 18th and 19th centuries. During the First World War (1914–18) Slovaks joined with Czechs in campaigning for an independent state, which would be composed of the Czech Lands and Slovakia. The Republic of Czechoslovakia was established on 28 October 1918, as one of the successor states to the Austro-Hungarian Empire. The country's boundaries were defined by the Treaty of Trianon of 1920, under which a large Hungarian minority was incorporated into Slovakia. Czechoslovakia's first Constitution, promulgated in 1920, made no provision for a proper federal system, and Slovak proposals for self-government were rejected by the central authorities in the capital, Prague. A further cause of Slovak disaffection was the fact that the Czech Lands were the focus of the country's economic development, while there was also an ideological divide: while the majority of Slovaks were strict Roman Catholics, the central Government in Prague was professedly anticlerical.

In October 1938, following the Munich Agreement of 29 September (whereby the predominantly German-populated areas of Czechoslovakia were ceded to Germany), nationalists declared Slovak autonomy. On 14 March 1939, one day before Nazi armed forces occupied the Czech Lands, Adolf Hitler agreed to the establishment of a separate Slovak state, under the pro-Nazi 'puppet' regime of Fr Jozef Tiso. Any opposition to the Tiso regime was ruthlessly suppressed, and the treatment of Jews was particularly severe. In August 1944 an armed resistance (the Slovak National Uprising) against Tiso's regime was begun, but it was suppressed within two months by German troops.

Following the restoration of the Czechoslovak state in 1945, at the end of the Second World War, certain concessions were made to Slovak demands for autonomy, including the establishment of a regional legislature with restricted powers (the Slovenská národná rada—Slovak National Council) and an executive, both in Bratislava, the Slovak capital. However, communists (led by Gustav Husák) seized power in Slovakia in late 1947, and in the whole of the country in 1948. In May 1948 a new Constitution was approved, which declared Czechoslovakia to be a 'people's democracy'. The communists' consolidation of power was completed in June with the election to the post of President of the Czech Klement Gottwald, leader of the Communist Party of Czechoslovakia (CPCz) and Prime Minister since 1946.

In the first years of communist rule there was widespread repression. Expressions of Slovak nationalism were harshly suppressed, and in 1954 Husák and other Slovaks were imprisoned on charges of separatism. The new Constitution of 1960 restricted Slovak autonomy: the executive in Bratislava was dissolved, and legislative authority was removed from the Slovenská národná rada. In January 1968 Alexander Dubček (a Slovak and hitherto leader of the Communist Party of Slovakia—CPS) was appointed First Secretary of the CPCz. The wide-ranging political and economic reforms introduced by Dubček and the new Government included plans for the creation of a federal system of two equal republics. This period of political tolerance and freedom of expression (subsequently known as the 'Prague Spring') was abruptly ended in August 1968 by the armed intervention of some 600,000 troops of the USSR and its allies. Dubček was replaced by Husák as First (subsequently General) Secretary of the CPCz, and there was a purge of party members, in particular reformists and associates of Dubček. Nevertheless, the federal system was realized in January 1969: separate Czech and Slovak Socialist Republics were established, each with its own government and legislature (Národná rada—National Council). Supreme legislative and executive power, meanwhile, were vested in the Federal Assembly and the Federal Government, respectively. However, the reimposition of centralized communist rule, under the leadership of Husák, left the new regional institutions largely powerless.

In 1975 Husák was appointed President of Czechoslovakia. In December 1987 he was replaced as General Secretary of the CPCz by Miloš Jakeš, a Czech member of the CPCz Presidium. Although the administration publicly avowed its commitment to introduce political and economic reforms similar to those taking place in the USSR under Mikhail Gorbachev, political liberalization was not forthcoming. The Government continued its repressive treatment of both the Roman Catholic Church and the several dissident groups that had been established since the late 1970s (the most important being Charter 77). Nevertheless, the dissident movement was instrumental in organizing a series of anti-Government demonstrations, beginning in 1988, which were to culminate in the anti-communist revolution of late 1989 (see the chapter on the Czech Republic).

Elections to the Federal Assembly and to the Czech and Slovak National Councils on 8–9 June 1990 were the first to be held freely since 1946. Of the Slovak parties and movements, Public Against Violence (PAV), which, with its Czech counterpart, Civic Forum, had been the principal force in effecting the end of communist rule, emerged with the largest representation at both federal and republican level. A coalition Slovak Government, dominated by PAV, was subsequently formed, with Vladimír Mečiar as Prime Minister.

The future of Czech-Slovak relations dominated political debate in the latter half of 1990, amid increasing support in Slovakia for a more decentralized form of the existing federation. Among the Slovak political parties, the Christian Democratic Movement (CDM), which formed part of the Slovak coalition Government, advocated greater Slovak autonomy within a common state; however, more radical parties—most notably the Slovak National Party (SNP), which held seats in both the federal and republican legislatures—advocated the complete secession of Slovakia from the federation. The debate over the future of the country (which since April 1990 had been officially known as the Czech and Slovak Federative Republic) led to increasing political turmoil in Slovakia during 1991. In March Mečiar was forced to resign as Slovak Prime Minister, accused of harming Czech-Slovak relations by his increasingly strident advocacy of full autonomy for Slovakia. Mečiar left PAV and formed a new party, the Movement for a Democratic Slovakia (MDS). He was replaced as Prime Minister by Ján Čarnogurský, the leader of the CDM. Proposals by the Czechoslovak President, Václav Havel, for a referendum to determine the country's future were repeatedly rejected by the Federal Assembly.

Following elections to the federal and republican legislatures on 5–6 June 1992, the MDS emerged as the largest Slovak party both in the Federal Assembly and the Slovenská národná rada.

In the latter body the MDS won 74 of the 150 seats available, compared with only 18 obtained by the CDM and 15 by the SNP. The Party of the Democratic Left (PDL—the successor to the CPS) secured the second largest representation (29 seats). In late June Mečiar was reinstated as Prime Minister, at the head of a new, MDS-dominated Slovak Government.

On 17 July 1992 the Slovenská národná rada approved a declaration of Slovak sovereignty, as a result of which the dismantling of the Czechoslovak federation appeared inevitable. In late July Mečiar and his Czech counterpart, Václav Klaus, reached agreement on the necessary measures to permit the separation of the two republics. On 1 September the new Slovak Constitution was adopted by the Slovenská národná rada. In November the Federal Assembly finally approved (albeit at the third attempt and by a margin of only three votes) legislation to permit the constitutional dissolution of Czechoslovakia (to be effected on 1 January 1993).

During the remainder of 1992 there was an acceleration of the process of dividing federal assets and liabilities, as well as the armed forces, between the Czech and Slovak Republics. In December the two republics signed a co-operation agreement, and subsequently established formal diplomatic relations. With the dissolution of all federal structures at midnight on 31 December, the Czech Republic and the Slovak Republic came into existence. Recognition was rapidly accorded to the new countries by all those states that had maintained relations with Czechoslovakia, as well as by various international bodies.

Slovakia's MDS-dominated Government and legislature remained in place. In February 1993 the Národná rada Slovenskej republiky (National Council of the Slovak Republic, as the legislature was redesignated—Národná rada) elected Michal Kováč, Deputy Chairman of the MDS and former Chairman of Czechoslovakia's Federal Assembly, as President. Internal divisions in the MDS culminated in March with the dismissal of Milan Kňažko, the strongest critic of Mečiar within the party, from his post of Deputy Prime Minister and Minister of Foreign Affairs. Kňažko subsequently formed an opposition liberal party, the Alliance of Democrats of the Slovak Republic (ADSR). Also in March the SNP leader, Ludovít Černák, resigned as Minister of the Economy, leaving the Government (with the exception of two independent ministers) composed exclusively of members of the MDS. However, as a result of several defections, the party (plus affiliates) lost its majority in the legislature. A new coalition Government, in which the SNP held several principal portfolios, was formed in November. One of Mečiar's ministerial nominees was rejected by Kováč, who had become severely critical of the Prime Minister. In December Mečiar ignored a demand by the President for his resignation.

Mečiar's position was further undermined in early 1994. In February six SNP deputies left the party to form what became the National Democratic Party—New Alternative (NDP—NA), led by Černák. In the same month the Minister of Foreign Affairs, Jozef Moravčík, and the Deputy Prime Minister, Roman Kováč, resigned from the Government, subsequently establishing the Democratic Union of Slovakia (DUS). In March the Národná rada approved a motion expressing no confidence in Mečiar's Government (the MDS and the SNP both abstained from voting). Following the resignation of Mečiar's administration, a new, five-party, interim coalition was installed. The new Government, with Moravčík as Prime Minister, comprised members of the CDM and the PDL, as well as the NDP—NA, the DUS and the ADSR (the last was subsequently absorbed into the DUS). Early legislative elections were scheduled for September.

The MDS emerged as the leading party at elections to the Národná rada, held on 30 September and 1 October 1994 (with the participation of some 76% of the electorate). The renewed success of the MDS (which, in alliance with the Farmers' Party of Slovakia, secured 35.0% of the total votes cast and 61 seats) was attributed to Mečiar's populist election campaign. The Common Choice bloc (an alliance of left-wing parties, led by the PDL) won 10.4% of the votes cast and 18 seats, followed by a coalition of Hungarian parties (17) and the CDM (also 17). The remaining seats were taken by the DUS (15), the Association of Workers of Slovakia (AWS—formed earlier in the year, following a split in the PDL—13 seats) and the SNP (nine seats).

Subsequent inter-party negotiations proved inconclusive, and in late October 1994 Kováč requested that Mečiar form a Government. A coalition of the MDS, the SNP and the AWS was announced in December. In January 1995 the new Government attempted to annul all decisions on privatization made by the previous administration and overturn a presidential veto. However, in May the Constitutional Court declared the suspension of the privatization programme to be illegal. The personal enmity between Mečiar and Kováč culminated in an unsuccessful motion of no confidence in the President, following allegations that the Slovak Intelligence Service (SIS, which had been under presidential control until April) had provided Kováč with confidential information concerning the activities of political parties, in particular the MDS, and of state officials.

In February 1996 President Kováč claimed that there was evidence to suggest that the SIS had been responsible for the abduction of one of his sons (also called Michal) from Bratislava. Michal Kováč had subsequently been detained by police on an international arrest warrant in Austria, in connection with allegations of embezzlement, but later permitted to return to Slovakia. Mečiar alleged that the President had also been involved in the embezzlement affair, and that his son had organized his own abduction in order to divert attention from the financial scandal; President Kováč subsequently filed libel charges against Mečiar. However, investigations into both the alleged abduction and the libel suit were adjourned owing to lack of evidence. (Although in April 1999 Ivan Lexa, the former head of the SIS, was arrested in connection with Michal Kováč's abduction, he was not convicted of any crime.)

The Ministers of the Economy, of Foreign Affairs and of the Interior were replaced in August 1996. Opposition deputies, meanwhile, campaigned for a referendum to be held on their proposals that the Head of State be elected by direct popular vote, rather than chosen by the legislature. President Kováč scheduled a referendum for 23–24 May 1997. However, when the poll took place, the question on presidential elections was omitted from the ballot papers. The majority of voters consequently boycotted the referendum, and the rate of electoral participation (at less than 10%) was too low to render the vote valid. The Minister of Foreign Affairs, Pavol Hamžík, resigned in protest at what he regarded as the Government's manipulation of the democratic process. In June several thousand people attended a rally to protest against the Government's intervention in the referendum. In February 1998, following a ruling by the Constitutional Court that government intervention had impeded citizens' rights to vote in the referendum, and in response to appeals from the opposition, Kováč announced that a new referendum would be held in April.

Meanwhile, the Slovak Democratic Coalition (SDC), a new grouping of five opposition parties (including the CDM and the DUS), demanded Mečiar's resignation, accusing his administration of endangering Slovakia's political and economic future, following the failure of Slovakia to be invited to join the North Atlantic Treaty Organization (NATO, see p. 351) or to be recommended by the European Commission for negotiations on membership of the European Union (EU, see p. 255) in mid-1997. In October, despite ongoing tension, Kováč and Mečiar issued a joint statement affirming Slovakia's commitment to future membership of the EU and other international organizations, amid increasing concern about the country's image abroad.

During January–March 1998 several attempts to elect a new President failed in the Národná rada, when candidates were unable to secure the required three-fifths' majority. The MDS had not contested the first rounds of voting, apparently confirming opposition fears that Mečiar was attempting to ensure that the presidency would remain vacant when Kováč left office, enabling him to assume a number of presidential powers. On 2 March Kováč's term expired, and certain presidential powers were transferred to the Government, in accordance with the Constitution. Mečiar immediately cancelled the referendum scheduled for April and announced the dismissal of some 28 of Slovakia's ambassadors abroad. He also granted an amnesty to various prisoners, including those suspected of abducting Kováč's son in 1995, and halted criminal proceedings relating to the May 1997 referendum. The Prime Minister's actions prompted a series of widely supported protest rallies organized by opposition parties, and were strongly criticized by the EU and the USA. In mid-April 1998 a further round of voting in the presidential election was contested for the first time by an MDS candidate; however, the Národná rada again failed to elect a new head of state. Subsequent attempts were also unsuccessful.

In May 1998, in preparation for legislative elections scheduled for September, the Národná rada approved amendments to the electoral law, including a stipulation that political parties obtain at least 5% of the votes cast to secure parliamentary representation. Legislation was also approved that restricted pre-election campaigning to the state-run media. In June three ethnic

Hungarian parties merged to create the Party of the Hungarian Coalition (PHC), and the SDC registered officially as a single party. In July a constitutional amendment providing for the transfer of a number of presidential powers to the Chairman of the Národná rada, in the event of the presidency becoming vacant, was supported by deputies from all parties.

The elections to the Národná rada were held on 25–26 September 1998, with the participation of 84.2% of the electorate. The MDS narrowly retained its position as the strongest party in the legislature, winning 43 seats (with 27.0% of the votes cast), but was unable to form a government, with its only possible ally, the SNP, holding 14 seats. The SDC obtained 42 seats (26.3% of the votes), the PDL 23 seats (14.7%), the PHC 15 seats and the Party of Civic Understanding (PCU—formed earlier that year) 13 seats. With a combined total of 93 seats, the SDC, the PDL, the PHC and the PCU agreed to form a new administration, and a new coalition Government, headed by Mikuláš Dzurinda, the leader of the SDC, was appointed at the end of October. Jozef Migaš, of the PDL, was elected Chairman of the Národná rada. The opposition's victory was welcomed both by Western institutions and by neighbouring countries, which anticipated improved relations with Slovakia. Dzurinda emphasized the new Government's intention to pursue early membership of the EU and NATO, pledged to combat organized crime, and outlined measures to improve Slovakia's economic situation. In December the European Parliament adopted a resolution on Slovakia's application for membership of the EU, recommending that the European Commission consider initiating entry talks in 1999.

In January 1999 the Národná rada approved a constitutional amendment providing for the introduction of direct presidential elections. The ruling coalition nominated Rudolf Schuster, the Chairman of the PCU, as its presidential candidate. Nine candidates contested the first round of the presidential election, which was held on 15 May. Schuster won 47.4% of the votes cast, and Mečiar obtained 37.2%. (Kováč had withdrawn his candidature in favour of Schuster.) Schuster defeated Mečiar in a second round of voting on 29 May, with 57.2% of the votes cast, and was duly inaugurated as President on 15 June, having resigned the chairmanship of the PCU.

In September 1999 a large demonstration was staged in Bratislava to protest against rising unemployment and declining living standards, resulting from a series of austerity measures implemented by the Government. In October Černák resigned as Minister of the Economy; the post was assumed by Lubomír Harach, the Chairman of the DUS. In January 2000, following several weeks of disputes over the future structure of the SDC, Dzurinda announced plans to form a new party, the Slovak Democratic and Christian Union (SDCU). The SDCU was officially registered in February, and was joined by several government ministers. Further SDC deputies subsequently resigned from the CDM and the DUS to join the SDCU. Following Dzurinda's election as SDCU Chairman at the party's opening congress in November, the SDC became effectively defunct.

Revisions to the Constitution, although opposed by the MDS and the SNP, were adopted by a narrow majority in the legislature in February 2001. The amendments (which officially entered into effect on 1 July) redefined the relationship between national and international law, thereby facilitating the process of joining foreign alliances; strengthened the powers of the Constitutional Court; granted greater independence to the judiciary; and provided for public administration reform. In May Schuster replaced Pavol Hamzik, the Deputy Prime Minister for European Integration, held responsible for the misuse of EU funds, which had led to the suspension of payments in the previous month. Also in May the Minister of the Interior tendered his resignation, following increasing criticism of an investigation into mismanagement under the Mečiar administration.

In July 2001 dissension increased between the government coalition parties over new legislation providing for the establishment of a higher level of regional self-administration. Following the adoption of the reforms, which provided for the creation of eight 'higher territorial units' (VÚCs), local government elections took place on 1 and 15 December. In a reflection of increasing popular support, MDS representatives secured 146 of the 401 seats in the regional councils and six of the eight gubernatorial posts. (However, voter participation in the second round was estimated at only 22% of the registered electorate.)

In January 2002 the PDL demanded the resignation of the reformist Minister of Finance, Brigita Schmögnerová (a PDL member), after she allegedly withheld information regarding the privatization programme. Although Dzurinda initially refused to dismiss her, threats by the PDL to withdraw from the coalition finally resulted in her replacement. Schmögnerová subsequently left the PDL and formed a new political party, the Social Democratic Alternative (SDA). In February the Deputy Prime Minister for the Economy, Ivan Mikloš, who was principally responsible for a programme of extensive structural reforms, survived a second motion of no confidence in the Národná rada.

In July 2002 members of the MDS who had not been selected by the party to contest the forthcoming legislative elections established a new party, the Movement for Democracy. At the elections to the Národná rada on 20–21 September, the MDS received the highest proportion of the votes cast (19.5%), obtaining 36 mandates. The SDCU received 15.1% of the votes cast and 28 seats; a centre-right party, Direction (Směr), 13.5% and 25 seats; the PHC 11.2% and 20 seats; and the CDM 8.3% and 15 seats. The New Citizens' Alliance (NCA), established in 2001, won 8.0% of the votes and 15 seats, while the Slovak Communist Party (SCP) significantly increased its share, securing 6.3% and 11 seats. However, Mečiar proved unable to form a coalition government, and in late September Schuster invited Dzurinda to establish a new administration. A coalition agreement was signed in early October by four reformist, centre-right parties (the SDCU, the PHC, the CDM and the NCA), which together held 78 of the 150 seats in the Národná rada. On 16 October Schuster formally appointed a new coalition Government. The leader of the Democratic Party (DP), which had supported the SDCU in the elections, was allocated a portfolio, although the party was not a coalition member. Mikloš was retained in the administration as the new Minister of Finance. The adoption of an austerity budget in November prompted popular protests. Local government elections took place on 6–7 December; mayoral offices were equally divided between the government coalition parties and the MDS.

In May 2003 a new party, the People's Union, was formed by disaffected members of the MDS. In the following month Mečiar was re-elected as Chairman of the MDS. At the same time, MDS members approved changing the party's name to the People's Party—Movement for a Democratic Slovakia (PP–MDS). Tensions emerged within the ruling coalition in July, after the Národná rada approved legislative amendments proposed by the NCA, easing restrictions on abortion, which were strongly opposed by the CDM. In late July Schuster vetoed the legislation, fearing the collapse of the Government. In September the Deputy Prime Minister and Minister of the Economy, Robert Nemcsics, officially resigned his post, after losing the support of the NCA, following his criticism of Pavel Rusko, the Chairman of the party. Later that month Rusko was appointed as Deputy Prime Minister and Minister of the Economy. In October Juraj Liska was appointed as Minister of Defence, replacing Ivan Šimko, who had been dismissed in September. A number of deputies subsequently left the SDCU to join Šimko's newly formed Free Forum, rendering the ruling coalition a minority Government, with just 68 parliamentary seats. In March 2004 Mikloš survived a further motion of no confidence.

In the first round of voting in the presidential election of 3 April 2004, Mečiar won 32.7% of the votes cast, followed by the Movement for Democracy leader (and former ally of Mečiar) Ivan Gašparovič, who won 22.3% of the votes. Eduard Kukan of the SDCU, the Minister of Foreign Affairs and the preferred candidate of Dzurinda's Government, took third place, with 22.1% of the votes, while Schuster, the incumbent, obtained just 7.4% of the votes. The failure of Kukan's presidential bid prompted demands in the Národná rada for the resignation of Dzurinda, whereas Mečiar's success was regarded as a potential threat to Slovakia's planned accession to the EU (due in May). In the second round of voting, held on 17 April, Gašparovič was elected as President, receiving 59.9% of the votes cast; the rate of participation by the electorate in the second round was 43.5%. Gašparovič, who subsequently resigned from the leadership of the Movement for Democracy, was inaugurated on 15 June. Meanwhile, at Slovakia's first elections to the European Parliament in mid-June, a rate of participation by the electorate of just 17.0% was recorded—the lowest rate recorded in any EU member state. The SDCU received 17.1% of the votes, the PP—MDS 17.0%, Direction 16.9% and the CDM 16.2%; the four parties were each allocated three seats in the European Parliament. The PHC, which won 13.2% of votes, obtained two seats.

In January 2005 a new party, Direction-Social Democracy, was formed by the merger of Direction, the Social Democratic Party of Slovakia, the SDA and the PDL. In November 2004, meanwhile, the National Memory Institute had announced that it was to publish thousands of hitherto secret official files from Slovakia's communist era, detailing names of collaborators with the former regime; a deputy minister resigned in January 2005, after he was revealed to be a former agent of the communist security services.

In July 2005 Dzurinda survived a motion of no confidence in the Národná rada, which had been proposed by the Chairman of Direction-Social Democracy, Robert Fico, and supported by PP—MDS Chairman Vladimír Mečiar. Fico had criticized Dzurinda for his failure to combat corruption, and argued that his reforms had increased poverty. In August President Gašparovič dismissed Rusko from his post as Deputy Prime Minister and Minister of the Economy, after he was implicated in a loan scandal, which revealed an apparent conflict of interest between his private business activities and his ministerial duties. (Rusko had refused to comply with an earlier request that he tender his resignation, after the CDM threatened to withdraw its 15 deputies from the Národná rada if he remained in the Government.) Deputy Prime Minister and Minister of Finance Ivan Mikloš assumed the economy portfolio, in an acting capacity. Rusko, who remained leader of the NCA, subsequently urged Dzurinda to dismiss the Minister of Health, Rudolf Zajac (who had been nominated by the NCA, but was not a party member), and the Minister of Culture, František Tóth (an NCA member), both of whom had supported Rusko's removal, threatening to withdraw the NCA from the Government should Dzurinda refuse. Members of the NCA opposed to Rusko's leadership, including two party Vice-Chairmen, Lubomír Lintner and Jirko Malchárek, and Tóth, formed a splinter faction, led by Lintner. At the beginning of September the SDCU, the CDM and the PHC agreed to expel the NCA from the ruling coalition; Zajac and Tóth were permitted to retain their posts. Lintner's group of deputies pledged its co-operation with the governing parties, and proposed Malchárek for the post of Minister of the Economy. On 11 September the NCA expelled nine members from the party, including Tóth and five Vice-Chairmen (among them Lintner and Malchárek). The following day the Government signed a co-operation agreement with Lintner's group of deputies. Opposition parties boycotted the Národná rada, but, after nine days, the Government narrowly managed to secure sufficient support to open a legislative session. In October Gašparovič appointed Malchárek as Deputy Prime Minister and Minister of the Economy.

In October 2005 DP leader Ľudovít Kaník resigned as Minister of Labour, Social Affairs and the Family. Kaník, who was replaced by Iveta Radičová, subsequently proposed a merger of the DP and the SDCU. In December a congress of the DP approved a draft agreement on the merger, which was confirmed in January 2006 at an extraordinary congress of the SDCU. The new political union was known as the SDCU-DP.

Meanwhile, on 26 November and 10 December 2005 an estimated 18% of the electorate took part in local government elections. Just 11% of the electorate participated in the second round, the lowest rate of participation in Slovakia's history. Of the parties represented in the Národná rada, the CDM secured 87 of the 412 seats in the VÚCs, Direction-Social Democracy took 70 and the SDCU won 64.

In January 2006 the Minister of Defence, Juraj Liška, tendered his resignation, after a military aircraft crashed on the Hungarian–Slovak border, killing some 42 people. Although the cause of the accident was unknown, the Government had been criticized for its decision to modernize Soviet-manufactured aircraft, rather than buying new equipment. Liška was replaced by Martin Fedor. In February the CDM announced the withdrawal of its three ministers from the Government, following Dzurinda's refusal to submit for discussion a proposal to approve a treaty with the Vatican that would enable workers to refuse to perform duties on the basis of religious objections. Dzurinda argued that any such treaty would permit the Roman Catholic Church to interfere in civil affairs. The leader of the CDM subsequently resigned as Chairman of the Národná rada, and was replaced, in an acting capacity, by the PHC leader and Deputy Chairman of the legislature, Béla Bugár. As a result of the CDM's withdrawal, the ruling coalition controlled just 53 seats in the legislature, and three days later the Národná rada approved a proposal by Dzurinda for legislative elections, originally due to take place in September, to be held on 17 June. Gašparovič subsequently appointed Martin Pado of the SDCU-DP as Minister of the Interior, László Szigeti of the PHC as Minister of Education, and Lucia Žitňanská, an independent, as Minister of Justice. In April Tóth was dismissed from his position as Minister of Culture, after being accused of misusing state funds; Rudolf Chmel, who held the position until May 2005, was subsequently reappointed to the culture portfolio.

In legislative elections held on 17 June 2006 the majority of seats (a total of 50) were won by Fico's Direction-Social Democracy, which secured 29.1% of the votes cast. The SDCU-DP obtained 18.4% of the votes (31 seats), while the SNP and the PHC both won 11.7% (20 seats). Fifteen seats were allocated to the PP—MDS, which attracted 8.8% of the ballot, while the CDM secured 14 seats, with 8.3%. The rate of participation in the elections was 54.7%. Three days later Fico was invited by President Gašparovič to form a government. On 28 June Direction-Social Democracy voted in favour of inviting the SNP and the PP—MDS to enter into a coalition; an agreement to this end was signed on 3 July. Fico's new administration predominantly comprised members of his own party, with the SNP and the PP—MDS being allocated just three and two cabinet posts, respectively. Neither Mečiar nor SNP Chairman Ján Slota were awarded cabinet positions. None the less, the Party of European Socialists (PES), in protest at Direction-Social Democracy's involvement with a far-right organization such as the SNP, voted temporarily to suspend the party's membership. (Direction-Social Democracy, whose contingent had been aligned with the PES in the European Parliament, was formally expelled from the PES in October.) Moreover, the European People's Party-European Democrats, the strongest conservative group within the European Parliament, agreed to create a monitoring team to observe developments in Slovakia, as proposed by Slovak MEPs within the group. Fico was formally appointed Prime Minister on 4 July; the new Národná rada was sworn in on the same day.

Assurances by Fico's administration that it would continue the foreign and domestic policies pursued by the previous Government, including those pertaining to Slovakia's planned accession to the euro zone (which was scheduled for 1 January 2009), were undermined in the weeks following the general election by highly contentious statements attributed to Slota in the domestic and international press on the issues of deportation and Slovakia's ethnic Hungarian population. While the PHC appealed to prosecutors to take legal action against Slota, the SNP threatened to sue controversial PHC deputy Miklos Duray for terming it a 'fascist' party. Following an attack in late August 2006 in the western town of Nitra by ultra-nationalists on a Hungarian student—one of a series of manifestations of anti-Hungarian sentiment—and subsequent pressure from the Hungarian Prime Minister, Ferenc Gyurcsány, Fico publicly condemned extremism in Slovakia. (Police later accused the student of fabricating the attack and abandoned their investigation into the incident.) An escalation in tension between Slovakia and Hungary prompted President Gašparovič to express his concerns regarding national intolerance in his country, but also to warn against excessive criticism of Slovakia. At the end of August the Chairman of the Parliamentary Assembly of the Council of Europe, Rane van der Linden, denounced the manifestations of racial intolerance in Slovakia. In early September Minister of Foreign Affairs Ján Kubiš and his Hungarian counterpart, Kinga Göncz, pledged to work together to improve bilateral relations. The head of the European Commission, José Manuel Barroso, also criticized the escalating tension in Slovakia with regard to its Hungarian minority, and reminded the country of its commitment to human rights as a member state of the EU. On 7 September the Národná rada adopted a declaration against extremism and intolerance (112 deputies voted in favour of the motion, while 28 abstained). In 2006 Slovakia granted asylum to just eight individuals, from a total of 2,871 applicants, the lowest figure since the country's inception in 1993.

Despite the turbulence of the first two months of his premiership, by the end of 2006 Fico appeared to have consolidated his position and introduced a period of political stability. Direction-Social Democracy performed well at the municipal elections of 2 December (in which 47.7% of the electorate participated). However, the appointment in that month of Radim Hreha, a strong supporter of Fico, as Director of Slovak Television (STV) prompted fears that the premier was applying pressure on the state media to adopt a pro-Government stance, fears that were fuelled in January 2007 by Hreha's dismissal of Editor-in-Chief Roland Kyska, who had recently been involved in a public disagreement with Fico. In April an internal dispute erupted within the PHC when Duray accused outgoing Chairman Béla Bugár of co-operating with the communist-era secret police. (Bugár had been replaced as Chairman at the beginning of that month by Pál Csáky, whom many expected to adopt a more radical stance on Hungarian autonomy.)

In November 2007 the PP—MDS threatened to withdraw from the Government, in protest at Fico's dismissal of the Minister of Agriculture (a representative of that party), after evidence emerged of an illicit land sale agreement involving the Slovak State Land Fund. However, in December the Národná rada approved the budget for 2008, by 85 votes to 61, in a motion that was also regarded as expressing confidence in Fico's administration. In January 2008 the new Minister of Agriculture, Zdenka Kramplová, ordered the dismissal of the entire board of the Slovak State Land Fund. Later that month the Minister of Defence, František Kašický, resigned, following allegations that his ministry had overpriced tenders for the maintenance of military barracks; he was succeed by Jaroslav Baška, also of Direction-Social Democracy. The formation of a new political party, the Conservative Democrats of Slovakia (CDS), was announced in March by four deputies who had recently defected from the CDM; the CDS was formally registered in July. Meanwhile, in April President Gašparovič signed into law new regulations that were expected severely to restrict the activities of the print media; the new legislation, which entered into effect in June, had been drafted by the Minister of Culture, following ongoing government criticism of press statements, and had attracted objections from international organizations.

Richard Raši of Direction-Social Democracy was appointed as Minister of Health in early June 2008, after the incumbent, Ivan Valentovič, resigned, citing personal reasons. Later that month the Minister of Finance, Ján Počiatek, survived a motion of no confidence proposed by the opposition, which alleged that plans to adjust the koruna's value against the euro had been disclosed to private investors ahead of the revaluation in May; Počiatek denied the accusations. However, further government changes were effected in August, when Ján Chrbet and Stanislav Becík were appointed as Minister of Agriculture and Minister of the Environment, respectively, replacing Kramplová and Jaroslav Izák. Kramplová had been dismissed over an alleged lack of transparency in the awarding of a tender, as well as controversial donations to the PP—MDS, of which she was Central Secretary, while Izák had been forced to resign for inappropriately disbursing environmental subsidies to individuals reported to be close to his party, the SNP. Ján Kubiš resigned as Minister of Foreign Affairs in January 2009 to become Executive Secretary of the UN Economic Commission for Europe; he was succeeded by Miroslav Lajčák, hitherto High Representative of the International Community and EU Special Representative in Bosnia and Herzegovina.

Seven candidates contested the first round of voting in a presidential election held on 21 March 2009. Gašparovič, the incumbent President, who was supported by the governing Direction-Social Democracy and SNP, secured the largest share of the valid votes cast, with 46.7%, followed by Iveta Radičová, a Vice-Chairperson of the SDCU-DP and also supported by the PHC and CDM, who won 38.1%. The other five candidates all won less than 6% of the valid votes cast, František Mikloško, representing the CDS, taking third place, with 5.4%. Gašparovič defeated Radičová in a second round of voting on 4 April 2009, receiving 55.5% of the valid votes cast. The rate of participation by the electorate was 43.6% in the first round and 51.7% in the second round. There was speculation that Radičová's strong performance in the presidential election would lead to continued co-operation between the opposition parties. In mid-April the Minister of Construction and Regional Development, Marian Janušek of the SNP, tendered his resignation, which had been requested by Fico after investigations by the Public Procurement Office and the Supreme Audit Office confirmed that Janušek's ministry had mishandled the tendering process for a €120m. contract that had been awarded to a consortium of two companies reported to have links to SNP Chairman Slota. The opposition parties swiftly initiated a vote of no confidence in Janušek's replacement, Igor Stefanov, on the grounds of his involvement in preparing the tender, but this was defeated.

In 1997 Mečiar appealed to the Roma population not to seek asylum abroad, after a number of Roma were repatriated from the United Kingdom. However, Slovakia's Roma continued to seek political asylum abroad (largely unsuccessfully), prompting several countries to introduce mandatory visa requirements, on a temporary basis, for Slovak citizens. Although, according to the 2001 census, there were some 89,900 Roma in Slovakia, the community was unofficially estimated to number around 200,000. In January 2004 a report by the Council of Europe (see p. 236) concluded that Slovakia's Roma were frequently victims of racial prejudice and were disadvantaged socially. In the following month proposed reductions in social welfare prompted violent protests by the Roma minority, and some 1,000 troops were deployed to control rioting. In July new legislation was introduced prohibiting discrimination on the grounds of ethnicity. In November 2006 the European Monitoring Centre on Racism and Xenophobia, based in Vienna, Austria, criticized Slovakia, along with the Czech Republic and Hungary, for segregating its Roma populations, particularly in the education sector, but also with regard to housing and the labour market.

Slovakia's relations with Hungary have been strained by the issue of the large Hungarian minority (numbering some 520,500 at the 2001 census) resident in Slovakia, who are campaigning for cultural and educational autonomy. The two countries are also involved in a dispute over the Gabčíkovo-Nagymaros hydroelectric project, a scheme initiated by the Governments of Czechoslovakia and Hungary in 1977, which involved the construction of two dams and the diversion of the River Danube. Despite Hungary's decision in 1989 to abandon the project (following pressure by environmentalist groups), the Czechoslovak Government announced that it would proceed unilaterally with its part of the construction. In early 1993 Slovakia and Hungary agreed to forward the dispute to the International Court of Justice (ICJ) in The Hague, Netherlands, and to operate a temporary water-management scheme in the mean time. In March 1995, none the less, an historic bilateral Treaty of Friendship and Co-operation was signed by the Prime Ministers of Hungary and Slovakia. The Treaty, notably, guaranteed the rights of ethnic minorities in each republic, while confirming the existing state border. However, the language law approved by the Slovak legislature in November, declaring Slovak the only official language and thereby potentially restricting the use of minority languages, was criticized both by Hungarian residents of Slovakia and by the Hungarian Government, as a violation of the Treaty. In August 1997 the Hungarian Prime Minister, Gyula Horn, and Mečiar agreed on the establishment of a joint commission to assess the implementation of the 1995 Treaty.

In September 1997 the ICJ pronounced its judgment on the Gabčíkovo-Nagymaros hydroelectric project, ruling that both countries had breached international law: Hungary was not justified in suspending work on the project, while the former Czechoslovakia should not have proceeded unilaterally. Both countries were to pay compensation for damages, and to negotiate regarding the realization of the original agreement. The participation of the PHC in the new Slovak Government, appointed in October 1998, improved prospects for the protection of minority rights. In February 1999 the first meeting of the joint minorities commission to monitor the implementation of the 1995 Treaty was held in Budapest, Hungary. In July 1999 the Národná rada approved legislation that provided for the use of an ethnic minority language in towns where the minority accounted for at least 20% of the population.

In December 1999 Hungary renounced any claim to a share of the hydroelectric energy produced by the Gabčíkovo-Nagymaros dam project, but requested an increase in the common flow of water along the Danube, for ecological reasons. In February 2001 Slovakia accepted that it had no legal means to compel Hungary to complete the project, but stated that it was to seek compensation. In December 2003 an intergovernmental commission was established to co-ordinate negotiations on the issue. Meanwhile, in January 2002 relations between Slovakia and Hungary had again become acrimonious, following Hungary's adoption of legislation that granted ethnic Hungarians resident in six neighbouring states, including Slovakia, education, employment and medical benefits. The Slovak Government protested that the new legislation violated Slovakia's sovereignty, and demanded that it be cancelled or amended. In March 2003 Hungary agreed to suspend the application of the law in Slovakia, and in December the Ministers of Foreign Affairs of Hungary and Slovakia signed an agreement on the issue. The provisions of the Hungarian 'status law' were effectively superseded by the accession of Hungary and Slovakia to the EU in May 2004 (see below). In February 2006 it was announced that Slovakia and Hungary had agreed to implement the 1997 ICJ ruling on the Gabčíkovo-Nagymaros hydroelectric project. The two Governments were to draft an agreement on the implementation of the ruling and amend the 1977 agreement on the construction and operation of the system.

SLOVAKIA

Relations with neighbouring Austria were strained by the issue of the partially constructed, Soviet-designed nuclear power station at Mochovce (north-east of Bratislava), operated by Slovenské elektrárne (Slovak Electricity), the completion of which was opposed by the Austrian Government, owing to safety concerns. An agreement on completion of the project was signed in April 1996, with Western European, Russian and Czech companies, according to which the first reactor would be commissioned by July 1998 and the second by March 1999. Tension increased in June 1998, when the first reactor was activated, despite a request from the Austrian Government that Slovakia delay the opening of the plant until an international team of inspectors, who had visited Mochovce in May, had submitted a final report on the plant's safety. In late 1999 the Slovak Government announced its decision to close two existing reactors at Jaslovské-Bohunice between 2006 and 2008, further antagonizing Austria, which had favoured closure by 2000. In May 2004, shortly after Slovakia's accession to the EU, tensions between the two countries heightened, following the Slovak Government's announcement that it intended to complete work on the Mochovce plant. Construction of Mochovce's two unfinished reactors by Slovenské elektrárne (majority owned by the Italian electricity group Enel since 2006) commenced in November 2008 and was scheduled to be completed by 2013, at an estimated cost of €2,800m. In January 2009 concern was raised by the Government's announcement that it planned to reactivate a reactor at Jaslovské-Bohunice, which had only been decommissioned at the end of 2008, in response to energy shortages caused by a cessation in supplies of natural gas from Russia, via Ukraine, following a dispute between those two countries over pricing; however, the plan to restart the reactor was subsequently abandoned, and gas supplies resumed later that month.

In December 1999 Slovakia was among six countries formally invited to commence talks on accession to the EU; entry negotiations opened in February 2000. Following the return to power of a reformist coalition Government in October 2002 (see above), at an EU summit meeting held in Copenhagen, Denmark, in December, Slovakia was one of 10 nations invited to become a member in 2004. At a national referendum, which was conducted on 16–17 May 2003, 92.5% of votes were cast in favour of membership of the EU; some 52% of the electorate participated in the ballot. Slovakia's Treaty of Accession was formally ratified by the Národná rada on 1 July, and the country became a full member of the EU on 1 May 2004. In December 2007 Slovakia, together with eight other EU member nations (including the Czech Republic, Hungary and Poland), implemented the Schengen Agreement on freedom of travel, effectively removing border controls between those states subject to the Agreement. In early 2008 the Slovak authorities announced a subsequent increase in the number of illegal immigrants detained. Following Kosovo's unilateral declaration of independence in February (see the chapter on Kosovo), Slovakia was among several EU member nations (including Spain, Romania and Cyprus) to refuse to recognize it as a sovereign state, although the Government offered it 'partnership'. The ratification of the EU's Lisbon Treaty, which was designed to reform the Union's institutions, was approved by the Národná rada in April and received presidential assent in May. The parliamentary vote had been delayed for several months as opposition parties withheld their support for the Treaty in protest at proposed domestic legislation regulating the print media (which was also adopted in April—see above); in the event, PHC deputies finally agreed to vote in favour of ratification, while the SDCU-DP and the CDM boycotted proceedings. In May the European Commission approved Slovakia's planned accession to the euro zone on 1 January 2009. This decision was confirmed by EU finance ministers in July 2008, and Slovakia became the 16th member of the euro zone as scheduled.

Meanwhile, in February 1994 Slovakia joined NATO's 'Partnership for Peace' programme (see p. 353). At a NATO summit meeting in Prague at the end of November 2002, Slovakia (together with six other countries) was formally invited to join the Alliance, and it became a full member on 29 March 2004. In May Slovakia hosted a plenary session of the NATO Parliamentary Assembly, and in February 2005 it hosted a summit meeting between US President George W. Bush and Russian President Vladimir Putin. President Bush praised the deployment of 100 Slovak troops to Iraq to participate in the US-led military operations there. However, in February 2007 Fico fulfilled one of his electoral promises by withdrawing his country's troops from Iraq. (This, in addition to controversial visits by the new premier to the People's Republic of China and Libya, was seen as an effort by Fico to distance himself from the pro-US stance of his predecessor.) Also in February it was agreed that some 60 Slovak troops stationed in Kabul, Afghanistan, as part of the NATO-led International Security Assistance Force (ISAF) mission, would be transferred to Kandahar, in the south of the country, by June. In June 2008 the Národná rada approved an increase in the maximum number of Slovakian troops authorized to be deployed in Afghanistan from 115 to 246; at early 2009 121 Slovakians were participating in ISAF. In March 2007 Slovakia joined the International Energy Agency (IEA).

Government

Supreme legislative power is vested in the Národná rada Slovenskej republiky (National Council of the Slovak Republic), the 150 members of which are elected for a term of four years by universal adult suffrage. The President of the Republic (Head of State) is directly elected by universal adult suffrage for a five-year term. The President, who is restricted to two consecutive terms of office, appoints the Prime Minister and, on the latter's recommendation, the other members of the Government (the supreme body of executive power). For administrative purposes, Slovakia is divided into eight 'higher territorial units' (VÚCs), each with a regional council (together totalling 401 seats), and 79 electoral districts.

Defence

As assessed at November 2008, the total active strength of Slovakia's armed forces was 17,445: army 7,297, air force 4,192, and some 5,956 centrally controlled personnel, logistical, and support staff. In July 2005 it was announced that compulsory military service was to be abandoned from 1 August, and in December the army became fully professional. Slovakia became a full member of the North Atlantic Treaty Organization (NATO, see p. 351) on 29 March 2004. The 2008 budget allocated 31,200m. koruny to defence.

Economic Affairs

In 2007, according to the World Bank, Slovakia's gross national income (GNI), measured at average 2005–07 prices, was US $63,324m., equivalent to $11,730 per head (or $19,340 per head on an international purchasing-power parity basis). During 2000–07, it was estimated, the population remained constant, while gross domestic product (GDP) per head increased, in real terms, by an average of 6.1% per year. Overall GDP increased, in real terms, at an average annual rate of 6.2% in 2000–07, according to preliminary official figures; real GDP increased by 10.4% in 2007.

The agricultural sector (including hunting, forestry and fishing) contributed 3.4% of GDP in 2008, and engaged 4.2% of the employed labour force. The principal crops are sugar beet, wheat and maize. Livestock-breeding is also important. During 2000–07 the GDP of the agricultural sector increased, in real terms, at an average annual rate of 8.4%. Agricultural GDP increased by 9.2% in 2007.

Industry (including mining, manufacturing, construction and power) contributed 36.8% of GDP in 2008, and engaged 39.4% of the employed labour force in 2007. The GDP of the industrial sector increased, in real terms, at an average annual rate of 10.9% during 2000–07. Industrial GDP increased by 12.2% in 2007.

Mining and quarrying contributed 0.6% of GDP in 2008, and engaged 0.7% of the employed labour force in 2007. The principal minerals extracted include brown coal and lignite, copper, zinc, lead, iron ore and magnesite. There are also deposits of crude petroleum, natural gas and mercury, as well as materials used in construction (including limestone, gravel and brick loam). The GDP of the mining and quarrying sector decreased at an average annual rate of 1.5% in 2000–07. Mining GDP declined by 33.1% in 2006, but increased by 48.0% in 2007.

The manufacturing sector contributed 22.1% of GDP in 2008, and engaged 26.9% of the employed labour force in 2007. The GDP of the manufacturing sector increased at an average annual rate of 13.7% in 2000–07. Manufacturing GDP increased by 19.5% in 2007.

Energy is derived principally from nuclear power, which provided some 56.5% of electricity generated in 2005. In that year coal accounted for 19.1% of electricity production, and hydroelectric power for 14.8%. A nuclear power station at Jaslovské-Bohunice has been in operation since the early 1980s, although two reactors there were closed in 2006 and 2008. In mid-1998 the first block of a new nuclear power installation, at Mochovce, commenced operations; construction work on two unfinished reactors there was due to be completed by 2013. Slovakia has been heavily dependent on imported fuel and energy products. Mineral fuels and lubricants, etc., accounted for 11.0% of the value of total merchandise imports in 2007.

The services sector contributed 59.7% of GDP in 2008, and engaged 56.4% of the employed labour force in 2007. During 2000–07 the GDP of the services sector increased, in real terms, at an average annual rate of 3.5%. Services GDP increased by 10.0% in 2007.

In 2007 Slovakia recorded a trade deficit of US $909m., and there was a deficit of some $4,103m. on the current account of the balance of payments. In 2007 the principal source of imports was Germany, which accounted for 19.9% of the total; other major suppliers were the Czech Republic, Russia and Hungary. Germany was also the principal market for exports in that year (accounting for 21.5%); other important purchasers were the Czech Republic, France, Italy, Poland, Austria and Hungary. The main exports in 2007 were machinery and transport equipment (particularly road vehicles, telecommunications and sound recording equipment, and electrical machinery, apparatus and appliances), basic manufactures (notably iron and steel) and miscellaneous manufactured articles. The principal imports were machinery and transport equipment, basic manufactures, mineral fuels and lubricants, miscellaneous manufactured articles, and chemicals and related products.

Slovakia's overall budgetary deficit was 36,110m. koruny in 2007, equivalent to 1.9% of GDP. At the end of 2006 Slovakia's total external debt was US $27,085m., of which $4,508m. was long-term public debt. In 2003 the cost of debt-servicing was equivalent to 13.8% of the value of exports of goods and services. The annual rate of inflation averaged 4.9% in 2000–08; consumer prices increased by 2.8% in 2007 and by 4.6% in 2008. According to official figures, the average rate of unemployment was 11.0% in 2007, but declined to 9.6% in 2008.

Slovakia is a member of the European Bank for Reconstruction and Development (EBRD, see p. 251). In 2000 Slovakia was admitted to the Organisation for Economic Co-operation and Development (OECD, see p. 358). Slovakia signed an association agreement with the European Community (now European Union—EU, see p. 255) in October 1993, and became a full member of the EU on 1 May 2004.

Following independence in 1993, the economy successfully shifted from its traditional reliance on industry to services, and from state to private ownership. The privatization programme was extended in 2000, and in November 2003 the Národná rada approved an amendment to existing legislation permitting the sale of majority stakes in large state-owned utilities and natural monopolies. In January 2004 a 19% uniform rate of income tax, corporate tax and value-added tax was introduced, the relatively low rate of corporate taxation subsequently leading to increased foreign direct investment. However, plans to privatize many state-run enterprises were halted by the Government of Robert Fico, which assumed power in July 2006. Slovakia was admitted to the EU's exchange rate mechanism (ERM II) in November 2005, when the koruny was linked to the common European currency, the euro. In May 2008 the European Commission agreed that Slovakia had fulfilled the Maastricht criteria for membership of the euro zone, a decision confirmed by EU finance ministers in July 2008, despite concerns from the European Central Bank regarding the rate of consumer price inflation, and Slovakia duly adopted the euro on 1 January 2009. Real GDP growth slowed to 6.4% in 2008, from a high of 10.4% in 2007, as a consequence of the global financial crisis. Slovakia's economic slowdown was expected to continue in 2009, owing to weaker domestic and external demand, resulting from tighter lending conditions and recession in many of the country's principal export markets. The unemployment rate, which had declined to 7.8% in November 2008 (although significant regional disparities remained), increased steadily in the following four months, reaching 10.3% in March 2009. In November 2008 the Government adopted a programme of 27 measures aimed at reducing the impact of the international downturn on Slovakia, which included improvements in the use of EU funds; reductions in public expenditure; investment in infrastructure projects; and new loan schemes for small and medium-sized enterprises. A €332m. plan to support employment and boost domestic demand was also announced in January 2009. None the less, in April the central bank forecast that real GDP would contract by 2.4% in 2009.

Education

Education in Slovakia is provided free of charge at all levels in state-controlled and church-affiliated schools. Children between the ages of three and six may attend kindergarten (materská škola). Compulsory education begins at six years of age, when children enter basic school (základná škola), which takes nine years to complete (although the ninth year is optional). In 2007 482,566 pupils were enrolled at primary schools. In 2005 enrolment at primary schools included 92% of pupils in the relevant age-group, according to UNESCO estimates. There are three types of secondary school: the grammar school (gymnázium), which prepares students for higher education, and of which there were 252 in 2007, secondary specialized school (stredná odborná škola, 242) and secondary vocational school (stredné odborné učilište, 181), with a total enrolment of 227,599 students. In 2006 secondary enrolment was equivalent to 96% of children in the relevant age-group. In 2007 there were 30 institutions of higher education, with a total enrolment of 132,499 students. Children who, owing to disabilities, cannot attend regular schools may receive instruction at special schools. There are also private schools (basic and secondary). Of total government expenditure in 2007, 62,4230m. koruny (9.6%) was allocated to education, according to preliminary figures.

Public Holidays

2009: 1 January (Anniversary of the Slovak Republic), 6 January (Epiphany), 10 April (Good Friday), 13 April (Easter Monday), 1 May (Labour Day), 8 May (Anniversary of Liberation), 5 July (Day of the Slav Apostles, Cyril and Methodius), 29 August (National Day, Anniversary of the Slovak National Uprising), 1 September (Constitution Day), 15 September (Our Lady of Seven Sorrows), 1 November (All Saints' Day), 17 November (Day of Freedom and Democracy), 24–26 December (Christmas).

2010: 1 January (Anniversary of the Slovak Republic), 6 January (Epiphany), 2 April (Good Friday), 5 April (Easter Monday), 1 May (Labour Day), 8 May (Anniversary of Liberation), 5 July (Day of the Slav Apostles, Cyril and Methodius), 29 August (National Day, Anniversary of the Slovak National Uprising), 1 September (Constitution Day), 15 September (Our Lady of Seven Sorrows), 1 November (All Saints' Day), 17 November (Day of Freedom and Democracy), 24–26 December (Christmas).

Weights and Measures

The metric system is in force.

Statistical Survey

Source: Statistical Office of the Slovak Republic, Miletičova 3, 824 67 Bratislava; tel. (2) 5023-6340; fax (2) 5556-1361; e-mail agnesa.kralikova@statistics.sk; internet www.statistics.sk.

Area and Population

AREA, POPULATION AND DENSITY

Area (sq km)	49,033*
Population (census results)	
3 March 1991	5,274,335
26 May 2001	
Males	2,612,515
Females	2,766,940
Total	5,379,455
Population (official estimates at 31 December)	
2006	5,393,637
2007	5,400,998
2008	5,412,254
Density (per sq km) at 31 December 2008	110.4

* 18,932 sq miles.

POPULATION BY ETHNIC GROUP
(at 2001 census)

	Number	%
Slovak	4,614,854	85.79
Hungarian	520,528	9.68
Gypsy (Roma)	89,920	1.67
Czech, Moravian, Silesian	46,968	0.87
Ruthenian, Ukrainian	35,015	0.65
German	5,405	0.10
Others (incl. undeclared)	66,765	1.24
Total	**5,379,455**	**100.00**

REGIONS
(at 31 December 2008)

	Area (sq km)	Population	Density (per sq km)
Banská Bystrica	9,455	653,697	69
Bratislava	2,053	616,578	300
Košice	6,753	775,509	115
Nitra	6,343	706,375	111
Prešov	8,993	803,955	89
Trenčín	4,501	599,859	133
Trnava	4,148	559,934	135
Žilina	6,788	696,347	103
Total	**49,034**	**5,412,254**	**110**

Note: Each region is named after its principal city.

PRINCIPAL TOWNS
(estimated population at 31 December 2002)

Bratislava (capital)	427,049	Trnava	69,868
Košice	235,509	Martin	60,017
Prešov	92,486	Trenčín	57,413
Nitra	86,958	Poprad	55,982
Žilina	85,347	Prievidza	52,658
Banská Bystrica	82,493	Zvolen	43,674

Mid-2007 ('000, incl. suburbs, UN estimate): Bratislava 424 (Source: UN, *World Urbanization Prospects: The 2007 Revision*).

BIRTHS, MARRIAGES AND DEATHS

	Registered live births Number	Rate (per 1,000)	Registered marriages Number	Rate (per 1,000)	Registered deaths Number	Rate (per 1,000)
2000	55,151	10.2	25,903	4.8	52,724	9.8
2001	51,136	9.5	23,795	4.4	51,980	9.7
2002	50,841	9.5	25,062	4.7	51,532	9.6
2003	51,713	9.6	26,002	4.8	52,230	9.7
2004	53,747	10.0	27,885	5.2	51,852	9.6
2005	54,430	10.1	26,149	4.9	53,475	9.9
2006	53,904	10.0	25,939	4.8	53,301	9.9
2007	54,424	10.1	27,437	5.1	53,856	10.0

Life expectancy (years at birth, WHO estimates): 74.4 (males 70.4; females 78.3) in 2006 (Source: WHO, *World Health Statistics*).

ECONOMICALLY ACTIVE POPULATION
(labour force surveys, '000 persons)

	2005	2006	2007
Agriculture, hunting, forestry and fishing	105.1	100.8	99.3
Mining and quarrying	14.7	16.0	16.4
Manufacturing	591.9	608.6	634.2
Electricity, gas and water	42.6	41.9	40.3
Construction	209.8	226.1	237.1
Wholesale and retail trade; repair of motor vehicles, motorcycles and personal and household goods	269.5	290.6	300.0
Hotels and restaurants	90.3	101.8	102.0
Transport, storage and communications	147.2	156.2	165.3
Financial intermediation	48.1	51.8	47.6
Real estate, renting and business services	129.2	131.6	145.7
Public administration and defence; compulsory social security	154.6	161.8	159.8
Education	163.7	166.8	163.4
Health and social work	150.0	154.5	154.7
Other community, social and personal service activities	88.4	85.3	82.1
Private households with employed persons	7.4	5.8	8.2
Extra-territorial organizations	0.2	0.2	0.8
Activities not adequately defined	3.8	1.9	0.5
Total	**2,216.2**	**2,301.4**	**2,357.3**
Unemployed	427.5	353.4	291.9
Total labour force	**2,643.7**	**2,654.8**	**2,649.2**
Males	1,456.6	1,470.7	1,465.1
Females	1,186.9	1,184.2	1,184.0

Source: ILO.

Health and Welfare

KEY INDICATORS

Total fertility rate (children per woman, 2006)	1.2
Under-5 mortality rate (per 1,000 live births, 2006)	8
HIV/AIDS (% of persons aged 15–49, 2007)	<0.1
Physicians (per 1,000 head, 2004)	3.1
Hospital beds (per 1,000 head, 2006)	6.8
Health expenditure (2006): US $ per head (PPP)	1,235
Health expenditure (2006): % of GDP	7.0
Health expenditure (2006): public (% of total)	73.9
Human Development Index (2006): ranking	41
Human Development Index (2006): value	0.872

For sources and definitions, see explanatory note on p. vi.

SLOVAKIA

Agriculture

PRINCIPAL CROPS
('000 metric tons)

	2005	2006	2007
Wheat	1,607.9	1,342.7	1,440.6
Barley	739.3	641.8	695.0
Maize	1,074.0	838.3	675.2
Rye	68.6	30.2	56.8
Oats	38.2	41.4	40.3
Triticale (wheat-rye hybrid)	52.4	30.4	38.5
Potatoes	301.2	263.1	381.7
Sugar beet	1,732.6	1,370.9	855.3
Peas, dry	28.2	22.8	16.4
Sunflower seed	195.3	228.6	135.4
Rapeseed	235.1	259.7	336.4
Cabbages and other brassicas	84.5	87.7	85.0*
Tomatoes	61.0	63.0	60.0*
Chillies and peppers, green	28.7	28.6	28.0*
Cucumbers and gherkins	32.4	32.0	32.0*
Onions, dry	27.1	26.9	27.0*
Carrots and turnips	37.6	37.8	37.0*
Apples	47.0	30.8	18.0
Grapes	54.1	52.0	50.7
Watermelons	10.7	7.5	8.0*
Tobacco, unmanufactured	1.0	0.7	0.4

* FAO estimate.

Aggregate production ('000 metric tons, may include official, semi-official or estimated data): Total cereals 3,585.3 in 2005, 2,928.8 in 2006, 2,949.8 in 2007; Total roots and tubers 301.2 in 2005, 263.1 in 2006, 381.7 in 2007; Total vegetables (incl. melons) 340.6 in 2005, 333.3 in 2006, 329.0 in 2007; Total fruits (excl. melons) 170.1 in 2005, 94.9 in 2006, 79.4 in 2007.

Source: FAO.

LIVESTOCK
('000 head, year ending 30 September)

	2005	2006	2007
Cattle	540	528	508
Pigs	1,149	1,108	1,105
Sheep	321	320	333
Goats	39	40	38
Horses	8	8	8
Chickens	13,262	13,619	13,038

Source: FAO.

LIVESTOCK PRODUCTS
('000 metric tons)

	2005	2006	2007*
Cattle meat	26.4	21.4	25.0
Pig meat	139.9	122.3	130.0
Chicken meat	87.2	86.1	85.0
Cows' milk	1,100.0	1,070.0	1,000.0
Goats' milk	8.9	8.2	8.5
Hen eggs	62.9	70.3	70.0
Other poultry eggs*	4.5	5.0	5.0

* FAO estimates.
Source: FAO.

Forestry

ROUNDWOOD REMOVALS
('000 cubic metres, excl. bark)

	2005	2006	2007
Sawlogs, veneer logs and logs for sleepers	4,845	4,102	4,862
Pulpwood	3,629	2,676	2,813
Other industrial wood	531	783	783
Fuel wood	297	307	417
Total	9,302	7,869	8,875

Source: FAO.

SAWNWOOD PRODUCTION
('000 cubic metres, incl. railway sleepers)

	2005	2006	2007
Coniferous (softwood)	1,984	1,760	1,872
Broadleaved (hardwood)	637	680	909
Total	2,621	2,440	2,781

Source: FAO.

Fishing

(metric tons, live weight)

	2004	2005	2006
Capture	1,603	1,693	1,718
Common carp	1,015	1,112	1,184
Northern pike	61	68	61
Pike-perch	78	83	65
Breams	98	105	95
Aquaculture	1,180	955	1,263
Common carp	345	169	414
Rainbow trout	818	742	784
Total catch (incl. others)	2,783	2,648	2,981

Source: FAO.

Mining

('000 metric tons, unless otherwise indicated)

	2004	2005	2006
Coal (brown and lignite)	2,952	2,511	2,500*
Crude petroleum	50	50	50
Natural gas (million cu metres)	200	200	200
Limestone and other calcareous stones for cement	4,501	6,034	6,611
Sands and gravel ('000 cubic metres)	1,300*	1,800	1,800

* Estimated production.
Source: US Geological Survey.

SLOVAKIA

Industry

SELECTED PRODUCTS
('000 metric tons, unless otherwise indicated)

	2001	2002	2003
Wheat flour	312	333	320
Bread	145	138	140
Refined sugar	38	35	38
Beer ('000 hectolitres)	4,520	4,800	4,630
Wine ('000 hectolitres)	450	374	345
Distilled alcoholic beverages ('000 hectolitres)	123	111	109
Cotton yarn	3.6	6.3	5.4
Footwear, excl. rubber footwear ('000 pairs)	8,994	9,555	13,496
Paper and paperboard	988	994	n.a.
Paints and enamels	32.9	34.6	32.7
Black-coal coke	1,697	1,806	1,886
Residual fuel oils	718	620	635
Gas-diesel (distillate fuel) oil	2,406	2,341	2,351
Cement	3,123	3,141	3,147
Pig-iron*	3,255	3,533	3,892
Crude steel*	3,989	4,275	4,709
Alumina*	111.6	132.1	156.9
Household refrigerators and freezers ('000 units)	27	2	n.a.
Passenger motor cars ('000 units)	277	226	n.a.
Lorries (number)	70	n.a.	n.a.
Colour television receivers ('000 units)	594	712	n.a.
Electric energy	32,046	32,427	31,179

* Source: US Geological Survey.

Source: UN, *Industrial Commodity Statistics Yearbook*.

Black-coal coke ('000 metric tons): 1,883 in 2004 (Source: UN, *Industrial Commodity Statistics Yearbook*).

Residual fuel oils ('000 metric tons): 585 in 2004 (Source: UN, *Industrial Commodity Statistics Yearbook*).

Gas-diesel (distillate fuel) oil ('000 metric tons): 2,598 in 2004 (Source: UN, *Industrial Commodity Statistics Yearbook*).

Cement ('000 metric tons, estimate): 3,158 in 2004; 3,499 in 2005 (Source: US Geological Survey).

Pig-iron ('000 metric tons, estimate): 3,980 in 2004; 3,681 in 2005 (Source: US Geological Survey).

Crude steel ('000 metric tons, estimate): 4,564 in 2004; 4,242 in 2005 (Source: US Geological Survey).

Aluminium ingot, primary (metric tons, estimates): 175 in 2004; 158 in 2005 (Source: US Geological Survey).

Electric energy (million kWh): 30,567 in 2004 (Source: UN, *Industrial Commodity Statistics Yearbook*).

Finance

CURRENCY AND EXCHANGE RATES

Monetary Units
100 halierov (singular: halier) = 1 slovenská koruna (Slovak crown or Sk).

Sterling, Dollar and Euro Equivalents (31 December 2008)
£1 sterling = 31.175 koruna;
US $1 = 21.385 koruna;
€1 = 29.761 koruna;
1,000 koruna = £32.08 = $46.76 = €33.60.

Average Exchange Rate (koruna per US $)
2006   29.697
2007   24.694
2008   21.361

Note: Slovakia adopted the euro on 1 January 2009, replacing the former national currency at a fixed exchange rate of €1 = 30.126 koruna

GOVERNMENT FINANCE
(general government transactions, non-cash basis, '000 million koruna)

Summary of Balances

	2005	2006*	2007*
Revenue	534.32	573.65	617.45
Less Expense	546.75	604.91	621.80
Net operating balance	−12.43	−31.27	−4.36
Less Net acquisition of non-financial assets	29.20	29.95	31.76
Net lending/borrowing	−41.63	−61.21	−36.11

Revenue

	2005	2006*	2007*
Taxes	271.66	283.76	319.81
Taxes on income, profits and capital gains	83.57	93.59	110.24
Taxes on goods and services	180.51	183.05	202.61
Social contributions	184.10	200.67	217.74
Grants	14.71	6.93	7.80
Other revenue	63.86	82.30	72.10
Total	534.32	573.65	617.45

Expense/Outlays

Expense by economic type	2005	2006*	2007*
Compensation of employees	107.47	126.22	125.21
Use of goods and services	77.84	90.45	83.06
Consumption of fixed capital	—	—	—
Interest	25.49	26.95	29.42
Subsidies	27.40	30.15	40.75
Grants	11.11	14.64	15.62
Social benefits	249.22	269.46	292.54
Other expense	48.21	47.04	35.21
Total	546.75	604.91	621.80

Outlays by functions of government†	2005	2006*	2007*
General public services	91.62	105.14	92.47
Defence	23.38	25.46	25.95
Public order and safety	30.00	32.23	35.94
Economic affairs	71.46	85.20	85.17
Environmental protection	10.50	11.46	12.74
Housing and community amenities	12.94	13.95	13.25
Health	95.79	107.02	116.70
Recreation, culture and religion	12.68	17.76	19.52
Education	57.42	62.73	62.42
Social protection	170.16	184.20	199.79
Statistical discrepancy	—	−10.27	−10.38
Total	575.95	634.86	653.56

* Preliminary.
† Including net acquisition of non-financial assets.

Source: IMF, *Government Finance Statistics Yearbook*.

INTERNATIONAL RESERVES
(US $ million at 31 December)

	2006	2007	2008
Gold (national valuation)	717	944	976
IMF special drawing rights	1	2	2
Foreign exchange	12,645	18,026	17,805
Total	13,363	18,972	18,783

Source: IMF, *International Financial Statistics*.

MONEY SUPPLY
(million koruna at 31 December)

	2006	2007	2008
Currency outside banks	131,171	141,713	48,214
Demand deposits at commercial banks	397,554	456,562	497,413
Total money (incl. others)	528,978	598,590	545,969

Source: IMF, *International Financial Statistics*.

SLOVAKIA

COST OF LIVING
(Consumer Price Index; base December 2000 = 100)

	2006	2007	2008
Foodstuffs and non-alcoholic beverages	113.5	118.0	127.1
Alcoholic beverages and tobacco	140.8	146.1	152.1
Clothing and footwear	106.3	107.1	108.1
Housing, water, electricity, gas and other fuels	185.0	196.0	210.1
All items (incl. others)	136.3	140.1	146.5

NATIONAL ACCOUNTS
(million koruna at current prices)

Expenditure on the Gross Domestic Product

	2006	2007	2008
Final consumption expenditure	1,261,162	1,356,010	1,494,120
Households	926,468	1,018,117	1,127,812
Non-profit institutions serving households	16,247	16,972	17,881
General government	318,447	320,921	348,427
Gross capital formation	461,909	515,769	584,027
Gross fixed capital formation	439,503	483,476	526,159
Changes in inventories	22,406	32,293	57,868
Total domestic expenditure	1,723,071	1,871,779	2,078,147
Exports of goods and services	1,400,964	1,602,151	1,675,234
Less Imports of goods and services	1,464,637	1,621,149	1,724,680
Statistical discrepancy	—	—	−286
GDP in purchasers' values	1,659,398	1,852,781	2,028,415

Gross Domestic Product by Economic Activity

	2006	2007	2008
Agriculture, hunting, forestry and fishing	53,192	59,160	62,859
Mining and quarrying	6,450	8,854	11,305
Manufacturing	360,945	411,455	405,749
Construction	114,914	131,981	159,792
Electricity, gas and water supply	101,021	102,171	100,618
Wholesale and retail trade; repair of motor vehicles	224,754	266,014	301,422
Hotels and restaurants	22,009	23,825	35,566
Transport and storage	109,673	118,349	143,971
Financial intermediation	62,447	63,140	68,067
Real estate, renting and business activities	204,331	218,875	257,858
Other services	237,618	263,620	291,805
Sub-total	1,497,354	1,667,444	1,839,012
Taxes, less subsidies, on products	162,044	185,337	189,403
GDP in purchasers' values	1,659,398	1,852,781	2,028,415

BALANCE OF PAYMENTS
(US $ million)

	2005	2006	2007
Exports of goods f.o.b.	31,851	41,735	57,806
Imports of goods f.o.b.	−34,214	−44,283	−58,715
Trade balance	−2,363	−2,549	−909
Exports of services	4,405	5,436	7,063
Imports of services	−4,078	−4,675	−6,531
Balance on goods and services	−2,036	−1,787	−376
Other income received	1,585	1,959	2,340
Other income paid	−3,570	−4,051	−5,628
Balance on goods, services and income	−4,021	−3,880	−3,665
Current transfers received	1,403	1,623	2,070
Current transfers paid	−1,386	−1,681	−2,508
Current balance	−4,005	−3,937	−4,103
Capital account	−18	−42	465

—continued	2005	2006	2007
Direct investment abroad	−145	−368	−403
Direct investment from abroad	2,411	4,167	3,363
Portfolio investment assets	−691	−186	−1,083
Portfolio investment liabilities	−246	1,741	349
Other investment assets	−498	−1,020	−1,535
Other investment liabilities	5,422	−3,017	6,281
Financial derivatives assets	−98	−442	265
Financial derivatives liabilities	64	279	−213
Net errors and omissions	324	167	302
Overall balance	2,521	−2,656	3,688

Source: IMF, *International Financial Statistics*.

External Trade

PRINCIPAL COMMODITIES
(distribution by SITC, US $ million)

Imports f.o.b.	2005	2006	2007
Food and live animals	1,650.9	1,882.7	2,488.7
Crude materials (inedible) except fuels	1,179.6	1,379.0	1,649.3
Mineral fuels, lubricants, etc.	4,509.6	6,027.5	6,362.7
Petroleum, petroleum products, etc.	2,547.6	3,470.8	4,047.4
Gas, natural and manufactured	1,363.2	1,970.0	1,603.2
Chemicals and related products	3,343.7	3,941.3	5,031.4
Medicinal and pharmaceutical products	966.3	1,056.1	1,393.2
Basic manufactures	6,150.8	7,633.5	10,072.7
Iron and steel	1,359.2	1,807.9	2,672.6
Metal manufactures	1,483.7	1,759.8	2,386.9
Machinery and transport equipment	12,936.6	17,240.9	25,319.6
General industrial machinery and equipment	1,426.8	2,061.1	2,512.3
Telecommunication and sound recording equipment	1,322.1	2,360.4	5,523.9
Electrical machinery, apparatus and appliances	2,949.2	3,540.4	4,361.3
Road vehicles	3,945.3	5,383.1	7,965.2
Miscellaneous manufactured articles	3,780.7	5,714.7	6,032.6
Professional, scientific and controlling instruments	1,174.1	2,495.6	1,818.7
Total (incl. others)	24,225.8	44,383.2	57,754.0

SLOVAKIA

Exports f.o.b.	2005	2006	2007
Food and live animals	1,272.0	1,535.7	1,900.3
Mineral fuels, lubricants, etc.	1,871.1	2,251.3	2,673.3
Petroleum, petroleum products, etc.	1,847.3	2,226.9	2,650.0
Chemicals and related products	1,747.8	2,200.5	2,695.7
Basic manufactures	7,823.0	9,842.9	12,120.6
Rubber manufactures	818.6	933.8	1,134.6
Paper, paperboard and articles of paper pulp	852.2	1,054.6	1,296.0
Iron and steel	2,837.1	3,531.3	4,361.1
Metal manufactures	1,218.4	1,518.2	2,119.4
Machinery and transport equipment	14,082.0	20,317.1	31,120.5
General industrial machinery and equipment	1,510.0	1,901.5	2,526.6
Telecommunications and sound recording equipment	1,683.1	4,036.5	7,272.8
Electrical machinery, apparatus and appliances	2,456.6	2,938.3	3,798.1
Road vehicles	5,841.6	8,535.5	14,029.1
Miscellaneous manufactured articles	3,369.3	3,920.6	5,223.8
Total (incl. others)	31,852.1	41,719.2	57,801.8

Source: UN, *International Trade Statistics Yearbook*.

PRINCIPAL TRADING PARTNERS
(US $ million)

Imports f.o.b.	2005	2006	2007
Austria	1,333.9	1,513.7	1,799.3
Belgium	488.7	553.8	703.2
China, People's Republic	1,114.1	1,731.9	2,989.6
Czech Republic	4,367.5	5,318.5	6,620.4
France (incl. Monaco)	1,118.5	1,455.5	2,277.1
Germany	7,055.7	9,054.9	11,478.3
Hungary	1,228.8	2,033.0	3,123.8
Italy	1,629.3	2,033.7	2,316.8
Japan	646.3	901.0	934.1
Korea, Republic	900.4	1,723.4	2,882.8
Netherlands	463.3	597.8	773.6
Poland	1,399.9	1,973.3	2,446.4
Russia	3,674.5	5,084.6	5,431.4
Spain	584.2	689.2	879.6
Switzerland (incl. Liechtenstein)	284.5	344.9	469.8
Ukraine	481.5	547.3	603.1
United Kingdom	611.5	661.0	780.6
USA	471.0	561.5	612.4
Total (incl. others)	34,225.8	44,383.2	57,754.0

Exports f.o.b.	2005	2006	2007
Austria	2,271.5	2,535.0	3,335.3
Belgium	625.5	777.6	1,236.0
Czech Republic	4,520.9	5,710.8	7,185.7
Denmark	224.3	362.7	569.2
France (incl. Monaco)	1,230.1	1,806.7	3,926.4
Germany	8,215.0	9,821.8	12,428.0
Hungary	1,891.8	2,444.6	3,316.6
Italy	2,112.9	2,716.8	3,695.1
Netherlands	1,090.1	1,776.7	2,053.3
Poland	2,001.0	2,580.0	3,592.2
Romania	502.6	633.1	1,060.4
Russia	494.7	685.6	1,308.7
Slovenia	301.9	363.3	464.8
Spain	654.6	1,203.9	1,834.9
Sweden	334.8	573.6	878.3
Switzerland (incl. Liechtenstein)	253.3	318.7	483.6
Turkey	305.8	407.0	657.1
Ukraine	412.8	544.3	781.2
United Kingdom	975.8	1,621.2	2,778.0
USA	1,004.6	1,325.7	1,441.9
Total (incl. others)	31,852.1	41,719.2	57,801.8

Source: UN, *International Trade Statistics Yearbook*.

Transport

SUMMARY

	2005	2006	2007
Railway transport:			
freight ('000 tons)	49,310	52,449	51,813
passengers ('000)	50,458	48,438	47,070
Public road transport:			
freight ('000 tons)	48,357	51,530	50,633
passengers ('000)	449,456	403,270	384,637
Waterway transport: freight ('000 tons)	1,526	1,713	1,806

ROAD TRAFFIC
(motor vehicles in use at 31 December)

	2005	2006	2007
Passenger cars ('000)	1,304	1,334	1,434
Buses and coaches ('000)	9	9	10
Goods vehicles ('000)	160	173	196

SHIPPING
Merchant Fleet
(registered at 31 December)

	2005	2006	2007
Number of vessels	47	54	57
Displacement ('000 gross registered tons)	211.2	232.7	233.3

Source: Lloyd's Register-Fairplay, *World Fleet Statistics*.

CIVIL AVIATION
(traffic on scheduled services)

	2005	2006	2007
Passengers carried ('000)	1,716	2,291	3,068
Freight carried ('000 metric tons)	230	41	1,318

Tourism

FOREIGN TOURIST ARRIVALS
(visitors at accommodation facilities)

Country of origin	2004	2005	2006
Austria	55,609	55,630	60,560
Czech Republic	419,273	424,900	455,381
France	37,006	42,668	41,095
Germany	188,067	194,158	190,422
Hungary	111,065	121,615	121,981
Italy	50,201	59,344	60,971
Poland	179,078	198,479	224,159
United Kingdom	34,349	51,720	63,137
USA	28,665	32,593	29,569
Total (incl. others)	1,401,189	1,514,980	1,611,808

Tourism receipts (US $ million, excl. passenger transport): 901 in 2004; 1,210 in 2005; 1,513 in 2006.
Source: World Tourism Organization.

SLOVAKIA

Communications Media

	2005	2006	2007
Telephones ('000 main lines in use)	1,197.0	1,167.4	1,150.7
Mobile cellular telephones ('000 subscribers)	4,540.5	4,893.2	6,068.1
Personal computers ('000 in use)	1,929	n.a.	n.a.
Internet users ('000)	1,905.2	2,255.6	2,350.0
Broadband subscribers ('000)	181.5	317.0	443.8
Newspapers: titles	426	464	498
Newspapers: circulation ('000 copies)	239,869	233,281	234,775
Periodicals: titles	962	952	1,047
Periodicals: circulation ('000 copies)	244,691	194,042	181,993

Radio receivers (licensed): 1,255,624 in 1998; 1,368,863 in 1999; 1,347,477 in 2000.

Television receivers (licensed): 1,392,883 in 1998; 1,241,663 in 1999; 1,211,773 in 2000.

Book production (number of titles): 2,064 in 1997; 4,386 in 1998; 3,153 in 1999.

Facsimile machines (number registered): 54,037 in 1998.

Sources: partly International Telecommunication Union and UNESCO Institute for Statistics.

Education

(2007, unless otherwise indicated)

	Institutions	Teachers	Students
Kindergarten	2,910	13,164	139,374
Primary (basic)	2,254	30,449	482,566
Secondary: grammar	252	6,894	99,915
Secondary: specialized	242	6,376	75,802
Secondary: vocational	181	2,589	51,882
Higher	30	9,510	132,499

Directory

The Constitution*

On 1 September 1992 the Slovenská národná rada (Slovak National Council) adopted the Constitution of the Slovak Republic (which entered into force on 1 January 1993), the main provisions of which, as amended in January 1999, are summarized below:

FUNDAMENTAL PROVISIONS

The Slovak Republic is a democratic and sovereign state, ruled by law. It is bound neither to an ideology, nor to a religion. State power belongs to the people, who exercise it either through their representatives or directly. The state authorities shall act only on the basis of the Constitution and to the extent and in the manner stipulated by law.

The territory of the Slovak Republic is integral and indivisible. The conditions for naturalization or deprival of state citizenship of the Slovak Republic are regulated by law. No person may be deprived of citizenship against his or her will. The Slovak language is the state language in the republic. The use of languages other than the state language in administrative relations is regulated by law. The capital of the republic is Bratislava.

BASIC RIGHTS AND FREEDOMS

The people are free and equal, and the rights and freedoms of every citizen are guaranteed, irrespective of sex, race, colour, language, faith, political or other conviction, national or social origin, nationality or ethnic origin. No person may be tortured, nor be subjected to cruel, inhuman or humiliating treatment or punishment. Capital punishment is not practised.

Every person has the right to own property. The place of abode is inviolable. The freedom of migration and the freedom of domicile are guaranteed.

The freedom of expression and the right to information are guaranteed. Censorship is prohibited. The right to assemble peacefully is guaranteed. Every person has the right to be a member of a union, community, society or any other association. Citizens have the right to found political parties and movements. Such parties and movements, as well as other associations, are separate from the State.

The citizens have the right to participate in the administration of public affairs, either directly or through the free election of their representatives. The right to vote is universal, direct and equal and is exercised by secret ballot.

The universal advancement of citizens who are members of national minorities and ethnic groups is guaranteed, above all the right to develop their own culture, to broadcast and receive information in their mother tongue, to join national associations and to found and maintain educational and cultural institutions. The languages of national minorities may also be used in administrative relations.

Every person has the right to the free choice of profession and vocational training, as well as to do business and to perform other commercial activities. Employees are entitled to fair and satisfactory working conditions. Citizens may form free associations to protect their economic and social interests. Trade unions are independent of the State. The right to strike is guaranteed.

Every citizen is entitled to adequate old-age and disability benefits; widow's allowances; free health care; family support; and education.

NÁRODNÁ RADA SLOVENSKEJ REPUBLIKY

Supreme legislative power is vested in the Národná rada Slovenskej republiky (National Council of the Slovak Republic—Národná rada), which has 150 deputies, elected for a four-year term. The deputies represent the citizens and are elected by them in general, equal and direct elections, by secret ballot.

The Národná rada has the power to: adopt the Constitution, constitutional and other laws and supervise their execution; decide on proposals to call a referendum; prior to their ratification, give consent to international political, economic or other agreements; establish ministries and other bodies of state administration; supervise the activities of the Government and approve a vote of confidence or censure on the Government or its members; approve the state budget and supervise its execution; elect judges, including the Chairman and Vice-Chairmen of the Supreme Court and of the Constitutional Court; adopt a resolution to declare war if the Slovak Republic is attacked, or if such a declaration ensues from the obligations of international treaties.

THE PRESIDENT OF THE REPUBLIC

The President is the Head of State of the Slovak Republic. He or she is directly elected by universal adult suffrage for a five-year term. The President is responsible to the Národná rada. He/she may not be elected for more than two consecutive terms.

The President represents the Slovak Republic internationally; negotiates and ratifies international agreements; receives and gives credentials to envoys; convenes constituent sessions of the Národná rada; may dissolve the Národná rada; signs laws; appoints and recalls the Prime Minister and other members of the Government and receives their resignation; grants amnesty, pardons and commutes sentences imposed by courts; may declare a state of emergency on the basis of constitutional law; may declare a referendum.

THE GOVERNMENT

The Government of the Slovak Republic is the highest organ of executive power. It is composed of the Prime Minister and Ministers.

SLOVAKIA

The Prime Minister is appointed by the President of the Republic. On the Prime Minister's recommendation, the President appoints and recalls the members of the Government and puts them in charge of their ministries. For the execution of office, the Government is responsible to the Národná rada.

The Government has the power to prepare bills; issue decrees; adopt fundamental provisions for economic and social policy; authorize drafts for the state budget and closing account of the year; decide international agreements; decide principal questions of internal and international policy; submit bills to the Národná rada; request the legislature for a vote of confidence.

*Further revisions to the Constitution were approved in February 2001 and officially entered into effect on 1 July. The amendments redefined the relationship between national and international law, incorporated Slovakia's aim of joining foreign alliances, strengthened the powers of the Constitutional Court, granted greater independence to the judiciary (by the establishment of a new judicial council), and provided for public administration reform, with the creation of a higher level of regional self-government.

The Government

HEAD OF STATE

President of the Republic: IVAN GAŠPAROVIČ (elected 17 April 2004; inaugurated 15 June 2004; re-elected 4 April 2009).

GOVERNMENT
(May 2009)

The Government comprises members of Direction-Social Democracy, the Slovak National Party (SNP) and the People's Party—Movement for a Democratic Slovakia (PP—MDS).

Prime Minister: ROBERT FICO (Direction-Social Democracy).

Deputy Prime Minister for Knowledge-Based Society, European Affairs, Human Rights and Minorities: DUŠAN ČAPLOVIČ (Direction-Social Democracy).

Deputy Prime Minister and Minister of the Interior: ROBERT KALIŇÁK (Direction-Social Democracy).

Deputy Prime Minister and Minister of Education: JÁN MIKOLAJ (SNP).

Deputy Prime Minister and Minister of Justice: ŠTEFAN HARABIN (PP—MDS).

Minister of Finance: JÁN POČIATEK (Direction-Social Democracy).

Minister of Foreign Affairs: MIROSLAV LAJČÁK (Independent).

Minister of the Economy: ĽUBOMÍR JAHNÁTEK (Direction-Social Democracy).

Minister of Defence: JAROSLAV BAŠKA (Direction-Social Democracy).

Minister of Culture: MAREK MAĎARIČ (Direction-Social Democracy).

Minister of Health: RICHARD RAŠI (Direction-Social Democracy).

Minister of Agriculture: STANISLAV BECÍK (PP—MDS).

Minister of Transport, Post and Telecommunications: ĽUBOMÍR VÁŽNY (Direction-Social Democracy).

Minister of Construction and Regional Development: IGOR ŠTEFANOV (SNP).

Minister of Labour, Social Affairs and the Family: VIERA TOMANOVÁ (Direction-Social Democracy).

Minister of the Environment: JÁN MIKOLAJ (SNP) (acting).

MINISTRIES

Office of the President: Hodžovo nám. 1, 810 00 Bratislava, POB 128; tel. (2) 5788-8200; fax (2) 5441-7010; e-mail informacie@prezident.sk; internet www.prezident.sk.

Office of the Government: nám. Slobody 1, 813 70 Bratislava; tel. (2) 5729-5111; fax (2) 5249-7595; e-mail urad@government.gov.sk; internet www.government.gov.sk.

Ministry of Agriculture: Dobrovičova 12, 812 66 Bratislava; tel. (2) 5926-6111; fax (2) 5926-6311; e-mail tlacove@land.gov.sk; internet www.land.gov.sk.

Ministry of Construction and Regional Development: Prievozská 2B, 825 25 Bratislava; tel. (2) 5831-7111; fax (2) 5293-1203; e-mail informacie@build.gov.sk; internet www.build.gov.sk.

Ministry of Culture: nám. SNP 33, 813 31 Bratislava; tel. (2) 2048-2155; fax (2) 2048-2174; e-mail mksr@culture.gov.sk; internet www.culture.gov.sk.

Ministry of Defence: Kutuzovova 7, 832 47 Bratislava; tel. (2) 4425-0320; fax (2) 4425-3242; e-mail tlacove@mod.gov.sk; internet www.mod.gov.sk.

Ministry of the Economy: Mierová 19, 827 15 Bratislava; tel. (2) 4854-1111; fax (2) 4333-7827; e-mail info@economy.gov.sk; internet www.economy.gov.sk.

Ministry of Education: Stromová 1, 813 30 Bratislava; tel. (2) 5937-4111; fax (2) 5937-4335; e-mail kancmin@minedu.sk; internet www.minedu.sk.

Ministry of the Environment: nám. Ľ. Štúra 1, 812 35 Bratislava; tel. (2) 5956-1111; fax (2) 5956-2031; e-mail info@enviro.gov.sk; internet www.enviro.gov.sk.

Ministry of Finance: Štefanovičova 5, POB 82, 817 82 Bratislava; tel. (2) 5958-1111; fax (2) 5958-3048; e-mail podatelna@mfsr.sk; internet www.finance.gov.sk.

Ministry of Foreign Affairs: Hlboká cesta 2, 833 36 Bratislava; tel. (2) 5978-1111; fax (2) 5978-2213; e-mail info@mzv.sk; internet www.mzv.sk.

Ministry of Health: Limbová 2, POB 52, 837 52 Bratislava; tel. (2) 5937-3111; fax (2) 5477-7983; e-mail office@health.gov.sk; internet www.health.gov.sk.

Ministry of the Interior: Pribinova 2, 812 72 Bratislava; tel. (2) 5094-1111; fax (2) 5094-4397; e-mail tokmv@minv.sk; internet www.minv.sk.

Ministry of Justice: Župné nám. 13, 813 11 Bratislava; tel. (2) 5935-3111; fax (2) 5935-3600; e-mail tlacove@justice.sk; internet www.justice.gov.sk.

Ministry of Labour, Social Affairs and the Family: Špitálska 4–6, 816 43 Bratislava; tel. (2) 5975-1617; fax (2) 5292-1258; e-mail tothova@employment.gov.sk; internet www.employment.gov.sk.

Ministry of Transport, Post and Telecommunications: nám. Slobody 6, POB 100, 810 05 Bratislava; tel. (2) 5949-4111; fax (2) 5249-4794; e-mail info@telecom.gov.sk; internet www.telecom.gov.sk.

President

Presidential Election, First Ballot, 21 March 2009

Candidates	Valid votes	%
Ivan Gašparovič	876,061	46.71
Iveta Radičová	713,735	38.05
František Mikloško	101,573	5.42
Zuzana Martináková	96,035	5.12
Milan Melník	45,985	2.45
Dagmara Bollová	21,378	1.14
Milan Sidor	20,862	1.11
Total	**1,875,629**	**100.00**

Second Ballot, 4 April 2009

Candidates	Valid votes	%
Ivan Gašparovič	1,234,787	55.53
Iveta Radičová	988,808	44.47
Total	**2,223,595**	**100.00**

Legislature

Národná rada Slovenskej republiky
(National Council of the Slovak Republic)

nám. Alexandra Dubčeka 1, 812 80 Bratislava; tel. (2) 5972-1111; fax (2) 5441-9529; e-mail info@nrsr.sk; internet www.nrsr.sk.

Chairman: PAVOL PAŠKA.

General Election, 17 June 2006

Party	Votes	% of votes	Seats
Direction-Social Democracy	671,185	29.14	50
Slovak Democratic and Christian Union-Democratic Party	422,815	18.36	31
Slovak National Party	270,230	11.73	20
Party of the Hungarian Coalition	269,111	11.68	20
People's Party—Movement for a Democratic Slovakia	202,540	8.79	15
Christian Democratic Movement	191,443	8.31	14
Others	275,815	11.98	—
Total valid votes	**2,303,049**	**100.00**	**150**

Election Commission

Ústredná volebná komisia, Ministerstva vnútra (Central Elections Commission, Ministry of the Interior): Drieňova 22, 826 86 Bratislava; tel. (2) 4859-1111; fax (2) 4333-3175; e-mail ovr.svs@mvsr.vs.sk; internet www.civil.gov.sk; organ of the Ministry of the Interior; Chair. EDITA PFUNDTNER.

Political Organizations

Christian Democratic Movement (CDM) (Kresťansko-demokratické hnutie—KDH): Bajkalská 25, 821 09 Bratislava; tel. (2) 5057-4101; fax (2) 5057-4049; e-mail tlacove@kdh.sk; internet www.kdh.sk; f. 1990; conservative; supports Christian and family values; Chair. PAVOL HRUŠOVSKY.

Civic Conservative Party (Občianska konzervatívna strana—OKS): Panenská 26, 811 03 Bratislava; e-mail oks@oks.sk; internet www.oks.sk; f. and regd 2001; Chair. PETER ZAJAC.

Communist Party of Slovakia (CPS) (Komunistická strana Slovenska—KSS): Ústredný výbor, Hattalova 12A, 831 03 Bratislava; tel. and fax (2) 4437-2540; e-mail sekr@kss.sk; internet www.kss.sk; f. 1992 following merger of two Marxist parties, the Union of Communists of Slovakia (Zväz komunistov Slovenska) and the Communist Party of Slovakia—91 (Komunistická strana Slovenska—91), which were established by Orthodox communists opposed to the transformation of the Communist Party of Slovakia into the non-Marxist Party of the Democratic Left (Strana demokratickej ľavice); Pres. JOZEF HRDLIČKA; 9,000 mems.

Conservative Democrats of Slovakia (CDS) (Konzervatívni demokrati Slovenska—KDS): Štefánikova 5, 811 06 Bratislava; e-mail spokesman@kdsonline.sk; internet www.kdsonline.sk; f. 2008 by fmr mems of Christian Democratic Movement; Chair. VLADIMÍR PALKO.

Direction-Social Democracy (Smer-Sociálna demokracia): Súmračná 27, 821 02 Bratislava; tel. and fax (2) 4342-6297; e-mail sekretariat.fico@strana-smer.sk; internet www.strana-smer.sk; f. and regd in 1999 as Direction (Smer); absorbed the Party of Civic Understanding in 2003; merged with the Party of the Democratic Left in Dec. 2004, and name changed as above; absorbed the Leftwing Bloc in Dec. 2007; Chair. ROBERT FICO.

Free Forum Party (Slobodné fórum) (SF): Bazová 9, 821 08 Bratislava; tel. (2) 5564-2494; fax (2) 5564-2496; e-mail sf@slobodneforum.sk; internet www.slobodneforum.sk; f. 2003; regd 2004; centre-right; in March 2006 reached agreement on co-operation with the Democratic Party of Slovakia, the Democratic Union of Slovakia and the Green Party, ahead of legislative elections in June; Chair. ZUZANA MARTINÁKOVÁ.

Green Party (Strana zelených): Sienkiewiczova 4, 811 09 Bratislava; tel. and fax (2) 5292-3231; e-mail sekretariat@stranazelenych.sk; internet www.stranazelenych.sk; f. 1989; regd 1991; in March 2006 reached agreement on co-operation with the Democratic Party of Slovakia, the Democratic Union of Slovakia and the Free Forum, ahead of legislative elections in June; Chair. PETER PILINSKÝ.

League—Civil Liberal Party (Liga—Občiansko liberálna strana): Hotel Most Slávy, 17 novembra 11, 914 51 Trenčianske Teplice; tel. (32) 655-2054; e-mail info@liga-ols.sk; internet www.liga-ols.sk; f. 2008 by fmr mems of New Citizens' Alliance; liberal; Pres. ROBERT NEMCSICS.

Liberal Party (Liberálna strana—LS): Račianska 66, 831 02 Bratislava; e-mail liberalna.strana@zoznam.sk; internet www.liberalnastrana.sk; f. 2003 by fmr mems of Movement for a Democratic Slovakia; regd 2003 as People's Union; name changed as above March 2007; Chair. GUSTÁV KRAJČI.

Movement for Democracy (Hnutie za demokraciu—HZD): Nevädzová 5, 821 01 Bratislava; tel. (2) 4828-7638; fax (2) 4828-7417; e-mail hzd@hzd.sk; internet www.hzd.sk; f. and regd 2002 by fmr mems of the Movement for a Democratic Slovakia; Chair. JOZEF GRAPA.

Party of the Hungarian Coalition (PHC) (Strana maďarskej koalície/Magyar Koalíció Pártja): Čajakova 8, 811 05 Bratislava; tel. (2) 5249-5546; fax (2) 5249-5264; e-mail smk@smk.sk; internet www.mkp.sk; f. 1998 by merger of Coexistence (Spolužitie/Együttélés), the Hungarian Christian Democratic Movement and the Hungarian Civic Party; Chair. PÁL CSÁKY.

People's Party—Movement for a Democratic Slovakia (PP—MDS) (Ľudová strana—Hnutie za Demokratické Slovensko—LS—HZDS): POB 49, Tomášikova 32A, 830 00 Bratislava; tel. (2) 4822-0203; fax (2) 4822-0223; e-mail krampl@hzds.sk; internet www.hzds.sk; f. 1991 as Movement for a Democratic Slovakia; present name adopted 2003; Chair. VLADIMÍR MEČIAR.

Slovak Democratic and Christian Union-Democratic Party (SDCU-DP) (Slovenská demokratická a kresťanská únia-Demokratická strana—SDKÚ-DS): Ružinovská 28, 827 35 Bratislava; tel. (2) 4341-4102; fax (2) 4341-4106; e-mail sdku@sdkuonline.sk; internet www.sdkuonline.sk; f. and regd 2000 as the Slovak Democratic and Christian Union; name changed as above following merger with the Democratic Party in Jan. 2006; Chair. MIKULÁŠ DZURINDA.

Slovak National Party (SNP) (Slovenská národná strana—SNS): Šafárikovo nám. 3, 814 99 Bratislava; tel. (2) 5292-4260; fax (2) 5296-6188; e-mail sns@sns.sk; internet www.sns.sk; f. 1871; regd 1990; right-wing; against ethnic-Hungarian representation in govt; Chair. JÁN SLOTA.

Diplomatic Representation

EMBASSIES IN SLOVAKIA

Angola: Jelenia 4, 811 05 Bratislava 1; tel. (2) 5441-2164; fax (2) 5441-2182; e-mail embangola1@chello.sk; Ambassador ALBERTO CORREIA NETO.

Austria: Ventúrska 10, 811 01 Bratislava; tel. (2) 5930-1500; fax (2) 5443-2486; e-mail pressburg-ob@bmeia.gv.at; internet www.rakusko.eu; Ambassador Dr HELMUT WESSELY.

Belarus: Jančova 5, 811 02 Bratislava; tel. (2) 6225-1052; fax (2) 6280-2026; e-mail slovakia@belembassy.org; internet www.belembassy.org/slovakia; Chargé d'affaires a.i. VIKTOR NAVROTSKY.

Belgium: Fraňa kráľa 5, 811 05 Bratislava; tel. (2) 5710-1211; fax (2) 5249-4296; e-mail ambabelbratis@stonline.sk; internet www.diplomatie.be/bratislava; Ambassador ALAIN COOLS.

Brazil: Radisson SAS Carlton Hotel, rms 630 & 632 & 634, Hviezdoslavovo nám. 3, 811 02 Bratislava; tel. (2) 5939-0696; fax (2) 5939-0904; e-mail bratislava@mre.gov.br; Ambassador MARÍLIA SARDENBERG ZELNER GONÇALVES.

Bulgaria: Kuzmányho 1, 811 06 Bratislava 1; tel. (2) 5441-5308; fax (2) 5441-2404; e-mail bulharskoet@stonline.sk; internet www.bulgarianembassy.sk; Ambassador OGNIAN GALKOV.

China, People's Republic: Jančova 8, 811 02 Bratislava; tel. and fax (2) 6280-4291; e-mail chinask@gtinet.sk; internet sk.chineseembassy.org; Ambassador JIANFU CHEN.

Croatia: Mišíkova 21, 811 06 Bratislava; tel. (2) 5720-2091; fax (2) 5443-5365; e-mail croemb.bratislava@mvpei.hr; internet sk.mvp.hr; Ambassador TOMISLAV CAR.

Cuba: Somolického 1A, 811 05 Bratislava; tel. (2) 5249-2777; fax (2) 5249-4200; e-mail embacuba@embacuba.sk; internet www.embacuba.sk; Ambassador DAVID PAULOVICH ESCALONA.

Czech Republic: POB 208, Hviezdoslavovo nám. 8, 810 00 Bratislava; tel. (2) 5920-3303; fax (2) 5920-3330; e-mail bratislava@embassy.mzv.cz; internet www.mzv.cz/bratislava; Ambassador VLADIMÍR GALUŠKA.

Denmark: Panská 27, 816 06 Bratislava; tel. (2) 5930-0200; fax (2) 5443-3656; e-mail btsamb@um.dk; internet www.ambbratislava.um.dk; Ambassador JØRGEN MUNK RASMUSSEN.

Egypt: Dunajská 4, POB 322, 811 08 Bratislava 1; tel. (2) 2421-0236; fax (2) 2421-0237; Ambassador HASSAN HANAFY MAHMOUD EL-LAITHY.

Finland: Palisády 29, 811 06 Bratislava; tel. (2) 5980-5111; fax (2) 5980-5120; e-mail sanomat.brt@formin.fi; internet www.finlandembassy.sk; Ambassador JUKKA JALMARI LEINO.

France: Hlavné nám. 7, 812 83 Bratislava; tel. (2) 5934-7111; fax (2) 5934-7199; e-mail diplo@france.sk; internet www.france.sk; Ambassador HENRY CUNY.

Georgia: Michalská 9, 811 01 Bratislava 1; tel. (2) 5464-6484; fax (2) 5464-6486; e-mail bratislava.emb@mfa.gov.ge; Ambassador NIKOLOZ NIKOLOZISHVILI.

Germany: Hviezdoslavovo nám. 10, 813 03 Bratislava; tel. (2) 5920-4400; fax (2) 5443-1480; e-mail info@germanembassy.sk; internet www.pressburg.diplo.de; Ambassador Dr JOCHEN TREBESCH.

Greece: Hlavné nám. 4, 811 01 Bratislava; tel. (2) 5443-4143; fax (2) 5443-4064; e-mail embassy@greece.sk; Ambassador NICOLAOS KANELLOS.

Holy See: Nekrasovova 17, 811 04 Bratislava; tel. (2) 5479-3528; fax (2) 5479-3529; e-mail nunziatura@nunziatura.sk; Apostolic Nuncio Most Rev. MARIO GIORDANA (Titular Archbishop of Minora).

Hungary: Sedlárska 3, 814 25 Bratislava; tel. (2) 5920-5200; fax (2) 5443-5484; e-mail mission.pzs@kum.hu; internet www.mfa.gov.hu/emb/bratislava; Ambassador ANTAL HEIZER.

India: Dunajská 4, 811 08 Bratislava; tel. (2) 5296-2915; fax (2) 5296-2921; e-mail eindia@slovanet.sk; internet www.indianembassy.sk; Ambassador HOMAI SAHA.

Indonesia: Mudroňova 51, 811 03 Bratislava; tel. (2) 5441-9886; fax (2) 5441-9890; e-mail indonesia@indonesia.sk; internet www.indonesia.sk; Ambassador HARSHA EDWANA JOESOEF (designate).

SLOVAKIA

Iraq: Korabinského 3, 811 02 Bratislava; tel. (2) 5413-1466; fax (2) 5413-1464; e-mail brtsemb@gmail.com; internet www.iraqembassy.sk; Chargé d'affaires a.i. HASSAN QASSIM HASSAN AHMED ESH-SHEIKH.

Ireland: Carlton Savoy Bldg, Mostavá 2, 811 02 Bratislava 1; tel. (2) 5930-9611; fax (2) 5443-0690; e-mail bratislava@dfa.ie; internet www.embassyofireland.sk; Ambassador KATHRYN COLL.

Israel: Sláviče údolie 106, POB 6, 811 02 Bratislava; tel. (2) 5441-0557; fax (2) 5441-0850; e-mail cao-sec@bratislava.mfa.gov.il; Ambassador ZEEV BOKER.

Italy: Palisády 49, 811 06 Bratislava; tel. (2) 5980-0011; fax (2) 5441-3202; e-mail amb.bratislava@esteri.it; internet www.ambbratislava.esteri.it; Ambassador BRUNELLA BORZI.

Japan: Hlavné nám. 2, 813 27 Bratislava; tel. (2) 5980-0100; fax (2) 5443-2771; e-mail info@jpembassy.sk; internet www.sk.emb-japan.go.jp; Ambassador YOSHIO NOMOTO.

Libya: Révova ul. 45, 811 02 Bratislava 1; tel. (2) 5441-0324; fax (2) 5441-0730; e-mail lpb@stonline.sk; Chargé d'affaires KHALIFA AHMED.

Netherlands: Fraňa Kráľa 5, 811 05 Bratislava; tel. (2) 5262-5081; fax (2) 5249-1075; e-mail btl@minbuza.nl; internet www.holandskoweb.com; Ambassador ROB SWARTBOL.

Norway: Palisády 29, 811 06 Bratislava; tel. (2) 5910-0100; fax (2) 5910-0115; e-mail emb.bratislava@mfa.no; internet www.norway.sk; Ambassador BRIT LØVSETH.

Poland: Hummelova 4, 814 91 Bratislava 1; tel. (2) 5949-0211; fax (2) 5441-3184; e-mail bratampl@nextra.sk; internet www.bratyslawa.polemb.net; Ambassador ANDRZEJ KRAWCZYK.

Portugal: Moskovská 10, 811 08 Bratislava 1; tel. (2) 5010-2211; fax (2) 5010-2222; e-mail embportbrat@stonlinek.sk; internet www.embport.sk; Ambassador JOSÉ ERNST HENZLER VIEIRA BRANCO.

Romania: Fraňa Kráľa 11, 811 05 Bratislava 1; tel. (2) 5249-1665; fax (2) 5244-4056; e-mail ro-embassy@mail.t-com.sk; internet bratislava.mae.ro; Ambassador FLORIN VODIȚĂ.

Russia: Godrova 4, 811 06 Bratislava; tel. (2) 5441-4436; fax (2) 5443-4910; e-mail info@rusemb.sk; internet www.rusemb.sk; Ambassador ALEKSANDR I. UDALTSOV.

Serbia: Búdková 38, 811 04 Bratislava; tel. (2) 5443-1927; fax (2) 5443-1933; e-mail embassy.serbia@internet.sk; internet bratislava.mfa.gov.yu; Ambassador DANKO PROKIĆ.

Slovenia: Moyzesova 4, POB 37, 813 15 Bratislava 1; tel. (2) 5726-7700; fax (2) 5245-0009; e-mail vbs@gov.si; Chargé d'affaires a.i. MIHA ROSSLER.

Spain: Prepoštská 10, 811 01 Bratislava; tel. (2) 5441-5724; fax (2) 5441-7565; e-mail embespsk@mail.mae.es; internet www.mae.es/Embajadas/bratislava; Ambassador JOSÉ ANGEL LÓPEZ JORRIN.

Sweden: Palisády 29, 811 06 Bratislava; tel. (2) 5910-2200; fax (2) 5910-2233; e-mail ambassaden.bratislava@foreign.ministry.se; internet www.swedenabroad.com/bratislava; Ambassador MIKAEL WESTERLIND.

Switzerland: Tolstého 9, 811 06 Bratislava; tel. (2) 5930-1111; fax (2) 5930-1100; e-mail bts.vertretung@eda.admin.ch; internet www.eda.admin.ch/bratislava; Ambassador JOSEF AREGGER.

Turkey: Holubyho 11, 811 03 Bratislava 1; tel. (2) 5441-5504; fax (2) 5441-3145; e-mail turkishembassy@nextra.sk; Ambassador TUNÇ ÜGDÜL.

Ukraine: Radvanská 35, 811 01 Bratislava; tel. (2) 5920-2810; fax (2) 5441-2651; e-mail ukremb@ukrembassy.sk; internet www.mfa.gov.ua/slovakia; Ambassador INNA V. OHNYIVETS.

United Kingdom: Panská 16, 811 01 Bratislava; tel. (2) 5998-2000; fax (2) 5998-2237; e-mail bebra@internet.sk; internet ukinslovakia.fco.gov.uk; Ambassador MICHAEL JOHN WYN ROBERTS.

USA: Hviezdoslavovo nám. 5, POB 309, 811 02 Bratislava; tel. (2) 5443-3338; fax (2) 5922-3026; e-mail cons@usembassy-bratislava.sk; internet slovakia.usembassy.gov; Chargé d'affaires a.i. KEITH ALAN EDDINS.

Judicial System

The judicial system of Slovakia has three levels: district courts (45), regional courts (eight) and the Supreme Court. Regional courts serve as courts of appeal to the district courts, as well as serving as courts of first instance in some cases; the Supreme Court is the highest judicial authority in the country, operating as a court of cassation and appeal for Regional Courts. There is also a Constitutional Court to ensure compliance with the Constitution. In April 2002 an 18-member Judicial Council was elected, all of whom were lawyers, and nine of whom were judges. Three members are nominated by the President, three by the legislature, three by the Government, and eight are elected by the judges themselves. The final member is the Chairman of the Supreme Court. The Council proposes candidates for judgeships, decides on the assignment of judges, comments on the budget, and elects the Chief Justice of the Supreme Court.

Supreme Court of the Slovak Republic
(Najvyšší súd Slovenskej republiky)

Župné nám. 13, Bratislava 81 490; tel. (2) 5935-3111; fax (2) 5441-1535; internet www.nssr.gov.sk.

Chairman: (vacant).

Office of the Prosecutor-General: Štúrova ul. 2, 812 85 Bratislava; tel. (2) 5953-2505; fax (2) 5953-2653; e-mail generalna.prokuratura@genpro.gov.sk; internet www.genpro.gov.sk; Prosecutor-General DOBROSLAV TRNKA.

Constitutional Court of the Slovak Republic
(Ustavný súd Slovenskej republiky)

Hlavná 110, 042 65 Košice; tel. (55) 720-7211; fax (55) 622-7639; e-mail ochodni@concourt.sk; internet www.concourt.sk.

Chairman: IVETTA MACEJKOVÁ.

Religion

The principal religion in Slovakia is Christianity, of which the largest denomination is the Roman Catholic Church. About 10% of the population profess no religious belief.

CHRISTIANITY

The Roman Catholic Church

In early 2008 changes to the organization of the Roman Catholic Church in Slovakia were implemented. Slovakia comprises four archdioceses (including one of the Slovak Byzantine Rite) and five Latin Rite dioceses, two Slovak Byzantine Rite eparchies and a Military Ordinariate. At 31 December 2006 there were an estimated 4,994,652 adherents, equivalent to 73.6% of the total population.

Bishops' Conference: Kapitulská 11, 81 499 Bratislava; tel. (2) 5443-5234; fax (2) 5443-5913; e-mail kbs@kbs.sk; internet www.kbs.sk; Pres. Rt Rev. FRANTIŠEK TONDRA (Bishop of Spiš).

Latin Rite

Archbishop of Bratislava: Most Rev. STANISLAV ZVOLENSKÝ, Špitálska 7, 814 92 Bratislava; tel. (2 5720-0611; internet www.abu-bratislava.sk.

Archbishop of Košice: Most Rev. ALOJZ TKÁČ, Hlavná 28, 041 83 Košice; tel. (55) 682-8111; fax (55) 622-1034; e-mail abukosice@kbs.sk; internet www.rimkat.sk.

Archbishop of Trnava: Most Rev. JÁN SOKOL, Jána Hollého 10, POB 78, 919 66 Trnava; tel. (33) 591-2111; fax (33) 591-2280; e-mail abu@abu.sk; internet www.abu.sk.

Slovak Rite

Archbishop of Prešov: Most Rev. JÁN BABJAK, Hlavná 1, POB 135, 081 35 Prešov; tel. (51) 773-4622; fax (51) 756-2625; e-mail mons.babjak@greckokat.sk; internet www.grkatpo.sk; 137,203 adherents, 166 parishes (Dec. 2006).

The Eastern Orthodox Church

Orthodox Church in the Czech Lands and Slovakia (Pravoslávna cirkev v českých krajinách a na Slovensku): Budovateľská 1, 080 01 Prešov; tel. (51) 773-2174; fax (51) 773-4045; e-mail dzugan@orthodox.sk; internet www.orthodox.sk; divided into two eparchies in Slovakia: Prešov and Michalovce (the first of which is an archbishopric); and two eparchies in the Czech Republic: Prague and Olomouc—Brno (q.v.); Archbishop of Prešov Rev. JÁN.

Protestant Churches

Apostolic Church in Slovakia (Apoštolská cirkev na Slovensku): Sreznevského 2, 831 03 Bratislava; tel. and fax (2) 4425-0913; e-mail rada@acs-net.sk; internet www.acs-net.sk; f. 1956; affiliated to international Assemblies of God; 4,000 mems; Pres. JÁN LACHO.

Baptist Union of Slovakia: Súlovská 2, 821 05 Bratislava; tel. and fax (2) 4342-1145; e-mail baptist@baptist.sk; internet www.baptist.sk; f. 1994; 1,973 mems (2005); Pres. Rev. TOMÁŠ KRIŠKA; Sec. Rev. TOMAS VALCHAŘ.

Evangelical Church of the Augsburg (Lutheran) Confession in Slovakia (Evanjelická cirkev augsburského vyznania na Slovensku): Palisády 46, POB 289, 811 00 Bratislava; tel. and fax (2) 5443-2940; e-mail sekretariat@ecav.sk; internet www.ecav.sk; 321 parishes in 14 seniorates and two districts; 372,858 mems (2009); Bishop-Gen. MILOS KLÁTIK; Gen. Superintendent DELINGA PAVEL.

Reformed Christian Church of Slovakia: Synodal Office, Hlavné nám. 23, 979 01 Rimavská Sobota; tel. (47) 562-1936; fax (47) 563-

3090; e-mail reformata@reformata.sk; 109,735 mems and 325 parishes (2001); Bishop LÁSZLÓ FAZEKAS.

JUDAISM

Central Union of the Jewish Religious Communities in the Slovak Republic (Ústredný zväz židovských náboženských obcí v Slovenskej republike): Kozia ul. 21, 814 47 Bratislava; tel. (2) 5441-2167; fax (2) 5441-1106; e-mail uzzno@netax.sk; c. 3,000 mems; Exec. Chair. FERO ALEXANDER; Rabbi BARUCH MYERS.

The Press

The publications listed below are in Slovak, unless otherwise indicated.

PRINCIPAL DAILIES

Banská Bystrica

Smer magazín (Direction Magazine): Horná 37, 974 01 Banská Bystrica; tel. (48) 415-1582; e-mail hospodarka.bb@petitpress.sk; internet www.regionalnenoviny.sk/?sek=rn_sdm; f. 1948; independent; Editor-in-Chief ZITA SURÁKOVÁ.

Bratislava

Hospodárske noviny (Economic News): POB 35, Seberíniho 1, 820 07 Bratislava 27; tel. (2) 5063-3627; fax (2) 5063-4724; e-mail hn@hnx.sk; internet www.hnonline.sk; morning; Editor-in-Chief ALICA ĎURIANOVÁ; circ. 40,000.

Nový čas (New Time): Bratislava; tel. (2) 536-3070; fax (2) 536-3104; f. 1991; morning; Editor-in-Chief ZUZANA RAČKOVÁ; circ. 230,000.

Pravda (Truth): Trnavská cesta 39A, 831 04 Bratislava; tel. (2) 4959-6111; internet www.pravda.sk; f. 1920; independent; left-wing; Editor-in-Chief PAVOL MINARIK; circ. 165,000.

Roľnícke noviny (Agricultural News): Bratislava; tel. (2) 368-449; fax (2) 321-282; f. 1946; Editor-in-Chief JURAJ SESTÁK; circ. 20,000.

Slovenská republika (Slovak Republic): Ružová dolina 6, 824 70 Bratislava; tel. (2) 5022-1505; fax (2) 5022-1500; e-mail redakcia@republika.sk; Editor-in-Chief EDUARD FAŠUNG; circ. 78,000.

Sme (We Are): Mytná 33, 810 05 Bratislava; tel. (2) 5923-3500; fax (2) 5923-3669; internet www.sme.sk; f. 1993; merged with Práca (Labour) in Oct. 2002; Editor-in-Chief MARTIN SIMECKA; circ. 95,613.

Šport (Sport): Svätoplukova 2, 819 23 Bratislava; tel. (2) 60-053; fax (2) 211-380; Editor-in-Chief ZDENO SIMONIDES; circ. 85,000.

Új szó (New Word): nám. SNP 30, 814 64 Bratislava; tel. (2) 5923-3459; fax (2) 523-8321; internet www.ujszo.com; f. 1948; midday; in Hungarian; Editor-in-Chief ATTILA LOVÁSZ; circ. 42,000.

Večerník (Evening Paper): Dunajská 4, 811 08 Bratislava; tel. (2) 5710-4021; fax (2) 5292-0741; e-mail vecernik@vecernikba.sk; internet www.vecernikba.sk; f. 1956; evening; Editor-in-Chief MÍCHAELA CONZAROVÁ; circ. 30,000.

Košice

Lúč (Ray): Košice; tel. (55) 633-2117; fax (55) 359-090; f. 1992; Editor-in-Chief EDITA PAČAJOVÁ-KARDOŠOVÁ; circ. 15,000.

Slovenský východ (Slovak East): Letná 45, 042 66 Košice; tel. (55) 53-979; fax (55) 53-950; Editor-in-Chief DUŠAN KLINGER; circ. 30,000.

Prešov

Prešovský večerník (Prešov Evening Paper): Jarkova 4, 080 01 Prešov; tel. (51) 772-4563; fax (51) 772-3398; internet www.vecernik.po.sk; f. 1990; Editor-in-Chief Dr PETER LIČÁK; circ. 13,000.

PRINCIPAL PERIODICALS

A Het (The Week): Bratislava; weekly; Hungarian-language magazine; Editor-in-Chief ATTILA LOVÁSZ.

Avízo: Seberíniho 1, 821 03 Bratislava 2; tel. and fax (2) 4823-2111; e-mail obchod@avizo.sk; internet www.avizo.sk; 3 a week; advertising and information; Gen. Dir OTO LANC; circ. 50,000 (2008).

Eurotelevízia (Eurotelevision): POB 47, 820 04 Bratislava 24; tel. (2) 5822-7124; fax (2) 5822-7143; e-mail eurotelevizia@eurotelevizia.sk; weekly TV and radio guide; Editor-in-Chief ELENA BUDINSKÁ; circ. 290,000.

International: Bratislava; tel. (2) 367-808; fax (2) 326-685; weekly; current affairs; Editor-in-Chief TATIANA JAGLOVÁ; circ. 60,000.

Kamarát (Friend): Bratislava; tel. and fax (2) 240-8777; f. 1950; fortnightly; magazine for teenagers; Editor-in-Chief VLADIMÍR TOPERCER; circ. 30,000.

Katolícke noviny (Catholic News): Matúšova 22, POB 9, 810 01 Bratislava; tel. (2) 5930-6911; e-mail posta@katnoviny.sk; internet online.katnoviny.sk; f. 1849; weekly; Editor-in-Chief MÁRIA KOTEŠOVÁ; circ. 116,000.

Krásy Slovenska (Beauties of Slovakia): Dúbravská cesta 9, POB 115, 840 05 Bratislava 45; tel. (2) 5465-2055; fax (2) 5465-2056; e-mail info@krasy-slovenska.sk; internet www.krasy-slovenska.sk; illustrated bi-monthly; Editor-in-Chief MILAN KUBIŠ; circ. 10,000.

Línia: Pribišova 19A, 841 05 Bratislava; tel. (2) 6025-1123; fax (2) 6025-1130; monthly; lifestyle; Editor-in-Chief JÁN HANUŠKA; circ. 25,000.

Romano nevo Ïil/Rómsky nový list (The New Romany Journal): Jarková 4, 080 01 Prešov; tel. (51) 772-5283; fax (51) 773-3439; e-mail redakcia@rnl.sk; internet www.rnl.sk; f. 1991; in Romany, Slovak and English; publ. by the Association Jekhetane-Spolu (Together); Chief Editors JOZEF FERENC, DENISA HAVRĽOVÁ, DANIELA HIVEŠOVÁ-ŠILANOVÁ, ROMAN ČONKA; circ. 8,500.

Slovenka (Slovak Woman): Jaskový rad 5, 833 80 Bratislava; tel. (2) 5478-9652; fax (2) 5477-6118; e-mail slovenka@slovenka.sk; f. 1948; weekly; illustrated magazine; Editor-in-Chief ZUZANA KRÚTKA; circ. 220,000.

Slovenské národné noviny (Slovak National News): Matica slovenská, Mudroňova 1, 036 52 Martin; tel. and fax (43) 413-4060; internet www.matica.sk/snn/snn.html; f. 1845; weekly; organ of Matica slovenská cultural organization; Editor-in-Chief PETER MIŠÁK; circ. 7,000.

Slovenský profit: Bratislava; tel. (2) 563-3817; fax (2) 563-4581; economic weekly; Editor-in-Chief IVETA SEIFERTOVÁ; circ. 25,000.

Stop: Exnárova 57, 820 12 Bratislava; tel. (2) 4342-5052; fax (2) 4342-0554; e-mail stop@ba.telecom.sk; fortnightly; motoring; Editor-in-Chief ĽUBOŠ KRÍŽ; circ. 47,000.

Szabad újság (Free Journal): Michalská 9, 814 99 Bratislava; tel. (2) 333-012; fax (2) 330-519; f. 1991; Hungarian-language economic weekly; Editor-in-Chief GÉZA SZABÓ; circ. 40,000.

Trend: Bratislava; tel. (2) 2082-2222; fax (2) 2082-2223; e-mail redakcia@trend.sk; internet www.etrend.sk; f. 1991; weekly; for entrepreneurs; publ. by Trend Holding; Editor-in-Chief RADOSLAV BAŤO; circ. 25,000.

Vasárnap (Sunday): SNP 30, 814 64 Bratislava 1; tel. (2) 5923-3235; fax (2) 5923-3295; e-mail reklama@ujsz.com; f. 1948; weekly; independent Hungarian-language magazine; Editor-in-Chief JÓZSEF SZILVÁSSY; circ. 97,000.

Život (Life): Pribinova 25, 819 37 Bratislava; tel. (2) 210-4135; fax (2) 210-4145; f. 1951; illustrated family weekly; Editor-in-Chief MILAN VÁROŠ; circ. 255,000.

NEWS AGENCIES

Rómska tlačová agentúra (Roma Press Agency): Slovenskej jednoty 44, 040 01 Košice; tel. (55) 632-1372; e-mail rpa@mecem.sk; internet www.mecem.sk/rpa; reports on matters relating to the Roma minority, and aims to bring attention to issues affecting the community; Dir-Gen. KRISTÍNA MAGDOLENOVÁ.

SITA: Mýtna 15, 811 07 Bratislava; tel. (2) 5249-6106; fax (2) 5249-3466; e-mail slovakam@sita.sk; internet www.sita.sk; f. 1997; independent; Dir-Gen. PAVOL MUDRY.

Tlačová agentúra Slovenskej republiky (TASR) (News Agency of the Slovak Republic): Pribinova 25, 819 28 Bratislava; tel. (2) 5921-0444; fax (2) 5296-3405; e-mail foreign@tasr.sk; internet www.tasr.sk; f. 1992; overseas bureaux in Belgium, Czech Republic, Hungary, Lebanon, Poland, Spain, United Kingdom and USA; Dir-Gen. JAROSLAV REZNÍK.

PRESS ASSOCIATION

Slovenský syndikát novinárov (Slovak Syndicate of Journalists): Župné nám. 7, 815 68 Bratislava; tel. (2) 5443-5071; fax (2) 5443-2438; e-mail krutka.zuzana@ssn.sk; internet www.ssn.sk; f. 1968; reorganized 1990; 2,600 mems; Chair. ZUZANA KRÚTKA.

Publishers

Academic Electronic Press: Bajzova 7, 821 08 Bratislava; tel. and fax (2) 5556-4495; non-fiction.

Dajama: Ľublanská 2, 831 02 Bratislava; tel. and fax (2) 4463-1702; e-mail info@dajama.sk; internet www.dajama.sk; guide-books about Slovakia in Slovak, Hungarian, German, Polish, Russian and English.

Enigma: Javorová 4, 949 01 Nitra 1; tel. (87) 655-5551; e-mail enigma@enigma.sk; internet www.enigma.sk; f. 1991; textbooks, translations of children's books, illustrated books; Dir VLADIMIR PRELOZNIK.

SLOVAKIA   Directory

Epos, Ing. Miroslav Mračko: Pečnianska 27, 851 01 Bratislava 5; tel. and fax (2) 6241-2357; e-mail epos@epos.sk; internet www.epos.sk; f. 1990; economics, law, non-fiction.

Kalligram, s.r.o.: Staromestská 6D, POB 223, 810 00 Bratislava 1; tel. and fax (2) 5441-5028; e-mail kalligram@kalligram.sk; internet www.kaligram.sk; f. 1990; Slovak and Central European and world literature, literary criticism, philosophy, religion, history, social sciences, science; Dir LÁSZLÓ SZIGETI.

Koloman Kertész Bagala (LCA Publishers Group): POB 99, 810 00 Bratislava 1; tel. (2) 5441-5366; fax (2) 5464-7393; e-mail lca@lca.sk; internet www.lca.sk; f. 1991; fiction; Dir KOLOMAN KERTÉSZ BAGALA.

Matica slovenská: J. C. Hronského, 036 52 Martin; tel. (43) 413-2454; fax (43) 413-3188; e-mail msba@matica.sk; internet www.matica.sk; f. 1863; literary science, bibliography, biography and librarianship; Chair. Ing. JOZEF MARKUŠ.

Poradca podnikateľa, spol. s.r.o. (Entrepreneur's Adviser): Martina Rázusa 23A, 010 01 Žilina; tel. (41) 705-3777; fax (41) 705-3214; internet www.epi.sk; books and CD-ROMs providing economic and legal information; Dir JÁN BRIGANT.

Príroda a.s. (Nature): Bratislava; tel. (2) 396-335; fax (2) 397-564; e-mail priroda@priroda.bts.sk; f. 1949; school textbooks, encyclopedias, reference books, etc. for children and young people; Chair. Ing. EMILIA JANKOVITSOVÁ.

Slovenské pedagogické nakladeteľstvo—Mladé letá, s.r.o. (Slovak Educational Publishing House—Young Years): Bratislava; tel. (2) 5022-7312; fax (2) 5542-5758; e-mail spn@spn.sk; internet www.spn-mladeleta.sk; f. 1920; pedagogical literature, educational, school texts, dictionaries; Exec. Man. DARINA TOROKOVA.

Slovenský spisovatel a.s. (Slovak Writer): Bratislava; tel. and fax (2) 499-736; e-mail slovspis@slovspis.sk; fiction, poetry; Dir MARTIN CHOVANEC.

Smena (Change): Bratislava; tel. (2) 498-018; fax (2) 493-305; f. 1949; fiction, literature for young people, newspapers and magazines; Dir Ing. JAROSLAV SIŠOLÁK.

Šport: Bratislava; tel. (2) 69-195; sport, physical culture, guidebooks, periodicals; Dir Dr BOHUMIL GOLIAN.

Tatran: Michalská 9, 815 82 Bratislava; tel. (2) 5443-5849; fax (2) 5443-5777; f. 1949; fiction, art books, children's books, literary theory; Dir Dr EVA MLÁDEKOVÁ.

Veda (Science): Bradáčova 7, 852 86 Bratislava; tel. and fax (2) 832-254; f. 1953; publishing house of the Slovak Academy of Sciences; scientific and popular scientific books and periodicals; Man. EVA MAJESKÁ.

PUBLISHERS' ASSOCIATION

Publishers' and Booksellers' Asscn of the Slovak Republic (Združenie vydavateľov a kníhkupcov Slovenskej republiky): Gregorovej 8, 821 03 Bratislava; tel. and fax (2) 4333-6700; e-mail alex.aust@post.sk; Pres. Dr ALEX AUST.

Broadcasting and Communications

TELECOMMUNICATIONS

Regulatory Authority

Telecommunications Office of the Slovak Republic: Továrenská 7, POB 18, 810 06 Bratislava 16; tel. (2) 5788-1552; fax (2) 5293-2096; e-mail roman.vavro@teleoff.gov.sk; internet www.teleoff.gov.sk; Chair. LADISLAV MIKUŠ.

Service Providers

Orange Slovensko (Orange Slovakia): Prievozská 6, 821 09 Bratislava; tel. (2) 5851-2345; e-mail info@orange.sk; internet www.orange.sk; f. 1997 as Globtel; present name adopted 2002; wholly owned by Orange (France); provides mobile cellular telecommunications services; Dir-Gen. PAVOL LANČARIČ.

T-Com, a.s.: nám. Slobody 6, 817 62 Bratislava 15; tel. (2) 5249-2324; fax (2) 5249-2492; e-mail sekr.gr@st.sk; internet www.t-com.sk; 51% owned by Deutsche Telekom (Germany), 34% owned by Ministry of Transport, Post and Telecommunications, 15% owned by the National Property Fund of the Slovak Republic; formerly Slovenské Telekomunikácie; name changed to Slovak Telecom in Jan. 2004; name changed as above in March 2006; Pres. and Chief Exec. MIROSLAV MAJOROŠ.

T-Mobile Slovensko, a.s.: Vajnorská 100A, 831 03 Bratislava; tel. (2) 4955-1111; internet www.t-mobile.sk; f. 1997; 100% owned by T-Com; provides mobile cellular telecommunications services; Gen. Dir ROBERT CHVÁTEL.

Telefónica O2 Slovakia s.r.o.: Einsteinova 24, Bratislava 851 01; tel. (2) 6202-0100; fax (2) 6202-0444; internet www.sk.o2.com; f. 2007; subsidiary of Telefónica (United Kingdom); mobile cellular telecommunications services; Gen. Man. JURAJ ŠEDIVÝ.

BROADCASTING

Radio

Slovenský rozhlas (Slovak Radio): Mýtna 1, POB 55, 817 55 Bratislava; tel. (2) 5727-3560; fax (2) 5249-8923; e-mail interrel@slovakradio.sk; internet www.slovakradio.sk; f. 1926; Chair. IGOR GALLO; Dir-Gen. MILOSLAVA ZEMKOVÁ.

Television

Slovenská televízia (STV) (Slovak Television): Mlynská dolina 28, 845 45 Bratislava; tel. (2) 6542-3001; fax (2) 6542-2341; internet www.stv.sk; f. 1956; public broadcasting co; Chair. of Council MARTIN KÁKOŠ; Gen. Man. ŠTEFAN NIŽŇANSKÝ.

TA3: Gagarinova 12, POB 31, 820 15 Bratislava; tel. (2) 4820-3511; fax (2) 4820-3549; e-mail ta3@ta3.com; internet www.ta3.com; f. 2001; privately owned; Dir-Gen. MATEJ RIBANSKÝ.

TV Joj: Grešákova 10, 040 01 Kosiče; tel. (55) 622-2664; fax (55) 622-1027; e-mail joj@joj.sk; internet www.joj.sk; f. 2002; privately owned subsidiary of Nova TV (Czech Republic); Dir-Gen. VLADIMÍR ŽELEZNÝ; Dir MILAN KNAŽKO.

TV Markíza: Bratislavská 1A, POB 7, 843 56 Bratislava 48; tel. (2) 6827-4111; fax (2) 6595-6824; e-mail markiza@markiza.sk; internet tv.markiza.sk; f. 1996; first privately owned television channel; 80% owned by Central European Media Enterprises Ltd (USA); Dir-Gen. VÁCLAV MIKA.

Finance

(cap. = capital; res = reserves; dep. = deposits; m. = million; brs = branches; amounts in Slovak koruna, unless otherwise indicated)

BANKING

Central Bank

National Bank of Slovakia (Národná banka Slovenska): Imricha Karvaša 1, 813 25 Bratislava; tel. (2) 5787-1111; fax (2) 5787-1100; e-mail webmaster@nbs.sk; internet www.nbs.sk; f. 1993; res −91,270.0m., dep. 404,636.0m., total assets 463,126.0m. (Dec. 2007); central bank; Gov. IVAN ŠRAMKO.

Commercial Banks

Citibank (Slovakia), a.s.: Mlynské nivy 43, 825 01 Bratislava; tel. (2) 5823-0111; fax (2) 5823-0200; e-mail citibank.slovakia@citibank.com; internet www.citibank.sk; f. 1995; cap. 1,650.0m., res 1,403.8m., dep. 28,401.2m. (Dec. 2007); CEO ERIC LEMMENS; 3 brs.

Dexia banka slovensko, a.s.: Hodžova 11, 010 11 Žilina; tel. (41) 511-1111; fax (41) 562-4129; e-mail info@dexia.sk; internet www.dexia.sk; f. 1993; present name adopted 2003; 84.4% owned by Dexia Kommunalkredit Bank AG (Austria); cap. 1,202.4m., res 517.3m., dep. 51,830.0m. (Dec. 2006), total assets 70,466.1m. (Dec. 2007); Chair. and CEO STEFAAN DEPAEPE; 53 brs.

Istrobanka, a.s.: Laurinská 1, POB 109, 810 00 Bratislava; tel. (2) 5939-7111; fax (2) 5443-1120; e-mail info@istrobanka.sk; internet www.istrobanka.sk; f. 1992; 100% owned by KBC Bank NV (Belgium); cap. 2,175.0m., res 0.0m., dep. 36,826.1m. (Dec. 2007); Chair. and Gen. Man. VOLKER PICHLER; 11 brs.

Komerční Banka Bratislava, a.s.: Hodžovo nám. 1A, POB 137, 810 00 Bratislava; tel. (2) 5927-7328; fax (2) 5296-1959; e-mail koba@koba.sk; internet www.koba.sk; f. 1995; cap. 500.0m., res 169.5m., dep. 7,755.0m. (Dec. 2007); Chair. and CEO JAROMÍR CHABR.

OTP Banka Slovensko, a.s. (Investment and Development Bank): Štúrová 5, 813 54 Bratislava; tel. (2) 5979-1111; fax (2) 5296-3484; e-mail info@otpbanka.sk; internet www.otpbanka.sk; f. 1992; present name adopted 2002; 97.2% owned by OTP Bank (Hungary); cap. 2,064.4m., res 733.5m., dep. 44,362.9m. (Dec. 2007); Chair. and CEO ERNÖ KELECSÉNYI; 72 brs.

Poštová banka, a.s. (Postal Bank): Prievozska 2B, 821 09 Bratislava; tel. (2) 5960-3333; fax (2) 5960-3344; e-mail postbank@pabk.sk; internet www.pabk.sk; f. 1993; cap. 2,489.9m., res 1,372.9m., dep. 30,388.7m. (Dec. 2007); Chair. and CEO ROMAN FEČÍK; 24 brs.

Privatbanka, a.s.: Suché Mýto 1, 811 03 Bratislava; tel. (2) 5920-6620; fax (2) 5443-3131; e-mail privatbanka@privatbanka.sk; internet www.privatbanka.sk; f. 1996; present name adopted 2005; cap. 756.9m., res 37.9m., dep. 8,735.5m. (Dec. 2007); Chair. and CEO ĽUBOŠ ŠEVČÍK.

SLOVAKIA

Tatra banka, a.s.: POB 42, Hodzovo nám. 3, 811 06 Bratislava; tel. (2) 5919-1111; fax (2) 5919-1110; e-mail tatrabanka@tatrabanka.sk; internet www.tatrabanka.sk; f. 1990; res 27,493.2m., dep. 196,025.8m., total assets 253,015.6m. (Dec. 2007); Chair. and Gen. Man. IGOR VIDA; 30 brs.

UniCredit Bank, a.s.: Sancová 1A, 813 33 Bratislava; tel. (2) 4950-2112; fax (2) 4437-3975; internet www.unicreditbank.sk; f. 1990; present name adopted 2007; 99.0% owned by Bank Austria Creditanstalt AG (Austria); cap. 7,095.5m., res 6,321.2m., dep. 121,077.8m. (Dec. 2007); Chair. of Bd and CEO JOZEF BARTA; 10 brs, 83 sub-brs.

Volksbank Slovensko, a.s.: Vysoká 9, POB 81, 810 00 Bratislava; tel. (2) 5965-1111; fax (2) 5441-2453; e-mail market@volksbank.sk; internet www.volksbank.sk; f. 1991 as Ľudová banka; name changed as above in 2007; 91% owned by Volksbank International AG (Austria); cap. 1,000.0m., res 3,052.1m., dep. 34,423.9m. (Dec. 2007); Chair. KURT KAPELLER; 47 brs.

Všeobecná úverová banka, a.s. (General Credit Bank): Mlynské Nivy 1, POB 90, 829 90 Bratislava; tel. (2) 5055-1111; fax (2) 5556-6650; e-mail contact@vub.sk; internet www.vub.sk; f. 1990; 96.5% owned by Intesa Holding International SA (Luxembourg); cap. 12,978m., res 3,012m., dep. 256,008m. (Dec. 2007); Chair. and CEO IGNACIO JAQUOTOT; 240 brs.

Savings Banks

Prvá stavebná sporiteľňa, a.s.: Bajkalská 30, POB 48, 829 48 Bratislava; tel. (2) 5855-5855; fax (2) 5341-1131; internet www.pss.sk; f. 1992; cap. 1,000m.; Chair. IMRICH BÉREŠ.

Slovenská sporiteľňa, a.s. (Slovak Savings Bank): Tomášikova 48, 832 37 Bratislava; tel. (2) 4862-1111; fax (2) 5957-4009; e-mail info@slsp.sk; internet www.slsp.sk; f. 1842; 100% owned by Erste Bank (Austria); dep. 272,481.0m., total assets 303,913.0m. (Dec. 2007); Chair. and CEO JAN ROLLO; 270 brs.

COMMODITY AND STOCK EXCHANGES

Bratislava Commodity Exchange (Komoditná burza Bratislava): Trnavská cesta 50A, 821 02 Bratislava; tel. (2) 5293-1010; fax (2) 5293-1007; e-mail sekretariat@kbb.sk; internet www.kbb.sk; Chair. ĽUDOVÍT SCHOLTZ.

Bratislava Stock Exchange (Burza cenných papierov v Bratislave, a.s.): Vysoká 17, POB 151, 814 99 Bratislava 1; tel. (2) 4923-6111; fax (2) 4923-6103; e-mail info@bsse.sk; internet www.bsse.sk; f. 1991; Chair. VLADIMÍR KOCOUREK; Dir-Gen. MÁRIA HURAJOVÁ.

INSURANCE

Allianz—Slovak Insurance Co (Allianz—Slovenská poisťovňa, a.s.): Dostojevského rad 4, 815 74 Bratislava; tel. (2) 5963-1111; fax (2) 5963-2740; e-mail info@allianzsp.sk; internet www.allianzsp.sk; 84.5% owned by Allianz AG (Germany), 15% owned by European Bank for Reconstruction and Development; majority stake divested to Allianz AG (Germany) in 2002; name changed from Slovenská poisťovňa to Allianz—Slovenská poisťovňa in 2003; Chair. TORSTEN LEUE; 2,900 employees.

Trade and Industry

GOVERNMENT AGENCIES

National Property Fund of the Slovak Republic (Fond Národného Majetku Slovenskej Republiky): Drieňová 27, 821 01 Bratislava; tel. (2) 4827-1111; fax (2) 4827-1289; e-mail fnm@natfund.gov.sk; internet www.natfund.gov.sk; f. 1993; supervises the privatization process; Pres. PETER ŠIMKO.

SARIO—Slovak Investment and Trade Development Agency (SARIO—Slovenská agentúra pre rozvoj investícií a obchodu): Martinčekova 17, 821 01 Bratislava; tel. (2) 5826-0100; fax (2) 5826-0109; e-mail sario@sario.sk; internet www.sario.sk; f. 1991; CEO PETER HAJAŠ.

CHAMBERS OF COMMERCE

Slovak Chamber of Commerce and Industry (Slovenská obchodná a priemyselná komora): Gorkého 9, 816 03 Bratislava; tel. (2) 5443-3291; fax (2) 5413-1159; e-mail sopkurad@scci.sk; internet www.scci.sk; Pres. Dr PETER MIHÓK.

Banská Bystrica Chamber of Commerce and Industry: nám. Š. Moysesa 4, 974 01 Banská Bystrica; tel. (48) 412-5634; fax (48) 412-5636; e-mail sopkrbb@sopk.sk; internet www.bb.scci.sk.

Košice Chamber of Commerce and Industry: Floriánska 19, 040 01 Košice; tel. (55) 7279-160; fax (55) 7279-156; e-mail sopkrkke@scci.sk; internet www.sopk.sk/ko/sk; Dir IVAN PEZLÁR.

Trenčín Chamber of Commerce and Industry: ul. Jilemnického 2, 911 01 Trenčín; tel. (32) 652-3834; fax (32) 652-1023; e-mail sopkrktn@scci.sk; internet www.sopk.sk/tn/an/index.html.

Žilina Chamber of Commerce and Industry: ul. Halková 31, 010 01 Žilina; tel. (41) 723-5655; fax (41) 723-5653; internet www.sopk.sk/za/sk; Dir JÁN MIŠURA.

UTILITIES

Electricity

Slovenské elektrárne, a.s. (SE) (Slovak Electricity): Hraničná 12, 827 36 Bratislava 212; tel. (2) 5866-1111; fax (2) 5341-7525; e-mail info@hq.seas.sk; internet www.seas.sk; fmr state-owned utility; 66% share acquired by Enel (Italy) in April 2006; 34% owned by the National Property Fund; Chair. and Dir-Gen. PAOLO RUZZINI; Deputy Chair. MARCO ARCELLI.

Stredoslovenská energetika, a.s. (SSE) (Central Slovakia Energy): Republiky 5, 010 47 Žilina; tel. (41) 519-1111; fax (41) 519-2575; e-mail sse@sse.sk; internet www.sse.sk; 51% owned by the National Property Fund of the Slovak Republic, 49% by Eléctricité de France; regional electricity distributor; Chair. and Dir-Gen. PIERRE CHAZERAIN.

Východoslovenská energetika, a.s. (VSE) (East Slovakia Energy): Mlynská 31, 042 91 Košice; tel. (55) 610-2111; fax (55) 678-6516; e-mail info@vse.sk; internet www.vse.sk; 51% owned by the National Property Fund of the Slovak Republic, 49% by RWE Energie AG (Germany); regional electricity distributor; Chair. and CEO NORBERT SCHÜRMANN.

Západoslovenská energetika (ZSE) (West Slovakia Energy): Čulenova 6, 816 47 Bratislava; tel. (2) 5296-1741; fax (2) 5061-3901; e-mail kontakt@zse.sk; internet www.zse.sk; f. 1922; 51% owned by National Property Fund of the Slovak Republic, 40% by E.ON Energie AG (Germany) and 9% by the European Bank for Reconstruction and Development; regional electricity distributor; Chair. of Bd of Dirs KONRAD KREUZER; Dir of Man. Bd Dr JÁN ORLOVSKÝ.

Gas

Slovenský Plynárenský Priemysel (SPP) (Slovak Gas Co): Mlynské nivy 44A, 825 11 Bratislava; tel. (2) 5869-1111; fax (2) 5869-2765; e-mail spp@spp.sk; internet www.spp.sk; partially privatized in July 2002; Chair. BERND WAGNER.

TRADE UNION CONFEDERATION

Confederation of Trade Unions of the Slovak Republic (Konfederácia odborových zväzov Slovenskej republiky): Odborárské nám. 3, 815 70 Bratislava; tel. (2) 5557-6065; fax (2) 5023-9102; e-mail press@kozsr.sk; internet www.kozsr.sk; Pres. MIROSLAV GAZDIK; 347,760 mems (2007).

Transport

RAILWAYS

In 2007 the total length of railways in Slovakia was estimated at 3,629 km, of which 1,578 km were electrified.

Železnice Slovenskej republiky (Slovak State Railways): Klemensova 8, 813 61 Bratislava; tel. (2) 2029-1111; fax (2) 5296-2296; e-mail gr@zsr.sk; internet www.zsr.sk; f. 1993; became a joint-stock co with responsibility for management of rail infrastructure in 2001, when responsibility for operations was transferred to the newly established state-owned concern, Železničná spoločnosť; Chair. JURAJ MRAVČÁK; Dir-Gen. ŠTEFAN HLINKA.

Železničná spoločnosť Cargo Slovakia, a.s. (ZSSK Cargo): Drieňová 24, 820 09 Bratislava; e-mail infoservis@zscargo.sk; internet www.zscargo.sk; f. 2005, following division into two of the state railway company, Železničná spoločnosť, a.s.; operation of rail freight transport and freight-related commercial activities; state-owned; Chair. of Bd of Dirs MATIEJ AUGUSTÍN.

Železničná spoločnosť Slovensko, a.s.: Železničná 1, 041 79 Košice; tel. (2) 2029-7362; fax (2) 5341-0128; e-mail info@slovakrail.sk; internet www.slovakrail.sk; f. 2005, following division into two of the state railway company, Železničná spoločnosť, a.s.; passenger transport; state-owned; Chair. and Dir-Gen. MILAN CHUPEK.

Dopravný podnik Bratislava, a.s. (Bratislava Transport): Olejkárska 1, 814 52 Bratislava; tel. (2) 5950-1411; fax (2) 5950-1400; e-mail sekretariat.gr@dpb.sk; internet www.dpb.sk; tramway being upgraded to light-rail system; 11 routes with 154 stops; Dir-Gen. ROBERT KADNÁR.

SLOVAKIA   *Directory*

ROADS

In 2004 the total length of the road system (including motorways) was estimated at 43,000 km, of which 87.3% was paved.

Slovak Road Administration (Slovenská správa ciest): Miletičova 19, 826 19 Bratislava; tel. (2) 5025-5111; fax (2) 5556-7976; e-mail info@ssc.sk; internet www.ssc.sk; f. 1996; Dir-Gen. Ing. ROMAN ZEMBERA.

INLAND WATERWAYS

The total length of navigable waterways in Slovakia (on the River Danube) is 172 km. The Danube provides a link with Germany, Austria, Hungary, Serbia, Bulgaria, Romania and the Black Sea. The main river ports are Bratislava and Komárno.

State Shipping Authority (Štátna plavebná správa): Prístavná 10, 821 09 Bratislava; tel. (2) 5556-6336; fax (2) 5556-6335; e-mail sekretariat@sps.sk; internet www.sps.sk; Dir Ing. JOZEF MORAVČÍK.

Slovak Shipping and Ports Co, a.s. (Slovenská plavba a prístavy, a.s.): Horárska 12, 815 24 Bratislava; tel. (2) 5827-1111; fax (2) 5827-1114; e-mail spap@spap.sk; internet www.spap.sk; Chair. of Bd JOZEF BLAŠKO; Gen. Man. JAROSLAV MICHALCO.

CIVIL AVIATION

There are five international airports in Slovakia: Bratislava (M. R. Štefánik Airport), Košice, Piešťany, Poprad and Sliač.

Air Slovakia: Pestovateľská ul. 2, 821 04 Bratislava; tel. (2) 4342-2744; fax (2) 4342-2742; e-mail airslovakia@airslovakia.sk; internet www.airslovakia.sk; f. 1993; scheduled passenger flights between Slovakia and Cyprus, India, Israel, Italy, Kuwait and the United Kingdom; charter and cargo services; Pres. HARJINDER SINGH SIDHU; Dir-Gen. MICHAEL HALPER.

SkyEurope Airlines, a.s.: Ivanská 30B, POB 24, 820 01 Bratislava 21; tel. (2) 4850-1111; fax (2) 4850-1000; e-mail info@skyeurope.com; internet www.skyeurope.com; f. 2001; first budget airline in Central Europe; scheduled passenger services; domestic and international services; Chair. and CEO JASON BITTER.

Tourism

Slovakia's tourist attractions include ski resorts in the High and Low Tatras and other mountain ranges, more than 20 spa resorts (with thermal and mineral springs), numerous castles and mansions, and historic towns, including Bratislava, Košice, Nitra, Bardejov, Kežmarok and Levoča. In 2006 1,611,808 foreign tourists visited Slovakia, compared with 975,105 in 1999. In 2006 revenue from tourism totalled US $1,513m.

Slovak Tourist Board: nám. L. Stura 1, POB 35, 974 05 Banská Bystrica; tel. (48) 413-6146; fax (48) 413-6149; e-mail sacr@sacr.sk; internet www.sacr.sk; Dir-Gen. SVETLANA GAVOROVÁ.

SLOVENIA

Introductory Survey

Location, Climate, Language, Religion, Flag, Capital

The Republic of Slovenia is situated in south-central Europe. It is bounded by Austria to the north, Hungary to the north-east, Croatia to the south and east, and Italy to the west, and it has a short western coastline on the Adriatic Sea. The climate is Alpine in the mountainous areas, Mediterranean along the coast and continental in the interior. Average temperatures range from between 0°C (32°F) and 22°C (71.6°F) inland, and between 2°C (35.6°F) and 24°C (75.2°F) on the coast. Average annual rainfall ranges from 800 mm (31.5 ins) in the east to 3,000 mm (118.1 ins) in the north-west. The official language is Slovene, and, in ethnically mixed regions, also Hungarian and Italian. The majority religion in Slovenia is Roman Catholicism, although there are small communities of other Christian denominations and of Muslims and Jews. The national flag (proportions 2 by 3) consists of three horizontal stripes of white, blue and red, with a shield in the upper hoist depicting a white three-peaked mountain (Triglav), below which are two horizontal wavy blue lines and above which are three six-pointed yellow stars. The capital is Ljubljana.

Recent History

Following the collapse of the Austro-Hungarian Empire, the Kingdom of Serbs, Croats and Slovenes was proclaimed on 4 December 1918. (The territory of Slovenia was formally ceded by Austria by the Treaty of Saint-Germain in 1919.) In 1929 the name of the country was changed to Yugoslavia. Yugoslavia collapsed under German attack in 1941, and, during the Second World War, Germany annexed lower Styria and Yugoslav Carinthia, while Italy annexed Istria and the territory around Ljubljana. (There was a continuing dispute with Italy over Istria; in 1954 Italy was awarded the city of Trieste, and Yugoslavia the remainder of the territory, giving Slovenia access to the sea.) Hungary occupied the plains along the Mura in north-eastern Slovenia.

The Slovene Liberation Front, formed in 1941, joined with the communist-led all-Yugoslav Partisan Army of Josip Broz (Tito), which was eventually recognized as an ally by the British and US Governments. Following the post-war proclamation of the Federal People's Republic of Yugoslavia (from 1963 the Socialist Federal Republic of Yugoslavia—SFRY), Slovenia became the most prosperous of the Yugoslav republics, but was increasingly suspicious of Serb domination. On 27 September 1989 the Slovene Assembly voted in favour of radical amendments to the Constitution of Slovenia, confirming Slovenia's sovereignty and its right to secede from the SFRY. The organization of multi-party elections was envisaged, and the establishment of opposition parties (the local League of Communists of Slovenia—LCS—having hitherto been the only legal party) was formally authorized. Slovenia was warned that the amendments contravened the Federal Constitution, and the Serbian leader, Slobodan Milošević, attempted to arrange protests in Slovenia against the Slovene leadership; however, the planned demonstrations were banned in November. Milošević subsequently instructed all Serbian enterprises to sever links with Slovenia, which retaliated by imposing reciprocal economic sanctions.

In January 1990 the Slovenian delegation withdrew from the 14th (Extraordinary) Congress of the League of Communists of Yugoslavia (LCY), following the overwhelming rejection of their proposals to reform the federal party and to give greater autonomy to the respective Leagues of Communists of the republics. The LCY suffered a further reverse in February, when its Central Committee was unable to secure the quorum necessary to set a date for the reconvening of the Congress. A boycott by the entire Slovene contingent was supported by members of the Leagues of Communists of Croatia and Macedonia. The LCS suspended its links with the LCY, and changed its name to the Party of Democratic Reform (PDR). In that month Štefan Korošec of Slovenia was removed from the position of Secretary of the Presidium of the LCY Central Committee, in advance of the expiry of his mandate, and was replaced by a Serb. In March Slovenia was redesignated the Republic of Slovenia. Meanwhile, opposition parties had been formed, and in December 1989 six of the main parties formed a coalition, the Democratic Opposition of Slovenia (DEMOS). In multi-party elections, held in April 1990, DEMOS won a majority in the republican parliament, and subsequently formed a Government under Lojze Peterle, the leader of the Slovenian Christian Democrats (SCD). However, the leader of the PDR, Milan Kučan (an opponent of Milošević), was elected President of the State Presidency, and the PDR remained the largest single party in the legislature.

On 2 July 1990 the Slovenian legislature declared the sovereignty of the republic. An amendment to the republican Constitution, resolving that republican laws should take precedence over federal laws, was approved by the legislature on 27 September. Slovenia also assumed control over the local territorial defence force, thereby bringing the republic into direct confrontation with the Serb-dominated federal army, which attempted to reassert its authority by confiscating weapons and seizing the headquarters of the republican force. Slovenian and Croatian proposals to reform the Yugoslav Federation were rejected, and Serbia imposed economic sanctions on imports from the secessionist states. None the less, in a referendum held in Slovenia on 23 December 1990, some 89% of those who voted (about 94% of the electorate) endorsed Slovenian independence.

Relations between Slovenia and the SFRY deteriorated further in January 1991, when the Slovenian authorities refused to implement an order by the SFRY Presidency to disarm all paramilitary groups. In the same month Slovenia and Croatia signed friendship and military co-operation agreements. Although the Slovenian Government approved a programme for Slovenian dissociation from the SFRY in February, both Slovenia and Croatia remained willing to consider a federation of sovereign states. However, following the Serbian-led crisis in the Federal State Presidency in March (see the chapter on Serbia), the Slovenian Government became more resolved to withdraw from the federation. In May Slovenia declared its intention to secede before the end of June, and legislation was adopted that would enable eventual independence, including the establishment of a Slovenian army. Tensions with the federal authorities were exacerbated when Slovenia attempted to take control of the collection of customs duties.

Slovenia and Croatia declared their independence from the SFRY on 25 June 1991. In response, Serb-dominated federal troops were mobilized on 27 June, and tanks were dispatched from Belgrade, the Serbian and Yugoslav capital. Sporadic fighting ensued, and, despite attempts by the European Community (EC—now European Union—EU, see p. 255) to arrange a cease-fire, there was an aerial bombardment of Brnik (Ljubljana) airport. On 7–8 July an EC-mediated cease-fire agreement between Slovenia and the SFRY ended all hostilities in Slovenia. According to official figures, 79 people were killed in the fighting in Slovenia. On 8 October (following the expiry of a three-month moratorium on dissociation, agreed as part of the EC cease-fire accord) Slovenia proclaimed its full independence, introduced its own currency, the tolar, and recalled all of its citizens serving in federal institutions. All federal army units had withdrawn from Slovenia by 26 October. A new Slovenian Constitution, providing for a bicameral legislature, was promulgated on 23 December. Slovenia was recognized by the EC in January 1992. The USA recognized the country in April, and withdrew sanctions against Slovenia (imposed on all states in the territory of the former SFRY in the previous year) in August. Slovenia was admitted to the UN in May.

Peterle's administration experienced increasing difficulties, as the struggle for independence became less of a unifying factor. In October 1991 the Slovenian Democratic Union, one of the larger and most influential DEMOS parties, split into two factions, both of which remained in the coalition. A liberal wing formed the Democratic Party (DP) under the Minister of Foreign Affairs, Dr Dmitrij Rupel, while the majority of the party's parliamentary delegates supported a more conservative programme and formed the National Democratic Party, led by the Minister of Justice and Administration, Dr Rajko Pirnat. DEMOS, undermined by such factionalism, was dissolved in December, although it was envisaged that the Peterle administration would remain in power pending the organization of elections (to take place under the terms of the new Constitution). However, the Government lost a parliamentary motion of no confidence in April 1992, and Peterle resigned. He was replaced by Dr Janez Drnovšek, the leader of the Liberal Democratic Party (LDP) and a former President of the SFRY Presidency.

Parliamentary and presidential elections took place on 6 December 1992. About 85% of the registered electorate participated in elections to the Državni zbor (National Assembly). Although the LDP returned the greatest number of deputies (22) to the 90-member body, it failed to secure a majority of seats in the legislature. Among the groupings that obtained representation were the SCD, with a total of 15 seats, the United List (a four-party electoral alliance), with 14 seats, and the extreme nationalist Slovenian National Party (SNP), which won 12 seats. In the presidential election, Kučan (standing as an independent candidate) was re-elected to what had become, under the terms of the 1991 Constitution, a largely ceremonial post, obtaining 63.9% of the votes cast. His nearest rival, Ivan Bizjak of the SCD, secured 21.1% of the votes. Voting was held concurrently for the 22 directly elected members of the advisory Državni svet (National Council); its remaining 18 members were chosen by an electoral college shortly afterwards.

In January 1993 Drnovšek formed a coalition Government, comprising members of the LDP, the SCD, the United List (later renamed the United List of Social Democrats—ULSD), the Greens of Slovenia and the Social Democratic Party of Slovenia (SDPS). Peterle was appointed Minister of Foreign Affairs, and Bizjak Minister of Internal Affairs. In July the Minister of Defence, Janez Janša, was among several senior politicians implicated in a scandal involving the sale of armaments to Bosnian Muslims (Bosniaks), in contravention of the UN embargo on the transfer of military equipment between the former Yugoslav republics. Earlier in the year Janša (the President of the SDPS) had accused Kučan of protecting former officials of the communist regime. Janša was dismissed from the Government in March 1994, after a ministerial commission found that security forces under the command of the Ministry of Defence had ill-treated a former ministry employee. The SDPS withdrew from the Government, protesting that the coalition agreement had been breached. In addition, the party cited as its reasons for leaving the Government continuing high-level corruption and the change in the coalition's structure, following the merger in March of the LDP with three other organizations to form a new party, Liberal Democracy of Slovenia (LDS). The LDS, led by Drnovšek, also included the DP and the Greens of Slovenia—Eco-Social Party (comprising the parliamentary members of the Greens of Slovenia), and numbered 30 deputies in the Državni zbor. Drnovšek subsequently formed a new coalition Government with the SCD and the ULSD. However, Bizjak resigned as Minister of Internal Affairs in May, following allegations that security forces controlled by his ministry had been involved in criminal activities in Austria. In September the appointment of an LDS member, Jožef Školjč, to the presidency of the Državni zbor prompted Peterle's resignation from the Government, in protest at what he regarded as the excessive concentration of authority among members of the LDS. Although the SCD remained within the government coalition, Drnovšek refused to accede to the party's demand that Peterle's successor should also be a member of the SCD. In January 1995 an agreement was finally reached whereby Zoran Thaler of the LDS was appointed Minister of Foreign Affairs, and Janko Deželak of the SCD assumed the post of Minister of Economic Relations and Development (a portfolio hitherto held by the LDS).

In January 1996 the ULSD withdrew from the governing coalition, following the Prime Minister's proposal to replace the ULSD Minister of Economic Affairs, Dr Maks Tajnikar. Tajnikar was subsequently replaced by an independent deputy, Metod Dragonja, and the three other positions left vacant by the ULSD withdrawal were allocated to one member of the LDS and two of the SCD. In May Thaler was defeated in a motion of no confidence, prompted by his acceptance of a compromise solution to a dispute with Italy (which had prevented Slovenia's accession to associate membership of the EU—see below) opposed by the SCD.

At the elections to the Državni zbor, which took place on 10 November 1996, the LDS returned 25 deputies to the chamber, and subsequently increased its overall strength to 45 seats, having gained the support of the ULSD, the Democratic Party of Pensioners of Slovenia (DeSUS), the SNP and the representatives of the Hungarian and Italian minorities. A newly formed opposition alliance, Slovenian Spring, comprising the Slovenian People's Party (SPP), the SCD and the SDPS, also held 45 seats in the Državni zbor. Consequently, Kučan's nomination that Drnovšek be returned to the office of Prime Minister failed to obtain the requisite majority of more than one-half of the deputies. Following a protracted delay, an SCD deputy withdrew from the party to become an independent deputy, and agreed to support Drnovšek's candidacy, and in January 1997 Drnovšek was re-elected as Prime Minister. However, the continued absence of a majority in the Državni zbor impeded the formation of a new government, with the parties belonging to Slovenian Spring refusing to accept an administration headed by Drnovšek. Drnovšek consequently failed to secure sufficient support for his proposed new coalition administration, which was to include representatives of all the parties in the legislature. In late February the SPP (which held 19 seats) finally agreed to join a coalition government with the LDS and DeSUS, which was subsequently approved by 52 votes in the Državni zbor.

Following an agreement in July 1997 by parliamentary party leaders to co-operate over the country's bid to join the EU, a two-thirds' majority of the Državni zbor voted to amend the Constitution, to allow foreigners to purchase land in Slovenia, thereby meeting the requirements for ratification of the EU association agreement. The agreement was ratified by the legislature on the following day. The European Commission subsequently recommended that the EU begin membership negotiations with Slovenia in 1998. Despite this positive development, in late July 1997 Thaler resigned as Minister of Foreign Affairs. Boris Frlec was appointed to the post in September.

A presidential election took place on 23 November 1997. Kučan won a second term of office, with 55.6% of the votes cast. His nearest rival, the President of the Državni zbor, Janez Podobnik, secured 18.4% of the votes. Indirect elections to the Državni svet followed on 26 November.

In January 2000 Frlec resigned as Minister of Foreign Affairs, following criticism of his failure to resolve long-standing disputes between the Governments of Slovenia and Croatia (particularly regarding the joint sea border and the Krško nuclear power station—see below). He was replaced in February by Dr Dmitrij Rupel. In March it was announced that the SPP and the SCD were to merge in the following month, and that the nine ministers belonging to the SPP would resign from the Government. Drnovšek was obliged to resign in April, after his proposed new government was rejected by the Državni zbor. The SPP and SCD merged as planned in mid-April, and subsequently formed a new alliance, Coalition Slovenia, with the SDPS. Coalition Slovenia nominated Andrej Bajuk as a candidate for the premiership, and in early May, having twice been narrowly rejected by the Državni zbor, Bajuk was endorsed as Prime Minister. The Government, which was approved by the Državni zbor in June, notably included Peterle as Minister of Foreign Affairs and Janša as Minister of Defence.

In July 2000 the approval by 70 of the 90 deputies in the Državni zbor of constitutional amendments, providing for the introduction of a system of proportional representation in the forthcoming elections, resulted in division within the SPP. Bajuk (who had opposed the new legislation) announced his resignation from the reconstituted SPP and his intention of establishing a new breakaway party. Kučan subsequently declared that the legislative elections would take place in October. In August Bajuk was elected Chairman of the newly formed New Slovenia—Christian People's Party (NSi), which was also joined by Peterle. The elections to the Državni zbor on 15 October were conducted under the new system, whereby 88 deputies were elected on the basis of proportional representation, and the remaining two deputies were elected as representatives of the Italian and Hungarian minority communities. The LDS secured 34 seats (an increase of nine seats compared with 1996), while the SDPS won 14 seats, the ULSD 11 seats, the SPP nine seats, and the NSi eight seats. Consequently, Drnovšek was re-elected to the premiership by the Državni zbor in early November. Following inter-party negotiations, a coalition agreement was reached by the LDS, the ULSD, the SPP and DeSUS. A new Government, which included several prominent members of Drnovšek's previous administrations, was endorsed by the legislature at the end of November. Drnovšek announced that administrative reforms essential to EU requirements were to be expedited.

The presidential election on 10 November 2002 was contested by nine candidates. (Kučan was prohibited, under the terms of the Constitution, from seeking election for a third term.) Drnovšek won the highest proportion of votes, with 44.4%, but failed to secure an outright majority; a second round between him and Barbara Brezigar, a state prosecutor, who was supported by the SDPS and the NSi (and had received 30.8% of the votes), was scheduled for 1 December. At this second ballot, Drnovšek was elected to the presidency, with 56.5% of the votes cast. Anton Rop, also a member of the LDS and hitherto Minister of Finance, was nominated to replace Drnovšek as Prime Minister, and on 19 December a new Government was approved by the Državni zbor. Drnovšek was inaugurated as President on 22 December. In September 2003 the SDPS was reconstituted as the Slovenian Democratic Party (SDP).

In early 2004 the Državni zbor approved legislation providing for the restoration of citizenship to 18,000 nationals of former Yugoslav republics, who (resident in Slovenia at the time of its independence) had been removed from population records and lost their residency rights. However, at a referendum, which was conducted in April, following pressure from the SNP and three right-wing parties, some 94% of the votes cast by 31% of the electorate rejected adoption of the new legislation. Following the referendum, the SPP, the only party in the governing coalition to have supported the referendum, withdrew from the Government (which was subsequently reorganized). Following the accession of Slovenia to full membership of the EU on 1 May (see below), the first elections to the European Parliament took place on 13 June, although only about 28% of the electorate participated. In the elections, the NSi, the SDP and the LDS each obtained two mandates, while the ULSD received one seat. In July Rop dismissed Rupel as Minister of Foreign Affairs; Rupel had announced that he was transferring his support to the opposition SDP prior to forthcoming legislative elections. Ivo Vajgl, hitherto ambassador to Germany, was subsequently appointed to the post.

At the legislative elections on 3 October 2004, the centre-right SDP secured 29.1% of votes cast and 29 seats in the 90-member Državni zbor, defeating the ruling LDS (with 22.8% of the votes and 23 seats). Janša was appointed Prime Minister on 9 November. Following lengthy inter-party negotiations, the SDP reached a coalition agreement with the SPP, the NSi and DeSUS, and a new Government was approved by 51 votes in the Državni zbor on 3 December. In April 2005 the ULSD was reconstituted as the Social Democrats (SD), under the continued leadership of Borut Pahor.

In late November 2005 trade unions organized a mass demonstration in Ljubljana (the largest to be staged since 1991), in protest at government plans for extensive economic reforms, including the proposed introduction of a uniform rate of value-added tax. In December the Državni zbor approved the appointment of an economist as Minister without Portfolio; Jože Damijan was to head a newly established government development office and be responsible for the implementation of the reform strategy that was intended to facilitate Slovenia's adoption of the common European currency, the euro, in January 2007. Later that month this strategy was approved by the Državni zbor. In March 2006 Damijan announced his resignation, but Janša announced that the reforms would continue as planned. In December the Minister of Labour, Family and Social Affairs, Janez Drobnič of the NSi, was removed by the Državni zbor, on the grounds that he had mismanaged dialogue over labour and social reforms.

In March 2007 dissent between Drnovšek and the Državni zbor resulted in failure to appoint a new Governor of the national bank to replace Mitja Gaspari, whose second term in the post expired at the end of that month. Drnovšek's nomination of Gaspari for a third term, and subsequently of his deputy, Andrej Rant, was rejected by the legislature. In June Janša finally agreed to support Drnovšek's nomination of a former Minister of Finance, Marko Kranjec, as Governor, which was subsequently approved by a substantial majority in the Državni zbor.

At a first round of voting in the presidential election on 21 October 2007, of the six candidates, Peterle, who contested the election as an independent with the support of the SDP, the SPP and the NSi, won 28.7% of the votes cast, while Danilo Türk, a former UN diplomat and independent candidate supported by DeSUS and the SD, won 24.5% and Gaspari obtained 24.1%. At the second round of voting, contested by Peterle and Türk on 11 November, Türk was elected President, with 68.0% of the votes cast. In mid-November the Government won a motion of confidence proposed by Janša, who had complained that opposition criticism was impeding preparations to adopt the rotational presidency of the EU. Türk was inaugurated on 22 December, upon the expiry of the mandate of Drnovšek (who had decided not to seek re-election and, following a period of prolonged ill health, died in early 2008).

Elections to the Državni zbor were conducted on 21 September 2008. The SD secured 29 seats in the chamber, with 30.5% of votes cast, narrowly defeating Janša's SDP, which won 28 seats (29.3% of votes); For Real—New Politics (Zares—a party established in 2007 by breakaway members of the LDS) received nine seats (9.4% of votes), DeSUS seven seats (7.5%), the SNP five seats (5.4%), the SPP (allied with the Youth Party of Slovenia) five seats (5.2%) and the LDS five seats (5.2%), while the NSi failed to achieve the minimum share for representation. Voter turn-out was 63.1%. Türk officially nominated Pahor as Prime Minister on 3 November; a coalition agreement was subsequently reached between the SD, Zares, DeSUS and the LDS, which together held 50 of the 90 seats in the legislature. Pahor's new Government was approved by the Državni zbor on 21 November; following his pledge to form a technocratic administration, it contained seven independent members, including Samuel Žbogar (hitherto the Slovenian ambassador in the USA) as the Minister of Foreign Affairs and Gaspari as Minister without Portfolio, responsible for Development and European Affairs. A new post, that of Minister without Portfolio, responsible for Slovenes Abroad, was also created. Pahor pledged that the introduction of measures to combat the effects of the international financial crisis would be a priority for the Government.

Areas of disputed border territory with Croatia, most notably the maritime boundary in the Bay of Piran in Istria, undermined otherwise harmonious relations between the two countries following independence. In July 1993 tensions between the two countries prevented the signing of agreements on friendship and co-operation and on the regulation of bilateral payments, although protocols governing other issues, including trade and economic relations, were concluded. In November Slovenian proposals to decommission the country's nuclear power plant, at Krško (constructed by the former federal authorities to supply energy to both Slovenia and Croatia), prompted protests by Croatia, which was reliant on the installation for one-quarter of its energy requirements. Little progress was achieved during 1994 in efforts to delineate the joint border, and the resumption of construction by Croatia of border facilities on Slovenian territory provoked renewed protests by the Slovenian Government. In October the Croatian Government submitted a formal protest to Slovenia, following the approval of legislation providing for a reorganization of local government boundaries in Slovenia, as part of which four villages in the disputed area were to be included within the Slovenian municipality of Piran (Pirano). The Državni zbor subsequently agreed to delay implementation of the law (and thus the holding of elections) in three villages, pending a resolution of the border issue. In February 1995 a meeting of the Slovenian-Croatian joint border commission agreed that, since the process of delineating the border would be lengthy, this should be pursued separately from other bilateral concerns. In March Slovenia and Croatia agreed to divide ownership of the Krško nuclear station equally between the two countries.

In July 1998 Slovenia ceased distributing electricity generated at the Krško nuclear power plant to Croatia, claiming that it had failed to pay for power, valued at some US $14m., already supplied. In the same month Slovenia privatized its share of the Krško power plant. Croatia was reported to have resumed payments to Slovenia in August, and subsequently the transfer of electricity was restored. In November it was announced that the dispute over the Krško nuclear power plant would be resolved on the basis of co-ownership. Following the election of a new Government in Croatia in early 2000, bilateral relations improved significantly. After lengthy negotiations between Drnovšek and the Croatian Prime Minister, Ivica Račan, an agreement resolving the outstanding issues of contention between Slovenia and Croatia was signed in July 2001. The accord (which required endorsement by the legislatures of the two countries) granted Slovenia access to the Adriatic Sea through the Bay of Piran, and provided for continued joint management of the Krško nuclear installation; the four disputed border villages were to remain under Croatian sovereignty. In 2003 a further dispute erupted between Slovenia and Croatia, after the Croatian Government announced plans to establish an economic zone in the Adriatic Sea, which would remove Slovenia's direct access to international waters. The Slovenian Government temporarily withdrew its ambassador in Croatia.

In August 2005 it was announced that Croatia had withdrawn its ambassador to Slovenia, following the Slovenian Government's decision to declare a fishing zone in the border region. (The ambassador was returned by early September.) After the Državni zbor approved the Government's decision, Croatia declared the fishing zone to be illegitimate and demanded that the issue be referred to international arbitration. The Slovenian Government demonstrated reluctance to enter into international arbitration and, following the official opening of Croatia's accession negotiations with the EU earlier that month, threatened to obstruct Croatian membership. The Slovenian Government also continued to reject claims by Croatia that it was liable for outstanding debts owed to Croatian citizens by the former Ljubljanska Banka of Slovenia. At the end of 2005 the Croatian national power utility submitted to an international centre for investment disputes a demand for compensation for undelivered electricity from the Krško installation. In January 2007 the dispute between Croatia and Slovenia over their joint maritime boundary was revived with a diplomatic protest by Slovenia that the Croatian Government had pre-empted a border demarcation by extending concessions for petroleum exploration in the disputed region. The Croatian Government reiterated demands that the dispute be referred to international arbitration. At the beginning of 2008 Croatia implemented legislation enforcing its environmental fishing zone in the Adriatic Sea, which it had declared in 2003 with the objective of protecting fishing stocks; Slovenia, together with Italy, opposed the measure, which would result in significant financial damage for their fleets. Slovenia (which had assumed the EU's rotational presidency) indicated that the issue would impede Croatia's ongoing EU integration process. In March 2008, following continued pressure from the EU, Croatia agreed that implementation of the environmental fishing zone would be postponed until its anticipated accession to the Union.

In October 2008 the Slovenian Government demanded that Croatia withdraw documentation submitted as part of its EU accession negotiations, which was considered to predetermine the common maritime border that remained under dispute. At an intergovernmental conference in December, Croatia was prevented by a Slovenian veto from making progress in 11 negotiating chapters. The Croatian Government issued a statement denying that the documentation predetermined the maritime border. The European Commission expressed concern at Slovenia's decision to impede the accession negotiations and urged both countries to resolve the issue through bilateral discussions; however, Croatian Prime Minister Ivo Sanader demanded that the dispute be referred to international arbitration. In early February 2009 the Državni zbor ratified the protocols for Croatia's accession to the North Atlantic Treaty Organization (NATO), which had been supported by Slovenia's governing coalition on the grounds that it would improve regional stability. Later in February, however, following an initiative by the SPP that a referendum be conducted on Croatia's prospective NATO membership, the Državni zbor adopted a declaration that Slovenia's national interests be protected during Croatia's NATO accession process and stating its territorial claim. Although the SPP proceeded with the organization of a petition in support of a referendum on Croatia's NATO membership, it failed to gather the 40,000 signatures required under the Slovenian Constitution for the scheduling of a national referendum. A meeting between Sanader and Pahor, in Mokrice, Slovenia, in late February failed to produce any agreement; Sanader continued to insist that the border issue be referred to the International Court of Justice, while the Slovenian Government announced its acceptance of a proposal by the European Commissioner responsible for Enlargement, Olli Rehn, that the European Commission mediate a resolution to the dispute. Nevertheless, Türk ratified Croatia's NATO accession protocol in late March; Croatia was admitted as a member of the Alliance in early April. After the EU indefinitely postponed an accession conference with Croatia later in April, pending progress in the outstanding dispute, it increasingly appeared that the impasse was endangering the Croatian Government's objective of completing negotiations by the end of 2009. Both Slovenia and Croatia were reported to have reacted favourably to a proposal by Rehn for the establishment of an arbitration court, comprising five judges to be nominated jointly by Croatia and Slovenia; Pahor and Sanader agreed to meet in early May, following internal consultations on the proposal.

Slovenia and Croatia are united in their opposition to movements for Istrian autonomy and to any revision to their detriment of the 1975 Treaty of Osimo, which had defined the borders between the SFRY and Italy, and had provided for the payment by the SFRY of compensation for Italian property transferred to Yugoslav sovereignty after 1947. In 1993 some 35,000 Italians were reported to be demanding compensation for, or the restitution of, property in Slovenia. Consequently, in July 1994 the Italian Government of Silvio Berlusconi stated that until the Slovenian authorities agreed to compensate Italian nationals who had fled after 1947 from territory now held by Slovenia, and whose property had been confiscated under communist rule, Italy would block efforts by Slovenia to achieve further integration with Western Europe. Italy thus prevented scheduled negotiations on an association agreement between Slovenia and the EU until March 1995, when the new Italian Government of Lamberto Dini withdrew the veto. However, it was not until May 1996 that Slovenia and Italy agreed to a compromise solution proposed by Spain, whereby Slovenia was to allow EU nationals to purchase property in Slovenia, on a reciprocal basis, within four years of the association agreement's ratification, and EU citizens who had previously permanently resided in Slovenia for a period of three years (thus including Italian nationals who had fled after the Second World War) would be permitted to buy immediately. In June Slovenia finally signed an association agreement with the EU, and simultaneously applied for full membership of the organization. In July 1997 the Državni zbor voted in favour of amending the Constitution in accordance with the agreement.

In April 1993 Slovenia signed a trade and economic co-operation accord with the EU, and it achieved associate membership of the organization in June 1996 (see above). Slovenia joined the Council of Europe (see p. 236) in May 1993, and in December was granted observer status at the Western European Union (see p. 442) conference in Paris, France. In March 1994 it was announced that Slovenia was to join NATO's 'Partnership for Peace' (see p. 353) programme. In January 1996 Slovenia was admitted to the Central European Free Trade Agreement (now Association). Formal accession negotiations with the EU commenced in November 1998. In December 2002, at a summit meeting in Copenhagen, Denmark, Slovenia was one of 10 nations officially invited to become members of the EU with effect from 2004. Meanwhile, at a summit meeting in Prague, Czech Republic, in November 2002, Slovenia was formally invited to join NATO in 2004. A national referendum on the issue of joining both organizations was conducted on 23 March 2003; some 89.6% of voters endorsed membership of the EU, and 66.1% membership of NATO. On 29 March 2004 Slovenia was officially admitted to NATO, together with Bulgaria, Estonia, Latvia, Lithuania, Romania and Slovakia, at a ceremony in Washington, DC, USA. Slovenia's accession to the EU followed on 1 May. In June 2006 EU leaders, meeting in Brussels, Belgium, approved Slovenia's application to adopt the European common currency, the euro, with effect from 1 January 2007. The decision was confirmed by EU Ministers of Finance on 11 July, and Slovenia joined the euro zone as scheduled. In December Slovenia implemented the EU's Schengen Agreement on freedom of travel, effectively removing border controls between those states subject to the Agreement. Ratification of the EU's Lisbon Treaty, which was designed to reform the Union's institutions, was approved by the Državni zbor in January 2008 and received presidential assent in the following month.

Government

Under the terms of the 1991 Constitution, as subsequently modified, legislative power is vested in the 90-member Državni zbor (National Assembly). Of the 90 deputies, who serve a term of four years, 88 are elected on the basis of proportional representation; two members are representatives of the Hungarian and Italian minorities. The Državni svet (National Council), which is elected for five years, comprises 22 directly elected members and 18 members chosen by an electoral college to represent various social, economic, trading, political and local interest groups; the Council's role is mainly advisory, but it is empowered to veto decisions of the Državni zbor. The Prime Minister, who is elected by the Državni zbor, nominates the Government (subject to the approval of the legislature). The President of the Republic has largely ceremonial powers, and is directly elected for a maximum of two five-year terms. For administrative purposes, Slovenia is divided into 193 municipalities, 11 of which are designated as city municipalities.

SLOVENIA

Defence

As assessed at November 2008, the active Slovenian armed forces numbered 7,200 (with 3,800 reserves). There was a paramilitary police force of 4,500 (with 5,000 reserves). In September 2003 the Government announced the abolition of compulsory military service, prior to the country's official accession to the North Atlantic Treaty Organization (NATO, see p. 351) on 29 March 2004. The budget for 2008 allocated €560m. to defence.

Economic Affairs

In 2007, according to the World Bank, Slovenia's gross national income (GNI), measured at average 2005–07 prices, was US $42,306m., equivalent to $20,960 per head (or $26,640 per head on an international purchasing-power parity basis). During 2000–07, it was estimated, the population increased at an average annual rate of 0.2%, while gross domestic product (GDP) per head increased, in real terms, by an average of 4.1% per year. Overall GDP increased, in real terms, at an average annual rate of 4.4% in 2000–07, according to official figures. Real GDP increased by 6.8% in 2007.

Agriculture (including hunting, forestry and fishing) contributed 2.4% of GDP and engaged 4.7% of the employed labour force in 2007. The principal crops are cereals (particularly maize and wheat), potatoes, sugar beet and fruits (especially grapes and apples). Slovenia's forests, which cover about one-half of the country, are an important natural resource. Agricultural GDP declined at an average rate of 2.2% per year during 2000–07. The GDP of the sector decreased by 11.0% in 2007.

Industry (including mining, manufacturing, construction and power) contributed 34.4% of GDP and engaged 37.7% of the employed labour force in 2007. Industrial GDP increased at an average rate of 5.4% per year in 2000–07. Sectoral GDP increased by 8.0% in 2007.

Mining and quarrying contributed 0.4% of GDP and engaged 0.4% of the employed labour force in 2007. The principal activity is coal-mining; lead and zinc are also extracted, together with relatively small amounts of natural gas, petroleum and salt. Slovenia also has small deposits of uranium. The GDP of the mining sector increased at an average rate of 2.6% per year in 2000–07. Mining GDP increased by 7.1% in 2006, but declined by 3.1% in 2007.

Manufacturing contributed 23.4% of GDP and engaged 26.6% of the employed labour force in 2007. Manufacturing GDP increased at an average rate of 5.5% per year in 2000–07. GDP in the manufacturing sector increased by 7.8% in 2007.

A nuclear power station was constructed in Slovenia by the former Yugoslav authorities to provide energy for both Slovenia and Croatia (see Recent History). In 2005 nuclear power stations provided 38.9% of energy requirements, coal-fired electricity-generating stations provided 34.9%, and hydroelectric power stations provided 22.9%. Imports of fuel products comprised 9.4% of the value of merchandise imports in 2007.

The services sector contributed 63.3% of GDP and engaged 57.7% of the employed labour force in 2007. Tourism is a significant source of revenue; tourist activity was adversely affected by the political instability of 1991, but the number of arrivals recovered, reaching 2,681,200 in 2007. The GDP of the services sector increased at an average rate of 4.4% per year in 2000–07. Growth in the services sector was 6.8% in 2007.

In 2007 Slovenia recorded a visible trade deficit of US $2,310m., and there was a deficit of $2,293m. on the current account of the balance of payments. In that year Slovenia's principal source of imports was Germany (accounting for 19.4% of the total); other major suppliers were Italy (18.3%), Austria and France. Germany was also the principal market for exports (taking 18.8% of the total in that year); Italy, Croatia, Austria and France were also significant purchasers. The major imports in 2007 were machinery and transport equipment, basic manufactures, chemical products, miscellaneous manufactured articles, mineral fuels and crude materials. The principal exports in that year were machinery and transport equipment (particularly road vehicles and parts, and electrical machinery), basic manufactures (notably metal manufactures), chemicals, and miscellaneous manufactured articles.

Slovenia's overall budgetary deficit for 2007 was €372.7m., equivalent to 1.1% of GDP. At the end of 2007 total central government debt amounted to US $10,866m. The annual rate of inflation averaged 4.8% in 2000–07. Consumer prices increased by 3.6% in 2007. An estimated 7.3% of the total labour force were unemployed in 2007.

Slovenia has joined several international organizations, including the IMF, the World Bank and (as a 'Country of Operations') the European Bank for Reconstruction and Development (see p. 251). The country became a full member of the World Trade Organization (see p. 410) in July 1995 and acceded to full membership of the European Union (EU, see p. 255) on 1 May 2004.

By the mid-1990s important advances in the transformation of the economy had allowed Slovenia to gain a favourable position among the countries chosen to participate in negotiations to join the EU. At April 2003 Slovenia had achieved sustained convergence in per-head income to about 70% of the EU average. Slovenia formally acceded to the EU on 1 May 2004 and, following the successful adoption of measures to reduce inflation, achieved entry into the exchange rate mechanism (ERM II) in June. The continued reduction of inflation in order to meet EU levels was central to government policy. Slovenia adopted the euro on 1 January 2007. In November 2005 the Government announced extensive economic reforms, including measures to increase competitiveness, reform the labour market and the pension and health systems, and resume the privatization of state-owned enterprises. Trade unions responded by organizing mass protests, in particular against plans to introduce a uniform rate of value-added tax, which they claimed would adversely affect the standard of living. Nevertheless, the economic reform strategy was officially approved by the legislature in December. Inflation increased to 3.6% in 2007. Observers largely attributed the rise in consumer prices to the rigid labour market, which placed constant upward pressure on wages and undermined the overall competitiveness of the economy. Consumer price inflation continued to rise, reaching an annual rate of 6.9% in July 2008, when Slovenia recorded the highest level of inflation in the euro zone, and an annual average rate of some 5.5% in 2008. However, a sharp contraction in demand for Slovenia's exports as a result of the global economic slowdown, particularly in the EU, in late 2008 and early 2009 and a subsequent reduction in domestic consumption and investment helped to contain inflation, which stood at an annual rate of 1.1% in April 2009. The IMF forecast that the budget deficit would increase from 0.3% of GDP in 2008 to 3.4% in 2009 as the Government increased spending to stimulate the economy. GDP growth of 3.5% was estimated in 2008, but it was forecast that the economy would contract by 1.5% in 2009 as the international economic crisis intensified.

Education

Primary education is free and compulsory for all children between the ages of six and 15 years. In ethnically mixed regions, two methods of schooling have been developed: bilingual or with instruction in the minority languages. Various types of secondary education, beginning at 15 and lasting between two and five years, are also available. In 2005/06 95% of children in the relevant age-group (males 96%; females 95%) were enrolled at primary schools, while enrolment in secondary education included 90% of children in the appropriate age-group (males 90%; females 91%). Slovenia's four universities are situated in Ljubljana, Maribor, Koper (the University of Primorska) and Nova Gorica, with 60,284, 23,363, 6,490 and 725 students, respectively, in 2008/09; a further 7,266 students were enrolled in other higher education institutions in that year. Expenditure on education by all levels of government in 2003 was estimated at SIT 350,062m., representing 6.1% of total government spending.

Public Holidays

2009: 1–2 January (New Year), 8 February (Prešeren Day, National Day of Culture), 10–13 April (Easter), 27 April (Resistance Day), 1–2 May (Labour Day), 25 June (National Statehood Day), 15 August (Assumption), 31 October (Reformation Day), 1 November (All Saints' Day), 25 December (Christmas Day), 26 December (Independence Day).

2010: 1–2 January (New Year), 8 February (Prešeren Day, National Day of Culture), 2–5 April (Easter), 27 April (Resistance Day), 1–2 May (Labour Day), 25 June (National Statehood Day), 15 August (Assumption), 31 October (Reformation Day), 1 November (All Saints' Day), 25 December (Christmas Day), 26 December (Independence Day).

Weights and Measures

The metric system is in force.

Statistical Survey

Source (unless otherwise indicated): Statistical Office of the Republic of Slovenia, 1000 Ljubljana, Vožarski pot 12; tel. (1) 2415104; fax (1) 2415344; e-mail info.stat@gov.si; internet www.stat.si.

Area and Population

AREA, POPULATION AND DENSITY

Area (sq km)	20,273*
Population (census results)	
31 March 1991	1,913,355
31 March 2002	
Males	958,576
Females	1,005,460
Total	1,964,036
Population (official estimates at 30 June)†	
2006	2,008,516
2007	2,019,406
2008	2,039,399
Density (per sq km) at 30 June 2008	100.6

* 7,827 sq miles.
† Estimates are calculated on a *de jure* basis.

POPULATION BY ETHNIC GROUP
(2002 census)

Ethnic group	Number	%
Slovenes	1,631,363	83.06
Serbs	38,964	1.98
Croats	35,642	1.81
Bosniaks	21,542	1.10
Muslims*	10,467	0.53
Others	226,058	11.51
Total (incl. others)	1,964,036	100.00

* Including persons claiming Muslim ethnicity rather than religious adherence.

PRINCIPAL TOWNS
(population at 2002 census)

Ljubljana (capital)	265,881		Koper (Capodistria)	47,539
Maribor	110,668		Novo mesto	40,925
Kranj	51,225		Nova Gorica	35,640
Celje	48,081			

Mid-2007 ('000, incl. suburbs, UN estimate): Ljubljana 244 (Source: UN, *World Urbanization Prospects: The 2007 Revision*).

BIRTHS, MARRIAGES AND DEATHS

	Registered live births		Registered marriages		Registered deaths	
	Number	Rate (per 1,000)	Number	Rate (per 1,000)	Number	Rate (per 1,000)
2000	18,180	9.1	7,201	3.6	18,588	9.3
2001	17,477	8.8	6,935	3.5	18,508	9.3
2002	17,501	8.8	7,064	3.5	18,701	9.4
2003	17,321	8.7	6,756	3.4	19,451	9.7
2004	17,961	9.0	6,558	3.3	18,523	9.3
2005	18,157	9.1	5,769	2.9	18,825	9.4
2006	18,932	9.4	6,368	3.2	18,180	9.1
2007	19,823	9.8	6,373	3.2	18,584	9.2

Life expectancy (years at birth, WHO estimates): 78.1 (males 74.4; females 81.7) in 2006 (Source: WHO, *World Health Statistics*).

IMMIGRATION AND EMIGRATION

	2005	2006	2007
Long-term immigrants	15,041	20,016	29,193
Long-term emigrants	8,605	13,749	14,943

ECONOMICALLY ACTIVE POPULATION
('000 persons aged 15 years and over, December)

	2005	2006	2007
Agriculture, hunting, forestry and fishing	38.6	38.4	40.2
Mining and quarrying	4.1	3.9	3.7
Manufacturing	228.3	228.7	229.7
Electricity, gas and water supply	11.3	11.4	11.3
Construction	65.2	71.9	80.9
Wholesale and retail trade; repair of motor vehicles, motorcycles, and personal and household goods	107.9	108.9	114.3
Hotels and restaurants	31.1	31.7	33.0
Transport, storage and communications	50.7	52.6	57.0
Financial intermediation	21.3	21.9	22.6
Real estate, renting and business activities	66.8	72.5	77.8
Public administration and defence; compulsory social security	49.8	49.9	50.4
Education	58.2	58.8	59.1
Health and social work	50.2	51.0	51.4
Other social and personal services	29.7	30.9	32.3
Private households with employed persons	0.5	0.4	0.5
Total employed	813.6	833.0	864.4
Unemployed	92.6	78.3	68.4
Total labour force	906.1	911.3	932.8

Health and Welfare

KEY INDICATORS

Total fertility rate (children per woman, 2006)	1.3
Under-5 mortality rate (per 1,000 live births, 2006)	4
HIV/AIDS (% of persons aged 15–49, 2007)	<0.1
Physicians (per 1,000 head, 2005)	2.4
Hospital beds (per 1,000 head, 2006)	4.8
Health expenditure (2006): US $ per head (PPP)	2,065
Health expenditure (2006): % of GDP	8.4
Health expenditure (2006): public (% of total)	73.0
Human Development Index (2006): ranking	26
Human Development Index (2006): value	0.923

For sources and definitions, see explanatory note on p. vi.

SLOVENIA

Agriculture

PRINCIPAL CROPS
('000 metric tons)

	2005	2006	2007
Wheat	141.3	134.4	133.3
Barley	61.2	61.6	67.9
Maize	351.2	276.1	308.3
Oats	7.6	6.3	5.5
Triticale (wheat-rye hybrid)	7.8	10.9	12.0
Potatoes	144.7	107.0	131.1
Sugar beet	260.1	262.0	260.0*
Cabbages and other brassicas	25.0	26.1	22.2
Lettuce and chicory	7.4	8.4	12.5
Tomatoes	6.6	4.6	4.4
Chillies and peppers, green	10.2	4.8	3.7
Onions, dry	7.2	5.4	4.5
Apples	106.2	119.2	114.5
Pears	8.2	11.4	11.8
Peaches and nectarines	13.3	11.2	9.3
Plums	4.3	5.4	6.3
Grapes	120.7	105.5	122.5

* FAO estimate.

Aggregate production ('000 metric tons, may include official, semi-official or estimated data): Total cereals 576.3 in 2005, 493.6 in 2006, 531.9 in 2007; Total roots and tubers 144.7 in 2005, 107.0 in 2006, 130.1 in 2007; Total vegetables (incl. melons) 89.1 in 2005, 80.3 in 2006, 66.4 in 2007; Total fruits (excl. melons) 260.0 in 2005, 260.2 in 2006, 271.2 in 2007.

Source: FAO.

LIVESTOCK
('000 head)

	2005	2006	2007
Cattle	451	453	451
Pigs	534	547	575
Sheep	119	129	132
Goats	23	25	28
Horses	20	21*	22*
Chickens	3,114	2,684	2,930
Turkeys	130	135	110

* FAO estimate.
Source: FAO.

LIVESTOCK PRODUCTS
('000 metric tons)

	2005	2006	2007*
Cattle meat	45.4	39.5	35.6
Pig meat	63.9	61.1	57.0
Sheep meat	1.6	1.6	1.9
Chicken meat	45.6	44.0	41.0
Duck meat*	1.2	1.2	1.2
Goose meat*	3.8	4.3	3.7
Turkey meat	9.3	5.5	8.2
Cows' milk	659.7	643.1	654.0
Hen eggs	14.3	15.8	17.1

* FAO estimate(s).
Source: FAO.

Forestry

ROUNDWOOD REMOVALS
('000 cubic metres, excl. bark)

	2005	2006	2007
Sawlogs, veneer logs and logs for sleepers	1,403	1,712	1,699
Pulpwood	288	445	353
Other industrial wood	99	39	41
Fuel wood	943	984	788
Total	2,733	3,180	2,881

Source: FAO.

SAWNWOOD PRODUCTION
('000 cubic metres, incl. railway sleepers)

	2005	2006	2007
Coniferous (softwood)	387	446	477
Broadleaved (hardwood)	140	134	151
Total	527	580	628

Source: FAO.

Fishing

(metric tons, live weight)

	2004	2005	2006
Capture	1,022	1,223	1,131
Common carp	83	76	80
European pilchard (sardine)	374	327	298
European anchovy	238	438	410
Aquaculture	1,571	1,346	1,369
Common carp	199	241	204
Rainbow trout	1,001	805	894
European seabass	78	25	30
Mediterranean mussel	164	201	163
Total catch	2,593	2,569	2,500

Source: FAO.

Mining

(metric tons, unless otherwise indicated)

	2004	2005	2006
Brown coal ('000 metric tons)	611	594	587
Lignite ('000 metric tons)	4,198	3,945	3,934
Natural gas ('000 cubic metres)	4,500	4,335	4,163
Crude petroleum	344	298	284
Bentonite*	1,000	140	130
Quartz and quartzite (incl. glass sand)*	200,000	200,000	200,000
Sand and gravel (excl. glass sand)	5,000,000*	3,750,707	6,871,519
Pumice*	40,000	40,000	40,000
Salt	1,000*	803	1,624

* Estimate(s).
Source: US Geological Survey.

Industry

SELECTED PRODUCTS
('000 metric tons, unless otherwise indicated)

	2004	2005	2006
Wine ('000 hectolitres)	361	293	255
Footwear (excl. rubber) ('000 pairs)	3,599	3,108	3,150
Veneer sheets ('000 cubic metres)	48	64	64
Plywood ('000 cubic metres)*	27	27	29
Mechanical wood pulp*	32	50	50
Chemical wood pulp*	121	111	62
Newsprint*	31	116	116
Household and sanitary paper*	161	63	39
Wrapping and packaging paper and paperboard	105	105	99
Cement†‡	1,300	1,500	1,500
Crude steel ingots (incl. crude steel for casting)§	566	583	628
Refined lead†	16.0	15.4	15.4
Passenger motor cars ('000)	140	185	n.a.
Electric energy (million kWh)	15,272	15,117	15,115

* Source: FAO.
† Source: US Geological Survey.
‡ Estimated production.
§ Source: International Iron and Steel Institute (Brussels).

Finance

CURRENCY AND EXCHANGE RATES

Monetary Units
100 cent = 1 euro (€).

Sterling, Dollar and Euro Equivalents (31 December 2008)
£1 sterling = 1.0475 euros;
US $1 = 0.7185 euros;
€10 = £9.55 = $13.92.

Average Exchange Rate (euros per US $)
2006   0.7971
2007   0.7306
2008   0.6827

The tolar was introduced in October 1991, replacing (initially at par) the Yugoslav dinar. Slovenia participated in the common European currency, the euro, with effect from 1 January 2007; a fixed exchange rate of €1 = 239.640 tolars was in operation. The euro and the tolar circulated alongside each other until 14 January, after which time the euro (comprising 100 cent) became the sole legal tender.

BUDGET
(€ '000)*

Revenue	2006	2007	2008†
Tax revenue	11,761,990	12,757,942	13,937,239
Taxes on income and profits	2,735,295	2,917,671	3,442,172
Taxes on payroll, property, etc.	472,935	418,141	258,038
Social security contributions	4,231,224	4,597,973	5,095,009
Domestic taxes on goods and services	4,077,290	4,498,577	4,805,271
Taxes on international trade and transactions	50,681	117,079	120,092
Other current revenue	633,312	709,227	853,193
Capital revenue and grants	172,165	148,422	124,971
Transferred revenues	42,811	42,500	54,225
Receipts from EU budget	348,416	347,997	365,374
Total	12,958,693	14,006,088	15,335,002

Expenditure‡	2006	2007	2008†
Current expenditure (excl. transfers)	5,688,953	5,950,896	6,555,674
Interest payments	376,392	356,983	335,119
Current transfers	5,925,824	6,143,945	6,741,108
Capital expenditure (excl. transfers)	901,419	1,130,466	1,251,964
Capital transfers	404,589	334,274	458,023
Payments to EU budget	287,892	355,904	427,915
Total	13,208,676	13,915,485	15,434,684

* Figures represent a consolidation of the accounts of the central Government (State Budget, Pension Fund and Health Insurance Fund) and local administrative authorities.
† Preliminary figures.
‡ Excluding net lending (€ '000): 46,301 in 2006; 463,352 in 2007; –86,284 in 2008.

Source: Ministry of Finance, Ljubljana.

INTERNATIONAL RESERVES
(US $ million at 31 December)

	2007	2008
Gold (market prices)	86.16	89.10
IMF special drawing rights	12.59	11.80
Reserve position in IMF	25.17	46.35
Foreign exchange	942.04	809.91
Total	1,065.96	957.16

Source: IMF, *International Financial Statistics*.

MONEY SUPPLY
(million tolars at 31 December)

	2003	2004	2005
Currency outside banks	156,040	167,920	187,230
Demand deposits at commercial banks	608,480	808,110	917,310
Total money (incl. others)	767,700	982,240	1,107,390

Note: Figures are rounded to the nearest 10,000 tolars.
Currency issued (€ million at 31 December): 2,947 in 2007; 3,257 in 2008.
Demand deposits (€ million at 31 December): 7,148 in 2007; 6,871 in 2008.
Other deposits (€ million at 31 December): 11,152 in 2007; 12,334 in 2008.
Source: IMF, *International Financial Statistics*.

COST OF LIVING
(Consumer Price Index for urban areas; base: 2000 = 100)

	2005	2006	2007
Food (incl. beverages)	124.3	127.2	136.8
Fuel and light	139.0	150.4	155.5
Clothing (incl. footwear)	113.2	112.4	114.9
Rent	187.7	195.9	201.6
All items (incl. others)	130.6	133.8	138.6

Source: ILO.

NATIONAL ACCOUNTS
(€ million at current prices)

SLOVENIA

Expenditure on the Gross Domestic Product

	2005	2006	2007
Final consumption expenditure	21,053	22,263	24,080
Households	15,324	16,135	17,691
Non-profit institutions serving households	277	303	293
General government	5,452	5,825	6,096
Gross capital formation	7,769	8,904	10,840
Gross fixed capital formation	7,263	8,161	9,478
Changes in inventories / Acquisitions, less disposals, of valuables	506	743	1,363
Total domestic expenditure	28,822	31,167	34,920
Exports of goods and services	17,860	20,661	24,187
Less Imports of goods and services	17,978	20,820	24,636
GDP in purchasers' values	28,704	31,008	34,471

Gross Domestic Product by Economic Activity

	2005	2006	2007
Agriculture, hunting and forestry	676.3	642.7	712.1
Fishing	3.6	3.7	3.3
Mining and quarrying	126.8	134.6	134.3
Manufacturing	5,983.7	6,412.3	7,070.3
Electricity, gas and water supply	761.7	818.0	781.8
Construction	1,694.9	1,980.1	2,407.4
Wholesale and retail trade; repair of motor vehicles, motorcycles and personal and household goods	2,994.7	3,178.4	3,673.0
Hotels and restaurants	573.9	627.0	752.6
Transport, storage and communications	1,853.7	2,041.2	2,340.9
Financial intermediation	1,085.1	1,326.6	1,370.4
Real estate, renting and business activities	4,256.0	4,597.5	5,300.8
Public administration and defence; compulsory social security	1,512.1	1,599.9	1,682.7
Education	1,421.1	1,496.1	1,565.3
Health and social work	1,277.6	1,331.2	1,382.6
Other community, social and personal services	918.6	979.3	1,032.5
Private households with employed persons	18.7	19.3	21.0
Gross value added at basic prices	25,158.7	27,187.9	30,231.2
Taxes on products	3,697.3	3,953.5	4,440.2
Less Subsidies	152.4	133.5	200.4
GDP in market prices	28,703.6	31,008.0	34,470.9

BALANCE OF PAYMENTS
(US $ million)

	2005	2006	2007
Exports of goods f.o.b.	18,146	21,397	27,123
Imports of goods f.o.b.	−19,404	−22,856	−29,432
Trade balance	−1,258	−1,458	−2,310
Exports of services	3,976	4,344	5,650
Imports of services	−2,915	−3,254	−4,231
Balance on goods and services	−198	−368	−891
Other income received	781	1,135	1,400
Other income paid	−1,143	−1,642	−2,400
Balance on goods, services and income	−560	−874	−1,890
Current transfers received	878	988	1,251
Current transfers paid	−998	−1,202	−1,654
Current balance	−681	−1,088	−2,293

—continued	2005	2006	2007
Capital account (net)	−138	−169	−72
Direct investment abroad	−629	−905	−1,574
Direct investment from abroad	540	649	1,483
Portfolio investment assets	−2,100	−2,677	−4,493
Portfolio investment liabilities	102	849	1,379
Financial derivatives assets	−13	−16	−31
Other investment assets	−1,899	−2,428	−6,271
Other investment liabilities	4,842	4,399	12,215
Net errors and omissions	181	−270	−541
Overall balance	206	−1,656	−199

Source: IMF, *International Financial Statistics*.

External Trade

PRINCIPAL COMMODITIES
(distribution by SITC, € million)

Imports c.i.f.	2005	2006	2007
Food and live animals	825.2	953.9	1,197.5
Crude materials (inedible) except fuels	833.8	1,028.6	1,218.2
Mineral fuels, lubricants, etc.	1,675.6	2,045.9	2,020.3
Petroleum, petroleum products, etc.	1,122.2	1,288.0	1,348.3
Chemicals and related products	2,028.1	2,228.8	2,560.6
Basic manufactures	3,571.3	4,213.7	4,850.1
Textile yarn, fabrics, etc.	458.6	446.8	444.6
Iron and steel	876.8	1,042.6	1,348.3
Non-ferrous metals	500.6	724.4	842.6
Other metal manufactures	576.6	747.8	843.9
Machinery and transport equipment	5,156.7	5,955.5	7,383.2
Machinery specialized for particular industries	437.3	539.7	616.8
General industrial machinery, equipment and parts	720.2	858.6	1,002.0
Electrical machinery, apparatus, etc.	904.8	1,021.2	1,206.4
Road vehicles (incl. air-cushion vehicles) and parts (excl. tyres, engines and electrical parts)	1,832.8	2,049.2	2,838.1
Miscellaneous manufactured articles	1,564.8	1,737.5	2,037.0
Clothing and accessories (excl. footwear)	302.3	341.1	409.8
Total (incl. others)	15,804.8	18,340.8	21,507.6

SLOVENIA

Exports f.o.b.	2005	2006	2007
Chemicals and related products	1,877.8	2,298.2	2,672.8
Medicinal and pharmaceutical products	913.9	1,161.3	1,395.8
Basic manufactures	3,621.4	4,313.5	4,855.1
Paper, paperboard and articles thereof	461.0	473.4	519.3
Textile yarn, fabrics, etc.	400.9	419.0	449.4
Iron and steel	562.5	668.9	833.8
Non-ferrous metals	532.8	733.8	785.4
Other metal manufactures	630.1	856.4	1,027.3
Machinery and transport equipment	5,647.2	6,395.8	7,848.7
General industrial machinery, equipment and parts	799.1	1,000.1	1,211.6
Electrical machinery, apparatus, etc.	1,514.3	1,664.8	1,865.1
Road vehicles (incl. air-cushion vehicles) and parts (excl. tyres, engines and electrical parts)	2,183.4	2,281.4	3,111.4
Miscellaneous manufactured articles	2,219.9	2,337.4	2,423.2
Furniture and parts; bedding mattresses, etc.	846.3	859.2	825.9
Clothing and accessories (excl. footwear)	283.8	270.5	281.2
Total (incl. others)	14,397.1	16,757.2	19,405.9

PRINCIPAL TRADING PARTNERS
(€ million)

Imports c.i.f.	2005	2006	2007
Austria	1,952.7	2,245.2	2,691.5
Belgium	336.5	409.8	494.9
China, People's Republic	196.8	245.8	346.0
Croatia	608.8	735.9	849.4
Czech Republic	379.7	399.5	506.2
France	1,156.6	1,128.8	1,151.6
Germany	3,163.2	3,743.4	4,177.9
Hungary	603.1	671.1	758.3
Italy	3,013.5	3,405.3	3,927.6
Japan	123.1	72.6	90.8
Netherlands	572.1	683.2	762.1
Poland	239.0	302.7	355.3
Russia	334.2	357.1	490.0
Slovakia	210.5	259.0	282.4
Spain	490.2	498.1	529.4
Sweden	126.2	144.7	165.2
Switzerland	205.0	255.8	210.5
Turkey	147.7	180.2	180.0
United Kingdom	235.7	302.0	347.2
USA	145.4	199.2	280.3
Total (incl. others)	15,804.8	18,340.8	21,507.6

Exports f.o.b.	2005	2006	2007
Austria	1,159.6	1,450.7	1,512.8
Belgium	158.7	185.6	185.0
Bosnia and Herzegovina	514.9	484.7	535.6
Croatia	1,304.2	1,464.4	1,569.7
Czech Republic	320.5	390.3	489.4
France	1,185.0	1,135.1	1,278.4
Germany	2,862.9	3,295.8	3,652.2
Hungary	284.3	385.1	647.1
Italy	1,818.5	2,157.0	2,565.4
Macedonia, former Yugoslav republic	134.1	125.7	144.2
Netherlands	207.4	235.5	316.1
Poland	364.0	487.9	616.5
Russia	467.5	599.5	691.6
Serbia	261.8	509.0	669.9
Slovakia	213.4	272.1	310.9
Spain	257.9	320.8	356.3
Switzerland	187.8	155.2	189.8
United Kingdom	358.4	468.7	526.2
USA	294.0	384.0	329.3
Total (incl. others)	14,397.1	16,757.2	19,405.9

Transport

RAILWAYS
(traffic)

	2005	2006	2007
Passenger journeys ('000)	15,742	16,131	16,123
Passenger-kilometres (million)	777	793	812
Freight carried ('000 metric tons)	16,344	17,052	17,575
Freight ton-kilometres (million)	3,245	3,373	3,603

ROAD TRAFFIC
(registered motor vehicles at 31 December)

	2005	2006	2007
Motorcycles	14,473	18,801	34,162
Mopeds	34,198	34,392	37,331
Passenger cars	960,213	980,261	1,014,122
Buses	2,255	2,277	2,330
Lorries	60,234	62,964	68,891
Agricultural tractors	85,021	86,304	80,193
Total (incl. others)	1,170,606	1,200,979	1,255,661

SHIPPING
Merchant Fleet
(at 31 December)

	2005	2006	2007
Number of vessels	5	6	6
Displacement (grt)	1,130	1,626	1,628

Source: Lloyd's Register-Fairplay, *World Fleet Statistics*.

International Sea-borne Freight Traffic
('000 metric tons)

	2005	2006	2007
Goods loaded	193	188	202
Goods unloaded	2,997	3,206	2,956

CIVIL AVIATION
(traffic)

	2005	2006	2007
Kilometres flown ('000)	17,814	19,367	22,087
Passengers carried ('000)	944	1,018	1,136
Passenger-kilometres (million)	1,019	1,043	1,186
Freight carried (metric tons)	3,035	4,193	4,510
Freight ton-kilometres ('000)	2,765	3,436	3,724

Tourism

FOREIGN TOURIST ARRIVALS
('000)*

Country of origin	2005	2006	2007
Austria	201.9	203.5	207.2
Croatia	94.0	101.8	106.4
France	55.9	54.0	60.5
Germany	219.3	204.8	211.1
Italy	338.3	357.1	368.7
Netherlands	53.6	51.8	56.8
United Kingdom	90.9	91.0	87.1
Total (incl. others)	2,395.0	2,484.6	2,681.2

* Figures refer to arrivals at accommodation establishments.

Receipts from tourism (US $ million, incl. passenger transport): 1,726 in 2004; 1,894 in 2005; 1,911 in 2006 (Source: World Tourism Organization).

SLOVENIA

Communications Media

	2005	2006	2007
Telephone subscribers ('000 main lines)*	816.4	837.5	857.1
Mobile cellular telephones ('000 subscribers)*	1,759.2	1,819.6	1,928.4
Television subscriptions ('000)	619	624	609
Personal computers ('000 in use)*	808	n.a.	n.a.
Internet users ('000)*	1,090	1,251	1,300
Broadband subscribers ('000)*	196.6	263.7	344.8
Daily newspapers	10	9	14
Non-daily newspapers	267	226	180
Other periodicals	1,539	1,425	1,429
Book production (titles published, including pamphlets)	4,394	4,684	5,129

* Source: International Telecommunication Union.

Facsimile machines (subscribers): 8,850 in 2002.

Education

(2007/08, unless otherwise indicated)

	Institutions	Teachers	Males	Females	Total
Pre-primary	811	7,708	32,044	29,315	61,359
Elementary*	473	18,107	85,925	80,561	166,486
Upper secondary*	268	12,168	54,296	53,733	108,029
Higher education†	49	5,673	37,066‡	54,163‡	91,229‡

* Including education of adults.
† 2006/07.
‡ Excluding post-graduate students.

Adult literacy rate (UNESCO estimates): 99.7% (males 99.7%; females 99.6%) in 2007 (Source: UNESCO Institute for Statistics).

Directory

The Constitution

The Constitution of the Republic of Slovenia was enacted on 23 December 1991. The following is a summary of the Constitution's main articles:

INTRODUCTION

Slovenia is a democratic republic, governed by the rule of law. Slovenia is a territorially indivisible state. Human rights and fundamental freedoms—including the rights of the autochthonous Italian and Hungarian ethnic communities—are protected. Slovenia attends to the welfare of Slovenian emigrants and migrant workers abroad.

The separation of church and state is guaranteed. Religious groups enjoy equal rights under the law and are guaranteed freedom of activity.

The autonomy of local government in Slovenia is guaranteed. The capital of the republic is Ljubljana. The official language of Slovenia is Slovene. In those areas where Italian or Hungarian ethnic communities reside, the official language is also Italian or Hungarian.

HUMAN RIGHTS AND FUNDAMENTAL FREEDOMS

All persons are guaranteed equal human rights and fundamental freedoms, irrespective of national origin, race, sex, language, religion, political or other beliefs, financial status, birth, education or social status, and all persons are equal before the law. Human life is inviolable, and there is no capital punishment. No person may be subjected to torture, inhuman or humiliating punishment or treatment. The right of each individual to personal liberty is guaranteed.

Respect for the humanity and dignity of the individual is guaranteed in all criminal or other proceedings. Except for certain situations (as determined by statute), all court proceedings are conducted in public. Each person is guaranteed the right of appeal. Any person charged with a criminal offence is presumed innocent until proven guilty.

Each person has the right to freedom of movement. The right to own and to inherit property is guaranteed. Freedom of expression of thought, freedom of speech, freedom to associate in public, and the freedom of the press are guaranteed. The right to vote is universal and equal. Each citizen who has attained the age of 18 years is eligible both to vote and to stand for election.

The freedom of work is guaranteed. The State regulates compulsory health, pension, disability and other social insurance, and ensures the proper administration thereof. Education is free, and the State provides the opportunity for all citizens to obtain a proper education.

Each person is entitled freely to identify with his national grouping or ethnic community, to foster and give expression to his culture, and to use his own language and script. All incitement to ethnic, racial, religious or other discrimination, as well as the inflaming of ethnic, racial, religious or other hatred or intolerance, is unconstitutional, as is incitement to violence or to war. The autochthonous Italian and Hungarian ethnic communities are guaranteed the right freely to use their national symbols. These two communities have the right to education and schooling in their own languages. They are also entitled to establish autonomous organizations in order to exercise their rights. The Italian and Hungarian communities are directly represented, both at the local level and in the Državni zbor (National Assembly). The status and special rights of Gypsy (Roma) communities living in Slovenia are determined by statute.

ECONOMIC AND SOCIAL RELATIONS

The State is responsible for the creation of opportunities for employment. Each person has the right to a healthy environment, and the State is responsible for such an environment.

Free enterprise is guaranteed. The establishment of trade unions, and the operation and membership thereof, is free. Workers enjoy the right to strike. The State creates the conditions necessary to enable each citizen to obtain proper housing.

ADMINISTRATION OF THE STATE

The Državni zbor (National Assembly)

The Državni zbor consists of 90 deputies, who serve a four-year term; 88 deputies are elected on a proportional basis from within eight regions, each of which is subdivided into 11 constituencies (although not all constituencies will necessarily obtain a direct representative). The remaining two deputies are elected as representatives of the Italian and Hungarian ethnic communities of Slovenia. The President of the Državni zbor (Speaker) is elected by a majority vote of all elected deputies.

The Državni zbor enacts laws; makes other decisions; authorizes adherence to international agreements; may call a referendum; may proclaim a state of war or a state of emergency, at the initiative of the Government; and may establish parliamentary inquiries with respect to matters of public importance.

The Državni svet (National Council)

The Državni svet represents social, economic, trade and professional, and local interests. It is composed of 40 councillors: four representing employers; four representing employees; four representing farmers, small business persons and independent professional persons; six representing non-profit-making organizations; and 22 representing local interests. Councillors are elected for a five-year term.

The Državni svet may: propose the enactment of statutes by the Državni zbor; demand that the Državni zbor reconsider statutes prior to their proclamation; demand the holding of a referendum; and demand the establishment of a parliamentary inquiry. The Državni zbor may require the Državni svet to provide its opinions on specific matters. A councillor of the Državni svet may not be simultaneously a deputy of the Državni zbor.

The President of the Republic

The President of the Republic of Slovenia is Head of State and Commander-in-Chief of the Defence Forces. The President is elected on the basis of universal, equal and direct suffrage by secret ballot. The President's term of office is five years (with a maximum of two consecutive terms). Only a citizen of Slovenia may be elected President of the Republic. Presidential elections are called by the President of the Državni zbor. The office of President of the Republic is incompatible with other public offices or other employment. In the event that the President of the Republic is permanently incapacitated, dies, resigns or is otherwise permanently unable to perform his functions, the President of the Državni zbor temporarily occupies the office of the President of the Republic until such time as a replacement is elected.

The President of the Republic is empowered to: call elections to the Državni zbor; proclaim statutes; appoint state officers and functionaries; accredit, and revoke the accreditation of, Slovenian ambassadors to foreign states, and to accept the credentials of foreign diplomatic representatives; grant amnesties; and confer state honours, decorations and honorary titles.

If, in the course of carrying out his office, the President of the Republic acts in a manner contrary to the Constitution or commits a serious breach of the law, he may be brought before the Constitutional Court upon the request of the Državni zbor. The President may be dismissed from office upon the vote of no less than two-thirds of all of the judges of the Constitutional Court.

The Government

The Government is composed of the Prime Minister and ministers. The Government is independent, and individual ministers are independent within their own particular portfolios. Ministers are accountable to the Državni zbor. After consultations with the leaders of the various political groups within the Državni zbor, the President of the Republic proposes to the Državni zbor a candidate for the office of Prime Minister. The Prime Minister is elected by the Državni zbor by a majority vote. Ministers in the Government are appointed or dismissed by the Državni zbor, upon the proposal of the Prime Minister. The Prime Minister is responsible for the political unity, direction and administrative programme of the Government and for the co-ordination of the work of the various ministers. The Državni zbor may, upon the motion of no fewer than 10 deputies and by a majority vote, elect a new Prime Minister (such a vote is deemed a vote of 'no confidence' in the Government). Furthermore, the Državni zbor may bring the Prime Minister or any minister before the Constitutional Court to answer charges relating to breaches of the Constitution.

The Judiciary

Judges independently exercise their duties and functions in accordance with the Constitution and with the law. The Supreme Court is the highest court for civil and criminal cases in the republic. The Državni zbor elects judges upon the recommendation of the Judicial Council, which is composed of 11 members. The office of a judge is incompatible with office in any other state body, local government body or organ of any political party.

The Office of the Public Prosecutor

The Public Prosecutor is responsible for the preferment of criminal charges, for prosecuting criminal matters in court and for the performance of such other duties as are prescribed by statute.

LOCAL SELF-GOVERNMENT

Slovenians exercise local government powers and functions through self-governing municipalities and other local government organizations. A municipality may comprise a single community or a number of communities, whose inhabitants are bound together by common needs and interests. The State supervises the proper and efficient performance of municipalities and wider self-governing local administrative bodies. Municipalities raise their own revenue. Municipalities are at liberty to join other municipalities in establishing wider self-governing local administrative bodies or regional local government bodies to exercise administrative powers and to deal with matters of wider common interest. Citizens may join together and form self-governing local bodies to further their common interests.

PUBLIC FINANCE

The Bank of Slovenia is the central bank. It is independent in its operations and accountable to the Državni zbor. The Governor of the Bank of Slovenia is appointed by the Državni zbor.

THE CONSTITUTIONAL COURT

The Constitutional Court is composed of nine judges, elected by the Državni zbor, upon the nomination of the President of the Republic, for a single term of nine years. The President of the Constitutional Court is elected by the judges from among their own number to hold office for a period of three years.

The Constitutional Court is empowered to decide upon matters relating to: the conformity of statutes with the Constitution and with international agreements; complaints of breaches of the Constitution involving individual acts infringing human rights and fundamental freedoms; juridical disputes between the state and local government bodies or among such local government bodies; juridical disputes between the Državni zbor, the President of the Republic and the Government; and unconstitutional acts or activities of political parties.

The Government

HEAD OF STATE

President: Dr Danilo Türk (elected 11 November 2007; inaugurated 22 December 2007).

GOVERNMENT
(April 2009)

A coalition comprising representatives of the Social Democrats (SD), For Real—New Politics (Zares), Liberal Democracy of Slovenia (LDS) and the Democratic Party of Pensioners of Slovenia (DeSUS).

Prime Minister: Borut Pahor (SD).
Minister of Finance: Dr Franc Križanič (SD).
Minister of Internal Affairs: Katarina Kresal (LDS).
Minister of Foreign Affairs: Samuel Žbogar (Independent).
Minister of Justice: Aleš Zalar (LDS).
Minister of Defence: Dr Ljubica Jelušič (SD).
Minister of Labour, Family and Social Affairs: Dr Ivan Svetlik (Independent).
Minister of the Economy: Dr Matej Lahovnik (Zares).
Minister of Agriculture, Forestry and Food: Dr Milan Pogačnik (Independent).
Minister of Culture: Majda Širca (Zares).
Minister of the Environment and Physical Planning: Karl Viktor Erjavec (DeSUS).
Minister of Transport: Dr Patrick Vlačič (SD).
Minister of Education and Sport: Dr Igor Lukšič (SD).
Minister of Health: Borut Miklavčič (Independent).
Minister of Public Administration: Irma Pavlinič-Krebs (Zares).
Minister of Higher Education, Science and Technology: Gregor Golobič (Zares).
Minister without Portfolio, responsible for Local Self-Government and Regional Policy: Zlata Ploštajner (Independent).
Minister without Portfolio, responsible for Development and European Affairs: Mitja Gaspari (Independent).
Minister without Portfolio, responsible for Slovenes Abroad: Dr Boštjan Žekš (Independent).

MINISTRIES

Office of the President: 1000 Ljubljana, Erjavčeva 17; tel. (1) 4781222; fax (1) 4781357; e-mail gp.uprs@up-rs.si; internet www.up-rs.si.

Office of the Prime Minister: 1000 Ljubljana, Gregorčičeva 20; tel. (1) 4781000; fax (1) 4781721; e-mail gp.kpv@gov.si; internet www.kpv.gov.si.

Government Office for Development and European Affairs: 1000 Ljubljana, Gregorčičeva 25; tel. (1) 4781180; fax (1) 4781191; e-mail go.svr@gov.si; internet www.svr.gov.si.

Government Office for Local Self-Government and Regional Policy: 1000 Ljubljana, Kotnikova 28; tel. (1) 3083178; fax (1) 4783619; e-mail gp.svlr@gov.si; internet www.svlr.gov.si.

Government Office for Slovenes Abroad: 1000 Ljubljana, Komenskega 11; tel. (1) 2308000; fax (1) 2308017; e-mail urad.slovenci@gov.si; internet www.uszs.gov.si.

Ministry of Agriculture, Forestry and Food: 1000 Ljubljana, Dunajska 56–58; tel. (1) 4789000; fax (1) 4789021; e-mail gp.mkgp@gov.si; internet www.mkgp.gov.si.

Ministry of Culture: 1000 Ljubljana, Maistrova 10; tel. (1) 3695900; fax (1) 3695901; e-mail gp.mk@gov.si; internet www.mk.gov.si.

Ministry of Defence: 1000 Ljubljana, Vojkova 55; tel. (1) 4712211; fax (1) 4712978; e-mail info@mors.si; internet www.mors.si.

Ministry of the Economy: 1000 Ljubljana, Kotnikova 5; tel. (1) 4003311; fax (1) 4001031; e-mail info.mg@gov.si; internet www.mg.gov.si.

Ministry of Education and Sport: 1000 Ljubljana, Masarykova 16; tel. (1) 4005400; fax (1) 4005329; e-mail gp.mss@gov.si; internet www.mss.gov.si.

Ministry of the Environment and Physical Planning: 1000 Ljubljana, Dunajska cesta 48; tel. (1) 4787400; fax (1) 4787422; e-mail gp.mop@gov.si; internet www.mop.gov.si.

Ministry of Finance: 1502 Ljubljana, Župančičeva 3; tel. (1) 3696610; fax (1) 3696619; e-mail gp.mf@gov.si; internet www.mf.gov.si.

Ministry of Foreign Affairs: 1001 Ljubljana, Prešernova 25; tel. (1) 4782000; fax (1) 4782340; e-mail info.mzz@gov.si; internet www.mzz.gov.si.

SLOVENIA

Ministry of Health: 1000 Ljubljana, Štefanova 5; tel. (1) 4786001; fax (1) 4786058; e-mail gp.mz@gov.si; internet www.mz.gov.si.

Ministry of Higher Education, Science and Technology: 1000 Ljubljana, Kotnikova 38; tel. (1) 4784600; fax (1) 4784719; e-mail gp.mvzt@gov.si; internet www.mvzt.gov.si.

Ministry of Internal Affairs: 1501 Ljubljana, Štefanova 2; tel. (1) 4284000; fax (1) 2514330; e-mail gp.mnz@gov.si; internet www.mnz.gov.si.

Ministry of Justice: 1000 Ljubljana, Županičeva 3; tel. (1) 3695200; fax (1) 3695783; e-mail gp.mp@gov.si; internet www.mp.gov.si.

Ministry of Labour, Family and Social Affairs: 1000 Ljubljana, Kotnikova 5; tel. (1) 3697700; fax (1) 3697832; e-mail gp.mddsz@gov.si; internet www.mddsz.gov.si.

Ministry of Public Administration: 1000 Ljubljana, Tržaška cesta 21; tel. (1) 4788330; fax (1) 4788331; e-mail gp.mju@gov.si; internet www.mju.gov.si.

Ministry of Transport: 1535 Ljubljana, Langusova 4; tel. (1) 4788000; fax (1) 4788139; e-mail gp.mpz@gov.si; internet www.mzp.gov.si.

President

Presidential Election, First Ballot, 21 October 2007

Candidate	Votes	% of votes
Lojze Peterle (Independent)	283,412	28.73
Danilo Türk (Independent)	241,349	24.47
Mitja Gaspari (Independent)	237,632	24.09
Zmago Jelinčič Plemeniti (Slovenian National Party)	188,951	19.16
Darko Krajnc (Youth Party of Slovenia)	21,526	2.18
Others	13,559	1.37
Total	**986,429**	**100.00**

Second Ballot, 11 November 2007

Candidate	Votes	% of votes
Danilo Türk (Independent)	677,333	68.03
Lojze Peterle (Independent)	318,288	31.97
Total	**995,621**	**100.00**

Legislature

The Slovenian legislature is bicameral, comprising the Državni zbor (National Assembly), the directly elected lower chamber, and the Državni svet (National Council), the indirectly elected upper chamber.

Državni zbor
(National Assembly)

1102 Ljubljana, Šubičeva 4; tel. (1) 4789400; fax (1) 4789845; e-mail gp@dz-rs.si; internet www.dz-rs.si.

President: Dr PAVEL GANTAR.

General Election, 21 September 2008

Party	Votes	% of votes	Seats
Social Democrats	320,248	30.45	29
Slovenian Democratic Party	307,735	29.26	28
For Real—New Politics	98,526	9.37	9
Democratic Party of Pensioners of Slovenia	78,353	7.45	7
Slovenian National Party	56,832	5.40	5
Slovenian People's Party–Youth Party of Slovenia	54,809	5.21	5
Liberal Democracy of Slovenia	54,771	5.21	5
Others*	80,553	7.65	2
Total	**1,051,827**	**100.00**	**90**

*Two of the 90 seats in the Državni zbor are reserved for representatives of the Italian and Hungarian minorities.

Državni svet
(National Council)

1000 Ljubljana, Šubičeva 4; tel. (1) 4789798; fax (1) 4789851; e-mail janez.susnik@ds-rs.si; internet www.ds-rs.si.

There are 40 councillors in the Državni svet, who are indirectly elected for a five-year term by an electoral college.

President: BLAŽ KAVČIČ.

Election Commission

Republic Electoral Commission: 1000 Ljubljana, Slovenska 54; tel. (1) 4322002; fax (1) 4331269; e-mail rvk@gov.si; internet volitve.gov.si; Chair. MARKO GOLUBIĆ.

Political Organizations

Democratic Party of Pensioners of Slovenia (DeSUS) (Demokratična stranka upokojencev Slovenije): 1000 Ljubljana, Kersnikova 6; tel. (1) 4397350; fax (1) 4314113; e-mail desus@siol.net; internet www.desus.si; Pres. KARL VIKTOR ERJAVEC.

For Real—New Politics (Zares—Nova Politika—Zares): 1000 Ljubljana, Županičeva 8; tel. (1) 2428750; e-mail info@zares.si; internet www.zares.si; f. 2007 by fmr mems of Liberal Democracy of Slovenia; Pres. GREGOR GOLOBIČ.

Greens of Slovenia (Zeleni Slovenije): 10000 Ljubljana, Komenskega 11; tel. (2) 7781071; fax (2) 7878543; e-mail zeleni@zeleni.si; internet www.zeleni.si; f. 1989; in 1993 the party split into two factions, one retaining the original name, the other, more radical, wing adopting the title, Greens of Slovenia—Eco-Social Party; Chair. Prof. VLADO CUŠ.

Liberal Democracy of Slovenia (LDS) (Liberalna demokracija Slovenije): 1000 Ljubljana, trg Republike 3; tel. (1) 2000310; fax (1) 2000311; e-mail lds@lds.si; internet www.lds.si; f. 1994 by a merger of the Liberal Democratic Party, the Greens of Slovenia—Eco-Social Party, the Democratic Party and the Socialist Party of Slovenia; Chair. KATARINA KRESAL; 18,000 mems.

New Slovenia—Christian People's Party (NSi) (Nova Slovenija—Krščanska ljudska stranka): 1000 Ljubljana, Cankarjeva 11; tel. (1) 2416650; fax (1) 2416670; e-mail tajnistvo@nsi.si; internet www.nsi.si; f. 2000 by mems of the Slovenian People's Party; Pres. LJUDMILA NOVAK.

Slovenian Democratic Party (SDP) (Slovenska Demokratska Stranka—SDS): 1000 Ljubljana, Komenskega 11; tel. (1) 4345450; fax (1) 4345452; e-mail sekretar@sds.si; internet www.sds.si; f. 1989 as Social Democratic Party of Slovenia; name changed in 2003; centre-right; Pres. JANEZ JANŠA; Sec.-Gen. DUŠAN STRNAD; 20,000 mems.

Slovenian National Party (SNP) (Slovenska nacionalna stranka—SNS): 1000 Ljubljana, Tivolska 13; tel. (1) 2529020; fax (1) 2529022; e-mail info@sns.si; internet www.sns.si; f. 1991; right-wing nationalist party; Pres. ZMAGO JELINČIČ; Sec.-Gen. MIŠA GLAŽAR; 7,500 mems (2007).

Slovenian People's Party (SPP) (Slovenska ljudska stranka) (SLS): 1000 Ljubljana, Beethovnova 4; tel. (1) 2418820; fax (1) 2511741; e-mail tajnistvo@sls.si; internet www.sls.si; f. 1989 as the Slovenian Farmers' Asscn; merged with the Slovenian Christian Democrats in April 2000; Pres. BOJAN ŠROT.

Social Democrats (SD) (Socialni demokrati): 1000 Ljubljana, Levstikova 15; tel. (1) 2444100; fax (1) 2444123; e-mail info@socialnidemokrati.si; internet www.socialnidemokrati.si; f. 1993 as United List of Social Democrats; renamed 2005; Pres. BORUT PAHOR; Gen. Sec. UROŠ JAUŠEVEC; 23,000 mems.

Diplomatic Representation

EMBASSIES IN SLOVENIA

Albania: 1000 Ljubljana, Zaloška cesta 69; tel. (1) 5473650; fax (1) 5473652; e-mail embassy.ljubljana@mfa.gov.al; Ambassador SANDËR KOVACI.

Austria: 1000 Ljubljana, Prešernova cesta 23; tel. (1) 4790700; fax (1) 2521717; e-mail laibach-ob@bmaa.gv.at; internet www.bmeia.gv.at/laibach; Chargé d'affaires a.i. ERIKA BERNHARD.

Belgium: 1000 Ljubljana, trg Republike 3/IX; tel. (1) 2006010; fax (1) 4266395; e-mail ljubljana@diplobel.org; internet www.diplomatie.be/ljubljanafr; Ambassador LOUIS MOURAUX.

Bosnia and Herzegovina: 1000 Ljubljana, Kolarjeva 26; tel. (1) 2343250; fax (1) 2343261; e-mail ambihlju@siol.net; Ambassador ZDRAVKO BEGOVIĆ.

Brazil: 1000 Ljubljana, Kongresni trg 3; tel. (1) 2442400; fax (1) 2442420; e-mail mail@brazil.si; Ambassador DÉBORA VAINER BARENBOIM.

Bulgaria: 1000 Ljubljana, Rožna dolina XV/18; tel. (1) 4232451; fax (1) 4258845; e-mail bgembassysl@siol.net; Ambassador FILIP BOKOV.

China, People's Republic: 1000 Ljubljana, Koblarjeva 3; tel. (1) 4202855; fax (1) 2822199; e-mail kitajsko.veleposlanistvo@siol.net; internet si.china-embassy.org; Ambassador ZHI ZHAOLIN.

Croatia: 1000 Ljubljana, Gruberjevo nabrežje 6; tel. (1) 2004401; fax (1) 4258106; e-mail croemb.slovenia@mvp.hr; internet si.mvp.hr; Ambassador Dr SVJETLAN BERKOVIĆ.

Cyprus: 1000 Ljubljana, Komenskega 12; tel. (1) 2321542; fax (1) 2302002; e-mail embassy.cyprus@siol.net; Ambassador CHARALAMBOS PANAYIDES.

Czech Republic: 1000 Ljubljana, Riharjeva 1; tel. (1) 4202450; fax (1) 2839259; e-mail ljubljana@embassy.mzv.cz; internet www.mzv.cz/ljubljana; Ambassador IVANA HLAVSOVÁ.

Denmark: 1000 Ljubljana, Tivolska 48, Eurocenter; tel. (1) 4380800; fax (1) 4317417; e-mail ljuamb@um.dk; internet www.ambljubljana.um.dk; Ambassador ANITA HUGAU.

Egypt: 1000 Ljubljana, Opekarska cesta 18A; tel. (1) 4295420; fax (1) 2839122; e-mail embassy.ljubljana@mfa.gov.eg; Ambassador AHMED FAROUK.

Finland: 1000 Ljubljana, Ajdovščina 4/8; tel. (1) 3002120; fax (1) 3002139; e-mail sanomat.lju@formin.fi; internet www.finland.si; Ambassador BIRGITTA STENIUS-MLADENOV.

France: 1000 Ljubljana, Barjanska cesta 1; tel. (1) 4790400; fax (1) 4790410; e-mail ambafrance_si@siol.net; internet www.ambafrance.si; Ambassador CHANTAL DE GHAISNE DE BOURMONT.

Germany: 1000 Ljubljana, Prešernova cesta 27; tel. (1) 4790300; fax (1) 4250899; e-mail germanembassy-slovenia@siol.net; internet www.ljubljana.diplo.de; Ambassador Dr HANS-JOACHIM GOETZ.

Greece: 1000 Ljubljana, Trnovski pristan 14; tel. (1) 4201400; fax (1) 2811114; e-mail gremb.lju@mfa.gr; Ambassador DIONYSSIOS COUNDOUREAS.

Holy See: 1000 Ljubljana, trg Krekov 1; tel. (1) 4339204; fax (1) 4315130; e-mail apostolska.nunciatura@rkc.si; Apostolic Nuncio Most Rev. ABRIL Y CASTELLÓ SANTOS (Titular Archbishop of Tamada).

Hungary: 1210 Ljubljana, ul. Konrada Babnika 5; tel. (1) 5121882; fax (1) 5121878; e-mail huemblju@siol.net; internet www.mfa.gov.hu/kulkepviselet/SLO/hu; Ambassador Dr JÓZSEF CZUKOR.

India: 1000 Ljubljana, Maurerjeva 29; tel. (1) 5133117; fax (1) 5133116; e-mail amb.ljubljana@mea.gov.in; Ambassador Dr VILLUR SUNDARARAJAN SESHADRI.

Ireland: 1000 Ljubljana, Palača kapitelj, Poljanski nasip 6; tel. (1) 3008970; fax (1) 2821096; e-mail ljubljanaembassy@dfa.ie; internet www.irishembassy.si; Ambassador PATRICK MCCABE.

Italy: 1000 Ljubljana, Snežniška 8; tel. (1) 4262194; fax (1) 4253302; e-mail archivio.lubiana@esteri.it; internet www.amblubiana.esteri.it; Ambassador ALESSANDRO PIETROMARCHI.

Japan: 1000 Ljubljana, trg Republike 3/XI; tel. (1) 2008281; fax (1) 2511822; internet www.si.emb-japan.go.jp; Ambassador SHIGEHARU MARUYAMA.

Latvia: 1000 Ljubljana, Ajdovščina 4; tel. (1) 4341620; fax (1) 4341622; e-mail juris.poikans@mfa.gov.lv; Ambassador JURIS POIKANS.

Lithuania: 1000 Ljubljana, Kongresni trg 3; tel. (1) 2442611; fax (1) 2442619; e-mail amb.si@urm.lt; Ambassador RIMUTIS KLEVEČKA.

Macedonia, former Yugoslav republic: 1000 Ljubljana, Prešernova 2; tel. (1) 4210021; fax (1) 4210023; e-mail makamb@siol.net; Ambassador SAMOIL JOSIF FILIPOVSKI.

Montenegro: 1000 Ljubljana, Njegoševa cesta 14; tel. (1) 4395364; fax (1) 4395360; e-mail embamon-lj@t-2.net; Ambassador RANKO MILOVIĆ.

Netherlands: 1000 Ljubljana, Palača Kapitelj, Polijanski nasip 6; tel. (1) 4201461; fax (1) 4201470; e-mail lju@minbuza.nl; internet www.netherlands-embassy.si; Ambassador JOHN C. M. GROFFEN.

Norway: 1000 Ljubljana, Ajdovščina 4/8; tel. (1) 3002140; fax (1) 3002150; e-mail emb.ljubljana@mfa.no; Ambassador GURO KATHARINA HELWIG VIKOR.

Poland: 1000 Ljubljana, Bežigrad 10; tel. (1) 4364712; fax (1) 4362521; e-mail ambpol.si@siol.net; internet www.lublana.polemb.net; Ambassador PIOTR KASZUBA.

Portugal: 1000 Ljubljana, trg Republika 3/10; tel. (1) 4790540; fax (1) 4790550; e-mail embportlju@siol.net; Ambassador MARIA DO CARMO ALLEGRO DE MAGALHÃES.

Romania: 1000 Ljubljana, Smrekarjeva 33A; tel. (1) 5058294; fax (1) 5055432; e-mail embassy.of.romania@siol.net; internet ljubljana.mae.ro; Ambassador DANA MANUELA CONSTANTINESCU.

Russia: 1000 Ljubljana, Tomšičeva 9; tel. (1) 4256875; fax (1) 4256878; e-mail ambrus.slo@siol.net; internet www.rus-slo.mid.ru; Ambassador MIKHAIL V. VANIN.

Serbia: 1000 Ljubljana, Slomškova 1; tel. (1) 4380111; fax (1) 4342688; e-mail amba.srbije.lju@siol.net; Ambassador PREDRAG FILIPOV.

Slovakia: 1000 Ljubljana, Tivolska cesta 4; tel. (1) 4255425; fax (1) 4210524; e-mail emb.ljubljana@mzv.sk; Ambassador Dr MARIANNA ORAVCOVÁ.

Spain: 1000 Ljubljana, Trnovski pristan 24; tel. (1) 4202330; fax (1) 4202333; e-mail emba.espa.eslovenia@siol.net; Ambassador CARMEN FONTES MUÑOZ.

Sweden: 1000 Ljubljana, Ajdovščina 4/8; tel. (1) 3000270; fax (1) 3000271; e-mail ambassaden.ljubljana@foreign.ministry.se; internet www.swedenabroad.com/ljubljana; Ambassador INGER ULTVEDT.

Switzerland: 1000 Ljubljana, trg Republike 3/VI; tel. (1) 2008640; fax (1) 2008669; e-mail lju.vertretung@admin.ch; internet www.eda.admin.ch/ljubljana; Ambassador STEFAN SPECK.

Turkey: 1000 Ljubljana, Livarska 4; tel. (1) 2364150; fax (1) 4365240; e-mail vrtucije@siol.net; internet www.turkish-embassy.si; Ambassador AYSE SEZGIN.

Ukraine: 1000 Ljubljana, Teslova 23; tel. (1) 4210604; fax (1) 4210603; e-mail emb_si@mfa.gov.ua; Ambassador VADYM V. PRYIMACHENKO.

United Kingdom: 1000 Ljubljana, trg Republike 3/IV; tel. (1) 2003910; fax (1) 4250174; e-mail info@british-embassy.si; internet ukinslovenia.fco.gov.uk; Ambassador ANDREW PAGE.

USA: 1000 Ljubljana, Prešernova cesta 31; tel. (1) 2005500; fax (1) 2005555; e-mail usembassyljubljana@state.gov; internet slovenia.usembassy.gov; Chargé d'affaires a.i. BRADLEY A. FREDEN.

Judicial System

The Slovenian Constitution guarantees the independence of the judiciary.

The 44 district courts decide minor cases. The 11 regional courts act as courts of the first instance in all cases other than those for which the district courts have jurisdiction. Four regional courts act as courts of the second instance. There are, in addition, labour courts and social courts, which adjudicate in disputes over pensions, welfare allocations and other social benefits. A Higher Labour and Social Court has jurisdiction in the second instance. The Supreme Court is the highest authority for civil and criminal law. There is also a Constitutional Court, composed of nine judges, each elected for a single term of nine years.

Constitutional Court of the Republic of Slovenia (Ustavno sodišča Republike Slovenije): 1000 Ljubljana, Beethovnova 10; tel. (1) 4776400; fax (1) 2510451; e-mail info@us-rs.si; internet www.us-rs.si; Pres. Dr JOŽE TRATNIK.

Supreme Court of the Republic of Slovenia (Vrhovno Sodišče Republike Slovenije): 1000 Ljubljana, Tavčarjeva 9; tel. (1) 3664200; fax (1) 3664301; e-mail franc.testen@sodisce.si; internet www.sodisce.si; Pres. FRANC TESTEN.

Office of the State Prosecutor-General: 1000 Ljubljana, trg OF 13; tel. (1) 4341935; fax (1) 4341945; e-mail dtrs@dt-rs.si; internet www.dt-rs.si; State Prosecutor-General BARBARA BREZIGAR.

Religion

Most of the population are Christian, predominantly adherents of the Roman Catholic Church. There are few Protestant Christians, despite the importance of a Calvinist sect (the Church of Carniola) to the development of Slovene literature in the 16th century. At the census of 2002 some 57.8% of the population described themselves as Roman Catholics, 10.1% as atheists, 2.4% as Muslims, 2.3% as Orthodox Christians and 0.8% as Protestants; 22.8% of all respondents did not respond to the question requesting their religious allegiance.

CHRISTIANITY

The Roman Catholic Church

The Roman Catholic Church in Slovenia comprises two archdioceses and four dioceses. At 31 December 2006 there were an estimated 1,605,384 adherents (equivalent to 79.8% of the total population).

Bishops' Conference

1000 Ljubljana, p.p. 121/III, Ciril Metodov trg 4; tel. (1) 2342600; fax (1) 2314169; e-mail ssk@rkc.si.

f. 1993; Pres. Most Rev. FRANC KRAMBERGER (Archbishop of Maribor).

Archbishop of Ljubljana: Most Rev. ALOJZIJ URAN, 1001 Ljubljana, p.p. 1990, Ciril Metodov trg 4; tel. (1) 2342600; fax (1) 2314169; e-mail nadskofija.ljubljana@rkc.si.

SLOVENIA

Archbishop of Maribor: Most Rev. FRANC KRAMBERGER, 2000 Maribor, Slomškov trg 19; tel. (2) 2290401; fax (2) 2523092; e-mail ordinariat@slomsek.net.

Protestant Church

Evangelical Lutheran Church of Slovenia: 9226 Moravske Toplice, 11 Levstikova; tel. (2) 5381323; fax (2) 5381324; e-mail evang.cerkev.si@siol.net; f. 1561; 20,000 mems; Chair. GEZA ERNIŠA.

ISLAM

Islamic Association in the Republic of Slovenia (Islamska Skupnost V Republiki Sloveniji): 1000 Ljubljana, Grabiovičeva 14; tel. (1) 2313625; fax (1) 2313626; internet www.islamska-skupnost.si; Dir NEVZET PORIĆ.

The Press

The publications listed below are in Slovene, unless otherwise indicated.

PRINCIPAL DAILIES

Delo (Event): 1509 Ljubljana, Dunajska 5; tel. (1) 4727402; fax (1) 4737406; e-mail webmaster@delo.si; internet www.delo.si; f. 1959; morning; Editor-in-Chief PETER JANCIC; circ. 93,781.

Dnevnik (Daily): 1510 Ljubljana, Kopitarjeva 2; tel. (1) 3082100; fax (1) 3082189; e-mail info@dnevnik.si; internet www.dnevnik.si; f. 1951; evening; independent; Man. Dir BRANKO BERGANT; Editor-in-Chief ZLATKO SETINC; circ. 63,000.

Slovenske novice (Slovene News): 1509 Ljubljana, Dunajska 5; tel. (1) 1737700; fax (1) 1737352; f. 1991; Editor-in-Chief MARJAN BAUER; Man. Editor TIT DOBERSEK; circ. 80,000.

Večer (Evening): 2000 Maribor, Svetozarevska 14; tel. (2) 2353500; fax (2) 2353368; internet www.vecer.si; f. 1945; Dir BORIS CEKOV; Editor-in-Chief MILAN PREDAN; circ. 70,000.

PERIODICALS

Avto magazin: 1000 Ljubljana, Dunajska 5; tel. (1) 1738251; fax (1) 1738220; f. 1967; fortnightly; cars, motorcycles and sports; Editor BOŠTJAN JEVŠEK; circ. 16,000.

Delavska enotnost: 1000 Ljubljana, Dalmatinova 4; tel. (1) 1310033; fax (1) 1313942; f. 1942; weekly; trade union issues; Dir and Editor-in-Chief MARJAN HORVAT; circ. 16,000.

Dolenjski list: 8000 Novo mesto, Glavni trg 24; tel. (7) 3323606; fax (7) 3322898; internet www.dol-list.si; f. 1950; weekly; general and local information; Editor-in-Chief MARJAN LEGAN; circ. 24,000.

Družina: 1000 Ljubljana, trg Krekov 1; tel. (1) 1316202; fax (1) 1316152; e-mail druzina@siol.net; internet www.druzina.si; f. 1952; Christian; Editor-in-Chief JANEZ GRIL; circ. 70,000.

Finance: 1509 Ljubljana, Dunajska 5; tel. (1) 1330137; fax (1) 1312223; internet www.finance.si; f. 1992; 2 a week; Editor-in-Chief JOŽE PETROVČIČ; circ. 8,500.

Gea: 1536 Ljubljana, Slovenska 29; tel. (1) 2413230; fax (1) 1252836; e-mail gea@mkz-lj.si; f. 1990; monthly; popular science; Editor-in-Chief JANA LESKOVEC; circ. 23,000.

Gorenjski glas: 4000 Kranj, Zoisova 1; tel. (4) 2014200; fax (4) 2014213; internet www.gorenjskiglas.si; f. 1947; 2 a week; general and regional information; Editor-in-Chief MARIJA VOLEJAK; circ. 23,300.

Jana: 1509 Ljubljana, Dunajska 5; tel. (1) 319260; fax (1) 1334320; f. 1972; weekly; women's interest; Editor-in-Chief BERNARDA JEKLIN; circ. 62,000.

Kaj: 62000 Maribor, Svetozarevska 14; tel. (2) 26951; fax (2) 227736; f. 1984; weekly; popular; Editor-in-Chief MILAN PREDAN; circ. 16,500.

Kmečki glas: 1000 Ljubljana, p.p. 47, Železna 14; tel. (1) 1735350; fax (1) 1735376; internet www.kmeckiglas.com; weekly; general and agricultural news; Dir BORIS DOLNIČAR; circ. 38,000.

Lipov list: 1000 Ljubljana, Miklosičeva 38/6; tel. (1) 4341682; fax (1) 4341680; e-mail tzs@siol.net; monthly; Editor-in-Chief MARJETICA NOVAK.

Mag: 1000 Ljubljana, Njegoševa 14; tel. (1) 319480; fax (1) 1329158; f. 1995; weekly; news and politics; Editor-in-Chief JANEZ MARKES.

Mladina: 1000 Ljubljana, Resljeva 16; tel. (1) 1328175; fax (1) 1331239; internet www.mladina.si; f. 1942; weekly; news magazine; Editor-in-Chief JANI SEVER; circ. 30,000.

Moj mikro: 1509 Ljubljana, Dunajska 5; tel. (1) 4738261; fax (1) 4738109; e-mail marjan.kodelja@delo-revije.si; internet www.mojmikro.si; monthly; personal computers; Editor-in-Chief MARJAN KODELJA.

Muska: 1000 Ljubljana, Kersnikova 4; tel. (1) 1317039; fax (1) 322570; e-mail kaja.sivic@kiss.uni_lj.si; monthly; music; Editor-in-Chief KAJA SIVIČ.

Naš Cas (Our Time): 63320 Velenje, Foltova 10; tel. (3) 855450; fax (3) 851990; f. 1956; weekly; general and regional information; Editor-in-Chief STANE VOVK; circ. 6,250.

Nedeljski dnevnik (Weekly Record): 1000 Ljubljana, Kopitarieva 2; tel. (1) 3082100; fax (1) 3082469; e-mail info@nedeljski.si; internet www.nedeljski.si; f. 1961; weekly; popular; Editor-in-Chief ZLATKO ŠETINC; circ. 145,000 (2006).

Novi tednik (New Weekly): 3000 Celje, Prešernova 19; tel. (3) 442500; fax (3) 441032; internet www.novitednik.com; f. 1945; weekly; general and local information; Editor-in-Chief BRANE STAMEJČIČ; circ. 16,980.

Obrtnik: 1000 Ljubljana, Celovška 71; tel. (1) 5830507; fax (1) 5193496; e-mail revija.obrtnik@ozs.si; internet www.ozs.si; f. 1971; monthly; small businesses; Editor-in-Chief MIRAN JAREC; circ. 60,000.

PIL: 1000 Ljubljana, Slovenska 29; tel. (1) 2413221; fax (1) 4252836; e-mail pil@mkz.si; internet www.pil-on.net; monthly; for children aged 9 to 12 years; Editor BARBARA JARC; circ. 21,000.

Podjetnik: 1000 Ljubljana, Dunajska 51; tel. (1) 1330102; fax (1) 1330450; internet www.podjetnik.si; f. 1992; monthly; business and management; Editor-in-Chief JOŽE VILFAN; circ. 8,500.

Primorske novice (News from the Primorska region): 6000 Koper, ul. OF 12; tel. (5) 6648100; fax (5) 6648110; e-mail editors@primorske.si; internet www.primorske.si; f. 1947; daily; general and regional information; Editor-in-Chief SILVA KRIŽMAN; circ. 23,000.

Profit: 1000 Ljubljana, Dunajska 7; tel. (1) 4304310; fax (1) 2318940; e-mail profit.uredmistvo@sid.net; 2 a month; business; Editor-in-Chief JOŽE SIMČIČ.

Rodna gruda (Native Breast): 1000 Ljubljana, Cankarjeva 1/II, Združenje Slovenska izseljenska matica; tel. (1) 2410288; fax (1) 4251673; e-mail rodna.gruda@druzenje-sim.si; internet www.zdruzenje-sim.si; f. 1951; monthly; national issues and news; Editor-in-Chief VIDA POSINKOVIĆ; circ. 2,100.

Slovenian Business Report: 1000 Ljubljana, Dunajska 5; tel. (1) 3091924; fax (1) 3091705; e-mail info@sbr.si; internet www.sbr.si; f. 1991; monthly; in English; economic affairs; Editor-in-Chief JOŽE PETROVČIČ; circ. 4,000.

Slovenija: 1000 Ljubljana, Cankarjeva 1/II; tel. (1) 2410284; fax (1) 4251673; e-mail sim@siol.net; f. 1987; quarterly; in English; news about Slovenia and Slovenes; Man. Editor JOŽE PREŠEREN; circ. 3,500.

Štajerski Tednik: 2250 Ptuj, Raičeva 6; tel. (2) 7493410; fax (2) 7493435; e-mail tednik@radio-tednik.si; internet www.radio-tednik.si; f. 1948; weekly; politics, local information; Editor-in-Chief JOŽE ŠMIGOC; circ. 12,000.

Stop: 1000 Ljubljana, Dunajska 5; tel. (1) 319190; fax (1) 1330403; f. 1967; weekly; leisure, film, theatre, pop music, radio and television programmes; Editor IGOR SAVIČ; circ. 44,600.

Tretji dan (Third Day): 1000 Ljubljana, Jurčičev trg 2; tel. (1) 1263071; fax (1) 223864; weekly; Editor-in-Chief Dr TONE JAMNIK.

Tribuna: 1000 Ljubljana, Kersnikova 4; tel. (1) 319496; fax (1) 319448; 3 a week; student newspaper; Editor-in-Chief BOJAN KORENINI.

Vestnik Murska Sobota (Murska Sobota Herald): 9000 Murska Sobota, ul. Arhitekta Novaka 13; tel. (2) 5311960; fax (2) 5321175; e-mail vestnik@eunet.si; internet www.p-inf.si; f. 1949; weekly; popular; Editor-in-Chief JANEZ VOTEK; circ. 20,000.

Zdravje (Health): 1000 Ljubljana, Smartinska 10; tel. (1) 2319360; monthly; Editor-in-Chief MARIJA MICA KOTNIK.

PRESS AGENCIES

Morel: 1000 Ljubljana, Reboljeva 13, statti Parmova 41–45; tel. (1) 4361222; fax (1) 4361223; e-mail morel@si21.com; internet www.morel.si; f. 1993; Dir and Chief Editor EMIL LUKANČIČ-MORI.

Slovenska Tiskovna Agencija (STA): 1000 Ljubljana, Cankarjeva 5, p.p. 145; tel. (1) 2410100; fax (1) 4266050; e-mail desk@sta.si; internet www.sta.si; f. 1991; Gen. Man. BOJAN VESELINOVIČ; Editor-in-Chief BORUT MEŠKO.

Publishers

Cankarjeva Založba: 1000 Ljubljana, Kopitarjeva 2; tel. (1) 3603720; fax (1) 3603787; e-mail import.books@cankarjeva-z.si; internet www.cankarjeva-z.si; f. 1945; philosophy, science and popular science, dictionaries and reference books, Slovenian and translated literature, international co-productions; Dir-Gen. JOŽE KORINŠEK.

DZS d.d.: 1538 Ljubljana, Dalmatinova 2; tel. (1) 3069700; fax (1) 3069877; e-mail info@dzs.si; internet www.dzs.si; f. 1945; textbooks, manuals, world classics, natural sciences, art books, encyclopedias, dictionaries, educational CD-ROMs; Exec. Dir ADA DE COSTA PETAN.

Mladinska Knjiga Založba: 1000 Ljubljana, Slovenska 29; tel. (1) 2413288; fax (1) 4252294; e-mail intsales@mkz-lj.si; f. 1945; books for youth and children, including general, fiction, science, travel and school books, language courses, magazines and videos; Dir MILAN MATOS.

Slovenska Matica: 1000 Ljubljana, Kongresni trg 8; tel. and fax (1) 4224340; e-mail drago.jancar@siol.net; f. 1864; poetry, science, philosophy; Pres. Prof. Dr MILČEK KOMELJ.

Založba Lipa Koper: Koper; tel. (5) 6274883; fiction; Dir Prof. JOŽE A. HOČEVAR.

Založba Obzorja d.d. Maribor: 2000 Maribor, Partizanska 3–5; tel. (2) 2348100; fax (2) 2348135; e-mail info@zalozba-obzorja.si; internet www.zalozba-obzorja.si; f. 1950; popular science, general literature, periodicals, etc.; Man. Dir GORAZD ZEMLJARIČ.

Broadcasting and Communications

TELECOMMUNICATIONS

Telecommunications Agency (Agencija za telekomunikacije, radiodifuzijo in pošto Republike Slovenije—ATRP): 1000 Ljubljana, Kotnikova 19A; tel. (1) 4734900; fax (1) 4328036; e-mail urst.box@gov.si; internet www.atrp.si; Dir JOŽE KLEŠNIK (acting).

Mobitel: 1537 Ljubljana, Vilharjeva 23; tel. (1) 4722200; fax (1) 4722990; e-mail info@mobitel.si; internet www.mobitel.si; f. 1991; 100% owned by Telekom Slovenije; mobile cellular telecommunications services; Chief Exec. KLAVDIJ GODNIČ.

Si.mobil–Vodafone: 1000 Ljubljana, Šmartinska cesta 134B; tel. (1) 5440000; fax (1) 5440099; e-mail info@simobil.si; internet www.simobil.com; f. 1999; subsidiary of Mobilkom Austria; Chair. of Bd DEJAN TURK; 370,000 subscribers (Mar. 2006).

T-2: 2000 Maribor, Streliška cesta 150; e-mail pr@t-2.net; internet www.t-2.net; f. 2004; mobile cellular telecommunications services.

Telekom Slovenije: 1000 Ljubljana, Cigaletova 15; tel. (1) 2341000; fax (1) 2314736; e-mail info@telekom.si; internet www.telekom.si; f. 1949; 52.5% state-owned; Pres. BOJAN DREMELJ.

Tušmobil: 3000 Celje, Resljeva ulica 16; tel. (1) 6000999; fax (1) 6002021; internet www.tusmobil.si; f. 2007; mobile cellular telecommunications services.

BROADCASTING

Regulatory Authority

Slovenian Broadcasting Council (Svet za Radiodifuzijo—SRDF): 1000 Ljubljana, Stegne 7; tel. (1) 5836300; fax (1) 5111101; e-mail srdf.box@apek.si; internet www.srdf.si; f. 1994; nine mems; protects independence of radio and television programmes; supervises the activities of broadcasting and cable operators; Chair. Dr DEJAN JELOVAC.

Radio

Radiotelevizija Slovenija (RTV Slo): 1550 Ljubljana, Kolodvorska 2; tel. (1) 4752154; fax (1) 4752150; e-mail webmaster@rtvslo.si; internet www.rtvslo.si; f. 1928; 3 radio programmes nationally; broadcasts in Slovene, Hungarian and Italian; Gen. Man. ANTON GUZEJ.

Radio Koper Capodistria: 6000 Koper, ul. OF 15; tel. (5) 6485483; fax (5) 6485488; e-mail radio.koper@rtvslo.si; internet www.rtvslo.si; Dir DRAGOMIR MIKELIĆ.

Radio Slovenia International: 2000 Maribor, Ilichova 33; tel. (2) 4299132; fax (2) 4299215; e-mail srecko.trglec@rtvslo.si; internet www.rtvslo.si; f. 2001; broadcasts in Slovene, English and German 24 hours a day; Editor-in-Chief SREČKO TRGLEC.

Television

Radiotelevizija Slovenija (RTV Slo): 1550 Ljubljana, Kolodvorska 2; tel. (1) 4752154; fax (1) 4752150; e-mail webmaster@rtvslo.si; internet www.rtvslo.si/html/radio-slo; f. 1928; 3 television programmes (TV1, TV2 and TV3) nationally; broadcasts in Slovene, Hungarian and Italian; Gen. Man. ANTON GUZEJ.

Kanal A: 1000 Ljubljana, Tivolska 50; tel. (1) 1334133; fax (1) 1334222; Pres. DOUGLAS FULTON.

Pop TV: 1000 Ljubljana, Kranjčeva 26; tel. (1) 1893200; fax (1) 1612222; Editor TOMAŽ PEROVIČ.

TV 3: 1210 Ljubljana, Štula 23; tel. (1) 1831200; fax (1) 1521512; Editor-in-Chief MLADEN SICHROVSKY.

Finance

BANKS

(cap. = capital; res = reserves; dep. = deposits; m. = million; amounts in euros, unless otherwise indicated; brs = branches)

In January 1999 new banking legislation allowed foreign banks to establish branches in Slovenia for the first time.

National Bank

Banka Slovenije (Bank of Slovenia): 1505 Ljubljana, Slovenska 35; tel. (1) 4719000; fax (1) 2515516; e-mail bsl@bsi.si; internet www.bsi.si; formerly National Bank of Slovenia, as part of the Yugoslav banking system; assumed central bank functions in 1991; cap. and res 799.9m., dep. 936.5m. (Dec. 2007); Gov. Dr MARKO KRANJEC.

Selected Banks

Abanka Vipa d.d.: 1517 Ljubljana, Slovenska 58, POB 368; tel. (1) 4718100; fax (1) 4325165; e-mail info@abanka.si; internet www.abanka.si; f. 1955 as Ljubljana Branch of Yugoslav Bank for Foreign Trade; present name adopted 1989; cap. 23.0m., res 427.5m., dep. 2,961.7m. (Dec. 2007); Pres. ALES ZAJDELA; 32 brs.

Banka Celje d.d.: 3001 Celje, Vodnikova 2, POB 431; tel. (3) 4221000; fax (3) 4221100; e-mail info@banka-celje.si; internet www.banka-celje.si; cap. 14.1m., res 51.5m., dep. 1,333.2m. (Dec. 2007); Pres. NIKO KAČ.

Banka Koper d.d.: 6502 Koper, Pristaniška 14; tel. (5) 6661000; fax (5) 6662006; e-mail info@banka-koper.si; internet www.banka-koper.si; f. 1955; cap. 29.7m., res 176.5m., dep. 1,411.5m. (Dec. 2007); Pres. of the Management Bd VOJKO COK; 14 brs.

Deželna banka Slovenije d.d.: 1000 Ljubljana, Kolodvorska 9; tel. (1) 4727100; fax (1) 4727411; e-mail info@dbs.si; internet www.dbs.si; f. 1990; present name adopted 2004; cap. 15.8m., res 38.0m., dep. 669.9m. (Dec. 2007); Pres. Dr DRAŠKO VESELINOVIČ; 10 brs.

Gorenjska Banka d.d. Kranj: 4000 Kranj, Bleiweisova cesta 1, POB 147; tel. (4) 2084000; fax (4) 2021718; e-mail info@gbkr.si; internet www.gbkr.si; f. 1955; cap. 13.8m., res 337.3m., dep. 1,337.5m. (Dec. 2007); Pres. and Chief Exec. ZLATKO KAVČIČ; 5 brs.

Hypo Alpe-Adria-Bank d.d.: 1000 Ljubljana, Dunajska cesta 117; tel. (1) 5804000; fax (1) 5804001; e-mail hypo-bank@hypo.si; internet www.hypo-alpe-adria.si; f. 1999; cap. 114.0m., res 21.9m., dep. 1,746.5m. (Dec. 2007); Pres. ANTON ROMIH.

Nova Kreditna banka Maribor d.d. (Nova KBM): 2505 Maribor, Vita Kraigherja 4; tel. (2) 2292290; fax (2) 2524333; e-mail info@nkbm.si; internet www.nkbm.si; f. 1955; present name adopted 1994; 42.3% state-owned; cap. 24.4m., res 261.6m., dep. 3,832.1m. (Dec. 2007); Pres. and CEO MATJAŽ KOVAČIČ; 90 brs and sub-brs.

Nova Ljubljanska banka d.d. (NLB): 1520 Ljubljana, trg Republike 2; tel. (1) 4250155; fax (1) 4250331; e-mail info@nlb.si; internet www.nlb.si; f. 1994; commercial, investment and savings bank; 35.4% state-owned, 34.0% owned by KBC Bank NV (Belgium); cap. 66.8m., res 1,460.5m., dep. 11,157.3m. (Dec. 2007); Pres. MARJAN KRAMAR; 198 brs.

Probanka d.d.: 2000 Maribor, Svetozarevska 12; tel. (2) 2520500; fax (2) 2526029; e-mail info@probanka.si; internet www.probanka.si; f. 1991; cap. 53.4m., res 17.8m., dep. 960.7m. (Dec. 2007); Pres. and Chair. ROMANA PAJENK.

Raiffeisen banka d.d: 2000 Maribor, Slomškov trg 18; tel. (2) 2293100; fax (2) 2223502; e-mail info@r-kb.si; internet www.r-kb.si; f. 1992; present name adopted 2007; cap. 14.1m., res 36.1m., dep. 796.2m. (Dec. 2007); Chair. KLEMENS NOWOTNY; 14 brs.

SKB Banka d.d.: 1000 Ljubljana, Ajdovščina 4; tel. (1) 4715918; fax (1) 4715513; e-mail info@skb.si; internet www.skb.si; f. 1978; 99.6% owned by Société Générale (France); cap. 52.8m., res 145.6m., dep. 2,199.6m. (Dec. 2007); Pres. and Chief Exec. CVETKA SELŠEK; 58 brs.

UniCredit Banka Slovenija d.d.: 1000 Ljubljana, Smartinska 140; tel. (1) 5876600; fax (1) 5411860; e-mail info@unicreditgroup.si; internet www.unicreditgroup.si; f. 1991; fmrly Bank Austria Creditanstalt d.d. Ljubljana; name changed as above Sept. 2007; cap. 3,898.9m. tolars, res 29,986.6m. tolars, dep. 482,666.7m. tolars (Dec. 2006); Chair. FRANCE ARHAR.

STOCK EXCHANGE

Ljubljana Stock Exchange (Ljubljanska Borza d.d.): 1000 Ljubljana, Slovenska 56; tel. (1) 4710211; fax (1) 4710213; e-mail info@ljse.si; internet www.ljse.si; f. 1989; operative 1990; Pres. ANDREJ SKETA.

INSURANCE

Adriatic Insurance Co: 6503 Koper, Ljubljanska cesta 3A; tel. (5) 6643100; fax (5) 6643303; e-mail info@adriatic.si; internet www.adriatic.si; f. 1990.

SLOVENIA

Grawe Insurance Co d.d.: 2000 Maribor, Gregorčičeva 39; tel. (2) 2285500; fax (2) 2285526; e-mail prima@prima.si.

Maribor Insurance Co: 2507 Maribor, Cankarjeva 3; tel. (2) 224111.

Merkur Insurance Co: 1000 Ljubljana, Dunajska 58; tel. (1) 3005450; fax (1) 4361092; e-mail info@merkur-zav.si; internet www.merkur-zav.si; f. 1992; Gen. Man. DENIS STROLIGO.

Triglav Insurance Co (Zavarovalnica Triglav d.d.): 1000 Ljubljana, Miklošičeva 19; tel. (1) 4747200; fax (1) 4326302; e-mail info-triglav@triglav.si; internet www.triglav.si; Chair. of Management Bd ANDREJ KOCIČ; Chair. of Supervisory Bd DAMJAN MIHEVC.

Trade and Industry

GOVERNMENT AGENCY

Agency of the Republic of Slovenia for Restructuring and Privatization (Agencija Republike Slovenije za Prestrukturiranje in Privatizacijo—ARSPIP): 1000 Ljubljana, Kotnikova 28; tel. (1) 1316030; fax (1) 1316011; e-mail webmaster@arspip.si; Dir MIRA PUC.

CHAMBERS OF COMMERCE

Chamber of Commerce and Industry of Slovenia (Gospodarska Zbornica Slovenije): 1504 Ljubljana, Dimičeva 13; tel. (1) 5898313; fax (1) 5898317; e-mail infolink@gzs.si; internet www.gzs.si; Pres. JOSKO CUK.

Chamber of Small Businesses of Slovenia: 1000 Ljubljana, Celovška 71; tel. (1) 4593241; fax (1) 4559270; Pres. MIHA GRAH; Sec. ANTON FILIPIČ; 50,000 mems.

UTILITIES

Electricity

Elektro-Slovenija d.o.o. (ELES): 1000 Ljubljana, Hajdrihova 2; tel. (1) 1301440; fax (1) 1250333; e-mail info@eles.si; internet www.eles.si; national electricity distributor; Dir-Gen. VITOSLAV TÜRK.

Nuklearna Elektrarna p.o. (NEK): 8270 Krško, Vrbina 12; tel. (7) 4802000; fax (7) 4921006; e-mail nek@nek.si; internet www.nek.si; f. 1974; 50% owned by GEN energija Ljubljana, 50% owned by Hrvatska Elektropriveda Zagreb (Croatia); production and distribution of electricity from nuclear power plant at Krško.

Gas

Geoplin d.o.o.: 1000 Ljubljana, Ljubljanska brigade 11; tel. (1) 5820600; fax (1) 5820601; e-mail info@geoplin.si; internet www.geoplin.si; f. 1975; national gas co; Gen. Man. ALOJZ STANA.

TRADE UNIONS

The Association of Independent Trade Unions of Slovenia: 1000 Ljubljana, Dalmatinova 4; tel. (1) 4317983; fax (1) 4318294; Pres. DUŠAN SEMOLIČ.

Independence—Confederation of New Trade Unions of Slovenia: Ljubljana; tel. (1) 4329141; fax (1) 4302868; Pres. FRANCE TOMŠIČ.

Transport

RAILWAYS

Slovenske Železnice (SŽ) (Slovenian Railways): 1506 Ljubljana, Kolodvorska 11; tel. (1) 2914001; fax (1) 2914800; e-mail boris.zjvec@slo-zeleznice.si; internet www.slo-zeleznice.si; Dir-Gen. BORIS ŽIVEC.

ROADS

In 2007 the country had 38,709 km of roads, of which 579 km were motorways and expressways and 975 km were highways, main or national roads. An 84-km motorway links Ljubljana with the coastal region in the south-west.

Directorate for Roads: Ministry of Transport, 1535 Ljubljana, Langusova 4; tel. (1) 1788000; fax (1) 1788139; e-mail drsc-info@gov.si.

SHIPPING

Slovenia's principal international trading port, at Koper, handles some 3m. tons of freight annually.

Luka Koper d.d.: 6501 Koper, Vojkovo nabrežje 38; tel. (5) 6656100; fax (5) 6395020; e-mail portkoper@luka-kp.si; internet www.luka-kp.si; f. 1957; Pres. of Management Bd ROBERT ČASAR.

Principal Shipping Company

Splošna Plovba: 6320 Portorož, Obala 55, POB 60; tel. (5) 6766000; fax (5) 6766130; e-mail plovba@5-plovba.si; transport of all types of cargo; regular liner service; Man. Dir ALDO KREJAČIČ.

CIVIL AVIATION

There are three international airports in Slovenia, at Brnik (Ljubljana), Maribor and Portorož.

Adria Airways: 1000 Ljubljana, Kuzmičeva 7; tel. (1) 3691000; fax (1) 4369233; e-mail info@adria.si; internet www.adria.si; f. 1961; operates international scheduled services to destinations in Europe and the Middle East; Pres. TADEJ TUFEK.

Tourism

Slovenia offers a variety of tourist attractions, including Mediterranean resorts to the west, the Julian Alps and the lakes of Bled and Bohinj to the north, and, in the south, the karst limestone regions, with more than 6,000 caves. The number of foreign tourist arrivals increased steadily from the mid-1990s, reaching 2,681,200 in 2007. Tourism receipts totalled US $1,911m. in 2006.

Slovenian Tourist Board: 1000 Ljubljana, Dunajska 156; tel. (1) 5891840; fax (1) 5891841; e-mail info@slovenia.info; internet www.slovenia.info; f. 1996; Gen. Man. DIMITRIJ PICIGA.

SOLOMON ISLANDS

Introductory Survey

Location, Climate, Language, Religion, Flag, Capital

Solomon Islands is a scattered Melanesian archipelago in the south-western Pacific Ocean, east of Papua New Guinea. The country includes most of the Solomon Islands (those to the north-west being part of Papua New Guinea), Ontong Java Islands (Lord Howe Atoll), Rennell Island and the Santa Cruz Islands, about 500 km (300 miles) to the east. The climate is equatorial, with small seasonal variations, governed by the trade winds. In Honiara the average temperature is about 27°C (81°F) and the average annual rainfall about 2,160 mm (85 ins). The official language is standard English, although pidgin English is more widely used and understood. More than 80 different local languages exist, and no vernacular is common to the whole country. More than 95% of the inhabitants profess Christianity, and most of the remainder follow traditional beliefs. The national flag (proportions 1 by 2) comprises two triangles, one of blue (with its base at the hoist and its apex in the upper fly) and one of dark green (with its base in the fly and its apex in the lower hoist), separated by a narrow yellow diagonal stripe (from lower hoist to upper fly), with five white five-pointed stars (arranged to form a diagonal cross) in the upper hoist. The capital is Honiara, on the island of Guadalcanal.

Recent History

The northern Solomon Islands became a German protectorate in 1885 and the southern Solomons a British protectorate in 1893. Rennell Island and the Santa Cruz Islands were added to the British protectorate in 1898 and 1899. Germany ceded most of the northern Solomons and Ontong Java Islands to the United Kingdom between 1898 and 1900. The whole territory, known as the British Solomon Islands Protectorate, was placed under the jurisdiction of the Western Pacific High Commission (WPHC), with its headquarters in Fiji.

The Solomon Islands were invaded by Japan in 1942, but, after a fierce battle on Guadalcanal, most of the islands were recaptured by US forces in 1943. After the Second World War the protectorate's capital was transferred from Tulagi Island to Honiara. In January 1953 the headquarters of the WPHC also moved to Honiara. Meanwhile, elected local councils were established on most of the islands, and by 1966 almost the whole territory was covered by such councils.

Under a new Constitution, introduced in October 1960, a Legislative Council and an Executive Council were established for the protectorate's central administration. Initially, all members of both bodies were appointed, but from 1964 the Legislative Council included elected members, and the elective element was gradually increased. Another Constitution, introduced in March 1970, established a single Governing Council of 17 elected members, three ex-officio members and (until the end of 1971) up to six public service members. A new Governing Council of 24 directly elected members was formed in 1973, when a ministerial system was introduced.

A further new Constitution, adopted in April 1974, instituted a single Legislative Assembly, containing 24 members who chose a Chief Minister with the right to appoint his own Council of Ministers. A new office of Governor of the Protectorate was also created, to assume almost all of the functions previously exercised in the territory by the High Commissioner for the Western Pacific. Solomon Mamaloni, leader of the newly founded People's Progressive Party (PPP), was appointed the first Chief Minister in August 1974. The territory was officially renamed the Solomon Islands in June 1975, although it retained protectorate status.

In January 1976 the Solomon Islands received internal self-government, with the Chief Minister presiding over the Council of Ministers in place of the Governor. In June elections were held for an enlarged Legislative Assembly, and in July the Assembly elected one of its new members, Peter Kenilorea, to the position of Chief Minister. Solomon Islands (as it was restyled) became an independent state, within the Commonwealth, on 7 July 1978. The Legislative Assembly became the National Parliament and designated Kenilorea the first Prime Minister. The main political issue confronting the new nation was the proposed decentralization of authority to the regions, support for which was particularly strong in the Western District, the most commercially developed part of the country. The first general election since independence took place in August 1980. Independent candidates won more seats than any of the three parties. Parliament again elected Kenilorea Prime Minister by an overwhelming majority. In August 1981, however, Parliament approved a motion expressing no confidence in Kenilorea, and chose Mamaloni, who now led the People's Alliance Party (PAP) following the merger of the PPP with the Rural Alliance Party in 1979, to succeed him as Prime Minister.

After legislative elections in October 1984, Sir Peter Kenilorea (as he had become) was again elected as Prime Minister. The new Government consisted of a coalition of nine members of Kenilorea's Solomon Islands United Party (SIUPA), three members of the newly formed Solomone Ano Sagufenua (SAS) party and three independents. The five provincial ministries, established by Mamaloni, were abolished, in accordance with Kenilorea's declared policy of restoring to central government control some of the powers held by the provincial governments.

In October 1985 a new political party, which sought a resolution of ongoing land disputes, the Nationalist Front for Progress (NFP), was formed, under the leadership of Andrew Nori. The SAS subsequently withdrew from the coalition, and Kenilorea formed a new Cabinet, comprising nine members of the SIUPA, three of the NFP and three independents. Kenilorea resigned following the approval of a motion of no confidence (two others having previously been defeated); in December Ezekiel Alebua, the former Deputy Prime Minister, assumed the premiership.

A report by a specially commissioned constitutional review committee, chaired by Mamaloni, was published in March 1988, and proposed that Solomon Islands become a federal republic within the Commonwealth, and that the President of the Republic be a native of the territory. In January 1989 the PAP announced that Solomon Islands would be declared a republic if the party won the next general election, scheduled to take place in February. At the election the PAP won 11 of the 38 seats, the largest representation obtained by any party, while Alebua's party, the United Party, won only four seats. In March Mamaloni was elected Prime Minister. His Cabinet included the former Governor-General of Solomon Islands, Sir Baddeley Devesi, and was described as the first since independence to comprise the members of a single party.

In October 1990 Mamaloni resigned as leader of the PAP, one week before Parliament was due to vote on another motion of no confidence in his premiership, declaring that he would remain as an independent Prime Minister. He dismissed five members of the Cabinet, replacing them with four members of the opposition and a PAP back-bencher. The Prime Minister defied persistent demands for his resignation by a majority of the members of Parliament. The remaining 10 ministers of the PAP were expelled from the party in February 1991, following their refusal to resign from their posts in the interests of party unity. Later that year, as a result of continuing economic decline, the Solomon Islands Council of Trade Unions issued an ultimatum demanding Mamaloni's resignation.

At elections to the recently enlarged National Parliament in May 1993 the Group for National Unity and Reconciliation (GNUR), led by Mamaloni, won 21 of the 47 seats. However, a newly formed coalition of opposition parties and independents, the National Coalition Partners (NCP), was successful in electing an independent member, Francis Billy Hilly, to the premiership in June. Hilly defeated Mamaloni by a single vote.

In October 1994 a constitutional crisis arose, following attempts by the Governor-General, Moses (later Sir Moses) Pitakaka, to dismiss Hilly on the grounds that he no longer held a parliamentary majority. However, Hilly remained in office, with the support of a High Court ruling, and confusion intensified when Pitakaka appointed the opposition leader, Mamaloni, to the position of Prime Minister. Hilly finally resigned at the end of October, and the post was declared vacant. In a parliamentary election to the premiership in early November, Mamaloni defeated the former Governor-General, Devesi, by 29 votes to 18.

In late 1995 and early 1996 Mamaloni's Government suffered a series of allegations of corruption and misconduct, particularly in relation to claims that seven ministers had received payments from foreign logging companies between 1993 and 1995, although in February 1996 all seven were acquitted.

Controversy over constituency payments by parliament members, and the reinstatement of the Constituency Development Fund, which entitled each member to US $66,000, and which had been widely used by members at the previous general election to secure re-election by purchasing gifts for voters, arose in mid-1996. In September the regional trades union organization, the South Pacific and Oceanic Council of Trade Unions (SPOCTU), cited the prevalence of corruption as the greatest obstacle to the islands' development, and stated that, in consequence, investors and aid donors would remain reluctant to make financial commitments to Solomon Islands. In February 1997 legislation to reform the provincial government system, which had been approved by the National Parliament but vehemently opposed by the larger provinces, was declared invalid by the High Court.

In May 1997 Mamaloni announced his intention to hold an early general election, following which he would resign as leader of the GNUR. Meanwhile, Alebua resigned from the leadership of the NCP, following accusations of misconduct, and was replaced by Edward Hunuehu. A general election took place on 6 August to a legislature that had recently been enlarged to 50 seats. The GNUR won 24 seats and a new grouping, the Solomon Islands Alliance for Change Coalition (SIACC), secured the remainder. In late August Bartholomew Ulufa'alu was elected Prime Minister, defeating the newly elected leader of the GNUR, Danny Philip, by 26 votes to 22. The new Government announced a programme of extensive structural reforms, including a rationalization of the public sector, a reduction in the number of ministerial portfolios (from 16 to 10), and measures to expand the private sector and to encourage greater participation of non-governmental organizations in the country's socio-economic development. The measures aimed to restore a degree of economic stability to Solomon Islands and to attract increased foreign investment. Legislation proposing that a politician seeking to change party allegiance would automatically lose his or her seat and be subject to a by-election was similarly intended to increase political stability.

In April 1998 Job Dudley Tausinga, whose Coalition for National Advancement (CNA) constituted the largest group outside the Government, was appointed Leader of the Opposition. Numerous defections between the Government and opposition in 1998 created ongoing political instability, which prompted the Government to reiterate its proposal for legislation to restrict the rights of elected members of the National Parliament to change party allegiance. In late September Solomon Mamaloni was elected Leader of the Opposition. Mamaloni died in January 2000 and was succeeded by Manasseh Sogavare, under whose leadership the CNA subsequently reverted to its original name of the PPP.

From April 1998 violent unrest in Honiara was attributed to ethnic tensions, mainly between the inhabitants of Guadalcanal and Malaita provinces. One underlying cause of the disturbances was the alienation of land by the Government since independence. Title to some land thus expropriated had been returned to Guadalcanal, but this had not allayed a widespread feeling of resentment in the province at the financial burden imposed by hosting the country's capital. It was reported that a group styling itself the 'Guadalcanal Revolutionary Army' (GRA) had begun a campaign of militancy to force the Government to relocate the capital. The unrest intensified in early 1999, prompting the Government to establish a peace committee for the province. In mid-1999 talks between the Premier of Guadalcanal Province, Ezekiel Alebua, and the Solomon Islands Prime Minister failed to alleviate inter-ethnic tensions in the province. Riots broke out in Honiara, and some 80 Malaitan immigrants were evacuated following threats by armed GRA militants. Following Ulufa'alu's demands that peace be restored to the province before the implementation of any further measures, the GRA ordered an immediate halt to its activities. The Guadalcanal Provincial Assembly subsequently declared that it had accepted an initial payment of SI $500,000 in compensation for accommodating the national capital. A reconciliation ceremony was held between the two parties, during which Alebua appealed to the GRA to lay down its arms. However, the Malaitans subsequently demanded that they too be compensated, to the sum of US $600,000, for damage to their property by the GRA militants.

Throughout 1999 violent clashes led to many deaths and forced thousands to abandon their villages, prompting the Government to announce a state of emergency in Guadalcanal. A Commonwealth Special Envoy and a UN peace-keeping force arrived to assist in the negotiation of a peace agreement with the Isatabu Freedom Movement (IFM, formerly the GRA, and also known in 1999 as the Isatabu Freedom Fighters—IFF), led by Andrew Te'e. A number of peace agreements reached throughout 1999 quickly broke down, and a peace-monitoring group from Fiji and Vanuatu, jointly funded by Australia and New Zealand, arrived in Guadalcanal in late October. In January 2000 a new guerrilla group emerged, the Malaita Eagle Force (MEF), and demanded US $40m. in compensation payments for loss of property incurred by Malaitans as a result of the conflict. Among their spokesmen was the former Minister of Finance, Andrew Nori.

Following further outbreaks of violence in the province that led to the death of four people, including two policemen, in February 2000, the Governor-General issued a decree outlawing membership of both the IFM and the MEF. Further clashes between the two rebel groups were reported in early March, and later that month riots took place in Honiara during which Malaitan immigrants stoned the headquarters of the Guadalcanal provincial government. In May the order that outlawed the groups was suspended. In early June members of the MEF, armed with weapons obtained in raids on police armouries, seized control of Honiara, placing Ulufa'alu under house arrest. The rebels demanded the immediate resignation of the Prime Minister, claiming that he, himself an ethnic Malaitan, had failed to compensate displaced Malaitans within the established deadline (allegedly set for that day) and also demanded the appointment of a new Commissioner of Police, the de facto head of national security. In renewed outbreaks of violence, up to 100 people were reportedly killed. The MEF, meanwhile, claimed to have gained control of the Police Force, 98% of the military-style weapons in the territory, broadcasting services and the telecommunications infrastructure. Ulufa'alu was released after four days, following an agreement between the MEF and government negotiators that a special parliamentary sitting would be convened during which Ulufa'alu would be subject to a motion of no confidence. A 14-day cease-fire was called to guarantee the safe passage of a Commonwealth monitoring team. In mid-June June Ulufa'alu resigned, one day before the scheduled no-confidence vote, but remained as 'caretaker' Prime Minister for a 14-day transitional period during which negotiations between the MEF, the IFM and a Commonwealth Special Envoy, Professor Ade Adefuye of Nigeria, were to take place. However, negotiations foundered following the MEF's refusal to hand over its weapons, pending the appointment of a new Prime Minister, which was to occur in an extraordinary parliamentary session in late June. As this session failed to raise the necessary quorum, the election of a new Prime Minister was delayed until the end of June, when Sogavare, the Leader of the Opposition, defeated Rev. Leslie Boseto, incumbent Minister for Lands and Housing, by 23 votes to 21. Sogavare declared that he would seek to establish peace without making significant changes to the policy of the previous Government. None the less, Sogavare announced a comprehensive reallocation of ministerial posts and restructuring of ministries. A new Ministry for National Unity, Reconciliation and Peace was established, and plans to create a Solomon Islands Defence Force and Ministry of Defence were announced. (Previously defence issues had fallen within the remit of the police service, which had become compromised because of alleged MEF infiltration, and by allegations that about 75% of officers were ethnic Malaitans.)

New negotiations in August 2000 resulted in the declaration of a 90-day cease-fire between the IFM and the MEF, although intermittent violent disorder continued in Guadalcanal. In late August IFM dissidents kidnapped the brother of Deputy Prime Minister Allan Kemakeza, demanding that SI $6.5m. in compensation be paid to the displaced persons of Guadalcanal. Kemakeza was released unharmed after 10 days without the payment of a ransom. In mid-September a breakaway group from the IFM, which had reverted to the former name of the GRA under the leadership of Harold Keke, held an airline pilot hostage with a demand for SI $2m.; he was released unharmed without the demands being acceded to, although Keke later claimed that the Government had paid him US $200,000.

A further round of talks in Queensland, Australia, led to the signing on 15 October 2000 of a treaty known as the Townsville Peace Agreement, by the MEF, the IFM, the Solomon Islands Government and the Provincial Governments of Malaita and Guadalcanal. An amnesty for all those involved in crimes associated with the ethnic conflict was to be granted, subject to the surrender of all weaponry within 30 days. The agreement also envisaged the creation of an international peace-monitoring team, and the repatriation to their home villages of all MEF and IFM soldiers at the expense of the Solomon Islands Government. Infrastructure and service in the two provinces would be restored and developed. The two provinces would also be granted a greater degree of administrative autonomy. Malaita Province was to receive additional funding to reflect the demands placed on the region by the influx of 20,000 displaced persons from Guadalcanal.

The implementation of the peace process, overseen by monitors from Australia and New Zealand, was threatened in mid-November 2000, when four people were killed in a shooting in Gizo, Western Province. Among the dead were two members of Papua New Guinea's Bougainville Revolutionary Army (BRA). Moreover, delays in the disarmament process involving the MEF and the IFM caused the deadline for the surrender of arms to be extended until 15 December. In mid-November, following an announcement that the Guadalcanal Provincial Government headquarters, which had been occupied by members of the MEF since June, was to be rehabilitated as a symbol of national unity, arsonists, believed to be linked with the MEF, attacked the building. Despite a series of ceremonies in late November and early December, in which members of the IFM and MEF surrendered weapons, it was believed that at least 400 illegally held weapons remained in circulation at the end of December. The legislation granting immunity to those who had committed crimes during the conflict was approved by Parliament in mid-December, and was criticized by the prominent human rights organization, Amnesty International. Also in December, new legislation permitted the appointment of two further ministers, a Minister of Rehabilitation, Reconstruction and Redirection, and a Minister of Economic Reform and Structural Adjustment. In late December one man was injured in an attack on a motel, in Honiara, in which disarmed former IFM rebels recruited to join the police were resident. Responsibility for the attack was attributed to a group calling itself the Marau Eagle Force, from the eastern Marau region of Guadalcanal, which was subject to separate peace negotiations. The Guadalcanal Liberation Force (GLF), as it was restyled, led by Harold Keke, also announced that it had not accepted the cease-fire. In early January 2001 concerns were expressed that, as a result of the ongoing economic crisis and a larger number of rebels having opted to join the police than had been anticipated, the Government might be unable to pay the former rebels, thus prompting further concerns about security.

In early January 2001 it was reported that the Government was contemplating an extension of the amnesty. Further violence broke out between Guadalcanal militants and members of the Marau Eagle Force. A peace agreement between the group and the IFM was signed in early February, although the Peace Monitoring Council observed that the infrastructure of the Marau region had been almost entirely destroyed since 1998 and that there was little immediate prospect of recovery. Violent incidents between the Marau Eagle Force, the GLF and government patrols throughout March–April 2001 led the International Peace Monitoring Team from Australia to state that the cease-fire arrangement reached under the Townsville Peace Agreement had been breached. In June the Premier of Guadalcanal, Ezekiel Alebua, was shot and seriously injured in an assassination attempt, apparently carried out on the orders of former leaders of the IFM. Harold Keke met the Deputy Prime Minister and the secretary of the Peace Monitoring Council in June and, in October, he voiced his support for the imminent general elections. However, the failure of former militia groups to surrender their guns was the main obstacle to a lasting peace throughout 2001, and officials estimated that there remained some 500 high-powered weapons in the community, in addition to hand-made weapons. The Government declared an 'arms amnesty' in April 2002. Militants surrendered some 2,000 guns with impunity. Weapons disposal began in June, coinciding with the International Peace Monitoring Team's departure from the country.

Meanwhile, in the second half of 2000 Western, Choiseul, and Temutu provinces all declared themselves to be semi-autonomous states within Solomon Islands. On 1 September the legislature of the latter, representing 20,000 inhabitants, approved a bill allowing for a referendum on the province's proposed independence; the worsening economic situation caused by the conflict in Guadalcanal was believed to be a determining factor. Additionally, movements in Guadalcanal and Makira provinces demanding greater autonomy were reported to have gained strength at this time. In late November the Minister of Provincial Government and Rural Development Nathaniel Waena announced that legislation to amend the Constitution would be submitted in 2001, in order to institute a federal system of government. Controversy arose following an announcement by the Government, in mid-March 2001, that it intended to introduce legislation to extend the life of Parliament for a further year, to expire in August 2002, stating that the social and economic position of the islands would not facilitate the holding of elections as scheduled in August 2001. This proposal attracted widespread opposition, including that of churches, trade unions, all provincial premiers, and the principal overseas aid donors to Solomon Islands. When it became apparent that he would not possess a parliamentary majority to support the legislation, Sogavare withdrew the bill from Parliament in early May; later that month it was announced that the elections would be held in December, funded wholly from overseas. In September the National Parliament approved a bill to increase national general election registration fees by 150%; Walter Folotalu, former member of the National Parliament for Baegu, successfully challenged the proposed legislation in the High Court in October. In the same month the High Court also began hearing the case brought by former Prime Minister Bartholomew Ulufa'alu; he had challenged the legality of the Government, seeking a ruling that the coup and subsequent election that ousted him were unconstitutional (he lost the case in November 2001).

In October 2001 public services deteriorated as nation-wide power cuts resulted from the inability of the Solomon Islands Electricity Authority (SIEA) to pay for its supplies of diesel fuel. The Government announced the introduction of health charges in order to maintain medical services, and was forced to appeal to Australia and New Zealand for assistance in policing, as violent crime was becoming endemic. A storage container holding weapons relinquished under the Townsville Peace Agreement was broken into and, in November, the revelation that compensation totalling SI $17.4m. had been paid to former members of the MEF for alleged property damage precipitated a violent demonstration by protesters demanding similar recompense. The Prime Minister was prevented from leaving his office (to attend a session of the UN General Assembly in New York), and the house of the Deputy Prime Minister was vandalized.

Accusations and rumours of bribery and intimidation were rife during the campaigning that preceded the general election, held on 5 December 2001. The electoral grouping of the SIACC won 12 seats, the PAP secured nine and the PPP six, while 22 seats were won by independent candidates. In the absence of a clear SIACC leader, 11 elected members of the coalition convened with 11 elected independents to decide upon a satisfactory premier. Following various shifts in allegiances, Sir Allan Kemakeza (as he had become), leader of the PAP and former Deputy Prime Minister, was declared Prime Minister. Despite having been previously accused of misappropriating state funds, the former Minister of Finance, Snyder Rini, was appointed Deputy Prime Minister and Minister for National Planning.

However, the new Government was unable to improve the increasingly desperate political and economic situation on the islands. A peace summit, organized by the Peace Monitoring Council, scheduled to be held in March 2002 was postponed until June, and, as the security situation in the country deteriorated further, numerous international peace monitors began withdrawing from the islands. In March Kemakeza dismissed Michael Maina, the Minister of Finance, after Maina failed to consult the Cabinet prior to announcing a number of drastic budgetary measures, the most significant of which was his decision to devalue the national currency by 25%. Maina was replaced by Laurie Chan, who in early April revalued the currency.

There were reports of further disturbances on the western coast of Guadalcanal in early June 2002 during which it was claimed that 11 Malaitans, who were part of a force attempting to capture the GLF leader, Harold Keke, had been killed. In mid-July water and electricity supplies to the capital were interrupted after the SIEA was once again unable to purchase fuel to power its generators, and the Solomon Islands Water Authority

(SIWA) had failed to pay rental arrears to the landowners of the Kongulai water source. The country was further adversely affected by a series of strikes in mid-August by public-sector workers in protest at the non-payment of their salaries. Later in that month the Minister for Youth and Sports and Women's Affairs, Rev. Augustin Geve, was assassinated. It was subsequently reported that Harold Keke had claimed responsibility for the murder. In September a church deacon was found beheaded on a beach on Guadalcanal's southern coast, an area considered to be a stronghold of the GLF. In a separate incident in the same month a woman and three children were shot dead and 11 others wounded in an assault which local chiefs attributed to Keke's organization. In late September Kemakeza made a formal request to the UN for a peace-keeping force to address the increasing state of lawlessness in the country and in the following month a delegation of four UN officials visited the islands to assess the situation.

In mid-October 2002 the Cabinet approved the establishment of the National Peace Council, an interim body, to replace the Peace Monitoring Council, the mandate of which expired on 15 October under the terms of the Townsville Peace Agreement. A permanent body was to be established after 16 January 2003. However, it was confirmed in the same month that more weapons were in circulation in the country than when the peace agreement was signed in October 2000. The National Peace Council expressed a belief that many of the weapons surrendered under the arms amnesty of April 2002 had been removed for use by police officers in their campaign to capture Keke.

In mid-December 2002 the Minister of Finance, Laurie Chan, resigned. The Government claimed that this action was in response to criticism of his budget, which had recently been approved by the Cabinet. However, Radio New Zealand reported that his resignation was in protest at the Government's decision to pay unscheduled allowances to the 'special constables' (former militants from the ethnic conflict who were allowed to join the police force as part of the peace agreement) who had demanded the payments with threats and violence. The latter had included an incident in which gunshots were fired at the Prime Minister's residence by a group of 'special constables'. The Government confronted a serious challenge in mid-December when six independent members of Parliament resigned because of what they described as a 'leadership problem' within the coalition. However, the Government defeated an opposition motion of no confidence by 28 votes to 17.

The country's precarious peace process suffered a major reversal in February 2003 when a leading member of the National Peace Council, Sir Frederick Soaki, was assassinated. There was speculation that the killing might have been connected to his involvement in a 'demobilization' programme for 'special constables'. A report by Amnesty International in March 2003 claimed that the country's 'special constables' had tortured and killed numerous people in the operation against Harold Keke along the southern coast of Guadalcanal. In April three of Keke's close associates deserted him and reported that they had witnessed him carry out nine murders in recent weeks. The killings were mostly thought to have involved his own supporters whom he had suspected of collaborating with the police. In May it was reported that Keke had taken six missionaries hostage in southern Guadalcanal. In a separate incident on Malaita, in the same month, an Australian missionary was beheaded.

In early June 2003 Kemakeza travelled to the Australian capital of Canberra for a meeting with Prime Minister John Howard, at which he reiterated the Solomon Islands' request for direct foreign intervention in order to address the country's worsening law and order crisis. (Former Prime Minister Manasseh Sogavare had made a similar appeal for Australia to send troops to the country at the time of the signing of the Townsville Peace Agreement in October 2000, but the request had been rejected.) In mid-June senior officials from Australia and New Zealand arrived in Solomon Islands to assess the possibility of mounting a regional intervention in the country. At a meeting of the Pacific Islands Forum (see p. 393) in Sydney, Australia, later that month, delegates from the 16 nations agreed unanimously to send a multinational intervention force to Solomon Islands; eight island members stated their intention to commit personnel to the force. The proposed action was to constitute the largest armed intervention in the South Pacific region since the Second World War.

Meanwhile, reports of violence and intimidation by Harold Keke and his rebel forces continued during June 2003. At least 23 people (including 11 members of a religious order) were taken hostage and several more were killed. An estimated 1,000 villagers fled their homes after Keke took control of a police post, thereby expanding the area under his control. The rebel leader also burned two villages where he believed that local people had informed the authorities of his activities. Furthermore, in the same month his militia forced some 1,200 people at gun-point to stand along several stretches of beach in order to serve as a human shield and thereby prevent a planned police landing in the area. Atrocities continued in the following month when another settlement (of some 500 people) was burned on Keke's orders and a number of people (including several children) were beaten to death or beheaded.

Following further discussions in July 2003 the Australian Government stated its requirements for the intervention to proceed, which included unhindered access to the country's financial records and the appointment of up to 100 foreign nationals to senior positions in the islands' public service and government sectors. The economic component of the proposed intervention would also provide for the payment of Solomon Islands' domestic and foreign debts through increased aid from Australia and New Zealand. Displaced villagers (estimated to total 20,000 since ethnic violence intensified in 2000) were to receive a specific allocation of $100,000 in aid from Australia. The Solomon Islands Government unanimously approved legislation to allow the Australian-led force, the Regional Assistance Mission to Solomon Islands (RAMSI) as it became known, into the country, and the Australian warship HMAS *Manoora* subsequently arrived in Honiara with 400 personnel, followed by a total of 2,225 troops and police from various other countries, including New Zealand, Papua New Guinea, Fiji, Tonga, Vanuatu and Samoa.

In early August 2003 the UN Secretary-General, Kofi Annan, commended the Pacific island countries for their efforts to support Solomon Islands and stated that the UN was prepared to contribute actively to any future peace process in the country. On 13 August Harold Keke surrendered and was arrested, along with 10 of his close associates. Thousands of villagers gathered to watch as Keke handed over a large number of firearms and was taken away on HMAS *Manoora* for his own safety. Later that month a 17-member 'economic assistance team' arrived in Solomon Islands, some of whom were to assume strategic roles in government and the public service in order to implement major reforms. The Australian Prime Minister also made a one-day visit to the islands. By early September the regional forces announced that they had collected a total of 3,850 weapons since the start of a firearms amnesty a month earlier. Australia began to withdraw its troops in late October and by early December more than one-half of its personnel had left the islands. In November 2004 Tuvalu sent two police officers to join the regional forces, bringing the number of countries involved in the operation to 11. The murder of an Australian soldier in the same month prompted Australia to increase the number of its defence personnel in Solomon Islands by 100.

The capture and arrest of members of various militia groups, including two individuals who had been signatories to the Townsville Peace Agreement, continued during late 2003. Police Superintendent Mannaseh Maelanga, who had served as the MEF's Supreme Commander, was arrested in November and sentenced to one year's imprisonment in March 2004. Andrew Te'e, former Supreme Commander of the IFM, was arrested and charged with the murder of three people. In February 2004 Keke and two of his associates were found guilty of the murder in 2002 of Augustine Geve (see above). He was expected to stand trial for other alleged offences, including the murder of seven missionaries, in the following months.

The Government was subject to considerable embarrassment in December 2003 when the Minister for Communications, Aviation and Meteorology, Daniel Fa'afunua, was arrested and charged with the assault of his wife and of a female police officer, with being drunk and disorderly and with demanding money with menaces. The former minister was found guilty in February 2004 and received a lengthy prison sentence. In September of that year the Minister for Agriculture and Livestock, Alex Bartlett, was arrested on charges relating to violent offences that had occurred during 2000, when he was involved in the leadership of the MEF. In June 2004 Nathaniel Waena, the former Minister for National Unity, Reconciliation and Peace, was elected Governor-General, with 27 parliamentary votes.

Further controversy within the Cabinet arose in early 2005 when the Minister for Provincial Government, Clement Rojumana, was arrested on 25 corruption charges and the Minister for Police, Michael Maina, was charged with theft. Both ministers were replaced in March. In April the former Minister for Finance, Francis Zama, was charged with official corruption over the alleged granting to himself of an exemption from the payment of goods tax during his period in office. Moreover, a police investigation in mid-2005 claimed that the Minister for Health, Benjamin Una, had been involved in two shooting incidents in 2004 that had targeted personnel from the regional intervention force, including the killing of an Australian officer. Una denied the allegations. In October 2005 the Minister for Fisheries and Marine Resources, Paul Maenu'u, was obliged to resign following his vote at a meeting of the International Whaling Commission in favour of a reintroduction of commercial whaling, in defiance of the Government's stated position. Mathias Taro was appointed to replace Maenu'u. In November Una submitted his resignation as Minister for Health, having been arrested and charged with stealing aid funds that had been donated for a development project in his parliamentary constituency. Johnson Koli was named as the new Minister for Health. Alfred Sasako was appointed as Minister for Infrastructure and Development in the same month, but was dismissed in March 2006 following allegations of misconduct. In January 2006, meanwhile, Simeon Bouro was named as Minister for Mines and Energy.

In November 2005 the Prime Minister became involved in controversy with regard to the allocation of loans from a Taiwanese bank. It was claimed that during his tenure of the post of Minister for National Unity and Reconciliation in 2001, Sir Allan Kemakeza had received compensation of US $121,000 for personal losses incurred during ethnic unrest. Following an audit, it was revealed that millions of dollars could not be accounted for and that the Cabinet had remained unaware of the situation.

In the legislative election held on 5 April 2006 around one-half of the incumbent members of the National Parliament lost their seats. It was believed that only 16 of the 50 incoming members had formally declared their party affiliation prior to the election, illustrating that electors tended to vote for individuals rather than for representatives of specific political parties. It was subsequently reported that independents occupied 29 seats and that the recently formed Solomon Islands Party for Rural Advancement (SIPRA), led by Job Dudley Tausinga, held four seats, the National Party four seats, the PAP four seats and the Solomon Islands Democratic Party three seats, with the remainder being distributed among various other parties. On 18 April three candidates participated in the contest for the post of Prime Minister, but none secured the requisite majority in the first session of voting in Parliament. Manasseh Sogavare was thus eliminated and a second ballot took place, at which Snyder Rini, leader of the Association of Independent Members of Parliament and former Deputy Prime Minister, received 27 parliamentary votes, while Job Dudley Tausinga won 23.

Rini's appointment as Prime Minister led to widespread protests. A group calling itself People's Power delivered a petition to the Governor-General demanding Rini's immediate resignation, claiming that he had been involved in corruption and bribery. It was variously alleged that Rini had accepted funding from the local Chinese business community and from both mainland Chinese and Taiwanese supporters who hoped to influence the electoral process. Snyder Rini was nevertheless sworn in on 20 April 2006. Public dissatisfaction culminated in two days of the most serious rioting witnessed in the country for many years. Much of the capital was left in ruins, and in particular many local Chinese businesses and homes were destroyed in arson attacks. It was reported that more than 300 citizens of the People's Republic of China had been evacuated from Honiara to their homeland. A curfew was imposed, and in an attempt to restore law and order in the capital Australia dispatched reinforcements of 110 soldiers and 70 police officers. Several opposition politicians were among those arrested in connection with the rioting. However, shortly before a parliamentary vote of no confidence was scheduled to take place, and after just eight days in the post of Prime Minister, Snyder Rini announced his decision to resign. The announcement led to scenes of jubilation in Honiara, although Rini remained in office in an acting capacity, pending a fresh parliamentary ballot to choose the next Prime Minister. On 4 May Manasseh Sogavare was elected, securing 28 votes; Fred Fono, who had briefly served as Deputy Prime Minister in the interim Government, received 22 votes. The majority of Solomon Islanders appeared to welcome the appointment of Manasseh Sogavare, who on the following day announced the composition of his Cabinet. Job Dudley Tausinga was appointed as Deputy Prime Minister, also assuming responsibility for the portfolio of forestry, environment and conservation. Bartholomew Ululfa'alu was named Minister for Finance and Treasury; Patteson Oti became Minister for Foreign Affairs; and Bernard Ghiro was appointed Minister for Home Affairs.

Following his assumption of office, the new Prime Minister announced that the country's economic strategies were to be reorientated and that a new policy regarding the management of Taiwanese financial aid to Solomon Islands was to be formulated, to permit greater transparency in the use of such funds (see above). Francis Billy Hilly was dismissed from the post of Minister of Commerce, Industries and Employment in August following his alleged refusal to denounce a memorandum of understanding signed by his National Party with China. In October a parliamentary no-confidence motion submitted by Fred Fono, the Leader of the Opposition, against Prime Minister Sogavare, failed to gain sufficient votes to succeed. Sogavare subsequently effected a minor reorganization of his cabinet, in which the Minister of Finance and Treasury, Bartholomew Ulufa'alu, was replaced by Gordon Darcy Lilo, hitherto Minister for National Reform and Aid Co-ordination, while Steve Abana became Minister for Planning and Aid Co-ordination. In December Deputy Prime Minister Job Tausinga resigned, apparently over a logging-related dispute, and was replaced by Toswell Kaua, who retained the agriculture and livestock portfolio.

In early April 2007 a large earthquake in the South Pacific caused a tsunami that resulted in more than 50 fatalities in Solomon Islands and destroyed the homes of thousands in the Western and Choiseul provinces. Aftershocks continued to hamper international and local relief efforts. Australia and Taiwan both supported emergency operations in the area.

In May 2007 Minister for Public Service Joses Sanga died. Sanga's portfolio was allocated to Deputy Prime Minister Toswell Kaua, while the agriculture and livestock portfolio, hitherto the responsibility of Kaua, was transferred to a new cabinet member, Severino Nuaiasi. In the same month Francis Zama was convicted of official corruption (see above), receiving a 20-month prison sentence. Zama's sentence was subsequently suspended, and in October he was appointed Minister for Justice and Legal Affairs, before being transferred to the finance and treasury portfolio, and later to education and human resources. In November Sir Allan Kemakeza, the former Prime Minister, was convicted of larceny, intimidation and demanding money with menaces, relating to the theft of vehicles from a local law firm in 2002.

In August 2007 a motion of no confidence against Sogavare was withdrawn amid reports of bribery allegations against a member of the opposition. Sogavare confronted a further challenge in November when 13 members of his Government resigned, including Deputy Prime Minister Toswell Kaua, Minister for Education and Human Resources Development Derek Sikua and other cabinet ministers. Together with the opposition, the group urged Sogavare himself to resign owing to the lack of confidence in his leadership. With the prospect of another motion of no confidence, a protracted period of uncertainty ensued. Sogavare's non-attendance at an earlier meeting of the Pacific Islands Forum, along with his handling of the Moti affair (see below), were criticized in some quarters. Both sides claimed to have the support of a parliamentary majority, and several defectors and members of the opposition reportedly joined the Government after being appointed to cabinet posts. However, in mid-December a no-confidence motion submitted against Sogavare succeeded by a narrow margin, and soon after, Derek Sikua was elected to replace him as Prime Minister. Sikua's Cabinet included several members of the Sogavare Government prior to the defections, including Toswell Kaua, who was appointed Minister for Law and Justice, and Gordon Darcy Lilo, who assumed responsibility for environment, conservation and meteorology. Other notable appointments included Fred Fono as Deputy Prime Minister and William Haomae as Minister for Foreign Affairs. The Government announced that it aimed to scale down the number of political appointments in an attempt to curb government spending.

In January 2008 the opposition was further weakened by the withdrawal of support of four of its members. It was reported in June that the Government was promoting the federalization of Solomon Islands and was soon to introduce legislation to that effect. In late July the opposition filed a motion of no confidence against the Government, citing public dissatisfaction with increasing food prices, among other factors. However, the motion, which was presented to the National Parliament in early August, was defeated by a considerable margin. Meanwhile, the conviction of Sir Allan Kemakeza (see above), Minister for Forestry and former Prime Minister, resulted in his departure from the Cabinet as well as from the National Parliament, which in turn precipitated a minor ministerial reorganization in September: Matthew Wale was appointed as Minister for Education and Human Resources Development, to replace Job Dudley Tausinga, who assumed responsibility for the forestry portfolio. In October Prime Minister Sikua was acquitted of drink-driving charges brought against him in January. In late April 2009, furthermore, Sikua and Secretary to Cabinet Jeremiah Manele filed a joint defamation suit in the High Court against the *Island Sun* newspaper, for an article which alleged that the two men had become intoxicated and behaved inappropriately at the UN General Assembly in New York in October 2008.

In May 2009 Sikua effected a major cabinet reorganization: Peter Tom became the Minister for Home Affairs, and James Tora was appointed Minister for Police, National Security and Correctional Services; Samuel Manetoali became Minister of Lands, Survey and Housing, while Martin Magga was transferred to the health portfolio; Manasseh Maelanga, MP for East Malaita, was brought into the Cabinet as Minister for Provincial Government and Institutional Strengthening; David Pacha was appointed Minister for Mines, Energy and Rural Electrification; Laurie Chan replaced Toswell Kaua as Minister for Justice and Legal Affairs, the latter reportedly being removed for health reasons; and Johnson Koli was allocated the portfolio of women, youth and children's affairs. Sikua also dismissed six Permanent Secretaries who had been appointed under the Sogavare Government. The dismissed secretaries successfully sued the Government for compensation, claiming breach of contract.

In late January and early February 2009 heavy rainfall resulted in severe flooding in areas including Malaita and Central provinces. The Government proclaimed a national disaster as the number of fatalities rose to 10.

In April 2009 the Government officially established the Solomon Islands Truth and Reconciliation Commission. The panel was charged with investigating the causes of the violent conflict in Guadalcanal that occurred between 1997 and 2003. The Commission was composed of five members and was headed by a former Vice-President of Fiji, Ratu Joni Madraiwiwi. However, Amnesty International expressed concern that the Commission might be detrimental to future court cases against alleged perpetrators of the violence, as any evidence brought before the Commission would thus become inadmissible in trials.

Also in April 2009, an official report into the 2006 riots (see above) found the Royal Solomon Islands Police responsible for the violence, owing to incompetence and a failure properly to fulfil its duty. However, the report concluded that there was no conspiracy connected to the violence. Following its release, the Government was accused of editing the report to remove information regarding specific individuals and groups found to be responsible for the riots; the Government denied this charge.

In regional affairs, relations between Solomon Islands and Australia became increasingly strained in 2006 over the extradition of Julian Moti, an Australian citizen who in September had been appointed as the Attorney-General of Solomon Islands. Moti, who was wanted by the Australian authorities on a charge of statutory rape (allegedly committed in Vanuatu several years previously), had been arrested in Papua New Guinea but contravened the conditions of his bail and gained refuge in the Solomon Islands' High Commission in Port Moresby in October. Shortly thereafter he was flown, reportedly on an aircraft of the Papua New Guinea Defence Force, to Solomon Islands, where he was arrested by police officers serving under RAMSI and charged with illegal immigration. In mid-October Prime Minister Sogavare declared his unwillingness to give assent to any Australian extradition requests and claimed that Moti's detention was unlawful. Sogavare's threat to suspend the mandate for RAMSI and reappraise Australia's role in the mission attracted criticism from the parliamentary opposition, and fears were raised about the repercussions of the dispute on the security and stability of Solomon Islands. Indeed, Australia suggested that its aid policy might be affected by the incident. The rift deepened when RAMSI officers carried out a forcible search of Sogavare's office to obtain evidence relating to the Moti case, while Sogavare was abroad attending a meeting of the Pacific Islands Forum. At the meeting Australia was accused by both Sogavare and the Papua New Guinean Prime Minister, Sir Michael Somare, of violating the sovereignty of their respective countries; one of the conclusions of the summit meeting was the establishment of a commission to review RAMSI and its operations. Peter Shanel, the Minister for Commerce, Employment and Trade, was arrested for allegedly having given misleading information with regard to Moti's entry into Solomon Islands; it was reported that the dismissal of Police Commissioner Shane Castles, an Australian citizen, in December, was related in part to Shanel's arrest and to the raid on Sogavare's office. In mid-December immigration charges against Moti were dismissed. The Solomon Islands Government then proposed a dialogue between Moti and the Australian authorities. In January 2007 Australia appointed a new High Commissioner to succeed Patrick Cole, who had been expelled from Solomon Islands in September 2006 because of his alleged interference in domestic politics; Sogavare hailed the appointment of Peter Hooton in March as a means to a resolution of the problems between the two countries. However, RAMSI remained a point of contention: in February 2007 the Australian Minister for Foreign Affairs, in an open letter published in a Solomon Islands newspaper, appealed to the islanders to support the mission; in the same month the Solomon Islands Minister for Foreign Affairs, Patteson Oti, urged the formulation of an exit strategy for RAMSI. At the end of February a RAMSI official reacted positively to the Government's assertion that it would not arm its police force as previously intimated. In July, having been suspended for several months, Moti was sworn in as Attorney-General, an act that was described by Australian Prime Minister John Howard as 'provocative and insensitive'. Sogavare, for his part, threatened to take Australia to the International Court of Justice, claiming that its pursuit of Moti was related to political interests. Australia applied for Moti's extradition, but was refused in September. Relations between the two countries improved following the replacement of Sogavare by Derek Sikua as Prime Minister, and the subsequent extradition of Julian Moti to Australia in December 2007. Sikua visited Australia in January 2008, reportedly assuring the new Australian Prime Minister, Kevin Rudd, of his approval of RAMSI; Rudd paid a reciprocal visit to Solomon Islands in March, and in April 2009 Australia's Minister for Trade, Simon Crean, visited the Solomons to discuss trade and economic development issues. Evidence of a further strengthening of relations between the two countries was demonstrated when the Solomon Islands Government donated aid to Australia to assist in the relief effort following the devastating bush fires in the state of Victoria that occurred in February 2009.

In 1990 relations between Papua New Guinea and Solomon Islands deteriorated, following allegations by the Solomon Islands' Government that patrol boats from Papua New Guinea were interfering with the traditional crossing between Bougainville Island (Papua New Guinea) and the Shortland Islands, while the Papua New Guinea Government accused Solomon Islands of harbouring members of the rebel BRA and of providing them with supplies. Despite the signing that year of an agreement on joint border surveillance and arrangements to host peace negotiations between the BRA and the Papua New Guinea Government, relations worsened considerably in 1992 when Papua New Guinea forces carried out several unauthorized incursions into the Shortland Islands, in which a fuel depot was destroyed and two Solomon Islanders were killed. Alleging Australian involvement in the incursions, Mamaloni suspended surveillance flights by the Australian air force over its territory, and relations between the two countries deteriorated significantly. Despite the initiation of discussions between Solomon Islands and Papua New Guinea in January 1993, further incursions were reported in April. Following the election of a new Government in May in Solomon Islands, relations appeared to improve, and subsequent negotiations between the two countries resulted in an agreement to close the BRA office in Honiara. However, tensions with Papua New Guinea increased in 1996 as violence on Bougainville intensified. Numerous incursions by Papua New Guinea defence forces into Solomon Islands' waters were reported, while the Papua New Guinea Government repeated accusations that Solomon Islands was harbouring BRA activists. Nevertheless, in June 1997 Papua New Guinea and Solomon Islands concluded a maritime border agreement, following several years of negotiations. The purpose of the agreement was not only to delineate the sea boundary between the two countries but also to provide a framework for co-operation in matters of security, natural disaster, customs, quarantine, immigration and conservation. In December 1997 the Prime Ministers of the two countries paid an extended visit to Bougainville to express support for the recently established truce agreement. Furthermore, the Governor of Bougainville was sympathetic to the problem of increasing numbers of Solomon Islanders from the Western Province crossing to Bougainville in late 2001. Many were trading goods in Bougainville in exchange for food and services. Discussions regarding the border of Papua New Guinea were held in April 2002; both Governments were concerned about the increase of weapons trafficking from Bougainville to the Western Province. Renewed border discussions took place between the two countries in June 2003. A development agreement that included joint infrastructural development, technical assistance and information sharing was signed by the two Governments in March 2005. In January 2008 the new Solomon Islands Prime Minister, Derek Sikua, visited Papua New Guinea to bolster relations between the two countries, which, he maintained, had been damaged by the Moti affair and its consequences.

In March 1988 Solomon Islands signed an agreement with Vanuatu and Papua New Guinea to form the Melanesian Spearhead Group. The new group regarded as its principal aims the preservation of Melanesian cultural traditions and the attainment of independence by the French Overseas Territory of New Caledonia. In March 1990 the Melanesian Spearhead Group admitted the Front de Libération Nationale Kanak Socialiste (FLNKS—the main Kanak, or Melanesian, political group in New Caledonia). In mid-1994 the group concluded an agreement regarded as the first stage in the establishment of a free trade area by the three countries. Fiji was admitted to the group in mid-1996. Solomon Islands announced its commitment to further economic integration with the countries of the Melanesian Spearhead Group in late 1997. The members of the Melanesian Spearhead Group signed a constitution in March 2007. In October 1995 Solomon Islands became a signatory of the Federated States of Micronesia Agreement on Regional Fisheries Access. In early 1997 Solomon Islands and Vanuatu agreed to undertake negotiations on the maritime boundaries between the two countries in an attempt to clarify uncertainty regarding fishing rights.

Diplomatic relations with Taiwan were established in 1983. A seven-member parliamentary delegation, including five cabinet ministers, travelled to Taiwan in September 2004 to discuss mutual co-operation and aid. In May 2006 it was announced that Taiwan's first quarterly payment in relation to the Rural Constituency Development Fund (RCDF) had been released. Total Taiwanese aid was projected at US $2.9m. annually. In August, during an official visit, the Solomon Islands Minister for Foreign Affairs, Patteson Oti, reaffirmed his country's strong links with Taiwan, and in December 2007 the new Prime Minister of Solomon Islands, Derek Sikua, pledged to continue his country's pro-Taiwan policy. In May 2009 Prime Minister Sikua embarked upon a tour of Taiwan, Indonesia and Japan, where he met with senior-level government officials and attended a number of regional summit meetings.

Solomon Islands' relations with Japan attracted international attention in mid-2005, when, following receipt of US $6.7m. from the Japanese Government for a major project to improve Honiara Airport, Solomon Islands voted with Japan (see above) to remove a 20-year moratorium on commercial whaling at a meeting of the International Whaling Commission (thereby reneging on a recent commitment to abstain from the vote). Its decision to support Japan's pro-whaling position resulted in the removal of Solomon Islands from a list of destinations promoted by several international diving organizations, which was likely to have a negative impact on the country's tourism industry.

The country's practice of capturing and exporting large numbers of live dolphins drew international criticism in mid-2003, when police mounted a large-scale security operation around Honiara Airport to prevent journalists from filming some 200 dolphins being loaded into a cargo aeroplane bound for Mexico. Several reports of harassment and violence against foreign journalists were received. It was believed that, owing to the high price commanded by the sale of the animals, senior Solomon Islands officials were likely to be involved. The trade in wild dolphins had been prohibited by most developed countries under a Convention on International Trade in Endangered Species of Wild Flora and Fauna. Furthermore, the trade was not only a cause for concern among foreigners: in late 2003 one of the country's important traditional houses of chiefs, the Gela, expressed disquiet over the treatment that the animals had received. In December 2004 a consignment of dolphins was prevented from being exported after representatives from the fishing industry complained that the trade was harming the reputation of the islands' important tuna industry (widely perceived by Western countries to be 'dolphin-friendly'). The export of dolphins was subsequently banned upon the entry into force in November 2005 of a new law, whereby those found to have contravened the regulations might receive a fine or a prison sentence of six months. In June 2007, however, the ban was removed, and in October of that year a consignment of 28 dolphins was sent to the United Arab Emirates, provoking criticism from environmentalists.

From 2004 the huge increase in the production of round logs in Solomon Islands led to considerable disquiet among community representatives, landowners and environmentalists. The total harvest of round logs in that year was estimated at more than 900,000 cu m, which was equivalent to five times the sustainable limit for timber production in the country. In November a petition of more than 1,000 signatures was delivered to the Government, demanding a reduction in the current rate of logging, increased regulation of logging activity by foreign companies and a greater role for local communities in decisions made about their forestry resources. The petition, which contained endorsements from every province in Solomon Islands, urged the Government to approve legislation known as the Forests Bill 2004, providing for the sustainable management of the forestry industry. However, the Government postponed consideration of the proposed legislation, and it was reported that logging rates had increased yet further in anticipation of its introduction. Concerns were again aroused in late 2005, and in December the people of Maniwiriwiri village on Makira island staged a peaceful protest, successfully preventing bulldozers from passing through the village and gaining access to a logging project located near the site of the residents' water supply and dam. This was one of many peaceful protests in an area where the local community was taking an increasingly strong stance against logging operations. In April 2008 the incoming Government of Derek Sikua announced that more stringent environmental controls were to be imposed on the country's logging operations (see Economic Affairs).

Government

Under the 1978 Constitution, executive authority is vested in the British monarch, as Head of State, and is exercisable by the monarch's representative, the Governor-General, who is appointed on the advice of Parliament and acts on the advice of the Cabinet. Legislative power is vested in the unicameral National Parliament, with 50 members elected by universal adult suffrage for four years (subject to dissolution) in single-member constituencies. The Cabinet is composed of the Prime Minister, elected by Parliament, and other ministers appointed by the Governor-General on the Prime Minister's recommendation. The Cabinet is responsible to Parliament. The country comprises four Districts, within which there are nine local government councils, elected by universal adult suffrage. The Constitution provides for further devolution of power to provincial authorities.

Defence

In July 2003, as the security situation on Guadalcanal deteriorated, the Regional Assistance Mission to Solomon Islands (RAMSI), an Australian-led force comprising more than 2,500 troops and police from various countries in the region, arrived in Solomon Islands to restore law and order. Assisting the local security forces, RAMSI personnel remained in the country in mid-2009.

Economic Affairs

In 2007, according to estimates by the World Bank, Solomon Islands' gross national income (GNI), measured at average 2005–07 prices, was US $363m., equivalent to US $730 per head (or US $1,680 on an international purchasing-power parity basis). During 2000–07, it was estimated, the population increased at an average annual rate of 2.5%, while gross domestic product (GDP) per head increased, in real terms, at an average annual rate of 0.2%. According to figures from the Asian Development Bank (ADB), overall GDP increased, in real terms, at an average annual rate of 2.3% in 2000–06. GDP increased by 10.3% in 2007 and by 6.4% in 2008.

Agriculture (including hunting, forestry and fishing) contributed 54.7% of GDP (at 1984/85 prices) in 2006, according to figures from the ADB. In 2004 an estimated 28.7% of those working in the formal sector of the economy were involved in agriculture. In 2005, according to FAO, more than 71% of the labour force, including the informal sector, were engaged in agricultural activities. The principal cash crops have traditionally included coconuts, cocoa, rice and oil palm. Earnings from copra (which was for many years the country's main export) decreased from SI $45.6m. in 2006 to $36.8m. in 2007. The value of cocoa exports increased from SI $30.3m. in 2006 to $70.8m. in 2007. Meanwhile, the rehabilitation of the palm oil industry involved plans to replant thousands of hectares of the former plantations and to clear other areas for new plantations. Spices are cultivated for export on a small scale. The production of tuna is important, and fish accounted for 11.8% of export earnings in 2007. The forestry sector is the leading source of revenue, timber exports accounting for 65.2% of total export receipts in 2007. However, the dramatic increase in the production of timber from the early 1990s prompted several international organizations to express alarm at the rate of logging in the country (see Recent History). Output of timber reached 1,148,000 cu m in 2007, in comparison with 536,000 cu m in 2000. The value of timber exports rose from SI $190.5m. in 2000 to $838.7 in 2007. The World Bank estimated that agricultural GDP expanded by an annual average of 5.9% during 2000–07, increasing by 7.4% in the latter year.

Industry (including mining, manufacturing, construction and power) contributed 7.8% of GDP in 2006 and employed 6.4% of wage-earners in 2004. The mining sector's contribution to GDP is negligible. Gold has been the sole mineral export of significance. The other (mainly undeveloped) mineral resources include deposits of copper, lead, zinc, silver, cobalt, asbestos, phosphates, nickel and high-grade bauxite. In 2008 a Japanese company was reported to have identified significant deposits of nickel on the island of Choiseul. The World Bank estimated that industrial GDP decreased at an average annual rate of 1.5% during 2000–07; however, the sector's GDP expanded by an estimated 6.9% in 2007.

Manufacturing contributed 3.0% of GDP 2006, and employed 15.6% of wage-earners in 1995. The most important branches are food-processing (notably fish-canning), coconut-based products, brewing, saw-milling, logging and handicrafts. The World Bank estimated that the GDP of the manufacturing sector contracted by an annual average of 3.6% during 2000–07, expanding by 1.9% in the latter year.

Energy is derived principally from hydroelectric power, with solar energy being increasingly utilized. Mineral fuels accounted for 23.7% of the total import costs in 2007. Several potential petroleum-producing areas in the islands have been identified. Electricity output totalled 75m. kWh in 2007.

Service industries contributed 37.6% of GDP in 2006 and engaged 64.9% of wage-earners in 2004. Earnings from the tourism sector reached only US $2m. in 2006, compared with $13m. in 1998. Tourist arrivals were estimated to have increased from 13,748 in 2007 to 16,264 in 2008. The World Bank estimated that during 2000–07 services GDP increased by an annual average of 1.0%, rising by 4.5% in 2007.

In 2007 there was a visible trade deficit of US $71.9m. and a deficit of $44.3m. on the current account of the balance of payments. In 2007 the principal sources of imports were Singapore (which accounted for 29.0%), Australia (26.5%), Japan and New Zealand, while the principal markets for exports were the People's Republic of China (51.0%), the Republic of Korea (8.4%), Thailand (6.6%), Japan, Italy and the Philippines. The principal exports in that year were timber, fish, palm oil, cocoa and copra. The principal imports were mineral fuels, foodstuffs, basic manufactures, beverages and tobacco.

The 2008 budget projected total expenditure of SI $1,400m. According to the ADB, the fiscal deficit increased from the equivalent of 0.3% of GDP in 2007 to 5.6% of GDP in 2008. Aid from Australia was projected at $A236.4m. in 2008/09, while financial assistance from New Zealand was budgeted at $NZ32.8m. for the same year. In 2007, according to the ADB, the country's external debt totalled US $147m. and the cost of debt-servicing was equivalent to 4.3% of the value of exports of goods and services. The average annual rate of inflation in Honiara in 2000–07 was 8.6%. The rate of inflation was estimated by the ADB to have risen from 7.6% in 2007 to 16.5% in 2008. The extent of the islands' informal sector impedes an accurate assessment of the rate of unemployment; however, youth unemployment, particularly in urban areas, has remained at a high level.

Solomon Islands is a member of the Pacific Community (see p. 391), the Pacific Islands Forum (see p. 393), the Asian Development Bank (see p. 191) and the UN Economic and Social Commission for Asia and the Pacific (ESCAP, see p. 36), and is a signatory to the Lomé Conventions and the successor Cotonou Agreement (see p. 311) with the European Union (EU). The country is also a member (with Fiji, Papua New Guinea and Vanuatu) of the Melanesian Spearhead Group, which provides for free trade among member countries, and of the World Trade Organization (WTO, see p. 410).

The economy of Solomon Islands remains one of the least developed in the Pacific region. Progress has been impeded by weak governance, inadequate infrastructure and a very high rate of population growth. The country's major agricultural and forestry exports are vulnerable to inclement weather and to fluctuations in commodity prices on international markets. The regional intervention of 2003 (see Recent History) included an economic recovery programme involving increased assistance from Australia (totalling some $A1,000m. over 10 years). The destruction of numerous businesses (owned predominantly by Chinese entrepreneurs) in the rioting of early 2006 was a deterrent to potential investors. Furthermore, the islands' heavy dependence upon forestry, with logging being the prime constituent of both taxation and export revenues, has become a major economic, as well as environmental, concern. With the industry having continued to operate at an unsustainable rate, in April 2008 the new Government announced various measures to counter the detrimental impact of logging activities on the nation's forests. Henceforth all companies, including those engaged in the mining and agricultural sectors, were to be required to obtain a public environment report prior to commencing operations. In the longer term, the depletion of the islands' timber reserves and inevitable decline in future revenues were expected to require the Government to adopt a more cautious programme of expenditure. A major challenge for the Government, therefore, was the development of alternative sources of revenue. The substantial rises in global prices for essential commodities such as rice and petroleum in the first half of 2008 greatly increased inflationary pressures; in September the rate of inflation was reported to have reached a high point of 23.5%. The ADB anticipated that GDP growth would decelerate to 2.2% in 2009. Despite the projected decline in the growth of the economy, the Government's budget for 2009, announced in December 2008, provided for a significant increase in expenditure, of which the education sector was to receive a large allocation. As global economic conditions continued to deteriorate, in March 2009 it was announced that all development projects were to be reviewed. Priority was to be given to maintaining the country's essential services.

Education

Education is not compulsory in Solomon Islands. Primary education generally begins at six years of age and lasts for six years. Secondary education, normally beginning at the age of 12, lasts for up to five years. In 2005 enrolment at primary schools was equivalent to 97% of children in the relevant age-group (males 99%; females 95%) while enrolment at secondary schools was equivalent to 30% of children from the relevant age-group (males 32%; females 27%). In 1993 there were 523 primary schools and 23 secondary schools. Primary pupils totalled 75,082 and secondary students numbered 22,487 in 2004/05. There are two teacher-training schools and a technical institute. Scholarships are available for higher education at various universities overseas. The Solomon Islands Centre of the University of the Pacific opened in Honiara in 1977. In 2005 plans to construct several new educational centres were announced. In an attempt to reduce the number of pupils abandoning their studies each year, many new community high schools were to be built over a period of 15 years. The islands were also granted funding for nine new distance learning centres, one to be built in each of the provinces. In November 2005 it was also announced that the University of the South Pacific was to establish a fourth campus in Solomon Islands, thereby reducing the amount of government funding needed to send students overseas.

Public Holidays

2009: 1 January (New Year's Day), 10–13 April (Easter), 1 June (Whit Monday), 8 June (Queen's Official Birthday), 7 July (Independence Day), 25 December (Christmas Day), 26 December (Boxing Day).

2010 (provisional): 1 January (New Year's Day), 2–5 April (Easter), 24 May (Whit Monday), 7 June (Queen's Official Birthday), 7 July (Independence Day), 25 December (Christmas Day), 26 December (Boxing Day).

Weights and Measures

The metric system is in force.

SOLOMON ISLANDS

Statistical Survey

Source (unless otherwise indicated): National Statistics Office, Ministry of Finance, P.O. Box G6, Honiara; tel. (677) 27835; fax (677) 23951; e-mail Stats_management@mof.gov.sb; internet www.spc.int/prism/country/sb/stats.

AREA AND POPULATION

Area: 27,556 sq km (10,639 sq miles).

Population: 285,176 at census of 23–24 November 1986; 409,042 (males 211,381, females 197,661) at census of 21–22 November 1999. *Mid-2008* (projected estimate): 506,992 (males 261,214, females 245,778).

Density (mid-2008): 18.4 per sq km.

Ethnic Groups (census of November 1986): Melanesians 268,536; Polynesians 10,661; Micronesians 3,929; Europeans 1,107; Chinese 379; Others 564.

Principal Towns (population at 1999 census): Honiara (capital) 49,107; Noro 3,482; Gizo 2,960 (Source: Thomas Brinkhoff, *City Population*—internet www.citypopulation.de). *Mid-2005* (incl. suburbs, UN estimate) Honiara 61,000 (Source: UN, *World Urbanization Prospects: The 2005 Revision*).

Births and Deaths (annual averages, 2000–05, UN estimates): Birth rate 33.5 per 1,000; Death rate 7.3 per 1,000 (Source: UN, *World Population Prospects: The 2008 Revision*).

Life Expectancy (years at birth, WHO estimates): 66.5 (males 65.3; females 67.9) in 2006. Source: WHO, *World Health Statistics*.

Employment (excluding informal sector, 2004, estimates): Agriculture 6,342; Forestry 3,482; Fishing 5,114; Manufacturing (incl. mining and quarrying) 1,476; Electricity and water 469; Construction 1,397; Trade, restaurants and hotels 3,274; Transport, storage and communications 1,246; Finance, insurance, real estate and business services 806; Administration 6,758; Other community, social and personal service activities 21,757; *Total* 52,121. *2005* (excluding informal sector, estimate): Total employed 56,559. Source: IMF, *Solomon Islands: Statistical Appendix* (October 2006). *Mid-2005* ('000, FAO estimates): Agriculture, etc. 178; Total labour force 250. Source: FAO.

HEALTH AND WELFARE
Key Indicators

Total Fertility Rate (children per woman, 2006): 4.0.

Under-5 Mortality Rate (per 1,000 live births, 2006): 79.

Physicians (per 1,000 head, 2003): 0.1.

Hospital Beds (per 1,000 head, 2005): 1.5.

Health Expenditure (2006): US $ per head (PPP): 107.

Health Expenditure (2006): % of GDP: 4.7.

Health Expenditure (2006): public (% of total): 93.0.

Access to Water (% of persons, 2006): 70.

Access to Sanitation (% of persons, 2006): 32.

Human Development Index (2006): ranking: 134.

Human Development Index (2006): value: 0.591.

For sources and definitions, see explanatory note on p. vi.

AGRICULTURE, ETC.

Principal Crops ('000 metric tons, 2007, FAO estimates unless otherwise indicated): Coconuts 276 (unofficial figure); Oil palm fruit 155; Rice, paddy 5.7; Cocoa beans 5.3; Sweet potatoes 86; Yams 30; Taro 40; Vegetables (incl. melons) 8.2; Fruits (excl. melons) 0.3.

Livestock ('000 head, year ending September 2007, FAO estimates): Cattle 13.6; Pigs 54; Chickens 235.

Livestock Products (metric tons, 2007, FAO estimates): Cattle meat 750; Pig meat 2,300; Chicken meat 300; Hen eggs 510; Cows' milk 1,400.

Forestry ('000 cu m, 2007): *Roundwood Removals* (excl. bark): Sawlogs and veneer logs 1,130; Fuel wood 124 (FAO estimate); Total 1,254. *Sawnwood Production:* 12 (FAO estimate, all broadleaved, incl. railway sleepers).

Fishing (metric tons, live weight, 2006): Skipjack tuna 18,557; Yellowfin tuna 10,466; Bigeye tuna 248; Total catch (incl. others, FAO estimate): 39,336 (excl. aquatic plants 120).

Source: FAO.

MINING

Production (kilograms, 2006): Gold 10. Source: US Geological Survey.

INDUSTRY

Production (metric tons unless otherwise indicated, 2007): Copra 28,000; Coconut oil 741,000; Palm oil 22,000; Electric energy 75 million kWh. Source: Asian Development Bank.

FINANCE

Currency and Exchange Rates: 100 cents = 1 Solomon Islands dollar (SI $). *Sterling, US Dollar and Euro Equivalents* (31 December 2008): £1 sterling = SI $11.681; US $1 = SI $8.013; €1 = SI $11.151; SI $100 = £8.56 = US $12.48 = €8.97. *Average Exchange Rate* (SI $ per US $): 7.6095 in 2006; 7.6520 in 2007; 7.7344 in 2008.

Budget (SI $ million, 2007): *Revenue*: Taxes 938.8; Non-tax revenue 154.4; Grants 116.7; Total 1,209.9. *Expenditure*: Total 1,246.2 (Current expenditure 1,080.3, Capital expenditure 165.9). Source: Asian Development Bank.

Official Development Assistance (US $ million, 2000): Bilateral 22.1; Multilateral 46.3; Total 68.4 (Grants 69.7, Loans −1.3). *2005:* Total 198. Source: UN, *Statistical Yearbook for Asia and the Pacific*.

International Reserves (US $ million at 31 December 2007): Reserve position in IMF 0.87; Foreign exchange 118.18; *Total* 119.05. Source: IMF, *International Financial Statistics*.

Money Supply (SI $ million at 31 December 2007): Currency outside banks 213.24; Demand deposits at deposit money banks 500.40; *Total money* (incl. others) 720.05. Source: IMF, *International Financial Statistics*.

Cost of Living (Consumer Price Index for Honiara, average of quarterly figures; base: October–December 1992 = 100): 308.2 in 2005; 342.8 in 2006; 369.0 in 2007. Source: Central Bank of Solomon Islands, *Quarterly Review* (December 2008).

Gross Domestic Product (US $ million at constant 1990 prices): 248 in 2001; 238 in 2002; 243 in 2003. Source: UN, *Statistical Yearbook*.

Gross Domestic Product by Economic Activity (SI $ million at constant 1984/85 prices, 2006): Agriculture 182.6; Mining 0.0; Manufacturing 10.0; Electricity, gas and water 5.5; Construction 10.4; Trade 29.7; Transport and communications 16.2; Finance 15.7; Other services (including public administration) 63.8; *GDP at factor cost* 333.8. Source: Asian Development Bank.

Balance of Payments (US $ million, 2007): Exports of goods f.o.b. 168.1; Imports of goods f.o.b. −240.0; *Trade balance* −71.9; Exports of services and income 83.7; Imports of services and income −67.4; *Balance on goods, services and income* −55.6; Current transfers received 49.4; Current transfers paid −38.1; *Current balance* −44.3; Capital account (net) 15.0; Direct investment 2.8; Other investments −8.0; Net errors and omissions −7.3; *Overall balance* −41.8. Source: Asian Development Bank.

EXTERNAL TRADE

Principal Commodities (SI $ '000, 2007): *Imports c.i.f.*: Food and live animals 231,381; Mineral fuels, etc. 434,324; Basic manufactures 95,429; Machinery and transport equipment 206,847; Total (incl. others) 1,836,334. *Exports f.o.b.*: Fish 151,392; Copra 36,768; Palm oil 105,281; Timber 838,693; Cocoa 70,838; Total (incl. others) 1,285,651.

Principal Trading Partners (US $ million, 2007): *Imports*: Australia 86.0; China, People's Republic 11.1; Fiji 13.0; Japan 14.7; New Zealand 14.9; Papua New Guinea 12.6; Singapore 94.2; USA 6.1; Total (incl. others) 324.6. *Exports*: China, People's Republic 164.1; Italy 12.0; Japan 19.5; Korea, Republic 26.9; Philippines 11.9; Thailand 21.2; Total (incl. others) 321.9. Note: Data reflect the IMF's direction of trade methodology and, as a result, the totals may not be equal to those presented for trade in commodities.

Source: Asian Development Bank.

TRANSPORT

Road Traffic (motor vehicles in use at 30 June 1986): Passenger cars 1,350; Commercial vehicles 2,026.

SOLOMON ISLANDS

Shipping: *Traffic* (international traffic, '000 metric tons, 1990): Goods loaded 278; Goods unloaded 349 (Source: UN, *Monthly Bulletin of Statistics*). *Merchant Fleet* (registered at 31 December 2007): Vessels 34; Total displacement ('000 grt) 11.8 (Source: Lloyd's Register-Fairplay, *World Fleet Statistics*).

Civil Aviation (traffic on scheduled services, 2004): Kilometres flown 3 million; Passengers carried 85,000; Passenger-km 73 million; Total ton-km 7. Source: UN, *Statistical Yearbook*.

TOURISM

Visitor Arrivals by Country (2007): Australia 5,960; Japan 572; New Zealand 987; Papua New Guinea 1,007; United Kingdom 318; USA 953; Vanuatu 950; Total (incl. others) 13,748.

Tourism Receipts (US $ million, excl. passenger transport): 4 in 2004; 2 in 2005; 2 in 2006.

Source: World Tourism Organization.

COMMUNICATIONS MEDIA

Non-daily Newspapers (1996): 3; estimated circulation 9,000.

Radio Receivers (1997): 57,000 in use.

Television Receivers (2001): 12,000 in use.

Telephones (2006): 7,600 main lines in use.

Mobile Cellular Telephones (2007): 10,900 subscribers.

Personal Computers (2005): 22,000 in use.

Internet Users (2006): 8,000.

Broadband subscribers (2007): 1,000.

Facsimile Machines (1999): 764 in use.

Sources: UNESCO, *Statistical Yearbook*; International Telecommunication Union.

EDUCATION

Pre-primary (2002/03): 16,469 pupils.

Primary: 523 schools (1993); 2,514 teachers (1994); 75,082 pupils (2004/05).

Secondary: 23 schools (1993); 618 teachers (1994); 22,487 pupils (2004/05).

Overseas Centres (1988): 405 students.

Source: UNESCO, *Statistical Yearbook*; UNESCO Institute for Statistics.

Adult Literacy Rate (estimate based on census data): 76.6% in 2003. Source: UN Development Programme, *Human Development Report*.

Directory

The Constitution

A new Constitution came into effect at independence on 7 July 1978.

The main provisions are that Solomon Islands is a constitutional monarchy with the British sovereign (represented locally by a Governor-General, who must be a Solomon Islands citizen) as Head of State, while legislative power is vested in the unicameral National Parliament composed of 50 members (increased from 47 in 1997), elected by universal adult suffrage for four years (subject to dissolution), and executive authority is exercised by the Cabinet, led by the Prime Minister. The Governor-General is appointed for up to five years, on the advice of Parliament, and acts in almost all matters on the advice of the Cabinet. The Prime Minister is elected by and from members of Parliament. Other ministers are appointed by the Governor-General, on the Prime Minister's recommendation, from members of Parliament. The Cabinet is responsible to Parliament. Emphasis is laid on the devolution of power, and traditional chiefs and leaders have a special role within these arrangements. Legislation approved in August 1996 provided for the abolition of the provincial government system and the transfer of legislative and administrative powers from the nine provincial governments to 75 area assemblies and councils controlled by central Government.

The Constitution contains comprehensive guarantees of fundamental human rights and freedoms, and provides for the introduction of a 'leadership code' and the appointment of an Ombudsman and a Public Solicitor. It also provides for 'the establishment of the underlying law, based on the customary law and concepts of the Solomon Islands people'. Solomon Islands citizenship was automatically conferred on the indigenous people of the islands and on other residents with close ties with the islands upon independence. The acquisition of land is reserved for indigenous inhabitants or their descendants.

In mid-1999 it was announced that two review committees had been established to amend the Constitution. They were expected to examine ways in which the traditions of the various ethnic groups could be better accommodated.

The Government

HEAD OF STATE

Monarch: HM Queen ELIZABETH II.

Governor-General: Sir NATHANIEL WAENA (sworn in 7 July 2004).

CABINET
(May 2009)

Prime Minister: Dr DEREK SIKUA.

Deputy Prime Minister and Minister for Rural Development and Indigenous Affairs: FRED FONO.

Minister for Agriculture and Livestock: SELWYN RIUMANA.

Minister for Commerce, Industry and Employment: FRANCIS BILLY HILLY.

Minister for Communication, Aviation and Meteorology: VARIAN LONAMEI.

Minister for Culture and Tourism: SETH GUKUNA.

Minister for Development Planning and Aid Co-ordination: STEVE ABANA.

Minister for Education and Human Resources Development: MATTHEW WALE.

Minister for Energy, Mines and Rural Electrification: DAVID PACHA.

Minister for Environment and Conservation: GORDON DARCY LILO.

Minister for Finance and Treasury: SNYDER RINI.

Minister for Fisheries and Marine Resources: NOLLEN LENI.

Minister for Foreign Affairs, External Trade and Immigration: WILLIAM HAOMAE.

Minister for Forestry: JOB DUDLEY TAUSINGA.

Minister for Health and Medical Services: MARTIN MAGGA.

Minister for Home Affairs: PETER TOM.

Minister for Infrastructure Development: STANLEY SOFU.

Minister for Justice and Legal Affairs: LAURIE CHAN.

Minister for Lands, Housing and Survey: SAMUEL MANETOALI.

Minister for National Unity, Peace and Reconciliation: SAM IDURI.

Minister for Police, National Security and Correctional Services: JAMES TORA.

Minister for Provincial Government and Institutional Strengthening: MANASSEH MAELANGA.

Minister for Public Service: MILNER TOZAKA.

Minister for Women, Youth and Children's Affairs: JOHNSON KOLI.

MINISTRIES

Office of the Prime Minister: POB G1, Honiara; tel. 21867; fax 26088; internet www.pmc.gov.sb.

Ministry of Agriculture and Livestock Development: POB G13, Honiara; tel. 27987; fax 28365; e-mail psagriculture@pmc.gov.sb.

Ministry of Commerce, Industry and Employment: Honiara; tel. 28614; fax 25084; e-mail pscommerce@pmc.gov.sb.

Ministry of Communication and Aviation: Honiara; tel. 28049; fax 28054.

Ministry of Culture and Tourism: Honiara; tel. 26848; fax 26875.

Ministry of Development, Planning and Aid Co-ordination: Honiara; tel. 28608; fax 30163.

Ministry of Education and Human Resources: POB G28, Honiara; tel. 28643; fax 22042; e-mail pseducation@pmc.gov.sb.

Ministry of Energy, Mines and Rural Electrification: Honiara; tel. 28609; fax 25811; e-mail psmines@pmc.gov.sb.

Ministry of Environment, Conservation and Meteorology: Honiara; tel. 28611; fax 28735; e-mail psforestry@pmc.gov.sb.

Ministry of Finance and Treasury: POB 26, Honiara; tel. 24102; fax 28619; e-mail psfinance@pmc.gov.sb.

Ministry of Fisheries and Marine Resources: Honiara; tel. 39143; e-mail psfisheries@pmc.gov.sb.

Ministry of Foreign Affairs and External Trade: POB G10, Honiara; tel. 28612; fax 20351; e-mail psforeign@pmc.gov.sb.

Ministry of Forestry: Honiara; tel. 28611; fax 28735.

Ministry of Health and Medical Services: POB 349, Honiara; tel. 20830; fax 20085.

Ministry of Home Affairs: Honiara; tel. 28602; fax 25591; e-mail psaffairs@pmc.gov.sb.

Ministry of Infrastructure Development: POB G30, Honiara; tel. 28605; fax 28705; e-mail kudu@mnpd.gov.sb.

Ministry of Justice and Legal Affairs: Honiara; tel. 21048; fax 28424; e-mail psjustice@pmc.gov.sb.

Ministry of Lands, Housing and Survey: Honiara; tel. 22750; fax 27298; e-mail pslands@pmc.gov.sb.

Ministry of National Unity, Reconciliation and Peace: Honiara; tel. 28616.

Ministry of Police, National Security and Correctional Services: POB 1723/404, Honiara; tel. 28607; fax 28423; e-mail pspolice@pmc.gov.sb.

Ministry of Provincial Government and Institutional Strengthening: POB G35, Honiara; tel. 28606; fax 28708.

Ministry of Public Service: Honiara; tel. 28617; fax 25559; e-mail pspublic@pmc.gov.sb.

Ministry of Rural Development and Indigenous Affairs: Honiara; tel. 25238; fax 22170.

Ministry of Women, Youth and Children's Affairs: Honiara; tel. 28602; fax 23547.

Legislature

National Parliament
POB G19, Honiara; tel. 21751; fax 23866.
Speaker: Sir PETER KENILOREA.
General Election, 5 April 2006

Party	Seats
Solomon Islands Party for Rural Advancement	4
National Party	4
People's Alliance Party	4
Solomon Islands Democratic Party	3
Social Credit Party	2
Solomon Islands Liberal Party	2
LAFARI Party	2
Independents and others	29
Total	50

Election Commission

Electoral Commission: Parliament House, POB G19, Honiara; tel. 20683; Dir MUSU KEVU.

Political Organizations

Parties in the National Parliament can have a fluctuating membership and an influence disproportionate to their representation. There is a significant number of independents who are loosely associated in the amorphous, but often decisive, 'Independent Group'. The following parties represent the main groupings:

LAFARI Party: c/o National Parliament, POB G19, Honiara; supports an increased role for tribal chiefs in society; Leader JOHN M. GARO.

National Party: c/o National Parliament, POB G19, Honiara; f. 1996; Leader FRANCIS BILLY HILLY.

People's Alliance Party (PAP): Honiara; f. 1979; est. by merger of People's Progressive Party (f. 1973) and Rural Alliance Party (f. 1977); advocates establishment of a federal republic; Leader CLEMENT KENGAVA; Sec. EDWARD KINGMELE.

Social Credit Party: c/o National Parliament, POB G19, Honiara; f. 2006; focuses on the underlying issues of communal tension and economic underdevelopment; Leader MANASSEH SOGAVARE.

Solomon Islands Democratic Party: c/o National Parliament, POB G19, Honiara; campaigns for self-reliance and for ending of country's dependence on external aid; Leader STEVE WILLIAM ABANA.

Solomon Islands Liberal Party (SILP): c/o National Parliament, POB G19, Honiara; f. 1976; est. as National Democratic Party (NADEPA); present name adopted in 1986; Leader JAPHET WAIPORA.

Solomon Islands Party for Rural Advancement (SIPRA): Honiara; f. 2006; advocates the decentralization of powers and the recognition of community governance structures and traditional values; Pres. and Leader JOB DUDLEY TAUSINGA; Sec.-Gen. SAM ALASIA.

Other parties that contested the 2006 election included the Christian Alliance Party, the Solomon Islands Labour Party, the Solomons First Party, the One Nation Party and the United Party.

Diplomatic Representation

EMBASSIES AND HIGH COMMISSIONS IN SOLOMON ISLANDS

Australia: Hibiscus Ave, POB 589, Honiara; tel. 21561; fax 23691; e-mail austhoniara.enquiries@dfat.gov.au; internet www.solomonislands.embassy.gov.au; High Commissioner FRANK INGRUBER (designate).

China (Taiwan): Panatina Plaza, POB 586, Honiara; tel. 38050; fax 38060; e-mail embroc@solomon.com.sb; Ambassador GEORGE CHAN.

Japan: National Provident Fund Bldg, Mendana Ave, POB 560, Honiara; tel. 22953; fax 21006; Chargé d'affaires IWANDA AKIRA.

New Zealand: Mendana Ave, POB 697, Honiara; tel. 21502; fax 22377; e-mail nzhicom@solomon.com.sb; High Commissioner MARK RAMSDEN (designate).

Papua New Guinea: POB 1109, Honiara; tel. 20561; fax 20562; High Commissioner PARAI TAMEI.

United Kingdom: Telekom House, Mendana Ave, POB 676, Honiara; tel. 21705; fax 21549; e-mail bhc@solomon.com.sb; High Commissioner TIMOTHY SMART.

Judicial System

The High Court is a Superior Court of Record with unlimited original jurisdiction and powers (except over customary land) as prescribed by the Solomon Islands Constitution or by any law for the time being in force in Solomon Islands. The Judges of the High Court are the Chief Justice, resident in Solomon Islands and employed by its Government, and the Puisne Judges (of whom there are usually three). Appeals from this Court go to the Court of Appeal, the members of which are senior judges from Australia, New Zealand and Papua New Guinea. The Chief Justice and judges of the High Court are ex officio members of the Court of Appeal.

In addition there are Magistrates' Courts staffed by qualified and lay magistrates exercising limited jurisdiction in both civil and criminal matters. There are also Local Courts staffed by elders of the local communities, which have jurisdiction in the areas of established native custom, petty crime and local government by-laws. In 1975 Customary Land Appeal Courts were established to hear land appeal cases from Local Courts, which have exclusive original jurisdiction over customary land cases.

Office of the Registrar: High Court and Court of Appeal, POB G21, Honiara; tel. 21632; fax 22702; Registrar and Commissioner of the High Court KELLY LEVI.

President of the Court of Appeal: Lord (GORDON) SLYNN.
Chief Justice of the High Court: Sir ALBERT ROCKY PALMER.
Attorney-General: GABRIEL SURI.

Religion

More than 95% of the population profess Christianity, and the remainder follow traditional beliefs. According to the census of 1976, about 34% of the population adhered to the Church of Melanesia (Anglican), 19% were Roman Catholics, 17% belonged to the

SOLOMON ISLANDS — Directory

South Seas Evangelical Church, 11% to the United Church (Methodist) and 10% were Seventh-day Adventists. Most denominations are affiliated to the Solomon Islands Christian Association. In many areas Christianity is practised alongside traditional beliefs, especially ancestor worship.

CHRISTIANITY

Solomon Islands Christian Association: POB 1335, Honiara; tel. 23350; fax 26150; e-mail essica@solomon.com.sb; f. 1967; five full mems, seven assoc. mem. orgs; Chair. Most Rev. ADRIAN SMITH; Gen. Sec. EMMANUEL IYABORA.

The Anglican Communion

Anglicans in Solomon Islands are adherents of the Church of the Province of Melanesia, comprising eight dioceses: six in Solomon Islands (Central Melanesia, Malaita, Temotu, Ysabel, Hanuato'o and Central Solomons, which was established in May 1997) and two in Vanuatu (one of which also includes New Caledonia). The Archbishop is also Bishop of Central Melanesia and is based in Honiara. The Church had an estimated 180,000 members in 1988.

Archbishop of the Province of Melanesia: (vacant), Archbishop's House, POB 19, Honiara; tel. 21892; fax 21098; e-mail epogo@comphq.org.sb.

General Secretary: GEORGE KIRIAU, Provincial Headquarters, POB 19, Honiara; tel. 21892; fax 21098; e-mail gkiriau@comphq.oeg.sb.

The Roman Catholic Church

For ecclesiastical purposes, Solomon Islands comprises one archdiocese and two dioceses. At 31 December 2006 there were an estimated 98,835 adherents in the country. The Bishops participate in the Bishops' Conference of Papua New Guinea and Solomon Islands (based in Papua New Guinea).

Archbishop of Honiara: Most Rev. ADRIAN THOMAS SMITH, Holy Cross, GPOB 237, Honiara; tel. 21943; fax 26426; e-mail chancery@solomon.com.sb.

Other Christian Churches

Assembly of God: POB 928, Honiara; tel. and fax 25512; f. 1971; Gen. Supt Rev. JERIEL OTASUI.

Christian Fellowship Church: Church, Paradise, Munda, Western Province; f. 1960; over 5,000 mems in 24 villages; runs 12 primary schools in Western Province.

Seventh-day Adventist Mission: POB 63, Honiara; tel. 21191; over 9,000 mems on Guadalcanal and over 6,800 on Malaita (Oct. 2000); Pres. of Western Pacific Region NEIL WATTS; Sec. Pastor J. PIUKI TASA.

South Seas Evangelical Church: POB 16, Honiara; tel. 22388; fax 20302; Pres. ERIC TAKILA; Gen. Sec. CHARLES J. RAFEASI.

United Church in Solomon Islands: POB 82, Munda, Western Province; tel. 61125; fax 61143; e-mail ucsihq@solomon.com.sb; a Methodist church; Bishop of Solomon Islands Region Rev. PHILEMON RITI; Gen. Sec. GINA TEBULU.

BAHÁ'Í FAITH

National Spiritual Assembly: POB 245, Honiara; tel. 22475; fax 25368; e-mail bahainsa@welkam.solomon.com.sb.

ISLAM

Solomon Islands Muslim League: POB 219, Honiara; tel. 21773; fax 24243; Gen. Sec. Dr MUSTAPHA RAMO; 66 mems.

The Press

Agrikalsa Nius (Agriculture News): POB G13, Honiara; tel. 21211; fax 21955; f. 1986; monthly; Editor ALFRED MAESULIA; circ. 1,000.

Citizens' Press: Honiara; monthly.

Link: Solomon Islands Development Trust, POB 147, Honiara; tel. 21130; fax 21131; pidgin and English; 3 or 4 a year.

Solomon Nius: POB 718, Honiara; tel. 22031; fax 26401; monthly; Dept of Information publication; Editor-in-Chief THOMAS KIVO; monthly; circ. 2,000.

Solomon Star: POB 255, Honiara; tel. 22062; fax 25290; e-mail solstar@solomon.com.sb; internet www.solomonstarnews.com; f. 1982; daily; English; Dir JOHN W. LAMANI; Editor PETER LOMAS (acting); circ. 4,000.

Solomon Times: POB 212, Honiara; tel. 23272; fax 39197; internet www.solomontimes.com; weekly; Chief Editor and Man. Dir EDWARD KINGMELE.

Solomon Voice: POB 1235, Honiara; tel. 20116; fax 20090; f. 1992; weekly; circ. 10,000; Editor CAROL COLVILLE.

Broadcasting and Communications

TELECOMMUNICATIONS

Telekom (Solomon Telekom Company Ltd): POB 148, Honiara; tel. 21576; fax 23110; e-mail sales@telekom.com.sb; internet www.solomon.com.sb; 64.74% owned by Solomon Islands National Provident Fund, 32.58% by Cable and Wireless plc, 2.68% by Investment Corpn of Solomon Islands; operates national and international telecommunications links; Chair. JOHN BEVERLEY; Chief Exec. LOYLEY NGIRA.

BROADCASTING

Radio

Solomon Islands Broadcasting Corporation: POB 654, Honiara; tel. 20051; fax 23159; e-mail sibcnews@solomon.com.sb; internet www.sibconline.com.sb; f. 1976; daily transmissions in English and pidgin; broadcasts total 112 hours per week; Chair. AUGUSTINE TANEKO; Gen. Man. CORNELIUS RATHAMANA; Editor WALTER NALANGU.

Finance

The financial system is regulated and monitored by the Central Bank of Solomon Islands. There are three commercial banks and a development bank. Financial statutory corporations include the Home Finance Corpn (which took over from the Housing Authority in 1990), the Investment Corporation of Solomon Islands (the state holding company) and the National Provident Fund. At the end of 2000 there were 165 credit unions, with total assets estimated at SI $27m.

BANKING

(cap. = capital; res = reserves; dep. = deposits; brs = branches; amounts in Solomon Islands dollars)

Central Bank

Central Bank of Solomon Islands: POB 634, Honiara; tel. 21791; fax 23513; e-mail info@cbsi.com.sb; internet www.cbsi.com.sb; f. 1983; sole bank of issue; cap. 2.6m., res 268.9m., dep. 512.3m. (Dec. 2006); Gov. DENTON RARAWA; Deputy Gov. GANE SIMBE.

Development Bank

Development Bank of Solomon Islands: POB 911, Honiara; tel. 21595; fax 23715; e-mail dbsi@welkam.solomon.com.sb; f. 1978; declared insolvent in Sept. 2004 and placed under the administration of the Central Bank of Solomon Islands; Chair. JOHN MICHAEL ASIPARA; Man. Dir LUKE LAYMAN ETA; 4 brs; 5 sub-brs.

Commercial Banks

Australia and New Zealand Banking Group Ltd (Australia): Mendana Ave, POB 10, Honiara; tel. 21111; fax 26937; e-mail solomons@anz.com; internet www.anz.com/SolomonIslands; Gen. Man. TAIT JENKIN.

Bank South Pacific Ltd (Papua New Guinea): tel. 21874; fax 24674; e-mail bsp@solomon.com.sb; internet www.bsp.com.sb; fmrly National Bank of Solomon Islands Ltd; became br. of Bank of South Pacific Ltd following acquisition in 2007; Gen. Man. MARK CORCORAN.

Westpac Banking Corporation (Australia): National Provident Fund Bldg, 721 Mendana Ave, POB 466, Honiara; tel. 21222; fax 23419; internet www.westpac.com.sb; Man. GIAN TAVIANI.

INSURANCE

A number of British and Australian insurance companies maintain agencies in Solomon Islands.

Trade and Industry

GOVERNMENT AGENCY

Investment Corporation of Solomon Islands: POB 570, Honiara; tel. 22511; fax 21263; holding company through which the Government retains equity stakes in a number of corporations; Chair. MATTHEW WALE.

SOLOMON ISLANDS
Directory

DEVELOPMENT ORGANIZATION

Solomon Islands Development Trust (SIDT): POB 147, Honiara; tel. 23409; fax 21131; e-mail sidt@welkam.solomon.com.sb; f. 1982; development org.; Exec. Dir ABRAHAM BAENESIA.

CHAMBER OF COMMERCE

Solomon Islands Chamber of Commerce and Industry: POB 650, Honiara; tel. 39542; fax 39544; e-mail chamberc@solomon.com.sb; internet www.solomonchamber.com; 69 member cos (July 2004); Chair. MIKE HEMMER; Gen. Sec. SALLY ZIKU.

INDUSTRIAL AND TRADE ASSOCIATIONS

Association of Mining and Exploration Companies: c/o POB G24, Honiara; f. 1988; Pres. NELSON GREG YOUNG.

Commodities Export Marketing Authority: POB 54, Honiara; tel. 22528; fax 21262; e-mail cema@solomon.com.sb; regulator of agricultural commodities such as coconut, cocoa, coffee, palm oil, spices and ngali nut products; agencies at Honiara, Noro and Yandina; Chair. MARTIN SOPAGE; Gen. Man. PITAKIA MOSES PELOMO.

Livestock Development Authority: POB 525, Honiara; tel. 29649; fax 22214; f. 1977; privatized 1996; Man. Dir WARREN TUCKER.

Solomon Islands Business Enterprise Centre: POB 972, Honiara; tel. 26651; fax 26650; e-mail simbec@solomon.com.sb.

Solomon Islands Forest Industries Association: POB 1617, Honiara; tel. 26026; fax 20267; Chair. and Sec. KAIPUA TOHI.

EMPLOYERS' ORGANIZATIONS

Chinese Association: POB 1209, Honiara; tel. 22351; fax 23480; asscn of business people from the ethnic Chinese community.

Federation of Solomon Islands Business: POB 320, Honiara; tel. 22902; fax 21477.

UTILITIES

Electricity

Solomon Islands Electricity Authority (SIEA): POB 6, Honiara; tel. 39422; fax 39472; e-mail mike@siea.com.sb; internet www.siea.com.sb; f. 1961; autonomous, govt-owned entity responsible for generation, transmission, distribution and sale of electrical energy; Chair. Hon. FRANCIS ZAMA; CEO MICHAEL NATION.

Water

Solomon Islands Water Authority (SIWA): POB 1407; Honiara; tel. 23985; fax 20723; f. 1994; Gen. Man. DONALD MAKINI.

CO-OPERATIVE SOCIETIES

Central Co-operative Association (CCA): Honiara.

Salu Fishing Cooperative Association: POB 1041, Honiara; tel. 26550.

Solomon Islands Consumers Co-operative Society Ltd: Honiara; tel. 21798; fax 23640.

Solomon Islands Farmers and Producers Cooperative Association Ltd: Honiara; tel. 30908.

Western General Co-operative Association (WGCA): Gizo, Western Province.

TRADE UNIONS

There are 14 registered trade unions in Solomon Islands.

Solomon Islands Council of Trade Unions (SICTU): National Centre for Trade Unions, POB 271, Honiara; tel. 22566; fax 23171; f. 1986; Pres. DAVID P. TUHANUKU; Sec. BENEDICT ESIBAEA; the principal affiliated unions are:

Media Association of Solomon Islands (MASI): POB 654, Honiara; tel. 20051; fax 23300; e-mail sibcnews@welkam.solomon.com.sb; Pres. JOHN LAMANI.

Solomon Islands Medical Association: Honiara.

Solomon Islands National Teachers' Association (SINTA): POB 967, Honiara; f. 1985; Pres. K. SANGA; Gen. Sec. BENEDICT ESIBAEA.

Solomon Islands National Union of Workers (SINUW): POB 14, Honiara; tel. 22629; Pres. DAVID P. TUHANUKU; Gen. Sec. TONY KAGOVAI.

Solomon Islands Post and Telecommunications Union: Honiara; tel. 21821; fax 20440; Gen. Man. SAMUEL SIVE.

Solomon Islands Public Employees' Union (SIPEU): POB 360, Honiara; tel. 21967; fax 23110; Pres. MARTIN KARANI; Sec.-Gen. PAUL BELANDE.

Solomon Islands Seamen's Association: POB G32, Honiara; tel. 24942; fax 23798.

Transport

ROADS

There are about 1,391 km of roads maintained by the central and provincial governments. In addition, there are 800 km of privately maintained roads mainly for plantation use. Honiara has a main road running about 65 km each side of it along the north coast of Guadalcanal, and Malaita has a road 157 km long running north of Auki and around the northern end of the island to the Lau Lagoon, where canoe transport takes over; and one running south for 35 km to Masa. On Makira a road links Kira Kira and Kakoranga, a distance of 35 km.

SHIPPING

Regular shipping services (mainly cargo) exist between Solomon Islands and Australia, New Zealand, Hong Kong, Japan, Singapore, Taiwan and European ports. The four main ports are at Honiara, Yandina, Noro and Gizo.

Solomon Islands Ports Authority: POB 307, Honiara; tel. 22646; fax 23994; e-mail ports@solomon.com.sb; f. 1956; responsible for the ports of Honiara and Noro; Chair. NELSON BOSO; Gen. Man. N. B. KABUI.

Sullivans (SI) Ltd: POB 3, Honiara; tel. 21643; fax 23889; e-mail shipping@sullivans.com.sb; shipping agents, importers, wholesalers; CEO KEVIN CHANT.

Tradco Shipping Ltd: POB 114, Honiara; tel. 22588; fax 23887; e-mail tradco@solomon.com.sb; f. 1984; shipping agents; Man. Dir GERALD STENZEL.

CIVIL AVIATION

Two airports are open to international traffic and a further 25 serve internal flights. Air Niugini (Papua New Guinea) and Qantas (Australia) fly to Honiara International Airport (located 13 km from the capital).

Director of Civil Aviation: DEMETRIUS T. PIZIKI.

Solomon Airlines Limited: POB 23, Honiara; tel. 20031; fax 20232; e-mail gzoleveke@solair.com.sb; internet www.flysolomons.com; f. 1968; govt-owned; international and domestic operator; scheduled services between Honiara and Port Moresby (Papua New Guinea), Nadi (Fiji), Brisbane (Australia) and Port Vila (Vanuatu); Chair. MATTHEW WALE; CEO RON SUMSUM.

Tourism

The development of the tourism sector is hindered by the relative inaccessibility of the islands and the inadequacy of tourist facilities. In 2006 tourism receipts (excl. passenger transport) amounted to US $2m. Tourist arrivals were reported to have risen from 13,748 in 2007 to 16,264 in 2008.

Solomon Islands Tourism Industry Association (SITIA): Honiara; tel. 26848; fax 26875; f. 2008; Pres. WILSON MAELAUA.

Solomon Islands Visitors Bureau: POB 321, Honiara; tel. 22442; fax 23986; e-mail info@sivb.com.sb; internet www.visitsolomons.com.sb; f. 1980; Gen. Man. MICHAEL TOKURU; Marketing Man. FREDA UNUSI.

SOMALIA

Introductory Survey

Location, Climate, Language, Religion, Flag, Capital

The Somali Democratic Republic lies on the east coast of Africa, with Ethiopia to the north-west and Kenya to the west. There is a short frontier with Djibouti to the north-west. Somalia has a long coastline on the Indian Ocean and the Gulf of Aden, forming the 'Horn of Africa'. The climate is generally hot and dry, with an average annual temperature of 27°C (80°F). It is hotter in the interior and on the Gulf of Aden, but cooler on the Indian Ocean coast. Average annual rainfall is less than 430 mm (17 ins). The national language is Somali, but Arabic is also in official use. English and Italian are widely spoken. The state religion is Islam, and the majority of Somalis are Sunni Muslims. There is a small Christian community, mostly Roman Catholics. The national flag (proportions 2 by 3) is pale blue, with a large five-pointed white star in the centre. The capital is Mogadishu.

Recent History

Somalia was formed by a merger of two former colonial territories: British Somaliland, in the north, and its larger and more populous neighbour, Italian Somaliland. The United Kingdom established a protectorate in British Somaliland in 1886. Italian Somaliland originated in 1889, when Italy concluded agreements with two local rulers, who placed their territories under Italian protection. Italy's occupation of the region was subsequently extended along the coast and inland, and Italian control was completed in 1927. During the Second World War British Somaliland was conquered temporarily by Italian troops, but in 1941 it was recaptured by a British counter-offensive, which also forced the Italians to withdraw from Eritrea, Italian Somaliland and Ethiopia. A British military administration was then established in British and Italian Somaliland.

Under the provisions of the post-war peace treaty of February 1947, Italy renounced all rights to Italian Somaliland. In December 1950, however, the pre-war colony became the UN Trust Territory of Somalia, with Italy returning as the administering power for a 10-year transitional period, prior to independence. The territory's first general election on the basis of universal adult suffrage was held in March 1959, when 83 of the 90 seats in the Legislative Assembly were won by the Somali Youth League (SYL), a pro-Western party led by the Prime Minister, Seyyid Abdullah Issa.

British Somaliland reverted to civilian rule in 1948. The British colonial authorities prepared the territory for self-government, and the first general election took place in March 1959. Fresh elections, for a new legislative council, were held in February 1960, with all parties in favour of early independence and the unification of all Somali territories. Representatives of British Somaliland and the Trust Territory of Somalia met in April and agreed on a merger of the two territories in an independent republic. British Somaliland was granted independence on 26 June, and the merger received unanimous approval by the legislature on the following day.

Accordingly, the union of former British and Italian Somaliland took effect on 1 July 1960, when the independent Somali Republic was proclaimed. Dr Aden Abdullah Osman, hitherto President of the legislature of the southern territory, was elected to be the first President of the new Republic, and the legislatures of the two Somali regions merged to create a single National Assembly. The two dominant parties in former British Somaliland joined with the SYL to form a tripartite coalition government. Dr Abd ar-Rashid Ali Shermarke of the SYL became Prime Minister. In June 1964 Shermarke resigned as Prime Minister and was replaced by Abd ar-Razak Hussein, who formed a cabinet exclusively from members of the SYL. In June 1967, however, Shermarke was elected by the National Assembly to replace President Osman. He appointed a new Cabinet, led by Mohamed Ibrahim Egal, the former Prime Minister of British Somaliland.

On 15 October 1969 President Shermarke was assassinated. Six days later the army seized control in a coup on the eve of a planned presidential election. Power was assumed by the armed forces Commander-in-Chief, Maj.-Gen. Mohamed Siad Barre, who proclaimed the Somali Democratic Republic. The 1960 Constitution was suspended, political parties were abolished and the National Assembly was dissolved. In October 1970 Siad Barre declared Somalia a socialist state and began a revolutionary programme of national unification and social and economic reform. In July 1976 power was transferred to the newly formed Somali Revolutionary Socialist Party (SRSP), with Siad Barre as Secretary-General.

A new Constitution came into force in September 1979. Elections were held in December for a new legislature, the People's Assembly, which, in January 1980, elected Siad Barre as President of the Republic. Constitutional amendments, approved by the Assembly in November 1984, effectively transferred all powers of government to the President. Despite continuing internal unrest, at elections to the Assembly, in December, a single list of SRSP candidates was reportedly endorsed by 99.9% of voters.

A presidential election, at which Siad Barre was the sole candidate, took place in December 1986, confirming his presidency for a further seven-year term by 99.9% of a reported 4.9m. votes cast. Although Lt-Gen. Mohamed Ali Samater was appointed to the newly created post of Prime Minister in February 1987, the President continued to dominate Somalia's political life.

Meanwhile, in October 1981 the Somali Salvation Front formed the Democratic Front for the Salvation of Somalia (DFSS, later renamed the Somali Salvation Democratic Front—SSDF) with two other opposition groups. Together with another group founded in 1981, the Somali National Movement (SNM), and with substantial Ethiopian military support, DFSS guerrillas invaded the central border area of Somalia in July 1982. The invasion was contained by the Somali national forces but, despite US and Italian military aid, they failed to expel the rebel troops from the country. Following a meeting between Siad Barre and Lt-Col Mengistu, the Ethiopian leader, in January 1986, Ethiopian military support for the insurgent groups was reduced, particularly in respect of the DFSS.

Anti-Government demonstrations in Mogadishu in July 1989, in protest at the arrest of several leading Muslim clerics, were violently suppressed by the armed forces, resulting in the deaths of more than 400 demonstrators. Two recently created opposition groups, the United Somali Congress (USC—composed of Hawiye clan intellectuals) and the National United Front of Somalia (allegedly dominated by disaffected army officers), were thought to have orchestrated the demonstrations. In August there were reports of fighting between government troops and members of the Ogadeni clan in southern Somalia, and Western sources claimed that the only areas of the country that remained under government control were Mogadishu, parts of Hargeysa and Berbera.

As Siad Barre's authority declined, in July 1990 the Council of Ministers endorsed earlier proposals for the democratization of Somalia's political system. It was decided that, following a review by the People's Assembly, a new constitution would be submitted to a national referendum in October, and that multi-party legislative and local government elections would be held in February 1991. In August 1990 the USC, the SNM and the Somali Patriotic Movement (SPM) agreed to co-ordinate their separate military campaigns to overthrow Siad Barre. In October the Government announced the immediate introduction of the new Constitution and a new electoral code. Siad Barre relinquished the post of Secretary-General of the SRSP, in accordance with the Constitution, which stipulated that the President should hold no responsibilities other than those of the presidency. Despite the apparent readiness of the new Government to hasten the process of political reform, the principal insurgent groups showed no signs of relaxing their military campaigns, and in November SPM forces seized control of Kismayu, in southern Somalia. On 25 December legislation was introduced to permit the establishment of political parties opposed to the Government.

On 1 January 1991 the USC announced that it had captured most areas of Mogadishu and that it had besieged the home of Siad Barre. On 27 January Siad Barre was reported to have fled the capital with those forces remaining loyal to him, and the USC took power. It immediately invited all former opposition groups to participate in a national conference to discuss the democratization of Somalia. On 29 January the USC appointed Ali Mahdi Mohamed (a government minister in the 1960s) as President, in a temporary capacity, and he, in turn, invited Umar Arteh Ghalib (a former foreign affairs minister) to form a government that would prepare the country for democracy. The provisional Government was approved by the President on 2 February.

By mid-March 1991, however, Somalia was close to anarchy. Opposition movements rejected the USC's invitation to take part in a national conference, and the SNM was reported to have formed an 11-member administration and a legislature to govern the former territory of British Somaliland. In May the SNM announced its official support for the secession of that territory, and later that month the SNM Central Committee elected Abd ar-Rahman Ahmed Ali 'Tur' as President of the self-proclaimed 'Republic of Somaliland'. In June the Committee approved a 17-member government to administer the territory for a period of two years, after which free elections were to be held.

The SNM declined an invitation issued by the USC to participate in a conference of national reconciliation in June 1991, stating that it did not concern 'Somaliland'. The conference, convened in Djibouti, was attended by representatives of the USC, the Somali Democratic Movement (SDM), the SPM and the DFSS, and mandated delegates from the four organizations to travel to 'Somaliland' to persuade the SNM to abandon its declaration of independence. The SNM insisted, however, that the secession of 'Somaliland' from Somalia was irreversible. At a second reconciliation conference in July the four groups that had met in June were joined by the United Somali Front (USF) and the SDA. The leaders of the six groups signed a manifesto, which, *inter alia*, committed them to defeat the forces of Siad Barre (which had regrouped as the Somali National Front—SNF), to readopt the 1960 Constitution, which Barre had suspended in 1969, and to implement a general cease-fire. The manifesto also confirmed Ali Mahdi in his position as Somalia's President for a period of two years pending free elections. Ali Mahdi was sworn in as President on 18 August 1991, and in September he reappointed Ghalib as Prime Minister; in October the latter announced the formation of a newly expanded Government, comprising 72 ministers and deputy ministers, in order to ensure equal representation for the six participating groups.

Meanwhile, in June 1991 a major rift had developed within the USC, and supporters of President Ali Mahdi clashed with those of the USC's military commander, Gen. Mohamed Farah Aidid, in Mogadishu. Aidid objected to Ali Mahdi's assumption of the presidency, since he had commanded the military campaign to overthrow Siad Barre. In July Aidid was elected Chairman of the USC. In October Aidid rejected the legitimacy of the Government appointed earlier that month, and in November his faction launched a major offensive on the President's positions in the capital. The fighting intensified, and in December Ali Mahdi appealed to the UN to send a peace-keeping force to intervene in the conflict. The UN responded by sending a special envoy to Mogadishu in January 1992. However, the envoy's attempts met with failure, and the mission was followed by an escalation in violence. In mid-January Aidid appointed his own, 21-member administration. By the end of March it was estimated that 14,000 people (mostly civilians) had been killed and 27,000 wounded in the hostilities in Mogadishu.

In January 1992 the UN imposed an embargo on the sale of armaments to Somalia. In the following month the UN, the Organization of African Unity (OAU, now the African Union—AU, see p. 172), the League of Arab States (the Arab League, see p. 344) and the Organization of the Islamic Conference (OIC, see p. 382) issued a joint appeal for a cease-fire, stating that it was a prerequisite for the granting of humanitarian aid to Somalia. Representatives from the rival factions in Mogadishu subsequently agreed to the terms of a cease-fire accord devised by the international organizations. In March, in discussions with a joint mission of the UN, the OAU, the OIC and the Arab League in Mogadishu, Aidid agreed to the monitoring of the cease-fire by a foreign observer mission. In April the UN Security Council approved the establishment of a 'UN Operation in Somalia' (UNOSOM), to comprise a 50-strong observer mission to monitor the cease-fire, while it also agreed, in principle, to dispatch a peace-keeping force to protect UN personnel and supplies at Mogadishu's port, and to escort food supplies to distribution points. However, the Security Council needed to obtain consent for the peace-keeping force from both parties involved in the conflict, and Aidid was opposed to the deployment of foreign military personnel in Somalia.

In April 1992 the SNF advanced on Mogadishu, with Siad Barre apparently intent on recapturing the capital. Forces of the SNF came to within 40 km of the capital, but Gen. Aidid's militias decisively repelled them, pursuing them to the south of the country. Siad Barre fled, with some 200 supporters, to Kenya. (Siad Barre was refused political asylum in Kenya, and in May he moved to Nigeria, where he died in January 1995.) In May Aidid's forces and those of the SPM, the SDM and the Southern Somali National Movement (SSNM), with which he had formed a military alliance known as the Somali Liberation Army (SLA), captured Kismayu, which had been held by the SNF. By June the SLA was in control of the majority of central and southern Somalia, making Aidid the most powerful of the country's warlords. In late June the UN secured agreement from the principal factions in Mogadishu for the deployment of the observer mission envisaged in the March cease-fire accord. In August Aidid agreed to the deployment of 500 UN troops entrusted with escorting food aid from Mogadishu's port and airport to distribution points.

Also in August 1992 the coalition of Gen. Aidid's faction of the USC with the SPM, the SDM and the SSNM was consolidated with the formation of the Somali National Alliance (SNA), of which Aidid was the leader. Meanwhile, Ali Mahdi strengthened ties with other armed groups hostile to Aidid, notably the SSDF and a faction of the SPM, and forged links with Gen. Mohamed Siad Hersi 'Morgan' (who had led the SNF since the departure of his father-in-law, Siad Barre).

By early November 1992 UNOSOM's 500 armed troops still had not been deployed. However, later in the month UNOSOM secured Mogadishu's airport with the agreement of the clan controlling it. The USA subsequently offered to lead a military operation in the country, with a US contingent of up to 30,000 men. The proposed US operation was sanctioned by the Security Council in early December. Shortly afterwards an advance contingent of 1,800 US marines landed on the beaches of Mogadishu and took control of the port and airport. Aidid and Ali Mahdi had instructed their supporters that the US forces were amicable, and consequently they encountered little resistance. The arrival of the foreign force, however, provoked fierce fighting in Kismayu, Baidoa and the north-east, with rival factions attempting to gain territory before the expected imposition of a cease-fire. The US members of the Unified Task Force (UNITAF) were reinforced subsequently by troops from 21 other countries.

In January 1993 14 of Somalia's political organizations attended peace negotiations in Addis Ababa, Ethiopia, held under the auspices of the UN. The talks resulted in agreements on an immediate cease-fire, disarmament under UN supervision and the holding of a conference of national reconciliation in March. Despite the cease-fire agreement, hostilities were resumed in various parts of the country almost immediately. In mid-March the national reconciliation conference opened in Addis Ababa and later that month an accord providing for the establishment of a Transitional National Council as the supreme authority in Somalia, with a mandate to hold elections within two years was agreed upon. The Council was to comprise 74 members: one from each of the 15 organizations represented at the conference, three from each of the 18 proposed administrative regions (inclusive of 'Somaliland') and five from Mogadishu.

Agreement on the future government of Somalia was reached hours after the UN Security Council approved the establishment of UNOSOM II, which was to take over responsibility for maintaining security from UNITAF by 1 May 1993. UNOSOM II was to be the UN's largest ever peace-keeping operation, comprising 28,000 military personnel and 2,800 civilian staff, and its first where peace-enforcement without consent from parties within the country was authorized. UNOSOM II was, in addition, to be responsible for overseeing the rehabilitation of the country and the repatriation of Somali refugees. In May the USA transferred responsibility for international efforts in Somalia to UNOSOM II whose forces embarked on a series of armed initiatives, including air strikes, against suspected strategic positions of the SNA. Despite the increased scale of UNOSOM operations, Aidid avoided injury or capture during June, prompting the Security Council to issue a formal warrant for his arrest. The violent deaths of three Italian UNOSOM soldiers in July provoked Italian media claims that the military emphasis of the mission, promoted by the USA in pursuit of Aidid, was threatening the security of UN personnel and jeopardizing diplomatic initiatives undertaken by the Italian Government. The situation was exacerbated by a US helicopter attack on a suspected pro-Aidid command centre, which resulted in the deaths of 50–100 Somalis, and the murder, in retaliation, of four foreign journalists by enraged Somali crowds.

Uncompromising media coverage of the aftermath of the deaths of three US soldiers in September 1993, and a violent exchange in the capital in October (which resulted in the deaths of some 300 Somalis, 18 US servicemen and the capture, by local militiamen, of a US helicopter pilot and a Nigerian soldier), prompted widespread public outrage in the USA. The US President, Bill Clinton, subsequently announced that all US troops were to be withdrawn by the end of March 1994, regardless of the outcome of attempts to negotiate a political settlement to the conflict by that date. Clinton's decision, announced in October, to withdraw the US Ranger élite forces (which had actively sought to apprehend Aidid) prompted speculation that the release of the US pilot and the Nigerian soldier, secured in mid-October following lengthy discussions between representatives of the US Government and Aidid, had been achieved as part of an undisclosed bilateral agreement. Despite Aidid's declaration of a unilateral cease-fire prior to the talks, and subsequent indications of his willingness to enter into negotiations with the USA (in preference to the UN), fighting between pro-Aidid and pro-Mahdi factions escalated. In December Aidid and Ali Mahdi (who in November reportedly assumed the leadership of the Somali Salvation Alliance—SSA, a coalition of 12 factions opposed to Aidid) attended negotiations in Addis Ababa, but discussions disintegrated with little progress.

In February 1994, in the context of the imminent withdrawal of UNOSOM contingents from the USA and several other Western nations, the UN Security Council revised UNOSOM's mandate, reducing the troop strength of the mission to a maximum of 22,000. In March, following protracted negotiations, initiated by the UN, an agreement on the restoration of peace was signed by Aidid and Ali Mahdi (on behalf of the SSA) in Nairobi, Kenya, committing both sides to a cease-fire, disarmament and the organization of a conference of national reconciliation in May to elect a president, vice-presidents and a prime minister. Electoral procedures and a future legislative structure were to be decided at a meeting of all signatories to the 1993 Addis Ababa agreement and the SNM, to be convened in April. By mid-1994, however, no such meeting had taken place, with accusations of failure to adhere to the terms of the Nairobi agreement proceeding from both Aidid and the SSA.

In June 1994 the UN Security Council agreed to renew UNOSOM's mandate by four months; in November it extended the mandate to a final date of 31 March 1995. As the deadline for UNOSOM's departure approached, the competition for control of installations currently held by the UN, in particular the port and airport, became the focus of factional hostility. In November 1994 UN forces began to withdraw from positions outside Mogadishu in the first stages of UNOSOM's departure. 'Operation United Shield', to ensure the safe evacuation of the UN troops and civilian personnel, as well as most of the equipment brought in under UNOSOM, was organized and led by the USA. The USA stationed several thousand marines in warships off the Somali coast in December, and in early 1995 they were joined by a multinational force of naval and air force units in order to protect departing UN employees (by early 1995 some 136 members of UNOSOM had been killed since the beginning of the operation).

In late February 1995 1,800 US and 400 Italian marines landed on Mogadishu's beaches, and command of the remaining 2,400 UN troops and of the whole operation was passed from the UN to the US commander. The marines secured the port and airport, and evacuated the remaining UN soldiers. The departure of the last UN personnel on 2 March (almost one month ahead of schedule) was closely followed by that of the US and Italian marines themselves. Somali looters overran the airport, but armoured cars from Aidid's faction, reportedly accompanied by UN-trained police officers, took control of the area. Ali Mahdi's Abgal clansmen gained control of the eastern section of the airport, and skirmishes were reported between the two sides. Aidid and Ali Mahdi subsequently agreed on the reopening of the port and set out detailed terms for the 'technical peace committee' that was to administer the port and airport; however, the terms of the agreement were promptly violated by both sides, and fighting for control of the crucial sites resumed.

Significant divisions within the SNA became more apparent in June 1995, following an attempt by disaffected members to replace Aidid with his former aide, Osman Hassan Ali 'Ato', as Chairman of the party. SNA members loyal to Aidid immediately rejected the legitimacy of the actions of the Ali 'Ato' faction and announced the expulsion of the faction from the SNA. In mid-June a conference of reconciliation, convened in southern Mogadishu by representatives of 15 pro-Aidid factions, elected Aidid President of the Republic of Somalia for a three-year term. Five Vice-Presidents, representing the interests of distinct clans, were also elected, and the composition of a comprehensive cabinet was subsequently announced. However, Aidid's presidency and mandate to govern were immediately rejected in a joint statement issued by Ali Mahdi and Ali 'Ato'. In September Aidid's forces seized Baidoa.

Fighting between Gen. Aidid's supporters and those loyal to Ali 'Ato' intensified in early 1996. In July pro-Aidid factions clashed with supporters of Ali Mahdi in Mogadishu, resulting in some 90 fatalities. Aidid was wounded during the skirmishes, and on 1 August he died as a result of his injuries. Despite initial hopes that Aidid's death might result in a cessation of hostilities and the resumption of peace negotiations, on 4 August one of his sons, Hussein Mohamed Aidid (a former US marine and hitherto Aidid's chief of security), was appointed interim President by the SNA leadership council. Hussein Aidid (who was subsequently elected Chairman of the SNA) vowed to continue his father's struggle, and factional fighting quickly resumed.

In December 1996 representatives of some 26 Somali factions (notably excluding the SNA) held protracted talks in Sodere, Ethiopia, under the auspices of the Ethiopian Government and the Intergovernmental Authority on Development (IGAD). The conference culminated in January 1997 in the formation of a 41-member National Salvation Council (NSC), with an 11-member executive committee and a five-member joint chairmanship committee, to act as an interim government charged with drafting a transitional charter and holding a national reconciliation conference. Aidid condemned the establishment of the NSC and accused the Ethiopian authorities of interfering in Somali affairs.

International mediation efforts continued, and in March 1997 representatives of Somali factions participated in talks in Cairo, Egypt, under the auspices of the Egyptian Government and the Arab League. In December, at the culmination of negotiations that began in November, 26 Somali faction leaders (including Aidid and Ali Mahdi) signed an accord in Cairo, establishing an end to all hostilities and providing for the eventual formation of a transitional government, charged with holding a general election within three years. A condition of the accord was that a national reconciliation conference be held in Baidoa in February 1998 in order to elect a 13-member presidential council (three representatives from each of Somalia's four principal clans and one from a minority group), a prime minister and a 189-seat legislature. The conference was later postponed on two occasions, not least because troops loyal to Aidid remained stationed in Baidoa.

In September 1999 the UN Secretary-General, Kofi Annan, announced that the UN Security Council was to consider a solution to the Somalia problem, following a proposal made by the Somali Peace Alliance (under the chairmanship of 'Puntland' Leader Abdullahi Yussuf) that central authority in Somalia be gradually rebuilt, beginning with regionally based administrations. This proposal was, however, immediately rejected by the Mogadishu faction leaders and President Egal of 'Somaliland'. In October IGAD delegates met in Addis Ababa to discuss President Ismael Omar Gelleh of Djibouti's proposed peace plan for Somalia. In February 2000 IGAD member states endorsed Gelleh's plan, which envisaged the staging of a Somali national reconciliation conference in Djibouti in late April and early May, to be attended by up to 1,500 delegates from various cross-sections of Somali society. Under the plan they would elect members to a new national legislature to be based in Mogadishu, which would, in turn, elect a President. The President would be responsible for choosing a Prime Minister, subject to the approval of the legislature, who would lead a transitional government for a period of no longer than two years, during which time a national constitution would be drafted and a date for elections would be selected. However, although the peace plan was unanimously approved by OAU foreign ministers in March, and also won the approval of the UN and the USA, Egal announced that 'Somaliland' would refuse any attempts to unite it with Somalia.

The Somali national reconciliation conference opened in Arta, Djibouti, on 2 May 2000, with some 400 delegates, representing various Somali clans and political and armed groups, in attendance. By mid-June the number of delegates had risen to around

900, although notably only one of the principal Somali faction leaders, Ali Mahdi, was present. In early July the conference produced a draft national charter, which envisaged the Somali Republic adopting a federal system of government, after a three-year interim period, comprising 18 regional administrations. Furthermore, it provided for the creation of the Somali Transitional National Assembly (TNA), which would consist of 225 members, of whom 25 would be women. Each of the four major Somali clans (Dir, Hawiye, Darod and Rahanwin) was allocated 44 parliamentary seats, and an alliance of small clans was to receive 24 seats; the remaining 25 seats were reserved for women from the four major clans and the alliance of small clans, each of which would receive five seats. However, disagreements between clans and sub-clans over the distribution of seats ensued, and in early August President Gelleh intervened, suggesting the appointment of a further 20 members to the assembly, thus increasing the total number to 245. Gelleh's proposal was accepted, and on 13 August the TNA held its inaugural session in Arta. On 26 August it was announced that Abdulkasim Salad Hasan, a member of the Hawiye clan, who had held several ministerial positions in the Siad Barre administration, had been elected President of Somalia by the members of the TNA. Hasan was sworn in as President on the following day at a ceremony in Arta.

On 30 August 2000 President Hasan returned to Mogadishu, where he was greeted by tens of thousands of Somalis. At the same time several Mogadishu faction leaders opposed to the outcome of the Djibouti conference, including Hussein Aidid, Ali 'Ato' and Hussein Haji Bod, met in San'a for talks with Yemeni President Ali Abdullah Saleh, who attempted to persuade them to lend their support to Hasan's administration. However, on his return to Somalia, Aidid implored the international community not to recognise the legitimacy of Hasan's appointment. On 8 October President Hasan appointed Ali Khalif Galaydh, a former Minister of Industry in the Siad Barre regime, to the post of Prime Minister; later that month Galaydh announced a 32-member Cabinet.

Relations between Somalia and Ethiopia deteriorated in January 2001, after Galaydh accused Ethiopia of providing arms to factions opposed to the Transitional National Government (TNG). Relations between the two countries were further strained in March, when the Ethiopian authorities allowed several Somali faction leaders to convene in Addis Ababa for a series of meetings, which resulted in the creation of the Somali Reconciliation and Restoration Council (SRRC), headed by Hussein Aidid.

In early May 2001 Galaydh appointed 25 members to a Peace and Reconciliation Committee (PRC), chaired by former Prime Minister Abd ar-Razak Hussein, which was charged with obtaining recommendations from a cross-section of Somali factions for ways of accelerating the reconciliation process, defining the most suitable means of establishing a federal system in the country and addressing property and land issues. In mid-July violent clashes were again reported to have taken place in Mogadishu between followers of Hussein Aidid and Ali 'Ato' and troops loyal to the TNG, resulting in numerous fatalities. In late July the new administration suffered a further major set-back after Abd ar-Razak Hussein resigned as Chairman of the PRC, claiming that Galaydh had demonstrated a lack of co-operation with the committee and had failed actively to support its work. Abdiqadir Muhammad Adan Zope was subsequently appointed acting Chairman of the PRC.

In mid-October 2001 a group of dissatisfied TNA members proposed a motion of 'no confidence' in the TNG, citing the administration's failure to promote the reconciliation process and its lack of progress regarding the constitution of regional administrations. Later that month 141 of the 174 TNA members participating in the vote approved the motion to dismiss the Galaydh administration.

In mid-November 2001 President Hasan appointed Col Hassan Abshir Farah, hitherto Minister of Water and Mineral Resources, as Prime Minister. Farah announced that his first priority was to implement a programme of national reconciliation, and thus the appointment of a new cabinet was delayed until after the conclusion of further peace talks between the SRRC and members of the TNA, which were scheduled to take place in Nairobi later that month. Although the talks were further postponed until mid-December, they were attended by senior members of the SNA (again with the notable exception of Hussein Aidid) and representatives of several other Mogadishu faction leaders. On 24 December, in the Kenyan town of Nakura, Farah, on behalf of the TNA, and Mowlid Ma'aneh Mohamed, the Secretary-General of the SRRC, signed a peace agreement, which provided for the formation of an 'all-inclusive government' to ensure equitable power-sharing among all Somali clans and the establishment of a Nairobi-based secretariat to oversee the implementation of the Somali peace process and to solicit funds for it.

In mid-February 2002 Farah formed a new 31-member Cabinet, which notably included Dr Hussein Mohamed Usman Jimbir, a former senior member of the SRRC, as Minister of Education. However, several members of factions that had signed the Nakura peace agreement in December 2001 were reported to have requested to be excluded from the new Government until a parliamentary committee, established to investigate a proposed increase in the number of parliamentary seats, had released its recommendations. The reconciliation process in Somalia was further endangered in early April 2002, when the Rahanwin Resistance Army (RRA) announced that it had established a new autonomous region in south-western Somalia, based in Baidoa, to be known as the 'State of South-western Somalia'. The Chairman of the RRA, Mohamed Hasan Nur Shatigadud, was elected as 'President' of the new region for a four-year period.

In late June 2002 the TNG confirmed that it would attend an IGAD-sponsored reconciliation conference scheduled to be held in Kenya in July. The conference was subsequently postponed until September, and early that month the authorities in 'Somaliland' announced that they would not attend the talks. Following a further delay, the conference opened in the Kenyan town of Eldoret in mid-October in the presence of representatives of the Governments of Ethiopia, Kenya, Uganda, Sudan, Djibouti and Eritrea. Following the conclusion of the first phase of the conference, the TNG and a number of Somali factions signed a temporary cease-fire and agreed to abide by the final outcome of the conference; to establish an all-inclusive federal system of government; to combat terrorism; and to enhance the safety of aid workers in the country. Further progress was slowed by continuing deadlock over the allocation of seats to the plenary session of the conference. However, by early December the TNG and Mogadishu-based faction leaders Hussein Aidid, Mohammed Qanyare Afrah, Yalahow and Ali 'Ato' signed a declaration committing themselves to ending violence in the Somali capital. In January 2003, however, Yalahow announced that he would no longer participate in the conference. Yalahow's departure followed the earlier withdrawal of Qanyare Afrah from the proceedings. In February the conference was moved to Nairobi, and, despite a number of cease-fire violations, in the following month the TNG and the remaining faction leaders provisionally agreed on the formation of an administration for Mogadishu and further measures to bring peace to the capital.

In early July 2003 delegates at the Nairobi conference reached a provisional agreement on the formation of an interim government. The arrangement provided for a transitional unicameral parliament, whose 351 members would be selected by political leaders, and which would remain in operation for four years. The nomination of members of parliament was to be made by the signatories of the December 2002 cease-fire declaration and politicians who were originally, and officially, invited to the conference. However, President Hasan rejected the agreement, which had been signed by Farah, stating that it would divide the country, and in August 2003 divisions between Hasan and Farah intensified. Later that month, just days before the expiry of the three-year mandate of the TNG, Hasan reportedly dismissed Farah and the Speaker of the TNA. Hasan insisted that the current governing institutions would remain in place, despite the expiry of their mandate, until a new President, government and parliament had been installed. Dr Abdi Guled Mohamed, the Minister of Air and Land Transport, was appointed premier, in an acting capacity.

In November 2003 the Somali National Salvation Council, a recently formed alliance of 12 factions, chaired by Yalahow, pledged to boycott any further talks in Nairobi. Despite the expiry of his mandate in August 2003, President Hasan appointed Mohamed Abdi Yusuf, hitherto Deputy Speaker of the TNA, as Prime Minister in early December. In the following month the TNA approved the appointment of a new 37-member TNG, which included three Deputy Prime Ministers. Also in January 2004 talks reconvened in Nairobi with the aim of restoring the faltering peace process. Following a period of intense negotiations, during which Yalahow and the leaders of the Juba Valley Alliance (JVA), the RRA and the SNF rejoined the discussions, later that month representatives from more than 20 factions in attendance agreed to establish a new transitional parliament, comprising 275 members (rather than the 351 previously agreed), who would serve a five-year term. Once formed, the parliament would appoint a President, who, in turn, would nominate a Prime Minister to form a government. It was envisaged that each of the four major Somali clans would select 61 members of the new legislature, while a coalition of smaller clans would be responsible for choosing the remaining 31 members. However, several faction leaders expressed concern at perceived favouritism towards certain groups on the part of the Kenyan and Djiboutian authorities overseeing the talks.

In mid-June 2004 an arbitration committee was formed in Nairobi to oversee the nomination of members to the new parliament, and by mid-August the majority of the new members of the Transitional Parliament (TP) had been nominated and inauguration ceremonies commenced in Nairobi. On 15 September Shariff Hassan Sheikh Adan, a Mogadishu-based business executive, was elected Speaker of the TP and later that month nominations were invited for the position of President. Following two rounds of voting by the 275 members of the TP on 10 October two presidential candidates remained: Col Abdullahi Yussuf Ahmed, the President of the autonomous region of 'Puntland' (see below), and Abdallah Ahmed Addow, a former Somali ambassador to the USA. At a third round of voting held later that day, Yussuf secured 189 of the 268 votes cast and was sworn in as President of Somalia at a ceremony in Nairobi on 14 October. In early November Yussuf appointed Ali Mohammed Ghedi, a member of the Hawiye clan and a former AU official, as Prime Minister.

On 7 December 2004 Ghedi unveiled a new 31-member Cabinet. Hussein Aidid was appointed Deputy Prime Minister and Minister of the Interior and Security, while Qanyare Afrah became Minister of National Security. However, the following day a number of ministers resigned from the Government, maintaining that the new administration was too large and did not fairly distribute power among the major clans, and on 12 December the TP, which remained based in Nairobi, overwhelmingly approved a motion of 'no confidence' in Ghedi, effectively dissolving the new Government. Two days later President Yussuf reappointed Ghedi as Prime Minister and in late December that decision was endorsed by 229 members of the TP. Ghedi was tasked with forming a government that more accurately represented the major clans and in early January 2005 Ghedi announced an amended Cabinet, which comprised some 90 ministers, assistant ministers and state ministers. Aidid and Qanyare Afrah retained the posts previously awarded to them, while Salim Aliow Ibrow was appointed Deputy Prime Minister and Minister of Finance, and Mahmud Abdullahi Jama Deputy Prime Minister and Minister of Information. Later in January 2005 the new Cabinet was approved by the TP.

Shortly after he had taken office, President Yussuf had appealed to the AU and the UN to approve the deployment of a peace-keeping force of up to 20,000 troops to assist with the relocation of the TP and the Government to Mogadishu and to disarm militias in the Somali capital. However, ongoing violence in the city caused plans to be stalled. In early January 2005 the AU stated its readiness 'in principle' to deploy a contingent of peace-keepers to Somalia, although no indication was given of the size of the force or the likely date of its arrival in the country. In mid-January Ghedi announced that the Government would begin the relocation to Mogadishu by the end of that month and envisaged that with the support of international peace-keepers the entire Government and Parliament would be settled in the capital by early May. Despite further concerns over the security situation in the capital, plans for the relocation of the Government and the Parliament proceeded, and in early February a delegation of 30 members of the TP, led by the Minister of Trade, Muse Sudi Yalahow, arrived in Mogadishu followed by a further 50 parliamentarians, led by Sheikh Adan, a few days later. It was subsequently announced, however, that members of the Cabinet would travel to various parts of Somalia to establish possible locations for the Government's new base and that ministers remained deeply divided on the most suitable course of action. As an AU mission arrived in Mogadishu in mid-February to assess the security situation, thousands of people staged protests against the proposed peace-keeping force and a bomb exploded in the capital killing two people and seriously injuring six others. In late February Yussuf and Ghedi arrived in Somalia to head a delegation, which would investigate potential bases for the new Government; notably, the President and the Prime Minister did not visit Mogadishu as part of their tour. The delegation returned to Kenya in early March and Ghedi's special adviser announced that other towns were being considered as a temporary base for the new Government until violence in the capital subsided.

In mid-March 2005 IGAD defence ministers agreed to deploy a 10,000-strong peace-keeping force, the IGAD Peace Support Mission to Somalia (IGASOM) in the country from 30 April, to be replaced at an unspecified later date by an AU force. Demonstrations were held days later in Mogadishu opposing the deployment of peace-keeping troops from neighbouring countries, and members of the TP were involved in a violent confrontation following a vote to reject the planned deployment. In an attempt to allay fears in Somalia, the IGAD Council of Ministers proposed a compromise solution, in which a reduced IGASOM force of 6,800 would initially be deployed, comprised solely of Sudanese and Ugandan troops. In late March the Somali Government announced that it would temporarily relocate to Baidoa and Jowhar, 90 km north of Mogadishu. However, heavy fighting in Baidoa later in March between supporters of Yussuf and militia opposed to the relocation of the Government outside of Mogadishu resulted in at least 14 fatalities, and in late April the 80 parliamentarians situated in Mogadishu rejected calls from the President and the UN-led Joint Co-ordination and Monitoring Committee to return to Nairobi, stating that a return to exile would jeopardize ongoing efforts to 'pacify' the capital.

At the end of April 2005 a bomb exploded in Mogadishu, killing 15 people and injuring at least 50 others, at a rally attended by Ghedi. In early May 100 members of the TP opposed to Yussuf's relocation plans, including Sheikh Adan, boycotted a parliamentary vote in Nairobi, where supporters of the President approved the planned relocation to Baidoa and Jowhar and the deployment of the proposed peace-keeping force. Days later Qanyare Afrah, Yalahow and Ali 'Ato' undertook to combine their militias and to withdraw militiamen and armoured vehicles from Mogadishu, and a partial disarmament of their forces took place at a ceremony in the capital. Also in April, the AU approved plans to send 1,700 peace-keeping troops to Somalia but stated that the force would only arrive when its security could be guaranteed. In mid-May 30 members of the TP accompanied Sheikh Adan upon his return to Mogadishu, while a spokesman for the President announced that Jama had been removed from office. In late May up to 19 people were reportedly killed during heavy fighting in Baidoa between militia affiliated to two opposing members of the TP. In mid-June Ghedi and the remaining ministers and members of parliament left Nairobi and arrived in Jowhar, despite the opposition of local militia. Fears of renewed conflict between the opposing factions were raised in early July as Yussuf announced plans to gather a group of militiamen in Jowhar and in August tensions escalated when the Mogadishu-based members of the TP accused Yussuf of planning a civil war with military assistance from Ethiopia. In September, speaking before the UN General Assembly, Yussuf urged the UN Security Council to lift the arms embargo, which he claimed had hindered the establishment of a national security force and had prevented the deployment of peace-keepers in Somalia. A convoy carrying Ghedi on a visit to Mogadishu was attacked with grenades and a land mine in early November. Three people were killed in the apparent assassination attempt, although Ghedi was uninjured in the attack. Later that month 11 people were killed during fighting in Mogadishu after the Union of Islamic Courts (UIC) of Mogadishu, which had established a court system in the capital based on *Shari'a* (Islamic) law, attempted to seize control of cinemas it had accused of encouraging immoral and criminal behaviour.

In early January 2006 Yussuf and Sheikh Adan signed an agreement for the TP to meet in Somalia within 30 days, following further talks held in San'a, and in late January members of the group led by Sheikh Adan signalled their willingness to support a process of reconciliation. Despite the absence of Ali 'Ato', Yalahow and several other prominent ministers opposed to Yussuf, 205 parliamentarians assembled in Baidoa on 26 February as the TP met for the first time since returning from Kenya. In late February a number of formerly opposed faction leaders, including Qanyare Afrah and Yalahow, formed a new political alliance—the Alliance for the Restoration of Peace and Counter-Terrorism (ARPCT)—which aimed to combat Islamist extremism in Somalia. Militia supported by the ARPCT were in conflict with forces loyal to the UIC in the south of Mogadishu and at least 33 people were killed before a cease-fire was negotiated by Somali elders. However, some 140 people were killed and thousands fled the capital in late March as fighting resumed, and attempts by elders to renegotiate a cease-fire between the two factions continued. Unrest continued in the capital during early May with more than 80 people reported to have been killed in clashes between the two sides.

In early June 2006 the UIC claimed to have seized control of Mogadishu. Later that month, at a meeting convened by the Arab League in Khartoum, Sudan, the Government signed an agreement of mutual recognition with the UIC in an attempt to avert a potential attack on Baidoa. Also in June four cabinet ministers, including Qanyare Afrah, were dismissed for refusing to end ongoing battles with Islamist extremists. Shortly after the agreement was signed the UIC underwent a reorganization and was renamed the Somali Supreme Islamic Courts Council (SSICC). The US-led Contact Group on Somalia urged the Somali Government to enter further discussions with the SSICC to avoid more widespread conflict. Talks were initially scheduled for mid-July, but the Government requested their postponement, accusing the SSICC of breaching cease-fire agreements. President Yussuf subsequently agreed to meet with SSICC leaders; however, they, in turn, refused to negotiate. In late July and early August some 40 ministers and assistant ministers resigned, citing their dissatisfaction with Prime Minister Ghedi's apparent unwillingness to negotiate with the SSICC. On 28 July the Minister of Constitutional and Federal Affairs, Abdallah Derow Isaq, was shot dead outside a mosque in Baidoa and two days later Prime Minister Ghedi narrowly defeated a vote of 'no confidence' in the TP. However, President Yussuf dissolved the Cabinet on 7 August and instructed Ghedi to form a new administration. In late August Ghedi nominated 31 Ministers, 31 Assistant Ministers and five State Ministers to form a new Government. Among the most notable appointments were Bare Adan Shire (hitherto Minister of Reconstruction and Resettlement) as Minister of Defence and Isma'il Muhammad Hurre 'Buba' as Minister of Foreign Affairs.

Tensions continued between the Government and the SSICC and during late August 2006 SSICC forces took control of several towns to the north of Mogadishu, and continued to demand the withdrawal of all Ethiopian troops stationed in Somalia, the presence of whom had repeatedly been denied by both the Somali and the Ethiopian Governments. Further peace talks took place in Khartoum on 4 September under the auspices of the Arab League and the following day IGAD convened a meeting in Nairobi at which regional leaders agreed to deploy an international peace force to Somalia, despite continued opposition to the proposal from the SSICC. IGAD also increased pressure on the UN to remove the arms embargo, which would allow President Yussuf to form a national security force; many observers feared that lifting the embargo would lead to a resurgence of fighting. In late September the remaining port outside SSICC control, at Kismayu, was seized by that organization. In November a UN arms report claimed that the mobilization of an IGAD peace-keeping mission to Somalia, as demanded by Ethiopian forces, would exacerbate existing tensions (see below) and would only be effective if the UN arms embargo was properly enforced.

Meanwhile, in mid-September 2006 President Yussuf narrowly escaped an assassination attempt outside the Parliament buildings. In exchanges of fire that followed the explosion 11 people were killed, including Yussuf's brother, which served further to increase tensions between the weakened Government and the SSICC, although the latter denied any involvement in the incident.

In mid-October 2006 the SSICC declared a *jihad* (holy war) on Ethiopia, which it accused of launching a military offensive against Islamist troops. The Ethiopian Government had hitherto denied any military presence in Somalia but later that month the Ethiopian Prime Minister, Meles Zenawi, announced that his country was at war with the Islamist forces. A US report claimed that Ethiopia had earlier breached the UN arms embargo by delivering a consignment of weapons to the Somali Government forces and that Ethiopia's military presence in Somalia could intensify Somali nationalism and provoke attacks against Ethiopians. It was also reported that Eritrea was supplying arms to the Islamist militia.

Further peace talks were scheduled to take place in Khartoum in October 2006, but the SSICC refused to enter into discussions while the Ethiopian military remained in Somalia, and in early November negotiations were postponed. The SSICC issued a peace initiative to the Somali Government on 11 November; however, the Government rejected this and the following day violent conflict erupted, igniting fears that the situation could escalate into a regional war. Ethiopian reinforcements arrived in Baidoa, while SSICC troops were deployed to positions close to the Ethiopian border. In early December the Ethiopian Government reported attacks by insurgents who had crossed the border. At the same time, violence escalated in the area surrounding Baidoa as opposing troops sought to exert control over the seat of government. The UN Security Council hurriedly adopted a resolution (No. 1725) providing for peace-keeping missions from other African nations to enter Somalia in support of government forces. Meanwhile, the SSICC, although lacking military strength in their comparatively limited number of soldiers, was securing wider popular support. The SSICC claimed that the majority of the country, under Islamist control, remained peaceful and that international intervention was the cause of much of the conflict. Nevertheless, in mid-December the SSICC issued an ultimatum to the Ethiopian forces to leave Somalia within seven days or face a full-scale war. Ethiopia rejected these demands and civilians fled Baidoa and the surrounding areas as fighting broke out once more; the SSICC maintained that it was not at war with the Somali Government forces. During a meeting with the European Union (EU) Commissioner for Development and Humanitarian Aid on 20 December the SSICC declared that it would honour its commitment to attending peace talks in Sudan and there followed reports that fighting had begun to subside. However, Ethiopian troops advanced towards Mogadishu forcing the SSICC to retreat. Pro-Government forces began to regain control over the capital and popular support for the SSICC reportedly waned.

On 1 January 2007, with the SSICC forces driven out of the capital, Prime Minister Ghedi announced a three-day amnesty during which civilians were to turn in their weapons. The UN warned that the continued presence of Eritrean forces in Somalia remained a threat to the fragile peace, and as Ethiopia began to withdraw troops from Somalia there was increased pressure on the AU to establish a peace-keeping force in the region. Remaining pro-Government troops were subjected to guerrilla attacks in the weeks that followed, although these were reported to be small in scale, and the success of the peace process remained uncertain. The USA launched a series of air strikes against Islamists who continued to pose a threat in southern areas of Somalia. In early January five Somali cabinet ministers were arrested in Kenya, having addressed a press conference and demanded that Ethiopian troops leave their country. The Kenyan Government issued a statement declaring that it would not tolerate actions which could disrupt the peace process. Further violence was reported in Mogadishu during late January, following the visit of an AU delegation to the capital to attend further talks on the deployment of a peace-keeping mission, causing many civilians to flee the area.

In mid-January 2007 Sheikh Adan was dismissed as Speaker of the TP amid allegations that he supported the Islamist extremists and had failed to attend parliamentary meetings. Shaykh Adan Madobe was elected to replace Sheikh Adan on 31 January. Meanwhile, in mid-January 154 members of the TP voted in favour of declaring martial law, to be imposed for a period of three months from 31 January. Two faction leaders had opposed the motion, claiming that the situation would worsen with the establishment of military control.

At the end of January 2007 the AU summit convened in Addis Ababa, Ethiopia, concluded, having secured less than 4,000 troops of the 8,000 pledged to constitute the peace force. However, President Yussuf agreed to stage a national reconciliation conference with the aim of bringing an end to the conflict in the war-torn country and in early February a week of political leaders' meetings began in the capital. It was agreed that the reconciliation conference would be held in mid-April. Later in February the UN Security Council adopted a resolution (No. 1744) authorizing the establishment of the AU Mission in Somalia (AMISOM) with an initial mandate of six months. It was envisaged that this force would replace the withdrawing Ethiopian troops and provide support to the Government. However, in early March insurgents attacked the first AMISOM contingent to arrive in Somalia. Days later a military plane carrying further peace-keeping personnel caught fire at an airport in Mogadishu, although no casualties were reported.

A tentative cease-fire was agreed on 22 March 2007 between elders of the Hawiye clan and Ethiopian military officials. However, it broke down almost immediately when Government forces attacked Islamist militia in the southern region of the capital in an attempt to consolidate their control and the fighting escalated into what many observers claimed was the most violent conflict in 15 years. Fighting continued into early April and by that time, according to the office of the UN High Commissioner for Refugees (UNHCR), some 47,000 people had fled Mogadishu and it was reported that some 1,500 people had been killed, while several thousand more had been injured. The reconciliation talks were postponed until June.

Meanwhile, in February 2007 Prime Minister Ghedi effected a cabinet reshuffle; four ministers were redesignated, including the Deputy Prime Minister and Minister of Interior and Security, Hussein Aidid, who was demoted to the position of Minister of Public Works and Housing. Further governmental changes were implemented in April, including the appointment of Husayn Elabe Fahiye as Minister of Foreign Affairs.

On 12 March 2007 the TP voted to relocate the Government and the following day the office of the President moved from Baidoa to the capital, Mogadishu. Cabinet ministers began preparations to transfer their offices to the capital but progress was hindered by continuing violence in the city. The Government announced in mid-March that additional security measures were to be implemented to quell the unrest, including deploying trained Ethiopian and AU troops to the worst affected areas. A UN agency reported that by late April more than 300,000 people—almost one-third of the city's population—had left Mogadishu, and in May Hawiye clan elders conceded defeat in the capital and the Government urged the group to enter into negotiations over disarmament. Meanwhile, the UN insisted on the need for investigations into alleged war crimes and human rights violations in Somalia.

The much-delayed reconciliation conference, scheduled for 14 June 2007, was further postponed as violence continued in Mogadishu. In mid-May a number of explosions were reported, and the following month the Prime Minister's residence came under attack when a bomb exploded killing several people. Ghedi escaped unharmed, however. The incident occurred after militants based in the north of Somalia were reported to have been killed when the USA launched a missile attack on a Somali village being used as a base. The reconciliation conference finally began in mid-July amid further violence and bomb attacks. Among the most pressing issues for discussion were the holding of future elections and the resolution of clan divisions, and the international community encouraged the Government to include moderate Islamists in the conference. However, Islamists and Hawiye clan elders refused to attend the meeting on the grounds that while Ethiopian troops remained in the country, the conference would not provide a neutral base for discussions. The outcome of the seven-week conference, largely considered successful by Somali organizers, was undermined by the absence of key parties, according to international observers. The Islamists planned to hold a separate conference in Asmara, Eritrea, although analysts agreed that an all-inclusive conference was needed to secure a lasting peace. In late August AMISOM's mandate was extended for a further six months.

The opposition conference began in early September 2007, attended by Sheikh Hassan Dahir Aweys, Chairman of the SSICC, who had been in hiding since being driven from Mogadishu by Ethiopian forces earlier that year. At the meeting, also attended by UN and EU observers, SSICC and opposition leaders formed a coalition known as the Alliance for the Re-liberation of Somalia (ARS). The ARS aimed to remove the Ethiopian-backed Government and would be guided by a 191-member committee, to function as a Parliament led by the former Speaker of the TP, Sheikh Adan. A 10-member executive committee was elected, with Sheikh Sharif Sheikh Ahmed named as Chairman.

Relations between President Yussuf, a member of the Darod clan, and Prime Minister Ghedi of the Hawiye clan, had become increasingly strained in 2007. Ghedi had opposed suggestions by Yussuf that cabinet ministers no longer needed to be members of the TP, while the two had also clashed over the control of petroleum concessions in 'Puntland' and funding pledged by Saudi Arabia. In late October Prime Minister Ghedi tendered his resignation following further outbreaks of violence involving insurgents and Ethiopian troops. Nur Hassan Hussein, the Secretary-General of the Somali Red Crescent humanitarian organization and a Hawiye, was named as the new Prime Minister and sworn into office on 24 November. Earlier in that month fighting in Mogadishu escalated, forcing thousands of residents to flee the capital.

Prime Minister Hussein announced his new Cabinet in December 2007, but his nominations were criticized by the Ethiopian Government, particularly that of Minister of Foreign Affairs and International Co-operation Mohamed Ali Hamud, who was believed to have close ties to Arab governments. Shortly after their appointment, five ministers submitted their resignation, claiming that the composition of the new administration did not fully represent their clans. Having failed to gain approval for his first Cabinet, Hussein formed a new Government in mid-January 2008, which included Ibrow as Minister of Justice and Religious Affairs and Acting Minister of Labour and Social Affairs, Aydid Abdullahi Ilka Hanaf as Minister of Education and Culture and Acting Minister of Health, and Muhammad Abdisalan Adan as Minister of Information, Youth Affairs and Sports; all three were also awarded the status of Deputy Prime Minister.

In late January 2008 AU security officials submitted a proposal for measures to establish lasting peace and security. The plan included increased efforts towards achieving reconciliation; ensuring a safe environment for humanitarian aid workers; and fostering greater co-operation from the international community in peace-keeping operations. In February Prime Minister Hussein conceded that the Government was willing to meet opposition leaders in an attempt to revive the faltering reconciliation process. The UN was considering the deployment of a UN peace-keeping force to replace AMISOM, which by mid-April comprised only 2,450 troops and had largely been restricted to protecting transport facilities in Mogadishu and providing security for government officials. In February the UN Security Council had authorized the extension of AMISOM's mandate until late August. In late March it was reported that at least 19 civilians were killed in Mogadishu when fighting broke out between government troops and Islamist insurgents. Meanwhile, rebel forces launched a raid on Jowhar and in the same month the USA formally designated the militant Islamist group, ash-Shabab ('The Youth'), which had been established in 2007 by former members of the UIC, as a terrorist organization, claiming that it was linked to the al-Qa'ida network (see below). In March the Somali representative of UNHCR announced that, owing to the continuing violence, about 20,000 civilians were fleeing Mogadishu each month, and around 1m. Somalis were living as refugees.

Islamist insurgents seized the town of Adado, in the central region of Galgudud, in April 2008, reportedly killing 15 people. In the same month Sudan Ali Ahmed, the Chairman of the Elman Human Rights Organization, claimed that fighting in Mogadishu had killed 81 people: according to Ahmed the deaths were as a result of Ethiopian troops using heavy artillery in residential areas. Meanwhile a report by Amnesty International accused Ethiopian forces of committing extrajudicial killings during a raid on a mosque in Mogadishu in which 21 people were alleged to have been killed. In early May the leader of ash-Shabab, Aden Hashi Ayro, was killed in an air strike launched by US forces on the town of Dhuusa Mareeb, which resulted in the deaths of at least seven other people. Later that month UN-sponsored peace talks between the TNG and the ARS commenced in Djibouti; however, Islamist leaders in Somalia, including hardline elements of the ARS led by Aweys, reiterated their refusal to enter into negotiations until Ethiopian forces had been withdrawn from Somalia. Also in mid-May the UN Security Council approved the establishment of a joint planning unit and recommended the relocation of the UN Political Office for Somalia (UNPOS) from Nairobi to Mogadishu. UNPOS was to support the TNG in the development of a constitution and prepare for the holding of a referendum and free and democratic elections in 2009. Meanwhile tens of thousands of people took to the streets of Mogadishu in violent protests against the sharp increase in food prices; the rioting lasted for two days and there were reports that five people were killed when security forces fired on the crowds.

In June 2008 an agreement was concluded by members of the TNG and a moderate faction of the ARS present in Djibouti, which included provisions for the withdrawal of Ethiopian troops from Somalia and the deployment of a UN peace-keeping force to replace them; it was also agreed that a cease-fire would be implemented within 30 days. (The agreement was officially signed in August.) Hardline Islamists in Somalia, who had boycotted the talks, dismissed the agreement and in July the group split into two separate factions (the moderate 'Djibouti wing' and the more hardline 'Asmara wing'). Despite the agreement, intense fighting continued between insurgents and government forces, with reports of clashes in Mogadishu that resulted in the deaths of at least 28 people. Furthermore, two policemen were killed when their vehicle was destroyed in a bomb attack in which three other people died, and in late June the SSICC claimed to have captured the cities of Hawdar, Wajid and Balad Weyn in central and south-west Somalia. In the

SOMALIA

Introductory Survey

following month the head of the UN Development Programme office in Mogadishu, Usman Ali Ahmad, was shot dead near his residence in the city, although it was not clear who was responsible for the killing. The attack was part of a wider campaign by insurgents, in particular those affiliated to ash-Shabab, to target aid workers in the country, at least 20 of whom were believed to have been murdered, and a further 17 kidnapped, between January and July.

The UN Security Council extended the mandate of AMISOM for a further six months in August 2008, while Meles announced plans to begin the withdrawal of Ethiopian troops from Somalia. Nevertheless, violence continued in Mogadishu: at least 20 civilians were reported to have been killed by a roadside bomb, and one Ugandan soldier serving with the AMISOM peace-keeping force died in a separate incident. Gunmen kidnapped two western journalists near the capital, and Islamists captured the southern port of Kismayu in the same month, after three days of intense fighting in which some 100 people were killed and thousands more were displaced. Meanwhile, on 2 August it was reported that nine ministers and one deputy minister had resigned from the TNG, apparently in response to Hussein's dismissal of the Governor of the Banaadir region, Mohammed Umar Habeeb; Hussein subsequently appointed six new ministers to the TNG. In October the security situation in Mogadishu deteriorated further and there were bombings in the capital of 'Somaliland' as well as co-ordinated suicide attacks against government buildings in 'Puntland'. None the less, a new peace treaty was signed between the TNG and the 'Djibouti wing' of the ARS, in which they agreed to implement an official cease-fire the following month. It was also revealed that Ethiopian troops would begin withdrawing from Somalia on 21 November; the Ethiopian Government subsequently announced that it would remove all of its forces by the end of the year. Meanwhile, ash-Shabab had taken control of large area of central and southern Somalia, and with the imminent withdrawal of Ethiopian forces there were concerns that it would succeed in capturing Mogadishu. Indeed, President Yussuf informed members of the TP meeting in Nairobi that effectively there was no longer a functional government in Somalia.

In mid-December 2008 Yussuf announced that he had dismissed Prime Minister Hussein following his attempts to establish a power-sharing administration with moderate Islamists. Hussein rejected this decision, insisting that only the TP had the power to remove him, but, despite the TP voting in favour of reinstating Hussein, the President later named Mohamed Mohamud Guled as the new Prime Minister. On 24 December Guled announced his resignation, stating that his appointment was causing dissension within the Government. President Yussuf in turn resigned on 29 December; he was replaced in an acting capacity by the Speaker of the TP, Adan Madobe.

On 30 January 2009 the TP elected Sheikh Sharif Sheikh Ahmed, the leader of the 'Djibouti wing' of the ARS, as President. Sheikh Ahmed defeated Gen. Maslah Mohamed Siyad (the son of Siad Barre) in a second round of voting by 293 votes to 126. The election was held in Djibouti as ash-Shabab insurgents had, following the withdrawal of Ethiopian troops, recently captured Baidoa, the seat of the TP. Prior to the vote, the TP had agreed to increase the composition of that body by 275 members to 550 deputies; 149 new members from the 'Djibouti wing' of the ARS were appointed to the TP.

Amid the uncertainty that followed Yussuf's resignation in December 2008 the violence continued as insurgents shelled government forces and AMISOM positions in Mogadishu, while a number of Islamist groups began to fight among themselves. New insurgent groups, seeking to take advantage of the potential power vacuum created by the departure of Ethiopian troops, had formed in late December, including the Ahlu-Sunna Wal-Jama, which declared a *jihad* against hardline Islamist factions: there were reports that it had captured two towns which were previously controlled by ash-Shabab. Ethiopian forces commenced their withdrawal in early January 2009, and on 16 January the UN Security Council adopted a resolution (No. 1863) agreeing in principle to deploy a peace-keeping force to Somalia to replace AMISOM; however, in April UN Secretary-General Ban Ki-Moon indicated that it was unlikely a force would be established for some time, owing to the danger peace-keeping troops would face.

Meanwhile, in February 2009 President Sheikh Ahmed appointed a new Prime Minister, Omar Abdirashid Ali Sharmarke (hitherto Somalia's ambassador-designate to the USA), and on 21 February Ali Sharmake formed a new Council of Ministers which included Shaykh Abdulqadir Ali Umar, a senior member of the SSICC, as Minister of Internal Affairs. Despite this, fighting continued in Mogadishu, where at least 11 Burundian troops serving with the AMISOM peace-keeping force were reported to have been killed, and ash-Shabab fighters captured the town of Hodur, near the border with Ethiopia. Sheikh Ahmed announced the introduction of *Shari'a* law in an attempt to defuse clashes between the Government and hardline Islamists factions; however, the violence persisted, and in April at least eight people were killed following a mortar attack on the TP building. (The legislative body had relocated to Mogadishu in March). With the effective collapse of central Government and ongoing insecurity, it was feared that the situation would only deteriorate further.

In May 1993 Egal, who had been Somalia's Prime Minister in 1967–69, was elected as the new President of 'Somaliland'. In June Egal announced the composition of a 14-member council of ministers for 'Somaliland'. By late September a two-year transitional programme for reconstruction had been approved by a 47-member bicameral parliament (comprising a council of elders and a council of representatives). The administration's hopes that the prevailing atmosphere of peace in the north-western region would inspire the international community's prompt recognition of 'Somaliland' were largely frustrated, in October, by the OAU Secretary-General's rejection of the territory's independent status. Relations between the Egal administration and UNOSOM officials improved in late 1993, following the assurances of the UN Secretary-General that the mission would not interfere in the region's affairs but would provide funding for reconstruction and the rehabilitation of the police force. Nevertheless, in August 1994 Egal expelled UN representatives from 'Somaliland', accusing them of interfering in internal affairs. This was apparently precipitated by talks between the new UN Special Representative to Somalia, James Victor Gbeho (appointed in July), and Ahmed Ali 'Tur', who was courted by both the UN and Gen. Aidid following his disavowal of secession for 'Somaliland'. In October the rift between Egal and Ahmed Ali 'Tur' culminated in violent confrontations in Hargeysa between military units remaining loyal to Egal and those defecting to support Ahmed Ali 'Tur'. By mid-December it was estimated that three-quarters of the population of Hargeysa had fled, many thousands of them seeking refuge in Ethiopia (see below). Fighting spread to other parts of 'Somaliland', and in April government forces were in conflict with fighters from the Garhadji clan who had recently formed an alliance with Issa militiamen belonging to the anti-secessionist USF. Despite Egal's weakened position, he persevered with the introduction of a new currency for the territory, the 'Somaliland shilling'.

In August 1995 four sub-committees were established to draft a new constitution for 'Somaliland'. A provisional document was published in March 1996. Peace talks between the territory's warring factions were conducted in December 1995, and in May 1996 it was reported that rebel armed forces had surrendered their weapons at an official disarmament ceremony in Hargeysa. In February 1997, shortly after it was announced that the constitution had become effective for a three-year interim period, Egal was re-elected (by an electoral college) President of 'Somaliland' for a five-year term.

At a referendum held in late May 2001, according to official results, 91.7% of the voters in 'Somaliland' approved a new constitution for the territory, which contained a clause confirming the self-declared state's independence. However, the outcome appeared unlikely to persuade the international community to grant recognition to 'Somaliland'. In mid-January 2002 Egal's term of office, which had been due to expire at the end of February, prior to scheduled presidential and parliamentary elections, was extended for one year by the council of elders. In early May, however, Egal died from complications following surgery at a military hospital in South Africa; a seven-day period of national mourning was declared, and the Vice-President, Dahir Riyale Kahin, was inaugurated as President of 'Somaliland'. Kahin appointed Ahmed Yusuf Yassin as Vice-President later that month, and in July Kahin announced that a presidential election would be held in January 2003. The election was delayed on a number of occasions, but finally proceeded on 14 April. According to results published by the 'Somaliland' Election Commission, Kahin defeated his nearest rival, Ahmad Muhammad Silanyo, by just 80 votes, securing 205,595 (42.1%) of the total 498,639 votes cast. A third candidate, Faysal Ali Warabe, received 77,433 votes (15.5%). Silanyo immediately contested the result of the election and announced his intention to appeal against the outcome. However, in the following month the 'Somaliland' constitutional court confirmed the legitimacy of Kahin's victory, and he was sworn in as President on 16 May.

During 2004–05 'Somaliland' continued its attempts to secure international recognition and reiterated that it would not participate in ongoing peace negotiations taking place in Kenya (see above). Indeed, following the election of Yussuf to the Somali presidency in mid-October 2004, Kahin again stated the readiness of 'Somaliland' to defend its territorial integrity and that it would seek to retain its independent status. Elections to the lower chamber of the legislature, the House of Representatives, scheduled to be held in late March 2005, were postponed by Kahin. Members of parliament had objected to the allocation of seats in the new legislature by clan, rather than on a one-person, one-vote basis, and demanded a national census to determine voter eligibility. Nevertheless, an amended elections bill was approved by the House of Representatives in early April. On 29 September candidates from three political parties contested the 82 seats in the House of Representatives. Kahin's Unity, Democracy and Independence Party (UDUB) emerged as the largest of the three parties with 33 seats, the Peace, Unity and Development Party (KULMIYE) won 28 seats and the Justice and Development Party (UCID) 21. At the official opening of parliament in November a disagreement over the election of a speaker developed into a physical confrontation between members of the Council. The role was eventually allocated to Abdirahman Mohamed Abdullahi of the UCID, and in mid-December the 'Somaliland' parliament held its first full session. In March 2009 it was announced that presidential elections, originally scheduled for August 2008 but postponed due to instability in the region, would instead be held in September 2009.

In July 1998 Col Abdullahi Yussuf Ahmed, a former leader of the SSDF, announced the formation of 'Puntland', a new autonomous administration in north-eastern Somalia. In August Abdullahi Yussuf, as President of the new administration, appointed a cabinet, which was subsequently approved by the recently inaugurated 69-member parliament (empowered to act as the legislature for a three-year transitional period, prior to the holding of regional elections). A charter for 'Puntland', released shortly afterwards, precluded 'Puntland' from seceding from Somalia, while it envisaged the adoption of a federal system of national government, with similar regional governments emerging around the country. Hussein Aidid declared his opposition to the administration, accusing the Ethiopian authorities of encouraging 'Puntland' to secede. In late June 2001 Yussuf's mandate was controversially extended for a further three years by the 'Puntland' parliament, at the behest of clan elders. The legality of the decision was challenged by several opposition figures, and the 'Puntland' High Court issued a decree, effective from 1 July, placing all security services and other government institutions under its supervision. The Chief Justice of 'Puntland', Yussuf Haji Nur, subsequently proclaimed himself President of the territory; senior clan elders confirmed Haji Nur as acting President until 31 August. However, Yussuf rejected this decision, and heavy fighting ensued between followers of Yussuf and Haji Nur. In late August a general congress, attended by representatives of all major 'Puntland' clans, opened in Garowe, the region's capital, to elect a new President and Vice-President, as well as members to a new 'Puntland' assembly, and in mid-November Jama Ali Jama and Ahmad Mahmud Gunle were sworn in as President and Vice-President, respectively. In April 2002 Yussuf and Ali Jama met for talks in Ethiopia, but no agreement was reached. Fighting continued in 'Puntland' during 2002 and early 2003, with numerous casualties reported on both sides. In May 2003 Yussuf sought to stabilize 'Puntland' by concluding a power-sharing agreement with opposition forces, under the terms of which opposition members were granted a number of ministerial portfolios. In July 2004, following a presidential decree which reduced the Government's term in office from two years to six months, Yussuf formed a new 15-member Government. In October Yussuf was elected President of Somalia (see above) and Mohamed Abdi Hashi succeeded him as President of 'Puntland' in an acting capacity. In early January 2005 Gen. Mohamud Muse Hersi 'Adde', a former Somali diplomat, secured the support of 35 members of the 'Puntland' parliament, thus defeating Hashi, who won 30 votes, and was elected President of 'Puntland'. Hassan Dahir Afqurac was elected Vice-President. In late February 2006 an armed confrontation near the parliament building between security forces and a group loyal to the Minister for Planning, Abdirahman Farole, resulted in at least three deaths. Security forces had surrounded the building, which the group had occupied the previous day. In early March members of parliament approved a new Cabinet, in which incumbent ministers retained their portfolios, with the exception of Farole, whom Hersi had dismissed following the siege. Meanwhile, in October 2005 it emerged that 'Puntland' had issued mineral and oil exploration rights to Range Resources of Australia in an agreement that included the regions of Sanaag and Sool, disputed by 'Puntland' and the neighbouring region of 'Somaliland', prompting vociferous criticism from the 'Somaliland' administration. From September 2004 troops from both regions had reportedly been engaged in heavy fighting near the border between the two self-declared states. In December 2007 Hersi effected a cabinet reshuffle in which Gen. Abdullahi Said Samatar was named Minister of Security. A new Ministry of Oil and Minerals was established. In January 2009 the parliament elected Farole as the new President of 'Puntland', with 49 of the 66 members voting for him, and the remaining 17 lending their support to Hersi. Farole named a new Cabinet in which only three members of the previous administration were retained.

The escalation of hostilities between the Siad Barre Government and the rebel forces increased the flow of refugees from Somalia to Ethiopia and Kenya. Following the SNM's assumption of control in northern Somalia in early 1991, thousands of refugees returned from Ethiopia. Many more returned to their home territory in 'Somaliland' in late 1991 and early 1992, as a result of the ethnic conflict in south-western Ethiopia. The intensification of hostilities in the south of Somalia from April 1992 precipitated a huge movement of refugees: by the end of 1992 there were approximately 400,000 Somali refugees in Kenya, more than 300,000 in Ethiopia, up to 100,000 in Yemen, and hundreds of thousands in the Persian (Arabian) Gulf region, in Europe and North America. In early 1993 the International Committee of the Red Cross estimated that three-quarters of Somalia's population had been internally displaced by the civil conflict, although by late 1994 many thousands had returned to their villages. However, in November some 30,000 civilians fled to Ethiopia to escape fighting in Hargeysa, 'Somaliland'. According to UNHCR, at the end of 2007 there were an estimated 455,356 Somali refugees world-wide, including 192,420 in Kenya, 110,616 in Yemen, 33,659 in the United Kingdom, and 25,843 in Ethiopia.

In April 1988 a decade of hostile relations between Somalia and Ethiopia, following the war in 1977–78 over the Ogaden area of Ethiopia (which is inhabited by ethnic Somalis), ended with a peace accord. It was agreed to re-establish diplomatic relations, to withdraw troops from border areas and to exchange prisoners of war. Following the overthrow of the Mengistu regime in May 1991, the new Government in Ethiopia declared itself neutral with regard to the factions fighting for control of Somalia. Ethiopia hosted peace conferences for the warring Somali factions in 1993, 1996 and 1997. The Egyptian, Kenyan and Libyan authorities also fostered peace initiatives for Somalia from the late 1990s.

In March 1998 Ethiopian troops reportedly occupied several towns in Somalia's Gedo region, following the capture of the SNF-controlled town of Elwak (in Kenya) by the Islamist, Somali-based group al-Ittihad al-Islam. In April 1999 the Ethiopian Government denied reports that its forces were occupying two districts in western Somalia, while Hussein Aidid and Ali Mahdi reiterated their claims that Ethiopia was encouraging the division of Somalia by providing armaments and ammunition to autonomous administrations in the country.

Following the outbreak of the Eritrean–Ethiopian border conflict in mid-1998, rival Somali factions were the recipients of increasingly large consignments of weapons from the two warring countries, which sought to secure Somali allegiance to their causes. Growing concern about the activities of Eritrean-supported Somali militias prompted Ethiopia to launch cross-border raids into Somalia against warlords, and in June 1999 the RRA, assisted by Ethiopian troops, captured the town of Baidoa from Hussein Aidid's SNA. Aidid's continuing support of the Eritrean Government and Ethiopian insurgent groups led neutral observers to believe that the conflict was in danger of spreading elsewhere in the Horn of Africa. The Ethiopian Government claimed, however, that its actions were merely attempts to protect the border from attacks initiated by Somali-based rebel opposition groups. In September Ali 'Ato' and Aidid attended a meeting with the Ethiopian Minister of Foreign Affairs, Seyoum Mesfin, in Libya where an agreement was reached whereby Aidid would withdraw support for Ethiopian Oromo rebels in return for Ethiopian disengagement from

SOMALIA

Introductory Survey

Somalia. In November the SNA announced that it had disarmed several hundred Oromo Liberation Front (OLF) rebels living in Somalia, had closed down their offices and had asked the OLF leaders to leave the country. It was, however, reported that Ethiopian incursions into Somalia continued in early 2000. During late 2000 and early 2001 relations between the two countries deteriorated after the Hasan administration accused Ethiopia of offering support to faction leaders hostile to the TNA (see above). Relations between the two countries improved following the visit of a Somali government delegation to Ethiopia in June 2001. However, in September it was reported that Ethiopia had ordered the closure of the common border, fearing an increase in terrorist activity in Somalia after the events of 11 September. In November the Prime Ministers of the two countries met for talks in Addis Ababa, at which Ethiopia reiterated its concern over the suspected presence of Islamist terrorist elements in Somalia. Nevertheless, both sides pledged to improve bilateral relations, and Ethiopia affirmed its support for a comprehensive reconciliation process in Somalia. In February 2003 relations between the two countries were again strained after the Ethiopian Prime Minister admitted sending Ethiopian troops into Somali territory in pursuit of members of al-Ittihad al-Islam.

Following the suicide attacks on New York and Washington, DC, on 11 September 2001, for which the USA held the al-Qa'ida (Base) organization of Osama bin Laden responsible, the USA 'froze' the foreign assets of Somalia's al-Barakat bank, as it suspected that much of the estimated US $500m. remitted from Somalis abroad to the bank was being funnelled to terrorist organizations. Furthermore, al-Ittihad al-Islam was among 27 groups designated as foreign terrorist organizations in September by the US Government, which believed that al-Ittihad al-Islam had links to al-Qa'ida. In November the new Somali Prime Minister, Hassan Abshir Farah, denied that his Government had any links to al-Ittihad al-Islam or to al-Qa'ida and stated that he would not object to the deployment of US troops inside Somalia to monitor and detect alleged terrorist activities. In the following month US officials were reported to have held talks with several Somali faction leaders regarding the possible existence of al-Qa'ida camps in areas under their control. US special forces raided a Mogadishu hospital in March 2003 and seized a suspected al-Qa'ida operative, who was believed to have been involved in the bombing of an Israeli-owned hotel in Mombasa, Kenya, in November 2002, which resulted in the deaths of 18 people. A report published by the UN in November 2003 stated that the al-Qa'ida cell that had launched the attack on the hotel had used Somalia as a base, and warned of the possibility of further acts of terrorism being plotted, after it discovered evidence of attempts by extremist groups to procure weapons in Mogadishu. US naval forces stationed in Djibouti and Bahrain conducted patrols along the coast of Somalia throughout 2005 following a reported increase in piracy, and in late January 2006 13 suspected pirates were captured following an armed pursuit near the coast involving a US guided missile destroyer. In early March US naval forces launched a missile attack on the southern town of Dobley, targeting a Kenyan national suspected of involvement with the bombings of the US embassies in Tanzania and Kenya in August 1998, and the November 2002 Mombassa attack.

According to a report published in October 2007 by the International Maritime Bureau (IMB), the number of maritime pirate attacks off the coast of Somalia increased significantly during the first nine months of 2007, with 26 reported incidents compared with eight during the same period of 2006. By early 2008, in response to increasingly frequent attacks, particularly in the busy shipping lanes in the Gulf of Aden, there were demands for an international response to the problem. The US and French Governments proposed amendments to international law that would allow naval forces to pursue pirates into Somalia's territorial waters, and arrest and prosecute them. In April pirates seized a French tourist yacht off the coast of Somalia with 30 crew members on board; all those taken hostage were freed after a ransom was paid. The Somali Government then granted France permission to pursue the pirates on to Somali territory, where they were caught and detained by a French navy helicopter. On 2 June the UN Security Council adopted Resolution 1816, which, for a period of six months, allowed any state, in co-operation with the Somali Government, to enter Somalia's territorial waters in order to combat piracy. In October the IMB announced that there had been 63 reported cases of pirate attacks off the coast of Somalia between January and September 2008, and that the attacks were increasingly ambitious in scale: in November pirates captured a Saudi-owned oil tanker, transporting some 2m. barrels of petroleum, and demanded a US $25m. ransom for its return. (The vessel was released in January 2009 following the reported payment of $3m.) The UN Security Council passed two further resolutions in December 2008, extending the mandate of states working with the TNG to fight piracy off the coast of Somalia. A number of countries, including the USA, Russia and India, deployed warships to patrol the waters and provide an escort for vessels; a North Atlantic Treaty Organization operation was launched in October and was replaced by an EU operation in December. None the less, pirate attacks continued into the following year. Despite the release of 23 Filipino crew members and their vessel in April 2009 and the rescue earlier that month by US naval commandos of the captain of a US ship taken hostage on a lifeboat off the Somali coast, it was reported at that time that a further 18 ships and over 310 crew members were still being held by Somali pirates.

Government

In July 2000 a Somali national reconciliation conference, sponsored by President Gelleh of Djibouti, approved a national Charter, which envisaged the Somali Republic adopting a federal system of government, comprising 18 regional administrations, after a three-year interim period. The Charter provided for the creation of a Transitional National Assembly (TNA), which was to exercise legislative power in Somalia during the interim period. The 245-member TNA, comprising members of the four major clans and of an alliance of smaller clans, as well as 20 influential Somalis, was inaugurated in August and elected a President of Somalia. In October the President nominated a Prime Minister, who formed a Cabinet. Despite the expiry of its mandate in August 2003, the TNA remained in place, pending the election of a new legislative body. In late January 2004, following protracted negotiations in Kenya, an agreement was signed that provided for the establishment of a new 275-member national parliament, to comprise 61 representatives from each of the four major clans and 31 from an alliance of smaller clans. Once established, the parliament elected a national President, who, in turn, nominated a Prime Minister to form a government.

Defence

Of total armed forces of 64,500 in June 1990, the army numbered 60,000, the navy 2,000 and the air force 2,500. In addition, there were 29,500 members of paramilitary forces, including 20,000 members of the People's Militia. Following the overthrow of the Siad Barre regime in January 1991, there were no national armed forces. Somalia was divided into areas controlled by different armed groups, which were based on clan, or sub-clan, membership. Following his election to the presidency in August 2000, Abdulkasim Salad Hasan announced his intention to recruit former militiamen into a new national force: by December some 5,000 Somalis had begun training under the supervision of Mogadishu's Islamic courts. However, efforts to establish a new national armed force have made little progress since the Government's return to Somalia from exile in 2005. In November 2008 it was estimated that the armed forces of the Transitional National Government (TNG) numbered around 2,000. The total armed forces of the self-proclaimed 'Republic of Somaliland' were estimated to number 15,000, while the armed forces of 'Puntland' were believed to number around 5,000–10,000. The AU Mission in Somalia had an estimated 3,400 troops present in the country (1,700 from Burundi and 1,700 from Uganda); during 2008 there were also 2,500–3,000 Ethiopian troops stationed in Somalia to support the TNG, but these were withdrawn in January 2009.

Economic Affairs

In 2007, according to estimates by the UN, Somalia's gross national income (GNI) was US $2,450m., equivalent to $282 per head. In 2007 gross domestic product (GDP) was an estimated $2,532m., equivalent to $291 per head. During 2000–07, it was estimated, the population increased at an average annual rate of 3.0%. GDP increased, in real terms, at an average annual rate of 5.7% in 2000–07; growth of 2.7% was recorded in 2007.

According to UN estimates, agriculture (including forestry and fishing) contributed 60.1% of GDP in 2007. According to FAO estimates, 68.8% of the working population were employed in agriculture in mid-2005. Agriculture is based on the breeding of livestock, which accounted for 49% of GDP in 1989 and 38.4% of the total value of exports in 1988. Bananas are the principal cash crop, accounting for 40.3% of export earnings in 1988. The GDP of the agricultural sector declined by an average of 4.1% per year in

1990–99; agricultural GDP increased by 12.0% in 1999. Total cereals production was 207,800 metric tons in 1999, the lowest annual yield since 1993, but recovered to an estimated 359,000 in 2005, before declining to 196,000 in 2007. Southern Somalia experienced severe drought in 2005, causing harvests to fail for the third consecutive year and provoking acute shortages of food among the population.

According to UN estimates, industry (including mining, manufacturing, construction and power) contributed 7.4% of GDP in 2007, and employed an estimated 12.0% of the working population in 2002. The combined GDP of the mining, manufacturing, construction and power sectors increased by an average of 5.7% per year in 2000–07; growth in 2007 was 2.6%. The GDP of the construction sector increased at an average annual rate of 5.8% in 2000–07; growth of 2.3% was recorded in 2007.

Mining contributed 0.3% of GDP in 1988. Somalia's mineral resources include salt, limestone, gypsum, gold, silver, nickel, copper, zinc, lead, manganese, uranium and iron ore. Deposits of petroleum and natural gas have been discovered, but remain unexploited: US petroleum companies were granted exploration rights covering two-thirds of the country by Siad Barre, and were expected to start investigations once there was a durable peace. In February 2001 it was reported that the French petroleum company TotalFinaElf had signed an agreement with the transitional Somali Government to carry out oil exploration in the south of the country. Discussions commenced in January 2003 between the 'Somaliland' administration and a British-based company regarding the possible granting of contracts for petroleum exploration. An Australian mining company, Range Resources, began mineral and petroleum exploration in 'Puntland' and in October 2005 it signed a contract with the 'Puntland' Government, granting it 50.1% of exploration rights for the entire region, including territory disputed by neighbouring 'Somaliland'. However, the Transitional Federal Government later declared the contract void.

According to UN estimates, manufacturing contributed almost 2.5% of GDP in 2007. The most important sectors are food-processing, especially sugar-refining, the processing of hides and skins, and the refining of petroleum. Manufacturing GDP increased by an average of 6.3% per year in 2000–07; growth in 2007 was 4.0%.

Energy is derived principally from oil-fired generators. Imports of fuel products comprised 14% of the value of merchandise imports in 1990.

The services sector contributed 32.5% of GDP in 2007, and engaged an estimated 21.1% of the employed labour force in 2002. Tourism accounted for some 9.3% of GDP in 1988, although since the outbreak of civil unrest there has been little tourist activity in Somalia.

In 1989 Somalia recorded a visible trade deficit of US $278.6m., and there was a deficit of $156.7m. on the current account of the balance of payments. In 1982 the principal source of imports (34.4%) was Italy, while Saudi Arabia was the principal market for exports (86.5%). Other major trading partners in that year were the United Kingdom, the Federal Republic of Germany and Kenya. The principal exports in 1988 were livestock and bananas. The principal imports were petroleum, fertilizers, foodstuffs and machinery. Livestock and bananas remained the principal exports in the late 1990s, while the United Arab Emirates emerged as Somalia's main trading partner.

In 1988 Somalia recorded a budget deficit of 10,009.4m. Somali shillings. A provisional budget for 1991 was projected to balance at 268,283.2m. Somali shillings. Somalia's total external debt was US $2,836m. at the end of 2006, of which $1,923m. was long-term public debt. In 1990–2001 the average annual rate of inflation was 20.6%. Consumer prices increased by 11.5% in 2001. The rate of unemployment was estimated at 47.4% in 2002.

Somalia is a member of the African Development Bank (see p. 170) and the Islamic Development Bank (see p. 340).

Somalia's long history of civil unrest, together with unreliable climatic conditions, have undermined the traditional agricultural base of the economy. In December 2001 the UN announced that Somalia was on the verge of an economic collapse unparalleled in modern history. This was attributed largely to the US Administration's decision to enforce the closure of the al-Barakat banking and telecommunications organization (see Recent History), owing to its suspected links to terrorist organizations, thus severing the remittance process on which so much of the country is heavily dependent. The formation of a new Government in late 2004 raised hopes that central authority would be restored to the country, thus enabling the possible creation of financial institutions and providing a degree of stability, which would, in turn, encourage the development of the economy. Indeed, in July 2004 Coca-Cola opened a soft drinks plant in Mogadishu, representing the largest single investment in the country, and in February 2005 Somalia signed a trade agreement with Kenya providing for co-operation in various sectors, including livestock farming, fisheries, telecommunications and industry. In mid-2007 the China National Offshore Oil Corporation signed an agreement with the Somali Government, which allowed the former the opportunity to explore any land with potential reserves of natural resources. The development was in contrast to the general policy of Western companies, which saw the exploitation of conflict areas as anathema to local interests. However, despite pledges of significant humanitarian aid by the international community, divisions within the Government and ongoing conflict continued to prevent the development of an economic infrastructure. Furthermore, the escalation of hostilities from early 2007 between government troops and Islamist forces resulted in around 1.1m. internal refugees by late 2008, while aid agencies estimated that one-half of the country's population was in need of emergency assistance. Meanwhile, a significant increase in piracy in the Gulf of Aden in 2008 has threatened trade and investment, while interrupting humanitarian supplies. In response the EU launched a naval and air defence force in late 2008 to patrol the busy sea lanes.

Education

All private schools were nationalized in 1972, and education is now provided free of charge. Primary education, lasting for seven years, is officially compulsory for children aged six to 13 years. However, in 2002 enrolment at primary schools was equivalent to only 16.9% of the school-age population (boys 20.8%; girls 12.7%). Secondary education, beginning at the age of 13, lasts for five years, but is not compulsory. In 1985 the enrolment at secondary schools included 3% of children (boys 4%; girls 2%) in the relevant age-group. Current expenditure on education in the Government's 1988 budget was 478.1m. Somali shillings (equivalent to 1.9% of total current spending). Following the overthrow of Siad Barre's Government in January 1991 and the descent of the country into anarchy, Somalia's education system collapsed. In January 1993 a primary school was opened in the building of Somalia's sole university, the Somali National University in Mogadishu (which had been closed in early 1991). The only other schools operating in the country were a number run by Islamist groups and some that had been reopened in 'Somaliland' in mid-1991.

Public Holidays

2009: 1 January (New Year's Day), 7 January*† (Ashoura), 9 March* (Mouloud, Birth of the Prophet), 1 May (Labour Day), 26 June (Independence Day), 1 July (Foundation of the Republic), 20 September* (Id al-Fitr, end of Ramadan), 27 November* (Id al-Adha, Feast of the Sacrifice), 27 December*† (Ashoura).

2010: 1 January (New Year's Day), 26 February* (Mouloud, birth of the Prophet), 1 May (Labour Day), 26 June (Independence Day), 1 July (Foundation of the Republic), 10 September* (Id al-Fitr, end of Ramadan), 16 November* (Id al-Adha, Feast of the Sacrifice), 16 December* (Ashoura).

* These holidays are dependent on the Islamic lunar calendar and may vary by one or two days from the dates given.

† This festival occurs twice (in the Islamic years AH 1430 and 1431) within the same Gregorian year.

Weights and Measures

The metric and imperial systems are both used.

SOMALIA

Statistical Survey

Sources (unless otherwise stated): Economic Research and Statistics Dept, Central Bank of Somalia, Mogadishu, and Central Statistical Dept, State Planning Commission, POB 1742, Mogadishu; tel. (1) 80385.

Area and Population

AREA, POPULATION AND DENSITY

Area (sq km)	637,657*
Population (census results)†	
7 February 1975	3,253,024
February 1986 (provisional)	
Males	3,741,664
Females	3,372,767
Total	7,114,431
Population (UN estimates at mid-year)‡	
2006	8,544,000
2007	8,733,000
2008	8,926,000
Density (per sq km) at mid-2008	14.0

* 246,201 sq miles.
† Excluding adjustment for underenumeration.
‡ Source: UN, *World Population Prospects: The 2008 Revision*.

PRINCIPAL TOWNS
(estimated population in 1981)

Mogadishu (capital)	500,000	Berbera	65,000
Hargeysa	70,000	Merca	60,000
Kismayu	70,000		

Mid-2007 ('000, including suburbs, UN estimate): Mogadishu 1,100 (Source: UN, *World Urbanization Prospects: The 2007 Revision*).

BIRTHS AND DEATHS
(annual averages, UN estimates)

	1990–95	1995–2000	2000–05
Birth rate (per 1,000)	45.5	45.9	45.7
Death rate (per 1,000)	20.6	17.9	16.2

Source: UN, *World Population Prospects: The 2008 Revision*.

Life expectancy (years at birth, WHO estimates): 54.6 (males 53.6; females 55.7) in 2006 (Source: WHO, *World Health Statistics*).

ECONOMICALLY ACTIVE POPULATION
(estimates, '000 persons, 1991)

	Males	Females	Total
Agriculture, etc.	1,157	1,118	2,275
Industry	290	46	336
Services	466	138	604
Total labour force	1,913	1,302	3,215

Source: UN Economic Commission for Africa, *African Statistical Yearbook*.

2002 (percentage distribution): Agriculture 66.9; Industry 12.0; Services 21.1 (Source: The World Bank and United Nations Development Programme, *Socio-Economic Survey 2002 Somalia*).

Mid-2005 (estimates in '000): Agriculture, etc. 2,572; Total labour force 3,737 (Source: FAO).

Health and Welfare

KEY INDICATORS

Total fertility rate (children per woman, 2006)	6.2
Under-5 mortality rate (per 1,000 live births, 2006)	145
HIV/AIDS (% of persons aged 15–49, 2007)	0.5
Physicians (per 1,000 head, 1997)	0.04
Hospital beds (per 1,000 head, 1997)	0.42
Health expenditure (2001): US $ per head (PPP)	18
Health expenditure (2001): % of GDP	2.6
Health expenditure (2001): public (% of total)	44.6
Access to water (% of persons, 2006)	29
Access to sanitation (% of persons, 2006)	23

For sources and definitions, see explanatory note on p. vi.

Agriculture

PRINCIPAL CROPS
('000 metric tons, FAO estimates unless otherwise indicated)

	2005	2006	2007
Rice, paddy	18	18	16
Maize	200	97	99
Sorghum	140	145*	80
Sweet potatoes	8	7	7
Cassava (Manioc)	85	82	82
Sugar cane	210	220	215
Groundnuts, with shell	9	5	6
Sesame seed	30	30	30
Watermelons	8	7	8
Grapefruit and pomelos	6	6	6
Bananas	38	38	38
Oranges	9	9	9
Lemons and limes	8	8	8
Dates	11	12	12

* Unofficial figure.

Aggregate production ('000 metric tons, may include official, semi-official or estimated data): Total cereals 359 in 2005, 261 in 2006, 196 in 2007; Total roots and tubers 93 in 2005, 89 in 2006, 89 in 2007; Total vegetables (incl. melons) 92 in 2005, 83 in 2006, 84 in 2007; Total fruits (excl. melons) 208 in 2005, 74 in 2006, 74 in 2007.

Source: FAO.

LIVESTOCK
('000 head, year ending September, FAO estimates)

	2004	2005	2006
Cattle	5,400	5,500	5,350
Sheep	14,500	14,700	13,100
Goats	13,800	14,600	12,700
Pigs	5	5	4
Asses and mules	44	44	n.a.
Camels	7,210	7,230	7,000
Chickens	3	3	3

2007: Production assumed to be unchanged from 2006 (FAO estimates).

Source: FAO.

SOMALIA

LIVESTOCK PRODUCTS
('000 metric tons, FAO estimates)

	2005	2006	2007
Cows' milk	450	437	435
Goats' milk	413	394	393
Sheep's milk	475	468	468
Cattle meat	68	66	66
Sheep meat	53	48	48
Goat meat	39	42	42
Hen eggs	3	3	3

Source: FAO.

Forestry

ROUNDWOOD REMOVALS
('000 cubic metres, excl. bark, FAO estimates)

	2005	2006	2007
Sawlogs, veneer logs and logs for sleepers*	28	28	28
Other industrial wood	82	82	82
Fuel wood	10,803	11,127	11,461
Total	10,913	11,237	11,571

* Annual output assumed to be unchanged since 1975.
Source: FAO.

SAWNWOOD PRODUCTION
('000 cubic metres, incl. railway sleepers)

	1973	1974	1975
Total (all broadleaved)	15*	10	14

* FAO estimate.
1976–2007: Production assumed to be unchanged from 1975 (FAO estimates).
Source: FAO.

Fishing

('000 metric tons, live weight, FAO estimates)

	1999	2000	2001
Marine fishes	23.5	19.8	26.3
Total catch (incl. others)	24.8	20.8	27.5

2002–06: Figures assumed to be unchanged from 2001 (FAO estimates).
Source: FAO.

Mining

('000 metric tons, estimates)

	2002	2003	2004
Salt	1	1	1
Gypsum	2	2	2

Source: US Geological Survey.

Industry

SELECTED PRODUCTS
('000 metric tons, unless otherwise indicated)

	1986	1987	1988
Sugar*	30.0	43.3	41.2
Canned meat (million tins)	1.0	—	—
Canned fish	0.1	—	—
Pasta and flour	15.6	4.3	—
Textiles (million yards)	5.5	3.0	6.3
Boxes and bags	15.0	12.0	5.0
Cigarettes and matches	0.3	0.2	0.1
Petroleum products	128	44	30
Electric energy (million kWh)†	253	255‡	257‡

* Data from FAO.
† Source: UN, *Industrial Commodity Statistics Yearbook*.
‡ Provisional figure.

Raw sugar ('000 metric tons): 20 in 2003; 20 in 2004; 15 in 2005 (Source: UN, *Industrial Commodity Statistics Yearbook*).

Electric energy (million kWh): 280 in 2003; 280 in 2004; 290 in 2005 (Source: UN, *Industrial Commodity Statistics Yearbook*).

Finance

CURRENCY AND EXCHANGE RATES

Monetary Units
100 cents = 1 Somali shilling (So. sh.).

Sterling, Dollar and Euro Equivalents (28 November 2008)
£1 sterling = 22,093 Somali shillings;
US $1 = 14,406 Somali shillings;
€1 = 18,335 Somali shillings;
100,000 Somali shillings = £4.53 = $6.94 = €5.45.

Average Exchange Rate (Somali shillings per US $)
1987 105.18
1988 170.45
1989 490.68

Note: A separate currency, the 'Somaliland shilling', was introduced in the 'Republic of Somaliland' in January 1995. The exchange rate was reported to be US $1 = 2,750 'Somaliland shillings' in March 2000.

CURRENT BUDGET
(million Somali shillings)

Revenue	1986	1987	1988
Total tax revenue	8,516.4	8,622.4	12,528.1
Taxes on income and profits	1,014.8	889.7	1,431.0
Income tax	380.5	538.8	914.8
Profit tax	634.3	350.9	516.2
Taxes on production, consumption and domestic transactions	1,410.4	1,274.2	2,336.4
Taxes on international transactions	6,091.2	6,458.5	8,760.6
Import duties	4,633.2	4,835.2	6,712.1
Total non-tax revenue	6,375.2	8,220.4	7,623.4
Fees and service charges	274.1	576.1	828.8
Income from government property	633.4	656.4	2,418.9
Other revenue	5,467.2	6,987.9	4,375.7
Total	14,891.6	16,842.8	20,151.5

Expenditure	1986	1987	1988
Total general services	11,997.7	19,636.7	24,213.6
Defence	2,615.9	3,145.0	8,093.9
Interior and police	605.0	560.7	715.4
Finance and central services	7,588.3	14,017.8	12,515.6
Foreign affairs	633.0	1,413.9	2,153.1
Justice and religious affairs	248.5	290.2	447.0
Presidency and general administration	93.0	148.0	217.4
Planning	189.0	24.9	24.3
National Assembly	25.0	36.2	46.9
Total economic services	1,927.6	554.1	600.3

SOMALIA

Statistical Survey

Expenditure—*continued*	1986	1987	1988
Transportation	122.2	95.2	94.5
Posts and telecommunications	94.3	76.7	75.6
Public works	153.9	57.5	69.8
Agriculture	547.2	59.4	55.3
Livestock and forestry	459.0	89.5	109.9
Mineral and water resources	318.8	85.2	93.1
Industry and commerce	131.0	45.1	43.9
Fisheries	101.2	45.5	58.2
Total social services	1,050.5	900.1	930.8
Education	501.6	403.0	478.1
Health	213.8	203.5	255.2
Information	111.5	135.0	145.8
Labour, sports and tourism	139.6	49.3	51.7
Other	84.0	109.3	—
Total	**14,975.8**	**21,091.0**	**25,744.7**

1989 (estimates): Budget to balance at 32,429.0m. Somali shillings.
1990 (estimates): Budget to balance at 86,012.0m. Somali shillings.
1991 (estimates): Budget to balance at 268,283.2m. Somali shillings.

CENTRAL BANK RESERVES
(US $ million at 31 December)

	1987	1988	1989
Gold*	8.3	7.0	6.9
Foreign exchange	7.3	15.3	15.4
Total	**15.6**	**22.3**	**22.3**

* Valued at market-related prices.
Source: IMF, *International Financial Statistics*.

MONEY SUPPLY
(million Somali shillings at 31 December)

	1987	1988	1989
Currency outside banks	12,327	21,033	70,789
Private-sector deposits at central bank	1,771	1,555	5,067
Demand deposits at commercial banks	15,948	22,848	63,971
Total money	**30,046**	**45,436**	**139,827**

Source: IMF, *International Financial Statistics*.

COST OF LIVING
(Consumer Price Index; base: 2000 = 100)

	2001	2002	2003
All items	111.5	133.8	133.8

2004–06: Consumer prices assumed to be unchanged from 2003.
Source: African Development Bank.

NATIONAL ACCOUNTS

Expenditure on the Gross Domestic Product*
(estimates, million Somali shillings at current prices)

	1988	1989	1990
Government final consumption expenditure	33,220	58,530	104,760
Private final consumption expenditure	240,950	481,680	894,790
Increase in stocks	14,770	n.a.	n.a.
Gross fixed capital formation	44,780	134,150	240,030
Total domestic expenditure	**333,720**	**674,360**	**1,239,580**
Exports of goods and services	7,630	8,890	8,660
Less Imports of goods and services	49,430	57,660	58,460
GDP in purchasers' values	**291,920**	**625,580**	**1,189,780**

* Figures are rounded to the nearest 10m. Somali shillings.
Source: UN Economic Commission for Africa, *African Statistical Yearbook*.

Gross Domestic Product by Economic Activity
(million Somali shillings at constant 1985 prices)

	1986	1987	1988
Agriculture, hunting, forestry and fishing	54,868	59,378	61,613
Mining and quarrying	291	291	291
Manufacturing	4,596	4,821	4,580
Electricity, gas and water	77	62	57
Construction	3,289	3,486	2,963
Trade, restaurants and hotels	8,587	9,929	8,599
Transport, storage and communications	6,020	6,153	5,873
Finance, insurance, real estate and business services	3,743	4,095	3,890
Government services	1,631	1,530	1,404
Other community, social and personal services	2,698	2,779	2,863
Sub-total	**85,800**	**92,524**	**92,133**
Less Imputed bank service charges	737	748	748
GDP at factor cost	**85,064**	**91,776**	**91,385**
Indirect taxes, *less* subsidies	5,301	4,250	3,262
GDP in purchasers' values	**90,365**	**96,026**	**94,647**

GDP at factor cost (estimates, million Somali shillings at current prices): 249,380 in 1988; 500,130 in 1989; 923,970 in 1990 (Source: UN Economic Commission for Africa, *African Statistical Yearbook*).

BALANCE OF PAYMENTS
(US $ million)

	1987	1988	1989
Exports of goods f.o.b.	94.0	58.4	67.7
Imports of goods f.o.b.	−358.5	−216.0	−346.3
Trade balance	**−264.5**	**−157.6**	**−278.6**
Imports of services	−127.7	−104.0	−122.0
Balance on goods and services	**−392.2**	**−261.6**	**−400.6**
Other income paid	−52.0	−60.6	−84.4
Balance on goods, services and income	**−444.2**	**−322.2**	**−485.0**
Current transfers received	343.3	223.7	331.2
Current transfers paid	−13.1	—	−2.9
Current balance	**−114.0**	**−98.5**	**−156.7**
Investment liabilities	−22.8	−105.5	−32.6
Net errors and omissions	39.0	22.4	−0.8
Overall balance	**−97.9**	**−181.7**	**−190.0**

Source: IMF, *International Financial Statistics*.

External Trade

PRINCIPAL COMMODITIES
(million Somali shillings)

Imports*	1986	1987	1988
Foodstuffs	1,783.3	3,703.6	1,216.1
Beverages and tobacco	298.1	183.6	6.2
Manufacturing raw materials	230.0	626.9	661.4
Fertilizers	1.8	238.0	2,411.4
Petroleum	2,051.0	3,604.2	3,815.9
Construction materials	981.4	2,001.9	307.8
Machinery and parts	1,098.3	1,203.6	957.1
Transport equipment	1,133.8	1,027.6	195.2
Total (incl. others)	**8,443.4**	**13,913.7**	**11,545.5**

* Figures cover only imports made against payments of foreign currencies. The total value of imports in 1986 was 20,474 million Somali shillings.

Exports	1986	1987	1988
Livestock	4,420.3	7,300.0	3,806.5
Bananas	1,207.2	2,468.8	3,992.3
Hides and skins	294.0	705.2	492.0
Total (incl. others)	**6,372.5**	**10,899.9**	**9,914.1**

1992 (estimates, US $ million): Imports 150; Exports 80.

SOMALIA

PRINCIPAL TRADING PARTNERS
('000 Somali shillings)

Imports	1980	1981	1982
China, People's Repub.	46,959	40,962	89,772
Ethiopia	43,743	146,853	155,775
Germany, Fed. Repub.	104,117	430,548	214,873
Hong Kong	5,351	13,862	3,972
India	41,467	19,638	4,801
Iraq	2,812	67,746	402
Italy	756,800	662,839	1,221,146
Japan	28,900	54,789	48,371
Kenya	86,515	105,627	198,064
Saudi Arabia	120,208	160,583	82,879
Singapore	18,569	15,592	73,652
Thailand	19,296	40,527	106,474
United Kingdom	172,613	935,900	238,371
USA	201,662	141,823	154,082
Total (incl. others)	2,190,627	3,221,715	3,548,805

Exports	1980	1981	1982
Djibouti	6,640	3,209	2,458
Germany, Fed. Repub.	11,376	1,956	20,086
Italy	107,661	58,975	77,870
Kenya	2,425	6,929	4,211
Saudi Arabia	583,768	803,631	1,852,936
United Kingdom	1,233	—	3,169
USA	1,301	—	6,970
Yemen, People's Dem. Repub.	3,182	—	—
Total (incl. others)	844,012	960,050	2,142,585

Source: the former Ministry of Planning, Mogadishu.

1986: *Imports* (estimates, million Somali shillings) USA 1,816; Japan 836; China, People's Repub. 553; United Kingdom 773; France 341; Germany, Fed. Repub. 1,481; Total (incl. others) 8,443; *Exports* (estimates, million Somali shillings) USA 5; China, People's Repub. 4; United Kingdom 31; France 27; Germany, Fed. Repub. 11; Total (incl. others) 6,373 (Source: UN Economic Commission for Africa, *African Statistical Yearbook*).

Transport

ROAD TRAFFIC
(estimates, '000 motor vehicles in use)

	1994	1995	1996
Passenger cars	2.8	2.0	1.0
Commercial vehicles	7.4	7.3	6.4

Source: International Road Federation, *World Road Statistics*.

SHIPPING
Merchant Fleet
(registered at 31 December)

	2005	2006	2007
Number of vessels	18	19	18
Total displacement ('000 grt)	2.8	10.3	9.9

Source: Lloyd's Register-Fairplay, *World Fleet Statistics*.

International Sea-borne Freight Traffic
('000 metric tons)

	1989	1990	1991
Goods loaded	325	324	n.a.
Goods unloaded	1,252*	1,118	1,007*

* Estimate.

Source: UN Economic Commission for Africa, *African Statistical Yearbook*.

CIVIL AVIATION
(traffic on scheduled services)

	1989	1990	1991
Kilometres flown (million)	3	3	1
Passengers carried ('000)	89	88	46
Passenger-km (million)	248	255	131
Freight ton-km (million)	8	9	5

Source: UN, *Statistical Yearbook*.

Tourism

	1996	1997	1998
Tourist arrivals ('000)	10	10	10

Source: World Bank.

Communications Media

	1995	1996	1997
Radio receivers ('000 in use)	400	450	470
Television receivers ('000 in use)	124	129	135
Telephones ('000 main lines in use)*	15	15	15
Daily newspapers	1	2	n.a.

* Estimates.

2003: Mobile cellular telephones (subscribers) 200,000; Telephones (main lines in use, estimate) 100,000; Internet users 30,000.

2004: Mobile cellular telephones (subscribers) 500,000; Telephones (main lines in use, estimate) 100,000; Internet users 86,000.

2005: Mobile cellular telephones (subscribers) 500,000; Telephones (main lines in use, estimate) 100,000; Internet users 90,000.

2006: Mobile cellular telephones (subscribers) 550,000; Internet users 94,000.

2007: Mobile cellular telephones (subscribers) 600,000; Internet users 98,000.

Sources: UNESCO, *Statistical Yearbook*; International Telecommunication Union.

Education

(1985, unless otherwise indicated)

	Institutions	Teachers	Pupils
Pre-primary	16	133	1,558
Primary	1,224	10,338	196,496
Secondary:			
general	n.a.	2,149	39,753
teacher training	n.a.	30*	613*
vocational	n.a.	637	5,933
Higher	n.a.	817†	15,672†

* Figure refers to 1984.
† Figure refers to 1986.

Source: UNESCO, *Statistical Yearbook*.

1990 (UN estimates): 377,000 primary-level pupils; 44,000 secondary-level pupils; 10,400 higher-level pupils.

1991: University teachers 549; University students 4,640.

Adult literacy rate (UNESCO estimates): 24.0% in 2002 (Source: UN Development Programme, *Human Development Report*).

Directory

The Constitution

The Constitution promulgated in 1979 and amended in 1990 was revoked following the overthrow of President Siad Barre in January 1991. In July 2000 delegates at the Somali national reconciliation conference in Arta, Djibouti, overwhelmingly approved a national Charter, which was to serve as Somalia's constitution for an interim period of three years. The Charter, which is divided into six main parts, guarantees Somali citizens the freedoms of expression, association and human rights, and distinctly separates the executive, the legislature and the judiciary, as well as guaranteeing the independence of the latter.

The Government

HEAD OF STATE

President: SHEIKH SHARIF SHEIKH AHMED (took office 31 January 2009).

CABINET
(April 2009)

Prime Minister: OMAR ABDIRASHID ALI SHARMARKE.
Deputy Prime Minister and Minister of Fisheries and Marine Resources: Prof. ABDIRAHMAN HAJI ADAN IBBI.
Deputy Prime Minister and Minister of Finance: SHARIF HASAN SHAYKH ADAN.
Deputy Prime Minister and Minister of Energy and Fuel: ABDIWAHID ILMI GONJEH.
Minister of Foreign Affairs: MUHAMMAD ABDULLAHI OMAAR.
Minister of Defence: MUHAMMAD ABDI GANDI.
Minister of National Planning and International Co-operation: ABDIRAHMAN ABDISHAKUR WARSAME.
Minister of Constitutional and Federal Affairs: MADOBE NUNOW MUHAMMAD.
Minister of Endowment and Religious Affairs: SHAYKH NUR ALI ADAN.
Minister of Gender and Family Affairs: FOWSIYA MUHAMMAD SHAYKH.
Minister of Rehabilitation and the Disabled: MUHAMMAD ALI IBRAHIM.
Minister of Humanitarian Assistance: Dr MAHMUD ABDI IBRAHIM.
Minister of Information: FARHAN ALI MAHMUD.
Minister of Research and Technology: MUHAMMAD ALI.
Minister of Health: QAMAR ADAN ALI.
Minister of Labour: MUHAMMAD ABDI MAREYE.
Minister of Somali Communities Abroad: ABDULLAHI AHMAD ABDULLE AZHARI.
Minister of Education: AHMAD ABDULLAHI WAYEL.
Minister of Works and Housing: MUHAMMAD ABDI YUSUF.
Minister of Rural Development: KHADIJA MUHAMMAD DIRIYE.
Minister of Sports and Youth Affairs: SALEBAN OLAD ROBLE.
Minister of Internal Affairs: SHAYKH ABDULQADIR ALI UMAR.
Minister of National Security: UMAR HASHI ADAN.
Ministry of Livestock Development: ABUKAR ALI USMAN.
Minister of Justice and Religious Affairs: ABDIRAHMAN MAHMUD FARAH JANAQOW.
Minister of Agriculture: HASAN MUHAMMAD NUR SHATIGADUD.
Minister of Ports and Sea Transport: MUHAMMAD IBRAHIM HABSADE.
Minister of National Heritage: MUHAMMAD MURSAL.
Minister of Culture and Higher Education: Prof. IBRAHIM HASAN ADOW.
Minister of Minerals and Water Resources: ABDALLA BOS AHMAD.
Minister of Reconstruction: HUSAYN ELABE FAHIYE.
Minister of Tourism and Wildlife: MUHAMMAD HUSAYN SA'ID.
Minister of Posts and Communications: ABDIRIZAK USMAN JURILE.
Minister of Commerce: ABDIRASHID IRO.
Minister of Industry: ABDIRAHMAN JAMA ABDALLA.
Minister of Air and Land Transport: ALI JAMA JINGELI.
Minister of the Environment and the Conservation of Trees: BUR'I MUHAMMAD HAMZI.

MINISTRIES

The new Somali Cabinet was sworn in in Djibouti on 21 February 2009, but relocated to Mogadishu later that month.

Legislature

TRANSITIONAL PARLIAMENT

Speaker: SHAYKH ADAN MADOBE.

In January 2004, following protracted negotiations in Kenya, an agreement was signed that provided for the establishment of a new 275-member transitional national parliament, to comprise 61 representatives from each of the four major clans and 31 from an alliance of smaller clans. Members were sworn in to the Transitional Parliament (TP) in August. In January 2009 it was agreed that the composition of the TP (which remained based in Baidoa, owing to the adverse security situation in Mogadishu) would be increased by a further 275 members.

Political Organizations

Alliance for the Re-liberation of Somalia (ARS): f. 2007; split into two factions in 2008; 'Djibouti wing' led by SHEIKH SHARIF SHEIKH AHMED signed a peace agreement with the TNG, while the 'Asmara wing' led by SHEIKH HASSAN DAHIR AWEYS remained in conflict with the Government.
Islamic Party (Hizb al-Islam): radical Islamist party; Chair. SHEIKH AHMAD QASIM.
Islamic Union Party (al-Ittihad al-Islam): aims to unite ethnic Somalis from Somalia, Ethiopia, Kenya and Djibouti in an Islamic state.
Juba Valley Alliance (JVA): f. 1999; alliance of militia and businessmen from the Habr Gedir and Marehan clans; Pres. BARE ADAN SHIRE.
National Democratic League: Beled Weyne; f. 2003; Chair. Dr ABDIRAHMAN ABDULLE ALI; Sec.-Gen. ABDIKARIM HUSAYN IDOW.
Peace and Development Party: Mogadishu; f. 2002; Chair. ABDULLAHI HASAN AFRAH.
Rahanwin Resistance Army (RRA): guerrilla force active around Baidoa; Chair. HASAN MUHAMMAD NUR SHATIGADUD.
Ash-Shabab (The Youth): f. 2007 by former members of the Union of Islamic Courts; leader IBRAHIM HAJI JAMA.
Somali Democratic Alliance (SDA): f. 1989; represents the Gadabursi ethnic grouping in the north-west; opposes the Isaaq-dominated SNM and its declaration of an independent 'Republic of Somaliland'; Leader MOHAMED FARAH ABDULLAH.
Somali Democratic Movement (SDM): represents the Rahanwin clan; movement split in early 1992, with this faction in alliance with Ali Mahdi Mohamed; Leader ABDULKADIR MOHAMED ADAN.
Somali Eastern and Central Front (SECF): f. 1991; opposes the SNM's declaration of the independent 'Republic of Somaliland'; Chair. HIRSI ISMAIL MOHAMED.
Somali National Alliance (SNA): f. 1992 as alliance between the Southern Somali National Movement (which withdrew in 1993) and the factions of the United Somali Congress, Somali Democratic Movement and Somali Patriotic Movement given below; Chair. HUSSEIN MOHAMED AIDID.
  Somali Democratic Movement (SDM): represents the Rahanwin clan; Chair. ADAM UTHMAN ABDI; Sec.-Gen. Dr YASIN MA'ALIM ABDULLAHI.
  Somali Patriotic Movement (SPM): f. 1989; represents Ogadenis (of the southern Darod clan); Chair. GEDI UGAS MADHAR.
Somali National Front (SNF): f. 1991; guerrilla force active in southern Somalia, promoting Darod clan interests and seeking restoration of SRSP Govt; a rival faction (led by OMAR HAJI MASALEH) is active in southern Somalia; Leader Gen. MOHAMED SIAD HERSI 'MORGAN'.
Somali National Salvation Council: f. 2003; Chair. MUSE SUDI YALAHOW.
Somali Patriotic Movement (SPM): f. 1989 in southern Somalia; represents Ogadenis (of the Darod clan) in southern Somalia; this faction of the SPM has allied with the SNF in opposing the SNA; Chair. Gen. ADEN ABDULLAHI NOOR ('Gabio').

SOMALIA

Somali Peace Loving Party: Mogadishu; f. 2002; Dr KHALID UMAR ALI.

Somali People's Democratic Union (SPDU): f. 1997; breakaway group from the SSDF; Chair. Gen. MOHAMED JIBRIL MUSEH.

Somali Reconciliation and Restoration Council (SRRC): f. 2001 by faction leaders opposed to the establishment of the Hasan administration; aims to establish a rival national govt; Co-Chair. HUSSEIN MOHAMED AIDID, HILOWLE IMAN UMAR, ADEN ABDULLAHI NOOR, HASAN MOHAMED NUR, ABDULLAHI SHAYKH ISMA'IL; Sec.-Gen. MOWLID MA'ANEH MOHAMED.

Somali Revolutionary Socialist Party (SRSP): f. 1976 as the sole legal party; overthrown in Jan. 1991; conducts guerrilla operations in Gedo region, near border with Kenya; Sec.-Gen. (vacant); Asst Sec.-Gen. AHMED SULEIMAN ABDULLAH.

Somali Salvation Democratic Front (SSDF): f. 1981 as the Democratic Front for the Salvation of Somalia (DFSS), as a coalition of the Somali Salvation Front, the Somali Workers' Party and the Democratic Front for the Liberation of Somalia; operates in cen. Somalia, although a smaller group has opposed the SNA around Kismayu in alliance with the SNF; Chair. MOHAMED ABSHIR MONSA.

Somali Solidarity Party: Mogadishu; f. 1999; Chair. ABD AR-RAHMAN MUSA MOHAMED; Sec.-Gen. SA'ID ISA MOHAMED.

Southern Somali National Movement (SSNM): based on coast in southern Somalia; Chair. ABDI WARSEMEH ISAR.

Supreme Somali Islamic Courts Council: formerly the Union of Islamic Courts; seeks to create a Somali state under the guiding principles of Shari'a (Islamic) law; Chair. Sheikh HASSAN DAHIR AWEYS.

United Somali Congress (USC): f. 1989 in cen. Somalia; overthrew Siad Barre in Jan. 1991; party split in 1991, with this faction dominated by the Abgal sub-clan of the Hawiye clan, Somalia's largest ethnic group; Leader ABDULLAHI MA'ALIN; Sec.-Gen. MUSA NUR AMIN.

  United Somali Congress—Somali National Alliance (USC—SNA): f. 1995 by dissident mems of the SNA's USC faction; represents the Habr Gedir sub-clan of the Hawiye; Leader OSMAN HASSAN ALI 'ATO'.

  United Somali Congress—Somali Salvation Alliance (USC—SSA): Leader MUSE SUDI YALAHOW.

United Somali Party (USP): opposes the SNM's declaration of the independent 'Republic of Somaliland'; Leader MOHAMED ABDI HASHI.

Unity for the Somali Republic Party (USRP): f. 1999; the first independent party to be established in Somalia since 1969; Leader ABDI NUR DARMAN.

Diplomatic Representation

EMBASSIES IN SOMALIA

Note: Following the overthrow of Siad Barre in January 1991, all foreign embassies in Somalia were closed and all diplomatic personnel left the country. Some embassies were reopened, including those of France, Sudan and the USA, following the arrival of the US-led Unified Task Force (UNITAF) in December 1992; however, nearly all foreign diplomats left Somalia in anticipation of the withdrawal of the UN peace-keeping force, UNOSOM, in early 1995.

Cuba: Mogadishu.

Djibouti: Mogadishu.

Iran: Via al-Mukarah, POB 1166, Mogadishu; tel. (1) 80881.

Korea, Democratic People's Republic: Via Km 5, Mogadishu; Ambassador KIM RYONG SU.

Kuwait: First Medina Rd, Km 5, POB 1348, Mogadishu.

Libya: Via Medina, POB 125, Mogadishu; Ambassador MOHAMED ZUBEYD.

Pakistan: Via Afgoi, Km 5, POB 339, Mogadishu; tel. (1) 80856.

Sudan: Via al-Mukarah, POB 552, Mogadishu; Chargé d'affaires a.i. FADIL AL-JASULI MUSTAFA.

Turkey: Via Km 6, POB 2833, Mogadishu; tel. (1) 81975.

United Arab Emirates: Via Afgoi, Km 5, Mogadishu; tel. (1) 23178.

Yemen: K4, Mogadishu; Ambassador AHMED HAMID ALI UMAR.

Judicial System

Constitutional arrangements in operation until 1991 provided for the Judiciary to be independent of the executive and legislative powers. Laws and acts having the force of law were required to conform to the provisions of the Constitution and to the general principles of Islam.

Attorney-General: ABDULLAH DAHIR BARRE.

Supreme Court: Mogadishu; the court of final instance in civil, criminal, administrative and auditing matters; Chair. Sheikh AHMAD HASAN.

Military Supreme Court: Mogadishu; f. 1970; tried mems of the armed forces.

National Security Court: Mogadishu; heard cases of treason.

Courts of Appeal: Mogadishu; sat at Mogadishu and Hargeysa, with two sections, General and Assize.

Regional Courts: There were eight Regional Courts, with two sections, General and Assize.

District Courts: There were 84 District Courts, with Civil and Criminal Divisions. The Civil Division had jurisdiction over all controversies where the cause of action had arisen under Shari'a (Islamic) Law or Customary Law and any other Civil controversies where the matter in dispute did not involve more than 3,000 shillings. The Criminal Division had jurisdiction with respect to offences punishable with imprisonment not exceeding three years, or fines not exceeding 3,000 shillings, or both.

Qadis: District Courts of civil jurisdiction under Islamic Law.

Following the withdrawal of the UN peace-keeping force, UNOSOM, in early 1995, most regions outside Mogadishu reverted to clan-based fiefdoms where Islamic (Shari'a) law (comprising an Islamic Supreme Council and local Islamic high courts) prevailed. In October 1996 Ali Mahdi Mohamed endorsed a new Islamic judicial system under which appeals could be lodged on all sentences passed by Islamic courts, and no sentence imposed by the courts could be implemented prior to an appeal court ruling. In April 2009 the Transitional Parliament voted in favour of the introduction of Shari'a throughout Somalia.

Religion

ISLAM

Islam is the state religion. Most Somalis are Sunni Muslims.

Imam: Gen. MOHAMED ABSHIR.

CHRISTIANITY

The Roman Catholic Church

Somalia comprises a single diocese, directly responsible to the Holy See. At 31 December 2006 there were an estimated 100 adherents.

Bishop of Mogadishu: (vacant), POB 273, Ahmed bin Idris, Mogadishu; tel. (1) 20184; e-mail evechcat@intnet.dj.

The Anglican Communion

Within the Episcopal Church in Jerusalem and the Middle East, the Bishop in Egypt has jurisdiction over Somalia.

The Press

The Country: POB 1178, Mogadishu; tel. (1) 21206; f. 1991; daily.

Dalka: POB 388, Mogadishu; tel. (1) 500533; e-mail dalka@somalinternet.com; internet www.dalka-online.com; f. 1967; current affairs; weekly.

Heegan (Vigilance): POB 1178, Mogadishu; tel. (1) 21206; f. 1978; weekly; English; Editor MOHAMOUD M. AFRAH.

Horseed: POB 1178, Mogadishu; tel. (1) 21206; e-mail horseednet@gmail.com; internet www.horseednet.com; weekly; in Somali and English.

Huuriya (Liberty): Hargeysa; daily.

Jamhuuriya (The Republic): Hargeysa; e-mail webmaster@jamhuuriya.info; internet www.jamhuuriya.info; independent; daily; Editor-in-Chief HASSAN SAÏD FAISAL ALI; circ. 2,500.

Al-Mujeehid: Hargeysa; weekly.

New Era: POB 1178, Mogadishu; tel. (1) 21206; quarterly; in English, Somali and Arabic.

Qaran Press (Maalinle Madaxbannaan): Mogadishu; tel. (1) 215305; internet www.qaranpress.com; financial information; daily; in Somali; Editor ABDULAHI AHMED ALI; circ. 2,000.

Riyaaq (Happiness): Bossaso.

Sahan (Pioneer): Bossaso; Editor MUHAMMAD DEEQ.

Somalia in Figures: Ministry of National Planning, POB 1742, Mogadishu; tel. (1) 80384; govt statistical publ; 3 a year; in English.

Somalia Times: POB 555, Mogadishu BN 03040; e-mail info@somalpost.com; internet www.somaliatimes.com; Somali; weekly; circ. 50,000.

SOMALIA

NEWS AGENCIES

Horn of Africa News Agency: Mogadishu; e-mail info@hananews.org; internet www.hananews.org; f. 1990.

Somali National News Agency (SONNA): POB 1748, Mogadishu; tel. (1) 24058; Dir Muhammad Hasan Kahin.

Publishers

Government Printer: POB 1743, Mogadishu.

Somalia d'Oggi: Piazzale della Garesa, POB 315, Mogadishu; law, economics and reference.

Broadcasting and Communications

TELECOMMUNICATIONS

Ministry of Information: POB 1748, Mogadishu; tel. (1) 999621; Dir-Gen. A. Ali Askar.

Somali Telecom (Olympic Telecommunications): Mogadishu.

Somaliland Telecommunications Corpn: Hargeysa; Dir Mohamed Arwo.

Telcom Somaliland: Telcom Somaliland Bldg, Togdheer St, Hargeysa; tel. (2) 300161; fax (2) 300162; e-mail info@telcomsomaliland.com; internet www.telcomsomaliland.com; f. 2003; provides local, national long distance and int. telecommunications, mobile communications and data services.

BROADCASTING

Radio

Holy Koran Radio: Mogadishu; f. 1996; religious broadcasts in Somali.

Radio Awdal: Boorama, 'Somaliland'; operated by the Gadabursi clan.

Radio Banaadir: Tahlil Warsame Bldg, 4 Maka al-Mukarama Rd, Mogadishu; tel. (5) 944176; e-mail rbb@radiobanadir.com; internet www.radiobanadir.com; f. 2000; serves Mogadishu and its environs.

Radio Free Somalia: tel. 2525630838; e-mail admin@radiofreesomalia.com; internet www.radiofreesomalia.com; f. 1993; operates from Galacaio in north-eastern Somalia; relays humanitarian and educational programmes.

Radio Gaalkayco: operates from 'Puntland'.

Radio Hargeysa, the Voice of the 'Republic of Somaliland': POB 14, Hargeysa; tel. 155; e-mail radiohargeysa@yahoo.com; internet www.radiosomaliland.com/radiohargeisa.html; serves the northern region ('Somaliland'); broadcasts in Somali, and relays Somali and Amharic transmission from Radio Mogadishu; Dir of Radio Idris Egal Nur.

Radio HornAfrique: Mogadishu; f. 1999; commercial independent station broadcasting music and programmes on social issues; Dir (vacant).

Radio Mogadishu, Voice of the Masses of the Somali Republic: southern Mogadishu; f. 1993 by supporters of Gen. Aidid after the facilities of the fmr state-controlled radio station, Radio Mogadishu (of which Gen. Aidid's faction took control in 1991), were destroyed by UNOSOM; broadcasts in Somali, Amharic, Arabic, English and Swahili; Chair. Farah Hasan Ayoboqore.

Radio Mogadishu, Voice of Somali Pacification: Mogadishu; f. 1995 by supporters of Osman Hassan Ali 'Ato'; broadcasts in Somali, English and Arabic; Dir-Gen. Muhammad Diriyeh Ilmi.

Radio Mogadishu, Voice of the Somali Republic: northern Mogadishu; f. 1992 by supporters of Ali Mahdi Mohamed; Chair. Farah Hassan Ayoboqore.

Radio Somaliland: internet www.radiosomaliland.com.

Voice of Peace: POB 1631, Addis Ababa, Ethiopia; f. 1993; aims to promote peace and reconstruction in Somalia; receives support from UNICEF and the AU.

Some radio receivers are used for public address purposes in small towns and villages.

Note: In January 2007 the Transitional National Government was granted emergency powers to proscribe four media companies in an attempt to restore order in Mogadishu. HornAfrique Media and Shabelle Media were believed to have ceased operations although others condemned the ban and refused to close.

Television

A television service, financed by Kuwait and the United Arab Emirates, was inaugurated in 1983. Programmes in Somali and Arabic are broadcast for three hours daily, extended to four hours on Fridays and public holidays. Reception is limited to a 30-km radius of Mogadishu.

Somali Television Network (STN): Mogadishu; f. 1999; broadcasts 22 channels in Somali, English, French, Hindi, Gujarati, Bengali, Punjabi, Italian and Arabic; Man. Dir Aburahman Robley Ulayereh.

Television HornAfrique: Mogadishu; f. 1999; broadcasts 6 channels in Somali and Arabic; CEO Ali Iman Sharmarkeh.

Finance

(cap. = capital; res = reserves; m. = million; brs = branches; amounts in Somali shillings unless otherwise stated)

BANKING

Central Bank

Central Bank of Somalia (Bankiga Dhexe ee Soomaaliya): Corso Somalia 55, POB 11, Mogadishu; tel. (1) 657733; fax (1) 215026; f. 1960; bank of issue; cap. and res 132.5m. (Sept. 1985); Gov. Bashir Isse Ali; Gen. Man Mohamed Mohamed Nur.

A central bank (with 10 branches) is also in operation in Hargeysa (in the self-proclaimed 'Republic of Somaliland').

Commercial Banks

Commercial Bank of Somalia: Via Primo Luglio, POB 203, Mogadishu; tel. (1) 22861; f. 1990 to succeed the Commercial and Savings Bank of Somalia; state-owned; cap. 1,000m. (May 1990); 33 brs.

Universal Bank of Somalia: Mogadishu; f. 2002; cap. US $10m.; Gen. Man. Mahad Adan Barkhadle (acting).

Private Bank

Somali-Malaysian Commercial Bank: Mogadishu; f. 1997; cap. US $4m.

Development Bank

Somali Development Bank: Via Primo Luglio, POB 1079, Mogadishu; tel. (1) 21800; f. 1968; state-owned; cap. and res 2,612.7m. (Dec. 1988); Pres. Mohamed Mohamed Nur; 4 brs.

INSURANCE

Cassa per le Assicurazioni Sociali della Somalia: POB 123, Mogadishu; f. 1950; workers' compensation; Dir-Gen. Hassan Mohamed Jama; 9 brs.

State Insurance Co of Somalia: POB 992, Mogadishu; f. 1974; Gen. Man. Abdullahi Ga'al; brs throughout Somalia.

Trade and Industry

DEVELOPMENT ORGANIZATIONS

Agricultural Development Corpn: POB 930, Mogadishu; f. 1971 by merger of fmr agricultural and machinery agencies and grain marketing board; supplies farmers with equipment and materials and purchases growers' cereal and oil seed crops; Dir-Gen. Mohamed Farah Anshur.

Livestock Development Agency: POB 1759, Mogadishu; f. 1966; Dir-Gen. Hassan Weli Sheikh Hussen; brs throughout Somalia.

Somali Co-operative Movement: Mogadishu; Chair. Hassan Hawadle Madar.

Somali Oil Refinery: POB 1241, Mogadishu; Chair. Nur Ahmed Darawish.

Water Development Agency: POB 525, Mogadishu; Dir-Gen. Khalif Haji Farah.

CHAMBER OF COMMERCE

Chamber of Commerce and Industry: Somali Chamber Bldg, nr Banadir Hotel, Shibis District, Mogadishu; tel. (1) 643081; fax (1) 221560; e-mail info@somalicci.com; internet www.somalicci.com; f. 1970.

TRADE ASSOCIATION

National Agency of Foreign Trade: POB 602, Mogadishu; tel. (1) 120485; major foreign trade agency; state-owned; brs in Berbera and over 150 centres throughout Somalia; Dir-Gen. Jama aw Muse.

SOMALIA

UTILITIES

Water Development Agency: POB 525, Mogadishu; Dir-Gen. KHALIF HAJI FARAH.

TRADE UNIONS

National Union of Somali Journalists (NUSOJ): Tree Biano Bldg, Via al-Mukarah Km 4, Mogadishu; fax (1) 859944; e-mail nusoj@nusoj.org; internet www.nusoj.org; f. 2002 as Somali Journalists' Network (SOJON) ; name changed as above in 2005; Sec.-Gen. OMAR FARUK OSMAN; 6 brs across Somalia.

Transport

RAILWAYS

There are no railways in Somalia.

ROADS

In 2000 there were an estimated 22,100 km of roads, of which some 11.8% were paved.

SHIPPING

Merca, Berbera, Mogadishu and Kismayu are the chief ports. An EU-sponsored development project for the port of Berbera (in 'Somaliland') was announced in February 1996. It was reported that the port of Mogadishu, which had been largely closed since 1995, was reopened to commercial traffic in August 2006. There was a large increase in piracy off the coast of Somalia during 2008 (see Recent History).

Somali Ports Authority: POB 935, Mogadishu; tel. (1) 30081; Port Dir AHMED HAGI ALI ADANI.

Juba Enterprises Beder & Sons Ltd: POB 549, Mogadishu; privately owned.

National Shipping Line: POB 588, Mogadishu; tel. (1) 23021; state-owned; Gen. Man. Dr ABDULLAHI MOHAMED SALAD.

Puntland Shipping Service: Bossaso.

Shosman Commercial Co Ltd: North-Eastern Pasaso; privately owned.

Somali Shipping Corpn: POB 2775, Mogadishu; state-owned.

CIVIL AVIATION

Mogadishu has an international airport. There are airports at Hargeysa and Baidoa and six other airfields. It was reported that a daily service had been inaugurated in April 1994 between Hargeysa (in the self-declared 'Republic of Somaliland') and Nairobi, Kenya. Mogadishu international airport (closed since 1995) was officially reopened in mid-1998, but continuing civil unrest hampered services. In August 2006 the airport reopened to commercial flights.

Air Somalia: Mogadishu; f. 2001; operates internal passenger services and international services to destinations in Africa and the Middle East; Chair. ALI FARAH ABDULLEH.

Jubba Airways: POB 6200, 30th St, Mogadishu; tel. (1) 217000; fax (1) 227711; e-mail jubbaair@emirates.net.ae; internet www.jubba-airways.com; f. 1998; operates domestic flights and flights to destinations in Djibouti, Saudi Arabia, the United Arab Emirates and Yemen.

SOUTH AFRICA

Introductory Survey

Location, Climate, Language, Religion, Flag, Capital

The Republic of South Africa occupies the southern extremity of the African mainland. It is bordered by Namibia to the north-west, by Botswana and Zimbabwe to the north, by Mozambique to the north-east, and by Swaziland to the east. Lesotho is completely surrounded by South African territory. The climate is generally sub-tropical, but with considerable regional variations. Temperatures in Cape Town, on the south-west coast, vary from 7°C (45°F) to 26°C (79°F), with an annual average of about 17°C (63°F). Annual rainfall averages 510 mm (20 ins) at Cape Town, and 1,101 mm (43 ins) at Durban, on the east coast. The official languages are Sepedi, Sesotho, Setswana, siSwati, Tshivenda, Xitsonga, Afrikaans, English, isiNdebele, isiXhosa and isiZulu. About 79.0% of the population are black, 9.6% are white, 8.9% are Coloured (of mixed race), and 2.5% are Asian (mainly of Indian origin). Most of the inhabitants profess Christianity, although traditional African religions are still adhered to. There are also small minorities of Hindus (nearly all Asians) and Muslims (mainly Coloureds and Asians). The national flag (proportions 2 by 3) has a green 'Y' shape extending from the upper and lower hoist corners to the centre of the fly end, bordered in white on its outer edges, and in light orange on its inner edges near the hoist; the areas above and below the horizontal band of the 'Y' are red and blue respectively, with a black triangle at the hoist. The administrative capital is Pretoria, the legislative capital is Cape Town, and the judicial capital is Bloemfontein.

Recent History

On 31 May 1910 four British dependencies were merged to form the Union of South Africa, a dominion under the British Crown. In 1931 the British Parliament recognized the Union as an independent country within the Commonwealth. From the establishment of South Africa until 1984, national administration was the exclusive preserve of the white population.

The National Party (NP), which acceded to power in 1948, introduced the doctrine of apartheid (in theory the separate, but equal, development of all racial groups, in practice leading to white, particularly Afrikaner, supremacy). The principal opposition to government policy during the 1950s took the form of a campaign of civil disobedience, led by the multiracial African National Congress of South Africa (ANC). In 1959 some members of the ANC formed the exclusively black Pan-Africanist Congress (PAC). In 1960 the ANC and the PAC protested against the 'pass laws' (which required blacks to be in possession of special documentation in designated white urban areas); at one demonstration, in Sharpeville, 67 blacks were killed by security forces, prompting international outrage, and further demonstrations within South Africa, as a result of which the ANC and the PAC were declared illegal. Both movements subsequently formed military wings, based outside South Africa, to conduct campaigns of sabotage. An influential leader of the ANC, Nelson Mandela, was detained in 1962 and sentenced to life imprisonment on a charge of sabotage in 1964, but remained a focus for opposition to apartheid.

On 31 May 1961, following a referendum among white voters in October 1960, South Africa became a republic, and left the Commonwealth. Dr Hendrik Verwoerd was Prime Minister from 1958 until his assassination in September 1966. He was succeeded by the former Minister of Justice, Balthazar Johannes (B. J.) Vorster.

As an integral part of the policy of apartheid, the territorial segregation of African ethnic groups was enforced, on the grounds that the Native Reserves (comprising only 13% of national territory) constituted the historic 'homelands' (Bantustans) of different African nations. In 1963 Transkei was accorded 'self-governing' status, with an Executive Council, headed by a Chief Minister, to be elected by a Legislative Assembly. Bophuthatswana (June 1972), Ciskei (August 1972), Lebowa (October 1972), Gazankulu (February 1973), KwaZulu (April 1973), Qwaqwa (November 1974), KwaNdebele (October 1977), and KaNgwane (August 1984) were subsequently granted 'self-government'. Transkei was declared 'independent' in October 1976, Bophuthatswana in December 1977, Venda in September 1979 and Ciskei in December 1981. The population of the 'independent homelands' was not entitled to South African citizenship. The 'independent homelands' were not recognized by any government other than that of South Africa.

The numerous discriminatory laws regulating the lives of the country's black, 'Coloured' (a term used to denote people of mixed race) and 'Indian' (Asian) populations, combined with stringent security legislation, led to the detention without trial of many of the Government's opponents, the banning of black political organizations outside the 'homelands', and the forced removal of hundreds of thousands of blacks in accordance with the provisions of the Group Areas Act of 1966 (which imposed residential segregation of the races) and the 'homelands' policy. In June 1976 violent riots occurred in Soweto (South-Western Townships), near Johannesburg, and rapidly spread to other black urban areas. Vorster used the executive's virtually limitless powers, conferred by the newly adopted Internal Security Act, to suppress riots and strikes. Several hundred people died in confrontations with the security forces, and many more were detained without trial. Allegations of human rights violations by security forces culminated in international indignation at the death in detention of a black community leader, Steve Biko, in September 1977. In 1978 black, Coloured and Indian activists founded the Azanian People's Organization (AZAPO).

In September 1978 Vorster resigned as Prime Minister, and was succeeded by Pieter Willem (P. W.) Botha, hitherto the Minister of Defence. In February 1981 a new, 60-member advisory body, the President's Council, comprising representatives of the white, Coloured and Indian population, was formed to consider constitutional reform. Its recommendations to include Coloureds and Indians (but not blacks) in a three-chamber Parliament, with a multiracial government (led by an executive President), exacerbated inter-party differences: the 'verligte' (liberal) wing of the NP, led by Botha, advocated the establishment of a confederation of South Africa and the 'homelands', with separate citizenships but a common South African nationality, and was strongly opposed by the 'verkrampte' (uncompromising) wing of the party. In March 1982 16 extreme right-wing parliamentary deputies who had opposed the constitutional recommendations were expelled from the NP; they subsequently formed the Conservative Party of South Africa (CP), in conjunction with other right-wing elements.

Throughout 1983 and 1984 Botha pursued his policy of constitutional reform. The majority vote of the Coloured Labour Party (LP) in 1983 to participate in the reform programme caused divisions within the party. The constitutional body representing the Indian population, the South African Indian Council (SAIC), provisionally agreed to the proposals, subject to approval by an Indian community referendum. This decision was opposed by the Transvaal Anti-SAIC Committee, an organization that had been formed in 1981 in protest at participation in elections to the SAIC. In August 1983 the Committee established the United Democratic Front (UDF), to organize resistance on a national scale to Indian and Coloured participation in the constitutional reforms. The UDF rapidly became the principal legal opposition movement.

The constitutional reforms were approved by the House of Assembly in September 1983, and by about 66% of voters in an all-white referendum in November. In the same month the Progressive Federal Party (PFP) decided to take part in the reformed system. However, six 'homeland' leaders, including Chief Mangosuthu Gatsha Buthelezi, the Chief Minister of KwaZulu (who had consistently opposed the 'homelands' policy), rejected the constitutional reforms on the grounds that blacks remained excluded from participation in the central Government. Despite a previous pledge by the Prime Minister to assess Coloured and Indian opinion on the reforms, elections to the Coloured and Indian chambers of the new Parliament, known as the House of Representatives and the House of Delegates, respectively, took place in August 1984, without prior referendums. As a result, the boycott that had been organized by the

UDF was widely observed: about 18% of the eligible Coloured population voted in the elections to the House of Representatives, with the LP winning 76 of the 80 directly elected seats, while only 16.6% of eligible Indian voters participated in the elections to the House of Delegates, with the National People's Party (NPP) winning 18 and the Solidarity Party 17 of the 40 directly elected seats. (The House of Assembly, as elected in 1981, remained in office.)

The new Constitution came into effect in September 1984. Under the terms of the Constitution, legislative power was vested in the State President and the tricameral Parliament, comprising the 178-member House of Assembly (for the representation of whites), the 85-member House of Representatives (for Coloureds) and the 45-member House of Delegates (for Indians). The post of Prime Minister was abolished and Botha was unanimously elected to the new office of State President (which combined the powers of Head of State and Prime Minister) by an electoral college, comprising members of all three parliamentary chambers. A President's Council, a new Cabinet and three Ministers' Councils (one for each population group) were subsequently established. The Cabinet comprised only two non-white members, the Chairmen of the Indian and Coloured Ministers' Councils, neither of whom was given a portfolio.

During 1985–86 a number of the laws on which apartheid was based were modified or repealed, prompting strong right-wing opposition. The Immorality Act (1927) and the Prohibition of Mixed Marriages Act (1949), which banned sexual relations and marriage between members of different races, were repealed in April 1985, and in the following month it was announced that the Prohibition of Political Interference Act (1967), prohibiting members of different racial groups from belonging to the same political party, was to be abrogated. In April 1986 the Government promulgated legislation that provided for the removal of a number of restrictions on the movement, residence and employment of blacks in white urban areas. On 1 July the 'pass laws' were officially repealed, with the introduction of uniform identity documents for all South African citizens. On the same day reforms concerning the structure of local and provincial government were implemented, and legislation granting blacks limited rights to own property in black urban areas entered into force. In the same month it was announced that citizens of the four 'independent homelands' who were residing and working permanently in South Africa were to regain South African citizenship; in effect, however, only a small proportion of the population of the 'homelands' was eligible. Following discussions, initiated by Buthelezi in April 1986, regarding the establishment of a joint authority for his 'homeland', KwaZulu, and the province of Natal, the Government agreed to the formation of an administrative body, the Joint Executive Authority (which was installed in November 1987).

The introduction of the new Constitution in September 1984 prompted severe rioting in the black townships. Factional clashes within the black community also occurred, notably between supporters of the ANC and of the Inkatha Movement, a Zulu organization led by Buthelezi. In July 1985 the Government declared a state of emergency in 36 districts; by March 1986 it was estimated that 757 people had been killed, and almost 8,000 arrested. In June of that year Botha declared a nation-wide state of emergency, on the grounds that national security was endangered by subversive elements. Press censorship subsequently became progressively stricter, and the powers of the security forces were extended. Opposition to the Government emerged from the influential Congress of South African Trade Unions (COSATU).

At a general election to the House of Assembly in May 1987, the NP secured 123 of the 166 directly-elective seats. The CP increased its representation from 17 to 22 elective seats, thereby replacing the PFP as the official opposition. In June the Government renewed the state of emergency, and further stringent press restrictions were imposed.

In January 1989 Botha withdrew from his official duties, owing to ill health; in February he resigned as leader of the NP, and was succeeded by Frederik Willem (F. W.) de Klerk, hitherto Minister of National Education. Despite almost unanimous demands from the party that he should share power with de Klerk before retiring at the next general election, Botha refused to allow his power as State President to be eroded, and in March he resumed his official duties. In April the PFP, the Independent Party (which had been formed by one of a number of 'verligte' defectors from the NP in 1988) and the National Democratic Movement (established by dissident PFP members in late 1987) merged to form the Democratic Party (DP).

The state of emergency was extended for a further 12 months in June 1989. In August Botha claimed that members of his Cabinet had omitted to inform him of a prospective visit by de Klerk to Zambia to meet with President Kenneth Kaunda (which he opposed, owing to Kaunda's support for the ANC). Following a confrontation with the Cabinet, Botha resigned as State President. Shortly afterwards de Klerk was appointed acting President.

Elections to the three Houses of Parliament took place in September 1989. The NP won 93 of the 166 elective seats in the House of Assembly, while the CP secured 39 seats, and the DP 33 seats. Less than 12% of the Coloured electorate voted in the general election to the House of Representatives, at which the LP won 69 of the 80 directly-elective seats. Some 20% of the Indian electorate voted in the general election to the House of Delegates: the Solidarity Party secured 16 of the 40 directly-elective seats, while the NPP won nine. In mid-September, following his inauguration as State President, de Klerk stated that the implementation of constitutional reforms was his highest priority.

On 2 February 1990 de Klerk announced several radical reforms, including the legalization of the ANC, the PAC, the South African Communist Party (SACP), the UDF and more than 30 other banned political organizations. Nelson Mandela and a further 120 political prisoners were to be released unconditionally. In addition, most emergency regulations restricting the media were to be removed, as were repressive measures imposed on former political detainees; detention without trial was to be limited to a maximum of six months. De Klerk confirmed that the Government intended to initiate negotiations with the black opposition, with the aim of drafting a new democratic constitution. Leaders of the extreme right-wing parties reacted to de Klerk's reforms with threats of violence.

Mandela's release from prison, on 11 February 1990, received much international attention. In March he was elected Deputy President of the ANC. In spite of appeals by Mandela for reconciliation between rival factions within the black community, the continuing violence in Natal between supporters of the Inkatha Movement and mainly Xhosa-speaking supporters of the ANC intensified in March and April, and unrest erupted in several black townships. In mid-May legislation was introduced that granted temporary immunity from prosecution to political exiles who had committed crimes, including leaders of the ANC. In June de Klerk repealed the state of emergency in all provinces except Natal. In July Buthelezi reconstituted the Inkatha Movement as the Inkatha Freedom Party (IFP), in order to participate in future constitutional negotiations. The following month the ANC and the Government reached an agreement whereby, in preparation for constitutional negotiations, the ANC was to suspend its guerrilla activities, and the Government was to release more than 3,000 political prisoners and to facilitate the return to South Africa of an estimated 40,000 exiles. However, the ANC subsequently continued to train recruits for its military wing (known as Umkhonto we Sizwe—MK) and to stockpile ammunition, thereby contravening the terms of its cease-fire and causing the Government to delay the release of political prisoners and the repatriation of exiles.

During August 1990 factional fighting between supporters of the IFP and of the ANC escalated in the black townships surrounding Johannesburg; more than 500 people were reported to have been killed by the end of that month. Nevertheless, in October the state of emergency was revoked in Natal. Also that month the Separate Amenities Act of 1953 (which had imposed racial segregation with regard to public amenities) was repealed, prompting right-wing protests, particularly from the Afrikaanse Weerstandsbeweging (AWB), a paramilitary organization that had been formed in 1973 under the leadership of Eugene Terre'Blanche. During October the NP opened its membership to all races.

In February 1991 de Klerk announced that he was to introduce draft legislation to repeal the principal remaining apartheid laws: the Land Acts of 1913 and 1936 (which stipulated that the black population was entitled to own only 13.6% of the land), the Group Areas Act, the Black Communities Act of 1984 (which enforced the separate status of black townships) and the Population Registration Act of 1950 (which decreed that all South Africans should be registered at birth according to race) were subsequently abolished. In the same month the Government agreed to assume joint administrative powers in Ciskei, following increasing pressure within the 'independent homeland' for its reincorporation into South Africa and for the resignation of its military ruler. In mid-February the Government and the ANC reached agreement on the release of political prisoners, the return of exiles and the curtailment of activities by the MK. However, increasing township violence continued to impede constitutional negotiations.

In May 1991 Winnie Mandela, the wife of Nelson Mandela, was found guilty of assaulting and kidnapping a young ANC activist, Stompie Moeketsi Seipei, in 1988, and was sentenced to six years' imprisonment, causing considerable embarrassment for the ANC. (Winnie Mandela, who separated from Nelson Mandela in 1992, remained at liberty, pending an appeal against the verdict; in June 1993 the conviction for assault was overturned, and her sentence was commuted to a fine and a suspended term of imprisonment.) In July 1991, at a national congress of the ANC, Nelson Mandela was elected as its President and Cyril Ramaphosa, hitherto leader of the National Union of Mineworkers, was elected Secretary-General of the organization.

In August 1991 the Government declared an amnesty for all political exiles. During that month the UDF was dissolved. In September the Government, the ANC, the IFP and 23 other political organizations signed a national peace accord, in an attempt to end township violence; however, unrest continued to escalate. In October a judicial commission of inquiry was established to assess the causes of civil violence.

A multi-party conference on South Africa's future, known as the Convention for a Democratic South Africa (CODESA), was convened in December 1991. CODESA was attended by the Government and 18 political organizations, including the ANC, the NP, the DP, the LP, the NPP, New Solidarity (formerly the Solidarity Party) and representatives of the 'homelands' (including the IFP, which represented KwaZulu); the conference was boycotted by the PAC, AZAPO and the CP. The negotiating body's stated aim to create an undivided South Africa was rejected by the IFP, which favoured the concept of a South African federation of independent states, and by the Bophuthatswana administration, which demanded total independence from South Africa.

In March 1992 a referendum of the white population resulted in an overwhelming mandate for the continuation of the process of reform. In May, however, constitutional negotiations were suspended, owing to the Government's insistence on having a majority vote in CODESA. The ANC subsequently organized a campaign of mass protests. Following a visit to the township by de Klerk, 30 demonstrators were killed as the security forces suppressed an anti-Government protest. The ANC subsequently withdrew from all bilateral discussions with the Government, pending the latter's agreement to a number of demands, including the immediate release of all remaining political prisoners and effective action to curtail township violence. In August the ANC, SACP and COSATU intensified their campaign of anti-Government protests. In the same month several parliamentary deputies belonging to the CP defected to form a new extreme right-wing party, the Afrikaner Volksunie (AVU).

In mid-1992 the ANC announced that it was to organize a series of demonstrations in protest against 'homeland' leaders who wished their territories (Bophuthatswana, Ciskei, KwaZulu and Qwaqwa) to retain a strong measure of autonomy in the future South Africa. In September Ciskei security forces killed 28 ANC demonstrators, and injured about 200, prompting international outrage. The ANC accused the South African security forces (some of whose members had been seconded to Ciskei) of complicity in the incident. In mid-September de Klerk announced that measures to reduce the 'independence' of the 'homelands' would be implemented. In late 1992 the leaders of Bophuthatswana, Ciskei and KwaZulu, in conjunction with the IFP, the AVU and the CP, formed a pressure group (the Concerned South Africans Group—COSAG) to campaign for a maximum degree of regional autonomy.

In late September 1992 the Government accepted the ANC's preconditions for the resumption of constitutional negotiations. A 'record of understanding' was signed, which stated that the new Constitution would be drafted by an elected constitutional assembly and that there would be a non-racial elected interim government. In October the Constitution was amended to permit blacks to serve in the Cabinet. Later in that month legislation was approved that granted immunity from prosecution to perpetrators of politically motivated offences committed prior to 8 October 1990. In December Buthelezi published a draft constitution for a planned state comprising the KwaZulu 'homeland' and the province of Natal, which would retain a strong measure of autonomy within a future South African federation.

In February 1993 the ANC and the Government agreed to the immediate resumption of multi-party discussions. In March, at a meeting between the Government and 25 delegations from national political parties (including the formerly unco-operative PAC, IFP and CP) and the 'homeland' Governments, it was decided that CODESA was to be reconstituted, with the PAC, the IFP and the CP granted equal status with the other representatives. In May an informal alliance was established of 21 right-wing organizations (including the AVU, the CP and the AWB), known as the Afrikaner Volksfront (AVF), to co-ordinate opposition to the negotiating process.

In June 1993 legislation providing for the abolition of the President's Council was approved by Parliament. The IFP, CP and KwaZulu delegations subsequently withdrew from the negotiating forum, while the remaining representatives continued discussions on the precepts of a multiracial interim constitution. The interim Constitution, promulgated in July, entrenched equal rights for citizens regardless of race, and vested executive power in a President and a Cabinet, which was to comprise representatives of the political parties that held a stipulated number of seats in the legislature. Legislative authority was vested in a bicameral Parliament, comprising a 400-member National Assembly (to be elected by proportional representation) and a Senate (with 10 members elected by each regional legislature). The National Assembly and Senate formed the Constitutional Assembly, which was to draft a new constitution, with adherence to the principles stipulated by the negotiating forum. Although the interim Constitution included provisions for the establishment of regional legislatures, it was rejected by COSAG (while the IFP, KwaZulu and CP delegations continued to boycott negotiations).

In early September 1993 the negotiating forum approved legislation providing for the establishment of a multiracial Transitional Executive Council (TEC), which was to rule in conjunction with the existing Government pending the elections, thereby allowing blacks to participate in central government for the first time. The TEC was to comprise representatives of the groups involved in the negotiating process; however, the IFP, the CP, the governments of Bophuthatswana, Ciskei and KwaZulu, and the PAC refused to participate. Later in September Parliament adopted legislation providing for the installation of the TEC, and the establishment of an Independent Electoral Commission (IEC), and an independent media commission and broadcasting authority.

In October 1993 the constituent members of COSAG, together with the AVF, formed the Freedom Alliance (FA), with the stated objective of negotiating concessions regarding regional autonomy. The Bophuthatswana and Ciskei delegations subsequently withdrew from the negotiating forum. In November the negotiating forum repealed legislation providing for detention without trial. Later that month agreement was reached regarding the establishment of a new security force, which was to be under the control of both central and provincial government, and a reconstituted national defence force, which was to comprise members of the existing armed forces of South Africa and the 'independent homelands', and the military wings of political organizations.

On 18 November 1993, following intensive discussions, 19 of the 21 delegations remaining in the negotiating forum approved the interim Constitution, which incorporated several amendments to the draft promulgated in July. A number of significant compromises between the Government and the ANC had been achieved: the Government abandoned its demand that cabinet decisions require a two-thirds' majority (thereby accepting that power-sharing would not be constitutionally entrenched), while the ANC agreed to a fixed five-year period for transition to majority rule. The President was to be elected by the National Assembly, and was to exercise executive power in consultation with at least two Deputy Presidents, who were to be nominated by parties with a minimum of 80 seats in the National Assembly (equivalent to 20% of the national vote). A Constitutional Court was to be appointed by the President from a list of candidates nominated by an independent judicial commission. As a concession to the FA, the interim Constitution included a provision that entitled the legislatures of the nine redesignated provinces to draft their own constitutions, subject to the principles governing the national Constitution. Nevertheless, the FA, together with the PAC, rejected the interim Constitution.

In early December 1993 the negotiating forum reached agreement on the reincorporation of the four 'independent homelands' into South Africa on 27 April 1994, when the interim Constitution was to enter into force. On 1 January South African citizenship was to be restored to the population of the 'homelands', who would be entitled to vote in the elections. However, the governments of Bophuthatswana and Ciskei refused to recognize the decision. On 7 December 1993 the TEC commenced sessions, but was, as expected, boycotted by a number of delegations. In mid-December the IEC was established. On 22 December Parliament ratified the interim Constitution, thereby effecting its own dissolution as an organ of the apartheid regime.

In January 1994 the military wing of the PAC, the Azanian People's Liberation Army (APLA), was implicated in indiscriminate killings of civilians; the PAC, however, denied responsibility for the violence and announced that it had suspended the activities of the APLA. In January the Ciskei government decided to join the TEC and subsequently withdrew from the FA.

In February 1994, in accordance with a decision by the TEC, de Klerk announced that the elections, which were to be monitored by international observers, would take place between 26 and 28 April. The IFP confirmed that it intended to boycott the elections, after the Zulu tribal monarch, King Goodwill Zwelithini (who was Buthelezi's nephew), rejected the interim Constitution and declared sovereignty over the territory traditionally owned by the Zulus. In mid-February Nelson Mandela announced a number of proposed amendments to the interim Constitution. The FA, however, rejected the concessions, on the grounds that the powers of regional government remained inadequate, and refused to attend discussions on the proposed amendments, which were, nevertheless, adopted by the negotiating forum. In early March, after the ANC and IFP agreed to accept international mediation regarding the issue of regional autonomy, Buthelezi announced that he was to register the IFP provisionally to contest the elections. The leader of the AVU, Gen. (retd) Constand Viljoen (who had increasingly dissociated himself from extreme right-wing elements in the AVF) also provisionally registered a new party, the Freedom Front (FF). Despite the insistence of the AVF that its constituent groups were to boycott the elections, the FF subsequently submitted a list of candidates, which included several prominent members of the CP. The IFP failed to present a list of candidates by the stipulated date, while Zwelithini continued to urge his followers to boycott the elections.

In March 1994 the President of Bophuthatswana, Lucas Mangope (a member of the FA), announced that the population of the 'homeland' would not participate in the elections. Following widespread protests in Bophuthatswana, Mangope fled from the capital, Mmabatho, after disaffected members of the security forces demanded that he allow participation in the elections and refused to take action against the demonstrators. At the apparent instigation of the AVF, some 5,000 armed right-wing extremists, principally members of the AWB, entered Bophuthatswana and occupied Mmabatho, with the aim of reinstating Mangope. Shortly afterwards the Government dispatched some 2,000 members of the armed forces to Bophuthatswana, which, together with disaffected local troops, regained control of the 'homeland'. The Government and the TEC formally deposed Mangope, whose removal signified the effective dissolution of the FA. Later in March members of the armed forces were deployed in Ciskei to maintain civil order, following the resignation of the 'homeland's' military ruler in response to a strike by reformist members of the security forces. (The TEC and the Government assumed joint responsibility for administration in Bophuthatswana and Ciskei pending the elections.)

In April 1994 an agreement was reached whereby the IFP was to participate in the elections, in exchange for guarantees that the institutions of the Zulu monarch and kingdom were to be recognized in the interim Constitution. Under the terms of a proposed draft constitution for KwaZulu/Natal (as Natal had been redesignated in February), the Zulu monarch was to be granted additional territorial powers and sovereignty with regard to traditional law and custom. However, the AVF announced that it would continue to boycott the elections. In April Terre'Blanche threatened that a campaign of recent bomb attacks would continue unless the Government acceded to demands for Afrikaner self-determination. Under the terms of an accord between the Government, the ANC and the FF earlier in April, the level of support for the FF in the elections was to be used to determine whether a separate Afrikaner state might be established in any region with the approval of the majority of the resident population. Prior to the elections, the Government also reached an agreement with the PAC, which provided for the inclusion of members of the APLA in the new national defence force, in exchange for a guaranteed cessation of hostilities.

On 27 April 1994 the interim Constitution came into force, with voting commencing on the previous day, as scheduled. Although a number of reports of electoral malpractice emerged, the IEC declared that the elections had been free and fair. The promulgation of the official results was delayed, owing, in part, to disputed ballots in KwaZulu/Natal; following negotiations between the IFP and the ANC, it was agreed that the IFP would be allocated 50.3% of the vote in the province, thereby allowing it a majority of one seat in the regional legislature. On 2 May, after partial results indicated a substantial majority in favour of the ANC, de Klerk conceded defeat, prompting widespread jubilation. Shortly afterwards it was announced that the ANC had secured 62.7% of votes cast, while the NP had won 20.4%, the IFP 10.5% and the FF 2.2%. Consequently, the ANC narrowly failed to obtain a parliamentary majority of two-thirds, which, under the terms of the interim Constitution, would have allowed its members to draft and adopt the new constitution without consulting other parties. The NP, which secured a majority in the province of Northern Cape, received the stipulated percentage of the national vote entitling it to nominate a Deputy President. Mandela subsequently appointed a senior official of the ANC, Thabo Mbeki, as First Deputy President, while de Klerk was nominated as Second Deputy President.

Mandela was officially elected as President by the National Assembly on 9 May 1994, and was inaugurated on the following day at a ceremony that was attended by a large number of international heads of state. A Cabinet of National Unity, comprising 18 representatives of the ANC, six of the NP and three of the IFP, was subsequently formed, with Buthelezi allocated the portfolio of home affairs. The appointment of Winnie Mandela (now President of the ANC's Women's League) as a deputy minister was widely interpreted as an attempt to prevent her from criticizing the new administration. Later in May the provincial legislatures elected a 90-member Senate, comprising 60 representatives of the ANC, 17 of the NP, five of the IFP and FF, respectively, and three of the DP. The ANC consequently held a slightly higher majority in the Constitutional Assembly than in the National Assembly, but failed, nevertheless, to obtain a two-thirds' majority. The Secretary-General of the ANC, Cyril Ramaphosa, was subsequently elected Chairman of the Constitutional Assembly.

The new Government adopted a Reconstruction and Development Programme (RDP), which comprised extensive measures for social and economic development, including the reform of the education and health services. The Government also announced plans to establish a 'Truth and Reconciliation Commission' (TRC), composed of eminent citizens, which would investigate violations of human rights perpetrated under the apartheid regime; the TRC was to be empowered to grant indemnity to individuals who confessed to politically motivated crimes committed before 5 December 1993 (when the TEC was effectively installed). Although the FF had failed to obtain the level of support in the elections stipulated as a precondition to the consideration of its demands, the Government subsequently agreed to the establishment of a 'volkstaat council', in which Viljoen and other right-wing Afrikaners were to debate the issue of self-determination. Meanwhile, it was disclosed that de Klerk had authorized the transfer of state-owned land (comprising one-third of the territory of KwaZulu/Natal) to Zwelithini shortly before the elections. The ANC denied knowledge of the agreement.

In June 1994 it was announced that the new South African National Defence Force (SANDF) was to be constituted over a period of three years (to allow the integration of former members of the MK and APLA). In mid-June a cabinet committee decided that Zwelithini was to remain the statutory trustee of the territory in KwaZulu/Natal that had been transferred to his control prior to the elections. In September the Government officially ended the state of emergency in KwaZulu/Natal that had been imposed in March. In October the IFP majority in the provincial legislature of KwaZulu/Natal adopted legislation that provided for the establishment of an advisory council of Zulu chiefs, the House of Traditional Leaders, in which Zwelithini would be equal in status to other chiefs (including Buthelezi).

In November 1994 the Government adopted legislation that formally restored the rights of land ownership to members of the black population who had been dispossessed following the introduction of discriminatory legislation beginning in 1913; the

Restitution of Land Rights Act provided for the establishment of a special commission and court to investigate and arbitrate claims.

In January 1995 the National Intelligence Service (NIS) was replaced with two new bodies, incorporating elements of the ANC's security department and agencies of the former 'homelands': the South African Secret Service, under the command of the former head of the NIS, was to control international intelligence, while the National Intelligence Agency (NIA), headed by a former ANC security official, was to be responsible for internal intelligence. In the same month, amid reports of increasing political violence between ANC and IFP supporters in KwaZulu/Natal, Buthelezi was elected Chairman of the House of Traditional Leaders.

An 11-member Constitutional Court was installed in February 1995; the Court was to ensure that the executive, legislative and judicial organs of government adhered to the principles entrenched in the interim Constitution, and was to endorse a final constitutional text with respect to these principles. In the same month Mandela confirmed that he would not contest the elections in 1999. In late March Mandela finally removed Winnie Mandela from the Cabinet, after she publicly criticized government expenditure on the visit to South Africa of the British monarch.

At a party conference on constitutional policy in April 1995, the ANC rejected NP proposals that the principle of power-sharing be entrenched in the final constitution, thereby extending the tenure of the coalition Government. The conference also failed to accept IFP demands for international mediation on regional autonomy, and adopted constitutional proposals that provided for a Senate comprising members of provincial legislatures, which would be empowered to veto provincial legislation. Buthelezi subsequently suspended IFP participation in the Constitutional Assembly, and indicated that the IFP would not accept a constitution that had been drafted by the remaining parties in the Assembly. In late May Mandela consented to foreign mediation on constitutional discussions. In the same month the National Assembly approved draft legislation providing for the establishment of the TRC; only the FF deputies opposed the enactment of the legislation.

At the local elections, which took place in most parts of the country on 1 November 1995, the ANC secured 66.4% of the votes cast and the majority of the seats on the local councils, while the NP won 16.2% and the FF 4.0%. Elections in KwaZulu/Natal were postponed until March 1996, owing to continuing violence in the region. Voting took place in some parts of Western Cape, but not in the metropolitan area of Cape Town, nor in some rural areas of the province, as a result of delays in the demarcation of electoral boundaries. After further delays, the local elections in KwaZulu/Natal took place on 26 June, amid relative calm. The IFP won the largest share (44.5%) of the votes cast.

Meanwhile, in November 1995 Gen. Magnus Malan, the Minister of Defence in 1980–91, and a further 10 prominent officials in the former armed forces were arrested on charges relating to the killing of 13 people in KwaMakutha (south of Durban) in 1987; they were accused of involvement in the establishment in 1985 of a military camp in Namibia where IFP commandos were trained to perpetrate attacks on prominent ANC supporters. The arrest and subsequent indictment of Gen. Malan and the other former officers provoked great controversy; Mandela was accused by members of the NP and FF of political bias in his refusal to grant temporary indemnity to the accused until their cases could be heard by the TRC, which was to commence sessions in April 1996. (In late November 1995 Archbishop Desmond Tutu was appointed as Chairman of the Commission.) Buthelezi was cited in the indictment as having in 1985 requested the assistance of the security forces in creating paramilitary units to combat the ANC.

Renewed violence in KwaZulu/Natal in December 1995 culminated in an attack by some 600 IFP supporters against the village of Shobashobane, an ANC enclave in the south of the province, in which some 19 people were killed. In early February 1996 the NP Minister of Provincial Affairs and Constitutional Development, Roelf Meyer, announced that he was to resign from the Government and would assume the new post of Secretary-General of the NP. Later that month Abraham Williams, also of the NP, resigned from the post of Minister of Welfare and Population Development, following allegations that he had defrauded social security funds. In March Mandela was granted a divorce from Winnie Mandela (who subsequently became known as Winnie Madikizela-Mandela). Also that month, in a cabinet reorganization, Mandela appointed Trevor A. Manuel, hitherto the Minister of Trade and Industry, to the finance portfolio.

The trial of Gen. Malan and his 19 co-defendants began in Durban in early March 1996. (In May charges were abandoned against three of the former security force commanders, owing to insufficient evidence.) In mid-March the Government withdrew indemnity from prosecution that had been granted by de Klerk's Government to 73 ANC members, including Mbeki and Modise. In April the TRC, comprising Archbishop Tutu (who retired from the archbishopric in June) and 16 other members drawn from all racial groups and a variety of professions, commenced hearings, which were to continue for up to two years. The Commission was empowered to grant judicial amnesties to perpetrators of human rights violations committed during the apartheid era, if it was satisfied that a full disclosure had been made and that the crime in question had been politically motivated (depending on the gravity of the crime). The TRC was also to advise on appropriate reparations to the victims (or to their families) of crimes committed.

On 8 May 1996 Parliament approved the final version of the Constitution, with the NP voting in favour, in spite of its reservations over some provisions. The IFP maintained its boycott of the Constitutional Assembly, while the 10 FF deputies abstained; only the two deputies of the African Christian Democratic Party (ACDP) voted against the adoption of the Constitution. The new Constitution incorporated an extensive Bill of Rights, and provided for the establishment of a commission to guarantee the rights of the white minority. A National Council of Provinces was to replace the existing Senate, and was designed to increase the influence of the provinces on the policy of the central Government (although falling short of the provincial powers demanded by the IFP). De Klerk subsequently announced that the NP was to withdraw from the Government of National Unity, attributing the decision to the diminishing influence of his party on government policy, the refusal of the ANC to include power-sharing arrangements in the new Constitution, and the necessity, in the interests of democracy, for an effective opposition. The NP later withdrew from all the Provincial Governments except for that of Western Cape (where it was in the majority). Mandela appointed members of his own party to the ministerial portfolios vacated by NP members and abolished the position of Second Deputy President.

In late August 1996 Mbeki made a statement to the TRC regarding violations of human rights perpetrated during the apartheid era, including the execution of 34 people at the ANC's camps in Angola, asserting that these were justified in the context of the struggle against apartheid. De Klerk apologized before the TRC for the suffering that the apartheid policies of the NP had caused, but denied that any violations of human rights had been authorized during his time in government. Also in late August Eugene de Kock, a former commander of the notorious counter-insurgency 'hit squad', the Vlakplaas, was convicted of 89 charges relating to the activities of the unit, including six charges of murder. In September de Kock detailed to the Supreme Court his involvement in the apartheid regime's campaign against his opponents, claiming that de Klerk and Botha had both had full knowledge of these operations, which included assassinations.

In early September 1996 the Constitutional Court ruled that the new Constitution failed to adhere to the principles enshrined in the interim Constitution in a number of respects, notably with regard to the powers of the provinces, which the Court deemed insufficient. The Constitutional Assembly was to amend the document accordingly within a period of 90 days. The amended Constitution was approved by both chambers of Parliament on 11 October, with the ANC and the NP having negotiated a slight increase in the powers of the provinces. The new Constitution was returned to the Constitutional Court for final endorsement, and was promulgated by the President at a ceremony in Sharpeville on 10 December. The new Constitution entered into force on 4 February 1997. On 6 February the inaugural session of the new National Council of Provinces, which replaced the Senate as the second chamber of Parliament, was held.

Meanwhile, in October 1996 Gen. Malan and his co-defendants were acquitted of all charges in connection with the massacre in Kwa-Makutha. Although it was accepted that the killings had been committed by IFP supporters who had been trained by the former armed forces, the prosecution failed to prove that the attack had been authorized by military or political leaders. The judgment was regarded as a set-back for the TRC, with Gen.

Malan urging former members of the armed forces not to seek amnesties from the TRC, but to submit to trial in the courts if charged (thus discouraging potential confessions to the Commission). Later in October the TRC proposed that the final date for indemnity be extended from 6 December 1993 to 10 May 1994 (the date of Mandela's inauguration as President). Shortly afterwards a former police commissioner submitted evidence to the TRC implicating Botha in an attack against the headquarters of the South African Council of Churches in 1988. Botha declared that he would not submit evidence to the Commission and denied involvement in any crimes for which he needed to apply for amnesty. Following discussions with Tutu, however, he agreed to co-operate with the TRC by means of correspondence. In late October Tutu criticized the ANC for failing to submit amnesty applications from its members, and subsequently threatened to resign from the TRC if such applications were not made. The ANC responded by assuring the TRC that applications by its members would be made where necessary.

On 13 December 1996 (the eve of the deadline for applications for amnesty from the TRC) Mandela announced that the final date for the period in which crimes had been committed and the deadline for the receipt of amnesty applications were to be extended, to 10 May 1994 and 10 May 1997, respectively. The ANC confirmed that some 360 of its members, including three cabinet ministers, had applied for amnesty.

By the 10 May 1997 deadline nearly 8,000 amnesty applications had been received. In mid-May Meyer resigned from the NP and from the National Assembly, following opposition from within the NP to his proposal that the party be reconstituted in order to attract black support. Meyer, in alliance with Bantu Holomisa, the former ruler of Transkei (who, in 1996, had been dismissed from the Government and expelled from the ANC for indiscipline, in connection with allegations he had made at a hearing of the TRC), subsequently established a new political movement, the United Democratic Movement (UDM). Also in May 1997 de Klerk made a second appearance before the TRC; his continued insistence that he had been unaware of the violations of human rights perpetrated during the period of apartheid prompted an angry response from Tutu, who accused de Klerk of being responsible for abuses. The NP subsequently suspended co-operation with the TRC, and initiated legal action against the TRC on the grounds of political bias.

In June 1997 Terre'Blanche received a custodial term of six years for the attempted murder of a black employee, and a further one-year sentence for assault; he was released on bail pending an appeal against his conviction. In the same month Buthelezi invited the ANC to enter into negotiations with the aim of reaching an agreement to end political violence in KwaZulu/Natal. However, in July the killing of five ANC members, including two newly elected municipal councillors, in KwaZulu/Natal reflected the continuing political tensions in the province. In early August the IFP withdrew from the peace discussions, after it was alleged during hearings of the TRC that Buthelezi had been aware of political killings perpetrated by supporters of the IFP during apartheid. At the end of August de Klerk resigned from the leadership of the NP and retired from active politics; he was subsequently replaced by Marthinus van Schalkwyk.

In September 1997 five members of the former security forces appeared before the TRC to apply for amnesty for the killing of Biko in 1977 (see below); it was admitted during the hearing that some of the evidence presented at the inquest into Biko's death had been fabricated. In the same month the publication of a book, based on statements by a former bodyguard of Madikizela-Mandela, Katiza Cebekhulu, attracted considerable publicity; Cebekhulu alleged that Madikizela-Mandela had been actively involved in the killing of Seipei in 1988, and that she had subsequently ordered that a physician who had examined the victim prior to his death be killed. Nevertheless, Madikizela-Mandela continued to receive widespread public support, and was nominated for the post of Deputy President of the ANC by the party's Women's League prior to the ANC's December 1997 congress. Later in September Madikizela-Mandela appeared before the TRC, having been implicated by previous applicants for amnesty in 18 incidences of human rights violations, including eight killings. The TRC subsequently acceded to Madikizela-Mandela's request that hearings of her testimony be conducted in public. In November representatives of the business community applied for amnesty for their involvement with the apartheid system; however, Tutu criticized the failure of much of the private business sector, including three multinational petroleum companies, to participate in the TRC. During hearings of the TRC regarding the allegations against Madikizela-Mandela later that month, a number of witnesses testified that she had assaulted and killed several people. Cebekhulu appeared before the TRC to reiterate the claims that had been published in September 1997. Madikizela-Mandela subsequently denied involvement in any violations of human rights, and initiated legal action against Cebekhulu for libel.

At the ANC congress in December 1997 Mandela resigned from the presidency of the party, as anticipated, and was succeeded by Mbeki, who was elected unopposed. Jacob Zuma was elected Deputy President of the party. Madikizela-Mandela, who had refused her nomination to contest the post of Deputy President, was, however, elected to the NEC.

In August 1998, following considerable delays, Botha, who had failed to comply with three subpoenas ordering him to testify at the TRC regarding his enforcement of apartheid through emergency rule in the 1980s, was convicted of being in contempt of the TRC, receiving a fine of R 10,000 and a one-year suspended sentence (which could be brought into effect if he failed to comply with a further TRC subpoena). In September Parliament adopted legislation guaranteeing employment equity, whereby corporations were required to employ a certain proportion of blacks, women and disabled people.

In October 1998 the TRC commenced reparation payments to victims of human rights violations under the apartheid system and at the end of that month Tutu presented to Mandela the TRC's interim report detailing human rights violations committed in 1960–64, based on statements from some 21,000 victims of abuses and about 7,000 amnesty applicants. The report concluded that the apartheid system constituted a crime against humanity; it was alleged that, while the State was primarily accountable for violations of human rights, the ANC had also committed abuses in its legitimate struggle against apartheid (notably in the MK's torture and execution of suspected dissidents in detention camps outside South Africa). Botha, as President of the State Security Council in 1978–89, was considered to be responsible for an increase in killings of government opponents and to have ordered the bomb attacks by state agents in the 1980s. Buthelezi was deemed accountable for human rights violations perpetrated by the IFP (which was responsible for the highest proportion of killings in 1990–94). The report also cited Viljoen, Terre'Blanche, and Madikizela-Mandela as being responsible for serious violations of human rights. It was stated that the South African business community had benefited from the apartheid system, and the introduction of a 'wealth tax' to assist in social reconstruction was proposed. The prosecution of those responsible for human rights violations who had not applied for amnesty, or who had been denied amnesty, was recommended. Buthelezi and Viljoen dismissed the findings of the report as reflecting pro-ANC bias in the TRC, and Buthelezi subsequently threatened to prosecute the Commission, particularly with regard to the report's allegation that the IFP had colluded with the apartheid regime. In November 1998 one of the members of the security forces implicated in the 1977 killing of Biko was refused amnesty, on the grounds that the killing was not politically motivated. Amnesty applications of the remaining four members of the security forces involved in the incident were rejected in early 1999. In December 1998 Mandela confirmed that perpetrators of crimes committed under the apartheid regime would not be granted a general amnesty, which had been urged by the NP, IFP and some members of the ANC. Under TRC regulations, applicants would only be granted amnesty after submitting a full confession and evidence that the crime was politically motivated. However, in October 2003 the Ministry of Justice and Constitutional Development announced that none of the men implicated in the killing of Biko would be prosecuted, largely owing to insufficient evidence.

In January 1999 the Secretary-General of the UDM, Sifiso Nkabinde, was assassinated (apparently by ANC supporters) in KwaZulu/Natal. Some 11 ANC members were killed in a retaliatory attack by armed assailants. Further clashes between UDM and ANC supporters around Richmond were reported. Also in January a bomb attack at a Cape Town police station was widely attributed to an Islamist group, People Against Gangsterism and Drugs (PAGAD). Meanwhile, an increasing number of attacks against farmers by organized armed groups were reported. The South African Agricultural Union claimed that the attacks (in which more than 550 members of the farming community had been killed in 1994–98) were part of a campaign to force farmers to abandon their land. In May the ANC and IFP signed an agreement to end hostilities between their supporters in KwaZulu/Natal during the forthcoming electoral period.

More than 16m. voters participated in legislative elections, which took place peacefully, at national and provincial level, on 2 June 1999. The ANC secured 266 of the 400 seats in the National Assembly, with 66.4% of votes cast; the DP increased its representation in the Assembly from seven to 38 seats, while the IFP won 34, and the New National Party (NNP, as the NP had been reconstituted), which had lost much support to the DP, only 28 seats. The ANC subsequently formed a coalition with an Indian party, the Minority Front, thereby securing a two-thirds' majority in the National Assembly. The IFP reached a coalition agreement with the ANC in KwaZulu/Natal, where the IFP Premier retained his post. In Western Cape no party won a majority of seats in the provincial legislature, and, after intensive negotiations, the NPP and DP established a coalition Government to prevent the ANC, which had obtained the highest number of votes, from gaining power. On 16 June Mbeki was inaugurated as President, in a ceremony also marking the formal retirement of Mandela. The IFP joined the ANC in a further coalition Government, in which Buthelezi remained Minister of Home Affairs. Zuma became Deputy President.

In June 1999 Botha's appeal against his conviction was upheld, on the technical grounds that the TRC's subpoena was invalid since its mandate had temporarily expired. In July the TRC released a report containing evidence from former members of the security forces that implicated Botha in the killing of eight anti-apartheid activists in 1988. (Botha died in October 2006.) In August the TRC granted amnesty to Vlok, the former Commissioner of Police, Gen. Johan van der Merwe, de Kock, and a further 14 members of the former security forces, in respect of ordering the bombing of the offices of the South African Council of Churches in 1988. In September the Minister of Justice announced that further cases were to be submitted to judges specially nominated by Mbeki. In October the trial of Wouter Basson, the head of the apartheid regime's chemical and biological armaments programme in 1982–92, on 64 charges (including responsibility for the killing of 200 members of the South West Africa People's Organisation of Namibia—SWAPO), commenced at the High Court in Pretoria. He was acquitted of 15 charges in June 2001, and the remaining charges in April 2002. Later in October 1999 the TRC granted amnesty to nine former members of the security forces, including de Kock, who had provided evidence regarding the bombing of the ANC offices in London in 1982. In December 1999 10 members of the AWB were granted amnesty for the bombing campaign in 1994.

In January 2000 the National Assembly adopted extensive legislation prohibiting discrimination on any grounds and the use of racist terms in language. Meanwhile, the principal opposition parties (the DP, NNP, UDM and the FA) announced their intention to form an alliance prior to local government elections due in November; the DP also signed an electoral agreement with the smaller ACDP. In February, however, seven senior UDM officials left the party to join the ANC (increasing the total number of defections from the UDM since late 1999 to 34). In March, following the rejection of an appeal in October 1999, Terre'Blanche was ordered by the Pretoria High Court to surrender to the authorities to serve the one-year sentence he had received for assault, pending a further appeal against his six-year sentence. He was subsequently released on parole from the shorter sentence, but the longer sentence was confirmed on appeal in March 2001. (Terre'Blanche was released on parole in June 2004 after serving three years of the sentence. In November 2003 he was also convicted of involvement in terrorist activities prior to the 1994 elections and received a further, suspended, six-year sentence.) In June 2000 it was announced that the NNP and DP were to form a new coalition, known as the Democratic Alliance (DA), to contest the local government elections.

In September 2001 the South African Medical Research Council reported that HIV/AIDS was the largest single cause of death in South Africa, responsible for approximately 40% of adult deaths, and estimated that, without effective treatment, up to 7m. people could die from the disease by 2010. Mbeki had attracted criticism in August 2001 after urging the Minister of Health to reduce the budget for HIV/AIDS treatment, citing mortality figures from 1995 (when the disease accounted for only 2.2% of deaths). In December the Ministry of Health lost a case brought by the Treatment Action Campaign (TAC), a group of AIDS activists, when the High Court in Pretoria ordered it to provide antiretroviral drugs to all pregnant women infected with HIV to reduce the chance of transmission to their children; the Government had argued that the drugs were toxic and excessively expensive to administer. (The Government lost its appeal against the ruling in April 2002.) In February 2002 Buthelezi, as Minister of Home Affairs, ordered the distribution of antiretroviral drugs in Kwazulu/Natal, in contravention of official government policy, and in March the High Court upheld the ruling that ordered state provision of antiretroviral drugs. The Government sought leave to appeal the ruling, but it was overturned by the Constitutional Court in July; in October the Government announced that it would investigate means of providing antiretroviral drugs through the public health system. In November 2003 the Government also announced that it would spend R 12,100m. on combating HIV/AIDS over the next four years; R 1,900m. was to be allocated for the provision of antiretroviral drugs. At that time the Government committed to providing free antiretroviral treatment to some 53,000 people by March 2004; however, by November of that year the number of people receiving treatment was estimated at only 18,500. In September 2004 the National Assembly approved legislation to regulate the country's 200,000 practitioners of traditional medicine, thereby granting them formal recognition; some 70% of the population were believed to consult traditional healers.

Meanwhile, in July 2001 the PAC drew attention to what it considered the Government's inadequate housing and land redistribution policies, by seizing land belonging to farmers and the Provincial Government in east Johannesburg and inviting thousands of homeless people to settle there; many constructed shacks, believing that they were part of a resettlement scheme. Within two weeks the Government had removed the estimated 7,000 squatters from the land, using armed police-officers. COSATU and affiliated unions organized a two-day general strike in August in protest at the proposed privatization of public assets, which, it claimed, would result in large-scale redundancies. COSATU estimated that 4m. workers had participated in the strike, a figure that the Government described as exaggerated. In August Agri South Africa, an organization representing commercial farmers (mainly white) and 'emerging' black farmers, reported that there had been more than 6,000 attacks on South African farms since 1991, resulting in the deaths of more than 1,000 people; it was widely feared that the motivation for the attacks was land redistribution, as had been the case in Zimbabwe since the late 1990s. The South African Government declared land seizures illegal in August.

The leader of the NNP, van Schalkwyk, announced in October 2001 that the party was suspending its participation in the DA, following differences with the DP; the DP had dismissed the mayor of Cape Town, a prominent figure in the NNP, while the DP suspected the NNP of attempting to increase membership in an attempt to take overall control of the DA. Van Schalkwyk announced that the NNP would seek an accommodation with the ANC, as the IFP had done, retaining its independence, but holding positions in the Cabinet. In late November the ANC and NNP announced a power-sharing agreement in Western Cape (the only province not previously under ANC control), and the NNP also took seats in seven of the eight other Provincial Governments (all except Kwazulu/Natal, where the ANC had an agreement with the IFP). Discord within the NNP emerged when Gerald Morkel resigned as Premier of Western Cape in November, after publicly refusing to support closer co-operation with the ANC; he was replaced by Peter Marais. Meanwhile, in October COSATU accused the ANC of attempting to discredit it and suppress criticism of the Government, after a leaked report from the ANC national executive suggested that COSATU intended to establish a rival, extreme left-wing party. Marais resigned in May over allegations of sexual harassment and was replaced by van Schalkwyk.

A ruling by the Constitutional Court in late 2002, allowing national and provincial deputies to change parties without losing their seats, led to significant changes in the political landscape: in April 2003 the ANC secured a two-thirds' parliamentary majority when members of the UDM and the NNP defected to the ruling party, while the FA and the Afrikaner Eenheidsbeweging lost all their seats. At provincial level, members of the IFP defected to the ANC in KwaZulu/Natal and assumed further positions in the Cabinet, although the premiership of the province remained under IFP control. In April Madikizela-Mandela, who had been re-elected to the NEC of the ANC in December, was convicted of fraud and theft for obtaining bank loans using the fabricated names of employees of the ANC Women's League, and sentenced to five years' imprisonment.

The TRC's final report was presented to Mbeki in March 2003. The Commission had granted amnesty to 1,200 people, but had rejected more than 5,000 applications. Tutu recommended that some US $240m. ($12,000 each) be paid to the 20,000 people identified as victims of apartheid, and urged companies that had benefited through their involvement with the apartheid regime to contribute to the reparations process. Publication of the final report had been delayed by a legal challenge brought by the IFP, which was heavily implicated in the perpetration of human rights violations. In April, having rejected the suggestion that a special tax be imposed on companies that had gained from apartheid, Mbeki announced that those designated victims by the TRC would receive single payments of just over $3,800 each.

An empowerment charter for the financial sector, released in October 2003, envisaged that within four years 25% of all company executives would be non-white; and that 50% of goods bought by financial companies would be sourced from black-owned suppliers, rising to 70% by 2014. The mining sector had released a similar charter in March 2003: this pledged that 26% of mines would be black-owned within 10 years; the first conversions of mineral rights were expected by the end of 2004. In 1994 the Government had promised to transfer 30% of white-owned farms to non-whites over the next five years, but by 2004 only 2% had been transferred. In October of that year the Minister of Agriculture and Land Affairs, Angela Thoko Didiza, announced that some R 30,000m. would be required to settle outstanding land claims by the Government's 2005 deadline. In February 2007 the first order was given for the sale of a white-owned farm in the Northern Cape province.

Elections to the National Assembly and the provincial legislatures took place concurrently on 14 April 2004. The ANC won 279 of the National Assembly's 400 seats, with 69.7% of the valid votes cast. The DA took 50 seats, with 12.4% of votes cast, and the IFP 28, with 7.0%. The ANC secured overall control of seven of the nine provincial assemblies; although it failed to win outright majorities in Kwazulu/Natal and Western Cape, the ANC subsequently nominated premiers to head all nine provincial governments. The IEC declared the elections to have been free and fair. On 23 April members of the National Assembly voted unanimously to re-elect Mbeki to the presidency. President Mbeki announced the composition of a new Cabinet, which included most senior members of the previous administration: Zuma was reappointed Deputy President, while Mantombanza (Manto) Tshabalala-Msimang retained the health portfolio despite the slow progress regarding the provision of antiretroviral drugs to combat HIV/AIDS. Kader Asmal was replaced as Minister of Education by G. Naledi Pandor and Buthelezi who had held the post of Minister of Home Affairs since 1994, was dismissed. The two IFP representatives who had been allocated ministerial portfolios did not take up their posts when the new Government was sworn in on 29 April.

In August 2004 van Schalkwyk announced that the NNP was to merge with ANC and that the NNP would be disbanded in September 2005. The NNP leader also stated his intention to join the ANC and urged all NNP members to do the same. Former President de Klerk subsequently announced his resignation from the NNP in protest at the decision. (The NNP officially ceased to exist at the end of February 2006.)

Meanwhile, in August 2003, the National Director of Public Prosecutions, Bulelani Ngcuka, had announced that Deputy President Zuma would not be prosecuted for alleged corruption in connection with an arms-procurement deal, despite an apparent recommendation from investigators that he be charged. This prompted accusations of government interference in the legal process and opposition demands for Zuma's resignation. Zuma repeatedly rejected the allegations against him; however, in early June 2005 his financial adviser, Schabir Shaik, was found guilty of corruption and fraud and sentenced to fifteen years' imprisonment by the Durban High Court. The Court found evidence of a corrupt relationship between Shaik and Zuma, and that a series of payments made by Shaik on behalf of Zuma were intended to influence Zuma to benefit Shaik's business. Although Zuma did not give evidence, the trial revealed that Zuma had been party to a bid to solicit a bribe from a French defence company involved in the arms-procurement deal. Shaik launched an appeal against his conviction but this was rejected by the Supreme Court of Appeal in November 2006.

President Mbeki came under increasing pressure to dismiss Zuma and on 14 June 2005 he announced that the Deputy President would be 'released' from his duties. Zuma was replaced by Phumzile Mlambo-Ngcuka, hitherto the Minister of Energy and Mineral Affairs; Lindiwe Hendricks assumed Mlambo-Ngucka's vacated portfolio. In early August it was reported that the new Deputy President advocated the forced expropriation of white farms to accelerate the process of land distribution. At an education conference later that month Mlambo-Ngcuka was also reported to have called for South Africa to model its land redistribution programme on that of Zimbabwe. Zuma's trial commenced in the High Court in late July 2006. In mid-September the High Court judge dismissed the case, stating that Zuma had suffered social prejudice as a result of the publicity the case had received. The judge also cited failures of the State to hear legal challenges to raids carried out on the property of Zuma and his advisers, adding that further investigations into the case should have been conducted. Zuma's supporters believed that the result would increase the likelihood of him being elected to the presidency in 2009, and urged President Mbeki, who was constitutionally prohibited from serving a third term, to reinstate him as Deputy President. Nevertheless, tensions remained between Mbeki and Zuma and differences continued to divide the ANC.

In November 2005 it was also reported that Zuma was under investigation for the alleged rape of a female family friend; he was charged with the offence in early December but strenuously denied the allegation and was acquitted in early May 2006. In a separate investigation into missing funds 16 current and former ministers were found guilty of theft and fraud in October 2006. As much as R 17m. had been stolen and parliamentary travel privileges had been abused. Earlier that year an investigation was launched in Germany into allegedly corrupt arms-procurement deals in South Africa.

In May 2007 Helen Zille, the Mayor of Cape Town, was elected leader of the DA, replacing Tony Leon who had led the party since its formation in 2000. In June 2007 the ANC held a national policy conference following which it was announced that both Mbeki and Zuma could contest the leadership of the party at its national conference in December. Internal tensions had continued to divide the ruling tripartite coalition, although Mbeki warned in June that he would not be dictated to regarding government policies by the SACP. Zuma had secured the support of senior members of the SACP, which was considering contesting the 2009 general election independently from the ANC if Mbeki retained the leadership of that party. In September 2007 Zuma received the endorsement of COSATU for his leadership campaign, although a number of leading South African business executives expressed concern that if Zuma were elected to the national presidency, he would reverse Mbeki's economic policies.

As the leadership contest gained momentum senior members of the ANC exerted pressure on both Mbeki and Zuma to withdraw their candidatures, claiming that their rivalry was causing a major rift within the party. Neither candidate was prepared to concede and in December 2007 ANC members elected Zuma to the party presidency after he secured 2,329 votes to Mbeki's 1,505; Kgalema Motlanthe was appointed ANC Deputy President. However, later that month the National Prosecuting Authority (NPA) indicted Zuma on charges of corruption and fraud. The Supreme Court of Appeal had ruled in November that Zuma could again be tried in connection with the arms-procurement deal. Zuma once more denied the allegations; however, the trial was scheduled to commence in August 2008, thus endangering his potential accession to the national presidency. In early 2008 differences between Mbeki and Zuma continued, deepening divides within both the ANC and the Government. In February the DA and the Independent Democrats announced their intention to seek a vote of no confidence in Mbeki and force an early general election. Zuma's impending trial threatened to damage his chances of success in the election and the ANC demanded that Motlanthe, considered a potential alternative candidate, be given a cabinet post. Reflecting the declining influence of Mbeki's power, in April he agreed to include Motlanthe in the National Assembly.

Public frustration escalated in May 2008 amid worsening economic conditions; rising food and fuel prices placed greater strain on resources and in mid-May clashes broke out in several townships between local residents and foreigners. It was in these areas that Mbeki was perceived to be failing in his responsibilities as President, and dissatisfaction with Mbeki's Government continued to increase. Some 20 people were killed in the fighting and several hundred more were injured, while aid workers in the area reported that as many as 30,000 people had been displaced by the violence. Mbeki received further criticism later that month from the DA which claimed that the country now lacked strong leadership, evidenced by Mbeki's delayed decision to deploy the armed forces to suppress the recent fighting and his continued stance of 'quiet diplomacy' in relation to the volatile situation in Zimbabwe (see below). Meanwhile, it was announced that Zuma's corruption trial would be delayed until early 2009. Zuma attended a court hearing in August to appeal to have the charges against him dropped and, with further appeals possible, it was becoming less likely that the trial would take place before the April election, improving Zuma's chances of succeeding Mbeki as President.

Mbeki's power continued to decline and in July 2008 the ANC National Executive Committee (NEC) appointed Motlanthe to the newly created post of Minister in the Presidency, responsible for Government Business. As such, Motlanthe assumed de facto control over the Government. At the same time the NEC dismissed three of Mbeki's allies, including Nosimo Balindlela, Premier of Eastern Cape, and Ebrahim Rasool, Premier of Western Cape, highlighting divisions within the ANC.

In September 2008 the High Court dismissed the charges brought against Zuma, and ruled that there was evidence of political interference from high-ranking officials in the investigation. This caused the rift within the ANC to widen and it was subsequently announced that Mbeki had relinquished the presidency at the party's request, effective from 25 September. His resignation was followed by that of 11 cabinet ministers, including Mlambo-Ngcuka and Manuel. A parliamentary vote elected Motlanthe as the new President with a clear majority and he was to remain in the post until the legislative elections in April 2009. It was rumoured that Zuma had not been elected for fear that it would appear he had assumed the role clandestinely. Widely thought to be the leading candidate for the presidency, the ANC preferred to have Zuma's legitimacy confirmed with a democratic election. Baleka Mbete, hitherto the Speaker of the National Assembly, was subsequently named Deputy President and Charles Nqakula was appointed Minister of Defence, while Manuel was reappointed Minister of Finance; Gwen Mahlangu-Nkabinde replaced Mbete as Speaker.

Divisions within the ANC deepened and in November 2008 a group of former ANC members and allies of Mbeki, led by Mosiuoa Lekota, formed a new political party, the Congress of the People (COPE). The ANC launched a formal complaint against the name of the new party, claiming that the ANC was regularly referred to in political spheres by the same name. Nevertheless, COPE was officially launched in December with members claiming that the party would provide a serious challenge to the ANC; COPE members won 12 seats in local by-elections that month.

As preparations for the general election began in early 2009, Zuma faced a further reverse when an appeal court overturned the earlier ruling that dismissed the corruption charges brought against him. Mbeki supported the decision, claiming that it had been inappropriate of the High Court judge to imply that a political rival had influenced the case against Zuma. However, the following month the trial date was postponed until August. It was later suggested that, should the ANC secure a large enough majority at the elections to enable it to amend the Constitution, legislation could be introduced to prevent the prosecution of the incumbent President. In March Zuma approached the prosecutor's office with a deal offering to refrain from appointing only close ANC allies to high-profile positions, should he be elected in April, in return for all charges against him being dismissed. Meanwhile, Mlambo-Ngcuka announced that she had left the ANC to join COPE.

On 22 April 2009 elections duly took place to the National Assembly and to South Africa's nine provincial legislatures. Final results, announced by the IEC on 25 April, confirmed the overwhelming victory of the ANC, which, with 65.9% of total votes cast, won 264 of the National Assembly's 400 seats. The DA took 67 seats, with 16.7% of votes cast, and COPE secured 30 seats with 7.4%. The ANC also secured overall control of eight provincial assemblies. More than 77% of the registered electorate participated. As expected, Zuma was elected President by the National Assembly with 277 votes and was inaugurated on 9 May. The following day Zuma announced his new Government and the reorganization of a number of ministries: a National Planning Commission and a performance monitoring and evaluation competency were created within the presidency, to be led by Manuel and Collins Chabane, respectively; the Ministry of Minerals and Energy was divided into two separate ministries; and the Ministry for Education was separated into the Ministry of Basic Education and the Ministry of Higher Education. Appointments made to the enlarged administration included Motlanthe as Deputy President, Pravin Gordhan (the Commissioner of the South African Revenue Service) as Minister of Finance and Jeff Radebe as Minister of Justice and Constitutional Development; the hitherto Minister of Foreign Affairs, Nkosazana Dlamini-Zuma was moved to the Ministry of Home Affairs. Also of note was the appointment of the leader of the Afrikaner nationalist Vryheidsfront Plus party, Dr Pieter Mulder, as Deputy Minister of Agriculture, Forestry and Fisheries.

South Africa became increasingly isolated politically in southern Africa after Zimbabwe (formerly Rhodesia) underwent the transition to independence in April 1980. During the 1980s South Africa's continued occupation of Namibia resulted in frequent clashes between SWAPO guerrillas and South African troops (see the chapter on Namibia). In 1971 the International Court of Justice had declared South Africa's presence in Namibia to be illegal and the UN had, in 1973, recognized SWAPO as the 'authentic representative of the Namibian people'. Following the collapse of the semi-autonomous internal administration, South Africa resumed direct rule of Namibia in January 1983. In February 1984 South Africa and Angola agreed on a cease-fire along the Angola–Namibia border, and established a joint commission to monitor the withdrawal of South African troops from Angola. On 22 December 1988 Angola, Cuba and South Africa signed a formal treaty designating 1 April 1989 as the commencement date for the process leading to Namibian independence, as well as a treaty requiring all 50,000 Cuban troops to be withdrawn from Angola by July 1991. Elections were held in Namibia in November 1989, and independence for the former South African territory was achieved on 21 March 1990, under a SWAPO-controlled Government. The strategic port of Walvis Bay and 12 offshore islands, to which Namibia laid claim, remained under South African jurisdiction until September 1991, when the two countries agreed to administer the disputed territories jointly. In August 1993 South Africa relinquished sovereignty over Walvis Bay and the 12 islands, which were officially transferred to Namibia in March 1994. In August 2001 the South African and Namibian foreign ministers met to discuss the issue of their joint border on the Orange river; Namibia claimed the border extended to the middle of the river, while South Africa claimed it lay on the northern bank, provoking differences over mineral and fishing rights.

In 1984 South Africa signed a mutual non-aggression pact with Mozambique (the Nkomati accord), which implied that South Africa would withdraw its covert support for the Resistência Nacional Moçambicana (Renamo), while Mozambique would prevent the ANC from using its territory as a base for attacks on South Africa. In September 1985 the South African Government conceded that there had been 'technical' violations of the accord. In May 1988 Mozambican and South African officials agreed to reactivate the Nkomati accord, and in September President Botha visited President Joaquim Chissano of Mozambique, his first state visit to a black African nation. Following his election as President, Mandela made an official visit to Mozambique in July 1994. In August of that year South Africa, Mozambique and Swaziland signed a security co-operation accord, in an effort to combat the continuing illicit transport of armaments. In February 1997 South Africa appealed to the Government of Swaziland to release Swazi trade union leaders from detention. The Swazi Government protested at action mounted by COSATU in support of its Swazi counterparts, stating that it represented interference in the internal affairs of Swaziland. In April 2006 protests were staged by COSATU, the SACP and its Youth League, and the Swaziland Solidarity Network in support of Swaziland's campaign for democracy and human rights. Demonstrators attempted to blockade several crossing points on the Swaziland border and more than 20 people were arrested.

In 1979 the Southern African Development Co-ordination Conference (SADCC) was established by southern African countries, to work towards a reduction of their economic dependence on South Africa. SADCC reformed in August 1992 as the Southern African Development Community (SADC, see p. 400), which aimed to achieve closer economic integration between its member states. South Africa was admitted to SADC in August 1994. In April 1997 members of the South African armed forces participated in military training exercises in Zimbabwe, as part of a nascent SADC regional peace-keeping force. In September 1998 about 600 South African and 200 Botswanan troops were dispatched to restore order in the Lesotho capital, Maseru, under the aegis of SADC, following a coup attempt by junior military officers. About 750 South African troops, together with some 350 Botswanan troops, remained in Lesotho to maintain civil order, before their withdrawal in May 2000.

In April 2000 Mbeki, together with the Presidents of Namibia and Mozambique, visited Zimbabwe to increase pressure on President Robert Mugabe to prevent the illegal occupation of white-owned farmland (see the chapter on Zimbabwe). Despite international condemnation of Mugabe and requests by a number of countries, most notably the United Kingdom, for more unequivocal criticism of President Mugabe's actions from South Africa, President Mbeki attempted to maintain 'constructive engagement' towards Zimbabwe. Following Mugabe's re-election as President in March 2002, the ANC issued a statement endorsing the ballot, despite allegations that Mugabe's party, the Zimbabwe African National Union—Patriotic Front, had intimidated voters and engaged in electoral fraud. The South African Government's position strained relations with the United Kingdom and the USA, and the latter threatened to withdraw support for the New Partnership for Africa's Development (NEPAD, see below) if the Government did not condemn Mugabe. However, later in March Mbeki was part of a Commonwealth troika (also comprising the President of Nigeria and the Prime Minister of Australia) that decided to suspend Zimbabwe from meetings of that organization for a period of one year. Mbeki had previously ignored pleas from Morgan Tsvangirai, the leader of the main opposition party in Zimbabwe, the Movement for Democratic Change, to impose sanctions on Zimbabwe prior to the election. In March 2003 Donald (Don) McKinnon, the Secretary-General of the Commonwealth, stated that the troika had concluded that Zimbabwe's suspension from the organization's meetings should remain in force for a further nine months. However, South Africa subsequently denied that it had agreed to the extension of the suspension. Zimbabwe withdrew from the Commonwealth in December 2003, shortly before the conclusion of the organization's Heads of Government meeting, at which the country's suspension had been extended indefinitely. Mbeki had criticized the decision to maintain the suspension, claiming that some Commonwealth members had failed to understand the question of land ownership in Zimbabwe. The Commonwealth appointed South Africa to a six-member advisory panel charged with monitoring the situation in Zimbabwe. Mbeki met separately with Mugabe and Tsvangirai in that month in an unsuccessful attempt to persuade them to form a coalition government. Mbeki continued to mediate between Mugabe and Tsvangirai prior to the Zimbabwean presidential and legislative elections held in March 2008, and brokered the introduction of new election legislation requiring electoral officials to post the number of votes cast at individual polling stations. However, following the decision of the Zimbabwe Electoral Commission not to release the results of the presidential election, in April Mugabe boycotted an emergency SADC summit in Zambia called to discuss the situation in Zimbabwe. Mbeki travelled to Harare for talks with Mugabe, but the former's policy of 'quiet diplomacy' attracted criticism from a number of international observers, while Tsvangirai appealed for Mbeki to relinquish his role as mediator to Zambian President Levy Mwanawasa. Despite his resignation from the South African presidency, Mbeki continued to chair negotiations between Tsvangirai and Mugabe and in September the two sides concluded the Interparty Political Agreement (see chapter on Zimbabwe), which provided for a power-sharing arrangement. Further discussions, again with mediation by Mbeki, resulted in the installation of a new Council of Ministers in February 2009 and the appointment of Tsvangirai to the Zimbabwean premiership.

In November 1996 South Africa was criticized for its approval of a substantial sale of weapons to Rwanda, which was believed to be providing military support to rebels in eastern Zaire who were engaged in conflict with the Zairean army. In response to international pressure, the South African Government subsequently decided to suspend the sale of armaments to Rwanda. During 1996 South Africa supported efforts to achieve reconciliation in Angola and in early 1997 was involved in intensive diplomatic activity, along with other African countries, with the aim of negotiating an end to the civil war in Zaire. Following the assumption of power by Alliance des forces démocratiques pour la libération du Congo-Zaïre, led by Laurent-Désiré Kabila, in May, South Africa became the first foreign government to recognize the new regime and pledged to assist in reconstruction efforts and in the holding of elections in the renamed Democratic Republic of the Congo (DRC). In October 2001 South African soldiers were dispatched to Burundi (q.v.) as part of a proposed 700-member peace-keeping mission, in an effort to enforce national security and to support the formation of a multi-ethnic transitional government. Mandela had been instrumental in negotiating a peace accord (signed in August 2000), whereby the Hutu and Tutsi ethnic groups, which had been engaged in civil conflict since 1993, were each to hold the presidency for 18 months during a three-year transitional period. In May 2003 1,400 South African troops were deployed in the DRC as part of a UN peace-keeping mission, rising to 1,750 at January 2004. In November 2004 President Mbeki was mandated by the African Union (AU, see p. 172) to lead peace negotiations in Côte d'Ivoire (q.v), following the breakdown of a cease-fire between the Government of that country and rebels. In March 2005 South Africa dispatched some 300 troops to Darfur, Sudan (q.v.), as part of an AU mission to investigate and monitor events in the region.

Following the implementation of political reforms in South Africa from February 1990, international sanctions imposed during the 1980s were reviewed. During 1991 South Africa was readmitted to international sporting competition, after many years of exclusion. In July the USA officially withdrew economic sanctions (which were, however, retained by a number of US states and cities). In October Commonwealth Heads of Government endorsed the withdrawal of cultural sanctions against South Africa; however, sanctions on finance, arms and trade and investment remained. Japan ended all its sanctions during that month. In 1992 the European Community (EC, now the European Union—EU) withdrew a number of sanctions against South Africa. In September 1993, following the adoption of legislation providing for the installation of a multiracial transitional administration (see above), the international community ended the remaining economic sanctions against South Africa. The UN Security Council ended its mandatory embargo on armaments, following the establishment of an interim Government of National Unity in May 1994; South Africa subsequently established diplomatic relations with more than 165 countries. South Africa became a member of the Commonwealth on 1 June, and joined the Organization of African Unity (OAU—now the AU) later that month. The People's Republic of China refused to establish formal diplomatic links while South Africa maintained relations with Taiwan. In November 1996 President Mandela announced that South Africa's diplomatic relations with Taiwan were to be severed in favour of the People's Republic of China, with effect from the end of 1997. In response, Taiwan withdrew its ambassador indefinitely and announced that the majority of its aid projects in South Africa would be suspended.

In December 1995 a joint US-South African commission was established, chaired by Mbeki and the US Vice-President, Al Gore. In February 1998 it was announced that South Africa and the USA were to normalize their defence trade agreement, thereby allowing South African armaments companies to trade with their US counterparts for the first time. In August 1998 two people were killed, and about 27 injured, in a bomb attack on a US restaurant in Cape Town. A supporter of an organization styled Muslims Against Global Oppression (MAGO) claimed to have perpetrated the bombing, apparently in retaliation for US air attacks on Sudan and Afghanistan (although MAGO officially denied responsibility for the incident). Several members of PAGAD were subsequently arrested in connection with the bombing. A series of further bombings in the Cape Town area, and the killing of a local magistrate in July 2000, were also attributed by the authorities to PAGAD.

In March 1998, following four years of negotiations, the EU approved the terms for a comprehensive free-trade agreement with South Africa. The agreement provisionally came into force on 1 January 2000; a continuing dispute with the Governments of Italy, Spain, Portugal and Greece, which had refused to sign the accord on wines and spirits, was resolved after South Africa agreed to discontinue the use of traditional European names for alcoholic drinks within five years. In December 2000 a framework agreement was reached on a free-trade accord with the Southern Common Market (known as Mercosur—Mercado Común del Sur, comprising Argentina, Brazil, Paraguay and Uruguay); trade negotiations were ongoing in early 2004.

In October 2001 the New Partnership for Africa's Development (NEPAD) was launched, as part of a long-term strategy for socio-economic recovery in Africa, in accordance with a decision taken at the OAU summit held in Lusaka, Zambia, in July. Mbeki formulated NEPAD's founding documents, in conjunction with the heads of state of Algeria, Egypt, Nigeria and Senegal, and South Africa was to host the Secretariat. In mid-2004 the AU agreed that the Pan-African Parliament (PAP) would be based in South Africa; the Government then announced that the PAP would be housed in Midrand (between Johannesburg and Pretoria). The second session of the PAP—its first in South Africa—took place at temporary headquarters in Midrand in mid-September that year.

In February 2007 South Africa signed a defence agreement with the Central African Republic committing to the provision of military training and the donation of surplus military supplies. The accord indicated that South Africa was becoming more lenient in its attitude towards involvement with countries threatened by regional conflict. In April 2008 South Africa signed a memorandum of understanding with the Republic of the Congo to develop co-operation between the two countries' military services, indicating that South Africa may be preparing to work more closely with other central African countries within the framework of the military organization established under the Communauté économique des états de l'Afrique centrale (see p. 425).

Government

Under the terms of the Constitution, which was adopted on 8 May 1996 and entered into force on 4 February 1997, legislative power is vested in a bicameral Parliament, comprising a National Assembly and a National Council of Provinces (formerly the Senate). The National Assembly is elected by universal adult suffrage under a system of proportional representation and has between 350 and 400 members. The 90-member National Council of Provinces comprises six permanent delegates and four special delegates from each of the provincial legislatures (see below). The President, who is elected by the National Assembly from among its members, exercises executive power in consultation with the other members of the Cabinet. Any party that holds a minimum of 80 seats in the National Assembly (equivalent to 20% of the national vote) is entitled to nominate an Executive Deputy President. A Constitutional Court ensures that the executive, legislative and judicial organs of government adhere to the provisions of the Constitution.

Each of the nine provinces has a legislature, which is elected under a system of proportional representation. Each legislature is entitled to draft a constitution for the province, subject to the principles governing the national Constitution, and to elect a Premier, who heads an Executive Council. Parties that hold a minimum of 10% of seats in the provincial legislature are entitled to a proportional number of portfolios in the Executive Council.

Defence

As assessed at November 2008, the South African National Defence Force (SANDF) totalled about 62,082: army 37,141, navy 6,244, air force 10,653 and a medical corps numbering 8,044. The SANDF comprised members of the former South African armed forces, together with personnel from the former military wings of the ANC and the Pan-Africanist Congress, and the former 'homelands'. In 2009 the military was undergoing a process of reform. Budgetary expenditure on defence was estimated at R 27,899m. in 2008/09.

Economic Affairs

In 2007, according to estimates by the World Bank, South Africa's gross national income (GNI), measured at average 2005–07 prices, was US $274,009m., equivalent to $5,760 per head (or $9,560 per head on an international purchasing-power parity basis). During 2000–07, it was estimated, the population increased at an average annual rate of 1.1%, while gross domestic product (GDP) per head, in real terms, increased by 3.0%. Overall GDP increased, in real terms, at an average annual rate of 4.3% in 2001–08, according to figures from the South African Reserve Bank; growth was 3.1% in 2008.

Agriculture (including forestry and fishing) contributed 3.3% of GDP in 2008. Some 8.8% of the employed labour force were engaged in the sector at September 2007. Maize (also the principal subsistence crop), fruit and sugar are exported, and livestock-rearing is also important; wool is another significant export. The GDP of the agricultural sector declined by an average of 0.4% per year in 2000–07, according to the World Bank. Agricultural GDP decreased by 13.1% in 2006, but increased by 4.8% in 2007.

Industry (including mining, manufacturing, construction and power) contributed 33.7% of GDP in 2008, and engaged 26.0% of the employed labour force at September 2007. Industrial GDP increased at an average annual rate of 3.4% in 2000–07, according to the World Bank. Industrial GDP increased by 4.8% in 2007.

Mining contributed 9.5% of GDP in 2008, and engaged 3.4% of the employed labour force at September 2007. South Africa was the world's second largest producer of gold in 2007, with the major mineral export accounting for about 10.9% of total world production. China overtook South Africa as the world's leading producer of gold in 2007. Coal, platinum, iron ore, diamonds, chromium, manganese, vanadium, vermiculite, antimony, limestone, asbestos, fluorspar, uranium, copper, lead and zinc are also important mineral exports. There are reserves of petroleum, natural gas, sillimanite, titanium and zirconium. The GDP of the mining sector increased by an average of 0.2% per year in 2001–08, according to figures from the South African Reserve Bank. However, mining GDP contracted by an estimated 6.5% in 2008.

Manufacturing contributed 18.8% of GDP in 2008, and engaged 13.6% of the employed labour force at September 2007. The GDP of the manufacturing sector increased at an average annual rate of 3.4% in 2000–07, according to the World Bank. Manufacturing GDP increased by 4.8% in 2007.

Energy is derived principally from coal-based electricity (94.1% in 2005); this is supplemented by nuclear power and by hydroelectric power (4.6% and 0.9%, respectively). The construction of a plant to convert natural gas into liquid fuel was completed in 1992. Exploitation of petroleum reserves in oilfields located 140 km south-west of the Southern Cape commenced in 1997. In 2001 substantial reserves of natural gas were discovered off the Western Cape. Imports of mineral fuels and lubricants comprised 18.6% of the value of total imports in 2007.

The services sector contributed 63.0% of GDP in 2008, and engaged 65.2% of the employed labour force at September 2007. The real GDP of the services sector increased by an average of 4.8% per year in 2000–07, according to the World Bank. Services GDP increased by 4.8% in 2007.

In 2007 South Africa recorded a visible trade deficit of US $5,741m., while there was a deficit of $20,780m. on the current account of the balance of payments. In 2007 the principal source of imports for South Africa was Germany (an estimated 11.7%); other major suppliers of imports were the People's Republic of China, the USA and Japan. The principal market for exports in that year was the USA (11.8%); other important purchasers were the United Kingdom, Japan, Germany the United Kingdom and China. The principal exports in 2007 were basic manufactures (particularly platinum, iron and steel and diamonds), road vehicles, mineral fuels, chemical products and food and live animals. The principal imports were road vehicles, mineral fuels (particularly petroleum) and chemical products.

In the financial year 2008/09 South Africa's estimated budget deficit was R 22,783.1m. At the end of 2006 South Africa's total foreign debt was US $35,549m., of which $13,940m. was long-term public debt. The cost of debt-servicing in that year was equivalent to 6.7% of the value of exports of goods and services. The annual rate of inflation averaged 5.3% in 2000–07; consumer prices increased by 7.1% in 2007. According to ILO, 23.0% of the labour force were unemployed at September 2007.

South Africa is a member of SACU (with Botswana, Lesotho, Namibia and Swaziland), of the Southern African Development Community (SADC, see p. 400) and of the African Development Bank (see p. 170). The Secretariat of the New Partnership for Africa's Development (see p. 178) is located in South Africa.

Following the removal of economic sanctions (imposed by the international community in protest at apartheid) in late 1993, and democratic elections in April 1994, foreign governments pledged considerable financial assistance to South Africa, and by 1999 financial market conditions had improved considerably, resulting in lower inflation, increased real GDP and greater investor confidence. Economic progress continued in the 2000s: real GDP growth of 5.4% and 5.1% were recorded in 2006 and 2007, respectively; public debt fell from 35.4% of GDP in 2003 to an estimated 29.9% in 2008; and business and consumer confidence grew. However, many problems remained, including the high level of unemployment (which stood at 21.9% in 2008), the uneven distribution of income (poverty was still widespread among vast sections of the population), and the devastating social and economic impact of the HIV/AIDS epidemic. Several initiatives aimed at reducing social disparities had been introduced, such as the Broad-Based Black Empowerment Act (instituted in 2004) to redistribute the nation's wealth among the black population, while the Government pledged that 26% of businesses would be led by blacks by 2014. The land reform initiative also aimed to transfer 30% of commercial agricultural land to previously disadvantaged groups by that date. Considerable resources were allocated to infrastructure projects, social expenditure and job creation, while the staging of the association football World Cup (to be held in mid-2010) was expected to boost employment opportunities and stimulate economic activity. However, the country was not immune to the effects of the global economic slowdown, with resultant GDP growth of only 3.1% in 2008, and a contraction of 1.6% forecast for 2009. Exports were adversely affected by falling commodity prices and weak demand, while there was reduced private sector investment and access to credit. Some 74,000 people became unemployed in the last quarter of 2008, with the number expected to rise in 2009. In response, the Government pledged to maintain planned expenditure, notably in infrastructure projects and social provision, in the hope of generating employment, reducing crime and fostering business confidence. It was anticipated that the current account deficit, which had risen to 8% of GDP in 2008, would decline to 5.3% in 2009, with inflation also falling, from some 12% at the end of 2008 to 6% in 2009.

Education

School attendance is compulsory for children of all population groups between the ages of seven and 16 years. From 1991 state schools were permitted to admit pupils of all races, and in 1995 the right to free state education for all was introduced. According to UNESCO estimates, in 2003/04 enrolment at primary schools included 88.3% of pupils in the relevant age-group (males 88.4%; females 88.2%), while in 1999/2000 secondary enrolment included 62.3% of pupils in the relevant age-group (males 58.9%; females 65.7%). During the 1980s universities, which were formerly racially segregated, began to admit students of all races. In 2006 there were 11 universities, five universities of technology, and six comprehensive institutions. Budget estimates for 2008/09 indicated the allocation of R 19,749.4m. (3.1% of total expenditure) to education.

Public Holidays

2009: 1 January (New Year's Day), 21 March (Human Rights Day), 10 April (Good Friday), 13 April (Family Day), 27 April (Freedom Day), 1 May (Workers' Day), 16 June (Youth Day), 9 August (National Women's Day), 24 September (Heritage Day), 16 December (Day of Reconciliation), 25 December (Christmas Day), 26 December (Day of Goodwill).

2010: 1 January (New Year's Day), 21 March (Human Rights Day), 2 April (Good Friday), 5 April (Family Day), 27 April (Freedom Day), 1 May (Workers' Day), 16 June (Youth Day), 9 August (National Women's Day), 24 September (Heritage Day), 16 December (Day of Reconciliation), 25 December (Christmas Day), 26 December (Day of Goodwill).

Weights and Measures

The metric system is in use.

Statistical Survey

Source (unless otherwise indicated): Statistics South Africa, Private Bag X44, Pretoria 0001; tel. (12) 3108911; fax (12) 3108500; e-mail info@statssa.pwv.gov.za; internet www.statssa.gov.za.

Area and Population

AREA, POPULATION AND DENSITY*

Area (sq km)	1,219,090†
Population (census results)	
9 October 1996	40,583,573
9 October 2001	
Males	21,434,033
Females	23,385,737
Total	44,819,770
Population (official estimates at mid-year)	
2006	47,391,029
2007	47,850,064
2008	48,687,300
Density (per sq km) at mid-2008	39.9

* Excluding data for Walvis Bay (area 1,124 sq km or 434 sq miles, population 22,999 in 1991), sovereignty over which was transferred from South Africa to Namibia on 1 March 1994.
† 470,693 sq miles.

ETHNIC GROUPS
(at census of October 2001)*

	Number	% of total
Africans (Blacks)	35,416,164	79.02
Europeans (Whites)	4,293,638	9.58
Coloureds	3,994,507	8.91
Asians	1,115,461	2.49
Total	**44,819,770**	**100.00**

* Figures exclude the effect of additional deaths caused by HIV/AIDS.

PROVINCES
(official estimates at mid-2008)

	Area (sq km)	Population	Density (per sq km)	Capital
Eastern Cape	169,580	6,579,300	38.8	Bisho
Free State*	129,480	2,877,700	22.2	Bloemfontein
Gauteng†	17,010	10,447,100	614.2	Johannesburg
KwaZulu/Natal	92,100	10,105,500	109.7	Pietermaritzburg
Limpopo‡	123,910	5,274,800	42.6	Pietersburg
Mpumalanga§	79,490	3,590,000	45.2	Nelspruit
Northern Cape	361,830	1,125,900	3.1	Kimberley
North-West	116,320	3,425,000	29.4	Mmabatho
Western Cape	129,370	5,262,000	40.7	Cape Town
Total	**1,219,090**	**48,687,300**	**39.9**	

* Formerly the Orange Free State.
† Formerly Pretoria-Witwatersrand-Vereeniging.
‡ Known as Northern Province (formerly Northern Transvaal) until February 2002.
§ Formerly Eastern Transvaal.

Note: Figures for population are rounded estimates based on the cohort-component compilation method.

SOUTH AFRICA

PRINCIPAL TOWNS
(metropolitan areas, population at 2001 census)

Johannesburg	3,225,812	Springs	80,776
Durban	3,090,122	Vanderbijlpark	80,201
Cape Town*	2,893,247	Vereeniging	73,288
Pretoria*	1,985,983	Uitenhage	71,668
Port Elizabeth	1,005,779	Rustenburg	67,201
Soweto	858,649	Kimberley	62,526
Tembisa	348,687	Brakpan	62,115
Pietermaritzburg	223,518	Witbank	61,092
Botshabelo	175,820	Somerset West	60,609
Mdantsane	175,783	Klerksdorp	59,511
Boksburg	158,650	Midrand	44,566
East London	135,560	Newcastle	44,119
Bloemfontein*	111,698	Welkom	34,158
Benoni	94,341	Potchefstroom	26,725
Alberton	89,394	Carletonville	18,362
Krugersdorp	86,618	Westonaria	8,440

* Pretoria is the administrative capital, Cape Town the legislative capital and Bloemfontein the judicial capital.

Mid-2007 ('000, incl. suburbs, UN estimates): Johannesburg 3,435; Cape Town 3,215; East Rand (Ekurhuleni) 2,986; Durban 2,729; Pretoria 1,338; Vereeniging 1,074; Port Elizabeth 1,021 (Source: UN, *World Urbanization Prospects: The 2007 Revision*).

BIRTHS AND DEATHS
(annual averages, UN estimates)

	1990–95	1995–2000	2000–05
Birth rate (per 1,000)	27.5	25.2	24.2
Death rate (per 1,000)	8.4	9.9	13.4

Source: UN, *World Population Prospects: The 2008 Revision*.

Registered live births ('000): 1,380 in 2005; 1,346 in 2006; 1,200 in 2007.

Registered deaths: 572,620 in 2004; 593,337 in 2005; 607,184 in 2006.

Registered marriages: 180,657 in 2005; 184,860 in 2006; 183,030 in 2007.

Life expectancy (years at birth, UN estimates): 51.3 (males 50.0; females 52.6) in 2006 (Source: WHO, *World Health Statistics*).

IMMIGRATION AND EMIGRATION

	2001	2002	2003
Immigrants:			
Africa	1,419	2,472	4,961
Europe	1,714	1,847	2,567
Asia	1,289	1,738	2,328
Americas	213	244	354
Oceania	51	65	99
Total (incl. others and unspecified)	4,832	6,545	10,578
Emigrants:			
Africa	1,584	1,461	2,611
Europe	5,316	4,637	6,827
Asia	226	218	445
Americas	1,713	1,473	2,090
Oceania	2,912	2,523	3,248
Total (incl. others and unspecified)	12,260	10,890	16,165

Immigrants (2004): Africa 5,235; Europe 2,638; Asia 2,225; Americas 343; Oceania 2,638; Total (incl. others) 10,714.

ECONOMICALLY ACTIVE POPULATION
('000 persons aged 15 to 65 years)

	2005	2006	2007
Agriculture, hunting, forestry and fishing	925	1,088	1,164
Mining and quarrying	411	398	455
Manufacturing	1,706	1,737	1,799
Electricity, gas and water	100	119	116
Construction	935	1,024	1,066
Trade, restaurants and hotels	3,024	3,055	2,952
Transport, storage and communications	616	611	596
Financing, insurance, real estate and business services	1,296	1,309	1,340
Community, social and personal services	2,192	2,319	2,452
Private households	1,067	1,108	1,244
Not classifiable by economic activity	29	33	51
Total employed	12,301	12,800	13,234
Unemployed	4,487	4,391	3,945
Total labour force*	16,788	17,191	17,179

* Figures have been assessed independently, so that totals are not always the sum of the component parts.

2006 ('000): Total labour force 17,191 (males 9,287, females 7,904).

Health and Welfare

KEY INDICATORS

Total fertility rate (children per woman, 2006)	2.7
Under-5 mortality rate (per 1,000 live births, 2006)	69
HIV/AIDS (% of persons aged 15–49, 2007)	18.1
Physicians (per 1,000 head, 2004)	0.8
Health expenditure (2006): US $ per head (PPP)	869
Health expenditure (2006): % of GDP	8.6
Health expenditure (2006): public (% of total)	41.9
Access to water (% of persons, 2006)	93
Access to sanitation (% of persons, 2006)	59
Human Development Index (2006): ranking	125
Human Development Index (2006): value	0.670

For sources and definitions, see explanatory note on p. vi.

Agriculture

PRINCIPAL CROPS
('000 metric tons)

	2005	2006	2007
Wheat	1,905.0	2,105.0	1,756.9
Barley	225.0	236.0	199.9
Maize	11,716	6,935	7,339
Oats	34.0	43.5	45.0*
Sorghum	260.0	96.0	166.0*
Potatoes	1,767.7	1,862.9	1,900.0*
Sweet potatoes	54.3	47.0	47.0*
Sugar cane	21,265.0	20,275.4	20,500.0*
Beans, dry	69.8	67.3	68.0*
Soybeans	272.5	424.0	430.0*
Groundnuts, with shell	64.0	74.0	75.0*
Sunflower seed	620.0	520.0	300.0†
Seed cotton	54.1	39.2	40.0*
Cabbages and other brassicas	155.3	141.5	145.0*
Tomatoes	462.2	441.8	445.0*
Pumpkins, squash and gourds	253.9	78.3	95.0*
Onions, dry	387.3	403.2	400.0*
Carrots and turnips	127.1	127.5	130.0*
Maize, green*	320	310	310*
Watermelons	74.8	65.3	65.0*
Bananas	351.6	343.7	345.0*
Oranges	1,246.5	1,334.4	1,400.0*
Tangerines, mandarins, clementines and satsumas	137.1	133.0	135.0*
Lemons and limes	184.3	217.0	220.0*
Grapefruit and pomelos	363.0	415.2	430.0*

SOUTH AFRICA

—continued

	2005	2006	2007
Apples	680.4	639.8	650.0*
Pears	312.8	316.1	325.0*
Apricots	43.7	83.6	85.0*
Peaches and nectarines	172.6	167.0	180.0*
Plums and sloes	53.6	39.0	38.0*
Grapes	1,682.8	1,550.4	1,600.0*
Mangoes, mangosteens and guavas	108.6	95.3	97.0*
Avocados	105.9	61.4	65.0*
Pineapples	180.6	166.3	166.0*
Tobacco, unmanufactured	20.0	17.5	20.0*

* FAO estimate(s).
† Unofficial figure.

Aggregate production ('000 metric tons, may include official, semi-official or estimated data): Total cereals 14,176 in 2005, 9,454 in 2006, 9,547 in 2007; Total roots and tubers 1,822 in 2005, 1,910 in 2006, 1,947 in 2007; Total vegetables (incl. melons) 2,243 in 2005, 2,006 in 2006, 2,033 in 2007; Total fruits (excl. melons) 5,714 in 2005, 5,590 in 2006, 5,765 in 2007.

Source: FAO.

LIVESTOCK
('000 head, year ending September)

	2005	2006	2007*
Cattle	13,790	13,532	13,500
Pigs	1,656	1,623	1,650
Sheep	25,334	24,983	25,000
Goats	6,356	6,400	6,400
Horses*	270	270	270
Asses*	150	n.a.	n.a.
Chickens	121,000	125,840	126,000
Ducks*	360	360	365
Geese and guinea fowls*	130	130	130
Turkeys*	500	500	500

* FAO estimates.
Source: FAO.

LIVESTOCK PRODUCTS
('000 metric tons)

	2005	2006	2007*
Cattle meat	705	804	805
Sheep meat	115	117	118
Goat meat*	36.5	36.2	36.5
Pig meat	147	151	150
Chicken meat	949	971	975
Cows' milk	2,871	2,971	3,000
Hen eggs	366	384	385
Wool, greasy*	45.0	45.0	45.0

* FAO estimates.
Source: FAO.

Forestry
(including Namibia)

ROUNDWOOD REMOVALS
('000 cubic metres, excl. bark, FAO estimates)

	2004	2005	2006
Sawlogs, veneer logs and logs for sleepers	5,237.1	2,282.8	2,131.1
Pulpwood	14,833.3	14,833.3	14,833.3
Other industrial wood	1,260.9	1,098.3	1,098.3
Fuel wood	12,000.0	12,000.0	12,000.0
Total	33,331.3	30,214.4	30,062.7

2007: Production assumed to be unchanged from 2006 (FAO estimates).
Source: FAO.

SAWNWOOD PRODUCTION
('000 cubic metres, incl. railway sleepers)

	2004	2005	2006
Coniferous (softwood)	2,689.0	2,014.7	2,011.3
Broadleaved (hardwood)	134.8	201.8	79.8
Total	2,823.8	2,216.5	2,091.1

2007: Production assumed to be unchanged from 2006 (FAO estimates).
Source: FAO.

Fishing
('000 metric tons, live weight)

	2004	2005	2006
Capture*	888.1	817.2	617.4
Cape hakes (Stokvisse)	153.3	144.0	132.1
Southern African pilchard	373.8	246.8	217.3
Whitehead's round herring	47.2	28.9	42.7
Southern African anchovy	190.1	282.7	134.4
Cape horse mackerel	34.1	35.1	27.0
Aquaculture	3.2	3.1	3.4*
Total catch*†	891.2	820.3	620.7

* FAO estimate(s).
† Excluding aquatic plants ('000 metric tons, FAO): 25.6 in 2004; 9.6 in 2005; 9.6 in 2006.

Note: Figures exclude aquatic animals, recorded by number rather than weight. The number of Nile crocodiles captured was: 35,760 in 2004; 25,526 in 2005; 37,868 in 2006. The number of toothed whales caught was 77 in 2004; 77 in 2005; 0 in 2006.

Source: FAO.

Mining
('000 metric tons, unless otherwise indicated)

	2004	2005	2006*
Hard coal	242,747	244,940	244,782
Crude petroleum ('000 barrels)	6,769	7,277	4,441
Natural gas	1,916	2,060	1,795
Iron ore†	24,800	24,900	26,000
Copper ore (metric tons)†	102,574	96,600	100,000‡
Nickel ore (metric tons)†	39,851	42,392	41,599
Lead concentrates (metric tons)†	37,485	42,159	48,273
Zinc ore (metric tons)†	32,001	32,112	34,444
Manganese ore and concentrates (metallurgical and chemical)§	4,282	4,611	5,213
Chromium ore§	7,677	7,494	7,418
Vanadium ore (metric tons)†	23,302	22,604	23,780
Zirconium concentrates (metric tons)‡	368,000	376,000	398,000
Antimony concentrates (metric tons)†	4,967	5,979	6,000‡
Cobalt ore (metric tons)‡†	460	400	400
Silver (kg)	71,600	87,874	86,951
Uranium oxide (metric tons)	887	795	639
Gold (kg)	337,223	294,671	272,128
Platinum-group metals (kg)	276,401	302,981	307,528
Kaolin	81.9	59.4	51.6
Magnesite—crude	65.9	54.8	55.0‡
Phosphate rock§	2,735	2,577	2,629
Fluorspar	265.0	266.0	270.0
Salt	332.7	399.1	464.9
Diamonds ('000 carats)	14,295	15,776	15,153
Gypsum—crude	524.0	547.6	554.0
Mica (metric tons)	285	924	828
Talc (metric tons)	8,141	8,469	10,966
Pyrophyllite (metric tons)	28,987	60,267	74,886

* Preliminary figures.
† Figures refer to metal content of ores and concentrates.
‡ Estimate.
§ Gross weight.

Source: US Geological Survey.

SOUTH AFRICA

Industry

SELECTED PRODUCTS
('000 metric tons, unless otherwise indicated)

	2002	2003	2004
Wheat flour*	1,898	1,943	2,016
Sugar—refined	1,141	1,653	n.a.
Footwear ('000 pairs)	19,699	17,317	n.a.
Chemical wood pulp	2,648	2,667	n.a.
Newsprint	338	336	336
Rubber tyres ('000)	12,038	12,804	n.a.
Motor spirit (petrol)	8,085	8,360	8,343
Kerosene	636	620	633
Jet fuel	1,637	1,874	1,778
Distillate fuel oils	7,383	7,593	7,141
Lubricating oils	412	446	376
Petroleum bitumen—asphalt	278	408	412
Cement (sales)†	9,624	10,163	13,784
Pig-iron†	5,823	6,234	6,011
Crude steel†	9,100	9,481	9,500
Refined copper—unwrought†	101.0	111.0	91.5
Colour television receivers ('000)	271	359	n.a.
Passenger motor cars—assembled ('000)	300	306	n.a.
Lorries—assembled ('000)	129	125	n.a.
Electric energy (million kWh)	217,712	234,229	244,607

* Twelve months ending September.
† Source: US Geological Survey.

2005 ('000 metric tons, data from US Geological Survey): Cement sales 13,000 (estimate); Pig-iron 6,130; Crude steel 9,493; Refined copper—unwrought 99,388.

2006 ('000 metric tons, data from US Geological Survey): Cement sales 13,000 (estimate); Pig-iron 6,160; Crude steel 9,721; Refined copper—unwrought 104.1.

Source: mostly UN, *Industrial Commodity Statistics Yearbook*.

Finance

CURRENCY AND EXCHANGE RATES

Monetary Units
100 cents = 1 rand (R).

Sterling, Dollar and Euro Equivalents (31 December 2008)
£1 sterling = 13.56 rand;
US $1 = 9.31 rand;
€1 = 12.95 rand;
100 rand = £7.37 = $10.75 = €7.72.

Average Exchange Rate (rand per US $)
2006   6.7716
2007   7.0454
2008   8.2612

BUDGET
(million rand, year ending 31 March)

Revenue	2006/07	2007/08	2008/09*
Tax revenue (gross)	495,515.1	572,814.6	627,692.8
Taxes on incomes and profits	279,990.5	332,058.3	383,635.0
Individuals	140,578.3	168,774.4	199,000.0
Companies (including secondary tax)	134,290.0	160,705.2	182,000.0
Retirement funds	3,190.5	285.4	230.0
Other	1,931.7	2,293.3	2,405.0
Taxes on payroll and workforce	5,597.4	6,330.9	7,255.6
Taxes on property	10,332.3	11,883.9	9,710.0
Domestic taxes on goods and services	174,637.9	194,690.3	202,064.0
Value-added tax	134,462.6	150,442.8	154,919.0
Excise duties	17,652.1	19,699.1	21,790.0

Revenue—continued	2006/07	2007/08	2008/09*
Levies on fuel	21,844.6	23,740.5	24,480.0
Air departure tax	484.8	540.6	580.0
Other	193.7	181.1	225.0
Stamp duties and fees	615.7	569.7	618.0
State Miscellaneous Revenue	339.2	612.0	630.0
Taxes on international trade and transactions	24,002.2	27,081.9	24,410.2
Departmental revenue	10,880.5	11,671.7	12,351.6
Sub-total	506,395.6	584,486.3	640,044.4
Less SACU payments†	25,194.9	24,712.6	28,920.6
Total	481,200.7	559,773.8	611,123.8

Expenditure	2006/07‡	2007/08	2008/09*
Central government administration	9,508.8	11,813.7	15,913.9
The Presidency	236.3	264.2	311.7
Parliament	755.1	835.7	913.8
Foreign affairs	2,944.7	4,069.7	5,569.8
Home affairs	2,546.9	3,241.7	4,816.6
Public works	3,025.8	3,402.3	4,302.0
Financial and administrative services	18,144.5	21,013.7	33,826.8
Government communication and information system	293.1	380.9	439.8
National treasury	16,171.0	18,966.2	31,424.2
Public services and administration	429.4	370.4	420.2
Public service commission	96.1	108.1	113.7
SA management development institute	58.3	131.1	105.5
Statistics South Africa	1,096.6	1,057.0	1,323.4
Social services	90,933.8	104,777.9	120,972.3
Arts and culture	1,329.9	1,585.8	2,160.3
Education	14,249.8	16,241.3	19,749.4
Health	11,338.0	12,762.7	15,851.2
Labour	1,453.5	1,948.6	1,747.6
Social development	61,676.1	67,191.4	76,554.2
Sport and Recreation South Africa	886.5	5,048.0	4,909.7
Justice and protection services	71,660.5	80,143.3	90,344.2
Correctional services	9,251.2	11,122.4	12,338.8
Defence	23,817.6	25,180.1	27,899.0
Independent complaints directorate	65.3	80.9	98.5
Justice and constitutional development	6,005.2	7,373.8	8,515.5
Safety and security	32,521.2	36,386.1	41,492.3
Economic services and infrastructure	70,346.8	90,233.4	109,136.4
Agriculture	2,224.0	3,328.4	2,937.7
Communications	1,319.6	1,911.8	2,331.5
Environmental affairs and tourism	2,059.7	2,788.8	3,206.6
Housing	7,166.0	8,586.3	10,928.5
Land affairs	3,720.5	5,897.5	6,659.4
Minerals and energy	2,607.7	2,947.4	3,786.2
Provincial and local government	24,575.7	30,029.7	35,639.0
Public enterprises	2,589.8	4,604.0	3,269.4
Science and technology	2,613.0	3,127.3	3,721.7
Trade and industry	3,804.7	5,295.4	5,126.9
Transport	13,360.4	16,331.6	24,492.8
Water affairs and forestry	4,305.7	5,385.4	7,036.6
Contingency reserve	—	—	−5,898.0
Sub-total	260,594.3	307,982.0	364,295.6
State debt costs	52,192.2	52,877.1	53,926.0
Provincial equitable share	150,752.9	172,861.5	204,009.9
Skills levy and seats	5,328.4	6,284.3	7,529.6
Members' remuneration	223.3	242.4	2,754.0
Judges' salaries	1,099.3	1,184.5	1,389.3
President and deputy-president salary	2.2	2.3	2.5
Total	470,192.5	541,434.1	633,906.9

* Estimates.
† Payments to Botswana, Lesotho, Namibia and Swaziland, in accordance with Southern African Customs Union agreements.
‡ Preliminary outcome.

Source: National Treasury, Pretoria.

SOUTH AFRICA

Statistical Survey

INTERNATIONAL RESERVES
(US $ million at 31 December)

	2006	2007	2008
Gold (national valuation)	2,530	3,354	3,485
IMF special drawing rights	355	352	344
Reserve position in IMF	1	2	2
Foreign exchange	22,720	29,234	30,238
Total	25,606	32,942	34,069

Source: IMF, *International Financial Statistics*.

MONEY SUPPLY
(million rand at 31 December)

	2006	2007	2008
Currency outside banks	49,951	53,606	57,362
Demand deposits at deposit money banks	287,612	344,691	352,185
Total	337,563	398,297	409,547

Source: IMF, *International Financial Statistics*.

COST OF LIVING
(Consumer Price Index; base: 2000 = 100)

	2005	2006	2007
Food	137.9	147.8	163.1
Clothing	92.3	84.6	76.8
Housing	113.4	118.2	129.7
Electricity, gas and other fuels	135.7	141.9	153.3
All items (incl. others)	128.0	134.0	143.5

Source: ILO.

NATIONAL ACCOUNTS
(million rand at current prices, preliminary)

National Income and Product

	2006	2007	2008
Compensation of employees	761,856	855,845	956,562
Net operating surplus	541,170	636,378	759,767
Consumption of fixed capital	219,506	256,373	306,946
Gross domestic product (GDP) at factor cost	1,522,532	1,748,596	2,023,275
Taxes on production	235,941	263,244	273,857
Less Subsidies	13,256	12,754	13,355
GDP at market prices	1,745,217	1,999,086	2,283,777
Primary incomes received from abroad	41,207	48,448	48,254
Less Primary incomes paid abroad	75,982	112,001	122,098
Gross national income at market prices	1,710,442	1,935,533	2,209,933
Current transfers received from abroad	1,792	1,839	2,917
Less Current transfers paid abroad	20,686	22,633	27,445
Gross national disposable income at market prices	1,691,548	1,914,739	2,185,405

Expenditure on the Gross Domestic Product

	2006	2007	2008
Government final consumption expenditure	344,758	394,653	464,791
Private final consumption expenditure	1,087,281	1,227,793	1,384,979
Increase in stocks	31,221	16,046	−9,878
Gross fixed capital formation	328,670	422,300	530,183
Residual item	9,816	23	−15,520
Total domestic expenditure	1,801,746	2,060,815	2,354,555
Exports of goods and services	517,549	629,092	807,704
Less Imports of goods and services	574,078	690,821	878,482
GDP at market prices	1,745,217	1,999,086	2,283,777
GDP at constant 2000 prices	1,174,078	1,233,930	1,271,717

Gross Domestic Product by Economic Activity

	2006	2007	2008
Agriculture, forestry and fishing	44,778	56,727	68,380
Mining and quarrying	127,144	148,215	196,094
Manufacturing	283,427	325,830	385,731
Electricity, gas and water	36,564	40,669	46,530
Construction (contractors)	41,842	51,968	63,755
Wholesale and retail trade, catering and accommodation	216,499	237,232	260,287
Transport, storage and communication	144,164	155,788	165,824
Finance, insurance, real estate and business services	329,533	392,257	444,910
Government services	231,262	260,223	304,552
Other community, social and personal services	93,595	106,063	117,424
Gross value added at basic prices	1,548,808	1,774,972	2,053,487
Taxes, less subsidies, on products	196,409	224,114	230,290
GDP at market prices	1,745,217	1,999,086	2,283,777

Source: South African Reserve Bank.

BALANCE OF PAYMENTS
(US $ million)

	2005	2006	2007
Exports of goods f.o.b.	55,284	64,163	75,920
Imports of goods f.o.b.	−56,279	−70,031	−81,661
Trade balance	−995	−5,868	−5,741
Exports of services	11,157	12,014	13,562
Imports of services	−12,155	−14,290	−16,563
Balance on goods and services	−1,993	−8,145	−8,742
Other income received	4,640	6,078	6,882
Other income paid	−9,569	−11,237	−15,967
Balance on goods, services and income	−6,922	−13,304	−17,827
Current transfers received	240	261	265
Current transfers paid	−3,041	−3,078	−3,218
Current balance	−9,723	−16,121	−20,780
Capital account (net)	30	30	28
Direct investment abroad	−909	−5,929	−2,982
Direct investment from abroad	6,522	−184	5,737
Portfolio investment assets	−911	−2,231	−3,439
Portfolio investment liabilities	5,698	21,814	15,074
Other investment assets	−3,503	−6,635	517
Other investment liabilities	5,686	8,456	7,130
Net errors and omissions	2,875	4,510	4,451
Overall balance	5,766	3,711	5,737

Source: IMF, *International Financial Statistics*.

External Trade

PRINCIPAL COMMODITIES
(distribution by SITC, US $ million)

Imports c.i.f.	2005	2006	2007
Food and live animals	1,750.6	2,127.1	2,839.6
Crude materials (inedible) except fuels	1,550.9	2,025.7	2,516.2
Mineral fuels, lubricants, etc.	7,846.1	12,547.0	14,847.3
Petroleum, petroleum products, etc.	7,620.2	12,242.1	14,317.6
Crude petroleum oils, etc.	6,474.2	9,487.5	10,917.9
Chemicals and related products	5,516.7	6,104.9	7,163.9
Basic manufactures	6,262.6	7,581.1	9,241.4
Non-metallic mineral manufactures	1,646.6	1,790.7	2,200.0
Machinery and transport equipment	21,672.1	25,890.3	29,795.2
Power generating machinery and equipment	1,116.0	1,960.0	1,696.5

SOUTH AFRICA

Statistical Survey

Imports c.i.f.—continued	2005	2006	2007
Machinery specialized for particular industries	2,324.6	2,865.7	4,158.7
General industrial machinery, equipment and parts	2,647.4	3,378.1	3,881.9
Office machines and automatic data-processing equipment	2,595.8	2,916.7	3,108.2
Telecommunications and sound equipment	3,288.9	3,744.6	3,818.2
Other electrical machinery, apparatus, etc.	2,211.0	2,756.6	3,259.2
Road vehicles	5,522.8	6,565.9	7,746.2
Passenger motor vehicles (excl. buses)	3,627.1	4,153.7	4,410.3
Other transport equipment	1,611.7	1,195.7	1,599.7
Miscellaneous manufactured articles	4,943.4	6,078.4	6,412.4
Total (incl. others)	55,032.6	68,469.1	79,872.6

Exports f.o.b.	2005	2006	2007
Food and live animals	3,074.8	2,882.3	3,196.8
Vegetables and fruit	1,641.0	1,553.2	1,883.6
Beverages and tobacco	852.1	805.2	967.8
Crude materials (inedible) except fuels	4,284.6	5,403.8	7,139.8
Metalliferous ores and metal scrap	2,607.2	3,856.3	5,305.1
Mineral fuels, lubricants, etc.	4,866.2	4,997.2	6,759.0
Coal, lignite and peat	3,273.1	3,139.2	3,386.4
Petroleum, petroleum products, etc.	1,581.0	1,827.9	3,226.0
Chemicals and related products	3,955.1	3,909.9	4,340.2
Basic manufactures	18,405.5	21,449.4	26,106.9
Non-metallic mineral manufactures	2,923.3	2,806.3	2,901.8
Pearl, precious and semi-precious stones, unworked or worked	2,584.6	2,460.3	2,533.8
Diamonds (non-industrial), not mounted or set	2,559.2	2,426.3	2,487.8
Iron and steel	5,864.1	5,647.9	7,460.1
Pig-iron, etc.	2,913.4	2,512.9	3,889.1
Non-ferrous metals	7,463.1	10,809.6	13,018.7
Silver, platinum and other platinum group metals	5,385.0	8,026.1	9,842.1
Platinum group metals, unwrought, unworked or semi-manufactured	5,316.2	8,012.1	9,823.1
Aluminium	1,609.7	2,055.7	2,201.4
Aluminium and aluminium alloys, unwrought	1,068.3	1,411.3	1,608.8
Machinery and transport equipment	9,574.4	11,293.3	13,411.6
General industrial machinery, equipment and parts	2,315.4	3,053.8	4,051.3
Road vehicles	4,200.2	4,719.5	5,164.9
Passenger motor vehicles (excl. buses)	2,860.2	2,718.3	2,635.5
Miscellaneous manufactured articles	1,601.4	1,500.0	1,628.9
Total (incl. others)	46,991.0	52,601.8	64,026.6

Source: UN, *International Trade Statistics Yearbook*.

PRINCIPAL TRADING PARTNERS
(US $ million)*

Imports f.o.b.	2005	2006	2007
Argentina	433.7	969.3	1,018.7
Australia	1,150.6	1,404.5	1,458.5
Belgium	746.3	842.3	988.0
Brazil	1,309.8	1,381.3	1,658.6
China, People's Repub.	4,945.6	6,879.5	8,562.7
France (incl. Monaco)	2,419.3	2,495.4	2,680.3
Germany	7,716.1	8,584.5	9,316.9
India	1,102.5	1,613.2	1,777.5
Iran	2,250.0	2,697.8	2,955.5
Ireland	639.8	634.6	809.1

Imports f.o.b.—continued	2005	2006	2007
Italy	1,624.4	2,045.7	2,218.1
Japan	3,715.9	4,458.1	5,249.4
Korea, Repub.	1,452.7	1,746.0	1,791.5
Malaysia	686.8	852.0	1,064.6
Netherlands	851.1	1,112.8	1,276.3
Nigeria	653.9	1,366.7	1,771.8
Saudi Arabia	3,046.8	3,612.5	3,606.3
Singapore	453.4	1,041.1	654.7
Spain	880.7	1,035.3	1,112.7
Sweden	762.9	864.1	1,152.3
Switzerland-Liechtenstein	708.1	603.6	710.2
Thailand	880.0	1,174.0	1,466.6
United Kingdom	3,036.5	3,396.5	3,863.5
USA	4,347.7	5,216.1	6,166.1
Total (incl. others)	55,032.6	68,469.1	79,872.6

Exports f.o.b.	2005	2006	2007
Angola	544.5	686.5	772.2
Australia	1,415.0	1,189.8	1,278.4
Belgium	1,416.5	1,493.5	1,748.8
Canada	352.6	440.5	779.0
China, People's Repub.	1,368.7	2,108.8	4,169.6
France (incl. Monaco)	1,068.4	1,262.1	1,382.9
Germany	3,329.7	3,944.3	5,106.0
Hong Kong	587.2	399.9	655.5
India	1,170.3	783.6	1,349.5
Israel	759.2	664.7	785.3
Italy	1,160.9	1,347.6	1,429.8
Japan	5,149.3	6,227.0	7,039.3
Kenya	458.7	471.0	643.3
Korea, Repub.	837.0	999.0	1,161.6
Mozambique	991.8	908.8	1,267.2
Netherlands	2,341.3	2,723.7	2,880.7
Nigeria	527.7	590.6	683.8
Spain	1,391.7	1,477.0	1,757.7
Switzerland-Liechtenstein	1,250.1	1,707.0	1,370.5
United Arab Emirates	437.1	556.5	708.6
United Kingdom	5,000.2	4,627.7	4,907.3
USA	4,893.2	6,058.2	7,528.7
Zambia	849.3	1,150.5	1,421.2
Zimbabwe	1,161.5	1,065.2	1,194.8
Total (incl. others)	46,991.0	52,601.8	64,026.6

* Imports by country of origin; exports by country of destination.

Source: UN, *International Trade Statistics Yearbook*.

Transport

RAILWAYS
(traffic, year ending 31 March)*

	1997/98	1998/99	1999/2000
Passenger-km (million)	1,775	1,794	3,930
Net ton-km (million)	103,866	102,777	106,786

* Including Namibia.

Source: UN, *Statistical Yearbook*.

ROAD TRAFFIC
(registered motor vehicles)

	2002
Heavy load vehicles	326,798
Heavy passenger motor vehicles	164,369
Light load vehicles	1,875,234
Light passenger motor vehicles	4,135,037
Motorcycles	159,266
Special vehicles	296,518
Other vehicles	17,955
Total (incl. others)	6,975,177

SOUTH AFRICA

SHIPPING

Merchant Fleet
(vessels registered at 31 December)

	2005	2006	2007
Number of vessels	243	242	250
Displacement ('000 grt)	180.6	173.1	192.6

Source: Lloyd's Register-Fairplay, *World Fleet Statistics*.

International Sea-borne Freight Traffic

	2003	2004	2005
Goods loaded (metric tons)	128,477,183	124,370,762	127,408,557
Goods unloaded (metric tons)	42,845,843	43,820,161	43,847,748
Containers loaded (TEU)	1,194,400	1,290,883	1,484,009
Containers unloaded (TEU)	1,220,167	1,341,888	1,530,227

Source: National Ports Authority of South Africa.

CIVIL AVIATION

(traffic on scheduled services)

	2002	2003	2004
Kilometres flown (million)	170	188	194
Passengers carried ('000)	8,167	9,160	9,879
Passenger-km (million)	22,914	24,666	26,048
Total ton-km (million)	2,853	3,125	3,270

Source: UN, *Statistical Yearbook*.

Tourism

FOREIGN VISITOR ARRIVALS*

Country of origin	2004	2005	2006
Botswana	806,820	798,455	765,705
France	111,636	103,674	108,713
Germany	249,564	253,471	263,225
Lesotho	1,479,802	1,668,826	1,919,889
Mozambique	405,579	648,526	926,496
Namibia	226,525	220,045	225,020
Netherlands	122,271	117,855	126,327
Swaziland	852,636	911,990	993,030
United Kingdom	463,176	476,627	494,955
USA	213,322	238,934	259,674
Zambia	122,512	128,390	160,984
Zimbabwe	558,093	783,100	n.a.
Total (incl. others and unspecified)	6,815,202	7,518,320	8,508,806

* Figures include same-day visitors (excursionists), but exclude arrivals of South African nationals resident abroad. Border crossings by contract workers are also excluded.

Tourism receipts (US $ million, incl. passenger transport): 7,380 in 2004; 8,448 in 2005; 8,967 in 2006.

Source: World Tourism Organization.

Communications Media

	2005	2006	2007
Telephones ('000 main lines in use)	4,729.0	4,700.0	4,642.0
Mobile cellular telephones ('000 subscribers)	33,960.0	39,662.0	42,300.0
Personal computers in use ('000)	3,966	n.a.	n.a.
Internet users ('000)	3,600.0	3,700.0	3,966.0
Broadband subscribers ('000)	165.3	335.1	n.a.

2001: Radio receivers ('000 in use): 11,696; Television receivers ('000 in use): 7,708.

2004: Daily newspapers (average circulation, '000): 1,408.0, (titles) 18.

Facsimile machines (number in use): 150,000 in 1997.

Book production: 5,418 titles in 1995.

Sources: partly UNESCO, *Statistical Yearbook*; UN, *Statistical Yearbook*; International Telecommunication Union.

Education

(2004)*

	Institutions	Teachers	Students
Primary	16,286	177,861	6,320,479
Secondary	5,887	114,755	3,717,780
Combined	3,911	53,305	1,755,083
Intermediate and middle	795	11,416	383,049
ABET centres†	2,339	15,954	272,725
ELSEN centres‡	408	7,392	86,388
Further education and training§	50	6,477	394,027
ECD‖	4,146	7,363	189,254
Higher education§	29	15,375	744,488

* Figures for public and independent institutions, unless otherwise indicated.
† Adult basic education and training.
‡ Education for learners with special needs.
§ Figures refer to public institutions only.
‖ Early childhood development.

Source: Department of Education.

Adult literacy rate (UNESCO estimates): 88.0% (males 88.9%; females 87.2%) in 2007 (Source: UNESCO Institute for Statistics).

Directory

The Constitution

The Constitution was adopted by the Constitutional Assembly (comprising the National Assembly and the Senate) on 8 May 1996, and entered into force on 4 February 1997. Its main provisions are summarized below:

FOUNDING PROVISIONS

The Republic of South Africa is one sovereign democratic state founded on the following values: human dignity, the achievement of equality and advancement of human rights and freedoms; non-racialism and non-sexism; supremacy of the Constitution and the rule of law; universal adult suffrage, a national common voters' roll, regular elections, and a multi-party system of democratic government, to ensure accountability, responsiveness and openness. There is common South African citizenship, all citizens being equally entitled to the rights, privileges and benefits, and equally subject to the duties and responsibilities of citizenship.

BILL OF RIGHTS

Everyone is equal before the law and has the right to equal protection and benefit of the law. The state may not unfairly discriminate directly or indirectly against anyone on one or more grounds, including race, gender, sex, pregnancy, marital status, ethnic or social origin, colour, sexual orientation, age, disability, religion, conscience, belief, culture, language and birth. The rights that are enshrined include: protection against detention without trial, torture or any inhuman form of treatment or punishment; the right to privacy; freedom of conscience; freedom of expression; freedom of assembly; political freedom; freedom of movement and residence; the right to join or form a trade union or employers' organization; the right to a healthy and sustainable environment; the right to prop-

SOUTH AFRICA

erty, except in the case of the Government's programme of land reform and redistribution, and taking into account the claims of people who were dispossessed of property after 19 June 1913; the right to adequate housing; the right to health care, food and water and social security assistance, if needed; the rights of children; the right to education in the official language of one's choice, where this is reasonably practicable; the right to use the language and to participate in the cultural life of one's choice, but not in a manner inconsistent with any provision of this Bill of Rights; access to state information; access to the courts; the rights of people who have been arrested or detained; and the right to a fair trial.

CO-OPERATIVE GOVERNMENT

Government is constituted as national, provincial and local spheres of government, which are distinctive, interdependent and inter-related. All spheres of government and all organs of state within each sphere must preserve the peace, national unity and indivisibility of the Republic; secure the well-being of the people of the Republic; implement effective, transparent, accountable and coherent government for the Republic as a whole; respect the constitutional status, institutions, powers and functions of government in the other spheres; not assume any power or function except those conferred on them in terms of the Constitution.

PARLIAMENT

Legislative power is vested in a bicameral Parliament, comprising a National Assembly and a National Council of Provinces. The National Assembly has between 350 and 400 members and is elected, in general, by proportional representation. National and provincial legislatures are elected separately, under a 'double-ballot' electoral system. Each provincial legislature appoints six permanent delegates and nominates four special delegates to the 90-member National Council of Provinces, which is headed by a Chairperson, who is elected by the Council and has a five-year term of office. Parliamentary decisions are generally reached by a simple majority, although constitutional amendments require a majority of two-thirds.

THE NATIONAL EXECUTIVE

The Head of State is the President, who is elected by the National Assembly from among its members, and exercises executive power in consultation with the other members of the Cabinet. No person may hold office as President for more than two terms. Any party that holds a minimum of 80 seats in the National Assembly (equivalent to 20% of the national vote) is entitled to nominate an Executive Deputy President. If no party, or only one party, secures 80 or more seats, the party holding the largest number of seats and the party holding the second largest number of seats in the National Assembly are each entitled to designate one Executive Deputy President from among the members of the Assembly. The President may be removed by a motion of no-confidence or by impeachment. The Cabinet comprises a maximum of 27 ministers. Each party with a minimum of 20 seats in the National Assembly (equivalent to 5% of the national vote) is entitled to a proportional number of ministerial portfolios. The President allocates cabinet portfolios in consultation with party leaders, who are entitled to request the replacement of ministers. Cabinet decisions are reached by consensus.

JUDICIAL AUTHORITY

The judicial authority of the Republic is vested in the courts, which comprise the Constitutional Court; the Supreme Court of Appeal; the High Courts; the Magistrates' Courts; and any other court established or recognized by an Act of Parliament. (See Judicial System.)

PROVINCIAL GOVERNMENT

There are nine provinces: Eastern Cape, Free State (formerly Orange Free State), Gauteng (formerly Pretoria-Witwatersrand-Vereeniging), KwaZulu/Natal, Limpopo (formerly Northern Transvaal, subsequently Northern Province), Mpumalanga (formerly Eastern Transvaal), Northern Cape, North-West and Western Cape. Each province is entitled to determine its legislative and executive structure. Each province has a legislature, comprising between 30 and 80 members (depending on the size of the local electorate), who are elected by proportional representation. Each legislature is entitled to draft a constitution for the province, subject to the principles governing the national Constitution, and elects a Premier, who heads a Cabinet. Parties that hold a minimum of 10% of seats in the legislature are entitled to a proportional number of portfolios in the Cabinet. Provincial legislatures are allowed primary responsibility for a number of areas of government, and joint powers with central government in the principal administrative areas.

LOCAL GOVERNMENT

The local sphere of government consists of municipalities, with executive and legislative authority vested in the Municipal Council. The objectives of local government are to provide democratic and accountable government for local communities; to ensure the provision of services to communities; to promote social and economic development, and a safe and healthy environment; and to encourage the involvement of communities and community organizations in the matters of local government. The National Assembly is to determine the different categories of municipality that may be established, and appropriate fiscal powers and functions for each category. Provincial Governments have the task of establishing municipalities, and of providing for the monitoring and support of local government in each province.

STATE INSTITUTIONS SUPPORTING CONSTITUTIONAL DEMOCRACY

The following state institutions are designed to strengthen constitutional democracy: the Public Protector (whose task is to investigate any conduct in state affairs, or in the public administration in any sphere of government, that is alleged or suspected to be improper); the Human Rights Commission; the Commission for the Protection and Promotion of the Rights of Cultural, Religious and Linguistic Communities; the Commission for Gender Equality; the Auditor-General; and the Electoral Commission.

TRADITIONAL LEADERS

The institution, status and role of traditional leadership, according to customary law, are recognized, subject to the Constitution. A traditional authority that observes a system of customary law may function subject to any applicable legislation and customs. National and provincial legislation may provide for the establishment of local or provincial houses of traditional leaders; the National Assembly may establish a national council of traditional leaders.

The Government

HEAD OF STATE

President: JACOB ZUMA (inaugurated 9 May 2009).
Deputy President: KGALEMA MOTLANTHE.

THE CABINET
(May 2009)

Minister of Agriculture, Forestry and Fisheries: TINA JOEMAT-PETTERSSON.

Minister of Arts and Culture: LULU XINGWANA.

Minister of Basic Education: ANGIE MOTSHEKGA.

Minister of Communications: SIPHIWE NYANDA.

Minister of Co-operative Governance and Traditional Affairs: SICELO SHICEKA.

Minister of Correctional Services: NOSIVIWE MAPISA-NQAKULA.

Minister of Defence and Military Veterans: LINDIWE. SISULU.

Minister of Economic Development: EBRAHIM PATEL.

Minister of Energy: DIPUO PETERS.

Minister of Finance: PRAVIN GORDHAN.

Minister of Health: Dr AARON MOTSOALEDI.

Minister of Higher Education and Training: Dr BLADE NZIMANDE.

Minister of Home Affairs: Dr NKOSAZANA DLAMINI-ZUMA.

Minister of Human Settlements: TOKYO SEXWALE.

Minister of International Relations and Co-operation: MAITE NKOANA-MASHABANE.

Minister of Justice and Constitutional Development: JEFF RADEBE.

Minister of Labour: MEMBATHISI MDLADLANA.

Minister of Mining: SUSAN SHABANGU.

Minister of Police: NATHI MTHETHWA.

Minister of Public Enterprises: BARBARA HOGAN.

Minister for the Public Service and Administration: RICHARD BALOYI.

Minister of Public Works: GEOFF DOIDGE.

Minister of Rural Development and Land Reform: GUGILE NKWINTI.

Minister of Science and Technology: NALEDI PANDOR.

Minister of Social Development: EDNA MOLEWA.

Minister of Sport and Recreation: MAKHENKESI STOFILE.

Minister of State Security: SIYABONGA CWELE.

SOUTH AFRICA

Ministers in the Presidency: TREVOR MANUEL (National Planning Commission), COLLINS CHABANE (Performance Monitoring, Evaluation and Administration).
Minister of Tourism: MARTHINUS VAN SCHALKWYK.
Minister of Trade and Industry: ROB DAVIES.
Minister of Transport: SBUSISO JOEL NDEBELE.
Minister of Water and Environmental Affairs: BUYELWA SONJICA.
Minister of Women, Youth, Children and People with Disabilities: NOLUTHANDO MAYENDE-SIBIYA.

In addition, there were 29 Deputy Ministers.

MINISTRIES

The Presidency: Union Bldgs, West Wing, Government Ave, Pretoria 0001; Private Bag X1000, Pretoria 0001; tel. (12) 3005200; fax (12) 3238246; e-mail president@po.gov.za; internet www.thepresidency.gov.za.

Ministry in The Presidency: National Planning Commission: Union Bldgs, 2nd Floor, Government Ave, Pretoria 0001; Private Bag X1000, Pretoria 0001; tel. (12) 3005200; fax (12) 3238246; e-mail minister@po.gov.za; internet www.thepresidency.gov.za.

Ministry in The Presidency: Performance Monitoring, Evaluation and Administration in The Presidency: Union Bldgs, 2nd Floor, Government Ave, Pretoria 0001; Private Bag X1000, Pretoria 0001; tel. (12) 3005200; fax (12) 3238246; e-mail samson@po.gov.za; internet www.thepresidency.gov.za.

Ministry of Agriculture, Forestry and Fisheries: Agriculture Bldg, 20 Beatrix St, Arcadia, Pretoria 0002; Private Bag X250, Pretoria 0001; tel. (12) 3197319; fax (12) 3218558; e-mail cco@nda.agric.za; internet www.doa.agric.za.

Ministry of Arts and Culture: 481 Church St, 10th Floor, cnr Church and Beatrix Sts, Kingsley Centre, Arcadia, Pretoria; Private Bag X899, Pretoria 0001; tel. (12) 4413709; fax (12) 4404485; e-mail sandile.memela@dac.gov.za; internet www.dac.gov.za.

Ministry of Basic Education: Sol Plaatje House, 123 Schoeman St, Pretoria 0002; Private Bag X603, Pretoria 0001; tel. (12) 3125501; fax (12) 3235989; internet www.education.gov.za.

Ministry of Communications: Nkululeko House, iParioli Office Park, 399 Duncan St, cnr Park St, Hatfield, Pretoria 0083; Private Bag X860, Pretoria 0001; tel. (12) 4278177; fax (12) 3626915; e-mail joe@doc.gov.za; internet www.doc.gov.za.

Ministry of Co-operative Governance and Traditional Affairs: 87 Hamilton St, Arcadia, Pretoria 0001; Private Bag X804, Pretoria 0001; tel. (12) 3340600; fax (12) 3340603.

Ministry of Correctional Services: Poyntons Bldg, West Block, cnr Church and Schubart Sts, Pretoria 0002; Private Bag X853, Pretoria 0001; tel. (12) 3072000; fax (12) 3286149; e-mail communications@dcs.gov.za; internet www.dcs.gov.za.

Ministry of Defence and Military Veterans: Armscor Bldg, Block 5, Nossob St, Erasmusrand 0181; Private Bag X427, Pretoria 0001; tel. (12) 3556101; fax (12) 3556134; e-mail mil@mil.za; internet www.dod.mil.za.

Ministry of Economic Development: Union Bldgs, Government Ave, Pretoria; Private Bag X1000, Pretoria 0001; tel. (012) 3005200; fax (86) 6835221.

Ministry of Energy: Mineralia Centre, 391 Andries St, Pretoria 0002; Private Bag X59, Pretoria 0001; tel. (12) 3179000; fax (12) 3204327; internet www.dme.gov.za.

Ministry of Health: 226 Prinsloo St, Pretoria 0001; Private Bag X399, Pretoria 0001; tel. (12) 3120546; fax (12) 3255526; e-mail bhengu@health.gov.za; internet www.health.gov.za.

Ministry of Higher Education and Training: Sol Plaatje House, 123 Schoeman St, Pretoria 0002; Private Bag X603, Pretoria 0001; tel. (12) 3125501; fax (12) 3235989; internet www.education.gov.za.

Ministry of Home Affairs: 270 Maggs St, Watloo; Private Bag X114, Pretoria 0001; tel. (12) 3148911; fax (12) 3216491; internet www.home-affairs.gov.za.

Ministry of Human Settlements: Govan Mbeki House, 240 Walker St, Sunnyside, Pretoria 0002; Private Bag X644, Pretoria 0001; tel. (12) 4211311; fax (12) 3418510.

Ministry of International Relations and Co-operation: Union Bldgs, East Wing, 1 Government Ave, Arcadia, Pretoria 0002; Private Bag X152, Pretoria 0001; tel. (12) 3510002; fax (12) 3231502; e-mail minister@foreign.gov.za; internet www.dfa.gov.za.

Ministry of Justice and Constitutional Development: Momentum Centre, 329 Pretorius St, cnr Pretorius and Prinsloo Sts, Pretoria 0001; Private Bag X276, Pretoria 0001; tel. (12) 3151332; fax (12) 3151749; e-mail znqayi@justice.gov.za; internet www.doj.gov.za.

Ministry of Labour: Laboria House, 215 Schoeman St, Pretoria 0002; Private Bag X117, Pretoria 0001; tel. (12) 3094000; fax (12) 3094030; e-mail page.boikanyo@labour.gov.za; internet www.labour.gov.za.

Ministry of Mining: Mineralia Centre, 391 Andries St, Pretoria 0002; Private Bag X59, Pretoria 0001; tel. (12) 3179000; fax (12) 3204327; internet www.dme.gov.za.

Ministry of Police: Wachthuis, 7th Floor, 231 Pretorius St, Pretoria; Private Bag X463, Pretoria 0001; tel. (12) 3932810; fax (12) 3932812; e-mail bloemb@saps.org.za.

Ministry of Public Enterprises: Infotech Bldg, Suite 401, 1090 Arcadia St, Hatfield, Pretoria 0083; Private Bag X15, Hatfield 0028; tel. (12) 4311000; fax (86) 5012624; e-mail vimla.maistry@dpe.gov.za; internet www.dpe.gov.za.

Ministry of Public Service and Administration: Batho Pele House, Proes St, Pretoria 0001; Private Bag X916, Pretoria 0001; tel. (12) 3361334; fax (12) 3361810; e-mail natasha@dpsa.gov.za; internet www.dpsa.gov.za.

Ministry of Public Works: Central Government Bldg, cnr Bosman and Vermeulen Sts, Pretoria 0002; Private Bag X65, Pretoria 0001; tel. (12) 3372000; fax (12) 3252856; internet www.publicworks.gov.za.

Ministry of Rural Development and Land Reform: Old Bldng, 184 cnr Jacob Mare and Paul Kruger Sts, Pretoria; Private Bag X833, Pretoria 0001; tel. (12) 3128911; fax (12) 3236072.

Ministry of Science and Technology: DST Bldg (No. 53), Meiring Naude Rd, Brummeria 0001; Private Bag X894, Pretoria 0001; tel. (12) 8436300; fax (12) 3242687; e-mail nelvis.qekema@dst.gov.za; internet www.dst.gov.za.

Ministry of Social Development: HSRC Bldg, North Wing, 134 Pretorius St, Pretoria 0002; Private Bag X901, Pretoria 0001; tel. (12) 3127479; fax (12) 3122502; e-mail lakelak@dsd.gov.za; internet www.welfare.gov.za.

Ministry of Sport and Recreation: cnr Vermeulen and Queen Sts, 66 Queen St, Pretoria; Private Bag X896, Pretoria 0001; tel. (12) 3045000; fax (12) 3238426; e-mail stofile@srsa.gov.za; internet www.srsa.gov.za.

Ministry of State Security: Bogare Bldg, 2 Atterbury Rd, Menlyn, Pretoria; POBag 1037, Menlyn 0077; tel. (12) 3670700; fax (12) 3670749; e-mail lornad@mweb.co.za; internet www.intelligence.gov.za.

Ministry of Tourism: Fedsure Forum Bldg, 10th Floor, North Tower, 315 Pretorius St, Pretoria; Private Bag X447, Pretoria, 0001; tel. (12) 3103611; fax (12) 3220082.

Ministry of Trade and Industry: 77 Meintjies St, Sunnyside, Pretoria 0002; Private Bag X84, Pretoria 0001; tel. (12) 3941508; fax (12) 3940337; e-mail contactus@thedti.gov.za; internet www.thedti.gov.za.

Ministry of Transport: 159 Forum Bldg, 159 Struben St, Pretoria 0002; Private Bag X193, Pretoria 0001; tel. (12) 3093000; fax (12) 3285926; e-mail khozac@dot.gov.za; internet www.transport.gov.za.

Ministry of Water and Environmental Affairs: Sedibeng Bldg, 10th Floor, 185 Schoeman St, Pretoria 0002; Private Bag X313, Pretoria 0001; tel. (12) 3368733; fax (12) 3284254; e-mail pagel@dwaf.gov.za; internet www.dwaf.gov.za.

National Treasury: 40 Church Sq., Pretoria 0002; Private Bag X115, Pretoria 0001; tel. (12) 3238911; fax (12) 3233262; e-mail dumisa.jele@treasury.gov.za; internet www.treasury.gov.za.

Legislature

PARLIAMENT

National Council of Provinces

Chairman: MNINWA JOHANNES MAHLANGU.

The National Council of Provinces (NCOP), which replaced the Senate under the new Constitution, was inaugurated on 6 February 1997. The NCOP comprises 90 members, with six permanent delegates and four special delegates from each of the nine provinces.

National Assembly

Speaker: MAX VUYISILE SISULU.

SOUTH AFRICA

General Election, 22 April 2009

Party	Votes	% of votes	Seats
African National Congress	11,650,748	65.90	264
Democratic Alliance	2,945,829	16.66	67
Congress of the People	1,311,027	7.42	30
Inkatha Freedom Party	804,260	4.55	18
Independent Democrats	162,915	0.92	4
United Democratic Movement	149,680	0.85	4
Vryheidsfront Plus	146,796	0.83	4
African Christian Democratic Party	142,658	0.81	3
United Christian Democratic Party	66,086	0.37	2
Pan-Africanist Congress of Azania	48,530	0.27	1
Minority Front	43,474	0.25	1
Azanian People's Organisation	38,245	0.22	1
African People's Convention	35,867	0.20	1
Others	134,614	0.76	—
Total	**17,680,729**	**100.00**	**400**

Provincial Governments
(May 2009)

EASTERN CAPE
Premier: Noxolo Kiviet (ANC).
Speaker of the Legislature: Fikile Xasa (ANC).

FREE STATE
Premier: Ace Magashule (ANC).
Speaker of the Legislature: Moeketsi Sesele (ANC).

GAUTENG
Premier: Nomvula Paula Mokonyane (ANC).
Speaker of the Legislature: Lindiwe Maseko (ANC).

KWAZULU/NATAL
Premier: Dr Zweli Lawrence Mkhize (ANC).
Speaker of the Legislature: Peggy Nkonyeni (ANC).

LIMPOPO
Premier: Cassel Mathale (ANC).
Speaker of the Legislature: Rudoph Phala (ANC).

MPUMALANGA
Premier: David D. Mabuza (ANC).
Speaker of the Legislature: Jackson Mthembu (ANC).

NORTHERN CAPE
Premier: Hazel Jenkins (ANC).
Speaker of the Legislature: Ghoolam Acharwaray (ANC).

NORTH-WEST
Premier: Maureen Modiselle (ANC).
Speaker of the Legislature: Nono Dumile Maloy (ANC).

WESTERN CAPE
Premier: Helen Zille (DA).
Speaker of the Legislature: Shahid Esau (DA).

Election Commission

Independent Electoral Commission: Election House, 260 Walker St, Sunnyside, Pretoria; tel. (12) 4285700; fax (12) 4285863; e-mail iec@elections.org.za; internet www.elections.org.za; f. 1996; Chair. Dr Brigalia Bam.

Political Organizations

A total of 26 parties contested the elections to the National Assembly in April 2009, while 38 parties presented candidates in the concurrent provincial elections.

African Christian Democratic Party (ACDP): Stats Building, 1st Floor, 2 Fore St, POB 1677, Alberton; tel. (11) 8693941; fax (11) 8693942; e-mail office@acdp.org.za; internet www.acdp.org.za; f. 1993; Leader Rev. Kenneth Meshoe.

African National Congress of South Africa (ANC): 54 Sauer St, Johannesburg 2001; POB 61884, Marshalltown 2107; tel. (11) 3761000; fax (11) 3761134; e-mail nmtyelwa@anc.org.za; internet www.anc.org.za; f. 1912; in alliance with the South African Communist Party (SACP) and the Congress of South African Trade Unions (COSATU); governing party since April 1994; Pres. Jacob Zuma; Deputy Pres. Kgalema Motlanthe; Sec.-Gen. Gwede Mantashe.

African People's Convention (APC): SAAU Bldg, cnr Andries and Schoeman Sts, Suite 610, 6th Floor, Pretoria 0001; tel. (11) 4985535; fax (11) 4985938; e-mail mmazibuko@gpl.gov.za; internet www.theapc.org.za; f. 2008; Pres. Themba Godi.

Afrikaner Weerstandsbeweging (AWB) (Afrikaner Resistance Movement): POB 274, Ventersdorp 2710, Johannesburg; tel. and fax (18) 2642516; e-mail awb@awb.co.za; internet www.awb.co.za; f. 1973; Afrikaner (Boer) nationalist group seeking self-determination for the Afrikaner people in South Africa; Leader Eugene Terre' Blanche.

Al Jama-ah: The Business Hub, 1A Forest Pl., Pinelands, Cape Town 7405; tel. (21) 5314273; internet www.aljama.co.za; Muslim party; Leader Mogamad Ganief Ebrahim Hendricks.

Azanian People's Organization (AZAPO): 141 Commissioner St, Kine Centre, 19th Floor, Johannesburg 2000; POB 4230, Johannesburg 2000; tel. (11) 3316430; fax (11) 3316433; e-mail azapo@mail.ngo.za; internet www.azapo.org.za; f. 1978; to seek the establishment of a unitary, democratic, socialist republic; excludes white mems; Pres. Mosibludi Mangena; Nat. Chair. Zithulele N. A. Cindi.

Boerestaat Party (Boer State Party): POB 4995, Luipaardsvlei 1743; tel. (11) 7623841; fax (11) 7623842; e-mail info@boerestaatparty.co.za; internet www.boerestaatparty.co.za; f. 1988; seeks the reinstatement of the Boer Republics in a consolidated Boerestaat; Leader Coen Vermaak.

Christian Democratic Alliance (CDA): Cape Town; tel. (21) 4033518; fax (21) 4033518; e-mail national.office@cda.org.za; internet www.cda.org.za; f. 2008; Leader Louis Michael Green; Sec.-Gen. Kevin Southgate.

Congress of the People (COPE): 34–36 Fricker Rd, Illovo, Sandton; tel. (11) 4476845; e-mail info@congressofthepeople.org.za; internet www.congressofthepeople.org.za; f. 2008 following split in the ANC; Chair. Mosiuoa Lekota.

Democratic Alliance (DA): POB 1475, Cape Town 8000; 2nd Floor, Theba Hosken House, cnr Breda and Mill Sts, Gardens, Cape Town; tel. (21) 4651431; fax (21) 4615559; e-mail info@da.org.za; internet www.da.org.za; f. 2000 by opposition parties, incl. the Democratic Party, the Federal Alliance and the New National Party (NNP), to contest that year's municipal elections; NNP withdrew in late 2001; Leader Helen Zille; Chair. Joe Seremane.

Herstigte Nasionale Party (HNP): 199 Neethling St, Eloffsdal, POB 1888, Pretoria 0001; tel. (12) 3358523; fax (12) 3358518; e-mail info@hnp.org.za; internet www.hnp.org.za; f. 1969 by fmr mems of the National Party; advocates 'Christian Nationalism'; Leader Jacob Jacobus Theart; Gen. Sec. Louis J. van der Schyff.

Independent Democrats (ID): Rm 28, Marks Bldg, Parliament Plein St, POB 751, Cape Town 8000; tel. (21) 4038696; fax (21) 4032350; e-mail id@id.org.za; internet www.id.org.za; f. 2003; Pres. Patricia de Lille; Chair. Mervyn Cirota.

Inkatha Freedom Party (IFP): 2 Durban Club Pl., Durban, 4000; POB 4432, Durban 4000; tel. (31) 3651300; fax (31) 3074964; e-mail ifpinfo@iafrica.com; internet www.ifp.org.za; f. 1975 as Inkatha National Cultural Liberation Movement with mainly Zulu support; reorg. in 1990 as a multiracial political party; Pres. Chief Mangosuthu Gatsha Buthelezi.

Minority Front: 347 Florence Nightingale Dr., Westcliff, Chatsworth; tel. (31) 4033360; fax (31) 4033354; e-mail mf@mf.org.za; internet www.mf.org.za; f. 1993; Indian support; Leader Amichand Rajbansi.

National Democratic Convention (NADECO): 1615 Commercial City, 40 Commercial Rd, Durban 4001; tel. (31) 3042098; fax (31) 3042944; e-mail mbathah@nadeco.org; internet www.nadeco.org; f. 2005; Pres. Rev. Hawu Mbatha; Chair. Themba Mbutho.

Pan-Africanist Congress of Azania (PAC): 10th Floor, Renaissance House, 16–22 New St, Ghandi Sq., Johannesburg; POB 6010, Johannesburg 2000; tel. (11) 8389380; fax (11) 8389384; e-mail pacazania@telkomsa.net; internet www.panafricanperspective.com/pac/index.html; f. 1959; Pres. Dr Motsoko Pheko; Nat. Exec. Sec. Mfanelo Skwatsha.

Progressive Independent Party (PIP): Indian support; Leader Faiz Khan.

South African Communist Party (SACP): Cosatu House, 3rd Floor, 1 Leyds St, Braamfontein; POB 1027, Johannesburg 2000; tel.

(11) 3393633; fax (11) 3396880; e-mail info@sacp.org.za; internet www.sacp.org.za; f. 1921; reorg. 1953; supports the ANC; Chair. GWEDE MANTASHE; Gen. Sec. BLADE NZIMANDE.

United Christian Democratic Party (UCDP): POB 3010, Mmabatho; tel. (18) 3815691; fax (18) 3817346; e-mail ucdpheadoff@ucdp.org.za; internet www.ucdp.org.za; f. 1972 as the Bophuthatswana Nat. Party; name changed to Bophuthatswana Dem. Party in 1974; present name adopted in 1991; multiracial; Leader KGOSI L. M. MANGOPE; Sec.-Gen. M. N. MATLADI; Nat. Chair. I. SIPHO MFUNDISI.

United Democratic Movement: Tomkor Bldg, 2nd Floor, cnr Vermeulen and Du Toit Sts, Pretoria; POB 26290, Arcadia 0007; tel. (12) 3210010; fax (12) 3210014; e-mail info@udm.org.za; internet www.udm.org.za; f. 1997; multiracial support; demands effective measures for enforcement of law and order; Pres. BANTU HOLOMISA; Sec.-Gen. HUMPHREY NOBONGOZA.

Vryheidsfront Plus (Freedom Front Plus—VF Plus/FF Plus): 203 Soutpansberg Ave, Rietondale, Pretoria; POB 74693, Lynnwood Ridge 0040; tel. (12) 3291220; fax (12) 3291229; e-mail info@vf.co.za; internet www.vryheidsfront.co.za; f. 1994 as Freedom Front; name changed after incorporating the Conservative Party and Afrikaner Eenheidsbeweging in Sept. 2003; right-wing electoral alliance; Leader Dr PIETER W. A. MULDER; Chair. ABRIE OOSTHUIZEN.

Diplomatic Representation

EMBASSIES AND HIGH COMMISSIONS IN SOUTH AFRICA

Algeria: 950 Arcadia St, Hatfield, Pretoria 0083; POB 57480, Arcadia 0007; tel. (12) 3425074; fax (12) 3426479; Ambassador MOURAD BENCHEIKH.

Angola: 1030 Schoeman St, Hatfield, Pretoria 0083; POB 8685, Pretoria 0001; tel. (12) 3420049; fax (12) 3427039; Ambassador MIGUEL GASPAR FERNANDES NETO.

Argentina: 200 Standard Plaza, 440 Hilda St, Hatfield, Pretoria 0083; POB 11125, Pretoria 0028; tel. (12) 4303524; fax (12) 4303521; e-mail argembas@global.co.za; Ambassador CARLOS SERSALE DI CERISANO.

Australia: 292 Orient St, Arcadia, Pretoria; Private Bag X150, Pretoria 0001; tel. (12) 4236000; fax (12) 3428442; e-mail pretoria.info@dfat.gov.au; internet www.australia.co.za; High Commissioner ANN JACQUELINE HARRAP.

Austria: Momentum Office Park, 1109 Duncan St, Brooklyn, Pretoria 0181; POB 95572, Waterkloof 0145; tel. (12) 4529155; fax (12) 4601151; e-mail pretoria-ob@bmeia.gv.at; internet www.bmeia.gv.at/pretoria; Ambassador Dr OTTO DITZ.

Bangladesh: 410 Farenden St, Sunnyside, Pretoria 0002; tel. (12) 3432105; fax (12) 3435222; e-mail bdoot@mweb.co.za; High Commissioner MD SHAHIDUL ISLAM.

Belarus: 327 Hill St, Arcadia, Pretoria 0083; POB 4107, Pretoria 0001; tel. (12) 4307664; fax (12) 3426280; e-mail sa@belembassy.org; Chargé d'affaires a.i. ALEKSEI LESNOY.

Belgium: 625 Leyds St, Muckleneuk, Pretoria 0002; tel. (12) 4403201; fax (12) 4403216; e-mail pretoria@diplobel.org; internet www.diplomatie.be/pretoria; Ambassador JAN MUTTON.

Benin: 900 Park St, cnr Orient and Park Sts, Arcadia, Pretoria 0083; POB 26484, Arcadia 0007; tel. (12) 3426978; fax (12) 3421823; e-mail embbenin@yebo.co.za; Chargé d'affaires a.i. PAMPHILE C. GOUTONDJI.

Bosnia and Herzegovina: 25 Stella St, Brooklyn, Pretoria 0181; POB 11464, Hatfield 0028; tel. (12) 3465547; fax (12) 3462295; e-mail bih@mweb.co.za; Ambassador DRAGAN PJEVIĆ.

Botswana: 24 Amos St, Colbyn, Pretoria 0083; POB 57035, Arcadia 0007; tel. (12) 4309640; fax (12) 3421845; High Commissioner MOTLHAGODI MOLOMO.

Brazil: Hillcrest Office Park, Woodpecker Pl., 1st Floor, 177 Dyer Rd, Hillcrest, Pretoria 0083; POB 3269, Pretoria 0001; tel. (12) 3665200; fax (12) 3665299; e-mail pretoria@brazilianembassy.org.za; internet www.brazilianembassy.org.za; Ambassador JOSÉ VICENTE DE SÁ PIMENTEL.

Bulgaria: 1071 Church St, Hatfield, Pretoria 0083; POB 29296, Arcadia 0007; tel. (12) 3423720; fax (12) 3423721; e-mail embulgsa@iafrica.com; internet www.bulgarianembassy.co.za; Ambassador VOLODYA CHANEV NEYKOV.

Burundi: 20 Glyn St, Colbyn, Pretoria 0083; POB 12914, Hatfield 0028; tel. (12) 3424881; fax (12) 3424885; Ambassador REGINE RWAMIBANGO.

Cameroon: 924 Pretorius St, Arcadia 0083; POB 13790, Hatfield 0028; tel. (12) 3624731; fax (12) 3424732; e-mail hicocam@cameroon.co.za; High Commissioner ADRIEN KOUAMBO JOMAGUE.

Canada: 1103 Arcadia St, cnr Hilda St, Hatfield, Pretoria 0083; Private Bag X13, Hatfield 0028; tel. (12) 4223000; fax (12) 4223052; e-mail pret@international.gc.ca; internet www.dfait-maeci.gc.ca/southafrica/menu-en.asp; High Commissioner RUTH ARCHIBALD.

Chile: Brooklyn Gardens, cnr Veale St and Middle St, Block B, 1st Floor, New Muckleneuk, Pretoria; POB 2449, Brooklyn Sq. 0075; tel. (12) 4608090; fax (12) 4608093; e-mail chile@iafrica.com; internet www.embchile.co.za; Ambassador CLAUDIO E. HERRERA ALAMOS.

China, People's Republic: 965 Church St, Arcadia, Pretoria 0083; POB 95764, Waterkloof 0145; tel. (12) 3424194; fax (12) 3424154; e-mail reception@chinese-embassy.org.za; internet www.chinese-embassy.org.za; Ambassador ZHONG JIANHUA.

Colombia: 1105 Park St, 3rd Floor, Hatfield, Pretoria 0083; POB 12791, Hatfield 0028; tel. (12) 3420211; fax (12) 3420216; e-mail info@embassyofcolombia.co.za; Ambassador EDGAR JOSÉ PEREA-ARIAS.

Comoros: 817 Thomas St, cnr Church and Eastwood Sts, Arcadia, Pretoria 0083; tel. (12) 3439483; fax (12) 3420138; Ambassador AHMED MOHAMED THABIT.

Congo, Democratic Republic: 791 Schoeman St, Arcadia, Pretoria 0083; POB 28795, Sunnyside 0132; tel. (12) 3446475; fax (12) 3444054; e-mail rdcongo@lantic.net; Ambassador BENE M'POKO.

Congo, Republic: 960 Arcadia St, Arcadia, Pretoria 0083; POB 40427, Arcadia 0007; tel. (12) 3425508; fax (12) 3425510; Ambassador ROGER ISSOMBO.

Côte d'Ivoire: 795 Government Ave, Arcadia, Pretoria 0083; POB 13510, Hatfield 0028; tel. (12) 3426913; fax (12) 3426713; Ambassador BOUBAKAR KONE.

Croatia: 1160 Church St, Colbyn, Pretoria 0083; POB 11335, Hatfield 0028; tel. (12) 3421206; fax (12) 3421819; Ambassador IVAN PICUKARIĆ.

Cuba: 45 Mackenzie St, Brooklyn, Pretoria 0181; POB 11605, Hatfield 0028; tel. (12) 3462215; fax (12) 3462216; e-mail sudafri@iafrica.com; Ambassador ANGEL VILLA HERNÁNDEZ.

Cyprus: cnr Church St and Hill St, Arcadia, Pretoria 0083; POB 14554, Hatfield 0028; tel. (12) 3425258; fax (12) 3425596; e-mail cyprusjb@mweb.co.za; High Commissioner ARGYROS ANTONIOU.

Czech Republic: 936 Pretorius St, Arcadia, Pretoria 0083; POB 13671, Hatfield 0028; tel. (12) 4312380; fax (12) 4302033; e-mail pretoria@embassymzv.cz; Ambassador MARTIN POHL.

Denmark: iParioli Office Park, Block B2, Ground Floor, 1166 Park St, Hatfield, Pretoria; POB 11439, Hatfield 0028; tel. (12) 4309340; fax (12) 3427620; e-mail pryamb@um.dk; internet www.ambpretoria.um.dk; Ambassador DAN E. FREDERIKSEN.

Dominican Republic: 270 Delphinus St, Waterkloof Ridge, Pretoria; tel. (12) 3463937; fax (12) 463807; e-mail embajadadominicana@telkomsa.net; Ambassador RAÚL FERNANDO BARRIENTOS-LARA.

Ecuador: 36 Selati St, Selati Park, Alphen Park, Pretoria; Chargé d'affaires a.i. J. P. NAVARRO LECARO.

Egypt: 270 Bourke St, Muckleneuk, Pretoria 0002; POB 30025, Sunnyside 0132; tel. (12) 3431590; fax (12) 3431082; e-mail egyptemb@global.co.za; Ambassador MOHAMED BADR ELDIN MOSTAFA ZAYED.

Equatorial Guinea: 48 Florence St, Colbyn, Pretoria; POB 12720, Hatfield 0028; tel. (12) 3429945; fax (12) 3427250; Ambassador JUAN ANTONIO BIBANG NCHUCHUMA.

Eritrea: 1281 Cobham Rd, Queenswood, Pretoria 0186; POB 11371, Queenswood 0121; tel. (12) 3331302; fax (12) 3332330; Chargé d'affaires a.i. T. M. GHEBRU.

Ethiopia: 47 Charles St, Bailey's Muckleneuk, Brooklyn 0181; POB 11469, Hatfield 0028; tel. (12) 3463542; fax (12) 3463867; e-mail ethiopia@sentechsa.com; Ambassador MELESE MARIMO MARASSO.

Finland: 628 Leyds St, Muckleneuk, Pretoria 0002; POB 443, Pretoria 0001; tel. (12) 3430275; fax (12) 3433095; e-mail sanomat.pre@formin.fi; internet www.finland.org.za; Ambassador HEIKKI TUUNANEN.

France: 250 Melk St, cnr Melk and Middle Sts, New Muckleneuk, Pretoria 0181; tel. (12) 4251600; fax (12) 4251689; e-mail france@ambafrance-rsa.org; internet www.ambafrance-rsa.org; Ambassador DENIS PIETTON.

Gabon: 921 Schoeman St, Arcadia, Pretoria 0083; POB 9222, Pretoria 0001; tel. (12) 3424376; fax (12) 3424375; Ambassador MARCEL-JULES ODONGUI-BONNARD.

Germany: 180 Blackwood St, Arcadia, Pretoria 0083; POB 2023, Pretoria 0001; tel. (12) 4278900; fax (12) 3433606; e-mail GermanEmbassyPretoria@gonet.co.za; internet www.pretoria.diplo.de; Ambassador DIETER WALTER HALLER.

Ghana: 1038 Arcadia St, Hatfield, Pretoria 0083; POB 12537, Hatfield 0028; tel. (12) 3425847; fax (12) 3425863; High Commissioner IBRAHIM ABASSA (acting).

Greece: 1003 Church St, Arcadia, Pretoria 0083; tel. (12) 3427136; fax (12) 4304313; e-mail embgrsaf@global.co.za; Ambassador ARISTIDIS SANDIS.

Guinea: 336 Orient St, Arcadia, Pretoria 0083; POB 13523, Hatfield 0028; tel. (12) 3420893; fax (12) 3427348; e-mail embaguinea@iafrica.com; Ambassador GAOUSSOU TOURÉ.

Haiti: 808 George St, Arcadia, Pretoria 0007; POB 14362, Hatfield 0028; tel. (12) 4307560; fax (12) 3427042; Ambassador YOLETTE AZOR-CHARLES.

Holy See: 800 Pretorius St, Arcadia, Pretoria 0083; POB 26017, Arcadia 0007; tel. (12) 3443815; fax (12) 3443595; e-mail nunziosa@iafrica.com; Apostolic Nuncio Most Rev. JAMES PATRICK GREEN.

Hungary: 959 Arcadia St, Hatfield, Pretoria 0083; POB 13843, Hatfield 0028; tel. (12) 4303030; fax (12) 4303029; e-mail mission.prt@kum.hu; Ambassador ISTVÁN EMRI.

India: 852 Schoeman St, Arcadia, Pretoria 0083; POB 40216, Arcadia 0007; tel. (12) 3425392; fax (12) 3425310; e-mail polinf@hicomind.co.za; High Commissioner R. K. BHATIA.

Indonesia: 949 Schoeman St, Arcadia, Pretoria 0082; POB 13155, Hatfield, Pretoria 0028; tel. (12) 3423350; fax (12) 3423369; e-mail fpanggabean@indonesia-pretoria.org.za; internet www.indonesia-pretoria.org.za; f. 1995; Ambassador SUGENG RAHARDJO.

Iran: 1002 Schoeman St, Hatfield, Pretoria 0083; POB 12546, Hatfield 0083; tel. (12) 3425880; fax (12) 3421878; internet www.iranembassy.org.za; Ambassador ASGHAR EBRAHIMI ASL.

Iraq: 803 Duncan St, Brooklyn, Pretoria 0181; POB 11089, Hatfield 0028; tel. (12) 3622048; fax (12) 3622027; Chargé d'affaires RASHEED MADHLOOM MUTLAK.

Ireland: Southern Life Plaza, 1st Floor, 1059 Schoeman St, cnr Festival and Schoeman Sts, Arcadia, Pretoria 0083; POB 4174, Arcadia 0001; tel. (12) 3425062; fax (12) 3424752; e-mail pretoria@dfa.ie; internet www.embassyireland.org.za; Ambassador COLIN WRAFTER.

Israel: 428 King's Hwy, Elizabeth Grove St, Lynnwood, Pretoria; POB 3726, Pretoria 0001; tel. (12) 3480470; fax (12) 3488594; e-mail operator@pretoria.mfa.gov.il; internet pretoria.mfa.gov.il; Ambassador DOV SEGEV-STEINBERG.

Italy: 796 George Ave, Arcadia, Pretoria 0083; tel. (12) 4230001; fax (12) 4305547; e-mail segreteria.pretoria@esteri.it; internet www.ambpretoria.esteri.it; Ambassador ELIO MENZIONE.

Jamaica: 1119 Burnett St, Hatfield, Pretoria 0083; tel. (12) 3626667; fax (12) 3668510; e-mail jhcpretoria@telkomsa.net; High Commissioner AUDLEY RODRIQUES (acting).

Japan: 259 Baines St, cnr Frans Oerder St, Groenkloof, Pretoria 0181; Private Bag X999, Pretoria 0001; tel. (12) 4521500; fax (12) 4603800; e-mail info@embjapan.org.za; internet www.japan.org.za; Ambassador TOSHIRO OZAWA.

Jordan: 252 Olivier St, Brooklyn, Pretoria 0075; POB 14730, Hatfield 0028; tel. (12) 346861517; fax (12) 3468611; e-mail embjordpta@telkomsa.net; Ambassador Dr MAZEN IZZEDINE TAL.

Kenya: 302 Brooks St, Menlo Park, Pretoria 0081; POB 35954, Menlo Park 0012; tel. (12) 3622249; fax (12) 3622252; e-mail info@kenya.org.za; High Commissioner THOMAS AMOLO.

Korea, Democratic People's Republic: 958 Waterpoort St, Faerie Glen, Pretoria; POB 1238, Garsfontein 0042; tel. (12) 9918661; fax (12) 9918662; e-mail dprkembassy@lantic.net; Ambassador AN HUI JONG.

Korea, Republic: Greenpark Estates, Bldg 3, 27 George Storrar Dr., Groenkloof, Pretoria 0081; POB 939, Groenkloof 0027; tel. (12) 4602508; fax (12) 4601158; e-mail korrsa@mweb.co.za; Ambassador KIM HAN-SOO.

Kuwait: 890 Arcadia St, Arcadia, Pretoria 0083; Private Bag X920, Pretoria 0001; tel. (12) 3420877; fax (12) 3420876; e-mail safarku@global.co.za; Ambassador HASSAN BADER KAREEM AL-OQAB.

Lebanon: 290 Lawley St, Waterkloof, Pretoria 0081; POB 941, Groenkloof 0027; tel. (12) 3467020; fax (12) 3467022; Ambassador MICHEL THOMAS KATRA.

Lesotho: 391 Anderson St, Menlo Park, Pretoria 0081; POB 55817, Arcadia 0007; tel. (12) 4607648; fax (12) 4607469; High Commissioner LINEO LYDIA KHECHANE-NTOANE.

Liberia: Suite 9 Section 7, Schoeman St Forum, 1157 Schoeman St, Hatfield, Pretoria; POB 14082, Hatfield, Pretoria; tel. (12) 3422734; fax (12) 3422737; e-mail libempta@pta.lia.net; Ambassador LOIS LEWIS BRUTHUS.

Libya: 900 Church St, Arcadia, Pretoria 0083; POB 40388, Arcadia 0007; tel. (12) 3423902; fax (12) 3423904; Ambassador Dr ABDULLAH ABDUSSALAM AZ-ZUBEDI.

Madagascar: 90B Tait St, Colbyn, Pretoria; POB 11722, Queenswood 0121; tel. (12) 3420983; fax (12) 3420995; e-mail consul@infodoor.co.za; Ambassador DENIS ANDRIAMANDROSO.

Malawi: 770 Government Ave, Arcadia, Pretoria 0083; POB 11172, Hatfield 0028; tel. and fax (12) 3421759; e-mail highcommalai@telkomsa.net; High Commissioner AGRINA MUSSA.

Malaysia: 1007 Schoeman St, Arcadia, Pretoria 0083; POB 11673, Hatfield 0028; tel. (12) 3425990; fax (12) 4307773; High Commissioner M. KENNEDY JAWAN.

Mali: 876 Pretorius St, Arcadia 0083; POB 12978, Hatfield, Pretoria 0028; tel. (12) 3427464; fax (12) 3420670; Ambassador SINALY COULIBALY.

Mauritania: 146 Anderson St, Brooklyn, Pretoria; tel. (12) 3623578; fax (12) 3623304; e-mail rimambapretoria@webmail.co.za; Chargé d'affaires AM DIAW.

Mauritius: 1163 Pretorius St, Hatfield, Pretoria 0083; tel. (12) 3421283; fax (12) 3421286; e-mail mhcpta@mweb.co.za; High Commissioner MOHAMED ISMAEL DOSSA.

Mexico: 570 Ferhsen St, Parkdev Bldg, Ground Floor, Brooklyn Bridge, Pretoria 0181; POB 9077, Pretoria 0001; tel. (12) 4601004; fax (12) 4609743; e-mail embamexza@mweb.co.za; Ambassador LUIS CABRERA CUARON.

Morocco: 799 Schoeman St, cnr Farenden St, Arcadia, Pretoria 0083; POB 12382, Hatfield 0028; tel. (12) 3430230; fax (12) 3430613; e-mail sifmapre@mwebbiz.co.za; Chargé d'affaires HABIB DEFOUAD.

Mozambique: 529 Edmund St, Arcadia, Pretoria 0083; POB 57465, Arcadia 0007; tel. (12) 4010300; fax (12) 3266388; e-mail embamoc.ras@minec.gov.mz; High Commissioner FERNANDO ANDRADE FAZENDA.

Myanmar: 201 Leyds St, Arcadia, Pretoria 0083; POB 12121, Queenswood 0121; tel. (12) 3415207; fax (12) 3413867; e-mail euompta@global.co.za; Chargé d'affaires a.i. WIN AUNG.

Namibia: 197 Blackwood St, Arcadia, Pretoria 0083; POB 29806, Sunnyside 0132; tel. (12) 4819100; fax (12) 3445998; e-mail secretary@namibia.org.za; High Commissioner PHILEMON KAMBALA.

Netherlands: 210 Queen Wilhelmina Ave, New Muckleneuk 0181, Pretoria; tel. (12) 4254500; fax (12) 3439950; e-mail pre@minbuza.nl; internet www.dutchembassy.co.za; Ambassador ROBERT GERARD DE VOS.

New Zealand: Block C, Hatfield Gardens, 1110 Arcadia St, Hatfield, Pretoria 0083; Private Bag X17, Hatfield 0028; tel. (12) 3428656; fax (12) 3428640; e-mail enquiries@nzhc.co.za; internet www.nzhc.co.za; High Commissioner GEOFFREY JOHN RANDAL.

Nigeria: 971 Schoeman St, Arcadia, Pretoria 0083; POB 27332, Sunnyside 0132; tel. (12) 3420805; fax (12) 3421668; High Commissioner Brig.-Gen. (retd) MOHAMMED BUBA MARWA.

Norway: iParioli Bldg, A2, 1166 Park St, Hatfield, Pretoria 0083; POB 11612, Hatfield 0028; tel. (12) 3426100; fax (12) 3426099; e-mail emb.pretoria@mfa.no; internet www.norway.org.za; Ambassador TOR CHRISTIAN HILDAN.

Oman: 42 Nicholson St, Muckleneuk, Pretoria 0081; POB 2650, Brooklyn 0075; tel. (12) 3460808; fax (12) 3461660; e-mail sult-oman@telkom.net; Ambassador KHALID BIN SULAIMAN BIN ABDUL RAHMAN BA'OMAR.

Pakistan: 312 Brooks St, Menlo Park, Pretoria 0181; POB 11803, Hatfield 0028; tel. (12) 3624072; fax (12) 3623967; e-mail pareppretoria@worldonline.co.za; High Commissioner ASHRAF QURESHI.

Panama: Pretoria; Ambassador ROBERTO E. CORDOVEZ CASTILLA.

Paraguay: 189 Strelitzia Rd, Waterkloof Heights, Pretoria 0181; POB 95774, Waterkloof 0145; tel. (12) 3471047; fax (12) 3470403; Chargé d'affaires GUSAVO LOPEZ-BELLO.

Peru: Brooklyn Gardens Bldg, Block A, 1st Floor, 235 Veale St, cnr Middel St, Nieuw Muckleneuk, Pretoria 0181; POB 907, Groenkloof 0027; tel. (12) 3468744; fax (12) 3468886; e-mail embaperu2@telkomsa.net; Ambassador DAÚL MATUTE-MEJÍA.

Philippines: 54 Nicholson St, Muckleneuk, Pretoria 0181; POB 2562, Brooklyn Sq. 0075; tel. (12) 3460451; fax (12) 3460454; e-mail pretoriape@mweb.co.za; internet mzone.mweb.co.za/residents/pretoriape; Ambassador VIRGILIO A. REYES, Jr.

Poland: 14 Amos St, Colbyn, Pretoria 0083; POB 12277, Queenswood 0121; tel. (12) 4302621; fax (12) 4302608; e-mail amb.pol@pixie.co.za; Ambassador MARCIN KUBIAK.

Portugal: 599 Leyds St, Muckleneuk, Pretoria 0002; POB 27102, Sunnyside 0132; tel. (12) 3412340; fax (12) 3413975; e-mail portemb@global.co.za; Ambassador JOÃO NUGENT RAMOS PINTO.

Qatar: 355 Charles St, Waterkloof, Pretoria 0181; Private Bag X13, Brooklyn Sq. 0075; tel. (12) 4521700; fax (12) 3466732; e-mail qatar-emb@lantic.net; Ambassador Dr BASHIR ISSA ASH-SHIRAWI.

Romania: 117 Charles St, Brooklyn, Pretoria 0181; POB 11295, Hatfield 0028; tel. (12) 4606940; fax (12) 4606947; e-mail rombembsa@global.co.za; Chargé d'affaires VALERIU NICOLAE.

Russia: 316 Brooks St, Menlo Park, Pretoria 0081; POB 6743, Pretoria 0001; tel. (12) 3621337; fax (12) 3620116; e-mail ruspospr@mweb.co.za; internet www.russianembassy.org.za; Ambassador ANATOLY A. MAKAROV.

Rwanda: 983 Schoeman St, Arcadia, Pretoria; POB 55224, Arcadia 0007; tel. (12) 3426536; fax (12) 3427106; e-mail ambapretoria@minaffet.gov.rw; Ambassador EUGÉNE MUNYAKAYANZA.

Saudi Arabia: 711 Duncan St, cnr Lunnon St, Hatfield, Pretoria 0083; POB 13930, Hatfield 0028; tel. (12) 3624230; fax (12) 3624239; Ambassador MOHAMMED MAHMOUD BIN ALI AL-ALI.

Senegal: Charles Manor, 57 Charles St, Baileys Muckleneuk, Pretoria 0181; POB 2948, Brooklyn Sq. 0075; tel. (12) 4605263; fax (12) 3465550; e-mail ambassenepta@telkomsa.za; Chargé d'affaires a.i. MOUSTAPHA DIENG.

Serbia: 163 Marais St, Brooklyn, Pretoria; POB 13026, Hatfield 0028; tel. (12) 4605626; fax (12) 4606003; e-mail info@scgembassy.org.za; internet www.scgembassy.org.za; Chargé d'affaires a.i. JASMINA SDAKOVIĆ-TATARAĆ.

Singapore: 980 Schoeman St, Arcadia, Pretoria 0083; POB 11809, Hatfield 0028; tel. (12) 4306035; fax (12) 3424425; e-mail sporehc@mweb.co.za; High Commissioner BERNARD WILLIAM BAKER.

Slovakia: 930 Arcadia St, Pretoria 0083; POB 12736, Hatfield 0028; tel. (12) 3422051; fax (12) 3423688; e-mail slovakemb@telkomsa.net; internet www.mfa.sk/zu; Ambassador LADISLAV STRAKA.

Spain: 337 Brooklyn Rd, Menlo Park, Pretoria 0181; POB 1633, Pretoria 0001; tel. (12) 4600123; fax (12) 4602290; e-mail emb.pretoria@mae.es; Ambassador PABLO BENAVIDES ORGAZ.

Sri Lanka: 410 Alexander St, Brooklyn, Pretoria 0181; tel. (12) 4607690; fax (12) 4607702; e-mail srilanka@global.co.za; internet www.srilanka.co.za; High Commissioner A. RAJAKARUNA.

Sudan: 1203 Pretorius St, Hatfield, Pretoria 0083; POB 25513, Monument Park 0105; tel. (12) 3424538; fax (12) 3424539; internet www.sudani.co.za; Ambassador KUOL ALOR.

Suriname: Suite No. 4, Groenkloof Forum Office Park, 57 George Storrar Drive, Groenkloof, 0181 Pretoria; POB 149, Pretoria; tel. (12) 3467627; fax (12) 3460802; e-mail embsur@lantic.net; Ambassador EDWARD RUDOLF BRAAFHEID.

Swaziland: 715 Government Ave, Arcadia, Pretoria 0007; POB 14294, Hatfield 0028; tel. (12) 3441910; fax (12) 3430455; High Commissioner PHILLIP NHLANHLA MUNTU MSWANE.

Sweden: iParioli Bldg, 1166 Park St, Hatfield 0083; POB 13477, Hatfield 0028; tel. (12) 4266400; fax (12) 4266464; e-mail sweden@iafrica.com; internet www.swedenabroad.com/pretoria; Ambassador PETER TEJLER.

Switzerland: 225 Veale St, Parc Nouveau, New Muckleneuk, Pretoria 0181; POB 2508, Brooklyn Sq. 0075; tel. (12) 4520660; fax (12) 3466605; e-mail pre.vertretung@eda.admin.ch; internet www.eda.admin.ch/pretoria; Ambassador RUDOLF BAERFUSS.

Syria: 963 Schoeman St, Arcadia, Pretoria 0083; POB 12830, Hatfield 0028; tel. (12) 3424701; fax (12) 3424702; e-mail syriaemb@telkomsa.net; Chargé d'affaires a.i. BASSAM DARWISH.

Tanzania: 822 George Ave, Arcadia, Pretoria 0007; POB 56572, Arcadia 0007; tel. (12) 3424393; fax (12) 4304383; e-mail thc@tanzania.org.za; internet www.tanzania.org.za; Chargé d'affaires PETER KABISSA.

Thailand: 428 cnr Hill and Pretorius Sts, Arcadia, Pretoria 0028; POB 12080, Hatfield 0083; tel. (12) 3424600; fax (12) 3424805; e-mail info@thaiembassy.co.za; internet www.thaiembassy.co.za; Chargé d'affaires a.i. WANCHAI JIAMCHOT-PATANAKUL.

Trinidad and Tobago: 258 Lawley St, Waterkloof, 0181 Pretoria; POB 95872, Waterkloof, Pretoria 0145; tel. (12) 4609688; fax (12) 3467302; e-mail tthepretoria@telkomsa.net; High Commissioner Dr WINSTON MAHABIR.

Tunisia: 850 Church St, Arcadia, Pretoria 0083; POB 56535, Arcadia 0007; tel. (12) 3426223; fax (12) 3426284; Ambassador Prof. Dr AHMED MAHJOUB.

Turkey: 1067 Church St, Hatfield, Pretoria 0083; POB 56014, Arcadia 0007; tel. (12) 3426055; fax (12) 3426052; e-mail pretbe@global.co.za; internet www.turkishembassy.co.za; Ambassador CEN ALTAN.

Uganda: 882 Church St, Pretoria 0083; POB 12442, Hatfield 0083; tel. (12) 3426031; fax (12) 3426206; e-mail ugacomer@mweb.co.za; High Commissioner KWERONDA RUHEMBA.

Ukraine: 398 Marais St, Brooklyn, Pretoria 0181; POB 36463, Menlo Park 0102; tel. (12) 4601943; fax (12) 4601944; e-mail emb_za@mfa.gov.ua; Ambassador VALERY HREBENIUK.

United Arab Emirates: 992 Arcadia St, Arcadia, Pretoria 0083; POB 57090, Arcadia 0007; tel. (12) 3427736; fax (12) 3427738; e-mail uae@mweb.co.za; Ambassador ISMAEL OBAID YUSUF AL-ALI.

United Kingdom: 255 Hill St, Arcadia, Pretoria 0002; tel. (12) 4217500; fax (12) 4217555; e-mail media.pretoria@fco.gov.uk; internet www.britain.org.za; High Commissioner Dr NICOLA BREWER.

USA: 877 Pretorius St, Arcadia, Pretoria 0083; POB 9536, Pretoria 0001; tel. (12) 4314000; fax (12) 3422299; e-mail embassypretoria@state.gov; internet southafrica.usembassy.gov; Chargé d'affaires a.i. HELEN LA LIME.

Uruguay: 301 MIB House, 3rd Floor, Hatfield Sq., 1119 Burnett St, Hatfield, Pretoria 0083; POB 3247, Pretoria 0001; tel. (12) 3626521; fax (12) 3626523; Ambassador GUILLERMO JOSÉ POMI BARIOLA.

Venezuela: Hatfield Gables South Bldg, 1st Floor, Suite 4, 474 Hilda St, Pretoria 0083; POB 11821, Hatfield 0028; tel. (12) 3626593; fax (12) 3626591; e-mail embasudaf@icon.co.za; Ambassador ANTONIO MONTILLA-SALDIVIA.

Viet Nam: 87 Brooks St, Brooklyn, Pretoria 0181; POB 13692, Hatfield 0028; tel. (12) 3628119; fax (12) 3628115; e-mail embassy@vietnam.co.za; Ambassador MANH HUNG NGUYEN.

Yemen: 329 Main St, Waterkloof 0181; POB 13343, Hatfield 0028; tel. (12) 4250760; fax (12) 4250762; e-mail info@yemenembassy.org.za; internet www.yemenembassy.org.za; Chargé d'affaires Dr ALI ABDUL-QAWI AL-GHAFFARI.

Zambia: 570 Ziervogel St, Arcadia, Pretoria 0083; POB 12234, Hatfield 0028; tel. (12) 3261854; fax (12) 3262140; High Commissioner LESLIE SAINOT MBULA.

Zimbabwe: Zimbabwe House, 798 Merton St, Arcadia, Pretoria 0083; POB 55140, Arcadia 0007; tel. (12) 3425125; fax (12) 3425126; e-mail zimpret@lantic.net; Ambassador SIMON KHAYA MOYO.

Judicial System

The common law of the Republic of South Africa is the Roman-Dutch law, the uncodified law of Holland as it was at the time of the secession of the Cape of Good Hope in 1806. The law of England is not recognized as authoritative, although the principles of English law have been introduced in relation to civil and criminal procedure, evidence and mercantile matters.

The Constitutional Court, situated in Johannesburg, consists of a Chief Justice, a Deputy Chief Justice and nine other justices. Its task is to ensure that the executive, legislative and judicial organs of government adhere to the provisions of the Constitution. It has the power to reverse legislation that has been adopted by Parliament. The Supreme Court of Appeal, situated in Bloemfontein, comprises a President, a Deputy President and a number of judges of appeal, and is the highest court in all but constitutional matters. There are also High Courts and Magistrates' Courts. A National Director of Public Prosecutions is the head of the prosecuting authority and is appointed by the President of the Republic. A Judicial Service Commission makes recommendations regarding the appointment of judges and advises central and provincial government on all matters relating to the judiciary.

Constitutional Court: cnr Queen and Sam Hancock/Hospital Sts, Constitution Hill, Braamfontein 2017; tel. (11) 3597400; fax (11) 4036524; e-mail cases@concourt.org.za; internet www.constitutionalcourt.org.za; f. 1995; Chief Justice PIUS N. LANGA.

Supreme Court of Appeal: cnr Elizabeth and President Brand Sts, Bloemfontein 9301; POB 258, Bloemfontein 9300; tel. (51) 4304128; fax (51) 4478098; e-mail astreet@justice.gov.za; internet www.supremecourtofappeal.gov.za; f. 1910; Pres. LEX MPATI.

Religion

Some 80% of the population profess the Christian faith. Other religions that are represented are Hinduism, Islam, Judaism and traditional African religions.

CHRISTIANITY

At mid-2000 there were an estimated 12.4m. Protestants and 18.7m. adherents of other forms of Christianity.

South African Council of Churches: POB 62098, Marshalltown 2107; tel. (11) 2417800; fax (11) 4921448; internet www.sacc.org.za; f. 1968; 26 mem. churches; Pres. Prof. RUSSEL BOTMAN; Gen. Sec. EDDIE MAKUE.

The Anglican Communion

Most Anglicans in South Africa are adherents of the Anglican Church of Southern Africa (formerly the Church of the Province of Southern Africa), comprising 25 dioceses (including Angola, Lesotho, Namibia, St Helena, Swaziland and two dioceses in Mozambique). The Church had an estimated 4.5m. communicant members at mid-2006.

Archbishop of Cape Town and Metropolitan of the Province of Southern Africa: Most Rev. THABO CECIL MAKGOBA, 20 Bishopscourt Dr., Bishopscourt, Claremont, Cape Town 7700; tel. (21) 7612531; fax (21) 7614193; e-mail archbish@bishopscourt-cpsa.org.za; internet www.anglicanchurchsa.org.

The Dutch Reformed Church (Nederduitse Gereformeerde Kerk–NGK)

In 2005/06, including confirmed and baptized members, the Dutch Reformed Churches in South Africa consisted of: the Dutch Reformed Church, with 1,155,001 (mainly white) members; the Uniting Reformed Church, with 1,039,606 (mainly Coloured and black) members; the Reformed Church in Africa, with 1,708 Indian members; and the Dutch Reformed Church in Africa, with an estimated 150,000 (mainly black) members. All congregations were desegregated in 1986.

General Synod: POB 13528, Hatfield, Pretoria 0028; tel. (12) 3420092; fax (12) 3420380; e-mail algemenesinode@ngkerk.org.za; internet www.ngkerk.org.za; Moderator Prof. PIET STRAUSS; Gen. Sec. Dr KOBUS GERBER.

The Lutheran Churches

Lutheran Communion in Southern Africa (LUCSA): POB 7170, Bonaero Park 1622; tel. (11) 9731873; fax (11) 3951615; e-mail info@lucsa.org; internet www.lucsa.org; f. 1991; co-ordinating org. for the Lutheran churches in southern Africa, incl. Angola, Botswana, Malawi, Mozambique, Namibia, South Africa, Swaziland, Zambia and Zimbabwe; 1,618,720 mems (1999); Pres. Bishop C. K. MOENGA; Exec. Dir Bishop Dr A. MOYO.

Evangelical Lutheran Church in Southern Africa (ELCSA): POB 7231, 1622 Bonaero Park; tel. (11) 9731853; fax (11) 3951888; e-mail elcsaadmin@mweb.co.za; f. 1975 by merger of four non-white churches; Presiding Bishop JOE RAMASHAPA; 580,377 mems (2009).

Evangelical Lutheran Church in Southern Africa (Cape Church): POB 3466, 7602 Matieland; tel. (21) 8869747; fax (21) 8869748; e-mail rohwernj@adept.co.za; Pres. Bishop NILS ROHWER; 4,083 mems (2009).

Evangelical Lutheran Church in Southern Africa (N-T): Church Council, 24 Geldenhuys Rd, Bonaero Park, Johannesburg; POB 7095, Bonaero Park 1622; tel. (11) 9731851; fax (11) 3951862; e-mail bishop@elcsant.org.za; internet www.elcsant.org.za; f. 1981; Pres. Bishop DIETER R. LILJE; 9,800 mems (2006).

Moravian Church in Southern Africa: POB 24111, Lansdowne 7779; tel. (21) 7614030; fax (21) 7614046; e-mail mcsa@iafrica.com; f. 1737; Pres. LENNOX MCBUSI; 50,000 mems (2009).

The Roman Catholic Church

South Africa comprises four archdioceses, 21 dioceses and one Apostolic Vicariate. At 31 December 2006 there were an estimated 3,209,852 adherents in the country, representing about 6.3% of the total population.

Southern African Catholic Bishops' Conference (SACBC)

Khanya House, 140 Visagie St, Pretoria 0001; POB 941, Pretoria 0001; tel. (12) 3236458; fax (12) 3266218; e-mail sacbclib@wn.apc.org; internet www.sacbc.org.za.

f. 1947; mems representing South Africa, Botswana and Swaziland; Pres. Archbishop BUTI TLHAGALE (Bishop of Johannesburg); Sec.-Gen. Fr RICHARD MENATSI.

Archbishop of Bloemfontein: JABULANI ADATUS NXUMALO, Archbishop's House, 7A Whites Rd, Bloemfontein 9301; POB 362, Bloemfontein 9300; tel. (51) 4481658; fax (51) 4472420; e-mail bfnarch@mweb.co.za.

Archbishop of Cape Town: Most Rev. LAWRENCE HENRY, Cathedral Place, 12 Bouquet St, Cape Town 8001; POB 2910, Cape Town 8000; tel. (21) 4622417; fax (21) 4619330; e-mail info@catholic-ct.org.za; internet www.catholic-ct.co.za.

Archbishop of Durban: Cardinal WILFRID NAPIER, Archbishop's House, 154 Gordon Rd, Durban 4001; POB 47489, Greyville 4023; tel. (31) 3031417; fax (31) 3121848; e-mail vg@catholic-dbn.org.za.

Archbishop of Pretoria: Most Rev. GEORGE FRANCIS DANIEL, Jolivet House, 140 Visagie St, Pretoria 0002; POB 8149, Pretoria 0001; tel. (12) 3265311; fax (12) 3253994; e-mail ptadiocese@absamail.co.za.

Other Christian Churches

In addition to the following Churches, there are a large number of Pentecostalist groups, and more than 4,000 independent African Churches.

African Gospel Church: POB 32312, 4060 Mobeni; tel. (31) 9074377; Moderator Rev. F. D. MKHIZE; Gen. Sec. O. MTOLO; 100,000 mems.

Afrikaanse Protestantse Kerk (Afrikaans Protestant Church): POB 11488, Hatfield 0028; tel. (12) 3621390; fax (12) 3622023; internet www.apkerk.co.za; f. 1987 by fmr mems of the Dutch Reformed Church (Nederduitse Gereformeerde Kerk) in protest at the desegregation of church congregations; c. 33,623 mems.

Apostolic Faith Mission of South Africa: Bldg no. 14, Central Office Park, 257 Jean Ave, POB 9450, Centurion; tel. (12) 6440490; fax (12) 6440732; e-mail admin@afm-ags.org; internet www.afm-ags.org; f. 1908; Pres. Dr ISAK BURGER; Gen. Sec. Pastor M. G. MAHLABO; 136,000 mems.

Assemblies of God: POB 51065, Musgrave 4062; tel. (21) 9144386; fax (21) 9144387; e-mail brian@assemblies.org.za; internet www.assemblies.org.za; f. 1915; Chair. Rev. ISAAC HLETA; Gen. Sec. Rev. C. P. WATT; 300,000 mems.

Baptist Union of Southern Africa: Private Bag X45, Wilropark 1731; tel. (11) 7685980; fax (11) 7685983; e-mail info@baptistunion.org.za; internet www.baptistunion.org.za; f. 1877; Pres. Rev. NIGEL D'AUBREY; Gen. Sec. Rev. ANGELO SCHEEPERS; 51,000 mems (2007).

Black Dutch Reformed Church: POB 137, Bergvlei 2012; Leader Rev. SAM BUTI; c. 1m. mems.

Church of England in South Africa: POB 2180, Clareinch 7740; tel. (21) 6717070; fax (21) 6712553; e-mail cameronb@cesa.org.za; internet www.cesa.org.za; Bishop Rt Rev. FRANK RETIEF (presiding), Bishop Rt Rev. MARTIN MORRISON, Bishop Rt Rev. Dr WARWICK COLE-EDWARDES, Bishop Rt Rev. DESMOND INGLESBY; 207 churches.

Evangelical Presbyterian Church in South Africa: POB 31961, Braamfontein 2017; tel. (11) 3391044; fax (11) 4034144; e-mail secretary@epcsa.org.za; internet www.epcsa.org.za; f. 1875; Gen. Sec. Rev. J. S. NGOBE; Treas. Rev. H. D. MASANGU; 60,000 mems.

The Methodist Church of Southern Africa: Methodist Connexional Office, POB 50216, Musgrave 4062; tel. (31) 2024214; fax (31) 2017674; e-mail general@mco.org.za; internet www.mco.org.za; f. 1883; Pres. Bishop I. M. ABRAHAMS; Sec. Rev. VUYANI G. NYOBOLE; 800,000 mems.

Nederduitsch Hervormde Kerk van Afrika: POB 2368, Pretoria 0001; tel. (12) 3228885; fax (12) 3203279; e-mail fanie@nhk.co.za; internet www.nhk.co.za; Gen. Sec. Dr S. P. PRETORIUS; 193,561 mems.

Nederduitse Gereformeerde Kerk in Afrika: Portland Pl., 37 Jorissen St, 2017 Johannesburg; tel. (11) 4031027; 6 synods (incl. 1 in Swaziland); Moderator Rev. S. P. E. BUTI; Gen. Sec. W. RAATH; 350,370 mems.

Presbyterian Church of Africa: POB 72, Nyanga, Cape Town 7755; tel. (21) 3850687; e-mail faleni@absamail.co.za; internet www.presbyterianchurchofafrica.co.za; f. 1898; 8 presbyteries (incl. 1 in Malawi and 1 in Zimbabwe); Moderator Rt Rev. ERIC NKOSIVUMILE MATOMELA; 1,231,000 mems.

Reformed Church in South Africa (Die Gereformeerde Kerke): POB 20004, Noordbrug 2522, Potchefstroom; tel. (18) 2973986; fax (18) 2931042; e-mail direkteur@gksa.org.za; internet www.gksa.org.za; f. 1859; Prin. Officer Dr C. J. SMIT; 158,973 mems.

Seventh-day Adventist Church: POB 468, Bloemfontein 9300; tel. (51) 4478271; fax (41) 4488059; e-mail sau.president@adventist.org.za; internet www.adventist.org.za; Pres. Pastor F. LOUW; Sec. Pastor T. KUNENE; 150,000 mems.

United Congregational Church of Southern Africa: POB 96014, Brixton; tel. and fax (21) 6839665; e-mail dave@uccsa.co.za; internet www.uccsa.org.za; f. 1799; Pres. Rev. IAN BOOTH; Gen. Sec. Rev. DES VAN DER WATER; 400,000 mems in 350 churches.

Uniting Presbyterian Church in Southern Africa: POB 96188, Brixton 2019; tel. (11) 3392471; fax (11) 3396938; e-mail gensec@presbyterian.org.za; internet www.upcsa.org.za; f. 1999; Moderator Rt Rev. W. D. POOL; Gen. Sec. Rev. V. S. VELLEM; Clerk of the Assembly T. W. COULTER; 130,000 mems.

Zion Christian Church: Zion City, Moria; f. 1910; South Africa's largest black religious group; Leader Bishop BARNABAS LEKGANYANE; c. 4m. mems.

ISLAM

In 2003 there were some 455 Mosques and 408 Muslim colleges in South Africa.

United Ulama Council of South Africa (UUCSA): POB 4118, Cape Town 8000; tel. (21) 6965150; fax (21) 6968502; f. 1994; Pres. SHEIKH EBRAHIM GABRIELS; Sec.-Gen. MOULANA YUSUF PATEL.

JUDAISM

According to the South African Jewish Board of Deputies, in 2006 there were about 80,000 Jews in South Africa, and about 200 organized Jewish communities.

African Jewish Congress: POB 51663, Raedene 2124; tel. (82) 4402621; fax (86) 6146724; e-mail moshe@beyachad.co.za; internet www.africanjewishcongress.com; f. 1994; co-ordinating body representing Jewish communities in sub-Saharan Africa; Pres. MERVYN SMITH; Spiritual Leader Rabbi MOSHE SILBERHAFT.

South African Jewish Board of Deputies: POB 87557, Houghton 2041; tel. (11) 6452523; fax (11) 6452559; e-mail sajbod@iafrica.com; internet www.jewish.org.za; f. 1903; the representative institution of

SOUTH AFRICA

South African Jewry; Pres. RUSSELL GADDIN; Chair. MICHAEL BAGRAIM; Nat. Dir WENDY KAHN.

BAHÁ'Í FAITH

National Spiritual Assembly: 209 Bellairs Dr., North Riding 2169, POB 932, Banbury Cross 2164; tel. (11) 4620100; fax (11) 4620129; e-mail nsa.sec@bahai.org.za; internet www.bahai.org.za; f. 1956; Gen. Sec. SHOHREH RAWHANI; 11,000 mems resident in 320 localities.

The Press

Government Communication and Information System (GCIS): Midtown Bldg, cnr Vermeulen and Prinsloo Sts, Pretoria; Private Bag X745, Pretoria 0001; tel. (12) 3142911; fax (12) 3252030; e-mail govcom@gcis.gov.za; internet www.gcis.gov.za; govt agency; CEO THEMBA MASEKO.

South African Press Ombudsman: POB 47221, Parklands 2121, Johannesburg; tel. (11) 7884837; fax (11) 7884990; e-mail pressombudsman@ombudsman.org.za; internet www.ombudsman.org.za; Ombudsman JOE THLOLOE.

DAILIES

Eastern Cape

Die Burger (Oos-Kaap): 52 Cawood St, POB 525, Port Elizabeth 6001; tel. (41) 5036111; fax (41) 5036138; e-mail kontak@dieburger.com; internet www.dieburger.com; f. 1937; morning; Afrikaans; Editor LEON VAN DER VYVER; circ. 23,849.

Daily Dispatch: 35 Caxton St, POB 131, East London 5200; tel. (43) 7022000; fax (43) 7022968; e-mail phyliciao@dispatch.co.za; internet www.dispatch.co.za; f. 1872; publ. by Dispatch Media (Pty) Ltd; afternoon; also publ. *Weekend Dispatch* (Sat.); English; Editor PHYLICIA OPPELT; circ. 33,338 (Mon.–Fri.), 27,927 (Sat.).

The Herald: Newspaper House, 19 Baakens St; POB 1117, Port Elizabeth 6000; tel. (41) 5047911; fax (41) 5853947; e-mail heraldletters@avusa.co.za; internet www.theherald.co.za; f. 1845; fmrly *Eastern Province Herald*; publ. by Johnnic Publishing Ltd; morning; English; Editor RIC WILSON; circ. 29,719 (Mon.–Fri.), 25,000 (Sat.).

Free State

Die Volksblad: 79 Voortrekker St, POB 267, Bloemfontein 9300; tel. (51) 4047600; fax (51) 4306949; e-mail nuus@volksblad.com; internet www.volksblad.com; f. 1904; publ. by Media 24; morning; Afrikaans; Editor JONATHAN CROWTHER; circ. 29,018 (Mon.–Fri.), 23,000 (Sat.).

Gauteng

Beeld: Media Park, Kingsway 69, Auckland Park, Johannesburg; POB 333, Auckland Park 2006; tel. (11) 7139000; fax (11) 7139960; e-mail nuus@beeld.com; internet www.beeld.com; f. 1974; publ. by Media 24; morning; weekly: *Kampus-Beeld*, student news and information, and *JIP* youth supplement; Afrikaans; Editor-in-Chief PEET KRUGER; Editor TIM DU PLESSIS; circ. 105,618 (Mon.–Fri.), 88,402 (Sat.).

Business Day: POB 1745, Saxonwold 2132; tel. (11) 2803000; fax (11) 2805505; internet www.bday.co.za; f. 1985; publ. by BDFM Publrs (Pty) Ltd; afternoon; English; financial; incl. *Wanted* arts and leisure magazine; Editor JIM JONES; circ. 40,451 (Mon.–Fri.).

The Citizen: POB 43069, Industria 2042; tel. (11) 2486000; fax (11) 2486213; e-mail news@citizen.co.za; internet www.citizen.co.za; f. 1976; publ. by Caxton Publrs & Printers Ltd; morning; English; Editor M. WILLIAMS; circ. 76,183 (Mon.–Fri.), 57,935 (Sat.).

The Pretoria News: 216 Vermeulen St, Pretoria 0002; POB 439, Pretoria 0001; tel. (12) 3002000; fax (12) 3257300; e-mail pta.newsdesk@inl.co.za; internet www.ptanews.co.za; f. 1898; publ. by Independent Newspapers Gauteng Ltd; afternoon; English; Editor ZINGISA MKHUMA; circ. 28,690 (Mon.–Fri.), 17,406 (Sat.).

Sowetan: 61 Commando Rd, Industria West, Johannesburg 2000; POB 6663, Johannesburg 2000; tel. (11) 4714000; fax (11) 4748834; e-mail editor@sowetan.co.za; internet www.sowetan.co.za; f. 1981; publ. by New Africa Publs (NAP) Ltd; morning; English; Editor THABO LESHILO; circ. 4,122,825 (Mon.–Fri.).

The Star: 47 Sauer St, POB 1014, Johannesburg 2000; tel. (11) 6339111; fax (11) 8343918; e-mail starnews@star.co.za; internet www.star.co.za; f. 1887; publ. by Independent Newspapers Gauteng Ltd; morning; English; also publ. *The Saturday Star*; Editor MOEGSIEN WILLIAMS; circ. 166,461 (Mon.–Fri.), 137, 385 (Sat.).

The Daily Sun: POB 121, Auckland Park 2006; tel. (11) 8776000; fax (11) 8776020; e-mail news@dailysun.co.za; internet www.dailysun.co.za; Editor THEMBA KHUMALO.

KwaZulu/Natal

The Daily News: 18 Osborne St, Greyville 4001; POB 47549, Greyville 4023; tel. (31) 3082106; fax (31) 3082185; internet www.iol.co.za; f. 1878; Mon.–Fri., afternoon; English; Editor ALAN DUNN; circ. 50,000.

The Mercury: 18 Osborne St, Greyville 4001; POB 47397, Greyville 4023; tel. (31) 3082472; fax (31) 3082662; e-mail mercnews@inl.co.za; internet themercury.co.za; f. 1852; publ. by Independent Newspapers KZN; morning; English; Editor DAVID CANNING; circ. 39,343 (Mon.–Fri.).

Witness: 45 Willowton Rd, POB 362, Pietermaritzburg 3200; tel. (33) 3551111; fax (33) 3551122; e-mail johnc@witness.co.za; internet www.witness.co.za; f. 1846; publ. by Natal Witness Printing and Publishing Co Ltd; morning; English; also publ. *Weekend Witness*; Editor J. CONYNGHAM; circ. 23,700 (Mon.–Fri.), 29,000 (Sat.).

Northern Cape

Diamond Fields Advertiser: POB 610, cnr Bean and Villiers Sts, Kimberley 8300; tel. (53) 8326261; fax (53) 8328902; e-mail pbe@independent.co.za; internet www.iol.co.za; publ. by Independent Newspapers Gauteng Ltd; morning; English; Editor KEVIN RITCHIE; circ. 8,948 (Mon.–Fri.).

North-West

Rustenburg Herald: 13 Coetzer St, POB 2043, Rustenburg 0300; tel. (14) 5928329; fax (14) 5921869; e-mail mailbag@rustenburgherald.co.za; internet www.mafikengmail.co.za/herald.htm; f. 1924; English and Afrikaans; Man. Editor C. THERON; circ. 20,368.

Western Cape

Die Burger: 40 Heerengracht, POB 692, Cape Town 8000; tel. (21) 4062222; fax (21) 4062913; e-mail kontak@dieburger.com; internet www.dieburger.com; f. 1915; publ. by Media 24; morning; Afrikaans; Editor HENRY JEFFREYS; circ. 104,102 (Mon.–Fri.), 117,092 (Sat.).

Cape Argus: 122 St George's St, POB 56, Cape Town 8000; tel. (21) 4884911; fax (21) 4884075; e-mail argusnews@ctn.independent.co.za; internet www.capeargus.co.za; f. 1857; publ. by Independent Newspapers Cape Ltd; afternoon; English; also publ. *Weekend Argus*; Editor CHRIS WHITFIELD; circ. 73,230 (Mon.–Fri.), 103,953 (Sat. and Sun.).

Cape Times: Newspaper House, 122 St George's Mall, Cape Town 8001; POB 11, Cape Town 8000; tel. (21) 4884776; fax (21) 4884744; e-mail alide.dasnois@inl.co.za; internet www.capetimes.co.za; f. 1876; publ. by Independent Newspapers Cape Ltd; morning; English; Dep. Editor ALIDE DASNOIS; circ. 49,526 (Mon.–Fri.).

WEEKLIES AND FORTNIGHTLIES

Eastern Cape

Weekend Post: Private Bag X6071, Port Elizabeth 6000; tel. (41) 5047251; fax (41) 5854966; e-mail weekend@johnnicec.co.za; internet www.weekendpost.co.za; publ. by Johnnic Publishing Co Ltd; English; Editor CHARMAIN NAIDOO; circ. 33,372 (Sat.).

Free State

Vista: POB 1027, Welkom 9460; tel. (57) 3571304; fax (57) 3532427; e-mail avaneck@volksblad.com; internet www.media24.com/eng/newspapers/vista.html; f. 1971; weekly; English and Afrikaans; Editor MARTI WILLN; circ. 38,000 (2005).

Gauteng

City Press: POB 3413, Johannesburg 2000; tel. (11) 7139002; fax (11) 7139977; e-mail news@citypress.co.za; internet www.citypress.co.za; f. 1983; publ. by RCP Media Bpk; weekly; English; Editor-in-Chief KHATHU MAMAILA; circ. 173,922 (Sun.).

Engineering News/Mining Weekly: POB 75316, Garden View 2047; tel. and fax (11) 6229350; e-mail newsdesk@engineeringnews.co.za; internet www.miningweekly.com; f. 1981; publ. by Creamer Media; weekly; Editor TERENCE CREAMER; circ. 20,000.

Financial Mail: Johncom Bldg, 4 Biermann Ave, Rosebank 2196; POB 1744, Saxenwold 2132; tel. (11) 2803016; fax (11) 2805800; e-mail fmmail@fm.co.za; internet www.financialmail.co.za; weekly; English; Editor BARNEY MTHOMBOTHI; circ. 33,000.

Mail and Guardian: POB 91667, Auckland Park 2006; tel. (11) 2507300; fax (11) 2507303; e-mail newsdesk@mg.co.za; internet www.mg.co.za; publ. by M&G Media (Pty) Ltd; weekly; English; CEO GOVIN REDDY; Editor FERIAL HAFFAJEE; circ. 40,162 (Fri.).

Noordwes Gazette: POB 515, Potchefstroom 2520; tel. (18) 2930750; e-mail potchherald@media24.com; weekly; English and Afrikaans; Editor H. STANDER; circ. 35,000.

SOUTH AFRICA

Northern Review: 16 Grobler St, POB 45, Pietersburg 0700; tel. (152) 2959167; fax (152) 2915148; weekly; English and Afrikaans; Editor R. S. DE JAGER; circ. 10,300.

Potchefstroom and Ventersdorp Herald: POB 515, Potchefstroom 2520; tel. (18) 2930750; fax (18) 2930759; e-mail potchherald@media24.com; internet www.potchefstroomherald.co.za; f. 1908; Friday; English and Afrikaans; Editor H. STANDER; Man. Dir RASSIE VAN ZYL; circ. 8,000.

Rapport: POB 333, Auckland Park 2006; tel. (11) 7139002; fax (11) 7139977; e-mail rapport@rapport.co.za; internet www.naspers.co.za/rapport; publ. by RCP Media; weekly; Afrikaans; Sr Gen. Man. and Publr SAREL DU PLESSIS; Editor LIZA ALBRECHT; circ. 322,731 (Sun.).

South African Jewish Report: Suite 175, Postnet X10039, Randburg 2125; tel. (11) 8860162; fax (11) 8864202; e-mail geoffs@icon.co.za; internet www.sajewishreport.co.za; weekly; publ. by SA Jewish Report (Pty) Ltd; Editor GEOFF SIFRIN.

Springs and Brakpan Advertiser: 48, 5th Ave, POB 761, Springs 1560; tel. (11) 8124800; fax (11) 8124823; e-mail springseditorial@caxton.co.za; f. 1916; English and Afrikaans; Editor CATHY GROSVENOR; circ. 13,000.

Sunday Times: POB 1742, Saxonwold 2132; tel. (11) 2805155; fax (11) 2805111; e-mail makhanyam@sundaytimes.co.za; internet www.sundaytimes.co.za; f. 1906; weekly; English; Editor-in-Chief MONDLI MAKHANYA; circ. 505,402 (Sun.).

Vaalweekblad: 27 Ekspa Bldg, D. F. Malan St, POB 351, Vanderbijlpark 1900; tel. (16) 817010; fax (16) 810604; internet www.vaalweekblad.com; weekly; Afrikaans and English; Editor W. J. BUYS; circ. 16,000.

Die Vrye Afrikaan: PO Box 675, Durbanville 7551; tel. (12) 3268646; e-mail redakteur@vryeafrikaan.co.za; internet www.vryeafrikaan.co.za; f. 2004; weekly; Afrikaans; Editor JOHANN ROUSSOUW; circ. 13,000.

KwaZulu/Natal

Farmers' Weekly: 368 Jan Smuts Ave, Craighall, Johannesburg 2196; tel. (11) 8890836; fax (11) 8890862; e-mail farmersweekly@caxton.co.za; internet www.farmersweekly.co.za; f. 1911; weekly; agriculture and horticulture; Editor CHRIS BURGESS; circ. 17,000.

Ilanga: 19 Timeball Blvd, The Point, Durban 4001; POB 2159 Durban 4000; tel. (31) 3374000; fax (31) 3379785; e-mail peterc@ilanganews.co.za; internet www.ilanganews.co.za; f. 1903; publ. by Mandla Matla Publishing Co (Pty) Ltd; 2 a week; also publ. *Ilanga Lange Sonto* (Sun. circ. 87,000); Zulu; Editor SIPHO NGOBESE; circ. 107,000; circ. 100,000 (Mon. and Thur.).

Independent On Saturday: 18 Osborne St, Greyville 4001; POB 47397, Greyville 4023; tel. (31) 3082900; fax (31) 3082185; e-mail satmail@inl.co.za; internet www.nn.independent.co.za; f. 1878; publ. by Independent Newspapers KZN; English; Editor CLYDE BAWDEN; circ. 56,216.

Kwana in the City: POB 35559, Northway 4065; tel. (31) 5641230; fax (31) 5649807; e-mail vrydag@eastcoast.co.za; internet www.kwana.co.za; f. 1995; publ. by Kwana Group; English; free community newspaper with focus on consumer and human rights issues; also publ. *Kwana on Track* (f. 2004, English and Zulu, circ. 50,000) aimed at rail commuters; Publr SHELLEY SEID; Editor Dr HILDA GROBLER; circ. 20,000.

Ladysmith Gazette: POB 10019, Ladysmith 3370; tel. (36) 6376801; fax (36) 6372283; f. 1902; weekly; English, Afrikaans and Zulu; Editor DIANA PROCTER; circ. 7,000.

Post: 18 Osborne St, Greyville, Durban 4000; POB 47397, Greyville 4023; tel. (31) 3082400; fax (31) 3082427; e-mail post@inl.co.za; internet www.thepost.co.za; f. 1955 as *Golden City Post*; publ. by Independent Newspapers KZN; weekly; English; focus on the Indian community; Editor BRIJLALL RAMGUTHEE; circ. 45,500 (Wed.).

Sunday Tribune: 18 Osborne St, POB 47549, Greyville 4023; tel. (31) 3082911; fax (31) 3082662; e-mail tribunenews@inl.co.za; internet www.sundaytribune.co.za; f. 1937; publ. by Independent Newspapers KZN; weekly; English; Editor ALAN DUNN; circ. 109,774 (Sun.).

Umafrika: 35A Intersite Ave, Umgeni Business Park, Durban; tel. (31) 2684500; fax (31) 2684545; e-mail editor@umafrika.co.za; f. 1911; owned by Izimpoondo Communications; Friday; Zulu and English; Editor and Publisher CYRIL MADLALA; circ. 32,000.

Northern Cape

Die Gemsbok: POB 60, Upington 8800; tel. 27017; fax 24055; English and Afrikaans; Editor D. JONES; circ. 8,000.

Western Cape

Drum: Naspers Bldg, 7th Floor, 5 Protea Place, Sandown 2096; POB 653284, Benmore 2010; tel. (11) 3220888; fax (11) 3220891; e-mail pmdluli@media24.com; f. 1951; English and Zulu; Editor ESMARE WEIDEMAN; Publr JOHN RELIHAN; circ. 79,895 (2006).

Eikestadnuus: 44 Alexander St, POB 28, Stellenbosch 7600; tel. (2231) 72840; fax (2231) 99538; internet www.news24.com/Eikestad; weekly; English and Afrikaans; Editor R. GERBER; circ. 7,000.

Fair Lady: POB 785266, Cape Town 2146; tel. (11) 3220858; fax (11) 8836611; e-mail flmag@fairlady.com; internet www.fairlady.com; fortnightly; English; Editor SUZY BROKENSHA; circ. 103,642.

Huisgenoot: 40 Heerengracht, POB 1802, Cape Town 8000; tel. (21) 4062115; fax (21) 4063316; e-mail hgnbrief@huisgenoot.com; internet www.huisgenoot.com; f. 1916; weekly; Afrikaans; Editor ESMARÉ WEIDEMAN; circ. 355,487.

Move! Magazine: Media City, 10th Floor, 1 Heerengracht St, Foreshore, Cape Town 8001; tel. (21) 4461232; fax (21) 4461206; e-mail move@media24.com; f. 2005; weekly; English; Editor SBU MPUNGOSE.

The Southern Cross: POB 2372, Cape Town 8000; tel. (21) 4655007; fax (21) 4653850; e-mail scross@global.co.za; internet www.thesoutherncross.co.za; f. 1920; publ. by Catholic Newspapers and Publishing Co Ltd; weekly; English; Roman Catholic interest; Editor GÜNTHER SIMMERMACHER; circ. 11,000 (Wed.).

tvplus: Media City, 10th Floor, 1 Heerengracht St, Cape Town 8001; POB 7197, Roggebaai 8012; tel. (21) 4461222; fax (21) 4461206; e-mail tvplus@media24.com; internet www.tvplus.co.za; f. 2000; weekly; English and Afrikaans; Editor WICUS PRETORIUS.

Tyger-Burger: 40 Heerengracht, POB 2271, Cape Town 8000; tel. (21) 4062121; fax (21) 4062913; weekly; Afrikaans and English; Editor ABIE VON ZYL.

Weekend Argus: 122 St George's Mall, POB 56, Cape Town 8000; tel. (21) 4884911; fax (21) 4884762; internet www.iol.co.za; f. 1857; Sat. and Sun.; English; Editor CHRIS WHITFIELD; circ. 108,294.

You Magazine: Naspers Bldg, 7th Floor, 40 Heerengracht St, Cape Town 8001; POB 7167, Roggebaai 8012; tel. (21) 4062166; fax (21) 4062937; e-mail you@you.co.za; internet www.you.co.za; f. 1987; weekly; English; Editor ESMARÉ WEIDEMAN; circ. 222,845 (2004).

MONTHLIES

Free State

Wamba: POB 1097, Bloemfontein; publ. in seven vernacular languages; educational; Editor C. P. SENYATSI.

Gauteng

Boxing World: 5A Dover St, Randburg, Gauteng; tel. (11) 8868558; e-mail info@boxingworld.co.za; f. 1976; Editor PETER LEOPENG; circ. 10,000.

Nursing News: POB 1280, Pretoria 0001; tel. (12) 3432315; fax (12) 3440750; f. 1978; English and Afrikaans; magazine of the Dem. Nursing Org; circ. 76,000.

KwaZulu/Natal

Bona: POB 32083, Mobeni 4060; tel. (31) 422041; fax (31) 426068; f. 1956; English, Sotho, Xhosa and Zulu; Editor DAIZER MQHABA; circ. 256,631.

Living and Loving: POB 218, Parklands, Johannesburg 2121; tel. (11) 8890621; fax (11) 8890668; e-mail livingandloving@caxton.co.za; internet www.livingandloving.co.za; publ. by Caxton Magazines; English; parenting magazine; Editor CARLIEN WESSELS; circ. 55,000.

Rooi Rose: POB 412982, Craighall 2024; tel. (11) 8890665; fax (11) 8890975; e-mail rooirose@caxton.co.za; internet www.rooirose.co.za; Afrikaans; women's interest; Editor MARTIE PANSEGROUW; circ. 122,296.

World Airnews: POB 35082, Northway 4065; tel. (31) 5641319; fax (31) 5637115; e-mail tom@airnews.co.za; internet www.airnews.co.za; f. 1973; aviation news; Man. Editor TOM CHALMERS; circ. 12,270 (2008).

Your Family: POB 473016, Parklands 2121; tel. (11) 8890749; fax (11) 8890642; e-mail yourfamily@caxton.co.za; internet www.yourfamily.co.za; f. 1973; English; cooking, crafts, DIY; Editor ANGELA WALLER-PATON; circ. 164,115.

Western Cape

Car: Ramsay, Son & Parker (Pty) Ltd, Digital Publishing, 3 Howard Dr., Pinelands, Cape Town; POB 180, Howard Place 7450; tel. (21) 5303100; fax (21) 5322698; e-mail car@rsp.co.za; internet www.cartoday.com; English; Editor J. BENTLEY; circ. 99,411 (2008).

Femina: 21 St John's St, POB 3647, Cape Town 8000; tel. (21) 4646248; fax (21) 4612501; Editor ROBYNNE KAHN; circ. 68,591.

Reader's Digest (South African Edition): 5 Protea Pl., Protea Park, Sandown, Johannesburg 2146; POB 785266, Sandton 2146; tel. (11) 3220700; fax (11) 8839495; e-mail magazine.sa@readersdigest.com;

internet www.readersdigest.co.za; f. 1948; English; Editor ANTHONY JOHNSON; circ. 62,399.

Sarie: POB 785266, Sandton 2146; tel. and fax (21) 4062366; e-mail mvanbre@sarie.com; internet www.natmags.com; monthly; Afrikaans; women's interest; Editor MICHELLE VAN BREDA; circ. 137,970 (2004).

South African Medical Journal: MASA House, Central House, Private Bag X1, Pinelands 7430; tel. (21) 5306520; fax (21) 5314126; e-mail danjn@telkomsa.net; internet www.samj.org.za; f. 1884; publ. by the South African Medical Asscn; Editor-in-Chief DANIEL J. NCAYIYANA; circ. 20,000.

Die Voorligter: Private Bag, Tyger Valley 7536; tel. (21) 9177000; fax (21) 9141333; e-mail lig@cnw-inter.net; internet www.christene.co.za; f. 1937; journal of the Dutch Reformed Church of South Africa; Editor Dr F. M. GAUM; circ. 50,000.

Wineland Magazine: VinPro, POB 1411, Suider-Paarl 7624; tel. (21) 8634524; fax (21) 8634851; e-mail cas@wineland.co.za; internet www.wineland.co.za; f. 1931; publ. by VinPro wine producers' org.; viticulture and the wine and spirit industry; incorporates *Wynboer* technical guide for wine producers; Editor CASSIE DU PLESSIS; circ. 10,000.

The Wisden Cricketer: POB 16368, Vlaeberg 8018; tel. (21) 4083813; e-mail aevlambi@touchline.co.za; internet www.wisdencricketer.co.za; f. 2005; Publr NIC WIDES; Editor ROB HOUWING.

Woman's Value: POB 1802, Cape Town 8000; tel. (21) 4062629; fax (21) 4062929; e-mail wvdited@womansvalue.com; internet www.women24.com; English; Editor and Publr TERENA LE ROUX; circ. 134,749.

PERIODICALS
Eastern Cape

African Journal of AIDS Research (AJAR): Centre for AIDS Development, Research and Evaluation, Institute of Social and Economic Research, Rhodes University, POB 94, Grahamstown 6140; tel. (46) 6038553; fax (46) 6038769; e-mail ajar@ru.ac.za; internet www.cadre.org.za; f. 2002; quarterly; Man. Editor KEVIN KELLY.

Gauteng

Africa Insight: Africa Institute of South Africa, POB 630, Pretoria 0001; tel. (12) 3049700; fax (12) 3261778; e-mail ngobenis@ai.org.za; internet www.ai.org.za; f. 1960; quarterly; journal of the Africa Institute of South Africa; Editor SOLANI NGOBENI; circ. 1,200.

African Journal of Political Science: 195 Beckett St, Arcadia, Pretoria; POB 13995, The Tramshed 0126; tel. (12) 3430409; fax (12) 3443622; e-mail program@aaps.org.za; 2 a year; articles in English and French; Editor ADEKUNLE AMUWO.

Africanus: Unisa Press, POB 392, UNISA, 0003 Pretoria; tel. (12) 4292953; fax (12) 4293449; e-mail delpoa@unisa.ac.za; 2 a year; journal of the Centre for Development Studies, Unisa; African and Third World developmental issues; Editor LINDA CORNWELL.

Codicillus: Unisa Press, POB 392, UNISA, 0003 Pretoria; tel. (12) 4292953; fax (12) 4293449; e-mail delpoa@unisa.ac.za; 2 a year; journal of the School of Law at the Univ. of South Africa; South African and international law; Editor Prof. H. C. ROODT.

The ScienceScope: POB 395, Pretoria 0001; tel. (12) 8414625; fax (12) 8413789; e-mail edaconceicao@csir.co.za; internet www.csir.co.za; f. 1991 as *Technobrief*; quarterly; publ. by the South African Council for Scientific and Industrial Research; Editor EUNICE DA CONCEIÇÃO; circ. 6,000.

South African Journal of Economics: 4.45 EBW Bldg, University of Pretoria, Pretoria 0002; POB 73354, Lynnwood Ridge 0040; tel. (12) 4203525; fax (12) 3625266; e-mail saje@up.ac.za; internet www.essa.org.za; f. 1933; quarterly; English and Afrikaans; journal of the Economic Soc. of South Africa; publ. by Blackwells; Man. Editor P. A. BLACK.

KwaZulu/Natal

African Journal on Conflict Resolution: ACCORD, Private Bag X018, Umhlanga Rocks 4320; tel. (31) 5023908; fax (31) 5024160; e-mail info@accord.org.za; internet www.accord.org.za/ajcr/intro.htm; f. 1999; annually; conflict transformation in Africa; Chair. Prof. JAKES GERWEL; Man. Editor RICHARD KAMIDZA; Editor JANNIE MALAN.

Indilinga: African Journal of Indigenous Knowledge Systems (IAJIKS): POB 13789, Cascades, Pietermaritzburg 3202; tel. (31) 9077000; fax (31) 9073011; e-mail nmkabela@hotmail.com; internet www.indilinga.org.za; f. 2002; 1–2 a year; issues relating to the transmission of local or traditional knowledge; Editor-in-Chief QUEENETH MKABELA.

South African Journal of Chemistry: School of Chemistry, University of KwaZulu-Natal, Durban 4000; tel. (31) 2601096; fax (31) 2603091; e-mail taford@vodamail.co.za; internet search.sabinet.co.za/sajchem; f. 1921; publ. by the South African Chemical Institute; digital; Co-ordinating Editor TONY FORD.

North-West

Historia: c/o Dept of Historical and Heritage Studies, Faculty of Humanities, Humanities Bldg (Main Campus), University of Pretoria, Pretoria 0002; tel. (12) 4202323; fax (12) 4202656; e-mail moutofa@unisa.ac.za; f. 1956; 2 a year; journal of the Historical Asscn of South Africa; South African and African history; Co-ordinating Editor ALEX MOULTON.

Western Cape

African Finance Journal: African Finance Association, ACIA, University of Stellenbosch Business School, POB 610, Bellville 7535; tel. (21) 9184347; fax (21) 9184262; e-mail afa@acia.sun.ac.za; f. 1999; 2 a year; finance, accounting and economics; Exec. Editor NICHOLAS BIEKPE.

Economic Prospects: Bureau for Economic Research, Economics and Management Sciences Bldg, 7th Floor, Bosman St, Stellenbosch 7600; Private Bag 5050, Stellenbosch 7599; tel. (21) 8872810; fax (21) 8839225; e-mail hhman@sun.ac.za; quarterly; forecast of the South African economy for the coming 18–24 months; Man. Editor P. LAUBSCHER.

Ecquid Novi: c/o South African Journal for Journalism Research, POB 106, Stellenbosch 7599; tel. (21) 8082625; fax (21) 8083488; e-mail novi@sun.ac.za; internet www.sun.ac.za/ecquidnovi; f. 1980; 2 a year; focus on role of the media in southern Africa and Africa; Editor ARNOLD S. DE BEER.

The Motorist: Highbury Monarch Pty, 8th Floor, Metlife Centre, 7 Coen Steytler Ave, Foreshore, 8001 Cape Town; tel. (21) 4160141; fax (21) 4187312; e-mail themotorist@monarchc.co.za; f. 1966; journal of the Automobile Asscn of SA; Editor FIONA ZERBST; circ. 131,584 (2000).

South African Law Journal: Faculty of Law, University of Cape Town, Private Bag Rondebosch 7700; POB 24299, Lansdowne 7779; tel. (21) 7633600; fax (21) 7970121; e-mail salj@law.uct.ac.za; f. 1884; Editor C. H. LEWIS; circ. 1,000.

NEWS AGENCIES

East Cape News (ECN) Pty Ltd: POB 897, Grahamstown 6140; tel. (46) 6361050; e-mail editor@ecn.co.za; internet www.ecn.co.za; f. 1997; fmrly East Cape News Agencies; Dir MIKE LOEWE.

South African Press Association (SAPA): Cotswold House, Greenacres Office Park, cnr Victory and Rustenburg Rds, Victory Park; POB 7766, Johannesburg 2000; tel. (11) 7821600; fax (11) 7821587; e-mail comms@sapa.org.za; internet www.sapa.org.za; f. 1938; Man. WIM J. H. VAN GILS; Editor MARK A. VAN DER VELDEN; 40 mems.

PRESS ASSOCIATIONS

Foreign Correspondents' Association of South Africa: POB 1136, Auckland Park 2006; tel. and fax (11) 4860490; e-mail fca@onwe.co.za; internet www.fcasa.co.za; represents 175 int. journalists; Chair. JOHN CHIAHEMEN; Sec. MARTINA SCHWIKOWSKI.

Newspaper Association of South Africa: Nedbank Gardens, 5th Floor, 33 Bath Ave, Rosebank 2196, Johannesburg; POB 47180, Parklands 2121; tel. (11) 7213200; fax (11) 7213254; e-mail na@printmedia.org.za; internet www.printmedia.org.za; f. 1882; represents 42 national daily and weekly newspapers, and 178 community newspapers; Pres. TREVOR NCUBE.

Print Media SA: 2nd Floor, 7 St David's, St David's Office Park, St David's Place, Parktown 2193; POB 47180, Parklands 2121; tel. (11) 7213200; fax (11) 7213254; e-mail mamosat@printmedia.org.za; internet www.printmedia.org.za; f. 1995 following the restructuring of the Newspaper Press Union of Southern Africa; represents all aspects of the print media (newspapers and magazines); over 700 mems; CEO INGRID LOUW.

Publishers

Acorn Books: POB 4845, Randburg 2125; tel. (11) 8805768; fax (11) 8805768; e-mail acorbook@iafrica.com; f. 1985; Africana, general, natural history; Propr and Publr ELEANOR-MARY CADELL.

Jonathan Ball Publishers: 10–14 Watkins St, Denver Ext. 4, Johannesburg 2094; POB 33977, Jeppestown 2043; tel. (11) 6222900; fax (11) 6018183; e-mail orders@jonathanball.co.za; internet www.jonathanball.co.za; acquired by Via Afrika (Naspers Group) in 1992; fiction, reference, bibles, textbooks, general; imprints incl. AD

SOUTH AFRICA

Donker (literature), Delta (general fiction and non-fiction) and Sunbird; Man. Dir JONATHAN BALL.

Bible Society of South Africa: Bible House, 134 Edward St, POB 5500, Tyger Valley 7536; tel. (21) 9108777; fax (21) 9108799; e-mail biblia@biblesociety.co.za; internet www.biblesociety.co.za; f. 1820; bibles and religious material in 11 official languages; CEO Rev. G. S. KRITZINGER.

Brenthurst Press (Pty) Ltd: Federation Rd, POB 87184, Houghton 2041; tel. (11) 5445400; fax (11) 4861651; e-mail orders@brenthurst.co.za; internet www.brenthurst.org.za; f. 1974; Southern African history; Dir MARCELLE GRAHAM.

Christelike Uitgewersmaatskappy (CUM): POB 1599, Vereeniging 1930; tel. (16) 4407000; fax (16) 4211748; e-mail orders@cabooks.co.za; internet www.cum.co.za; religious fiction and non-fiction.

Clever Books: POB 13816, Hatfield 0028; tel. (12) 3423263; fax (12) 4302376; e-mail info@cleverbooks.co.za; internet www.cleverbooks.co.za; f. 1981; subsidiary of MacMillan Publrs; Gen. Man. ELNA HARMSE.

Fisichem Publishers: 19 Hofmeyer St, Private Bag X3, Matieland 7602; tel. (21) 8870900; fax (21) 8839635; e-mail info@fisichem.co.za; internet fisichem.co.za; f. 1985; owned by FRJ Trust; science, maths and accounting study guides; Man. RETHA JORDAAN.

Flesch Publications: 11 Peninsula Rd, Zeekoevlei, Cape Town 7941; POB 31353, Grassy Park 7888; tel. (21) 7054317; fax (21) 7060766; e-mail sflesch@iafrica.com; f. 1954; biography, cookery, aviation; CEO STEPHEN FLESCH.

Fortress Books: POB 2475, Knysna 6570; tel. (44) 3826805; fax (44) 3826848; e-mail fortress@iafrica.com; internet www.uys.com/fortress; f. 1973; military history, biographies, financial; Man. Dir I. UYS.

Heinemann Publishers (Pty) Ltd: Heinemann House, Grayston Office Park, Bldg 3, 128 Peter Rd, Atholl Ext. 12, Sandton 2196; POB 781940, Sandown, Sandton 2146; tel. (11) 3228600; fax (11) 3228715; e-mail customerliaison@heinemann.co.za; internet www.heinemann.co.za; educational; incl. imprints Lexicon, Isando and Centaur; Man. Dir ORENNA KRUT.

Home Economics Publishers (Huishoudkunde Uitgewers): POB 7091, Stellenbosch 7599; tel. and fax (21) 8864722; e-mail mcv1@sun.ac.za; Man. M. C. VOSLOO.

Juta and Co Ltd: POB 14373, Lansdowne 7780, Cape Town; tel. (11) (21) 7633500; fax (21) 7633560; e-mail cserv@juta.co.za; internet www.juta.co.za; f. 1853; academic, educational, law, electronic; imprints incl. Double Storey (general contemporary), and University of Cape Town Press (scholarly and academic); CEO R. J. WILSON.

LAPA Publishers (Lees Afrikaans Praat Afrikaans): 380 Bosman St, POB 123, Pretoria 0001; tel. (12) 4010700; fax (12) 3244460; f. 1996 as the publishing arm of the Afrikaans Language and Culture Asscn; present name adopted in 2000; Afrikaans; general fiction and non-fiction; CEO WIM DE WET.

Learning Matters Africa: 341 West St, Durban 4001; POB 466, Durban 4000; tel. (31) 3053791; fax (31) 3077356; e-mail padams@adamsbooks.co.za; educational; CEO BRYAN PHILLIPS.

Lemur Books (Pty) Ltd (The Galago Publishing (1999) (Pty) Ltd): POB 1645, Alberton 1450; tel. (11) 9072029; fax (11) 8690890; e-mail lemur@mweb.co.za; internet www.galago.co.za; f. 1980; military, political, history, hunting, general; Man. Dir F. STIFF.

LexisNexis Butterworths SA: 215 North Ridge Rd, Morningside, Durban 4001; POB 792, Durban 4000; tel. (31) 2683111; fax (31) 2683108; e-mail customercare@lexisnexis.co.za; internet www.lexisnexis.co.za; f. 1948 as Butterworths; adopted LexisNexis name in 2001; jtly owned by Reed Elsevier, USA, and Kagiso Media; law, tax, accountancy; Chair. W. ROGER JARDINE; CEO WILLIAM J. LAST.

Lux Verbi-BM: POB 1822, Cape Town 8000; tel. (21) 8648237; fax (21) 8648292; e-mail jmc@luxverbi-bm.co.za; internet www.luxverbi-bm.com; f. 1818 as the Dutch Reformed Church Publishing Co; merged with Bible Media in 1999; subsidiary of the Naspers Group; imprints incl. Hugenote, NG Kerk Uitgewers, Protea, and Waterkant; Christian media; Man. Dir H. S. SPIES; Editor-in-Chief D. FOURIE.

Maskew Miller Longman (Pty) Ltd: cnr Forest Dr. and Logan Way, Pinelands 7405; POB 396, Cape Town 8000; tel. (21) 5326000; fax (21) 5310716; e-mail customerservices@mml.co.za; internet www.mml.co.za; f. 1893 as Miller Maskew; merged with Longman in 1983; jtly owned by Pearson Education and Caxton Publrs and Printers Ltd; imprints incl. Kagiso Publishing (f. 1994; fmrly De Jager-HAUM) and Phumelela Books; educational and general; CEO JAPIE PIENAAR.

Methodist Publishing House: POB 13128, Woodstock, Cape Town 7915; tel. (21) 4483640; fax (21) 4483716; e-mail george@methbooks.co.za; f. 1894; religion and theology; Gen. Man. GEORGE VINE (acting).

Nasou—Via Afrika: 40 Heerengracht, Cape Town 8001; POB 5197, Cape Town 8000; tel. (21) 4063005; fax (21) 4063086; e-mail CGillitt@nasou.com; internet www.nasou-viaafrika.com; f. 1963; subsidiary of Via Afrika (Naspers Group); educational; imprints incl. Acacia, Action Publrs, Afritech, Afro, Atlas, Era, Juta, KZN Books, Gariep, Idem, Phoenix Education, Shortland and Y-Press Grade R-3; Man. Dir CLIVE GILLITT.

NB Publishers: Naspers Bldg, 12th Floor, 40 Heerengracht, Roggebai 8012; POB 879, Cape Town 8000; tel. (21) 4063033; fax (21) 4063812; e-mail nb@nb.co.za; internet www.nb.co.za; English, Afrikaans, Xhosa and Zulu; Human & Rousseau (f. 1959; general, children's and youth literature, cookery and self-help), Kwela (f. 1994; fiction), Pharos (dictionaries), Tafelberg (f. 1950; fiction and non-fiction, politics, children's and youth literature) and Best Books (educational texts); Head of Publishing C. T. BREYTENBACH.

Oxford University Press: POB 12119, N1 City, Cape Town 7463; tel. (21) 5962300; fax (21) 5961234; e-mail oxford.za@oup.com; internet www.oxford.co.za; f. 1914; Man. Dir LIEZE KOTZE.

Protea Book House: 1067 Burnett St, Hatfield, Pretoria; POB 35110, Menlo Park, 0102 Pretoria; tel. (12) 3623444; fax (12) 3625688; e-mail protea@intekom.co.za; internet www.proteaboekhuis.co.za; f. 1997; art and photography, Afrikaans fiction, South African history, spiritual, academic and general; Dir NICOL STASSEN.

Random House Struik (Pty) Ltd South Africa: POB 2002, Houghton 2041; tel. (11) 4843538; fax (11) 4846180; e-mail lindad@randomstruik.co.za; f. 1966; general fiction; Man. Dir S. E. JOHNSON.

Shuter & Shooter Publishers (Pty) Ltd: 110CB Downes Rd, Pietermaritzburg; POB 13016, Cascades, Pietermaritzburg 3202; tel. (33) 8468700; fax (33) 8468701; e-mail sales@shuters.com; internet www.shuters.com; f. 1921; educational, general and African languages and trade books; Man. Dir PRIMI CHETTY.

University of KwaZulu-Natal Press (UKZN Press): Private Bag X01, Scottsville 3209; tel. (33) 2605226; fax (33) 2605801; e-mail books@ukzn.ac.za; internet www.ukznpress.co.za; academic and scholarly; Publr GLENN COWLEY; Editor SALLY HINES.

Van Schaik Publishers: 1064 Arcadia St, POB 12681, Hatfield 0028; tel. (12) 3422765; fax (12) 4303563; e-mail vanschaik@vanschaiknet.com; internet www.vanschaiknet.com; f. 1915; acquired by Nasionale Pers, latterly Via Afrika-Naspers Group in 1986; English and Afrikaans; academic and scholarly; CEO LEANNE MARTINI.

Wits University Press: PO Wits, Johannesburg 2050; tel. (11) 4845910; fax (11) 4845971; e-mail Veronica.Klipp@wits.ac.za; internet witspress.wits.ac.za; f. 1922; general trade, non-fiction and scholarly; Publr VERONICA KLIPP.

PUBLISHERS' ASSOCIATION

Publishers' Association of South Africa (PASA): Suite 305, 2nd Floor, The Foundry, Prestwich St, Green Point, Cape Town 8005; tel. (21) 4252721; fax (21) 4213270; e-mail pasa@publishsa.co.za; internet www.publishsa.co.za; f. 1992; promotes and protects the rights and responsibilities of the independent publishing sector in South Africa; Exec Dir. DUDLEY H. SCHROEDER.

Broadcasting and Communications

REGULATORY AUTHORITY

Independent Communications Authority of South Africa (ICASA): Pinmill Farm, Blocks A, B, C and D, 164 Katherine St, Sandton 2146; Private Bag X10002, Marlboro 2063; tel. (11) 5663000; fax (11) 4441919; e-mail info@icasa.org.za; internet www.icasa.org.za; f. 2000 as successor to the Independent Broadcasting Authority (f. 1993) and South African Telecommunications Regulatory Authority (f. 1996); regulates telecommunications and broadcasting; Chair. PARIS MASHILE.

TELECOMMUNICATIONS

Cell C (Pty) Ltd: 150 Rivonia Rd, Sandown 2196; Private Bag X36, Benmore 2010, Johannesburg; tel. (11) 3244000; fax (11) 3244009; e-mail customerservice@cellc.co.za; internet www.cellc.co.za; f. 2000; subsidiary of 3C Telecommunications (60% owned by Oger Telecom South Africa, 40% by CellSAf); mobile cellular telecommunications provider; Chair. TALAAT LAHAM; CEO JEFFREY HEDBERG.

Mobile Telephone Networks (Pty) Ltd (MTN): 3 Alice Lane, Ext. 38, PMB 9955, Sandton 2146; tel. (11) 3016000; fax (11) 3018448; internet www.mtn.co.za; f. 1994; mobile cellular telecommunications provider; operations in 21 countries in Africa and the Middle East; 11m. subscribers in South Africa (2006); Chair. MATAMELA CYRIL RAMAPHOSA; Group Pres. and CEO PHUTHUMA NHLEKO.

SOUTH AFRICA

Neotel: 28 Saddle Dr., Woodmead Office Park, Woodmead, Johannesburg 2191; PostNet Suite 612, Private Bag X29, Gallo Manor, Johannesburg, 2052; tel. (11) 585 1000; fax (11) 585 0001; e-mail info@neotel.co.za; internet www.neotel.co.za; Man. Dir and CEO AJAY PANDEY.

Telkom SA Ltd: Telkom Towers North, 152 Proes St, Pretoria 0002; POB 925, Pretoria 0001; tel. (12) 3111007; fax (12) 3114031; e-mail letlapll@telkom.co.za; internet www.telkom.co.za; f. 1991; 38% govt-owned; ICT solutions service provider; Chair. SHIRLEY LUE ARNOLD; Exec. Dir REUBEN SEPTEMBER.

Virgin Mobile South Africa (Pty) Ltd (VMSA): CitiGroup Bldg, 2nd Floor, 145 West St, Sandton, Johannesburg; POB 78331, Sandton 2146; tel. (11) 3244000; fax (11) 3244113; e-mail CustomerCare@virginmobile.co.za; internet www.virginmobile.co.za; f. 2006; jt venture btwn Cell C and Virgin Mobile Telecoms Ltd, United Kingdom; mobile cellular telecommunications provider; CEO SAJEED SACRANIE.

Vodacom Group (Pty) Ltd: Vodacom Corporate Park, 082 Vodacom Blvd, Vodavalley, Midrand 1685; tel. (11) 6535000; e-mail corporate.affairs@vodacom.co.za; internet www.vodacom.co.za; f. 1993; 50% owned by Telkom SA Ltd, 50% by Vodafone Group PLC, United Kingdom; subsidiaries in the DRC (f. 2002), Lesotho (f. 1996), Mozambique (f. 2003) and Tanzania (f. 1999); Chair. OYAMA MABANDLA; CEO ALLAN KNOTT CRAIG.

BROADCASTING

Radio

South African Broadcasting Corpn (SABC)—Radio: Private Bag X1, Auckland Park 2006, Johannesburg; tel. (11) 7149111; fax (11) 7149744; e-mail rpsales@sabc.co.za; internet www.sabc.co.za; f. 1936; comprises 15 public radio stations and three commercial radio stations broadcasting in 11 languages; Chair. Prof. PAULUS ZULU; CEO CHARLOTTE MAMPANE.

Domestic Services

Radio South Africa; Afrikaans Stereo; Radio 5; Radio 2000; Highveld Stereo; Good Hope Stereo; Radio Kontrei; RPN Stereo; Jacaranda Stereo; Radio Algoa (regional services); Radio Lotus (Indian service in English); Radio Metro (African service in English); Radio Lebowa; Radio Ndebele; Radio Sesotho; Setswana Stereo; Radio Swazi; Radio Tsonga; Radio Xhosa; Radio Zulu.

External Service

Channel Africa Network: POB 91313, Auckland Park 2006; tel. (11) 7142255; fax (11) 7142072; e-mail molotod@sabc.co.za; internet www.channelafrica.org; f. 1966; external service of SABC; broadcasts 217 hours per week in English, French, Portuguese, Kiswahili, Chinyanja and Silozi; Gen. Man. DAVID MOLOTO.

Television

In February 2007 the Government announced that the country would begin digital terrestrial broadcasting in November 2008 and that the country's analogue signal would be switched off in 2011.

e.tv: 5 Summit Rd, Hyde Park, Johannesburg 2196; Private Bag, X9944, Sandton 2146; tel. (11) 5379300; e-mail info@etv.co.za; internet www.etv.co.za; f. 1998; CEO MARCEL GOLDING.

Naspers: 40 Heerengracht, Cape Town 8001; tel. (21) 4062121; e-mail GKGreen@multichoice.co.za; internet www.naspers.co.za; provides subscription television through Multichoice, M-Net and SuperSport packages; CEO COBUS STOFBERG.

South African Broadcasting Corpn (SABC)—Television: Private Bag X41, Auckland Park 2006; tel. (11) 7149111; fax (11) 7145055; e-mail enterpri@sabc.co.za; internet www.sabc.co.za; transmissions began in 1976; broadcasts television services in 11 languages over three channels; SABC1 broadcasts in English, isiZulu, isiXhosa, isiNdebele and siSwati; SABC2 broadcasts in English, Afrikaans, Sesotho, Setswana, Sepedi, Xitsonga and Tshivendi; SABC3 broadcasts documentaries, educational programmes and sport in English; Chair. Prof. PAULUS ZULU; CEO DALI MPOFU.

Finance

(cap. = capital; auth. = authorized; res = reserves; dep. = deposits; m. = million; brs = branches; amounts in rand)

BANKING

In 2006 there were 30 commercial banks and 1,354 microfinance institutions operating in South Africa. The five largest banks—Standard Bank, Nedbank, ABSA, FirstRand and Investec—controlled some 86% of total banking assets.

Central Bank

South African Reserve Bank: 370 Church St, POB 427, Pretoria 0002; tel. (12) 3133911; fax (12) 3133197; e-mail info@resbank.co.za; internet www.reservebank.co.za; f. 1921; cap. 2.0m., res 8,026.2m., dep. 103,970.9m. (March 2007); Gov. TITO T. MBOWENI; Sen. Dep. Gov. X. P. GUMA; 7 brs.

Commercial Banks

ABSA Bank Ltd: ABSA Towers East, 3rd Floor, 170 Main St, Johannesburg 2001; tel. (11) 3504000; fax (11) 3504625; e-mail absa@absa.co.za; internet www.absa.co.za; cap. 303m., res 9,888m., dep. 400,310m. (Dec. 2006); Chair. Dr DANIE CRONJÉ; CEO STEVE F. BOOYSEN; 726 brs.

African Bank Investments Ltd: 59 16th Rd, Private Bag X170, Midrand 1685; tel. (11) 2569000; fax (11) 2569217; e-mail CBrighten@africanbank.co.za; internet www.abil.co.za; f. 1975; cap. 1,876.4m., res 186.7m., dep. 706.2m. (Sept. 2002); CEO LEONIDAS KIRKINIS; 268 brs.

Albaraka Bank Ltd: 134 DR A B Xuma St, Durban 4001; POB 4395, Durban 4000; tel. (31) 3662800; fax (31) 3052631; e-mail marketing@albaraka.co.za; internet www.albaraka.co.za; f. 1989; operates according to Islamic principles; cap. 150.0m., dep. 1,443.5m., total assets 1,686.3m. (Dec. 2007); Chair. ADNAN AHMED YOUSIF; CEO SHABIR CHOHAN.

AMB Holdings Ltd: 135 Daisy St, Sandown 2196; tel. (11) 6667300; fax (11) 6667325; e-mail asprague@amb.co.za; internet www.amb.co.za; Exec. Dir ZENZO LUSENGO; CEO ANDREW SPRAGUE.

Bidvest Bank Ltd: Rennie House, 11th Floor, 19 Ameshoff St, Braamfontein 2001, Johannesburg; POB 185, Johannesburg 2000; tel. (11) 4073000; fax (11) 4073322; e-mail letstalk@bidvestbank.co.za; internet www.bidvestbank.co.za; f. 1850 as Rennies Bank Ltd; renamed as above in 2007; subsidiary of Bidvest Group Ltd; foreign exchange, trade finance and related activities; cap. 1.8m., res 301.5m., dep. 466.9m. (June 2008); Chair. J. L. PAMENSKY; CEO A. C. SALOMON; over 60 brs.

Brait South Africa Ltd: 9 Fricker Rd, Illovo Blvd, Illovo, Sandton 2196; Private Bag X1, Northlands 2116; tel. (11) 5071000; fax (11) 5071001; internet www.brait.com; f. 1998; subsidiary of Brait SA, Luxembourg; total assets 802.3m. (Mar. 2004); CEO JOHN COULTER.

FirstRand Bank Ltd: 4th Floor, 4 First Place, cnr Fredman Dr. and Rivonia Rd, Bank City, Sandton 2196; POB 786273, Sandton 2146; tel. (11) 2821808; fax (11) 2828088; e-mail information@firstrand.co.za; internet www.firstrand.co.za; f. 1971 as First National Bank of Southern Africa; merged with Rand Bank in 1998; cap. 4m., res 24,945m., dep. 392,385m. (June 2007); Exec. Chair. RONNIE WATSON; CEO PAUL HARRIS; 600 brs.

GBS Mutual Bank: 18–20 Hill St, Grahamstown 6139; POB 114, Grahamstown 6140; tel. (46) 6227109; fax (46) 6228855; e-mail gbs@gbsbank.co.za; internet www.gbsbank.co.za; f. 1877; total assets 659.0m. (Mar. 2003); Chair. C. K. M. STONE; CEO A. M. VORSTER; 4 brs.

Habib Overseas Bank Ltd: N77 Oriental Plaza, Fordsburg, Johannesburg 2092; POB 62369, Marshalltown, Johannesburg 2107; tel. (11) 8347441; fax (11) 8347446; e-mail habib@global.co.za; internet www.habiboverseas.co.za; f. 1992; cap. 20m., dep. 447m., total assets US $68.5m. (Dec. 2006); Chair. HABIB MOHAMED D. HABIB; 5 brs.

HBZ Bank Ltd: 135 Jan Hofmeyr Rd, Westville, Durban 3631; POB 1536, Wandsbeck 3631; tel. (31) 2674400; fax (31) 2671193; e-mail sazone@hbzbank.co.za; internet www.hbzbank.co.za; f. 1995; subsidiary of Habib Bank Ltd; cap. 10.0m., res 72.9m., 1,080.3m. (Dec. 2006); Chair. MUHAMMAD HABIB; CEO ZAFAR ALAM KHAN; 4 brs.

Imperial Bank Ltd: 24 Achter Rd, cnr Witkoppen, Paulshof, Sandton 2021; POB 6093, Rivonia 2128; tel. (11) 2753000; fax (11) 2754488; e-mail phassim@imperialbank.co.za; internet www.imperialbank.co.za; f. 1996; 51.1% owned by Nedbank, 49.9% by Imperial Holdings; total assets 12,955.0m. (Dec. 2003); Chair. H. R. BRODY; CEO R. VAN WYK.

Meeg Bank Ltd: Absa Bldg, 5th Floor, 85 Oxford St, cnr Oxford and Gladstone Sts, East London 5201; POB 429, East London 5200; tel. (43) 7029600; fax (43) 7029700; e-mail marketing@meegbank.co.za; internet www.meegbank.co.za; f. 1977; fmrly Bank of Transkei; name changed Oct. 1998; total assets 1,253.4m. (March 2008); Chair. Prof. WISEMAN LUMKILE NKUHLU; Man. Dir M. D. LEGODU; 5 brs.

Mercantile Bank Ltd: Mercantile Lisbon House, 142 West St, Sandown 2196; POB 782699, Sandton 2146; tel. (11) 3020300; fax (11) 7844081; internet www.mercantile.co.za; f. 1965; subsidiary of Mercantile Lisbon Bank Holdings; cap. 1,483.3m., res 56.1m., dep. 3,571.2m. (Dec. 2006); Chair. Dr JOAQUIM A. S. DE ANDRADE CAMPOS; CEO D. J. BROWN; 14 brs.

Nedbank Ltd: 135 Rivonia Rd, Sandown 2196, Johannesburg 2001; POB 1144, Johannesburg 2000; tel. (11) 2940999; fax (11) 2950999; e-mail Gawien@nedbank.co.za; internet www.nedbankgroup.co.za;

SOUTH AFRICA

f. 1988; name changed from Nedcor Bank Ltd Nov. 2002; subsidiary of Nedbank Group Ltd; cap. 4,052m., res 24,005m., dep. 350,713m. (Dec. 2006); Chair. REUEL J. KHOZA; CEO TOM BOARDMAN; 472 brs.

South African Bank of Athens Ltd: Bank of Athens Bldg, 116 Marshall St, Johannesburg 2001; POB 7781, Johannesburg 2000; tel. (11) 6344300; fax (11) 8381001; e-mail info@bankofathens.co.za; internet www.bankofathens.co.za; f. 1947; 99.51% owned by National Bank of Greece; cap. 9.3m., res 92.5m., dep. 732.3m. (Dec. 2006); Chair. A. LEOPOULOS; CEO HECTOR ZARCA; 11 brs.

The Standard Bank of South Africa Ltd: Standard Bank Centre, 5 Simmonds St, Johannesburg 2001; POB 7725, Johannesburg 2000; tel. (11) 2994701; fax (11) 6364207; e-mail information@standardbank.co.za; internet www.standardbank.co.za; f. 1862; cap. 60m., res 25,825m., dep. 470,939m. (Dec. 2006); Chair. DEREK E. COOPER; CEO J. H. MAREE; 951 brs.

Teba Bank Ltd: Sanhill Park, 1 Eglin Rd, Sunninghill; Private Bag X101, Sunninghill 2157; tel. (11) 5185000; fax (86) 6415809; e-mail corpcomm@tebabank.com; internet www.tebabank.co.za; f. 2000; fmrly Teba Savings Fund; specializes in microfinance and providing financial services to mining communities; total assets 2,200.0m. (Feb. 2006); CEO MARK WILLIAMS; 90 brs, 29 agencies.

Merchant Bank

Marriott Merchant Bank Ltd: 2 Delamore Rd, Hillcrest 3610; POB 2099, Hillcrest 3650; tel. (31) 7650700; fax (31) 3661222; e-mail info@marriott.co.za; internet www.marriott.co.za; f. 1994; CEO SIMON PEARSE.

Investment Banks

Cadiz Investment Bank Ltd: Fernwood House, 1st Floor, The Oval, 1 Oakdale Rd, Newlands 7700; POB 44547, Claremont 7735; tel. 6578300; fax 6578301; e-mail reception@cadiz.co.za; internet www.cadiz.co.za; f. 1993; 15% owned by Investec, 11% by Makana Financial Services; total assets 298.1m. (Dec. 2003); Chair. RAY CADIZ; CEO RAM BARKAI.

Investec Bank Ltd: 100 Grayston Dr., Sandown, Sandton 2196; POB 785700, Sandton 2146; tel. (11) 2867000; fax (11) 2867777; e-mail investorrelations@investec.com; internet www.investec.com; f. 1974; cap. 19m., res 11,400m., dep. 125,000m. (Mar. 2008); CEO S. KOSEFF; 6 brs.

Sasfin Bank Ltd: Sasfin Pl., 13–15 Scott St, Waverley 2090; POB 95104, Grant Park 2051; tel. (11) 8097500; fax (11) 8872489; e-mail info@sasfin.com; internet www.sasfin.com; f. 1951; subsidiary of Sasfin Holdings Ltd; total assets 2,545m. (2007); Chair. MARTIN GLATT; CEO ROLAND SASSOON.

Development Bank

Development Bank of Southern Africa (DBSA): 1258 Lever Rd, Headway Hill; POB 1234, Halfway House, Midrand 1685; tel. (11) 3133911; fax (11) 3133086; e-mail info@dbsa.org; internet www.dbsa.org; total assets 23,684.5m. (March 2004); f. 1983; Chair. JAYASEELAN NAIDOO; CEO PAUL BALOYI.

Bankers' Association

Banking Association South Africa: Sunnyside Office Park, Bldg D, 3rd Floor, 32 Princess of Wales Terrace, Parktown 2193; tel. (11) 6456700; fax (11) 6456800; e-mail webmaster@banking.org.za; internet www.banking.org.za; f. 1993; fmrly Banking Council of South Africa; name changed as above in 2005; 15,000 mems; Chair. S. BOOYSEN; Man. Dir CASSIM COOVADIA.

STOCK EXCHANGE

JSE Ltd: One Exchange Sq., 2 Gwen Lane, Sandown, Sandton; Private Bag X991174, Sandton 2146; tel. (11) 5207000; fax (11) 5208584; e-mail info@jse.co.za; internet www.jse.co.za; f. 1887 as Johannesburg Stock Exchange; present name adopted in 2005; in late 1995 legislation was enacted providing for the deregulation of the Stock Exchange; automated trading commenced in June 1996; demutualized in July 2005 and became a listed co in June 2006; CEO R. M. LOUBSER.

INSURANCE

In 2003 South Africa was served by 96 short-term and 69 long-term insurers, and six reinsurance firms.

Allianz Insurance Ltd: 40 Ashford Rd, Parkwood, Johannesburg 2001; POB 62228, Marshalltown 2107; tel. (11) 4421111; fax (11) 4421125; e-mail baini@allianz.co.za; internet www.allianz.co.za; Chair. D. DU PREEZ; Man. Dir IAN BAIN.

Clientèle Life Assurance Co: Clientèle House, Morning View Office Park, cnr Rivonia and Alon Rds, Morningside, Johannesburg; POB 1316, Rivonia 2128; tel. (11) 3203333; e-mail services@clientelelife.com; internet www.clientelelife.com; f. 1997; subsidiary of Hollard Insurance Group; Chair. GAVIN ROUTLEDGE; Man. Dir G. BASIL REEKIE.

Credit Guarantee Insurance Corpn of Africa Ltd: 31 Dover St, POB 125, Randburg 2125; tel. (11) 8897000; fax (11) 8861027; e-mail info@cgic.co.za; internet www.creditguarantee.co.za; f. 1956; Chair. KEITH KENNEDY; Man. Dir MIKE C. TRUTER.

Discovery: 16 Fredman Dr., Sandton 2146; POB 784262, Sandton 2146; tel. (11) 5292888; fax (11) 5293590; e-mail worldinfo@discovery.co.za; internet www.discoveryworld.co.za; f. 1992; 64% owned by FirstRand; health and life assurance; Chair. LAURITZ L. DIPPENAAR; CEO ADRIAN GORE.

Liberty Life: Liberty Life Centre, 1 Ameshoff St, Braamfontein, Johannesburg 2001; POB 10499, Johannesburg 2000; tel. (11) 4083911; fax (11) 4082109; e-mail info@liberty.co.za; internet www.liberty.co.za; f. 1958; Chair. D. E. COOPER; CEO BRUCE HEMPHILL.

Metropolitan Life Ltd: Parc du Cap Complex, Mispel Rd, POB 2212, Cape Town; POB 2212, Bellville 7535; tel. (21) 9405911; fax (21) 9406142; e-mail info@metropolitan.co.za; internet www.metropolitan.co.za; Chair. D. E. MOSENEKE; Man. Dir P. R. DOYLE.

Momentum Life Assurers Ltd: 268 West Ave, Centurion, Gauteng 0157; POB 7400, Centurion 0046; tel. (12) 6718911; fax (12) 6636288; e-mail corporate@momentum.co.za; internet www.momentum.co.za; f. 1967; Chair. LAURIE DIPPENAAR; Man. Dir HILLIE P. MEYER.

Mutual & Federal Insurance Co Ltd: Mutual Federal Centre, 75 President St, POB 1120, Johannesburg 2000; tel. (31) 5086396; fax (31) 5026760; e-mail contact@mf.co.za; internet www.mf.co.za; f. 1970; Chair. J. B. MAGWAZA; Man. Dir K. N. KENNEDY.

Old Mutual (South African Mutual Life Assurance Society): Mutualpark, Jan Smuts Dr., POB 66, Cape Town 8001; tel. (21) 5099111; fax (21) 5094444; e-mail contact@oldmutual.com; internet www.oldmutual.com; f. 1845; Chair. MICHAEL J. LEVETT; CEO JAMES SUTCLIFFE.

Regent Insurance Co Ltd: 146 Boeing Rd East, Elma Park, POB 674, Edenvale 1609; tel. (11) 8795000; fax (11) 4539533; e-mail email@bob.co.za; internet www.regent.co.za; f. 1989; 100% owned by Imperial Holdings; Gen. Man. JONO SOAMES.

Santam Ltd: Santam Head Office, 1 Sportica Cres., Bellville 7530; POB 3881, Tyger Valley 7536; tel. (21) 9157000; fax (21) 9140700; e-mail info@santam.co.za; internet www.santam.co.za; f. 1918; Chair. D. K. SMITH; CEO IAN KIRK.

South African National Life Assurance Co Ltd (SANLAM): 2 Strand Rd, Bellville; POB 1, Sanlamhof 7532; tel. (21) 9479111; fax (21) 9479440; e-mail life@sanlam.co.za; internet www.sanlam.co.za; f. 1918; Chair. Dr J. VAN ZYL.

Zurich Insurance Co South Africa Ltd: 70 Fox St, Johannesburg 2001; tel. (11) 3709111; fax (11) 8368018; e-mail info@insurance.za.org; internet www.saeagle.co.za; fmrly South African Eagle Insurance Co Ltd; rebranded as above in 2007; Chair. M. C. SOUTH; CEO N. V. BEYERS.

Association

South African Insurance Association (SAIA): JCC House, 3rd Floor, 27 Owl St, Milpark; POB 30619, Braamfontein 2017; tel. (11) 7265381; fax (11) 7265351; e-mail adele@saia.co.za; internet www.saia.co.za; f. 1973; represents short-term insurers; Chair. RONNIE NAPIER; CEO BARRY SCOTT.

Trade and Industry

DEVELOPMENT ORGANIZATIONS

Business Partners Ltd: 3 Caxton Rd, POB 43297, Industria, Johannesburg 2193; tel. (11) 4703000; fax (11) 4703123; e-mail enquiries@businesspartners.co.za; internet www.businesspartners.co.za; f. 1981 as Small Business Devt Corpn; invests in, and provides services to, small and medium-sized enterprises; Chair. JOHANN RUPERT; Man. Dir JO' SCHWENKE.

Independent Development Trust: Glenwood Office Park, cnr Oberon and Sprite Sts, Faerie Glen, Pretoria; POB 73000, Lynnwood Ridge 0043; tel. (12) 8452000; fax (12) 3480894; internet www.idt.org.za; f. 1990; advances the national. devt programme working with govt and communities in fields incl. poverty relief, infrastructure, empowerment, employment and capacity building; CEO THEMBI NWEDAMUSTWU.

Industrial Development Corpn of South Africa Ltd (IDC): 19 Fredman Dr., Sandown 2196; POB 784055, Sandton 2146; tel. (11) 2693000; fax (11) 2693116; e-mail callcentre@idc.co.za; internet www.idc.co.za; f. 1940; promotes entrepreneurship and competitiveness; total assets 90,421m. (March 2008); Chair. Dr WENDY Y. N. LUHABE; CEO G. M. QHENA.

SOUTH AFRICA

Productivity SA: Private Bag 235, Midrand 1685; tel. (11) 8485300; fax (11) 8485555; e-mail info@productivitysa.co.za; internet www.productivitysaco.za; f. 1968; Chair. Dr J. M. LAUBSCHER (acting); Exec. Dir Dr BONGANI COKA (acting).

CHAMBERS OF COMMERCE

Bloemfontein Chamber of Commerce and Industry: 1st Floor, Tourism Centre, 30 Park Rd, Bloemfontein; POB 87, Bloemfontein 9301; tel. (51) 4473369; fax (51) 4475064; internet www.bcci.co.za; f. 2004; Pres. MOSS MOTSHUMI; c. 550 mems (2006).

Cape Town Regional Chamber of Commerce and Industry: Cape Chamber House, 19 Louis Gradner St, Foreshore, Cape Town 8001; tel. (21) 4024300; fax (21) 4024302; e-mail info@capechamber.co.za; internet www.capechamber.co.za; f. 1804; Pres. JEREMY WILEY; 4,632 mems.

Chamber of Commerce and Industry–Johannesburg: JCC House, 6th Floor, 27 Owl St, cnr Empire Rd, Milpark; Private Bag 34, Auckland Park 2006; tel. (11) 7265300; fax (11) 4822000; e-mail info@jcci.co.za; internet www.jcci.co.za; f. 1890; CEO KEITH BREBNOR; 3,800 mems.

Durban Chamber of Commerce and Industry: Chamber House, 190 Stanger St, POB 1506, Durban 4000; tel. (31) 3351000; fax (31) 3321288; e-mail chamber@durbanchamber.co.za; internet www.durbanchamber.co.za; CEO GUGU MAZIBUKO; 3,500 mems.

Gauteng North Chamber of Commerce and Industry (GNCCI): Tshwane Events Centre, Soutter St, Pretoria; POB 2164, Pretoria 0001; tel. (12) 3271487; fax (12) 3271490; internet www.gncci.co.za; f. 1929; fmrly Pretoria Business and Agricultural Centre; merged with Pretoria Sakekamer in 2004; Chair. BERT BADENHORST; CEO WIM DU PLESSIS; over 900 mems.

Pietermaritzburg Chamber of Business (PCB): POB 11734, Dorpspruit, Pietermaritzburg 3206; tel. (33) 3452747; fax (33) 3944151; e-mail pcb@pcb.org.za; internet www.pcb.org.za; f. 2002 as successor to the Pietermaritzburg Chamber of Commerce and Industries (f. 1910); CEO ANDREW LAYMAN; 880 mems.

Port Elizabeth Regional Chamber of Commerce and Industry (PERCCI): 200 Norvic Dr., Greenacres, Port Elizabeth 6045; KPMG House, POB 63866, Greenacres 6057; tel. (41) 3731122; fax (41) 3731142; e-mail info@pechamber.org.za; internet www.percci.co.za; f. 1994; Pres. SIYA MHLALUKA; 814 mems.

South African Chamber of Commerce and Industry (SACCI): 24 Sturdee Ave, Rosebank, Johannesburg 2196; POB 213, Saxonwold 2132; tel. (11) 4463800; fax (11) 4463850; e-mail info@sacci.org.za; internet www.sacci.org.za; f. 1990 by merger of Asscn of Chambers of Commerce and Industry and South African Federated Chamber of Industries; fmrly known as South African Chamber of Business; Pres. Prof. ALWYN LOUW; CEO NEREN RAU.

Wesvaal Chamber of Business (WESCOB): POB 7167, Flamwood 2572; tel. (18) 4627109; fax (86) 6936365; e-mail chamber@gds.co.za; internet www.wesvaalchamber.co.za; f. 1898; Pres. JOHAN SMIT; c. 100 mems.

INDUSTRIAL AND TRADE ORGANIZATIONS

Association of Cementitious Material Producers: POB 10181, Centurion 0046; tel. (12) 6635146; fax (12) 6636036; e-mail naudek.acmp@mweb.co.za; f. 2002; Chair. ORRIE FENN.

Cape Wools: POB 2191, Port Elizabeth 6056; tel. (41) 544301; fax (41) 546760; e-mail onav@capewools.co.za; internet www.capewools.co.za; f. 1997; Section 21 service company; seven mems: three appointed by wool producer orgs, two by the Wool Textile Council, one by Wool Brokers and Traders and one by Labour; Chair. GEOFF KINGWILL; Gen. Man. ANDRÉ STRYDOM.

Chamber of Mines of South Africa: Chamber of Mines Bldg, 5 Hollard St, POB 61809, Marshalltown 2107; tel. (11) 4987100; fax (11) 8341884; e-mail webmaster@bullion.org.za; internet www.bullion.org.za; f. 1889; Pres. SIPHO NKOSI.

Clothing Trade Council (CloTrade): 35 Siemers Rd, 6th Floor, Doornfontein; POB 2303, Johannesburg 2000; tel. (11) 4020664; fax (11) 4020667; f. 2002; successor to the Clothing Fed. of South Africa; Pres. JACK KIPLING.

Grain Milling Federation: POB 7262, Centurion 0046; tel. (12) 6631660; fax (12) 6633109; e-mail gmf@grainmilling.org.za; internet www.grainmilling.org.za; f. 1944; Exec. Dir JANNIE DE VILLIERS.

Master Builders South Africa (MBSA): POB 1619, Halfway House, Midrand 1685; tel. (11) 2059000; fax (11) 3151644; e-mail info@mbsa.org.za; internet www.mbsa.org.za; f. 1904; fmrly known as Building Industries Fed. South Africa; President EUNICE FORBES; CEO PIERRE FOURIE; 4,000 mems.

Master Diamond Cutters' Association of South Africa: Private Bag X1, Suite 105, Excom 2023; tel. (11) 3341930; fax (11) 3341933; e-mail info@masingita.co.za; f. 1928; Pres. MACDONALD TEMANE; 76 mems.

National Association of Automobile Manufacturers of South Africa: Nedbank Plaza, 1st Floor, cnr Church and Beatrix Sts, Pretoria 0002; POB 40611, Arcadia 0007; tel. (12) 3232980; fax (12) 3263232; e-mail naamsa@iafrica.com; internet www.naamsa.co.za; f. 1935; Dir N. M. W. VERMEULEN; 19 full mems and 21 assoc. mems.

National Chamber of Milling, Inc: POB 7262, Centurion 0046; tel. (12) 6631660; fax (12) 6633109; e-mail info@grainmilling.org.za; internet www.grainmilling.org.za; f. 1936; Exec. Dir JANNIE DE VILLIERS.

National Textile Manufacturers' Association: POB 81, New Germany 3620; tel. (31) 7104410; fax (31) 7056257; f. 1947; Sec. PETER MCGREGOR; 9 mems.

Plastics Federation of South Africa: 18 Gazelle Rd, Corporate Park South, Old Pretoria Rd, Midrand; Private Bag X68, Halfway House, Midrand 1685; tel. (11) 3144021; fax (11) 3143764; internet www.plasticsinfo.co.za; f. 1979; Exec. Dir DAVID HUGHES; 10 mems.

Printing Industries Federation of South Africa (PIFSA): Printech Ave, Laser Park, POB 1084, Honeydew 2040; tel. (11) 6993000; fax (11) 6993010; e-mail pifsa@pifsa.org; internet www.pifsa.org; f. 1916; CEO C. W. J. SYKES; c. 900 mems (representing 65% of printers in South Africa); six additional regional brs.

Retail Motor Industry Organization (RMI): POB 2940, Randburg 2125; tel. (11) 8866300; fax (11) 7894525; e-mail rmi@rmi.org.za; internet www.rmi.org.za; f. 1908; affiliates throughout southern Africa; CEO JEFF OSBORNE; 7,800 mems.

South African Dairy Foundation: POB 72300, Lynnwood Ridge, Pretoria 0040; tel. (12) 3485345; fax (12) 3486284; e-mail dairy-foundation@pixie.co.za; f. 1980; Sec. S. L. VAN COLLER; 59 mems.

South African Federation of Civil Engineering Contractors (SAFCEC): 12 Skeen Blvd, POB 644, Bedfordview 2008; tel. (11) 4090900; fax (11) 4501715; e-mail admin@safcec.org.za; internet www.safcec.org.za; f. 1939; Exec. Dir H. P. LANGENHOVEN; 300 mems.

South African Fruit and Vegetable Canners' Association (Pty) Ltd (SAFVCA): Hoofstraat 258 Main St, POB 6175, Paarl 7620; tel. (21) 8711308; fax (21) 8725930; e-mail info@safvca.co.za; internet www.safvca.co.za; f. 1953; Gen. Man. JILL ATWOOD-PALM; 9 mems.

South African Inshore Fishing Industry Association (Pty) Ltd: POB 2066, Cape Town 8000; tel. (21) 4252727; e-mail safish@new.co.za; f. 1953; Chair. W. A. LEWIS; Man. S. J. MALHERBE; 4 mems.

South African Oil Expressers' Association: Cereal Centre, 6th Floor, 11 Leyds St, Braamfontein 2017; tel. (11) 7251280; f. 1937; Sec. Dr R. DU TOIT; 14 mems.

South African Paint Manufacturers' Association: POB 751605, Gardenview, Johannesburg 2047; tel. (11) 4552503; e-mail sapma@sapma.org.za; internet www.sapma.org.za; Chair. BARON SCHREUDER; 87 mems.

South African Petroleum Industry Association (SAPIA): ABSA Centre, 14th Floor, Adderley St, Cape Town 8001; POB 7082, Roggebai 8012; tel. (21) 4198054; fax (21) 4198058; internet www.sapia.co.za; f. 1994; represents South Africa's six principal petroleum cos; Chair. JAMES SEUTLOADI; Dir AVHAPFANI TSHIFULARO.

South African Sugar Association (SASA): 170 Flanders Dr., POB 700, Mount Edgecombe 4300; tel. (31) 5087000; fax (31) 5087199; internet www.sugar.org.za; Exec. Dir M. K. TRIKAM.

Includes:

South African Sugar Millers' Association Ltd (SASMAL): POB 1000, Mt Edgecombe 4300; tel. (31) 5087300; fax (31) 5087310; e-mail sasmal@sasa.org.za; represents interests of sugar millers and refiners within the operations of SASA; Exec. Dir D. W. HARDY; 6 mem. cos.

Sugar Manufacturing and Refining Employers' Association (SMREA): POB 1000, Mount Edgecombe 4300; tel. (31) 5087300; fax (31) 5087310; e-mail sasmal@sasa.org.za; f. 1947; regulates relations between mems and their employees; participates in the Bargaining Council for the sugar manufacturing and refining industry; Chair. B. V. LANE; 6 mem. cos.

South African Wool Textile Council: POB 2201, North End, Port Elizabeth 6056; tel. (41) 4845252; fax (41) 4845629; Sec. BEATTY-ANNE STARKEY.

Steel and Engineering Industries Federation of South Africa (SEIFSA): 42 Anderson St, POB 1338, Johannesburg 2000; tel. (11) 2989400; fax (11) 2989500; e-mail info@seifsa.co.za; internet www.seifsa.co.za; f. 1943; Exec. Dir BRIAN ANGUS; 38 affiliated trade asscns representing 2,350 mems.

VinPro (SA): POB 1411, Suider-Paarl 7624; tel. (21) 8073322; fax (21) 8632079; e-mail info@vinpro.co.za; internet www.vinpro.co.za; f. 1979; represents wine producers; Chair. ABRIE BOTHA; Exec. Dir JOS LE ROUX.

UTILITIES

Electricity

Electricity Supply Commission (ESKOM): POB 1091, Johannesburg 2000; tel. (11) 8008111; fax (11) 8004390; e-mail PAIA@eskom.co.za; internet www.eskom.co.za; f. 1923; state-controlled; CEO P. J. MAROGA.

Gas

SASOL Gas: POB 4211, Randburg 2125; tel. (11) 8897600; fax (11) 8897955; e-mail gascustomercare@sasol.com; internet www.sasol.com; f. 1964; Man. Dir HANS NAUDÉ.

Water

Umgeni Water: 310 Burger St, Pietermaritzburg 3201; POB 9, Pietermaritzburg 3200; tel. (331) 3411111; fax (331) 3411167; e-mail info@umgeni.co.za; internet www.umgeni.co.za; f. 1974; CEO MZIMKULU MSIWA.

Water Research Commission: Private Bag X03, Gezina 0031; tel. (12) 3300340; fax (12) 3312565; e-mail orders@wrc.org.za; internet www.wrc.org.za; Chair. Prof. J. B. ADAMS; CEO Dr RIVKA KFIR.

TRADE UNIONS

According to COSATU, some 40% of workers were unionized at March 2005. Under amendments to the Labour Relations Act (LRA), 1995, introduced in 2002, the Government sought to eliminate illegitimate trade unions and employers' organizations. The provisions of the LRA also stipulated that organizations that failed to provide annual audited financial accounts would be deregistered.

Trade Union Federations

Confederation of South African Workers' Unions (CONSAWU): 21 Adriana Cres., Gateway Industrial Park, Rooishuiskraal X25, Centurion; tel. (12) 6614265; fax (12) 6611793; e-mail consawu@mweb.co.za; internet www.consawu.co.za; f. 2003; affiliated to World Confed. of Labour and Dem. Org. of African Workers' Trade Unions; Pres. JOEL MFINGWANA; Gen. Sec. KHULILE NKUSHUBANA; 290,000 mems (2007).

Affiliates with 20,000 or more mems include:

National Union of Public Service and Allied Workers (NUPSAW): NUPSAW House, 814 Church St, Eastwood, Pretoria; POB 11459, Tramshed 0126; tel. (12) 3421674; fax (86) 6724354; e-mail generalsecretary@nupsaw.co.za; internet www.nupsaw.co.za; f. 1998; Pres. EZRA MFINGWANA; Gen. Sec. SUCCESS MATAITSANE; c. 42,000 (2005).

Other organizations affiliated to CONSAWU include: the Asscn of Metal, Iron and General Workers' Union; the Asscn Trade Union of South African Workers; the Brick and General Workers' Union; Building, Wood and Allied Workers' Union of South Africa; the Building Workers' Union; the Food and Gen. Workers' Union; the Commercial Workers' Union of South Africa; the Food, Cleaning and Security Workers' Union; the Fed. Council of Retail and Allied Workers; the Hotel and Allied Restaurant Workers' Union; the Movement for Social Justice; the Nat. Certified Fishing and Allied Workers' Union; the Nat. Construction, Building and Allied Workers' Union; the Nat. Union of Tertiary Education of South Africa; the Professional Educators' Union; the Professional Employees' Trade Union of South Africa; the Progressive Gen. Employees' Asscn of South Africa; the Progressive Trade Union of South Africa; Solidarity; the South African Building and Allied Workers' Org.; the South African Domestic and Gen. Workers' Union; the South African Food, Retail and Agricultural Workers' Union; the Transport Action, Retail and Gen. Workers' Union; the Trawler and Line Fishermen's Union; the Westcoast Workers' Union; and the Workers' Labour Council–South Africa.

Congress of South African Trade Unions (COSATU): COSATU House, 4th Floor, 1–5 Leyds St, Braamfontein; POB 1019, Johannesburg 2000; tel. (11) 3394911; fax (11) 3396940; e-mail patrick@cosatu.org.za; internet www.cosatu.org.za; f. 1985; 21 trade union affiliates representing c. 1.8m. paid-up mems; Pres. SDUMO DLAMINI; Gen. Sec. ZWELINZIMA VAVI.

Affiliates with 20,000 or more mems include:

Chemical, Energy, Paper, Printing, Wood and Allied Workers' Union (CEPPWAWU): Umoya House, 3rd Floor, 2–6 New St, South Ghandi Sq., Johannesburg 2001; POB 3219, Johannesburg 2000; tel. (11) 8332870; fax (11) 8332883; e-mail secretariat@ceppwawu.org.za; f. 1999 by merger of the Chemical Workers' Industrial Union and Paper, Printing, Wood and the Allied Workers' Union; represents workers in the petrochemical, consumer chemical, rubber, plastics, glass and ceramics, printing, pulp and paper, furniture and woodworking industries; Pres. PASCO DYANI; Gen. Sec. WELILE NOLINGO; Nat. Treas. MARY NXUMALO; 61,768 mems (2006).

Communication Workers' Union (CWU): 29 Rissik St, 3rd Floor, Johannesburg 2001; POB 10248, Johannesburg 2000; tel. (11) 8384848; fax (11) 8385962; e-mail membership@cwu.org.za; internet www.cwu.org.za; f. 1996 by merger of the Post Office Employees' Asscn, the Post and Telecommunication Workers' Asscn and the South African Post Telecommunication Employees' Asscn; Pres. JOE CHAUKE; Gen. Sec. GALLANT ROBERTS; 44,000 mems (2006).

Democratic Nursing Organisation of South Africa (DENOSA): 605 Church St, Pretoria 0001; POB 1280, Pretoria 0001; tel. (12) 3432315; fax (12) 3440750; e-mail info@denosa.org.za; internet www.denosa.org.za; f. 1996; Pres. EPHRAIM P. MAFALO; Gen. Sec. THEMBEKA T. GWAGWA; 64,165 mems (2006).

Food and Allied Workers' Union (FAWU): Vuyisile Mini Centre, cnr NY1 and NY110, Guguletu, Cape Town; POB 1234, Woodstock 7915; tel. (21) 6379040; fax (21) 6379190; e-mail admin@fawu.org.za; affiliated to the Int. Union of Food, Agricultural, Hotel, Restaurant, Catering, Tobacco and Allied Workers' Asscns; Pres. (vacant); Gen. Sec. KATISHI MASEMOLA; 111,029 mems (2006).

National Education, Health and Allied Workers' Union (NEHAWU): 56 Marshall St, Marshalltown, Johannesburg; POB 10812, Johannesburg 2000; tel. (11) 8332902; fax (11) 8330757; e-mail bongi@nehawu.org.za; internet www.nehawu.org.za; f. 1987; affiliated to the Public Services Int.; Pres. NOLUTHANDO MAYENDE-SIBIYA; Gen. Sec. FIKILE MAJOLA; 192,739 mems (2006).

National Union of Metalworkers of South Africa (NUMSA): NUMSA Bldg, 153 Bree St, cnr Becker St, Newtown, Johannesburg 2001; POB 260483, Excom 2023; tel. (11) 6891700; fax (11) 8336408; e-mail mziwakheh@numsa.org.za; internet www.numsa.org.za; affiliated to the Int. Metalworkers' Fed.; represents workers in the engineering, motor, tyre, rubber and automobile assembly industries; Pres. MTHUTHUZELI TOM; Gen. Sec. SILUMKO NONDWANGU; 216,808 mems (2006).

National Union of Mineworkers (NUM): 7 Rissik St, cnr Frederick St, Johannesburg 2000; POB 2424, Johannesburg 2000; tel. (11) 3772000; fax (11) 8360367; e-mail Tmlabatheki@num.org.za; internet www.num.org.za; f. 1982; represents workers in the mining, energy, construction, building material manufacturing, civil engineering and building industries; Pres. SENZENI ZOKWANA; Gen. Sec. FRANS BALENI; 262,042 mems (2006).

Police and Prisons Civil Rights Union (POPCRU): 1 Marie Rd, Auckland Park 0183; tel. 861403040; fax (11) 7268834; e-mail gs@popcru.org.za; internet www.popcru.org.za; Pres. ZIZAMELE MAKHAZA; Gen. Sec. ABBEY WITBOOI; 95,864 mems (2006).

SASBO: The Finance Union: SASBO House, Fourmall Office Park West, 1 Percy St, Fourways; Private Bag X84, Bryanston 2021; tel. (11) 4670192; fax (11) 4670188; e-mail michelek@sasbo.org.za; internet www.sasbo.org.za; f. 1916 as the South African Soc. of Bank Officials; Gen. Sec. SHAUN OELSCHIG; 65,500 mems (2009).

Southern African Clothing and Textile Workers' Union (SACTWU): Industria House, 350 Victoria Rd, Salt River, Cape Town; POB 1194, Woodstock 7915; tel. (21) 4474570; fax (21) 4474593; e-mail headoffice@sactwu.org.za; internet www.sactwu.org.za; affiliated to the Int. Textile, Garment and Leather Workers' Fed.; Pres. THEMBA KHUMALO; Gen. Sec. EBRAHIM PATEL; 110,216 mems (2006).

South African Commercial, Catering and Allied Workers' Union (SACCAWU): SACCAWU House, 11 Leyds St, Braamfontein; POB 10730, Johannesburg 2000; tel. (11) 4038333; fax (11) 4030309; e-mail secretariatadmin@saccawu.org.za; f. 1975; affiliated to the Union Network Int.; represents workers in the service industry, commercial, catering, tourism, hospitality and finance sectors; Pres. AMOS MOTHAPO; Gen. Sec. BONES SKULU; 107,553 mems (2006).

South African Democratic Teachers' Union (SADTU): Matthew Goniwe House, cnr Goud and Marshall Sts, Johannesburg 2000; POB 6401, Johannesburg 2000; tel. (11) 3344830; fax (11) 3344836; e-mail dmbetse@sadtu.org.za; internet www.sadtu.org.za; f. 1990; affiliated to Education Int.; Pres. THOBILE NTOLA; Gen. Sec. THULAS NXESI; 224,387 mems (2006).

South African Municipal Workers' Union (SAMWU): Trade Union House, 8 Beverly St, Athlone, Cape Town; Private Bag X9, Athlone 7760; tel. (21) 6971151; fax (21) 6969175; e-mail soraya.solomon@samwu.org.za; internet www.samwu.org.za; f. 1987; affiliated to the Public Services Int.; Pres. PETRUS MASHISHI; Gen. Sec. MTHANDEKI NHLAPO; 118,973 (2006).

South African Transport and Allied Workers' Union (SATAWU): Marble Towers, 6th Floor, cnr Jeppe and Von Wielligh Sts, Johannesburg 2000; POB 9451, Johannesburg 2001; tel. (11) 3336127; fax (11) 3338918; e-mail cecilia@satawu.org.za; internet www.satawu.org.za; f. 2000; affiliated to the Int. Trans-

SOUTH AFRICA

port Workers' Fed.; Pres. Ezrom Mabyana; Gen. Sec. Randall Howard; 134,000 mems (2006).

Other organizations affiliated to COSATU include: the Musicians' Union of South Africa; the Performing Arts Workers' Equity; the Public and Allied Workers' Union of South Africa; the South African Democratic Nurses' Union; the South African Football Players' Union; the South African Medical Association; and the South African State and Allied Workers' Union.

Federation of Unions of South Africa (FEDUSA): Fedusa House, 10 Kingfisher St, Horizon Park, Roodepoort 1725; POB 7779, Westgate 1734; tel. (11) 2791800; fax (11) 2791821; e-mail dennis@fedusa.org.za; internet www.fedusa.org.za; f. 1997 by merger of the Fed. of South African Labour Unions and Fed. of Civil Servants; 22 mem. unions; politically non-aligned; proposed 'super fed.' with the Nat. Council of Trade Unions and Confed. of South African Workers' Unions delayed in 2006; Pres. Danie Carstens; Gen. Sec. Dennis George; 360,000 mems (2007).

Affiliated unions with 10,000 or more mems include:

Health and Other Service Personnel Trade Union of South Africa (HOSPERSA): POB 12266, Queenswood, Pretoria 0121; tel. (12) 3652021; fax (12) 3652043; e-mail gs@hospersa.co.za; internet www.hospersa.co.za; f. 1958; affiliated to the Public Services Int.; represents workers in the public and private health, welfare and services sectors, and the public safety and security and education sectors; Pres. Godfrey Selematsela; Gen. Sec. Noel Desfontaines; 71,700 mems (2009).

National Security and Unqualified Workers' Union (NASAWU): United Bldg, 10th Floor, 58 Field St, Durban; POB 63015, Bishopsgate, Durban 4008; tel. (31) 3059320; fax (31) 3059621; Gen. Sec. Harold Mdineka; 13,000 mems (2006).

National Union of Leather and Allied Workers (NULAW): Mercury House, 6th Floor, Rm 67, 320 Smith St, Durban; POB 839, Durban 4000; tel. (31) 3076420; fax (31) 3043077; e-mail nulaw.mar@mweb.co.za; internet www.nulaw.org.za; affiliated to the Int. Textile, Garment and Leather Workers' Fed.; Gen. Sec. Martin Paulsen; 13,180 mems (2005).

Professional Transport Workers' Union (PTWU): Sable Centre, 3rd Floor, 41 De Korte St, Braamfontein, Johannesburg; POB 31415, Braamfontein 2017; tel. (11) 3394249; fax (11) 6820444; e-mail ptwu@wol.co.za; represents workers in the road freight, private security and cleaning sectors; Gen. Sec. Paul wa Malema; c. 10,000 mems (2002).

South African Typographical Union (SATU): SATU House, 166 Visagie St, Pretoria 0001; POB 1993, Pretoria 0001; tel. (12) 3236097; fax (12) 3231284; e-mail martind@satu.co.za; internet www.satu.co.za; f. 1982; represents workers in the printing, newspaper and packaging industries; Gen. Sec. Martin Deysel; 17,796 mems (2001).

Suid-Afrikaanse Onderwysersunie (SAOU) (South African Teachers' Union): SAOU Bldg, 278 Serene St, Garsfontein, Pretoria; POB 90120, Garsfontein 0042; tel. (12) 3489641; fax (12) 3489658; e-mail saou@saou.co.za; internet www.saou.co.za; Pres. Johannes S. Roux; CEO Edward H. Davies; 24,247 (2006).

UASA—The Union: UASA Office Park, 42 Goldman St, Florida 1709; POB 565, Florida 1710; tel. (11) 4723600; fax (11) 6744057; e-mail andre.venter@uasa.org.za; internet www.uasa.org.za; f. 1998 by merger of the Administrative, Technical and Electronic Asscn of South Africa and Officials' Asscn of South Africa; fed. of 31 unions incl. the fmr Nat. Employees' Trade Union; represents workers in the mining, motor, transport, manufacturing and engineering industries; fmrly United Association of South Africa; CEO J. P. L. 'Koos'! Bezuidenhout; 86,000 mems (2008).

Other organizations affiliated to FEDUSA include: the Airline Pilots' Association of South Africa; the Care, Catering and Retail Allied Workers' Union of South Africa; the Construction and Engineering Industrial Workers' Union; the Insurance and Banking Staff Association; the Internal Staff Association; the Jewellers and Goldsmiths' Union; the Millennium Workers Union; the Mouth Peace Workers' Union; the National Democratic Change and Allied Workers' Union; the National Teachers' Union; the National Union of Hotel, Restaurant, Catering, Commercial, Health and Allied Workers; the South African Communications Union; the South African Parastatal and Tertiary Institutions Union; the United National Public Servants Association of South Africa and Allied Workers' Union; and the United Transport and Allied Trade Union.

National Council of Trade Unions (NACTU): Metropolitan Life Centre, 4th Floor, 108 Fox St, Johannesburg; POB 10928, Johannesburg 2000; tel. (11) 8331040; fax (11) 8331032; e-mail info@nactu.org.za; internet www.nactu.org.za; f. 1986 by merger of the Council of Unions of South Africa and Azanian Confed. of Trade Unions; fed. of 22 African trade unions; aligned to the Pan-Africanist Congress of Azania party; Pres. Joseph Maqhekeni; Gen. Sec. Manene Samela; 310,000 mems (2007).

Affiliates with 10,000 or more mems include:

Building, Construction and Allied Workers' Union (BCAWU): Glencairn Bldg, 8th Floor, 73 Market St, Johannesburg; POB 96, Johannesburg 2000; tel. (11) 3339180; fax (11) 3339944; e-mail bcawu@netactive.co.za; f. 1974; affiliated to the Building and Wood Workers Int.; Gen. Sec. Narius Moloto; c. 25,000 mems (2003).

Media Workers' Association of South Africa (MWASA): 208-212 cnr Jeppe and von Wielligh Sts, POB 11136, Johannesburg; tel. (11) 3371019; fax (11) 3371806; f. 1978 as the Writers' Asscn of South Africa, successor to the Union of Black Journalists; present name adopted in 1986; affiliated to the Int. Fed. of Journalists and Union Network Int.; applied to become a political party in 2005; Pres. Tuwani Gumani; Sec.-Gen. Albert Makgoba; c. 27,000 mems (1998).

Metal and Electrical Workers' Union of South Africa (MEWUSA): Elephant House, 5th Floor, 107 Market St, Johannesburg; POB 3669, Johannesburg 2000; tel. and fax (11) 3369425; e-mail mewusa@lantic.net; internet www.mewusa.org.za; f. 1989; affiliated to the Int. Metalworkers' Fed.; Pres. Daniel Lengoabala; Gen. Sec. Nkrumah Raymond Kgagudi; c. 10,000 paid-up mems (2005).

National Union of Food, Beverages, Wine, Spirit and Allied Workers (NUFBWSAW): 8 Stannic Bldg, 4th Floor, New St, South Ghandi Sq., Johannesburg; POB 5718, Johannesburg 2000; tel. (11) 8331140; fax (11) 8331503; Pres. Armstrong Ntoyakhe; Nat. Organizer Anthony Hendricks; c. 10,000 mems (2005).

South African Chemical Workers' Union (SACWU): 29 Klerk St, btwn Harrison and Dirk Sts, 11th Floor, Johannesburg; POB 236, Johannesburg 2000; tel. (11) 8386581; fax (11) 8386622; e-mail samela@sacwu.co.za; Pres. Joseph Maqhekeni; c. 40,000 mems (2003).

Other organizations affiliated to NACTU include: the Banking, Insurance and Finance Workers' Union; the Hospitality Industry and Allied Workers' Union; the Hotel, Liquor, Catering, Commercial and Allied Workers' Union of South Africa; the Municipality, Education, State, Health and Allied Workers' Union; the National Clothing and Textile Workers' Union of South Africa; the National Services and Allied Workers' Union; the National Union of Farm Workers; the National Union of Furniture and Allied Workers; the Parliamentary Staff Union; the Transport and Allied Workers Union; and the Transport and Omnibus Workers' Union.

Non-affiliated Union

Public Servants' Association of South Africa (PSA): PSA Head Office Bldg, 563 Belvedere St, Arcadia, Pretoria; POB 40404, Arcadia 0007; tel. (12) 3036500; fax (12) 3036652; e-mail ask@psa.co.za; internet www.psa.co.za; withdrew affiliation from FEDUSA in 2006; Chair. Paul Sello; Pres. Koot Myburgh; Gen. Man. Danny Adonis; 185,500 mems (2006).

Transport

Most of South Africa's railway network and the harbours and airways are administered by the state-owned Transnet Ltd. There are no navigable rivers. Private bus services are regulated to complement the railways.

Transnet Ltd: Carlton Centre, 150 Commissioner St, Johannesburg 2001; POB 72501, Parkview 2122; tel. (11) 3083000; fax (11) 3082638; e-mail thandi.mlangeni@transnet.net; internet www.transnet.co.za; Chair. F. Phaswana; CEO C. F. Wells (acting).

RAILWAYS

With the exception of commuter services, the South African railways system is operated by Transnet Freight Rail Ltd (formerly Spoornet), the rail division of Transnet. The network comprised 31,400 track-km in 1996, of which 16,946 km was electrified. Extensive rail links connect Transnet Freight Rail with the rail networks of neighbouring countries.

Transnet Freight Rail: Inyanda House, 21 Wellington Rd, Parktown 2193; Private Bag X47, Johannesburg 2000; tel. (11) 5449368; fax (11) 5449515; e-mail dan.motaung@transnet.net; internet www.spoornet.co.za; fmrly Spoornet; renamed as above in 2007; CEO Siyabonga Gama.

ROADS

In 2001 there were an estimated 364,131 km of classified roads, including 239 km of motorways.

South African National Roads Agency Ltd (SANRAL): Ditsela Pl., 1204 Park St, cnr Duncan St, Hatfield, Pretoria; POB 415, Pretoria 0001; tel. (12) 4266000; fax (12) 3622116; e-mail info@nra.co.za; internet www.nra.co.za; f. 1998; responsible for design, construction, management and maintenance of 16,150 km of the national road network (2008); Chair. LOT NDLOVU; CEO NAZIR ALLI.

SHIPPING

The principal harbours are at Richards Bay, Durban, Saldanha, Cape Town, Port Elizabeth, East London Ngqura (Coega), and Mossel Bay. The deep-water port at Richards Bay has been extended and its facilities upgraded. Both Richards Bay and Saldanha Bay are major bulk-handling ports, while Saldanha Bay also has an important fishing fleet. More than 30 shipping lines serve South African ports.

South African Maritime Safety Authority (SAMSA): 161 Lynnwood Rd, cnr Duncan St, Brooklyn, Pretoria; POB 13186, Hatfield 0028; tel. (12) 3662600; fax (12) 3662601; e-mail info@samsa.org.za; internet www.samsa.org.za; advises the Govt on matters connected with sea transport to, from or between South Africa's ports, incl. safety at sea, and prevention of pollution by petroleum; CEO TSIETSI MOKHELE.

Transnet National Ports Authority: POB 32696, Braamfontein 2017; tel. (11) 2429003; fax (11) 2424027; internet www.transnet.co.za/NPAuthority.aspx; f. 2000; fmrly part of Portnet; subsidiary of Transnet; controls and manages the country's eight major seaports; CEO KHOMOTSO PHIHLELA.

Transnet Port Terminals: Kingsmead Office Park, cnr Stalwart and Stanger Sts, Durban 4001; tel. (86) 1204485; fax (31) 3088352; e-mail tptwebmaster@transnet.net; internet www.transnetportterminals.net; f. 2000 as South African Port Terminals, renamed as above in 2008; fmrly part of Portnet; subsidiary of Transnet; operates 13 container, bulk, breakbulk and car terminals at six of the country's major ports; CEO TAU MORWE.

CIVIL AVIATION

Civil aviation is controlled by the Minister of Transport. The Chief Directorate: Civil Aviation Authority at the Department of Transport is responsible for licensing and control of domestic and international air services.

Airports Company South Africa (ACSA): 24 Johnson Rd, Riverwoods, Bedfordview 2008; POB 75480, Gardenview 2047; tel. (11) 9216262; internet www.airports.co.za; f. 1993; owns and operates South Africa's 12 principal airports, of which six (at Johannesburg, Cape Town, Durban, Lanseria, Mmabatho and Pilanesburg) are classified as international airports; Chair. TOMMY OLIPHANT; Man. Dir MONHLA HLAHLA.

Civil Aviation Authority (CAA): Ikhaya Lokundiza, Bldg 16, Treur Close, Waterfall Park, Bekker St, Midrand; Private Bag X73, Halfway House 1685; tel. (11) 5451000; fax (12) 5451465; e-mail mail@caa.co.za; internet www.caa.co.za; CEO COLIN JORDAAN.

Airlink Airline: POB 7529, Bonaero Park 1622; tel. (11) 9611700; fax (11) 3951076; e-mail info@flyairlink.com; internet www.saairlink.co.za; f. 1992; internal and external scheduled services and charters in Southern Africa; Man. Dirs RODGER FOSTER, BARRIE WEBB.

COMAIR Ltd: cnr Atlas Rd and Marignane Dr., POB 7015, Bonaero Park 1622; tel. (11) 9210111; fax (11) 9733913; e-mail cr@comair.co.za; internet www.comair.co.za; f. 1946; scheduled domestic, regional and international services; Chair. D. NOVICK; Jt CEOs ERIK VENTER, GIDON NOVICK.

Interair South Africa: Private Bag 8, POB JHB Int. Airport 1627; Ground Floor, Finance House, Ernest Oppenheimer Rd, Bruma Lake Office, Bruma, Johannesburg; tel. (11) 6160636; fax (11) 6160930; e-mail info@interair.co.za; internet www.interair.co.za; Exec. Chair. DAVID P. TOKOPH.

Safair (Pty) Ltd: POB 938, Kempton Park 1620; tel. 9280000; fax 3951314; e-mail marketing@safair.co.za; internet www.safair.co.za; f. 1965; subsidiary of Imperial Holdings Ltd; aircraft leasing, engineering and maintenance services; CEO CHRISTO KOK.

South African Airways (SAA): Airways Park, Jones Rd, Private Bag X13, Johannesburg 1627; tel. (11) 9782888; fax (11) 9789567; e-mail voyager@flysaa.com; internet www.flysaa.com; f. 1934; state-owned; internal passenger services linking all the principal towns; international services to Africa, Europe, North and South America and Asia; Chair. JAKES GERWEL; CEO CHRIS SMYTH (acting).

Tourism

Tourism is an important part of South Africa's economy. The chief attractions for visitors are the climate, scenery and wildlife reserves. In 2006 some 8.5m. tourists visited South Africa. In that year receipts from tourism amounted to US $8,967m.

South African Tourism: Bojanala House, 90 Protea Rd, Chislehurston, Johannesburg 2196; Private Bag X10012, Sandton 2146; tel. (11) 8953000; fax (11) 8953001; internet www.southafrica.net; f. 1947; 11 overseas brs; CEO MOEKETSI MOSOLA.

SPAIN

Introductory Survey

Location, Climate, Language, Religion, Flag, Capital

The Kingdom of Spain, in south-western Europe, forms more than four-fifths of the Iberian peninsula. The country also includes the Balearic Islands in the Mediterranean Sea, the Canary Islands in the Atlantic Ocean and a few small enclaves in North Africa. Mainland Spain is bounded to the north by Andorra and France and to the west by Portugal. To the east is the Mediterranean Sea, and Morocco lies 30 km to the south. The climate is less temperate than in most of western Europe, with hot summers and, in the hilly interior, cold winters. The official national language is Spanish. Catalan, and its close relative Valencian, are widely spoken in the north-east, Basque in the north and Galician in the north-west; all have co-official status in their respective regions. The overwhelming majority of the population are Roman Catholics, but the 1978 Constitution laid down that Spain had no official state religion. The national flag (proportions 2 by 3) carries three horizontal stripes, of red, yellow (half the depth) and red. The state flag carries, in addition, the national coat of arms. The capital is Madrid.

Recent History

After winning the civil war of 1936–39, the Nationalist forces, led by Gen. Francisco Franco y Bahamonde, established an authoritarian rule which restricted individual liberties and severely repressed challenges to its power. In 1942 Gen. Franco revived the traditional legislative assembly, the Cortes (Courts), with limited powers. After keeping Spain neutral in the Second World War, Franco announced in 1947 that the monarchy (abolished in 1931) would be restored after his death or retirement. In 1967, in the first elections since the civil war, a portion of the Cortes was directly elected under a limited franchise. In July 1969 Franco nominated Prince Juan Carlos de Borbón (grandson of the last reigning monarch, King Alfonso XIII) as his successor, and in June 1973 relinquished the post of President of the Council of Ministers to Adm. Luis Carrero Blanco, who was killed in December. Responsibility for the assassination was claimed by Euskadi ta Askatasuna (ETA—Basque Homeland and Liberty), the Basque separatist organization. Carlos Arias Navarro became President of the Government (Prime Minister) in January 1974.

Franco died in November 1975. He was succeeded as Head of State by King Juan Carlos, and in December a more liberal Council of Ministers was formed. In 1976 restrictions on political activity were lifted. In July Arias Navarro resigned at the King's request, and was replaced by Adolfo Suárez González. The introduction of democratic government then proceeded rapidly, and an elected bicameral legislature was established. Most of the numerous de facto political parties were able to take part in the general elections for the Cortes, held in June 1977. An overall majority was won by the Unión de Centro Democrático (UCD), a coalition party headed by the Prime Minister. In December 1978 a new Constitution was endorsed by referendum and ratified by the King. It confirmed Spain as a parliamentary monarchy, with freedom for political parties, and guaranteed the right of Spain's 'nationalities and regions' to autonomy.

A general election was held in March 1979, resulting in little change in the distribution of seats in the Cortes. The new Government was again headed by Suárez. Basque and Catalan autonomous parliaments were established in March 1980 and, in elections to both parliaments, the UCD was heavily defeated by the moderate regionalist parties. Confidence in Suárez diminished and in January 1981 he resigned. Leopoldo Calvo-Sotelo Bustelo, hitherto the Deputy Prime Minister, succeeded him.

In February 1981 a group of armed civil guards, led by Lt-Col Antonio Tejero Molina, stormed into the Cortes, taking hostage 350 deputies. The military commander of Valencia, Lt-Gen. Jaime Milans del Bosch, declared a state of emergency in that region and sent tanks on to the streets of the city of Valencia. King Juan Carlos acted swiftly to secure the loyalty of other military commanders, and by the following morning had been able to persuade Milans himself to stand down. Tejero surrendered, and the deputies were released unharmed. More than 30 military officers were subsequently brought to trial, and both Tejero and Milans received lengthy prison sentences. Milans was released in 1990, and Tejero was released in 1996.

Immediately after the attempted coup, Calvo-Sotelo formed a new Council of Ministers, resisting pressure to establish a coalition government. The Prime Minister addressed various contentious issues during his term of office, including his decision to take Spain into the North Atlantic Treaty Organization (NATO, see p. 351). At the election for the first Galician Parliament, held in October 1981, the Alianza Popular (AP) won two seats more than the UCD. The overwhelming Socialist victory at the election for the Parliament of Andalucía (Andalusia) in May 1982 was a grave set-back for the central Government. Following Calvo-Sotelo's replacement as party leader by Landelino Lavilla Alsina in July, Suárez defected to found a rival party, the Centro Democrático y Social (CDS). Desertion from the UCD continued and by August the party no longer commanded a workable majority, and an early general election was called. In October, however, shortly before the election, a right-wing plot to stage a pre-emptive military coup was uncovered. Four colonels were arrested (three of whom were subsequently sentenced to prison terms), and Milans was also implicated. The election resulted in a decisive victory for the Partido Socialista Obrero Español (PSOE—Spanish Socialist Workers' Party), led by Felipe González Márquez, who formed a new Council of Ministers in December 1982.

One of the most serious problems facing the new Government was the continuing tension in the Basque region (see below). Moreover, in June 1985 hundreds of thousands of workers, motivated by the Unión General de Trabajadores (UGT) and supported by the Confederación Sindical de Comisiones Obreras (CCOO), protested against proposed reforms in the social security system and consequent reductions in pension rights. Following large-scale demonstrations against Spain's membership of NATO, in March 1986 a long-awaited referendum on the question of Spain's continued membership of the alliance was held. Contrary to expectations, the Spanish people voted to remain within NATO, following Prime Minister González's reversal on the issue and an extensive campaign by the Government.

In an early general election held in June 1986 the PSOE was returned to power, winning 184 of the 350 seats in the Congreso de los Diputados (Congress of Deputies), 18 fewer than at the 1982 election, while the conservative Coalición Popular (CP), which incorporated the AP, the Partido Demócrata Popular (subsequently Democracia Cristiana) and the Partido Liberal, won 105 seats. A new Council of Ministers was appointed in late July, again led by González. Following its defeat, the CP fell into disarray, and in December Manuel Fraga, the leader of the AP, resigned.

In June 1987 the results of the European Parliament, regional and municipal elections confirmed the continuing decline in support for the PSOE. The AP also sustained losses, while the centre-left CDS was able to strengthen its position. The growing rift between the Prime Minister and the UGT (a trade union traditionally allied to the PSOE) became increasingly evident, and in October Nicolás Redondo, the UGT leader, and a union colleague resigned from their seats as PSOE deputies in the Cortes, in protest against the Government's economic policies. The UGT and CCOO then combined forces to organize a new campaign of protests against the Government, which continued throughout 1988, culminating in December in a one-day general strike, which was supported by almost 8m. workers. Similar strikes in Madrid and elsewhere followed.

In January 1989 Fraga returned to the leadership of the AP, which was relaunched as the Partido Popular (PP) and which was subsequently joined by Democracia Cristiana and the Partido Liberal. The unity of the PSOE was undermined by the establishment of a dissident faction and by the defection to Izquierda Unida (IU—United Left, an alliance comprising the Partido Comunista de España and other left-wing parties) of 100 PSOE members. Nevertheless, at the general election, held eight months early, in late October, the PSOE was returned to power on a provisional basis, pending investigations into allegations of polling irregularities. After several months of controversy, the

PSOE's representation in the Congreso de los Diputados was reduced to 175 of the 350 seats, the PP holding 107 seats. The PSOE, however, was able to retain a majority by subsequently entering into a tactical alliance with the CDS, the Catalan nationalist Convergència i Unió (CiU) and the Euzko Alderdi Jeltzalea/Partido Nacionalista Vasco (EAJ/PNV—the Basque Nationalist Party).

Various corruption scandals involving both main parties were revealed over the course of the new legislative term. In April 1990 a number of PP officials and business executives were arrested in connection with allegations of bribery and in 1991 a PSOE official resigned, following revelations of illegal donations to that party. Public concern at apparent widespread corruption increased in February 1992 when the Governor of the central bank, the Banco de España, Mariano Rubio, was accused of irregularities relating to his personal investments. In early 1993 the PSOE's reputation was further damaged by new revelations concerning the party's financing. Having refused to permit inspection of its accounts, in late 1992 the PSOE headquarters had been forcibly searched on the orders of the judge investigating the allegations. Following a Supreme Court inquiry into the affair, PSOE officials, business executives and bankers were charged, and in October 1997 eight defendants were sentenced to terms of imprisonment.

At the general election in June 1993 the PSOE failed to obtain an absolute majority in the Congreso de los Diputados, where its strength declined to 159 of the 350 seats. The PP increased its representation to 141 seats, while IU won 18 seats, CiU 17 and the EAJ/PNV five. The CDS lost all of its seats. The PSOE's negotiations with CiU and with the EAJ/PNV failed to result in the conclusion of a formal coalition agreement. In July, therefore, González commenced his fourth term as Prime Minister, at the head of a minority administration. With the Spanish economy in recession the Prime Minister appealed for support for drastic measures to address the economic crisis. In November, however, thousands of protesters demonstrated against the Government's economic policies. Controversial labour legislation, as amended to comply with CiU requests, was approved by the Congreso in March 1994.

In 1994–95 the Government came under increasing pressure over suggestions that it had been involved in the establishment of the Grupos Antiterroristas de la Liberación (GAL), a counter-terrorist grouping which had been formed in 1983 with the aim of combating ETA. It was alleged that members of the Ertzaintza (Basque Country police force) had given support to the organization, which was suspected of responsibility for the murders of numerous ETA members exiled in France. Investigations into the affair had begun in 1988, and in 1991 a senior police officer in Bilbao, José Amedo, and an accomplice, Michel Domínguez, were convicted of organizing the groups of mercenaries and imprisoned. In December 1994, following further questioning of the pair and the reopening of the case, Julián Sancristóbal, a former director-general of state security in the Ministry of the Interior, was arrested on suspicion of financing and assisting GAL. The Prime Minister denied that the Government had been connected in any way with the so-called 'dirty war' of the 1980s against ETA. In February 1995, however, the investigating judge Baltasar Garzón ordered the arrest of Rafael Vera, the former Secretary of State for Security, on suspicion of involvement in the kidnapping in 1983 of Segundo Marey, a French business executive mistaken for an ETA member, and of misuse of public funds. In April 1995, concluding that GAL had been established and financed by the Ministry of the Interior, Garzón indicted a total of 14 former officials, including Vera and Sancristóbal, both of whom were subsequently released on bail. Garzón's final report into the origins and financing of GAL implicated González along with the former Deputy Prime Minister and Minister of Defence, Narcís Serra, the Minister of the Interior during 1982–88, José Barrionuevo, the Basque socialist leader, Txiki Benegas, and other PSOE officials.

In September 1995 Judge Eduardo Móner was appointed by the Supreme Court to examine the allegations against the Prime Minister and the other senior politicians. Móner subsequently heard declarations from Sancristóbal that the abduction of Marey in 1983 had been approved by both Barrionuevo and Vera. In October 1995 José Luis Corcuera (who had succeeded Barrionuevo as Minister of the Interior), Sancristóbal and Vera were charged with misuse of public funds. In January 1996, his parliamentary immunity having been removed, Barrionuevo was indicted by the Supreme Court on three charges: illegal detention; misuse of public funds; and association with an armed group. In April Judge Móner reported that he had found no evidence linking González to the activities of the death squads, believed to be responsible for the murders of 27 ETA members, while Serra and Benegas were also exonerated.

In April 1997 Judge Móner concluded his inquiry into the abduction of Marey. In September the Supreme Court confirmed that 12 defendants were to stand trial: Barrionuevo, Vera, Sancristóbal, Amedo, Domínguez and seven others. At the conclusion of the trial in July 1998, Barrionuevo, Vera and Sancristóbal were found guilty of kidnapping and misappropriation of public funds; each received a prison sentence of 10 years. The sentences of the other nine defendants ranged from two to nine years. By the end of December, however, 11 of the prisoners had been set free, their sentences having been suspended, while the 12th was released in June 2000. A further trial began in September 2001, with González among some 100 witnesses called upon to testify. In January 2002 Barrionuevo and Corcuera were absolved of the charges of misappropriation of funds; however, Vera was sentenced to seven years' imprisonment and barred from holding public office for 18 years.

At the general election, held 15 months early, in March 1996, and in which 78% of the electorate participated, the PP took 156 of the 350 seats in the Congreso de los Diputados, thus falling short of an outright majority. The PSOE, its reputation severely damaged by the ongoing Marey affair, won 141 seats, IU 21 and CiU 16. In the Senado (Senate) the PP received 132 of the 256 seats (winning 111 by direct election), while the PSOE took 96 (81 by direct election). The King invited José María Aznar, the President of the PP, to form a government. After protracted negotiations, the PP and CiU reached agreement on a pact enabling Aznar to take office. Having also secured the support of the five EAJ/PNV deputies and of the four representatives of Coalición Canaria (CC), the new Prime Minister's investiture finally took place in early May. (However, the EAJ/PNV abandoned its pact with the Government in September 1997, before withdrawing its support entirely in December 1999.)

One of the new administration's main priorities was the reduction of the budget deficit. Several aspects of the Government's policies, however, aroused intense opposition. In December 1996 civil servants took part in a 24-hour strike to protest against the Government's imposition of a pay 'freeze', while in February 1997 a two-week strike by truck drivers, in support of improved working conditions, caused severe disruption and led to the closure of the country's road borders. In early 1998 one miner died during violent protests in northern Spain, where the coal-miners of Asturias were demonstrating against proposed job losses (the Government having been obliged to plan decreases in coal output in order to comply with European Union (EU, see p. 255) directives regarding reductions in subsidies to state-owned industries). At the end of January, after a month-long strike that attracted much public sympathy, agreement was reached when the Government granted concessions on the terms of early retirement for miners.

At the PSOE congress in June 1997, having led the party for 23 years, González unexpectedly announced his resignation as Secretary-General. Joaquín Almunia, hitherto the party's parliamentary spokesman and a loyal associate of González, was chosen to succeed him. In April 1998, in a new procedure that required the holding of primary elections in the contest for the selection of the PSOE's next prime ministerial candidate, Almunia was defeated by Josep Borrell, a former government minister. Almunia's offer of resignation from the party leadership was rejected. In November, in a bid to restore party unity, the PSOE designated Borrell as party leader and sole spokesman, while Almunia was to remain responsible for political affairs, at the head of the party's federal executive committee. However, in May 1999 Borrell resigned following the revelation of a financial scandal involving allegations of malpractice by two former colleagues during the 1980s. He was replaced in July by Almunia, who was selected unopposed as the party's prime ministerial candidate.

In April 1998, meanwhile, after an inquiry lasting three years, Judge Gómez de Liaño concluded his investigation into the fate of two ETA activists allegedly killed by GAL members in 1983. Criminal proceedings were instigated against seven suspects, including Vera, Elgorriaga and Gen. Rodríguez Galindo. In April 2000 Galindo and Elgorriaga were found guilty of involvement in the abduction and murder of the two activists, and were each sentenced to 71 years' imprisonment.

The ruling party's strong performance at the legislative election held on 12 March 2000 was largely attributed to the Government's record of economic success (in particular its reduction of the unemployment rate). In the lower house the PP won 183 of the 350 seats, thus unexpectedly securing an absolute majority. The PSOE's representation was reduced to 125 seats, while IU, which had conducted a joint campaign with the PSOE, suffered a sharp decline in support, losing 13 of its 21 seats in the Congreso de los Diputados. The moderate regional parties, CiU and the EAJ/PNV, took 15 and seven seats, respectively. In the Senado the PP increased its strength to 127 of the 208 directly elected seats, whereas the PSOE's representation decreased to 61 seats. The level of voter participation was less than 70%. Almunia immediately conceded defeat and resigned as leader of the PSOE. At the party congress in July José Luis Rodríguez Zapatero, a lawyer, was elected to the leadership of the PSOE. Zapatero, who excluded left-wingers from the new national executive committee, declared his intention to modernize the party in order to form an effective opposition.

At the end of April 2000, with the support of the 15 CiU and four CC deputies, Aznar, who expressed a desire to govern largely by consensus, was sworn in for a second term of office. The Prime Minister announced the composition of the new Council of Ministers on the following day. Mariano Rajoy, hitherto Minister of Education, was appointed Deputy Prime Minister and Minister of the Presidency. Rodrigo Rato also remained a Deputy Prime Minister, retaining the economy portfolio, while that of finance was allocated to Cristóbal Montoro. Josep Piqué i Camps became Minister of Foreign Affairs. The incoming Government's programme included the reduction of taxes, reforms in the financing of the Autonomous Communities and improvements in the judicial system.

During 2001 the Government suffered from the alleged involvement of several PP members in corruption cases. In mid-June the Supreme Court decided to proceed with an investigation into the role of the Minister of Foreign Affairs, Josep Piqué, in the fraudulent sale of Ertoil, a subsidiary of the Spanish fuel company Ercros, of whose board Piqué was a member, to the French company Elf Aquitaine. In mid-2001 the Government's reputation was undermined by the collapse of the Antonio Camacho Gescartera stockbroking company, as a result of which several prominent charities and organizations lost significant sums of money. In September the President of the National Securities and Exchange Commission (Comisión Nacional del Mercado de Valores—CNMV), Pilar Valiente, was remanded in custody following the publication of her personal diaries, in which it was revealed that she had long been aware of discrepancies in the stockbroker's accounts. Since Valiente had been appointed by the Deputy Prime Minister and Minister of the Economy, Rodrigo Rato, his position also came under scrutiny and a full reorganization of the CNMV was ordered in early 2002, following the implication of several more of its members in the case. In November 2002 a €2.1m. fine was imposed on the Spanish arm of the British HSBC bank, for its role in 'laundering' Gescartera funds worth some €100m. in 138 numbered accounts.

In January 2002 the PP re-elected Aznar as its President, but he made clear his intention not to seek a third term as Prime Minister in 2004. In May 2002, after the trial of Arnaldo Otegi of Batasuna (the political wing of ETA—see below) was dismissed by the Supreme Court, a request by Aznar for reconsideration was strongly criticized by the judiciary as misplaced government intervention. Also in May, as a result of the failure of negotiations between the Government, trade unions and employers' representatives over proposed reforms to employment law, the CCOO and the UGT announced plans to hold the first general strike since 1988; the following day the Government approved the imposition of reforms to unemployment subsidies by decree. The general strike proceeded in mid-June 2002, with the UGT claiming a rate of participation of 80%. In June disagreements between Aznar and Jordi Pujol i Soley, the President of CiU and of the Generalitat (the autonomous administration of Catalonia—Cataluña or Catalunya), in which Aznar accused the latter of disloyalty to the Government and support for the general strike, led to a freezing of relations between the PP and CiU for a 'period of reflection'. The resultant resignation of the Minister of Labour prompted a cabinet reorganization, in which, most notably, Ana Palacio replaced Piqué as Minister of Foreign Affairs. Revised legislation on labour reform, which annulled the main provisions of the controversial decree, was approved by the Congreso de los Diputados in October.

In mid-November 2002 the Aznar Government was faced with a serious crisis following the sinking of the Liberian-registered, Greek-owned oil tanker *Prestige* 240 km off the coast of Galicia.

The vessel, which had reported to the authorities that its hull had ruptured and that it was leaking oil, had been refused landfall and had been towed out to sea, where it split in two and sank six days later. An estimated 12,000 metric tons of the vessel's 77,000-ton capacity was believed to have been released into the sea in the first slick, around one-half of which soon reached the Galician coast, requiring the imposition of a prohibition of fishing in that area. It was subsequently revealed that the oil remaining in the wreck was still leaking (in early January 2003 the total amount of spillage was revised to 25,000 tons). Massive clean-up operations were launched, mostly by environmental groups and by the local population; a significant lack of aid from the Spanish military aroused widespread public discontent. Demonstrations were attended by some 150,000 people in Santiago de Compostela in December and by around 100,000 people in Vigo in January 2003, at which participants protested at the perceived mishandling of the disaster by both the regional and national PP authorities and demanded the resignation of Aznar. A local commission launched by the regional Government of Galicia met with obstruction from the central Government, which also delayed the setting up of a national investigation. Meanwhile, the oil slicks spread to the Basque region, and also reached the coastlines of France and Portugal.

Amid the increasing likelihood of US-led military action against the Iraqi regime of Saddam Hussain in early 2003, Aznar was one of eight European leaders to sign a declaration at the end of January in support of US moves towards an ultimatum. Public opinion, however, already swayed against the PP by the Government's handling of the *Prestige* disaster, was, in general, strongly against military action, with 3m. people participating in anti-war demonstrations in mid-February, and opinion polls suggesting that at least 80% of the population was against the launching of armed conflict in Iraq. None the less, in late February Aznar expressed his support for US-led military action with a UN mandate. As the US intention to commence armed intervention with or without UN approval became clear, Aznar assured the Spanish people that Spain would not contribute to any military coalition. A summit meeting hosted in the Azores in March led to a joint declaration by Aznar, the British Prime Minister, Tony Blair, and the US President, George W. Bush, condemning the regime of Saddam Hussain and expressing support for necessary military actions. The subsequent announcement by the USA of its intention to act, if need be, without international ratification received the PP Government's concerted support. Although the PP Government strongly supported Aznar's policy on Iraq, by 1 April six parliamentary motions rejecting the war (which had commenced on 20 March) had been proposed by opposition parties, and on 29 March a number of non-governmental organizations filed charges against Aznar before the Supreme Court, accusing him of exceeding his authorities. Public demonstrations continued in March and April, with a march in Madrid on 6 April supported by the prominent judge Garzón, and another comprising up to 200,000 protesters in Barcelona on 12 April. In April seven diplomatic staff at the Iraqi embassy in Madrid were expelled at the request of the USA, ostensibly on the grounds of alleged espionage.

The scale of public protest against the Iraqi conflict prompted the drafting of legislation by the PP in April 2003 that would extend the jurisdiction of military courts to include trial (with a maximum sentence of six years) for acts of protest staged to discredit Spain's participation in international armed conflict. In July, despite the level of popular feeling against the war and the dissent of all the opposition parties, the Government committed 1,300 troops to the peace-keeping force. In November seven Spanish intelligence officers were killed in Iraq, bringing the total number of Spaniards to have died as a direct result of the conflict to 10. Opinion polls reported that an estimated 90% of the Spanish population believed that the instigation of armed conflict in Iraq by the US-led coalition had been a mistake, and Zapatero, the leader of the PSOE, stated that if his party won the general election in March 2004, Spanish troops would be withdrawn from Iraq. In September 2003 the Deputy Prime Minister, Rajoy, was appointed as the PP's prime ministerial candidate for the general election following his nomination by Aznar.

Four days before the general election, on 11 March 2004, 10 bombs exploded in four commuter trains in Madrid, killing 191 people and injuring more than 1,500. The Minister of the Interior, Acebes, immediately indicated that ETA was the principal suspect; Batasuna, however, was swift to condemn the attacks. Campaigning for the election was suspended, and three days of national mourning were declared. On 12 March demonstrations against the atrocity were held throughout Spain, and more than 2m. people marched through the centre of Madrid. Despite the Government's initial supposition that the bombings had been carried out by ETA, suspicion increasingly came to rest on Islamist militants; in the days following the attacks three Moroccans suspected of having links to the al-Qa'ida (Base) organization of the Saudi-born militant Islamist Osama bin Laden and to the May 2003 suicide bombings in Casablanca, Morocco, were arrested.

Opinion polls conducted before the general election had widely predicted that the PP would win with a reduced majority. However, the bombings became the central issue in the election, which took place as scheduled on 14 March 2004. Following the emergence of evidence suggesting that Islamists had perpetrated the attacks, the Government was criticized for its premature response in blaming ETA and its unwillingness to consider other possibilities. In the event, the PSOE secured an unexpected victory in the elections to the lower house, winning 42.7% of the votes (164 seats), while the PP obtained 37.7% of the votes (148 seats). The PP retained its majority in the Senado, however, winning 102 of the directly elected seats, compared with the 93 directly elected seats secured by the PSOE. The PP held 126 seats in the final composition of the Senado, and the PSOE 111. The election turn-out, at 77.2%, was nine percentage points higher than in 2000. Immediately after his party's victory Zapatero reiterated his pledge to withdraw Spanish troops from Iraq if control in that country were not handed over by the US-led coalition authorities to the UN by 30 June. However, on assuming office he announced that the troops would be withdrawn as quickly as possible, and the Spanish withdrawal was completed by the end of May. Zapatero announced that he did not intend to form a coalition government; rather, the PSOE made pacts with smaller parties in the two legislative chambers, effectively isolating the PP. Having won a congressional vote of confidence, Zapatero and his new Council of Ministers were inaugurated on 17 April. Miguel Ángel Moratinos assumed the position of Minister of Foreign Affairs and Co-operation, and José Antonio Alonso was appointed Minister of the Interior. Pedro Solbes, previously the EU Commissioner for Economic and Monetary Affairs, was appointed Second Deputy Prime Minister and Minister of the newly reunited departments of the economy and finance. The new Government's programme included constitutional reform, transforming the Senado into a more regionally representative body, fiscal reform, the implementation of a co-ordinated anti-terrorism policy and a focus on improving gender equality and reducing domestic violence.

On 2 April 2004, meanwhile, a bomb of the same type discovered on the trains involved in the earlier Madrid attacks was defused on the railway line between Madrid and Seville (Sevilla). The following day seven men who were suspected of involvement in the bombings apparently blew themselves up, killing one police officer, during a police raid on an apartment in Leganés, a suburb of Madrid; Abdelmajid Farkhet, the man suspected of organizing the 11 March attacks, was among the dead. In May a parliamentary commission of inquiry into the train bombings was established. Specifically, the commission was to investigate information on the attacks provided by the PP Government, that Government's anti-terrorist policy, and the trafficking of illegal arms in Spain. In late November the former Prime Minister, Aznar, was questioned by the commission. Aznar maintained that ETA was linked to the Islamist militants suspected of carrying out the bomb attacks. Zapatero, who subsequently appeared before the commission, alleged that the PP administration had deleted all government computer records relating to the train bombings before leaving office. In March 2005 the preliminary findings of the commission, supported by all the parliamentary groups except the PP, were published. Recommendations included an increase in the implementation of security measures; however, the commission was criticized by some observers for being overly political in its handling of the inquiry.

During its first two years in office Zapatero's Government relied less on support from the opposition in major policy areas than had the previous Government. In particular, the PP did not support the Government in its attempts to begin negotiations with ETA, or on the Catalan Statute of Autonomy (see below), and the Government passed its legislative agenda mainly with the support of Esquerra Republicana de Catalunya (ERC) and IU. In December 2004 the Government's budget was approved by the Congreso de los Diputados, despite having been vetoed in the PP-dominated Senado.

Despite opposition from leaders of the Roman Catholic church, legislation permitting marriage between couples of the same sex was adopted by the Senado in June 2005, following its approval by the Congreso de los Diputados in April. In November new defence legislation was passed that required any deployment of Spanish troops abroad to be approved by the Cortes, and limited the circumstances in which such a deployment might occur.

In February 2006 Spain's highest consultative body, the Council of State, voted to support the Government's proposed amendments to the Constitution. Among the changes anticipated were the alteration of the law of royal succession, removing the preference for a male heir, a restructuring of the Senado and an increase in the power of the Autonomous Communities in the upper house; also to be addressed was the contentious issue of whether the Autonomous Communities should be regarded as 'nations'. However, in May 2007 Zapatero announced that the Government was abandoning constitutional reform for the duration of the current legislature owing to lack of support from the PP.

In April 2006 Zapatero announced an unexpected reorganization of the Government, prompted by the resignation of the Minister of Defence, José Bono; he was replaced by Alonso, who was in turn succeeded as Minister of the Interior by Alfredo Pérez Rubalcaba. Further cabinet changes occurred in early September after the Minister of Industry, Tourism and Trade, José Montilla, announced his intention to stand for election as President of the Generalitat in the forthcoming Catalan elections; he was replaced by Joan Clos. In February 2007 Juan Fernando López Aguilar relinquished the post of Minister of Justice to stand for the presidency of the regional government of the Canary Islands (Islas Canarias), and was replaced by Mariano Fernández Bermejo, the former Chief Prosecutor of Madrid.

The Government came under pressure in early 2007 over its handling of the situation in the Basque Country, following ETA's breach of its cease-fire and the subsequent collapse of nascent peace talks (see below). In early March the prison sentence of Iñaki de Juana Chaos, an ETA militant who had been on hunger strike for nearly four months in protest at his continued detention, was commuted to house arrest on humanitarian grounds. (De Juana's 18-year sentence had been due to end in 2004, but had been extended after he was convicted of making terrorist threats.) The Government had feared that de Juana would come to be regarded as a martyr for Basque nationalism if he were allowed to die in gaol. However, his release prompted protests from the opposition, which urged Zapatero to resign, while some 500,000 people participated in an anti-Government demonstration in Madrid, organized by the PP. However, following the declaration by ETA in early June that its cease-fire had ended, de Juana was returned to prison near Madrid. The Government attracted criticism again in late March, following the release of Otegi, the leader of Batasuna, who had been brought to trial in Madrid on charges of glorifying terrorism, after the prosecution withdrew the charges. Otegi was re-arrested later in the year, when he began serving a 15-month prison sentence in relation to the same charges.

During 2007 a principal topic of political debate concerned proposals, presented personally by Zapatero as Prime Minister, to introduce a 'law on historic memory' that was intended to provide formal recognition to those who had lost their lives during and immediately before the civil war, and to those who had been the victims of political repression under the Franco regime. The draft legislation was subject to criticism from both the PP, which regarded the proposals contained within the law as potentially socially divisive and unwarranted, and from human rights groups and the Catalan nationalist allies of the Government, the ERC, which considered the measures to be insufficiently rigorous. None the less, the Congreso de los Diputados approved the legislation at the end of October. Public funds were to be provided to organizations involved in locating mass graves, and to identifying, exhuming and re-burying the dead. Trials on political charges conducted during the period of Franco's rule were to be declared illegitimate (sentences passed were not, however, to be repealed outright), while political rallies at Franco's place of burial were to be prohibited. Meanwhile, also in late October, tens of thousands of Spanish pilgrims paraded in the Vatican City, to commemorate the beatification by the Roman Catholic Church of some 498 priests and members of religious orders killed during the Civil War, principally by Republican forces. In November 2008 Spain's leading investigating judge, Garzón, launched a criminal investigation into the disappearance of tens of thousands of Spaniards during the civil war and Franco's dictatorship, and ordered the exhumation of several mass graves. Garzón claimed jurisdiction on the grounds that the crimes committed during this period constituted 'crimes against humanity' rather than political crimes, and were consequently not covered by an amnesty law of 1977 nor by any statute of limitations. Later that month, however, the country's highest criminal court, the Audiencia Nacional, ruled that Garzón did not have the authority to launch such an investigation and that inquiries into such crimes must be carried out by courts in the regions where the crimes were committed. Also in November it was announced that some 500,000 descendants of those Spaniards who fled the country during the civil war and Franco's reign would be permitted to apply for Spanish citizenship.

Meanwhile, in September 2007 Zapatero announced that a general election was to be held on 9 March 2008. Campaigning for the election by the PSOE and PP was suspended one day early, following the assassination, seemingly by ETA, of a former PSOE candidate in local elections in Mondragon, the Basque Country. At the elections, both the PSOE and PP increased their share of the votes cast, and their representation in the Congreso de los Diputados, compared with the results of the 2004 election, to 43.6% and 169 seats, and 40.1% and 154 seats, respectively. The representation of IU and of the ERC decreased, to two and three seats, respectively, while CiU won 10 seats and the EAJ/PNV six. Four other parties, mostly representing regional interests, obtained representation in the chamber. As in the outgoing lower chamber, no party controlled an overall majority of seats, although it was anticipated that the PSOE would again form a minority government. In concurrent elections to the Senado, the PP remained the largest faction, with 98 of the directly elected seats, and (following the appointment, in the following month, of senators to represent the Autonomous Community of Andalusia, in which an election to the regional legislature had been held concurrently with the general election) a further 24 appointed seats. The PSOE obtained 79 directly elected seats, and held 14 appointees.

On 9 April 2008 Zapatero narrowly failed to obtain the requisite two-thirds' majority in the Congreso de los Diputados (176 deputies) to be confirmed as Prime Minister, although he succeeded in obtaining the simple majority required at a second vote held two days later. The appointment of a new Government, including the formation of two new ministries—of Equality and of Science and Innovation—was announced later in the month. Several principal positions remained unchanged from the outgoing administration: Moratinos retained his post as Minister of Foreign Affairs and Co-operation; Rubalcaba remained as Minister of the Interior; María Teresa Fernández de la Vega as First Deputy Prime Minister, Minister of the Presidency and Government Spokesperson; and Solbes as Second Deputy Prime Minister and Minister of the Economy and Finance. New appointments included Carme Chacón Piqueras as Minister of Defence—the first woman to assume that post in Spain. Indeed, excluding the premiership, women accounted for exactly one-half of the ministerial appointments.

Zapatero's new Government was faced with growing problems precipitated by the world economic slowdown. In the year to March 2009 unemployment in the country nearly doubled as some 2m. people lost their jobs and the construction industry collapsed. In June 2008 road hauliers began an indefinite national strike in protest at the effects of high fuel prices, which caused widespread disruption across the country as roads were blocked and supplies disrupted. The Government, which deployed thousands of police to clear the roads, leading to arrests and violent clashes between police and protesters, rejected requests to set a minimum price for haulage, but introduced measures to reduce the impact of the price rises. In response to the economic downturn, Zapatero introduced stimulus plans in April, August and November. Faced with growing levels of unemployment, in January 2009 the Government announced an incentive aimed at unemployed immigrants in Spain, under the terms of which they could cash in their unemployment benefits for a lump sum of some €10,000, on condition that they returned to their home countries and agreed not to return to Spain to seek work for at least three years.

Meanwhile, in early 2009 allegations of corruption were brought against the PP. It was claimed that several of the party's members, including the head of the regional government in Valencia, Francisco Camps, had accepted bribes from business executives who donated money to the party. In February the Minister of Justice, Bermejo, resigned from his post after it was claimed that he had interfered in the investigation by going on a hunting trip with Garzón, the judge in charge of the investigation. Bermejo was replaced by Francisco Caamaño Domínguez, hitherto Zapatero's Secretary for Parliamentary Affairs. In April Zapatero effected a cabinet reorganization in order to boost the PSOE's flagging popularity amid the economic crisis and prior to the European Parliament elections, scheduled to take place in June. Among the most notable appointments was the replacement of the Second Deputy Prime Minister and Minister of the Economy and Finance, Pedro Solbes, by Elena Salgado Méndez. Solbes had openly disagreed with Zapatero over future fiscal stimulus plans, opposing a further widening of the country's budget deficit. The PSOE suffered losses at a number of regional elections held in March (see below), seemingly due to public dissatisfaction with the Government's response to the economic downturn.

Autonomous regional parliaments were established in the Basque Country and in Catalonia in 1980. The parliaments of Galicia and Andalucía were established in October 1981 and May 1982, respectively, and the remaining 13 Legislative Assemblies of the Autonomous Communities (Comunidades Autónomas) were elected in May 1983. In 2001 proposals were announced to complete the development process of the Autonomous Communities with a policy of co-operation between the communities, through meetings and conferences. The presidents of each Autonomous Community were to be incorporated into the Senado, thus making it more representative of Spain as a whole. (See Legislative Assemblies of the Autonomous Communities for details of the most recent elections to all regional parliaments.)

Prior to the regional elections in Catalonia in 2003, Jordi Pujol, who had been President of a CiU-led Government in Catalonia for 23 years, announced that he would retire. No party won an absolute majority in the Catalan regional elections held on 16 November, and the two leading parties, CiU and the Partit dels Socialistes de Catalunya (PSC), each entered negotiations to form a coalition with the separatist ERC, which, having almost doubled its representation to 23 seats, held the balance of power. A coalition was subsequently formed comprising the PSC, ERC and the ecologist Iniciativa per Catalunya-Verds (IC-V). The PSC candidate, Pasqual Maragall, was inaugurated as President of the Generalitat on 15 December.

In September 2005 the Catalan Parliament overwhelmingly approved the draft of a revised Statute of Autonomy, to replace the existing document which had been in force since 1979. The proposed statute provoked considerable controversy elsewhere in the country over its definition of Catalonia as a 'nation' and its provision for greater fiscal and judicial independence. In 2006 Prime Minister Zapatero bypassed the PSC, traditionally allied to the national PSOE, and negotiated an agreement with the centre-right CiU to revise the proposed statute, significantly reducing the extent of financial independence that would be granted to Catalonia. In late March the Congreso de los Diputados approved the statute, despite the opposition of ERC, which favoured full independence, and the PP, which claimed that the statute violated the Constitution. In May Maragall dismissed the ERC members of the Catalan Government in response to the party's refusal to support the autonomy statute, and announced that early elections would take place following the referendum on the statute to be held on 18 June. At the referendum the new Statute of Autonomy was approved by 73.2% of voters in Catalonia; voter participation was 48.9%. The statute came into force in August. Meanwhile, in June Maragall declared that he would not be standing for the presidency of the Generalitat in the forthcoming elections; instead, the PSC's First Secretary, José Montilla, was elected as the party's candidate. At the elections, held on 1 November, CiU emerged as the largest party, having won 48 of the 135 seats in the legislature. However, the PSC, which won 37 seats, was able to retain power by forming a left-wing coalition with ERC and IC-V, with Montilla as President of the Generalitat.

Several other autonomous communities, including Aragón, the Balearic Islands (Islas Baleares or Illes Balears), the Canary Islands, Castilla-La Mancha and Galicia, began proceedings to reform their statutes of autonomy in 2005 and 2006. In April 2006 a new statute for Valencia entered into force, which, *inter alia*, defined Valencia as an 'historic nationality' (a term traditionally applied to Catalonia, the Basque Country and Galicia), made Valencian an official language and increased judicial and tax-raising independence. A new statute for Andalucía, which also defined the region as an 'historic nationality', took effect in

March 2007, after being approved by 87% of the participating electorate in a referendum in February.

In the Basque region, meanwhile, terrorist activity by the separatist organization, ETA, founded in 1959, continued. Having claimed its first victim in 1961, between 1978 and 1992 alone a total of 711 murders was attributed to the group. Despite bomb attacks in Bilbao in February 1983 and Madrid in July 1986, the central Government maintained its offer of social reintegration, instigated in mid-1984, to former ETA members. The explosion in June 1987 of a bomb beneath a crowded Barcelona supermarket, which killed 21 and injured 45, was the most devastating attack committed by the organization, prompting Herri Batasuna (HB), ETA's political wing, to issue its first condemnation of a terrorist attack. Co-operation with the authorities of France and Algeria (where numerous ETA members were discovered to be living) was strengthened, and in October the French police arrested 67 Basque suspects. In December five children were among the 12 killed in a bomb attack on the married quarters of a Civil Guard barracks in Zaragoza, which provoked a further public outcry and prompted the Government to break off negotiations with ETA early in the following year. In January 1988, after protracted negotiations, six Basque parties (excluding HB) signed the Ajuria Enea Pact, rejecting terrorism as a means of determining the region's future. In January 1989 ETA declared a unilateral truce in an effort to reopen negotiations with the Government. Subsequent discussions between representatives of the Government and of ETA collapsed in April. A resolution declaring the right of the Basque people to self-determination was approved by the Basque Parliament in February 1990.

During the early and mid-1990s the authorities achieved considerable success in their counter-terrorist activities against ETA, particularly with increased co-operation from France. In July 1992 ETA's offer of a truce (to coincide with the forthcoming Olympic Games in Barcelona), in return for the reopening of dialogue, was rebuffed by the Government, which continued to insist upon the group's permanent renunciation of violence. Moreover, between then and February 1993 (when a major arsenal was discovered in France and ETA's operational head was captured) more than 500 ETA suspects were arrested. However, hopes of thereby forcibly and judicially terminating ETA's campaign of violence were ended in June by two car bomb explosions (one of which killed seven people) in Madrid.

The results of the election to the Basque Parliament in October 1994 demonstrated the continuing decline in support for HB and the Basque electorate's growing revulsion at the actions of ETA. Several senior ETA leaders were captured in late 1994 and in mid-1995, but attacks on police officers continued. In January 1995 Gregorio Ordóñez, a member of the Basque Parliament and the PP candidate for the mayoralty of San Sebastián at the forthcoming municipal elections, was shot dead, the first politician since 1992 to be murdered by ETA. Thousands of Basque citizens took to the streets of San Sebastián and Bilbao to protest against the assassination. In April 1995 Aznar, leader of the opposition PP, narrowly survived a car-bomb attempt on his life in Madrid, which injured 19 others. In August the authorities announced that a plot to assassinate King Juan Carlos had been foiled. Successive murders of politicians in early 1996 provoked a public outcry. Some 1m. citizens, including Prime Minister González and many other political leaders, attended an anti-ETA march in Madrid. As the general election approached, Jon Idígoras, the veteran HB leader, was arrested, amid controversy arising from a campaign video that apparently supported the activities of ETA.

In July 1996, following a brief truce and the new PP Government's conditional offer of dialogue in the previous month, ETA renewed its bombing campaign, this time targeting the tourism industry. However, the authorities continued to arrest and convict ETA activists. A resurgence of violence in 1997 culminated in the abduction in July of Miguel Angel Blanco, a PP councillor in the Basque town of Ermua. ETA issued an ultimatum that prisoners belonging to the separatist organization be transferred to gaols in the Basque Country. Despite numerous appeals, including a message from the Pope, Blanco was duly shot upon the expiry of ETA's 48-hour deadline. His death provoked an unprecedented display of public outrage. In the largest demonstration since the attempted military coup of 1981, millions of Spaniards took to the streets, including Prime Minister Aznar, who led a protest march in Madrid. The Prime Minister vowed to intensify the Government's campaign against ETA, while urging (along with the moderate Basque parties) the isolation of HB. In October 2007 an attempt to plant remote-controlled grenades outside the new Guggenheim Museum in Bilbao, which was due to be inaugurated by the King, was thwarted by the police, but resulted in the death of one officer.

In December 1997 the 23 members of the collective leadership of HB were each sentenced to seven years' imprisonment for collaborating with an armed group. In a significant development, for the first time the direct relationship between ETA and HB, which continued to claim to be independent of the terrorist organization, was recognized by the judiciary. The members of the collective leadership were released in July 1999, when their imprisonment was ruled unconstitutional. Meanwhile, in early 1998 a new HB leadership was elected, pledging to continue with the policies of its predecessors. ETA's campaign of targeting PP councillors continued, extending beyond the Basque region for the first time in January, when a councillor and his wife were murdered in Seville. The capture of several ETA activists in San Sebastián, as they prepared to launch mortar bombs at a police barracks, resulted in the discovery of another plot to assassinate King Juan Carlos.

Following a dispute regarding a proposal to oblige all members of the Basque Parliament to accord formal recognition to the Spanish Constitution, in June 1998 the Partido Socialista de Euskadi-Euskadiko Ezkerra (PSE-EE) withdrew from the Basque coalition Government after 12 years of co-operation. In early September, apparently attempting to pre-empt any ban on its activities and while still declining to renounce the use of violence, HB announced that it was to contest the forthcoming elections as Euskal Herritarrok (EH). In mid-September both the PP and the opposition PSOE expressed reservations at the conclusion of an agreement (the 'Lizarra Pact') by the EAJ/PNV, Eusko Alkartasuna (EA), HB and IU on proposals for unconditional discussions with ETA. Nevertheless, following several months of secret talks between representatives of the EAJ/PNV and HB, on 16 September ETA declared an indefinite truce. In a conciliatory gesture, the Prime Minister indicated his willingness to transfer a number of ETA convicts to prisons in the Basque Country.

At the Basque elections held in October 1998, the EAJ/PNV again received the greatest support, while the PP supplanted the PSE-EE as the party with the second largest representation in the regional parliament. At the end of October it was announced that the State was to assume responsibility for compensation of the victims of ETA, the total sum in question now estimated at 60,000m. pesetas. However, the Government refused to compensate members of GAL. The Prime Minister also stated that, while being required to renounce the use of violence, ETA would not be obliged to relinquish all its weapons. In November the central Government announced the inauguration of direct contact with representatives of ETA, which reaffirmed its commitment to the cease-fire. In December, with the support of EH, an entirely nationalist coalition Government was established, under Juan José Ibarretxe of the EAJ/PNV as Lehendakari.

In February 1999, in France, the first arrest since the cease-fire of an ETA suspect was made. In March the police arrested six ETA activists, including the alleged head of ETA's military wing (who was convicted in April 2002). However, in May the Spanish Government announced that 304 (of an estimated 550) exiles, who had been obliged to leave Spain on account of their alleged connections to ETA, were to be permitted to return to their homeland.

In July 1999, for the first time, EH joined other Basque parties in signing a declaration rejecting the use of violence. In early September, as the first anniversary of the truce approached, it was revealed that a total of 180 ETA prisoners had been released within the last year. However, official monitoring of ETA activity continued and at the end of September three ETA suspects were arrested in France. On 28 November, on the eve of the opening in Paris of the trial of 13 ETA defendants, the terrorist organization announced the end of the 14-month cease-fire. Thousands of citizens took to the streets to urge that the truce be maintained. Hours before the expiry of the truce on 3 December, the EAJ/PNV, along with other signatories of the Lizarra Pact, invited EH to sign a document demanding full sovereignty for the Basque Country and criticizing the policies of both the Spanish and French Governments.

Despite successful official action against ETA activities, in January 2000 the organization successfully exploded two car-bombs in Madrid, one of which killed an army officer. More than 1m. people, led by the Prime Minister, participated in a protest march in the capital. At the end of the month it was reported that ETA's international network, responsible for the co-ordination of financial and logistical support, had been dismantled. In February, however, a Basque socialist politician and his bodyguard were killed in a bomb attack in Vitoria, prompting Ibarretxe to sever all links with EH, which subsequently announced that it was withdrawing from the Basque Parliament.

In June 2000 a PP politician was assassinated, resulting in the abolition of local government pacts between the EAJ/PNV and EH. In September 20 financial and political organizers of EKIN, ETA's fund-raising wing, were arrested. Seven of these were convicted in April 2001, on the same day that Judge Garzón pronounced EKIN illegal, owing to its associations with ETA. Meanwhile, on 15 September 2000 the French authorities arrested the suspected former leader of ETA Ignacio Gracia Arregui (Iñaki de Rentería) on charges of terrorism and attempting to assassinate the King in 1995. In December he was sentenced to five years' imprisonment, added to a previous sentence of 11 years. Later that month the assassination of a PP politician in Barcelona prompted a demonstration attended by 100,000 protesters, which was led by Aznar.

In September 2000 EH abandoned the ruling coalition, leaving the EAJ/PNV without a majority in the Basque Government. In October–November several public officials were killed in attacks perpetrated by ETA. During 2000 some 100 members or collaborators of ETA were detained following covert Civil Guard operations; six command units were dismantled; and 12 members of ETA were successfully extradited. However, street disturbances in Basque cities continued to escalate, many caused by Haika (Rise Up), the youth wing of ETA, and there were 23 fatalities resultant from ETA attacks. The violence continued into 2001, as did arrests of ETA suspects by the Spanish and French authorities.

On 20 February 2001 Ibarretxe announced that Basque regional elections would be held early, on 13 May. The PP and PSOE had proposed an all-party anti-terrorist pact to follow the elections, and a co-ordinating committee was established to form anti-terrorist policy. In March 16 people who were believed to be leaders of Haika were arrested and in May Judge Garzón pronounced Haika illegal. Following retaliatory attacks throughout March, ETA warned that it was to target holiday resorts. At elections to the Basque Parliament held in May, the EAJ/PNV-EA electoral coalition, led by Ibarretxe, retained power, taking 33 of the 75 seats. The PP obtained 19 seats, while the PSE-EE won 13, EH seven and IU-EB three seats. The EAJ/PNV and the EA now controlled more seats than the combined forces of the PP and the PSOE. Following its losses in the elections, HB elected new members to its leadership and declared that, henceforth, it wished to be known as Batasuna (Unity).

Violence continued through mid-2001, with the assassination of the financial director of the *El Diario Vasco* newspaper and various attempted bombings, including a parcel bomb in Madrid, which killed one person. In July Spain secured an agreement with Mexico for the extradition of 20 suspected ETA members and further co-operation against ETA. Less than two weeks later, however, the inauguration of Ibarretxe as Lehendakari was accompanied by ETA action in Tolosa, where a member of the Ertzaintza was assassinated, and in Leitxa, Navarra, where a local councillor was killed in a bomb attack. Two days later 50,000 people demonstrated in Pamplona to protest at the violence. In late July several bomb attacks took place across Spain. On 30 July two former leading ETA members were sentenced to 1,128 years' imprisonment for various crimes, including 46 counts of murder. At the end of August it was estimated that, so far in 2001, some 51 arrests of alleged ETA members had been made.

In October 2001 Ibarretxe warned that he was determined to hold a referendum on self-determination for the Basque Country, should the Government in Madrid continue to reject dialogue and ETA continue its campaign of violence. However, Prime Minister Aznar condemned the proposal as unconstitutional, and the violence resumed with the bombing of a courthouse in Vitoria. In mid-October a car-bomb exploded in Madrid, injuring 17 people. It was later reported that the bomb had been intended to be detonated at a military parade earlier in the day, at which members of the royal family were present, to commemorate the National Day. In November some 35,000 people marched through Bilbao to demand the right for self-determination for the Basque region. This followed two high-profile bomb attacks on Madrid earlier that month, one of which injured 95 people.

Basque groups took advantage of the beginning of Spain's presidency of the EU in January 2002 to demand greater representation in the European Parliament. The central Government, however, welcomed the introduction of an EU-wide arrest warrant, due to come into effect in 2004, which it hoped would help capture ETA suspects. In May 2002 the trial of Otegi of Batasuna for vocal support of ETA was dismissed by the Supreme Court, to the consternation of the Government which attempted to intervene. After a number of ETA actions during the EU summit in Seville in June, however, the Senado approved measures to outlaw political parties deemed to support terrorist organizations. The legislation was widely seen as targeting Batasuna, and, indeed, in August a parliamentary vote outlawed the party, while a separate Supreme Court order enforced the closure of party offices and a three-year suspension of party activities. Subsequently, in March 2003, the Supreme Court officially outlawed Batasuna. (The party was banned for a further two years in early 2006.) In December 2003 an attempt to circumvent the delegalization of Batasuna led the party to establish another organization, Sozialista Abertzaleak (Patriotic Socialists), in the hope of contesting regional elections later that year. A total of 122 ETA members were arrested during 2002.

In January 2003 the national legislature approved anti-terrorist legislation, extending the maximum sentence for terrorist activities from 30 to 40 years, and in February the Basque-language newspaper *Euskaldunon Egunkaria* was shut down on the grounds of its alleged links with ETA. Prime Minister Aznar's hope for external support in the eradication of ETA was widely believed to have been one of the reasons for his backing of US-led military action in Iraq during 2003 (see above). Prior to regional and municipal elections in May, the central Government banned some 1,500 candidates from standing on the grounds of their alleged links with ETA. In response, ETA urged the lodging of protest votes in support of the banned politicians. In July two members of ETA were given terms of imprisonment of 790 years and six months for the 1987 bombing of a supermarket in Barcelona, in which 21 people had died.

In September 2003 Ibarretxe presented to the regional legislature his plan for shared sovereignty over the Basque Country, which proposed the 'free association' of the Basque Country with Spain, the creation of a separate judiciary and education system and the right of the Basque Country to conduct international relations. The proposals—known as the Ibarretxe plan—were not widely supported in the region, and were strongly criticized by Madrid-based politicians and media, including Aznar, who accused Ibarretxe of treason. In December Spanish police foiled a planned attack by suspected ETA terrorists on a railway station in Madrid, and in February 2004, in the run-up to the general election in March, two men were captured driving towards Madrid with 500 kg of explosives. In the same month ETA declared a cease-fire in Catalonia.

In January 2004 the Constitutional Court rejected Batasuna's appeal for legalization. Immediately following the PSOE's victory in the general election in March, ETA expressed a desire to begin a dialogue with the new Government; this was rejected, however, by the incoming administration of premier Zapatero. In late 2004, following the establishment of a Franco-Spanish anti-terrorism police force in September, a series of arrests of suspected members of ETA took place in France and Spain, including the capture in October of the alleged leader of the organization, Mikel 'Antza' Albizu Iriarte, in France. Subsequently Batasuna announced that it was prepared to negotiate. However, in December and January 2005 a series of bombs were detonated around Spain, and in early February ETA exploded a car bomb, injuring over 40 people, at a conference centre in Madrid, which was due to be visited by the King and President Vicente Fox of Mexico. In 2004 a total of 135 suspected members of ETA were arrested, 74 in Spain and the others in France and Belgium. In December Judge Garzón published a report stating that in the previous 10 years ETA had been responsible for the deaths of more than 800 people, and had caused some €8,000m. of damage; however, 2004 was notable for being the first year since the early 1970s in which ETA had not been responsible for any deaths.

In December 2004 the Basque Parliament voted in favour of the Ibarretxe plan, with the last-minute support of Sozialista Abertzaleak, the perceived successor to Batasuna, and thus the new political wing of ETA. In early February 2005 the plan was debated by the Congreso de los Diputados and rejected by an overwhelming majority, although Zapatero declared that he was prepared to enter into negotiations on the status of the Basque Country within Spain. Ibarretxe responded by bringing the date of the Basque regional elections forward to 17 April, and declaring that he would go ahead with plans for a referendum on the Ibarretxe plan, despite claims by the central Government that this was unconstitutional. The election was seen as a gauge of the popularity of the Ibarretxe plan. Prior to the poll, Aukera Guztiak, a nationalist party, was banned on the grounds of being close to ETA. In the event, Ibarretxe's EAJ/PNV-EA coalition won a reduced majority of 29 seats, equivalent to 38.7% of votes cast.

In May 2005 the Congreso de los Diputados approved government plans to open negotiations with ETA, should the group consent to disarm. An estimated 300,000 demonstrators opposed to talks with ETA marched in Madrid in early June. In October Harriet Aguirre, an alleged senior leader of ETA, was arrested in France, and in November, in the largest ever such prosecution, the trial commenced of 56 people suspected of belonging to, or aiding, ETA. Nevertheless, ETA continued its bombing campaign around Spain during 2005 and early 2006, although no fatalities were caused. However, on 22 March 2006 ETA declared a 'permanent cease-fire', the first time in its history that it had taken such a step. It was speculated that the cease-fire had been prompted by the arrest of many of the organization's leaders. Zapatero responded to ETA's unilateral declaration by stating in May that the Government intended to enter into peace talks with the group; in June the Prime Minister confirmed that negotiations would, eventually, take place. Despite these advances, during late 2006 ETA issued a number of statements indicating that it was not prepared to abandon violence or relinquish its weapons until the Basque Country became independent of Spain. In October the theft of 360 pistols from an arms depot near Nîmes, France, was attributed to ETA by the French and Spanish authorities, casting further doubt on the future of the peace process. On 30 December, less than two weeks after the Government held its first formal meeting with ETA officials, a car bomb exploded at Barajas airport in Madrid, killing two people. Although ETA claimed responsibility for the attack, it claimed that its permanent cease-fire remained intact; none the less, Zapatero suspended talks in the wake of the bombing.

In the approach to the municipal elections of 27 May 2007, a number of separatist political parties were prevented from standing because of suspected links with Batasuna. Following a failed attempt by Batasuna members in late March to register a party called Abertzale Sozialisten Batasuna (Patriotic Socialist Union) with the Ministry of Interior, in April Acción Nacionalista Vasca (ANV), a legal political party founded in 1930 as an offshoot of the EAJ/PNV but whose activity had become very limited, fielded candidates in municipalities throughout the Basque Country and Navarra. Concurrently, an electoral list bearing the name Abertzale Sozialistak (AS) stood for election in 232 municipalities. After it emerged that large numbers of candidates for both ANV and AS were members of Batasuna, in early May the Constitutional Court annulled all the AS lists and 133 (around one-half) of those fielded by ANV; however, it stopped short of recommending that ANV be banned entirely. Both AS and ANV were also prevented from standing in the elections to the parliament of Navarra, held on 27 May.

On 5 June 2007 ETA announced an immediate end to its cease-fire, issuing a statement accusing the Government of 'pursuing detentions, torture and persecution' of its members. Several days later Otegi was re-arrested and began serving a 15-month prison sentence on charges of glorifying terrorism. In late August an explosion in Durango, the Basque Country, in which two police officers were injured, was reported to constitute the first attack by ETA since the expiry of its cease-fire. Another car bomb later in the month resulted in no injuries. In early September, in a joint French-Spanish operation, four suspected members of ETA, who were believed to have been responsible for the attack at Barajas Airport in Madrid in December 2006 were arrested, and 350 kg of explosives were seized.

In early September 2007, in response to a request by Judge Garzón, some 23 senior members of Batasuna were arrested during a clandestine meeting of the organization in Segura. Batasuna described the arrests as constituting a 'declaration of war' by the Spanish authorities; the EAJ/PNV were also critical of the arrests. In early December two Spanish civil guards were shot by suspected members of ETA in Southern France; one of the officers was killed and the other left in a coma. The killing was believed to constitute the first killing perpetrated by ETA in France for some 30 years. Further bomb attacks against court buildings in the Basque country occurred in mid-December and in early February 2008, but in both instances no-one was injured. At the beginning of February another senior member of Batasuna, Pernando Barrena, was arrested. Later in the month, in response to a further request by Garzón, the High Court suspended the operations, for a period of three years, of two political parties that favoured the independence of the Basque Country from Spain. Garzón declared that the parties—the ANV and the Partido Comunista de la Tierra Vasca (PCTV—Communist Party of the Basque Lands)—were linked to Batasuna.

Violence by ETA continued throughout 2008: in mid-April a bomb exploded outside PSOE offices in Bilbao injuring seven police officers, and in mid-May a truck bomb was detonated outside a civil guard barracks in Legutiano, the Basque Country, killing one officer and injuring four others. For the first time since June 2006, when the PP withdrew its support for the Government's fight against ETA following the Government's agreement to participate in peace talks with the group, the PP lent its support to Zapatero in endorsing a joint statement condemning the attack. In May 2008, after some 20 years in hiding, Francisco Javier López Peña, the suspected political leader of ETA, was arrested in Bordeaux, France.

In July 2008 it was announced by the Spanish authorities that the most active ETA cell, the 'Vizcaya commando' had been dismantled. Nine people were arrested, including Arkaitz Goikoetxea, the suspected cell leader. Nevertheless, bomb attacks continued in mid-2008, principally in tourist areas, and in September a car bomb exploded at a military academy in Santona killing one soldier and injuring eight other people. In August Otegi was released from prison having served a 15-month sentence for glorifying terrorism. A referendum in the Basque Country, planned for 25 October, was in early September ruled as unconstitutional by the Tribunal Constitucional. The referendum had planned to gauge support for Basque self-determination from Spain and a negotiated settlement with ETA. On the day the referendum was due to take place, thousands of protesters marched in the Basque Country demanding that a referendum on Basque self-determination take place. Meanwhile, later in September the Audiencia Nacional sentenced 21 members of a Basque prisoner support group to terms of imprisonment of between eight and 10 years for belonging to ETA.

Several arrests of senior ETA members were made from late 2008. In November Miguel de Garikoitz Aspiazu Rubina, the suspected military leader of ETA who had allegedly ordered the truck bombing of Barajas Airport in Madrid in December 2006, was arrested in the French Pyrenees. In December 2008 Rubina's apparent successor as military leader, Aitzol Irionda, was arrested in Gerde, France, and only four months later Irionda's successor Jurdan Martitegi was also arrested near Perpignan, France.

At elections to the Basque Parliament held in March 2009 the EAJ/PNV won 30 of the 75 seats in the regional legislature. The PSE-EE performed well, winning 25 seats, while the PP took 13; the nationalist Aralar won four seats and two other nationalist parties, Eusko Alkartasuna and Ezker Batua-Berdeak, each won one seat. The Unión Progreso y Democracia (UPD) also took one seat. Prior to the poll, several radical separatist parties had been excluded from the election on the basis that they were linked with ETA. In September 2008 the Tribunal Supremo had banned the ANV and the left-wing Euskal Herrialdeetako Alderdi Komunista, while in February 2009 Askatasuna and the newly-established Demokrazia Hiru Milioi were also banned. One month after the elections, and with the EAJ/PNV unable to achieve the required absolute majority of 38 seats, a non-nationalist coalition of the PSE-EE and the PP took power in the Basque Country for the first time since 1979. The new Government, under the PSE-EE's Patxi López as Lehendakari, set out as its priority the fight against ETA. With the Basque Parliament free of any pro-ETA groups and with ETA's weakened state in mid-2009, following the capture of three of its successive leaders, many commentators remarked on the potential for successful peace talks to take place later that year.

Catalan and Galician nationalist extremists pursued a limited terrorist campaign in the 1980s and 1990s. The Catalan organization, Terra Lliure (Free Land), claimed its first victim in 1987, and the Galician Exército Guerrilheiro do Povo Galego Ceive (EGPGC—Free Galician People's Guerrilla Army) carried out its only murder, of a civil guard, in early 1989. In mid-1989 the Catalan Government was reported to be negotiating with Terra Lliure, and in July 1991 the group's dissolution was announced, following its renunciation of the use of violence. In mid-1992, however, a dissident faction planted several bombs. The trial of 24 alleged members of Terra Lliure concluded in July 1995, 18 being found guilty; 15 were pardoned in June 1996. The EGPGC's campaign continued intermittently. In September

1991 the alleged leader of the group was apprehended by the authorities and, upon the arrest in November of eight suspected EGPGC members, it was believed that the organization had been dissolved. In June 1994 six EGPGC activists received prison sentences, while two others were acquitted.

Following the suicide attacks in the USA on 11 September 2001, it was reported that 16 Islamist activists had been arrested in Spain in late 2001. They were accused of belonging to al-Qa'ida, which was held principally responsible for the attacks, and charged with terrorist activities. Further arrests were made during April and June 2002. In January 2003 16 North Africans, mostly from Algeria, were arrested near Barcelona and Girona following the discovery of a cache of chemicals and explosives, which were purportedly intended to be used in attacks around Europe. In September five men of Syrian origin were arrested in Spain on suspicion of having links with al-Qa'ida. Baltasar Garzón issued an arrest warrant for Osama bin Laden, and a further 34 individuals were charged with belonging to a terrorist organization. The trial of 24 alleged members of al-Qa'ida, some of whom were charged with organizing the 11 September attacks, commenced in Madrid in April 2005. In September 18 of the defendants were found guilty of being members of al-Qa'ida; Syrian-born Imad Yarkas was sentenced to 27 years' imprisonment for involvement in the 11 September attacks, while the others received prison sentences of between six and 11 years for a range of terrorism offences.

In late March 2004 international arrest warrants were issued for six suspected terrorists with Moroccan connections, including Abdelmajid Farkhet, a Tunisian, who was suspected of having masterminded the 11 March train bombings in Madrid (see above) and who was known to have been preaching *jihad* (Islamic holy war) in the capital since mid-2003. Throughout the rest of 2004 and in early 2005 further arrests were made in Spain and in other European countries in connection with the Madrid train bombings; by early April 2005 a total of 24 people, mainly North Africans, had been charged on counts of terrorism and murder. In October and November 2004 some 33 suspected Islamist militants, reportedly with links to Moroccan fundamentalist groups, were arrested in connection with an alleged plot to detonate explosive devices in the high court and other public buildings in Madrid. In March 2006 32 people were charged in connection with the plot.

The first trial in connection with the train bombings was held in November 2004, and a 16-year-old Spaniard received a prison sentence of six years for trafficking explosives that were subsequently used in the attacks. In December Rabei Osman as-Sayed, one of the suspected leaders of the plot to blow up the trains in Madrid, was extradited from Italy, and in the same month Hassan al-Haski, who was alleged to be a leader of the Moroccan Islamist group, Groupe islamique combattant Marocain (GICM), was arrested and charged with 191 counts of murder. The GICM was reportedly connected to the May 2003 suicide bombings in Casablanca, Morocco. In November and December 2005 17 people were arrested on suspicion of providing logistical and financial assistance to an Algerian-based Islamist militant group, the Groupe salafiste pour la prédication et le combat. It was reported that a total of around 90 suspected Islamist militants were arrested in Spain during 2005, some of whom were alleged to have been involved in recruiting other radicals to join the insurgency in Iraq. In April 2006 29 people, mostly Moroccan nationals, but including three Spanish citizens (who had supplied the explosives used in the bombings), were charged with involvement in the Madrid train bombings. The trial of the suspects began in February 2007 and, at the end of October, 21 of the suspects were convicted of the attacks, while seven were acquitted, including an Egyptian citizen who had been accused of organizing the attacks. (Charges had been dropped against the remaining person charged, on grounds of lack of evidence.) Three defendants were sentenced to the equivalent of the maximum permissible prison term of 40 years, having been found guilty of murdering 191 people, procuring two involuntary abortions (as two of the people killed in the attacks were pregnant women) and conspiring to cause the deaths of the 1,856 people injured in the attacks. A further principal suspect in the attacks was arrested in January 2008 in Morocco, where he was to be brought to trial. In July four of the 21 men convicted of being involved in the 2001 terrorist attacks in Madrid were cleared by the Tribunal Supremo, and this court upheld the decision of a lower court to acquit Rabei Ousmane Sayed Ahmed, allegedly one of those responsible for planning the attacks. In early December 2008 a Moroccan man, Hicham Ahmidan, was sentenced to 10 years' imprisonment having been convicted of providing logistical support to the March 2004 bombers. Later that month another Moroccan national, Abdelilah Ahriz, was sentenced to 20 years' imprisonment, having been convicted of belonging to the group that carried out the attack and of raising money to fund terrorist activities.

In the late 1990s there was growing concern over the increasing number of illegal immigrants entering Spain, mostly from Latin America and North Africa. In 2000 some 14,893 people were apprehended, compared with 3,569 in the previous year. The influx of illegal immigrants had resulted in social unrest in some areas, with anti-immigration protests and violent attacks against the immigrant population. Despite intense opposition from the other parties in the Congreso de los Diputados, in July 2000 the Government announced proposals for the reform of the immigration law (adopted by the Congreso in December 1999), introducing severe penalties for illegal immigrants, and for traffickers and employers of illegal immigrants. Those entering the country illegally could be deported within 48 hours. Illegal workers would be deprived of the right to strike and to join a trade union, and their use of public services would be limited. They would gain the right to remain in the country only after five years of employment, rather than the two years previously specified. The reforms entered into force in January 2001, at which time there were an estimated 200,000 illegal immigrants in Spain. Demonstrations against the reforms were staged across the country, and in Barcelona 300 illegal immigrants locked themselves into the Santa María del Pi Church and declared a hunger strike. In June the Government agreed to grant the protesters legal status. Despite criticism from the opposition, amendments to the electoral legislation received parliamentary approval in late July: these specified modalities whereby immigrants who could prove that they had been working in Spain since January 2001 could obtain residency.

In January 2003 changes to immigration legislation, allowing South Americans of Spanish ancestry to apply for Spanish citizenship, were expected to lead to some 1m. applications. At the same time, greater strictures were placed on applications from other non-EU countries.

In February 2005 an amnesty was granted to the estimated 800,000 illegal immigrants in Spain, the terms of which required employers to register illegal immigrants, thereby allowing them to receive working permits. Immigration was becoming an increasingly important factor in the Spanish economy, with the number of registered immigrants living in Spain rising from 900,000 in 2000 to 3.7m. in 2005—equivalent to 8.4% of the resident population. In March 2006 the Spanish Government announced its intention to open the Spanish labour market from May to citizens of the eight central and eastern European countries that joined the EU in May 2004, removing restrictions that had been imposed at that time. Meanwhile, large numbers of Africans continued to attempt to enter Spain, often by highly dangerous routes. In October 2005 hundreds of would-be immigrants attempted to climb the barriers separating Morocco from the Spanish exclaves of Ceuta and Melilla, while in March 2006 it was estimated that some 1,200 Africans had died in the previous four months attempting to sail from Mauritania to the Canary Islands. Spain and Mauritania subsequently agreed to tighten their borders in an effort to deter African migrants from trying to enter Europe. Nevertheless, large numbers of immigrants landed in the Canary Islands between May and September 2006—many of whom were repatriated by the Spanish authorities—and in the latter month it was reported that 27,000 immigrants had arrived in the islands so far that year, five times as many as in 2005.

In December 1988 Spain and the USA renewed their bilateral defence agreement, permitting the USA's use of bases in Spain for a further eight years from May 1989. In late 1996 the accord was extended until May 1998. In November 1999 the US Administration requested permission to establish their principal base in southern Europe in Cádiz. Spain was admitted to Western European Union (WEU, see p. 442) in November 1988. In November 1992 Spain dispatched a substantial contingent of troops to Bosnia and Herzegovina, the first Spanish soldiers to serve in a UN peace-keeping operation. Continuing to assume a greater international role, Spain contributed troops to the multinational force deployed in Albania in April 1997, and again in April 1999 during the NATO offensive against Yugoslavia (Serbia and Montenegro). Spain committed 1,200 ground troops to the international peace-keeping force deployed in the Serbian Province of Kosovo in June 1999. In mid-2003, despite widespread public opposition, Spain sent 1,300 peace-keeping troops to Iraq to join the US-led coalition forces, and in October of that year pledged €250m. to the reconstruction process in Iraq. Following the election of the PSOE Government in March 2004, however, the withdrawal of the Spanish troops was completed by the end of May. In June 2007 US Secretary of State Condoleezza Rice visited Madrid, becoming the first senior official of the US Administration to visit Spain since the PSOE Government took office. In early 2007 Spain was contributing to a number of international peace-keeping missions, including the United Nations Interim Force in Lebanon, in which some 1,100 Spanish troops were serving and the International Security Assistance Force in Afghanistan, in which some 742 Spanish troops were serving. In March 2009 it was announced that the remaining 600 Spanish troops in Kosovo would be withdrawn later that year. Spain was one of five EU countries that did not recognize Kosovo's unilateral declaration of independence from Serbia in 2008. NATO criticized the announcement, which had been made without prior consultation.

From 1998, under Spanish law persons accused of crimes against humanity, no matter where they had taken place, could be tried in a Spanish court. In the late 1990s criminal proceedings continued in Spain against former Argentine and Chilean officials of the military dictatorships of Argentina (1976–83) and of Chile (1979–90), during which numerous Spanish citizens had been killed. In November 1999 the investigating judge, Garzón, issued international arrest warrants for 98 citizens of Argentina. In January 2000, however, the judge's request for the extradition of 48 Argentines, accused of various atrocities, was refused. In August 2003 Ricardo Cavallo, an Argentine former naval officer, was extradited from Mexico on charges of human rights abuses. In November 1998, following the arrest in the United Kingdom of Gen. Augusto Pinochet and the instigation by Garzón of extradition proceedings against the former Chilean President, Chile's ambassador to Madrid was recalled for consultations. In October 1999 a British judge ruled that the former Chilean President could be extradited to Spain to answer 35 charges of torture and conspiracy. In March 2000, however, Pinochet was permitted to return to Chile from the United Kingdom, where he had remained under house arrest, extradition proceedings having been abandoned on medical grounds. In early 2005, following an indictment by Garzón, Adolfo Scilingo, an Argentine former army officer, was given a prison sentence of 640 years for crimes against humanity under the military rule in Argentina during 1976–83.

The PSOE Government elected in 2004 implemented a shift in foreign relations emphasis from the USA to Europe, and accords were signed on the creation of a joint anti-terrorism police force with France, and on increased military co-operation between EU member states, including the creation of a European rapid-reaction force. In late 2005 tensions arose with the USA over a Spanish agreement to sell military equipment to Venezuela. In April 2006 the foreign affairs committee of the Congreso de los Diputados requested that the Government compile a detailed report on alleged flights by the USA's Central Intelligence Agency (CIA) via Spain. This followed reports that the CIA had used European airports to transport suspected Islamist militants to third countries for interrogation. In December 2008 letters written by Miguel Aguirre de Cárcer, then Director-General of the Ministry of Foreign Affairs, were leaked to the Spanish daily newspaper *El País*, which apparently indicated that the Aznar administration had assisted the Bush Administration in the arrangement of transfers of prisoners from Afghanistan to the US military detention facility at Guantánamo Bay, Cuba, in 2001. The Minister of Foreign Affairs and Co-operation, Miguel Angel Moratinos, denied that any secret CIA flights had actually landed in Spain, despite the fact that the Aznar Government had granted permission to the US authorities.

Spanish ratification of the Treaty on European Union (the Maastricht Treaty) was completed in November 1992. A dispute between Spain and the United Kingdom over the sovereignty of the neighbouring British dependency of Gibraltar remained unresolved. Relations deteriorated in 1995 upon Spain's announcement that, in protest at the apparent inadequacy of British efforts, it was to implement stricter border controls to combat the problem of drugs- and tobacco-smuggling from Gibraltar. In May 1996, upon the election of a new Government in the territory, border controls were further strengthened by the Spanish authorities leading to renewed protests from the British Government. In 1997 the United Kingdom rejected Spanish initiatives entailing joint sovereignty for up to 100 years prior to an eventual transfer of power to Spain. In December Spanish proposals that, following a period of joint sovereignty, Gibraltar became an Autonomous Community were similarly rebuffed by the British Government. In 1998 tension was renewed over the issue of access to fishing grounds. The seizure of a Spanish fishing vessel in early 1999 led to a serious escalation of the dispute and the imposition of new border controls and travel restrictions by Spain. In April 2000 Spain and the United Kingdom signed an agreement relating to the administrative status of Gibraltar. The territory's identity cards would henceforth be accepted by Spain as valid for travel within the EU. Furthermore, the agreement permitted the implementation of numerous EU directives, long obstructed by Spain, which had refused to recognize the Government of Gibraltar as a 'competent authority' in EU affairs. It was also agreed that Spain and Gibraltar would communicate indirectly through a facility, based in London, provided by the British authorities. In March 2001 Spain condemned plans by the political parties of Gibraltar to request reforms to the 1969 Constitution, allowing self-determination, and to hold a referendum on decolonization. Following a meeting between Spanish and British officials in Brussels in mid-2001, the Minister of Foreign Affairs, Josep Piqué, and his British counterpart, Jack Straw, held discussions in October, during which they agreed to work towards solving the dispute by December 2002. The issue of the right of Gibraltarians to vote on any agreement reached by the two Governments continued to impede the progress of the discussions, Piqué warning the British Government that Spain would not accept the results of such a referendum. At further talks in November, however, Piqué announced plans to increase the number of telephone lines available to Gibraltar, from 35,000 to 100,000, and provide access to Spanish health care for the inhabitants of the territory. The deadline for achieving a solution was also brought forward to September 2002. In January 2002 it was reported that the Spanish Government had agreed to modify its demand for outright sovereignty over the territory and reconsider the option of sharing sovereignty over the territory with the United Kingdom for an indefinite period. In an open letter published in the Gibraltarian press, Piqué attempted to persuade the citizens of Gibraltar of the advantages of Spanish sovereignty and urged its Chief Minister, Peter Caruana, to join the discussions; Caruana had hitherto boycotted the negotiations. During May, however, Aznar announced that Spain would never withdraw its territorial claim to the British exclave. Negotiations progressed in mid-2002, although a stalemate emerged when Spain disagreed with the British conditions for joint sovereignty—that it be permanent, that the military base would remain under British control, and that all changes be approved by a referendum put to the people of Gibraltar. In a referendum organized by the local administration of Gibraltar in November, which was not, however, recognized by the Spanish or British Governments, the electorate voted overwhelmingly (by 99%, of a turn-out of 87.9%) against joint sovereignty with Spain. Relations were further strained in November 2003 when the Spanish Government ordered that the frontier with Gibraltar be closed for the first time since 1985. The Spanish authorities maintained that this action was taken as a precautionary measure when a cruise-ship carrying passengers suffering from a virulent stomach virus was docked in Gibraltar. Following informal talks between Spanish and Gibraltarian officials in September 2004, Spain lifted its ban on cruise ships from outside the EU visiting both Gibraltar and Spain and announced that it would be seeking to reopen negotiations with the United Kingdom. In December the first of what was to be an annual tripartite meeting between the United Kingdom, Spain and Gibraltar was held in the United Kingdom, and it was subsequently announced that henceforth decisions on the territory's future must be agreed by all three parties. In early 2006 Spain opposed the inclusion of references to the right to self-determination of Gibraltarians in a proposed new constitution for Gibraltar. However, in March Straw assured the Spanish Government that the draft constitution would not change the current international status or sovereignty of the territory, nor affect Spanish rights over Gibraltar under the Treaty of Utrecht, which would constrain the right to self-determination, in the view of the British Government, and that independence would therefore only be a future option for Gibraltar with Spain's consent. The Constitution was subsequently approved in a referendum in the territory in December. Meanwhile, in September 2006 a meeting was held in Córdoba between the Spanish Minister of Foreign Affairs and Co-operation, Moratinos, the British Minister of State for Europe, Geoff Hoon, and Caruana, the first ever meeting between members of all three Governments. An agreement was signed which, *inter alia*, envisaged the expansion of Gibraltar Airport, with a new terminal building straddling the border, and allowed Spain to open a branch of the Spanish cultural organization, the Instituto Cervantes, in Gibraltar, over which the Spanish flag would fly. While relations between Spain and the United Kingdom improved from 2006, tensions still remained. In January 2009 several Spanish opposition parliamentarians accused a Gibraltarian development company of 'illegal incursion' into Spanish waters, after it proposed to erect platforms on the seabed. In March the Spanish Government made a formal complaint to the British authorities over a proposed visit to the territory by a member of the British royal family, describing it as 'an affront' to Spain.

A national referendum on the EU Treaty establishing a Constitution for Europe took place in Spain on 20 February 2005, with 76.2% of the votes cast being in favour of ratifying the treaty. The turn-out, however, was equivalent to only 42.3% of the electorate. Following the rejection of this treaty by France and the Netherlands later that year, in December 2007 a new, amended treaty was signed in Lisbon, Portugal by the heads of state or of government of the 27 EU member countries. Spain ratified the resultant Treaty of Lisbon by parliamentary approval in July 2008, despite its rejection by the Irish electorate in a referendum in June.

Relations with Morocco have been dominated by the issues of sovereignty of the Spanish exclaves of Ceuta and Melilla, illegal immigration and drugs-trafficking, and by disputes over fishing rights. By early 2000 the problems of illegal immigration (not only via Spanish North Africa but increasingly via the Canary Islands) had become a major political issue. In May, during a visit to Morocco, the Spanish Prime Minister confirmed that the recently implemented immigration law, one of the most liberal within the EU, was to be reformed (see above). Since its entry into force earlier in the year, the new legislation had encouraged more than 82,000 illegal migrants to apply for Spanish residency permits. Protests against the reforms were staged in Spanish North Africa as well as in mainland Spain. Negotiations on the renewal of the fishing agreement between Morocco and the EU, permitting Spanish vessels access to Moroccan waters, commenced in September 1999. The agreement expired in November and Morocco indicated that it would not be renewed. In October 2001 Morocco recalled its ambassador to Spain, declaring that it was dissatisfied with the level of bilateral relations following the failure of the EU negotiations. In the following month a Spanish fishing vessel was apprehended by the Moroccan authorities and charged with fishing without a licence. In early April 2002, however, it was reported that the two Governments were preparing to reinstate their respective ambassadors. Relations were threatened again in July, following the occupation of a small uninhabited islet near Ceuta, the Isla de Perejil (Laila), by 12 Moroccan soldiers. Spain lodged a formal protest against this action on 12 July, but Morocco refused to withdraw its men, claiming that Perejil had been a part of Morocco since independence in 1956. Spanish soldiers reoccupied the island on 17 July, and a subsequent US-mediated agreement between Spain and Morocco left the island unoccupied. Issues over the sovereignty of Ceuta and Melilla continued to be problematic, however, and in September Morocco accused Spain of repeated violations of its airspace and territorial waters and reasserted its claims over the exclaves before the UN. Relations improved somewhat in November, however, when Morocco offered the temporary use of its territorial waters to 64 Spanish fishing boats after the *Prestige* oil disaster. Meetings in December 2002 and January 2003 contributed to the re-establishment of diplomatic relations between the two countries in February. During an official visit by Aznar to Morocco in December Spain and Morocco agreed to instigate a feasibility survey for a tunnel linking the two countries. A report on the survey's findings was expected to be submitted to the EU in 2009.

Government

Under the Constitution approved in 1978, Spain is an hereditary monarchy, with the King as Head of State. He appoints the President of the Government (Prime Minister) and, on the latter's recommendation, other members of the Council of Ministers. Legislation is initiated for discussion in the Cortes (national assembly) in Madrid, in the Parliaments of the Autonomous Communities, or by popular petition. The King's actions in state affairs must receive the prior approval of the Cortes, to which the Government is responsible. The Council of State is the supreme consultative organ of the Government.

Legislative power is vested in the Cortes Generales, comprising two Houses, elected by direct universal adult suffrage for four years (subject to dissolution). The Congreso de los Diputados (Congress of Deputies) has 350 members, elected by proportional representation, and the Senado (Senate) has 208 directly elected members, plus 51 regional representatives, elected by the autonomous parliaments. A party can gain representation only if it obtains at least 3% of the votes.

Regional self-government was established in the 1978 Constitution. In October 1979 the statutes of the first of 17 Autonomous Communities were approved by referendum. The first Legislative Assemblies (Basque and Catalan) were elected in March 1980. The Galician Legislative Assembly was elected in October 1981 and that of Andalucía in May 1982. The remaining 13 were constituted in May 1983, thus completing the process of devolution. The regions possess varying degrees of autonomy. Each Legislative Assembly is elected for four years.

Spain comprises 50 provinces, each with its own Council (Diputación Provincial). The system of Civil Governors was replaced (by royal decree) in April 1997: a government sub-delegate is appointed by each Autonomous Community's government delegate.

Defence

Plans for the gradual abolition of military service and for the establishment of professional armed forces were announced in early 1996; conscription was abolished in 2000, while the final stages of professionalization were completed in 2003. Legislation to permit the entry of women to all sections of the armed forces took effect in early 1989. As assessed at November 2008, the total strength of the armed forces was 149,150, comprising: army 95,600; navy 23,200 (including 5,300 marines); air force 20,900; and 9,450 in joint service. The paramilitary Guardia Civil (Civil Guard) numbered 72,600. Spain became a member of the North Atlantic Treaty Organization (NATO, see p. 351) in May 1982. In December 1997 Spain's full integration into the military structure of NATO (with effect from January 1999) was approved by the alliance. Spain joined Western European Union (WEU, see p. 442) in November 1988. In September 2004 an agreement to form a gendarmerie comprising 3,000 troops was signed by Spain, France, Italy, Portugal and the Netherlands. In November of the same year the European Union (EU) ministers responsible for defence agreed to create a number of 'battlegroups' (each comprising about 1,500 men), which could be deployed at short notice to crisis areas around the world. The EU battlegroups, two of which were to be ready for deployment at any one time, following a rotational schedule, reached full operational capacity from 1 January 2007. Spain was the sole contributor to one battlegroup and led another with the participation of Germany, France and Portugal. Spain also participated in the Spanish-Italian Amphibious battlegroup, which was led by Italy. The budget for defence was €8,140m. in 2008.

Economic Affairs

In 2007, according to estimates by the World Bank, Spain's gross national income (GNI), measured at average 2005–07 prices, was US $1,321,756m., equivalent to $29,450 per head (or $30,820 per head on an international purchasing-power parity basis). During 2000–07, it was estimated, the population increased at an average annual rate of 1.6%, while gross domestic product (GDP) per head increased, in real terms, by an average of 1.8% per year. Overall GDP increased, in real terms, at an average annual rate of 3.4% in 2000–07; growth was 3.8% in 2007.

Agriculture (including forestry and fishing) contributed an estimated 2.9% of GDP in 2007 and engaged 4.5% of the employed labour force in the same year. The principal crops are barley, wheat, sugar beet, vegetables, citrus fruits, grapes and olives; wine and olive oil are important products. The fishing industry is significant. The Spanish fishing fleet is one of the largest in the world. Agricultural GDP shrank at an average annual rate of 1.8% in 2000–06, according to the World Bank; it declined by 10.0% in 2005, mainly owing to severe drought, but increased by 0.3% in 2006.

Industry (including mining, manufacturing, power and construction) contributed an estimated 30.3% of GDP in 2007, and engaged 29.3% of the employed labour force in the same year. According to the World Bank, industrial GDP increased at an average annual rate of 2.9% in 2000–06; it increased by 3.8% in 2006.

The mining and quarrying industry provided less than 1.0% of GDP in 2004 and engaged 0.3% of the employed labour force in 2007. The principal minerals produced include cement, industrial sand and gravel, aluminium, copper, gold, silver and zinc. Although coal is plentiful in Spain, the production costs are relatively high. Subsidies to the industry were likely to end in 2010.

Manufacturing contributed an estimated 15.1% of GDP in 2007 and engaged 15.2% of the employed labour force in the same year. In 2005 Spain was the world's fifth largest exporter of passenger cars. In that year exports of passenger vehicles numbered 2.25m. units. Other important industries are ship-building, chemicals, steel, textiles and footwear; some of these sectors underwent a process of rationalization in the 1980s. Investment is being made in new manufacturing industries, such as information technology and telecommunications equipment. Manufacturing GDP increased at an average annual rate of 0.8% in 2000–05, according to the World Bank; the rate of growth was 0.3% in 2005.

Energy (comprising mining and power) contributed an estimated 3.0% of GDP in 2007, and employed 0.5% of the labour force in the same year. Energy is derived principally from petroleum, most of which is imported. In 2007 imports of mineral fuels and lubricants accounted for 14.9% of total import costs. Natural gas became an increasingly important fuel source in the late 1990s. Some natural gas requirements are obtained from the Bay of Biscay, the remainder being imported by pipeline from Algeria. Nuclear energy provided 53.9% of total electricity production in 2007, while coal provided 22.0% and hydroelectric power 8.8%. Wind and solar power together accounted for 9.1% of the electricity supply in the same year. According to official estimates, energy GDP increased by 2.0% annually in 2000–07; energy GDP grew by 0.8% in 2007.

In 2007 the services sector accounted for an estimated 66.8% of GDP, while it engaged 66.2% of the employed labour force in the same year. The tourism industry makes an important contribution to the Spanish economy. In 2007 the number of tourist arrivals was estimated at 59.2m. (27.5% from the United Kingdom), and receipts from tourism reached €49,946m. Remittances from emigrants are also significant; in 2007 remittances amounted to €5.3m. According to the World Bank, the GDP of the services sector increased at an average annual rate of 3.5% in 2000–06; services GDP increased by 3.6% in 2006.

In 2007 Spain recorded a visible trade deficit of US $123,515m. and there was a deficit of $145,355m. on the current account of the balance of payments. In 2007 the principal sources of imports were Germany (15.3%) and France (12.3%). France was the main export market in that year, purchasing 18.8%, followed by Germany (10.8%). Italy, Portugal and the United Kingdom. Other members of the European Union (EU, see p. 255) are also important trading partners. The principal imports in 2007 were machinery and transport equipment, mineral fuels and lubricants, basic manufactures, chemical products, and food and live animals. The main exports were machinery and transport equipment, basic manufactures, chemicals and related products, and food and live animals (particularly fruit and vegetables).

In 2008 the budget deficit was equivalent to 3.8% of GDP. The annual rate of inflation averaged 3.1% in 2002–07; consumer prices increased by an average of 4.1% in 2008. The unemployment rate was 8.3% in 2007.

Spain became a member of the EU in January 1986, and participated in the introduction of the European single currency, the euro, on 1 January 1999. Spain is also a member of the Organisation for Economic Co-operation and Development (OECD, see p. 358).

The Government of José Luis Rodríguez Zapatero that took office in April 2004 pledged to continue the fiscal policies of the previous administration, which had taken Spain into the single European currency (introduced in 1999) and had predicted annual budgetary surpluses for 2004–07. By the time Zapatero had won a second term in early 2008, however, Spain was entering a period of economic downturn, prompted for the most part by the effects of the global financial crisis. Spain's extended period of rapid expansion from the 1990s had been driven by consumer demand based on the availability of inexpensive credit and a rapid rise in property prices. The contraction of credit had a dramatic impact on the housing market, which was already saturated with new properties. With the construction sector accounting for 13.3% of the working population and contributing some 11.0% of GDP in 2007, the effect on the economy was great. During the expansionary period inflation was higher than in neighbouring countries, leading to a loss of competitiveness and a large current account deficit. The country officially entered a recession at the end of 2008, following declines in GDP of 0.2% and 1.9% in the third and fourth quarters, respectively. In March 2009 it was announced that unemployment in Spain had reached 17.4%, the highest level in the EU, with more than 100,000 people losing their jobs every month from September 2008. Furthermore, the global economic slowdown had begun to affect the tourism industry, notably arrivals from the main market for Spanish tourism, the United Kingdom, as a result of the weakness of British sterling against the euro. In April 2008 the newly re-elected Government approved stimulus measures to support the economy, including tax rebates. Further stimulus measures were introduced in August and November, which included increased investment in public infrastructure projects, notably public housing. The fiscal balance deteriorated from a surplus of 2.3% in 2007 to a deficit of 3.8% of GDP in 2008, which was predicted by the Banco de España to increase to 8.3% in 2009, significantly above the EU's deficit limit of 3% of GDP. In April 2009 the central bank warned the Government against further spending and tax cuts in an attempt to revive the economy. None the less, the Prime Minister appeared favourable toward further fiscal stimulus plans. Also in April Pedro Solbes, who had criticized the Prime Minister's response to the economic crisis, was replaced as Minister of the Economy and Finance. The Spanish Government estimated that GDP would contract by 1.6% in 2009, although the IMF speculated that the actual figure could be significantly higher, at 3.0%.

Education

In 2007/08 some 1.62m. children were attending pre-school institutions. In that year 2.60m. children were enrolled at primary schools and a total of 2.95m. were enrolled in secondary education. Under reforms implemented in 1991, basic education is compulsory, and available free of charge, from the ages of six to 16 years. It comprises primary education, which begins at six years of age and lasts for six years, and secondary education, composed of two two-year cycles, followed between the ages of 12 and 16. Thereafter, students may take either a vocational training course, lasting one or two years, or the two-year *Bachillerato* course, in preparation for university entrance. Private schools, many of which are administered by the Roman Catholic Church, are responsible for the education of more than 30% of Spanish children. In the Autonomous Communities the teaching of languages other than Spanish (such as Catalan) is regulated by decree. In 2006/07 enrolment at primary schools included 100% of children (males 100%; females 99%) in the relevant age-group, while enrolment at secondary schools in that year included 91% of children (males 90%; females 91%) in the appropriate age-group. In 2004 the Government announced a reform of the education system, part of which included the designation of religious education as an optional, rather than compulsory, subject.

Some 1.38m. students were attending university in 2007/08. In that year there were 72 universities, including the open university (UNED, established in 1972). There are three cycles within university education. The first cycle lasts for three years and leads to the degree of *Diplomatura*. The second cycle lasts for two or three years and leads to the degree of *Licenciatura*. The degree of Doctor is awarded upon completion of the two-year third cycle and the writing of a thesis. Higher technical studies in engineering and architecture are followed at *Escuelas Técnicas de Grado Medio* and *Escuelas Técnicas de Grado Superior*. In 2008 total public expenditure on education was estimated at €49,887.2m.

Public Holidays

2009: 1 January (New Year's Day), 6 January (Epiphany), 9 April (Maundy Thursday), 10 April (Good Friday), 1 May (Labour Day), 15 August (Assumption), 12 October (National Day, anniversary of the discovery of America), 1 November (All Saints' Day), 6 November (Constitution Day), 8 December (Immaculate Conception), 25 December (Christmas Day).

2010: 1 January (New Year's Day), 6 January (Epiphany), 1 April (Maundy Thursday), 2 April (Good Friday), 1 May (Labour Day), 15 August (Assumption), 12 October (National Day, anniversary of the discovery of America), 1 November (All Saints' Day), 6 November (Constitution Day), 8 December (Immaculate Conception), 25 December (Christmas Day).

Some of the above holidays are not observed in all the Autonomous Communities. In addition, various local holidays are established by regional and municipal authorities, giving an annual total of 14 public holidays.

Weights and Measures

The metric system is in force.

Statistical Survey

Source (unless otherwise stated): Instituto Nacional de Estadística, Paseo de la Castellana 183, 28071 Madrid; tel. (91) 5839100; fax (91) 5839158; internet www.ine.es.

Area and Population

AREA, POPULATION AND DENSITY*

Area (sq km)	505,988†
Population (census results)	
1 March 1991	38,872,268
1 November 2001	
Males	20,021,850
Females	20,825,521
Total	40,847,371
Population (official estimates at 1 July)	
2006	44,068,244
2007	44,873,567
2008	45,593,385
Density (per sq km) at 1 July 2008	90.1

* Including the Spanish External Territories (Spanish North Africa—area 33 sq km), an integral part of Spain. Ceuta had a population of 72,353 on 1 July 2008, while Melilla's population was 69,347.
† 195,363 sq miles.

PROVINCES
(population at 1 July 2008)*†

Alava	307,203		Lugo	346,759
Albacete	395,083		Madrid	6,245,883
Alacant (Alicante)	1,866,277		Málaga	1,548,424
Almería	672,619		Murcia	1,430,986
Avila	169,274		Navarra	610,384
Badajoz	673,410		Ourense	328,086
Illes Balears (Balearic Is)	1,058,668		Oviedo (Principado de Asturias)	1,059,089
Barcelona	5,346,715		Palencia	170,965
Burgos	365,015		Las Palmas	1,064,151
Cáceres	406,315		Pontevedra	941,411
Cádiz	1,205,692		Salamanca	347,651
Castellón (Castelló) de la Plana	584,455		Santa Cruz de Tenerife	997,348
			Santander (Cantabria)	573,758
Ciudad Real	514,945		Segovia	161,013
Córdoba	784,797			
A Coruña (La Coruña)	1,121,842		Sevilla	1,840,055
Cuenca	213,830		Soria	93,064
Girona (Gerona)	718,875		Tarragona	781,065
Granada	898,933		Teruel	145,529
Guadalajara	231,681		Toledo	646,104
Guipúzcoa	692,171		Valencia	2,499,834
Huelva	500,043		Valladolid	521,279
Huesca	221,396		Vizcaya	1,139,079
Jaén	655,045		Zamora	194,412
La Rioja	313,772		Zaragoza	939,706
León	483,781			
Lleida (Lérida)	423,813		**Total**	**45,451,685**

* Excluding the Spanish External Territories (Spanish North Africa).
† Including residents temporarily abroad.

PRINCIPAL TOWNS*
(population at 1 January 2005)

Madrid (capital)	3,155,359		Vitoria-Gasteiz	226,490
Barcelona	1,593,075		Santa Cruz de Tenerife	221,567
Valencia	796,549		Badalona	218,553
Sevilla	704,154		Elche	215,137
Zaragoza	647,373		Oviedo	212,174
Málaga	558,287		Móstoles	204,463
Murcia	409,810		Cartagena	203,945
Las Palmas de Gran Canaria	378,628		Alcalá de Henares	197,804
Palma de Mallorca	375,773		Sabadell	196,971
Bilbao	353,173		Jerez de la Frontera	196,275
Córdoba	321,164		Fuenlabrada	195,131
Valladolid	321,001		Terrassa	194,947
Alacant (Alicante)	319,380		Pamplona	193,328
Vigo	293,725		Santander	183,955
Gijón	273,931		Donostia-San Sebastián	182,930
Hospitalet de Llobregat	252,884		Almería	181,702
A Coruña (La Coruña)	243,349		Leganés	181,284
Granada	236,982		Burgos	172,421

* Population figures refer to *municipios*, each of which may contain some rural area as well as the urban centre.

BIRTHS, MARRIAGES AND DEATHS

	Registered live births		Registered marriages		Registered deaths	
	Number	Rate (per 1,000)	Number	Rate (per 1,000)	Number	Rate (per 1,000)
2000	397,632	9.9	216,451	5.4	360,391	9.0
2001	406,380	10.1	208,057	5.1	360,131	8.9
2002	418,846	10.1	211,522	5.1	368,618	8.9
2003	441,881	10.5	212,300	5.0	384,828	9.2
2004	454,591	10.7	216,149	5.1	371,934	8.7
2005	466,371	10.8	209,125	4.8	387,019	8.9
2006	482,957	11.0	203,453	4.6	371,478	8.4
2007*	491,183	10.9	203,697	4.5	384,442	8.6

* Provisional.

Life expectancy (years at birth, WHO estimates): 80.8 (males 77.5; females 84.1) in 2006 (Source: WHO, *World Health Statistics*).

ECONOMICALLY ACTIVE POPULATION
('000 persons aged 16 years and over)

	2005	2006	2007
Agriculture, hunting and forestry	940.6	893.0	873.3
Fishing	60.1	51.3	52.2
Mining and quarrying	60.4	66.4	60.1
Manufacturing	3,113.0	3,106.9	3,089.8
Electricity, gas and water supply	106.6	118.8	111.9
Construction	2,357.2	2,542.9	2,697.3
Wholesale and retail trade; repair of motor vehicles, motorcycles and personal and household goods	2,886.8	2,983.5	3,128.6
Hotels and restaurants	1,291.1	1,402.7	1,450.5
Transport, storage and communications	1,117.2	1,158.2	1,177.1
Financial intermediation	457.3	472.5	500.0
Real estate, renting and business activities	1,678.4	1,857.4	2,017.1
Public administration and defence; compulsory social security	1,196.7	1,221.6	1,238.4

SPAIN

—continued	2005	2006	2007
Education	1,090.5	1,108.8	1,112.3
Health and social work	1,134.6	1,180.8	1,229.2
Other community, social and personal service activities	793.7	815.3	846.2
Private households with employed persons	682.8	760.6	770.0
Extra-territorial organizations and bodies	6.1	7.0	2.1
Total employed	18,973.2	19,747.7	20,356.0
Total unemployed	1,912.5	1,837.1	1,833.9
Total labour force	20,885.7	21,584.8	22,189.9
Males	12,251.7	12,534.1	12,802.5
Females	8,634.1	9,050.7	9,387.4

Health and Welfare

KEY INDICATORS

Total fertility rate (children per woman, 2006)	1.4
Under-5 mortality rate (per 1,000 live births, 2006)	4
HIV/AIDS (% of persons aged 15–49, 2007)	0.5
Physicians (per 1,000 head, 2004)	3.3
Hospital beds (per 1,000 head, 2005)	3.4
Health expenditure (2006): US $ per head (PPP)	2,388
Health expenditure (2006): % of GDP	8.1
Health expenditure (2006): public (% of total)	72.5
Human Development Index (2006): ranking	16
Human Development Index (2006): value	0.949

For sources and definitions, see explanatory note on p. vi.

Agriculture

PRINCIPAL CROPS
('000 metric tons)

	2005	2006	2007
Wheat	4,027	5,576	6,377
Rice, paddy	824	746	701
Barley	4,626	8,318	11,684
Maize	4,120	3,461	3,648
Oats	542	918	1,274
Potatoes	2,563	2,502	2,502
Sugar cane	43	55*	60*
Sugar beet	7,291	6,045	5,141
Olives	4,022	5,473	5,788
Sunflower seed	381	607	743
Lettuce	993	1,070	1,070*
Tomatoes	4,810	3,679	3,615*
Chillies and peppers, green	1,064	1,074	1,065
Onions, dry	1,006	1,151	1,177
Oranges	2,376	2,360	2,691
Tangerines, mandarins, clementines and satsumas	1,957	2,634	2,081
Lemons and limes	945	853	880*
Apples	774	661	672
Pears	640	590	537
Peaches and nectarines	1,231	1,256	1,150
Grapes	6,054	6,402	6,013
Watermelons	720	718	796
Cantaloupes and other melons	1,087	1,042	1,082

* FAO estimate.

Aggregate production ('000 metric tons, may include official, semi-official or estimated data): Total cereals 14,364 in 2005, 19,353 in 2006, 24,135 in 2007; Total roots and tubers 2,595 in 2005, 2,538 in 2006, 2,537 in 2007; Total vegetables (incl. melons) 13,349 in 2005, 12,562 in 2006, 12,676 in 2007; Total fruits (excl. melons) 15,548 in 2005, 16,120 in 2006, 15,293 in 2007.

Source: FAO.

LIVESTOCK
('000 head, year ending September)

	2005	2006	2007
Horses*	240	245	250
Asses, mules or hinnies	252	n.a.	n.a.
Cattle	6,463	6,184	6,456
Pigs	24,884	26,219	26,034
Sheep	22,749	22,452	21,847
Goats	2,905	2,957	2,847
Chickens*	130,000	135,000	137,000

* FAO estimates.

Source: FAO.

LIVESTOCK PRODUCTS
('000 metric tons)

	2005	2006	2007
Cattle meat	715	671	705
Sheep meat	224	230	225
Goat meat	14	12	12
Pig meat	3,168	3,219	3,222
Horse meat	5	5	6
Rabbit meat	71	72	99
Chicken meat	1,084	1,062	1,067
Cows' milk	6,553	6,469	6,717
Sheep's milk	423	403	360
Goats' milk	423	450	489
Hen eggs	828	850	884
Honey	27	30	31
Wool, greasy	22	22	22

* FAO estimate(s).

Source: FAO.

Forestry

ROUNDWOOD REMOVALS
('000 cubic metres, excl. bark)

	2005	2006	2007
Sawlogs, veneer logs and logs for sleepers	7,343	5,860	4,532
Pulpwood	5,207	7,544	7,531
Other industrial wood	801	705	483
Fuel wood	2,180	1,607	1,982
Total	15,532	15,716	14,528

Source: FAO.

SAWNWOOD PRODUCTION
('000 cubic metres, incl. railway sleepers)

	2005	2006	2007
Coniferous (softwood)	2,750	2,860	2,180
Broadleaved (hardwood)	910	946	1,152
Total	3,660	3,806	3,332

Source: FAO.

Fishing

('000 metric tons, live weight)

	2004	2005	2006
Capture*	807.6	846.1	949.5
European pilchard (sardine)	64.4	66.0	70.1
Skipjack tuna	122.0	139.9	168.6
Yellowfin tuna	107.6	92.6	88.7
Jack and horse mackerels	39.9	38.5	30.9
Aquaculture	293.8	219.8	293.3
Blue mussel	231.6	158.1	228.8
Total catch*	**1,101.4**	**1,065.9**	**1,242.8**

* FAO estimates.

Note: Figures exclude Sardinia coral (metric tons): 8 in 2004; 7 in 2005; 6 in 2006.

Source: FAO.

Mining

('000 metric tons, unless otherwise indicated, estimates)

	2004	2005	2006
Anthracite	8,923	8,553	8,354
Lignite	8,147	7,587	6,822
Crude petroleum ('000 barrels)	1,913	1,261	1,300*
Natural gas (million cu m)	370.0	330.0*	330.0*
Copper†	1.4	7.9	8.7
Kaolin	438.0	450.0*	450.0*
Potash salts (crude)*	590.0	575.0	580.0
Sepiolite	851.6	800.0*	800.0*
Dolomite	14,489	15,000*	15,000*
Fluorspar‡	145.7	144.0	150.0
Salt (unrefined)	3,993	4,550	4,600
Gypsum (crude)	12,534	13,000*	11,500*

* Estimated production.
† Figures refer to the metal content of ores.
‡ Figures refer to total CaF_2 content (acid and metallurgical grades).

Source: US Geological Survey.

Industry

SELECTED PRODUCTS
('000 metric tons, unless otherwise indicated)

	2003	2004	2005
Fish (tinned)	371.0*	398.7	384.1
Wheat flour	2,950	2,965	3,073
Vinegar	934	910	1,002
Distilled alcohol ('000 hectolitres)	3,936	4,297	4,815
Wine ('000 hectolitres)	29,569	36,228	40,302
Beer ('000 hectolitres)	31,028	31,467	31,156
Soft drinks ('000 hectolitres)	49,502	71,090	59,889
Cigarettes (million units)	n.a.	48,651	47,506
Washing powders and detergents	2,398.7	2,289.0	2,225.0
Aluminium (primary)†	389.1	397.5	394.2
Refined copper (primary)†	307.0	243.2	302.3
Pig-iron†	3,645	4,036	4,200
Cement (Portland)†	44,747	45,593	50,347
Motorcycles ('000)	88	119	197
Passenger cars ('000)	n.a.	2,482.3	2,375.4
Electricity (million kWh)	260,727	280,007	294,077

* Data from FAO.
† Data from the US Geological Survey.

Source: mainly UN, *Industrial Commodity Statistics Yearbook*.

2006 ('000 metric tons unless otherwise stated): Ham and other prepared meats 858.9; Tuna, bonito and other tinned fish 212.1; Olive oil 979.3; Wheat flour 3,035.6; Wine ('000 hectolitres) 9,415.7; Beer ('000 hectolitres) 34,031.7; Mineral water 5,363.1; Soft drinks ('000 litres) 4,579.1; Cement (Portland) 49,301.5; Concrete 201,253.

Finance

CURRENCY AND EXCHANGE RATES

Monetary Units
100 cent = 1 euro (€).

Sterling and Dollar Equivalents (31 December 2008)
£1 sterling = 1.0475 euros;
US $1 = 0.7185 euros;
€10 = £9.55 = $13.92.

Average Exchange Rate (euros per US $)
2006   0.7971
2007   0.7306
2008   0.6827

Note: The national currency was formerly the peseta. From the introduction of the euro, with Spanish participation, on 1 January 1999, a fixed exchange rate of €1 = 166.386 pesetas was in operation. Euro notes and coins were introduced on 1 January 2002. The euro and local currency circulated alongside each other until 28 February, after which the euro became the sole legal tender.

BUDGET
(€ million)

Revenue	2007	2008	2009
Current operations	144,840	156,201	139,962
Direct taxation	83,925	90,753	77,041
Indirect taxation	50,740	53,363	50,202
Rates and other revenue	2,486	2,780	3,732
Current transfers	5,757	6,013	5,807
Estate taxes	1,933	3,293	3,181
Capital operations	1,707	2,556	1,148
Transfer of real investments	109	126	120
Capital transfers	1,598	2,431	1,028
Financial assets	998	2,798	2,340
Total	**147,545**	**161,555**	**143,450**

Expenditure*	2007	2008	2009
Current	120,402	129,144	133,528
Social security	5,913	6,739	7,386
Autonomous communities	36,010	39,628	38,644
Autonomous organs	3,395	1,938	4,315
Local corporations	13,746	14,690	14,848
Private companies	175	222	225
Foreign contributions	12,053	12,803	12,742
Families	2,997	3,136	3,096
Personnel	23,686	25,378	26,848
Purchase of goods and services	3,431	3,563	3,502
Interest	15,946	16,631	17,424
Contingency fund	3,028	3,100	3,251
Capital	19,497	20,287	21,125
Investment	9,956	10,588	10,408
Capital transfers	9,541	9,699	10,717
Financial assets	12,112	14,981	34,292
Financial liabilities	33,378	34,509	33,973
Total	**188,417**	**202,021**	**226,169**

* Calculated according to recognized obligations rather than payments made.

Source: Ministerio de Economía y Hacienda, Madrid.

INTERNATIONAL RESERVES
(US $ million at 31 December)

	2006	2007	2008
Gold*	8,518	7,574	7,832
IMF special drawing rights	335	369	223
Reserve position in IMF	399	319	650
Foreign exchange*	10,088	10,792	11,540
Total	**19,340**	**19,054**	**20,245**

* Figures for gold and foreign exchange exclude deposits made with the European Monetary Institute (now the European Central Bank). Gold is valued at market-related prices.

Source: IMF, *International Financial Statistics*.

SPAIN

MONEY SUPPLY
(€ '000 million at 31 December)

	2006	2007	2008
Currency issued*	65.93	70.92	79.44
Demand deposits at banking institutions	493.65	485.30	464.09

* Currency put into circulation by the Banco de España was €90,040m. in 2006, €88,820m. in 2007 and €86,430m. in 2008.

Source: IMF, *International Financial Statistics*.

COST OF LIVING
(Consumer Price Index; base: 2006 = 100)

	2005	2007	2008
Food (excl. alcoholic beverages and tobacco)	96.1	103.7	109.8
Alcohol and tobacco	98.2	107.0	111.2
Household expenses	97.5	102.6	105.2
Clothing (incl. footwear)	98.8	101.1	101.7
Rent	93.9	103.7	110.6
Transport	95.7	102.1	108.0
All items (incl. others)	96.6	102.8	107.0

NATIONAL ACCOUNTS
(€ million at current prices)

National Income and Product

	2005*	2006*	2007†
Compensation of employees	427,402	456,059	488,323
Gross operating surplus and mixed income	381,903	415,644	451,782
Gross domestic product (GDP) at factor cost	809,305	871,703	940,105
Taxes, *less* subsidies on production and imports	99,145	109,251	109,743
GDP in market prices	908,450	980,954	1,049,848
Primary incomes (net)	−12,745	−16,710	−26,958
Gross national income	895,705	964,244	1,022,890
Less Consumption of fixed capital	138,692	152,355	166,697
Net national income	757,013	811,889	856,193
Current transfers (net)	−6,940	−9,364	−9,340
Gross national disposable income	750,073	802,525	846,853

* Preliminary.
† Estimates.

Expenditure on the Gross Domestic Product

	2005*	2006*	2007†
Final consumption expenditure	688,611	741,194	789,842
Households	516,818	554,495	587,713
Non-profit institutions serving households	8,053	8,721	9,391
General government	163,740	177,978	192,783
Gross capital formation	267,938	300,036	328,659
Gross fixed capital formation	266,624	298,189	326,433
Changes in inventories	1,314	1,847	2,226
Total domestic expenditure	956,549	1,041,230	1,118,501
Exports of goods and services	233,460	255,315	275,024
Less Imports of goods and services	281,559	315,591	343,677
GDP in market prices	908,450	980,954	1,049,848

* Preliminary.
† Estimates.

Gross Domestic Product by Economic Activity

	2005*	2006*	2007†
Agriculture, hunting, forestry and fishing	25,877	25,114	27,342
Mining and quarrying; electricity, gas and water supply‡	25,352	26,775	27,807
Manufacturing	124,568	132,419	141,838
Construction	94,042	106,361	115,181
Private sector service industries	425,776	455,643	490,098
Public sector service industries	117,819	127,391	138,529
Gross value added in basic prices	813,434	873,703	940,795
Import duties, value-added tax and other taxes, *less* subsidies on products	95,016	107,251	109,053
GDP in market prices	908,450	980,954	1,049,848

* Preliminary.
† Estimates.
‡ Including refinery products.

BALANCE OF PAYMENTS
(US $ million)

	2005	2006	2007
Exports of goods f.o.b.	196,580	220,774	256,681
Imports of goods f.o.b.	−281,784	−325,444	−380,197
Trade balance	−85,204	−104,670	−123,515
Exports of services	94,663	106,628	129,303
Imports of services	−67,129	−78,423	−98,900
Balance on goods and services	−57,669	−76,465	−93,112
Other income received	39,445	55,855	72,688
Other income paid	−60,701	−81,814	−115,931
Balance on goods, services and income	−78,925	−102,424	−136,355
Current transfers received	20,194	21,563	26,058
Current transfers paid	−24,656	−29,263	−35,058
Current balance	−83,388	−110,124	−145,355
Capital account (net)	10,107	7,857	6,291
Direct investment abroad	−41,922	−99,492	−127,777
Direct investment from abroad	24,573	27,250	60,122
Portfolio investment assets	−119,356	−11,253	−6,574
Portfolio investment liabilities	172,713	244,210	124,167
Financial derivatives liabilities	273	2,419	−9,529
Other investment assets	−42,198	−99,778	−51,347
Other investment liabilities	79,803	41,595	144,942
Net errors and omissions	−2,524	−2,106	5,275
Overall balance	−1,920	578	215

Source: IMF, *International Financial Statistics*.

SPAIN

External Trade

PRINCIPAL COMMODITIES
(distribution by SITC, US $ million)

Imports c.i.f.	2005	2006	2007
Food and live animals	20,668.8	22,053.4	27,298.0
Fish, crustaceans and molluscs, and products thereof	5,695.8	6,426.2	7,075.6
Vegetables and fruit	3,490.1	3,647.8	4,677.9
Beverages and tobacco	4,010.8	3,618.4	4,316.8
Alcoholic beverages	1,634.0	1,830.7	2,074.1
Tobacco and tobacco manufactures	2,130.3	1,546.1	1,870.6
Mineral fuels and lubricants	40,673.8	51,803.1	58,399.6
Petroleum, petroleum products etc.	31,224.0	39,728.8	45,230.7
Gas, natural and manufactured	7,003.2	9,942.8	10,643.0
Chemicals and related products	33,464.6	36,445.5	43,233.0
Organic chemicals	7,890.7	8,622.7	9,529.8
Medicinal and pharmaceutical products	8,985.5	9,628.9	12,171.3
Basic manufactures	36,143.4	43,194.3	53,649.3
Paper, paperboard and related products	4,413.9	4,674.9	5,480.0
Textile yarn, fabrics and articles thereof	4,483.7	4,771.1	5,356.8
Iron and steel	9,644.0	12,127.2	15,623.6
Non-ferrous metals	3,859.5	5,841.9	7,528.9
Manufactures of metal	6,120.2	7,108.2	8,955.5
Machinery and transport equipment	109,837.3	120,981.2	142,727.0
Telecommunications, sound recording and reproducing equipment	11,006.2	13,284.7	15,090.5
Electrical machinery, apparatus and appliances	12,232.9	14,190.6	19,304.6
Road vehicles	44,673.9	48,034.8	58,170.6
Passenger cars	23,024.8	24,175.4	29,105.9
Miscellaneous manufactured articles	31,417.0	35,353.4	42,124.6
Total (incl. others)	289,610.8	329,975.8	391,236.9

Exports f.o.b.	2005	2006	2007
Food and live animals	21,814.7	23,332.6	27,363.7
Vegetables and fruit	11,741.2	12,411.3	14,152.9
Tomatoes	1,057.9	1,009.9	1,179.1
Oranges, mandarins, clementines etc.	2,352.4	2,388.2	2,929.7
Beverages and tobacco	2,916.8	2,972.2	3,614.6
Wine	1,977.9	2,059.8	2,568.7
Mineral fuels and lubricants	8,379.4	9,852.5	11,976.8
Animals and vegetable oils, fats and waxes	2,413.8	2,665.7	3,168.5
Olive oil	2,036.2	2,271.2	2,605.3
Chemicals and related products	23,061.1	25,563.0	31,655.4
Medicinal and pharmaceutical products	6,722.2	7,595.7	9,819.5
Basic manufactures	32,229.6	37,910.4	45,782.1
Ceramic products	2,707.3	2,949.3	3,357.4
Iron and steel	7,045.7	8,380.0	11,444.7
Machinery and transport equipment	77,489.2	84,784.6	97,800.1
Electrical machinery, apparatus and appliances	8,719.8	9,191.5	10,082.1
Road vehicles	41,335.4	44,245.5	53,178.3
Miscellaneous manufactured articles	17,429.8	18,558.2	21,571.4
Total (incl. others)	192,798.2	214,061.2	253,753.9

Source: UN, *International Trade Statistics Yearbook*.

PRINCIPAL TRADING PARTNERS
(US $ million)

Imports c.i.f.	2005	2006	2007
Algeria	5,072.0	5,766.6	6,145.3
Belgium	8,832.8	9,638.8	10,955.6
China, People's Republic	14,557.2	18,050.4	25,382.7
France (incl. Monaco)	40,841.0	42,106.0	48,041.7
Germany	42,712.9	46,830.4	59,906.2
Italy	24,746.7	27,296.5	34,108.8
Japan	7,363.0	7,433.4	8,348.6
Netherlands	11,680.6	13,200.4	15,578.8
Portugal	9,339.5	10,718.5	12,720.5
Russia	6,452.2	9,325.3	10,830.4
Sweden	3,710.3	4,286.7	4,871.0
United Kingdom	16,454.6	16,688.4	19,416.3
USA	9,305.8	10,790.0	13,802.8
Total (incl. others)	289,610.8	329,975.8	391,236.9

Exports f.o.b.	2005	2006	2007
Belgium	5,452.1	6,253.0	7,155.6
France (incl. Monaco)	36,990.7	40,058.2	47,708.9
Germany	21,901.1	23,350.4	27,282.1
Greece	2,137.9	2,396.1	3,032.1
Italy	16,128.0	18,265.6	22,595.3
Mexico	3,293.5	3,791.4	4,364.5
Morocco	2,789.4	3,269.1	4,203.3
Netherlands	6,027.1	7,079.7	8,287.7
Portugal	18,456.1	19,056.5	21,947.5
Turkey	3,352.2	3,498.3	4,041.6
United Kingdom	16,201.6	17,054.7	19,582.6
USA	7,952.6	9,453.8	10,208.0
Total (incl. others)	192,798.4	214,061.2	253,753.9

Source: UN, *International Trade Statistics Yearbook*.

Transport

RAILWAYS
(RENFE only)

	2002	2003	2004
Number of passengers ('000)	484,460	490,440	484,461
Passenger-km (million)	19,480	19,309	19,017
Freight ('000 metric tons)	26,359	26,929	26,806
Freight ton-km (million)	11,660	11,866	11,927

Source: Red Nacional de los Ferrocarriles Españoles (RENFE), Madrid.

ROAD TRAFFIC
('000 motor vehicles in use at 31 December)

	2005	2006	2007
Passenger cars	20,250.4	20,636.7	21,760.2
Buses	58.2	58.3	61.0
Lorries	4,655.4	4,835.7	5,140.6
Motorcycles	1,805.8	2,042.3	2,311.3
Tractors	194.2	196.9	212.7
Other vehicles	693.2	761.3	832.6

SHIPPING
Merchant Fleet
(registered at 31 December)

	2005	2006	2007
Number of vessels	1,612	1,638	1,648
Displacement (grt)	2,361,683	3,004,626	3,061,813

Source: Lloyd's Register-Fairplay, *World Fleet Statistics*.

SPAIN

International Sea-borne Freight Traffic

	2003	2004	2005
Goods loaded ('000 metric tons)	68,227	74,576	81,066
Goods unloaded ('000 metric tons)	221,455	236,200	259,214

Source: partly Puertos del Estado, Ministerio de Fomento, Madrid.

CIVIL AVIATION
(domestic and international traffic on scheduled services)

	2005	2006	2007
Passengers carried ('000)	179,047	191,125	208,510
Goods carried ('000 metric tons)	610,145	582,876	607,129

Source: Dirección General de Aviación Civil, Ministerio de Fomento, Madrid.

Tourism

FOREIGN TOURIST ARRIVALS
('000 persons, incl. Spaniards resident abroad)

Country of residence	2005	2006	2007
Belgium	1,822	1,825	1,681
France	8,875	9,220	9,331
Germany	9,918	10,118	10,047
Ireland	1,365	1,507	1,633
Italy	2,957	3,362	3,633
Netherlands	2,435	2,515	2,448
Portugal	1,992	2,193	2,364
Switzerland	1,155	1,381	1,388
United Kingdom	16,090	16,185	16,271
USA	884	921	1,124
Total (incl. others)	55,914	58,190	59,193

Receipts from tourism (€ million): 46,060 in 2005; 48,243 in 2006; 49,946 in 2007.

Source: Instituto de Estudios Turísticos, Madrid.

Communications Media

	2005	2006	2007
Telephones ('000 main lines in use)	18,004.0	18,384.7	18,583.3
Mobile cellular telephones ('000 subscribers)	42,694.1	46,152.0	48,813.0
Personal computers ('000 in use)	12,000	n.a.	n.a.
Internet users ('000)	17,233	18,578	19,690
Broadband subscribers ('000)	5,035.2	6,690.7	7,944.7

Facsimile machines (1996): 700,000 in use (estimate).
Radio receivers ('000 in use, 1997): 13,100.
Book production (2003): titles ('000) 72.0; copies (million) 238.7.
Daily newspapers (2004): 151 (with combined average circulation of 6,183,000 copies per issue).
Non-daily newspapers (1999): 11 (with combined average circulation of 5,371,000).

Sources: partly UN, *Statistical Yearbook*; UNESCO Institute for Statistics; UNESCO, *Statistical Yearbook*; and International Telecommunication Union.

Education

(2007/08 forecasts, unless otherwise indicated)

	Institutions*	Teachers	Students
Pre-primary	3,985	19,237†	1,620,505
Primary	9,805‡	117,753†	2,603,175
Special education	486	6,396†	29,555
Secondary: general	} 4,569‡	} 216,361†§	{ 1,826,825
Secondary: vocational and university entrance			{ 1,125,820
Universities, etc.	72	107,905	1,381,749

* 2005/06 figures.
† 2003/04 figure.
‡ Excluding institutions providing primary education and the first cycle of secondary education (2,475), or institutions providing both primary and secondary education (1,268).
§ Excluding personnel teaching at institutions that provide both primary and secondary education (147,300).

Source: Ministerio de Educación y Ciencia, Madrid.

Directory

The Constitution

The Constitution of the Kingdom of Spain was approved by popular referendum on 6 December 1978, and promulgated on 29 December 1978.

According to the final provisions, all the fundamental laws of the Franco regime are repealed, together with all measures incompatible with the Constitution.

The following is a summary of the main provisions:

PRELIMINARY PROVISIONS

Spain is a social and democratic State whose supreme values are freedom, justice, equality and political pluralism. National sovereignty and power reside with the Spanish people, the political form of the State being a parliamentary Monarchy.

The Constitution is based on the indissoluble unity of the Spanish nation, and recognizes and guarantees the right to autonomy of the nationalities and regions.

FUNDAMENTAL RIGHTS, DUTIES AND FREEDOMS

Standards concerning fundamental rights and freedoms recognized in the Constitution are to be interpreted in accordance with the Universal Declaration of Human Rights and other international treaties and agreements of a similar nature ratified by Spain.

All Spaniards are equal under the law and no Spaniard by birth may be deprived of his nationality. The age of majority is 18, suffrage is free and universal and every person has a right to public service.

The main freedoms listed are described below, bearing in mind that the Constitution contains the proviso that no person, group or action pose a threat to public order and safety. Free entry to and exit from Spain, freedom of thought, belief and expression are guaranteed, as is the right of access to state and public communications media by significant social and political groups and to administrative archives and registers by individuals, except in matters concerning state security and defence, and the private life and home of the individual, which are inviolable.

There is no state religion, but the state will maintain co-operation with the Roman Catholic Church and other religious groups.

Freedom of association is guaranteed, except for criminal, paramilitary and secret associations, all associations being bound to inscribe themselves in a public register; the right to form trade unions and to strike is also guaranteed, military personnel being subject to special laws in these cases.

Every person has a right to work for a just remuneration, under conditions of safety, hygiene and a healthy environment. The State is to be run on the principles of a market economy. Social security payments are provided for and it is stipulated that special care be taken of the handicapped and the elderly.

In criminal matters, the death penalty is abolished except under military criminal law in time of war. Extradition functions on the principle of reciprocity but the terms do not apply to political crimes, acts of terrorism, however, not being considered as such. All persons are presumed innocent before trial, and a habeas corpus clause provides for a detainee to be freed within 72 hours of arrest or to be brought before a court.

SPAIN

THE CROWN

The King is the Head of State, the symbol of its unity and permanence, and the highest representative of the Spanish State in international relations. His decisions and acts must be approved by the Government, and responsibility for the King's actions is borne by those who approve them. The Crown is hereditary descending to the sons of the Sovereign in order of seniority or, if there are no sons, to the daughters. Persons marrying against the wishes of the King or Cortes Generales (national assembly) are excluded from the succession. The Constitution lays down the procedure for establishing the Regency.

The King's duties are as follows:

to approve and promulgate laws;

to convene and dissolve the Cortes and to call elections and referendums (according to the Constitution);

to propose a candidate for the presidency of the Government and dismiss him;

to appoint the members of the Government on the proposal of the President (Prime Minister);

to issue decrees approved by the Council of Ministers, and to confer civil and military posts and grant honours and distinctions in accordance with the laws;

to be informed of the affairs of State, and to preside over the Council of Ministers when he deems it necessary on the request of the President of the Government;

to command the Armed Forces;

to grant mercy according to the law (which may not authorize general pardons);

to accredit ambassadors and other diplomatic representatives;

to express the State's assent to bind itself to international treaties;

to declare war and peace on the prior authorization of the Cortes.

THE CORTES GENERALES

The Cortes represent the Spanish people and comprise the Congreso de los Diputados (Congress of Deputies—lower house) and the Senado (Senate—upper house).

The Congreso has a minimum of 300 deputies and a maximum of 400, elected by universal, free, equal, direct and secret suffrage. Each province forms one constituency, the number of deputies in each one being determined according to population and elected by proportional representation for four years, Ceuta and Melilla having one deputy each. Elections must be held between 30 and 60 days after the end of each parliamentary mandate, and the Congreso convened within 25 days of the elections.

The Senado is based on territorial representation. Each province elects four senators for four years. Each island or group of islands forms one constituency. Gran Canaria, Mallorca and Tenerife return three senators each, the others one each. The Autonomous Communities return, in addition, one senator, plus one more for each million inhabitants, appointed by the legislative assembly of the community.

Each House lays down its own rules of procedure and elects its own president and governing body. Each year there are two ordinary sessions of the Cortes, of four and five months each, and a standing committee of 21 members in each House looks after affairs while the Cortes are in recess or during electoral periods. Measures are adopted by a majority in both Houses providing that a majority of the members is present. If agreement is not reached between the Congreso and the Senado, a joint committee must attempt to solve the differences by drawing up a text to be voted on again by both Houses. In the case of further non-agreement, the issue is decided by an absolute majority vote in the Congreso.

LEGISLATION

Laws may not be retroactive.

Organic laws concern the development of fundamental rights and public freedoms, the approval of statutes of autonomy, the general electoral system, and other matters specified in the Constitution. Any approval, modification or repeal of these laws requires an absolute majority in the Congreso. The Cortes may delegate the power to issue measures called Legislative Decrees with the status of law to a governmental legislative body. In urgent cases the Government may issue provisional measures in the form of Decree-Laws not affecting the fundamental laws and rights of the nation, which must be voted upon by the Cortes within 30 days.

All laws must be sanctioned by the King within 15 days of their approval by the Cortes.

Provision is made for the popular presentation of bills if they are supported by 500,000 reputable signatures.

THE GOVERNMENT

The Government is the executive power and is composed of a President proposed by the King on the Cortes' approval and voted into office by the Congreso by absolute majority. If no President is elected within two months, the King will dissolve the Cortes and convene new elections with the approval of the President of the Congreso. The President of the Government designates the Ministers.

The Council of State is the supreme consultative organ of the Government. (An organic law will regulate its composition.)

Further articles provide for the procedure for declaring a state of alarm, emergency or siege.

THE JUDICIARY

Justice derives from the people and is administered in the name of the King by judges and magistrates subject only to the law. The principle of jurisdictional unity is the basis of the organization and functioning of the Courts, which are established in an organic law of judicial power.

The Judiciary is governed by the General Council of Judicial Power, presided over by the President of the Supreme Court and made up of 20 members elected by the Cortes and appointed by the King for five years. Of those 20 members, 12 are judges or magistrates, four are nominated by the Congreso and four by the Senado, these eight being elected by a three-fifths' majority from lawyers and jurists of more than 15 years' professional service.

The Attorney-General is appointed by the King on the Government's approval.

TERRITORIAL ORGANIZATION

The State is organized into municipalities, provinces and Autonomous Communities, all of which have local autonomy.

THE AUTONOMOUS COMMUNITIES

The peripheral provinces, with their own historical, cultural and economic characteristics, are entitled to accede to self-government, but the Constitution states that in no case will the federation of the Autonomous Communities be permitted.

The matters in which the Communities may assume competence include: land use and building, public works and transport, ports, agriculture, environment, minerals, economic development, culture, tourism, social aid, health and local policing, all within the framework of national laws and policy and as long as nothing outside the regional boundaries is involved. In the specific case of financial autonomy, revenue proceeds from the State and from each Autonomous Community's own taxes, and a State Compensation Fund acts to correct any imbalances between the Communities. State competence will always prevail over regional competence should conflict arise over matters not under the exclusive control of the Autonomous Communities.

The State may pass laws by absolute majority to establish the principles for the harmonization of measures taken by the Autonomous Communities, even concerning matters directly under their authority.

THE CONSTITUTIONAL COURT

This court monitors observance of the Constitution and comprises 12 members appointed by the King, of whom four are elected by the Congreso and four by the Senado by three-fifths' majority, two on the proposal of the Government and two on the proposal of the General Council of Judicial Power. They are appointed for nine years, with three members resigning every three years.

The Government

HEAD OF STATE

King of Spain, Head of State, Commander-in-Chief of the Armed Forces and Head of the Supreme Council of Defence: HM King JUAN CARLOS I (acceded to the throne 22 November 1975).

COUNCIL OF MINISTERS
(April 2009)

President of the Government (Prime Minister): JOSÉ LUIS RODRÍGUEZ ZAPATERO.

First Deputy Prime Minister, Minister of the Presidency and Government Spokesperson: MARÍA TERESA FERNÁNDEZ DE LA VEGA SANZ.

Second Deputy Prime Minister and Minister of the Economy and Finance: ELENA SALGADO MÉNDEZ.

Third Deputy Prime Minister and Minister for Public Administration: MANUEL CHAVES GONZÁLEZ.

SPAIN

Minister of Foreign Affairs and Co-operation: MIGUEL ÁNGEL MORATINOS CUYAUBÉ.

Minister of Justice: FRANCISCO CAAMAÑO DOMÍNGUEZ.

Minister of Defence: CARME CHACÓN PIQUERAS.

Minister of the Interior: ALFREDO PÉREZ RUBALCABA.

Minister of Development: JOSÉ BLANCO LÓPEZ.

Minister of Education: ÁNGEL GABILONDO PUJOL.

Minister of Labour and Immigration: CELESTINO CORBACHO CHAVES.

Minister of Industry, Tourism and Trade: MIGUEL SEBASTIÁN GASCÓN.

Minister of the Environment, Agriculture and Marine Affairs: ELENA ESPINOSA MANGANA.

Minister of Culture: ÁNGELES GONZÁLEZ-SINDE REIG.

Minister of Health and Social Policy: TRINIDAD JIMÉNEZ GARCÍA-HERRERA.

Minister of Housing: BEATRIZ CORREDOR SIERRA.

Minister of Science and Innovation: CRISTINA GARMENDIA MÉNDIZABAL.

Minister of Equality: BIBIANA AÍDO ALMAGRO.

MINISTRIES

Office of the President of the Government: Complejo de la Moncloa, Avda de Puerta de Hierro s/n, 28071 Madrid; fax (91) 3900217; e-mail jlrzapatero@presidencia.gob.es; internet www.la-moncloa.es.

Ministry of Culture: Plaza del Rey 1, 28071 Madrid; tel. (91) 7017000; fax (91) 7017352; e-mail contacte@mcu.es; internet www.mcu.es.

Ministry of Defence: Paseo de la Castellana 109, 28071 Madrid; tel. (91) 3955000; e-mail infodefensa@mde.es; internet www.mde.es.

Ministry of Development: Paseo de la Castellana 67, 28071 Madrid; tel. (91) 5978787; fax (91) 5978573; e-mail fomento@fomento.es; internet www.fomento.es.

Ministry of the Economy and Finance: Alcalá 9, 28014 Madrid; tel. (91) 5958348; fax (91) 5958486; e-mail informacion.alcala@meh.es; internet www.meh.es.

Ministry of Education: Alcalá 36, 28071 Madrid; tel. (91) 7018000; fax (91) 7018648; e-mail prensa@mepsyd.es; internet www.mepsyd.es.

Ministry of the Environment, Agriculture and Marine Affairs: Paseo Infanta Isabel 1, 28071 Madrid; tel. (91) 3475368; fax (91) 4675854; e-mail sministr@marm.es; internet www.marm.es.

Ministry of Equality: Alcalá 37, 28014 Madrid; tel. (91) 5243220; fax (91) 5243597; e-mail contratacion@migualdad.es; internet www.migualdad.es.

Ministry of Foreign Affairs and Co-operation: Plaza de la Provincia 1, 28012 Madrid; tel. (91) 3799700; e-mail informaec@maec.es; internet www.maec.es.

Ministry of Health and Social Policy: Paseo del Prado 18–20, 28014 Madrid; tel. 901 400100; fax (91) 5964480; e-mail oiac@msc.es; internet www.msc.es.

Ministry of Housing: Paseo de la Castellana 112, 28071 Madrid; tel. (91) 7284004; fax (91) 7284861; e-mail portal.vivienda@vivienda.es; internet www.mviv.es.

Ministry of Industry, Tourism and Trade: Paseo de la Castellana 160, 28071 Madrid; tel. (902) 446006; fax (91) 4578066; e-mail info@mityc.es; internet www.mityc.es.

Ministry of the Interior: Paseo de la Castellana 5, 28046 Madrid; tel. (91) 5371111; fax (91) 5371003; e-mail estafeta@mir.es; internet www.mir.es.

Ministry of Justice: San Bernardo 45, 28015 Madrid; tel. (91) 3904500; internet www.mjusticia.es.

Ministry of Labour and Immigration: Nuevos Ministerios, Agustín de Bethencourt 4, 28071 Madrid; tel. (91) 3630000; e-mail gprensa@mtin.es; internet www.mtin.es.

Ministry of the Presidency: Complejo de la Moncloa, Avda de Puerta de Hierro s/n, 28071 Madrid; tel. (91) 3214000; e-mail sec@mpr.es; internet www.mpr.es.

Ministry of Public Administration: Paseo de la Castellana 3, 28071 Madrid; tel. (91) 2731029; fax (91) 2731012; e-mail portal@map.es; internet www.map.es.

Ministry of Science and Innovation: Albacete 5, 28027 Madrid; tel. (90) 2218600; e-mail informa@micinn.es; internet web.micinn.es.

COUNCIL OF STATE

Consejo de Estado: Mayor 79, 28013 Madrid; tel. (91) 5166262; fax (91) 5166244; e-mail tinfo@consejo-estado.es; internet www.consejo-estado.es.

President: FRANCISCO RUBIO LLORENTE.

Legislature

LAS CORTES GENERALES

Congreso de los Diputados (Congress of Deputies)

Carrera de San Jerónimo s/n, 28071 Madrid; tel. (91) 3906000; fax (91) 4298707; e-mail servicio.informacion@sgral.congreso.es; internet www.congreso.es.

President: JOSÉ BONO MARTÍNEZ (PSOE).

First Vice-President: TERESA CUNILLERA I MESTRES (PSOE).

General Election, 9 March 2008

	%	Seats
Partido Socialista Obrero Español (PSOE)*	43.87	169
Partido Popular (PP)†	39.93	154
Convergència i Unió (CiU)	3.03	10
Euzko Alderdi Jeltzalea/Partido Nacionalista Vasco (EAJ/PNV)	1.19	6
Esquerra Republicana de Catalunya (ERC)	1.13	3
Izquierda Unida (IU)	3.77	2
Bloque Nacionalista Galego (BNG)	0.83	2
Coalición Canaria—Partido Nacionalista Canario (CC-PNC)	0.69	2
Union Progreso y Democracia (UPyD)	1.19	1
Nafarroa Bai (Na-Bai)	0.24	1
Total (incl. others)	100.00	350

* Including Partit dels Socialistes de Catalunya.
† Including Unión del Pueblo Navarro.

Senado (Senate)

Plaza de la Marina Española 8, 28071 Madrid; tel. (91) 5381000; fax (91) 5381003; e-mail informacion@senado.es; internet www.senado.es.

President: FRANCISCO JAVIER ROJO GARCÍA (PSE-EE).

First Vice-President: ISIDRE MOLAS I BATLLORI (PSC-PSOE).

The Senate comprises 264 members, 208 of whom are directly elected for a term of four years. The remaining 56 regional representatives are chosen by the assemblies of the autonomous regions and are renewed following legislative elections in those regions. Following the general election held on 9 March 2008, and the appointment, in the following month, of seven senators to represent the Autonomous Community of Andalusia, the strength of the parties was as follows:

Grouping	Directly elected	Appointed	Total
Partido Popular (PP)	98	23	121
Partido Socialista Obrero Español (PSOE)	79	17	96
Entesa Catalana de Progrés*	12	4	16
Partido Socialista de Euskadi-Euskadiko Ezkerra	6	1	7
Convergència i Unió (CiU)	4	3	7
Euzko Alderdi Jeltzalea/Partido Nacionalista Vasco (EAJ/PNV)	2	2	4
Unión del Pueblo Navarro	3	—	3
Partido dos Socialistas de Galicia-PSOE	2	1	3
Coalición Canaria (CC)	1	1	2
Independent	1	1	2
Bloque Nacionalista Galego (BNG)	—	1	1
Partido Aragonés (PAR)	—	1	1
Partit Socialista de Mallorca-Entesa Nacionalista	—	1	1
Total	208	56	264

* An alliance of the Esquerra Republicana de Catalunya, the Esquerra Unida i Alternativa, the Iniciativa per Catalunya Verds and the Partit dels Socialistes de Catalunya.

Legislative Assemblies of the Autonomous Communities

(For full names of political parties, see Political Organizations)

ANDALUCÍA (ANDALUSIA)

President of the Government (Junta): José Antonio Griñán Martínez (PSOE).
President of the Parliament: Fuensanta Coves (PSOE).
Election, 9 March 2008

	Seats
PSOE	56
PP	47
IU-LV-CA*	6
Total	109

*Convocatoria por Andalucía.

ARAGÓN

President of the Government: Marcelino Iglesias Ricou (PSOE).
President of the Parliament (Cortes): Francisco Pina Cuenca (PSOE).
Election, 27 May 2007

	Seats
PSOE	30
PP	23
PAR	9
ChA	4
IU	1
Total	67

ASTURIAS

President: Vicente Alberto Álvarez Areces (PSOE).
President of the Parliament (Junta General del Principado): María Jesús Álvarez González (PSOE).
Election, 27 May 2007

	Seats
PSOE	21
PP	20
IU	4
Total	45

BALEARIC ISLANDS (SEE ISLAS BALEARES)
BASQUE COUNTRY (SEE PAÍS VASCO)

CANARIAS (CANARY ISLANDS)

President of the Government: Paulino Rivero Baute (CC).
President of the Parliament: Antonio A. Castro Cordobez (CC).
Election, 27 May 2007

	Seats
PSOE	26
CC-PNC	17
PP	15
CC-AHI	2
Total	60

CANTABRIA

President: Miguel Ángel Revilla Roiz (PRC).
President of the Parliament: Miguel Ángel Palacio García (PSOE).
Election, 27 May 2007

	Seats
PP	17
PSOE	10
PRC	12
Total	39

CASTILLA Y LEÓN (CASTILE AND LEON)

President of the Government (Junta): Juan Vicente Herrera Campo (PP).
President of the Parliament (Cortes): José Manuel Fernández Santiago (PP).
Election, 27 May 2007

	Seats
PP	48
PSOE	33
UPL	2
Total	83

CASTILLA-LA MANCHA (CASTILE-LA MANCHA)

President of the Government (Junta de Comunidades): José María Barreda Fontes (PSOE).
President of the Parliament (Cortes): Francisco José Pardo Piqueras (PSOE).
Election, 27 May 2007

	Seats
PSOE	26
PP	21
Total	47

CATALUÑA/CATALUNYA (CATALONIA)

President of the Government (Generalitat): José Montilla Aguilera (PSC).
President of the Parliament: Ernest Benach i Pascual (ERC).
Election, 1 November 2006

	Seats
CiU	48
PSC-PSOE	37
ERC	21
PP	14
ICV-EUiA*	12
Ciutadans	3
Total	135

*Coalition of Iniciativa per Catalunya Verds (ICV) and Esquerra Unida i Alternativa (EUiA).

COMUNIDAD VALENCIANA/COMUNITAT VALENCIANA (VALENCIA)

President of the Government (Generalitat): Francisco Enrique Camps Ortiz (PP).
President of the Parliament (Corts): María Milagrosa Martínez Navarro (PP).
Election, 27 May 2007

	Seats
PP	55
PSPV-PSOE	37
Compromís pel País Valencià*	7
Total	99

*A coalition of EUPV, Bloc Nacionalista Valenciana and Els Verds del País Valencià.

EXTREMADURA

President of the Government (Junta): Guillermo Fernández Vara (PSOE).
President of the Parliament (Asamblea): Juan Ramón Ferreira Díaz (PSOE).
Election, 27 May 2007

	Seats
PSOE	38
PP	27
Total	65

SPAIN

GALICIA

President of the Government (Xunta): ALBERTO NÚÑEZ FEIJÓO (PP).
President of the Parliament: PILAR ROJO NOGUERA (PP).
Election, 1 March 2009

	Seats
PP	39
PS de G-PSOE	24
BNG	12
Total	75

ISLAS BALEARES/ILLES BALEARS (BALEARIC ISLANDS)

President of the Government: FRANCESC ANTICH I OLIVER (PSOE).
President of the Parliament: MARIA ANTÒNIA MUNAR I RIUTORT (UM).
Election, 27 May 2007

	Seats
PP	28
PSOE	16
PSOE-ExC	6
PSM-Bloc per Mallorca*	4
UM	3
PSM-Els Verds de Menorca	1
AIPF†	1
Total	59

* An alliance of PSM, Alternativa Esquerra Unida-Els Verds and ERC.
† Agrupació Independent Popular de Formentera.

MADRID

President: ESPERANZA AGUIRRE GIL DE BIEDMA (PP).
President of the Parliament (Asamblea): ELVIRA RODRÍGUEZ HERRER (PP).
Election, 27 May 2007

	Seats
PP	67
PSOE	42
IU	11
Total	120

MURCIA

President of the Government: RAMÓN LUIS VALCÁRCEL SISO (PP).
President of the Parliament (Asamblea Regional): FRANCISCO CELDRÁN VIDAL (PP).
Election, 27 May 2007

	Seats
PP	29
PSOE	15
IU-LV	1
Total	45

NAVARRA (NAVARRE)

President of the Government: MIGUEL SANZ SESMA (UPN).
President of the Parliament: MARÍA ELENA TORRES MIRANDA (PSN-PSOE).
Election, 27 May 2007

	Seats
UPN	22
Nafarroa Bai	12
PSN-PSOE	12
CDN	2
IU/NEB*	2
Total	50

* Nafarroako Ezker Batua.

PAÍS VASCO/EUSKADI (BASQUE COUNTRY)

Lehendakari (President): PATXI LÓPEZ (PSE-EE/PSOE).
President of the Parliament: ARANTZA QUIROGA CIA (PP).
Election, 1 March 2009

	Seats
EAJ-PNV	30
PSE-EE/PSOE	24
PP	13
Aralar	4
EA	2
EB-B	1
UPyD	1
Total	75

LA RIOJA

President of the Government: PEDRO MARÍA SANZ ALONSO (PP).
President of the Parliament: JOSÉ IGNACIO CENICEROS GONZÁLEZ (PP).
Election, 27 May 2007

	Seats
PP	17
PSOE	14
PR	2
Total	33

VALENCIA (SEE COMUNIDAD VALENCIANA)

Political Organizations

In 2005 around 500 political parties were officially registered.

PRINCIPAL NATIONAL PARTIES

Izquierda Unida (IU) (United Left): Olimpo 35, 28043 Madrid; tel. (91) 7227500; fax (91) 3880405; e-mail secretariaorganizacion@izquierda-unida.es; internet www.izquierda-unida.es; f. 1986 as coalition of Partido Comunista de España and other left-wing parties; Co-ordinator-Gen. CAYO LARA.

    Partido Comunista de España (PCE) (Communist Party of Spain): Olimpo 35, 28043 Madrid; tel. (91) 3004969; fax (91) 3004744; e-mail webmasterpce@pce.es; internet www.pce.es; f. 1922; Euro-communist; absorbed Partido Comunista Obrero Español (PCOE) in 1986, and most of Partido Comunista de los Pueblos de España (PCPE) in Jan. 1989; Sec.-Gen. FRANCISCO FRUTOS GRAS.

Partido Popular (PP) (People's Party): Génova 13, 28004 Madrid; tel. (91) 5577300; fax (91) 3122322; e-mail partidopopular@pp.es; internet www.pp.es; f. 1976; fmrly Alianza Popular, name changed 1989; absorbed Democracia Cristiana (fmrly Partido Demócrata Popular) and Partido Liberal in early 1989; centre-right, Christian Democrat; 750,000 mems (2008); Pres. MARIANO RAJOY BREY; Sec.-Gen. MARÍA DOLORES DE COSPEDAL GARCIA.

Partido Socialista Obrero Español (PSOE) (Spanish Socialist Workers' Party): Ferraz 68 y 70, 28008 Madrid; tel. (91) 5820444; fax (91) 5820422; e-mail infopsoe@psoe.es; internet www.psoe.es; f. 1879; affiliated to the Socialist International; merged with the Partido Socialista Popular in 1978; joined by Partido de los Trabajadores de España-Unidad Comunista (PTE-UC) in 1991 and Partido de Nueva Izquierda (PDNI) in 2001; 551,469 mems (2006); Pres. MANUEL CHAVES GONZÁLEZ; Sec.-Gen. JOSÉ LUIS RODRÍGUEZ ZAPATERO.

Unión Progreso y Democracia (UPyD): Orense 25, 6°, 628080 Madrid; tel. (91) 5982286; fax (91) 7700078; e-mail informacion@upyd.es; internet www.upyd.es; f. 2007; Spokesperson ROSA DÍEZ GONZÁLEZ.

Los Verdes (LV) (The Greens): C/ Imagen nº 6, 4º B1, 41003 Sevilla; tel. (95) 4214756; fax (95) 4226888; e-mail losverdes@verdes.es; internet www.verdes.es; f. 1984; confederation of various regional environmentalist parties.

REGIONAL PARTIES

There are branches of the main national parties in most autonomous communities, some of which bear alternative or additional names. There are also numerous regional parties, including the following:

Andalucía
(Andalusia)

Partido Andalucista (PA): Vidrio 32, 41003 Sevilla; tel. (95) 4502157; fax (95) 4210446; e-mail prensa@partidoandalucista.org; internet www.partidoandalucista.org; f. 1965; Sec.-Gen. PILAR GONZÁLEZ MODINO.

Aragón

Chunta Aragonesista (ChA): Conde de Aranda 14–16, 1°, 50003 Zaragoza; tel. (976) 284242; fax (976) 281311; e-mail sedenacional@chunta.com; internet www.chunta.com; f. 1986; left-wing; Pres. NIEVES IBEAS VUELTA.

Partido Aragonés (PAR): Coso 87, 50001 Zaragoza; tel. (976) 200616; e-mail sugerencias@partidoaragones.es; internet www.partidoaragones.es; f. 1977; fmrly Partido Aragonés Regionalista; centre-right; Pres. JOSÉ ANGEL BIEL; Sec.-Gen. ALFREDO BONÉ PUEYO.

Asturias

Unión Renovadora Asturiana (URAS): Menéndez Valdés 2, 1°, 33201 Gijón; tel. (98) 5353245; e-mail correo@uras.org; internet www.uras.org; f. 1998 following split in PP of Asturias; in 2004 formed coalition, Unión Asturianista, with Partíu Asturianista (PAS); Pres. JAVIER LÓPEZ ALONSO; Sec.-Gen. FERNANDO EXPÓSITO VENAYAS.

Canarias
(Canary Islands)

Agrupación Herreña Independiente (AHI): La Constitución 4, 38900 Valverde, El Hierro, Santa Cruz de Tenerife; tel. (922) 551134; fax (922) 551224; party of El Hierro island; Pres. TOMÁS PADRÓN HERNÁNDEZ.

Coalición Canaria (CC): Buenos Aires 24, 35001 Las Palmas, Gran Canaria; tel. (928) 363142; e-mail lagomera@coalicioncanaria.org; internet www.coalicioncanaria.org; f. 1993 as coalition of Canary Islands parties incl. Agrupaciones Independientes de Canarias, Centro Canario Nacionalista, Iniciativa Canaria and Asamblea Majorera; united as a single party in 2005; Pres. CLAUDINA MORALES.

Partido Nacionalista Canario (PNC): Méndez Núñez 27, 35008 38001, Santa Cruz de Tenerife; tel. and fax (922) 292475; internet www.pnc-canarias.eu; f. 1977; National Pres. JUAN MANUEL GARCÍA RAMOS; National Sec.-Gen. GUSTAVO DAVILA DE LEÓN.

Cantabria

Partido Regionalista de Cantabria (PRC): Amós de Escalante 2, 2°D, 39002 Santander; tel. (942) 229177; fax (942) 362337; e-mail prc@prc.es; internet www.prc.es; f. 1978; centre-right; Sec.-Gen. MIGUEL ÁNGEL REVILLA ROIZ.

Castilla y León
(Castile and Leon)

Unión del Pueblo Leonés (UPL): Avda República Argentina 13, 1°, 24004 León; tel. (987) 263309; fax (987) 204499; internet www.uniondelpuebloleones.com; f. 1986 as Unión Leonesista; advocates autonomy for León region; 4,000 mems; Pres. MELCHOR MORENO DE LA TORRE; Sec.-Gen. JOAQUÍN OTERO PEREIRA.

Cataluña/Catalunya
(Catalonia)

Ciutadans-Partit de la Ciutadania/Ciudadanos-Partido de la Ciudadanía (Citizens-Citizenship Party): Plaza Urquinaona 6, planta 16 B, 08010 Barcelona; tel. (90) 2140306; e-mail info@ciudadanos-cs.org; internet www.ciudadanos-cs.org; f. 2006; opposes Catalan nationalism; Pres. ALBERT RIVERA; Sec.-Gen. MANUEL GARCÍA BOFILL.

Convergència i Unió (CiU): Còrsega 331, 08037 Barcelona; tel. (93) 2363100; e-mail ciu@ciu.info; internet www.ciu.info; f. 1978 as an electoral alliance; became confederation of parties in March 2001; Catalan nationalist, conservative; Pres. ARTUR MAS I GAVARRÓ; Sec.-Gen. JOSEP ANTONI DURAN I LLEIDA; an alliance of the following two parties:

Convergència Democràtica de Catalunya (CDC): Còrsega 331–333, 08037 Barcelona; tel. (93) 2363100; fax (93) 2363115; e-mail cdc@convergencia.org; internet www.convergencia.org; f. 1974; Catalan nationalist, centrist; Pres. JORDI PUJOL I SOLEY; Sec.-Gen. ARTUR MAS I GAVARRÓ.

Unió Democràtica de Catalunya (UDC): Travessera de Gràcia 17–21, àtic, 08021 Barcelona; tel. (93) 2402200; fax (93) 2402201; e-mail info@unio.org; internet www.unio.org; f. 1931; Christian democrat; Pres. JOSEP ANTONI DURAN I LLEIDA; Sec.-Gen. JOSEP MARIA PELEGRÍ I AIXUT.

Esquerra Republicana de Catalunya (ERC) (Republican Left of Catalonia): Calàbria 166, 08015 Barcelona; tel. (93) 4536005; fax (93) 3237122; e-mail info@esquerra.org; internet www.esquerra.cat; f. 1931; advocates independence for Catalonia within European context, a just society and national solidarity of Catalan people; Pres. JOAN PUIGCERDÓS; Sec.-Gen. JOAN RIDAO.

Esquerra Unida i Alternativa (EUiA): Doctor Aiguader 10-12, 08003 Barcelona; tel. (93) 3170034; fax (93) 3179251; e-mail euia@euia.cat; internet www.euia.cat; federation of five communist and left-wing parties in Catalonia; republican; affiliated to Izquierda Unida; Co-ordinator-Gen. JORDI MIRALLES I CONTE.

Iniciativa per Catalunya Verds (ICV): Ciutat 7, 08002 Barcelona; tel. (93) 3010612; fax (93) 4124252; e-mail iniciativa@iniciativa.cat; internet www.iniciativa.cat; f. 1987 as Iniciativa per Catalunya, a federation of left-wing parties; adopted current name in 1998 following alliance with Els Verds (Confederació Ecologista de Catalunya); Pres. JOAN SAURA LAPORTA; Sec.-Gen. JOAN HERRERA TORRES.

Partit dels Socialistes de Catalunya (PSC-PSOE): Nicaragua 75, 08029 Barcelona; tel. (93) 4955400; fax (93) 4955435; e-mail info@socialistes.org; internet www.socialistes.cat; f. 1978 by merger of various Catalan parties of socialist ideology; allied to PSOE; Pres. JOSÉ MONTILLA AGUILERA.

Comunidad Valenciana/Comunitat Valenciana
(Valencia)
(see also Cataluña)

Bloc Nacionalista Valencià: Sant Jacint 28, entresòl, 46008 Valencia; tel. (96) 3826606; fax (96) 3826276; e-mail bloc@bloc.ws; internet www.bloc.ws; f. 1998 as federation of Unitat del Poble Valencià (f. 1982), Partit Valencià Nacionalista (f. 1990) and Nacionalistes d'Alcoi (f. 1994); progressive Valencian nationalist party; Pres. JOSEP MARIA PAÑELLA ALCACER; Sec. Gen. ENRIC XAVIER MORERA CATALÀ.

Esquerra Unida del País Valencià (EUPV): Gran Via Ramón i Cajál 55, 2°, 46007 Valencia; e-mail eu.pvalencia@izquierda-unida.es; tel. (963) 841888; fax (963) 847678; e-mail eupv@eupv.org; internet www.eupv.org; left-wing; affiliated to Izquierda Unida; Co-ordinator GLÒRIA MARCOS I MARTÍ.

Esquerra Valenciana (EV): 13129-4621994 Valencia; internet www.esquerra-valenciana.org; f. 1934 as part of Front Popular; Pres. ROBERTO MORO; Sec.-Gen. VÍCTOR BAETA SUBIAS.

Partido Socialista del País Valenciano (PSPV-PSOE) (Valencian Socialist Party): Palau de les Corts Valencianes, Plaza San Lorenzo 4, 46003 Valencia; internet www.pspv-psoe.net; affiliated to PSOE; Pres. DIEGO MACÍA ANTÓN; Sec.-Gen. (vacant).

Galicia

Bloque Nacionalista Galego (BNG): Avda Rodríguez de Viguri 16, baixo, 15703 Santiago de Compostela; tel. (981) 555850; fax (981) 555851; e-mail sedenacional@bng-galiza.org; internet www.bng-galiza.org; f. 1982; Galician nationalist; Leader ANXO QUINTANA GONZÁLEZ.

Partido dos Socialistas de Galicia (PS de G-PSOE) (Galician Socialist Party): Rua do Pino 1–9, 15704 Santiago de Compostela; tel. (981) 552030; fax (981) 588708; e-mail ceng@psdeg-psoe.org; internet www.psdeg-psoe.org; Galician branch of the PSOE; Sec.-Gen. EMILIO PÉREZ TOURIÑO.

Islas Baleares/Illes Balears
(Balearic Islands)
(see also Cataluña)

Alternativa Esquerra Unida-Els Verds: Sindicat 74, 1r 2a, 07001 Palma de Mallorca; tel. (971) 724488; fax (971) 971711836; internet www.alternativa-euev.cat; alliance of Esquerra Unida de les Illes Balears (affiliated to Izquierda Unida) and Els Verds de Mallorca; Spokespersons EBERHARD GROSSKE, MIQUEL ANGEL LLAUGER.

Eivissa pel Canvi (ExC) (Ibiza for Change): Apdo Correos 40, Santa Gertrudis, Santa Eulària des Riu, Eivissa; internet www.eivissapelcanvi.org; f. 2006; opposes municipal corruption.

PSM-Entesa Nacionalista (PSM-EN): Isidoro Antillón 9, baixos, 07006 Palma de Mallorca; tel. (971) 775252; fax (971) 774848; e-mail federacio@psm-entesa.cat; internet www.psm-entesa.org; f. 1989 as Federació de l'Esquerra Nacionalista de les Illes Balears (FENIB); federation of PSM-Entesa Nacionalista de Mallorca (f. 1976 as Partit Socialista de les Illes, renamed Partit Socialista de Mallorca—PSM in 1977), PSM-Entesa Nacionalista de Menorca (f. 1977 as Partit Socialista de Menorca), Entesa Nacionalista i Ecologista d'Eivissa (f. 1989) and other groups; Socialist, Catalan nationalist, environmentalist; Sec.-Gen. BARTOLOMEU CARRIÓ TRUJILLANO.

Unió Mallorquina (UM): Sindicat 21, 07001 Palma de Mallorca; tel. (971) 726336; fax (971) 728116; e-mail um@unio-mallorquina.com; internet www.unio-mallorquina.com; f. 1982 as continuation of Unión de Centro Democrático in Mallorca; liberal, centrist; Pres. MIQUEL NADAL I BUADES.

SPAIN

Navarra
(Navarre)
(see also País Vasco)

Aralar: Aduanaren txokoa 16–18, behea, 31001 Pamplona; tel. (948) 206362; fax (948) 206003; e-mail nafarroa@aralar.net; internet www.aralar.net; f. 1990; Basque separatist, left-wing; rejects violence; Co-ordinator-Gen. PATXI ZABALETA.

Batzarre (Assembly): Navarrería 15, 1°C, 31001 Pamplona; tel. (948) 224757; fax (948) 210063; e-mail info@batzarre.org; internet www.batzarre.org; f. 1987; left-wing Basque nationalist party of Navarre.

Convergencia de Demócratas de Navarra (CDN): Avda Carlos III 7, 1°, 31002 Pamplona; tel. (948) 228185; fax (948) 227336; e-mail cdn@cdn.es; internet www.cdn.es; f. 1995; progressive centrist party; promotes Navarrese identity and opposes integration with Basque Country; Pres. JOSÉ ANDRÉS BURGUETE TORRES; Sec. CARLOS PÉREZ-NIEVAS LÓPEZ DE GOICOECHEA.

Nafarroa Bai (Na Bai) (Navarre Yes): Plaza del Castillo 32, 1° izqda, 31001 Pamplona; tel. (948) 203033; fax (948) 203034; e-mail nafarroabai@nafarroabai.net; internet www.nafarroabai.org; coalition of Basque nationalist parties in Navarre: Aralar, Batzarre, Eusko Alkartasuna and EAJ-PNV; Leader PATXI ZABALETA.

Partido Socialista de Navarra (PSN): Paseo de Sarasate 15, 2°, 31002 Pamplona; tel. (948) 225003; fax (948) 221534; e-mail info@psn-psoe.org; internet www.psn-psoe.org; Navarrese branch of PSOE; Sec.-Gen. ROBERTO JIMÉNEZ ALLI.

Unión del Pueblo Navarro (UPN): Plaza Príncipe de Viana 1, 4° dcha 31002 Pamplona; tel. (948) 223402; fax (948) 210810; e-mail info@upn.org; internet www.upn.org; f. 1979; allied to Partido Popular; centre-right; opposes closer ties between Navarre and Basque Country; Pres. YOLANDA BARCIA; Sec.-Gen. CARLOS GARCÍA ADANERO.

País Vasco/Euskadi
(Basque Country)

Aralar: see Navarra above.

Euskal Herrialdeetako Alderdi Komunista (EHAK): f. 2002; communist, Basque separatist; participated in 2005 elections to Basque Parliament, adopting programme of the banned party Aukera Guztiak; banned in Sept. 2008; Leader JUAN CARLOS RAMOS.

Eusko Abertzale Ekintza-Acción Nacionalista Vasca (EAE-ANV): Santa Maria 2, 48920 Portugalete (Vizcaya); tel. (944) 955899; e-mail info@eae-anv.org; internet www.eae-anv.org; f. 1930 by a faction of Partido Nacionalista Vasco; left-wing, republican, Basque separatist; barred from contesting 2008 general election; banned in Sept. 2008; Sec.-Gen. ANTXON GÓMEZ.

Eusko Alkartasuna (EA) (Basque Solidarity): Camino de Portuetxe 23, 1°, 20018 San Sebastián; tel. (943) 020130; fax (943) 020131; e-mail gipuzkoa@euskoalkartasuna.org; internet www.euskoalkartasuna.org; f. 1985 (as Eusko Abertzaleak—Basque Nationalists) by dissident group of progressive EAJ-PNV mems; Pres. UNAI ZIARRETA BILBAO; Sec.-Gen. JOSEBA AZKARRAGA RODERO.

Euzko Alderdi Jeltzalea-Partido Nacionalista Vasco (EAJ-PNV): Sabin Etxea, Ibáñez de Bilbao 16, 48001 Bilbao; tel. (94) 4039400; fax (94) 4039415; e-mail idazkaria.ebb@eaj-pnv.com; internet www.eaj-pnv.com; f. 1895; Basque nationalist; seeks to achieve autonomy through peaceful means; 32,000 mems; Pres. IÑIGO URKULLU RENTERIA; Sec. BELLEN GREAVES BADILLO.

Ezker Batua-Berdeak (EB-B): Fernández del Campo 24, 48010 Bilbao; tel. (94) 4702100; fax (94) 4701012; internet www.ezkerbatua-berdeak.org; f. 1986 as a coalition of left-wing, social democratic and environmentalist parties; Pres. JAVIER MADRAZO.

Partido Socialista de Euskadi-Euskadiko Ezkerra (PSE-EE) (Basque Socialist Party-Basque Left): Alameda de Recalde 27, 4°, 48009 Bilbao; tel. (94) 4242142; fax (94) 4238904; e-mail info@socialistasvascos.com; internet www.socialistasvascos.com; f. 1993 by merger of PSE-PSOE (Basque branch of PSOE) and Euskadiko Ezkerra; affiliated to PSOE; Pres. JESÚS EGUIGUREN; Sec.-Gen. PATXI LÓPEZ.

La Rioja

Partido Riojano (PR): Portales 17, 1°, 26001 Logroño; tel. (941) 238199; fax (941) 254396; e-mail partidoriojano@partidoriojano.es; internet www.partidoriojano.es; Pres. MIGUEL GÓMEZ IJALBA; Sec.-Gen. JAVIER SÁENZ TORRE MERINO.

ILLEGAL ORGANIZATIONS

Illegal terrorist organizations include the Basque separatist Euskadi ta Askatasuna (ETA, Basque Homeland and Liberty, f. 1959) and the extreme left-wing Grupos de Resistencia Antifascista Primero de Octubre (GRAPO, First of October Anti-Fascist Resistance Groups, f. 1975). It was reported in June 2007 that the latter had been put out of action following a successful police operation. After the Madrid train bombings in March 2004 it was revealed that fundamentalist Islamist groups, thought to be connected to the Moroccan Groupe islamique combattant Marocain (GICM), were operating in Spain. A 2002 law facilitated the banning of political parties deemed to support violence or terrorism. The legislation was employed against a number of parties in the Basque Country, most notably Batasuna (f. 1978 as Herri Batasuna), a separatist party led by Arnaldo Otegi Mondragón, which was banned by the Supreme Court in March 2003 due to its links to ETA. A number of parties and lists deemed to be alternatives to Batasuna have also been prevented from standing for election. In February 2009 Askatasuna (Freedom) and the newly-established Demokrazia Hiru Milioi were banned.

Election Commission

Junta Electoral Central: Congreso de los Diputados, Carretera de San Jerónimo 36, 28071 Madrid; tel. (91) 3906367; fax (91) 4297778; internet www.juntaelectoralcentral.es; independent; Pres. ANTONIO MARTÍN VALVERDE'.

Diplomatic Representation

EMBASSIES IN SPAIN

Afghanistan: Umbría 8, 28043 Madrid; tel. (91) 7218581; fax (91) 7216832; e-mail embajadadeafganistanenmadrid@gmail.com; Chargé d'affaires GUL AHMAD SHERZADA.

Albania: María de Molina 64, 5°B, 28006 Madrid; tel. (91) 5612118; fax (91) 5613775; e-mail embassy.madrid@mfa.gov.al; Ambassador ANILA BITRI LANI.

Algeria: General Oraá 12, 28006 Madrid; tel. (91) 5629705; fax (91) 5629877; e-mail embargel@tsai.es; Ambassador MOHAMMED HANECHE.

Andorra: Alcalá 73, 28009 Madrid; tel. (91) 4317453; fax (91) 5776341; e-mail embajada@embajadaandorra.es; Ambassador XAVIER ESPOT MIRÓ.

Angola: Serrano 64, 3°, 28001 Madrid; tel. (91) 4356430; fax (91) 5779010; e-mail gabinete@embajadadeangola.com; internet www.embajadadeangola.com; Ambassador ARMANDO DA CRUZ NETO.

Argentina: Pedro de Valdivia 21, 28006 Madrid; tel. (91) 7710519; fax (91) 7710526; e-mail embajada@portalargentino.net; internet www.portalargentino.net; Ambassador CARLOS ANTONIO BETTINI.

Australia: Plaza del Descubridor Diego de Ordás 3, 28003 Madrid; tel. (91) 3536600; fax (91) 3536692; e-mail pilar.sanchez@dfat.gov.au; internet www.spain.embassy.gov.au; Ambassador NOEL CAMPBELL.

Austria: Paseo de la Castellana 91, 9°, 28046 Madrid; tel. (91) 5565315; fax (91) 5973579; e-mail madrid-ob@bmeia.gv.at; internet www.bmeia.gv.at/madrid; Ambassador Dr ULRIKE TILLY.

Azerbaijan: Ronda de la Avutarda 38, 28043 Madrid; tel. (91) 7596010; fax (91) 7597056; Ambassador MAMMAD NOVRUZ OĞLU ALIYEV.

Bangladesh: Diego de León 69, 2°D, 28006 Madrid; tel. (91) 4019932; fax (91) 4029564; e-mail chancery@bdoot-mad.e.telefonica.net; Ambassador SAIFUL AMIN KHAN.

Belgium: Paseo de la Castellana 18, 6°, 28046 Madrid; tel. (91) 5776300; fax (91) 4318166; e-mail madrid@diplobel.org; internet www.diplobel.org/spain; Ambassador JOHAN SWINNEN.

Bolivia: Velázquez 26, 3°, 28001 Madrid; tel. (91) 5780835; fax (91) 5773946; e-mail embajada@embajadadebolivia.es; internet www.embajadadebolivia.es; Ambassador MARÍA DEL CARMEN ALMENDRAS CAMARGO.

Bosnia and Herzegovina: Lagasca 24, 2°, 28001 Madrid; tel. (91) 5750870; fax (91) 4355056; e-mail admin@embajadabih.es; Ambassador ZELJANA ZOVKO.

Brazil: Fernando el Santo 6, 28010 Madrid; tel. (91) 7004650; fax (91) 7004660; e-mail adm@embajadadebrasil.es; internet www.brasil.es; Ambassador PAULO CESAR DE OLIVEIRA CAMPOS.

Bulgaria: Santa María Magdalena 15, 28016 Madrid; tel. (91) 3455761; fax (91) 3591201; e-mail embulmad@tyahoo.es; Ambassador IVAN YANKOV HRISTOV.

Cameroon: Rosario Pino 3, 28020 Madrid; tel. (91) 5711160; fax (91) 5712504; e-mail ambcammadrid@telefonica.net; internet ambacam-madrid.com; Ambassador MARTIN MBARGA NGUELE.

Canada: Núñez de Balboa 35, 28001 Madrid; tel. (91) 4233250; fax (91) 4233251; e-mail madrid@international.gc.ca; internet www.canada-es.org; Ambassador MALCOLM MCKECHNIE.

SPAIN
Directory

Chile: Lagasca 88, 6°, 28001 Madrid; tel. (91) 4319160; fax (91) 5775560; e-mail echilees@tsai.es; Ambassador Osvaldo Puccio Huidobro.

China, People's Republic: Arturo Soria 113, 28043 Madrid; tel. (91) 5194242; fax (91) 5192035; e-mail embajadachina@embajadachina.es; internet www.embajadachina.es; Ambassador Zhu Bangzao.

Colombia: General Martínez Campos 48, 28010 Madrid; tel. (91) 7004770; fax (91) 3102869; e-mail emadrid@cancilleria.gov.co; internet www.embacol.com; Ambassador Carlos Rodado Noriega.

Congo, Democratic Republic: Paseo de la Castellana 255, 1°, 28046 Madrid; tel. (91) 7332647; fax (91) 3231575; e-mail ambardcmadrid@hotmail.com; Ambassador (vacant).

Costa Rica: Paseo de la Castellana 164, 17°, 28046 Madrid; tel. (91) 3459622; fax (91) 3533709; e-mail embajada@embcr.org; Ambassador Melvin Alfredo Sáenz Biolley.

Côte d'Ivoire: Serrano 154, 28006 Madrid; tel. (91) 5626916; fax (91) 5622193; e-mail costamarfil@ic1.inycom.es; Ambassador Jeanne Guehe Moulot.

Croatia: Claudio Coello 78, 2°, 28001 Madrid; tel. (91) 5776881; fax (91) 5776905; e-mail croemb.madrid@mvp.hr; internet es.mvp.hr; Ambassador Filip Vučak.

Cuba: Paseo de la Habana 194, 28036 Madrid; tel. (91) 3592500; fax (91) 3596145; e-mail secreembajada@ecubamad.com; internet emba.cubaminrex.cu/espana; Ambassador Alberto Velazco San José.

Cyprus: Paseo de la Castellana 45, 4–5°, 28046 Madrid; tel. (91) 5783114; fax (91) 5782189; e-mail embajadachipre@telefonica.net; internet www.mfa.gov.cy/embassymadrid; Ambassador Nearchos Palas.

Czech Republic: Avda Pío XII 22–24, 28016 Madrid; tel. (91) 3531880; fax (91) 3531885; e-mail madrid@embassy.mzv.cz; internet www.mfa.cz/madrid; Ambassador Martin Košatka.

Denmark: Serrano 26, 7°, 28001 Madrid; tel. (91) 4318445; fax (91) 4319168; e-mail madamb@um.dk; internet www.ambmadrid.um.dk; Ambassador Niels Pultz.

Dominican Republic: Paseo de la Castellana 30, 28046 Madrid; tel. (91) 4315395; fax (91) 4358139; e-mail embajada@embajadadominicana.es; internet www.embajadadominicana.es; Ambassador Alejandro González Pons.

Ecuador: Velázquez 114, 2°, 28006 Madrid; tel. (91) 5627215; fax (91) 7450244; e-mail embajada@mecuador.es; Ambassador Nicolás Issa Obando.

Egypt: Velázquez 69, 28006 Madrid; tel. (91) 5776308; fax (91) 5781732; Ambassador Yasser Morad Hossny.

El Salvador: General Oraá 9, 28006 Madrid; tel. (91) 5628002; fax (91) 5630584; e-mail madrid@embasalva.com; Ambassador Dr Enrique Borgo Bustamante.

Equatorial Guinea: Avda Pío XII 14, 28016 Madrid; tel. (91) 3532169; fax (91) 3532165; Ambassador Ignacio Milan Tang.

Estonia: Claudio Coello 91, 28006 Madrid; tel. (91) 4261671; fax (91) 4261672; e-mail embassy.madrid@mfa.ee; internet www.estemb.es; Ambassador Andres Rundu.

Finland: Paseo de la Castellana 15, 28046 Madrid; tel. (91) 3196172; fax (91) 3083901; e-mail sanomat.mad@formin.fi; internet www.finlandia.es; Ambassador Maija Lahteenmaki.

France: Salustiano Olózaga 9, 28001 Madrid; tel. (91) 4238900; fax (91) 4238908; e-mail chancellerie@ctv.es; internet www.ambafrance-es.org; Ambassador Bruno Delaye.

Gabon: Francisco Alcántara 3A, 28002 Madrid; tel. (91) 4138211; fax (91) 4131153; e-mail emb-gabon-es@nemo.es; Ambassador Carlos Victor Boungou.

Georgia: Felipe IV 10, 28014 Madrid; tel. (91) 4293329; fax (91) 4296883; e-mail embassymadrid@mfa.gov.ge; internet www.spain.mfa.gov.ge; Ambassador Zurab Pololikashvili.

Germany: Fortuny 8, 28010 Madrid; tel. (91) 5579000; fax (91) 3102104; e-mail zreg@madri.auswaertiges-amt.de; internet www.madrid.diplo.de; Ambassador Wolf-Ruthart Born.

Ghana: Capitán Haya 38, 10°A, 28020 Madrid; tel. (91) 5670390; fax (91) 5670393; e-mail mission@ghanaembassyspain.com; Ambassador Francis Tsegah.

Greece: Avda Dr Arce 24, 28002 Madrid; tel. (91) 5644653; fax (91) 5644668; e-mail embajadadegrecia@telefonica.net; internet www.embagrec.org; Ambassador Geórgios Gabrielides.

Guatemala: Rafael Salgado 3, 10° dcha, 28036 Madrid; tel. (91) 3441722; fax (91) 4587894; e-mail informacion@embajadaguatemala.es; internet www.embajadaguatemala.es; Ambassador Guísela Atalida Godínez Sazo.

Haiti: Marques del Duero 3, 1°, 28001 Madrid; tel. (91) 5752624; fax (91) 4314600; e-mail ambhaities@yahoo.es; Ambassador Yolette Azor Charles.

Holy See: Avda Pío XII 46, 28016 Madrid; tel. (91) 7668311; fax (91) 7667085; e-mail nunap@planalfa.es; Apostolic Nuncio Most Rev. Manuel Monteiro de Castro (Titular Archbishop of Benevento).

Honduras: Rafael Calvo 15, 6°D, 28010 Madrid; tel. (91) 7025157; fax (91) 7025158; e-mail info@embahonduras.es; internet www.embahonduras.es; Ambassador José Eduardo Martell Mejía.

Hungary: Fortuny 6, 4°, 28010 Madrid; tel. (91) 4137011; fax (91) 4134138; e-mail info@embajada-hungria.org; internet www.mfa.gov.hu/emb/madrid; Ambassador Edit Bucsi Szabó.

India: Avda Pío XII 30–32, 28016 Madrid; tel. (91) 1315114; fax (91) 3451112; internet www.embajadaindia.com; Ambassador Suryakanthi Tripatthi.

Indonesia: Agastia 65, 28043 Madrid; tel. (91) 4130294; fax (91) 4138994; e-mail kbri@embajadadeindonesia.es; internet www.embajadadeindonesia.es; Ambassador Slamet Santoso Mustafa.

Iran: Jerez 5, Villa El Altozano, Chamartín, 28016 Madrid; tel. (91) 3450112; fax (91) 3451190; e-mail embiran@hotmail.com; Ambassador Seyed Davoud Mohseni Salehi Monfared.

Iraq: Ronda de Sobradiel 67, 28043 Madrid; tel. (91) 7591282; fax (91) 7593180; e-mail mdremb@iraqmofamail.net; Ambassador Talal H. Al-Khudairi.

Ireland: Paseo de la Castellana 46, 4°, 28046 Madrid; tel. (91) 4364093; fax (91) 4351677; internet www.irlanda.es; Ambassador Peter Gunning.

Israel: Velázquez 150, 7°, 28002 Madrid; tel. (91) 7829500; fax (91) 7829555; e-mail embajada@embajada-israel.es; internet www.embajada-israel.es; Ambassador Raphael Schutz.

Italy: Lagasca 98, 28006 Madrid; tel. (91) 4233300; fax (91) 5757776; e-mail archivio.ambmadrid@esteri.it; internet www.ambmadrid.esteri.it; Ambassador Pasquale Terracciano.

Japan: Serrano 109, 28006 Madrid; tel. (91) 5907600; fax (91) 5901321; internet www.es.emb-japan.go.jp; Ambassador Motohide Yoshikawa.

Jordan: General Martínez Campos 41, 28010 Madrid; tel. (91) 3191100; fax (91) 3082536; e-mail jordania@telefonica.net; internet www.embjordaniaes.org; Ambassador Zaid M. Al-Lozi.

Kazakhstan: Cascanueces 25, 28043 Madrid; tel. (91) 7216290; fax (91) 7219374; e-mail embajada@kazesp.org; internet www.kazesp.org; Ambassador Yergali Bulegenov.

Korea, Republic: González Amigó 15, 28033 Madrid; tel. (91) 3532000; fax (91) 3532001; e-mail embspain.adm@mofa.go.kr; Ambassador Chun-seun Lee.

Kuwait: Paseo de la Castellana 141, 16°, 28046 Madrid; tel. (91) 5792467; fax (91) 5702109; Ambassador Adil Hamad M. al-Ayyar.

Latvia: Alfonso XII 52, 1°, 28014 Madrid; tel. (91) 3691362; fax (91) 3690020; e-mail lespan@telefonica.net; Ambassador Mārtiņš Perts.

Lebanon: Paseo de la Castellana 178, 3° izqda, 28046 Madrid; tel. (91) 3451368; fax (91) 3455631; e-mail leem-e@teleline.es; Chargé d'affaires a.i. Choucri Abboud.

Libya: Pisuerga 12, 28002 Madrid; tel. (91) 5635753; fax (91) 5643986; e-mail oficinapopularlibia-madrid@hotmail.com; Ambassador Abdulwahed R. Gammudi.

Lithuania: Pisuerga 5, 28002 Madrid; tel. (91) 7022116; fax (91) 3104018; e-mail amb.es@urm.lt; internet es.mfa.lt; Chargé d'affaires a.i. Lycra Puisyte-Bostroem.

Luxembourg: Claudio Coello 78, 1°, 28001 Madrid; tel. (91) 4359164; fax (91) 5774826; e-mail madrid.amb@mae.etat.lu; internet www.mae.lu/espagne; Ambassador Jean A. Welter.

Macedonia, former Yugoslav republic: Don Ramón de la Cruz 107, 2°B, 28006 Madrid; tel. (91) 5717298; fax (91) 5713481; e-mail emb.mkd.madrid@gmail.com; Ambassador Metodija Belevski.

Malaysia: Paseo de la Castellana 91, Edif. Centro 23, 10°, 28046 Madrid; tel. (91) 5550684; fax (91) 5555208; e-mail mwmadrid@adv.es; Ambassador Naimun Ashakli.

Malta: Paseo de la Castellana 45, 6° dcha, 28046 Madrid; tel. (91) 3913061; fax (91) 3913066; e-mail maltaembassy.madrid@gov.mt; Ambassador Tanya Vella.

Mauritania: Velázquez 90, 3°, 28006 Madrid; tel. (91) 5757006; fax (91) 4359531; Ambassador Salem Ould Memmou.

Mexico: Carrera de San Jerónimo 46, 28014 Madrid; tel. (91) 3692814; fax (91) 4202292; e-mail embamex@embamex.es; internet www.embamex.es; Ambassador Jorge Zermeño Infante.

Monaco: Villanueva 12, 28001 Madrid; tel. (91) 5782048; fax (91) 4357132; e-mail espagne@ambassade-monaco.org; Ambassador (vacant).

Morocco: Serrano 179, 28002 Madrid; tel. (91) 5631090; fax (91) 5617887; e-mail correo@embajada-marruecos.es; internet www.embajada-marruecos.es; Ambassador Omar Azziman.

SPAIN

Mozambique: Goya 67, 1° izqda, 28001 Madrid; tel. (91) 5776382; fax (91) 5776705; e-mail embamocmadrid@worldonline.es; Ambassador ALVARO MANUEL T. DA SILVA.

Netherlands: Avda del Comandante Franco 32, 28016 Madrid; tel. (91) 3537500; fax (91) 3537565; e-mail nlgovmad@telefonica.net; internet spanje.nlambassade.org; Ambassador COMO VAN HELLENBERG HUBAR.

New Zealand: Pinar 7, 3°, 28006 Madrid; tel. (91) 5230226; fax (91) 5230171; e-mail embnuevazelanda@telefonica.net; internet www.nzembassy.com/spain; Ambassador ROBERT MOORE-JONES.

Nicaragua: Paseo de la Castellana 127, 1° B, 28046 Madrid; tel. (91) 5555510; fax (91) 4555737; e-mail augusto.zamora@orange.es; Ambassador AUGUSTO C. ZAMORA RODRÍGUEZ.

Nigeria: Segre 28, 28002 Madrid; tel. (91) 5630911; fax (91) 5636320; e-mail nigerian-emb-sp@jet.es; internet www.nigeriainspain.org; Ambassador OBED WADZANI.

Norway: Serrano 26, 28001 Madrid; tel. (91) 4363840; fax (91) 3190969; e-mail emb.madrid@mfa.no; internet www.noruega.es; Ambassador PER LUDVIG MAGNUS.

Oman: Mirasierra Suite Hotel, hab. 416–17, Alfredo Marquerie 43, 28034 Madrid; tel. (91) 7277932; fax (91) 7277933; Ambassador HILAL B. MARHOON SALIM ALMAMARY.

Pakistan: Avda Pío XII 11, 28016 Madrid; tel. (91) 3458995; fax (91) 3458158; e-mail cancilleria@embajada-pakistan.org; internet www.embajada-pakistan.org; Ambassador HUMAIRA HASAN.

Panama: Claudio Coello 86, 1° dcha, 28006 Madrid; tel. (91) 5765001; fax (91) 5767161; Ambassador HUMBERTO LÓPEZ TIRONE.

Paraguay: Doctor Fleming 3, 1°, 28036 Madrid; tel. (91) 3082746; fax (91) 3085319; e-mail embapar@arrakis.es; Ambassador OSCAR J. CABELLO SARUBBI.

Peru: Príncipe de Vergara 36, 5° dcha, 28001 Madrid; tel. (91) 4314242; fax (91) 5776861; e-mail lepru@embajadaperu.es; Ambassador JOSÉ LUIS PÉREZ SÁNCHEZ-CERRO.

Philippines: Eresma 2, 28002 Madrid; tel. (91) 7823830; fax (91) 4116606; e-mail madridpe@terra.es; internet www.philmadrid.com; Ambassador JOSEPH DELANO BERNARDO Y MEDINA.

Poland: Guisando 23 bis, 28035 Madrid; tel. (91) 3736605; fax (91) 3736624; e-mail embajada@polonia.es; internet www.madrid.polemb.net; Chargé d'affaires a.i. BARBARA SOŚNICKA.

Portugal: Pinar 1, 28006 Madrid; tel. (91) 7824960; fax (91) 7824972; e-mail embmadrid@emb-portugal.es; internet www.embajadaportugal-madrid.org; Ambassador JOSÉ FILIPE MORAES CABRAL.

Qatar: Paseo de la Castellana 92, Hotel Villamagna, 28046 Madrid; tel. (91) 3106926; fax (91) 3104851; Ambassador Sheikh FAHAD BIN AWIDA ATH-THANI.

Romania: Avda Alfonso XIII 157, 28016 Madrid; tel. (91) 3501881; fax (91) 3452917; e-mail secretariat@embajadaderumania.es; internet madrid.mae.ro; Ambassador MARIA LIGOR.

Russia: Velázquez 155, 28002 Madrid; tel. (91) 4110807; fax (91) 5629712; e-mail embrues@infonegocio.com; internet www.spain.mid.ru; Ambassador ALEKSANDR I. KUZNETSOV.

San Marino: Padre de Jesús Ordóñez 18, 3°, 28002 Madrid; tel. (91) 5639000; fax (91) 5631931; e-mail sm_madrid@accessnet.es; Ambassador ENRICO MARIA PASQUINI.

Saudi Arabia: Dr Alvarez Sierra 3, 28033 Madrid; tel. (91) 3834300; fax (91) 3021145; e-mail info@arabiasaudi.org; internet www.arabiasaudi.org; Ambassador Prince SA'UD BIN NAIF BIN ABD AL-AZIZ AS-SA'UD.

Serbia: Velázquez 162, 28002 Madrid; tel. (91) 5635045; fax (91) 5630440; e-mail office@embajada-serbia.es; internet www.embajada-serbia.es; Ambassador JELA BAĆOVIĆ.

Slovakia: Pinar 20, 28006 Madrid; tel. (91) 5903861; fax (91) 5903868; e-mail mail@embajadaeslovaquia.es; Ambassador JÁN VALKO.

Slovenia: Hermanos Bécquer 7, 2°, 28006 Madrid; tel. (91) 4116893; fax (91) 5646057; e-mail vma@gov.si; Ambassador PETER REBERC.

South Africa: Claudio Coello 91, 28006 Madrid; tel. (91) 4363780; fax (91) 5777414; e-mail embassy@sudafrica.es; internet www.sudafrica.com; Ambassador VUSI BRUCE KOLOANE.

Sudan: Paseo de la Castellana 115, 11° izqda, 28046 Madrid; tel. (91) 4174903; fax (91) 5972516; e-mail sudani49@hotmail.com; Ambassador ELUZAI MOGA YOKWE.

Sweden: Caracas 25, 28010 Madrid; tel. (91) 7022000; fax (91) 7022040; e-mail ambassaden.madrid@foreign.ministry.se; internet www.swedenabroad.com/madrid; Ambassador ANDERS RÖNQUIST.

Switzerland: Núñez de Balboa 35A, 7°, 28001 Madrid; tel. (91) 4363960; fax (91) 4363980; e-mail vertretung@mad.rep.admin.ch; internet www.eda.admin.ch/madrid; Ambassador JÜRG BONO.

Syria: Plaza de Platerías Martínez 1, 1°, 28014 Madrid; tel. (91) 4203946; fax (91) 4202681; Ambassador MAKRAM OBEID.

Thailand: Joaquín Costa 29, 28002 Madrid; tel. (91) 5632903; fax (91) 5640033; e-mail madthai@temb.e.telefonica.net; Ambassador BUSBA BUNNAG.

Tunisia: Avda Alfonso XIII 64–68, 28016 Madrid; tel. (91) 4473508; fax (91) 5938416; Ambassador MUHAMMAD RIDHA KECHRID.

Turkey: Rafael Calvo 18, 2°, 28010 Madrid; tel. (91) 3198111; fax (91) 3086602; e-mail info@tcmadridbe.org; internet www.tcmadridbe.org; Ambassador ENDER ARAT.

Ukraine: Ronda de la Abubilla 52, 28043 Madrid; tel. (91) 7489360; fax (91) 3887178; e-mail emb_es@mfa.gov.ua; Ambassador ANATOLIY A. SHCHERBA.

United Arab Emirates: Capitán Haya 40, 28020 Madrid; tel. (91) 5701003; fax (91) 5715176; e-mail ambassadormadrid@uae.e.telefonica.net; Ambassador Dr HASSA ABDULLAH AL-OTAIBAH.

United Kingdom: Fernando el Santo 16, 28010 Madrid; tel. (91) 7008200; fax (91) 7008210; e-mail enquiries.madrid@fco.gov.uk; internet ukinspain.fco.gov.uk; Ambassador DENISE MARY HOLT.

USA: Serrano 75, 28006 Madrid; tel. (91) 5872200; fax (91) 5872303; internet www.embusa.es; Ambassador ARNOLD A. CHACÓN, Jr.

Uruguay: Paseo del Pintor Rosales 32, 1°, 28008 Madrid; tel. (91) 7580475; fax (91) 5428177; e-mail urumatri@urumatri.com; Ambassador RICARDO GONZÁLEZ ARENAS.

Uzbekistan: Madrid.

Venezuela: Avda Capitán Haya 1, 13°, Edif. Eurocentro, 28020 Madrid; tel. (91) 5981200; fax (91) 5971583; e-mail embajada@espana.gob.ve; internet espana.gob.ve; Ambassador ALFREDO TORO HARDY.

Viet Nam: Arturo Soria 201, 1°A, 28043 Madrid; tel. (91) 5102867; fax (91) 4157067; e-mail claudiomes@yahoo.com; internet www.embavietnam-madrid.org; Ambassador NGUYEN XUAN PHONG.

Yemen: Paseo de la Castellana 117, 8°, 28046 Madrid; tel. (91) 4119950; fax (91) 5623865; e-mail secretaria@embajadayemen.es; internet www.embajadayemen.es; Chargé d'affaires a.i. ABDULRAHMAN KAMARAMI.

Judicial System

Consejo General del Poder Judicial (CGPJ) (General Council of Judicial Power)
Marqués de la Ensenada 8, 28071 Madrid; tel. (91) 7006100; fax (91) 7006358; e-mail webmaster@cgpj.es; internet www.poderjudicial.es. The highest governing body of the judiciary; comprises a President, 20 members elected by the Cortes and appointed by the King for a five-year term (10 by the Congress of Deputies and 10 by the Senate); supervises the judicial system; independent of the Ministry of Justice; Pres. FRANCISCO JOSÉ HERNANDO SANTIAGO

General Prosecutor: CÁNDIDO CONDE-PUMPIDO.

CONSTITUTIONAL COURT

Tribunal Constitucional: Domenico Scarlatti 6, 28003 Madrid; tel. (91) 5508000; fax (91) 5449268; e-mail buzon@tribunalconstitucional.es; internet www.tribunalconstitucional.es; Pres. MARÍA EMILIA CASAS BAAMONDE.

SUPREME COURT

Tribunal Supremo: Palacio de Justicia, Plaza de la Villa de París s/n, 28071 Madrid; tel. (91) 3971200; e-mail webmaster@cgpj.es; internet www.poderjudicial.es; Composed of five courts: civil; criminal; litigation; company; and military, each with its president and its respective judges; Pres. FRANCISCO JOSÉ HERNANDO SANTIAGO.

HIGH COURTS

Audiencia Nacional (National Court): García Gutiérrez 1, 28004 Madrid; tel. (91) 3973339; fax (91) 3973306; established in 1977; consists of three divisions: Penal; Social; and Contencioso-Administrativo, each with its president and respective judges; attached to Second Court of Supreme Court; deals primarily with crimes associated with a modern industrial society, such as corruption, forgery, drugs-trafficking and also terrorism; Pres. ANGEL JUANES.

OTHER COURTS

The Higher Courts of Justice in the Autonomous Communities comprise civil, criminal, administrative and labour divisions, while Provincial Courts hear proceedings for prosecutions of offences by lengthy prison terms, and appeals against the rulings of lower courts. The lower courts are the Criminal, Administrative, Labour, Juvenile and Prison Supervisory Courts of First Instance and Trial Courts. In municipalities where there are no Courts of First Instance and Trial, there is a Magistrates' Court.

Religion

CHRISTIANITY

About 90% of Spain's inhabitants profess adherence to Roman Catholicism, and the country contains some 61,000 churches, with about 500 persons in each parish. Opus Dei, which seeks to integrate religious faith and professional work, plays an important role in Spanish society. There are some 30,000 Protestants in Spain.

The Roman Catholic Church

For ecclesiastical purposes, Spain (including Spanish North Africa) comprises 14 metropolitan archdioceses and 55 dioceses. At 31 December 2006 there were an estimated 40.8m. adherents, equivalent to 92.0% of the population.

Bishops' Conference

Conferencia Episcopal Española, Añastro 1, 28033 Madrid; tel. (91) 3439600; fax (91) 3439602; e-mail conferenciaepiscopal@planalfa.es; internet www.conferenciaepiscopal.es.
f. 1977; Pres. Cardinal ANTONIO MARÍA ROUCO VARELA (Archbishop of Madrid); Sec.-Gen. JUAN ANTONIO MARTÍNEZ CAMINO.

Archbishop of Barcelona: Cardinal LLUÍS MARTÍNEZ SISTACH.
Archbishop of Burgos: Most Rev. FRANCISCO GIL HELLÍN.
Archbishop of Granada: Most Rev. FRANCISCO JAVIER MARTÍNEZ FERNÁNDEZ.
Archbishop of Madrid: Cardinal ANTONIO MARÍA ROUCO VARELA.
Archbishop of Mérida-Badajoz: Most Rev. SANTIAGO GARCÍA ARACIL.
Archbishop of Oviedo: (vacant).
Archbishop of Pamplona and Tudela: Most Rev. FRANCISCO PÉREZ GONZÁLEZ.
Archbishop of Santiago de Compostela: Most Rev. JULIÁN BARRIO BARRIO.
Archbishop of Sevilla: Cardinal CARLOS AMIGO VALLEJO.
Archbishop of Tarragona: Most Rev. JAUME PUJOL BALCELLS.
Archbishop of Toledo: Most Rev. BRAULIO RODRÍGUEZ PLAZA.
Archbishop of Valencia: Most Rev. CARLOS OSORO SIERRA.
Archbishop of Valladolid: (vacant).
Archbishop of Zaragoza: Most Rev. MANUEL UREÑA PASTOR.

Other Christian Churches

Iglesia Española Reformada Episcopal (IERE) (Spanish Reformed Episcopal Church): Beneficencia 18, 28004 Madrid; tel. (91) 4452560; fax (91) 5944572; e-mail eclesiae@arrakis.es; internet www.anglicanos.org; f. 1860; mem. of the Anglican Communion; 17 congregations (2004); Bishop Rt Rev. CARLOS LÓPEZ LOZANO.

Unión Evangélica Bautista Española (UEBE) (Baptist Evangelical Union of Spain): San Jacinto 26, 3°, 46008 Valencia; tel. (963) 591633; fax (963) 134581; e-mail secretaria@uebe.org; internet www.uebe.org; f. 1922; Pres. Rev. ROBERTO VELERT; Gen. Sec. Rev. MANUEL SARRIAS.

ISLAM

It is estimated that there are some 1m. Muslims in Spain, many of whom are Moroccan migrant workers.

Comisión Islámica de España: Anastasio Herrero 5, 28020 Madrid; tel. (91) 5714040; fax (91) 5708889; e-mail cie@teleline.es; umbrella org.; negotiates with Govt on Islamic affairs; Sec.-Gen. RIAY TATARY BAKRY.

  Federación Española de Entidades Religiosas Islámicas (FEERI): Madrid; f. 1989; 57 mem. groups; Pres. FÉLIX ANGEL HERRERO.

  Unión de Comunidades Islámicas de España (UCIDE): Anastasio Herrero 5, Madrid 28020; tel. (91) 5714040; e-mail webmaster@islamhispania.org; internet www.islamhispania.org; Pres. RIAY TATARY BAKRY.

Comunidad Ahmadía del Islam en España: La Mezquita Basharat, 14630 Pedro Abad (Córdoba); tel. (957) 186203; fax (957) 186300; e-mail info@alislam.org; internet www.alislam.org; Pres. MUBARIK AHMAD KHAN.

JUDAISM

There are an estimated 48,000 Jews in Spain.

Federación de Comunidades Judías de España (Federation of Jewish Communities of Spain): Miguel Angel 7, 1° C, 28010 Madrid; tel. (91) 7001208; fax (91) 3915717; e-mail fcje@fcje.org; internet www.fcje.org; 30 communities; Pres. JACOBO ISRAEL GARZÓN.

The Press

The most widely read newspapers are *ABC*, *El Mundo*, *El País* and *La Razón*, published in Madrid, and *La Vanguardia*, published in Barcelona. Important regional newspapers include *El Periódico de Catalunya* (Barcelona), *El Correo* (Bilbao) and *La Voz de Galicia* (A Coruña). Sporting dailies, notably *Marca* and *As*, enjoy very high circulation figures. Much of the Spanish media is owned by large corporations, of which the most prominent are Grupo PRISA (*El País*) and Vocento (*ABC* and various regional titles).

PRINCIPAL DAILIES
(arranged by province)

Albacete

La Tribuna de Albacete: Paseo de la Cuba 14, 02005 Albacete; tel. (967) 191000; fax (967) 240386; e-mail redaccion@latribunadealbacete.es; internet www.latribunadealbacete.es; Propr Promecal; Dir FRANCISCO JAVIER MARTÍNEZ GARCÍA.

Alicante

Información: Avda Dr Rico 17, Apdo 214, 03005 Alicante; tel. (96) 5989100; fax (96) 5989165; e-mail redaccion@epi.es; internet www.diarioinformacion.com; f. 1940; Propr Editorial Prensa Ibérica; Dir JUAN R. GIL; circ. 32,303.

Almería

La Voz de Almería: Avda Mediterráneo 159, 1°, Edif. Cadena Ser, 04007 Almería; tel. (950) 280036; fax (950) 256458; e-mail lavoz@lavozdealmeria.com; internet www.lavozdealmeria.com; morning; Dir PEDRO MANUEL DE LA CRUZ ALONSO; circ. 10,575.

Asturias

El Comercio: Diario El Comercio 1, 33207 Gijón; tel. (98) 5179800; fax (98) 5340955; e-mail elcomercio@elcomerciodigital.es; internet www.elcomerciodigital.com; f. 1878; Propr Vocento; Dir ÍÑIGO NORIEGA GÓMEZ; circ. 26,102.

La Nueva España: Calvo Sotelo 7, Edif. Sedes, 33007 Oviedo; tel. (98) 5279700; fax (98) 5279711; e-mail pam@lne.es; internet www.lne.es; f. 1937; Propr Editorial Prensa Ibérica; Dir ISIDORO NICIEZA; circ. 60,469.

El Periódico—La Voz de Asturias: La Lila 6, bajo, 33002 Oviedo; tel. (98) 5101500; fax (98) 5101505; e-mail vozredaccion@elperiodico.com; internet www.lavozdeasturias.es; f. 1923; Propr Grupo Zeta; Dir LUIS MUGUETA SAN MARTÍN; circ. 10,077.

Badajoz

Hoy—Diario de Extremadura: Carretera Madrid–Lisboa 22, 06008 Badajoz; tel. (924) 252511; fax (924) 205297; e-mail hoyredaccion@hoy.es; internet www.hoy.es; f. 1933; Catholic; Badajoz and Cáceres editions; Propr Vocento; Dir JULIÁN QUIRÓS; circ. 23,365.

Barcelona

Avui: Enric Granados 84, entresòl, 08008 Barcelona; tel. (93) 3163900; fax (93) 3163936; e-mail info@avui.cat; internet www.avui.cat; f. 1976; Catalan; Exec. Pres. ANTONI CAMBREDÓ; Dir XAVIER BOSCH; circ. 28,591.

Mundo Deportivo: Avda Diagonal 577, 5°, 08036 Barcelona; tel. (93) 3444100; fax (93) 3444250; e-mail contacto@elmundodeportivo.es; internet www.elmundodeportivo.es; f. 1906; sport; Propr Grupo Godó; Dir SANTI NOLLA ZAYAS; circ. 96,561.

El Periódico de Catalunya: Consell de Cent 425–427, 08009 Barcelona; tel. (93) 2655353; fax (93) 4846512; e-mail atencion.lector@elperiodico.com; internet www.elperiodico.com; daily; f. 1978; parallel edns in Spanish and Catalan; Propr Grupo Zeta; Dir RAFAEL NADAL; circ. 177,830.

Sport: Consell de Cent 425–427, 6°, 08009 Barcelona; tel. (93) 2279400; fax (93) 2279410; e-mail redaccion@diariosport.com; internet www.sport.es; Propr Grupo Zeta; Dir JOAN VEHILS; circ. 104,987.

La Vanguardia: Avda Diagonal 477, 08036 Barcelona; tel. (93) 4812200; fax (93) 3185587; e-mail lavanguardia@lavanguardia.es; internet www.lavanguardia.es; f. 1881; Propr Grupo Godó; Dir JOSÉ ANTICH; circ. 209,735.

SPAIN

Burgos

Diario de Burgos: Avda Castilla y León 62–64, 09006 Burgos; tel. (947) 268375; fax (947) 268003; e-mail redaccion@diariodeburgos.es; internet www.diariodeburgos.es; f. 1891; Catholic; Propr Promecal; Dir Antonio José Mencía Gullón; circ. 14,266.

Cádiz

Diario de Cádiz: Edif. Fénix, Avda de El Puerto 2, 11007 Cádiz; tel. (956) 297900; fax (956) 261460; e-mail redaccion@diariodecadiz.es; internet www.diariodecadiz.es; f. 1867; Propr Grupo Joly; Dir José Joaquín León; circ. 26,073.

Diario de Jerez: Patricio Garvey s/n, Apdo 316, 11402 Jerez de la Frontera; tel. (956) 321411; fax (956) 349904; e-mail redaccion@diariojerez.es; internet www.diariodejerez.com; f. 1984; Propr Grupo Joly; Dir Rafael Navas Renedo; circ. 8,695.

Cantabria

Alerta—el Diario de Cantabria: 1 de Mayo s/n, Barrio San Martín, 39011 Peñacastillo; tel. (942) 320033; fax (942) 322046; e-mail administracion@eldiarioalerta.com; internet www.eldiarioalerta.com; f. 1937; independent; Dir Ciriaco Díaz Porras; circ. 30,619.

El Diario Montañés: La Prensa s/n, La Albericia, 39012 Santander; tel. (942) 354000; fax (942) 341806; e-mail redaccion.dm@eldiariomontanes.es; internet www.eldiariomontanes.es; f. 1902; Propr Vocento; Dir Manuel Angel Castañeda Pérez; circ. 39,901.

Castellón

El Periódico Mediterráneo: Carretera de Almassora s/n, 12005 Castellón de la Plana; tel. (964) 349500; fax (964) 349505; e-mail mediterraneo@elperiodico.com; internet www.elperiodicomediterraneo.com; f. 1938; Propr Grupo Zeta; Dir José Luis Valencia; circ. 10,810.

Ciudad Real

El Día de Ciudad Real: Plaza Cervantes 6, 13001 Ciudad Real; tel. (926) 223033; fax (926) 227185; e-mail redaccion@eldiadeciudadreal.com; internet www.eldiadeciudadreal.com; f. 2002; independent; Dir Santiago Mateo Sahuquillo; circ. 4,500.

La Tribuna de Ciudad Real: Pedro Muñoz 3, 13005 Ciudad Real; tel. (926) 215301; fax (926) 215306; e-mail ciudadreal@diariolatribuna.com; internet www.diariolatribuna.com; Propr Promecal; Dir Oscar Gálvez Maté; circ. 3,976.

Córdoba

Córdoba: Ing. Juan de la Cierva 18 (Polígono Torrecilla), Apdo 2, 14013 Córdoba; tel. (957) 420302; fax (957) 204648; e-mail cordoba2@elperiodico.com; internet www.diariocordoba.com; f. 1941; Propr Grupo Zeta; Dir Francisco Luis Córdoba Berjillos; circ. 15,503.

A Coruña

El Correo Gallego: Preguntoiro 29, 15704 Santiago de Compostela; tel. (981) 543700; fax (981) 543701; e-mail grupocorreogallego@elcorreogallego.es; internet www.elcorreogallego.es; f. 1878; Propr Grupo Correo Gallego; Dir José Manuel Rey Nóvoa; circ. 18,238.

Galicia Hoxe: Preguntoiro 29, 15704 Santiago de Compostela; tel. (981) 543700; fax (981) 543701; e-mail info@galicia-hoxe.com; internet www.galicia-hoxe.com; f. 1994 as *O Correo Galego*; refounded under current name 2003; Galician; Propr Grupo Correo Gallego; Dir José Manuel Rey Nóvoa.

El Ideal Gallego: Polígono de Pocomaco, C12, 15190 Mesoiro; tel. (981) 173040; fax (981) 299327; e-mail elidealgallego@elidealgallego.com; internet www.elidealgallego.com; f. 1917; independent; Dir Juan Ramón Díaz García; circ. 15,500 (Sun. 20,000).

La Voz de Galicia: Avda de la Prensa 84–85, Polígono de Sabón, 15142 Arteixo; tel. (981) 180180; fax (981) 180410; e-mail redac@lavoz.com; internet www.lavozdegalicia.es; f. 1882; Propr Grupo Voz; Dir Xosé Luis Vilela Conde; circ. 103,702.

Girona

El Punt: Santa Eugènia 42, 17005 Girona; tel. (972) 186400; fax (972) 186420; e-mail elpunt@elpunt.com; internet www.vilaweb.cat/www/elpunt; f. 1979; Catalan; various regional edns; also publishes weekly edns covering Valencia and Perpignan (France); Dir Emili Gispert; circ. 25,531.

Granada

Ideal: Huelva 2, Polígono de Asegra, 18210 Peligros; tel. (958) 809809; fax (958) 402480; e-mail cartasdirector@ideal.es; internet www.ideal.es; f. 1932; Propr Vocento; Dir Eduardo Peralta de Ana; circ. 32,887; edns in Granada, Jaén and Almería.

Guipúzcoa

El Diario Vasco: Camino de Portuetxe 2, Barrio de Ibaeta, Apdo 201, 20018 San Sebastián; tel. (943) 410700; fax (943) 410814; e-mail redacción@diariovasco.com; internet www.diariovasco.com; f. 1934; Propr Vocento; Dir José Gabriel Mujika; circ. 98,700 (Sat./Sun. 121,000).

Gara: Camino Portuetxe 23, 2°, 20018 San Sebastián; tel. (943) 316999; fax (943) 316998; internet www.gara.net; f. 1999; Basque and Spanish; left-wing Basque nationalist; independent; Dir Josu Juaristi.

Illes Balears

Diari de Balears: Paseo Mallorca, 9°A, 07011 Palma de Mallorca; tel. (971) 788300; fax (971) 455740; e-mail redaccio@ddbalears.cat; internet dbalears.cat; f. 1939 as *Baleares*; refounded as Catalan daily in 1996; Propr Grupo Serra; Dir Miquel Serra Magraner.

Diario de Ibiza: Avda de la Paz, 07800 Ibiza; tel. (971) 190000; fax (971) 190322; e-mail diariodeibiza@epi.es; internet www.diariodeibiza.es; Propr Editorial Prensa Ibérica; Dir Joan Serra Tur; circ. 7,615.

Diario de Mallorca: Puerto Rico 15, Polígono de Levante, 07006 Palma de Mallorca; tel. (971) 170300; fax (971) 170301; e-mail secretaria.diariodemallorca@epi.es; internet www.diariodemallorca.es; f. 1953; Propr Editorial Prensa Ibérica; Dir José Eduardo Iglesias Barca; circ. 22,350.

Menorca, Diario Insular: Cap de Cavalleria 5, 07714 Mahón, Menorca; tel. (971) 351600; fax (971) 351983; e-mail redaccion@menorca.info; internet www.menorca.info; f. 1941; Dir Joan Bosco Marquès Bosch; circ. 6,609.

Última Hora: Paseo Mallorca 9A, 07011 Palma de Mallorca; tel. (971) 788333; fax (971) 454190; e-mail master@ultimahora.es; internet www.ultimahora.es; f. 1893; Propr Grupo Serra; Dir Pedro Comas Barceló; circ. 36,487.

León

Diario de León: Carretera León–Astorga, Km 4,5, 24010 León; tel. (987) 840300; fax (987) 840340; e-mail web@diariodeleon.com; internet www.diariodeleon.es; Dir Fernando Aller González; circ. 16,100.

Lleida (Lérida)

Segre: Riu 6, Apdo 543, 25007 Lérida; tel. (973) 248000; fax (973) 246031; e-mail redaccio@diarisegre.com; internet www.diarisegre.com; f. 1982; Catalan and Spanish edns; independent; Dir Juan Cal Sánchez; circ. 13,184.

Lugo

El Progreso: Ribadeo s/n, 27002 Lugo; tel. (982) 298100; fax (982) 298102; e-mail correo@elprogreso.es; internet www.elprogreso.es; f. 1908; Dir Luis Rodríguez García; Editor-in-Chief Blanca García Montenegro; circ. 15,509.

Madrid

ABC: Juan Ignacio Luca de Tena 7, 28027 Madrid; tel. (91) 3399000; fax (91) 3203680; e-mail cartas@abc.es; internet www.abc.es; f. 1905; conservative, monarchist; various regional edns; Propr Vocento; Dir José Antonio Zarzalejos; circ. 230,422.

As: Albasanz 14, 4°, 28037 Madrid; tel. (91) 3752500; fax (91) 3752558; e-mail diarioas@diarioas.es; internet www.as.com; f. 1967; sport; Propr Grupo PRISA; Dir Alfredo Relaño Estapé; circ. 225,670.

Cinco Días: Gran Vía 32, 2°, 28013 Madrid; tel. (91) 3537900; fax (91) 3537991; e-mail redaccion@cinodias.com; internet www.cincodias.com; f. 1978; economic; Propr Grupo PRISA; Dir Jorge Rivera; circ. 37,945.

El Economista: Condesa de Venadito 1, 3°, 28027 Madrid; tel. (91) 3246700; fax (91) 3246727; e-mail comunicacion@eleconomista.es; internet www.eleconomista.es; f. 2006; originally f. 1886 as weekly; daily; Pres. Alfonso de Salas; Dir Amador G. Ayora; circ. 22,516.

Expansión: Paseo de la Castellana 66, 28046 Madrid; tel. (91) 3373220; fax (91) 3373266; e-mail expansion@recoletos.es; internet www.expansion.es; economic; Propr Unidad Editorial, SA; Dir Jesús Martínez de Rioja Vázquez; circ. 50,394.

La Gaceta de los Negocios: Pantoja 14, 28002 Madrid; tel. (91) 4327600; fax (91) 4327733; e-mail jpv@negocios.com; internet www.negocios.com; f. 1989; daily; business and finance; Dir José María García Hoz; circ. 37,902.

Marca: Paseo de la Castellana 66, 2°, 28046 Madrid; tel. (91) 3373220; fax (91) 3373276; e-mail marca.com@unidadeditorial.es; internet www.marca.com; f. 1938 as weekly in San Sebastián, 1942

SPAIN

as daily in Madrid; sport; Propr Unidad Editorial, SA; Dir RAFAEL ALIQUE; circ. 310,793.

El Mundo (del Siglo Veintiuno): Pradillo 42, 28002 Madrid; tel. (91) 5864800; fax (91) 5864848; internet www.elmundo.es; f. 1989; centre-right; various regional edns; Propr Unidad Editorial, SA; Pres. CARMEN IGLESIAS; Dir PEDRO J. RAMÍREZ CODINA; circ. 337,172.

El País: Miguel Yuste 40, 28037 Madrid; tel. (91) 3378200; fax (91) 3377758; e-mail redaccion@elpais.com; internet www.elpais.com; f. 1976; centre-left; regional edns in Andalusia, Basque Country, Catalonia, Galicia and Valencia; Propr Grupo PRISA; Pres. IGNACIO POLANCO MORENO; Dir JAVIER MORENO BARBER; circ. 425,927.

Qué!: Orense 81, 3°, 28020 Madrid; tel. (91) 5726200; fax (91) 5710085; e-mail redaccion@quediario.com; internet www.quediario.com; f. 2005; free; 15 local edns; Propr Vocento; Dir ANA I. PEREDA; circ. 959,283.

La Razón: Josefa Valcárcel 42, 28027 Madrid; tel. (91) 3247000; fax (91) 7423604; e-mail sugerencias@larazon.es; internet www.larazon.es; f. 1998; conservative; Pres. MAURICIO CASALS; Dir JOSÉ ALEJANDRO VARA; circ. 149,559.

20 Minutos: Condesa de Venadito 1, 1°, 28027 Madrid; tel. (91) 7015600; fax (91) 7015660; e-mail nosevende@20minutos; internet www.20minutos.es; f. 2000; free; 15 regional edns; Dir ARSENIO ESCOLAR; circ. 850,000.

Málaga

La Opinión de Málaga: Granada 42, 29015 Málaga; tel. (95) 2126200; fax (95) 2126255; e-mail secretaria@epi.es; internet www.laopiniondemalaga.es; f. 1999; Propr Editorial Prensa Ibérica; Dir JOAQUÍN MARÍN ALARCÓN; circ. 7,589.

Sur: Avda Dr Marañón 48, 29009 Málaga; tel. (95) 2649600; fax (95) 2279508; e-mail redaccion.su@diariosur.es; internet www.diariosur.es; f. 1937; Propr Vocento; Dir JOSÉ ANTONIO FRÍAS RUIZ; circ. 60,000 (also publishes free English weekly, circ. 32,293).

Murcia

La Verdad: Camino Viejo de Monteagudo s/n, 30160 Murcia; tel. (968) 369100; fax (968) 369147; e-mail lectores@laverdad.es; internet www.laverdad.es; f. 1903; local edns published in Albacete and Alicante; propr Vocento; Dir JOSÉ MARÍA ESTEBAN IBÁÑEZ; circ. 29,794.

Navarra

Diario de Navarra: Carretera Zaragoza s/n, 31191 Cordovilla (Navarra); tel. (948) 236050; fax (948) 150320; e-mail cartas@diariodenavarra.es; internet www.diariodenavarra.es; f. 1903; conservative; independent; Dir INÉS ARTAJO AYESA; circ. 57,893.

Diario de Noticias: Altzutzate 8, Polígono Areta, 31620 Huarte; tel. (948) 332533; fax (948) 332518; e-mail cad@noticiasdenavarra.com; internet www.noticiasdenavarra.com; f. 1994; independent; Dir JOSEBA SANTAMARÍA; circ. 18,135.

Ourense

La Región: Polígono Industrial de San Cibrao das Viñas C4, 32091 Ourense; tel. (988) 600102; e-mail info@laregion.es; internet www.laregion.es; f. 1910; independent; Pres. JOSÉ LUIS OUTEIRIÑO RODRÍGUEZ; Dir ALFONSO SÁNCHEZ IZQUIERDO; circ. 11,405.

Las Palmas de Gran Canaria

Canarias 7: Profesor Lozano 7, Urbanización El Sebadal, 35008 Las Palmas; tel. (928) 301300; fax (928) 301434; e-mail infocan@canarias7.es; internet www.canarias7.es; f. 1982; Dir FRANCISCO SUÁREZ ALAMO; circ. 30,544.

La Provincia—Diario de las Palmas: Alcalde Ramírez Bethencourt 8, 35003 Las Palmas; tel. (928) 479410; fax (928) 479401; e-mail laprovincia@epi.es; internet www.laprovincia.es; *La Provincia* f. 1911, *Diario de las Palmas* f. 1895; Propr Editorial Prensa Ibérica; Dir ANGEL TRISTÁN PIMIENTA; circ. 30,990.

Pontevedra

Faro de Vigo: Factoría de Chapela, 36320 Redondela; tel. (986) 814600; fax (986) 814615; e-mail redaccion@farodevigo.es; internet www.farodevigo.es; f. 1853; Propr Editorial Prensa Ibérica; Dir JUAN CARLOS DA SILVA; circ. 40,263.

La Rioja

La Rioja: Vara del Rey 74, Apdo 28, 26002 Logroño; tel. (941) 279107; fax (941) 279106; e-mail redaccion@larioja.com; internet www.diariolarioja.com; f. 1889; Propr Vocento; Dir RAMÓN ALONSO; circ. 16,780.

Salamanca

La Gaceta Regional de Salamanca: Avda de los Cipreses 81, 37004 Salamanca; tel. (923) 252020; fax (923) 256155; e-mail admon@lagacetadesalamanca.com; internet www.lagacetadesalamanca.es; f. 1920; independent; Dir IÑIGO DOMÍNGUEZ DE CALATAYUD; circ. 14,985.

Santa Cruz de Tenerife

El Día: Avda de Buenos Aires 71, Apdo 97, 38005 Santa Cruz; tel. (922) 238300; fax (922) 214247; e-mail redaccioneldia@eldia.es; internet www.eldia.es; f. 1910; Dir JOSÉ E. RODRÍGUEZ RAMÍREZ; circ. 24,352.

Diario de Avisos: Salamanca 5, 38006 Santa Cruz; tel. (922) 272350; fax (922) 241039; e-mail redaccion@diariodeavisos.com; internet www.diariodeavisos.com; f. 1890; refounded 1976; Dir LEOPOLDO FERNÁNDEZ CABEZA DE VACA; circ. 12,293.

La Opinión de Tenerife: Plaza Santa Cruz de la Sierra 2, 38003 Santa Cruz; tel. (922) 471800; fax (922) 471801; e-mail tenerife@laopinion.es; internet www.laopinion.es; Propr Editorial Prensa Ibérica; Dir CARMEN RUANO; circ. 6,317.

Sevilla
(Seville)

El Correo de Andalucía: Américo Vespucio 39, Isla de la Cartuja. 41092 Sevilla; tel. (95) 4999251; fax (95) 4517635; e-mail redaccion@correoandalucia.es; internet www.correoandalucia.es; f. 1899; independent; Pres. JOSÉ RODRÍGUEZ DE LA BORBOLLA CAMOYÁN; Dir ANTONIO HERNÁNDEZ-RODICIO; circ. 15,470.

Diario de Sevilla: Rioja 14, 41001 Sevilla; tel. (95) 4506200; fax (95) 4506222; e-mail secretaria@diariodesevilla.es; internet www.diariodesevilla.es; f. 1999; Propr Grupo Joly; Dir MANUEL JESÚS FLORENCIO; circ. 22,378.

Tarragona

Diari de Tarragona: Domènech Guansé 2, 43005 Tarragona; tel. (977) 299700; fax (977) 223013; e-mail diari@diaridetarragona.com; internet www.diaridetarragona.com; f. 1808; Spanish and Catalan; Dir RAMON PEDRÓS; circ. 14,082.

Valencia

Levante—El Mercantil Valenciano: Traginers 7, 46014 Valencia; tel. (96) 3992200; fax (96) 3992276; e-mail levante-emv@epi.es; internet www.levante-emv.es; f. 1872; Propr Editorial Prensa Ibérica; Dir PEDRO MUELAS NAVARRETE; circ. 44,345.

Mini Diario: Jesús 40, 1°, 46007 Valencia; tel. (96) 3462624; fax (96) 3462620; e-mail redaccion@minidiario.com; internet www.minidiario.com; f. 1992; free; edns in Valencia and Alicante; Dir JUAN PÉREZ; circ. 56,360.

Las Provincias: Polígono Industrial Vara de Quart, Gremis 1, 46014 Valencia; tel. (96) 3502211; fax (96) 3590188; e-mail lasprovincias@lasprovincias.es; internet www.lasprovincias.es; f. 1866; rightist; Propr Vocento; Dir PEDRO ORTIZ SIMARRO; circ. 41,487.

Valladolid

El Día de Valladolid: Edif. Promecal, Los Astros s/n, 47009 Valladolid; tel. (983) 325045; fax (983) 325047; e-mail redaccion@diavalladolid.es; internet www.eldiadevalladolid.com; f. 2000; Propr Promecal; Pres. ANTONIO MÉNDEZ POZO.

El Norte de Castilla: Vázquez de Menchaca 10 (Polígono de Argales), 47008 Valladolid; tel. (983) 412100; fax (983) 412111; e-mail redaccion.nc@nortecastilla.es; internet www.nortecastilla.es; f. 1854; Propr Vocento; Dir CARLOS ROLDÁN SAN JUAN; circ. 36,422.

Vizcaya (Bizkaia)

El Correo: Pintor Losada 7, Apdo 205, 48004 Bilbao; tel. (94) 4870100; fax (94) 4870111; e-mail info@diario-elcorreo.es; internet www.elcorreodigital.com; f. 1910; edns in Vizcaya and Álava; Propr Vocento; Dir ÁNGEL ARNEDO GIL; circ. 119,601.

Deia: Carretera Bilbao Galdácano 8 (Bolueta), 48004 Bilbao; tel. (94) 4599100; fax (94) 4599120; e-mail cartas@deia.com; internet www.deia.com; f. 1997; Basque nationalist, associated with the EAJ-PNV; publishes weekly satirical supplement, *Caduca Hoy*; circ. 21,179.

Zaragoza

Heraldo de Aragón: Paseo de la Independencia 29, Apdo 175, 50001 Zaragoza; tel. (976) 765000; fax (976) 765001; e-mail redaccion@heraldo.es; internet www.heraldo.es; f. 1895; independent; also publishes edn in Huesca; Dir GUILLERMO FATÁS CABEZA; circ. 53,865.

El Periódico de Aragón: Hernán Cortés 37, bajo, 50005 Zaragoza; tel. (976) 700400; fax (976) 700458; e-mail eparagon@elperiodico

SPAIN

.com; internet www.elperiodicodearagon.com; f. 1990; Propr Grupo Zeta; Dir JAIME ARMENGOL; circ. 12,481.

SELECTED PERIODICALS

The Arts

Arquitectura y Diseño: RBA Revistas, SA, Pérez Galdós 36 bis, 08012 Barcelona; internet www.rba.es; monthly; architecture and design; Dir-Gen. ARIADNA HERNÁNDEZ; circ. 47,741 (June 2007).

Claves de Razón Práctica: Julián Camarillo 29B, 1°, 28004 Madrid; tel. (91) 5386104; fax (91) 5222291; e-mail claves@progresa.es; internet claves.progresa.es/claves; f. 1990; monthly; books and culture; Dirs JAVIER PRADERA, FERNANDO SAVATER; circ. 4,500.

El Croquis: Avda de los Reyes Católicos 9, El Escorial, 28280 Madrid; tel. (91) 8969414; fax (91) 8969415; e-mail elcroquis@elcroquis.es; internet www.elcroquis.es; six a year; architecture, in Spanish and English; Dirs FERNANDO MÁRQUEZ CECILIA, RICHARD LEVENE; circ. 17,837 (June 2007).

Experimenta: Churruca 27, 4° ext. dcha, 28004 Madrid; tel. (91) 5214049; fax (91) 5213212; e-mail info@experimenta.es; internet www.experimenta.es; f. 1989; architecture and design; Dir PIERLUIGI CATTERMOLE FIORAVANTI.

Insula: Complejo Atica, Edif. 4, Vía de las Dos Castillas 33, 28224 Pozuelo de Alarcón, Madrid; tel. (91) 7848200; fax (91) 3589505; internet www.insula.es; f. 1946; monthly; literature and social sciences; Editor ARANTXA GÓMEZ SANCHO; circ. 6,000.

Letra Internacional: Monte Esquinza 30, 3° dcha, 28010 Madrid; tel. (91) 3104313; fax (91) 3194585; e-mail editorial@fpi.es; internet www.fpabloiglesias.es; f. 1986; quarterly; culture; Dir SALVADOR CLOTAS I CIERCO.

Magisterio: Javier Ferrero 2, 28002 Madrid; tel. (91) 5199131; fax (91) 4151124; e-mail informacion@magisnet.com; internet www.magisnet.com; f. 1866; Wed.; education; Dir JOSÉ MARÍA DE MOYA ANEGÓN; circ. 24,200.

Ritmo: Isabel Colbrand 10, Oficina 87, 28050 Madrid; tel. (91) 3588774; fax (91) 3588944; e-mail correo@ritmo.com; internet www.ritmo.com; monthly; classical music; Dir ANTONIO RODRÍGUEZ MORENO.

Qué Leer: Gran Vía de les Corts Catalanes 133, 2°, 08014 Barcelona; tel. (93) 2232136; fax (93) 4322907; e-mail queleer@hachette.es; internet www.que-leer.com; f. 1996; monthly; book news, etc.; Dir JORGE DE COMINGES; circ. 26,608.

Current Affairs, History, Religion, etc.

A Nosa Terra: Rúa Príncipe 22, 36202 Vigo; tel. (986) 222405; fax (986) 223101; e-mail info@anosaterra.com; internet www.anosaterra.com; f. 1907; weekly; Galician; Dir MANUEL VEIGA TABOADA.

Aceprensa: Núñez de Balboa 125, 6°, 28006 Madrid; tel. (91) 5158975; fax (91) 5631243; e-mail redaccion@aceprensa.com; internet www.aceprensa.com; f. 1973; weekly; news and features; Editorial Dir IGNACIO ARÉCHAGA DUQUE; circ. 4,000.

Boletín Oficial del Estado (BOE): Avda de Manoteras 54, 28050 Madrid; tel. (902) 365303; fax (91) 3841555; internet www.boe.es; f. 1936; successor of *Gaceta de Madrid*, f. 1661; daily except Sun.; laws, decrees, orders, etc.; Dir-Gen. JULIO SEAGE MARIÑO; circ. 60,000.

Cambio 16: Arroyo de Fontarrón 51, 28030 Madrid; tel. (91) 4201199; fax (91) 3601302; e-mail cambio16@cambio16.info; internet www.cambio16.info; f. 1972; weekly, Wed.; general; Pres., Editorial Bd MANUEL DOMÍNGUEZ MORENO.

El Ciervo: Calvet 56, 08021 Barcelona; tel. (93) 2005145; fax (93) 2011015; e-mail redaccion@elciervo.es; internet www.elciervo.es; f. 1951; monthly; politics and culture; Dir ROSARIO BOFILL; circ. 5,000.

Ciudad Nueva: José Picón 28, 28028 Madrid; tel. (91) 7259530; fax (91) 7130452; e-mail revista@ciudadnueva.com; internet www.ciudadnueva.com; f. 1958; monthly; Dir JAVIER RUBIO; circ. 7,000.

La Clave: Avda de Argón 336, 28022 Madrid; tel. (91) 8373131; fax (91) 8373136; e-mail redaccion@laclave.com; internet www.laclave.com; f. 2001; weekly; news magazine; Dir JOSÉ LUIS BALBIN; circ. 60,000.

Clío: Gran Vía de les Corts Catalanes 133, 2°, 08014 Barcelona; tel. (93) 2232136; fax (93) 4322907; e-mail clio@hachette.es; internet www.cliorevista.com; f. 2001; monthly; history; Dir JOSEP A. BORRELL; circ. 36,401.

Ecclesia: Alfonso XI 4, 28014 Madrid; tel. (91) 5315400; fax (91) 5225561; e-mail ecclesia@planalfa.es; f. 1941; weekly; religious information; Dir JESÚS DE LAS HERAS MUELA; Editor-in-Chief MIGUEL DE SANTIAGO; Propr Conferencia Episcopal Española; circ. 24,000.

Época: Paseo de la Castellana 36–38, 28046 Madrid; tel. (91) 5109100; fax (91) 5109149; e-mail epoca@epoca.es; internet www.epoca.es; weekly; Dir CARLOS DAVILA.

Historia 16: Rufino González 13,1°, 28037 Madrid; tel. (91) 3271171; fax (91) 3271220; e-mail h16redaccion@telefonica.net; f. 1976; monthly; history; Dir MARÍA ALDAVE; circ. 25,000.

El Jueves: Avda Diagonal 468, 5°, 08006 Barcelona; tel. (93) 2922217; fax (93) 2375824; e-mail redaccion@eljueves.es; internet www.eljueves.es; f. 1977; weekly, Wed.; satirical; Dir MANEL FONTDEVILA; circ. 73,454 (2006).

Mundo Cristiano: Paseo de la Castellana 210, 2°B, 28046 Madrid; tel. (91) 3507739; fax (91) 3590230; e-mail mundoc@edicionespalabra.es; f. 1963; monthly; Dir DARIO CHIMENO CANO; Editor-in-Chief JOSÉ M. NAVALPOTRO; circ. 12,747 (June 2007).

Nueva Revista: Javier Ferrero 2, 28002 Madrid; tel. (91) 5199756; fax (91) 4151254; e-mail nuevarevista@tst.es; internet www.nuevarevista.net; f. 1990; six a year; politics, culture, art; Pres. ANTONIO FONTÁN PÉREZ.

Política—Revista Republicana: Ríos Rosas 10, 1°B, 28003 Madrid; tel. (902) 158935; fax (91) 4411165; e-mail ir@bitmailer.net; internet www.izquierdarepublicana.com; f. 1935; bi-monthly; organ of Izquierda Republicana; Dir ISABELO HERREROS.

Revista de Estudios Políticos: Plaza de la Marina Española 9, 28071 Madrid; tel. (91) 4228927; fax (91) 5419574; e-mail editer@cepc.es; internet www.cepc.es; f. 1941; quarterly; Dirs PEDRO DE VEGA, JUAN J. SOLOZÁBAL ECHAVARRÍA; publ. by Centro de Estudios Políticos y Constitucionales; circ. 1,000.

El Socialista: Gobelas 31, 28023 Madrid; tel. (91) 5820044; fax (91) 5820045; e-mail elsocialista@elsocialista.es; internet www.elsocialista.es; f. 1866; monthly; general information; Dir JOAQUÍN TAGAR; circ. 185,000.

El Temps: Octubre, Centre de Cultura Contemporània, Sant Ferran 12, 46001 Valencia; tel. (96) 3535100; fax (96) 3534569; e-mail eltemps@eltemps.net; internet www.eltemps.net; f. 1984; weekly; general information; in Catalan; Dir JORDI FORTUNY I BATALLA; circ. 25,000.

Tiempo de Hoy: O' Donnell 12, 3°, 28009 Madrid; tel. (91) 5863300; fax (91) 5863346; e-mail contacta.tiempo@zetadigital.es; internet www.tiempodehoy.es; weekly; Dir JESÚS RIVASÉS; circ. 43,408 (June 2007).

Treball: Ciutat 7, 08002 Barcelona; tel. (93) 3010612; fax (93) 4124252; e-mail treball@iniciativa.cat; internet www.iniciativa.cat; f. 1991; 6 a year; organ of Iniciativa per Catalunya Verds; Dir MARC RIUS; circ. 6,000.

Vida Nueva: Impresores 15, Urbanización Prado del Espino, 28660 Boadilla del Monte, Madrid; tel. (91) 4226255; fax (91) 4226118; e-mail juan.antonio.rubio@ppc-editorial.com; internet www.vidanueva.com; f. 1958; weekly; society and religion; Dir JUAN RUBIO; circ. 20,000.

Finance

Actualidad Económica: Paseo de la Castellana 66, 3°, 28046 Madrid; tel. (91) 3370346; fax (91) 5628415; e-mail aeconomica@recoletos.es; internet www.actualidad-economica.com; f. 1958; weekly, Mon.; Dir MIGUEL ÁNGEL BELLOSO; circ. 46,000.

Capital: Albasanz 15, Edif. A, 28037 Madrid; tel. (91) 4369800; fax (91) 5767881; e-mail mmoreno@gyj.es; internet www.capital.es; f. 2000; monthly; business and economics; publ. by Grupo G+J; Dir JOSÉ LUIS GÓMEZ; circ. 35,088 (June 2007).

Dinero: Sepúlveda 7 B, 28108 Madrid; tel. (91) 4327672; fax (91) 4327765; e-mail cgarcia@negocios.com; monthly; business and finance; Dir MIGUEL ORMAETXEA ARROYO; circ. 11,586 (June 2007).

El Empresario: Diego de León 50, 3°, 28006 Madrid; tel. (91) 4116161; fax (91) 5645269; e-mail elempresario@cepyme.es; internet www.cepyme.es; monthly; economics and business; circ. 15,000.

Información Comercial Española—Revista de Economía: Paseo de la Castellana 162, 5°, 28046 Madrid; tel. (91) 3493627; fax (91) 3493634; 8 a year; published by Ministry of the Economy and Finance; Dir ANTONIO HERNÁNDEZ GARCÍA.

Mi Cartera de Inversión: José Abascal 56, 7°, 28003 Madrid; tel. (91) 4563320; fax (91) 4563328; e-mail r.rubio@inverca.com; internet www.hoyinversion.com; Dir RAFAEL RUBIO GÓMEZ-CAMINERO; circ. 16,788 (Dec. 2006).

El Mundo Financiero: Peña Sacra 1, 28260 Madrid; tel. and fax (91) 8583547; e-mail jlbarcelo@elmundofinanciero.com; internet www.elmundofinanciero.com; f. 1946; monthly; Dir JOSÉ LUIS BARCELÓ MEZQUITA; circ. 15,000.

El Nuevo Lunes de la Economía y la Sociedad: Ferrocarril 37, dpdo, 28045 Madrid; tel. (91) 5160803; fax (91) 5160819; e-mail nuevolunes@elnuevolunes.com; internet www.elnuevolunes.es; weekly; Pres. JOSÉ GARCÍA ABAD.

SPAIN

Home, Fashion and General

Casa Diez: Avda Cardenal Herrera Oria 3, 28034 Madrid; tel. (91) 7287000; fax (91) 7289144; e-mail malvarez@hachette.es; internet www.casadiez.orange.es; monthly; home decoration; Dir MILAGROS ÁLVAREZ GORTARI; circ. 172,360 (June 2007).

Clara: Muntaner 40–42, 08011 Barcelona; tel. (93) 5087000; fax (93) 4545949; e-mail clara@hymsa.com; internet www.clara.es; f. 1992; monthly; Dir HORTÈNSIA GALÍ PÉREZ; circ. 133,388 (June 2007).

Cosmopolitan: Albasanz 15, Edif. A, 28037 Madrid; tel. (91) 4369820; fax (91) 4358701; e-mail cosmopolitan@gyj.es; internet www.cosmohispano.com; f. 1990; monthly; Dir SARAH GLATTSTEIN FRANCO; circ. 197,792 (June 2007).

Diez Minutos: Avda Cardenal Herrera Oria 3, 28034 Madrid; tel. (91) 7287000; fax (91) 7289132; e-mail diezminutos@hachette.es; internet www.diezminutos.es; f. 1951; weekly; celebrity gossip; Dir CRISTINA ACEBAL; circ. 376,797 (June 2007).

Elle: Avda Cardenal Herrera Oria 3, 28034 Madrid; tel. (91) 7287000; fax (91) 7289135; e-mail elle@hachette.es; internet www.elle.es; f. 1986; monthly; Dir SUSANA MARTÍNEZ VIDAL; circ. 221,425 (June 2007).

Elle Deco: Avda Cardenal Herrera Oria 3, 28034 Madrid; tel. (91) 7287000; fax (91) 7289144; e-mail elledeco@hachette.es; internet www.elledeco.es; f. 1989; 5 a year; Dir MILAGROS ALVAREZ GORTARI.

Gaceta Internacional: Alonso Cano 66, 1°, 28003 Madrid; tel. (91) 5547354; fax (91) 5539395; e-mail info@aphis.org; internet www.aphis.org; monthly; international magazine produced by the Asociación de la Prensa Hispanoamericana; Dir ARMANDO RESTREPO BRETÓN; Editor-in-Chief YOLANDA ARRATIA GARCÍA; circ. 16,500 in Spain, 150,000 internationally.

GEO: Albasanz 15, Edif. A, 28037 Madrid; tel. (91) 4369800; fax (91) 4369781; e-mail geo@gyj.es; internet www.georevista.es; f. 1987; monthly; geography, nature, people, photo-journalism, travel; Dir DAVID CORRAL; circ. 36,858 (June 2007).

GQ: Paseo de la Castellana 9–11, 28046 Madrid; tel. (91) 7004170; fax (91) 3199325; e-mail gq@condenast.es; internet www.revistagq.com; monthly; men's magazine; Dir JAVIER FERNÁNDEZ DE ANGULO; circ. 40,000 (July 2008).

¡Hola!: Miguel Angel 1, 4°, 28010 Madrid; tel. (91) 7021300; fax (91) 3196444; internet www.hola.com; f. 1944; weekly; general illustrated; Dir EDUARDO SÁNCHEZ JUNCO; circ. 540,902 (June 2007).

Interviú: O'Donnell 12, 5°, 28009 Madrid; tel. (91) 5863300; fax (91) 5863555; e-mail interviu@grupozeta.es; internet www.interviu.es; f. 1976; weekly; Dir TERESA VIEJO; circ. 98,500 (June 2007).

Labores del Hogar: Muntaner 40–42, 08011 Barcelona; tel. (93) 5087000; fax (93) 4540551; e-mail labores@hymsa.com; f. 1926; monthly; home textile crafts; Dir EULÀLIA UBACH; circ. 59,695 (June 2007).

Lecturas: Muntaner 40–42, 08011 Barcelona; tel. (93) 5087000; fax (93) 4541322; e-mail lecturas@hymsa.com; internet www.lecturas.es; f. 1921; weekly, Fri.; Dir JAVIER DE MONTINI; circ. 208,149 (June 2007).

Man: Consejo de Ciento 425, 5°, 08009 Barcelona; tel. (93) 4846600; fax (93) 2324542; internet www.revistaman.es; monthly; men's fashion, etc.; Dir JUAN CARLOS DE LA IGLESIA GONZÁLEZ; circ. 54,865 (June 2007).

Marie Claire: Albasanz 15, Edif. A, 28037 Madrid; tel. (91) 4369800; fax (91) 5767881; e-mail cplanchuelo@gyj.es; internet www.marie-claire.es; f. 1987; monthly; Dir JOANA BONET CAMPRUBÍ; circ. 112,825 (June 2007).

Mía: Albasanz 15, Edif. A, 28037 Madrid; tel. (91) 4369889; fax (91) 5758880; e-mail mia@gyj.es; internet www.miarevista.es; f. 1986; weekly; Dir KETTY RICO OLIVER; circ. 169,686 (June 2007).

Nuevo Estilo: Avda Cardenal Herrera Oria 3, 28034 Madrid; tel. (91) 7287000; fax (91) 7289338; e-mail nuevoestilo@hachette.es; internet www.nuevo-estilo.es; f. 1977; monthly; home decoration; Dir MARTA RIOPÉREZ; circ. 76,000 (June 2008).

Nuevo Vale: Gran Vía de Carlos III 124, 5°, 08034 Barcelona; tel. (93) 2061540; fax (93) 2805555; e-mail buzon@publicacioneseres.com; weekly; Dir ESTHER GIRALT; circ. 104,445 (June 2007).

Pronto: Gran Vía de Carlos III 124, 5°, 08034 Barcelona; tel. (93) 2061540; fax (93) 2805555; e-mail pronto@publicacioneseres.com; f. 1972; weekly; general information; Dir ANTONIO GÓMEZ ABAD; circ. 976,892 (June 2007).

Semana: Cuesta de San Vicente 28, 28008 Madrid; tel. (91) 5472300; fax (91) 5414488; e-mail redaccion@semana.es; internet www.semana.es; f. 1942; weekly; general, illustrated; Dir CHARO CARRACEDO ARMADA; circ. 206,349 (June 2007).

Ser Padres Hoy: Albasanz 15, Edif. A, 28037 Madrid; tel. (91) 4369800; fax (91) 5767881; e-mail publicidad@gyj.es; internet www.serpadres.es; f. 1974; monthly; for parents; Dir JAVIER J. GARCÍA GONZÁLEZ; circ. 37,462 (June 2008).

Súper Pop: Gran Vía Carlos III 124, 1°, 08034 Barcelona; tel. (93) 2521452; fax (93) 2521450; e-mail info@superpop.es; f. 1976; fortnightly; teenage magazine; Dir SILVIA ALEMÁN; circ. 196,207 (June 2007).

Telva: Avda de San Luis 25, 28033 Madrid; tel. (91) 4436333; fax (91) 3373143; e-mail telva@telva.com; internet www.telva.com; f. 1963; beauty, fashion, weddings, interviews, cookery and fitness; monthly; Dir NIEVES FONTANA LÍBANO; circ. 186,600 (June 2008).

Tu Bebé: Muntaner 40–42, 08011 Barcelona; tel. (93) 5087000; fax (93) 4541322; e-mail tu_bebe@hymsa.com; f. 1993; monthly; for parents; Dir PEDRO RIAÑO MARTÍNEZ; circ. 60,000.

Vogue España: Paseo de la Castellana 9–11, 28046 Madrid; tel. (91) 7004170; fax (91) 3199325; e-mail vogue@condenast.es; internet www.vogue.es; f. 1988; monthly; Dir YOLANDA SACRISTÁN; circ. 123,696 (June 2007).

Woman: Bailén 84, 2°, 08009 Barcelona; tel. (93) 4846600; fax (93) 2324630; e-mail woman@grupozeta.es; internet www.woman.es; f. 1992; monthly; Dir EMPAR PRIETO; circ. 142,308 (June 2007).

Leisure Interests and Sport

Automóvil: Ancora 40, 28045 Madrid; tel. (91) 3470100; fax (91) 3470135; e-mail automovil@mpib.es; internet www.motorpress-iberica.es; monthly; motoring; Dir FERNANDO GÓMEZ BLANCO; circ. 234,849 (June 2007).

Autopista: Ancora 40, 28045 Madrid; tel. (91) 3470100; fax (91) 3470135; e-mail autopista@mpib.es; internet www.motorpress-iberica.es; weekly; motoring; Editor ARANCHA PATO; circ. 29,291 (June 2007).

Cinemanía: Progresa (Grupo Prisa), Julián Camarillo 29B, 1°, 28037 Madrid; tel. (91) 5386104; fax (91) 5222291; e-mail cinemania@progresa.es; internet www.progresa.es; f. 1995; monthly; films; Dir CARLOS MARAÑÓN; circ. 48,654 (June 2008).

Coche Actual: Ancora 40, 28045 Madrid; tel. (91) 3470100; fax (91) 3470119; e-mail cocheactual@mpib.es; internet www.motorpress-iberica.es; weekly; cars; Dir ANTONIO RONCERO FERNÁNDEZ; circ. 26,343 (June 2007).

Don Balón: Avda Diagonal 435, 1–2°, 08036 Barcelona; tel. (93) 2092000; fax (93) 2412358; e-mail info@donbalon.org; internet www.donbalon.com; f. 1975; weekly; sport; Editor-in-Chief ANTONIO CASALS; circ. 10,480 (June 2006).

Fotogramas: Gran Vía de les Corts Catalanes 133, 2°, 08014 Barcelona; tel. (93) 2232790; fax (93) 4322907; e-mail fotogramas@hachette.es; internet www.fotogramas.es; f. 1946; monthly; cinema; Dir TONI ULLED NADAL; circ. 107,598.

Guía del Ocio—La Semana de Barcelona: Muntaner 492, bajos, 08022 Barcelona; tel. (93) 4185005; fax (93) 4179471; e-mail redaccion@guiadelociobcn.com; internet www.guiadelociobcn.com; f. 1977; weekly, Friday; listings and reviews of events; Dir XAVIER MUNIESA CALDERÓ; circ. 50,000.

Guía del Ocio—La Semana de Madrid: Alcalá 106, 2°, 28009 Madrid; tel. (91) 4316080; fax (91) 5769307; e-mail guiadelocio@guiadelociomad.com; internet www.guiadelocio.com; weekly, Fri.; listings and reviews of events; Dir-Gen. JUAN MIGUEL ALONSO SECO.

Motociclismo: Ancora 40, 28045 Madrid; tel. (91) 3470100; fax (91) 3470152; e-mail motociclismo@mpib.es; internet www.motociclismo.es; f. 1951; weekly; motorcycling; Dir and Editor AUGUSTO MORENO DE CARLOS; circ. 35,147 (June 2007).

Sport Life: Ancora 40, 28045 Madrid; tel. (91) 3470100; fax (91) 3470236; e-mail sportlife@mpib.es; internet www.motorpress-iberica.es; monthly; Editor FRANCISCO JESÚS CHICO; circ. 55,412 (June 2007).

Supertele: Avda Cardenal Herrera Oria 3, 28034 Madrid; tel. (91) 7287000; fax (91) 7289129; e-mail supertele@hachette.es; internet www.supertele.es; f. 1992; weekly; TV magazine; Dir PURIFICACIÓN BLANCO PAÍNO; circ. 80,673 (June 2007).

Tele Digital: Vallehermoso 32, 28015 Madrid; tel. (91) 4451950; fax (91) 4450621; internet www.sateliteinfos.com; Dir JOSÉ DA CUNHA.

Tele Indiscreta: Avda Cardenal Herrera Oria 3, 28034 Madrid; tel. (91) 7287000; fax (91) 3581348; e-mail teleindiscreta@hachette.es; internet www.teleindiscreta.es; weekly; popular illustrated; TV programmes; Dir PURIFICACIÓN BLANCO PAÍNO; circ. 31,852 (June 2007).

Telenovela: Avda Cardenal Herrera Oria 3, 28034 Madrid; tel. (91) 7287051; fax (91) 3581348; e-mail telenovela@hachette.es; internet www.tele-novela.orange.es; f. 1993; TV series; Dir AGUSTÍN DE TENA; circ. 64,946 (June 2007).

TP Teleprograma: Avda Cardenal Herrera Oria 3, 28034 Madrid; tel. (91) 7287000; fax (91) 7289129; e-mail tp@hachette.es; internet www.t-p.es; f. 1966; weekly; TV, cinema and video; Dir PURIFICACIÓN BLANCO PAÍNO; circ. 156,280 (June 2007).

SPAIN

Viajar: O'Donnell 12, 3°, 28009 Madrid; tel. (91) 5863630; fax (91) 5863411; e-mail mlopez.viajar@grupozeta.es; internet www.revistaviajar.es; f. 1978; monthly; travel; Dir MARIANO LÓPEZ; circ. 75,000.

Vinos de España: Islas Marquesas 28B, 28035 Madrid; tel. (91) 3865152; fax (91) 3860265; e-mail vinos@mundonatura.es; f. 1996; wines and viniculture; bi-monthly; also tri-monthly in German; Dir ALBERTO HUERTA; circ. 30,000.

Medicine, Science and Technology

Arbor: Vitruvio 8, 28006 Madrid; tel. (91) 5616651; fax (91) 5855326; e-mail arbor@csic.es; internet www.csic.es/arbor; f. 1944; monthly; science, thought and culture; publ. by Consejo Superior de Investigaciones Científicas (CSIC); Dir ALBERTO SÁNCHEZ ÁLVAREZ-INSUA.

Avión Revue: Ancora 40, 28045 Madrid; tel. (91) 3470100; fax (91) 3470174; e-mail avionrevue@mpib.es; f. 1982; monthly; aeroplanes; Dir JOSÉ MARÍA PARÉS; circ. 14,081 (June 2007).

Computerworld: Fortuny 18, 4°, 28010 Madrid; tel. (91) 3496600; fax (91) 3196104; e-mail computerworld@idg.es; internet www.idg.es/computerworld; f. 1981; weekly; also available: *CIO, Comunicaciones World, Dealer World, iWorld, MacWorld, PC World Digital, PC World PRO*; Editor-in-Chief MARÍA JOSÉ MARZAL; circ. 10,327.

El Ecologista: Marqués de Laganés 12, 28004 Madrid; tel. (91) 5312389; fax (91) 5312611; e-mail comunicacion@ecologistasenaccion.org; internet www.ecologistasenaccion.org; f. 1979; quarterly; ecological issues; Dir JOSÉ LUIS GARCÍA CANO; circ. 13,000.

Gaceta Médica de Bilbao: Lersundi 9, Apdo 5073, 48009 Bilbao; tel. (94) 4233768; fax (94) 4232161; e-mail gacetamedica@telefonica.net; f. 1894; quarterly; official publication of the Academia de Ciencias Médicas de Bilbao/Bilboko Sendalarintz Jakindia; Dir Dr JUAN IGNACIO GOIRIA ORMAZABAL; circ. 5,000.

Investigación y Ciencia: Muntaner 339, Pral 1°, 08021 Barcelona; tel. (93) 4143344; fax (93) 4145413; e-mail precisa@investigacionyciencia.es; internet www.investigacionyciencia.es; f. 1976; quarterly; Dir JOSÉ MARÍA VADERAS GALLARDO; circ. 20,866 (Dec. 2006).

Mundo Científico: Pérez Galdós 36, 08012 Barcelona; tel. (93) 4157374; fax (93) 2177378; monthly; Dir JORGE ALCALDE.

Muy Interesante: Albasanz 15, 28037 Madrid; tel. (91) 4369800; fax (91) 5767881; e-mail publicidad@gyj.es; internet www.muyinteresante.es; f. 1981; monthly; history, medicine, nature, science; Dir JOSÉ PARDINA CANCER; circ. 241,454 (June 2008).

Natura: Islas Marquesas 28B, 28035 Madrid; tel. (91) 3865152; fax (91) 3860265; e-mail redaccion@mundonatura.es; f. 1983; bi-monthly; wildlife, archaeology, research, travel, food; Dir JESÚS INIESTA; circ. 69,913.

PC Actual: López de Hoyos 141, 5°, 28002 Madrid; tel. (91) 5106600; fax (91) 5194813; e-mail javier-perez@rba.es; internet www.pc-actual.com; monthly; Dir JAVIER PÉREZ CORTIJO.

Tiempos Médicos: Editores Médicos, SA, Alsasua 16, 28023 Madrid; tel. (91) 3768140; fax (91) 3739907; e-mail edimsa@edimsa.es; internet www.edimsa.es; 10 a year; Dir Dr A. CHICHARRO PAPIRI; circ. 10,000.

NEWS AGENCIES

Agencia EFE, SA: Esproncceda 32, 28003 Madrid; tel. (91) 3467100; fax (91) 3467134; e-mail efe@efe.es; internet www.efe.es; f. 1939; national and international news; 140 bureaux and correspondents abroad; sports, features, radio and television, and photographic branches; Pres. ÁLEX GRIJELMO; Gen. Man. LOLA ÁLVAREZ.

Colpisa: José Abascal 56, 1°, 28003 Madrid; tel. (91) 4564600; fax (91) 4564701; f. 1972; Pres. JOSÉ MARÍA BERGARECHE; Dir ROGELIO RODRÍGUEZ.

Europa Press Noticias: Paseo de la Castellana 210, 3°, 28046 Madrid; tel. (91) 3592600; fax (91) 3503251; e-mail noticias@europapress.es; internet www.europapress.es; Dir ANGEL EXPÓSITO MORA.

Iberia Press: Velázquez 46, 1°, 28001 Madrid; tel. and fax (91) 8155319; e-mail press-bulletin@jet.es; f. 1977; Dir JOSÉ RAMÓN ALONSO.

PRESS ASSOCIATIONS

National Organizations

Asociación de Corresponsales de Prensa Extranjera (ACPE): Monte Esquinza 41, 1°, 28010 Madrid; tel. (91) 3101433; fax (91) 3080950; e-mail acpe.corresponsales@wanadoo.es; internet www.acpe-corresponsales.com; f. 1923; foreign correspondents' asscn; Pres. SAID IDA HASSAN; Sec.-Gen. CARLOS MEZA; 150 mems.

Directory

Asociación de Editores de Diarios Españoles (AEDE): Orense 69, 2°, 28020 Madrid; tel. (91) 4251085; fax (91) 5796020; e-mail maribel@aede.es; internet www.aede.es; f. 1978; 33 mems, representing 95 daily newspapers (2008); Pres. PILAR DE YARZA.

Asociación de Revistas Culturales en España (ARCE): Hortaleza 75, 28004 Madrid; tel. (91) 3086066; fax (91) 3199267; e-mail info@arce.es; internet www.arce.es; f. 1983.

Federación de Asociaciones de Periodistas de España (FAPE): Juan Bravo 6, 28006 Madrid; tel. (91) 5850038; fax (91) 5850035; e-mail fape@fape.es; internet www.fape.es; f. 1922; Pres. FERNANDO GONZÁLEZ URBANEJA; Sec.-Gen. LUIS SERRANO ALTIMIRAS; 48 mem. asscns.

Unión de Escritores y Periodistas Españoles: Madrid; f. 1978; journalists' asscn; Pres. ANTONIO ARIAS PIQUERAS; Sec.-Gen. ELOY S. CASTAÑARES; 4,000 mems.

Provincial Organizations

Barcelona

Centre Internacional de Premsa de Barcelona: Rambla de Catalunya 10, 1°, 08007 Barcelona; tel. (93) 4121111; fax (93) 3178386; e-mail cipb@periodistes.org; internet www.periodistes.org; f. 1988; facilities and services for journalists; Pres. XAVIER BATALLA GARCÍA; Dir MÓNICA VIÑAS.

Bilbao

Asociación de Periodistas de Bizkaia (Bizkaiko Kazetarien Elkartea): Dr Achucarro 10, 1°, 48011 Bilbao; tel. and fax (94) 4168748; e-mail asociacion@periodistasvascos.com; internet www.periodistasvascos.com; Pres. JOSÉ MANUEL ALONSO; Sec. BLANCA GARCÍA-EGOCHEAGA.

Madrid

Asociación de la Prensa de Madrid: Juan Bravo 6, 28006 Madrid; tel. (91) 5850010; fax (91) 5850050; e-mail apm@apmadrid.es; internet www.apmadrid.es; f. 1895; Pres. FERNANDO GONZÁLEZ URBANEJA; Sec.-Gen. LUIS SERRANO ALTIMIRAS; 7,000 mems.

Centro de Prensa de Madrid: Claudio Coello 98, 28006 Madrid; tel. (91) 5850010; fax (91) 5850050; Sec.-Gen. JOSÉ MARÍA LORENTE TORIBIO.

Sevilla

Asociación de la Prensa de Sevilla: Plaza de San Francisco 9, 1°, 41004 Sevilla; tel. (95) 4500468; fax (95) 4225299; e-mail aps@asociacionprensa.org; internet www.asociacionprensa.org; f. 1909; Pres. ANA MARÍA CARVAJAL LLORENS; Sec.-Gen. PILAR SURIÑACH MUÑOZ.

Zaragoza

Centro de Prensa de Zaragoza: Cinco de Marzo 9, 50004 Zaragoza; tel. (976) 223210; fax (976) 222963; e-mail aparagon@aparagon.es; internet www.aparagon.es/centrop.asp; Pres. RAMÓN J. BUETAS CORONAS; Sec. ROBERTO GARCÍA BERMEJO.

Publishers

Alianza Editorial: Juan Ignacio Luca de Tena 15, 28027 Madrid; tel. (91) 3938888; fax (91) 7414343; e-mail alianzaeditoriale@anaya.es; internet www.alianzaeditorial.es; f. 1959; advanced textbooks, fiction, general non-fiction, reference, paperbacks; imprint of Grupo Anaya; Gen. Man. VALERIA CIOMPI.

Barcino Editorial: Montseny 9, 08012 Barcelona; tel. and fax (93) 2186888; e-mail info@editorialbarcino.com; internet www.editorialbarcino.com; f. 1924; Catalan classics, general; Dir CARLES DUARTE MONTSERRAT.

Carroggio, SA de Ediciones: Pelai 28–30, 08001 Barcelona; tel. (93) 4949922; fax (93) 4949923; e-mail carroggio@carroggio.com; internet www.carroggio.com; f. 1911; art, literature, reference books, multimedia; Man. Dir SANTIAGO CARROGGIO GUERIM.

Columna Edicions: Peu de la Creu 4, 08001 Barcelona; tel. (93) 4437100; fax (93) 4417130; e-mail info@columnaedicions.cat; internet www.columnaedicions.cat; f. 1985; imprint of Grup 62; fiction and non-fiction in Catalan.

Durvan, SA de ediciones: Colón de Larreátegui 13, 3°, 48001 Bilbao; tel. (94) 4230777; fax (94) 4243832; e-mail editorial@durvan.com; internet www.durvan.com; f. 1960; Dir JAVIER PEREDA PRADO.

EDHASA (Editora y Distribuidora Hispano-Americana, SA): Avda Diagonal 519–521, 2°, 08029 Barcelona; tel. (93) 4949720; fax (93) 4194584; e-mail info@edhasa.es; internet www.edhasa.com; f. 1946; contemporary fiction, non-fiction, pocket books, historical fiction and non-fiction, crime, philosophy; Editorial Dir and Man. DANIEL FERNÁNDEZ.

Ediciones Cátedra: Juan Ignacio Luca de Tena 15, 28027 Madrid; tel. (91) 3938787; fax (91) 7412118; e-mail catedra@catedra.com; internet www.catedra.com; f. 1973; imprint of Grupo Anaya; literature, literary criticism, history, humanities, linguistics, arts, cinema, music, feminism; Pres. JOSÉ MANUEL GÓMEZ.

Ediciones de Cultura Hispánica: General Pardiñas 55, 28006 Madrid; tel. (91) 37999494; fax (91) 5838311; internet www.aeci.es; f. 1943; arts, law, history, economics for circulation in Latin America; Literary and Artistic Dir ANTONIO PAPELL.

Ediciones Destino: Provenza 260, 5°, 08008 Barcelona; tel. (93) 4967001; fax (93) 4967002; e-mail edicionesdestino@stl.logicontrol.es; internet www.edestino.es; f. 1942; imprint of Grupo Planeta; general fiction, history, art, children's books.

Ediciones Deusto: Alameda Recalde 27, 7°, 48009 Bilbao; tel. (94) 4356161; fax (94) 4356166; e-mail deustomail@ediciones-deusto.es; internet www.ediciones-deusto.es; f. 1960; management and law; Man. Dir ENRIQUE IGLESIAS MONTEJO.

Ediciones Encuentro: Ramírez de Arellano 17, 10°, 28043 Madrid; tel. (91) 5322607; fax (91) 5322346; e-mail encuentro@ediciones-encuentro.es; internet www.ediciones-encuentro.es; f. 1978; theology, philosophy, art, history, biography, society, politics, literature.

Ediciones Mensajero, SAU: Sancho de Azpeitia 2, 48014 Bilbao; tel. (94) 4470358; fax (94) 4472630; e-mail mensajero@mensajero.com; internet www.mensajero.com; f. 1915; arts, biography, theology, psychology, pedagogy, social science and paperbacks; Dir ANGEL ANTONIO PÉREZ GÓMEZ.

Ediciones Morata, SL: Mejía Lequerica 12, 28004 Madrid; tel. (91) 4480926; fax (91) 4480925; e-mail morata@edmorata.es; internet www.edmorata.es; f. 1920; psychology, psychiatry, pedagogics, sociology; Dir FLORA MORATA.

Ediciones Obelisco: Pedro IV 78, 3 y 5°, 08005 Barcelona; tel. (93) 3098525; fax (93) 3098523; e-mail info@edicionesobelisco.com; internet www.edicionesobelisco.com; f. 1981; general fiction and non-fiction; Dir JULI PERADEJORDI.

Ediciones Omega: Platón 26, 08006 Barcelona; tel. (93) 2010599; fax (93) 2097362; e-mail omega@ediciones-omega.es; internet www.ediciones-omega.es; f. 1948; biology, field guides, geography, geology, agriculture, photography; Chair. ANTONIO PARICIO.

Ediciones Pirámide: Juan Ignacio Luca de Tena 15, 28027 Madrid; tel. (91) 3938989; fax (91) 7423661; e-mail piramide@anaya.es; internet www.edicionespiramide.es; f. 1973; scientific and technical books, business, economics, psychology; imprint of Grupo Anaya; Man. Dir MARIANO JOSÉ NORTE.

Ediciones Polígrafa: Balmes 52, 08009 Barcelona; tel. (93) 4882381; fax (93) 4877392; e-mail info@edicionespoligrafa.com; internet www.edicionespoligrafa.com; f. 1960; arts, leisure; Man. Dir JUAN DE MUGA DÒRIA; Editor-in-Chief FRANCISCO REI.

Ediciones Siruela: Almagro 25, 28010 Madrid; tel. (91) 3555720; fax (91) 3552201; e-mail atencionlector@siruela.com; internet www.siruela.com; f. 1982; history, literature, art, children's books, translations; Dir JACOBO FITZ-JAMES STUART.

Ediciones Universidad de Navarra (EUNSA): Plaza de los Sauces 1 y 2, 31010 Barañain (Navarra); tel. (948) 256850; fax (948) 256854; e-mail info@eunsa.es; internet www.eunsa.es; f. 1967; architecture, natural sciences, law, history, social sciences, theology, philosophy, medical, engineering, journalism, education, economics and business administration, biology, literature, library science, paperbacks, etc.; Chair. GUIDO STEIN.

Edicións Xerais de Galicia: Doutor Marañón 12, 36211 Vigo; tel. (986) 214888; fax (986) 201366; e-mail xerais@xerais.es; internet www.xerais.es; f. 1979; imprint of Grupo Anaya; literature, education, history and reference books in Galician.

Editorial Anagrama: Pedró de la Creu 58, 08034 Barcelona; tel. (93) 2037652; fax (93) 2037738; e-mail anagrama@anagrama-ed.es; internet www.anagrama-ed.es; f. 1969; fiction, essays, foreign literature in translation; Editor and Dir JORGE HERRALDE.

Editorial Bosch: Comte d'Urgell 51 bis, Apdo 928, 08011 Barcelona; tel. (93) 4521050; fax (93) 4521057; e-mail bosch@bosch.es; internet www.bosch.es; f. 1934; law, social science, classics; Man. ALBERT FERRÉ.

Editorial Castalia: Zurbano 39, 28010 Madrid; tel. (91) 3195857; fax (91) 3102442; e-mail castalia@castalia.es; internet www.castalia.es; f. 1945; classics, literature; Pres. AMPARO SOLER GIMENO.

Editorial CEAC: Perú 164, 08020 Barcelona; tel. (93) 2660247; fax (93) 3084392; e-mail info@ceacedit.com; internet www.editorialceac.com; f. 1947; imprint of Grupo Planeta; textbooks, education, leisure; Man. JAIME PINTANEL.

Editorial Desclée de Brouwer: Henao 6, 3° dcha, 48009 Bilbao; tel. (94) 4246843; fax (94) 4237594; e-mail info@edesclee.com; internet www.edesclee.com; f. 1945; general non-fiction in Spanish and Basque; Pres. JAVIER GOGEASKOETXEA.

Editorial Edaf: Jorge Juan 30, 1°, 28001 Madrid; tel. (91) 4358260; fax (91) 4315281; e-mail edaf@edaf.net; internet www.edaf.net; f. 1967; literature, dictionaries, occult, natural health, paperbacks; Dir-Gen. JOSÉ ANTONIO FOSSATI SEDDON.

Editorial Everest: Carretera León–Coruña, Km 5, Apdo 339, 24080 León; tel. (987) 844200; fax (987) 844202; e-mail info@everest.es; internet www.everest.es; f. 1957; general; Dir-Gen. JOSÉ ANTONIO LÓPEZ MARTÍNEZ.

Editorial Galaxia: Avenida de Madrid 44, 36204 Vigo (Pontevedra); tel. (986) 432100; fax (986) 223205; e-mail galaxia@editorialgalaxia.es; internet www.editorialgalaxia.es; f. 1950; literary works, reviews, popular, children's, Galician literature; Dir VÍCTOR F. FREIXANES.

Editorial Gredos: Sánchez Pacheco 85, 28002 Madrid; tel. (91) 7444920; fax (91) 5192033; e-mail comercial@editorialgredos.com; internet www.editorialgredos.com; f. 1944; linguistics, philology, humanities, art, literature, dictionaries; Dir MANUEL OLIVEIRA CALVET.

Editorial Gustavo Gili: Rosselló 87–89, 08029 Barcelona; tel. (93) 3228161; fax (93) 3229205; e-mail info@ggili.com; internet www.ggili.com; f. 1902; photography, art, architecture, design, fashion; Dirs GABRIEL GILI, MÓNICA GILI.

Editorial Hispano-Europea: Bori y Fontestá 6, 08021 Barcelona; tel. (93) 2018500; fax (93) 4142635; e-mail hispanoeuropea@hispanoeuropea.com; internet www.hispanoeuropea.com; f. 1954; technical, scientific, sport, pets and reference; Propr and Man. Dir JORGE J. PRAT ROSAL.

Editorial Juventud: Provença 101, 08029 Barcelona; tel. (93) 4441800; fax (93) 4398383; e-mail info@editorialjuventud.es; internet www.editorialjuventud.es; f. 1923; general fiction, biography, history, art, music, reference, dictionaries, travel books, children's books, paperbacks, in Catalan and Spanish; Dir LUIS ZENDRERA.

Editorial Marfil: San Eloy 17, 03804 Alcoy; tel. (96) 5523311; fax (96) 5523496; e-mail editorialmarfil@editorialmarfil.com; internet www.editorialmarfil.com; f. 1947; textbooks, psychology, pedagogy, university texts, literature; Man. RAFAEL LLORÉNS FIGUEROLA.

Editorial Nerea: Aldamar, 36 bajo, 20007 San Sebastián; tel. (943) 432227; fax (943) 433379; e-mail nerea@nerea.net; internet www.nerea.net; f. 1987; architecture, art, history. photography; Chair. MARTA CASARES.

Editorial Reus, SA: Preciados 23, 2°, 28013 Madrid; tel. (91) 5213619; fax (91) 5312408; e-mail reus@editorialreus.es; internet www.editorialreus.es; f. 1852; law; Pres. JESÚS M. PINTO VARELA.

Editorial Reverté: Loreto 13–15, Local B, 08029 Barcelona; tel. (93) 4193336; fax (93) 4195189; e-mail reverte@reverte.com; internet www.reverte.com; f. 1947; scientific and technical; Dir JAVIER REVERTÉ MASCÓ.

Editorial Seix Barral: Avda Diagonal 662–664, 7°, 08034 Barcelona; tel. (93) 4967003; fax (93) 4967004; e-mail editorial@seix-barral.es; internet www.seix-barral.es; f. 1911; literary fiction.

Editorial Tecnos: Juan Ignacio Luca de Tena 15, 28027 Madrid; tel. (91) 3938550; fax (91) 7426631; e-mail foro_tecnos@anaya.es; internet www.tecnos.es; f. 1947; law, social and political science, philosophy and economics; imprint of Grupo Anaya; Man. MANUEL GONZÁLEZ MORENO.

Editorial Teide: Viladomat 291, 08029 Barcelona; tel. 902 233030; fax (93) 3212646; e-mail info@editorialteide.com; internet www.editorialteide.es; f. 1942; educational, scientific, technical and art; Man. Dir FEDERICO RAHOLA.

La Esfera de los Libros: Avda de Alfonso XIII 1, bajos, 28002 Madrid; tel. (91) 2960200; fax (91) 2960206; e-mail laesfera@esferalibros.com; internet www.esferalibros.com; history, journalism, biography; Dir-Gen. JOSÉ MARÍA CALVÍN.

Espasa: Complejo Ática, Edif. 4, Vía de las Dos Castillas 33, 28224 Pozuelo de Alarcón (Madrid); tel. (91) 7848200; fax (91) 3525020; e-mail surgerencias@espasa.es; internet www.espasa.com; f. 1860; encyclopaedias, history, dictionaries, literature, biographies, paperbacks, etc.; CEO EDUARDO BOFILL.

Fondo de Cultura Económica de España, SL (FCE España): Librería Juan Rulfo México, Fernando el Católico 86, 28015 Madrid; tel. (91) 7632800; e-mail directora.general@fondodeculturaeconomica.com; internet www.fondodeculturaeconomica.com; f. 1974; sciences, literature, children's books, history, academic; Dir JUAN GUILLERMO LÓPEZ.

Galaxia Gutenberg: Travessera de Gràcia 47–49, 08021 Barcelona; tel. (93) 3660100; fax (93) 3660104; e-mail galaxiagutenberg@circulo.es; internet www.galaxiagutenberg.com; f. 1995; literary fiction, poetry, economics.

Grup 62: Peu de la Creu 4, 08001 Barcelona; tel. (93) 4437100; fax (93) 4437130; e-mail correu@grup62.com; internet www.grup62.com; f. 1962; 18 imprints publishing titles in Catalan and Spanish, including Art 62, Edicions 62, Editorial Empúries, Editorial Selecta, Ediciones Península, El Aleph Editores, Enciclopèdia Catalana, Luciérnaga, Nous Negocis, Planeta, Pòrtic i Mina, Proa, Salsa Books; Pres. J. M. MARTOS.

Grupo Anaya: Juan Ignacio Luca de Tena 15, 28027 Madrid; tel. (91) 3554405; fax (91) 3933937; e-mail administrador@anaya.es; internet www.anaya.es; f. 1959; imprints include Algaida, Alianza Editorial, Anaya, Barçanova, Clé Internacional, Del Prado, Ediciones Cátedra, Ediciones Pirámide, Edicións Xerais de Galicia, Editorial Tecnos, Eudema, Larousse and Oberon; reference, sciences, arts, literature, education; Pres. JOSÉ MANUEL GÓMEZ.

Grupo Edebé: Paseo San Juan Bosco 62, 08017 Barcelona; tel. (93) 2037408; fax (93) 2054670; e-mail informacion@edebe.net; internet www.edebe.com; f. 1968; imprints include Giltza, Rodeira, Marjal and Guadiel; children's and educational publications; Man. JOSÉ ALDUNATE JURÍO.

Grupo Editorial Bruño: Maestro Alonso 21, 28028 Madrid; tel. (91) 7244800; fax (91) 3613133; e-mail informacion@editorial-bruno.es; internet www.editorial-bruno.es; f. 1898; education, children's books; Dir-Gen. JOSÉ ANTONIO CAMACHO.

Grupo Editorial Luis Vives: Xaudaró 25, 28034 Madrid; tel. (91) 3344883; fax (91) 3344882; e-mail dediciones@edelvivies.es; internet www.grupoeditorialluisvives.com; f. 1890; imprints include Edelvives, Baula (Catalan), Alhucema, Ibaizabal (Basque) and Tambre (Galician); children's books, textbooks, reference under the imprints.

Grupo Editorial Santillana: Torrelaguna 60, 28043 Madrid; tel. (91) 7449060; fax (91) 7449019; e-mail grupo@santillana.es; internet www.gruposantillana.com; f. 1960; part of Grupo PRISA; imprints include Aguilar, Alfarguara, Altea, Richmond Publishing and Taurus; Pres. EMILIANO MARTÍNEZ.

Grupo Océano: Milanesado 21–23, 08017 Barcelona; tel. (93) 2802020; fax (93) 2041073; e-mail info@oceano.com; internet www.oceano.com; f. 1950; imprints include Circe, Instituto Gallach de Librería y Ediciones and Oceano; general; Chair. JOSÉ LLUIS MONREAL.

Grupo Planeta: Avda Diagonal 662–664, 08034 Barcelona; tel. (93) 4928000; fax (93) 4928565; internet www.planeta.es; f. 1949; imprints include Ediciones Destino, Ediciones Deusto, Ediciones Minotauro, Ediciones Temas de Hoy, Editorial CEAC, Editorial Crítica, Editorial Planeta, Emcé Editores, GeoPlaneta, MR Ediciones, Timun Mas; Pres. JOSÉ MANUEL LARA BOSCH.

Herder Editorial, SA: Provença 388, 08025 Barcelona; tel. (93) 4762626; fax (93) 2073448; e-mail herder@herdereditorial.com; internet www.herdereditorial.com; f. 1944; literature, language, theology, sociology, psychology.

Iberoamericana de Libros y Ediciones, SL: Amor de Dios 1, 28014 Madrid; tel. (91) 4293522; fax (91) 4295397; e-mail info@iberoamericanalibros.com; internet www.ibero-americana.net; f. 1996; owned by Verveut Verlagsgesellschaft (Germany); academic books.

Larousse Editorial: Mallorca, 45, 3°, 08029 Barcelona; tel. (93) 2413505; fax (93) 241351; e-mail larousse@larousse.es; internet www.larousse.es; f. 1912; encyclopaedias, dictionaries, atlases, linguistics.

Marcombo, SA de Boixareu Editores: Gran Vía de les Corts Catalanes 594, 08007 Barcelona; tel. (93) 3180079; fax (93) 3189339; e-mail info@marcombo.com; internet www.marcombo.com; f. 1945; reference, sciences, textbooks; Pres. and Man. Dir JOSEP M. BOIXAREU VILAPLANA.

Montagud Editores: Ausiàs Marc 25, 1°, 08010 Barcelona; tel. (93) 3182082; fax (93) 3025083; e-mail montagud@montagud.com; internet www.montagud.com; f. 1906; business; Chair. FRANCISCO ANTOJA GIRALT.

MR Ediciones, SA: Recoletos 4, 3°, 28001 Madrid; tel. (91) 4230314; fax (91) 4230306; e-mail info@ediciones-martinez-roca.es; internet www.edicionesmartinezroca.com; f. 1965; fmrly Ediciones Martínez Roca; fiction, New Age, spirituality, sport, 'how-to' books, psychology, psychiatry; Dir LAURA FALCÓ.

Narcea, SA de Ediciones: Avda Dr Federico Rubio y Galí 9, 28039 Madrid; tel. (91) 5546484; fax (91) 5546487; e-mail narcea@narceaediciones.es; internet www.narceaediciones.es; f. 1968; humanities, pedagogy, psychology, spirituality, textbooks; Man. Dir MONICA B. GONZÁLEZ NAVARRO.

Nivola Libros y Ediciones, SL: Sector Islas 12, Local 3B, Tres Cantos, 28760 Madrid; tel. (91) 8045817; fax (91) 8041482; e-mail nivola@nivola.com; internet www.nivola.com; science.

Noguer y Caralt Editores: Santa Amèlia 22, bajos, 08034 Barcelona; tel. (93) 2801399; fax (93) 2801993; e-mail contact@noguercaralt.com; internet www.noguercaralt.com; f. 1993; dictionaries, children's, philosophy, art; Man. EMILIO ARDÉVOL.

Plaza y Janés: Travessera de Gràcia 47–49, 08021 Barcelona; tel. (93) 3660300; fax (93) 2002219; internet www.plaza.es; f. 1959; fiction and non-fiction, reference; imprint of Random House Mondadori; Dir-Gen. JUAN PASCUAL.

Random House Mondadori: Travessera de Gràcia 47–49, 08021 Barcelona; tel. (93) 3660300; fax (93) 3660449; e-mail gestionweb@rhm.es; internet www.randomhousemondadori.es; f. 2001; imprints include Areté, Beascoa, Debate, Electa, Lumen, Montena, Plaza y Janés, Rosa dels Vents, and co listed below; Gen. Man. RICARDO CAVALLERO.

Siglo XXI de España, Editores: Menéndez Pidal 3 bis, 28036 Madrid; tel. (91) 5617748; fax (91) 5615819; e-mail sigloxxi@sigloxxieditores.com; internet www.sigloxxieditores.com; f. 1967; pocket collections, reference, history, social sciences; Pres. PABLO GARCÍA-ARENAL.

SM Grupo: Impresores 2, Urbanización Prado del Espino, 28660 Boadilla del Monte, Madrid; tel. (91) 4228800; fax (91) 5089927; e-mail clientes@grupo-sm.com; internet www.grupo-sm.com; f. 1940; textbooks, children's, reference, travel, literature; Pres. JUAN DE ISASA GONZÁLEZ UBIETA; Man. Dir JAVIER CORTÉS SORIANO.

Thomson Reuters Aranzadi: Camino de Galar 15, 31190 Cizur Menor (Navarra); tel. (948) 297297; fax (948) 297200; e-mail clientes@aranzadi.es; internet www.aranzadi.es; f. 1929; fmrly Editorial Aranzadi; law; Dir JUAN CARLOS FRANQUET.

Tusquets Editores: Cesare Cantú 8, 08023 Barcelona; tel. (93) 2530400; fax (93) 4176703; internet www.tusquets-editores.es; art, general fiction and non-fiction.

Vicens Vives: Polígono Industrial Pratense, 111, parcela 16, El Prat de Llobregat, 08820 Barcelona; tel. (93) 4782755; fax (93) 4783659; e-mail e@vicensvives.es; internet www.vicensvives.es; f. 1961; school and university, educational; Dir ROSARIO RAHOLA DE ESPONA.

PUBLISHERS' ASSOCIATIONS

Asociación de Editores de Madrid: Santiago Rusiñol 8, 28040 Madrid; tel. (91) 5544745; fax (91) 5532553; e-mail editoresmadrid@editoresmadrid.org; internet www.editoresmadrid.org; f. 1977; Pres. JOSÉ MARÍA GUTIÉRREE DE LA TORRE; Sec.-Gen. AMALIA MARTÍN PEREDA.

Asociación de Editoriales Universitarias Españolas (AEUE): Plaza de las Cortes 2, 7°, 28014 Madrid; tel. (91) 3600698; fax (91) 3601201; e-mail secretariatecnica@une.es; internet www.aeue.es; Pres. MAGDA POLO PUJADAS; Sec. ISABEL TERROBA PASCUAL.

Associació d'Editors en Llengua Catalana (Association of Publishers in Catalan Language): València 279, 1°, 08009 Barcelona; tel. (93) 2155091; fax (93) 2155273; e-mail info@editorsencatala.org; internet www.catalanpublishers.org; f. 1978; Pres. MANUEL SANGLAS MUCHART; Sec.-Gen. SEGIMON BORRÀS.

Federación de Gremios de Editores de España (Federation of Publishers' Associations of Spain): Cea Bermúdez 44, 2° dcha, 28003 Madrid; tel. (91) 5345195; fax (91) 5352625; e-mail fgee@fge.es; internet www.federacioneditores.org; f. 1978; Pres. JORDI ÚBEDA I BAULÓ; Exec. Dir ANTONIO MARÍA AVILA.

Gremi d'Editors de Catalunya: València 279, 1°, 08009 Barcelona; tel. (93) 2155091; fax (93) 2155273; e-mail info@gremieditorscat.es; internet www.gremieditorscat.es; Pres. JOSEP M. PUIG DE LA BELLACASA; Sec.-Gen. SEGIMON BORRÀS.

Gremio de Editores de Euskadi/Euskadiko Editoreen Elkartea: Lehendakari Aguirre 11, 3°, 48014 Bilbao; tel. (94) 4764313; fax (94) 4761980; internet www.editores-euskadi.com; Pres. JAVIER GOGEASCOECHEA ARRIEN; Man. Dir ANDRÉS FERNÁNDEZ SECO.

Broadcasting and Communications

TELECOMMUNICATIONS

The telecommunications market was fully deregulated in December 1998.

BT España: Edif. Herre, Salvador de Madariaga 1, 28027 Madrid; tel. (91) 270800; fax (91) 2708888; internet www.btglobalservices.com/business/es/es/index.html; Dir-Gen. JACINTO CAVESTANY VALLEJO.

Euphony: Plaza de la Independencia 10, 28001 Madrid; tel. (91) 5239577; e-mail serviciocliente@euphony.com; internet www.euphony.es; fixed-line and mobile cellular telecommunications services, internet service provider; Chief Exec. GILES REDPATH.

Euskaltel: Parque Tecnológico Edificio 809, 48160 Derio (Vizcaya); tel. (94) 4011000; fax (94) 4011020; internet www.euskaltel.com; f. 1995; offers fixed-line and mobile cellular telecommunications, digital cable television, and broadband internet services in the Basque Country; Chair. JOSÉ ANTONIO ARDANZA GARRO; CEO ALBERTO GARCÍA ERAUZKIN.

Jazztel: Anabel Segura 11, Edificio, 28108 Alcobendas, Madrid; tel. (91) 1839000; fax (91) 1839943; e-mail contact@jazztel.com; internet www.jazztel.com; Pres. LEOPOLDO FERNÁNDEZ PUJALS.

ONO: Basauri 7 y 9, 28023 Madrid; tel. (91) 1809300; internet www.ono.es; f. 1998; broadband internet, telephone and television; owns Grupo Auna; Pres. EUGENIO GALDÓN; CEO RICHARD ALDEN.

Orange: Parque Empresarial La Finca, Paseo del Club Deportivo 1, Edif. 8, 28223 Pozuelo de Alarcón (Madrid); internet www.orange.es; owned by France Telecom España; fmrly Uni2 and Amena.

Telefónica: Gran Vía 28, 28013 Madrid; tel. (91) 7406918; e-mail prensa@telefonica.es; internet www.telefonica.es; f. 1924; privatized in 1997; monopoly on telephone services removed in 1998; incl. mobile network Telefónica Móviles; provides services in 41 countries (2007); Pres. CÉSAR ALIERTA; CEO JULIO LINARES.

Vodafone España: Avda Europa 1 (Central), Parque Empresarial La Moraleja, 28108 Alcobendas, Madrid; tel. 607 133333; internet www.vodafone.es; f. 1998; fmrly Airtel; mobile services; Pres. VITTORIO COLAO; CEO FRANCISCO ROMÁN.

Xfera Moviles: Avda de la Vega 15, Alcobendas, 28100 Madrid; tel. (91) 1315200; fax (91) 1315202; e-mail prensa@yoigo.com; internet www.yoigo.com; f. 2006; 76.6% owned by TeliaSonera (Sweden); provides mobile cellular communications services under the brand name 'Yoigo'.

Regulatory Authorities

Comisión del Mercado de las Telecomunicaciones (CMT): Alcalá 37, 28014 Madrid; tel. (91) 3724300; fax (91) 3724205; e-mail cmt@cmt.es; internet www.cmt.es; f. 1996; Pres. REINALDO RODRÍGUEZ ILLERA; Sec. IGNACIO REDONDO ANDREU.

Secretaría de Estado de Telecommunicaciones y para la Sociedad de la Información: Ministerio de Industria, Turismo y Comercio, Capitán Haya 41, 2°, 28071 Madrid; tel. (91) 3461583; fax (91) 3461520; internet www.setsi.mityc.es.

BROADCASTING

Corporación Radio Televisión Española (RTVE): Edif. Prado del Rey, 28223 Pozuelo de Alarcón, Madrid; tel. (91) 5815461; fax (91) 5815454; e-mail direccion.comunicacion@rtve.es; internet www.rtve.es; state-owned company; controls and co-ordinates radio and television; incorporates Televisión Española, Televisión Española Internacional, Televisión Española Temática, Radio Nacional de España, Instituto Oficial de Radio y Televisión and the Orquesta Sinfónica y Coro; formerly Ente Público Radio Televisión Española; renamed and reformed in 2007 to become independent of govt influence; Pres. LUIS FERNÁNDEZ FERNÁNDEZ.

Independent Companies

Compañía de Radio y Televisión de Galicia (CRTVG): Bando-San Marcos, 15820 Santiago de Compostela (A Coruña); tel. (981) 540640; fax (981) 540829; internet www.crtvg.es; f. 1985; Galician language station; Dir-Gen. BENIGNO SÁNCHEZ GARCÍA.

Corporació Catalana de Mitjans Audiovisuals (CCMA): Ganduxer 117, 08022 Barcelona; tel. (93) 4444800; fax (93) 4444824; e-mail comunicacio@ccma.cat; internet www.ccma.cat; f. 1983; Catalan language station; six television channels and four radio stations; Pres. ALBERT SÁEZ I CASAS; Sec.-Gen. ROSA CULLELL I MUNIESA.

Euskal Irrati Telebista (EITB)/Radiotelevisión Vasca: 48215 Iurreta (Vizcaya); tel. (94) 6031000; fax (94) 6031095; e-mail info@eitb.com; internet www.eitb.com; f. 1982; Basque station; two television channels, two international television channels and five radio stations; Dir-Gen. ANDONI ORTUZAR ARRUABARRENA.

Onda Regional de Murcia: Avda Libertad 6, bajo, 30009 Murcia; tel. (968) 200000; fax (968) 230850; e-mail felipe.nicolas@orm.es; internet www.orm.es; Dir-Gen. JOAQUIN AZPARREN IRIGOYEN.

Ràdiotelevisió Valenciana (RTVV): Polígono Accés Ademús s/n, 46100 Burjassot (Valencia); tel. (96) 3183000; fax (96) 3183001; e-mail dgen@rtvv.es; internet www.rtvv.es; f. 1984; Dir-Gen. PEDRO GARCÍA GIMENO.

Radio Televisión de Andalucía (RTVA): Sede Central RTVA, Pabellón de Canal Sur (Antigua Pabellón de Andalucía), José de Gálvez s/n, 41090 San Juan de Aznalfarache (Sevilla); tel. (95) 5054600; fax (95) 5054937; e-mail comunicacion@rtva.es; internet www.rtva.es; Dir-Gen. RAFAEL CAMACHO.

Radio Televisión Madrid (RTVM): Paseo del Príncipe 3, Ciudad de la Imagen, 28223 Pozuelo de Alarcón (Madrid); tel. (91) 5128200; fax (91) 5128300; e-mail prensa@telemadrid.es; internet www.telemadrid.es; Dir-Gen. FRANCISCO GIMÉNEZ-ALEMÁN.

Radiotelevisión Canaria (RTVC): Avda Bravo Murillo 5, Edif. Mapfre, 1°, 38003 Santa Cruz de Tenerife; tel. (922) 470200; fax (922) 273173; e-mail tvcanaria@tvcanaria.tv; internet www.tvcanaria.tv; f. 1997; broadcasts in the Canaries; Dir-Gen. FRANCISCO MORENO GARCÍA.

Radiotelevisión Castilla-La Mancha (RTVCM): Río Alberche s/n, Edif. RTVCM, Polígono Santa María de Benquerencia, 45007 Toledo; tel. (925) 288600; fax (925) 287883; e-mail comunicacion@rtvcm.es; internet www.rtvcm.es; Dir-Gen. JORDI GARCÍA CANDAU.

Federation

Federación de Asociaciones de Radio y Televisión de España: Evaristo San Miguel 8, 28008 Madrid; tel. (91) 5481222; fax (91) 5593630; e-mail artv@jazzfree.com; Pres. FEDERICO SÁNCHEZ AGUILAR; Sec.-Gen. JOSÉ ESTEBAN VERDES.

RADIO

Radio Nacional de España (RNE): Casa de la Radio, Prado del Rey, 28223 Pozuelo de Alarcón (Madrid); tel. (91) 5817000; fax (91) 5183240; e-mail secretario_general.rne@rtve.es; internet www.rne.es; broadcasts Radio 1, Radio Clásica, Radio 3, Radio 4, Radio 5 Todo Noticias; 17 regional stations; Dir-Gen. JAVIER ARENAS; Sec.-Gen. EDUARDO HERNÁNDEZ.

Radio Exterior de España (REE): Apdo 156.202, 28080 Madrid; tel. (91) 3461081; fax (91) 3461815; e-mail dir_radioexterior.rne@rtve.es; overseas service of RNE; broadcasts in 10 languages; includes a world service in Spanish; Dir FRANCISCO JAVIER GARRIGÓS.

Independent Stations

Ambiente Musical: Paseo de la Castellana 210, 10°, 28046 Madrid; tel. (91) 3454000; fax (91) 3591321; e-mail estudio@musicam.net; Dir-Gen. MANEL SALLÉS CARCELLER.

Cadena 100: Alfonso XI 4, 28014 Madrid; tel. (91) 5951244; fax (91) 5225454; e-mail contacto@cadena100.es; internet www.cadena100.es; Dir JAVIER LLANO ABRIL.

Cadena M80: Gran Vía 32, 8°, 28013 Madrid; tel. (91) 3470700; fax (91) 5228693; e-mail programas@m80radio.com; internet www.m80radio.com; Dir MANUEL DÁVILA MORENO.

Cadena Dial: Gran Vía 32, 8°, 28013 Madrid; tel. (91) 3470700; fax (91) 5211753; internet www.cadenadial.com; e-mail direccion@cadenadial.com; Dir JUAN CARLOS CHAVES.

Cadena Ona Catalana: Aragón 390–394, 2°, 08013 Barcelona; tel. (93) 2449990; fax (93) 2459459; e-mail onacatalana@onacatalana.com; internet www.onacatalana.com; Dir-Gen. JOSEP PUIGBÓ.

Cadena Ondacero RadioVoz Galicia: Ronda de Outeiro 1, bajo, 15006 A Coruña; tel. (981) 180600; fax (981) 180477; e-mail manuel.mantilla@radiovoz.es; internet www.radiovoz.es; Dir MANTILLA MANUEL.

Cadena de Ondas Populares Españolas/Radio Popular, SA (COPE): Alfonso XI 4, 3°, 28014 Madrid; tel. (91) 5951200; fax (91) 5322008; e-mail comunicacion@cope.es; internet www.cope.es; f. 1959; controlled by Roman Catholic Church; numerous medium-wave and FM stations; Pres. and CEO ALFONSO CORONEL DE PALMA.

Cadena Radio España/Radio España Madrid: Manuel Silvela 9, 28010 Madrid; tel. (91) 4475300; fax (91) 5938413; Pres. and Dir-Gen. JOSÉ ANTONIO SÁNCHEZ.

Cadena Radio Estudio: Pasaje de la Radio 1, Alcobendas, 28100 Madrid; tel. (91) 6531199; fax (91) 6533072; e-mail radioestudio@futurnet.es; Dir-Gen. ROMÁN BEITIA ALONSO.

Cadena Radiolé: Gran Vía 32, 7°, 28013 Madrid; tel. (91) 3470740; Dir JUAN CARLOS CHAVES.

Cadena TOP Radio España: Manuel Silvela 9, 28010 Madrid; tel. (91) 4475300; fax (91) 4477026; internet www.topradio.es; Pres. JOSÉ ANTONIO SÁNCHEZ.

Catalunya Ràdio, SRG, SA: Avda Diagonal 614–616, 08021 Barcelona; tel. (93) 3069200; fax (93) 3069201; e-mail correo@catradio.cat; internet www.catradio.cat; f. 1983; run by Catalan autonomous govt; four channels: Catalunya Ràdio, Catalunya Música, Catalunya Informació, iCat; six internet channels; Dir OLEGUER SARSANEDAS PICAS.

COMRàdio: Pavelló Cambó, Recinte de la Maternitat, Travessera de les Corts 131–159, 08028 Barcelona; tel. (93) 5080600; fax (93) 5080810; e-mail comradio@comradio.com; internet www.comradio.com; Dir-Gen. JORDI LLONCH MASSANÉS.

EITB Radio: Miramón Pasealekua 172, 20014 San Sebastián; tel. (943) 012300; fax (943) 012295; e-mail info@eitb.com; internet www.eitb.com; run by Basque autonomous govt; broadcasts on FM and MW as Euskadi Irratia, Radio Euskadi (Bilbao), Radio Vitoria (Vitoria-Gasteiz) and EITB Irratia; Dir JULIAN BELOKI GERRA.

Europa FM: Bueso Pineda 7, 28043 Madrid; tel. (91) 4134361; fax (91) 4137175; e-mail europafm@europafm.es; internet europafm.com; Pres. FRANCISCO GAYA GONZÁLEZ.

Grupo Pavesa Comunicación, SL—Radio Ondas Riojanas: Sabto Domingo 5, 26580 Arnedo; tel. (941) 383350; fax (941)

SPAIN

383383; e-mail ondarioja@ondarioja.com; internet www.ondarioja.com; Pres. PEDRO VEGA HERNÁNDEZ.

Los 40 Principales: Gran Vía 32, 8°, 28013 Madrid; tel. (91) 3470705; fax (91) 5317370; internet www.los40.com; Dir JAUME BARÓ GARRIGA.

Muinmo, SL: Apolonio Morales 6–10, 28036 Madrid; tel. (91) 3536017; fax (91) 3536019; Dir-Gen. MIGUEL ANGEL MONTERO QUEVEDO.

Onda Cero Radio (OCR): José Ortega y Gasset 22–24, 28006 Madrid; tel. (91) 436400; fax (91) 436101; e-mail ondacero@ondacero.es; internet www.ondacero.es; owned by Telefónica; Dir-Gen. JOSÉ LUIS OROSA ROLDAN.

Radio Autonomía Madrid, SA: Paseo del Príncipe 3, Ciudad de la Imagen, 28223 Pozuelo de Alarcón, Madrid; tel. (91) 5128649; fax (91) 5123752; e-mail ondamadrid@ondamadrid.com; internet www.ondamadrid.es; f. 1985; Dir MIGUEL PÉREZ-PLA DE VIU.

Ràdio Autonomia Valenciana, SA/Ràdio Nou: Avda Blasco Ibáñez 136, 46022 Valencia; tel. (96) 3183600; fax (96) 3183602; internet www.radionou.com; Dir JAVIER GOMAR ALBERT.

Radio ECCA: Avda Escaleritas 64, 1°, 35011 Las Palmas de Gran Canaria; tel. (928) 257400; fax (928) 207395; e-mail info@radioecca.org; internet www.radioecca.org; adult education; Dir-Gen. LUCAS LÓPEZ PÉREZ.

Radio Galega (RG): San Marcos, 15780 Santiago de Compostela; tel. (981) 540940; fax (981) 540919; e-mail radiogalega@crtvg.es; internet www.crtvg.es; f. 1985; run by Galician autonomous Govt; Man. Dir VIRGILIO COSTAS PUMAR.

Radio Surco-Castilla La Mancha: Concordia 14, Bajo C, 13700 Tomelloso (Ciudad Real); tel. (926) 505959; fax (926) 505961; e-mail r.surco@retemail.es; internet www.radiosurco.es; Dir FRANCISCO CASTELLANOS CUELLAR.

Punto Radio: e-mail info@puntoradio.com; internet www.puntoradio.com; f. 2005; Pres. JOSÉ MARÍA BERGARECHE.

Sociedad Española de Radiodifusión (Cadena SER): Gran Vía 32, 28013 Madrid; tel. (91) 3477700; fax (91) 3470709; internet www.cadenaser.com; f. 1924; 235 regional stations; owned by Grupo PRISA; Dir-Gen. RAÚL RODRÍGUEZ.

Digital Radio

In March 1999 two digital radio licences were awarded for the frequencies MF-1 and MF-2. MF-1 was controlled by Cope, Intereconomía, Recoletos and El Mundo, while MF-2 was controlled by SER, Onda Rambla-Planeta, Onda Cero, Radio España, Onda Digital and Prensa Española. MF-1 began broadcasting in Madrid and Barcelona in July 2000.

Radio Association

Asociación Española de Radiodifusión Comercial (AERC): Plaza Independencia 2, 4° dcha, 28001 Madrid; tel. (91) 4357072; fax (91) 4356196; e-mail aerc@retemail.es; groups nearly all commercial radio stations; Pres. RAFAEL PÉREZ DEL PUERTO; Sec.-Gen. ALFONSO RUÍZ DE ASSIN.

TELEVISION

Legislation relating to the ending of TVE's monopoly and the regulation of private TV stations was approved in April 1988. In 2005–06 the existing private terrestrial broadcasters—Antena 3, Telecinco and Canal+—were joined by Cuatro (operated by Sogecable) and La Sexta. It was envisaged that analogue broadcasts would cease in 2010.

Televisión Española (TVE): Edif. Prado del Rey, 28223 Pozuelo de Alarcón, Madrid; tel. (91) 3464968; fax (91) 3463055; e-mail consultas@rtve.es; internet www.tve.es; broadcasts on TVE-1 and La 2; production centres in Barcelona and Las Palmas de Gran Canaria and 15 regional centres; broadcasts to Europe and the Americas on Canal Internacional; Dir JAVIER PONS.

Independent Stations

Antena 3 Televisión: Avda de Isla Graciosa s/n, 28700 San Sebastián de los Reyes, Madrid; tel. (91) 6230500; fax (91) 6230994; e-mail antena3tv@antena3tv.com; internet www.antena3tv.com; f. 1989; owned by Grupo Planeta; Pres. JOSÉ MANUEL LARA BOSCH.

Canal 9—Televisió Autonómica Valenciana (TVV): Polígon Accés Ademús, 46100 Burjassot (Valencia); tel. (96) 3183000; fax (96) 3183001; e-mail wmaster@rtvv.es; internet www.rtvv.es; f. 1989; second channel commenced operations in 1997; Dir GENOVEVA REIG.

Canal Sur Televisión: Carretera San Juan de Aznalfarache, Apdo 132, 41920 San Juan de Aznalfarache, Sevilla; tel. (95) 5607600; fax (95) 5054740; e-mail csalinas@cica.es; internet www.canalsur.es; f. 1989; regional station for Andalusia; Dir-Gen. RAFAEL CAMACHO.

Euskal Telebista—ETB (TV Vasca): 48215 Iurreta (Vizcaya); tel. (94) 6031000; fax (94) 6031095; e-mail info@eitb.com; internet www.eitb.com; f. 1982; 2 channels broadcasting to Basque Country, one in Basque, one in Spanish; Dir BINGEN ZUPIRIA GOROSTIDI.

Popular TV: Alfonso XI 4, 28014 Madrid; tel. (91) 3096669; e-mail populartv@populartv.net; internet www.populartv.net; broadcasts on a local and national level; Pres. BERNARDO HERRÁEZ RUBIO; Dir-Gen. ALEJANDRO SAMANES PRAT.

Sogecable: Avda de los Artesanos 6, 28760 Tres Cantos (Madrid); tel. (91) 7367000; internet www.sogecable.es; f. 1989; satellite and digital television, internet services; operates Cuatro (national terrestrial channel), Digital+, (digital provider), Canal Satélite Digital, CNN+, Compañía Independiente de Televisión, Gestsport, Sogecine; 43.2% owned by Grupo PRISA, 16.7% by Telefónica; Pres. RODOLFO MARTÍN VILLA.

Grupo Telecinco: Carretera de Irún, Km 11,700, 28049 Madrid; tel. (91) 155555; e-mail oinf@telecinco.es; internet www.telecinco.es; f. 1990; private commercial national network; jt owned by Grupo Mediaset (Italy), Grupo Correo de Comunicación, Ice Finance (The Netherlands); Pres. ALEJANDRO ECHEVARRÍA.

Televisió de Catalunya: Carrer de la TV3, s/n, 08970 Sant Joan Despi, Barcelona; tel. (93) 4999333; fax (93) 4730671; internet www.tv3.cat; f. 1983; broadcasts in Catalan; Dir FRANCESC ESCRIBANO.

Televisión de Galicia (TVG): San Marcos, Apdo 707, 15820 Santiago de Compostela; tel. (981) 540640; fax (981) 540719; e-mail crtvg@crtvg.es; internet www.crtvg.es; f. 1985; broadcasts in Galician; Man. Dir ANGEL QUINTANILLA LOUZAO.

Televisión Autonomía Madrid, SA (Telemadrid): Paseo del Príncipe de España 1, 28223 Pozuelo de Alarcón (Madrid); tel. (91) 5128200; fax (91) 5128300; e-mail correo@telemadrid.es; internet www.telemadrid.es; commenced transmissions in 1989; controlled by RTVM; cultural channel, laOtra, commenced transmission in March 2001; Dir-Gen. FRANCISCO GIMÉNEZ ALEMÁN; Man. Dir FERNANDO JEREZ.

Other Satellite, Cable and Digital Television

By 2000 more than 2m. Spanish homes and businesses were served by cable telecommunications and some 900,000 received digital television, at which time there were more than 100 satellite, cable and digital television broadcasters in Spain. Many of these were operated by existing broadcasting companies. Others include:

Chello Multicanal: Saturno 1, Pozuelo de Alarcón, 28224 Madrid; tel. (91) 7141080; fax (91) 3516873; e-mail lineadirecta@chellomulticanal.com; internet www.chellomulticanal.com/es; f. 1996; cable; operates nine channels; Dir-Gen. EDUARDO ZULUETA.

Grupo Auna: Avda Diagonal 579–585, 08014 Barcelona; internet www.auna.es; part of ONO; telecommunications, internet and cable TV; operates the cable telecommunications providers Aragón de Cable, Cabletelca, Cable i Televisió de Catalunya, Madritel, Supercable de Andalucía, Supercable Sevilla and Supercable Almería.

Hispasat: Gobelas 41, 28023 Madrid; tel. (91) 7102540; fax (91) 3729000; e-mail comunicacion@hispasat.es; internet www.hispasat.com; satellite; Pres. PETRA MATEOS.

Telecable de Asturias: Marqués de Pidal 11, bajo, 33004 Oviedo, Asturias; tel. (985) 081111; fax (985) 081112; e-mail info@telecable.es; internet www.telecable.es; cable; f. 1995; operator for Asturias.

Telefónica Cable: Calle Virgilio 2, Edif. 2, 2°, 28223 Pozuelo de Alarcón (Madrid); tel. (91) 5129510; e-mail cac@tcable.es; internet www.telefonica-cable.com; f. 1997; cable.

Veo TV: Plaza de la Castellana 40, 28046 Madrid; internet www.veo.es; f. 2001; digital; Dir EDUARDO SÁNCHEZ ILLANA.

Associations

Agrupación de Operadores de Cable (AOC): Obenque 4, 28042 Madrid; f. 1998; by CYC Madrid, Retecal, Telecable and Grupo Cable; group of cable telecommunications operators; Dir JESÚS PELEGRÍN.

Promoción e Identificación de Servicios Emergentes de Telecomunicaciones Avanzadas (PISTA): Secretaría de Estado de Telecomunicaciones y para la Sociedad de la Información, Capitán Haya 41, 28071 Madrid; tel. (91) 3462820; fax (91) 3461567; e-mail jmontalban@mityc.es; part of Ministry of Industry, Tourism and Trade; initiative for the promotion and identification of emerging advanced telecommunications.

Unión de Televisiones Comerciales Asociadas (UTECA): Maldonado 4, bajo C, 28006 Madrid; tel. (91) 5759778; fax (91) 5776754; e-mail uteca@uteca.com; internet www.uteca.com; f. 1998; represents commercial television interests; Pres. JOSÉ MANUEL LARA BOSCH; Sec.-Gen. JORGE DEL CORRAL Y DÍEZ DEL CORRAL.

SPAIN   *Directory*

Finance

(cap. = capital, res = reserves, dep. = deposits, brs = branches, m. = million, amounts in euros)

BANKING

Central Bank

Banco de España: Alcalá 48, 28014 Madrid; tel. (91) 3386063; fax (91) 3385884; e-mail bde@bde.es; internet www.bde.es; f. 1782; granted exclusive right of issue in 1874; nationalized 1962; granted a degree of autonomy in 1994; cap. 1,000.0m., res 5,793.6m., dep. 38,344.6m. (Dec. 2006); Gov. MIGUEL ÁNGEL FERNÁNDEZ ORDÓÑEZ; 22 brs.

Principal Commercial and Development Banks

Banca March SA: Avda Alejandro Rosselló 8, 07002 Palma de Mallorca; tel. (971) 779100; fax (971) 779187; e-mail divinter@bancamarch.es; internet www.bancamarch.es; f. 1926; cap. 29.2m., res 1,576.6m., dep. 7,573.4m. (Dec. 2006); Pres. JOSÉ CARLOS MARCH DELGADO; Man. Dir FRANCISCO VERDÚ PONS; 271 brs.

Banco de Andalucía: Fernández y González 4, 41001 Sevilla; tel. (95) 4594700; fax (95) 4594802; internet www.bancoandalucia.es; f. 1844; 80.1% owned by Grupo Banco Popular; cap. 16.3m., res 938.0m., dep. 11,153.2m. (Dec. 2007); Pres. MIGUEL DE SOLÍS Y MARTÍNEZ CAMPOS; Gen. Man. FRANCISCO PARDO MARTÍNEZ; 298 brs.

Banco Bilbao Vizcaya Argentaria (BBVA): Paseo de la Castellana 81, 28046 Madrid; tel. (91) 4876000; fax (91) 4876417; internet www.bbva.es; f. 2000 by merger; cap. 1,837.0m., res 20,761.0m., dep. 450,733.4m. (Dec. 2007); Pres. JOSÉ IGNACIO GOIRIGOLZARRI TELLAECHE; Chair. and Chief Exec. FRANCISCO GONZÁLEZ RODRÍGUEZ; 3,375 brs.

Banco Caixa Geral: Juan Ignacio Luca de Tena 1, 28027 Madrid; tel. (91) 3099000; fax (91) 3209275; e-mail extranjero@bancaixageral.es; internet www.bancocaixageral.es; f. 1969; present name adopted 2006; 99.6% owned by Caixa Geral de Depósitos (Portugal); cap. 360.3m., res −45.4m., dep. 3,750.7m. (Dec. 2006); Pres. ANTÓNIO MALDONADO GONELHA; Chief Exec. FERNANDO FARIA DE OLIVEIRA.

Banco de Castilla: Plaza de los Bandos 10, 37002 Salamanca; tel. (923) 290000; fax (923) 211902; internet www.bancocastilla.es; f. 1915; 95.2% owned by Grupo Banco Popular; cap. 26.0m., res 404.2m., dep. 4,272.8m. (Dec. 2006); Pres. GABRIEL GANCEDO DE SERAS; Gen. Man. JOSÉ BRAVO JIMÉNEZ; 199 brs.

Banco Cooperativo Español: Virgen de los Peligros 6, 28013 Madrid; tel. (91) 5956700; fax (91) 5956800; internet www.cajarural.com; f. 1990; cap. 72.9m., res 123.1m., dep. 8,252.5m. (Dec. 2007); Chair. JOSÉ LUIS GARCÍA PALACIOS; Gen. Man. JAVIER PETIT ASUMENDI; 4,100 brs.

Banco Español de Crédito S.A. (Banesto): Gran Vía de Hortaleza 3, 28043 Madrid; tel. (91) 3383100; fax (91) 3381883; e-mail uninternac@banesto.es; internet www.banesto.es; f. 1902; cap. 548.5m., res 2,631.2m., dep. 96,240.2m. (Dec. 2006); Chair. ANA PATRICIA BOTÍN-SANZ DE SAUTUOLA Y O'SHEA; CEO JOSÉ A. GARCÍA CANTERA; 1,703 brs.

Banco de Galicia: Policarpo Sanz 23, Pontevedra, 36202 Vigo; tel. (986) 822100; fax (986) 822101; internet www.bancogalicia.es; f. 1918; part of Grupo Banco Popular Español; cap. 9.1m., res 337.7m., dep. 3,624.3m. (Dec. 2006); Pres. JESÚS PLATERO; Gen. Man. JUAN J. RUBIO; 141 brs.

Banco Gallego S.A.: Avda Linares Rivas 30, 15005 A Coruña; tel. (981) 127950; fax (981) 126582; e-mail intervenciongeneral@bancogallego.com; internet www.bancogallego.es; f. 1847; cap. 83.4m., res 66.9m., dep. 3,786.9m. (Dec. 2007); Pres. JUAN MANUEL URGOITI LÓPEZ-OCAÑA; Gen. Man. JOSÉ LUIS LOSADA RODRÍGUEZ; 163 brs.

Banco Guipuzcoano, SA: Avda de la Libertad 21, 20004 San Sebastián; tel. (943) 418100; fax (943) 418337; e-mail bgintnal@bancogui.com; internet www.bancogui.es; f. 1899; cap. 37.4m., res 539.5m., dep. 9,099.3m. (Dec. 2007); Pres. JOSÉ MARÍA AGUIRRE GONZÁLEZ; Gen. Man. JUAN LUIS ARRIETA; 265 brs.

Banco Pastor: Cantón Pequeño 1, Edif. Pastor, 15003 La Coruña; tel. (981) 127600; fax (981) 210301; internet www.bancopastor.es; f. 1776; cap. 86.4m., res 1,068.2m., dep. 21,604.3m. (Dec. 2006); Chair. JOSÉ MARÍA ARIAS MOSQUERA; Chief Exec. JORGE GOST GIJÓN; 568 brs.

Banco Popular Español: Velázquez 34, 28001 Madrid; tel. (91) 5207000; fax (91) 5783274; internet www.bancopopular.es; f. 1926; cap. 5,274.0m., dep. 97,801.5m. (Dec. 2007); Pres. ÁNGEL CARLOS RON GÜIMIL; Chief Exec. JOSÉ MARIA LUCIA; 2,224 brs.

Banco de Sabadell: POB 1, Plaza Sant Roc 20, Sabadell, 08201 Barcelona; tel. (93) 7289289; fax (93) 7270606; e-mail info@bancsabadell.com; internet www.bancsabadell.com; f. 1881; cap. 153.0m., res 3,232.8m., dep. 63,643.6m. (Dec. 2006); Chair. JOSEP OLIU; 1,186 brs.

Banco Santander: Plaza de Canalejas 1, 28014 Madrid; tel. (91) 5581111; internet www.santander.com; f. 1857; cap. 3,127.1m., res 44,550.3m., dep. 812,543.0m. (Dec. 2007); Chair. EMILIO BOTÍN-SANZ DE SAUTUOLA Y GARCÍA DE LOS RÍOS; Man. Dir JUAN BOTÍN; 8,848 brs.

Banco Urquijo, SA: Príncipe de Vergara 131, 28002 Madrid; tel. (91) 3372000; fax (91) 3372096; internet www.bancourquijo.es; f. 1870; part of Grupo Banco de Sabadell; cap. 92.7m., res 148.7m., dep. 3,675.0m. (Dec. 2004); Pres. FERDINAND VERDONCK; CEO ALFONSO TOLCHEFF; 60 brs.

Banco de Valencia: Pintor Sorolla 2–4, 46002 Valencia; tel. (96) 3984500; fax (96) 3984570; e-mail division.internacional@bancodevalencia.es; internet www.bancodevalencia.es; f. 1900; cap. 102.9m., res 747.7m., dep. 14,550.4m. (Dec. 2006); Pres. JOSÉ LUIS OLIVAS MARTÍNEZ; Gen. Man. DOMINGO PARRA SORIA; 428 brs.

Banco de Vasconia: Plaza del Castillo 39, 31001 Pamplona; tel. (948) 179600; fax (948) 179665; e-mail servicioscentrales@bancovasconia.es; internet www.bancovasconia.es; f. 1901; 96.9% owned by Banco Popular Español; cap. 9.6m., res 173.5m., dep. 3,351.4m. (Dec. 2006); Pres. JOSÉ R. RODRÍGUEZ GARCÍA; Gen. Man. MIGUEL MOZO LOBATO; 121 brs.

Bankinter: Paseo de la Castellana 29, 28046 Madrid; tel. (91) 3397500; fax (91) 3397556; e-mail international@bankinter.es; internet www.bankinter.com; f. 1965; finances industrial and business dealings with medium- and long-term loans and investments; cap. 117.9m., res 1,333.5m., dep. 43,174.4m. (Dec. 2006); Chair. JUAN ARENA DE LA MORA; CEO JAIME ECHEGOYEN; 253 brs.

Barclays Bank SA: Plaza de Colón 1, 28046 Madrid; tel. (91) 3361000; fax (91) 3361134; internet www.barclays.es; f. 1974; cap. 157.8m., res 666.5m., dep. 19,251.6m. (Dec. 2005); 99.7% owned by Barclays Bank PLC (United Kingdom); Chair. C. MARTÍNEZ DE CAMPOS; 163 brs.

Savings Banks

Bilbao Bizkaia Kutxa (Caja de Ahorros Municipal de Bilbao/Caja de Ahorros Vizcaina): Gran Vía 30–32, 48009 Bilbao; tel. (94) 4017000; fax (94) 4017800; e-mail bbktelefono@bbk.es; internet www.bbk.es; f. 1907; cap. 0.0m., res 3,517.8m., dep. 23,066.9m. (Dec. 2007); Chair. and Chief Exec. XABIER DE IRALA; 330 brs.

CAIXANOVA (Caixa de Aforros de Vigo, Ourense e Pontevedra): Avda García Barbon 1–3, 36201 Vigo; tel. (986) 828200; fax (986) 828238; e-mail internacionalcx@caixanova.com; internet www.caixanova.com; f. 1929; present name adopted 2000; cap. 0.0m., res 1,543.4m., dep. 20,0506.5m. (Dec. 2006); Pres. and Chair. JULIO FERNÁNDEZ GAYOSO; Gen. Man. JOSÉ LUIS PEGO ALONSO; 526 brs.

Caixa d'Estalvis de Catalunya (Caixa Catalunya): Plaza Antonio Maura 6, 08003 Barcelona; tel. (93) 4845000; fax (93) 4845141; e-mail international.services@caixacatalunya.es; internet www.caixacatalunya.es; f. 1926; res 2,664.8m., dep. 60,631.4m., total assets 67,551.4m. (Dec. 2006); Pres. NARCÍS SERRA; Gen. Man. JOSEP ADOLF TODÓ; 936 brs.

Caixa d'Estalvis de Sabadell (Caixa Sabadell): Gràcia 17, Sabadell, 08201 Barcelona; tel. (93) 7286700; fax (93) 7286555; e-mail info@caixasabadell.es; internet www.caixasabadell.com; f. 1859; res 503.4m., dep. 9,845.1m., total assets 11,808.8m. (Dec. 2006); Pres. LLUÍS BRUNET BERCH; Gen. Man. JORDI MESTRE GONZÁLEZ; 334 brs.

Caixa d'Estalvis de Tarragona (Caixa Tarragona): Plaza Imperial Tàrraco 6, 43005 Tarragona; tel. (977) 299200; fax (977) 299250; e-mail liniapreferent@caixatarragona.es; internet www.caixatarragona.es; f. 1952; res 438.0m., dep. 6,460.3m., total assets 7,065.7m. (Dec. 2006); Pres. GABRIEL FERRATÉ PASCUAL; Gen. Man. RAFAEL JENÉ VILLAGRASA; 289 brs.

Caixa d'Estalvis de Terrassa (Caixaterrassa): Ramble d'Ègara 350, 08221 Terrasa; tel. (93) 7397700; fax (93) 7397777; e-mail ct.0560.3@caixaterrassa.es; internet www.caixaterrassa.es; f. 1877; res 586.5m., dep. 7,848.9m., total assets 10,121.1m. (Dec. 2006); Pres. FRANCES ASTALS COMA; Gen. Man. ENRIC MATA TARRAGÓ; 164 brs.

Caja de Ahorros de Asturias (CAJASTUR): Plaza de la Escandalera 2, 33003 Oviedo; tel. (98) 5102222; fax (98) 5215649; e-mail extranjero@cajastur.es; internet www.cajastur.es; f. 1945; res 1,707.8m., dep. 9,614.9m., total assets 11,946.5m. (Dec. 2006); Pres. and CEO MANUEL MENÉNDEZ MENÉNDEZ; 343 brs.

Caja de Ahorros de Castilla la Mancha (CCM): Parque San Julián 20, 16002 Cuenca; tel. (969) 177314; fax (969) 177606; e-mail webmaster@ccm.es; internet www.ccm.es; f. 1992; management assumed by Banco de España in March 2009; cap. 0.0m., res 997.2m., dep. 17,174.4m. (Dec. 2006); Pres. (vacant); 390 brs.

Caja de Ahorros de Galicia (Caixa Galicia): Rúa Nueva 30, 15003 A Coruña; tel. (981) 188000; fax (981) 188001; internet www.caixagalicia.es; f. 1978; cap. 0.0m., res 2,225.9m., dep. 43,568.9m. (Dec. 2007); Pres. MAURO VARELA PÉREZ; Gen. Man. JOSÉ LUIS MÉNDEZ LÓPEZ; 866 brs.

Caja de Ahorros de la Inmaculada de Aragón (CAI): Paseo Independencia 10, 50004 Zaragoza; tel. (976) 718100; fax (976)

SPAIN
Directory

718377; e-mail info.corporativa@cai.es; internet www.cai.es; f. 1905; res 687.4m., dep. 7,865.4m., total assets 8,743.9m. (Dec. 2006); Pres. ANTONIO AZNAR GRASA; 238 brs.

Caja de Ahorros del Mediterráneo (CAM): San Fernando 40, 03001 Alicante; tel. (96) 5905000; fax (96) 5905044; e-mail cam@cam.es; internet www.cam.es; f. 1875; cap. 3.0m., res 2,980.3m., dep. 65,369.2m. (Dec. 2007); Chair. VICENTE SALA BELLÓ; Gen. Man. ROBERTO LÓPEZ ABAD; 1,067 brs.

Caja de Ahorros y Monte de Piedad de las Baleares 'Sa Nostra': Ramón Llull 2, 07001 Palma de Mallorca; tel. (971) 171717; fax (971) 171797; e-mail sanostra@sanostra.es; internet www.sanostra.es; res 543.7m., dep. 8,693.8m., total assets 10,099.2m. (Dec. 2006); Chair. FERNANDO ALZAMORA CARBONELL; Gen. Man. PEDRO BATLE MAYO; 229 brs.

Caja de Ahorros y Monte de Piedad del Círculo Católico de Obreros de Burgos (CajaCírculo): Avda de los Reyes Católicos 1, 09005 Burgos; tel. (947) 288200; fax (947) 288210; internet www.cajacirculo.es; f. 1909; res 471.1m., dep. 3,902.2m., total assets 4,547.4m. (Dec. 2006); Chair. JOSÉ IGNACIO MIJANGOS LINAZA; Gen. Man. SANTIAGO RUIZ DIEZ; 176 brs.

Caja de Ahorros y Monte de Piedad de Guipúzcoa y San Sebastián (Gipuzkoa eta Donstiako Aurrezki Kutxa): Garibai 15, Apdo 1389, 20004 San Sebastián; tel. (943) 001000; fax (943) 001045; e-mail infokutxa@kutxa.es; internet www.kutxa.es; f. 1896; cap. 215.6m., res 2,427.6m., dep. 20,835.1m. (Dec. 2007); Pres. and Chair. XABIO ITURBE OTAEGI; 330 brs.

Caja de Ahorros y Monte de Piedad de Madrid (Caja Madrid): Plaza de Celenque 2, 28013 Madrid; tel. (91) 3792000; fax (91) 5216980; e-mail bvegasga@cajamadrid.es; internet www.cajamadrid.es; f. 1869; cap. and res 6,775.0m., dep. 145,175.4m. (Dec. 2007); Pres. MIGUEL BLESA DE LA PARRA; 1,914 brs.

Caja de Ahorros y Monte de Piedad de Navarra (Caja Navarra): Avda de Carlos III 8, 31002 Pamplona; tel. (948) 222333; fax (948) 208269; e-mail sac@can.es; internet www.can.es; f. 1921; cap. 0.0m., res 766.6m., dep. 11,554.7m. (Dec. 2006); Pres. MIGUEL SANZ SESMA; Gen. Man. ENRIQUE GOÑI BELTRÁN DE GARIZURIETA; 323 brs.

Caja de Ahorros y Monte de Piedad de Zaragoza, Aragón y Rioja (IBERCAJA): Plaza del Paraíso 2, 50008 Zaragoza; tel. (976) 767676; fax (976) 214417; internet www.ibercaja.es; f. 1876; res 1,995.5m., dep. 32,420.1m., total assets 35,237.2m. (Dec. 2006); Chair. AMADO FRANCO LAHOZ; Gen. Man. JOSÉ LUIS AGUIRRE LOASO; 1,008 brs.

Caja de Ahorros de Murcia (Cajamurcia): Gran Vía Escultor Salzillo 23, 30005 Murcia; tel. (968) 361600; fax (968) 306160; internet www.cajamurcia.es; f. 1965; cap. 0.0m., res 1,248.7m., dep. 14,649.8m., total assets 16,719.6m. (Dec. 2006); Pres. JUAN ROCA GUILLAMÓN; Gen. Man. CARLOS EGEA KRAUEL; 415 brs.

Caja de Ahorros y Pensiones de Barcelona (La Caixa): Avda Diagonal 621–629, 08028 Barcelona; tel. (93) 4046000; fax (93) 3395703; e-mail estudis@lacaixa.es; internet www.lacaixa.es; f. 1990; res 11,186.1m., dep. 172,754.9m., total assets 209,123.2m. (Dec. 2006); Chair. RICARDO FORNESA; Pres. and Chief Exec. ISIDRO FAINÉ; 5,053 brs.

Caja de Ahorros de Valencia, Castellón y Alicante (BANCAJA) (Caixa d'Estalvis de València, Castelló i Alacant): Pintor Sorolla, 8, 46002 Valencia; tel. (96) 3875500; fax (96) 3527550; internet www.bancaja.es; f. 1878; res 3,533.9m., dep. 89,390.1m., total assets 99,584.9m. (Dec. 2007); Chair. JOSÉ LUIS OLIVAS MARTÍNEZ; Gen. Man. JOSÉ FERNANDO GARCÍA CHECA; 1,055 brs.

Caja Duero (Caja de Ahorros de Salamanca y Soria): Plaza de los Bandos 15–17, 37002 Salamanca; tel. (923) 279300; fax (923) 270680; internet www.cajaduero.es; f. 1881; res 1,092.3m., dep. 14,843.6m., total assets 16,774.3m. (Dec. 2006); Pres. and Chair. JULIO FERMOSO; Gen. Man. LUCAS HERNÁNDEZ; 563 brs.

Caja España (Caja España de Inversiones, Caja de Ahorros y Monte de Piedad): Ordoño II 17, 24001 León; tel. (987) 218683; fax (987) 218067; e-mail buzon@cajaespana.es; internet www.cajaespana.es; f. 1900; res 978.8m., dep. 20,100.0m., total assets 22,377.4m. (Dec. 2007); Chair. SANTOS LLAMAS LLAMAS; Gen. Man. JOSÉ IGNACIO LAGARTOS RODRÍGUEZ; 538 brs.

Caja Insular de Ahorros de Canarias (La Caja de Canarias): Triana 20, 35002 Las Palmas; tel. (928) 442254; fax (928) 442599; e-mail ciac@lacajadecanarias.es; internet www.lacajadecanarias.es; f. 1939; res 304.4m., dep. 5,376.4m., total assets 5,843.8m. (Dec. 2005); Pres. ANTONIO MARRERO HERNÁNDEZ.

Caja Laboral Popular Coop. de Crédito (Caja Laboral): Paseo José María Arizmendiarrieta s/n, Guipúzcoa, 20500 Mondragón; tel. (943) 719500; fax (943) 719778; e-mail cajalaboral.net@cajalaboral.es; internet www.cajalaboral.es; f. 1959; cap. 418.7m., res 966.6m., dep. 17,806.7m. (Dec. 2006); Pres. JUAN M. OTAEGUI MURUA; Gen. Man. ELIAS ATUCHA ARESTI; 389 brs.

Confederación Española de Cajas de Ahorros (CECA): Alcalá 27, 28014 Madrid; tel. (91) 5965000; fax (91) 5965742; e-mail admin@ceca.es; internet www.ceca.es; f. 1928; national asscn of savings banks; cap. 30.1m., res 596.2m., dep. 13,706.3m. (Dec. 2007); Pres. and Dir-Gen. JUAN RAMÓN QUINTÁS SEOANE; 22,445 brs.

Deutsche Bank SAE: Avda Diagonal 446, 08006 Barcelona; tel. (93) 3673788; fax (93) 3673311; internet www.deutsche-bank.es; f. 1950; present name adopted 1994; 99.7% owned by Deutsche Bank AG (Germany); cap. 67.4m., res 525.9m., dep. 13,964.9m. (Dec. 2006); Chair. HERMANN-JOSEF LAMBERTU.

Montes de Piedad y Caja de Ahorros de Ronda, Cádiz, Almería, Málaga y Antequera (Unicaja): Avda Andalucía 10–12, 29007 Málaga; tel. (952) 138000; fax (952) 138130; e-mail info@personal.unicaja.es; internet www.unicaja.es; f. 1991; cap. 0.0m., res 2,151.8m., dep. 24,145.4m. (Dec. 2006); Pres. BRAULIO MEDEL CAMARÁ; Gen. Man. MIGUEL ANGEL CABELLO JURADO; 870 brs.

Banking Associations

Asociación Española de Banca (AEB): Velázquez 64–66, 28001 Madrid; tel. (91) 7891311; fax (91) 7891310; f. 1977; Pres. MIGUEL MARTÍN; Sec.-Gen. PEDRO PABLO VILLASANTE.

Fondo de Garantía de Depósitos (FGD): José Ortega y Gasset 22, 28006 Madrid; tel. (91) 4316645; fax (91) 5755728; e-mail fogade@fgd.es; internet www.fgd.es; f. 1977; deposit guarantee fund; Pres. JOSÉ MARÍA VIÑALS IÑÍGUEZ.

STOCK EXCHANGES

Bolsas y Mercados Españoles (BME): Palacio de la Bolsa, Plaza de la Lealtad 1, 28014 Madrid; tel. (91) 7095000; fax (91) 5326816; e-mail accionista@bolsasymercados.es; internet www.bolsasymercados.es; integrates cos that manage securities market and financial system; Pres. ANTONIO J. ZOIDO MARTÍNEZ.

Bolsa de Barcelona: Paseo de Gracia 19, 08007 Barcelona; tel. (93) 4013555; fax (93) 4013650; e-mail informacion@borsabcn.es; internet www.borsabcn.es; f. 1915; Pres. JOAN HORTALÀ I ARAU.

Bolsa de Bilbao: José M. Olabarri 1, 48001 Bilbao; tel. (94) 4034400; fax (94) 4034430; e-mail bolsabil@bolsabilbao.es; internet www.bolsabilbao.es; f. 1890; CEO JOSÉ LUIS DAMBORENEA.

Bolsa de Madrid: Plaza de la Lealtad 1, 28014 Madrid; tel. (91) 5891161; fax (91) 5312290; e-mail internacional@bolsamadrid.es; internet www.bolsamadrid.es; f. 1831; 49 mems; Chair. and CEO ANTONIO ZOIDO MARTÍNEZ.

Bolsa de Valores de Valencia: Libreros 2 y 4, 46002 Valencia; tel. (96) 3870100; fax (96) 3870133; e-mail webmaster@bolsavalencia.es; internet www.bolsavalencia.es; f. 1980; Vice-Pres. and CEO MANUEL ESCÁMEZ SÁNCHEZ.

Regulatory Authority

Comisión Nacional del Mercado de Valores (CNMV): Miguel Ángel 11, 28010 Madrid; tel. (91) 5851500; fax (91) 3193373; e-mail inversores@cnmv.es; internet www.cnmv.es; f. 1988; national securities and exchange commission; Pres. JULIO SEGURA SÁNCHEZ.

INSURANCE

Aegon Unión Aseguradora: Príncipe de Vergara 156, 28002 Madrid; tel. (91) 5636222; fax (91) 5639715; internet www.aegon.es; f. 1944; owned by Aegon NV (The Netherlands); life, property, health and personal insurance and reinsurance; Chair. ALEJANDRO ROYO-VILLANOVA PAYÁ; CEO JESÚS QUINTANAL SAN EMETERIO.

Allianz, Compañía de Seguros y Reaseguros: Paseo de la Castellana 39, 28046 Madrid; tel. (91) 5960400; fax (91) 5578702; internet www.allianz.es; f. 1999; total premiums 2,292m. (2004); Pres. DETLEV BREMKAMP; CEO VICENTE TARDÍO.

Ascat Vida: Provença 398–404, 08025 Barcelona; tel. (93) 484600; tel. (93) 4846002; e-mail info_ascat@ascat.es; internet www.ascat.es; f. 1986; subsidiary of Caixa Catalunya.

Asistencia Sanitaria Interprovincial de Seguros (ASISA): Caracas 12, 28010 Madrid; tel. (91) 3190191; fax (91) 4103836; e-mail asisa.informacion@asisa.es; internet www.asisa.es; Pres. FRANCISCO CARREÑO CASTILLA.

Axa: Paseo de la Castellana 79, 28046 Madrid; tel. (91) 5388200; fax (91) 5553197; internet www.axa.es; Pres. EDUARDO DE AGUIRRE ALONSO-ALLENDE.

Banco Vitalicio de España, Compañía Anónima de Seguros: Paseo de Gracia 11, 08007 Barcelona; tel. (93) 4840100; fax (93) 4840239; internet www.vitalicio.es; f. 1880; total premiums 1,221.2m. (2004); Pres. JOSÉ MARÍA AMUSÁTEGUI DE LA CIERVA.

BBVA Seguros: Alcalá 17, 28014 Madrid; tel. (91) 5379231; fax (91) 3747266; e-mail seguros@grupobbva.com; internet www.bbvaseguros.com.

Bilbao, Cía Anónima de Seguros y Reaseguros (Seguros Bilbao): Paseo del Puerto 20, 48990 Neguri-Getxo (Vizcaya); tel. (94) 4898100; fax (94) 4898263; internet www.segurosbilbao.com; f. 1918;

gen. insurance, represented throughout Spain; part of Grupo Catalana Occidente; Pres. FRANCISCO JOSÉ ARREGUI; Man. Dir IÑAKI ALVARES.

Caja de Seguros Reunidos, Cía de Seguros y Reaseguros (Caser Seguros): Plaza de la Lealtad 4, 28014 Madrid; tel. (91) 5955000; fax (91) 5955018; e-mail informacion@caser.es; internet www.caser.es; f. 1942; represented throughout Spain; total premiums 1,587.9m. (2005); Dir-Gen. IGNACIO EYRIES GARCÍA DE VINUESA.

Crédito y Caución (Compañía Española de Seguros y Reaseguros): Paseo de la Castellana 4, 28046 Madrid; tel. (91) 4326300; fax (91) 4326506; e-mail sac@creditoycaucion.es; internet www.creditoycaucion.com; f. 1929; total premiums 361m. (2005); Pres. JESÚS SERRA FARRÉ; CEO ISIDRO UNDA URZAIZ.

Estrella Seguros: Orense 2, 28020 Madrid; tel. (91) 5905656; fax (91) 5907674; e-mail clientes@laestrella.es; internet www.laestrella.es; f. 1901; all classes of insurance and reinsurance; total premiums 1,007.3m. (2005); Pres. Duque CARLOS ZURITA DELGADO; CEO MÓNICA MONDARDINI.

Grupo Catalana Occidente: Avda Alcalde Barnils 63, 08174 Sant Cugat del Vallés (Barcelona); tel. (93) 5820500; fax (93) 5820560; e-mail calidad@catalanaoccidente.com; internet www.catalanaoccidente.com; insurance and reinsurance; Pres. JOSÉ MARÍA SERRA FARRÉ.

Mapfre Mutualidad (Mapfre Mutualidad de Seguros y Reaseguros): Carretera de Pozuelo a Majadahonda, Km 3800, 28820 Majadahonda, Madrid; tel. (91) 6262100; fax (91) 6262308; internet www.mapfre.com; f. 1933; car insurance; Pres. JOSÉ A. REBUELTA GARCÍA.

Mapfre Seguros Generales: Paseo de Recoletos 23, 28004 Madrid; tel. (91) 5816300; fax (91) 5815252; internet www.mapfre.com; Pres. RAFAEL GALARRAGA SOLORES.

Mapfre Vida: Avda General Perón 40, 28020 Madrid; tel. (91) 5811400; fax (91) 5811592; internet www.mapfre.com; life; Man. Dir SEBASTIÁN HOMET DUPRA.

Mutua General de Seguros (MGS): Avda Diagonal 543, 08029 Barcelona; tel. (93) 3221212; fax (93) 3220971; e-mail sac@mgs.es; internet www.mgs.es; f. 1907; Pres. JORGE LUQUE VICO.

Mutua Madrileña: Paseo de la Castellana 33, 28046 Madrid; tel. (902) 555555, (91) 5578200; fax (91) 3105223; internet www.mutua-mad.es; f. 1930; Pres. IGNACIO GARRALDA RUÍZ DE VELASCO.

Ocaso, SA, Compañía de Seguros y Reaseguros: Princesa 23, 28008 Madrid; tel. (91) 5380100; fax (91) 5418509; e-mail ocaso@ocaso.es; internet www.ocaso.es; f. 1920; total premiums 513m., cap. 100m. (2002); 370 brs in Spain, 1 in London, 1 in Puerto Rico; Pres. ISABEL CASTELO D'ORTEGA; Dir-Gen. D. ANTONIO DOMÍNGUEZ CUERDO.

Sanitas de Seguros: Ribera del Loira 52, 28042 Madrid; tel. 902 230220; fax (91) 5852516; e-mail iferrando@sanitas.es; internet www.sanitas.es; health; Pres. JUAN JOSÉ LÓPEZ-IBOR.

SantaLucía Seguros: Plaza de España 15, 28008 Madrid; tel. (91) 5419387; fax (91) 5410133; e-mail atencion@santalucia.es; internet www.santalucia.es; f. 1922; Pres. CARLOS J. ALVAREZ NAVARRO.

Vidacaixa: General Almirante 6, 08014 Barcelona; tel. (93) 2278700; fax (93) 3324441; internet www.vidacaixa.es; subsidiary of Grupo CaiFor; Pres. TOMÁS MUNIESA ARANTEGUI.

Zurich: Vía Augusta 192–200, 08021 Barcelona; tel. (93) 2099111; fax (93) 2014849; e-mail zurich.seleccion-es@zurich.com; internet www.zurichspain.com.

Regulatory Authority

Dirección General de Seguros y Fondos de Pensiones: Paseo de la Castellana 44, 28046 Madrid; tel. (91) 3397000; fax (91) 3397113; e-mail dirseguros@meh.es; internet www.dgsfp.meh.es; supervisory body; part of Ministry of the Economy and Finance; Dir-Gen. RICARDO LOZANO ARAGÜÉS.

Insurance Association

Unión Española de Entidades Aseguradoras y Reaseguradoras (UNESPA): Núñez de Balboa 101, 28006 Madrid; tel. (91) 7451530; fax (91) 7451531; internet www.unespa.es; f. 1977; Pres. PILAR GONZÁLEZ DE FRUTOS; Sec.-Gen. MIRENCHU DEL VALLE; c. 300 mem. cos.

Trade and Industry

GOVERNMENT AGENCIES

Comisión Nacional de la Competencia (CNC): Barquillo 5, 28004 Madrid; tel. (91) 5680510; fax (91) 5680590; e-mail informacion@cncompetencia.es; internet www.cncompetencia.es; f. 2007 by merger of the Servicio de Defensa de la Competencia and the Tribunal de Defensa de la Competencia; investigates anti-competitive practices and enforces competition law; Pres. LUIS BERENGUER FUSTER.

Instituto Español de Comercio Exterior (ICEX): Paseo de la Castellana 14, 28046 Madrid; tel. (91) 3496100; fax (91) 4316128; internet www.icex.es; f. 1982; institute for foreign trade; Pres. SILVIA IRANZO GUTIÉRREZ.

Secretaría General de Comercio Exterior: Secretaría de Estado de Comercio y Turismo, Paseo de la Castellana 160, 28046 Madrid; tel. 902 446006; fax (91) 4578066; part of Ministry of Industry, Tourism and Trade; Sec.-Gen. ALFREDO BONET BAIGET.

DEVELOPMENT ORGANIZATIONS

Instituto Andaluz de la Reforma Agraria (IARA): Tabladilla s/n, 41013 Sevilla; tel. (95) 5032271; fax (95) 5032149; empowered to expropriate land under the agricultural reform programme; Pres. JUAN ÁNGEL FERNÁNDEZ BATANERO.

Instituto Galego de Promoción Económica (IGAPE): Complejo Administrativo Barrio de San Lázaro s/n, 15703 Santiago de Compostela (A Coruña); tel. (981) 541147; fax (981) 558844; e-mail igape@igape.es; internet www.igape.es; promotes devt in Galicia; overseas brs in P.R. China, Germany, Japan, Poland and USA; Dir-Gen. ÁLVARO ÁLVAREZ-BLÁZQUEZ FERNÁNDEZ; Sec.-Gen. JOSÉ MARÍA PENELAS FIGUEIRA.

Instituto Madrileño de Desarrollo (IMADE): José Abascal 57, 28003 Madrid; tel. (91) 3997400; e-mail informacion@imade.es; internet www.imade.es; f. 1984; public devt institution for Madrid region; Dir AURELIO GARCÍA DE SOLA Y ARRIAGA.

Sociedad de Desarrollo de Navarra (SODENA): Avda Carlos III el Noble 36, 1° dcha, 31003 Pamplona; tel. (848) 421942; fax (848) 421943; e-mail info@sodena.com; internet www.sodena.com; promotes devt in Navarra; Pres. JOSÉ ROIG ALDASORO.

Sociedad para el Desarrollo Económico de Canarias (Sodecan): Villalba Hervás 4, 6°, 38002 Santa Cruz de Tenerife; tel. (922) 298020; fax (922) 298131; e-mail sodecantf@sodecan.es; internet www.sodecan.es; promotes devt in the Canary Islands; Pres. EUSEBIO BAUTISTA VIZCAINO.

Sociedad para el Desarrollo Industrial de Castilla y León (SODICAL): Doctrinos 6, 4°, 47001 Valladolid; tel. (983) 343811; fax (983) 330702; e-mail sodical@sodical.es; internet www.sodical.es; f. 1982; promotes devt in Castile and Leon; Dir-Gen. MANUEL FERNÁNDEZ DÍEZ.

Sociedad para el Desarrollo Industrial de Extremadura (Sodiex): Avda Virgen de Guadalupe, 10001 Cáceres; tel. (927) 224878; fax (927) 243304; e-mail sodiex@sodiex.es; internet www.sodiex.es; f. 1977; promotes industrial devt in Extremadura.

Sociedad para el Desarrollo Industrial de Galicia (SODIGA): Orense 6, La Rosaleda, 15701 Santiago de Compostela; tel. (981) 541621; fax (981) 566183; promotes industrial devt in Galicia.

CHAMBERS OF COMMERCE

Cámara de Comercio Internacional (International Chamber of Commerce): Avda Diagonal 452-4, 08006 Barcelona; tel. (93) 4169300; fax (93) 4169301; e-mail iccspain@cambrabcn.es; internet www.iccspain.org; f. 1922; Pres. GUILLERMO DE LA DEHESA; Sec.-Gen. LUIS SOLÁ VILARDELL.

Confederación Española de Comercio (CEC): Orense 25, 2°C, 28020 Madrid; tel. (91) 5981050; fax (91) 5520967; e-mail cec@confespacomercio.com; internet www.confespacomercio.com; Pres. PERE LLORENS LORENTE; Sec.-Gen. MIQUEL ÁNGEL FRAILE VILLAGRASA; 400,000 mems.

Consejo Superior de Cámaras Oficiales de Comercio, Industria y Navegación de España (High Council of Official Chambers of Commerce, Industry, and Navigation of Spain): Ribera del Loira 12, 28042 Madrid; tel. (91) 5906900; fax (91) 5906913; e-mail info@cscamaras.es; internet www.camaras.org; f. 1922; Pres. JOSÉ ANTONIO QUIROGA Y PIÑEYRO; Dir-Gen. EDOUARDO MORENO; comprises 85 Chambers throughout Spain, incl. the following:

Cámara de Comercio de Bilbao/Bilboko Merkataritza Ganbera: Gran Vía 13, 48001 Bilbao; tel. (94) 4706500; fax (94) 4436171; e-mail atencionalcliente@camarabilbao.com; internet www.camarabilbao.com; Pres. IGNACIO MARÍA ECHEBERRIA MONTEBERRIA; Dir-Gen. JUAN LUIS LASKURAIN ARGARATE.

Cámara Oficial de Comercio e Industria de Madrid: Ribera del Loira 56–58, 28042 Madrid; tel. (91) 5383500; fax (91) 5383677; e-mail camara@camaramadrid.es; internet www.camaramadrid.es; f. 1887; Pres. SALVADOR SANTOS CAMPANO; Dir-Gen. MIGUEL GARRIDO; 370,000 mems.

Cámara Oficial de Comercio, Industria y Navegación de Sevilla: Plaza de la Contratación 8, 41004 Sevilla; tel. (954) 211005; fax (954) 225619; e-mail ccinsevilla@camaradesevilla.com; internet www.camaradesevilla.com; f. 1886.

SPAIN

Cámara Oficial de Comercio, Industria y Navegación de Valencia: Poeta Querol 15, 46002 Valencia; tel. (96) 3103900; fax (96) 3531742; e-mail info@camaravalencia.com; internet www.camaravalencia.com; f. 1886; Pres. ARTURO VIROSQUE RUÍZ; Dir FERNANDO ZÁRRAGA QUINTANA.

Cambra de Comerç de Barcelona: Avda Diagonal 452–454, 08006 Barcelona; tel. (90) 2448448; fax (93) 4169301; internet www.cambrabcn.es; f. 1886; Pres. MIQUEL VALLS MASEDA; Dir XAVIER CARBONELL I ROURA.

INDUSTRIAL AND TRADE ASSOCIATIONS

Agrupación de Exportadores del Centro de España (AGRECE) (Group of Exporters of Central Spain): Ribera del Loira 56–58, 28042 Madrid; tel. (91) 5383500; fax (91) 5383677; e-mail cex2@camaramadrid.es; internet www.camaramadrid.es; part of Cámara Oficial de Comercio e Industria de Madrid; exporters.

Agrupación de Fabricantes de Cemento de España (OFICEMEN): José Abascal 53, 28003 Madrid; tel. (91) 4411688; fax (91) 4423817; e-mail direccion@oficemen.com; internet www.oficemen.com; cement manufacturers; Pres. JEAN MARTIN-SAINT-LÉON; Dir-Gen. ANICETO ZARAGOZA.

Asociación de Comercio de Cereales y Oleaginosas de España (ACCOE) (Spanish Association of Oilseeds and Cereals Traders): Doctor Fleming 56, 3°D, 28036 Madrid; tel. (91) 3504305; fax (91) 3455009; e-mail info@accoe.org; internet www.accoe.org; f. 1977; cereal traders; Pres. PELAYO MORENO SÁNCHEZ; Sec.-Gen. JOSÉ M. ALVAREZ BLASCO.

Asociación de Criadores Exportadores de Sherry (ACES): Eguiluz 2, 11402 Jerez de la Frontera (Cádiz); tel. (956) 341046; fax (956) 346081; sherry exporters; Pres. FRANCISCO VALENCIA JAÉN.

Asociación de Empresas de Electrónica, Tecnologías de la Información y Telecomunicaciones de España (AETIC): Príncipe de Vergara 74, 4°, 28006 Madrid; tel. (91) 5902300; e-mail aetic@aetic.es; internet www.aetic.es; f. 1984; electronic, information and telecommunication industries; Pres. JESÚS BANEGAS NÚÑEZ; Dir-Gen. GONZALO CARO SANTA CRUZ; c. 1,000 mem. cos.

Asociación Española de Comercio Exterior de Cereales y Productos Análogos (AECEC): Orense 85, Edif. Lexington, 28020 Madrid; tel. (91) 678400; fax (91) 5714244; e-mail aecec@arrakis.es; cereal exporters; Pres. J. CORNEJO; Sec.-Gen. DIEGO PAZOS.

Asociación Española de Exportadores de Electrónica e Informática (SECARTYS): Gran Vía de les Corts Catalanes 774, 4°, 08013 Barcelona; tel. (93) 2478560; fax (93) 2478561; e-mail secartys@secartys.org; internet www.secartys.org; f. 1968; electronics exporters; Pres. JOSEP ROF; Dir-Gen. CARLOS VIVAS.

Asociación Española de Fabricantes de Automóviles y Camiones (ANFAC): Fray Bernardino Sahagún 24, 28036 Madrid; tel. (91) 3431343; fax (91) 3450377; e-mail prensa@anfac.com; internet www.anfac.es; car and lorry manufacturers; Pres. FRANCISCO JAVIER GARCÍA SANZ.

Asociación Española de Fabricantes de Equipos y Componentes para Automoción (SERNAUTO): Castelló 120, 28006 Madrid; tel. (91) 5621041; e-mail sernauto@sernauto.es; internet www.sernauto.es; f. 1967; asscn of manufacturers of equipment and components for automobile industry; Pres. JOSÉ MARÍA PUJOL ARTIGAS; Dir-Gen. JOSÉ ANTONIO JIMÉNEZ SACEDA.

Asociación Española de la Industria y Comercio Exportador de Aceite de Oliva (ASOLIVA): José Abascal 40, 2°, 28003 Madrid; tel. (91) 4468812; fax (91) 5931918; e-mail asoliva@asoliva.es; internet www.asoliva.es; f. 1928; olive oil exporters; Pres. JOSÉ PONT AMENOS.

Asociación Española de Productoras de Fibras Químicas (PROFIBRA): Via Laietana 46, 2°, 08003 Barcelona; tel. and fax (93) 3196534; e-mail profibra@profibra.com; f. 1977; chemical fibre producers; Pres. RAFAEL ESPAÑOL NAVARRO; Sec.-Gen. GUILLERMO GRAELL DENIEL.

Asociación de Exportadores de Pescado y Cefalopodos Congelados (AEPYCC): Diego de León 44, 28006 Madrid; tel. (91) 4112407; fax (91) 5618178; fish exporters; Pres. RAMÓN MASO; Sec. IGNACIO MONTENEGRO GONZÁLEZ.

Asociación Industrial Textil de Proceso Algodonero (AITPA): Gran Vía de les Corts Catalanes 670, 08010 Barcelona; tel. (93) 3189200; fax (93) 3026235; e-mail aitpa@aitpa.es; internet www.aitpa.es; cotton textile industry; Pres. ADRIA SERRA.

Asociación Nacional Española de Fabricantes de Hormigón Preparado (ANEFHOP): Bretón de los Herreros 43, bajo, 28003 Madrid; tel. (91) 4416634; fax (91) 3993497; e-mail info@anefhop.es; internet www.anefhop.com; f. 1968; concrete manufacturers; Pres. MANUEL A. SOBRAL CRUZ; Dir-Gen. FRANCISCO JAVIER MARTÍNEZ DE EULATE.

Asociación Nacional de Fabricantes de Pastas Papeleras, Papel y Cartón (ASPAPEL): Avda de Baviera 15, 28028 Madrid; tel. (91) 5763003; fax (91) 5774710; e-mail aspapel@aspapel.es; internet www.aspapel.es; f. 1977; paper and cardboard manufacturers; Pres. IÑIGO ECHEVARRIA; Dir-Gen. CARLOS REINOSO TORRES.

Comité de Gestión de Cítricos (CGC): Monjas de Santa Catalina 8, 4°, 46002 Valencia; tel. (96) 3521102; fax (96) 3510718; e-mail comite@citricos.org; internet www.citricos.org; citrus fruit exporters; Pres. VICENTE BORDILS RAMÓN; Dir JOSÉ MARTÍNEZ SERRANO.

Confederación de Cooperativas Agrarias de España (CCAE) (Confederation of Spanish Agrarian Co-operatives): Agustín de Bethencourt 17, 4°, 28003 Madrid; tel. (91) 5351035; fax (91) 5540047; e-mail ccae@ccae.es; internet www.ccae.es; Pres. RICARDO MARTÍN GUTIÉRREZ; Dir-Gen. EDUARDO BAAMONDE NOCHE.

Confederación Española de Organizaciones Empresariales del Metal (CONFEMETAL): Príncipe de Vergara 74, 5°, 28006 Madrid; tel. (91) 5625590; fax (91) 5635758; e-mail informacion@confemetal.es; internet www.confemetal.es; metal asscns; Pres. CARLOS PÉREZ DE BRICIO OLARIAGA; Sec.-Gen. ANDRÉS SÁNCHEZ DE APELLÁNIZ.

Confederación Nacional de la Construcción (CNC): Diego de León 50, 2°, 28006 Madrid; tel. (91) 5619715; fax (91) 5615269; e-mail cnc@cnc.es; internet www.cnc.es; f. 1977; construction industry; Pres. JUAN FRANCISCO LAZCANO ACEDO.

Consejo Intertextil Español (CIE): Gran Via de les Corts Catalanes 670, 08010 Barcelona; tel. (93) 3189200; fax (93) 3026235; e-mail cie@consejointertextil.com; internet www.consejointertextil.com; textile industry; Pres. JOSEP CASAS; Sec.-Gen. JORDI FONT; 7 mem. asscns.

Federación Empresarial de la Industria Química Española (FEIQUE): Hermosilla 31, 1°, 28001 Madrid; tel. (91) 4317964; fax (91) 5763381; e-mail info@feique.org; internet www.feique.org; chemical industry; Pres. FERNANDO ITURRIETA; Dir-Gen. FERNANDO GALBIS.

Federación Española de Asociaciones de Productores y Exportadores de Frutas, Hortalizas, Flores y Planta Vivas (FEPEX): Miguel Angel 13, 4A, 28010 Madrid; tel. (91) 3191050; fax (91) 3103812; e-mail fepex@fepex.es; internet www.fepex.es; fruit and vegetable producers and exporters; Pres. ANDRÉS CUARTERO RUIZ; Dir JOSÉ MARÍA POZANCOS; 26 mem. asscns.

Federación Española de Exportadores de Frutos Cítricos (FECIT): Hernan Cones 4E, 46004 Valencia; tel. (96) 3521284; fax (96) 3513187; citrus fruit exporters; Pres. ANTONIO PELUFO; Sec. LUIS RIBERA PERIS.

Federación Española de Industrias de la Alimentación y Bebidas (FIAB): Diego de León 44, 1° izqda, 28006 Madrid; tel. (91) 4117211; fax (91) 4117344; e-mail fiab@fiab.es; internet www.fiab.es; f. 1977; food and drink industries; Pres. ARTURO GIL PÉREZ ANDUJAR; Sec.-Gen. JORGE JORDANA BUTTICAZ DE POZAS.

Federación de Industrias del Calzado Español (FICE): Núñez de Balboa 116, 3°, 28006 Madrid; tel. (91) 5627003; fax (91) 5620094; e-mail info@fice.es; internet www.fice.es; f. 1977; footwear; Pres. RAFAEL CALVO RODRÍGUEZ.

Fundación Cotec: Marqués de Salamanca 11, 2° izqda, 28006 Madrid; tel. (91) 4364774; fax (91) 4311239; internet www.cotec.es; f. 1990; promotes technological innovation and understanding; Pres. JOSÉ ANGEL SÁNCHEZ ASIAÍN; Dir JUAN MULET.

Sociedad Estatal de Participaciones Industriales (SEPI): Velázquez 134, 28006 Madrid; tel. (91) 3961000; fax (91) 5628789; e-mail informacion@sepi.es; internet www.sepi.es; f. 1996; asscn of state-owned cos; Pres. ENRIQUE MARTÍNEZ ROBLES; Sec.-Gen. FERNANDO SEQUEIRA FUENTES; 36 mems.

Unión de Empresas Siderúrgicas (UNESID): Castelló 128, 3°, 28006 Madrid; tel. (91) 5624010; fax (91) 5626584; e-mail unesid@unesid.org; internet www.unesid.org; f. 1968; asscn of Spanish producers of steel; Chair. GONZALO URQUIJO; Dir-Gen. JUAN I. BARTOLOMÉ.

EMPLOYERS' ORGANIZATIONS

Círculo de Empresarios: Paseo de la Castellana 15, 6°, 28001 Madrid; tel. (91) 5781472; fax (91) 5774871; e-mail asociacion@circulodeempresarios.org; internet www.circulodeempresarios.org; f. 1977; comprises CEOs of more than 180 major cos; Pres. CLAUDIO BOADA PALLERÉS; Sec.-Gen. PEDRO MORENÉS EULATE.

Confederación Española de Organizaciones Empresariales (CEOE) (Spanish Confederation of Employers' Organizations): Diego de León 50, 28006 Madrid; tel. (91) 5663400; fax (91) 5622562; e-mail ceoe@ceoe.es; internet www.ceoe.es; f. 1977; covers industry, agriculture, commerce and service sectors; comprises 210 orgs; Pres. GERARDO DÍAZ FERRÁN; Vice-Pres. and Sec.-Gen. JUAN JIMÉNEZ DE AGUILAR.

Confederación Empresarial de Madrid (CEIM): Diego de León 50, 1°, 28006 Madrid; tel. (91) 4115317; fax (91) 5627537; internet info@ceim.es; internet www.ceim.es; small, medium and large businesses; Pres. ARTURO FERNÁNDEZ ÁLVAREZ; Sec. ALEJANDRO COUCEIRO.

Confederación Empresarial Valenciana (CEV): Plaza Conde de Carlet 3, 46003 Valencia; tel. (96) 3155720; fax (96) 3923199; e-mail cev@cev.es; internet www.cev.es; f. 1977; Pres. JOSÉ VICENTE GONZÁLEZ PÉREZ; Sec.-Gen. ENRIQUE SOTO RIPOLL.

Confederación Empresarial Vasca/Euskal Entrepresarien Konfederakuntza (CONFEBASK): Gran Vía 45, 2°, 48011 Bilbao; tel. (94) 4021331; fax (94) 4021333; e-mail confebask@confebask.es; internet www.confebask.es; f. 1983; Pres. MIGUEL LAZPIUR; Sec.-Gen. JOSÉ GUILLERMO ZUBÍA GUINEA.

Confederación Española de la Pequeña y Mediana Empresa (CEPYME): Diego de León 50, 3°, 28006 Madrid; tel. (91) 4116161; fax (91) 5645269; e-mail cepyme@cepyme.es; internet www.cepyme.es; small and medium businesses; Pres. ANTONIO MASA GODOY; Sec.-Gen. ELÍAS APARICIO BRAVO.

Fomento del Trabajo Nacional/Foment del Treball Nacional—Confederación Empresarial de Catalunya: Vía Laietana 32, 08003 Barcelona; tel. (93) 4841200; fax (93) 4841230; e-mail foment@foment.com; internet www.foment.com; f. 1771 as Real Compañía de Hilados de Algodón del Principado de Catalunya; devt of national labour; Pres. JOAN ROSELL LASTORTRAS; Sec.-Gen. JUAN PUJOL SEGARRA.

UTILITIES

Comisión Nacional de Energía (CNE): Alcalá 47, 28014 Madrid; tel. (91) 4329600; fax (91) 5776218; e-mail dre@cne.es; internet www.cne.es; f. 1999; part of Ministry of Industry, Tourism and Trade; regulates energy systems; Pres. MARÍA TERESA COSTA CAMPI.

Instituto para la Diversificación y Ahorro de la Energía (IDAE): Madera 8, 28004 Madrid; tel. (91) 4564900; fax (91) 5230414; e-mail comunicacion@idae.es; internet www.idae.es; f. 1974 as Centro de Estudios de la Energía; under control of General Secretariat of Energy (Ministry of Industry, Tourism and Trade); Dir-Gen. ENRIQUE JIMÉNEZ LARREA.

Secretaría General de Energía: Paseo de la Castellana 160, 28071 Madrid; tel. (91) 3494819; fax (91) 4587704; e-mail secgenenergia@mityc.es; internet www.mityc.es/energia; part of Ministry of Industry, Tourism and Trade; Sec.-Gen. PEDRO MARÍN URIBE.

Electricity

Asociación Española de la Industria Eléctrica (UNESA): Francisco Gervás 3, 28020 Madrid; tel. (91) 5674800; fax (91) 5674987; e-mail info@unesa.es; internet www.unesa.es; f. 1944; groups principal electricity cos; Pres. PEDRO RIVERO; Sec.-Gen. PASCUAL SALA.

Operador del Mercado Ibérico de Energía—Polo Español (OMEL): Alfonso XI 6, 4° y 5°, 28014 Madrid; e-mail info@omel.es; internet www.omel.es; f. 2003; Spanish branch of the Iberian Energy Market; Pres. and CEO MARÍA LUISA HUIDOBRO Y ARREBA.

Red Eléctrica de España (REE): Paseo del Conde de los Gaitanes 177, 28109 La Moraleja (Madrid); tel. (91) 6508500; fax (91) 6504542; e-mail redelectrica@ree.es; internet www.ree.es; manages and operates the national grid; Pres. LUIS ATIENZA SERNA.

Principal Electricity Companies

Endesa: Ribera del Loira 60, Campo de las Naciones, 28042 Madrid; tel. (91) 2131000; fax (91) 5638181; internet www.endesa.es; f. 1983; generator, distributor and vendor of electricity; also provides gas; 67% owned by Enel (Italy), 25% owned by Acciona (Spain); Pres. JOSÉ MANUEL ENTRECANALES DOMECQ.

E.ON España: Medio 12, 39003 Santander; tel. (942) 246000; fax (942) 246034; e-mail informacion@eon.com; internet www.eon-espana.com; f. 2008 following the acquisition of Enel Viesgo; subsidiary of E.ON AG (Germany); generation, distribution and supply; also provides gas; CEO MIGUEL ANTOÑANZAS.

HC Energía: Plaza de la Gesta 2, 33007 Oviedo (Asturias); tel. (98) 5230300; e-mail hcenergia@hcenergia.com; internet www.hcenergia.com; f. 1919; fmrly Hidroeléctrica del Cantábrico; generation, distribution and supply; also provides gas; owned by Electricidade de Portugal; Pres. MANUEL MENÉNDEZ MENÉNDEZ.

Iberdrola: Cardenal Gardoqui 8, 48008 Bilbao; tel. (944) 151411; fax (944) 663194; e-mail informacion@iberdrola.com; internet www.iberdrola.com; generation, distribution and supply; supplies mainly hydroelectric power; also provides gas; Pres. and CEO JOSÉ IGNACIO SÁNCHEZ GALÁN.

Unión Fenosa: Avda San Luis 77, 28033 Madrid; tel. (91) 5676000; fax (91) 5676658; e-mail unionfenosa@unionfenosa.es; internet www.unionfenosa.es; generation, distribution and supply; also provides gas; Chair. PEDRO LÓPEZ JIMÉNEZ; CEO HONORATO LÓPEZ ISLA.

Gas

Enagás: Paseo de los Olmos 19, 28005 Madrid; tel. (902) 443700; e-mail contacta@enagas.es; internet www.enagas.es; operates gas transportation network; f. 1972; Pres. ANTONI LLARDÉN CARRATLÁ.

Endesa Gas: Aznar Molina 2, 50002 Zaragoza; tel. (976) 760000; fax (976) 760044; internet www.endesa.es; distributor of gas; comprises five subsidiaries; also provides electricity; subsidiary of Endesa; Pres. AMADO FRANCO LAHOZ; Dir-Gen. FERNANDO CORTINA GONZÁLEZ.

Gas Natural SDG: Avda Portal de l'Angel 22, 08002 Barcelona; tel. (93) 4025100; fax (93) 4029317; internet www.gasnatural.com; distributor of gas; also provides electricity and communications; comprises regional distribution cos; Pres. SALVADOR GABARRÓ SERRA; CEO RAFAEL VILLASECA MARCO.

Naturgas Energía: Plaza Pío Baroja 3, 48001 Bilbao; tel. (94) 4035700; fax (94) 4249733; e-mail webnaturgas@naturgasenergia.com; internet www.naturgasenergia.com; f. 1982; 65.6% owned by HC Energía; distributor of gas and electricity; Pres. MANUEL MENÉNDEZ.

Water

Dirección General del Agua: Plaza de San Juan de la Cruz s/n, 28071 Madrid; tel. (91) 5976660; part of Ministry of the Environment, Agriculture and the Marine; co-ordinates water policy and supervises water management; Dir-Gen. JAIME PALOP PIQUERAS.

Grupo Agbar: Torre Agbar, Avda Diagonal 211, 08009 Barcelona; tel. (93) 3422000; fax (93) 3422662; e-mail comunicacion@agbar.es; internet www.agbar.es; treatment of water and waste liquid; provision of sanitation and certification services; Pres. JORGE MERCADER MIRÓ; Dir-Gen. ANGEL SIMÓN GRIMALDOS.

Grupo Aguas de Valencia: Gran Vía Marqués del Turia 19, 46005 Valencia; tel. (96) 3860600; e-mail aquas.valencia@aquasvalencia.es; internet www.aguasdevalencia.es; water and sewerage services; Chair. V. BOLUDA FOS.

TRADE UNIONS

Central Sindical Independiente y de Funcionarios (CSI-CSIF): Maudes 15, 1°, 28003 Madrid; tel. (91) 2735900; fax (91) 2735991; e-mail s.presidencia@csi-csif.es; internet www.csi-csif.es; Pres. DOMINGO FERNÁNDEZ VEIGUELA; Sec.-Gen. LOURDES BLANCO AMILLATEGUI.

Confederación General de Trabajo (CGT) (General Confederation of Labour): Sagunto 15, 28010 Madrid; tel. (91) 4475769; fax (91) 4453132; e-mail sp-comunicacion@cgt.es; internet www.cgt.es; Sec.-Gen. ELADIO VILLANUEVA SARAVIA.

Confederación Intersindical Galega (CIG): Rua Miguel Ferro Caaveiro 10, 3°, 15073 Santiago de Compostela; tel. (981) 564300; fax (981) 571082; e-mail secretarioxeral@galizacig.net; internet www.galizacig.com; Galician confederation; Sec.-Gen. XÉSUS E. SEIXO FERNÁNDEZ.

Confederación Nacional del Trabajo (CNT) (National Confederation of Labour): Secretariado Permanente del Comité Nacional, Imagen 8, 5°B, 41003 Sevilla; tel. (945) 562395; e-mail sp_cn@cnt.es; internet www.cnt.es; Sec.-Gen. RAFAEL CORRALES.

Confederación Sindical de Comisiones Obreras (CCOO) (Workers' Commissions): Fernández de la Hoz 12, 28010 Madrid; tel. (91) 7028000; fax (91) 3104804; e-mail ccoo@ccoo.es; internet www.ccoo.es; f. 1956; independent left-wing; Sec.-Gen. JOSÉ MARÍA FIDALGO VELILLA; 1,050,000 mems (2005).

Eusko Langilleen Alkartasuna/Solidaridad de Trabajadores Vascos (ELA—Euskal Sindikatua) (Basque Workers' Solidarity): Barrainkua 13, 48009 Bilbao; tel. (94) 4037700; fax (94) 4037777; e-mail naziorte@elasind.org; internet www.ela-sindikatua.org; f. 1911; legally recognized 1977; independent; Sec.-Gen. JOSÉ ELORRIETA AURREKOETXEA; 106,000 mems (2006).

Unión General de Trabajadores (UGT) (General Union of Workers): Hortaleza 88, 28004 Madrid; tel. (91) 5897601; fax (91) 5897603; e-mail info@cec.ugt.org; internet www.ugt.es; f. 1888; eight affiliated federations; Sec.-Gen. CÁNDIDO MÉNDEZ RODRÍGUEZ.

Unión Sindical Obrera (USO) (Workers' Trade Union): Príncipe de Vergara 13, 7°, 28001 Madrid; tel. (91) 5774113; fax (91) 5772959; e-mail uso@uso.es; internet www.uso.es; f. 1960; independent; Sec.-Gen. JULIO SALAZAR MORENO; 105,000 mems.

SPAIN   *Directory*

Transport

RAILWAYS

In August 2000 it was announced that rail transport was to be liberalized by 2008, with private operators using the state rail infrastructure. Construction of a high-speed railway linking Madrid with the Portuguese capital, Lisbon, was expected to be completed by 2013. A further high-speed link from Madrid to the French border, via Barcelona, was scheduled to be completed in 2009. There were also plans for high-speed links between Madrid and Valencia, and between Barcelona and Málaga, along with a new railway between Valencia and the Basque Country. From January 2005 the state railway company, RENFE, was divided into an operating and a management division, and the goods transport sector was open to competition. RENFE's monopoly on passenger transport was to end in 2010. In 2005 the total rail network was 12,624.5 km, 483.7 km of which was high-speed track.

Administrador de Infraestructuras Ferroviarias (Adif): Paseo del Rey 30, 28008 Madrid; tel. (91) 3008080; e-mail vialia@adif.es; internet www.adif.es; f. 2005; state-owned; fmrly part of state-owned railway co, Red Nacional de los Ferrocarriles Españoles (RENFE); manages railway infrastructure; Pres. ANTONIO GONZÁLEZ MARÍN; Sec.-Gen. MARÍA ROSA SANZ CEREZO.

RENFE Operadora: Avda Pío XII 110, 28036 Madrid; tel. (91) 3006600; e-mail comunicacion@renfe.es; internet www.renfe.es; f. 2005 following liberalization of railway sector; fmrly Red Nacional de los Ferrocarriles Españoles (RENFE); state-owned; Pres. JOSÉ SALGUEIRO CARMONA; Sec.-Gen. JOSÉ L. MARROQUÍN MOCHALES.

Eusko Trenbideak—Ferrocarriles Vascos (ET/FV) (EuskoTren): Atxuri 6, 48006 Bilbao; tel. (94) 4019900; fax (94) 4019901; e-mail attcliente@euskotren.es; internet www.euskotren.es; f. 1982; controlled by the Basque Govt; 188 km of 1,000 mm gauge; Dir-Gen. JOSÉ MIGUEL MÚGICA PERAL.

Ferrocarriles de Vía Estrecha (Feve) (Narrow Gauge Railways): Plaza de los Ferroviarios, 33012 Oviedo; tel. (98) 5297656; fax (98) 5281708; e-mail info@feve.es; internet www.feve.es; f. 1965 by integration of private cos; operates mainly in suburban areas of northern cities; 1,194 km (2006) of narrow-gauge track (of which 317 km were electrified); Pres. ANGEL VILLALBA ALVAREZ; Dir-Gen. AMADOR RUBLES TASCÓN.

Ferrocarrils de la Generalitat de Catalunya (FGC): Pau Casals 24, 8°, 08021 Barcelona; tel. (93) 3663000; fax (93) 3663350; e-mail nalba@fgc.net; internet www.fgc.net; f. 1979; 290 km, of which 161 km are electrified; Pres. JOAN TORRES I CAROL.

Ferrocarrils de la Generalitat de Valencia (FGV): Partida de Xirivelleta, 46014 Valencia; tel. (96) 3976565; fax (96) 3976580; e-mail webmaster_fgv@gva.es; internet www.fgv.es; f. 1986; 237 km of track; also operates Valencia Metro, with four lines and 143 km of track, and Tram Alicante (93 km); Pres. MARIO FLORES LANUZA; Dir-Gen. MARISA GRACIA GIMÉNEZ.

Metro de Bilbao: Navarra 2, 48001 Bilbao; tel. (94) 4254000; e-mail info@metrobilbao.net; internet www.metrobilbao.com; f. 1995; 38.9 km; 2 lines and 36 stations; Dir-Gen. RAFAEL SARRIA ANSOLEAGA.

Metro de Madrid: Cavanilles 58, 28007 Madrid; tel. 902 444403; fax (91) 7212957; e-mail prensa@metromadrid.es; internet www.metromadrid.es; 283 km, 13 lines, 231 stations, also light railway network (Metro Ligero) of 28 km, 3 lines, 38 stations; Pres. MANUEL MELIS MAYNAR; Dir ILDEFONSO DE MATÍAS JIMÉNEZ.

Transports Metropolitans de Barcelona (TMB): Carrer 60, 21–31, Sector A. Polígono industrial Zona Franca, 08040 Barcelona; tel. (93) 2987000; e-mail tmb@tmb.net; internet www.tmb.net; 85.8 km, 6 lines, 104 stations (2008); Chair. ASSUMPTA ESCARP GILBERT TINTORÉ.

ROADS

The total road network at December 2003 was 666,292 km, including 12,609 km of motorway and 24,858 km of main roads.

Dirección General de Carreteras: Paseo de la Castellana 67, 28071 Madrid; tel. (91) 5977000; fax (91) 5978535; part of Ministry of Development; Dir-Gen. JUAN FRANCISCO LAZCANO ACEDO.

SHIPPING

Spain has many ports. Among the most important are Algeciras, Barcelona, Valencia, Tarragona, Bilbao, Cartagena, Gijón, Huelva and Santa Cruz de Tenerife. The 1,638 ships of the merchant fleet totalled 3,061,813 grt in December 2007.

Asociación de Navieros Españoles (ANAVE): Dr Fleming 11, 1° dcha, 28036 Madrid; tel. (91) 4580040; fax (91) 4579780; e-mail anave@anave.es; internet www.anave.es; shipowners' asscn; Pres. JUAN RIVA FRANCOS; Dir MANUEL CARLIER DE LAVALLE.

Dirección General de la Marina Mercante: Ruíz de Alarcón 1, 28014 Madrid; tel. (91) 5979118; fax (91) 5979120; part of Ministry of Development; Dir-Gen. FELIPE MARTÍNEZ MARTÍNEZ.

Puertos del Estado: Avda del Partenón 10, 28042 Madrid; tel. (91) 5245500; fax (91) 5245501; e-mail webmaster@puertos.es; internet www.puertos.es; Pres. MARIANO NAVAS GUTIÉRREZ.

Principal Shipping Companies

Acciona Trasmediterránea: Avda de Europa 10, Parque Empresarial La Moraleja, 28018 Alcobendas (Madrid); tel. (91) 4238500; fax (91) 4238555; e-mail info@trasmediterranea.es; internet www.trasmediterranea.es; f. 1917; Spanish ports, Balearic and Canary Is and Spanish North African, Algerian and Moroccan ports; Pres. MIGUEL ANGEL FERNÁNDEZ VILLAMANDOS; Dir-Gen. JOSÉ MANUEL FERNÁNDEZ VILLAMANDOS.

Agencia Marítima Española Evge: Avda Francesc Cambó 17, 08003 Barcelona; tel. (93) 3905800; fax (93) 2681750; e-mail evge@evgebcn.com; internet www.evgebcn.com; f. 1959; international shipping agents; Man. Dir RAMÓN OLIETE COSSIO.

Auximar, SL (Marítima del Norte): Miño 4, 28002 Madrid; tel. (91) 7454300; fax (91) 7454303; e-mail central@auximar.es; internet www.auximar.es; f. 1957; ship management, refrigerated cargo vessels, liquefied gas tankers; Dirs IÑIGO DE SENDAGORTA, JAVIER DE SENDAGORTA.

Compañía Remolcadores Ibaizabal: Muelle de Tomás Olabarri 4, 5°, 48930 Las Arenas (Vizcaya); tel. (94) 4645133; fax (94) 4645565; e-mail ibaizabal@ibaizabal.org; internet www.remolcadoresibaizabal.com; f. 1906; ocean-going, coastal, harbour, salvage; Pres. ALEJANDRO AZNAR SAINZ.

Compañía Trasatlántica Española: José Abascal 58, 3°, 28003 Madrid; tel. (91) 4514244; fax (91) 3993736; internet www.trasatlantica.com; f. 1850; freight services to Europe, North Africa, Caribbean, South America; Man. Dir JAVIER VILLASANTE.

Empresa Naviera Elcano S.A.: José Abascal, 4°, 28003 Madrid; tel. (91) 5369800; fax (91) 4451324; e-mail elcanox@xelcano.sa.es; internet www.navieraelcano.com; Pres. JOSÉ SILVERA.

Ership: Lagasca 88, 28001 Madrid; tel. (91) 4263400; fax (91) 5750883; e-mail chart@ership.com; internet www.ership.com; fmrly TAC; CEO GONZALO ALVARGONZÁLEZ.

Naviera Pinillos: Capitán Haya 21, 28020 Madrid; tel. (91) 5556711; fax (91) 5569777; e-mail pinillos@pinillos.com; internet www.pinillos.com; f. 1840; part of Grupo Boluda; services between Canary Is and other Spanish ports; Pres. VICENTE BOLUDA; Dir ANGEL MATO.

Nenufar Shipping: Manuel Ferreo 13, 28036 Madrid; tel. (91) 3158393; fax (91) 3158384; e-mail nenufar@nenufar.com; internet www.nenufar.com; f. 1983; part of Grupo Boluda; services to Spanish ports, Canary Is, Italy, Portugal, the United Kingdom, Morocco and Mauritania.

Repsol Naviera Vizcaina: Juan de Aguriaguerra 35, 2°, 48009 Bilbao; tel. (94) 4251100; fax (94) 4251143; f. 1956; world-wide, but particularly Mediterranean, Near East and Persian (Arabian) Gulf to Spain and transatlantic trade; Man. Dir JAVIER GONZÁLEZ JULIÁ.

CIVIL AVIATION

In 2008 there were more than 50 airports, almost all of which were equipped to receive international flights.

Dirección General de Aviación Civil: Paseo de la Castellana 67, 28071 Madrid; tel. (91) 5975356; fax (91) 5975357; internet www.fomento.es/aviacioncivil; Dir-Gen. MANUEL BAUTISTA PÉREZ.

Aeropuertos Españoles y Navegación Aérea (AENA): Arturo Soria 109, 28043 Madrid; tel. (91) 3211000; fax (91) 3212571; e-mail servicios-aeroportuarios@aena.es; internet www.aena.es; f. 1990; network of airports in Spain; Pres. MANUEL AZUAGA MORENO.

Principal Airlines

In mid-2006 a total of 30 Spanish airlines were registered with the Ministry of Development.

Air Europa Líneas Aéreas: Centro Empresarial Globalia, Apdo. Correos-132, 07620 Llucmajor; tel. (971) 178190; fax (971) 178353; internet www.air-europa.com; f. 1986; charter and scheduled services to Canary and Balearic Is, North Africa, Central, Southern and Eastern Europe; also Mexico, Cuba and Dominican Republic; Pres. JUAN JOSÉ HIDALGO ACERA; Dir-Gen. MANUEL PANADERO.

Binter Canarias: Aeropuerto de Gran Canaria, Parcela 9, del ZIMA Apdo 50, Gran Canaria; tel. (928) 579601; fax (928) 579603; e-mail info@bintercanarias.es; internet www.bintercanarias.com; f. 1988; scheduled services within Canary Islands and to Madeira, Morocco, Western Sahara and Mauritania; subsidiary of Grupo Iberia; Pres. PEDRO AGUSTÍN DEL CASTILLO; CEO RODOLFO NÚÑEZ RUANO.

Clickair: Solsones 2, Esc. B., 3° 1, Parc de Negocis Mas Blau, Prat de Llobregat, 08820 Barcelona; tel. (93) 3784400; e-mail info@clickair.com; internet www.clickair.com; f. 2006; low-cost airline; flights from Barcelona to other Spanish destinations (incl. Canary Islands), and to destinations in Europe, Israel, Russia and North Africa; Dir-Gen. ALEX CRUZ DE LLANO.

Grupo Iberia: Velázquez 130, 28006 Madrid; tel. (91) 5877462; fax (91) 5877949; e-mail prensaintl@iberia.es; internet www.iberia.com; f. 1927; domestic and international passenger and freight services to 101 destinations in 40 countries; partner in airline alliance OneWorld; Chair. and CEO FERNANDO CONTE GARCÍA.

Iberworld Airlines: Gran Vía Asima 23, Polígono Son Castelló, 07009 Palma de Mallorca; tel. (91) 229144; fax (91) 713184; e-mail iberworld@iberworld.com; internet www.iberworld.com; domestic, international and intercontinental charter flights.

LTE International Airways: Carrer del Ter 27, Polígono Son Fuster, 07009 Palma de Mallorca; tel. (971) 475700; fax (971) 478874; e-mail info@lte.es; internet www.lte.es; f. 1987; charter flights between Spanish islands, metropolitan Spain and Italy; Pres. JOSÉ M. GOYA; Dir CASIMIRO BERMÚDEZ.

Spanair: Edif. Spanair, 07611 Palma de Mallorca; tel. (971) 745020; fax (971) 492553; e-mail spanair@spanair.es; internet www.spanair.com; f. 1986; passenger scheduled and charter services within Spain, incl. Canary and Balearic Islands and within Europe, and to Algeria and The Gambia; 80.1% stake acquired by Iniciatives Empresarials Aeronàutiques in Jan. 2009; 19.9% owned by SAS Group (Denmark/Norway/Sweden); Pres. FERRAN SORIANO; CEO MARCUS HEDBLOM.

Vueling Airlines: Edif. Muntadas, Berguedà 1, Parque de Negocios Mas Blau, El Prat de Llobregat, 08820 Barcelona; tel. (93) 3787878; fax (93) 3787879; e-mail clients@vueling.com; internet www.vueling.com; f. 2004; low-cost airline; domestic and international flights; Pres. JOSEP PIQUÉ; CEO LARS NYGAARD.

Tourism

Spain's tourist attractions include its climate, beaches and historic cities. Tourism makes an important contribution to the country's economy. In 2007 59.2m. foreign tourists visited Spain. Receipts from tourism totalled €49,946m. in that year.

Instituto de Turismo de España (Turespaña): José Lázaro Galdiano 6, 28036 Madrid; tel. (91) 3433500; e-mail infosmile@tourspain.es; internet www.tourspain.es; promotes tourism; offices in Spain and abroad; Pres. JOAN MESQUIDE FERRANDO; Dir-Gen. ANTONIO BERNABÉ GARCÍA.

Secretaría de Estado de Comercio y Turismo: Paseo de la Castellana 160, 28071 Madrid; fax (91) 4578066; internet www.comercio.es; Sec. PEDRO MEJÍA GÓMEZ.

SPANISH EXTERNAL TERRITORIES

The Spanish External Territories comprise mainly Ceuta and Melilla, two enclaves within Moroccan territory on the north African coast. Attached to Melilla, for administrative purposes, are Peñón de Vélez de la Gomera, a small fort on the Mediterranean coast, and two groups of islands, Peñón de Alhucemas and the Chafarinas. Ceuta and Melilla are seen as integral parts of Spain by the Spanish Government and have the status of autonomous cities, although Morocco has put forward a claim to both. Sovereignty over the uninhabited island of Perejil (known as Laila to the Moroccans) is disputed between Spain and Morocco.

CEUTA

Introductory Survey

Location, Climate, Language, Religion

Ceuta, one of the two main enclaves of Spanish North Africa, is situated on the north African coast opposite Gibraltar, the Strait here being about 25 km wide. The average temperature is 17°C. Spanish and Arabic are spoken. The majority of Europeans are Roman Catholic, most North Africans being Muslim. There are small Hindu and Jewish communities.

Recent History

The population of the enclave is mostly Spanish. The proportion of Arab residents, however, has increased, owing to the large number of immigrants from Morocco. Those born in the territory are Spanish citizens and subjects. An ancient port and walled city, Ceuta was retained by Spain upon Moroccan independence from France in 1956. Having developed as a military and administrative centre for the former Spanish Protectorate in Morocco, Ceuta now functions as a bunkering and fishing port. In 1974 the town became the seat of the Capitanía General de Africa. Two-thirds of Ceuta's land area are used exclusively for military purposes.

In November 1978 King Hassan of Morocco stated his country's claim to Ceuta and the other main Spanish enclave in North Africa, Melilla, a claim that was reiterated following the opening of the Spanish frontier with Gibraltar in early 1985. In October 1981 Spain declared before the UN that Ceuta and Melilla were integral parts of Spanish territory. Spain rejects any comparison between the two enclaves and Gibraltar. From 1984 there was increasing unease over Spanish North Africa's future, following rioting in Morocco in January and the signing of the treaty of union between Libya and Morocco in August. In July 1985 the joint Libyan-Moroccan assembly passed a resolution calling for the 'liberation' of Ceuta and Melilla.

Details of Ceuta and Melilla's new draft statutes, envisaging the establishment of two local assemblies, with jurisdiction over such matters as public works, agriculture, tourism, culture and internal trade, were approved by the central Government in December 1985. Unlike Spain's other regional assemblies, however, those of Ceuta and Melilla were not to be vested with legislative powers. After negotiations with representatives of the Muslim community, in May 1986 the central Government agreed to grant Spanish nationality to more than 2,400 Muslims resident in the enclaves. At the general election held in June the ruling Partido Socialista Obrero Español (PSOE) was successful in Ceuta.

In February 1988 it was announced that, in accordance with regulations of the European Community (EC, now European Union—EU, see p. 255), to which Spain had acceded in 1986, Moroccan citizens would in due course require visas to enter Spain. Entry to Spanish North Africa, however, was to be exempt from the new ruling.

In March 1988, after several months of negotiations, the central Government and principal opposition parties in Madrid reached a broad consensus on draft autonomy statutes for Spanish North Africa. Although it was envisaged that Spain would retain the territories, the possibility of a negotiated settlement with Morocco was not discounted. In July, seven years after the enclaves' first official request for autonomy, the central Government announced that the implementation of the territories' autonomy statutes was to be accelerated. Meanwhile, in October Morocco's Minister of Foreign Affairs formally presented his country's claim to Ceuta and Melilla to the UN General Assembly. In 1989 Spain and Morocco agreed to hold annual summit meetings in an effort to improve relations. At the general election held in October 1989 the ruling PSOE retained its Ceuta seats, despite allegations by the opposition Partido Popular (PP) that many names on the electoral register were duplicated.

In April 1990 the Spanish Government presented the autonomy statutes for discussion in the territories. It was confirmed that the enclaves were to remain an integral part of Spain, and that they were to be granted self-government at municipal, rather than regional, level. Moroccan political parties were united in their denunciation of what they considered an attempt to legalize Spanish possession of the territories. The draft autonomy statutes of Ceuta and Melilla were submitted to the Congreso de los Diputados (Congress of Deputies) in Madrid for discussion in October 1991. In November thousands of demonstrators, many of whom had travelled from the enclaves, attended a protest march in Madrid (organized by the Governments of Ceuta and Melilla), in support of demands for full autonomy for the territories. In early 1992, however, the central Government confirmed that the assemblies of Ceuta and Melilla were not to be granted full legislative powers. At the general election of June 1993 the PSOE of Ceuta lost its one seat in the Congreso and its two seats in the Senado (Senate) to the PP.

The final statutes of autonomy were approved by the Spanish Government in September 1994, in preparation for their presentation to the Cortes (parliament). The statutes provided for 25-member local assemblies with powers similar to those of the municipal councils of mainland Spain. Each assembly would elect from among its members a city president. The proposals for limited self-government were not well received in Ceuta where, in October, a general strike received widespread support, while demonstrations subsequently took place in both Ceuta and Madrid. Following their approval by the Congreso de los Diputados in December, the autonomy statutes were ratified by the Senado in February 1995. Approval of the statutes by the Spanish Cortes was denounced by Morocco, which declared that the recovery of Ceuta and Melilla was to be one of its major objectives.

Elections for the new local assemblies were held in May 1995. In Ceuta the PP won nine of the 25 seats, Progreso y Futuro de Ceuta (PFC) six, the nationalist Ceuta Unida (CEU) four and the PSOE three. Basilio Fernández López of the PFC was re-elected Mayor/President, heading a coalition with CEU and the PSOE. Mustafa Mizziam Ammar, leader of the Partido Democrático y Social de Ceuta (PDSC), became the first Muslim candidate ever to be elected in the territory.

In February 1996 the Spanish and Moroccan Prime Ministers met in Rabat, Morocco, for their first summit meeting since December 1993. At the general election held in March 1996 the three PP delegates to the Cortes in Madrid were re-elected. In July Mayor/President Fernández López resigned after seven months at the head of a minority administration, and was replaced by Jesús Fortes Ramos of the PP, who urged that the enclave be considered a fully autonomous region.

In mid-1996 attention focused once again on the issue of illegal immigration from Africa. Both Ceuta and Melilla appealed to the EU for financial assistance to counter the problems arising from the enclaves' attractive location as an entry point to Europe and from the recent implementation of the EU's Schengen Agreement permitting the free movement of persons among the accord's signatory countries. Negotiations in Madrid in October between the Spanish Minister of the Interior and his Moroccan counterpart resulted in an agreement on the establishment of two joint commissions to address the specific problems of illegal immigration and drugs-trafficking. At further discussions in December, for the first time since the signing of a joint accord in 1992, Morocco agreed to the readmission of illegal immigrants held in the Spanish enclaves. In September the Secretary-General of the North Atlantic Treaty Organization (NATO) confirmed that Ceuta and Melilla would remain outside the alliance's sphere of protection if Spain were to be fully integrated into NATO's military structure.

At the elections of June 1999 the most successful party was the Grupo Independiente Liberal (GIL), which secured 12 of the 25 seats in the Assembly. Antonio Sampietro Casarramona of the GIL replaced Jesús Fortes Ramos of the PP as Mayor/President in August, following the latter's removal from office by a motion of censure supported by a rebel PSOE deputy, Susana Bermúdez. The defection to the GIL of the socialist deputy was ostensibly due to the PSOE's apparent refusal to allocate her the education and culture portfolio, as desired. The authorities subsequently announced that a judicial inquiry into the defection of Bermúdez was to be conducted.

Both the PSOE and the PP accused the GIL of having bribed the deputy to transfer her allegiance. In March 2000 Sampietro and Bermúdez were charged with bribery. At the general election held on 12 March Ceuta's three PP representatives in Madrid, one deputy and two senators, all secured re-election.

In early 1999 it was conceded that the security barrier along Ceuta's border with Morocco was proving inadequate. The EU-funded project had been initiated five years previously but remained unfinished. Between January and July alone a total of 21,411 illegal immigrants were apprehended on Ceuta's frontier and returned to Morocco. In November border security was reinforced by the army. Further improvements to the barrier were completed in February 2000. The implementation in that month of new legislation relating to immigrants' rights obliged the border post at Ceuta to provide legal assistance to those being denied entry to Spain by the police. In May the Government of Ceuta estimated that more than 25,000 potential immigrants, mainly Moroccans, were concentrated on the north African coast, awaiting an opportunity to travel to southern Spain. It was also revealed that during 1999 a total of 700,000 illegal immigrants had been refused admission to Spanish North Africa.

In Morocco, meanwhile, King Hassan died in July 1999. In January 2000 Prime Minister José María Aznar visited Ceuta and Melilla (although in his capacity as President of the PP, rather than President of the Government), describing the enclaves as constant parts of Spain's future. Morocco subsequently cancelled a scheduled official visit of the Spanish Minister of Foreign Affairs (although the official reason given by the Moroccan authorities for the cancellation was that King Muhammad was on holiday). In May Aznar declared that the controversial immigration law, which had taken effect in February, would need to be reviewed, as, since its entry into force, more than 82,000 immigrants had applied for Spanish residency permits. Large numbers of immigrants continued to enter the two enclaves illegally throughout 2000, and further clashes between migrants and the security forces were reported. The immigration law reforms, which entered into force in January 2001, intended to assist those seeking asylum but offered severe penalties to illegal immigrants and to traffickers in and employers of illegal immigrants. Protests against the reforms were staged in Spanish North Africa, as in Spain.

In September 2000, following a ruling in the Spanish courts that Ceuta and Melilla could not be considered to be autonomous communities, the ruling GIL proposed in the Ceuta Assembly that the Spanish Government grant Ceuta greater autonomy. Discussions on the proposal, which proved highly emotive, led to disturbances within the Assembly. However, the motion was subsequently carried by a majority vote.

In January 2001 five Ceuta councillors resigned their posts and announced their departure from the GIL, thus depriving the party of its majority in the Assembly. Former PSOE deputy Bermúdez subsequently withdrew her support for the GIL, which had previously enabled the party to assume office. A motion of censure against Sampietro, proposed by the PP, the PSOE, the PDSC and one of the former GIL councillors, was carried in February, with the support of 17 of the 25 deputies, and Juan Jesús Vivas Lara of the PP was appointed Mayor/President. A new Council was subsequently announced, including the five 'rebel' councillors (now members of the Grupo Mixto). The Vice-President of the Council, Jesús Simarro Marín, resigned in July; Cristina Bernal Durán was appointed to replace him.

The Government announced in September 2001 that the identification papers of Moroccans wishing to enter Ceuta and Melilla would be examined more closely and increased the police presence at the frontiers. In August the human rights organization Amnesty International had accused the Spanish Government of the systematic abuse of the rights of homeless children from Morocco and Algeria, citing Melilla and Ceuta as regions where the worst offences occurred.

Relations with Morocco remained tense in late 2001, especially following that country's abrupt withdrawal of its ambassador from Madrid in October. A confrontation developed between Moroccan and Spanish police in December when the Spanish authorities attempted to seize a vessel, allegedly laden with narcotics, which the Moroccans had already been pursuing through their own waters. Relations were threatened again in July 2002, after the occupation of Perejil, a small islet near Ceuta, by 12 Moroccan soldiers. Madrid made a formal protest to Rabat on 12 July, but Morocco refused to withdraw its men, claiming that Perejil (known as Laila to the Moroccans) had been a part of Morocco since independence in 1956. Four Spanish gunboats were dispatched to patrol the locality and Spanish soldiers reoccupied the island on 17 July. A subsequent US-mediated arrangement resulted in agreement by both countries to leave the islet unoccupied. However, in September Morocco reasserted its claims to Ceuta and Melilla at the UN. Later in the month Morocco additionally accused Spain of violating its airspace and territorial waters more than 90 times since July, and cancelled a scheduled meeting with Spain in protest against the alleged landing of a Spanish military helicopter on Perejil; Spain denied the claim. In response to several border incidents and in an attempt to halt illegal immigration, Spain ordered the permanent closure of the border with Morocco at Benzu in October.

A bilateral immigration accord signed by Spain and Morocco in February 2003 proposed the repatriation to Morocco of 200 illegal immigrant minors from Ceuta and Melilla in March. Early 2003 saw an increase in measures to strengthen border security. Moreover, a series of suicide bombings launched against Western targets in Casablanca in May, killing up to 45 people, resulted in a further tightening of border security. It was believed that one of the leaders of the militant Islamist group thought to be responsible for the attacks was a resident of Ceuta, and that others involved in the bombings had subsequently fled to mainland Spain via Ceuta. In June the Spanish Government's delegate in Ceuta initiated a request to the Ministry of Foreign Affairs in Madrid to withdraw citizenship from any dual-nationals in the enclave who were proven criminals, members of fundamentalist groups or pro-Moroccan. At the regional elections held in May 2003 the PP achieved an absolute majority in Ceuta for the first time, winning 19 out of 25 seats, while the Unión Demócrata Ceutí (UDCE), which represented the Muslim population, secured three. Juan Jesús Vivas Lara remained as Mayor/President.

In September 2003 Aznar visited Morocco for bilateral discussions, although the issue of sovereignty over Spain's North African possessions was reportedly avoided. In 2003 it was estimated that around 3,000 immigrants passed through Ceuta, and the enclave received more than 1,400 asylum requests, compared with 372 in 2002 and 82 in 2001. Official figures stated that 18% of the requests processed in 2003 were successful. In December 2003 Morocco and Spain made progress towards reaching an accord on the repatriation of illegal immigrant minors; however, a final agreement was not signed. Human rights groups criticized the two centres provided by the Spanish Government for immigrants as inadequate.

At the general election held on 14 March 2004 the PP retained the deputy and senators elected by Ceuta. In September the Mayor/President, Vivas Lara, met with the newly elected Spanish Prime Minister, José Luis Rodríguez Zapatero, to discuss the possible change in status of Ceuta from Ciudad Autónoma (Autonomous City) to Comunidad Autónoma (Autonomous Community), in line with other areas of Spain. In that year the height of the barrier separating Ceuta and Morocco reached 6 m. In November the central Government unveiled plans to build reception centres for immigrants on the mainland, to which illegal immigrants arrested in Ceuta and Melilla would be transported.

In 2005 potential immigrants continued to attempt to gain access to Europe through Ceuta and Melilla, with a succession of groups of would-be immigrants attempting to scale the walls separating the enclaves from Morocco. In September five would-be immigrants were killed by security forces during an attempt by some 600 people to climb the wall into Ceuta. It was announced at a Spanish-Moroccan summit held in late September in Seville, Spain, that security on both sides of the border would be increased following the attempts; however, the waves of immigration continued in early October, and more deaths resulted. Concern arose that immigrants captured by Moroccan security forces were being abandoned in Morocco's south-western desert. In October the Spanish Government authorized €3m. to improve facilities for immigrants in the enclaves. Heightened security reduced the number of attempts being made to climb the walls, but it appeared that immigrants were looking for new (and potentially more dangerous) routes to Europe via the Canary Islands.

In October 2005 the Congreso de los Diputados in Madrid reaffirmed the integral Spanish nature of the enclaves. In early 2006 Zapatero made the first official visit by a Prime Minister to the enclaves in over 25 years. His visit was condemned by the Moroccan authorities as a provocation, despite the fact that relations between Spain and Morocco had been favourable during the first two years of Zapatero's administration, with increasing co-operation on immigration issues. In May the Councillor of Development, Elena Sánchez, died suddenly. She was replaced by Juan António Rodríguez Ferrón, hitherto Councillor of the Interior. In the same month the Government Delegate in Ceuta, Jerónimo Nieto, was replaced by José Jenaro García-Arreciado Batanero.

In February 2007 the Spanish Government reached an agreement with the Governments of Ceuta and Melilla to abandon plans to change the cities' status to that of Autonomous Communities. In return, more powers would be devolved to the cities in the areas of employment and social services, and their budgets would be increased. At elections held on 27 May the PP retained its absolute majority in the Assembly, again winning 19 of the 25 seats; the UDCE, in alliance with the left-wing Izquierda Unida, secured four seats, while the PSOE won two. Vivas Lara resumed office as Mayor/President. The entire regional executive of the PSOE, headed by Secretary-General Antonia Palomo, resigned as a result of the party's poor performance in the elections. In October ongoing divisions within the local branch of the PSOE led to its dissolution, and the party's national leadership delegated a commission to assume temporary responsibility for PSOE activities in Ceuta. (The local

SPANISH EXTERNAL TERRITORIES   Ceuta

branch of the PSOE resumed activities under a newly elected Secretary-General, José Antonio Carracao, in December 2008.)

In early November 2007 a two-day visit to Ceuta and Melilla by King Juan Carlos, his first since acceding to the throne in 1975, was warmly welcomed by residents, but provoked considerable anger in Morocco. The Moroccan Government recalled its ambassador from Madrid for consultations ahead of the visit, which it deemed regrettable and provocative. The Spanish Prime Minister sought to defuse tensions, insisting that relations with Morocco, which had improved in recent years, remained strong. However, Morocco's King Muhammad VI noted that Spain risked jeopardizing bilateral relations, and urged Spain to engage in dialogue with Morocco over the disputed enclaves. Later in November the Moroccan Government postponed a planned visit to Rabat by the Spanish Minister of Development. The Moroccan ambassador to Spain returned to Madrid in January 2008, following a visit to Rabat by the Spanish Minister of Foreign Affairs and Co-operation, Miguel Angel Moratinos, who delivered a conciliatory letter from Prime Minister Zapatero to King Muhammad.

At the general election held on 9 March 2008 the PP retained Ceuta's one seat in the Congreso de los Diputados and its two seats in the Senado. In April the Government of Ceuta opposed plans to reorganize the Spanish armed forces, amid fears that they would result in a substantial reduction in the number of troops stationed in the city. However, the central Government rejected this suggestion, insisting that the composition of the forces deployed in its North African territories would change, but that it did not intend to reduce overall numbers. In the following month José Fernández Chacón was appointed to replace José Jenaro García-Arreciado Batanero as Government Delegate in Ceuta.

Late 2008 saw an increase in measures to strengthen border security after a militant Islamist group, al-Qa'ida in the Islamic Maghreb, announced that it intended to intensify its campaign of violence against the governments of North Africa. (Previously confined largely to Algeria, the group had latterly staged several bomb attacks in neighbouring countries, and its leader, Abu Musab Abd al-Wadud, had reportedly stated his intention to expand its activities into Europe.)

Government

Following the adoption of statutes of autonomy and the establishment of local assemblies in 1995, Ceuta and Melilla remain integral parts of Spain, but have greater jurisdiction over matters such as public works, internal trade and tourism. Each enclave has its own Mayor/President. Ceuta, Melilla and the island dependencies are known as *plazas de soberanía*, fortified enclaves over which Spain has full sovereign rights. In both Ceuta and Melilla civil authority is vested in an official (Delegado del Gobierno) directly responsible to the Ministry of the Interior in Madrid. This official is usually assisted by a government sub-delegate. There is also one delegate from each of the Ministries in Madrid.

Defence

Military authority is vested in a commandant-general. The enclaves are attached to the military region of Seville. Spain had 8,100 troops deployed in its North African territories in August 2003.

Economic Affairs

In 2007, according to official estimates, the gross domestic product (GDP) of Ceuta was equivalent to €21,994 per head, ranking 10th (in terms of GDP per head) in a list of the 19 Spanish autonomous regions. According to preliminary official estimates, total GDP was €1,613.9m. in 2008. The population of Ceuta increased by an annual average of 0.2% in 2002–08, while GDP grew by 3.0% during 2000–08; GDP increased, in real terms, by an estimated 3.8% in 2007, but growth for 2008 was estimated at just 1.8%.

Agricultural activity in Ceuta is negligible, as is employment in the sector; according to preliminary estimates, the sector contributed just 0.2% of GDP in 2008. Agricultural GDP decreased, in real terms, by an annual average of 4.2% during 2000–08; the sector's GDP decreased by an estimated 8.2% in 2008.

Industry is on a limited scale (although there is a local brewery), but the sector contributed 15.7% of GDP in 2008, and 9.8% of the employed population were engaged in the sector, on average, during the first quarter of 2009. Manufacturing GDP increased, in real terms, by an annual average of 1.0% during 2000–08; the GDP of the manufacturing sector increased by 3.2% in 2007, but was estimated to have declined by 0.7% in 2008. A small decline (0.3%) was also recorded in the construction sub-sector in 2008, although the energy sub-sector recorded a small increase of 1.5% in that year, according to official estimates.

Services contributed an estimated 84.1% of GDP in 2008, and some 90.2% of the employed population were engaged in the sector, on average, in the first quarter of 2009. Services GDP increased, in real terms, by an annual average of 2.9% during 2000–08; the sector's GDP increased by 4.7% in 2007, and by an estimated 2.3% in 2008.

Most of the population's food is imported, with the exception of fish, which is obtained locally (sardines and anchovies are among the most significant catches). A large proportion of the tinned fish is sold outside Spain. More important to the economies of Ceuta and Melilla is the port activity; most of their exports take the form of fuel supplied—at very competitive rates—to ships. Most of the fuel comes from the Spanish refinery in Tenerife. Ceuta's port received a total of 8,506 ships in 2005. The main exports are frozen and preserved fish, foodstuffs and beer. Most trade is conducted with other parts of Spain. In 2008 Ceuta's trade deficit was €293.9m. In that year the principal source of imports (accounting for some 25% of the total value) was the Netherlands; other major suppliers were the People's Republic of China (around 16%), Belgium and France. Mexico was the principal market for exports (taking some 85% of the total value). The principal imports in 2008 were mineral fuels and oils, accounting for more than 50% of the total, and textiles and clothing. The principal exports were pharmaceutical products (accounting for more than 80% of the total value). Tourism makes a significant contribution to the territory's economy. In 2004 68,205 tourists visited Ceuta, attracted by duty-free goods. In 2006 89,931 overnight stays were recorded by tourist visitors to Ceuta and Melilla. In 2004 there was an estimated budget surplus of €750,000, equivalent to 0.1% of GDP. The annual rate of inflation averaged 3.1% in 2002–08; the rate was 3.8% in 2008. According to provisional estimates, on average, some 15.8% of the labour force were unemployed during the first quarter of 2009.

Upon the accession in January 1986 of Spain to the European Community (EC, now European Union—EU, see p. 255), Ceuta was considered a Spanish city and therefore as European territory, and joined the organization as part of Spain. It retained its status as a free port. The statute of autonomy, adopted in early 1995, envisaged the continuation of the territory's fiscal benefits. Euro notes and coins became the sole legal tender on 28 February 2002.

Sustained Spanish economic growth in the 2000s and successive enlargements of the EU that took place during that decade limited Spain's access to EU aid, with the result that, although income in the enclave had not improved significantly, subsidies for Ceuta would be progressively reduced during the period 2007–13, with a view to their eventual withdrawal. The city's consolidated budget for 2008 included current and capital transfers from the Spanish state of €64.8m and €28.5m., respectively. Ceuta's economy relies heavily on a transient Moroccan work-force; unofficial estimates of unemployment among Ceuta's permanent residents suggest a rate of some 35%, the highest in Spain.

Education

The education system is similar to that of mainland Spain; however, there are also teachers of the Islamic religion in the city.

Statistical Survey

Sources (unless otherwise stated): Administración General del Estado, Beatriz de Silva 4, 51001 Ceuta; tel. (956) 512616; fax (956) 511893; Instituto Nacional de Estadística, Paseo de la Castellana 183, 28071 Madrid; tel. (91) 5839100; fax (91) 5839158; internet www.ine.es; *Memoria Socioeconómico y Laboral de 2004:* Consejo Económico y Social, Edif. La Tahoma, Esquina Salud Tejero y Dueñas, Ceuta; tel. (956) 519131; fax (956) 519146; e-mail ces-ceuta@ceuta.es.

AREA AND POPULATION

Area: 19.7 sq km (7.6 sq miles).

Population (census results): 67,615 at 1 March 1991; 71,505 at 1 November 2001 (males 35,991, females 35,514). *2009* (official estimate at 1 January): 72,561 (males 36,284, females 36,277).

Density (1 January 2009): 3,683 per sq km.

Births, Marriages and Deaths (2007): Live births 1,136 (birth rate 15.8 per 1,000); Marriages 374 (marriage rate 5.2 per 1,000); Deaths 537 (death rate 7.5 per 1,000).

Life Expectancy (years at birth): Total 78.6 (males 75.7; females 81.6) in 2005.

Immigration and Emigration (2007): Immigrants 460; Emigrants 112.

Economically Active Population ('000 persons aged 16 years and over, January–March 2009, estimates): Agriculture, hunting, forestry and fishing 0.0; Construction 1.4; Other industry 1.4; Services 25.9; *Total employed* 28.7; Unemployed 5.4; *Total labour force* 34.1 (males 20.8, females 13.4).

AGRICULTURE, ETC.

Livestock (animals slaughtered, 2004): Sheep 1,025; Goats 108.

SPANISH EXTERNAL TERRITORIES

Fishing (metric tons, live weight of catch): 304.1 in 2002; 310.8 in 2003; 236.8 in 2004.

FINANCE

Currency and Exchange Rates: 100 cent = 1 euro (€). *Sterling and Dollar Equivalents* (31 December 2008): £1 Sterling = 1.047 euros; US $1 = 0.719 euros; 10 euros = £9.55 = $13.92. *Average Exchange Rate* (euros per US $): 0.7971 in 2006; 0.7306 in 2007; 0.6827 in 2008. Note: The local currency was formerly the Spanish peseta. From the introduction of the euro, with Spanish participation, on 1 January 1999, a fixed exchange rate of €1 = 166.386 pesetas was in effect. Euro notes and coins were introduced on 1 January 2002. The euro and local currency circulated alongside each other until 28 February, after which the euro became the sole legal tender.

Budget (€ '000, 2004): *Revenue:* Current operations 170,621.8 (Direct taxation 6,397.6, Indirect taxation 90,247.4, Rates and other revenue 14,342.8, Current transfers 54,106.2, Estate taxes 5,527.7); Capital operations 49,002.7 (Capital transfers 31,715.2, Transfers of real investments 3,073.4, Assets 704.3, Liabilities 13,509.7); Total 219,624.5. *Expenditure:* Current operations 153,214.7 (Wages and salaries 74,948.9, Goods and services 55,016.6, Financial 3,561.4, Current transfers 19,687.8); Capital operations 65,659.8 (Real investments 53,365.5, Capital transfers 0.0, Assets 1,705.0, Liabilities 10,589.2); Total 218,874.5.

Cost of Living (Consumer Price Index; base: 2006 = 100): All items 96.9 in 2005; 101.9 in 2007; 105.8 in 2008.

Gross Domestic Product (€ million at current prices, provisional): 1,447.8 in 2006; 1,555.5 in 2007; 1,613.9 in 2008.

Gross Domestic Product by Economic Activity (€ million at current prices, 2008, provisional): Agriculture, hunting, forestry and fishing 3.2; Energy 75.4; Construction 119.1; Other industry 37.9; Services 1,241.9; *Sub-total* 1,477.5; Net taxes on products 136.4; *GDP at market prices* 1,613.9.

EXTERNAL TRADE

Principal Commodities (€ million, 2008): *Imports:* Milk and dairy products, eggs, honey, etc. 17.1; Mineral fuels and oils, and products thereof 150.9; Textile and clothing 37.8; Footwear 11.2; Electrical machinery and equipment, and parts thereof 14.0; Vehicles (excl. rail or tram), and parts thereof 10.9; Total (incl. others) 296.5. *Exports:* Pharmaceutical products 2.2; Total (incl. others) 2.6.

Principal Trading Partners (€ million, 2008): *Imports:* Belgium 34.2; China, People's Republic 48.4; France 32.4; Netherlands 75.4; Total (incl. others) 296.5. *Exports:* Mexico 2.2; Total (incl. others) 2.6.

Source: Foreign Trade Database, Agencia Tributaria (Madrid).

TRANSPORT

Road Traffic (Ceuta and Melilla, 2007): Vehicles registered 107,258 (Passenger cars 76,801, Buses, etc. 115, Lorries and vans 16,675, Motorcycles 11,637, Tractors 195, Other 1,835).

Shipping (domestic and international, 2006, provisional): Vessels entered 10,498; Goods handled ('000 metric tons) 1,855; Passenger movements ('000) 2,377.

Civil Aviation (2006, preliminary): Journeys made 2,343; Passengers carried ('000) 21; Goods transported 3 metric tons.

TOURISM

Visitor Arrivals (by country of residence, 2002): France 2,653; Germany 700; Italy 1,076; Portugal 1,062; Spain 41,593; United Kingdom 1,430; USA 2,939; Total (incl. others) 61,356. *2004:* Foreign visitors 17,243; Spanish visitors 50,962; Total visitors 68,205. *2006* (Ceuta and Melilla): 89,931 overnight stays by tourists.

COMMUNICATIONS MEDIA

Telephones (main lines in use, 2004): 24,849.

EDUCATION

(2005/06)

Pre-primary: 24 schools; 149 teachers; 2,961 students.

Primary: 22 schools; 411 teachers (excl. 42 engaged in both pre-primary and primary teaching); 5,948 students.

Secondary: First Cycle: 16 schools (of which 6 schools also provided second-cycle education and 5 provided vocational education, see below); 209 teachers (excl. 34 engaged in both secondary and primary teaching and 234 engaged in more than one cycle of secondary); 3,874 students.

Secondary: Second Cycle: 34 teachers; 1,298 students.

Secondary: Vocational: 83 teachers; 970 students.

Source: Ministry of Education and Science, Madrid.

Directory

Government

Government Delegate in Ceuta: JOSÉ FERNÁNDEZ CHACÓN.

Deputy elected to the Congress in Madrid: FRANCISCO ANTONIO GONZÁLEZ PÉREZ (PP).

Representatives to the Senate in Madrid: NICOLÁS FERNÁNDEZ CUCURULL (PP), LUZ ELENA SANÍN NARANJO (PP).

COUNCIL OF GOVERNMENT
(April 2009)

Mayor/President: JUAN JESÚS VIVAS LARA.

Vice-President and Councillor of the Presidency: PEDRO GORDILLO DURÁN.

Councillor of Development: JUAN MANUEL DONCEL DONCEL.

Councillor of the Economy and Employment: GUILLERMO MARTÍNEZ ARCAS.

Councillor of Education, Culture and Women: MARÍA ISABEL DEU DEL OLMO.

Councillor of the Environment and Urban Services: YOLANDA BEL BLANCA.

Councillor of Health and Consumer Affairs: ADELA MARÍA NIETO SÁNCHEZ.

Councillor of the Interior: JOSÉ ANTONIO RODRÍGUEZ GÓMEZ.

Councillor of Finance: FRANCISCO MÁRQUEZ DE LA RUBIA.

Councillor of Social Affairs: CAROLINA PÉREZ GÓMEZ.

Councillor of Youth, Sports and New Technology: KISSY CHANDIRAMANI RAMESH.

GOVERNMENT OFFICES

Delegación del Gobierno: Beatriz de Silva 4, 51001 Ceuta; tel. (956) 984400; fax (956) 513671; e-mail roberto@ceuta.map.es.

Office of the Mayor/President: Plaza de Africa s/n, Asamblea, 1°, 51001 Ceuta; tel. and fax (956) 528309; e-mail presidencia@ceuta.es; internet www.ceuta.es.

Council of Development: Plaza de Africa s/n, Asamblea, 3°, 51001 Ceuta; tel. and fax (956) 528240; e-mail fomento@ceuta.es.

Council of the Economy and Employment: Edif. Ceuta Center, 1°, 51001 Ceuta; tel. and fax (956) 528262; e-mail economia@ceuta.es.

Council of Education, Culture and Women: Plaza de Africa s/n, Asamblea, 2°, 51001 Ceuta; tel. and fax (956) 528166; e-mail educacion@ceuta.es.

Council of the Environment and Urban Services: Plaza de Africa s/n, Asamblea, 3°, 51001 Ceuta; tel. and fax (956) 528164; e-mail medioambiente@ceuta.es; internet www.ceuta.es/medioambiente.

Council of Finance: Edif. Ceuta Center, 51001 Ceuta; e-mail hacienda@ceuta.es.

Council of Health and Consumer Affairs: Carretera San Amaro 12, Ceuta; tel. and fax (856) 200680; fax (856) 200723; e-mail sanidad@ceuta.es.

Council of the Interior: Edif. Polifuncional, Avda España, 51001 Ceuta; tel. (956) 528076.

Council of Social Affairs: Carretera San Amaro 12, Ceuta; tel. (856) 200680; fax (856) 200723.

Council of Youth, Sports and New Technologies: Avda de Africa s/n, Ceuta; tel. (956) 518844; fax (956) 510295.

Assembly

Election, 27 May 2007

	Seats
Partido Popular (PP)	19
Unión Demócrata Ceutí (UDCE)-Izquierda Unida (IU)	4
Partido Socialista Obrero Español (PSOE)	2
Total	**25**

SPANISH EXTERNAL TERRITORIES   *Ceuta*

Election Commission

Junta Electoral de Zona y Provincial de Ceuta: Ceuta; Sec. Francisco Javier Izquierdo Carbonero.

Political Organizations

Izquierda Unida (IU): General Yaque, 4-1°, 11701 Ceuta; tel. and fax (956) 513558; e-mail izquierdaunidaceuta@hotmail.com; internet www.izquierda-unida.es; alliance of left-wing parties; Leader Mohammed Haddu Musa.

Partido Democrático y Social de Ceuta (PDSC): Bolivia 35, 51001 Ceuta; Muslim party; Leader Mustafa Mizziam Ammar.

Partido Popular (PP): Teniente Arrabal 4, Edif. Ainara, Bajo, 51001 Ceuta; tel. (956) 511636; fax (956) 513218; e-mail ceuta@pp.es; internet www.ppceuta.es; fmrly Alianza Popular; national-level, centre-right party; Pres. Pedro Gordillo Durán; Sec.-Gen. María Dolores Pastilla Gómez.

Partido Socialista Obrero Español (PSOE): Daóiz 1, 51001 Ceuta; tel. (956) 515553; internet www.ceuta.psoe.es; national-level, left-wing party; Sec.-Gen. José Antonio Carracao.

Partido Socialista del Pueblo de Ceuta (PSPC): Echegarray 1, Local 1D, 51001 Ceuta; tel. and fax (956) 518869; e-mail pspc@pspc.info; internet www.pspc.es; f. 1986 by dissident members of PSOE and others; Sec.-Gen. Iván Chaves.

Unión Demócrata Ceutí (UDCE): Avda Teniente-Coronel Gautier 22, 2° dcha, Ceuta; Muslim party; Leader Muhammad Alí.

There are also various civic associations.

Judicial System

Tribunal Superior de Justicia de Andalucía, Ceuta y Melilla: Plaza Nueva, 10, Palacio de la Real Chancillería, 18071 Granada, Spain; tel. (958) 002600; fax (958) 002720; e-mail webmaster.ius@juntadeandalucia.es; internet www.juntadeandalucia.es; Pres. Augusto Méndez de Lugo y López De Ayala.

Religion

CHRISTIANITY

The Roman Catholic Church

Bishop of Cádiz and Ceuta: Antonio Ceballos Atienza (resident in Cádiz), Vicar-General Francisco Correro Tocón, Obispado de Ceuta, Plaza de Nuestra Señora de Africa, 51001 Ceuta; tel. (956) 517732; fax (956) 513208; e-mail obispadoceuta@planalfa.es; internet www.obispadodecadizyceuta.org.

OTHER RELIGIONS

Ceuta has a large Muslim population (estimated at around 30,000), as well as Jewish and Hindu communities.

The Press

El Faro de Ceuta: Sargento Mena 8, 51001 Ceuta; tel. (956) 524035; fax (956) 524147; e-mail ceuta@grupofaro.es; internet www.elfaroceutamelilla.es; f. 1934; morning; Pres. Rafael Montero Palacios; Editors-in-Chief José M. Gallardo, Tamara Crespo; circ. 5,000.

El Pueblo de Ceuta: Independencia 11, 1°, 51001 Ceuta; tel. (956) 514367; fax (956) 517650; e-mail elpuebloredaccion@telefonica.net; internet www.elpubloceuta.es; f. 1995; daily; Dir and Editor-in-Chief Salvador Vivancos Canales.

NEWS AGENCY

Agencia EFE: Milán Astray 1, 1°, Of. 8, 51001 Ceuta; tel. (956) 517550; fax (956) 516639; e-mail ceuta@agenciaefe.net; Correspondent Rafael Peña Soler.

PRESS ASSOCIATION

Asociación de la Prensa: Beatriz de Silva 14, 1° E, 51001 Ceuta; tel. (639) 403713; fax (956) 528205; Pres. Francisco Ruiz Jiménez Carmona.

Broadcasting

RADIO

Onda Cero Radio Ceuta: Delgado Serrano 1, 1° dcha, 51001 Ceuta; tel. (956) 200068; fax (956) 200179; internet www.ondacero.es; Dir Rafael Romaguera Mena.

Radio Nacional de España: Real 90, 51001 Ceuta; tel. (956) 524688; fax (956) 519067; e-mail prensa@rtve.es; internet www.rtve.es; Dir Eduardo Sánchez Dorado.

Radio Popular de Ceuta/COPE: Sargento Mena 8, 1°, 11701 Ceuta; tel. (956) 524200; fax (956) 524202; internet www.cope.es; Dir Daniel Oliva.

Radio Televisión Ceuta: Real 90, Portón 4, 1° dcha, 51001 Ceuta; tel. (956) 511820; fax (956) 516820; e-mail televidente@rtvce.es; internet www.rtvce.es; f. 1934; commercial; owned by Sociedad Española de Radiodifusión; Dir Antonio Rosa Guerrero.

TELEVISION

Radio Televisión Ceuta: Real 90, Portón 4, 1° dcha, 51001 Ceuta; tel. (956) 511820; fax (956) 516820; internet www.rtvce.es; Dir Manuel González Bolorino.

Finance

BANKING

In 2007 there were nine banks operating in Ceuta, all of which were based in mainland Spain.

Banco Bilbao Vizcaya Argentaria (BBVA): Gonzalez de la Vega 8, 51001 Ceuta; tel. (956) 201238; fax (956) 510585; internet www.bbva.es; 4 brs.

Banco de España: Plaza de España 2, 51001 Ceuta; tel. (956) 513253; fax (956) 513108; internet www.bde.es.

Banco Español de Crédito (Banesto): Camoens 5, 51001 Ceuta; tel. (956) 524028; internet www.banesto.es.

Banco Popular Español: Paseo del Revellín 1, 51001 Ceuta; tel. (956) 515340; fax (956) 512970; internet www.bancopopular.es.

Banco Santander Central Hispano (BSCH): Paseo del Revellín 17–19, 51001 Ceuta; tel. (956) 511371; internet www.gruposantander.es; 2 brs.

Caja de Ahorros y Pensiones de Barcelona (La Caixa): Gran Vía s/n, 51001 Ceuta; tel. (956) 515886; fax (956) 513972; internet www.lacaixa.es; 4 brs.

Caja Duero: Sargento Coriat 5, 51001 Ceuta; tel. (956) 518040; fax (956) 517019; tel. www.cajaduero.es; 1 br.

Caja Madrid: Plaza de los Reyes s/n, 51001 Ceuta; tel. (956) 524016; fax (956) 524017; internet www.cajamadrid.es; 6 brs.

Montes de Piedad y Caja de Ahorros de Ronda, Cádiz, Almería, Málaga y Antequera (Unicaja): Paseo Revellín 21, 51001 Ceuta; tel. (956) 518340; fax (956) 519561; internet www.unicaja.es; 2 brs.

INSURANCE

MAPFRE: Paseo Marina Española 92, Edif. Patio Paramo, 51001 Ceuta; tel. (956) 519638; fax (956) 513916; e-mail balfaro@mapfre.com; internet www.mapfre.com; Commercial Man. Borja Alfaro Infante; 3 offices.

Trade and Industry

Cámara Oficial de Comercio, Industria y Navegación: Dueñas 2, 51001 Ceuta; tel. (956) 509590; fax (956) 509589; e-mail camerceuta@camaras.org; internet www.camaraceuta.org; chamber of commerce; Pres. Luis Moreno Naranjo; Sec.-Gen. María del Rosario Espinosa Suárez.

Confederación de Empresarios de Ceuta: Paseo de las Palmeras, Edif. Corona 26–28, 51001 Ceuta; tel. (856) 200038; fax (956) 512010; e-mail info@confeceuta.es; internet www.confeceuta.es; employers' confed; Pres. Rafael Montero Avalos; Sec.-Gen. Josefa Guerrero Ríos.

UTILITIES

Aguas de Ceuta Empresa Municipal, SA (ACEMSA): Solis 1, Edif. San Luis, Ceuta; tel. (956) 524619; e-mail aguasdeceuta@acemsa.es; internet www.acemsa.es; Pres. Yolanda Bel Blanco; Dir-Gen. Manuel Gómez Hoyos.

Empresa de Alumbrado Eléctrico de Ceuta SA: Beatriz de Silva 2, Ceuta; tel. (956) 511901; e-mail info@electricadeceuta.com; internet www.electricadeceuta.com; generates and transmits electricity; Rep. Alberto Ramón Gaitán Rodríguez.

TRADE UNION

Confederación Sindical de Comisiones Obreras (CCOO): Alcalde Fructuoso Miaja 1, 51001 Ceuta; tel. (956) 516243; fax (956) 517991; e-mail ccoo.ce@ceuta.ccoo.es; internet www.ccoo.es; 3,214 mems (2004); Sec.-Gen. José Luis Aróstegui Ruiz.

SPANISH EXTERNAL TERRITORIES

Transport

Much of the traffic between Spain and Morocco passes through Ceuta; there are ferry services to Algeciras, Melilla, Málaga and Almería. Plans for an airport are under consideration. Helicopter services to Málaga are provided by Helisureste. There were 28 km of paved roads in Ceuta in 2006. Construction of a highway between the Port of Ceuta and the Moroccan border was due to be completed in 2010. The Port of Ceuta is one of the most important in the Mediterranean. In 2006 1.9m. metric tons of goods, 2.4m. passengers and 10,498 boats passed through the port.

Port of Ceuta: Autoridad Portuaria de Ceuta, Muelle de España s/n, 51001 Ceuta; tel. (956) 527000; fax (956) 527001; e-mail apceuta@puertodeceuta.com; internet www.puertodeceuta.com; Pres. José Francisco Torrado López.

Acciona Trasmediterránea: Muelle Cañorero Dato 6, 51001 Ceuta; tel. (956) 505390; fax (956) 504714; e-mail info@trasmediterranea.es; internet www.trasmediterranea.es; f. 1917; services between Algeciras and Ceuta.

Euroferrys: Muelle Cañorero Dato, 51001 Ceuta; tel. (956) 507070; fax (956) 505588; e-mail clientes@euroferrys.com; internet www.euroferrys.com; f. 1998; owned by Acciona Trasmediterránea; passenger and cargo services between Algeciras and Ceuta; Pres. Joaquín González Sanjuán.

Tourism

Visitors are attracted by the historical monuments, the Parque Marítimo and the museums, as well as by the Shrine of Our Lady of Africa. There were 68,205 visitors to Ceuta in 2004, of whom 50,962 were from mainland Spain. In that year Ceuta had five hotels.

Servicios Turísticos de Ceuta: Baluarte de los Mallorquines, Edrissis s/n, 51001 Ceuta; tel. (856) 200560; fax (856) 200565; e-mail turismo@ceuta.es; internet www.turismodeceuta.es.

MELILLA

Introductory Survey

Location, Climate, Language, Religion

Melilla is situated on a small peninsula jutting into the Mediterranean Sea. The average temperature is 17°C. Spanish and Arabic are spoken. The majority of Europeans are Roman Catholic, most North Africans being Muslim.

Recent History

The population of Melilla is mostly Spanish. The proportion of Arab residents, however, has greatly increased, owing to the large number of immigrants from Morocco. Those born in the territory are Spanish citizens and subjects. Melilla was the first Spanish town to rise against the Government of the Popular Front in July 1936, at the beginning of the Spanish Civil War. Like Ceuta, Melilla was retained by Spain when Morocco became independent in 1956. In addition to its function as a port, Melilla now serves as a military base, more than one-half of the enclave's land area being used solely for military purposes. In October 1978 King Hassan of Morocco attempted to link the question of the sovereignty of Melilla to that of the return of the British dependent territory of Gibraltar to Spain. (See the chapter on Ceuta for details on Morocco's relationship with Spain and the North African enclaves.)

After negotiations with representatives of the Muslim community, in May 1986 the central Government in Madrid agreed to grant Spanish nationality to more than 2,400 Muslims resident in Melilla and Ceuta, under the terms of legislation introduced in July 1985 requiring all foreigners resident in Spain to register with the authorities. At that time only some 7,000 of the estimated 27,000-strong Muslim community in Melilla held Spanish nationality. In response to protests, particularly in Melilla, the central Government had given assurances that it would assist the full integration into Spanish society of Muslims in the enclaves. By mid-1986, however, the number of Muslims applying for Spanish nationality in Melilla had reached several thousand. As a result of delays in the processing of the applications, Aomar Muhammadi Dudú, the leader of the newly founded Muslim Partido de los Demócratas de Melilla (PDM), accused the Government of failing to fulfil its pledge to the Muslim residents.

At the general election of June 1986 the ruling Partido Socialista Obrero Español (PSOE) was defeated by the centre-right Coalición Popular (CP) in Melilla, the result indicating the strong opposition of the Spanish community to the Government's plan to integrate the Muslim population. Tight security surrounded the elections, and 'parallel elections', resulting in a vote of confidence in the PDM leader, were held by the Muslim community. Polling was accompanied by several days of unrest. Talks in Madrid between representatives of the main political parties in Melilla and the Ministry of the Interior resulted in concessions to the enclave. In September Dudú agreed to accept a senior post in the Ministry, with responsibility for relations with the Muslim communities of Spain. In November, however, Muslim leaders in Melilla announced that they wished to establish their own administration in the enclave, in view of the Madrid Government's failure to fulfil its promise of Spanish citizenship for Muslim residents. The Spanish Minister of the Interior reiterated assurances of the Government's commitment to integrating the Muslim community. Later in the month thousands of Muslims took part in a peaceful demonstration in support of Dudú, who had resigned his Madrid post after only two months in office. (He subsequently went into exile in Morocco and lost the support of Melilla's Muslim community.)

In February 1987 police reinforcements were dispatched from Spain, in response to a serious escalation of inter-racial tensions in Melilla. Numerous demonstrators were detained, and several prominent Muslims were charged with sedition and briefly held in custody. King Hassan reaffirmed his support for the Muslims of the Spanish enclaves.

In March 1988, after several months of negotiations, the central Government and main opposition parties in Madrid reached a broad consensus on draft autonomy statutes for the Spanish External Territories. (See the chapter on Ceuta for details of the statutes.)

At the general election held in October 1989 the election results were declared invalid, following the discovery of serious irregularities. At the repeated ballot, in March 1990, both seats in the Senado (Senate) and the one seat in the Congreso de los Diputados (Congress of Deputies) were won by the Partido Popular (PP), the latter result depriving the PSOE of its overall majority in the Madrid lower chamber. By 1990 almost all residents were in possession of an identity card.

At elections to the municipal council held in May 1991, the PP secured 12 of the 25 seats and Ignacio Velázquez Rivera of the right-wing Partido Nacionalista de Melilla (PNM) was elected Mayor of the enclave, replacing the previous PSOE mayor. At the general election of June 1993 the PSOE candidate defeated the incumbent PP member in the Congreso de los Diputados; the PP also lost one of its two seats in the Senado.

The final statutes of autonomy for Ceuta and Melilla were approved by the Spanish Government in September 1994, in preparation for their presentation to the Cortes (parliament—see the chapter on Ceuta). At elections for the new local assembly, held in May 1995, the level of participation was less than 62%. The PP won 14 of the 25 seats, the PSOE five seats, the Coalición por Melilla (CpM), a new Muslim grouping, four seats and the right-wing Unión del Pueblo Melillense (UPM) two seats. Ignacio Velázquez (PP/PNM) returned to the position of Mayor/President.

At the general election held in March 1996, the PSOE lost its seat in the lower house to the PP, which also took both seats in the Senado. In the same month thousands of Muslims took part in a demonstration, organized by the CpM, to protest against their position on the margins of society.

In March 1997 a motion of censure against Ignacio Velázquez resulted in the Mayor/President's defeat, owing to the defection to the opposition of two PP councillors, Enrique Palacios and Abdelmalik Tahar. The opposition then declared Palacios to be Mayor/President, although the central Government continued to recognize Velázquez as the rightful incumbent. In May, for the first time, the Mayor/Presidents of both Ceuta and Melilla attended a conference of the autonomous regions' presidents, held in Madrid. Despite the attempted 'coup' in Melilla, the territory was represented by Ignacio Velázquez. In November, from Tenerife, Abdelmalik Tahar accused Velázquez and five associates of having subjected him to blackmail and threats, as a result of which he had relinquished his seat on the Council, thereby permitting the PP to replace him and to regain its majority. In December Tahar, who was now under police protection, declared to the investigating judge that he had been offered 50m. pesetas (of which he had received 3m.) and a monthly sum of 200,000 pesetas. Following a judicial ruling leading to the successful revival of the motion of censure against Velázquez in February 1998, Palacios took office as Mayor/President of Melilla, accusing his predecessor of serious financial mismanagement. A new motion of censure, presented by the PP urging that (despite the bribery charges against him) Velázquez be restored to office, was deemed to be illegal and therefore rejected in a decree issued by Palacios, who also ordered the temporary closure of the local assembly. In July Palacios accused the PP of having employed public funds, amounting to more than 200m. pesetas, to secure the votes of some 2,500 Muslims at the 1995 local elections. The allegations were denied by the PP.

During 1997 there was increased concern regarding the numbers of illegal immigrants. In June police reinforcements were drafted into Melilla, following renewed disturbances in which one immigrant died. More than 100 illegal immigrants were immediately returned to Morocco as part of a special security operation, and on the same day a total of 873 Moroccans were denied entry to Melilla. (More than 10,000 Moroccans continued to cross the border legally each day, in order to work in the enclave.) In August the Spanish General Prosecutor demanded emergency measures to address the immigration crisis, having urged the Ministry of the Interior in June to find an immediate solution. In the same month various non-governmental organizations condemned the rudimentary conditions in which more than 900 illegal immigrants, mainly from sub-Saharan Africa and Algeria, were being held in Melilla. In December the Spanish Government announced that 1,206 sub-Saharan Africans were to be transferred from Ceuta and Melilla to the mainland.

In January 1999, after 12 years' exile in Morocco, Aomar Muhammadi Dudú returned to Melilla, in preparation for the local elections to be held in June. At the elections the Grupo Independiente Liberal (GIL), recently founded by Jesús Gil, the controversial Mayor of Marbella, Spain, secured seven of the 25 seats in the assembly of Melilla. In July the two newly elected PSOE councillors defied a central directive to vote with the five PP delegates (in order to obstruct the accession of the GIL to the city presidency), and instead gave their support to Mustafa Aberchán Hamed of the CpM, which had won five seats. The Muslim Aberchán was thus elected to replace Enrique Palacios as Mayor/President of Melilla. In mid-July Aberchán and the GIL agreed to form a minority Government. The two rebel PSOE councillors subsequently relinquished their seats. In October, following a disagreement between the CpM and the GIL, Aberchán was able to reach a broad agreement with members of the PP and UPM, enabling him to remain in office. In November the Melilla branch of the GIL announced that henceforth it was to operate independently of the mainland party. In the same month, a new agreement between Aberchán and the GIL having been concluded, the latter grouping declared its intention to renew its participation in the Government of Melilla. As a result, the socialist councillors withdrew from the administration.

In December 1999 the Mayor/President announced the composition of a new coalition Government, the post of First Vice-President being allocated to Crispin Lozano, the local leader of the GIL, while Enrique Palacios of the newly founded Partido Independiente de Melilla (PIM) became Second Vice-President. In the same month Ignacio Velázquez, the former PP Mayor/President, was barred from public office for six years, having been found guilty of neglecting his duty during his tenure of office. The conviction was in respect of an incident in 1992 when Velázquez had convened a session of the Council, which was scheduled to vote on a motion of censure against him, in full knowledge of the fact that at least one member was due to be in Madrid that day, thus rendering any vote invalid. However, he was acquitted of charges of misappropriation of public funds. In May 2000, following the defection to the opposition of two GIL deputies and one UPM representative, Aberchán declared that, despite the Government's loss of its majority, he would not resign. The opposition subsequently announced that they would request a vote of 'no confidence' in Aberchán's Government at the earliest opportunity. Later in the month the national leadership of the PP and the PSOE met in Madrid in an attempt to negotiate a solution to the political crisis in Melilla. The two parties agreed that, if Aberchán's Government was removed from office, they would form a coalition government in partnership with the UPM, whose leader, Juan José Imbroda Ortiz, would be nominated Mayor/President. In July the remaining five GIL members left the Government and joined the opposition. The opposition subsequently introduced a motion of censure against Aberchán, whom they accused of nepotism, of a lack of transparency, and of harassment of the opposition. Aberchán, who described the accusations as being racially motivated, announced that the CpM was to withdraw from the legislature. In mid-July some 2,000 Muslim citizens of Melilla demonstrated in support of Aberchán. At the same time Palacios suspended the motion of censure by decree, reportedly without having consulted Aberchán. (Palacios was subsequently barred from public office for seven years, having been found guilty of perversion of the course of justice.) The opposition later successfully overturned the decree in the courts, and the vote on the motion of censure against Aberchán was therefore able to proceed. The motion was adopted in September, with the support of 16 of the 25 deputies, and Imbroda was elected as Mayor/President. In late 2000 four members of the GIL announced their departure from the party. In January 2002 Velázquez resigned as Councillor of the Presidency, after the Supreme Court upheld his 1999 conviction.

At the regional elections held in May 2003 a coalition of the PP and the UPM won 15 seats, with the CpM taking seven. The incumbent Mayor/President, Juan José Imbroda Ortiz, remained in power. The PP's success was, in part, the result of a concerted effort to prevent the perpetuation of unstable government that had characterized the previous four years under the GIL. A rising fear of immigration was another likely factor.

At the general election held on 14 March 2004, meanwhile, the PP retained Melilla. In September Imbroda met the recently elected Spanish Prime Minister, José Luis Rodríguez Zapatero, to discuss the possibility that Melilla would become a 'Comunidad Autónoma' (Autonomous Community), a move that would give legislative powers to the government of the territory. The plan was, however, abandoned in February 2007, owing to disagreement over the content of the proposed statute of autonomy; instead, the Spanish Government agreed to devolve more powers to Ceuta and Melilla in the areas of education and social services.

In May 2004, meanwhile, the Government of Melilla announced plans to improve security along the border with Morocco. In August, however, in the first mass entry for three years, some 450 people attempted to enter Melilla illegally by climbing the security fence; as many as 40 people were believed to have succeeded in entering the territory. During August–October 2005 increasing numbers of would-be migrants attempted to scale the security barriers separating Melilla from Morocco. A number of deaths were said to have resulted from these attempts, and in October it was reported that six people had been shot during violent clashes with Moroccan security forces. It was subsequently announced that one barrier would be doubled in height (to 6 m), and that border security would be increased. Meanwhile, the Spanish Government announced funding of €17m. for security in Melilla.

At the local election held on 27 May 2007 the PP (which had absorbed its coalition partner, the UPM) obtained 15 seats in the Assembly, the same number as previously, thereby retaining its overall majority; the CpM and the PSOE each won five seats. The constitution of the Assembly was delayed until early July owing to an appeal against the election result levied by the CpM, which alleged that the PP had engaged in acts of electoral fraud, including the falsification of postal ballots. The appeal was rejected by the Supreme Court of Justice of Andalusia, which ruled that the evidence presented by the CpM was not sufficient to indicate irregularity. Imbroda was subsequently re-elected as Mayor/President.

A two-day visit to Melilla and Ceuta by King Juan Carlos and Queen Sofía in early November 2007 was strongly condemned by the Moroccan authorities (see the chapter on Ceuta). Several thousand Moroccans, including politicians and trade union representatives, took part in a demonstration at the border with Melilla to protest against the presence of the Spanish King. The Government of Melilla issued a statement accusing the Moroccan Government of interfering in Spanish domestic affairs by criticizing the visit.

At the general election held on 9 March 2008 the PP retained Melilla's one seat in the Congreso de los Diputados, although only by a narrow margin, as well as its two seats in the Senado. Later that month Esther Donoso García-Sacristán was appointed as Councillor of Contracting and Heritage to replace María del Carmen Dueñas Martínez, who had been elected to the Senado. In April Gergorio Escobar was appointed to replace José Fernández Chacón as Government Delegate in Ceuta. At the regional PP congress held in late October 2008, Juan José Imbroda Ortiz was appointed to succeed Arturo Esteban Albert as local President of the PP.

In April 2008 the Government of Melilla urged the Spanish Ministry of Defence to suspend plans to restructure the armed forces, claiming that these would entail a reduction in the number of troops stationed in the city. For its part, the central Government maintained that although there would be changes in the composition of the forces deployed in Melilla, overall numbers would not be reduced.

Two suspected Islamist militants were detained in Melilla at the beginning of April 2008, in accordance with international arrest warrants issued by the Moroccan Government in connection with their alleged involvement in terrorist activities, including a series of suicide bombings against Western targets in Casablanca in May 2003, in which 45 people died.

Attempts by illegal migrants to cross the border between Melilla and Morocco increased in late October 2008 after heavy flooding damaged the recently fortified fence separating the two territories. Although additional security forces were deployed to patrol the damaged areas, it was reported that in one incident almost half of a group of some 60 sub-Saharan Africans succeeded in entering Melilla; 17 others were reportedly arrested. In the weeks that followed further attempts were made to breach the fence: more than 150 people were reported to have tried to enter Melilla during November; and a number of people were injured in clashes with Moroccan and Spanish security forces (including several members of the security forces).

Government

See the chapter on Ceuta.

SPANISH EXTERNAL TERRITORIES

Defence
See the chapter on Ceuta.

Economic Affairs
In 2007, according to official estimates, the gross domestic product (GDP) of Melilla was equivalent to €21,089 per head, ranking 13th (in terms of GDP per head) in a list of the 19 Spanish autonomous regions. In 2008, according to preliminary figures, GDP totalled €1,489.5m. The population of Melilla increased by an annual average of 0.7% in 2002–08, while GDP grew by an average of 3.2% per year, in real terms, during 2000–08; real GDP increased by an estimated 3.5% in 2007, but growth was estimated at just 1.2% for 2008.

Agricultural activity in Melilla is negligible, as is employment in that sector (at around 0.3% of the total); according to preliminary estimates, the sector contributed just 0.7% of GDP in 2008. Agricultural GDP decreased, in real terms, by an annual average of 0.5% during 2000–08; the sector's GDP increased by an estimated 3.1% in 2007, before recording an estimated decline of 1.7% in 2008.

Although industry is on a limited scale, the sector contributed 14.5% of GDP in 2008, and 11.5% of the employed population were engaged in the sector, on average, during the first quarter of 2009. Manufacturing GDP increased, in real terms, by an annual average of 0.7% during 2000–08; the GDP of the manufacturing sector increased by 4.2% in 2007, but declined by an estimated 5.9% in 2008. A small decrease, in real terms, of 0.8% was also registered in the construction sub-sector in that year, although the energy sub-sector recorded estimated growth of 2.1%, according to official estimates.

Services contributed an estimated 84.8% of GDP in 2008, and some 87.0% of the employed population were engaged in the sector, on average, in the first quarter of 2009. Services GDP increased, in real terms, by an annual average of 3.2% during 2000–08; the sector's GDP increased by 4.2% in 2007, and by an estimated 1.8% in 2008.

Most of the population's food is imported, with the exception of fish, which is obtained locally (sardines and anchovies are among the most significant catches). A large proportion of the tinned fish is sold outside Spain. More important to the economies of Melilla and Ceuta is the port activity; most of their exports take the form of fuel supplied—at very competitive rates—to ships. Most of the fuel comes from the Spanish refinery in Tenerife. Apart from the ferries from Málaga and Almería in mainland Spain, Melilla's port is not busy—a total of 1,163 vessels entered in 2006—and its exports are correspondingly low. Most trade is conducted with other parts of Spain. In 2008 Melilla recorded a trade deficit of €145.5m. In 2008 the principal source of imports (accounting for almost 35% of the total value) was the People's Republic of China; other major suppliers were the USA and Germany. Morocco was the principal market for exports, taking more than 90% of the total value. The principal imports in 2008 were fruits and vegetables (some 20% of the total value), textiles and clothing and vehicles. The principal exports were clothing and made-up textile articles (almost 30% of the total value) and man-made filaments. Tourism makes a significant contribution to the territory's economy. In 2006 89,931 overnight stays were recorded by tourist visitors to Ceuta and Melilla. The annual rate of inflation averaged 3.6% in 2002–08; the rate was 3.9% in 2008. On average, some 25.4% of the labour force were unemployed during the first quarter of 2009.

Upon the accession in January 1986 of Spain to the European Community (EC, now European Union—EU, see p. 255), Melilla was considered a Spanish city and European territory, and joined the organization as part of Spain. It retained its status as a free port. The statute of autonomy, adopted in early 1995, envisaged the continuation of the territory's fiscal benefits. Euro notes and coins became the sole legal tender on 28 February 2002.

In June 1994 the EU announced substantial regional aid: between 1995 and 1999 Melilla was to receive a total of ECU 45m., of which ECU 18m. was to be in the form of direct aid. However, successive enlargements of the EU and sustained Spanish economic growth during the 2000s limited Spain's access to EU aid, with the result that, although income in the enclave had not improved significantly, subsidies for Melilla would be progressively reduced during the period 2007–13, with a view to their eventual withdrawal. The city's consolidated budget for 2008 included current and capital transfers from the Spanish state of €81.0m. and €14.8m., respectively. In May 2009 it was reported that the Spanish Government was considering increasing existing tax concessions to the aviation industry in some non-peninsular regions of Spain, including Melilla, as part of a new initiative to stimulate economic growth.

Education
The education system is similar to that of mainland Spain. In addition to the conventional Spanish facilities, the Moroccan Government finances a school for 600 Muslim children, the languages of instruction being Arabic and Spanish. The curriculum includes Koranic studies. In 1982 only 12% of Muslim children were attending school, but by 1990 the authorities had succeeded in achieving an attendance level of virtually 100%. The open university (Universidad Nacional de Educación a Distancia—UNED) maintains a branch.

The Peñón de Vélez de la Gomera, Peñón de Alhucemas and Chafarinas Islands
These rocky islets, situated, respectively, just west and east of al-Hocima (Alhucemas) and east of Melilla off the north coast of Morocco, are administered with Melilla. The three Chafarinas Islands lie about 3.5 km off Ras el-Ma (Cabo de Agua). The Peñón de Alhucemas is situated about 300 m from the coast. The Peñón de Vélez de la Gomera is situated about 80 km further west, lying 85 m from the Moroccan shore, to which it is joined by a narrow strip of sand. A small military base is maintained on the Peñón de Vélez, while a military garrison of fewer than 100 men is stationed on the Peñón de Alhucemas, and a garrison of about 100 Spanish soldiers is maintained on the Isla del Congreso, the most westerly of the Chafarinas Islands. A supply ship calls at the various islands every two weeks. Prospective visitors must obtain the necessary military permit in Ceuta or Melilla.

Statistical Survey

Source (unless otherwise stated): Instituto Nacional de Estadística, Paseo de la Castellana 183, 28071 Madrid; tel. (91) 5839100; fax (91) 5839158; internet www.ine.es.

AREA AND POPULATION

Area: 12.5 sq km (4.8 sq miles).

Population (census results): 56,600 at 1 March 1991; 66,411 at 1 November 2001 (males 33,224, females 33,187). *2009* (official estimate at 1 January): 70,076 (males 34,700, females 35,376).

Density (1 January 2009): 5,606 per sq km.

Births, Marriages and Deaths (2007): Live births 1,112 (birth rate 16.3 per 1,000); Marriages 529 (marriage rate 7.7 per 1,000); Deaths 433 (death rate 6.3 per 1,000).

Life Expectancy (years at birth): Total 79.3 (males 76.7; females 81.9) in 2005.

Immigration and Emigration (2007): Immigrants 1,243; Emigrants 343.

Economically Active Population ('000 persons aged 16 years and over, January–March 2009, estimates): Agriculture, hunting, forestry and fishing 0.3; Construction 1.8; Other industry 0.6; Services 18.1; *Total employed* 20.8; Unemployed 7.1; *Total labour force* 27.9 (males 16.8, females 11.0).

FINANCE

Currency and Exchange Rates: 100 cent = 1 euro (€). *Sterling and Dollar Equivalents* (31 December 2008): £1 Sterling = 1.047 euros; US $1 = 0.719 euros; 10 euros = £9.55 = $13.92. *Average Exchange Rate* (euros per US $): 0.7971 in 2006; 0.7306 in 2007; 0.6827 in 2008. Note: The local currency was formerly the Spanish peseta. From the introduction of the euro, with Spanish participation, on 1 January 1999, a fixed exchange rate of €1 = 166.386 pesetas was in effect. Euro notes and coins were introduced on 1 January 2002. The euro and local currency circulated alongside each other until 28 February, after which the euro became the sole legal tender.

Cost of Living (Consumer Price Index, annual averages; base: 2006 = 100): All items 95.8 in 2005; 102.7 in 2007; 106.7 in 2008.

Gross Domestic Product (€ million at current prices, provisional): 1,348.3 in 2006; 1,447.4 in 2007; 1,489.5 in 2008.

Gross Domestic Product by Economic Activity (€ million at current prices, 2008, provisional): Agriculture, hunting, forestry and fishing 9.5; Energy 34.3; Construction 133.9; Other industry 29.7; Services 1,156.2; *Sub-total* 1,363.6; Net taxes on products 125.9; *GDP at market prices* 1,489.5.

EXTERNAL TRADE

Principal Commodities (€ million, 2008): *Imports:* Fruits and vegetables 29.5; Coffee, tea, maté and spices 12.5; Cereals 7.7; Mineral fuels and oils, and products thereof 7.4; Textile and clothing 23.6; Footwear 9.3; Vehicles (excl. rail or tram), and parts thereof 14.8; Total (incl. others) 155.3. *Exports:* Man-made filaments 2.0; Man-made staple fibres 1.4; Clothing and made-up textile articles 2.8; Electrical machinery and equipment, and parts thereof 1.7; Total (incl. others) 9.8.

Principal Trading Partners (€ million, 2008): *Imports:* China, People's Republic 52.1; Germany 12.9; Thailand 8.2; USA 19.1; Viet

Nam 8.6; Total (incl. others) 155.3. *Exports:* Morocco 9.2; Total (incl. others) 9.8.

Source: Foreign Trade Database, Agencia Tributaria (Madrid).

TRANSPORT

Road Traffic (Ceuta and Melilla, 2007): Vehicles registered 107,258 (Passenger cars 76,801, Buses, etc. 115, Lorries and vans 16,675, Motorcycles 11,637, Tractors 195, Other 1,835).

Shipping (domestic and international, 2006, provisional): Vessels entered 1,163; Goods handled ('000 metric tons) 811; Passenger movements ('000) 443.

Civil Aviation (2006, preliminary): Journeys made 9,742; Passengers transported ('000) 305; Goods transported 430 metric tons.

TOURISM

Tourist Arrivals (by country of residence, 2002): France 476; Germany 432; Italy 331; Netherlands 425; Spain 23,648; Total (incl. others) 31,812. *2006* (Ceuta and Melilla): 89,931 overnight stays by tourists.

EDUCATION

(2005/06)

Pre-primary: 20 schools; 159 teachers, 3,237 students.

Primary: 15 schools; 422 teachers (excl. 20 engaged in both pre-primary and primary teaching); 5,996 students.

Secondary: First Cycle: 9 schools (of which 4 schools also provided second-cycle education and 5 provided vocational education); 255 teachers (excl. 10 engaged in both primary and secondary teaching, and 198 engaged in more than one secondary cycle, and excl. 33 specialists); 3,923 students.

Secondary: Second Cycle: 53 teachers; 1,339 students.

Secondary: Vocational: 703 students; 65 teachers.

Source: Ministry of Education and Science, Madrid.

Directory

Government

Government Delegate in Melilla: GREGORIO ESCOBAR.

Deputy elected to the Congress in Madrid: ANTONIO GUTIÉRREZ MOLINA (PP).

Representatives to the Senate in Madrid: MARÍA DEL CARMEN DUEÑAS MARTÍNEZ (PP), JUAN JOSÉ IMBRODA ORTIZ (PP).

COUNCIL OF GOVERNMENT
(April 2009)

Mayor/President of Melilla: JUAN JOSÉ IMBRODA ORTIZ.

First Vice-President and Councillor of Public Administration: MIGUEL MARÍN COBOS.

Second Vice-President and Councillor of the Presidency and Civic Participation: ABDELMALIK EL-BARKANI ABDELKADER.

Councillor of Finance and Budgeting: GUILLERMO FRÍAS BARERRA.

Councillor of the Economy, Employment and Tourism: DANIEL CONESA MÍNGUEZ.

Councillor of Development: RAFAEL RICARDO MARÍN FERNÁNDEZ.

Councillor of Social Welfare and Health: MARÍA ANTONIA GARBÍN ESPIGARES.

Councillor of the Environment: RAMÓN GAVILÁN ARAGÓN.

Councillor of Culture: SIMI CHOCRÓN CHOCRÓN.

Councillor of Civic Security: RAMÓN ANTÓN MOTA.

Councillor of Education and Voluntary Organizations: ANTONIO MIRANDA MONTILLA.

Councillor of Contracting and Heritage: ESTHER DONOSO GARCÍA-SACRISTÁN.

Councillor of Youth and Sport: FRANCISCO ROBLES FERRÓN.

GOVERNMENT OFFICES

Delegación del Gobierno: Avda de la Marina Española 3, 52001 Melilla; tel. (95) 2675840; fax (95) 2672657; e-mail puri@melilla.map.es.

Office of the Mayor/President: Palacio de la Asamblea, Plaza de España, 52001 Melilla; tel. (95) 2699287; fax (95) 2679230; e-mail presidencia@melilla.es; internet www.melilla.es.

Council of Civic Security: Jefatura Policía Local, General Astilleros 25, Melilla; tel. (95) 2698110; fax (95) 2698121; e-mail policialocal@melilla.es.

Council of Contracting and Heritage: Palacio de la Asamblea, Plaza de España, 52001 Melilla; tel. (95) 2699157; fax (95) 2699160; e-mail consejeriacontratacion@melilla.es.

Council of Culture: Palacio de la Asamblea, Plaza de España, 52001 Melilla; tel. (95) 2699193; fax (95) 2699158; e-mail consejeriacultura@melilla.es.

Council of Development: Antiguo Edif. Mantelete, Duque de Ahumada s/n, Melilla 52071; tel. (95) 2699223; fax (95) 2699224; e-mail consejeriafomento@melilla.es.

Council of the Economy, Employment and Tourism: Justo Sancho Miñano 2, 52801 Melilla; tel. (95) 2676241; fax (95) 2676242; e-mail consejeriaeconomia@melilla.es.

Council of Education and Voluntary Organizations: Querol 7, 52001 Melilla; tel. (95) 2699214; fax (95) 2699279; e-mail educacion@melilla.es.

Council of the Environment: Palacio de la Asamblea, Plaza de España, 52001 Melilla; tel. (95) 2699134; fax (95) 2699161; e-mail consejeriamedioambiente@melilla.es.

Council of Finance and Budgeting: Palacio de la Asamblea, Plaza de España, 52001 Melilla; tel. (95) 2699157; fax (95) 2699160; e-mail conserjeriahacienda@melilla.es.

Council of the Presidency and Civic Participation: Palacio de la Asamblea, Plaza de España, 52001 Melilla; tel. (95) 2699207; fax (95) 2699137; e-mail consejeriapresidencia@melilla.es.

Council of Public Administration: Palacio de la Asamblea, Plaza de España, 52001 Melilla; tel. (95) 2699102; fax (95) 2699103; e-mail cap@melilla.es.

Council of Social Welfare and Health: Carlos Ramírez de Arellano 10, Melilla; tel. (95) 2699301; fax (95) 2699302; e-mail consejeriabienstarsocial@melilla.es.

Council of Youth and Sport: Palacio de la Asamblea, Plaza de España, 52001 Melilla; tel. (95) 2699225; fax (95) 2699208; e-mail consejeriadeporteyjuventud@melilla.es.

Assembly

Election, 27 May 2007

	Seats
Partido Popular (PP)	15
Coalición por Melilla (CpM)	5
Partido Socialista Obrero Español (PSOE)	5
Total	**25**

Election Commission

Junta Electoral de Zona y Provincial de Melilla: Melilla; Sec. RUPERTO MANUEL GARCÍA HERNÁNDEZ.

Political Organizations

Partido Popular (PP): Roberto Cano 2, 1° izqda, POB 384, 52001 Melilla; tel. (95) 2681095; fax (95) 2684477; e-mail melilla@pp.es; internet www.ppmelilla.es; national-level, centre-right party; absorbed the Unión del Pueblo Melillense in 2007; Pres. JUAN JOSÉ IMBRODA ORTIZ; Sec. Gen. MARÍA CARMEN DUEÑAS MARTÍNEZ.

Partido Socialista de Melilla-Partido Socialista Obrero Español (PSME-PSOE): Doctor García Martínez 3, 52006 Melilla; tel. (95) 2677807; fax (95) 2679857; e-mail infopsoe@psoe.es; internet www.psoe.es; national-level, left-wing party; Pres. ANDRÉS VISIEDO SEGURA; Sec.-Gen. DIONISIO MUÑOZ PÉREZ.

There are also various civic associations in Melilla.

Religion

As in Ceuta, most Europeans are Roman Catholics. The registered Muslim community numbered 20,800 in 1990. The Jewish community numbered 1,300. There is also a Hindu community.

ISLAM

Comisión Islámica de Melilla (CIM): García Cabrelles 13, Melilla; Sec.-Gen. ABDERRAMÁN BENYAHYA.

CHRISTIANITY
The Roman Catholic Church
Melilla is part of the Spanish diocese of Málaga.

The Press

El Faro de Melilla: Castelar 5, 1°, Melilla; tel. (95) 2690029; fax (95) 2683992; e-mail melilla@grupofaro.es; internet www.elfaroceutamelilla.es; Pres. RAFAEL MONTERO PALACIOS; Editor-in-Chief ANGELA M. PERAZZI.

Melilla Hoy: Polígono Industrial SEPES, La Espiga, Naves A-1/A-2, 52006 Melilla; tel. (95) 2690000; fax (95) 2675725; e-mail redaccion@melillahoy.es; internet www.melillahoy.es; f. 1985; Pres. ENRIQUE BOHÓRQUEZ LÓPEZ-DÓRIGA; Editor-in-Chief MUSTAFA HAMED; circ. 2,000.

Sur: Músico Granados 2, 52001 Melilla; tel. (95) 2691283; fax (95) 2673674; e-mail surmelilla@rusadirmedia.com; internet www.diariosur.es; local edn of Málaga daily; Perm. Rep. AVELINO GUTIÉRREZ PÉREZ.

El Telegrama de Melilla: Polígono La Espiga, Nave A-8, 52006 Melilla; tel. (95) 2691443; fax (95) 2691469; e-mail telegramademelilla@yahoo.es; internet www.eltelegrama.com; Dir JUAN CARLOS HEREDIA.

NEWS AGENCY

Agencia EFE: Cándido Lobera 4, 1° izqda, 52001 Melilla; tel. (95) 2685235; fax (95) 2680043; e-mail melilla@efe.es; Correspondent (vacant).

PRESS ASSOCIATION

Asociación de la Prensa: Apartado de Correos 574, 29880 Melilla; tel. (95) 2681854; fax (95) 2675725; Pres. MIGUEL GÓMEZ BERNARDI.

Broadcasting

RADIO

Cadena Dial Melilla: Muelle Ribera 18B, 52005 Melilla; tel. (95) 2682328; fax (95) 2681573; e-mail radiomelilla@unionradio.es; internet www.cadenadial.com; Rep. ROCÍO GONZÁLEZ JUSTO.

Onda Cero Radio Melilla: Músico Granados 2, 52004 Melilla; tel. (95) 2691283; e-mail ondaceromelilla@ondaceromelilla.net; internet www.ondaceromelilla.net; Dir JOSÉ JESÚS NAVAJAS TROBAT.

Radio Melilla: Muelle Ribera s/n, 52005 Melilla; tel. (95) 2681708; fax (95) 2681573; e-mail radiomelilla@unionradio.es; internet www.cadenaser.com; commercial; owned by Sociedad Española de Radiodifusión; Dir ANTONIA RAMOS PELÁEZ.

Radio Nacional de España (RNE): Duque de Ahumada 5, 52001, Melilla; tel. (95) 2681907; fax (95) 2683108; internet www.rtve.es; state-controlled; Rep. MONTSERRAT COBOS RUANO.

TELEVISION

A fibre optic cable linking Melilla with Almería was laid in 1990. From March 1991 Melilla residents were able to receive three private TV channels from mainland Spain: Antena 3, Canal+ and Tele 5.

Antena 3: Edif. Melilla, Urbanización Rusadir, 29805 Melilla; tel. (95) 2688840; internet www.antena3.com.

Finance

BANKING

There were seven banks operating in Melilla in 2007, all of which were based in mainland Spain.

Banco Bilbao Vizcaya Argentaria (BBVA): Teniente Aguilar De Mera 3 52001 Melilla; tel. (952) 686076; fax (952) 685249; internet www.bbva.es; 5 brs.

Banco de España: Plaza de España 3, 52001 Melilla; tel. (95) 2683940; internet www.bde.es.

Banco Español de Crédito (Banesto): Avda Juan Carlos I 12, 52001 Melilla; tel. (95) 2684348; internet www.banesto.es; 2 brs.

Banco Popular Español: Avda Juan Carlos I 14, 52001 Melilla; tel. (95) 2684847; fax (95) 2676844; internet www.bancopopular.es.

Banco Santander Central Hispano (BSCH): Ejército Español 1, 52001 Melilla; tel. (95) 2681422; internet www.gruposantander.es; 3 brs.

Caja de Ahorros y Pensiones de Barcelona (La Caixa): Avda Juan Carlos I 28, 52001 Melilla; tel. (95) 2685760; fax (95) 2960276; internet www.lacaixa.es; 2 brs.

Montes de Piedad y Caja de Ahorros de Ronda, Cádiz, Almería, Málaga y Antequera (Unicaja): Ejército Español 9, 52001 Melilla; tel. (952) 682595; fax (952) 683684; internet www.unicaja.es; 4 brs.

INSURANCE

MAPFRE: Avda Democracia 9, 52004 Melilla; tel. (95) 2673189; fax (95) 2674977; e-mail maberna@mapfre.com; internet www.mapfre.com; Commercial Man. BERNABE ESCOZ; 2 offices.

Trade and Industry

Cámara Oficial de Comercio, Industria y Navegación: Cervantes 7, 52001 Melilla; tel. (95) 2684840; fax (95) 2683119; e-mail info@camaramelilla.es; internet www.camaramelilla.es; f. 1906; chamber of commerce; Pres. MARGARITA LÓPEZ ALMENDÁRIZ; Vice-Pres. HAMED MAANAN BENAISA BOUJI.

Confederación de Empresarios de Melilla (CEME-CEOE): Plaza 1 de Mayo, Bajo Dcha, 52003 Melilla; tel. (95) 2673696; fax (95) 2676175; e-mail ceme@cemelilla.org; internet www.cemelilla.org; f. 1979; employers' confed; Pres. MARGARITA LÓPEZ ALMENDÁRIZ; Sec.-Gen. JERÓNIMO PÉREZ HERNÁNDEZ.

UTILITIES

The Spanish electricity company Endesa operates an oil-fired power station in Melilla. In 2007 a new 12.6-MW generator was installed, increasing capacity by 22%.

TRADE UNION

Confederación Sindical de Comisiones Obreras (CCOO): Plaza 1° de Mayo s/n, 2°, 52004 Melilla; tel. (95) 2676535; fax (95) 2672571; e-mail orga.melilla@melilla.ccoo.es; internet www.ccoo.es; Sec.-Gen. ANGEL GUTIÉRREZ GÓMEZ.

Transport

There is a daily ferry service to Málaga and a service to Almería. Melilla airport, situated 4 km from the town, is served by daily flights to various destinations on the Spanish mainland, operated by Iberia Regional/Air Nostrum. There were 30 km of paved roads in Melilla in 2006. The Port of Melilla handled 811,000 metric tons of goods and 443,000 passengers in 2006; 1,163 boats passed through the port in that year.

Port of Melilla: Autoridad Portuaria de Melilla, Avda de la Marina Española 4, 52001 Melilla; tel. (95) 2673600; fax (95) 2674838; e-mail puertodemelilla@puertodemelilla.es; internet www.puertomelilla.es; Pres. ARTURO ESTEBAN; Dir JOSÉ LUIS ALMAZÁN.

Acciona Trasmediterránea: Avda General Marina 1, 52001 Melilla; tel. (95) 2681635; fax (95) 2682685; e-mail correom@trasmediterranea.es; internet www.trasmediterranea.es; operates ferry service between Melilla and Almería and Málaga, in mainland Spain.

Tourism

There is much of historic interest to the visitor, while Melilla is also celebrated for its modernist architecture. Several new hotels, including a luxury development, were constructed in the 1990s. In 2002 tourist arrivals, including visitors from mainland Spain, numbered 31,812.

Oficina Provincial de Turismo: Pintor Fortuny 21, 52004 Melilla; tel. (95) 2675444; fax (95) 2679616; e-mail info@melillaturismo.com; internet www.melillaturismo.com.

SRI LANKA

Introductory Survey

Location, Climate, Language, Religion, Flag, Capital

The Democratic Socialist Republic of Sri Lanka lies in southern Asia. It comprises one large island and several much smaller ones, situated in the Indian Ocean, about 80 km (50 miles) east of the southern tip of India. The climate is tropical, with an average annual temperature of about 27°C (81°F) in Colombo. There is very little seasonal variation in temperature: the monthly average in Colombo ranges from 25°C (77°F) to 28°C (82°F). The south-western part of the island receives rain from both the south-west and the north-east monsoons: average annual rainfall in Colombo is 2,365 mm (93 ins). Sinhala and Tamil are recognized national languages. One of the official languages, Sinhala, is spoken by more than 70% of the population. Tamil was made the country's second official language in 1988. According to the 2001 census, in 18 out of 25 districts 76.7% of the population are Buddhist, 8.5% are Muslim, 7.9% are Hindu and 6.1% are Roman Catholic. The census results did not cover the Tamil-dominated (and therefore mainly Hindu) northern and eastern districts. The national flag (proportions 1 by 2) consists mainly of a dark crimson rectangular panel, with a yellow border, in the fly. In the centre of the panel is a gold lion, carrying a sword, while in each corner (also in gold) there is a leaf of the bo (bodhi) tree, which is sacred to Buddhists. At the hoist are two vertical stripes, also edged in yellow, to represent Sri Lanka's minorities: one of green (for Muslims) and one of orange (for Tamils). The commercial capital is Colombo. In 1982 the ancient capital of Sri Jayawardenepura (Kotte) became the administrative capital.

Recent History

Sri Lanka, known as Ceylon until 1972, gained its independence from the United Kingdom in February 1948. From then until 1956, for a brief period in 1960 and from 1965 to 1970 the country was ruled, latterly in coalition, by the United National Party (UNP), which was concerned to protect the rights of the Tamils, Hindu members of an ethnic minority (closely linked with the inhabitants of the southern Indian state of Tamil Nadu), who are concentrated in the north (and, to a lesser extent, in the east) of the main island. The socialist Sri Lanka Freedom Party (SLFP), formed in 1951 by Solomon Bandaranaike, emphasized the national heritage, winning the support of groups that advocated the recognition of Sinhala as the official language and the establishment of Buddhism as the predominant religion. The SLFP won the 1956 elections decisively and remained in power, except for a three-month interruption in 1960, until 1965, having formed a coalition Government with the Lanka Sama Samaj Party (LSSP), a Trotskyist group, in 1964. Following the assassination of Solomon Bandaranaike in 1959, his widow, Sirimavo Bandaranaike, assumed the leadership of the SLFP. At the 1970 elections the SLFP became the leading partner of a United Front coalition Government with the LSSP and the Communist Party of Sri Lanka. In 1971 the United Front Government suppressed an uprising led by the left-wing Janatha Vimukthi Peramuna (JVP—People's Liberation Front). A state of emergency was declared, and the party was banned.

In 1976 the main Tamil party, the Federal Party, and other Tamil groups formed the Tamil United Liberation Front (TULF), demanding a separate Tamil state ('Eelam') in the northern and eastern parts of the country. In December of that year the communists supported strikes of transport unions, which were initiated by the UNP and the LSSP (the latter had been expelled from the coalition in 1975). The strikes ended in January 1977, and in February Sirimavo Bandaranaike prorogued the National State Assembly until May. Several members of the SLFP resigned, and seven members of the Communist Party left the coalition Government, forming an independent group within the opposition. In February the state of emergency, which had been imposed in 1971, was lifted and the JVP was legalized again. A general election was held in July 1977, accompanied by widespread violence. The UNP won the election, with an overwhelming majority, and the party's leader, Junius Richard Jayewardene, became Prime Minister. In August riots broke out between the Sinhalese majority and the Tamil minority. The TULF, which had become the main opposition party, increased its demands for an independent Tamil state. In October a constitutional amendment was passed to establish a presidential system of government, and in February 1978 Jayewardene became the country's first executive President.

Continued violence and pressure from the Tamils during 1978 led the Government to make some concessions, such as the recognition of the Tamil language, in the new Constitution of the Democratic Socialist Republic of Sri Lanka, which came into force in September. In view of this, the Ceylon Workers' Congress (CWC) joined the Government, but the TULF remained undecided, mainly for fear of reprisals by Tamil extremists. Further violence prompted the declaration of a state of emergency in July 1979 in the northern district of Jaffna, where the Tamils are in a majority. At the same time, stringent anti-terrorist legislation was passed in Parliament (as the National State Assembly had been renamed in 1978), and a presidential commission was established to study the Tamil issue.

In June 1980 a general strike, called by left-wing trade unions seeking higher wages, led to the declaration of a state of emergency between July and August, and more than 40,000 government workers lost their jobs. In August the TULF agreed to the establishment of District Development Councils, providing for a wide measure of regional autonomy. Elections to these, held in June 1981, were boycotted by the SLFP, the LSSP and the Communist Party, and the UNP won control of 18 of the 24 Councils. Subsequent communal disturbances between Sinhalese and Tamils led to the imposition of a state of emergency in the north for five days in June, and throughout the country from August 1981 to January 1982. Tamil MPs proposed a motion of no confidence in the Government and subsequently boycotted Parliament until November 1981, when a peace initiative to ease racial tension was proposed by the Government.

Meanwhile, in October 1980 the former Prime Minister, Sirimavo Bandaranaike, was found guilty of having abused power by a special presidential commission, which deprived her of all civic rights and effectively prevented her from standing in the next elections.

In August 1982 Parliament approved an amendment to the 1978 Constitution which enabled President Jayewardene to call a presidential election before his term of office expired, i.e. after four years instead of six. Sri Lanka's first presidential election was held in October 1982, and Jayewardene was returned to office with 53% of the votes cast. The SLFP candidate, Hector Kobbekaduwa, polled 39%, despite his party's disarray and Sirimavo Bandaranaike's loss of civic rights.

Following this success, the President announced, with the approval of Parliament and the Supreme Court, that, instead of a general election, a referendum would be held to decide whether to prolong the life of Parliament for a further six years after the session ended in July 1983. A state of emergency was in force between October 1982 and January 1983, and all opposition newspapers were closed by the Government. Sirimavo Bandaranaike was allowed to campaign in the referendum, which took place in December 1982 and resulted in approval of the proposal to prolong Parliament until 1989. On a 71% turn-out, 55% (3.1m.) voted in favour, with the dissenting minority of 2.6m. being concentrated mainly in and around Jaffna.

A state of emergency was declared in May 1983 to combat mounting terrorism, and in June Tamil terrorist activity led to army reprisals and the worst outbreak of violence for many years, with more than 400 deaths and particularly severe rioting in Jaffna and Colombo. A curfew and press censorship were imposed, and three left-wing parties (including the JVP) were banned. In July the 16 TULF MPs resigned in protest at the extension of Parliament, as approved by the referendum. In August Parliament passed a 'no-separation' amendment to the Constitution, depriving those espousing Tamil separatism of their civic rights. In October the TULF MPs were found to have forfeited their seats because of their parliamentary boycott. After much discussion and with the informal mediation of India, an All-Party Conference (APC) began in January 1984. The APC comprised representatives of the Buddhist, Christian and Muslim faiths as well as political leaders from the Sinhalese and Tamil communities. The Government proposed to establish provincial councils, with some regional autonomy, throughout the country. The TULF, however, demanded regional devolution that would enable the northern province, with its Tamil majority, to amalgamate with the eastern province where the Tamils were in a minority and thus create a Tamil state within the framework of a united Sri Lanka. The Sinhalese and the Muslims were implacably opposed to this proposal. The APC was finally abandoned in December, without agreement on the crucial question of the extent of regional autonomy.

Further violent outbursts in the northern part of the island in November and December 1984 led to the proclamation of another state of emergency. There were widespread accusations of gross military indiscipline, along with condemnation of government-sponsored settlement of Sinhalese in Tamil areas in the eastern province. A restricted zone was established between Mannar and Mullaitivu, to prevent contact with the Indian state of Tamil Nadu, where many of the Tamil militants were based.

In February 1986 there was a resurgence of violence in the northern and eastern provinces. In May a series of explosions in Colombo was widely believed to have been carried out by Tamil terrorists. The Government intensified its campaign against the insurgents by increasing defence expenditure and by launching an offensive against the militant Tamils in the Jaffna peninsula. This offensive made little headway, but the government cause was helped by internecine fighting between two of the principal Tamil militant groups, the Tamil Eelam Liberation Organization (TELO) and the Liberation Tigers of Tamil Eelam (LTTE—also known as the Tamil Tigers), the latter of which, over the year, emerged as the dominant Tamil separatist group under the leadership of Velupillai Prabhakaran. In May Tamil terrorists renewed their attacks on Sinhalese villagers who had been settled by the Government in Tamil-dominated areas in the eastern province. In June the Government presented fresh devolution proposals to a newly convened APC, in which the TULF was not invited to participate, while the SLFP boycotted the talks. The proposals again envisaged the formation of provincial councils, but did not satisfy the Tamils' demand for amalgamation of the northern and eastern provinces. The proposals were also rejected by the SLFP, on the grounds that they conceded too much to the Tamils.

In January 1987, in response to an announcement by the LTTE that they intended to seize control of the civil administration of Jaffna, the Government suspended, indefinitely, the distribution of all petroleum products to the peninsula. In the same month all the powers previously vested in the Prime Minister, Ranasinghe Premadasa, as Minister of Emergency Civil Administration were transferred to a new Ministry of National Security, directly supervised by the President. In February the Government launched an offensive against the terrorists in the Batticaloa district of the eastern province. The situation worsened in April, when the LTTE, having rejected an offer of a cease-fire by the Sri Lankan Government, carried out a series of outrages against the civilian population, including a bomb explosion in Colombo's main bus station, which killed more than 100 people. In response, the Government attempted to regain control of the Jaffna peninsula, the stronghold of the LTTE. During the resultant struggle between the LTTE and government forces, India demonstrated its support for the Tamils by violating Sri Lankan airspace to drop food and medical supplies in Jaffna. On 29 July, however, an important breakthrough was made when President Jayewardene and the Indian Prime Minister, Rajiv Gandhi, signed an accord regarding an attempted settlement of the country's ethnic crisis. The main points were: the provision of an Indian Peace-Keeping Force (IPKF) to oversee its proper implementation; a complete cessation of hostilities, and the surrender of all weapons held by the Tamil militants; the amalgamation of the northern and eastern provinces into one administrative unit, with an elected provincial council (together with the creation of provincial councils in the seven other provinces); the holding of a referendum in the eastern province at a date to be decided by the Sri Lankan President, to determine whether the mixed population of Tamils, Sinhalese and Muslims supported an official merger with the northern province into a single Tamil-dominated north-east province; a general amnesty for all Tamil militants; the repatriation of some 130,000 Tamil refugees from India to Sri Lanka (by early 1991 the number of Tamil refugees in India had risen to an estimated 210,000, and in early 1992 the Indian Government began to repatriate them, allegedly on a voluntary basis); the prevention of the use of Indian territory by Tamil militants for military or propaganda purposes; the prevention of the military use of Sri Lankan ports by any country in a manner prejudicial to Indian interests; and the provision that Tamil and English should have equal status with Sinhala as official languages. The accord encountered widespread disapproval among the Sinhalese population and from the SLFP, which claimed that it granted too much power to the Tamil minority.

In July and August 1987 more than 7,000 Indian troops were dispatched to Sri Lanka. After a promising start in August, the surrender of arms by the Tamil militant groups became more sporadic in September, and the implementation of the peace accord was impeded by further internecine fighting among the Tamil militias (involving the LTTE in particular), which necessitated direct intervention by the IPKF. Under arrangements reported to have been negotiated in September with the Indian authorities, the LTTE were to be allocated a majority of seats on an interim council, which was to administer the northern and eastern provinces, pending the holding of elections. Despite this concession, the surrender of arms by the LTTE had virtually ceased by early October; the group had resumed its terrorist attacks on Sinhalese citizens, and had declared itself to be firmly opposed to the peace accord. In response to the resurgence in violence, the IPKF launched an offensive against the LTTE stronghold in the Jaffna peninsula in October. The Indian troops encountered fierce and prolonged resistance from the Tamil militants, which resulted in the deployment of thousands of reinforcements. By the end of the month, however, the IPKF had gained control of Jaffna city, while most of the LTTE militants had escaped to establish a new base for guerrilla operations, in the Batticaloa district of the eastern province. Both sides had suffered heavy casualties.

Because of the continuing violence, the Sri Lankan Government abandoned its plan to create an interim administrative council for the northern and eastern provinces. However, in November 1987, despite strong opposition from the SLFP (which vehemently opposed the proposed merger of the northern and eastern provinces), Parliament adopted the legislation establishing provincial councils.

Another major threat to the successful implementation of the peace accord was the re-emergence in 1987 of the outlawed Sinhalese group, the JVP, which had been officially banned in August 1983 and which was based mainly in the south of the island. This group claimed that the accord conceded too much power to the Tamils. As part of its anti-accord campaign, the JVP was widely believed to have been responsible for an assassination attempt on President Jayewardene in August, in which one MP was killed and several cabinet ministers were seriously wounded, and to have murdered more than 200 UNP supporters by February 1988, including the Chairman of the UNP, Harsha Abeywardene, and the leader of the left-wing Sri Lanka Mahajana (People's) Party (SLMP), Vijaya Kumaratunga, who supported the accord. In May 1988 the Government revoked the five-year ban on the JVP in return for an agreement by the party to end its campaign of violence, but JVP leaders disowned the agreement as a hoax.

In February 1988 a new opposition force emerged when an alliance, named the United Socialist Alliance (USA), was formed between the SLMP, the LSSP, the Communist Party of Sri Lanka, the Nava Sama Samaja Party, and (most notably) the Tamil rights group entitled the Eelam People's Revolutionary Liberation Front (EPRLF). Although the USA group, led by Chandrika Bandaranaike Kumaratunga (the widow of the SLMP leader and the daughter of Sirimavo Bandaranaike), comprised opposition parties, it expressed support for the peace accord.

Elections to seven of the new provincial councils were held in April and June 1988 (in defiance of the JVP's threats and violence); elections in the northern and eastern provinces were postponed indefinitely. The UNP won a majority and effective control in all seven, while the USA emerged as the main opposition group. The SLFP boycotted the elections, in protest at the continuing presence of the IPKF (which now numbered about 50,000) in Sri Lanka. In September President Jayewardene officially authorized the merger of the northern and eastern provinces into a single north-eastern province, prior to provincial council elections there. The JVP reacted violently, and was widely believed to have been responsible for the murder of the Minister of Rehabilitation and Reconstruction at the end of the month. In protest against the proposed elections in the new north-eastern province and the presidential election (due to be held in December), the JVP organized a series of disruptive strikes and violent demonstrations in the central, western and southern provinces in October. In an effort to curb the increasing violence, the Government applied extensive emergency regulations, imposed curfews in areas of unrest, and deployed armed riot police. Despite boycotts and threats by both the JVP and the LTTE, elections to the new north-eastern provincial council took place in November. The moderate and pro-accord Tamil groups, the EPRLF and the Eelam National Democratic Liberation Front (ENDLF), together with the Sri Lanka Muslim Congress (SLMC), were successful in the elections, while the UNP won only one seat. In early December Parliament unanimously approved a Constitution Amendment Bill to make Tamil one of the country's two official languages (with Sinhala), thus fulfilling one of the major commitments envisaged in the peace accord. On 19 December the presidential election took place, in circumstances of unprecedented disruption, and was boycotted by the LTTE and the JVP. None the less, about 55% of the total electorate was estimated to have voted. The Prime Minister, Ranasinghe Premadasa (the UNP's candidate), won by a narrow margin, with 50.4% of the total votes, while Sirimavo Bandaranaike, the President of the SLFP (whose civil rights had been restored in January 1986), received 44.9%. On the following day, as promised earlier in the month by the Government, Parliament was dissolved in preparation for a general election.

In early January 1989 Premadasa was sworn in as Sri Lanka's new President, and an interim Cabinet was appointed. In the same month, the Government repealed the state of emergency, which had been in force since May 1983, and abolished the Ministry of National Security. Concurrently, however, special security measures were invoked in an attempt to arrest the escalating violence. Shortly after his inauguration, Premadasa offered to confer with the extremists and invited all groups to take part in the electoral process. The JVP and the LTTE, however, intensified their campaigns of violence in protest at the forthcoming general election. In early February 1989 the moderate, pro-accord Tamil groups, the EPRLF, the ENDLF and the TELO, formed a loose alliance, under the leadership of the TULF, to contest the general election. In the election, which was held on 15 February and which was, again, marred by widespread violence, the UNP won 125 of the 225 contested seats. The new system of proportional representation, which was introduced at this election, was especially advantageous to the SLFP, which became the major opposition force in Parliament, with 67 seats. The comparatively low electoral participation of 64% confirmed, again, that intimidatory tactics, employed by the LTTE and the JVP, had had an effect on the voters. A few days later President Premadasa installed a new Cabinet, and in March he appointed the Minister of Finance, Dingiri Banda Wijetunga, as the country's new Prime Minister. Although both the LTTE and the JVP rejected a conciliatory offer made by the President in April, in a surprising development, representatives of the LTTE began discussions with government officials in Colombo in the following month.

Between January and April 1989 five battalions of the IPKF left Sri Lanka, and in May the Sri Lankan Government announced that it wanted all Indian troops to have left Sri Lanka by the end of July. In response, Rajiv Gandhi stressed that the timetable for a complete withdrawal would have to be decided mutually, and that, before the Indian forces left, he wanted to ensure the security of the Tamils and the devolution of real power to the elected local government in the north-eastern province. In protest against the continued presence of the IPKF in Sri Lanka, the JVP organized a series of demonstrations and strikes. As a result of the escalating unrest, the Government reimposed a state of emergency on 20 June. In the same month, shortly after the murders of several prominent Tamil leaders, the peace negotiations between the Sri Lankan Government and the LTTE were temporarily discontinued. In September the Governments of Sri Lanka and India signed an agreement in Colombo, under which India promised to make 'all efforts' to withdraw its remaining 45,000 troops from Sri Lanka by the end of the year, and the IPKF was to declare an immediate unilateral cease-fire. In turn, the Sri Lankan Government pledged immediately to establish a peace committee for the north-eastern province in an attempt to reconcile the various Tamil groups and to incorporate members of the LTTE into the peaceful administration of the province.

The JVP suffered a very serious set-back when its leader, Rohana Wijeweera, and his principal deputy were shot dead by the security forces in November 1989. In the following month the leader of the military wing of the JVP, Saman Piyasiri Fernando, was killed in an exchange of gunfire in Colombo. Between September 1989 and the end of January 1990 the Sri Lankan security forces effectively destroyed the JVP as a political force, thus substantially transforming the country's political scene. All but one member of the JVP's political bureau and most leaders at district level had been killed. It was estimated, however, that the number of civilians killed in the lengthy struggle between the JVP and the Government might have been as high as 25,000–50,000.

As the Indian troops increased the speed of their withdrawal from Sri Lanka in the latter half of 1989, the LTTE initiated a campaign of violence against its arch-rivals, the more moderate Indian-supported EPRLF, which was mustering a so-called Tamil National Army, with Indian help, in the north-eastern province, to resist the LTTE. The LTTE accused the EPRLF and its allies of forcibly conscripting thousands of Tamil youths into the Tamil army. Following months of peace talks with the Government, however, the political wing of the LTTE was recognized as a political party by the commissioner of elections in December. The LTTE leaders then proclaimed that the newly recognized party would take part in the democratic process (it demanded immediate fresh elections in the north-eastern province) under the new name of the People's Front of the Liberation Tigers (PFLT). By the end of 1989 the inexperienced and undisciplined Tamil National Army had been virtually destroyed by the LTTE, who now appeared to have the tacit support of the central Government and had taken control of much of the territory in the north-eastern province.

Following further talks between the Governments of Sri Lanka and India, the completion date for the withdrawal of the IPKF was postponed until the end of March 1990. In early March the EPRLF-dominated north-eastern provincial council, under the leadership of Annamalai Varadharajah Perumal, renamed itself the 'National Assembly of the Free and Sovereign Democratic Republic of Eelam' and gave the central Government a one-year ultimatum to fulfil a charter of demands. Two weeks later, however, Perumal was reported to have fled to southern India. The last remaining IPKF troops left Sri Lanka on 24 March, a week ahead of schedule. In the next month the Government eased emergency regulations (including the ban on political rallies) in an effort to restore a degree of normality to the country after years of violence. At the same time, Sri Lanka's security forces, encouraged by the relative lull in violence, halted all military operations against the now much-weakened JVP and the Tamil militant groups. A fragile peace was maintained until June, when the LTTE abandoned their negotiations with the Government and renewed hostilities with surprise attacks on military and police installations in the north and north-east. Consequently, the Sri Lankan security forces were compelled to launch a counter-offensive. In mid-June the Government dissolved the north-eastern provincial council (despite protests by the EPRLF), and the holding of fresh elections in the province was postponed indefinitely pending the LTTE's agreement to participate in them (as earlier promised). In August the LTTE intensified their campaign of violence in the eastern province against the Muslim population, which retaliated with counter-attacks. At the end of August the Government launched a major offensive against the Tamil strongholds in the Jaffna peninsula. In March 1991 it was widely suspected that the LTTE were responsible for the assassination of a senior Sri Lankan cabinet member, the Minister of Plantation Industries and Minister of State for Defence, Ranjan Wijeratne (who had been in charge of both the government forces' successful offensive against the JVP, several years earlier, and the ongoing offensive against the LTTE), and for the bomb attack on an armed-forces building in Colombo in June. More significantly, for its regional implications, the LTTE were believed to have been responsible for the assassination of the former Indian Prime Minister, Rajiv Gandhi, near Madras (now known as Chennai), the state capital of Tamil Nadu, in May. In early 1992 the Indian Government proscribed the LTTE in India and banned their activities on Indian territory.

In May 1991 President Premadasa consolidated his political position when the UNP won a decisive victory in the local government elections. In August, however, the opposition, with the support of a number of UNP parliamentary members, began proceedings for the impeachment of the President. The impeachment motion listed 24 instances of alleged abuse of power and constituted a serious challenge to the authority of Premadasa and to the stability of his Government. However, it was rejected in October by the Speaker of Parliament on the grounds that some of the signatures on the resolution were invalid. Eight erstwhile UNP parliamentary members, including two former cabinet members, Lalith Athulathmudali and Gamini Dissanayake, who were expelled from the party (thus losing their parliamentary seats as well) by Premadasa for supporting the impeachment motion, formed a new party in December, called the Democratic United National Front (DUNF), to which they hoped to attract dissident members of the UNP.

The security forces suffered a serious reversal in August 1992, when 10 senior officers, including the northern military commander and the Jaffna peninsula commander, were killed in a land-mine explosion near Jaffna. Tension between the Muslim and Tamil populations in the north-eastern district of Polonnaruwa drastically increased following the massacre of more than 170 Muslim villagers by suspected LTTE guerrillas in October. In the next month the LTTE were also widely believed to have been responsible for the murder of the naval commander, Vice-Admiral Clancy Fernando, in Colombo. The LTTE themselves lost one of their most senior leaders when Velupillai Prabhakaran's chief deputy was killed at sea in January 1993.

In late April 1993 the opposition DUNF accused Premadasa's Government of having been responsible for the assassination of the party's leader, Lalith Athulathmudali. In response, Premadasa alleged that the perpetrators of the murder had been LTTE terrorists; the LTTE, however, denied any responsibility for the killing. The country was thrown into greater political turmoil on 1 May, when President Premadasa was assassinated in a bomb explosion in Colombo. The LTTE were officially blamed for the murder, although, again, they strenuously denied any involvement. A few days later Parliament unanimously elected the incumbent Prime Minister, Dingiri Banda Wijetunga, to serve the remaining presidential term (expiring in December 1994), and the erstwhile Minister of Industries, Science and Technology, Ranil Wickremasinghe, was appointed to replace him in the premiership. In provincial elections held in mid-May 1993 the UNP won control of four of the seven councils; no polling was carried out in the area covered by the now defunct north-eastern province (the province was officially declared invalid by the Supreme Court in October 2006). Although the ruling party received 47% of the votes, it was the first time since 1977 that its percentage of total votes had fallen below 50%, an indication of an erosion of its support base that became more pronounced in the early part of 1994.

The Sri Lankan forces achieved considerable success in their fight against ethnic violence in the eastern province in 1993, but were forced to abandon a massive military offensive in the Jaffna peninsula in October owing to the ferocity of the LTTE resistance. In the following month both sides suffered heavy casualties in the course of the battle over the military base at Pooneryn on the Jaffna lagoon. As a result of this military débâcle, in which, according to official figures, more than 600 army and naval personnel were either killed or captured, the Government established a new combined security forces command for the Jaffna and Kilinochchi districts to counter the LTTE threat.

Despite the continuing violence, provincial elections were held in the eastern province and in the northern town of Vavuniya in early March 1994; the UNP secured the greatest number of seats, while independent Tamil groups also performed well. The LTTE and the TULF boycotted the poll. The ruling party suffered its first major electoral reverse for 17 years at the end of the month, however, when an opposition grouping known as the People's Alliance (PA, of which the main constituents were the SLFP and the traditional Marxist left and which was headed by the former leader of the USA group, Chandrika Kumaratunga) won a clear majority in elections to the southern provincial council. On 24 June, in an apparent attempt to catch the opposition by surprise, the President dissolved Parliament and announced that early legislative elections were to be held on 16 August, ahead of the presidential election. Wijetunga's ploy failed, however: the PA obtained 48.9% of the votes, thus securing a narrow victory over the UNP, which received 44% of the poll. Under the prevailing system of proportional representation, this translated to 105 seats for the PA and 94 for the UNP in the 225-seat Parliament. The 17-year rule of the UNP had thus come to an end. On 18 August President Wijetunga abandoned hope of forming a UNP minority Government and appointed Kumaratunga as Prime Minister, the PA having secured the support of the SLMC, the TULF, the Democratic People's Liberation Front and a small, regional independent group. A new Cabinet was appointed on the following day, almost all members of which belonged to the SLFP. In line with her electoral pledge to abolish the executive presidency and to establish a parliamentary system in its place, the Prime Minister removed the finance portfolio from the President and assumed responsibility for it herself. Although Wijetunga retained the title of Minister of Defence, actual control of the ministry was expected to be exercised by the Deputy Minister of Defence. The Prime Minister's mother, Sirimavo Bandaranaike, was appointed as Minister without Portfolio. With regard to the Tamil question, overtures were made between the new Government and the LTTE concerning unconditional peace talks (these commenced in mid-October) and at the end of August, as a gesture of goodwill, the Government partially lifted the economic blockade on LTTE-occupied territory. In addition, the Prime Minister created a new Ministry of Ethnic Affairs and National Integration and assumed the portfolio herself, thus revealing her determination to seek an early solution to the civil strife.

In September 1994 Kumaratunga was unanimously elected by the PA as its candidate for the forthcoming presidential poll, while Gamini Dissanayake, the leader of the opposition (who had left the DUNF and returned to the UNP in 1993), was chosen as the UNP's candidate. The election campaign was thrown into confusion, however, on 24 October 1994, when Dissanayake was assassinated by a suspected LTTE suicide bomber in a suburb of Colombo; more than 50 other people, including the General Secretary of the UNP, Gamini Wijesekara, and the leader of the SLMP, Ossie Abeyagoonasekera, were also killed in the blast. The Government declared a state of emergency and suspended the ongoing peace talks with the LTTE. Dissanayake had been an outspoken critic of these talks and had been one of the architects of the 1987 Indo-Sri Lankan accord. His widow, Srima Dissanayake, was chosen by the UNP to replace him as the party's presidential candidate. The state of emergency was revoked on 7 November (with the exception of the troubled areas in the north and east) to facilitate the fair and proper conduct of the presidential election, which was held on 9 November. Kumaratunga won the election, with 62.3% of the votes, while Srima Dissanayake obtained 35.9%. The Government viewed the victory as a clear mandate for the peace process initiated earlier that year. Sirimavo Bandaranaike was subsequently appointed Prime Minister for the third time. The new President pledged to abolish the executive presidency before mid-July 1995, on the grounds that she believed that the post vested too much power in one individual, and promised to initiate a programme of social, economic and constitutional change.

The Government and the LTTE resumed peace talks in early January 1995, which resulted in the drawing up of a preliminary agreement on the cessation of hostilities as a prelude to political negotiations. This important development constituted the first formal truce since fighting was renewed in the north-east in June 1990. In April 1995, however, following several rounds of deadlocked negotiations, with both sides accusing each other of making unreasonable demands and proposals, the LTTE unilaterally ended the truce, withdrew from the peace talks and resumed hostilities against the government forces. In response, the Government cancelled all the concessions made to the guerrillas during the peace negotiations and placed the security forces on alert. A disturbing escalation in the violence was demonstrated at the end of the month by the LTTE's deployment, for the first time, of surface-to-air missiles.

In July 1995 the Government launched another major offensive in the Jaffna peninsula. As the offensive was intensified in mid-October, tens of thousands of civilians were compelled by the LTTE to flee the area. In retaliation against the army's attack, rather than actively confronting the troops, the LTTE detonated explosives on the country's two largest oil storage facilities near Colombo, which received virtually all of Sri Lanka's imported petroleum. As a result, about 20% of the island's petroleum supply was destroyed. In November two LTTE suicide bombers caused 18 deaths and more than 50 injuries in Colombo. In early December, however, the Sri Lankan army achieved a major victory in capturing the city of Jaffna and subsequently much of the Jaffna peninsula. Although the LTTE's military strength and morale were undermined, the rebels, as expected, reverted to guerrilla warfare and further terrorist activity. The day after the armed forces had raised the national flag above Jaffna, the LTTE rejected the President's offer of an amnesty in exchange for disarmament and announced a new recruitment drive. The Government's short-term strategy with regard to the Jaffna peninsula was to attempt to persuade the tens of thousands of civilians now living in refugee camps to return there and to establish a fully functional civil administration in the region. As widely feared, there was an escalation in LTTE-organized terrorist activity following the recapture of Jaffna; at the end of January 1996 more than 100 people were killed and about 1,400 were injured as a result of a suicide bomb attack on the Central Bank in Colombo. This devastating attack appeared to be the LTTE's response to the Government's release of the legal draft of devolution proposals earlier that month. Against a background of continuing conflict between the Tamil militants and the government forces in the north and east of the country, the President extended the state of emergency to cover the whole country in April (since coming to power in November 1994, the PA administration had restricted the emergency provisions to the troubled northern and eastern regions and Colombo). In mid-May 1996 the army announced that it now controlled the whole of the Jaffna peninsula and claimed that, of the 300,000 Tamil civilians who had been displaced by the ethnic violence, about 250,000 had returned to the government-held areas. Despite the army's controlling presence in the Jaffna peninsula, the LTTE were by no means a spent force. In mid-July the Tamil militants attacked and overran the isolated military base at Mullaitivu on the north-eastern coast of Sri Lanka, inflicting very heavy casualties on the army (according to the LTTE, at least 1,200 government soldiers were killed; according to official figures, the army death toll was about 300). About one week later the LTTE were suspected of planting a bomb on a crowded suburban train near Colombo, which killed more than 70 people. In September the army seized control of the northern town of Kilinochchi, which had served as the LTTE's new headquarters since April. In the following month Prabhakaran and nine other militants were charged with more than 700 criminal acts of terrorism, including the bombing of the Central Bank in January. This constituted the first occasion that the Government had taken legal action against the LTTE leader. Fierce fighting between the Tamil militants and government troops continued into 1997, both in the north and east of the country; in early March it was estimated that more than 50,000 people had died and about one million people had been displaced as a result of the 14-year civil war.

The Government was given a considerable boost in March 1997, following its overwhelming success in local elections, in which it won more than 80% of the contested bodies (voting did not take place in the troubled northern and eastern provinces). However, although the Government secured control over a majority of the local bodies, its share of the total vote decreased to 48%, compared with the 62% it achieved in the presidential election of November 1994. The UNP obtained nearly 42% of the poll. None the less, the Government viewed the election results as a mandate to continue preparing its devolution plans offering limited autonomy to the Tamil secessionists (plans that had, so far, been blocked by the UNP). In May the Government launched a fresh military offensive against the LTTE, with the aim of gaining control of the 75-km stretch of the A9 highway between Vavuniya and Elephant Pass, which is the point of entry to the Jaffna peninsula. In late August the Government announced that it would submit its devolution proposals for parliamentary debate in October. In mid-October, however, 18 people were killed and more than 100 injured (including about 35 foreigners) when a bomb exploded in the car park of a Colombo hotel. It was widely believed that the LTTE deliberately targeted foreigners in this attack following the US Administration's decision a few days earlier to place the organization on its official proscribed list of international terrorist groups. At the end of the month, despite protests from the UNP, the draft of the proposed constitutional amendments was presented to Parliament. The prospect of peace, however, appeared increasingly remote in late January 1998, when 16 people were killed in a suspected LTTE suicide bombing in Kandy at Sri Lanka's most sacred Buddhist temple, the Dalada Maligawa ('Temple of the Tooth'). The following day the Government retaliated by formally outlawing the LTTE, thus apparently ruling out the prospect of further peace negotiations in the near future and focusing instead on a military solution. The Government suffered another set-back in late January when the UNP effectively rejected the proposed devolution package. The UNP disagreed with the Government's proposal to devolve wide-ranging powers to regional councils—including a Tamil-administered area—and favoured the concept of power-sharing at the centre. Also at the end of January, polls were conducted in Jaffna for the first time in 15 years. The local authority elections, which were monitored by tens of thousands of troops, were contested by a number of moderate Tamil political parties but were, not surprisingly, boycotted by the LTTE. The largest number of seats was won by the Eelam People's Democratic Party, but the turn-out was a mere 28%, owing to LTTE threats to disrupt the voting.

In mid-May 1998 the recently elected mayor of Jaffna (the first person to hold that position in 14 years), Sarojini Yogeswaran, who was a member of the moderate TULF, was assassinated by two suspected LTTE gunmen after refusing demands by Tamil militants to resign. In September Yogeswaran's replacement, Ponnuthurai Sivapalan, who was also a leading member of the TULF, was killed, along with 19 others, in a suspected LTTE bomb explosion in Jaffna city hall.

In early June 1998 the Government imposed an indefinite 'total ban' on news coverage (both local and foreign) of the ongoing civil war. In late September hundreds of troops on both sides were killed when the LTTE recaptured Kilinochchi and the army seized Mankulam, the last major town held by the guerrillas on the vital northern highway. By the end of the year, despite fierce fighting and large numbers of casualties on both sides, the army had still failed to capture completely the northern highway, which, if opened, would provide the military with a vital land route to the Jaffna peninsula (hitherto during the civil war, all government troops and supplies had had to be transported by sea or air). In early December the Government announced its decision to cancel the operation to capture the highway, which, since it was launched in May 1997, had cost the lives of more than 3,000 government troops. There were also indications that the army had a serious manpower problem (it needed to recruit 20,000 fresh troops), caused partly by desertions and growing numbers of casualties.

In late January 1999 the ruling PA won the elections to the north-western provincial council by a significant margin, but amid allegations of widespread electoral fraud and violence against opposition activists. A few days later the Supreme Court in Colombo overruled an order made by President Kumaratunga in August 1998 postponing elections to five other provincial councils. The Court stated that the presidency had no constitutional right to postpone the elections through the declaration of a state of emergency, as it had done, and asked the election commission to hold the polls within the next three months and to hold all five of them on a single day. In the provincial elections, which were eventually held in early April, the PA won control in four provinces and retained power in the fifth—the polls were very keenly contested, however, with the PA achieving about 43% of the total votes and the UNP obtaining around 41%. Elections to the southern province, which were held in May, also resulted in a PA-led administration. One noteworthy feature of this series of provincial polls was the resurgence of the JVP as a credible political force (it won 8% of the vote in all of the contested provincial councils, and, specifically, as much as 20% in the Hambantota district of the southern province).

Meanwhile, in March 1999 the army launched another offensive against the LTTE in the northern province, the objective of which was to reduce the area under the effective control of the Tamil guerrillas. In mid-June, in an unprecedented order, the President temporarily dissolved the powerful National Security Council and divested the Chief of Defence Staff of sweeping powers. Prospects of achieving a peace settlement in Sri Lanka appeared even more distant in late July, following the assassination by a suspected LTTE suicide bomber in Colombo of the TULF Vice-President, Neelan Tiruchelvam, who was a leading peace campaigner and human rights activist. In the same month Kumaratunga promoted 15 PA members to the position of deputy minister, in a move that was widely interpreted as an attempt to ensure that politicians remained loyal to the Alliance prior to and during the forthcoming general election. The promotions were heavily criticized by the opposition as financially profligate.

In October 1999 President Kumaratunga announced the holding of an early presidential election in December (about 11 months ahead of schedule), prompting the opposition to claim that her decision was aimed at bolstering the foundering ruling coalition prior to the legislative elections, which were due to be held in October 2000. In November 1999, however, the Government suffered a debilitating set-back following a rapid series of LTTE victories in the north-eastern Wanni region, thus reversing more than two years of territorial gains by the military. Following these demoralizing defeats and amid reports of large-scale desertions and mutiny in the army ranks, the Government announced a tightening of existing military censorship on domestic news coverage in an attempt to stem adverse publicity and reorganized the northern military command.

A few days before the presidential election, which was held on 21 December 1999, Kumaratunga survived an assassination attempt by a suspected LTTE suicide bomber in Colombo; the explosion killed more than 20 people and injured more than 100, while the President sustained wounds to her right eye. The election, which was contested by 13 candidates and attracted a 73% turn-out of the electorate, was marred by widespread allegations of vote-rigging, intimidation and violence. Kumaratunga was returned to power by a narrow majority (possibly having garnered a considerable sympathy vote), winning 51% of the total votes, while her main rival, Ranil Wickremasinghe of the UNP, secured 43%.

At the end of January 2000, in a dramatic reversal of policy, Wickremasinghe announced that, in spite of reservations, the UNP would henceforth offer legislative support to the Government's proposed constitutional amendments regarding devolution (first unveiled in 1995), which were designed to prepare the ground for peace talks with the LTTE; the opposition party, however, later appeared to vacillate with regard to its support, following indications that Kumaratunga intended to retain the executive presidency for a further six years. In early 2000 the Government confirmed that, at Kumaratunga's request, the Norwegian Government had agreed to play an intermediary role in any peace negotiations. The Norwegian Minister of Foreign Affairs, Knut Vollebæk, arrived in Colombo in February to discuss with Kumaratunga and Wickremasinghe the modalities for commencing direct peace talks between the Sri Lankan Government and the LTTE. Earlier that month Vollebæk had met a senior LTTE official in London, United Kingdom, to assess the separatists' opinions regarding peace negotiations. According to commentators, the preconditions of both sides (respectively, the withdrawal of all government troops from Tamil areas and the abandonment by the LTTE of their demand for an independent state) were the most serious obstacles to the commencement of talks.

Despite the steps being taken towards the instigation of peace talks, heavy fighting continued between the army and the LTTE in the north. In April 2000, having made several significant gains, the LTTE announced that they had captured the large military base at Elephant Pass at the strategic entrance point to the peninsula (the garrison had been under government control since the IPKF's withdrawal in 1990). In early May President Kumaratunga came under intense pressure from various quarters to seek Indian assistance in an attempt to halt the rapid LTTE march to recapture Jaffna; the Indian Government firmly ruled out military intervention, but offered to provide humanitarian aid (including mediation and the evacuation of troops). India also announced that it was extending its ban on the outlawed LTTE for a further two years. In response to the escalating military crisis, the Government imposed draconian security measures, banning all activities perceived as a threat to national security and giving extensive powers to the armed forces and police, and renewed press censorship on the foreign media. By mid-May the LTTE claimed to be only 1 km from the administrative centre of Jaffna, and thousands of terrified civilians were reported to be fleeing from the embattled city. In late May, as the army and the LTTE continued to struggle for control of the peninsula, the Government appealed for new army recruits, and Norway launched a fresh diplomatic initiative to find a peaceful solution to the ethnic crisis. In early June the Minister of Industrial Development, Clement V. Gunaratna, and more than 20 others were killed by a suspected LTTE suicide bomber in Colombo. At the end of the month President Kumaratunga and the leader of the opposition UNP, Ranil Wickremasinghe, began discussions on the draft of the new Constitution designed to resolve the conflict with the LTTE. The LTTE, however, immediately denounced the proposals. At the same time, the Supreme Court ruled that the recently renewed press censorship was illegal as the appointment of the official censor had not been approved by Parliament. Nevertheless, the President reimposed a series of restrictions on the local and foreign press and reappointed the official censor under the same emergency regulations employed in May. The Government and UNP then agreed on a draft constitution, which recommended converting the country into a *de facto* federal state through the establishment of eight semi-autonomous regional councils. However, the Tamil parliamentary parties, the TULF, PLOTE and Eelam People's Democratic Party (EPDP), rejected the proposals as providing inadequate autonomy to the Tamil regions of the country. Senior Buddhist monks rejected the reforms, owing to fears that devolution would threaten the Sinhalese-dominated population and prominence of Buddhism in Sri Lanka. In late July the UNP withdrew its support for the reforms. Street demonstrations were held in protest at the proposals. In August the President indefinitely postponed a parliamentary vote on the issue, and hence any further discussion of the reform programme, once it became clear that the Government would not obtain the two-thirds' majority required to secure the passage of the requisite legislation. The LTTE intensified attacks on security forces. On 10 August Sirimavo Bandaranaike announced her resignation as Prime Minister, owing to ill health. She was replaced by Ratnisiri Wickremanayake, the erstwhile Minister of Public Administration, Home Affairs and Plantation Industries. Parliament was dissolved in preparation for a general election.

Meanwhile, a report issued by the University Teachers for Human Rights in mid-July 2000 claimed that there had been a dramatic increase in the number of child soldiers forcibly recruited by the LTTE, in preparation for a major assault on Jaffna city. In September heavy fighting between the LTTE and Sri Lankan army continued; the army reclaimed a naval base and Jaffna's second largest town, Chavakachcheri. By the end of September, however, the LTTE had managed to regain some territory. In the same month the Minister of Shipping and Shipping Development, Mohammad H. M. Ashraff, and the President of the SLMC, along with 14 others, were killed in a helicopter crash in Kegalle District. A high-level investigation into the incident was ordered; there was widespread speculation that the aircraft had been shot down by LTTE guerrillas.

The parliamentary elections of 10 October 2000 were marred by allegations of electoral malpractice and by systematic violence and intimidation (particularly on the part of the incumbent PA). Nevertheless, the elections attracted a turn-out of 75% of the electorate. Despite the electoral irregularities, neither the PA nor the UNP won an absolute majority (taking 107 and 89 of the 225 parliamentary seats, respectively), but, having gained the support of the EPDP and National Unity Alliance (NUA—primarily a constituent of the SLMC), the PA was able to form a new, expanded coalition under the premiership of Wickremanayake. Former Prime Minister Sirimavo Bandaranaike died shortly after casting her vote. On 18 October Parliament elected Anura Bandaranaike, a member of the UNP and the President's estranged brother, as parliamentary Speaker; this was the first time in 40 years that the position had been held by a member of the opposition. This development was followed by an agreement between the PA and UNP to preserve the stability of the new Government for the next two years. On 19 October a new Cabinet was announced. In exchange for its support, the NUA established a 100-day deadline for the President to introduce a new constitution and to open negotiations with the LTTE. At the end of the month the JVP announced its willingness to support the Government in order to prevent the NUA from wielding excessive influence.

In late October 2000 negotiations between the leader of the LTTE, Velupillai Prabhakaran, and the Norwegian peace envoy, Erik Solheim, commenced. Discussions between Solheim and the President were also initiated. In early November Prabhakaran proposed direct peace negotiations with the Government, without any preconditions, but demanded a reduction in fighting and the lifting of an economic embargo on areas controlled by the LTTE to create a suitable atmosphere for talks. In mid-December the Government announced that it was prepared to enter immediate peace negotiations, but would not scale down its offensive or lift the embargo until talks were under way. The LTTE rejected peace talks without the prior implementation of a cease-fire and later declared a unilateral one-month cease-fire, to begin from 24 December, as a 'goodwill gesture' to assist the peace process. Shortly afterwards, however, government troops launched an offensive in the Jaffna peninsula, and violence continued. The Government rejected the cease-fire, dismissing it as a strategic manoeuvre, and insisted that it would not discuss a cease-fire until the two parties entered peace negotiations. On 23 January 2001, and at regular intervals thereafter, the LTTE extended the cease-fire by one month, but the Government refused to reciprocate likewise. Despite dialogue between Solheim and representatives of the LTTE and Government, respectively, being resumed in late January, in mid-March violence escalated and continued into April.

In June 2001 the President dismissed the leader of the SLMC, Abdul Rauf Hakeem, from his position as Minister of Internal and International Trade, Commerce, Muslim Religious Affairs and Shipping Development, later accusing him of making anti-

Government statements and refusing to support government policies. The President's strategy foundered, however, when Hakeem and six other members of the SLMC withdrew their support for the ruling PA, thereby reducing the coalition Government to a minority in Parliament. Immediately afterwards, opposition parties challenged the Government with a no-confidence motion. In order to prevent the motion from being debated in Parliament in mid-July, the President suspended the legislature on 10 July until 7 September, and announced that a referendum on a new constitution would take place on 21 August. The rulings, which were undemocratic and unconstitutional, respectively, caused a constitutional crisis. The UNP-led opposition organized a series of demonstrations against the President's decision to prorogue Parliament. The President also faced opposition within the Cabinet, particularly to the referendum. As a result, Kumaratunga announced in early August that the referendum would be postponed until mid-October.

In the mean time, in early June 2001 the Norwegian Minister of Foreign Affairs, Thorbjørn Jagland, arrived in Colombo, at the request of the President, in an attempt to bolster the peace initiative. The LTTE, however, protested against this development, claiming that it was an effort to undermine Solheim's position. In early July President Kumaratunga circumvented Parliament and reimposed a state of emergency under anti-terrorist regulations. The President also extended a ban on the LTTE. On 24 July, the 18th anniversary of the launch of the LTTE's separatist campaign, Tamil militants attacked the capital's international airport and an adjacent airbase. Several hours of shooting between Tamil militants and the army ended with all 13 guerrillas and seven soldiers killed. During the attack the LTTE destroyed eight military aircraft and three civilian aircraft, and damaged a number of others. The assault on the country's only international airport, renowned for its impenetrable security, adversely affected the tourist industry and, thus, the economy, and raised questions about the air force and airport's defence system. Following the incident, the army launched a retaliatory air attack on LTTE bases; violence between the army and guerrillas escalated. At the end of August the LTTE rejected the Government's offer of a cease-fire, dismissing it as a strategic manoeuvre.

In an attempt to resolve the political crisis, the Prime Minister and senior cabinet members conducted negotiations with the UNP on the possible establishment of a coalition government. The UNP, however, opted to form a UNP-led coalition with other opposition parties. Consequently, the President entered into negotiations with the left-wing, radical JVP. On 5 September 2001 the JVP formally agreed to support the minority Government for one year (but not to join the administration), in return for a set of conditions laid out in a 28-point memorandum of understanding. The JVP's 10 seats in Parliament raised the Government's share to a majority of 119 out of 225 seats. The President had already granted the JVP two of its demands by cancelling the referendum and announcing that Parliament would be reconvened one day earlier. In addition, the President agreed to suspend negotiations with the LTTE for one year and to postpone the privatization programme. In accordance with the JVP's demands, in mid-September the size of the Cabinet was halved to 22 members. However, three senior cabinet members resigned, refusing to participate in an administration supported by the left-wing party. Several members of the PA criticized the pact and doubted its longevity. Later that month Parliament approved an item of legislation to establish a Constitutional Council, which would be responsible for removing political influence from major institutions and appointing independent commissions for public service, the judiciary, the police and elections. At the end of September a motion of no confidence in the Government was resubmitted to Parliament. On 10 October 13 members of the PA, including several ministers, defected to the opposition, reducing the coalition to a minority. In order to forestall defeat in the vote of no confidence due to take place the next day, President Kumaratunga dissolved Parliament. The opposition condemned the decision, although the dissolution was constitutional (one year had passed since the previous legislative elections).

The general election on 5 December 2001, reportedly one of the most violent in Sri Lanka's history, was marred by incidents of vote-rigging and other electoral malpractices. Some tens of thousands of Tamil voters were barred from voting after the army prevented them from leaving LTTE-controlled areas to cast their vote. The outgoing Government claimed that the UNP had signed a secret pact with the LTTE, an allegation strongly denied by the opposition. Nevertheless, 72% of the electorate voted. The UNP won 109 of the 225 seats (with 45.6% of the vote) and the PA received 77 seats (37.2%). The JVP secured 16 seats (9.1%) and the Tamil Nationalist Alliance (TNA—a Tamil opposition alliance comprising the TULF, TELO, EPRLF and All Ceylon Tamil Congress formed prior to the election) won 15 seats (3.9%). The UNP leader, Ranil Wickremasinghe, formed the United National Front (UNF) with the SLMC to ensure a majority of 114 seats in Parliament, and on 9 December he was sworn in as Prime Minister. For the first time since 1984, the Prime Minister and the President were from two opposing parties. The President was at first reluctant to relinquish her defence and finance portfolios, which she eventually gave up in return for full control over the élite Presidential Security Division that was deployed for her personal protection, and refused initially to allow members of her former administration who had defected to the UNP to join the Government. After lengthy negotiations, a new coalition Government, including the TNA and 12 members of the former PA administration, was sworn in on 12 December. In 2002 the right of the President to dissolve Parliament after one year from the date of the last election loomed over the new Government. In an attempt to curb the President's powers and to ensure stability for the peace process (see below), the Government recommended that parliamentary resolutions determine future elections; however, the President refused to support this suggestion. In September the Government introduced to Parliament a proposed constitutional amendment that would restrict the right of the President to dissolve the legislature when the governing party had a majority in Parliament. In October, however, the Supreme Court ruled that the proposed statute required not only a two-thirds' majority in the legislature, but also endorsement by a national referendum.

The UNP's victory in December 2001 was largely attributed to the party's keenness to resume negotiations with the LTTE; on his accession, the Prime Minister reiterated this willingness. Significantly, the TNA was a member of the coalition Government. Although the LTTE launched major attacks against army troops and the police, during which 26 were killed, to mark the inauguration of the new Cabinet, on 19 December the Tamil extremists announced a unilateral one-month cease-fire from 25 December. On 21 December the Government responded with the declaration of a cease-fire as a 'gesture of goodwill'. The Prime Minister also announced that the free movement of food, medicine and other non-military supplies into the Tamil-controlled areas would be allowed; a concession refused, hitherto, by the President. In early January 2002 the Government announced the reduction of economic sanctions on the northern areas controlled by the LTTE. One week later a delegation of Norwegian diplomats, led by Norway's Deputy Minister of Foreign Affairs, Vidar Helgesen, arrived in Colombo to conduct negotiations with the Prime Minister and President, and eventually to facilitate peace talks between the Government and the LTTE. At the end of January both sides extended the cease-fire by one month. At the same time, the LTTE released 10 army and civilian prisoners. As a further confidence-building measure, the Government restored the electricity supply to part of the northern Tamil-controlled Vavuniya district.

On 22 February 2002 the Government and LTTE signed an agreement on an internationally monitored indefinite cease-fire to take effect the following day. Norway was requested to monitor the cease-fire. It was hoped that this breakthrough would lead to peace negotiations and end years of fighting in which more than 60,000 people had been killed. However, in mid-February there were several reports that the LTTE was continuing forcibly to recruit Tamil children.

In mid-March 2002 Prime Minister Wickremasinghe visited Jaffna, the first premier to do so since 1982. In early April the Government lifted a six-year ban on domestic flights and allowed commercial airlines to resume flights to Jaffna. A week later an important road linking the Jaffna peninsula with the rest of the country was opened for the first time in 12 years. On 10 April Prabhakaran addressed an international press conference for the first time in more than 10 years. He demanded the lifting of the ban on the LTTE as a prerequisite to negotiations and declared his commitment to peace and full support of the cease-fire. A few days later he signed a pact with the SLMC, allowing the largest Muslim party in Sri Lanka to participate in proposed negotiations with the Government. It was also agreed that nearly 100,000 Muslims expelled from the north by the LTTE about 10 years ago would be allowed to return to their homes. At the end of April the Prime Minister rejected the LTTE's demand for an independent Tamil state, or 'eelam', raising doubts about resolving the ethnic conflict. Meanwhile, Kumaratunga, who had reportedly criticized the Government for making too many concessions to the Tamil militants, expressed her support in late April for a public demonstration against the proposal to grant legal status to the LTTE.

In May 2002 a Tamil-owned trawler, reported to have been illegally importing weapons, was destroyed by the Sri Lankan navy in an exchange of gunfire off the coast of the eastern Batticaloa district—the first major violation of the cease-fire to have occurred. The LTTE refuted allegations that they had been smuggling arms and accused the army of attacking a civilian fishing boat in an effort to undermine the cease-fire. Later in the month the Norwegian-led Sri Lanka Monitoring Mission (SLMM) issued a statement conveying concern over the increasing number of cases of civilians being harassed by the LTTE. In June incidents of violence between Hindu Tamils and Muslims in eastern Sri Lanka resulted in eight deaths and several injuries.

Meanwhile, also in May 2002, the first direct talks for seven years between the Government and the LTTE took place on the Jaffna peninsula. Although the August deadline for the commencement of formal peace negotiations was not achieved, the cease-fire was upheld. According to the office of the UN High Commissioner for Refugees (UNHCR, see p. 69), by mid-August 103,000 displaced families had returned to their homes since the beginning of the cease-fire in February. On 4 September the Government lifted the official ban on the LTTE, a prerequisite to negotiations set by the LTTE. (The President, however, firmly opposed the removal of the ban until the talks were under way.) The first round of negotiations took place on 16–18 September in Thailand. The Minister of Constitutional Affairs, Prof. G. L. Peiris, was chief negotiator for the Government; Anton Balasingham led negotiations on behalf of the LTTE. The talks were successful: both sides agreed to establish a joint committee to deal with security issues, and a joint task force to concentrate on the reconstruction of areas destroyed by war, the clearing of land-mines and the resettling of 800,000 internally displaced people to high-security zones. On the last day of negotiations Balasingham unexpectedly renounced the LTTE's long-standing demand for independence, instead agreeing to consider regional autonomy and self-government.

In early October 2002 four people were killed and 15 injured in clashes between government and LTTE forces in Ampara district, in one of the most serious violations of the cease-fire to date. On 31 October a Sri Lankan court convicted *in absentia* Prabhakaran for his role in a 1996 truck bombing in Colombo and sentenced him to 200 years' imprisonment. The sentencing did not have an effect on the second round of negotiations, which began on 31 October in Thailand. The four-day talks concentrated mainly on humanitarian issues, but concluded in a breakthrough, with both sides agreeing to create a subcommittee to examine a political solution to the conflict. Balasingham announced that the LTTE were willing to participate in the democratic process, would allow other political parties to operate in the areas under their control and would cease the recruitment of child soldiers. The LTTE also abandoned their demand for an interim government in the north-east. Both sides agreed to establish subcommittees to deal with rehabilitation and military de-escalation. However, while the talks progressed, a curfew was imposed in large parts of Colombo after three days of rioting between the majority Sinhalese and members of the Muslim community. Meanwhile, Sinhalese nationalists opposed to the peace process questioned the sincerity of the LTTE, dismissing the progress at the negotiations as an attempt to win publicity and international favour. Nevertheless, the peace process gained momentum in late November when Balasingham arrived in Norway to enter negotiations with the Prime Minister on the eve of a one-day international donor conference in support of Sri Lanka's quest for a lasting peace. A few days later Prabhakaran confirmed in his annual address that the LTTE were prepared to accept regional autonomy rather than an independent state, but warned that violence would resume if negotiations collapsed.

In December 2002, at the third round of peace talks, held in Oslo, Norway, the two sides agreed on 'internal self-determination' based on a federal system of government within a united Sri Lanka. Peiris and Balasingham described the developments as unprecedented and historic. However, in order to achieve the two-thirds' majority required in Parliament to pass a constitutional amendment, the Government needed to secure the support of the President. Although Kumaratunga welcomed the peace agreement, she had repeatedly criticized the Government for making too many concessions during the peace process. In mid-December a close adviser of the President stated that the PA would not support a political solution unless the LTTE disarmed. However, at the fourth round of negotiations, held in Thailand in early January 2003, Balasingham refused to yield to pressure to disarm the Tamil guerrillas prior to a political settlement and rejected Kumaratunga's demand that the LTTE's squad of suicide bombers disband. The talks concluded with an agreement to accelerate the rate of return and resettlement of up to 250,000 displaced people. Meanwhile, despite Tamil promises to halt the forced recruitment of children, the SLMM reported that the LTTE had enlisted hundreds of child soldiers since the instigation of the cease-fire. The fifth round of negotiations, held in Germany in early February, was overshadowed by a serious violation of the cease-fire. On 7 February three LTTE guerrillas committed suicide by setting fire to their trawler after the Sri Lankan navy intercepted the vessel and Norwegian peace monitors discovered arms on board. The two-day negotiations focused on human rights issues; it was agreed that UNICEF would monitor a joint programme to rehabilitate child soldiers.

Meanwhile, the SLMC split in early December 2002 after two members of the party mounted a challenge to Hakeem's leadership. In early February 2003 President Kumaratunga censured the Prime Minister for granting a licence to the LTTE radio station, Voice of Tigers, amid rising tension in the 'cohabitation Government'. On 7 February the PA and JVP began negotiations to form a joint front against the UNF Government. The JVP strongly opposed the LTTE and attempted to persuade the President to dismiss the governing coalition. Prabhakaran failed to attend a meeting with Norwegian peace mediators in mid-March, reportedly owing to the sinking of a civilian Tamil ship by the Sri Lankan navy several days earlier. The LTTE declared that they were considering abandoning the peace talks as a result of the incident. Furthermore, the sixth round of negotiations, held in Japan on 18–21 March, ended without agreement, amid reports of renewed violence in Sri Lanka. An international donor meeting in Washington, DC, USA, to consider aid for Sri Lanka's reconstruction in preparation for a major donor conference to be held in Japan in June, took place in mid-April. The LTTE, however, were not invited: the USA had not yet lifted its ban on the Tamil organization; neither had India, one of the attendees at the meeting. On 21 April the LTTE announced that they were temporarily withdrawing from the peace negotiations and that they would not attend the donor conference in Japan in June because they were excluded from the aid conference in the USA. They were also dissatisfied with the manner in which the cease-fire had been implemented (government troops remained stationed in many parts of the Tamil-controlled areas in a clear violation of the cease-fire) and the way in which the Government was carrying out rehabilitation and relief measures. Following the LTTE announcement, the President placed the security forces on high alert; however, the LTTE expressed its intention to uphold the cease-fire and there were no signs of renewed tension.

Efforts to revive the peace process suffered a set-back in May 2003. In a letter to the Prime Minister, Balasingham demanded that the Government establish an interim administration for the north-east of the country. The Government refused to agree, offering instead a 'development-orientated' structure for the area, with greater financial authority for the LTTE. The LTTE rejected this proposal as not extensive enough, and attempts to resume the peace negotiations failed. Informal talks, however, continued to take place. In mid-June a senior leader of the EPRLF, Subathran, was shot dead. Subathran was the most senior of 30 politicians from rival Tamil parties and suspected army informants to have been assassinated since the beginning of the cease-fire; the LTTE were believed to have been responsible for the attack, creating serious doubts over the Tamil organization's commitment to multi-party politics. At the same time, an LTTE oil tanker exploded and sank during a confrontation with a Sri Lankan navy patrol. The LTTE and Government offered conflicting versions of the incident: military officials reported that the ship was smuggling weapons and that Tamil militants aboard the vessel refused to stop despite several warnings and caused the explosion to avoid being caught; the LTTE denied the charges, claiming that the Sri Lankan navy fired at the ship after capturing the crew. At the end of the month the LTTE organized a demonstration to demand the return of thousands of homes on the Jaffna peninsula occupied by the Sri Lankan army as high-security zones since the 1980s; some

150,000 people attended the rally. Although the Government was committed to vacating these zones, the army believed a sudden withdrawal would give the LTTE the opportunity to seize complete control of the Jaffna peninsula. Meanwhile, in early June an international donor Conference on the Reconstruction and Development of Sri Lanka took place in Tokyo, Japan, despite the refusal of the LTTE to attend. The international community agreed to give Sri Lanka US $4,500m. in aid over four years as long as the stalled peace process was revived.

In July 2003 the Government requested Norwegian peace envoy Jon Westbørg to inform the LTTE of the Government's new proposals for an interim administration, which reportedly included greater financial and political powers for the LTTE. The LTTE agreed to consider the offer. In the same month the Sri Lankan administration decided to grant Sri Lankan citizenship to more than 160,000 Tamils of Indian origin who had been unable to return home since the beginning of the civil war. In August the SLMM reported that the Tamil militants had failed to comply with the terms of the cease-fire agreement by refusing to dismantle a camp in the north-eastern district of Trincomalee. Following talks with Norwegian monitors, and under pressure from the international community, the LTTE agreed to reconsider their position. However, at the end of August the Tamil rebels refused to dismantle the camp, insisting that it had existed before the cease-fire agreement was reached and should, therefore, be allowed to remain. This claim was rejected by the security forces and independent truce monitors. Controversy over the issue continued with allegations by the military and opposition that the LTTE had established 13 new camps since the beginning of the cease-fire; the Tamil militants denied the charges. The matter had also become a source of contention between the Prime Minister and President. Wickremasinghe censured the President for discussing security issues publicly, while President Kumaratunga continued to criticize the Government's conduct in the peace process. Meanwhile, the Kumaratunga-led PA and left-wing JVP failed to form an alliance owing to differences over their approach to the peace process and devolution of power.

Despite the political wrangling and the LTTE's increasingly rigid stance, the Prime Minister remained optimistic in late September 2003 that the stalled peace process would resume. However, in early October the Minister of Defence accused the LTTE of having increased their military strength two-fold and of having continued to conscript child soldiers since the beginning of the truce in February 2002. In late October 2003 the LTTE revealed a detailed plan for an Interim Self-Governing Authority (ISGA) to administer north-eastern Sri Lanka. The LTTE demanded an authority with a guaranteed Tamil majority and full control over regional administration for five years pending the achievement and implementation of a final settlement. The Government reacted cautiously to the plan; nevertheless, the Government announced that it would request Norwegian mediators to facilitate the resumption of talks. President Kumaratunga, however, condemned the offer, claiming that it was the first step towards a separate state.

On 4 November 2003 the country was plunged into a constitutional crisis when Kumaratunga took advantage of the Prime Minister's absence (he was attending trade negotiations in the USA) and suspended the legislature for a period of two weeks, dismissed the Minister of Interior and Christian Affairs, the Minister of Defence and of Transport, Highways and Aviation, and the Minister of Mass Communication, assuming these portfolios herself, and deployed troops to key positions in the capital in the stated interest of preserving national security. It was reported that Kumaratunga had declared a state of emergency on 5 November, but withdrew the decree two days later on Wickremasinghe's return from the USA. The President claimed that the Prime Minister had made too many concessions to the LTTE during peace negotiations. Kumaratunga and Wickremasinghe held two meetings in an attempt to resolve the crisis, with little success: Wickremasinghe rejected the offer to form a government of national unity and suggested that, since the President had assumed the defence portfolio, Kumaratunga should lead the peace negotiations. However, the two leaders agreed to appoint a committee to establish by mid-December new power-sharing arrangements. In the mean time, in mid-November the Norwegian peace negotiators announced that they would withdraw from the peace process until it was made clear who held power and authority in Sri Lanka.

In mid-January 2004 the crisis worsened when Kumaratunga declared that she had held an undisclosed swearing-in ceremony in 2000 to give herself another year in office, thereby extending her term to December 2006. Analysts debated whether the action was constitutional. Later in January the Kumaratunga-led SLFP and the JVP formed the United People's Freedom Alliance (UPFA). The UPFA was joined by four other left-wing parties, which had been members of the erstwhile PA, in early February. On 7 February Kumaratunga dissolved Parliament and called a general election for 2 April, almost four years ahead of schedule. Hours before the dissolution, the President created two new cabinet appointments for her supporters; the existing Cabinet was to operate in an acting capacity prior to the general election. Both the Cabinet and the LTTE condemned the decision, amid fears that the election would further undermine the peace process with the LTTE. The LTTE, however, pledged to maintain the cease-fire. Meanwhile, it was reported in late January that a Christian church at Mattegoda, near Colombo, had been attacked. The incident was the latest of at least 30 attacks on Christian churches since November 2003, which had allegedly been encouraged by hardline Buddhist clergy. Christians had been accused of sympathizing with the LTTE and carrying out unethical conversions. President Kumaratunga warned that anyone guilty of promoting religious tension would be severely punished.

In early March 2004 a rift within the LTTE appeared after a senior Tamil eastern regional commander declared his independence from the rest of the group. V. Muralitharan (commonly known as Col Karuna) withdrew his 6,000 fighters from the 15,000-strong LTTE in a dispute with the northern-based LTTE leader, Prabhakaran. Karuna, who accused northern Tamil groups of ignoring and discriminating against eastern groups, made it clear that he would not resume violence. However, he would not recognize the cease-fire agreement between the Government and Prabhakaran, and instead demanded a separate truce agreement with the Sri Lankan administration. Analysts feared that the schism might escalate into factional war; the split also raised questions about Prabhakaran's control over the LTTE and undermined the Tamil militants' claims that the main obstacle in the peace process was political divisions among Sinhalese political parties. The rift also adversely affected Norway's fresh attempt to revive the peace initiative. In late March the LTTE vowed to remove Karuna from Sri Lanka. The Tamil political candidate and supporter of Karuna, Rajan Sathyamoorthy, was shot dead by suspected Tamil militants in the eastern town of Batticaloa, raising fears of factional fighting. Although the LTTE denied any involvement in the killing, government troops were deployed to Batticaloa to maintain law and order. On 9 April fighting between the two Tamil factions broke out. The conflict ended on 13 April with Karuna reported to have fled from his base and gone into hiding, his forces having dispersed and the LTTE assuming full control of the eastern areas.

At the general election, which took place on 2 April 2004, the UPFA won 105 of the 225 seats, having taken 45.6% of the votes cast; Wickremasinghe's UNP retained 82 seats (with 37.8% of the votes), while the TNA won 22 seats (with 7.0%). In an unexpected development, the Buddhist Jathika Hela Urumaya (JHU—National Heritage Party) won nine seats. The LTTE had openly supported the TNA during the election campaign and described the large number of seats won by the alliance as an endorsement and recognition of the LTTE as 'the sole representative' of the Tamil population. Participation at the election was reported to have reached 75% of eligible voters and the poll concluded peacefully. However, there were claims of voter intimidation and electoral malpractice, particularly in the north and east of the country. The UPFA, which had not secured an outright majority of seats in Parliament, undertook negotiations with a view to forming a coalition administration. Meanwhile, Mahinda Rajapakse, a senior member of the UPFA and former fisheries minister, was sworn in as Prime Minister on 6 April. By 10 April the UPFA still needed the support of at least eight legislators to achieve an absolute majority in Parliament; nevertheless, a 31-member Cabinet was sworn in. While Kumaratunga retained the defence portfolio, Lakshman Kadirgamar was appointed Minister of Foreign Affairs. In late April, having resolved a dispute with the UPFA, four members of the JVP were also sworn in as ministers.

Meanwhile, the LTTE responded to the election result with a threat to return to violence if their demands for self-rule were not met. They later requested the Government to open negotiations on the basis of the proposed ISGA that they had submitted in late October 2003. President Kumaratunga had already agreed to abide by the cease-fire and pledged to resume negotiations with the LTTE; however, it was widely acknowledged that neither the President nor the JVP would be willing to grant the degree of devolution that was desired by the Tamil organization.

From June 2004 onwards the cease-fire between the LTTE and the Government came under increasing pressure. During discussions with the Norwegian team monitoring the ongoing peace process, the LTTE accused the Sri Lankan armed forces of sheltering Col Karuna and of assisting him in waging a campaign against them. Despite initially denying it, the armed forces eventually admitted that they had helped Karuna to escape, while insisting that the plan had been carried out without government knowledge. Fears that the cease-fire was close to collapse were heightened when a suicide bomber blew herself up during questioning at a police station in Colombo in early July, having first attempted to meet the Tamil Secretary-General of the EPDP, Douglas Devananda, who was a long-standing opponent of the LTTE. Although the LTTE denied any involvement in the attack, they were widely believed to have been responsible both for the bombing, and for the assassination of an EPDP politician in Ampara district later in that month. Meanwhile, clashes continued to occur between the LTTE and members of the faction that had broken away under the leadership of Karuna. In September it was reported that Norwegian envoy Erik Solheim had failed in his attempts to instigate new peace talks between the Government and the LTTE.

In September 2004 the UPFA Government achieved a legislative majority for the first time since its formation in April when the CWC, which had eight seats in Parliament, announced that it would join the ruling coalition. Muttu Sivalingam of the CWC was subsequently appointed Minister of Community Development and Estate Infrastructure. In the following month three members of the opposition SLMC defected to the UPFA, further strengthening the Government.

In December 2004 the LTTE formally rejected a new proposal by the Government that the two sides restart peace negotiations. The LTTE attributed their decision to the fact that the JVP, one of the members of the coalition Government, opposed their condition that any negotiations should be based upon their proposed ISGA. The LTTE had warned in November that they would return to their violent struggle for self-rule unless the Government agreed to discuss the ISGA. Concerns were raised by several prominent donor countries that the JVP's stance was undermining the peace process.

Sri Lanka was one of the countries most seriously affected by the devastating tsunami caused by a massive earthquake in the Indian Ocean on 26 December 2004. More than 31,000 Sri Lankans were killed in the disaster, which also left thousands homeless and without livelihoods. The tourism industry was badly affected by the catastrophe, with many hotels and resorts being damaged or destroyed. It was initially hoped that the scale of the disaster would serve to ease tensions between the Government and the LTTE, particularly as the Tamil areas of the island were amongst those worst hit. However, conflicts soon surfaced over the distribution of aid; the LTTE claimed that the Government was restricting the flow of international aid into Tamil-controlled areas and demanded that it be delivered directly to them. Talks intended to resolve the dispute held at the end of January 2005 ended without agreement. The situation deteriorated further in the following month, when it was revealed that around 70% of the survivors of the tsunami disaster had yet to receive any government relief, apparently owing to a combination of bureaucratic incompetence and corruption. The Tamil Relief Organization (TRO), controlled by the LTTE, alleged that only one-third of the aid was reaching the Tamil-controlled northern and eastern areas, despite government claims that two-thirds of the aid was destined for these areas.

In June 2005 the Government finally signed an agreement—entitled the Post-Tsunami Operational Management Structure (P-TOMS)—that would allow the LTTE to participate in the distribution of aid for the reconstruction effort. The agreement had been reached only following the withdrawal from the ruling coalition of the JVP, which had remained stringently opposed to any deal with the LTTE. The JVP's withdrawal left the Government with a minority in the legislature, although the opposition UNP had assured the Government of its support for the aid-sharing mechanism. In the following month, however, in response to a petition from the JVP and the JHU, the Supreme Court suspended the implementation of the P-TOMS, ruling that several of its clauses were illegal. Meanwhile, increasing tensions between the LTTE and government forces, complicated by the former's ongoing clashes with the rebel Karuna faction, led to an upsurge in violence that prompted international donors to warn the two sides that the ongoing cease-fire was under threat. At the end of May the chief of military intelligence in Colombo, Maj. Nizam Muthalif, had become the most senior official to have been assassinated by the LTTE since the agreement of the cease-fire in February 2002.

In August 2005 the peace process between the Government and the LTTE was further jeopardized when the Minister of Foreign Affairs, Lakshman Kadirgamar, was assassinated by unidentified gunmen at his home in Colombo. Although they denied involvement, the LTTE were held responsible for the attack. In the aftermath of the murder, President Kumaratunga declared a state of emergency, granting the security forces broad powers of detention. Amid widespread fears that the cease-fire would collapse, both sides announced their commitment to its maintenance, and the LTTE agreed to meet with the Government to review the truce agreement. Later in August Kumaratunga announced the appointment of her brother, Anura Bandaranaike, the incumbent Minister of Tourism, as Kadirgamar's successor. Bandaranaike retained the tourism portfolio. In September the LTTE declined a Norwegian proposal that the talks should be held at the international airport near Colombo, while the Government rejected the LTTE's suggestion that they be held in Kilinochchi, the political centre of LTTE-controlled northern Sri Lanka. Later in the same month the European Union (EU) issued a statement banning LTTE delegations from visiting any of its member states. Sporadic violence continued throughout the following months.

Meanwhile, there was controversy over the schedule for the next presidential election. While, under the terms of the Constitution, the next election was due to be held in December 2005, President Kumaratunga claimed that the holding of an undisclosed swearing-in ceremony in 2000 (see above) had actually extended her second term until December 2006. In July the SLFP announced that its presidential candidate would be Prime Minister Rajapakse. In August the Supreme Court brought an end to the controversy, ruling that the election should be held by 22 November 2005. In September it was announced that the election would take place on 17 November. Former Prime Minister Ranil Wickremasinghe subsequently declared that he would stand as the candidate of the UNP. The JVP offered its support to Rajapakse, on the condition that were he to secure victory he would commit his government to the retention of a unitary state, renegotiate the ongoing cease-fire with the LTTE and end the privatization of state assets. Rajapakse concluded a similar agreement with the JHU.

On 17 November 2005 14 candidates contested the presidential election. Rajapakse secured a narrow victory over his closest rival, Wickremasinghe, winning 50.3% of the vote, compared with 48.4% for Wickremasinghe. The election was notable for the low turn-out amongst the country's Tamil population, particularly in the LTTE-controlled northern and eastern areas; this was thought to have played a significant part in Wickremasinghe's defeat, as he had stressed his commitment to the ongoing cease-fire agreement during the electoral campaign. While the LTTE had stated that they would not prevent people from voting, there was widespread evidence that they had done so. Rajapakse subsequently nominated Minister of Agriculture, Public Security, Law and Order and of Buddha Sasana, Ratnasiri Wickremanayake, as Prime Minister. In the new Cabinet, announced shortly afterwards, Minister of Ports and Aviation Mangala Samaraweera was additionally allocated the foreign affairs portfolio, while Bandaranaike continued as Minister of Tourism. Neither the JVP nor the JHU were awarded any cabinet portfolios.

In December 2005 violence in the country escalated. At least 60 people died over the course of the month as a result of various attacks believed to have been co-ordinated by the LTTE. In early January 2006 a suicide bomb attack on a naval patrol vessel resulted in the deaths of 13 sailors, constituting the largest loss of military life since the cease-fire began. A further nine sailors were killed in a land-mine explosion later in that month, as the number of violent incidents continued to increase. In February negotiators representing the LTTE and the Government convened in Geneva, Switzerland, to hold talks on how to control the recent upsurge in violence. A joint statement issued following the conclusion of the talks committed both sides to uphold the cease-fire which appeared in imminent danger of collapse. The LTTE agreed to attempt to prevent further attacks on the security forces, while the Government pledged to try to disarm the Karuna faction of the LTTE, which was believed to have been acting on behalf of the armed forces against its erstwhile comrades. However, in April the LTTE stated that it would not attend the second round of talks scheduled to be held in Geneva that month, alleging that government forces had carried out attacks on Tamil civilians and that the Sri Lankan navy had prevented the LTTE commanders in the east of the country from meeting the LTTE political leaders in the north. In late April a suicide bombing believed to have been perpetrated by the LTTE at the army headquarters in Colombo killed at least 11 people and seriously injured the Chief of Staff of the Army, Lt-Gen. Sarath Fonseka. The Government subsequently ordered a number of air strikes on alleged LTTE bases near Trincomalee, which, according to the LTTE, caused the displacement of approximately 15,000 people. The violence continued, further jeopardizing the ongoing cease-fire: in May the SLMM acknowledged that a 'low intensity war' was taking place. At the end of the month the EU classified the LTTE as a terrorist organization, which entailed a suspension of LTTE fund-raising in EU member states, a 'freeze' on the organization's assets and a ban on travel to the EU. The LTTE responded by demanding the withdrawal of EU members of the SLMM, resulting in the departure of Danish, Finnish and Swedish monitors in July and August. Amid escalating violence the LTTE withdrew from peace talks planned for June. In mid-June fears about the intensification of the conflict were realized when landmine explosions killed some 64 civilians, including several children, on a crowded bus in Kebithigollewa. Despite the LTTE's condemnation of the attack, the Government retaliated by launching air attacks on Kilinochchi. A new front in the fighting opened up over access to the Maavil-Aru waterway, which became the scene of a number of air and ground offensives in July. The violence spread to the town of Muttur, north of the waterway, forcing thousands of inhabitants, many of them Muslims, to flee in August. Clashes between LTTE fighters and army troops continued in the north and east of the country, with rising death tolls of civilians, rebels and government forces. At the end of September the SLMM estimated that the resumption of hostilities had resulted in the displacement of some 200,000 people. In October, following a suicide bombing near Habarana that killed approximately 100 naval officers, it was feared that relatively unaffected areas of the country would be drawn into the conflict when the LTTE attacked a naval base in the southern town of Galle. Little progress was made at peace talks held in Geneva at the end of October, although both sides agreed to uphold the terms of the cease-fire agreement. In November it was reported that an army attack on a Tamil refugee camp in LTTE-held territory had resulted in at least 65 civilian fatalities. Shortly afterwards a TNA member of Parliament was assassinated in Colombo, with no group immediately claiming responsibility. At the end of November Prabhakaran declared the cease-fire to be 'defunct' and blamed the Government for failing to find a solution. In early December the Government amended existing laws to extend the powers of security officials and support anti-terrorist operations. Anton Balasingham, the chief LTTE negotiator, died in mid-December. In the same month Col. Karuna's forces were reported to have killed around 35 LTTE fighters in eastern Sri Lanka, while 24 children were kidnapped and later released by the LTTE, supposedly in error.

The violence continued into 2007, with government forces reportedly securing the eastern town of Vakarai in January after a series of battles and the displacement of an estimated 30,000 people. According to SLMM estimates published in February, the conflict had resulted in almost 4,000 fatalities over the preceding 15 months. In late February the ambassadors of Italy and the USA were injured in mortar fire during a visit to Batticaloa; the attack was blamed on the LTTE. In March there was a renewal of hostilities in eastern areas, reportedly as part of a larger government drive to secure the east of the country, as concerns mounted for the estimated 155,000 civilians left homeless by the fighting. In late March the strengthened capability of LTTE forces was demonstrated by an air attack on the government airbase at Katunayake, which was followed in late April by air bombings of fuel depots in the Colombo area.

Meanwhile, at the end of June 2006 Rajapakse was elected unopposed to replace Kumaratunga as President of the SLFP. In January 2007 more than 20 dissident politicians from the opposition parties joined the Government, thus giving it a parliamentary majority. This, in turn, precipitated a cabinet reshuffle in which UNP defectors and SLMC members were allocated several portfolios. Shortly after the defections from the UNP the party reportedly indicated that the memorandum of understanding signed between the UNP and the SLFP in October of the previous year to ensure co-operation on several issues of national importance, including the LTTE conflict, had been invalidated. Appointments to the new Cabinet, which now numbered more than 50 ministers, included the former Deputy Leader of the UNP, Karu Jayasuriya, as Minister of Public Administration and Home Affairs, and Rohitha Bogollagama as Minister of Foreign Affairs. Further ministerial changes were reported in the following month, when Minister of Ports and Aviation Mangala Samaraweera, Minister of National Heritage Anura Bandaranaike and Minister of Port Development Sripathi Sooriyarachchi were dismissed (Bandaranaike was, however, later reinstated). In June Samaraweera and Sooriyarachchi founded a new political party, the Sri Lanka Freedom Party—Mahajana Wing (SLFP—M), in reaction to the 'path of extremism' they believed the SLFP to be taking. In the following month the UNP and the SLFP—M signed an agreement, pledging to resolve the civil conflict within nine months should they come to power. (Sooriyarachchi was killed in a car accident in February 2008.) In December 2007 the SLMC withdrew its support for the governing coalition, and the party's leader, Abdul Rauf Hakeem, resigned from his position as Minister of Posts and Telecommunication.

As fighting continued in the north and east of the country, it became increasingly difficult to determine accurate death tolls from the varying statements of the military and the LTTE; however, in mid-2007 it was estimated that the resumption of hostilities had resulted in approximately 5,000 fatalities since 2005. There were frequent reports of human rights violations on both sides. In June 2007 hundreds of Tamils were apparently forced to leave Colombo by the police, and accounts of abductions and disappearances were commonplace. The LTTE, in turn, was criticized for its alleged recruitment of children, forced recruitment and abduction of adults, and political killings. The UN High Commissioner for Human Rights also expressed concern over human rights violations reportedly committed by Col Karuna's TMVP. However, the Government declined the Commissioner's offer to establish an office in the country.

In July 2007 the army claimed that its operations in the eastern province had resulted in a decisive victory over the LTTE and had led to its recapture of the region, prompting the Government to announce a development package worth Rs 6,500m. Government spending on defence had increased as the conflict escalated, resulting in reduced funding elsewhere. The front line shifted as fighting intensified in the north of the country. Both sides suffered set-backs in late 2007 and early 2008. In October 2007 the LTTE conducted an aerial and land attack on the Anuradhapura airbase, reportedly killing tens of military officers and destroying eight aircraft. S. P. Thamilselvan, the head of the LTTE's political wing and a leading member of its negotiating team, was killed in an aerial bombardment by the military in the following month. In early January 2008 a senior LTTE intelligence official was reportedly killed in a landmine explosion; his death was followed within days by that of D. M. Dassanayake, the Minister of Nation Building, in a bomb attack. The Government had given notice of its intention to withdraw from the cease-fire agreement, an action that was formalized on 16 January and that appeared to confirm the Government's preference for a military solution to the conflict. As a result, the SLMM announced the end of its activities in Sri Lanka. Also in January, Col Karuna, who had been apprehended while attempting to enter the United Kingdom on a false passport in late 2007, was sentenced to nine months' imprisonment by a British court on charges of identity fraud. Speculation had arisen over the links between Karuna's faction and the Sri Lankan Government, and the role that this alleged alliance had played in the Government wresting control of the eastern province from the LTTE. In July 2008 the British authorities repatriated Karuna from the United Kingdom. In March 2009, having left the TMVP to join first the UPFA and subsequently the SLFP, Karuna (using his civilian name, Vinayagamoorthy Muralidharan) was appointed as Minister of National Integration and Reconciliation (a non-cabinet post).

Following the collapse of the cease-fire agreement in January 2008, the All Party Representatives' Committee (APRC), which had been established in 2006 to work towards finding a political solution to the conflict, urged Rajapakse to create provincial councils as part of a devolution process in the affected regions. Observers noted that the APRC had excluded the TNA from its proceedings and lacked the support of certain sections of the opposition. The Government subsequently announced the formation of a Temporary Interim Advisory Council in the northern province, which, it was claimed, would have a diverse composition and address minority issues. In March 2008 local elections were conducted in the Batticaloa district of the eastern province, at which the TMVP, campaigning under the UPFA banner, secured victory. However, the TMVP was criticized for alleged violence and intimidation in the run-up to the elections, and the poll was boycotted by the UNP and the TNA. Full provincial council elections were held in May; the UPFA, with the support of the TMVP, secured a majority in the provincial council, although some observers claimed that the election was not free and fair. Meanwhile, the violence continued unabated; in early April the Minister of Highways and Road Development, Jeyaraj Fernandopulle, (together with at least 14 other people) was killed in a suspected LTTE suicide bombing carried out near Colombo, while a suicide attack in the centre of the capital itself in mid-May left around 10 people dead. According to estimates published by the British Broadcasting Corporation (BBC) that month, the civil conflict had caused more than 70,000 deaths since 1983.

In the latter half of 2008 the Sri Lankan army made considerable advances against the LTTE, which, nevertheless, put up fierce resistance and increasingly resorted to terrorist attacks across the country. Both sides suffered heavy casualties, although, owing to stringent restrictions placed on the media by the Government, exact numbers were impossible to confirm. There was also growing international concern over the mounting casualties among (mainly) Tamil civilians as a result of the army's offensive against the LTTE. In response, the Government claimed that the retreating LTTE was using the civilian population as a human shield. In early January 2009 the rebels lost control of their *de facto* capital, Kilinochchi, and later that month their last remaining stronghold, Mullaitivu, fell to the advancing government troops. By April the LTTE were cornered in a small stretch of coastal territory in the north-east of the country. Despite the Government having established a designated 5 sq km safe zone for the thousands of civilians fleeing from the violence, there were reports of hundreds of innocent people being killed by both sides in the conflict. The LTTE and the army both denied any responsibility for civilian deaths and the latter claimed to have stopped using heavy artillery (although the evidence of intensive shelling suggested otherwise). The humanitarian crisis facing the Government in mid-May was very serious, with more than 200,000 refugees living in makeshift accommodation and medical and food provisions in short supply. There were growing demands from the international community (including the US Administration and the UN) for an immediate cease-fire to allow the safe evacuation of the 50,000 civilians trapped in the conflict zone. However, the government forces, in their determination to rout the LTTE, refused to halt their bombardment, while the rebels, for their part, continued to attempt to prevent the refugees from leaving the conflict zone. On 17 May the Government reported that all the civilians remaining in the war zone had been freed and claimed to have defeated the last remnants of the rebel forces (who were holding out in a small area on the coast), thus bringing the 26-year civil conflict to its conclusion. The LTTE were reported to have finally laid down their arms and released a statement that their struggle had 'reached its bitter end'. The following day there were unconfirmed reports that Prabhakaran, together with several other senior LTTE officials, had been killed while attempting to escape the advancing army. Amid scenes of jubilation on the streets of Colombo, President Rajapakse formally announced the army's victory over the LTTE on 19 May and declared the following day as a public holiday. In an attempt to allay the concerns of the Tamil population, Rajapakse pledged immediately to address the political issues arising from the conflict's conclusion by negotiating some form of power-sharing agreement with the Tamils in the north and east of the island.

In foreign policy, Sri Lanka has adopted a non-aligned role. Sri Lanka is a founder member of the South Asian Association for Regional Co-operation (SAARC, see p. 397), formally established in 1985.

Government

A presidential form of government was adopted in October 1977 and confirmed in the Constitution of September 1978. The Constitution provides for a unicameral Parliament as the supreme legislative body, its members being elected by a system of modified proportional representation. Executive powers are vested in the President, who is Head of State. The President is directly elected for a term of six years and is not accountable to Parliament. The President has the power to appoint or dismiss the Prime Minister and members of the Cabinet; may assume any portfolio; and is empowered to dismiss Parliament. In 1982 the Constitution was amended, allowing the President to call a presidential election before his/her first term of office was completed. In 1983 the Constitution was further amended to include a 'no-separation' clause, making any division of Sri Lanka illegal, and any advocates of separatism liable to lose their civic rights.

Sri Lanka comprises nine provinces and 25 administrative districts, each with an appointed Governor and elected Development Council. A network of 68 Pradeshiya Sabhas (district councils) was inaugurated throughout the country in January 1988.

Defence

As assessed at November 2008, the armed forces totalled 150,900 (including recalled reservists): army 117,900, navy 15,000, air force 18,000. There were also paramilitary forces of around 88,600 (including 13,000 Home Guard, an estimated 15,000 National Guard and a 3,000-strong anti-guerrilla unit). Budgetary expenditure on defence, public security and law and order for 2008 was estimated at Rs 166,447m. (equivalent to 11.0% of total estimated spending). Military service is voluntary.

Economic Affairs

In 2007, according to estimates by the World Bank, Sri Lanka's gross national income (GNI), measured at average 2005–07 prices, was US $30,785m., equivalent to $1,540 per head (or $4,210 per head on an international purchasing-power parity basis). During 2000–07, it was estimated, the population increased at an average annual rate of 0.4%, while gross domestic product (GDP) per head grew, in real terms, by an average of 4.4% per year. Overall GDP increased, in real terms, at an average annual rate of 4.9% in 2000–07. According to the Asian Development Bank (ADB), real GDP rose by 7.7% in 2006, by 6.8% in 2007 and by 6.0% in 2008.

In 2008 agriculture (including hunting, forestry and fishing) contributed an estimated 13.4% of GDP, while 31.3% of the employed labour force (excluding inhabitants of the northern and eastern provinces) were engaged in the sector in 2007. The principal cash crops are tea (which accounted for 17.3% of total export earnings in 2007), rubber and coconuts. In 2004 Sri Lanka was the world's second largest tea exporter, having been overtaken by Kenya in that year. Rice production is also important. Cattle, buffaloes, goats and poultry are the principal livestock. During 2000–07 agricultural GDP increased at an average annual rate of 1.7%. According to the ADB, agricultural GDP expanded by 6.3% in 2006, by 3.4% in 2007 and by 7.5% in 2008.

Industry (including mining and quarrying, manufacturing, construction and power) contributed an estimated 29.4% of GDP in 2008, and engaged 26.6% of the employed labour force (excluding inhabitants of the northern and eastern provinces) in 2007. During 2000–07 industrial GDP increased at an average annual rate of 4.6%. According to the ADB, industrial GDP rose by 8.1% in 2006, by 7.6% in 2007 and by 5.9% in 2008.

Mining and quarrying contributed an estimated 1.6% of GDP in 2008, and, according to the ADB, engaged 1.8% of the employed labour force in 2001. Diamonds are the major mineral export (accounting for an estimated 5.9% of total export earnings in 2007). Another commercially important mineral in Sri Lanka is graphite, and there are also deposits of iron ore, monazite, uranium, ilmenite sands, limestone and clay.

Manufacturing contributed an estimated 18.0% of GDP in 2008, and engaged 1.9% of the employed labour force (excluding inhabitants of the northern and eastern provinces) in 2007. The principal branches of manufacturing include wearing apparel (excluding footwear), textiles, food products, and also petroleum and coal products. The garment industry is Sri Lanka's largest earner of foreign exchange, with sales of garments and textiles providing an estimated 56.4% of total export earnings in 2007. During 2000–07 manufacturing GDP increased by an average of 3.5% per year. The GDP of the manufacturing sector rose by 5.5% in 2006 and by an estimated 6.4% in 2007, according to official figures.

Energy is derived principally from petroleum, which accounted for 60.6% of electricity production in 2005. In the same year hydroelectric power accounted for 39.4% of electricity produced. In 2007 construction of a coal-fired electricity plant commenced; once operational, the plant was expected to alter significantly the structure of the energy sector. Imports of petroleum comprised 22.1% of the value of total imports in 2007.

The services sector, which is dominated by tourism, contributed an estimated 57.3% of GDP in 2008, and engaged 38.7% of the employed labour force (excluding inhabitants of the northern and eastern provinces) in 2007. During 2000–07 services GDP increased at an average annual rate of 5.8%. According to the ADB, the sector's GDP grew by 7.7% in 2006, by 7.1% in 2007 and by 5.6% in 2008.

In 2007 Sri Lanka recorded a visible trade deficit of US $2,430m. and there was a deficit of $1,465m. on the current account of the balance of payments. In 2007 the principal source of imports (21.7%) was India, while the USA was the principal market for exports (23.4%). Other major trading partners were the People's Republic of China, Singapore and the United Kingdom. The principal exports in 2007 were textiles and garments, and agricultural products (principally tea). The principal imports were petroleum, textiles and machinery and transport equipment.

The estimated budgetary deficit for 2008 totalled Rs 740,853m. (equivalent to 6.8% of GDP). Sri Lanka's total external debt was US $15,077m. at the end of 2008. In that year the cost of debt-servicing was equivalent to 14.3% of earnings from the exports of goods and services. During 1997–2007 the average annual rate of inflation was 10.0%; according to the ADB, the rate was 10.0% in 2006, 15.8% in 2007 and 22.6% in 2008. According to the ADB, an estimated 5.2% of the labour force were unemployed in 2008.

Sri Lanka is a member of the ADB (see p. 191), a founder member of the South Asian Association for Regional Co-operation (SAARC, see p. 397), which seeks to improve regional co-operation, particularly in economic development, a founder member of the Colombo Plan (see p. 425), which seeks to promote economic and social development in Asia and the Pacific, and a member of the UN Economic and Social Commission for Asia and the Pacific (ESCAP, see p. 36).

Following the declaration of a cease-fire between the Government and the Liberation Tigers of Tamil Eelam (LTTE) in February 2002, the economy showed clear signs of recovery. The export sector improved, and tourist arrivals increased. A privatization programme was also under way: the insurance, utilities, petroleum and telecommunications sectors were opened to private investment. In 2003 substantial progress was also made in public enterprise reform: several key public corporations were privatized and the electricity sector was opened to private investment. Donors at an international conference in June of that year pledged US $4,500m. in aid over the next five years to help rebuild the country's economy and infrastructure. The prerequisites to the assistance were a serious commitment from the Government to a restructuring programme and a permanent peace agreement between the LTTE and the Government. The reconstruction effort necessitated by the devastating effect upon much of Sri Lanka's coastline of the massive tsunami in late December 2004 impeded the country's economic performance to an extent in 2005. The fisheries and tourism sectors sustained extensive damage, resulting in the loss of many livelihoods. However, the more commercial areas in the west of the country were unaffected, limiting the economic impact of the disaster. Furthermore, the provision of substantial aid from the international community generated a strong momentum in the rehabilitation effort and real GDP consequently rose by 6.2% in 2005. The persistent fiscal deficit remained a considerable obstacle to Sri Lanka's development, however, rising from 7.9% of GDP in 2004 to 8.4% in 2005. The Government increasingly relied on external creditors to finance this deficit, thus contributing to escalating levels of public debt and higher rates of inflation. More prudent budgetary operations led to a reduction in the deficit in 2006 to 8.0% and it was hoped that the authorities' decision to remove costly petrol subsidies would strengthen the fiscal position in the medium to long term. According to the ADB, a fiscal deficit equivalent to 7.7% of GDP was realized in 2007, owing largely to the broadening of Sri Lanka's tax base. However, in March 2008 the IMF warned that, despite improving fiscal conditions, rising inflation required the continued use of firm monetary policies and therefore discouraged the printing of further money. Moreover, escalating security problems and the official lifting of the cease-fire in early 2008 (see Recent History) were expected to engender additional expenditure on defence and to deter foreign investment. Despite the global economic downturn and the intensification of the conflict in the north of the country in 2008, the economy proved resilient (aided by strong growth in the agricultural sector). However, on the downside, there was a substantial rise in the rate of inflation and an increase in the trade deficit, largely owing to higher international food and petroleum prices. As the global economy continued to suffer in early 2009, the rate of growth in GDP in Sri Lanka was forecast to fall to 4.5% that year. However, following the apparent resolution of the bloody civil conflict in May, it was widely hoped that the subsequent rehabilitation and reconstruction programmes (with the requisite funding) would give the economy a real boost, and would attract greater levels of domestic and foreign investment.

Education

Education is officially compulsory for 11 years between five and 15 years of age, and it is available free of charge from lower kindergarten to university age. There are three types of school: state-controlled schools (mostly co-educational), denominational schools and Pirivenas (for Buddhist clergy and lay students). Primary education begins at the age of five and lasts for five years. Secondary education, beginning at 10 years of age, lasts for up to eight years, comprising a first cycle of six years and a second of two years. In 2003/04 the total enrolment at primary and secondary schools was equivalent to an estimated 88.1% of the school-age population (boys 88%; girls 90%). Primary enrolment in that year included an estimated 97.1% of children in the relevant age-group, while secondary enrolment was equivalent to an estimated 82.5% (boys 82%; girls 83%) of pupils. There are 26 teacher-training colleges, 12 universities, 13 polytechnic institutes, eight junior technical colleges and an open university. Budgeted expenditure on education by the central Government in 2005 was Rs 63,360m. (11.2% of total government spending).

Public Holidays

2009: 15 January (Tamil Thai Pongal Day), 4 February (Independence Commemoration Day), 23 February (Maha Shivaratri), 9 March (Milad un-Nabi, Birth of the Prophet), 10 April (Good Friday), 13 April (Sinhala and Tamil New Year's Eve), 14 April (Sinhala and Tamil New Year's Day), 1 May (May Day), 20 May (Victory over the LTTE), 21 September (Id al-Fitr, Ramazan Festival Day), 17 October (Diwali—Festival of Lights), 27 November (Id al-Adha, Hadji Festival Day), 25 December (Christmas Day).

2010: 15 January (Tamil Thai Pongal Day), 4 February (Independence Commemoration Day), 12 February (Maha Shivaratri), 25 February (Milad un-Nabi, Birth of the Prophet), April (Sinhala and Tamil New Year's Eve), April (Sinhala and Tamil New Year's Day), 2 April (Good Friday), 1 May (May Day), 11 September (Id al-Fitr, Ramazan Festival Day), 5 November (Diwali—Festival of Lights), 16 November (Id al-Adha, Hadji Festival Day), 25 December (Christmas Day).

Note: A number of Hindu, Muslim and Buddhist holidays depend on lunar sightings. There is a holiday every lunar month on the day of the full moon.

Weights and Measures

Legislation passed in 1974 provided for the introduction of the metric system, but imperial units are still used for some purposes.

SRI LANKA

Statistical Survey

Source (unless otherwise stated): Department of Census and Statistics, 15/12 Maitland Crescent, POB 563, Colombo 7; tel. (11) 2682176; fax (11) 2697594; e-mail dcensus@lanka.com.lk; internet www.statistics.gov.lk.

Area and Population

AREA, POPULATION AND DENSITY

Area (sq km)	65,525*
Population (census results)	
17 March 1981	14,846,750
17 July 2001 (provisional)†	
Males	8,343,964
Females	8,520,580
Total	16,864,544
Population (official estimates at mid-year)	
2005	19,668,000
2006	19,886,000
2007	20,010,000
Density (per sq km) at mid-2007	305.4

* 25,299 sq miles. This figure includes inland water (3,189 sq km).
† Figures refer to 18 out of 25 districts where enumeration was carried out completely. Enumeration was only partially conducted in Mannar, Vavuniya, Batticaloa and Trincomalee districts, owing to security concerns; data from these districts brought the total enumerated population to approximately 17,560,000. The census was not conducted in the districts of Jaffna, Mullaitivu and Kilinochchi, also owing to security concerns. The total estimated population for the entire country at July 2001 was 18,732,255.

ETHNIC GROUPS
(census results)

	1981	2001*†
Sinhalese	10,979,561	13,810,664
Sri Lankan Tamil	1,886,872	736,484
Indian Tamil	818,656	855,888
Sri Lankan Moors	1,046,926	1,349,845
Others	114,735	111,663
Total	14,846,750	16,864,544

* Provisional.
† Figures refer to 18 out of 25 districts.

DISTRICTS
(population estimates at mid-2007)

	Area (sq km, excl. inland water)*	Population ('000)	Density (persons per sq km)
Colombo	676	2,456	3,633
Gampaha	1,341	2,140	1,596
Kalutara	1,576	1,111	705
Kandy	1,917	1,380	720
Matale	1,952	477	244
Nuwara Eliya	1,706	742	435
Galle	1,617	1,052	651
Matara	1,270	813	640
Hambantota	2,496	552	221
Jaffna	929	599	645
Mannar	1,880	101	54
Vavuniya	1,861	166	89
Mullaitivu	2,415	147	61
Kilinochchi	1,205	146	121
Batticaloa	2,610	523	200
Ampara	4,222	615	146
Trincomalee	2,529	355	140
Kurunegala	4,624	1,524	330
Puttalam	2,882	752	261
Anuradhapura	6,664	801	120
Polonnaruwa	3,077	395	128
Badulla	2,827	850	301
Moneragala	5,508	425	77
Ratnapura	3,236	1,086	336
Kegalle	1,685	802	476
Total	62,705	20,010	319

* As at 1988; revised total land area is 62,336 sq km.

PRINCIPAL TOWNS
(provisional, population at 2001 census)

Colombo (Kolamba)*	642,020	Sri Jayawardenepura (Kotte)†	115,826
Dehiwala-Mount Lavinia	209,787	Kandy (Maha Nuwara)	110,049
Moratuwa	177,190	Kalmunai (Galmune)	94,457
Jaffna (Yapanaya)	145,600‡	Galle (Galla)	90,934
Negombo (Migamuwa)	121,933		

* Commercial capital.
† Administrative capital.
‡ Estimated population at mid-1997 (Source: Provincial Councils, Department of Elections).

Source: Thomas Brinkhoff, *City Population* (internet www.citypopulation.de).

BIRTHS, MARRIAGES AND DEATHS
(year of registration, provisional)

	Registered live births		Registered marriages	Registered deaths	
	Number	Rate (per 1,000)	Number	Number	Rate (per 1,000)
2000	340,144	18.4	186,548	112,569	6.1
2001	354,101	18.9	186,698	111,100	5.9
2002	363,549	19.1	190,832	110,637	5.8
2003	363,343	18.9	193,387	114,310	5.9
2004	360,220	18.5	191,985	112,568	5.8
2005	370,424	18.8	194,352	129,822	6.6
2006	371,264	18.7	197,458	115,424	5.8
2007	380,069	19.0	195,193	116,883	5.8

Life expectancy (years at birth, WHO estimates): 72.4 (males 68.7; females 76.3) in 2006 (Source: WHO, *World Health Statistics*).

ECONOMICALLY ACTIVE POPULATION
('000 persons aged 10 years and over, excluding northern and eastern provinces)

	2005	2006	2007
Agriculture, hunting, forestry and fishing	2,059.3	2,287.3	2,202.1
Manufacturing	1,292.9	1,363.1	1,331.4
Mining and quarrying			
Electricity, gas and water	417.2	526.9	542.5
Construction			
Wholesale and retail trade, repair of motor vehicles, motorcycles and personal household goods	817.1	955.0	932.1
Restaurants and hotels	115.0	129.4	118.5
Transport, storage and communications	448.4	430.3	456.8
Financing, insurance, real estate and business services	226.1	221.1	215.2
Public administration and defence	465.4	400.5	433.0
Education	254.4	276.8	259.5
Health and social work	120.9	109.7	115.9
Other community, social and personal services	113.0	123.9	104.6
Private households with employed persons	48.3	80.2	87.4
Activities not adequately defined	410.2	201.2	242.9
Total employed	6,788.1	7,105.3	7,041.9
Unemployed	523.7	493.4	447.0
Total labour force	7,311.8	7,598.8	7,488.9

SRI LANKA

Health and Welfare

KEY INDICATORS

Total fertility rate (children per woman, 2006)	1.9
Under-5 mortality rate (per 1,000 live births, 2006)	13
HIV/AIDS (% of persons aged 15–49, 2007)	<0.1
Physicians (per 1,000 head, 2006)	0.6
Hospital beds (per 1,000 head, 2000)	2.9
Health expenditure (2006): US $ per head (PPP)	213
Health expenditure (2006): % of GDP	4.2
Health expenditure (2006): public (% of total)	49.2
Access to water (% of persons, 2006)	82
Access to sanitation (% of persons, 2006)	86
Human Development Index (2006): ranking	104
Human Development Index (2006): value	0.742

For sources and definitions, see explanatory note on p. vi.

Agriculture

PRINCIPAL CROPS
('000 metric tons)

	2005	2006	2007
Rice, paddy	3,246	3,342	3,131
Maize	42	48	56
Potatoes	79	78	77
Sweet potatoes	41	42	49
Cassava (Manioc)	223	226	220
Sugar cane	992	1,137	783
Beans, dry	9	8	8*
Cow peas, dry	11	10	11
Coconuts	1,912	913	954
Cabbages	64	59	69
Tomatoes	57	61	65
Pumpkins, squash and gourds	87	78	97
Cucumbers and gherkins	27	25	28
Aubergines (Eggplants)	84	88	93
Chillies and peppers, green	67	67	63
Onions, dry	109	134	149
Beans, green	41	41	41
Carrots and turnips	37	36	38
Plantains	545	504	519
Lemons and limes	5	5	5
Guavas, mangoes and mangosteens	93	85	85
Pineapples	58	57	53
Coffee, green	7	6	6
Tea	317	311	305
Pepper	18	19	19
Cinnamon	13	13	13
Natural rubber	104	109	118

* FAO estimate.

Aggregate production ('000 metric tons, may include official, semi-official or estimated data): Total cereals 3,295 in 2005, 3,396 in 2006, 3,193 in 2007; Total roots and tubers 344 in 2005, 346 in 2006, 346 in 2007; Total vegetables (incl. melons) 640 in 2005, 658 in 2006, 714 in 2007; Total fruits (excl. melons) 768 in 2005, 658 in 2006, 668 in 2007.

Source: FAO.

LIVESTOCK
('000 head, year ending September)

	2005	2006	2007
Buffaloes	308	314	319
Cattle	1,185	1,215	1,223
Sheep	10	14	16
Goats	395	382	389
Pigs	85	92	94
Chickens	11,636	13,313	13,779

Source: FAO.

LIVESTOCK PRODUCTS
('000 metric tons)

	2005	2006	2007
Cattle meat	29.3	26.3	26.5*
Buffalo meat*	3.6	3.7	3.7
Goat meat	1.5	1.5	1.4*
Pig meat	2.2	2.3	2.4*
Chicken meat	97.3	78.8	65.0*
Cows' milk	136.7	139.3	143.4
Buffaloes' milk	26.1	26.7	27.3
Goats' milk*	4.7	5.1	5.0
Hen eggs	49.0	51.1	51.9

* FAO estimate(s).

Source: FAO.

Forestry

ROUNDWOOD REMOVALS
('000 cubic metres, excl. bark, FAO estimates)

	2005	2006	2007
Sawlogs, veneer logs and logs for sleepers	117	117	117
Other industrial wood	577	577	577
Fuel wood	5,584	5,584	5,431
Total	6,278	6,278	6,125

Source: FAO.

SAWNWOOD PRODUCTION
('000 cubic metres, incl. railway sleepers)

	1999*	2000	2001
Coniferous (softwood)	—	—	30
Broadleaved (hardwood)	5	29	31
Total	5	29	61

* FAO estimates.

2002–07: Production assumed to be unchanged from 2001 (FAO estimates).

Source: FAO.

Fishing

('000 metric tons, live weight)

	2004	2005	2006
Capture	309.2	167.7	230.6
Tilapias	22.2	21.6	19.3
Demersal percomorphs	17.5	10.6	11.2
Clupeoids	54.4	24.9	56.2
Skipjack tuna	62.3	32.5	33.8
Carangids	13.6	6.0	9.6
Mackerels	18.4	9.7	15.6
Sharks, rays, skates etc.	23.4	5.3	5.7
Aquaculture	2.5	1.7	3.8
Total catch	311.7	169.4	234.3

Source: FAO.

Mining

('000 metric tons, unless otherwise indicated, estimates)

	2005	2006	2007
Natural graphite (metric tons)	3,000	3,200	3,300
Salt—unrefined	80	81	82
Kaolin	9	10	10
Phosphate rock (gross weight)	43	44	45

Ilmenite concentrates ('000 metric tons): 34.1 in 1998.

Zirconium concentrates ('000 metric tons): 13 in 1999.

Sources: US Geological Survey; UN, *Industrial Commodity Statistics Yearbook*.

SRI LANKA

Industry

SELECTED PRODUCTS
('000 barrels, unless otherwise indicated)

	2005	2006	2007
Raw sugar ('000 metric tons)	14	19	17
Cigarettes (million units)	4,832	4,832	4,719
Jet fuel*	650	700	700
Motor gasoline—petrol*	2,200	2,200	2,300
Kerosene*	1,500	1,500	1,500
Distillate fuel oil*	5,200	5,300	5,400
Residual fuel oil*	5,100	5,000	5,000
Cement ('000 metric tons)*	1,500	1,600	1,700
Plywood ('000 cu m)†	14	14	14
Electric energy (million kWh)	8,769	9,389	9,814

* Estimates.
† FAO estimates.

Naptha ('000 metric tons): 99 in 2003; 103 in 2004; 118 in 2005.

Sources: US Geological Survey; Asian Development Bank, *Key Indicators of Developing Asian and Pacific Countries*; FAO; UN, *Industrial Commodity Statistics Yearbook*.

Finance

CURRENCY AND EXCHANGE RATES

Monetary Units
100 cents = 1 Sri Lanka rupee (R).

Sterling, Dollar and Euro Equivalents (31 December 2008)
£1 sterling = Rs 164.936;
US $1 = Rs 113.140;
€1 = Rs 157.457;
1,000 Sri Lanka rupees = £6.06 = $8.84 = €6.35.

Average Exchange Rate (rupees per US $)
2006 103.914
2007 110.626
2008 108.332

BUDGET
(Rs million)

Revenue	2006	2007*	2008*
Taxation	424,899	541,849	653,109
Taxes on income and profits	47,389	55,044	141,291
Taxes on domestic goods and services	263,728	323,464	390,352
Value-added tax	164,277	201,643	251,770
Excise duty (ordinance)	20,660	24,996	27,155
Excise duty (special provisions)	70,523	84,350	95,185
Stamp duty	1,495	4,200	6,251
Taxes on international trade	80,497	100,206	115,914
Import duties	53,006	60,432	69,551
Licence taxes and other	2,967	4,355	5,552
Non-tax revenue	66,938	82,289	93,619
Capital revenue	14,455	11,482	11,738
Other	52,483	70,807	81,881
Foreign grants	19,911	25,750	28,750
Total	511,748	649,888	775,477

Expenditure by category	2006	2007*	2008*
Recurrent expenditure	579,040	632,836	725,440
Personal emoluments	121,842	156,006	168,244
Salaries and wages	81,250	108,816	113,109
General public services	18,234	25,851	40,955
Transfers	244,040	220,386	241,133
Retirement benefits	58,726	68,922	73,293
Provincial councils	63,032	74,985	82,537
Interest payments	150,778	176,843	209,845
Other purposes	44,147	53,751	65,264
Capital expenditure	197,012	380,346	417,577
Public debt repayments	295,693	339,903	373,314
Domestic	246,843	268,969	287,499
Foreign	48,851	70,935	85,814
Total expenditure	1,071,745	1,353,085	1,516,330

Expenditure by institution	2006	2007*	2008*
Special spending units	7,727	7,305	9,217
Ministries	1,064,018	1,345,780	1,507,113
Finance and planning	533,129	587,539	675,056
Defence, public security, law and order	110,230	155,704	166,447
Nation building and estate infrastructure development	38,855	50,792	54,282
Health care and nutrition	37,482	50,993	57,800
Public administration and home affairs	66,845	87,209	92,000
Local government and provincial councils	82,936	102,932	114,770
Total expenditure	1,071,745	1,353,085	1,516,330

* Estimates.

Source: Ministry of Finance and Planning, Colombo.

INTERNATIONAL RESERVES
(excluding gold, US $ million at 31 December)

	2005	2006	2007
IMF special drawing rights	2	3	7
Reserve position in IMF	68	72	76
Foreign exchange	2,581	2,762	3,433
Total	2,651	2,837	3,516

Source: IMF, *International Financial Statistics*.

MONEY SUPPLY
(Rs million at 31 December)

	2005	2006	2007
Currency outside banks	114,070	135,020	147,183
Demand deposits at commercial banks	116,620	124,657	119,407
Total money (incl. others)	231,621	261,033	268,005

Source: IMF, *International Financial Statistics*.

COST OF LIVING
(Consumer Price Index for Colombo; base: 2000 = 100)

	2005	2006	2007
Food (incl. beverages)	163.0	184.6	218.2
Fuel and light	178.1	228.3	286.3
Clothing (excl. footwear)	117.6	122.2	127.8
Rent	100.0	100.0	100.0
All items (incl. others)	159.7	181.5	213.3

Source: ILO.

SRI LANKA

NATIONAL ACCOUNTS
(Rs million at current prices)

Expenditure on the Gross Domestic Product

	2006	2007	2008*
Government final consumption expenditure	451,438	546,545	713,788
Private final consumption expenditure	1,988,378	2,403,167	3,073,651
Increase in stocks	91,330	115,632	99,498
Gross fixed capital formation	730,910	884,688	1,115,310
Total domestic expenditure	3,262,056	3,950,032	5,002,247
Exports of goods and services	885,381	1,041,935	1,098,376
Less Imports of goods and services	1,208,757	1,413,278	1,690,056
GDP at market prices	2,938,680	3,578,688	4,410,567
GDP at factor cost, at constant 2002 prices	2,090,564	2,232,656	2,365,500

* Provisional.

Gross Domestic Product by Economic Activity

	2006	2007	2008*
Agriculture, hunting, forestry and fishing	333,137	418,104	589,998
Mining and quarrying	46,202	56,645	71,768
Manufacturing	564,987	661,983	791,898
Construction	216,833	264,104	327,138
Electricity, gas and water	72,457	88,005	104,666
Transport, storage and communications	344,909	423,820	530,980
Wholesale and retail trade	659,597	790,628	949,372
Hotels and restaurants	16,646	18,367	20,611
Finance, real estate and	266,972	328,158	413,322
Ownership of dwellings	103,201	126,212	141,794
Public administration	257,837	333,758	380,765
Private services	55,902	68,905	88,255
GDP at market prices	2,938,680	3,578,688	4,410,567

* Provisional.

BALANCE OF PAYMENTS
(US $ million)

	2005	2006	2007
Exports of goods f.o.b.	6,347	6,883	7,741
Imports of goods f.o.b.	−7,977	−9,228	−10,170
Trade balance	−1,630	−2,345	−2,430
Exports of services	1,540	1,625	1,712
Imports of services	−2,089	−2,394	−2,603
Balance on goods and services	−2,179	−3,114	−3,321
Other income received	76	312	449
Other income paid	−375	−700	−807
Balance on goods, services and income	−2,478	−3,502	−3,679
Current transfers received	1,968	2,161	2,502
Current transfers paid	−233	−258	−288
Current balance	−743	−1,599	−1,465
Capital account (net)	250	291	269
Direct investment abroad	−38	−29	−55
Direct investment from abroad	272	480	603
Portfolio investment assets	276	355	326
Portfolio investment liabilities	−216	−304	−322
Other investment assets	−223	297	−281
Other investment liabilities	−4	−111	−257
Net errors and omissions	−73	−96	−192
Overall balance	−498	−717	−1,374

Source: IMF, *International Financial Statistics*.

External Trade

PRINCIPAL COMMODITIES
(Rs million)

Imports c.i.f.	2005	2006	2007
Consumer goods	165,221	206,141	221,371
Wheat	14,200	20,679	25,891
Durables	89,611	106,607	103,627
Intermediate goods	534,804	620,131	721,473
Petroleum	166,562	215,168	276,775
Textiles	153,957	160,987	180,689
Investment goods	188,081	233,637	297,266
Machinery and transport equipment	119,310	148,781	178,325
Total (incl. others)	891,359	1,066,689	1,251,135

Exports f.o.b.	2005	2006	2007*
Agricultural products	116,045	134,481	166,945
Tea	81,482	91,667	113,565
Petroleum products	13,169	19,580	18,693
Rubber based products	13,169	19,580	53,318
Diamonds	26,594	32,440	38,588
Textiles and garments	291,087	320,829	369,696
Total (incl. others)	497,695	562,450	655,170

* Provisional.

Source: Central Bank of Sri Lanka, Colombo.

PRINCIPAL TRADING PARTNERS
(US $ million)

Imports c.i.f.	2005	2006	2007
China, People's Republic	630.6	1,218.2	1,514.4
Hong Kong	648.2	486.7	491.3
India	1,835.4	2,268.5	2,707.6
Iran	523.9	658.6	749.8
Japan	379.7	470.2	435.8
Korea, Republic	210.3	195.8	233.8
Malaysia	393.5	587.5	412.6
Singapore	736.9	1,013.8	920.1
United Arab Emirates	296.3	372.5	424.1
United Kingdom	276.5	212.2	212.9
Total (incl. others)	8,863.2	11,579.4	12,484.1

Exports f.o.b.	2005	2006	2007
France	121.4	110.6	148.2
Germany	271.8	299.8	381.8
India	566.4	700.0	835.6
Italy	199.6	248.6	351.3
Japan	144.6	186.1	187.9
Russia	157.7	185.2	225.9
United Arab Emirates	170.3	210.2	273.7
United Kingdom	777.3	850.3	981.3
USA	1,988.1	2,074.8	1,980.5
Total (incl. others)	6,383.7	7,491.9	8,458.5

Source: Asian Development Bank, *Key Indicators of Developing Asian and Pacific Countries*.

Transport

RAILWAYS

	2005	2006	2007
Passengers (million)	114.4	105.4	110.5
Freight carried ('000 metric tons)*	1,502	1,551	1,707

* Excluding livestock.

Source: Sri Lanka Railways.

SRI LANKA

ROAD TRAFFIC
(motor vehicles in use at 31 December)

	2000	2001	2002
Passenger cars	233,018	241,444	253,447
Buses and coaches	64,963	66,273	67,702
Lorries and vans	300,712	312,495	328,913
Road tractors	133,092	138,879	146,043
Motorcycles and mopeds	834,586	868,705	923,467
Total	1,566,371	1,627,796	1,719,572

Source: International Road Federation, *World Road Statistics*.

SHIPPING

Merchant Fleet
(registered at 31 December)

	2005	2006	2007
Number of vessels	82	81	85
Displacement ('000 grt)	177.8	174.1	163.3

Source: Lloyd's Register-Fairplay, *World Fleet Statistics*.

International Sea-borne Shipping
(freight traffic, '000 metric tons, Colombo, Trincomalee and Galle only)

	2005	2006	2007
Goods loaded	13,155	15,622	17,724
Goods unloaded	24,145	27,039	28,621

CIVIL AVIATION
(traffic on scheduled services)

	2002	2003	2004
Kilometres flown (million)	29	34	43
Passengers carried ('000)	1,741	1,958	2,413
Passenger-km (million)	6,327	6,910	8,310
Total ton-km (million)	778	864	1,068

Source: UN, *Statistical Yearbook*.

Tourism

FOREIGN TOURIST ARRIVALS*

Country of residence	2004	2005	2006
Australia	24,471	25,836	21,665
Belgium	5,718	3,891	6,373
Canada	14,974	21,335	14,863
France	30,422	26,641	22,703
Germany	58,932	46,320	47,296
India	104,390	113,023	128,520
Italy	17,984	10,147	12,353
Japan	19,747	17,163	16,217
Maldives	15,201	24,396	24,505
Netherlands	21,487	15,252	19,460
Pakistan	9,629	11,056	11,165
Switzerland	10,687	8,339	7,729
United Kingdom	107,042	92,929	88,531
USA	15,680	25,392	20,825
Total (incl. others)	566,202	549,308	559,603

* Excluding Sri Lanka nationals residing abroad.

Tourism receipts (US $ million, incl. passenger transport): 808 in 2004; 729 in 2005; 733 in 2006.

Sources: Ceylon Tourist Board; World Tourism Organization.

Communications Media

	1999	2000	2001
Television receivers ('000 in use)	1,900	2,100	2,200
Telephones ('000 main lines in use)	669.1	767.4	822.1
Mobile cellular telephones ('000 subscribers)	256.7	430.2	667.7
Personal computers ('000 in use)	105	135	175
Internet users ('000)	65.0	121.5	150.0
Newspapers	174	180	189
Books published: titles	4,655	1,818	n.a.
Books published: copies ('000)	n.a.	25,459.3	7,439.1

Facsimile machines (number in use, estimate): 11,000 in 1994.

Radio receivers ('000 in use): 3,850 in 1997.

2002 ('000): Telephones (main lines in use) 881.4; Mobile cellular telephones (subscribers) 931.6; Personal computers (number in use) 250; Internet users 200.0.

2003 ('000): Telephones (main lines in use) 939.0; Mobile cellular telephones (subscribers) 1,393.4; Personal computers (number in use) 325; Internet users 280.0; Broadband subscribers 3.4.

2004 ('000): Telephones (main lines in use) 993.4; Mobile cellular telephones (subscribers) 2,213.6; Personal computers (number in use) 530; Internet users 280.0; Broadband subscribers 20.4.

2005 ('000): Telephones (main lines in use) 1,244.0; Mobile cellular telephones (subscribers) 3,361.8; Personal computers (number in use) 530; Internet users 350.0; Broadband subscribers 26.1.

2006 ('000): Telephones (main lines in use) 1,884.1; Mobile cellular telephones (subscribers) 5,412.5; Internet users 500.0; Broadband subscribers 22.9.

2007 ('000): Telephones (main lines in use) 2,742.1; Mobile cellular telephones (subscribers) 7,983.5; Internet users 771.7; Broadband subscribers 63.3.

Sources: UN, *Statistical Yearbook*; UNESCO, *Statistical Yearbook*; Telecommunications Regulatory Commission of Sri Lanka and International Telecommunication Union.

Education

(1995)

	Institutions	Teachers	Students
Primary	9,657	70,537	1,962,498
Secondary	5,771*	103,572	2,314,054
Universities and equivalent	n.a.	2,344	40,035
Distance learning	n.a.	206	20,601

* 1992 figure.

1996: Primary: 9,554 institutions, 66,339 teachers, 1,843,848 students.

1997: Primary: 60,832 teachers, 1,807,751 students; Secondary: 2,313,511 students.

1998: Primary: 1,798,162 students.

2001: Universities: 12 institutions, 2,999 teachers, 48,899 students.

2002: Universities: 12 institutions, 3,225 teachers (excl. open university), 48,667 students (excl. open university).

2003 (provisional): Universities: 12 institutions, 3,386 teachers (excl. open university), 59,734 students (excl. open university).

Sources: UNESCO, *Statistical Yearbook*; Ministry of Education, Colombo.

Adult literacy rate (UNESCO estimates): 91.5% (males 93.2%; females 89.9%) in 2007 (Source: UNESCO Institute for Statistics).

Directory

The Constitution

The Constitution of the Democratic Socialist Republic of Sri Lanka was approved by the National State Assembly (renamed Parliament) on 17 August 1978, and promulgated on 7 September 1978. The following is a summary of its main provisions:

FUNDAMENTAL RIGHTS

The Constitution guarantees the fundamental rights and freedoms of all citizens, including freedom of thought, conscience and worship and equal entitlement before the law.

THE PRESIDENT

The President is Head of State, and exercises all executive powers, including defence of the Republic. The President is directly elected by the people for a term of six years, and is eligible for re-election. The President's powers include the right to:

(i) choose to hold any portfolio in the Cabinet;
(ii) appoint or dismiss the Prime Minister or any other minister;
(iii) preside at ceremonial sittings of Parliament;
(iv) dismiss Parliament at will; and
(v) submit to a national referendum any Bill or matter of national importance which has been rejected by Parliament.

LEGISLATURE

The Parliament is the legislative power of the people. It consists of such number of representatives of the people as a Delimitation Commission shall determine. The members of Parliament are directly elected by a system of modified proportional representation. By-elections are abolished, successors to members of Parliament being appointed by the head of the party which nominated the outgoing member at the previous election. Parliament exercises the judicial power of the people through courts, tribunals and institutions created and established or recognized by the Constitution or established by law. Parliament has control over public finance.

OTHER PROVISIONS

Religion

Buddhism has the foremost place among religions and it is the duty of the State to protect and foster Buddhism, while assuring every citizen the freedom to adopt the religion of their choice.

Language

The Constitution recognizes two official languages, Sinhala and Tamil. Either of the national languages may be used by all citizens in transactions with government institutions.

Amendments

Amendments to the Constitution require endorsement by a two-thirds' majority in Parliament. In February 1979 the Constitution was amended by allowing members of Parliament who resigned or were expelled from their party to retain their seats, in certain circumstances. In January 1981 Parliament amended the Constitution to increase its membership from 168 to 169. An amendment enabling the President to seek re-election after four years was approved in August 1982. In February 1983 an amendment providing for by-elections to fill vacant seats in Parliament was approved. An amendment banning parties that advocate separatism was approved by Parliament in August 1983. In November 1987 Parliament adopted an amendment providing for the creation of eight provincial councils (the northern and eastern provinces were to be merged as one administrative unit); although the northern and eastern provinces were subsequently merged, the Supreme Court announced the merger to be officially invalid in October 2006. In December 1988 Parliament adopted an amendment affording Tamil the same status as Sinhala, as one of the country's two official languages.

The Government

HEAD OF STATE

President: MAHINDA RAJAPAKSE (sworn in 19 November 2005).

THE CABINET
(April 2009)

Prime Minister and Minister of Internal Administration: RATNASIRI WICKREMANAYAKE.
Minister of Foreign Affairs: ROHITHA BOGOLLAGAMA.
Minister of Defence, of Public Security, Law and Order, of Highways and Road Development, of Religious Affairs and Moral Upliftment, of Finance and Planning, and of Nation Building: MAHINDA RAJAPAKSE.
Minister of Tourism: MILINDA MORAGODA.
Minister of Posts and Telecommunication, and of Special Projects: MAHINDA WIJESEKERA.
Minister of Justice: AMARASIRI DODANGODA.
Minister of Healthcare and Nutrition: NIMAL SIRIPALA DE SILVA.
Minister of Transport: DULLAS ALAHAPERUMA.
Minister of Trade, Marketing Development, Co-operatives and Consumer Affairs: BANDULA GUNAWARDENA.
Minister of Agricultural Development and Agrarian Services Development: MAITHRIPALA SIRISENA.
Minister of Power and Energy: JOHN SENEVIRATNA.
Minister of Child Development and Women's Affairs: SUMEDHA G. JAYASENA.
Minister of Mass Media and Information, and of Enterprise Development and Investment Promotion: ANURA PRIYADARSHANA YAPA.
Minister of Urban Development and Sacred Area Development: DINESH GUNAWARDENA.
Minister of Social Services and Social Welfare: DOUGLAS DEVANANDA.
Minister of Public Administration and Home Affairs: Dr SARATH AMUNUGAMA.
Minister of Housing and Common Amenities: FERIAL ASHRAFF.
Minister of Education: SUSIL PREMAJAYANTHA.
Minister of Labour Relations and Manpower: ATHAUDA SENEVIRATNE.
Minister of Rural Industries and Self-Employment Promotion: R. M. S. B. NAVINNE.
Minister of Vocational and Technical Training: PIYASENA GAMAGE.
Minister of Local Government and Provincial Councils: JANAKA BANDARA THENAKOON.
Minister of Fisheries and Aquatic Resources: FELIX PERERA.
Minister of Science and Technology: Prof. TISSA VITHARANA.
Minister of Constitutional Affairs and National Integration: D. E. W. GUNASEKERA.
Minister of Disaster Management and Human Rights: MAHINDA SAMARASINGHE.
Minister of Plantation Industries: D. M. JAYARATNE.
Minister of Petroleum and Petroleum Resources Development: A. H. M. FOWZIE.
Minister of Youth Empowerment and Socio-Economic Development: ARUMUGAN THONDAMAN.
Minister of Community Development and Social Inequity Eradication: P. CHANDRASEKERAN.
Minister of Water Supply and Drainage: A. L. M. ATHAULLAH.
Minister of Resettlement and Disaster Relief Services: ABDUL RISATH BATHIYUTHEEN.
Minister of Plan Implementation: P. DAYARATNE.
Minister of Supplementary Crops Development: R. M. DHARMADASA BANDA.
Minister of Parliamentary Affairs: M. H. MOHOMED.
Minister of Export Development and International Trade: Prof. G. L. PEIRIS.
Minister of Public Estate Management and Development: MILROY FERNANDO.
Minister of Land and Land Development: JEEWAN KUMARANATUNGA.
Minister of Youth Affairs: PAVITHRA WANNIARACHCHI.
Minister of Indigenous Medicine: TISSA KARALIYADDE.
Minister of Sports and Public Recreation: GAMINI LOKUGE.
Minister of Construction and Engineering Services: RAJITHA SENARATNE.

SRI LANKA

Minister of Foreign Employment Promotion and Welfare: KEHELIYA RAMBUKWELLE.

Minister of Livestock Development: R. M. C. B. RATHNAYAKE.

Minister of Cultural Affairs: MAHINDA YAPA ABEYWARDENA.

Minister of Higher Education: Prof. WISWA WARNAPALA.

Minister of Irrigation and Water Management, and of Ports and Aviation: CHAMAL RAJAPAKSA.

Minister of Industrial Development: KUMARA WELGAMA.

Minister of Environment and Natural Resources: CHAMPIKA RANAWAKA.

MINISTRIES

President's Secretariat: Republic Sq., Colombo 1; tel. (11) 2324801; fax (11) 2331246; e-mail gosl@presidentsl.org; internet www.presidentsl.org.

Prime Minister's Office: 58 Sir Ernest de Silva Mawatha, Colombo 7; tel. (11) 2575317; fax (11) 2575454; internet www.pmoffice.gov.lk.

Ministry of Agricultural Development and Agrarian Services: 'Govijana Mandiraya', 80/5 Rajamalwatta Rd, Battaramulla, Colombo; tel. (11) 2869553; fax (11) 2868919; e-mail agmin@sltnet.lk; internet www.mimrd.gov.lk.

Ministry of Child Development and Women's Empowerment: 177 Nawala Rd, Narahenpita, Colombo 5; tel. (11) 2505584; fax (11) 2369294; e-mail mwa@sltnet.lk.

Ministry of Community Development and Social Inequity Eradication: 35/A Dr N. M. Perera Mawatha, Colombo 8.

Ministry of Constitutional Affairs and National Integration: 310 Galle Rd, Colombo 3; tel. (11) 2375178; fax (11) 2375181; e-mail consas@constitution.gov.lk; internet www.constitution.gov.lk.

Ministry of Construction and Engineering Services: 'Sethsiripaya', 2nd Floor, Battaramulla, Colombo; internet (11) 2867954.

Ministry of Cultural Affairs: 'Sethsiripaya', 8th Floor, Battaramulla, Colombo; tel. (11) 2872001; fax (11) 2872021; e-mail mcasec@sltnet.lk.

Ministry of Defence, Public Security, Law and Order: 15/5 Baladaksha Mawatha, POB 572, Colombo 3; tel. (11) 2430860; fax (11) 2446300; e-mail secretary@defence.lk; internet www.defence.lk.

Ministry of Disaster Management and Human Rights: 2 Wijerama Mawatha, Colombo 7; tel. (11) 2695013; fax (11) 2681980; e-mail info@dmhr.gov.lk; internet www.dmhr.gov.lk.

Ministry of Education: 'Isurupaya', Pelawatte, Battaramulla, Colombo; tel. (11) 2785141; fax (11) 2785162; e-mail minedu@moe.gov.lk; internet www.moe.gov.lk.

Ministry of Enterprise Development and Investment Promotion: World Trade Centre, West Tower, 25th Level, Echelon Sq, Colombo 1; tel. (11) 2394951; fax (11) 2424960; e-mail secedip@sltnet.lk.

Ministry of Environment and Natural Resources: 82 Sampath Paya, Rajamalwatte Rd, Battaramulla, Colombo; tel. (11) 2882112; fax (11) 2863652; e-mail promotion@menr.lk; internet www.menr.lk.

Ministry of Export Development and International Trade: 'Rakshana Mandiraya', 6th Floor, 21 Vauxhall St, Colombo 2; tel. (11) 2435002.

Ministry of Finance and Planning: Galle Face Secretariat, Colombo 1; tel. (11) 2484500; fax (11) 2449823; e-mail mfsa@sltnet.lk; internet www.treasury.gov.lk.

Ministry of Fisheries and Aquatic Resources: Maligawatta, Colombo 10; tel. (11) 2446183; fax (11) 2541184; e-mail secretary@fisheries.gov.lk; internet www.fisheries.gov.lk.

Ministry of Foreign Affairs: Republic Bldg, Colombo 1; tel. (11) 2328040; fax (11) 2389484; e-mail publicity@formin.gov.lk; internet www.slmfa.gov.lk.

Ministry of Foreign Employment Promotion and Welfare: Level 33, West Tower, World Trade Centre, Colombo 1; tel. (11) 2438734; fax (11) 2438736; e-mail fep_gov@sltnet.lk; internet www.minfep.gov.lk.

Ministry of Healthcare and Nutrition: 'Suwasiripaya', 385 Wimalawansha Himi Mawatha, Colombo 10; tel. (11) 2694033; fax (11) 2692694; e-mail dhi@health.gov.lk; internet www.health.gov.lk.

Ministry of Higher Education: 18 Ward Place, Colombo 7; tel. (11) 2694486; fax (11) 2697239; e-mail mioh.hied@sltnet.lk; internet www.mohe.gov.lk.

Ministry of Highways and Road Development: Sethsiripaya Office Complex, 'C' Wing, 9th Floor, POB 53, Battaramulla, Colombo; tel. (11) 2871821; fax (11) 2862705; e-mail hiwaysec@sltnet.lk; internet www.mohsl.gov.lk.

Ministry of Housing and Common Amenities: 'Sethsiripaya', 2nd Floor, Sri Jayawardanapura Kotte, Battaramulla, Colombo; tel. (11) 2861586; fax (11) 2888151; e-mail ministry@mhc.gov.lk.

Directory

Ministry of Indigenous Medicine: 80/5 'Govijana Mandiraya', Rajamalwatta Road, Battaramulla, Colombo; tel. (11) 2872093; fax (11) 2885126; e-mail inmed@dialogsl.net.

Ministry of Industrial Development: 73/1 Galle Rd, Colombo 3; tel. (11) 2392149; fax (11) 2449402; e-mail misec@sltnet.lk; internet www.industry.gov.lk.

Ministry of Internal Administration: 51 Sir Ernest de Silva Mawatha, Colombo 7; tel. (11) 2301235.

Ministry of Irrigation and Water Management: 11 Jawatta Rd, Colombo 5; tel. (11) 2554000.

Ministry of Justice and Law Reforms: Superior Courts Complex Bldg, Colombo 12; tel. (11) 2323022; fax (11) 2320785; internet www.justiceministry.gov.lk.

Ministry of Labour Relations and Manpower: Labour Secretariat, 2nd Floor, Narahenpita, Colombo 5; tel. (11) 2581149; fax (11) 2588950; e-mail slmol@slt.lk.

Ministry of Land and Land Development: 'Govijana Mandiraya', 80/5 Rajamalwatta Rd, Battaramulla, Colombo; tel. (11) 2887410; fax (11) 2887404; e-mail nips@sltnet.lk.

Ministry of Livestock Development: 45 St Michael's Rd, POB 562, Colombo 3; tel. (11) 2541369; fax (11) 2541377; e-mail geethacb@hotmail.com; internet www.livestock.gov.lk.

Ministry of Local Government and Provincial Councils: 330 Union Place, Colombo 2; tel. (11) 2305326; fax (11) 2347529; e-mail secpl@minhaprolo.gov.lk; internet www.minhaprolo.gov.lk.

Ministry of Mass Media and Information: 163 Kirulapone Mawatha, Polhengoda, Colombo 5; tel. (11) 2513459; fax (11) 2514053; e-mail mediasecretary@media.gov.lk; internet www.media.gov.lk.

Ministry of Nation Building and Estate Infrastructure Development: 177 Galle Rd, Colombo 3; tel. (11) 2390895; fax (11) 2382069; e-mail secmdrrn@sltnet.lk.

Ministry of National Heritage: 'Sethsiripaya', 8th Floor, Battaramulla, Colombo 3; tel. (11) 2872001.

Ministry of Parliamentary Affairs: 464/B Pannipitiya Rd, Pelewatta, Battaramulla; tel. (11) 2786988; fax (11) 2787895; e-mail mpasl@sltnet.lk.

Ministry of Petroleum and Petroleum Resources Development: 80 Sir Ernest De Silva Mawatha, Colombo 7; tel. (11) 2564355.

Ministry of Plan Implementation: Central Bank Building, 5th Tower, 12th Floor, 30 Janadhipathi Mawatha, Colombo 1; tel. (11) 2477000; fax (11) 2477959; e-mail bhaila@slt.lk.

Ministry of Plantation Industries: 55/75 Vauxhall Lane, Colombo 2; tel. (11) 2320901; fax (11) 2303022; e-mail dpmpi@sltnet.lk; internet www.plantationindustries.gov.lk.

Ministry of Ports and Aviation: 19 Chaithiya Rd, Colombo 1; tel. (11) 2439350; fax (11) 2431658; e-mail specd@slpa.lk; internet www.ports-aviation.gov.lk.

Ministry of Posts and Telecommunication: World Trade Centre, West Tower, Level 18, Colombo 1; tel. (11) 2422591; fax (11) 2323465; e-mail spostele@sltnet.lk.

Ministry of Power and Energy: 493/1 T. B. Jaya Mawatha, Colombo 10; tel. (11) 2687768; fax (11) 2681248; e-mail secrepe@sltnet.lk; internet www.mope.gov.lk.

Ministry of Public Administration and Home Affairs: Independence Sq., Colombo 7; tel. (11) 2696211; fax (11) 2697410; e-mail info@pubad.gov.lk; internet www.pubad.gov.lk.

Ministry of Public Estate Management and Development: 320 T. B. Jayah Mawatha, Colombo 10; tel. (11) 2672505; fax (11) 2672501; e-mail secpemd@sltnet.lk.

Ministry of Religious Affairs and Moral Upliftment: 115 Wijerama Mawatha, Colombo 7; tel. (11) 2690736; fax (11) 2690897; e-mail herathmudi@yahoo.com.

Ministry of Resettlement and Disaster Relief Services: 146 Galle Rd, Colombo 3; tel. (11) 2395109; fax (11) 2395517; e-mail acmrazik@gmail.com; internet www.resettlementmin.gov.lk.

Ministry of Rural Industries and Self Employment Promotion: 780 Maradana Rd, Colombo 10; tel. (11) 2669280; fax (11) 2669281; e-mail secofficerisep@sltnet.lk; internet www.risepmin.gov.lk.

Ministry of Science and Technology: 561/3 Etvigala Mawatha, POB 1571, Colombo 5; tel. (11) 2554848; fax (11) 2510565; e-mail mstsasad@sltnet.lk; internet www.most.gov.lk.

Ministry of Social Services and Social Welfare: 'Sethsiripaya', 5th Floor, Battaramulla, Colombo; tel. (11) 2887349; fax (11) 2877381; e-mail msssec@sltnet.lk; internet www.socialwelfare.gov.lk.

Ministry of Sports and Public Recreation: 420 Bauddhaloka Mawatha, Colombo 7; tel. (11) 2669237; fax (11) 2683569; e-mail info@sportsministry.gov.lk.

SRI LANKA

Ministry of Supplementary Plantation Crops Development: 561/3 Elvitigala Mawatha, Colombo 8; tel. (11) 2150722; fax (11) 2375378.

Ministry of Tourism: 64 Galle Rd, Colombo 3; tel. (11) 2385241; fax (11) 2399274; e-mail slmts@sltnet.lk; internet www.slmts.slt.lk.

Ministry of Trade, Marketing Development, Co-operatives and Consumer Services: 'Rakshana Mandiraya', 7th Floor, 21 Vauxhall St, Colombo 2; tel. (11) 2300341; fax (11) 2447669; e-mail comsec@commerce.gov.lk; internet www.commerce.gov.lk.

Ministry of Transport: 1 D. R. Wijewardene Mawatha, POB 588, Colombo 10; tel. (11) 2687105; fax (11) 2687108; e-mail mintrans@sltnet.lk; internet www.transport.gov.lk.

Ministry of Urban Development and Sacred Area Development: 'Sethsiripaya', 3rd Floor, Battaramulla, Colombo 3; tel. (11) 2877002; fax (11) 2871835; e-mail secudws@sltnet.lk.

Ministry of Vocational and Technical Training: 'Nipunatha Piyasa', 354/2 Elwitigala Mawatha, Narahenpita, Colombo 5; tel. (11) 2597677; fax (11) 2597691; e-mail sec_sdvte@sltnet.lk; internet www.nipunatha.gov.lk.

Ministry of Water Supply and Drainage: 34 Thakahashi Bldg, Narahenpita Rd, Nawala; tel. (11) 2808135.

Ministry of Youth Affairs: 420 Bouddhaloka Mawatha, Colombo 7; tel. (11) 2665291; e-mail yendammika@gmail.com.

Ministry of Youth Empowerment and Socio-Economic Development: 43 Jawatta Rd, Colombo 5; tel. (11) 2169507.

President and Legislature

PRESIDENT

Presidential Election, 17 November 2005

Candidate	Valid votes	% of votes
Mahinda Rajapakse (UPFA)	4,887,152	50.29
Ranil Wickremasinghe (UNP)	4,706,366	48.43
Total (incl. others)	9,717,039	100.00

PARLIAMENT

Speaker: W. J. M. LOKUBANDARA.
Deputy Speaker: PRIYANKARA JAYARATNE.

General Election, 2 April 2004

Party	Seats
United People's Freedom Alliance (UPFA)*	105
United National Party (UNP)	82
Tamil National Alliance (TNA)	22
Jathika Hela Urumaya (JHU)	9
Sri Lanka Muslim Congress (SLMC)	5
Others	2
Total	225

*Coalition comprising the Sri Lanka Freedom Party, Janatha Vimukthi Peramuna, Communist Party of Sri Lanka, Democratic United National Front, Lanka Sama Samaja Party and Sri Lanka Mahajana Party.

Note: Direct elections were held for 196 of the 225 seats on the basis of a proportional representation system involving preferential voting; the remaining 29 were chosen from party lists according to each party's national share of the vote.

Election Commission

Department of Elections: Elections Secretariat, Sarana Mawatha, Rajagiriya, Jayawardenapura; tel. (11) 2868441; fax (11) 2868445; e-mail comelesl@sltnet.lk; internet www.slelections.gov.lk; f. 1947; govt dept; establishment of independent commission pending in 2008; Commr of Elections DAYANANDA DISSANAYAKE.

Political Organizations

Akhila Ilankai Tamil United Front (AITUK): e-mail secretary@tamilunitedfront.com; internet www.tamilunitedfront.com; f. 2006; Tamil; advocates federal solution to ethnic conflict; Gen. Sec. K. VIGNESWARAN.

Ceylon Workers' Congress (CWC): 'Savumia Bhavan', 72 Ananda Coomarasamy Mawatha, POB 1294, Colombo 7; tel. (11) 2301359; fax (11) 2301355; e-mail cwconline@sltnet.lk; f. 1939; represents the interests of workers in the mercantile and local government sectors and of workers on tea, rubber and coconut plantations; 250,000 mems; Pres. and Gen. Sec. S. R. ARUMUGAN THONDAMAN.

Democratic People's Front: 72 Bankshall St, Colombo 11; tel. (11) 2473511; fax (11) 2435961; has operated as a national political party since Sept. 1988; Sec.-Gen. NALLIASH KUMARAGURUPARAN.

Democratic Workers' Congress (DWC) (Political Wing): 70 Bankshall St, POB 1009, Colombo 11; tel. (11) 2439199; fax (11) 2435961; f. 1978 as political wing of DWC trade union (f. 1939); aims to eliminate discrimination against the Tamil-speaking Sri Lankans of recent Indian origin; 201,382 mems (1994); Pres. and Gen. Sec. MANO GANESHAN.

Desha Vimukthi Janatha Pakshaya (National Liberation People's Party): 63/24, Wewewatte, Weliweriya; tel. 338812; has operated as a national political party since Sept. 1988; Sec. P. M. PODIAPPUHAMY.

Deshapriya Janatha Viyaparaya (DJV) (Patriotic People's Movement): militant, Sinhalese group; associated with the JVP.

Eelam National Democratic Liberation Front (ENDLF): 315 Kandy Rd, Kilinochchi; Tamil; supports 1987 Indo-Sri Lankan peace accord; has operated as a national political party since Sept. 1988; Pres. G. GNANASEKARAN; Dep. Gen. Sec. P. RAJARATNAM.

Eelam People's Democratic Party (EPDP): 121 Park Rd, Colombo 5; tel. (11) 2551015; fax (11) 2585255; e-mail epdp@sltnet.lk; internet www.epdpnews.com; Tamil; Sec.-Gen. DOUGLAS DEVANANDA.

Eksath Lanka Podujana Pakshaya: 43/5 Galle Rd, Colombo 4; tel. (77) 2313321; Sec. U. LALITH WIJETHUNGA.

Janatha Vimukthi Peramuna (JVP) (People's Liberation Front): 198/19 Panchikawattha Rd, Colombo 10; tel. (11) 4400511; fax (11) 2786050; e-mail jvplanka@sltnet.lk; internet www.jvpsrilanka.com; f. 1964; banned following a coup attempt in 1971, regained legal status in 1977, banned again in 1983, but regained legal status in 1994; Marxist; Sinhalese support; Leader SOMAWANSA AMARASINGHE.

Jathika Hela Urumaya (JHU) (National Heritage Party): 253/C, 'Ravindu', Vihara Mawatha, Weboda; tel. (11) 2810185; fax (11) 2811504; e-mail helaurumaya@gmail.com; internet www.jathikahelaurumaya.org; f. 2004; Buddhist; Sinhalese nationalist; Asst Sec. G. D. D. GUNATHILAKE.

Liberal Party: 88/1 Rosmead Place, Colombo 7; tel. (11) 2691589; fax (11) 2699772; e-mail libparty@sri.lanka.net; internet www.liberalparty-srilanka.org; Pres. SWARNA AMARATUNGA; Sec.-Gen. KAMAL NISSANKA.

Mahajana Eksath Peramuna (MEP) (People's United Front): 31/27 Narahenpita Rd, Nawala, Rajagiriya; tel. 872318; f. 1956; Sinhalese and Buddhist support; left-wing; advocates economic self-reliance; Pres. DINESH C. R. GUNAWARDENA.

Muslim National Unity Alliance (MNUA): Sama Mandiraya, 53 Vauxhall Lane, Colombo 2; tel. (11) 2424187; affiliate party of the Sri Lanka Muslim Congress; has operated as a national political party since 1986; Leader FARIEL ASHRAFF.

Muslim United Liberation Front: 134 Hulftsdorp St, Colombo 12; tel. (11) 2501198; has operated as a national political party since Sept. 1988.

National Freedom Front (NFF): 377/4 Ratnarama Rd, Hokandara North; tel. (60) 2071340; e-mail info@nffsrilanka.com; internet www.nffsrilanka.com; f. 2008 as a breakaway faction of the JVP; Chair. WIMAL WEERAWANSA; Gen. Sec. NANDANA GUNATILAKA.

Nava Sama Samaja Party (NSSP) (New Equal Society Party): Left Front, 17 Barracks Lane, Colombo 2; tel. (11) 2430621; fax (11) 2305963; e-mail nssp@nssp.info; internet www.nssp.info; f. 1977; Trotskyist; operates under the New Left Front; Gen. Sec. LINUS JAYATILAKE; Presidium Member Dr VICKRAMABAHU KARUNARATHNE.

New Democratic Party (NDP): C. C. S. M. Complex, 3rd Floor, S-47, Colombo 11; tel. (71) 4302909; fax (11) 2473757; e-mail info@ndpsl.org; internet www.ndpsl.org; f. 1978 as the Sri Lanka Communist Party; adopted current name in 1991; upholds Marxist-Leninist-Mao Zedong philosophy in anti-imperialist campaigning for social justice; publs monthly party newsletter Puthiya Poomi; Gen. Sec. S. K. SENTHIVEL.

Singhalaye Nithahas Peramuna (Sinhalese Freedom Front): Sri Panchananda Charity Bldg, Kelani Railway Station Rd, Colombo; f. 1994; nationalist, Buddhist; Pres. ARYA SENA TERA; Sec. Prof. NALIN DE SILVA.

Sri Lanka Freedom Party—Mahajana Wing (SLFP—M): Colombo; f. 2007 as breakaway faction of the Sri Lanka Freedom Party, under the leadership of fmr Minister of Foreign Affairs and fmr Minister of Port Development; advocates constitutional reform, incl. revisions to the Executive President's authority; memorandum of understanding signed with United National Party in July 2007 whereby the two parties pledged to contest future elections as a broad

SRI LANKA

coalition (the 'National Congress'); Founder and Leader MANGALA SAMARAWEERA.

Sri Lanka Muslim Congress: Sama Mandiraya, 53 Vauxhall Lane, Colombo 2; tel. (11) 2431711; internet www.slmc.org; Leader RAUF HAKEEM.

Sri Lanka Progressive Front: 7, 7th Lane, Pagoda Rd, Nugegoda; tel. (11) 826564; f. 1996 following split from Janatha Vimukthi Peramuna; leftist nationalist party; Sec. ROHAN JAYATUNGA.

Tamileela Makkal Viduthalai Pulikal (TMVP) (Tamileela Peoples Liberation Tigers—Karuna Group): Colombo; internet www.tmvp.org; f. 2004; political and paramilitary group, fmrly of LTTE; joint asscn with the Eelam National Democratic Liberation Front (India); Leader SIVANESATHURAI CHANDRAKANTHAN ('PILLAYAN'); Gen.-Sec. A. KAILESVARARAJAH.

Tamil National Alliance (TNA): 3rd Floor, Parliamentary Complex, Sri Jeyawardanapura Kotte, Colombo; e-mail enquiries@tamilalliance.net; internet www.tamilalliance.net; f. 2001; alliance of Tamil parties.

Eelam People's Revolutionary Liberation Front (EPRLF): 310 Hospital Rd, Jaffna; tel. (21) 2222022; internet www.eprlf.net; Tamil rights group; the party split into two factions, one led by ANNAMALAI VARADHARAJAH PERUMAL, known as the Varadharajah faction, and the other by SURESH K. PREMACHANDRAN, known as the Premachandran faction; c. 1,000 mems.

Tamil Eelam Liberation Organization (TELO): 34 Ammankovil Rd, Pandarikulam, Vavuniya; tel. (24) 2222977; fax (24) 2224457; e-mail teloheadoffice@yahoo.com; internet www.telo.org; supports 1987 Indo-Sri Lankan peace accord; has operated as a national political party since Sept. 1988; pro-LTTE; Leader SELVAM ADAIKALANTHAN.

Tamil United Liberation Front (TULF): 30/1B Alwis Place, Colombo 3; tel. (11) 2347721; fax (11) 2347721; e-mail tulf2000@yahoo.com; f. 1976 following merger of All Ceylon Tamil Congress (f. 1945) and Federal Party (f. 1949); Pres. VEERASINGHAM ANANDASANGAREE; Sec.-Gen. R. SAMPANTHAN.

United National Party (UNP): 30 Sir Marcus Fernando Mawatha, Colombo 7; tel. (11) 5636551; fax (11) 2682905; e-mail info@unp.lk; internet www.unp.lk; f. 1946; democratic socialist; aims at a non-aligned foreign policy, supports Sinhala and Tamil as the official languages and state aid to denominational schools; Leader RANIL WICKREMASINGHE; Chair. RUKMAN SENANAYAKE; Gen. Sec. TISSA ATTANAYAKE.

United People's Freedom Alliance (UPFA): 121 Wijerama Mawatha, Colombo 7; tel. (11) 268047; f. 2004; left wing coalition incl. communists and Trotskyists; Chair. (vacant).

Communist Party of Sri Lanka (CPSL): 91 Dr N. M. Perera Mawatha, Colombo 800; tel. (11) 2695328; fax (11) 2691610; e-mail dew128@dialogsl.net; f. 1943; advocates establishment of socialist society; seeks broadening of democratic rights and processes, political solution to ethnic problem, defence of social welfare and presses for social justice; supports national sovereignty, territorial integrity and national unity of the country; Gen. Sec. DEW GUNASEKERA.

Democratic United National Front (DUNF): 60 1st Lane, Rawathawatte, Moratuwa; tel. (11) 2645566; f. 1991 by dissident group of UNP politicians; 500,000 mems; Pres. D. M. G. EKANAYAKE; Gen. Sec. ARIYAWANSA DISSANAYAKE.

Lanka Sama Samaja Party (LSSP) (Lanka Equal Society Party): 457 Dr Colvin R. de Silva Mawatha, Colombo 2; tel. (11) 2676770; f. 1935; Trotskyist; Gen. Sec. WIMALASIRI DE MEL.

Sri Lanka Freedom Party (SLFP): 301 T. B. Jayah Mawatha, Colombo 10; tel. (11) 2679113; fax (11) 2685563; e-mail slfp@srilankafreedomparty.org; internet www.srilankafreedomparty.org; f. 1951; democratic socialist; advocates a non-aligned foreign policy, industrial development in both the state sector and the private sector, rapid modernization in education and in the economy, and safeguards for minorities; Chair. MAHINDA RAJAPAKSE; Gen. Sec. MAITHRIPALA SIRISENA.

Sri Lanka Mahajana (People's) Party (SLMP): 196 Kolonnawa Rd, Wellampitiya; f. 1984 by fmr mems of the SLFP; social democrats; Leader SARATH KONGAHAGE; Gen. Sec. PREMASIRI PERERA.

Upcountry People's Front: 56, Rosita Housing Scheme, Kotagala; tel. (52) 28286; represents interests of workers (mainly of Indian Tamil origin) on tea plantations; Sec. P. CHANDRASEKARAN.

Tamil separatist groups also include the Liberation Tigers of Tamil Eelam (LTTE), the Tamil Eelam Liberation Front (TELF; Gen. Sec. M. K. EELAVENTHAN), the People's Liberation Organization of Tamil Eelam (PLOTE); Leader DHARMALINGAM SIDDHARTHAN; Vice-Pres. KARUVAI A. SRIKANTHASAMI), the People's Revolutionary Action Group, the Ellalan Force and the Tamil People's Protection Party.

Diplomatic Representation

EMBASSIES AND HIGH COMMISSIONS IN SRI LANKA

Australia: 21 Gregory's Rd, Colombo 7; tel. (11) 2463200; fax (11) 2686453; e-mail austcom@sltnet.lk; internet www.srilanka.embassy.gov.au; High Commissioner KATHY KLUGMAN.

Bangladesh: 5 Ward Pl., Colombo 7; tel. (11) 2303943; fax (11) 2695556; e-mail bdootlanka@eureka.lk; High Commissioner MAHBUB UZ ZAMAN.

Canada: 6 Gregory's Rd, Cinnamon Gdns, POB 1006, Colombo 7; tel. (11) 5326232; fax (11) 5226299; e-mail clmbo@international.gc.ca; internet www.dfait-maeci.gc.ca/world/embassies/srilanka; High Commissioner ANGELA BOGDAN.

China, People's Republic: 381/A Bauddhaloka Mawatha, Colombo 7; tel. (11) 2694491; fax (11) 2693799; e-mail chinaemb_lk@mfa.gov.cn; internet lk.china-embassy.org; Ambassador YANG XIUPING.

Cuba: 15/9 Maitland Crescent, Colombo 7; tel. (11) 2677170; fax (11) 2669380; e-mail cubaembalk@sltnet.lk; internet embacuba.cubaminrex.cu/srilankaing; Ambassador NIRSIA CASTRO GUEVARA.

Egypt: 39 Dickman's Rd, Colombo 5; tel. (11) 2583621; fax (11) 2585292; e-mail egyptemb@sltnet.lk; Ambassador GIHAN AMIN MOHAMED ALI.

France: 89 Rosmead Pl., POB 880, Colombo 7; tel. (11) 2698815; fax (11) 2699039; e-mail ambfrclb@sltnet.lk; internet www.ambafrance-lk.org; Ambassador MICHEL LUMMAUX.

Germany: 40 Alfred House Ave, POB 658, Colombo 3; tel. (11) 2580431; fax (11) 2580440; e-mail info@colombo.diplo.de; internet www.colombo.diplo.de; Ambassador JÜRGEN WEERTH.

Holy See: 220 Bauddhaloka Mawatha, Colombo 7 (Apostolic Nunciature); tel. (11) 2582554; fax (11) 2580906; e-mail nuntius@sltnet.lk; Apostolic Nuncio Most Rev. Dr JOSEPH SPITERI (Titular Archbishop of Serta).

India: 36–38 Galle Rd, Colombo 3; tel. (11) 2421605; fax (11) 2446403; e-mail cpic@sltnet.lk; internet www.hcicolombo.org; High Commissioner ALOK PRASAD.

Indonesia: 400/50 Sarana Rd, off Bauddhaloka Mawatha, Colombo 7; tel. (11) 2674337; fax (11) 2678668; e-mail pensosbud@kbrilk.org; internet indonesia-colombo.lk; Ambassador DJAFAR HUSEIN.

Iran: 17 Bullers Lane, Colombo 7; tel. (11) 2501137; fax (11) 2502691; e-mail emb_colombo@mfa.gov.ir; Ambassador BEHNAM BEHRUZ.

Italy: 55 Jawatta Rd, Colombo 5; tel. (11) 2588388; fax (11) 2596344; e-mail ambasciata.colombo@esteri.it; internet www.ambcolombo.esteri.it; Ambassador PIO MARIANI.

Japan: 20 Gregory's Rd, POB 822, Colombo 7; tel. (11) 2693831; fax (11) 2698629; e-mail cultujpn@sltnet.lk; internet www.lk.emb-japan.go.jp; Ambassador KIYOSHI ARAKI.

Korea, Democratic People's Republic: Colombo; Ambassador HAN CHANG-ON.

Korea, Republic: 98 Dharmapala Mawatha, Colombo 7; tel. (11) 2699036; fax (11) 2696699; e-mail kesl@koreanembassy.net; Ambassador CHOI KI-CHUL.

Kuwait: 292 Bauddhaloka Mawatha, Colombo 7; tel. (11) 2597958; fax (11) 2597954; e-mail cmb@kuwaitembassysl.org; Ambassador FAHID HAJAR SHAOUF AL-MUTAIRI.

Libya: 120 Horton Pl., POB 155, Colombo 7; tel. (11) 2693700; fax (11) 2695671; e-mail libya@eureka.lk; Sec. of the People's Bureau ABD-AL KARIM ALI ABD-AL KARIM.

Malaysia: 33 Bagatalle Rd, Colombo 3; tel. (11) 2554681; fax (11) 2554684; e-mail malcolmbo@eureka.lk; internet www.kln.gov.my/perwakilan/colombo; High Commissioner ROSLI ISMAIL.

Maldives: 25 Melbourne Ave, Colombo 4; tel. (11) 2587827; fax (11) 2581200; e-mail info@maldiveshighcom.lk; internet www.maldiveshighcom.lk; High Commissioner ALI HUSSAIN DIDI.

Myanmar: 4A Rosmead Ave, Rosmead Place, Colombo 7; tel. (11) 2696440; fax (11) 2682052; e-mail mmembcmb@eureka.lk; Ambassador U THAN TUN.

Nepal: 153 Kynsey Rd, Colombo 8; tel. (11) 2689657; fax (11) 2689629; e-mail nepalembassy@eureka.lk; Ambassador DURGA PRASAD BHATTARAI.

Netherlands: 25 Torrington Ave, Colombo 7; tel. (11) 2596914; fax (11) 2502855; e-mail col@minbuza.nl; internet www.hollandinsrilanka.org; Ambassador LEUNI CUELENAERE.

Norway: 34 Ward Place, Colombo 7; tel. (11) 2469611; fax (11) 2695009; e-mail emb.colombo@mfa.no; internet www.norway.lk; Ambassador TORE HATTREM.

Pakistan: 211 De Saram Place, Colombo 10; tel. (11) 2696301; fax (11) 2695780; e-mail parepcolombo@sltnet.lk; High Commissioner SHAHEEN GILANI.

SRI LANKA

Qatar: 11 Rajakeeya Mawatha, Old Race Course Ave, Colombo 7; tel. (11) 2690440; fax (11) 2690443; Ambassador SAED BIN ABDULLA AL-MANSOORI.

Romania: 9–11 Queens Terrace, Colombo 3; tel. (11) 2505005; fax (11) 2505006; e-mail romania@sltnet.lk; internet www.romania.lk; Chargé d'affaires a.i. IONEL GOMBOS.

Russia: 62 Sir Ernest de Silva Mawatha, Colombo 7; tel. (11) 2573555; fax (11) 2574957; e-mail rusemb@itmin.net; internet www.sri-lanka.mid.ru; Ambassador VLADIMIR P. MIKHAYLOV.

Saudi Arabia: 39 Sir Ernest de Silva Mawatha, Colombo 7; tel. (11) 2682087; fax (11) 2682088; e-mail lkemb@mofa.gov.sa; Ambassador ABDUL ASIA BIN AL JEMAZ.

South Africa: 114 Rosmead Place, Colombo 7; tel. (11) 2689926; fax (11) 2688670; e-mail sahc_info@sltnet.lk; High Commissioner BUYISIWE MAUREEN PHETO.

Sweden: 49 Bullers Lane, POB 1072, Colombo 7; tel. (11) 4795400; fax (11) 4795450; e-mail ambassaden.colombo@foreign.ministry.se; internet www.swedenabroad.com/colombo; Chargé d'affaires BÖRJE MATTSSON.

Switzerland: 63 Gregory's Rd, POB 342, Colombo 7; tel. (11) 2695117; fax (11) 2695176; e-mail col.vertretung@eda.admin.ch; internet www.eda.admin.ch/colombo; Ambassador RUTH FLINT.

Thailand: Greenlanka Towers, 9th Floor, 46/46 Nawam Mawatha, Colombo 2; tel. (11) 2302500; fax (11) 2304511; e-mail thaicmb@sltnet.lk; internet www.thaiembassy.org/colombo; Ambassador THINAKORN KANASUTA.

United Arab Emirates: 44 Ernest de Silva Mawatha, Colombo 7; tel. (11) 2565052; fax (11) 2564104; Ambassador M. M. MOHAMOUD AL-MAHMOUD.

United Kingdom: 389 Bauddhaloka Mawatha, Colombo 7; tel. (11) 5390629; fax (11) 5390694; e-mail colombo.general@fco.gov.lk; internet www.ukinsrilanka.fco.gov.uk; High Commissioner Dr PETER HAYES.

USA: 210 Galle Rd, POB 106, Colombo 3; tel. (11) 2441272; fax (11) 2429070; internet srilanka.usembassy.gov; Ambassador ROBERT O. BLAKE.

Judicial System

The judicial system consists of the Supreme Court, the Court of Appeal, the High Court, District Courts, Magistrates' Courts and Primary Courts. The last four are Courts of the First Instance and appeals lie from them to the Court of Appeal and from there, on questions of law or by special leave, to the Supreme Court. The High Court deals with all criminal cases and the District Courts with civil cases. There are Labour Tribunals to decide labour disputes.

The Judicial Service Commission comprises the Chief Justice and two judges of the Supreme Court, nominated by the President. All judges of the Courts of First Instance (except High Court Judges) and the staff of all courts are appointed and controlled by the Judicial Service Commission. The Supreme Court consists of the Chief Justice and not fewer than six and not more than 10 other judges. The Court of Appeal consists of the President and not fewer than six and not more than 11 other judges.

Chief Justice of the Supreme Court: SARATH NANDA SILVA.

Attorney-General: MOHAN PIERIS.

Religion

According to the 2001 census, the distribution of the population by religion in 18 out of 25 districts was: Buddhist 76.7%, Muslim 8.5%, Hindu 7.9%, Roman Catholics 6.1% and other Christians 0.8%. The census results did not cover the Tamil-dominated northern and eastern districts, where a higher proportion of Hindus could be expected.

BUDDHISM

Theravada Buddhism is the predominant sect. There are an estimated 53,000 Buddhist *Bhikkhus* (monks), living in about 6,000 temples.

All Ceylon Buddhist Congress: 380 Bauddhaloka Mawatha, Colombo 7; tel. (11) 2688517; fax (11) 2691695; e-mail acbc@isplanka.lk; internet www.acbc.lk; f. 1919; Pres. JAGATH SUMATHIPALA; Jt Secs Maj.-Gen. (retd) JALIYA NAMMUNI, RANJITH EKANAYAKE.

Sri Lanka Regional Centre of the World Fellowship of Buddhists: 380 Bauddhaloka Mawatha, Colombo 7; tel. (11) 2681886; fax (11) 2833362; e-mail nationlanka@sltnet.lk; Pres. D. M. JAYATILAKA DISSANAYAKE; Sec. Prof. JAYANTHA WEERAKOON.

HINDUISM

The majority of the Tamil population are Hindus. According to the 2001 census the Hindu population in 18 out of 25 districts was 1,329,020.

CHRISTIANITY

National Christian Council of Sri Lanka: 368/6 Bauddhaloka Mawatha, Colombo 7; tel. (11) 2671723; fax (11) 2671721; e-mail sec@nccsl.org; internet www.nccsl.org; f. 1945; 13 mem. bodies; Gen. Sec. Rev. Dr JAYASIRI PEIRIS.

The Anglican Communion

The Church of Ceylon (Sri Lanka) comprises two Anglican dioceses. In 1985 there were about 78,000 adherents.

Bishop of Colombo: Rt Rev. DULEEP KAMIL DE CHICKERA, Bishop's House, 358/2 Bauddhaloka Mawatha, Colombo 7; tel. (11) 2684810; fax (11) 2684811; e-mail bishop@eureka.lk; diocese f. 1845.

Bishop of Kurunegala: Rt Rev. KUMARA BANDARA SAMUEL ILLANGASINGHE, Bishop's House, Kandy Rd, Kurunegala; tel. (37) 22191; fax (37) 26806; e-mail bishopkg@sltnet.lk; diocese f. 1950.

The Roman Catholic Church

For ecclesiastical purposes, Sri Lanka comprises one archdiocese and 10 dioceses. At 31 December 2007 there were an estimated 1,403,989 adherents in the country.

Catholic Bishops' Conference in Sri Lanka: 19 Balcombe Place, Cotta Rd, Borella, Colombo 8; tel. (11) 2697062; fax (11) 2699619; e-mail conferencesl@sltnet.lk; internet www.cbcsl.com; f. 1975; Pres. Most Rev. VIANNEY FERNANDO (Bishop of Kandy); Sec.-Gen. Rt Rev. Dr NORBERT M. ANDRADI.

Archbishop of Colombo: Most Rev. Dr OSWALD THOMAS COLMAN GOMIS, Archbishop's House, 976 Gnanartha Pradeepaya Mawatha, Colombo 8; tel. (11) 2695471; fax (11) 2692009; e-mail sunilde@sltnet.lk; internet www.archdioceseofcolombo.com.

The Church of South India

The Church comprises 21 dioceses, including one, Jaffna, in Sri Lanka. The diocese of Jaffna, with an estimated 18,500 adherents in 1997, was formerly part of the South India United Church (a union of churches of the Congregational and Presbyterian/Reformed traditions), which merged with the Methodist Church in South India and the four southern dioceses of the (Anglican) Church of India to form the Church of South India in 1947.

Bishop in Jaffna: Rt Rev. Dr DANIEL S. THIAGARAJAH, 36 5/2, Sinsapa Rd, Colombo 6; tel. (11) 2150795; fax (11) 2505805; e-mail bishop@csijaffnadiocese.com; internet csijaffnadiocese.com.

Other Christian Churches

Christian Reformed Church: General Consistory Office, 363 Galle Rd, Colombo 6; tel. (11) 2360861; fax (11) 2582469; e-mail drc1642@sltnet.lk; f. 1642; Pres. of Gen. Consistory Rev. N. ROSHAN MENDIS; Admin. Mgr GODFREY B. EBENEZER.

Methodist Church: Methodist Headquarters, 252 Galle Rd, Colombo 3; tel. (11) 2575630; fax (11) 2436090; e-mail methhq@sltnet.lk; internet www.gbgm-umc.org/methchsrilan; 30,139 mems (2000); Pres. of Conference Rev. W. P. EBENEZER JOSEPH; Sec. of Conference Rev. J. C. S. ROHITHA DE SILVA.

Other denominations active in the country include the Sri Lanka Baptist Sangamaya.

BAHÁ'Í FAITH

Spiritual Assembly: Bahá'í National Centre, 65 Havelock Rd, Colombo 5; tel. and fax (11) 2587360; e-mail nsasrilanka@sltnet.lk.

The Press

NEWSPAPERS

Newspapers are published in Sinhala, Tamil and English. There are five main newspaper publishing groups:

Associated Newspapers of Ceylon Ltd: Lake House, 35 D. R. Wijewardene Mawatha, POB 248, Colombo 10; tel. (11) 2435641; fax (11) 2449069; e-mail webmgr@sri.lanka.net; internet www.lakehouse.lk; f. 1926; nationalized 1973; publr of *Daily News*, *Evening Observer*, *Thinakaran*, *Lak Janatha* and *Dinamina* (dailies); three Sunday papers: *Sunday Observer*, *Silumina* and *Thinakaran Vaara Manjari*; and 11 periodicals; Chair. BANDULA PADMAKUMARA; CEO TIKIRI KOBBEKADUWA.

Express Newspapers (Ceylon) Ltd: 185 Grandpass Rd, POB 160, Colombo 14; tel. (11) 2323841; fax (11) 2439987; e-mail md@expressnewspapers.lk; internet www.virakesari.lk; f. 1930; publr of

SRI LANKA

Virakesari Daily, *Mithran Varamalar*, *Metro News* and *Virakesari Weekly* (Sunday); Chair. HARI SELVANATHAN; Man. Dir KUMAR NADESAN.

Leader Publications (Pvt) Ltd: 24 Katukurunduwatte Rd, Ratmalana; tel. (75) 2365892; fax (75) 2365891; e-mail editor@thesundayleader.lk; internet www.thesundayleader.lk; publr of *The Sunday Leader* and *Irida Peramuna*.

Upali Newspapers Ltd: 223 Bloemendhal Rd, POB 133, Colombo 13; tel. (11) 2497500; e-mail prabath@unl.upali.lk; f. 1981; publr of *The Island*, *Divaina* (dailies), two Sunday papers, *Sunday Island* and *Sunday Divaina*, four weeklies, *Vidusara*, *Navaliya*, *Bindu* and *The Island International* (for sale abroad only), and one bi-weekly, *Vathmana–News Magazine* ; English and Sinhala; Editor-in-Chief PRABATH SAHABANDU; Chair. LAKMENI WIJAYWARDANA WELGAMA.

Wijeya Newspapers Ltd: 8 Hunupitiya Cross Rd, Colombo 2; tel. (11) 2314714; fax (11) 2449504; e-mail pradeep@wijeya.lk; internet www.wijeya.lk; f. 1979; publr of *Daily Mirror*, *The Sunday Times*, *Lankadeepa*, *Irida Lankadeepa* and *Sirikatha*; Sinhala and English; Chair. RANJIT SUJIVA WIJEWARDENE.

Dailies

Daily Mirror: 8 Hunupitiya Cross Rd, Colombo 2; tel. (11) 2314714; fax (11) 2449504; e-mail mirror@wijeya.lk; internet www.dailymirror.lk; f. 1996; English and Sinhala; Editor CHAMPIKA LIYANAARACHCHI; circ. 30,000.

Daily News: Lake House, D. R. Wijewardene Mawatha, POB 248, Colombo 10; tel. (11) 2429429; fax (11) 2343694; e-mail editor@dailynews.lk; internet www.dailynews.lk; f. 1918; morning; English; Editor GEOFF WIJEYESINGHE; circ. 65,000.

Dinakara: 95 Maligakanda Rd, Colombo 10; tel. (11) 2595754; f. 1978; morning; Sinhala; publ. by Rekana Publrs; official organ of the Sri Lanka Freedom Party; Editor MULEN PERERA; circ. 12,000.

Dinamina: Lake House, D. R. Wijewardene Mawatha, POB 248, Colombo 10; tel. (11) 2221181; internet www.dinamina.lk; f. 1909; morning; Sinhala; Editor G. S. PERERA; circ. 140,000.

Divaina: 223 Bloemendhal Rd, POB 133, Colombo 13; tel. (11) 2224001; fax (11) 2448103; e-mail gamini@unl.upali.lk; internet www.divaina.com; f. 1982; morning and Sunday; Chief Editor GAMINI SUMANASEKERA.

Eelanadu: Jaffna; tel. (21) 22389; f. 1959; morning; Tamil; Chair. S. RAVEENTHIRANATHAN; Editor M. SIVANANTHAM; circ. 15,000.

The Island: 223 Bloemendhal Rd, Colombo 13; tel. (11) 2497574; fax (11) 2497543; e-mail prabath@unl.upali.lk; internet www.island.lk; f. 1981; English; Editor PRABATH SAHABANDU; circ. 80,000.

Lak Janatha: Lake House, D. R. Wijewardene Mawatha, Colombo 10; tel. (11) 2421181; f. 2005; evening; Sinhala; Editor SUJEEWA DISSANAYAKE.

Lankadeepa: 8 Hunupitiya Cross Rd, Colombo 2; tel. (11) 2448321; fax (11) 2438039; e-mail siri@wijeya.lk; internet www.lankadeepa.lk; f. 1986; Sinhala and English; Editor SIRI RANASINGHE; circ. 160,000.

Namathu Eelanadu: Jaffna; f. 2002; Tamil; Editor SIVASUBRAMANIAM RAGURAM.

Peraliya: Borella Supermarket Complex, 2nd Floor, Colombo 8; Editor SUJEEWA GAMAGE.

Thinakaran: Lake House, D. R. Wijewardene Mawatha, POB 248, Colombo 10; tel. (11) 2221181; internet www.thinakaran.lk; f. 1932; morning; Tamil; Editor R. SIVAGURUNATHAN; circ. daily 14,000.

Thinakkural: 68 Ellie House Rd, Colombo 15; internet www.thinakkural.com; Tamil; also publ. from Jaffna; Editor A. SIYANESACHELVAN.

Uthayan: Jaffna; e-mail uthayandaily@gmail.com; internet www.uthayan.com; Tamil; Chief Editor M. V. KAANAMYLNATHAN; circ. 22,000.

Valampuri: 3, 2nd Lane, Brown Rd, Jaffna; tel. (21) 2227829; fax (21) 2223378; e-mail valampurii@yahoo.com; f. 1999; Tamil; Chief Editor N. VIJAYASUNTHARAM.

Virakesari Daily: 185 Grandpass Rd, POB 160, Colombo 14; tel. (11) 2320881; fax (11) 2439987; e-mail kesari10@virakesari.lk; internet www.virakesari.lk; f. 1931; morning; Tamil; Man. Dir KUMAR NADESAN; Editor R. PRABAGAN; circ. 60,000.

Sunday Newspapers

Irida Lankadeepa: 8 Hunupitiya Cross Rd, Colombo 2; tel. (11) 2448321; fax (11) 2438039; e-mail siri@wijeya.lk; internet www.lankadeepa.lk; Sinhala; Chief Editor SIRI RANSINGHE.

Janasathiya: 47 Jayantha Weerasekara Mawatha, Colombo 10; f. 1965; Sinhala; publ. by Suriya Publishers Ltd; Editor SARATH NAWANA; circ. 50,000.

Mithran Varamalar: 185 Grandpass Rd, Colombo 14; tel. (11) 2320881; fax (11) 2448205; e-mail kesari25@virasekari.lk; internet www.virakesari.lk; f. 1969; Tamil; Man. Dir KUMAR NADESAN; Editor V. THEVARAJ; circ. 29,000.

Silumina: Lake House, 35 D. R. Wijewardene Mawatha, Colombo 10; tel. (11) 2324772; fax (11) 2449069; e-mail editor@silumina.lk; internet www.silumina.lk; f. 1930; Sinhala; Editor NIWAL HORANA; circ. 264,000.

Sunday Island: 223 Bloemendhal Rd, POB 133, Colombo 13; tel. (11) 2421599; fax (74) 2497543; e-mail manik@unl.upali.lk; f. 1981; English; Editor MANIK DE SILVA; circ. 40,000.

The Sunday Leader: 24 Katukurunduwatte Rd, Ratmalana; tel. (75) 2365892; fax (75) 2365891; e-mail editor@thesundayleader.lk; internet www.thesundayleader.lk; English; Editor (vacant).

Sunday Observer: D. R. Wijewardene Mawatha, POB 248, Colombo 10; tel. (11) 2429231; fax (11) 2429230; e-mail editor@sundayobserver.lk; internet www.sundayobserver.lk; f. 1923; English; Editor JAYATILLEKE DE SILVA; circ. 125,000.

Sunday Thinakkural: 68 Ellie House Rd, Colombo 15; internet www.thinakkural.com/sundaythinakkural; Tamil; also publ. from Jaffna; Editor A. SIYANESACHELVAN.

The Sunday Times: 8 Hunupitiya Cross Rd, Colombo 2; tel. (11) 2326247; fax (11) 2423922; e-mail editor@sundaytimes.wnl.lk; internet www.sundaytimes.lk; f. 1986; English and Sinhala; Editor SINGHA RATNATUNGA; circ. 116,000.

Thinakaran Vaara Manjari: Lake House, 35 D. R. Wijewardene Mawatha, Colombo 10; tel. (11) 2221181; f. 1948; Tamil; Editor R. SRIKANTHAN; circ. 35,000.

Virakesari Weekly: 185 Grandpass Rd, Colombo 14; tel. (11) 2320881; fax (11) 2448205; e-mail webmaster@virakesari.lk; internet www.virakesari.lk; f. 1931; Tamil and English; Man. Dir KUMAR NADESAN; Editor MURUGESAMPILLAI SUBRAMANIAM; circ. 110,000.

PERIODICALS
(weekly unless otherwise stated)

Athavan: Colombo; Tamil.

Aththa: 91 Dr N. M. Perera Mawatha, Colombo 8; tel. (11) 2691450; fax (11) 2691610; e-mail dew128@dialogsl.net; f. 1964; Sinhala; publ. by the Communist Party of Sri Lanka; Editor GUNASENA VITHANA; circ. 28,000.

Business Lanka: Trade Information Service, Sri Lanka Export Development Board, Level 7, 42 Navam Mawatha, POB 1872, Colombo 2; tel. (11) 2300677; fax (11) 2300715; e-mail tisinfo@tradenetsl.lk; f. 1981; quarterly; information for visiting business executives, etc.; Editor S. D. ISAAC.

Ceylon Commerce: National Chamber of Commerce of Sri Lanka, NCCSL Bldg, 450 D. R. Wijewardene Mawatha, POB 1375, Colombo 10; tel. (11) 2689597; fax (11) 2689596; e-mail nccsl@slt.lk; monthly.

Ceylon Medical Journal: 6 Wijerama Mawatha, Colombo 7; tel. (11) 2693324; fax (11) 2698802; e-mail office@cmj.slma.lk; internet www.cmj.slma.lk; f. 1887; quarterly; Editors Prof. H. JANAKA DE SILVA, Dr A. ABEYGUNASEKERA.

The Economic Times: 130/C/8 Jothikarama Mawatha, Kalalgoda, Pannipitiya; tel. (11) 2796134; fax (11) 4305787; f. 1970; Editor THIMSY FAHIM.

The Financial Times: 323 Union Place, POB 330, Colombo 2; tel. (11) 2226181; quarterly; commercial and economic affairs; Man. Editor CYRIL GARDINER.

Gnanarthapradeepaya: Colombo Catholic Press, 2 Gnanarthapradeepaya Mawatha, Borella, Colombo 8; tel. (11) 2695984; fax (11) 2692586; e-mail pradeepaya@sltnet.lk; f. 1866; Sinhala; Roman Catholic; Chief Editor Rev. Fr CYRIL GAMINI FERNANDO; Exec. Dir Rev. Fr ROHAN DE ALWIS; circ. 26,000.

Irudina: Lithira Publications (Pvt) Ltd, 98 Ward Place, Colombo 7; tel. (11) 5344202; fax (11) 5344200; e-mail editor@irudina.lk; internet www.irudina.lk; f. 2004; Sinhala; Editor MOHAN LAL PIYADASA.

Janakavi: 47 Jayantha Weerasekera Mawatha, Colombo 10; fortnightly; Sinhala; Assoc. Editor KARUNARATNE AMERASINGHE.

Manasa: 150 Dutugemunu St, Dehiwala, Colombo; tel. (11) 2553994; f. 1978; Sinhala; monthly; science of the mind; Editor SUMANADASA SAMARASINGHE; circ. 6,000.

Mihira: Lake House, 35 D. R. Wijewardene Mawatha, Colombo 10; tel. (11) 2419583; f. 1964; Sinhala children's magazine; Editor M. NEWTON PINTO; circ. 145,000.

Morning Star: 39 Fussels Lane, Colombo 6; tel. (11) 2511233; fax (11) 2584836; e-mail jdcsiacm@panlanka.net; f. 1841; English and Tamil; publ. by the Jaffna diocese of the Church of South India.

Nava Yugaya: Lake House, 35 D. R. Wijewardene Mawatha, Colombo 10; tel. (11) 2419581; f. 1956; literary fortnightly; Sinhala; Editor SUJEEWA DISSANAYAKE; circ. 57,000.

SRI LANKA

Navaliya: 223 Bloemendhal Rd, Colombo 13; tel. (11) 2324001; fax (11) 2448103; internet www.navaliya.com; Sinhala; women's interest; Editor CHANDANI WIJETUNGE; circ. 148,260.

Pathukavalan: POB 2, Jaffna; tel. (21) 22300; f. 1876; Tamil; publ. by St Joseph's Catholic Press; Editor Rev. Fr RUBAN MARIAMPILLAI; circ. 7,000.

Puthiya Ulaham: 115 4th Cross St, Jaffna; tel. (21) 22627; f. 1976; Tamil; six a year; publ. by Centre for Better Society; Editor Rev. Dr S. J. EMMANUEL; circ. 1,500.

Ravaya: Colombo; Sinhala; Editor VICTOR IVAN.

Samajawadhaya: 91 Dr N. M. Perera Mawatha, Colombo 8; tel. (11) 2595328; monthly; theoretical; publ. by the Communist Party of Sri Lanka.

Sarasaviya: Lake House, 35 D. R. Wijewardene Mawatha, Colombo 10; tel. (11) 2429586; internet www.sarasaviya.lk; f. 1963; Sinhala; films; Editor GRANVILLE SILVA; circ. 56,000.

Sinhala Bauddhaya: Maha Bodhi Mandira, 130 Rev. Hikkaduwe Sri Sumangala Nahimi Mawatha, Colombo 10; tel. and fax (11) 1677626; e-mail mahabodhi@asia.com; f. 1906; publ. by The Maha Bodi Society of Ceylon; Hon. Sec. KIRTHI KALAHE; circ. 25,000.

Sirikatha: 8 Hunupitiya Cross Rd, Colombo 2; tel. (11) 2314714; fax (11) 2449504; Sinhala women's magazine; Editor SIRI RANASINGHE.

Sri Lanka Government Gazette: Government Press, POB 507, Colombo; tel. (11) 2293611; f. 1802; Sinhala and Tamil; official govt bulletin; circ. 54,000.

Sri Lanka Today: Government Dept of Information, 7 Sir Baron Jayatilaka Mawatha, Colombo 1; tel. (11) 2228376; English; quarterly; Editor MANEL ABHAYARATNE.

Subasetha: Lake House, 35 D. R. Wijewardene Mawatha, Colombo 10; tel. (11) 2221181; internet www.subasetha.lk; f. 1967; Sinhala; astrology, the occult and indigenous medicine; Editor Capt. K. CHANDRA SRI KULARATNE; circ. 100,000.

Tharunee: Lake House, 35 D. R. Wijewardene Mawatha, Colombo 10; tel. (11) 2429588; fax (11) 2449069; f. 1969; Sinhala; women's journal; Editor SUMANA SAPRAMADU; circ. 95,000.

Vidusara: 223 Bloemendhal Rd, Colombo 13; tel. (11) 2324001; fax (11) 2448103; internet www.vidusara.com; Sinhala; Editor ANURA SIRIWARDENA; circ. 103,992.

NEWS AGENCIES

Lankapuvath (National News Agency of Sri Lanka): 30/75A, Longdon Pl., Colombo 07; tel. (11) 2585927; fax (11) 2585930; e-mail office@lankapuvath.net; internet www.lankapuvath.lk; f. 1978; Chair. PRADEEP GUNAWARDENA; Editor G. L. W. WIJESINHA.

TamilNet: e-mail tamilnet@tamilnet.com; internet www.tamilnet.com; f. 1997; reports on Tamil affairs.

PRESS ASSOCIATIONS

Foreign Correspondents' Association of Sri Lanka: 20 1/1 Regent Flats, Sir Chittampalan Gardiner Mawatha, Colombo; tel. (11) 2231224.

Sri Lanka Press Association: Colombo; Pres. B. H. S. JAYEWARDENE.

Publishers

W. E. Bastian and Co (Pvt) Ltd: 23 Canal Row, Fort, Colombo 1; tel. (11) 2432752; f. 1904; art, literature, technical; Dirs H. A. MUNIDEVA, K. HEWAGE, N. MUNIDEVA, G. C. BASTIAN.

Buddhist Publication Society: 54 Sangaraja Mawatha, POB 61, Kandy; tel. (81) 2237283; fax (81) 2238901; e-mail bps@sltnet.lk; internet www.bps.lk; f. 1958; philosophy, religion and theology; Pres. Bhikkhu BODHI; Editor BHIKKU NYANATUSITA.

Colombo Catholic Press: 2 Gnanarthapradeepaya Mawatha, Borella, Colombo 8; tel. (11) 2678106; fax (11) 2692586; e-mail colombocp@sltnet.lk; f. 1865; religious; publrs of *The Messenger*, *Gnanarthapradeepaya*, *The Weekly*; Exec. Dir Rev. Fr ROHAN DE ALWIS.

M. D. Gunasena and Co Ltd: 217 Olcott Mawatha, POB 246, Colombo 11; tel. (11) 2323981; fax (11) 2323336; e-mail publishingmgr@mdgunasena.com; internet www.mdgunasena.com; f. 1913; educational and general; Chair M. D. PERCY GUNASENA; Man. Dir M. D. ANANDA GUNASENA.

Lake House Printers and Publishers Ltd: 41 W. A. D. Ramanayake Mawatha, POB 1458, Colombo 2; tel. (11) 2433271; fax (11) 2449504; e-mail wnl@wijeya.lk; f. 1965; Chair. R. S. WIJEWARDENE; Sec. D. P. ANURA NISHANTHA KUMARA.

Pradeepa Publishers: 34/34 Lawyers' Office Complex, Colombo 12; tel. and fax (11) 2435074; academic and fictional; Propr K. JAYATILAKE.

Saman Publishers Ltd: 49/16 Iceland Bldg, Colombo 3; tel. (11) 2223058; fax (11) 2447972.

Sarexpo International Ltd: Caves Bookshop, 81 Sir Baron Jayatilleke Mawatha, POB 25, Colombo 1; tel. (11) 2422676; fax (11) 2447854; e-mail sarexpo@eureka.lk; f. 1876; history, arts, law, medicine, technical, educational; Man. Dir C. J. S. FERNANDO.

K. V. G. de Silva and Sons (Colombo) Ltd: Shop No. 5, Liberty Plaza, Colombo 3; tel. (11) 7455646; fax (11) 7555543; f. 1898; art, philosophy, scientific, technical, academic, 'Ceyloniana', fiction; Man. FREDERICK JAYARATNAM.

PUBLISHERS' ASSOCIATION

Sri Lanka Association of Publishers: 112 S. Mahinda Mawatha, Maradana, Colombo 10; tel. (11) 2695773; fax (11) 2696653; Pres. DAYAWANSA JAYAKODY; Sec.-Gen. GAMINI WIJESURIYA.

Broadcasting and Communications

TELECOMMUNICATIONS

Dialog Telekom PLC: 475 Union Pl., Colombo 2; tel. (11) 7678678; fax (11) 2678692; e-mail dialog@dialog.lk; internet www.dialog.lk; operates Dialog GSM, Sri Lanka's largest mobile telephone network; Chief Exec. Dr SHRIDHIR SARIPUTTA HANSA WIJAYASURIYA.

Lanka Communication Services (Pvt) Ltd: 65C Dharmapala Mawatha, Colombo 7; tel. (11) 2437545; fax (11) 2537547; e-mail webmaster@lankacom.net; internet www.lankacom.net; f. 1991; subsidiary of Singapore Telecom International; Man. Dir ROHITH UDALAGAMA.

Sri Lanka Telecom Ltd: Telecom Headquarters, 7th Floor, Lotus Rd, POB 503, Colombo 1; tel. (11) 2329711; fax (11) 2440000; e-mail pr@slt.lk; internet www.slt.lk; 35% owned by Nippon Telegraph and Telephone Corpn (Japan), 49.5% by Govt of Sri Lanka and 3.5% by employees; Chair. LEISHA DE SILVA CHANDRASENA.

Regulatory Authority

Telecommunications Regulatory Commission of Sri Lanka: 276 Elvitigala Mawatha, Manning Town, Colombo 8; tel. (11) 2689345; fax (11) 2689341; e-mail dgtsl@trc.gov.lk; internet www.trc.gov.lk; f. 1996; Chair. LALITH WEERATHUNGA; Dir-Gen. PRIYANTHA KARIYAPPERUMA.

RADIO

Sri Lanka Broadcasting Corpn: Independence Sq., POB 574, Colombo 7; tel. (11) 2697491; fax (11) 2691568; e-mail dg@slbc.lk; internet www.slbc.lk; f. 1967; under Ministry of Information and Media; controls all broadcasting in Sri Lanka; regional stations at Anuradhapura, Kandy and Matara; transmitting stations at Ambewela, Amparai, Anuradhapura, Diyagama, Ekala, Galle, Kanthalai, Mahiyangana, Maho, Matara, Puttalam, Ratnapura, Seeduwa, Senkadagala, Weeraketiya; home service in Sinhala, Tamil and English; foreign service also in Tamil, English, Sinhala, Hindi, Kannada, Malayalam, Nepali and Telugu; 893 broadcasting hours per week: 686 on domestic services, 182 on external services and 126 on education; Chair. HUDSON SAMARASINGHE; Dir-Gen. SAMANTHA WELIWERIYA.

Asura FM: No. 52, 5th Lane, Colombo 3; tel. (11) 2575000; fax (11) 2301082; internet www.asurafm.com; broadcasts 24 hrs daily in Sinhala; Chair. NIRAJ WICKREMESINGHE.

Colombo Communications (Pvt) Ltd: 686 Galle Rd, Colombo 3; tel. (11) 5577777; fax (11) 2505796; e-mail info@efm.lk; internet www.efm.lk; commercial station; three channels broadcast 24 hrs daily in English, Sinhala and Tamil.

Lite FM: No. 52, 5th Lane, Colombo 3; tel. (11) 2575000; fax (11) 2301082; e-mail litefm@tnlradio.com; internet www.litefm.me; f. 1999; commercial station; broadcasts 24 hrs daily in English; Chair. NIRAJ WICKREMESINGHE.

MBC Networks (Pvt) Ltd: 7 Braybrooke Place, Colombo 2; tel. (11) 5340111; fax (11) 5340116; e-mail info@media.maharaja.lk; internet www.capitalmaharaja.com; commercial station comprising four channels; broadcasts 24 hrs daily in English, Sinhala and Tamil; Dir NEDRA WEERASINGHE.

TNL Radio: No. 52, 5th Lane, Colombo 3; tel. (11) 2575000; fax (11) 2301082; internet www.tnlrocks.com; f. 1993; commercial station; broadcasts 24 hrs daily in English; Chair. NIRAJ WICKREMESINGHE.

Trans World Radio: Orchid Pl., off Swarnadisi Pl., Koswatte, Nawala; tel. (5) 559321; fax (11) 2877750; e-mail rkoch@twr.org; internet www.twr.org; f. 1978; religious station; broadcasts 2–3 hrs

SRI LANKA

every morning and six and a half hrs each evening to Indian subcontinent; Dir (Finance/Administration) ROGER KOCH; Eng. P. VELMURUGAN.

TELEVISION

Sri Lanka Rupavahini Corpn (SLRC): Independence Sq., POB 2204, Colombo 7; tel. (11) 2587722; fax (11) 2580929; e-mail ict@rupavahini.lk; internet www.rupavahini.lk; f. 1982; studio at Colombo; transmitting stations at nine locations; broadcasts 18 hrs daily on Channel I, 15 hrs daily on Channel II; Chair. and Dir-Gen. ARIYARATNE ATHUGALA.

Independent Television Network (ITN): Wickremasinghepura, Battaramulla; tel. (11) 2774424; fax (11) 2774591; e-mail itn@slt.lk; internet www.itn.lk; broadcasts about 19 hrs daily; operates Lakhanda Radio (24 hrs; daily); Chair. ANURA SIRIWARDENA; Gen. Man. W. P. A. M. WIJESINGHE.

EAP Network (Pvt) Ltd: 676 Galle Rd, Colombo 3; tel. (11) 2503819; fax (11) 2503788; e-mail eapnet@slt.lk; Chair. SOMA EDIRISINGHE; Man. Dir JEEVAKA EDIRISINGHE.

MTV Channel (Pvt) Ltd: Araliya Uyana, Depanama, Pannipitiya; tel. (11) 5340111; e-mail info@media.maharaja.lk; internet www.capitalmaharaja.com/mtvchannels.html; f. 1992; broadcasts on three channels in English, Sinhala and Tamil.

National Television of Tamil Eelam (NTT): e-mail ntt_news@yahoo.com; f. 2005; broadcasts for two hrs daily.

Telshan Network (Pvt) Ltd (TNL): 9D Tower Bldg, 25 Station Rd, Colombo 4; tel. (11) 2596241; fax (11) 2706125; e-mail tnltvr@slt.lk; Chair. and Man. Dir SHANTILAL NILKANT WICKREMESINGHE.

Finance

(cap. = capital; res = reserves; dep. = deposits; m. = million; brs = branches; amounts in Sri Lanka rupees, unless otherwise indicated)

BANKING
Central Bank

Central Bank of Sri Lanka: 30 Janadhipathi Mawatha, POB 590, Colombo 1; tel. (11) 2477000; fax (11) 2477712; e-mail cbslgen@cbsl.lk; internet www.cbsl.gov.lk; f. 1950; sole bank of issue; cap. US $138,058m., res US $943.8m., dep. US $1,359.2m. (Dec. 2008); Gov. and Chair. of the Monetary Board AJITH NIVARD CABRAAL; Dep. Govs Dr RANEE JAYAMAHA, W. A. WIJEWARDENA, M. A. R. C. COORAY; 3 regional offices.

Commercial Banks

Bank of Ceylon: 4 Bank of Ceylon Mawatha, POB 241, Colombo 1; tel. (11) 2446811; fax (11) 2447171; e-mail boc@boc.lk; internet www.boc.lk; f. 1939; 100% state-owned; cap. 4,000m., res 3,614m., dep. 310,923.6m. (Dec. 2006); Chair. Dr GAMINI WICKRAMASINGHE; Gen. Man. B. A. C. FERNANDO; 303 brs in Sri Lanka, 3 brs abroad.

Commercial Bank of Ceylon PLC: Commercial House, 21 Bristol St, POB 856, Colombo 1; tel. (11) 2430416; fax (11) 2449889; e-mail e-mail@combank.net; internet www.combank.net; f. 1969; 29.77% owned by DFCC Bank, 29.91% by govt corpns and 40.32% by public; cap. 20,514.8m., res 13,421.2m., dep. 206,452.2m. (Dec. 2007); Chair. M. J. C. AMARASURIYA; Man. Dir A. L. GOONERATNE; 136 brs.

Hatton National Bank Ltd: 479 T. B. Jayah Mawatha, POB 837, Colombo 10; tel. (11) 2664664; fax (11) 2446523; e-mail moreinfo@hnb.net; internet www.hnb.net; f. 1970; 27.1% owned by individuals, 72.9% by institutions; cap. 5,059.4m., res 10,612.2m., dep. 182,894.3m. (Dec. 2007); Chair. RIENZIE T. WIJETILLEKE; Man. Dir and CEO RAJENDRA THEAGARAJAH; 160 brs.

Nations Trust Bank Ltd: 242 Union Place, Colombo 2; tel. (11) 4313131; fax (11) 2307854; e-mail info@nationstrust.com; internet www.nationstrust.com; f. 1999; privately owned; acquired Mercantile Leasing Ltd by merger to form Nations Leasing business; cap. 2,061.6m., res 517.3m., dep. 30,559.5m. (Dec. 2007); Chair. AJIT GUNEWARDENE; CEO ZULFIQAR ZAVAHIR.

Pan Asia Banking Corpn Ltd: 450 Galle Rd, Colombo 3; tel. (11) 2565556; fax (11) 2565558; e-mail pabc@pabcbank.com; internet www.pabcbank.com; f. 1995; 100% privately-owned (82.9% owned by local shareholders, 17.1% by foreign shareholders); cap. 1,106.4m., res 128.7m., dep. 10,082.5m. (Dec. 2006); Chair. A. G. WEERASINGHE; Man. Dir and CEO KIMARLI FERNANDO; 18 brs.

People's Bank: 75 Sir Chittampalam A. Gardiner Mawatha, POB 728, Colombo 2; tel. (11) 2327841; fax (11) 2433127; e-mail info@peoplesbank.lk; internet www.peoplesbank.lk; f. 1961; 92% owned by Govt, 8% by co-operatives; cap. 4,202.0m. (incl. special lending rights 4,152.0m. capital pending allotment), res 6,254.4m., dep. 269,947.2m. (Dec. 2006); Chair. W. KARUNAJEEWA; CEO and Gen. Man. P. V. PATHIRANA; 324 brs.

Sampath Bank Ltd: Sampath Centre Bldg, 110 Sir James Peiris Mawatha, POB 997, Colombo 2; tel. (11) 2303050; fax (11) 2303085; e-mail info@sampath.lk; internet www.sampath.lk; f. 1987; cap. 1,581.7m., res 6,987.4m., dep. 100,614.4m. (Dec. 2007); Chair. I. W. SENANAYAKE; Exec. Dir/CEO HARRIS PREMARATNE; 100 brs.

Seylan Bank PLC: Ceylinco Seylan Towers, 90 Galle Rd, POB 400, Colombo 3; tel. (11) 2456789; fax (11) 2456456; e-mail info@seylan.lk; internet www.eseylan.com; f. 1988 as Seylan Bank Ltd; cap. 2,542.4m., res 4,493.8m., dep. 114,421.3m. (Dec. 2007); Chair. EASTMAN NARANGODA; Exec. Dir R. NADARAJAH; 116 brs.

Union Bank of Colombo Ltd: 15A Alfred Place, Colombo 3; tel. (11) 2370870; fax (11) 2370692; e-mail ubc@unionb.com; internet www.unionb.com; f. 1995; cap. 1,630.0m., res 10.5m., dep. 8,932.5m. (Dec. 2007); Chair. AJITA DE ZOYSA; CEO and Dir MAHENDRA FERNANDO.

Development Banks

Agricultural and Industrial Credit Corpn of Ceylon: POB 20, Colombo 3; tel. (11) 2223783; f. 1943; loan cap. 30m.; Chair. V. P. VITTACHI; Gen. Man. H. S. F. GOONEWARDENA.

DFCC Bank: 73/5 Galle Rd, POB 1397, Colombo 3; tel. (11) 2442442; fax (11) 2440376; e-mail info@dfccbank.com; internet www.dfccbank.com; f. 1956 as Development Finance Corpn of Ceylon; name changed as above 1997; provides long- and medium-term credit, investment banking and consultancy services; cap. 1,302.0m., res 11,661.2m., dep. 7,811.5m. (March 2008); Chair. RAJAN BRITO; Gen. Man. and CEO NIHAL FONSEKA; 3 brs.

National Development Bank Ltd: DHPL Bldg, 42 Nawam Mawatha, POB 1825, Colombo 2; tel. (11) 2314640; fax (11) 2314642; e-mail contact@ndbbank.com; internet www.ndbbank.com; f. 1979 by an Act of Parliament as National Development Bank of Sri Lanka; subsequently privatized and name changed as above in June 2005; provides long-term finance for projects, equity financing and merchant banking services; cap. 818.6m., res 7,736.2m., dep. 27,183.1 (Dec. 2006); Chair. P. M. NAGAHAWATTE; CEO ERAN WICKRAMARATNE.

State Mortgage and Investment Bank: 269 Galle Road, POB 156, Colombo 3; tel. (11) 2573561; fax (11) 2573346; e-mail agmit@smib.lk; internet www.smib.lk; f. 1979; Chair. CHANDIMA WEERAKKODY; Gen. Man. AJITH WEERASINHE.

Merchant Banks

Merchant Bank of Sri Lanka Ltd: Bank of Ceylon Merchant Tower, 28 St Michael's Rd, POB 1987, Colombo 3; tel. (11) 4711711; fax (11) 2565666; e-mail mbslbank@mbslbank.com; internet www.mbslbank.com; f. 1982; 53.8% owned by Bank of Ceylon; public ltd liability co; cap. p.u. 2,500m., total assets 2,128m. (2003); Chair. JANAKA RATNAYAKE; CEO GAMINI KARUNATHILEKA; 3 brs.

People's Merchant Bank Ltd: Hemas House, Level 2, 75 Braybrooke Place, Colombo 2; tel. (11) 2300191; fax (11) 2300190; e-mail pmbank@sltnet.lk; internet www.pmblk.com; f. 1984 as a subsidiary of People's Bank; Chair. Dr G. FERNANDO.

Financial Association

The Finance Houses' Association of Sri Lanka: 181/1A Dharmapala Mawatha, Colombo 7; tel. (11) 2665865; fax (11) 2665864; e-mail finass@sltnet.lk; f. 1958; represents the finance cos registered and licensed by the Central Bank of Sri Lanka; Chair. SHILEY PERERA; Sec.-Gen. DENNIS VISWASAM.

STOCK EXCHANGES

Securities and Exchange Commission of Sri Lanka: 11–01 East Tower, 28th and 29th Floors, World Trade Centre, Echelon Sq., Colombo 1; tel. (11) 2439144; fax (11) 2439149; e-mail mail@sec.gov.lk; internet www.sec.gov.lk; f. 1987; Dir-Gen. CHANNA DE SILVA; Chair. UDAYASRI KARIYAWASAM.

Colombo Stock Exchange: 04–01, West Block, World Trade Centre, Echelon Sq., Colombo 1; tel. (11) 2446581; fax (11) 2445279; e-mail cse@cse.lk; internet www.cse.lk; f. 1896; stock market; 21 mem. firms and 234 listed cos; Chair. A. N. FONSEKA; CEO SUREKHA SELLAHEWA.

INSURANCE

Ceylinco Insurance Co Ltd: Ceylinco House, 4th Floor, 69 Janadhipathi Mawatha, Colombo 1; tel. (11) 2485757; fax (11) 2485769; e-mail jagath@lanka.com.lk; internet www.ceylinco-insurance.com; f. 1987; general and life insurance; Chair. and Man. Dir J. L. B. KOTELAWALA.

Eagle Insurance Co Ltd: 'Eagle House', 75 Kumaran Ratnam Rd, Colombo 2; tel. (11) 2437090; fax (11) 2447620; e-mail info@eagle.com.lk; internet www.eagle.com.lk; f. 1988 as CTC Eagle Insurance Co Ltd; general and life insurance; mem. of Aviva International Holdings Ltd; Man. Dir DEEPAL SOORIYAARACHCHI.

SRI LANKA   *Directory*

Hayleys PLC: Hayley Bldg, 400 Deans Rd, Colombo 10; tel. (11) 2695729; fax (11) 2699299; internet www.hayleys.com; f. 1952; Chair. N. G. WICKREMERATNE; Dep. Chair. A. M. PANDITHAGE.

National Insurance Corpn Ltd: 47 Muttiah Rd, POB 2202, Colombo 2; tel. (11) 2445738; fax (11) 2445733; e-mail nicopl@slt.lk; general; Chair. T. M. S. NANAYAKKARA; Sec. A. C. J. DE ALWIS.

Sri Lanka Insurance Corporation Ltd: 'Rakshana Mandiraya', 21 Vauxhall St, POB 1337, Colombo 2; tel. (11) 2357537; fax (11) 2447742; e-mail slic@srilankainsurance.com; internet www.srilankainsurance.com; f. 1961; privatized in 2003; all classes of insurance; Chair. D. H. S. JAYAWARDENE; CEO NALAKA GODAHEWA.

Union Assurance Ltd: Union Assurance Centre, 20 St Michael's Rd, Colombo 3; tel. (11) 2428428; fax (11) 2343065; e-mail unionassurance@ualink.lk; internet www.ualink.lk; f. 1987; general and life insurance; Chair. AJIT GUNEWARDENE; CEO MARINA THARMARATNAM.

Trade and Industry

GOVERNMENT AGENCIES

Board of Investment of Sri Lanka: World Trade Centre, West Tower, 26th Floor, Echelon Sq., Colombo 1; tel. (11) 2435027; fax (11) 2422407; e-mail infoboi@boi.lk; internet www.boi.lk; f. 1978 as the Greater Colombo Economic Commission; promotes foreign direct investment and administers the eight Export Processing Zones at Katunayake, Biyagama, Koggala, Mirigama, Malwatta, Horana, Mawathagama and Polgahawela; also administers industrial township at Watupitiwala and industrial parks at Seetawaka and Kandy; Chair. and Dir-Gen. DHAMMIKA PERERA.

Public Enterprises Reform Commission (PERC): World Trade Centre, West Tower, 11th Floor, Colombo 1; tel. (11) 2346831; fax (11) 2326116; e-mail info@perc.gov.lk; f. 1995 to advise Govt on privatization and restructuring of loss-making state-sector enterprises and to promote national economic development; Chair. W. M. BANDUSENA; Dir-Gen. LEEL WICKREMARACHCHI.

Sri Lanka Gem and Jewellery Exchange: World Trade Centre, East Low Block, Levels 4 and 5, Echelon Sq., Colombo 1; tel. (11) 2390645; fax (11) 2390648; e-mail gemautho@sltnet.lk; internet www.srilankagemautho.com; f. 1990; testing and certification of gems, trading booths; Dir-Gen. D. L. P. R. ABEYARATNE.

National Gem and Jewellery Authority: 25 Galle Face Terrace, Colombo 3; tel. and fax (11) 2390650; fax (11) 2329352; e-mail chngja@sltnet.lk; internet www.srilankagemautho.com; f. 1971 as State Gem Corpn; Chair. W. HASITHA TILLEKERATNE; Dir-Gen. S. J. S. CHANDRAGUPTHA.

Trade Information Service: Sri Lanka Export Development Board, Level 7, 42 Navam Mawatha, POB 1872, Colombo 2; tel. (11) 2300675; fax (11) 2300676; e-mail tisinfo@edb.tradenetsl.lk; internet www.srilankabusiness.com; f. 1981 to collect and disseminate commercial information and to provide advisory services to trade circles; Dir W. M. D. S. WEERAKOON.

DEVELOPMENT ORGANIZATIONS

Coconut Development Authority: 54 Nawala Rd, Narahenpita, POB 1572, Colombo 5; tel. (11) 2502502; fax (11) 2508729; e-mail info@cda.lk; internet www.cda.lk; f. 1972; state body; promotes the coconut industry through financial assistance for mfrs of coconut products, market information, consultancy services and quality assurance; Chair. D. J. U. PURASINGHE.

Industrial Development Board of Ceylon (IDB): 615 Galle Rd, Katubedda, POB 09, Moratuwa; tel. (11) 2605326; fax (11) 2607002; e-mail idb@sltnet.lk; internet www.idb.lk; f. 1969; under Ministry of Rural Industries and Self Employment Promotion; promotes industrial development through provincial network; Chair. GAMINI GUNADESA; Gen. Man. A. M. Y. J. MANAPPERUMA.

Centre for Entrepreneurship Development and Consultancy Services: 615 Galle Rd, Katubedda, POB 09, Moratuwa; tel. (11) 2632156; f. 1989; Dir T. M. KULARATHNE (acting).

Centre for Industrial and Technology Information Services (CITIS): 615 Galle Rd, Katubedda, POB 09, Moratuwa 10400; tel. (11) 2605326; fax (11) 2607002; e-mail idb@sltnet.lk; internet www.idb.lk; f. 1989; disseminates information to small and medium-sized enterprises; Chair. GAMINI GUNADESA.

Information and Communication Technology Association of Sri Lanka (ICTA): 160/24 Kirimandala Mawatha, Colombo 5; tel. (11) 2369100; fax (11) 2369091; e-mail info@icta.lk; internet www.icta.lk; f. 2003; govt-owned; responsible for development of information communication technology in Sri Lanka; Chair. Prof. P. W. EPASINGHE (acting).

Janatha Estates Development Board: 55/75 Vauxhall St, Colombo 2; tel. (11) 2320901; fax (11) 2446577; f. 1975; manages 18 tea and spice plantations; 10,164 employees; 1 regional office.

Sri Lanka Export Development Board: Trade Information Service, Level 7, 42 Navam Mawatha, Colombo 2; tel. (11) 2300705; fax (11) 2300715; e-mail tisinfo@edb.tradenetsl.lk; internet www.tradenetsl.lk/edb; f. 1979; Chair. ROHANTHA ATHUKORALA.

CHAMBERS OF COMMERCE

Federation of Chambers of Commerce and Industry of Sri Lanka: 53 Vauxhall Lane, 3rd Floor, Colombo 2; tel. (11) 2304253; fax (11) 2304255; e-mail fccisl@fccisl.lk; internet www.fccisl.lk; f. 1973; a central org. of 53 chambers of commerce and industry and trade asscns representing 12,500 cos throughout Sri Lanka; Pres. KOSALA WICKRAMANAYAKE; Sec.-Gen. SAMANTHA ABEYWICKRAMA.

All Ceylon Trade Chamber: 212/45 1/3 Bodhiraja Mawatha, Colombo 11; tel. (11) 2432428; Pres. MUDLIYAR N. W. J. MUDALIGE; Gen. Sec. Y. P. MUTHUKUMARANA.

Ceylon Chamber of Commerce: 50 Navam Mawatha, POB 274, Colombo 2; tel. (11) 2421745; fax (11) 2449352; e-mail info@chamber.lk; internet www.chamber.lk; f. 1839; 517 mems; Chair. JAYAMPATHI BANDARANAYAKE; Sec.-Gen. and CEO HARIN MALWATTE.

Ceylon National Chamber of Industries: Galle Face Court 2, Rm 20, 1st Floor, POB 1775, Colombo 3; tel. (11) 2423734; fax (11) 2331443; e-mail info@cnci.biz; f. 1960; 325 mems; Chair. A. K. RATNARAJAH; Sec.-Gen. and CEO UPALI SAMARASINGHE.

International Chamber of Commerce Sri Lanka: Ground Floor, 53 Vauxhall St, POB 1733, Colombo 2; tel. (11) 2307825; fax (11) 2307841; e-mail iccsl@sltnet.lk; internet www.iccsrilanka.com; f. 1955; Chair. TARIQ M. RANGOONWALA; CEO GAMINI PEIRIS.

National Chamber of Commerce of Sri Lanka: NCCSL Bldg, 450 D. R. Wijewardena Mawatha, POB 1375, Colombo 10; tel. (11) 2689600; fax (11) 2689596; e-mail sg@nccsl.lk; internet www.nccsl.lk; f. 1948; Pres. CHANDRA LAL DE ALWIS; Hon. Sec. TILAK GODAMANNA.

INDUSTRIAL AND TRADE ASSOCIATIONS

Association of Computer Training Organizations: 51 Sir Marcus Fernando Mawatha, Colombo 7; tel. (11) 2665261; fax (11) 4713821; e-mail actos@infotel.lk; internet www.actos.lk; f. 1991; 30 mems; Pres. KAPILA GIRAGAMA.

Ceylon Coir Fibre Exporters' Association: c/o Volanka Ltd, 193 Minuwangoda Rd, Kotugoda; tel. (11) 2232475; fax (11) 2232477; e-mail com@volanka.com; internet www.volanka.com; Chair. INDRAJITH PIYASENA.

Ceylon Hardware Merchants' Association: 159 1/5 Mahavidyalaya Mawatha, Colombo 13; tel. (11) 2433085; fax (11) 2423342; 191 mems; Pres. S. T. S. ARULANANTHAN.

Ceylon Planters' Society: 40/1 Sri Dhammadara Mawatha, Ratmalana; tel. (11) 2715656; fax (11) 2716758; e-mail plansoty@yahoo.com; f. 1936; 1,133 mems (plantation mans); 25 brs and nine regional organizations; Pres. D. K. BENEDICT; Sec. D. N. R. WIJEWARDENA.

Coconut Products Traders' Association: c/o Ceylon Chamber of Commerce, 50 Navam Mawatha, POB 274, Colombo 2; tel. (11) 2421745; fax (11) 2449352; e-mail info@chamber.lk; internet www.chamber.lk; f. 1925; Chair. THARAKA DADAGAMUWA; Sec. E. P. A. COORAY.

Colombo Rubber Traders' Association: c/o Ceylon Chamber of Commerce, 50 Navam Mawatha, POB 274, Colombo 2; tel. (11) 2421745; fax (11) 2449352; e-mail info@chamber.lk; internet www.chamber.lk; f. 1918; Chair. A. L. WEERASINGHE; Sec. E. P. A. COORAY.

Colombo Tea Traders' Association: c/o Ceylon Chamber of Commerce, 50 Navam Mawatha, POB 274, Colombo 2; tel. (11) 2421745; fax (11) 2449352; e-mail info@chamber.lk; internet www.chamber.lk; f. 1894; 203 mems; Chair. TYEAB AKBARALLY; Sec. E. P. A. COORAY.

Exporters Association of Sri Lanka (EASL): 50 Navam Mawatha, Colombo 2; tel. (11) 2421745; fax (11) 2449352; e-mail sushani@chamber.lk; internet www.exporterssrilanka.org; f. 1997; Chair. M. MENDIS.

Free Trade Zone Manufacturers' Association: Plaza Complex, Unit 6 (Upper Floor), IPZ, Katunayake; tel. (11) 2259875; fax (11) 2252813; internet www.ftzma.lk; Chair. BEAUNO FERNANDO.

Joint Apparel Association Forum (JAAF): 16 De Fonseka Rd, Colombo 5; tel. (11) 4528494; fax (11) 2501753; e-mail info@jaafsl.com; internet www.jaafsl.com; f. 2002; co-ordinates and develops apparel industry; Chair. AJITH DIAS; Sec.-Gen. T. G. ARIYARATNE.

Sea Food Exporters' Association: c/o Tropic Frozen Foods Ltd, 16/1 Thammita Rd, Negombo; tel. (31) 2222959.

Software Exporters' Association: c/o Ceylon Chamber of Commerce, 50 Navam Mawatha, Colombo 2; tel. (11) 2421745; fax (11)

SRI LANKA

2449352; e-mail gayani@chamber.lk; internet www.islandsoftware.org; f. 1999; 52 mems; Chair. JAYANTHA DE SILVA.

Sri Lanka Apparel Exporters' Association: 45 Rosmead Place, Colombo 7; tel. (11) 2670778; fax (11) 2683118; e-mail srilanka-apparel@sltnet.lk; internet www.srilanka-apparel.com; f. 1982; Chair. KUMAR MIRCHANDANI; Sec. HEMAMALI SIRISENA.

Sri Lanka Association of Manufacturers and Exporters of Rubber Products (SLAMERP): 425 Thimbirigasyaya Rd, Colombo 5; tel. (11) 2521200; fax (11) 2521222; e-mail slamerp@panlanka.net; f. 1984; Chair. ANANDA CALDERA; Sec.-Gen. C. DIAS BANDARANAYAKE.

Sri Lanka Association of Printers: 290 D. R. Wijewardena Mawatha, Colombo 10; tel. (11) 2472315; fax (11) 2386716; e-mail slap@sltnet.lk; f. 1956; 390 mems; publs quarterly magazine *Printceylon*; Pres. KOSALA TILLEKERATNE; Sec. SHAMAL JAYATHILLEKE.

Sri Lanka Chamber of the Pharmaceutical Industry: 15 Tichbourne Passage, Colombo 10; tel. (11) 2231560; fax (11) 2671877; e-mail aperera@sol.lk; internet www.slcpi.org; Pres. ADRIAN BASNAYAKE; Sec. PALITHA JAYATILLEKE.

Sri Lanka Fruit and Vegetables Producers, Processors and Exporters' Association: c/o Sri Lanka Export Development Board, 42 Navam Mawatha, Colombo 2; tel. (11) 2300705; fax (11) 2304879; Pres. SARATH DE SILVA.

Sri Lanka Importers, Exporters and Manufacturers' Association (SLIEMA): POB 12, Colombo; tel. (11) 2696321; fax (11) 2684480; e-mail tradelink@slt.lk; f. 1955; Pres. WILLIAM JOHN TERRENCE PERERA.

Sri Lanka Jewellery Manufacturing Exporters' Association: Colombo; tel. (11) 2445141; fax (11) 2445105; Pres. IFTHIKHAR AZIZ; Sec. CHANAKA ELLAWELA.

Sri Lanka Shippers' Council: c/o Ceylon Chamber of Commerce, 50 Nawam Mawatha, POB 274, Colombo 2; tel. (11) 2421745; fax (11) 2449352; internet www.slsc.ws; Pres. RANDOLPH PERERA.

Sri Lanka Tea Board: 574 Galle Rd, POB 1750, Colombo 3; tel. (11) 2587814; fax (11) 2587341; e-mail promotion@pureceylontea.com; internet www.pureceylontea.com; f. 1976 for development of tea industry through quality control and promotion in Sri Lanka and in world markets; Chair. LALITH HETTIARACHCHI; Dir-Gen. H. D. HEMARATNE.

Sri Lanka Wooden Furniture and Wood Products Manufacturers' and Exporters' Association: c/o E. H. Cooray & Sons Ltd, 411 Galle Rd, Colombo 3; tel. (11) 2509227; fax (11) 2575198; Pres. PATRICK AMARASINGHE; Sec. PINSIRI FERNANDO.

Sugar Importers' Association of Sri Lanka: c/o C. W. Mackie & Co Ltd, 36 D. R. Wijewardena Mawatha, POB 89, Colombo 10; tel. (11) 2423554; fax (11) 2438069; e-mail nalin@export.cwmackie.com; Pres. M. THAVAYOGARAJAH; Sec. C. KAPUWATTA.

EMPLOYERS' ORGANIZATION

Employers' Federation of Ceylon: 385 J3 Old Kotte Rd, Rajagiriya, Colombo; tel. (11) 2867966; fax (11) 2867942; e-mail luckys@empfed.lk; internet www.empfed.lk; f. 1929; mem. of International Organization of Employers and Confederation of Asia Pacific Employers; 510 mems; Chair. H. D. S. AMARASURIYA; Dir-Gen. R. L. P. PEIRIS.

UTILITIES

Electricity

Ceylon Electricity Board: 50 Sir Chittampalam A. Gardiner Mawatha, POB 540, Colombo 2; tel. (11) 2324471; fax (11) 2323935; e-mail admin@ceb.lk; internet www.ceb.lk; f. 1969; Chair. UDAYASRI KARIYAWASAM.

Water

National Water Supply and Drainage Board (NWSDB): Galle Rd, Ratmalana, Colombo; tel. (11) 2638999; fax (11) 2636449; e-mail gm@waterboard.lk; internet waterboard.lk; f. 1975; govt corpn; Chair. S. C. AMARASINGHE.

CO-OPERATIVES

In 2000 there were an estimated 11,793 co-operative societies in Sri Lanka, with membership totalling 17,235,000. In January 2008 the top five co-operatives in Sri Lanka were:

Mahiyangana Multi-Purpose Co-operative: Mahiyanganaya; f. 1971; food and agriculture; Chair. P. M. C. BANDARA.

Matara District Tea Producers' Co-operative: f. 1998; food and agriculture; c. 3,000 mems (2003); Chair. B. RANWAKA.

Morawakkorale Tea Producers' Co-operative Society: Deniyaya Rd, Kotapola; tel. (77) 3970670; e-mail pleenas@yahoo.com; internet kotapola.com/mtpcs.htm; f. 1953; 4,013 mems (2008); Gen. Man. W. W. LEENAS PRIYASHANTHA.

Negombo Multi-Purpose Co-operative: 358 Main St, Negombo; tel. (31) 2238846; f. 1971; diversified financials.

Polonnaruwa District Milk Producers' Co-operative: Polonnaruwa; f. 1979; food and agriculture.

TRADE UNIONS

At the end of 2000 there were 1,588 trade unions functioning in Sri Lanka.

All Ceylon Trade Union Federation (ACTUF): 198/19 Panchikawatte Rd, Colombo 10; tel. (11) 2595566; fax (11) 5358783; e-mail editor@unions.lk; internet www.unions.lk; f. 1941; Pres. K. D. LAL KANTHA.

All Ceylon Federation of Free Trade Unions (ACFFTU): 94-1/6 York Bldg, York St, Colombo 1; tel. (11) 2431847; fax (11) 2470874; e-mail nwc@itmin.com; 10 affiliated unions; 84,000 mems; Pres. MARCELL C. RAJAHMONEY; Sec.-Gen. ANTON LODWICK.

Ceylon Federation of Labour (CFL): 457 Union Place, Colombo 2; tel. (11) 2694273; f. 1957; 16 affiliated unions; 155,969 mems; Pres. Dr COLVIN R. DE SILVA; Gen. Sec. S. S. SIRIWARDANE.

Ceylon Mercantile, Industrial and General Workers' Union (CMU): 3 22nd Lane, Colombo 3; tel. (11) 2328157; fax (11) 2434025; e-mail cgscmu@sltnet.lk; Gen. Sec. BALA TAMPOE.

Ceylon Workers' Congress (CWC): 'Savumia Bhavan', 72 Ananda Coomarasamy Mawatha, POB 1294, Colombo 7; tel. (11) 2301359; fax (11) 2301355; e-mail cwconline@sltnet.lk; f. 1939; political entity; represents mainly plantation workers of recent Indian origin; 50 district offices and seven regional offices; 250,000 mems; Pres. MUTHU SIVALINGAM; Gen. Sec. S. ARUMUGAN THONDAMAN.

Democratic Workers' Congress (DWC): 70 Bankshall St, POB 1009, Colombo 11; tel. (11) 2423746; fax (11) 2435961; f. 1939; 201,382 mems (1994); Pres. MANO GANESHAN; Gen. Sec. R. KITNAN.

Government Workers' Trade Union Federation (GWTUF): 457 Union Place, Colombo 2; tel. (11) 2295066; 52 affiliated unions; 100,000 mems; Leader P. D. SARANAPALA.

Jathika Sevaka Sangamaya (JSS) (National Employees' Union): 416 Kotte Rd, Pitakotte, Colombo; tel. (11) 2565432; f. 1959; 357,000 mems; represents over 70% of unionized manual and clerical workers of Sri Lanka; Pres. W. A. NEVILLE PERERA; Sec. SIRINAL DE MEL.

Lanka Jathika Estate Workers' Union (LJEWU): 60 Bandaranayakepura, Sri Jayawardenepura Mawatha, Welikada, POB 1918, Rajagiriya; tel. (11) 2865138; fax (11) 2862262; e-mail ljewusl@gmail.com; f. 1958; 350,000 mems; Pres. RAVINDRA SAMARAWEERA; Gen. Sec. K. VELAYUDAM.

National Workers' Congress: 1/6 York Bldg, 94 York St, Colombo 1; tel. (11) 2431847; fax (11) 2470874; e-mail nwc@itmin.net; internet www.slnwc.org; f. 1947; Pres. M. C. RAJAHMONEY.

Public Services National Trade Union Federation (PSNTUF): Colombo; internet www.psntuf.lk; f. 1973; 100 affiliated unions; 100,000 mems; Pres. JOSEPH M. PERERA.

Sri Lanka Nidahas Sewaka Sangamaya (Sri Lanka Free Workers' Union): 301 T. B. Jayah Mawatha, POB 1241, Colombo 10; tel. and fax (11) 2694074; f. 1960; 478 br. unions; 193,011 mems; Gen. Sec. LESLIE DEVENDRA.

Trade Union Confederation: Colombo; f. 2008; 40 affiliated unions; Pres. K. S. WEERASEKERA; Sec. H. M. NAWARATNE BANDARA.

Transport

RAILWAYS

Sri Lanka Railways Authority (SLRA): Colombo; f. 2003; responsible for running of national railway network; Gen. Man. T. LALITHASIRI GUNARUWAH.

Sri Lanka Railways (SLR): Olcott Mawatha, POB 335, Colombo 10; tel. (11) 2431177; fax (11) 2446490; e-mail gmr-slr@sltnet.lk; internet www.railway.gov.lk; f. 1864; under Ministry of Transport; operates 1,447 track-km; there are ten railway lines across the country and 164 stations, with 134 sub-stations (2008); Gen. Man. T. L. GUNARUWAN.

ROADS

In 1999 there were an estimated 96,695 km of roads in Sri Lanka, of which 11,462 km were main roads, while in 2003 the road network was estimated to have expanded to 97,286 km, of which 81% was paved. In April 2002 a major highway linking the Jaffna peninsula with the rest of the country was opened for the first time in 12 years. Delayed construction of a four-lane Southern Expressway, extending from Colombo to Matara and jointly funded by the Asian Development Bank (ADB) and Japanese Bank for International Co-operation, was in progress in 2006 at a revised cost of US $600m. Completion of the 126-km road was tentatively scheduled for

SRI LANKA

Directory

2010, although by mid-2008 only some 35% of the highway had been constructed. There were also plans to extend the highway, once completed, to Hambantota, where Sri Lanka's second international airport was to be constructed. The ADB agreed a $150m. loan to Sri Lanka for the widening and rehabilitation of 350 km of national highways in December 2006, and the Government allocated Rs 3,720m. in 2008 for improvements to 1,208 km of rural roads.

Ministry of Transport: 1 D. R. Wijewardene Mawatha, POB 588, Colombo 10; tel. (11) 2687105; fax (11) 2684930; e-mail mintrans@sltnet.lk; internet www.transport.gov.lk; maintains 11,661 km of national highways and 4,429 bridges through the Road Development Authority.

Department of Motor Traffic: 581-341 Elvitigala Mawatha, POB 533, Colombo 5; tel. (11) 2694331; fax (11) 2694338; e-mail dmtsl@sltnet.lk; internet www.motortraffic.gov.lk.

Sri Lanka Transport Board: 200 Kirula Rd, Narahenpita, POB 1435, Colombo 5; tel. (11) 2581120; fax (11) 2368921; e-mail chairmanctb@sltnet.lk; f. 1958; nationalized organization responsible for road passenger transport services consisting of a central transport board, 11 Cluster Bus Cos and one regional transport board; fleet of 4,077 buses (2006); Chair. TUDER CAYARATNE; Sec. D. P. W. DE LIVERA.

SHIPPING

Colombo is one of the most important ports in Asia and is situated at the junction of the main trade routes. The other main ports of Sri Lanka are Trincomalee, Galle and Jaffna. Trincomalee is the main port for handling tea exports.

Ceylon Association of Ships' Agents (CASA): 56 Ward Place, Colombo 7; tel. (11) 2696227; fax (11) 2698648; e-mail casa@sltnet.lk; internet www.casa.lk; f. 1944; primarily a consultative organization; represents mems in dealings with govt authorities; 120 mems; Chair. Capt. AJITH PEIRIS; Sec.-Gen. DHAMMIKA WALGAMPAYA.

Sri Lanka Ports Authority: 19 Chaithya Rd, POB 595, Colombo 1; tel. (11) 2421201; fax (11) 2440651; e-mail info@slpa.lk; internet www.slpa.lk; f. 1979; responsible for all cargo handling operations and harbour development and maintenance in the ports of Colombo, Galle, Kankasanthurai, Trincomalee, Oluvil, Point Pedro and Hambantota; Chair. PRIYATH BANDU WICKRAMA; Man. Dir W. G. SAMARATUNGA.

Shipping Companies

Ceylon Ocean Lines Ltd: 'Sayuru Sevana', 46/12 Nawam Mawatha, Colombo 2; tel. (11) 2434928; fax (11) 2439245; e-mail oceanlines@col.lk; f. 1956; shipping agents, freight forwarders, charterers, container freight station operators and bunkers; Dirs Capt. L. P. WEINMAN, Capt. A. V. RAJENDRA.

Ceylon Shipping Corpn Ltd: 6 Sir Baron Jayatilaka Mawatha, POB 1718, Colombo 1; tel. (11) 2328772; fax (11) 2449486; e-mail cscl@cscl.lk; internet www.cscl.lk; f. 1971 as a govt corpn; became govt-owned limited liability co in 1992; operates fully-containerized service to Europe, the Far East, the Mediterranean, USA and Canada (East Coast); Chair. Y. L. S. HAMEED.

Ceylon Shipping Lines Ltd: 450 D. R. Wijewardena Mawatha, POB 891, Colombo 10; tel. (11) 2689500; fax (11) 2689510; e-mail cslmgmt@sltnet.lk; internet www.ceylonshippinglines.com; shipping agents, travel agents, off dock terminal operators; Chair. ARMYNE WIRASINHA; Man. Dir D. P. C. LAWRENCE.

Ceyoceanic Ltd: 80 Reclamation Rd, POB 795, Colombo 11; tel. (11) 2236071; Dir M. T. G. ANAAM.

Colombo Dockyard Ltd: Port of Colombo, Graving Docks, POB 906, Colombo 15; tel. (11) 2429000; fax (11) 2446441; e-mail coldock@cdl.lk; internet www.cdl.lk; f. 1974; 51% owned by Onomichi Dockyard Co Ltd, Japan, and 49% by Sri Lankan public and government institutions; four dry-docks, seven repair berths (1,200 m), repair of ships up to 125,000 dwt, and builders of steel/aluminium vessels of up to 3,000 dwt; Chair. S. TATEBE; Man. Dir and CEO M. P. B. YAPA.

Mercantile Shipping Co Ltd: Bohen House, 108 Aluthmawatha Rd, Colombo 15; tel. (11) 2331792; fax (11) 2331799; e-mail info@mscl.lk; internet www.mscl.lk.

Sri Lanka Shipping Co Ltd: 46/5 Navam Mawatha, POB 1125, Colombo 2; tel. (11) 2336853; fax (11) 2437420; e-mail lankaship@slsc.lk; internet www.srilankashipping.com; f. 1956.

INLAND WATERWAYS

There are more than 160 km of canals open for traffic.

CIVIL AVIATION

Civil aviation is controlled by the Government's Department of Civil Aviation. There are airports at Batticaloa, Colombo (Bandaranaike for external flights and Ratmalana for internal), Gal Oya, Palali, Jaffna and Trincomalee. In April 2002 the Government lifted a six-year ban on domestic flights and permitted commercial airlines to resume services to Jaffna. Construction work on a second international airport, located about 180 km south of Colombo at Hambantota, was due to commence in mid-2009 and was scheduled to be completed in 2011.

Civil Aviation Authority of Sri Lanka: Supreme Bldg, 64 Galle Rd, Colombo 3; tel. (11) 2433213; fax (11) 2440231; e-mail seccaa@caa.lk; internet www.caa.lk; f. 2002; under the supervision of the Ministry of Ports and Aviation; Chair. LAL LIYANARACHCHI; CEO and Dir-Gen. Civil Aviation AJANTHA MARASINGHE.

SriLankan Airlines Ltd: World Trade Centre, East Tower, 22nd Floor, Echelon Sq., Colombo 1; tel. (11) 97335555; fax (11) 97335122; e-mail ulweb@srilankan.aero; internet www.srilankan.aero; f. 1979 as Air Lanka Ltd, name changed as above in 1999; international services to Europe, the Middle East, South Asia and the Far East; Chair. NISHANTA WICKREMASINGHE; CEO MANOJ GUNAWARDENA.

Helitours: Air Headquarters, POB 594, Colombo 2; tel. (11) 2342577; fax (11) 2343969; e-mail ops1@slaf.gov.lk; internet www.slaf.lk; commercial wing of Sri Lankan Air Force; charter services to domestic destinations; Dir Wing-Commdr DAYAL WIJERATNE.

Lionair (Pvt) Ltd: Asian Aviation Centre, Colombo Airport, Ratmalana, Colombo; tel. (11) 2622622; fax (11) 2611540; e-mail citadeld@sierra.lk; f. 1994; scheduled and charter services to eight domestic destinations; Chair. CHANDRAN RUTNAM; Man. Dir ASOKA PERERA.

Mihin Lanka: 4-109, Bandaranaike Memorial International Conference Hall, Bauddhaloka Mawatha, Colombo 7; tel. (11) 2699305; fax (11) 2697525; e-mail info@mihinlanka.com; internet www.mihinlanka.com; f. 2007; govt-owned; international services to India, the Maldives, United Arab Emirates, Thailand and Singapore; Chair. SAJIN VAS GUNAWARDENA.

Tourism

As a stopping place for luxury cruises and by virtue of the spectacle of its Buddhist festivals, ancient monuments and natural scenery, Sri Lanka is one of Asia's most important tourist centres. Good motor roads connect Colombo to the main places of interest.

Sri Lanka's tourism industry has been adversely affected by the ongoing intercommunal violence. Following a deterioration in the security situation in 2007 and the subsequent collapse of the cease-fire agreement in early 2008, according to figures from the Sri Lanka Tourism Development Authority, tourist arrivals decreased from 494,008 in 2007 to 438,475 in 2008 and tourist receipts fell from US $384m. to $320m. over the same period.

Sri Lanka Tourism Promotion Bureau: 80 Galle Rd, Colombo 3; tel. (11) 2426967; fax (11) 2440001; e-mail info@srilanka.travel; internet www.srilanka.travel; f. 1966; Chair. BERNARD GOONETILLEKE; Man. Dir DILEEP MUDADENIYA.

SUDAN

Introductory Survey

Location, Climate, Language, Religion, Flag, Capital

The Republic of Sudan lies in north-eastern Africa. It is bordered by Egypt to the north, by the Red Sea, Eritrea and Ethiopia to the east, by the Central African Republic, Chad and Libya to the west, and by Kenya, Uganda and the Democratic Republic of the Congo (formerly Zaire) to the south. The climate shows a marked transition from the desert of the north to the rainy equatorial south. Temperatures vary with altitude and latitude. The annual average for the whole country is about 21°C (70°F). Arabic is the official language, although other languages are spoken and English is widely understood. Most northern Sudanese are Muslims, while in the south most of the inhabitants are animists or Christians. The national flag (proportions 1 by 2) has three equal horizontal stripes, of red, white and black, with a green triangle at the hoist. The capital is Khartoum.

Recent History

The Sudan (as the country was known before 1975) achieved independence as a parliamentary republic on 1 January 1956. After a military coup in November 1958, a Supreme Council of the Armed Forces was established and ruled until October 1964, when it was overthrown in a civilian revolution. In May 1969 power was seized by a group of officers, led by Col Gaafar Muhammad Nimeri. All existing political institutions and organizations were abolished, and the 'Democratic Republic of the Sudan' was proclaimed, with supreme authority in the hands of the Revolutionary Command Council (RCC). In October 1971 a referendum confirmed Nimeri's nomination as President. A new Government was formed, the RCC was dissolved, and the Sudanese Socialist Union (SSU) was recognized as the only political party.

An early problem facing the Nimeri Government concerned the disputed status of the three southern provinces (Bahr al-Ghazal, Equatoria and Upper Nile), whose inhabitants are racially and culturally distinct from most of the country's population. Rebellion against rule from the north had first broken out in 1955, and fighting continued until March 1972, when an agreement to give the three provinces a degree of autonomy was concluded between members of the Government and representatives of the South Sudan Liberation Movement. A High Executive Council (HEC) for the Southern Region was established in April 1972, and Sudan's permanent Constitution was endorsed in April 1973. Elections to the Regional People's Assembly for southern Sudan took place in November 1973, followed by elections to the National People's Assembly in April 1974.

In October 1981 the National People's Assembly was dissolved. When new elections were held in December, its membership had been reduced from 366 to 151, as many powers had been devolved to the regions. At the same time, the southern HEC was dissolved. The entire Sudanese Government was dismissed in November, although many individuals were later reinstated. In April 1982 a new Southern Region People's Assembly was elected.

In April 1983 President Nimeri was re-elected for a third six-year term. During that year Sudan's north–south conflict escalated, and in June Nimeri finally decided to redivide the south into three smaller regions, each with its own assembly, in an effort to quell the unrest. In September Nimeri suddenly announced the imposition of strict Islamic law (the *Shari'a*), provoking anger in the largely non-Muslim south, and in April 1984 Nimeri proclaimed a state of emergency. The stringent application of *Shari'a* law aggravated tensions within the country and strained relations between Sudan and its allies, Egypt and the USA.

In May 1984 Nimeri replaced his Council of Ministers with a 64-member Presidential Council, in accordance with the '*Shoura*' (consultation) principle of *Shari'a* law. In July, however, the National People's Assembly rejected his proposed constitutional amendments to make Sudan a formal Islamic state. In October Nimeri ended the state of emergency and offered to revoke the redivision of the south, if a majority of southerners desired it. The situation in the south continued to deteriorate, with the emergence of the Sudan People's Liberation Movement (SPLM), whose armed forces, the Sudan People's Liberation Army (SPLA), rapidly gained military control over large areas of the provinces of Bahr al-Ghazal and Upper Nile.

On 6 April 1985, while Nimeri was visiting the USA, he was deposed in a bloodless military coup. The country's new leader, Gen. Abdel-Rahman Swar ad-Dahab (who had recently been made Minister of Defence and Commander-in-Chief of the army by Nimeri), appointed a Transitional Military Council (TMC) to govern the country, but he pledged a return to civilian rule after a one-year transitional period. The SSU and the National People's Assembly were dissolved, and hundreds of Nimeri's officials were arrested; Nimeri went into exile in Cairo, Egypt. A transitional Constitution was introduced in October 1985 that allowed new political groupings to emerge in preparation for a general election, and in December the name of the country was officially changed to 'the Republic of Sudan'.

In a general election in April 1986 the Umma Party (UP), led by Sadiq al-Mahdi, won 99 of the 264 seats in the new National Assembly, followed by the Democratic Unionist Party (DUP), with 63 seats. A coalition Government was formed by the UP and DUP, with four portfolios in the Council of Ministers allocated to southern parties. Al-Mahdi became Prime Minister and Minister of Defence, and a six-member Supreme Council assumed the functions of Head of State. With these appointments, the TMC was dissolved, signifying a return to civilian rule.

In response to the April 1985 coup, the SPLM initially declared a cease-fire, but presented the new regime with a series of demands concerning the southern region. Despite Swar ad-Dahab's offer of various concessions to the south, the SPLM refused to negotiate with the TMC, and fighting resumed. In May 1987 a temporary Council for the Southern Sudan (CSS) was established. Its influence on the army and the SPLM, the two contending de facto ruling powers that now existed in the south, was, however, negligible. In June al-Mahdi announced that the coalition parties had agreed that laws based on a 'Sudanese legal heritage' would replace those unacceptable to non-Muslims, who would be exempted from Islamic taxation and special penalties. However, the SPLM continued to demand a total abrogation of Islamic law, while the National Islamic Front (NIF) demanded that the Islamic code be imposed on the whole country. On 25 July the Government imposed a 12-month state of emergency, aimed at bringing under control the worsening economic situation.

In May 1988 a new Government of National Unity, comprising members of the UP, the DUP, the NIF and some southern Sudanese political parties, was formed. In November representatives of the SPLM met senior members of the DUP and reached agreement on proposals to end the civil war. A statement issued by the two sides stipulated that, prior to the convening of a national constitutional conference, the Islamic legal code should be suspended, that military agreements between Sudan and other countries should be abandoned, and that the state of emergency be lifted and a cease-fire implemented in the south. In December, however, a state of emergency was again declared amid reports of an attempted military coup, and the DUP withdrew from the Government.

In February 1989 Dr Hassan at-Turabi, the leader of the NIF, was appointed Deputy Prime Minister. Although the peace agreement concluded by the DUP and the SPLM in November had been widely endorsed, the NIF opposed its provision for the suspension of Islamic laws as a prelude to the negotiation of a peace settlement. The NIF was consequently excluded from a new Government formed in March. Peace negotiations between a government delegation and the SPLM commenced in Ethiopia in April, and at the beginning of May the SPLM leader, Col John Garang, proclaimed a one-month cease-fire (subsequently extended to 30 June), renewing hopes for peace and aiding the work of famine relief. The negotiations culminated in an agreement to suspend Islamic laws, pending the proposed convening, in September, of a constitutional conference.

On 30 June 1989 a bloodless coup, led by Brig. (later Lt-Gen.) Omar Hassan Ahmad al-Bashir, removed al-Mahdi's Government. Al-Bashir formed a 15-member Revolutionary Command

Council for National Salvation (RCC), which declared its primary aim to be the resolution of the southern conflict. Al-Bashir, who became Head of State, Chairman of the RCC, Prime Minister and Minister of Defence, and Commander-in-Chief of the armed forces, abolished the Constitution, the National Assembly and all political parties and trade unions, and declared a state of emergency.

The SPLM's response to the coup was cautious. In July 1989 Lt-Gen. al-Bashir declared a one-month unilateral cease-fire and offered amnesty to those opposing the Government 'for political reasons'. By August the SPLM's terms for a negotiated settlement to the conflict included the immediate resignation of the RCC, prior to the establishment of an interim government, in which the SPLM, the banned political parties and other groupings would be represented. However, the new regime's proximity to the NIF had become apparent, and the negotiations collapsed immediately over the issue of Islamic law. Hostilities, which had been in abeyance since the beginning of May, resumed at the end of October.

In February 1991 the RCC enacted a decree instituting a new, federal system of government. Sudan was divided into nine states, each of which had its own governor, deputy governor and cabinet of ministers, and assumed responsibility for local administration and the collection of some taxes. The central Government retained control over foreign policy, military affairs, the economy and the other principal areas of administration. At the beginning of February it had been announced that a new penal code, based on *Shari'a* law, would take effect in March, but would not apply in the three southern states, pending the establishment there of elected assemblies to resolve the issue. The SPLM nevertheless regarded the application of Islamic law in the northern states as unacceptable, citing the large numbers of non-Muslims resident there.

The overthrow, in May 1991, of the Ethiopian Government, led by Mengistu Haile Mariam, had implications for the SPLA forces, who had previously enjoyed Ethiopian support. In late May armed clashes were reported within Ethiopia between SPLA forces and those of the new Ethiopian Government, and the Sudanese Government declared its recognition of, and support for, the new Ethiopian regime. In October Sudan and Ethiopia signed a treaty of friendship and co-operation.

In February 1992 al-Bashir appointed all 300 members of a new transitional National Assembly, which included the entire RCC, all government ministers and the governors of Sudan's nine states. The Assembly was accorded legislative authority, with the power to examine all decrees issued by the RCC, and responsibility for preparing the country for parliamentary elections.

In early 1993 the NIF was reported to be opposed to the continued military character of the Government, and to favour the dissolution of the RCC. In January al-Bashir effected an extensive reorganization of the Cabinet, but stated that the RCC would not be dissolved. Rather, in 1994 the gradual transfer of power to the regional councils would begin. Talks between the Government and the SPLA ended inconclusively in January 1993. By this time the SPLA was reported to have split into three factions.

In mid-October 1993 al-Bashir announced political reforms in preparation for presidential and legislative elections in 1994 and 1995, respectively. The RCC was dissolved after it had appointed al-Bashir as President and as head of a new civilian Government. Cabinet ministers were requested to remain in office until elections took place. Later in October al-Bashir appointed a new Minister of Defence—a portfolio that he had formerly held himself—and a new Vice-President.

In January 1994 the two principal rival factions of the SPLA were reported to have agreed on a cease-fire. In February Sudan was redivided into 26 states instead of the nine that had formed the basis of administration since 1991. The executive and legislative powers of each state government were to be expanded, and southern states were to be exempted from *Shari'a* law. In March delegations representing the Government and two factions of the SPLA participated in peace talks held in Nairobi, Kenya, under the auspices of the Intergovernmental Authority on Drought and Development (IGADD—superseded in 1996 by the Intergovernmental Authority on Development—IGAD, see p. 321), which in September 1993 had formed a committee on the Sudanese conflict comprising the Heads of State of Kenya, Ethiopia, Uganda and Eritrea. All parties to the talks agreed to allow the free passage of relief supplies to southern Sudan. In April 1994 the Government adopted legislation providing for the appointment, by the President, of an independent commission to supervise legislative elections scheduled to take place in the second half of 1994, and for a constitutional referendum.

A further round of IGADD-sponsored peace negotiations was held in Nairobi on 18–28 July 1994. On 23 July the Government announced a unilateral cease-fire, to which Garang's faction of the SPLA reportedly responded on 28 July with a cease-fire of its own. However, when the negotiations resumed in early September, divergent positions on the issues of the governance of the south and the role of religion in government quickly led to deadlock. The severing, in December, of diplomatic relations between Sudan and Eritrea led Sudan to inform the IGADD in early 1995 that it no longer considered Eritrea to be a suitable intermediary in the Sudanese conflict. A cabinet reshuffle in February suggested a reinforcement of the Islamic character of the Government.

In mid-March 1995 Garang announced that his faction of the SPLA was to mount a new northern offensive in collaboration with other northern rebels. The New Sudan Brigade aimed to unite other insurgent groups against the Government, but did not appear to gain the support of rival SPLA factions. In late March it was reported that former US President Jimmy Carter had persuaded the Government to declare a unilateral cease-fire for a period of two months, and to offer rebel groups an amnesty if they surrendered their weapons. The SPLA and the South Sudan Independence Movement (SSIM) responded by also declaring cease-fires. In late May the Government extended its cease-fire for two months. However, it soon became apparent that the army was continuing to conduct military operations. In June a conference of groups and parties opposed to the Sudanese Government commenced in Asmara, Eritrea. The conference, hosted by the Eritrean People's Front for Democracy and Justice and organized by the Asmara-based National Democratic Alliance (NDA), was attended, among others, by representatives of the DUP, the UP and the Sudanese Communist Party. It was agreed that, once the al-Bashir regime had been ousted, religion would be separated from politics and that a referendum would be held regarding the secession of the southern provinces. The conference was also reported to have achieved a rapprochement between the SPLA and other opposition groups.

In August 1995 a reshuffle of the Cabinet was announced. The DUP claimed that those ministers who had been dismissed had been involved in the attempted assassination of President Mubarak of Egypt in June (see below). Later in August President al-Bashir announced that legislative and presidential elections would be held in 1996. At the end of January 1996 the USA announced the withdrawal of its diplomatic personnel from Sudan, owing to doubts about the Government's ability to guarantee their safety. Prior to their withdrawal, the UN Security Council had unanimously adopted Resolution 1044, which accused Sudan of supporting terrorism and condemned its role in the attempted assassination of Mubarak. The resolution also demanded that Sudan immediately extradite three individuals implicated in the attempted assassination.

Legislative and presidential elections took place in March 1996. Some 5.5m. of Sudan's 10m. eligible voters were reported to have participated in the election of 275 deputies to a new, 400-seat National Assembly. The remaining 125 deputies had been appointed at a national conference in January. Representatives of opposition groups and parties alleged that electoral malpractice had been widespread. In the presidential election al-Bashir (who was reportedly opposed only by token candidates) obtained 75.7% of the total votes cast, and formally commenced a five-year term of office on 1 April. On the same day Dr Hassan at-Turabi, the Secretary-General of the NIF, was unanimously elected President of the National Assembly.

Rumours of an attempted *coup d'état* in late March 1996 prejudiced the newly constituted regime's claim that the elections signified the beginning of a new period of stability and reconciliation, as did reports of serious unrest in Khartoum in early April and the decision not to appoint a new Cabinet until it became clear whether the UN would impose sanctions on Sudan for its failure to comply with the terms of UN Security Council Resolution 1044. On 10 April a 'political charter for peace' was signed by the Government, the SSIM and the SPLA-United, pledging to preserve Sudan's national unity and to take joint action to develop those areas of the country that had been affected by the civil war. The charter also provided for the holding of a referendum as 'a means of realizing the aspirations of southern citizens' and affirmed that Islamic law would be the basis of future legislation. On 17 April Sudan's First Vice-

President was reported to have invited Garang to sign the charter on behalf of his faction of the SPLA, prompting speculation that this was part of an ongoing attempt to form a new government of national unity. However, the new Cabinet, announced on 21 April, retained the military, Islamist cast of its predecessor. On 28 April the UN Security Council imposed diplomatic sanctions on Sudan for failing to comply with the terms of Resolution 1044. In October al-Bashir appointed eight deputies to the National Assembly to represent constituencies in the south where, owing to the civil war, it had not been possible to hold elections in March.

In April 1997 a peace accord, covering major issues such as power-sharing and *Shari'a* law, and promising a referendum on southern secession after a four-year transition period, was signed by six rebel groups. Both the NDA and the SPLA, however, rejected the agreement. In August, in accordance with the terms of the agreement, the Southern States Co-ordination Council (SSCC) was established; Dr Riek Mashar Teny-Dhurgon, the leader of the Southern Sudan Defence Force (SSDF), was sworn in as its Chairman. At the beginning of September the SPLA-United declared a cease-fire, and its commander, Dr Lam Akol, returned to Khartoum in the following month.

In March 1998 al-Bashir announced a government reorganization in which a number of former rebel leaders were appointed to the Cabinet, including Akol as Minister of Transport. In April a new Constitution was approved by the National Assembly and endorsed by 96.7% of voters in a referendum held between 1 and 20 May. Under its terms, executive power would be vested in the Council of Ministers, which would be appointed by the President but responsible to the National Assembly. Legislative power was to be vested in the National Assembly. The Constitution also guaranteed freedom of thought and religion, and the right to lawful political association. New legislation approved in November 1998 provided for the establishment of an independent election commission and of a Constitutional Court, and for the legalization of political associations. Registration of political parties began in January 1999.

In May 1999 former President Nimeri returned to Sudan after 14 years in exile in Egypt. His return was welcomed by the Government, although opposition parties demanded his prosecution for crimes he had allegedly committed while President. In the same month at-Turabi held talks in Switzerland with Sadiq al-Mahdi, with the aim of initiating a process of reconciliation. At the end of May a meeting took place in Kampala, Uganda, between al-Mahdi, Garang and Mubarak al-Mahdi (of the NDA), to discuss several issues regarding their conflict with the Sudanese Government.

In August 1999 the Government accepted a Libyan peace initiative, which envisaged a cease-fire, an end to media propaganda, direct talks through a conference of national dialogue and the establishment of a preparatory committee. The peace effort was to be co-ordinated jointly by Egypt and Libya. The Government did, however, express reservations over a number of conditions proposed by the NDA, which included the suspension of articles in the Constitution that restricted public liberty and the release of political prisoners. In September the SPLA stated that it supported the Egyptian-Libyan peace initiative 'in principle', although after a meeting with the US Secretary of State in October (see below) Garang discounted the Egyptian-Libyan initiative in favour of the IGAD-sponsored peace process.

At a conference, held in Cairo in October 1999, the leaders of the NDA decided to examine ways of combining the peace initiative sponsored by IGAD and the Egyptian-Libyan initiative, in order to unite the parties of the NDA, a number of whom opposed the pursuit of two parallel initiatives. At the end of November Djibouti hosted a regional IGAD summit meeting, attended by Kenya, Ethiopia and Sudan, to discuss issues related to development and stability in the region. While in Djibouti, President al-Bashir met the UP leader, al-Mahdi, following which the Sudanese Government and the UP signed a declaration of principles, which envisaged a federal system of government and the holding of a referendum within four years to allow southerners to choose between the division of the country or unity with decentralized powers. The agreement was welcomed by many parties; however, the NDA responded by stating that it would escalate the war in the south, not end it. Garang later condemned and disavowed the Djibouti agreement.

During 1999 there were increasing reports of rivalry between al-Bashir and at-Turabi, particularly following the introduction of a bill in the National Assembly that sought to remove the President's power to appoint and dismiss state governors. Consideration of the draft legislation was repeatedly delayed, but a vote was scheduled to be held in mid-December in which the National Assembly was widely expected to approve it. However, on 12 December al-Bashir dissolved the National Assembly and imposed a three-month state of emergency, claiming that he had taken these measures in order to end the 'duality' in the administration. An emergency order suspended some articles of the Constitution, although provincial councils and governors were to continue working. At-Turabi accused al-Bashir of having carried out a *coup d'état*, although a legal challenge, mounted against the measures, was later rejected by the Constitutional Court.

IGAD-sponsored talks held in Nairobi in January 2000 made some progress on the issue of a referendum. At the end of January al-Bashir appointed a new Cabinet and state governors. An emergency development programme, formulated by the SSCC, for the southern states was approved by the Government in February. Teny-Dhurgon resigned as Chairman of the SSCC in February in protest at the Government's failure to implement the terms of the peace accords and at al-Bashir's disregard for the Constitution. In mid-February Teny-Dhurgon claimed a major victory over government forces and announced the establishment of the Sudan People's Defence Force (SPDF).

In March 2000 the Government extended the state of emergency until the end of the year, and approved a law allowing the formation of political parties (superseding the 1998 law), although this was rejected by the opposition, as it still incorporated provisions to suspend the activities of any party. In the same month the UP announced its decision to suspend its membership of the NDA during a meeting in Asmara. In April 2000 it was reported that a presidential election was planned for October; the ruling National Congress (NC) had nominated al-Bashir as its candidate in October 1999. However, most opposition parties, including the UP, indicated that they would not participate in any elections prior to the convening of a national conference to discuss the problems in Sudan. In May 2000 al-Bashir announced the suspension of the secretariat of the NC, including the activities of at-Turabi and his deputies, and affirmed his intention to restructure the party.

IGAD-sponsored peace talks, held in April 2000, ended inconclusively, and in May the SPLM suspended its participation in protest at the Government's alleged continued bombing of civilian targets. It reaffirmed its commitment to the unification of the IGAD process and the Egyptian-Libyan initiative, but did not indicate on what conditions it would resume talks. The next round of IGAD-sponsored talks had been scheduled to begin on 17 May. In June the SPLM announced it would rejoin the peace talks, and in that month al-Bashir declared a general amnesty for all opponents of the Government; however, it was rejected by a number of opposition groups, including the SPLM. Later that month at-Turabi announced the formation of a new political party, the Popular National Congress (PNC), whose registration was formally approved in August.

In September 2000 al-Mahdi confirmed the withdrawal of the UP from the NDA alliance. Later that month al-Bashir visited Asmara, where he met with an NDA delegation. The two parties discussed possible political settlements to the situation in Sudan and agreed to meet for further direct talks, although no date for such discussions was set. In October it was reported that al-Bashir had dismissed Maj.-Gen. George Kongor Arop from the post of Second Vice-President. The following month al-Mahdi returned to Sudan from his four-year self-imposed exile in Eritrea and Egypt, but announced that he would not participate in the forthcoming elections.

Presidential and legislative elections were held concurrently over a 10-day period in mid-December 2000, although they were boycotted by the main opposition parties. As expected, al-Bashir was re-elected President, with 86.5% of the votes cast, comfortably defeating his nearest rival, former President Nimeri, who obtained 9.6% of the vote. Voting did not take place in the three southern states. The NC secured 355 seats in the new 360-member National Assembly; the remaining five seats were won by small opposition parties. On 3 January 2001 al-Bashir extended the state of emergency for a further year.

On 21 February 2001 at-Turabi was arrested at his home in Khartoum after it was announced that the PNC and the SPLM had signed a memorandum of understanding in Switzerland urging the Sudanese people to participate in 'peaceful popular resistance' against the al-Bashir regime. In early March at-Turabi and several other members of the PNC's leadership council were reported to have been charged with criminal conspiracy, undermining the constitutional order, waging war on the state and calling for violent opposition to public authority. (In late May at-Turabi was released from prison and placed under house arrest.) Meanwhile, the day after at-Turabi's arrest, al-Bashir implemented a major reorganization of the Cabinet and replaced many of the country's state governors. Several new ministries were created, and, although the new, 32-member Cabinet was dominated by NC members, al-Bashir incorporated four members of two minor opposition parties into the Government. Two members of the UDSF retained their positions in the Cabinet, but the UP, despite earlier indications to the contrary, refused to participate in the new administration and officially stated that it would not accept ministerial posts before the holding of free and fair elections in the south of the country and the resolution of the armed conflict in that region.

In early July 2001 it was reported that the Sudanese Government and the NDA had both provisionally accepted a renewed Libyan-Egyptian peace initiative, which provided for an immediate cease-fire, the establishment of a transitional government and a number of constitutional reforms. Later that month the leadership council of the NC approved the Libyan-Egyptian plan. However, al-Bashir maintained that he would not support any proposals that involved the separation of state and religion or the partition of the country, thus endangering the success of the initiative, as the NDA concurrently reiterated its demand for the right of the southern states to be granted self-determination.

In late September 2001 the UN Security Council voted to remove the sanctions imposed on Sudan in 1996 (see above) and praised the country's recent efforts to combat terrorism. Notably, the USA, which had previously used its vote to veto the lifting of sanctions, abstained, enabling the motion to be carried. In mid-December the state of emergency was again extended for a further 12 months. In January 2002 Teny-Dhurgon and Garang announced the merger of the SPDF and the SPLA. Teny-Dhurgon had defected from the SPLM/SPLA in 1991 and had signed a peace accord with the Government in 1997 (as leader of the SSDF); however, this agreement had collapsed in early 2001.

In mid-January 2002 talks sponsored jointly by the USA and Switzerland commenced in Buergenstock, Switzerland. Following six days of intensive discussions, the Sudanese Government and the SPLA agreed to observe a six-month cease-fire, to be supervised by a joint military commission, in the central Nuba region in order to facilitate the delivery of vital aid supplies to the area. However, the following month the USA announced that it had suspended discussions with the Sudanese Government, after two separate incidents earlier that month in which Sudanese air force planes had bombed civilians collecting food supplies in the Bahr al-Ghazal province. The Sudanese Minister of External Relations subsequently issued an apology for the attack and in mid-March the USA brokered an agreement between the SPLA and the Sudanese Government, which aimed to guarantee the protection of civilians from military attacks; the agreement was to be monitored by two teams of international observers. In early July the cease-fire was extended for a further six months, and in late December it was agreed that it would continue until July 2003.

In May 2002 the Minister of Finance, Adb ar-Rahim Muhammad Hamdi, reportedly resigned owing to ill health. There was, however, speculation that he had been dismissed by al-Bashir following the implementation of several unpopular economic measures. Hamdi was subsequently replaced by Muhammad al-Hasan az-Zubayr. In June three members of the NC, including Akol, resigned from the party in protest at the increasing dominance of al-Bashir. In mid-August al-Bashir renewed the detention order that had been placed on at-Turabi the previous year for a further 12 months, and in September at-Turabi was transferred to prison. In the previous month al-Bashir had effected a minor reorganization of the Council of Ministers, and in September Akol was dismissed as Minister of Transport; Akol was one of a number of former NC members who had, earlier that month, established a new political party, the Justice Party. In November al-Bashir carried out a further reshuffle of the Council of Ministers and created two new ministries. In December the state of emergency was once again extended for a further 12 months.

Meanwhile, in mid-June 2002 a new round of IGAD-sponsored peace talks between the Government and the SPLM opened in Machakos, Kenya. A major breakthrough in the conflict was achieved on 20 July, when delegations from the SPLM and the Government signed an accord, known as the Machakos Protocol, which provided for a six-year period of autonomy for the south, to be followed by an internationally monitored referendum on self-determination. The Protocol also stated that Sudan's Constitution would be rewritten to ensure that *Shari'a* law would not be applied to non-Muslim southerners. Government and SPLM delegations reconvened in Machakos in mid-August for talks. However, further outbreaks of fighting between the two sides were reported, and in early September, in response to the SPLA's capture of Torit, the Government announced that it had suspended talks with the SPLM and launched an offensive to try and reclaim the town. Despite agreeing to cease hostilities and resume peace talks, government forces recaptured Torit in early October. Later that month the two sides reconvened in Machakos and signed a cease-fire agreement for the duration of the ongoing discussions. Negotiations between the Government and the SPLM were halted in mid-November, after no agreement could be reached on the number of government and civil service posts to be allocated to southerners and the distribution of petroleum revenues. Disputes also remained over control of the Abyei, Blue Nile and Nuba Mountains provinces in central Sudan and the religious status of Khartoum. The two sides did, however, agree to extend the cease-fire until the end of March 2003.

Talks resumed in Nairobi in mid-January 2003, and the following month a memorandum of understanding was signed under which the Government and the SPLM agreed to allow international observers to monitor the cease-fire. In April al-Bashir and Garang met for only the second time in 20 years and announced that they anticipated that the peace talks would be concluded by the end of June; they also reaffirmed their commitment to the Machakos Protocol and pledged to facilitate unrestricted delivery of humanitarian assistance to those in the south of the country. However, in May it became apparent that the talks would not be concluded as expected, after negotiations between the Government and the SPLM ended with a number of key issues, including wealth- and power-sharing, still unresolved. In July the government delegation rejected a document presented by the IGAD mediators, providing for a separate army and an independent central bank for the south, as it maintained that this was in conflict with the Machakos Protocol, which had enshrined the unity of Sudan. In mid-August talks between the Government and the SPLM recommenced in the Kenyan town of Nanyuki, and later that month the discussions were extended until mid-September in order to give both sides additional time to resolve their outstanding differences.

In mid-September 2003 the SPLA and the Sudanese Government agreed to extend their cease-fire for a further two months, and days later the two sides signed a landmark security agreement. Under the terms of the arrangement, two separate armed forces were to be created, as well as a number of integrated units, comprising both government and SPLA troops. Both sides agreed to contribute 12,000 soldiers to a joint force to be deployed in southern Sudan, and a further 6,000 soldiers from each side were to be dispatched to the disputed Nuba Mountains and Blue Nile provinces. Furthermore, 80% of the government forces in southern Sudan would be withdrawn to the north no later than two and a half years after the signing of a comprehensive peace agreement. It was also agreed that both sides' forces would be reduced at a later, unspecified date and that they would be placed under the command of a joint defence board composed of SPLM and government officials. In October the US Secretary of State, Colin Powell, secured assurances from the Sudanese Government and the SPLM that a comprehensive settlement would be reached by the end of the year. Nevertheless, later in October US sanctions on Sudan (see below) were extended for a further 12 months. Also in October at-Turabi was released from detention, and all restrictions on the NPC's activities were lifted. In late March 2004 the Sudanese security forces arrested some 27 people, among them at-Turabi, five other members of the PNC and 10 military officers, on suspicion of plotting to overthrow the Government. In January 2005 a number of those apprehended were released; however, at-Turabi remained in detention along with some 12 other PNC members. Meanwhile, in October 2004 al-Bashir dismissed the Assistant President, Mubarak al-Fadil al-Mahdi, who was reportedly not replaced.

In early December 2003 SPLM delegates visited Khartoum for the first time since the escalation of the north–south conflict in 1983, prior to convening for further talks with the Government in Naivasha, Kenya. On 7 January 2004 the two sides signed an accord on wealth- and revenue-sharing, which also provided for the establishment of two separate banking systems for the north and the south, as well as a new national currency on the signing of a final peace settlement. Although talks resumed in Kenya in mid-February, progress on other matters remained stalled, and by mid-May, despite intense international pressure, the two sides had still not concluded a definitive peace agreement. Furthermore, in mid-April the UN announced it had been forced to suspend aid operations in southern Sudan, owing to renewed violence, and that some 50,000 people had fled their homes in the region during the previous month.

The Government and the SPLM signed three protocols on 26 May 2004, which removed the remaining obstacles to the conclusion of a comprehensive peace accord. Specifically, the protocols stated that the SPLM and other southern groups would hold 30% of government seats in the north, while holding 70% of seats in the south; that the contested regions of the Blue Nile and the Nuba Mountains would be governed by an administration in which 55% of the seats would be taken by government officials and 45% by the SPLM, while the petroleum-rich region of Abyei would be granted special status and be governed by the presidential office; and that Khartoum would remain under Islamic law with certain protections for non-Muslims.

The final round of the IGAD-sponsored talks began in Naivasha in late June 2004, although progress was delayed by the Sudanese authorities' attempts to involve other pro-government southern militias in the talks. Talks eventually resumed in October and on 31 December a permanent cease-fire was agreed by the Sudanese Government and the SPLM. On 9 January 2005 Garang and Vice-President Ali Osman Muhammad Taha signed the Comprehensive Peace Agreement (CPA) in Nairobi in the presence of Powell and representatives from the UN, the European Union (EU, see p. 255), the African Union (AU, see p. 172) and IGAD, thus formally bringing an end to more than 20 years of civil conflict between the SPLA and successive governments. Under the agreement Garang was to assume the position of Sudanese Vice-President in late February and would act as President of southern Sudan during the six-year period of autonomy, after which a referendum on secession would be held. However, by mid-April Garang had yet to take up either position and it was announced that the commission charged with formulating a new constitution would not be appointed until later that month. Meanwhile, in mid-January the Government signed a peace accord with the NDA in Cairo, Egypt, which allowed for the return of NDA leaders to Sudan and granted them the right to conduct their political activities in the country.

In late January 2005 it was announced that the administrative capital of southern Sudan would be established at Rumbek, a town with limited electricity and running water, which had been extensively damaged by bombing during the civil conflict. The UN appealed for the international community to assist with the reconstruction of southern Sudan's infrastructure. On 25 January the UN announced that it had restored diplomatic ties with Sudan and would contribute some €50m. in aid, to be divided equally between the north and the south, and in early February the UN Secretary-General, Kofi Annan, announced plans to deploy some 10,000 peace-keeping troops to Sudan to monitor the cease-fire and assist with the disarmament process. In mid-March the Government launched its six-year recovery and development plan, the main priority of which was to rebuild the country's infrastructure, predicted to cost US $8,000m. over two years. In late March the UN Security Council unanimously approved Resolution 1590, which provided for the establishment of the UN Mission in Sudan (UNMIS), comprising up to 10,000 peace-keeping troops and 715 civilian personnel and to be deployed in southern Sudan for an initial period of six months; a contingent of Nepalese soldiers duly commenced duties at the end of the month.

In early June 2005 the UP, the PNC and 14 smaller opposition parties signed an agreement to form a new coalition, styled the National Forces Coalition. At a meeting held in Cairo in mid-June Taha and the NDA leaders signed an agreement for the NDA to join a power-sharing administration and the NDA subsequently nominated 27 of its members to the commission charged with drafting the new interim Constitution. In late June al-Bashir announced the release of 'all political detainees', among them at-Turabi. Earlier that month the President had lifted the ban prohibiting all political activity by the PNC. On 6 July the National Assembly ratified the new interim Constitution (see below) and on 9 July Garang was appointed First Vice-President of the new presidential council, replacing Taha who took the role of Vice-President, and as President of Southern Sudan. In mid-July Government troops withdrew from Juba and the surrounding area in accordance with the CPA, which stipulated that 17% of Government troops be redeployed within six months of signing the agreement, and Garang named the SPLM deputy leader, Commdr Salva Kiir Mayardit, as Vice-President of the new southern administration. Interim governors were also appointed to each of the 10 states in southern Sudan. On 1 August it was announced that Garang had been killed in a helicopter crash as he travelled to Rumbek from Kampala. Salva Kiir succeeded Garang as leader of the SPLA/SPLM, and was later appointed as First Vice-President of Sudan and President of Southern Sudan. Also in early August al-Bashir announced the formation of a committee to investigate the circumstances surrounding Garang's death.

During August 2005 differences regarding wealth-sharing and the allocation of the energy portfolio continued to obstruct the formation of a government of national unity. However, in late September an agreement was reached and the list of government ministers was announced, in which 16 portfolios (including those of defence, interior, finance and energy and mining) were awarded to members of the NC, nine to the SPLM and four to members of smaller opposition parties. In late January 2006, at the sixth AU summit, which took place in Khartoum, the emergence of al-Bashir as the leading candidate for the chairmanship of the organization provoked widespread criticism from the international community and proved unacceptable to representatives from a number of AU member states. Following two days of negotiations, it was agreed that the President of the Republic of Congo, Gen. Denis Sassou-Nguesso, would assume the chairmanship in 2006, to be succeeded by al-Bashir in 2007. Faced with unanimous opposition, in January 2007 al-Bashir withdrew his candidacy and the President of Ghana, John Kufuor, assumed the role of Chairman.

Meanwhile, in February 2003 a new area of conflict emerged in the Darfur region of western Sudan. The Sudan Liberation Movement (SLM) announced the commencement of an armed campaign to end Darfur's political and economic marginalization and to combat the Government's 'ethnic cleansing' activities in the region. The SLM, which was reported to have some 1,500 troops and received support from Eritrea, subsequently attacked the provincial capital, Al-Fasher. In an attempt to suppress the revolt the Sudanese authorities armed pro-Government ethnic Arab militias, known as the *Janjaweed*, who systematically razed entire villages to the ground and carried out indiscriminate killings. In April the Sudanese authorities refused offers of talks with the rebels, dismissed senior security officials in the region, and deployed additional forces to Darfur to retake most of the territory that had been lost to the SLM. Fighting continued in the area until early September, when, following mediation from the Chadian Government, a cease-fire was agreed. Under the accord, the Government agreed to release more than 50 suspected SLM members from detention. However, there were reports of ongoing incidents in Darfur during late 2003, with large numbers of Sudanese, fleeing alleged human rights abuses, crossing the border into Chad to seek refuge. In December aid agencies maintained that the Sudanese Government was preventing food and medical supplies from reaching the Darfur region, and in January 2004 Sudanese planes reportedly bombed a number of villages in the border area, just weeks after the rebels claimed to have killed some 700 government troops. By March it was estimated that more than 130,000 Sudanese had entered Chad and as many as 900,000 people had been displaced as a result of the ongoing conflict and the rapidly deteriorating humanitarian situation. At the end of that month indirect peace talks between the Government, the SLM and the Sudan Justice and Equality Movement (SJEM), attended by international observers, commenced in Chad, and on 8 April a 45-day humanitarian cease-fire was signed by representatives of the three parties. By early June it was estimated that as a result of continued violence in Darfur more than 30,000 people had been killed and a further 1m. people had been displaced, with 350,000 of those at risk from starvation and disease.

Following visits from Annan and Powell to refugee camps in Darfur in late June 2004 and the threat of the imposition of UN sanctions on the *Janjaweed*, in early July the Sudanese authorities committed to a series of actions, including the more aggressive use of the security forces to deal with the militia, the easing of travel restrictions for aid workers and the deployment of AU troops in Darfur. There followed a marginal improvement in access granted to humanitarian aid agencies but the security situation remained precarious as militias continued to attack civilian populations. In mid-July AU-sponsored peace talks between the Sudanese Government and the rebels opened in Addis Ababa, Ethiopia. The talks swiftly collapsed after the Government rejected the preconditions set out by the SLM and the SJEM for further negotiations, which included the disarmament of the *Janjaweed* and the removal of those *Janjaweed* fighters absorbed by the police and army; the observation of the April cease-fire agreement; the prosecution of the perpetrators of crimes and an inquiry into allegations of genocide; unimpeded humanitarian access for aid agencies; the release of prisoners of war; and a 'neutral' venue for future talks. In late July the US House of Representatives approved a resolution declaring the human rights abuses in Darfur a 'genocide' and on 30 July the UN Security Council adopted a resolution (No. 1556), that called on the Sudanese Government to end the conflict in Darfur, to facilitate the delivery of humanitarian aid, and to grant AU peace monitors access to the region. The resolution was rejected by the Sudanese Government and the armed forces spokesman, Gen. Muhammad Bashir Suleiman, described it as a 'declaration of war'.

In early August 2004 the UN Special Envoy to Sudan, Jan Pronk, agreed a number of measures with the Sudanese Government, aimed at averting the imposition of sanctions if certain conditions were fulfilled. However, in mid-August aid workers continued to report government-imposed travel restrictions and incidences of government-assisted violence occurring across the Darfur region. On 20 August the Sudanese Government admitted to the UN that it had control over certain *Janjaweed* members and stated that it would divulge the names of those fighters of which it was aware. On 25 August the Government agreed to allow further foreign troops into Darfur. However, as the UN Security Council resolution expired at the end of the month, observers of the cease-fire reported that the government forces had launched attacks on civilians in Darfur only one week previously and Annan announced that the Sudanese authorities had failed to meet the requirements set out by the UN.

In mid-September 2004 the UN Security Council approved a second resolution (No. 1564), stating that it would consider imposing sanctions affecting Sudan's petroleum industry should it fail to take steps to disarm the *Janjaweed* and protect civilians from further attacks. The UN was also to establish a commission to investigate claims that the human rights abuses in Darfur amounted to genocide, while the AU planned to increase the size of its monitoring force in the region (the African Union Mission in Sudan—AMIS) from 350 to some 3,500. Further peace talks held days earlier between the Government, the SLA and the SJEM in Abuja, Nigeria, ended without agreement. In early October 2004 the British Prime Minister, Anthony (Tony) Blair, arrived in Sudan for talks with President al-Bashir in an attempt to resolve the Darfur issue. A five-point peace plan, proposed by Blair, was accepted by the President. In agreeing to the plan, the Sudanese Government pledged to allow an increase in the number of AU troops in the country; to identify its forces in Darfur to enable the effective monitoring of the cease-fire; to commit to a cessation of hostilities in Darfur within three months and to negotiate a comprehensive agreement to the ongoing conflict in southern Sudan (see above) by the end of 2004; and to assist with the distribution of humanitarian aid.

In mid-November 2004, following talks in Abuja, the Government agreed to establish a 'no-fly' zone over the Darfur region (the rebels had accused government forces of using aircraft to support *Janjaweed* attacks). In mid-December AU cease-fire monitors reported that they had witnessed large quantities of arms and ammunition being delivered to government forces in Darfur. Days later, following the expiry of a deadline imposed by the AU for both sides to cease all hostilities, the Sudanese authorities agreed to end military operations in Darfur on the condition that the rebels also refrained from acts of violence. Despite the agreement, the AU reported later in December that government forces had attacked the village of Labado in the south of the Darfur region. Continued attacks were reported and in early February 2005 a UN commission of inquiry revealed that although serious crimes against humanity had taken place, these did not amount to genocide. It did, however, identify 51 suspected war criminals and recommended that they be tried by the International Criminal Court (ICC, see p. 324), which was to undertake preparatory analysis of the situation prior to deciding whether to commence a full investigation into allegations of war crimes committed in Darfur. Al-Bashir pledged not to send any Sudanese nationals abroad for trial, but the Minister of External Relations, Dr Mustafa Osman Ismail, subsequently offered to hold any future ICC trial in Sudan. In late April the AU confirmed that additional peace-keeping troops would arrive in Darfur by the end of September, increasing the number of AMIS troops to 7,731.

In mid-May 2005 the SLM and the SJEM agreed to maintain a cease-fire and to engage in further talks with the Government. However, according to the UN there was an increase in the number of reported instances of rape and kidnapping in the region during the month of April and attacks on civilians by *Janjaweed* fighters continued. In late May a conference for international donor countries was held in Addis Ababa and US $200m. was pledged to fund the enlarged AU peace-keeping operation in Darfur. NATO had previously announced that it would provide training, logistics and technical support to the mission. In early June the ICC commenced an investigation into allegations that the Sudanese Government and the *Janjaweed* had committed crimes against humanity in the Darfur region. Talks between rebels and the Government resumed in Abuja in mid-June, after which the two sides signed a declaration of principles. Meanwhile, in mid-June the Government established a court at which 162 people accused of committing crimes against humanity in the Darfur region were to be tried, and referred to the institution as 'an alternative' to the ICC. The court was rejected by rebel groups in Darfur, who claimed that Sudanese officials would escape trial, and Pronk dismissed the notion that the court could replace the ICC. In mid-July the SLM and SJEM signed an agreement to end their dispute and to normalize relations following a meeting in Tripoli, Libya. Despite the absence of an SLM faction, talks resumed in mid-September amid reports of increasing violence in Darfur. In early October a rebel faction captured 18 AU peace-keeping staff close to the border with Chad, although most were released after one day. Also in early October four AU peace-keepers were killed in southern Darfur and in mid-October concerns over escalating violence prompted the UN to withdraw all non-essential staff from Darfur. In late November Annan reported a further increase in violence against civilians in the region and the AU called for an end to the killing of civilians as peace talks resumed in Abuja. The human rights organization Human Rights Watch (HRW) released a report in mid-December, which accused al-Bashir, Taha and several other senior Government officials of involvement in crimes against humanity committed in Darfur. The report also called for them to be investigated by the ICC and added to a UN list of suspects eligible for sanctions. Later in December ICC investigators were refused permission by the Government to visit Darfur to gather evidence of alleged crimes against humanity.

In mid-January 2006 Annan called upon the USA and European countries to contribute logistical support and troops for a planned UN peace-keeping mission in Darfur. The AU had earlier warned that a lack of funds would lead to the eventual withdrawal of AMIS from the region. Sudan declared its vehement opposition to the proposal and al-Bashir reportedly stated that Darfur would become a 'graveyard' for any foreign troops deployed in the region. In late January the SLM and the SJEM announced the formation of the Alliance of Revolutionary Forces in West Sudan, in a move intended to strengthen the rebels' position in the Abuja negotiations. In early March the AU voted to extend the mandate of AMIS until September, when a UN force was expected to assume peace-keeping duties. However, Arab League heads of state, meeting in Khartoum in late March, agreed to provide funds for the AU force to remain and voted to support Sudanese opposition to the deployment of non-African peace-keeping troops. In late April the UN Security Council approved Resolution 1672, imposing sanctions on four individuals suspected of involvement in crimes committed in the Darfur region: Maj.-Gen. Gaafar Muhammad el-Hassan, Commander of the Western Military Region for the Sudanese Air Force; the Commander of the SLA, Adam Yacub Shant; the Field Commander of the rebel National Movement for Reform and Development, Gabril Abdulkareem Badri; and Sheikh Musa Hilal of the *Janjaweed* militia were banned from travelling outside of Sudan and any assets they held abroad were to be 'frozen'. Also in late April the Government agreed to accept an AU peace agreement. However, the 30 April deadline was twice extended by two days, and officials from the USA and United Kingdom arrived in Abuja to aid the negotiations.

On 4 May 2006 the SJEM and the SLM faction led by Abd al-Wahid Muhammad an-Nur rejected the agreement. Nevertheless, the faction led by Minni Minawi announced that it had accepted the proposals, despite reservations regarding certain conditions, and the Darfur Peace Agreement (DPA) was signed on 5 May. The measures stipulated in the document included, *inter alia*, a Government undertaking to disarm completely the *Janjaweed* by mid-October; the establishment of buffer zones around refugee camps and access routes for humanitarian aid organizations; the integration of rebel forces into the Sudanese armed forces and police; the allocation of eight seats in the National Assembly to Minawi's group; and the transfer of US $300m. to a reconstruction and development fund for Darfur, and further annual transfers of $200m. for two years thereafter. The agreement also proposed that a referendum be held in 2008 to decide upon the issue of Darfur being recognized as a region rather than as three separate states. In mid-May 2006 the deadline for the two remaining rebel groups to accept the DPA was extended until the end of May and negotiations continued. However, the deadline passed and the two remaining factions maintained their opposition to the DPA.

In June 2006 a joint AU-UN delegation arrived in Darfur to assess the needs of AMIS and the feasibility of its replacement by a UN force. In July, at an AU Summit in Banjul, The Gambia, the UN Secretary-General announced that President al-Bashir had refused to allow UN troops to take over from AMIS. It was also announced that the AU would withdraw its peace-keeping force from the region at the end of September. A conference convened in mid-July under the auspices of the UN also failed to convince the Sudanese Government to accept a UN peace-keeping force, although participating countries pledged some US $200m. in funds, the majority of which would be used to assist the increasingly overwhelmed AU troops. Concerns began to emerge that UN peace-keepers would eventually be deployed but under a weaker mandate, thus limiting the force's scope to protect civilians. Minawi repeatedly called for UN forces to be sent to the troubled region and in mid-June he threatened to withdraw from the peace agreement, claiming that the deal would collapse without the immediate support of the international community. In July the two signatories of the DPA, the Government and Minawi's faction of the SLM, launched violent attacks on the rebel groups who had rejected the peace agreement. New factions had begun to emerge to challenge Minawi's increasing power in the north of Darfur, joining forces to form the National Redemption Front (NRF). Fighting subsequently spread from northern Darfur towards the west of the region.

On 31 August 2006 the UN Security Council adopted a resolution (No. 1706), which provided for some 17,300 additional military personnel and 3,300 civilian police to be dispatched to Sudan to support UNMIS, and for its mandate to be extended to assume the responsibilities of AMIS in Darfur. Violence in the region had escalated during that month and the UN, the AU and humanitarian agencies alleged that Minawi's troops had joined Government forces and the *Janjaweed* militia in fighting the rebel groups. The Sudanese Government continued to refuse to allow UN forces into Darfur and reinforcements were deployed to the region; AU forces remaining in the area reported that Government troops had bombed rebel-held villages, threatening the delivery of aid supplies. In response the AU increased the number of peace-keeping personnel and stated that AMIS would remain in Darfur until the end of the year.

On 27 September 2006 President al-Bashir issued a decree establishing an interim authority in Darfur, in accordance with the terms of the DPA. The authority was to be headed by Minawi, in his capacity as senior assistant to the President, a position to which he was appointed following the signing of the CPA. He was to be supported by a group of advisers, including the Governors of the three states in Darfur.

In an unprecedented move to deter the deployment of UN troops Sudan allegedly issued a warning to neighbouring countries in October 2006 that any offer to provide peace-keeping personnel would be considered a 'hostile act'. The Government denied this claim, but maintained that it would only accept UN assistance given under the auspices of the AU, despite the AU's continued warnings that it was unable to cope under the pressure of limited funding and resources. Following alleged attacks by government forces, rebel groups in Darfur stated that they were obliged to take appropriate action to defend themselves since the Government had refused to allow UN troops into the region to protect civilians. A spokesman for the NRF claimed that the new rebel force was not bound by any previous cease-fire agreement and the conflict continued.

In October 2006, the Government issued a statement that a plan had been devised to fulfil the commitments of the DPA, including the disarmament of the Arab militia group. The plan was submitted to the AU and was to be implemented over a two-month period, extending the original deadline for disarming the militia group by two months. The following month, Minawi alleged that the Government was rearming and mobilizing the *Janjaweed* and called for the international community to act swiftly to find a resolution to the conflict. In December 2006 Jan Eliasson, hitherto the Swedish Minister for Foreign Affairs, replaced Pronk as UN Special Envoy to Sudan.

In November 2006 discussions took place in Addis Ababa on measures to reinforce the AMIS forces, which had thus far failed to halt the violence in Darfur. Proposals were made for a hybrid AU-UN force with a greater role to be assumed by the UN troops. Sudan again reiterated its opposition to the presence of UN troops; however, later that month Sudan announced that it accepted, in principle, the proposal of a hybrid force, but requested further discussions on key issues before any changes could be implemented. Meanwhile, the AU agreed to extend the mandate of AMIS until mid-2007 as the UN temporarily withdrew non-essential staff from the capital of Northern Darfur state amid fears of escalating violence between rebel fighters and the *Janjaweed*.

The UN Security Council continued with efforts to persuade Sudan to accept a joint AU-UN mission in Darfur, and in late December 2006 al-Bashir accepted the proposals, stating that UN plans required immediate implementation. However, it was stipulated that the AU was to remain in command of the hybrid force. A three-part UN plan was initiated: the first phase included reinforcing the much-weakened AU force with UN troops and supplies, to be followed by further support packages. The third phase required the overhaul of the size and command of the force, in favour of a greater UN role, to which Sudan remained resolutely opposed. Nevertheless, by 31 December the AU had secured a tentative cease-fire agreement from rebel groups in northern Darfur.

Peace efforts were undermined in January 2007 when the day after the cease-fire was agreed insurgent-held positions were bombed. A Government spokesman initially denied any involvement in the attacks; however, al-Bashir subsequently admitted that Government troops had bombed rebel forces, but claimed that this did not breach the cease-fire agreement since they were defending themselves from rebel attacks. The Government appeared to relent and agreed to measures to restore peace, including a 60-day cease-fire and an AU-UN-sponsored peace summit, to be held in Ethiopia later that month. Journalists were once more permitted to enter the region after a two-month ban. In late January the ICC dispatched a team of officials to Khartoum to investigate crimes committed during the conflict in Darfur and in late February the ICC indicted the former Minister of State for the Interior, Ahmad Muhammad Harun, and the leader of the *Janjaweed* militia, Ali Muhammad Ali Abd ar-Rahman, on multiple charges of war crimes and crimes against humanity. The following month the Sudanese authorities announced that they had suspended all co-operation with the ICC. In May that body issued arrest warrants for Harun and ar-Rahman, who was reported to be in Sudanese custody. Meanwhile, a further shift in the stance of the Sudanese Government was reported in early February when al-Bashir appointed two members of rebel factions to executive positions in the Council of Ministers and in the Darfur administration. In July 2008 the Chief Prosecutor of the ICC, Luis Moreno Ocampo, presented evidence against al-Bashir in respect of 10 charges of genocide, crimes against humanity and war crimes committed in Darfur from March 2003, and requested the issuance of a warrant for Bashir's arrest. The Sudanese Government, in response, displayed a more united front and considered handing over Harun and ar-Rahman in return for the suspension of the case against al-Bashir; in September ar-Rahman was arrested and detained. In March 2009 an international arrest warrant for al-Bashir was formally issued. It was the first time charges of war crimes and genocide had been brought against a Head of State at the ICC, and the matter prompted a mixed response from regional leaders and the international community; some claimed that the decision would create further instability in the region and would not facilitate progress towards peace and reconciliation.

With increasingly widespread acceptance that the DPA signed in May 2006 had broken down, rebel factions agreed upon a need to collaborate in order to challenge the power of the ruling NC. By the end of December an alliance had formed, uniting many of the rebel groups that had refused to sign the DPA, styled the Non-Signatory Factions (NSF). A conference of NSF and remaining NRF commanders, due to be held in early 2007 to renegotiate the terms of the failed peace agreement, was delayed as government forces carried out a series of bomb attacks in the area where the conference was to take place. An-Nur's faction of the SLM, fearful of being overpowered by the NSF, joined with remaining non-signatories to threaten the credibility of the impending conference. Despite further clashes, the conference eventually commenced in February 2007.

Meanwhile, in January 2006 the National Assembly adopted controversial legislation governing the registration of political parties. The legislation prohibited any member of the armed forces (excluding al-Bashir and the First Vice-President Salva Kiir), the police, the security forces or the SPLA, and judges, judicial advisers, diplomats and high-ranking civil servants from joining any political party. The new law also made provisions for any party to be dissolved, or prevented from participating in elections, if it was believed to be undertaking activities that breached the CPA. The legislation was proposed by the SPLM and approved by the NC. Claiming that this contravened the Constitution and defied democratic rule, the NDA withdrew from the National Assembly in protest.

As the conflict in western Sudan continued, the people of eastern Sudan, including the Rashaida and the Beja communities, expressed their increasing resentment towards the Government. The eastern regions had been severely affected by drought and famine and, encouraged by the success of the SPLA in forcing negotiations with the Government, some of the Beja launched an armed struggle, supported by NDA and SPLA forces. The Beja Congress, which emerged during the 1960s, was joined during the 1990s by the Rashaida Free Lions group, and in 2005 the two groups merged to form the Eastern Front (EF). Although their forces were much smaller than those rebel groups fighting in Darfur, they occupied strategic points, launching attacks on the road and rail routes that provided access to the only port on the coast of Sudan, and threatened to destabilize the country's economy. Military offensives by government forces failed to prevent the EF from launching more attacks on eastern Sudan's transport and economic infrastructure and in 2006 the Government agreed to negotiate with the group. In June 2006 talks were held in Asmara, presided over by the Eritrean authorities, and on 19 June the Government and the EF signed an agreement on a set of principles for developing a peace agreement; a cease-fire was also implemented, to be monitored by Eritrean military officials. Peace talks resumed in July and, after lengthy negotiations, a power-sharing agreement was signed on 9 October. The following day the positions of presidential assistant and presidential adviser were assigned to members of the rebel group, along with other positions in the Government at both national and regional level. The peace deal was ratified by the Sudanese authorities on 18 October, ending several years of conflict between the Government and the EF.

Concerns were raised in late 2005 that the ongoing conflict in Darfur could spread to neighbouring Chad. In late November Sudan accused the Chadian air force of violating Sudanese airspace by flying over the Darfur region and claimed that Chadian armed forces had crossed the border into Darfur to steal cattle. Chad responded with accusations that Sudan had provided weapons to a group of soldiers who had deserted the Chadian army and were planning to overthrow the President of Chad, Gen. Idriss Deby. In mid-December Chadian rebels based in Darfur attacked the border town of Adre and the Chadian Government declared 'a state of belligerence' with Sudan, which it held ultimately responsible for the assault. In February 2006 the two countries held talks in Libya aimed at preventing further escalation in the dispute and agreement was reached to restore diplomatic relations and to prevent rebels from using territory to launch cross-border raids. However, in March Deby publicly questioned Sudan's commitment to the accord following a series of attacks on villages in Chad by the *Janjaweed*, allegedly with Sudanese 'material and financial' assistance. In mid-April Deby expelled the Sudanese ambassador to Chad and ordered the closure of the land border between the two countries following an attack on the Chadian capital, N'Djamena, by rebel forces. However, a threat to forcibly return Sudanese refugees was subsequently withdrawn. In early August, at a meeting convened in N'Djamena the two countries agreed to restore diplomatic relations and reopen border crossings and embassies. By November it had become apparent that the conflict in Darfur had spread into the Central African Republic (CAR). In the north of that country, groups of rebel fighters had begun to form, forming allegiances with Chadian factions and providing a route through to Chad for the Sudanese rebels. As the conflict spread many aid workers began to withdraw, leaving the inhabitants of eastern Chad facing a potential health crisis. In February 2007 a summit was held under the auspices of French President Jacques Chirac, during which the CAR, Chad and Sudan agreed that they would cease support for rebel fighters in either of the three countries. In early May, following mediation by Saudi Arabia's King Abdallah, Presidents al-Bashir and Deby agreed to co-operate with the AU and the UN in their attempts to stabilize the Chad–Sudan border. Both countries approved the formation of a joint border force, and pledged to cease training and funding rebel groups and to stop all cross-border attacks.

Also in April 2007 the UN Security Council approved the extension of the mandate of UNMIS until October. In mid-June 2007, following further discussions in Addis Ababa, the Government of Sudan agreed to accept a joint AU-UN peace-keeping force, comprising up to 20,000 troops. However, shortly after issuing a statement accepting the deployment of peace-keeping personnel, the Government began to delay the process, questioning the command structure of the operation. Nevertheless, the following month the UN Security Council adopted Resolution 1769 establishing UNAMID, the UN-AU hybrid operation in Darfur, with an initial mandate of 12 months. Further disagreements threatened to disrupt the process when, in August, the AU announced that UNAMID peace-keeping forces would comprise only African personnel, safeguarding the AU's lead role in Sudan. UNAMID assumed peace-keeping operations on 31 December but was severely under-resourced with less than one-half of the pledged 20,000 troops deployed. In February 2008 a legal framework was agreed, which would allow UNAMID peace-keepers to move freely within the country without fear of attacks by government forces. In July the UN Security Council extended UNAMID's mandate until July 2009 by 14 votes to one, with the notable abstention of the USA in protest over the indictments for war crimes in the Darfur conflict (see above). Meanwhile, further peace negotiations were initiated by President Abdoulaye Wade of Senegal and in March 2008, at a meeting in Dakar, Senegal, attended by regional leaders and EU and UN representatives, Chad and Sudan signed a non-aggression agreement renewing their commitment to restoring peace. Nevertheless, violence in the region continued and thousands more civilians were reported to have crossed the border into Chad to escape the conflict. In May Sudan accused Chadian rebels of involvement in an attack on Sudan's largest city, Omdurman, and severed diplomatic relations with Chad. Chad subsequently accused Sudan of attacking a town on the common border, although Sudan denied the allegations. In June military leaders from Chad and Sudan met in Senegal to discuss mechanisms for ensuring security in the border region, including the deployment of troops at strategic positions along the border, and diplomatic ties were later restored. However, in August hundreds of people implicated in the Omdurman attack remained in detention without charge.

Reports emerged in September 2008 that government forces had launched a renewed campaign of violence in eastern Darfur, attacking rebel strongholds in an attempt to secure access to oil reserves and transport routes to Chad. Rebels in the nearby oil-rich province of Kordofan were mobilized to support the offensive, evoking concerns that the crisis in Darfur could spread eastwards. Located on the border with Southern Sudan, the region is vital for oil supplies to the south; however, jurisdiction of the area remains with Khartoum and the people of Kordofan were expected to play an important role in both the forthcoming general election and the referendum on the status of Southern Sudan. As fighting continued in Darfur, al-Bashir announced a unilateral cease-fire in November, including the disarmament of pro-Government militia, on the condition that sufficient measures for monitoring the situation were implemented. However, the failure of previous attempts to impose cease-fire in the region led many to doubt the sincerity of the announcement and rebel leaders demanded that the *Janjaweed* be disarmed before they would consider laying down their own weapons. Reinforcements from Pakistan and Ethiopia were deployed to Darfur in December to assist the peace-keeping operation, taking the number of UNAMID troops to some 12,737, only 60% of the numbers authorized at its inception. Additional African troops were pledged in early 2009 with UNAMID expected to be operating at full strength by October of that year. In February the SJEM signed a accord with the Sudanese Government, laying the foundation for renewed peace negotiations in Darfur, but talks stalled the following month when the SJEM withdrew from the accord after humanitarian aid workers were expelled from the country.

Meanwhile, Salva Kiir effected a minor ministerial reshuffle of the Government of Southern Sudan (GOSS) in July 2007 in an attempt to consolidate his cabinet's power, suggesting that the

SPLM planned to take a firmer approach to dealing with the ruling NC. In September Salva Kiir accused the Government in Khartoum of undermining the CPA by failing to withdraw troops from the southern oilfields and refusing to pay Southern Sudan its due revenues.

In September 2007 the UN Secretary General, Ban Ki-Moon, announced that a further round of peace talks on Darfur had been scheduled for the following month, to take place in Tripoli. The Government later agreed to comply with the terms of a cease-fire agreement, to be enforced during the peace negotiations. Al-Bashir also urged rebel leaders to attend the talks, although it was not immediately apparent which of the rebel groups had agreed to participate. In late September 10 AU peacekeepers in Darfur were killed in an attack believed to have been carried out by a breakaway rebel faction, while further attacks were reported in other parts of the country. Talks commenced in Tripoli on 27 October; however, in response to continued attacks by government forces, many rebel groups declined to attend the meeting and instead held separate talks in Juba, convened by the Government of Southern Sudan. The Tripoli talks had been further hindered by the collapse of the coalition Government in Khartoum earlier that month. In mid-October the SPLM withdrew from the Government in protest against delays in implementing the CPA. Al-Bashir subsequently reorganized the Council of Ministers, naming SPLM members Deng Alor Kol as Minister of Foreign Affairs and Mansur Khaled as Minister of Foreign Trade among the new appointments. Salva Kiir also effected changes to the GOSS in which two ministers were dismissed and two new presidential advisers were appointed. Additional governmental changes were implemented in December when seven SPLM members were appointed to the central Government. Akol, who had been demoted from the position of Minister of Foreign Affairs to Minister of Cabinet Affairs in the October reshuffle, was dismissed from the cabinet and replaced by Pagan Amum of the SPLM. Akol had been accused by fellow SPLM members of developing close ties with the NC. Al-Bashir carried out a further minor reorganization of the Government in mid-February 2008. Lt-Gen. Nhial Deng Nhial was named GOSS Minister of SPLA Affairs following the death of his predecessor, Dominic Dim Deng, in a plane crash in May; a presidential adviser was also killed in the incident.

Renewed violence in the Abyei region broke out in early 2008 after a period of relative calm, once again highlighting the prevalence of the north–south divide. Clashes between the SPLA and members of the Misseriya tribe (supported by the NC) threatened to ignite the situation in Darfur and to derail progress towards holding presidential and legislative elections planned for July 2009. A referendum on the status of the Darfur region, which had already been postponed until 2011, would potentially be further delayed if the 2009 elections were not held as scheduled. Nevertheless, a national census commenced in April 2008 in an attempt to ensure the general election could take place, although rebel groups opposed the census. It was also agreed that the dispute over Abyei's status should be referred for arbitration at the International Court of Justice (ICJ) in The Hague, Netherlands. An interim administration was established in the Abyei region in August; Arop Moyak of the SPLM was named Chief Administrator, while the NC's Rahama Abuldrahman an-Nur was appointed Deputy Chief Administrator. In April 2009 the elections were postponed until November of that year.

In addition to civil war and economic crisis, Sudan has experienced drought and famine, and the problem has been compounded by a very large number of refugees in the southern provinces, mainly from Ethiopia and Chad. At the end of 2007, according to estimates from the office of the UN High Commissioner for Refugees (UNHCR), there were some 523,032 Sudanese refugees abroad, of whom 242,555 were in Chad, 162,063 in Uganda, 45,261 in Kenya, and 35,493 in Ethiopia. Sudan was also host to some 222,722 refugees at that time, of whom 160,488 were originally from Eritrea. During 1997 there had been large-scale refugee repatriation, particularly to Ethiopia and the DRC, but in 1998 a further 37,000 refugees arrived in Sudan, including 10,300 from Kenya and 9,500 from Uganda. During 2000 more than 94,000 Eritrean refugees fleeing the border war with Ethiopia entered Sudanese territory; by the end of that year, however, some 68,000 had been repatriated. In early 2003 the US Committee for Refugees stated that Sudan possessed the largest internally displaced population in the world, officially estimated at 4m. people. By late 2004, as a result of the Darfur conflict, it was estimated by UNHCR that some 1.6m. people were displaced within Darfur and that some 200,000 people had fled to neighbouring Chad. In December 2002 the refugee status of Eritreans living in Sudan expired, and in the following month UNHCR convoys, which would return Eritreans to their country, recommenced. It was reported that since May 2001 more than 100,000 Eritreans had been repatriated. In 2002 some 18,000 Sudanese were repatriated from Kenya. In late December 2005 UNHCR announced that some 500,000 refugees were to be repatriated to southern Sudan from neighbouring countries. The process commenced earlier that month when 90,000 Sudanese refugees left northern Kenya.

Meanwhile, in June 1997 the Government banned relief flights to the south—an act that caused concern to aid agencies; the UN Children's Fund stated that thousands of children were at risk and announced that there had been a rise in the infant mortality rate in that area. By April 1998 many aid agencies were warning of widespread famine in the south if immediate action was not taken. The Government initially refused to act, as it claimed that aid would fall into rebel hands. However, in May the Government agreed to reopen all relief corridors in the worst affected areas and to allow the aid agencies to operate a total of 22 food distribution sites. In March 1999 further warnings were issued of impending famine. Hostilities again escalated in the south in August 2000, and the Sudanese Government was accused of deliberately bombing relief facilities in that region. In response, the UN announced the suspension of all aid flights under the Operation Lifeline Sudan programme. However, later that month, following personal assurances from al-Bashir that measures were being taken to ensure the safety of all humanitarian workers in the region, the UN agreed to resume relief flights. In February 2001 the UN World Food Programme launched an appeal for US $135m. of food aid, required to feed the estimated 2.9m. people in Sudan under threat of starvation as a result of the ongoing civil war and severe drought. However, in May the International Committee of the Red Cross temporarily suspended all aid deliveries, after the co-pilot of one of its planes was killed while flying over southern Sudan. Aid flights were subsequently resumed later that month. In mid-April 2005 donors from the international community, including the USA, the European Commission and the United Kingdom, pledged $4,500m. in aid which was to go directly to southern Sudan. By March 2006, however, the UN Special Envoy to Sudan, Jan Pronk, acknowledged that only a small portion of the money pledged had thus far been spent.

Following an unsuccessful coup attempt in 1976, Sudan severed diplomatic relations with Libya and established a mutual defence pact with Egypt. Diplomatic links between Sudan and Libya were restored in 1978, but relations became strained in 1981, during Libya's occupation of Chad, and President Nimeri frequently accused Libya of supporting plots against him. After the 1985 coup, Libya was the first country to recognize the new regime, and relations between the two countries improved significantly. Although Libya's military involvement in Chad declined, some Libyan forces remained in north-western Sudan, despite repeated Sudanese demands for their withdrawal. The regime that took power in Sudan in 1985 adopted a foreign policy of non-alignment, in contrast to Nimeri's strongly pro-Western attitude, and sought improved relations with Ethiopia and the USSR, to the concern of Sudan's former allies, Egypt and the USA. In 1990, after Lt-Gen. al-Bashir had visited Col Qaddafi, the Libyan leader, in Tripoli, Sudan and Libya signed a 'declaration of integration' that envisaged the complete union of the two countries within four years. In 1995 Sudan, Libya and Chad were reported to be discussing integration after eventual legislative elections in Chad. Tension subsequently arose between Libya and Sudan as a result of Libya's expulsion of Sudanese expatriate workers, but did not, apparently, detract from the two countries' commitment to integration, reiterated in 1996.

In September 1995 Ethiopia accused Sudan of harbouring terrorists implicated in the attempted assassination of President Mubarak in June and, in response, announced the closure of some Sudanese diplomatic facilities in the country and of non-governmental organizations connected with Sudan. In April 1996 Sudan claimed that Ethiopian government forces had collaborated with the SPLA in attacks on two towns in south-eastern Sudan, while in June Ethiopia accused Sudan of attempting to destabilize the region. In January 1997 relations deteriorated further when, following alleged attacks on Sudan, President al-Bashir declared a *jihad* (holy war) against Ethiopian aggression and ordered a general mobilization. Ethiopia, however, denied any involvement in the attacks. An improvement in relations was reported during 1998, although in December the Ethiopian Minister of Foreign Affairs stated that relations between the two countries would not improve until Sudan handed over those responsible for the attempted assassination of the Egyptian President. One of the suspects was extradited in 1999 (see below), and in November, on his return from a visit to Ethiopia, al-Bashir stated that relations with that country were fully normalized. The common border was reopened in early 2000, and in March the Sudanese and Ethiopian Governments signed a number of agreements, which provided for increased co-operation in political, cultural, commercial and transport sectors. Further agreements regarding border security were signed in the following month. Relations between the two countries were temporarily strained in late April 2001 after an internal Ethiopian flight was hijacked and diverted to Khartoum. Although the incident was brought to a swift conclusion, and all passengers on board the aircraft were released unharmed, the Sudanese authorities refused Ethiopia's request for the hijackers to be extradited to Ethiopia for trial. A seven-year dispute over border demarcation appeared to have been resolved in June 2008 when an accord was concluded, under which Ethiopia returned small pockets of land to the al-Qadaref region. However, Ethiopians complained that the Ethiopian Government had failed to consult its citizens on the matter and that the agreement granted Sudanese nationals the right to occupy certain areas of holy or historic importance. The chair of the joint border committee declared he would repeal the decision, although the Sudanese Government insisted that progress on the issue had been made.

Sudan's relations with Eritrea deteriorated after 1991, and in December 1994 Eritrea severed diplomatic relations with Sudan. Eritrea has sponsored meetings of the principal groups opposed to the Sudanese regime, which it accuses of lending support to the insurgent Eritrean Islamic Jihad. In December 1994 Eritrea sponsored a meeting between various Sudanese opposition groups, which resulted in a 'Declaration of Political Agreement'. The signatories included the SPLA, the UP and the DUP. In January 1995 Sudan demanded that Eritrea withdraw from the IGADD peace committee (see above), which also included Ethiopia, Kenya and Uganda. A further deterioration in relations occurred after a conference of the Sudanese opposition, organized by the NDA, was held in Asmara in June (see above). In July 1996 Sudanese government forces claimed that attacks had been launched against them from within Eritrea. In April 1997 Sudan protested to the UN over Eritrean aggression on its territory. In June Sudan denied Eritrean accusations that the Sudanese Government had masterminded a plot to assassinate the Eritrean President. The border was closed in June 1997, and again in February 1998, as a result of the violence; further attacks were reported in the border area by both Eritrea and Sudan throughout 1998. Following talks held in November 1998, in Qatar, the two sides signed an agreement for the open discussion of bilateral issues. A further meeting, held in May 1999, resulted in an accord, signed by the Presidents of Sudan and Eritrea, in which they agreed to restore diplomatic relations, to refrain from hostile propaganda and to establish joint committees, both to implement the terms of the accord and to study any further issues that might arise between the two countries, although tensions between the two countries remained. In June the two countries established joint committees in accordance with the terms of the Doha agreement. A further agreement was signed in Asmara in January 2000, providing for the immediate reopening of the two countries' borders and embassies and the resumption of flights between their airports. In February the Presidents of Eritrea and Sudan held talks in Khartoum, and it was agreed to issue passports to residents in the border area. Furthermore, they declared that they would not allow opposition groups located in their respective countries to launch cross-border raids. However, relations between the two countries deteriorated in July, when the Sudanese Government accused Eritrea of assisting the NDA with a planned offensive in eastern Sudan. In October President Afewerki visited Khartoum, where he held talks with al-Bashir, during which both sides expressed their desire for a fresh beginning to their bilateral relations and agreed to take measures to settle differences between the two countries in a peaceful manner. In July 2001 Eritrea and Sudan signed an agreement on border security, which aimed to eradicate smuggling and illegal infiltration, as well as ensure the safe passage of people and goods. Relations between the two countries deteriorated again in mid-2002, and in October the Sudanese authorities closed the common border, claiming that Eritrea had been involved in an NDA offensive in eastern Sudan. Following a meeting with the Yemeni President, Ali Abdullah Saleh, and the Ethiopian Prime Minister, Meles Zenawi, in December 2003, President al-Bashir accused Eritrea of arming and training rebels in the Darfur region of Sudan and maintained that Eritrea was a destabilizing force in the region. Eritrea refuted the allegations. In mid-October 2004 Eritrea accused Sudan of complicity in an attempt to assassinate President Afewerki, while Sudan maintained that Eritrea had provided rebels with arms in an attempt to destabilize the Sudanese Government. In mid-March 2005 it was announced that talks between the NDA and Sudanese authorities would take place in a further attempt to normalize relations. Relations between the two countries were again strained in late June when Sudan accused Eritrea of providing assistance to rebel forces who had attacked Sudanese government troops in eastern Sudan earlier that month. However, at a meeting in Khartoum in October Akol, who had earlier been appointed Minister of Foreign Affairs, signed an agreement with his Eritrean acting counterpart to work towards normalizing relations between Sudan and Eritrea. In August 2006 Second Vice-President Taha received a ministerial delegation from Eritrea; the two parties discussed the possibility of joint co-operation in fields such as agriculture and economics. Having been actively involved in securing a deal between the Sudanese Government and the EF (see above), Eritrea expressed its regret at Sudan's decision in mid-2008 to ban all political activity by Eritrean opposition movements.

Sudan and Uganda have accused each other of supporting groups opposed to their respective regimes, and in 1995 Uganda broke off diplomatic relations with Sudan. A further deterioration in relations in December brought the two countries to the brink of open war. In 1996 Sudan and Uganda agreed to restore diplomatic relations, provided that each side undertook to cease its support for rebel factions operating from the other's territory, and to participate in an international committee to monitor the agreement. In February 1997, in response to protests about its deployment of troops on the Sudan–Uganda border, Uganda denied accusations that it intended to invade Sudan. In late April Sudan denied allegations that its forces had invaded northern Uganda and, at the end of the month Dr Riek Mashar Teny-Dhurgon, the Chairman of the SSCC, visited Uganda to discuss relations between the two countries prior to the forthcoming IGAD summit meeting, which was later cancelled owing to a concurrent meeting of leaders of the Organization of African Unity (OAU, now the AU). In August President Mandela of South Africa hosted talks between the two countries. Relations between Sudan and Uganda improved during 1999, and in December, following a meeting in Nairobi, mediated by former US President Jimmy Carter, the two countries signed an accord in which they agreed to restore diplomatic relations and to end support to each other's rebel groups; shortly afterwards it was announced that eight leaders of the Lord's Resistance Army (LRA) were to be relocated from Sudan to a country of their choice in accordance with the agreement. In February 2000, however, Uganda expressed its dissatisfaction with Sudan's implementation of the accord and called for Sudan to disarm the LRA and to disband all LRA camps within Sudan. Sudan reaffirmed its commitment to the agreement and in June 2001 the two countries exchanged diplomats. In August the Ugandan embassy in Khartoum reopened and a chargé d'affaires was appointed. In March 2002 the two countries signed an agreement whereby Sudan temporarily authorized Ugandan troops to pursue LRA rebels within Sudan, and later that month the Ugandan Government announced that its troops had captured all four main bases in Sudan belonging to the LRA. In late November the Sudanese authorities agreed to extend permission for Ugandan troops to remain on its territory for as long as Uganda deemed necessary. Meanwhile, the two countries upgraded relations to ambassadorial level.

President Nimeri was one of very few Arab leaders to support President Sadat of Egypt's initiative for peace with Israel in 1978. Sudan's close relations with Egypt were consolidated in 1982, when a 'charter of integration' was signed. The first session of the joint 'Nile Valley Parliament', created by the charter, was convened in 1983 with 60 Sudanese and 60 Egyptian members. After the 1985 coup, the leaders of the two countries reaffirmed links between Khartoum and Cairo, despite the change of government in Sudan. Relations with Egypt deteriorated in 1991, as a result of the Sudanese Government's support for Iraq during the Gulf crisis. Egypt also expressed concern at the perceived growth of Islamic 'fundamentalism' in Sudan. The two countries are involved in a dispute over the Halaib border area, and in early 1992 relations deteriorated sharply following the announcement that Sudan had awarded a Canadian company a concession to explore for petroleum there. Relations deteriorated further, as Egypt repeatedly accused Sudan of supporting illegal Islamic fundamentalist groups in Egypt, while Sudan alleged that Egypt was supporting the SPLA. In August the Sudanese Government sought international arbitration on the Halaib issue, claiming that Egypt had been settling families in the area in an effort to bring it under Egyptian control. In January 1993 Sudan complained to the UN Security Council that Egyptian troops had infringed Sudan's territorial integrity. In March Egypt announced the construction of a new road link to Halaib. Sudan retaliated by appropriating the Khartoum campus of the University of Cairo. In June Sudan announced that it was closing two Egyptian consulates in Sudan and two of its own consulates in Egypt. A meeting between Lt-Gen. al-Bashir and President Mubarak of Egypt, during a summit session of the OAU at the end of June appeared, however, to ease tensions between the two countries, and was followed by a meeting of their respective Ministers of Foreign Affairs at the end of July. In May 1994 Sudan accused Egypt of establishing military posts on Sudanese territory, and at the end of the month the Sudanese Ministry of Foreign Affairs announced that Sudan wished to refer its dispute with Egypt to the ICJ for arbitration. In January 1995 Egypt rejected a request by Sudan to refer the dispute over the Halaib border area to a meeting of the OAU's council of Ministers of Foreign Affairs in Addis Ababa. On 26 June relations suffered a further, serious setback after the attempted assassination of President Mubarak of Egypt on his arrival in Addis Ababa to attend the annual conference of the OAU. The Egyptian Government immediately accused Sudan of complicity in the attack, and the OAU made the same allegation in September. In January 1996 the UN Security Council condemned Sudan's role in the attempted assassination and adopted Resolution 1044 seeking the extradition of three individuals implicated in the attack. Relations between Sudan and Egypt appeared to improve in 1997; in December talks were held between President al-Bashir and senior Egyptian officials, and in January 1998 it was agreed that a joint chamber of commerce would be established. In May a joint Sudanese-Egyptian technical committee met in Khartoum to finalize details for the return of several institutions in Sudan to Egyptian control. Both sides agreed that the institutions should be returned, although differences remained over the time period for this operation. In October Sudan and Egypt agreed on a plan to hasten the normalization of relations, and a further meeting was held in Cairo in January 1999 to discuss bilateral relations. In June it was announced that diplomatic relations between the two countries were to be upgraded. Relations improved further in July when it was announced that Sudan had extradited one of the three suspects implicated in the attempted assassination of Mubarak. In December the two countries agreed to normalize their relations and to resolve their dispute over the Halaib issue amicably. In March 2000 it was announced that the University of Cairo in Khartoum was to be reopened, and later that month Egypt appointed an ambassador to Sudan for the first time since the assassination attempt on Mubarak. In September the Sudanese and Egyptian ministers responsible for foreign affairs held the first session of the Egyptian-Sudanese Commission for 10 years, at which the two countries expressed their commitment to further bilateral economic development. In May 2003 Mubarak visited Khartoum for the first time since the attempted assassination and held talks with al-Bashir, during which the two leaders reaffirmed their commitment to improving relations between Egypt and Sudan.

The USA has been one of the severest critics of the present Sudanese Government, frequently expressing concern about Sudan's links with Iran. Allegations of Sudanese involvement in terrorism resulted in the detention in the USA, in 1993, of five Sudanese residents suspected of plotting to blow up buildings and road tunnels in New York, and to assassinate President Mubarak of Egypt on a visit to the USA; the USA subsequently added Sudan to its list of countries accused of sponsoring terrorism. In August 1997 the USA imposed economic sanctions against Sudan, owing to its alleged continued support for terrorism. In late August 1998 the USA launched a missile attack on what it claimed was a chemical weapons factory in Khartoum. Immediately after the attack, however, the Sudanese Government denied these claims and stated that it was, in fact, a private pharmaceuticals plant. Sudan recalled its ambassador to the USA and refused permission for US aircraft to use its airspace; its requests for a UN inquiry into the attack were unanimously refused by the Security Council, despite backing from the League of Arab States (see p. 344) and the Organization of the Islamic Conference (see p. 382). By February 1999 it had become evident that the US intelligence on which the attack had been based was fundamentally flawed. In May Sudan requested compensation for the damage caused by the bomb attack, and in July 2000 the proprietor of the factory announced his intention to sue the US Government for damages. Meanwhile, in April 1999 the USA had announced its decision to ease sanctions on the export of food and medicine to Sudan, and at the end of May Sudan fulfilled one of the conditions set by the USA for a review of the sanctions regime by signing a treaty banning chemical weapons. In November, however, the USA enacted controversial legislation allowing food aid to be delivered directly to the Sudanese rebels. An improvement in relations was evident in March 2000 following a visit to Sudan by a US diplomat to discuss the possibility of reopening the US embassy in Khartoum; in mid-April the embassy was duly reopened. However, relations once again deteriorated in December, when Sudan lodged an official complaint with the UN after the US Assistant Secretary of State, Susan Rice, visited rebel-held areas of southern Sudan in November, without the permission of the Sudanese Government. Following the election of a new US Administration, under the leadership of President George W. Bush, in January 2001, there was some uncertainty regarding the USA's policy towards Sudan. In July the Bush administration outlined its three main policy objectives for Sudan: to deal with the humanitarian crisis, to end Sudan's role as a sanctuary for terrorism, and to promote a just peace by bringing the warring parties together. In September Bush appointed a former senator, John Danforth, as his special envoy to Sudan.

Following the September 2001 suicide attacks on New York and Washington, DC, Sudan agreed to assist the USA with its search for terrorist suspects, and by late September the Sudanese authorities had arrested some 30 individuals resident in Sudan who were suspected of having links to Osama bin Laden, a Saudi-born Islamist activist exiled in Afghanistan, and the al-Qa'ida (Base) organization, which the USA held responsible for the attacks. Nevertheless, US sanctions remained in place, and Sudan continued to be listed by the US Department of State as a sponsor of terrorism. Furthermore, two Sudanese banks were among numerous institutions under US investigation as possible sources of financial support for bin Laden. Sudan expressed criticism of the US-led military strikes on Afghanistan, which commenced in November, and later that month the USA extended sanctions until November 2002. In October 2002 Bush approved legislation that allowed the USA to impose further sanctions, including the suspension of multilateral loans, on the Sudanese Government, should it fail to negotiate in good faith with the southern rebels or interfere with humanitarian efforts in the south of the country. The USA also froze the financial assets of 12 Sudanese companies, including the National Broadcasting Corporation. Under the Sudan Peace Act, conditions in Sudan would be evaluated every six months, although the law also made provision for the expenditure of US $100m. a year by the USA until 2005 in areas of Sudan not under the Sudanese Government's control. In October 2003 the US Agency for International Development pledged a further $40m. to finance initiatives to assist Sudan to recover from the civil war. However, the additional aid was conditional on the implementation of a comprehensive peace agreement. In mid-November the US embassy in Khartoum was temporarily closed in response to a 'specific threat' to US interests in Sudan. The conflict in Darfur (see above) resulted in the deterioration of relations between Sudan and the USA and in September 2004 the US Administration accused the Sudanese Government of committing genocide. The USA subsequently proposed a draft UN resolution, which threatened to impose sanctions on Sudan's petroleum industry if the Sudanese authorities did not act to end the violence in the region. In late July 2005 the US Secretary of State, Condoleezza Rice, met with al-Bashir in Khartoum and also visited the Abu Shouk refugee camp in the Darfur region, and called for 'actions, not words' from the Sudanese administration to resolve the conflict in Darfur. During the visit, Rice also indicated that the USA was to send an ambassador to Khartoum for the first time since 1997. In early August 2005, two US envoys arrived in Sudan tasked with assisting the reinforcement of the Comprehensive Peace Agreement following the death of Garang. In mid-October 2006 President Bush approved the Darfur Peace and Accountability Act of 2006, which provided for the imposition of sanctions against those responsible for genocide, war crimes, and crimes against humanity, and supported humanitarian efforts and measures to secure peace in the region of Darfur. He also issued an executive order freezing the assets and property of the Sudanese Government and prohibiting financial transactions with that body. The USA threatened to impose economic sanctions on state-controlled companies in Sudan in April 2007 unless the Government agreed to co-operate in restoring peace to the Darfur region. The following month President Bush implemented measures to exclude Sudanese companies from the US financial system.

Sudan's relations with the United Kingdom deteriorated in May 1998, following a statement made by the British Secretary of State for International Development in which she accused Sudan of using food aid as a weapon in Bahr al-Ghazal. The Sudanese Government vehemently denied this and accused the United Kingdom of having a negative attitude towards forthcoming peace negotiations. The British Government played an active role in attempting to end the violence in Darfur—the British Secretary of State for Foreign and Commonwealth Affairs, Jack Straw, visited the region in August 2004, and Prime Minister Blair visited Khartoum in October to increase diplomatic pressure on the Sudanese Government. In December 2006 Prime Minister Blair announced his intention to support plans to impose a 'no-fly zone' and stated that he would seek UN approval for the measure, which was to be enforced by US and British troops.

Government

In October 1993 the Revolutionary Command Council for National Salvation, which had assumed power after the military coup of 30 June 1989, was dissolved after appointing Lt-Gen. al-Bashir as President and head of a new civilian Government. In April 1998 a new Constitution was endorsed by the National Assembly, and was presented to President al-Bashir. The document was endorsed by 96.7% of voters in a national referendum held in May. Under its terms, executive power is vested in the Council of Ministers, which is appointed by the President, but is responsible to the National Assembly. Legislative power is vested in the National Assembly. The 360-member National Assembly serves a term of four years. Of its 360 members, 270 are directly elected in single seat constituencies, 35 members represent women, 26 represent university graduates and 29 represent trade unions.

In February 1994 Sudan was redivided into 26 states (rather than the nine that had formed the basis of administration since 1991). A governor assumed responsibility for each state, assisted by five—in the case of the southern states six—state ministers.

In early July 2005 the National Assembly approved an interim Constitution as part of the Comprehensive Peace Agreement signed in January between the Sudanese Government and the Sudan People's Liberation Movement (SPLM). The interim Constitution provided for the establishment of a Government of National Unity, representation in which was to be divided between northerners and southerners, with the former holding 70% of the posts and the latter 30%. The interim Constitution also stipulated that, pending legislative elections, which were to be held no later than the end of the fourth year of the interim period, the National Assembly shall be composed of 450 members who shall be appointed by the President of the Republic in consultation with the First Vice-President, according to the 70%:30% north to south ratio.

Provision was also made in the interim Constitution for the election of the President of the Government of Southern Sudan and the establishment of a transitional Southern Sudan Assembly. The President of Government of Southern Sudan shall be elected directly by the people of southern Sudan for a five-year mandate, renewable only once. The transitional Southern Sudan Assembly shall be an inclusive, constituent legislature composed of 170 appointed members with 70% representing the SPLM; 15% representing the National Congress; and 15% representing the other southern Sudanese political forces.

Defence

As assessed at November 2008, the armed forces comprised: army an estimated 105,000, navy an estimated 1,300, air force 3,000. A paramilitary Popular Defence Force included 17,500 active members and 85,000 reserves. Budgeted defence expenditure in 2007 was an estimated US $579m. Military service is compulsory for males aged 18–30 years and lasts for up to two years. It was announced in early 2009 that a private British company, Adam Smith International, was to be involved in reforming and professionalizing Sudan's armed forces.

Economic Affairs

In 2007, according to estimates by the World Bank, Sudan's gross national income (GNI), measured at average 2005–07 prices, was US $37,031m., equivalent to $960 per head (or $1,880 on an international purchasing-power parity basis). During 2000–07, it was estimated, the population increased at an average annual rate of 2.1%, while gross domestic product (GDP) per head increased, in real terms, by an average of 5.1% per year. Overall GDP increased, in real terms, at an average annual rate of 7.3% in 2000–07; growth in 2007 was 10.2%.

Agriculture (including forestry and fishing) contributed 35.5% of GDP in 2007 (at constant 1981/82 prices) and employed about 56.5% of the labour force in mid-2005, according to FAO estimates. The principal cash crop is sesame seed (including oilcake), which accounted for 2.6% of total export earnings in 2006. The principal subsistence crops are sorghum, millet and wheat. The GDP of the agricultural sector increased by an average of 3.6% per year in 2000–07, according to the World Bank. Agricultural GDP increased by 8.5% in 2007.

Industry (including mining, manufacturing, construction and power) contributed 30.5% of GDP in 2007 (at constant 1981/82 prices), and employed 7.9% of the labour force in 1983. In 2000–07 industrial GDP increased at an average annual rate of 11.9%, according to the World Bank. Industrial GDP increased by 8.2% in 2007.

Mining accounted for only 0.1% of employment in 1983 and an estimated 19.2% of GDP in 2007 (at constant 1981/82 prices). Sudan has reserves of petroleum, chromite, gypsum, gold, iron ore and wollastonite. Sudan began to develop its petroleum reserves in the mid-1990s; proven reserves totalled 6,600m. barrels at the end of 2007, sufficient to sustain production at current levels for almost 40 years. In that year Sudan was the sixth largest producer of petroleum in Africa. In 2006 petroleum and petroleum products accounted for 87.5% of total export earnings. The GDP of the mining sector increased by 34.6% in 2007.

Manufacturing contributed 6.3% of GDP in 2007. The most important branch of the sector is food-processing, especially sugar-refining, while the textile industry, cement production and petroleum-refining are also significant. Some 4.6% of the labour force were employed in manufacturing in 1983. According to the World Bank, in 2000–07 manufacturing GDP increased at an average annual rate of 7.7%. Manufacturing GDP increased by 8.0% in both 2007.

Energy is derived from petroleum (which contributed 70.0% of total output in 2005) and hydroelectric power (30.0%). In May 2004 the Government announced plans to provide 90% of the country with electricity over the following five years by harnessing more of the hydro-electric potential of the Nile. Sudan is a net exporter of fuels, with imports of refined petroleum products comprising an estimated 0.3% of the total value of imports in 2007, compared to 5.0% in 2006.

Services contributed 34.1% of GDP in 2007 (at constant 1981/82 prices), and employed 18.8% of the labour force in 1983. During 2000–07, according to the World Bank, the GDP of the services sector increased at an average annual rate of 8.2%. In 2007 the GDP of the services sector rose by 15.4%.

In 2006 Sudan recorded a visible trade surplus of US $1,156.8m., but there was a deficit of $3,447.1m. on the current account of the balance of payments. In 2007 the principal sources of imports were the People's Republic of China (accounting for 16.4% of the total), Saudi Arabia, Japan, the United Arab Emirates (UAE) and the United Kingdom. In 2006 the principal market for Sudanese exports was also the People's Republic of China (taking 78.9%); Japan and the UAE were the other major purchasers. The principal exports in 2006 were mineral products (especially petroleum and petroleum products). The principal imports in 2007 were machinery and transport equipment, chemicals and related products, and food and live animals.

In 2007 Sudan recorded an overall budget deficit of 2,859m. new Sudanese pounds. At the end of 2006 Sudan's total external debt was US $19,158m., of which $11,609m. was long-term public debt. In that year the cost of debt-servicing was equivalent to 4.1% of the total value of exports of goods and services. In 2000–07 the average annual rate of inflation was 7.7%. Consumer prices increased by an average of 8.0% in 2007.

Sudan is a member of the AfDB (see p. 170), the Arab Bank for Economic Development in Africa (see p. 345), the Council of Arab Economic Unity (see p. 233) and the Islamic Development Bank (see p. 340). In 1997 Sudan's membership of both the Arab Fund for Economic and Social Development (AFESD, see p. 183) and the Arab Monetary Fund (see p. 184) was suspended. Membership of the AFESD was restored in April 2000.

Sudan's formidable economic problems can be traced back to the 1970s, when the country's agricultural potential was neglected. The problems were compounded by civil conflict, which, in addition to depressing economic activity in the areas where it was waged, caused a massive waste of state resources. Sudan began exporting petroleum in late 1999 and further discoveries of petroleum in 2001 led to a vast increase in export revenues; however, much of these earnings were used by the Government to fund the war against the rebels in the south of the country. Much of Sudan's proven reserves of oil are located in southern Sudan and, following the Comprehensive Peace Agreement (CPA) signed by the Government and the SPLM in January 2005, levels of foreign investment were expected to increase, thus providing capital for reconstruction programmes in the regions affected by the civil war. However, in recent years international financial institutions have been reluctant to provide funding and the donor community remained deeply concerned by the ongoing conflict and humanitarian crisis in the Darfur region. In November 2008 the UN requested some $2,000m. of humanitarian aid to fund projects in 2009, one-half of which would target the Darfur region, where conflict has displaced around 50% of the region's population since 2001. Furthermore, since the issuing of an arrest warrant for President al-Bashir by the International Criminal Court in mid-2008, humanitarian agencies have been expelled from the country, raising fears of further population displacement. Significantly, while many companies from Europe and North America have been reluctant to invest in Sudan, due in part to events in Darfur, companies from the People's Republic of China, India and Malaysia have acquired major stakes in a number of Sudanese oil concessions. In February 2007 China and Sudan signed a US $1,150m. agreement to construct a new railway linking Khartoum and Port Sudan in the east of the country (where there are significant gold and natural gas reserves). In late 2008 officials were seeking some $1,000m. from Middle-Eastern and Asian countries to finance projects in the agriculture sector. Uganda and Sudan, meanwhile, opened a new trading centre in Juba, which was expected to facilitate a large increase in commerce between southern Sudan and Uganda. Juba has emerged as a major distribution centre for the south of the country since the signing of the CPA. GDP growth of 6.8% was estimated in 2008, although the IMF forecast that this rate would slow to 4.0% in 2009 as the global economic downturn continued to worsen.

Education

The Government provides free primary education from the ages of six to 12 years. Secondary education begins at 13 years of age and lasts for up to five years. In 2000/01 enrolment at primary schools included 49% of children in the relevant age-group (boys 54%; girls 45%), according to UNESCO estimates, while in 1998/99 enrolment at secondary schools was equivalent to 30% of children in the relevant age-group (boys 31%; girls 29%). There are 26 public universities in Sudan.

Public Holidays

2009: 1 January (Independence Day), 9 March* (Mouloud, Birth of the Prophet), 6 April (Uprising Day, anniversary of 1985 coup), 20 April (Sham an-Nassim, Coptic Easter Monday), 30 June (Revolution Day), 20 September* (Id al-Fitr, end of Ramadan), 27 November* (Id al-Adha, Feast of the Sacrifice), 18 December* (Muharram, Islamic New Year), 25 December (Christmas).

2010: 1 January (Independence Day), 26 February* (Mouloud, Birth of the Prophet), 6 April (Uprising Day, anniversary of the 1985 coup), 5 April (Sham an-Nassim, Coptic Easter Monday), 30 June (Revolution Day), 10 September* (Id al-Fitr, end of Ramadan), 16 November* (Id al-Adha, Feast of the Sacrifice), 7 December* (Muharram, Islamic New Year), 25 December (Christmas).

* The dates of Islamic holidays are determined by sightings of the moon, and may be slightly different from those given above.

Weights and Measures

The metric system is gradually replacing traditional weights and measures.

Statistical Survey

Source (unless otherwise stated): Department of Statistics, Ministry of Finance and National Economy, POB 735, Khartoum; tel. (183) 777563; fax (183) 775630; e-mail info@mof-sudan.net; internet www.mof-sudan.net.

Area and Population

AREA, POPULATION AND DENSITY

Area (sq km)	2,505,813*
Population (census results)†	
1 February 1983	20,594,197
15 April 1993‡	
Males	12,518,638
Females	12,422,045
Total	24,940,683
Population (UN estimates at mid-year)§	
2006	39,545,000
2007	40,432,000
2008	41,348,000
Density (per sq km) at mid-2008	16.5

* 967,500 sq miles.
† Excluding adjustments for underenumeration, estimated to have been 6.7% in 1993.
‡ Provisional result.
§ Source: UN, *World Population Prospects: The 2008 Revision*.

PROVINCES
(1983 census, provisional)*

	Area (sq miles)	Population	Density (per sq mile)
Northern	134,736	433,391	3.2
Nile	49,205	649,633	13.2
Kassala	44,109	1,512,335	34.3
Red Sea	84,977	695,874	8.2
Blue Nile	24,009	1,056,313	44.0
Gezira	13,546	2,023,094	149.3
White Nile	16,161	933,136	57.7
Northern Kordofan	85,744	1,805,769	21.1
Southern Kordofan	61,188	1,287,525	21.0
Northern Darfur	133,754	1,327,947	9.9
Southern Darfur	62,801	1,765,752	28.1
Khartoum	10,883	1,802,299	165.6
Eastern Equatoria	46,073	1,047,125	22.7
Western Equatoria	30,422	359,056	11.8
Bahr al-Ghazal	52,000	1,492,597	28.7
Al-Buhayrat	25,625	772,913	30.2
Sobat	45,266	802,354	17.7
Jonglei	47,003	797,251	17.0
Total	**967,500**	**20,564,364**	**21.3**

* In 1991 a federal system of government was inaugurated, whereby Sudan was divided into nine states, which were sub-divided into 66 provinces and 281 local government areas. A constitutional decree, issued in February 1994, redivided the country into 26 states.

SUDAN

PRINCIPAL TOWNS
(population at 1993 census)

Omdurman	1,271,403	Nyala		227,183
Khartoum (capital)	947,483	El-Gezira		211,362
Khartoum North	700,887	Gedaref		191,164
Port Sudan	308,195	Kosti		173,599
Kassala	234,622	El-Fasher		141,884
El-Obeid	229,425	Juba		114,980

Source: UN, *Demographic Yearbook*.

Mid-2007 ('000, including suburbs, UN estimate): Khartoum 4,754 (Source: UN, *World Urbanization Prospects: The 2007 Revision*).

BIRTHS AND DEATHS
(annual averages, UN estimates)

	1990–95	1995–2000	2000–05
Birth rate (per 1,000)	40.2	38.1	34.5
Death rate (per 1,000)	13.2	12.0	11.0

Source: UN, *World Population Prospects: The 2008 Revision*.

Life expectancy (years at birth, WHO estimates): 60 (males 59; females 61) in 2006 (Source: WHO, *World Health Statistics*).

ECONOMICALLY ACTIVE POPULATION*
(persons aged 10 years and over, 1983 census, provisional)

	Males	Females	Total
Agriculture, hunting, forestry and fishing	2,638,294	1,390,411	4,028,705
Mining and quarrying	5,861	673	6,534
Manufacturing	205,247	61,446	266,693
Electricity, gas and water	42,110	1,618	43,728
Construction	130,977	8,305	139,282
Trade, restaurants and hotels	268,382	25,720	294,102
Transport, storage and communications	209,776	5,698	215,474
Financing, insurance, real estate and business services	17,414	3,160	20,574
Community, social and personal services	451,193	99,216	550,409
Activities not adequately defined	142,691	42,030	184,721
Unemployed persons not previously employed	387,615	205,144	592,759
Total	**4,499,560**	**1,843,421**	**6,342,981**

* Excluding nomads, homeless persons and members of institutional households.

Mid-2005 (estimates in '000): Agriculture, etc. 8,220; Total 14,558 (Source: FAO).

Health and Welfare

KEY INDICATORS

Total fertility rate (children per woman, 2006)	4.4
Under-5 mortality rate (per 1,000 live births, 2006)	89
HIV/AIDS (% of persons aged 15–49, 2007)	1.4
Physicians (per 1,000 head, 2005)	0.3
Hospital beds (per 1,000 head, 2005)	0.7
Health expenditure (2006): US $ per head (PPP)	61
Health expenditure (2006): % of GDP	3.8
Health expenditure (2006): public (% of total)	37.1
Access to water (% of persons, 2006)	70
Access to sanitation (% of persons, 2006)	35
Human Development Index (2006): ranking	146
Human Development Index (2006): value	0.526

For sources and definitions, see explanatory note on p. vi.

Agriculture

PRINCIPAL CROPS
('000 metric tons)

	2005	2006	2007
Wheat*	415	642	642
Rice, paddy	20	35†	30†
Maize†	45	70	60
Millet*	745	792	792
Sorghum*	4,275	5,203	5,048
Potatoes	385	260*	320†
Cassava (Manioc)†	11	10	10
Yams†	138	137	137
Sugar cane	7,186	7,500†	7,500
Beans, dry	15	23†	18†
Broad beans, horse beans, dry	112	138†	150†
Groundnuts, with shell	520	364*	460*
Sunflower seed	12	12*	14*
Sesame seed	277	200*	260*
Melonseed†	46	46	46
Seed cotton	311	240†	240†
Tomatoes	484	600†	580†
Pumpkins, squash and gourds†	69	68	68
Aubergines (Eggplants)†	230	230	230
Onions, dry†	60	59	59
Garlic†	18	18	18
Canteloupes (incl. other melons)†	28	28	28
Watermelons†	145	145	145
Dates	328	330†	330†
Oranges†	18	18	18
Lemons and limes†	64	63	63
Grapefruits and pomelos†	68	68	68
Guavas, mangoes and mangosteens†	195	195	195
Bananas†	75	74	74

* Unofficial figure(s).
† FAO estimate(s).

Aggregate production ('000 metric tons, may include official, semi-official or estimated data): Total cereals 5,500 in 2005, 6,742 in 2006, 6,572 in 2007; Total roots and tubers 552 in 2005, 416 in 2006, 476 in 2007; Total vegetables (incl. melons) 1,825 in 2005, 2,122 in 2006, 2,139 in 2007; Total fruits (excl. melons) 1,165 in 2005, 754 in 2006, 754 in 2007.

Source: FAO.

LIVESTOCK
('000 head, year ending September)

	2005	2006*	2007*
Horses*	26	26	26
Asses*	750	n.a.	n.a.
Cattle	40,468	39,300	39,500
Camels	3,908	3,700	3,700
Sheep	49,797	48,500	49,000
Goats	42,526	42,000	42,000
Chickens*	37,000	37,000	35,000

* Estimates.

Source: FAO.

LIVESTOCK PRODUCTS
('000 metric tons)

	2005	2006*	2007*
Cattle meat	350	350	340
Sheep meat*	148	148	148
Goat meat	186	186	186
Chicken meat*	31	30	28
Cows' milk	5,480	5,200	5,300
Sheep's milk	487	487	480
Goats' milk	1,519	1,519	1,450
Hen eggs*	47	47	47
Wool, greasy*	46	46	46

* Estimates.

Source: FAO.

SUDAN

Forestry

ROUNDWOOD REMOVALS
('000 cubic metres, FAO estimates)

	2005	2006	2007
Sawlogs, veneer logs and logs for sleepers	123	123	123
Other industrial wood	2,050	2,050	2,050
Fuel wood	17,698	17,901	18,110
Total	19,871	20,074	20,283

Source: FAO.

Gum arabic ('000 metric tons, year ending 30 June): 24 in 1993/94; 27 in 1994/95; 25 in 1995/96 (Source: IMF, *Sudan—Recent Economic Developments*, March 1997).

Fishing

('000 metric tons, live weight, FAO estimates)

	2004	2005	2006
Capture	57.0	62.0	63.0
Nile tilapia	20.0	21.5	21.8
Other freshwater fishes	32.0	35.0	35.5
Marine fishes	4.9	5.4	5.6
Aquaculture	1.6	1.6	1.6
Total catch	58.6	63.6	64.6

Source: FAO.

Mining

('000 metric tons, unless otherwise stated)

	2005	2006	2007*
Crude petroleum ('000 barrels)	126,000	158,000*	176,600
Salt (unrefined)*	65.0	68.0	68.0
Chromite	21.7	28.8	15.5
Gold ore (kilograms)†	3,625	3,158	2,787

* Estimated production.
† Figures refer to the metal content of ores.

Source: US Geological Survey.

Industry

PETROLEUM PRODUCTS
(metric tons)

	2005	2006	2007*
Motor spirit (petrol)	7,827	9,717	9,700
Naphtha	248	216	220
Jet fuels	1,596	1,445	1,400
Kerosene	340	320	320
Gas-diesel (distillate fuel) oils	9,965	13,554	14,000
Residual fuel oils	2,589	2,566	2,600

* Estimates.
Source: US Geological Survey.

SELECTED OTHER PRODUCTS
('000 metric tons)

	2003	2004	2005
Wheat flour	890	870	n.a.
Raw sugar	686	789	728
Cement	320	244	244

2002 ('000 metric tons): Refined sugar 674; Vegetable oils 63.

Source: UN, *Industrial Commodity Statistics Yearbook*.

Finance

CURRENCY AND EXCHANGE RATES

Monetary Units
100 piastres = 1 Sudanese dinar.

Sterling, Dollar and Euro Equivalents (31 December 2008)
£1 sterling = 2.992 dinars;
US $1 = 2.053 dinars;
€1 = 2.857 dinars;
1,000 Sudanese dinars = £3.34 = $4.87 = €3.50.

Average Exchange Rate (Sudanese dinars per US $)
2006   2.1715
2007   2.0161
2008   2.0770

Note: On 1 March 1999 the Sudanese pound (£S) was replaced by the Sudanese dinar (SDD), equivalent to £S10. The pound was withdrawn from circulation on 31 July 1999. A new Sudanese pound (SDG), equivalent to 100 dinars (and 1,000 old pounds) was introduced on 10 January 2007. The new currency was to circulate along with previous currencies (the old pound had continued to circulate in some regions) for a transitional period, but became the sole legal tender on 1 July 2007.

CENTRAL GOVERNMENT BUDGET
(million new Sudanese pounds)

Revenue	2005	2006	2007*
Tax revenue	4,721	5,099	5,777
Direct taxes	922	952	1,097
Indirect taxes	3,799	4,147	4,680
Non-tax revenue	10,008	10,332	12,256
Oil revenue	9,010	8,794	10,893
Other	997	1,538	1,363
Total†	14,729	15,431	18,033

Expenditure	2005	2006	2007*
Current expenditure	13,827	15,846	17,612
Wages, salaries and pensions	3,011	3,945	4,901
Other current spending	6,510	6,143	5,352
Debt service paid	862	930	897
Goods and services	724	930	1,127
General reserve	1,233	1,254	938
Other obligations	3691	2,808	1,971
Transfers to states	4,307	5,758	7,359
Capital expenditure	2,276	3,118	3,801
Locally financed	1,781	2,324	2,625
Foreign financed	495	794	1,177
Statistical discrepancy	−164	267	—
Total	15,939	19,231	21,414

* Preliminary figures.
† Excluding grants totalling (million new Sudanese pounds): 0.0 in 2005; 361 in 2006; 522 in 2007 (preliminary).

Source: IMF, *Sudan: First Review of Performance Under the 2007-08 Staff-Monitored Program* (June 2008).

INTERNATIONAL RESERVES
(US $ million at 31 December)

	2005	2006	2007
IMF special drawing rights	0.1	—	—
Foreign exchange	1,868.5	1,659.9	1,377.9
Total	1,868.6	1,659.9	1,377.9

Source: IMF, *International Financial Statistics*.

SUDAN

MONEY SUPPLY
(million Sudanese dinars at 31 December)

	2005	2006	2007
Currency outside banks	3,761.34	5,355.32	5,639.76
Demand deposits at deposit money banks	3,937.19	4,813.87	5,440.54
Total money (incl. others)	8,130.06	10,524.09	11,374.63

Source: IMF, *International Financial Statistics*.

COST OF LIVING
(Consumer Price Index; base: 1992 = 100)

	1998	1999	2000
Food, beverages and tobacco	3,930.8	4,670.3	4,883.3
Clothing and footwear	3,615.7	4,010.5	3,985.6
Housing	3,826.8	5,257.2	6,192.9
Household operations	3,677.7	3,899.3	3,706.4
Health care	5,277.9	6,313.5	6,984.7
Transport and communications	7,107.7	8,661.7	9,082.8
Entertainment	2,261.2	3,046.0	4,149.7
Education	5,947.8	7,057.0	8,048.7
All items (incl. others)	4,299.8	5,077.0	5,451.9

Source: Bank of Sudan.

All items (Consumer Price Index; base: 2000 = 100): 145.5 in 2005; 155.9 in 2006; 168.4 in 2007 (Source: IMF, *International Financial Statistics*).

NATIONAL ACCOUNTS
Expenditure on the Gross Domestic Product
(US $ million at current prices)

	2005	2006	2007
Government final consumption expenditure	4,675.05	6,089.25	6,613.65
Private final consumption expenditure	19,839.60	27,190.75	32,720.23
Gross fixed capital formation	6,109.09	8,226.54	10,013.87
Total domestic expenditure	30,623.74	41,506.54	49,347.75
Exports of goods and services	4,972.80	6,052.25	6,847.82
Less Imports of goods and services	7,701.14	9,994.69	10,470.14
GDP in purchasers' values	27,895.39	37,564.10	45,725.43
GDP at constant 2000 prices	16,219.32	18,133.20	20,164.12

Source: African Development Bank.

Gross Domestic Product by Economic Activity
('000 million new Sudanese pounds at constant 1981/82 prices)

	2006	2007
Agriculture and forestry	8,177	8,670
Mining and quarrying	3,500	4,710
Manufacturing	1,440	1,540
Electricity and water	280	300
Construction	890	950
Government Services	2,833	3,031
Other services	5,097	5,352
Gross domestic product	22,217	24,553

Source: Bank of Sudan, Khartoum.

BALANCE OF PAYMENTS
(US $ million)

	2005	2006	2007
Exports of goods f.o.b.	4,824.3	5,656.6	8,879.2
Imports of goods f.o.b.	−5,946.0	−7,104.7	−7,722.4
Trade balance	−1,121.7	−1,448.1	1,156.8
Exports of services	113.9	247.1	384.3
Imports of services	−1,844.4	−2,799.9	−2,938.7
Balance on goods and services	−2,852.2	−4,000.9	−1,397.6
Other income received	44.1	89.3	183.7
Other income paid	−1,405.9	−2,103.3	−2,436.8
Balance on goods, services and income	−4,214.0	−6,014.9	−3,650.7
Current transfers received	1,680.5	1,899.9	2,321.5
Current transfers paid	−479.6	−1,083.6	−2,117.9
Current balance	−3,013.1	−5,198.7	−3,447.1
Direct investment from abroad	2,304.6	3,534.1	2,425.6
Portfolio investment assets	50.6	−0.1	62.1
Portfolio investment liabilities	—	−35.3	−16.6
Other investment assets	1,134.7	208.2	−535.3
Investment liabilities	−605.3	1,031.7	1,060.6
Net errors and omissions	726.5	−130.9	26.9
Overall balance	598.0	−590.9	−423.8

Source: IMF, *International Financial Statistics*.

External Trade

PRINCIPAL COMMODITIES
(US $ million)

Imports c.i.f.	2005	2006	2007
Food and live animals	800.0	945.9	465.4
Cereals and cereal preparations	459.3	403.8	205.2
Unmilled durum wheat	367.0	326.4	161.2
Mineral fuels, lubricants, etc.	363.6	443.4	32.3
Refined petroleum products	355.3	443.2	32.2
Chemicals and related products	650.8	647.1	1,027.8
Medicinal and pharmaceutical products	187.0	184.2	814.7
Basic manufactures	1,545.2	1,549.0	1,017.1
Textiles and textile products (excl. clothing)	185.3	218.2	152.9
Cement	160.2	145.7	91.5
Iron and steel	654.1	584.5	211.5
Machinery and transport equipment	3,269.7	4,389.3	6,264.3
Power generating machinery and equipment	280.4	381.2	649.7
Machinery specialized for particular industries	797.6	1,068.3	1,110.5
Miscellaneous industrial machinery	404.4	418.5	260.5
Telecommunication and recording equipment	261.2	469.9	1,310.8
Road vehicles	1,024.0	1,387.1	1,043.9
Passenger vehicles (excl. buses)	301.9	345.2	301.3
Lorries and special purpose vehicles	377.7	519.8	495.6
Miscellaneous manufactured articles	492.4	609.0	898.1
Total (incl. others)	7,366.8	8,844.5	9,853.6

SUDAN

Exports f.o.b.	2004	2005	2006
Food and live animals	209.8	186.8	150.8
Live animals	136.6	106.5	109.9
Sheep and goats	121.3	101.5	106.5
Sheep	118.8	98.5	103.2
Crude materials (inedible) except fuels	307.5	337.5	291.2
Oil seeds and oleaginous fruit	145.8	112.1	147.5
Sesame seeds	134.1	100.9	143.7
Cotton	87.7	103.6	71.1
Mineral fuels, lubricants, etc.	2,792.1	3,745.3	4,796.1
Petroleum and petroleum products	2,779.8	3,738.5	4,791.7
Machinery and transport equipment	194.5	99.3	58.3
Other commodities and transactions	100.4	128.7	174.2
Non-monetary gold, unwrought	74.5	108.1	148.2
Total (incl. others)	3,612.0	4,505.8	5,478.7

Source: UN, *International Trade Statistics Yearbook*.

PRINCIPAL TRADING PARTNERS
(US $ million)

Imports c.i.f.	2005	2006	2007
Australia	239.3	242.0	116.0
Canada	78.5	76.7	136.7
China, People's Repub.	1,316.2	1,662.4	1,614.0
Egypt	405.8	476.9	357.2
France (incl. Monaco)	204.5	292.6	258.3
Germany	370.6	447.3	481.9
India	320.1	591.2	276.6
Indonesia	52.8	66.1	196.0
Italy	299.9	301.9	192.7
Japan	539.2	712.7	744.7
Jordan	46.3	55.0	268.3
Korea, Repub.	195.8	283.9	265.3
Malaysia	157.7	87.5	22.1
Netherlands	92.8	137.2	218.9
Saudi Arabia	591.3	789.5	1,429.6
Sweden	93.9	108.0	476.7
Switzerland (incl. Liechtenstein)	66.7	98.6	57.3
Turkey	165.5	200.6	65.2
United Arab Emirates	440.0	491.1	714.2
United Kingdom	358.3	420.4	564.0
USA	106.9	105.8	59.1
Total (incl. others)	7,366.8	8,844.5	9,853.6

Exports f.o.b.	2004	2005	2006
Canada	7.6	56.3	66.8
China, People's Repub.	2,319.4	3,323.8	4,324.3
Egypt	75.0	52.0	68.6
France	19.6	28.2	15.2
Germany	31.7	25.9	21.3
India	29.9	24.7	22.2
Indonesia	41.3	14.6	5.1
Japan	328.0	372.2	299.0
Saudi Arabia	250.0	183.3	154.7
Singapore	113.6	3.5	12.2
United Arab Emirates	78.4	120.2	280.5
United Kingdom	78.0	84.6	50.8
Total (incl. others)	3,612.0	4,505.8	5,478.7

Source: UN, *International Trade Statistics Yearbook*.

Transport

RAILWAY TRAFFIC*

	1991	1992	1993
Freight ton-km (million)	2,030	2,120	2,240
Passenger-km (million)	1,020	1,130	1,183

*Estimates.

Source: UN Economic Commission for Africa, *African Statistical Yearbook*.

2000 (passengers carried): 258,000 (Source: Sudan Railways).

ROAD TRAFFIC
(motor vehicles in use)

	2000	2001	2002
Passenger cars	46,000	46,400	47,300
Commercial vehicles	60,500	61,800	62,500

Source: UN, *Statistical Yearbook*.

SHIPPING

Merchant Fleet
(registered at 31 December)

	2005	2006	2007
Number of vessels	17	19	19
Displacement (grt)	15,650	25,904	25,904

Source: Lloyd's Register-Fairplay, *World Fleet Statistics*.

International Sea-borne Freight Traffic
(estimates, '000 metric tons)

	1991	1992	1993
Goods loaded	1,290	1,387	1,543
Goods unloaded	3,800	4,200	4,300

Source: UN Economic Commission for Africa, *African Statistical Yearbook*.

CIVIL AVIATION
(traffic on scheduled services)

	2002	2003	2004
Kilometres flown (million)	6	7	8
Passengers carried ('000)	409	420	473
Passenger-km (million)	767	786	898
Total ton-km (million)	98	103	116

Source: UN, *Statistical Yearbook*.

Tourism

	2004	2005	2006
Foreign visitor arrivals	60,577	245,798	328,148
Tourism receipts (US $ million, excl. passenger transport)	21	89	n.a.

Source: World Tourism Organization.

Communications Media

	2005	2006	2007
Telephones ('000 main lines in use)	570.0	767.2	345.2
Mobile cellular telephones ('000 subscribers)	1,828	4,288	7,464
Personal computers ('000 in use)	3,250	n.a.	n.a.
Internet users ('000)	500	850	1,500

Source: International Telecommunication Union.

1996: Daily newspapers 5 (average circulation 737,000 copies) (Source: UNESCO, *Statistical Yearbook*).

1997: Radio receivers ('000 in use) 7,550 (Source: UNESCO, *Statistical Yearbook*).

1998: Non-daily newspapers 11 (average circulation 5,644,000); Periodicals 54 (average circulation 68,000 copies) (Source: UN, *Statistical Yearbook*).

2000: Television receivers ('000 in use) 8,500 (Source: International Telecommunication Union).

Education

(2006/07, unless otherwise stated)

	Institutions*	Teachers	Males	Females	Total
Pre-primary	5,984	28,185	244,233	246,575	490,808
Primary	11,982	107,933	2,165,233	1,794,077	3,959,310
Secondary	3,512	79,122	771,681	691,117	1,462,798
Universities, etc.	n.a.	4,486†	n.a.	n.a.	200,538†

* Figures refer to 1998.
† Estimates for 2000.

Source: UNESCO Institute for Statistics.

Adult literacy rate (UNESCO estimates): 60.9% (males 71.1%; females 51.8%) in 2000 (Source: UNESCO Institute for Statistics).

Directory

The Constitution

Following the coup of 6 April 1985, the Constitution of April 1973 was abrogated. A transitional Constitution, which entered into force in October 1985, was suspended following the military coup of 30 June 1989. In April 1998 a new Constitution was approved by the National Assembly, and presented to President al-Bashir. At a referendum held in June, the new Constitution was endorsed by 96.7% of voters. This Constitution, which entered into force on 1 July 1998, vests executive power in the Council of Ministers, which is appointed by the President but responsible to the National Assembly. Legislative power is vested in the National Assembly. The Constitution guarantees freedom of thought and religion, and the right to political association, provided that such activity complies with the law.

On 9 July 2005 the National Assembly approved an interim Constitution, as part of the Comprehensive Peace Agreement signed in January between the Sudanese Government and the Sudan People's Liberation Movement (SPLM). The Interim National Constitution provided for the establishment of a Government of National Unity (GONU), representation in which was to be divided between northerners and southerners, with the former holding 70% and the latter 30% of the posts. In the GONU, the National Congress shall be represented by 52% (49% northerners and 3% southerners); the SPLM shall be represented by 28% (21% southerners and 7% northerners); other northern political forces shall be represented by 14%; and other southern political forces shall be represented by 6%.

The Interim National Constitution also stipulated that, pending legislative elections, which were to be held by no later than the end of the fourth year of the interim period, the National Assembly shall be composed of 450 members who shall be appointed by the President of the Republic in consultation with the First Vice-President, according to the 70%:30% north-south ratio.

Provision was also made in the Interim National Constitution for the election of the President of the Government of Southern Sudan and for the establishment of a transitional Southern Sudan Assembly. The President of Government of Southern Sudan shall be elected directly by the people of Southern Sudan for a five-year mandate, renewable only once. The transitional Southern Sudan Assembly shall be an inclusive, constituent legislature composed of 170 appointed members with 70% representing the SPLM, 15% representing the National Congress, and 15% representing the other southern Sudanese political forces.

The Government

HEAD OF STATE

President: Lt-Gen. OMAR HASSAN AHMAD AL-BASHIR (took power as Chairman of the Revolutionary Command Council for National Salvation (RCC) on 30 June 1989; appointed President by the RCC on 16 October 1993; elected President in March 1996; re-elected in December 2000).

First Vice-President: Commdr SALVA KIIR MAYARDIT.

Second Vice-President: ALI OSMAN MUHAMMAD TAHA.

COUNCIL OF MINISTERS
(April 2009)

Prime Minister: Lt-Gen. OMAR HASSAN AHMAD AL-BASHIR (National Congress).

Minister of Foreign Affairs: DENG ALOR KOL (SPLM).

Minister of the Interior: IBRAHIM MOHAMMED HAMED.

Minister of the Presidency: Maj.-Gen. BAKRI HASSAN SALEH (National Congress).

Minister of Cabinet Affairs: PAGAN AMUM (SPLM).

Minister of Defence: Maj.-Gen. Eng. ABD AR-RAHIM MUHAMMAD HUSSEIN (National Congress).

Minister of Justice: ABD AL-BASIT SALEH SABDARAT (National Congress).

Minister of Information and Communication: ZAHAWI IBRAHIM MALEK (UP).

Minister of Federal Government: Lt-Gen. ABD AR-RAHMAN SAID (NDA).

Minister of Finance and National Economy: Dr AWAD AHMAD AL-JAZ (National Congress).

Minister of Foreign Trade: JAMES KOCK RONA (SPLM).

Minister of International Co-operation: AT-TIJANI SALEH FEDAIL (National Congress).

Minister of Industry: JALAL YUSUF MUHAMMAD AD-DUQAYR (DUP).

Minister of Investment: KOSTI MANYEBI (SPLM).

Minister of Agriculture and Forestry: Prof. ZUBEIR BESHIR TAHA (National Congress).

Minister of Animal Resources: MOHAMMED AHMED TAHER ABU KALABISH (National Congress).

Minister of Irrigation and Water Resources: Eng. KAMAL ALI MUHAMMAD (National Congress).

Minister of Energy and Mining: AZ-ZOBEIR AHMED HASSAN (National Congress).

Minister of Transport, Roads and Bridges: PHILIP THON (SPLM).

Minister of Culture, Youth and Sport: MUHAMMAD YUSSUF ABDALLAH (National Congress).

Minister of Tourism and Wildlife: JOSEF MALWAL (UDSF).

Minister of Scientific Research and Technology: IBRAHIM MUHAMAD OMAR (NC).

Minister of Education: HAMID MUHAMAD IBRAHIM (NDA).

Minister of Labour, Public Services and Development of Human Resources: Maj.-Gen. (retd) ALISON MANANI MAGAYA (National Congress).

Minister of Health: Dr TABITA SOKAYA (SPLM).

Minister of Humanitarian Affairs: JAMES HARUN RUN LUAL (SPLM).

Minister of Religious Affairs and Waqf: AZHARI AT-TIGANI AWAD AS-SID (National Congress).

SUDAN

Minister of Welfare and Social Development: SAMIA AHMAD MUHAMMAD.

Minister of the Environment and Urban Development Construction: AHMED BABKIR NAHAR (National Congress).

Minister of Parliamentary Affairs: JOSEPH OKELLO (USAP).

In addition, there is one presidential adviser and 39 Ministers of State. The President also has 14 special advisers who are considered part of the Government.

GOVERNMENT OF SOUTHERN SUDAN
(April 2009)

President: Commdr SALVA KIIR MAYARDIT.
Vice-President: Dr RIEK MACHAR.
Minister for Cabinet Affairs: Dr LUKA MONOJA TOMBEKAN.
Minister for Presidential Affairs: Dr LUKA BIONG DENG.
Minister for SPLA Affairs: Lt-Gen. NHIAL DENG NHIAL.
Minister for Regional Co-operation: Dr BARNABA MARIAL BENJAMIN.
Minister for Finance and Economic Planning: KUOL ATHIAN MAWIEN.
Minister for Internal Affairs: PAUL MAYOM AKEC.
Minister for Legal Affairs and Constitutional Development: MICHAEL MAKUEI LUETH.
Minister for Health: Dr JOSEPH MONYTUIEL AKOL.
Minister for Education, Science and Technology: Prof. JOB DHORUAI.
Minister for Labour, Public Services and Human Resource Development: AWUT DENG ACUIL.
Minister for Telecommunications and Postal Services: Maj.-Gen. GIER CUANG ALUONG.
Minister for Information and Broadcasting: GABRIEL CHANGSON CHENG.
Minister for Environment, Wildlife and Tourism: AGNES LUKUDU.
Minister for Agriculture and Forestry: Dr SAMSON LUKARE KWAJE.
Minister for Roads and Transport: DAVID DENG ATHORBEI.
Minister for Gender, Social Welfare and Religious Affairs: MARY KIDEN KIMBO.
Minister for Rural Development and Co-operatives: Prof. PHILIP YONA JAMBI.
Minister for Animal Resources and Fisheries: Dr FESTO FAUSTINO KUMBANIDWA.
Minister for Culture, Youth and Sports: Maj.-Gen. (retd) ALBINO AKOL AKOL.
Minister for Industry and Mining: Dr JOHN LUK JUK.
Minister for Commerce, Trade and Supplies: ANTHONY LINO MAKANA.
Minister for Housing, Land and Public Utilities: MARTIN OKERUK.
Minister of Parliamentary Affairs: Dr MARTIN ELIA LOMURO.

In addition, there are five presidential advisers.

MINISTRIES

Ministry of Agriculture and Forestry: POB 285, al-Gamaa Ave, Khartoum; tel. (183) 780951; e-mail moafcc@sudanmail.net.
Ministry of Animal Resources: Khartoum.
Ministry of Cabinet Affairs: POB 931, Khartoum; tel. (183) 784205; fax (183) 771331; e-mail info@sudan.gov.sd; internet www.sudan.gov.sd/en.
Ministry of Culture, Youth and Sport: Khartoum.
Ministry of Defence: POB 371, Khartoum; tel. (183) 774910.
Ministry of Education: Khartoum; tel. (183) 772808; e-mail moe-sd@moe-sd.com; internet www.moe-sd.com.
Ministry of Energy and Mining: POB 2087, Khartoum; tel. (183) 775595; fax (183) 775428.
Ministry of the Environment and Urban Development Construction: POB 300, Khartoum; tel. (183) 462604.
Ministry of Federal Government: Khartoum.
Ministry of Finance and National Economy: POB 735, Khartoum; tel. (183) 777563; fax (183) 775630; e-mail info@mof-sudan.net; internet mof-sudan.com.
Ministry of Foreign Affairs: POB 873, Khartoum; tel. (183) 773101; fax (183) 772941; e-mail ministry@mfa.gov.sd; internet www.sudanmfa.com.
Ministry of Foreign Trade: Khartoum; tel. (183) 772793; fax (183) 773950.
Ministry of Health: POB 303, Khartoum; tel. (183) 773000; e-mail inhsd@sudanet.net; internet www.fmoh.gov.sd.
Ministry of Higher Education and Scientific Research: POB 2081, Khartoum; tel. (183) 779312; e-mail mhesr@sudanmail.net.
Ministry of Humanitarian Affairs: POB 1976, Khartoum; tel. (183) 780675; e-mail human@mha.gov.sd; internet www.mha.gov.sd.
Ministry of Industry: POB 2184, Khartoum; tel. (183) 777830.
Ministry of Information and Communication: Khartoum.
Ministry of the Interior: POB 2793, Khartoum; tel. (183) 776554.
Ministry of International Co-operation: POB 2092, Khartoum; tel. (183) 772169; fax (183) 780115; e-mail info@micsudan.com; internet www.micsudan.com.
Ministry of Investment: POB 6286, Khartoum; tel. (183) 787194; fax (183) 787199; internet www.sudaninvest.gov.sd.
Ministry of Irrigation and Water Resources: POB 878, Khartoum; tel. (183) 783221; fax (183) 773388; e-mail oehamad@hotmail.com.
Ministry of Justice: POB 302, an-Nil Ave, Khartoum; tel. (183) 774842; fax (183) 771479.
Ministry of Labour, Public Services and Development of Human Resources: Khartoum.
Ministry of Parliamentary Affairs: Khartoum.
Ministry of Religious Affairs and Waqf: Khartoum.
Ministry of Tourism and Wildlife: POB 2424, Khartoum; tel. (183) 471329; fax (183) 471437; e-mail admin@sudan-tourism.com.
Ministry of Transport, Roads and Bridges: POB 300, Khartoum; tel. (183) 781629; fax (183) 780507.
Ministry of Welfare and Social Development: Khartoum.

STATE GOVERNORS
(April 2009)

Al-Buhayrat: Lt-Gen. DANIEL WET AKOT.
Bahr al-Jabal: Maj.-Gen. CLEMENT WANI KONGA.
Blue Nile: ABDALLAH UTHMAN AL-HAJ.
Eastern Equatoria: ALOYSIO AMOR.
Gadarif: AD-DAW OSMAN HASSAN AL-FAKI.
Gezira: Lt-Gen. (retd) ABD AR-RAHMAN SIR AL-KHATIM.
Jonglei: PHILLIP THON LEEK.
Kassala: Lt-Gen. FARUQ HASAN MUHAMMAD NUR.
Khartoum: Dr ABD AL-HALIM ISMAIL AL-MUTA'AFI.
Northern: ADIL AWAD SULIMAN.
Northern Bahr al-Ghazal: MARYANG AKOI AGO.
Northern Darfur: OSMAN MUHAMMAD YUSUF KIBIR.
Northern Kordofan: GHULAM AD-DIN UTHMAN.
Red Sea: Maj.-Gen. (retd) HATIM AL-WASIL ASH-SHAYKH AS-SAMMANI.
River Nile: AHMED MAGZOB AHMED.
Sennar: AHMED ABBAS.
Southern Darfur: ADAM HAMID MUSA.
Southern Kordofan: SOMI ZAYDAN ATTIYAH.
Upper Nile: Dr DAK DOK BISHOK.
Wahdah: Brig. TABAN DENG GAI.
Warab: ANTHONY BOL MADUT.
Western Bahr al-Ghazal: MARK NABIBOSH OBONG.
Western Darfur: Staff Maj.-Gen. (retd) SULAYMAN ABDALLAH ADAM.
Western Equatoria: Commdr SAMUEL ABU JOHN KABASHI.
Western Kordofan: Maj.-Gen. AT-TAYIB ABD AR-RAHMAN MUKHTAR.
White Nile: MAJDHUB YUSUF BABIKIR.

SUDAN
Directory

President

PRESIDENT

Election, 13–22 December 2000

Candidate	% of total votes cast
Omar Hassan Ahmad al-Bashir (National Congress)	86.5
Gaafar Muhammad Nimeri (Alliance of the People's Working Forces)	9.6
Malik Hussain	1.6
as-Samawi'it Husayn Osman Mansur (Independent Democrats)	1.0
Mahmoud Ahmad Juna	1.0

Legislature

MAJLIS WATANI
(National Assembly)

Speaker: AHMAD IBRAHIM AT-TAHIR.
Deputy Speakers: ANGELO BEDA, ABDALLAH AL-HARDELLO.
Election, 13–22 December 2000

	Seats
National Congress	355
Others	5
Total	**360***

* Of the 360 members, 270 are directly elected in single seat constituencies, 35 members represent women, 26 represent university graduates and 29 represent trade unions.

According to the interim Constitution approved by the National Assembly in July 2005, the National Assembly shall be composed of 450 members who shall be appointed by the President of the Republic in consultation with the First Vice-President. Legislative elections were to be held by no later than the end of the fourth year of the interim period.

Election Commission

General Election Commission (GEC): PO 14416, Omdurman; tel. (15) 558537; fax (15) 560950; e-mail info@sudan-parliament.org; comprises a chairman and two mems appointed for the election period only; mems appointed by the President, subject to the approval of the National Assembly; responsible for the election of the President, provincial magistrates, and national, provincial and local assembly mems; Chairman ABD AL-MUN'IM AZ-ZAYN AN-NAHHAS.

Political Organizations

National Congress: Khartoum; successor to National Islamic Front; Pres. Lt-Gen. OMAR HASSAN AHMAD AL-BASHIR; Sec.-Gen. Prof. IBRAHIM AHMAD UMAR.

The right to political association, subject to compliance with the law, was guaranteed in the Constitution approved by referendum in June 1998. (All political organizations had been banned following the military coup of 30 June 1989.) The registration of parties began in January 1999. The following parties are among the most active:

Alliance of the People's Working Forces: Khartoum; Head GAAFAR MUHAMMAD NIMERI; Sec.-Gen. KAMAL AD-DIN MUHAMMAD ABDULLAH (acting).

Democratic Unionist Party (DUP): Khartoum; Leader OSMAN AL-MIRGHANI; participates in National Democratic Alliance (see below).

Free Sudanese National Party (FSNP): Khartoum; Chair. Fr PHILIP ABBAS GHABBUSH.

Independent Democrats: Khartoum; Leader AS-SAMAWITT HUSAYN OSMAN MANSUR.

Islamic-Christian Solidarity: Khartoum; Founder HATIM ABDULLAH AZ-ZAKI HUSAYN.

Islamic Revival Movement: Khartoum; Founder SIDDIQ AL-HAJ AS-SIDDIQ.

Islamic Socialist Party: Khartoum; Leader SALAH AL-MUSBAH.

Islamic Ummah Party: Khartoum; Chair. WALI AD-DIN AL-HADI AL-MAHDI.

Justice Party: Khartoum; f. 2002 by fmr members of the National Congress.

Moderate Trend Party: Khartoum; Leader MAHMUD JIHA.

Muslim Brotherhood: Khartoum; Islamic fundamentalist; Leader Dr HABIR NUR AD-DIN.

National Democratic Party: Khartoum; f. 2002 following merger of the Union of Nationalistic Forces, the Communist Party and the National Solidarity Party.

Nile Valley Conference: Khartoum; Founder Lt-Gen. (retd) UMAR ZARUQ.

Popular Masses' Alliance: Khartoum; Founder FAYSAL MUHMAD HUSAYN.

Popular National Congress (PNC): Khartoum; f. 2000; Founder HASSAN AT-TURABI.

Socialist Popular Party: Khartoum; Founder SAYYID KHALIFAH IDRIS HABBANI.

Sudan Green Party: Khartoum; Founder Prof. ZAKARAIA BASHIR IMAM.

Sudan People's Liberation Movement (SPLM): Khartoum; e-mail info@splmtoday.com; internet www.splmtoday.com; Leader Commdr SALVA KIIR MAYARDIT; Sec.-Gen. PAGAN AMOUN.

Sudanese Central Movement: Khartoum; Founder Dr MUHAMMAD ABU AL-QASIM HAJ HAMAD.

Sudanese Initiative Party: Khartoum; Leader J'AFAR KARAR.

Sudanese National Party (SNP): Khartoum; Leader HASAN AL-MAHI; participates in the National Democratic Alliance (see below).

Umma Party (UP): internet www.umma.org; f. 1945; Mahdist party based on the Koran and Islamic traditions; Chair. Dr UMAR NUR AD-DA'IM; Leader SADIQ AL-MAHDI; withdrew from the National Democratic Alliance (see below) in March 2000.

Union of Sudan African Parties (USAP): f. 1987; Chair. JOSEPH OKELLO; Sec.-Gen. Prof. AJANG BIOR.

United Democratic Salvation Front (UDSF): Khartoum; political wing of the Sudan People's Defence Force; Chair. Dr RIEK MASHAR TENY-DHURGON.

A number of opposition movements are grouped together in the Asmara-based **National Democratic Alliance (NDA)** (Chair. OSMAN AL-MIRGHANI; Sec.-Gen. JOSEPH OKELU). These include the **Beja Congress** (Sec.-Gen. Amna Dirar), the **Legitimate Command (LC)**, the **Sudan Alliance Forces (SAF)** (f. 1994; Commdr-in-Chief Brig. ABD AL-AZIZ KHALID OSMAN), the **Sudan Federal Democratic Alliance (SFDA)** (f. 1994; advocates a decentralized, federal structure for Sudan; Chair. AHMAD DREIGE).

In 2003 two rebel groups, the **Sudan Liberation Movement (SLM)** (Leader MINNI ARKUA MINAWI) and the **Sudan Justice and Equality Movement (SJEM)**, began an armed rebellion in the Darfur region of western Sudan.

At a meeting convened in Asmara, Eritrea, in 2006 the **National Redemption Front (NRF)** was formed by the leader of the SJEM, Dr KHALIL IBRAHIM MOHAMED, his counterpart, AHMAD DREIGE of the SFDA, and KHAMIS ABDALLA ABAKAR, the former Deputy Chairman of Abd al-Wahid Muhammad an-Nur's faction of the SLM, and leader of the **Group of 19 (G-19)**. The G-19 emerged as the principal faction of the NRF, originally formed as a group of commanders who defected from an-Nur's faction during the Abuja negotiations. In December 2006 a group of Arab rebels, opposed to the Sudanese army and the *Janjaweed*, formed an alliance called the **Popular Forces Troops (PFT)**.

Diplomatic Representation

EMBASSIES IN SUDAN

Afghanistan: Madinatol Riyadh, Shareol Moshtal Sq. 10, House No. 81, Khartoum; tel. (183) 221852; fax (183) 222059; e-mail afembsudan@hotmail.com; Chargé d'affaires a.i. KHALILURRAHMAN HANANI.

Algeria: Blvd El-Mechtel Eriad, POB 80, Khartoum; tel. (183) 234773; fax (183) 224190; Ambassador SALIH BEN KOBBI.

Bulgaria: St 31, House No. 9, Block 10, al-Amarat, POB 1690, 11111 Khartoum; tel. (183) 560106; fax (183) 560107; e-mail bgembsdn@yahoo.co.uk; Chargé d'affaires a.i. SVILEN BOZHANOV.

Chad: St 57, al-Amarat, Khartoum; tel. (183) 471612; Ambassador BAHARADINE HAROUNE IBRAHIM.

China, People's Republic: POB 1425, Khartoum; tel. (183) 272730; fax (183) 271138; e-mail ssddssgg@yahoo.com.cn; Ambassador LI CHENGWEN.

Congo, Democratic Republic: St 13, Block 12 CE, New Extension, 23, POB 4195, Khartoum; tel. (183) 471125; Chargé d'affaires a.i. BAWAN MUZURI.

Egypt: University St, POB 1126, Khartoum; tel. (183) 777646; fax (183) 778741; e-mail sphinx-egysud@yahoo.com; Ambassador AFIFI ABD AL-WAHAB.

Eritrea: St 39, House No. 26, POB 1618, Khartoum 2; tel. (183) 483834; fax (183) 483835; e-mail erena@sudanet.net; Ambassador Gen. ISSA AHMED ISSA.

Ethiopia: Plot No. 4, Block 384BC, POB 844, Khartoum; tel. (183) 471379; fax (183) 471141; e-mail eekrt@hotmail.com; Ambassador ATO ALI ABDO.

France: al-Amarat, St 13, Plot No. 11, Block 12, POB 377, 11111 Khartoum; tel. (183) 471082; fax (183) 465928; e-mail cad.khartoum@diplomatie.gouv.fr; internet www.ambafrance-sd.org; Ambassador PATRICK NICOLOSO.

Germany: 53 Baladia St, Block No. 8D, Plot 2, POB 970, Khartoum; tel. (183) 777990; fax (183) 777622; e-mail regl@khar.auswaertiges-amt.de; internet www.khartum.diplo.de; Ambassador RAINER EBERLE.

Holy See: Kafouri Belgravia, POB 623, Khartoum (Apostolic Nunciature); tel. (183) 330037; fax (183) 330692; e-mail kanuap@yahoo.it; Apostolic Nuncio Most Rev. LEO BOCCARDI (Titular Archbishop of Bitettum).

India: 61 Africa Rd, POB 707, Khartoum II; tel. (183) 574001; fax (183) 574050; e-mail ambassador.office@indembsdn.com; internet www.indembsdn.com; Ambassador DEEPAK VOHRA.

Indonesia: St 60, 84, Block 12, ar-Riyadh, POB 13374, Khartoum; tel. (183) 225106; fax (183) 225528; e-mail kbri_khartoum@sudanmail.com; Ambassador SYAMSUDIN YAHYA.

Iran: Sq. 15, House No. 4, Mogran, POB 10229, Khartoum; tel. (183) 781490; fax (183) 778668; e-mail iransud@yahoo.com; Ambassador REZA AMERI.

Iraq: Sharia ash-Shareef al-Hindi, POB 1969, Khartoum; tel. (183) 271867; fax (183) 271855; e-mail krtemb@iraqmofamail.net; Ambassador SAMIR KHAIREE ALNEEMA.

Italy: St 39, Block 61, POB 793, Khartoum; tel. (183) 471615; fax (183) 471217; e-mail ambasciata.khartoum@esteri.it; internet www.ambkhartoum.esteri.it; Ambassador ROBERTO CANTONE.

Japan: St 43, House No. 67, POB 1649, Khartoum; tel. (183) 471601; fax (183) 471600; Ambassador YUICHI ISHII.

Jordan: St 33, House No. 13, POB 1379, Khartoum; tel. (183) 483125; fax (183) 471038; Ambassador MUNTHER QUBAAH.

Kenya: Plot No. 516, Block 1 West Giraif, POB 8242, Khartoum; tel. (155) 772800; fax (155) 772802; e-mail kenemb@yahoo.com; Ambassador ROBERT MUTUA NGESU.

Korea, Republic: House No. 2, St 1, New Extension, POB 2414, Khartoum; tel. (183) 451136; fax (183) 452822; e-mail ssudan@mofat.go.kr; Ambassador DONG EOK KIM.

Kuwait: Africa Ave, near the Tennis Club, POB 1457, Khartoum; tel. (183) 781525; Ambassador MUNTHIR BADR SALMAN.

Lebanon: St 5, Al-Amarat, Khartoum; tel. (183) 461320; fax (113) 461246; e-mail amliban@hotmail.com; Ambassador SHARBEL STEPHAN.

Libya: 50 Africa Rd, POB 2091, Khartoum; Secretary of People's Bureau ABDURRAHMAN MOHAMED SHALGHAM.

Malaysia: St 3, Block 2, al-Amarat, POB 11668, Khartoum; tel. (183) 482763; fax (183) 482762; e-mail malkhtoum@kln.gov.my; Ambassador HAJI ZAINAL HAMZAH.

Morocco: St 19, 32, New Extension, POB 2042, Khartoum; tel. (183) 473068; fax (183) 471053; e-mail sifmasoud@sudan.mail.net; Ambassador MUHAMMAD MAA EL-AININE.

Netherlands: St 47, House No. 76, POB 391, Khartoum; tel. (183) 471200; fax (183) 471204; e-mail kha@minbuza.nl; internet www.mfa.nl/kha; Ambassador N. W. M. BRAAKHUIS.

Nigeria: St 17, Sharia al-Mek Nimr, POB 1538, Khartoum; tel. (183) 779120; fax (183) 771491; Ambassador IBRAHIM KARLI.

Norway: St 49, House No. 63, POB 13096, Khartoum; tel. (183) 578336; fax (183) 577180; e-mail emb.khartoum@mfa.no; internet www.norway-sudan.org; Ambassador SVEIN SEVJE.

Oman: St 1, New Extension, POB 2839, Khartoum; tel. (183) 471606; fax (183) 471017; Ambassador SALIM BIN FANKHAR ASH-SHANFARI.

Pakistan: Dr Mehmood Sharif St, House No. 78, Block 25, POB 1178, Khartoum; tel. (183) 265599; fax (183) 273777; e-mail embkhartoum@yahoo.com; Ambassador MUHAMMAD ALAM BROHI.

Qatar: Elmanshia Block 92H, POB 223, Khartoum; tel. (183) 261113; fax (183) 261116; e-mail qatarembkht@yahoo.com; Ambassador ALI HASSAN ABDULLAH AL-HAMADI.

Romania: Kassala Rd, Plot No. 172–173, Kafouri Area, POB 1494, Khartoum North; tel. (185) 338114; fax (185) 341497; e-mail ambro_khartoum@hotmail.com; Ambassador Dr EMIL GHITULESCU.

Russia: A10 St, B1, New Extension, POB 1161, Khartoum; tel. (183) 471042; fax (183) 471239; e-mail rfsudan@hotmail.com; Ambassador ENVARBIK M. FAZELIYANOV.

Saudi Arabia: St 11, New Extension, Khartoum; tel. (183) 741938; Ambassador SHEIKH ABDULLAH AL-MALHOUK.

Somalia: St 23–25, New Extension, POB 1857, Khartoum; tel. (183) 744800; Ambassador Prof. MAHDI ABUKAR.

South Africa: St 11, House No. 16, Block B9, al-Amarat, POB 12137, Khartoum; tel. (183) 585301; fax (183) 585082; e-mail khartoum@foreign.gov.za; Ambassador Dr MANELISI GENGE.

Switzerland: St 15, House No. 7, Amarat, POB 1707, Khartoum; tel. (183) 471010; fax (183) 471115; e-mail kha.vertretung@eda.admin.ch; internet www.eda.admin.ch/khartoum; Ambassador ANDREJ MOTYL.

Syria: St 3, New Extension, POB 1139, Khartoum; tel. (183) 471152; fax (183) 471066; Ambassador MOHAMMED AL-MAHAMEED.

Tunisia: St 15, 35, al-Amarat, Khartoum; tel. (183) 487947; fax (183) 487950; e-mail at_khartoum@yahoo.fr; Ambassador SAÏD NACEUR BENROMDHANE.

Turkey: Baladia St, House No. 21, Block 8H, POB 771, Khartoum; tel. (183) 794215; fax (183) 794218; e-mail hartumbe@gmail.com; Ambassador MEHMET FATIH CEYLAN.

Uganda: POB 2676, Khartoum; tel. (183) 158571; fax (183) 797868; e-mail ugembkht@hotmail.com; Ambassador MULL KATENDE.

United Arab Emirates: St 3, New Extension, POB 1225, Khartoum; tel. (183) 744476; e-mail uaembassy@sudanmail.net; Ambassador ISA ABDULLAH AL-BASHAR AN-NUAIMI.

United Kingdom: St 10, off Baladia St, POB 801, Khartoum; tel. (183) 777105; fax (183) 776457; e-mail Media.Khartoum@fco.gov.uk; internet www.britishembassy.gov.uk/sudan; Ambassador Dr ROSALIND MARY MARSDEN.

USA: Ali Abd al-Latif St, POB 699, Khartoum; tel. (183) 774701; internet khartoum.usembassy.gov; Chargé d'affaires a.i. ALBERTO M. FERNANDEZ.

Yemen: St 11, New Extension, POB 1010, Khartoum; tel. (183) 743918; Ambassador SALAH AL-ANSI.

Judicial System

Until September 1983 the judicial system was divided into two sections, civil and Islamic, the latter dealing only with personal and family matters. In September 1983 President Nimeri replaced all existing laws with Islamic (*Shari'a*) law. Following the coup in April 1985, the *Shari'a* courts were abolished, and it was announced that the previous system of criminal courts was to be revived. In June 1986 the Prime Minister, Sadiq al-Mahdi, reaffirmed that the *Shari'a* law was to be abolished. It was announced in June 1987 that a new legal code, based on a 'Sudanese legal heritage', was to be introduced. In July 1989 the military Government established special courts to investigate violations of emergency laws concerning corruption. It was announced in June 1991 that these courts were to be incorporated in the general court administration. Islamic law was reintroduced in March 1991, but was not applied in the southern states of Equatoria, Bahr al-Ghazal and Upper Nile.

Chief Justice: GALAL ED-DIN MUHAMMAD OSMAN.

Religion

The majority of the northern Sudanese population are Muslims, while in the south the population are principally Christians or animists.

ISLAM

Islam is the state religion. Sudanese Islam has a strong Sufi element, and is estimated to have more than 15m. adherents.

CHRISTIANITY

Sudan Council of Churches: Inter-Church House, St 35, New Extension, POB 469, Khartoum; tel. (183) 742859; f. 1967; 12 mem. churches; Chair. Most Rev. PAOLINO LUKUDU LORO (Roman Catholic Archbishop of Juba); Gen. Sec. Rev. CLEMENT H. JANDA.

Roman Catholic Church

Latin Rite

Sudan comprises two archdioceses and seven dioceses. At 31 December 2006 there were an estimated 5,049,011 adherents, representing about 10.7% of the total population.

Sudan Catholic Bishops' Conference

General Secretariat, POB 6011, Khartoum; tel. (183) 225075. f. 1971; Pres. Mgr RUDOLF DENG MAJAK (Bishop of Wau); Sec.-Gen. JOHN DINGI MARTIN.

Archbishop of Juba: Most Rev. PAOLINO LUKUDU LORO, Catholic Church, POB 32, Juba, Equatoria State; tel. 820303; fax 820755; e-mail archbishopofjuba@hotmail.com.

Archbishop of Khartoum: Cardinal GABRIEL ZUBEIR WAKO, Catholic Church, POB 49, Khartoum; tel. (183) 782174; fax (183) 783518; e-mail ayuong@yahoo.com.

Maronite Rite

Maronite Church in Sudan: POB 244, Khartoum; Rev. Fr YOUSEPH NEAMA.

Melkite Rite

Patriarchal Vicariate of Egypt and Sudan: Greek Melkite Catholic Patriarchate, 16 Sharia Daher, 11271 Cairo, Egypt; tel. (2) 5905790; fax (2) 5935398; e-mail grecmelkitecath_egy@hotmail.com; General Patriarchal Vicar in Egypt and Sudan Mgr (JOSEPH) JULES ZEREY (Titular Archbishop of Damietta); Patriarchal Vicar in Sudan Mgr Exarkhos GEORGE BANNA; POB 766, Khartoum; tel. (183) 777910.

Syrian Rite

Syrian Church in Sudan: Under the jurisdiction of the Patriarch of Antioch; Protosyncellus Rt Rev. JOSEPH-CLÉMENT HANNOUCHE (Bishop of Cairo).

Orthodox Churches

Coptic Orthodox Church

Metropolitan of Khartoum, Southern Sudan and Uganda: Rt Rev. ANBA DANIAL, POB 4, Khartoum; tel. (183) 770646; fax (183) 785646; e-mail metaous@email-sudan.net.

Bishop of Atbara, Omdurman and Northern Sudan: Rt Rev. ANBA SARABAMON, POB 628, Omdurman; tel. (183) 550423; fax (183) 556973.

Greek Orthodox Church

Metropolitan of Nubia: POB 47, Khartoum; tel. (183) 772973; Archbishop DIONYSSIOS HADZIVASSILIOU.

The Ethiopian Orthodox Church is also active.

The Anglican Communion

Anglicans are adherents of the (Episcopal) Church of the Province of the Sudan. The Province, with 24 dioceses and about 1m. adherents, was established in 1976.

Archbishop in Sudan and Bishop of Juba: Most Rev. DANIEL DENG BUL YAK, ECS Liaison Office, POB 604, Khartoum; tel. (11) 485720; fax (11) 485717; e-mail ecsprovince@hotmail.com.

Other Christian Churches

Evangelical Church: POB 57, Khartoum; c. 1,500 mems; administers schools, literature centre and training centre; Chair. Rev. RADI ELIAS.

Presbyterian Church: POB 40, Malakal; autonomous since 1956; 67,000 mems (1985); Gen. Sec. Rev. THOMAS MALUIT.

The Africa Inland Church, the Sudan Interior Church and the Sudanese Church of Christ are also active.

The Press

DAILIES

Press censorship was imposed following the 1989 coup.

Abbar al-Youm: Khartoum; tel. (183) 779396; daily; Editor AHMED AL-BALAL AT-TAYEB.

Al-Anbaa: Khartoum; tel. (183) 466523; f. 1998; Editor-in-Chief NAJIB ADAM QAMAR AD-DIN.

Al-Wan: Khartoum; tel. (183) 775036; e-mail alwaan@cybergates.net; daily; independent; pro-Govt; Editor HOUSSEN KHOGALI.

An-Nasr: Khartoum; tel. (183) 772494; Editor Col YOUNIS MAHMOUD.

Ar-Rai al-Akhar: Khartoum; tel. (183) 777934; daily; Editor MOHI AD-DIN TITTAWI.

Ar-Rai al-Amm: Khartoum; tel. (183) 778182; fax (183) 772176; e-mail info@rayaam.net; internet www.rayaam.net; daily; Editor SALAH MUHAMMAD IBRAHIM.

Khartoum Monitor: St 61, New Extension, Khartoum; e-mail Khartoummonitor@hotmail.com; Chair. and Editor ALFRED TABAN; Man. Editor WILLIAM EZEKIEL.

Sudan Mirror: POB 59163, 00200 Nairobi, Kenya; tel. and fax (20) 3876439; e-mail info@sdt.co.ke; e-mail daneiffe@gmail.com; internet www.sudanmirror.com; f. 2003; Dir DANIEL EIFFE.

Sudan Standard: Ministry of Information and Communication, Khartoum; daily; English.

PERIODICALS

Al-Guwwat al-Musallaha (The Armed Forces): Khartoum; f. 1969; publs a weekly newspaper and monthly magazine for the armed forces; Editor-in-Chief Maj. MAHMOUD GALANDER; circ. 7,500.

New Horizon: POB 2651, Khartoum; tel. (183) 777913; f. 1976; publ. by the Sudan House for Printing and Publishing; weekly; English; political and economic affairs, devt, home and international news; Editor AS-SIR HASSAN FADL; circ. 7,000.

Sudanow: POB 2651, Khartoum; tel. (183) 777913; f. 1976; publ. by the Sudan House for Printing and Publishing; monthly; English; political and economic affairs, arts, social affairs and diversions; Editor-in-Chief AHMED KAMAL ED-DIN; circ. 10,000.

NEWS AGENCIES

Sudan News Agency (SUNA): Sharia al-Gamhouria, POB 1506, Khartoum; tel. (183) 775770; e-mail suna@sudanet.net; internet www.suna-sd.net; Dir-Gen. ALI ABD AR-RAHMAN AN-NUMAYRI.

Sudanese Press Agency: Khartoum; f. 1985; owned by journalists.

Publishers

Ahmad Abd ar-Rahman at-Tikeine: POB 299, Port Sudan.

Al-Ayyam Press Co Ltd: Aboulela Bldg, POB 363, United Nations Sq., Khartoum; f. 1953; general fiction and non-fiction, arts, poetry, reference, newspapers, magazines; Man. Dir BESHIR MUHAMMAD SAID.

As-Sahafa Publishing and Printing House: POB 1228, Khartoum; f. 1961; newspapers, pamphlets, fiction and govt publs.

As-Salam Co Ltd: POB 944, Khartoum.

Claudios S. Fellas: POB 641, Khartoum.

Khartoum University Press: POB 321, Khartoum; tel. (183) 776653; f. 1964; academic, general and educational in Arabic and English; Man. Dir ALI EL-MAK.

GOVERNMENT PUBLISHING HOUSE

El-Asma Printing Press: POB 38, Khartoum.

Broadcasting and Communications

TELECOMMUNICATIONS

Canar Telecommunication (Canartel): Al-Qibla Centre, Block 37, cnr As-Sahafa and Madani Rds, POB 8182, Khartoum; tel. (15) 5550000; fax (15) 5550055; e-mail support@canar.sd; internet www.canar.sd; f. 2005; operates fixed-line telephone and internet services; Man. Dir. SAOOD AL-JENAIBI.

Ministry of Information and Communication: Khartoum; regulatory body; Sec.-Gen. Eng. AWAD E. WIDAA.

MTN-Sudan: 264 Garden City, POB 34611111, Khartoum; tel. (92) 1111111; internet www.mtn.sd; f. 2005; mobile cellular telephone provider; CEO IMAD KREIDIEH; 1.4m. subscribers (2007).

Posts and Telegraphs Public Corpn: Khartoum; tel. (183) 770000; fax (183) 772888; e-mail sudanpost@maktoob.com; regulatory body; Dir-Gen. AHMAD AT-TIJANI ALALLIM.

Sudan Telecom Co (SUDATEL): Sudatel Tower, POB 11155, Khartoum; tel. (183) 797400; fax (183) 782322; e-mail info@sudatel.net; internet www.sudatel.sd; f. 1993; service provider for Sudan; CEO IMAD ADDIN HUSSIEN AHMED.

Zain: Khartoum; tel. 91230000; e-mail info@sd.zain.com; internet www.sd.zain.com; f. 1997 as MobiTel; name changed as above in 2007; provides mobile cellular telephone services.

BROADCASTING

Radio

Sudan Radio: POB 572, Omdurman; tel. (187) 559315; fax (187) 560566; e-mail info@sudanradio.info; internet www.sudanradio.info; f. 1940; state-controlled service broadcasting daily in Arabic, English, French and Swahili; Dir-Gen. MUTASIM FADUL USUD.

SUDAN

Voice of Sudan: e-mail informationsec@ndasudan.org; active since 1995; run by the National Democratic Alliance; Arabic and English.

Television

An earth satellite station operated on 36 channels at Umm Haraz has much improved Sudan's telecommunications links. A nation-wide satellite network is being established with 14 earth stations in the provinces. There are regional stations at Gezira (Central Region) and Atbara (Northern Region).

Sudan Television: POB 1094, Omdurman; tel. (15) 550022; internet www.sudantv.net; f. 1962; state-controlled; 60 hours of programmes per week; Head of Directorate HADID AS-SIRA.

Finance

(cap. = capital; res = reserves; dep. = deposits; m. = million; brs = branches; amounts in Sudanese dinars, unless otherwise indicated)

BANKING

All domestic banks are controlled by the Bank of Sudan. Foreign banks were permitted to resume operations in 1976. In December 1985 the Government banned the establishment of any further banks. It was announced in December 1990 that Sudan's banking system was to be reorganized to accord with Islamic principles. In 2000 there were a total of 25 banks in Sudan. In May 2000 the Bank of Sudan issued new policy guidelines under which Sudan's banks were to merge into six banking groups to improve their financial strength and international competitiveness; the mergers were to be implemented during the period 2007–09.

Central Bank

Bank of Sudan: Gamhoria St, POB 313, Khartoum; tel. (183) 782246; fax (183) 787226; e-mail sudanbank@sudanmail.net; internet www.bankofsudan.org; f. 1960; bank of issue; cap. 1,200.0m., res 7,474.9m., dep. 772,433.7m. (Dec. 2004); Gov. Dr SABIR MUHAMMAD HASSAN; 13 brs.

Commercial Banks

Al-Baraka Bank: Baraka Tower, Zubeir Pasha St, POB 3583, Khartoum; tel. (183) 785810; fax (183) 778948; e-mail khairy@albarakasudan.com; internet www.albarakasudan.com; f. 1984; 87.8% owned by Al-Baraka Banking Group (Bahrain); investment and export promotion; cap. 3,353.6m., res 4,042.7m., dep. 37,220.2m. (Dec. 2006); Chair. OSMAN AHMED SULIMAN; Gen. Man. ABDALLAH KHAIRY HAMID; 24 brs.

Ash-Shamal Islamic Bank: Ash-Shamal Islamic Tower, as-Sayid Abd ar-Rahman St, POB 10036, 11111 Khartoum; tel. (183) 779078; fax (183) 772661; e-mail info@alshamalbank.com; internet www.alshamalbank.com; f. 1990; total assets 18,258.0m. (Dec. 2003); Pres. GAFAAR OSMAN FAGIR; Gen. Man. ABDELMONEIM HASSAN SAYED (acting); 17 brs.

Bank of Khartoum: Intersection Gamhouria St and El-Gaser St, POB 1008, Khartoum; tel. 156660000; fax (183) 781120; e-mail info@bok.sd; internet www.bok-sd.com; f. 1913; 60% owned by Dubai Islamic Bank PJSC (United Arab Emirates); absorbed National Export/Import Bank and Unity Bank in 1993; cap. 11,800m., res 450.1m., dep. 48,600m. (Dec. 2003); Chair. Dr KHALID M. ALI AL KAMDA; Gen. Man. FADI SALIM AL-FAQIH; 118 brs.

Blue Nile Mashreg Bank: Barlaman St, POB 984, Khartoum; tel. (183) 776092; fax (183) 782562; e-mail info@bluemashreg.com; internet www.bluemashreg.com; cap. 1,531.8m., res 872.8m., dep. 18,822.9m. (Dec. 2006); Chair. MUHAMMAD ISMAIL MUHAMMAD; Gen. Man. ISAAM USMAN MAHGOUB.

Buffalo Commercial Bank: BCB Junction, Juba; e-mail info@buffalocommercialbank.com; internet www.buffalocommercialbank.com; f. 2008; Chair. Dr LUAL ACUEK LUAL DENG; CEO BISWASH GAUCHAN.

Farmers Commercial Bank: POB 11984, Al-Qasr Ave, Khartoum; tel. (183) 774960; fax (183) 773687; e-mail mozarea@alnlilin.com; internet www.fcbsudan.com; f. 1960 as Sudan Commercial Bank; name changed as above in 1999 following merger with Farmers Bank for Investment and Rural Development; cap. 4,140.1m., res 1,335.0m., dep. 21,375.5m. (Dec. 2006); Chair. AT-TAYB ELOBEID BADR; Pres. SULIMAN HASHIM MOHAMED TOUM; 28 brs.

National Bank of Sudan: Kronfli Bldg, Zubeir Pasha St, POB 1183, Khartoum; tel. (183) 789410; fax (183) 779545; f. 1982; 70% owned by Bank Audi SAL, Lebanon; cap. 1,991.9m., res 86.7m., dep. 9,048.4m. (Dec. 2005); Chair. Dr IMAD ITANI; 13 brs in Sudan, 2 abroad.

Omdurman National Bank: Al-Qaser Ave, POB 11522, Khartoum; tel. (183) 770400; fax (183) 777263; e-mail info@omd-bank.com; internet www.omd-bank.com; f. 1993; cap. 6,096.3m., res 8,362.2m., dep. 342,391.2m. (Dec. 2005); Gen. Man. ABDEL RAHMAN HASSAN ABDEL RAHMAN; 17 brs; 852 employees.

Sudanese French Bank: Plot No. 6, Block A, Al-Qasr St, POB 2775, Khartoum; tel. (183) 771730; fax (183) 790391; e-mail info@sfbank.net; internet www.sfbank.net/englishsfb; f. 1978 as Sudanese Investment Bank; name changed as above in 1993; cap. £S 67m., res £S 21.3m., dep. £S 648.9m. (Dec. 2007); Chair. OSMAN SALMAN MOHAMED NOUR; Gen. Man. MASSAD MOHAMMED AHMED ABDUL KARIM; 20 brs.

Tadamon Islamic Bank: Baladia St, POB 3154, Khartoum; tel. (183) 771505; fax (183) 773840; e-mail info@tadamonbank-sd.com; internet www.tadamonbank-sd.com; f. 1981; cap. 6,775.5m., res 1,363.9m., dep. 66,768.0m. (Dec. 2006); Chair. Dr HASSAN OSMAN SAKOTA; Gen. Man. ABDALLAH NOGD ALLAH AHMAIDI; 18 brs.

Foreign Banks

Byblos Bank Africa Ltd: 21 al-Amarat St, POB 8121, Khartoum; tel. (183) 566444; fax (183) 566454; e-mail Byblosbankafrica@byblosbank.com; internet www.byblosbank.com.lb; 65% owned by Byblos Bank SAL, Beirut; f. 2003; cap. 6,375.2m., res 554.3m., dep. 25,814.2m. (Dec. 2006); Chair. Dr FRANÇOIS S. BASSIL; Gen. Man. NADIM GHANTOUS.

Faisal Islamic Bank (Sudan) (Saudi Arabia): Faih'a Bldg, Ali al-Latif St, POB 2415, Khartoum; tel. (183) 777920; fax (183) 780193; e-mail fibsudan@fibsudan.com; internet www.fibsudan.com; f. 1977; cap. 6,000.0m., res 862.5m., dep. 55,634.2m. (Dec. 2006); Chair. Prince MUHAMMAD AL-FAISAL AS-SAUD; Gen. Man. ALI OMAR IBRAHIM FARAH; 30 brs.

National Bank of Abu Dhabi (United Arab Emirates): Taka Bldg, Atbara St, POB 2465, Khartoum; tel. (183) 778517; fax (183) 774892; e-mail gamalaldin.alkheir@nbad.com; internet www.nbad.com; f. 2007; cap. and res £S 16.9m., total assets £S 12.5m. (Dec. 1987); Regional Man. OMER SID AHMED (acting).

Saudi Sudanese Bank: Baladia St, POB 1773, Khartoum; tel. (183) 780307; fax (183) 781836; e-mail saudi-sud@saudisb.sd; internet www.saudisb.sd; f. 1986; cap. 422.6m., res 2,736.5m., dep. 35,017.0m. (Dec. 2005); Chair. ABDEL GALIL EL-WASIA; Gen. Man. MUDATHIR ALI AL-BASHIR (acting); 13 brs.

Development Banks

Agricultural Bank of Sudan: Ghoumhoria Ave, POB 1263, Khartoum; tel. (183) 777432; fax (183) 778296; e-mail agribank@yahoo.com; f. 1957; cap. 5,200.0m., res 3,609.4m., dep. 18,864.9m. (Dec. 2003); provides finance for agricultural projects; Pres. AS-SAYID GAFFAR MUHAMMAD AL-HASSAN; Gen. Man. AS-SAYID AL-KINDI MUHAMMAD OSMAN; 40 brs.

Islamic Co-operative Development Bank (ICDB): Et-Tanmha Tower, Kolyat Eltib St, POB 62, Khartoum; tel. (183) 780223; fax (183) 777715; f. 1983; cap. and res 3,821.0m., total assets 28,250.4m. (Dec. 2003); Chair. El-Haj ATTA EL-MANAN IDRIS; 6 brs.

En-Nilein Bank: United Nations Sq., POB 1722, Khartoum; tel. (183) 771984; fax (183) 785811; e-mail info@nidbg.com; internet www.nidbg.com; f. 1993 by merger of En-Nilein Bank and Industrial Bank of Sudan; name changed as above in 2007; 99% owned by Central Bank of Sudan; provides tech. and financial assistance for private-sector industrial projects and acquires shares in industrial enterprises; cap. 3,282.6m., res −861.4m., dep. 54,046.9m. (Dec. 2005); Man. Dir MOHAMED ABBAS AGAB; 37 brs.

NIMA Development and Investment Bank: Hashim Hago Bldg, As-Suk al-Arabi, POB 665, Khartoum; tel. (183) 779496; fax (183) 781854; f. 1982 as National Devt Bank; name changed as above 1998; 90%-owned by NIMA Groupe, 10% private shareholders; finances or co-finances economic and social devt projects; cap. £S 4,000m., res £S 106m. (Dec. 1998); Dir-Gen. SALIM AS-SAFI HUGIR; 6 brs.

Sudanese Estates Bank: Baladia St, POB 309, Khartoum; tel. (183) 777917; fax (183) 779465; f. 1967; mortgage bank financing private-sector urban housing devt; cap. and res £S 1,700m., total assets £S 9,500m. (Dec. 1994); Chair. Eng. MUHAMMAD ALI EL-AMIN; 6 brs.

STOCK EXCHANGE

Sudanese Stock Exchange: Al-Baraka Tower, 5th Floor, POB 10835, Khartoum; tel. (183) 776235; fax (183) 776134; f. 1995; Chair. HAMZA MUHAMMAD JENAWI; 27 mems.

INSURANCE

African Insurance Co (Sudan) Ltd: New Abu Ella Bldg, Parliament Ave, Khartoum; tel. (183) 173402; fax (183) 177988; f. 1977; fire, accident, marine and motor; Gen. Man. AN-NOMAN AS-SANUSI.

Blue Nile Insurance Co (Sudan) Ltd: Al-Qasr Ave, Blue Nile Insurance Bldg, POB 2215, Khartoum; tel. (183) 170580; fax (183)

172405; internet www.blue-nile-insurance.com; f. 1965; Gen. Man. MUHAMMAD AL-AMIN MIRGHANI.

Foja International Insurance Co Ltd: POB 879, Khartoum; tel. (183) 784470; fax (183) 783248; fire, accident, marine, motor and animal; Gen. Man. MAMOON IBRAHIM ABD ALLA.

General Insurance Co (Sudan) Ltd: El-Mek Nimr St, POB 1555, Khartoum; tel. (183) 780616; fax (183) 772122; f. 1961; Gen. Man. AS-SAMAWL AS-SAYED HAFIZ.

Islamic Insurance Co Ltd: Al-Faiha Commercial Bldg, Ali Abdul-latif St, POB 2776, Khartoum; tel. (183) 772656; f. 1979; all classes; CEO Dr OTHMAN ABDUL WAHAB.

Khartoum Insurance Co Ltd: Al-Taminat Bldg, Al-Jamhouriya St, POB 737, Khartoum; tel. (183) 778647; f. 1953; Chair. MUDAWI M. AHMAD; Gen. Dir YOUSIF KHAIRY.

Juba Insurance Co Ltd: Al-Baladiya St, Sayen Osnam Al-Amin Bldg, 2nd Floor, POB 10043, Khartoum; tel. (183) 783245; fax (183) 781617; Gen. Man. ABDUL AAL AD-DAWI.

Middle East Insurance Co Ltd: Al-Qasr St, Kuronfuli Bldg, 1st Floor, POB 3070, Khartoum; tel. (183) 772202; fax (183) 779266; f. 1981; fire, marine, motor and general liability; Chair. AHMAD I. MALIK; Gen. Dir ALI MUHAMMAD AHMED EL-FADL.

Sudanese Insurance and Reinsurance Co Ltd: Al-Gamhouria Ave, Nasr Sq., Abd Al-Rahman Makawi Bldg, 3rd Floor, POB 2332, Khartoum; tel. (183) 770812; e-mail info@sudinreco.com; internet www.sudinreco.com; f. 1967; Gen. Man. HASSAN ES-SAYED MUHAMMAD ALI.

United Insurance Co (Sudan) Ltd: Makkawi Bldg, Al-Gamhouria St, POB 318, Khartoum; tel. (183) 776630; fax (183) 770783; e-mail abdin@unitedinsurance.ws; internet www.unitedinsurance.ws; f. 1968; Chair. HASHIM EL-BERIER; Dir-Gen. MUHAMMAD ABDEEN BABIKER.

Trade and Industry

GOVERNMENT AGENCIES

Agricultural Research Corpn: POB 126, Wadi Medani; tel. (51) 1842226; fax (51) 1843213; e-mail arcdg@sudanmail.net; internet www.arcsudan.sd; f. 1967; Dir-Gen. Prof. AZHARI ABDELAZIM HAMADA.

Animal Production Public Corpn: POB 624, Khartoum; tel. (183) 778555; Gen. Man. Dr FOUAD RAMADAN HAMID.

General Petroleum Corpn: POB 2649, Khartoum; tel. (183) 777554; fax (183) 773663; e-mail secretarygeneral@spc.sd; f. 1976; Chair. Dr AWAD AHMED AL-JAZZ; Sec.-Gen. Dr OMER MOHAMED KHEIR.

Gum Arabic Co Ltd: POB 857, Khartoum; tel. (183) 462111; fax (183) 467923; e-mail info@gac-arabicgum.com; internet www.gac-arabicgum.com; f. 1969; Chair. ABD EL-HAMID MUSA KASHA; Gen. Man. HASSAN SAAD AHMED.

Industrial Production Corpn: POB 1034, Khartoum; tel. (183) 771278; f. 1976; Dir-Gen. OSMAN TAMMAM.

Cement and Building Materials Sector Co-ordination Office: POB 2241, Khartoum; tel. (183) 774269; Dir T. M. KHOGALI.

Food Industries Corpn: POB 2341, Khartoum; tel. (183) 775463; Dir MUHAMMAD AL-GHALI SULIMAN.

Leather Industries Corpn: POB 1639, Khartoum; tel. (183) 778187; f. 1986; Man. Dir IBRAHIM SALIH ALI.

Oil Corpn: POB 64, Khartoum North; tel. (183) 332044; Gen. Man. BUKHARI MAHMOUD BUKHARI.

Spinning and Weaving General Co Ltd: POB 765, Khartoum; tel. (183) 774306; f. 1975; Dir MUHAMMAD SALIH MUHAMMAD ABDALLAH.

Sudan Tea Co Ltd: POB 1219, Khartoum; tel. (183) 781261.

Sudanese Mining Corpn: POB 1034, Khartoum; tel. (183) 770840; f. 1975; Dir IBRAHIM MUDAWI BABIKER.

Sugar and Distilling Industry Corpn: POB 511, Khartoum; tel. (183) 778417; Man. MIRGHANI AHMAD BABIKER.

Mechanized Farming Corpn: POB 2482, Khartoum; Man. Dir AWAD AL-KARIM AL-YASS.

National Cotton and Trade Co Ltd: POB 1552, Khartoum; tel. (183) 80040; f. 1970; Chair. ABD EL-ATI A. MEKKI; Man. Dir ABD AR-RAHMAN A. MONIEM; Gen. Man. ZUBAIR MUHAMMAD AL-BASHIR.

Port Sudan Cotton Trade Co Ltd: POB 590, Port Sudan; POB 590, Khartoum; Gen. Man. SAÏD MUHAMMAD ADAM.

Public Agricultural Production Corpn: POB 538, Khartoum; Chair. and Man. Dir ABDALLAH BAYOUMI; Sec. SAAD AD-DIN MUHAMMAD ALI.

Public Corpn for Building and Construction: POB 2110, Khartoum; tel. (183) 774544; Dir NAIM AD-DIN.

Public Corpn for Irrigation and Excavation: POB 619, Khartoum; tel. (183) 780167; Gen. Sec. OSMAN AN-NUR.

Public Corpn for Oil Products and Pipelines: POB 1704, Khartoum; tel. (183) 778290; Gen. Man. ABD AR-RAHMAN SULIMAN.

Rahad Corpn: POB 2523, Khartoum; tel. (183) 775175; financed by the World Bank, Kuwait and the USA; Man. Dir HASSAN SAAD ABDALLA.

State Trading Corpn: POB 211, Khartoum; tel. (183) 778555; Chair. E. R. M. TOM.

Automobile Corpn: POB 221, Khartoum; tel. (183) 778555; importer of vehicles and spare parts; Gen. Man. DAFALLA AHMAD SIDDIQ.

Captrade Engineering and Automobile Services Co Ltd: POB 97, Khartoum; tel. (183) 789265; fax (183) 775544; e-mail cap1@sudanmail.net; f. 1925; importers and distributors of engineering and automobile equipment; Gen. Man. ESSAM MOHD EL-HASSAN KAMBAL.

Gezira Trade and Services Co: POB 17, Port Sudan; tel. (311) 825109; fax (311) 822029; e-mail gtsportsudan@hotmail.com; f. 1980; importer of agricultural machinery, spare parts, electrical and office equipment, foodstuffs, clothes and footwear; exporter of oilseeds, grains, hides and skins and livestock; provides shipping insurance and warehousing services; agents for Lloyds and P & I Club; Chair. NASR ED-DIN M. OMER.

Khartoum Commercial and Shipping Co: POB 221, Khartoum; tel. (183) 778555; f. 1982; import, export and shipping services, insurance and manufacturing; Gen. Man. IDRIS M. SALIH.

Silos and Storage Corpn: POB 1183, Khartoum; stores and handles agricultural products; Gen. Man. AHMAD AT-TAIEB HARHOOF.

Sudan Cotton Co Ltd: POB 1672, Khartoum; tel. (183) 775755; fax (183) 770703; e-mail sccl@sudanmail.net; internet www.sudan-cotton.com; f. 1970; exports and markets cotton; Chair. ABBAS ABD AL-BAGI HAMMAD; Dir-Gen. Dr ABDIN MUHAMMAD ALI.

Sudan Gezira Board: POB 884, HQ Barakat Wadi Medani, Gezira Province; tel. 2412; Sales Office, POB 884, Khartoum; tel. (183) 740145; f. 1950; responsible for Sudan's main cotton-producing area; the Gezira scheme is a partnership between the Govt, the tenants and the board. The Govt provides the land and is responsible for irrigation. Tenants pay a land and water charge and receive the work proceeds. The Board provides agricultural services at cost, technical supervision and execution of govt agricultural policies relating to the scheme. Tenants pay a percentage of their proceeds to the Social Development Fund. The total potential cultivable area of the Gezira scheme is c. 850,000 ha and the total area under systematic irrigation is c. 730,000 ha. In addition to cotton, groundnuts, sorghum, wheat, rice, pulses and vegetables are grown for the benefit of tenant farmers; Man. Dir Prof. FATHI MUHAMMAD KHALIFA.

Sudan Oilseeds Co Ltd: Parliament Ave, POB 167, Khartoum; tel. (183) 780120; f. 1974; 58% state-owned; exporter of oilseeds (groundnuts, sesame seeds and castor beans); importer of foodstuffs and other goods; Chair. SADIQ KARAR AT-TAYEB; Gen. Man. KAMAL ABD AL-HALIM.

DEVELOPMENT CORPORATIONS

Sudan Development Corpn (SDC): 21 al-Amarat, POB 710, Khartoum; tel. (183) 472151; fax (183) 472148; f. 1974 to promote and co-finance devt projects with special emphasis on projects in the agricultural, agri-business and industrial sectors; cap. p.u. US $200m.; Man. Dir ABDEL WAHAB AHMED HAMZA.

Sudan Rural Development Co Ltd (SRDC): POB 2190, Khartoum; tel. (183) 773855; fax (183) 773235; e-mail srdfc@hotmail.com; f. 1980; SDC has 27% shareholding; cap. p.u. US $20m.; Gen. Man. EL-AWAD ABDALLA H. HIJAZI (designate).

Sudan Rural Development Finance Co (SRDFC): POB 2190, Khartoum; tel. (183) 773855; fax (183) 773235; f. 1980; Gen. Man. OMRAN MUHAMMAD ALI.

CHAMBER OF COMMERCE

Union of Sudanese Chambers of Commerce: POB 81, Khartoum; tel. (183) 772346; fax (183) 780748; e-mail chamber@sudanchamber.org; internet www.sudanchamber.org; f. 1908; Pres. AT-TAYEB AHMED OSMAN; Sec.-Gen. IBRAHIM MUHAMMAD OSMAN.

INDUSTRIAL ASSOCIATION

Sudanese Chambers of Industries Association: Africa St, POB 2565, Khartoum; tel. (183) 471716; fax (183) 471720; e-mail info@sudanindustries.org; internet www.sudanindustry.org; f. 1974; Chair. NOUR ELDIN SAEED AS-SAID.

UTILITIES

Public Electricity and Water Corpn: POB 1380, Khartoum; tel. (183) 81021; Dir Dr YASIN AL-HAJ ABDIN.

CO-OPERATIVE SOCIETIES

There are about 600 co-operative societies, of which 570 are officially registered.

Central Co-operative Union: POB 2492, Khartoum; tel. (183) 780624; largest co-operative union operating in 15 provinces.

TRADE UNIONS

All trade union activity was banned following the 1989 coup. The following organizations were active prior to that date.

Federations

Sudan Workers Trade Unions Federation (SWTUF): POB 2258, Khartoum; tel. (183) 777463; includes 42 trade unions representing c. 1.75m. public service and private sector workers; affiliated to the Int. Confed. of Arab Trade Unions and the Org. of African Trade Union Unity; Pres. MUHAMMAD OSMAN GAMA; Gen. Sec. YOUSUF ABU SHAMA HAMED.

Sudanese Federation of Employees and Professionals Trade Unions: POB 2398, Khartoum; tel. (183) 773818; f. 1975; includes 54 trade unions representing 250,000 mems; Pres. IBRAHIM AWADALLAH; Sec.-Gen. KAMAL AD-DIN MUHAMMAD ABDALLAH.

Transport

RAILWAYS

The total length of railway in operation in 2002 was 5,978 route-km. The main line runs from Wadi Halfa, on the Egyptian border, to al-Obeid, via Khartoum. Lines from Atbara and Sinnar connect with Port Sudan. There are lines from Sinnar to Damazin on the Blue Nile (227 km) and from Aradeiba to Nyala in the south-western province of Darfur (689 km), with a 445-km branch line from Babanousa to Wau in Bahr al-Ghazal province. In 2001 plans were announced for the construction of a rail link between Port Sudan and Moyale, Ethiopia.

Sudan Railways Corpn (SRC): POB 65, Atbara; tel. 2000; f. 1875; Gen. Man. OMAR MUHAMMAD NUR.

ROADS

Roads in northern Sudan, other than town roads, are only cleared tracks and often impassable immediately after rain. Motor traffic on roads in the former Upper Nile province is limited to the drier months of January–May. There are several good gravelled roads in the Equatoria and Bahr al-Ghazal provinces which are passable all the year, but in these districts some of the minor roads become impassable after rain.

Over 48,000 km of tracks are classed as 'motorable'; there were 3,160 km of main roads and 739 km of secondary roads in 1985. A 1,190-km tarmac road linking the capital with Port Sudan was completed during 1980. In 1996, according to World Bank estimates, some 36.3% of Sudan's roads were paved. By 1997 a 270-km road linking Jaili with Atbara had been completed, as part of a scheme to provide an alternative route from Khartoum to the coast. A 484-km highway links Khartoum, Haiya and Port Sudan.

National Transport Corpn: POB 723, Khartoum; Gen. Man. MOHI AD-DIN HASSAN MUHAMMAD NUR.

Public Corpn for Roads and Bridges: POB 756, Khartoum; tel. (183) 770794; f. 1976; Chair. ABD AR-RAHMAN HABOUD; Dir-Gen. ABDOU MUHAMMAD ABDOU.

INLAND WATERWAYS

The total length of navigable waterways served by passenger and freight services is 4,068 km, of which approximately 1,723 km is open all year. From the Egyptian border to Wadi Halfa and Khartoum navigation is limited by cataracts to short stretches, but the White Nile from Khartoum to Juba is almost always navigable.

River Transport Corpn (RTC): POB 284, Khartoum North; operates 2,500 route-km of steamers on the Nile; Chair. ALI AMIR TAHA.

River Navigation Corpn: Khartoum; f. 1970; jtly owned by Govts of Egypt and Sudan; operates services between Aswan and Wadi Halfa.

SHIPPING

Port Sudan, on the Red Sea, 784 km from Khartoum, and Suakin are the only commercial seaports.

Axis Trading Co Ltd: POB 1574, Khartoum; tel. (183) 775875; f. 1967; Chair. HASSAN A. M. SULIMAN.

Red Sea Shipping and Services Co: POB 308, Khartoum; tel. (183) 580885; fax (183) 5119090; e-mail rredseaco@redsea-sd.com; internet www.redsea-sd.com; Gen. Man. AWAD HAG ALI HAMED.

Sea Ports Corpn: Port Sudan; tel. (183) 779114; fax (183) 779338; e-mail spcp11@sudanports.gov.sd; internet sudanports.gov.sd; f. 1906; Gen. Man. MUHAMMAD TAHIR AILA.

Sudan Shipping Line Ltd: POB 426, Port Sudan; tel. 2655; POB 1731, Khartoum; tel. (183) 780017; f. 1960; 10 vessels totalling 54,277 dwt operating between the Red Sea and western Mediterranean, northern Europe and United Kingdom; Chair. ISMAIL BAKHEIT; Gen. Man. SALAH AD-DIN OMER AL-AZIZ.

United African Shipping Co: POB 339, Khartoum; tel. (183) 780967; Gen. Man. MUHAMMAD TAHA AL-GINDI.

CIVIL AVIATION

In June 2005 the Government announced that preliminary construction work had been completed for a new international airport at a site 40 km south-west of Khartoum. Work to build runways and two passenger terminals was scheduled to be completed by 2008. The airport was expected to open in 2010.

Civil Aviation Authority: Sharia Sayed Abd ar-Rahman, POB 430, Khartoum; tel. (183) 787757; fax (183) 779715; e-mail info@caa.gov.sd; internet www.caa-sudan.net; f. 1936; Dir-Gen. ABOU BAKR GAAFAR AHMAD.

Azza Transport: Mak Nimir St, POB 11586, Khartoum; tel. (183) 783761; fax (183) 770408; e-mail info@azzatransport.com; internet www.azzatransport.com; f. 1993; charter and dedicated freight to Africa and the Middle East; Man. Dir Dr GIBRIL I. MOHAMED.

Sudan Airways Co Ltd: Sudan Airways Complex, 161 Obeid Khatim St, Riadh Nlock No. 10, POB 253 Khartoum; tel. (183) 243738; fax (183) 115951; e-mail gm@sudanair.com; internet www.sudanair.com; f. 1947; internal flights and international services to Africa, the Middle East and Europe; Man. Dir AHMED OMER ABDELRAHMAN.

Sudanese Aeronautical Services (SASCO): POB 8260, al-Amarat, Khartoum; tel. (183) 7463362; fax (183) 4433362; fmrly Sasco Air Charter; chartered services; Chair. M. M. NUR.

Trans Arabian Air Transport (TAAT): POB 1461, Africa St, Khartoum; tel. (183) 451568; fax (183) 451544; e-mail ftaats@sudanmail.net; f. 1983; dedicated freight; services to Africa, Europe and Middle East; Man. Dir Capt. EL-FATI ABDIN.

United Arabian Airlines: POB 3687, Office No. 3, Elekhwa Bldg, Atbara St, Khartoum; tel. (183) 773025; fax (183) 784402; e-mail krthq@uaa.com; f. 1995; charter and dedicated freight services to Africa and the Middle East; Man. Dir M. KORDOFANI.

Tourism

Although tourism in Sudan remains relatively undeveloped, the eastern Red Sea coast and Nile tributaries offer opportunities for water sports. Other attractions include ancient Egyptian remains and the Ad-Dinder National Tourist Park, a game reserve established in 1935. In 1991 Sudan's first Marine National Park opened on Sanganeb atoll. A total of 328,148 tourists visited Sudan in 2006. Receipts from tourism in 2005 were US $89m.

Public Corpn of Tourism and Hotels: POB 7104, Khartoum; tel. (183) 781764; f. 1977; Dir-Gen. Maj.-Gen. EL-KHATIM MUHAMMAD FADL.

SURINAME

Introductory Survey

Location, Climate, Language, Religion, Flag, Capital

The Republic of Suriname lies on the north-east coast of South America. It is bordered by Guyana to the west, by French Guiana to the east, and by Brazil to the south. The climate is sub-tropical, with fairly heavy rainfall and average temperatures of between 21°C (70°F) and 30°C (86°F). Average annual rainfall varies from 3,720 mm (146 ins) in the north to 804 mm (32 ins) in the south. The official language is Dutch. The other main languages are Hindustani and Javanese. The majority of the people can speak the native language Sranang Tongo, a Creole language known as Negro English or taki-taki, while Chinese, English, French and Spanish are also used. The principal religions are Christianity (professed by about 48% of the population), Hinduism (24%) and Islam (16%). The national flag (proportions 2 by 3) has five horizontal stripes: a broad central band of red (with a five-pointed yellow star in the centre), edged with white, between bands of green. The capital is Paramaribo.

Recent History

Settlers from England landed in Suriname in the 1630s, and the territory was alternately a British and a Dutch colony until it was eventually awarded to the Netherlands by the Treaty of Vienna in 1815. The colony's economy depended on large sugar plantations, for which labour was provided by slaves of African origin. Following the abolition of slavery in 1863, immigration of labourers from India and the then Dutch East Indies was encouraged, and many of them settled permanently in Suriname. This history explains the country's current ethnic diversity: there are small communities of the original Amerindian population (mainly in the interior) and of ethnic Chinese and Europeans; a Creole population, largely of African descent, constitutes about one-third of the population, as do the Asian-descended 'East' Indians (known locally as Hindustanis); the Indonesian-descended 'Javanese' form about 15% of the population, and another Creole group, the 'boschnegers' or Bush Negroes, forms a further 10% (the Bush Negroes are the Dutch-speaking descendants of escaped slaves, long-established in the rainforest as a tribalized society of four clans). Under a Charter signed in December 1954, Suriname (also known as Dutch Guiana) became an equal partner in the Kingdom of the Netherlands, with the Netherlands Antilles and the Netherlands itself, and gained full autonomy in domestic affairs.

The Hindustani-dominated Government, in power since 1969 and led by Dr Jules Sedney, resigned in February 1973. General elections in November were won by an alliance of parties, the Nationale Partij Kambinatie (NPK), which favoured complete independence from the Netherlands, and in December Henck Arron, leader of the Nationale Partij Suriname (NPS—a predominantly Creole party), became Prime Minister. Suriname became independent on 25 November 1975. Dr Johan Ferrier, hitherto the Governor of Suriname, became the new republic's first President. Some 40,000 Surinamese emigrated to the Netherlands after independence, leaving Suriname with a severely underskilled work-force. Border disputes with French Guiana and Guyana also ensued. The general election of October 1977 resulted in a clear majority for the NPK, and Henck Arron continued as Prime Minister.

The Arron administration was overthrown in February 1980 by a group of soldiers, who formed a military council, the Nationale Militaire Raad (NMR). President Ferrier refused to agree to the retention of supreme power by the NMR, and in March he appointed a civilian administration led by Dr Henk Chin-A-Sen, a former leader of the Partij Nationalistische Republiek. In August the Army Chief of Staff, NMR member Sgt-Maj. (later Lt-Col) Désiré (Desi) Bouterse (subsequently Commander-in-Chief of the armed forces), led a coup. Ferrier was replaced by Chin-A-Sen; the legislature was dissolved, and a state of emergency declared. A Hindustani-inspired counter-coup, led by Sgt-Maj. Wilfred Hawker, failed in March 1981. In September the President announced details of a draft Constitution, which sought to limit the army to a supervisory role in government. The army responded with the formation of the Revolutionary People's Front, a comprehensive political alliance headed by Bouterse and two other members of the NMR, Maj. Roy Horb and Lt (later Commdr) Iwan Graanoogst, together with three leaders of workers' and students' organizations. In February 1982 the NMR, led by Bouterse, seized power from Chin-A-Sen and his civilian Government. The Vice-President of the Supreme Court, L. Fred Ramdat Misier, was appointed interim President. Hawker was executed after attempting a further coup in March. (Chin-A-Sen left for the Netherlands, where, in January 1983, he formed the Movement for the Liberation of Suriname, which aimed to remove Bouterse from power by peaceful means.)

A state of siege was declared, and martial law was imposed, as a result of the attempted coup of March 1982. In order to prevent the Netherlands from suspending its aid, a 12-member Cabinet of Ministers with a civilian majority was appointed, and a moderate economist, Henry Neyhorst, became Prime Minister, although Bouterse remained effectively in control. Failure to effect promised social and economic changes lost Bouterse the support of left-wing groups and trade unions, which supported the business community in demanding a return to constitutional rule. In October the arrest of Cyriel Daal, the leader of Suriname's principal trade union (De Moederbond), prompted strikes and demonstrations. In order to avert a general strike, Bouterse agreed to arrange for the election of a constituent assembly to draft a new constitution by March 1983 (to be followed by the establishment of an elected government), but he later reneged on this commitment. In December 1982 members of the armed forces burned down several buildings used by the opposition. During the ensuing disturbances, 15 prominent citizens, including Daal, were killed, in what became known as the 'December Murders'. The Government resigned, the Netherlands and the USA halted all aid, and the country was placed under rule by decree; an interim, military-dominated Government was appointed. An attempted coup in January 1983, the sixth since February 1980, resulted in the dismissal of two-thirds of the officers of the armed forces and the death of Maj. Horb. In February 1983 Dr Errol Alibux, a former Minister of Social Affairs, was appointed Prime Minister. He formed a new Cabinet of Ministers, composed of members of two left-wing parties, the Progressieve Arbeiders en Landbouwers Unie (PALU) and the Revolutionaire Volkspartij. The new Government immediately ended the restrictions imposed in December 1982.

In January 1984, after a series of widely observed strikes in support of demands for the restoration of civilian rule and the organization of free elections, Bouterse dismissed the Cabinet of Ministers. Agreement was reached with the strike organizers, following the withdrawal of proposals to increase taxation rates. An interim Government, with Wim Udenhout, a former adviser to Bouterse, as Prime Minister, was created in February to formulate a timetable for the gradual restoration of constitutional rule. Nominees of the trade unions and business sector were also included in the new Government. Bouterse hoped to consolidate his position by securing a political base through Standvaste (the 25 February Movement), which he had founded in November 1983. In December 1984 plans for a nominated National Assembly (comprising representatives of Standvaste, the trade unions and the business community) were announced. The Netherlands Government, however, refused to consider the changes as a significant move towards democratic rule, deeming them insufficient to merit the resumption of aid. None the less, the National Assembly was inaugurated in January 1985. A new Cabinet of Ministers, based on the previous administration, was formed by Udenhout.

The tripartite administration collapsed in April 1985, after the withdrawal from the Cabinet of Ministers of three of the four trade union nominees. A reconstituted Cabinet, formed in June, contained new members with links to traditional political parties. In November the ban on political parties was revoked, and in the same month, former NPS Prime Minister Arron, together with Jaggernath Lachmon of the Hindustani-based Vooruitstrevende Hervormings Partij (VHP) and Willy Soemita of the Kaum-Tani Persuatan Indonesia (KTPI), accepted an invitation to join the NMR, renamed the Topberaad (Supreme Council). By

July 1986 only two military officers remained on the Topberaad. In that month Bouterse appointed a new Cabinet of Ministers, including representatives from industry, business, political parties, trade unions and Standvaste. Pretaap Radhakishun, a business executive and member of the VHP, was appointed Prime Minister. The Cabinet drafted a new Constitution, which was approved by a national referendum in September 1987.

From July 1986 anti-Government guerrillas began a series of attacks on military posts on the eastern border of the country. The guerrillas were led by Ronnie Brunswijk (a former presidential bodyguard). Mainly Bush Negroes, they claimed that government resettlement policies threatened the autonomy of their tribal society, as guaranteed by treaties, signed in 1760, with the former Dutch authorities. It was reported that financial support for the guerrillas (known as the Jungle Commando, or Surinamese Liberation Army—SLA) was being provided by Surinamese exiles in the Netherlands, in particular by members of the Movement for the Liberation of Suriname. By November most of the eastern district of Marowijne was under guerrilla control, and the rebels had also occupied the area near Zanderij (later renamed Johan Adolf Pengel) International Airport, south of Paramaribo. Rebel attacks on the mining town of Moengo forced the closure of the country's principal bauxite mines. The town was recaptured by the armed forces in December, but the mines remained closed. At the beginning of December a state of emergency was declared in eastern and southern Suriname, and a curfew was imposed. Reports that some 200 civilians had been massacred by government troops in the search for guerrillas led to protests by the Netherlands and US Governments.

In February 1987 five members of the Cabinet of Ministers, including Radhakishun, resigned. Jules Wijdenbosch, hitherto the Minister of Internal Affairs and a member of Standvaste, was appointed Prime Minister. The entire Cabinet resigned at the end of March 1987, and a new Cabinet, led by Wijdenbosch, was appointed by Bouterse in April.

In 1987, in preparation for the general election that was to be held in November, several political parties resumed their activities. Standvaste was reconstituted, under Wijdenbosch, as the Nationale Democratische Partij (NDP—National Democratic Party). Three major opposition parties, the NPS, the VHP and the KTPI (whose name was changed to the Kerukanan Tulodo Pranatan Ingil in October 1987), announced an electoral alliance, the Front voor Demokratie en Ontwikkeling (FDO—Front for Democracy and Development). Brunswijk's SLA observed a cease-fire for the duration of the voting.

The FDO won a decisive victory in elections to the 51-seat National Assembly held in November 1987. In January 1988 the National Assembly unanimously elected Ramsewak Shankar (a former Minister of Agriculture) as President of the Republic, and Henck Arron was elected Vice-President and thus (in accordance with the new Constitution) Prime Minister. In December 1987 Bouterse was appointed leader of a five-member Military Council, established under the new Constitution to 'guarantee a peaceful transition' to democracy. In July 1988 the Netherlands Government agreed to resume aid to Suriname, but under more restrictive conditions than hitherto. Aid was to be provided only on a project-by-project basis until the Suriname Government implemented the IMF's structural-adjustment programme, considered necessary to correct the economic crisis. However, relations remained tense, largely owing to the Dutch administration's mistrust of the intentions of the Surinamese army.

In July 1989 representatives of the Government and the SLA, meeting in French Guiana, signed an agreement at Kourou, which was ratified by the National Assembly in August. The main provisions of the Kourou Accord were: a general amnesty for those involved in the recent conflicts; the ending of the state of emergency; the incorporation of many members of the SLA into a special police unit for the interior of the country; and significant investment in the interior. The armed forces declared their opposition to the Accord, but took no direct action against continuing negotiations. However, at the end of August there was a further outbreak of guerrilla activity, in the west of the country, by an Amerindian group critical of some of the provisions of the Accord. The group, known as the Tucayana Amazonica, principally opposed the involvement of the SLA in the proposed police force for the interior; it also requested the restoration of the Bureau for Amerindian Affairs. Several of the group's demands were similar to those of the army command, and there were allegations that Tucayana were being armed and encouraged by the military, exploiting the traditional antipathy between the Amerindians and many of the Bush Negroes. In October, however, the Tucayana spokesmen were augmented by elected representatives of the Amerindian communities (the Commission of Eight) and the two groups met representatives of the National Assembly, who stated that the Government was prepared to supplement, but not rescind, the Kourou Accord.

Also in October 1989 Tucayana received the support of another new insurgent group, the Mandela Bush Negro Liberation Movement (BBM), which declared itself to be dissatisfied with the Kourou Accord. The BBM was formed by members of the most westerly (and, hitherto, least involved in the civil war) of the Bush Negro clans, the Matauriërs. In the same month, however, Brunswijk's SLA secured the support of another new insurgent group, the Union for Liberation and Democracy (UBD), which occupied the mining town of Moengo. Apparently composed of radical former members of the SLA, the UBD declared its support for the Accord.

On 22 December 1990 Bouterse resigned as Commander-in-Chief of the armed forces, after President Shankar failed to issue an official protest at the Netherlands' treatment of Bouterse, who was denied access to the country while in transit at Amsterdam's airport. Suspicions that Bouterse's resignation might portend a military coup were realized two days later, when the acting Commander-in-Chief of the armed forces, Graanoogst, seized power from the Government. The coup was immediately condemned by the Dutch Government, which suspended development aid to Suriname. Johan Kraag (honorary chairman of the NPS and a former Minister of Labour) was appointed provisional President on 29 December, and promptly invited Bouterse to resume command of the armed forces, thus substantiating speculation that Kraag was merely acting on behalf of Bouterse. A transitional Government (led by Jules Wijdenbosch) was sworn in on 7 January 1991, and it was announced that a general election would take place within 100 days, later extended to 150 days. In March Brunswijk and Bouterse (who had continued negotiations intermittently since 1989) signed a peace accord in the rebel stronghold of Drietabbetje. In April four rebel groups, the SLA, Tucayana, the BBM and Angula (or 'Defiance', led by Carlos Maassi), signed a further agreement with the Government, promising to respect the law and not to obstruct the conduct of free elections.

The elections, which were monitored by a delegation from the Organization of American States (OAS, see p. 373), were held in May 1991. The Nieuw Front (NF), an electoral alliance comprising the members of the former FDO and the Surinaamse Partij van de Arbeid, secured 30 seats in the National Assembly, while the NDP won 12. The remaining nine seats were won by a new coalition, Democratisch Alternatief 1991 (DA '91), mainly comprising former members of the FDO critical of the Government's failure to curb the political influence of the military. Despite the fact that it had not secured the two-thirds' majority in the Assembly necessary to elect automatically its presidential candidate, Runaldo R. Venetiaan, the NF refused to consider the possibility of any agreement involving the formation of a coalition government or the cession of ministerial posts or policy commitments to either the NDP or DA '91. When a series of meetings of the National Assembly in July failed to result in any one presidential candidate securing a majority, the Chairman of the Assembly, Jaggernath Lachman, in accordance with provisions incorporated in the Constitution, convened the Vereinigde Volksvergadering (United People's Assembly), a body comprising the members of the National Assembly and representatives of the municipal and district councils, in order to elect a President. On 7 September Venetiaan was elected with an overwhelming 79% of the votes. One of Venetiaan's first acts as President was to announce, in October, the reduction of the armed forces by two-thirds and a reduction in the defence budget of 50%. These measures were introduced as part of a government programme of 'socialization' of the armed forces. In addition, amendments to the Constitution, approved in March 1992, included measures to curb the political influence of the military, removing all its constitutional duties except those of national defence and the combating of organized subversion, and banning serving members of the security forces from holding representative public office. In April the Military Council, established under the 1987 Constitution, was abolished.

In August 1992 a peace agreement was signed by the Government and the SLA and the Tucayana; the BBM also committed itself to the agreement. Under the terms of the agreement, the amnesty law envisaged under the Kourou Accord of 1989, covering all civil conflicts since 1985 and amended to include insurgent groups formed since the ratification of the Kourou Accord, was to be implemented. All weapons were to be surrendered to the Government, under OAS supervision. Following disarmament, members of all the groups would be eligible for recruitment into a special police force for the interior of the country. In addition, the Government gave assurances that the interior would receive priority in its programmes for economic development and social welfare. However, in March 2005 former guerrillas claimed that the Government had not fulfilled its pledge to provide them with jobs and medical care.

In November 1992 Bouterse resigned as Commander-in-Chief of the armed forces, prompting public concern that the move might once again signal a coup. Venetiaan's appointment of Col (retd) Arthy Gorré as Bouterse's successor resulted in a confrontation between the Government and senior military officers in April 1993. (Gorré had supported the 1980 coup staged by Bouterse, but had resigned from the armed forces in 1987, following a disagreement with the latter.) Graanoogst, who had occupied the position of Commander-in-Chief on an interim basis since Bouterse's resignation, refused to concede the post to Gorré. He was supported by his fellow members of the military high command and by Bouterse, who, despite his resignation, remained effectively in control of the armed forces. Venetiaan subsequently deferred Gorré's appointment until May, when it was endorsed by a majority in the National Assembly, despite veiled threats of a military coup and an attack on the national television station, which had allegedly been instigated by Bouterse. All four members of the military high command subsequently acceded to a request by the National Assembly for their resignations. Three of them, including Graanoogst, later accepted posts as advisers to the Government, thus assuaging fears of an escalation of the conflict. Indications that the Netherlands might intervene to assist the Government were also considered influential in averting further military defiance of civilian rule.

At a general election conducted in May 1996 no single party secured a legislative majority, much less the two-thirds' majority necessary to elect its presidential candidate. The NF secured 24 seats, the NDP 16, DA '91 and Pendawa Lima four each and Alliantie the remaining three seats. Venetiaan, having rejected an offer from Bouterse to form a coalition government, began negotiations with the three other parties with representation in the legislature. However, the negotiations failed to produce agreement on a coalition. Neither Venetiaan nor the candidate of the NDP, former Prime Minister Jules Wijdenbosch, were able to command the two-thirds' majority in the National Assembly necessary to secure the presidency, and responsibility for electing the president consequently passed to the Vereinigde Volksvergadering. Wijdenbosch obtained the simply majority required to win and was inaugurated as President on 14 September. The KTPI and a dissident faction of the VHP, the Beweging voor Vernieuwing en Democratie (BVD), subsequently left the NF alliance, joining an NDP-led coalition. However, the support of the KTPI and the BVD was conditional upon Bouterse's exclusion from the new Government. The parties also stipulated that the portfolios of foreign affairs, finance, defence and internal affairs should not be allocated to the NDP. The new coalition Government, appointed in September, comprised members of the NDP, KTPI, BVD and the Hernieuwde Progressieve Partij (HPP).

In August 1997 the Government recalled its ambassador to the Netherlands for consultations, following the decision by the Dutch Government to seek an international arrest warrant for Bouterse on charges of illegal drugs-trafficking. Bouterse was reportedly in hiding following the issue of the warrant. Talks aimed at improving relations between the Governments of Suriname and the Netherlands were conducted, at ministerial level, in New York, USA, in April 1998. However, the fact that Bouterse was continuing to serve on the Council of State, as part of the Suriname Government, remained a serious source of dissatisfaction for the Netherlands' delegation, which resisted pressure from Suriname's police force to withdraw the warrant for Bouterse's arrest. In March 1999 the Dutch authorities began legal proceedings against Bouterse *in absentia*, on charges of corruption and drugs-trafficking. Similar *in absentia* court proceedings were initiated in the Netherlands against the guerrilla leader Ronnie Brunswijk (who was found guilty on charges of drugs-trafficking in April, and sentenced to eight years' imprisonment) and the President of the Central Bank of Suriname, Henk Goedschalk, who was accused of deliberate financial mismanagement. Despite the Suriname Government's refusal to accede to the demands of the Netherlands Government for the apprehension and extradition of Bouterse, in April President Wijdenbosch dismissed Bouterse from the Council of State, claiming that he represented a divisive force in Surinamese politics. In July Bouterse was convicted and sentenced, *in absentia*, to 16 years in prison (later reduced to 11 years) and fined US $2.3m. The Attorney-General of the Netherlands filed further charges (this time for torture resulting in death) against Bouterse in January 2000. The new charges concerned the 1982 December Murders and arose because of a complaint filed by relatives of the victims.

Dissatisfaction with the Government's management of the economy increased in 1998 and 1999. In June 1998 widespread industrial action brought chaos to the country for several days. There was further labour unrest in the agriculture and mining sectors later in the year. Following another national strike, which brought the country to a virtual standstill, the entire Cabinet resigned in May 1999. In June the National Assembly passed a vote of no confidence in the President. However, the result fell short of the two-thirds' majority needed to force him from office and Wijdenbosch refused to tender his own resignation. Instead he called for early elections to be held by 25 May 2000 and asked the cabinet members to remain in office. However, in December the Government resubmitted its resignation after several of its members were implicated in financial and sexual scandals. President Wijdenbosch accepted several ministers' resignations, distributing their portfolios among the remaining ministers. Prior to the election, in an apparent attempt to distance himself from Bouterse, Wijdenbosch left the NDP and formed a new electoral coalition, Democratisch Nationaal Platform 2000 (DNP 2000).

Voting proceeded on 25 May 2000, when Venetiaan's NF (an electoral alliance comprising the NPS, the Pertajah Luhur, the Surinaamse Partij van de Arbeid, and the VHP) secured 33 of the 51 seats; the Millenium Combinatie (an alliance including the NDP) took 10, and DNP 2000 three. Having narrowly failed to secure the two-thirds' majority to appoint a new President directly, the NF entered into coalition negotiations with the smaller parties. On 4 August Venetiaan was elected to the presidency for the second time, winning 37 of the 51 votes cast in the National Assembly. On assuming office on 12 August, the new President pledged to fight corruption, accelerate economic development and reduce debt. In October the Dutch Government agreed to resume aid to Suriname, which had been suspended since 1998.

On 1 November 2000 the Suriname Court of Justice ruled that Bouterse must stand trial in Suriname in connection with the December Murders. In May 2001 a key witness in the case against Bouterse, the former activist and founder of the Labour Party, Fred Derby, died. In September the Dutch High Court ruled that Bouterse could not be prosecuted in the Netherlands under the UN's Convention on Torture, as the legislation had not been ratified in that country until 1989, seven years after the atrocities took place. However, in the following month it upheld Bouterse's 1999 conviction for drugs-trafficking and demanded he be extradited to serve his 11-year prison sentence—a measure that could not be enacted, as the Surinamese Constitution prohibited extradition of its citizens.

The arrival of a detachment of Dutch marines in June 2002 prompted speculation that the Dutch Government would attempt to arrest Bouterse; the Netherlands claimed that the troops were merely engaged in a joint military exercise. However, in the same month, the Dutch Government dispatched forensic specialists to assist Surinamese police officers investigating the December Murders. In December a judge presiding over the case ordered the exhumation of the remains of the 15 murder victims. As a result of a four-year investigation, a military court indicted Bouterse and 25 other suspects for the 1982 December Murders in December 2004. In mid-March 2007 Bouterse publicly apologized to the families of the 15 victims and advocated an amnesty for the suspects. At a preliminary hearing of the military tribunal on 30 November, the judge rejected an appeal by Bouterse's lawyer that, as a former head of state, his client was entitled to stand trial in a civilian court. All other formal objections had been rejected by April 2008, when the hearings were adjourned until further notice, but in February 2009 proceedings began against Bouterse and 23 other suspects formally accused of the December Murders. In August 2005 the OAS's Inter-American Court of Human Rights instructed the Government to investigate a massacre that occurred in the Maroon village of Moiwana in 1986, during Bouterse's presidency, and to pay US $13,000 compensation to the 130 survivors. President Venetiaan formally apologized for the massacre at a ceremony in Moengo on 15 July 2006.

The illegal trafficking of drugs continued to be a problem in Suriname. The UN's Drug Control Programme estimated that some 22 metric tons of cocaine were transported annually to Europe via Suriname. In March 2002 three Surinamese, three Brazilians and one Colombian were sentenced to up to 14 years' imprisonment for attempting to bring 1,198 kg of cocaine into the country. The men had been arrested in March 2001 in what had been the largest ever seizure of illegal drugs by the Surinamese police. In October 2002 the Netherlands announced the provision of training and equipment to assist the Surinamese security forces' campaign against drugs-trafficking and funds for the construction of a new police headquarters in Paramaribo. Following negotiations held in January 2004 the two Governments agreed to co-operate on intelligence-gathering and sea patrols; it was also agreed that security would be increased on both passenger and cargo flights from Suriname. By 2008 the US Department of State's International Narcotics Control Strategy Report asserted that efforts to combat drugs-trafficking had yielded results during the previous year. The publication noted that in 2007 206 kg of cocaine were seized and 667 people were arrested for drugs-related offences. However, it identified a lack of resources, limited law enforcement capabilities and corruption in the judicial system as inhibitors in the Government's ongoing progress in addressing the problem.

Legislative elections were scheduled to be held on 25 May 2005. In March the NDP formally nominated Bouterse as its candidate in the indirect presidential election that was to follow the legislative ballot, in June. The USA reacted to the NDP's nomination by threatening to sever diplomatic links with Suriname in the event of Bouterse being re-elected President. The NDP accused the USA of political interference and lodged a formal complaint with the Caribbean Community and Common Market (CARICOM, see p. 206) and the OAS. The other main contenders for the presidency were the incumbent Venetiaan, who was seeking a third term in office, and former President Jules Wijdenbosch, representing the Volksalliantie Voor Vooruitgang (VVV—People's Alliance for Progress), an alliance comprising the DNP 2000, the BVD and the Democratisch Alternatief.

The ruling NF's popularity waned in the months preceding the election. Mounting political pressure regarding allegations of corruption led, in May 2005, to the resignation of Minister of Public Works Dewanand Balesar, pending an investigation into his alleged participation in a scheme that awarded contracts to fictitious contractors. (In September the National Assembly voted to remove Balesar's immunity from prosecution and in late March 2007 Balesar was brought to trial charged with defrauding the state.) Nevertheless, at the election the NF retained its position as the largest party in the National Assembly, attracting 39.4% of the votes cast and securing 23 of the 51 seats. The NDP also performed well, obtaining 22.2% of total votes and 15 seats, while the VVV secured just five seats (13.8%). Bouterse and former guerrilla leader Ronnie Brunswijk were both elected to the legislature.

Following the election the NF entered into negotiations with smaller parties in order to garner the two-thirds' parliamentary majority needed to re-elect Venetiaan to the presidency. As a result, on 13 July 2005 Venetiaan was nominated by a coalition of the NF, the DA '91 and the A-Combinatie (a coalition that included the Algemene Bevrijdings- en Ontwikkeling Partij—General Liberation and Development Party—led by Brunswijk). In an unexpected move, two days later the NDP presidential candidate Bouterse withdrew from the contest, nominating his former running mate Rabin Parmessar in his stead. The NDP and the VVV formed a coalition, nominating Wilfried Roseval, formerly Wijdenbosch's running mate, for the vice-presidency. However, neither Venetiaan nor Parmessar secured the requisite two-thirds' majority during the two rounds of voting held on 19 and 26 July. Responsibility for electing the new head of state subsequently passed to the 891-member Vereinigde Volksvergadering. With only a simple majority required, on 3 August Venetiaan secured the presidency with 560 votes, compared with 315 for Parmessar. At his inauguration on 12 August President Venetiaan pledged to combat criminal activity and to continue to pursue established financial policies and budgetary discipline to secure economic stability.

In an attempt to reduce the cost of imported petroleum, in July 2005 the Government signed the PetroCaribe energy accord with Venezuela, thereby gaining access to favourable energy concessions and the option of preferential terms should the price of petroleum exceed US $40 per barrel. However, the steep increases in the retail cost of petroleum products, and consequently of transportation, led to civil unrest in the latter half of 2005 and early 2006. Public transport was disrupted across the country in September 2005 as a result of industrial action by bus drivers, and in January 2006 teachers, angry at the Government's failure to increase transport subsidies, staged demonstrations outside government buildings. Power shortages in the west of the country in February prompted further protests.

There were a number of cabinet changes in 2006 and early 2007. In January 2006 the Minister of Trade and Industry, Siegfried Gilds, resigned following accusations of money-laundering and membership of a criminal organization. Meanwhile, in mid-March the Surinamese ambassador to the Netherlands, Edgar Amanh, tendered his resignation following an incident at Schiphol Airport, Amsterdam, during which the Surinamese Minister of Transport, Communications and Tourism, Alice H. Amafo, was requested to undergo an unexpected security inspection. Amanh was reportedly held responsible for failing to inform the Government about the new Dutch security measures. Amafo tendered her own resignation in March 2007 following allegations of financial misconduct related to an official expenses claim for her birthday celebrations (totalling US $13,000). Her ministerial responsibilities were subsequently added to the portfolio of Minister of the Interior Maurits S. H. Hassankhan.

A number of international agreements were reached in 2007. In April the Surinamese Government acceded to the UN Development Assistance Framework agreement, under which US $40m. would be made available for social development initiatives in the country in 2008–11. Suriname also benefited from the assistance of the European Union (see p. 255), which, in July 2007, approved various contracts for the upgrade and development of the country's tourism and transport sectors, totalling allocations of €1.5m. and €3.2m., respectively.

Workers from four different sectors staged strikes in late 2007 and early 2008, causing disruption and drawing attention to their poor working conditions. In November 2007 over 1,000 teachers left their positions, seeking higher wages and a fair system of benefits. The strike continued until early 2008, when the Government agreed to increase wages by 10%, with further talks due to take place between the Government and union representatives later in the year to resolve outstanding issues. Airports had to operate a revised schedule in late 2007 when air traffic controllers initiated strike action to demand new equipment and improved safety standards, as well as increased allowances. In March 2008 the Jarikaba banana plant was forced to close for a week when workers protested at what they considered to be an unacceptable pay increase of 5%. In the following month bauxite workers went on strike in support of demands for a more substantial salary increase.

In January 2009 Bouterse was formally expelled from Parliament after persistent non-attendance, dating back to 2007, rendered his membership invalid.

Suriname has a territorial dispute with Guyana over an estimated 15,000 sq km (6,000 sq miles) of land in the Corentije region, and another with French Guiana over land to the east of the Litani river. In April 1990, with the mediation of the UN High Commissioner for Refugees, France and Suriname agreed terms providing for the repatriation of an estimated 10,000 Surinamese refugees from French Guiana. In October French Guiana was reported to have begun forcible repatriation of Surinamese refugees. In April 1992, under a plan agreed between France, Suriname and the UN, some 6,000 Surinamese refugees were offered voluntary repatriation. In July the Suriname Government delivered an official protest to the French authorities concerning the alleged compulsory repatriation of refugees. By that time some 2,500 Surinamese refugees had returned to Suriname. Relations with France deteriorated in early 2007 when the French Government designated a 2m.-ha region along the disputed border with French Guiana as a national park. Under its new protected status, the traditional hunting and fishing practices of the indigenous Surinamese communities were strictly prohibited in the park. The Organization of Indigenous People in Suriname (OIS) protested against the restrictions to the French Government in July, and in February 2008 it was reported that Suriname and France were due to resume talks, with France seeking to expand the maritime boundary by lodging a claim with the UN Convention on the Law of the Sea.

SURINAME

Introductory Survey

In 1995 Guyana and Suriname reached agreement on the establishment of a joint commission in order to seek a resolution of the countries' territorial dispute. In June 1998 Guyana granted the Canadian-based company CGX Energy Inc a concession to explore for petroleum and gas along the continental margin off Guyana, part of which lay within the disputed maritime area. In May 2000 Suriname formally claimed that Guyana had violated its territorial integrity, and invited Guyana to begin negotiations regarding the maritime boundary. In June the Surinamese Navy forced CGX to remove the drilling platform. In June 2001 the Ministers of Foreign Affairs of the two countries issued a declaration of their Governments' commitment to peace and co-operation and in the following year revived the Guyana–Suriname Bilateral Co-operation Council. The two Governments agreed to investigate the possibility of a joint exploration for petroleum in the disputed territory and to improve co-operation in trade, investments and joint ventures. However, relations again became strained in 2003 when the Surinamese Government decreed that maps of the country circulated by diplomatic missions in Paramaribo must include the disputed territory. Guyana lodged a formal protest and sent a naval detachment to patrol the Corentijn River. Both countries subsequently strengthened their military presence in the area and in February 2004 two Surinamese gunboats expelled a Canadian company, exploring for oil with Guyana's permission, from the area. At the end of that month Guyana referred the maritime boundary dispute to arbitration at the UN's International Tribunal for the Law of the Sea, in Hamburg, Germany. In September 2007 the Tribunal ruled in favour of Guyana, granting sovereignty over 33,152 sq km (12,800 sq miles) of coastal waters; Suriname was awarded 17,891 sq km (6,900 sq miles). Guyana's subsequent claims for compensation of US $34m. for damage arising from the expulsion of the oil rig were dismissed by the UN Permanent Court of Arbitration, which ruled that Suriname had not used armed force.

In March 2002 the Surinamese and Dutch Ministers of Foreign Affairs approved the establishment of a Returned Emigration Committee to oversee the voluntary repatriation of Surinamese with Dutch nationality without the loss of social benefits. In October 2004 customs officials in Suriname and the Netherlands reached an agreement to share information in an attempt to reduce tax evasion on imports from the Netherlands.

Government

Under the provisions of the 1987 Constitution, legislative power is held by the National Assembly, with 51 members, elected by universal adult suffrage for a five-year term. The Assembly elects the President and the Vice-President of the Republic. Executive power is vested in the President, who appoints the Cabinet of Ministers, led by the Vice-President, who is also the Prime Minister. The Cabinet is responsible to the National Assembly. A Council of State, comprising civilians and members of the armed forces, advises the President and the Cabinet of Ministers on policy, and has power of veto over legislation approved by the Assembly. Suriname comprises 10 administrative districts.

Defence

Suriname's armed forces numbered 1,840 men and women, as assessed at November 2008. There is an army of 1,400, a navy of 240, and an air force of about 200. Defence expenditure in 2007 was budgeted at US $22m.

Economic Affairs

In 2007, according to estimates by the World Bank, Suriname's gross national income (GNI), measured at average 2005–07 prices, was US $2,166m., equivalent to $4,730 per head (or $7,640 per head on an international purchasing-power parity basis). During 2000–07, it was estimated, the population increased at an average annual rate of 0.7%, while gross domestic product (GDP) per head increased, in real terms, by an average of 5.0% per year over the same period. According to World Bank figures, overall GDP increased, in real terms, at an average annual rate of 5.7% in 2000–07; growth was estimated at 5.4% in 2007.

Agriculture (including hunting, forestry and fishing) contributed 5.2% of GDP (excluding the informal sector) in 2006, and the sector engaged 8.0% of the employed population at the census conducted in 2004. The principal crop is rice, which supplies domestic demand and provided 1.3% of export earnings in 2007. Bananas are cultivated for export, together with plantains, sugar cane and citrus fruits, while Suriname also produces coconuts, maize and vegetables. In April 2002 the Government closed the state-run banana company Surland after it accumulated debt of some US $8m. However, the company was subsequently restructured with the aid of a US $6m. loan from the Inter-American Development Bank (IDB, see p. 318), and production and exports resumed in March 2004. In January 2005 some US $23m. was granted by the Dutch Government to assist the diversification of the agricultural sector and to improve rural roads and irrigation systems. Livestock is being developed, as are the extensive timber reserves (more than 80% of Suriname's total land area is covered by forest). Commercial fishing is important (exports of shrimp and fish providing an estimated 6.1% of total export revenue in 2005). In January 2007 it was announced that Japan was to fund construction of a US $8m. fisheries centre. According to the World Bank, agricultural GDP increased by 2.0% per year in 2000–06; the sector grew by 0.9% in 2006.

Industry (including mining, manufacturing, public utilities and construction) contributed 38.1% of GDP (excluding the informal sector) in 2006, and the sector engaged some 22.9% of the employed labour force at the 2004 census. The principal activity is the bauxite industry, which dominates both the mining and manufacturing sectors. In the early 2000s there were plans to build an industrial development zone near to Johan Adolf Pengel International Airport at Zanderij. According to the World Bank, industrial GDP increased by an annual average of 10.0% in 2000–06; the sector increased by 8.9% in 2006.

Mining and quarrying contributed 9.3% of GDP (excluding the informal sector) in 2006, and the sector engaged 5.9% of the employed labour force at the 2004 census. The principal product is bauxite (used in the manufacture of aluminium), of which Suriname is one of the world's leading producers (producing an estimated 4.8m. metric tons in 2005). In 2003 the US-based aluminium company Alcoa reached an accord with the Government to allow Alcoa to increase the capacity of its existing bauxite operations in the country. Alcoa was also granted permission for a joint venture with the Australian company BHP for an aluminium melting plant and hydroelectric dam in the Backhuis Mountains. In November 2004 Alcoa and BHP Billiton announced joint plans to invest in two new bauxite mines, which began operations in 2006. The large-scale exploitation of gold in central-eastern Suriname was postponed in the late 1990s, owing to falling gold prices; gold reserves at the Gross Rosebel mine, situated some 80 km south of Paramaribo, were estimated at 2.4m. oz. In late 2002 the Canadian gold-mining corporation Cambior began construction of new facilities at Gross Rosebel. Extraction began in January 2004, and in that year gold production reportedly reached a record 8,513 kg, rising to 10,619 kg in 2005. In 2007 gold contributed some 35.9% of total export revenue. Reserves of petroleum in Suriname are exploited at a rate of around 12,500 barrels per day. Some 40% of production is for export, but much is used domestically in the bauxite industry. Unproven reserves are also thought to exist in the Saramacca district. Suriname also has extensive deposits of iron ore and reserves of manganese, copper, nickel, platinum and kaolin. According to government estimates, the GDP of the mining sector increased by an average of 10.6% per year in 2000–04; sectoral GDP increased by a dramatic 31.3% in 2004.

Manufacturing contributed 20.2% of GDP (excluding the informal sector) in 2006, and the sector engaged an estimated 7.0% of the employed labour force in the same year, according to the 2004 census. Bauxite refining and smelting is the principal industry (alumina accounted for an estimated 47.5% of export revenue in 2007), but there are also important food-processing industries and manufacturers of cigarettes, beverages and chemical products. According to the World Bank, manufacturing GDP increased by an estimated average of 11.1% per year in 2000–06; the sector expanded by 1.6% in 2006.

Energy is derived principally from hydroelectricity and hydrocarbon fuels, which are mainly imported; in 2007 mineral fuels and lubricants accounted for 14.1% of total merchandise imports. The country has considerable potential for the further development of hydroelectric power. In April 2004 the Government announced plans to install a major power line from the Afobakka hydroelectric dam to Paramaribo. The three-year project was undertaken by two companies based in India and financed by a loan from the Indian Government. In 2005 Suriname produced 1,571m. kWh of electricity, derived mostly from hydroelectric power.

The services sector contributed 56.6% of GDP (excluding the informal sector) in 2006, and the sector engaged an estimated

SURINAME

64.3% of the employed labour force at the 2004 census. According to the World Bank, the GDP of the services sector increased by an average of 6.1% per year in 2000–06; sectoral growth was 4.9% in 2006.

In 2007 Suriname recorded a visible trade surplus of US $173.7m., and there was a surplus of $184.9m. on the current account of the balance of payments. The principal source of imports in 2005 was the USA (providing 24.4% of total imports); other significant suppliers in that year were the Netherlands, Trinidad and Tobago and Japan. The principal markets for exports in 2005 were Norway (some 23.9% of the value of total exports), the USA and France. The principal imports in 2007 were machinery and transport equipment, basic manufactures, mineral fuels and lubricants and food and live animals. The principal exports the same year were alumina, gold, shrimp and fish and crude petroleum.

In 2007 there was an estimated budgetary surplus of 195.5m. Surinamese dollars (equivalent to around 3.0% of GDP, excluding the contributions of the informal sector). At the end of 2002 the total external public debt stood at an estimated US $319.8m., of which $161.9m. was long-term public debt. By the end of December 2007 total external public debt had declined to US $161.1m. According to the IMF, the annual rate of inflation averaged 12.1% in 2000–07. According to official figures, consumer prices increased by an average of 14.7% in 2008. According to official sources, the rate of unemployment was 9.5% in 2004. The informal sector contributed around 14.3% of GDP in 2006.

In February 1995 Suriname was granted full membership of the Caribbean Community and Common Market (CARICOM, see p. 206). It was also one of the six founder members of CARICOM's Caribbean Single Market and Economy (CSME), established on 1 January 2006. The CSME was intended to enshrine the free movement of goods, services and labour throughout the CARICOM region. Forecasts in January 2007 indicated that the CSME would be fully operational by 31 December 2008.

On assuming office in September 2000, the Government of Runaldo Venetiaan discovered that most of the country's gold reserves had been converted into US dollars. With the country nearing bankruptcy, in October the new President announced a series of measures intended to stabilize the exchange rate and the domestic inflation rate. The official exchange rate was devalued by 89% and tariffs on utilities were raised. As a result, the annual inflation rate fell to 38.6% in 2001 and to 15.5% in 2002. The stricter fiscal regime implemented by Venetiaan's administration contributed to a stable economic outlook. Economic activity is relatively diversified in range, but the dominant sector is the bauxite industry. In 2005 the IMF highlighted Suriname's dependence on a non-renewable resource and recommended that the Government establish a revenue stabilization fund in preparation for the eventual depletion of bauxite deposits. In October 2008 the Australian-based mining company BHP Billiton announced that deposits in its three mines in Suriname would be depleted by 2010 and that it would cease all mining activities by that date. The IMF estimated economic growth at 5.4% in 2007, in part due to a €1.5m. grant from the European Union (see p. 255), which enabled an increase in capacity in the tourism sector, and strong growth in the mineral sector. The Government achieved a budget surplus of 3.0% of GDP that year. However, the rate of inflation increased threefold between March 2007 and 2008, to 13.8%, as a result of rising fuel and food prices, an increase in the availability of credit and the unofficial linking of the Surinamese dollar to the depreciating US dollar. GDP growth was estimated to have increased by 6.5% in 2008, but was expected to slow in 2009 in response to the global economic crisis.

Education

Primary education is compulsory for children between seven and 12 years of age. Primary education begins at six years of age and lasts for six years. Secondary education comprises a first cycle of four years and a second cycle of three years. All education in government and denominational schools is provided free of charge. In 2006/07 enrolment in primary education included an estimated 94.1% of children in the relevant age-group, while in 2004/05 enrolment in secondary education included an estimated 67.7% of children in the relevant age-group. The traditional educational system, inherited from the Dutch, was amended after the 1980 revolution to place greater emphasis on serving the needs of Suriname's population. This included a literacy campaign and programmes of adult education. Higher education is provided by technical and vocational schools and by the University of Suriname at Paramaribo, which has faculties of law, economics, medicine, social sciences and technology. Of total expenditure by the Central Government in 1996, an estimated Sf 3,480.5m (3.2%) was for education. In March 2003 the Inter-American Development Bank (IDB, see p. 318) approved a US $12.5m. loan to fund the reform of the basic education system into a single 10-year cycle. It was also intended to provide for a modernized curriculum with redesigned text books and a reform of the examination system. It was hoped that the funds would result in a 10% increase in the number of pupils who finished sixth grade and a 20% reduction in drop-out and repetition rates. A further $13m. grant for the sector was approved by the Dutch Government in January 2005.

Public Holidays

2009: 1 January (New Year's Day), March* (Phagwa), 10–13 April (Easter), 1 May (Labour Day), 1 July (National Union Day), 20 September (Id al-Fitr, end of Ramadan), 25 November (Independence Day), 25–26 December (Christmas).

2010: 1 January (New Year's Day), March* (Phagwa), 2–5 April (Easter), 1 May (Labour Day), 1 July (National Union Day), 10 September (Id al-Fitr, end of Ramadan), 25 November (Independence Day), 25–26 December (Christmas).

*Exact date dependent upon sightings of the moon.

Weights and Measures

The metric system is in force.

Statistical Survey

Sources (unless otherwise stated): Algemeen Bureau voor de Statistiek, Kromme Elleboogstraat 10, POB 244, Paramaribo; tel. 473927; fax 425004; e-mail info@statistics-suriname.org; internet www.statistics-suriname.org; Ministry of Trade and Industry, Havenlaan 3, POB 9354, Paramaribo; tel. 402080; fax 402602.

AREA AND POPULATION

Area: 163,820 sq km (63,251 sq miles).

Population: 355,240 (males 175,814, females 179,426) at census of 1 July 1980; 492,829 (males 247,846, females 244,618, not known 365) at census of 2 August 2004. *Mid-2008* (estimate): 515,000. Source: UN, *World Population Prospects: The 2008 Revision*.

Density (at mid-2008): 3.1 per sq km.

Ethnic Groups (1980 census, percentage): Creole 34.70; Hindustani 33.49; Javanese 16.33; Bush Negro 9.55; Amerindian 3.10; Chinese 1.55; European 0.44; Others 0.84.

Administrative Districts (population at census of 2 August 2004): Paramaribo 242,946; Wanica 85,986; Nickerie 36,639; Coronie 2,887; Saramacca 15,980; Commewijne 24,649; Marowijne 16,642; Para 18,749; Brokopondo 14,215; Sipaliwini 34,136; *Total* 492,829.

Principal Towns (census of 2 August 2004): Paramaribo (capital) 205,000; Lelydorp 15,600; Nieuw Nickerie 11,100. Source: Thomas Brinkoff, *City Population* (internet www.citypopulation.de).

Births, Marriages and Deaths (2004): Registered live births 9,062 (birth rate 18.6 per 1,000); Marriages 1,951 (4.0 per 1,000); Registered deaths 3,319 (death rate 6.8 per 1,000). *2007:* Birth rate 19.5 per 1,000; Death rate 6.9 per 1,000. *2008:* Birth rate 19.2 per 1,000. Sources: UN, *Demographic Yearbook*; Pan American Health Organization.

Life Expectancy (years at birth, WHO estimates): 68.0 (males 64.9; females 71.3) in 2006. Source: WHO, *World Health Statistics*.

Economically Active Population ('000 persons aged 15–64 years, census of 2004): Agriculture, hunting, forestry and fishing 12,593; Mining and quarrying 9,308; Manufacturing 10,971; Utilities 1,659; Construction 14,031; Trade 25,012; Hotels, restaurants and bars 4,833; Transport, storage and communication 8,711; Financial inter-

SURINAME

mediation 2,723; Real estate, renting and business activities 6,350; Public administration and defence 27,995; Education 8,355; Health and social work 6,797; Other community, social and personal service activities 9,911; Unknown 7,456; *Total employed* 156,705 (males 101,919, females 54,768, unknown 18); Unemployed 16,425; *Total labour force* 173,130.

HEALTH AND WELFARE
Key Indicators

Total Fertility Rate (children per woman, 2006): 2.5.

Under-5 Mortality Rate (per 1,000 live births, 2006): 39.

HIV/AIDS (% of persons aged 15–49, 2007): 2.4.

Physicians (per 1,000 head, 2000): 0.5.

Hospital Beds (per 1,000 head, 2004): 3.1.

Health Expenditure (2006): US $ per head (PPP): 361.

Health Expenditure (2006): % of GDP: 7.4.

Health Expenditure (2006): public (% of total): 41.9.

Access to Water (% of persons, 2006): 92.

Access to Sanitation (% of persons, 2006): 82.

Human Development Index (2006): ranking: 89.

Human Development Index (2006): value: 0.770.

For sources and definitions, see explanatory note on p. vi.

AGRICULTURE, ETC.

Principal Crops ('000 metric tons, 2007, FAO estimates): Rice, paddy 195; Roots and tubers 5; Sugar cane 120; Coconuts 9; Vegetables 22; Bananas 44; Plantains 12; Oranges 13; Other citrus fruit 3.

Livestock ('000 head, 2007, FAO estimates): Cattle 137; Sheep 8; Goats 7; Pigs 25; Chickens 3,800.

Livestock Products ('000 metric tons, 2007, FAO estimates): Cattle meat 2; Pig meat 2; Chicken meat 6; Cows' milk 9; Hen eggs 3.

Forestry ('000 cu metres, 2007, FAO estimates): *Roundwood Removals:* Sawlogs, veneer logs and logs for sleepers 165; Other industrial wood 3; Fuel wood 46; Total 214. *Sawnwood Production:* Total (incl. railway sleepers) 57.

Fishing ('000 metric tons, 2006): Capture 30.6 (Marine fishes 19.1; Penaeus shrimps 1.0; Atlantic seabob 10.3); Aquaculture 0.2; *Total catch* 30.8.

Source: FAO.

MINING

Selected Products (2005, estimates): Crude petroleum ('000 barrels) 4,380; Bauxite ('000 metric tons) 4,757; Gold (Au content, kg) 10,619. Source: US Geological Survey.

INDUSTRY

Selected Products ('000 metric tons unless otherwise indicated, 2005 unless otherwise indicated): Gold-bearing ores 300 (kg, 2004); Gravel and crushed stone 85 (2002); Distillate fuel oil 41; Residual fuel oils 349; Cement 65 (estimate); Alumina 1,944 (estimate); Beer of barley 21 (2007); Coconut oil 0.94 (2007); Palm oil 0.22 (2007); Cigarettes 483 (million, 1996); Plywood 1 ('000 cubic metres); Electricity 1,571 (million kWh). Sources: mainly UN, *Industrial Commodity Statistics Yearbook* and FAO.

FINANCE

Currency and Exchange Rates: 100 cents = 1 Surinamese dollar. *Sterling, Dollar and Euro Equivalents* (31 December 2008): £1 sterling = 4.002 Surinamese dollars; US $1 = 2.745 Surinamese dollars; €1 = 3.820 Surinamese dollars; 100 Surinamese dollars = £24.99 = US $36.43 = €26.18. *Average Exchange Rate* (Surinamese dollars per US $): 2.744 in 2006; 2.745 in 2007; 2.745 in 2008. *Note:* Between 1971 and 1993 the official market rate was US $1 = 1.785 guilders. A new free market rate was introduced in June 1993, and a unified, market-determined rate took effect in July 1994. A mid-point rate of US $1 = 401.0 guilders was in effect between September 1996 and January 1999. A new currency, the Surinamese dollar, was introduced on 1 January 2004, and was equivalent to 1,000 old guilders. Some data in this survey are still presented in terms of the former currency.

Budget (million Surinamese dollars, 2007, estimates): *Revenue:* Direct taxation 778.8; Indirect taxation 804.0 (Domestic taxes on goods and services 368.8, Taxes on international trade 430.9, Other taxes (incl. bauxite levy) 4.3); Non-tax revenue 319.7; Total 1,902.5 (excl. grants 99.5). *Expenditure:* Wages and salaries 678.4; Subsidies and transfers 217.0; Goods and services 590.1; Interest payments 94.5; Capital 225.4; Total 1,805.4 (excl. net lending 1.1). Source: IMF, *Suriname: Statistical Appendix* (August 2008).

International Reserves (US $ million at 31 December 2008): Gold (national valuation) 40.08; IMF special drawing rights 0.56; Reserve position in IMF 9.43; Foreign exchange 423.28; Total 473.35. Source: IMF, *International Financial Statistics*.

Money Supply ('000 Surinamese dollars at 31 December 2007): Currency outside banks 409,242; Demand deposits at deposit money banks 696,343; Total money (incl. others) 1,145,554. Source: IMF, *International Financial Statistics*.

Cost of Living (Consumer Price Index for Paramaribo area; base: October–December 2000 = 100): 197.4 in 2006; 210.0 in 2007; 240.9 in 2008.

Gross Domestic Product ('000 Surinamese dollars at constant 1990 prices, preliminary figures): 5,430 in 2005; 5,675 in 2006; 5,981 in 2007.

Expenditure on the Gross Domestic Product ('000 Surinamese dollars at current prices, 2004, preliminary figures): Public consumption 1,015,201; Private consumption 2,105,154; Public investment 146,514; Private investment 764,342; Exports of goods and non-factor services 1,059,242; *Less* Imports of goods and non-factor services 1,952,281; GDP in purchasers' values 3,138,172. Source: IMF, *Suriname: Statistical Appendix* (February 2006).

Gross Domestic Product by Economic Activity ('000 Surinamese dollars at current prices, 2006): Agriculture, hunting and forestry 253,586; Fishing 33,464; Mining and quarrying 511,138; Manufacturing 1,107,891; Electricity, gas and water 272,180; Construction 200,675; Wholesale and retail trade 500,891; Hotels and restaurants 93,133; Transport, storage and communications 380,096; Financial intermediation 321,986; Real estate, renting and business activities 357,800; Public administration 340,246; Education 220,196; Health and social work 32,447; Other community, social and personal services 71,915; Informal sector 786,647; Sub-total 5,484,291; *Less* Imputed bank service charge 214,127; *Gross value added in basic prices* 5,270,164; Taxes on products, less subsidies 603,229; GDP at market prices 5,873,393. Source: IMF, *Suriname: Statistical Appendix* (August 2008).

Balance of Payments (US $ million, 2007): Exports of goods f.o.b. 1,359.0; Imports of goods f.o.b. –1,185.3; *Trade balance* 173.7; Exports of services 244.7; Imports of services –317.2; *Balance on goods and services* 101.2; Other income received 43.6; Other income paid –35.4; *Balance on goods, services and income* 109.4; Current transfers received 137.9; Current transfers paid –62.4; *Current balance* 184.9; Capital account (net) 8.1; Direct investment from abroad –246.7; Portfolio investment liabilities –1.3; Other investment assets 83.5; Other investment liabilities –12.6; Net errors and omissions 161.0; *Overall balance* 176.9. Source: IMF, *International Financial Statistics*.

EXTERNAL TRADE

Principal Commodities (US $ million, 2007): *Imports c.i.f.:* Food and live animals 124.2; Mineral fuels, lubricants, etc. 166.5; Chemicals 86.8; Basic manufactures 185.4; Machinery and transport equipment 345.4; Total (incl. others) 1,184.7. *Exports f.o.b.:* Alumina 645.7; Gold 488.8; Shrimp and fish 99.2; Crude oil 107.5; Rice 18.1; Total (incl. others) 1,360.8. Sources: UN, *International Trade Statistics Yearbook* and IMF, *Suriname: Statistical Appendix* (August 2008).

Principal Trading Partners (US $ million, 2005): *Imports c.i.f.:* Belgium 23.6; Brazil 39.3; Canada 10.1; China, People's Repub. 59.5; Germany 23.9; Japan 47.5; Netherlands 160.0; Trinidad and Tobago 116.0; United Kingdom 18.3; USA 267.9; Total (incl. others) 1,099.9. *Exports f.o.b.:* Barbados 6.6; France 74.8; Iceland 26.9; Japan 10.7; Netherlands 24.2; Norway 222.4; Trinidad and Tobago 20.7; USA 155.6; Total (incl. others) 929.1. Source: IMF, *Suriname: Statistical Appendix* (May 2007).

TRANSPORT

Road Traffic (registered motor vehicles, 2000 estimates): Passenger cars 61,365; Buses and coaches 2,393; Lorries and vans 20,827; Motorcycles and mopeds 30,598.

Shipping: *International Sea-borne Freight Traffic* (estimates, '000 metric tons, 2001): Goods loaded 2,306; Goods unloaded 1,212. *Merchant Fleet* (registered at 31 December 2007): Number of vessels 9; Total displacement 4,721 grt. Source: Lloyd's Register-Fairplay, *World Fleet Statistics*.

Civil Aviation (traffic on scheduled services, 2004): Kilometres flown (million) 5; Passengers carried ('000) 289; Passenger-km (mil-

SURINAME

lion) 1,616; Total ton-km (million) 201. Source: UN, *Statistical Yearbook*.

TOURISM

Tourist Arrivals (number of non-resident arrivals at national borders, '000): 137.8 in 2004; 160.0 in 2005.

Tourism Receipts (US $ million, excl. passenger transport): 52 in 2004; 96 in 2005; 109 in 2006.

Source: World Tourism Organization.

COMMUNICATIONS MEDIA

Radio Receivers (1997): 300,000 in use.
Television Receivers (2000): 110,000 in use.
Telephones (2006): 81,500 main lines in use.
Facsimile Machines (1996): 800 in use.
Mobile Cellular Telephones (2006): 320,000 subscribers.
Personal Computers (2001): 20,000 in use.
Internet Users (2007): 44,000.
Broadband Subscribers (2006): 2,700.
Daily Newspapers (2005): 4.
Non-daily Newspapers (2000): 10.

Sources: mainly UNESCO, *Statistical Yearbook*; UN, *Statistical Yearbook*; International Telecommunication Union.

EDUCATION

Pre-primary (2006/07): 813 teachers; 16,292 pupils.

Primary (2006/07 unless otherwise stated, incl. special education): 308 schools (2001/02); 4,913 teachers; 65,020 pupils.

Secondary (2006/07 unless otherwise stated, incl. teacher-training): 141 schools (2001/02); 3,373 teachers; 47,235 pupils.

University (2001/02): 1 institution; 350 teachers; 3,250 students.

Other Higher (2001/02): 3 institutions; 200 teachers; 1,936 students.

Adult Literacy Rate (UNESCO estimates): 90.4% (males 92.7%; females 88.1%) in 2007.

Source: mainly UNESCO Institute for Statistics.

Directory

The Constitution

The 1987 Constitution was approved by the National Assembly on 31 March and by 93% of voters in a national referendum in September.

THE LEGISLATURE

Legislative power is exercised jointly by the National Assembly and the Government. The National Assembly comprises 51 members, elected for a five-year term by universal adult suffrage. The Assembly elects a President and a Vice-President and has the right of amendment in any proposal of law by the Government. The approval of a majority of at least two-thirds of the number of members of the National Assembly is required for the amendment of the Constitution, the election of the President or the Vice-President, the decision to organize a plebiscite and a People's Congress and for the amendment of electoral law. If it is unable to obtain a two-thirds' majority following two rounds of voting, the Assembly may convene a United People's Assembly (Vereinigde Volksvergadering) and supplement its numbers with members of local councils. The approval by a simple majority is sufficient in the United People's Assembly.

THE EXECUTIVE

Executive authority is vested in the President, who is elected for a term of five years as Head of State, Head of Government, Head of the Armed Forces, Chairman of the Council of State, the Cabinet of Ministers and the Security Council.

The Government comprises the President, the Vice-President and the Cabinet of Ministers. The Cabinet of Ministers is appointed by the President from among the members of the National Assembly. The Vice-President is the Prime Minister and leader of the Cabinet, and is responsible to the President.

In the event of war, a state of siege, or exceptional circumstances to be determined by law, a Security Council assumes all government functions.

THE COUNCIL OF STATE

The Council of State comprises the President (its Chairman) and 14 additional members, composed of two representatives of the combined trade unions, one representative of the associations of employers, one representative of the National Army and 10 representatives of the political parties in the National Assembly. Its duties are to advise the President and the legislature and to supervise the correct execution by the Government of the decisions of the National Assembly. The Council may present proposals of law or of general administrative measures to the Government. The Council has the authority to suspend any legislation approved by the National Assembly which, in the opinion of the Council, is in violation of the Constitution. In this event, the President must decide within one month whether or not to ratify the Council's decision.

The Government

HEAD OF STATE

President: RUNALDO RONALD VENETIAAN (assumed office 12 August 2000; re-elected by vote of the United People's Assembly 3 August 2005).

Council of State: Chair. RUNALDO RONALD VENETIAAN (President of the Republic); 14 mems; 10 to represent the political parties in the National Assembly, one for the Armed Forces, two for the trade unions and one for employers.

CABINET OF MINISTERS
(April 2009)

Vice-President: RAMDIEN SARDJOE (VHP).
Minister of Finance: HUMPHREY HILDENBERG (NPS).
Minister of Foreign Affairs: LYGIA L. KRAAG-KETELDIJK (NPS).
Minister of Defence: IVAN C. FERNALD (NPS).
Minister of Home Affairs: MAURITS S. H. HASSANKHAN (VHP).
Minister of Justice and the Police: CHANDRIKAPERSAD SANTOKHI (VHP).
Minister of Planning and Foreign Aid: RICARDO OTTO VAN RAVENSWAAY (DA '91).
Minister of Agriculture, Animal Husbandry and Fisheries: KERMECHEND STANLEY RAGHOEBARSING (VHP).
Minister of Transport, Communications and Tourism: RICHEL APENSA (AC).
Minister of Public Works: GANESHKOEMAR KANDHAI (VHP).
Minister of Social Affairs and Housing: HENDRIK SOERAT SETROWIDJOJO (PL).
Minister of Trade and Industry: CLIFFORD MARICA (SPA).
Minister of Regional Development: MICHEL FELISIE (AC).
Minister of Education and Community Development: EDWIN TOEKIDJAN WOLF (PL).
Minister of Health: CELCIUS WALDO WATERBERG (AC).
Minister of Labour, Technological Development and the Environment: JOYCE AMARELLO-WILLIAMS (SPA).
Minister of Natural Resources: GREGORY ALLAN RUSLAND (NPS).
Minister of Physical Planning and of Land and Forestry Management: MICHAEL JONG TJIEN FA (PL).

MINISTRIES

Ministry of Agriculture, Animal Husbandry and Fisheries: Letitia Vriesdelaan 7, Paramaribo; tel. 477698; fax 470301; e-mail minlvv@sr.net.

Ministry of Defence: Kwattaweg 29, Paramaribo; tel. 474244; fax 420055; e-mail defensie@sr.net.

Ministry of Education and Community Development: Dr Samuel Kafiluddistraat 117–123, Paramaribo; tel. 498383; fax 495083; e-mail minond@sr.net.

SURINAME

Ministry of Finance: Tamarindelaan 3, Paramaribo; tel. 472610; fax 476314; e-mail financien@sr.net; internet www.minfin.sr.

Ministry of Foreign Affairs: Lim A. Postraat 25, POB 25, Paramaribo; tel. 471209; fax 410411; e-mail buza@sr.net.

Ministry of Health: Henck Arronstraat 64, POB 201, Paramaribo; tel. 410441; fax 473923; e-mail info@volksgezondheid.gov.sr; internet www.volksgezondheid.gov.sr.

Ministry of Home Affairs: Wilhelminastraat 3, Paramaribo; tel. 476461; fax 421170; e-mail gensur@sr.net.

Ministry of Justice and the Police: Henck Arronstraat 1, Paramaribo; tel. 475805; fax 412109; e-mail ipoffsur@sr.net.

Ministry of Labour, Technological Development and the Environment: Wagesweegstraat 22, POB 911, Paramaribo; tel. 477045; fax 410465; e-mail arbeid@sr.net.

Ministry of Land and Forestry Management: Paramaribo.

Ministry of Natural Resources: Dr J. C. de Mirandastraat 11–13, Paramaribo; tel. 410160; fax 472911; e-mail minnh@sr.net.

Ministry of Physical Planning: Cornelis Jongbawstraat 10–12, Paramaribo; tel. 470728; fax 473316; e-mail mpjong@datsunsuriname.com.

Ministry of Planning and Foreign Aid: Dr S. Redmondstraat 118, Paramaribo; tel. 471108; fax 421056; e-mail plos@sr.net; internet www.plos.sr.

Ministry of Public Works: Verlengde Jagernath Lachmonstraat 167, Paramaribo; tel. 462500; fax 464901; e-mail minow@sr.net.

Ministry of Regional Development: Van Rooseveltkade 2, Paramaribo; tel. 471269; fax 424333; e-mail regon@sr.net.

Ministry of Social Affairs and Housing: Waterkant 30–32, Paramaribo; tel. 472340; fax 470516; e-mail soza@sr.net.

Ministry of Trade and Industry: Havenlaan 3, POB 9354, Paramaribo; tel. 402886; fax 402602; e-mail dhisur@yahoo.com.

Ministry of Transport, Communications and Tourism: Prins Hendrikstraat 24–26, Paramaribo; tel. 420905; fax 420100; e-mail odc@mintct.sr; internet www.mintct.sr; Dir THELMA DOUGLAS-PINAS.

Legislature

NATIONAL ASSEMBLY

Chairman: PAUL SALAM SOMOHARDJO.

General Election, 25 May 2005

Party	Seats	% of votes cast
Nieuwe Front*	23	39.37
Nationale Democratische Partij	15	22.20
Volksalliantie Voor Vooruitgang†	5	13.79
A-Combinatie‡	5	7.21
A1§	3	5.86
Unie van Progressieve Surinamers/Partij voor Democratie en Ontwikkeling in Eenheid	—	4.67
Nieuw Suriname	—	1.57
Progressieve Arbeiders en Landbouwers Unie	—	0.89
Progressieve Politieke Partij	—	0.17
Total	**51**	**100.00**‖

* An alliance of the Nationale Partij Suriname (NPS), the Pertajah Luhur (PL), the Surinaamse Partij van de Arbeid (SPA) and the Vooruitstrevende Hervormingspartij (VHP).
† An alliance of the Democratisch Nationaal Platform 2000 (DNP 2000), the Basispartij voor Vernieuwing en Democratie (BVD), the Kerukanan Tulodo Pranatan Ingigil (KTPI) and the Democratisch Alternatief.
‡ Including candidates of the Algemene Bevrijdings- en Ontwikkelingspartij (ABOP) and the Broederschap en Eenheid in Politiek (BEP).
§ Including candidates from the Democratisch Alternatief 1991 (DA '91), the Democraten van de 21 (D21) and the Politieke Vleugel van de FAL (PVF).
‖ Including invalid votes.

Election Commission

Centraal Hoofdstembureau (CHS) (Central Polling Authority): Wilhelminastraat 3, Paramaribo; tel. 410362; independent; Chair. LOTHAR BOKSTEEN.

Political Organizations

Algemene Bevrijdings- en Ontwikkelingspartij (ABOP) (General Liberation and Development Party): Jaguarstraat 15, Paramaribo; internet www.abop-suriname.net; f. 1986; contested the 2005 election as part of the A-Combinatie (AC) electoral list; Pres. RONNIE BRUNSWIJK.

Alternatief Forum (AF) (Alternative Forum): Gladiolenstraat 26–28, Paramaribo; tel. 432342; Chair. GERARD BRUNINGS.

Amazone Partij Suriname (APS) (Suriname Amazon Party): Wilhelminastraat 91, Paramaribo; tel. 452081; Pres. KENNETH VAN GENDEREN.

Broederschap en Eenheid in Politiek (BEP): Ariestraat BR 34, S. O. B. Projekt, Paramaribo; tel. 494466; f. 1986; contested the 2005 election as part of the A-Combinatie (AC) electoral list; Chair. CAPRINO ALLENDY.

Democraten van de 21 (D21) (Democrats of the 21st Century): Goudstraat 22, Paramaribo; f. 1986; contested the 2005 election as part of the A1 electoral list; Chair. SOEWARTO MUSTADJA.

Democratisch Alternatief 1991 (DA '91) (Democratic Alternative 1991): POB 91, Paramaribo; tel. 470276; fax 493121; e-mail info@da91.sr; f. 1991; contested the 2005 election as part of the A1 electoral list; social-democratic; Chair. W. JESSERUN.

Hernieuwde Progressieve Partij (HPP) (Renewed Progressive Party): Tourtonnelaan 51, Paramaribo; tel. 426965; e-mail hpp@cq-link.sr; f. 1986; Chair. HARRY KISOENSINGH.

Nationale Democratische Partij (NDP) (National Democratic Party): Dr H. D. Benjaminstraat 38, Paramaribo; tel. 499183; fax 432174; e-mail ndpsur@sr.net; internet www.ndp.sr; f. 1987 by Standvaste (the 25 February Movt); army-supported; Chair. DESIRÉ (DESI) DELANO BOUTERSE.

Nationale Partij Voor Leiderschap en Ontwikkeling (NPLO) (National Party for Leaderhip and Development): Tropicaweg 1, Paramaribo; tel. 551252; f. 1986; Chair. OESMAN WANGSABESARIE.

Naya Kadam (New Choice): Naarstraat 5, Paramaribo; tel. 482014; fax 481012; e-mail itsvof@sr.net; Chair. INDRA DJWALAPERSAD; Sec. WALDO RAMDIHAL.

Nieuw Front (NF) (New Front): Paramaribo; f. 1987 as Front voor Demokratie en Ontwikkeling (FDO—Front for Democracy and Devt); name changed as above in 1991; Pres. RUNALDO R. VENETIAAN; an alliance comprising:

Nationale Partij Suriname (NPS) (Suriname National Party): Wanicastraat 77, Paramaribo; tel. 477302; fax 475796; e-mail nps@sr.net; internet www.nps-suriname.com; f. 1946; predominantly Creole; Sec. OTMAR ROEL RODGERS.

Pertijajah Luhur (PL) (Full Confidence Party): Hoek Gemenlandsweg-Daniel Coutinhostraat, Paramaribo; tel. 401087; fax 420394; Pres. PAUL SALAM SOMOHARDJO.

Surinaamse Partij van de Arbeid (SPA) (Suriname Labour Party): Rust en Vredestraat 64, Paramaribo; tel. 425912; fax 420394; f. 1987; affiliated with C-47 trade union; social democratic party; joined NF in 1991; Leader SIEGFRIED F. GILDS.

Vooruitstrevende Hervormings Partij (VHP) (Progressive Reformation Party): Jagernath Lachmanstraat 130, Paramaribo; tel. 425912; fax 420394; internet www.parbo.com/vhp; f. 1949 as Verenigde Hindostaanse Partij (United Indian Party); name changed as above in 1973; leading left-wing party; predominantly Indian; Leader R. SARDJOE.

Nieuw Suriname (NS) (New Suriname): Paramaribo; contested the 2005 election.

Partij voor Demokratie en Ontwikkeling in Eenheid (DOE) (Party for Democracy through Unity and Development): Kamperfoeliestraat 23, Paramaribo; internet www.angelfire.com/nv/DOE; f. 1999.

Pendawa Lima: Bonistraat 115, Geyersvlij, Paramaribo; tel. 551802; f. 1975; predominantly Indonesian; Chair. RAYMOND SAPOEN.

Politieke Vleugel van de FAL (PVF): Keizerstraat 150, Paramaribo; political wing of farmers' org. Federatie van Agrariërs en Landarbeiders; contested the 2005 election as part of the A1 electoral list; Chair. JIWAN SITAL.

Progressieve Arbeiders en Landbouwers Unie (PALU) (Progressive Workers' and Farm Labourers' Union): Dr S. Kafiluddistraat 27, Paramaribo; tel. 400115; e-mail palu@sr.net; socialist party; Chair. JIM K. HOK; Vice-Chair. HENK RAMNANDANLAL.

Progressieve Bosneger Partij (PBP): f. 1968; resumed political activities 1987; represents members of the Bush Negro (Boschneger) ethnic group; associated with the Pendawa Lima (see above).

Progressieve Politieke Partij (PPP) (Progressive Political Party): Paramaribo; contested the 2005 election; Chair. SURINDER MUNGRA.

SURINAME

Progressieve Surinaamse Volkspartij (PSV) (Suriname Progressive People's Party): Keizerstraat 122, Paramaribo; tel. 472979; f. 1946; resumed political activities 1987; Christian democratic party.

Seeka: Paramaribo; contested the 2005 election as part of the A-Combinatie (AC) electoral list; Chair. PAUL ABENA.

Unie van Progressieve Surinamers/Partij voor Democratie en Ontwikkeling in Eenheid (UPS/DOE): Paramaribo; contested the 2005 election.

Volksalliantie Voor Vooruitgang (People's Alliance for Progress): Paramaribo; contested the 2005 election; Leader JULES WIJDENBOSCH; alliance comprising:

Basispartij voor Vernieuwing en Democratie (BVD) (Base Party for Renewal and Democracy): Hoogestraat 28–30, Paramaribo; tel. 422231; e-mail info@bvdsuriname.org; internet www.bvdsuriname.org; Chair. TJAN GOBARDHAN.

Democratisch Alternatief (Democratic Alternative): Jadnanansinghlaan 5, Paramaribo.

Democratisch Nationaal Platform 2000 (DNP 2000) (National Democratic Platform 2000): Gemenlandsweg 83, Paramaribo; f. 2000; Pres. JULES WIJDENBOSCH.

Kerukunan Tulodo Pranatan Inggil (KTPI) (Party for National Unity and Solidarity): Bonistraat 64, Geyersvlijt, Paramaribo; tel. 456116; f. 1947 as the KaumTani Persuatan Indonesia; largely Indonesian; Leader WILLY SOEMITA.

Partij Pembangunan Rakat Suriname (PPRS): Paramaribo; Chair. R. KAAIMAN.

Diplomatic Representation

EMBASSIES IN SURINAME

Brazil: Maratakkastraat 2, POB 925, Paramaribo; tel. 400200; fax 420774; e-mail brasemb@sr.net; internet www2.mre.gov.br/suriname/index.asp; Ambassador JOSÉ LUIZ MACHADO E COSTA.

China, People's Republic: Anton Dragtenweg 154, POB 3042 Paramaribo; tel. 451570; fax 452540; e-mail chinaemb_sr@mfa.gov.cn; internet sr.chineseembassy.org; Ambassador SU GE.

Cuba: Brokopondolaan 4, Paramaribo; tel. 434917; fax 432626; e-mail embacubasuriname@gmail.com; internet embacu.cubaminrex.cu/surinaming; Ambassador ANDRÉS MARCELO GONZÁLEZ GARRIDO.

France: Henck Arronstraat 5–7, POB 2648, Paramaribo; tel. 476455; fax 471208; e-mail ambafrance.paramaribo@diplomatie.gouv.fr; internet www.ambafrance-sr.org; Ambassador RICHARD BARBEYRON.

Guyana: Gravenstraat 82, POB 785, Paramaribo; tel. 477895; fax 472679; e-mail guyembassy@sr.net; Chargé d'affaires a.i. YVONNE LESPERANS.

India: Rode Kruislaan 10, POB 1329, Paramaribo; tel. 498344; fax 491106; e-mail india@sr.net; internet www.indembassysuriname.com; Ambassador KANWAL JIT SINGH SODDHI.

Indonesia: Van Brussellaan 3, Uitvlugt, POB 157, Paramaribo; tel. 431230; fax 498234; e-mail indonemb@sr.net; Ambassador SUPRIJANTO MUHADI.

Japan: Henck Arronstraat 23–25, POB 2921, Paramaribo; tel. 474860; fax 412208; e-mail eojparbo@sr.net; Ambassador YASUO MATSUI (resident in Venezuela).

Netherlands: Van Roseveltkade 5, POB 1877, Paramaribo; tel. 477211; fax 477792; e-mail prm@minbuza.nl; Ambassador TANYA VAN GOOL.

Russia: Anton Dragtenweg 7, POB 8127, Paramaribo; tel. and fax 472387; Ambassador PAVEL SERGIEV.

USA: Dr Sophie Redmondstraat 129, POB 1821, Paramaribo; tel. 472900; fax 425690; e-mail embuscen@sr.net; internet suriname.usembassy.gov; Ambassador LISA BOBBIE SCHREIBER HUGHES.

Venezuela: Henck Arronstraat 23–25, POB 3001, Paramaribo; tel. 475401; fax 475602; e-mail embajador@suriname.gob.ve; internet www.suriname.gob.ve; Ambassador FRANCISCO DE JESÚS SIMANCAS.

Judicial System

The administration of justice is entrusted to a Court of Justice, the six members of which are nominated for life, and three Cantonal Courts. Suriname recognized the Caribbean Court of Justice (CCJ) on matters of original jurisdiction pertaining to international trade. The CCJ was inaugurated in Port of Spain, Trinidad and Tobago, on 16 April 2005.

President of the Court of Justice: JOHN VON NIESEWAND.

Attorney-General: MAUREEN K. DAYALA.

Religion

Many religions are represented in Suriname. According to the census at August 2004, Christians represented approximately 48.3% of the population, Hindus 23.6% and Muslims 16.0%. The Bahá'í faith is also represented.

CHRISTIANITY

Committee of Christian Churches: Paramaribo; Chair. Rev. JOHN KENT (Praeses of the Moravian Church).

The Roman Catholic Church

For ecclesiastical purposes, Suriname comprises the single diocese of Paramaribo, suffragan to the archdiocese of Port of Spain (Trinidad and Tobago). The Bishop participates in the Antilles Episcopal Conference (currently based in Port of Spain, Trinidad and Tobago). At 31 December 2006 there were 126,460 adherents to the Roman Catholic faith, representing some 25% of the population.

Bishop of Paramaribo: WILHELMUS ADRIANUS JOSEPHUS MARIA DE BEKKER, Bisschopshuis, Henck Arronstraat 12, POB 1230, Paramaribo; tel. 425918; fax 471602; e-mail cabisdom@sr.net.

The Anglican Communion

Within the Church in the Province of the West Indies, Suriname forms part of the diocese of Guyana. The Episcopal Church is also represented.

Anglican Church: St Bridget's, Hoogestraat 44, Paramaribo.

Protestant Churches

Evangelisch-Lutherse Kerk in Suriname: Waterkant 102, POB 585, Paramaribo; tel. 425503; fax 481856; e-mail elks@sr.net; Pres. WIM LOOR; 4,000 mems.

Moravian Church in Suriname (Evangelische Broeder Gemeente): Maagdenstraat 50, POB 1811, Paramaribo; tel. 473073; fax 475794; e-mail ebgs@sr.net; f. 1735; Praeses MAARTEN MINGOEN; 40,000 mems (2004).

Adherents to the Moravian Church consitute some 15% of the population. Also represented are the Christian Reformed Church, the Dutch Reformed Church, the Baptist Church, the Evangelical Methodist Church, Pentecostal Missions, the Seventh-day Adventists and the Wesleyan Methodist Congregation.

HINDUISM

Arya Dewaker: Johan Adolf Pengelstraat 210, Paramaribo; tel. 400706; e-mail aryadewaker@sr.net; members preach the Vedic Dharma; disciples of Maha Rishi Swami Dayanand Sarswati, the founder of the Arya Samaj in India; f. 1929; Chair. INDERDATH TILAKDHARIE.

Sanatan Dharm: Koningstraat 31–33, POB 760, Paramaribo; tel. 404190; f. 1930; Pres. Dr R. M. NANNAN PANDAY; over 150,000 mems.

ISLAM

Federatie Islamitische Gemeenten in Suriname: Paramaribo; Indonesian Islamic org.; Chair. K. KAAIMAN.

Stichting der Islamitische Gemeenten Suriname: Verlengde Mahonielaan 39, Paramaribo; Indonesian Islamic org.

Surinaamse Islamitische Organisatie (SIO): Watermolenstraat 10, POB 278, Paramaribo; tel. 475220; fax 472075; e-mail ijamaludin@hotmail.com; f. 1978; Pres. Dr I. JAMALUDIN; Sec. Dr K. M. MOENNE; 6 brs.

Surinaamse Moeslim Associatie: Kankantriestraat 55–57, Paramaribo; Javanese Islamic org.

JUDAISM

The Dutch Jewish Congregation and the Dutch Portuguese-Jewish Congregation are represented in Suriname.

Jewish Community: The Synagogue Neve Shalom, Keizerstraat, POB 1834, Paramaribo; tel. 400236; fax 402380; e-mail rene-fernandes@cq-link.sr; internet www.ujcl.org; f. 1854; mem. of Union of Jewish Congregations of Latin America and the Caribbean (UJCL); Officiant JACQUES VAN NIEL; 300 mems (2005).

The Press

DAILIES

Dagblad Suriname: Zwartenhovenbrugstraat 154, POB 975, Paramaribo; tel. 426336; fax 471718; e-mail general@dbsuriname.com; internet www.dbsuriname.com; f. 2002; Dir FARIED PIERKHAN; Editor LAL MAHOMED JAMES.

SURINAME

De Ware Tijd: Malebatrumstraat 9, POB 1200, Paramaribo; tel. 472833; fax 411169; e-mail infodwt@dwt.net; internet www.dwtonline.com; f. 1957; morning; Dutch; independent/liberal; Dir STEVE JONG TJIEN FA; Editor-in-Chief RICARDO CARROT.

De West: Dr J. C. de Mirandastraat 2–6, POB 176, Paramaribo; tel. 473327; fax 470322; e-mail dewest@cq-link.sr; internet www.dewestonline.cq-link.sr; f. 1909; midday; Dutch; liberal; Editor GEORGE D. C. FINDLAY; circ. 15,000–18,000.

PERIODICALS

Advertentieblad van de Republiek Suriname: Henck Arronstraat 120, POB 56, Paramaribo; tel. 473501; fax 454782; f. 1871; 2 a week; Dutch; govt and official information bulletin; Editor E. D. FINDLAY; circ. 1,000.

CLO Bulletin: Gemenelandsweg 95, Paramaribo; f. 1973; irreg.; Dutch; labour information publ. by civil servants' union.

Kerkbode: Burenstraat 17–19, POB 219, Paramaribo; tel. 473079; fax 475635; e-mail stadje@sr.net; f. 1906; weekly; religious; circ. 2,000.

Omhoog: Henck Arronstraat 21, POB 1802, Paramaribo; tel. 425992; fax 426782; e-mail rkomhoog@sr.net; f. 1952; Dutch; weekly; Catholic bulletin; Editor S. MULDER; circ. 5,000.

Xtreme Magazine: Uranusstraat 49, Paramaribo; tel. 456969.

Publishers

Afaka International NV: Residastraat 23, Paramaribo; tel. and fax 530640; e-mail info@afaka.biz; internet www.afaka.biz; f. 1996; Dir GERRIT BARRON.

Educatieve Uitgeverij Sorava NV: Latourweg 10, POB 8382, Paramaribo; tel. and fax 480808.

IMWO, Universiteit van Suriname: Universiteitscomplex, Leysweg 1, POB 9212, Paramaribo; tel. 465558; fax 462291; e-mail bmhango@yahoo.com.

Ministerie van Onderwijs en Volksontwikkeling (Ministry of Education and Community Development): Dr Samuel Kafilludistraat 117–123, Paramaribo; tel. 498850; fax 495083.

Okopipi Publ. (Publishing Services Suriname): Van Idsingastraat 133, Paramaribo; tel. 472746; e-mail pssmoniz@sr.net; fmrly I. Krishnadath.

Papaya Media Counseling: Plutostraat 30, POB 8304, Paramaribo; tel. and fax 454530; e-mail roy_bhikharie@sr.net; f. 2002; Man. Dir ROY BHIKHARIE.

Stichting Wetenschappelijke Informatie (Foundation for Information and Development): Prins Hendrikstraat 38, Paramaribo; tel. 475232; fax 422195; e-mail swin@sr.net; f. 1977.

Tabiki Productions: Weidestraat 34, Paramaribo; tel. 478525; fax 478526; e-mail insightsuriname@yahoo.com.

VACO, NV: Domineestraat 26, POB 1841, Paramaribo; tel. 472545; fax 410563; f. 1952; Dir EDUARD HOGENBOOM.

PUBLISHERS' ASSOCIATION

Publishers' Association Suriname: Domineestraat 32, POB 1841, Paramaribo; tel. 472545; fax 410563.

Broadcasting and Communications

TELECOMMUNICATIONS

Regulatory Authority

Telecommunications Authority Suriname (TAS): Heerenstraat 13–15, 1°, Paramaribo; tel. 421463; fax 421465; e-mail tasur@sr.net; f. April 2006 under new Telecommunication Provisions Act; regulatory authority; Dir JETTIE OLFF.

Major Service Providers

Digicel Suriname: Henck Arronstraat 27–29, POB 1848, Paramaribo; tel. 473169; fax 551533; mobile operating licence granted in Aug. 2006; operations commenced Dec. 2007; Dir MITCHELL TJIN A. DJIE; Country Man. PHILIP VAN DALSEN.

International Telecommunication Suriname NV (IntelSur NV): Paramaribo; mobile operating licence granted in August 2006 formalized in April 2007; CEO ERIC LELIENHOF.

Telecommunication Corporation Suriname (Telesur): Heiligenweg 1, POB 1839, Paramaribo; tel. 473944; fax 404800; internet www.telesur.sr; liberalization of the telecommunications sector ended Telesur's monopoly in April 2007; supervisory function of Telesur assumed by new regulatory body, Telecommunication Authority Suriname (q.v.); Man. Dir DIRK M. R. CURRIE.

BROADCASTING

Radio

ABC Radio (Ampie's Broadcasting Corporation): Maystraat 57, Paramaribo; tel. 464609; fax 464680; e-mail info@abcsuriname.com; internet www.abcsuriname.com; f. 1975; re-opened in 1993; commercial; Dutch and some local languages.

Radio Apintie: Verlengde Gemenelandsweg 37, POB 595, Paramaribo; tel. 498855; fax 400684; e-mail apintie@sr.net; internet www.apintie.sr; f. 1958; commercial; Dutch and some local languages; Gen. Man. CHARLES VERVUURT.

Radio Bersama: Bonniestraat 115, Paramaribo; tel. 551804; fax 551803; f. 1997; Dir AJOEB MOENTARI.

Radio Boskopou: Roseveltkade 1, Paramaribo; tel. 410300; govt-owned; Sranang Tongo and Dutch; Head Mr VAN VARSEVELD.

Radio Garuda: Goudstraat 14–16, Paramaribo; tel. 422422; Dir TOMMY RADJI.

Radio Nickerie (RANI): Waterloostraat 3, Nieuw Nickerie; tel. 231462; commercial; Hindi and Dutch.

Radio Paramaribo (Rapar): Verlengde Jagernath Lachmonstraat 34, POB 975, Paramaribo; tel. 499995; fax 493121; e-mail rapar@sr.net; f. 1957; commercial; Dutch and some local languages; Dir FARIED PIERKHAN.

Radio Radika: Indira Gandhiweg 165, Paramaribo; tel. 482800; fax 482910; e-mail radika@sr.net; re-opened in 1989; Dutch and Hindi; Dir ROSHNI RADHAKISHUN.

Radio Sangeet Mala: Indira Gandhiweg 73, Paramaribo; tel. 485893; Dutch and Hindi; Dirs RADJEN SOEKHRADJ, SOEDESH RAMSARAN.

Radio SRS (Stichting Radio Omroep Suriname): Jacques van Eerstraat 20, POB 271, Paramaribo; tel. 498115; fax 498116; e-mail radiosrs@sr.net; f. 1965; commercial; govt-owned; Dutch and some local languages; Dir LEOPOLD DARTHUIZEN.

Radio Ten: Letitia Vriesdelaan 5, Paramaribo; tel. 410881; fax 410885; e-mail radio10@cq-link.sr; internet www.radio10.cq-link.sr.

Other stations include: Radio KBC, Radio Koyeba, Radio Pertjaya, Radio Shalom, Radio Zon, Ramasha Radio, Rasonic Radio and Trishul Radio.

Television

ABC Televisie (Ampie's Broadcasting Corporation): Maystraat 57, Paramaribo; tel. 464555; fax 464680; e-mail info@abcsuriname.com; internet www.abcsuriname.com; Channel 4.

Algemene Televisie Verzorging (ATV): Adrianusstraat 55, POB 2995, Paramaribo; tel. 404611; fax 402660; e-mail info@atv.sr; internet www.atv.sr; f. 1985; govt-owned; commercial; Dutch, English, Portuguese, Spanish and some local languages; Channel 12; Man. GUNO COOMAN.

STVS (Surinaamse Televisie Stichting): Letitia Vriesdelaan 5, POB 535, Paramaribo; tel. 473031; fax 477216; e-mail adm@stvs.info.sr; internet www.parbo.com/stvs; f. 1965; govt-owned; commercial; local languages, Dutch and English; Channel 8; Dir KENNETH OOSTBURG.

Finance

(cap. = capital; res = reserves; dep. = deposits; m. = million; brs = branches; amounts in Surinamese dollars unless otherwise specified)

BANKING

Central Bank

Centrale Bank van Suriname: 18–20 Waterkant, POB 1801, Paramaribo; tel. 473741; fax 476444; e-mail info@cbvs.sr; internet www.cbvs.sr; f. 1957; Gov. ANDRÉ E. TELTING.

Commercial Banks

Finabank NV: Dr Sophie Redmondstraat 59–61, Paramaribo; tel. 472266; fax 422672; e-mail finabank@sr.net; internet www.finabanknv.com; f. 1991; Gen. Man. MERLEEN ATMODIKROMO.

Handels-Krediet- en Industriebank (Hakrinbank NV): Dr Sophie Redmondstraat 11–13, POB 1813, Paramaribo; tel. 477722; fax 472066; e-mail hakrindp@sr.net; internet www.hakrinbank.com; f. 1936; cap. 0.1m., res 33.2m., dep. 552.5m. (Dec. 2006); Pres. and Chair. A. K. R. SHYAMNARAIN; Man. Dirs M. TJON-A-TEN, J. D. BOUSAID; 6 brs.

Landbouwbank NV: FHR Lim A Postraat 34, POB 929, Paramaribo; tel. 475945; fax 411965; e-mail lbbank@sr.net; f. 1972; govt-owned; agricultural bank; Chair. D. FERRIER; Pres. R. MERHAI; 5 brs.

RBTT Bank NV: Kerkplein 1, Paramaribo; tel. 471555; fax 411325.

De Surinaamsche Bank NV: Henck Arronstraat 26–30, POB 1806, Paramaribo; tel. 471100; fax 411750; e-mail info@dsbbank.sr; internet www.dsbbank.sr; f. 1865; cap. 0.8m., res 93.5m., dep. 1,178.3m. (Dec. 2007); Chair. S. SMIT; 8 brs.

Surinaamse Postspaarbank: Knuffelsgracht 10–14, POB 1879, Paramaribo; tel. 472256; fax 472952; e-mail spsbdir@sr.net; f. 1904; savings and commercial bank; cap. and res Sf 1,044m., dep. Sf 66,533m. (Dec. 2004); Man. ALWIN R. BAARH (acting); 2 brs.

Surinaamse Volkscredietbank: Waterkant 104, POB 1804, Paramaribo; tel. 472616; fax 473257; e-mail btlsvcb@sr.net; f. 1949; cap. and res Sf 170.3m. (Dec. 1997); Man. Dir THAKOERDIEN RAMLAKHAN; 3 brs.

Development Bank

Nationale Ontwikkelingsbank van Suriname NV: Jagernath Lachmonstraat 160–162, POB 677, Paramaribo; tel. 465000; fax 497192; f. 1963; govt-supported; cap. and res Sf 34m. (Dec. 1992).

INSURANCE

Assuria NV: Grote Combeweg 37, POB 1501, Paramaribo; tel. 477955; fax 472390; e-mail assuria@sr.net; internet www.assuria .sr; f. 1961; life and indemnity insurance; Man. Dir Dr S. SMIT.

Assuria Schadeverzekering NV: Henck Arronstraat 5–7, POB 1030, Paramaribo; tel. 473400; fax 476669; e-mail assuria@sr.net; internet www.assuria.sr; Chair. J. J. HEALY; Man. Dir Dr S. SMIT.

CLICO Life Insurance Company Ltd: Klipstenenstraat 29, POB 3026, Paramaribo; tel. 472525; fax 476777; e-mail clicosur@sr.net; internet www.clico.com/suriname; CEO CLAUDIUS DACON; Dir KAREN-ANN GARDIER.

Fatum Levensverzekering NV: Noorderkerkstraat 5–7, Paramaribo; tel. 471541; fax 410067; e-mail fatum@sr.net; internet www.fatum-suriname.com.

Hennep Verzorgende Verzekering NV: Dr Sophie Redmondstraat 246, Paramaribo; tel. 425205; fax 425209; e-mail hennep@sr .net; internet www.uitvaarthennep.com; f. 1896; Man. Dir H. J. HENNEP.

Parsasco NV: Henck Arronstraat 117, Paramaribo; tel. 421212; fax 421325; e-mail parsasco@sr.net; internet www.parsasco.com; f. 1955; Man. Dir AMAR RANDJITSING.

Self Reliance: Heerenstraat 48–50 en Henck Arronstraat 69–71, Paramaribo; tel. 472582; fax 472475; e-mail self-reliance@sr.net; internet www.self-reliance.sr; f. 1980; general and life insurance; Pres. MAURICE L. ROEMER.

Trade and Industry

DEVELOPMENT ORGANIZATIONS

Centre for Industry and Export Development: Rust en Vredestraat 79–81, POB 1275, Paramaribo; tel. 474830; fax 476311; f. 1981; Man. R. A. LETER.

Stichting Planbureau Suriname (National Planning Office of Suriname): Dr Sophie Redmondstraat 118, POB 172, Paramaribo; tel. 447408; fax 475001; e-mail dirsps@sr.net; internet www .planbureau.net; f. 1951; responsible for regional and socio-economic long- and short-term planning; Man. Dir LILIAN J. M. MONSELS-THOMPSON.

CHAMBERS OF COMMERCE

Kamer van Koophandel en Fabrieken (Chamber of Commerce and Industry): Dr J. C. de Mirandastraat 10, POB 149, Paramaribo; tel. 474536; fax 474779; e-mail chamber@sr.net; f. 1910; Pres. R. L. A. AMEERALI; 16,109 mems.

Surinaams–Nederlandse Kamer voor Handel en Industrie (Suriname–Netherlands Chamber of Commerce and Industry): Jagernath Lachmonstraat 158, Paramaribo; tel. and fax 476909.

INDUSTRIAL AND TRADE ASSOCIATIONS

Associatie van Surinaamse Fabrikanten (ASFA) (Suriname Manufacturers' Asscn): Jaggernath Lachmonstraat 187, POB 3046, Paramaribo; tel. 439797; fax 439798; e-mail asfa@sr.net; Chair. KATHLEEN LIEUW KIE SONG; 317 mems.

Vereniging Surinaams Bedrijfsleven (Suriname Trade and Industry Association): Prins Hendrikstraat 18, POB 111, Paramaribo; tel. 475286; fax 475287; e-mail info@vsbstia.org; internet www .vsbstia.org; Pres. MARCEL A. MEYER; 290 mems.

UTILITIES

Electricity

Staatsolie Maatschappij Suriname: Dr Ir Adhinstraat 21, POB 4069, Paramaribo; tel. 499649; fax 491105; e-mail mailstaatsolie@ staatsolie.com; internet www.staatsolie.com; state-owned electricity supplier; Man. Dir M. C. H. WAALDIJK.

TRADE UNIONS

Council of the Surinamese Federation of Trade Unions (RAVAKSUR): f. 1987; Sec. FREDDY WATERBERG; comprises:

Algemeen Verbond van Vakverenigingen in Suriname 'De Moederbond' (AVVS) (General Confederation of Trade Unions): Verlengde Jagernath Lachmonstraat 134, POB 2951, Paramaribo; tel. 465116; fax 463501; e-mail avvsmoederbonds51@hotmail.com; right-wing; Pres. ERROLL G. SNIJDERS; Gen. Sec. ALESSANDRO SPRONG; 15,000 mems.

Centrale Landsdienaren Organisatie (CLO) (Central Organization for Civil Service Employees): Gemenelandsweg 743, Paramaribo; tel. 499839; Pres. RONALD HOOGHART; 13,000 mems.

Organisatie van Samenwerkende Autonome Vakbonden (OSAV): Noorderkerkstraat 2–10, Paramaribo; fax 478548; Pres. SONNY CHOTKAN; Gen. Sec. RONNY HEK.

Progressieve Werknemers Organisatie (PWO) (Progressive Workers' Organization): Limesgracht 80, POB 406, Paramaribo; tel. 475840; f. 1948; covers the commercial, hotel and banking sectors; Pres. ANDRE KOORNAAR; Sec. EDWARD MENT; 4,000 mems.

Progressive Trade Union Federation (C-47): Wanicastraat 230, Paramaribo; tel. 401120; fax 401149; e-mail c47@sr.net; Pres. ROBBY BERENSTEIN; Gen. Sec CLAUDETTE ETNEL.

Federation of Civil Servants Organization (CLO): Verlengde Gemenelandsweg 74, Paramaribo; tel. 464200; fax 493918; Pres. RONALD HOOGHART; Gen. Sec. DOROTHY TELTING.

Federation of Farmers and Agrarians (FAL): Keizerstraat 150, Paramaribo; tel. 420833; fax 474517; Pres. JIWAN SITAL; Gen. Sec. ANAND DWARKA.

Nickerie Banana Workers' Union (BABN): Paramaribo; f. 2008; Pres. DAYANAND DWARKA.

Transport

RAILWAYS

There are no public railways operating in Suriname.

ROADS

In 2003 Suriname had an estimated 4,304 km (2,674 miles) of roads, of which 26.3% were paved. The principal east–west road, 390 km in length, links Albina, on the eastern border, with Nieuw Nickerie, in the west.

SHIPPING

Suriname is served by many shipping companies and has about 1,500 km (930 miles) of navigable rivers and canals. A number of shipping companies conduct regular international services (principally for freight) to and from Paramaribo including EWL, Fyffesgroup, the Alcoa Steamship Co, Marli Marine Lines, Bic Line, Nedlloyd Line, Maersk Lines and Tecmarine Lines (in addition to those listed below). There are also two ferry services linking Suriname with Guyana, across the Corentijn river, and with French Guiana, across the Marowijne river.

Maritieme Autoriteit Suriname (Suriname Maritime Authority): Cornelis Jongbawstraat 2, POB 888, Paramaribo; tel. 476733; fax 472940; e-mail info@mas.sr; internet www.mas.sr; fmrly Dienst voor de Scheepvaart; govt authority supervising and controlling shipping in Surinamese waters; Man. of Maritime Operations A. EDENBURG.

Scheepvaart Maatschappij Suriname NV (SMS) (Suriname Shipping Line Ltd): Waterkant 44, POB 1824, Paramaribo; tel. 472447; fax 474814; e-mail surinam_line@sr.net; f. 1936; state-owned; passenger services in the interior; Chair. A. T. EDENBURG.

Suriname Coast Traders NV: Flocislaan 4, Industrieterrein Flora, POB 9216, Paramaribo; tel. 463040; fax 463831; internet www .pasonsgroup.com; f. 1981; subsidiary of Pasons Group.

NV VSH United Suriname Shipping Company: van 't Hogerhuysstraat 9–11, POB 1860, Paramaribo; tel. 402558; fax 403515; e-mail sales@vshunited.com; internet www.vshunited.com/shipping .html; shipping agents and freight carriers; Man. RICHARD STEENLAND.

CIVIL AVIATION

The main airport is Johan Adolf Pengel International Airport (formerly Zanderij International Airport), 45 km from Paramaribo. Domestic flights operate from Zorg-en-Hoop Airport, located in a suburb of Paramaribo. There are 35 airstrips throughout the country.

Surinaamse Luchtvaart Maatschappij NV (SLM) (Suriname Airways): Mr Jagernath Lachmonstraat 136, POB 2029, Paramaribo; tel. 465700; fax 491213; e-mail publicrelations@slm.firm.sr; internet www.slm.nl; f. 1962; services to Amsterdam (Netherlands) and to destinations in North America, South America and the Caribbean; Vice-Pres. CLYDE CAIRO.

Gonini Air Service Ltd: Doekhiweg 1, Zorg-en-Hoop Airport, POB 1614, Paramaribo; tel. 499098; fax 498363; f. 1976; privately owned; licensed for scheduled and unscheduled national and international services (charters, lease, etc.); Man. Dir GERARD BRUNINGS.

Gum Air NV: Doekhieweg 3, Zorg-en-Hoop Airfield, Paramaribo; tel. 498888; fax 497670; e-mail info@gumair.com; internet www.gumair.com; privately owned; unscheduled domestic and regional flights; Man. HENK GUMMELS.

Tourism

Efforts were made to promote the previously undeveloped tourism sector in the 1990s. Attractions include the varied cultural activities, a number of historical sites and an unspoiled interior with many varieties of plants, birds and animals. There are 13 nature reserves and one nature park. There were an estimated 162,509 stop-over arrivals in 2007, of which a majority came from the Netherlands. In 2006 tourism receipts totalled US $109m.

Suriname Tourism Foundation: Dr J. F. Nassylaan 2, Paramaribo; tel. 424878; fax 477786; e-mail info@suriname-tourism.org; internet www.suriname-tourism.org; f. 1996; Exec. Dir ARMAND LI-A-YOUNG.

SWAZILAND

Introductory Survey

Location, Climate, Language, Religion, Flag, Capital

The Kingdom of Swaziland is a land-locked country in southern Africa, bordered by South Africa to the north, west, south and south-east, and by Mozambique to the east. The average annual temperature is about 16°C (61°F) on the Highveld, and about 22°C (72°F) in the sub-humid Lowveld, while annual rainfall ranges from 1,000 mm (40 ins) to 2,280 mm (90 ins) on the Highveld, and from 500 mm (20 ins) to 890 mm (35 ins) in the Lowveld. English and siSwati are the official languages. About 60% of the population profess Christianity, while most of the remainder adhere to traditional beliefs. The national flag (proportions 2 by 3) is blue, with a yellow-edged horizontal crimson stripe (one-half of the depth) in the centre. On this stripe is a black and white Swazi shield, superimposed on two spears and a staff, all lying horizontally. The capital is Mbabane.

Recent History

Swaziland, which was previously under the joint rule of the United Kingdom and the South African (Transvaal) Republic, became a British protectorate in 1903, and one of the High Commission Territories in 1907, the others being the colony of Basutoland (now the Kingdom of Lesotho) and the protectorate of Bechuanaland (now the Republic of Botswana). The British Act of Parliament that established the Union of South Africa in 1910 also provided for the inclusion in South Africa of the three High Commission Territories, subject to consultation with the local inhabitants.

Swaziland's first Constitution, which was introduced by the British Government, entered into force in January 1964. The Paramount Chief (iNgwenyama—the Lion), King Sobhuza II, subsequently established a traditionalist political party, the Imbokodvo National Movement (INM), which secured all of the seats in the new Legislative Council at elections in June of that year. In 1965, in response to continued pressure from the INM, the British Government established a committee to draft proposed constitutional amendments. A new Constitution, which was promulgated in 1966 and came into effect in April 1967, provided for the introduction of internal self-government pending the attainment of full independence by the end of 1969. Executive power was vested in King Sobhuza as the hereditary monarch and constitutional Head of State. The Legislative Council was dissolved in March 1967, and elections to the new bicameral Parliament took place in April. The INM secured all 24 elective seats in the House of Assembly, although the Ngwane National Liberatory Congress (NNLC) received 20% of the votes cast. In May King Sobhuza formed Swaziland's first Cabinet, appointing the leader of the INM, Prince Makhosini Dlamini, as Prime Minister. On 6 September 1968 Swaziland was granted full independence within the Commonwealth, and a new Constitution (based on the existing Constitution) was adopted.

In April 1973, in accordance with a parliamentary resolution, King Sobhuza repealed the Constitution, imposed a state of emergency under which all political activity was suspended, introduced legislation providing for detention without trial for a period of 60 days, and announced the formation of a national army. A new Constitution, promulgated on 13 October 1978, confirmed the King's control of executive and legislative decisions. The functions of the bicameral parliament, comprising a House of Assembly and a Senate, were confined to debating government proposals and advising the King. The existing 40 traditional local councils (Tinkhundla—singular: Inkhundla) were each to nominate two members to an 80-member electoral college, which was, in turn, to elect 40 deputies to the House of Assembly. Members of the House of Assembly were to select 10 members of the Senate, while the King was to nominate a further 10 members to each chamber. All political parties (including the INM) were prohibited. Legislative elections took place later that year, and the parliament was inaugurated in January 1979. In June 1982 the Swaziland National Council, an advisory body on matters of Swazi tradition, comprising members of the royal family, was redesignated as the Supreme Council of State (Liqoqo).

King Sobhuza died in August 1982. In accordance with Swazi tradition, the powers of Head of State devolved upon the Queen Mother (Ndlovukazi—Great She Elephant) Dzeliwe, who was authorized to act as Regent until King Sobhuza's designated successor, Prince Makhosetive (born in 1968), attained the age of 21. Shortly afterwards Queen Regent Dzeliwe appointed the Liqoqo, which was to advise her in all affairs of State. Competition to secure supreme executive power subsequently emerged between the Prime Minister, Prince Mabandla N. F. Dlamini, and several prominent members, led by Prince Mfanasibili Dlamini, of the Liqoqo. In March 1983 Prince Mabandla was replaced as Prime Minister by a traditionalist, Prince Bhekimpi Dlamini. In August, under the powers of the 'Authorized Person' (an important hereditary post, held by Prince Sozisa Dlamini, the Chairman of the Liqoqo), Queen Regent Dzeliwe was deposed, apparently as a result of her reluctance to dismiss Prince Mabandla. Following an attempt by Queen Regent Dzeliwe to appeal against her deposition, Prince Mfanasibili and his followers obtained an official declaration that the High Court had no jurisdiction in matters concerning Swazi custom and tradition. Widespread opposition to the deposition of Queen Regent Dzeliwe was suppressed, and in September Queen Ntombi, the mother of Prince Makhosetive, was officially invested as Regent. In November elections to the Libandla took place, and a new Cabinet was appointed, in which only Prince Bhekimpi and the Minister of Foreign Affairs, Richard Dlamini, were retained.

In October 1985, following protests by prominent members of the royal family at the Liqoqo's monopoly of power, Queen Regent Ntombi dismissed Prince Mfanasibili. It was subsequently announced that the Liqoqo was to be reconstituted in its former capacity as an advisory body on matters pertaining to traditional law and custom. In December all those convicted of conspiracy in late 1984 were pardoned and released. In January 1986 it was announced that Prince Makhosetive was to be crowned in April, three years earlier than expected, in order to end the competition for power among vying royal factions.

Prince Makhosetive was crowned on 25 April 1986, and assumed the title of King Mswati III. In May King Mswati dissolved the Liqoqo, thereby consolidating his power. In July the King reorganized the Cabinet, and in October he appointed a former senior member of the security forces, Sotsha Dlamini, as Prime Minister. In May 1987 12 prominent officials, including Prince Bhekimpi and Prince Mfanasibili, were charged with sedition and treason, in connection with the removal from power of Queen Regent Dzeliwe in 1983. In November King Mswati established a special tribunal to preside over all cases involving alleged offences against the King or the Queen Regent; defendants appearing before the tribunal were not to be granted the right to legal representation or appeal. In March 1988 10 of those accused of involvement in the deposition of Queen Regent Dzeliwe were convicted of treason by the special tribunal, and received custodial sentences; two defendants were acquitted. In July, however, it was reported that the 10 convicted in March had been released.

In November 1987 elections to the legislature took place, one year earlier than scheduled. In July 1998 King Mswati dismissed Sotsha Dlamini for alleged disobedience, replacing him with Obed Dlamini, a former leader of the Swaziland Federation of Trade Unions (SFTU).

In early 1990 the People's United Democratic Movement (PUDEMO), which had been established in 1983, distributed tracts questioning the legitimacy of the monarchy in its existing form and demanding constitutional reform. Security forces subsequently arrested a number of suspected members of PUDEMO, who were variously charged with treason, sedition or conspiring to form a political party. All the defendants were acquitted of the principal charges, although five were convicted of illegally attending a political gathering (the sentences of two of the five were annulled on appeal in October 1991). In November King Mswati dismissed the reformist Minister of Justice, Reginald Dhladhla, reportedly on the advice of the Swaziland National Council (which had been reconstituted from the former

Liqoqo), prompting public concern that it continued to exert undue influence on government policies. Later in November five members of PUDEMO (who had previously been acquitted of all charges) were arrested under legislation enabling the detention of suspects without trial. In March 1991 the prisoners were released, as a result of international pressure. In an attempt to advance its objectives through legal bodies, PUDEMO subsequently established a number of affiliated organizations, including the Human Rights Association of Swaziland (HUMARAS) and the Swaziland Youth Congress (SWAYOCO), but these were not accorded official recognition.

In September and October 1991 a committee, termed Vusela (Greetings), conducted a series of public forums throughout the country to elicit popular opinion on political reforms. Widespread demands for the abolition of the existing electoral system were reported, while there was substantial criticism of the composition of the Vusela committee itself. In subsequent months several peaceful demonstrations, organized by SWAYOCO to demand the establishment of a democratic system of government, were suppressed by security forces. In October King Mswati announced an extensive reorganization of the Cabinet. In February 1992 PUDEMO declared itself a legal opposition party (in contravention of the prohibition on political association), rejected King Mswati's efforts to institute political reform, and demanded a constitutional referendum. Two further opposition movements, the Swaziland United Front (SUF) and the Swaziland National Front (SWANAFRO), subsequently re-emerged. In February King Mswati appointed a second committee (Vusela 2), which was to present recommendations for consideration by the King, based on the conclusions of the first committee.

In October 1992 King Mswati approved several proposals submitted by Vusela 2. The House of Assembly (redesignated the National Assembly) was to be expanded to 65 deputies (of whom 55 were to be directly elected by secret ballot from candidates nominated by the Tinkhundla, and 10 appointed by the King), and the Senate to 30 members (10 selected by the National Assembly and 20 appointed by the King); in addition, the legislation providing for detention without trial was to be abrogated, and a new constitution, incorporating the amendments, enshrining an hereditary monarchy and confirming the fundamental rights of the individual and the independence of the judiciary, was to be drafted. However, opposition groups protested at the committee's failure to recommend the immediate restoration of a multi-party political system: the issue was to be postponed until the forthcoming elections, in order to determine the extent of public support. PUDEMO announced its opposition to the electoral reforms, and demanded that the Government organize a national convention to determine the country's constitutional future. King Mswati subsequently dissolved parliament, and announced that he was to rule by decree, with the assistance of the Council of Ministers (as the Cabinet had been restyled), pending the adoption of a new constitution and the holding of parliamentary elections. Later in October King Mswati announced that elections to the National Assembly would take place in the first half of 1993. At a series of public meetings doubts were expressed as to the viability of the reformed electoral system; in early 1993, in response to public concern, it was announced that legislation preventing the heads of the Tinkhundla from exerting undue influence in the nomination of candidates had been introduced.

The first round of elections to the expanded National Assembly took place on 25 September 1993. The second round of parliamentary elections, on 11 October, was contested by the three candidates in each Inkhundla who had obtained the highest number of votes in the first poll; the majority of members of the former Council of Ministers (which had been dissolved in late September), including Obed Dlamini, failed to secure seats in the Assembly. Later in October King Mswati nominated a further 10 deputies to the National Assembly, which elected 10 of its members to the Senate; King Mswati subsequently appointed the remaining 20 senators, among them Obed Dlamini and Prince Bhekimpi. In November the former Minister of Works and Construction, Prince Jameson Mbilini Dlamini, considered a traditionalist, was appointed Prime Minister, and a new Council of Ministers was formed.

In February 1994 it was announced that King Mswati was to appoint a 15-member commission, comprising representatives of organs of State and non-governmental organizations, to draft a new constitution, and a national policy council, which was to prepare a manifesto of the Swazi people. Elections to the Tinkhundla (which had been postponed from March) finally took place, although a high rate of abstention by voters was reported. (The heads of the Tinkhundla had previously been appointed by the King.)

In January 1996 PUDEMO announced a campaign of protests and civil disobedience, owing to the Government's failure to respond to demands for the installation of a multi-party system and for the adoption of a constitution restricting the monarch to a largely ceremonial role. Security forces intervened to suppress demonstrations by SFTU members, and violent clashes ensued, in which three people were reported to have been killed. The SFTU refused to enter into negotiations with the Government, stipulating that the 1973 decree and restrictions on trade unions be revoked prior to discussions. Meanwhile, it was reported that some members of the Government, including Obed Dlamini, also favoured political reform. King Mswati accused the trade unions of attempting to overthrow the monarchy, and threatened to order his traditional warriors to suppress the strike. The SFTU subsequently suspended strike action to allow negotiations to proceed with the Government (which continued to reject the unions' preconditions for discussions). In February 1996 King Mswati announced that the process of drafting a new constitution would be initiated later that year, and that the ban on political activity would also be reviewed. In May King Mswati indicated that a 'People's Parliament', comprising a series of consultative meetings between citizens and government leaders, had been initiated to solicit public opinion regarding constitutional reform. At the same time King Mswati dismissed Prince Mbilini as Prime Minister, and announced that he would appoint his successor in consultation with the Swaziland National Council.

In late July 1996, following an emergency meeting (attended by the Heads of State of Mozambique, Botswana, Zimbabwe and South Africa) to discuss Swaziland's political situation, King Mswati appointed a Constitutional Review Commission, comprising chiefs, political activists and trade unionists, to collate submissions from the Swazi people and subsequently draft proposals for a new constitution. (The Commission received substantial funds from international donors.) At the same time, Dr Barnabas Sibusiso Dlamini, an IMF Executive Director and former Minister of Finance, was appointed Prime Minister.

In December 1996 the Prime Minister announced that a 'task force', composed of workers, employers and government representatives, had discussed the SFTU's demands made in March 1995, and that the implementation of the recommendations outlined in the resulting report was to be overseen by the Labour Advisory Board. In January 1997, however, the SFTU claimed that there had been no response to its demands for democratic reform, and resolved to begin indefinite strike action from February. Meanwhile, the PUDEMO President, Mario Masuku, declared that Swaziland's leaders were not committed to change, and withdrew from the Constitutional Review Commission. At the end of January the four main leaders of the SFTU were arrested and subsequently charged with intimidating bus owners into joining the forthcoming strike. The strike, pronounced illegal by the Government, proceeded, and was apparently observed by approximately one-half of the labour force. On the ninth day of industrial action six strikers were seriously injured in violent clashes with the security forces. The SFTU leaders declined the Government's offer to release them on condition that they end the strike; their trial was dismissed in February, owing to lack of evidence. At the beginning of March the Congress of South African Trade Unions (COSATU), which had asserted its support for the SFTU throughout the strike, initiated a one-day blockade of the Swazi border. The SFTU decided to suspend the strike shortly afterwards, as the Government had agreed to commence negotiations, but resolved to continue industrial action on the first two days of each month until its 27 demands had been met. In April 1997 the SFTU postponed a further blockade indefinitely, in order to allow the Government adequate time to review the situation.

In August 1998 King Mswati dissolved the National Assembly, in preparation for elections scheduled for October. Opposition groups urged voters to boycott the polls, in the absence of the immediate legalization of political parties. Some 350 candidates were nominated by the Tinkhundla to contest the 55 elective seats in the Assembly. Voting took place on 16 and 24 October; turn-out was reportedly low. A new Cabinet, with Sibusiso Dlamini as Prime Minister, was appointed in mid-November, and a new Senate and Swaziland National Council were formed.

In April 1999 the NNLC, PUDEMO and the SFTU united to form the Swaziland Democratic Alliance (SDA). The NNLC leader, Obed Dlamini, was elected Chairman. The formal launch of the SDA was scheduled for 11 April, to coincide with the end of the Southern African Development Community (SADC, see p. 400) labour conference in Mbabane. However, following warnings from the police that the proposed inauguration, which had been rescheduled for 19 April, was illegal and would not be permitted to take place, the executive of the SDA met and cancelled the event.

A judicial crisis developed in late 2002 when, with reference to decrees issued by the King in connection with the evictions of some 200 people from their homes in October 2000, the six South African judges of the Swaziland Court of Appeal resigned in protest at the Government's refusal to accept two rulings that the King had no power to overrule the National Assembly. The judges of the High Court subsequently announced that they would refuse to sit or set dates for hearings, and a strike by members of the legal profession ensued. In April 2003 a report by the International Bar Association attributed the judicial crisis to the lack of clearly defined roles for the executive, legislature and judiciary. In May the Government withdrew a statement in which it had accused the judges of being under external influence. In mid-September 2004 the Government reversed its position on the rulings which had provoked the crisis. Hearings were scheduled to resume at the Court of Appeal in November on condition that those evicted were allowed to return to their villages.

Meanwhile, in June 2001 King Mswati provoked international criticism by promulgating a decree that, it was claimed, effectively amounted to the declaration of a state of emergency; the legislation ensured that no person or body, including the courts, had the authority to challenge the King, prevented newspapers from challenging publishing bans, allowed the King to appoint judges and traditional chiefs personally, and made ridiculing or impersonating the King a criminal offence. Opposition groups in Swaziland condemned the decree as reinforcing tyrannical rule, and criticized the international community's lack of interest in the country's political situation. The King revoked the decree in July, in response to international diplomatic pressure, notably a threat by the USA to impose economic sanctions. However, at the same time the King issued a new decree that retained certain sections of the original decree, including a provision allowing the detention of Swazi citizens without the option of bail for some offences.

In August 2001 the Constitutional Review Commission submitted its report, which recommended that the King's powers be extended and political parties remain outlawed, but stated that the introduction of a bill of rights that was not in conflict with Swazi laws and customs was a possibility. In February 2002 a 15-member committee, appointed by the King, began drafting a new constitution; PUDEMO criticized the Government for allegedly manipulating the Commission's report and selecting members of the drafting committee who were sympathetic to government policy. In May Prince David, the King's brother, and Chairman of the constitution-drafting committee, announced a new draft constitution, which, *inter alia*, envisaged the retention of the Tinkhundla system for forthcoming elections to the National Assembly.

King Mswati introduced the Internal Security Bill in June 2002, intended to suppress political dissent. It provided variously for fines and prison sentences for those found guilty of carrying or wearing banners or flags of banned political formations, or of participating in mass strikes or boycotts. Training abroad to commit acts of insurgency in Swaziland would be punishable by up to 20 years' imprisonment. The bill was severely criticized by the SFTU, PUDEMO and various foreign governments, which considered it to be inconsistent with the bill of rights and the proposed constitutional reform.

In October 2002 the King was the subject of a legal challenge from the mother of a girl chosen to be his 10th wife; the woman alleged that her daughter had been abducted by two of the King's emissaries. However, she withdrew the case in early November, when her daughter stated that she had no objection to becoming a queen. Further controversy arose over the King's order for a private aircraft costing around US $45m. The National Assembly voted against the purchase of the aircraft in November, after it was revealed that development funds from international donors had been diverted to pay for it, but the vote was overruled by the Council of Ministers. The European Union (EU) had previously suspended financial aid to the country over the issue in September 2002. In August 2003 the Prime Minister denied newspaper reports that claimed that the aircraft had been purchased. In January 2004 the King's request for funds to construct a new palace for each of his wives provoked further controversy.

In May 2003 King Mswati announced the dissolution of the National Assembly. Pending elections to a new Assembly, scheduled for October, a council, styled the King's Order-in-Council, was charged with debating and enacting legislation in collaboration with the King. The elections to the National Assembly, duly held in October, were reportedly marked by a very low turn-out, many voters having apparently heeded an appeal by pro-democracy groups for a boycott of the polls. Although several members of proscribed political organizations stood as independent candidates, a Commonwealth monitoring team subsequently declared that the elections had been largely meaningless, in view of the lack of basic democratic freedoms that prevailed in Swaziland. In November the King appointed Themba Dlamini, a former incumbent on various parastatal bodies and a close associate of the royal family, as the new Prime Minister. At the same time, the King accepted a new draft constitution that, observers noted, safeguarded many of the monarchy's existing prerogatives. Among the provisions of the proposed new basic law was that the King should remain the head of the executive and retain responsibility for appointing the Prime Minister. He would, furthermore, retain a power of veto over any bill that received parliamentary approval. However, the draft Constitution did propose the removal of the King's power to rule by decree and provided for the replacement of the Court of Appeal by a new Supreme Court as Swaziland's highest judicial body.

Meanwhile, in March 2004 Marwick Khumalo resigned as Speaker of the National Assembly and was replaced, in May, by Charles S'gayoyo Magongo. Khumalo claimed that he had been forced to resign, owing to his opposition to government attempts to purchase a private aircraft for the King. In May the National Assembly voted to suspend itself in protest at the Government's stated intention to review the Industrial Court's ruling that the Clerk of Parliament had been illegally dismissed by the previous Prime Minister and should be reinstated. Also in May the National Constituent Assembly (NCA—a pressure group composed of churches, political parties, labour and human rights organizations) announced a legal challenge to what it claimed was the King's intention of promulgating the proposed new Constitution by decree. In mid-June the NCA petitioned the High Court, demanding that the constitution-drafting committee should be required to hold public hearings and receive submissions from interested parties. The High Court agreed that it would hear the petition in August, although no date was fixed.

In January 2005 the SFTU commenced a two-day general strike in protest at the proposed constitutional reform, which it maintained entrenched the power of the monarchy. The new Constitution was finally approved by a joint sitting of the Senate and the National Assembly in early June. It was ratified by King Mswati on 26 July and came into effect on 7 February 2006. The Constitution was viewed as being socially progressive, according greater rights to women—legally recognized as adults for the first time—and guaranteeing the right to primary education, but politically conservative: executive power was concentrated in the King and the Tinkhundla remained as the basis of the parliamentary system; the King would also continue to appoint the Prime Minister and the Cabinet, Chiefs and High Court judges and could dissolve the legislature. A bill of rights guaranteed freedom of assembly and speech; however, these rights could be suspended by the King if he considered it to be in the public interest. Furthermore, while there existed provision for the judiciary to interpret the Constitution, ultimate authority was vested with the King. There also remained considerable ambiguity regarding the legality of political parties, although the Constitution stated that the 'people of Swaziland have a right to be heard through and represented by their own freely chosen representatives in the government of the country'.

In late February 2006 the King effected a reshuffle of the Cabinet. Moses Mathendele Dlamini was appointed Minister of Foreign Affairs and Trade, replacing Mabili Dlamini, who assumed the housing and urban development portfolio vacated by Dumsile Sukati. Sukati was appointed Minister of Natural Resources and Energy, replacing Mfofmfo Nkambule, who took over the health and social welfare portfolio from Chief Sipho Shongwe. A minor government reshuffle was carried out in May in which Nkambule was replaced by Njabulo Mabuza.

In September 2006 the Deputy Prime Minister, Albert Shabangu, collapsed and died at his private residence in Mhlosheni, in the south of the country. He was accorded a state funeral in early October, having served the Government as a cabinet minister for over 15 years. Later that month it was announced that Constance Simelane, hitherto the Minister of Education, had been appointed as the new Deputy Prime Minister. Themba Msibi assumed responsibility for the education portfolio, while Magongo replaced him as Minister of Public Service and Information.

In February 2008 six opposition parties announced that they would boycott forthcoming legislative elections, which were scheduled for later that year, and demanded the introduction of a system of multi-party democracy. A spokesman for PUDEMO stated that it was important to 'deny the state legitimacy' by refusing to take part. In April the Deputy President of that party, Gabriel Mkhumane, was shot dead in South Africa, where he had lived in exile for 24 years. The following month the Elections and Boundaries Commission announced that voter registration had begun for the election, which was scheduled for September, although political parties were still effectively proscribed. In June the King dissolved the House of Assembly (as the lower legislative body had been redesignated in the 2006 Constitution), and on 19 September the election proceeded as scheduled, despite demonstrations by pro-democracy activists who denounced it as a farce. The SFTU organized a march in Mbabane, and a further demonstration was planned on the border with South Africa, however this was suppressed by the security forces and a number of activists were arrested. In the same month an extravagant ceremony was held to celebrate the King's 40th birthday and the 40th anniversary of Swaziland's independence.

Following the announcement of the election results there were reports that two men had been killed, and a third injured, when a bomb exploded on a road close to the King's Lozitha palace, east of Mbabane: it was believed that the men were planning to detonate the bomb near the royal palace but that it exploded prematurely. The injured man, a South African national, was taken into custody and charged with treason, while a fourth man who was involved managed to escape; one of those who died in the attempted bombing, Jack Govender, was a founding member of the anti-royalist Swaziland Solidarity Network (SSN). In October 2008 the King reappointed Sibusiso Dlamini as Prime Minister, and a new Council of Ministers was subsequently formed with a number of new appointments, including Themba Masuku as Deputy Prime Minister. Lutfo Dlamini succeeded Moses Mathendele Dlamini as Minister of Foreign Affairs, and Benedict Xaba replaced Mabuza as Minister of Health, while Princess Tsandzile (one of five female appointments to the Cabinet) was named as Minister of Natural Resources and Energy, in place of Sukati.

In November 2008 the President of PUDEMO, Mario Masuku, was arrested and charged under new anti-terrorism laws in connection with the attempted bomb attack on the royal palace. In the same month Prime Minister Dlamini formally listed four opposition organizations (PUDEMO, the Swaziland Liberation Army, the SSN and SWAYOCO) as terrorist groups. The Attorney-General, Majahenkhaba Dlamini, also warned journalists that reports in which they criticized the Government could lead to their arrest under the Suppression of Terrorism Act 2008. In February 2009 SWAYOCO Secretary-General, Thabile Zwane, was arrested for alleged terrorist activities while Mario Masuku was still awaiting trial after several months in custody.

Swaziland has been severely affected by the HIV/AIDS pandemic. The Government has been criticized for its reluctance to confront the problem directly; proposed measures have included sterilizing or branding those infected with HIV. In an attempt to prevent the spread of the disease, in September 2001 the Government ordered women aged 18 years or younger to remain celibate and avoid shaking hands with men for a period of five years. In February 2004 the Prime Minister declared a national disaster, brought about by Swaziland's high incidence of HIV infection in combination with drought, land degradation and rising poverty. Following a visit to the country, in mid-March 2006 the UN Secretary-General's special envoy reported that 42.6% of the adult population (aged between 15 and 49 years) was infected with HIV; a recent survey of pregnant women between the ages of 25 and 29 had indicated a prevalence rate of 56.3%. It was anticipated that by 2010 orphaned children would represent between 10% and 15% of the population. New legislation was proposed in April 2006 to prohibit direct or indirect discrimination against employees; most notably, the bill contained a clause relating to discrimination against those infected with HIV. In August 2007 a new national health policy was launched, aimed at addressing the decline in the quality of health care services by 2015 and limiting the spread of HIV/AIDS. In January 2008 nurses voted to begin strike action in protest over the Government's failure to address poor working conditions and delayed payment of salaries. Meanwhile, in September 2007 it was announced that a new, decentralized strategy for combating HIV/AIDS was to be implemented, affording communities the responsibility of determining the action required in that area. Basic centres were to be established, from which a secretary, heading an HIV/AIDS committee elected from the community, would identify those in need of specific medical care and co-ordinate aid response from non-governmental organizations.

During the apartheid era Swaziland pursued a policy of dialogue and co-operation with South Africa. In 1982 the two countries signed a secret non-aggression pact; several members of the African National Congress of South Africa (ANC), which had increasingly used Swaziland as a base for guerrilla attacks into South Africa, were subsequently arrested and expelled from Swaziland. The signing, in March 1984, of the Nkomati accord between South Africa and Mozambique (which banned both countries from harbouring dissidents) led many ANC members to flee from Mozambique to neighbouring Swaziland. Following the murder, in 1984, of the deputy chief of the Swazi security police, the Government initiated a campaign to arrest all ANC fugitives remaining in the country (the ANC denied involvement in the killing). In 1986 leading Swazi politicians expressed opposition to the imposition of economic sanctions against South Africa, owing to the dependence of Swaziland's own economy on that country. Detentions and deportations of ANC members by the Swazi Government continued, while several suspected ANC members were abducted by South African security forces or killed in Swaziland by gunmen who were widely assumed to be South African. Following the legalization of the ANC in 1990, the Swazi Prime Minister, Obed Dlamini, pledged to conduct an inquiry (which, however, he failed to initiate) into state operations against ANC members. Formal diplomatic relations were established in 1993. From the late 1990s prominent South African organizations, including the ANC and COSATU, expressed support for the SFTU's demands for political reform, prompting the Swazi Government to protest of interference in its domestic affairs. In April 1995 the South African Government announced that it had rejected a long-standing claim by Swaziland to a region in the Mpumalanga province (formerly Eastern Transvaal). However, King Mswati declared in a letter to South African President, Thabo Mbeki, in early 2001 that he had not abandoned his intention to reincorporate parts of Mpumalanga and KwaZulu/Natal provinces into Swaziland. In 2003 the Chairperson of the Swaziland Border Adjustment Committee, Prince Khuzulwandle, criticized Mbeki for declining to discuss realignments of the border. During pro-democracy protests in April 2007 at five crossing points on the border with South Africa, at least six PUDEMO members were arrested.

Following the ratification of the October 1992 peace accord in Mozambique (q.v.), an agreement signed by the Governments of Swaziland and Mozambique and the office of the UN High Commissioner for Refugees in August 1993 provided for the repatriation of some 24,000 Mozambican nationals from Swaziland. In December the number of Swazi troops deployed at the border with Mozambique was increased, following clashes between Swazi and Mozambican forces in the region. Mozambique subsequently protested at alleged border incursions by members of the Swazi armed forces. In early 1994 discussions took place between Swazi and Mozambican officials to seek mutually satisfactory arrangements for the joint patrol of the border, and in 1995 it was announced that the Mhlumeni border post, closed since the 1970s, would reopen as the second official transit point between the two countries. In September 1997, during the first visit to Swaziland made by a Mozambican Prime Minister, a bilateral extradition agreement was signed, with the aim of reducing cross-border crime. In December 1999 the Swazi authorities expelled some 500 Mozambican citizens who had been declared illegal immigrants. In the following month a campaign began to encourage Mozambicans living in Swaziland to register for military service there.

Government

The Constitution of 7 February 2006 vests supreme executive power in the hereditary King, who is the Head of State, and provides for a bicameral legislature, comprising a House of

Assembly and a Senate. The functions of the legislature are confined to debating government proposals and advising the King. Executive power is exercised through the Cabinet, which is appointed by the King.

The Parliament of Swaziland consists of the Senate, comprising not more than 31 members (of whom 20 are appointed by the King—at least eight of these are women—and 10 elected by the House of Assembly, one-half of which are women) and the House of Assembly, which comprises not more than 76 members. Of these, 60 are directly elected from candidates nominated by traditional local councils, known as Tinkhundla, and 10 are appointed by the King, one-half of which are women. Additionally one women is selected from each of the four regions of Swaziland and the Attorney-General is also an ex officio member.

The King appoints the Prime Minister and the Cabinet and has the power to dissolve the bicameral legislature. The Swazi National Council (Sibaya) constitutes the highest policy and advisory council of the nation and functions as the annual general meeting of the nation. A Council of Chiefs, composed of 12 chiefs drawn from the four regions of Swaziland advises the King on customary issues and any matter relating to chieftancy.

Defence

The Umbutfo Swaziland Defence Force, created in 1973, totalled 2,657 regular troops in November 1983. Swaziland also has a paramilitary police force. Military service is compulsory and lasts for two years. Of total current expenditure by the central Government in 2001/02, E 168m. (6.6%) was allocated to defence.

Economic Affairs

In 2007, according to estimates by the World Bank, Swaziland's gross national income (GNI), measured at average 2005–07 prices, was US $2,951m., equivalent to $2,580 per head (or $4,930 per head on an international purchasing-power parity basis). During 2000–07, it was estimated, the population increased at an average annual rate of 1.3%, while gross domestic product (GDP) per head declined, in real terms, by an average of 0.1% per year. Overall GDP increased, in real terms, at an average annual rate of 1.2% in 2000–07; growth in 2007 was 2.4%.

Agriculture (including forestry) contributed 8.1% of GDP in 2007, according to World Bank estimates. About 31.6% of the labour force were employed in the agricultural sector in mid-2005 (including subsistence farming), according to FAO. However, according to IMF estimates, at June 2005 only 20.8% of those in paid employment were engaged in agriculture. The principal cash crops are sugar cane (sugar accounted for 14.1% of domestic export earnings in 2007), cotton, citrus fruits, pineapples and maize. Tobacco and rice are also cultivated. Livestock-rearing is traditionally important. Substantial food imports were required in 2004, owing to low cereal production caused by drought. An estimated 70% of the maize crop was destroyed by drought in February 2005. At that time the UN World Food Programme was supplying food aid to some 260,000 people. Commercial forestry (which employs a significant proportion of the population) provides wood for the manufacture of pulp. During 2000–07, according to the World Bank, agricultural GDP increased by an average of 0.5% per year. Agricultural GDP declined by 2.4% in 2006, but increased by 2.8% in 2007.

According to the World Bank, industry (including mining, manufacturing, construction and power) contributed 46.4% of GDP in 2007, and engaged 28.8% of those in paid employment in June 2005. During 2000–06, according to the World Bank, industrial GDP increased at an average annual rate of 0.4%. Industrial GDP declined by 0.8% in 2005, but increased by 2.4% in 2006.

Mining contributed 0.4% of GDP in 2006 and engaged 1.3% of those in paid employment in June 2005. Swaziland has extensive reserves of coal, much of which is exported. Asbestos is also an important mineral export. In addition, Swaziland has reserves of tin, kaolin, talc, iron ore, pyrophyllite and silica. During 2000–04, according to the IMF, mining GDP declined by an average of 5.0% per year; mining GDP declined by 20.2% in 2003 but increased by 9.0% in 2004.

Manufacturing contributed 39.9% of GDP in 2006, and in June 2005 engaged 21.2% of those in paid employment. Manufacturing is mainly based on the processing of agricultural, livestock and forestry products. During 2000–07, according to the World Bank, manufacturing GDP increased at an average annual rate of 1.7%. Manufacturing GDP increased by 3.0% in 2007.

Swaziland imports most of its energy requirements from South Africa. The Swazi Government aimed to increase domestic energy output to cover approximately 50% of the country's needs, following the construction of a hydroelectric power station on the Maguga Dam, which began operations in 2002. However, in 2005 80.7% of total electrical energy generated and imported was obtained from South Africa and Mozambique, compared with 77.1% in 2002. Mineral fuels and lubricants accounted for an estimated 15.6% of imports in 2007. In the mid-2000s plans were being discussed for the construction of a 100-MW thermal power station in the Lowveld using bagasse, the waste left from processing sugar cane.

The services sector contributed 45.5% of GDP in 2007 and engaged 50.3% of those in paid employment in June 2005. According to the World Bank, the GDP of the services sector increased by an average of 7.4% per year in 2000–07. Services GDP increased by 2.3% in 2007.

In 2007, according to the IMF, Swaziland recorded a visible trade deficit of US $271.1m., while there was a deficit of $65.5m. on the current account of the balance of payments. In 2007 the principal source of imports was South Africa (92.9%) which was also the principal market for exports (45.2%); Botswana and the United Kingdom were also important markets. The principal imports in 2007 were machinery and transport equipment, food and live animals, basic manufactures and mineral fuels and lubricants; the principal exports in 2007 were chemicals and chemical products, and food and live animals.

In the financial year ending 31 March 2008 there was an estimated overall budgetary surplus of E 1,348m. Swaziland's external debt totalled US $544.4m. at the end of 2006, of which $493.7m. was long-term public debt. In that year the cost of debt-servicing was equivalent to 1.8% of the value of exports of goods and services. In 2000–07, according to the African Development Bank, annual inflation averaged 6.5%; consumer prices increased by an average of 6.9% in 2007. It was estimated that 40% of the labour force were unemployed in 1995.

Swaziland is a member of the Common Market for Eastern and Southern Africa (see p. 215), of the Southern African Development Community (SADC, see p. 400) and of the Southern African Customs Union (SACU), which also includes Botswana, Lesotho, Namibia and South Africa.

Swaziland's economy is vulnerable to fluctuations in international prices for some major exports, including sugar, as well as to the effects of unfavourable weather conditions. In addition, prevailing economic conditions in neighbouring South Africa have a pronounced impact on the Swazi economy: although Swaziland may determine the exchange rate of its currency, the lilangeni, this has remained at par with the South African rand. At the beginning of 2004 the new Prime Minister, Themba Dlamini, made a number of proposals for the improvement of Swaziland's economic prospects, including a review of government spending, the encouragement of foreign investment and the promotion of small businesses; however, any progress was expected to be slow. The removal in January 2005 of World Trade Organization quotas for textile exports to the USA brought Swaziland into direct competition with exporters based in Asia, while the EU's proposals to reduce the price at which it purchased sugar from Swaziland by some 36% by 2007 was expected to cost the industry some E 370m. during 2007–10. The EU did, however, allocate €100m. to assist Swazi farmers in diversifying into alternative crops, such as cotton, while the Government continued to encourage farmers to grow geraniums for their essential oils. Furthermore, in early 2008 the European Commission granted Swazi sugar producers €15m. to protect them from the lowering in prices for that commodity. The significant decline in export revenues, owing to the strength of the currency, the decline in textile production and the lowering of sugar prices resulted in GDP growth averaging only some 2.0% per year in 2000–07, and the poor performance has been compounded by lack of investment and slow implementation of economic reforms, which have done little to reduce unemployment and poverty levels. However, the IMF praised the Government for its fiscal restraint, the result of which were budget surpluses in 2006 and 2007. Nevertheless, inflation continued to increase during 2008 as a result of high food and petroleum prices, and the medium-term prospects of the Swazi economy were also seriously threatened by the global financial crisis that began in 2008 and the extremely high rate of HIV/AIDS infection among the labour force. Meanwhile, the securing of significant amounts of much-needed foreign investment in Swaziland remained dependent on a satisfactory political settlement. The IMF forecast GDP growth of 0.5% in 2009 and 2.6% in 2010.

SWAZILAND

Education

Education is neither free nor compulsory in Swaziland. Primary education begins at six years of age and lasts for seven years; the Government announced in the 2001 budget that it hoped to provide free primary education in the future. Secondary education begins at 13 years of age and lasts for up to five years, comprising a first cycle of three years and a second of two years. According to UNESCO estimates, in 2005/06 76% of children in the relevant age-group (males 76%; females 77%) were enrolled at primary schools, while in that year secondary enrolment included 33% of children in the appropriate age-group (males 31%; females 35%). In 2005/06 5,692 students were enrolled at the University of Swaziland, which has campuses at Luyengo and Kwaluseni; there are also a number of other institutions of higher education. According to the IMF, of total expenditure by the central Government in the financial year 2004/05, E 27.9m. (5.0%) was for education.

Public Holidays

2009: 1 January (New Year's Day), 10–13 April (Easter), 19 April (Birthday of King Mswati), 25 April (National Flag Day), 1 May (Workers' Day), 21 May (Ascension Day), 22 July (Birthday of the late King Sobhuza), 6 September (Somhlolo—Independence—Day), 24 October (UN Day), 25–26 December (Christmas and Boxing Day).

2010: 1 January (New Year's Day), 2–5 April (Easter), 19 April (Birthday of King Mswati), 25 April (National Flag Day), 1 May (Workers' Day), 13 May (Ascension Day), 22 July (Birthday of the late King Sobhuza), 6 September (Somhlolo—Independence—Day), 24 October (UN Day), 25–26 December (Christmas and Boxing Day).

The Incwala and Umhlanga Ceremonies are held in December or January, and August or September (respectively), but the exact dates are variable each year.

Statistical Survey

Source (unless otherwise stated): Central Statistical Office, POB 456, Mbabane; internet www.gov.sz/home.asp?pid=75.

Area and Population

AREA, POPULATION AND DENSITY

Area (sq km)	17,363*
Population (census results)†	
11–12 May 1997	929,718
11 May 2007 (provisional)‡§	
Males	460,498
Females	493,026
Total	953,524
Population (UN estimate at mid-year)‖	
2008	1,168,000
Density (per sq km) at mid-2008	67.3

* 6,704 sq miles.
† Excluding absentee workers.
‡ Source: UN, *Population and Vital Statistics Report*.
§ Population data are *de jure*, although the totals were the subject of some dispute on publication; in early 2009 the Ministry of Economic Planning and Development published the State of Swaziland Population Report which contained a revised population estimate of 1,018,449 for 2007.
‖ Source: UN, *World Population Prospects: The 2008 Revision*.

ETHNIC GROUPS
(census of August 1986)

Swazi	661,646
Other Africans	14,468
European	1,825
Asiatic	228
Other non-Africans	412
Mixed	2,403
Unknown	77
Total	**681,059**

REGIONS
(population at census of May 2007; provisional figures)

	Area (sq km)	Population	Density (per sq km)
Hhohho	3,569	263,761	73.9
Manzini	5,945	293,260	49.3
Shiselweni	4,070	202,686	49.8
Lebombo	3,779	193,817	51.3
Total	**17,363**	**953,524**	**54.9**

Source: UN 2010 World Population and Housing Census Programme.

PRINCIPAL TOWNS
(population at census of May 1997)

Mbabane (capital)	57,992		Manzini	25,571

Mid-2007 (incl. suburbs, UN estimate): Mbabane 78,000 (Source: UN, *World Urbanization Prospects: The 2007 Revision*).

BIRTHS AND DEATHS
(annual averages, UN estimates)

	1990–1995	1995–2000	2000–05
Birth rate (per 1,000)	40.0	34.3	31.9
Death rate (per 1,000)	8.8	10.4	15.4

Source: UN, *World Population Prospects: The 2008 Revision*.

Life expectancy (years at birth, WHO estimates): 42.1 (males 41.3; females 42.7) in 2006 (Source: WHO, *World Health Statistics*).

EMPLOYMENT
(persons in paid employment at June)

	2003	2004	2005
Agriculture, hunting, forestry and fishing	21,491	20,804	19,955
Mining and quarrying	1,153	1,407	1,283
Manufacturing	19,485	19,874	20,272
Electricity, gas and water	1,418	1,389	859
Construction	4,824	5,293	5,115
Distribution	9,021	9,988	11,454
Transportation	2,491	2,265	3,007
Finance	6,422	5,202	6,430
Social services	26,758	27,247	27,228
Total employed	**93,063**	**93,469**	**95,603**

Source: IMF, *Kingdom of Swaziland: Selected Issues and Statistical Appendix* (March 2008).

Mid-2005 (estimates in '000): Agriculture, etc. 115; Total labour force 370 (Source: FAO).

SWAZILAND

Health and Welfare

KEY INDICATORS

Total fertility rate (children per woman, 2006)	3.6
Under-5 mortality rate (per 1,000 live births, 2006)	164
HIV/AIDS (% of persons aged 15–49, 2007)	26.1
Physicians (per 1,000 head, 2004)	0.16
Health expenditure (2006): US $ per head (PPP)	353
Health expenditure (2006): % of GDP	5.9
Health expenditure (2006): public (% of total)	62.0
Access to water (% of persons, 2006)	60
Access to sanitation (% of persons, 2006)	50
Human Development Index (2006): ranking	141
Human Development Index (2006): value	0.542

For sources and definitions, see explanatory note on p. vi.

Agriculture

PRINCIPAL CROPS
('000 metric tons)

	2005	2006	2007
Maize	74.5	67.1*	68.0*
Potatoes*	6.7	6.0	6.0
Sweet potatoes*	2.6	2.3	2.3
Sugar cane	5,200	5,000	5,000*
Groundnuts, with shell*	4.3	4.1	4.1
Tomatoes*	3.6	3.4	3.4
Oranges*	40	36	36
Grapefruit and pomelos*	40	37	37
Pineapples*	32	31	31

* FAO estimate(s).

Aggregate production ('000 metric tons, may include official, semi-official or estimated data): Total cereals 76 in 2005, 68 in 2006, 69 in 2007; Total roots and tubers 56 in 2005, 54 in 2006, 54 in 2007; Total vegetables (incl. melons) 11 in 2005, 11 in 2006, 11 in 2007; Total fruits (excl. melons) 119 in 2005, 108 in 2006, 108 in 2007.

Source: FAO.

LIVESTOCK
('000 head, year ending September, FAO estimates)

	2005	2006	2007
Horses	1.4	1.4	1.5
Asses	14.8	n.a.	n.a.
Cattle	615	580	585
Pigs	37	30	30
Sheep	27	27	28
Goats	274	275	276
Chickens	3,600	3,200	3,200

Source: FAO.

LIVESTOCK PRODUCTS
('000 metric tons, FAO estimates)

	2005	2006	2007
Cattle meat	14.3	12.5	12.5
Goat meat	1.9	1.9	1.9
Pig meat	1.4	1.2	1.2
Chicken meat	7.4	5.0	5.0
Cows' milk	38.7	37.5	39.0

Source: FAO.

Forestry

ROUNDWOOD REMOVALS
('000 cubic metres, excl. bark, FAO estimates)

	2005	2006	2007
Sawlogs, veneer logs and logs for sleepers	260	260	260
Other industrial wood	70	70	70
Fuel wood	560	996	1,012
Total	890	1,326	1,342

Source: FAO.

SAWNWOOD PRODUCTION
('000 cubic metres, incl. railway sleepers, FAO estimates)

	1995	1996	1997
Total (all coniferous)	90	100	102

1998–2007: Production assumed to be unchanged from 1997 (FAO estimates).

Source: FAO.

Fishing

(metric tons, live weight)

	1999	2000*	2001*
Capture	70*	70	70
Aquaculture	61	69	72
Common carp	18	20	20
Mozambique tilapia	20	25	25
Redbreast tilapia	12	13	15
North African catfish	5	6	6
Red claw crayfish	6	5	6
Total catch	131*	139	142

* FAO estimate(s).

2002–06 (metric tons, live weight, FAO estimate): Capture 70.

Source: FAO.

Mining

(metric tons, unless otherwise indicated)

	2005	2006	2007*
Coal	220,000	310,570	241,283
Ferrovanadium	345	491	500
Quarrystone ('000 cu m)	567	535	208

* Estimated production.

Source: US Geological Survey.

Industry

SELECTED PRODUCTS

	2003	2004	2005
Raw sugar ('000 metric tons)*	616	594	653
Electrical energy (million kWh)	475	475	475

* Source: International Sugar Organization (London).

Source: UN, *Industrial Commodity Statistics Yearbook*.

Wood pulp ('000 metric tons, FAO estimates): 167.7 in 2003; 180.6 in 2004; 172.0 in 2005; 167.0 in 2006; 172.0 in 2007 (Source: FAO).

SWAZILAND

Statistical Survey

Finance

CURRENCY AND EXCHANGE RATES

Monetary Units
100 cents = 1 lilangeni (plural: emalangeni).

Sterling, Dollar and Euro Equivalents (31 December 2008)
£1 sterling = 13.5648 emalangeni;
US $1 = 9.3050 emalangeni;
€1 = 12.9498 emalangeni;
100 emalangeni= £7.37 = $10.75 = €7.72.

Average Exchange Rate (emalangeni per US $)
2006   6.772
2007   7.045
2008   8.261

Note: The lilangeni is at par with the South African rand.

BUDGET
(million emalangeni, year ending 31 March)

Revenue*	2004/05	2005/06	2006/07
Tax revenue	4,627.8	5,189.5	7,683.3
Taxes on net income and profits.	1,164.0	1,267.4	1,534.0
Companies	324.0	472.5	598.0
Individuals	742.0	761.7	891.9
Non-resident dividends and interest	98.0	33.3	44.1
Taxes on property	12.0	13.3	17.4
Taxes on goods, services, and international trade	3,445.8	3,894.4	6,118.7
Receipts from Southern African Customs Union	2,772.8	3,101.1	5,321.8
Levies on sugar exports	22.0	21.1	33.1
Hotel and gaming taxes	5.0	7.8	9.6
Sales tax	549.0	734.9	620.1
Licences and other taxes	97.0	29.4	134.0
Other taxes	6.0	14.4	13.3
Other current revenue	98.0	137.3	172.1
Property income	46.0	53.4	88.6
Fees, fines, and non-industrial sales	52.0	83.9	83.5
Total	4,725.8	5,326.8	7,855.4

Expenditure†	2004/05	2005/06	2006/07
Current expenditure	4,295.0	4,416.3	4,661.8
Wages and salaries	1,964.0	2,443.0	2,621.8
Other purchases of goods and services	1,421.0	995.8	1,051.6
Interest payments	168.0	194.4	163.4
Domestic	49.0	31.6	35.3
Foreign	119.0	162.9	128.1
Subsidies and other current transfers	742.0	783.1	824.9
Capital expenditure	1,259.0	1,409.7	1,411.8
Health	82.6	47.8	95.4
Education	27.9	18.9	32.9
Agriculture	104.5	171.6	122.7
Transport and communications	347.6	387.0	381.1
Other	696.4	784.4	779.7
Total	5,554.0	5,826.0	6,073.7

* Excluding grants received (million emalangeni): 116.0 in 2004/05; 172.2 in 2005/06; 165.6 in 2006/07.

† Excluding net lending (million emalangeni): 3.0 in 2004/05; −68.3 in 2005/06; −21.6 in 2006/07.

Source: IMF, *Kingdom of Swaziland: Statistical Appendix* (March 2008).

2007/08 (million emalangeni, year ending 31 March, estimated): Total revenue (incl grants) 8,341; Total expenditure (incl. net lending) 6,993 (Source: IMF, *The Kingdom of Swaziland: 2008 Article IV Consultation-Staff Report; Public Information Notice on the Executive Board Discussion; and Statement by the Executive Director*—November 2008).

INTERNATIONAL RESERVES
(excl. gold, US $ million at 31 December)

	2005	2006	2007
IMF special drawing rights	3.55	3.74	3.96
Reserve position in IMF	9.38	9.87	10.37
Foreign exchange	230.97	358.91	759.86
Total	243.90	372.52	774.19

Source: IMF, *International Financial Statistics*.

MONEY SUPPLY
(million emalangeni at 31 December)

	2005	2006	2007
Currency outside banks	242.08	250.51	248.64
Demand deposits at deposit money banks	1,046.03	1,106.01	1,417.33
Total (incl. others)	1,294.76	1,358.14	1,666.78

COST OF LIVING
(Consumer Price Index; base: 2000 = 100)

	2003	2004	2005
Food	145.7	155.7	169.2
Fuel	114.0	119.2	123.9
Clothing	114.4	115.2	116.9
Housing	105.7	117.5	119.6
All items (incl. others)	129.0	133.5	139.9

Source: ILO.

NATIONAL ACCOUNTS
(million emalangeni at current prices)

Expenditure on the Gross Domestic Product

	2004	2005	2006
Government final consumption expenditure	3,422.6	3,449.1	3,683.9
Private final consumption expenditure	9,496.4	11,665.3	11,397.0
Gross fixed capital formation	2,831.6	2,983.3	2,986.4
Change in inventories	—	—	1.0
Total domestic expenditure	15,750.6	18,097.7	18,068.3
Exports of goods and services	13,279.8	12,062.8	12,009.8
Less Imports of goods and services	13,677.1	13,543.8	13,461.5
Statistical discrepancy	—	—	2,237.5
GDP in purchasers' values	15,353.4	16,616.6	18,854.1
GDP in constant 2000 prices	9,729.4	9,958.7	10,240.2

Gross Domestic Product by Economic Activity

	2004	2005	2006
Agriculture and forestry	1,083.7	1,139.1	1,151.7
Mining	57.0	44.2	56.6
Manufacturing	4,820.2	5,042.0	5,798.3
Electricity and water	124.6	132.1	138.9
Construction	655.8	568.3	588.2
Wholesale and retail trade	813.5	919.8	1,048.6
Hotels and restaurants	206.9	211.4	264.2
Transport and communications	1,004.4	1,086.8	1,131.9
Banking, finance and insurance	382.4	443.6	491.6
Real estate	559.3	597.6	637.3
Government services	2,222.5	2,434.3	2,711.8
Other services	226.5	242.0	251.4
Owner-occupied dwellings	232.7	239.4	248.6
Sub-total	12,389.5	13,100.7	14,519.1
Less Imputed bank service charge	258.4	299.7	332.1
GDP at factor cost	12,131.1	12,800.7	14,186.8
Indirect taxes / *Less* Subsidies	3,222.3	3,816.0	4,667.2
GDP at purchasers' values	15,353.4	16,616.6	18,854.1

Source: IMF, *Kingdom of Swaziland: Statistical Appendix* (March 2008).

SWAZILAND

BALANCE OF PAYMENTS
(US $ million)

	2005	2006	2007
Exports of goods f.o.b.	1,636.5	1,662.9	1,744.8
Imports of goods f.o.b.	−1,894.6	−1,914.9	−2,015.9
Trade balance	−258.1	−252.0	−271.1
Exports of services	282.5	283.3	454.7
Imports of services	−402.8	−373.4	−506.8
Balance on goods and services	−378.4	−342.1	−323.3
Other income received	271.3	241.7	280.8
Other income paid	−93.0	−227.7	−217.0
Balance on goods, services and income	−200.1	−328.1	−259.5
Current transfers received	339.6	366.3	403.5
Current transfers paid	−242.1	−234.8	−209.5
Current balance	−102.6	−196.6	−65.5
Capital account (net)	−3.5	24.8	−30.2
Direct investment abroad	22.0	0.6	−23.2
Direct investment from abroad	−45.9	121.0	37.5
Portfolio investment assets	3.7	−9.5	4.2
Portfolio investment liabilities	0.8	5.5	1.0
Other investment assets	84.3	101.2	357.8
Other investment liabilities	83.1	41.8	53.7
Net errors and omissions	−40.8	−237.8	−700.8
Overall balance	1.1	−148.9	−365.5

Source: IMF, *International Financial Statistics*.

External Trade

PRINCIPAL COMMODITIES
(US $ million)

Imports c.i.f.	2005	2006	2007
Food and live animals	249.0	176.7	212.2
Beverages and tobacco	29.8	22.7	21.9
Crude materials (inedible)	29.6	23.8	24.2
Minerals, fuels and lubricants	190.3	173.7	181.2
Chemicals and chemical products	223.5	175.2	158.0
Basic manufactures	334.5	263.8	199.5
Machinery and transport equipment	339.7	298.7	221.8
Miscellaneous manufactures	196.2	148.1	134.0
Total (incl. others)	1,654.0	1,321.8	1,164.2

Exports f.o.b. (incl. re-exports)	2005	2006	2007
Food and live animals	254.1	388.3	227.0
Beverages and tobacco	11.8	2.4	0.9
Crude materials (inedible)	124.1	140.1	83.6
Minerals, fuels and lubricants	10.3	14.2	13.4
Chemicals and chemical products	769.6	728.6	598.4
Basic manufactures	36.5	31.3	29.4
Machinery and transport equipment	80.8	31.0	30.7
Miscellaneous manufactures	240.4	205.4	97.0
Total (incl. others)	1,569.8	1,544.5	1,082.3

Source: UN, *International Trade Statistics Yearbook*.

PRINCIPAL TRADING PARTNERS
(US $ million)

Imports c.i.f.	2005	2006	2007
China, People's Repub.	38.0	55.5	4.6
Hong Kong	16.7	26.6	10.1
Japan	14.0	22.3	0.3
Korea, Republic	2.3	17.2	0.0
Mozambique	12.9	13.6	2.5
Namibia	0.0	11.7	25.7
Singapore	6.0	31.2	5.6
South Africa	1,460.6	996.4	1,081.1
Switzerland (incl. Liechtenstein)	0.0	21.4	0.0
United Kingdom	4.1	17.3	0.3
USA	7.2	8.3	5.1
Zimbabwe	0.0	14.7	0.0
Total (incl. others)	1,654.0	1,321.8	1,164.2

Exports f.o.b.	2005	2006	2007
Angola	4.7	0.0	0.0
Australia	29.9	220.7	2.9
Botswana	0.1	26.8	342.3
China, People's Repub.	6.7	0.0	0.0
Japan	1.9	0.0	28.6
Kenya	27.7	3.8	0.2
Malawi	3.2	445.8	0.2
Mozambique	84.8	28.3	5.0
Namibia	2.3	25.0	0.8
New Zealand	30.9	4.3	1.3
South Africa	1,171.5	567.4	489.7
Thailand	0.0	91.1	0.0
United Kingdom	5.5	0.2	153.4
USA	117.6	50.6	34.3
Zambia	3.4	24.1	1.5
Total (incl. others)	1,569.8	1,544.5	1,082.3

Source: UN, *International Trade Statistics Yearbook*.

Transport

RAILWAYS
(traffic)

	2002	2003	2004
Net total ton-km (million)	728	726	710

Source: UN, *Statistical Yearbook*.

ROAD TRAFFIC
(motor vehicles in use at 31 December 2003)

Passenger cars	44,113
Buses and coaches	6,424
Lorries and vans	42,576
Motorcycles and mopeds	3,184

Source: International Road Federation, *World Road Statistics*.

CIVIL AVIATION
(traffic on scheduled services)

	1998	1999	2000
Kilometres flown (million)	1	1	2
Passengers carried ('000)	41	12	90
Passenger-km (million)	43	13	68
Total ton-km (million)	4	1	6

Source: UN, *Statistical Yearbook*.

SWAZILAND

Tourism

TOURIST ARRIVALS
(at hotels)

Country of residence	2004	2005	2006
Australia	1,725	1,527	4,192
Mozambique	17,619	15,597	11,702
Portugal	828	733	8,188
South Africa	112,027	99,176	130,783
United Kingdom	17,776	15,737	11,948
Total (incl. others)	352,040	311,656	316,082

Tourism receipts (US $ million, incl. passenger transport): 75.1 in 2004; 78.3 in 2005; 74.1 in 2006.

Source: World Tourism Organization.

Communications Media

	2004	2005	2006
Telephones ('000 main lines in use)	44.5	35.0	44.0
Mobile cellular telephones ('000 subscribers)	145.0	200.0	250.0
Personal computers ('000 in use)	36	n.a.	n.a.
Internet users ('000)	36.0	41.6	42.0

2007: Mobile cellular telephones ('000 subscribers) 380.0.

Source: International Telecommunication Union.

Radio receivers (year ending 31 March 1998): 155,000 in use (Source: UN, *Statistical Yearbook*).

Television receivers (2002): 32,000 in use (Source: International Telecommunication Union).

Daily newspapers (2004): 2 (estimated circulation 27,000) (Source: UNESCO Institute for Statistics).

Education

(2004/05, unless otherwise indicated)

	Institutions	Teachers	Students
Pre-primary	n.a.	451	14,554
Primary	541*	6,741	221,596
Secondary	182*	4,241	71,124
University†	1‡	462§	5,692§

* Figure for 2001/02.
† Figures exclude vocational, technical and teacher-training colleges. In 2000 there were 1,822 students enrolled at these institutions, which numbered 10 in 2003.
‡ Figure for 2000.
§ Figure for 2005/06.

Source: UNESCO Institute for Statistics.

Adult literacy rate (UNESCO estimates): 79.6% (males 80.9%; females 78.3%) in 2000 (Source: UNESCO Institute for Statistics).

Directory

The Constitution

A new Constitution entered into force on 7 February 2006, replacing that of October 1978. It vests supreme executive power in the hereditary King (iNgwenyama—the Lion) and succession is governed by traditional law and custom. In the event of the death of the King, the powers of Head of State are transferred to the constitutional dual monarch, the Queen Mother (Ndlovukazi—Great She Elephant), who is authorized to act as Regent until the designated successor, the Crown Prince (Umntfwana), attains the age of 21.

The Parliament of Swaziland consists of the Senate, comprising not more than 31 members, of whom 20 are appointed by the King—at least eight of these are women—and 10 elected by the House of Assembly, one-half of which are women, and the House of Assembly, which comprises not more than 76 members. Of these, not more than 60 are directly elected from candidates nominated by traditional local councils, known as Tinkhundla, and not more than 10 are appointed by the King, one-half of which are women. Additionally, one woman is selected from each of the four regions of Swaziland and the Attorney-General is also an ex officio member.

The King appoints the Prime Minister and the Cabinet and has the power to dissolve the bicameral legislature. The Swazi National Council (Sibaya) constitutes the highest policy and advisory council of the nation and functions as the annual general meeting of the nation. A Council of Chiefs, composed of 12 chiefs drawn from the four regions of Swaziland, advises the King on customary issues and any matter relating to chieftancy.

The Constitution affirms the fundamental human rights and freedoms of the individual.

The Government

HEAD OF STATE

King: HM King MSWATI III (succeeded to the throne 25 April 1986).

COUNCIL OF MINISTERS
(April 2009)

Prime Minister: BARNABAS SIBUSISO DLAMINI.
Deputy Prime Minister: THEMBA MASUKU.
Minister of Economic Planning and Development: Prince SIHLANGUSEMPHI.
Minister of Finance: MAJOZI SITHOLE.
Minister of Foreign Affairs: LUTFO DLAMINI.
Minister of Public Works and Transport: NTUTHUKO DLAMINI.
Minister of Health: BENEDICT XABA.
Minister of Commerce, Industry and Trade: JABULILE MASHWAMA.
Minister of Agriculture and Co-operatives: MTITI FAKUDZE.
Minister of Local Government and Housing: Pastor LINDIWE GWEBU.
Minister of Education and Training: WILSON NTJANGASE.
Minister of Agriculture: CLEMENT DLAMINI.
Minister of Tourism and Environmental Affairs: MACFORD SIBANDZE.
Minister of Labour and Social Security: PATRICK MAGWEBETANE MAMBA.
Minister of Natural Resources and Energy: Princess TSANDZILE.
Minister of Sports, Culture and Youth Affairs: HLOBSILE NDLOVU.
Minister of Information Communications Technology: NEL'SIWE SHONGWE.
Minister of Home Affairs: Chief MGWAGWA GAMEDZE.
Minister of Public Service: MTITI FAKUDZE.
Minister of Justice: NDUMISO MAMBA.

MINISTRIES

Office of the Prime Minister: POB 433, Swazi Plaza, Mbabane; tel. 4042251; fax 4043943; internet www.gov.sz.

Office of the Deputy Prime Minister: POB 433, Swazi Plaza, Mbabane; tel. 4042723; fax 4044085.

Ministry of Agriculture: POB 162, Mbabane; tel. 4042731; fax 4044700.

Ministry of Commerce, Industry and Trade: Mbabane.

Ministry of Economic Planning and Development: POB 602, Mbabane; tel. 4043765; fax 4042157.

Ministry of Education and Training: POB 39, Mbabane; tel. 4042491; fax 4043880.

Ministry of Finance: POB 443, Mbabane; tel. 4048148; fax 4043187.

Ministry of Foreign Affairs: POB 518, Mbabane; tel. 4042661; fax 4042669.

Ministry of Health: POB 5, Mbabane; tel. 4042431; fax 4042092.

Ministry of Home Affairs: POB 432, Mbabane; tel. 4042941; fax 4044303.

Ministry of Information Communication Technology: Mbabane.

Ministry of Justice: POB 924, Mbabane; tel. 4046010; fax 4043533; e-mail ps@justice.gov.sz.

Ministry of Labour and Social Security: Mbabane.

Ministry of Local Government and Housing: POB 1832, Mbabane; tel. 4041739; fax 4045290.

Ministry of Natural Resources and Energy: POB 57, Mbabane; tel. 4046244; fax 4042436; e-mail nergyswa@realnet.co.sz.

Ministry of Public Service: POB 338, Mbabane; tel. 4042761; fax 4042774.

Ministry of Public Works and Transport: POB 58, Mbabane; tel. 4042321; fax 4042364.

Ministry of Sports, Culture and Youth Affairs: Phutfumani Bldg, Warner St, Mbabane.

Ministry of Tourism and Environmental Affairs: POB 2652, Mbabane; tel. 4046556; fax 4045415; internet www.mintour.gov.sz.

Legislature

SENATE

The Senate comprises not more than 31 members, of whom 20 are appointed by the King—at least eight of these are women—and 10 elected by the House of Assembly, one-half of which are women.

President: MUNTU MSAWANE.

HOUSE OF ASSEMBLY

The House of Assembly comprises not more than 76 members. Of these, not more than 60 are directly elected from candidates nominated by traditional local councils, known as Tinkhundla, and not more than 10 are appointed by the King, one-half of which are women. Additionally, one woman is selected from each of the four regions of Swaziland and the Attorney-General is also an ex officio member. The latest elections to the House of Assembly took place on 19 September 2008.

Speaker: PRINCE GUDUZA.

Election Commission

Elections and Boundaries Commission: POB 4842, Mbabane; tel. 4162813; fax 4161970; five mems; Chair. Chief GIJA DLAMINI.

Political Organizations

Party political activity was banned by royal proclamation in April 1973, and formally prohibited under the 1978 Constitution. Since 1991, following indications that the Constitution was to be revised, a number of political associations have re-emerged. Following the introduction of the new Constitution in February 2006, the legal status of party political activity remained unclear.

African United Democratic Party (AUDP): f. 2006; advocates full democratization of Swaziland; Pres. STANLEY MAUNDZISA; Sec.-Gen. SIBUSISO DLAMINI.

Imbokodvo National Movement (INM): f. 1964 by King Sobhuza II; traditionalist movement, which also advocates policies of devt and the elimination of illiteracy; Leader (vacant).

Ngwane National Liberatory Congress (NNLC): Ilanga Centre, Martin St, Manzini; tel. 5053935; f. 1962 by fmr mems of the SPP; advocates democratic freedoms and universal suffrage, and seeks abolition of the Tinkhundla electoral system; Pres. OBED DLAMINI; Sec.-Gen. DUMISA DLAMINI.

People's United Democratic Movement (PUDEMO): POB 4588, Manzini; tel. and fax 5054181; internet www.members.nbci.com/pudemo; f. 1983; seeks constitutional limitation of the powers of the monarchy; affiliated orgs include the Human Rights Asscn of Swaziland and the Swaziland Youth Congress (SWAYOCO—Pres. ALEX LANGWENYA; Sec.-Gen. KENNETH KUNENE); Pres. MARIO BONGANI MASUKU; Sec. SIKHUMBUZO PHAKATHI.

Swaziland National Front (SWANAFRO): Mbabane; Pres. ELMOND SHONGWE; Sec.-Gen. GLENROSE DLAMINI.

Swaziland Progressive Party (SPP): POB 6, Mbabane; tel. 2022648; f. 1959; Pres. J. J. NQUKU.

Swaziland United Front (SUF): POB 14, Kwaluseni; f. 1962 by fmr mems of the SPP; Leader MATSAPA SHONGWE.

Diplomatic Representation

EMBASSIES IN SWAZILAND

China (Taiwan): Makhosikhosi St, Mbabane; tel. 4044739; fax 4046688; e-mail rocembassy@africaonline.co.sz; Ambassador LEONARD CHAO.

Mozambique: Princess Dr., POB 1212, Mbabane; tel. 4041296; fax 4048482; e-mail moz.high@swazi.net; Ambassador TIAGO CATIGO RECIBO.

South Africa: The New Mall, 2nd Floor, Dr Sishayi Rd, POB 2507, Mbabane; tel. 4044651; fax 4044335; e-mail sahc@africaonline.co.sz; High Commissioner Dr MZOLISI MABUDE.

USA: 2350 Mbabane Pl., Mbabane; tel. 4046441; fax 4045959; internet swaziland.usembassy.gov; Ambassador MAURICE S. PARKER.

Judicial System

Following the introduction of the new Constitution, the Swaziland Superior Court of Judicature comprised the Supreme Court and the High Court, which replaced the existing Court of Appeal and the High Court. The Supreme Court is headed by the Chief Justice and consists of not fewer than four other Justices of the Supreme Court, and is the final Court of Appeal. The High Court consists of the Chief Justice and not fewer than four Justices of the High Court, and has unlimited original jurisdiction in civil and criminal matters.

Religion

About 60% of the adult Swazi population profess Christianity. Under the new Constitution, which came into effect on 7 February 2006, Christianity ceased to be recognized as the country's official religion. At mid-2005 there was a growing Muslim population, reported to number some 10,000 adherents. Most of the remainder of the population hold traditional beliefs.

CHRISTIANITY

At mid-2000 there were an estimated 153,000 Protestants and 466,000 adherents professing other forms of Christianity.

Council of Swaziland Churches: Mandlenkosi Ecumenical House, 142 Esser St, Manzini; POB 1095, Manzini; tel. 5053697; fax 5055841; e-mail c.o.c@africaonline.co.sz; f. 1976; Chair. Bishop MESHACK MABUZA; Gen. Sec. KHANGEZILE I. DLAMINI; 10 mem. churches incl. Roman Catholic, Anglican, Kukhany'okusha Zion Church and Lutheran.

League of African Churches: POB 230, Lobamba; asscn of 48 independent churches; Chair. SAMSON HLATJWAKO.

Swaziland Conference of Churches: 175 Ngwane St, POB 1157, Manzini; tel. and fax 5055253; e-mail scc@africaonline.co.sz; internet www.swazilandcc.org; f. 1929; Pres. Rev. JOHANNES V. MAZIBUKO; Gen. Sec. Rev. S. F. DLAMINI.

The Anglican Communion

Swaziland comprises a single diocese within the Church of the Province of Southern Africa. The Metropolitan of the Province is the Archbishop of Cape Town, South Africa. The Church had some 40,000 members at mid-2000.

Bishop of Swaziland: Rt Rev. MESHACK BOY MABUZA, Bishop's House, Muir St, POB 118, Mbabane; tel. 4043624; fax 4046759; e-mail anglicanchurch@africaonline.co.sz.

The Roman Catholic Church

The Roman Catholic Church was established in Swaziland in 1913. For ecclesiastical purposes, Swaziland comprises the single diocese of Manzini, suffragan to the archdiocese of Pretoria, South Africa. At

31 December 2006 there were an estimated 56,000 adherents in Swaziland (some 5.1% of the total population). The Bishop participates in the Southern African Catholic Bishops' Conference (based in Pretoria, South Africa).

Bishop of Manzini: Rt Rev. LOUIS NCAMISO NDLOVU, Bishop's House, Sandlane St, POB 19, Manzini; tel. 5056900; fax 5056762; e-mail bishop@africaonline.co.sz.

Other Christian Churches

Church of the Nazarene: POB 832, Manzini; tel. 5054732; f. 1910; 7,649 adherents (1994).

The Evangelical Lutheran Church in Southern Africa: POB 117, Mbabane; tel. 4043411; fax 4041847; f. 1902; Bishop JEREMIAH BHEKI MAGAGULA; 2,800 adherents in Swaziland (1994).

Mennonite Central Committee: POB 329, Mbabane; tel. 4042805; fax 4044732; f. 1971; Co-ordinator HLOB'SILE NXUMALO.

The Methodist Church in Southern Africa: POB 42, Mbabane; tel. 6321975; e-mail brianj@bcmc.co.za; internet www.methodist.org.za; f. 1880; Bishop BRIAN C. JENNINGS; 2,578 adherents (1992).

United Christian Church of Africa: POB 1345, Nhlangano; tel. 2022648; f. 1944; Pres. Rev. WELLINGTON B. MKHALIPHI; Founder and Gen. Sec. Dr J. J. NQUKU.

The National Baptist Church, the Christian Apostolic Holy Spirit Church in Zion and the Religious Society of Friends (Quakers) are also active.

BAHÁ'Í FAITH

National Spiritual Assembly: POB 298, Mbabane; tel. 5052689; f. 1960; mems resident in 153 localities.

ISLAM

Ezulwini Islamic Institute: Al Islam Dawah Movement of Swaziland, POB 133, Ezulwini; c. 3,000 adherents (1994).

The Press

PRINCIPAL NEWSPAPERS

The Guardian of Swaziland: POB 4747, Mbabane; tel. 404838; f. 2001; daily newspaper; publ. suspended May 2001, resumed Sept. 2001; Editor THULANI MTHETHWA.

The Swazi News: Sheffield Rd, POB 156, Mbabane; tel. 4042520; fax 4042438; e-mail swazinews@times.co.sz; internet www.times.co.sz; f. 1983; weekly; English; owned by *The Times of Swaziland*; Editor THULANI THWALA; circ. 24,000.

Swazi Observer: Observer House, 3 West St, POB A385, Swazi Plaza, Mbabane; tel. 4049600; fax 4045503; e-mail info@observer.org.sz; internet www.observer.org.sz; f. 1981; owned by Tibiyo Taka Ngwane; Mon.–Sat.; *Weekend Observer* (Sun.); publ. suspended Feb. 2000, resumed March 2001; CEO S. MYZO MAGAGULA; Editor-in-Chief MUSA NDLANGAMANDLA.

Swaziland Today: POB 395, Mbabane; tel. 4041432; fax 4043493; weekly; govt newsletter.

The Times of Swaziland: Sheffield Rd, POB 156, Mbabane; tel. 4042211; fax 4042438; e-mail editor@times.co.sz; internet www.times.co.sz; f. 1897; Mon.–Fri., Sun.; also monthly edn; English; other publs incl. *What's Happening* (tourist interest); Editor MARTIN DLAMINI; circ. 18,000.

PRINCIPAL PERIODICALS

Farming in Swaziland: POB 592, Mbabane; tel. and fax 4041839; e-mail cft@realnet.co.sz; quarterly; Editor CHRISTINA FORSYTH-THOMPSON; circ. 3,000.

The Nation: Mbabane House, 3rd Floor, Mahlokohla St, POB 4547, Mbabane; tel. and fax 4046611; e-mail thenation@realnet.co.sz; f. 1997; monthly; independent news magazine; publ. suspended briefly May 2001; Editor BHEKI MAKHUBU.

Swaziview: Mbabane; tel. 4042716; monthly magazine; general interest; circ. 3,500.

UNISWA Research Journal of Agriculture, Science and Technology: Private Bag 4, Kwaluseni; tel. 5274418; fax 5274428; e-mail research@uniswa.sz; internet www.uniswa.sz; 2 a year; publ. of the Faculties of Agriculture, Health Sciences and Science of the Univ. of Swaziland; Chair. Prof. E. M. OSSOM.

Publishers

Apollo Services (Pty) Ltd: POB 35, Mbabane; tel. 4042711.

GBS Printing and Publishing (Pty) Ltd: POB 1384, Mbabane; tel. 5052779.

Jubilee Printers: POB 1619, Matsaka; tel. 5184557; fax 5184558.

Longman Swaziland (Pty) Ltd: POB 2207, Manzini; tel. 5053891.

Macmillan Boleswa Publishers (Pty) Ltd: POB 1235, Manzini; tel. 5184533; fax 5185247; e-mail macmillan@africaonline.co.sz; f. 1978; textbooks and general; CEO DUSANKA STOJAKOVIC.

Swaziland Printing & Publishing Co Ltd: POB 28, Mbabane; tel. 4042716; fax 4042710.

Whydah Media Publishers Ltd: Mbabane; tel. 4042716; f. 1978.

Broadcasting and Communications

TELECOMMUNICATIONS

MTN Swaziland: Smuts St, POB 5050, H100 Mbabane; tel. 4060000; fax 4046217; e-mail yellohelp@mtn.co.sz; internet www.mtn.co.sz; f. 1998; jt venture between MTN Group, South Africa, and Swaziland Posts and Telecommunications Corpn; operates mobile cellular telephone network; 213,000 subscribers (2005); CEO THEMBA KHUMALO.

Swaziland Posts and Telecommunications Corpn (SPTC): Phutfumani Bldg, Mahlokohla St, POB 125, H100 Mbabane; tel. 4052000; fax 4052001; e-mail info@sptc.co.sz; internet www.sptc.co.sz; f. 1983; Chair. SABELO MASUKU; Man. Dir E. NATHI DLAMINI.

BROADCASTING

Radio

Swaziland Broadcasting and Information Service: POB 338, Mbabane; tel. 4042763; fax 4046953; e-mail sbisnews@africaonline.co.sz; f. 1966; broadcasts in English and siSwati; Dir STAN MOTSA.

Swaziland Commercial Radio (Pty) Ltd: POB 1586, Alberton 1450, South Africa; tel. (11) 4344333; fax (11) 4344777; privately owned commercial service; broadcasts to Southern Africa in English and Portuguese; music and religious programmes; Man. Dir A. DE ANDRADE.

Trans World Radio: POB 64, Manzini; tel. 5052781; fax 5055333; internet www.twr.org; f. 1974; religious broadcasts from five transmitters in 30 languages to Southern, Central and Eastern Africa and to the Far East.

Television

Swaziland Television Authority (Swazi TV): POB A146, Swazi Plaza, Mbabane; tel. 4043036; fax 4042093; e-mail swazitv.eng@africaonline.co.sz; f. 1978; state-owned; broadcasts seven hours daily in English; CEO VUKANI MAZIYA.

Finance

(cap. = capital; res = reserves; dep. = deposits; m. = million; brs = branches; amounts in emalangeni)

BANKING

Central Bank

Central Bank of Swaziland: POB 546, Mahlokohla St, Mbabane; tel. 4082000; fax 4048296; e-mail info@centralbank.org.sz; internet www.centralbank.org.sz; f. 1974; bank of issue; cap. 21.8m., res 31.4m., dep. 1,388.7m. (March 2006); Gov. MARTIN G. DLAMINI; Dep. Gov. S. G. MDLULI.

Commercial Banks

First National Bank of Swaziland Ltd: Sales House Bldg, 2nd Floor, POB 261, Mbabane; tel. 4045401; fax 4044735; e-mail hnsibande@fnb.co.sz; f. 1988; fmrly Meridien Bank Swaziland Ltd; wholly owned by FirstRand Bank Holdings Ltd, Johannesburg; cap. and res 61.5m., dep. 484.5m. (June 2002); Chair. Dr D. M. J. VON WISSEL; Man. Dir I. J. M. LEYENAAR; 7 brs.

Nedbank (Swaziland) Ltd: cnr Plaza-Dr Sishayi St and Bypass Rd, POB 68, Mbabane; tel. 4081000; fax 4044060; e-mail info@nedbank.co.sz; internet www.nedbank.co.sz; f. 1974; fmrly Standard Chartered Bank Swaziland Ltd; 23.1% state-owned; cap. 11.9m., res 134.6m., dep. 1,006.2m. (Dec. 2007); Chair. C. N. MAMBA; Man. Dir AMBROSE DLAMINI; 6 brs and 1 agency.

Development Banks

Standard Bank Swaziland Ltd: Standard House, 1st Floor, Swazi Plaza, POB A294, Mbabane; tel. 4046587; fax 4045899; e-mail standardbankswaziland@iafricaonline.co.sz; internet www.standardbank.co.sz; f. 1988; fmrly Stanbic Bank Swaziland, present name adopted 1997; merged with Barclays Bank of Swaziland in Jan. 1998; 25% state-owned; cap. 14.6m., res 89.3m., dep. 1,454.3m. (Dec.

SWAZILAND — Directory

2005); Chair. R. J. Rossouw (acting); Man. Dir Mervyn Lubbe; 10 brs, 1 agency.

Swaziland Development and Savings Bank (SwaziBank—Libhange LeSive): Engungwini Bldg, Gwamile St, POB 336, Mbabane; tel. 4042551; fax 4041214; e-mail swazibank@swazibank.sz; internet www.swazibank.sz; f. 1965; state-owned; taken over by central bank in 1995; under independent management since 2000; cap. and res 143.0m., total assets 557.9m. (March 2002); Chair. Tom Mbelu; Man. Dir Stanley M. N. Matsebula; 8 brs.

Financial Institution

Swaziland National Provident Fund: POB 1857, Manzini; tel. 5082000; fax 5082001; internet www.snpf.co.sz; f. 1974; provides benefits for employed persons on retirement from regular employment or in the event of becoming incapacitated; employers are required by law to pay a contribution for every eligible staff member; total assets 290m. (June 1996); CEO Prince Lonkhokhela Dlamini.

STOCK EXCHANGE

Swaziland Stock Exchange: Capital Markets Development Unit, Infumbe Bldg, 1st Floor, Warner St, POB 546, Mbabane; tel. 4082164; fax 4049493; e-mail info@ssx.org.sz; internet www.ssx.org.sz; f. 1990 as Swaziland Stock Market (SSM); state-owned; Chair. Martin G. Dlamini.

INSURANCE

Between 1974 and 1999 the state-controlled Swaziland Royal Insurance Corpn (SRIC) operated as the country's sole authorized insurance company, although cover in a number of areas not served by SRIC was available from several specialized insurers. In 1999 it was proposed that legislation would be enacted to end SRIC's monopoly and provide for the company's transfer to private sector ownership. The legislation was adopted as the Insurance Act in 2005.

Insurance Company

Swaziland Royal Insurance Corpn (SRIC): SRIC House, Somhlolo Rd, Gilfillan St, POB 917, H100 Mbabane; tel. 4043231; fax 4046415; e-mail sric@sric.sz; internet www.sric.sz; f. 1974; 41% state-owned, 59% owned by Munich-Reinsurance Co of Africa Ltd, Mutual and Fed. Insurance Co of South Africa Ltd, Swiss Re Southern Africa Ltd, S.A. Eagle Insurance Co Ltd, Old Mutual, and Mutual and Federal; Chair. Dr E. T. Gina; Gen. Man. Zombodze R. Magagula.

Insurance Association

Insurance Brokers' Association of Swaziland (IBAS): POB 222, Mbabane H100; tel. 4043226; fax 4046412; e-mail mzamo_dlamini@aon.co.sz; f. 1983; Chair. Mzamo Elliot Dlamini; 4 mems.

Trade and Industry

GOVERNMENT AGENCIES

Small Enterprise Development Co (SEDCO): POB A186, Swazi Plaza, Mbabane; tel. 4042811; fax 4040723; e-mail business@sedco.co.sz; internet www.sedco.biz; f. 1970; devt agency; supplies workshop space, training and expertise for 165 local entrepreneurs at eight sites throughout the country; CEO Dorrington Matiwane.

Swaziland Investment Promotion Authority (SIPA): Mbandzeni House, 7th Floor, Church St, POB 4194, Mbabane; tel. 4040472; fax 4043374; e-mail info@sipa.org.sz; internet www.sipa.org.sz; f. 1998; Gen. Man. Bhekie R. Dlamini.

DEVELOPMENT ORGANIZATIONS

National Industrial Development Corpn of Swaziland (NIDCS): POB 866, Mbabane; tel. 4043391; fax 4045619; f. 1971; state-owned; administered by Swaziland Industrial Devt Co; Admin. Dir P. K. Thamm.

Swaziland Coalition of Concerned Civic Organisations (SCCCO): Smithco Industrial Centre, Mswati III Ave, 11th St, Matsapha; POB 4173, Mbabane; tel. and fax 5187688; e-mail webmaster@swazicoalition.org.sz; internet www.swazicoalition.org.sz; f. 2003; promotes constitutional democracy, poverty alleviation, fiscal discipline, economic stability, competitive regional and international trade, social justice, and the rule of law; Sec.-Gen. Musa Hlope; 9 mems incl.:

Coordinating Assembly of Non-Governmental Organisations (CANGO): POB A67, Swazi Plaza, Mbabane; tel. 4044721; fax 4045532; e-mail director@cango.org.sz; internet www.cango.org.sz; f. 1983; Exec. Dir Emmanuel Ndlangamandla; over 70 mem. orgs.

Federation of Swaziland Employers and Chamber of Commerce (FSECC): POB 72, Mbabane; tel. 4040768; fax 4090051; e-mail fsecc@business-swaziland.com; internet www.business-swaziland.com; f. 2003 by merger of Fed. of Swaziland Employers (f. 1964) and Swaziland Chamber of Commerce (f. 1916); CEO Zodwa Mabuza; c. 500 mems (2005).

Swaziland Industrial Development Co (SIDC): Dhlan'Ubeka House, 5th Floor, cnr Tin and Walker Sts, POB 866, Mbabane; tel. 4044010; fax 4045619; e-mail info@sidc.co.sz; internet www.sidc.co.sz; f. 1986; 34.9% state-owned; finances private sector projects and promotes local and foreign investment; cap. E24.1m., total assets E178.4m. (June 1999); Chair. Tim Zwane; Man. Dir Tambo Gina.

Swaki (Pty) Ltd: Liqhaga Bldg, 4th Floor, Nkoseluhlaza St, POB 1839, Manzini; tel. 5052693; fax 5052001; e-mail info@swaki.co.sz; jtly owned by SIDC and Kirsh Holdings; comprises a number of cos involved in manufacturing, services and the production and distribution of food.

Swaziland Solidarity Network (SSN): c/o COSATU House, 3rd Floor, 1–5 Leyds St, Braamfontein, South Africa; POB 1027, Johannesburg 2000, South Africa; tel. (11) 3393621; fax (11) 3394244; e-mail ssnnetwork@gmail.org.za; internet www.swazisolidarity.org; f. 1997; umbrella org. promoting democracy; incorporates mems from Swaziland and abroad incl. PUDEMO, SWAYOCO, and the Swaziland Democratic Alliance (f. 1999); also incl., from South Africa, the ANC, SACP and COSATU.

Tibiyo Taka Ngwane (Bowels of the Swazi Nation): POB 181, Kwaluseni, Manzini; tel. 5184306; fax 5184399; internet www.tibiyo.com; f. 1968; national devt agency, with investment interests in all sectors of the economy; participates in domestic and foreign jt investment ventures; total assets: E604m. (1999); Chair. Prince Mangaliso; Man. Dir Ndumiso Mamba.

CHAMBERS OF COMMERCE

Sibakho Chamber of Commerce: POB 2016, Manzini; tel. and fax 5057347.

Swaziland Chamber of Commerce and Industry: see Fed. of Swaziland Employers and Chamber of Commerce.

INDUSTRIAL AND TRADE ASSOCIATIONS

National Agricultural Marketing Board: POB 4261, Manzini; tel. 5055314; fax 5054072; internet www.namboard.co.sz; Chair. Dr Micah B. Masuku; CEO Obed Hlongwane.

National Maize Corpn: POB 158, Manzini; tel. 5187432; fax 5184461; f. 1985.

Swaziland Citrus Board: Sokhamila Bldg, cnr Dzeliwe and Mdada Sts, POB 343, Mbabane H100; tel. 4044266; fax 4043548; e-mail citrus@realnet.co.sz; f. 1969; Chair. H. C. Noddeboe.

Swaziland Commercial Board: POB 509, Mbabane; tel. 4042930; Man. Dir J. M. D. Fakudze.

Swaziland Cotton Board: POB 220, Manzini; tel. and fax 5052775; e-mail dlaminiaa@gov.sz; f. 1967; CEO Tom Jele.

Swaziland Dairy Board: Enguleni Bldg, 3rd Floor, 287 Mahleka St, POB 2975, Manzini; tel. 5058262; fax 5058260; e-mail ceo-swazidairy@africaonline.co.sz; internet swazidairy.org; f. 1971; Gen. Man. N. T. Gumede.

Swaziland Sugar Association: 4th Floor, cnr Dzeliwe and Msakato Sts, POB 445, Mbabane; tel. 4042646; fax 4045005; e-mail info@ssa.co.sz; internet www.ssa.co.sz; CEO Dr Michael Matsebula.

EMPLOYERS' ORGANIZATIONS

Building Contractors' Association of Swaziland: POB 518, Mbabane; tel. 4040071; fax 4044258; e-mail soconswad@realnet.co.sz.

Swaziland Association of Architects, Engineers and Surveyors: Swazi Plaza, POB A387, Mbabane; tel. 4042227.

Swaziland Institute of Personnel and Training Managers: c/o UNISWA, Private Bag, Kwaluseni; tel. 5184011; fax 5185276.

UTILITIES

Electricity

Swaziland Electricity Board: Mhlambanyatsi Rd, Eluvatsini House, POB 258, Mbabane; tel. 4042521; fax 4042335; internet www.seb.co.sz; statutory body; f. 1963; Man. Dir (vacant).

Water

Swaziland Water Services Corpn: Emtfonjeni Bldg, Below Gables Shopping Complex, Ezulwini, MR103, POB 20, Mbabane H100; tel. 4163621; fax 4163617; e-mail headoffice@swsc.co.sz; internet www.swsc.co.sz; state authority; Chair. Esau N. Zwane; CEO Peter N. Bhembe.

CO-OPERATIVE ASSOCIATIONS

Swaziland Central Co-operatives Union: POB 551, Manzini; tel. 5052787; fax 5052964.

There are more than 123 co-operative associations, of which the most important is:

Swaziland Co-operative Rice Co Ltd: handles rice grown in Mbabane and Manzini areas.

TRADE UNIONS

At mid-2005 there were 55 organizations recognized by the Department of Labour. Only non-managerial workers may belong to a union.

Trade Union Federations

Swaziland Amalgamated Trade Unions (SATU): POB 7138, Manzini; tel. 5059544; fax 5052684; f. 2003 by merger of five industrial unions; affiliated to the Int. Metalworkers' Fed.; Sec.-Gen. FRANK NKULULEKO MNCINA; 3,500 mems (2005).

Swaziland Federation of Labour (SFL): Swazi Plaza, POB 1173, Mbabane; tel. 4045216; fax 4044261; e-mail sufiaw@realnet.co.sz; affiliated to the Int. Trade Union Confed.; Sec.-Gen. VINCENT V. NCONGWANE; 10,900 mems (2007).

Swaziland Federation of Trade Unions (SFTU): POB 1158, Manzini; tel. and fax 5056575; internet www.cosatu.org.za/sftu; f. 1973; affiliated to the Int. Trade Union Confed.; prin. trade union org. since mid-1980s; represents workers in the agricultural, private and public sectors; Pres. RICHARD NXUMALO; Sec.-Gen. JAN SITHOLE; 83,000 mems (2007).

21 affiliated mem. unions incl.:

Swaziland Agriculture and Plantation Workers' Union (SAPWU): POB 2010, Manzini; tel. 4526010; fax 4526106.

Swaziland Communications Workers' Union (SCWU): c/o Swaziland Post and Telecommunications Corpn, POB 125, Mbabane; fax 4042093; fmrly Swaziland Post and Telecommunications Workers' Union; present name adopted in 2006; Pres. KENNEDY DLAMINI; Sec.-Gen. MANDLA MDLULI.

Swaziland Manufacturing and Allied Workers' Union (SMAWU): Agora Shopping Complex, King Mswati III Ave, Matsapha, POB 2379, Manzini; tel. 5186503; fax 5187028; e-mail smawu@realnet.co.sz; affiliated to the Int. Textile, Garment and Leather Workers' Fed.; Gen. Sec. SIPHO PETERSON MAMBA; 7,000 mems (2004).

Swaziland National Association of Civil Service (SNACS): POB 2811, Manzini M200; tel. 557882; fax 557887; e-mail snacs@swazi.net; f. 1980; reportedly suspended from the SFTU in 2006; affiliated to the Public Services Int.; Pres. CHARLES KHUMALO; Gen. Sec. ABSOLOM DLAMINI; 3,855 mems (2002).

Swaziland Nurses' Association (Swaziland National Association of Nurses): POB 6191, Manzini; tel. and fax 5058070; f. 1965; affiliated to the Public Services Int.; Pres. PATRICK MASITSELA MHLANGA; Gen. Sec. JULIA JABULILE ZIYANÉ.

Swaziland Transport and Allied Workers' Union (STAWU): POB 3362, Manzini; affiliated to the Int. Transport Workers' Fed.

Other unions affiliated to the SFTU include the Building and Construction Workers' Union of Swaziland; the Swaziland Commercial and Allied Workers' Union; the Swaziland Conservation Workers' Union; the Swaziland Electricity Supply, Maintenance and Allied Workers' Union; the Swaziland Hotel, Catering and Allied Workers' Union; the Swaziland Manufacturing and Allied Workers' Union; the Swaziland Media and Publications Workers' Union; the Swaziland Mining, Quarrying and Allied Workers' Union; the Swaziland Motor Engineering Allied Workers' Union; the Swaziland Union of High Learning Institutions; the Workers' Union of Swaziland Security Guards; the Workers' Union of Town Councils; and the Swaziland Water and Co-operation Workers' Union.

Swaziland National Association of Teachers (SNAT): POB 1575, M200 Manzini; tel. 5052603; fax 5060386; e-mail snatcentre@africaonline.co.sz; internet www.snat.org.sz; affiliated to Education Int.; Pres. SIMON BRIAN MAKHANYA; Sec.-Gen. MUZI GLADWELL MHLANGA; 9,000 mems.

Swaziland Union of Financial Institutions and Allied Workers (SUFIAW): 100 Johnson St, Mbabane; tel. 4044261; fax 4045216; e-mail sufiaw@realnet.co.sz; Pres. VINCENT V. NCONGWANE.

Other registered unions include the Association of Lecturers and Academic Personnel of the University of Swaziland; and the University of Swaziland Workers' Union.

Staff Associations

Three staff associations exist for employees whose status lies between that of worker and that of management: the Nyoni Yami Irrigation Scheme Staff Association, the Swazican Staff Association and the Swaziland Electricity Board Staff Association.

Transport

Buses are the principal means of transport for many Swazis. Bus services are provided by private operators who are required to obtain annual permits for each route from the Road Transportation Board, which also regulates fares.

RAILWAYS

The rail network, which totalled 297 km in 1998–99, provides a major transport link for imports and exports. Railway lines connect with the dry port at Matsapha, the South African ports of Richards Bay and Durban in the south, the South African town of Komatipoort in the north and the Mozambican port of Maputo in the east. Goods traffic is mainly in wood pulp, sugar, molasses, coal, citrus fruit and canned fruit. In June 1998 the Trans Lebombo rail service was launched to carry passengers from Durban to Maputo via Swaziland. The service was terminated in May 2000, owing to insufficient demand. In August 2004 the Government announced plans to privatize Swaziland Railways.

Swaziland Railways: Swaziland Railway Bldg, cnr Johnston and Walker Sts, POB 475, Mbabane; tel. 4047211; fax 4047210; internet www.swazirail.co.sz; f. 1962; Chair. B. A. G. FITZPATRICK; CEO GIDEON J. MAHLALELA.

ROADS

In 2002 there were an estimated 3,594 km of roads, including 1,465 km of main roads and 2,129 km of secondary roads. About 30% of the road network was paved in that year. The rehabilitation of about 700 km of main roads and 600 km of district gravel-surfaced roads began in 1985, financed by World Bank and US loans totalling some E18m. In 1991 work commenced on the reconstruction of Swaziland's main road artery, connecting Mbabane to Manzini, via Matsapha, and in 2001 the Government announced the construction of two main roads in the north of the country, financed by Japanese loans.

Roads Department: Ministry of Public Works and Transport, POB 58, Mbabane; tel. 4042321; fax 4045825; e-mail tshabalalatr@gov.sz; Chief Roads Engineer T. M. TSHABALALA.

SHIPPING

Royal Swazi National Shipping Corpn Ltd: POB 1915, Manzini; tel. 5053788; fax 5053820; f. 1980 to succeed Royal Swaziland Maritime Co; 76% owned by Tibiyo Taka Ngwane; owns no ships, acting only as a freight agent; Gen. Man. M. S. DLAMINI.

CIVIL AVIATION

Swaziland's only airport is at Matsapha, near Manzini, about 40 km from Mbabane. In mid-1997 the Government initiated a three-year programme to upgrade the airport. In early 2003 construction began of an international airport at Sikhupe, in eastern Swaziland. In March 2006 Swaziland Airlink was one of 92 airlines banned from landing at European Union airports owing to safety concerns.

Swaziland Airlink: POB 939, Matsapha Airport, Manzini; tel. 5186155; fax 5186148; f. 1999; fmrly Royal Swazi Nat. Airways Corpn; jt venture between SA Airlink, South Africa (40%) and the Govt of Swaziland; scheduled passenger services from Manzini to Johannesburg, South Africa; Chair. LINDIWE KHUMALO-MATSE.

Tourism

Swaziland's attractions for tourists include game reserves (at Malolotja, Hawane, Mlawula and Mantenga) and magnificent mountain scenery. In 2006 tourist arrivals totalled 316,082; receipts from tourism amounted to US $74.1m. in that year.

Hotel and Tourism Association of Swaziland: Oribi Court, 1st Floor, Gwamile St, POB 462, Mbabane; tel. 4042218; fax 4044516; e-mail aliand@realnet.co.sz; internet www.visitswazi.com/tourismassoc; f. 1979.

Swaziland National Trust Commission (SNTC): POB 100, Lobamba; tel. 4161516; fax 4161875; e-mail director@sntc.org.sz (parks and wildlife); e-mail curator@sntc.org.sz (museums and monuments); internet www.sntc.org.sz; f. 1972; parastatal org. responsible for conservation of nature and cultural heritage (national parks, museums and monuments); CEO S. MAMBA.

Swaziland Tourism Authority: POB A1030, Swazi Plaza, Mbabane; tel. 4049693; fax 4049683; e-mail secretary@tourismauthority.org.sz; internet www.welcometoswaziland.com; f. 2001; CEO ERIC SIPHO MASEKO.

SWEDEN

Introductory Survey

Location, Climate, Language, Religion, Flag, Capital

The Kingdom of Sweden lies in north-western Europe, occupying about two-thirds of the Scandinavian peninsula. It is bordered by Finland to the north-east, and by Norway to the north-west and west. About 15% of Sweden's area lies north of the Arctic Circle. The Baltic Sea and the Gulf of Bothnia are to the east, the Skagerrak and Kattegat channels to the south-west. The country is relatively flat and is characterized by thousands of inland lakes and small coastal islands. There is a mountain range, the Kjolen mountains, in the north-west. Winters are cold and summers mild. In Stockholm the mean summer temperature is 18°C (64°F) and the mean winter temperature −3°C (27°F). The national language is Swedish, but there are Finnish and Lapp (Sámi) minorities (the latter numbering between 17,000 and 20,000), retaining their own languages. A majority of the inhabitants profess Christianity, and about 78% are adherents of the Evangelical Lutheran Church of Sweden. The national flag (proportions 5 by 8) is light blue with a yellow cross, the upright of the cross being to the left of centre. The capital is Stockholm.

Recent History

Sweden has been a constitutional monarchy, traditionally neutral, since the early 19th century. During this time the country has not participated in any war or entered any military alliance. Norway, formerly united with Sweden, became independent in 1905. Sweden adopted parliamentary government in 1917, and universal adult suffrage was introduced in 1921. From 1932 until 1976, except for a short break in 1936, Sweden was governed by the Socialdemokratiska Arbetareparti (SAP—Social Democratic Labour Party), either alone or as the senior partner in coalitions (1936–45 and 1951–57). During those 44 years the country had only three Prime Ministers, all Social Democrats. Since the Second World War Sweden has become an active member of many international organizations, including the UN (to which it has given military support), the Council of Europe (see p. 236) and, from 1995, the European Community (EC, now European Union—EU, see p. 255).

Olof Palme succeeded Dr Tage Erlander as Prime Minister and leader of the SAP in October 1969. After a general election in September 1970, Palme formed a minority Government. Under a constitutional reform, the Riksdag (Parliament) was reconstituted from January 1971, its two chambers being replaced by a unicameral assembly. King Gustaf VI Adolf, who had reigned since 1950, died in September 1973 and was succeeded by his grandson, Carl XVI Gustaf. A revised Constitution, effective from January 1975, ended the monarch's prerogative to appoint the Prime Minister: the Speaker of the Riksdag was to have this responsibility in future.

At the September 1976 election, dissatisfaction with high rates of taxation, necessary to maintain the advanced social welfare system that Sweden had developed, brought about the defeat of the SAP. Thorbjörn Fälldin, leader of the Centerpartiet (CP—Centre Party), formed a centre-right coalition in October. The wish of the CP to abandon Sweden's nuclear power programme caused serious controversy in June 1978, when an independent commission recommended its continuation. This view was endorsed by the Folkpartiet (FP—Liberals) and Moderata Samlingspartiet (MS—Moderates), whose rejection of a proposal by Fälldin to submit the nuclear issue to a national referendum precipitated the Government's resignation in October 1978. The FP formed a minority Government, led by Ola Ullsten. Following a general election in September 1979, Fälldin returned as Prime Minister of a coalition comprising members of the CP, the MS and the FP, with an overall parliamentary majority of only one seat. A referendum on the future of nuclear power was held in March 1980, at which a narrow majority of the electorate approved a limited programme of nuclear reactor development, to be progressively eliminated by 2010 and replaced by alternative energy resources.

During 1980 the Government's economic policies came under attack, mainly because of the rising rate of inflation, and there was severe industrial unrest. The MS, who disagreed with proposed tax reforms, left the coalition in May 1981. At the next general election, held in September 1982, the SAP was returned to power, winning 45.6% of the votes cast (securing 166 of the 349 seats in the Riksdag), but gaining an overall majority over the three non-socialist parties. In October Palme formed a minority Government, following an undertaking by the Vänsterpartiet—Kommunisterna (VpK—Left Party—Communists), which held 20 seats, to support the SAP. Palme's Government was returned to power in September 1985, with the support of the VpK. The SAP and the VpK together won 50.0% of the votes cast (178 seats), while the three main non-socialist parties won 48.0% (171 seats). The FP increased its share of seats in the legislature from 21 to 51, attracting voters from all of the other main parties. Palme undertook to continue to follow his 'third way' economic policy, seeking to combat inflation and recession while avoiding both excessively high levels of public spending and reductions in social welfare benefits.

In February 1986 Palme was murdered by an unknown assailant in Stockholm. In March the Deputy Prime Minister, Ingvar Carlsson, took office as Prime Minister and was also appointed acting Chairman of the SAP, pending ratification by the National Congress in 1987. Carlsson retained Palme's Cabinet and declared that he would continue the policies of his predecessor. In December 1988 Christer Pettersson, a man with a history of mental illness and violent crime, was arrested, and in mid-1989 he was tried for the murder of Palme. He was convicted amid some controversy, only to be acquitted on appeal in October. In December 1997 the public prosecutor's office petitioned the Supreme Court to re-examine the case against Pettersson in light of the discovery of new, allegedly incriminating, evidence. In May 1998, however, the Supreme Court ruled that there was insufficient new evidence to conduct a retrial.

Meanwhile, ecological concerns were heightened in 1988 by two disasters affecting the marine environment along Sweden's coast, both of which were attributed to the effects of pollutants. At the general election in September the environmentalist Miljöpartiet de Gröna (MP—Green Party) gained parliamentary representation for the first time, but the SAP remained in power with the continued support of the VpK. The MS remained the second largest party in the Riksdag. In February 1990 the VpK (subsequently restyled the Vänsterpartiet—VP—Left Party) and the MP refused to support the Government's proposed austerity measures. Carlsson resigned, but, having secured support for a more moderate set of proposals, he formed another minority Government.

During 1990 the Swedish economy entered into recession, and in December the Riksdag approved a new programme of austerity measures, intended to reduce inflation and to restore confidence in the economy. The Government was forced to abandon the long-held belief that the commitment to full employment and the defence of the welfare state (supported by high levels of taxation and of public expenditure) should be overriding priorities.

However, the popularity of the SAP continued to decline, and in the general election of September 1991 the party did not win enough seats to form a government, although, with 138 seats, it remained the largest party in the Riksdag. The MS increased their representation to 80 seats, while the Kristdemokratiska Samhällspartiet (KdS—Christian Democrats) and a recently formed right-wing party, Ny demokrati (ND—New Democracy), won 26 and 25 seats respectively, at the expense of the FP and the CP; the MP failed to secure 4% of the total votes cast, and thereby lost its seats. Carlsson resigned as Prime Minister for the second time, and in early October Carl Bildt, the leader of the MS (the largest non-socialist party in the legislature), formed a coalition government comprising members of four non-socialist parties—the MS, the CP, the FP and the KdS. Since these four parties, even in combination, still formed a minority in the Riksdag, they were obliged to rely on the ND for support in securing approval for legislation. Without delay, the new Government began to accelerate the deregulation of the economy already undertaken by its predecessor.

SWEDEN

During 1992 the recession continued in Sweden. Although the Government's austerity measures succeeded in reducing inflation, the high level of the budgetary deficit was a cause of concern. In September speculation on the international currency markets caused a rapid outflow of capital, and in November a fresh outflow of capital, following the SAP's refusal to approve reductions in public expenditure, forced the Government to allow the krona to 'float' in relation to other currencies, thereby effectively devaluing it by some 10%. In March 1993 the Government was defeated in the Riksdag when the ND refused to support budgetary proposals, but later in the same month the Government won a parliamentary vote of confidence (the ND abstained from voting).

At the general election in September 1994 the SAP secured 45.3% of the votes cast, increasing its representation to 161 seats. The VP won 22 seats (compared with 16 in 1991) and the MP 18. Although the MS maintained the level of support they had gained at the previous election, the other parties in the incumbent coalition Government fared badly. Bildt resigned as Prime Minister, and in October 1994 Carlsson formed a minority SAP Government. The results appeared to indicate a trend of increased support for parties opposed to Sweden's joining the EU (as the EC had become). Despite opposition to EU membership within the SAP, Carlsson declared that a major objective of his Government would be to secure a mandate for Sweden to join the EU in the forthcoming national referendum (see below). He also emphasized the need for stringent economic measures to reduce unemployment, stabilize the budgetary deficit and safeguard welfare provisions.

In March 1996 Carlsson relinquished his dual posts as Prime Minister and leader of the SAP, in order to retire from political life. Göran Persson, hitherto Minister of Finance, was elected unopposed as Prime Minister and leader of the SAP. Persson immediately initiated a broad cabinet reorganization.

In October 1996 Persson urged that the process to enlarge the EU be accelerated in order to strengthen European security. In November an independent study group, which had been commissioned by the Government to consider Sweden's proposed participation in Economic and Monetary Union (EMU, see p. 296), recommended that Sweden should not join EMU until the unemployment rate had been significantly reduced. In February 1997, however, the central bank advocated membership of EMU from its inception in 1999. Nevertheless, in June 1997 the Government announced that Sweden would not be participating in the first wave of EMU, citing a lack of public support for the project. The Government reiterated this stance in October, when it was also announced that Sweden had no intention of participating in the European Exchange Rate Mechanism (ERM).

In August 1997 details of a national programme of enforced sterilization conducted during 1935–75 against some 60,000 individuals assessed to be of inferior intellectual or physical capabilities, reported in the Swedish daily newspaper *Dagens Nyheter*, provoked national outrage and prompted the Government to announce the creation of a comprehensive public inquiry into the country's post-First World War eugenics programme. It was subsequently revealed that minimal compensation had been paid to just 16 victims of the programme during the previous 10 years. In March 1999 the Ministry of Health and Social Affairs announced that compensation amounting to a maximum of 175,000 kronor would be paid to each surviving victim of the programme. In August 2001 the State Sterilization Compensation Board stated that some 2,000 people had sought financial reparation, and that, of these, about 1,500 had received compensation, the total amount paid out being approximately 256m. kronor.

In March 1991 the Swedish and Danish Governments agreed to construct a 16-km combined bridge and tunnel for road and rail traffic, across the Öresund strait, between Malmö and Copenhagen (to be known as the Öresund Link). The plan aroused opposition in Sweden, on the grounds that the link might hinder the flow of water into the Baltic Sea, as well as increasing pollution by emissions from vehicles. In May 1994 a Swedish marine commission concluded that plans for the link did not provide sufficient guarantees to protect the flow of water into the Baltic. In the following month, however, the Swedish Government approved construction plans, prompting the resignation from the Government of the Minister of the Environment and leader of the CP, Olof Johansson. The link was opened in July 2000.

Prior to Sweden's membership of the EU (see below), trade with EU countries was conducted by means of a free-trade area, the European Economic Area (EEA), created in 1994 under the aegis of the European Free Trade Association (EFTA, see p. 426). Negotiations on admission to the EU began in February 1993, when the Bildt Government declared that the country's tradition of neutrality would not prevent Sweden from participating fully in the common foreign and security policy of the EU. The negotiations were concluded in March 1994. Sweden obtained safeguards for its traditional policy of freedom of official information, and for its strict environmental standards, and won concessions on the maintenance of subsidies for agriculture in remote areas. A national referendum on membership was held on 13 November, producing a 52.2% majority in favour of joining the EU. The Riksdag formally ratified membership in December, and Sweden's accession to the EU took effect from 1 January 1995 (whereupon Sweden withdrew from EFTA). It was widely held that concern about the possible effects on the domestic economy of remaining outside the EU, together with fears regarding Sweden's ability to influence international affairs, such as the maintenance of effective environmental controls, had been major factors in the outcome of the referendum. Following the vote, the Carlsson Government reiterated that Sweden would retain its non-aligned policy within the EU and therefore remain outside the North Atlantic Treaty Organization (NATO, see p. 351), although it would apply for observer status within Western European Union (WEU, see p. 442).

At the general election held in September 1998 the SAP maintained its position as the largest party in the Riksdag (winning 131 seats), despite a substantial reduction in its parliamentary representation compared with 1994. This was the SAP's worst electoral performance for some 70 years, and the party required the support of the VP and the MP to remain in government. The MS retained the position of second largest party in the Riksdag, obtaining 82 seats. Like the CP and the Kristdemokraterna (Kd, as the KdS had been renamed), the MS indicated their unwillingness to support the SAP in government. At about 81%, the participation rate at the election was the lowest for some 50 years. Post-electoral analysis identified the SAP's pursuit of financial regularity at the perceived expense of socialist policies as the probable cause of its poor performance: many voters had transferred their allegiance from the SAP to the VP. It was reported that, in return for its support, the VP would seek to persuade the Government to increase expenditure on social welfare and employment, and would encourage the slower repayment of Sweden's national debt, higher taxes, the complete decommissioning of Sweden's nuclear power stations, and a less stringent programme of privatization. Both the VP and the MP remained strongly opposed to any future participation by Sweden in EMU. In early October the new Government presented its statement of policy, which envisaged a more active role in Europe for Sweden. The Government would also seek to achieve sustainable economic growth in order to increase labour-force participation to a targeted 80% by 2004. Following the announcement of former premier Bildt's retirement from party politics, in August 1999 Bo Lundgren was elected to succeed him as leader of the MS.

In late 1999 it was reported that public spending on defence equipment was to be reduced drastically. Additionally, proposed reform of the national defence system was likely to result in the loss of some 10,000 military and civilian jobs. Earlier in the year the military high command had indicated that the Government's programme of defence rationalization would lead to an eventual halving of the strength of the armed forces, in terms of both personnel and hardware, prompting speculation that Sweden might be about to reconsider its non-aligned status with regard to regional security. In November 2000 Persson announced proposals to that effect. He asserted that neutrality was no longer relevant after the end of the Cold War, and that it did not cover all aspects of Sweden's security policy, such as disarmament, the non-proliferation of nuclear weapons and stability in Europe. However, Persson ruled out any move to join NATO, asserting that it was essential for the stability of northern Europe that Sweden remain non-aligned.

At the general election held on 15 September 2002 the SAP maintained its position as the largest party in the Riksdag, winning 39.8% of the votes cast and securing 144 of the 349 seats. Persson formed a minority SAP Government with the parliamentary support of the MP and the VP. In return for their support, the MP and the VP required the Government to espouse some of their policies, including, among others, a reduction of 6,000m. kronor in defence expenditure over five years and a moratorium on cod-fishing in the Baltic Sea from 1 January 2003, with compensation for the fishing industry.

In March 2000 a national congress of the SAP endorsed the adoption of future EMU entry as official party policy, despite a significant degree of opposition. Following the 2002 general election, Persson announced that a referendum would be held on the adoption of the euro in September 2003. In December 2002 opinion polls reported equal proportions in favour of and against adopting the euro, but by May 2003 the proportion of those opposing the euro had increased to 47%, while the proportion of those in favour had fallen to 40% and the number of undecided voters had increased to 13%. Meanwhile, the SAP remained sharply divided on the issue; the MS and other parties of the centre-right supported Sweden's entry into EMU. The campaign for the adoption of the euro was supported by the national media and the business community, whereas opposition to the new currency was focused in the trade unions, the MP and the VP. Most Swedes, and especially those in rural and northern areas or in public-sector employment, wanted to keep their generous social welfare provisions, which were funded through high taxation, and opponents of EMU feared that membership would force Sweden to reduce public spending so as not to breach the 3% budget deficit limit imposed by the EU's Stability and Growth Pact.

In September 2003, four days prior to the referendum on entry into EMU, the Minister for Foreign Affairs, Anna Lindh, was stabbed in central Stockholm; she died of her injuries the following day. Prior to her death, she had been one of the Government's most effective campaigners for entry into EMU, and was widely seen as a potential future SAP leader. The referendum was held as planned on 14 September, and speculation that support for the euro would be enhanced as a result of sympathy following Lindh's death, thereby undermining the legitimacy of the decision, proved unfounded, as voters decisively rejected the adoption of the euro. The result of the referendum, for which turn-out was 82.6%, was 42.0% in favour, 55.9% against and 2.1% blank. Only in Stockholm did the proposal to adopt the euro receive a majority of votes cast.

Mijail Mijailović, a Swede of Serbian origin, was arrested in September 2003 on suspicion of Lindh's murder. Mijailović, who had a history of mental illness and claimed there was no political motive for the attack, was tried in January 2004, and was convicted of murder and sentenced to life imprisonment. Mijailović appealed against his conviction, and in July the Court of Appeal in Stockholm ruled that he should be sent to a psychiatric institution rather than serving a prison sentence. The Lindh family challenged the decision in the Supreme Court, which in December confirmed Mijailović's sentence of life imprisonment.

With the prospect of the enlargement of the EU from 15 to 25 countries on 1 May 2004, concerns arose that the Swedish welfare system would be unduly burdened by an influx of workers from the new member states. In March of that year, following similar action by other EU member countries, the Government introduced legislation in the Riksdag proposing welfare and labour restrictions for migrant workers from the 10 accession countries for at least two years. However, the Riksdag rejected the bill at the end of April by 187 votes to 137. This defeat was seen as a major reverse for the Government, and meant that Sweden was one of the few EU countries without any restrictions limiting access to jobs or social security to citizens of the new member states.

The perceived failure of the main political parties adequately to address the strong current of EU scepticism expressed in Sweden's rejection of the euro led to the formation, in February 2004, of a new political grouping, the Junilistan (June List), which opposed further integration with the EU, but did not advocate withdrawal. The grouping stressed that it was not itself a political party, and went as far as appending its candidates' usual party affiliation to their names on the ballots for the forthcoming elections to the European Parliament. Thus voters would be able to support the June List on the issue of the EU while not altogether abandoning their usual party. This strategy proved successful, allowing the June List to draw support from across the political spectrum. At the elections, held on 13 June, the June List won 14.4% of the votes cast and three of Sweden's 19 seats in the European Parliament. The SAP, in contrast, suffered its worst electoral result since 1912, obtaining just 24.7% (five seats), while the MS won 18.2% (four seats). The VP and FP each won two seats, and the CP, MP and Kd one apiece. It was widely believed that the June List's success in the European elections might increase pressure on the Government to consider holding a national referendum on the ratification of the EU constitutional treaty, which had finally been approved by the Council of the EU in June 2004. However, the Government chose to present the treaty for approval (or otherwise) in the Riksdag: legislation was to be presented by September 2005, with a view to adoption in December of that year. However, following the rejection of the treaty at national referendums in France and the Netherlands in mid-2005, Sweden was one of several member states to decide to delay the ratification process indefinitely. At a meeting of the European Council in Brussels in June 2007, a preliminary agreement was reached to replace the rejected constitutional treaty. In December EU leaders met in Lisbon, Portugal, to sign the new Reform Treaty, which was to amend existing treaties. The Treaty of Lisbon, as it was subsequently known, was ratified by the Riksdag in November 2008. However, the future of the treaty remained uncertain, following its rejection by the Irish electorate at a referendum in June.

Meanwhile, in late October 2005 Persson effected a number of changes to the Government. The reorganization was widely viewed as an attempt by Persson (following the SAP's poor performance in the European parliamentary elections) to renew, and revive support for, his administration in advance of the general election scheduled for 2006.

In May 2005 the UN Committee against Torture ruled that Sweden had violated the 1984 UN Convention against Torture and Other Cruel, Inhuman or Degrading Treatment or Punishment in December 2001 by returning an asylum seeker to Egypt, where he had been convicted *in absentia* of membership of a terrorist group; the Committee stated that the Swedish authorities should have known at the time of the expulsion that Egypt used torture against detainees. Human rights groups had earlier expressed concern at the treatment of the asylum seeker and another Egyptian national deported at the same time; the two men had controversially been flown to Egypt in a US-leased aircraft, having been handed over to US security officials by the Swedish authorities. In November 2005 the Swedish Government ordered the Civil Aviation Authority to investigate media reports that aircraft used by the US Central Intelligence Agency (CIA) had landed at Swedish airports while transporting suspected terrorists to third countries for interrogation. In the following month the Authority, which examined the period from January 2002, reported that it could not substantiate the claims.

In September 2005 the Riksdag rejected a proposed amnesty for illegal immigrants living in Sweden, despite considerable public support for such a measure. Following the vote, a number of protests took place and 150,000 signatures were collected in favour of an amnesty. In November the Riksdag approved legislation allowing failed asylum seekers to reapply for a residence permit before the end of March 2006. It was estimated that 20,000 asylum seekers whose deportation orders had not been carried out owing to conditions in their home countries, or who had gone into hiding after having their original applications refused, would be eligible to submit new applications under the law.

In February 2006 the Government announced its intention for Sweden to overcome its dependency on petroleum within 15 years, without constructing any further nuclear power stations. A committee of industrialists, academics, farmers, vehicle manufacturers, civil servants and others was charged with devising a plan to achieve this, and was to report to the Riksdag later that year. The Government hoped to protect Sweden from the adverse economic effects of climate change and from fluctuations in the price of petroleum, which had increased substantially in recent years.

In March 2006 Laila Freivalds resigned as Minister for Foreign Affairs, following criticism of her ministry's involvement in forcing the temporary closure, in February, of the website of *SD-Kuriren*—the newspaper of the far-right Sverigedemokraterna (SD, Swedish Democrats)—which had asked readers to submit cartoons of the Prophet Muhammad. (The publication of caricatures depicting the Prophet in a Danish newspaper in late 2005, and in a number of other European newspapers in early 2006, had led to world-wide protests by Muslims—see the chapter on Denmark.) Freivalds had already come under pressure to resign in December 2005 after an independent commission held her partly responsible for the Government's slow response to the tsunamis in South-East Asia on 26 December 2004 (which killed more than 500 Swedes). Jan Eliasson, the President of the UN General Assembly, was appointed as the new Minister for Foreign Affairs; he was to hold both positions until the expiry of his UN term in September 2006.

At the general election, held on 17 September 2006, the centre-right Alliance for Sweden, comprising the MS, the FP, the CP and the Kd, emerged as the largest group in the Riksdag, the four parties together winning 178 seats. Of those, the MS, led by Fredrik Reinfeldt, won 97 seats (compared with 55 seats in the 2002 elections), the CP 29, the FP 28 and the Kd 24. The four main non-socialist parties had presented a joint programme for government, which included plans to reduce welfare dependency and increase the labour supply by means of tax cuts for the lower paid and reductions in the levels of unemployment benefit, to reduce the role of the state in the economy through the privatization of state-owned companies and to introduce private sector competition in health care and education. In contrast to its partners in the Alliance, the FP suffered a significant decline in support, recording a loss of 20 seats, compared with the 2002 elections. The revelation of a scandal regarding a group of FP activists, who, during the election campaign, had gained illegal access to the computer network of the SAP and distributed information they had obtained to fellow activists in the FP, was considered to have been a decisive factor in the party's poor electoral performance. The SAP, despite remaining the largest party in the Riksdag (with 130 seats), recorded its worst electoral result since 1914. Persson immediately resigned as Prime Minister and announced that he would relinquish the leadership of the SAP in March 2007. As the leader of the largest party in the Alliance, Reinfeldt assumed the role of Prime Minister.

Reinfeldt's appointments to the new coalition Government in October 2006 included Maud Olofsson, of the CP, as Deputy Prime Minister and Minister for Enterprise and Energy, and the former Prime Minister, Bildt, as Minister for Foreign Affairs. The appointment of Nyamko Sabuni, a former refugee from Zaire (now the Democratic Republic of the Congo), as Minister for Integration and Gender Equality in the new Cabinet was controversial, with Muslim groups organizing a petition calling for her resignation. Her outspoken views on integration, including a proposal for a ban on the wearing of the *hijab* (Islamic headscarf) by girls under the age of 15 years, compulsory checks for genital mutilation and the termination of state funding for religious schools, provoked criticism from immigrant communities. Shortly after assuming office the Minister for Culture, Cecilia Stegö Chilò, and the Minister for Foreign Trade, Maria Borelius, both of the MS, were forced to resign, following allegations of irregularities in their personal finances. Lena Adelsohn Liljeroth and Sten Tolgfors, both of the MS, assumed the culture and foreign trade portfolios, respectively.

At the SAP party conference held in mid-March 2007, Mona Sahlin was elected to succeed Persson as party leader. The trial of six people on charges relating to the illegal accessing of SAP computer data by FP activists, commenced in early April. Later that month three of the defendants were convicted and received substantial fines, while three members of the FP, including a former party secretary, were acquitted. None the less, the reputation of the party had been severely damaged. In that month, Lars Leijonborg, the Minister for Education and Research, whose leadership of the FP had been the subject of criticism for several months, announced that he would resign as party leader following the party conference, scheduled for September, as he could no longer command sufficient support within the party to remain in his post.

A Swedish artist, Lars Vilks, provoked anger among Muslim communities in August 2007, when he depicted the head of the Prophet Muhammad on a dog's body. The satirical image was deemed particularly offensive, not only for infringing Islamic tradition (which prohibits the representation of the Prophet) but because dogs are widely considered to be unclean in Islamic culture. The decision by Swedish newspaper *Nerikes Allehanda* to print the caricature resulted in formal protests by Egypt, Iran and Pakistan. In September Reinfeldt met with diplomats from a number of Muslim countries in an effort to defuse the tension. He apologized for any offence the image may have caused, but defended the right of Swedish citizens to freedom of expression. Vilks was subsequently placed under police protection, following reports that the head of al-Qa'ida in Iraq, Abu Omar al-Baghdadi, had offered a US $100,000 reward for his murder.

A minor government reorganization took place in September 2007. Sten Tolgfors, the Minister for Foreign Trade, was appointed Minister for Defence, following Mikael Odenberg's decision to resign from the post over government proposals to reduce the defence budget by up to 4,000m. kronor by 2010. Ewa Björling succeeded Tolgfors as the Minister for Foreign Trade. In November 2007 Ulrica Schenström resigned from her position as State Secretary to the Prime Minister, following revelations that she had consumed a significant quantity of alcohol with a journalist, while officially on call for the Government's emergency response unit. Hans Gustaf Wessberg was appointed as her successor.

Six people were arrested in Sweden and Norway in February 2008, on suspicion of financing militant organizations and planning terrorist acts. Three of the suspects, who were reported to be Swedish citizens, were apprehended at separate locations in Stockholm. The arrests were part of a co-ordinated action by the Swedish and Norwegian security forces. In June the Riksdag narrowly passed a controversial bill (by 143 votes to 138) to allow for all cross-border emails and telephone calls to be monitored for reasons of national security. The law took effect from 1 January 2009 and was strongly criticized by many commentators as an attack on civil liberties.

The country's opposition parties in December 2008 announced plans to form a coalition government if they were to win sufficient votes in the general election, scheduled for September 2010. The SAP, MP and VP stated that they would campaign as separate parties but would present a joint economic policy prior to the election. This followed previous attempts to form a coalition, which had been frustrated by the VP's reluctance to accept certain areas of the SAP-MP agreement, particularly in relation to economic policy.

In February 2009, despite divisions between the four governing parties on the issue, Reinfeldt announced the reversal of the decision to phase out the country's remaining nuclear power stations, as part of a new programme to combat global warming and increase energy security. Although the phased decommissioning of nuclear plants had been ratified in a referendum in 1980, by 2009 only two of the country's 12 nuclear reactors had been closed. Reinfeldt claimed that as the referendum result had not specified the means by which nuclear power would be replaced, the Government should not be bound by it. The new programme, which proposed the replacement of the 10 ageing reactors with new models, also aimed to ensure that the country would use 50% renewable energy by 2020, reduce greenhouse gas emissions by 40% and become carbon neutral by 2050. The VP, however, remained opposed to the development of nuclear energy.

The Swedish Government expressed its opposition to the US-led military operation against the regime of Saddam Hussain in Iraq from early 2003. However, Sweden contributed funds towards the reconstruction of Iraq, in addition to humanitarian aid.

Government

Sweden is a constitutional monarchy. The hereditary monarch is Head of State but has very limited formal prerogatives. Executive power rests with the Cabinet (Regeringen), which is responsible to the legislature (Riksdag). The unicameral Riksdag was introduced in January 1971. It has 349 members, elected by universal adult suffrage for four years, on the basis of proportional representation. The Prime Minister is nominated by the Speaker of the Riksdag and later confirmed in office by the whole House. The country is divided into 21 counties (Län) and 288 municipal districts (Kommun). Both counties and municipalities have popularly elected councils.

Defence

Proposals for a significant reduction in defence spending and resources were announced during 1999 (see Recent History). As assessed at November 2008, Sweden maintained total armed forces of 16,900, compared with 53,100 in 1999. The army consisted of 10,200 men, of whom 5,800 were conscripts; the navy 3,100 men, including 700 conscripts, and the air force 3,600 men, including 900 conscripts. In addition, there were voluntary defence reservists totalling 262,000, compared with 570,000 in 1999. Military service for males (aged between 19 and 47 years) lasts between seven and 15 months in the army and navy, and between eight and 12 months in the air force. Basic training for women is voluntary. In 2008 defence was allocated 43,713m. kronor in the budget. In November 2004 the European Union (EU, see p. 255) ministers responsible for defence agreed to create a number of 'battlegroups' (each comprising about 1,500 troops), which could be deployed at short notice to crisis areas around the world. The EU battlegroups, two of which were to be ready for deployment at any one time, following a rotational schedule, reached full operational capacity from 1 January 2007. Sweden leads a joint Nordic battle group, with contributions from Finland, Norway, Estonia and Ireland.

Economic Affairs

In 2007, according to estimates by the World Bank, Sweden's gross national income (GNI), measured at average 2005–07 prices, was US $421,342m., equivalent to $46,060 per head (or $36,590 on an international purchasing-power parity basis). During 2000–07, it was estimated, the population grew at an average annual rate of 0.4%, while gross domestic product (GDP) per head increased, in real terms, by an average of 2.2% per year. Sweden's overall GDP increased, in real terms, by an average of 2.6% per year in 2000–07. According to official figures, GDP increased by 2.5% in 2007.

Agriculture (including hunting, forestry and fishing) contributed 1.4% of GDP and employed 2.3% of the working population in 2007. The main agricultural products are dairy produce, meat, cereals and potatoes, primarily for domestic consumption. In 2007 forestry products (wood, pulp and paper) accounted for 10.5% of total merchandise exports. Agricultural GDP increased by an average of 2.6% per year during 2000–06; it contracted by 1.4% in 2007.

Industry (including mining, manufacturing, construction and power) provided 28.3% of GDP and employed 21.7% of the working population in 2007. Industrial GDP increased by an average of 3.9% per year in 2000–06. Industrial GDP grew by 2.7% in 2007.

Mining contributed 0.6% of GDP and employed 0.2% of the working population in 2007. The principal product is iron ore, but there are also large reserves of uranium (some 15% of the world's total known reserves), copper, lead and zinc. The GDP of the mining and quarrying sector declined, in real terms, by an average of 2.8% per year in 2003–07, according to Statistics Sweden; it decreased by 9.4% in 2006 but increased by 5.3% in 2007.

Manufacturing contributed 20.0% of GDP and employed 14.5% of the working population in 2007. Sweden's principal manufactures were paper and paper products, motor vehicles, chemicals, basic iron and steel, television and radio transmitters and other communications apparatus and general purpose machinery. Manufacturing GDP increased, in real terms, by an average of 4.7% per year in 2003–07, according to Statistics Sweden; it rose by 2.3% in 2007.

Energy is derived principally from hydroelectric power and nuclear power, which provided 46.0% and 45.7% of electricity generated in 2005, respectively. In February 2009, despite a resolution to phase out nuclear power that was approved in a referendum in 1980, the Swedish Government announced proposals to replace the 10 remaining nuclear reactors in Sweden as they become obsolete. The decision reflected ambitious targets for climate change and the desire for energy security. Alternative sources of energy are also being developed. Imports of petroleum and petroleum products accounted for 9.7% of total imports in 2007.

The services sector contributed 70.3% of GDP and engaged 76.1% of the employed population in 2007. The GDP of the services sector increased, in real terms, at an average annual rate of 2.2% during 2000–06; it grew by 3.7% in 2007.

In 2007 Sweden recorded a visible trade surplus of US $18,232m., and there was a surplus of $38,416m. on the current account of the balance of payments. The European Union (EU, see p. 255) dominates Swedish trade: in 2007 it provided 71.6% of imports and took 61.3% of exports. The European Free Trade Association (EFTA, see p. 426) is also an important trading partner. In 2007 the principal single source of imports was Germany (contributing 18.4% of total imports); other major suppliers were Denmark (9.2%), Norway (8.6%), the United Kingdom (6.9%), the Netherlands (6.1%) and Finland (6.1%). Germany was also the principal market for exports in that year (accounting for 10.4% of total exports); other major purchasers were Norway (9.4%), the USA (7.6%), Denmark (7.4%), the United Kingdom (7.1%) and Finland (6.4%). The principal exports in 2007 were machinery and transport equipment, basic manufactured goods and chemicals. The principal imports in 2007 were machinery and transport equipment, and basic and other manufactures.

In 2007 there was a budget surplus of 103,209m. kronor, equivalent to 3.4% of GDP. In 2007 the central Government's total debt was 1,168,013m. kronor, equivalent to 38.2% of GDP. The annual rate of inflation averaged 1.8% in 2000–08. Consumer prices increased by an average of 3.4% in 2008. The unemployment rate averaged 6.2% in 2007.

Sweden is a member of the Nordic Council (see p. 440) and the Nordic Council of Ministers (see p. 440). In January 1995 Sweden became a full member of the EU.

Sweden is a small open economy, which is more diversified than is usual for a country of its size, with important sectors such as engineering, high technology, domestic aviation, nuclear power, automotive manufacturing, armaments and telecommunications; Sweden also has major pharmaceutical and medical research capabilities. High levels of taxation in the country finance a generous social welfare system. However, this has also proved an obstacle to entrepreneurship and to the attraction and retention of skilled labour from abroad. In the late 1990s, following the country's most serious economic recession in some 60 years (triggered by high inflation and public sector salary bills), Sweden experienced a considerable economic recovery. Expansion in the high-technology sector fuelled exports and helped to achieve robust GDP growth. In 2002–03 Sweden's economy compared favourably with the members of the euro area, arguably influencing its rejection of participation in European Economic and Monetary Union (EMU) in a national referendum in 2003. With the advent of a new centre-right coalition Government in 2006 came attempts to reduce welfare dependency and increase the labour supply, through cuts in income taxes for low- and medium-income groups and curtailing unemployment benefits, while there were plans to sell stakes in many state-owned companies and lower the level of public debt. However, the economic programme encountered significant difficulties as the global financial and economic crisis adversely affected the economy, with GDP growth slowing to 2.7% in 2007 and contracting by 0.5% in 2008. Sweden officially entered recession in late 2008, after GDP declined in the second, third and fourth quarters of 2008. In October the Riksdag passed a plan worth up to 1,500,000m. kronor to guarantee new medium-term bank loans up to April 2009; the plan was extended by a further six months at that date. Also in October 2008 the Government announced it was to set aside a further 15,000m. kronor as a financial stabilization fund to be used to buy shares in failing banks. In early 2009 official sources indicated that the recession, exacerbated by the country's exposure to the ailing Baltic economies, was more profound than previously thought. Consumer spending and fixed investment plummeted, exports declined and productivity deteriorated, while the rate of unemployment rose as major companies reduced their workforce (including Volvo and Ericsson—the latter dismissing 4,000 employees in 2008 and announcing plans in early 2009 for an additional 5,000 redundancies). The central bank, meanwhile, reduced interest rates (to a record 0.5% in April 2009) in an attempt to mitigate the effects of the financial crisis. Nevertheless, it was anticipated that GDP would contract by more than 5% in 2009.

Education

Basic education, which is compulsory, extends for nine years, starting at the age of six or seven years, and is received at the comprehensive school (*grundskolan*). At the end of this period a pupil may enter the integrated upper secondary school (*gymnasieskolan*). In accordance with legislation implemented in 1992–95, courses at upper secondary schools last three years, and are organized into 16 nationally defined study programmes, comprising two university entrance programmes and 14 vocational programmes. All publicly funded schools follow a national curriculum. However, most schools are operated by municipal authorities, which have some autonomy over the profile of each school. In addition, parents have the right to send their children to independent schools, which are publicly funded and must share the same objectives as municipally-run schools, but may differ in character and methods. Enrolment at pre-primary level included 80% of children in the relevant age-group in 2003/04. Enrolment at primary schools in that year included 99% of children (100% of boys; 99% of girls) in the relevant age-group, while the comparable ratio for secondary enrolment was 98% (98% of boys; 99% of girls). There are some 39 higher education institutions in Sweden, including 10 that are privately owned. Slightly more than 30% of young people in Sweden proceed to higher education within five years of completing their upper secondary schooling. In 2003/04 enrolment in higher education was equivalent to 82% of people in the relevant age-group (males 65%; females 100%). The budget for 2007 allocated 44,200m.

SWEDEN

kronor (5.7% of total expenditure) to education and university research.

Public Holidays*

2009: 1 January (New Year's Day), 6 January (Epiphany), 10 April (Good Friday), 12 April (Easter), 13 April (Easter Monday), 1 May (May Day), 21 May (Ascension Day), 31 May (Whit Sunday), 6 June (National Day), 20 June (Midsummer Holiday), 31 October (All Saints' Day), 25 December (Christmas), 26 December (Boxing Day).

2010: 1 January (New Year's Day), 6 January (Epiphany), 2 April (Good Friday), 4 April (Easter), 5 April (Easter Monday), 1 May (May Day), 13 May (Ascension Day), 23 May (Whit Sunday), 6 June (National Day), 26 June (Midsummer Holiday), 6 November (All Saints' Day), 25 December (Christmas), 26 December (Boxing Day).

* The eve of a holiday is as important or more so than the holiday itself. Most Swedes have the day off, including those working in the civil service, banks, public transport, hospitals, shops and the media. Others have at least a half-day. This applies especially to Midsummer's Eve, All Saints' Day Eve and Christmas Eve. The eve of May Day is sometimes called Valborg Eve or St Walpurgis. When a holiday falls on a Thursday many Swedes have the following Friday off in addition. When a holiday falls on a Saturday or Sunday it is not taken on the following Monday.

Weights and Measures

The metric system is in force.

Statistical Survey

Sources (unless otherwise stated): Statistics Sweden, Klostergatan 23, 701 89 Örebro; tel. (19) 17-60-00; fax (19) 17-70-80; e-mail information@scb.se; internet www.scb.se; Nordic Statistical Secretariat (Copenhagen), *Yearbook of Nordic Statistics*.

Area and Population

AREA, POPULATION AND DENSITY

Area (sq km)	
Land	410,335
Inland waters	39,960
Total	450,295*
Population (census results)†	
1 November 1985	8,360,178
1 November 1990	
Males	4,242,351
Females	4,345,002
Total	8,587,353
Population (official estimates at 31 December)†	
2006	9,113,257
2007	9,182,927
2008	9,256,347
Density (per sq km) at 31 December 2008	22.6‡

* 173,859 sq miles.
† Population is *de jure*.
‡ Density refers to land area only.

COUNTIES
(31 December 2008)

	Land area (sq km)*	Population	Density (per sq km)
Stockholms län	6,519.3	1,981,263	303.9
Uppsala län	7,036.7	327,188	46.5
Södermanlands län	6,103.1	267,524	45.5
Östergötlands län	10,604.6	423,169	39.9
Jönköpings län	10,495.4	335,246	31.9
Kronobergs län	8,467.3	182,224	21.5
Kalmar län	11,219.1	233,397	20.8
Gotlands län	3,151.4	57,004	18.1
Blekinge län	2,946.7	152,259	51.7
Skåne län	11,035.4	1,214,758	110.1
Hallands län	5,461.6	293,572	53.8
Västra Götalands län	23,956.1	1,558,130	65.0
Värmlands län	17,591.3	273,374	15.5
Örebro län	8,546.3	277,732	32.5
Västmanlands län	6,317.9	249,976	39.6
Dalarnus län	28,195.6	275,867	9.8
Gävleborgs län	18,200.1	275,908	15.2
Västernorrlands län	21,684.5	243,372	11.2
Jämtlands län	49,343.1	126,897	2.6
Västerbottens län	55,189.7	257,812	4.7
Norrbottens län	98,249.0	249,677	2.5
Total†	410,335.4	9,256,347	22.6

* According to new estimates for land area.
† Including area of 21.2 sq km outside of existing county boundaries.

PRINCIPAL TOWNS
(estimated population of municipalities at 31 December 2008)*

Stockholm (capital)	810,120	Örebro	132,277
Göteborg (Gothenburg)	500,197	Norrköping	128,060
Malmö	286,535	Helsingborg	126,754
Uppsala	190,668	Jönköping	125,154
Linköping	141,863	Umeå	112,728
Västerås	134,684	Lund	107,351

* According to the administrative subdivisions of 1 January 2006.

BIRTHS, MARRIAGES AND DEATHS

	Registered live births		Registered marriages		Registered deaths	
	Number	Rate (per 1,000)	Number	Rate (per 1,000)	Number	Rate (per 1,000)
2001	91,446	10.3	35,778	4.0	93,752	10.5
2002	95,815	10.7	38,012	4.3	95,009	10.6
2003	99,157	11.0	39,041	4.3	92,961	10.4
2004	100,928	11.2	43,088	4.8	90,532	10.0
2005	101,346	11.2	44,381	n.a.	91,710	10.1
2006	105,913	11.6	45,551	n.a.	91,177	10.0
2007	107,421	11.7	47,898	n.a.	91,729	10.0
2008	109,301	n.a.	50,332	n.a.	91,449	n.a.

Life expectancy (years at birth, WHO estimates): 80.9 (males 78.7; females 83.0) in 2006 (Source: WHO, *World Health Statistics*).

IMMIGRATION AND EMIGRATION

	2006	2007	2008
Immigrants	95,750	99,485	101,171
Emigrants	44,908	45,418	45,294

SWEDEN

Statistical Survey

ECONOMICALLY ACTIVE POPULATION
(sample surveys, '000 persons aged 16 to 64 years)

	2005	2006	2007
Agriculture, hunting and forestry	84	84	99
Fishing	2	2	3
Mining and quarrying	7	8	9
Manufacturing	652	653	658
Electricity, gas and water supply	27	25	25
Construction	253	270	290
Wholesale and retail trade, repair of motor vehicles, motorcycles and personal and household goods	535	536	557
Hotels and restaurants	117	128	143
Transport, storage and communications	269	274	281
Financial intermediation	81	84	89
Real estate, renting and business activities	582	603	664
Public administration and defence, compulsory social security, extra-territorial organizations and bodies	238	249	260
Education	472	480	491
Health and social work	707	701	724
Other community, social and personal service activities, private households with employed persons	228	233	240
Activities not adequately defined	10	9	8
Total employed	**4,263**	**4,341**	**4,541**
Unemployed	270	246	298
Total labour force	**4,533**	**4,587**	**4,839**
Males	2,373	2,404	2,539
Females	2,161	2,181	2,300

Source: ILO.

Health and Welfare

KEY INDICATORS

Total fertility rate (children per woman, 2006)	1.8
Under-5 mortality rate (per 1,000 live births, 2006)	4
HIV/AIDS (% of persons aged 15–49, 2007)	0.1
Physicians (per 1,000 head, 2004)	3.3
Hospital beds (per 1,000 head, 1997)	5.2
Health expenditure (2006): US $ per head (PPP)	3,119
Health expenditure (2006): % of GDP	8.9
Health expenditure (2006): public (% of total)	81.2
Human Development Index (2006): ranking	7
Human Development Index (2006): value	0.958

For sources and definitions, see explanatory note on p. vi.

Agriculture

PRINCIPAL CROPS
('000 metric tons; holdings of more than 2 ha of arable land)

	2005	2006	2007
Wheat	2,246.8	1,967.4	2,254.7
Rye	112.3	115.4	127.5
Barley	1,592.9	1,110.6	1,439.0
Oats	746.3	624.4	892.3
Triticale (wheat-rye hybrid)	271.5	255.9	276.3
Potatoes	947.3	772.6	790.1
Rapeseed	198.2	220.0	223.0
Sugar beets	2,381.2	2,189.0	2,000.0†

* Unofficial figure.
† FAO estimate.

Aggregate production ('000 metric tons, may include official, semi-official or estimated data): Total cereals 5,050.6 in 2005, 4,128.4 in 2006, 5,058.9 in 2007; Total roots and tubers 947.3 in 2005, 772.6 in 2006, 790.1 in 2007; Total vegetables (incl. melons) 325.9 in 2005, 342.0 in 2006, 323.4 in 2007; Total fruits (excl. melons) 36.0 in 2005, 33.2 in 2006; 34.8 in 2007.

Source: FAO.

LIVESTOCK
('000 head, year ending September; holdings of more than 2 ha of arable land, or with large numbers of livestock)

	2005	2006	2007
Cattle	1,604.9	1,590.4	1,560.7
Sheep	456	480	505
Pigs	1,811.2	1,680.5	1,694.6
Horses*	95.7	96.0	95.0
Chickens	6,762	6,170	6,500*
Turkeys*	200	200	200

* FAO estimate.
Source: FAO.

LIVESTOCK PRODUCTS
('000 metric tons)

	2005	2006	2007*
Cattle meat	135.0	137.4	140.0
Horse meat	1.0	1.0	1.0
Sheep meat	4.1	4.2	4.1
Pig meat	275.1	264.4	270.0
Chicken meat	96.2	95.5	97.0
Game meat*	18.0	19.0	19.0
Cows' milk	3,206.0	3,175.0	3,000.0
Hen eggs	102.0	99.0†	102.0

* FAO estimates.
† Unofficial figure.
Source: FAO.

Forestry

ROUNDWOOD REMOVALS
('000 cubic metres; rounded figures)

	2005	2006	2007
Sawlogs, veneer logs and logs for sleepers	56,500	31,700	40,000
Pulpwood	35,300	26,500	30,800
Fuel wood*	5,900	5,900	5,900
Other industrial wood*	500	500	500
Total	**98,200**	**64,600**	**77,200**

* FAO estimates.
Source: FAO.

SWEDEN

SAWNWOOD PRODUCTION
('000 cubic metres, incl. railway sleepers; rounded figures)

	2005	2006	2007
Coniferous (softwood)	17,440	18,190	18,490
Broadleaved (hardwood)*	160	110	110
Total	17,600	18,300	18,600

* FAO estimates.

Source: FAO.

Fishing

('000 metric tons, live weight)

	2004	2005	2006
Capture	269.9	256.4	269.3
Atlantic cod	16.4	11.7	13.2
Blue whiting (Poutassou)	20.0	4.4	0.3
Sandeels (Sandlances)	34.6	8.8	32.8
Atlantic herring	89.0	105.6	103.4
European sprat	90.7	109.4	102.7
Aquaculture	6.0	5.9	7.5
Total catch	275.9	262.2	276.8

Note: Figures exclude aquatic mammals, recorded by number rather than by weight. The number of harbour porpoises caught was: 1 in 2004; nil in 2005; 2 in 2006.

Source: FAO.

Mining

('000 metric tons, unless otherwise indicated)

	2004	2005	2006
Iron ore*	14,700	15,300	16,000
Copper ore	90.6	97.8	86.7
Gold (kilograms)	5,200	6,600	4,500
Silver (metric tons)	319.6	309.9	292.0
Zinc ore	197.0	215.7	208.6
Lead ore	54.3	60.4	55.6

* Estimates.

Note: Figures relate to the metal content of ores.

Source: US Geological Survey.

Industry

SELECTED PRODUCTS
('000 metric tons, unless otherwise indicated)

	2004	2005	2006
Pig-iron and sponge-iron*	3,871	3,500†	3,500†
Crude steel*	5,949	6,692	5,435†
Aluminium*‡	130.4	132.6	133.2†
Copper (refined)*‡	236	247	248†
Lead (refined)*‡	73.5	78.9	65.2†
Mechanical wood pulp§	3,397.0	3,445.0	3,489
Chemical wood pulp§	8,417	8,216	8,292
Newsprint§	2,649.0	2,572.0	2,541
Printing and writing paper§	3,033.0†	3,119.0	3,414
Other paper and paperboard§	5,907.0†	6,084.0	6,111
Cement (hydraulic)*	2,588	2,600†	2,600†
Dwellings completed (number)	25,283	23,068	29,832
Electricity (million kWh)	148,824	154,982	140,307

* Source: US Geological Survey.
† Estimate.
‡ Primary and secondary metals.
§ Source: FAO.

Finance

CURRENCY AND EXCHANGE RATES

Monetary Units
100 öre = 1 Swedish krona (plural: kronor).

Sterling, Dollar and Euro Equivalents (31 December 2008)
£1 sterling = 11.386 kronor;
US $1 = 7.811 kronor;
€1 = 10.870 kronor;
100 Swedish kronor = £8.78 = $12.80 = €9.20.

Average Exchange Rate (kronor per US $)
2006 7.3783
2007 6.7588
2008 6.5911

STATE BUDGET
(million kronor)

Revenue	2006	2007	2008*
Tax revenue	744,461	755,919	783,683
Other current revenue	43,450	66,524	53,804
Capital revenue	56	18,016	52,617
Loan repayment	2,144	2,046	1,868
Computed revenue	7,763	8,174	8,713
Contributions from the European Union	12,441	13,037	10,896
Total	810,315	863,716	911,581

Expenditure	2006	2007	2008*
Justice	28,505	30,627	32,001
Defence	43,771	46,530	43,713
Health	42,176	46,665	50,356
Social insurance for the sick and disabled	125,683	119,464	115,199
Social insurance for the elderly	45,019	43,738	42,570
Social insurance for families and children	60,066	61,568	66,319
Social insurance for the unemployed / Employment	69,496	59,121	55,435
Education and university research	46,495	42,198	44,716
Community planning and housing	8,742	5,800	2,178
Communications	31,133	44,290	37,073
Agriculture, forestry and fisheries	20,985	15,478	15,583
General grants to municipalities	60,246	72,975	64,766
Interest on central government debt	49,472	47,255	41,490
Contributions to the European Union	25,920	26,635	29,513
Total (incl. others)	791,942	760,507	761,755

* Forecasts.

INTERNATIONAL RESERVES
(US $ million at 31 December)

	2006	2007	2008
Gold	3,245	3,993	3,821
IMF special drawing rights	386	406	306
Reserve position in IMF	318	257	463
Foreign exchange	24,074	26,382	25,127
Total	28,023	31,038	29,717

Source: IMF, *International Financial Statistics*.

SWEDEN

MONEY SUPPLY
(million kronor at 31 December)*

	2005	2006	2007
Currency outside banks	100,370	100,770	100,460
Demand deposits	973,110	1,103,460	1,201,780
Total money	1,073,480	1,204,230	1,302,240

* Figures are rounded to the nearest 10m. kronor.

2008 (million kronor at 31 December): Total money 1,485,300.

Source: IMF, *International Financial Statistics*.

COST OF LIVING
(Consumer Price Index; base: 1980 = 100)

	2006	2007	2008
Food and non-alcoholic beverages	239.9	244.8	261.7
Alcoholic beverages and tobacco	356.4	382.6	412.2
Clothing and footwear	164.7	168.7	166.9
Housing, water, electricity and fuels	338.8	352.4	376.4
Furniture and household goods	220.3	221.3	221.9
Health	752.3	772.7	763.1
Transport	368.0	372.1	386.5
Communication	188.1	181.9	173.5
Recreation and culture	188.5	187.8	182.3
Restaurants and hotels	407.2	420.2	442.8
Miscellaneous goods and services	317.4	327.1	332.9
All items	284.2	290.5	300.5

NATIONAL ACCOUNTS
(million kronor at current prices)

National Income and Product

	2005	2006	2007*
Compensation of employees	1,500,028	1,557,349	1,674,424
Net operating surplus	} 493,137	548,780	546,141
Net mixed income			
Domestic factor incomes	1,993,165	2,106,129	2,220,565
Consumption of fixed capital	336,152	354,045	374,323
Gross domestic product (GDP) at factor cost	2,329,317	2,460,174	2,594,888
Taxes, *less* subsidies, on production and imports	405,901	440,616	466,561
GDP in market prices	2,735,218	2,900,790	3,061,449
Primary incomes received from abroad (net)	−4,123	48,542	60,238
Gross national income	2,731,095	2,949,332	3,121,687
Less Consumption of fixed capital	336,152	354,045	374,323
Net national income	2,394,943	2,595,287	2,747,364
Other current transfers from abroad (net)	−40,853	−38,132	−38,382
Net national disposable income	2,354,090	2,557,155	2,708,982

Expenditure on the Gross Domestic Product

	2005	2006	2007*
Final consumption expenditure	2,051,050	2,135,212	2,222,956
Households	} 1,328,353	1,372,754	1,430,136
Non-profit institutions serving households			
General government	722,697	762,458	792,820
Gross capital formation	471,680	528,724	603,616
Gross fixed capital formation	475,885	528,473	581,710
Changes in inventories	−4,574	3	21,687
Acquisitions, less disposals, of valuables	369	248	219
Total domestic expenditure	2,522,730	2,663,936	2,826,572
Exports of goods and services	1,333,379	1,494,038	1,609,249
Less Imports of goods and services	1,120,891	1,257,184	1,374,372
GDP in market prices	2,735,218	2,900,790	3,061,449
GDP at constant 2000 prices	2,552,597	2,660,992	2,728,665

Gross Domestic Product by Economic Activity

	2005	2006	2007*
Agriculture, forestry and fishing	26,200	36,254	38,023
Mining and quarrying	11,694	16,161	16,722
Manufacturing	470,025	499,657	535,828
Electricity, gas and water	70,107	72,034	74,662
Construction	109,005	120,299	132,232
Wholesale and retail trade	267,405	282,747	298,070
Hotels and restaurants	35,379	37,782	39,881
Transport, storage and communications	162,613	166,591	172,672
Financial intermediation	106,576	93,418	97,661
Real estate and business services†	488,713	536,265	568,417
Government services	490,624	512,535	535,874
Education, health and social services	64,707	70,839	75,119
Other community, social and personal services	48,648	54,049	57,625
Other services‡	36,466	37,621	38,180
Gross value added in basic prices	2,388,734	2,536,252	2,680,966
Taxes on products	359,503	378,224	395,347
Less Subsidies on products	12,447	13,686	14,864
GDP in market prices	2,735,790	2,900,790	3,061,449

* Provisional figures.
† Including imputed rents of owner-occupied dwellings.
‡ Domestic services and non-profit institutions serving households.

Note: Financial intermediation services indirectly measured data are distributed to production sectors.

BALANCE OF PAYMENTS
(US $ million)

	2005	2006	2007
Exports of goods f.o.b.	131,976	148,789	170,462
Imports of goods f.o.b.	−112,274	−128,290	−152,230
Trade balance	19,701	20,498	18,232
Exports of services	42,887	49,797	63,587
Imports of services	−35,273	−39,571	−47,953
Balance on goods and services	27,316	30,724	33,865
Other income received	38,196	50,619	62,457
Other income paid	−35,412	−43,241	−52,923
Balance on goods, services and income	30,100	38,103	43,399
Current transfers received	5,027	5,107	4,741
Current transfers paid	−9,601	−10,051	−9,724
Current balance	25,526	33,159	38,416
Capital account (net)	308	−2,556	−441

SWEDEN

—continued

	2005	2006	2007
Direct investment abroad	−26,658	−20,186	−28,568
Direct investment from abroad	10,018	22,608	12,286
Portfolio investment assets	−12,942	−33,761	−49,973
Portfolio investment liabilities	13,608	13,159	59,636
Financial derivatives assets	29,417	54,071	39,239
Financial derivatives liabilities	−30,347	−53,935	−40,412
Other investment assets	−13,301	−50,621	−48,540
Other investment liabilities	1,722	36,649	34,258
Net errors and omissions	2,899	2,702	−16,348
Overall balance	250	1,289	−447

Source: IMF, *International Financial Statistics*.

OFFICIAL ASSISTANCE TO DEVELOPING COUNTRIES
(million kronor)

	2005	2006	2007
Bilateral assistance	16,857	21,028	19,814
Multilateral assistance	8,263	8,133	9,506
Total	25,120	29,161	29,320

External Trade

PRINCIPAL COMMODITIES
(distribution by SITC, million kronor)

Imports c.i.f.	2005	2006	2007
Food and live animals	52,733	59,744	64,570
Fresh fruit and vegetables	13,499	14,996	15,726
Crude materials (inedible) except fuels	27,097	31,384	37,292
Mineral fuels, lubricants, etc.	98,110	117,475	113,581
Petroleum, petroleum products, etc.	85,435	99,626	98,905
Chemicals and related products	89,007	98,202	110,526
Organic chemicals	15,269	17,204	18,860
Medical and pharmaceutical preparations	20,684	23,648	25,092
Unprocessed plastics	15,142	17,468	19,702
Basic manufactures	126,387	143,639	165,496
Iron and steel	38,465	39,547	50,051
Machinery and transport equipment	328,919	366,350	398,836
Power-generating machinery and equipment	24,800	25,337	27,396
Telecommunications and sound equipment	48,510	52,225	54,565
Other electrical machinery, apparatus, etc.	51,500	58,560	65,477
Road vehicles and parts*	90,514	102,010	111,744
Miscellaneous manufactured articles	101,603	111,433	118,702
Clothing and accessories (excl. footwear)	22,259	24,107	25,019
Other miscellaneous manufactured articles	33,825	36,239	37,784
Total (incl. others)	833,757	939,730	1,021,230

Exports f.o.b.	2005	2006	2007
Crude materials (inedible) except fuels	54,613	63,880	69,711
Wood, lumber and cork	24,116	27,162	30,027
Pulp and waste paper	14,367	15,243	16,449
Mineral fuels, lubricants, etc.	52,879	64,360	63,016
Petroleum, petroleum products, etc.	45,505	58,126	57,518
Chemicals and related products	109,128	125,183	126,069
Medical and pharmaceutical preparations	54,003	64,420	59,223
Basic manufactures	198,666	218,268	238,480
Paper, paperboard and manufactures	69,143	72,640	73,173
Iron and steel	57,868	61,819	77,376
Manufactures of metals	27,422	31,148	33,893
Machinery and transport equipment	441,435	481,165	502,235
Power-generating machinery and equipment	34,247	38,919	45,275
Machinery specialized for particular industries	41,737	46,572	52,252
General industrial machinery, equipment and parts	63,358	71,894	81,709
Telecommunications and sound equipment	92,691	90,953	76,967
Other electrical machinery, apparatus, etc.	42,708	49,060	53,596
Road vehicles and parts*	133,653	146,550	154,800
Miscellaneous manufactured articles	83,369	94,307	97,843
Total (incl. others)	977,280	1,089,095	1,141,515

* Data on parts exclude tyres, engines and electrical parts.

PRINCIPAL TRADING PARTNERS
(million kronor)

Imports c.i.f.	2005	2006	2007
Austria	8,996	9,872	11,034
Belgium	32,997	39,325	42,660
China, People's Repub.	22,491	28,996	35,635
Denmark	79,227	90,610	93,661
Estonia	6,925	7,502	7,875
Finland	50,050	55,286	62,230
France	42,784	44,476	50,635
Germany	151,518	168,623	188,180
Hong Kong	7,901	8,751	8,560
Ireland	11,498	12,285	12,406
Italy	27,476	31,806	36,292
Japan	17,433	18,112	17,676
Netherlands	54,966	58,907	62,678
Norway	68,166	80,225	87,643
Poland	20,358	25,184	29,607
Russia	24,820	33,093	29,685
Spain	13,551	14,518	14,935
Switzerland	8,523	9,293	8,939
United Kingdom	57,777	60,620	70,423
USA	28,342	31,595	31,896
Total (incl. others)	833,757	939,730	1,021,230

Exports f.o.b.	2005	2006	2007
Australia	11,184	14,376	13,022
Austria	9,124	10,406	11,653
Belgium	41,736	49,828	52,397
Canada	10,536	11,420	11,000
China, People's Repub.	18,844	20,172	22,170
Denmark	67,022	78,339	84,835
Finland	58,582	68,040	72,567
France	46,874	53,685	57,352
Germany	100,868	108,069	119,097
Italy	32,785	36,720	36,014

SWEDEN   *Statistical Survey*

Exports f.o.b.—*continued*	2005	2006	2007
Japan	14,849	16,865	13,942
Netherlands	44,209	52,229	57,797
Norway	83,701	99,370	107,012
Poland	17,508	22,554	27,994
Russia	15,987	17,865	22,684
Spain	27,803	33,547	32,162
Switzerland	9,229	9,658	10,241
United Kingdom	75,735	78,426	81,402
USA	102,783	100,896	86,471
Total (incl. others)	977,280	1,089,095	1,141,515

Transport

RAILWAYS
(traffic)

	2004	2005	2006
Passengers (million)	147	150	159
Passenger-km (million)	8,658	8,936	9,642
Freight (million metric tons)	60	63	65
Freight ton-km (million)	20,856	21,675	22,271

Freight ton-km (million): 20,856 in 2004.

ROAD TRAFFIC
('000 motor vehicles in use at 31 December)

	2005	2006	2007
Passenger cars	4,154	4,202	4,258
Buses and coaches	13	14	13
Lorries and vans	461	480	504
Motorcycles	250	269	287

SHIPPING

Merchant Fleet
(registered at 31 December)

	2005	2006	2007
Number of vessels	567	564	572
Total displacement ('000 grt)	3,765.7	3,876.5	4,044.9

Source: Lloyd's Register-Fairplay, *World Fleet Statistics*.

International Sea-borne Freight Traffic

	2004	2005	2006
Vessels entered ('000 grt)	106,690	115,715	119,917
Vessels cleared ('000 grt)	102,311	110,059	115,788
Goods loaded ('000 metric tons)	65,547	69,275	74,494
Goods unloaded ('000 metric tons)	79,088	82,641	83,267

CIVIL AVIATION
(traffic on scheduled services)*

	2002	2003	2004
Kilometres flown (million)	130	129	133
Passengers carried ('000)	12,421	11,873	11,624
Passenger-kilometres (million)	11,663	11,638	11,976
Total ton-kilometres (million)	1,427	1,410	1,452

* Including an apportionment (3/7) of the international services of Scandinavian Airlines System (SAS), operated jointly with Denmark and Norway.

Source: UN, *Statistical Yearbook*.

Tourism

VISITORS BY ORIGIN
(nights in all types of tourist accommodation)

	2004	2005	2006
Denmark	959,983	974,300	1,038,498
Finland	385,121	417,045	428,219
France	208,891	224,989	238,919
Germany	1,753,518	1,942,223	2,123,566
Italy	243,806	251,071	244,413
Japan	118,177	114,935	112,313
Netherlands	583,086	557,615	716,702
Norway	2,531,570	2,464,157	2,709,794
Russia	132,016	132,536	167,128
United Kingdom	603,972	641,892	642,792
USA	383,202	420,944	421,230
Total (incl. others)	9,723,676	10,077,859	10,951,666

Tourism receipts (US $ million, incl. passenger transport): 7,686 in 2004; 8,580 in 2005; 10,437 in 2006.

Source: World Tourism Organization.

Communications Media

	2005	2006	2007
Telephones ('000 main lines in use)	5,458.0	5,551.0	5,506.0
Mobile cellular telephones ('000 subscribers)	9,104	9,607	10,371
Internet users ('000)	6,890.0	6,981.2	7,000.0
Broadband subscribers ('000)	1,918.0	2,346.3	3,131.0
Daily newspapers:			
titles	168	166	169
average net circulation ('000 copies)	3,998	3,928	3,833
Weekly newspapers and periodicals:			
titles	423	443	443
average net circulation ('000 copies)	22,800	21,950	22,121
Book production (titles)	21,413	21,765	22,785

Television receivers ('000 in use, 2001): 8,600.

Radio receivers ('000 in use, 1997): 8,250.

Facsimile machines (estimated '000 in use, 1996): 450.

Sources: mainly International Telecommunication Union, UN, *Statistical Yearbook*, and UNESCO, *Statistical Yearbook*.

Education

(2004/05, unless otherwise indicated)

	Institutions	Teachers[1]	Students
Primary: grades 1–6	4,963	108,233	650,342
Secondary: grades 7–9			373,292
Integrated upper secondary schools	641[2]	37,640	347,713[3]
Higher education	64	20,000[4]	397,679[5]
People's colleges	147[2]	n.a.	108,742[6]
Municipal adult education	400[7]	6,593	226,851[5]

[1] Full-time and part-time teachers and teachers on leave.
[2] 1996/97.
[3] At 15 October 2004.
[4] 1994/95.
[5] 2003/04.
[6] Autumn term.
[7] 1993/94.

Directory

The Constitution

The Swedish Constitution is based on four fundamental laws and the Riksdag Act. The four fundamental laws are the Instrument of Government (originally dating from 6 June 1809), the Act of Succession (1810), the Freedom of the Press Act (1949) and the Fundamental Law on Freedom of Expression (1992). Following partial reforms in 1968 and 1969, a new Instrument of Government and a new Riksdag Act were adopted in 1973 and 1974, and a new Constitution, summarized below, came into force on 1 January 1975. The Riksdag Act, which contains detailed rules as to the functioning of the Riksdag (parliament), was formerly a fundamental law, but since 1974 has occupied an intermediate position between that of a fundamental law and that of an ordinary law.

GOVERNMENT

The Cabinet governs Sweden and is responsible to the Riksdag (parliament). The Constitution of 1975 formalized the position of the Monarch relative to the Cabinet and the Riksdag, and laid down rules on the selection and resignation of the Cabinet. In 1978 the Riksdag amended the constitutional law of succession to allow the first-born royal child, whether male or female, to be heir to the throne, with effect from 1980.

As Head of State, the Monarch has representative and ceremonial duties only. The Monarch does not participate in the government of the country, which is conducted rather by the Cabinet at meetings not attended by the Monarch. Decisions of government do not require the Monarch's signature, and it is the Speaker of the Riksdag, and not the Monarch, who leads the procedure resulting in the formation of a new Government. Following consultations within the Riksdag, the Speaker nominates a candidate for Prime Minister. If not more than one-half of the total number of members of the Riksdag vote against the proposed candidate, he or she is approved. Failing this approval, the procedure has to be repeated. After four unsuccessful attempts to secure Riksdag approval of a candidate for the premiership, a new election to the Riksdag must be held within three months. A candidate for the premiership approved by the Riksdag nominates the other members of the Government.

The Prime Minister can be dismissed at his or her own request, by the Speaker of the Riksdag, or in the event of a vote of no confidence in the Riksdag. Other ministers can be dismissed at their own request, by the Prime Minister or by a vote of no confidence. If the Prime Minister should resign or die, all of the ministers in the Cabinet must resign. A Cabinet that is due to resign shall, however, remain in power until a new Prime Minister has been appointed.

A demand for a vote of no confidence will be considered only if it is supported by 10% of the members of the Riksdag. A vote of no confidence requires the support of more than one-half of the Riksdag members. If the Riksdag decides upon a vote of no confidence, the Cabinet can avoid resigning if it calls for an extra general election within one week. The Riksdag may continue its business, or be summoned to convene, even after a decision has been made to hold new elections. A Riksdag session may, however, be terminated by a special decision of the Cabinet. Existing terms of office do not expire until the new terms of office have begun.

LEGISLATURE

The Riksdag is the prime representative of the Swedish people. It enacts laws, decides the amount and use of taxation and examines the Government's actions. The Riksdag contains 349 members, elected for four years.

In accordance with tradition, the work of the Swedish Riksdag is, to a great extent, carried on in a non-partisan atmosphere. This is largely the result of the thorough attention given to all questions by numerous standing committees elected by the Riksdag on a basis of proportional representation. Besides the Utrikesnämnden (Advisory Council on Foreign Affairs) and Special Committees, every Riksdag appoints from within the assembly a Constitution Committee, a Finance Committee, a Taxation Committee and at least 12 other committees.

The Constitution Committee examines the minutes of the Cabinet and deals with or initiates proposals concerning alterations of the fundamental laws and of laws regulating local government.

ELECTORAL SYSTEM

In order that local and national government terms of office should coincide, the Constitution calls for local and general elections to be held on the same day. In both cases the term of office for the elected candidate is four years. Proportional representation was introduced in Sweden between the years 1906 and 1909, universal and equal suffrage by 1921. Under the provisions of legislation passed in 1976, all aliens resident in the country for three years are permitted to vote in local elections. The minimum voting age is 18 years. In allocating the 349 seats in the Riksdag, the seats are divided into two groups. The first group of 310 'constituency seats' is distributed among the constituencies according to the number of eligible voters, and within each constituency among the parties. The remaining 39 seats are distributed as 'adjustment seats'. First, it is calculated how many seats each party would have obtained if the whole country had been treated as a single constituency and if the distribution of seats had taken place according to a modified Sainte-Laguë method. From this figure is subtracted the number of 'constituency seats' received, the result being the number of 'compensatory seats' to be allocated to each party. These seats are filled by candidates nominated in the constituencies. There is a check to the emergence of small parties in that only parties that have received at least 4% of the total votes cast are entitled to a seat. However, any party that receives 12% or more of the votes in any constituency will be allowed to compete for a permanent seat in that constituency.

The Government

HEAD OF STATE

Monarch: HM King CARL XVI GUSTAF (succeeded to the throne 15 September 1973).

THE CABINET
(April 2009)

A coalition of the Moderata Samlingspartiet (MS), the Centerpartiet (CP), the Folkpartiet Liberalerna (FP) and the Kristdemokraterna (Kd).

Prime Minister: FREDRIK REINFELDT (MS).

Deputy Prime Minister and Minister for Enterprise and Energy: MAUD OLOFSSON (CP).

Minister for Finance: ANDERS BORG (MS).

Minister for the Environment: ANDREAS CARLGREN (CP).

Minister for Justice: BEATRICE ASK (MS).

Minister for Foreign Affairs: CARL BILDT (MS).

Minister for EU Affairs: CECILIA MALMSTRÖM (FP).

Minister for Social Security: CRISTINA HUSMARK PEHRSSON (MS).

Minister for Agriculture: ESKIL ERLANDSSON (CP).

Minister for Foreign Trade: EWA BJÖRLING (MS).

Minister for International Development Co-operation: GUNILLA CARLSSON (MS).

Minister for Health and Social Affairs: GÖRAN HÄGGLUND (Kd).

Minister for Education: JAN BJÖRKLUND (FP).

Minister for Higher Education and Research: LARS LEIJONBORG (FP).

Minister for Culture: LENA ADELSOHN LILJEROTH (MS).

Minister for Elderly Care and Public Health: MARIA LARSSON (Kd).

Minister for Local Government and Financial Markets: MATS ODELL (Kd).

Minister for Integration and Gender Equality: NYAMKO SABUNI (FP).

Minister for Defence: STEN TOLGFORS (MS).

Minister for Employment: SVEN OTTO LITTORIN (MS).

Minister for Migration and Asylum Policy: TOBIAS BILLSTRÖM (MS).

Minister for Communications: ÅSA TORSTENSSON (CP).

MINISTRIES

Prime Minister's Office: Rosenbad 4, 103 33 Stockholm; tel. (8) 405-10-00; fax (8) 723-11-71; e-mail registrator@primeminister.ministry.se; internet www.regeringen.se; incl. EU Affairs.

Ministry of Agriculture: Fredsgt. 8, 103 33 Stockholm; tel. (8) 405-10-00; fax (8) 20-64-96; e-mail registrator@agriculture.ministry.se; internet www.regeringen.se/sb/d/1473.

Ministry of Culture: Drottninggt. 16, 103 33 Stockholm; tel. (8) 405-10-00; fax (8) 21-68-13; e-mail registrator@culture.ministry.se; internet www.regeringen.se/sb/d/8339.

Ministry of Defence: Jakobsgt. 9, 103 33 Stockholm; tel. (8) 405-10-00; fax (8) 723-11-89; e-mail registrator@defence.ministry.se; internet www.regeringen.se/sb/d/495.

SWEDEN   Directory

Ministry of Education and Research: Drottninggt. 16, 103 33 Stockholm; tel. (8) 405-10-00; fax (8) 723-11-92; e-mail registrator@educcult.ministry.se; internet www.regeringen.se/sb/d/1454.

Ministry of Employment: Mäster Samuelsgt. 70, 103 33 Stockholm; tel. (8) 405-10-00; fax (8) 411-36-16; internet www.regeringen.se/sb/d/8270.

Ministry of Enterprise, Energy and Communications: Mäster Samuelsgt. 70, 103 33 Stockholm; tel. (8) 405-10-00; fax (8) 411-36-16; e-mail registrator@industry.ministry.se; internet www.regeringen.se/sb/d/1470.

Ministry of the Environment: Tegelbacken 2, 103 33 Stockholm; tel. (8) 405-10-00; fax (8) 24-16-29; e-mail registrator@environment.ministry.se; internet www.regeringen.se/sb/d/1471.

Ministry of Finance: Drottninggt. 21, 103 33 Stockholm; tel. (8) 405-10-00; fax (8) 21-73-86; e-mail registrator@finance.ministry.se; internet www.regeringen.se/sb/d/1468.

Ministry for Foreign Affairs: Gustav Adolfs torg 1, 103 39 Stockholm; tel. (8) 405-10-00; fax (8) 723-11-76; e-mail registrator@foreign.ministry.se; internet www.regeringen.se/sb/d/1475.

Ministry of Health and Social Affairs: Fredsgt. 8, 103 33 Stockholm; tel. (8) 405-10-00; fax (8) 723-11-91; e-mail registrator@social.ministry.se; internet www.regeringen.se/sb/d/1474.

Ministry of Integration and Gender Equality: Fredsgt. 8, 103 33 Stockholm; tel. (8) 405-10-00; fax (8) 543-560-39; e-mail registrator@integration.ministry.se; internet www.regeringen.se/sb/d/8324.

Ministry of Justice: Rosenbad 4, 103 33 Stockholm; tel. (8) 405-10-00; fax (8) 20-27-34; e-mail registrator@justice.ministry.se; internet www.regeringen.se/sb/d/584.

Legislature

SVERIGES RIKSDAG

100 12 Stockholm; tel. (8) 786-40-00; e-mail riksdagsinformation@riksdagen.se; internet www.riksdagen.se.
Speaker: PER WESTERBERG.

General Election, 17 September 2006

Party	Votes	% of votes	Seats
Sveriges Socialdemokratiska Arbetareparti (SAP)	1,942,625	34.99	130
Moderata Samlingspartiet (MS)*	1,456,014	26.23	97
Centerpartiet (CP)*	437,389	7.88	29
Folkpartiet Liberalerna (FP)*	418,395	7.54	28
Kristdemokraterna (Kd)*	365,889	6.59	24
Vänsterpartiet (VP)	324,722	5.85	22
Miljöpartiet de Gröna (MP)	291,121	5.24	19
Others	315,014	5.67	—
Total	5,551,278	100.00	349

*Contested the elections as the Alliance for Sweden.

Election Commission

Valmyndigheten (Election Authority): Solna Strandväg 78, POB 4210, 171 04 Solna; tel. (8) 635-69-00; fax (8) 635-69-20; e-mail valet@val.se; internet www.val.se; independent; Dir GUNNAR SKARELL.

Political Organizations

Centerpartiet (CP) (Centre Party): Stora Nygt. 4, POB 2200, 103 15 Stockholm; tel. (8) 617-38-00; fax (8) 617-38-10; e-mail info@centerpartiet.se; internet www.centerpartiet.se; f. 1910 as an agrarian party; aims at social, environmental and progressive development and decentralization; Leader MAUD OLOFSSON; 68,000 mems.

Feministiskt initiativ (F!) (Feminist Initiative): POB 498, 101 29 Stockholm; tel. (0) 706-100-190; e-mail info@feministisktinitiativ.se; internet www.feministisktinitiativ.se; f. 2005; Principal Speakers STINA SUNDBERG, GUDRUN SCHYMAN.

Folkpartiet Liberalerna (FP) (Liberal Party): POB 2253, Stora Nygt. 2A, 103 16 Stockholm; tel. (8) 410-242-00; fax (8) 509-116-60; e-mail info@liberal.se; internet www.folkpartiet.se; f. 1902; advocates market-orientated economy and social welfare system; Chair. JAN BJÖRKLUND.

Junilistan (June List): Vasagt. 40, 111 20 Stockholm; tel. and fax (8) 23-01-11; e-mail kg.svenson@junilistan.se; internet www.junilistan.se; f. 2004 to contest elections to the European Parliament; opposes further powers for EU; Pres ANNIKA ERIKSSON, SÖREN WIBE.

Kristdemokraterna (Kd) (Christian Democratic Party): POB 2373, Munkbron 1, 103 18 Stockholm; tel. (8) 723-25-00; fax (8) 723-25-10; e-mail info@kristdemokraterna.se; internet www.kristdemokraterna.se; f. 1964 as Kristdemokratiska Samhällspartiet (KdS); promotes emphasis on Christian values in political life; Chair. GÖRAN HÄGGLUND; 24,000 mems.

Miljöpartiet de Gröna (MP) (Green Party): International Secretary, Swedish Parliament, 100 12 Stockholm; tel. (8) 786-57-86; fax (8) 786-53-75; e-mail international@mp.se; internet www.mp.se; f. 1981; Principal Speakers MARIA WETTERSTRAND, PETER ERIKSSON; c. 9,400 mems.

Moderata Samlingspartiet (MS) (Moderate Party): POB 2080, Stora Nygt. 30, 103 12 Stockholm; tel. (8) 676-80-00; fax (8) 21-61-23; e-mail info@moderat.se; internet www.moderat.se; f. 1904; advocates liberal-conservative policies and market-orientated economy; Chair. FREDRIK REINFELDT; 100,000 mems.

Piratpartiet (Pirate Party): POB 307, 101 26 Stockholm; tel. (8) 720-04-00; e-mail info@piratpartiet.se; internet www.piratpartiet.se; f. 2006; advocates the citizen's right to complete and exclusive control of information pertaining to his or her private life and the abolition of copyright on all material for non-commercial use; Chair. RICKARD FALKVINGE.

Sverigedemokraterna (SD) (Sweden Democrats): POB 200 85, 104 60 Stockholm; tel. (8) 50-00-00-50; fax (8) 643-92-60; e-mail info@sverigedemokraterna.se; internet www.sverigedemokraterna.se; f. 1988; nationalist, anti-immigration; currently unrepresented in the Riksdag, but has won representation at local level; Leader JIMMIE ÅKESSON.

Sveriges Socialdemokratiska Arbetareparti (SAP) (Swedish Social Democratic Party): Sveavägen 68, 105 60 Stockholm; tel. (8) 700-26-00; fax (8) 20-42-57; e-mail info@sap.se; internet www.socialdemokraterna.se; f. 1889; egalitarian; Chair. MONA SAHLIN; Sec.-Gen. IBRAHIM BAYLAN; 100,000 mems.

Vänsterpartiet (VP) (Left Party): Kungsgt. 84, POB 12660, 112 93 Stockholm; tel. (8) 654-08-20; fax (8) 653-23-85; e-mail vansterpartiet@riksdagen.se; internet www.vansterpartiet.se; f. 1917 as Left Social Democratic Party of Sweden; renamed the Communist Party 1921; renamed Left Party—Communists 1967; renamed Left Party 1990; policies based on the principles of Marxism, feminism and other theories; Chair. LARS OHLY.

Diplomatic Representation

EMBASSIES IN SWEDEN

Albania: Capellavägen 7, 181 32 Lidingö; tel. (8) 731-09-20; fax (8) 767-65-57; Ambassador RUHI HADO.

Algeria: Danderydsgt. 3–5, POB 26027, 100 41 Stockholm; tel. (8) 679-91-30; fax (8) 611-49-57; e-mail embassy.algeria@telia.com; internet www.embalgeria.se; Ambassador MERZAK BEDJAOUI.

Angola: Skeppsbron 8, POB 3199, 103 64 Stockholm; tel. (8) 24-28-90; fax (8) 34-31-27; e-mail info@angolaemb.se; internet www.angolaemb.se; Ambassador DOMINGOS CULOLO.

Argentina: POB 14039, 104 40 Stockholm; Narvavägen 32, 3rd Floor, Apartment 3, 115 22 Stockholm; tel. (8) 663-19-65; fax (8) 661-00-09; e-mail cancilleria@argemb.se; Ambassador HERNÁN MASSINI EZCURRA.

Australia: Sergels Torg 12, POB 7003, 103 86 Stockholm; tel. (8) 613-29-00; fax (8) 613-29-82; e-mail reception@austemb.se; internet www.sweden.embassy.gov.au; Ambassador (vacant).

Austria: Kommendörsgt. 35, 5th Floor, 114 58 Stockholm; tel. (8) 665-17-70; fax (8) 662-69-28; e-mail stockholm-ob@bmeia.gv.at; internet www.aussenministerium.at/stockholm; Ambassador Dr STEPHAN TOTH.

Azerbaijan: Karlavägen 60, 114 49 Stockholm; tel. (8) 411-24-55; fax (8) 411-24-58; e-mail azerembassy@gmail.com; Ambassador RAFAEL IBRAHIMOV.

Bangladesh: Anderstorpsvägen 12, 1st Floor, 171 54 Solna; tel. (8) 730-58-50; fax (8) 730-58-70; e-mail banijya@bangladeshembassy.se; Ambassador MUHAMMAD AZIZUL HAQUE.

Belarus: Herserudsvägen 5, 4th Floor, 181 34 Lidingö; tel. (8) 731-57-41; fax (8) 767-07-46; e-mail belarusambassador@telia.com; internet www.belembassy.org/sweden; Ambassador ANDREI M. GRINKEVICH.

Belgium: POB 1040, 101 38 Stockholm; Kungsbroplan 2, 2nd Floor, 112 27 Stockholm; tel. (8) 534-802-00; fax (8) 534-802-07; e-mail stockholm@diplobel.org; internet www.diplomatie.be/stockholm; Ambassador MARC BAPTIST.

SWEDEN — Directory

Bolivia: Södra Kungsvägen 60, 181 32 Lidingö; tel. (8) 731-58-30; fax (8) 767-63-11; e-mail embolivia-estocolmo@telia.com; Chargé d'affaires a.i. SISSY N. L. TORRICO CALVIMONTES.

Bosnia and Herzegovina: Birger Jarlsgt. 55, POB 7102, 103 87 Stockholm; tel. (8) 440-05-40; fax (8) 24-98-30; e-mail amb.bih.sto@telia.com; Ambassador DARKO ZELENIKA.

Botswana: Tyrgt. 11, POB 26024, 100 41 Stockholm; tel. (8) 545-258-00; fax (8) 723-00-87; Ambassador BERNADETTE SEBAGE RATHEDI.

Brazil: Odengt. 3, 114 24 Stockholm; tel. (8) 545-163-00; fax (8) 545-163-14; e-mail stockholm@brazilianembassy.se; internet www.brazilianembassy.se; Ambassador ANTONINO LISBOA MENA GONÇALVES.

Bulgaria: Karlavägen 29, 114 31 Stockholm; tel. (8) 723-09-38; fax (8) 21-45-03; e-mail bg.embassy@telia.com; internet www.bulgarien.se; Ambassador IVAN TZVETKOV.

Canada: Tegelbacken 4, 7th Floor, POB 16129, 103 23 Stockholm; tel. (8) 453-30-00; fax (8) 453-30-16; e-mail stkhm@international.gc.ca; internet www.canadaemb.se; Ambassador ALEXANDRA VOLKOFF.

Chile: Sturegt. 8, 3rd Floor, 114 35 Stockholm; tel. (8) 679-82-80; fax (8) 679-85-40; e-mail echilese@embassyofchile.se; internet www.embassyofchile.se; Ambassador JOSÉ MIGUEL CRUZ SÁNCHEZ.

China, People's Republic: Lidovägen 8, 115 25 Stockholm; tel. (8) 579-364-37; fax (8) 579-364-54; e-mail protocol@chinaembassy.se; internet www.chinaembassy.se; Ambassador CHEN MINGMING.

Colombia: Östermalmsgt. 46, 3rd Floor, POB 5627, 114 86 Stockholm; tel. (8) 21-43-20; fax (8) 21-84-90; e-mail embcol@telia.com; Chargé d'affaires a.i. ROBERTO EDUARDO MORA SARASTI.

Congo, Democratic Republic: Stockholmsvägen 33, 4th Floor, POB 1171, 181 23 Lidingö; tel. (8) 765-83-80; fax (8) 765-85-91; e-mail rdcongo6@hotmail.com; Chargé d'affaires a.i. HENRI MBAYAHE NDUNGO.

Croatia: Birger Jarlsgt. 13, 1st Floor, 111 45 Stockholm; tel. (8) 678-42-20; fax (8) 678-83-20; e-mail croemb.stockholm@mvpei.hr; Ambassador Dr SVJETLAN BERKOVIĆ.

Cuba: Sturevägen 9, 182 73 Stocksund; tel. (8) 545-83-277; fax (8) 545-83-270; e-mail primero.enero59@swipnet.se; internet home.swipnet.se/embacubasuecia; Ambassador ERNESTO MÉLENDEZ BACHS.

Cyprus: Birger Jarlsgt. 37, 4th Floor, POB 7649, 103 94 Stockholm; tel. (8) 24-50-08; fax (8) 24-45-18; e-mail info@cyprusemb.se; internet www.cyprusemb.se; Ambassador PAVLOS ANASTASIADES.

Czech Republic: Villagt. 21, POB 26156, 100 41 Stockholm; tel. (8) 440-42-10; fax (8) 440-42-11; e-mail stockholm@embassy.mzv.cz; internet www.mzv.cz/stockholm; Ambassador JAN KÁRA.

Denmark: Jakobs Torg 1, POB 16119, 103 23 Stockholm; tel. (8) 406-75-00; fax (8) 791-72-20; e-mail stoamb@um.dk; internet www.ambstockholm.um.dk; Ambassador TOM RISDAHL JENSEN.

Dominican Republic: Kungsholmsgt. 10, 5th Floor, POB 5584, 114 85 Stockholm; tel. (8) 667-46-11; fax (8) 667-51-05; e-mail stockholm@domemb.se; Ambassador MARINA ISABEL CACERES DE ESTÉVEZ.

Ecuador: Engelbrektsgt. 13, 114 32 Stockholm; tel. (8) 679-60-43; fax (8) 611-55-93; e-mail suecia@embajada-ecuador.se; internet www.embajada-ecuador.se; Ambassador ROBERTO BETANCOURT RUALES.

Egypt: Strandvägen 35, POB 14230, 104 40 Stockholm; tel. (8) 459-98-60; fax (8) 661-26-64; e-mail embassyofegypt@telia.com; Ambassador SAMAH MUHAMMAD SOTOUHI.

El Salvador: Herserudsvägen 5A, 5th Floor, 181 34 Lidingö; tel. (8) 765-86-21; fax (8) 731-72-42; e-mail embassy@elsalvador.se; internet www.elsalvador.se; Ambassador MARTIN RIVERA GÓMEZ.

Eritrea: Stjärnvägen 2B, 4th Floor, POB 1164, 181 23 Lidingö; tel. (8) 441-71-70; fax (8) 446-73-40; e-mail info@eritrean-embassy.se; internet www.eritrean-embassy.se; Chargé d'affaires a.i. YONAS MANNA BAIRU.

Estonia: Tyrgt. 3, 114 27 Stockholm; POB 26076, 100 41 Stockholm; tel. (8) 545-122-80; fax (8) 545-122-99; e-mail info@estemb.se; internet www.estemb.se; Ambassador ALAR STREIMANN.

Ethiopia: Löjtnantsgt. 17, POB 10148, 100 55 Stockholm; tel. (8) 665-60-30; fax (8) 660-81-77; e-mail ethio.all@telia.com; internet www.ethemb.se; Ambassador DINA MUFTI.

Finland: Gärdesgt. 11, POB 24285, 104 51 Stockholm; tel. (8) 676-67-00; fax (8) 20-74-97; e-mail info@finland.se; internet www.finland.se; Ambassador ALEC AALTO.

France: Kommendörsgt. 13, POB 5135, 102 43 Stockholm; tel. (8) 459-53-00; fax (8) 459-53-41; e-mail presse@ambafrance-se.org; internet www.ambafrance-se.org; Ambassador JOËL DE ZORZI.

Georgia: Humlegårdsgt. 19, 1st Floor, 114 46 Stockholm; tel. (8) 678-02-60; fax (8) 678-02-64; e-mail geoemb.sweden@telia.com; internet www.sweden.mfa.gov.ge; Ambassador AMIRAN KAVADZE.

Germany: Artillerigt. 64, POB 27832, 115 93 Stockholm; tel. (8) 670-15-00; fax (8) 670-15-72; e-mail info@stockholm.diplo.de; internet www.stockholm.diplo.de; Ambassador Dr JOACHIM RÜCKER.

Greece: Kommendörsgt. 16, POB 55565, 102 04 Stockholm; tel. (8) 545-660-10; fax (8) 660-54-70; e-mail grembstockholm@greekembassy.se; internet www.greekembassy.se; Ambassador EVANGELOS CAROKIS.

Guatemala: Munkbron 3, 111 28 Stockholm; tel. (8) 660-52-29; fax (8) 660-42-29; e-mail embassy@guatemala.se; internet www.guatemala.se; Ambassador FERNANDO MOLINA GIRÓN.

Holy See: Svalnäsvägen 10, 182 63 Djursholm; tel. (8) 446-51-10; fax (8) 622-51-10; e-mail nunciature@telia.com; Apostolic Nuncio Most Rev. EMIL PAUL TSCHERRIG (Titular Archbishop of Volitanus).

Honduras: Stjärnvägen 2, 7th Floor, 181 34 Lidingö; tel. (8) 731-50-84; fax (8) 636-99-83; e-mail hondurasembassy@telia.com; internet www.hondurasembassy.se; Ambassador ILIANA WALESKA PASTOR MELGHEM.

Hungary: Dag Hammarskjölds Väg 10, POB 24125, 104 51 Stockholm; tel. (8) 661-67-62; fax (8) 660-29-59; e-mail embassy.stockholm@kum.hu; internet www.mfa.gov.hu/kulkepviselet/se; Ambassador GÁBOR IKLÓDY.

Iceland: Kommendörsgt. 35, 114 58 Stockholm; tel. (8) 442-83-00; fax (8) 660-74-23; e-mail icemb.stock@utn.strj.is; internet www.iceland.org/se; Ambassador GUÐMUNDUR ÁRNI STEFÁNSSON.

India: Adolf Fredriks Kyrkogt. 12, POB 1340, 111 83 Stockholm; tel. (8) 10-70-08; fax (8) 24-85-05; e-mail information@indianembassy.se; internet www.indianembassy.se; Ambassador DEEPA GOPALAN WADHWA.

Indonesia: Sysslomansgt. 18/I, POB 12520, 102 29 Stockholm; tel. (8) 545-55-880; fax (8) 650-87-50; e-mail kbri@indonesiskaambassaden.se; internet www.indonesiskaambassaden.se; Ambassador LINGGAWATY HAKIM.

Iran: Västra Yttringe Gård, Elfviksvägen, POB 6031, 181 06 Lidingö; tel. (8) 636-36-77; fax (8) 636-36-13; internet www.iran.se; Ambassador RASOUL ESLAMI.

Iraq: Baldersgt. 6A, POB 26031, 100 41 Stockholm; tel. (8) 411-44-43; fax (8) 796-83-66; Ambassador AHMAD A. BAMARNI.

Ireland: Östermalmsgt. 97, POB 10326, 100 55 Stockholm; tel. (8) 661-80-05; fax (8) 660-13-53; e-mail stockholmembassy@dfa.ie; internet www.embassyofireland.se; Ambassador BARRIE ROBINSON.

Israel: Storgt. 31, POB 14006, 104 40 Stockholm; tel. (8) 528-065-00; fax (8) 528-065-55; e-mail info@stockholm.mfa.gov.il; internet stockholm.mfa.gov.il; Ambassador BENNY DAGAN.

Italy: Oakhill, Djurgården, 115 21 Stockholm; tel. (8) 545-671-00; fax (8) 660-05-05; e-mail info.stockholm@esteri.it; internet www.ambstoccolma.esteri.it; Ambassador ANNA DELLA CROCE DI DOJOLA.

Japan: Gärdesgt. 10, 115 27 Stockholm; tel. (8) 579-353-00; fax (8) 661-88-20; e-mail protocol@japansamb.se; internet www.se.emb-japan.go.jp; Ambassador AKIRA NAKAJIMA.

Kenya: Birger Jarlsgt. 37, 2nd Floor, POB 7694, 103 95 Stockholm; tel. (8) 21-83-04; fax (8) 20-92-61; e-mail kenya.embassy@telia.com; Ambassador PURITY W. MUHINDI.

Korea, Democratic People's Republic: Norra Kungsvägen 39, 181 31 Lidingö; tel. (8) 767-38-36; fax (8) 767-38-35; e-mail koryo@telia.com; Ambassador RI HUI CHOL.

Korea, Republic: Laboratoriegt. 10, POB 27237, 102 53 Stockholm; tel. (8) 545-894-00; fax (8) 660-28-18; e-mail koremb.sweden@mofat.go.kr; internet www.mofat.go.kr; Ambassador CHO HEE-YONG.

Kuwait: Banérgt. 37, POB 10030, 100 55 Stockholm; tel. (8) 450-99-80; fax (8) 450-99-55; e-mail kuwaitambassad@telia.com; Ambassador SAMI MUHAMMAD AL-SULAIMAN.

Laos: Badstrandsvägen 11, POB 34050, 112 65 Stockholm; tel. (8) 618-20-10; fax (8) 618-20-01; e-mail laoembassy.se; internet www.laoembassy.se; Ambassador DONE SOMVORACHIT.

Latvia: Odengt. 5, POB 19167, 104 32 Stockholm; tel. (8) 700-63-00; fax (8) 14-01-51; e-mail embassy.sweden@mfa.gov.lv; internet www.stockholm.mfa.gov.lv; Ambassador ELITA KUZMA.

Lebanon: Kommendörsgt. 35, POB 5360, 102 49 Stockholm; tel. (8) 665-19-65; fax (8) 662-68-24; internet www.lebanonembassy.se; Ambassador NASRAT AL-ASSAD BASSILE.

Libya (People's Bureau): Valhallavägen 74, POB 10133, 100 55 Stockholm; tel. (8) 14-34-35; fax (8) 10-43-80; e-mail libyanembassy06@hotmail.com; Chargé d'affaires a.i. HAGI DHAN.

Lithuania: Grevgt. 5, 114 53 Stockholm; tel. (8) 667-54-55; fax (8) 667-54-56; e-mail info@litemb.se; internet www.litemb.se; Ambassador REMIGIJUS MOTUZAS.

Macedonia, former Yugoslav republic: Riddargt. 35, POB 10128, 100 55 Stockholm; tel. (8) 661-18-30; fax (8) 661-03-25; e-mail macedonian.embassy@telia.com; Ambassador AGON DEMJAHA.

Malaysia: Karlavägen 37, POB 26053, 100 41 Stockholm; tel. (8) 440-84-00; fax (8) 791-87-60; e-mail mwstholm@algohotellet.se; Ambassador DATO' KAMARUDIN MUSTAFA.

Mexico: Grevgt. 3, 114 53 Stockholm; tel. (8) 663-51-70; fax (8) 663-24-20; e-mail suecia.embamex@telia.com; internet www.sre.gob.mx/suecia; Ambassador NORMA BERTHA PENSADO MORENO.

Moldova: Engelbrektsgt. 10, 114 32 Stockholm; tel. (8) 411-40-64; fax (8) 411-40-74; e-mail stockholm@moldovaembassy.se; internet www.moldovaembassy.se; Ambassador NATALIA GHERMAN.

Morocco: Kungsholmstorg 16, 112 21 Stockholm; tel. (8) 545-511-30; fax (8) 545-511-39; e-mail sifamastock@stockholm.mail.telia.com; Ambassador ZOHOUR ALAOUI.

Mozambique: Sturegt. 46, 4th Floor, POB 5801, 102 48 Stockholm; tel. (8) 666-03-50; fax (8) 663-67-29; e-mail info@embassymozambique.se; internet www.embassymozambique.se; Ambassador PEDRO COMISSÁRIO AFONSO.

Namibia: Luntmakargt. 86–88, POB 19151, 104 32 Stockholm; tel. (8) 442-98-00; fax (8) 612-66-55; e-mail info@embassyofnamibia.se; internet www.embassyofnamibia.se; Ambassador THERESIA SAMARIA.

Netherlands: Götgt. 16A, POB 15048, 104 65 Stockholm; tel. (8) 556-933-00; fax (8) 556-933-11; e-mail sto@minbuza.nl; internet www.nlemb.se; Ambassador JAN EDWARD CRAANEN.

New Zealand: Stureplan 4C, 4th Floor, 114 35 Stockholm; tel. (8) 463-31-16; fax (8) 463-10-10; e-mail nzemb.skm@mft.net.nz; Ambassador BARBARA BRIDGE.

Nicaragua: Sandhamnsgt. 40, 6th Floor, 115 28 Stockholm; tel. (8) 667-18-57; fax (8) 662-41-60; e-mail embajada.nicaragua@swipnet.se; Chargé d'affaires a.i. ALVARO BACA RODRÍGUEZ.

Nigeria: Tyrgt. 8, POB 628, 101 32 Stockholm; tel. (8) 24-63-90; fax (8) 24-63-98; e-mail nigerian.embassy@swipnet.se; internet nigerianembassy.se; Ambassador Dr GODKNOWS BOLADEI IGALI.

Norway: Skarpögt. 4, POB 27829, 115 27 Stockholm; tel. (8) 665-63-40; fax (8) 782-98-99; e-mail emb.stockholm@mfa.no; internet www.norge.se; Ambassador ODD LAURITZ FOSSEIDBRÅTEN.

Pakistan: Karlavägen 65, 1st Floor, POB 5872, 102 40 Stockholm; tel. (8) 20-33-00; fax (8) 24-92-33; e-mail info@pakistanembassy.se; internet www.pakistanembassy.se; Chargé d'affaires a.i. MUHAMMAD AAMAR AFTAB QURESHI.

Panama: Östermalmsgt. 59, POB 55547, 102 04 Stockholm; tel. (8) 662-65-35; fax (8) 662-89-91; e-mail panaembasuecia@tele2.se; Ambassador CECILIO EDUARDO SIMON ENGLISH.

Peru: Brunnsgt. 21B, 2nd Floor, 111 38 Stockholm; tel. (8) 440-87-40; fax (8) 20-55-92; e-mail info@peruembassy.se; internet www.peruembassy.se; Ambassador GILBERT CHAUNY DE PORTURAS-HOYLE.

Philippines: Skeppsbron 20, 1st Floor, POB 2219, 103 15 Stockholm; tel. (8) 23-56-65; fax (8) 14-07-14; e-mail stockholm@philembassy.se; internet www.philembassy.se; Ambassador MARIA ZENEIDA ANGARA COLLINSON.

Poland: Karlavägen 35, 114 31 Stockholm; tel. (8) 505-750-00; fax (8) 505-750-86; e-mail info.polen@tele2.se; internet www.sztokholm.polemb.net; Ambassador MICHAŁ CZYŻ.

Portugal: Narvavägen 32, 2nd Floor, POB 10194, 100 55 Stockholm; tel. (8) 545-670-60; fax (8) 662-53-29; e-mail portugal@embassyportugal.se; internet www.embassyportugal.se; Ambassador JOSÉ CARLOS JÚLIO DA CRUZ ALMEIDA.

Romania: Östermalmsgt. 36, POB 26043, 100 41 Stockholm; tel. (8) 10-86-03; fax (8) 10-28-52; e-mail info@romanianembassy.se; internet stockholm.mae.ro; Ambassador VICTORIA POPESCU.

Russia: Gjörwellsgt. 31, 112 60 Stockholm; tel. (8) 13-04-41; fax (8) 618-27-03; e-mail rusembassy@telia.com; internet www.ryssland.se; Ambassador ALEKSANDR M. KADAKIN.

Saudi Arabia: Sköldungagt. 5, POB 26073, 100 41 Stockholm; tel. (8) 23-88-00; fax (8) 796-99-56; Ambassador Dr ABD AR-RAHMAN GDAIA.

Senegal: Birger Jarlsgt. 37, 3 tr., POB 7384, 111 45 Stockholm; tel. (8) 411-71-60; fax (8) 411-71-68; e-mail senegalembassy@telia.com; Ambassador HENRI-ANTOINE TURPIN.

Serbia: Valhallavägen 70, POB 26209, 100 41 Stockholm; tel. (8) 21-84-36; fax (8) 21-84-95; e-mail serbiaemb@telia.com; Ambassador Prof. Dr NINOSLAV D. STOJADINOVIĆ.

Slovakia: Arsenalsgt. 2, 3rd Floor, POB 7183, 103 88 Stockholm; tel. (8) 545-039-61; fax (8) 545-039-69; e-mail emb.stockholm@mzv.sk; internet www.mzv.sk/stockholm; Ambassador PETER KMEC.

Slovenia: Styrmansgt. 4, 1st Floor, 114 54 Stockholm; tel. (8) 545-65-885; fax (8) 662-92-74; e-mail vst@mzz-dkp.gov.si; Ambassador VOJISLAV SUC.

South Africa: Fleminggt. 20, 4th Floor, 112 26 Stockholm; tel. (8) 24-39-50; fax (8) 660-71-36; e-mail saemb.swe@telia.com; internet www.southafricanemb.se; Ambassador SOPHONIA RAPHULANE MAKGETLA.

Spain: Djurgårdsvägen 21, Djurgården, POB 10295, 100 55 Stockholm; tel. (8) 667-94-30; fax (8) 663-79-65; e-mail emb.estocolmo@mae.es; internet www.mae.es/embajadas/estocolmo; Ambassador ENRIQUE VIGUERA RUBIO.

Sri Lanka: Strandvägen 39, POB 24055, 104 50 Stockholm; tel. (8) 663-65-23; fax (8) 660-00-89; e-mail slembassy@comhem.se; internet www.slembassy.se; Ambassador RANJITH PEMSIRI JAYASOORIYA.

Sudan: POB 26142, 100 41 Stockholm; Stockholmsvägen 33, 181 33 Lidingö; tel. (8) 611-77-80; fax (8) 611-77-82; e-mail sudanembassy@telia.com; Ambassador MOSES MOJWOK AKOL.

Switzerland: Valhallavägen 64, POB 26143, 100 41 Stockholm; tel. (8) 676-79-00; fax (8) 21-15-04; e-mail sto.vertretung@eda.admin.ch; internet www.eda.admin.ch/stockholm; Ambassador ROBERT REICH.

Syria: Vendevägen 90, 5th Floor, POB 42, 182 11 Danderyd; tel. (8) 660-88-10; fax (8) 660-88-05; e-mail info@syrianembassy.se; internet www.syrianembassy.se; Chargé d'affaires a.i. AYMAN ALLOUSH.

Tanzania: Näsby Allé 6, 183 55 Täby; tel. (8) 732-24-30; fax (8) 732-24-32; e-mail mailbox@tanemb.se; internet www.tanemb.se; Chargé d'affaires a.i. JACIB PIUS MSEKWA.

Thailand: Floragt. 3, POB 26220, 100 40 Stockholm; tel. (8) 791-73-40; fax (8) 791-73-51; e-mail info@thaiembassy.se; internet www.thaiembassy.se; Ambassador APICHART CHINWANNO.

Tunisia: Narvavägen 32, 1st Floor, POB 24030, 104 50 Stockholm; tel. (8) 545-855-20; fax (8) 662-19-75; e-mail at.stockholm@swipnet.se; Chargé d'affaires a.i. NARJES DRIDI.

Turkey: Dag Hammarskjölds Väg 20, POB 24105, 104 51 Stockholm; tel. (8) 23-08-40; fax (8) 663-55-14; e-mail turkbe@turkemb.se; internet www.turkemb.se; Ambassador NECIP EGÜZ.

Ukraine: Stjärnvägen 2A, 181 34 Lidingö; tel. (8) 731-76-90; fax (8) 731-56-90; e-mail emb_se@mfa.gov.ua; internet www.mfa.gov.ua/sweden; Ambassador YEVGEN PEREBYINIS.

United Arab Emirates: Norrlandsgt. 20, POB 7485, 103 92 Stockholm; tel. (8) 411-12-44; fax (8) 411-12-45; Ambassador Sheikh NAJLA MOHAMED SALEM AL-QASSIMI.

United Kingdom: Skarpögt. 6–8, POB 27819, 115 93 Stockholm; tel. (8) 671-30-00; fax (8) 671-31-04; e-mail info@britishembassy.se; internet ukinsweden.fco.gov.uk; Ambassador ANDREW J. MITCHELL.

USA: Dag Hammarskjölds Väg 31, 115 89 Stockholm; tel. (8) 783-53-00; fax (8) 661-19-64; e-mail stockholmweb@state.gov; internet www.usemb.se; Chargé d'affaires a.i. ROBERT J. SILVERMAN.

Uruguay: Kommendörsgt. 35, POB 10114, 100 55 Stockholm; tel. (8) 660-31-96; fax (8) 665-31-66; e-mail urustoc@uruemb.se; Ambassador MANUEL VIEIRA MEROLA.

Venezuela: Engelbrektsgt. 35B, POB 26012, 100 41 Stockholm; tel. (8) 411-09-96; fax (8) 21-31-00; e-mail venezuela.embassy@comhem.se; Chargé d'affaires a.i. ZULIMA ROJAS MAVARES.

Viet Nam: Örby Slottsvägen 26, 125 71 Älvsjö; tel. (8) 556-210-70; fax (8) 556-210-80; e-mail info@vietnamemb.se; internet www.vietnamemb.se; Ambassador TRINH QUANG THANH.

Zambia: Gårdsvägen 18, 3rd Floor, POB 3056, 169 03 Solna; tel. (8) 679-90-40; fax (8) 679-68-50; e-mail info@zambiaembassy.se; internet www.zambiaembassy.se; Ambassador JOYCE MUSENGE.

Zimbabwe: Herserudsvägen 5A, 7th Floor, 181 34 Lidingö; POB 3253, 103 65 Stockholm; tel. (8) 765-53-80; fax (8) 21-91-32; e-mail mbuya@stockholm.mail.telia.com; Ambassador MARY SIBUSISIWE MUBI.

Judicial System

The judiciary and the executive are separate, although judges are appointed by the Government. A judge can be removed by an authority other than a court, but may, in such an event, request a judicial trial of the decision.

To supervise the courts in administrative matters, there is a central authority, the Domstolsverket, in Jönköping. This authority has no control over the judicial process, in which the court is independent even of the legislature and Government.

There are state officers who exercise control over the judiciary as well as the administrative authorities. The Justitiekansler (Chancellor of Justice or Attorney-General) and the four Justitieombudsmän supervise the courts and the general administration including the armed forces. The Justitiekansler performs his functions on behalf of the Government. The Justitieombudsmän are appointed by and act on behalf of the legislature.

Attorney-General (Justitiekansler): GÖRAN LAMBERTZ.

SUPREME COURT

Högsta domstolen (Supreme Court in Stockholm): Riddarhustorget 8, POB 2066, 103 12 Stockholm; tel. (8) 561-666-00; fax (8) 561-666-86; e-mail hogsta.domstolen@dom.se; internet www

SWEDEN

.hogstadomstolen.se; the Supreme Court in Stockholm, consisting of a minimum of 14 members, is the Court of Highest Instance. The Court works in three chambers, each of which is duly constituted of five members. Certain cases are decided by full session of the Court. There are also special divisions with three members (or, in simple cases, one member) which decide whether the Court is to consider a case.

Chairman of the Supreme Court: JOHAN MUNCK.
Justices: GERTRUD LENNANDER, LEIF THORSSON, DAG VICTOR, SEVERIN BLOMSTRAND, TORGNY HÅSTAD, MARIANNE LUNDIUS, LARS DAHLLÖF, ANN-CHRISTINE LINDEBLAD, ELLA NYSTRÖM, KERSTIN CALISSENDORFF, PER VIRDESTEN, ANNA SKARHED, GUDMUND TOIJER, STEFAN LINDSKOG, LENA MOORE.

APPELLATE COURTS

The Court of Appeal, the Court of Second Instance, consists of a president, judges of appeal and associate judges of appeal. The work is apportioned between various divisions, each of which has five or six members. In criminal cases the bench consists of three professional judges and two lay assessors; in petty and civil cases there are three professional judges only. There are six Courts of Appeal (hovrätt).

President of the Court of Appeal (Stockholm): FREDRIK WERSÄLL.
President of the Court of Appeal (Jönköping): KATHRIN FLOSSING.
President of the Court of Appeal (Malmö): LARS-GÖRAN ENGSTRÖM.
President of the Court of Appeal (Göteborg): GUNNEL WENNBERG.
President of the Court of Appeal (Sundsvall): STEN ANDERSSON.
President of the Court of Appeal (Umeå): ANDERS IACOBÆUS.

DISTRICT COURTS

The District Court acts as a Court of First Instance in both civil and criminal cases. At mid-2007 there were 68 District Courts (tingsrätt). In criminal cases the court is composed of a presiding professional judge and three or, in serious cases, five lay assessors; in petty cases the court consists of the professional judge only. In civil cases the court is ordinarily composed of three professional judges; however, preparatory sessions are conducted by one professional judge. In family law cases, the court is composed of a professional judge and three lay assessors. The lay assessors are elected for a period of four years (during which they are on duty for about 10 days a year). They act as members of the bench and should consequently be distinguished from the jurors of other countries. In certain types of case technical experts may sit alongside the judges.

ADMINISTRATIVE COURTS

In each of the 23 administrative districts of the country there is a County Administrative Court (länsrätten). This Court handles appeal cases concerning the assessment of social security and welfare. The bench ordinarily consists of a professional judge and three lay assessors, although in simple cases a professional judge may preside alone.

Appeals against decisions by the County Administrative Courts may be made to Administrative Courts of Appeal (kammarrätter) consisting of a president, judges of appeal and associate judges of appeal. The courts work in divisions, each of which normally has six members. The bench consists of at least three and not more than four judges. In certain cases there are, however, three professional judges and two lay assessors. There are four Administrative Courts of Appeal.

The Supreme Administrative Court of Sweden (Regeringsrätten) in Stockholm, consisting of 19 members, is the Court of Highest Instance in Administrative cases. The composition of the Court is governed by rules very similar to those that apply to the Supreme Court.

Chairman of the Supreme Administrative Court: STEN HECKSCHER.
President of the Administrative Court of Appeal (Stockholm): THOMAS ROLÉN.
President of the Administrative Court of Appeal (Göteborg): HANS-JÖRGEN ANDERSSON.
President of the Administrative Court of Appeal (Sundsvall): MARGARETA ÅBERG.
President of the Administrative Court of Appeal (Jönköping): PETER ROSÉN.

SPECIAL COURTS

Special courts exist for certain categories of cases, e.g. fastighetsdomstolar (real estate courts) for cases concerning real estate.

OMBUDSMEN

The post of Justitieombudsman was created in 1800 to supervise the manner in which judges, government officials and other civil servants observe the laws, and to prosecute those who act illegally, misuse their position or neglect their duties. The Ombudsman is allowed access to all documents and information and has the right to be present at the considerations of the courts and other authorities. Government ministers in Sweden are not subject to supervision by the Ombudsman. The term of office is four years.

Ombudsmen: MATS MELIN, KERSTIN ANDRÉ, HANS-GUNNAR AXBERGER, CECILIA NORDENFELT.

Religion

CHRISTIANITY

About 78% of the population were members of the Svenska Kyrkan (Church of Sweden) in 2004. Since the constitutional link between the Church and the state was severed in 2000 a significant number of people have left the Church each year.

Sveriges Kristna Råd (Christian Council of Sweden): Ekumeniska Centret, Starrbäcksgt. 11, 172 99 Sundbyberg; tel. (8) 453-68-00; fax (8) 453-68-29; e-mail info@skr.org; internet www.skr.org; f. 1993; 27 mem. churches; Chair. Rev. KARIN WIBORN; Gen. Sec. SVEN-BERNHARD FAST.

Church of Sweden

Svenska kyrkan

Kyrkans Hus, Sysslomansgt. 4, 751 70 Uppsala; tel. (18) 16-95-00; fax (18) 16-96-07; e-mail info@svenskakyrkan.se; internet www.svenskakyrkan.se.

Evangelical Lutheran; 13 dioceses, 2,200 parishes, 3,300 active clergy (including missionaries in the mission fields); the Archbishop of Uppsala is head of the Church.

Archbishop of Uppsala: Most Rev. ANDERS WEJRYD, 751 70 Uppsala; tel. (18) 16-95-00; fax (18) 16-96-25.

Evangeliska Fosterlands-Stiftelsen (Swedish Evangelical Mission): Sysslomansgt. 4, 751 70 Uppsala; tel. (18) 16-98-00; fax (18) 16-98-01; e-mail efs@efs.svenskakyrkan.se; internet www.efs.nu; f. 1856; an independent mission org. within the Church of Sweden; 17,994 mems; Chair. RAY RAWALL; Mission Dir ANDERS SJÖBERG.

Other Protestant Churches

Eesti Evangeeliumi Luteri Usu Kirik (Estonian Evangelical Lutheran Church): POB 450 74, 104 30 Stockholm 45; tel. (8) 20-69-78; e-mail ingo.jaagu@bredband.net; 12,000 mems; Dean INGO TIIT JAAGU; Gen. Sec. IVAR NIPPAK.

Metodistkyrkan i Sverige (United Methodist Church): Danska vägen 20, 412 66 Göteborg; tel. (31) 733-78-40; fax (31) 733-87-49; e-mail info@metodistkyrkan.se; internet www.metodistkyrkan.se; f. 1868; 3,565 mems; Bishop ØYSTEIN OLSEN; Pres. of Conference Board ANDERS SVENSSON.

Sjundedags Adventistsamfundet (Seventh-day Adventists): POB 536, 101 30 Stockholm; tel. (8) 545-297-70; fax (8) 20-48-68; e-mail info@adventist.se; internet www.adventist.se; f. 1880; 2,800 mems; Pres. BOBBY SJÖLANDER; Sec. AUDREY ANDERSSON.

Svenska Baptistsamfundet (Baptist Union of Sweden): Starrbäcksgt. 11, 172 99 Sundbyberg; tel. (8) 564-827-00; fax (8) 564-827-27; e-mail info@baptist.se; internet www.baptist.se; f. 1848; 223 churches, 17,195 mems (2007); mem. European Baptist Fed., Baptist World Alliance and Christian Council of Sweden (Sveriges Kristna Råd); Pres. Rev. KARIN WIBORN; Gen. Sec. LARS DALESJÖ.

Svenska Missionskyrkan (Mission Covenant Church of Sweden): Tegnérgt. 8, POB 6302, 113 81 Stockholm; tel. (8) 674-07-00; fax (8) 674-07-93; e-mail info@missionkyrkan.se; internet www.missionskyrkan.se; f. 1878; 61,769 mems; Pres. GÖRAN ZETTERGREN; Chair. of Board ULF HÅLLMARKER.

The Roman Catholic Church

For ecclesiastical purposes, Sweden comprises the single diocese of Stockholm, directly responsible to the Holy See. At 31 December 2006 there were 140,000 adherents in the country, representing 1.5% of the total population.

Scandinavian Bishops' Conference

POB 135, 421 22 Västra Frölunda; tel. (31) 709-57-15; fax (31) 49-21-70; e-mail nbk@bishopsoffice.org; internet www.nordiskabiskopskonferensen.org.

f. 1960 new statutes approved 2000; covers Sweden, Norway, Denmark, Finland and Iceland; Pres. Rt Rev. ANDERS ARBORELIUS; Sec.-Gen. Rt Rev. GEORG MÜLLER.

SWEDEN

Bishop of Stockholm: Rt Rev. ANDERS ARBORELIUS, Götgt. 68, POB 4114, 102 62 Stockholm; tel. (8) 462-66-00; fax (8) 702-05-55; e-mail biskop@katolskakyrkan.se; internet www.katolskakyrkan.se.

Other Denominations

Other Christian Churches include the Pentecostal Movement (with an estimated 90,000 mems in 2004), the Orthodox Churches of the Greeks, Romanians, Russians, Serbians and Finnish (together numbering about 100,000 mems in 2004), the Church of Jesus Christ of Latter-day Saints (Mormons—9,000 mems in 2004), the Swedish Alliance Missionary Society (12,895 mems in 1997), the Jehovah's Witnesses (23,000 mems in 2004) and the Salvation Army (25,531 mems in 1997).

ISLAM

In 2004 there were approximately 300,000 to 350,000 Muslims in Sweden, of whom around 100,000 were believed to be religiously active. Muslim affiliations represented among immigrant groups are predominantly with the Shi'a and Sunni branches of Islam.

Islamiska Radet i Sverige (Islamic Council of Sweden—IRIS): POB 3053, 14503 Norsborg; tel. (8) 531-707-95; fax (8) 531-706-65; f. 1986.

Islamiska Kulturcenterunionen i Sverige (Union of the Islamic Cultural Centres in Sweden—IKUS): POB 3053, 145 03 Norsborg; tel. (8) 531-707-95; fax (8) 531-706-65; f. 1984.

Sveriges Muslimska Förbund (SMUF): Stockholms Moske, Kapellgränd 10, 116 25 Stockholm; tel. and fax (8) 643-10-04; e-mail aldebe@arabia.com.

JUDAISM

In 2004 the total number of Jews living in Sweden was estimated to be approximately 18,500–20,000; however, the Jewish community estimated 10,000 active, or practising, members. There are Orthodox, Conservative and Reform Jewish synagogues. The largest Jewish community is in Stockholm.

Jewish Community in Stockholm: Wahrendorffsgt. 3B, POB 7427, 103 91 Stockholm; tel. (8) 587-858-00; fax (8) 587-858-58; e-mail info@jfst.se; internet www.jfst.se; f. 1776; c. 4,500 mems; Exec. Dir THOMAS BAB.

OTHER RELIGIONS

In 2004 there were approximately 3,000–4,000 Buddhists and a similar number of Hindus in Sweden.

The Press

Press freedom in Sweden dates from a law of 1766. The 1949 Freedom of the Press Act, a fundamental law embodying the whole of the press legislation in the Constitution, guarantees the Press's right to print and disseminate ideas; protects those supplying information by forbidding editors to disclose sources under any circumstances; authorizes all public documents to be publicly available, official secrets being the only exception; and contains provision for defamation. Press offences are to be referred to common law, and all cases against the Press must be heard by jury.

In 1916 the Press Council was founded by press organizations to monitor ethical matters within the Press. Lacking judicial status, it has powers to rehabilitate persons wronged by the Press who refuse to apply to courts of law. Its judgments are widely published and highly respected.

In 1969 the office of Press Ombudsman was established to supervise adherence to ethical standards. Public complaints shall be directed to the Press Ombudsman, who is also entitled to act on his own initiative. He may dismiss a complaint if unfounded, or if the newspaper agrees to publish a retraction or rectification acceptable to the complainant. When he finds that the grievance is of a more serious nature, he will file a complaint with the Press Council, which will then publish a statement acquitting or criticizing the newspaper. The findings of the Council are published in the newspaper concerned.

The dominating influence of the few major dailies is largely confined to Stockholm, the provinces having a strong Press of their own. The major dailies are: *Aftonbladet*, *Dagens Nyheter*, *Expressen*, *Svenska Dagbladet*, *Dagens Industri* (all Stockholm), *Göteborgs-Posten* (Gothenburg), *Sydsvenskan* (Malmö). In 2006 there were 166 daily newspapers with a combined circulation of 3.9m.

The two principal magazine publishers in Sweden are the Bonnier group (also a large book publisher and the majority shareholder in the newspapers *Dagens Nyheter*, *Expressen* and *Sydsvenskan*) and the Aller company. Four other companies produce most of the remainder of Sweden's magazine circulation. The most popular weekly periodicals include the family magazines *Året Runt*, *Hemmets Veckotidning*, *Allers* and *Hemmets Journal*, and the home and household magazine *ICA Kuriren*. *Vi* caters for serious cultural and political discussion, and *Bonniers Litterära Magasin* specializes in literary topics.

PRINCIPAL NEWSPAPERS

Newspapers with a circulation exceeding 15,000 are listed below.

Ängelholm

Nordvästra Skånes Tidningar: 262 83 Ängelholm; tel. (431) 84-000; fax (431) 26-177; f. 1847; daily; Conservative; Editor-in-Chief BENNIE OHLSSON.

Borås

Borås Tidning: 501 85 Borås; tel. (33) 700-07-00; fax (33) 10-14-36; f. 1826; morning; Conservative; Editor JAN ÖJMERTZ; circ. 53,000 (2001).

Eksjö

Smålands-Tidningen: POB 261, 575 23 Eksjö; tel. (381) 13-200; fax (381) 17-145; f. 1899; morning; independent; Editor BENGT WENDLE.

Eskilstuna

Eskilstuna-Kuriren Strengnäs Tidning: POB 120, 631 02 Eskilstuna; tel. (16) 15-60-00; fax (16) 51-63-04; e-mail redaktion@ekuriren.se; internet www.ekuriren.se; f. 1890; morning; Liberal; Editor PEO WÄRRING; circ. 33,000 (2006).

Falkenberg

Hallands Nyheter: 311 81 Falkenberg; tel. (346) 29-000; fax (346) 29-115; e-mail redaktionen@hn.se; internet www.hn.se; f. 1905; morning; Centre; Editor ANNA KARIN LITH; circ. 31,000 (2001).

Falun

Dala-Demokraten: POB 825, Stigaregat. 17, 791 29 Falun; tel. (23) 47-500; fax (23) 20-668; e-mail redaktionen@deladem.se; internet www.daladomokraten.se; f. 1917; morning; Social Democrat; Editor GÖRAN GREIDER.

Falu-Kuriren: POB 265, 791 26 Falun; tel. (23) 93-500; fax (23) 12-073; e-mail red@falukuriren.se; internet www.falukuriren.se; f. 1894; morning; Liberal; Editor CHRISTER GRUHS.

Gävle

Arbetarbladet: POB 287, 801 04 Gävle; tel. (26) 15-93-00; fax (26) 12-14-06; f. 1902; morning; Social Democrat; Editor KENNET LUTTI.

Gefle Dagblad: POB 367, 801 05 Gävle; tel. (26) 15-95-00; fax (26) 15-97-00; f. 1895; morning; Liberal; Editor ROBERT ROSÉN.

Göteborg
(Gothenburg)

Göteborgs-Posten: Polhemsplatsen 5, 405 02 Göteborg; tel. (31) 62-40-00; fax (31) 62-45-85; e-mail redaktion@gp.se; internet www.gp.se; f. 1858; morning; Liberal; Editor-in-Chief PETER HJORNE; circ. 245,600 (2006).

Halmstad

Hallandsposten: 301 81 Halmstad; tel. (35) 14-75-00; fax (35) 14-76-88; e-mail redaktionen@hallandsposten.se; internet www.hallandsposten.se; f. 1850; morning; Liberal; Editor VIVEKA HEDBJÖRK.

Hässleholm

Norra Skåne: 281 81 Hässleholm; tel. (451) 74-50-00; fax (451) 74-50-32; e-mail chefred@nsk.se; internet www.nsk.se; f. 1899; morning; Centre; Editor BILLY BENGTSSON; circ. 21,800 (2001).

Helsingborg

Helsingborgs Dagblad: Vasatorpsvägen 1, 251 83 Helsingborg; tel. (242) 489-90-00; e-mail redaktionen@hd.se; internet hd.se; f. 1867; morning; independent; Editor-in-Chief LARS JOHANSSON.

SD-Kuriren: POB 130 45, 250 13 Helsingborg; tel. (73) 62-60-661; fax (455) 151-33; e-mail redaktion@sdkuriren.se; internet www.sdkuriren.se; f. 1988; organ of the Sverigedemokraterna; Editor-in-Chief RICHARD JOMSHOF; circ. 30,000.

Hudiksvall

Hudiksvalls Tidning: POB 1201, 824 15 Hudiksvall; tel. (650) 355-00; fax (650) 355-60; e-mail redaktion@ht.se; internet www.ht.se; f. 1909; includes *Hälsinglands Tidning*; morning; Centre; Man. Dir RUBEN JACOBSSON; Editor JÖRGEN BENGTSON.

SWEDEN   Directory

Jönköping

Jönköpings-Posten/Smålands Allehanda: 551 80 Jönköping; tel. (36) 30-40-50; fax (36) 12-61-11; f. 1865; morning; independent; Editor STIG FREDRIKSSON.

Kalmar

Barometern med Oskarshamns-Tidningen: 391 88 Kalmar; tel. (480) 59-100; fax (480) 59-131; f. 1841; morning; Conservative; Editor GUNILLA ANDREASSON.

Karlskrona

Blekinge Läns Tidning: 371 89 Karlskrona; tel. (455) 77-000; fax (455) 82-170; e-mail kudcenter@blt.se; internet www.blt.se; f. 1869; morning; Liberal; Editor-in-Chief KERSTIN JOHANSSON; circ. 36,800 (2003).

Sydöstra Sveriges Dagblad: Landbrogt. 17, 371 88 Karlskrona; tel. (455) 19-000; fax (455) 82-237; f. 1903; morning; Social Democrat; Editor ANDERS HAGQUIST.

Karlstad

Nya Wermlands-Tidningen: POB 28, 651 02 Karlstad; tel. (54) 19-90-00; fax (54) 19-96-00; e-mail redaktion@nwt.se; internet www.nwt.se; f. 1836; morning; Conservative; Editor STAFFAN ANDER.

Värmlands Folkblad: POB 67, 651 03 Karlstad; tel. (54) 17-55-06; fax (54) 15-16-59; e-mail kundtjanst@vf.se; internet www.vf.se; f. 1918; morning; Social Democrat; Editor PETER FRANKE.

Kristianstad

Kristianstadsbladet: 291 84 Kristianstad; tel. (44) 18-55-00; fax (44) 21-17-01; e-mail kb@kristianstadsbladet.se; internet www.kristianstadsbladet.se; f. 1856; morning; Liberal; Man. Dir BO WIGERNÄS; Editor HAKAN BENGTSSON; circ. 31,900 (2004).

Lidköping

Nya Läns-Tidningen: 531 81 Lidköping; tel. (510) 89-700; fax (510) 89-796; e-mail post@nlt.se; f. 1903; morning; 3 a week; Liberal; Editor LENNART HÖRLING.

Linköping

Östgöta Correspondenten: 581 89 Linköping; tel. (13) 28-00-00; fax (13) 28-03-24; e-mail nyhet@corren.se; internet www.corren.se; f. 1838; morning; Liberal; Editor OLA SIGVARDSSON; circ. 59,300 (2006).

Luleå

Norrbottens-Kuriren: 971 81 Luleå; tel. (920) 37-500; fax (920) 67-107; f. 1861; morning; Conservative.

Norrländska Socialdemokraten: 971 83 Luleå; tel. (920) 36-000; fax (920) 36-279; f. 1919; morning; Social Democrat; Editor LENNART HÅKANSSON.

Malmö

Kvällsposten: 205 26 Malmö; tel. (40) 28-16-00; fax (40) 93-92-24; f. 1990; evening; Liberal; Editor LARS KLINT.

Skånska Dagbladet: Östergt. 11, POB 165, 201 21 Malmö; tel. (40) 660-55-00; fax (40) 97-47-70; f. 1888; morning; Centre; Editor JAN A. JOHANSSON.

Sydsvenskan: 205 05 Malmö; tel. (40) 28-12-00; fax (40) 93-54-75; e-mail sydsvenskan@sydsvenskan.se; internet sydsvenskan.se; f. 1848; morning; Liberal independent; Editors JONAS GRUVÖ, HEIDI AVELLAN; circ. 136,400 (2003).

Norrköping

Norrköpings Tidningar: 601 83 Norrköping; tel. (11) 20-00-00; fax (11) 20-02-40; e-mail redaktionen@nt.se; internet www.nt.se; f. 1758; morning; Conservative; Editor CHARLI NILSSON; circ. 49,900 (2000).

Nyköping

Södermanlands Nyheter: 611 79 Nyköping; tel. (155) 76-700; fax (155) 26-88-01; e-mail redaktionen@sn.se; internet www.sn.se; f. 1893; morning; Editor GÖRAN CARLSTORP; circ. 25,300 (2006).

Örebro

Nerikes Allehanda: 701 92 Örebro; tel. (19) 15-50-00; fax (19) 12-03-83; e-mail redaktionen@na.se; internet www.na.se; f. 1843; morning; Liberal; Editor KRISTER LINNER.

Örnsköldsvik

Örnsköldsviks Allehanda: POB 110, 891 23 Örnsköldsvik; tel. (660) 29-50-00; fax (660) 15-064; e-mail lars.nordstrom@allehanda.se; f. 1843; morning; Liberal; Editor LARS NORDSTRÖM; circ. 20,800 (2001).

Östersund

Länstidningen: 831 89 Östersund; tel. (63) 15-55-00; fax (63) 15-55-95; f. 1924; morning; Social Democrat; Editors PETER SWEDENMARK, CHRISTER SJÖSTRÖM; circ. 17,000 (2003).

Östersunds-Posten: POB 720, 831 28 Östersund; tel. (63) 16-16-00; fax (63) 10-58-02; f. 1877; morning; Centre; Editors BOSSE SVENSSON, HÅKAN LARSSON.

Piteå

Piteå-Tidningen: POB 193, 941 24 Piteå; tel. (911) 64-500; fax (911) 64-650; f. 1915; morning; Social Democrat; Editor OLOV CARLSSON.

Skara

Skaraborgs Läns Tidning: POB 214, 532 23 Skara; tel. (511) 13-010; fax (511) 18-815; f. 1884; morning; Liberal; Editor HANS OLOFSSON.

Skellefteå

Norra Västerbotten: POB 58, 931 21 Skellefteå; tel. (910) 57-700; fax (910) 57-875; e-mail redaktionsavderlning@norran.se; internet www.norran.se; f. 1910; morning; 6 days a week; Liberal; Editor OLA THEANDER; circ. 30,500 (2000).

Skövde

Skaraborgs Allehanda: POB 407, 541 28 Skövde; tel. (500) 46-75-00; fax (500) 48-05-82; e-mail redaktion@sla.se; internet www.sla.se; f. 1884; morning; Conservative; Editor MÅNS JOHNSON.

Södertälje

Länstidningen: 151 82 Södertälje; tel. (8) 550-921-00; fax (8) 550-877-72; e-mail redaktion@lt.se; f. 1861; morning; 6 a week; Centre; Editor TORSTEN CARLSSON; circ. 17,600 (2002).

Stockholm

Aftonbladet: 105 18 Stockholm; tel. (8) 725-20-00; fax (8) 600-01-70; e-mail redaktion@aftonbladet.se; internet www.aftonbladet.se; f. 1830; evening; Social Democrat independent; Editor-in-Chief KALLE JUNGKVIST.

Dagen: 105 36 Stockholm; tel. (8) 619-24-00; fax (8) 619-60-51; e-mail info@dagen.se; f. 1945; morning; 4 a week; Christian independent; Editor DANIEL GRAHN; circ. 20,200 (2003).

Dagens Industri: 113 90 Stockholm; tel. (8) 736-50-00; fax (8) 31-19-06; internet di.se; f. 1976; 6 a week; business news; Editor LINUS PAULSSON.

Dagens Nyheter: 105 15 Stockholm; tel. (8) 738-10-00; fax (8) 738-21-80; e-mail info@dn.se; internet www.dn.se; f. 1864; morning; independent; Editor-in-Chief THORBJÖRN LARSSON; CEO LENA HERRMANN; circ. 344,000 (2007).

Expressen: Gjörwellsgt. 30, 105 16 Stockholm; tel. (8) 738-30-00; fax (8) 738-33-40; e-mail redaktionen@expressen.se; internet www.expressen.se; f. 1945; evening; Liberal; Editor OTTO SJÖBERG; circ. 353,000 (2003).

Svenska Dagbladet: 105 17 Stockholm; tel. (8) 13-50-00; fax (8) 13-56-80; e-mail svd@svd.se; internet www.svd.se; f. 1884; morning; Conservative; Editor-in-Chief LENA K. SAMUELSSON; circ. 170,000 (2000).

Sundsvall

Sundsvalls Tidning: 851 72 Sundsvall; tel. (60) 19-70-00; fax (60) 15-44-33; e-mail redaktion@st.nu; internet www.st.nu; f. 1841; morning; Liberal; Editor KJELL CARNBRO; circ. 35,700 (2005).

Trollhättan

Trollhättans Tidning: POB 54, 461 22 Trollhättan; tel. (520) 49-42-00; fax (520) 49-43-19; f. 1906; morning; 5 a week; independent; Editor TORBJÖRN HÅKANSSON.

Uddevalla

Bohusläningen med Dals Dagblad: 451 83 Uddevalla; tel. (522) 99-000; fax (522) 51-18-88; f. 1878; morning; Liberal; Editor ULF JOHANSSON.

SWEDEN	Directory

Umeå

Västerbottens-Kuriren: 901 70 Umeå; tel. (90) 15-10-00; fax (90) 77-00-53; e-mail info@vk.se; internet www.vk.se; f. 1900; morning; Liberal.

Uppsala

Upsala Nya Tidning: POB 36, Danmarksgt. 28, 751 03 Uppsala; tel. (18) 478-00-00; fax (18) 12-95-07; e-mail hakan.holmberg@unt.se; internet www.unt.se; f. 1890; morning; Liberal; Editor-in-Chief LARS NILSSON; circ. 62,800 (2002).

Värnamo

Värnamo Nyheter: 331 84 Värnamo; tel. (370) 30-19-56; fax (370) 493-95; e-mail redaktion@varnamonyheter.se; internet www.varnamonyheter.se; f. 1917; morning; independent; Editor STIG-ERIC EINARSSON; circ. 23,000 (2000).

Västerås

Vestmanlands Läns Tidning: POB 3, 721 03 Västerås; tel. (21) 19-90-00; fax (21) 19-90-60; e-mail nyheter@vlt.se; internet www.vlt.se; f. 1831; morning; Liberal; Editor ELISABETH BÄCK; circ. 48,000 (2003).

Växjö

Smålandsposten: 351 70 Växjö; tel. (470) 77-05-00; fax (470) 209-49; f. 1866; morning; Conservative; Editor CLAES-GÖRAN HEGNELL.

Ystad

Ystads Allehanda: 271 81 Ystad; tel. (411) 55-78-00; fax (411) 13-955; e-mail nyheter@ystadsallehanda.se; internet www.ystadsallehanda.se; f. 1873; morning; Liberal; Editor MARGARETHA ENGSTRÖM; circ. 26,100 (2004).

POPULAR PERIODICALS

Allas Veckotidning: Allers Förlag, 205 35 Malmö; tel. (40) 38-59-00; fax (40) 38-59-64; e-mail allas@aller.se; f. 1931; weekly; family; Editor-in-Chief TINA JANSSON; circ. 138,400.

Allers: 251 85 Helsingborg; tel. (42) 17-35-00; fax (42) 17-35-68; e-mail redaktionen@allers.se; f. 1877; weekly; family; Editor-in-Chief LOTTA HYLANDER; circ. 217,000.

Allt om Mat: Sveavägen 53, 105 44 Stockholm; tel. (8) 736-53-00; fax (8) 34-00-88; e-mail red@aom.bonnier.se; internet www.alltommat.se; f. 1970; 18 a year; food specialities; Editor-in-Chief JAN HOLMSTRÖM; circ. 125,800.

Antik och Auktion: Landskronåvagen 23, 251 85 Helsingborg; tel. (42) 12-35-00; fax (42) 17-37-40; e-mail carin.stentorp@aller.se; internet www.antikochauktion.se; f. 1978; monthly; antiques; Editor CARIN STENTORP; circ. 57,900.

Året Runt: 105 44 Stockholm; tel. (8) 736-52-00; fax (8) 30-49-00; f. 1946; weekly; family; Editor LILLIAN EHRENHOLM-DAUN; circ. 243,500.

Bilsport: POB 529, 371 23 Karlskrona; tel. (455) 33-53-25; fax (455) 291-75; e-mail bilsport@fabas.se; internet www.bilsport.se; f. 1962; fortnightly; motor-sport, cars; Editor-in-Chief FREDRIK SJÖQVIST; circ. 67,300.

Damernas Värld: 105 44 Stockholm; tel. (8) 736-53-00; fax (8) 24-46-46; e-mail red@dv.bonnier.se; f. 1940; monthly; women's interest; Editor MONA JOHANSSON; circ. 118,800.

Elle: St Eriksplan 2, 113 93 Stockholm; tel. (8) 457-80-00; fax (8) 457-80-80; e-mail ellered@hachette.se; internet www.elle.se; f. 1988; monthly; women's interest; Editor KRISTINA ADOLFSSON; circ. 81,900.

Femina Månadens Magasin: 251 85 Helsingborg; tel. (42) 17-35-00; fax (42) 17-36-82; e-mail femina@aller.se; f. 1981; monthly; women's interest; Editor LISBETH LUNDAHL; circ. 118,000.

Frida: Hammarby Kajväg 14, 120 30 Stockholm; tel. (8) 587-481-00; fax (8) 587-481-07; e-mail frida@frida.forlag.se; internet www.frida.se; fortnightly; for teenage girls; Editor-in-Chief KAROLINA OLOVSSON; circ. 67,000.

Hänt Extra: POB 27704, 115 91 Stockholm; tel. (8) 679-46-00; fax (8) 679-46-77; f. 1986; weekly; family; Editors-in-Chief JAN BARD, THORD SKÖLDEKRANS; circ. 113,300.

Hänt i Veckan: POB 27704, 115 91 Stockholm; tel. (8) 679-46-00; fax (8) 679-46-33; f. 1964; weekly; family; Editor-in-Chief STEN HEDMAN; circ. 132,800.

Hemmets Journal: Egmont Tidskrifter AB, 205 07 Malmö; tel. (40) 38-52-00; fax (40) 38-53-98; e-mail red.hj@egmont.se; internet www.hj.egmont.se; f. 1920; weekly; family; Editor-in-Chief JANNE WALLES; circ. 231,800.

Hemmets Veckotidning: Allers Förlag AB, 205 35 Malmö; tel. (40) 38-59-00; fax (40) 38-59-14; f. 1929; weekly; family; Editor ULLA COCKE; circ. 215,300.

Hus & Hem: ICA Förlaget AB, POB 6630, 113 84 Stockholm; tel. (8) 728-23-00; fax (8) 34-56-37; e-mail kundtjanst.husohem@formapg.se; internet www.husohem.se; 12 a year; for house-owners; Editor ANNA LILJEBERG; circ. 153,000.

ICA Kuriren: POB 6630, 113 84 Stockholm; tel. (8) 728-23-00; fax (8) 728-23-50; e-mail red.kuriren@forlaget.ica.se; internet www.icakuriren.se; f. 1942; weekly; home and household; Editor ÅSA LUNDEGÅRD; circ. 364,300.

Kalle Anka & Co: 205 08 Malmö; tel. (40) 693-94-00; fax (40) 693-94-95; e-mail kalle.anka@egmont.se; internet www.ankeborg.egmont.se; f. 1948; weekly; comics; Editor TORD JÖNSSON; circ. 138,000.

Kvällsstunden: Tidningshuset Kvällsstunden AB, POB 1080, 721 27 Västerås; tel. (21) 19-04-00; fax (21) 13-62-62; e-mail info@tidningshuset.com; internet www.tidningshuset.com; weekly; family magazine; Editor ÅKE LINDBERG; circ. 54,300.

Må Bra: POB 27780, 115 93 Stockholm; tel. (8) 679-46-00; fax (8) 667-34-39; f. 1978; monthly; health and nutrition; Editor-in-Chief INGER RIDSTRÖM; circ. 97,900.

OKEJ: Egmont Kärnan AB, Ö Förstadsgt. 34, 205 08 Malmö; tel. (40) 693-94-00; fax (40) 693-94-94; e-mail okej@egmont.se; internet www.okej.se; f. 1980; monthly; pop-music magazine; Editor ANDERS TENGNER; circ. 44,400.

Premium Motor: POB 6019, 175 06 Järfälla; tel. (8) 761-09-50; fax (8) 761-09-49; motoring; Editor STAFFAN SWEDENBORG; circ. 44,615.

Privata Affärer: Sveavägen 53, 105 44 Stockholm; tel. (8) 736-53-00; fax (8) 31-25-60; e-mail pren@privataaffarer.se; internet www.privataaffarer.se; f. 1978; monthly; personal money management; Editor-in-Chief HANS BOLANDER; circ. 111,200.

Röster i Radio/TV: POB 27704, 115 91 Stockholm; tel. (8) 679-46-00; fax (8) 679-46-33; f. 1934; weekly; family magazine and programme guide to radio and television; Editor-in-Chief EDGAR ANTONSSON; circ. 140,000.

Sköna hem: 105 44 Stockholm; tel. (8) 736-52-00; fax (8) 33-74-11; e-mail skonahem@skh.bonnier.se; internet www.skonahem.com; f. 1979 (Sköna Hem), 1956 (Allt i Hemmet), merged 1992; monthly; interior decoration; Editor-in-Chief EVA ABRAHAMSSON; circ. 98,800.

Svensk Damtidning: POB 27710, 115 91 Stockholm; tel. (8) 679-46-00; fax (8) 679-47-50; f. 1980; weekly; women's interest; Editor-in-Chief KARIN LENMOR; circ. 132,400.

Teknikens Värld: 105 44 Stockholm; tel. (8) 736-53-00; fax (8) 736-00-11; internet www.teknikensvarld.com; f. 1948; fortnightly; motoring; Editor-in-Chief DANIEL FRODIN; circ. 48,100.

Vår bostad: POB 12651, 112 93 Stockholm; tel. (8) 692-02-00; fax (8) 650-06-41; e-mail info@varbostad.se; internet www.varbostad.se; f. 1924; 11 a year; house and home; Editor ULRICA AMBJÖRN; circ. 928,700.

Vecko-Revyn: Kungsgt. 34, 105 44 Stockholm; tel. (8) 736-52-00; fax (8) 24-16-02; e-mail ebba@veckorevyn.com; internet veckorevyn.net; f. 1935; weekly; young women's interest; Editor EBBA VON SYDOW; circ. 91,100.

Vi Bilägare: POB 23800, 104 35 Stockholm; tel. (8) 736-12-00; fax (8) 736-12-49; e-mail redaktionen@vibilagare.se; internet www.vibilagare.se; f. 1930; fortnightly; auto and travel; Editor NILS-ERIC FRENDIN; circ. 170,000.

Vi Föräldrar: 105 44 Stockholm; tel. (8) 736-53-00; fax (8) 34-00-43; e-mail red@vf.bonnier.se; internet www.viforaldrar.se; f. 1968; monthly; parents' magazine; Editor-in-Chief HELENA RÖNNBERG; circ. 59,500.

SPECIALIST PERIODICALS

Aktuellt i Politiken: Sveavägen 68, 105 60 Stockholm; tel. (8) 700-26-00; fax (8) 11-65-42; weekly; social, political and cultural affairs; organ of Social Democratic Labour Party; circ. 55,000.

Allt om Jakt & Vapen: POB 3263, 103 65 Stockholm; tel. (8) 30-16-30; fax (8) 28-59-74; e-mail jaktochvapen@pressdata.se; internet www.jaktovapen.com; 11 a year; hunting; Editor ERIK WALLIN; circ. 41,500.

Arbetsledaren: POB 12069, 102 22 Stockholm; tel. (8) 652-01-20; fax (8) 653-99-68; f. 1908; 10 a year; journal for foremen and supervisors; Editor INGRID ASKEBERG; circ. 87,400.

Barn: 107 88 Stockholm; tel. (8) 698-90-00; fax (8) 698-90-14; e-mail barn@rb.se; internet www.rb.se/barn; owned by Rädda Barnen (Save the Children Sweden); 6 a year; children's rights; Editor-in-Chief SOFIE ARNÖ; circ. 125,700.

Båtliv: POB 8097, 371 38 Karlskrona; tel. (445) 297-80; fax (455) 36-97-99; e-mail info@batliv.se; internet www.batliv.se; 5 a year; for boat-owners and boat-club members; Editor LARS-ÅKE REDÉEN; circ. 126,300.

Byggnadsarbetaren: 106 32 Stockholm; tel. (8) 728-49-00; fax (8) 728-49-80; e-mail k.p@byggnadsarbetaren.se; internet www

SWEDEN

.byggnadsarbetaren.se; f. 1949; 15 a year; building; Editor KENNETH PETTERSON; circ. 119,700 (2008).

Dina Pengar: Konsument Göteborg, POB 11364, 404 28 Göteborg; tel. (8) 573-650-60; e-mail redaktionen@dinarpengar.se; internet www.di.se; 9 a year; finance; Editor BJÖRN HEDENSJÖ; circ. 83,000.

Du&jobbet: Hornsgatan 174, POB 17550, 118 91 Stockholm; tel. (8) 442-46-00; fax (8) 442-46-08; e-mail redaktionen@duochjobbet.se; internet www.duochjobbet.se; f. 1912; monthly; working environment, health, management; Editor-in-Chief EVA BERLIN; circ. 25,000.

Handelsnytt: POB 1146, 111 81 Stockholm; tel. (8) 412-68-00; fax (8) 21-43-33; e-mail handelsnytt@handels.se; internet www.handelsnytt.se; f. 1906; 11 a year; organ of the Union of Commercial Employees; circ. 71,300.

Hundsport: POB 11141, 100 61 Stockholm; tel. (8) 642-37-20; fax (8) 641-00-62; monthly; for dog-owners; Editor TORSTEN WIDHOLM; circ. 101,300.

Jaktmarker och Fiskevatten: Västra Torggt. 18, 652 24 Karlstad; tel. (54) 10-03-70; fax (54) 10-09-83; 11 a year; hunting and fishing; circ. 48,100.

Kommunalarbetaren: POB 19034, 104 32 Stockholm; tel. (8) 728-28-00; fax (8) 30-61-42; e-mail kommunalarbetaren@kommunal.se; internet www.ka.se; 22 a year; organ of the Union of Municipal Workers; Editor LIV BECKSTRÖM; circ. 605,000.

Kyrkans Tidning: POB 15412, 104 65 Stockholm; tel. (8) 462-28-00; fax (8) 644-76-71; e-mail redaktionen@kyrkanstidning.com; internet www.kyrkanstidning.com; f. 1982; weekly; organ of the Church of Sweden; Man. Dir THOMAS GRAHL; Editor DAG TUVELIUS; circ. 46,700.

LAND-Familjetidningen: Gävlegt. 22, 113 92 Stockholm; tel. (8) 588-365-10; fax (8) 588-369-59; e-mail land@lrfmedia.lrf.se; internet www.tidningenland.com; f. 1971; weekly; organ of the farmers' asscn; circ. 234,000 (2006).

LAND Lantbruk: Gävlegt. 22, 113 92 Stockholm; tel. (8) 787-51-00; fax (8) 787-55-02; e-mail internetredaktionen@lantbruk.com; internet www.lantbruk.com; f. 1971; weekly; organ of the farmers' asscn; agriculture, forestry; circ. 121,800.

Lärarförbundet: Segelbåtsvägen 15, POB 12229, 102 26 Stockholm; tel. (8) 737-65-00; e-mail sten.svensson@lararforbundet.se; internet www.lararforbundet.se; 22 a year; for teachers; Editor-in-Chief STEN SVENSSON; circ. 225,000.

Lön & Jobb: POB 30102, 104 25 Stockholm; tel. (8) 737-80-00; fax (8) 618-67-22; e-mail lonjobb@htf.se; internet www.lon-jobb.nu; 18 a year; organ of the Union of Commercial Salaried Employees; Editor-in-Chief CARL VON SCHÉELE; circ. 147,300.

Metallarbetaren: Olof Palmesgt. 11, 105 52 Stockholm; tel. (8) 10-68-30; fax (8) 11-13-02; f. 1888; weekly; organ of Swedish Metal Workers' Union; Editor PER AHLSTRÖM; circ. 415,400.

Motor: POB 23142, 104 35 Stockholm; tel. (8) 690-38-00; fax (8) 690-38-22; monthly; cars and motoring; circ. 141,700.

Motorföraren: Heliosgt. 11, 120 30 Stockholm; tel. (8) 555-765-55; fax (8) 555-765-95; e-mail motorforaren@mhf.se; internet www.mhf.se; f. 1927; 8 a year; motoring and tourism; Editor SÖREN SEHLBERG; circ. 41,300.

Musiktidningen Musikomanen: POB 6903, 102 39 Stockholm; tel. (8) 31-00-07; e-mail alexander.scarlat@chello.se; f. 1964; 4 a year; classical and modern music; Senior Editor ALEXANDER SCARLAT; circ. 3,000.

Ny Teknik: Mäster Samuelsgt. 56, 106 12 Stockholm; tel. (8) 796-66-00; fax (8) 613-30-28; e-mail redaktion@nyteknik.se; internet www.nyteknik.se; f. 1967; weekly; technical publication owned by the two largest engineering societies of Sweden; Editor-in-Chief LARS NILSSON; circ. 150,500.

PRO-Pensionären: POB 3274, 103 65 Stockholm; tel. (8) 701-67-00; fax (8) 20-33-58; e-mail info@pro.se; internet www.pro.se; f. 1942; 10 a year; magazine for pensioners; Editor AGNETA BERG-WAHLSTEDT; circ. 293,900.

SEKO-magasinet: Barnhusgt. 10, POB 1102, 111 81 Stockholm; tel. (8) 791-41-00; fax (8) 21-16-94; f. 1955; 11 a year; organ of the National Union of Services and Communications Employees; Editor-in-Chief JESPER BENGTSSON; circ. 154,700.

SIA-Skogsindustriarbetaren: Olof Palmesgt. 31, POB 1138, 111 81 Stockholm; tel. (8) 701-77-90; fax (8) 411-27-42; e-mail sia@skogstrafacket.org; monthly; forestry; circ. 69,100.

SIF-Tidningen: SIF-huset, Olof Palmesgt. 17, 105 32 Stockholm; tel. (8) 508-970-00; fax (8) 508-970-12; e-mail bjorn.oijer@sif.se; internet www.siftidn.sif.se; 19 a year; organ of the Union of Clerical and Technical Employees; Editor-in-Chief BJORN OIJER; circ. 331,800.

Skog & Såg: Sag i Syd, POB 37, 551 12 Jönköping; tel. (36) 34-30-00; fax (36) 12-86-10; f. 1966; 4 a year; sawmills and forestry; Editor HENRIK ASPLUND; circ. 75,000.

SKTF-Tidningen: POB 7825, 103 97 Stockholm; tel. (8) 789-63-00; fax (8) 789-64-79; e-mail sktftidningen@sktf.se; internet www.sktftidningen.nu; 20 a year; organ of the Union of Municipal Employees; Editor KENT KÄLLQVIST; circ. 182,800.

Sunt Förnuft: 114 95 Stockholm; tel. (8) 613-17-00; fax (8) 21-38-58; 8 a year; tax-payers' magazine; circ. 175,100.

Svensk Bokhandel (Journal of the Swedish Book Trade): Birkagt. 16C, POB 6888, 113 86 Stockholm; tel. (8) 545-417-70; fax (8) 545-417-75; e-mail redaktion@svb.se; internet www.svb.se; co-publ. by Swedish Publrs' Asscn and Swedish Booksellers' Asscn, for booksellers, publishers, antiquarians and librarians; Editor LARS WINKLER; circ. 4,400.

Svensk Golf: POB 84, 182 11 Danderyd; tel. (8) 622-15-00; fax (8) 622-69-30; e-mail info@golf.se; internet www.golf.se; monthly; golf; Editor TOBIAS BERGMAN; circ. 353,000.

Svensk Jakt: Skedhults Säteri, 575 96 Eksjö; tel. (381) 371-80; fax (381) 371-85; e-mail svenskjakt@telia.com; internet www.jagareforbundet.se/svenskjakt; f. 1862; 11 a year; for hunters and dog-breeders; circ. 157,800 (2004).

Sveriges Natur: POB 4625, 116 91 Stockholm; tel. (8) 702-65-00; fax (8) 702-27-02; e-mail sveriges.natur@snf.se; internet www2.snf.se/sveriges-natur; f. 1909; 5 a year; organ of Swedish Society for Nature Conservation; Editor CARL-AXEL FALL; circ. 120,000.

Tidningen C: POB 2200, 103 15 Stockholm; tel. (8) 617-38-30; fax (8) 617-38-10; e-mail c.redaktionen@centrepartiet.se; f. 1929; 10 a year; organ of the Centre Party; Editor EVA-KANN LIND; circ. 68,000.

Transportarbetaren: POB 714, 101 33 Stockholm; tel. (8) 723-77-00; fax (8) 723-00-76; 11 a year; organ of the Swedish Transport Workers' Union; Editor JAN LINDKVIST; circ. 72,000.

Turist: 101 20 Stockholm; tel. (8) 463-21-00; 6 a year; tourism and travel; Editor MONIKA TROZELL; circ. 215,000.

NEWS AGENCIES

Svenska Nyhetsbyrån (Swedish Conservative Press Agency): POB 3553, 103 69 Stockholm; tel. (8) 14-07-50; fax (8) 10-10-48; e-mail red@snb.se; internet www.snb.se; Pres. FREDRIK HAAGE; Editor-in-Chief and Dir PER SELSTAM.

Svensk-Internationella Pressbyrån AB (SIP) (Swedish-International Press Bureau): Stymansgt. 4, 114 54 Stockholm; tel. (8) 528-088-10; fax (8) 528-088-30; e-mail ld@publicitet.com; internet www.publicitet.se; f. 1927; Editor-in-Chief CHRISTER LIEDHOLM.

Tidningarnas Telegrambyrå (Swedish News Agency): Katarinavägen 15, 105 12 Stockholm; tel. (8) 692-26-00; fax (8) 692-28-55; e-mail redaktionen@tt.se; internet www.tt.se; f. 1921; co-operative news agency, working in conjunction with Reuters, AFP and other agencies; Chair. RAOUL GRÜNTHAL; Gen. Man. and Editor-in-Chief THOMAS PETERSSOHN.

PRESS ASSOCIATIONS

Pre Cent (Centre Party's Press Agency): POB 2033, 103 11 Stockholm; tel. (8) 786-48-84; fax (8) 24-30-04; e-mail red@precent.se; f. 1987; Editor-in-Chief JIMMY DOMINIUS; 33 mems.

Svenska Journalistförbundet (Swedish Union of Journalists): POB 1116, 111 81 Stockholm; tel. (8) 613-75-00; fax (8) 21-26-80; e-mail kansliet@sjf.se; internet www.sjf.se; f. 1901; Pres. AGNETA LINDBLOM HULTHÉN; 19,000 mems.

Svenska Tidningsutgivareföreningen (Swedish Newspaper Publishers' Asscn): Kungsholmstorg 5, POB 22500, 104 22 Stockholm; tel. (8) 692-46-00; fax (8) 692-46-38; e-mail info@tu.se; internet www.tu.se; f. 1898; Man. Dir PÄR FAGERSTRÖM; 200 mems.

Sveriges Tidskrifter (Swedish Magazine Publishers' Asscn): Vasagt. 50, 111 20 Stockholm; tel. (8) 545-298-90; fax (8) 14-98-65; e-mail info@sverigestidskrifter.se; internet www.sverigestidskrifter.se; f. 1943; Man. Dir LARS STRANDBERG.

Sveriges Vänsterpressförening (Liberal Press Asscn): 901 70 Umeå; tel. (90) 15-10-00; fax (90) 77-46-47; f. 1905; Pres. OLOF KLEBERG; Sec. MATS OLOFSSON; c. 130 mems.

Publishers

Alfabeta Bokförlag AB: Bondegt. 21, POB 4284, 102 66 Stockholm; tel. (8) 714-36-30; fax (8) 643-24-31; e-mail info@alfamedia.se; internet www.alfamedia.se; fiction, psychology, biography, cinema, art, music, travel guides, children's books; Man. Dir DAG HERNRIED.

Bokförlaget Atlantis AB: Sturegt. 24, 114 36 Stockholm; tel. (8) 545-660-70; fax (8) 545-660-71; e-mail mail@atlantisbok.se; internet

SWEDEN

www.atlantisbok.se; f. 1977; fiction, non-fiction, art; imprint: Signum; Man. Dir PETER LUTHERSSON.

Berghs Förlag AB: Observatoriegt. 10, POB 45084, 104 30 Stockholm; tel. (8) 31-65-59; fax (8) 32-77-45; e-mail info@berghsforlag.se; internet www.berghsforlag.se; f. 1954; non-fiction for adults and children, picture books and fiction for children, craft books, popular science, 'New Age' literature; Man. Dir ERIK JOHANSSON.

Bonnier Carlsen Bokförlag AB: Sveavägen 56, POB 3159, 103 63 Stockholm; tel. (8) 696-89-30; fax (8) 696-89-31; e-mail info@carlsen.bonnier.se; internet www.bonniercarlsen.se; picture books, juvenile books, non-fiction, board books, comics; Man. Dir ANNA BORNÉ MINBERGER.

Bonnierförlagen AB: Sveavägen 56, POB 3159, 103 63 Stockholm; tel. (8) 696-80-00; fax (8) 696-80-46; e-mail info@bok.bonnier.se; internet www.bok.bonnier.se; f. 1837; fiction, non-fiction, encyclopaedias, reference books, quality paperbacks; includes Albert Bonniers Förlag AB, Bonnier Utbildning AB, Bokförlaget Forum AB, Wahlström & Widstrand, Autumn Publishing, Bonnier Audio, Bonnier Carlsen, Bokförlaget Rebus, Bokförlaget Max Ström; Chair. JACOB DALBORG.

Bokförlaget Bra Böcker: Ångbåtsbron 1, POB 892, 201 80 Malmö; tel. (40) 665-46-00; internet www.bbb.se; f. 1965; fiction, biography, books in translation; Man. Dir ERIK JOHANSSON.

Brombergs Bokförlag AB: Hantverkargt. 26, POB 12886, 112 98 Stockholm; tel. (8) 562-620-80; fax (8) 562-620-85; e-mail info@brombergs.se; internet www.brombergs.se; literary fiction, non-fiction; Man. Dir DOROTEA BROMBERG.

Brutus Östlings Bokförlag Symposion: POB 148, 241 22 Eslöv; tel. (413) 606-10; fax (413) 109-48; e-mail order@symposion.se; internet www.symposion.se; poetry, drama, non-fiction.

Carlsson Bokförlag AB: Stora Nygt. 31, 111 27 Stockholm; tel. (8) 411-23-49; fax (8) 796-84-57; e-mail info@carlssonbokforlag.se; internet www.carlssonbokforlag.se; art, photography, ethnology, history, politics; Man. Dir TRYGVE CARLSSON.

Bokförlaget DN: POB 703 21, 107 23 Stockholm; tel. (8) 696-87-90; fax (8) 696-83-67; e-mail marknad@forum.se; internet www.bokforlagetdn.se; publishing division of Dagens Nyheter newspaper; Publr and Pres. ALBERT BONNDER.

Eriksson & Lindgren Bokförlag AB: Tryckerigt. 4, POB 2052, 102 12 Stockholm; tel. (8) 769-88-11; fax (8) 769-88-13; e-mail info@eriksson-lindgren.se; internet www.eriksson-lindgren.se; f. 1990; children's; Man. Dir GUNILLA HALKJÆR OLOFSSON.

Bokförlaget T. Fischer & Co: Svartmangt. 18, POB 2036, 103 11 Stockholm; tel. (8) 643-38-46; fax (8) 643-38-98; e-mail bokforlaget@fischer-co.se; internet www.fischer-co.se; non-fiction; owned by Lind & Co.

Forma Publishing Group: Port-Anders-Gt., T3, 721 85 Västerås; tel. (21) 19-40-00; fax (21) 19-41-36; e-mail patrik.widlund@formapg.se; internet www.formapg.se; f. 1945 as ICA Förlaget AB; present name adopted 2004; non-fiction, cookery, handicrafts, gardening, natural history, popular psychology, health, domestic animals, sports; magazine publisher; Chair. CLAES-GÖRAN SYLVÉN; Man. Dir PATRIK WIDLUND.

Forum Publishers: Gamla Brogt. 26, POB 70321, 107 23 Stockholm; tel. (8) 696-84-40; fax (8) 696-83-67; e-mail brittinger.nordstrand@forum.se; internet www.forum.se; f. 1943; general fiction, non-fiction; Man. Dir MAGNUS NYTELL.

Gedins Förlag: Tystagt. 10, 115 20 Stockholm; tel. (8) 662-15-51; fax (8) 663-70-73; e-mail gedins@perigab.se; fiction, non-fiction, poetry, food, psychology, politics; Man. Dir PER I. GEDIN.

Gehrmans Musikförlag AB: POB 42026, 126 12 Stockholm; Västberga allé 5, 126 30 Hägersten; tel. (8) 610-06-00; fax (8) 610-06-27; e-mail info@gehrmans.se; internet www.gehrmans.se; f. 1893; orchestral and choral music; general music publishing; Pres. JOE LINDSTRÖM; CEO KETTIL SKARBY.

Informationsförlaget: Sveavägen 61, POB 6884, 113 86 Stockholm; tel. (8) 545-560-50; fax (8) 31-39-03; e-mail red@informationsforlaget.se; internet www.informationsforlaget.se; f. 1979; publishers of books for cos and orgs on demand; reference, encyclopaedias, gastronomy, illustrated books; Man. Dir ULF HEIMDAHL.

Liber AB: 113 98 Stockholm; tel. (8) 690-90-00; fax (8) 690-94-70; e-mail export@liber.se; internet www.liber.se; general and educational publishing; owned by Wolters Kluwer NV (Netherlands); Man. Dir JERKER NILSSON.

Liber Hermods AB: Råsundavägen 18, 113 98 Stockholm; tel. (8) 690-94-00; e-mail keith.fransson@liber.se; internet www.liberhermods.se; f. 1993; further and higher education; Man. Dir KEITH FRANSSON.

J. A. Lindblads Bokförlags AB: Warfvingesväg 30, POB 30195, 104 25 Stockholm; tel. (8) 618-78-98; e-mail bertil.wahlstrom@lindblads.se; fiction, non-fiction, juvenile, paperbacks; Man. Dir BERTIL WAHLSTRÖM.

Abraham Lundquist AB Musikförlag: POB 93, 182 11 Danderyd; tel. (8) 732-92-35; fax (8) 732-92-38; e-mail info@abrahamlundquist.se; internet www.abrahamlundquist.se; f. 1838; music; Man. Dir (vacant).

Bokförlaget Natur och Kultur: Karlavägen 31, POB 27323, 102 54 Stockholm; tel. (8) 453-86-00; fax (8) 453-87-90; e-mail info@nok.se; internet www.nok.se; f. 1922; textbooks, general literature, fiction; Man. Dir GUNN JOHANSSON.

Norstedts Förlag AB: Tryckerigt. 4, POB 2052, 103 12 Stockholm; tel. (8) 769-88-50; fax (8) 769-88-64; e-mail info@norstedts.se; internet www.norstedts.se; f. 1823; fiction, non-fiction; imprints: Norstedts, Prisma, Nautiska, Norstedts Pocket and Norstedts Audio; part of Norstedts Förlagsgrupp; Man. Dir MARIA HAMREFORS.

Norstedts Förlagsgrupp: Tryckerigt. 4, POB 2052, 103 12 Stockholm; tel. (8) 769-87-00; fax (8) 769-88-64; e-mail info@panorstedt.se; internet www.panordstedt.se; subsidiaries: Norstedts Förlag, Norstedts Akademiska Förlag, Rabénförlagen; Man. Dir MARIA HAMREFORS.

Norstedts Juridik AB: 106 47 Stockholm; tel. (8) 690-90-90; fax (8) 690-91-91; e-mail info.fritzes@nj.se; internet www.nj.se; f. 1837; owned by Wolters Kluwer NV (Netherlands); fmrly C. E. Fritzes AB; CEO PATRIK HOGBERG.

Bokförlaget Opal AB: Tegelbergsvägen 31, POB 20113, 161 02 Bromma; tel. (8) 28-21-79; fax (8) 29-66-23; e-mail opal@opal.se; internet www.opal.se; f. 1973; Man. Dir BENGT CHRISTELL.

Ordfront Förlag AB: Bellmansgt. 30, POB 17506, 118 91 Stockholm; tel. (8) 462-44-00; fax (8) 462-44-90; e-mail info@ordfront.se; internet www.ordfront.se; fiction, history, politics; Man. Dir JAN-ERIK PETTERSSON.

Prisma Bokförlaget: Tryckerigt. 4, POB 2052, 103 12 Stockholm; tel. (8) 769-89-00; fax (8) 769-89-13; e-mail info@prismabok.se; internet www.prismabok.se; f. 1963; imprint of Nordstedt Bokförlag AB; Dir VIVECA EKELUND.

Rabénförlagen: Tryckerigt. 4, POB 2052, 103 12 Stockholm; tel. (8) 769-88-00; fax (8) 769-88-13; e-mail info@raben.se; internet www.raben.se; f. 1942; general, juvenile; imprints: Rabén & Sjögren, Gammafon, Tiden, Eriksson & Lindgren; part of Norstedts Förlagsgrupp; Dir ERIK LIEDBERG.

Bokförlaget Semic: Esplanaden 3B, POB 1243, 172 25 Sundbyberg; tel. (8) 799-30-50; fax (8) 799-30-64; e-mail info@semic.se; internet www.semic.se; handbooks, calendars, comic magazines, juvenile; Pres. RICKARD EKSTRÖM.

Stenströms Bokförlag AB: Linnégt. 98, POB 24086, 104 50 Stockholm; tel. (8) 663-76-01; fax (8) 663-22-01; f. 1983; Man. Dir BENGT STENSTRÖM.

Streiffert Förlag AB: Skeppargt. 27, POB 5334, 102 47 Stockholm; tel. (8) 661-58-80; fax (8) 783-04-33; e-mail info@streiffert.se; internet www.streiffert.se; f. 1990; Man. Dir BO STREIFFERT.

Svenska Förlaget liv & ledarskap AB: POB 3313, 103 66 Stockholm; e-mail kundservice@svenskaforlaget.com; internet www.svenskaforlaget.com; non-fiction.

Timbro Förlag/SFN: Kungsgt. 60, POB 5234, 102 45 Stockholm; tel. (8) 587-898-00; fax (8) 667-00-37; e-mail info@timbro.se; internet www.timbro.se; economics, political science; Dir BILLY MCCORMAC.

Verbum Förlag AB: St Paulsgt. 2, POB 15169, 104 65 Stockholm; tel. (8) 743-65-00; fax (8) 641-45-85; e-mail info.forlag@verbum.se; internet www.verbum.se; f. 1911; theology, fiction, juvenile, music; Man. Dir CLAES-GÖRAN GUNNARSSON.

Wahlström & Widstrand: Kungsgt. 60, POB 5587, 114 85 Stockholm; tel. (8) 696-84-80; fax (8) 696-83-80; e-mail christina.enell.eriksson@bonnierforlagen.se; internet www.wwd.se; f. 1884; fiction, non-fiction, biography, history, science, paperbacks; owned by Bonnierförlagen AB; Man. Dir KERSTIN ANGELIN.

PUBLISHERS' ASSOCIATIONS

Föreningen Svenska Läromedel (Swedish Asscn of Educational Publishers): Drottninggt. 97, 113 60 Stockholm; tel. (8) 736-19-40; fax (8) 736-19-44; e-mail fsl@fsl.se; internet www.fsl.se; f. 1973; Chair. JERKER NILSSON; Dir MONA HILLMAN PINHEIRO; 15 mems.

Svenska Förläggareföreningen (Swedish Publishers' Asscn): Drottninggt. 97, 113 60 Stockholm; tel. (8) 736-19-40; fax (8) 736-19-44; e-mail info@forlaggare.se; internet www.forlaggare.se; f. 1843; Chair. KJELL BOHLUND; Man. Dir KRISTINA AHLINDER; 68 mems.

SWEDEN   *Directory*

Broadcasting and Communications

TELECOMMUNICATIONS

Regulatory Authority

Post-och Telestyrelsen (PTS): POB 5398, Birger Jarlsgt. 16, 102 49 Stockholm; tel. (8) 678-55-00; fax (8) 678-55-05; e-mail pts@pts.se; internet www.pts.se; Dir-Gen. MARIANNE TRESCHOW.

Major Service Providers

Tele 2 AB: Skeppsbron 18, POB 2094, 103 13 Stockholm; tel. (85) 562-000-60; fax (85) 562-000-40; e-mail press.relations@tele2.com; internet www.tele2.com; f. 1993; Pres. and CEO LARS-JOHAN JARNHEIMER.

Telefonaktiebolaget LM Ericsson: Torshamngt. 23, 164 83 Stockholm; tel. (8) 719-00-00; fax (8) 719-19-76; e-mail investor.relations.se@ericsson.com; internet www.ericsson.com; parent co of the Ericsson group; mobile and fixed network provider; represented in 140 countries; Chair. MICHAEL TRESCHOW; CEO CARL-HENRIC SVANBERG.

Telenor Sverige AB: Campus Gräsvik 12, 371 80 Karlskrona; tel. (4) 553-310-00; fax (4) 553-312-22; internet www.telenor.se; fmrly Vodafone Sverige AB; provides mobile cellular communications under brand name *Djuice*, as well as broadband internet access and digital television services; acquired by Telenor AS (Norway) in 2005; Man. Dir JOHAN LINDGREN.

TeliaSonera AB: Sturegt. 1, 106 63 Stockholm; tel. (8) 504-550-00; fax (8) 504-550-01; e-mail teliasonera@teliasonera.se; internet www.teliasonera.se; f. by merger of Telia AB (Sweden) with Sonera Ltd (Finland); 37.3% owned by Govt of Sweden, 13.7% by Govt of Finland, 49.0% by individual and institutional investors; Chair. TOM VON WEYMARN; Pres. and CEO LARS NYBERG.

Teracom AB: Esplanaden 9, POB 1366, 172 27 Sundbyberg; tel. (8) 555-420-00; fax (8) 555-420-01; e-mail webmaster@teracom.se; internet www.teracom.se; provides digital television and radio services, fixed-line telephony and broadband internet access; Pres. ÅSA SUNDBERG; Dir CRISTER FRITZSON.

BROADCASTING

Until the end of 1992 public service radio and television were organized within the state broadcasting corporation, Sveriges Radio AB, a public service organization financed by licence fees; this operated two national television channels and three national radio channels, together with 24 local radio stations. On 1 January 1993 the state corporation was replaced by three companies, Sveriges Radio AB, Sveriges Television AB, and Sveriges Utbildningsradio AB, responsible for radio, television, and educational radio and television, respectively. The operations of these companies are regulated by law and by agreements with the Government. From 1 January 1994 the three companies came into the ownership of three foundations.

Radio

There are four public service radio channels, as well as neighbourhood radio stations and private local radio stations (financed by advertising).

IBRA Radio AB: POB Regulatorvägen 11, Flemingsberg, 141 99 Stockholm; tel. (8) 608-96-00; fax (8) 608-96-50; e-mail info@ibra.se; internet www.ibra.se; non-commercial private Christian co broadcasting to all continents; Pres. JACK-TOMMY ARDENFORS; Dir HANS OLOFSSON.

Sveriges Radio AB (SR): Oxenstiernsgt. 20, 105 10 Stockholm; tel. (8) 784-50-00; fax (8) 784-15-00; e-mail mikael.nilsson@sr.se; internet www.sr.se; f. 1993; independent co responsible for national radio broadcasting; Man. Dir KERSTIN BRUNNBERG.

Sveriges Utbildningsradio AB: 113 95 Stockholm; tel. (8) 784-40-00; fax (8) 784-43-91; e-mail Kundtjanst@ur.se; internet www.ur.se; f. 1978; public service co responsible for educational broadcasting on radio and television; CEO CHRISTINA BJÖRK.

Television

There are two public service television channels (SVT 1 and SVT 2). The broadcasts are financed by licence fees. In 1991 the Government awarded the licence for a third terrestrial nation-wide television channel to TV 4 (which is financed by advertising). Television channels transmitted by satellite and cable, and directed at the Swedish audience, include: TV 3, Kanal 5, TV 6, Kanal 9, Z-TV, and the film channels TV 1000, FilmMax, Filmnet Plus and Filmnet Movie.

Kanal 5: Rådmansgt. 42, 114 99 Stockholm; tel. (8) 674-15-00; fax (8) 612-05-95; e-mail info@kanal5.se; internet kanal5.se; commercial satellite channel; owned by ProSiebenSat1 (Germany); Dir-Gen. JONAS SJÖGREN.

Sveriges Television AB (SVT): TH T2, Oxenstiernsgt. 26-34, 105 10 Stockholm; tel. (8) 784-00-00; fax (8) 784-15-00; e-mail eva.hamilton@svt.se; internet www.svt.se; f. 1956; independent; operates seven channels: SVT1, SVT2, SVT24, SVT Barnkanalen, Kunskapskanalen, SVT Europa and SVT HD; Dir-Gen. EVA HAMILTON.

Sveriges Utbildningsradio AB: see RadioTV 3: Stockholm; tel. (8) 562-023-00; fax (8) 562-023-30; e-mail info@tv3.se; internet www.tv3.se; commercial satellite channel.

TV 4: Tegeluddsvägen 3–5, 115 79 Stockholm; tel. (8) 459-40-00; fax (8) 459-44-44; internet www.tv4.se; commercial terrestrial channel; Man. Dir TORSTEN LARSSON.

Finance

(cap. = capital; res = reserves; dep. = deposits; m. = million; brs = branches; amounts in kronor unless otherwise stated)

SUPERVISORY BODY

Finansinspektionen (Financial Supervisory Authority): POB 7821, Brunnsgt. 3, 103 97 Stockholm; tel. (8) 787-80-00; fax (8) 24-13-35; e-mail finansinspektionen@fi.se; internet www.fi.se; f. 1991 by merger of Bankinspektionen (Bank Inspection Board, f. 1907) and Försäkringsinspektionen (Private Insurance Supervisory Service, f. 1904), for the supervision of commercial and savings banks, financial companies, insurance companies, insurance brokers, friendly societies, mortgage institutions, securities firms and unit trusts, the stock exchange and clearing functions, the securities registry centre and the information registry centre; Chair. BENGT WESTERBERG; Dir-Gen. MARTIN ANDERSSON.

BANKING

At the end of 2007 there were 126 banks in Sweden, comprising 28 commercial banks, 31 foreign banks, 65 savings banks and two co-operative banks.

Central Bank

Sveriges Riksbank: Brunkebergstorg 11, 103 37 Stockholm; tel. (8) 787-00-00; fax (8) 21-05-31; e-mail registratorn@riksbank.se; internet www.riksbank.se; f. 1668; bank of issue; led by an executive board of six members (including a Governor), appointed by a General Council of 11 members, all of whom are, in turn, appointed by the Riksdag; cap. 1,000m., res 57,247m., dep. 12,272m. (Dec. 2007); Chair., Gen. Council JOHAN GERNANDT; Gov. STEFAN INGVES; 2 brs.

Commercial Banks

Danske Bank i Sverige: Norrmalmstorg 1, POB 7523, 103 92 Stockholm; tel. (8) 524-800-00; internet www.danskebank.se; f. 1837 as Östgöta Enskilda Bank; subsidiary of Den Danske Bank (Denmark); Chair. PETER STRAARUP; Pres. and CEO ULF LUNDAHL; 30 brs.

Nordea Bank AB: Hamngt. 10, 105 71 Stockholm; tel. (8) 614-78-00; fax (8) 20-08-46; internet www.nordea.com; f. 1974 as Post- och Kreditbanken; present name adopted 2001; part of Nordea Group; 19.9% owned by Swedish Govt; cap. €2,597m., res -€160m., dep. €337,178m. (Dec. 2007); Chair. HANS DALBORG; Pres. and CEO CHRISTIAN CLAUSEN; 252 brs in Sweden.

Skandinaviska Enskilda Banken AB (SEB): Kungsträdgårdsgt. 8, 106 40 Stockholm; tel. (8) 763-80-00; fax (8) 763-83-89; internet www.seb.se; f. 1972; cap. 6,872m., res 29,479m., dep. 1,908,309m. (Dec. 2007); Chair. MARCUS WALLENBERG; Pres. and Group CEO ANNIKA FALKENGREN; 260 brs.

Svenska Handelsbanken AB: Kungsträdgårdsgt. 2, 106 70 Stockholm; tel. (8) 701-10-00; fax (8) 701-24-37; e-mail info@handelsbanken.se; internet www.handelsbanken.se; f. 1871 as A. B. Stockholms Handelsbank; present name adopted 1956; cap. 2,888m., res 50,210m., dep. 1,630,212m. (Dec. 2006); Chair. HANS LARSSON; Pres. and CEO PÄR BOMAN; 459 brs in Sweden.

Swedbank AB: Brunkebergstorg 8, 105 34 Stockholm; tel. (8) 585-900-00; fax (8) 796-80-92; internet www.swedbank.se; f. 1997 by merger of Föreningsbanken and Sparbanken Sverige; present name adopted 2006; cap. 10,823m., res 6,489m., dep. 635,810m. (Dec. 2006); Chair. CARL ERIC STÅLBERG; Pres. and CEO JAN LIDÉN; 470 brs in Sweden.

Banking Organization

Svenska Bankföreningen (Swedish Bankers' Asscn): Regeringsgt. 38, POB 7603, 103 94 Stockholm; tel. (8) 453-44-00; fax (8) 796-93-95; e-mail info@bankforeningen.se; internet www.bankforeningen.se; f. 1880; Pres. JAN LIDÉN; Man. Dir PÄR BOMAN; 29 mems.

SWEDEN *Directory*

STOCK EXCHANGE

NASDAQ OMX Nordic Exchange Stockholm: Tullvaktsvägen 15, 105 78 Stockholm; tel. (8) 405-60-00; fax (8) 405-60-01; internet www.nasdaqomx.com; f. 1863 under govt charter; automated trading system introduced by 1990; Stockholmsbörsen merged with OMX AB in 1998; acquired by NASDAQ Stock Market, Inc (USA) in 2008; part of OMX Nordic Exchange with the Copenhagen (Denmark), Helsinki (Finland) and Reykjavík (Iceland) exchanges; Group CEO ROBERT GREIFELD; Group Pres. MAGNUS BÖCKER.

INSURANCE

The total assets of Swedish insurance companies in 2005 was 440,147m. kronor.

Principal Insurance Companies

Folksam: Bohusgt. 14, 106 60 Stockholm; tel. (8) 772-60-00; fax (8) 702-99-22; e-mail info@floksam.se; internet www.folksam.se; f. 1908; all branches of life and non-life insurance; Pres. and CEO ANDERS SUNDSTRÖM.

Skandia Insurance Co Ltd: Sveavägen 44, 103 50 Stockholm; tel. (8) 788-10-00; fax (8) 788-30-80; e-mail contact@oldmutual.com; internet www.skandia.com; f. 1855; owned by Old Mutual PLC (United Kingdom); all branches of life insurance; Chair. LARS OTTERBECK; Pres. and CEO JULIAN ROBERTS.

Trygg-Hansa: Flemminggt. 18, 106 26 Stockholm; tel. (8) 693-10-00; fax (8) 650-93-67; internet www.trygghansa.se; f. 1828; all branches of non-life insurance; owned by Codan Forsikring A/S (Denmark); CEO RICKARD GUSTAFSON.

Insurance Associations

Konsumernternas försäkringsbyrå (Swedish Consumers' Insurance Bureau): Karlavägen 108, 104 51 Stockholm; tel. (8) 22-58-00; fax (8) 24-88-91; e-mail angela.olsson@konsumenternas.se; internet www.konsumenternas.se; f. 1979; provides free advice to consumers on various insurance matters; principles are the Konsumentverket (Swedish Consumer Agency), the Finansinpektionen (Financial Supervisory Authority) and the Sveriges Försäkringsförbund (Swedish Insurance Fed.); Chair. GUNNAR OLSSON.

Svenska Försäkringsföreningen (Swedish Insurance Society): Karlavägen 108, POB 24213, 104 51 Stockholm; tel. (8) 522-789-00; fax (8) 522-789-95; e-mail info@forsakringsforeningen.se; internet www.forsakringsforeningen.se; f. 1875; promotes sound development of the Swedish insurance business; Chair. LARS ROSÉN; Sec. SARA RÅSMAR.

Sveriges Försäkringsförbund (Swedish Insurance Federation): Karlavägen 108, POB 24043, 104 50 Stockholm; tel. (8) 522-785-00; fax (8) 522-785-15; e-mail info@forsakringsforbundet.com; internet www.forsakringsforbundet.com; Chair. TORBJÖRN MAGNUSSON; Man. Dir CHRISTINA LINDENIUS.

Trade and Industry

GOVERNMENT AGENCIES

Arbetsförmedlingen (Public Employment Service): Hälsingegt. 38, 113 43, Stockholm; tel. (8) 508-801-00; e-mail registrator@arbetsformedlingen.se; internet www.arbetsformedlingen.se; f. 2008 to replace Arbetsmarknadsverket and Arbetsmarknadsstyrelsen; central agency, responsible for administration of Sweden's labour market; main aims: to match those seeking employment to suitable vacancies, to encourage those outside the labour market to seek employment, and to maintain a high level of employment within the labour market; managed by a nine-mem. board, appointed by Govt; Chair. THOMAS FRANZÉN; Dir-Gen. ANGELES BERMUDEZ-SVANKVIST.

Exportrådet (Swedish Trade Council): World Trade Center, Klarabergsviadukten 70, POB 240, 101 24 Stockholm; tel. (8) 588-660-00; fax (8) 588-661-90; e-mail info@swedishtrade.se; internet www.swedishtrade.se; f. 1972; Chair. BO DANKIS; Man. Dir ULF BERG.

Nutek (Swedish Agency for Economic and Regional Growth): Götgatan 74, 11621 Stockholm; tel. (8) 681-91-00; fax (8) 19-68-26; e-mail nutek@nutek.se; internet www.nutek.se; Dir-Gen. SUNE HALVARSSON (acting).

CHAMBERS OF COMMERCE

Handelskammaren Jönköpings Län: Elmiavägen 11, 554 54 Jönköping; tel. (36) 30-14-30; fax (36) 12-95-79; e-mail info@jonkoping.cci.se; internet www.jonkoping.cci.se; f. 1975; Pres. JOHAN SVEDBERG; Man. Dir GÖRAN KINNANDER; 400 mems.

Handelskammaren Mälardalen: Drottninggt. 26, POB 8044, 700 08 Örebro; tel. (19) 16-61-60; fax (19) 11-77-50; e-mail info@handelskammarenmalardalen.se; internet www.handelskammarenmalardalen.se; f. 1907; Pres. CHRISTER HENEBÄCK; Man. Dir MERIT ISRAELSSON.

Handelskammaren Mittsverige (Mid-Sweden Chamber of Commerce): Kyrkogt. 26, 852 32 Sundsvall; tel. (60) 17-18-80; fax (60) 61-86-40; e-mail sdl@midchamber.se; internet www.midchamber.se; f. 1913; Chair. ROLF JOHANNESSON; Man. Dir DICK JANSSON; 400 mems.

Handelskammaren Värmland: Södra Kyrkogt. 6, 652 24 Karlstad; tel. (54) 22-14-80; fax (54) 22-14-90; e-mail info@handelskammarenvarmland.se; internet www.handelskammarenvarmland.se; f. 1912; Pres. JOHAN ENGSTRÖM; Sec. ULF LJUNGDAHL; 1,200 mems.

Mellansvenska Handelskammaren: POB 296, 801 04 Gävle; tel. (26) 66-20-80; fax (26) 66-20-99; e-mail chamber@mhk.cci.se; internet www.mhk.cci.se; f. 1907; Pres. OVE ANONSEN; Man. Dir ANDERS FRANCK; 465 mems.

Norrbottens Handelskammare: Kyrkogt. 13, 972 38 Luleå; tel. (920) 45-56-60; fax (920) 45-56-66; internet www.north.cci.se; f. 1904; Chair. HANS ERIKSSON; Man. Dir ANDREAS LIND.

Östsvenska Handelskammaren: Nya Rådstugugt. 3, 60224 Norrköping; tel. (11) 28-50-30; fax (11) 13-77-19; e-mail info@east.cci.se; internet www.east.cci.se; f. 1913; covers Östergötland, Södermanland and Gotland; c. 600 mem. cos; Chair. ANN KRUMLINDE; Man. Dir LARS ERICHS.

Stockholms Handelskammare: V. Trädgårdsgt. 9, POB 16050, 103 21 Stockholm; tel. (8) 555-100-00; fax (8) 566-316-20; e-mail info@chamber.se; internet www.chamber.se; f. 1902; Pres. JENS SPENDRUP; Dir PETER EGARDT.

Sydsvenska Industri- och Handelskammaren: Skeppsbron 2, 211 20 Malmö; tel. (40) 690-24-00; fax (40) 690-24-90; e-mail info@handelskammaren.com; internet www.handelskammaren.com; f. 1905; Pres. LARS FRITHIOF; Man. Dir STEPHAN MÜCHLER; 2,500 mems.

Västsvenska Industri- och Handelskammaren: Mässans Gt. 18, POB 5253, 402 25 Göteborg; tel. (31) 83-59-00; fax (31) 83-59-36; e-mail info@handelskammaren.net; internet www.handelskammaren.net; f. 1661; Chair. FINN JOHNSSON; Man. Dir ANDERS KÄLLSTRÖM; c. 2,600 mems.

INDUSTRIAL AND TRADE ASSOCIATIONS

Svenskt Näringsliv (Confederation of Swedish Enterprise): Storgt. 19, 114 82 Stockholm; tel. (8) 553-430-00; fax (8) 553-430-99; e-mail info@svensktnaringsliv.se; internet www.svensktnaringsliv.se; f. 2001 by merger of Sveriges Industriförbund (f. 1910) and Svenska Arbetsgivareföreningen (f. 1902); central org. representing Swedish business and industry; Pres. SIGNHILD ARNEGÅRD HANSEN; Dir-Gen. URBAN BÄCKSTRÖM; consists of 50 mem. asscns, representing c. 54,000 cos.

Företagarna (Federation of Private Enterprises): Regeringsgt. 52, 106 67 Stockholm; tel. (8) 406-17-00; fax (8) 24-55-26; e-mail info@foretagarna.se; internet www.foretagarna.se; f. 1990; Chair. JAN CARLZON; Man. Dir ANNA-STINA NORDMARK NILSSON; 55,000 mems.

Grafiska Företagens Förbund (Graphic Companies' Federation): Karlavägen 108, POB 24184, 104 51 Stockholm; tel. (8) 762-68-00; fax (8) 611-08-28; e-mail info@grafiska.se; internet www.grafiska.se; Chair. GÖRAN GUSTAFSSON; Man. Dir LARS JOSEFSSON.

Jernkontoret (Steel Producers' Asscn): Kungsträdgårdsgt. 10, POB 1721, 111 87 Stockholm; tel. (8) 679-17-00; fax (8) 611-20-89; e-mail office@jernkontoret.se; internet www.jernkontoret.se; f. 1747; Chair. OLOF FAXANDER; Man. Dir ELISABETH NILSSON.

Lantbrukarnas Riksförbund (LRF) (Federation of Swedish Farmers): Franzéngt. 6, 105 33 Stockholm; tel. (0) 771-573-573; e-mail info@lrf.se; internet www.lrf.se; Chair. LARS-GÖRAN PETTERSSON; Man. Dir KARL-GUNNAR BURMAN; 167,743 mems.

Plast- & Kemiföretagen (Swedish Plastics and Chemicals Asscn): Storgt. 19, POB 5501, 114 85 Stockholm; tel. (8) 783-86-00; fax (8) 663-63-23; e-mail info@plastkemiforetagen.se; internet www.plastkemiforetagen.se; f. 2003 by merger of the Asscn of Swedish Chemical Industries and the Plastics and Chemicals Fed.; Pres. JAN SVÄRD; Man. Dir MAGNUS HUSS; c. 300 mems.

Skogsindustrierna (Swedish Forest Industries' Federation): POB 55525, 102 04 Stockholm; tel. (8) 762-72-60; fax (8) 611-71-22; e-mail terese.sundberg@skogsindustrierna.org; internet www.forestindustries.se; Chair. LEIF BRODÉN; Dir-Gen. MARIE S. ARWIDSON.

SveMin (Föreningen för gruvor, mineral- och metallproducenter i Sverige) (Swedish Asscn of Mines, Mineral and Metal Producers): Kungsträdgårdsgt. 10, POB 1721, 111 87 Stockholm; tel. (8) 762-67-55; fax (8) 678-02-10; e-mail info@svemin.se; www.svemin.se; f. 2004; Pres. LENNART EVRELL; Man. Dir BENGT HULDL; 40 mem. cos.

SWEDEN

Directory

Svensk Handel (Swedish Federation of Trade): Regeringsgt. 60, 103 29 Stockholm; tel. (8) 762-77-00; fax (8) 762-77-77; e-mail info@svenskhandel.se; internet www.svenskhandel.se; Chair. KENNETH BENGTSSON; Man. Dir DAG KLACKENBERG; 13,000 mems.

Svensk Industriförening (Swedish Industry Asscn): Klara Norra Kyrkogt. 31, POB 22307, 104 22 Stockholm; tel. (8) 440-11-70; fax (8) 440-11-71; e-mail info@sinf.se; internet www.sinf.se; f. 1941; Man. Dir ANDERS EKDAHL; 1,500 mems.

TEKO (Textile and Clothing Industries' Asscn): Storgt. 5, POB 5510, 114 85 Stockholm; tel. (8) 762-68-80; fax (8) 762-68-87; e-mail teko@teko.se; internet www.teko.se; f. 1907; Chair. SVEN GATENHEIM; Man. Dirs OLA TOFTEGAARD, KARL OLOF STENQVIST; 263 mems.

EMPLOYERS' ORGANIZATIONS

Almega: Sturegat. 11, POB 55545, 102 04 Stockholm; tel. (8) 762-69-00; fax (8) 762-69-48; e-mail almega.epost@almega.se; internet www.almega.se; f. 1921; seven mem. asscns: Swedish IT and Telecom Industries, Almega Samhall Employers' Asscn, Almega Service Asscns, Almega Service Employers' Asscn, Media and Information Employers' Asscn, Asscn of Private Care Providers, Swedish Asscn of Staff Agencies; Chair. HÅKAN BRYNGELSON; Dir-Gen. JONAS MILTON; 8,900 mems.

Byggnadsämnesförbundet (Building Material Manufacturers Employers): Storgt. 19, POB 16347, 102 15 Stockholm; tel. (8) 762-65-35; fax (8) 762-65-12; e-mail info@baf.se; internet www.baf.se; Chair. JOHAN SKOGLUND; Man. Dir LARS DICANDER; c. 200 mem. cos.

Elektriska Installatörsorganisationen EIO (The Swedish Electrical Contractors' Association): Rosenlundsgt. 40, POB 17537, 118 91 Stockholm; tel. (8) 762-75-00; fax (8) 668-86-17; e-mail info@eio.se; internet www.eio.se; Chair. THOMAS CARLSSON; Man. Dir HANS ENSTRÖM; 2,500 mem. cos.

Försäkringsbranschens Arbetsgivareorganisation (Insurance Employers): Karlavägen 108, POB 24168, 104 51 Stockholm; tel. (8) 522-786-00; fax (8) 522-786-70; e-mail info@fao.se; internet www.fao.se; Chair. TORBJÖRN MAGNUSSON; Man. Dir CHRISTINA LINDENIUS; 145 mem. cos.

Livsmedelsföretagen (Li) (Food Industry): Storgt. 19, POB 16105, 102 15 Stockholm; tel. (8) 762-69-00; fax (8) 762-69-48; e-mail info@li.se; internet www.li.se; f. 2001 by merger of Livsmedelsbranschens Arbetsgivareförbund and Livsmedelsindustrierna; Chair. PER STENSTRÖM; Man. Dir AGNETA DREBAR; c. 1,000 mems.

Maskinentreprenörerna (Earth-Moving Contractors): Storgt. 19, POB 1609, 111 86 Stockholm; tel. (8) 762-70-65; fax (8) 611-85-41; e-mail kaisa.makiranta@me.se; internet www.maskinentreprenorerna.se; Chair. HÅKAN NORÉN; Man. Dir HAMPE MOBÄRG; c. 3,600 mem. cos.

Medie- och Informationsarbetsgivarna (Media and Information Employers' Association): POB 55545, 102 04 Stockholm; tel. (8) 762-70-30; fax (8) 611-41-47; internet www.almega.se; Chair. LENNART WIKLUND; Man. Dir CHARLOTT RICHARDSON; 400 mem. cos.

Plåtslageriernas Riksförbund (Platers): Rosenlundsgt. 40, POB 17536, 118 91 Stockholm; tel. (8) 762-75-85; fax (8) 616-00-72; e-mail info@plr.se; internet www.plr.se; Chair. PER ANDERSSON; Man. Dir GITTE LEGER; 900 mem. cos.

Stål och Metall Arbetsgivareförbundet (Steel and Metal Industry Employers): Kungsträdgårdsgt. 10, POB 1721, 111 87 Stockholm; tel. (8) 762-67-35; fax (8) 611-62-64; e-mail info@metallgruppen.se; internet www.stalometall.se; f. 1906; Pres. PETER GOSSAS; Man. Dir BENGT HULDT; 200 mems with 44,000 employees.

SVEMEK (Welding Engineering): POB 1721, 111 87 Stockholm; tel. (8) 762-67-35; fax (8) 611-62-64; e-mail info@metallgruppen.se; internet www.svemek.se; fmrly Svets Mekaniska Arbetsgivareförbundet; Pres. PER LINDE; Man. Dir BENGT HULDT; 414 mems with 4,629 employees.

Sveriges Bageriförbund (Bakery and Confectionery Employers): Storgt. 19, POB 55680, 102 15 Stockholm; tel. (8) 762-60-00; fax (8) 678-66-64; e-mail bjorn@bageri.se; internet www.bageri.se; f. 1900; Chair. MATS ROSÉN; Man. Dir BJÖRN HELLMAN; 530 mems.

Sveriges Byggindustrier (Swedish Construction Federation): Storgat. 19, POB 5054, 102 42 Stockholm; tel. (8) 698-58-00; fax (8) 698-59-00; e-mail info@bygg.org; internet www.bygg.org; Chair. LEIF STRIDH; Man. Dir BO ANTONI; c. 3,000 mem. cos.

Teknikföretagen (Asscn of Swedish Engineering Industries): Storgt. 5, POB 5510, 114 85 Stockholm; tel. (8) 782-08-00; fax (8) 782-09-00; e-mail info@teknikforetagen.se; internet www.teknikforetagen.se; f. 1896 as VI Sveriges Verkstadsindustrier; Pres. HANS-OLOV OLSSON; Man. Dir ANDERS NARVINGER; 3,400 mem. cos.

TransportGruppen (Transport Industry): Storgt. 19, POB 5384, 102 49 Stockholm; tel. (8) 762-71-00; fax (8) 611-46-99; e-mail info@transportgruppen.se; internet www.transportgruppen.se; eight mem. asscns: Swedish Road Transport Employers' Asscn, Swedish Bus and Coach Employers' Asscn, Swedish Air Transport Industry Employers' Asscn, Swedish Motor Trade Employers' Asscn, Employers' Asscn of the Swedish Petroleum Industry, Swedish Shipowners Employers' Asscn, Asscn Ports of Sweden, Swedish International Freight Asscn; Chair. PER OLOF JANSSON; Dir PETER JEPPSSON.

Trä- och Möbelindustriförbundet (Swedish Wood Products Industry Employers' Asscn): Storgt. 19, POB 16006, 103 21 Stockholm; tel. (8) 762-72-50; fax (8) 762-72-24; e-mail info@tmf.se; internet www.tmf.se; Chair. ULF ADOLFSSON; Man. Dir LEIF G. GUSTAFSSON; 800 mem. cos.

VVS Företagen (Heating, Plumbing, Refrigeration and Insulation Employers): Mejerivägen 3, POB 47160, 100 74 Stockholm; tel. (8) 762-75-00; fax (8) 669-41-19; e-mail info@vvsforetagen.se; internet www.vvsforetagen.se; f. 1918; Chair. ÖSTEN LINDGREN; Man. Dir ROINE KRISTIANSON; c. 1,400 mems.

UTILITIES

Regulatory Authority

Energimyndigheten (Swedish Energy Agency): Kungsgt. 43, POB 310, 631 04 Eskilstuna; tel. (16) 544-20-00; fax (16) 544-20-99; e-mail registrator@energimyndigheten.se; internet www.energimyndigheten.se; f. 1998; monitors and advises electricity and natural gas cos, also undertakes research into renewable energy; Dir-Gen. TOMAS KÅBERGER.

Electricity and Gas

E.ON Sverige AB: Carl Gustafs väg 1, 205 09 Malmö; tel. (40) 25-50-00; e-mail info@eon.se; internet www.eon.se; f. 2001; frmly Sydkraft AB; part of E.ON Group (Germany); generation, distribution and supply of electricity and natural gas; Pres. and CEO HÅKAN BUSKHE.

Fortum AB: Hangövägen 19, 115 77 Stockholm; tel. (8) 671-70-00; fax (8) 671-77-77; e-mail res.koncernkommunikationsverige@fortum.com; internet www.fortum.se; f. 1998 by merger of Imatran Voima and Neste Oyj (both Finland); mem. of Fortum Corpn (Finland), international energy co with core businesses in gas, power and heat; electricity production, distribution and supply; Chair. PETER FAGERNÄS; Dir-Gen. MIKAEL LILIUS.

Göteborg Energi AB: POB 53, 401 20 Gothenberg; tel. (31) 62-60-00; fax (31) 15-25-01; internet www.goteborgenergi.se; distribution of electricity and natural gas; co-owns electricity supplier *Plusenergi* with Vattenfall; Man. Dir ANDERS HEDENSTEDT.

Lunds Energi AB: Trollebergsvägen 5, 221 00 Lund; tel. (46) 35-60-00; fax (46) 18-92-62; e-mail kundtjanst@lundsenergi.se; internet www.lundsenergi.se; f. 1907; distribution, supply of electricity and natural gas; subsidiaries incl.: Billinge Energi AB, Kraftringen Service AB, KREAB Energi AB, Nynäshamn Energi; Man. Dir JAN SAMUELSSON.

Öresundskraft AB: Västra Sandgt. 4, 251 06 Helsingborg; tel. (42) 490-30-00; fax (42) 490-30-60; e-mail info@oresundskraft.se; internet www.oresundskraft.se; distribution and supply of electricity and natural gas; Man. Dir ANDERS ÖSTLUND.

Umeå Energi AB: Storgt. 34, POB 224, 901 05 Umeå; tel. (90) 16-38-00; fax (90) 16-39-59; e-mail umea.energi@umeaenergi.se; internet www.umeaenergi.se; production, distribution and supply of electricity; Man. Dir KURT ÅSTRÖM.

Vattenfall AB: 162 87 Stockholm; tel. (8) 739-50-00; fax (8) 739-51-29; e-mail info@vattenfall.se; internet www.vattenfall.se; f. 1909; became limited liability co in 1992; state-owned; power generation and distribution; co-owns electricity supplier *Plusenergi* with Göteborg Energi AB; some 90 directly or indirectly owned operational subsidiaries; interests in Denmark, Finland, Germany and Poland; Pres. and CEO LARS G. JOSEFSSON.

Water

Responsibility for water supply lies with the municipalities. Since the 1990s many municipalities have formed limited companies under public ownership to manage water supply, such as the supplier for the capital (Stockholm Vatten AB). Several municipalities have contracted private companies to manage water supply.

TRADE UNIONS

The three principal trade union bodies are the Swedish Trade Union Confederation (LO), the Confederation of Professional Employees (TCO) and the Confederation of Professional Associations (SACO).

Landsorganisationen i Sverige (LO) (Swedish Trade Union Confederation): Barnhusgt. 18, 105 53 Stockholm; tel. (8) 796-25-00; fax (8) 796-28-00; e-mail mailbox@lo.se; internet www.lo.se; f. 1898; affiliated to ITUC; Pres. WANJA LUNDBY-WEDIN.

Fifteen affiliated unions, with a total membership of 1,586,729 (June 2007):

Byggnads (Building Workers): Hagagt. 2, 106 32 Stockholm; tel. (8) 728-48-00; fax (8) 34-50-51; e-mail forbundet@byggnads.se; internet www.byggnads.se; Pres. HANS TILLY; 117,000 mems.

Fastighetsanställdas Förbund (Building Maintenance Workers): Upplandsgt. 4, 2nd Floor, POB 70446, 107 25 Stockholm; tel. (8) 696-11-50; fax (8) 24-46-90; e-mail info.fk@fastighets.se; internet www.fastighets.se; f. 1936; Pres. HANS ÖHLUND; 39,243 mems (Dec. 2005).

Grafiska Fackförbundet—Mediafacket (Graphic and Media Workers): Barnhusgt. 20, 3rd Floor, POB 1101, 111 81 Stockholm; tel. (8) 791-16-00; fax (8) 411-41-01; e-mail gf@gf.se; internet www.gf.se; f. 1973; Pres. TOMMY ANDERSSON; 23,000 mems (Dec. 2005).

Handelsanställdas Förbund (Commercial Employees): Upplandsgt. 5, POB 1146, 111 81 Stockholm; tel. (8) 412-68-00; fax (8) 10-00-62; e-mail handels@handels.se; internet www.handels.se; f. 1906; Pres. LARS-ANDERS HÄGGSTRÖM; 172,000 mems (Dec. 2005).

Hotell- och Restaurang Facket (Hotel and Restaurant Workers): Olof Palmesgt. 31, 3rd Floor, POB 1143, 111 81 Stockholm; tel. (0) 771-57-58-59; fax (8) 411-71-18; internet www.hrf.net; f. 1918; Pres. ELLA NIIA; 60,000 mems (Dec. 2005).

IF Metall: Olof Palmesgt. 11, 105 52 Stockholm; tel. (8) 786-80-00; fax (8) 240-86-74; e-mail postbox.fk@ifmetall.se; internet www.ifmetall.se; f. 2006 by merger of Industrifacket and Svenska Metallindustriarbetareförbundet; Pres. STEFAN LÖFVEN; c. 415,000 mems.

Kommunal—Svenska Kommunalarbetareförbundet (Swedish Municipal Workers' Union): Hagagt. 2, 1st Floor, POB 19039, 104 32 Stockholm; tel. (8) 728-28-00; fax (8) 31-87-45; e-mail kommunal.forbundet@kommunal.se; internet www.kommunal.se; Pres. YLVA THÖRN; 573,600 mems.

SEKO—Facket för Service och Kommunikation (Services and Communications Employees): Barnhusgt. 6–10, POB 1105, 111 81 Stockholm; tel. (8) 791-41-00; fax (8) 21-89-53; e-mail seko@seko.se; internet www.seko.se; f. 1970; present name since 1995; Pres. JANNE RUDÉN; c. 153,000 mems.

Skogs- och Träfacket (Swedish Forest and Wood Trade Union): Olof Palmesgt. 31, 5th Floor, POB 1152, 111 81 Stockholm; tel. (8) 701-77-00; fax (8) 20-79-04; e-mail postbox.fk@skogstrafacket.org; internet www.skogstrafacket.org; f. 1998 by merger of Svenska Skogsarbetareförbundet and Svenska Träindustriarbetareförbundet; Chair. and Pres. KJELL DAHLSTRÖM; 55,000 mems.

Svenska Elektrikerförbundet (Electricians): Upplandsgt. 14, 1st Floor, POB 1123, 111 81 Stockholm; tel. (8) 412-82-82; fax (8) 412-82-01; e-mail postbox.fk@sef.com; internet www.sef.com; f. 1906; Pres. STIG LARSSON; 26,000 mems.

Svenska Livsmedelsarbetareförbundet (Food Workers): Upplandsgt. 3, POB 1156, 111 81 Stockholm; tel. (8) 769-29-00; fax (8) 796-29-03; e-mail info@livs.se; internet www.livs.se; f. 1896; Pres. HANS-OLOF NILSSON; 48,285 mems (Dec. 2005).

Svenska Målareförbundet (Painters): Olof Palmesgt. 31, POB 1113, 111 81 Stockholm; tel. (8) 587-274-00; fax (8) 587-274-99; e-mail post@malareforbundet.se; internet www.malareforbundet.se; f. 1887; Chair. LARS-ÅKE LUNDIN; 15,900 mems.

Svenska Musikerförbundet (Musicians): Alströmergt. 25B, POB 49144, 101 29 Stockholm; tel. (8) 587-060-00; fax (8) 16-80-20; e-mail info@musikerforbundet.se; internet www.musikerforbundet.se; f. 1907; Pres. JAN GRANVIK; 3,700 mems (Dec. 2001).

Svenska Pappersindustriarbetareförbundet (Swedish Paperworkers' Union): Olof Palmesgt. 11, 5th Floor, POB 1127, 111 81 Stockholm; tel. (8) 796-61-00; fax (8) 411-41-79; e-mail info@pappers.se; internet www.pappers.se; f. 1920; Pres. JAN-HENRIK SANDBERG; 25,090 mems (2002).

Svenska Transportarbetareförbundet (Transport Workers): Olof Palmesgt. 29, 6th Floor, POB 714, 101 33 Stockholm; tel. (10) 480-30-00; fax (8) 24-03-91; e-mail transport.fk@transport.se; internet www.transport.se; f. 1897; Chair. PER WINBERG; c. 73,000 mems.

SACO (Confederation of Professional Asscns): POB 2206, Lilla Nygt. 14, 103 15 Stockholm; tel. (8) 613-48-00; fax (8) 24-77-01; e-mail kansli@saco.se; internet www.saco.se; f. 1947; affiliated to ITUC and ETUC; Chair. ANNA EKSTRÖM; 430,300 mems (Dec. 2007).

There are 24 affiliated unions and professional orgs, of which the following are the largest:

Jusek: Nybrogt. 30, POB 5167, 102 44 Stockholm; tel. (8) 665-29-00; fax (8) 662-79-23; e-mail vaxel@jusek.se; internet www.jusek.se; asscn of graduates in law, business administration and economics, computer and systems science, personnel management and social science; Pres. GÖRAN ARRIUS; 65,000 mems.

Lärarnas riksförbund (National Union of Teachers in Sweden): Sveavägen 50, POB 3529, 103 69 Stockholm; tel. (8) 613-27-00; fax (8) 21-91-36; e-mail lr@lr.se; internet www.lr.se; f. 1884; Pres. METTA FJELKNER; 80,000 mems.

Sveriges Ingenjörer (Swedish Asscn of Graduate Engineers): Malmskillnadsgt. 48, POB 1419, 111 84 Stockholm; tel. (8) 613-80-00; fax (8) 796-71-02; e-mail info@sverigesingenjorer.se; internet www.sverigesingenjorer.se; Pres. ULF BENGTSSON; 120,000 mems.

Tjänstemännens Centralorganisation (TCO) (Confederation of Professional Employees): Linnégt. 14, 114 94 Stockholm; tel. (8) 782-91-00; fax (8) 663-75-20; e-mail info@tco.se; internet www.tco.se; f. 1944; affiliated to ITUC, European Trade Union Confed. and Council of Nordic Trade Unions; Pres. STURE NORDH.

17 affiliated unions with total membership of 1,026,000 (June 2007), of which the following are the largest:

Fackförbundet ST (Civil Servants): Sturegt. 15, POB 5308, 102 47 Stockholm; tel. (8) 790-51-00; fax (8) 24-29-24; e-mail st@st.org; internet www.st.org; f. 1904; fmrly Statstjänstemannaförbundet; Pres. ANNETTE CARNHEDE; 93,000 mems.

Finansförbundet (Bank Employees): Olof Palmesgt. 17, POB 720, 101 34 Stockholm; tel. (8) 614-03-00; fax (8) 611-38-98; e-mail info@finansforbundet.se; internet www.finansforbundet.se; Pres. LILLEMOR SMEDENVALL; 39,000 mems.

Lärarförbundet (Teachers): Segelbåtsvägen 15, POB 12229, 102 26 Stockholm; tel. (8) 737-65-00; fax (8) 656-94-15; e-mail kansli@lararforbundet.se; internet www.lararforbundet.se; Pres. EVA-LIS SIRÉN; 225,000 mems.

Ledarna—Sveriges chefsorganisation (Professional and Managerial Staff): St Eriksgt. 26, POB 12069, 102 22 Stockholm; tel. (8) 598-990-00; fax (8) 598-990-10; e-mail ledarna@ledarna.se; internet www.ledarna.se; f. 1905; Pres. ANNIKA ELIAS; 70,000 mems.

Sif (Clerical and Technical Employees in Industry): Olof Palmesgt. 17, 105 32 Stockholm; tel. (8) 508-970-00; fax (8) 508-970-01; e-mail koc@sif.se; internet www.sif.se; f. 1920 as Sveriges Verkstäders Tjänstemannaförening, restyled Svenska Industritjänstemannaförbundet 1932; present name adopted 2000; Pres. MARI-ANN KRANTZ; 350,000 mems.

SKTF—Sveriges Kommunaltjänstemannaförbund (Local Government Officers): Kungsgt. 28A, POB 7825, 103 97 Stockholm; tel. (8) 789-63-00; fax (8) 789-64-81; e-mail sktf@sktf.se; internet www.sktf.se; Pres. EVA NORDMARK; 170,000 mems.

Tjänstemannaförbundet HTF (Commercial Salaried Employees): Franzéngt. 5, POB 30102, 104 25 Stockholm; tel. (8) 737-80-00; fax (8) 618-77-19; e-mail htf@htf.se; internet www.htf.se; f. 1937; fmrly Handelstjänstemannaförbundet; Pres. BENGT OLSSON; 158,436 mems (Feb. 2004).

Vårdförbundet (Swedish Asscn of Health Professionals): Adolf Fredriks Kyrkogt. 11, POB 3260, 103 65 Stockholm; tel. (8) 14-77-00; fax (8) 411-42-29; e-mail info@vardforbundet.se; internet www.vardforbundet.se; fmrly Svenska Hälso- och Sjukvårdens Tjänstemannaförbund; Pres. ANNA-KARIN EKLUND; 108,480 mems (June 2007).

Transport

RAILWAYS

In mid-2007 there were 11,904 km of standard- and narrow-gauge railways, of which 9,683 km of track was electrified. In mid-2008 a railway line extending 190 km, connecting Nyland and Umeå on the north-eastern coast of Sweden, was under construction and was scheduled to be completed by late 2010.

SJ AB (Statens Järnvägar): 105 50 Stockholm; tel. (10) 751-50-00; fax (10) 751-54-24; e-mail sjinfo@sj.se; internet www.sj.se; f. 1856; state-owned; runs passenger traffic on all state-owned railway track; Chair. ULF ADELSOHN; CEO JAN FORSBERG.

Banverket: Jussi Björlings väg 2, 781 85 Borlänge; tel. (243) 44-50-00; e-mail banverket@banverket.se; internet www.banverket.se; primarily govt funded; manages Sweden's state-owned railway infrastructure; Dir-Gen. MINOO AKHTARZAND.

Malmö-Limhamns Järnvägs AB: POB 30022, 200 61 Limhamn; tel. (40) 36-15-04; fax (40) 15-86-24; 5 km of 1,435-mm gauge; Dir UWE JÖHNSON; Traffic Man. K. HOLMBERG.

TGOJ Trafik AB: Gredbyvägen 3–5, 632 21 Eskilstuna; tel. (16) 17-26-61; fax (16) 17-26-66; e-mail info@tgojtrafik.se; internet www.tgojtrafik.se; f. 1877; 300 km of 1,435-mm gauge electrified railways; Chair. JAN SUNDLING; Pres. BENGT FORS.

ROADS

At 31 December 2004 there were an estimated 424,597 km of roads, of which 1,591 km were motorways, 15,385 km were main or national roads and 82,883 km of secondary or regional roads. In 2000 a road-rail link between Malmö and Copenhagen (Denmark), across the 16-km Öresund strait, was opened. A bridge linking Sweden and Norway, at Svinesund, was opened in 2005.

SHIPPING

The principal ports in terms of cargo handled are Göteborg (Gothenberg), Brofjorden, Trelleborg, Luleå and Malmö. Stockholm is also an important port. At 31 December 2007 the Swedish merchant fleet numbered 572 vessels, with a combined displacement of 4.0m. grt.

Principal Shipping Companies

Broström Ship Management AB: POB 39, 471 21 Skärhamn; tel. (304) 67-67-00; fax (304) 67-11-10; e-mail info@brostrom.se; internet www.brostrom.se; 97.3% owned by Maersk Product Tankers AB; management co, operating specialized tanker services; Man. Dir LENART SIMONSSON.

Broström Tankers AB: 403 30 Göteborg; tel. (31) 61-60-00; fax (31) 61-60-12; e-mail brotank@brostrom.se; internet www.brostrom.se; f. 1990; specializes in transporting petroleum products, in north-west Europe and world-wide; Man. Dir TORE ANGERVALL.

Rederi AB Transatlantic: Södra Hamnen 27, POB 32, 471 21 Skärhamn; tel. (304) 67-47-00; fax (304) 67-47-70; e-mail info@rebt.se; internet www.rabt.se; f. 2005 by merger of B&N Nordsjöfrakt AB (f. 1972) and Gorthon Lines AB (f. 1915); freight shipping, forwarding, storage, agency, ice-breaking; Man. Dir CARL-JOHAN HAGMAN.

Stena AB: Masthuggskajen, 405 19 Göteborg; tel. (31) 85-50-00; fax (31) 12-06-51; e-mail info@stenaline.com; internet www.stena.com; f. 1939; parent co of Stena Line, Stena Bulk, Stena RoRo, Stena Teknik, Concordia Maritime and Northern Marine Management; CEO DAN STEN OLSSON.

Wallenius Lines AB: Swedenborgsgt. 19, POB 17086, 104 62 Stockholm; tel. (8) 772-05-00; fax (8) 640-68-54; e-mail info@walleniuslines.com; internet www.walleniuslines.com; f. 1934; car and truck carriers; Pres. LONE FØNSS SCHRØDER.

Associations

Föreningen Sveriges Sjöfart och Sjöförsvar (Swedish Maritime League): Kastellet, Kastellholmen, 111 49 Stockholm; tel. (8) 611-74-81; fax (8) 611-74-76; e-mail fsss@algonet.se; f. 1983 by merger of Swedish General Shipping Asscn and Swedish Navy League; Pres. CLAES TORNBERG; Gen. Sec. STEN GÖTHBERG; 2,000 mems.

Sveriges Redareförening (Swedish Shipowners' Asscn): Södra Hamngt. 53, POB 330, 401 25 Göteborg; tel. (31) 62-95-25; fax (31) 15-23-13; e-mail srf@sweship.se; internet www.sweship.se; f. 1906; Pres. LARS HØGLAND; Man. Dir HÅKAN FRIDBERG.

CIVIL AVIATION

The main international airport is at Arlanda, 42 km from Stockholm. Gothenburg (Göteborg) and Malmö are also served by international airports. There are regular flights between the main cities in Sweden. Many domestic flights operate from Bromma (Stockholm's city airport).

Luftfartsstyrelsen (Swedish Civil Aviation Authority): Vikboplan 7, 601 73 Norrköping; tel. (11) 415-20-00; e-mail luftfartsstyrelsen@luftfartsstyrelsen.se; internet www.luftfartsstyrelsen.se; f. 1923 as Luftfartsverket; present name adopted 2005; state body; central govt authority for matters concerning civil aviation; Dir-Gen. NILS GUNNAR BILLINGER.

Scandinavian Airlines System (SAS): Frösundavik Allé 1, Solna, 195 87 Stockholm; tel. (8) 797-00-00; fax (8) 797-15-15; internet www.sas.se; f. 1946; the national carrier of Denmark, Norway and Sweden. It is a consortium owned two-sevenths by SAS Danmark A/S, two-sevenths by SAS Norge ASA and three-sevenths by SAS Sverige AB. Each parent org. is a limited co owned 50% by Govt and 50% by private shareholders. The SAS group includes the consortium and the subsidiaries in which the consortium has a majority or otherwise controlling interest; the Board consists of two members from each of the parent cos and the chairmanship rotates among the three national chairmen on an annual basis. SAS absorbed Linjeflyg AB (domestic passenger, newspaper and postal services in Sweden) in 1993; strategic alliance with Lufthansa (Germany) formed in 1995; Chair. FRITZ H. SCHUR; Pres. and CEO MATS JANSSON.

Transwede Airways AB: POB 2011, 438 11 Landvetter; tel. (31) 94-79-80; fax (31) 94-79-90; e-mail trygve.gjertsen@transwede.com; internet www.transwede.se; f. 1985 as Aerocenter Trafikflyg AB; current name adopted 1986; relaunched 2005; operates charter passenger services within Scandinavia; CEO TRYGVE GJERTSEN.

West Air Sweden: Prästgårdsgt. 1, POB 5433, 402 29 Göteborg; tel. (31) 703-04-50; fax (31) 703-04-55; e-mail info@westair.se; internet www.westair.se; f. 1963; present name adopted 1993; Pres. GUSTAF THUREBORN.

Tourism

Sweden offers a variety of landscape, from the mountains of the 'Midnight Sun', north of the Arctic Circle, to the white sandy beaches of the south. There are many lakes, waterfalls and forests, and Stockholm is famed for its beautiful situation and modern architecture. Most tourists come from the other Scandinavian countries, Germany and the United Kingdom. In 2007 tourism receipts totalled an estimated US $12,000m.

Svenska Turistföreningen (Swedish Touring Club): Ameralitetsbacken 1, POB 25, 101 20 Stockholm; tel. (8) 463-21-00; fax (8) 678-19-58; e-mail info@stfturist.se; internet www.stfturist.se; f. 1885; 300,000 mems; owns and operates mountain hotels and youth hostels; co-ordinates nature and cultural activities in local clubs; Pres. TORGNY HÅSTAD; Sec.-Gen. YVONNE ARENTOFT.

Turistdelegationen: POB 4044, 102 61 Stockholm; tel. (8) 681-90-00; e-mail nutek@nutek.se; internet www.nutek.se/turistnaringen; f. 1995; Swedish Tourist Authority became part of Nutek, the Swedish Agency for Economic and Regional Growth, in January 2006; state-owned; promotes enterprise and entrepreneurship in the tourist industry in Sweden and produces and disseminates tourism information; Dir DENNIS BEDEROFF.

SWITZERLAND

Introductory Survey

Location, Climate, Language, Religion, Flag, Capital

The Swiss Confederation lies in central Europe, bounded to the north by Germany, to the east by Austria and Liechtenstein, to the south by Italy and to the west by France. The climate is generally temperate, but varies considerably with altitude and aspect. In Zürich the average temperature ranges from −1°C (30°F) in winter to 16°C (61°F) in summer. There are four national languages: German, French, Italian and Romansh (Rumantsch), spoken by 72.5%, 21.0%, 4.3% and 0.6% of resident Swiss nationals, respectively, in 2000. Other languages are spoken by the remaining 1.6% of the population. Including resident aliens, the linguistic proportions in 2000 were: German 63.7%, French 20.4%, Italian 6.5%, Romansh 0.5% and other languages 9.0%. Most Swiss citizens profess Christianity: in 2000 42.7% were Protestants and 41.2% Roman Catholics. Of the total resident population in 2000, 35.3% were Protestants and 41.8% Roman Catholics. The Federal flag, which is square, consists of a white upright cross in the centre of a red ground. The capital is Bern (Berne).

Recent History

Switzerland, whose origins date back to 1291, has occupied its present area since its borders were fixed by treaty in 1815. At the same time, it was internationally recognized as a neutral country. Despite the strategic importance of Switzerland, its 'permanent neutrality' has never since been violated. The country has not entered any military alliances, and it avoided participation in both World Wars. Executive authority is exercised on a collegial basis by the Federal Council (cabinet), with a President who serves, for only one year at a time, as 'the first among equals'. Owing to the restricted powers of the Federal Council, initiatives and referendums form the core of the political process. Switzerland is a confederation of 20 cantons and six half-cantons. In 1979 the mainly French-speaking region of Jura seceded from the predominantly German-speaking canton of Bern, becoming the first new canton to be established since 1815.

Despite the fact that Switzerland has long been the headquarters of many international organizations, the country did not join the UN until 2002, owing to concerns that it would conflict with the country's traditional neutrality. Switzerland was a founder member of the European Free Trade Association (EFTA, see p. 426) in 1960 and joined the Council of Europe (see p. 236) in 1963.

Since 1959 government posts have been divided between the members of the Social Democratic Party, the Radical Democratic Party, the Christian Democratic People's Party and the Swiss People's Party. This coalition holds more than 80% of the seats in the National Council (the lower house of the Federal Assembly), and all but three of the 46 seats in the Council of States (the upper house). The ruling coalition dominated the National Council at elections held between 1975 and 1995, although it lost some support to the Green Party of Switzerland, which grew to become the fifth largest party as public concern regarding ecological issues increased.

Switzerland began to emerge from its traditional isolation in the early 1990s. This was largely due to economic pressures resulting from the world recession and the further integration of the European Community (EC, now European Union—EU, see p. 255). In May 1992 the Government's proposal for Switzerland to join the IMF and the World Bank was approved in a referendum. On the following day, the Federal Council announced that it was to apply for membership of the EC. In a referendum on 6 December, however, the Swiss electorate voted against ratification of an agreement, signed in May, to create a free-trade zone encompassing both EC and EFTA member states. (The European Economic Area was established, without Switzerland, in January 1994.) Despite this setback, the Government declared its intention to continue to pursue its application for membership of the EC. During 1993 Switzerland confined itself to seeking bilateral negotiations with the EC on issues of particular national interest. Agreement was reached in December 1996 to phase out Swiss work permits for citizens of EU member states over a period of six years. At the beginning of December 1998 Switzerland and the EU concluded a bilateral trade agreement, having settled a lengthy dispute over the imposition of tolls on road freight traffic through Switzerland. By February 2000 the Government had negotiated seven bilateral free-trade agreements with the EU. The accords included the gradual elimination of immigration controls between Switzerland and the EU over a period of 12 years. Although the Government insisted that Swiss sovereignty was not affected by the trade agreements, opponents of Swiss membership of the EU submitted a petition, thereby forcing a referendum on the agreements. At the referendum, which was held in May, 67.2% of those who voted approved the agreements. Following the submission of a petition by pro-EU lobbyists, a referendum was held in March 2001 on whether to begin 'fast-track' accession negotiations with the EU; the ballot attracted an unusually high participation rate and the motion was rejected by 77% of the voters. The result was believed to have been influenced in part by a letter from the European Commission in February, widely perceived as coercive, which urged the acceleration of negotiations with the EU regarding co-operation against customs fraud and tax evasion. The Government insisted that the vote did not represent a rejection of the EU, but rather reflected the desire to move towards accession at a slower pace, and that its plans for eventual membership of the EU remained unchanged.

The enfranchisement of women in federal elections was approved at a referendum in February 1971. However, the half-cantons of Appenzell Ausserrhoden and Appenzell Innerrhoden introduced female suffrage only in 1989 and 1990, respectively. In October 1984 the Federal Assembly elected Switzerland's first female cabinet minister, Dr Elisabeth Kopp of the Radical Democratic Party, who became Head of the Federal Department of Justice and Police. In December 1988 the Assembly elected Kopp, by a large majority, to be Vice-President of the Swiss Confederation for 1989, concurrently with her other duties in the Federal Council. In the same month, however, she announced her resignation from her post as Head of the Federal Department of Justice and Police, following allegations that she had violated regulations concerning official secrecy. In February 1989, following an official investigation of the case, Kopp was replaced as Vice-President; in February 1990, however, she was acquitted by the Federal Supreme Court.

In January 1993 the Head of the Federal Department of Foreign Affairs, René Felber, resigned. Under the terms of the coalition, Felber was to be replaced by another francophone member of the Social Democratic Party. In March the party's official candidate, Christiane Brunner, a trade union leader, was rejected by other members of the coalition in favour of a male candidate, Francis Matthey, who, however, following pressure from within the party, refused the nomination. The Social Democratic Party subsequently reconfirmed Brunner's candidacy but presented another female candidate in addition, Ruth Dreifuss, also a trade union activist. Following three rounds of voting, Dreifuss was elected to the Federal Council. In December 1998 the Federal Assembly elected Dreifuss (by then Head of the Federal Department of Home Affairs) as President of the Confederation for 1999. A female Christian Democratic People's Party candidate, Ruth Metzler, was elected Head of the Federal Department of Justice and Police in March 1999. In the following month 59.2% of voters in a national referendum approved a revised draft Constitution that included new provision for the right to undertake strike action by the labour force.

The commission that had investigated the allegations against Kopp during 1989 subsequently revealed that the office of the Federal Public Prosecutor held about 900,000 secret files on some 200,000 Swiss citizens and foreigners. In March 1990 riots ensued when around 30,000 people demonstrated in Bern in protest at the existence of such files. The Government subsequently announced that it would commission a report on the activities of the security services and introduce new laws regulating state security; it also opened most of the files to public scrutiny. Published in June 1993, the report found that security service observation had been largely restricted to left-wing groups since 1945 and that security service personnel had at times behaved in an unprofessional manner.

Meanwhile, during 1986 the Government introduced legislation that aimed to restrict the number of refugees who were to be granted political asylum in Switzerland. However, the new legislation was criticized by socialist, religious and humanitarian groups, and in April 1987 a national referendum on the issue was held. Of the 41.8% of the electorate who voted at the referendum, a substantial majority was in favour of the new restrictions. In March 1994, in an attempt to control increasing drugs-related crime (following allegations that immigrants trading in illicit drugs were exploiting the asylum laws to avoid extradition), the Government approved legislation restricting the rights of asylum seekers and immigrants, which included provisions for their arrest and detention without trial for failure to possess the requisite identification documents; further stringent measures against foreigners suspected of trafficking in illegal drugs were approved by national referendum in December. Civil rights groups accused the Government of yielding to popular xenophobic sentiment in an effort to divert attention from its failure to overcome the drugs problem. In December 1996 a proposal sponsored by the Swiss People's Party to confiscate the earnings of asylum seekers in Switzerland and to expel automatically all those without sufficient documentation was narrowly rejected in a national referendum. In a referendum held in September 2000 63.7% of voters rejected a motion to reduce the number of foreigners allowed to settle in Switzerland from 20% of the total population to 18%. At a referendum held in November 2002, 51.1% of voters rejected proposals, drawn up by the Swiss People's Party, under which would-be refugees arriving in Switzerland via any country free of political persecution (in practice, all neighbouring countries) would automatically be denied refugee status and returned to that country.

The results of elections to the National Council and the Council of States, held in October 1999, challenged, initially at least, some of the assumptions generally made about the Swiss political process. They were characterized, above all, by the strong performance of the Swiss People's Party, which, in terms of votes gained, became the country's largest party. In the National Council the Swiss People's Party overtook both the Radical Democratic Party and the Christian Democratic People's Party to become the second largest party after the Social Democratic Party. Seats in the National Council are allotted in proportion to votes gained. However, the complex, 'cantonal' nature of the electoral system ensured ultimate victory for the Social Democratic Party. In the Council of States, the Swiss People's Party obtained a total of seven seats, thereby becoming the third largest party (after the Radical Democrats and the Christian Democrats).

In the early years of the 21st century the stability of the 'grand coalition' that had governed Switzerland since 1959 was increasingly threatened by the growing influence of the Swiss People's Party. Under the so-called 'magic formula' traditionally used to determine the distribution of government seats among the coalition partners, the Social Democratic Party, the Radical Democratic Party and the Christian Democratic People's Party each received two seats and the Swiss People's Party received only one. However, at the general election held on 19 October 2003 the Swiss People's Party received the largest share of the votes cast and thus for the first time became the largest party in the National Council, with 55 seats. The party demanded a second seat on the Federal Council to reflect this (to be taken by Christoph Blocher), and threatened to withdraw from the coalition, effectively ending the era of consensus politics, if its demand was not met. (Traditionally, Swiss ministers are reappointed at each election, and keep their seats until such time as they resign.) When the Federal Assembly elected the Federal Council on 10 December, however, Blocher contested the seat held by Metzler and, after three ballots, won with a majority of just five votes. This was the first ministerial deselection for 130 years, and the first time the composition of the governing coalition had been changed in 44 years. When the new Federal Council took office on 1 January 2004, Blocher became Head of the Federal Department of Justice and Police, which carried with it responsibility not only for policy on immigration and asylum but also for negotiating with the EU on Swiss membership of the Schengen Agreement (which binds signatories to the abolition of border controls) and the Dublin Convention on Asylum (relating to common formal arrangements on asylum).

In December 2004 the Federal Assembly approved a second set of bilateral agreements with the EU, which had been signed in October. Under the agreements Switzerland was to introduce (incrementally between 1 July 2005 and 2011) a withholding tax of 35% on the income of EU citizens' savings held in Switzerland, with banking secrecy to be retained. The agreements also provided for co-operation against customs fraud and for Switzerland's associate membership of the Schengen Agreement and Dublin Convention, as well as for the extension of the first set of bilateral agreements (see above) to the 10 states (mostly in Central and Eastern Europe) that had acceded to full membership of the EU earlier in the year. The National Council voted against submitting the agreement on the Schengen/Dublin accords to an obligatory referendum. However, the Swiss People's Party gathered sufficient signatures to force a referendum on the issue. At the referendum, held on 5 June 2005, 54.6% of participating voters (56.6% of the electorate) supported Switzerland's adherence to the Schengen/Dublin accords. (The Schengen/Dublin accords were duly implemented on 12 December 2008.) The extension of existing bilateral agreements to the new EU member states was approved by 56.0% of voters at a referendum held on 25 September 2005; a participation rate of 54.5% was recorded.

In June 2004 the National Council approved a two-tier immigration policy whereby priority was to be given to EU and EFTA nationals, with immigration otherwise restricted to only highly skilled workers in the agricultural, construction, health and tourism sectors. At a national referendum held in September, a government plan to ease citizenship procedures for Swiss-born second-generation immigrants was opposed by 56.8% of those who participated, while a plan to grant automatic citizenship to third-generation immigrants was rejected by 51.6%. (Foreigners comprise approximately 20% of Switzerland's population.) In November voters in a referendum approved a programme of fiscal reform for the redistribution of funds between the Federal Government and the cantons, and a federal resolution that extended the Government's power to levy direct federal and value-added taxes to 2020 (this mandate had been due to expire in 2006).

A referendum on the registration of same-sex partnerships was held on 5 June 2005, at which 58.0% of voters supported proposals to grant registered same-sex couples similar legal rights to married couples in areas such as taxation and pensions (although they would not be allowed to adopt children, nor would they be eligible for fertility treatment). The participation rate was 56.5%.

In April 2006 Josef Deiss, of the Christian Democratic People's Party, unexpectedly announced his resignation as Head of the Federal Department for Economic Affairs. He was replaced in June by party colleague Doris Leuthard. At a national referendum, held on 24 September, 67.8% of the valid votes cast were in favour of a proposal, supported by the Swiss People's Party, further to curtail the rights of asylum seekers and foreign migrants to Switzerland. Under the proposals, refugees would be required to present valid identification documents to the authorities within two days of their arrival in Switzerland and the issuance of work permits to non-skilled individuals from non-EU and -EFTA countries would effectively be ended.

Campaigning for a general election, scheduled for late October 2007, was characterized by the increased polarization of the electorate. In mid-September controversy arose following accusations of racism against the Swiss People's Party by a UN official in Switzerland, which followed that party's use of images deemed to be xenophobic in its campaign posters. In early October the campaign was marred by violent clashes in the capital, Bern, between police and left-wing activists who had attempted to disrupt a rally held by the Swiss People's Party.

At the election, which was held on 21 October 2007, the Swiss People's Party strengthened its position as the largest party, winning 62 seats in the National Council. The Social Democratic Party performed poorly, taking just 43 seats, while the Radical Democratic Party and the Christian Democratic People's Party won 31 seats apiece. The Green Party increased its representation, winning 20 seats. Opposition to the Swiss People's Party centred increasingly on Blocher, who was due to become Vice-President of the Confederation for 2008. A large number of Federal Assembly members opposed Blocher's re-election to the Federal Council, in particular the Green Party, which announced its intention to propose its own candidate. However, prior to the vote, which took place on 12 December 2007, the Green Party withdrew its candidate in favour of a moderate member of the Swiss People's Party, Eveline Widmer-Schlumpf, who eventually defeated Blocher after two rounds of voting. In defiance of the party leadership, Widmer-Schlumpf announced that she would accept a role in the Federal Council. The Swiss People's Party subsequently announced the withdrawal of its support for the Government, in protest at Blocher's deselection. On 1 January 2008 Widmer-Schlumpf took office as Head of the Federal Department of Justice and Police.

Following Blocher's deselection, both Widmer-Schlumpf and the Head of the Federal Department of Defence, Civil Protection and Sports, Samuel Schmid, were excluded from the party's parliamentary group, on the grounds that their moderate views conflicted with those of the majority of the party's supporters. In March 2008 the party leadership accused Widmer-Schlumpf of betraying the party and initiated measures to expel her. In accordance with the party's constitution, the national executive requested that the Graubünden cantonal organization—of which Widmer-Schlumpf was a leading figure—formally revoke her membership of the party. However, the cantonal executive refused to comply and it, in turn, was expelled and replaced by a committee of more right-wing members. The attempt by the Swiss People's Party to impose discipline upon its regional organizations prompted the secession, in June, of executives in other traditionally moderate cantonal sections, notably Bern, where dissident members formed a new party, styled the Conservative Democratic Party. The former Swiss People's Party executives in Glarus and Graubünden subsequently formed parties under the same name in their respective cantons. The new parties immediately gained representation in the Government, as Widmer-Schlumpf and Schmid were among the leading members. The Conservative Democratic Party was formally inaugurated as a national party at a special conference held in Glarus in November 2008; a member of the Bern cantonal parliament, Hans Grunder, was elected as party President.

In early November 2008 Schmid unexpectedly announced his intention to resign from the Government, with effect from the end of December. (He had been subject to media criticism since mid-2008, following an incident at a military training camp in which six soldiers died, and the resignation of the head of the armed forces in July, following allegations of personal misconduct.) At the election for Schmid's successor in early December, the list of candidates included three members of the Swiss People's Party, notably Blocher and the head of the Zürich cantonal organization, Ueli Maurer; Maurer was elected to the role after three rounds of voting, defeating the President of the Swiss Farmers' Union, Hansjörg Walter, by a margin of just one vote. Following his election, Maurer confirmed his commitment to bipartisan government, although the President of the Swiss People's Party, Toni Brunner, called for the party to receive a second cabinet seat. The result underscored the marginalization of Blocher, who withdrew his candidacy after the first round of voting.

Meanwhile, in July 2008 the Radical Democratic Party and the Liberal Party of Switzerland announced plans for a formal merger and, at a special conference held in Bern in October, delegates representing the two parties overwhelmingly approved the proposals. The formal merger of the two parties, as FDP.The Liberals, was completed on 1 January 2009; Fulvio Pelli, previously the leader of the Radical Democratic Party, became President of the new formation. Hans Rudolf Merz, of FDP.The Liberals, became President of the Confederation for 2009.

Swiss laws denying investigators access to information regarding bank accounts held with Swiss banks were severely criticized from late 2008. In July the US Internal Revenue Service (IRS) issued a summons to the Swiss bank UBS, demanding that it release the confidential details of US clients suspected by the US Department of Justice of tax evasion. In November a senior UBS executive was indicted by US officials, on charges of aiding US citizens to evade the payment of tax. In return for the abandonment of criminal investigations into the activities of a number of employees at an 'offshore' banking subsidiary in the USA, in February 2009 UBS admitted to facilitating the concealment of assets by clients in the USA. Under the terms of the agreement, the bank paid a fine of some US $780m. and pledged to reveal the details of 255 accounts held by foreign customers. However, following accusations that the agreement violated Swiss laws on banking secrecy, the President of the Confederation, Merz, insisted that the agreement only concerned information regarding clients suspected of fraud, rather than of tax evasion—which is considered a civil offence in Switzerland. (A separate, civil investigation by the IRS into some 52,000 UBS accounts held by US citizens was ongoing in April 2009.)

Throughout early 2009 the Swiss Government was subject to intense pressure from several other governments, notably including France and Germany, over its continued reluctance to implement changes to the country's laws on banking secrecy. In February the Federal Council appointed a committee of financial and legal experts to recommend measures designed to uphold banking secrecy. In mid-March, however, the cabinet approved proposals to relax the legislation to permit the sharing of information on accounts held in Swiss banks with investigators in certain individual cases where allegations of tax evasion could be proven. Nevertheless, the Government insisted that it continued to endorse the principle of banking secrecy and that the reform would affect a very small number of cases. The announcement followed media reports earlier that month that the Organisation for Economic Co-operation Development (OECD, see p. 358) had recommended that Switzerland be placed on a list of countries considered to be 'unco-operative tax havens'.

At a national referendum held in early February 2009, 59.6% of the valid votes cast were in favour of the extension of an agreement with the EU permitting the free movement of EU citizens within Switzerland to include migrants from Bulgaria and Romania, both of which had joined the EU in 2007. The Swiss People's Party and other right-wing groups had campaigned against the treaty's extension, claiming that it would prompt a significant increase in the number of Eastern European migrants arriving in Switzerland, while the other parties represented in the Federal Council, trade unions and groups representing Swiss businesses all supported the proposal.

In November 1989 64.4% of voters in a referendum rejected a proposal to abolish the armed forces by 2000. The referendum, which had been instigated by the Group for Switzerland Without an Army (an alliance of socialist, pacifist, youth and ecological organizations), attracted an unusually high level of participation, almost 70% of the electorate. Following the referendum, the Federal Military (Defence) Department established a working party to examine proposals for reforms in the armed forces; consequently, the strength of the armed forces was considerably reduced during the early 1990s. In June 1993 the Federal Assembly approved legislation that sought permission for Swiss forces to be included in future UN peace-keeping operations. However, at a referendum on the issue, which took place in June 1994, 57.3% of voters rejected the proposal. Switzerland did subsequently join the 'Partnership for Peace' (see p. 353) programme of the North Atlantic Treaty Organization (NATO) in 1996. Swiss peace-keepers have participated in operations in Bosnia and Herzegovina, while Swiss truce-verifiers have worked in Kosovo under the Organization for Security and Co-operation in Europe (OSCE, see p. 366). In November 2000 a referendum was held on proposals to reduce the military budget by one-third; the motion was rejected by 62.4% of voters. A further proposal to abolish the armed forces was rejected by 78.1% of voters in a referendum held in December 2001; 76.8% of voters also rejected a replacement civilian force.

Until 2002, although Switzerland maintained a permanent observer at the UN and had joined the organization's non-political specialized agencies, it was not a full member of the UN. At a referendum in 1986, although the Government campaigned in its favour, some 75.7% of voters had rejected full membership of the UN; the plebiscite was characterized by a relatively high rate of participation rate, at 50.2%. In March 2000 a petition favouring membership of the UN forced a further future referendum on the issue, to take place in 2002. In September 2001 the Federal Assembly approved proposals for Switzerland to join the UN. At the referendum, which was held on 3 March 2002, the proposals required not only the support of the majority of voters, but also the approval of at least one-half of the cantons in order to be adopted. In the event, 54.6% of voters and 12 (of 23) cantons supported the proposals; the participation rate at the referendum was 57.8%. Switzerland was formally admitted as a member of the UN in September of that year.

At a national referendum held in February 2003 70.3% of voters cast their ballots in favour of two proposed reforms whereby voters would be given the automatic right to challenge treaties signed between Switzerland and other countries (although, in practice, all important agreements are already subject to a referendum), and petitions with the requisite number of signatures could be used to introduce legislation, rather than solely constitutional amendments as was already the case. The rate of participation in the referendum, however, was markedly low, at only 28%.

In September 1995 the Swiss Bankers' Association (SBA) announced the introduction of measures that would enable relatives to trace and recover the assets deposited in Swiss bank accounts by victims of the Nazi massacre of Jews in the Second World War. To assist in this process an accord was signed in May 1996 by the SBA and the World Jewish Congress establishing an Independent Committee of Eminent Persons (ICEP), which was to be responsible for auditing all dormant Swiss bank accounts. In September controversial documents were released from British and US archives, claiming that gold valued at several thousand million dollars, at current prices, had been deposited in Swiss banks during the Second World War. Much of it was suspected to have belonged to Jews killed in the Holocaust. The Swiss Federal Assembly subsequently approved legislation establishing an independent panel to investigate the ownership of these assets, and legislation ordering banks to release all records that might pertain to dealings with the Nazi regime in Germany or its victims. In December the Federal Government appointed an international commission to conduct a broad historical investigation of Switzerland's role as a financial centre during the Second World War.

Meanwhile, the issue of 'Nazi gold' had received much coverage in the international press. Jewish organizations threatened to boycott Swiss financial institutions, claiming that insufficient efforts were being made to recover their assets. In March 1997 three of Switzerland's most prominent banks, Crédit Suisse, Swiss Bank Corporation and Union Bank of Switzerland, established a special humanitarian fund for impoverished survivors of the Holocaust, under the administration of the Federal Government; the first payments from the fund were made in November. In December Swiss banks issued the first payments to claimants of funds from dormant accounts that had been opened prior to and during the Second World War.

In March 1998 senior US public finance officials, threatening an imminent boycott of Swiss banks and industrial interests, placed the former under increasing pressure to agree to a swift 'global settlement' of the issue of Holocaust victims' accounts, involving the establishment of a victims' fund and a timetable for payment; soon afterwards (against the wishes of the Swiss Government, which believed the ICEP to be making adequate progress in assessing claims) Swiss Bank Corporation and Union Bank of Switzerland, which subsequently merged to form UBS, and Crédit Suisse announced their intention to negotiate such a settlement. In August UBS and Crédit Suisse agreed to pay US $1,250m. to the World Jewish Congress as compensation for the role of Swiss financial institutions in retaining dormant Jewish assets, handling gold deposited by the Nazis and lending money during the Second World War to German companies that had utilized Jewish slave labour. In return, all threats of boycotts and legal action against Swiss concerns were withdrawn.

In December 1999 the ICEP reported that its audit of all dormant Swiss bank accounts had shown that some 54,000 of these might have belonged to Jews murdered in the Holocaust (although the figure was subsequently reduced to 36,000). The Committee recommended that details of 25,000 of the 54,000 accounts should be publicized in order to alert survivors of the Holocaust or their heirs to their existence. The Committee did not attempt to value the funds held in the accounts, but stated that the total would probably not exceed the US $1,250m. already committed by UBS and Crédit Suisse to the World Jewish Congress. The publication of the ICEP report was followed, almost immediately, by that of the international historical commission appointed in December 1996. The commission concluded that, by closing its border to an estimated 24,500 fugitive Jews from 1942, Switzerland bore partial responsibility for their deaths at the hands of the Nazis. Following the release of the historical commission's report, the Government formally apologized for Switzerland's role in the Second World War. Further details emerged in August 2001, which indicated that several of Switzerland's largest companies, including Nestlé, had ignored reports of Nazi atrocities and had continued to trade with Germany during the Second World War. Moreover, it was revealed that, despite Switzerland's neutrality, the Government had issued Germany and Italy with credits to buy Swiss-made machinery and weapons. In December a further report indicated that Switzerland had harboured substantial amounts of Nazi funds and assets, and even concealed entire German companies, during the Second World War. The report also stated that Switzerland had provided a refuge for several prominent Nazi war criminals following the end of hostilities.

In May 2000 UBS and Crédit Suisse agreed to allow researchers to examine records of more than 2m. bank accounts in order to verify or reject claims by Holocaust survivors. The proposed settlement of US $1,250m. to end the threat of litigation by Holocaust survivors against Swiss banks was approved by a judge in the USA in July. The two banks formally agreed the settlement in August; four Swiss insurers added a further $50m. in response to claims that the insurance policies of Holocaust survivors had not been honoured. Swiss companies that had used forced labour during the Second World War were also required to contribute. In February 2001 Swiss banks published lists of dormant bank accounts, thought to be linked to the Holocaust, to be claimed by the account-holders or their heirs.

In January 2004 legislation entered into force pardoning many Swiss citizens who were condemned and punished for illegally helping refugees during the Second World War. Although almost 30,000 Jews took refuge in Switzerland during the war, more than 20,000 were turned away, many of whom later died in Nazi concentration camps. Many Swiss citizens who helped refugees across the border or hid them after their arrival were prosecuted and imprisoned and, in most cases, their criminal records were allowed to stand. The new legislation allowed those prosecuted, or their relatives and other organizations, to apply for a pardon via a parliamentary commission. There was, however, no provision for compensation.

Relations with Israel were strained from early 2008. Both the Israeli Government and the US Administration of President George W. Bush criticized Switzerland's friendly relations with Iran, following a visit in March by the Head of the Federal Department of Foreign Affairs, Micheline Calmy-Rey, to the Iranian capital, Tehran, during which she met with the Iranian President, Mahmoud Ahmadinejad. Calmy-Rey had earlier witnessed the signature of a 25-year contract between the National Iranian Gas Export Company and the Swiss energy firm, Elektrizitäts-Gesellschaft Laufenburg AG, for the supply of natural gas from 2012. In late April 2009 the newly elected Israeli coalition Government recalled its ambassador to Switzerland, following a meeting between the President of the Swiss Confederation, Hans-Rudolf Merz, and Ahmadinejad to discuss bilateral relations. The previous day, at a UN summit meeting on racism held in Geneva, several delegates had walked out of the chamber during a speech given by Ahmadinejad, in which he referred to Israel as a 'racist country'; Israel, the USA and several other countries had declined to attend the summit, in protest against Ahmadinejad's participation. The Israeli ambassador returned to Switzerland a week later.

In the late 1990s a series of high-profile money-laundering cases threatened to damage Switzerland's reputation as a stable financial centre. Most notably, these included the freezing of assets and accounts linked to Gen. Sani Abacha and Slobodan Milošević, the former leaders of Nigeria and Yugoslavia respectively, and the former head of the Peruvian secret service, Vladimiro Montesinos. Suspect funds found in Swiss bank accounts were linked to missing IMF aid paid to Russia and also to the former leader of the Philippines, Ferdinand Marcos. The total value of suspect funds under investigation in Switzerland increased from 333m. Swiss francs in 1999 (representing 160 cases) to 1,543m. Swiss francs (representing 370 cases) in 2000.

In August 2003 Switzerland declared itself willing to co-operate with Nigeria's efforts to recover funds stolen by Abacha. The Nigerian Government estimated that Abacha had embezzled some US $2,000m., of which about $700m. was believed to have been deposited in Switzerland. The Swiss Government announced in April 2006 that it had returned all of the funds to the Nigerian Government. Appeals from the Abacha family for ownership of the money had been rejected. According to an agreement reached between Switzerland and Nigeria, the World Bank was to ensure the returned funds were used for development projects in health, education and basic infrastructure. In 2006 the Federal Supreme Court ruled that indefinite freezes imposed by the Government on privately-held assets in Swiss banks were unconstitutional. Non-governmental organizations expressed fears that the ruling could lead to the release of further assets whose provenance was suspected to be illegal, including an estimated 7.7m. Swiss francs believed to have been deposited by former President Mobutu Sese Seko of Zaire (now Democratic Republic of Congo). In mid-April 2009 the Swiss federal prosecutor ruled that, owing to the statute of limitations, assets believed to have been deposited by former President Mobutu should be returned to his family upon the expiry of the order freezing those funds at the end of April. However, a week later the order was extended until 31 October, following an appeal to the Federal Criminal Court by a private individual against the decision to release the funds.

Government

The Swiss Confederation, composed of 20 cantons and six half-cantons, has a republican federal Constitution. Legislative power is held by the bicameral Federal Assembly: the Council of States, with 46 members representing the cantons (two for each canton and one for each half-canton), elected for three to four years; and the National Council, with 200 members directly elected by universal adult suffrage for four years, on the basis of proportional representation. Executive power is held by the Federal Council, which has seven members elected for four years by a joint session of the Federal Assembly. The Assembly also elects one of the Federal Councillors to be President of the Confederation (Head of State) for one year at a time.

National policy is the prerogative of the Federal Government, but considerable power is vested in the cantons. Under the Constitution, the autonomous cantons hold all powers not specifically delegated to the federal authorities. The Swiss citizen shares three distinct allegiances—communal, cantonal and national. Direct participation is very important in communal government, and all adult Swiss residents may take part in the communal assemblies or referendums, which decide upon local affairs. Each canton has its own written constitution, government and legislative assembly. The referendum, which can be on a communal, cantonal or national scale, further ensures the possibility of direct public participation in decision-making.

Defence

National defence is based on compulsory military service. Switzerland maintains no standing army except for a small permanent personnel of commissioned and non-commissioned officers primarily concerned with training. Military service consists of 18 weeks' compulsory recruit training for males at the age of 19–20 years, followed by seven three-week 'refresher' training courses between the ages of 20 and 30 years. Each soldier keeps his equipment in his own home, and receives compulsory marksmanship training between periods of service. As assessed at November 2008, the total strength of the armed forces, when mobilized, was 211,023, comprising an active force of 22,823 and reserves of 188,200 (army 131,700; air force 33,300; command support organization 10,800; and logistics organization 12,400). In addition, there is a civil defence force numbering 85,000. The Confederation belongs to no international defence organizations, and the strategy of the army and air force is defensive. In December 1996 Switzerland signed the 'Partnership for Peace' (see p. 353) framework document of the North Atlantic Treaty Organization (NATO). Defence expenditure for 2008 was budgeted at 3,902m. Swiss francs.

Economic Affairs

In 2007, according to estimates by the World Bank, Switzerland's gross national income (GNI), measured at average 2005–07 prices, was US $452,121m., equivalent to $59,880 per head (or $43,870 per head on an international purchasing-power parity basis). During 2000–07, it was estimated, the population grew by an average of 0.7% per year, while gross domestic product (GDP) per head increased, in real terms, at an average annual rate of 0.9%. Overall GDP increased, in real terms, by an average of 1.7% per year in 2000–07; real GDP increased by 3.1% in 2007.

Agriculture (including forestry and fishing) contributed an estimated 1.2% of GDP in 2007, and engaged 4.0% of the employed labour force in 2008. The principal cash crops are sugar beet, potatoes and wheat. Dairy products, notably cheese, are also important. At a national referendum held in November 2005, 55.7% of voters approved a five-year ban on the use of genetically modified crops. According to the World Bank, agricultural GDP declined at an average annual rate of 2.1% in 2000–05; it increased by 10.0% in 2004, but contracted by 2.1% in 2005.

Industry (including mining and quarrying, manufacturing, power and construction) contributed an estimated 28.0% of GDP in 2007, and engaged 23.3% of the employed labour force in 2008. In 2000–05 industrial GDP increased by an average of 1.3% per year. It rose by 2.5% in 2005.

Switzerland is not richly endowed with mineral deposits, and only rock salt and building materials are mined or quarried in significant quantities. In 2008 only 0.1% of the working population were employed in mining and quarrying. The sector contributed an estimated 0.2% of GDP in 2006.

The manufacturing sector, which contributed an estimated 19.9% of GDP in 2006, engaged 15.8% of the employed labour force in 2008. The most important branches are precision engineering (in particular clocks and watches, which provided 8.1% of export revenue in 2007), heavy engineering, machine-building, textiles, chocolate, chemicals and pharmaceuticals.

Of total electricity output in 2005, 54.1% was provided by hydroelectric power and 40.4% by nuclear power (from five reactors with a total generating capacity of 3,077 MW). Imports of mineral fuels comprised 6.8% of the value of total imports in 2007 (including Liechtenstein). Switzerland is a net exporter of electricity.

The services sector contributed an estimated 70.8% of GDP in 2007, and engaged 72.7% of the employed labour force in 2008. Switzerland plays an important role as a centre of international finance, and Swiss markets account for a significant share of international financial transactions. The insurance sector is also highly developed, and Swiss companies are represented throughout the world. Switzerland draws considerable revenue from tourism; receipts from tourism totalled 13,334m. Swiss francs in 2006.

In 2007 Switzerland recorded a visible trade surplus of US $12,750m., and there was a surplus of $43,946m. on the current account of the balance of payments. The European Union (EU, see p. 255) accounted for the majority of Switzerland's trade, providing 81.2% of the country's imports and taking 62.0% of exports in 2008. In that year the principal source of imports was Germany (providing 34.7% of total imports), followed by Italy (11.4%), France (9.7%) and the USA (4.8%). Germany was also the principal market for exports (accounting for 20.3% of total exports), followed by the USA (9.4%), Italy (8.8%) and France (8.6%). The principal exports in 2008 were chemicals, machinery and clocks and watches. The main imports in that year were chemicals, machinery, motor vehicles, and textiles, clothing and footwear.

Switzerland recorded a consolidated budgetary surplus of 10,421m. Swiss francs (equivalent to 2.0% of GDP) in 2007. There was a consolidated budgetary surplus of 5,592m. Swiss francs in 2008. Total government debt was an estimated 120,843m. Swiss francs in 2007, equivalent to 23.6% of GDP. The annual rate of inflation averaged 0.8% in 2000–07; consumer prices increased by 2.5% in 2008. The rate of unemployment averaged 3.2% in 2008. Of all the major European countries, Switzerland has the highest percentage of foreign workers (25.6% of the working population in 2006).

Switzerland is a founder member of the European Free Trade Association (EFTA, see p. 426).

Switzerland is a prosperous country, despite its small size, with a high level of income per head. Its economic success, built around financial services and a modern industrial sector, is in large part due to a highly educated labour force and a flexible labour market. Although Switzerland is not a member of the EU, it is nevertheless largely dependent on the euro area for economic growth and enjoys privileged access to the EU's internal market through numerous bilateral agreements. Inflation and unemployment in Switzerland are low as a result of sound monetary and fiscal policies. From 2004 Switzerland enjoyed continued growth in real GDP, partly owing to the success of the private banking and insurance sectors. However, the prominence of the financial services sector in the Swiss economy left the country vulnerable to the effects of the global financial crisis in 2008. In October the Swiss National Bank (SNB) provided some 6,000m. Swiss francs of additional capital to the country's largest bank, UBS, which subsequently revealed losses of some 20,000m. Swiss francs for the year. In November the Government proposed a package of measures valued at 900m. Swiss francs, to take effect in early 2009, which was intended to facilitate the creation of jobs. A fall in demand, concomitant with a strengthening of the Swiss franc against the euro, precipitated a steep decline in the value of exports in the late 2008, while an attendant decline in consumer spending prompted the SNB to reduce interest rates, in an attempt to offset the risk of deflation. In February 2009 the cabinet introduced a further package of stimulus measures valued at 710m. Swiss francs, principally comprising investment in infrastructure projects and research; the measures received parliamentary approval in March. Switzerland officially entered into recession in the second half of 2008 as economic growth contracted in the two final quarters of the year, leading overall GDP growth for the year at an estimated 1.6%. GDP was forecast to contract by 0.8% in 2009, before returning to limited growth in 2010.

SWITZERLAND

Education

Primary and secondary education are controlled by the cantons, with the result that there are 26 different systems in operation. Responsibility for higher education is shared between the cantons and the Federal Government. Education is compulsory for children between the ages of seven and 16 years. Primary education, which commences at the age of six or seven, lasts for up to six years. The duration and system of secondary education depends on individual cantonal policy. Some 20% of 17-year-olds continue their studies at a higher secondary school (*Gymnasium/Collège*), and a leaving certificate (*Matura/Maturité*) from one of these is a prerequisite for entry to academic higher education. About 70% proceed to vocational training (trade and technical) for a period of three to four years. There are 10 cantonal universities, two Federal Institutes of Technology (of university standing) and one Academic Institute (a teacher-training college of university standing), as well as seven universities of applied sciences. Numerous private schools exist, as well as one private university of applied sciences. In 2004/05 enrolment at pre-primary level included 72% of children in the relevant age-group; the comparable ratios for primary and secondary education were 89% and 82% (males 84%; females 80%), respectively. Enrolment at tertiary level in that year was equivalent to 46% of those in the relevant age-group (males 48%; females 43%). In 2006 federal, cantonal and communal expenditure on education amounted to 27,802m. Swiss francs (19.6% of total public expenditure).

Public Holidays

2009: 1 January (New Year's Day), 10 April (Good Friday)*, 13 April (Easter Monday)*, 21 May (Ascension Day), 1 June (Whit Monday)*, 1 August (National Day), 25 December (Christmas), 26 December (St Stephen's Day)*.

2010: 1 January (New Year's Day), 2 April (Good Friday)*, 5 April (Easter Monday)*, 13 May (Ascension Day), 24 May (Whit Monday)*, 1 August (National Day), 25 December (Christmas Day), 26 December (St Stephen's Day)*.

In addition, various cantonal and local holidays are observed.

* Observation varies by canton.

Weights and Measures

The metric system is in force.

Statistical Survey

Source (unless otherwise stated): Federal Statistical Office, Information Service, 10 Espace de l'Europe, 2010 Neuchâtel; tel. 327136011; fax 327136012; e-mail info@bfs.admin.ch; internet www.bfs.admin.ch.

Area and Population

AREA, POPULATION AND DENSITY

Area (sq km)	41,284*
Population (census results)	
4 December 1990	6,873,687
5 December 2000	
Males	3,567,567
Females	3,720,443
Total	7,288,010
Population (official estimates at 31 December)†	
2006	7,508,739
2007	7,593,500
2008‡	7,700,200
Density (per sq km) at 31 December 2008‡	186.5

* 15,940 sq miles.
† Figures refer to permanent resident population, and have not been adjusted to take the results of the 2000 census into account.
‡ Provisional.

LANGUAGES
(Swiss nationals, %)

	1980	1990	2000
German	73.5	73.4	72.5
French	20.1	20.5	21.0
Italian	4.5	4.1	4.3
Romansh	0.9	0.7	0.6
Others	1.0	1.3	1.6

REGIONS AND CANTONS

Region/Canton	Area (sq km)*	Population ('000, 2008†) Total	Per sq km	Capital (with population, 2000‡)
Région lémanique	8,718.7	1,437.5	164.9	—
Genève	282.4	445.8	1,578.6	Genève (177,964)
Valais	5,224.4	303.2	58.0	Sion (27,171)
Vaud	3,211.9	688.5	214.4	Lausanne (124,914)
Espace Mittelland	10,062.0	1,729.3	171.9	—
Bern	5,959.3	969.1	162.6	Bern (128,634)
Fribourg	1,670.6	268.1	160.5	Fribourg (35,547)
Jura	838.5	70.0	83.5	Delémont (11,353)
Neuchâtel	802.9	170.3	212.1	Neuchâtel (32,914)
Solothurn	790.7	251.7	318.3	Solothurn (15,489)
Nordwestschweiz	1,958.2	1,049.4	535.9	—
Aargau	1,403.6	591.7	421.6	Aarau (15,470)
Basel-Stadt	37.0	186.0	5,027.0	Basel (166,558)
Basel-Landschaft	517.6	271.7	524.9	Liestal (12,930)
Zürich	1,728.9	1,332.9	771.0	Zürich (363,273)
Ostschweiz	11,521.1	1,085.3	94.2	—
Appenzell Ausserrhoden	242.8	52.8	217.5	Herisau (15,882)
Appenzell Innerrhoden	172.5	15.6	90.4	Appenzell (5,447)
Glarus	685.1	38.4	56.1	Glarus (5,556)
Graubünden	7,105.5	190.6	26.8	Chur (32,989)
St Gallen	2,025.7	470.9	232.5	St Gallen (72,626)
Schaffhausen	298.5	75.3	252.3	Schaffhausen (33,628)
Thurgau	991.0	241.6	243.8	Frauenfeld (21,954)
Zentralschweiz	4,483.6	733.2	163.5	—
Luzern	1,493.5	368.8	246.9	Luzern (59,496)
Nidwalden	275.9	40.6	147.2	Stans (6,983)
Obwalden	490.6	34.3	69.9	Sarnen (9,145)
Schwyz	908.2	143.5	158.0	Schwyz (13,802)
Uri	1,076.7	35.1	32.6	Altdorf (8,541)
Zug	238.7	110.8	464.2	Zug (22,973)
Ticino	2,812.2	332.6	118.3	Bellinzona (16,463)
Total	**41,284.2**	**7,700.2**	**186.5**	—

* Figures exclude lakes larger than 5 sq km (total area 1,289.5 sq km). Also excluded are special territories (total area 7.2 sq km).
† Estimated permanent resident population at 31 December.
‡ Census figures.

SWITZERLAND

PRINCIPAL TOWNS
(estimated population at 31 December 2005)

Zürich (Zurich)	347,517	Biel (Bienne)	48,735
Genève (Genf or Geneva)	178,722	Thun (Thoune)	41,138
Basel (Bâle)	163,930	Köniz	37,250
Bern (Berne, capital)	122,178	La Chaux-de-Fonds	36,809
Lausanne	117,388	Schaffhausen (Schaffhouse)	33,569
Winterthur (Winterthour)	93,546	Fribourg (Freiburg)	33,008
St Gallen (Saint-Gall)	70,316	Chur (Coire)	32,409
Luzern (Lucerne)	57,533	Neuchâtel (Neuenburg)	32,117

BIRTHS, MARRIAGES AND DEATHS

	Registered live births Number	Rate (per 1,000)	Registered marriages Number	Rate (per 1,000)	Registered deaths Number	Rate (per 1,000)
2001	73,509	10.2	35,987	5.0	61,287	8.5
2002	72,372	9.9	40,213	5.5	61,768	8.5
2003	71,848	9.8	40,056	5.4	63,070	8.6
2004	73,082	9.9	39,460	5.3	60,180	8.1
2005	72,903	9.8	40,139	5.4	61,124	8.2
2006	73,371	9.8	39,817	5.3	60,283	8.1
2007	74,494	9.8	40,330	5.3	61,089	8.0
2008*	76,900	10.0	41,700	5.4	61,700	8.0

* Provisional figures.

Life expectancy (years at birth, WHO estimates): 81.8 (males 79.1; females 84.2) in 2006 (Source: WHO, *World Health Statistics*).

ECONOMICALLY ACTIVE POPULATION*
(April–June, '000 persons aged 15 years and over)

	2006	2007	2008†
Agriculture, hunting, forestry and fishing	162	172	178
Mining and quarrying	5	5	5
Manufacturing	690	704	711
Electricity, gas and water supply	25	26	25
Construction	303	310	307
Wholesale and retail trade; repair of motor vehicles, motorcycles and personal and household goods	652	666	671
Hotels and restaurants	244	249	257
Transport, storage and communications	274	277	280
Financial intermediation	219	229	231
Real estate, renting and business activities	520	541	565
Public administration and defence; compulsory social security	185	192	189
Education	280	284	289
Health and social work	497	506	523
Other community, social and personal service activities	195	199	203
Private households with employed persons	53	52	61
Total employed	**4,304**	**4,413**	**4,495**
Unemployed	169	156	147
Total labour force	**4,473**	**4,569**	**4,642**
Males	2,463	2,515	2,538
Females	2,010	2,054	2,103

* Refers to workers who are employed for at least one hour per week, and includes foreign workers ('000): 1,106 in 2006; 1,156 in 2007; 1,201 in 2008 (provisional).
† Provisional.

Health and Welfare

KEY INDICATORS

Total fertility rate (children per woman, 2006)	1.4
Under-5 mortality rate (per 1,000 live births, 2006)	5
HIV/AIDS (% of persons aged 15–49, 2007)	0.6
Physicians (per 1,000 head, 2006)	4.0
Hospital beds (per 1,000 head, 2005)	5.7
Health expenditure (2006): US $ per head (PPP)	4,312
Health expenditure (2006): % of GDP	11.3
Health expenditure (2006): public (% of total)	60.3
Human Development Index (2006): ranking	10
Human Development Index (2006): value	0.955

For sources and definitions, see explanatory note on p. vi.

Agriculture

PRINCIPAL CROPS
('000 metric tons)

	2005	2006	2007
Wheat	531.2	540.7	562.2
Barley	231.2	229.4	218.1
Maize	198.9	151.1	186.0
Rye	9.4	8.6	10.4
Oats	15.3	12.0	10.6
Triticale (wheat-rye hybrid)	68.4	64.5	59.4
Potatoes	485.0	392.0	490.0
Sugar beet	1,409.4	1,242.7	1,584.0
Rapeseed	58.8	56.3	67.7
Cabbages and other brassicas	34.4	28.5	30.0
Lettuce and chicory	65.0	57.0	60.0
Tomatoes	27.1	26.9	27.0*
Onions and shallots, green	23.2	1.8	1.7*
Carrots and turnips	59.0	53.0	55.0*
Apples	204.8	266.3	250.0*
Pears	64.6	83.0	80.0*
Grapes	126.9	128.1	130.0*

* FAO estimate.

Aggregate production ('000 metric tons, may include official, semi-official or estimated data): Total cereals 1,057 in 2005, 1,008 in 2006, 1,049 in 2007; Total roots and tubers 485 in 2005, 392 in 2006, 490 in 2007; Total vegetables (incl. melons) 313 in 2005, 288 in 2006, 193 in 2007; Total fruits (excl. melons) 432 in 2005, 513 in 2006, 497 in 2007.

Source: FAO.

LIVESTOCK
('000 head, year ending September)

	2005	2006	2007
Cattle	1,544.5	1,554.7	1,565.0
Horses	55.1	56.3	55.0*
Pigs	1,609.5	1,652.0	1,650.0*
Sheep	446.4	449.3	450.0*
Goats	74.0	76.9	75.0*
Chickens	8,117	7,805	8,000*

* FAO estimate.
Source: FAO.

SWITZERLAND

LIVESTOCK PRODUCTS
('000 metric tons)

	2005	2006	2007*
Cattle meat	132.3	134.9	135.0
Sheep meat	6.2	5.8	6.0
Pig meat	236.3	243.5	250.0
Chicken meat	58.0	51.7	50.0
Cows' milk	3,933.8	3,922.5	4,000.0
Goats' milk	20.0	21.0	20.0
Hen eggs	38.9	38.8	39.0

* FAO estimates.

Source: FAO.

Forestry

ROUNDWOOD REMOVALS
('000 cubic metres, excluding bark)

	2005	2006	2007
Sawlogs, veneer logs and logs for sleepers	3,421	3,630	3,648
Pulpwood	584	634	689
Other industrial wood	29	20	23
Fuel wood	1,251	1,417	1,329
Total	5,285	5,702	5,691

Source: FAO.

SAWNWOOD PRODUCTION
('000 cubic metres, including railway sleepers)

	2005	2006	2007
Coniferous (softwood)	1,500	1,580	1,463
Broadleaved (hardwood)	91	88	78
Total	1,591	1,668	1,541

Source: FAO.

Fishing

(metric tons, live weight)

	2004	2005	2006
Capture	1,602	1,475	1,422
Roach	167	163	166
European perch	359	281	267
Whitefishes	912	865	822
Aquaculture	1,205	1,214	1,214
Rainbow trout	1,110	1,107	1,107
Total catch	2,807	2,689	2,636

Source: FAO.

Industry

SELECTED PRODUCTS
('000 metric tons, unless otherwise indicated)

	2002	2003	2004
Cement*	3,771	3,613	3,851
Cigars (million)	167	166	n.a.
Cigarettes (million)	37,160	38,140	39,059
Aluminium (unwrought, primary)*†	40.0	43.5	44.5
Flour (wheat)	395	395	395
Chocolate and chocolate products	142.2	139.7	148.2
Motor spirit (petrol, '000 barrels)*	9,928	9,089	10,000
Distillate fuel oils ('000 barrels)*	15,002	14,126	14,000
Residual fuel oil ('000 barrels)*	4,782	4,891	5,000
Electric energy (million kWh)‡	66,649	67,166	65,299

* Source: US Geological Survey.
† Source: World Metal Statistics, London.
‡ Including Liechtenstein.

Source (unless otherwise indicated): UN, *Industrial Commodity Statistics Yearbook*.

Watches ('000 exported): 17,840 in 1984; 25,137 in 1985; 28,075 in 1986.

New dwellings (units completed): 35,961 in 1997; 33,734 in 1998; 33,108 in 1999.

2005 ('000 barrels, unless otherwise indicated): Cement 4,022,000 metric tons; Aluminium (primary, unwrought) 44,458 metric tons; Motor spirit (petrol) 10,000; Distillate fuel oils 20,000; Residual fuel oil 30,000 (Source: US Geological Survey).

2006 ('000 barrels, unless otherwise indicated): Cement 4,000,000 metric tons; Aluminium (primary, unwrought) 40,000 metric tons; Motor spirit (petrol) 10,000; Distillate fuel oils 20,000; Residual fuel oil 30,000 (Source: US Geological Survey).

2007 ('000 barrels, unless otherwise indicated): Cement 4,000,000 metric tons; Aluminium (primary, unwrought) 40,000 metric tons; Motor spirit (petrol) 10,000; Distillate fuel oils 20,000; Residual fuel oil 30,000 (Source: US Geological Survey).

Finance

CURRENCY AND EXCHANGE RATES

Monetary Units
 100 Rappen (centimes) = 1 Schweizer Franken (franc suisse) or Swiss franc.

Sterling, Dollar and Euro Equivalents (31 December 2008)
 £1 sterling = 1.5507 francs;
 US $1 = 1.0637 francs;
 €1 = 1.4804 francs;
 100 Swiss francs = £64.49 = $94.01 = €67.55.

Average Exchange Rates (Swiss francs per US $)
 2006   1.2538
 2007   1.2004
 2008   1.0831

SWITZERLAND

BUDGET
(million Swiss francs)*

Revenue†	2002	2003	2004
Taxes	95,697	94,568	97,643
Taxes on income and wealth	64,935	63,418	65,412
Income and wealth tax	45,591	45,986	46,590
Corporation and capital gains tax	12,615	12,118	12,218
Pre-paid tax	2,628	1,641	2,628
Other taxes on income and wealth	4,101	3,673	3,976
Stamp duty	2,819	2,624	2,755
Taxes on property and goods	1,895	1,937	1,960
Taxes on motor vehicles	1,774	1,820	1,851
Taxes on consumption	23,735	24,204	25,052
Value-added tax	16,857	17,156	17,666
Taxes on traffic	1,067	999	993
Customs duty	1,091	1,090	1,054
Agricultural duty	3	3	4
Duty from drivers	86	105	124
Duty from casinos	65	189	291
Other revenue	38,913	35,246	36,581
Total	**134,610**	**129,814**	**134,224**

Expenditure	2002	2003	2004
General administration	8,818	9,204	8,855
Public order and safety	7,514	7,872	7,970
Defence	5,162	5,066	4,979
Foreign relations	2,373	2,365	2,427
Education	25,786	26,560	27,684
Culture and leisure activities	4,187	4,212	4,249
Health	18,047	18,839	19,326
Social welfare	25,411	26,481	27,742
Transport and administration	14,671	14,024	14,411
Environment	4,909	4,897	4,907
National economy	7,058	6,466	6,344
Finances and taxes	10,317	9,825	9,486
Total	**134,253**	**135,811**	**138,379**

* Incorporates federal, cantonal and communal budgets, but excludes social security obligations. The consolidated accounts (including social security obligations) were (million Swiss francs): *Revenue:* 162,213 in 2002; 161,932 in 2003; 165,097 in 2004. *Expenditure:* 163,687 in 2002; 167,981 in 2003; 170,738 in 2004.

† Not including parish taxes.

2005 (million Swiss francs): Total revenue 141,581; Total expenditure 140,147 (Source: Swiss National Bank).

2006 (million Swiss francs, estimates): Total revenue 150,993; Total expenditure 141,803 (Source: Swiss National Bank).

2007 (million Swiss francs, estimates): Total revenue 158,758; Total expenditure 148,337 (Source: Swiss National Bank).

2008 (million Swiss francs, estimates): Total revenue 163,642; Total expenditure 158,050 (Source: Swiss National Bank).

INTERNATIONAL RESERVES
(US $ million at 31 December)

	2006	2007	2008
Gold (national valuation)	26,404	30,898	29,013
IMF special drawing rights	275	248	229
Reserve position in IMF	455	359	681
Foreign exchange	37,364	43,867	44,151
Total	**64,498**	**75,372**	**74,074**

Source: IMF, *International Financial Statistics*.

MONEY SUPPLY
('000 million Swiss francs at 31 December)

	2006	2007	2008
Currency outside banks	45.71	46.85	49.16
Demand deposits at deposit money banks	186.90	194.85	239.04
Total money (incl. others)	**232.61**	**241.70**	**292.00**

Source: IMF, *International Financial Statistics*.

COST OF LIVING
(Consumer Price Index; annual averages; base: December 2005 = 100)

	2006	2007	2008
Foodstuffs	101.2	101.8	104.9
Alcoholic beverages and tobacco	100.1	102.1	104.8
Clothing and footwear	94.1	94.3	98.1
Housing and energy	101.4	103.6	108.6
Household equipment, etc.	100.4	100.8	101.6
Health	100.1	99.9	99.7
Transport	101.6	102.7	106.3
Communication	98.4	95.5	92.7
Education	100.5	102.1	103.7
Recreation and culture	99.5	99.0	99.6
Restaurants and hotels	101.2	102.5	104.9
Other goods and services	100.8	100.8	101.7
All items	**100.5**	**101.2**	**103.7**

NATIONAL ACCOUNTS
(million Swiss francs at current prices)

National Income and Product

	2005	2006*	2007*
Compensation of employees	287,393	302,512	318,666
Operating surplus	78,125	82,460	85,936
Domestic factor incomes	**365,518**	**384,972**	**404,602**
Consumption of fixed capital	83,190	86,163	90,732
Gross domestic product (GDP) at factor cost	**448,708**	**471,135**	**495,334**
Indirect taxes	33,026	34,604	35,702
Less Subsidies	18,596	18,698	18,895
GDP in purchasers' values	**463,139**	**487,041**	**512,142**
Factor income received from abroad	127,494	132,453	151,617
Less Factor income paid abroad	83,779	88,097	117,675
Gross national product	**506,853**	**531,397**	**546,084**
Less Consumption of fixed capital	83,190	86,163	90,732
National income in market prices	**423,663**	**445,234**	**455,352**

* Provisional figures.

Expenditure on the Gross Domestic Product

	2005	2006*	2007*
Final consumption expenditure	332,839	341,310	351,161
Households and non-profit institutions serving households	278,641	286,723	296,055
General government	54,198	54,587	55,106
Gross capital formation	100,124	108,323	113,857
Gross fixed capital formation	98,197	104,328	112,426
Changes in inventories	−510	−1	511
Acquisitions, *less* disposals, of valuables	2,436	3,997	920
Total domestic expenditure	**432,963**	**449,633**	**465,018**
Exports of goods and services	226,250	255,272	286,191
Less Imports of goods and services	196,074	217,864	239,067
GDP in market prices	**463,139**	**487,041**	**512,142**

* Provisional figures.

SWITZERLAND

Gross Domestic Product by Economic Activity

	2004	2005	2006*
Agriculture, hunting, forestry and fishing	5,934	5,478	5,441
Mining	750	785	779
Manufacturing	80,365	83,999	91,120
Electricity, gas and water	8,313	8,627	9,315
Construction	23,821	24,913	25,543
Wholesale and retail trade	57,505	58,594	60,616
Hotels and restaurants	10,105	10,239	10,683
Transport; storage and communications	28,239	28,948	29,554
Financial intermediation; insurance, real estate and business activities	95,966	98,131	106,037
Public administration	47,381	48,109	48,720
Education	2,420	2,433	2,471
Health and social work	27,385	28,162	28,940
Other community and social activities	10,467	10,611	10,923
Personal service activities	26,101	26,840	28,010
Sub-total	424,751	435,870	458,153
Taxes on products	29,929	30,423	31,904
Less Subsidies on products	3,302	3,154	3,016
GDP in market prices	451,379	463,139	487,041

* Provisional figures.

2007 (provisional figures): Agriculture, hunting, forestry and fishing 5,607; Industry 134,951 (Construction 26,409); Services 341,511; *Sub-total* 482,069; Taxes, *less* subsidies, on products 30,073; *GDP in market prices* 512,142.

BALANCE OF PAYMENTS
(US $ million)

	2005	2006	2007
Exports of goods f.o.b.	151,309	167,221	200,490
Imports of goods f.o.b.	−145,442	−162,213	−187,740
Trade balance	5,867	5,008	12,750
Exports of services	49,766	55,274	66,374
Imports of services	−27,411	−28,317	−33,373
Balance on goods and services	28,222	31,965	45,751
Other income received	101,978	108,873	126,193
Other income paid	−67,955	−75,429	−118,592
Balance on goods, services and income	62,245	65,410	53,351
Current transfers received	15,504	17,639	22,883
Current transfers paid	−26,464	−26,989	−32,288
Current balance	51,284	56,060	43,946
Capital account (net)	−665	−2,770	−2,299
Direct investment abroad	−50,844	−76,553	−50,635
Direct investment from abroad	−525	31,950	49,730
Portfolio investment assets	−53,263	−41,700	−20,344
Portfolio investment liabilities	5,636	68	1,626
Financial derivatives assets	—	−2,168	−3,794
Financial derivatives liabilities	—	−707	−6,605
Other investment assets	−70,498	−42,975	−293,599
Other investment liabilities	83,312	61,394	293,858
Net errors and omissions	17,348	17,771	−8,423
Overall balance	−18,215	370	3,461

Source: IMF, *International Financial Statistics*.

External Trade

Note: Swiss customs territory includes the Principality of Liechtenstein, the German enclave of Büssingen and the Italian commune of Campione, but excludes the free zone of the Samnaun Valley.

PRINCIPAL COMMODITIES
(million Swiss francs)

Imports c.i.f.	2003	2004	2005
Agricultural and forestry products	10,368.7	10,505.2	10,997.4
Mineral fuels	6,905.7	7,767.7	11,194.4
Textiles and items of clothing	8,611.5	8,699.3	8,846.2
Clothing (excl. footwear)	5,384.9	5,435.2	5,655.5
Paper, paperboard and graphics	4,478.2	4,901.0	5,049.5
Leather, rubber and plastic products	4,453.1	4,835.9	5,198.8
Chemical products	27,489.4	29,606.7	32,796.5
Chemical elements and unmoulded plastics	6,603.4	7,499.4	8,933.6
Pharmaceutical products	16,104.3	17,411.5	19,166.4
Metal products	9,789.9	11,571.9	12,367.2
Machinery (incl. electrical)	26,009.6	27,659.7	29,972.3
Industrial machinery	9,105.2	9,631.8	10,548.6
Office machines	5,929.2	5,796.3	6,019.7
Electronics	7,439.9	8,375.8	9,311.0
Passenger cars	7,639.0	7,761.6	7,790.3
Precision instruments	4,463.3	4,882.4	5,373.6
Precious metals and gemstones	5,202.9	5,698.2	6,499.6
Total (incl. others)	134,986.7	143,996.2	157,544.5

Exports f.o.b.	2003	2004	2005
Agricultural and forestry products	4,427.0	4,863.4	5,192.2
Chemical products	45,193.6	49,601.9	54,838.0
Chemical elements and unmoulded plastics	5,815.7	6,331.8	6,425.0
Pharmaceutical products	30,947.8	34,819.8	39,792.5
Metals and metal products	9,976.0	11,112.5	11,663.7
Machinery (incl. electrical)	31,183.3	33,839.3	35,172.0
Industrial machinery	20,047.7	21,650.8	21,803.8
Electronics	8,488.6	9,513.1	10,715.1
Precision instruments	9,757.6	10,204.6	11,500.2
Clocks and watches	10,216.9	11,157.9	12,390.3
Precious metals and gemstones	4,521.9	5,085.2	4,791.1
Total (incl. others)	141,157.5	152,756.5	162,991.1

2006 (million Swiss francs): *Imports:* Machinery, equipment and electronics 32,018; Precision instruments, watches and jewellery 12,171; Chemicals 35,785; Textiles, clothing and footwear 9,392; Motor vehicles 15,495; Total (incl. others) 165,410. *Exports:* Machinery, equipment and electronics 38,630; Precision instruments 12,925; Watches 13,743; Chemicals 62,975; Textiles, clothing and footwear 4,405; Metals 13,424; Total (incl. others) 177,475 (Source: Swiss National Bank).

2007 (million Swiss francs): *Imports:* Machinery, equipment and electronics 35,118; Precision instruments, watches and jewellery 13,678; Chemicals 41,260; Textiles, clothing and footwear 10,040; Motor vehicles 17,098; Total (incl. others) 183,578. *Exports:* Machinery, equipment and electronics 43,065; Precision instruments 13,977; Watches 15,956; Chemicals 68,811; Textiles, clothing and footwear 4,637; Metals 15,498; Total (incl. others) 197,533 (Source: Swiss National Bank).

2008 (million Swiss francs): *Imports:* Machinery, equipment and electronics 35,609; Precision instruments, watches and jewellery 15,108; Chemicals 38,270; Textiles, clothing and footwear 10,039; Motor vehicles 16,750; Total (incl. others) 186,850. *Exports:* Machinery, equipment and electronics 43,806; Precision instruments 14,910; Watches 17,030; Chemicals 71,948; Textiles, clothing and footwear 4,469; Metals 15,277; Total (incl. others) 206,680 (Source: Swiss National Bank).

SWITZERLAND

PRINCIPAL TRADING PARTNERS
(million Swiss francs)*

Imports c.i.f.	2003	2004	2005
Austria	5,662.6	6,085.7	7,219.9
Belgium	4,031.0	4,249.5	4,793.7
China, People's Republic	2,423.0	2,840.9	3,378.4
France	15,297.8	15,107.2	15,804.4
Germany	42,738.3	46,341.9	49,732.2
Ireland	4,796.1	4,692.5	5,652.4
Italy	14,076.4	15,848.3	16,530.1
Japan	2,845.8	3,046.6	2,918.1
Netherlands	6,555.6	6,989.6	7,551.5
Russia	1,202.8	1,042.0	1,023.1
Spain	3,193.5	3,440.1	3,980.4
Sweden	1,675.3	1,676.1	1,484.5
United Kingdom	5,609.3	5,842.1	6,951.0
USA	7,356.6	7,253.6	8,328.0
Total (incl. others)	134,986.7	143,996.2	157,544.5

Exports f.o.b.	2003	2004	2005
Austria	4,660.6	4,901.2	5,169.1
Belgium	2,757.8	2,855.9	2,932.5
Canada	1,437.6	1,994.2	2,268.6
China, People's Republic	2,485.1	3,107.0	3,466.8
France	12,416.9	13,511.7	14,136.3
Germany	29,224.1	30,922.2	31,691.8
Hong Kong	4,144.4	4,237.0	4,011.8
Israel	710.1	746.5	776.6
Italy	12,782.6	13,712.0	14,816.2
Japan	5,408.9	5,722.3	5,892.1
Netherlands	4,484.6	4,462.8	5,548.2
Singapore	1,365.3	1,500.7	1,633.1
Spain	4,903.8	5,975.9	6,595.2
Sweden	1,628.6	1,651.0	1,605.8
Turkey	1,692.7	1,997.1	2,054.4
United Kingdom	6,768.2	7,676.8	8,803.2
USA	15,442.4	15,780.0	17,513.2
Total (incl. others)	141,157.5	152,756.5	162,991.1

* Imports by country of production; exports by country of consumption.

2006 (million Swiss francs): *Imports:* Austria 7,496.6; Belgium 5,093.3; China, People's Republic 3,918.6; France 17,096.7; Germany 55,099.8; Ireland 4,613.1; Italy 18,426.0; Netherlands 8,267.0; Spain 4,038.4; United Kingdom 6,006.6; USA 8,308.4; Total (incl others) 165,410.3. *Exports:* Austria 5,829.1; China, People's Republic 3,753.0; France 15,224.8; Germany 35,827.6; Hong Kong 3,562.0; Italy 15,913.8; Japan 6,361.0; Netherlands 6,034.1; Spain 6,880.7; United Kingdom 8,343.1; USA 18,255.0; Total (incl others) 177,474.8 (Source: Swiss National Bank).

2007 (million Swiss francs): *Imports:* Austria 8,047.8; Belgium 5,332.2; China, People's Republic 4,765.7; France 17,857.7; Germany 62,170.8; Ireland 6,023.8; Italy 20,588.6; Netherlands 8,748.3; Spain 4,123.5; United Kingdom 7,076.3; USA 9,426.2; Total (incl others) 183,577.8. *Exports:* Austria 6,254.7; China, People's Republic 4,786.1; France 16,662.2; Germany 41,149.2; Hong Kong 4,196.8; Italy 17,524.2; Japan 6,165.7; Netherlands 6,126.1; Spain 7,524.1; United Kingdom 9,413.1; USA 18,406.8; Total (incl others) 197,532.7 (Source: Swiss National Bank).

2008 (million Swiss francs): *Imports:* Austria 6,029.8; Belgium 4,015.5; China, People's Republic 5,529.0; France 17,823.7; Germany 41,959.9; Ireland 846.9; Italy 18,239.5; Netherlands 6,265.9; Spain 7,332.4; United Kingdom 6,029.8; USA 19,465.1; Total (incl others) 206,679.6. *Exports:* Austria 7,905.6; China, People's Republic 4,978.1; France 18,061.6; Germany 64,815.1; Hong Kong 1,021.6; Italy 21,246.0; Japan 2,943.9; Netherlands 8,999.6; Spain 3,906.3; United Kingdom 7,905.6; USA 9,448.1; Total (incl others) 186,849.7 (Source: Swiss National Bank).

Transport

RAILWAY TRAFFIC

	2003	2004	2005
Passengers carried (million)*	327	336	364
Passenger-km (million)	14,509	14,914	16,144
Freight carried (million metric tons)	62.4	69.3	67.9
Freight ton-km (million)†	10,598	11,489	11,677

* Excluding multiple journeys.
† Net ton-km (excl. weight of containers, etc.): 9,534 in 2003; 10,245 in 2004; 10,149 in 2005.

ROAD TRAFFIC
(motor vehicles in use at 30 September)

	2004	2005	2006
Passenger cars	3,811,351	3,863,807	3,899,917
Buses and coaches	44,784	45,785	46,445
Lorries and vans	298,193	307,264	314,020
Agricultural vehicles	180,898	182,093	185,450
Other industrial vehicles	50,957	51,860	53,437
Motorcycles	583,010	592,194	608,648

INLAND WATERWAYS
(freight traffic at port of Basel, '000 metric tons)

	1996	1997	1998
Goods loaded	876.9	837.5	688.4
Goods unloaded	6,283.4	7,002.4	7,420.3

Source: Federal Department of Transport.

SHIPPING

Merchant Fleet
(at 31 December)

	2005	2006	2007
Number of vessels	26	29	32
Displacement ('000 grt)	479.6	510.0	588.6

Source: Lloyds Register-Fairplay, *World Fleet Statistics*.

CIVIL AVIATION
(traffic on scheduled services)

	2002	2003	2004
Km flown (million)	256	218	172
Passengers carried ('000)	13,292	10,118	9,287
Passenger-km (million)	26,704	23,295	20,602
Total ton-km (million)	3,720	3,617	2,986

Source: UN, *Statistical Yearbook*.

SWITZERLAND

Tourism

FOREIGN TOURIST ARRIVALS
(at hotels, and similar establishments)

Country of residence	2005	2006
Austria	149,826	160,031
Belgium	207,644	218,743
France	542,502	585,472
Germany	2,007,203	2,106,860
Italy	460,982	498,702
Japan	335,199	347,277
Netherlands	312,546	329,022
Spain	163,981	189,121
United Kingdom	709,155	784,963
USA	657,060	725,497
Total (incl. others)	7,228,851	7,863,957

Tourism receipts (million Swiss francs): 12,549 in 2005; 13,334 in 2006.

Source: mainly World Tourism Organization.

Communications Media

	2005	2006	2007
Telephones ('000 main lines in use)	5,149.7	5,022.0	5,000.0
Mobile cellular telephones ('000 subscribers)	6,834.2	7,436.2	8,096.0
Personal computers ('000 in use)	6,430	n.a.	n.a.
Internet users ('000)	3,800	4,360	4,610
Broadband subscribers ('000)	1,624.2	1,988.1	2,400.0
Books published (titles)	10,128	11,875	11,410
Newspapers:			
number	206	205	201
circulation ('000)	2,290.5	2,239.5	2,202.7

Source: mainly International Telecommunication Union.

Television receivers ('000 in use): 4,000 in 2001.

Facsimile machines ('000 in use, 1996): 207.

Radio licences ('000, 1996): 2,805.

Education

(2007)

	Institutions	Teachers	Students
Pre-primary	5,006	13,800	151,699
Compulsory primary*	} 6,141	{ 43,791	} 788,072
Compulsory secondary*		35,712	
Upper secondary	893	13,100	
General	n.a.	13,100	} 329,890
Vocational	n.a.	n.a.	
Higher	382	81,143	
Vocational	n.a.	n.a.	} 225,862
Specialty	n.a.	34,472†	
Universities	n.a.	46,671†	

* Excluding schools with special curriculums.
† Including teaching assistants and administrative and technical personnel.

Directory

The Constitution

A revised Constitution (summarized below) was adopted by referendum on 18 April 1999 and entered into force on 1 January 2000, replacing that of 1874.

Switzerland is divided into federated cantons, which have sovereign authority except where the Constitution defines limits to their powers or accords responsibility to the Federal authority. After a referendum in September 1978, the Constitution was amended to allow for the formation of the canton of Jura, increasing the number of cantons to 26.

Principally, the Federal authority is responsible for civil, penal and commercial law, legislation concerning marriage, residence and settlement, export and import duties, defence, postal and telecommunications services, the mint, forestry, hunting and fishing, hydroelectric power, the economy, railways, important roads and bridges, social insurance, and international affairs. Administration is largely in the hands of the cantons, and in the combined management of Federal authorities and cantons. The cantons derive their revenue from direct taxation. The Federal authority draws its revenue from direct and indirect taxation. The profits from Federal enterprises and customs duties are received by the Federal authorities.

COMMUNES

Each of the more than 3,000 communes of Switzerland has local autonomy over such matters as public utilities and roads, and grants primary citizenship. Decisions are made by communal assemblies. The smallest communes have fewer than 20 inhabitants, while the largest, Zürich, has around 360,000.

CANTONS

The 26 cantons of the Swiss Confederation each have their own constitution and their own method of choosing the members of the cantonal assembly and cantonal government and the State Councillors who represent them at the federal level. Two cantons, Glarus and Appenzell Innerrhoden, retain the Landsgemeinde, an annual assembly open to all citizens of the canton of voting age, as their supreme decision-making authority. Elsewhere, democracy is less direct, the secret ballot and the referendum having replaced the mass assembly.

FEDERAL ASSEMBLY

The Federal Assembly (Bundesversammlung/Assemblée Fédérale) is the supreme governing body of the Confederation. It is composed of two bodies, the National Council (Nationalrat/Conseil National) and the Council of States (Ständerat/Conseil des Etats), which deliberate separately. The 200 members of the National Council are elected directly, by proportional representation, every four years. The minimum age for voting and eligibility for election in the Confederation is 18 years. Women gained full political rights at federal level and in almost all of the cantons in 1971; female suffrage had been introduced in all 26 cantons by 1990. The Council of States is composed of representatives of the cantons, elected by the people in various ways, according to the cantonal constitutions. The six half-cantons of Appenzell Ausserrhoden, Appenzell Innerrhoden, Nidwalden, Obwalden, Basel-Landschaft and Basel-Stadt each send one member and the remaining cantons each send two. Legislative and fiscal measures must be accepted by both houses in order to be adopted. The Federal Assembly supervises the army, the civil service and the application of the law, exercises the right of pardon and elects the

SWITZERLAND

Federal Supreme Court, the General who commands the army in times of crisis, and the Federal Council.

FEDERAL COUNCIL

Executive authority is vested in the Federal Council, whose seven members are each in charge of a Federal Department. Each year the Federal Assembly appoints the President and Vice-President of the Confederation from among the Federal Councillors. Generally, the Councillors are chosen from the members of the Federal Assembly for four years after every general election. The various regions and language communities of Switzerland should have equal representation within the Federal Council.

REFERENDUMS AND INITIATIVES

Referendums are held on both cantonal and federal levels. In many cantons all legislation has to be accepted by a majority of the voters, and in some cantons major financial matters have to be submitted to the popular vote. In federal affairs the consent of a majority of the voters and of the cantons must be obtained for amendments to the Federal Constitution, for extraconstitutional emergency legislation and for the decision to join collective security organizations or international bodies, but referendums are optional for other legislation. A petition from 50,000 voters, or of eight cantons, is needed to bring about a national referendum, which can accept or reject any legislation that has been passed by parliament. The initiative gives voters in many cantons the right to propose a constitutional or legislative amendment and to demand a popular vote on it. A petition by 100,000 voters is needed to initiate a vote on an amendment to the Federal Constitution, but as federal laws cannot be proposed by means of an initiative, some constitutional amendments introduced in this manner concern relatively unimportant matters and participation of the voters is, on average, 30% to 45%. The initiative is also used by the political opposition to effect changes in government policy.

The Government

FEDERAL COUNCIL
(April 2009)

President of the Swiss Confederation for 2009 and Head of the Federal Department of Finance: HANS-RUDOLF MERZ (FDP.The Liberals).

Vice-President of the Swiss Confederation for 2009 and Head of the Federal Department of Economic Affairs: DORIS LEUTHARD (Christian Democratic People's Party).

Head of the Federal Department of Foreign Affairs: MICHELINE CALMY-REY (Social Democratic Party).

Head of the Federal Department of Home Affairs: PASCAL COUCHEPIN (FDP.The Liberals).

Head of the Federal Department of Justice and Police: EVELINE WIDMER-SCHLUMPF (Conservative Democratic Party).

Head of the Federal Department of Defence, Civil Protection and Sports: UELI MAURER (Swiss People's Party).

Head of the Federal Department of the Environment, Transport, Energy and Communications: MORITZ LEUENBERGER (Social Democratic Party).

Chancellor of the Swiss Confederation: CORINA CASANOVA (Christian Democratic People's Party).

FEDERAL DEPARTMENTS

Federal Chancellery: Bundeshaus West, 3003 Bern; tel. 313223791; fax 313223706; e-mail webmaster@admin.ch; internet www.bk.admin.ch.

Federal Department of Defence, Civil Protection and Sports: Bundeshaus Ost, 3003 Bern; tel. 313245058; fax 313245104; e-mail postmaster.vbs@gs-vbs.admin.ch; internet www.vbs.admin.ch.

Federal Department of Economic Affairs: Bundeshaus Ost, 3003 Bern; tel. 313222007; fax 313222194; e-mail info@gs-evd.admin.ch; internet www.evd.admin.ch.

Federal Department of the Environment, Transport, Energy and Communications: Bundeshaus Nord, Kochergasse 10, 3003 Bern; tel. 313222111; fax 313222692; e-mail info@gs-uvek.admin.ch; internet www.uvek.admin.ch.

Federal Department of Finance: Bernerhof, Bundesgasse 3, 3003 Bern; tel. 313226033; fax 313233852; e-mail info@gs-efd.admin.ch; internet www.efd.admin.ch.

Federal Department of Foreign Affairs: Bundeshaus West, 3003 Bern; tel. 313222111; fax 313225994; e-mail info@eda.admin.ch; internet www.eda.admin.ch.

Federal Department of Home Affairs: Bundeshaus, Inselgasse 1, 3003 Bern; tel. 313228041; fax 313227901; e-mail info@gs-edi.admin.ch; internet www.edi.admin.ch.

Federal Department of Justice and Police: Bundeshaus West, 3003 Bern; tel. 313222111; fax 313227832; e-mail info@gs-ejpd.admin.ch; internet www.ejpd.admin.ch.

Legislature

BUNDESVERSAMMLUNG/ASSEMBLÉE FÉDÉRALE
(Federal Assembly)

Nationalrat/Conseil National
(National Council)

Parlamentsgebäude, 3003 Bern; tel. 313228790; e-mail information@pd.admin.ch.

President: CHIARA SIMONESCHI-CORTESI (2008/09).

General Election, 21 October 2007

	Seats
Swiss People's Party	62†
Social Democratic Party	43
Radical Democratic Party	31*
Christian Democratic People's Party	31
Green Party	20
Liberal Party	4*
Green Liberal Party	3
Evangelical People's Party	2
Workers' Party	1
Union of Federal Democrats	1
Ticino League	1
Christian Socialist Party	1
Total	**200**

* The Radical Democratic Party and the Liberal Party merged, as FDP.The Liberals, on 1 January 2009.
† In September 2008 four representatives of the Swiss People's Party left that party and joined the Conservative Democratic Party.

Ständerat/Conseil des Etats
(Council of States)

Parlamentsgebäude, 3003 Bern; tel. 313228790; e-mail information@pd.admin.ch.

President: ALAIN BERSET (2008/09).

Elections, 2007

	Seats
Christian Democratic People's Party	15
Radical Democratic Party	12*
Social Democratic Party	9
Swiss People's Party	7†
Green Party	2
Green Liberal Party	1
Total	**46**

Note: Members are elected by canton; method and period of election differs from canton to canton
* The Radical Democratic Party and the Liberal Party merged to form FDP.The Liberals on 1 January 2009.
† In September 2008 a representative of the Swiss People's Party left that party and joined the Conservative Democratic Party.

Political Organizations

Bürgerlich-Demokratische Partei (BDP) (Conservative Democratic Party): Postfach 119, 3000 Bern 6; tel. 313521482; fax 313521471; e-mail mail@bdp.info; internet www.bdp.info; f. Nov. 2008 by fmr mems of Swiss People's Party (q.v.); cantonal orgs in Aargau, Bern, Glarus, Graubünden, St Gallen, Thurgau and Valais; Pres. HANS GRUNDER.

Christlichdemokratische Volkspartei der Schweiz—Parti démocrate-chrétien suisse (Christian Democratic People's Party): Klaraweg 6, Postfach 5835, 3001 Bern; tel. 313573333; fax 313522430; e-mail info@cvp.ch; internet www.cvp.ch; f. 1912; advocates a Christian outlook on world affairs, federalism and Christian social reform by means of professional asscns; non-sectarian; Pres. CHRISTOPHE DARBELLAY; Gen. Sec. TIM FREY; Leader of Parliamentary Group URS SCHWALLER.

SWITZERLAND

Christlichsoziale Partei—Parti chrétien-social (Christian Social Party): Eichenstr. 79, 3184 Wünnewil; tel. 264963074; e-mail info@csp-pcs.ch; internet www.csp-pcs.ch; f. 1997; Pres. Monika Bloch Süss; Sec. Marlies Schafer-Jungo.

Eidgenössisch-Demokratische Union—Union Démocratique Fédérale (Federal Democratic Union): Frutigenstr. 8, Postfach 2144, 3601 Thun; tel. 332223637; fax 332223744; e-mail info@edu-schweiz.ch; internet www.edu-schweiz.ch; Pres. Hans Moser.

Evangelische Volkspartei der Schweiz—Parti évangélique suisse (Evangelical People's Party): Josefstr. 32, Postfach 3467, 8021 Zürich; tel. 442727100; fax 442721437; e-mail info@evppev.ch; internet www.evppev.ch; f. 1919; Pres. Heiner Studer; Gen. Sec. Joel Blunier.

FDP.Die Liberalen/PLR.Les Libéraux-Radicaux (FDP.The Liberals): Neuengasse 20, Postfach 6136, 3001 Bern; tel. 313203535; fax 313203500; e-mail info@fdp.ch; internet www.fdp.ch; f. 2009 by merger of the Radical Democratic Party and the Liberal Party of Switzerland; predecessor org. led the movement that gave rise to the Federative State and the Constitution of 1848; promotes a strong Fed. Govt, while respecting the legitimate rights of the cantons and all the minorities; liberal democratic principles; Pres. Dr Fulvio Pelli; Leader of Parliamentary Group Gabi Huber; Gen. Sec. Stefan Brupbacher.

Freiheits-Partei der Schweiz/Die Auto-Partei (Freedom Party of Switzerland/The Automobile Party): Eigasse 13, Postfach, 4622 Egerkingen; tel. 623983838; fax 623984848; e-mail zs@freiheits-partei.ch; internet www.freiheits-partei.ch; f. 1985 to support motorists' rights; subsequently campaigned for restricted immigration; Pres. Peter Commarmot; Sec. Walter Müller.

Grüne Partei der Schweiz—Parti écologiste suisse (Green Party of Switzerland): Waisenhauspl. 21, 3011 Bern; tel. 313126660; fax 313126662; e-mail gruene@gruene.ch; internet www.gruene.ch; f. 1983; Pres. Ueli Leuenberger; Leader of Parliamentary Group Therese Frösch; Gen. Sec. Hubert Zurkinden.

Grünliberale Partei Schweiz (Green Liberal Party of Switzerland): Postfach 367, 3000 Bern 7; tel. 313230530; e-mail schweiz@grunliberale.ch; internet www.grunliberale.ch; f. 2007; represented in Federal Assembly and Zürich cantonal council; Pres. Martin Bäumle; Gen. Sec. Jan Flückiger.

Lega dei Ticinesi (Ticino League): via Monte Boglia 7, CP 2311, 6901 Lugano; tel. 919731048; fax 919731040; internet www.legaticinesi.ch; f. 1991; Pres. Giuliano Bignasca; Sec. Mauro Malandra.

Liberal-Demokratische Partei Basel-Stadt (Die Liberalen) (Liberal-Democratic Party Basel-City): Postfach, 4010 Basel; tel. 612721236; fax 612721743; e-mail info@ldp.ch; internet www.ldp.ch; Pres. Christoph Bürgenmeier.

Mouvement Citoyens Genevois (Geneva Citizens' Movement): CP 340, 1211 Geneva 17; tel. 228497333; fax 223214507; e-mail info@mcge.ch; internet www.mcge.ch; f. 2005; Pres. Eric Stauffer.

Partei der Arbeit der Schweiz—Parti suisse du travail (Parti ouvrier et populaire) (Workers' Party): Postfach 533, 3000 Bern 22; e-mail secret-pst-pda@gouvernement.ch; internet www.pst.ch; f. 1944; Pres. Nelly Buntschu.

Schweizer Demokraten—Démocrates suisses (Swiss Democrats): Postfach 8116, 3001 Bern; tel. 319742010; fax 319742011; e-mail sd-ds@bluewin.ch; internet www.schweizer-demokraten.ch; f. 1961 as Nationale Aktion gegen die Überfremdung von Volk und Heimat—Action nationale; present name adopted 1990; 6,000 mems; main objectives are preservation of the country's political independence and of individual freedom, protection of the environment, and restriction of immigration; Pres. Bernhard Hess; Gen. Sec. Roland Schöni.

Schweizerische Volkspartei—Union démocratique du centre (Swiss People's Party—SPP): Brückfeldstr. 18, 3000 Bern 26; tel. 313005858; fax 313005859; e-mail gs@svp.ch; internet www.svp.ch; f. 1971; Pres. Toni Brunner; Leader of Parliamentary Group Caspar Baader; Gen. Sec. Silvia Bär (acting).

Sozialdemokratische Partei der Schweiz—Parti socialiste suisse (Social Democratic Party): Spitalgasse 34, 3001 Bern; tel. 313296969; fax 313296970; e-mail plauener@sp-ps.ch; internet www.sp-ps.ch; f. 1888; bases its policy on democratic socialism; mem. of Socialist International and assoc. mem. of Party of European Socialists; c. 40,000 mems; Pres. Christian Levrat; Leader of Parliamentary Group Ursula Wyss; Sec.-Gen. Thomas Christen.

> **Partito Socialista, sezione ticinese del PSS** (Socialist Party): piazza Governo 4, 6500 Bellinzona; tel. 918259462; fax 918259601; e-mail segreteria@ps-ticino.ch; internet www.ps-ticino.ch; f. 1992; fmrly the Partito Socialista Unitario; Pres. Manuele Bertoli.

Directory

Diplomatic Representation

EMBASSIES IN SWITZERLAND

Afghanistan: 63 rue de Lausanne, 1202 Geneva; tel. 227311616; fax 227314510; e-mail mission.afghanistan@bluewin.ch; internet www.mission-afghanistan.ch; Ambassador Nanguyulai Tarzi.

Albania: Pourtalèsstr. 45A, 3074 Muri bei Bern; tel. 319526010; fax 319526012; e-mail emalb.ch@bluewin.ch; Ambassador Mehmet Elezaj.

Algeria: Willadingweg 74, 3000 Bern 15; tel. 313501050; fax 313501059; e-mail info@ambassade-algerie.ch; internet www.ambassade-algerie.ch; Ambassador El-Haoués Riache.

Angola: Laubegstr. 18, 3006 Bern; tel. 313518585; fax 313518586; e-mail berna@ambassadeangola.ch; internet www.ambassadeangola.ch; Ambassador Apolinario Jorge Correia.

Argentina: Jungfraustr. 1, 3005 Bern; tel. 313564343; fax 313564340; e-mail esuiz@mrecic.gov.ar; internet www.suiza.embajada-argentina.gov.ar; Chargé d'affaires a.i. Fernando Raúl Lerena.

Armenia: 28 ave du Mail, 1205 Geneva; tel. 223201100; fax 223206148; e-mail arm.mission@deckpoint.ch; Ambassador Charles Aznavour.

Austria: Kirchenfeldstr. 77–79, 3005 Bern; tel. 313565252; fax 313515664; e-mail bern-ob@bmeia.gv.at; internet www.aussenministerium.at/bern; Ambassador Hans Peter Manz.

Azerbaijan: Dalmaziquai 27, 3005 Bern; tel. 313505040; fax 313505041; e-mail bern@mission.mfa.gov.az; internet www.azembassy.ch; Ambassador Elchin Amirbayov.

Belarus: Quartierweg 6, CP 438, 3074 Muri bei Bern; tel. 319527914; fax 319527616; e-mail swiss@belembassy.org; Chargé d'affaires a.i. Andrei Kulazhanka.

Belgium: Jubiläumsstr. 41, 3005 Bern; tel. 313500150; fax 313500165; e-mail bern@diplobel.fed.be; internet www.diplomatie.be/bern; Ambassador Régine De Clercq.

Bosnia and Herzegovina: Thorackerstr. 3, 3074 Muri bei Bern; tel. 313511052; fax 313511079; e-mail emb-ch-brn@vtxmail.ch; Ambassador Jakob Finci.

Brazil: Monbijoustr. 68, 3007 Bern; tel. 313718515; fax 313710525; e-mail info@brasbern.ch; internet www.brasbern.ch; Ambassador Maria Stela Pompeu Brasil Frota.

Bulgaria: Bernastr. 2–4, 3005 Bern; tel. 313511455; fax 313510064; e-mail bulembassy@bluewin.ch; internet www.bulembassy.ch; Ambassador Atanas Pavlov.

Burundi: 44 rue de Lausanne, 1201 Geneva; tel. 227327705; fax 227327734; e-mail mission.burundi@bluewin.ch; Ambassador Pierre Barusasiyeko.

Cameroon: Brunnadernrain 29, 3006 Bern; tel. 313524734; fax 313524760; e-mail secretariat@ambacamberne.ch; internet www.ambacamberne.ch; Ambassador Léonard Henri Bindzi.

Canada: Kirchenfeldstr. 88, 3005 Bern; tel. 313573200; fax 313573210; e-mail bern@international.gc.ca; internet www.switzerland.gc.ca; Ambassador Robert Collette.

Chile: Eigerpl. 5, 12th Floor, 3007 Bern; tel. 313700058; fax 313720025; e-mail embajada@embachile.ch; Ambassador María Carolina Rosetti Gallardo.

China, People's Republic: Kalcheggweg 10, 3006 Bern; tel. 313527333; fax 313514573; e-mail chinaemb_ch@mfa.gov.cn; internet www.china-embassy.ch; Ambassador Dong Jinyi.

Colombia: Dufourstr. 47, 3005 Bern; tel. 313511700; fax 313511710; e-mail eberna@cancilleria.gov.co; internet www.emcol.ch; Chargé d'affaires a.i. Jean-Philippe Pening Gaviria.

Congo, Democratic Republic: Sulgenheimweg 21, 3007 Bern; tel. 313713538; fax 313727466; e-mail rdcambassy@bluewin.ch; Ambassador Kesia-Mbe Mindua.

Congo, Republic: 8 rue Chabray, 1201 Geneva; tel. 227318821; fax 227318826; e-mail missioncongo@bluewin.ch; Chargé d'affaires a.i Jean Marcellin Megot.

Costa Rica: Schwarztorstr. 11, 3007 Bern; tel. 313727887; fax 313727834; e-mail costa.rica@bluewin.ch; Ambassador Edgar Mohs Villalta.

Côte d'Ivoire: Thormannstr. 51, 3005 Bern; tel. 313508080; fax 313508081; e-mail acibe-1@acibe.org; internet www.acibe.org; Ambassador Mamadou Diarrassouba.

Croatia: Thunstr. 45, 3005 Bern; tel. 313520275; fax 313520373; e-mail croemb.bern@mvpei.hr; Ambassador Jakša Muljačić.

Cuba: Gesellschaftsstr. 8, CP 5275, 3012 Bern; tel. 313022111; fax 313029830; e-mail embacuba.berna@bluewin.ch; internet emba.cubaminrex.cu/suiza; Ambassador Isaac Roberto Torres Barrios.

SWITZERLAND

Czech Republic: Muristr. 53, Postfach 537, 3000 Bern 31; tel. 313504070; fax 313504098; e-mail bern@embassy.mzv.cz; internet www.mfa.cz/bern; Ambassador Dr BORIS LAZAR.

Denmark: Thunstr. 95, 3006 Bern; tel. 313505454; fax 313505464; e-mail brnamb@um.dk; internet www.ambbern.um.dk; Ambassador LARS MØLLER.

Dominican Republic: Weltpoststr. 4, Postfach 22, 3000 Bern 15; tel. 313511585; fax 313511587; e-mail embaj.rep-dom@sunrise.ch; Ambassador JOSÉ TOMÁS ARES GERMÁN.

Ecuador: Kramgasse 54, 3011 Bern; tel. 313516254; fax 313512771; e-mail embecusuiza@bluewin.ch; Ambassador RAFAEL ALFONSO PAREDES PROANO.

Egypt: Elfenauweg 61, 3006 Bern; tel. 313528012; fax 313520625; Ambassador MAGDY GALAL SHARAWY.

Ethiopia: 56 rue de Moillebeau, CP 338, 1211 Geneva 19; tel. 229197010; fax 229197029; e-mail mission.ethiopia@ties.itu.int; internet www.ethiopianmission.ch; Ambassador FISSEHA YIMER.

Finland: Weltpoststr. 4, Postfach 11, 3015 Bern; tel. 313504100; fax 313504107; e-mail sanomat.brn@formin.fi; internet www.finlandia.ch; Ambassador PEKKA OJANEN.

France: Schosshaldenstr. 46, 3006 Bern; tel. 313592111; fax 313592191; e-mail scac@ambafrance-ch.org; internet www.ambafrance-ch.org; Ambassador JOËLLE BOURGEOIS.

Georgia: 1 rue Richard Wagner, 1202 Geneva; tel. 229191010; fax 227339033; e-mail geomission.geneva@bluewin.com; internet www.switzerland.mfa.gov.ge; Ambassador GIORGI GORGILADZE.

Germany: Willadingweg 83, Postfach 250, 3000 Bern 15; tel. 313594111; fax 313594444; e-mail info@bern.diplo.de; internet www.bern.diplo.de; Ambassador Dr AXEL BERG.

Ghana: Belpstr. 11, Postfach, 3001 Bern; tel. 313817852; fax 313814941; e-mail ghanaemb@tcnet.ch; internet www.ghanaembassy.ch; Ambassador ELLEN SERWAA NEE-WHANG.

Greece: Weltpostr. 4, 3015 Bern; tel. 313561414; fax 313681272; e-mail gremb.brn@mfa.gr; internet www.greekembassy.ch; Ambassador CONSTANTINE TRITARIS.

Holy See: Thunstr. 60, 3006 Bern (Apostolic Nunciature); tel. 313526040; fax 313525064; e-mail nunziaturach@yahoo.com; Apostolic Nuncio Most Rev. FRANCESCO CANALINI (Titular Archbishop of Valeria).

Hungary: Muristr. 31, Postfach 216, 3000 Bern 15; tel. 313528572; fax 313512001; e-mail mission.brn@kum.hu; internet www.mfa.gov.hu/emb/bern; Ambassador ERZEBET NAGY.

India: Kirchenfeldstr. 28, 3006 Bern; tel. 313511110; fax 313511557; e-mail india@indembassybern.ch; internet www.indembassybern.ch; Ambassador CHITRA NARAYANAN.

Indonesia: Elfenauweg 51, 3006 Bern; tel. 313520983; fax 313516765; e-mail kbribern@bgb.ch; internet www.indonesia-bern.org; Ambassador LUCIA HELWINDA RUSTAM.

Iran: Thunstr. 68, 3006 Bern; tel. 313510801; fax 313515652; e-mail secretariat@iranembassy.ch; internet www.iranembassy.ch; Ambassador KEYVAN IMANI.

Iraq: Elfenstr. 6, 3006 Bern; tel. 313514043; fax 313518312; e-mail bernemb@iraqmofamail.net; internet www.irakembassy.ch; Chargé d'affaires a.i. AHMED KHALIL AHMED AL-ANI.

Ireland: Kirchenfeldstr. 68, 3005 Bern; tel. 313521442; fax 313521455; e-mail berne@dfa.ie; internet www.embassyofireland.ch; Chargé d'affaires a.i. JANE ANN DUFFY.

Israel: Alpenstr. 32, 3006 Bern; tel. 313563500; fax 313563556; e-mail info@bern.mfa.gov.il; internet bern.mfa.gov.il; Ambassador ILAN ELGAR.

Italy: Elfenstr. 14, 3000 Bern 16; tel. 313500777; fax 313500711; e-mail ambasciata.berna@esteri.it; internet www.ambberna.esteri.it; Ambassador GIUSEPPE DEODATO.

Japan: Engestr. 53, 3000 Bern 9; tel. 313002222; fax 313002255; e-mail eojs@bluewin.ch; internet www.ch.emb-japan.go.jp; Ambassador ICHIRO KOMATSU.

Jordan: Belpstr. 11, 3007 Bern; tel. 313840404; fax 313840405; e-mail info@jordanembassy.ch; Ambassador SHEHAB AD-DIN MADI.

Kazakhstan: Alleeweg 15, 3006 Bern; tel. 313517972; fax 313517975; e-mail kasachische.botschaft@freesurf.ch; Ambassador AMANZHOL ZHANKULIYEV.

Korea, Democratic People's Republic: Pourtalèsstr. 43, 3074 Muri bei Bern; tel. 319516621; fax 319515704; e-mail dprk.embassy@bluewin.ch; Ambassador RI CHOL.

Korea, Republic: Kalcheggweg 38, 3006 Bern; tel. 313562444; fax 313562450; e-mail swiss@mofat.go.kr; internet www.mofat.go.kr/switzerland; Ambassador CHANG CHUL-KYOON.

Kosovo: Amthausgasse 3, 3011 Bern; tel. 313100690; fax 313100691; e-mail embassy.switzerland@ks-gov.net; Chargé d'affaires a.i. NAIM MALAJ.

Kuwait: Brunadernrain 19, 3006 Bern; tel. 313567000; fax 313567001; e-mail info@kuwaitembassy.ch; internet www.kuwaitembassy.ch; Ambassador SUHAIL KHALIL YOUSEF SHUHAIBER.

Kyrgyzstan: 4–6 rue du Lac, 1ère étage; tel. 227079220; fax 227079221; e-mail kyrgyzmission@bluewin.ch; internet www.kyrgyzmission.net; Ambassador MUKTAR DJUMALIEV.

Lebanon: Thunstr. 10, 3074 Muri bei Bern; tel. 319506565; fax 319506566; e-mail ambalibch@hotmail.com; Ambassador HUSSEIN RAMMAL.

Libya: Tavelweg 2, 3006 Bern; tel. 313513076; fax 313511325; Chargé d'affaires a.i. IBRAHIM AD-DREDI.

Liechtenstein: Willadingweg 65, Postfach, 3000 Bern 15; tel. 313576411; fax 313576415; e-mail info@brn.rep.llv.li; internet www.bern.liechtenstein.li; Ambassador HUBERT FERDINAND BÜCHEL.

Lithuania: Kramgasse 12, 3011 Bern; tel. 313525291; fax 313525292; e-mail amb.ch@urm.lt; internet ch.mfa.lt; Ambassador VYTAUTAS PLEČKAITIS.

Luxembourg: Kramgasse 45, 3000 Bern 8; tel. 313114732; fax 313110019; e-mail berne.am@mae.etat.lu; Ambassador GÉRARD PHILIPPS.

Macedonia, former Yugoslav republic: Kirchenfeldstr. 30, 3005 Bern; tel. 313520002; fax 313520037; e-mail makedamb@bluewin.ch; Chargé d'affaires a.i. JASMIN KJAHIL.

Madagascar: 32 ave de Riant-Parc, 1209 Geneva; tel. 227401650; fax 227401616; e-mail ambamadsuisse@bluewin.ch; internet www.madagascar-diplomatie.ch; Ambassador RAJEMISON RAKOTOMAHARO.

Malaysia: Jungfraustr. 1, 3005 Bern; tel. 313504700; fax 313504702; e-mail malberne@kln.gov.my; Ambassador Dato' MOHD YUSOF BIN AHMAD.

Mexico: Weltpoststr. 20, 3015 Bern; tel. 313574747; fax 313574748; e-mail embamex1@swissonline.ch; internet www.sre.gob.mx/suiza; Ambassador LUCIANO JOUBLANC MONTANO.

Monaco: Hallwylstr. 34, 3005 Bern; tel. 313562858; fax 313562855; e-mail ambassademonaco@bluewin.ch; Ambassador ROBERT FILLON.

Montenegro: 147 rue de Lausanne, 1202 Geneva; tel. 227326680; fax 227326682; e-mail missionofmontenegro@bluewin.ch; Ambassador MILOMIR MIHALJEVIĆ.

Morocco: Helvetiastr. 42, 3005 Bern; tel. 313510362; fax 313510364; e-mail sifamaberne2@bluewin.ch; internet www.amb-maroc.ch; Ambassador MUHAMMAD SAÏD BENRYANE.

Netherlands: Seftigenstr. 7, 3007 Bern; tel. 313508700; fax 313508710; e-mail ben@minbuza.nl; internet www.nlembassy.ch; Ambassador PETER SCHÖNHERR.

Nigeria: Zieglerstr. 45, Postfach 574, 3007 Bern; tel. 313842600; fax 313842626; e-mail info@nigerianbern.org; internet www.nigerianbern.org; Ambassador Dr MARTIN I. UHOMOIBHI.

Norway: Bubenbergpl. 10, Postfach 5264, 3011 Bern; tel. 313105555; fax 313105550; e-mail emb.bern@mfa.no; internet www.amb-norwegen.ch; Ambassador ROLF TROLLE ANDERSEN.

Pakistan: Bernastr. 47, 3005 Bern; tel. 313501790; fax 313501799; e-mail parepberne@bluewin.ch; Ambassador AYESHA RIYAZ.

Paraguay: Kramgasse 58, Postfach 523, 3000 Bern 8; tel. 313123222; fax 313123432; e-mail embapar@embapar.ch; Chargé d'affaires RAÚL ALBERTO FLORENTÍN ANTOLA.

Peru: Thunstr. 36, 3005 Bern; tel. 313518555; fax 313518570; e-mail embajadaperu@bluewin.ch; Ambassador ELIZABETH ASTETE RODRÍGUEZ.

Philippines: Kirchenfeldstr. 73–75, 3005 Bern; tel. 313501717; fax 313522602; e-mail info@philembassyberne.ch; internet www.philembassyberne.ch; Ambassador MARIA THERESA LAZARO.

Poland: Elfenstr. 20A, 3000 Bern 15; tel. 313580240; fax 313580216; e-mail sek.ambasada@bluewin.ch; internet www.berno.polemb.net; Ambassador JAROSŁAW STARZYK.

Portugal: Weltpoststr. 20, 3015 Bern; tel. 313528602; fax 313514432; e-mail embpt.berna@scber.dgaccp.pt; Ambassador EURICO JORGE HENRIQUES PAES.

Romania: Kirchenfeldstr. 78, 3005 Bern; tel. 313523522; fax 313526455; e-mail ambasada@roamb.ch; internet berna.mae.ro; Ambassador IONEL NICU SAVA.

Russia: Brunnadernrain 37, 3006 Bern; tel. 313520566; fax 313525595; e-mail rusbotschaft@bluewin.ch; internet www.switzerland.mid.ru; Ambassador IGOR B. BRATCHIKOV.

Saudi Arabia: Kramburgstr. 12, 3006 Bern; tel. 313521555; fax 313514581; e-mail chemb@mofa.gov.sa; Ambassador HAZEM M. S. KARAKOTLY.

Serbia: Seminarstr. 5, 3006 Bern; tel. 313526353; fax 313514474; e-mail info@ambasadasrbije.ch; internet www.ambasadasrbije.ch; Chargé d'affaires a.i. VLADIMIR NESIĆ.

SWITZERLAND

Slovakia: Thunstr. 99, 3006 Bern 1; tel. 313563930; fax 313563933; e-mail slovak@spectraweb.ch; internet www.bern.mfa.sk; Ambassador STEFAN SCHILL.

Slovenia: Schwanengasse 9, 3011 Bern; tel. 313109000; fax 313124414; e-mail vbe@gov.si; internet bern.embassy.si; Chargé d'affaires a.i. BRANKO ZUPANC.

South Africa: Alpenstr. 29, Postfach, 3000 Bern 6; tel. 313501313; fax 313513944; e-mail bern.admin@foreign.gov.za; internet www.southafrica.ch; Chargé d'affaires a.i. NGWAKO SOLOMON TSHIVHULA.

Spain: Kalcheggweg 24, Postfach 99, 3000 Bern 15; tel. 313505252; fax 313505255; e-mail emb.berna@mae.es; internet www.maec.es/embajadas/berna; Ambassador FERNANDO RIQUELME LIDÓN.

Sweden: Bundesgasse 26, Postfach, 3001 Bern; tel. 313287000; fax 313287001; e-mail ambassaden.bern@foreign.ministry.se; internet www.swedenabroad.com/bern; Ambassador PER THÖRESSON.

Thailand: Kirchstr. 56, 3097 Liebefeld-Bern; tel. 319703030; fax 319703035; e-mail thai.bern@bluewin.ch; Ambassador CHAIYONG SATJIPANON.

Tunisia: Kirchenfeldstr. 63, 3005 Bern; tel. 313528226; fax 313510445; e-mail at.berne@bluewin.ch; Ambassador RAFIA LIMAM BAOUENDI.

Turkey: Lombachweg 33, 3006 Bern; tel. 313597070; fax 313528819; e-mail tcbern@tr-botschaft.ch; internet www.tr-botschaft.ch; Ambassador ALEV KILIÇ.

Ukraine: Feldeggweg 5, 3005 Bern; tel. 313522316; fax 313516416; e-mail emb_ch@mfa.gov.ua; internet www.ukremb.ch; Ambassador IHOR DIR.

United Kingdom: Thunstr. 50, 3000 Bern 15; tel. 313597700; fax 313597701; e-mail info@britishembassy.ch; internet ukinswitzerland.fco.gov.uk; Ambassador JOHN NICHOLS.

USA: Sulgeneckstr. 19, 3007 Bern; tel. 313577011; fax 313577320; internet bern.usembassy.gov; Chargé d'affaires a.i. LEIGH GABRIELLE CARTER.

Uruguay: Kramgasse 63, 3011 Bern; tel. 313122226; fax 313112747; e-mail uruhelve@bluewin.ch; Ambassador CARLOS BRUGNINI GARCÍA LAGOS.

Venezuela: Schosshaldenstr. 1, Postfach 1005, 3000 Bern 23; tel. 313505757; fax 313505758; e-mail embavenez@greenmail.ch; internet www.embavenez-suiza.com; Chargé d'affaires a.i. FÁTIMA MAJZOUB EL-MAJZOUB.

Viet Nam: Schlösslistr. 26, 3008 Bern; tel. 313887878; fax 313887879; e-mail info@vietnam-embassy.ch; internet www.vietnam-embassy.ch; Ambassador HOANG VAN NHA.

Judicial System

Switzerland has possessed a common Civil Code since 1912, but the Penal Code was only unified in 1942. Under the Code capital punishment was abolished by the few cantons that still retained it. The individual cantons continue to elect and maintain their own magistracy, and retain certain variations in procedure. The canton of Zürich, for example, has justices of the peace (Friedensrichter—normally one for each commune), District Courts (Bezirksgerichte), Labour Courts (Arbeitsgerichte), Courts for Tenancy Matters, an Appeal Court (Obergericht) with various specialized benches, a Cassation Court (Kassationsgericht), and, for the more important cases under penal law, a Jury Court (Geschworenengericht).

At the federal level, the Federal Supreme Court has, in principle, jurisdiction over judicial matters. However, federal appeals commissions adjudicate appeals against rulings by the federal authority. From 1997 a revision of the federal judicial system was undertaken that saw the establishment of two new judicial bodies of first instance, in order to alleviate the burden on the Federal Supreme Court. These were the Federal Criminal Court (from April 2004) and the Federal Administrative Court (from January 2007). In January 2007 the competences of the Federal Insurance Court were merged with the Federal Supreme Court. There are also military courts at the federal level.

Most disputes relating to the application of federal administrative law are first judged by the Federal Administrative Court. In January 2007 the Federal Administrative Court replaced some 30 federal appeals commissions as well as the current departmental appeals services.

FEDERAL SUPREME COURT

Schweizerisches Bundesgericht—Tribunal fédéral

Schweizerhofquai 6, 6004 Luzern; 29 ave du Tribunal fédéral, 1000 Lausanne 14; tel. 213189111; fax 213233700; e-mail direktion@bger.admin.ch; internet www.bger.ch.

Composed of 38 judges elected for a six-year term by the Federal Assembly. According to the Constitution any citizen eligible for election to the National Council can theoretically be elected Justice to the Court, but in practice only lawyers are considered for this office. All of the official Swiss languages must be represented in the Court. The President of the Federal Supreme Court is elected by the Federal Assembly for a two-year term, with no possibility of re-election, from among the senior judges of the Court. The Court is divided into six permanent branches or chambers, each of which has jurisdiction over cases pertaining to a specific subject, namely: (a) two 'Public', i.e. Constitutional and Administrative Law Divisions, being composed of seven and six judges, respectively; (b) two Civil or Private Law Divisions of six judges each, which serve mainly as Courts of Appeal in civil matters; (c) the Debt Execution and Bankruptcy Law Chamber of three judges (members of the Second Civil Law Division); (d) the Criminal Law Division, the so-called Court of Cassation, which is composed of five judges and which hears mainly appeals in criminal law matters. There are also four non-permanent divisions hearing exclusively cases that involve certain crimes against the Confederation, certain forms of terrorism, and other offences related to treason.

President: LORENZ MEYER.

Vice-President: SUZANNE LEUZINGER.

FEDERAL CRIMINAL COURT

Bundesstrafgericht—Tribunal pénal fédéral

CP 2720, 6501 Bellinzona; Viale Stefano Franscini 3, 6500 Bellinzona; tel. 918226262; fax 918226242; e-mail info@bstger.admin.ch; internet www.bstger.ch.

f. 2004; composed of 13 judges elected by the Federal Assembly; court of first instance for criminal cases assigned to federal jurisdiction; in particular, may adjudicate offences such as crimes and misdemeanours against the Confederation's interests, offences committed using explosives, economic crime, organized crime or money-laundering beyond the internal or external borders of Switzerland.

President: ALEX STAUB.

Vice-President: ANDREAS J. KELLER.

FEDERAL ADMINISTRATIVE COURT

Bundesverwaltungsgericht—Tribunal administratif fédéral

Postfach, 3000 Bern 14; tel. 587052626; fax 587052980; e-mail info@bvger.admin.ch; internet www.bvger.ch.

Composed of 72 judges elected by the Federal Assembly for a renewable period of six years; court of first instance for cases arising from administrative decisions at the federal level; appeals in some cases relating to civil and public law matters may be heard in the Federal Supreme Court.

President: CHRISTOPH BANDLI.

Vice-President: PHILIPPE WEISSENBERGER.

Religion

According to the 2000 census, the religious adherence of the total resident population was as follows: Roman Catholic 41.8%, Protestant 35.3%, Orthodox Church 1.8%, Old Catholic 0.2%, Muslim 4.3%, Jewish 0.2%, other religions (including Buddhist and Hindu) 0.8% and those without religion 11.1%.

CHRISTIANITY

The Roman Catholic Church

For ecclesiastical purposes, Switzerland comprises six dioceses and two territorial abbacies. All of the dioceses and abbacies are directly responsible to the Holy See. At 31 December 2006 there were an estimated 3,183,081 adherents (some 44.4% of the total population).

Bishops' Conference

Secrétariat de la Conférence des Evêques Suisses, 21 ave du Moléson, CP 122, 1706 Fribourg; tel. 263224794; fax 263224993; e-mail sbk-ces@gmx.ch; internet www.kath.ch/sbk-ces-cvs.

f. 1863; Pres. Rt Rev. KURT KOCH (Bishop of Basel); Sec.-Gen. Abbé FELIX GMÜR.

Bishop of Basel: Rt Rev. KURT KOCH, Bischöfliches Ordinariat, Baselstr. 58, Postfach 216, 4501 Solothurn; tel. 326255825; fax 326255845; e-mail generalvikariat@bistum-basel.ch; internet www.bistum-basel.ch.

Bishop of Chur: Rt Rev. VITUS HUONDER, Bischöfliches Ordinariat, Hof 19, Postfach 133, 7002 Chur; tel. 812586000; fax 812586001; e-mail kanzlei@bistum-chur.ch; internet www.bistum-chur.ch.

Bishop of Lausanne, Geneva and Fribourg: Rt Rev. BERNARD GENOUD, 86 rue de Lausanne, CP, 1701 Fribourg; tel. 263474850; fax 263474851; e-mail chancellerie@diocese-lgf.ch; internet www.diocese-lgf.ch.

SWITZERLAND

Bishop of Lugano: Rt Rev. PIER GIACOMO GRAMPA, CP 5382, Via Borghetto 6, 6901 Lugano; tel. 919138989; fax 919138990; e-mail segretaria.vescovo@catt.ch; internet www.catt.ch.

Bishop of Sankt Gallen: Rt Rev. MARKUS BÜCHEL, Bischöfliches Ordinariat, Klosterhof 6B, Postfach 263, 9001 Sankt Gallen; tel. 712273340; fax 712273341; e-mail kanzlei@bistum-stgallen.ch; internet www.bistum-stgallen.ch.

Bishop of Sion: Rt Rev. NORBERT BRUNNER, 12 rue de la Tour, CP 2124, 1950 Sion 2; tel. 273291818; fax 273291836; e-mail diocese.sion@cath-vs.ch; internet www.cath-vs.ch.

Protestant Churches

Federation of Swiss Protestant Churches (Schweizerischer Evangelischer Kirchenbund—Fédération des Eglises protestantes de Suisse): Sulgenauweg 26, Postfach, 3000 Bern 23; tel. 313702525; fax 313702580; e-mail info@sek-feps.ch; internet www.sek-feps.ch; f. 1920; comprises the 26 reformed cantonal churches of Aargau, Appenzell (incl. Appenzell Ausserhoden and Appenzell Innerhoden), Basel-Landschaft, Basel-Stadt, Bern-Jura-Solothurn, Fribourg, Geneva, Glarus, Graubünden, Luzern, Neuchâtel, Nidwalden, Obwalden, St Gallen, Schaffhausen, Schwyz, Solothurn, Thurgau, Ticino, Uri, Valais, Vaud, Zug, Zürich, the Free Evangelical Church of Geneva and the United Methodist Church; the exec. organ is the Council of the Federation (Rat des Schweizerischen Evangelischen Kirchenbundes—Conseil de la Fédération); Pres. Rev. THOMAS WIPF.

ISLAM

According to the 2000 census there were 310,807 Muslims recorded in Switzerland, making Islam the second largest religion in the country. There are two major mosques, one in Zürich and one in Geneva, and approximately 200 Islamic centres located throughout the country.

Federation of Islamic Organizations in Switzerland (Föderation Islamischer Dachorganisationen in der Schweiz—Fédération d'Organisations Islamiques de Suisse): Poststr. 8, 9325 Roggwil; tel. 714551383; fax 714551387; e-mail hmaizar@fids.ch; internet www.fids.ch; f. 2006; 12 mem. orgs; Pres. Dr HISHAM MAIZAR.

Föderation Islamischer Gemeinschaften in der Schweiz: Hohlstrasse 615A, 8050 Zürich; tel. 443013151; f. 1978.

JUDAISM

According to the 2000 census there were 17,900 Jews in Switzerland.

Schweizerischer Israelitischer Gemeindebund—Fédération suisse des communautés israélites: Gotthardstr. 65, Postfach 2105, 8027 Zürich; tel. 433050777; fax 433050766; e-mail info@swissjews.org; internet www.swissjews.org; f. 1904; Pres. Dr HERBERT WINTER; Gen. Sec. (vacant).

The Press

Freedom of the press in Switzerland is guaranteed by Article 17 of the amended 1999 Constitution, and the only formal restrictions on the press are the legal restraints concerned with abuses of this freedom.

Switzerland's federal constitutional structure and the coexistence of diverse languages and religions have tended to produce a decentralized press, fragmented into numerous local papers, often with very low circulations. The majority of newspapers are regional, even such high circulation ones as *Berner Zeitung*, *Tages-Anzeiger* and national dailies such as *Neue Zürcher Zeitung*. About 67% of newspapers are printed in German, 27% in French, 4% in Italian and less than 1% in Romansh. Some 100,000 copies of French, German, Italian and Spanish newspapers are imported daily.

PRINCIPAL DAILIES

Baden

Aargauer Zeitung: Stadtturmstr. 19, 5400 Baden; tel. 582005858; fax 582005859; e-mail azredaktion@azag.ch; internet www.aargauerzeitung.ch; f. 1996 by merger of *Aargauer Tagblatt* and *Badener Tagblatt*; Editor-in-Chief PETER BURI; circ. 129,321 (2007).

Basel/Bâle

Basler Zeitung: Aeschenpl. 7, 4002 Basel; tel. 616391111; fax 616311582; e-mail redaktion@baz.ch; internet www.baz.ch; f. 1976; liberal; Editor-in-Chief MATTHIAS GEERING; circ. 94,084 (2007).

Bellinzona

La Regione Ticino: Via Ghiringhelli 9, 6500 Bellinzona; tel. 918211121; fax 918211122; e-mail info@laregione.ch; internet www.laregione.ch; f. 1992; Editor GIACOMO SALVIONI; circ. 33,308 (2007).

Bern/Berne

Berner Zeitung: Nordring/Dammweg 9, 3001 Bern; tel. 3133003111; fax 313327724; e-mail redaktion@bernerzeitung.ch; internet www.bzonline.ch; f. 1844; independent; Editors-in-Chief MARKUS EISENHUT, MICHAEL HUG; circ. 213,544 (2007).

Der Bund: Bubenbergpl. 8, 3001 Bern; tel. 313851111; fax 313851112; e-mail redaktion@derbund.ch; internet www.ebund.ch; f. 1850; liberal; Editor-in-Chief ARTUR K. VOGEL; circ. 60,500 (2005).

Biel/Bienne

Bieler Tagblatt: Robert-Walser-Pl. 7, 2502 Biel; tel. 323219111; fax 323219119; e-mail btredaktion@bielertagblatt.ch; internet www.bielertagblatt.ch; independent; Editor-in-Chief CATHERINE DUTTWEILER; circ. 27,576 (2007).

Brig

Walliser Bote: Furkastr. 21, 3900 Brig; tel. 279229988; fax 279229989; e-mail info@walliserbote.ch; internet www.walliserbote.ch; Catholic; Editor-in-Chief PIUS RIEDER; circ. 26,727 (2007).

La Chaux-de-Fonds

L'impartial: 14 rue Neuve, 2300 La Chaux-de-Fonds; tel. 329102000; fax 329102009; e-mail redaction@limpartial.ch; internet www.limpartial.ch; f. 1880; independent; Editor-in-Chief NICOLAS WILLEMIN; circ. 15,182 (2007).

Chur/Coire

Bündner Tagblatt: Comercialstr. 22, 7007 Chur; tel. 812555000; fax 812555123; e-mail redaktion-bt@suedostschweiz.ch; internet www.suedostschweiz.ch/medien/bt; f. 1852; independent; Editor-in-Chief CHRISTIAN BUXHOFER.

La Quotidiana: Via Centrala 4, 7130 Glion; tel. 819200710; fax 819200715; e-mail redaktion-lq@suedostschweiz.ch; f. 1997; in Romansh; Publr Südostschweiz Presse AG; Editor-in-Chief MARTIN CABALZAR.

Die Südostschweiz: Comercialstr. 22, 7007 Chur; tel. 812255050; fax 812255102; e-mail zentralredaktion@suedostschweiz.ch; internet www.suedostschweiz.ch; publ. regional editions for Gaster und See and Glarus; independent; Publr Südostschweiz Presse AG; Editor-in-Chief ANDREA MASÜGER; circ. 126,697 (2007).

Delémont

Le Quotidien Jurassien: 6 route de Courroux, 2800 Delémont; tel. 324211818; fax 324211890; e-mail lqj@lqj.ch; internet www.lqj.ch; f. 1993; independent; Editor-in-Chief PIERRE-ANDRÉ CHAPATTE; circ. 21,246 (2007).

Dielsdorf

Zürcher Unterländer: Schulstr. 12, 8157 Dielsdorf; tel. 18548282; fax 18530690; e-mail redaktion@zuonline.ch; internet www.zuonline.ch; Editor-in-Chief CHRISTINE FIVIAN; circ. 22,544 (2007).

Frauenfeld

Thurgauer Zeitung: Promenadenstr. 16, 8501 Frauenfeld; tel. 527235757; fax 527235707; e-mail redaktion@thurgauerzeitung.ch; internet www.thurgauerzeitung.ch; f. 1798; independent; Publrs Huber & Co AG; Editor-in-Chief URSULA FRAEFEL; circ. 39,406 (2007).

Freiburg/Fribourg

La Liberté: 42 blvd de Pérolles, 1705 Fribourg; tel. 264264411; fax 264264444; e-mail redaction@laliberte.ch; internet www.laliberte.ch; Editor-in-Chief LOUIS RUFFIEUX; circ. 38,735 (2007).

Genève
(Geneva)

Le Temps: 3 pl. de Cornavin, CP 2570, 1211 Geneva 2; tel. 227995858; fax 227995859; e-mail info@letemps.ch; internet www.letemps.ch; f. 1998; Dir and Editor-in-Chief JEAN-JACQUES ROTH; circ. 45,103 (2007).

Tribune de Genève: CP 5115, 11 rue des Rois, 1211 Geneva 11; tel. 223224000; fax 227810107; e-mail alain.giroud@edipresse.ch; internet www.tdg.ch; f. 1879; independent; morning; Editor-in-Chief PIERRE RUETSCHI; circ. 62,003 (2007).

Herisau

Appenzeller Zeitung: Kasernenstr. 64, 9100 Herisau; tel. 713546474; fax 713546475; e-mail redaktion@appon.ch; internet www.appenzellerzeitung.ch; radical democratic; f. 1828; Publrs

SWITZERLAND

Appenzeller Medienhaus Schläpfer AG; Editor-in-Chief MONIKA EGLI.

Lausanne

Le Matin: 33 ave de la Gare, 1001 Lausanne; tel. 213494949; fax 21494929; internet www.lematin.ch; f. 1862; independent; Editor-in-Chief PETER ROTHENBÜHLER; circ. 70,012 (2007).

24 heures: 33 ave de la Gare, 1001 Lausanne; tel. 213494444; fax 213494419; internet www.24heures.ch; f. 1762; independent; Editor-in-Chief THIERRY MAYER; circ. 89,102 (2007).

Lugano

Corriere del Ticino: Via Industria, 6933 Muzzano; tel. 919603131; fax 919682779; e-mail cdt@cdt.ch; internet www.cdt.ch; f. 1891; independent; Dir GIANCARLO DILLENA; circ. 38,108 (2007).

Giornale del Popolo: Via San Gottardo 50, 6900 Lugano; tel. 919223800; fax 919223805; e-mail redazione@gdp.ch; internet www.gdp.ch; f. 1926; independent; Pres. PIER GIACOMO GRAMPA; circ. 18,057 (2007).

Luzern/Lucerne

Neue Luzerner Zeitung: Maihofstr. 76, 6006 Lucerne; tel. 414295252; fax 414295181; e-mail redaktion@neue-lz.ch; internet www.zisch.ch; f. 1996; Editor-in-Chief THOMAS BORNHAUSER; circ. 130,213 (2007).

Neuchâtel/Neuenburg

L'Express: 39 rue de la Pierre-à-Mazel, 2000 Neuchâtel; tel. 327235300; fax 327235209; e-mail redaction@lexpress.ch; internet www.lexpress.ch; f. 1738; independent; Editor-in-Chief NICOLAS WILLEMIN; circ. 23,344 (2007).

Sankt Gallen/Saint-Gall

St Galler Tagblatt: Fürstenlandstr. 122, 9001 St Gallen; tel. 712727711; fax 712727476; e-mail zentralredaktion@tagblatt.ch; internet www.tagblatt.ch; f. 1839; liberal; Editor-in-Chief GOTTLIEB F. HÖPLI; circ. 101,732 (2007).

Schaffhausen/Schaffhouse

Schaffhauser Nachrichten: Vordergasse 58, 8201 Schaffhausen; tel. 526333111; fax 526333401; e-mail redaktion@shn.ch; internet www.shn.ch; f. 1861; liberal; Editor-in-Chief NORBERT NEININGER; circ. 24,657 (2007).

Sion

Le Nouvelliste: 13 rue de l'Industrie, 1950 Sion; tel. 273297511; fax 273297578; e-mail redaction@nouvelliste.ch; internet www.lenouvelliste.ch; Catholic; Editor-in-Chief JEAN-FRANÇOIS FOURNIER; circ. 42,671 (2007).

Stäfa

Zürichsee-Zeitung: Seestr. 86, 8712 Stäfa; tel. 19285555; fax 19285550; e-mail redstaefa@zsz.ch; internet www.zsz.ch; f. 1845; radical democratic; Editor-in-Chief BENJAMIN GEIGER; circ. 45,519 (2007).

Thun/Thoune

Berner Oberländer: Rampenstr. 1, 3602 Thun; tel. 332251515; fax 332251505; e-mail redaktion-bo@bom.ch; internet www.berneroberlaender.ch; f. 1898; independent; Publrs Berner Oberland Medien AG; Editor-in-Chief RENÉ E. GYGAX; circ. 23,500 (2005).

Thuner Tagblatt: Rampenstr. 1, 3602 Thun; tel. 332251515; fax 332251505; e-mail redaktion-tt@bom.ch; internet www.thunertagblatt.ch; independent; publ. by Berner Oberland Medien AG; Editor-in-Chief RENÉ E. GYGAX; circ. 24,000 (2005).

Wetzikon

Zürcher Oberländer: Rapperswilerstr. 1, 8620 Wetzikon; tel. 19333333; fax 19323232; e-mail redaktion@zol.ch; internet www.zo-medien.ch; f. 1852; liberal; Editor-in-Chief CHRISTOPH VOLLENWEIDER; circ. 38,663 (2007).

Winterthur/Winterthour

Der Landbote: Garnmarkt 1–10, Postfach, 8401 Winterthur; tel. 522669901; fax 522669911; e-mail redaktion@landbote.ch; internet www.landbote.ch; f. 1836; independent; morning; Editor-in-Chief COLETTE GRADWOHL; circ. 35,898 (2007).

Zofingen

Zofinger Tagblatt: Vordere Hauptgasse 33, 4800 Zofingen; tel. 627459350; fax 627459419; e-mail ztredaktion@ztonline.ch; internet www.zofingertagblatt.ch; f. 1873; liberal; Editor BEAT KIRCHHOFER.

Zürich

Blick: Dufourstr. 23, 8008 Zürich; tel. 442596262; fax 442596665; e-mail redaktion@blick.ch; internet www.blick.ch; independent; Editor-in-Chief BERNHARD WEISSBERG; circ. 240,066 (2007).

Neue Zürcher Zeitung: Falkenstr. 11, Postfach, 8021 Zürich; tel. 442581111; fax 442521329; e-mail redaktion@nzz.ch; internet www.nzz.ch; f. 1780; independent-liberal; Editor-in-Chief MARKUS SPILLMANN; circ. 143,875 (2007).

Tages-Anzeiger: Werdstr. 21, 8021 Zürich; tel. 442484411; fax 442484471; e-mail redaktion@tages-anzeiger.ch; internet www.tagesanzeiger.ch; f. 1893; independent; Editors-in-Chief MARKUS EISENHUT, RES STREHLE; circ. 216,411 (2007).

20 Minuten: Werdstr. 21, Postfach, 8021 Zürich; tel. 442486820; fax 442486821; e-mail redaktion@20minuten.ch; internet www.20min.ch; f. 1999; distributed free of charge; six regional editions: Bern/Basel, Geneva, Luzern, Région, St Gallen and Zürich; Editor-in-Chief MARCO BOSELLI; circ. 435,460 (2007).

PERIODICALS AND JOURNALS

Allgemeine Schweizerische Militärzeitschrift: Brunnenstr. 7, 8604 Volketswil; tel. 449084560; fax 449084540; e-mail redaktion@asmz.ch; internet www.asmz.ch; f. 1834; 11 a year; Editor-in-Chief ROLAND BECK; circ. 21,000.

Die Alpen: Monbijoustr. 61, Postfach, 3000 Bern 23; tel. 313701885; fax 313701890; e-mail alpen@sac-cas.ch; internet www.sac-cas.ch; monthly; publ. by Schweizer Alpen-Club; circ. 95,000.

Annabelle création: Baslerstr. 30, 8048 Zürich; tel. 444046333; fax 444046218; e-mail redaktion@an-creation.ch; f. 1998; creative lifestyle and living magazine; monthly; circ. 102,866.

Auto & Lifestyle (ACS Clubmagazin): Wasserwerkgasse 39, 3000 Bern 13; tel. 313283111; fax 313110310; e-mail acszv@acs.ch; internet www.acs.ch; publ. by the Automobile Club of Switzerland; 10 a year; circ. 63,200.

Automobil Revue: Dammweg 9, 3001 Bern; tel. 313303034; fax 313303032; e-mail office@automobilrevue.ch; internet www.automobilrevue.ch; f. 1906; weekly publ. in German and French (*Revue automobile*); Editor PIERRE-ANDRÉ SCHMIDT; circ. 67,412.

Beobachter: Förrlibuckstr. 70, 8021 Zürich; tel. 434445252; fax 434445353; e-mail redaktion@beobachter.ch; internet www.beobachter.ch; f. 1927; 2 a month; circ. 315,081.

Bilanz: Förrlibuckstr. 70, 8021 Zürich; tel. 434445520; fax 434445521; internet www.bilanz.ch; f. 1977; review of business in Switzerland; circ. 57,548.

Courrier neuchâtelois: 2013 Colombier; tel. 328417250; fax 328411521; e-mail administration@editionsduchateau.ch; weekly; Editor RENÉ GESSLER; circ. 88,087.

Du—Zeitschrift für Kultur: Du Verlags AG, Holbeinstr. 8, 8008 Zürich; tel. 432434600; fax 432434611; e-mail redaktion@dumag.ch; internet www.dumag.ch; f. 1941; monthly art review; Editor ANDREAS KLÄUI; circ. 31,915.

Echo Magazine: 12 rue de Meyrin, CP 80, 1211 Geneva 7; tel. 225930303; fax 225930319; e-mail abo.echo.magazine@saripress.ch; internet www.echomagazine.ch; f. 1929; weekly; circ. 22,000; Editor-in-Chief BERNARD LITZLER.

L'Eco dello Sport: via San Gottardo 25, 6500 Bellinzona; tel. 919603131; fax 91575750; circ. 44,000.

Finanz und Wirtschaft: Verlag Finanz und Wirtschaft AG, Hallwylstr. 71, Postfach, 8021 Zürich; tel. 442983535; fax 442983500; e-mail verlag@fuw.ch; internet www.fuw.ch; f. 1928; 2 a week; finance and economics; circ. 34,604 (2007).

Freisinn: Postfach 6136, 3001 Bern; tel. 313203535; fax 313203500; e-mail zila@fdp.ch; internet www.fdp.ch; f. 1979; monthly; politics; Editor-in-Chief NICO ZILA; circ. 71,160.

Glücks-Post: Dufourstr. 49, 8008 Zürich; tel. 442596912; fax 442596930; e-mail glueckspost@ringier.ch; internet www.gluecksposts.ch; women's interest; f. 1977; weekly; Editor-in-Chief BÉATRICE ZOLLINGER; circ. 148,737.

Handels Zeitung: Seestr. 37, 8027 Zürich; tel. 442883555; fax 442883575; e-mail redaktion@handelszeitung.ch; internet www.handelszeitung.ch; f. 1862; financial, commercial and industrial weekly; Publr RALPH BÜCHI; Chief Editor MARTIN SPIELER; circ. 33,044.

L'Hebdo: Pont Bessières 3, POB 6682, 1002 Lausanne; tel. 213317600; fax 213317601; e-mail courrier.hebdo@ringier.ch; internet www.hebdo.ch; f. 1981; weekly; news magazine; Editor-in-Chief ALAIN JEANNET; circ. 48,451 (2007).

L'Illustré: 3 Pont Bessières, POB 6505, 1002 Lausanne; tel. 213317500; fax 213317501; e-mail illustre@ringier.ch; internet www.illustre.ch; f. 1921; weekly; Chief Editor Frederico Campomodo; circ. 97,974.

Museum Helveticum: Steinentorstr. 13, 4010 Basel; tel. 612789565; fax 612789566; e-mail verlag@schwabe.ch; internet www.schwabe.ch; f. 1944; quarterly; Swiss journal for classical philology, ancient history and classical archaeology; Editors Prof. M. Billerbeck, Prof. A. Giovannini, Prof. Th. Gelzer, Prof. H. Harich-Schwarzbauer; publ. by Schwabe AG.

Music Scene: 5401 Baden; tel. 562032200; fax 562032299; e-mail info@music-scene.ch; internet www.music-scene.ch; f. 1924; young people's fortnightly; circ. 50,000.

Nebelspalter: Bahnhofstr. 17, 9326 Horn; tel. 718468876; fax 718468879; e-mail redaktion@nebelspalter.ch; internet www.nebelspalter.ch; f. 1875; 10 a year; satirical; Editor-in-Chief Marco Ratschiller; publ. by Engeli & Partner Verlag; circ. 12,600.

Revue médicale suisse: Editions Médecine et Hygiène, 46 chemin de la Mousse, POB 475, 1225 Chêne-Bourg 4; tel. 227029311; fax 227029355; e-mail redac@revmed.ch; internet www.revmed.ch; f. 2005 to replace Revue médicale de la suisse romande and Médecine et Hygiène; monthly; circ. 5,600.

Revue militaire suisse: 3 ave de Florimont, 1006 Lausanne; tel. 213114817; fax 213119709; e-mail info@jcrc.ch; internet www.revuemilitairesuisse.ch; f. 1856; 8 a year; Editor-in-Chief Maj. Alexandre Vautravers.

Revue suisse de zoologie: Muséum d'Histoire Naturelle, CP 6434, 1211 Geneva 6; tel. 224186300; fax 224186301; e-mail danielle.decrouez@mhn.ville-ge.ch; f. 1893; quarterly; Dir Danielle Decrouez.

Schweizer Archiv für Neurologie und Psychiatrie (Archives Suisses de Neurologie et de Psychiatrie): Schwabe AG Verlag, Steinentorstr. 13, 4010 Basel; tel. 612789565; fax 612789566; e-mail e.vonwartburg@schwabe.ch; internet www.sanp.ch; f. 1917; 8 a year.

Schweizer Familie: Werdstr. 21, Postfach, 8021 Zürich; tel. 442486106; fax 444284096; internet www.schweizerfamilie.ch; f. 1893; weekly; Editor Andreas Durisch; Man. Dir Josef Burch; circ. 205,529.

Schweizer Illustrierte: Dufourstr. 23, 8008 Zürich; tel. 442596363; fax 442620442; internet www.schweizer-illustrierte.ch; f. 1911; illustrated weekly; Chief Editor Dominic Geisseler; circ. 232,519.

Schweizer Monatshefte: Vogelsangstr. 52, 8006 Zürich; tel. 443612606; fax 443637005; e-mail info@schweizermonatshefte.ch; internet www.schweizermonatshefte.ch; f. 1921; political, economic and cultural monthly; Editors Robert Nef, Suzann Renninger; circ. 2,500.

Schweizerisches Handelsamtsblatt (Feuille officielle suisse du commerce): Effingerstr. 1, Postfach 8164, 3001 Bern; tel. 313240992; fax 313240961; e-mail info@shab.ch; internet www.shab.ch; f. 1883; commercial daily; publ. by State Secretariat for Economic Affairs (SECO); Editor-in-Chief Markus Tanner; circ. 10,000.

Snowactive: Strike Media Schweiz AG, Gösgerstr. 15, 5012 Schönenwerd; tel. 326247685; fax 326247251; e-mail j.weibel@snowactive.ch; internet www.snowactive.ch; f. 1968; 7 a year; German and French/Italian editions; Editor Joseph Weibel; circ. 85,000.

Swiss Engineering (STZ): Les Cerisiers, 1585 Bellerive; tel. 266773270; fax 266773269; e-mail mediakom@bluewin.ch; internet www.swissengineering-stz.ch; 1 a year; technical journal in German; Editor-in-Chief Hannes Gysling; circ. 20,000.

Swiss Journal of Psychology/ Schweizerische Zeitschrift für Psychologie/ Revue suisse de psychologie: Unitobler, Muesmattstr. 45, 3000 Bern 9; e-mail margit.oswald@psy.unibe.ch; internet www.verlag-hanshuber.com; f. 1942; quarterly; Editor-in-Chief Prof. Dr Friedrich Wilkening.

Swiss Medical Weekly: EMH Swiss Medical Publrs Ltd, Steinentorstr. 13, 4010 Basel; tel. 614678555; fax 614678556; e-mail red@smw.ch; internet www.smw.ch; f. 1871; fortnightly; Man. Editor Dr Natalie Marty.

TCS-Zürich: Geissbüelstr. 24–26, 8604 Volketswil; tel. 442868613; fax 442868637; official organ of the Zürich Touring Club; monthly; Chief Editor Reto Cavegn; circ. 200,000.

Tele: Dufourstr. 23, 8008 Zürich; tel. 442596111; fax 442598697; e-mail telesekr@ringier.ch; internet www.tele.ch; f. 1967; television, cinema and multimedia; weekly; Editor Klaus Kriesel; circ. 214,214.

Touring: Maulbeerstr. 10, 3001 Bern; tel. 313805000; fax 313805006; f. 1935; fortnightly; German, French and Italian editions; Chief Editor Stefan Senn; circ. 1,306,000.

TV 8: 3 Pont Bessières, 1005 Lausanne; tel. 213317700; fax 213317701; e-mail tv8@ringier.ch; weekly; circ. 83,119 (2007).

Vox Romanica: Centre de dialectologie, Université de Neuchâtel, 6 ave DuPeyrou, 2000 Neuchâtel; tel. 327181720; fax 327181721; e-mail vox.romanica@unine.ch; internet www.unine.ch/dialectologie/vox/vox.html; f. 1936; annual review of Romance linguistics and medieval literature; publ. by Collegium Romanicum (Swiss Association of Romanists); Editors Prof. Dr Rita Franceschini, Prof. Andres Kristol.

Weltwoche: Förrlibuckstr. 70, 8021 Zürich; tel. 434445111; fax 434445669; e-mail redaktion@weltwoche.ch; internet www.weltwoche.ch; f. 1933; weekly; independent; Editor-in-Chief Roger Köppel; circ. 92,337.

Werk, Bauen + Wohnen: Talstr. 39, 8001 Zürich; tel. 442181430; fax 442181434; e-mail wbw.zh@bluewin.ch; internet www.werkbauenundwohnen.ch; f. 1913; monthly; architecture; circ. 8,000.

NEWS AGENCY

Schweizerische Depeschenagentur AG/Agence Télégraphique Suisse SA (SDA/ATS) (Swiss News Agency): Länggassstr. 7, 3001 Bern; tel. 313093333; fax 313093030; e-mail sekretariat.reda@sda.ch; internet www.sda.ch; f. 1894; agency for political and general news; Chair., Management Bd Markus Schwab; Chief Editor Bernard Maissen.

PRESS ASSOCIATIONS

Impressum—Die Schweizer Journalistinnen/Les journalistes suisses/I giornalisti svizzeri: Grand'Places 14A, 1701 Fribourg; tel. 263471500; fax 263471509; e-mail info@impressum.ch; internet www.impressum.ch; Pres Antoine Gessler, Stefan Rohrbach.

Presse Suisse: 1 ave de Florimont, 1006 Lausanne; tel. 213434090; fax 213434099; e-mail admin@pressesuisse.ch; internet www.pressesuisse.ch; f. 1921 as Union Romande des éditeurs de journaux et de périodiques; present name adopted 2006; 54 mems and 6 assoc. mems; Pres. Valérie Boagno.

Verband Schweizer Presse: Konradstr. 14, Postfach 1202, 8021 Zürich; tel. 3186464; fax 3186462; e-mail contact@schweizerpresse.ch; internet www.schweizerpresse.ch; f. 1899; Pres. Hanspeter Lebrument; c. 150 mems.

Publishers

FRENCH-LANGUAGE PUBLISHING HOUSES

Academic Press Fribourg: 42 blvd de Pérolles, CP 176, 1705 Fribourg; tel. 264264311; fax 264264300; e-mail info@paulusedition.ch; internet www.paulusedition.ch; Dir Felix C. Furrer.

Editions l'Age d'Homme SA: 10 rue de Genève, 1003 Lausanne 9; tel. 213120095; fax 213208440; e-mail info@agedhomme.com; internet www.lagedhomme.com; f. 1966; fiction, biography, music, art, social sciences, science fiction, literary criticism; Man. Dir Vladimir Dimitrijevic.

Editions de l'Aire SA: 15 rue de l'Union, BP 57, 1800 Vevey; tel. 219236836; fax 219236823; e-mail editionaire@bluewin.ch; internet www.editions-aire.ch; f. 1978; literature, history, philosophy, religion; Man. Michel Moret.

La Bibliothèque des Arts: 55 ave de Rumine, 1005 Lausanne; tel. 213123667; fax 213123615; e-mail webmaster@bibliotheque-des-arts.com; internet www.bibliotheque-des-arts.com; f. 1952; art, culture; Dir Olivier Daulte.

Librairie Droz SA: 11 rue Firmin-Massot, 1211 Geneva 12; tel. 223466666; fax 223472391; e-mail droz@droz.org; internet www.droz.org; f. 1924; history, medieval literature, French literature, linguistics, social sciences, economics, archaeology; Dir Max Engammare.

Edipresse Publications SA: 33 ave de la Gare, 1001 Lausanne; tel. 213494545; fax 213494110; e-mail epsa.info@edipresse.ch; internet www.edipresse.com; f. 1988; newspapers, magazines; Pres. Pierre Lamunière.

Editions Eiselé SA: 42 Confrérie, CP 128, 1008 Prilly; tel. 21623650; fax 216236359; e-mail jleisele@worldcom.ch; internet www.eisele.ch; arts, education, popular science, textbooks.

Editions d'En Bas: 12 rue du Tunnel, 1005 Lausanne; tel. 213233918; fax 213123240; e-mail enbas@bluewin.ch; internet www.enbas.ch; literature, politics, memoirs, travel, poetry; Dir Jean Richard.

Françoise Gonin Editions d'Art: 1 chemin du Grand-Praz, 1012 Lausanne; tel. 217285948; fax 217285948; internet www.gonin.org/editions; f. 1926; art books.

SWITZERLAND

current affairs programmes from **SF1**, **SF2** and **Presse TV** in hourly and half-hourly blocks; Dir INGRID DELTENRE.

Télévision suisse romande (TSR): 20 quai Ernest-Ansermet, CP 234, 1211 Geneva 8; tel. 227082020; fax 223204813; e-mail tsr@tsr.ch; internet www.tsr.ch; operates **TSR1** and **TSR2**; Dir GILLES MARCHAND.

Televisione svizzera di lingua italiana (TSI): CP, 6903 Lugano; tel. 918035111; fax 918035355; e-mail info@rtsi.ch; internet www.rtsi.ch; operated by Radiotelevisione svizzera di lingua italiana (RTSI); two Italian-language channels: **TSI1** full-service channel aimed at a broad audience, **TSI2** complementary channel with sport, children's programmes and repeats of news programmes from **TSI1**; Dir of TV RENIGIO RATTI.

Televisiun Rumantscha (TvR): Via da Masans 2, 7002 Chur; tel. 812557575; fax 812557500; e-mail contact@rtr.ch; internet www.rtr.ch; operated by Radio e Televisiun Rumantscha (RTR); provides programming in Romansh (*Telesguard* and *Cuntrasts*) which is broadcast on SF1; Dir BERNARD CATHOMAS.

There are also 83 local and regional television stations, 18 of which have high transmission activity.

Finance

(cap. = capital; res = reserves; dep. = deposits; m. = million; brs = branches; all values are in Swiss francs)

REGULATORY AUTHORITY

Eidgenössische Finanzmarktaufsicht (FINMA) (Swiss Financial Market Supervisory Authority): Schwanengasse 2, 3003 Bern; tel. 313279100; fax 313279101; e-mail info@finma.ch; internet www.finma.ch; f. 2009 by merger of the Federal Office of Private Insurance, the Swiss Federal Banking Commission and the Anti-Money Laundering Control Authority; supervises banks, insurance cos, stock exchanges, securities dealers and other financial intermediaries; Pres. Dr EUGEN HALTINER; Dir Dr PATRICK RAAFLAUB.

BANKING

Switzerland's banks have a long-standing reputation as a secure repository for foreign capital. The Swiss Banking Law of 1934 declared it a penal offence for a bank to provide information about its clients without their explicit authorization, unless a court had ordered otherwise. When foreign authorities wish to investigate Swiss accounts, criminal charges must have been made in a foreign court and accepted as valid by Switzerland. The system of numbered accounts has also shielded depositors' shares from investigation. However, the abuse of bank secrecy by organized crime led Switzerland and the USA to sign a treaty in May 1973, whereby banking secrecy rules may be waived in the case of common-law crime (although not for non-criminal tax evasion and anti-trust law infringements). Further amendments to banking secrecy legislation were introduced in 1990 and 1998.

In June 1977 the Swiss banks agreed a code of practice which required the introduction of stricter controls over the handling of foreign funds. The opening of numbered accounts was subjected to closer scrutiny and the practice of actively encouraging the flow of foreign money into the country was checked. The agreement was modified in 1982. In 1987, following the withdrawal from the agreement of the Swiss National Bank, the code was adapted by the Swiss Bankers' Association into rules of professional conduct; further modifications to the code were introduced in 1992. In 1978, in view of the steady increase in Swiss banks' international business, the Federal Banking Commission was given greater supervisory powers. Banks were required for the first time to submit consolidated balance sheets to the Commission and new consolidation requirements forced banks to raise capital to between 6% and 8% of total liabilities. The capital requirement is now one of the highest in the world.

On 1 January 2009 the Federal Banking Commission merged with two other federal bodies to form the Swiss Financial Market Supervisory Authority (FINMA), which assumed responsibility for regulating the entire financial services sector.

At the end of 2007 there were 330 banks operating in Switzerland. The 24 cantonal banks are mostly financed and controlled by the cantons, and their activities are co-ordinated by the Association of Swiss Cantonal Banks. In 2007 they had 796 branches and controlled more than one-third of Switzerland's savings deposits.

Central Bank

Schweizerische Nationalbank/Banque nationale suisse (Swiss National Bank): Börsenstr. 15, Postfach 2800, 8022 Zürich; tel. 446313111; fax 446313911; e-mail snb@snb.ch; internet www.snb.ch; f. 1907; conducts the country's monetary policy as an independent central bank; obliged by the Constitution and statute to act in accordance with the interests of the country as a whole; primary goal is to ensure price stability, while taking due account of economic developments; Dept I handles international affairs, economic affairs, legal and administrative affairs, human resources and communications; Dept II handles cash, finance and controlling, financial stability and oversight, and security; Dept III handles financial markets, asset management, risk management, banking operations and information technology; cap. 25m., res 16,473m., dep. 8,359m. (Dec. 2006); Chair., Governing Bd Dr JEAN-PIERRE ROTH (until 31 December 2009), PHILIPP HILDEBRAND (from 1 January 2010).

Canton Banks

There are 24 cantonal banks, of which the following are the largest:

Aargauische Kantonalbank: Bahnhofstr. 58, 5001 Aarau; tel. 628357777; fax 628357778; e-mail akb@akb.ch; internet www.akb.ch; f. 1913; cap. 200m., res 332m., dep. and bonds 15,111m. (Dec. 2007); Pres. ARTHUR ZELLER; CEO RUDOLF DELLENBACH; 30 brs.

Banca dello Stato del Cantone Ticino: Viale H. Guisan 5, 6501 Bellinzona; tel. 918037111; fax 918037170; internet www.bancastato.ch; f. 1915; cap. 100m., res 125m., dep. and bonds 6,277m. (Dec. 2006); Chair. FULVIO PELLI; Pres., Exec. Bd DONATO BARBUSCIA; 4 brs.

Banque Cantonale de Fribourg: 1 blvd de Pérolles, 1701 Fribourg; tel. 848223223; fax 263507709; e-mail info@bcf.ch; internet www.bcf.ch; f. 1892 as Banque de l'Etat de Fribourg; present name adopted 1996; cap. 70m., res 350m., dep. and bonds 8,097m. (Dec. 2006); Chair. GILBERT MONNERON; CEO ALBERT MICHEL; 26 brs.

Banque Cantonale de Genève: 17 quai de l'Ile, CP 2251, 1211 Geneva; tel. 582112100; fax 582112199; e-mail info@bcge.ch; internet www.bcge.ch; f. 1994; cap. 360m., res 366m., dep. and bonds 11,453m. (Dec. 2007); Chair. MICHEL MATTACCHINI; CEO BLAISE GOETSCHIN; 23 brs.

Banque Cantonale du Jura: 10 rue de la Chaumont, CP 278, 2900 Porrentruy; tel. 324651301; fax 324651495; e-mail bcj@bcj.ch; internet www.bcj.ch; f. 1979; cap. 45m., res 61m., dep. and bonds 1,618m. (Dec. 2007); Chair. Dr PAUL-ANDRÉ SANGLARD; Gen. Man. BERTRAND VALLEY; 12 brs.

Banque Cantonale du Valais: 8 pl. des Cèdres, CP 133, 1951 Sion; tel. 273246111; fax 273246666; e-mail info@bcvs.ch; internet www.bcvs.ch; f. 1917; cap. 150m., res 275m., dep. and bonds 7,318m. (Dec. 2007); Chair. MAURICE DE PREUX; CEO JEAN-DANIEL PAPILLOUD; 20 brs.

Banque Cantonale Neuchâteloise: 4 pl. Pury, 2001 Neuchâtel; tel. 327236111; fax 327236236; e-mail info@bcn.ch; internet www.bcn.ch; f. 1883; cap. 125m., res 145m., dep. 4,345m. (Dec. 2006); Pres. JEAN-PIERRE GHELFI; Gen. Man. JEAN-NOËL DUC; 1 br.

Banque Cantonale Vaudoise: 14 pl. St François, CP 300, 1003 Lausanne; tel. 212121000; fax 212121596; e-mail info@bcv.ch; internet www.bcv.ch; f. 1845; cap. 537m., res 2,209m., dep. and bonds 29,966m. (Dec. 2007); Chair. OLIVIER STEIMER; CEO PASCAL KIENER; 66 brs.

Basellandschaftliche Kantonalbank: Rheinstr. 7, 4410 Liestal; tel. 619259494; fax 619259674; e-mail info@blkb.ch; internet www.blkb.ch; f. 1864; cap. 240m., res 573m., dep. and bonds 13,588m. (Dec. 2007); Pres. WILHELM HANSEN; CEO Dr BEAT OBERLIN; 8 brs.

Basler Kantonalbank: Spiegelgasse 2, 4002 Basel; tel. 612662555; fax 612662915; e-mail bkb@bkb.ch; internet www.bkb.ch; f. 1899; cap. 254m., res 381m., dep. and bonds 13,195m. (Dec. 2007); Chair. Dr ANDREAS C. ALBRECHT; CEO HANS-RUDOLF MATTER; 19 brs.

BEKB/BCBE (Berner Kantonalbank/Banque Cantonale Bernoise): Bundespl. 8, 3001 Bern; tel. 316661111; fax 316666040; e-mail bekb@bekb.ch; internet www.bekb.ch; f. 1834 as Banque Cantonale de Berne; present name adopted 1991; cap. 280m., res 690m., dep. and bonds 18,308m. (Dec. 2007); Pres. Dr JÜRG RIEBEN; CEO JEAN-CLAUDE NOBILI; 78 brs.

Graubündner Kantonalbank: Postfach, 7002 Chur; tel. 812569111; fax 812526729; e-mail info@gkb.ch; internet www.gkb.ch; f. 1870; cap. 200m., res 221m., dep. and bonds 12,121m. (Dec. 2007); Pres. Dr HANS HATZ; CEO ALOIS VINZENS; 74 brs.

Luzerner Kantonalbank: Pilatusstr. 12, 6002 Lucerne; tel. 844822811; fax 412062090; e-mail info@lukb.ch; internet www.lukb.ch; f. 1850; cap. 357m., res 670m., dep. and bonds 16,883m. (Dec. 2007); Chair. FRITZ STUDER; CEO BERNARD KOBLER; 26 brs.

Schwyzer Kantonalbank (SKZB): Bahnhofstr. 3, 6431 Schwyz; tel. 588002020; fax 588002021; e-mail kundenzentrum@szkb.ch; internet www.szkb.ch; f. 1889 as Kantonalbank Schwyz, present name adopted 1997; cap. 78m., res 252m., dep. and bonds 9,233m. (Dec. 2007); Pres. ALOIS CAMENZIND; CEO GOTTFRIED WEBER; 27 brs.

St Galler Kantonalbank: St Leonhardstr. 25, Postfach 2063, 9001 St Gallen; tel. 712313131; fax 712313232; e-mail info@sgkb.ch; internet www.sgkb.ch; f. 1868; cap. 557m., res 871m., dep. and bonds 17,623m. (Dec. 2006); Chair. Dr FRANZ-PETER OESCH; Pres., Exec. Bd ROLAND LEDERGERBER; 37 brs.

SWITZERLAND

Thurgauer Kantonalbank: Bankpl. 1, Postfach 160, 8570 Weinfelden; tel. 848111444; fax 848111445; e-mail info@tkb.ch; internet www.tkb.ch; f. 1871; cap. 400m., res 218m., dep. and bonds 13,256m. (Dec. 2007); Chair. RENÉ BOCK; CEO HANSPETER HERGER; 30 brs.

Urner Kantonalbank: Bahnhofstr. 1, 6460 Altdorf; tel. 418756000; fax 418756313; e-mail info@urkb.ch; internet www.urkb.ch; f. 1915; cap. 30m., res 51m., dep. and bonds 1,734m. (Dec. 2007); Pres. Dr HANSRUEDI STADLER; CEO PETER ZGRAGGEN; 9 brs.

Zuger Kantonalbank: Baarerstr. 37, 6301 Zug; tel. 417091111; fax 417091555; e-mail service@zugerkb.ch; internet www.zugerkb.ch; f. 1892; cap. 144m., res 254m., dep. and bonds 5,862m. (Dec. 2006); Chair. and Pres. BEAT BERNET; Gen. Man. TONI LUGINBÜHL; 10 brs.

Zürcher Kantonalbank: Bahnhofstr. 9, 8010 Zürich; tel. 442939393; fax 442923802; e-mail info@zkb.ch; internet www.zkb.ch; f. 1870; cap. 1,925m., res 4,566m., dep. and bonds 86,391m. (Dec. 2007); Chair. Dr URS OBERHOLZER; CEO MARTIN SCHOLL; 103 brs.

Commercial Banks (Selected List)

Baloise Bank SoBa: Amthauspl. 4, 4502 Solothurn; tel. 326260202; fax 326233692; e-mail bank@baloise.ch; internet www.baloise.ch; f. 1994; subsdidiary of Bâloise-Gruppe; Group Chair. Dr ROLF SCHÄUBLE; Group CEO MARTIN STROBEL.

Bank Julius Baer & Co Ltd: Bahnhofstr. 36, 8010 Zürich; tel. 588881111; fax 588881122; internet www.juliusbaer.com; f. 1890; cap. 575m., res 2,428m., dep. and bonds 34,171m. (Dec. 2007); Chair. RAYMOND J. BAER; Pres., Exec. Bd and CEO BORIS COLLARDI; 13 brs.

Banque Thaler SA: 3 rue Pierre-Fatio, 1211 Geneva 3; tel. 227070909; fax 227070910; e-mail info@banquethaler.ch; internet www.banquethaler.ch; f. 1982 as KBC Bank (Suisse) SA; present name adopted 2000; cap. 20m., res 7m., dep. 60m. (Dec. 2007); Pres. ROBERT CUYPERS; Gen. Man. DIRK EELBODE.

BNP Paribas (Suisse) SA: 2 pl. de Hollande, 1204 Geneva; tel. 582122111; fax 582122222; internet www.bnpparibas.ch; f. 1961 as United Overseas Bank SA; present name adopted 2001; cap. 320m., res 1,619m., dep. and bonds 34,860m. (Dec. 2006); Chair. GEORGE CHODRON DE COURCEL; CEO PASCAL BORIS; 5 brs.

BSI SA: Via Franscini 8, 6900 Lugano; tel. 588093111; fax 588093678; e-mail info@bsibank.com; internet www.bsibank.com; f. 1873 as Banca della Svizzera italiana; present name adopted 1998; absorbed Banca del Gottardo in 2008; cap. 440m., res 363m., dep. and bonds 10,317m. (Dec. 2007); Chair. Dr GIORGIO GHIRINGHELLI; CEO Dr ALFREDO GYSI; 7 brs.

Clariden Leu AG: Bahnhofstr. 32, 8001 Zürich; tel. 582052111; fax 582052191; e-mail info@claridenleu.com; internet www.claridenleu.com; f. 2007 by merger of Bank Hofmann, Bank Leu, BGP Banca di Gestione Patrimoniale, Clariden Bank and Crédit Suisse Fides; Chair. PETER ECKERT; CEO HANS NÜTZI; 8 brs.

Crédit Suisse Group: Postfach 100, 8070 Zürich; Paradepl. 8, 8001 Zürich; tel. 442121616; fax 443332587; internet www.credit-suisse.ch; f. 1856; cap. 46m., res 43,153m., dep. 1,136,420m. (Dec. 2007); Group CEO BRADY W. DOUGAN; CEO, Switzerland HANS-ULRICH MEISTER; 290 brs.

Migros Bank AG: Seidengasse 12, 8023 Zürich; tel. 442298111; fax 442298715; e-mail info@migros.ch; internet www.migrosbank.ch; f. 1958; cap. 700m., res 1,442m., dep. 26,163m. (Dec. 2007); Chair. HERBERT BOLLIGER; Pres., Exec. Bd Dr HARALD NEDWED; 54 brs.

Neue Aargauer Bank: Bahnhofstr. 49, 5001 Aarau; tel. 564627100; fax 564627542; e-mail webmaster@nab.ch; internet www.nab.ch; f. 1989; 98.6% owned by Crédit Suisse Group; cap. 137m., res 679m., dep. and bonds 16,936m. (Dec. 2007); Pres. JOSEF MEIER; CEO PETER BÜHLMANN; 33 brs.

Raiffeisen Schweiz Genossenschaft/Raiffeisen Switzerland Cooperative: Raffeisenpl., 9001 St Gallen; tel. 712258888; fax 712258887; e-mail direct@raiffeisen.ch; internet www.raiffeisen.ch; f. 1902; cap. 467m., res 6,234m., dep. 113,342m. (Dec. 2007); Chair., Bd of Dirs FRANZ MARTY; Chair., Exec. Bd Dr PIERIN VINCENZ; 367 associated banks.

RBS Coutts Bank Ltd: Stauffacherstr. 1, 8022 Zürich; tel. 432455111; fax 432455396; internet www.rbscoutts.com; f. 1930; fmrly Coutts Bank von Ernst; current name adopted 2008; cap. 110m., res 1,029m., dep. 15,914m. (Dec. 2008); Chair. DAVID DOUGLAS-HOME, Earl of Home; 5 brs.

Swissquote Bank: 33 chemin de la Créteaux, 1196 Gland; tel. 229999411; fax 229999412; e-mail info@bank.swissquote.ch; internet www.swissquote.ch; f. 2000; Chair. MARIO FONTANA; CEO MARC BÜRKI.

UBS AG: Bahnhofstr. 45, 8021 Zürich; tel. 442341111; fax 442399111; e-mail info@ubs.com; internet www.ubs.com; f. 1998 by merger of Union Bank of Switzerland (f. 1912) and Swiss Bank Corpn (f. 1872); cap. 207m., res -2,703m., dep. 1,925,342m. (Dec. 2007); Chair. KASPAR VILLIGER; Group CEO OSWALD GRÜBEL; 357 brs.

Union Bancaire Privée: 96–98 rue du Rhône, CP 1320, 1211 Geneva 1; tel. 588192111; fax 588192200; e-mail ubp@ubp.ch; internet www.ubp.ch; f. 1990 by merger of TDB American Express Bank (f. 1956) and Compagnie de Banque et d'Investissements (f. 1969); cap. 300m., res 1,145m., dep. and bonds 16,789m. (Dec. 2008); Chair. EDGAR DE PICCIOTTO; CEO GUY DE PICCIOTTO; 6 brs.

Valiant Bank: Bundespl. 4, Postfach 5333, 3001 Bern; tel. 313209111; fax 313209112; internet www.valiant.ch; f. 2001 by merger of Spar- und Leihkasse in Bern, Gewerbekasse in Bern, bank in Langnau, BB Bank Belp and Ersparnikasse Murten; cap. 110m., res 1,006m., dep. and bonds 15,787m. (Dec. 2007); Chair. Prof. Dr ROLAND VON BÜREN; CEO MICHAEL HOBMEIER; 88 brs.

Private Banks

Switzerland's private banking sector is the largest, in terms of assets, in the world. In 2007 there were 14 privately owned banks in Switzerland, of which the following are among the most important:

Banque Privée Edmond de Rothschild SA: 18 rue de Hesse, 1204 Geneva; tel. 588189111; fax 588189121; e-mail contact@bper.ch; internet www.lcf-rothschild.ch; f. 1924; cap. 45m., res 493m., dep. and bonds 1,414m. (Dec. 2007); Chair. Baron BENJAMIN DE ROTHSCHILD; Gen. Man. CLAUDE MESSULAM; 2 brs.

EFG Bank: Bahnhofstr. 16, Postfach 2255, 8022 Zürich; tel. 442261717; fax 442261726; e-mail enquiries_ch@efgbank.com; internet www.efgbank.com; f. 1997 as EFG Private Bank SA; present name adopted 2005; cap. 62m., res 247m., dep. 9,228m. (Dec. 2006); Chair. JEAN-PIERRE CUONI; CEO MARKUS CADUFF.

HSBC Private Bank (Suisse) SA: 2 quai Général Guisan, CP 3580, 1211 Geneva 3; tel. 587055555; fax 587055151; internet www.hsbcprivatebank.com; f. 1988 as Republic National Bank New York (Suisse) SA; present name adopted 2004; cap. 683m., res 1,979m., dep. 61,178m. (Dec. 2007); Chair. PETER WIDMER; CEO PETER F. BRAUNWALDER; 3 brs.

Hyposwiss Private Bank AG: Schützengasse 4, 8021 Zürich; tel. 442143111; fax 442115223; e-mail info@hyposwiss.ch; internet www.hyposwiss.ch; f. 1889 as Schweizerische Hypothekenbank; present name adopted 2002; cap. 26m., res 72m., dep. and bonds 654m. (Dec. 2007); Chair. ROLAND LEDERGERBER; CEO SIEGFRIED R. PEYER.

Lombard Odier Darier Hentsch & Cie: 11 rue de la Corraterie, 1211 Geneva 11; tel. 227092111; fax 227092911; e-mail contact@lodh.com; internet www.lodh.com; f. 2002 by merger of Lombard Odier & Cie (f. 1798) and Darier Hentsch & Cie (f. 1991); Snr Partners PIERRE DARIER, THIERRY LOMBARD; Man. Partners PATRICK ODIER, JEAN PASTRÉ, BERNARD DROUX, ANNE-MARIE DE WECK, CHRISTOPHE HENTSCH, HUBERT KELLER.

Pictet & Cie Banquiers: 60 route des Acacias, 1211 Geneva 73; tel. 583232323; fax 583232324; e-mail info@pictet.com; internet www.pictet.com; f. 1805; Snr Partner IVAN PICTET; Partners CLAUDE DEMOLE, JACQUES DE SAUSSURE, NICOLAS PICTET, PHILIPPE BERTHERAT, JEAN-FRANÇOIS DEMOLE, RENAUD DE PLANTA, RÉMY BEST.

Central Co-operative Credit Institution

Bank Coop AG: Aeschenpl. 3, 4002 Basel; tel. 612862121; fax 612714595; e-mail info@bankcoop.ch; internet www.bankcoop.ch; f. 1927 as Co-operative Central Bank; present name adopted 2001; 56.3% stake owned by Basler Kantonalbank; cap. 338m., res 324m., dep. and bonds 11,213m. (Dec. 2007); Chair. WILLI GERSTER; Pres., Exec. Bd ANDREAS WÄSPI; 33 brs.

Bankers' Organizations

Association of Foreign Banks in Switzerland: Löwenstr. 51, Postfach 1211, 8021 Zurich; tel. 442244070; fax 442210029; e-mail info@foreignbanks.ch; internet www.foreignbanks.ch; f. 1972; 144 mems (Dec. 2007); Chair. Dr ALFREDO GYSI; Sec. Gen. Dr MARTIN MAURER.

Schweizerische Bankiervereinigung/Association Suisse des Banquiers (Swiss Bankers' Asscn): Aeschenpl. 7, Postfach 4182, 4002 Basel; tel. 612959393; fax 612725382; e-mail office@sba.ch; internet www.swissbanking.org; f. 1912; 363 institutional mems and 16,000 individual mems; Chair. PIERRE MIRABAUD; CEO Dr URS P. ROTH.

Verband Schweizerischer Kantonalbanken/Union des Banques Cantonales Suisses (Asscn of Swiss Cantonal Banks): Wallstr. 8, 4002 Basel; tel. 612066666; fax 612066667; e-mail vskb@vskb.ch; internet www.kantonalbank.ch; f. 1907; perm. office est. 1971; Chair. PAUL NYFFELER; Dir HANSPETER HESS.

STOCK EXCHANGES

BX Berne eXchange (Berner Börsenverein): Aarbergergasse 36, 3011 Bern; tel. 313114042; fax 313115309; e-mail office@berne-x.com; internet www.bernerboerse.ch; f. 1884; 9 mems, 6 assoc. mems; Dir JÜRG NIEDERHÄUSER.

SWITZERLAND

SIX Swiss Exchange: Selnaustr. 30, 8021 Zürich; tel. 588545454; fax 588545455; e-mail six@six.com; internet www.six-swiss-exchange.com; f. 1873; 51 mems; Pres. Prof. Dr PETER GOMEZ; CEO CHRISTIAN KATZ.

INSURANCE

In December 2008 there were 259 insurance companies in Switzerland.

Allianz Suisse: Bleicherweg 19, Postfach, 8022 Zürich; tel. 583587111; fax 583584042; e-mail contact@allianz-suisse.ch; internet www.allianz-suisse.ch; subsidiaries: Allianz Suisse Versicherungen, Allianz Suisse Leben, Allianz Suisse Personal Financial Services; Chair. ULRICH ZIMMERLI; CEO Dr MANFRED KNOF.

AXA Winterthur: Gen. Guisan-Str. 40, Postfach 357, 8401 Winterthur; tel. 522611111; fax 522136620; e-mail info.ch@axa-winterthur.ch; internet www.axa-winterthur.ch; f. 1875; fmrly Winterthur Schweizerische Versicherungs-Gesellschaft; owned by AXA Group (France); Pres. ALFRED BOUCKAERT; CEO PHILIPPE EGGER.

Basler Versicherungen: Aeschengraben 21, 4002 Basel; tel. 612858585; fax 612857070; e-mail insurance@baloise.ch; internet www.baloise.ch; f. 1864; all classes; part of Bâloise-Gruppe; CEO MARTIN STROBEL.

Generali (Schweiz) Holding AG: Soodmattenstr. 10, 8134 Adliswil 1; tel. 447124040; fax 447124425; e-mail info@generali.ch; internet www.generali.ch; life and non-life; part of Generali Group (Italy); CEO ALFRED LEU.

Helvetia Versicherungen: St Alban-Anlage 26, 4002 Basel; tel. 582801000; fax 582801001; internet www.helvetia.ch; f. 1861; owned by Helvetia Holding; life, fire, burglary, accident liability, motor; Chair. Dr ERICH WALSER; CEO, Switzerland PHILIPP GMÜR.

Schweizerische Mobiliar Versicherungsgesellschaft (Die Mobiliar): Bundesgasse 35, 3001 Bern; tel. 313896111; fax 313896852; e-mail info@mobi.ch; internet www.mobi.ch; f. 1826; accident, sickness, fire and damage by the elements, theft, valuables, damage by water, glass breakage, machines, construction work, interruption of business, epidemics, warranty, guarantee, third-party liability, motor vehicles, travel, transport; CEO URS BERGER.

Schweizerische National-Versicherungs-Gesellschaft (Nationale Suisse): Steinengraben 41, 4003 Basel; tel. 612752111; fax 612752656; internet www.nationalesuisse.ch; CEO HANS KÜNZLE.

SCOR Holding (Switzerland) Ltd: General Guisan-Quai 26, Postfach, 8022 Zürich; tel. 446399335; fax 446399334; internet www.converium.ch; fmrly Converium; acquired by SCOR Group (France) in 2007; Group Chair. DENIS KESSLER; CEO BENJAMIN GENTSCH.

Swiss Life: General Guisan-Quai 40, POB 2831, 8022 Zürich; tel. 432843311; fax 432846311; e-mail info.com@swisslife.ch; internet www.swisslife.com; f. 1857; specializes in international employee benefit and pension plans; brs in France, Germany, Liechtenstein, Luxembourg and Singapore; Group CEO BRUNO PFISTER.

Swiss Re (Schweizerische Rückversicherungs-Gesellschaft) (Swiss Reinsurance Co): Mythenquai 50/60, 8022 Zürich; tel. 442852121; fax 442852999; e-mail contact@swissre.com; internet www.swissre.com; f. 1863; world-wide reinsurance; Chair. WALTER KIELHOLZ; CEO STEFAN LIPPE.

Vaudoise Assurances: Pl. de Milan, 1001 Lausanne; internet www.vaudoise.ch; f. 1895; subsidiaries: Vaudoise Générale (non-life), Vaudoise Vie (life); Pres. ROLF MEHR.

Zürich Versicherungs-Gesellschaft: Thurgauerstrasse 80, 8085 Zürich; tel. 446282828; fax 446288444; e-mail kontakt@zurich.ch; internet www.zurich.ch; f. 1922; part of Zurich Financial Services group; life; Group CEO JAMES J. SCHIRO.

Insurance Organization

Schweizerischer Versicherungsverband—Association suisse d'assurances (SVV—ASA) (Swiss Insurance Asscn): C. F. Meyer-Str. 14, Postfach 4288, 8022 Zürich; tel. 442082828; fax 442082800; e-mail info@svv.ch; internet www.svv.ch; f. 1901; Pres. ERICH WALSER; Dir LUCIUS DÜRR; 72 mems.

Trade and Industry

GOVERNMENT AGENCIES

Osec Business Network Switzerland: Stampfenbachstr. 85, Postfach 2407, 8035 Zürich; tel. 443655151; fax 443655221; e-mail contact@osec.ch; internet www.osec.ch; offices in Lausanne and Lugano; promotes trade; CEO DANIEL KÜNG.

Directory

PRINCIPAL CHAMBERS OF COMMERCE

Aargauische Industrie- und Handelskammer: Entfelderstr. 11, 5001 Aarau; tel. 628371818; fax 628371819; e-mail info@aihk.ch; internet www.aihk.ch; Pres. DANIEL KNECHT.

Berner Handelskammer: Gutenbergstr. 1, 3001 Bern; tel. 313888787; fax 313888788; e-mail hk@bern-cci.ch; internet www.bern-cci.ch; Pres. NIKLAUS J. LÜTHI.

Camera di commercio, dell'industria, dell'artigianato e dei servizi del Cantone Ticino (Cc-Ti): Corso Elvezia 16, 6901 Lugano; tel. 919115111; fax 919115112; e-mail cciati@cci.ch; internet www.cciati.ch; f. 1917; Dir LUCA ALBERTONI; 804 mems.

Chambre de commerce Fribourg (CCF): 37 route du Jura, 17061 Fribourg; tel. 263471220; fax 263471239; e-mail info@ccfribourg.ch; internet www.ccfribourg.ch; f. 1917; Pres. CHARLES PHILLOT; Dir VIVIANE COLLAUD (acting).

Chambre de commerce et d'industrie du Jura: 23 rue de l'Avenir, CP 274, 2800 Delémont 1; tel. 324214545; fax 324214540; e-mail ccjura@cci.ch; internet www.ccij.ch; Pres. JEAN-PAUL RENGGLI; Dir JEAN-FRÉDÉRIC GERBER; 400 mems.

Chambre neuchâteloise du commerce et de l'industrie: 4 rue de la Serre, 2001 Neuchâtel; tel. 327221515; fax 327221520; internet www.cnci.ch; Pres. FRÉDÉRIC GEISSBUHLER; Dir PIERRE HILTPOLD.

Chambre valaisanne de commerce et d'industrie: 6 rue Pré-Fleuri, CP 288, 1951 Sion; tel. 273273535; fax 273273536; e-mail info@cci-valais.ch; internet www.cci-valais.ch; Pres. BERNARD BRUTTIN; Dir VINCENT RIESEN; 479 mems.

Chambre vaudoise du commerce et de l'industrie: 47 ave d'Ouchy, CP 315, 1001 Lausanne; tel. 216133535; fax 216133505; e-mail cvci@cvci.ch; internet www.cvci.ch; Pres. BERNARD RÜEGER; Dir CLAUDINE AMSTEIN; 2,500 mems.

Chambre de commerce, d'industrie et des services de Genève (CCIG): 4 blvd du Théâtre, 1211 Geneva 11; tel. 228199111; fax 228199100; e-mail ccig@cci.ch; internet www.ccig.ch; f. 1865; Pres. FRANÇOIS NAEF; Dir JACQUES JEANNERAT; 1,700 mems.

Glarner Handelskammer: Spielhof 14A, 8750 Glarus; tel. 556401173; fax 556403639; e-mail glhk@landolt-althaus.ch; internet www.glarusnet.ch/glhk; Pres. ANDERS HOLTE; Sec. Dr KARLJÖRG LANDOLT.

Handelskammer beider Basel: Aeschenvorstadt 67, Postfach, 4010 Basel; tel. 612706060; fax 612706005; e-mail hkbb@hkbb.ch; internet www.hkbb.ch; Pres. THOMAS STAEHELIN; 800 mems.

Handelskammer und Arbeitgeberverband Graubünden: Hinterm Bach 40, 7000 Chur; tel. 812543800; fax 812543809; e-mail info@hkgr.ch; internet www.hkgr.ch; Pres. LUDWIG LOCHER.

Handelskammer und Arbeitgebervereinigung Winterthur (HAW): Neumarkt 15, 8401 Winterthur; tel. 522130763; fax 522089934; e-mail info@haw.ch; internet www.haw.ch; f. 1992; Pres. THOMAS ANWANDER; Dir CHRISTIAN MODL.

Industrie- und Handelskammer St Gallen-Appenzell: Gallusstr. 16, Postfach, 9001 St Gallen; tel. 712241010; fax 712241060; e-mail sekretariat@ihk.ch; internet www.ihk.ch; f. 1466; Pres. Dr KONRAD HUMMLER; Dir Dr KURT WEIGELT; 1,300 mems.

Industrie- und Handelskammer Thurgau: Schmidstr. 9, Postfach 396, 8570 Weinfelden; tel. 716221919; fax 716226257; e-mail info@ihk-thurgau.ch; internet www.ihk-thurgau.ch; Pres. PETER A. SCHIFFERLE; Dir PETER MAAG; 600 mems.

Solothurner Handelskammer: Grabackerstr. 6, Postfach 1554, 4502 Solothurn; tel. 326262424; fax 326262426; e-mail info@sohk.ch; internet www.sohk.ch; f. 1874; Pres. KURT LOOSLI; Dir ROLAND FÜRST.

Zentralschweizerische Handelskammer: Kapellpl. 2, 6002 Lucerne; tel. 414106865; fax 414105288; e-mail info@hkz.ch; internet www.hkz.ch; f. 1889; Pres. Dr WERNER STEINEGGER; Dir ALEX BRUCKERT; 500 mems.

Zürcher Handelskammer: Bleicherweg 5, Postfach 3058, 8022 Zürich; tel. 442174050; fax 442174051; e-mail direktion@zurichcci.ch; internet www.zurichcci.ch; f. 1873; represents businesses in Zürich, Schaffhausen and Zug cantons; Pres. PETER QUADRI; CEO Dr LUKAS BRINER; 1,800 mems.

INDUSTRIAL AND TRADE ASSOCIATIONS

Associazione Industrie Ticinesi: Corso Elvezia 16, 6901 Lugano; tel. 919118486; fax 919234636; e-mail info@aiti.ch; internet www.aiti.ch; Pres. PAOLO FIORAVANTI; Dir SANDRO LOMBARDI.

Chocosuisse—Verband Schweizerischer Schokoladefabrikanten: Münzgraben 6, 3000 Bern 7; tel. 313100990; fax 313100999; e-mail info@chocosuisse.ch; internet www.chocosuisse.ch; f. 1901; asscn of chocolate mfrs; Pres. WALTER ANDERAU; Dir Dr FRANZ SCHMID; 18 mems, 2 assoc. mems.

Economiesuisse (Swiss Business Federation): Hegibachstr. 47, Postfach 1072, 8032 Zürich; tel. 444213535; fax 444213434; e-mail info@economiesuisse.ch; internet www.economiesuisse.ch; f. 1870; as Schweizerischer Handels- und Industrie-Verein; present name adopted 2000; Pres. GEROLD BÜHRER; Exec. Dir Dr PASCAL GENTINETTA; 163 mems.

Electrosuisse: Luppmenstr. 1, 8320 Fehraltorf; tel. 19561111; fax 19561122; e-mail info@electrosuisse.ch; internet www.electrosuisse.ch; f. 1889 as Swiss Electrotechnical Association; electronics; Chair. MAURICE JACOT; Man. Dir Dr UELI BETSCHART; 1,750 mem. cos.

Fédération de l'Industrie Horlogère Suisse (FH): 6 rue d'Argent, 2501 Bienne; tel. 323280828; fax 323280880; e-mail info@fhs.ch; internet www.fhs.ch; f. 1982 by merger of Swiss Chamber of Watchmaking and Swiss Watchmaking Fed.; watch industry; Pres. JEAN-DANIEL PASCHE; 542 mems.

Föderation der Schweizerischen Nahrungsmittel-Industrien: Thunstr. 82, Postfach 1009, 3000 Bern 6; Münzgraben 6, 3000 Bern 7; and Elfenstrasse 19, 3000 Bern 6; tel. 313562121; fax 313510065; e-mail info@thunstrasse82.ch; internet www.fial.ch; foodstuffs; Secs BEAT HODLER, GUY EMMENEGGER, Dr FRANZ URS SCHMID; 199 mems.

Schweizerischer Baumeisterverband (SBV): Weinbergstr. 49, Postfach, 8035 Zürich; tel. 442588111; fax 442588335; e-mail verband@baumeister.ch; internet www.baumeister.ch; f. 1897; building contractors; Pres. WERNER MESSMER; Dir DANIEL LEHMANN; 3,000 mems.

Schweizerischer Gewerbeverband (SGV) (Swiss Union of Small and Medium Enterprises): Schwarztorstr. 26, 3007 Bern; tel. 313801414; fax 313801415; e-mail info@sgv-usam.ch; internet www.sgv-usam.ch; f. 1879; Pres. EDI ENGELBERGER; Dir Dr PIERRE TRIPONEZ; 257 mems and 25 cantonal sections.

Schweizerischer Verband für visuelle Kommunikation (Viscom): Alderstr. 40, Postfach, 8034 Zürich; tel. 414212828; fax 414212829; e-mail info@viscom.ch; internet www.viscom.ch; f. 1869; printing industry; Pres. PETER EDELMANN; Dir THOMAS GSPONER; 730 mems.

Schweizerischer Versicherungsverband: (see under Insurance).

SGCI Chemie Pharma Schweiz (Swiss Society of Chemical Industries): Nordstr. 15, Postfach, 8021 Zürich; tel. 443681711; fax 443681770; e-mail mailbox@sgci.ch; internet www.sgci.ch; f. 1882; chemical and pharmaceutical industry; Pres. C. MÄDER; Dir-Gen. Dr B. MOSER; c. 250 mems.

Swiss Cigarette: 15 route des Arsenaux, CP 137, 1705 Fribourg; tel. 264255050; fax 264255055; e-mail office@swiss-cigarette.ch; internet www.swiss-cigarette.ch; f. 1933; formerly Communauté de l'industrie suisse de la cigarette; cigarette mfrs; Dir CHANTAL AEBY PÜRRO; three mem. cos.

Swiss Retail Federation: Marktgasse 50, 3000 Bern 7; tel. 313124040; fax 313124041; e-mail info@swiss-retail.ch; internet www.swiss-retail.ch; formerly Verband der Schweizerischen Waren- und Kaufhäuser; Pres. BRUNO FRICK; 33 mem. cos.

Textilverband Schweiz: Beethovenstr. 20, Postfach 2900, 8022 Zürich; tel. 442897979; fax 442897980; e-mail zuerich@swisstextiles.ch; internet www.swisstextiles.ch; f. 1874; textiles and fashion; Pres. MAX R. HUNGERBÜHLER; Dir Dr THOMAS SCHWEIZER; 220 mems.

Verband Schweizerischer Kreditbanken und Finanzierungsinstitute (VSKF): Toblerstr. 97/Neuhausstr. 4, 8044 Zürich; tel. 442504340; fax 442504349; e-mail office@gigersimmen.ch; internet www.vskf.org; asscn of credit banks and finance institutes; Pres. HEINZ HOFER; Sec. Dr ROBERT SIMMEN; 13 mems.

Verband Schweizerische Ziegelindustrie: Elfenstr. 19, 3006 Bern; tel. 313521188; fax 313521185; e-mail mail@domoterra.ch; internet www.domoterra.ch; f. 1874; heavy clay; Sec.-Gen. Dr PETER R. BURKHALTER; 11 mem. cos.

EMPLOYERS' ORGANIZATIONS

Central Organizations

Schweizerischer Arbeitgeberverband (Confed. of Swiss Employers): Hegibachstr. 47, Postfach, 8032 Zürich; tel. 444211717; fax 444211718; e-mail verband@arbeitgeber.ch; internet www.arbeitgeber.ch; f. 1908; Pres. Dr RUDOLF STÄMPFLI; Dir THOMAS DAUM; 78 mems.

Schweizerischer Bauernverband (Union Suisse des Paysans, Lega svizzera dei contadini, Swiss Farmers' Union): Laurstr. 10, 5201 Brugg; tel. 564625111; fax 564415348; e-mail info@sbv-usp.ch; internet www.bauernverband.ch; f. 1897; Pres. HANSJÖRG WALTER; Dir JACQUES BOURGEOIS.

Principal Regional Organizations

Arbeitgeberverband Basel: Aeschenvorstadt 71, Postfach 4010 Basel; tel. 612059600; fax 612059609; e-mail info@arbeitgeberbasel.ch; internet www.arbeitgeberbasel.ch; f. 2007 by merger of Basler Volkswirtschaftsbund and Arbeitgeber-Verband Basel; Pres. MARC R. JAQUET; Dir BARBARA GUTZWILLER-HOLLIGER; 2,500 mems.

Fédération des entreprises romandes: 98 rue de Saint-Jean, CP 5278, 1211 Geneva 11; tel. 227153111; fax 227153213; e-mail info@fer-ge.ch; internet www.fer-ge.ch; Pres. DANIEL DELAY; Sec.-Gen. BLAISE MATTHEY.

Luzerner Industrie-Vereinigung: Kapellpl. 2, Postfach 3142, 6002 Lucerne; tel. 4106889; e-mail info@hkz.ch; internet www.hkz.ch; Pres. WERNER STEINEGGER; Dir ALEX BRUCKERT.

Union des associations patronales genevoises: 98 rue de Saint-Jean, 1211 Geneva 11; tel. 227153241; fax 227380434; e-mail uapg@uapg.ch; internet www.uapg.ch; union of employers' asscns in Geneva; Pres. ANDRÉ GALIOTTO.

Union des industriels valaisans: 6 rue de Lausanne, 1950 Sion; tel. 273232992; fax 273232288; e-mail info@uiv.ch; internet www.uiv.ch; Pres. GONZAGUE OVERNEY.

Verband der Arbeitgeber Region Bern (VAB): Kapellenstr. 14, Postfach 6916, 3001 Bern; tel. 313902581; fax 313902582; e-mail info@berner-arbeitgeber.ch; internet www.berner-arbeitgeber.ch; f. 1919; employers' asscn for the Bern region; Pres. CHRISTIAN KAUTER; Dir Dr CLAUDE THOMANN.

Vereinigung Zürcherischer Arbeitgeberorganisationen: Selnaustr. 30, 8021 Zürich; tel. 588542801; fax 588542801; e-mail dieter.sigrist@swx.com; f. 1947; asscn of Zürich employers' orgs; Pres. THOMAS ISLER; Sec. DIETER SIGRIST.

Sectional Organizations

Arbeitgeberverband Schweizerischer Papier-Industrieller: Bergstr. 110, 8032 Zürich; tel. 442669920; fax 442669949; e-mail zpk@zpk.ch; internet www.zpk.ch; paper mfrs; Pres. FRANK RUEPP; Dir MAX FRITZ; 11 mems.

Convention Patronale de l'Industrie Horlogère Suisse: 65 ave Léopold-Robert, 2301 La Chaux-de-Fonds; tel. 329100383; fax 329100384; e-mail info@cpih.ch; internet www.cpih.ch; f. 1937; watch mfrs; Pres. ELISABETH ZÖLCH; Gen. Sec. FRANÇOIS MATILE; seven mems.

Swissmem (ASM and VSM) (Swiss Mechanical and Electrical Engineering Industries): Kirchenweg 4, Postfach, 8032 Zürich; tel. 443844111; fax 443844242; internet www.swissmem.ch; f. 1905; Pres. JOHANN NIKLAUS SCHNEIDER-AMMANN; Dir PETER DIETRICH; c. 930 mems.

UTILITIES

Electricity

Verband Schweizerischer Elektrizitätsunternehmen: Hintere Bahnhofstr. 10, Postfach, 5001 Aarau; tel. 628252525; fax 628252526; e-mail info@strom.ch; internet www.strom.ch; electricity producers' asscn; f. 1895; Pres. Dr RUDOLF STEINER; Dir JOSEF DÜRR.

Gas

Verband der Schweizerischen Gasindustrie: Grütlistr. 44, Postfach, 8027 Zürich; tel. 412883131; fax 412021834; e-mail vsg@erdgas.ch; f. 1920; Pres. Dr HAJO LEUTENEGGER; Dir JEAN-MARC HENTSCH.

Water

The cantons are responsible for the supply of water, but delegate to the municipalities and communes. As a result Switzerland has some 3,000 water companies. Water is usually supplied by a public company or co-operative, such as the municipal water suppliers for Basel, Winterthur and Zürich (Industrielle Werke Basel, Stadtwerk Winterthur, Wasserversorgung Zürich).

TRADE UNIONS

National Federations

Schweizerischer Gewerkschaftsbund (SGB) (Swiss Fed. of Trade Unions): Monbijoustr. 61, 3007 Bern; tel. 313770101; fax 313770102; e-mail info@sgb.ch; internet www.sgb.ch; f. 1880; main trade union org.; 16 affiliated unions; affiliated to ITUC; Pres. PAUL RECHSTEINER; c. 390,000 mems.

Travail.Suisse: Hopfenweg 21, Postfach 5775, 3001 Bern; tel. 313702111; fax 313702109; e-mail info@travailsuisse.ch; internet www.travailsuisse.ch; f. 2002 by merger of Confédération des Syndicats Chrétiens de Suisse and Fédération des Sociétés Suisses d'Employés; 12 affiliated unions; Pres. MARTIN FLÜGEL; 168,352 mems (Jan. 2008).

Principal Unions

Angestellte Schweiz (Employees Switzerland): Rigipl. 1, Postfach, 8033 Zürich; tel. 443601111; fax 443601112; e-mail info@angestellte

.ch; internet www.angestellte.ch; fed. of 80 unions representing workers in engineering, electrical, metal, chemical and pharmaceutical industries; mem. union of Travail.Suisse; Pres. BENNO VOGLER; 24,237 mems (Jan. 2008).

Comedia (Media): Monbijoustr. 33, Postfach 6336, 3001 Bern; tel. 313906611; fax 313906691; e-mail info@comedia.ch; internet www.comedia.ch; f. 1858; mem. union of SGB; Pres DANIÈLE LENZIN, ROLAND KREUZER; c. 15,000 mems.

Gewerkschaft Kommunikation (Communications): Looslistr. 15, Postfach 370, 3027 Bern; tel. 319395211; fax 319395262; e-mail zentralsekretariat@syndicom.ch; internet www.gewerkschaftkom.ch; f. 1999; represents workers in postal service, telecommunications, ICT and air-traffic control sectors; mem. union of SGB; Pres. ALAIN CARRUPT; c. 37,000 mems.

Hotel & Gastro Union (Hotel and Restaurant Workers): Adligenswilerstr. 22, 6006 Luzern; tel. 414182222; fax 414120372; internet www.hotelgastrounion.ch; f. 1886 as Union Helvetia; present name adopted 2000; mem. union of Travail.Suisse; Pres. BRUNO POMA; 17,721 mems (Jan. 2008).

Organizzazione Christiano-Sociale Ticinese (OCST): Via Balestra 19, 6900 Lugano; tel. 919211551; fax 919235365; e-mail segretariato.cantonale@ocst.com; internet www.ocst.com; f. 1919; Pres. ROMANO ROSSI; 37,086 mems (Jan. 2008).

Schweizerischer Eisenbahn- und Verkehrspersonal-Verband (SEV) (Railway and Transport Workers): Steinerstr. 35, Postfach, 3000 Bern 6; tel. 313575757; fax 313575858; internet www.sev-online.ch; f. 1919; mem. union of SGB; Pres. JÜRG HURNI; c. 48,000 mems.

Schweizerischer Verband des Personals öffentlicher Dienste (Public Services): Birmensdorferstr. 67, Postfach 8279, 8036 Zürich; tel. 442665252; fax 442665253; e-mail vpod@vpod-ssp.ch; internet www.vpod-ssp.ch; f. 1905; mem. union of SGB; Pres. CHRISTINE GOLL; Gen. Sec. STEFAN GIGER; c. 35,000 mems.

Syna (Syndicat Interprofessionnel/Sindicato Interprofessionale): Josefstr. 59, 8031 Zürich; tel. 442797171; fax 442797172; e-mail zuer@syna.ch; internet www.syna.ch; f. 1998 to replace Landesverband freier Schweizer Arbeitnehmer (f. 1919); represents workers in all sectors; mem. union of Travail.Suisse; Pres. KURT REGOTZ; 65,924 mems (Jan. 2008).

Unia: Weltpoststr. 20, Postfach 272, 3000 Bern 15; tel. 313502111; fax 313502211; e-mail info@unia.ch; internet www.unia.ch; f. 2004 by merger of Gewerkschaft Bau und Industrie (GBI), Gewerkschaft Industrie, Gewerbe, Dienstleistungen (SMUV), Gewerkschaft Verkauf, Handel, Transport, Lebensmittel (VHTL) and Gewerkschaft unia; represents construction and engineering industries as well as employees in the retail and catering sectors; mem. union of SGB; Pres RENZO AMBROSETTI, ANDREAS RIEGER; c. 200,000 mems (2007).

Transport

RAILWAYS

Construction of the 35-km Lötschberg rail tunnel was completed in June 2007, shortening travel time between Germany and the Italian city of Milan by about one hour. Excavation of a further 57-km rail tunnel, the Gotthard Base Tunnel, began in 2003; the tunnel was scheduled to become operational in 2016. The Saint Gotthard rail tunnel was opened in 1982.

Schweizerische Bundesbahnen (SBB) (Chemins de fer fédéraux suisses): Hochschulstr. 6, 3000 Bern 65; tel. 512201111; fax 512204265; e-mail railinfo@sbb.ch; internet www.sbb.ch; f. 1902; 3,034 km in 2007 (of which 1,707 km were multiple track); Chair. THIERRY LALIVE D'EPINAY; CEO ANDREAS MEYER.

Small private companies control private railways in Switzerland, chiefly along short mountain routes, with a total length of around 2,032 km. The following are among the principal private railways:

BLS AG: Genfergasse 11, Postfach, 3001 Bern; tel. 313272727; fax 313272910; e-mail info@bls.ch; internet www.bls.ch; f. 1906; 449 km; 11 passenger routes; cargo services on Lötschberg–Simplon route; direct car-train connection from Bern to the Valais and Italy; boat services on Lakes Thun and Brienz; 7 commuter rail services in Bern; Man. Dir Dr MATHIAS TROMP.

Centovalli Railway: Via Franzoni 1, CP 146, 6601 Locarno; tel. 917560400; fax 917560499; e-mail fart@centovalli.ch; internet www.centovalli.ch; f. 1923; 19 km of track in Switzerland; Locarno–Camedo-Domodossola (Italy); Dir MAURO CARONNO.

Matterhorn Gotthard Bahn AG: Nordstr. 20, 3900 Brig; tel. 279277777; fax 279277779; e-mail info@mgbahn.ch; internet www.mgbahn.ch; f. 2003 by merger of BVZ Zermatt-Bahn AG and Furka Oberalp Bahn AG; 25% state-owned, 75% owned by BVZ Holding AG; Zermatt–Brig–Disentis and Andermatt–Göschenen; 144 km; Chair. DANIEL LAUBER; Dir HANS-RUDOLF MOOSER.

Matterhorn Gotthard Bahn Infrastruktur AG: Nordstr. 20, 3900 Brig; tel. 279277777; fax 279277779; e-mail info@mgbahn.ch; internet www.mgbahn.ch; 100% state-owned; responsible for track, overhead catenary equipment, operating control centres, station bldgs and workshops; Pres. ROLF ESCHER.

Matterhorn Gotthard Bahn Verkehrs AG: Nordstr. 20, 3900 Brig; tel. 279277777; fax 279277779; e-mail info@mgbahn.ch; internet www.mgbahn.ch; 75% owned by BVZ Holding AG, 25% state-owned; controls all railway operations, incl. rolling stock, depots and related maintenance; Pres. DANIEL LAUBER.

Montreux-Oberland Bernois: CP 1426, 1820 Montreux; tel. 219898181; fax 219898100; e-mail mob@mob.ch; internet www.mob.ch; f. 1899; 75 km; Montreux–Château d'Oex–Gstaad–Zweisimmen–Lenk i/S; operates tour services incl. GoldenPass Panoramic, GoldenPass Classic, Belle Epoque, Rochers-de-Naye, Les Pléiades and the Chocolate Train; operates funicular railways on Vevey–Chardonne–Mont-Pèlerin and Les Avants–Sonloup routes; Dir R. KUMMROW.

Rhätische Bahn AG (Rhaetian Railway): Bahnhofstr. 25, 7002 Chur; tel. 812549100; fax 812549118; internet www.rhb.ch; f. 1889; 375 km; the most extensive of the privately run railways; Chair., Management Bd ERWIN RUTISHAUSER.

Südostbahn AG: Bahnhofpl. 1A, 9001 St Gallen; tel. 712282323; fax 712282333; e-mail info@sob.ch; internet www.sob.ch; f. 1889; f. 2001 by merger of Schweizerische Südostbahn and Bodensee–Toggenburg-Bahn; 35.8% owned by Federal Govt; 120 km; Pres. GEORG HESS.

ROADS

In 2006 Switzerland had 71,298 km of roads, including 1,758 km of motorways and expressways. The construction of a national network of approximately 1,857 km of motorways is scheduled for completion by 2010. The 17-km road tunnel through the Saint Gotthard Pass, a European road link of paramount importance, was opened in 1980.

Swiss Federal Roads Office (Bundesamt für Strassen/Office fédéral des routes): Mühlestr. 2, Ittigen, 3003 Bern; tel. 313229411; fax 313232303; e-mail info@astra.admin.ch; internet www.astra.admin.ch; Dir RUDOLF DIETERLE.

INLAND WATERWAYS

Inland navigation legislation is the responsibility of the Confederation, but sovereignty over the waterways rests with the cantons. This means, in practice, that the Confederation limits its activities to the supervision of the licensed shipping companies (passenger ships and the related infrastructure, such as landing stages) and pilots; the cantons supervise pleasure-boat navigation (sports boats, i.e. sail and motor boats, etc.) and the non-licensed passenger vessels and goods shipping on the lakes and rivers.

SHIPPING

In 2007 Switzerland's registered merchant fleet comprised 32 vessels, with an aggregate displacement of 588,622 grt. The principal shipping companies in Switzerland are:

ABCmaritime: 1 rue Perdtemps, 1260 Nyon; tel. 223657100; fax 223657111; e-mail info@abcmaritime.ch; internet www.abcmaritime.ch; f. 1982; ship management; Man. Dir PETER ZÜRCHER.

Agility Logistics AG: Sankt Jakobs-Str. 220, 4002 Basel; tel. 613165151; fax 613133133; e-mail oceanfreight@natural.info; internet www.agilitylogistics.com; fmrly Natural van Dam AG; shipping management and freight forwarder; CEO, Europe BEAT SIMON.

Keller Shipping Ltd: Holbeinstr. 68, Postfach 3479, 4002 Basel; tel. 612818686; fax 612818679; e-mail info@lloydsagency.ch; internet www.lloydagency.ch; agency of Lloyds of London (United Kingdom) in Switzerland and Liechtenstein; Pres. A. R. KELLER.

Mediterranean Shipping Co SA: 40 ave Eugène-Pittard, 1206 Geneva; tel. 227038888; fax 227038787; e-mail info@mscgva.ch; internet www.mscgva.ch; f. 1970; operates 376 container vessels (March 2008); Dir G. APONTE.

Reederei Zürich AG: Bergstr. 109, 8030 Zürich; tel. 4112571040; fax 616393466; e-mail webmaster@reedereizurich.com; internet www.reedereizurich.com; ship management.

Suisse-Atlantique, Société de Navigation Maritime SA: 7 ave des Baumettes, CP 48, 1020 Renens 1; tel. 216372201; fax 216372202; e-mail activity@suisat.com; world-wide tramping services; Pres. E. ANDRE; Dir C. DIDAY.

CIVIL AVIATION

Switzerland's principal airports are situated at Zürich and Geneva. A major airport at Basel-Mulhouse-Freiburg (EuroAirport) serves northern Switzerland, but is situated across the border in France.

Darwin Airline: Lugano Airport, 6982 Agno; tel. 916124500; fax 916124520; e-mail info@darwinairline.com; internet www

SWITZERLAND

.darwinairline.com; f. 2003; low-cost airline; flights from four Swiss airports to destinations in Italy and Spain; Pres. SERGIO ERMOTTI; CEO FABIO PARINI.

Edelweiss Air: Operations Center, Postfach, 8058 Zürich-Flughafen; tel. 438165060; fax 438165061; e-mail office@edelweissair.ch; internet www.edelweissair.ch; f. 1995; operates charter flights to destinations in Italy, Spain, eastern Europe and north Africa; acquired by Swiss in 2008; CEO KARL KISTLER.

Swiss (Swiss International Air Lines): Postfach, 4002 Basel; tel. 615820000; fax 615823333; e-mail communications@swiss .com; internet www.swiss.com; f. 1979 as Crossair, took over operations from Swissair and adopted current name in 2002; national carrier operating routes to 76 destinations in 42 countries; subsidiary of Deutsche Lufthansa AG (Germany); CEO CHRISTOPH FRANZ (until 31 May 2009), HARRY HOHMEISTER (from 1 June 2009).

Tourism

Switzerland's principal attractions are the lakes and lake resorts and the mountains. Walking, mountaineering and winter sports are among the chief pastimes. Foreign tourist arrivals at hotels and similar establishments totalled 7.9m. in 2006. Receipts from tourism in that year were 13,334m. Swiss francs.

Switzerland Tourism: Tödistr. 7, 8027 Zürich; tel. 442881111; fax 442881205; e-mail info@myswitzerland.com; internet www .myswitzerland.com; f. 1917; Dir JÜRG SCHMID.

SYRIA

Introductory Survey

Location, Climate, Language, Religion, Flag, Capital

The Syrian Arab Republic lies in western Asia, with Turkey to the north, Iraq to the east and Jordan to the south. Lebanon and Israel are to the south-west. Syria has a coastline on the eastern shore of the Mediterranean Sea. Much of the country is mountainous and semi-desert. The coastal climate is one of hot summers and mild winters. The inland plateau and plains are dry but cold in winter. Average temperatures in Dimashq (Damascus) range from 2°C to 12°C (36°F to 54°F) in January and from 18°C to 37°C (64°F to 99°F) in August. The national language is Arabic, with Kurdish a minority language. According to the UN Relief and Works Agency for Palestine Refugees in the Near East (UNRWA), at December 2008 there were 461,897 Palestinian refugees registered in Syria. More than 80% of the population are Muslims (mostly Sunnis), but there is a substantial Christian minority of various sects. The national flag (proportions 2 by 3) has three equal horizontal stripes, of red, white and black, with two five-pointed green stars in the centre of the white stripe. The capital is Damascus.

Recent History

Syria was formerly part of Turkey's Ottoman Empire. Turkish forces were defeated in the First World War (1914–18) and Syria was occupied in 1920 by France, in accordance with a League of Nations mandate. Syrian nationalists proclaimed an independent republic in September 1941. French powers were transferred in January 1944, and full independence was achieved on 17 April 1946. In December 1949 Syria came under a military dictatorship, led by Brig. Adib Shishekly. He was elected President in July 1953, but was overthrown by another army coup in February 1954.

In February 1958 Syria merged with Egypt to form the United Arab Republic (UAR). In September 1961, following a military coup in Damascus, Syria seceded and formed the independent Syrian Arab Republic. In 1963 Maj.-Gen. Amin al-Hafiz formed a Government in which members of the Arab Socialist Renaissance (Baath) Party were predominant. In February 1966 the army deposed the Government of President al-Hafiz, replacing him with Dr Nur ed-Din al-Atasi. However, in November 1970, after a bloodless coup, the military (moderate) wing of the Baath Party seized power, led by Lt-Gen. Hafiz al-Assad, who was elected President in March 1971. In March 1972 the National Progressive Front (NPF), a grouping of the five main political parties (including the Baath Party), was formed under the leadership of President Assad.

Increasing border tension between Syria and Israel was a major influence leading to the Six-Day War of June 1967, when Israel attacked its Arab neighbours in reprisal for the closure of the Strait of Tiran by the UAR (Egypt). Israeli forces made swift territorial gains, including the Golan Heights region of Syria, which remains under Israeli occupation. An uneasy truce lasted until October 1973, when Egyptian and Syrian forces launched simultaneous attacks on Israeli-held territory. On the Syrian front, there was fierce fighting in the Golan Heights until a cease-fire was agreed after 18 days. In May 1974 the US Secretary of State, Henry Kissinger, secured an agreement for the disengagement of forces. Israel's formal annexation of the Golan Heights in December 1981 effectively impeded the prospect of a negotiated Middle East settlement at this time.

Syria disapproved of the second interim Egyptian-Israeli Disengagement Agreement, signed in September 1975, but agreed to acknowledge it as a *fait accompli* in return for Egypt's acceptance of Syria's role in Lebanon. Syria had progressively intervened in the Lebanese civil war during 1976, finally providing the bulk of the 30,000-strong Arab Deterrent Force (ADF). Syria condemned the Egyptian President, Anwar Sadat, for Egypt's peace initiative with Israel in November and December 1977, the Camp David agreements signed by Egypt and Israel in September 1978, and the subsequent peace treaty concluded between them.

From 1977 frequent assassinations of Alawites (the minority Islamic sect to which Assad belonged) indicated sectarian tension within Syrian society. Assad attributed much of the opposition to the Muslim Brotherhood, a conservative Islamist group, and he ordered the brutal suppression of an uprising in Hamah (Hama), led by the outlawed Brotherhood, in February 1982. From November 1983, after Assad suffered a heart attack, rivals to the succession—including Col Rifaat al-Assad, the President's brother—vied for pre-eminence. In March 1984, following Assad's recovery, the appointment of three Vice-Presidents had the effect of equally distributing power among the President's potential successors and giving none the ascendancy. Assad was also able to rely on a cadre of loyal officers who ensured the army's continued support for the President.

The ADF, based in northern Lebanon, was unable to act when Israel invaded southern Lebanon in June 1982 and surrounded Beirut, trapping Syrian troops and fighters of the Palestine Liberation Organization (PLO). The Syrian and Palestinian forces in Beirut were evacuated in August, under the supervision of a multinational peace-keeping force, and some 50,000 Syrian troops, deployed in the Beka'a valley and northern Lebanon, faced 25,000 Israelis in the south of the country, even though the ADF's mandate had expired. Syria rejected the May 1983 Israel-Lebanon peace agreement, formulated by US Secretary of State George Shultz, refusing to withdraw its forces from Lebanon and continuing to supply the militias of the Lebanese Druze and Shi'ite factions in their fight against the Lebanese Government and the Christian Phalangists. From May 1983 Syria supported a revolt against Yasser Arafat and the leadership of Fatah (the Palestine National Liberation Movement) and by November Syrian and rebel PLO forces had cornered Arafat, the PLO Chairman, in the Lebanese port of Tarabulus (Tripoli). Arafat and some 4,000 of his supporters were eventually evacuated, under UN protection, in December.

In March 1984 President Amin Gemayel of Lebanon capitulated to Syria's influence over Lebanese affairs, and abrogated the May 1983 agreement with Israel. In April President Assad approved Gemayel's plans for a Lebanese government of national unity, giving equal representation to Muslims and Christians. In September Syria arranged a truce to end fighting in Tripoli between the pro-Syrian Arab Democratic Party and the Sunni Tawhid Islami (Islamic Unification Movement). The Lebanese army entered the city in late 1984, under the terms of a Syrian-backed extended security plan, to assert the authority of the Lebanese Government. Syria also authorized Lebanon's participation in talks with Israel to co-ordinate the departure of the Israeli Defence Force (IDF) from southern Lebanon (with that of other security forces), in order to prevent an outbreak of civil violence. After the final stage of the Israeli withdrawal in June 1985, several hundred Israeli troops and advisers remained in Lebanon to assist the Israeli-backed 'South Lebanon Army' (SLA) in policing a narrow buffer zone along the Lebanese side of the international border. Syria removed 10,000–12,000 troops from the Beka'a valley in July, leaving some 25,000 in position.

President Assad was re-elected for a third seven-year term of office in February 1985, and in early 1985 Syria involved itself in seeking to resolve Lebanon's sectarian unrest. Through its proxy, Amal, Syria sought to prevent Yasser Arafat from re-establishing a power base in Beirut, and around 650 people died in the fighting before a cease-fire was agreed in Damascus in June. In December the three main Lebanese militias—the Druze, Amal and Lebanese Forces (LF) Christian militia—met in Damascus to sign a Syrian-brokered accord outlining a politico-military settlement of the civil war. However, the Shi'ite Hezbollah and Sunni Murabitoun militias were not party to the accord and President Gemayel, who had not been consulted during the drafting of the agreement, refused to endorse it. Opposition to the accord was further manifested following Samir Gaegea's promotion to the leadership of the LF in January 1986. Syria brokered another cease-fire in June, this time in the Palestinian refugee camps around Beirut (where fighting between Palestinian guerrillas and Shi'ite Amal militiamen had recently escalated); this proved to be the first stage in a Syrian-sponsored peace plan for Muslim west Beirut. The co-operation of the Amal, Druze and Sunni militias was dependent upon the deployment of uniformed Syrian troops in Beirut for the first time since 1982. Though the activities of the militias in west Beirut were temporarily curbed, the plan was strongly opposed in Christian east Beirut and was not extended to the predominantly Shi'ite southern suburbs, where most of the city's Palestinian refugees lived. By early 1987 heavy fighting had resumed in west Beirut, between Amal forces and an alliance of Druze, Murabitoun and Communist Party militias. Syrian troops (soon numbering some 7,500) succeeded in enforcing a cease-fire in the central and northern areas of west Beirut, but were not deployed in the southern suburbs.

At a general election held in February 1986 the Baath Party and other members of the NPF (excluding the Communist Party, which contested the poll independently) obtained 151 of the 195 seats in the People's Assembly. The communists won nine seats, and independents 35. In November 1987, following the resignation of Abd ar-Rauf al-Kassem as Prime Minister, Mahmoud az-Zoubi, the Speaker of the Assembly, was appointed premier. In May 1988 Syria's interest in the Lebanese presidential election, scheduled to be held in August of that year, prompted an intense period of fighting between Amal and Hezbollah in Beirut's southern suburbs. Overt Syrian support for the candidacy of Sulayman Franjiya (President of Lebanon during 1970–76), and later for Mikhail ad-Daher (after the first postponement of the election), aroused the opposition of Lebanese Christian leaders, who objected to candidates imposed by foreign powers. Consequently, Syria refused to recognize the interim military administration appointed by President Gemayel shortly before his term of office expired. From March 1989 Christian forces, commanded by Gen. Michel Aoun (the head of the interim Lebanese Government), attempted to expel Syrian forces from Lebanon, thereby provoking one of the most violent confrontations of the entire civil war.

In October 1989, under the auspices of the League of Arab States (the Arab League, see p. 344), the Lebanese National Assembly endorsed a charter of national reconciliation (the Ta'if agreement). The Lebanese authorities envisaged a continuing role for the Syrian army in Lebanon by stipulating that it should assist in the implementation of two security plans incorporated in the accord, which also included the constitutional amendments that Syria had long sought to effect in Lebanon. (For further details concerning the Ta'if agreement, see the chapter on Lebanon.) In May 1991 Syria and Lebanon signed a treaty of 'fraternity, co-operation and co-ordination', which was immediately denounced by Israel as a further step towards the formal transformation of Lebanon into a Syrian protectorate. Israel responded by deploying armed forces inside the buffer zone in southern Lebanon, and any likelihood of Israel's compliance with UN Security Council Resolution 425 (adopted in March 1978), which demanded the withdrawal of Israeli armed forces from southern Lebanon, diminished. Syria was the only Arab state which refused to recognize the independent Palestinian state (proclaimed by the Palestine National Council in November 1988), in accordance with its long-standing policy of preventing any other force in Lebanon from acquiring sufficient power to challenge Syrian interests. Meanwhile, Syria persistently denied claims, principally by the USA, that it was sponsoring international terrorism, and refused to restrict the activities of Palestinian groups on its territory. Following a series of bomb attacks in Europe in 1985–86, in November 1986 members of the European Community (EC, now European Union—EU, see p. 255), excluding Greece, imposed limited diplomatic and economic sanctions against Syria, as did the USA and Canada. However, the EC (with the exception of the United Kingdom) ended its ban on ministerial contacts with Syria in July 1987; financial aid was resumed in September, although a ban on the sale of weapons to Syria remained in force.

At elections to the People's Assembly (now expanded to 250 seats) in May 1990, the Baath Party won 134 seats and other parties 32, while 84 seats were reserved for independent candidates. In December 1991 it was announced that 2,864 political prisoners were to be released; this was regarded as the first indication of President Assad's intention to liberalize Syria's political system. In March 1992 Assad indicated that new political parties might in future be established, but he rejected the implementation of foreign democratic frameworks as unsuited to the country's level of economic development. In January 1994 Basel al-Assad, President Assad's eldest son and presumed successor, was killed in a road accident; the President's second son, Bashar, was reportedly instructed to assume the role of his late brother in order to avoid a power struggle. In August senior government officials, including the Commander of the Special Forces, were removed from office in an apparent attempt by Assad to consolidate his position and improve Syria's international standing.

The ruling Baath Party and its NPF allies reinforced their dominance of Syrian affairs at elections to the People's Assembly in August 1994, winning 167 of the 250 seats. In November 1995—the 25th anniversary of President Assad's seizure of power—some 1,200 political prisoners, including members of the banned Muslim Brotherhood, were released under an amnesty, while a number of the Brotherhood's leaders were allowed to return from exile. During 1996 there were reports of several explosions in Damascus, in addition to a number of attacks on Syrian targets in Lebanon. In January 1997 the Syrian-based Islamic Movement for Change claimed responsibility for a bomb attack in central Damascus in December 1996, in which 11 people died.

In February 1998 President Assad unexpectedly dismissed his brother, Col Rifaat al-Assad, as Vice-President (a post he had held since 1984, although he had spent much of the intervening period overseas). In July President Assad appointed new chiefs of both the Syrian army and the intelligence service, prompting speculation that he was seeking to extend the political influence of his second son, Bashar.

Elections to the People's Assembly were held on 30 November and 1 December 1998, at which the NPF, led by the ruling Baath Party, again won 167 of the 250 seats. On 11 February 1999 a national referendum ratified the incoming Assembly's decision to nominate President Assad for a fifth term of office. It was widely speculated that Bashar would be promoted to the vice-presidency in a new administration, having already been promoted to the rank of army colonel in January, and reportedly granted new powers over important domestic matters. In June the Syrian authorities were said to be undertaking an 'unprecedented' campaign, led by Bashar al-Assad, to counter corruption in public office. Several leading officials and businessmen were subsequently incarcerated, and in October, following a nine-month trial, a former director of Syria's intelligence service received a lengthy prison sentence for alleged corruption and embezzlement of public funds. Details emerged in September of large-scale arrests (involving 1,000 people, according to some reports) by security forces in Damascus and Al-Ladhiqiyah (Latakia) against supporters and relatives of Rifaat al-Assad. Subsequent closures of Rifaat's interests (including port facilities in Latakia) provoked several days of violent clashes between his supporters and the security forces, in which, according to reports rejected by the Government, hundreds of people were killed or injured.

Having accepted the resignation of Mahmoud az-Zoubi and his administration in March 2000, President Assad named Muhammad Mustafa Mero, formerly governor of Halab (Aleppo), as Prime Minister. A new Cabinet was subsequently inaugurated, with a programme to accelerate social and economic reforms, to strengthen anti-corruption measures, and to resume peace negotiations with Israel. In all, 22 new ministers were appointed (including a number of younger technocrats and supporters of Bashar al-Assad), although the foreign affairs, defence and interior portfolios remained unchanged. In May az-Zoubi was expelled from the Baath Party for alleged 'irregularities and abuses' during his period in office. His assets were subsequently seized, and he was expected to stand trial on corruption charges. However, in late May official sources reported that az-Zoubi had committed suicide.

President Assad died on 10 June 2000. Shortly after his death the People's Assembly amended the Constitution, lowering the minimum age required of a president from 40 to 34 years, thus enabling Bashar al-Assad to assume the presidency. Bashar al-Assad was also nominated as Commander-in-Chief of the Armed Forces, and his military rank was upgraded to that of Lieutenant-General. Following approval of Bashar's nomination for the presidency by the People's Assembly in late June (the Baath Party having already endorsed his candidacy), a nation-wide referendum on the succession was scheduled for July; the First Vice-President, Abd al-Halim Khaddam, assumed the role of acting President. In mid-June Bashar al-Assad was elected Secretary-General of the Baath Party. Rifaat al-Assad claimed that the assumed succession by Bashar was unconstitutional, and declared that he would challenge his nephew for the presidency. (The Syrian authorities reportedly issued a warrant for Rifaat's arrest should he attempt to enter the country from exile.) At the national referendum held on 10 July, Bashar al-Assad (the sole presidential candidate) received the endorsement of a reported 97.29% of voters. In his inaugural address to the People's Assembly on 17 July, President Assad emphasized as priorities for his administration economic reform, the elimination of official corruption and the conclusion of a peace treaty with Israel.

In July 2000 the new President released a significant number of political prisoners, the majority of whom were communists and members of the Muslim Brotherhood. Nevertheless, in September a statement by 99 Syrian intellectuals, published in the Lebanese press, demanded increased democracy and freedom of expression, an end to the state of emergency (in force since 1963) and the release of political detainees. In November the army deployed tanks and armoured vehicles in the southern region of As-Suweida, in order to quell three days of violent clashes between members of the Sunni bedouin and Druze communities; 20 people died in the fighting, and some 200 were injured. On the 30th anniversary of his father's seizure of power, commemorated in mid-November, President Bashar al-Assad declared an amnesty for about 600 political detainees, as well as a general amnesty for several non-political offences. The decision to free as many as 100 Lebanese prisoners was widely viewed as a gesture of goodwill at a time when influential elements within Lebanon were demanding a lessening of Syrian influence in Lebanese political life.

In January 2001 a group of at least 1,000 intellectuals, among them a prominent businessman and deputy, Riad Seif, urged the Syrian regime to approve political reforms. They demanded the suspension of martial law, the holding of free elections, a free press, the release of political prisoners and an end to discrimination against women. Later that month a new 'liberal' political organization, the Movement for Social Peace, was reportedly established under Seif's leadership; there were, however, reports that it had subsequently been disbanded. Meanwhile, following a decision by the Baath Party in November 2000 to permit the other political parties in the NPF to issue their own newspapers, it was announced in early 2001 that the first non-state-controlled newspaper for several decades was to be published by the Communist Party. Syria's first privately owned newspaper for almost 40 years was also issued from February, while the launch was announced of the official newspaper of the Syrian Arab Socialist Union.

In August 2001 an independent deputy, Mamoun al-Homsi, was detained after starting a hunger strike in protest at official corruption and the Government's failure to end martial law. In September the leader of the Communist Party, Riad at-Turk, was taken into custody on charges of defaming the presidency (he had reportedly criticized the system of 'hereditary succession'). A few days later Riad Seif, who had held an 'illegal' discussion forum on political reform (the authorities had recently required that such forums be approved in advance), was arrested. Trial proceedings began in October against al-Homsi and Seif, and in March 2002 al-Homsi was convicted of 'attempting to change the Constitution by illegal means' and sentenced to a five-year custodial term. Seif also received a five-year gaol sentence in April, having been convicted on similar charges; he was released from prison in January 2006. In June 2002 at-Turk was sentenced to two-and-a-half years' imprisonment, although he was freed by President Assad in November, reportedly on 'humanitarian grounds'. Meanwhile, in November 2001 some 120 political prisoners were released under a general amnesty. In January 2002 legislation relating to private broadcasting was relaxed.

President Assad effected an extensive reorganization of the Government in December 2001. Prime Minister Mero retained his post, as did the Ministers of Defence and Foreign Affairs (the long-serving Minister of Foreign Affairs, Farouk ash-Shara', additionally became the fourth Deputy Prime Minister), although a new Minister of the Interior, Maj.-Gen. Ali Hammoud (former head of the intelligence service), was named. However, several 'pro-reform' ministers were appointed to strategic portfolios relating to the economy, among them Muhammad al-Atrash as Minister of Finance.

Elections to the People's Assembly were held on 2 and 3 March 2003, at which the NPF, led by the ruling Baath Party, again won 167 of the 250 seats, with the remaining 83 going to independents. Electoral turn-out was estimated to be 63.5%. Opposition parties, under an umbrella grouping called the National Democratic Rally, boycotted the election on the grounds that it was undemocratic. On 9 March the newly reconvened legislature elected the Deputy Prime Minister in charge of Public Services, Muhammad Naji al-Otari, as the new Speaker of the People's Assembly. Al-Otari was replaced as Deputy Prime Minister by Muhammad Safi Abu Wdan in late March.

In July 2003 it was reported that President Bashar al-Assad had adopted a decree effectively ending the Baath Party's monopoly on government, military and public sector positions. In September Prime Minister Mero resigned, along with his Cabinet, apparently as a result of his failure to accelerate the process of political reform. Al-Otari was appointed as the new Prime Minister, and his first Cabinet was announced at the end of the month. Notable new appointments included Dr Muhammad al-Hussain, a former Deputy Prime Minister, as Minister of Finance, and Ahmad al-Hassan as Minister of Information. Soon afterwards at least 16 government officials were dismissed as part of a new anti-corruption campaign. In September assets belonging to the former Minister of Industry in the Government of Prime Minister Mero, Dr Issam az-Zaim, were seized in connection with alleged corruption at a state-owned textile plant in Latakia. In May 2004 Maj.-Gen. Mustafa Tlass retired from the posts of Minister of Defence and Deputy Commander-in-Chief of the Armed Forces; he was succeeded in both posts by armed forces Chief of Staff Hasan at-Turkmani, who was in turn replaced by Gen. Ali Habib (hitherto Special Forces Commander).

Issues of civil rights came to the fore in early 2004. In February a prominent lawyer and human rights activist, Haitham Malih, was prevented from travelling to the United Arab Emirates; the Syrian Human Rights Association claimed that Malih was being punished for having criticized the ongoing state of emergency (in force since 1963) in a speech he made to the German Bundestag (Federal Assembly) two months earlier. At the same time the Lebanese newspaper *An-Nahar* published a petition signed by 1,500 Syrian intellectuals, democratic activists and lawyers urging the Government to instigate radical reforms, including the lifting of the state of emergency and the release of political prisoners. At the end of the month foreigners were banned from studying at the 20 Islamic schools licensed by the Ministry of Labour and Social Affairs; they would henceforth only be allowed to study Islamic law at Damascus University. Although the official reason given was that the degrees awarded by the schools were not yet officially recognized, the decision was widely regarded as a crackdown by the secular regime on foreign Islamists who were using their studies as a cover for militant, fund-raising or recruitment activities.

There was a widespread outbreak of violent, predominantly Kurdish, protest in March 2004. The unrest started in the north-eastern town of Al-Qamishli, close to the border with Turkey, when fighting at a football match escalated into large-scale anti-Government protests and fighting between the Arab majority and Kurdish minority; a number of deaths were reported. Minister of the Interior Hammoud travelled to the region to oversee the quelling of the violence, and the Government accused Kurdish political groups of deliberately inciting the riots. However, the unrest quickly spread to the town of Al-Hasakah, and Kurdish émigrés in many European countries staged demonstrations of solidarity with the Kurds outside Syrian embassies. There were also outbreaks of violence at commemorations of the anniversary of a chemical attack by the former Iraqi regime of Saddam Hussain on the Kurdish town of Halabja, in northern Iraq, in 1988, and at least seven Kurds were reported to have been killed in Aleppo and Afrin. By April 2004 it appeared that hundreds of Kurds were still being detained by the authorities in connection with the previous month's clashes, and Amnesty International called for an independent inquiry into the unrest and for any remaining detainees to be either charged or released. In connection with the violence, in June it was alleged that Syrian military intelligence had announced to three senior Kurdish leaders the end of state tolerance of the actitivities of unlicensed Kurdish parties; hundreds of Kurds allegedly remained in custody, having been arrested on suspicion of involvement in the March incident. Meanwhile, in April 2004 a car bomb exploded outside the former offices of the UN Disengagement Observer Force in Damascus; an exchange of fire between police and four people fleeing the scene resulted in the deaths of two assailants, a police officer and a bystander; the other two attackers were arrested by the authorities.

In July and August 2004, as part of an amnesty declared by President Assad, 251 political prisoners were freed, including members of the Muslim Brotherhood and Imad Shiash, who had been serving a prison sentence since 1975 for his membership of the proscribed Arab Communist Organization. In October Assad announced a significant reorganization of the Council of Ministers, dismissing eight ministers from their posts. Prominent appointees included Maj.-Gen. Ghazi Kanaan, a former head of Syrian military intelligence in Lebanon, who assumed the interior portfolio from Hammoud, and Mahdi Dakhlallah, a well-known journalist, who was appointed Minister of Information. In February 2005 it was reported that Maj.-Gen. Khalil had reached retirement age, and had been replaced as military intelligence chief by Brig.-Gen. Asef Shawkat. (For further details regarding internal political developments, see below.)

In July 1991, following a meeting with the US Secretary of State, James Baker, President Assad agreed for the first time to participate in direct negotiations with Israel at a regional peace conference, for which the terms of reference would be a comprehensive settlement based on UN Security Council Resolutions 242 (of 1967) and 338 (1973). In August 1991 the Israeli Cabinet formally agreed to attend a peace conference on terms proposed by the USA and the USSR. An initial, 'symbolic' session of the conference was held in Madrid, Spain, in October, and attended by Israeli, Syrian, Egyptian, Lebanese and Palestinian-Jordanian delegations. Syria's principal aim was to recover the Golan Heights, occupied by Israel since 1967. However, it emphasized that it was not prepared to achieve national goals at the expense of a comprehensive Middle East peace settlement. Syria regarded the Declaration of Principles on Palestinian Self-Rule in the Occupied Territories—the basis of a peace settlement signed by Israel and the PLO in September 1993—as deeply flawed. Furthermore, President Assad viewed the secret negotiations between Israel and the PLO prior to the Declaration of Principles as having undermined the united Arab position in the peace process, and Syria gave no indication that it would cease to support those Palestinian factions, such as the Damascus-based Popular Front for the Liberation of Palestine—General Command (PFLP—GC), which actively opposed the accord.

President Assad met US President Bill Clinton in Geneva, Switzerland, in January 1994—his first such meeting with a US leader since 1977—in an attempt to give fresh impetus to the Syrian track of the peace process. In June Syria reacted warily to the signing by Jordan and Israel of 'sub-agendas' for future bilateral discussions, and continued to adhere to the principle of a united Arab approach to negotiation with Israel. In September Israel published details of a plan for the partial withdrawal of its armed forces from the Golan Heights; Syria rejected the proposals, although President Assad continued to affirm his willingness to achieve peace with Israel. Clinton visited Damascus in October for talks with Assad (the first visit by a US President to Syria for some 20 years), in a further attempt to facilitate the resumption of dialogue between Syria and Israel. However, it was not until March 1995 that bilateral negotiations finally resumed.

In May 1995 Israel and Syria concluded a 'framework understanding on security arrangements', in order to facilitate the participation in the discussions of the two countries' military Chiefs of Staff. Israel stated publicly that it had proposed a four-year timetable for the withdrawal of its armed forces from the Golan Heights, but that Syria had insisted on one of 18 months. In June the Israeli and Syrian Chiefs of Staff held talks in Washington, DC. Negotiations became deadlocked once again, however, and the situation was aggravated by political turmoil in Israel following the assassination of the Prime Minister, Itzhak Rabin, in November. The acting Israeli Prime Minister, Shimon Peres, indicated that no further discussions would take place until after the Israeli general election in May, owing to Syria's refusal to condemn the violence in Israel and to take firmer action against terrorism generally. Following the election to the Israeli premiership of Likud leader Binyamin Netanyahu, an emergency Arab League summit meeting, held in Cairo, Egypt, in June, urged the new right-wing Government in Israel not to abandon the principle of negotiating 'land-for-peace', and demanded the removal of all Israeli settlements in the Golan Heights and their return to Syria. Netanyahu rejected the 'land-for-peace' policies of his Labour predecessor and also insisted that continued Israeli sovereignty over the Golan Heights must be the basis of any peace settlement with Syria. The redeployment, in September, of Syrian armed forces in Lebanon to positions in the Beka'a valley gave rise to speculation in Israel that Syria, frustrated at the lack of progress in the peace process, might be preparing an attack on Israeli forces.

The Israeli-Syrian peace initiative was further interrupted by the construction of a controversial new Jewish settlement at Jabal Abu Ghunaim (Har Homa) in Arab East Jerusalem in March 1997. Prospects of a resumption in negotiations were further frustrated after the Israeli Knesset approved a preliminary reading of proposed legislation stipulating that the return of land to Syria would require the approval of at least two-thirds of deputies. In March 1998 Syria accused Israel of attempting to sabotage its relationship with Lebanon after the Israeli Prime Minister offered to withdraw from southern Lebanon in exchange for a security arrangement before reaching a formal agreement with Syria regarding the Golan Heights. Both Syria and Lebanon reiterated that any withdrawal must be unconditional, in compliance with UN Security Council Resolution 425. Syria was sceptical regarding the likely success of the US-brokered Wye Memorandum, signed in October by Israel and the Palestinian (National) Authority (PA), towards achieving a lasting peace in the Middle East, and President Assad again demanded a resumption of 'land-for-peace' negotiations.

Syria welcomed the success of Ehud Barak and his Labour-led One Israel coalition in the Israeli elections of May 1999. Barak reportedly proposed a five-phase plan to negotiate peace with Syria and to effect an Israeli withdrawal from southern Lebanon. Syria responded with the demand that Barak uphold his pre-election pledge to withdraw from Lebanon within one year of his election, and to resume peace talks from their point of deadlock in 1996. At the inauguration of the new Israeli Cabinet in early July 1999, Barak promised to negotiate a bilateral peace with Syria, based on UN Security Council Resolutions 242 and 338, thus apparently signalling to the Assad regime his intention to return most of the occupied Golan Heights to Syria in exchange for peace and normalized relations. In mid-July, prior to a meeting in Washington, DC, between Barak and President Clinton, Syria was reported to have warned dissidents of Damascus-based Palestinian organizations to cease their military operations against Israel, and to have interrupted the supply of Iranian weapons to Hezbollah guerrillas in southern Lebanon. Moreover, in late July Syria reported a 'cease-fire' with Israel, although mutual disagreements remained, most notably over the point at which previous negotiations had been suspended. In September, as Israel and the PA signed the Sharm esh-Sheikh Memorandum (or Wye Two—see the chapter on Israel) in Egypt, US Secretary of State Madeleine Albright held talks with President Assad in Damascus.

In early December 1999 Israel and Syria agreed to resume negotiations from the point at which they had stalled in 1996 (this was following mediation by Clinton). The first round of discussions between the Syrian Minister of Foreign Affairs, Farouk ash-Shara', and the Israeli premier, Ehud Barak, was opened by the US President in mid-December 1999 in Washington, DC. Both sides agreed to resume discussions in the following month, and in late December Syria and Israel were reported to have agreed an informal 'cease-fire' in order to limit the conflict in Lebanon. A second round of talks between ash-Shara' and Barak proceeded in early January 2000 (with the involvement of Clinton) in Shepherdstown, West Virginia. Syria and Israel had agreed meanwhile on the establishment of committees to discuss simultaneously the issues of borders, security, normalization of relations, and water sharing. However, in mid-January the peace talks were postponed indefinitely. Syria declared that it required a 'written' commitment from Israel to withdraw from the Golan Heights prior to a resumption of talks, while Israel demanded the personal involvement of President Assad in the negotiating process, and that Syria take action to restrain Hezbollah in southern Lebanon. In March the Israeli Cabinet voted unanimously to withdraw its forces from Lebanon by July, even in the absence of a peace settlement with Syria, while the Knesset voted to change the majority required in the event of an Israeli withdrawal from the Golan from 50% of participating voters to 50% of the registered electorate.

In May 2000 ash-Shara' hosted discussions in Palmyra with his Egyptian and Saudi Arabian counterparts in an effort to co-ordinate a united Arab position towards the USA and Israel prior to the planned Israeli withdrawal from southern Lebanon. Reports following the talks suggested that Saudi Arabia and Egypt had pledged military support to Syria in the event of Israeli aggression. The accelerated withdrawal of Israeli armed forces from southern Lebanon was completed on 24 May, several weeks ahead of the original Israeli deadline. Following the death, in June, of President Assad, and the succession of his second son, Bashar al-Assad, in July, the Israeli-Syrian track of the Middle East peace process remained stalled. Nevertheless, Bashar indicated a desire to resume negotiations in the near future, although he emphasized that Syrian policy on the Golan Heights remained unchanged. The escalation of the Palestinian al-Aqsa *intifada* from September strained Syria's relations with Israel and, as tensions increased throughout the Middle East, Israel accused Syria of involvement in the abduction of Israeli military personnel by Hezbollah in the disputed Shebaa Farms area of southern Lebanon. (Shebaa Farms has been designated by the UN as being part of Syria, and thus subject to the Syrian track of the peace process.) During an emergency summit meeting of the Arab League held in Cairo in October, Farouk ash-Shara' urged all Arab countries to sever diplomatic ties with Israel.

Following the election of Likud leader Ariel Sharon to the Israeli premiership in February 2001, President Assad again reiterated Syria's position: namely that negotiations would only be resumed upon a full Israeli withdrawal from the Golan Heights. Tensions between the two sides increased in April following an attack by Israeli forces on a Syrian radar station in eastern Lebanon, in which at least one Syrian soldier died. In December, following talks in Damascus between Egypt's President Hosni Mubarak and President Assad, Egypt and Syria issued a joint statement condemning Israeli military actions in the West Bank and Gaza, and called on the international community to put pressure on Israel to halt its 'aggression'. In January 2003 a Syrian soldier was killed during a rare exchange of gunfire between Israeli and Syrian forces in the Golan Heights. In November 2004 Assad announced that he was willing to resume peace talks with Israel unconditionally (although it was unclear whether the Syrian President intended for negotiations to resume from where they had collapsed in 2000—see above); however, Israel refused to conduct talks with Syria until it closed the headquarters of Hamas and Islamic Jihad, and Assad rejected Israel's setting of conditions as unacceptable.

In April 2003 US President George W. Bush handed to the Israeli and Palestinian leaderships the so-called 'roadmap' peace plan, which had been drawn up by the Quartet group (comprising the USA, the UN, Russia and the EU). The plan envisaged an end to the Arab–Israeli conflict and the creation of a sovereign Palestinian state by 2005–06 (for full details of the roadmap, see the chapter on Israel). A fully negotiated peace settlement between Israel and Syria was one of the objectives of the roadmap, but Syria was keen to emphasize that the new plan must run in tandem with the Syrian track of negotiations on the Golan Heights issue; however, in May 2003 President Assad reportedly assured Javier Solana, the EU's High Representative for the Common Foreign and Security Policy, that Syria would unconditionally accept the roadmap. An offer from Syria to resume peace talks with Israel in July was firmly rejected by Israeli Prime Minister Ariel Sharon as 'insincere'. In the following month Israel accused Syria of masterminding an attack by Hezbollah in Shebaa Farms. In October Israel launched an air attack against an alleged Palestinian militant training camp inside Syria. Israel claimed that the camp at Ain Saheb near Damascus was being used by Hamas and Islamic Jihad, which the latter group denied, while another Palestinian militant group, the Popular Front for the Liberation of Palestine (PFLP), stated that the facility at Ain Saheb was in fact not in use. Israel insisted that the attack was not directed against Syria, but was in retaliation for a suicide bomb attack in Haifa, Israel, in which 19 Israelis were killed. In January 2004 President Assad rejected Israeli offers to resume peace negotations, describing them as a 'media manouevre'. Following an Israeli warning of military action against Syria for its presumed involvement in suicide attacks in Israel that killed 16 people in August, a senior Hamas official was assassinated in Damascus in September, provoking an angry response from Syrian officials.

There was increasing agitation in Lebanon for a cessation of Syrian influence on Lebanese political affairs after the inauguration of a new Syrian President and the Israeli withdrawal from southern Lebanon. In July 2000 Maronite Christian leaders in Lebanon requested that President Assad release all Lebanese political prisoners held in Syria, and in the following month a coalition of Christian political parties in Lebanon urged voters there to boycott the forthcoming parliamentary elections, on the grounds that Syria would predetermine the outcome of the poll. The results of the elections, at which former premier Rafik Hariri resoundingly defeated the Syrian-sponsored Government of Selim al-Hoss, served to intensify speculation about Syria's future role in Lebanese affairs. Syrian officials reacted angrily when the Lebanese Druze leader and traditional ally of Syria, Walid Joumblatt, demanded a 're-evaluation' of Syria's role in Lebanon. In December 46 Lebanese prisoners (many of whom were Christians detained by Syrian troops during the civil war) were released from Syrian detention; hitherto Syria had never confirmed that it was holding Lebanese political prisoners.

In June 2001 Syria withdrew some 6,000–10,000 of its armed forces from predominantly Christian districts of east and south Beirut, and from Mount Lebanon; some of the troops were redeployed in the Beka'a valley. However, Syria retained a number of military bases in strategic areas of the Lebanese capital. President Assad's discussions with President Emile Lahoud in March 2002 reportedly centred on the forthcoming Arab League conference in Beirut, at which Saudi Arabia's Crown Prince Abdullah was formally to submit his proposals for a Middle East peace settlement (for further details, see the chapter on Lebanon). The two leaders reportedly demanded that any peace deal should include the right of return for Palestinian refugees. Redeployments of Syrian troops from central Lebanon took place in April 2002, and from northern Lebanon in February 2003. The new Lebanese Government formed under Hariri in April was widely considered to be the most pro-Syrian administration in Lebanon for more than a decade. In June unidentified assailants fired rockets at the studios of Hariri's Future Television in central Beirut. Syria was blamed for having organized the attack, chiefly as a warning to the Lebanese Prime Minister following remarks he made on a state visit to Brazil in which Hariri appeared to call for an improvement in Arab–Israeli relations. Moreover, the attack coincided with a further redeployment of Syrian troops from Lebanon.

Syrian influence on Lebanese political affairs continued during 2004: following meetings with Syrian officials, Lebanon decided not to effect any government changes in response to a strike in the southern suburbs of Beirut in late May, and Prime Minister Hariri, also following meetings with Syrian officials, withdrew his objection to the extension, in August, of President Lahoud's mandate by three years. However, international pressure on Syria increased following the adoption in early September of UN Security Council Resolution 1559, which, without referring to Syria explicitly, demanded that Lebanon's sovereignty be respected and that all foreign forces leave the country. (See the chapter on Lebanon for further details of Lebanese domestic affairs and of the UN resolution.) The Syrian army subsequently redeployed about 3,000 special forces from positions south of Beirut, and further troops were withdrawn in December from the northern town of Batrun and from Beirut's southern suburbs and airport to the Beka'a valley. However, the new Lebanese Government approved by the legislature in November (in which Rafik Hariri had been replaced as Prime Minister by Omar Karami) was regarded as being even more favourable than its predecessor to continued Syrian influence in Lebanese affairs. In December a number of Lebanese political parties issued a joint statement demanding the cessation of foreign interference in the country.

Former Lebanese Prime Minister Rafik Hariri was killed in a car bombing in Beirut on 14 February 2005. Although President Assad condemned the attack, the USA, without accusing Syria of involvement in the incident, withdrew its ambassador to Syria for consultations, and later demanded the complete withdrawal of Syrian troops from Lebanon and a thorough and transparent investigation into the attack. Meanwhile, Syria and Iran agreed to form a 'united front' against foreign threats to their states. Syria declared later in the month that it would redeploy all of its troops in Lebanon to the Beka'a valley. Mass protests against Syria's influence on Lebanese affairs, and against the Syrian military presence in Lebanon, followed, and in late February President Bush demanded that Syria: withdraw all troops and security service personnel from Lebanon; stop using its territory to support militant groups; support free and fair elections in Lebanon; and adhere to UN Security Council Resolution 1559 (see above). The UN Secretary-General, Kofi Annan, called on Syria to withdraw its troops from Lebanon by April.

In late February 2005 Karami announced the resignation of his administration, but, under President Lahoud's request, he and his ministers remained in office pending the appointment of a new government. Opposition groups continued to demand that Syrian army and intelligence personnel withdraw from Lebanon, and that senior Lebanese security officials resign. In early March the US Secretary of State, Condoleezza Rice, reiterated Bush's demands and warned Syria that it was threatening peace and preventing change in the Middle East. She also stated that there was evidence of the involvement of Islamic Jihad in a bombing in Tel-Aviv, Israel, in February. Meanwhile, Presidents Assad and Lahoud agreed at a summit meeting to the withdrawal of Syrian troops to the Beka'a valley by the end of March;

Syria later promised to withdraw all troops before Lebanon's general election in May, and to provide the UN with a timetable for the withdrawal. Rice praised the decision, but urged the two countries to accelerate the process. Syria reportedly withdrew 4,000–6,000 of its troops from Lebanon to Syria in mid-March, removing Syrian soldiers and intelligence agents from their barracks and offices around Tripoli and Beirut; 8,000–10,000 troops reportedly remained in the Beka'a valley. A UN report released in late March blamed Syria for allowing political tension in Lebanon to mount before the murder of Hariri; it also criticized Lebanon's initial attempts to investigate the incident. In early April the UN Security Council approved Resolution 1595, which established an International Independent Investigation Commission (UNIIIC) to investigate Hariri's murder. The German prosecutor Detlev Mehlis was appointed to head the commission. The formation of a new Lebanese administration, headed by newly appointed Prime Minister Najib Mikati, was announced in mid-April. Later in the month Syria declared that it had withdrawn all of its troops and security forces from Lebanon, and in early May a UN team dispatched to Lebanon to confirm the withdrawal announced that thus far it had not found a single Syrian soldier in areas that it had inspected.

Legislative elections were held in Lebanon in four rounds between 29 May and 19 June 2005 (see the chapter on Lebanon). A broad anti-Syrian alliance, led by Rafik Hariri's son, Saad ed-Din al-Hariri, secured the highest number of seats in the National Assembly (72 of 128 seats). A pro-Syrian bloc that included Hezbollah and Amal secured 35 seats, and a bloc led by a former Commander-in-Chief of the Lebanese army, Gen. Michel Aoun, who had allied himself with pro-Syrian factions immediately prior to the elections, won 21 seats. Pro-Syrian Nabih Berri was re-elected as President of the National Assembly in late June, and Fouad Siniora, a close ally of Rafik Hariri, was appointed as Prime Minister. A new Cabinet was installed in July. Syrian President Assad and Prime Minister Otari met Fouad Siniora in Syria in August. The two states reportedly agreed to improve relations based on mutual respect, and Siniora emphasized Lebanon's support of Syria and its commitment to bilateral agreements. Various prominent Lebanese figures opposed to Syrian influence in Lebanon were killed or injured in bomb attacks during mid- to late 2005, including the former Secretary-General of the Parti communiste libanais (Lebanese Communist Party), who was killed in a car bombing in Beirut in June.

At the 10th national congress of the Baath Party in June 2005, President Assad was re-elected as Secretary-General. Vice-President and member of the party leadership Abd al-Halim Khaddam reportedly asked to be relieved of all of his duties, citing a wish to allow more young people to be represented in the party and state leadership. Although there was no confirmation that Khaddam's resignation as Vice-President had been accepted, it was announced that he had not been re-elected to the party leadership. The political committee of the Baath Party endorsed proposals to relax laws relating to the state of emergency, and to produce legislation allowing the formation of independent parties and increased freedom of the press; however, by mid-2009 the proposed reforms had yet to be introduced.

In December 2005 Khaddam, who had been living in exile in Paris since his resignation, held an interview with the Dubai-based satellite television station *Al-Arabia* in which he accused Assad of having personally threatened Rafik Hariri a few months prior to his assassination. Khaddam subsequently declared that, in his view, Assad had ordered Hariri's killing, although he awaited the final decision of the investigating commission. He declared that the current Syrian regime could not be reformed, and called on opposition groups in Syria to co-operate to defeat it. In early January 2006 the Baath Party announced that it had formally expelled Khaddam, accusing him of treachery against the party, his country and the Arab nation for his accusations against the Syrian President. Meanwhile, in December 2005 the People's Assembly unanimously approved a motion calling for Khaddam to be brought to trial on charges of treason and corruption. In January 2006 the Syrian Government froze Khaddam's assets, and in April a military court formally charged the former Vice-President with a series of offences, including inciting a foreign attack on Syrian soil and plotting to seize political and civil power.

In response to reports that Syrian intelligence agents might not have completely withdrawn from Lebanon, the UN announced in June 2005 that it was considering sending a commission to the country to investigate the claims. (Syria continued to assert that it had removed all of its security personnel.) UNIIIC began its inquiry into Rafik Hariri's assassination in mid-June, with a three-month mandate. In August UNIIIC arrested three former Lebanese security officials with close ties to Syria, who had tendered their resignations in April, for questioning regarding the assassination. A fourth security chief, who had retained his post after Hariri's murder, subsequently handed himself in to the organization. A former, pro-Syrian parliamentary deputy was also detained. In mid-October, shortly before UNIIIC issued its first report on the investigation, the official Syrian Arab News Agency announced the death, by suicide, of the Minister of the Interior, Maj.-Gen. Ghazi Kanaan; a formal investigation subsequently confirmed the cause of death. Shortly before his apparent suicide, Kanaan had issued a statement to a Lebanese radio station defending Syria's role in Lebanon and announcing that he had been questioned by UNIIIC, but had not given any evidence against Syria. Some analysts noted that Kanaan, a potential alternative to the Syrian President who had opposed the decision to extend Lebanese President Lahoud's tenure by three years in 2004 (see above), had been seen as a threat to Assad.

According to its first report, issued in October 2005, UNIIIC had found evidence that Lebanese and Syrian intelligence and security services were directly involved in the assassination of Rafik Hariri. Moreover, the report reasoned, the act was too complex and too well planned to have taken place without the approval of senior Syrian security officials and their Lebanese counterparts. UNIIIC expressed its extreme concern at the lack of co-operation of the Syrian authorities. Lebanon and Syria both rejected the report, criticizing the investigation's findings as politically motivated, and Syria announced that it had established a special judicial commission to deal with all matters relating to UNIIIC's mission. The UN commission was granted an extension to its mandate to mid-December. The UN Security Council reacted to the report by adopting Resolution 1636 at the end of October, establishing measures against suspects in the assassination, including prohibitions on travel and the freezing of assets, and urging Syria to co-operate fully with the investigation commission and to detain suspects identified by the inquiry as suspects in Hariri's assassination, threatening unspecified 'further action' should Syria not fulfil the resolution's demands. The Security Council gave Syria until 15 December to comply with the resolution, which was sponsored by the USA, France and the United Kingdom. Syria reported in November that it had arrested six government officials for questioning. Meanwhile, in late October, the UN Special Envoy, Terje Roed-Larsen, published his report on compliance with UN Security Council Resolution 1559, in which he commended Syria's withdrawal of its troops from Lebanon, but criticized Lebanon for not complying with the resolution's demands.

In his second report to the UN Security Council, issued in December 2005, Mehlis noted that Syria had presented five officials suspected of involvement in the murder of Hariri to UNIIIC for interrogation in Vienna, Austria. However, the report again accused Syria of reluctance to co-operate with the investigating body and of hindering the investigation. UNIIIC had found further evidence of the involvement of the Lebanese and Syrian intelligence and security services in the assassination, and Mehlis identified 19 suspects, six of whom were Syrian (of which five were those currently under interrogation in Vienna). Mehlis resigned as head of UNIIIC shortly after he presented the report, citing personal and professional reasons; he was replaced by Serge Brammertz. UNIIIC's mandate was extended to 15 June 2006.

In January 2006, after Abd al-Halim Khaddam accused President Assad of having personally threatened Hariri (see above), UNIIIC investigators declared that they wished to question President Assad and Syria's Minister of Foreign Affairs ash-Shara'. However, the Minister of Information, Mahdi Dakhlallah, declared that Syria would not permit UNIIIC to interview the President. Brammetz met ash-Shara' and other unspecified Syrian officials in late February. Ash-Shara' announced in March that he had reached an agreement with UNIIIC providing for full Syrian co-operation with the investigation, while maintaining the country's 'sovereignty and dignity'. (Khaddam reiterated his claims that Assad was ultimately responsible for Hariri's assassination throughout 2006, and called for a popular revolt to effect the President's removal from office.)

President Assad effected a comprehensive reorganization of the Council of Ministers in February 2006. Ash-Shara' was appointed as Vice-President to replace Khaddam, and given additional responsibility for Foreign Affairs and Information; he was replaced as Minister of Foreign Affairs by Walid Mouallem. Brig.-Gen. Bassam Abd al-Majid was accorded the Interior portfolio, vacant since the death of Ghazi Kanaan in October 2005. In March 2006 Dr Najah al-Attar was also named as a Vice-President.

In May 2006 274 Lebanese and Syrian intellectuals and activists signed the Beirut-Damascus Declaration, a petition urging the Syrian Government to reassess its policy on Lebanon, to respect the sovereign independence of that country and to establish normal diplomatic relations; many of those who signed the Declaration were subsequently arrested. In April 2007 Anwar al-Bunni, a well-known advocate for democratic reform in Syria, was convicted on charges of disseminating false information and thereby damaging national morale, and was sentenced to five years' imprisonment. Four other prominent Syrian activists, all of whom, like al-Bunni, had signed the Declaration, were convicted on similar charges in the following month; two received three-year prison sentences, while the other two (convicted *in absentia*) were sentenced to 10 years' imprisonment. Human rights groups quickly denounced the convictions, which they claimed were a violation of the right of free speech and part of an ongoing process of intimidation by means of which the Syrian Government hoped to silence dissidents.

Meanwhile, the third and fourth UNIIIC reports on the assassination of Hariri were published in March and June 2006, respectively. Recent Syrian co-operation was described as 'generally satisfactory', and the investigators claimed to have made considerable progress with regard to their understanding both of the circumstances surrounding the murder and of the links between the planners and the perpetrators of the killing. However, the report acknowledged that more thorough investigation was required into alleged links between Hariri's assassination and 14 other attacks against anti-Syrian figures in Lebanon since October 2004. In mid-June 2006 UNIIIC's mandate was extended for another year. The fifth UNIIIC report was released by Brammertz in September, and again described Syrian co-operation with the investigation as 'general satisfactory'.

Syria was forced to deny accusations that it had orchestrated the assassination of Pierre Gemayel, the Lebanese Minister of Industry, renowned for his anti-Syrian disposition, who was shot dead in his car on the outskirts of Beirut in November 2006 (see the chapter on Lebanon). Among those quick to apportion the blame firmly on Syria was Saad ed-Din Hariri, the son of Rafik. The US ambassador to the UN, John Bolton, while refraining from making any explicit accusations, also suggested that Syria might logically be considered a likely suspect in Gemayel's killing. During 2007 the Syrian leadership continued to oppose demands by the international community, including the US Administration, that an international tribunal be established in order to try suspects in Hariri's murder. In response to the adoption by the UN Security Council, in May, of Resolution 1757, establishing a special tribunal for this purpose, Syria emphasized its position that the tribunal represented a violation of Lebanese sovereignty, and that it would refuse to hand over any Syrian suspects to the new body.

In January 2007, in preparation for legislative elections scheduled to take place in April, President Assad approved amendments to electoral legislation, including the introduction of stricter regulations on the financing of campaigns. No changes were made to the quota system by which 167 of the 250 seats were reserved for the NPF, despite widespread demands for its abolition from reformists. Ten days before the polls the Government announced that the number of seats reserved for the NPF would actually be increased to 170, thus reducing the number of seats set aside for independent candidates to just 80. At the elections to the People's Assembly on 22–23 April, voter turn-out was officially reported at 56.1% of the registered electorate; however, opponents of the Government claimed that the true rate of participation was, at most, 10%–20%. Speaking at an official press conference on 26 April, the Minister of the Interior announced that the NPF had secured 172 seats, two more than its recently allocated share and five more than its original two-thirds' quota; the number of independents thus fell to 78. The opposition, which had boycotted the polls, called upon the international community to condemn the elections and to acknowledge the illegitimacy of the newly installed legislature, and both domestic and external human rights groups (as well as even government-controlled newspapers) denounced the elections as undemocratic. In the following month the legislature unanimously approved the Baath Party's nomination of Bashar al-Assad for a second term as President, a national referendum on which was duly held on 27 May. Assad was endorsed for another seven-year term of office by a reported 97.6% of votes; turn-out was officially declared to have been more than 95.8%.

In October 2005 a coalition of political activists and members of banned political organizations had issued a document entitled the Damascus Declaration for Democratic National Change, which urged the establishment, through peaceful means, of a democratic state, built on moderate Islamic principles, with a new constitution to guarantee liberty and human rights for all. The Declaration also appealed for a democratic solution to the issue of Kurdish nationalism. In December 2007 168 signatories convened to re-affirm the Declaration's message and to elect a National Council; Fida' al-Hourani, daughter of Akram al-Hourani, one of the founders of the Baath Party, was elected President. In the weeks following the meeting up to 40 members of the movement were detained; at least 12 senior activists remained in custody in early 2008, among them al-Hourani and other prominent dissidents and human rights campaigners such as Riad Seif, Ali al-Abdullah, Muhammad Darwish, and Akram and Walid al-Bunni (brothers of gaoled activist Anwar al-Bunni). Legal proceedings against 12 dissidents were initiated in July on charges including spreading false information and weakening national morale. The accused, who had pleaded not guilty to all charges, were convicted in October and accorded sentences of between two and two-and-a-half years' imprisonment. A court ruling that granted early release to two of the jailed signatories of the Beirut-Damascus Declaration, was overturned on appeal in November. The decision provoked criticism from international human rights organizations and from the EU. In a report published in February 2009, the US-based Human Rights Watch appealed for the abolition of the Supreme State Security Court, an extra-judicial organ of state which, the organization stated, was used primarily to try suspected dissidents without granting them proper legal representation or the right of appeal.

In mid-February 2008 Imad Mughniyeh, a senior Hezbollah member, was killed in a car bombing in Damascus. Hezbollah claimed the attack had been carried out by Israeli secret service operatives, an allegation that was denied by Israel. The Syrian authorities immediately launched an investigation into the incident. However, the fact that no findings were released prompted widespread speculation concerning the possible involvement of Syrian or other Arab nationals in the bombing. Brig.-Gen. Muhammad Suleiman, a senior adviser and close ally of President Assad, was shot dead near the port city of Tartous in early August. After an initial refusal to comment on Suleiman's death, the Government confirmed the assassination some days later. Suleiman had allegedly acted as a liaison with Hezbollah, as well as with the International Atomic Energy Agency (IAEA—which was investigating Syria's alleged nuclear facility, see below). An inquiry into the assassination was apparently launched by Syrian intelligence services, but no findings had been announced by mid-2009. In late September 2008 a car bomb, detonated close to both a security forces' base and an important Shi'a shrine, on the outskirts of Damascus, killed 17 people and injured at least 14. The bombing was the deadliest attack on Syrian territory for more than 20 years. In November Syrian state television broadcast what it claimed were the confessions of 11 militants responsible for the September bomb attack. The 10 men and one woman, as well as a 12th operative who had carried out the suicide attack, were described as members of Fatah al-Islam, a militant Sunni Islamist group active in the Palestinian refugee camps in Lebanon (q.v.). The confessions also contained the allegation that the group had been funded by Saad ed-Din Hariri's Tayar al-Mustaqbal (Future Movement). Tayar al-Mustaqbal strongly denied this allegation, and countered with the claim that Fatah al-Islam was, in fact, funded by the Syrian intelligence authorities. Unsubstantiated reports in December suggested that the leader of Fatah al-Islam, Shakir al-Abssi, had been either captured or killed by security forces in Syria. In mid-October, meanwhile, there were violent clashes between Syrian security forces and suspected militants at the Yarmuk Palestinian refugee camp, close to Damascus, in which two Iraqi men and a police officer were reportedly killed.

A protracted political crisis in Lebanon, during which pro-Syrian factions, including Hezbollah, obstructed a new presidential election (the tenure of President Lahoud having ended in November 2007), threatened to escalate into civil war in that country during 2008. Syria was swift to deny claims by many Western governments that it was preventing the presidential vote from taking place, and that it was seeking to bring about the collapse of Lebanon's Western-backed Government by providing military assistance to Hezbollah and its allies. However, following the signing of the Qatari-brokered Doha Agreement in May 2008, which ended the political deadlock in Lebanon and led to the formation of a national unity administration and the election of Michel Suleiman as President, renewed rapprochement between Syria and Lebanon became possible. In fact, Syria's support for the agreement was regarded as providing the catalyst for a marked improvement in its international standing generally. A landmark agreement was reached between Lebanon and Syria in mid-July, when the two countries announced that they were to enter into diplomatic relations and open embassies in one another's capitals for the first time. Syria's Minister of Foreign Affairs, Walid Mouallem, visited Beirut in July for further talks on bilateral relations, and President Suleiman made a two-day state visit to Syria in mid-August. During Suleiman's visit it was announced that the work of a committee to demarcate the Lebanese–Syrian border would be resumed. The countries also agreed jointly to investigate the issue of persons missing since Lebanon's civil war and to review existing bilateral agreements. President Assad issued a decree formally establishing diplomatic relations with Lebanon in mid-October. Ziad Baroud, Lebanon's Minister of the Interior, visited his Syrian counterpart in Damascus for talks on security co-operation in November, and, in an unexpected development, Gen. Michel Aoun, leader of the Christian opposition in Lebanon and a former adversary of Syria (see above), was a guest of President Assad in December. By late March 2009 both countries had opened their respective embassies and approved the nominations of the ambassadors: Michel el-Khoury, Lebanon's envoy in Damascus; and Ali Abd al-Karim Ali, Syria's counterpart in Beirut. The Special Tribunal for Lebanon, established to try those suspected of involvement in the assassination of Rafik Hariri (see above) began operating in early March 2009 near The Hague, Netherlands. One of the main suspects in the case, Zuhair as-Siddiq, a former officer in the Syrian intelligence service, was reportedly arrested in Dubai in April 2009.

President Assad announced a significant reorganization of the Council of Ministers in late April 2009, appointing six new ministers. Notable changes included the appointment of Gen. Saeed Muhammad Sammour, a senior military intelligence officer, as Minister of the Interior, in place of Brig.-Gen. Bassam Abd al-Majid, and the appointment of Ahmad Hammoud Younis, a judge and former deputy in the People's Assembly, as the new Minister of Justice. The Ministry of Local Administration and Environment was divided into two separate ministries: Kawkab as-Sabagh Muhammad Jamil ad-Dayeh was appointed to the new post of Minister of State for Environmental Affairs; and Tamer Fouad al-Hijeh became Minister of Local Administration.

The Syrian Government condemned the suicide attacks carried out in New York and Washington, DC, on 11 September 2001. However, Syria was openly critical of the decision of the US Administration of George W. Bush—as part of its world-wide 'war on terror'—to launch a military campaign against targets in Afghanistan linked to the Taliban regime and to the militant Islamist organization held principally responsible for the attacks, the al-Qa'ida (Base) network of Osama bin Laden. In October the British Prime Minister, Tony Blair, undertook an official visit to Syria, to garner Arab support for the US-led campaign in Afghanistan, and asked the Syrian leadership to end its support for militant groups such as Hezbollah and the PFLP. However, President Assad condemned the West's bombing of Afghan civilians and stated that organizations engaged in fighting the Israeli occupation were 'legitimate'. In December 2002 President Bashar al-Assad became the first Syrian leader to visit the United Kingdom, where he expressed his opposition to a US-led military campaign to bring about 'regime change' in Iraq, and rejected Blair's demand to curb militant Palestinian groups operating in Syria. In April of that year US Secretary of Defense Donald Rumsfeld had accused Syria, Iran and Iraq of involvement in terrorism against Israeli civilians. Relations between Syria and the USA deteriorated further during late 2002 and early 2003. Several members of the US Administration proposed the imposition of economic sanctions against Syria as punishment for its continued support for militant Palestinian organizations such as Islamic Jihad, Hamas and the PFLP. US officials also accused Syria of involvement in the illegal purchase of oil from Iraq. In November 2002 the Syrian leadership refused US demands that it close the Damascus office of Islamic Jihad, following a renewed campaign by that organization against targets in Israel.

As the US-led coalition forces launched a military campaign to oust the regime of Saddam Hussain in Iraq in March 2003, the USA also increasingly hinted that Syria might be the next target for a US-imposed 'regime change'. Damascus referred to the campaign in Iraq as an 'illegal invasion'. Moreover, Syrians were angered in late March when a bus close to the border with Iraq was hit by a stray US missile, killing five Syrian civilians. Damascus strongly denied claims by the Bush Administration that it was providing military equipment to Iraq during the conflict. The USA alleged that Syria had assisted leading members of the Iraqi Baath Party to flee the country after the collapse of Saddam Hussain's regime and that Iraqi weapons of mass destruction might have been transported to cross the border into Syria. However, in April President Bush declared that Syria was co-operating with the US-led coalition, having recently sealed its border with Iraq. Nevertheless, US officials from the Department of the Treasury estimated that US $3,000m. of Iraqi money was being held by Syrian-controlled banks in Damascus and Lebanon, in contravention of a UN resolution calling on all Iraqi funds held abroad to be handed over to the US-controlled Iraqi Fund for Development.

In December 2003 US President Bush signed the Syria Accountability Act, which allowed the USA to impose a range of sanctions on Syria unless the country met a series of conditions (including ending its support for terrorist groups). The sanctions were eventually put in place on 11 May 2004; they included a ban on all US exports to Syria other than food or medicine, and a halt to flights between the two countries. Syria rejected the sanctions, asserting that they would not affect the country or its economy, and in October Syria signed a bilateral agreement with the EU for greater economic co-operation, with Syria agreeing to renounce proliferation of nuclear weapons. In December it was reported that evidence had been found that Syria was permitting the training on its territory of militants to be used as insurgent fighters in Iraq, as well as allowing insurgents across the border between the two countries; Syria denied the claims. In May 2005, following reports that Iraqi militants had planned recent bombings at a meeting in Syria, the USA and Iraq urged Syria to prevent foreign fighters from crossing the border into Iraq.

In March 2007 Syria called for a 'serious dialogue' with the USA on a wide range of concerns pertaining to the Middle East. In the following month Nancy Pelosi, Speaker of the US House of Representatives (the third highest ranking elected official in the USA after the President and Vice-President), visited Damascus as part of a wider tour of the region, thus becoming the most senior US official to visit Syria since 2003. Pelosi's unauthorized visit drew strong criticism from President Bush, who, stung by the challenge to his Administration's policy of isolation towards the Syrian Government, accused Pelosi of usurping executive powers and of sending 'mixed signals' to a 'state sponsor of terrorism'. Pelosi, of the Democratic Party, dismissed such censure, pointing out that three Republican congressmen had also visited Syria very recently without attracting any disapproval from the Bush Administration. The Syrian ambassador to the USA, Imad Moustapha, described Pelosi's overture as a 'positive step', but one that offered little likelihood of a change in US policy. However, in May 2007 US Secretary of State Condoleezza Rice held landmark talks with Syrian Minister of Foreign Affairs Mouallem on the sidelines of a major summit meeting held in Egypt, intended to address the situation in Iraq. The sideline negotiations represented the first official high-level talks between the two countries since the murder of Rafik Hariri. During the talks Rice urged the Syrian leadership to take further action to prevent foreign fighters from crossing into Iraq from Syria in order to participate in the anti-US insurgency.

It was hoped that Syrian–US tensions would be eased when in November 2007 Syria agreed to send a low-level delegation to the international peace meeting held under US auspices in Annapolis, Maryland, USA, with the aim of relaunching the Middle East peace process. However, such optimism proved to be short-lived. In February 2008 President Bush approved an expanded range of sanctions against the Syrian regime, which he accused of destabilizing both Iraq and Lebanon. The new sanctions included a freeze on the assets of prominent Syrian officials or businessmen deemed to have benefited from corrupt practices. In March the US Administration also announced that maritime vessels docking in US ports that had previously visited Syrian ports would henceforth be placed on a Port Security Advisory List, amid US concerns regarding Syrian links with international terrorist networks. The Bush Administration extended sanctions further against Syria in May, imposing an embargo on exports of certain goods to the country. This tighter sanctions regime was imposed following allegations by US intelligence agencies that there existed a covert nuclear co-operation between Syria and the Democratic People's Republic of Korea (North Korea—see below).

Notwithstanding President Bush's reassertion, in a speech to the UN in late September 2008, that Syria was a state sponsor of terrorism, Secretary of State Rice held further talks on regional affairs with Walid Mouallem in New York later the same week. However, in an incident that threatened to curtail the potential progress in US-Syrian relations, four US military helicopters, flying from Iraq, carried out a covert raid some 10 km inside Syrian territory in late October, targeting a building under construction in the Abu Kamal district. Official Syrian sources claimed that eight civilians, among them children, had been killed, and several others injured. However, an unnamed US intelligence source asserted that the operation had successfully targeted a prominent associate of al-Qa'ida, Abu Ghadiya, who was allegedly responsible for smuggling foreign militants and weapons across the Syrian border into Iraq, and that all those killed were militants. Mouallem, who was in the United Kingdom at the time of the raid for talks on improving Syria's ties with Europe, described the operation as a 'criminal and terrorist act'. At the end of October thousands of protesters took part in a demonstration close to the US embassy in Damascus, which was protected by a cordon of Syrian riot police.

Following the inauguration of Barack Obama as the new US President in January 2009, there was renewed optimism concerning US-Syrian relations. In the opening weeks of his presidency Obama announced his intention to pursue a pragmatic and reconciliatory foreign policy approach in the Middle East. During late January and February three separate US congressional delegations visited Damascus for talks with President Assad on improving bilateral relations. The final delegation was led by John Kerry, Chairman of the US Senate Foreign Relations Committee, who stated that he was optimistic about the prospects for US-Syrian co-operation on several regional issues, including the formation of a Palestinian unity government. Imad Moustapha, Syria's ambassador to the USA, held talks in Washington, DC with Jeffrey Feltman, Acting Assistant Secretary of the Bureau of Near Eastern Affairs at the US Department of State in late February; Moustapha described the meeting as constructive. The process of dialogue continued to grow in significance when Feltman, along with Daniel Shapiro, a senior White House official who had been involved in drafting the Syria Accountability Act in 2003, held talks in Damascus with Minister of Foreign Affairs Mouallem. While both sides emphasized the positive aspects of the dialogue, neither denied that there remained significant obstacles to a full normalization of relations—notably Syria's support for Hamas and Hezbollah, and its relationship with Iran, and the USA's continued policy of sanctions against Syria and support for Israel.

In August 1999 a diplomatic crisis developed between Syria and the Palestinian authorities after the Syrian Deputy Prime Minister and Minister of Defence, Maj.-Gen. Mustafa Tlass, publicly accused Yasser Arafat of having 'sold Jerusalem and the Arab nation' in peace agreements concluded with Israel since 1993, and made other personal insults against the Palestinian leader. The PA demanded that Tlass resign (and Fatah reportedly issued a death warrant against Tlass), while President Assad was apparently angered by the minister's remarks. Arafat attended the funeral of President Hafiz al-Assad, and in mid-2000 the PA renewed its demand that Syria free all remaining Palestinian prisoners from its gaols; seven Palestinians were released into Lebanese custody in December. Amid Syrian efforts to support the Palestinians in their escalating conflict with the Israelis, and following talks between Bashar al-Assad and Arafat during the summit meeting of Arab League states in Jordan in March 2001, the two leaders declared that they had achieved a reconciliation. In December 2004 PLO leader Mahmud Abbas made the first official Palestinian visit to Damascus since 1996. Abbas, the Palestinian Prime Minister, Ahmad Quray, the Minister of Foreign Affairs, Dr Nasser al-Kidwa, and President Assad discussed the current situation in the Palestinian territories and preparations for the presidential election scheduled to be held there in January 2005. Assad emphasized Syria's support for the Palestinian people and their struggle for national unity, while Abbas stressed the importance of co-operation between Syria and the PA. By the end of 2008 there were 461,897 Palestinian refugees registered in Syria.

In October 1998 the Jordanian Government demanded 'immediate answers' from Syria concerning a list of 239 Jordanians allegedly missing in Syria, and a further 190 who it claimed were being held in Syrian prisons. The Syrian authorities agreed to investigate the matter, but stated that most of those listed were in fact members of Palestinian organizations linked with Jordan and had violated Syrian laws. In February 1999 President Assad unexpectedly attended the funeral of King Hussein of Jordan, and reportedly held a private meeting with the new monarch. Syria had welcomed the succession of King Abdullah, and the new Jordanian King made his first official visit to Syria in April. The two leaders urged a resumption of the peace process and increased bilateral co-operation; Syria agreed to supply Jordan with water during 1999, as the latter was undergoing a drought, and both sides agreed to hold future discussions regarding the Jordanian prisoners in Syria. King Abdullah made an unscheduled visit to Syria in July, at a time when Jordan was concerned that any separate peace settlement between Syria and Israel might undermine the Palestinian position in future negotiations. The joint Syrian-Jordanian Higher Committee met in August in Amman, under the chairmanship of both countries' premiers—the first time in almost a decade that a senior Syrian delegation had visited Jordan's capital. Meanwhile, the Syrian Government stated that many of the Jordanian prisoners held in Syria had been released under a general amnesty granted in July (see above) and that the 'very few' who remained in Syrian gaols were non-political detainees. Later in August Syria ended a 10-year ban on the free circulation of Jordanian newspapers and publications in the country. A further 17 Jordanian prisoners were reportedly released from Syrian gaols in March 2000. Following the death of President Assad in June, King Abdullah visited Damascus in July for talks with Syria's new President, Bashar al-Assad; Syria again agreed to supply Jordan with water during that summer. It was reported in November that Syria had upgraded its diplomatic representation in Jordan to ambassadorial level. In February 2004 Syria and Jordan launched the Wahdah Dam project on Jordan's River Yarmuk. The project, which was completed in September 2006, aimed to provide Jordan with water and Syria with electricity.

Relations between Syria and Iraq had been strained since the early 1970s due to a rivalry between the respective factions of the Baath Party in Damascus and Baghdad. Notably, Syria supported Iran in its war with Iraq in 1980–88. Although an extraordinary summit meeting of the Arab League in November 1987 produced a unanimous statement expressing solidarity with Iraq and condemning Iran for prolonging the war and for its occupation of Arab territory, Syria announced subsequently that a reconciliation with Iraq had not taken place, and that Syrian relations with Iran remained fundamentally unchanged. Syria also used its veto to prevent the adoption of an Iraqi proposal to readmit Egypt to the Arab League, but it could not prevent the inclusion in the final communiqué of a clause permitting individual member nations to re-establish diplomatic relations with Egypt. However, Egypt's recognition of the newly proclaimed Palestinian state in November 1988 gave fresh impetus to attempts to achieve a reconciliation between Egypt and Syria. These culminated in the restoration of bilateral relations in December 1989, and in the visit of Egypt's President Hosni Mubarak to Damascus.

Syria appeared keen to take advantage of the diplomatic opportunities arising from Iraq's invasion of Kuwait in August 1990, and in particular to improve its relations with the USA. Syria endorsed Egypt's efforts to co-ordinate an Arab response to the invasion, and agreed to send troops to Saudi Arabia as part of a pan-Arab deterrent force, supporting the US-led effort to deter an Iraqi invasion of Saudi Arabia; Syria also committed itself to the demand for an unconditional Iraqi withdrawal from Kuwait. Indications that Syria's participation in the multinational force was transforming its relations with the West were confirmed in November when diplomatic ties were restored with the United Kingdom. Iraq's overwhelming military defeat by the US-led multinational force in February 1991 strengthened Syria's position with regard to virtually all its major regional concerns. In March the Ministers of Foreign Affairs of the members of the Co-operation Council for the Arab States of the Gulf (Gulf Co-operation Council, see p. 229) met their Egyptian and Syrian counterparts in Damascus to discuss regional security. The formation of an Arab peace-keeping force, comprising mainly Egyptian and Syrian troops, was subsequently announced. (In

May, however, Egypt declared its intention to withdraw its forces from the Gulf region within three months, thus casting doubt on the future of joint Syrian-Egyptian security arrangements.) Moreover, Syria's decision to ally itself, in opposition to Iraq, with the Western powers and the 'moderate' Arab states led the USA to realize that it could no longer seek to exclude Syria from any role in the resolution of the Arab-Israeli conflict. A shift in Syria's relations with the USSR, a major source of military assistance but whose programmes of political liberalization President Assad had recently criticized, provided another reason for its realignment with the West.

After Iraq's defeat by the multinational force in February 1991, Syria became a centre for elements of the Iraqi opposition. However, it remains committed to the territorial integrity of Iraq, fearing that disintegration might encourage minorities within Syria (particularly the Kurds) to pursue their own autonomy. Three crossing points on the Syria-Iraq border were reopened in June 1997 to facilitate bilateral trade (Syria closed its border with Iraq in 1980), and in September 1998 Iraq, Iran and Syria agreed to establish a joint forum for foreign policy co-ordination (particularly with regard to the USA). In the same month Syria and Iraq reopened commercial centres in one another's capitals, and in April 1999 a series of mutual agreements were signed, as part of the process of normalizing relations. Throughout 1998–2002 the Syrian Government criticized US and British air-strikes against Iraqi air defence targets, as well as the maintenance of UN sanctions against Iraq.

In August 2000 a rail link between Aleppo and the Iraqi capital was reopened after an interval of some 20 years, and in December the Syrian authorities reportedly removed all restrictions on Iraqi citizens travelling to Syria. In November, furthermore, Iraq was reported to have begun transporting crude petroleum to Syria via a pipeline not used since the early 1980s. When the US Secretary of State, Colin Powell, visited Damascus in February 2001, his discussions with the Syrian President apparently centred on Syria's alleged violation of UN sanctions regarding the supply of petroleum from Iraq; in January 2002 British officials publicly accused Syria of sanctions violations. In August 2001 the Syrian Prime Minister, leading a ministerial and commercial delegation, became the most senior Syrian official to visit Iraq for two decades. Syria was particularly concerned (as was Turkey) by the potential ascendance of Iraqi Kurdish groups should the incumbent regime in Baghdad be overthrown, although, visiting these countries in March 2002, the Patriotic Union of Kurdistan leader, Jalal Talabani, gave assurances that Iraq's Kurdish groups had no intention of establishing their own state. There were reports in mid-2002 that Syria was involved in mediation efforts between Iraq and Kuwait. (In October 2001 Syria had been elected as a non-permanent member of the UN Security Council for 2002–03.) Despite its unexpected support for UN Security Council Resolution 1441, approved in November, which imposed strict terms according to which Iraq must disarm or else face probable military action, Syria expressed its firm opposition to the US-led military campaign against the Iraqi regime which began in March 2003 (see the chapter on Iraq).

In February 2006 Syria and Iraq announced that they were to restore full diplomatic relations and exchange ambassadors as soon as a new government was installed in Iraq. Relations were formally restored in November, ending a hiatus of more than 20 years, and the two sides also agreed to co-operate on security issues. It was hoped that the renewal of diplomatic ties would facilitate the policing of the shared border, across which a large number of militants were still reported to be entering Iraq. In February 2007 a spokesman for the Iraqi Government claimed that 50% of those who had committed suicide bomb attacks in Iraq had entered the country from Syria, although this was staunchly denied by the Syrian Government. A report by the office of the UN High Commissioner for Refugees, published in April 2007, estimated the number of displaced Iraqis in Syria at some 1.2m. people. New regulations requiring Iraqi citizens to obtain a visa before entering Syria were introduced in October 2007; access to Syria from Iraq had been unrestricted since 2000. Following a visit to Baghdad by Minister of Foreign Affairs Mouallem in March 2009, Prime Minister al-Otari led a ministerial delegation on a two-day visit to Iraq in April, during which talks were held on border security, economic co-operation and regional affairs.

Allegations about Syria's involvement in the assassination of Rafik Hariri, in February 2005, and its role in Lebanon generally, led to increasing international and regional isolation, which, in turn, increased the strategic importance of Syria's ties with Iran. In August 2005 President Assad visited the Iranian President, Mahmoud Ahmadinejad, in Tehran; the first such visit by a foreign head of state since the election of Ahmadinejad earlier that year. The two leaders announced their solidarity in the face of common foreign threats. Several presidential summits were subsequently held in both Tehran and Damascus between early 2006 and late 2008. Meanwhile, in March 2007 it was reported that Iran and Syria had, during a visit to the Syrian capital by the Iranian Minister of Defence and Armed Forces Logistics, signed a memorandum of understanding with regard to defence co-operation, and in July President Ahmadinejad undertook a high-profile visit to Damascus.

A summit meeting of Arab League member states, held in Damascus in March 2008, was boycotted by several leading officials; notable absentees were Egypt's President Mubarak and Saudi Arabia's King Abdullah, both of whom blamed Syria and Iran for contributing to the crisis in Lebanon through their support for the Hezbollah-led opposition. When Saudi Arabia had transferred its ambassador in Damascus to Qatar in February, it declined to appoint a new ambassador to Syria, demonstrating apparent disapproval at Syria's role in the Lebanese political crisis. Relations with Saudi Arabia remained strained throughout 2008, and the two countries' conflicting interests in the region were highlighted again by their divergent responses to Israel's military offensive in Gaza, launched in late December 2008 (see below). President Assad attended an emergency Arab League meeting in Doha in mid-January 2009, convened by Qatar with the stated aim of formulating a unified Arab response to the crisis in Gaza. However, the Doha summit was boycotted by several nations, notably Egypt and Saudi Arabia, and did not achieve the quorum of 15 participating states required to grant the meeting official status. Shortly afterwards, however, during the Arab Economic, Social and Development Summit in Kuwait, Assad attended a private meeting hosted by the Saudi King and also attended by the leaders of Qatar, Egypt and Kuwait, which was heralded as achieving significant progress towards greater Arab unity. Unofficial reports in February suggested that Saudi Arabia might be preparing to appoint a new ambassador to Syria. In early March 2009 the Saudi Minister of Foreign Affairs, Prince Sa'ud al-Faisal, met with President Assad in Damascus for talks on Arab reconciliation and other regional issues. Al-Faisal extended an invitation to Assad to visit Saudi Arabia, and both sides described the talks as positive and constructive. On 11 March King Abdullah hosted a one-day summit on regional affairs attended by President Assad (in his first visit to Saudi Arabia for four years), President Mubarak of Egypt and the Kuwaiti Amir, Sheikh as-Sabah. Foremost among the objectives of the summit were the promotion of Arab unity and support for the Egyptian-brokered reconciliation talks between the rival Palestinian factions, Fatah and Hamas.

Relations between Syria and Turkey became increasingly strained in the 1990s, owing to disagreements over the sharing of water from the Euphrates river. No permanent agreement on this resource has been concluded, and both Syria and Iraq are concerned that new dams in Turkey will reduce their share of water from the Euphrates. Syria's relations with Turkey deteriorated sharply in April 1996 after it was revealed that Turkey and Israel had concluded a military co-operation agreement earlier in the year. In August 1997 Syria condemned the decision by the USA, Israel and Turkey to conduct joint naval manoeuvres, although the three countries claimed that the exercises (carried out in January 1998) were solely for humanitarian purposes. Tension between Syria and Turkey increased considerably in October 1998, when Turkey threatened to invade Syria if its demands for an end to alleged Syrian support for the separatist Kurdistan Workers' Party (Partiya Karkeren Kurdistan—PKK) were not met. The Turkish authorities also demanded the extradition of the PKK leader, Abdullah Öcalan (who, they claimed, was directing PKK operations from Damascus), and insisted that Syria renounce its historic claim on the Turkish province of Hatay. Turkey's aggressive stance was viewed by Syria as evidence of a Turkish-Israeli military and political alliance, and as a result both Syria and Turkey ordered troops to be deployed along their joint border. Diplomatic efforts to defuse the crisis by Egypt, Iran and the UN, and Syrian assurances that Öcalan was not residing in Syria, allowed a degree of normalization in bilateral relations. In late October, following two days of negotiations in southern Turkey, representatives of the two countries signed an agreement whereby the PKK was to be banned from entering Syrian territory, while the organization's active bases in Syria and Lebanon's Beka'a valley were to be closed. Turkey and Syria also agreed mutual security guarantees, and resolved to invite Lebanon to participate in further discussions regarding the issue of PKK activity.

Despite persistent Syrian concerns regarding the close nature of Turkish-Israeli relations, it was reported in March 2000 that Syrian and Turkish officials were holding discussions in Damascus on a memorandum of principles, intended to establish a new framework for future bilateral relations. In September Syria and Turkey signed a co-operation agreement relating to countering terrorism and organized crime, and in June 2002 they signed two military co-operation accords. Moreover, reports in February that the Turkish army was to begin the clearance of landmines along its border with Syria were seen as evidence of a steady improvement in bilateral relations. In December 2003 relations were strengthened by Syria's decision to hand over 22 suspects sought by the Turkish authorities in connection with four suicide bomb attacks in Istanbul in November, in which at least 60 people were killed. In early January 2004 President Assad made the first ever visit by a Syrian Head of State to Turkey. Turkey's membership of NATO, and hence its relatively close relationship with the USA, as well as shared concerns about a possible 'ripple-effect' of increased Kurdish autonomy in northern Iraq following the removal of the regime of Saddam Hussain, were believed to be among the principal reasons for Syria's initiative to improve its relations with Turkey. In December Syria and Turkey agreed to create a bilateral free trade zone, and the agreement took effect in January 2007. A Joint Technical Committee on water resources, involving Syria, Turkey and Iraq, was reconvened in May 2007, after some 15 years of inactivity, and by early 2009 various joint initatives aimed at resolving disagreements over water resources were under discussion; these included a proposed joint Turkish-Syrian dam on the Orontes River at the border between Syria and Turkey. Meanwhile, political and economic relations with Turkey continued to progress in 2008, with Turkey's role as mediator for indirect Syrian-Israeli peace talks (see below) and the signing of several new agreements on trade and investment co-operation in December 2008.

In January 2005 Assad visited Russia for official talks with President Vladimir Putin. Earlier in the month reports that Russia was to sell missiles to Syria that could be used against targets in Israel provoked anger in that country. Russia subsequently confirmed its intention to sell missiles to Syria in February, asserting that the weapons would only be used for defensive purposes. President Assad again visited Russia in late August 2008, where discussions were held with President Dmitrii Medvedev on defence co-operation: the Russian authorities announced their readiness to supply Syria with a new consignment of defensive weapons. Reports that the countries were negotiating an agreement to deploy offensive Russian missiles on Syrian soil, in response to a planned US missile shield in Central Europe, were subsequently denied by an official Syrian source. Following the defence summit, work commenced on the development of an extensive Russian naval facility at the Syrian port of Tartous.

Syria's relations with France became increasingly strained following the killing of Rafik Hariri in February 2005. French President Jacques Chirac, a friend and supporter of Hariri, accused Syria of involvement in the assassination, and Chirac's successor, Nicolas Sarkozy, announced in December 2007 that his Government would cease all diplomatic contacts with Syria until the regime demonstrated that it was committed to enabling the Lebanese National Assembly to elect a successor to President Lahoud (see the chapter on Lebanon). However, after the signing of the Doha Agreement in May 2008 (see above) there was a rapid rapprochement of Syria and France. In mid-July President Assad was invited to Paris by Sarkozy to attend a summit on the French President's new Union for the Mediterranean initiative. In August Syria appointed a new ambassador to France—the post having been vacant since the retirement of the previous envoy some 18 months previously. In the same week, the French Minister of Foreign Affairs, Bernard Kouchner, launched what he termed a 'new era of relations' when he held talks with his Syrian counterpart and President Assad in Damascus. President Sarkozy began a two-day official visit to Syria in September, the first visit by a French President since 2002. During the visit a quadripartite summit was held by the leaders of France, Syria, Turkey and Qatar; foremost on the agenda were the ongoing Turkish-mediated indirect talks between Syria and Israel.

The EU had resumed a formal dialogue with Syria in March 2007, when Javier Solana, the Secretary-General of the Council of the EU and High Representative for the Common Foreign and Security Policy, met with Mouallem and President Assad. In October 2008 Solana made his first visit to Damascus in over two years, signalling the resumption of negotiations on an EU association agreement which had stalled after the assassination of Rafik Hariri in 2005. Abdullah ad-Dardari, the Deputy Prime Minister, responsible for Economic Affairs, held two days of negotiations in Brussels with Benita Ferrero-Waldner, the EU Commissioner responsible for External Relations and European Neighbourhood Policy, in late November. These negotiations led to the signing, in mid-December, of a draft co-operation agreement, with ratification of an association agreement anticipated by mid-2009. In October, meanwhile, Walid Mouallem made an official visit to the United Kingdom, and in November the British Secretary of State for Foreign and Commonwealth Affairs, David Miliband, visited Damascus for talks with President Assad: their discussions encompassed bilateral relations, intelligence co-operation and regional affairs. The visit was the first by a senior member of the British Government since 2001.

In December 2006 Israeli Prime Minister Ehud Olmert rejected an appeal from President Assad for a resumption of formal peace negotiations with Syria. Olmert accused Assad of merely trying to curry international favour at a time when Syria was under intense scrutiny for its alleged complicity in the assassinations in Lebanon of Rafik Hariri and Pierre Gemayel (see above). Vice-Premier Shimon Peres stated that Israel would welcome negotiations with Syria, but only when that country had ceased its support of militant organizations such as Hamas and Hezbollah. In January 2007 a former Israeli diplomat claimed that Israel and Syria had in fact conducted secret negotiations concerning a possible peace deal between September 2004 and July 2006, in which month the outbreak of the conflict between Israel and Hezbollah (see the chapters on Israel and Lebanon) had abruptly brought the proceedings to a close. (According to reports in the Israeli media, prior to the collapse of talks, mutual understandings had been reached with regard to an Israeli withdrawal from the Golan Heights and other issues of contention.) The diplomat's claims were strongly denied by the Syrian Government; however, Israeli officials acknowledged that meetings might have been held between non-governmental representatives from the two countries. In March 2007 President Assad was reported to have confirmed that in fact secret talks had taken place between 'non-official' channels.

In June 2007, amid reports that Olmert had established a ministerial committee whose task would be to examine Israel's military preparedness for a potential conflict with Syria, the Israeli premier was said to have declared that he was ready to engage in direct negotiations with the Syrian regime, without preconditions first being met. The Israeli media commented that Olmert had relayed to Syria, through Turkish and German officials, the proposal that Israel withdraw from the Golan Heights in exchange for Syria's undertaking to 'gradually dissolve' its links with Iran and militant organizations in Lebanon and the Palestinian territories. Tensions between Israel and Syria worsened in early September, after Israel carried out an air-strike on a military installation at al-Kibar, 'deep within' Syrian territory. In October President Assad stated that the Israeli strike had hit a military building that was under construction and denied media reports speculating that it might have been a concealed nuclear reactor. In April 2008 US intelligence officials reportedly presented evidence that the target of the Israeli air-strike was in fact a nuclear facility that was being constructed with assistance from North Korea; the Syrian authorities again strongly rejected the claims. An investigation of the site was carried out by the IAEA in June; however, the remains of the original building had been razed and buried under the concrete foundations of a new construction. The IAEA investigators stated in November that traces of uranium had been discovered, although the source of the material remained uncertain. While the IAEA insisted its findings warranted further investigation, the Syrian authorities refused to grant the agency additional access to al-Kibar, or to a number of other sites, stating that the source of the uranium was Israeli missiles used in the bombing of the installation. In a report issued in February 2009 the IAEA contended there was a 'low probability' that Israeli munitions were the source of the radioactive material, and described Syria's co-operation with their investigation as unsatisfactory.

Meanwhile, in May 2008 Turkey's Minister of Foreign Affairs, Ali Babacan, confirmed that indirect talks aimed at achieving a comprehensive peace agreement between Israel and Syria, through Turkish mediation, were to begin in İstanbul. Four rounds of talks were held between May and August. However, a fifth round of talks, scheduled for September, was postponed due to the political uncertainty in Israel following the resignation of Prime Minister Olmert (see the chapter on Israel). Following Israel's military offensive against Hamas targets in the Gaza Strip, launched on 27 December 2008 and code-named 'Operation Cast Lead' (see the chapters on Israel and the Palestinian Autonomous Areas), President Assad formally suspended the talks with Israel. Several large public demonstrations against Israel's actions in Gaza took place in Damascus, targeting locations such as the representative offices of the UN and the EU and the Egyptian embassy. During the campaign for Israel's general election, which took place in February 2009, the Likud leader, Binyamin Netanyahu, declared his outright opposition to the surrender of the Golan Heights as part of any peace agreement with Syria. After a new Israeli coalition Government was sworn in, under Netanyahu's premiership, in early April, his Minister of Foreign Affairs, Avigdor Lieberman (leader of Israel Beytenu) ruled out any Israeli withdrawal from the Golan Heights.

Government

Under the 1973 Constitution (as subsequently amended), legislative power is vested in the unicameral People's Assembly, with 250 members elected by universal adult suffrage to serve a four-year term. Executive power is vested in the President, elected by direct popular vote for a seven-year term. (Following the death of President Hafiz al-Assad on 10 June 2003, the Constitution was amended to allow his son, Lt-Gen. Bashar al-Assad, to accede to the presidency). He governs with the assistance of an appointed Council of Ministers, led by the Prime Minister. Syria has 14 administrative districts (*mohafazat*).

Defence

National service, which normally lasts for 30 months, is compulsory for men. As assessed at November 2008, the regular armed forces totalled 292,600 men: an army of 215,000 (including conscripts), an air defence command of 40,000, a navy of 7,600 and an air force of 30,000. In addition, Syria had 314,000-strong reserve forces (army 280,000; air force 10,000; air defence 20,000; navy 4,000). Paramilitary forces included a gendarmerie (connected to the Ministry of the Interior) of 8,000 and a Baath Party Workers' Militia of an estimated 100,000. Some 8,000–10,000 Syrian troops were deployed in Lebanon in March 2005; however, in April Syria claimed to have withdrawn all of its forces from that country (see the chapter on Lebanon). Defence expenditure for 2007 was budgeted at £S74,900m.

Economic Affairs

In 2007 according to estimates by the World Bank, Syria's gross national income (GNI), measured at average 2005–07 prices, was US $34,993m., equivalent to $1,760 per head (or $4,370 per head on an international purchasing-power parity basis). During 2000–07, it was estimated, the population increased at an average annual rate of 2.7%, while gross domestic product (GDP) per head increased, in real terms, by an average of 1.9% per year. Overall GDP increased, in real terms, at an average annual rate of 4.7% in 2000–07; growth was 6.3% in 2007, according to official figures.

Agriculture (including forestry and fishing) contributed 20.2% of GDP in 2007, and engaged 26.2% of the employed labour force (excluding foreign workers) in 2003. The principal cash crops are cotton (which accounted for about 2.4% of export earnings in 2003) and fruit and vegetables. Agricultural GDP increased at an average annual rate of 5.3% in 2000–07; the sector's GDP increased by 10.2% in 2006 but declined by 10.3% in 2007.

Industry (comprising mining, manufacturing, construction and utilities) provided 35.0% of GDP in 2007, and engaged 24.8% of the employed labour force (excluding foreign workers) in 2003. The GDP of the industrial sector increased at an annual average rate of 0.9% during 2000–07; industrial GDP increased by 3.7% in 2007.

Mining contributed an estimated 19.7% of GDP in 2003, and employed 0.3% of the working population (excluding foreign workers) in 1999. Crude petroleum is the major mineral export, accounting for 58.5% of total export earnings in 2003, and phosphates are also exported. Syria also has reserves of natural gas and iron ore. At the end of 2007 Syria had proven oil reserves of 3,000m. barrels, and estimated average oil production was 394,000 barrels per day (b/d), having declined from 596,000 b/d in 1995. Syria was estimated to have 290,000m. cu m of proven natural gas reserves at the end of 2007, and in that year production of natural gas reached an estimated daily average of 5,300m. cu m. In 2001 Syria and Lebanon signed an agreement under which Syria was to supply gas to northern Lebanon. However, although the pipeline intended to supply the natural gas was completed in 2005, the two countries did not implement the agreement owing to political differences.

Manufacturing contributed an estimated 7.3% of GDP in 2004, and employed 12.7% of the working population in 1999. The principal branches of manufacturing, measured by gross value of output, are: food products, beverages and tobacco; chemicals, petroleum, coal, rubber and plastic products; textiles, clothing, leather products and footwear; metal products, machinery, transport equipment and appliances; and non-metallic mineral products. The GDP of the manufacturing sector increased by an average of 13.8% per year during 2000–07; manufacturing GDP increased by 5.0% in 2007.

Energy is derived principally from petroleum (providing 53.0% of total electricity production in 2005), and also natural gas (37.1%) and hydroelectric power (9.9%). Imports of mineral fuels and lubricants comprised 33.0% of the value of total imports in 2007.

Services accounted for 44.7% of GDP in 2007, and engaged 49.0% of the employed labour force (excluding foreign workers) in 2003. The GDP of the services sector increased at an average rate of 7.2% per year in 2000–07; growth of the sector was 19.2% in 2007.

In 2006 Syria recorded a visible trade surplus of US $886m., and there was a surplus of $890m. on the current account of the balance of payments. In 2006 the principal source of imports (10.2%) was Russia; other important suppliers were the People's Republic of China, Egypt, Saudi Arabia, Italy and Turkey. Italy was the primary market for exports in that year (19.6%); other major purchasers were France, Saudi Arabia, the United Kingdom and Jordan. The principal exports in 2007 were mineral fuels and lubricants, food and live animals, basic manufactures and chemicals, while the principal imports were mineral fuels and lubricants, machinery and transport equipment, basic manufactures, chemicals, and food and live animals.

A budget deficit of £S61,900m. was recorded in 2007, while a balanced budget was projected for 2008. At the end of 2006 Syria's total external debt was US $6,508m., of which $5,640m. was long-term public debt. The cost of debt-servicing in that year was equivalent to 1.9% of the total value of exports of goods and services. Annual inflation averaged 4.9% in 2000–07. Consumer prices increased by 4.5% in 2007. According to the IMF, 8.3% of the labour force were unemployed in 2006; however, other sources estimated unemployment to be more than double this rate.

Syria is a member of the UN Economic and Social Commission for Western Asia (ESCWA, see p. 45), the Arab Fund for Economic and Social Development (AFESD, see p. 183), the Arab Monetary Fund (see p. 184), the Council of Arab Economic Unity (see p. 233), the Islamic Development Bank (see p. 340) and the Organization of Arab Petroleum Exporting Countries (OAPEC, see p. 379).

Since July 2000 the regime under President Bashar al-Assad has implemented a bolder programme of economic reforms than his predecessor, Hafiz al-Assad, although progress has remained slow. The reduction of the economy's dependence on revenue from petroleum became a priority as it was considered likely that Syria could become a net importer of petroleum as early as 2010, and that its reserves would be exhausted by 2030. The authorities' economic plan for 2006–10 focused on improving the country's financial and business climate, liberalizing trade and stimulating GDP growth. Other planned reforms included the introduction, with IMF assistance, of a value-added tax by 2008 (subsequently deferred until 2010), and the phasing out of petroleum price subsidies. By early 2008 the country's first two Islamic banks were operational, with a further six having been granted licences. The opening of a stock exchange in March 2009 was aimed at fostering an expanded commercial sector. Meanwhile, unemployment remained high, at more than 20% according to some sources. Moreover, the rapid rate of population growth required the Government to create sufficient employment opportunities for the greatly expanding labour force. In 2006 the Government decreed that all public and private sector foreign currency transactions be carried out in euros rather than US dollars, apparently in order to make foreign assets more secure under the economic sanctions regime imposed by the US Administration of George W. Bush in 2004. (In May 2008 the US sanctions were tightened—see Recent History.) The country's economic performance in 2007 and 2008 was influenced by the presence of more than 1m. refugees from Iraq, with the consequent increased levels of demand and rise in inflation. The IMF, assessing the economy in late 2008, estimated growth of 5.2% in 2008 and projected growth of 3.9% in 2009. It was anticipated that Syria's economic performance in 2009 would reflect the impact of the global economic crisis, which was likely to constrict the tourism and industrial sectors and also result in a decline in remittances from abroad. Agricultural output, meanwhile, was expected to have been adversely affected by drought in late 2008 and early 2009.

Education

Primary education, which begins at six years of age and lasts for six years, is officially compulsory. In 2004/05 total enrolment at primary and secondary level was equivalent to 86.8% of children in the relevant age-group. In 2001/02 primary enrolment included 94.5% of children in the appropriate age-group. Secondary education, beginning at 12 years of age, lasts for a further six years, comprising two cycles of three years each. In 2006/07 enrolment at secondary schools included 65.7% of children in the relevant age-group. There are agricultural and technical schools for vocational training, and five state-run universities. In 2003 the decision was made to end the state monopoly on education, imposed by the Baath Party in 1963. By 2006/07 there were eight private universities and numerous private schools; in that year there were 380,000 students enrolled in Syrian universities: 250,000 at state institutions, 6,000 at private institutions and a further 2,500 at the Syrian Virtual University (established in 2002, and which offers degree courses via the internet). Total government expenditure on education in 2007 totalled £S98,308m. (16.7% of total government expenditure).

The UN Relief and Works Agency (UNRWA) provides education for Palestinian refugees in Syria. During the academic year 2008/09 UNWRA operated 119 elementary and preparatory schools in Syria, with a total enrolment of 65,479 pupils.

Public Holidays

2009: 1 January (New Year's Day), 8 March (Revolution Day), 9 March* (Mouloud/Yum an-Nabi, Birth of Muhammad), 21 March (Mother's Day), 17 April (Independence Day), 17–20 April (Greek Orthodox Easter), 1 May (Labour Day), 6 May (Martyrs' Day), 19 July* (Leilat al-Meiraj, Ascension of Muhammad), 20 September* (Id al-Fitr, end of Ramadan), 6 October (Anniversary of October War), 27 November* (Id al-Adha, Feast of the Sacrifice), 18 December* (Muharram, Islamic New Year), 25 December (Christmas Day).

2010: 1 January (New Year's Day), 26 February* (Mouloud/Yum an-Nabi, Birth of Muhammad), 8 March (Revolution Day), 21 March (Mother's Day), 2–5 April (Greek Orthodox Easter), 17 April (Independence Day), 1 May (Labour Day), 6 May (Martyrs' Day), 8 July* (Leilat al-Meiraj, Ascension of Muhammad), 10 September* (Id al-Fitr, end of Ramadan), 6 October (Anniversary of October War), 16 November* (Id al-Adha, Feast of the Sacrifice), 7 December* (Muharram, Islamic New Year), 25 December (Christmas Day).

* These holidays are dependent on the Islamic lunar calendar and may vary by one or two days from the dates given.

Weights and Measures

The metric system is in force.

Statistical Survey

Sources (unless otherwise stated): Central Bureau of Statistics, rue Abd al-Malek bin Marwah, Malki Quarter, Damascus; tel. (11) 3335830; fax (11) 3322292; e-mail cbs@mail.sy; internet www.cbssyr.org; Central Bank of Syria, place du 17 avril, Damascus; tel. (11) 2216802; fax (11) 2248329; e-mail info@bcs.gov.sy; internet www.banquecentrale.gov.sy.

Area and Population

AREA, POPULATION AND DENSITY

Area (sq km)	
Land	184,050
Inland water	1,130
Total	185,180*
Population (census results)†	
8 September 1981	9,052,628
3 September 1994	
Males	7,048,906
Females	6,733,409
Total	13,782,315
Population (UN estimates at mid-year)‡	
2006	19,789,000
2007	20,504,000
2008	21,227,000
Density (per sq km) at mid-2008	114.6

* 71,498 sq miles.
† Official estimates at mid-year, including Palestinian refugees. According to the United Nations Relief and Works Agency for Palestine Refugees in the Near East (UNRWA), there were 461,897 Palestinian refugees in Syria at 30 December 2008.
‡ Source: UN, *World Population Prospects: The 2008 Revision*.

PRINCIPAL TOWNS
(official estimates at 1 December 2008)

Halab (Aleppo)	5,315,000	Deir ez-Zor		1,511,000
Hims (Homs)	1,977,000	Al-Hasakah		1,445,000
		Al-Ladhiqiyah		
Hamah (Hama)	1,938,000	(Latakia)		1,161,000
Idleb	1,865,000	Ar-Raqqah (Rakka)		903,000
Dimashq (Damascus, capital)	1,684,000			

BIRTHS, MARRIAGES AND DEATHS
(excl. nomad population and Palestinian refugees, estimates)

	Registered live births		Registered marriages	Registered deaths
	Number	Rate (per 1,000)		
1997	496,140	32.9	128,146	53,366
1998	505,008	32.4	130,835	57,893
1999	503,473	31.3	136,157	56,564
2000	505,484	31.0	139,843	57,759
2001	524,212	31.4	153,842	60,814
2002	471,970	27.6	174,449	53,252
2003	492,639	28.1	n.a.	53,778
2004	491,476	n.a.	178,166	57,855

Source: UN, *Demographic Yearbook*.

Life expectancy (years at birth, WHO estimates): 72.5 (males 70.1; females 75.0) in 2006 (Source: WHO, *World Health Statistics*).

SYRIA

ECONOMICALLY ACTIVE POPULATION
(labour force sample survey, persons aged 15 years and over, 2003)*

	Males	Females	Total
Agriculture, hunting, forestry and fishing	816,598	352,145	1,168,743
Mining and quarrying; manufacturing; and electricity, gas and water	558,324	50,381	608,705
Construction	492,657	7,727	500,384
Trade, restaurants and hotels	650,835	26,394	677,229
Transport, storage and communications	258,541	6,946	265,487
Financing, insurance, real estate and business services	78,585	11,162	89,747
Community, social and personal services	851,357	306,922	1,158,279
Total employed	3,706,897	761,677	4,468,574
Unemployed	334,066	214,372	548,438
Total labour force	4,040,963	976,049	5,017,012

* Figures refer to Syrians only, excluding armed forces.

2006 ('000 persons): Total employed 4,899 (males 4,286, females 613); Unemployed 443 (males 254, females 189); Total labour force 5,342 (Source: IMF, *Syrian Arab Republic: Statistical Appendix—February 2009*).

Health and Welfare

KEY INDICATORS

Total fertility rate (children per woman, 2006)	3.2
Under-5 mortality rate (per 1,000 live births, 2006)	13
HIV/AIDS (% of persons aged 15–49, 2003)	<0.1
Physicians (per 1,000 head, 2006)	0.5
Hospital beds (per 1,000 head, 2006)	1.4
Health expenditure (2006): US $ per head (PPP)	109
Health expenditure (2006): % of GDP	3.9
Health expenditure (2006): public (% of total)	47.6
Access to water (% of persons, 2006)	89
Access to sanitation (% of persons, 2006)	92
Human Development Index (2006): ranking	105
Human Development Index (2006): value	0.736

For sources and definitions, see explanatory note on p. vi.

Agriculture

PRINCIPAL CROPS
('000 metric tons)

	2005	2006	2007*
Wheat	4,668.8	4,900.0*	4,500.0
Barley	767.4	700.0	730.0
Maize	187.2	215.0*	215.0
Potatoes	608.4	620.0*	640.0
Sugar beet	1,096.3	1,140.0*	1,150.0
Chick-peas	65.2	65.0*	65.5
Lentils	153.7	165.0*	165.0
Almonds*	130.0	131.0	132.0
Olives	501.0	510.0*	550.0
Cabbages and other brassicas	39.5	43.0*	45.0
Lettuce and chicory	51.7	52.0*	57.0
Tomatoes	945.5	950.0*	950.0
Cauliflowers	45.5	46.0*	48.0
Pumpkins, squash and gourds*	127.0	129.5	136.0
Cucumbers and gherkins	146.7	147.0*	147.0
Aubergines (Eggplants)	154.4	155.0*	156.0
Chillies and peppers, green*	45.0	41.0	41.0
Onions and shallots, green	47.6	48.0*	47.0
Onions, dry	125.1	125.0*	127.0

—continued	2005	2006	2007*
Oranges*	450.0	450.0	430.0
Lemons and limes*	111.0	111.0	105.0
Apples*	296.0	365.0	365.0
Apricots*	65.5	85.0	87.0
Sweet cherries	53.4	41.7*	42.0
Peaches and nectarines	51.6	53.0*	52.0
Grapes*	306.4	310.0	310.0
Watermelons	588.3	590.0*	600.0
Cantaloupes and other melons	105.9	105.0*	105.0
Figs	49.8	50.5*	51.0

* FAO estimate(s).

Aggregate production ('000 metric tons, may include official, semi-official or estimated data): Total cereals 5,631 in 2005, 5,823 in 2006, 5,453 in 2007; Total roots and tubers 608 in 2005, 620 in 2006, 640 in 2007; Total oilcrops 234 in 2005, 241 in 2006, 255 in 2007; Total vegetables (incl. melons) 2,765 in 2005, 2,832 in 2006, 2,853 in 2007; Total fruits (excl. melons) 1,751 in 2005, 1,846 in 2006, 1,824 in 2007.

Source: FAO.

LIVESTOCK
('000 head, year ending September)

	2005	2006*	2007*
Horses	15.0	15.0	15.5
Asses	111.8	n.a.	n.a.
Cattle	1,082.6	1,100.0	1,150.0
Camels	23.4	24.0	24.5
Sheep	1,965.1	2,000.0	2,100.0
Goats	1,295.7	1,300.0	1,350.0
Chickens	23,795	24,000	24,500

* FAO estimates.

Source: FAO.

LIVESTOCK PRODUCTS
('000 metric tons)

	2005	2006	2007*
Cattle meat	55.2	56.0*	57.0
Sheep meat	179.9	200.0	200.0
Chicken meat*	120.0	124.0	125.0
Cows' milk*	1,400.0	1,250.0	1,300.0
Sheep's milk*	700.0	605.0	610.0
Goats' milk*	70.2	62.0	65.0
Hen eggs*	155.2	155.0	170.0
Wool, greasy*	44.0	34.0	34.0

* FAO estimate(s).

Source: FAO.

Forestry

ROUNDWOOD REMOVALS
('000 cubic metres, excl. bark)

	2005	2006	2007
Sawlogs, veneer logs and logs for sleepers	16	16	16
Other industrial wood	24	24	24
Fuel wood	15	20	21
Total	55	60	61

* FAO estimate.

Sawnwood production ('000 cubic metres): *1980*: Coniferous (softwood) 6.6; Broadleaved (hardwood) 2.4; Total 9.0. *1981–2007*: Production as in 1980 (FAO estimates).

Source: FAO.

Fishing

(metric tons, live weight)

	2004	2005	2006
Capture	8,528	8,447	8,264
Freshwater fishes	5,451	4,770	4,869
Aquaculture	8,682	8,533	8,902
Common carp	4,245	3,920	4,387
Tilapias	3,650	3,363	3,460
Total catch	17,210	16,980	17,166

Source: FAO.

Mining

('000 metric tons, unless otherwise indicated)

	2004	2005*	2006*
Phosphate rock	2,883	3,500	3,664
Salt (unrefined)	141	110	133
Gypsum	432	467	444
Natural gas (million cu m)	9,700	8,300	8,600
Crude petroleum ('000 42-gallon barrels)*	181,000	167,000	152,000

* Estimates.

Source: US Geological Survey.

Industry

SELECTED PRODUCTS
('000 metric tons, unless otherwise indicated)

	2004	2005	2006
Plywood (cu m)*	7.8	7.8	7.8
Paper and paperboard	75	75	75
Cement (hydraulic)	4,757	4,700	4,700†
Olive oil (virgin)‡	145.8	167.0	130.3
Soybean oil*	23.5	31.3	47.6
Cottonseed oil	61.0‡	71.9‡	60.7*
Motor spirit (petrol, '000 barrels)	11,413	11,000†	11,000†
Distillate fuel oils ('000 barrels)	30,758	31,000†	31,000†
Residual fuel oils ('000 barrels)	30,210	30,000†	30,000†
Electric energy (million kWh)	32,077	34,935	n.a.

* FAO estimate(s).
† Estimated production.
‡ Unofficial figure(s).

2003 ('000 metric tons unless otherwise indicated): Cotton yarn (pure and mixed) 98.4; Glass and pottery products 73.4; Soap 16.5.

2007 ('000 metric tons unless otherwise indicated): Cottonseed oil 61.0 (FAO estimate); Olive oil (virgin) 152.0 (unofficial figure); Soybean oil 50.0 (FAO estimate); Plywood (cu m) 7.8 (FAO estimate); Paper and paperboard 75 (FAO estimate).

Sources: FAO; US Geological Survey; UN, *Industrial Commodity Statistics Yearbook*.

Finance

CURRENCY AND EXCHANGE RATES

Monetary Units
100 piastres = 1 Syrian pound (£S).

Sterling, Dollar and Euro Equivalents (31 December 2008)
£1 sterling = £S16.364;
US $1 = £S11.225;
€1 = £S15.622;
£S1,000 = £61.11 sterling = $89.09 = €64.01.

Exchange Rate: Between April 1976 and December 1987 the official mid-point rate was fixed at US $1 = £S3.925. On 1 January 1988 a new rate of $1 = £S11.225 was introduced. In addition to the official exchange rate, there is a promotion rate (applicable to most travel and tourism transactions) and a flexible rate.

BUDGET
(£S '000 million)

Revenue	2005	2006	2007
Oil-related proceeds	106.2	127.0	99.6
Non-oil tax revenue	160.3	196.3	221.4
Income and profits	59.3	65.0	74.2
International Trade	30.7	32.9	33.4
Excises	4.5	6.6	9.1
Other	65.8	91.9	104.7
Non-oil non-tax revenue	89.9	111.5	137.5
Total	356.3	434.9	458.6

Expenditure	2005	2006	2008
Current expenditure	277.0	317.2	325.7
Wages and salaries	157.0	207.0	223.2
Goods and services	21.5	22.5	24.3
Interest payments	29.0	29.5	30.0
Subsidies and transfers	69.5	51.2	41.6
Development expenditure	154.4	176.5	194.8
Social	60.3	65.7	68.8
Agriculture	15.5	17.9	22.5
Extractive industries	8.1	11.6	16.7
Manufacturing industries	8.4	9.4	7.7
Utilities	34.6	39.9	39.3
Construction	0.4	0.9	0.7
Trade	1.8	3.9	2.6
Transport and communications	21.3	24.8	31.2
Finance	2.4	3.3	4.4
Other	1.5	0.2	1.0
Total	431.4	493.7	520.5

2008 (£S '000 million, estimates): Total revenue 600.0; Total expenditure 600.0.

Source: Ministry of Finance, Damascus.

CENTRAL BANK RESERVES
(US $ million at 31 December)

	1986	1987	1988
Gold*	29	29	29
Foreign exchange	144	223	193
Total	173	252	222

* Valued at $35 per troy ounce.

1989–2006 (US $ million, national valuation): Gold 29.

Source: IMF, *International Financial Statistics*.

MONEY SUPPLY
(£S million at 31 December)

	2005	2006	2007
Currency outside banks	384,719	399,093	422,357
Demand deposits at commercial banks	287,637	241,543	303,202
Total money (incl. others)	688,276	660,804	731,661

Source: IMF, *International Financial Statistics*.

COST OF LIVING
(Consumer Price Index; base: 2000 = 100)

	2001	2002	2003
Food and beverages	100.2	99.6	107.3
Electricity, gas and other fuels (incl. water)	100.0	111.2	119.5
Clothing and footwear	100.5	96.5	102.9
Rent	100.7	102.9	124.0
All items (incl. others)	100.4	101.4	109.3

2004: Food and beverages 112.8; All items (incl. others) 114.1.
2005: Food and beverages 122.4; All items (incl. others) 122.6.
2006: Food and beverages 138.0; All items (incl. others) 134.1.
2007: All items 140.1.

Source: ILO.

SYRIA

NATIONAL ACCOUNTS
(£S million at current prices)

Expenditure on the Gross Domestic Product

	2005	2006	2007
Government final consumption expenditure	206,631	194,937	248,300
Private final consumption expenditure	993,118	1,122,666	1,205,181
Gross fixed capital formation	359,909	363,639	422,221
Changes in stocks	−95,294	−48,670	127,758
Total domestic expenditure	1,464,364	1,632,572	2,003,460
Exports of goods and services	618,278	673,495	779,923
Less Imports of goods and services	588,876	607,587	763,573
GDP in market prices	1,493,766	1,698,480	2,019,810
GDP at constant 2000 prices	1,151,462	1,211,338	1,288,000

Gross Domestic Product by Economic Activity

	2005	2006	2007
Agriculture, hunting, forestry and fishing	305,351	347,361	413,877
Mining and quarrying / Manufacturing / Electricity, gas and water	418,888	543,946	645,003
Construction	40,320	61,805	72,676
Wholesale and retail trade	302,605	286,357	352,774
Transport and communications	160,851	182,195	201,155
Finance and insurance	73,969	84,433	112,328
Government services	159,460	150,578	200,662
Other community, social and personal services	37,162	42,511	48,307
Non-profit private services	795	908	954
Sub-total	1,499,401	1,700,094	2,047,736
Import duties	22,904	32,877	18,850
Less Imputed bank service charges	−28,539	−34,491	−46,776
GDP in market prices	1,493,766	1,698,480	2,019,810

BALANCE OF PAYMENTS
(US $ million)

	2004	2005	2006
Exports of goods f.o.b.	7,220	8,602	10,245
Imports of goods f.o.b.	−6,957	−8,742	−9,359
Trade balance	263	−140	886
Exports of services	2,613	2,910	2,924
Imports of services	−2,235	−2,359	−2,520
Balance on goods and services	642	411	1,290
Other income received	385	395	428
Other income paid	−1,114	−1,258	−1,363
Balance on goods, services and income	−88	−452	355
Current transfers received	690	763	770
Current transfers paid	−16	−16	−235
Current balance	587	295	890
Capital account (net)	18	18	18
Direct investment from abroad	275	500	600
Other investment assets	−237	−524	−733
Other investment liabilities	−135	−138	−919
Net errors and omissions	−256	−137	−588
Overall balance	251	14	−732

Source: IMF, *International Financial Statistics*.

External Trade

PRINCIPAL COMMODITIES
(distribution by SITC major group, £S million)

Imports	2005	2006	2007
Food and live animals	54,709	56,856	68,802
Beverages and tobacco	2,746	4,694	5,651
Crude materials, inedible, except fuels	22,236	21,376	25,696
Mineral fuels and lubricants	123,650	143,926	225,666
Animal and vegetable oils and fats	3,788	3,754	5,370
Chemicals and related products	59,061	59,677	78,368
Basic manufactures	106,775	111,669	147,949
Machinery and transport equipment	99,593	112,685	117,840
Total (incl. others)	502,368	531,324	684,557

Exports	2005	2006	2007
Food and live animals	31,899	75,470	93,079
Beverages and tobacco	3,096	3,166	5,040
Crude materials, inedible, except fuels	13,754	15,256	9,296
Mineral fuels and lubricants	211,775	203,756	219,541
Animal and vegetable oils and fats	5,001	9,120	13,595
Chemicals and related products	9,288	24,765	28,755
Basic manufactures	18,111	56,217	70,321
Machinery and transport equipment	3,785	23,861	26,936
Total (incl. others)	424,300	505,012	579,034

PRINCIPAL TRADING PARTNERS
(£S million)

Imports c.i.f.	2004	2005	2006
China, People's Republic	22,909	29,414	34,566
Egypt	9,283	12,963	27,523
France	6,486	8,499	18,702
Germany	9,686	10,870	15,423
India	6,605	8,689	16,688
Italy	12,790	13,871	25,971
Japan	7,613	11,556	15,867
Lebanon	5,934	8,292	7,229
Netherlands	3,111	3,427	4,812
Romania	5,148	4,207	3,769
Russia	15,885	13,765	54,353
Saudi Arabia	15,278	15,903	27,218
Spain	2,921	3,550	3,463
Turkey	13,923	15,564	21,322
United Kingdom	4,257	3,052	2,299
USA	13,869	11,824	12,120
Total (incl. others)	389,006	502,369	531,324

Exports f.o.b.	2004	2005	2006
Egypt	5,136	6,731	19,197
France	47,743	52,424	44,473
Germany	1,307	4,675	6,625
Italy	60,007	89,031	98,967
Jordan	7,050	7,036	19,940
Kuwait	2,611	2,555	12,218
Lebanon	9,221	8,778	18,995
Netherlands	5,869	13,054	5,244
Russia	404	444	2,307
Saudi Arabia	16,493	17,120	44,166
Spain	9,494	14,163	16,424
Turkey	17,047	13,414	16,259
United Kingdom	4,425	12,017	21,914
USA	8,392	14,164	10,451
Total (incl. others)	301,553	424,300	505,012

SYRIA   Directory

Transport

RAILWAYS
(traffic)

	2002	2003	2004
Passenger-km ('000)	384,321	525,357	691,916
Freight ('000 metric tons)	5,927	6,414	7,232

ROAD TRAFFIC
(motor vehicles in use)

	2002	2003	2004
Passenger cars	175,918	200,933	227,639
Buses	4,758	4,767	4,758
Lorries, trucks, etc.	362,392	376,543	388,716
Motorcycles	99,009	104,732	122,323

SHIPPING
Merchant Fleet
(registered at 31 December)

	2005	2006	2007
Number of vessels	162	151	139
Total displacement ('000 grt)	412.5	388.7	361.0

Source: Lloyd's Register-Fairplay, *World Fleet Statistics*.

International Sea-borne Traffic

	1996	1997	1998
Vessels entered ('000 net reg. tons)	2,901*	2,640	2,622
Cargo unloaded ('000 metric tons)	4,560	4,788	5,112
Cargo loaded ('000 metric tons)	1,788	2,412	2,136

* Excluding Banias.

Vessels entered ('000 net registered tons): 2,928 in 1999; 2,798 in 2000; 2,827 in 2001.

Source: mainly UN, *Monthly Bulletin of Statistics* and *Statistical Yearbook*.

CIVIL AVIATION
(traffic on scheduled services)

	2002	2003	2004
Kilometres flown (million)	16	9	11
Passengers carried ('000)	824	940	1,170
Passenger-km (million)	1,609	744	2,212
Total ton-km (million)	169	173	219

Source: UN, *Statistical Yearbook*.

Tourism

FOREIGN VISITOR ARRIVALS
(incl. excursionists)*

Country of nationality	2004	2005	2006
Iran	196,699	247,662	270,915
Iraq	804,131	913,266	1,289,250
Jordan	851,095	940,413	882,501
Kuwait	105,715	103,474	98,892
Lebanon	2,262,733	1,681,158	1,786,943
Saudi Arabia	461,035	469,118	408,186
Turkey	658,581	688,978	480,553
Total (incl. others)	6,153,653	5,837,980	6,009,483

* Figures exclude Syrian nationals resident abroad.

2007 ('000): Total arrivals 6,004.

Tourism receipts (US $ million, incl. passenger transport): 1,883 in 2004; 2,035 in 2005; 2,113 in 2006.

Source: World Tourism Organization.

Communications Media

	2005	2006	2007
Telephones ('000 main lines in use)	2,903	3,243	3,452
Mobile cellular telephones ('000 in use)	2,950	4,675	6,700
Personal computers ('000 in use)	800	n.a.	n.a.
Internet users ('000)	1,100	1,550	3,470
Broadband subscribers ('000)	1.2	7.9	n.a.

1992: Book production 598 titles.

1996: Daily newspapers 8 (average circulation 287,000 copies).

1997 ('000 in use): Radio receivers 4,150.

1998 ('000 in use): Facsimile machines 22.

2000 ('000 in use): Television receivers 1,080.

Sources: UNESCO, *Statistical Yearbook*; UN, *Statistical Yearbook*; International Telecommunication Union.

Education

(2005/06, unless otherwise indicated)

	Institutions*	Teachers	Males	Females	Total
Pre-primary	1,431	6,541	82,185	73,296	155,481
Primary		124,665†	1,189,066	1,090,479	2,279,545
Secondary: general	1,140	26,273*	1,223,259	1,127,435	2,350,694
Secondary: vocational	595	17,368†	66,596	47,398	113,994
Higher*	5	8,084	141,310	138,304	279,614

* Excluding private universities; data for 2006/07.
† 2003/04 figure.

Source: mainly UNESCO Institute for Statistics.

Adult literacy rate (UNESCO estimates): 83.1% (males 89.7%; females 76.5%) in 2007 (Source: UNESCO Institute for Statistics).

Directory

The Constitution

A new and permanent Constitution was endorsed by 97.6% of voters in a national referendum held on 12 March 1973. The 157-article Constitution defines Syria as a 'Socialist popular democracy' with a 'pre-planned Socialist economy'. Under the new Constitution, Lt-Gen. Hafiz al-Assad remained President, with the power to appoint and dismiss his Vice-President, Premier and government ministers, and also became Commander-in-Chief of the Armed Forces, Secretary-General of the Baath Socialist Party and President of the National Progressive Front. According to the Constitution, the President is elected by direct popular vote for a seven-year term. Legislative power is vested in the People's Assembly, with 250 members elected for a four-year term by universal adult suffrage.

SYRIA

Following the death of President Hafiz al-Assad on 10 June 2000, the Constitution was amended to allow his son, Lt-Gen. Bashar al-Assad, to accede to the presidency. Bashar al-Assad also became Commander-in-Chief of the armed forces, Secretary-General of the Baath Socialist Party and President of the National Progressive Front.

The Government

HEAD OF STATE

President: Lt-Gen. BASHAR AL-ASSAD (assumed office 17 July 2000).

Vice-President, responsible for Foreign Affairs and Information: FAROUK ASH-SHARA'.

Vice-President: Dr NAJAH AL-ATTAR.

COUNCIL OF MINISTERS
(April 2009)

Prime Minister: MUHAMMAD NAJI AL-OTARI.
Deputy Prime Minister, responsible for Economic Affairs: ABDULLAH AD-DARDARI.
Minister of Defence: Lt-Gen. HASSAN AT-TURKMANI.
Minister of Foreign Affairs: WALID MOUALLEM.
Minister of Information: MOHSEN BILAL.
Minister of the Interior: Gen. SAEED MUHAMMAD SAMMOUR.
Minister of Local Administration: TAMER FOUAD AL-HIJEH.
Minister of Education: ALI SA'D.
Minister of Higher Education: GHIATH BARAKAT.
Minister of Electricity: AHMAD QUSAY KAYYALI.
Minister of Culture: RIYAD NA'ASAN AGHA.
Minister of Transport: YAAROB SULEIMAN BADR.
Minister of Petroleum and Mineral Resources: SUFIAN ALLAW.
Minister of Industry: FOUAD ISSA AL-JONI.
Minister of Finance: Dr MUHAMMAD AL-HUSSEIN.
Minister of Economy and Trade: AMER HOSNI LUFTI.
Minister of Housing and Construction: OMAR IBRAHIM GHALAWANJI.
Minister of Justice: AHMAD HAMMOUD YOUNIS.
Minister of Agriculture and Agrarian Reform: Dr ADEL SAFAR.
Minister of Irrigation: NADER AL-BUNI.
Minister of Communications and Technology: IMAD ABD AL-GHANI SABOUNI.
Minister of Health: RIDA ADNAN SAEED.
Minister of Awqaf (Islamic Endowments): MUHAMMAD ABD AS-SATTAR AS-SAYYID.
Minister of Labour and Social Affairs: DIALA HAJ-AREF.
Minister of Tourism: Dr SAADALLAH AGHA AL-QALLA.
Minister of Presidential Affairs: MANSOUR AZZAM.
Minister of Expatriates: JOSEPH SWEID.
Minister of State for Environmental Affairs: KAWKAB AS-SABAGH MUHAMMAD JAMIL AD-DAYEH.
Ministers of State: YOUSUF SULEIMAN AL-AHMAD, BASHAR ASH-SH'AR, HUSSEIN MAHMOUD FARZAT, HASSAN AS-SARRI, GHIATH JARAATLY.

MINISTRIES

Office of the President: Damascus.
Office of the Prime Minister: rue Chahbandar, Damascus; tel. (11) 2226000.
Ministry of Agriculture and Agrarian Reform: rue Jabri, place Hedjaz, Damascus; tel. (11) 2213613; fax (11) 2216627; e-mail agre-min@syriatel.net; internet www.syrian-agriculture.org.
Ministry of Awqaf (Islamic Endowments): place al-Misat, Damascus; tel. (11) 4470005; fax (11) 4470006; e-mail admin@syrianawkaf.org; internet www.syrianawkaf.org.
Ministry of Communications and Technology: rue Abed, Damascus; tel. (11) 3320807; fax (11) 2246403; e-mail admin@moct.gov.sy; internet www.moct.gov.sy.
Ministry of Culture: rue George Haddad, Rawda, Damascus; tel. (11) 3331556; fax (11) 3320804; e-mail info@moc.gov.sy; internet www.moc.gov.sy.
Ministry of Defence: place Omayad, Damascus; tel. (11) 7770700; fax (11) 2237842.
Ministry of Economy and Trade: rue Maysaloun, Damascus; tel. (11) 2213514; fax (11) 2225695; e-mail econ-min@net.sy; internet www.syrecon.org.
Ministry of Education: rue Shahbander, al-Masraa, Damascus; tel. (11) 4444800; fax (11) 4420435; e-mail info@syrianeducation.org.sy; internet www.syrianeducation.org.sy.
Ministry of Electricity: BP 4900, rue al-Kouatly, Damascus; tel. (11) 2223086; fax (11) 2223686.
Ministry of Expatriates: Island 20, Dummar, Damascus; tel. (11) 3193999; fax (11) 3134301; e-mail webmaster@moex.gov.sy; internet ministryofexpatriates.gov.sy.
Ministry of Finance: BP 13136, rue Jule Jammal, Damascus; tel. (11) 2239624; fax (11) 2224701; e-mail mof@net.sy; internet www.syrianfinance.org.
Ministry of Foreign Affairs: rue ar-Rashid, Damascus; tel. (11) 3331200; fax (11) 3327620.
Ministry of Health: rue Majlis ash-Sha'ab, Damascus; tel. (11) 3311020; fax (11) 3311114; e-mail health-min@net.sy; internet www.moh.gov.sy.
Ministry of Higher Education: BP 9251, place Mezzeh Gamarik, Damascus; tel. (11) 2119865; fax (11) 2128919; e-mail mhe@shern.net; internet www.mhe.gov.sy.
Ministry of Housing and Construction: place Yousuf al-Azmeh, as-Salheyeh, Damascus; tel. (11) 2217571; fax (11) 2459400; e-mail diwan@mhc.gov.sy; internet www.mhc.gov.sy.
Ministry of Industry: BP 12835, rue Maysaloun, Damascus; tel. (11) 2231834; fax (11) 2231096; e-mail industry-min@mail.sy; internet www.syrianindustry.org.
Ministry of Information: Immeuble Dar al-Baath, Autostrade Mezzeh, Damascus; tel. and fax (11) 6664681; e-mail info@moi.gov.sy; internet www.moi.gov.sy.
Ministry of the Interior: rue al-Bahsah, al-Marjeh, Damascus; tel. (11) 2313471; fax (11) 2324835; e-mail admin@civilaffair-moi.gov.sy; internet www.civilaffair-moi.gov.sy.
Ministry of Irrigation: BP 4451, rue Fardoss; tel. (11) 2212741; fax (11) 3320691; e-mail ministry@irrigation.gov.sy; internet www.irrigation.gov.sy.
Ministry of Justice: rue an-Nasr, Damascus; tel. (11) 2214105; fax (11) 2246250.
Ministry of Labour and Social Affairs: place Yousuf al-Azmeh, as-Salheyeh, Damascus; tel. (11) 2210355; fax (11) 2247499; internet www.molsa.gov.sy.
Ministry of Local Administration: BP 3311, Damascus; tel. (11) 2317911; fax (11) 2316921; e-mail info@mlae-sy.org; internet www.mlae-sy.org.
Ministry of Petroleum and Mineral Resources: BP 40, al-Adawi, Insha'at, Damascus; tel. (11) 4451624; fax (11) 4463942; e-mail mopmr@net.sy.
Ministry of State for Environmental Affairs: Damascus.
Ministry of Tourism: BP 6642, rue Barada, Damascus; tel. (11) 2210122; fax (11) 2242636; e-mail min-tourism@mail.sy; internet www.syriatourism.org.
Ministry of Transport: BP 33999, rue al-Jala'a, Damascus; tel. (11) 3316840; fax (11) 3323317; e-mail min-trans@net.sy; internet www.mot.gov.sy.

Legislature

MAJLIS ASH-SHA'AB
(People's Assembly)

Speaker: MAHMOUD AREF AL-ABRASH.

Election, 22 and 23 April 2007

Party	Seats
National Progressive Front*	172
Independents	78
Total	**250**

*The National Progressive Front reportedly comprised 10 political parties, headed by the Baath Arab Socialist Party.

Political Organizations

The **National Progressive Front (NPF—Al-Jabha al-Wataniyah at-Taqadumiyah)**, headed by the late President Hafiz al-Assad, was formed in March 1972 as a coalition of five political parties. The Syrian Constitution defines the Baath Arab Socialist Party as 'the leading party in the society and the state'. At mid-2007 the NPF consisted of 10 parties:

SYRIA

Arab Democratic Unionist Party (Hizb al-Ittihad al-'Arabi ad-Dimuqrati): f. 1981, following split from the Arab Socialist Union; considers the concerns of the Arab world in general as secondary to those of Syria itself in the pursuit of pan-Arab goals; Chair. GHASSAN AHMAD OSMAN.

Arab Socialist Movement (Harakat al-Ishtiraki al-'Arabi): Damascus; f. 1963, following split from Arab Socialist Union; contested the 2007 election to the People's Assembly as two factions (see also National Vow Movement); Leader AHMAD AL-AHMAD.

Arab Socialist Union (al-Ittihad al-Ishtiraki al-'Arabi): Damascus; f. 1973, following the separation of the Syrian branch from the international Arab Socialist Union; Nasserite; supportive of the policies of the Baath Arab Socialist Party; Leader SAFWAN AL-QUDSI.

Baath Arab Socialist Party (al-Hizb al-Ba'th al-'Arabi al-Ishtiraki): National Command, BP 9389, Autostrade Mezzeh, Damascus; tel. (11) 6622142; fax (11) 6622099; e-mail baath@baath-party.org; internet www.baath-party.org; Arab nationalist socialist party; f. 1947, as a result of merger between the Arab Revival (Baath) Movement (f. 1940) and the Arab Socialist Party (f. 1940); in power since 1963; supports creation of a unified Arab socialist society; approx. 1m. mems in Syria; brs in most Arab countries; Sec.-Gen. Lt-Gen. BASHAR AL-ASSAD.

Democratic Socialist Unionist Party (al-Hizb al-Wahdawi al-Ishtiraki ad-Dimuqrati): f. 1974, following split from the Arab Socialist Union; Chair. FADLALLAH NASR AD-DIN.

National Vow Movement (Harakat al-'ahd al-Watani): a breakaway party from the Arab Socialist Union; was part of the Arab Socialist Movement; awarded three seats in 2007 election to the People's Assembly; Leader GHASSAN ABD AL-AZIZ OSMAN.

Socialist Unionists (Al-Wahdawiyyun al-Ishtirakiyyun): f. 1961, through split from the Baath Arab Socialist Party following that organization's acceptance of Syria's decision to secede from the United Arab Republic; Nasserite; aims for Arab unity, particularly a new union with Egypt; produces weekly periodical *Al-Wehdawi*; Chair. FAYEZ ISMAIL.

Syrian Arab Socialist Union Party: Damascus; tel. (11) 239305; Nasserite; Sec.-Gen. SAFWAN KOUDSI.

Syrian Communist Party (Bakdash) (al-Hizb ash-shuyu'i as-suri): POB 7837, Damascus; tel. (11) 4455048; fax (11) 4446390; e-mail info@syriancp.org; internet www.syriancp.org; f. 1924 by Fouad Shamal in Lebanon and Khalid Bakdash (died 1995); until 1943 part of joint Communist Party of Syria and Lebanon; party split into two factions under separate leaders, Bakdash and Faisal (q.v.), in 1986; Marxist-Leninist; publishes fortnightly periodical *Sawt ash-Shaab*; Sec.-Gen. WISSAL FARHA BAKDASH.

Syrian Communist Party (Faisal) (al-Hizb ash-shuyu'i as-suri): Damascus; f. 1986, following split of Syrian Communist Party into two factions under separate leaders, Faisal and Bakdash (q.v.); aims to end domination of Baath Arab Socialist Party and the advantages given to mems of that party at all levels; advocates the lifting of the state of emergency and the release of all political prisoners; publishes weekly periodical *An-Nour*; Sec.-Gen. YOUSUF RASHID FAISAL.

Syrian Social Nationalist Party (Centralist Wing) (al-Hizb as-Suri al-Qawmi al-Ijtima'i): e-mail webmaster@ssnp.info; internet www.ssnp.com; f. 1932 in Beirut, Lebanon; joined the NPF in 2005; also known as Parti populaire syrien; seeks creation of a 'Greater Syrian' state, incl. Syria, Lebanon, Jordan, the Palestinian territories, Iraq, Kuwait, Cyprus and parts of Egypt, Iran and Turkey; advocates separation of church and state, the redistribution of wealth, and a strong military; supports Syrian involvement in Lebanese affairs; has brs world-wide, and approx. 90,000 mems in Syria; Chair. ISSAM MAHAYIRI.

There are numerous opposition parties, within Syria or in exile, which are forced to operate on a clandestine basis. Formed in 1980, the **National Democratic Rally** (NDR—Tajammu' al-Watani ad-Dimuqrati) is an alliance of banned, secularist opposition parties, several of which are opposition wings of parties that joined the ruling NPF.

A current member of the NDR, the **Syrian Democratic People's Party** (al-Hizb ash-Sha'ab as-Suri ad-Dimuqrati—leader ABULLAH HOSHA) was founded in 1973 as the Syrian Communist Party (Political Bureau), following the decision by founder Riad at-Turk to split from that party after its leader, Khalid Bakdash, decided to allow the organization to join the NPF. The party adopted its current name in 2005. The party publishes an online newsletter (www.arraee.com).

There is also a **Marxist-Leninist Communist Action Party**, which regards itself as independent of all Arab regimes.

An illegal Syrian-based organization, the **Islamic Movement for Change (IMC)**, claimed responsibility for a bomb attack in Damascus in December 1996.

Diplomatic Representation

EMBASSIES IN SYRIA

Algeria: Immeuble Noss, Raouda, Damascus; tel. (11) 3331446; fax (11) 3334698; Ambassador SALEH BOUSHEH.

Argentina: BP 116, Damascus; tel. (11) 3334167; fax (11) 3327326; e-mail easir@net.sy; Ambassador HERNÁN ROBERTO PLORUTTI.

Armenia: BP 33241, Ibrahim Hanono St, Malki, Damascus; tel. (11) 6133560; fax (11) 6130952; e-mail am309@net.sy; Ambassador ARCHAD BOLADIAN.

Austria: BP 5634, Immeuble Mohamed Naim ad-Deker, 1 rue Farabi, Mezzeh Est, Damascus; tel. (11) 61380100; fax (11) 6116734; e-mail damaskus-ob@bmeia.gv.at; Ambassador MARIA KUNZ.

Bahrain: BP 36225, Damascus; tel. (11) 6132314; fax (11) 6130502; e-mail damascus.mission@mofa.gov.bh; Ambassador ABD AR-RAHMAN MUBARAK AS-SULEITTI.

Belarus: BP 16239, 27 rue Qurtaja, Mezzeh Est, Damascus; tel. (11) 6118097; fax (11) 6132802; e-mail syria@belembassy.org; Ambassador OLEG YERMALOVICH.

Belgium: 3 rue Salaam, Bâtiment 101, 2e–3e étage, Mezzeh Est, Damascus; tel. (11) 61399931; fax (11) 61399977; e-mail damascus@diplobel.fed.be; internet www.diplomatie.be/damascus; Ambassador DERRICK LUNCK.

Brazil: BP 2219, 39 rue Al-Farabi, Mezzeh Est, Damascus; tel. (11) 6124551; fax (11) 6124553; e-mail braemsyr@net.sy; Ambassador EDGAR ANTONIO CASIANO.

Bulgaria: BP 2732, 8 rue Pakistan, place Arnous, Damascus; tel. (11) 3318445; fax (11) 4419854; e-mail bul_emb@abv.bg; Ambassador GEORGI YANKOV.

Canada: BP 3394, Damascus; tel. (11) 6116692; fax (11) 6114000; e-mail dmcus@dfait-maeci.gc.ca; internet www.dfait-maeci.gc.ca/syria; Ambassador GLENN DAVIDSON.

Chile: 6 rue Ziad Bin Abi Soufian, Rawda, Damascus; tel. (11) 3338443; fax (11) 3331563; e-mail echilesy@scs-net.org; Ambassador RICARDO FIEGELIST SCHMIDT.

China, People's Republic: BP 2455, 83 rue Ata Ayoubi, Damascus; tel. (11) 3339594; fax (11) 3338067; e-mail chinaemb_sy@mfa.gov.cn; internet sy.chineseembassy.org; Ambassador LI HUAXIN.

Cuba: Immeuble Istouani and Charbati, 40 rue ar-Rachid, Damascus; tel. (11) 3339624; fax (11) 3333802; e-mail embacubasy@net.sy; Ambassador LUIS ERINEL MARISY FIGUEREDO.

Cyprus: BP 9269, 278G rue Malek bin Rabia, Mezzeh Ouest, Damascus; tel. (11) 6130812; fax (11) 6130814; e-mail syriapio@scs-net.org; Ambassador EFSTATHIOS ORPHANIDES.

Czech Republic: BP 2249, place Abou al-Ala'a al-Maari, Damascus; tel. (11) 3331383; fax (11) 3338268; e-mail damascus@embassy.mzv.cz; internet www.mzv.cz/damascus; Ambassador TOMÁŠ ULIČNÝ.

Denmark: BP 2244, Fatmeh Idriss 6, rue al-Ghazzawi, Mezzeh Ouest, Damascus; tel. (11) 61909000; fax (11) 61909033; e-mail damamb@um.dk; internet www.ambdamaskus.um.dk; Ambassador OLE EGBERG MIKKELSEN.

Egypt: BP 12443, rue al-Gala'a, Abou Roumaneh, Damascus; tel. (11) 3330756; fax (11) 3337961; fax egyemb@syria.net; Ambassador SHAWKI ISMAIL ALI SOLIMAN.

Eritrea: BP 12846, Autostrade Al-Mazen West, 82 rue Akram Mosque, Damascus; tel. (11) 6112357; fax (11) 6112358; Chargé d'affaires a.i. HUMMED MOHAMED SAEED KULU.

Finland: BP 3893, Immeuble 164A, rue Doha, Area 3, Mezzeh Est, Damascus; tel. (11) 6127570; fax (11) 6119777; e-mail sanomat.dam@formin.fi; Ambassador HARRI MÄKI-REINIKKA.

France: BP 769, rue Ata al-Ayoubi, al-Afif, Damascus; tel. (11) 3390200; fax (11) 3390221; e-mail ambafr@net.sy; internet www.ambafrance-sy.org/spip.php?rubrique=1; Ambassador MICHEL DUCLOS.

Germany: BP 2237, 16 rue Abd al-Mun'im Riyad, al-Malki, Damascus; tel. (11) 37900000; fax (11) 3323812; e-mail info@damaskus.diplo.de; internet www.damaskus.diplo.de; Ambassador ANDREAS REINICKE.

Greece: BP 30319, Immeuble Pharaon, 11 rue Farabi, Mezzeh Est, Damascus; tel. (11) 6113035; fax (11) 6114920; e-mail gremb.dam@mfa.gr; Ambassador KONSTANTINA ZAGORIANOU-PRIFTI.

Holy See: BP 2271, 1 place Ma'raket Ajnadin, al-Malki, Damascus (Apostolic Nunciature); tel. (11) 3332601; fax (11) 3327550; e-mail noncesy@mail.sy; Apostolic Nuncio Most Rev. MARIO ZENARI (Titular Archbishop of Iulium Carnicum).

Hungary: BP 2607, 12 rue as-Salam, Mezzeh Est, Damascus; tel. (11) 6117966; fax (11) 6117917; e-mail mission.dam@kum.hu; internet www.mfa.gov.hu/kulkepviselet/sy; Ambassador Prof. PÉTER MEDGYES.

SYRIA

India: BP 685, 3455 Ibn Al-Haitham St, Abou Roumaneh, Damascus; tel. (11) 3347351; fax (11) 3347912; e-mail indemcom@scs-net.org; Ambassador V. PRANATHARTHI HARAN.

Indonesia: BP 3530, Immeuble 26, Bloc 270A, 132 rue Al-Madina al-Munawar, Mezzeh Est, Damascus; tel. (11) 6119630; fax (11) 6119632; e-mail kbridams@net.sy; internet kbri-damascus.go.id; Ambassador MUHAMMAD BASYOUNI.

Iran: BP 2691, Autostrade Mezzeh, nr ar-Razi Hospital, Damascus; tel. (11) 6117675; fax (11) 6110997; e-mail iran-dam@net.sy; Ambassador SAYED AHMAD MOUSSAVI.

Iraq: Damascus; tel. (11) 3341290; fax (11) 3341291; e-mail dmkemb@iraqmofamail.net; Ambassador Dr ALA'A HUSSAIN AL-JAWADI.

Italy: BP 2216, rue al-Ayoubi, Damascus; tel. (11) 3338338; fax (11) 3320325; e-mail ambasciata.damasco@esteri.it; internet www.ambdamasco.esteri.it; Ambassador ACHILLE FRANCO LUIGI AMIRIO.

Japan: BP 3366, 3537 Sharkasiya, rue al-Jala'a, Abou Roumaneh, Damascus; tel. (11) 3338273; fax (11) 3339920; Ambassador MASAKI KUNEIDA.

Jordan: rue Abou Roumaneh, Damascus; tel. (11) 3334642; fax (11) 3336741; internet www.jordanembassydemascus.gov.jo; Ambassador OMAR AL-OMAR.

Korea, Democratic People's Republic: rue Fares al-Khouri-Jisr Tora, Damascus; Ambassador CHOE SU HON.

Kuwait: rue Ibrahim Hanano, Damascus; tel. (11) 6118511; fax (11) 6117640; e-mail damascus@mofa.gov.kw; Ambassador FAHED AHMAD AL-AWADHI.

Lebanon: Abou Roumaneh, Damascus; Ambassador MICHEL EL-KHOURY.

Libya: Abou Roumaneh, Damascus; Head of People's Bureau AHMAD ABD AS-SALAM BIN KHAYAL.

Malaysia: 117 Farabi St, Mezzeh East Villas, Damascus; tel. (11) 6122811; fax (11) 6122814; e-mail malsyria@kln.gov.my; Ambassador IBRAHIM ABDULLAH.

Mauritania: ave al-Jala'a, rue Karameh, Damascus; Ambassador AAL OULD AHMADO.

Morocco: 35 rue Abu Bakr Al Karkhi-Villas, Mezzeh Ouest, Damascus; tel. (11) 6110451; fax (11) 6117885; e-mail sifmar@scs-net.org; Ambassador ABDELOUAHAB BELLOUKI.

Netherlands: BP 702, Immeuble Tello, rue al-Jala'a, Abou Roumaneh, Damascus; tel. (11) 3336871; fax (11) 3339369; e-mail dmc@minbuza.nl; Ambassador DÉSIRÉE BONIS.

Norway: BP 7703, Immeuble 2, rue Shafei, Mezzeh Est, Damascus; tel. (11) 6122941; fax (11) 6131159; e-mail emb.damascus@mfa.no; internet www.norway.org.sy; Ambassador ROLF WILLY HANSEN.

Oman: BP 9635, rue Ghazzawi, Mezzeh Ouest, Damascus; tel. (11) 6110408; fax (11) 6114589; e-mail oman-em@scs-net.org; Ambassador MUHAMMAD BIN SALEM BIN SAID ASH-SHANFARI.

Pakistan: BP 9284, rue al-Farabi, Mezzeh Est, Damascus; tel. (11) 6132694; fax (11) 6132662; e-mail parepdam@scs-net.org; Ambassador MUNZER SHAFIQ.

Panama: BP 2548, Apt 7, Immeuble az-Zein, rue al-Bizm, Malki, Damascus; tel. (11) 224743; Chargé d'affaires CARLOS A. DE GRACIA.

Philippines: BP 36849, 56 rue Hamzeh bin al-Mutaleb, Mezzeh, Damascus; tel. (11) 6115893; e-mail pe.damascus@dfa.gov.ph; Ambassador WILFREDO R. CUYUGAN.

Poland: BP 501, rue Baha Eddin Aita, Abou Roumaneh, Damascus; tel. (11) 3333010; fax (11) 3315318; e-mail damaszek.amb.sekretariat@msz.gov.pl; internet www.damaszek.polemb.net; Ambassador MICHAŁ MURKOCIŃSKI.

Qatar: BP 4188, rue Ahmed Shouki, Abou Roumaneh, Damascus; e-mail damascus@mofa.gov.qa; tel. (11) 3336717; fax (11) 3342455; Ambassador MAJED GHANEM AL-ALI AL-MAADEED.

Romania: BP 4454, 8 rue Ibrahim Hanano, Damascus; tel. (11) 3327570; fax (11) 3327571; e-mail damascamb@gmail.com; Ambassador DANTOS FLORIN SANDOVETCH.

Russia: rue Umar bin al-Khattab, ad-Dawi, Damascus; tel. (11) 4423155; fax (11) 4423182; e-mail rusemb@scs-net.org; Ambassador SERGEI KIRPICHENKO.

Saudi Arabia: rue al-Jala'a, Abou Roumaneh, Damascus; tel. (11) 3334914; fax (11) 3337383; e-mail syemb@mofa.gov.sa; Ambassador (vacant).

Serbia: BP 739, 18 rue al-Jala'a, Abou Roumaneh, Damascus; tel. (11) 3336222; fax (11) 3333690; e-mail ambasada@srbija-damask.org; internet www.srbija-damask.org; Ambassador Dr GORDANA ANIČIĆ.

Slovakia: BP 33115, 158 rue ash-Shafei, Mezzeh Est, Damascus; tel. (11) 6132114; fax (11) 6132598; e-mail slovemb@scs-net.org; internet www.damascus.mfa.sk; Ambassador OLDRICH HLAVÁČEK.

Somalia: ave Ata Ayoubi, al-Afif, Damascus; Ambassador (vacant).

South Africa: BP 9141, rue al-Ghazaoui, 7 Jadet Kouraish, Mezzeh Ouest, Damascus; tel. (11) 61351520; fax (11) 6111714; e-mail admin.damascus@foreign.gov.za; Ambassador MUHAMMAD DANGOR.

Spain: BP 392, rue ash-Shafi, Mezzeh Est, Damascus; tel. (11) 6132900; fax (11) 6132941; e-mail emb.damasco@mae.es; Ambassador JUAN RAMÓN SERRAT CUENCA-ROMERO.

Sudan: Damascus; tel. (11) 6111036; fax (11) 6112904; e-mail sud-emb@net.sy; Ambassador ABD AR-RAHMAN DIRAR.

Sweden: BP 4266, Immeuble du Patriarcat Catholique, rue Chakib Arslan, Abou Roumaneh, Damascus; tel. (11) 33400700; fax (11) 3327749; e-mail ambassaden.damaskus@foreign.ministry.se; internet www.swedenabroad.com/damascus; Ambassador NICHOLAS KIPPON.

Switzerland: BP 234, 2 rue ash-Shafi, Mezzeh Est, Damascus; tel. (11) 6111972; fax (11) 6111976; e-mail dam.vertretung@eda.admin.ch; internet www.eda.admin.ch/damascus; Ambassador MARTIN AESCHBACHER.

Tunisia: BP 4114, 6 rue ash-Shafi, blvd Fahim, Mezzeh, Damascus; tel. (11) 6132700; fax (11) 6132704; e-mail at.damas@net.sy; Ambassador MUHAMMAD AOUITI.

Turkmenistan: Miset, 4097 Ruki ed-Din, 2e étage, Damascus; tel. (11) 2241834; fax (11) 3320905.

Turkey: BP 3738, 56–58 ave Ziad bin Abou Soufian, Damascus; tel. (11) 33501930; fax (11) 3339243; e-mail turkemb.damascus@mfa.gov.tr; internet damascus.emb.mfa.gov.tr; Ambassador Y. HALIT ÇEVIK.

Ukraine: BP 33944, 14 rue as-Salam, Mezzeh Est, Damascus; tel. (11) 6113016; fax (11) 6121355; e-mail emb_sy@mfa.gov.ua; internet www.mfa.gov.ua/syria; Ambassador OLEH SEMENETS.

United Arab Emirates: Immeuble Housami, 62 rue Raouda, Damascus; tel. (11) 3330308; fax (11) 3327961; e-mail emirate-damas@net.sy; Ambassador SALEM AL-QATAM AZ-ZA'ABI.

United Kingdom: BP 37, Immeuble Kotob, 11 rue Muhammad Kurd Ali, Malki, Damascus; tel. (11) 3391535; fax (933) 214342; e-mail british.embassy.damascus@fco.gov.uk; internet ukinsyria.fco.gov.uk; Ambassador SIMON COLLIS.

USA: BP 29, 2 rue al-Mansour, Abou Roumaneh, Damascus; tel. (11) 33914444; fax (11) 33913999; e-mail damasweb-query@state.gov; internet syria.usembassy.gov; Chargé d'affaires MAURA CONNELLY.

Venezuela: BP 2403, Immeuble at-Tabbah, 5 rue Lisaneddin bin al-Khateb, place Rauda, Damascus; tel. (11) 6124835; fax (11) 6124833; e-mail embavenez@tarassul.sy; internet www.embavensiria.com; Ambassador DIA NADER AL-ANDARI.

Yemen: Abou Roumaneh, Charkassieh, Damascus; Ambassador ABD AL-WAHAB HADI MOHSIN TAWAF.

Judicial System

The Courts of Law in Syria are principally divided into two juridical court systems: Courts of General Jurisdiction and Administrative Courts. Since 1973 the Supreme Constitutional Court has been established as the paramount body of the Syrian judicial structure.

THE SUPREME CONSTITUTIONAL COURT

This is the highest court in Syria. It has specific jurisdiction over: (i) judicial review of the constitutionality of laws and legislative decrees; (ii) investigation of charges relating to the legality of the election of members of the Majlis ash-Sha'ab (People's Assembly); (iii) trial of infractions committed by the President of the Republic in the exercise of his functions; (iv) resolution of positive and negative jurisdictional conflicts and determination of the competent court between the different juridical court systems, as well as other bodies exercising judicial competence. The Supreme Constitutional Court is composed of a Chief Justice and four Justices. They are appointed by decree of the President of the Republic for a renewable period of four years.

Chief Justice of the Supreme Court: ADNAN ZUREIQ, Damascus; tel. (11) 3331902.

COURTS OF GENERAL JURISDICTION

The Courts of General Jurisdiction in Syria are divided into six categories: (i) The Court of Cassation; (ii) The Courts of Appeal; (iii) The Tribunals of First Instance; (iv) The Tribunals of Peace; (v) The Personal Status Courts; (vi) The Courts for Minors. Each of the above categories (except the Personal Status Courts) is divided into Civil, Penal and Criminal Chambers.

(i) The Court of Cassation: This is the highest court of general jurisdiction. Final judgments rendered by Courts of Appeal in penal and civil litigations may be petitioned to the Court of Cassation by the Defendant or the Public Prosecutor in penal and criminal litigations, and by any of the parties in interest in civil litigations, on grounds of defective application or interpretation of the law as stated in the challenged judgment, on grounds of irregularity of form or procedure, or violation of due process, and on grounds of defective reasoning of judgment rendered. The Court of Cassation is composed of a President, seven Vice-Presidents and 31 other Justices (Councillors).

(ii) The Courts of Appeal: Each court has geographical jurisdiction over one governorate (Mouhafazat). Each court is divided into Penal and Civil Chambers. There are Criminal Chambers which try felonies only. The Civil Chambers hear appeals filed against judgments rendered by the Tribunals of First Instance and the Tribunals of Peace. Each Court of Appeal is composed of a President and sufficient numbers of Vice-Presidents (Presidents of Chambers) and Superior Judges (Councillors). There are 54 Courts of Appeal.

(iii) The Tribunals of First Instance: In each governorate there are one or more Tribunals of First Instance, each of which is divided into several Chambers for penal and civil litigations. Each Chamber is composed of one judge. There are 72 Tribunals of First Instance.

(iv) The Tribunals of Peace: In the administrative centre of each governorate, and in each district, there are one or more Tribunals of Peace, which have jurisdiction over minor civil and penal litigations. There are 227 Tribunals of Peace.

(v) Personal Status Courts: These courts deal with marriage, divorce, etc. For Muslims each court consists of one judge, the 'Qadi Shari'i'. For Druzes there is one court consisting of one judge, the 'Qadi Mazhabi'. For non-Muslim communities there are courts for Roman Catholics, Orthodox believers, Protestants and Jews.

(vi) Courts for Minors: The constitution, officers, sessions, jurisdiction and competence of these courts are determined by a special law.

PUBLIC PROSECUTION

Public prosecution is headed by the Attorney-General, assisted by a number of Senior Deputy and Deputy Attorneys-General, and a sufficient number of chief prosecutors, prosecutors and assistant prosecutors. Public prosecution is represented at all levels of the Courts of General Jurisdiction in all criminal and penal litigations and also in certain civil litigations as required by the law. Public prosecution controls and supervises enforcement of penal judgments.

ADMINISTRATIVE COURTS SYSTEM

The Administrative Courts have jurisdiction over litigations involving the state or any of its governmental agencies. The Administrative Courts system is divided into two courts: the Administrative Courts and the Judicial Administrative Courts, of which the paramount body is the High Administrative Court.

MILITARY COURTS

The Military Courts deal with criminal litigations against military personnel of all ranks and penal litigations against officers only. There are two military courts: one in Damascus, the other in Aleppo. Each court is composed of three military judges. There are other military courts, consisting of one judge, in every governorate, which deal with penal litigations against military personnel below the rank of officer. The different military judgments can be petitioned to the Court of Cassation.

Religion

The majority of Syrians follow a form of Islamic Sunni orthodoxy. There are also a considerable number of religious minorities: Shi'a Muslims; Isma'ili Muslims; the Isma'ili of the Salamiya district, whose spiritual head is the Aga Khan; a large number of Druzes, the Nusairis or Alawites of the Jebel Ansariyeh (a schism of the Shi'ite branch of Islam, to which about 11% of the population, including President Assad, belongs) and the Yezidis of the Jebel Sinjar; and a minority of Christians.

The Constitution states only that 'Islam shall be the religion of the head of the state'. The original draft of the 1973 Constitution made no reference to Islam at all, and this clause was inserted only as a compromise after public protest. The Syrian Constitution is thus unique among the constitutions of Arab states (excluding Lebanon) with a clear Muslim majority in not enshrining Islam as the religion of the state itself.

ISLAM

Grand Mufti: Sheikh AHMAD BADER ED-DIN HASSOUN, POB 7410, Damascus; tel. (11) 2688601; fax (11) 2637650; e-mail info@drhassoun.com; internet www.drhassoun.com.

CHRISTIANITY

Orthodox Churches

Greek Orthodox Patriarchate of Antioch and all the East: BP 9, Damascus; tel. (11) 5424400; fax (11) 5424404; e-mail info@antiochpat.org; internet www.antiochpat.org; Patriarch of Antioch and all the East His Beatitude IGNATIUS HAZIM; has jurisdiction over Syria, Lebanon, Iran and Iraq.

Syrian Orthodox Patriarchate of Antioch and all the East: BP 22260, Bab Touma, Damascus; tel. (11) 54498989; e-mail patriarch-z-iwas@scs-net.org; Patriarch of Antioch and all the East His Holiness IGNATIUS ZAKKA I IWAS; the Syrian Orthodox Church includes one Catholicose (of India), 37 Metropolitans and one Bishop, and has an estimated 4m. adherents throughout the world.

The Armenian Apostolic Church is also represented in Syria.

The Roman Catholic Church

Armenian Rite

Patriarchal Exarchate of Syria: Exarchat Patriarcal Arménien Catholique, BP 22281, Bab Touma, Damascus; tel. (11) 5413820; fax (11) 5419431; f. 1985; represents the Patriarch of Cilicia (resident in Beirut, Lebanon); 4,500 adherents (31 December 2008); Exarch Patriarchal Bishop JOSEPH ARNAOUTIAN.

Archdiocese of Aleppo: Archevêché Arménien Catholique, BP 97, 33 at-Tilal, Aleppo; tel. (21) 2123946; fax (21) 2116637; e-mail armen.cath@mail.sy; 17,500 adherents (31 December 2006); Archbishop BOUTROS MARAYATI.

Diocese of Kamichlié: Evêché Arménien Catholique, BP 17, Al-Qamishli; tel. (53) 424211; fax (53) 426211; 4,000 adherents (31 December 2006); Bishop JOSEPH ARNAOUTI.

Chaldean Rite

Diocese of Aleppo: Evêché Chaldéen Catholique, BP 4643, 1 rue Patriarche Elias IV Mouawwad, Soulémaniyé, Aleppo; tel. (21) 4441660; fax (21) 4600800; e-mail audoa@scs–net.org; 15,000 adherents (31 December 2006); Bishop ANTOINE AUDO.

Latin Rite

Apostolic Vicariate of Aleppo: BP 327, 19 rue Al-Fourat, Aleppo; tel. (21) 2682399; fax (21) 2689413; e-mail vicariatlatin@mail.sy; f. 1762; 12,000 adherents (31 December 2008); Vicar Apostolic GIUSEPPE NAZZARO (Titular Bishop of Forma).

Maronite Rite

Archdiocese of Aleppo: Archevêché Maronite, BP 203, 57 rue Fares-El-Khoury, Aleppo; tel. and fax (21) 2118048; fax (21) 2123048; e-mail maronite@scs-net.org; 4,000 adherents (31 December 2006); Archbishop YOUSSEF ANIS ABI-AAD.

Archdiocese of Damascus: Archevêché Maronite, BP 2179, 6 rue ad-Deir, Bab Touma, Damascus; tel. (11) 5412888; fax (11) 5436002; e-mail psamirn@cyberia.net.lb; f. 1527; 14,000 adherents (31 December 2006); Archbishop SAMIR NASSAR.

Diocese of Latakia: Evêché Maronite, BP 161, rue Hamrat, Tartous; tel. (43) 223433; fax (43) 322939; 33,000 adherents (31 December 2006); Bishop YOUSSEF-MASSOUD MASSOUD.

Melkite Rite

Melkite Greek Catholic Patriarchate of Antioch: Patriarcat Grec-Melkite Catholique, BP 22249, 12 avenue az-Zeitoun, Bab Charki, Damascus; tel. (11) 5441030; fax (11) 5417900; e-mail pat.melk@scs-net.org; internet www.pgc-lb.org; or BP 70071, Antélias, Lebanon; tel. (4) 413111; fax (4) 418113; f. 1724; jurisdiction over 1.5m. Melkites throughout the world (including 290,000 in Syria); Patriarch of Antioch and all the East, of Alexandria and of Jerusalem His Beatitude GREGORIOS III LAHAM; the Melkite Church includes the patriarchal sees of Damascus, Cairo and Jerusalem and four other archdioceses in Syria; seven archdioceses in Lebanon; one in Jordan; one in Israel; and six eparchies (in the USA, Brazil, Canada, Australia, Venezuela, Argentina and Mexico).

Archdiocese of Aleppo: Archevêché Grec-Catholique, BP 146, 9 place Farhat, Aleppo; tel. (21) 2119307; fax (21) 2119308; e-mail gr.melkcath@mail.sy; 17,000 adherents (31 December 2006); Archbishop JEAN-CLÉMENT JEANBART.

Archdiocese of Busra and Hauran: Archevêché Grec-Catholique, Khabab, Hauran; tel. (15) 855012; e-mail derbosra@hotmail.com; 27,000 adherents (31 December 2006); Archbishop BOULOS NASSIF BORKHOCHE.

Archdiocese of Homs: Archevêché Grec-Catholique, BP 1525, rue El-Mo'tazila, Boustan ad-Diwan, Homs; tel. (31) 2482587; fax (31) 2464587; e-mail isidore_battikha@yahoo.fr; 30,000 adherents (31 December 2006); Archbishop ISIDORE BATTIKHA.

Archdiocese of Latakia: Archevêché Grec-Catholique, BP 151, rue al-Moutannabi, Latakia; tel. (41) 460777; fax (41) 476002; e-mail saouafnicolas@yahoo.fr; 10,000 adherents (31 December 2006); Archbishop NICOLAS SAWAF.

SYRIA

Syrian Rite

Archdiocese of Aleppo: Archevêché Syrien Catholique, place Mère Teresa de Calcutta, Azizié, Aleppo; tel. (21) 2126750; fax (21) 2126752; e-mail a_chahda@hotmail.com; 8,000 adherents (31 December 2005); Archbishop DENYS ANTOINE CHAHDA.

Archdiocese of Damascus: Archevêché Syrien Catholique, BP 2129, 157 rue Al-Mustaqeem, Bab Charki, Damascus; tel. and fax (11) 5445343; e-mail psamirm@cyberia.met.lb; 9,000 adherents (31 December 2006); Archbishop GRÉGOIRE ELIAS TABÉ.

Archdiocese of Hassaké-Nisibi: Archevêché Syrien Catholique, BP 6, Hassaké; tel. (52) 320812; 35,000 adherents (31 December 2006); Archbishop JACQUES BEHNAN HINDO.

Archdiocese of Homs: Archevêché Syrien Catholique, BP 303, rue Hamidieh, Homs; tel. (31) 221575; fax (21) 224350; 10,000 adherents (31 December 2006); Archbishop THÉOPHILE GEORGES KASSAB.

The Anglican Communion

Within the Episcopal Church in Jerusalem and the Middle East, Syria forms part of the diocese of Jerusalem (see the chapter on Israel).

Other Christian Groups

Protestants in Syria are largely adherents of either the National Evangelical Synod of Syria and Lebanon or the Union of Armenian Evangelical Churches in the Near East (for details of both organizations, see the chapter on Lebanon).

The Press

Since the Baath Arab Socialist Party came to power, the structure of the press has been modified according to socialist patterns. Most publications are issued by political, religious or professional associations (such as trade unions), and several are published by government ministries. However, two privately owned daily newspapers have been launched in recent years. Anyone wishing to establish a new paper or periodical must apply for a licence.

The major dailies are *Al-Baath* (the organ of the party), *Tishreen*, *Ath-Thawra* and the *Syria Times*, all published in Damascus.

PRINCIPAL DAILIES

Al-Baath (Renaissance): BP 9389, Autostrade Mezzeh, Damascus; tel. (11) 6622142; fax (11) 6622099; e-mail baath@baath-party.org; internet www.albaath.news.sy; f. 1946; morning; Arabic; organ of the Baath Arab Socialist Party; Editor ILYAS MURAD; circ. 45,000.

Baladna: BP 2000, al-Huda Bldg, al-Eskandaria St, Damascus; tel. (11) 6122515; fax (11) 6122514; e-mail info@ug.com.sy; internet www.baladnaonline.net; Arabic; privately owned; publ. by United Group for Publishing, Advertising and Marketing; Chief Editor SAMIR ASH-SHIBANI.

Barq ash-Shimal (The Syrian Telegraph): rue Aziziyah, Aleppo; morning; Arabic; Editor MAURICE DJANDJI; circ. 6,400.

Champress: Immeuble Arnos, place Arnos, Damascus; tel. (11) 44681199; fax (11) 44681190; e-mail mail@champress.com; internet www.champress.com; privately owned; political; online only; Arabic; Dir ALI JAMALO.

Al-Fida' (Redemption): Hama; Al-Wahda Foundation for Press, Printing and Publishing, BP 2448, Dawar Kafr Soussat, Damascus; tel. (11) 225219; fax (11) 2216851; e-mail fedaa@thawra.com; internet fedaa.alwehda.gov.sy; morning; Arabic; political; Editor A. AULWANI; circ. 4,000.

Al-Furat: Deir ez-Zor; Al-Wahda Foundation for Press, Printing and Publishing, BP 2448, Dawar Kafr Soussat, Damascus; tel. (51) 224494; fax (51) 218418; e-mail furat@thawra.com; internet furat.alwehda.gov.sy; Editor ADNAN OWAID.

Al-Horubat: Homs; Al-Wahda Foundation for Press, Printing and Publishing, BP 2448, Dawar Kafr Soussat, Damascus; tel. (11) 225219; fax (11) 2216851; e-mail ouroba@thawra.com; internet ouruba.alwehda.gov.sy; morning; Arabic; political; circ. 5,000.

Al-Jamahir (The People): Aleppo; Al-Wahda Foundation for Press, Printing and Publishing, BP 2448, Dawar Kafr Soussat, Damascus; tel. (21) 214309; fax (21) 214308; e-mail jamahir@thawra.com; internet jamahir.alwehda.gov.sy; Arabic; political; Chief Editor MORTADA BAKACH; circ. 10,000.

Syria Times: BP 5452, Medan, Damascus; tel. (11) 2247359; fax (11) 2231374; e-mail syriatimes@teshreen.com; internet syriatimes.tishreen.info; English; publ. by Tishreen Foundation for Press and Publishing; Editor FOUAD MARDOUD; circ. 15,000.

Ath-Thawra (Revolution): Al-Wahda Foundation for Press, Printing and Publishing, BP 2448, Dawar Kafr Soussat, Damascus; tel. (11) 2210850; fax (11) 2216851; e-mail admin@thawra.com; internet thawra.alwehda.gov.sy; f. 1963; morning; Arabic; political; Editor ASAAD ABBOUD; circ. 40,000.

Tishreen (October): BP 5452, Medan, Damascus; tel. (11) 2131100; fax (11) 2246860; e-mail tnp@mail.sy; internet www.tishreen.info; Arabic; publ. by the Tishreen Foundation for Press and Publishing; Chief Editor KHALAF AL-JARAAD; circ. 50,000.

Al-Wahda (Unity): Latakia; Al-Wahda Foundation for Press, Printing and Publishing, BP 2448, Dawar Kafr Soussat, Damascus; tel. (11) 225219; fax (11) 2216851; e-mail wehda@thawra.com; internet wehda.alwehda.gov.sy; Arabic; political.

Al-Watan: Duty Free Zone, Damascus; tel. (11) 2137400; fax (11) 2139928; internet www.alwatan.sy; f. 2006; Arabic; political; privately owned; Chief Editor WADDAH ABED RABBO.

WEEKLIES AND FORTNIGHTLIES

Abyad wa Aswad (White and Black): 8 rue Hekmat Alasale, Almastaba 4, Muhajirin; tel. (11) 3739968; fax (11) 3739949; e-mail a-and-a@scs-net.org; internet www.awaonline.net; f. 2002; weekly; Arabic; political; privately owned; Editor AYMAN AD-DAQUQ.

Al-Ajoua' (The Air): Compagnie de l'Aviation Arabe Syrienne, BP 417, Damascus; fortnightly; Arabic; aviation; Editor AHMAD ALLOUCHE.

Al-Esbou ar-Riadi (The Sports Week): Immeuble Tibi, ave Fardoss, Damascus; weekly; Arabic; sports; Asst Dir and Editor HASRAN AL-BOUNNI; circ. 14,000.

Al-Fursan (The Cavalry): Damascus; Arabic; political magazine; Editor RIFAAT AL-ASSAD.

Al-Iqtisadiya: rue Abd al-Munim Riyad 13, Damascus; tel. (11) 3737344; fax (11) 3737348; e-mail info@iqtissadiya.com; internet www.iqtissadiya.com; f. 2001; weekly; Arabic; economic; privately owned; Editor WADDAH ABD AR-RABBO.

Kantsasar: POB 133, Aleppo; tel. (21) 2246753 (also fax); e-mail kantsasar@excite.com; internet www.periotem.com; weekly; publ. by Armenian Prelacy of Aleppo; Editor MARY MERDKHANIAN.

Kassioun: BP 35033, Damascus; tel. (11) 3346681; fax (11) 3346681; e-mail general@kassioun.org; internet www.kassioun.org; weekly; publ. by the Syrian Communist Party (Bakdash).

Kifah al-Oummal al-Ishtiraki (The Socialist Workers' Struggle): Fédération Générale des Syndicats des Ouvriers, rue Qanawat, Damascus; weekly; Arabic; labour; publ. by General Federation of Labour Unions; Editor SAID AL-HAMAMI.

Al-Maukef ar-Riadi (Sport Stance): Al-Wahda Foundation for Press, Printing and Publishing, BP 2448, Dawar Kafr Soussat, Damascus; tel. (11) 225219; e-mail riadi@thawra.com; internet riadi.alwehda.gov.sy; weekly; Arabic; sports; circ. 50,000.

An-Nas (The People): BP 926, Aleppo; f. 1953; weekly; Arabic; Publr VICTOR KALOUS.

Nidal al-Fellahin (Peasants' Struggle): Fédération Générale des Laboureurs, BP 9389, Autostrade Mezzeh, Damascus; weekly; Arabic; Editor MANSOUR ABU AL-HOSN; circ. 8,100.

An-Nour (Light): BP 7394 Damascus; tel. (11) 3324914; fax (11) 3342571; e-mail annour@mail.sy; internet www.an-nour.com; f. 2001; weekly; Arabic; political and cultural; organ of the Syrian Communist Party (Faisal); Editor-in-Chief YAQUB GARRO.

Ar-Riada (Sport): BP 292, nr Electricity Institute, Damascus; weekly; Arabic; sports; Dir NOUREDDINE RIAL; Publr and Editor OURFANE UBARI.

As-Sakafat al-Usbouiya (Weekly Culture): BP 2570, Soukak as-Sakr, Damascus; weekly; Arabic; cultural; Publr, Dir and Editor MADHAT AKKACHE.

Sawt ash-Shaab (Voice of the People): Damascus; f. 1937, but publ. suspended in 1939, 1941, 1947 and 1958; relaunched in 2001; fortnightly; Arabic; organ of the Syrian Communist Party (Bakdash).

Al-Yanbu al-Jadid (New Spring): Immeuble Al-Awkaf, Homs; weekly; Arabic; literary; Publr, Dir and Editor MAMDOU AL-KOUSSEIR.

OTHER PERIODICALS

Al-Arabieh (The Arab Lady): Syrian Women's Association, BP 3207, Damascus; tel. (11) 3316560; monthly; Editor S. BAKOUR.

Ad-Dad: rue Tital, Wakf al-Moiriné Bldg, Aleppo; monthly; Arabic; literary; Dir RIAD HALLAK; Publr and Editor ABDULLAH YARKI HALLAK.

Al-Fikr al-Askari (The Military Idea): BP 4259, blvd Palestine, Damascus; fax (11) 2125280; f. 1950; 6 a year; Arabic; official military review publ. by the Political Administration Press.

Al-Ghad (Tomorrow): Association of Red Cross and Crescent, BP 6095, rue Maysat, Damascus; tel. (11) 2242552; fax (11) 7777040; monthly; environmental health; Editor K. ABED-RABOU.

Al-Irshad az-Zirai (Agricultural Information): Ministry of Agriculture, rue Jabri, Damascus; tel. (11) 2213613; fax (11) 2216627; 6 a year; Arabic; agriculture.

SYRIA

Jaysh ash-Sha'ab (The People's Army): Ministry of Defence, BP 3320, blvd Palestine, Damascus; fax (11) 2125280; f. 1946; monthly; Arabic; army magazine; publ. by the Political Department of the Syrian Army.

Al-Kalima (The Word): Al-Kalima Association, Aleppo; monthly; Arabic; religious; Publr and Editor FATHALLA SAKAL.

Layalina: Damascus; tel. (11) 6122515; fax (11) 6122514; e-mail info@layalinamag.com; internet layalina.sy.pressera.com; monthly; Arabic; social and lifestyle; publ. by United Group for Publishing, Advertising and Marketing; Chair. MAJD SULEIMAN.

Al-Kanoun (The Law): Ministry of Justice, rue an-Nasr, Damascus; tel. (11) 2214105; fax (11) 2246250; monthly; Arabic; juridical.

Al-Maaloumatieh (Information): National Information Centre, BP 11323, Damascus; tel. (11) 2127551; fax (11) 2127648; e-mail nice@net.sy; f. 1994; quarterly; computer magazine; Editor ABD AL-MAJID AR-RIFAI; circ. 10,000.

Al-Ma'arifa (Knowledge): Ministry of Culture, rue ar-Rouda, Damascus; tel. (11) 3336963; f. 1962; monthly; Arabic; literary; Editor ABD AL-KARIM NASIF; circ. 7,500.

Al-Majalla al-Batriarquia (The Magazine of the Patriarchate): Syrian Orthodox Patriarchate, BP 914, Damascus; tel. (11) 4447036; f. 1962; monthly; Arabic; religious; Editor SAMIR ABDOH; circ. 15,000.

Al-Majalla at-Tibbiya al-Arabiyya (Arab Medical Magazine): rue al-Jala'a, Damascus; tel. (11) 3331890; e-mail kfkallas@net.sy; internet www.arabmedmag.com; monthly; Arabic and English; publ. by Arab Medical Commission; Dir KHALID KALLAS; Editor Dr AL-LOUJAMI MAZEN.

Majallat Majma' al-Lughat al-Arabiyya bi-Dimashq (Magazine of the Arab Language Academy of Damascus): Arab Academy of Damascus, BP 327, Damascus; tel. (11) 3713145; fax (11) 3733363; e-mail mla@net.sy; f. 1921; quarterly; Arabic; Islamic culture and Arabic literature, Arabic scientific and cultural terminology; Chief Editor Dr SHAKER FAHAM; circ. 1,600.

Al-Maukef al-Arabi (The Arab Situation): Ittihab al-Kuttab al-Arab, rue Murshid Khatir, Damascus; monthly; Arabic; literary.

Monthly Survey of Arab Economics: BP 2306, Damascus; BP 6068, Beirut; f. 1958; monthly; English and French editions; published by Centre d'Etudes et de Documentation Economiques, Financières et Sociales; Dir Dr CHAFIC AKHRAS.

Al-Mouallem al-Arabi (The Arab Teacher): National Union of Teachers, BP 2842-3034, Damascus; tel. (11) 225219; f. 1948; monthly; Arabic; educational and cultural.

Al-Mouhandis al-Arabi (The Arab Engineer): Order of Syrian Engineers and Architects, BP 2336, Immeuble Dar al-Mouhandisen, place Azme, Damascus; tel. (11) 2214916; fax (11) 2216948; e-mail lbosea@net.sy; f. 1961; 4 a year; Arabic; scientific and cultural; Dir Eng. M. FAYEZ MAHFOUZ; Chief Editor Dr Eng. AHMAD AL-GHAFARI; circ. 50,000.

Al-Munadel (The Militant): c/o BP 11512, Damascus; fax (11) 2126935; f. 1965; monthly; Arabic; magazine of Baath Arab Socialist Party; Dir Dr FAWWAZ SAYYAGH; circ. 100,000.

An-Nashra al-Iktissad (Economic Bulletin): Damascus Chamber of Commerce; tel. (11) 2218339; fax (11) 2225874; e-mail dcc@dcc-sy.com; f. 1922; quarterly; finance and investment; Editor GHASSAN KALLA; circ. 3,000.

Risalat al-Kimia (Chemistry Report): BP 669, Immeuble al-Abid, Damascus; monthly; Arabic; scientific; Publr, Dir and Editor HASSAN AS-SAKA.

Ash-Shourta (The Police): Directorate of Public Affairs and Moral Guidance, Damascus; monthly; Arabic; juridical.

As-Sinaa (Industry): Damascus Chamber of Commerce, BP 1305, rue Mou'awiah, Harika, Damacus; tel. (11) 2222205; fax (11) 2245981; e-mail dcc@dcc-sy.com; monthly; commerce, industry and management; Editor Y. HINDI.

Souriya al-Arabiyya (Arab Syria): Ministry of Information, Immeuble Dar al-Baath, Autostrade Mezzeh, Damascus; tel. (11) 6622141; fax (11) 6617665; monthly; publicity; in four languages.

Syria Today: Baramkeh, Free Zone, Damascus; tel. (11) 88270310; fax (11) 2137343; e-mail info@syria-today.com; internet www.syria-today.com; monthly; English; economic and social development; Chair. LOUMA TARABINE; Man. Editor FRANCESCA DE CHÂTEL.

At-Tamaddon al-Islami (Islamic Civilization Society): Darwichiyah, Damascus; tel. (11) 2240562; fax (11) 3733563; e-mail isltmddn@hotmail.com; f. 1932; monthly; Arabic; religious; published by At-Tamaddon al-Islami Association; Pres. of Asscn AHMAD MOUAZ AL-KHATIB.

At-Taqa Wattanmiya (Energy and Expansion): BP 7748, rue al-Moutanabbi, Damascus; tel. (11) 233529; e-mail spccom1@scs-net.org; monthly; Arabic; publ. by the Syrian Petroleum Co.

Al-Yakza (The Awakening): Al-Yakza Association, BP 6677, rue Sisi, Aleppo; f. 1935; monthly; Arabic; literary social review of charitable institution; Dir HUSNI ABD AL-MASSIH; circ. 12,000.

Az-Zira'a (Agriculture): Ministry of Agriculture and Agrarian Reform, rue Jabri, Damascus; tel. (11) 2213613; fax (11) 2244023; f. 1985; monthly; Arabic; agriculture; circ. 12,000.

NEWS AGENCY

Syrian Arab News Agency (SANA): BP 2661, Baramka, Damascus; tel. (11) 2129702; fax (11) 2228265; e-mail public-relation@sana.sy; internet www.sana.sy; f. 1966; supplies bulletins on Syrian news to foreign news agencies; 16 offices abroad; 16 foreign correspondents; Dir-Gen. Dr ADNAN MAHMOUD.

Publishers

Arab Advertising Organization: BP 2842-3034, 28 rue Moutanabbi, Damascus; tel. (11) 2225219; fax (11) 2220754; e-mail sy-adv@net.sy; f. 1963; exclusive govt establishment responsible for advertising; publishes Directory of Commerce and Industry, Damascus International Fair Guide, Daily Bulletin of Official Tenders; Dir-Gen. MONA F. FABAH.

Damascus University Press: Baramkeh, Damascus; tel. (11) 2119890; fax (11) 2235779; internet www.damasuniv.net; f. 1923; medicine, engineering, social sciences, law, agriculture, arts, etc.; Dir FADI ASH-SHALABI.

Dar Al-Awael: BP 10181, Damascus; tel. (11) 44676270; fax (11) 44676273; e-mail alawael@daralawael.com; internet www.daralawael.com; f. 1999; academic publr; Dir-Gen. ISMAIL ABDULLAH.

Dar al-Fikr: POB 962, Damascus; tel. (11) 2211166; fax (11) 2239716; e-mail fikr@fikr.com; internet www.fikr.com; f. 1957; Islamic studies, academic and gen. non-fiction; Dir-Gen. MUHAMMAD ADNAN SALIM.

Institut Français du Proche-Orient: BP 344, Damascus; tel. (11) 3330214; fax (11) 3327887; e-mail secretariat@ifporient.org; internet www.ifporient.org; f. 1922; sociology, anthropology, Islamic studies, archaeology, history, language and literature, arts, philosophy, geography, religion; publs include Syria (bi-annual journal), Bulletin d'Etudes Orientales (annual journal), Bibliotheque Archeologique et Historique (series), Publications de l'Instituit Français de Damas (series); Dir FRANÇOIS BURGAT.

OFA-Business Consulting Center—Documents Service: BP 3550, 3 place Chahbandar, Damascus; tel. (11) 3318237; fax (11) 4426021; e-mail ofa1@net.sy; internet www.ofa-bcc.com; f. 1964; numerous periodicals, monographs and surveys on political and economic affairs; Dir-Gen. SAMIR A. DARWICH; has one affiliated branch, OFA-Business Consulting Centre (foreign co representation and services).

The Political Administration Press: BP 3320, blvd Palestine, Damascus; fax (11) 2125280; publishes Al-Fikr al-Askari (six a year) and Jaysh ash-Sha'ab (monthly).

Syrian Documentation Papers: BP 2712, Damascus; f. 1968; publishers of Bibliography of the Middle East (annual), General Directory of the Press and Periodicals in the Arab World (annual), and numerous publications on political, economic, literary and social affairs, as well as legislative texts concerning Syria and the Arab world; Dir-Gen. LOUIS FARÈS.

Tishreen Foundation for Press and Publishing: BP 5452, Medan, Damascus; tel. (11) 2131100; fax (11) 2246860; publishes Syria Times and Tishreen (dailies).

United Group for Publishing, Advertising and Marketing: Immeuble al-Huda, rue al-Eskandaria, Mazzeh, Damascus; tel. (11) 6122515; fax (11) 6122514; e-mail info@ug.com.sy; internet www.ug.com.sy; publs Baladna newspaper, Layalina magazine, What's On magazine; Chair. MAJD SULEIMAN.

Al-Wahda Foundation for Press, Printing and Publishing (Institut al-Ouedha pour l'impression, édition et distribution): BP 2448, Dawar Kafr Soussat, Damascus; tel. (11) 225219; internet www.thawra.com; publs Al-Fida', Al-Horubat, Al-Jamahir, Ath-Thawra and Al-Wihdat (dailies), Al-Maukef ar-Riadi (weekly) and other commercial publs; Dir-Gen. FAHD DIYAB.

Broadcasting and Communications

TELECOMMUNICATIONS

Syrian Telecommunications Establishment (STE—Syrian Telecom): BP 11774, Autostrade Mezzeh, Damascus; tel. (11) 2240000; fax (11) 6110000; e-mail ste-gm@net.sy; internet www.ste.gov.sy; f. 1975; Dir.-Gen. Dr NAZEM BAHSAS.

SYRIA
Directory

MTN Syria: BP 34474, Immeuble Al-Mohandis al-Arabi, Autostrade Mezzeh, Damascus; fax (11) 6667483; e-mail customercare@mtn.com.sy; internet www.mtnsyria.com; f. 2001 as Spacetel Syria; name changed to Areeba Syria in 2004; present name adopted in 2007 following the acquisition of a 75% stake by MTN Group (South Africa); provider of mobile telephone services; Chair. JAMAL RAMADAN; CEO ISMAIL JAROUDI; 3.5m. subscribers (Dec. 2008).

Syriatel: Immeuble STE, 6e étage, rue Thawra, Damascus; tel. (11) 3341910; fax (11) 3341917; e-mail info@syriatel.com.sy; internet www.syriatel.com; f. 2000; provider of mobile telephone services; Chair. RAMI MAKHLOUF; CEO NADER KALAI; 3.5m. subscribers (Oct. 2007).

BROADCASTING
Radio

General Organization of Radio and Television (ORTAS—Organisme de la Radio-Télévision Arabe Syrienne): place Omayyad, Damascus; tel. (11) 720700; fax (11) 2234930; e-mail contact@rtv.gov.sy; internet www.rtv.gov.sy; radio broadcasts started in 1945, television broadcasts in 1960; radio directorate consists of four departments: Radi, Shaab, Shabab FM, and a multilingual news service; television directorate operates one satellite and two terrestrial channels, broadcasting in Arabic, English and French; Dir-Gen. FAYEZ AS-SAYEGH; Dirs NAIF HAMMOUD (Radio), Dr FOUAD SHERBAJI (Television).

Television

General Organization of Radio and Television: see Radio.

Addounia TV: Damascus; tel. (11) 4472630; fax (11) 4472632; e-mail info@addounia.tv; internet www.addounia.tv; privately owned news channel; awarded broadcasting licence mid-2007; began broadcasting October 2008; Gen. Man. FOUAD ASH-SHARBAJI.

Finance

(cap. = capital; res = reserves; dep. = deposits; m.= million; brs = branches; amounts in £S unless otherwise indicated)

BANKING
Central Bank

Central Bank of Syria: place du 17 avril, Damascus; tel. (11) 2212642; fax (11) 2248329; e-mail info@bcs.gov.sy; internet www.banquecentrale.gov.sy; f. 1956; cap. and res 119,067m., dep. 413,591m. (Dec. 2006); Gov. Dr ADIB MAYALEH; 12 brs.

Other Banks

Agricultural Co-operative Bank: BP 4325, rue at-Tajehiz, Damascus; tel. and fax (11) 2213461; fax (11) 2241261; e-mail syrianagrobank@gmail.com; internet www.agrobank.org; f. 1888; cap. 10,000m., res 671m., dep. 12,000m. (Dec. 2001); Chair. and Dir-Gen. YASSER AS-SAMOR; 106 brs.

Arab Bank Syria SA (ABS): BP 38, rue Al-Mahdi bin Barakeh, Abou Roumaneh, Damascus; tel. (11) 3348130; fax (11) 3349844; e-mail ali.zatar@arabbank-syria.com; internet www.arabbank-syria.com; f. 2005; jt venture between Syrian investors (51%) and Arab Bank (Jordan—49%); private commercial bank; cap. 1,500.0m., res –44.9m., dep. 19,246.2m. (Dec. 2007); Chair. Dr KHALID WASSIF AL-WAZANI; Gen. Man. ALI ZATAR; 4 brs.

Bank Audi Syria sa: BP 6228, Damascus; e-mail contactus.syria@banqueaudi.com; internet www.banqueaudi.com/basy/syria.html; f. 2005; 47% owned by Audi Saradar Group (Lebanon), 26% by Syrian investors, 2% by a Saudi investor; remaining 25% oversubscribed in an initial public offering in Aug. 2005; private commercial bank; cap. 2,500.0m., res –50.7m., dep. 32,960.8m. (Dec. 2007); Chair. GEORGES ACHI; Dep. Chair. and Gen. Man. BASSEL S. HAMWI; 19 brs.

Bank of Syria and Overseas: BP 3103, Harika-Bab Barid, Lawyers' Syndicate Bldg, nr Chamber of Commerce, Damascus; tel. (11) 2460560; fax (11) 2460555; e-mail bsomail@bso.com.sy; internet www.bso.com.sy; f. 2004; jt venture between Banque du Liban et d'Outre Mer (BLOM, Lebanon—39%), the World Bank's International Finance Corporation (10%) and Syrian investors (51%); private commercial bank; cap. 3,000.0m., dep. 44,320.3m., total assets 49,743.1m. (Dec. 2006); Pres. Dr RATEB ASH-SHALLAH; Gen. Man. GEORGES SAYEGH; 11 brs.

Banque BEMO Saudi Fransi SA (BBSF): 39 rue Ayyar, Salhiah, Damascus; tel. (11) 2317778; fax (11) 2318778; e-mail bbsf@mail.sy; internet www.bbsfbank.com; f. 2004; jt venture between Syrian investors (51%), Banque Saudi Fransi (Saudi Arabia—27%) and Banque Européenne pour le Moyen-Orient (Lebanon—22%); private commercial bank; cap. 1,750m., res 67.4m., dep. 74,382.0m. (Dec. 2007); Chair. ABD AR-RAHMAN JAWA; Vice-Chair. and CEO RIAD OBEGI; 15 brs.

Byblos Bank Syria: POB 5424, Al-Chaalan, rue Amin Loutfi Hafez, Damascus; tel. (11) 3348240; fax (11) 3348207; e-mail byblosbanksyria@byblosbank.com; internet www.byblosbank.com.lb/aboutbbkgroup/bbk_sa/board/index.shtml; f. 2005; 41.5% owned by Byblos Bank SAL (Lebanon), 51% by Syrian investors and 7.5% by the Organization of Petroleum Exporting Companies Fund for International Development; private commercial bank; cap. US $40m.; Chair. SEMAAN BASSIL; CEO NADIM F. GHANTOUS; 6 brs.

CHAM Bank: POB 33979, pl. al-Nijmeh, Damascus; tel. (11) 3348720; fax (11) 3348731; e-mail info@chambank.com; internet www.chambank.com; f. 2006; jt venture between Dar Investment Company (Kuwait—12.5%), Commercial Bank of Kuwait (10%), Islamic Development Bank (Kuwait—9%) and several Syrian and other Gulf investors; cap. 5,000m.; private commercial bank run on Islamic principles; Chair. JAMAL ABD AL-HAMID AL-MUTAWA'A; Gen. Man. MUHAMMAD SALMAN.

Commercial Bank of Syria: BP 933, place Yousuf al-Azmeh, Damascus; tel. (11) 2218890; fax (11) 2216975; e-mail cbos@mail.sy; internet www.cbs-bank.com; f. 1967; govt-owned bank; cap. 70,000m., res 17,451m., dep. 473,667m. (Dec. 2006); Chair. and Gen. Man. Dr DOURAID AHMAD DERGHAM; 53 brs.

Industrial Bank: BP 7578, Immeuble Dar al-Mohandessin, rue Maysaloon, Damascus; tel. (11) 2228200; fax (11) 2228412; e-mail ind-bank@mail.sy; f. 1959; nationalized bank providing finance for industry; cap. 257m., total assets 8,131m. (Dec. 2001); Chair. and Gen. Man. MUHAMMAD ABU AN-NASSER; 13 brs.

The International Bank for Trade and Finance: place Hejazz, Damascus; tel. (11) 2460500; fax (11) 2460505; e-mail info@ibtf.com; internet www.ibtf.com.sy; f. 2004; 49% owned by Housing Bank for Trade and Finance (Jordan), 51% by Syrian investors; cap. 1,500m., res 59.1m., dep. 23,389.7m. (Dec. 2006); private commercial bank; Chair. MICHEL MARTO; Gen. Man. SULTAN AZ-ZU'BI; 16 brs.

Popular Credit Bank: BP 2841, 6e étage, Immeuble Dar al-Mohandessin, rue Maysaloon, Damascus; tel. (11) 2227604; fax (11) 2211291; f. 1967; govt-owned bank; provides loans to the services sector and is sole authorized issuer of savings certificates; Pres. and Gen. Man. MUHAMMAD HASSAN AL-HOUJJEIRI; 50 brs.

Real Estate Bank: BP 2337, place Yousuf al-Azmeh, Damascus; tel. (11) 2218602; fax (11) 2233107; e-mail realestate@realestate-sy.com; f. 1966; govt-owned bank; provides loans and grants for housing, schools, hospitals and hotel construction; cap. 1,000m. (Dec. 2001); Chair. and Gen. Man. MUHAMMAD AHMAD MAKHLOUF; 15 brs.

Syria International Islamic Bank: BP 35494, Damascus; tel. (11) 2241135; fax (11) 2241132; e-mail info@siib.sy; internet www.siib.sy; f. 2007; 49% Qatari-owned (including Qatar International Islamic Bank—30%); cap. 5,000m., res –151m., dep. 4,878m. (Dec. 2007); private commercial bank run on Islamic principles; Chair. YOUSUF AHMAD AN-NAAMA.

Syrian Lebanese Commercial Bank SAL (SLCB): c/o Commercial Bank of Syria, BP 933, Immeuble G.M., 6e étage, place Youssef Azmeh, Damascus; tel. (11) 2225206; fax (11) 2243224; e-mail hamra@slcbk.com; internet www.slcb.com.lb; f. 1974; head office is in Beirut, Lebanon; cap. £L90,000m., res £L14,860m., dep. £L330,854.0m. (Dec. 2006); Pres., Chair. and Gen. Man. Dr DOURAID AHMAD DERGHAM.

STOCK EXCHANGE

Six companies were listed on the Damascus Securities Exchange when it opened for trading in March 2009.

Damascus Securities Exchange: BP 6564, Damascus; tel. (11) 5190000; fax (11) 5190099; e-mail info@dse.sy; internet www.dse.sy; f. 2009; Chair. RATEB ASH-SHALLAH.

Supervisory Body

Syrian Commission on Financial Markets and Securities: BP 31845, Damascus; tel. (11) 3310487; fax (11) 3310722; e-mail info@scfms.sy; internet www.scfms.sy; f. 2005; Chair. MUHAMMAD AL-IMADY.

INSURANCE

A legislative decree, issued in 2005, allowed for the establishment of privately owned insurance companies.

General Social Security Organization: BP 2684, rue Port Said, Damascus; tel. (11) 2316932; fax (11) 2323115; e-mail taminat@gov.sy; internet www.taminat.gov.sy; Dir-Gen. KHALAF AL-ABDULLAH.

Syrian General Organization for Insurance (Syrian Insurance Co): BP 2279, 29 rue Ayyar, Damascus; tel. (11) 2218430; fax (11) 2220494; e-mail syrinsur@syrian-insurance.com; internet www.syrian-insurance.com; f. 1953; auth. cap. 1,000m.; nationalized co; operates throughout Syria; Chair. ADEL AL-KADAMANI; Dir-Gen. SULAYMAN AL-HASSAN.

SYRIA

Syrian Kuwaiti Insurance Co: BP 5778, Immeuble 4, King Abd al-aziz as-Saud St, Abu Rummaneh, Damascus; tel. (11) 3328060; fax (11) 3328061; e-mail info@skicins.com; internet www.skicins.com; f. 2006; cap. 850m.; all classes of insurance; owned by Gulf Insurance Company of Kuwait; Chair. KHALID SAUD AL-HASSAN.

United Insurance Co: BP 4419, Damascus; tel. (11) 3330241; fax (11) 3341934; e-mail info@uic.com.sy; internet www.uic.com.sy; awarded Syria's first-ever private insurance co licence in 2006.

Trade and Industry

STATE ENTERPRISES

Syrian industry is almost entirely under state control. There are national organizations responsible to the appropriate ministry for the operation of all sectors of industry, of which the following are examples:

Cotton Marketing Organization: BP 729, rue Bab al-Faraj, Aleppo; tel. (21) 2238486; fax (21) 2218617; e-mail cmo-aleppo@mail.sy; internet www.cmo.gov.sy; f. 1965; governmental authority for purchase of seed cotton, ginning and sales of cotton lint; Pres. and Dir-Gen. Dr AHMAD SOUHAD GEBBARA.

General Company for Phosphate and Mines (GECOPHAM): BP 288, Homs; tel. (31) 2751122; fax (31) 2751123; e-mail gecopham@net.sy; internet www.gecopham.com; f. 1970; production and export of phosphate rock; Gen. Dir Eng. FARHAN AL-HUHSSIN.

General Organization for Engineering Industries: POB 3120, Damascus; tel. (11) 2121834; fax (11) 2116201; e-mail g.o.eng.ind@net.sy; internet www.handasieh.org; 13 subsidiary cos.

General Organization for the Exploitation and Development of the Euphrates Basin (GOEDEB): Rakka; Dir-Gen. Dr Eng. AHMAD SOUHAD GEBBARA.

General Organization for Food Industry (GOFI): BP 105, rue al-Fardous, Damascus; tel. (11) 2457008; fax (11) 2457021; e-mail foodindustry@mail.sy; internet www.syriafoods.net; f. 1975; food-processing and marketing; Chair. and Gen. Dir KHALIL JAWAD.

General Organization for the Textile Industries: BP 620, rue al-Fardoss, Bawabet As-Salhieh, Damascus; tel. (11) 2216200; fax (11) 2216201; e-mail syr-textile@mail.syr; internet textile.org.sy; f. 1975; control and planning of the textile industry and supervision of textile manufacture; 27 subsidiary cos; Dir-Gen. Dr JAMAL ALOMAR.

Syrian Petroleum Company (SPC): BP 2849, Damascus; tel. (11) 3137935; fax (11) 3137979; e-mail spccom1@scs-net.org; internet www.spc-sy.com; f. 1958; state agency; holds the oil and gas concession for all Syria; exploits the Suweidiya, Karatchouk, Rumelan and Jbeisseh oilfields; also organizes exploring, production and marketing of oil and gas nationally; Chair. and Man. Dir Dr Eng. OMAR AL-HAMAD.

Al-Furat Petroleum Company: BP 7660, Damascus; tel. (11) 6183333; fax (11) 6184444; e-mail afpc@afpc.net.sy; internet www.afpc-sy.com; f. 1985; owned 50% by SPC and 50% by a foreign consortium of Syria Shell Petroleum Development B.V. and Deminex Syria GmbH; exploits oilfields in the Euphrates river area; Chair. SAID HUNEDI; Gen. Man. OLE MYKLESTAD.

DEVELOPMENT ORGANIZATIONS

State Planning Commission: Rukeneddin, Damascus; tel. (11) 5161015; fax (11) 5161010; e-mail info@planning.gov.sy; internet www.planning.gov.sy; Head TAYSIR RADDAWI.

Syrian Consulting Bureau for Development and Investment: BP 12574, 2nd Floor, Bldg 1, cnr Zuheir Ben Abi Sulma St and Ibin al-Khateeb St, Rawda, Damascus; tel. (11) 3345757; fax (11) 3340711; e-mail scb@scbdi.com; internet www.scbdi.com; f. 1991; independent; Man. Dir NABIL SUKKAR.

CHAMBERS OF COMMERCE AND INDUSTRY

Federation of Syrian Chambers of Commerce: BP 5909, rue Mousa Ben Nousair, Damascus; tel. (11) 3337344; fax (11) 3331127; e-mail syr-trade@mail.sy; internet www.fedcommsyr.org; f. 1975; Pres. Dr RATEB ASH-SHALLAH; Sec.-Gen. BASHAR NOURI.

Aleppo Chamber of Commerce: BP 1261, Aleppo; tel. (21) 2238236; fax (21) 2213493; e-mail alepchmb@mail.sy; internet www.aleppochamber.org; f. 1885; Pres. Dr HASSAN ZEIDO; Gen. Sec. MUHAMMAD MANSOUR.

Aleppo Chamber of Industry: BP 1859, rue al-Moutanabbi, Aleppo; tel. (21) 3620601; fax (21) 3620040; e-mail info@aleppo-coi.org; internet www.aleppo-coi.org; f. 1935; Pres. SALEH AL-MALLAH; Gen. Man. MUHAMMAD GHREWATI; 7,705 mems.

Damascus Chamber of Commerce: BP 1040, rue Mou'awiah, Damascus; tel. (11) 2211339; fax (11) 2225874; e-mail dcc@scs-net.org; internet www.dcc-sy.com; f. 1890; Pres. MUHAMMAD GHASSAN AL-QALLAA; Gen. Sec. BASHAR NOURI; 11,500 mems.

Damascus Chamber of Industry: BP 1305, rue Harika Mou'awiah, Damascus; tel. (11) 2215042; fax (11) 2245981; e-mail dci@mail.sy; internet www.dci-syria.org; Pres. Eng. IMAD GHRIWATI; Sec. Eng. AYIMEN MAOULAWI.

Hama Chamber of Commerce and Industry: BP 147, rue al-Kouatly, Hama; tel. (33) 525203; fax (33) 517701; e-mail hamacham@scs-net.org; internet hama-chamber.org; f. 1934; Pres. MU'TAZ GHANDOUR; Man. Dir ABD AR-RAZZAK AL-HAIT.

Homs Chamber of Commerce and Industry: BP 440, rue Abou al-Of, Homs; tel. (31) 2471000; fax (31) 2464247; e-mail homs-cc@aloola.sy; internet www.homschamber.org.sy; f. 1928; Pres. Dr Eng. ADEL TAYYARA; Gen. Man. M. FARES AL-HUSSAMY.

Latakia Chamber of Commerce and Industry: 8 rue Attar, Latakia; tel. (41) 479531; fax (41) 478526; e-mail lattakia@chamberlattakia.com; internet www.chamberlattakia.com; Pres. KAMAL ISMAIL AL-ASSAD.

Tartous Chamber of Commerce and Industry: POB 403, Tartous; tel. (43) 329852; fax (43) 329728; e-mail info@tcci-sy.com; internet tcci-sy.net; Pres. WAHIB KAMEL MERI; Gen. Man. MANAH ASSAF.

EMPLOYERS' ORGANIZATIONS

Fédération Générale à Damas: Damascus; f. 1951; Dir TALAT TAGLUBI.

Fédération de Damas: Damascus; f. 1949.

Fédération des Patrons et Industriels à Lattaquié: Latakia; f. 1953.

Order of Syrian Engineers and Architects: BP 2336, Immeuble Al Mohandessin, place Azmeh, Damascus; tel. (11) 2214916; fax (11) 2216948; e-mail osea@net.sy; internet www.syrianengineers.com; Pres. M. FAYEZ MAHFOUZ.

UTILITIES

Electricity

Public Establishment for Electricity Generation and Transmission (PEEGT): BP 3386, rue Nessan 17, Damascus; tel. (11) 2229654; fax (11) 2229062; e-mail peegt@net.sy; f. 1965; renamed 1994; state-owned; operates 11 power stations through subsidiary companies; Dir-Gen. Dr AHMAD AL-ALI; Gen. Man. HISHAM MASIAJ.

Gas

Syrian Gas Company: BP 4499, Homs; tel. (31) 2451925; fax (31) 2451933; e-mail info@sgc.gov.sy; internet www.sgc.gov.sy; f. 2003; state-owned; responsible for production, processing and distribution of gas supplies; Dir-Gen. ALI ABBAS.

Water

The Ministry of Housing and Construction is responsible for planning and regulation in the Syrian water sector; it oversees the operations of 14 regional water establishments who manage the provision of drinking water and sewerage facilities. The Ministry of Irrigation is responsible for the management of water resources and the provision of irrigation water, while the Ministry of Local Administration and Environment monitors water quality. An Integrated Water Resource Management Project, co-ordinated by the State Planning Commission, was initiated in 2006 with the aim of modernizing and integrating the various authorities responsible for the sector (see www.water.co.sy).

TRADE UNIONS

General Federation of Labour Unions (Ittihad Naqabat al-'Ummal al-'Am fi Suriya): BP 2351, rue Qanawat, Damascus; f. 1948; Chair. MUHAMMAD SHAABAN AZZOUZ; Sec. MAHMOUD FAHURI.

Transport

RAILWAYS

In 2007 the main railway system totalled 2,495 km of track. A new railway line linking Aleppo with Mersin in southern Turkey began operating in March 2009. Another new line connecting Aleppo with Gaziantep, also in southern Turkey, was anticipated in mid-2009. Plans for a mixed underground/elevated metro system in Damascus are at the planning stages. Construction work on the Green Line, consisting of a 16.5-km line and 17 stations, is scheduled to commence in 2012, with completion anticipated by 2016.

General Establishment of Syrian Railways: Ministry of Transport, BP 182, Aleppo; tel. (21) 2294602; fax (21) 2283162; e-mail cfs-syria@net.sy; internet www.cfssyria.org; f. 1897; Dir-Gen. GEORGE MAKABARI.

General Organization of the Hedjaz-Syrian Railway: BP 2978, rue Hedjaz, Damascus; tel. (11) 3331625; e-mail generaldirector@hijazerail.com; internet hijazerail.com; f. 1908; the Hedjaz Railway has 347 km of track (gauge 1,050 mm) in Syria; services operate between Damascus and Amman, on a branch line of about 24 km from Damascus to Katana, and there is a further line of 64 km from Damascus to Serghaya; Dir-Gen. S. AHMED.

ROADS

Arterial roads run across the country linking the north to the south and the Mediterranean to the eastern frontier. In 2007 Syria's total road network was 55,041 km, including 40,032 km of highways, main or national roads and 11,146 km of secondary roads. In the late 1990s work was scheduled to commence on the first stage of a project costing £S1,800m. to improve the road linking Rakka with Deir ez-Zor. In 2001 the Syrian Government awarded a contract for the construction of a 100-km, four-lane highway, connecting the eastern port town of Latakia with Ariba in the northern governorate of Aleppo, at an estimated cost of US $207m. The project was to be financed by loans from the Kuwaiti-based Arab Fund for Economic and Social Development and the Kuwait Fund for Arab Economic Development. Plans to construct a Damascus Ring Highway, at an estimated cost of US $380m., were being finalized in early 2009.

Public Establishment for Road Communications: BP 34203, Damascus; tel. (11) 2458411; fax (11) 2452682; e-mail director-g@perc.gov.sy; internet www.perc.gov.sy; f. 2003; Dir-Gen. HUSSAIN AL-ARNOUS.

PIPELINES

The Syrian Company for Oil Transport operates a network of domestic oil and gas pipelines, including a 560-km crude oil pipeline linking fields in Al-Hasakah province with Tartous, as well as some 2,000 km of gas pipelines. A 1,200-km Arab Gas Pipeline, to distribute Egyptian gas in the region, was announced by Egypt, Syria, Lebanon and Jordan in 2004. The first stage of the Syrian section was completed in 2008.

Syrian Co for Oil Transport (SCOT): BP 13, Banias; tel. (43) 711300; fax (43) 710418; e-mail scot50@scs-net.org; internet www.scot-syria.com; f. 1972; Gen. Man. NUMIR HABIB MAKHLOUF.

SHIPPING

Latakia is Syria's principal port; it has a 972-m quay with draughts ranging between 11.8 m–13.3 m. A concession to manage and operate the container terminal at Latakia was awarded to a consortium led by the French CMA CGM Group in March 2009. The concessionaire announced plans to increase capacity to 1m. 20-ft equivalent units (TEU) by 2012. Latakia handled 8m. tons of cargo in 2007 and 0.6m. TEUs in 2008. The other major ports are at Banias and Tartous. Tartous handled 12.5m. tons of cargo in 2007.

General Directorate of Syrian Ports: BP 505, Latakia; tel. (41) 473333; fax (41) 475805; e-mail gdp-itm@syrianport.com; internet www.syrianports.com; Dir-Gen. Rear-Adm. MOHSEN HASSAN.

Syrian General Authorities for Maritime Transport (SYRIAMAR): BP 314, place Zat as-Sawary, Latakia; tel. (41) 370681; fax (41) 371013; internet syriamar.net.

Abdulkader, Abu Bakr: Arwad, Latakia; operates a fleet of 5 general cargo vessels.

Delta Marine Transport: POB 1908, rue de Baghdad, Latakia; tel. (41) 222426; fax (41) 226047.

Ismail, A. M., Shipping Agency Ltd: BP 74, rue al-Mina, Tartous; tel. (43) 221987; fax (43) 318949; operates 8 general cargo vessels; Man. Dir MAHMOUD ISMAIL.

Latakia Port Authority: BP 220, rue Baghdad, Latakia; tel. (41) 476452; fax (41) 475760; e-mail lattakiaport@lattakiaport.com; internet www.lattakiaport.gov.sy; Gen. Man. SULEIMAN A. BALOUCH.

Muhieddine Shipping Co: BP 779, rue al-Mina, Tartous; tel. (43) 323090; fax (43) 317139; internet www.muhieddineshipping.net; operates 7 general cargo ships.

Riamar Shipping Co Ltd: Al Kornish ash-Sharki, BP 284, Immeuble Tarwin, rue du Port, Tartous; tel. (43) 314999; fax (43) 212616; e-mail aksabra@riamar.org; operates 6 general cargo vessels; Chair. and Man. Dir ABD AL-KADER SABRA.

Samin Shipping Co Ltd: BP 62, rue al-Mina, Tartous; tel. (43) 318835; fax (43) 318834; operates 10 general cargo ships.

Syro-Jordanian Shipping Co: BP 148, rue Port Said, Latakia; tel. (41) 471635; fax (41) 470250; e-mail syjomar@net.sy; f. 1976; operates 2 general cargo ships; transported 70,551 metric tons of goods in 1992; Chair. OSMAN LEBBADY; Tech. Man. M. CHOUMAN.

Tartous International Container Terminal JSC: BP 870, Tartous; tel. (43) 328882; fax (43) 328831; e-mail info@ictsi.sy; internet ictsi-sy.com; f. 2006; owned by International Container Terminal Services, Inc.; awarded 10-year concession to operate a container terminal at Tartous; Gen. Man. ROMEO A. SALVADOR.

Tartous Port Authority: BP 86, Tartous; tel. (43) 225150; fax (43) 315602; e-mail ta-pco@mail.sy; internet www.tartousport.com; Gen. Man. ZAKI E. NAJIB.

CIVIL AVIATION

There are international airports at Damascus and Aleppo. Plans to expand the capacity of Damascus airport were announced in 2005; in early 2009 the expansion work was still under way. Syrianair also operate domestic flights from airports in Al-Qamishli and Deir ez-Zor. Extensive renovation work at Deir ez-Zor was completed in 2008. Damascus International Airport handled 3.4m. passengers in 2007, while Aleppo handled 0.4m. passengers in the same year.

Directorate-General of Civil Aviation: BP 6257, place Nejmeh, Damascus; tel. (11) 3331306; fax (11) 2232201; Dir HAZEM AL-KHADRA.

Cham Wings Airlines: Immeuble Phillps, 4e étage, rue Alfardous, Damascus; tel. (11) 2244086; fax (11) 2454506; e-mail info@chamairlines.com; internet www.chamairlines.com; f. 2007; first private int. airline in Syria; flights from Damascus serving Baghdad, Istanbul, Jeddah, Sharm esh-Sheikh, Kyiv, Malmö; Vice Pres. SALIM SODA.

Syrian Arab Airlines (Syrianair): BP 417, 5th Floor, Social Insurance Bldg, Youssef al-Azmeh Sq., Damascus; tel. (11) 2220700; fax (11) 224923; e-mail syr-air@syriatel.net; internet www.syriaair.com; f. 1946; refounded 1961 to succeed Syrian Airways, after revocation of merger with Misrair (Egypt); domestic passenger and cargo services (from Damascus, Aleppo, Latakia and Deir ez-Zor) and routes to Europe, the Middle East, North Africa and the Far East; Chair. and Man. Dir NACHAAT NUMIR; Dir-Gen. GHAYDA ABD AL-LATIF.

Tourism

Syria's tourist attractions include a pleasant Mediterranean coastline, the mountains, town bazaars and antiquities of Damascus and Palmyra, as well as hundreds of deserted ancient villages in the north-west of the country. In 2006 some 6.0m. tourists visited Syria, and tourism receipts totalled US $2,113m.

Ministry of Tourism: BP 6642, rue Barada, Damascus; tel. (11) 2210122; fax (11) 2242636; e-mail min-tourism@mail.sy; internet www.syriatourism.org; f. 1972; Counsellor to the Minister SAWSAN JOUZY; Dir of Tourism Promotion and Marketing NIDAL MACHFEJ.

Middle East Tourism: BP 201, rue Fardoss, Damascus; tel. (11) 3325655; fax (11) 2246545; e-mail daadouche@net.sy; internet www.daadouche.com; f. 1952; Pres. MAHER DAADOUCHE; 7 brs.

Syrian Arab Co for Hotels and Tourism (SACHA): BP 5549, Mezzeh, Damascus; tel. (11) 2223286; fax (11) 2219415; f. 1977; Chair. DIRAR JUMA'A; Gen. Man. ELIAS ABOUTARA.

TAJIKISTAN

Introductory Survey

Location, Climate, Language, Religion, Flag, Capital

The Republic of Tajikistan is situated in the south-east of Central Asia. To the north and west it borders Uzbekistan, to the north-east Kyrgyzstan, to the east the People's Republic of China and to the south Afghanistan. The climate varies considerably according to altitude. The average temperature in January in Khujand (lowland) is −0.9°C (30.4°F); in July the average is 27.4°C (81.3°F). In the southern lowlands the temperature variation is somewhat more extreme. Rainfall is low in the valleys, in the range of 150–250 mm (6–10 ins) per year. In mountain areas winter temperatures can fall below −45°C (−51°F); the average January temperature in Murgab, in the mountains of south-east Kuhistoni Badakhshon, is −19.6°C (−3.3°F). Levels of rainfall are very low in mountain regions, seldom exceeding 60–80 mm (2–3 ins) per year. The official language is Tajik, an Iranian language; the Constitution grants Russian the status of a language of inter-ethnic communication, and all ethnic groups are guaranteed the right to use their native languages freely. The major religion is Islam. Most Tajiks and ethnic Uzbek residents follow the Sunni tradition, but the Pamiris are mostly Isma'ilis, a Shi'ite sect. The national flag (proportions 1 by 2) consists of three horizontal stripes from top to bottom of red, white and green, with a stylized gold crown surmounted by seven gold stars arranged in a semicircle in the centre of the white stripe. The capital is Dushanbe.

Recent History

In 1918 northern Tajikistan (which had been part of the Russian Empire since the 19th century) was conquered by the Bolsheviks, and the territory was incorporated into the Turkestan Autonomous Soviet Socialist Republic (ASSR). However, Dushanbe and the other southern regions of Tajikistan (which were subject to the Emirate of Bukhara) did not come under the control of the Bolsheviks until 1921. Opposition to Soviet rule was led by the *basmachis* (local guerrilla fighters) and foreign interventionists. In 1924 the Tajik ASSR was established as a part of the Uzbek Soviet Socialist Republic (SSR), and in January 1925 the south-east of Tajikistan was designated a Special Pamir Region (later renamed the Kuhistoni Badakhshon—Gornyi Badakhshan Autonomous Viloyat) within the Tajik ASSR. On 16 October 1929 the Tajik ASSR became a full Union Republic of the USSR and was slightly enlarged by the addition of the Khujand district from the Uzbek SSR. Soviet rule brought economic and social benefits to Tajikistan, but living standards remained low, and cattle-breeding, the main occupation in the uplands, was severely disrupted by collectivization. During the repressions of the 1930s almost all ethnic Tajiks in the republican Government were replaced by Russians.

During the 1970s increased Islamic influence was reported, as was violence towards non-indigenous nationalities. In 1978 there were reports of an anti-Russian riot, involving some 13,000 people, and after 1979 there were arrests of some activists opposed to Soviet intervention in Afghanistan. As in other Central Asian republics of the USSR, the first manifestation of the policies of Mikhail Gorbachev, who came to power as Soviet leader in 1985, was a campaign against corruption. Rakhmon Nabiyev, who had been First Secretary of the Communist Party of Tajikistan (CPT) since 1982, was replaced in late 1985 by Kakhar Makhkamov, who accused his predecessor of tolerating nepotism and corruption. Censorship was relaxed, and there was increased debate in the media of perceived injustices—such as alleged discrimination against Tajiks in Uzbekistan, and the legitimacy of the Uzbekistani–Tajikistani boundary. Greater freedom of expression encouraged interest in Tajik (and Iranian) culture and in 1989 Tajik was declared the state language.

In February 1990, following reports that Armenian refugees from the conflict in Nagornyi Karabakh (see the chapter on Azerbaijan) were to be settled in the capital, Dushanbe, violence broke out at a protest rally, when about 3,000 demonstrators clashed with police. A state of emergency was declared, and more than 5,000 troops suppressed the demonstrations; 22 people were reported dead and 565 injured. Two nascent opposition parties, Rebirth (Rastokhez), which had been involved in the February demonstrations, and the Democratic Party of Tajikistan (DPT), were refused official registration, and the Islamic Rebirth Party (IRP) was denied permission to hold a founding congress. Opposition politicians were barred from contesting the elections to the republic's Supreme Soviet (Supreme Council—legislature), held in March; 94% of the deputies elected were members of the CPT. None the less, in an apparent concession to growing Tajik nationalism the Supreme Soviet adopted a declaration of sovereignty on 25 August. In November Makhkamov was elected to the new post of executive President of the Republic by the Supreme Soviet; his only opponent was Nabiyev.

The Tajikistani Government, possibly anxious about increased Turkic dominance in Central Asia, displayed enthusiasm for a new Union Treaty (effectively preserving the USSR), and 90.2% of eligible voters in the republic were reported to have voted for the preservation of the USSR in the all-Union referendum in March 1991. In August, however, before the Treaty could be signed, conservative communists staged a coup in the Soviet and Russian capital, Moscow. Makhkamov did not oppose the coup, and on 31 August, after it had collapsed, he resigned as President, following demonstrations, which continued throughout much of September. On 9 September, following the declarations of independence by neighbouring Uzbekistan and Kyrgyzstan, the Tajikistani Supreme Soviet voted to proclaim an independent state, the Republic of Tajikistan. Kadriddin Aslonov, the Chairman of the Supreme Council and acting President, issued a decree that banned the CPT and nationalized its assets. In response, the communist majority in the Supreme Council demanded Aslonov's resignation, declared a state of emergency in the republic and rescinded the prohibition of the CPT. Aslonov resigned, and was replaced by Nabiyev. Nabiyev was, however, rapidly obliged to make substantial concessions to the opposition, and in early October the Supreme Council revoked the state of emergency, suspended the CPT and legalized the IRP. Shortly afterwards he resigned as acting President, in advance of the presidential election.

Seven candidates contested the direct presidential election, which took place on 24 November 1991. Attracting strong support in rural areas, Nabiyev won 57% of the votes cast, compared with 30% for the candidate favoured by the main opposition parties, Davlat Khudonazarov. Nabiyev took office in December. In late December Tajikistan signed the declaration establishing the Commonwealth of Independent States (CIS, see p. 225), the successor body to the USSR. In January 1992 a new Prime Minister, Akbar Mirzoyev, was appointed.

Anti-Government demonstrations began in Dushanbe in March 1992, initially prompted by Nabiyev's dismissal of Mamadayez Navzhuvanov, a prominent Badakhshoni, from the post of Minister of Internal Affairs. Protests against his dismissal were led by the group Lale Badakhshon, which advocated greater autonomy for the Pamiri peoples of the southern Kuhistoni Badakhshon Autonomous Viloyat. It was joined by Rebirth, the IRP and the DPT. Protesters demanding the resignation of Nabiyev and the Government remained encamped in the centre of Dushanbe for nearly two months; in response, the Government organized rival demonstrations, bringing supporters to the capital from the southern region of Kulob (Kulyab) and from Leninabad (later Khujand), in the north—the traditional areas of support for the CPT. In April members of the newly formed national guard loyal to Nabiyev opened fire on the demonstrators, killing at least eight people. In the following month the National Security Committee (NSC—the successor to the Soviet Committee for State Security—KGB) allegedly distributed weapons to pro-communist supporters, and the ensuing violent clashes escalated into civil war. Fighting in Dushanbe ended after Nabiyev negotiated a truce with opposition leaders and formed a new 'Government of National Reconciliation' led by Mirzoyev, in which eight of the 24 ministers were members of opposition parties. However, violent clashes erupted in Kulob Viloyat between pro-communist Kulobi forces, who opposed the President's compromise with the opposition, and members of Islamist and democratic groups. In late May the conflict spread into Qurgonteppa Viloyat (the main base of support for the

Islamist and democratic groups), where a Kulobi militia, the Tajik People's Front (TPF), led by Sangak Safarov, attempted to suppress the local forces of the informal Islamist-democratic coalition. The Kulobis alleged that their opponents were receiving weapons and assistance from Islamist groups in Afghanistan, and there were reports that Gulbuddin Hekmatyar, the leader of the Afghan *mujahidin* group, Hizb-i Islami, had established training camps in Afghanistan for Tajikistani fighters. The Islamist-democratic alliance, for its part, claimed that the ex-Soviet (Russian) garrisons were arming the pro-Government militias.

In August 1992 several members of the DPT and Lale Badakhshon were killed by Kulobi militia forces in Qurgonteppa. A violent conflict ensued between local members of the opposition and Kulobis, in which several hundred people were reportedly killed. Meanwhile, in Dushanbe anti-Government demonstrations resumed, and at the end of August demonstrators entered the presidential palace and took 30 officials hostage. In September Nabiyev was seized by opposition forces at Dushanbe airport, and was forced to announce his resignation. Akbarsho Iskandarov, the Chairman of the Supreme Council, temporarily assumed the responsibilities of Head of State. Mirzoyev also resigned, and Abdumalik Abdullojonov, a communist from Leninabad (later Soghd) Viloyat, was appointed acting Prime Minister. Iskandarov's administration, which had the support of all the main Islamist and democratic groups, had little influence, however, outside Dushanbe; much of the south of the country was under the control of the TPF militia, and some leaders of Leninabad Viloyat (which had a large Uzbek community) threatened to secede from Tajikistan if there was any attempt to introduce an Islamic state. In October the Islamist-democratic alliance's control of Dushanbe was threatened when forces led by Safarali Kenjayev, a former Chairman of the Supreme Soviet and a supporter of Nabiyev, entered the capital and attempted to seize power. Kenjayev briefly proclaimed himself Head of State, but his troops were forced to retreat by forces loyal to the regime. During the ensuing two months, however, Kenjayev's militias effectively enforced an economic blockade of the capital.

In November 1992, having failed to end the civil war, Iskandarov and the Government resigned. The legislature abolished the office of President, and Emomali Rakhmonov, a collective-farm chairman from Kulob Viloyat, was appointed Chairman of the Supreme Council (equivalent to Head of State). The legislature appointed a new Government, in which Abdullojonov retained the post of Prime Minister. However, all members of the opposition parties lost their portfolios, and the majority of the new ministers were Kulobis or supporters of Nabiyev. The Supreme Council also voted to combine Qurgonteppa and Kulob Viloyats into one unit, based in Qurgonteppa, and to be known as Khatlon Viloyat, in an apparent attempt to ensure control of the south of the country by pro-communist Kulobi forces.

In December 1992 forces loyal to the new Government, the TPF and Kulobi militias, captured Dushanbe, hitherto under the control of the Popular Democratic Army (PDA), a recently formed military coalition of Islamist and democratic groups. Between December 1992 and January 1993 some 60,000 Tajikistanis fled to Afghanistan, after alleged reprisals against supporters of the democratic and Islamist forces. Among those who fled was the influential *qazi* (Islamic judge) of Tajikistan, Akbar Turajonzoda, a senior member of the IRP, who was accused by the new Government of attempting to establish an Islamist state. In February he was replaced as spiritual leader of Tajikistan's Muslims by Fatkhullo Sharifzoda, who was given the title of *mufti*.

In February 1993 insurgents in the central region of Garm attempted to declare an 'autonomous Islamic republic', but the Government had secured control of most of the country by March. The Government estimated that 30,000 people had been killed and some 800,000 people displaced during the civil war; however, other sources claimed that as many as 100,000 people had died. Although the civil war effectively ended in early 1993, the continued insurgency of Islamist-democratic forces, notably from across the Afghan border, continued to destabilize the country. Rebel resistance near Garm was ended in March. In June the Supreme Court formally proscribed the IRP, Lale Badakhshon, Rebirth and the DPT, leaving the CPT as the only legal party. Two new parties established later in the year—the Party of Economic Freedom and the People's Democratic Party of Tajikistan (PDPT)—were founded or sponsored by members of the Government or its associates.

In December 1993 Abdullojonov resigned as premier; he was replaced by Abdujalil Samadov. From the end of 1993 Rakhmonov, who secured for his own office responsibility for the powerful Ministries of Defence and Internal Affairs, as well as for the NSC (and, in February 1994, operational supervision of the broadcast media), began to show signs of compromise. In March he announced his willingness to negotiate with the Islamist-democratic opposition, and talks began in April in Moscow, under the auspices of the UN and in the presence of representatives from Iran, Pakistan, Russia and the USA. The negotiations resulted in a protocol on the establishment of a joint commission on refugees. However, reconciliation was far from having been achieved: from March border incursions from Afghanistan intensified, resulting in clashes with the CIS troops stationed on the frontier (see below), and there was renewed insurgency in Kuhistoni Badakhshon. The continuing conflict along the Tajikistani–Afghan border was interpreted by some observers as being partly a battle for control of drugs-smuggling routes: since securing independence Tajikistan had become a major conduit for illicit drugs (chiefly opium) from Pakistan, Iran and Afghanistan to Russia and western Europe.

In August 1994 the forthcoming presidential election was postponed, to allow time for opposition candidates to be included in the poll. The implementation of a temporary cease-fire, agreed in September, was deferred until the following month after rebel forces launched a large-scale offensive in Tavil Dara, which was repelled by government troops. In December the UN Security Council authorized the deployment of a Mission of Observers in Tajikistan (UNMOT). When the election eventually took place on 6 November, the only two candidates were Rakhmonov and Abdullojonov. Some 85% of eligible voters were reported to have participated in the election, which was won by Rakhmonov, with some 58% of the votes cast; Abdullojonov received about 35% of the votes. The result reflected regional loyalties; Rakhmonov (a Kulobi) secured most of his support in the south, and Abdullojonov received a large proportion of the votes in Khujand and in Kuhistoni Badakhshon. In a concurrent referendum, some 90% of voters approved a new constitution. In December Jamshed Karimov was appointed as Chairman of the Council of Ministers.

In February 1995 renewed peace talks opened in Almaty, Kazakhstan, but little progress was achieved. Also in February the newly formed Party of Popular Unity and Accord (PPUA—led by Abdullojonov) announced that it would not contest the legislative elections scheduled to take place later that month, after Abdullojonov's candidature had been disallowed by the electoral authorities. The Organization for Security and Co-operation in Europe (OSCE, see p. 366) refused to send observers to the elections, claiming that the electoral law was severely flawed. Despite the opposition boycott, elections to the new Majlisi Oli (Supreme Assembly) took place on 26 February, with the participation of an estimated 84% of the electorate. In some 40% of constituencies there was only one candidate, and most of those elected were reported to be state officials loyal to the President, largely without party affiliation. A second round of voting was held on 12 March to elect representatives to 19 seats that had not been filled.

In March 1995 the opposition announced a unilateral, 50-day extension of the cease-fire, but later that month there were further attacks on border posts on the Tajikistani–Afghan frontier. In early April there was a serious escalation of the conflict in the region, and 34 border guards and 170 rebel troops were reportedly killed during one week of fighting. The opposition forces (comprising the IRP and Lale Badakhshon) claimed that they were responding to a large deployment of Tajikistani government troops and Russian border guards in Kuhistoni Badakhshon, in violation of the cease-fire agreement. The cease-fire was extended in late April, and again, for three months, in May. An exchange of prisoners was agreed at further talks in May. In July Rakhmonov met the leader of the IRP, Sayed Abdullo Nuri, and other opposition leaders for talks in Tehran, Iran, and in August the cease-fire was extended for six months. During the second half of 1995 conflict continued in the south of the country and on the border with Afghanistan. In September fighting was reported in Qurgonteppa between two military units, both formerly loyal to the Government. By the end of that month, when government forces regained control of the town, some 300 people had reportedly died. Further peace negotiations were convened, under UN auspices, in Asgabat, Turkmenistan, in November. However, the opposition withdrew, in response to the Government's refusal to accede to its demand for the formation of a national reconciliation council to govern the country alongside Rakhmonov during a two-year transition period.

In January 1996 Sharifzoda was killed by gunmen. Although the Government accused the IRP of responsibility for his death, the opposition denied any involvement. At the end of January opposition forces began a major offensive in the Tavil Dara region of Kuhistoni Badakhshon, and military commanders of the government troops initiated rebellions in two towns. The western town of Tursunzoda was taken by forces under Ibodullo Boitmatov, and Makhmoud Khudoberdiyev took control of Qurgonteppa. The commanders (both ethnic Uzbeks) demanded changes to the Government, notably the removal of several Kulobi ministers. In early February Khudoberdiyev's troops approached Dushanbe, but retreated when they encountered government forces. Following negotiations, Rakhmonov agreed to the commanders' demands; Karimov was replaced as premier by Yakhyo Azimov.

Despite the announcement of an indefinite extension of the cease-fire, fighting intensified in March and April 1996 near Tavil Dara, where it was reported that Russian border guards and aircraft were supporting Tajikistani government troops in attacks on rebel forces; in May opposition forces captured the town of Tavil Dara. Talks resumed in Aşgabat in July. A cease-fire was brokered in Tavil Dara, and agreement was reached on the conduct of further peace negotiations and on a gradual exchange of prisoners of war. However, large-scale hostilities resumed around Tavil Dara and opposition forces regained control of the town in mid-August; meanwhile, government and rebel troops fought for command of the strategic central region of Tajikistan. A further cease-fire agreement was reached, but was almost immediately violated as fierce fighting continued around Garm. However, later that month, in Moscow, Rakhmonov and Nuri agreed to form a National Reconciliation Council (NRC), to be headed by a representative of what had come to be known as the United Tajik Opposition (UTO), comprising both Islamists and supporters of democracy. The NRC was to have extensive executive powers to revise legislation on elections, political parties and the media, to debate constitutional amendments and to monitor the implementation of the peace agreement. A general amnesty was agreed, as were terms for an exchange of prisoners and the repatriation of refugees.

Negotiations were held in Tehran in January 1997 to determine the structure and composition of the NRC, and at further UN-mediated peace talks held in Mashhad, Iran, in February, it was agreed that the NRC was to comprise 26 seats divided equally between the Government and the UTO. Negotiations on the reintegration of opposition forces into Tajikistan's military structures, the exchange of prisoners and the legalization of opposition parties were held in Moscow and Tehran throughout March and April. In April Rakhmonov was wounded in an assassination attempt in Khujand. The UTO denied any involvement and condemned the attack. Following talks held in Tehran later that month, a protocol was signed by government and UTO representatives, which guaranteed the provisions of the December 1996 peace agreement. These were confirmed in the General Agreement on Peace and National Accord in Tajikistan, signed by Rakhmonov and Nuri in Moscow on 27 June 1997, which formally ended the five-year civil conflict. In July Nuri was elected Chairman of the NRC, at its inaugural session; a policy of 'mutual forgiveness' was concluded, as well as an amnesty to allow UTO fighters to return to Tajikistan.

In September 1997, for the first time in five years, Nuri arrived in Dushanbe, to participate in the NRC. Some 200 UTO fighters were deployed in the capital to guard members of the NRC, sessions of which formally commenced in mid-September. Meanwhile, opposition to the agreement led to a series of minor bomb explosions in Dushanbe in early September. In October an attack on the barracks of the presidential guard, attributed to Makhmoud Khudoberdiyev, resulted in the deaths of at least 14 servicemen.

By mid-November 1997 some 10,000 Tajikistani refugees had been repatriated from Afghanistan. Meanwhile, negotiations were held between Nuri and Rakhmonov to determine the allocation of portfolios in the new government (under the terms of the peace agreement, the UTO was to receive one-third of posts in both the central and regional administrations). In January 1998 the UTO delegation to the NRC temporarily suspended its participation in the Council, claiming that the Government had failed to implement the terms of the peace agreement. In February, however, three portfolios, including those of Labour and Employment and of the Economy and Foreign Economic Relations, were formally allocated to UTO members. Turajonzoda, the deputy leader of the UTO, who had been living in exile in Iran, made his return to Tajikistan conditional on his appointment to the Government as a Deputy Chairman; he arrived in Tajikistan in late February, and was appointed First Deputy Chairman, with responsibility for relations with CIS countries.

In March 1998 several people, including the brother of the former Prime Minister, Abdullojonov, were sentenced to death for their part in the attempted assassination of Rakhmonov in April 1997. An upsurge in fighting between government and opposition forces, in the vicinity of Dushanbe, resulted in many civilian deaths. In April 1998 Rakhmonov, who had joined the PDPT in March, was elected Chairman of the party. In May a cease-fire was agreed, following the outbreak of fighting between government and opposition forces close to Dushanbe. In August Rakhmonov confirmed the appointment of several UTO members to government posts. However, other opposition appointments were rejected by the President, bringing the number of UTO members in the Government to 11, rather than the 14 agreed under the terms of the peace accord. At the end of August five local officials in western Tajikistan were killed; the Government reportedly blamed supporters of Khudoberdiyev. In September the trial of four men, said to be associates of Khudoberdiyev, accused of attempting to overthrow the Government in August 1997, began in Dushanbe. In late September 1998 a senior opposition member, Otakhon Latifi, was assassinated in the capital. Meanwhile, accusations by the Government of opposition involvement in the deaths of the four UNMOT workers in July prompted the UTO to announce its withdrawal from the Government and the NRC at the end of September. The crisis was defused after intensive talks between Rakhmonov and UTO representatives resulted in agreement on a 10-point programme (which included measures to ensure the safety of opposition groups and the formation of a joint commission to investigate Latifi's death) to accelerate the peace process. (In June 2000 a militant was imprisoned, having been found guilty of Latifi's murder.)

In October 1998 an operation by government forces against two rebel factions in Dushanbe resulted in some 13 deaths and the detention of six rebels. Heavy fighting was reported around Khujand in early November, in what was regarded as the most violent uprising since the 1997 peace agreement, following the seizure by Khudoberdiyev's forces of police and security headquarters and a nearby airport. An estimated 100–300 people were killed; some 500 were injured and a number of police-officers were taken hostage. Khudoberdiyev's forces were reportedly defeated after five days of fighting. President Rakhmonov accused Abdullojonov of having instigated the rebellion. Criminal proceedings were initiated against the former premier shortly afterwards, as well as against Khudoberdiyev and two other prominent figures.

In mid-November 1998 the Majlisi Oli endorsed the appointment of several UTO members to the Council of Ministers, including Zokir Vazirov as a Deputy Chairman and Davlat Usmon as Minister of the Economy and Foreign Economic Relations. In December 1998 Nuri announced that the UTO would disband its armed forces in early 1999. In March 1999 the re-registration of political parties was effected by the Ministry of Justice: of the eight parties previously registered, only five received new licences. Criminal charges against leading opposition party members, including Nuri and Turajonzoda, were abandoned, in accordance with the 1997 amnesty; 360 UTO members were thus granted immunity from prosecution. At the end of the month the Supreme Court sentenced seven supporters of Khudoberdiyev to 10–14 years' imprisonment, following their conviction on charges of involvement in the attack on government forces in October 1997.

The Majlisi Oli adopted a resolution in mid-May 1999 whereby the estimated 5,500 opposition fighters registered were to receive a general amnesty. In late May the UTO leadership withdrew from the NRC: among its demands were the holding of elections to the Majlisi Oli in 1999, in advance of the presidential election scheduled for November, and further UTO appointments to government posts (so that it held one-third of all government positions, as specified by the 1997 peace agreement). In June 1999 President Rakhmonov and Nuri signed an agreement outlining a timetable for the implementation of the provisions of the peace agreement; furthermore, four UTO members were appointed to government posts. In July Rakhmonov appointed another five UTO representatives to government positions. In the same month the President reportedly announced that 21 of the 69 local government posts would be offered to opposition members. In August the UTO leadership announced that the integration of its fighters into the regular armed forces had been completed. Rakhmonov responded later that month by lifting a ban on opposition parties, and their media, that had been imposed in 1993.

At a referendum held on 26 September 1999, some 72% of the votes cast by an estimated 92% of the electorate gave their endorsement to amendments to the Constitution, proposed by President Rakhmonov, which included: the formation of a bilateral legislature; the extension of the presidential mandate from five to seven years; and the legalization of religiously-based political parties. The IRP was subsequently permitted to register as a political party. In October the UTO again temporarily withdrew from the NRC, alleging that pledges made by the Government had not been met and seeking a postponement of the forthcoming presidential election, owing to the fact that three of its candidates had been prevented from contesting the presidency. Meanwhile, it was reported in mid-October that the First Deputy Prime Minister and deputy leader of the UTO, Turajonzada, had been expelled from the organization and its largest constituent party, the IRP, after dissenting from party policy.

In the presidential election, held on 6 November 1999, Rakhmonov received some 97.0% of the total votes cast, according to official sources, defeating his only opponent, Usmon. The rate of participation by the electorate was reported to be almost 99%. However, the opposition demanded that the election be declared invalid, owing to alleged electoral malpractice; the OSCE had again refused to send any monitors to the election. Following the inauguration of President Rakhmonov on 16 November, the Government tendered its resignation, although ministers remained in office until the formation of a new Government in late December. Akil Akilov was appointed Chairman of the Council of Ministers (Prime Minister).

In December 1999 the legislature approved the reorganization of the Majlisi Oli as a bicameral parliament. Although six political parties were registered to participate in forthcoming elections to the upper and lower chambers, it was reported that a number of opposition parties had been barred from contesting the poll. (Further re-registration of parties was carried out during that month.) In the elections to the new Majlisi Namoyandagon (Assembly of Representatives), the lower chamber of the Majlisi Oli, held on 27 February 2000, Rakhmonov's PDPT (with its allies) was reported to have won 64.5% of the total votes cast and secured 45 of the 63 seats. The CPT won around 20.6% of the votes (13 seats), while the IRP secured about 7.5% (two seats). According to official sources, some 93% of eligible voters participated in the election. There were claims by the OSCE and opposition parties that electoral malpractice had been widespread. Following the elections, Nuri made a formal complaint to Rakhmonov, the UN and the OSCE, alleging that the President had reneged on pledges he had made in November 1999 regarding electoral procedures. A second round of voting took place on 12 March 2000 for 11 constituencies in which the requisite quorum of 50% had not been achieved. Results in a further three constituencies had been declared invalid at the first round of voting; re-elections for two seats took place in April and December, respectively. Meanwhile, on 23 March indirect elections to the Majlisi Milliy (National Assembly), the legislative upper chamber, were held for the first time (25 members of the chamber were elected by regional deputies, with eight further members appointed by the President of the Republic). At the end of the month the NRC was dissolved. In May UNMOT announced the cessation of its peace-keeping activities and withdrew from the country. On 1 June it was succeeded, with the authorization of the UN Security Council, by the UN Tajikistan Office of Peacebuilding (UNTOP). In October a new currency, the somoni, was introduced, replacing the Tajikistani rouble, which had been in use since May 1995.

In December 2000 the Supreme Court suspended the activities of the Justice (Adolatkhoh) Party for six months; the party claimed that the ruling was a consequence of its opposition to the President during the legislative elections. In August 2001 the party was banned, after it failed to re-register its members during its period of suspension. Meanwhile, in April several bomb attacks took place, which killed at least four people. In June state security forces launched an attack against a group of militants, led by a former UTO field commander, Rakhmon Sanginov, near Dushanbe; it was reported that some 36 rebels were killed. In August Sanginov was killed by security forces, and at the end of the month officials claimed that only about 10 of his supporters remained at large.

In September 2001 the Minister of Culture, Press and Information, Abdurakhim Rakhimov, was assassinated; Karomatullo Olimov was appointed as his successor in October. It was reported in December that 10 men had been sentenced to between eight and 25 years' imprisonment on charges of treason, terrorism and sedition, relating to the November 1998 insurrection in Khujand. In January 2002 two new ministries were created—the Ministries of Industry and of State Revenues and Tax Collection. In March a public accord agreement, signed in 1996 by pro-Government political parties and non-governmental organizations to express support for the peace process, and renewed in 1999, was extended indefinitely; the accord was signed by a representative of the IRP for the first time.

Drugs-smuggling remained a significant problem in Tajikistan, at times apparently involving government officials as well as Islamist militants. In August 2002 the former Deputy Minister of Defence, Col Nikolai Kim, was sentenced to 13 years' imprisonment for drugs-trafficking and embezzlement while in office in 1998. Organized crime also remained a problem: in October 2002 a senior police official was sentenced to 25 years' imprisonment on charges of murder, fraud and extortion. Also in October two men were sentenced to death, and a further six were reported to have received terms of imprisonment of between two and 25 years, after being found guilty of belonging to an armed grouping loyal to Khudoberdiyev. It was reported that almost 75 supporters of Khudoberdiyev had been convicted since 1999.

In January 2003 President Rakhmonov carried out a major reorganization of the Council of Ministers and other government structures. On 22 June an estimated 96% of the electorate participated in a referendum on proposed amendments to the Constitution, which were approved by 93% of the votes cast. The amendments approved included: an extension of judges' terms of office from five to 10 years; the removal from the Constitution of references to religious parties; and the abolition of the right to both free health care and higher education. Significantly, Rakhmonov would also be permitted to stand for two further seven-year terms of office upon the expiry of his existing mandate in 2006.

A Deputy Chairman of the IRP, Shamsiddin Shamsiddinov, was arrested in May 2003, and in October he became the first person to be tried on charges relating to the period of civil conflict. Shamsiddinov's detention and trial was widely interpreted as a new initiative by the Government to suppress Islamist groups by accusing them of war crimes. Following a closed trial, in January 2004 Shamsiddinov was sentenced to 16 years' imprisonment. Meanwhile, in October 2003 the former commander of the interior ministry rapid-reaction forces, Maj. Shodi Alimadov, was sentenced to eight years in prison, after being convicted on charges of corruption, extortion and abuse of office. In December and in January 2004 Rakhmonov effected a number of high-level government changes, notably including the appointment of Jurabek Nurmakhmadov as Minister of Energy, in place of Abdullo Yorov.

In September 2004 20 members of the banned transnational militant Islamist group Hizb-ut-Tahrir al-Islami (Party of Islamic Liberation—Hizb-ut-Tahrir) were sentenced to prison terms ranging from six months to 15 years. (According to the Office of the Prosecutor-General, between 2000 and July 2005 209 people were convicted of membership of Hizb-ut-Tahrir; no person arrested on suspicion of belonging to the organization had been acquitted. In January 2006 it was reported that 99 suspected members of the movement had been detained in 2005, of whom 40 had been tried and sentenced.)

In January 2005 Rakhmonov removed Kozidavlat Koimdodov from the post of Deputy Prime Minister, appointing him ambassador to Turkmenistan. Zokir Vazirov was dismissed as Deputy Prime Minister in February, and appointed Minister of Labour, Employment and Social Welfare. Meanwhile, in January the Chairman of the DPT, Makhmadruzi Iskandarov, was denied permission to register as a candidate in the parliamentary elections scheduled for 27 February, owing to criminal charges; Iskandarov had been arrested in Moscow in December 2004, accused of corruption and involvement in an attack on the offices of a prosecutor and of a regional branch of the Ministry of Internal Affairs in August; the DPT asserted that the arrest was politically motivated. Sulton Kuvvatov, the leader of the Union and Development Party (which had been denied registration in March 2004), was also detained and refused permission to register as a candidate in the elections, having been accused of insulting Rakhmonov and inciting ethnic hatred. In January 2005 a car bomb explosion outside the Ministry of Emergency Situations and Civil Defence in Dushanbe killed the driver of the vehicle and injured several others. A further bomb outside the same ministry in June injured four people. In January 2006 the Minister of Internal Affairs, Khomiddin Sharipov, announced the completion of an investigation into the two bombings. At least two people suspected of organizing the attacks were still to be apprehended, but a number of others, believed to be members of the militant Islamist group, the Islamic Movement of Uzbekistan (IMU), had been imprisoned.

Six political parties participated in the elections to the Majlisi Namoyandagon held on 27 February and 13 March 2005. Rakhmonov's PDPT reportedly won 74% of the votes cast nation-wide to decide the allocation of seats on the basis of party lists, securing a total of 52 of the 63 seats in the chamber. The CPT won 13% of the national vote on the basis of party lists (four seats in total), while the IRP secured 8% (two seats). A reported 92.6% of the electorate participated in the poll. The OSCE (and opposition parties) claimed that electoral malpractice was widespread and that amendments to the constitutional law on elections adopted in July 2004 had not been fully implemented. Several members of the IRP and other opposition parties received prison sentences, widely believed to be politically motivated, after being found guilty of charges of hooliganism, defamation and embezzlement. The first session of the newly elected Majlisi Namoyandagon was held on 17 March 2005. Indirect elections to the Majlisi Milliy took place on 24 March, and the eight presidential nominees were announced the following day. The first session of the new upper chamber convened on 15 April.

In late April 2005 it was reported that a former Minister of the Interior, Yakub Salimov, who had been extradited from Russia in February 2004, had been sentenced to 15 years' imprisonment for treason after a five-month closed trial. Meanwhile, in early April 2005 the Russian authorities released Iskandarov, owing to a lack of evidence, after refusing a request by Tajikistan for his extradition. However, Iskandarov was arrested in Dushanbe later that month; he claimed to have been kidnapped in Russia and brought to Tajikistan by unknown individuals. After the Russian and Tajikistani authorities failed to clarify the details of Iskandarov's transfer to Tajikistan, the DPT announced in May its temporary withdrawal from the Public Council (a body established in 1994 by Rakhmonov, and usually comprising social and cultural organizations and five of Tajikistan's six officially registered parties); in addition, the DPT criticized alleged malpractice during the legislative elections. The IRP and CPT subsequently also announced their withdrawal from the Public Council, in protest at the conduct of the elections.

In June 2005 the deputy leader of the Union and Development Party was found guilty of provoking ethnic discord and insulting President Rakhmonov, whom he had accused of genocide: he was sentenced to almost six years' imprisonment. In October the Supreme Court sentenced Iskandarov to 23 years' imprisonment, after he was found guilty on charges of terrorism, embezzlement and the possession of illegal weapons. Iskandarov vehemently denied the charges, but in January 2006 the verdict was upheld by the court of appeal. In March the Chairman of the opposition Social Democratic Party of Tajikistan (SDPT), Rakhmatullo Zoyirov, declared that there were some 1,000 political prisoners in Tajikistan. Also in March the European Union (EU, see p. 255) released a statement in which it expressed concern at the unclear circumstances surrounding Iskandarov's transfer from Russia to Tajikistan, and at allegations that he was mistreated prior to his trial.

There was considerable concern regarding the freedom of the media in 2005. Media representatives accused state officials of withholding information from and threatening journalists, and no independent newspapers or magazines were registered. The authorities reportedly prevented several independent newspapers and printing houses from publishing, and in April a privately owned television station was closed, ostensibly for failing to submit the requisite documentation. Meanwhile, in November two new political parties were registered: the Party of Economic Reforms and the Agrarian Party of Tajikistan. Zoyirov asserted that the organizations were instruments of the Government. In August 2006 the former commander of the presidential guard, Lt-Gen. Gaffor Mirzoyev, was sentenced to life imprisonment, following his conviction, by a closed trial, on charges of terrorism and of conspiring to overthrow the Government. Also in August Nuri died, and in the following month Muhiddin Kabiri was elected as Chairman of the IRP in his stead

A presidential election, which was contested by five candidates, took place on 6 November 2006; Rakhmonov was re-elected to office, with 79.3% of the votes cast, while Olimjon Boboyev of the Party of Economic Reforms, with only 6.2% of votes cast, was the second-placed candidate. The OSCE declared that the elections failed to meet international standards. A new Council of Ministers was announced by presidential decree on 1 December and approved by the Majlisi Oliy on 16 December; additionally, 10 ministries and government agencies were either dissolved or merged with other ministries and agencies. Ministers who retained their portfolios from the previous Government included Prime Minister Akilov (who was appointed, additionally, as Minister of Construction), Deputy Prime Minister Asadullo Ghulomov and Minister of Defence Maj.-Gen. Sherali Khayrulloyev. Notable changes included the appointment of Hamrokhon Zaripov, former Tajikistani ambassador to the USA, as Minister of Foreign Affairs, and that of Mahmadnazar Solehov as Minister of Internal Affairs, succeeding Sharipov. Izbillo Khojayev became Chairman of the Constitutional Court, and was replaced as Chairman of the Supreme Court by Nasratullo Abdulloyev. In January 2007 a new Agency for State Financial Control and Suppression of Corruption was established by presidential decree; Sherkhon Salimov, a representative of the PDPT in the Majlisi Namoyandagon, was chosen to head the new agency. Also in January Procurator-General Bobojon Bobokhonov announced that 10 opposition and Islamist organizations had been banned, owing to their alleged extremist disposition. In early February the DPT was refused registration by the Ministry of Justice, on the grounds of apparently inconsistent statements within the party's founding statute. At the same time a reorganization of the Ministry of Internal Affairs, including the foundation of a new Migration Service, was announced.

In March 2007 President Rakhmonov announced that he was to abandon the Russian-derived '-ov' suffix from his surname and that henceforth he wished to be known as Emomali Rakhmon, on the grounds that it was more 'Tajik'. Minister of Foreign Affairs Zaripov made a similar declaration in April, stating that he wished to be known as Hamrokhon Zarifi, and parents were encouraged to follow this example when naming their children. Other presidential decrees issued at this time were aimed primarily at schools, including the introduction of a new dress-code (reinforcing, *inter alia*, a prohibition on women wearing headscarves that had been introduced in 2005) and the abolition of Soviet-era holidays. In July the mandate of UNTOP was officially concluded. In November it was reported that the central government offices complex in Dushanbe had been damaged in a bomb explosion, in which one civilian had been killed; the perpetrators of the attack remained unknown. In January 2008 President Rakhmon removed three ministers in a government reorganization and also replaced a number of public senior state officials, after criticizing their failure to address increasing energy shortages. By February a critical humanitarian situation had developed in the country, as a result of severe weather conditions, together with continuing energy shortages, necessitating substantial humanitarian assistance. In April the authorities ordered the closure of an independent radio station, Radio Imruz, purportedly on technical grounds; Radio Imruz, having reported on public discontent, and social and economic difficulties since it commenced broadcasting in Dushanbe in the previous year, had been perceived as unusually critical of the authorities. In September the Tajikistani authorities announced the institution of criminal proceedings against a prominent opposition journalist and leader of the Vatandor (Patriot) Movement, Dodojon Atovullo, on charges of anti-state activities and public defamation of the President; Atovullo, who had been exiled in Moscow since 1992, was reported to have fled to Germany following an extradition request from Tajikistan.

At the beginning of March 2009 the State Committee for Television and Radio Broadcasting suspended operations of a Russian state television channel, RTR-Planeta (the only terrestrial broadcaster of Russian-language programming operating in Tajikistan), on the grounds that it had accrued debt equivalent to some US $130,000, and that a new broadcasting contract would be negotiated; the decision followed a visit by President Rakhmon in Moscow in February (see below) and a significant increase in anti-Russian sentiment in the Tajikistani media. In April the results were announced of an independent audit of the National Bank, conducted by a British company in late 2008 following the discovery that Tajikistan had received IMF loans based on false information; it was alleged that Deputy Prime Minister Murodali Alimardon, the Chairman of the National Bank in 1996–2008, was responsible for the misappropriation of at least $856m. of state funds allocated to support the cotton industry, which had been transferred to private enterprises headed by his relatives.

After the dissolution of the USSR, Russian troops remained in Tajikistan, officially adopting a neutral stance during the civil war. However, following the communist victory in Dushanbe in December 1992, they openly assisted pro-communist troops in quelling the opposition forces, and the Tajikistani Government became increasingly dependent on Russia, both militarily and economically. In January 1993 Russia, Kazakhstan, Kyrgyzstan and Uzbekistan committed themselves to the defence of Tajikistan's southern frontiers, thus supporting the Government in the continuing conflict on the Tajikistani–Afghan border. In practice, mainly Russian troops were responsible for repelling rebel fighters entering Tajikistan, with Russia defending the southern CIS border as if it were its own. In August Russia and the Central Asian states (excluding Turkmenistan) signed an agreement establishing a CIS peace-keeping force to police Tajikistan's border with Afghanistan.

Despite Russia's involvement in the civil conflict in Tajikistan, it also sought to mediate between the Government and the opposition leadership in exile. During 1994–95 relations between the Russian authorities and the Rakhmonov regime deteriorated. However, in 1996 and 1997 Russia hosted several rounds of the UN-sponsored negotiations for a political settlement in Tajikistan, which culminated in the signature of the peace agreement in Moscow in June 1997. In April 1999 Russia and Tajikistan signed an agreement on the establishment of a Russian military base in Tajikistan; in the same month nine major bilateral agreements were signed, including a Treaty of Alliance and Co-operation. In October 2004 Russia officially opened a military base in Tajikistan and took formal control of the Nurek space monitoring centre, after a meeting between the Russian President, Vladimir Putin, and President Rakhmonov; in return, Russia agreed to cancel US $242m. of Tajikistan's $300m. debt to Russia.

During the civil conflict in Tajikistan, the leadership of Uzbekistan provided military and political support to the Rakhmonov administration. In October 1994 Tajikistan and Uzbekistan signed a Co-operation Agreement envisaging greater bilateral co-ordination, especially in foreign policy and security. However, the Uzbekistani Government reportedly criticized the treatment of the Uzbek ethnic minority in Tajikistan, alleging that many ethnic Uzbeks had been replaced in their posts by Kulobis. None the less, Uzbekistan continued to provide considerable technical and military support for the Tajikistani administration. Following the signature of the peace agreement in June 1997, the Uzbekistani leadership expressed renewed concern at the possible Islamicization of Tajikistan. Further tensions arose in August 1999, when northern Tajikistan came under attack by unidentified aircraft, which, according to the Tajikistani leadership, belonged to Uzbekistani forces; an Uzbekistani military contingent was assisting Kyrgyzstan in repelling a group of Islamist militants in that country's nearby Osh region, in the Farg'ona valley. (The Uzbekistani Government subsequently admitted that its forces might accidentally have bombed the territory.) In April 2000 Tajikistan was strongly criticized by the Uzbekistani and Kyrgyzstani Governments for failing to expel the leader of a group of Uzbek anti-Government Islamist rebels, who had allegedly established a permanent base in Tajikistan. Armed incursions into those two countries by insurgents commenced in August. By the end of 2000 hostilities had subsided, although occasional violent incidents continued to be reported. In March 2001, in response to a claim by the Kyrgyzstani Government that Tajikistan harboured some 2,500 international terrorists, the Tajikistani Government declared there to be no members of any militant organization on its territory, and invited the Kyrgyzstani Government to examine its borders. The Uzbekistan authorities, which had begun to lay landmines along its border with Tajikistan from mid-2000, in an effort to prevent cross-border incursions by Islamist insurgents, officially informed Tajikistan of this only in May 2001. However, bilateral relations subsequently improved. President Rakhmonov visited President Karimov of Uzbekistan in December; it was announced that a crossing between the Penjakent region of Tajikistan and Uzbekistan's Samarqand region was to reopen, and the two leaders also agreed to collaborate to combat terrorism, crime and drugs-trafficking. In February 2002, at a meeting of the Tajikistani and Uzbekistani premiers, an agreement on border-crossing procedures was reached. In October a border agreement was signed by Presidents Rakhmonov and Karimov, although four areas in the northern Soghd Viloyat remained in dispute.

Tajikistani-Uzbekistani relations, which had become increasingly strained, deteriorated sharply following the suspension at the beginning of 2009 of Turkmenistan's electricity exports to Tajikistan, resulting from the continued failure of the Tajikistani and Uzbekistani authorities to agree a transit rate. Tajikistan accused Uzbekistani state utility Uzbekenergo of interrupting deliveries of Turkmenistani electricity, and threatened to limit the amount of water flowing downstream to Uzbekistan, in order to maintain levels in its reservoirs. (A complete absence of energy supplies in parts of Tajikistan was reported.) An additional matter of contention was the construction of a hydroelectric plant at Roghun, in central Tajikistan, of critical importance domestically but strongly opposed by Uzbekistan, owing to concerns regarding the potential impact of the project on its own water supplies. Later in January Uzbekistan President Islam Karimov and Russian President Dmitrii Medvedev issued a joint declaration, stating that any hydroengineering projects with transboundary implications were required to meet international laws and standards. However, in February Karimov unexpectedly announced that Uzbekistan was prepared to reconsider its opposition to the project, provided that international auditors verified its viability. On 19 February Uzbekistani First Deputy Prime Minister Rustam Azimov visited Tajikistan to attend the first bilateral high-level commission meeting in seven years; it was reported that negotiations resulted in agreement on a debt repayment schedule, and on a protocol regarding a reservoir in northern Tajikistan, although a number of the fundamental issues remained unresolved. Electricity supplies from Turkmenistan were subsequently resumed.

Tajikistan had begun to develop relations outside the USSR before its dissolution in 1991, notably with Iran, with which the Tajiks have strong ethnic and linguistic ties. However, the effective collapse of central authority in Tajikistan in 1992 severely hindered further development of foreign relations, although several states attempted to influence the progress of the country's civil war. Anti-Islamist groups in Tajikistan asserted that Iran was supplying armaments and other goods to Islamist elements in Tajikistan, but the Iranian authorities insisted that they were providing only cultural and humanitarian assistance. In July 1995 President Rakhmonov visited Tehran, where a number of agreements on cultural and economic co-operation were signed. Further agreements were signed in late 1996, providing for Iranian investment in Tajikistan's industrial and agricultural sectors, followed by economic, cultural and defence accords in late 1998. UN-sponsored peace negotiations between Tajikistani government and opposition representatives were held in Tehran in 1996 and 1997. In April 2002 Tajikistan and Iran signed nine protocols on co-operation in economic, political and social affairs. In April 2005 the two countries signed a memorandum of understanding on enhanced co-operation in defence matters, and for the provision, *inter alia*, of equipment and training for Tajikistani military personnel. Iran explained the agreement as an attempt to prevent 'external powers' from increasing their military presence in the region and threatening Iranian national security, widely interpreted as an intention to prevent the USA from securing control of additional military bases in Central Asia.

Relations with Afghanistan were strained by the apparent inability of the Afghan Government to prevent *mujahidin* fighters and consignments of weapons from crossing the frontier into Tajikistan. The election of the largely pro-communist Tajikistani Government in late 1992 further strained bilateral relations, and in April 1993 the Tajikistani Government protested to the Afghan authorities about alleged incursions across the border by Afghans, apparently to assist rebel troops. In December the Afghan President, Burhanuddin Rabbani, made an official visit to Tajikistan, which resulted in the signature of a bilateral friendship and co-operation treaty, as well as agreements on economic co-operation and border security. A tripartite agreement was signed, together with the office of the UN High Commissioner for Refugees, on the safety of refugees returning to Tajikistan. In April 1995 Afghanistan protested strongly against alleged Russian attacks on rebel bases within Afghanistan, and continued to deny any official support of rebel Tajik factions within the country. The widespread victory of Taliban forces in Afghanistan in that year threatened to destabilize the fragile situation in Tajikistan and, as the Taliban increased their territorial gains in northern Afghanistan, there was increasing concern in Tajikistan and neighbouring countries, which feared an influx of large numbers of refugees. In July 1998, while heavy fighting occurred close to Tajikistan's border with Afghanistan, the frontier was reinforced by Russian troops. As fighting escalated in Afghanistan in September 2000, the Tajikistani Government closed its border with that country.

Following the suicide attacks on the USA of 11 September 2001, attributed to the al-Qa'ida (Base) organization of the Saudi Arabian-born Islamist militant Osama bin Laden, Russian troops along the Tajikistani–Afghan border were placed on a state of alert in anticipation of military strikes against Afghanistan by the USA and allied countries. Although Rakhmonov announced his willingness to co-operate with the USA, both Tajikistan and Russia initially dismissed the possibility of Tajikistani territory being used as a base for any US-led military action; however, US specialists were granted entry to the country to oversee the distribution of humanitarian aid to Afghanistan. The Tajikistani Government declared its support for the aerial bombardment of Taliban and al-Qa'ida targets in Afghanistan, which commenced on 7 October, and in early November it was confirmed that Tajikistan had permitted US troops and forces of the North Atlantic Treaty Organization (NATO, see p. 351) to utilize three of its airbases. In January 2002 it was announced that US restrictions on the transfer of defence equipment to Tajikistan, imposed in 1993, had been lifted. In February 2002 Tajikistan joined NATO's 'Partnership for Peace' programme of military co-operation. In October 2004 the Secretary-General of NATO, Jaap de Hoop Scheffer, signed a bilateral transit agreement with Rakhmonov in support of NATO's International Security Assistance Force in Afghanistan. In December Russia began to transfer military control of the Pamir stretch of the Tajikistani–Afghan border to the Tajikistani authorities. The transfer was completed in September 2005; however, a Russian task force was to remain in Tajikistan, and Russia was to continue to train Tajikistan's border guards. Throughout the transfer, concern had been expressed at a possible increase in the cross-border smuggling of drugs from Afghanistan, and later in September international donors signed an agreement with Tajikistan on the security of the Tajikistani–Afghan border, according to which Tajikistan was to be provided with installations, equipment and training to help manage its borders. In early October the Majlisi Namoyandagon ratified a bilateral security agreement with Afghanistan on co-operation in countering terrorism, extremism and transnational organized crime. In August 2007 the Presidents of Tajikistan and Afghanistan inaugurated a bridge across the river Pyanzh at the border between the two countries; construction of the 680m-long bridge, which had cost US $37m., was funded principally by the US authorities. In February 2009, after Kyrgyzstan announced the closure of the US airbase on its territory that had been used by forces operating in Afghanistan, Tajikistan offered the use of its airspace for the transport of non-military NATO supplies; a potential increase in Tajikistani support for the coalition forces in Afghanistan was discussed with European Commission and NATO officials during a visit by President Rakhmon to Brussels, Belgium, in that month (see below). The first official visit to Tajikistan by a high-level NATO delegation took place in April. Tajikistan agreed to act as a transit route for non-military supplies and pledged further assistance in stabilization and reconstruction efforts in Afghanistan, beyond that provided by existing initiatives of the Tajikistani Ministry of Defence (which included a role in the US-sponsored training of Afghan army officers).

In the mid-1990s Tajikistan sought to develop relations with other Asian states, in particular the People's Republic of China. In April 1996 Tajikistan signed (together with Russia, Kazakhstan and Kyrgyzstan) a wide-ranging border agreement with China. This was supplemented by a further border accord, signed in August 1999. In January 2002 Tajikistan signed a further treaty with China, resolving contentious issues regarding the two countries' joint border on the edge of Kuhistoni Badakhshon, and in mid-May Tajikistan signed a border agreement, conceding 1,000 sq km of disputed territory to China. Meanwhile, in April 1997 an agreement on confidence-building measures in the military sphere was concluded. Members of the Shanghai Co-operation Organization (SCO, see p. 440), comprising China, Kazakhstan, Kyrgyzstan, Russia, Tajikistan and Uzbekistan, signed the Shanghai Convention on Combating Terrorism, Separatism and Extremism in mid-2001. At an emergency meeting in October of that year, the members agreed to establish an anti-terrorism centre. In September 2004 members of the SCO, meeting in Bishkek, Kyrgyzstan, agreed to increase co-operation in trade, science, technology, and humanitarian projects, as well as to improve anti-terrorism measures.

In March 2000 joint military exercises were conducted in southern Tajikistan by Kazakhstan, Kyrgyzstan, Tajikistan, Uzbekistan and Russia, as part of a joint commitment to combat international terrorism in the region. In May 2001 the signatory countries of the Collective Security Treaty—Armenia, Belarus, Kazakhstan, Kyrgyzstan, Russia and Tajikistan—formed a Rapid Reaction Force to combat Islamist militancy in Central Asia; in January 2002 it was announced that the force was ready to undertake combat missions. In March the Central Asian Economic Community, which Tajikistan joined in March 1998, was superseded by the Central Asian Co-operation Organization (CACO). In April 2003 the signatories of the Collective Security Treaty inaugurated a successor organization, known as the Collective Security Treaty Organization (CSTO). In April 1998 Tajikistan joined a customs union, already comprising Russia, Belarus, Kazakhstan and Kyrgyzstan. In October 2000 a new economic body, the Eurasian Economic Community (EURASEC, see p. 426), was established to supersede the customs union, and this organization merged with CACO in January 2006. In October 2007 EURASEC held a meeting in Dushanbe, when Tajikistan assumed the rotational chairmanship of the organization. EURASEC leaders approved the legal basis for the establishment of a new customs union that was initially to comprise Belarus, Kazakhstan and Russia, with Kyrgyzstan, Tajikistan and Uzbekistan expected to join by 2011. In February 2009 President Rakhmon visited Moscow to attend an unofficial CIS summit meeting; a strain in relations between Tajikistan and Russia had been widely attributed to Russian support for Uzbekistan in a dispute over water resources (see above). Rakhmon notably failed to secure pledges of financial support from Russia for Tajikistan's hydroelectric sector, while the large number of Tajik migrants resident in Russia continued to be an issue of contention. Also in February Rakhmon for the first time visited Brussels, Belgium, where he met the President of the European Commission, José Manuel Durão Barroso, to discuss co-operation in a number of areas; Barroso, who welcomed an offer by the Tajikistan Government of support for NATO operations in Afghanistan, announced an upgrade in the European Commission's representation in Dushanbe and an increase in EU financial assistance for Tajikistan, in view of its contribution to regional stability.

Government

Under the Constitution of November 1994 (to which a number of amendments were passed in September 1999 and June 2003), Tajikistan has a presidential system of government. The President is Head of State and also heads the executive branch of power. The President appoints a Prime Minister (or Chairman) to head the Government (Council of Ministers). Legislative power is vested in the 63-member lower chamber, the Majlisi Namoyandagon (Assembly of Representatives), and the upper chamber, the Majlisi Milliy (National Assembly), which has a minimum of 33 members. For administrative purposes, the country is divided into three viloyats (regions or oblasts): Soghd (known as Leninabad in 1936–92, and subsequently Khujand, until 2000), in the north; Khatlon (formerly the two viloyats of Kulob and Kurgan-Tyube), in the south; and the nominally autonomous viloyat of Kuhistoni Badakhshon. These regions are further subdivided into districts and towns. The city of Dushanbe has a separate status. Three cities and 10 districts of central Tajikistan are not incorporated into any of the viloyats, and are known as the Regions of Republican Subordination.

Defence

Following the dissolution of the USSR in December 1991, Tajikistan became a member of the Commonwealth of Independent States (CIS, see p. 225) and its Collective Security Treaty. In April 2003 the Collective Security Treaty Organization (CSTO) was inaugurated as the successor to the CIS collective security system, with the participation of Armenia, Belarus, Kazakhstan, Kyrgyzstan, Russia and Tajikistan. A Ministry of Defence was established in September 1992; in December it was announced that Tajikistan's national armed forces were to be formed on the basis of the Tajik People's Front and other paramilitary units supporting the Government. Integration of United Tajik Opposition (UTO) force members into the Tajikistani armed forces took place from 1998. Military service lasts for 24 months (12 months for those with higher-education degrees). As assessed at November 2008, the armed forces numbered 8,800, comprising an army of 7,300 and an air force of 1,500. Some 7,500 paramilitary border guards were attached to the Ministry of Internal Affairs. There were plans to form an Air Force squadron. The budget for 2007 allocated an estimated 300m. somoni to defence. Tajikistan became a member of the North Atlantic Treaty Organization's 'Partnership for Peace' programme of military co-operation (see p. 353) in February 2002.

Economic Affairs

In 2007, according to estimates by the World Bank, Tajikistan's gross national income (GNI), measured at average 2005–07 prices, was US $3,103m., equivalent to $460 per head (or $1,710 per head on an international purchasing-power parity basis). During 2000–07, it was estimated, the population increased by an annual average of 1.3%, while gross domestic product (GDP) per head increased by an annual average of 7.4%, in real terms. Overall GDP increased, in real terms, by an average of 8.8% per year during 2000–07. According to the Asian Development Bank (ADB, see p. 191), GDP increased by 7.9% in 2008.

Agriculture contributed 22.4% of GDP and provided 66.5% of employment in 2007. According to IMF estimates, the rural population accounted for some 72.4% of the total in 2000–03. Only 7% of Tajikistan's land is arable, the remainder being largely mountainous. The principal crop is grain, followed in importance by cotton, vegetables and fruit. Approximately 95% of the country's arable land is irrigated. Although in mid-1998 legislation was passed to establish a centre to aid farm privatization, agricultural reform has proceeded slowly. The IMF estimated that 51% of Tajikistan's arable land was privately owned at the end of 2001. According to the World Bank, during 2000–07 agricultural GDP increased, in real terms, by an average of 8.9% annually. Real agricultural GDP increased by 6.0% in 2007.

Industry (comprising manufacturing, mining, utilities and construction) contributed 27.4% of GDP and provided 8.2% of employment in 2007. There is little heavy industry, except for mineral extraction, aluminium production and power generation. Light industry concentrates on food-processing, textiles and carpet-making. According to the World Bank, industrial GDP increased, in real terms, by an average annual rate of 10.4% in 2000–07. Sectoral GDP increased by 6.0% in 2007.

Tajikistan has considerable mineral deposits, including gold, antimony, silver, aluminium, iron, lead, mercury and tin. There are deposits of coal as well as reserves of petroleum and natural gas. Mineral extraction is hampered by the mountainous terrain.

The GDP of the manufacturing sector increased, in real terms, by an annual average rate of 9.4% in 2000–07, according to the World Bank. Real manufacturing GDP increased by 6.0% in 2007.

Although imports of natural gas and petroleum products comprised 13.3% of the value of merchandise imports in 2001 (mainly supplied by Turkmenistan, Uzbekistan, Kazakhstan and Russia), Tajikistan is believed to have sufficient unexploited reserves of petroleum and natural gas to meet its requirements. The mountain river system is widely used for hydroelectric power generation, and Tajikistan is one of the largest producers of hydroelectric power world-wide. In 2005 hydroelectricity accounted for 97.7% of energy production. In January 2005 Tajikistan signed a protocol with Russia and Iran on the construction of two hydroelectric power plants, Sangtuda-1 and Sangtuda-2. In March an agreement was signed with Pakistan on the construction of a 700-km transmission line to transport electricity from Tajikistan's Roghun plant to Pakistan, from 2009. Construction work on Sangtuda-2 commenced in 2006; both power stations were scheduled for completion in 2009. The completion of Sangtuda-1 was to be fully funded by Russia, and Iran was to provide significant funding for the construction of the Sangtuda-2 plant, ownership of which was to be secured by Tajikistan in 2018. Tajikistan imports some 90% of its gas requirements, principally from Uzbekistan.

The services sector contributed 50.2% of GDP in 2007, and provided 25.3% of employment in the same year. The GDP of the services sector increased, in real terms, by an annual average of 7.9% in 2000–07; real services GDP increased by 12.1% in 2007.

In 2007, according to the IMF, Tajikistan recorded a visible trade deficit of US $1,558.0m., and there was a deficit of $495.1m. on the current account of the balance of payments. In 2007 the principal source of imports was Russia (accounting for 21.1% of the total); other important suppliers were the People's Republic of China (20.7%), Kazakhstan, Uzbekistan and Azerbaijan. The major market for exports in that year was Norway (accounting for 15.6% of the total); Turkey, Italy, Iran, Russia and Uzbekistan were also significant purchasers. The principal exports in 2002 were non-precious metals and mineral products; the principal imports were mineral products and chemicals.

The state budget for 2007 provided for an overall deficit of 1,037.4m. somoni, equivalent to 8.1% of GDP. Tajikistan's total external debt was US $1,154m. at the end of 2006, of which $982m. was long-term public debt. The cost of debt-servicing in that year was equivalent to 5.1% of the value of exports of goods and services. The average annual rate of inflation was 303.4% in 1990–2000. The rate of inflation was 12.5% in 2001 and 14.5% in 2002. According to the ADB, the rate of inflation was 19.7% in 2007. National figures from the ADB indicated that the rate of unemployment was 2.3% in 2007; however, other sources estimated the rate to be much higher.

In 1992 Tajikistan joined the Economic Co-operation Organization (ECO, see p. 249) and the European Bank for Reconstruction and Development (EBRD, see p. 251), as a 'Country of Operations'; it became a member of the IMF and the World Bank in 1993. In November 1996 Tajikistan joined the Islamic Development Bank (see p. 340) and it became a member of the ADB in 1998. In 2001 Tajikistan was granted observer status at the World Trade Organization (WTO, see p. 410).

The poorest of the republics of the former USSR, the Tajikistani economy was severely affected by the civil war that broke out in 1992. Following the conclusion of a peace agreement in 1997, international financial organizations allocated credit to assist in rebuilding the country's infrastructure. The country's economic performance improved significantly from 2000, although poverty remained widespread, and the economy highly dependent on remittances from abroad (which comprised about one-half of GDP in 2008, according to the ADB). Tajikistan succeeded in significantly reducing its external debt between 2000 and 2007. Cotton production, a central component of the domestic economy, declined in both 2007 and 2008, owing to chronic underinvestment and low productivity. Areas previously designated for cotton were increasingly appropriated for other crops, in response to high international food prices during early 2008. In March 2008 the IMF demanded that Tajikistan repay some US$48m., following the discovery that the National Bank had supplied the Fund with misleading financial information in order to obtain credits. In April 2009 an independent audit of the National Bank prescribed by the IMF revealed misappropriation of at least $856m. in state funds, which had been allocated to support the cotton industry. Analysts expressed concern that major Tajikistani banks, unable to repay IMF credits, would be bankrupted. Later in April the IMF, which welcomed the Government's decision to publish a report on the audit, approved a three-year arrangement to extend some $120m. under a Poverty Reduction and Growth Facility, thereby granting Tajikistan immediate access to funds of $38.7m. Following high-level discussions, the EU announced in February that it was to provide some $42.8m. to support the Tajikistani economy; an agreement to prevent dual taxation and income and capital tax evasion was also signed. The European Bank for Reconstruction and Development, which had demanded greater transparency in the operations of major state enterprises, subsequently announced the resumption of investment in Tajikistan; funds totalling some $70m. were to be provided to finance projects, particularly in the banking sector, in 2009. The IMF expressed concern that the economy was badly placed to withstand adverse conditions arising from the international financial crisis, citing an overreliance on remittances, high levels of state influence and the underdeveloped energy sector (which frequently suffered critical shortages, with a strongly detrimental impact on agricultural production).

Education

Education is officially compulsory for nine years, to be undertaken between seven and 17 years of age. Primary education begins at seven years of age and lasts for four years. Secondary education, beginning at the age of 11, lasts for up to seven years, comprising a first cycle of five years and a second of two years. In 2005/06 total enrolment at primary schools included 97.3% of the relevant age-group (males 99.4%; females 95.0%). In that year total enrolment at secondary schools included 80.4% of the relevant age-group (males 87.1%; females 73.5%). The majority of pupils received their education in Tajik (66.0% of pupils in general day schools in 1988). Following the adoption of Tajik as the state language, greater emphasis was placed in the curriculum on Tajik language and literature, including classical Persian literature. From 2003 the compulsory teaching of Russian was reintroduced to schools from September of that year. In 2007/08 there were 154,200 students enrolled at 34 institutes of higher education. Agreement on the establishment of a joint Russian-Tajik Slavonic University in Dushanbe was reached in 1997. In 2000 the Presidents of Kazakhstan, Kyrgyzstan and Tajikistan co-signed a charter of foundation for a new University of Central Asia, which was to be established in Khorog (in Kuhistoni Badakhshon Autonomous Viloyat) and administered by the Aga Khan Development Network, based in Geneva, Switzerland. Budgetary expenditure on education by all levels of government was 437.0m. somoni (12.5% of total government budgetary expenditure) in 2007.

Public Holidays

2009: 1 January (New Year's Day), 8 March (International Women's Day), 21–24 March (Navrus, Spring Holiday), 1 May (International Labour Day), 9 May (Victory Day), 27 June (National Accord Day), 9 September (Independence Day), 20 September* (Id-al-Fitr, end of Ramadan), 6 November (Constitution Day), 27 November* (Id-al-Adha, Feast of the Sacrifice).

2010: 1 January (New Year's Day), 8 March (International Women's Day), 21–24 March (Navrus, Spring Holiday), 1 May (International Labour Day), 9 May (Victory Day), 27 June (National Accord Day), 9 September (Independence Day), 10 September* (Id-al-Fitr, end of Ramadan), 6 November (Constitution Day), 16 November* (Id-al-Adha, Feast of the Sacrifice).

* These holidays are dependent on the Islamic lunar calendar and may vary by one or two days from the dates given.

Weights and Measures

The metric system is in force.

Statistical Survey

Source (unless otherwise indicated): State Committee for Statistics, 734001 Dushanbe, Kuchai Boxtar 17; tel. (372) 23-25-53; fax (372) 21-43-75; e-mail stat@tojikiston.com; internet www.stat.tj.

Area and Population

AREA, POPULATION AND DENSITY

Area (sq km)	143,100*
Population (census results)†	
12 January 1989	5,092,603
20 January 2000	
Males	3,069,100
Females	3,058,393
Total	6,127,493
Population (estimates at 31 December)	
2005	6,920,300
2006	7,063,800
2007	7,215,700
Density (per sq km) at 31 December 2007	50.4

* 55,251 sq miles.
† Figures refer to *de jure* population. The *de facto* total at the 1989 census was 5,108,576.

POPULATION BY ETHNIC GROUP
(2000 census)

	Number ('000 persons)	%
Tajik	4,898.4	79.9
Uzbek	936.7	15.3
Russian	68.2	1.1
Kyrgyz	65.5	1.1
Others	158.7	2.6
Total	**6,127.5**	**100.0**

ADMINISTRATIVE DIVISIONS
(31 December 2006, official estimates)

	Area (sq km)	Population	Density (per sq km)	Capital city
Viloyats				
Khatlon	24,800	2,519,600	101.6	Qurgonteppa
Soghd	25,400	2,095,700	82.5	Khujand
Autonomous Viloyat				
Kuhistoni Badakhshon	64,200	220,400	3.4	Khorog
Capital City				
Dushanbe	100	660,900	6,609.0	—
Regions of Republican Subordination *	28,600	1,567,200	54.8	—
Total	**143,100**	**7,063,800**	**49.4**	

* The Regions of Republican Subordination comprise 3 cities (Gissar; Kofarnikhon; Roghun) and 10 raions or districts (Faizabad; Garm; Gissar; Darban; Jirgital; Lenin; Shakhrinav; Tajikabad; Tavildara; and Varzov) in central Tajikistan where there is no higher tier of local government.

PRINCIPAL TOWNS
(population at 1 January 2002)

Dushanbe (capital)	575,900	Kanibadam	45,100
Khujand*	147,400	Kofarnihon‡	45,100
Kulob	79,500	Tursunzade	38,100
Qurgonteppa	61,200	Isfara	37,300
Istravshan†	51,700	Panjakent	33,200

* Known as Leninabad between 1936 and 1992.
† Also known as Urateppa (Ura-Tyube).
‡ Formerly Ordzhonikidzeabad.

Mid-2007 (incl. suburbs, UN estimate): Dushanbe 553,000 (Source: UN, *World Urbanization Prospects: The 2007 Revision*).

TAJIKISTAN

BIRTHS, MARRIAGES AND DEATHS*

	Registered live births Number	Rate (per 1,000)	Registered marriages Number	Rate (per 1,000)	Registered deaths Number	Rate (per 1,000)
2000	167,246	27.0	26,257	4.2	29,387	4.7
2001	171,623	27.2	28,827	4.6	32,015	5.1
2002	175,600	27.3	32,299	5.0	31,100	4.8
2003	177,900	27.1	39,102	6.0	33,200	5.0
2004	179,600	26.8	47,320	7.1	29,700	4.4
2005	180,800	26.4	52,352	7.6	31,500	4.6
2006	186,500	26.7	57,278	8.2	32,000	4.6
2007	200,000	28.0	97,713	13.5	33,700	4.7

* From 2002 onwards, figures for registered births and deaths are rounded to the nearest 100.

Life expectancy (years at birth, WHO estimates): 64.4 (males 62.6; females 66.3) in 2006 (Source: WHO, *World Health Statistics*).

IMMIGRATION AND EMIGRATION

	2005	2006	2007
Immigrants	17,962	19,646	24,283
Emigrants	27,311	30,554	38,761

ECONOMICALLY ACTIVE POPULATION
(annual averages, '000 persons)

	2005	2006	2007
Activities of the material sphere	1,770	1,790	1,784
Agriculture*	1,424	1,432	1,430
Industry†	121	118	114
Construction	62	64	63
Trade and catering‡	101	110	115
Transport and communications	62	66	62
Activities of the non-material sphere	342	341	366
Housing and municipal services	33	33	48
Health care, social security, physical culture and sports	72	74	76
Education, culture and arts	186	186	186
Science, research and development	4	4	4
Government and finance	31	34	34
Other non-material	16	10	18
Statistical discrepancy	—	6	—
Total employed	2,112	2,137	2,150
Unemployed	42	48	51
Total labour force	2,154	2,185	2,201

* Including forestry.
† Comprising manufacturing (except printing and publishing), mining and quarrying, electricity, gas, water, logging and fishing.
‡ Including material and technical supply.

Health and Welfare

KEY INDICATORS

Total fertility rate (children per woman, 2006)	3.5
Under-5 mortality rate (per 1,000 live births, 2006)	68
HIV/AIDS (% of persons aged 15–49, 2007)	0.3
Physicians (per 1,000 head, 2006)	2.0
Hospital beds (per 1,000 head, 2006)	6.1
Health expenditure (2006): US $ per head (PPP)	71
Health expenditure (2006): % of GDP	5.0
Health expenditure (2006): public (% of total)	22.6
Access to water (% of persons, 2006)	67
Access to sanitation (% of persons, 2006)	92
Human Development Index (2006): ranking	124
Human Development Index (2006): value	0.684

For sources and definitions, see explanatory note on p. vi.

Agriculture

PRINCIPAL CROPS
('000 metric tons)

	2005	2006	2007
Wheat	618	625*	612*
Rice, paddy	62	49	62*
Barley	64	65*	63*
Maize	156	139	158*
Potatoes	555	574	656
Cabbages and other brassicas	47†	50*	54*
Tomatoes	209†	221*	241*
Onions, dry	188†	199*	217*
Carrots	117†	124*	135*
Watermelons	170	218	254
Apples	107*	115*	85*
Apricots	11†	42*	31*
Peaches and nectarines	16†	32*	24*
Grapes	91	107	117
Seed cotton	448	440	420
Tobacco, unmanufactured	2	2*	2*

* FAO estimate.
† Unofficial figure.

Aggregate production ('000 metric tons, may include official, semi-official or estimated data): Total cereals 903 in 2005, 880 in 2006, 896 in 2007; Total roots and tubers 555 in 2005, 574 in 2006, 660 in 2007; Total vegetables (incl. melons) 888 in 2005, 978 in 2006, 1,083 in 2007; Total fruits (excl. melons) 239 in 2005, 302 in 2006, 261 in 2007.

Source: FAO.

LIVESTOCK
('000 head at 1 January)

	2005	2006	2007
Horses	75	75	76
Asses	164	n.a.	n.a.
Cattle	1,303	1,372	1,418
Camels*	40	42	42
Sheep	1,782	1,894	1,922
Goats	1,040	1,160	1,250
Chickens	2,296	2,451	2,500*

* FAO estimate(s).

Source: FAO.

LIVESTOCK PRODUCTS
('000 metric tons)

	2005	2006	2007
Cattle meat	26.7	25.3	26.9
Sheep meat	26.9	27.6	29.4
Chicken meat	0.2	0.6	0.7
Cows' milk	488	494*	529*
Goats' milk	45.0	50.9*	54.6*
Hen eggs	5.5	5.9	6.2*
Wool, greasy	4.4	4.0*	3.7*

* FAO estimate.

Source: FAO.

Forestry

ROUNDWOOD REMOVALS
('000 cubic metres, excluding bark)

	2005*	2006†	2007†
Total (all fuel wood)	90	90	90

* Unofficial estimate.
† FAO estimate.

Source: FAO.

Fishing

(metric tons, live weight)

	2002	2003	2004
Capture	181	158	184
Freshwater bream	25	24	28
Common carp	51	52	45
Crucial carp	17	11	8
Silver carp	16	12	14
Sichel	4	2	10
Asp	5	3	9
Other cyprinids	27	23	32
Wels (Som) catfish	12	9	18
Pike-perch	24	22	20
Aquaculture	143	167	26
Common carp	17	47	12
Grass carp (White amur)	29	30	3
Silver carp	95	88	7
Total catch	324	325	210

2005–06: Production assumed to be unchanged from 2004 (FAO estimates).
Source: FAO.

Mining

(metric tons, unless otherwise indicated)

	2003	2004	2005
Coal	46,500	88,30000	94,900
Crude petroleum	17,700	18,900	21,600
Natural gas (million cu m)	32.8	35.6	29.3
Lead concentrate*†	800	800	800
Antimony ore*†	1,800	2,000	2,000
Mercury*†	30	30	30
Silver (kilograms)†	5,000	5,000	5,000
Gold (kilograms)*†	2,700	3,000	3,000
Gypsum (crude)*	50,100	57,200	8,300

* Estimated production.
† Figures refer to the metal content of ores and concentrates.

Source: US Geological Survey.

2006 ('000 metric tons, unless otherwise indicated): Coal 105; Crude petroleum 24; Natural gas (million cu m) 20 (Source: Asian Development Bank).

2007 ('000 metric tons, unless otherwise indicated): Coal 165; Crude petroleum 26; Natural gas (million cu m) 17 (Source: Asian Development Bank).

Industry

SELECTED PRODUCTS
('000 metric tons, unless otherwise indicated)

	2005	2006	2007
Cottonseed oil (refined)*	44	38	38
Wheat flour†	459	457	470
Wine‡	0.5	6.2	6.1
Woollen garments ('000)	30,000	10,000	100,000
Woven cotton fabrics (million sq metres)	24.1	21.3	30.5
Rugs and carpets (million sq metres)	0.5	0.6	0.9
Stockings, etc (million pairs)	5.9	6.1	6.2
Fertilizer	40.5	32.3	24.5
Clay building bricks (million)	45.9	47.0	48.9
Slate (million sheets)	2.3	1.6	2.7
Cement	253.1	281.5	313.1
Aluminium (unwrought): primary§	379.6	n.a.	n.a.
Electric energy (million kWh)†	17,100	16,900	17,500

* Unofficial figures) from FAO.
† Source: Asian Development Bank.
‡ Estimates from FAO.
§ Source: US Geological Survey.

Finance

CURRENCY AND EXCHANGE RATES

Monetary Units
100 diram = 1 somoni.

Sterling, Dollar and Euro Equivalents (31 December 2008)
£1 sterling = 5.032 somoni;
US $1 = 3.452 somoni;
€1 = 4.804 somoni;
100 somoni = £19.87 = $28.97 = €20.82.

Average Exchange Rate (somoni per US $)
2006   3.2984
2007   3.4425
2008   3.4307

Note: The Tajikistani rouble was introduced in May 1995, replacing the Russian (formerly Soviet) rouble at the rate of 1 Tajikistani rouble = 100 Russian roubles. A new currency, the somoni (equivalent to 1,000 Tajikistani roubles), was introduced in October 2000.

BUDGET
(million somoni)*

Revenue†	2005	2006	2007
Tax revenue	1,192.5	1,567.4	2,288.7
Income and profit tax	150.9	194.1	304.9
Social duties	151.5	213.9	254.8
Property taxes	60.6	76.7	92.3
Internal taxes on goods and services	626.3	849.6	1,278.3
International trade and operations tax	57.1	68.1	106.3
Non-tax revenue	190.9	233.1	132.2
Income from property and enterprise activities	136.7	170.6	37.5
Administrative fees and levies	24.6	25.3	35.5
Total	1,383.4	1,800.5	2,420.9

Expenditure	2005	2006	2007
General government administration	204.4	225.7	421.1
Education	253.1	317.7	437.0
Health	82.4	105.4	145.2
Social security and welfare	232.4	317.0	355.6
Housing and communal services	80.2	101.6	216.6
Sporting and religious associations	41.9	61.7	76.2
Energy and fuel sector	17.7	38.2	51.8
Agriculture, forestry, fisheries and hunting	37.9	44.4	76.9
Natural resources, mining, construction	23.3	44.6	27.6
Transport and communications	78.8	87.2	94.3
Total (incl. others)	1,402.7	1,778.8	3,494.8

* Figures refer to the consolidated operations of the State Budget, comprising the budgets of the central (republican) Government and local authorities, and the Social Security Fund.
† Excluding grants received (million somoni): 31.2 in 2005; 22.9 in 2006; 36.5 in 2007.

INTERNATIONAL RESERVES
(US $ million at 31 December)

	2004	2005	2006
Gold (national valuation)	14.6	20.7	28.7
IMF special drawing rights	1.3	5.4	3.5
Foreign exchange	156.2	162.8	171.6
Total	172.1	188.9	203.8

2007 (US $ million at 31 December): Gold (national valuation) 44.8; IMF special drawing rights 3.6.

2008 (US $ million at 31 December): Gold (national valuation) 59.3; IMF special drawing rights 15.7.
Source: IMF, *International Financial Statistics*.

TAJIKISTAN

MONEY SUPPLY
(million somoni at 31 December)

	2005	2006	2007
Currency outside banks	155.3	166.4	1,029.9
Demand deposits	84.8	146.2	86.3
Total money (incl. others)	241.0	314.2	1,138.9

Source: IMF, *International Financial Statistics*.

COST OF LIVING
(Consumer Price Index; base: previous year = 100)

	2005	2006	2007
Food	108.3	113.9	125.5
Non-food	102.7	105.3	107.5
All items	107.1	112.5	119.7

Source: Asian Development Bank.

NATIONAL ACCOUNTS
(million somoni at current prices)

Expenditure on the Gross Domestic Product

	2004	2005	2006
Final consumption expenditure	5,292.8	6,899.4	8,773.8
Households			
Non-profit institutions serving households	4,566.0	5,847.1	7,502.1
General government	726.8	1,052.3	1,271.7
Gross capital formation	752.6	839.4	1,490.5
Gross fixed capital formation	640.0	801.3	1,445.3
Acquisitions, less disposals, of valuables			
Changes in inventories	112.6	38.1	45.2
Total domestic expenditure	6,045.4	7,738.8	10,264.3
Exports of goods and services	3,624.3	3,910.7	5,429.0
Less Imports of goods and services	4,293.1	5,245.0	7,748.0
Sub-total	5,376.6	6,404.5	7,945.3
Statistical discrepancy*	790.7	802.1	1,390.0
GDP in market prices	6,167.2	7,206.6	9,335.2

* Referring to the difference between the sum of the expenditure components and official estimates of GDP, compiled from the production approach.

Gross Domestic Product by Economic Activity

	2005	2006	2007
Agriculture	1,527.1	2,002.5	2,527.4
Mining, manufacturing and electricity, gas and water	1,637.5	1,986.9	1,966.9
Construction	334.7	567.5	1,115.6
Transport and communications	533.3	673.1	646.4
Trade	1,166.9	1,578.6	2,529.3
Other sectors of material production	48.7	38.2	43.4
Market and non-market services	1,127.1	1,428.8	2,431.0
GDP at factor cost	6,375.4	8,275.6	11,260.0
Indirect taxes, less subsidies	831.2	1,059.6	1,519.7
GDP in purchasers' values	7,206.6	9,335.3	12,779.7

BALANCE OF PAYMENTS
(US $ million)

	2005	2006	2007
Exports of goods f.o.b.	1,108.1	1,511.8	1,556.9
Imports of goods c.i.f.	−1,430.9	−1,954.6	−3,115.0
Trade balance	−322.8	−442.8	−1,558.0
Exports of services	146.3	134.2	148.7
Imports of services	−251.5	−394.5	−592.1
Balance on goods and services	−428.0	−703.1	−2,001.5
Other income received	9.6	12.4	22.4
Other income paid	−50.4	−76.4	−73.2
Balance on goods, services and income	−468.8	−767.0	−2,052.3
Current transfers received	599.9	1,146.0	1,794.3
Current transfers paid	−150.0	−400.4	−237.1
Current balance	−18.9	−21.4	−495.1
Capital account (net)	—	—	32.8
Direct investment (net)	54.5	338.6	360.0
Portfolio investment (net)	—	n.a.	0.2
Other investment assets	−71.3	−301.9	−386.7
Other investment liabilities	118.3	239.2	837.9
Net errors and omissions	−76.3	−264.7	−362.9
Overall balance	6.3	−10.1	−13.8

Source: IMF, *International Financial Statistics*.

External Trade

PRINCIPAL COMMODITIES
(US $ million, excl. alumina and aluminium)

Imports c.i.f.*	2005	2006	2007
Natural gas	27	35	65
Petroleum products	126	191	275
Electricity	58	67	66
Grain and flour	76	77	135
Total (incl. others)	1,330	1,725	2,547

Exports f.o.b.†	2005	2006	2007
Cotton fibre	144	129	138
Electricity	53	49	60
Total (incl. others)	909	1,399	1,468

* These figures do not include separate data for imports of alumina, one of Tajikistan's principal import goods. The most recent data available were for 2001, when imports of alumina accounted for US $184m. of $688m. in total imports (c.i.f.).
† These figures do not include separate data for exports of aluminium, Tajikistan's principal export item. The most recent data available were for 2001, when imports of aluminium accounted for US $397m. of $909m. in total exports (f.o.b.).

PRINCIPAL TRADING PARTNERS
(US $ million)

Imports	2005	2006	2007
Azerbaijan	114.9	138.2	164.9
China, People's Rep.	92.5	148.9	493.8
Italy	51.7	61.5	14.2
Kazakhstan	168.3	186.7	222.9
Russia	256.5	423.7	503.5
Turkey	21.9	36.5	129.4
Turkmenistan	53.8	60.3	71.9
Ukraine	82.0	64.3	76.8
USA	11.7	12.0	58.0
Uzbekistan	152.9	176.4	210.5
Total (incl. others)	1,330.0	1,725.3	2,384.6

TAJIKISTAN

Exports	2005	2006	2007
Iran	36.7	76.1	99.1
Italy	15.6	16.5	99.4
Kazakhstan	19.7	27.8	33.2
Latvia	44.2	35.1	0.8
Netherlands	423.4	569.4	26.0
Norway	—	—	152.4
Russia	82.8	65.4	85.8
Switzerland	27.0	24.5	27.1
Turkey	143.4	442.8	130.3
Uzbekistan	66.5	67.4	80.5
Total (incl. others)	908.7	1,398.9	979.0

Note: Data reflect the IMF's direction of trade methodology and, as a result, the totals may not be equal to those presented for trade in commodities.

Source: Asian Development Bank.

Transport

RAILWAYS

	2003	2004	2005
Passengers (million journeys)	0.5	0.7	0.7
Freight carried ('000 metric tons)	11,720.5	12,268.3	12,114.2

Passenger-km (million): 32 in 2001.

Freight ton-km (million): 1,248 in 2001.

CIVIL AVIATION
(traffic on scheduled services)

	2003	2004	2005
Passengers carried ('000)	400	600	500
Freight carried ('000 metric tons)	3.8	4.1	3.7

Kilometres flown (million): 4 in 1999.

Passenger-km (million): 229 in 1999.

Freight ton-km (million): 23 in 1999.

Source: partly UN, *Statistical Yearbook*.

Communications Media

	2003	2004	2005
Telephones ('000 main lines in use)	245.2	n.a.	280.2
Mobile cellular telephones ('000 subscribers)	240.0	n.a.	265.0
Internet users ('000)	4.1	5.0	19.5

2006–07: Data estimated to be unchanged from 2005.

Television receivers ('000 in use): 2,000 in 2000.

Facsimile machines (number in use): 2,100 in 1999.

Books published (titles): 150 in 1997.

Books published (copies): 997,000 in 1996.

Daily newspapers (estimates): 2 titles and 120,000 copies (average circulation) in 1996.

Non-daily newspapers: 73 titles and 153,000 copies (average circulation) in 1996.

Other periodicals: 11 titles and 130,000 copies (average circulation) in 1996.

Radio receivers ('000 in use): 850 in 1997.

Sources: UNESCO, *Statistical Yearbook*; International Telecommunication Union.

Education

(2007/08, unless otherwise indicated)

	Males	Females	Total
Pre-primary	33,400	27,500	60,900
Primary			
Secondary:			
Lower	n.a.	n.a.	1,690,600*
General			
Vocational	14,300	19,700	34,000
Professional technical	16,984	6,300	23,284
Higher (incl. universities)	110,700	43,500	154,200

* Figures exclude 1,500 pupils at evening classes (including those conducted by correspondence).

Institutions (2007/08, unless otherwise indicated): Pre-primary 482; Primary 662; Secondary—Lower 790; Secondary—General 2,349; Secondary—Vocational 52; Professional Technical 70; Higher (incl. universities) 33. Figures exclude 10 schools for pupils with mental or physical disabilities and 9 evening schools.

Teachers Pre-primary 6,615 (1996/97); Primary *and* Secondary—Lower, Upper *and* Vocational 99,400 (2007/08); Professional Technical n.a.; Higher (incl. universities) 6,100 (2001/02).

Directory

The Constitution

Tajikistan's Constitution entered into force on 6 November 1994, when it was approved by a majority of voters in a nation-wide plebiscite. It replaced the previous Soviet republican Constitution, adopted in 1978. The following is a summary of its main provisions (including amendments approved by referendum on 26 September 1999 and 22 June 2003).

PRINCIPLES OF THE CONSTITUTIONAL SYSTEM

The Republic of Tajikistan is a sovereign, democratic, law-governed, secular and unitary state. The state language is Tajik, but Russian is accorded the status of a language of communication between nationalities.

Recognition, observance and protection of human and civil rights and freedoms is the obligation of the State. The people of Tajikistan are the expression of sovereignty and the sole source of power of the State, which they express through their elected representatives.

Tajikistan consists of Kuhistoni Badakhshon Autonomous Viloyat (Region), viloyats, towns, districts, settlements and villages. The territory of the State is indivisible and inviolable. Agitation and actions aimed at disunity of the State are prohibited.

No ideology, including religious ideology, may be granted the status of a state ideology.

The Constitution of Tajikistan has supreme legal authority and its norms have direct application. Laws and other legal acts which run counter to the Constitution have no legal validity. The State, its bodies and officials are bound to observe the provisions of the Constitution.

Tajikistan will implement a peaceful policy, respecting the sovereignty and independence of other states of the world, and will determine foreign relations on the basis of international norms. Agitation for war is prohibited.

The economy of Tajikistan is based on various forms of ownership. The State guarantees freedom of economic activity, entrepreneurship, equality of rights and the protection of all forms of ownership, including private ownership. Land and natural resources are under state ownership.

FUNDAMENTAL DUTIES OF INDIVIDUALS AND CITIZENS

The freedoms and rights of individuals are protected by the Constitution, the laws of the republic and international documents to which Tajikistan is a signatory. The State guarantees the rights and freedoms of every person, regardless of nationality, race, sex, language, religious beliefs, political persuasion, social status, knowledge and property. Men and women have the same rights. Every person has the right to life. No one may be subjected to torture, punishment or inhuman treatment. No one may be arrested, kept in custody or exiled without a legal basis, and no one is adjudged guilty of a crime except by the sentence of a court in accordance with the law. Every person has the right freely to choose their place of residence, to leave the republic and return to it. Every person has the right to profess any religion, individually or with others, or not to profess any, and to take part in religious ceremonies. Every citizen has the right to take part in political life and state administration; to elect and be elected from the age of 18; to join and leave political parties, trade unions and other associations; to take part in meetings, rallies or demonstrations. Every person is guaranteed freedom of speech. State censorship is prohibited.

Every person has the right: to ownership and inheritance; to work; to housing; to social security in old age, or in the event of sickness or disability. Basic general education is compulsory.

A state of emergency is declared as a temporary measure to ensure the security of citizens and of the State in the instance of a direct threat to the freedom of citizens, the State's independence, its territorial integrity, or natural disasters. The period of a state of emergency is up to three months; it can be prolonged by the President of the Republic.

MAJLISI OLI (SUPREME ASSEMBLY)

The Majlisi Oli (Supreme Assembly) is the highest representative and legislative body of the republic. It is a bicameral legislative body, comprising a 63-member lower chamber, the Majlisi Namoyandagon (Assembly of Representatives), and an upper chamber, the Majlisi Milliy (National Assembly). The members of the Majlisi Namoyandagon are elected for a five-year term, 22 by proportional representation and 41 in single-mandate constituencies. Twenty-five members of the Majlisi Milliy are indirectly elected for a term of five years by regional deputies. Eight members of the chamber are appointed by the President of the Republic. Additionally, former Heads of State of the Republic of Tajikistan are entitled to a seat in the chamber.

The powers of the Majlisi Oli include: enactment and amendment of laws, and their annulment; interpretation of the Constitution and laws; determination of the basic direction of domestic and foreign policy; ratification of presidential decrees on the appointment and dismissal of the Chairman of the National Bank, the Chairman and members of the Constitutional Court, the Supreme Court and the Supreme Economic Court; ratification of the state budget; determining and altering the structure of administrative territorial units; ratification and annulment of international treaties; ratification of presidential decrees on a state of war and a state of emergency.

Laws are adopted by a majority of the legislative deputies. If the President does not agree with the law, he may return it to the Majlisi Oli. If the legislature once again approves the law, with at least a two-thirds' majority, the President must sign it.

THE PRESIDENT OF THE REPUBLIC

The President of the Republic is the Head of State and the head of the executive. The President is elected by the citizens of Tajikistan on the basis of universal, direct and equal suffrage for a seven-year term. Any citizen who knows the state language and has lived on the territory of Tajikistan for the preceding 10 years may be nominated to the post of President of the Republic.

The President has the authority: to represent Tajikistan inside the country and in international relations; to establish or abolish ministries with the approval of the Majlisi Oli; to appoint or dismiss the Prime Minister and other members of the Council of Ministers and to propose them for approval to the Majlisi Oli; to appoint and dismiss chairmen of regions, towns and districts, and propose new appointments for approval to the relevant assemblies of people's deputies; to appoint and dismiss members of the Constitutional Court, the Supreme Court and the Supreme Economic Court (with the approval of the Majlisi Oli); to appoint and dismiss judges of lower courts; to sign laws; to lead the implementation of foreign policy and sign international treaties; to appoint diplomatic representatives abroad; to be Commander-in-Chief of the armed forces of Tajikistan; to declare a state of war or a state of emergency (with the approval of the Majlisi Oli).

In the event of the President's death, resignation, removal from office or inability to perform his duties, the duties of the President will be carried out by the Chairman of the Majlisi Oli until further presidential elections can be held. New elections must be held within three months of these circumstances. The President may be removed from office in the case of his committing a crime, by the decision of at least two-thirds of deputies of the Majlisi Oli, taking into account the decisions of the Constitutional Court.

THE COUNCIL OF MINISTERS

The Council of Ministers consists of the President as Chairman, the Prime Minister, the First Deputy Prime Minister, Deputy Prime Ministers, Ministers and Chairmen of State Committees. The Council of Ministers is responsible for implementation of laws and decrees of the Majlisi Oli and decrees and orders of the President. The Council of Ministers leaves office when a new President is elected.

LOCAL GOVERNMENT

The local representative authority in regions, towns and districts is the assembly of people's deputies. Assemblies are elected for a five-year term. Local executive government is the responsibility of the President's representative: the chairman of the assembly of people's deputies, who is proposed by the President and approved by the relevant assembly. The Majlisi Oli may dissolve local representative bodies, if their actions do not conform to the Constitution and the law.

KUHISTONI BADAKHSHON AUTONOMOUS VILOYAT

Kuhistoni Badakhshon Autonomous Viloyat is an integral and indivisible part of Tajikistan, the territory of which cannot be changed without the consent of the regional assembly.

JUDICIARY

The judiciary is independent and protects the rights and freedoms of the individual, the interests of the State, organizations and institutions, and legality and justice. Judicial power is implemented by the Constitutional Court, the Supreme Court, the Supreme Economic Court, the Military Court, the Court of Kuhistoni Badakhshon Autonomous Viloyat, and courts of viloyats, the city of Dushanbe, towns and districts. The term of judges is 10 years. The creation of emergency courts is not permitted.

Judges are independent and are subordinate only to the Constitution and the law. Interference in their activity is not permitted.

THE OFFICE OF THE PROCURATOR-GENERAL

The Procurator-General and procurators subordinate to him ensure the control and observance of laws within the framework of their authority in the territory of Tajikistan. The Procurator-General is responsible to the Majlisi Oli and the President, and is elected for a five-year term.

PROCEDURES FOR INTRODUCING AMENDMENTS TO THE CONSTITUTION

Amendments and addenda to the Constitution are made by means of a referendum. A referendum takes place with the support of at least two-thirds of the people's deputies. The President, or at least one-third of the people's deputies, may submit amendments and addenda to the Constitution. The form of public administration, the territorial integrity and the democratic, law-governed and secular nature of the State are irrevocable.

The Government

HEAD OF STATE

President: EMOMALI RAKHMON (elected by popular vote 6 November 1994; re-elected 6 November 1999 and 6 November 2006).

COUNCIL OF MINISTERS
(April 2009)

Chairman of the Government: EMOMALI RAKHMON.
Prime Minister: AKIL AKILOV.
First Deputy Prime Minister: ASADULLO GHULOMOV.
Deputy Prime Minister: RUQIYA QURBONOVA.
Deputy Prime Minister: MURODALI ALIMARDON.
Minister of Justice: BAKHTIYOR KHUDOYOROV.
Minister of Agriculture: QOSIM QOSIMOV.
Minister of Internal Affairs: ABDURAHIM QAHOROV.
Minister of Foreign Affairs: HAMROKHON ZARIFI.
Minister of Education: ABDUJABBOR RAHMONOV.
Minister of Land Reclamation and Water Resources: SAIDI YOKUBZOD.
Minister of Labour and Social Welfare: SHUKURJON ZUHUROV.
Minister of Finance: SAFARALI NAJMIDDINOV.
Minister of Defence: Maj.-Gen. SHERALI KHAYRULLOYEV.

TAJIKISTAN

Minister of Transport and Communications: ABDURAHIM ASHUR.

Minister of Economic Development and Trade: GHULOMJON BOBOZODA.

Minister of Health: NUSRATULLO SALIMOV.

Minister of Culture: MIRZOSHOHRUKH ASRORI.

Minister of Energy and Industry: SHERALI GUL.

Note: The Chairmen of the State Committees for National Security, Statistics, and Investment and the Management of State Property are also members of the Council of Ministers.

MINISTRIES

Office of the President: 734023 Dushanbe, Xiyoboni Rudaki 80; tel. (372) 21-04-18; fax (372) 21-18-37; e-mail mail@president.tj; internet www.president.tj.

Secretariat of the Prime Minister: 734023 Dushanbe, Xiyoboni Rudaki 80; tel. (372) 21-18-71; fax (372) 21-51-10.

Ministry of Agriculture: 734025 Dushanbe, Xiyoboni Rudaki 14; tel. (372) 21-15-96; fax (372) 21-57-94.

Ministry of Culture: 734025 Dushanbe, Xiyoboni Rudaki 34; tel. (372) 21-03-05; fax (372) 21-47-01.

Ministry of Defence: 734025 Dushanbe, Kuchai Bokhtar 59; tel. (372) 23-18-97; fax (372) 23-19-37.

Ministry of Economic Development and Trade: 734002 Dushanbe, Kuchai Bokhtar 37; tel. (372) 27-34-34; fax (372) 21-04-04; e-mail sharipov_jamshed@hotmail.com; internet www.met.tj.

Ministry of Education: 734025 Dushanbe, Kuchai Chexov 13A; tel. (372) 21-46-05; fax (372) 21-70-41; internet www.education.tj.

Ministry of Energy and Industry: 734025 Dushanbe, Kuchai Boxtar 10; tel. (372) 21-50-64; fax (372) 27-90-10; e-mail energo@rs.tj; internet www.minenergo.tj.

Ministry of Finance: 734067 Dushanbe, Nazarov 64/14; tel. (37) 881-25-79; e-mail nii_finance@mail.tj; internet www.minfin.tj.

Ministry of Foreign Affairs: 734051 Dushanbe, Xiyoboni Rudaki 42; tel. (372) 21-18-08; fax (372) 21-02-59; e-mail dushanbe@mfaumo.td.silk.org; internet www.mid.tj.

Ministry of Health: 734025 Dushanbe, Kuchai Shevchenko 69; tel. (372) 21-30-64; fax (372) 21-48-71.

Ministry of Internal Affairs: 734025 Dushanbe, Kuchai Texron 29; tel. (372) 21-17-40; fax (372) 21-26-05.

Ministry of Justice: 734025 Dushanbe, pr. Rudaki 25; tel. (372) 21-44-05; fax (372) 21-80-66.

Ministry of Labour and Social Welfare: 734028 Dushanbe, Kuchai A. Navoi 52; tel. (372) 36-18-37; fax (372) 36-24-15.

Ministry of Land Reclamation and Water Resources: 734001 Dushanbe, Xiyoboni Rudaki 78; tel. (372) 35-35-66.

Ministry of Transport and Communications: 734025 Dushanbe, Xiyoboni Rudaki 57; tel. (37) 221-22-84; fax (37) 221-29-53; e-mail info@mincom.tj; internet www.mincom.tj.

President

Presidential Election, 6 November 2006, provisional results

Candidates	%
Emomali Rakhmonov* (People's Democratic Party of Tajikistan)	79.3
Olimjon Boboyev (Party of Economic Reforms)	6.2
Amirkul Karakulov (Agrarian Party of Tajikistan)	5.3
Ismoil Talbakov (Communist Party of Tajikistan)	5.1
Abdukhalim Gafforov (Socialist Party of Tajikistan)	2.8
Total†	100.0

* Known as Emomali Rakhmon from 2007.
† Including invalid votes, equivalent to 1.3% of the total.

Legislature

Constitutional amendments approved by a referendum in September 1999 provided for the establishment of a bicameral legislative body, the Majlisi Oli (Supreme Assembly), comprising a 63-member lower chamber, the Majlisi Namoyandagon (Assembly of Representatives), and an upper chamber, the Majlisi Milliy (National Assembly), which has a minimum of 33 members.

Majlisi Milliy
(National Assembly)

734051 Dushanbe, Xiyoboni Rudaki 42; tel. (372) 23-19-33; fax (372) 21-51-10; e-mail mejparl@parliament.tojikiston.com.

President: MAKHMADSAID UBAYDULLOYEV.

The Majlisi Milliy has a minimum of 33 members, of whom 25 (five from each of the five administrative regions of Tajikistan) are indirectly elected for a term of five years by regional deputies. Eight members of the chamber, who also serve for a term of five years, are appointed by the President of the Republic. All former Presidents of Tajikistan are also entitled to a seat in the Majlisi Milliy. Elections to the Majlisi Milliy were held on 24 March 2005, and the eight presidential nominees were announced on 25 March. The new chamber convened on 15 April.

Majlisi Namoyandagon
(Assembly of Representatives)

734051 Dushanbe, Xiyoboni Rudaki 42; tel. (372) 21-23-66; fax (372) 21-92-81; e-mail mejparl@parliament.tojikiston.com.

President: SAIDULLO KHAIRULLAYEV.

Elections, 27 February and 13 March 2005*

		Seats		
Parties	%†	A‡	B‡	Total
People's Democratic Party of Tajikistan (PDPT)	74	17	35	52
Communist Party of Tajikistan (CPT)	13	3	1	4
Islamic Rebirth Party of Tajikistan (IRP)	8	2	—	2
Independents	.	—	5	5
Total (incl. others)	100	22	41	63

* Final provisional results.
† Percentage refers to the share of the vote cast for seats awarded on the basis of party lists.
‡ Of the 63 seats in the Majlisi Namoyandagon, 22 (A) are awarded according to proportional representation on the basis of party lists, and 41 (B) are elected in single-mandate constituencies.

Election Commission

Central Commission for Elections and Referenda: 734051 Dushanbe, Xiyoboni Rudaki 42; tel. (372) 21-13-75; comprises Chair., Sec. and 13 mems, elected by the Majlisi Namoyandagon at the proposal of the President of the Republic; Chair. MIRZOALI BOLTUYEV.

Political Organizations

In September 2006 there were eight registered parties in Tajikistan.

Agrarian Party of Tajikistan (Agrarnaya partiya Tadzhikistana): 734000 Dushanbe; f. 2005; supports creation of a civil society and aims to protect the interests of the agricultural sector and its workers; Chair. AMIRKUL KARAKULOV; 1,300 mems (Jan. 2005).

Communist Party of Tajikistan (CPT) (Kommunisticheskaya partiya Tadzhikistana): 734002 Dushanbe, Kuchai F. Niyazi 37; tel. (372) 23-29-53; e-mail talbhakov_555@mail.ru; internet www.kpt.freenet.tj; f. 1924; sole registered party until 1991; Chair. SHODI D. SHABDOLOV; Sec. of Central Cttee ISMOIL TALBAKOV; 60,000 mems (Jan. 2005).

Democratic Party of Tajikistan (DPT) (Khizbi demokrati Tochikiston): 734000 Dushanbe, Kuchai Pushkin 64; tel. (372) 21-77-87; internet www.democrat-tj.org; f. 1990; banned in 1993; permitted to re-register 1996 and 1999; secular nationalist and pro-Western; Chair. SAIDJAFAR ISMONOV (acting) (Chair. of Vatan—Fatherland faction registered by the Ministry of Justice in Sept. 2006); Chair. (of unregistered faction) RAHMATULLO VALIEV; c. 4,500 mems (Jan. 2005).

Islamic Rebirth Party of Tajikistan (IRP): 734000 Dushanbe, pos. Kalinina, Kuchai Tukhagul 55; tel. (372) 27-25-30; fax (372) 27-53-93; f. 1990 by split from the All-Union Islamic Renaissance Party of the USSR; leadership fmrly based in Tehran, Iran; registered in 1991; banned 1993–99; Chair. MUHIDDIN KABIRI; 20,000 mems (Jan. 2005).

Justice (Adolatkoh): 734000 Dushanbe, Kuchai S. Nosirov 41; tel. (372) 24-90-55; f. 1996; campaigns for the establishment of social justice and construction of a state based on the rule of law; registration revoked 2001; Leader ABDURAKHMON KARIMOV.

Party of Economic Reforms (Partiya ekonomicheskikh reform): 734000 Dushanbe; f. 2005; supports establishment of a market economy on the basis of democratic principles; aims to reduce pov-

TAJIKISTAN

erty, undertake privatization and increase foreign investment; Chair. OLIMJON BOBOYEV; c. 1,000 mems (2005).

Party of Popular Unity and Accord (PPUA): 734000 Dushanbe; f. 1994; represents interests of northern Tajikistan; banned 1998; Leader ABDUMALIK ABDULLOJONOV.

People's Democratic Party of Tajikistan (PDPT) (Xizbi Xalkii Demokratii Tojikston): 734000 Dushanbe, Xiyoboni Rudaki 107; tel. (372) 21-63-21; e-mail ndpt1994@yahoo.com; internet www.hhdt.tj; f. 1994; campaigns for a united and secular state; Chair. EMOMALI SH. RAKHMON; First Dep. Chair. DAVLATALI DAVLATZODA; 100,000 mems (2008).

Social Democratic Party of Tajikistan (SDPT/KhSDT): 734000 Dushanbe, Xiyoboni Rudaki 81/49; tel. (372) 23-47-40; internet www.hsdt-tj.org; f. 1998; registered 2003; fmrly Justice and Progress of Tajikistan; Chair. RAKHMATULLO KH. ZOYIROV; 5,000 mems (Dec. 2004).

Socialist Party of Tajikistan: 734000 Dushanbe, Xiyoboni Rudaki 137; tel. (372) 34-77-11 (officially registered faction led by A. Gafforov); tel. (372) 27-39-59 (unregistered faction led by M. Narziyev); f. 1996; split into two factions in 2003, only one of which was registered by the Ministry of Justice; Chairmen ABDUKHALIM GAFFOROV (Chair. of faction registered by the Ministry of Justice), MIRKHUSEYN NARZIYEV (Chair. of unregistered faction); 15,000 mems (2003).

Union and Development Party (Xizb-i Ittihod va Taraqqiyot—Taraqqiyot): 734000 Dushanbe; f. 2000; unregistered; fmrly a faction of the Democratic Party of Tajikistan; Chair. SULTON KUVVATOV; 3,000 mems (2001).

Unity Party (Hizb-i-Vahdat): 734000 Dushanbe; f. 2001; unregistered.

The transnational militant Islamist **Hizb-ut-Tahrir al-Islami** (Party of Islamic Liberation—Hizb-ut-Tahrir) was believed to be operative in Tajikistan. As in neighbouring states, the organization was banned in Tajikistan, and a number of people have received gaol sentences for their alleged membership of the group, despite its stated intention of using only peaceful means of pursuing its goals, notably the restoration of a caliphate.

Diplomatic Representation

EMBASSIES IN TAJIKISTAN

Afghanistan: 734000 Dushanbe, Kuchai Pushkin 34; tel. (372) 221-67-35; fax (372) 251-00-96; e-mail afghanemintj@yahoo.com; Ambassador SAYED MUHAMMAD KHAIRKHA.

Azerbaijan: 734000 Dushanbe, Kuchai Farhor 1; tel. (372) 227-11-90; fax (372) 227-66-51; e-mail dushanbe@mission.mfa.gov.az; Ambassador MAGERRAM ABYSH OGLÜ ALIYEV.

China, People's Republic: 734002 Dushanbe, Xiyoboni Rudaki 143; tel. (372) 224-20-07; fax (372) 251-00-24; e-mail chinaembassy@tajnet.com; internet tj.china-embassy.org; Ambassador ZUO XUELIANG.

France: 734025 Dushanbe, Kuchai Rakhimi 17; tel. (372) 21-78-55; fax (372) 51-00-82; e-mail ambassade.douchanbe@diplomatie.gouv.fr; Ambassador HENRY ZIPPER DE FABIANI.

Germany: 734064 Dushanbe, Kuchai Somoni 59/1; tel. (372) 377-30-00; fax (372) 377-30-81; e-mail info@duschanbe.diplo.de; internet www.duschanbe.diplo.de; Ambassador DORIS HERTRAMPF.

India: 734000 Dushanbe, Kuchai Buxoro 45; tel. (372) 221-18-03; fax (372) 251-00-45; e-mail hocdushanbe@tojikiston.com; Ambassador AMAR SINHA.

Iran: 734000 Dushanbe, Kuchai Boxtar 18; tel. (372) 221-00-74; fax (372) 251-00-89; e-mail iranembassy.tj@gmail.com; internet www.iranembassy-tj.com; Ambassador ALIASGHAR SHERDOOST.

Japan: 734000 Dushanbe, Kuchai X. Nazarov 80A; tel. (372) 21-39-70; fax (44) 600-54-78; e-mail embjpn@embjpn.tojikiston.com; Ambassador YUICHI KUSUMOTO.

Kazakhstan: 734000 Dushanbe, Kuchai Xuseinzoda 31/1; tel. (372) 221-11-08; fax (372) 251-01-08; e-mail dipmiskz7@tajnet.com; Ambassador ABUTALIL I. AKHMETOV.

Korea, Republic: Dushanbe; Ambassador KIM HYNG-SU.

Kyrgyzstan: 734000 Dushanbe, Kuchai Said-Nusur 56; tel. and fax (372) 224-26-11; e-mail info@kgembassy.tj; internet www.kgembassy.tj; Ambassador TURATBEK E. JUNUSHALIYEV.

Pakistan: 734000 Dushanbe, Kuchai Azizbekov 20A; tel. (372) 227-62-55; fax (372) 221-17-29; e-mail parepdushanbe_taj@yahoo.com; Ambassador KHALID USMAN QAISER.

Russia: 734000 Dushanbe, Kuchai Abu Ali ibni Sino 29/31; tel. (372) 235-70-65; fax (372) 235-88-06; e-mail rambtadjik@rambler.ru; internet www.rusemb.tj; Ambassador RAMAZAN G. ABDULATIPOV.

Turkey: 734019 Dushanbe, Xiyoboni Rudaki 17/2; tel. (372) 21-22-08; fax (372) 51-00-12; e-mail turemdus@tajik.net; Ambassador AKIF AYHAN.

Turkmenistan: 734000 Dushanbe, Kuchai Chexov 22; tel. and fax (372) 221-68-84; e-mail embturkm@tjinter.com; Ambassador NURBERDY AMANMURADOV.

United Kingdom: 734002 Dushanbe, Kuchai M. Tursunzoda 65; tel. (372) 224-22-21; fax (372) 227-17-26; e-mail dushanbe.reception@fco.gov.uk; internet ukintajikistan.fco.gov.uk; Ambassador TREVOR CHARLES MOORE.

USA: 734019 Dushanbe, Xiyoboni I. Somoni 109A; tel. (372) 229-20-00; fax (372) 229-20-50; e-mail usembassydushanbe@state.gov; internet dushanbe.usembassy.gov; Ambassador TRACEY ANN JACOBSON.

Uzbekistan: 734003 Dushanbe, Kuchai L. Sherali 15; tel. (372) 21-21-84; fax (372) 24-90-77; e-mail ruzintaj@rambler.ru; internet www.uzembassy-tadjik.mfa.uz; Ambassador SHOQOSIM I. SHOISLOMOV.

Judicial System

Chairman of the Constitutional Court: IZBILLO KHOJAYEV, 734025 Dushanbe, Kuchai Boxtar 48; tel. (372) 21-61-96.

Chairman of the Supreme Court: NASRATULLO ABDULLOYEV, 734000 Dushanbe, Xiyoboni N. Karabayev 1; tel. (372) 73-40-18.

Procurator-General: BOBOJON BOBOKHONOV, 734000 Dushanbe, Kuchai Abu Ali ibni Sino 126; tel. (372) 35-19-72.

Higher Economic Court: 734000 Dushanbe, Kuchai F. Niyazi 37; tel. (372) 21-15-58; f. 1995; Chair. AMIRKHOJA GOIBNAZAROV.

Religion

ISLAM

The majority of Tajiks are adherents of Islam and are mainly Sunnis (Hanafi school). Many of the Pamiri peoples, however, are Isma'ilis (followers of the Aga Khan), a Shi'ite sect. Under the Soviet regime the Muslims of Tajikistan were subject to the Muslim Board of Central Asia and a muftiate, both of which were based in Tashkent, Uzbekistan. The senior Muslim cleric in Tajikistan was the *qazi* (supreme judge). In 1992 the incumbent *qazi* fled to Afghanistan, and in 1993 the Government appointed an independent *mufti* (expert in Islamic law). The Tajikistani Government, however, abolished the post of *mufti* in 1996, following the murder of the incumbent, and established a Council of Islamic Scholars (or *ulema*), as the highest Islamic religious authority in the country.

Council of Islamic Scholars (Ulema): 734000 Dushanbe; Chair. QARI AMANULLOH NEMATZADE.

CHRISTIANITY

Most of the minority Christian population is Slav, the main denomination being the Russian Orthodox Church. There are some Protestant and other groups, notably a Baptist Church in Dushanbe.

Roman Catholic Church

The Church is represented in Tajikistan by a Mission, established in September 1997. There were an estimated 300 adherents at 31 December 2006.

Superior: Rev. CARLOS AVILA, 734006 Dushanbe, Xiyoboni Titova 21/10; tel. (372) 21-21-90; fax (372) 23-26-77; e-mail catholic@tajik.net; internet www.catholic.tj.

The Russian Orthodox Church (Moscow Patriarchate)

The Church in Tajikistan comes under the jurisdiction of the Eparchy of Tashkent and Central Asia, based in Uzbekistan and headed by the Metropolitan of Tashkent and Central Asia, VLADIMIR (IKIM).

JUDAISM

In the late 2000s there were an estimated 350 Jews in Dushanbe. In 2008 the only synagogue remaining in Tajikistan was demolished by order of the Government, which planned to construct state buildings on its site. A new synagogue was opened elsewhere in Dushanbe in May 2009.

Leader of the Religious Society of Jews of Tajikistan: Rabbi MIHAIL ABURAHMANOV, 734001 Dushanbe, Kuchai N. Xikmata 26; tel. (372) 21-76-58.

TAJIKISTAN

The Press

In 2000 there were four national newspapers. In 1996 two daily newspapers and 73 non-daily newspapers were published in Tajikistan. There were also 11 periodicals published in that year.

PRINCIPAL NEWSPAPERS

Adabiyet va sanat (Literature and Art): 734001 Dushanbe, Kuchai I. Somoni 8; tel. (372) 24-57-39; f. 1959; weekly; organ of Union of Writers of Tajikistan and Ministry of Culture; in Tajik; Editor GULNAZAR KELDI; circ. 4,000.

Adolat (Justice): 731000 Dushanbe; in Tajik; organ of the Democratic Party of Tajikistan; publication suspended by Ministry of Culture in Sept. 2006, and again in Oct. 2006; Editor-in-Chief RAJAB MIRZO; circ. 1,000 (2006).

Biznes i Politika (Business and Politics): 734025 Dushanbe, Kuchai M. Tursunzoda 30; tel. (372) 23-52-50; e-mail b_p@rambler.ru; f. 1992; weekly; in Russian; Editor-in-Chief U. RAHMON; circ. 10,000.

Charxi Gardun (Wheel of Fortune): 734018 Dushanbe, Xiyoboni S. Sherozi 16; tel. (372) 33-56-72; e-mail gazeta@tojikiston.com; internet www.gazeta.tj; f. 1996; weekly; in Tajik; general; Editor-in-Chief AKBARALI SATTAROV.

Daijest Press (Press Digest): 734018 Dushanbe, Xiyoboni S. Sherozi 16; tel. (372) 33-25-03; e-mail gazeta@tojikiston.com; f. 1994; weekly; in Russian; overview of world press, incl. economics, popular culture; Editor-in-Chief AKBARALI SATTAROV.

Djavononi Tochikiston (Youth of Tajikistan): 734000 Dushanbe, Kuchai F. Niyazi 32; tel. (372) 23-38-01; f. 1930; weekly; organ of the Union of Youth of Tajikistan; in Tajik; Editor DAVLAT NAZRIYEV; circ. 3,000.

Ittixod (Unity): 734000 Dushanbe, Xiyoboni Rudaki 137; tel. (372) 34-77-11; organ of the Socialist Party of Tajikistan.

Jumhuriyat (Republic): 734018 Dushanbe, Xiyoboni S. Sherozi 16; tel. (372) 33-08-11; e-mail jumhuriyat@tojikiston.com; f. 1925; 3 a week; organ of the Govt and presidential administration; in Tajik; Editor-in-Chief KAMOL ABDURAHIMOV; circ. 8,000.

Kurer Tadzhikistana (Tajikistan Courier): 734018 Dushanbe, Xiyoboni S. Sherozi 16; tel. (372) 33-08-15; e-mail ttemirov@td.silk.org; weekly; independent; in Russian; Editor KH. YUSIPOV; circ. 40,000.

Millat (Nation): 734000 Dushanbe; f. 2005; in Tajik; independent; Editor ADOLAT UMAROVOI.

Minbari Xalk (People's Tribune): 734018 Dushanbe, Xiyoboni S. Sherozi 16; tel. (372) 33-79-07; fax (372) 33-72-10; organ of the People's Democratic Party of Tajikistan; Editor MANSUR SAIFIDDINOV; circ. 20,000.

Najot (Salvation): 734000 Dushanbe, Kuchai Toktogul 55; tel. (372) 31-47-38; weekly; organ of the Islamic Rebirth Party of Tajikistan; Editor-in-Chief SIDUMAR KHUSAINI.

Narodnaya Gazeta (People's Newspaper): 734018 Dushanbe, Xiyoboni S. Sherozi 16; tel. (372) 33-08-30; e-mail narodnaja@mail.ru; f. 1929; fmrly Kommunist Tadzhikistana (Tajik Communist); weekly; organ of the Govt; in Russian; Editor VLADIMIR VOROBIYEV; circ. 3,000.

Nerui Sukhan (Power of the Word): 734018 Dushanbe, Xiyoboni S. Sherozi 16; f. 2003; weekly; Editor-in-Chief MUKHTOR BOKIZODA.

Nidoi ranchbar (Call of the Workers): 734018 Dushanbe, Xiyoboni S. Sherozi 16; tel. (372) 33-38-50; f. 1992; weekly; organ of the Communist Party of Tajikistan; in Tajik; Editor-in-Chief KHABIBULLO YOROV; circ. 6,000.

Odamu olam (Person and World): 734000 Dushanbe; weekly; in Tajik; independent; socio-political; Editor-in-Chief MIRAHMAD AMIRSHO.

Oila: 734018 Dushanbe, Xiyoboni S. Sherozi 16; tel. (372) 33-32-51; weekly; independent; Editor-in-Chief FIRUZA SATTORI.

Omuzgor (Teacher): 734000 Dushanbe, Kuchai Aini 45; tel. (372) 21-63-36; f. 1932; weekly; organ of the Ministry of Education; in Tajik; Editor-in-Chief SAMIULLO SAIFULLOYEV; circ. 3,000.

Ruzi Nav (New Day): 734018 Dushanbe, Xiyoboni S. Sherozi 16; tel. (37) 233-14-40; f. 2003; weekly; independent; politics and govt; Chief Editor RAJABI MIRZO.

Sadoi Mardum (The Voice of the People): 734018 Dushanbe, Xiyoboni S. Sherozi 16; tel. (372) 33-89-22; e-mail sadoimardum@yandex.ru; f. 1991; 3 a week; organ of the legislature; in Tajik; Chief Editor JUMAHON NABOTOV; circ. 8,000.

Tojikiston (Tajikistan): 734018 Dushanbe, Xiyoboni S. Sherozi 16; tel. (372) 34-94-11; e-mail nt@tajnet.com; f. 1938; weekly; social and political; in Tajik; Editor-in-Chief SHARIF KHAMDAMPUR; circ. (annual) 9,000.

Tojikiston ovozi/Golos Tadzhikistana (Voice of Tajikistan): 734018 Dushanbe, Xiyoboni S. Sherozi 16; tel. (372) 33-06-08; f. 1992; weekly; organ of the Central Committee of the Communist Party of Tajikistan; in Tajik and Russian; Editors SULAYMAN ERMATOV, INOM MUSOYEV; circ. 24,700.

Tribun.tj: 731000 Dushanbe, Xiyoboni Rudaki 107; tel. (372) 21-05-45; fax (372) 24-27-59; e-mail tribun.tj@mail.ru; internet www.tribun.tj; f. 2005; daily; online only; in Russian; organ of the People's Democratic Party of Tajikistan.

Vechernii Dushanbe (Dunshanbe Evening News): 734018 Dushanbe, Xiyoboni S. Sherozi 16; tel. (372) 33-08-15; fax (372) 33-30-25; e-mail anush@tajnet.com; f. 1968; weekly; social and political; in Russian; Editor-in-Chief AKBARALI SATTAROV.

ViD—Den za Dnem (Day After Day): 734018 Dushanbe, Xiyoboni S. Sherozi 16; tel. (372) 38-53-84; general; Editor-in-Chief AKBARALI SATTOROV.

Xalk ovozi (Voice of the People): 734018 Dushanbe, Xiyoboni S. Sherozi 16; tel. (372) 33-05-04; f. 1929; 3 a week; organ of the President; in Uzbek; Editor I. MUKHSINOV; circ. 8,600.

Zindagi (Life): 734000 Dushanbe; f. 2004; weekly; in Tajik; independent; politics; Editor-in-Chief KHURSHED ATOVULLO.

PRINCIPAL PERIODICALS

Monthly, unless otherwise indicated.

Adab: 734025 Dushanbe, Kuchai Chexov 13; tel. (372) 23-49-36; organ of the Ministry of Education; in Tajik; Editor SH. SHOKIRZODA; circ. (annual) 24,000.

Avitsenna: 734018 Dushanbe, Xiyoboni S. Sherozi 16; tel. (372) 34-34-44; e-mail gazeta@tojikiston.com; weekly; in Russian; medicine; Editor-in-Chief AKBARALI SATTAROV.

Bunyod-i Adab (Culture Fund): 734000 Dushanbe; f. 1996 to foster cultural links among the country's Persian-speaking peoples; weekly; Editor ASKAR KHAKIM.

Djashma (Spring): 734018 Dushanbe, Xiyoboni S. Sherozi 16; tel. (372) 33-08-48; f. 1986; journal of the Ministry of Culture; for children; Editor KAMOL NASRULLO; circ. (annual) 10,000.

Farxang (Culture): 734003 Dushanbe, Xiyoboni Rudaki 124; tel. (372) 24-02-39; f. 1991; journal of the Culture Fund and Ministry of Culture; in Tajik; Editor-in-Chief J. AKOBIR; circ. 15,000.

Firuza: 734018 Dushanbe, Xiyoboni S. Sherozi 16; tel. (372) 33-89-10; f. 1932; organ of the Ministry of Culture; social and literary journal for women; Editor ZULFIYA ATOI; circ. (annual) 29,400.

Ilm va khayot (Science and Life): 734025 Dushanbe, Xiyoboni Rudaki 34; tel. (372) 27-48-61; f. 1989; organ of the Academy of Sciences; popular science; Editor T. BOIBOBO; circ. (annual) 12,000.

Istikbol: 734018 Dushanbe, Xiyoboni S. Sherozi 16; tel. (372) 33-14-52; f. 1952; organ of the Ministry of Culture; in Tajik; Chief Editor L. KENJAYEVA; circ. (annual) 10,000.

Marifat: 734024 Dushanbe, Kuchai Aini 45; tel. (372) 23-42-84; organ of the Ministry of Education; in Tajik; Editor O. BOZOROV; circ. (annual) 40,000.

Pamir: 734001 Dushanbe, Kuchai I. Somoni 8; tel. (372) 24-56-56; f. 1949; journal of the Union of Writers of Tajikistan; fiction; in Russian; Editor-in-Chief BORIS PSHENICHNYI.

Sadoi shark (Voice of the East): 734001 Dushanbe, Kuchai I. Somoni 8; tel. (372) 24-56-79; f. 1927; journal of the Union of Writers of Tajikistan; fiction; in Tajik; Editor URUN KUKHZOD; circ. 1,600.

NEWS AGENCIES

Asia-Plus TV-Radio Company: 734002 Dushanbe, Kuchai Boxtar 35/1, 8th Floor; tel. (372) 23-59-95; fax (372) 23-01-07; e-mail manager@asiaplus.tj; internet www.asiaplus.tj; f. 2002; independent; reports in Tajik and Russian; Gen. Dir UMED BABAKHANOV.

Avesta News Agency: 734025 Dushanbe, Xiyoboni Sherozi 16A; tel. (372) 27-10-84; e-mail zafar@avesta.tj; internet www.avesta.tj; f. 2004; Dir ZAFAR ABDULLAYEV.

Khovar (East): 737025 Dushanbe, Xiyoboni Rudaki 40; tel. (372) 23-23-83; fax (372) 21-21-37; e-mail khovar@tojikiston.com; internet www.khovar.tj; f. 1925; govt information agency; Dir ZAFAR SAIDOV.

Varorud: 735700 Soghd Viloyat, Khujand, Kuchai Ferdovsi 123; tel. and fax (342) 24-09-33; e-mail varorud@varorud.org; internet www.varorud.org; f. 2000; independent; Dir ILKHOM JAMOLOV.

PRESS ASSOCIATION

Internews Network—Tajikistan: 734025 Dushanbe, Kuchai Ak. Rajabov 7/1/4; tel. (372) 21-99-33; fax (372) 21-99-34; e-mail chuck@internews.tj; internet www.internews.tj; f. 1995; non-governmental org.; provides support and funding to media organizations, and in the training of journalists; Country Dir CHARLES RICE.

TAJIKISTAN
Directory

Publishers

Adib (Writer): 734000 Dushanbe, Xiyoboni Rudaki 37; tel. (372) 23-08-92; fax (372) 23-37-94; state-owned; Tajik and Russian; fiction, incl. poetry, and non-fiction, incl. books on Tajikistani and Central Asian culture.

Donish (Knowledge): 734000 Dushanbe, Xiyoboni Akademiya Nauk 33; state-owned; Russian and Tajik; non-fiction, incl. geography, literature, history, and art; associated with the Academy of Sciences.

Irfon (Light of Knowledge) Publishing House: 734018 Dushanbe, Kuchai N. Karabayev 17; tel. (372) 33-39-06; e-mail irfon_company@mail.ru; f. 1925; politics, social sciences, economics, agriculture, medicine and technology; Dir J. SHARIFOV; Editor-in-Chief A. OLIMOV.

Maorif va Farxang (Education and Culture) Publishing House: 734018 Dushanbe, Kuchai N. Karabayev 17; tel. and fax (372) 33-93-97; e-mail najmidin@netrt.org; f. 1958; educational, academic; Gen. Dir NAJMIDDIN ZAYNIDDINOV.

Sarredaksiyai Ilmii Entsiklopediyai Millii Tajik (Tajik National Scientific Encyclopaedia) Publishing House: 731000 Dushanbe, Kuchai Aini 126; tel. (372) 25-81-55; e-mail encyclopedia@yahoo.com; f. 1969; Editor-in-Chief A. QURBONOV.

Sharki Ozod Publishing House: 734018 Dushanbe, Xiyoboni S. Sherozi 16; tel. (372) 34-94-11; e-mail tadjikis@tajnet.com; state-owned; Dir MANZURHON DODOHONOV.

Surushan Publishing House: 734025 Dushanbe, Xiyoboni Rudaki 37; tel. and fax (372) 21-54-62; e-mail surushan@net.org; f. 1997; literary fiction, educational; Dir NURIDDIN ZAYNIDDINOV.

Broadcasting and Communications

TELECOMMUNICATIONS

Babilon-Mobil (Babilon-M): 734012 Dushanbe, Kuchai I. Somoni 8; tel. (44) 600-10-10; fax (4) 600-20-20; e-mail info@babilon-m.tj; internet www.babilon-m.com; f. 2002; mobile cellular telecommunications.

Beeline TJ: Dushanbe; e-mail pr@beeline.tj; internet www.beeline.tj; f. 2006; fmrly Tacom; 60% owned by VympelKom-Bilain (Russia); mobile cellular telecommunications services.

Indigo Somonkom: Khujand; internet www.somoncom.com; f. 2000; provides mobile cellular telecommunications in northern regions, particularly Soghd Viloyat; 130,000 subscribers (2006).

Indigo Tajikistan: 734000 Dushanbe, Kuchai M. Tursunzoda 23; tel. (372) 23-21-21; fax (372) 23-21-23; e-mail sales@indigo.tajnet.com; internet www.indigo.tj; f. 2001; mobile cellular telecommunications.

MLT (Mobile Lines of Tajikistan): 734025 Dushanbe, Xiyoboni Rudaki 57; tel. (372) 21-42-24; internet www.mlt.tj; f. 2001; fmrly TT Mobile; mobile cellular telecommunications.

Tajiktelecom: 734025 Dushanbe, Xiyoboni Rudaki 57A; tel. (372) 21-31-78; fax (372) 23-21-19; e-mail ttelecom@rs.tj; internet www.tajiktelecom.tj; f. 1996; national telecommunications operator; Dir-Gen. GULMAHMAD KAYUMOV.

BROADCASTING

In December 2001 there were some 20 independent television stations.

Regulatory Authority

State Committee for Television and Radio Broadcasting: 734000 Dushanbe; Chair. ASADULLO K. RAKHMONOV.

Radio

State TV-Radio Broadcasting Co of Tajikistan: 734025 Dushanbe, Kuchai Chapayev 31; tel. (372) 27-75-27; fax (372) 21-34-95; e-mail soro@ctvrtj.td.silk.org; Chair. ABDODZHABBOR RAKHMONOV.

Asia-Plus: 734018 Dushanbe, Xiyoboni Saadi Sherozi, 13th Floor; tel. and fax (44) 600-71-07; e-mail manager@asiaplus.tj; internet www.asiaplusradio.tj; f. 2002; radio and television station; broadcasts 24 hours a day in Russian and Tajik; Gen. Dir UMED BABAKHANOV.

Tajik Radio: 734025 Dushanbe, Kuchai Chapayev 31; tel. (372) 27-65-92; broadcasts in Russian, Tajik and Uzbek.

Tiroz: 735700 Soghd Viloyat, Khujand, Mikroraion 27; tel. (342) 25-66-89; e-mail trrktiroz@sugdien.com; internet www.tiroz.sugdien.com; Dir KHURSHED ULMASOV.

Television

State TV-Radio Broadcasting Co of Tajikistan: 734025 Dushanbe, Kuchai Chapayev 31; tel. (372) 27-75-27; fax (372) 21-34-95; e-mail soro@ctvrtj.td.silk.org; Chair. ABDODZHABBOR RAKHMONOV.

Poitaxt: 734013 Dushanbe, Kuchai Azizbekov 20; tel. (372) 23-26-29; independent; Dir RAKHMON OSTONOV.

Tajik Television (TTV): 734013 Dushanbe, Kuchai Behzod 7; tel. (372) 22-43-57.

Finance

(cap. = capital; res = reserves; dep. = deposits; brs = branches; m. = million; amounts in somoni, unless otherwise stated)

BANKING

Central Bank

National Bank of the Republic of Tajikistan (Bonki Millii Tochikiston): 734025 Dushanbe, Xiyoboni Rudaki 23/2; tel. (372) 21-26-28; fax (372) 51-00-68; e-mail info@natbank.tajnet.com; internet www.nbt.tj; f. 1991; cap. 0.8m., res 25.4m., dep. 604.8m. (Oct. 2003); Chair. SHARIF RAHIMZODA.

State Savings Bank

Amonatbonk: 734018 Dushanbe, Kuchai Loxuti 24; tel. (372) 221-70-81; fax (372) 223-14-16; e-mail info@amonatbonk.tj; internet www.amonatbonk.tj; f. 1991; fmrly br. of USSR Sberbank; licensed by presidential decree and not subject to the same controls as the commercial and trading banks; Chair. of Bd MAXMADAMIN B. MAXMADAMINOV; 58 brs, 480 sub-brs.

Other Banks

In June 2005 President Rakhmonov announced the removal of all restrictions on the activities of foreign banks in Tajikistan. There were reported to be 16 commercial banks in operation in Tajikistan in early 2005, including the following:

Agroinvestbank: 734018 Dushanbe, Xiyoboni S. Sherozi 21; tel. (372) 233-21-14; fax (372) 236-51-66; e-mail pressa@agroinvestbank.tj; internet www.agroinvestbank.tj; f. 1992; fmrly Agroprombank; cap. US $22.4m., res $5.7m., dep. $118.6m. (Dec. 2007); Chair. NIYOZMUROD M. SAIDMURODOV; 62 brs.

Orienbank: 734001 Dushanbe, Xiyoboni Rudaki 95/1; tel. (372) 21-09-20; fax (372) 21-18-77; e-mail info@orienbank.com; internet www.orienbank.com; f. 1922; cap. 60m., res 25m., dep. 216m. (Aug. 2008); commercial bank; Chair. of Bd HASAN ASADULLOZODA; Chair. of Bank Council SHERMALIK MALIKOV; 32 brs.

Tajbank: 734064 Dushanbe, Kuchai I. Somoni 59/1; tel. (372) 27-46-54.

Tajprombank (Tajik Joint-Stock Bank for Reconstruction and Development): 734025 Dushanbe, Kuchai X. Dexlavi 12/3; tel. (372) 21-27-20; e-mail tpb@tjinter.com; cap. US $1m., res $3m., dep. $4m.; Chair. DZHAMSHED ZIYAYEV; 8 brs.

Tojiksodirotbonk (Bank for Foreign Economic Affairs of the Republic of Tajikistan): 734012 Dushanbe, Kuchai X. Dexlavi 4; tel. (372) 21-59-52; fax (372) 21-47-38; e-mail sham@sodirotbonk.com; fmrly br. of USSR Vneshekonombank; underwent restructuring in 1999; Chair. I. L. LALBEKOV; 6 brs.

COMMODITY EXCHANGES

Tajik Republican Commodity Exchange (NAVRUZ): 734001 Dushanbe, Kuchai Orjonikidze 37; tel. (372) 23-48-74; fax (372) 27-03-91; f. 1991; Chair. SULEYMAN CHULEBAYEV.

Vostok-Mercury Torgovyi Dom: 734000 Dushanbe; tel. and fax (372) 24-60-61; f. 1991; trades in a wide range of goods.

INSURANCE

Muin Insurance Co: 734025 Dushanbe, Kuchai Sh. Rustaveli 16/1; tel. (372) 21-32-80; fax (372) 21-72-09; e-mail info@muin.tj; internet www.muin.tj; f. 1992; Dir-Gen. SHARIFJON ISHAKOV.

Orien Insurance: 734001 Dushanbe, Xiyoboni Rudaki 100; tel. and fax (372) 21-12-30; e-mail info@orieninsurance.tj; internet www.orieninsurance.tj; f. 2004; life and non-life; Dir ISKANDAR KH. SHARIPOV.

Tojiksurguta State Insurance Co: 734025 Dushanbe, Kuchai Chexov 4A; tel. (372) 21-75-07.

Trud Insurance Co: 734000 Dushanbe, Kuchai Bekzod 70; tel. (372) 227-24-24; fax (372) 221-72-21; e-mail info@trud.tj; internet www.trud.tj; f. 2004; life and non-life.

Trade and Industry

CHAMBER OF COMMERCE

Chamber of Commerce and Industry of the Republic of Tajikistan: 734012 Dushanbe, Kuchai Valamatzade 21; tel. (372) 21-52-84; fax (372) 21-14-80; e-mail chamber@tpp.tj; internet www.tpp.tj; f. 1960; brs in Khujant, Qurgonteppa, Khorog, and Chamber of Services in Dushanbe; Chair. SHARIF S. SAIDOV.

INDUSTRIAL ASSOCIATION

Tajikvneshtorg (Tajik External Trade) Industrial Asscn: 734035 Dushanbe, Xiyoboni Rudaki 25, POB 48; tel. (372) 23-29-03; fax (372) 22-81-20; f. 1988; co-ordinates trade with foreign countries in a wide range of goods; Pres. ABDURAKHMON MUKHTASHOV.

EMPLOYERS' ORGANIZATION

National Asscn of Small and Medium-Sized Businesses of Tajikistan: 734000 Dushanbe, Kuchai Bofanda 9; tel. (372) 27-79-78; fax (372) 21-17-26; f. 1993 with govt support; independent org.; Chair. MATLJUBA ULJABAEVA.

UTILITIES

Electricity

Barqi Tojik (Tajik Electricity): 734000 Dushanbe, Kuchai I. Somoni 64; tel. (372) 35-86-68; fax (372) 35-86-92; e-mail barkitojik@tajnet.com; Gen. Dir SANAT RAKHIMOV.

Pamir Energy Co (PamirEnergy): 736100 Kuhistoni Badakhshon, Khorog; tel. (352) 22-33-83; fax (352) 22-25-19; e-mail daler.jumaev@pamirenergy.com; f. 2002; jt venture between Governments of Tajikistan and Switzerland, the Aga Khan Fund for Economic Development, the International Finance Corpn and the International Development Association to provide electricity to Kuhistoni Badakhshon; Gen. Dir DALER JUMAYEV.

Gas

Dushanbegaz: 734000 Dushanbe; tel. (372) 27-89-28; supplies gas to Dushanbe City.

Soghdgaz: 735700 Soghd Viloyat, Khujand, 20 Kvartal; tel. (342) 22-53-95; fax (342) 24-35-16; supplies gas to Soghd Viloyat.

Tojikgaz: 734012 Dushanbe, Xiyoboni Rudaki 6; tel. (372) 21-66-68; fax (372) 21-28-16; state-controlled gas utility co.

TRADE UNIONS

Federation of Trade Unions: 734012 Dushanbe, Xiyoboni Rudaki 20; tel. (372) 23-17-79; fax (372) 23-25-06; f. 1926; present name adopted 1992; Chair. MURODALI S. SALIKHOV; 1.3m. mems.

Transport

RAILWAYS

There are few railways in Tajikistan. Lines link the major centres of the country with the railway network of Uzbekistan, connecting Khujand to the Farg'ona (Fergana) valley lines, and the cotton-growing centre of Qurgonteppa to Termiz. A new line, between the town of Isfara, in Soghd Viloyat, and Xavast, in Uzbekistan, was opened in 1995 and in 1997 a passenger route between Dushanbe and Volgograd, Russia, was inaugurated. The first section of a new line between Qurgonteppa and Kulob, in the south-west of Tajikistan, was inaugurated in 1998. In October 2002 a route from Kulob to Astrakhan, Russia, was opened. In 2009 the total length of the rail network in use was 679.9km.

Tajik Railways: 734012 Dushanbe, M. Nazarshoeva 35; tel. (372) 21-60-59; fax (372) 21-83-34; e-mail tajrwv@rs.tj; Dir AMONULLO KH. KHUKUMATULLO.

ROADS

In mid-2002 Tajikistan's road network totalled an estimated 30,000 km, including 13,747 km of highways. The principal highway links the northern city of Khujand, across the Anzob Pass (3,372 m), with the capital, Dushanbe, continuing to Khorog (Kuhistoni Badakhshon), before wending through the Pamir Mountains, to the east and north, to Osh, Kyrgyzstan, across the Akbaytal Pass (4,655 m). This arterial route exhibits problems common to much of the country's land transport: winter weather is likely to cause the road to be closed by snow for up to eight months of the year. In 2000 Tajikistan and the Asian Development Bank signed a memorandum of understanding for the rehabilitation of the road linking Dushanbe to the south-western cities of Qurgonteppa and Kulob. In the same year a road linking eastern Tajikistan with the People's Republic of China was completed, giving Tajikistan access to the Karakorum highway, which connects China and Pakistan.

CIVIL AVIATION

The main international airport is at Dushanbe, and there is also a major airport at Khujand. The country is linked to cities in Russia and other former Soviet republics, and to a growing number of destinations in Europe and Asia.

TajikAir: 734006 Dushanbe, Kuchai Titova 32/1; tel. (372) 21-21-45; fax (372) 21-86-85; e-mail tt_gart@tajnet.com; internet www.tajikair.tj; state-owned; operates flights to destinations in Afghanistan, the People's Republic of China (Xinjiang Uygur autonomous region), Germany, India, Iran, Kazakhstan, Kyrgyzstan, Pakistan, Russia, Turkey and the United Arab Emirates; Dir VALERII S. SHARIPOV.

Tourism

There was little tourism in Tajikistan even before the 1992–97 civil war. There is some spectacular mountain scenery, hitherto mainly visited by climbers, and, particularly in the Farg'ona (Fergana) valley, in the north of the country, there are sites of historical interest, notably the city of Khujand.

State Committee for Youth, Sports and Tourism: 734000 Dushanbe; f. 2006.

TANZANIA
Introductory Survey

Location, Climate, Language, Religion, Flag, Capital

The United Republic of Tanzania consists of Tanganyika, on the African mainland, and the nearby islands of Zanzibar and Pemba. Tanganyika lies on the east coast of Africa, bordered by Uganda and Kenya to the north, by Rwanda, Burundi and the Democratic Republic of the Congo (formerly Zaire) to the west, and by Zambia, Malawi and Mozambique to the south. Zanzibar and Pemba are in the Indian Ocean, about 40 km (25 miles) off the coast of Tanganyika, north of Dar es Salaam. The climate varies with altitude, ranging from tropical in Zanzibar and on the coast and plains to semi-temperate in the highlands. The official languages are Swahili and English and there are numerous tribal languages. There are Muslim, Christian and Hindu communities. Many Africans follow traditional beliefs. The national flag (proportions 2 by 3) comprises two triangles, one of green (with its base at the hoist and its apex in the upper fly) and the other of blue (with its base in the fly and its apex at the lower hoist), separated by a broad, yellow-edged black diagonal stripe, from the lower hoist to the upper fly.

Recent History

Tanganyika became a German colony in 1884, and was later incorporated into German East Africa, which also included present-day Rwanda and Burundi. In 1918, at the end of the First World War, the German forces in the area surrendered, and Tanganyika was placed under a League of Nations mandate, with the United Kingdom as the administering power. In 1946 Tanganyika became a UN Trust Territory, still under British rule. At a general election in September 1960 the Tanganyika African National Union (TANU) won 70 of the 71 seats in the National Assembly, and the party's leader, Dr Julius Nyerere, became Chief Minister. Internal self-government was achieved in May 1961, when Nyerere became Prime Minister. Tanganyika became independent, within the Commonwealth, on 9 December 1961, but Nyerere resigned as Prime Minister in January 1962, in order to devote himself to the direction of TANU. He was succeeded as premier by Rashidi Kawawa. On 9 December 1962, following elections in November, Tanganyika became a republic, with Nyerere as the country's first President. Kawawa became Vice-President. Zanzibar (including the island of Pemba), a British protectorate since 1890, became an independent sultanate in December 1963. Following an armed uprising by the Afro-Shirazi Party (ASP) in January 1964, the Sultan was deposed and a republic proclaimed. The new Government signed an Act of Union with Tanganyika in April 1964, thus creating the United Republic. The union was named Tanzania in October 1964, and a new Constitution was introduced in July 1965, which provided for a one-party state (although, until 1977, TANU and the ASP remained the respective official parties of mainland Tanzania and Zanzibar, and co-operated in affairs of state). Nyerere was elected President of the United Republic in September 1965, and was subsequently re-elected in 1970, 1975 and 1980.

Despite its incorporation into Tanzania, Zanzibar retained a separate administration, which ruthlessly suppressed all opposition. A separate Constitution for Zanzibar was adopted in October 1979, providing for a popularly elected President and a House of Representatives elected by delegates of the ruling party. The first elections to the 40-member Zanzibar House of Representatives were held in January 1980. Aboud Jumbe won an overwhelming majority at Zanzibar's first presidential election, held in October; however, mounting dissatisfaction among Zanzibaris concerning the union with Tanganyika culminated in the resignation, in January 1984, of Jumbe and three of his ministers. In April Ali Hassan Mwinyi, a former Zanzibari Minister of Natural Resources and Tourism, was elected unopposed as President of Zanzibar, winning 87.5% of the votes cast. A new Constitution for Zanzibar came into force in January 1985, providing for the House of Representatives to be directly elected by universal adult suffrage.

In February 1977 TANU and the ASP were amalgamated to form Chama Cha Mapinduzi (CCM), the Revolutionary Party of Tanzania. In April the National Assembly approved a permanent Constitution for Tanzania; this provided for the election to the National Assembly of representatives from Zanzibar, in addition to those from the Tanzanian mainland. Major changes to the Constitution were approved by the National Assembly in October 1984, limiting the President's powers and increasing those of the National Assembly.

President Nyerere retired in November 1985, and was succeeded by Mwinyi, who, as the sole candidate, had won 96% of the votes cast at a presidential election in October. Elections to the National Assembly were held on the same day. Mwinyi appointed Joseph Warioba (previously Minister of Justice) as Prime Minister and First Vice-President. At presidential and legislative elections in Zanzibar, also held in October, Idris Abdul Wakil (formerly Speaker of the Zanzibar House of Representatives) was elected President of Zanzibar to replace Mwinyi; although the sole candidate, he received only 61% of the votes. Nyerere remained Chairman of the CCM until August 1990 when he resigned and Mwinyi was appointed in his place.

In early 1988 tension began to increase in Zanzibar, reflecting underlying rivalries between the inhabitants of the main island and those of the smaller island of Pemba, between Zanzibar's African and Arab populations, and between supporters and opponents of unity with Tanganyika. In January Wakil suspended the islands' Government, the Supreme Revolutionary Council, and assumed control of the armed forces from the office of his main rival, Chief Minister Seif Sharrif Hamad, following earlier claims by Wakil that a group of dissidents, including members of the Council, had been plotting the overthrow of his administration. Hamad was replaced later that month by Dr Omar Ali Juma and in May Hamad and six other officials were expelled from the CCM for allegedly opposing the party's aims and endangering Tanzanian unity.

In October 1990 concurrent parliamentary and presidential elections were held in Zanzibar. Wakil did not stand for re-election; the sole presidential candidate, Dr Salmin Amour, was elected as Wakil's successor by 97.7% of the votes cast. Amour subsequently reappointed Juma as Chief Minister of Zanzibar. At the end of October national parliamentary and presidential elections took place. Mwinyi, the sole candidate in the presidential election, was re-elected for a second term, taking 95.5% of the votes cast. In November Mwinyi replaced Warioba as Prime Minister with John Malecela, previously the Tanzanian High Commissioner to the United Kingdom. In December 1994 Mwinyi reorganized the Cabinet. Malecela was replaced as Prime Minister and First Vice-President by Cleopa Msuya, hitherto the Minister of Industry and Trade and previously Prime Minister in 1980–83.

Meanwhile, in December 1991 a presidential commission published recommendations for the establishment of a multi-party political system. In February 1992 proposed constitutional amendments to this effect were ratified by a special congress of the CCM, which stipulated that, in order to protect national unity, all new political organizations should command support in both Zanzibar and mainland Tanzania, and should be free of tribal, religious and racial bias. In May the Constitutions of both the United Republic and Zanzibar were amended to enshrine a multi-party system. Several political organizations were officially registered from mid-1992.

In October 1995 multi-party legislative elections were held for the first time, concurrently with presidential elections, both in Zanzibar and throughout the Tanzanian union. At elections on 22 October the CCM secured 26 of the 50 elective seats in the Zanzibari House of Representatives, while the Civic United Front (CUF, campaigning for increased Zanzibari autonomy) took 24 seats. Amour was re-elected President of the islands by 50.2% of the votes cast, only narrowly defeating Hamad, who represented the CUF. Amour appointed a new ruling council, with Dr Mohamed Gharib Bilali, formerly a government official, as Chief Minister. The CUF contested the election results, accusing the Zanzibari authorities of electoral malpractice and refusing to recognize the legitimacy of the new Amour administration, while party delegates initially declined to take up their seats in the House of Representatives. The Tanzanian national elections, on 29 October, were disrupted by a combination of apparent organizational chaos and further allegations by opposition parties of electoral fraud. Administrative inefficiency led to the cancellation of the election results in seven constituencies in Dar es Salaam; these polls were repeated in mid-November. The opposition parties, alleging that the CCM was manipulating the voting process, refused to re-run, withdrew their candidates from the presidential election, and unsuccessfully petitioned the High Court to declare all results null and void. The Government proceeded to publish the results, whereby the CCM won 186 of the 232 elective seats in the National Assembly, the CUF 24, the National Convention for Reconstruction and Reform (NCCR—Mageuzi) 16, and Chama Cha Democrasia na Maendeleo (Chadema) and the United Democratic Party (UDP) three seats each. Benjamin Mkapa, hitherto Minister of Science, Technology and Higher Education, was deemed to have been elected President, winning 61.8% of the votes cast. The former Minister of Home Affairs, Augustine Mrema, took 27.8% of the votes. President Mkapa was inaugurated in late November; Juma (hitherto Chief Minister of Zanzibar) was appointed Vice-President. Shortly afterwards Mkapa announced a new Cabinet, with Frederick Sumaye (formerly Minister of Agriculture) as Prime Minister.

In his election campaign Mkapa had pledged to tackle corruption in high public office, and appointed a special presidential commission which in December 1996 issued a report asserting that corruption was widespread in the public sector. In September a parliamentary select committee investigating bribery allegations against the Minister of Finance, Simon Mbilinyi, had published a report recommending that he be made accountable for having illegally granted tax exemptions. Mbilinyi subsequently resigned. In October Mrema unexpectedly won a parliamentary by-election in a Dar es Salaam constituency for NCCR—Mageuzi, of which he had become Chairman following his dismissal from Government in 1995; although his campaign had focused on financial impropriety in government, Mrema had recently been accused of having presented false evidence to the parliamentary select committee on corruption in order to undermine the Government's credibility.

In August 1998 a car bomb exploded outside the US embassy in Dar es Salaam (concurrently with a similar attack at the US mission in Nairobi, Kenya); 11 people were killed in Dar es Salaam and some 75 were injured. The attacks were believed to have been co-ordinated by international Islamist terrorists led by a Saudi-born dissident, Osama bin Laden, and the USA retaliated by launching air-strikes against targets in Afghanistan and Sudan. Four men were convicted of involvement in the bombings by a court in New York, USA, in May 2001 and were later sentenced to life imprisonment.

A committee was appointed by the Government in July 1998 to assess public opinion on constitutional reform. In September Mkapa reorganized the Cabinet, following the nullification of the election to the National Assembly, in 1995, of two ministers and the resignation in August of the Minister of State in the President's Office, Hassy Kitine, who was alleged to have used state funds to finance medical treatment abroad for his wife. In April 1999 Mrema and his faction of NCCR—Mageuzi defected to the Tanzania Labour Party (TLP). Mrema initially assumed the chairmanship of the TLP, but in May he was banned by the High Court from holding any official post in that party. There was speculation that the death in October of former President Nyerere might give rise to increased pressure for a restructuring of the United Republic of Tanzania. This was, to some extent, reinforced by the release in December of the report of the committee charged with assessing public opinion on constitutional reform. While it found that some 96.3% of Zanzibaris and 84.8% of mainland Tanzanians favoured a 'two-tier' government for the United Republic, the committee itself recommended the establishment of a 'three-tier' system. In so doing it was adjudged by President Mkapa to have exceeded its mandate. In February 2000 the National Assembly approved draft legislation to amend the Constitution in accordance with citizens' recommendations as reported by the committee. Among these recommendations was one that the President should henceforth be elected by a majority vote.

At a presidential election held on 29 October 2000 Benjamin Mkapa was re-elected as President, securing 71.7% of votes cast; Prof. Ibrahim Lipumba, the Chairman of the CUF, won 16.3% of the votes cast, Augustine Mrema 7.8% and John Cheyo 4.2%. The participation rate was 84%. In the following month the CUF and Chadema agreed to form a five-year alliance and field joint candidates for the presidential elections in both the United Republic of Tanzania and in Zanzibar. It was agreed that if either candidate (both from the CUF) won, the respective prime minister would be drawn from Chadema. Candidates from the TLP and NCCR—Mageuzi failed to secure the minimum 200 referees and thus were not allowed to stand for election. At legislative elections, held concurrently, the CCM secured 244 seats in the National Assembly. The largest opposition group to obtain representation was the CUF, with 15 seats; the three other opposition parties (Chadema, the TLP and the UDP) won four, three and two seats, respectively. The polls were declared by international observers to have been freely and fairly conducted. In November Mkapa appointed a new Cabinet, reappointing Frederick Sumaye as Prime Minister.

In marked contrast, presidential and legislative elections were also held in Zanzibar and Pemba on 29 October 2000, amid widespread accusations of electoral fraud. Voting in 16 of the islands' 50 constituencies was annulled owing to a lack of ballot papers and voter registration lists. The Zanzibar Electoral Commission (ZEC) announced that new polls would be held in the 16 constituencies (all areas where the CUF enjoyed strong support), and that counting for the presidential elections for both Zanzibar and the United Republic would be delayed until the new results were received. Opposition parties and Commonwealth electoral observers called for a full re-run of the elections, but this was rejected by the ZEC. Following a week of confusion and violent clashes between the police and opposition supporters, the repeated polls were held on 5 November. Accusations of electoral fraud persisted, and the participation rate was reported to be low. Following the poll, the CCM claimed that it had won 67% of the votes cast (thereby winning 34 seats in the House of Representatives). The CUF refused to recognize the results of the ballot. Despite the concerns of the opposition parties and international observers, the ZEC proclaimed Amani Abeid Karume of the CCM as President of Zanzibar. The CUF refused to recognize Karume as President and demanded that a repeat election be held within four months.

In April 2001 an estimated 60,000 supporters of 12 opposition parties gathered peacefully in Dar es Salaam to demand that the Government hold fresh elections in Zanzibar, draft a new Constitution for the United Republic and establish independent electoral commissions. A similar, peaceful demonstration in Zanzibar later that month was attended by an estimated 60,000–85,000 protesters. President Karume, however, continued to reject the opposition's demands. In May 11 members of the Zanzibar House of Representatives and five members of the National Assembly were dismissed from their respective legislatures for having boycotted three successive sittings—their actions were part of the CUF's ongoing refusal to recognize the 2000 election results. The Attorney-General rejected subsequent demands from the CUF for their reinstatement. By-elections were held on 15 May 2003, at which the CUF won every seat it contested (amounting to 15 in the National Assembly and 11 in the Zanzibar House of Representatives). CUF candidates were disqualified from contesting six seats in the House of Representatives; these were won by CCM candidates.

In June 2001 it emerged that, following the violence of the 2000 elections, the CCM and the CUF had been holding a series of secret negotiations intended to resolve the political impasse in Zanzibar. The negotiations concluded with the signing of a *muafaka* (peace accord) between the two parties in Zanzibar in October 2001. Shortly afterwards the State withdrew all legal cases related to the post-election demonstrations.

In accordance with the CCM-CUF accord signed in October 2001, amendments to the Zanzibari Constitution were approved by the House of Representatives in April 2002. The amendments provided for the restructuring of the electoral commission to include opposition representatives (duly appointed in October 2002), the creation of a permanent voters' register and the removal of legislation requiring a person to live in a particular area for five consecutive years in order to qualify as a voter. Also included were the introduction of the right to appeal against High Court decisions and the appointment of a separate director of public prosecutions for Zanzibar.

In late 2003 and early 2004 political tension in Zanzibar intensified ahead of the elections due in late 2005. Supporters of the CUF were keen to avoid a repetition of the irregularities that had marred the elections of 1995 and 2000. Zanzibaris were reportedly particularly anxious as, according to the prevailing custom of the United Republic, they were to elect the next President. However, following remarks from President Mkapa that this custom was not guaranteed by law, many Zanzibaris feared their marginalization. In November 2003 the CUF Chairman, Lipumba, threatened to obtain a court injunction blocking the 2005 elections unless the register of voters was completed in time, and in April 2004 the leader of the Democratic Party made a similar threat, stating his intention to sue the National Electoral Commission (NEC) and the ZEC unless both bodies were reformed to include members of parties other than the CCM and the CUF. Opposition supporters were also concerned that the Government's efforts to encourage mainlanders who had been living in Zanzibar for more than 10 years to register for Zanzibari citizenship (thus making them eligible to vote in Zanzibar) constituted an attempt to manipulate voter registration in favour of the CCM. The Government, in contrast, deplored the circulation of leaflets throughout Zanzibar urging mainlanders to leave and alleged intimidation of mainlanders.

In early 2004 Islamism appeared to be exerting an increasing influence on politics in Zanzibar. Members of religious groups from Pakistan and Afghanistan were reported to have entered Zanzibar in March 2003 and begun spreading 'seditious teachings'. Moderate Zanzibari Muslim leaders expressed concern about rising extremism, and in March 2004 the island's Mufti, Sheikh Harith bin Kalef, denounced a radical Islamic group, the Zanzibar Union for Awakening and Islamic Forums Community (also known as Uamsho), as a political organization that used religion to disguise its efforts to destabilize Zanzibar. Police banned a demonstration by Uamsho, which insisted that the Mufti should be elected by Muslims rather than appointed by the Government and, it was claimed, advocated killing secular leaders who refused to impose Islamic law in Zanzibar. The demonstration proceeded, but was dispersed by the security forces. A series of bomb attacks followed, targeting Zanzibari power-stations, schools, and other government and private property. In late March two bombs exploded in Stone Town, outside the residences of the Mufti and the Minister of Communications and Transport, Zubeir Ali Maulid, while a third bomb was defused in a bar. A number of Uamsho leaders were subsequently arrested in connection with the bombings.

It was reported in February 2004 that the Government was to prepare, for the first time in 10 years, a supplementary budget, in order to cover additional costs associated with the 2005 elections (including the introduction of identity cards and the establishment of a permanent register of voters), as well as to counteract the effects of drought. In August, amid growing tension in Zanzibar, the CUF petitioned the UN to dispatch observers to the 2005 elections. The CUF noted that a permanent voters' register had yet to be established, and that the reformed ZEC still lacked a director. Moreover, the Joint Presidential Supervisory Commission (JPSC), established to implement the 2001 *muafaka*, was being investigated following allegations of embezzlement. The JPSC was partly funded by international donors, who suspended their contributions following the allegations.

In February 2005 Lipumba declared his candidacy for the presidential election, at which he would represent the CUF. The CCM elected Jakaya Mrisho Kikwete as its presidential candidate at its national party congress in May. (Under the terms of the Constitution, Mkapa was prohibited from standing for re-election to the presidency.) There were sporadic outbreaks of civil unrest on Zanzibar during the voter registration period, where new legislation requiring voters to have lived in their constituencies for at least three years resulted in some 32,000 potential voters being disqualified. Hamad, the CUF's presidential candidate in Zanzibar, had initially been barred from registering (which would have disqualified him from standing in the election) but appealed successfully against the decision.

Following the death of a candidate, it was announced in October 2005 that the elections on the mainland would be delayed until December. The elections in Zanzibar proceeded as scheduled on 30 October 2005 at which Karume was elected President, securing 53.2% of the valid votes cast; Hamad received 46.1% and the four other candidates who contested the presidential election received negligible support. In the legislative elections the CCM won 31 seats in the House of Representatives, and the CUF 18. The ballot in the one remaining constituency was rerun on 14 December, although the result was not made available. The ZEC declared the poll to have been free and fair, while observers from the Commonwealth generally agreed, but recommended investigations into violence and irregularities in voting in Stone Town. There were reports of sporadic violence and numerous unsubstantiated claims of fraud. However, the extreme violence of previous elections was avoided. Karume was sworn in as President of Zanzibar on 2 November.

On mainland Tanzania the delayed presidential and legislative elections were held concurrently on 14 December 2005. Turn-out was officially recorded at 72% and voting proceeded without notable incident. Kikwete was elected President with 80.3% of the votes cast, while Lipumba received 11.7%. The CCM won 207 seats in the National Assembly, the CUF 18, Chadema five and the TLP and UDP one seat each. The CCM received a further 59 of the 75 seats reserved for women (of the remainder the CUF received 10 and Chadema six) and six of the 10 seats reserved for presidential nominees (four remained vacant). Of the five representatives sent from the Zanzibari legislature, three were from the CCM and two from the CUF. The Attorney-General was also a CCM member. Thus, the CCM's final strength in the National Assembly came to 276 seats and the CUF's 30; Chadema secured 11 seats and the TLP and UDP one each. At his inauguration, on 21 December, Kikwete stated that his main priority as President would be to resolve the tensions on Zanzibar, while he also pledged to continue Mkapa's free-market economic policies. On 4 January 2006 Kikwete unveiled his new Cabinet, appointing Edward Lowassa, hitherto the Minister of Water Livestock and Development, as Prime Minister. In late June Kikwete assumed the chairmanship of the CCM.

In mid-October 2006 Kikwete effected a reshuffle in which 10 cabinet ministers were reassigned to new portfolios. Among those affected by the reorganization was the Minister of Home Affairs, Capt. John Zefania Chiligati, who was replaced by Joseph James Mungai, hitherto the Minister of Agriculture, Food Security and Co-operatives; Chiligati became the new Minister of Labour, Employment and Youth Development, replacing Prof. Jumanne Abdallah Maghembe. Further changes to the Cabinet were implemented in early January 2007, following the death of Juma Akukweti, the Minister of State in the Prime Minister's Office, responsible for Parliamentary Affairs; Dr Batilda Burian was named as his replacement. It was also announced that Dr Asha Rose Migiro had been appointed as Deputy Secretary-General of the UN. Bernard Kamillius Membe assumed her vacated foreign affairs and international co-operation portfolio.

The issue of corruption featured prominently in Tanzanian political events in 2008. In January President Kikwete dismissed the Governor of the central bank, Daudi Balali, after an external audit revealed that some US $116m. worth of fraudulent payments had been made from the bank's External Payment Arrears account during the 2005/06 financial year. Balali was replaced by his hitherto deputy, Prof. Beno Ndulu, and died in the USA in May. Some 20 bank employees and a number of prominent businessmen were arrested in connection with the case. In early February 2008 Prime Minister Lowassa tendered his resignation in response to the findings of a parliamentary investigation into his administration's awarding of a power-generation contract in 2006; the Minister of Energy and Minerals and the Minister of East African Co-operation also resigned as a result of their alleged role. Lowassa denied any wrongdoing and no criminal charges were brought against him. President Kikwete named Mizengo Pinda, hitherto Minister of State in the Prime Minister's Office, as Lowassa's successor. Pinda subsequently named a new Cabinet, which included Membe as Minister of Foreign Affairs and International Co-operation and Mwinyi as Minister of Defence and National Service. In April Andrew Chenge resigned as Minister of Infrastructure Development, following reports that he was being investigated in relation to corruption inquiries against the UK-based arms manufacturer, BAE Systems. He was replaced the following month by Dr Shukuru Kawambwa, hitherto Minister of Communication, Science and Technology; that portfolio was assumed by Prof. Peter Msolla. Stephen Wassira was named as the new Minister of Agriculture, Food Security and Co-operatives.

Meanwhile, at a meeting of representatives from the ruling CCM and the CUF in Zanzibar in February 2008, a proposed power-sharing accord between the two parties was discussed. The CUF approved the arrangement in mid-March, while the CCM did not immediately issue a statement on the agreement; however, the CCM was due to hold a meeting later that month at which the proposal was expected to be adopted. Several issues were to be discussed at the meeting, including Zanzibar governance issues and the composition of the ZEC. However, despite earlier indications of acceptance of the deal, the CCM rejected the proposal, claiming that the issue of power-sharing should be decided at a referendum. In early April the CUF staged demonstrations in opposition to the proposed referendum in an attempt to exert pressure on the CCM to accept the power-sharing agreement.

In March 2008 78 workers were killed when heavy rainfall flooded mine shafts at the Mererani tanzanite mine, causing some to collapse. There had been similar disasters at Mererani in the past: in 1998 over 100 miners had died in flooding, and in June 2002 40 workers were killed when they became trapped inside tunnels and were poisoned by carbon monoxide gas.

In October 2008 a peaceful demonstration was held in Dar es Salaam by albino Tanzanians, in response to an alarming number of murders and mutilations committed against people with albinism over the previous year. President Kikwete announced that there would be a campaign to end these killings, which were carried out by people who believed that the body parts of albinos could be used for ritual medicine and witchcraft. In February 2009 it was reported that at least 40 murders had been committed since mid-2007, and that more than 90 people had been arrested on suspicion of killing albino people or trading in their body parts.

Tanzania's relations with Uganda and Kenya were strained throughout the 1970s, particularly after the dissolution of the East African Community (EAC, see p. 425) in 1977. Uganda briefly annexed the Kagera salient from Tanzania in November 1978. In early 1979 Tanzanian troops supported the Uganda National Liberation Front in the overthrow of President Idi Amin Dada. In June 2000 Tanzania called on Uganda to pay 98,500m. shillings to cover the cost of the operation. President Mkapa later stated that the amount was to be regarded as a military debt and not, as some claimed, as compensation for those killed during the war. The Tanzania–Kenya border, closed since 1977, was reopened in November 1983, following an agreement on the distribution of the EAC's assets and liabilities. In the following month Tanzania and Kenya agreed to establish full diplomatic relations. The two countries reached agreement on a trade treaty and on the establishment of a joint co-operation commission in 1986. Tanzania pledged its support for the Government of Yoweri Museveni, which took power in Uganda in January of that year, and in November Tanzania began to send military instructors to Uganda to organize the training of Ugandan government troops. In November 1994, meeting in Arusha, the Presidents of Tanzania, Kenya and Uganda established a commission for co-operation; in March 1996 they met again in Nairobi, Kenya, to inaugurate formally the Secretariat of the Permanent Tripartite Commission for East African Co-operation, which aimed to revive the EAC. A treaty for the re-establishment of the EAC, providing for the creation of a free trade area (with the eventual introduction of a single currency), for the development of infrastructure, tourism and agriculture within the Community, and for the establishment of a regional legislative assembly and court, was formally ratified by the Tanzanian, Kenyan and Ugandan Heads of State in November 1999. The new East African Council of Ministers held its first meeting in Tanzania in January 2001. Talks on integrating the economies of the three EAC members followed, and in March 2004 Mkapa, Museveni, and President Mwai Kibaki of Kenya signed a protocol on the creation of a customs union, eliminating most duties on goods within the EAC, which came into force on 1 January 2005.

In August 1993, following a protracted mediation effort by the Mwinyi Government, a peace agreement was signed in Arusha by the Rwandan authorities and the rebel Front patriotique rwandais. In April 1994, however, following the assassination of the Rwandan President, Juvénal Habyarimana, hundreds of thousands of Rwandans fled to Tanzania to escape the atrocities being perpetrated in their homeland. In May the Tanzanian authorities appealed for international emergency aid to assist in the care of the refugees, many of whom were sheltering in makeshift camps in the border region. In March 1995 Tanzania banned the admission of further refugees from both Rwanda and Burundi (where violent unrest had erupted in late 1994); some 800,000 Rwandan and Burundian refugees were reportedly sheltering in Tanzania in September 1995. The International Criminal Tribunal for Rwanda, authorized by the UN to charge and try Rwandan nationals accused of direct involvement in the genocide perpetrated in that country during 1994, was inaugurated in June 1995 in Arusha. After the Tutsi-led military coup, which took place in Burundi in July 1996 (following the failure of peace talks mediated by former President Nyerere), the Mkapa administration imposed economic sanctions against the new regime of President Pierre Buyoya, in co-operation with other regional governments. Relations between Tanzania and Burundi remained strained, owing both to the presence of Burundian rebels in northern Tanzania, which the Buyoya regime accused the Mkapa administration of supporting, and to the increasing numbers of Burundians seeking refuge in Tanzania throughout 1996 and 1997. Talks between the Buyoya Government and opposition politicians, once again mediated by Nyerere, were convened in Arusha in 1998 and early 1999. The regional economic sanctions that were imposed against Burundi in 1996 were suspended in January 1999. In July 2002, following a meeting between President Mkapa and the Burundian Vice-President, Domitien Ndayizeye, the two countries stated that they were to normalize their relations. Peace negotiations between the Burundian transitional Government and rebel groups took place in Dar es Salaam in August and October of that year.

In December 1996 some of the Rwandan refugees remaining in Tanzania were repatriated, following the threat of forcible repatriation by the Tanzanian Government; however, 200,000 refugees, unwilling to return to Rwanda, reportedly fled their camps. In March 1997 the Tanzanian Government appealed for further international assistance in coping with the remaining refugees (an estimated 200,000 Burundians and 250,000 Zaireans). In June 1997 it was agreed to repatriate some 100,000 refugees to the Democratic Republic of the Congo (DRC—formerly Zaire). At the end of December 2007 the office of the UN High Commissioner for Refugees (UNHCR) estimated that some 74,300 refugees from the DRC remained in Tanzania, while the number of Burundian refugees was believed to have increased to 459,400.

In February 2000 the Government announced that nine refugee camps in the Kigoma region of west Tanzania had become saturated. Instability in Burundi and the DRC had recently led to further heavy influxes of refugees from those countries. At that time the number of officially registered refugees in west Tanzania reportedly totalled 468,000, but it was claimed that an additional 200,000 unregistered refugees were also present in the region. Burundians accounted for 70% of all refugees, and refugees from the DRC for 29%. In August 2000 a peace accord was signed in Arusha between the Burundian Government and various rebel groups; however, the main rebel groups refused to sign the agreement. Although the agreement neither stopped the fighting in Burundi, nor allowed the refugees to return home, it nevertheless resulted in a serious decline in the level of aid donations (for example, the UNHCR allocation for refugee camps in Tanzania was reduced by 55%). In May 2001 UNHCR and the Governments of Tanzania and Burundi signed an agreement to establish a tripartite commission for the voluntary repatriation of Burundian refugees in Tanzania, of whom there were an estimated 800,000 at that time. In August 2003 Burundi and Tanzania agreed to open additional border crossings to facilitate the return of refugees. An estimated 494,200 Burundian refugees remained in Tanzania in December of that year; by April 2004 a further 34,000 had returned to Burundi, and UNHCR aimed to repatriate a further 122,000 by the end of the year, in view of progress in the peace process and the improved security situation. At the end of 2006 there remained 352,640 Burundian refugees in Tanzania. In February 2004 the remaining Rwandan refugees in Tanzanian camps were repatriated. However, it was reported that an estimated 20,000 Rwandans were illegally resident in Tanzania at this time. At the end of 2007 there were some 99,099 refugees from the DRC in Tanzania. Remaining refugee camps were to close in January 2008; however, by April, it was estimated that some 100,000 Burundian refugees and more than 90,000 from the DRC remained in Tanzania. In August Tanzania began to process citizenship applications of around 76,000 Burundian refugees, following the contribution of US $4.6m. from the European Commission Development Fund.

In January 2009 it was reported that the Tanzanian Government had pledged to send up to 800 soldiers to assist the joint UN-African Union peace-keeping mission in Darfur, UNAMID. Minister of Defence and National Service, Dr Hussein Ali Mwinyi, announced that the troops would be despatched on completion of their training, although he did not give an exact date for their deployment.

Government

Under the provisions of the 1977 Constitution, with subsequent amendments, legislative power is held by the unicameral National Assembly, whose members serve for a term of five years. There is constitutional provision for both directly elected members (chosen by universal suffrage) and nominated members (including five members elected by and from the Zanzibar House of Representatives). The number of directly elected members exceeds the number of nominated members. The Electoral Commission may review and, if necessary, increase the number of constituencies before every general election. Executive power lies with the President, elected by popular vote for five years. The President must be at least 40 years of age and his mandate is limited to a maximum of two five-year terms. The President appoints a Vice-President, to assist him in carrying out his functions, and presides over the Cabinet, which is composed of a Prime Minister and other ministers who are appointed from among the members of the National Assembly.

Zanzibar has its own administration for internal affairs, and the amended Zanzibar Constitution, which came into force in January 1985, provides for the President, elected by universal adult suffrage, to hold office for a maximum of two five-year terms, and for the House of Representatives, of 45–55 members, to be directly elected by universal adult suffrage. The President of Zanzibar appoints the Chief Minister, and the two co-operate in choosing the other members of the Supreme Revolutionary Council, which has a maximum of 20 members.

In May 1992 the United Republic's Constitution was amended to legalize a multi-party political system.

Defence

As assessed at November 2008, the total active armed forces numbered an estimated 27,000, of whom about 23,000 were in the army, 1,000 in the navy and 3,000 in the air force. There are also paramilitary forces including a 1,400-strong Police Field Force and an 80,000-strong reservist Citizens' Militia. The estimated defence budget was 200,000m. shillings in 2007.

Economic Affairs

In 2007, according to estimates by the World Bank, mainland Tanzania's gross national income (GNI), measured at average 2005–07 prices, was US $16,287m., equivalent to $400 per head (or $1,200 per head on an international purchasing-power parity basis). During 2000–07, it was estimated, the population of the country as a whole increased at an average annual rate of 2.6%, while gross domestic product (GDP) per head increased, in real terms, by an average of 4.1% per year. Overall GDP increased, in real terms, at an average annual rate of 6.7% in 2000–07; growth was 7.1% in 2007.

Agriculture (including hunting, forestry and fishing) contributed an estimated 21.4% of mainland Tanzania's non-monetary GDP in 2007 and employed some 74.6% of the engaged labour force (including Zanzibar) in 2006. The principal cash crops are coffee (which provided 5.5% of export revenues in 2007), cotton, cashew nuts and cloves (Zanzibar's most important export, cultivated on the island of Pemba—they provided 0.4% of export revenues in 2007). Tobacco farming has increased steadily in recent years, and, in 2007, Tanzania had become the third largest producer in Africa, according to official sources. In that year exports of tobacco accounted for 4.0% of export revenue. Other cash crops include tea, sisal, pyrethrum, coconuts, sugar and cardamom. Exports of cut flowers (grown in the vicinity of Kilimanjaro Airport and freighted to Europe) commenced in the mid-1990s. Seaweed production is an important activity in Zanzibar. Farmers have been encouraged to produce essential food crops, most importantly cassava and maize. Cattle-rearing is also significant. A large proportion of agricultural output is produced by subsistence farmers. The predominance of illegal logging activities remain a concern, and timber exports have consequently been subject to intermittent bans, owing to the threat of deforestation and lost revenues through official foreign sales. Tanzania's agricultural GDP increased at an average annual rate of 4.9% during 2000–06, according to the World Bank; agricultural GDP increased by 3.8% in 2006.

Industry (including mining, manufacturing, construction and power) contributed an estimated 26.1% of mainland Tanzania's non-monetary GDP in 2007; the sector employed 5.0% of the United Republic's working population in 2006. During 2000–06 industrial GDP increased by an average of 9.3% per year, according to the World Bank; growth in 2006 was 8.6%.

Mining provided an estimated 4.6% of mainland Tanzania's non-monetary GDP in 2007. The sector employed 0.6% of the working population on both Zanzibar and mainland Tanganyika in 2006. Gold, diamonds, other gemstones (including rubies and sapphires), salt, phosphates, coal, gypsum, tin, kaolin, limestone and graphite are mined, and it is planned to exploit reserves of natural gas. Other mineral deposits include nickel, silver, cobalt, copper, soda ash, iron ore and uranium. Petroleum was discovered on Tanzania's coastal belt in the 1960s, but was only recently being considered seriously by companies searching for sources of petroleum outside the Middle East. According to the IMF, the GDP of the mining sector increased by an average of 12.9% per year in 1990–99; it grew by 9.1% in 1999.

Manufacturing contributed an estimated 10.2% of mainland Tanzania's non-monetary GDP in 2007. The sector employed 3.1% of the working population on Zanzibar and mainland Tanganyika in 2006. The most important manufacturing activities are food-processing, textile production, cigarette production and brewing. Pulp and paper, fertilizers, cement, clothing, footwear, tyres, batteries, pharmaceuticals, paint, bricks and tiles and electrical goods are also produced, while other activities include oil-refining, metal-working, vehicle assembly and engineering. Tanzania's manufacturing GDP increased at an average annual rate of 7.7% in 2000–06, according to the World Bank; it grew by 7.1% in 2006.

Energy is derived principally from hydroelectric power, which supplied 58.6% of Tanzania's electricity in 2005; however, dependence upon this source meant that the electricity supply remains vulnerable to drought conditions. The contribution of petroleum to the national grid increased from 1.5% of total supply to in 2004 to 38.2% in 2005. In September 2008 a 70-MW gas-fired power plant on Songo Songo Island became operational. Another plant, with a projected capacity of 45 MW, was scheduled for completion in Tegeta during 2009. Natural gas had not previously been used to generate electricity in any significant quantity in Tanzania. Imports of petroleum and petroleum products accounted for 29.7% of the total value of imports in 2007.

The services sector contributed an estimated 52.5% of mainland Tanganyika's non-monetary GDP in 2007; the sector employed 20.3% of the United Republic's working population in 2006. Tourism is an important potential growth sector: tourism receipts were approximately US $950m. in 2006. According to the World Bank, the GDP of the services sector increased by an average of 6.3% per year in 2000–07. Growth in the sector was 7.2% in 2006.

In 2007 Tanzania recorded a visible trade deficit of US $2,634.1m., and there was a deficit of $1,855.8m. on the current account of the balance of payments. In 2007 the principal sources of imports were United Arab Emirates (providing 13.2% of total imports), South Africa, India and the People's Republic of China. The main markets for exports were Switzerland and Liechtenstein (which, together, purchased 20.5% of total exports), South Africa and Kenya. The principal exports in 2007 were gold, metalliferous ores and metal scrap, fish and fish products and coffee. The principal imports were petroleum and petroleum products, machinery and transport equipment, chemicals and related products, and food and live animals.

A budgetary deficit of 2,410,000m. shillings was envisaged for the financial year ending 30 June 2009. At the end of 2006 Tanzania's external debt totalled US $4,240m., of which $2,929m. was long-term public debt. In that year the cost of debt-servicing was equivalent to 3.4% of the value of exports of goods and services. On 14 January 2005 the British Chancellor of the Exchequer, Gordon Brown, signed a memorandum of understanding with the Government under which the United Kingdom would service 10% of the debt (both interest and capital repayments) owed by Tanzania to the World Bank, IMF and African Bank for Reconstruction. It was part of a wider move to ease the debt burden of heavily indebted poor countries, and it was hoped his decision would persuade other wealthy nations to act similarly. However, the United Kingdom would cease to service Tanzanian debt if the Tanzanian Government breached undertakings on good governance and democracy. The annual rate of inflation for Tanganyika averaged 4.5% in 2000–06; consumer prices there increased by 9.1% in 2006. The annual rate of inflation for Zanzibar averaged 6.4% in 2000–05; consumer prices on the islands increased by 9.8% in 2005.

Tanzania is a member of the African Development Bank (see p. 170) and of the Southern African Development Community (see p. 400). Tanzania is a founder member (with Kenya and Uganda) of the restored East African Community (EAC, see p. 425).

By the mid-2000s Tanzania had become one of Africa's better-performing economies: since 2000 real GDP growth has averaged over 6.0% per year, of which agriculture and services (mostly trade, tourism and hotels) each accounted for about one-third. Tourism has been particularly successful: between 1990 and 2006 the number of tourist arrivals more than quadrupled, from

TANZANIA

150,000 to 644,124, and receipts rose dramatically, reaching US $950m. in the latter year. However, this economic improvement was accompanied by only a modest reduction in poverty, and in terms of GNI per head, Tanzania remains one of the world's poorest countries. One of the country's greatest economic problems is the very high level of its external debt and there was concern about Tanzania's continued dependence on foreign aid. The new President, Jakaya Kikwete, stated that he would continue the free-market policies of his predecessor; thus, it seemed likely that Tanzania's strong economic performance and good relations with donors would continue. Concerns were nevertheless raised that increased government spending on education and training to counteract a lack of skills in the labour force could prove insufficient, and it was feared that HIV/AIDS could constrain productivity improvements. The economy grew by an estimated 7.5% in 2008, owing to recovery of agriculture (which had experienced severe drought in 2007) and expansion in the mining, transport, construction and tourism sectors. High international commodity prices during the first half of the year increased revenues from a number of Tanzania's key exports (notably cotton), although the authorities imposed a temporary ban on maize exports in early 2008, following concerns that domestic supply was under threat. The slowdown in global economic activity that ensued in the aftermath of the US banking crisis in September 2008 was likely to temper inward investment, tourist arrivals and export revenues. The horticulture sector was of particular concern, as lower international prices eroded the profitability of exporting cut flowers. Although, the IMF commended the Government on its economic programme in its fourth review of a policy support instrument approved in February 2007, and growth of 8% was forecast for both 2009 and 2010, there remained little discernible improvement in the standard of living for the majority of the population.

Education

In 2004/05 enrolment at pre-pimary level was 23% (23% of both boys and girls). Education at primary level is officially compulsory and is provided free of charge. In secondary schools a government-stipulated fee is paid: from January 1995 this was 8,000 shillings per year for day pupils at state-owned schools and 50,000–60,000 shillings per year for day pupils at private schools. Villages and districts are encouraged to construct their own schools with government assistance. Almost all primary schools are government-owned. Primary education begins at seven years of age and lasts for seven years. According to UNESCO estimates, in 2005/06 enrolment at primary level included 97.8% of pupils in the appropriate age-group (98.5% of boys; 97.2% of girls). Secondary education, beginning at the age of 14, lasts for a further six years, comprising a first cycle of four years and a second of two years. Secondary enrolment in 1999/2000 included only 6% of children in the appropriate age-group (males 6%; females 5%), according to UNESCO estimates. In November 2001 it was announced that approximately 7m. children were to be enrolled in primary schools, under the Government's five-year plan to reintroduce universal primary education by 2005. Enrolment at tertiary level included just 1% of those in the relevant age-group in 2004/05 (males 2%; females 1%). There are 10 universities, including one on Zanzibar. Tanzania also has a number of vocational training centres and technical colleges. The 2008/09 budget allocated 19.8% of total Government expenditure for education.

Public Holidays

2009: 1 January (New Year's Day), 12 January (Zanzibar Revolution Day), 5 February (Chama Cha Mapinduzi Day), 9 March* (Maulid, Birth of the Prophet), 10–13 April (Easter), 26 April (Union Day), 1 May (International Labour Day), 7 July (Saba Saba, Industry's Day), 8 August (Peasants' Day), 26 August (Sultan's Birthday)†, 20 September* (Id El Fitr, end of Ramadan), 29 October (Naming Day), 27 November* (Id El Haji, Feast of the Sacrifice), 9 December (Independence Day), 18 December* (Muharram, New Year), 25–26 December (Christmas).

2010: 1 January (New Year's Day), 12 January (Zanzibar Revolution Day), 5 February (Chama Cha Mapinduzi Day), 26 February* (Maulid, Birth of the Prophet), 2–5 April (Easter), 26 April (Union Day), 1 May (International Labour Day), 7 July (Saba Saba, Industry's Day), 8 August (Peasants' Day), 26 August (Sultan's Birthday)†, 10 September* (Id El Fitr, end of Ramadan), 29 October (Naming Day), 16 November* (Id El Haji, Feast of the Sacrifice), 7 December* (Muharram, New Year), 9 December (Independence Day), 25–26 December (Christmas).

* These holidays are dependent on the Islamic lunar calendar and may vary by one or two days from the dates given.

† Zanzibar only.

Weights and Measures

The metric system is in force.

Statistical Survey

Source (unless otherwise stated): Economic and Research Policy Dept, Bank of Tanzania, POB 2939, Dar es Salaam; tel. (22) 2110946; fax (22) 2113325; e-mail info@hq.bot-tz.org; internet www.bot-tz.org.

Area and Population

AREA, POPULATION AND DENSITY

Area (sq km)	945,087*
Population (census results)	
28 August 1988	23,126,310
25 August 2002	
Males	16,910,321
Females	17,658,911
Total	34,569,232
Population (UN estimates at mid-year)†	
2006	40,177,000
2007	41,276,000
2008	42,484,000
Density (per sq km) at mid-2008	45.0

* 364,900 sq miles. Of this total, Tanzania mainland is 942,626 sq km (363,950 sq miles), and Zanzibar 2,461 sq km (950 sq miles).

† Source: UN, *World Population Prospects: The 2008 Revision*.

ETHNIC GROUPS
(private households, census of 26 August 1967)

African	11,481,595	Others	839
Asian	75,015	Not stated	159,042
Arabs	29,775	**Total**	11,763,150
European	16,884		

REGIONS
(at census of 25 August 2002)

Arusha	1,292,973	Mwanza	2,942,148
Dar es Salaam	2,497,940	Pwani	889,154
Dodoma	1,698,996	North Pemba†	186,013
Iringa	1,495,333	North Unguja†	136,953
Kagera	2,033,888	Rukwa	1,141,743
Kigoma	1,679,109	Ruvuma	1,117,166
Kilimanjaro	1,381,149	Shinyanga	2,805,580
Lindi	791,306	Singida	1,090,758
Manyara*	603,691	South Pemba†	176,153
Mara	1,368,602	South Unguja†	94,504
Mbeya	2,070,046	Urban West†	391,002
Morogoro	1,759,809	Tabora	1,717,908
Mtwara	1,128,523	Tanga	1,642,015

* Before the 2002 census Manyara was included in the region of Arusha.

† Part of the autonomous territory of Zanzibar.

TANZANIA

PRINCIPAL TOWNS
(estimated population at mid-1988)

Dar es Salaam	1,360,850	Mbeya		152,844
Mwanza	223,013	Arusha		134,708
Dodoma	203,833	Morogoro		117,760
Tanga	187,455	Shinyanga		100,724
Zanzibar	157,634			

Source: UN, *Demographic Yearbook*.

Mid-2007 ('000, incl. suburbs, UN estimate): Dar es Salaam 2,930 (Source: UN, *World Urbanization Prospects: The 2007 Revision*).

BIRTHS AND DEATHS
(annual averages, UN estimates)

	1990–1995	1995–2000	2000–05
Birth rate (per 1,000)	43.3	41.9	41.8
Death rate (per 1,000)	15.0	14.7	13.3

Source: UN, *World Population Prospects: The 2008 Revision*.

Life expectancy (years at birth, WHO estimates): 50.3 (males 50.0; females 50.6) in 2006 (Source: WHO, *World Health Statistics*).

ECONOMICALLY ACTIVE POPULATION
('000 persons aged 15 years and over, labour force survey, 2006)

	Males	Females	Total
Agriculture, hunting and forestry	6,064.8	7,120.3	13,185.1
Fishing	184.6	25.0	209.6
Mining and quarrying	90.8	14.1	104.9
Manufacturing	332.9	232.2	565.1
Electricity, gas and water supply	13.5	3.5	17.0
Construction	204.8	6.7	211.5
Wholesale and retail trade and restaurants and hotels	907.7	665.0	1,572.7
Hotel and restaurants	98.5	279.0	377.5
Transport, storage and communications	245.0	13.1	258.1
Financial intermediation	11.3	6.2	17.5
Real estate, renting and business activities	69.0	13.0	82.0
Public administration and defence; compulsory social security	157.4	27.3	184.7
Education	126.9	98.7	225.6
Health and social work	46.1	59.1	105.2
Community, social and personal services	88.3	38.2	126.5
Households with employed persons	138.2	563.3	701.5
Total employed	**8,779.8**	**9,164.7**	**17,944.6**
Unemployed	274.3	602.7	877.0
Total labour force	**9,054.2**	**9,767.4**	**18,821.5**

Source: ILO.

Health and Welfare

KEY INDICATORS

Total fertility rate (children per woman, 2006)	5.3
Under-5 mortality rate (per 1,000 live births, 2006)	118
HIV/AIDS (% of persons aged 15–49, 2007)	6.2
Physicians (per 1,000 head, 2004)	0.02
Hospital beds (per 1,000 head, 2006)	1.1
Health expenditure (2006): US $ per head (PPP)	45
Health expenditure (2006): % of GDP	5.5
Health expenditure (2006): public (% of total)	59.2
Access to water (% of persons, 2006)	55
Access to sanitation (% of persons, 2006)	33
Human Development Index (2006): ranking	152
Human Development Index (2006): value	0.503

For sources and definitions, see explanatory note on p. vi.

Agriculture

PRINCIPAL CROPS
('000 metric tons)

	2005	2006	2007
Wheat	115.0	110.0	115.0*
Rice, paddy	957.0	1,206.0	1,240.0*
Maize	3,288.0	3,373.0	3,400.0*
Millet*	155.0	185.0	219.0
Sorghum†	890.0	900.0	900.0
Potatoes*	260.0	240.0	240.0
Sweet potatoes*	970.0	960.0	960.0
Cassava (Manioc)*	7,000	6,500	6,600
Sugar cane*	2,750.0	2,750.0	2,750.0
Beans, dry*	290.0	290.0	290.0
Cashew nuts, with shell	72.0	90.4	92.0*
Groundnuts, with shell	54.0†	54.0†	55.0*
Coconuts*	370.0	370.0	370.0
Oil palm fruit*	65.0	65.0	65.0
Seed cotton*	350.0	290.0	210.0
Tomatoes*	145.0	145.0	145.0
Onions, dry*	55.0	51.5	52.0
Bananas*	150.0	150.0	150.0
Plantains*	600.0	600.0	600.0
Guavas, mangoes and mangosteens*	200.0	220.0	220.0
Pineapples*	78.0	78.0	78.0
Coffee, green	54.0	34.3	52.0†
Tea	30.7	30.3	31.0*
Cloves*	10.2	9.8	9.9
Tobacco, unmanufactured	47.0	52.0	53.0*

* FAO estimate(s).
† Unofficial figure(s).

Aggregate production ('000 metric tons, may include official, semi-official or estimated data): Total cereals 5,422.3 in 2005, 5,793.3 in 2006, 5,894.5 in 2007; Total roots and tubers 8,238.0 in 2005, 7,708.2 in 2006, 7,808.5 in 2007; Total vegetables (incl. melons) 1,245.9 in 2005, 1,242.4 in 2006, 1,242.9 in 2007; Total fruits (excl. melons) 1,338.3 in 2005, 1,102.2 in 2006, 1,102.3 in 2007.

Source: FAO.

LIVESTOCK
('000 head, year ending September)

	2005	2006	2007
Asses*	182.0	n.a.	n.a.
Cattle	17,719.1	17,700.0*	18,000.0*
Pigs*	455.0	455.0	455.0
Sheep*	3,521.0	3,500.0	3,550.0
Goats*	12,550.0	12,550.0	12,550.0
Chickens*	30,000	30,000	30,000

* FAO estimate(s).
Source: FAO.

LIVESTOCK PRODUCTS
('000 metric tons, FAO estimates)

	2005	2006	2007
Cattle meat	246.3	247.0	247.0
Sheep meat	10.3	10.4	10.4
Goat meat	30.6	30.6	30.5
Pig meat	13.0	13.0	13.0
Chicken meat	45.6	45.7	45.7
Cows' milk	840.0	840.0	850.0
Goats' milk	104.0	104.0	105.0
Hen eggs	35.1	35.1	35.1
Honey	27.0	27.0	27.0

Source: FAO.

TANZANIA

Forestry

ROUNDWOOD REMOVALS
('000 cubic metres, excluding bark, FAO estimates)

	2005	2006	2007
Sawlogs, veneer logs and logs for sleepers	317	317	317
Pulpwood	153	153	153
Other industrial wood	1,844	1,844	1,844
Fuel wood	21,712	21,914	22,127
Total	24,026	24,228	24,441

Source: FAO.

SAWNWOOD PRODUCTION
('000 cubic metres, including railway sleepers, FAO estimates)

	1992	1993	1994
Coniferous (softwood)	26	21	13
Broadleaved (hardwood)	22	18	11
Total	48	39	24

1995–2007: Production assumed to be unchanged from 1994 (FAO estimates).

Source: FAO.

Fishing

('000 metric tons, live weight)

	2004	2005	2006
Capture	362.5	375.5	341.1
Tilapias	51.7	35.3	44.4
Nile perch	98.5	124.3	95.5
Other freshwater fishes	113.8	109.0	122.6
Dagaas	40.0	45.0	22.0
Sardinellas	15.0	15.5	3.1
Aquaculture*	0.0	0.0	0.0
Total catch	362.5	375.5	341.1

* FAO estimates.

Note: Figures exclude aquatic plants ('000 metric tons): 6.2 (capture 0.2, aquaculture 6.0) in 2004; 6.0 (capture 0.0, aquaculture 6.0) in 2005; 0.3 (capture 0.0, aquaculture 0.3) in 2006. Also excluded are aquatic mammals, recorded by number rather than by weight. The number of Risso's dolphins caught was: 1 in 2004; nil in 2005; nil in 2006. The number of Indo-Pacific hump-backed dolphins caught was: 6 in 2004; nil in 2005; nil in 2006. The number of Spinner dolphins caught was: 3 in 2004; nil in 2005; nil in 2006. The number of other spotted dolphins caught was: 1 in 2004; nil in 2005; nil in 2006. The number of Nile crocodiles caught was: 1,560 in 2004; 1,427 in 2005; 1,100 in 2006.

Source: FAO.

Mining

('000 metric tons, unless otherwise indicated)

	2005	2006	2007
Coal (bituminous)	75	18	27
Diamonds ('000 carats)*	220	272	283
Gold (refined, kilograms)	52,236	47,000†	40,193
Salt	135	35	35
Gypsum and anhydrite	64	33	3
Limestone, crushed	2,006	1,608	1,322
Pozzolanic materials	163	129	184
Sand	5,800†	7,577	8,400†

* Estimated at 85% gem-quality and 15% industrial-quality stones. Excluding smuggled artisanal production.
† Estimate.

Source: US Geological Survey.

Industry

SELECTED PRODUCTS
(Tanganyika, '000 metric tons unless otherwise indicated)

	2005	2006	2007*
Refined sugar	268.8	173.4	251.4
Cigarettes (million)	4.5	5.0	7.7
Beer (million litres)	216.6	274.1	311.2
Textiles (million sq metres)	110.5	124.7	143.0
Cement	1,366.0	1,431.9	1,513.0
Rolled steel	47.6	53.8	48.7
Iron sheets	25.1	30.3	36.5
Sisal ropes	5.9	5.9	9.1
Paints*	16.2	18.4	22.5

* Provisional.

Finance

CURRENCY AND EXCHANGE RATES

Monetary Units
100 cents = 1 Tanzanian shilling.

Sterling, Dollar and Euro Equivalents (31 December 2008)
£1 sterling = 1,866.42 Tanzanian shillings;
US $1 = 1,280.30 Tanzanian shillings;
€1 = 1,781.79 Tanzanian shillings;
10,000 Tanzanian shillings = £5.36 = $7.81 = €5.61.

Average Exchange Rate (Tanzanian shillings per US $)
2006 1,251.90
2007 1,245.04
2008 1,196.31

BUDGET
('000 million shillings, year ending 30 June)*

Revenue†	2006/07	2007/08‡	2008/09§
Tax revenue	2,529	3,359	4,485
Import duties	246	289	421
Value-added tax	832	1,042	1,256
Excises	520	661	932
Income tax	714	984	1,393
Other taxes	219	383	483
Non-tax revenue	210	275	243
Total	2,739	3,635	4,729

Expenditure	2006/07	2007/08‡	2008/09§
Recurrent expenditure	3,296	3,398	4,648
Wages	976	1,135	1,570
Interest	216	265	282
Goods, services and transfers	2,105	1,998	2,795
Development expenditure and net lending	1,179	1,819	2,491
Local	504	974	1,359
Foreign	675	845	1,132
Total	4,475	5,217	7,139

* Figures refer to the Tanzania Government, excluding the revenue and expenditure of the separate Zanzibar Government.
† Excluding grants received.
‡ Preliminary.
§ Programmed budget.

Source: IMF, *United Republic of Tanzania: Fourth Review Under the Policy Support Instrument - Staff Report; Press Release on the Executive Board Discussion; and Statement by the Executive Director for United Republic of Tanzania* (January 2009).

TANZANIA

INTERNATIONAL RESERVES
(excl. gold, US $ million at 31 December)

	2005	2006	2007
IMF special drawing rights	0.7	0.1	0.2
Reserve position in IMF	14.3	15.0	15.8
Foreign exchange	2,033.8	2,244.2	2,870.4
Total	**2,048.8**	**2,259.3**	**2,886.4**

Source: IMF, *International Financial Statistics*.

MONEY SUPPLY
('000 million shillings at 31 December)

	2006	2007	2008
Currency outside banks	1,033.99	1,162.51	1,438.64
Demand deposits at commercial banks	969.55	1,424.81	1,715.74
Total money	**2,003.54**	**2,587.32**	**3,154.38**

Source: IMF, *International Financial Statistics*.

COST OF LIVING
(Consumer Price Index)

Tanganyika
(base: 2000 = 100)

	2003	2004	2005
Food (incl. beverages)	112.0	118.6	125.6
Fuel, light and water	107.7	112.9	107.6
Clothing (incl. footwear)	106.6	109.0	113.2
Rent	111.2	113.8	122.4
All items (incl. others)	**109.8**	**114.5**	**119.4**

2006 (base: 2000 = 100): Food (incl. beverages) 140.5; All items 130.3.

Source: ILO.

Zanzibar
(base: 2001 = 100)

	2002	2003
Food (incl. beverages)	106.9	116.7
Fuel, light and water	100.0	106.0
Clothing (incl. footwear)	106.7	128.3
Rent	104.9	118.0
All items (incl. others)	**105.2**	**114.7**

2004: Food (incl. beverages) 128.6; All items (incl. others) 124.0.

2005: Food (incl. beverages) 143.7; All items (incl. others) 136.1.

Source: ILO.

NATIONAL ACCOUNTS
(Tanzania mainland, current prices)

National Income and Product
(million shillings, provisional)

	1992	1993	1994
Compensation of employees	88,230	119,119	148,194
Operating surplus	906,923	1,132,774	1,462,193
Domestic factor incomes	**995,153**	**1,251,894**	**1,610,387**
Consumption of fixed capital	35,802	36,697	49,542
Gross domestic product (GDP) at factor cost	**1,030,955**	**1,288,591**	**1,659,929**
Indirect taxes	109,442	183,389	260,039
Less Subsidies	9,801	67,611	97,398
GDP in purchasers' values	**1,130,596**	**1,404,369**	**1,822,570**
Factor income received from abroad	2,563	7,934	8,648
Less Factor income paid abroad	72,969	67,842	78,173
Gross national product (GNP)	**1,060,190**	**1,344,460**	**1,753,045**
Less Consumption of fixed capital	35,802	36,697	49,542
National income in market prices	**1,024,387**	**1,307,593**	**1,703,504**
Other current transfers from abroad (net)	282,813	291,673	308,518
National disposable income	**1,307,200**	**1,599,436**	**2,084,022**

Expenditure on the Gross Domestic Product
(US $ million)

	2005	2006	2007
Government final consumption expenditure	2,484.23	2,512.09	2,848.14
Private final consumption expenditure	9,373.40	9,680.62	9,358.10
Gross capital formation	3,544.14	3,960.21	4,794.92
Total domestic expenditure	**15,401.77**	**16,152.92**	**17,001.16**
Exports of goods and services	2,944.76	3,136.60	3,795.18
Less Imports of goods and services	4,204.55	5,111.40	6,292.83
GDP at market prices	**14,141.97**	**14,178.11**	**14,503.51**

Source: African Development Bank.

Gross Domestic Product by Economic Activity
('000 million shillings)

	2005	2006	2007*
Agriculture, forestry and hunting	2,589,263	2,737,686	3,154,263
Fishing	219,930	235,045	269,831
Mining and quarrying	457,431	576,363	742,932
Manufacturing	1,269,145	1,395,282	1,625,504
Electricity, gas and water	319,621	331,787	393,714
Construction	1,103,096	1,212,496	1,411,592
Trade and repairs	1,752,826	2,044,421	2,416,506
Hotels and restaurants	394,417	459,584	559,722
Transport and communications	983,507	1,144,071	1,373,976
Public administration	1,278,881	1,440,913	1,652,556
Financial and business services	1,245,921	1,420,200	1,663,834
Education	251,022	268,594	289,617
Health	233,032	275,726	327,658
Other services	107,542	117,284	129,482
Sub-total	**12,205,634**	**13,659,452**	**16,011,187**
Less Financial intermediation services indirectly measured	141,723	169,661	208,281
Total monetary GDP	**12,063,911**	**13,489,791**	**15,802,906**
Non-monetary GDP	2,533,855	2,788,434	3,186,941
Agriculture, hunting and forestry	1,821,215	1,970,870	2,258,995
Fishing	5,727	6,409	7,358
Water	20,909	20,937	27,166
Construction	146,555	187,113	230,149
Real estate and business services	539,449	603,105	663,273
Total GDP at factor cost	**14,597,766**	**16,278,225**	**18,989,847**
Net taxes	1,367,527	1,663,043	1,958,559
Total GDP at market prices	**15,965,293**	**17,941,268**	**20,948,403**

*Provisional figures.

BALANCE OF PAYMENTS
(US $ million)

	2005	2006	2007
Exports of goods f.o.b.	1,679.1	1,917.6	2,226.6
Imports of goods f.o.b.	−2,997.6	−3,864.1	−4,860.6
Trade balance	**−1,318.5**	**−1,946.5**	**−2,634.1**
Exports of services	1,269.2	1,528.1	1,714.0
Imports of services	−1,207.3	−1,249.4	−1,473.6
Balance on goods and services	**−1,256.6**	**−1,667.8**	**−2,393.6**
Other income received	80.9	53.7	80.8
Other income paid	−185.0	−146.8	−159.8
Balance on goods, services and income	**−1,360.7**	**−1,760.9**	**−2,472.7**
Current transfers received	563.9	655.2	689.4
Current transfers paid	−67.5	−65.9	−72.5
Current balance	**−864.3**	**−1,171.6**	**−1,855.8**
Capital account (net)	393.2	5,217.7	957.8
Direct investment from abroad	494.1	597.0	647.0
Portfolio investment liabilities	2.5	2.6	2.8
Other investment assets	−61.5	−175.0	114.8
Other investment liabilities	230.2	−4,376.8	266.4
Net errors and omissions	−417.7	367.2	282.6
Overall balance	**−223.6**	**461.1**	**415.6**

Source: IMF, *International Financial Statistics*.

TANZANIA

External Trade

PRINCIPAL COMMODITIES
(US $ million)

Imports c.i.f.	2005	2006	2007
Food and live animals	190.4	292.6	384.9
Cereals and cereal preparations	118.8	211.7	267.1
Wheat and meslin, unmilled	86.3	120.4	233.5
Mineral fuels, lubricants, etc.	722.9	1,086.4	1,768.6
Petroleum, petroleum products, etc.	716.9	1,079.9	1,758.0
Petroleum products, refined	704.7	1,062.9	1,740.6
Animal and vegetable oils, fats and waxes	99.6	228.5	274.3
Fixed vegetable oils and fats	90.1	216.6	247.5
Palm oil	87.1	208.1	227.2
Chemicals and related products	499.6	517.0	682.3
Medicinal and pharmaceutical products	112.0	92.9	172.7
Plastics in primary forms	131.1	151.5	191.6
Basic manufactures	503.5	705.4	805.3
Iron and steel	162.0	209.2	245.5
Other metal manufactures	97.8	116.8	157.9
Machinery and transport equipment	987.1	1,427.9	1,627.3
Power generating machinery and equipment	49.0	128.1	218.2
Rotating electric plant, and parts thereof	18.7	97.7	135.2
Machinery specialized for particular industries	203.8	272.5	220.4
General industrial machinery, equipment and parts	119.8	158.1	169.6
Telecommunications, sound recording and reproducing equipment	120.0	189.0	251.7
Telecommunication equipment, parts and accessories	110.5	164.2	235.7
Other electrical machinery, apparatus and appliances, and parts	87.6	128.8	126.6
Road vehicles	315.8	457.1	502.7
Passenger motor vehicles, excl. buses	118.7	166.4	175.2
Lorries and special purpose motor vehicles	98.8	143.7	158.1
Vehicles for the transportation of goods or materials	86.8	130.2	147.1
Miscellaneous manufactured articles	177.3	199.1	236.4
Total (incl. others)	3,246.8	4,526.7	5,919.0

Exports f.o.b.	2005	2006	2007
Food and live animals	440.2	475.9	570.4
Fish, crustaceans, molluscs and preparations thereof	151.1	189.5	165.6
Fish, fresh, chilled or frozen	132.3	175.3	151.3
Fish fillets, fresh or chilled	79.7	129.8	82.9
Fish fillets, frozen	49.6	43.3	66.9
Cereals and cereal preparations	51.8	53.7	90.9
Vegetables and fruit	87.6	77.8	93.6
Fruit and nuts, fresh, dried	39.4	26.5	60.1
Cashew nuts, fresh or dried	45.8	49.9	27.4
Coffee, tea, cocoa, spices, and manufactures thereof	127.5	129.3	181.3
Coffee and coffee substitutes	83.6	77.1	117.6
Coffee, not roasted; coffee husks and skins	79.3	73.9	113.1
Spices	9.6	8.9	9.3
Cloves	8.5	8.0	8.6
Beverages and tobacco	141.1	110.4	101.8
Tobacco and tobacco manufactures	136.7	105.0	96.7
Tobacco, wholly or partly stripped	103.6	96.5	86.3
Crude materials, inedible, except fuels	289.7	334.5	435.5

Exports f.o.b.—continued	2005	2006	2007
Textile fibres (not wool tops) and their wastes (not in yarn)	121.3	81.3	96.2
Raw cotton, excl. linters, not carded or combed	68.2	46.5	40.4
Metalliferous ores and metal scrap	103.8	184.1	211.9
Ores and concentrates of precious metals	102.1	178.0	201.0
Basic manufactures	120.8	125.1	220.4
Non-metallic mineral manufactures	44.3	41.9	78.8
Pearl, precious and semi-precious stones, unworked or worked	33.2	34.4	61.5
Diamonds cut or otherwise worked, but not mounted or set	6.0	21.4	16.7
Gold, non-monetary, unwrought or semi-manufactured	551.3	610.7	553.8
Total (incl. others)	1,671.8	1,864.7	2,139.3

Source: UN, *International Trade Statistics Yearbook*.

PRINCIPAL TRADING PARTNERS
(US $ million)

Imports c.i.f.	2005	2006	2007
Australia	47.2	33.5	26.8
Bahrain	509.2	409.9	171.9
Belgium	48.8	77.0	109.9
Canada	36.4	37.4	35.9
China, People's Repub.	222.7	307.5	415.9
France	72.4	56.9	131.9
Germany	89.5	152.9	156.2
India	190.5	239.7	512.7
Indonesia	91.4	141.3	129.3
Italy	41.5	92.2	83.2
Japan	208.5	260.1	262.8
Kenya	174.4	217.8	103.6
Korea, Repub.	34.6	66.9	75.9
Malaysia	21.1	94.9	148.0
Netherlands	68.9	86.0	85.6
Saudi Arabia	43.9	246.4	220.9
South Africa	401.4	571.7	595.6
Sweden	73.0	53.2	104.9
Switzerland-Liechtenstein	26.2	67.5	254.6
Thailand	25.9	37.1	59.4
United Arab Emirates	205.4	497.8	782.5
United Kingdom	124.4	158.9	173.7
USA	103.2	125.1	189.0
Total (incl. others)	3,246.8	4,526.7	5,919.0

Exports f.o.b.	2005	2006	2007
Belgium	36.8	29.1	39.6
Congo, Democratic Repub.	62.3	58.4	83.8
France	8.3	11.9	12.6
Germany	77.9	112.8	100.7
Hong Kong	10.2	7.6	14.5
India	78.1	63.3	79.0
Italy	40.4	35.1	57.1
Japan	72.3	82.4	64.2
Kenya	93.5	103.8	123.4
Malawi	11.9	20.0	22.7
Netherlands	100.0	104.1	104.3
Saudi Arabia	35.5	49.3	97.6
Singapore	20.1	5.5	4.8
South Africa	294.8	274.6	204.0
Switzerland-Liechtenstein	145.9	359.8	438.0
Uganda	48.9	44.2	46.1
United Arab Emirates	35.5	49.3	97.6
United Kingdom	132.1	70.1	29.5
USA	18.2	22.5	62.5
Zambia	22.7	30.7	30.0
Total (incl. others)	1,671.8	1,864.7	2,139.3

Source: UN, *International Trade Statistics Yearbook*.

TANZANIA

Transport

RAILWAYS

	2004	2005	2006
Passengers ('000)	464	514	594
Freight ('000 metric tons)	1,002	1,169	775

Source: National Bureau of Statistics, *Tanzania in Figures 2006*.

ROAD TRAFFIC
(estimates, '000 motor vehicles in use)

	1994	1995	1996
Passenger cars	28.0	26.0	23.8
Buses and coaches	78.0	81.0	86.0
Lorries and vans	27.2	27.7	29.7
Road tractors	6.7	6.7	6.6

Source: IRF, *World Road Statistics*.

SHIPPING
Merchant fleet
(registered at 31 December)

	2005	2006	2007
Number of vessels	50	52	53
Displacement ('000 grt)	36.8	37.5	38.1

Source: Lloyd's Register-Fairplay, *World Fleet Statistics*.

International sea-borne traffic

	2004	2005	2006
Vessels docked	2,898	3,895	4,154
Cargo ('000 metric tons)	4,179	4,307	6,320
Passengers ('000)	525	1,072	664

Source: National Bureau of Statistics, *Tanzania in Figures 2006*.

CIVIL AVIATION
(traffic on scheduled services)

	2002	2003	2004
Kilometres flown (million)	3	4	5
Passengers carried ('000)	134	150	243
Passenger-km (million)	136	151	216
Total ton-km (million)	14	16	22

Source: UN, *Statistical Yearbook*.

Tourism

FOREIGN VISITOR ARRIVALS
(by country of origin)

	2004	2005	2006
Burundi	3,157	5,767	10,631
Canada	10,613	10,922	12,536
Congo, Democratic Repub.	8,030	9,479	9,792
France	21,849	23,547	19,643
Germany	19,222	18,170	19,651
India	14,804	17,598	13,020
Italy	44,045	49,829	50,287
Kenya	124,967	112,766	127,016
Malawi	16,868	19,999	17,247
Netherlands	14,594	15,805	262
Rwanda	6,089	17,037	13,056
South Africa	25,849	28,922	28,961
Spain	11,168	11,709	11,575
Uganda	24,253	25,373	35,521
United Kingdom	59,547	52,442	69,160
USA	40,248	47,621	55,687
Zambia	25,405	29,120	31,132
Total (incl. others)	582,807	612,754	644,124

Tourism receipts (US $ million, incl. passenger transport): 762 in 2004; 835 in 2005; 950 in 2006.

Source: World Tourism Organization.

Communications Media

	2005	2006	2007
Telephones ('000 main lines in use)	154.4	157.3	236.5
Mobile cellular telephones ('000 subscribers)	3,389.8	5,766.6	8,252.3
Personal computers ('000 in use)	278	n.a.	n.a.
Internet users ('000)	384	390	400

Source: International Telecommunication Union.

Television receivers ('000 in use, 2000): 700.

Radio receivers ('000 in use, estimate, 1997): 8,800 (Source: UNESCO, *Statistical Yearbook*).

Daily newspapers (2004): 14; average circulation ('000 copies, estimate) 60 (Source: UNESCO Institute for Statistics).

Education

(2006)

	Institutions	Teachers	Students
Primary (state)	14,440	148,607	1,993,000
Primary (private)	260	3,275	20,622
Secondary (state)	1,690	15,911	268,877
Secondary (private)	599	7,341	94,289
Higher (state)*	64	n.a.	50,021
Higher (private)†	39	n.a.	5,272

* Comprising 31 teacher training colleges, 5 technical colleges, 5 full universities, 4 constituent universities and 19 other higher institutions.
† Comprising 22 teacher training colleges and 17 universities.

Source: National Bureau for Statistics, *Tanzania in Figures 2006*.

Adult literacy rate (UNESCO estimates): 72.3% (males 79.0%; females 65.9%) in 2007 (Source: UNESCO Institute for Statistics).

Directory

The Constitution

The United Republic of Tanzania was established on 26 April 1964, when Tanganyika and Zanzibar, hitherto separate independent countries, merged. An interim Constitution of 1965 was replaced, on 25 April 1977, by a permanent Constitution for the United Republic. In October 1979 the Revolutionary Council of Zanzibar adopted a separate Constitution, governing Zanzibar's internal administration, with provisions for a popularly elected President and a legislative House of Representatives elected by delegates of the then ruling party. A new Constitution for Zanzibar, which came into force in January 1985, provided for direct elections to the Zanzibar House of Representatives. The provisions below relate to the 1977 Constitution of the United Republic, as subsequently amended.

GOVERNMENT

Legislative power is exercised by the Parliament of the United Republic, which is vested by the Constitution with complete sovereign power, and of which the present National Assembly is the legislative house. The Assembly also enacts all legislation concerning the mainland. Internal matters in Zanzibar are the exclusive jurisdiction of the Zanzibar executive, the Supreme Revolutionary Council of Zanzibar, and the Zanzibar legislature, the House of Representatives.

National Assembly

The National Assembly comprises both directly elected members (chosen by universal adult suffrage) and nominated members (including five members elected from the Zanzibar House of Representatives). The number of directly elected members exceeds the number of nominated members. The Electoral Commission may review and, if necessary, increase the number of electoral constituencies before every general election. The National Assembly has a term of five years.

President

The President is the Head of State, Head of the Government and Commander-in-Chief of the Armed Forces. The President has no power to legislate without recourse to Parliament. The assent of the President is required before any bill passed by the National Assembly becomes law. Should the President withhold his assent and the bill be repassed by the National Assembly by a two-thirds' majority, the President is required by law to give his assent within 21 days unless, before that time, he has dissolved the National Assembly, in which case he must stand for re-election.

The President appoints a Vice-President to assist him in carrying out his functions. The President presides over the Cabinet, which comprises a Prime Minister and other ministers who are appointed from among the members of the National Assembly.

JUDICIARY

The independence of the judges is secured by provisions which prevent their removal, except on account of misbehaviour or incapacity when they may be dismissed at the discretion of the President. The Constitution also makes provision for a Permanent Commission of Enquiry, which has wide powers to investigate any abuses of authority.

CONSTITUTIONAL AMENDMENTS

The Constitution can be amended by an act of the Parliament of the United Republic, when the proposed amendment is supported by the votes of not fewer than two-thirds of all the members of the Assembly.

The Government

HEAD OF STATE

President: Lt-Col (Retd) JAKAYA MRISHO KIKWETE (took office 21 December 2005).

Vice-President: Dr ALI MOHAMMED SHEIN.

CABINET
(April 2009)

President and Commander-in-Chief of the Armed Forces: Lt-Col (Retd) JAKAYA MRISHO KIKWETE.

Prime Minister: MIZENGO KAYANZA PETER PINDA.

Minister of Foreign Affairs and International Co-operation: BERNARD KAMILLIUS MEMBE.

Minister of East African Co-operation: Dr DIODORUS BUBERWA KAMALA.

Minister of Finance and Economic Affairs: MUSTAFA MKURO.

Minister of Industry, Trade and Marketing: Dr MARY MICHAELL NAGU.

Minister of Agriculture, Food Security and Co-operatives: STEPHEN MASATU WASSIRA.

Minister of Natural Resources and Tourism: SHAMSA MWANGUNGA.

Minister of Water and Irrigation: Prof. MARK JAMES MWANDOSYA.

Minister of Energy and Minerals: WILLIAM NGELEJE.

Minister of Infrastructure Development: Dr SHUKURU JUMANNE KAWAMBWA.

Minister of Communication, Science and Technology: Prof. PETER MAHAMOUD MSOLLA.

Minister of Health and Social Welfare: Prof. DAVID HOMELI MWAKYUSA.

Minister of Education and Vocational Training: Prof. JUMANNE ABDALLAH MAGHEMBE.

Minister of Labour, Employment and Youth Development: Prof. JUMA ATHUMANI KAPUYA.

Minister of Land, Housing and Human Settlements Development: Capt. JOHN ZEFANIA CHILIGATI.

Minister of Information, Culture and Sports: GEORGE MKUCHIKA.

Minister of Defence and National Service: Dr HUSSEIN ALI MWINYI.

Minister of Home Affairs: LAWRENCE KEGO MASHA.

Minister of Justice and Constitutional Affairs: MATHIAS MEINRAD CHIKAWE.

Minister of Community Development, Gender and Children: MARGARETH SIMWANZA SITTA.

Minister of Livestock and Fisheries Development: JOHN POMBE JOSEPH MAGUFULI.

Ministers of State in the President's Office: HAWA ABDULRAHMAN GHASIA (Public Service Management), SOFIA MNYAMBI SIMBA (Good Governance).

Ministers of State in the Vice-President's Office: MUHAMMED SEIF KHATIB (Union Affairs), Dr BATILDA SALHA BURIAN (Environment).

Ministers of State in the Prime Minister's Office: CELINA OMPESHI KOMBANI (Regional Administration and Local Governments), PHILIP SANG'KA MARMO (Parliamentary Affairs).

MINISTRIES

Office of the President: State House, POB 9120, Dar es Salaam; tel. (22) 2116538; fax (22) 2113425; internet www.tanzania.go.tz/poffice.htm.

Office of the Vice-President: POB 5380, Dar es Salaam; tel. (22) 2113857; fax (22) 2113856; e-mail makamu@twiga.com; internet www.tanzania.go.tz/vpoffice.htm.

Office of the Prime Minister: POB 980, Dodoma; tel. (26) 233201; internet www.tanzania.go.tz/pmoffice.htm.

Ministry of Agriculture, Food Security and Co-operatives: Kilimo I Building, Temeke, POB 9192, Dar es Salaam; tel. (22) 2862480; fax (22) 2865951; e-mail psk@kilimo.go.tz; internet www.kilimo.go.tz.

Ministry of Communication, Science and Technology: POB 2645, Dar es Salaam; tel. (22) 2111254; fax (22) 2112533; e-mail mst@mst.go.tz; internet www.mst.go.tz.

Ministry of Community Development, Gender and Children: POB 3448, Dar es Salaam; tel. (22) 2111459; fax (22) 2110933; e-mail info_wic@uccmail.co.tz; internet www.mcdcg.go.tz.

Ministry of Defence and National Service: POB 9544, Dar es Salaam; tel. (22) 2117153; fax (22) 2116719.

Ministry of East African Co-operation: POB 9280, Dar es Salaam; tel. (22) 2126827; fax (22) 2126651; internet www.meac.go.tz.

Ministry of Education and Vocational Training: POB 9121, Dar es Salaam; tel. (22) 2120403; fax (22) 2113271; e-mail psmoevt@moe.go.tz; internet www.moe.go.tz.

Ministry of Energy and Minerals: POB 2000, Dar es Salaam; tel. (22) 2112791; fax (22) 2121606; e-mail madini@africaonline.co.tz; internet www.mem.go.tz.

TANZANIA   *Directory*

Ministry of Finance and Economic Affairs: POB 9111, Dar es Salaam; tel. (22) 2111174; fax (22) 2110326; internet www.mof.go.tz.
Ministry of Foreign Affairs and International Co-operation: Kivukoni Front, POB 9000, Dar es Salaam; tel. (22) 2111906; fax (22) 2116600; e-mail nje@foreign.go.tz; internet www.mfaic.go.tz.
Ministry of Health and Social Welfare: 36/37 Samore Ave, POB 9083, Dar es Salaam; tel. (22) 2120261; fax (22) 2139951; e-mail moh@moh.go.tz; internet www.moh.gov.tz.
Ministry of Home Affairs: POB 9223, Dar es Salaam; tel. (22) 2119050; fax (22) 2119050; e-mail permsec@moha.go.tz; internet www.moha.go.tz.
Ministry of Industry, Trade and Marketing: POB 9503, Dar es Salaam; tel. (22) 2181397; fax (22) 2182481; e-mail tnwinfo@plancom.go.tz; internet www.mitm.go.tz.
Ministry of Information, Culture and Sports: Dar es Salaam; internet www.hum.go.tz.
Ministry of Infrastructure Development: Pamba Rd, Tancot House, POB 9144, Dar es Salaam; tel. (22) 2137650; fax (22) 2112751; e-mail permsec@infrastructure.go.tz; internet www.infrastructure.go.tz.
Ministry of Justice and Constitutional Affairs: POB 9050, Dar es Salaam; tel. (22) 2117099.
Ministry of Labour, Employment and Youth Development: POB 1422, Dar es Salaam; tel. (22) 2120419; fax (22) 2113082.
Ministry of Lands, Housing and Human Settlements Development: POB 9132, Dar es Salaam; tel. (22) 2121241; fax (22) 2113224; internet www.ardhi.go.tz.
Ministry of Livestock and Fisheries Development: Dar es Salaam; internet www.mifugo.go.tz.
Ministry of Natural Resources and Tourism: POB 9372, Dar es Salaam; tel. (22) 2111061; fax (22) 2110600; e-mail nature.tourism@mnrt.org; internet www.mnrt.org.
Ministry of Water and Irrigation: POB 9153, Dar es Salaam; tel. (22) 2117153; fax (22) 37138; e-mail dppmaj@raha.com; internet www.maji.go.tz.

SUPREME REVOLUTIONARY COUNCIL OF ZANZIBAR
(April 2009)

President and Chairman and Minister of Finance and Economic Planning: AMANI ABEID KARUME.
Chief Minister: SHAMSI VUAI NAHODHA.
Deputy Chief Minister and Minister of Information, Culture and Sport: ALI JUMA SHAMHUNA.
Minister of Communication and Transport: MACHANO OTHMAN SAIDI.
Minister of Education and Vocational Training: HAROUN ALI SULEIMAN.
Minister of Employment, Youth, Women and Children: ASHA ABDALLAH JUMA.
Minister of Agriculture, Livestock and Co-operatives: BURHANI SAADAT HAJI.
Minister of Water, Works, Energy and Land: MANSOUR YUSSUF HIMID.
Minister of Tourism, Trade and Investment: SAMIA SULUHU HASSAN.
Ministers of State in the President's Office: MWINYIAHJI MAKAME MWADINI (Finance and Economic Affairs), SULEIMAN OTHMAN NYANGA (Regional Administration, Local Government and Special Forces), RAMADHAN ABDALLAH SHAABAN (Constitutional Affairs and Good Governance).
Minister of State in the Chief Minister's Office: HAMZA HASAN JUMA.

MINISTRIES

Office of the President: POB 776, Zanzibar; tel. (24) 2230814; fax (24) 2233722.
Office of the Chief Minister: POB 239, Zanzibar; tel. (24) 2311126; fax (24) 233788.
Ministry of Agriculture, Livestock and Co-operatives: Zanzibar; tel. (24) 232662.
Ministry of Communication and Transport: POB 266, Zanzibar; tel. (24) 2232841.
Ministry of Education and Vocational Training: POB 394, Zanzibar; tel. (24) 232827.
Ministry of Employment, Youth, Women and Children: POB 884, Zanzibar; tel. (24) 30808.
Ministry of Finance and Economic Planning: POB 1154, Zanzibar; tel. (24) 231169.
Ministry of Information, Culture and Sport: POB 236, Zanzibar; tel. (24) 232640.
Ministry of Tourism, Trade and Investment: POB 772, Zanzibar; tel. (24) 232321.
Ministry of Water, Works, Energy and Land: Zanzibar.

President and Legislature

PRESIDENT
Election, 14 December 2005

Candidate	Votes	% of votes
Lt-Col (Retd) Jakaya Mrisho Kikwete (CCM)	9,123,952	80.28
Prof. Ibrahim Haruna Lipumba (CUF)	1,327,125	11.68
Freeman Mbowe (Chadema)	668,756	5.88
Augustine Lyatonga Mrema (TLP)	84,901	0.75
Sengondo Mvungi (NCCR—Mageuzi)	55,819	0.49
Others	104,924	0.92
Total	**11,365,477**	**100.00**

NATIONAL ASSEMBLY
Speaker: SAMUEL SITTA.
Election, 14 December 2005

Party	Seats*
Chama Cha Mapinduzi (CCM)	266
Civic United Front (CUF)	28
Chama Cha Demokrasia na Maendeleo (Chadema)	11
Tanzania Labour Party (TLP)	1
United Democratic Party (UDP)	1
Total	**307**

*In addition to the 232 elective seats, 75 seats are reserved for women (included in the figures above). Furthermore, 10 seats are reserved for presidential nominees and five for members of the Zanzibar House of Representatives; the Attorney-General is also an ex officio member of the National Assembly.

ZANZIBAR PRESIDENT
Election, 30 October 2005

Candidate	Votes	% of votes
Amani Abeid Karume	239,832	53.18
Seif Sharif Hamad	207,733	46.06
Haji Mussa Kitole	2,110	0.47
Others	1,293	0.29
Total	**450,968**	**100.00**

ZANZIBAR HOUSE OF REPRESENTATIVES
Speaker: PANDU AMEIR KIFICHO.
Election, 30 October 2005

Party	Seats*
Chama Cha Mapinduzi (CCM)	31
Civic United Front (CUF)	18
Total	**49**

*In addition to the 50 elective seats, five seats are reserved for regional commissioners, 10 for presidential nominees, 15 for women (on a party basis in proportion to the number of elective seats gained) and one for the Attorney-General. Results in one constituency were invalidated; a fresh ballot was held on 14 December 2005 in which the CCM won 53% of the votes cast.

Election Commission

National Election Commission of Tanzania (NEC): Posta House, POB 10923, Ghana/Ohio St, 6th and 7th Floor, Dar es Salaam; tel. (22) 2114963; fax (22) 2116740; e-mail info@nec.go.tz; internet www.nec.go.tz; f. 1993; Chair. LEWIS M. MAKAME; Dir of Elections R. R. KIRAVU.

TANZANIA *Directory*

Political Organizations

Bismillah Party: Pemba; seeks a referendum on the terms of the 1964 union of Zanzibar with mainland Tanzania.

Chama Cha Amani na Demokrasia Tanzania (CHADETA): House No. 41, Sadan St Ilala, POB 15809, Dar es Salaam; tel. (744) 889453; granted temporary registration in 2003.

Chama Cha Demokrasia na Maendeleo (Chadema—Party for Democracy and Progress): House No. 170 Ufipa St, POB 31191, Dar es Salaam; tel. (22) 2668866; e-mail info@chadema.net; internet www.chadema.net; supports democracy and social development; Chair. Freeman Mbowe; Sec.-Gen. Wilibrod Slaa.

Chama Cha Haki na Usitawi (Chausta—Party for Justice and Development): Drive Inn Oysterbay, POB 5450, Dar es Salaam; tel. (741) 247266; f. 1998; officially regd 2001; Chair. James Mapalala.

Chama Cha Mapinduzi (CCM) (Revolutionary Party of Tanzania): Kuu St, POB 50, Dodoma; tel. 2180575; e-mail katibumkuu@ccmtz.org; internet www.ccmtz.org; f. 1977 by merger of the mainland-based Tanganyika African National Union (TANU) with the Afro-Shirazi Party, which operated on Zanzibar and Pemba; sole legal party 1977–92; socialist orientation; Chair. Jakaya Mrisho Kikwete; Vice-Chair. Pius Msekwa, Amani A. Karume; Sec.-Gen. Yusuf Makamba.

Civic United Front (CUF): Mtendeni St at Malindi, POB 3637, Zanzibar; tel. (24) 2237446; fax (24) 2237445; e-mail headquarters@cuftz.org; internet www.cuftz.org; f. 1992 by merger of Zanzibar opposition party Kamahuru and the mainland-based Chama Cha Wananchi; commands substantial support in Zanzibar and Pemba, for which it demands increased autonomy; Chair. Prof. Ibrahim Haruna Lipumba; Sec.-Gen. Seif Sharif Hamad.

Democratic Party (DP): Ilala Mchikichini, POB 63102, Dar es Salaam; tel. (713) 430516; e-mail dp_watanganyika@yahoo.com; f. 2002; Chair. Rev. Christopher Mtikila.

Demokrasia Makini (MAKINI): Kibo Ubungo, POB 75636, Dar es Salaam; tel. (744) 295670; officially regd 2001.

Forum for Restoration of Democracy (FORD): House No. 6, Rufiji St, Kariakoo, POB 15587, Dar es Salaam; tel. (741) 292271; f. 2002.

Movement for Democratic Alternative (MDA): Zanzibar; seeks to review the terms of the 1964 union of Zanzibar with mainland Tanzania; supports democratic institutions and opposes detention without trial and press censorship.

National Convention for Construction and Reform (NCCR—Mageuzi): Plot No. 2 Kilosa St, Ilala, POB 72444, Dar es Salaam; tel. (744) 318812; f. 1992; Chair. Dr Kassim Magutu; Sec.-Gen. Mabere Marando.

National League for Democracy (NLD): Plot No. 7310 Sinza, POB 352, Dar es Salaam; f. 1993; Chair. Emmanuel J. E. Makaidi; Sec.-Gen. Michael E. A. Mhina.

National Reconstruction Alliance (NRA): Bububu St, Tandika Kilimahewa, POB 45197, Dar es Salaam; tel. (744) 496724; f. 1993; Chair. Ulotu Abubakar Ulotu; Sec.-Gen. Salim R. Matinga.

Popular National Party (PONA): Plot 104, Songea St, Ilala, POB 21561, Dar es Salaam; Chair. Wilfrem R. Mwakitwange; Sec.-Gen. Nicolaus Mchaina.

Tanzania Democratic Alliance Party (TADEA): Buguruni Malapa, POB 482, Dar es Salaam; tel. (22) 2865244; f. 1993; Pres. John D. Lifa-Chipaka; Sec.-Gen. Charles Dotto Lubala.

Progressive Party of Tanzania (PPT-Maendeleo): Wibu St, Kinondoni, POB 31932, Dar es Salaam; tel. (744) 300302; f. 2003; Leader Peter Mziray; Sec.-Gen. Ahmed Hamad.

Tanzania Labour Party (TLP): Argentina Manzese, POB 7273, Dar es Salaam; tel. (22) 2443237; f. 1993; Chair. Augustine Mrema.

Tanzania People's Party (TPP): Mbezi Juu, Kawe, POB 60847, Dar es Salaam; removed from register of political parties 2002; Chair. Alec H. Che-Mponda; Sec.-Gen. Gravel Limo.

United Democratic Party (UDP): Mbezi Juu, SLP 5918, Dar es Salaam; tel. (748) 613723; f. 1994; Leader John Momose Cheyo.

United People's Democratic Party (UPDP): Mtaa wa Shariff Muss, POB 3121, Zanzibar; tel. (744) 753075; f. 1993; Chair. Khalfani Ali Abdullah; Sec.-Gen. Ahmed M. Rashid.

Union for Multi-Party Democracy (UMD): House No. 84, Plot No. 630, Block No. 5, Kagera St. Magomeni, POB 2985, Dar es Salaam; tel. (744) 478153; f. 1993; Chair. Abdallah Fundikira.

Diplomatic Representation

EMBASSIES AND HIGH COMMISSIONS IN TANZANIA

Algeria: 34 Ali Hassan Mwinyi Rd, POB 2963, Dar es Salaam; tel. (22) 2117619; fax (22) 2117620; e-mail algemb@twiga.com; Ambassador Abdelmoun'aam Ahriz.

Angola: Plot 78, Lugalo Rd, POB 20793, Dar es Salaam; tel. (22) 2117674; fax (22) 2132349; Ambassador Ambrósio Lukoki.

Belgium: Ocean Rd, POB 9210, Dar es Salaam; tel. (22) 2112688; fax (22) 2117621; e-mail daressalaam@diplobel.be; internet www.diplomatie.be/dar-es-salaam; Ambassador Paul Jansen.

Canada: 38 Mirambo St, Garden Ave, POB 1022, Dar es Salaam; tel. (22) 2163300; fax (22) 2116897; e-mail dslam@international.gc.ca; internet www.dfait-maeci.gc.ca/tanzania; High Commissioner Janet Siddall.

China, People's Republic: 2 Kajificheni Close at Toure Dr., POB 1649, Dar es Salaam; tel. (22) 2667212; Ambassador Liu Xisheng.

Congo, Democratic Republic: 438 Malik Rd, POB 975, Upanga, Dar es Salaam; tel. (22) 2150282; fax (22) 2153341; Chargé d'affaires a.i. Nsingi Zi Lubaki.

Cuba: Plot 313, Lugalo Rd, POB 9282, Upanga, Dar es Salaam; tel. (22) 2115928; fax (22) 2128639; e-mail embajador@ctvsatcom.net; Ambassador Ernesto Gómez Díaz.

Denmark: Ghana Ave, POB 9171, Dar es Salaam; tel. (22) 2113887; fax (22) 2116433; e-mail daramb@um.dk; internet www.ambdaressalaam.um.dk; Ambassador Bjarne Henneberg Sørensen.

Egypt: 24 Garden Ave, POB 1668, Dar es Salaam; tel. (22) 2117622; fax (22) 2112543; e-mail egypt.emb.tz@Cats-net.com; Ambassador Sabry Magdy Sabry.

Finland: cnr Mirambo St and Garden Ave, POB 2455, Dar es Salaam; tel. (22) 2196565; fax (22) 2196573; e-mail sanomat.dar@formin.fi; internet www.finland.or.tz; Ambassador Juhani Toivonen.

France: Ali Hassan Mwinyi Rd, POB 2349, Dar es Salaam; tel. (22) 2198800; fax (22) 2198815; e-mail ambfrance@africaonline.co.tz; internet www.ambafrance-tz.org; Ambassador Jacques Champagne de Labriolle.

Germany: Umoja House, Mirambo St/Garden Ave, 2nd Floor, POB 9541, Dar es Salaam; tel. (22) 2117409; fax (22) 2112944; e-mail german.embassy@bol.co.tz; internet www.daressalam.diplo.de; Ambassador Dr Guido Herz.

Holy See: Oyster Bay, Plot 146, Haile Selassie Rd, POB 480, Dar es Salaam (Apostolic Nunciature); tel. (22) 2666422; fax (22) 2668059; e-mail nunzio@cats-net.com; Apostolic Nuncio Most Rev. Joseph Chennoth (Titular Archbishop of Milevum).

Indonesia: 299 Ali Hassan Mwinyi Rd, POB 572, Dar es Salaam; tel. (22) 2119119; fax (22) 2115849; e-mail kbridsm@raha.com; Ambassador Trijono Marjono.

Ireland: 353 Toure Dr., POB 9612, Oyster Bay, Dar es Salaam; tel. (22) 2602355; fax (22) 2602362; e-mail embassydaresalaam@dfa.ie; Ambassador Anne Barrington.

Italy: Plot 316, Lugalo Rd, POB 2106, Dar es Salaam; tel. (22) 2115935; fax (22) 2115938; e-mail segr.dar@esteri.it; internet www.ambdaressalaam.esteri.it; Ambassador Francesco Catania.

Japan: 1018 Ali Hassan Mwinyi Rd, POB 2577, Dar es Salaam; tel. (22) 2115827; fax (22) 2115830; e-mail embassyofjapan_tz@raha.com; internet www.tz.emb-japan.go.jp; Ambassador Hiroshi Nakagawa.

Kenya: Plot 127 Mafinga St, Kinondoni, POB 5231, Dar es Salaam; tel. (22) 2668285; fax (22) 2668213; e-mail info@kenyahighcomtz.org; internet www.kenyahighcomtz.org; High Commissioner Boaz Kidiga Mbaya.

Korea, Democratic People's Republic: Plot 5, Ursino Estate, Kawawa Rd, Msasani, POB 2690, Dar es Salaam; tel. (22) 2775395; fax (22) 2700838; Ambassador Soon Chun Lee.

Korea, Republic: Plot 97, Msese Rd, Kingsway, Kinondoni, POB 1154, Dar es Salaam; tel. (22) 2668788; fax (22) 2667509; e-mail embassy-tz@mofat.go.kr; internet tza.mofat.go.kr; Ambassador Kim Young-Jun.

Libya: 386 Mtitu St, POB 9413, Dar es Salaam; tel. (22) 2150188; fax (22) 2150068; Secretary of People's Bureau Dr Ahmed Ibrahim el-Ashhab.

Malawi: Plot 38, Ali Hassan Mwinyi Rd, POB 7616, Dar es Salaam; tel. (22) 2666284; fax (22) 2668161; e-mail mhc@africaonline.co.tz; High Commissioner (vacant).

Mozambique: 25 Garden Ave, POB 9370, Dar es Salaam; tel. and fax (22) 2124673; fax (22) 2116502; e-mail embamoc.tanzania@minec.gov.mz; High Commissioner Zacarias Kupela.

TANZANIA

Netherlands: Umoja House, 4th Floor, Garden Ave, POB 9534, Dar es Salaam; tel. (22) 2110000; fax (22) 2110044; e-mail dar@minbuza.nl; internet tanzania.nlembassy.org; Ambassador KAREL VAN KESTEREN.

Nigeria: 83 Haile Selassie Rd, POB 9214, Oyster Bay, Dar es Salaam; tel. (22) 2666000; fax (22) 2668947; e-mail nhc-dsm@raha.com; High Commissioner AHMED M. USMAN.

Norway: 160/50 Mirambo St, POB 2646, Dar es Salaam; tel. (22) 2113366; fax (22) 2116564; e-mail emb.daressalaam@mfa.no; internet www.norway.go.tz; Ambassador JON LOMØY.

Russia: Plot No. 73, Ali Hassan Mwinyi Rd, POB 1905, Dar es Salaam; tel. (22) 2666005; fax (22) 2666818; e-mail embruss@bol.co.tz; Ambassador LEONARD ALEKSEEVIC.

Rwanda: Plot 32, Ali Hassan Mwinyi Rd, POB 2918, Dar es Salaam; tel. (22) 2115889; fax (22) 2115888; e-mail ambadsm@minaffet.gov.rw; Ambassador ZEPHYR MUTANGUHA.

South Africa: Plot 1338/1339, Mwaya Rd, Msaski, POB 10723, Dar es Salaam; tel. (22) 2601800; fax (22) 2600684; e-mail ntombelal@foreign.gov.za; High Commissioner S. G. MFENYANA.

Spain: 99B Kinondoni Rd, POB 842, Dar es Salaam; tel. (22) 2666936; fax (22) 2666938; e-mail embesptz@mail.mae.es; Ambassador JUAN MANUEL GONZÁLEZ DE LINARES PALAU.

Sudan: 'Albaraka', 64 Ali Hassan Mwinyi Rd, POB 2266, Dar es Salaam; tel. (22) 2117641; fax (22) 2115811; e-mail sudan.emb.dar@raha.com; Ambassador ELMUGHIRA ALI OMAR.

Sweden: Mirambo St and Garden Ave, POB 9274, Dar es Salaam; tel. (22) 2196500; fax (22) 2196503; e-mail ambassaden.dar-es-salaam@foreign.ministry.se; internet www.swedenabroad.se/daressalaam; Ambassador STAFFAN HERRSTROM.

Switzerland: 79 Kinondoni Rd/Mafinga St, POB 2454, Dar es Salaam; tel. (22) 2666008; fax (22) 2666736; e-mail dar.vertretung@eda.admin.ch; Ambassador (vacant).

Syria: 246 Alykhan Rd, Upanga, POB 2442, Dar es Salaam; tel. (22) 2117656; fax (22) 2115860; Chargé d'affaires a.i. M. B. IMADI.

Uganda: Extelcom Bldg, 7th Floor, Samora Ave, POB 6237, Dar es Salaam; tel. (22) 2116754; fax (22) 2112974; e-mail ugadar@intafrica.com; High Commissioner IBRAHIM MUKIIBI.

United Arab Emirates: 2415 Kaunda Drive House, Dar es Salaam; tel. (22) 2669999; fax (22) 2669996; e-mail uaeembassy@bol.co.tz; Ambassador MALALLAH MUBARAK SUWAID AL-AMIRI.

United Kingdom: Umoja House, Garden Ave, POB 9200, Dar es Salaam; tel. (22) 2110101; fax (22) 2110102; e-mail bhc.dar@fco.gov.uk; internet ukintanzania.fco.gov.uk; High Commissioner DIANE LOUISE CORNER.

USA: 686 Old Bagamoyo Rd, Msasani, POB 9123, Dar es Salaam; tel. (22) 2668001; fax (22) 2668238; e-mail embassyd@state.gov; internet tanzania.usembassy.gov; Chargé d'affaires a.i. LARRY ANDRÉ.

Yemen: 353 United Nations Rd, POB 349, Dar es Salaam; tel. (22) 2117650; fax (22) 2115924; Chargé d'affaires a.i. MOHAMED ABDULLA ALMAS.

Zambia: 5–6 Ohio St/Sokoine Dr. Junction, POB 2525, Dar es Salaam; tel. and fax (22) 2112977; e-mail zhcd@raha.com; High Commissioner JOHN KASHONKA CHITAFU.

Zimbabwe: 2097 East Upanga, off Ali Hassan Mwinyi Rd, POB 20762, Dar es Salaam; tel. (22) 2116789; fax (22) 2112913; e-mail zimdares@cats-net.com; Ambassador J. M. SHAVA.

Judicial System

Permanent Commission of Enquiry: POB 2643, Dar es Salaam; tel. (22) 2113690; fax (22) 2111533; Chair. and Official Ombudsman Prof. JOSEPH F. MBWILIZA; Sec. A. P. GUVETTE.

Court of Appeal

Consists of the Chief Justice and four Judges of Appeal.

Chief Justice of Tanzania: AUGUSTINO RAMADHANI.

Chief Justice of Zanzibar: HAMID MAHMOUD HAMID.

High Court: headquarters at Dar es Salaam, but regular sessions held in all Regions; consists of a Jaji Kiongozi and 29 Judges.

District Courts: situated in each district and presided over by either a Resident Magistrate or District Magistrate; limited jurisdiction, with a right of appeal to the High Court.

Primary Courts: established in every district and presided over by Primary Court Magistrates; limited jurisdiction, with a right of appeal to the District Courts and then to the High Court.

Attorney-General: JOHNSON PAULO MATHIAS MWANYIKA.

Director of Public Prosecutions: KULWA MASSABA.

People's Courts were established in Zanzibar in 1970. Magistrates are elected by the people and have two assistants each. Under the Zanzibar Constitution, which came into force in January 1985, defence lawyers and the right of appeal, abolished in 1970, were reintroduced.

Religion

Religious surveys were eliminated from all government census reports after 1967. However, religious leaders and sociologists generally believe that the country's population is 30%–40% Christian and 30%–40% Muslim, with the remainder consisting of practitioners of other faiths, traditional indigenous religions and atheists. Foreign missionaries operate in the country, including Roman Catholics, Lutherans, Baptists, Seventh-day Adventists, Mormons, Anglicans and Muslims.

ISLAM

The Muslim population is most heavily concentrated on the Zanzibar archipelago and in the coastal areas of the mainland. There are also large Muslim minorities in inland urban areas. Some 99% of the population of Zanzibar is estimated to be Muslim. Between 80% and 90% of the country's Muslim population is Sunni; the remainder consists of several Shi'a groups, mostly of Asian descent. A large proportion of the Asian community is Isma'ili.

Ismalia Provincial Church: POB 460, Dar es Salaam.

National Muslim Council of Tanzania: POB 21422, Dar es Salaam; tel. (22) 234934; f. 1969; supervises Islamic affairs on the mainland only; Chair. Sheikh HEMED BIN JUMA BIN HEMED; Exec. Sec. Alhaj MUHAMMAD MTULIA.

Supreme Muslim Council: Zanzibar; f. 1991; supervises Islamic affairs in Zanzibar; Mufti Sheikh HARITH BIN KALEF.

Wakf and Trust Commission: POB 4092, Zanzibar; f. 1980; Islamic affairs; Exec. Sec. YUSUF ABDULRAHMAN MUHAMMAD.

CHRISTIANITY

The Christian population is composed of Roman Catholics, Protestants, Pentecostals, Seventh-day Adventists, members of the Church of Jesus Christ of Latter-day Saints (Mormons) and Jehovah's Witnesses.

Jumuiya ya Kikristo Tanzania (Christian Council of Tanzania): Church House, POB 1454, Dodoma; tel. (26) 2324445; fax (26) 2324352; f. 1934; Chair. Rt Rev. DONALD LEO MTETEMELA (Bishop of the Anglican Church); Gen. Sec. Rev. Dr LEONARD AMOS MTAITA.

The Anglican Communion

Anglicans are adherents of the Church of the Province of Tanzania, comprising 16 dioceses.

Archbishop of the Province of Tanzania and Bishop of Ruaha: Most Rev. DONALD LEO MTETEMELA, POB 1028, Iringa; fax (26) 2702479; e-mail ruaha@maf.or.tz.

Provincial Secretary: Dr R. MWITA AKIRI (acting), POB 899, Dodoma; tel. (26) 2321437; fax (26) 2324265; e-mail cpt@maf.org.

Greek Orthodox

Archbishop of East Africa: NICADEMUS OF IRINOUPOULIS (resident in Nairobi, Kenya); jurisdiction covers Kenya, Uganda and Tanzania.

Lutheran

Evangelical Lutheran Church in Tanzania: POB 3033, Boma Rd, Arusha; tel. (57) 8855; fax (57) 8858; e-mail elcthq@elct.or.tz; internet www.elct.or.tz; 1.5m. mems; Presiding Bishop ALEX G. MALASUSA; Exec. Sec. AMANI MWENEGOHA; 4.6m. mems (2009).

The Roman Catholic Church

Tanzania comprises five archdioceses and 25 dioceses. There were an estimated 11,366,935 adherents at 31 December 2006, equivalent to about 27.2% of the total population.

Tanzania Episcopal Conference

Catholic Secretariat, Mandela Rd, POB 2133, Dar es Salaam; tel. (22) 2851075; fax (22) 2851133; e-mail tec@cats-net.com; internet www.rc.net/tanzania/tec.

f. 1980; Pres. Mgr JUDE THADDAEUS RUWA'ICHI (Bishop of Dodoma).

Archbishop of Arusha: Most Rev. JOSAPHAT LOUIS LEBULU, Archbishop's House, POB 3044, Arusha; tel. (27) 2544361; fax (27) 2548004; e-mail angelo.arusha@habari.co.tz.

Archbishop of Dar es Salaam: Cardinal POLYCARP PENGO, Archbishop's House, POB 167, Dar es Salaam; tel. (22) 2113223; fax (22) 2125751; e-mail nyumba@cats-net.com.

TANZANIA

Archbishop of Mwanza: Most Rev. ANTHONY MAYALA, Archbishop's House, POB 1421, Mwanza; tel. and fax (28) 2501029; e-mail archmwz@mwanza-online.com.

Archbishop of Songea: Most Rev. NORBERT WENDELIN MTEGA, Archbishop's House, POB 152, Songea; tel. (25) 2602004; fax (25) 2602593; e-mail songea-archdiocese@yahoo.com.

Archbishop of Tabora: PAUL R. RUZOKA, Archbishop's House, Private Bag, PO Tabora; tel. (26) 2665608; fax (26) 2604000; e-mail archbishops-office@yahoo.co.uk.

Other Christian Churches

Baptist Mission of Tanzania: POB 9414, Dar es Salaam; tel. (22) 2170130; fax (22) 2170127; f. 1956; Admin. FRANK PEVEY.

Christian Missions in Many Lands (Tanzania): German Branch, POB 34, Tunduru, Ruvuma Region; f. 1957; Gen. Sec. THOMAS MÜHLING.

Moravian Church in Tanzania: POB 377, Mbeya; 113,656 mems; Gen. Sec. Rev. O. M. T. MPAYO.

Pentecostal Church: POB 34, Kahama.

Presbyterian Church: POB 2510, Dar es Salaam; tel. (22) 229075.

BAHÁ'Í FAITH

National Spiritual Assembly: POB 585, Dar es Salaam; tel. and fax (22) 2152766; e-mail bahaitz@africaonline.tz; mems resident in 2,301 localities.

OTHER RELIGIONS

Many people follow traditional beliefs. There are also some Hindu communities.

The Press

NEWSPAPERS

Daily

The African: Sinza Rd, POB 4793, Dar es Salaam; Editor-in-Chief JOHN KULEKANA.

Alasiri: POB 31042, Dar es Salaam; Swahili; Editor LUCAS MNUBI.

Daily News: POB 9033, Dar es Salaam; tel. (22) 2110165; fax (22) 2112881; f. 1972; govt-owned; Man. Editor SETHI KAMUHANDA; circ. 50,000.

The Democrat: Dar es Salaam; independent; Editor IDRISS LUGULU; circ. 15,000.

The Guardian: POB 31042, Dar es Salaam; tel. (22) 275250; fax (22) 273583; e-mail guardian@ipp.co.tz; internet www.ippmedia.com; f. 1994; English and Swahili; Man. Dir KIONDO MSHANA; Man. Editor PASCAL SHIJA.

Kipanga: POB 199, Zanzibar; Swahili; publ. by Information and Broadcasting Services.

Majira: POB 71439, Dar es Salaam; tel. (22) 238901; fax (22) 231104; independent; Swahili; Editor THEOPHIL MAKUNGA; circ. 15,000.

Nipashe: POB 31042, Dar es Salaam; Swahili; Editor HAMISI MZEE.

Uhuru: POB 9221, Dar es Salaam; tel. (22) 2182224; fax (22) 2185065; f. 1961; official publ. of CCM; Swahili; Man. Editor SAIDI NGUBA; circ. 100,000.

Weekly

Business Times: POB 71439, Dar es Salaam; tel. (22) 238901; fax (22) 231104; e-mail majira@bcsmedia.com; internet www.bcstimes.com; independent; English; Editor ALLI MWAMBOLA; circ. 15,000.

The Express: POB 20588, Dar es Salaam; tel. (22) 2180058; fax (22) 2182665; e-mail express@raha.com; internet www.theexpress.com; independent; English; Editor FAYAZ BHOJANI; circ. 20,000.

The Family Mirror: Faru/Nyamwezi St, Karikoo Area, POB 6804, Dar es Salaam; tel. (22) 181331; Editor ZEPHANIAH MUSENDO.

Gazette of the United Republic: POB 9142, Dar es Salaam; tel. (22) 231817; official announcements; Editor H. HAJI; circ. 6,000.

Government Gazette: POB 261, Zanzibar; f. 1964; official announcements.

Kasheshe: POB 31042, Dar es Salaam; Swahili; Editor VENANCE MLAY.

Leta Raha: POB 31042, Dar es Salaam; Swahili; Editor EDMOND MSANGI.

Mfanyakazi (The Worker): POB 15359, Dar es Salaam; tel. (22) 226111; Swahili; trade union publ; Editor NDUGU MTAWA; circ. 100,000.

Directory

Mzalendo: POB 9221, Dar es Salaam; tel. (22) 2182224; fax (22) 2185065; e-mail uhuru@udsm.ac.tz; f. 1972; publ. by CCM; Swahili; Man. Editor SAIDI NGABA; circ. 115,000.

Nipashe Jumapili: POB 31042, Dar es Salaam; Swahili.

Sunday News: POB 9033, Dar es Salaam; tel. (22) 2116072; fax (22) 2112881; f. 1954; govt-owned; Man. Editor SETHI KAMUCHANDA; circ. 50,000.

Sunday Observer: POB 31042, Dar es Salaam; e-mail guardian@ipp.co.tz; Man. Dir VUMI URASA; Man. Editor PETER MSUNGU.

Taifa Letu: POB 31042, Dar es Salaam; Swahili.

PERIODICALS

The African Review: POB 35042, Dar es Salaam; tel. (22) 2410130; e-mail mubakar@udsm.ac.tz; 2 a year; journal of African politics, development and international affairs; publ. by the Dept of Political Science, Univ. of Dar es Salaam; Chief Editor Dr MOHAMMED BAKARI; circ. 1,000.

Eastern African Law Review: POB 35093, Dar es Salaam; tel. (22) 243254; f. 1967; 2 a year; Chief Editor N. N. N. NDITI; circ. 1,000.

Elimu Haina Mwisho: POB 1986, Mwanza; monthly; circ. 45,000.

Habari za Washirika: POB 2567, Dar es Salaam; tel. (22) 223346; monthly; publ. by Co-operative Union of Tanzania; Editor H. V. N. CHIBULUNJE; circ. 40,000.

Jenga: POB 2669, Dar es Salaam; tel. (22) 2112893; fax (22) 2113618; journal of the National Development Corpn; circ. 2,000.

Kiongozi (The Leader): POB 9400, Dar es Salaam; tel. (22) 229505; f. 1950; fortnightly; Swahili; Roman Catholic; Editor ROBERT MFUGALE; circ. 33,500.

Kweupe: POB 222, Zanzibar; weekly; Swahili; publ. by Information and Broadcasting Services.

Mlezi (The Educator): POB 41, Peramiho; tel. 30; f. 1970; every 2 months; Editor Fr DOMINIC WEIS; circ. 8,000.

Mwenge (Firebrand): POB 1, Peramiho; tel. 30; f. 1937; monthly; Editor JOHN P. MBONDE; circ. 10,000.

Nchi Yetu (Our Country): POB 9142, Dar es Salaam; tel. (22) 2110200; f. 1964; govt publ; monthly; Swahili; circ. 50,000.

Nuru: POB 1893, Zanzibar; f. 1992; bi-monthly; official publ. of Zanzibar Govt; circ. 8,000.

Safina: POB 21422, Dar es Salaam; tel. (22) 234934; publ. by National Muslim Council of Tanzania; Editor YASSIN SADIK; circ. 10,000.

Sikiliza: POB 635, Morogoro; tel. and fax (23) 2604374; quarterly; Seventh-day Adventist; Editor MIKA D. MUSA; circ. 100,000.

Taamuli: POB 899, Dar es Salaam; tel. (22) 243500; 2 a year; journal of political science; publ. by the Dept of Political Science, Univ. of Dar es Salaam; circ. 1,000.

Tantravel: POB 2485, Dar es Salaam; tel. (22) 2111244; fax (22) 2116420; e-mail safari@ud.co.tz; internet www.tanzaniatouristboard.com; f. 1987; quarterly; publ. by Tanzania Tourist Board; Editor GERVAS TATAH MLOLA.

Tanzania Education Journal: POB 9121, Dar es Salaam; tel. (22) 227211; f. 1984; 3 a year; publ. by Institute of Education, Ministry of Education; circ. 8,000.

Tanzania Trade Currents: POB 5402, Dar es Salaam; tel. (22) 2851706; fax (22) 851700; e-mail betis@intafrica.com; bi-monthly; publ. by Board of External Trade; circ. 2,000.

Uhuru na Amani: POB 3033, Arusha; tel. (57) 8855; fax (57) 8858; quarterly; Swahili; publ. by Evangelical Lutheran Church in Tanzania; Editor ELIZABETH LOBULU; circ. 15,000.

Ukulima wa Kisasa (Modern Farming): Farmers' Education and Publicity Unit, POB 2308, Dar es Salaam; tel. (22) 2116496; fax (22) 2122923; e-mail fepu@twiga.com; f. 1955; bi-monthly; Swahili; publ. by Ministry of Food and Agriculture; Editor H. MLAKI; circ. 15,000.

Ushirika Wetu: POB 2567, Dar es Salaam; tel. (22) 2184081; e-mail ushirika@covision2000.com; monthly; publ. by Tanzania Federation of Co-operatives; Editor SIMON J. KERARYO; circ. 40,000.

Wela: POB 180, Dodoma; Swahili.

NEWS AGENCY

Press Services Tanzania (PST) Ltd: POB 31042, Dar es Salaam; tel. and fax (22) 2119195.

Publishers

Central Tanganyika Press: POB 1129, Dodoma; tel. (26) 2390015; fax (26) 2324565; e-mail ctp@anglican.or.tz; internet www.anglican.or.tz/ctp.htm; f. 1954; religious; Man. PETER MANG'ATI MAKASSI.

TANZANIA

DUP (1996) Ltd: POB 7028, Dar es Salaam; tel. and fax (22) 2410137; e-mail director@dup.udsm.ac.tz; f. 1979; educational, academic and cultural texts in Swahili and English; Dir Dr N. G. MWITTA.

Eastern Africa Publications Ltd: POB 1002 Arusha; tel. (57) 3176; f. 1979; general and school textbooks; Gen. Man. ABDULLAH SAIWAAD.

Inland Publishers: POB 125, Mwanza; tel. (68) 40064; general non-fiction, religion, in Kiswahili and English; Dir Rev. S. M. MAGESA.

Oxford University Press: Maktaba Rd, POB 5299, Dar es Salaam; tel. (22) 229209; f. 1969; literature, literary criticism, essays, poetry; Man. SALIM SHAABAN SALIM.

Tanzania Publishing House: 47 Samora Machel Ave, POB 2138, Dar es Salaam; tel. (22) 2137402; e-mail tphhouse@yahoo.com; f. 1966; educational and general books in Swahili and English; Gen. Man. PRIMUS ISIDOR KARUGENDO.

GOVERNMENT PUBLISHING HOUSE

Government Printer: Office of the Prime Minister, POB 9124, Dar es Salaam; tel. (22) 2860900; fax (22) 2866955; e-mail gptz@pmo.go.tz; Dir KASSIAN C. CHIBOGOYO.

Broadcasting and Communications

TELECOMMUNICATIONS

Tanzania Communications Regulatory Authority (TCRA): POB 474, Dar es Salaam; tel. (22) 2118947; fax (22) 2116664; e-mail dg@tcra.go.tz; internet www.tcra.go.tz; f. 1993; licenses postal and telecommunications service operators; manages radio spectrum; acts as ombudsman; Dir-Gen. Prof. JOHN NKOMA.

MIC Tanzania Ltd: Lugoda St, POB 2929, Dar es Salaam; tel. (741) 800800; fax (741) 123064; e-mail mobitel@mobitel.co.tz; operates mobile cellular telecommunications services through Mobitel network.

Tanzania Telecommunications Co Ltd (TTCL): Extelcoms House, Samora Ave, POB 9070, Dar es Salaam; tel. (22) 2142000; fax (22) 2113232; e-mail ttcl@ttcl.co.tz; internet www.ttcl.co.tz; 35% sold to consortium of Detecon (Germany) and Mobile Systems International (Netherlands) in Feb. 2001; CEO BILL BECKMAN.

Vodacom (Tanzania) Ltd: 14th Floor PPF Towers, POB 2369, Dar es Salaam; tel. (754) 705000; fax (754) 704014; e-mail feedback@vodacom.co.tz; internet www.vodacom.co.tz; mobile cellular telephone operator.

Zain Tanzania: Zain House, Ali Hassan Mwinyi Rd, Dar es Salaam; tel. (22) 2748181; e-mail helpdesktz@zain.com; internet www.tz.zain.com; f. 2001; Man. Dir KHALED MUHTADI.

Zanzibar Telecom (Zantel): POB 3459, Zanzibar; tel. (24) 2234823; fax (24) 2234850; e-mail customerservices@zantel.co.tz; internet www.zantel.co.tz; f. 1999; mobile cellular telephone operator for Zanzibar; Chair. SALEM AL SHARHAN; CEO NOEL HERRITY.

BROADCASTING

Radio

Radio FM Zenj 96.8: Zanzibar; f. 2005; owned by Zanzibar Media Corpn; broadcasts to 60% of Zanzibar, to be extended to all of Zanzibar and mainland coast from southern Tanzania to Kenya; Gen. Man. AUSTIN MAKANI.

Radio Kwizera: N'Gara; tel. (28) 2223679; fax (28) 2223795; e-mail rkngara@jrstz.co.tz; f. 1995; station's objective is to educate, entertain and inform refugee and local communities, with the aim of bringing about peace and reconciliation; Dir DAMAS S. J. MISSANGA.

Radio One: POB 4374, Dar es Salaam; tel. (22) 275914; e-mail itv@ipp.co.tz; internet www.ippmedia.com; subsidiary of ITV (see Television).

Radio Tanzania Zanzibar: state-owned.

Radio Tumaini (Hope): 1 Bridge St, POB 167, Dar es Salaam; tel. (22) 2117307; fax (22) 2112594; e-mail tumaini@africaonline.co.tz; broadcasts in Swahili within Dar es Salaam; operated by the Roman Catholic Church; broadcasts on religious, social and economic issues; Dir Fr JEAN-FRANÇOIS GALTIER.

Sauti Ya Tanzania Zanzibar (The Voice of Tanzania Zanzibar): POB 1178, Zanzibar; f. 1951; state-owned; broadcasts in Swahili on three wavelengths; Dir SULEIMAN JUMA.

Tanzania Broadcasting Corporation (TBC): Broadcasting House, Nyerere Rd, POB 9191, Dar es Salaam; tel. (22) 2860760; fax (22) 2865577; e-mail info@tbcorp.org; internet www.tbcorp.org; f. 2008; incorporates Radio Tanzania Dar es Salaam and the national TV network, Televisheni ya Taifa; Dir-Gen. DUNSTAN TIDO MHANDO.

Radio Tanzania Dar es Salaam (RTD): POB 9191, Dar es Salaam; tel. (22) 2860760; fax (22) 2865577; e-mail info@tbcorp.org; internet www.tbcorp.org; f. 1951; state-owned; subsidiary of TBC; domestic services in Swahili; external services in English; Gen. Man. EDDA SANGA.

Television

Dar es Salaam Television (DTV): POB 21122, Dar es Salaam; tel. (22) 2116341; fax (22) 2113112; e-mail franco.dtv@raha.com; f. 1994; Man. Dir FRANCO TRAMONTANO.

Independent Television (ITV): Mikocheni Light Industrial Area, POB 4374, Dar es Salaam; tel. (22) 2775914; fax (22) 2775915; e-mail itv@ipp.co.tz; internet www.ippmedia.com; f. 1994; wholly owned by IPP Ltd; 65% of programmes are locally produced and in Kiswahili; Man. Dir JOYCE MHAVILLE.

Star TV: POB 1732, Mwanza; tel. (28) 2503262; fax (28) 2500713; e-mail marketing@startvtz.com; internet www.startvtz.com; f. 2000.

Tanzania Broadcasting Corporation (TBC): see radio

Televisheni ya Taifa (TVT): POB 31519, Dar es Salaam; tel. (22) 2700011; fax (22) 2773078; e-mail info@tbcorp.org; internet www.tbcorp.org; f. 2000; state-owned; subsidiary of TBC since 2008; Gen. Man. CLEMENT MSHANA.

Television Zanzibar: POB 314, Zanzibar; tel. and fax (24) 22315951; e-mail karumehouse@tvz.co.tz; internet www.tvz.co.tz; f. 1973; Dir JAMA SIMBA.

Finance

(cap. = capital; res = reserves; dep. = deposits; m. = million; brs = branches; amounts in Tanzanian shillings, unless otherwise indicated)

BANKING

Central Bank

Bank of Tanzania (Benki Kuu Ya Tanzania): 10 Mirambo St, POB 2939, Dar es Salaam; tel. (22) 2110946; fax (22) 2113325; e-mail info@hq.bot-tz.org; internet www.bot-tz.org; f. 1966; bank of issue; cap. 10,000m., res 578,811m., dep. 1,346,560m. (June 2006); Gov. and Chair. Prof. BENNO NDULU; 4 brs.

Principal Banks

African Banking Corpn (Tanzania) Ltd: Barclays House, 1st Floor, Ohio St, POB 31, Dar es Salaam; tel. (22) 2119303; fax (22) 2112402; e-mail abct@africanbankingcorp.com; internet www.africanbankingcorp.com; wholly owned by African Banking Corpn Holdings Ltd; cap. 5,404m. (Dec. 2003); Chair. Dr JONAS KIPOKOLA.

Akiba Commercial Bank Ltd: TDFL Bldg, Upanga Rd, POB 669, Dar es Salaam; tel. (22) 2118340; fax (22) 2114173; e-mail akiba@cats-net.com; internet www.acb-bank.com; f. 1997; cap. 3,283.0m., res 517.5m., dep. 29,913.2m. (Dec. 2006); Chair. Dr IDRIS RASHIDI; Man. Dir J. LWANDE.

Azania Bancorp Ltd: POB 9271, Dar es Salaam; tel. (22) 2117997; fax (22) 2118010; e-mail info@azaniabank.co.tz; internet www.azaniabank.co.tz; 55% owned by National Social Security Fund, 31% owned by Parastatal Pension Fund, 9% owned by East African Development Bank, 5% owned by individuals; cap. 6,168m. (Dec. 2003); Chair. N. NSEMWA; CEO CHARLES SINGILI.

Bank M (Tanzania) Ltd: POB 96, 8 Ocean Rd, Dar Es Salaam; tel. (22) 2127825; fax (22) 2127824; e-mail ganpath.pillai@bankm.co.tz; f. 2007; 20% owned by Negus Holdings, 20% by Equity & Allied Ltd, 20% by Africarriers Ltd, 20% by Noble Investment Ltd; Gen. Man. SANJEEV KUMAR.

Barclays Bank (Tanzania) Ltd: Barclays House, Ohio St, POB 5137, Dar es Salaam; tel. (22) 2129381; fax (22) 2129757; e-mail karl.stumke@barclays.com; 99.9% owned by Barclays PLC (United Kingdom), 0.1% owned by Ebbgate Holdings Ltd; cap. 18,750m. (Dec. 2003); Chair. J. K. CHANDE; Man. Dir KARL STUMKE.

BOA Bank (Tanzania) Ltd: NDC Development House, cnr Kivukoni Front and Ohio St, POB 3054, Dar es Salaam; tel. (22) 2111229; fax (22) 2113740; e-mail eab@eurafricanbank-tz.com; internet www.boatanzania.com; f. 1994 as Eurafrican Bank (Tanzania) Ltd, name changed as above in 2007; 36.68% owned by Bank of Africa Kenya Ltd, 25.01% by Aureos Capital East Africa LLC, 25.01% by Belgian Investment Co; total assets 89,486m. (Dec. 2007); Chair. FULGENCE M. KAZAURA; Man. Dir KOBBY ANDAH.

Capital Finance Ltd: TDFL Bldg, 5th Floor, 1008 Ohio St/Upanga Rd, POB 9032, Dar es Salaam; tel. (22) 2135152; fax (22) 2135150; e-mail mail@cfl.co.tz; wholly owned by Tanzania Development Finance Co Ltd; cap. 4,000m. (Dec. 2003); Chair. H. K. SENKORO; CEO J. H. MCGUFFOG.

CF Union Bank Ltd: Jivan Hirji Bldg, Indira Gandhi/Mosque St, POB 1509, Dar es Salaam; tel. (22) 2110212; fax (22) 2118750; e-mail cfunionbank@raha.com; f. 2002 by merger of Furaha Finance Ltd and Crown Finance & Leasing Ltd; cap. 4m. (Dec. 2006); Chair. MUNIR ASGARALI BHARWANI; CEO SUBRAMANIAN GOPALAN.

Citibank Tanzania Ltd: Ali Hassan Mwinyi Rd, POB 71625, Dar es Salaam; tel. (22) 2117575; fax (22) 2113910; 99.98% owned by Citibank Overseas Investment Corpn; Chair. EMEKA EMUWA.

CRDB Bank: Azikiwe St, POB 268, Dar es Salaam; tel. (22) 2117442; fax (22) 2116714; e-mail crdb@crdbbank.com; internet www.crdbbank.com; f. as Co-operative and Rural Development Bank in 1947, transferred to private ownership and current name adopted 1996; 30% owned by DANIDA Investment; provides commercial banking services and loans for rural development; cap. 12,367m., res 30,551m., dep. 815,587m. (Dec. 2006); Chair MARTIN J. MMARI; Man. Dir Dr CHARLES S. KIMEI; 38 brs.

Dar es Salaam Community Bank Ltd (DCB): Arnautoglu Bldg, Bibi Titi Mohamed St, POB 19798, Dar es Salaam; tel. (22) 2180253; fax (22) 2180239; e-mail dcb@africaonline.co.tz; f. 2001; cap. 1,796m. (Dec. 2003); Chair. PAUL MILVANGE RUPIA; Man. Dir EDMUND PANCRAS MKWAWA.

Diamond Trust Bank Tanzania Ltd: POB 115, 9th Floor, Harbour View Towers, Dar es Salaam; tel. (22) 2114891; fax (22) 2124244; internet www.dtbafrica.com; f. 1946 as Diamond Jubilee Investment Trust; converted to bank and adopted current name in 1996; 55% owned by Diamond Trust Bank Kenya Ltd, 23% owned by Aga Khan Fund for Economic Development SA (Switzerland); cap. 1,108m., res 222m., dep. 64,054m. (Dec. 2006); Chair. MAHMOOD MANJI; CEO A. J. SMILES.

EXIM Bank (Tanzania) Ltd: NIC Investment House, Samora Ave, POB 1431, Dar es Salaam; tel. (22) 2113091; fax (22) 2119737; e-mail marketing@eximbank-tz.com; internet www.eximbank-tz.com; cap. 12,900m., res 793m., dep. 221,298m. (Dec. 2006); Chair. YOGESH MANEK; Man. Dir S. M. J. MWAMBENJA.

FBME Bank Ltd: POB 8298, Samora Ave, Dar es Salaam; tel. (22) 2126000; fax (22) 2126006; e-mail headoffice@fbme.com; internet www.fbme.com; f. 1982 in Cyprus as Federal Bank of the Middle East Ltd, subsidiary of Federal Bank of Lebanon SAL (Lebanon); changed country of incorporation to Cayman Islands in 1986, and to Tanzania in 2003; present name adopted 2005; cap. US $43m., res US $3m., dep. US $1,026m. (Dec. 2007); Chair. AYOUB-FARID M. SAAB, FADI M. SAAB; Gen. Man. (Tanzania) ANDREW B. STEPHENS; 5 brs.

Habib African Bank Ltd: India St, POB 70086, Dar es Salaam; tel. (22) 2111107; fax (22) 2111014; e-mail hasanrizvi@habibafricanbank.co.tz; f. 1998; cap. 7,332m., dep. 58,517m. (Dec. 2008); Chair. HABIB MOHAMMED D. HABIB; Man. Dir SYED HASAN RIZVI; 2 brs.

International Bank of Malaysia (Tanzania) Ltd: Upanga/Kisutu St, POB 9363, Dar es Salaam; tel. (22) 2110518; fax (22) 2110196; e-mail ibm@afsat.com; Chair. JOSEPHINE PREMLA SIVARETNAM; CEO M. RAHMAT.

International Commercial Bank (Tanzania) Ltd: 1st Floor, Jamhuri St/Morogoro Rd, Dar es Salaam; tel. (22) 2134989; fax (22) 2134286; e-mail enquiry@icbank-tz.com; f. 1998; 5 brs.

Kenya Commercial Bank (Tanzania) Ltd: National Audit House, Samora/Ohio St, POB 804, Dar es Salaam; tel. (22) 2115386; fax (22) 2115391; internet www.kcb.co.ke; cap. 6,000m. (Dec. 2003); Chair. S. MUDHUME; Man. Dir BAZRA TABULO.

Kilimanjaro Co-operative Bank Ltd: Mawenzi Rd, POB 1760, Moshi; tel. (27) 54470; fax (27) 53570; Chair. A. P. KAVISHE; Gen. Man. J. KULAYA.

Mufindi Community Bank: POB 147, Mafinga; tel. and fax (26) 2772165; e-mail mucoba@africaonline.co.tz; cap. 100m. (Dec. 2003); Chair. J. J. MUNGAI; Gen. Man. DANY MPOGOLE.

Mwanga Community Bank: Mwanga Township, POB 333, Mwanga, Kilimanjaro; tel. and fax (27) 2754235; Man. Dir CHRIS HALIBUT.

National Microfinance Bank Ltd (NMB): Samora Ave, POB 9213, Dar es Salaam; tel. (22) 2124048; fax (22) 2110077; e-mail ceo@nmbtz.com; internet www.nmbtz.com; f. 1997 following disbandment of The National Bank of Commerce; Chair. M. NGATUNGA; CEO JOHN R. GILES.

NBC Ltd (National Bank of Commerce Ltd): NBC House, Sokoine Drive, POB 1863, Dar es Salaam; tel. (22) 2112082; fax (22) 2112887; e-mail nbcltd@nbctz.com; internet www.nbctz.com; f. 1997 following disbandment of National Bank of Commerce; 55% owned by ABSA Group Ltd (South Africa), 30% by Govt and 15% by International Finance Corpn; cap. 10,000m., res 71,871m., dep. 683,798m. (Dec. 2006); Man. Dir CHRISTO DE VRIES; 47 brs, 2 agencies.

People's Bank of Zanzibar Ltd (PBZ): POB 1173, Stone Town, Zanzibar; tel. (24) 2231119; fax (24) 2231121; e-mail pbzltd@zanlik.com; f. 1966; controlled by Zanzibar Govt; cap. 16m. (June 1991); Chair. ABDUL RAHMAN M. JUMBE; Man. Dirs J. M. AMOUR, N. S. NASSOR; 3 brs.

Savings & Finance Ltd: Mission St/Samora Ave, POB 20268, Dar es Salaam; tel. (22) 2118625; fax (22) 2116733; 51% owned by National Industrial Credit Bank Ltd (Kenya); Man. Dir SURANJAN GHOSH.

Stanbic Bank Tanzania Ltd: Sukari House, cnr AH Mwinyi/Kinondoni Rd, POB 72647, Dar es Salaam; tel. (22) 2666430; fax (22) 2666301; e-mail tanzaniainfo@stanbic.com; internet www.stanbic.co.tz; f. 1993; wholly owned by Standard Africa Holdings Ltd; cap. 2,000m., res 871m., dep. 230,804m. (Dec. 2005); Chair ARNOLD B. S. KILEWO; Man. Dir BASHIR AWALE; 4 brs.

Standard Chartered Bank Tanzania Ltd: International House, 1st Floor, cnr Shaaban Robert St and Garden Ave, POB 9011, Dar es Salaam; tel. (22) 2122125; fax (22) 2113770; f. 1992; wholly owned by Standard Chartered Holdings (Africa) BV, Netherlands; cap. 1,000m., res −52m., dep. 489,269m. (Dec. 2006); Man. Dir H. SHAH.

Tanzania Development Finance Co Ltd (TDFL): TDFL Bldg, Plot 1008, cnr Upanga Rd and Ohio St, POB 2478, Dar es Salaam; tel. (22) 2116417; fax (22) 2116418; e-mail mail@tdfl.co.tz; f. 1962; owned by Govt (32%), govt agencies of the Netherlands and Germany (5% and 26%, respectively), the Commonwealth Development Corpn (26%) and the European Investment Bank (11%); cap. 3,303m. (Dec. 2001); Chair. H. K. SENKORO; CEO J. McGUFFOG.

Tanzania Investment Bank (TIB): cnr Zanaki St and Samora Machel Ave, POB 9373, Dar es Salaam; tel. (22) 2111708; fax (22) 2113438; e-mail tib-tz@intafrica.com; internet www.tib.co.tz; f. 1970; provides finance, tech. assistance and consultancy, fund administration and loan guarantee for economic devt; 99% govt-owned; cap. 7,641m., res 2,823m., dep. 45,746m. (Dec. 2005); Man. Dir WILLIAM A. MLAKI.

Tanzania Postal Bank (TPB): Extelecoms Annex Bldg, Samora Ave, POB 9300, Dar es Salaam; tel. (22) 2112358; fax (22) 2114815; e-mail md@postalbank.co.tz; internet www.postalbank.co.tz; f. 1991; state-owned; cap. 1,041m. (Dec. 2003); Chair. PAUL JUSTIN MKANGA; Man. Dir and CEO ALPHONSE R. KIHWELE; 4 brs and 113 agencies.

Ulc (Tanzania) Ltd: POB 31, Dar es Salaam; tel. (22) 2119422; fax (22) 2112402; e-mail jmacharia@ulc.co.tz; cap. 2,204m. (Dec. 1999); Chair. Dr JONAS KIPOKOLA; CEO JAMES MACHARIA.

United Bank of Africa Ltd: PPF House, Ground/Mezzanine Floors, Samora Ave/Morogoro Rd, POB 9640, Dar es Salaam; tel. (22) 2130113; fax (22) 2130116; e-mail uba@cats-net.com; cap. 2,532m. (Dec. 2002); Chair. N. N. KITOMARI; Man. Dir I. J. MITCHELL.

STOCK EXCHANGE

Dar es Salaam Stock Exchange: Twigga Bldg, 4th Floor, Samora Ave, POB 70081, Dar es Salaam; tel. (22) 2135779; fax (22) 2133849; e-mail info@darstockexchange.com; internet www.dse.co.tz; f. 1998; Chair. PETER MACHUNDE; Chief Exec. Dr HAMISI S. KIBOLA.

INSURANCE

Jubilee Insurance Co of Tanzania Ltd (JICT): Dar es Salaam; 40% owned by Jubilee Insurance Kenya, 24% by local investors, 15% by the IFC, 15% by the Aga Khan Fund for Economic Devt, 6% by others; cap. US $2m.

National Insurance Corporation of Tanzania Ltd (NIC): POB 9264, Dar es Salaam; tel. (22) 2113823; fax (22) 2113403; e-mail info-nic@nictanzania.com; internet www.nictanzania.com; f. 1963; state-owned; all classes of insurance; Chair. Prof. J. L. KANYWANYI; Man. Dir OCTAVIAN W. TEMU; 30 brs.

Niko Insurance (Tanzania) Ltd: PPF House, 8th Floor, Morogoro Rd/Samora Ave, POB 21228, Dar es Salaam; tel. (22) 2120188; fax (22) 2120193; e-mail info@nikoinsurance.co.tz; internet www.nikoinsurance.co.tz; f. 1998; subsidiary of NICO Holdings Ltd (based in Malawi); Gen. Man. MANFRED Z. SIBANDE.

Trade and Industry

GOVERNMENT AGENCIES

Board of External Trade (BET): POB 5402, Dar es Salaam; tel. (22) 2851706; fax (22) 2851700; e-mail betis@intafrica.com; internet www.bet.co.tz; f. 1978; trade and export information and promotion, market research, marketing advisory and consultancy services; Dir-Gen. MBARUK K. MWANDORO.

Board of Internal Trade (BIT): POB 883, Dar es Salaam; tel. (22) 228301; f. 1967 as State Trading Corpn; reorg. 1973; state-owned; supervises seven national and 21 regional trading cos; distribution of general merchandise, agricultural and industrial machinery, pharmaceuticals, foodstuffs and textiles; shipping and other transport services; Dir-Gen. J. E. MAKOYE.

Parastatal Sector Reform Commission (PSRC): Sukari House, POB 9252, Dar es Salaam; tel. (22) 2115482; fax (22) 2113065; e-mail masalla@raha.com.

TANZANIA

Tanzania Investment Centre (TIC): POB 938, Dar es Salaam; tel. (22) 2116328; fax (22) 2118253; e-mail information@tic.co.tz; internet www.tic.co.tz; f. 1997; promotes and facilitates investment in Tanzania; Exec. Dir EMMANUEL OLE NAIKO.

CHAMBERS OF COMMERCE

Dar es Salaam Chamber of Commerce: Kelvin House, Samora Machel Ave, POB 41, Dar es Salaam; tel. (744) 270438; fax (22) 2112754; e-mail dcc1919@yahoo.com; f. 1919; Exec. Dir Y. P. MSEKWA.

Tanzania Chamber of Commerce, Industry and Agriculture: 2nd Floor, Twiga House, Samora Ave, POB 9713, Dar es Salaam; tel. (22) 2119436; fax (22) 2119437; e-mail info@tccia.com; internet www.tccia.co.tz; f. 1988; Pres. E. MUSIBA.

Zanzibar Chamber of Commerce: POB 1407, Zanzibar; tel. (24) 2233083; fax (24) 2233349.

DEVELOPMENT CORPORATIONS

Capital Development Authority: POB 1, Dodoma; tel. (26) 2324053; f. 1973 to develop the new capital city of Dodoma; govt-controlled; Dir-Gen. EVARIST BABISI KEWBA.

Economic Development Commission: POB 9242, Dar es Salaam; tel. (22) 2112681; f. 1962 to plan national economic development; state-controlled.

National Development Corporation: Kivukoni Front, Ohio St, POB 2669, Dar es Salaam; tel. (22) 2112893; fax (22) 2113618; e-mail epztz@ndctz.com; internet www.ndctz.com; f. 1965; state-owned; cap. Ts. 30.0m.; promotes progress and expansion in production and investment.

Small Industries Development Organization (SIDO): Mfaume/Fire Rd, Upanga, POB 2476, Dar es Salaam; tel. (22) 2151947; fax (22) 2152070; e-mail dg@sido.go.tz; internet www.sido.go.tz; f. 1973; parastatal; promotes and assists development of small-scale enterprises in public, co-operative and private sectors, aims to increase the involvement of women in small businesses; Chair. JAPHET S. MLAGALA; Dir-Gen. MIKE LAISOR.

Sugar Development Corporation: Dar es Salaam; tel. (22) 2112969; fax (22) 230598; Gen. Man. GEORGE G. MBATI.

Tanzania Petroleum Development Corporation (TPDC): POB 2774, Dar es Salaam; tel. (22) 2181407; fax (22) 2180047; internet www.tpdc-tz.com; f. 1969; state-owned; oversees petroleum exploration and undertakes autonomous exploration, imports crude petroleum and distributes refined products; Man. Dir YONA S. M. KILLAGANE.

There is also a development corporation for textiles.

INDUSTRIAL AND TRADE ASSOCIATIONS

Cashewnut Board of Tanzania: POB 533, Mtwara; tel. (23) 2333303; fax (23) 2333536; e-mail info@cashewnut-tz.org; internet www.cashewnut-tz.org; govt-owned; regulates the marketing, processing and export of cashews; Chair. KITWANA KONDO; Dir-Gen. A. BENO MHAGAMA.

Confederation of Tanzania Industries (CTI): POB 71783, Dar es Salaam; tel. (22) 2114954; fax (22) 2115414; e-mail cti@cti.co.tz; internet www.cti.co.tz; f. 1991; Chair. REGINALD MENGI; Exec. Dir CHRISTINE KILINDU.

National Coconut Development Programme: POB 6226, Dar es Salaam; tel. (22) 2700552; fax (22) 275549; e-mail mari@mari.or.tz; f. 1979 to revive coconut industry; processing and marketing via research and devt in disease and pest control, agronomy and farming systems, breeding and post-harvest technology; based at Mikocheni Agricultural Research Inst; Dir Dr ALOIS K. KULLAYA.

Tanganyika Coffee Growers' Association Ltd: POB 102, Moshi.

Tanzania Horticultural Association (TAHA): Kanisa Rd, House No. 49, POB 3003, Arusha; tel. and fax (27) 2544568; e-mail taha@habari.co.tz; internet www.tanzaniahorticulture.com; f. 2004; Exec. Dir JACQUELINE MKINDI.

Tanzania Coffee Board (TCB): Kahawa House, POB 732, Moshi; tel. (27) 272324; fax (27) 270998; e-mail enquiries@tanzaniacoffee.co.tz; internet tanzaniacoffeeboard.org; Chair. PIUS NGEZE; Dir-Gen. ADOLPH KUMBURU.

Tanzania Cotton Board: Pamba House, Garden Ave, POB 9161, Dar es Salaam; tel. (22) 2122564; fax (22) 2112894; e-mail tclb@tancotton.co.tz; internet www.tancotton.co.tz; f. 1984; regulates, develops and promotes the Tanzanian cotton industry; Dir Gen. Dr JOE KABISSA.

Tanzania Exporters' Association: Plot No. 139, Sembeti Rd, POB 1175, Dar es Salaam; tel. (22) 2781035; fax (22) 2112752; e-mail smutabuz@hotmail.com.

Tanzania Pyrethrum Board: POB 149, Iringa; f. 1960; Chair. Brig. LUHANGA; CEO P. B. G. HANGAYA.

Tanzania Sisal Authority: POB 277, Tanga; tel. (53) 44401; fax (53) 42759; Chair. W. H. SHELLUKINDO; Man. Dir S. SHAMTE.

Tanzania Tobacco Board: POB 227, Mazimbu Rd, Morogoro; tel. (23) 2603364; fax (23) 2604401; Chair. V. KAWAWA; CEO FRANK S. URIO.

Tanzania Wood Industry Corporation: POB 9160, Dar es Salaam; Gen. Man. E. M. MNZAVA.

Tea Association of Tanzania: POB 2177, Dar es Salaam; tel. (22) 2122033; e-mail trit@twiga.com; f. 1989; Chair. Dr NORMAN C. KELLY; Exec. Dir DAVID E. A. MGWASSA.

Tea Board of Tanzania: TETEX House, Pamba Rd, POB 2663, Dar es Salaam; tel. and fax (22) 2114400; Chair. ROSTAM AZIZI; Dir-Gen. MATHIAS ASSENGA BENEDICT.

Zanzibar State Trading Corporation: POB 26, Zanzibar; internet www.zstczanzibar.com; govt-controlled since 1964; sole exporter of cloves, clove stem oil, chillies, copra, copra cake, lime oil and lime juice; Gen. Man. ABDULRAHMAN RASHID.

UTILITIES

Electricity

Tanzania Electric Supply Co Ltd (TANESCO): POB 9024, Dar es Salaam; tel. (22) 2451130; fax (22) 2113836; e-mail info@tanesco.com; internet www.tanesco.com; state-owned; placed under private management in May 2002; privatization pending; Chair. FULGENCE M. KAZAURA; Man. Dir Dr IDRIS RASHIDI.

Gas

Enertan Corpn Ltd: POB 3746, Dar es Salaam.

Songas Ltd: POB 6342, Dar es Salaam; tel. (22) 2117313; fax (22) 2113614; internet www.songas.com; f. 1998; Gen. Man. JIM MCCARDLE.

Water

Dar es Salaam Water and Sanitation Authority: POB 1573, Dar es Salaam; e-mail dawasapiu@raha.com; privatization pending.

National Urban Water Authority: POB 5340, Dar es Salaam; tel. (22) 2667505.

CO-OPERATIVES

There are some 1,670 primary marketing societies under the aegis of about 20 regional co-operative unions. The Co-operative Union of Tanzania is the national organization to which all unions belong.

Tanzania Federation of Co-operatives Ltd: POB 2567, Dar es Salaam; tel. (22) 2184082; fax (22) 2184081; e-mail ushirika@ushirika.co.tz; internet www.ushirika.coop; f. 1962; Exec. Sec. GERALD P. MALIMA; 700,000 mems.

Department of Co-operative Societies: POB 1287, Zanzibar; f. 1952; promotes formation and development of co-operative societies in Zanzibar.

Principal Societies

Kagera Co-operative Union Ltd: POB 5, Bukoba; tel. (28) 2220229; fax (28) 2221168; e-mail kcu@africaonline.co.tz; internet www.kcu-tz.com; 74 affiliated societies; 75,000 mems.

Kilimanjaro Native Co-operative Union (1984) Ltd: POB 3032, Moshi; tel. (27) 2752785; fax (27) 2754204; e-mail kncu@kilinet.co.tz; f. 1984; represents smallhold farmers and coffee-producers; 68 regd co-operative societies; Gen. Man. RAYMOND KIMARO.

Nyanza Co-operative Union Ltd: POB 9, Mwanza.

TRADE UNIONS

Union of Tanzania Workers (Juwata): POB 15359, Dar es Salaam; tel. (22) 226111; f. 1978; Sec.-Gen. JOSEPH C. RWEGASIRA; Dep. Secs-Gen. C. MANYANDA (Tanganyika), I. M. ISSA (Zanzibar).

Agricultural Workers: Sec. G. P. NYINDO.

Central and Local Government and Medical Workers: Sec. R. UTUKULU.

Communications and Transport Workers: POB 13920, Dar es Salaam; Sec. M. E. KALUWA.

Domestic, Hotels and General Workers: Sec. E. KAZOKA.

Industrial and Mines Workers: Sec. J. V. MWAMBUMA.

Railway Workers: Sec. C. SAMMANG' OMBE.

Teachers: Sec. W. MWENURA.

Principal Unaffiliated Unions

Organization of Tanzanian Trade Unions (OTTU): Dar es Salaam; Sec.-Gen. BRUNO MPANGAL.

TANZANIA

Workers' Department of Chama Cha Mapinduzi: POB 389, Vikokotoni, Zanzibar; f. 1965.

Transport

RAILWAYS

Tanzania Railways Corporation (TRC): POB 468, Dar es Salaam; tel. and fax (22) 2110599; e-mail ccm_shamte@trctz.com; internet www.trctz.com; f. 1977 after dissolution of East African Railways; privatization pending; operates 2,600 km of lines within Tanzania; Chair. J. K. CHANDE; Dir-Gen. LINFORD MBOMA.

Tanzania-Zambia Railway Authority (Tazara): POB 2834, Dar es Salaam; tel. (22) 2862191; fax (22) 2862474; e-mail acistz@twiga.com; internet www.tazara.co.tz; jtly owned and administered by the Tanzanian and Zambian Govts; operates a 1,860-km railway link between Dar es Salaam and New Kapiri Mposhi, Zambia, of which 969 km are within Tanzania; Chair. SALIM MSOMA; Man. Dir K. MKANDAWIRE; Regional Man. (Tanzania) A. F. S. NALITOLELA.

ROADS

In 2004 Tanzania had an estimated 85,000 km of classified roads, of which some 5,169 km were paved. A 1,930-km main road links Zambia and Tanzania, and there is a road link with Rwanda. A 10-year Integrated Roads Programme, funded by international donors and co-ordinated by the World Bank, commenced in 1991. Its aim was to upgrade 70% of Tanzania's trunk roads and to construct 2,828 km of roads and 205 bridges, at an estimated cost of US $650m.

The island of Zanzibar has 619 km of roads, of which 442 km are bituminized, and Pemba has 363 km, of which 130 km are bituminized.

INLAND WATERWAYS

Steamers connect with Kenya, Uganda, the Democratic Republic of the Congo, Burundi, Zambia and Malawi. A joint shipping company was formed with Burundi in 1976 to operate services on Lake Tanganyika. A rail ferry service operates on Lake Victoria between Mwanza and Port Bell.

SHIPPING

Tanzania's major harbours are at Dar es Salaam (eight deep-water berths for general cargo, three berths for container ships, eight anchorages, lighter wharf, one oil jetty for small oil tankers up to 36,000 gross tons, offshore mooring for oil supertankers up to 100,000 tons, one 30,000-ton automated grain terminal) and Mtwara (two deep-water berths). There are also ports at Tanga (seven anchorages and lighterage quay), Bagamoyo, Zanzibar and Pemba. A programme to extend and deepen the harbour entrance at Dar es Salaam commenced in 1997.

Tanzania Ports Authority (TPA): POB 9184, Dar es Salaam; tel. (22) 2116258; fax (22) 232066; e-mail dp@tanzaniaports.com; internet www.tanzaniaports.com; f. 2005 to replace the Tanzania Harbours Authority, in preparation for privatization; Dir-Gen. EPHRAIM MGAWE.

Chinese-Tanzanian Joint Shipping Co: POB 696, Dar es Salaam; tel. (22) 2113389; fax (22) 2113388; e-mail admin@sinotaship.com; f. 1967; services to People's Republic of China, South East Asia, Eastern and Southern Africa, Red Sea and Mediterranean ports.

National Shipping Agencies Co Ltd (NASACO): POB 9082, Dar es Salaam; f. 1973; state-owned shipping co; Man. Dir D. R. M. LWIMBO.

Tanzania Central Freight Bureau (TCFB): POB 3093, Dar es Salaam; tel. (22) 2114174; fax (22) 2116697; e-mail tcfb@cats-net.com.

Tanzania Coastal Shipping Line Ltd: POB 9461, Dar es Salaam; tel. (22) 237034; fax (22) 2116436; regular services to Tanzanian coastal ports; occasional special services to Zanzibar and Pemba; also tramp charter services to Kenya, Mozambique, the Persian (Arabian) Gulf, Indian Ocean islands and the Middle East; Gen. Man. RICHARD D. NZOWA.

CIVIL AVIATION

There are 53 airports and landing strips. The major international airport is at Dar es Salaam, 13 km from the city centre, and there are also international airports at Kilimanjaro, Mwanza and Zanzibar. The management of Kilimanjaro International Airport was privatized in 1998. In 2005 it was reported that privatization was to be extended to the management of airports at Dar es Salaam, Mtware and Mwanza.

Tanzania Civil Aviation Authority (TCAA): IPS Bldg, cnr Samora Machel Ave and Azikiwe St, POB 2819, Dar es Salaam; tel. (22) 2115079; fax (22) 2118905; e-mail tcaa@tcaa.go.tz; internet www.tcaa.go.tz; f. 2003; replaced Directorate of Civil Aviation (f. 1977); ensures aviation safety and security, provides air navigation services; Dir-Gen. MARGARET T. MUNYAGI.

Air Tanzania: ATC House, Ohio St/Garden Ave, POB 543, Dar es Salaam; tel. (22) 2197200; fax (22) 2125221; e-mail bookings@airtanzania.com; internet www.airtanzania.com; f. 1977; operates an 18-point domestic network and international services to Africa, the Middle East and Europe; Chair. MUSTAFA NYANG'ANYI; CEO DAVID MATTAKA.

Air Zanzibar: POB 1784, Zanzibar; f. 1990; operates scheduled and charter services between Zanzibar and destinations in Tanzania, Kenya and Uganda.

New ACS Ltd: Peugeot House, 36 Upanga Rd, POB 21236, Dar es Salaam; fax (22) 237017; operates domestic and regional services; Dir MOHSIN RAHEMTULLAH.

Precision Air Services Ltd: Quality Plaza Bldg, Nyerere Rd, POB 70770, Dar es Salaam; tel. (22) 2168000; fax (22) 2860725; e-mail contactcentre@precisionairtz.com; internet www.precisionairtz.com; f. 1993; operates scheduled and charter domestic and regional services; Man. Dir and CEO ALFONSE KIOKO.

Tanzanair: Julius Nyerere Int. Airport, POB 364, Dar es Salaam; tel. (22) 2843131; fax (22) 2844600; e-mail info@tanzanair.com; internet www.tanzanair.com; f. 1969; operates domestic and regional charter services, offers full engineering and maintenance services for general aviation aircraft; Dep. Man. Dir JOHN SAMARAS.

Tourism

Mount Kilimanjaro is a major tourist attraction. Tanzania has set aside about one-quarter of its land area for 12 national parks, 17 game reserves, 50 controlled game areas and a conservation area. Other attractions for tourists include beaches and coral reefs along the Indian Ocean coast, and the island of Zanzibar (which received 86,495 tourists in 1997 and is expanding and upgrading its tourism facilities). Visitor arrivals totalled 644,124 in 2006, and in that year revenue from tourism was US $950m.

Tanzania Tourist Board: IPS Bldg, 3rd Floor, POB 2485, Dar es Salaam; tel. (22) 2111244; fax (22) 2116420; e-mail safari@ud.co.tz; internet www.tanzaniatouristboard.com; f. 1993; state-owned; supervises the development and promotion of tourism; Man. Dir PETER J. MWENGUO.

Tanzania Wildlife Co Ltd: POB 1144, Arusha; tel. (78) 7787459; e-mail info@tanzaniawildlifecompany.com; internet www.tanzaniawildlifecompany.com; f. 1974; organizes hunting, photographic, horseback and adventure safaris; Man. Dir LEON LAMPRECHT.

Zanzibar Tourist Corporation: POB 216, Zanzibar; tel. (24) 2238630; fax (24) 2233417; e-mail ztc@zanzinet.com; internet www.zanzibartouristcorporation.com; f. 1985; operates tours and hotel services; Gen. Man. SABAAH SALEH ALI.

THAILAND

Introductory Survey

Location, Climate, Language, Religion, Flag, Capital

The Kingdom of Thailand lies in South-East Asia. It is bordered to the west and north by Myanmar (Burma), to the north-east by Laos and to the south-east by Cambodia. Thailand extends southward, along the isthmus of Kra, to the Malay Peninsula, where it borders Malaysia. The isthmus, shared with Myanmar, gives Thailand a short coastline on the Indian Ocean, and the country also has a long Pacific coastline on the Gulf of Thailand. The climate is tropical and humid, with an average annual temperature of 29°C (85°F). There are three main seasons: hot, rainy and cool. Temperatures in Bangkok are generally between 20°C (68°F) and 35°C (95°F). The national language is Thai. There are small minorities of Chinese, Malays and indigenous hill peoples. The predominant religion is Buddhism, mainly of the Hinayana (Theravada) form. About 4% of the population, predominantly Malays, are Muslims, and there is also a Christian minority, mainly in Bangkok and the north. The national flag (proportions 2 by 3) has five horizontal stripes, of red, white, blue, white and red, the central blue stripe being twice as wide as each of the others. The capital is Bangkok.

Recent History

Formerly known as Siam, Thailand took its present name in 1939. Under the leadership of Marshal Phibul Songkhram, Thailand entered the Second World War as an ally of Japan. Phibul was deposed in 1944, but returned to power in 1947 after a military coup. His influence declined during the 1950s, and in 1957 he was overthrown in a bloodless coup, led by Field Marshal Sarit Thanarat. Elections took place, but in 1958 martial law was declared and all political parties were dissolved. Sarit died in 1963 and was succeeded as Prime Minister by Gen. (later Field Marshal) Thanom Kittikachorn, who had served as Deputy Prime Minister since 1959. Thanom continued the combination of military authoritarianism and economic development instituted by his predecessor. A Constitution was introduced in 1968, and elections to a National Assembly took place in 1969, but in November 1971, following an increase in communist insurgency and internal political unrest, Thanom annulled the Constitution, dissolved the National Assembly and imposed martial law.

During 1972 there were frequent student demonstrations against the military regime, and in October 1973 the Government was forced to resign, after the army refused to use force to disperse student protesters, and King Bhumibol withdrew his support from the administration. An interim Government was formed under Dr Sanya Dharmasakti, the President of the Privy Council. In October 1974 a new Constitution, legalizing political parties, was promulgated, and in January 1975 elections were held to the new House of Representatives. A coalition Government was formed in February by Seni Pramoj, the leader of the Democrat Party (DP), but it was defeated by a vote of no confidence in the following month.

A new right-wing coalition Government, headed by the leader of the Social Action Party (SAP), Kukrit Pramoj (brother of Seni), was unable to maintain its unity, and Kukrit resigned in January 1976. After further general elections in April, a four-party coalition Government was formed, with Seni as Prime Minister. However, following violent student demonstrations in October during which the security forces killed hundreds of demonstrators, the Seni Government was dissolved, and a right-wing military junta, the National Administrative Reform Council (NARC), seized power. Martial law was declared, the Constitution was annulled, political parties were banned and strict press censorship was imposed. A new Constitution was promulgated, and a new Cabinet was announced, with Thanin Kraivixien, a Supreme Court judge, as Prime Minister.

Under the Thanin Government there was considerable repression of students and political activists. In October 1977 the Government was overthrown in a bloodless coup by a Revolutionary Council (later known as the National Policy Council—NPC) of military leaders, most of whom had been members of the NARC. The 1976 Constitution was abrogated, and the Secretary-General of the NPC (who was also the Supreme Commander of the Armed Forces), Gen. Kriangsak Chomanan, became Prime Minister. Many detainees were released, censorship was partially relaxed and the King nominated a National Assembly on the advice of the NPC. In December 1978 the National Assembly approved a new Constitution, and elections to a new House of Representatives were held in April 1979. However, members of the Senate were all nominated by the Prime Minister, and were almost all military officers. Kriangsak remained Prime Minister and formed a new Council of Ministers, after which the NPC was dissolved. When Kriangsak resigned in March 1980, he was replaced by Gen. Prem Tinsulanonda, the Commander-in-Chief of the Army and the Minister of Defence. A new coalition Government, composed largely of centre-right politicians acceptable to the armed forces, was formed.

Prem's administration survived an abortive coup attempt in April 1981. In December Prem effected a ministerial reorganization, reincorporating members of the SAP (who had been excluded from the Government in March), in order to repulse a challenge from the new National Democracy Party (NDP), established by Kriangsak. In April 1983 no single party won an overall majority in elections to the House of Representatives, and a coalition Government was formed by the SAP, Prachakorn Thai, the DP and the NDP, despite Chart Thai being the party with the largest number of seats. Prem was again appointed Prime Minister.

In September 1985 a group of military officers carried out a coup attempt in Bangkok. Troops loyal to the Government quickly suppressed the revolt, but at least five people were killed during the fighting. The leader of the revolt, Col Manoon Roopkachorn (who had also led the coup attempt in 1981), fled the country, but 40 others, including Kriangsak, were put on trial in October, accused of inciting sedition and rebellion. Gen. Arthit Kamlang-ek, the Supreme Commander of the Armed Forces and Commander-in-Chief of the Army (who was believed to have been sympathetic to the aims of the coup leaders), was replaced in his posts by Gen. Chavalit Yongchaiyudh, hitherto the army Chief of Staff.

In September 1985 and January 1986 there were extensive changes in the Government, including the replacement of all members of the SAP, following the resignation of Kukrit as the party's leader. In May 1986, following a parliamentary defeat for the Government over proposed vehicle taxation, the House of Representatives was dissolved. At a general election for an enlarged legislature in July, the DP won 100 of the 347 seats (compared with 56 of the 324 seats at the previous election). A coalition Government was formed, including members of the DP, Chart Thai, the SAP, Rassadorn and seven 'independent' ministers. Prem remained Prime Minister.

In April 1988 the rejection by dissident members of the DP of proposed legislation on copyright prompted 16 ministers belonging to the DP to resign for failing to maintain party unity. The King dissolved the House of Representatives, at Prem's request, and new elections were held in July. Internal disputes weakened support for the DP (25 dissidents had resigned in May), and Chart Thai won the largest number of seats (87). Gen. Chatichai Choonhavan, the leader of Chart Thai, was appointed Prime Minister in August, after Prem declined an invitation to remain in the post. A new Council of Ministers was formed, comprising members of Chart Thai, the DP, the SAP, Rassadorn, the United Democratic Party and the Muan Chon party. In April 1989 Ruam Thai, the Community Action Party, the Prachachon Party and the Progressive Party merged to form an opposition grouping called Ekkaparb (Solidarity). Nine members of the Prachachon Party subsequently defected to Chart Thai, giving the ruling coalition control of 229 of the 357 seats in the House of Representatives.

In March 1990 Chavalit resigned as acting Supreme Commander of the Armed Forces; he also resigned as Commander-in-Chief of the Army, in which post he was succeeded by Gen. Suchinda Kraprayoon, hitherto his deputy. In July, despite growing criticism of Chatichai's administration, following a number of corruption scandals and labour unrest, the House of Representatives overwhelmingly rejected an opposition motion of no confidence in the Government. In August, however,

THAILAND

Chatichai reorganized the Council of Ministers, incorporating Puangchon Chao Thai in the ruling coalition, and reducing the influence of the SAP, following the implication of many of its members in allegations of corruption.

In November 1990 Chatichai demoted the leader of the Muan Chon party, Chalerm Yoobamrung, an outspoken critic of the armed forces, from his position as Minister to the Prime Minister's Office. The leadership of the armed forces had demanded Chalerm's dismissal, threatening unspecified intervention if government changes did not take place. In early December Chatichai resigned as Prime Minister; he was reappointed on the next day and subsequently formed a coalition Government comprising Chart Thai, Rassadorn, Puangchon Chao Thai and former opposition parties Prachakorn Thai and Ekkaparb, which provided him with reduced support (227 of the 357 seats) in the House of Representatives.

On 23 February 1991 Chatichai's Government was ousted in a bloodless military coup. Gen. Sunthorn Kongsompong, the Supreme Commander of the Armed Forces, assumed administrative power as the Chairman of the newly created National Peace-keeping Council (NPC). The NPC was actually dominated by the effective head of the armed forces, Gen. Suchinda, one of four Deputy Chairmen of the NPC. The coup leaders cited government corruption and abuse of power to justify their action; however, the coup was also widely believed to have been organized in response to the recent erosion of military influence.

Under the NPC, the Constitution was abrogated, the House of Representatives, the Senate and the Council of Ministers were dissolved, and martial law was imposed. The NPC won unprecedented royal approval, and in March 1991 an interim Constitution was published. Anand Panyarachun, a business executive and former diplomat, was appointed acting Prime Minister pending fresh elections. Anand appointed a predominantly civilian interim Cabinet, composed mainly of respected technocrats and former ministers. Chatichai and Arthit, who had been arrested at the time of the coup, were released after two weeks. The NPC appointed a 292-member National Legislative Assembly, which included 149 serving or former military personnel, as well as many civilians known to have connections with the armed forces.

In May 1991 martial law was repealed in most areas, and political activity was permitted to resume. The New Aspiration Party (NAP—formed in October 1990 by Gen. Chavalit) gathered support as the traditional parties were in disarray, largely owing to investigations of corruption by the newly created Assets Examination Committee. In June 1991 the Commander-in-Chief of the Air Force, Air Chief Marshal Kaset Rojananin, sponsored the creation of a new party, Samakkhi Tham, led by Narong Wongwan, a former leader of Ekkaparb. In August Suchinda assumed, in addition to the post of Commander-in-Chief of the Army, the role of Supreme Commander of the Armed Forces.

In November 1991 the Constitution Scrutiny Committee, which had been effectively nominated by the NPC, presented a draft Constitution to the National Legislative Assembly. Following public criticism of the draft (including a demonstration by 50,000 protesters in Bangkok), the document was amended to reduce the number of nominated senators from 360 to 270, and to abolish provisions that allowed the Senate the right to participate in the selection of the Prime Minister. Opposition parties, including the NAP and Palang Dharma (led by the popular and influential Governor of Bangkok, Maj.-Gen. Chamlong Srimuang), continued to oppose the draft, claiming that it perpetuated the power of the NPC. The National Legislative Assembly approved the new Constitution in December, but campaigners continued to express concern over certain provisional clauses (which were to remain in effect for four years), under which the NPC was to appoint the Prime Minister and the Senate, and regarding the Senate's right to vote jointly with the elected House on motions of no confidence, thus enabling the Senate to dismiss a government with the support of only 46 elected representatives.

A general election took place on 22 March 1992, when 15 parties contested the 360 seats; 59.2% of the electorate voted. Samakkhi Tham and Chart Thai secured the largest number of seats, 79 and 74 respectively. The NAP secured 72 seats and Palang Dharma won 41 seats, 32 of which were in Bangkok. On the day of the election the NPC appointed the 270 members of the Senate, 154 of whom were officers of the armed forces or police. In late March it was announced that Narong Wongwan would lead a coalition government comprising his own party (Samakkhi Tham), Chart Thai, Prachakorn Thai, the SAP and Rassadorn.

Introductory Survey

However, US allegations of Narong's involvement in illicit drugs-trafficking caused the nomination to be rescinded. In early April Suchinda was named as Prime Minister, despite his assurances before the election that he would not accept the post. He was replaced as Supreme Commander of the Armed Forces by Kaset and as Commander-in-Chief of the Army by his brother-in-law, Gen. Issarapong Noonpakdi. Suchinda's accession to the premiership prompted an immediate popular protest by more than 50,000 demonstrators against the appointment of an unelected Prime Minister. Later in April Suchinda appointed eight other unelected members to a new Cabinet, retaining several technocrats from Anand's interim Government.

In early May 1992 Chamlong announced, at a rally attended by 100,000 demonstrators, that he would fast until death unless Suchinda resigned. The demonstrations continued uninterrupted for one week until the government parties agreed to amend the Constitution to prevent an unelected Prime Minister (including the incumbent Suchinda) from taking office, and to limit the power of the unelected Senate. Chamlong abandoned his hunger strike, and temporarily suspended the demonstration. However, violent anti-Government demonstrations erupted in Bangkok when it appeared that the Government might renege on its commitments. The Government declared a state of emergency in Bangkok and neighbouring provinces. Chamlong was arrested and more than 3,000 people were detained by security forces in a brutal attempt to suppress the riots, which continued for several days.

Following unprecedented intervention by King Bhumibol, Suchinda ordered the release of Chamlong, announced a general amnesty for those involved in the protests and pledged to introduce amendments to the Constitution. On 24 May 1992 Suchinda resigned, after failing to retain the support of the five coalition parties. On 10 June the National Assembly approved constitutional amendments, whereby the Prime Minister was required to be a member of the House of Representatives, the authority of the Senate was restricted and the President of the House of Representatives was to be the President of the National Assembly. On the same day the King, contrary to expectations, named Anand as Prime Minister. Anand appointed a politically neutral, unelected Cabinet, and dissolved the National Assembly in preparation for a general election. At the end of June the four parties that had opposed the military Government (the DP, the NAP, Palang Dharma and Ekkaparb) formed an electoral alliance, the National Democratic Front. In July Chatichai declined the leadership of Chart Thai and formed a new party, Chart Pattana, which quickly gained widespread support.

During mid-1992 Anand introduced measures to curb the political power of the armed forces, reduce military control of state enterprises, and remove the authority of the armed forces to intervene in situations of social unrest. In August Kaset and Issarapong were dismissed from their positions and demoted to inactive posts. The new Commander-in-Chief of the Army, Gen. Wimol Wongwanit, pledged that the army would not interfere in politics under his command.

The general election took place on 13 September 1992, when 12 parties contested the 360 seats in the House of Representatives; 62.1% of the electorate voted. 'Vote-buying' and violence persisted, especially in the north-eastern region. The DP won the largest number of seats (79), while Chart Thai and Chart Pattana secured 77 and 60 seats respectively. The DP was able to form a coalition with its allies, the NAP, Palang Dharma and Ekkaparb, which commanded 185 of the 360 seats. Despite its participation in the previous administration, the SAP (with 22 seats) was also subsequently invited to join the Government. On 23 September Chuan Leekpai, the leader of the DP, was formally approved as Prime Minister. Chuan declared his intention to eradicate corrupt practices, to decentralize government, to enhance rural development and to reduce the powers of the Senate.

Although Chuan's integrity as Prime Minister remained unquestioned, dissatisfaction with his style of leadership emerged in early 1993. In June, however, two motions of no confidence in the Cabinet were rejected by a considerable margin. Following its announcement in September that it was to merge with four opposition parties, including Chart Pattana, under the leadership of Chatichai, the SAP (which had been critical of Chuan's alleged indecisiveness) was expelled from the Government and replaced by the Seritham Party.

In September 1994 Chamlong resumed the leadership of Palang Dharma in party elections, and subsequently persuaded the party executive committee to approve the replacement of the party's 11 cabinet members. Chamlong's nominations for inclusion in the Cabinet included Thaksin Shinawatra, a prominent business executive, as Minister of Foreign Affairs. Despite some opposition to the selection of unelected candidates, the appointments were confirmed in October, when Chamlong was named a Deputy Prime Minister.

In December 1994 the NAP withdrew from the ruling coalition over a constitutional amendment providing for the future election of local government representatives, including village headmen. The NAP voted against the Government to protect the vested interests of incumbent local administrators who would control many votes at the next election. In order to secure a parliamentary majority, Chuan was obliged to include Chatichai's Chart Pattana in the governing coalition, although this severely compromised the Government's claims to represent honesty and reform.

In January 1995 Chuan finally obtained the approval of the National Assembly for a series of amendments to the Constitution to expand the country's democratic base. The reforms included a reduction in the size of the appointed Senate to two-thirds of that of the elective House of Representatives, the lowering of the eligible voting age from 20 years to 18, equality for women, the establishment of an administrative court, the introduction of parliamentary ombudsmen and the prohibition of senators and members of the Government from holding monopolistic concessions with government or state bodies. This last amendment necessitated the resignation of Thaksin as Minister of Foreign Affairs, owing to his extensive business interests.

In May 1995, dissatisfied with the Government's response to revelations that a land reform programme had been used to benefit wealthy landowners, the opposition tabled a motion of no confidence in the Government. (The scandal had already prompted the resignation of the Minister of Agriculture and Co-operatives in December 1994.) Following an announcement by Chamlong that Palang Dharma would not support the coalition in the no confidence vote, Chuan dissolved the House of Representatives on 19 May 1995.

At elections to an enlarged House of Representatives, which took place on 2 July 1995, 12 political parties contested 391 seats; 62.0% of eligible voters participated in the election. Chart Thai won the largest number of seats (92), followed by the DP (86) and the NAP (57). Support for these parties was based on provincial patronage politics and allegations of 'vote-buying' were widespread. The leader of Chart Thai, Banharn Silapa-Archa (who had been accused of 'possessing unusual wealth' by the military junta in 1991), formed a coalition Government comprising Chart Thai, the NAP, Palang Dharma, the SAP, Prachakorn Thai, Muan Chon and later Nam Thai (a business-orientated party formed in 1994 by Amnuay Viravan, a former minister). Thaksin (who had relinquished majority control of his company) had been elected to the leadership of Palang Dharma in May 1995, following the resignation of Chamlong. Banharn appointed all the leaders of the coalition parties (except for the Muan Chon party) as Deputy Prime Ministers. The composition of Banharn's Cabinet was widely criticized, owing to the predominance of professional politicians (who were often subject to allegations of corruption and 'vote-buying').

In March 1996 Banharn announced the composition of the new Senate, the first to be appointed by a democratically elected Prime Minister. In contrast to the previous Senate, only 39 active military officers were named as senators; other appointees included academics and business executives.

In May 1996 10 government ministers, including the Prime Minister, survived motions of no confidence, despite opposition revelations of financial irregularities at the Bangkok Bank of Commerce, including loans extended without collateral to members of the Thai Cabinet, notably the Deputy Minister of the Interior, Suchart Tancharoen, and the Deputy Minister of Finance, Newin Chidchob, both members of Chart Thai. Palang Dharma refused to support Suchart in the debate. In order to pre-empt the withdrawal of Palang Dharma from the ruling coalition, five members of Chart Thai, including Suchart and Newin, resigned from their government positions. Palang Dharma subsequently agreed to remain in the coalition. A cabinet reorganization at the end of May included the dismissal of Surakiart Surakiart, the Minister of Finance, who had failed to take action to prevent huge losses at the Bangkok Bank of Commerce.

In August 1996 the Government suffered a set-back following the withdrawal of Palang Dharma from the ruling coalition. This defection, which was the apparent result of a cabinet dispute over alleged bribery in the awarding of bank licences, reduced the Government's legislative majority by 23 seats. In September Banharn was able to secure the support of his coalition partners in a scheduled motion of no confidence in his administration only by undertaking to resign from the premiership. However, the inability of the coalition partners to agree on the appointment of a new Prime Minister led to the dissolution of the House of Representatives on 27 September.

In the general election, which was held on 17 November 1996 and was marred by violence and alleged extensive irregularities, the NAP won 125 of the 393 seats, while the DP secured 123 seats. The majority of NAP seats were gained through provincial patronage politics, while the more politically aware electorate of Bangkok returned the DP to 29 of the city's 37 seats. Chavalit, the leader of the NAP, was appointed Prime Minister, heading a coalition that incorporated Chart Pattana, the SAP, Prachakorn Thai, Muan Chon and the Seritham Party. The ruling coalition thus held 221 seats in the House of Representatives. Chatichai was appointed as the Chairman of the Prime Minister's special advisory group on economic and foreign affairs, and the majority of the other influential cabinet posts were assigned to other members of Chart Pattana and the NAP. Thaksin resigned as leader of Palang Dharma following the party's failure to win more than one seat in the House of Representatives.

As evidence of Chavalit's avowed intention to revive the economy, he allocated the finance portfolio and the deputy premiership with responsibility for economic affairs to Amnuay, a respected technocrat. However, Chavalit subsequently failed to give Amnuay the necessary support to overcome the obstacles imposed by other coalition members anxious to prevent the implementation of austere fiscal policies. In June 1997 Amnuay resigned and was replaced by the little-known Thanong Bidaya, the President of the Thai Military Bank. The Government's indecisive handling of the economy contributed to a financial crisis in mid-1997, following a series of sustained assaults on the Thai baht by currency speculators, which led to the baht's effective devaluation in early July. At the end of July the Governor of the Central Bank, Rerngchai Marakanonda, also resigned, citing political interference. The deterioration in the state of the economy in 1997 was reflected in an increase in popular protests. The Government introduced measures in June to constrain media attacks on the authorities and to limit mass protests.

In August 1997 Chavalit implemented a cabinet reorganization in an attempt to regain public confidence. On the advice of former Prime Minister Prem, the former Minister of Finance, Virabongsa Ramangkura, an outspoken critic of the Government's handling of the economic crisis, was appointed Deputy Prime Minister with responsibility for economic affairs, while Thaksin joined the Cabinet as Deputy Prime Minister with responsibility for regional development and trade.

Meanwhile, in January 1997 an assembly of 99 members was elected by the legislature to draft a new constitution following the unanimous approval of a constitution amendment bill by the National Assembly in September 1996. The draft Constitution included provisions for: a directly elected Senate; the replacement in the House of Representatives of 393 deputies from multi-member constituencies by 400 deputies from single-member constituencies and 100 deputies elected by proportional representation; the resignation of cabinet ministers from the legislature; the establishment of a minimum educational requirement for members of the National Assembly; the formation of an Election Commission to supervise elections (in place of the Ministry of the Interior); the centralization of vote-counting; compulsory voting; and the guarantee of press freedom. Although the draft gained the support of opposition parties and the media, there was considerable opposition to the new charter from within the ruling administration. Chavalit himself reneged on his pledge to support the draft, but then finally gave it his endorsement following the application of pressure by both business representatives and the armed forces.

Chavalit ensured his survival of a no confidence motion tabled by the opposition by scheduling the censure debate prior to the vote on the draft Constitution. If defeated, Chavalit could thus dissolve the National Assembly rather than resign, delaying the vote on the draft Constitution and forcing fresh elections under the existing Constitution. In the event the Government won the no confidence vote and the draft Constitution was approved on 27 September 1997. The new Constitution was promulgated on 11 October.

In October 1997 Thanong resigned as Minister of Finance, citing obstruction of his attempts to implement the extensive economic reforms required. Following popular demonstrations demanding the resignation of Chavalit, a cabinet reorganization was announced at the end of October. The new appointments failed to restore public or investor confidence in the Government, however, and the Thai currency continued to depreciate. At the beginning of November Chavalit's announcement that he would resign from the premiership on 6 November, following the adoption of important electoral and financial legislation, caused a slight recovery of the Thai baht. On 9 November Chuan, who maintained his reputation for integrity, assumed the premiership, following the formation of a coalition comprising Chuan's DP, Chart Thai, the SAP, Ekkaparb, the Seritham Party, Palang Dharma and the Thai Party (as well as 12 of the 18 members of Prachakorn Thai), which commanded the support of 210 of the 393 seats in the House of Representatives.

The transfer of power to Chuan, under the terms of the new Constitution, without the intervention of the armed forces or resort to a non-elected leader, received widespread approval and represented significant democratic progress. The new Cabinet included Tarrin Nimmanhaeminda as Minister of Finance (a post he had occupied in Chuan's previous administration) and the former Deputy Prime Minister, Supachai Panichpakdi, as Minister of Commerce. However, the baht continued to depreciate, causing intermittent social unrest. In March a vote of no confidence in Chuan's Government, which retained popular support, was defeated.

In May 1998 the Governor of the Central Bank, Chaiyawat Wibulsawadi, resigned, shortly before the publication of an independent report into the alleged mismanagement of the economy preceding the devaluation of the baht in July 1997 and the onset of the subsequent financial crisis. The report attributed much blame for the country's difficulties to the economic strategy followed by Chaiyawat, his predecessor, former Prime Minister Chavalit and former Minister of Finance Amnuay. Also in May new electoral legislation was approved, enabling polls to be held six months later. There were fears that, under the new legislation, the 12 members of the ruling coalition who had defected from Prachakorn Thai to help form the Government in November 1997 might lose their legal status as legislators. (The 12 were formally expelled from Prachakorn Thai in October 1998 but continued to form part of the coalition Government.) In July a new political party, Thai Rak Thai, was established by the former Deputy Prime Minister, Thaksin Shinawatra.

By August 1998 Thailand's economy appeared to have stabilized, and Chuan received rare public praise from Queen Sirikit. However, the Government was beset by allegations of corruption. In October Chuan reorganized his Government, bringing the Chart Pattana party into the ruling coalition and thereby increasing to 257 the number of seats held by the coalition in the House of Representatives. Five new ministers were appointed to the Cabinet, including the Secretary-General of Chart Pattana, Suwat Liptapanlop, who was assigned the industry portfolio. In December the opposition filed a motion to remove Chuan and Tarrin from office, on the grounds that they had allegedly acted in breach of the Constitution by submitting four Letters of Intent to the IMF (see p. 135) without first securing the approval of the House of Representatives; the motion was unsuccessful.

In July 1999 the SAP withdrew from the governing coalition, following disputes within the party concerning the allocation of cabinet positions, prompting a reorganization of the Cabinet. By August, however, public approval of the Government appeared to be in decline, and the coalition was placed under increasing pressure from the opposition to dissolve the House of Representatives and call elections. Thai Rak Thai intensified its recruitment campaign from mid-1999; a public debate on the alleged use of financial inducements by Thai Rak Thai to recruit members of other parties was initiated by members of the DP. In November Chavalit pledged his willingness to support Thai Rak Thai in the forthcoming general election in the event of his own NAP performing poorly.

In August 1999 a report on the state-owned Krung Thai Bank, which exposed the bank's dubious loan policies and other irregularities, was disclosed to the Senate and the press. The report led to allegations of corruption being made against Tarrin, whose brother, Sirin Nimmanhaeminda, had been the President of Krung Thai Bank until his resignation in January. Although the Government was reported in October to have exonerated a number of senior Krung Thai executives, including Sirin, of allegations of inefficiency and dishonesty, the controversy surrounding the bank continued and constituted the main focus of a no confidence motion filed by the opposition against the Government in December, in which the ruling coalition was accused of mismanagement of the economy and of condoning corruption. Although the Government survived the censure debate, the proceedings exposed divisions within the governing coalition (particularly between the DP and Chart Thai).

The DP fared badly in provincial elections held in February 2000, possibly owing to discontent among the rural population with the Government's refusal to subsidize crop prices. Allegations of corruption against the ruling coalition re-emerged in 2000. In March the Deputy Prime Minister and Minister of the Interior, Maj.-Gen. (retd) Sanan Kajornprasart, was accused by the National Anti-Corruption Committee (NACC) of having falsified his assets declaration statement (recently required of all cabinet ministers). Pending a ruling on the case by the Constitutional Court, Sanan resigned from his ministerial positions, being replaced by Banyat Bantadtan. In August Sanan was convicted of corruption by the Constitutional Court.

On 4 March 2000 elections to the new 200-member Senate were contested by more than 1,500 candidates. The level of voter participation was reported at 70%, with voting being compulsory for the first time. Although an increased focus on the suitability of the candidates themselves was reported, the widespread practice of 'vote-buying' persisted, and on 21 March the Election Commission disqualified 78 of the 200 winning candidates (including the wives of two cabinet ministers). A second round of polling was held in the 78 affected constituencies on 29 April, in which all but two of the disqualified contestants were permitted to stand again. However, there were further allegations of electoral fraud following the second round of voting, with 34 of the previously disqualified candidates being accused of various electoral violations. The Election Commission responded by declaring that a second re-run of the polls would be held in at least nine of the affected constituencies. (While the final results of the elections remained in dispute, none of the declared winners were able to assume their seats as they lacked the necessary quorum, resulting in a backlog of legislation and obliging the outgoing Senate to remain in office in an interim capacity.) Although in May it was reported that 22 senatorial candidates had been cleared of allegations of fraud by the Election Commission owing to lack of evidence, a third round of polling was scheduled to be held in June in a number of constituencies. Further allegations of electoral fraud necessitated a fourth and fifth round of polling in June and July respectively. Despite the resignation of almost 100 NAP deputies from the House of Representatives in June and July in support of an early dissolution of the House, Chuan reiterated his intention to dissolve the House in October. The SAP also withdrew from the House of Representatives in July in a similar attempt to gain an early dissolution. On 1 August Thailand's first-ever democratically elected Senate was formally inaugurated.

In November 2000 it was announced that elections to the House of Representatives would be held in January 2001. In December 2000 the NACC recommended that Thaksin Shinawatra should be indicted for having violated the Constitution by concealing financial assets and seeking to avoid the payment of taxes. One notable feature of Thai Rak Thai's electoral campaign was its targeting of rural votes by pledging grants of 1m. baht for each of Thailand's 70,000 villages and offering a debt-relief scheme for farmers. At the legislative elections held on 6 January 2001 Thai Rak Thai won 248 of the 500 seats in the House of Representatives, thereby almost gaining an unprecedented absolute majority. However, the elections were marred by widespread allegations of malpractice; indeed, many domestic and international observers declared that, despite the vigilance of the Election Commission, they had been the most corrupt ever held in Thailand. In late January repolling was held in more than 60 constituencies where the Election Commission had found evidence of fraudulent practice. In February a new Cabinet nominated by Thaksin was formally approved by the King. All but five of the appointees were members of Thai Rak Thai, with which the Seritham Party had merged since the election, thus affording Thai Rak Thai an absolute majority in the House of Representatives. With the support of its coalition partners, the NAP and Chart Thai, the incoming Thai Rak Thai administration controlled 339 of the 500 seats in the House.

In April 2001 the Constitutional Court formally commenced hearing charges of corruption brought against the Prime Minister, Thaksin, as recommended by the NACC. In the same month two bombs exploded in southern Thailand, killing a child and injuring 42 people. The involvement of a militant Islamist separatist organization, the Pattani United Liberation Organization (PULO), was suspected. The PULO belonged to Bersatu, an umbrella organization of three separatist movements, which, the Government claimed, was seeking to establish a Muslim state in southern Thailand.

On 30 June 2001 by-elections were held in seven constituencies to fill seats in the House of Representatives vacated by members disqualified for breaches of campaign rules after the January elections. However, the polls were again marred by allegations of corruption.

The Prime Minister was acquitted of the charges against him regarding concealment of his assets in August 2001. The judges ruled by a narrow eight-to-seven majority in his favour. His exoneration was welcomed by his many supporters, who had conducted a popular campaign that was thought to have exerted some influence over the court's verdict.

In October 2001 the Government introduced a plan to provide low-cost health care for the nation's poorest people, thus implementing one of the Prime Minister's election pledges. Doubts remained over the quality of the service provided. Later in the same month the limits to the Government's reform efforts were highlighted when army Sub-Lt Duangchalerm Yoobamrung, son of Chalerm Yoobamrung (now an influential NAP member of the House of Representatives), allegedly murdered a police officer during a fight in a night-club. Duangchalerm subsequently fled to Cambodia. As a result of his son's actions and subsequent popular criticism of the Government for its ineffectual attempts to bring him to justice, Chalerm was forced to resign from the deputy leadership of the NAP, although he retained an influential position within the Government. In May 2002 Duangchalerm surrendered himself to the Thai embassy in Malaysia and agreed to return home. In March 2004 Duangchalerm was acquitted of all the charges against him, allegedly owing to insufficient evidence.

In December 2002 King Bhumibol made a speech to mark his birthday in which he publicly criticized the Prime Minister, commenting that his Government's 'double standards' were effectively leading Thailand towards 'catastrophe'. His criticism was thought to be linked to his reported disapproval of the business relationship that existed between the Prime Minister and the King's son, Crown Prince Vajiralongkorn.

In January 2002 the NAP voted to merge with its coalition partner, Thai Rak Thai. Despite opposition from several NAP politicians, the party was legally dissolved in March. In the same month the Government was further strengthened when Chart Pattana joined the ruling coalition; a minor cabinet reorganization took place shortly afterwards in which Suwat Liptapanlop, Secretary-General of Chart Pattana, was allocated a ministerial position. Meanwhile, by-elections were held in 14 constituencies where the January 2001 general election results had been invalidated owing to electoral fraud and corruption. Thai Rak Thai lost five seats as a result, but retained its commanding majority in the National Assembly. Shortly afterwards six policemen died after gunmen attacked three security outposts—two in Pattani province and one in Yala province. The attacks were suspected to have been carried out by one of the militant Islamist separatist organizations known to exist in the area. Two bombs later exploded in Yala province, coinciding with a tour of the region by the Minister of the Interior. A Thai military official attributed the attacks to the Gerakan (or Guragan) Mujahideen Islam Pattani, a constituent group of Bersatu thought to be linked to the international terrorist network al-Qa'ida. In April 2002 the Constitutional Court formally granted the NAP's request that it be permitted to merge with Thai Rak Thai.

In May 2002 the Government succeeded in defeating no confidence motions that had been brought by the opposition against 15 of its ministers, including nine members of the Cabinet. In October Prime Minister Thaksin implemented an extensive cabinet reorganization, in which, among other changes, Chavalit Yongchaiyudh was replaced as Minister of Defence by Thammarak Isarangura, while former Minister of Transport Wan Muhamad Nor Matha became Minister of the Interior. Six ministers were also appointed to take responsibility for new ministries that had been created as part of the Government's ongoing bureaucratic reforms.

In February 2003 a further redistribution of cabinet portfolios took place. The Minister of Finance, Somkid Jatusripitak, and the Minister of Justice, Purachai Piemsomboon, were both appointed Deputy Prime Ministers; Somkid was replaced by his deputy, Suchart Jaovisidha, while Purachai was succeeded by former Minister of Energy Pongthep Thepkanjana. Meanwhile, the Government announced the commencement of an intensive anti-drugs campaign intended to eliminate Thailand's drug problem within three months. As the campaign continued, the huge number of suspected drug dealers being killed prompted criticism from both local and international human rights groups, which claimed that the Thai authorities were operating an illegal 'shoot to kill' policy and effectively condoning extra-judicial violence. The Government rejected a request from the Office of the UN High Commissioner for Human Rights (OHCHR, see p. 51) that it be permitted to send a representative to the country to investigate the killings. In March Thaksin acknowledged that mistakes had been made during the campaign, but denied that the police had been responsible for any extra-judicial killings. However, later in that month Thaksin ordered that the campaign should henceforth be concentrated upon provinces along the border with Myanmar, where the majority of drugs-smuggling activity was believed to take place. By mid-April 2003, according to a statement issued by police, as a result of the campaign some 2,275 people had been killed, of whom the police admitted to shooting 51 fatally for reasons of self-defence. At the end of April Thaksin stated that the campaign had eradicated 'about 90%' of the country's drugs problem. Meanwhile, two attacks on army bases in the south of the country were reportedly carried out by the PULO. In the following month, owing to the success of the anti-drugs offensive, Thaksin announced the commencement of a 'war on dark influences' intended to eradicate criminal networks operating in the country.

In April 2003 the DP elected Banyat Bantadtan as its new leader, following the retirement of Chuan Leekpai. In May five cabinet ministers evaded censure, following the tabling of an opposition no confidence motion accusing them of corruption. In the following month Thai Rak Thai defeated the DP at a by-election in Si Sa Ket. Later in June three men were arrested on suspicion of being members of the regional terrorist organization Jemaah Islamiah; they later confessed to having plotted to attack embassies and tourist destinations in the country. A further suspect was arrested in July. In the following month, in response to the perceived terrorist threat to Thailand, the Cabinet approved two anti-terrorism laws by decree, circumventing the legislature owing to the reported gravity of the threat. Shortly afterwards, the alleged former operational head of Jemaah Islamiah, the Indonesian citizen Riduan Isamuddin, also known as Hambali, was apprehended in Thailand; he was later taken into custody by the USA. In September the four suspected members of Jemaah Islamiah arrested earlier in the year were officially charged with membership of the organization and with plotting terrorist attacks in Thailand. Those charged, together with a fifth man being detained in Singapore, pleaded not guilty to the charges against them. Their trials began in November.

In October 2003, following the conclusion of its anti-drugs offensive five months previously, the Government announced the commencement of a 60-day campaign intended to rid Thailand of 'social evils' such as drug addiction, poverty and organized crime. In November a cabinet reorganization took place, which resulted in the removal of Chart Pattana from the Government. In consequence, Deputy Prime Minister Korn Dabbaransi and Minister of Labour and Social Welfare Suwat Liptapanlop were ousted from the Cabinet; they were succeeded by, respectively, Bhokin Bhalakula and Uraiwan Thienthong.

In January 2004 an outbreak of violence in the south of the country, which resulted in the deaths of several members of the security forces and included arson attacks on several schools, prompted the Government to declare martial law in the predominantly Muslim provinces of Pattani, Yala and Narathiwat, on the border with Malaysia. The violence was suspected by the Government to have been perpetrated by Gerakan Mujahideen Islam Pattani, although involvement by militants affiliated to Jemaah Islamiah was not discounted as a possibility. Two suspects arrested in January were believed to be members of Bersatu. The unrest continued into the following months, resulting in the temporary closure of approximately 1,000 schools in the area. Meanwhile, the Government responded by arresting local Islamic leaders and conducting army raids on *madrasahs* (Islamic religious schools), angering many members of the local Muslim population.

In March 2004 a further cabinet reorganization was implemented, in which the Ministers of Finance, Defence and the Interior—Suchart Jaovisidha, Thammarak Isarangura and

Wan Muhamad Nor Matha—were replaced by, respectively, Somkid Jatusripitak, Chettha Thanajaro and Bhokin Bhalakula. Korn Dabbaransi returned to the Cabinet as Minister of Science and Technology. The changes were believed to have been made in response to the ongoing deterioration in the security situation in the south of the country, together with a decline in the performance of the Stock Exchange of Thailand and public protests at the Government's planned privatization of the Electricity Generating Authority of Thailand. Candidates supported by Thai Rak Thai performed well in local elections in mid-March, securing control of 47 of 74 newly created Provincial Administrative Organizations.

In mid-March 2004, following further arson attacks in the south, which had destroyed some 36 government buildings, Prime Minister Thaksin dismissed the national police chief and the army commander for the southern region. Later in that month a bomb explosion in Sungai Kolok, in Narathiwat province, which injured 29 people, including 10 Malaysian tourists, prompted the Government to suspend a US $300m. development aid programme intended for Narathiwat, Pattani and Yala. In early April four police officers were arrested in connection with the recent disappearance of Somchai Neelapaijit, a prominent Muslim human rights lawyer who was defending the men charged in September 2003 with plotting attacks for Jemaah Islamiah.

The violence in the south escalated at the end of April 2004, when more than 100 suspected Islamic militants staged a series of raids on police and army bases. The security forces suppressed the attacks, killing 108 of the insurgents, including 32 who had taken refuge in a mosque in Pattani. Five security officials also died in the fighting. After the UN, human rights groups and some Muslim leaders had questioned the level of force used by the security forces to quash the attacks, in May the Government established an independent commission to investigate the incident at the mosque. Meanwhile, a censure motion tabled by the DP against eight cabinet ministers on the grounds of alleged incompetence, corruption and abuse of power was rejected by the House of Representatives.

In late May 2004 the Government announced that it had established unofficial contact with the leader of Bersatu, Wan Kadir Che Man, with the aim of holding peace talks. Wan Kadir, who was living in exile in Malaysia, had recently stated that he was willing to abandon Bersatu's demand for a separate homeland in southern Thailand. None the less, religious tension in the south persisted, as the body of a Buddhist farmer was found decapitated and a Buddhist shrine in Pattani was ransacked. The proposed talks with Wan Kadir were indefinitely suspended at the end of the month, following strong opposition from Deputy Prime Minister Chavalit Yongchaiyudh, who feared the meeting could be regarded as formal recognition of Bersatu and its leader. In mid-June some 3,000 teachers attended a rally in Pattani in support of demands for improved security following the killing of a colleague. At the end of the month more than 4,000 teachers in Narathiwat commenced strike action after a further shooting, but returned to work after two days in response to assurances of increased protection from the security forces.

At the end of June 2004 Chart Pattana rejoined the Government when Suwat Liptapanlop was appointed as a Deputy Prime Minister, in what was regarded as an attempt by Thaksin to consolidate support ahead of the legislative elections due to be held in early 2005. A number of deputies from Chart Thai and the DP subsequently defected to Thai Rak Thai, and in August 2004 Chart Pattana merged into Thaksin's party. Meanwhile, several former senior members of the DP formed a new party, Mahachon. In early August, in its first report since its establishment in 2001, the National Human Rights Commission claimed that human rights violations had increased under Thaksin's administration, notably during the anti-drugs campaign in 2003, and accused the Government of becoming increasingly authoritarian. Thaksin rejected the report's criticisms, and declared a second anti-drugs offensive in October, which was to last for one year. The election of the DP candidate, Apirak Kosayodhin, as Governor of Bangkok in late August represented a set-back for Thaksin, who had favoured the candidature of Paveena Hongsakul, the former Secretary-General of Chart Pattana, who had stood as an independent.

More than 300 suspected insurgents had surrendered to the authorities by mid-July 2004 in response to a government campaign; they were transferred to a detention facility at a military camp to undergo a re-education programme. Nevertheless, violent attacks and minor bomb explosions continued to occur in the southern provinces, with killings of public officials, police officers, Buddhist monks and civilians regularly reported. In August the independent commission investigating the deaths at the mosque in April released its report, which criticized the security forces for using grenades and concluded that troops had used disproportionate force. The Government announced that unspecified compensation would be paid to the families of those killed. At the end of August Thaksin visited Narathiwat, Pattani and Yala provinces, one day after a bomb had exploded at a market in Sukhirin, in Narathiwat, killing one person and injuring 31. The Government conceded that it had failed to control the violence in the south, and pledged to develop new strategies to quell the unrest.

In October 2004 Thaksin effected a reorganization of the Cabinet, which included the replacement of the Minister of Defence and the Minister of Agriculture and Co-operatives in an apparent response to the ongoing crisis in the south and an outbreak of avian influenza. The violence in southern Thailand continued throughout late 2004. One of the most serious incidents occurred in late October when troops fired tear gas to disperse more than 2,000 Muslim protesters who were demonstrating in Tak Bai, in Narathiwat province, against the detention of six suspected militants. Seven of the protesters were killed in the ensuing clashes and 78 of 1,300 demonstrators who were arrested later died, many from suffocation, as they were transported in overcrowded trucks to an army barracks. Amid increasing international concern at events in southern Thailand and at the Government's response to the unrest, Prime Minister Thaksin ordered an independent inquiry into the deaths. Most of those detained in connection with the protests were later released. A few days later two people were killed and 20 injured in a bomb attack in Sungai Kolok. The deteriorating security situation prompted rare interventions from the monarchy. King Bhumibol urged the Government to use more restraint in the southern provinces, and Queen Sirikit called for an end to the violence. In the first two weeks of November around 30 Buddhists were killed in apparent revenge attacks by suspected Islamic militants. The PULO had earlier vowed to retaliate in response to the deaths in Tak Bai. Later in that month an alleged leader of Bersatu was killed in a gunfight with the security forces in Panare, in the province of Pattani.

In December 2004 four Islamic teachers, who were suspected of being leaders of the separatist group Barisan Revolusi Nasional (part of Bersatu), were charged with terrorism and treason. Meanwhile, the inquiry into the incident at Tak Bai in October, in which 85 protesters died, concluded that the deaths had not been caused deliberately, but that the dispersal of the crowd and the transport of the prisoners had been mishandled and that senior officials had been negligent; three army commanders were subsequently transferred to inactive posts. The Cabinet later approved compensation worth more than 30m. baht for families of the dead and those injured. In late December at least two people were killed and several injured after a bomb exploded in Sungai Kolok. Following the fatal shooting of two of their colleagues, thousands of teachers in the south went on indefinite strike, urging the authorities to do more to protect them from attacks by Muslim militants.

The west coast of Thailand, in particular the province of Phang Nga, was severely affected by a series of tsunamis caused by a massive earthquake in the Indian Ocean on 26 December 2004. More than 5,300 people, including at least 1,700 foreigners from some 36 countries, were killed, and a further 2,900 were reported missing. The Thai Government largely refused international relief aid, but did accept considerable technical assistance in identifying the dead, a task that was made more difficult by the large number of foreign victims.

Thai Rak Thai won an overwhelming victory in legislative elections held on 6 February 2005, securing a large majority with 377 of the 500 seats in the House of Representatives. Although 20 parties contested the elections, only three other parties secured representation: the DP took 96 seats, Chart Thai 25 and Mahachon only two. The rate of voter participation was reported at 72%. Thai Rak Thai's success, which enabled it to form a single-party government for the first time, was widely attributed to Thaksin's prompt response to the devastation caused by the tsunamis in December and the strong performance of the economy under his premiership. However, as in previous election campaigns, there were allegations of widespread 'vote-buying', and numerous complaints of electoral malpractice were made. The election results prompted the immediate resignation of Banyat Bantadtan as leader of the DP; Abhisit Vejjajiva was

THAILAND

Introductory Survey

elected as his replacement in March. Prime Minister Thaksin began an unprecedented second consecutive term in office in March, following his formal re-election to the premiership by the House of Representatives. Somkid Jatusripitak retained his position as Minister of Finance in the new Cabinet, and was also appointed as a Deputy Prime Minister, while Kantathee Supamongkol, hitherto a trade representative, was allocated the foreign affairs portfolio, replacing Surakiart Sathirathai, who became a Deputy Prime Minister. Thammarak Isarangura, who had served as Minister of Defence during part of Thaksin's first term before being appointed as a Deputy Prime Minister, resumed the defence portfolio.

The violence in southern Thailand continued unabated throughout early 2005, and by early March more than 690 people had died since January 2004. In February 2005 the Government approved the formation of a new 12,000-strong army regiment to be stationed in the south. The troops were to focus on development work, as well as on improving security, but local Islamic leaders warned that an increased military presence in the region (where Thai Rak Thai had failed to secure a single seat in the recent elections) would only heighten disillusionment with the Government. During a three-day visit to the south in mid-February Thaksin announced controversial proposals to allocate development aid to villages in the region depending on the degree of violence found there. Some 1,580 villages had already been surveyed and categorized as red, yellow or green. The 358 villages where violent incidents were deemed to occur frequently were classified as 'red zones' and were to be deprived of funding. However, Thaksin later appeared to have abandoned the plans, which were widely criticized. As the Prime Minister's visit came to an end, a car bomb in Sungai Kolok killed six people and injured more than 40. In March Thaksin indicated that he was considering adopting a more moderate approach towards the insurgency in the south. He appointed former Prime Minister Anand Panyarachun to chair a 48-member National Reconciliation Commission (NRC), which was charged with restoring peace, and announced his intention to reduce the number of troops deployed in the region. In April two people were killed and more than 60 injured in three bomb explosions in the southern province of Songkhla, the first major attacks to occur outside the provinces of Narathiwat, Pattani and Yala. In November Thaksin extended martial law, already in force in the three southernmost provinces (see above), to encompass the districts of Chana and Thepha in Songkhla province.

Meanwhile, in May 2005 a major corruption scandal was revealed concerning Minister of Transport Suriya Jungrungreangkit's alleged improprieties during the purchase of baggage-scanning equipment for the new Suvarnabhumi International Airport. Suriya was the subject of a no confidence motion instigated by the DP, which, although easily defeated in the House of Representatives, caused considerable damage to the reputation of the ruling party. In a cabinet reorganization effected in August, Suriya was transferred to the less prominent position of Minister of Industry.

In June 2005 a delegation from the Organization of the Islamic Conference (OIC, see p. 382) was dispatched to Thailand on a fact-finding mission, at the invitation of Prime Minister Thaksin. In their subsequent report, the members of the delegation concluded, contrary to the claims of Islamic nations and rights groups, that religious issues were not the predominant factor in the ongoing militant attacks in the south of the country.

In January 2006, in the largest corporate take-over in Thailand's history, Prime Minister Thaksin's family sold its 49.6% holding stake in national telecommunications firm Shin Corporation Public Co Ltd (Shin Corp) to Singapore's state investment wing, Temasek Holdings, at a price of 70,000m. baht (US $1,900m.). The transaction took place on the same day on which a new law raising the limit on foreign ownership in telecommunication firms from 25% to 49% came into effect. The sale provoked outrage within Thailand. Many Thais were angered by the massive tax-free gains made by the Shinawatra family; there were demands for the Prime Minister to donate to the state the 26,000m. baht that had been waived in tax, rather than to profit in this way and thus effectively condone tax evasion. Considerable suspicion was also aroused by the fact that Thaksin's son and daughter had purchased shares in Shin Corp from Ample Vision (an investment company established by the Prime Minister in the British Virgin Islands) at a cost of one baht per share and yet had been able to sell them, just three days later, at a price of 49.25 baht per share. Furthermore, there was widespread concern about the sale of a telecommunications firm to a foreign company on account of the potential threat to national security. Thaksin denied any wrongdoing.

In early February 2006 the Minister of Culture, Uraiwan Thienthong, tendered her resignation from the Cabinet, citing 'the decline in political morality' as the reason for her decision. Later in that month, and without prior warning, Prime Minister Thaksin announced that the House of Representatives was being dissolved in preparation for an early election; it was subsequently declared that the poll was to be held in early April. While there was little doubt that the ruling Thai Rak Thai would win the election, the question of whether the party would attract a sufficient proportion of the vote to ease the pressure on Thaksin to resign was less certain. The premier's tactics were countered in an unexpected manner by the three main opposition parties—DP, Chart Thai and Mahachon—all of which announced that they were to boycott the proceedings. In an attempt to defuse the political tension, Thaksin offered to include the three parties within a national coalition government, regardless of whether or not they participated in the election; however, the offer was rejected. Thaksin also declared his intention to resign if Thai Rak Thai failed to secure more than 50% of the votes cast. During the period prior to the election demonstrators demanded the removal from power of the Prime Minister at numerous protest rallies in the capital, which were organized by the People's Alliance for Democracy (PAD), a loose coalition of anti-Thaksin groups and individuals (including royalists, academics, trade unionists and political activists) that had been established in 2005 by Sondhi Limthongkul, the founder of the Manager Media Group. The political tension was accompanied by an intensification of violence in the southern regions. Hundreds of schools in Yala were closed temporarily following the killing of three Buddhist teachers, allegedly by Muslim militants. In March the Prime Minister's son, Phantongtae Shinawatra, was adjudged to have been guilty of securities violations relating to the sale of Shin Corp, and was fined 5.98m. baht (US $153,000), by the Securities and Exchange Commission (SEC); Phantongtae was deemed to have failed fully to disclose transactions pertaining to his stock-holdings.

On 2 April 2006 the legislative election was held and, as expected, Thai Rak Thai secured victory, winning approximately 57% of votes cast. Turn-out was an estimated 64.8% of registered voters. However, 33.1% of those who voted selected the 'no vote' option on ballot papers. Owing to the boycott of the poll by the three main opposition parties, the House of Representatives was unable to convene by the end of the month as a significant number of seats remained vacant, despite the holding of several by-elections. Soon after the election Thaksin announced that he would not seek to return to the office of Prime Minister on a permanent basis and appointed the Deputy Prime Minister, Gen. Chidchai Wannasathit, to the role in an acting capacity. In May the Constitutional Court annulled the results of the election, declaring that they were invalid as the poll had been organized too quickly following the dissolution of the House of Representatives. The Election Commission subsequently announced that a new legislative election would take place in October. At the end of May Thaksin confirmed that he was returning to the post of interim Prime Minister.

Mounting tension between Prime Minister Thaksin and King Bhumibol, who was becoming increasingly vocal on the subject of the country's troubled political situation, was temporarily alleviated in June 2006 by celebrations to commemorate the 60th anniversary of the King's accession to the throne. In the same month militants carried out a series of co-ordinated attacks over a period of several days, detonating in excess of 50 bombs that targeted more than 30 locations across the three southernmost provinces; the attacks were reported to have killed at least four people and injured more than 20 others. In August almost two dozen bank branches in the province of Yala were targeted in another spate of co-ordinated explosions, which killed two people and injured a further 28. Meanwhile, at the end of June a team of prosecutors from the Attorney-General's office urged the disbandment of various parties, including Thai Rak Thai and the DP, on charges related to the April election, the former being accused of funding token opposition candidates, while the latter was alleged to have instigated a boycott of the poll. In July the Chairman of the Election Commission and two commissioners were found guilty of election law contravention and sentenced to four years' imprisonment by the Criminal Court.

On 19 September 2006, while Thaksin Shinawatra was out of the country, the Government was ousted from power in a bloodless military coup led by the Commander-in-Chief of the

Army, Gen. Sonthi Boonyaratglin. Gen. Sonthi, acting as part of the so-called Council for Democratic Reform, imposed martial law and suspended the Constitution, the Government and the legislature. In a statement to the media the Council claimed to have the support of King Bhumibol and ordered the cessation of activities by political parties, promising the imminent appointment of an interim Prime Minister with a mandate to oversee fresh elections. Within a week the Council had initiated an investigation into allegations of corruption within the Thaksin Government. At the beginning of October, following the signing of an interim Constitution by King Bhumibol, Gen. (retd) Surayud Chulanont was sworn in as Prime Minister by the military leadership, which had been renamed the Council for National Security and retained significant powers over the Government and the Constitution. Elections were projected for 2007, upon the drafting and approval of a new constitution. The Governor of the Bank of Thailand, Pridiyathorn Devakula, and the chairman of Bangkok Bank, Kosit Panpiemras, were appointed Deputy Prime Ministers in the Cabinet that was subsequently announced, taking additional charge of the finance and industry portfolios respectively. The National Legislative Assembly, comprising the Council's appointees, was approved by the King and convened in mid-October 2006. In November martial law was rescinded in approximately 40 provinces (although this did not take effect until January 2007). Meanwhile, Thaksin, who had remained overseas since the coup, announced his resignation from Thai Rak Thai in October 2006, following a large number of resignations from the party, which were said to have been prompted by the military leadership's assertion that those associated with political organizations guilty of electoral malpractice would be punished. In November Thaksin's son and daughter were ordered to pay tax on their share of the proceeds of the Shin Corp sale.

Hopes of a resolution to the ongoing insurgency in the south were raised by Gen. Sonthi's announcement in October 2006 that the military leadership was willing to engage in dialogue with certain groups. In the following month Prime Minister Surayud apologized for the deaths of the Muslim protesters in Tak Bai in 2004 (see above), and it was later announced that charges against several demonstrators would be rescinded. However, despite the apparent progress towards reconciliation, the violence continued in 2007: by March it was estimated that the conflict had caused more than 2,100 fatalities, of which more than 400 had occurred since the coup. At the end of December 2006 a series of eight bomb explosions in Bangkok killed three people and injured several others, but the attacks were not immediately attributed to the insurgents; rather, it was implied by some sources that associates of Thaksin were responsible, a claim he subsequently denied. In January 2007 the Government suspended Thaksin's diplomatic passport and requested a media ban on his lawyer's statements. Surayud later affirmed that Thaksin would be permitted to return to Thailand on the condition that he did not engage in political activity. Doubts were expressed at the end of February about the stability of the Government after the Deputy Prime Minister and Minister of Finance, Pridiyathorn Devakula, resigned, citing internal discord among other reasons. The interim Government's economic policies, which were based on a principle of 'self-sufficiency' advocated by the King and had thus far included measures to restrict the movement of foreign capital and foreign ownership of Thai companies, had been widely criticized and had damaged investor confidence. In the cabinet reorganization that followed, Chalongphob Sussangkarn succeeded Pridiyathorn as Minister of Finance. Paiboon Wattanasiritham, while retaining the social development and human security portfolio, was promoted to the position of Deputy Prime Minister. At the end of March Thaksin's wife, Pojaman Shinawatra, was charged with tax evasion in relation to a 1997 share transaction of the company that later became known as Shin Corp. Meanwhile, Gen. Sonthi was reported to have requested the enforcement of emergency rule to address the alleged threat of instability posed by regular anti-coup demonstrations in Bangkok. Surayud denied the request and announced that elections would be held in December 2007, following a constitutional referendum which was to be conducted by September.

In late May 2007 the Constitutional Tribunal (which had replaced the Constitutional Court under the interim Constitution) found Thai Rak Thai guilty of violating electoral legislation prior to the April 2006 poll, but acquitted the DP of all charges of malpractice. The Tribunal ordered the dissolution of Thai Rak Thai and a ban on 111 party members, including Thaksin, from participating in politics for five years. Thai Rak Thai had been accused of funding minor opposition parties to field candidates in constituencies in which it would have been unlikely to achieve the 20% of the vote required to secure election in uncontested seats. A number of demonstrations by the party's supporters in Bangkok followed the verdict. The ban on activities by political organizations was removed in early June 2007 to allow parties to begin campaigning for the forthcoming legislative election. In mid-June the Assets Examination Committee 'froze' bank accounts held by Thaksin (some jointly with his wife, Pojaman) containing a total of 52,900m. baht; the Committee later ordered additional assets to be 'frozen' as investigations continued into the former Prime Minister, who remained in self-imposed exile. A week later corruption charges were filed against Thaksin and Pojaman in relation to Pojaman's purchase in 2003 of a plot of land in Bangkok from a state agency for a sum allegedly far lower than its true value. Thaksin was also accused of concealing his assets.

The Constitution Drafting Assembly (the members of which had effectively been appointed by the Council for National Security) approved the final draft of a new constitution in early July 2007. The proposed constitution was designed to curb the powers of the Prime Minister, who would be limited to serving two four-year terms and barred from owning large stakes in private companies. In addition, the threshold for initiating a debate on a motion of no confidence in the Prime Minister would be reduced from two-fifths of the members of the House of Representatives in favour to one-fifth (although such a motion would still require the support of more than one-half of deputies to be endorsed). The Senate would be transformed from a fully elected body of 200 senators to one in which 74 of its 150 senators would be selected by a seven-member committee of judges and other senior state officials (such as the President of the Constitutional Court and the Chairperson of the Election Commission), with the remainder directly elected in each province, while the number of deputies in the House of Representatives would be reduced from 500 to 480 (400 to be elected on a multi-member constituency basis and 80 on a proportional representation basis). Further notable provisions committed the state to the implementation of the 'sufficient economy philosophy' and guaranteed an amnesty for those involved in the coup of September 2006. Critics of the draft claimed that it was 'anti-Thaksin' and less democratic than the 1997 Constitution. However, while acknowledging its flaws, the DP and Chart Thai supported the draft in the interest of restoring democracy as swiftly as possible. The draft Constitution was endorsed by 57.8% of those voting in a referendum on 19 August 2007. A relatively low turn-out, of 57.6% of eligible voters, was recorded. More detailed results suggested that the country remained politically divided, with the charter rejected by nearly 63% of voters in the rural north-east, a stronghold of the dissolved Thai Rak Thai, but approved by some 88% of voters in the south. After receiving royal assent, the new Constitution took effect on 24 August. Meanwhile, in late July a demonstration against military rule by several thousand people in Bangkok ended in violence, as protesters clashed with police after staging a rally outside the house of former Prime Minister Prem Tinsulanonda, now a senior royal adviser, whom they claimed had been involved in co-ordinating the coup. Nine alleged leaders of the demonstration, reported to be either allies of Thaksin or pro-democracy activists, were subsequently arrested and charged with illegal assembly and inciting violence.

In late July 2007 the National Legislative Assembly adopted legislation prohibiting new political parties from using the same names, logos or acronyms as parties dissolved by the Constitutional Tribunal for a period of five years. Many former Thai Rak Thai deputies subsequently joined the little-known People's Power Party (PPP), while others participated in the formation of new parties, such as Puea Pandin and Ruam Jai Thai (the latter later merging with Chart Pattana); Samak Sundaravej, a right-wing political veteran and former Governor of Bangkok, was elected leader of the PPP in August. In mid-August the Supreme Court issued arrest warrants for Thaksin and Pojaman after they failed to answer a summons to appear before the Court to answer the corruption charges relating to the land purchase in 2003. Further arrest warrants were issued for the couple by a criminal court in Bangkok in early September 2007 in connection with a police inquiry into alleged violations of stock-trading legislation. In late August it was announced that elections to the House of Representatives would be held on 23 December. Meanwhile, the insurgency in the south continued unabated. A report released by the US-based Human Rights Watch stated that 2,463 people (including 2,196 civilians) had been killed in attacks between January 2004 and July 2007.

Gen. Sonthi was appointed Deputy Prime Minister in charge of Security in early October 2007, having retired as Commander-in-Chief of the Army and resigned as Chairman of the Council for National Security, prompting speculation that he intended to remain in political office beyond the elections scheduled for December. He was replaced as Chairman of the Council for National Security by Air Chief Marshal Chalit Pukpasuk, the Commander-in-Chief of the Air Force. Sonthi's appointment was part of a wider cabinet reorganization necessitated by the recent resignations of five ministers who were under investigation by the National Counter Corruption Commission for allegedly breaching a 5% limit on ministerial shareholdings in private companies. Prime Minister Surayud and Deputy Prime Minister and Minister of Industry, Kosit Panpiemras, assumed additional responsibility for the interior and information and communications technology portfolios, respectively. In late October the Cabinet ordered martial law to be revoked in 221 districts, but maintained in 179 districts in 31 provinces.

During the week preceding the election, amid protests outside the parliament building by students and civil society activists, the National Legislative Assembly adopted many new pieces of legislation, most notably a controversial act giving the Internal Security Operations Command, an agency comprising military and civilian representatives, wide-ranging powers to counter perceived threats to national security. These enhanced powers, which were strongly criticized by human rights groups, included the ability to order curfews, detain suspects without trial, restrict freedom of movement and override the authority of government officials.

Some 74.5% of registered voters participated in the legislative elections, which took place, as scheduled, on 23 December 2007. Polls were repeated in the following month in a number of constituencies where the Election Commission had annulled results owing to 'vote-buying' and other irregularities. The PPP emerged as the largest party in the House of Representatives, securing 233 of the 480 seats, while the DP won 164, Chart Thai 34, Puea Pandin 24, Matchimathipataya 11, Ruam Jai Thai Chart Pattana nine and Pracharaj five. Essentially the successor to Thai Rak Thai, the PPP achieved greatest success in the north and north-east of the country, and its victory was regarded as a rejection of the 2006 coup and the outgoing military leadership. None the less, its failure to secure an outright majority of seats forced the PPP to negotiate with other parties to establish a coalition administration.

In mid-January 2008 the PPP leader, Samak Sundaravej, officially announced the formation of a six-party coalition controlling 316 of the 480 seats in the House of Representatives, leaving the DP as the sole opposition party in the legislature. The new House of Representatives was convened two days later, subsequently electing Yongyuth Tiyapairat, the deputy leader of the PPP, as its new Speaker and Samak as Prime Minister. Meanwhile, the Council for National Security was disbanded. Samak's new Cabinet was sworn in by King Bhumibol in early February. Many strategic posts in the new Government were allocated to personal allies of Thaksin. Samak assumed personal responsibility for the defence portfolio, while Surapong Suebwonglee, the Secretary-General of the PPP, was appointed Deputy Prime Minister and Minister of Finance. Noppadon Pattama, Thaksin's legal adviser, and Chalerm Yoobamrung, another close associate of the deposed Prime Minister, became Minister of Foreign Affairs and Minister of the Interior, respectively. Later in that month the Government announced plans to resume several populist policies initiated by Thaksin and to commence a new anti-drugs campaign, similar to those conducted under the former Prime Minister (which had resulted in some 2,500 deaths). Amendments to the Constitution were also envisaged. Thaksin returned to Thailand in late February after 17 months in exile, insisting that he had retired from active politics. He was immediately taken to hear the corruption charges against him and was granted bail. In mid-March he pleaded not guilty before the Supreme Court to using his influence to assist his wife with her land purchase in 2003. Thaksin's wife, Pojaman, had already returned in January 2008, when she was also granted bail and denied the charges against her. Elections to fill 76 of the 150 seats in the Senate were held on 2 March, the remaining 74 members having been appointed in the previous month by the selection committee. Electoral turn-out was estimated at 55.9%. The appointed senators were considered to be closer to the outgoing military leadership, while many of the elected senators were reported to be allies of Thaksin. Prasobsuk Boondech, an appointed senator and former Chief Justice of the Court of Appeals, was elected Speaker of the Senate in mid-March.

Despite the restoration of civilian rule, political uncertainty persisted in early 2008. In late February the new administration suffered a set-back when the Election Commission voted in favour of disqualifying Speaker Yongyuth from office, concluding that he had bribed local officials in exchange for votes during the general election campaign, and referred the case to the Supreme Court. There was a possibility that the PPP might be disbanded by the Constitutional Court if the Supreme Court were to find Yongyuth guilty and judge that the party was aware of 'vote-buying'. Yongyuth stood down as Speaker pending the Supreme Court's verdict. In mid-April the Election Commission recommended the dissolution of Chart Thai and Matchimathipataya on the grounds of electoral fraud allegedly committed by senior party officials; the case was referred to the Constitutional Court. The Commission was also investigating a complaint that the PPP and Thaksin had violated legislation governing political parties, the former by allegedly acting as a 'nominee' of Thai Rak Thai and the latter through his alleged involvement with the PPP, despite being barred from participating in politics. Meanwhile, the DP accused the coalition Government of self-interest in its plans to revise the Constitution, particularly its desire to amend the article allowing for an entire party to be held responsible for the wrongdoing of a single party executive. In April martial law was rescinded in all areas of the country except for the southern provinces of Narathiwat, Yala, Pattani and part of Songkhla, where the death toll in the ongoing insurgency had recently surpassed 3,000.

Political tensions rose in May 2008, as the PAD (which had led the campaign against Thaksin in 2006—see above) resumed its anti-Government demonstrations in Bangkok, protesting against the plans for constitutional reform. The Minister in the Prime Minister's Office, Chakrapob Penkair, a close ally of Thaksin, was forced to resign from the Cabinet in late May, after it emerged that he was to be charged under *lèse-majesté* legislation (prohibiting criticism of the monarch) in connection with a speech he gave at the Foreign Correspondents' Club in Bangkok in August 2007. Despite Chakrapob's resignation, which the royalist PAD had demanded, and Samak's decision to refer the issue of constitutional change to a parliamentary committee, daily demonstrations continued, albeit on a smaller scale than those of 2006, amid speculation regarding the possibility of another military coup. The Government also provoked criticism by endorsing an application made by the Cambodian Government to UNESCO (see p. 144) seeking World Heritage status for Preah Vihear, an 11th-century temple in an area of disputed sovereignty on the Thai–Cambodian border (see below). None the less, in late June 2008 DP-proposed motions of no confidence in Samak and seven of his ministers were easily defeated in the House of Representatives, owing to the ruling coalition's strong majority. However, the controversy over Preah Vihear persisted, leading to the resignation of the Minister of Foreign Affairs, Noppadon, in mid-July, after the Constitutional Court ruled that he had violated the Constitution by signing an agreement supporting Cambodia's (recently successful) bid without securing legislative approval; Tej Bunnag, hitherto adviser to the Office of His Majesty's Principal Private Secretary, was appointed as Noppadon's replacement. Meanwhile, earlier in July the Supreme Court found Yongyuth guilty of electoral fraud, banning him from participating in politics for five years.

The trial of Thaksin and his wife on charges related to Pojaman's 2003 purchase of a plot of state-owned land commenced in the Supreme Court in July 2008, a fortnight after three of Thaksin's lawyers had been convicted of attempting to bribe Court officials and sentenced to six months' imprisonment. Later in that month the Supreme Court announced that it would also hear allegations that Thaksin had abused his power by introducing a state lottery in 2003 and by instructing a state-controlled bank to offer a low-interest loan to Myanmar in 2004 for the purchase of telecommunications equipment from a subsidiary of Shin Corp. At the end of July, in a separate case, Pojaman and her brother were convicted of failing to pay tax of 546m. baht on a Shin Corp share transaction in 1997 and sentenced to three years' imprisonment; Pojaman's secretary received a two-year sentence. All three were released on bail, pending an appeal. In mid-August the Supreme Court issued an arrest warrant for Thaksin and Pojaman, who had absconded to the United Kingdom shortly before they were due to appear before the Court;

Thaksin announced that he would not return to Thailand, claiming that the charges against him were politically motivated and that he would not be tried fairly. The Supreme Court issued a second arrest warrant for Thaksin in September, after he failed to appear at the beginning of his trial on charges related to the alleged low-interest loan to Myanmar. In October the Supreme Court convicted Thaksin *in absentia* of violating an article of the Constitution concerning conflict of interest in relation to his involvement in his wife's purchase of state land in 2003, sentencing him to two years' imprisonment; Pojaman was acquitted of the corruption charges against her in this case.

Meanwhile, a cabinet reorganization was effected in early August 2008; notable changes included the appointment of Kowit Wattana, the national police chief during 2004–07, as Deputy Prime Minister and Minister of the Interior. Anti-Government protests in Bangkok escalated later that month, with the number of demonstrators rising to an estimated 30,000, as PAD supporters invaded several government buildings and the studios of the state-run National Broadcasting of Thailand, before occupying the grounds of Government House and refusing to leave. About 85 people were detained, and arrest warrants were subsequently issued for nine PAD leaders who were accused of illegal assembly and inciting unrest. Samak, who was forced to move his office initially to the military's headquarters and later to the former international airport at Don Muang, rejected demands for his resignation. As well as a change of government, the PAD advocated the introduction of what it termed 'new politics', which would involve a controversial reform of the House of Representatives, whereby 70% of its members would be appointed and only 30% elected. As tensions mounted, with police reportedly using tear gas to repel 2,000 demonstrators attempting to enter the police headquarters in Bangkok, the protests also extended beyond the capital, resulting in the temporary closure of three blockaded regional airports and disruption to rail services. At an emergency session of the National Assembly held at the end of August, Samak maintained his position that he would not resign from office. On 2 September the Prime Minister declared a state of emergency in Bangkok, after one person died in confrontations between rival protesters from the PAD and the pro-Government United Front for Democracy against Dictatorship (UDD). In a further set-back for the Government, on the following day Tej Bunnag resigned as Minister of Foreign Affairs, just over a month after his appointment. Meanwhile, moreover, the Election Commission recommended that the Constitutional Court dissolve the PPP on the grounds of the electoral fraud committed by former Speaker Yongyuth.

On 9 September 2008 the Constitutional Court ordered Samak and his Cabinet to resign, ruling that the Prime Minister had violated the Constitution by accepting payment for presenting a television cookery programme while in office. After a failed attempt by the PPP to secure the re-election of Samak as Prime Minister, owing to opposition from the party's coalition partners, on 17 September Somchai Wongsawat, a brother-in-law of Thaksin as well as Deputy Prime Minister and Minister of Education in the outgoing Cabinet, was elected to the premiership. A new Cabinet was sworn in on 25 September; Prime Minister Somchai assumed additional responsibility for the defence portfolio, while Sompong Amornwiwat was appointed Deputy Prime Minister and Minister of Foreign Affairs, and Suchart Thadathamrongvech became Minister of Finance. Somchai replaced Samak as leader of the PPP at the end of the month. Meanwhile, the state of emergency in Bangkok was rescinded on 14 September, but the PAD-led protesters continued their occupation of the Government House compound, vowing to remain as long as the PPP retained power. Two of the nine protest organizers for whom arrest warrants had been issued were detained in early October. Deputy Prime Minister Chavalit Yongchaiyudh, the Government's chief negotiator with the PAD, resigned on 7 October, after two people died and more than 400 were injured during violent clashes that occurred when police used tear gas to disperse several thousand PAD demonstrators who were besieging the legislative building. The remaining seven PAD leaders sought by police surrendered a few days later after treason charges against them were withdrawn; all nine PAD detainees were subsequently released on bail, still charged with lesser offences.

An estimated 40,000 people attended a rally in Bangkok in support of Thaksin and the PPP-led Government at the beginning of November 2008, demonstrating the continued popularity of the former Prime Minister and the deep divisions between his supporters and opponents. Also in early November two bomb explosions in Narathiwat killed one person and injured more than 70 people. A week earlier Prime Minister Somchai had visited the southern provinces, noting that separatist violence in the region, which had caused more than 3,400 deaths since January 2004, appeared to have eased. The United Kingdom revoked the visas of Thaksin and Pojaman in November 2008, while they were both out of the country; later that month it was announced that the couple had divorced. The Governor of Bangkok, Apirak Kosayodhin of the DP, who had been re-elected to the position in October, resigned in mid-November, after being indicted (together with a number of other officials and former Governor and Prime Minister Samak) in connection with alleged irregularities in the purchase of fire-fighting equipment for the capital; Sukhumbhand Paripatra of the DP was elected to replace Apirak as Governor of Bangkok in January 2009.

Several thousand PAD demonstrators again surrounded the parliament building on 24 November 2008, before moving to the Cabinet's temporary offices at Don Muang airport, in what they described as a 'final battle' to oust the Government. Thousands of PAD protesters then seized control of Suvarnabhumi, Bangkok's main international airport, which led to the cancellation of all flights, leaving passengers stranded and severely damaging the tourism industry. The PAD declared that its occupation of Suvarnabhumi would continue until Somchai resigned, prompting the Commander-in-Chief of the Army, Gen. Anupong Paochinda, to suggest that the Prime Minister should relinquish his position and call fresh elections, but Somchai insisted that he would remain in office. The PAD subsequently also forced the closure of Don Muang airport. On 27 November Somchai declared a state of emergency around Bangkok's two airports, following a meeting of the Cabinet in the northern city of Chiang Mai—where the Prime Minister's flight had been forced to land on his return the previous day from a summit meeting of the Asia-Pacific Economic Co-operation (APEC, see p. 185) in Peru. A stand-off subsequently ensued between police surrounding the airports and the protesters within. At the end of November some 20,000 government supporters attended a rally in the capital. Meanwhile, after three months, PAD protesters began to disperse from their encampment at Government House, where several small bomb attacks in late October and November had resulted in one death and injured around 90 people.

On 2 December 2008 the PAD announced that it was ceasing its protests and airport occupations, after the Constitutional Court ordered the dissolution of the PPP, Chart Thai and Matchimathipataya on the grounds of electoral fraud and barred the executives of the three parties from engaging in politics for five years, thus forcing Somchai to leave office. Many PPP deputies who were not disqualified from participating in politics joined Puea Thai, which had been formed in anticipation of the Court's decision; Yongyuth Wichaidith was elected as the new party's leader. Chart Thai and Matchimathipataya were similarly regrouped, as Chart Thai Pattana and Bhum Jai Thai, respectively. However, the DP succeeded in securing the support of a significant number of deputies from the dissolved parties, as well as that of several former coalition partners of the PPP, and on 15 December the DP's leader, Abhisit Vejjajiva, was elected as the new Prime Minister by a margin of 37 votes, defeating Pracha Promnok, the leader of Puea Pandin, who was supported by Puea Thai. In response to Abhisit's election, supporters of Somchai's outgoing administration protested outside the parliament building and the DP's headquarters. The new Prime Minister appealed for national unity, pledging to address the country's economic difficulties and to continue some of the more populist policies pursued by previous Governments. A new Cabinet took office on 22 December, comprising members of the DP, Friends of Newin (a breakaway faction of the former PPP, led by Newin Chidchob), Chart Thai Pattana, Puea Pandin (12 deputies from which had voted for Abhisit's election as Prime Minister), Ruam Jai Thai Chart Pattana, Bhum Jai Thai and the SAP (which had been revived in mid-2008 by its former leader, Suwit Khunkitti, following his departure from Puea Pandin). Observers generally welcomed the appointment of Korn Chatikavanij, a respected former investment banker, as Minister of Finance, but expressed concern regarding the lack of experience of several new ministers, while the selection of Kasit Piromya as Minister of Foreign Affairs was also controversial owing to his prominent support for the PAD protests. Thousands of demonstrators loyal to Thaksin and his allies, led by the UDD, staged protests against the legitimacy of Abhisit's Government in late December, forcing the Prime Minister to make his inaugural policy speech to the National Assembly at the offices of the Ministry of Foreign

Affairs; the parliament building was surrounded by protesters for two days.

By-elections were held on 11 January 2009 to fill the seats made vacant by the disqualification of deputies from the parties dissolved in the previous month. The governing coalition increased its majority in the House of Representatives, with the DP winning seven of the 29 seats contested, Chart Thai Pattana 10 and Puea Pandin three, while Puea Thai secured five seats and Pracharaj four. During its first few weeks in office the new Government focused its attention on measures to stimulate the economy, notably securing legislative approval of a 116,700m. baht supplementary budget that included provision for a payment of 2,000 baht to workers earning less than 15,000 baht per month. The new administration also expressed its determination to protect the monarchy, establishing a website urging people to inform on anyone perceived to be criticizing the King, and creating an internet security centre to co-ordinate the blocking of websites deemed to be offensive to the monarchy, with access to about 5,000 sites reportedly being denied during its first day in operation. Meanwhile, the number of prosecutions under the country's lèse-majesté legislation was reported to be increasing; the conviction of an Australian writer, who was sentenced to three years' imprisonment, attracted particular media attention, although, as in previous cases involving foreigners, he was subsequently granted a royal pardon.

It was reported in January 2009 that the Government intended to appoint a new civilian body to administer the south of the country and supervise military activities in the region. A report published by the human rights organization Amnesty International in that month claimed that the use of torture by the security forces in the counter-insurgency campaign in the southern provinces was widespread. The Thai military was also accused that month of mistreating Myanma and Bangladeshi migrants attempting to reach Thailand (see below).

The UDD organized an anti-Government rally at Government House at the end of January 2009 in support of its demands for the resignation of Abhisit's Cabinet, the dissolution of the House of Representatives, the organization of new elections, the reinstatement of the 1997 Constitution, and the prosecution of the PAD leadership (for the damage caused to the economy by the occupation of Bangkok's airports in 2008). A further protest outside Government House, lasting three days, was attended by up to 10,000 UDD supporters in late February 2009. In the following month the Government easily defeated motions of no confidence in Abhisit and five of his ministers, including Korn and Kasit, which had been tabled in the House of Representatives by Puea Thai. However, the UDD protests continued, and in late March at least 20,000 people again gathered outside Government House to demand the Prime Minister's resignation, forcing the cancellation of the Cabinet's weekly meeting at the end of the month. Meanwhile, the Thai authorities were seeking Thaksin's extradition from Hong Kong, where he was now believed to be based.

In early April 2009 UDD protesters forced the postponement of an Association of South East Asian Nations (ASEAN, see p. 194) summit meeting being held in Pattaya after blocking the route to the conference hall. Abhisit declared an extreme state of emergency as visiting Asian leaders were airlifted from the venue. In the same month violent altercations took place in Bangkok between UDD protesters and the authorities, culminating in the death of two protesters, with more than 120 injured. Thousands of Thai soldiers were mobilized following the violence to implement a security cordon around the Government House demonstrators, ultimately prompting protest leaders to appeal for an end to the movement. Arrest warrants were subsequently issued for 13 protest leaders on charges of inciting public disturbance and illegal assembly. Shortly after the ending of the protests, Sondhi Limthongkul, founder of the PAD, was shot in Bangkok in an apparent assassination attempt. Sondhi survived the shooting, in which his driver and aide were also injured.

In foreign affairs Thailand is a member of the Association of South East Asian Nations (ASEAN, see p. 194) and generally maintains good relations with the other member states. In September 2008 Thailand ratified the ASEAN Charter, which codified the principles and purposes of the Association and came into effect in December of that year. Its former dependence on the USA has been greatly reduced by the increasing importance of regional trade and diplomatic relations. In the late 1980s Prime Minister Chatichai adopted a new business-orientated policy towards Cambodia, Laos, Viet Nam and Myanmar, encouraging investment in their developing economies; this policy was successfully pursued by subsequent premiers. In April 1995, following lengthy discussions with Viet Nam, Cambodia and Laos, the four countries established the Mekong River Commission (see p. 427) to promote the joint development of the Mekong's resources. Relations with the People's Republic of China also improved as Thailand became one of China's most significant trading partners. In October 1993 Thailand was accepted as a full member of the Non-aligned Movement (see p. 439).

In January 1993, despite its previous reluctance to do so, Thailand officially closed its border with Cambodia to trade with areas controlled by the communist Cambodian insurgent group, the Party of Democratic Kampuchea (known as the Khmers Rouges), in compliance with UN sanctions against the movement. Nevertheless, violations of the embargo (mainly exports of logs and gems from Cambodia through Thailand) were widely reported during 1993. Accusations by representatives of the Cambodian Government that Thai complicity with the Khmers Rouges was undermining Cambodian attempts to end the insurgency were substantiated by reports from UN peace-keeping troops that members of the Thai armed forces were providing transport, medical care and other support for the Khmers Rouges. Official Thai government policy was to support the elected Government of Cambodia, but the armed forces controlled the border and were unwilling to jeopardize their lucrative business relations with the Khmers Rouges.

In January 1994 Chuan Leekpai made an official visit to Cambodia (the first such visit by a Thai premier), following which more strenuous efforts were made to control illicit border trade and to prevent members of the armed forces from co-operating with the Khmers Rouges. However, clashes between Thai and Cambodian troops continued as a result of incursions into Thai territory by Cambodian government forces in pursuit of the Khmers Rouges. In September 1995 Thailand and Cambodia signed an agreement to establish a border co-ordination committee. At its first meeting in November three border checkpoints, which had been closed in April, were reopened. In the latter half of 1997 intense fighting in Cambodia between forces loyal to the First Prime Minister, Hun Sen, and those of the former Second Prime Minister, Prince Norodom Ranariddh, led to further incursions, across Thailand's eastern border with Cambodia, and resulted in an influx of refugees to Thailand. In May 1998 Hun Sen visited Bangkok to hold discussions with Prime Minister Chuan. In January 1997, meanwhile, the Thai Government adopted a potentially controversial resolution unilaterally to extend Thailand's maritime jurisdiction over waters that were also claimed by Cambodia and Viet Nam. However, the Thai Government insisted that its decision was legal under international practice.

In January 2003 Thai-Cambodian relations were severely strained when the Thai embassy and several Thai businesses situated in the Cambodian capital, Phnom-Penh, were attacked by Cambodian demonstrators. Those who perpetrated the attacks were protesting against remarks, allegedly made by a Thai actress, claiming that the temples at Angkor Wat in Cambodia in fact belonged to Thailand. In response to the rioting, Prime Minister Thaksin downgraded diplomatic relations with Cambodia and announced plans to evacuate all Thai citizens from the country and to expel illegal Cambodian immigrants living in Thailand; the joint border was subsequently closed. The Cambodian Government issued a formal apology for the incident and promised compensation for those who had been affected by the violence. The Thai Government permitted a limited reopening of the border for commercial reasons in February. In early March Cambodia's Prime Minister, Hun Sen, ordered the border to be closed again, owing to alleged security concerns and in protest at the economic inequality between the two countries. However, later in that month the border was fully reopened and, in April, diplomatic relations were upgraded.

Tension arose between Thailand and Cambodia in July 2008, when the Preah Vihear temple, located on the border between the two countries, was declared a World Heritage Site by UNESCO, and both countries subsequently deployed troops to the area. Although the International Court of Justice had awarded ownership of the temple to Cambodia in a ruling in 1962, sovereignty of the surrounding area remained contentious, and the Thai Government's endorsement of Cambodia's application to UNESCO had provoked considerable controversy within Thailand. Bilateral talks aimed at resolving the situation commenced in late July, leading to agreement in August on the withdrawal of the majority of the soldiers deployed in the region, but in October three Cambodian troops and one Thai soldier were killed in exchanges of gunfire in the area. In mid-November, following three days of talks, the two Governments agreed to withdraw troops from the disputed area and to begin the demarcation of the joint border.

Following a military coup in Burma (now Myanmar) in September 1988, thousands of Burmese students fled to Thailand to avoid government repression. Amnesty International subsequently accused the Thai Government of coercing the students to return (resulting in their arrest and, in some cases, execution). In 1990 Myanma soldiers achieved unprecedented success in attacks on the strongholds of ethnic minorities on the Thai–Myanma border, since they were able to launch offensives from inside Thailand. The attacks resulted in a new influx of Myanma students and members of rebel ethnic groups seeking refuge in Thailand. The Thai Government refused to recognize those fleeing from Myanmar as refugees or to offer them aid. This refusal was motivated by its wish not to jeopardize the preferential treatment that it received from the Myanma Government, which had recently granted many licences to Thai businesses for the exploitation of Myanmar's natural resources.

In 1992 Myanma forces intensified their attacks on rebel bases near the Thai border. In March the Myanma Government warned Thai armed forces to withdraw from nearby border areas, but later in the month Thai troops clashed with Myanma forces which had entered Thailand to attack a nearby rebel base. In early December King Bhumibol appealed for a peaceful agreement to end the tension caused by the continued occupation by Myanma forces of Hill 491 in Chumphan province. In accordance with a bilateral agreement signed shortly afterwards, Myanma troops were withdrawn from the hill by late December. In February 1993 the two countries resolved to demarcate their common border. In April 1994 Thailand invited Myanmar to attend the annual ASEAN meeting of ministers responsible for foreign affairs, in Bangkok. In early 1995, however, relations with Myanmar were strained by the persistent border incursions into Thailand by forces of the Myanma Government during their offensive to capture the headquarters of the rebel Karen (Kayin) National Union (KNU) and subsequent attacks on disarmed Kayin refugees held in Thai camps along the border. In August Myanmar closed its land border with Thailand in protest at the alleged killing of a substantial number of Myanma seamen by Thai fishermen. A visit by Prime Minister Chavalit to Yangon, the capital of Myanmar, in September failed to resolve the situation and further discussions were held in November. In October 1996 the Thai Government approved the opening of three border checkpoints.

In late 1996 and early 1997 attacks allegedly carried out by breakaway Kayin rebels on Kayin refugee camps in Thailand resulted in a number of minor clashes between the Thai army and the rebels. In December 1997 the Thai and Myanma Governments agreed jointly to establish a panel to determine the legitimacy of an estimated 98,000 Kayin refugees sheltered along Thailand's border with Myanmar. In the same month, relief agencies operating along the border accused the Thai military authorities of using oppressive tactics to encourage the refugees to return to Myanmar, although the Thai military had earlier denied reports of its involvement in the forced repatriation of Kayin refugees. In March 1998 the Thai Government announced plans for the forced repatriation of several hundred thousand Myanma immigrants working illegally in Thailand, in response to the economic crisis afflicting the country. In the same month one of the largest Kayin refugee camps along the Thai–Myanma border was destroyed in a cross-border attack by the pro-Government rebel grouping, the Democratic Karen (Kayin) Buddhist Organization.

Relations between Thailand and Myanmar were placed under some strain in late 1999 when a group of armed Myanma student activists seized control of the Myanma embassy in Bangkok in early October, taking 89 people hostage and demanding the release of all political prisoners in Myanmar and the opening of a dialogue between the military Government and the opposition. All the hostages were released by the gunmen within 24 hours, in exchange for the Thai Government's provision of helicopter transport to give the hostage-takers safe passage to the Thai–Myanmar border. The Thai Government's release of the hostage-takers angered the ruling military junta in Myanmar, prompting the country to close its border with Thailand. In November, in a further indication of a deterioration in relations between the two countries, Thai forces expelled thousands of illegal Myanma migrant workers from the town of Mai Sot on the Thai–Myanma border, despite threats made by Myanma government troops to shoot the returnees. Although the border was reopened to commerce in late November, relations between the two countries remained fraught.

In January 2000 10 armed Myanma rebels took control of a hospital in Ratchaburi, Thailand, holding hundreds of people hostage. The hostage-takers, reported by some sources to be linked to the Kayin insurgent group, God's Army (a small breakaway faction of the KNU—the main KNU denied any connection with the gunmen), issued several demands, including that the shelling of their base on the Thai–Myanma border by the Thai military be halted, that co-operation between Thai and Myanma government forces against the Kayins should cease, and that their people be allowed to seek refuge in Thailand. However, in contrast to its peaceful handling of the siege of the Myanma embassy in Bangkok in October 1999, the response of the Thai Government to this second hostage crisis (which raised doubts about Thailand's national security and provoked further criticism from both the Thai political opposition and the general population of the Thai Government's relative tolerance of Myanma dissident activity in Thailand) was severe: government forces stormed the hospital, killing all 10 of the hostage-takers and releasing all of the hostages unharmed. This uncompromising resolution of the incident was praised by the military Government in Myanmar, and was regarded by many observers as the signal of a broader campaign by the Thai authorities against dissident activity by ethnic Myanma opposition groups operating in Thailand.

In February 2001 a border incident erupted between Thailand and Myanmar after Myanma forces pursued rebels belonging to the Shan State Army (SSA) into the northern Thai province of Chiang Rai, prompting reprisals by Thai troops. Despite the agreement of a cease-fire, Thailand sealed its border with Myanmar, and the situation was aggravated by Myanmar's assertion that Thailand was assisting the SSA. In April officials belonging to a non-governmental organization in Thailand claimed that the number of refugees of Myanma origin in Thailand had been underestimated and that, as of early April, they totalled almost 131,000. In May the Minister of Foreign Affairs, Surakiart Sathirathai, visited Myanmar in an effort to resolve the ongoing border tensions, but with little success. In the same month the United Wa State Army (UWSA), a Myanma ethnic militia, captured Hua Lone Hill near Chiang Mai; Thai troops recaptured the hill following a four-day battle in which at least 20 members of the UWSA were killed. The Government later lodged a formal protest with the Myanma Government after its forces allegedly bombed a Thai outpost situated near the hill. The Myanma Government responded by accusing the Thai armed forces of having launched air strikes into its territory. The problems were exacerbated when an article appeared in a Myanma newspaper that the Thai authorities claimed was insulting to the monarchy. In June 2001, after repeatedly denying reports that he intended to visit Myanmar, Thaksin Shinawatra became the first Thai Prime Minister to visit Yangon since 1997. While the subsequent discussions succeeded in defusing the immediate tensions, the two sides failed to come to any firm agreement as to how they would overcome the problems affecting bilateral relations. In July the Minister of Defence, Chavalit Yongchaiyudh, also visited Myanmar, and the two countries agreed to work together to expedite the repatriation of refugees on the common border. In September Gen. Khin Nyunt of Myanmar visited Thailand on a trip considered by many to constitute a starting point for a new era of improved relations. In January 2002 a joint Thai-Myanma commission met for the first time since 1999 to discuss plans to establish a task force that would aid in the repatriation of illegal Myanma immigrants. Further talks were held in February 2002, intended to facilitate bilateral co-operation in controlling the cross-border narcotics trade.

In March 2002 Thai-Myanma relations were placed under severe strain when Thai soldiers clashed with members of the UWSA in Chiang Mai. Following the incident, in which one Thai soldier and 12 UWSA guerrillas were killed, the Thai Government lodged a formal protest with Myanmar's ruling military junta. In April a bomb exploded on the so-called 'Friendship Bridge' linking the two countries, resulting in the deaths of at least seven people. Later in the same month the Vice-Chairman of Myanmar's ruling State Peace and Development Council (SPDC) visited Thailand to hold talks with the Government concerning drugs-smuggling and the continued border tensions. However, in May fresh fighting broke out along the joint border between Myanma government troops, together with their UWSA allies, and the SSA; subsequently, the SPDC again accused the Thai Government of supporting the SSA, following which it closed the shared border, owing to the deterioration of bilateral relations. Meanwhile, following the commencement of a Myanma military campaign on the border, intended to reclaim outposts and camps in the country's Shan State, Thai troops fired across the frontier when two Thai soldiers were allegedly injured by Myanma shells. The Government denied that it supported Myanma insurgent ethnic militias but admitted that it had allowed refugees from Myanmar to cross into Thailand. Shortly afterwards Thaksin claimed that bilateral relations had deteriorated to a new low point and that only an apology from Myanmar would improve the situation. In August the Thai Minister of Foreign Affairs stated that the two countries had agreed to hold talks in an effort to resolve the ongoing bilateral tensions; the joint border finally reopened in October. Relations continued to improve in 2003 and, in February, Thaksin paid a visit to Myanmar, during which the possibility of bilateral co-operation to address the problems posed by the cross-border narcotics trade and illegal immigration were discussed. In July the Thai Government announced plans to relocate all Myanma political refugees resident in Thailand to refugee camps near the joint border, where it was believed they could more easily be controlled and would thus present less of a threat to Thailand's relations with Myanmar. In early 2004 Myanmar announced that it was to award Thailand fishing concessions in its waters for one year. Fishing rights had been terminated in May 2001 following tensions on the joint border. In June 2004 Prime Minister Gen. Khin Nyunt of Myanmar visited Thailand and discussed various economic, development and border issues with Prime Minister Thaksin. In December Thaksin paid a visit to Myanmar, his first since the ousting of Khin Nyunt in October, and held talks with the new Prime Minister, Lt-Gen. Soe Win. In January 2005 Thailand increased security along the border with Myanmar, amid concerns that fighting between Myanma troops and insurgents might encroach upon Thai territory. At the end of March the Thai Government ordered the relocation of about 3,000 Myanma political refugees to camps near the joint border. However, about 1,000 of the refugees failed to meet a deadline to register with the Thai authorities, and they were to be detained and deported to Myanmar. In April Thailand again increased security along the border with Myanmar, in response to renewed fighting between rival Myanma ethnic rebel groups close to Thai territory. In January 2009 the office of the UN High Commissioner for Refugees (UNHCR, see p. 69) reported that around 110,000 Myanma refugees remained resident in nine camps in Thailand. Also in that month UNHCR expressed concern regarding allegations that Thai troops had intercepted large groups of Myanma and Bangladeshi migrants attempting to reach Thailand and forced them back out to sea in boats without engines; the Thai Government initiated an investigation into the claims.

Relations with Malaysia were adversely affected in November 1995 by the killing of two Thai fishermen by a Malaysian patrol vessel. In December an understanding was reached on the issue and it was agreed to establish a joint committee to resolve a longstanding dispute over fishing rights. Relations were also strained in early 1996 by Thai opposition to the Malaysian construction of a wall along the countries' common border. In late 1996 and early 1997 Thailand co-operated with Malaysia to prevent illegal Bangladeshi workers from entering Malaysia. Relations between the two countries continued to improve during 1998: by April, Prime Minister Chuan and his Malaysian counterpart, Mahathir Mohamad, had met five times in as many months to discuss bilateral issues. In January the Malaysian authorities arrested, and transferred to the Thai authorities, three alleged Muslim separatist leaders wanted in Thailand in connection with terrorist activities in the southern provinces of the country. In February 1997 Malaysia and Thailand established the Kolok river as the border demarcation between the two countries. In April 2001 the two countries agreed to co-operate to find those responsible for two bomb attacks in southern Thailand. In the same month Prime Minister Thaksin paid an official visit to Malaysia, during which the two countries discussed border demarcation issues and agreed that the planned construction of a gas pipeline between Thailand and Malaysia would proceed as originally intended. Relations remained cordial and, in December 2002, the cabinets of the two countries held an historic joint meeting, during which trade and security issues were discussed. In early 2004 the Malaysian Government co-operated with Thailand in an attempt to bring an end to the escalating violence in the south of the latter country. In February the Thai Government mooted plans to construct a security fence along parts of the joint border, in the hope of preventing militants from seeking refuge in Malaysia. As unrest in southern Thailand continued, Prime Minister Thaksin visited Malaysia in April for talks with his counterpart, Abdullah Badawi, on security along the border and the economic development of the surrounding area. None the less, the Malaysian Government rejected suggestions that the suspected perpetrators of the violence in southern Thailand had escaped to Malaysia. Bilateral relations were strained in December, when the Thai Government claimed to have photographic evidence that militants in southern Thailand had received training in Malaysia. In January 2005 the Malaysian authorities arrested Abdul Rahman Ahmad, whom Thailand held responsible for organizing much of the separatist violence in the south. A diplomatic dispute arose between the two countries in October concerning the fate of 131 Muslim asylum-seekers, who had fled from the violence-stricken southern province of Narathiwat to neighbouring Malaysia (see the chapter on Malaysia). Although the issue was eventually resolved in February 2006 when the Thai Government announced that it was to allow the refugees to remain in Malaysia, relations between the two countries had by that stage descended to their lowest point in recent years. In November 2005 former Malaysian Prime Minister Mahathir Mohamad visited Thailand for discussions with Prime Minister Thaksin regarding the ongoing insurgency in southern Thailand. The negotiations made some progress towards easing the tension that had been caused by Thai security officials' accusations that the Malaysian authorities were failing to prevent insurgents from crossing the border into Thailand. Thaksin and Mahathir agreed that the two countries should cease their 'war of words' and Mahathir was to stop advocating autonomy for Thailand's southern regions. In December Manasae Saeloh, a suspected leader of PULO, was arrested in Malaysia and relinquished to the Thai authorities, by which he was wanted in connection with numerous bomb attacks and other acts of violence. Gen. (retd) Surayud Chulanont visited Malaysia soon after taking office as interim Prime Minister in October 2006, holding talks with Abdullah Badawi on the insurgency in Thailand's southern provinces. An official visit to Thailand by Abdullah Badawi in February 2007 was reciprocated by Surayud in August. In December the two Prime Ministers officially opened a new bridge across the Kolok river, which it was hoped would lead to a reduction in violence in the border region by improving economic prospects.

In November 1996 the Government approved a proposal for the establishment of a Joint Thai-Lao Border Committee. In December 1997 it was announced by UNHCR that the review of the status of the last remaining group of Laotian refugees at the Ban Napho refugee camp in the Nakhan Phanom province of Thailand was scheduled to be completed by January 1998, after which the refugees were to be either allowed to settle in a third country or repatriated. In September 1999 282 Laotian refugees who had been residing at the camp were compulsorily repatriated by Thai officials and UNHCR after having been refused refugee status; a further 291 Laotian refugees were repatriated in December. In December 2003 the USA agreed to accept around 15,000 Laotian Hmong refugees living in refugee camps in Thailand. The first group of refugees was resettled in the USA in June 2004, under the aegis of the International Organization for Migration. Meanwhile, in August 2000 a border dispute arose between Thailand and Laos after Laos apparently attempted to assert sovereignty over all islands in the Mekong river, as it claimed was its right under the Siam-Franco treaty of 1926. The occupation by Laotian armed forces of the Mano I and Mano II islands took place during the demarcation of the river boundary (due to be completed by the end of 2000) between the two countries. In March 2002 a Thai court convicted 28 people, including 17 Laotian nationals, of charges relating to the dispute. Despite the existence of a bilateral extradition treaty, concluded in 2001, it was thought unlikely that Thailand would comply with a Lao Government request to extradite its citizens to Laos. In March 2004 the Thai and Laotian Governments held a joint cabinet meeting to discuss bilateral co-operation. In August 2006 the Ministries of Foreign Affairs of Thailand and of Laos indicated that the two countries would co-operate to find a solution to the Hmong refugee issue, although neither side claimed responsibility. Through a joint process, the two countries were later reported to be verifying the origin of the migrants. In January 2007 the Thai Government decided against the forcible repatriation to Laos of some 153 Hmong migrants who had been arrested in Bangkok in 2006, following offers of asylum from several Western countries. However, the group of Hmong, now numbering 158, and all recognized as refugees, remained in an immigration detention centre in Thailand in early 2009, according to UNHCR, which urged the Thai authorities to release them so that they could take up the previous offers of asylum in other countries. Meanwhile, in February 2008, following a visit to Laos, the Thai Minister of Foreign Affairs announced that the Thai authorities had almost completed the process of verifying the identity of the Hmong remaining in refugee camps in Phetchabun province (estimated at some 7,000). Later in that month 10 Hmong were repatriated to Laos ahead of an official visit to that country by the new Thai Prime Minister, Samak Sundaravej. In June UNHCR expressed concern regarding the conditions under which a group of 837 Hmong had recently been returned to Laos from Ban Huay Nam Khao camp in Phetchabun province, amid reports that they had been forcibly deported following a mass protest at the camp; in July, after a further 391 Hmong were repatriated, UNHCR urged the Thai authorities to allow it access to the camp. A total of 1,809 Hmong were returned to Laos during 2008. In January 2009 the Thai Government confirmed its intention to complete the repatriation of the 5,000 Hmong remaining at Ban Huay Nam Khao camp by June, prompting fears among human rights organizations that the process would not be conducted on a voluntary basis. Also in January, in an indication that the new administration in Thailand hoped to strengthen relations with Laos, Thai Prime Minister Abhisit Vejjajiva and Minister of Foreign Affairs Kasit Piromya both made that country the destination of their first official foreign visits. Kasit and his Lao counterpart agreed to make efforts to finalize the demarcation of their land border in 2009, followed by that of the maritime border in 2010. A rail link on a bridge connecting Thailand and Laos over the Mekong river was opened in March 2009.

In 1999 Thailand contributed 1,500 troops to the multinational peace-keeping force in the UN-administered territory of East Timor (now Timor-Leste), following the territory's vote for independence from Indonesia in a referendum held in August. The country also maintained a cordial bilateral relationship with Indonesia.

In December 2001 the Prime Minister paid an official visit to the USA. During his stay he held talks with US President George W. Bush and assured him that Thailand would remain a strong ally in the US-led 'war on terror' in the aftermath of the September terrorist attacks (see the chapter on the USA). In response, the US President praised the Thai Government for its consistent support throughout the campaign. In June 2003 Thaksin met with President Bush again in Washington, DC, to discuss counter-terrorism issues. In October President Bush attended an APEC summit meeting in Bangkok, having paid an official state visit to Thailand in the days preceding the summit. The two heads of state announced that they were to enter into formal negotiations with regard to the signing of a bilateral free trade agreement. The terms of the deal were expected to be comprehensive, including measures intended to liberalize trade in consumer goods, agricultural products, services and investment, as well as intellectual property rights. However, following the completion of the sixth round of talks between the two countries, held in January 2006, scant progress had been made. Furthermore, the political upheaval of 2006–08 led to further delays. In early 2009 the recently appointed Government of Abhisit Vejjajiva expressed hope that free trade negotiations with the USA would resume once the new administrations in both countries had fully settled into office. Meanwhile, in February 2008, following the return to civilian rule in Thailand, the USA announced the ending of its suspension of military aid to Thailand, which had been imposed following the coup of September 2006.

Following the terrorist attack on the Indonesian island of Bali in October 2002 (see the chapter on Indonesia), the Thai Government increased security in the country owing to speculation that Thailand, and in particular the tourist resort of Phuket, might be the target of further regional terrorist activity. Evidence was discovered that suggested southern Thailand as one of the locations used by those responsible for planning the Bali attack. Meanwhile, several foreign governments issued advisory warnings against unnecessary travel to the country. However, the Thai Government expressed its concern that such warnings were excessive and urged that they be rescinded.

Government

Thailand is a constitutional monarchy. In December 1991 a new Constitution was promulgated, which provided for a National Assembly (comprising an elected House of Representatives and an appointed Senate) and a Cabinet headed by a Prime Minister. In June 1992 the National Assembly approved a constitutional amendment requiring the Prime Minister to be a member of the House of Representatives. In January 1995 the National Assembly approved a constitutional charter, which provided for a number of amendments; these included lowering the voting age from 20 to 18 years and reducing the membership of the Senate to two-thirds of that of the House of Representatives.

A new draft Constitution was promulgated on 11 October 1997 (see Constitution, below); enabling legislation for the new Constitution was completed within 240 days. In September 2006, following the military coup (see Recent History, above), the Council for Democratic Reform (CDR) released an interim Constitution; this came into effect in the following month. A permanent Constitution was later drafted by a committee appointed by the CDR, and in August 2007 was put to a national referendum, wherein it was approved by 57.8% of voters, and duly became law.

The bicameral National Assembly of Thailand consists of the House of Representatives (Sapha Poothaen Rassadorn) and the Senate (Woothi Sapha). The House of Representatives has 480 members, of whom 400 are directly elected by constituency voting, while the remainder are elected by a party list system of proportional representation. Members are elected for a term of four years. The Senate consists of 150 members, of whom 76 are elected (one from each of Thailand's 76 provinces) and 74 are appointed by a selection committee. Senators serve six-year terms.

Defence

As assessed at November 2008, the Thai armed forces had a total strength of 306,600: 190,000 in the army, 70,600 in the navy and an estimated 46,000 in the air force. Military service is compulsory for two years between the ages of 21 and 30. Paramilitary forces, including a volunteer irregular force, numbered an estimated 113,700. The defence budget was 143,000m. baht for 2008.

Economic Affairs

In 2007, according to estimates by the World Bank, Thailand's gross national income (GNI), measured at average 2005–07 prices, was US $217,348m., equivalent to $3,400 per head (or $7,880 per head on an international purchasing-power parity basis). During 2000–07, it was estimated, the population increased at an annual average rate of 0.7%, while gross domestic product (GDP) per head increased, in real terms, by an average of 4.3% per year. Overall GDP increased, in real terms, at an average annual rate of 5.0% in 2000–07. According to the Asian Development Bank (ADB), GDP increased by 4.9% in 2007 and by 2.6% in 2008.

Agriculture (including forestry, hunting and fishing) contributed an estimated 11.6% of GDP in 2008. In 2007 41.8% of the employed labour force were engaged in the sector. Thailand's staple crop and principal agricultural export commodity is rice (Thailand became the world's largest exporter of rice in 1981). Rice exports accounted for 3.5% of the total value of exports in 2008. Other major crops include sugar cane, cassava (tapioca), oil palm fruit, maize, natural rubber, bananas, mangoes and pineapples. Fisheries products and livestock (mainly cattle, buffaloes, pigs and poultry) are also important. Thailand is one of the world's largest exporters of farmed shrimp. During 2000–07 agricultural GDP increased by an estimated annual average of 2.6%. Agricultural GDP was estimated to have risen by 1.8% in 2007 and by 5.1% in 2008.

Industry (including mining, manufacturing, construction and utilities) provided an estimated 45.1% of GDP in 2008. In 2007 20.7% of the employed labour force were engaged in industrial activities. During 2000–07 industrial GDP increased at an annual average rate of 6.1%. The GDP of the industrial sector increased by an estimated 5.7% in 2007 and by 3.4% in 2008.

Mining and quarrying contributed an estimated 3.5% of GDP in 2008 and engaged less than 0.2% of the employed labour force in 2007. Gemstones, notably diamonds, are the principal mineral export. Natural gas and, to a lesser extent, petroleum are also exploited, and production of these fuels increased substantially from the late 1990s. Tin, lignite, gypsum, tungsten, antimony, manganese, gold, zinc, iron and fluorite are also mined. During 2000–07 the GDP of the mining sector increased at an estimated average annual rate of 5.7%. Mining GDP increased by an estimated 3.8% in 2007 and by 2.4% in 2008.

Manufacturing provided an estimated 36.0% of GDP in 2008. In 2007 15.1% of the employed labour force were engaged in the sector. In 1999 manufacturing's contribution to export earnings was 80%. Textiles and garments and electronics and electrical goods (particularly semiconductors) constitute Thailand's principal branches of manufacturing. Other manufacturing activities include the production of cigarettes, chemicals, cement and beer, sugar and petroleum refining, motor vehicle production, rubber production and the production of iron and steel. During 2000–07 manufacturing GDP increased by an estimated annual average of 6.4%. The GDP of the sector increased by an estimated 6.2% in 2007 and by 3.9% in 2008.

Energy is derived principally from hydrocarbons. In 2006 47.1m. barrels of crude petroleum and 27,466m. cu m of natural gas were produced. In 2006 petroleum accounted for 44.3% of total fuel consumption, natural gas for 27.5%, coal for 12.4% and hydroelectricity for 1.8%. Lignite is also exploited. In 2003 solar and wind energy accounted for about 1% of electric power. However, Thailand remains dependent on imported petroleum and electricity. In 2008 imports of mineral fuels comprised 20.8% of the value of merchandise imports.

Services (including transport and communications, commerce, banking and finance, public administration and other services) contributed an estimated 43.3% of GDP in 2008 and 37.5% of the employed labour force were engaged in the services sector in 2007. Tourism has become a major source of foreign exchange. The number of tourist arrivals totalled 13.8m. in 2006, and receipts reached US $15,653m. However, the tourism sector has been intermittently affected by unrest in Bangkok and by the violence in southern Thailand (see Recent History). During 2000–07 the GDP of the services sector expanded by an estimated annual average of 4.6%. The GDP of the sector increased by 4.7% in 2007 and by 1.2% in 2008.

In 2007 Thailand recorded a visible trade surplus of US $25,547m.; in the same year there was a surplus of $15,755m. on the current account of the balance of payments. In 2008 the principal source of imports (18.7%) was Japan; other major suppliers in that year were the People's Republic of China (11.2%), the USA, the United Arab Emirates and Malaysia. The principal markets for exports in 2008 were the USA (11.4%), Japan (11.3%) and China (9.1%); other major purchasers were Singapore, Hong Kong and Malaysia. The principal imports in 2008 were machinery (31.8%), mineral fuels and lubricants, basic manufactures and chemical products. The principal exports were machinery (42.3%), food, basic manufactures, miscellaneous manufactured goods (including clothing and accessories) and chemicals and related products.

The 2008/09 budget projected a deficit of 349,500m. baht, equivalent to an estimated 3.5% of GDP. According to the ADB, Thailand's external debt totalled US $64,805m. at the end of 2008; in that year the cost of debt-servicing was equivalent to 6.7% of the value of exports of goods and services. The annual rate of inflation averaged 2.6% in 2000–07. Consumer prices increased by 5.4% in 2008. In 2008 1.4% of the labour force were unemployed.

Thailand is a member of the World Trade Organization (WTO, see p. 410), the UN Economic and Social Commission for Asia and the Pacific (ESCAP, see p. 36), the Asian Development Bank (ADB, see p. 191), the Association of South East Asian Nations (ASEAN, see p. 194), the Colombo Plan (see p. 425) and Asia-Pacific Economic Co-operation (APEC, see p. 185). In January 1993 the establishment of the ASEAN Free Trade Area (AFTA) commenced; the reduction of tariffs to between 0% and 5% was originally to be implemented by 2008 but this was subsequently brought forward to 2002. The target date for zero tariffs was advanced from 2015 to 2010 in November 1999. AFTA was formally established on 1 January 2002.

Thailand's steady recovery from the regional economic crisis of the late 1990s was jeopardized by the removal of the democratically elected Government in October 2006 and the subsequent political instability (see Recent History), which significantly weakened business confidence. According to the ADB, foreign direct investment decreased from US $9,381m. in 2007 to $7,703m. in 2008. Strong global demand for commodities such as rice increased activities in the agricultural sector during 2007/08, although the concomitant rise in the country's export revenues exacerbated the already rapid appreciation of the Thai baht. The onset of the global financial crisis in the latter part of 2008 contributed to a sharp reduction in levels of public expenditure and private investment, both of which had accounted for a significant portion of growth during the first half of the year. The overall value of the stock market was reported to have declined by 48% during the course of 2008. Owing to higher costs for fuel and foodstuffs, the rate of inflation accelerated rapidly in the first months of 2008, exceeding 9% in July. This prompted the Bank of Thailand to raise its interest rate, before implementing a series of reductions; the central bank's interest rate stood at 1.25% in April 2009. The deceleration of the global economy, combined with the disruption by demonstrators of the operations of Bangkok airport (see Recent History), had a major impact on the tourism industry in 2008. In an effort to mitigate the repercussions of global recessionary conditions, in January 2009 the Government announced an economic stimulus plan. The programme envisaged expenditure of 116,700m. baht and included provision for an increase in financial support for the most impoverished of Thai households, low interest loans to small businesses and training opportunities for the unemployed. The ADB forecast that GDP would contract by 2.0% in 2009.

Education

From January 2003, education became officially compulsory for 10 years, to be undertaken between the ages of seven and 16 years. In October 2002 12 years of free basic education was granted to students throughout the country for the first time, and in May 2004 this was expanded to 14 years, with the two years of pre-primary schooling henceforth also being offered free to all. Primary education begins at six years of age and lasts for six years. In 2006/07 enrolment in pre-primary schools was equivalent to 94% of children from the relevant age-group (males 93%; females 94%). In 2004/05 enrolment within primary education was equivalent to 97.1% of children in the relevant age group (males 100%; females 95%). Secondary education, beginning at 12 years of age, also lasts for six years, divided into two equal cycles. In 2004/05 total secondary enrolment was equivalent to 83% of children within the relevant age-group (males 79%; females 87%). There were 20 state universities (12 of which were in Bangkok) and 26 private universities and colleges in 1995. In 2003 a total of approximately 1.9m. students were enrolled within the tertiary education sector. Budgetary expenditure on education by the central Government was forecast to be 334,400m. baht (20.3% of total spending and equivalent to about 3.9% of GDP) in the financial year ending 30 September 2007, according to preliminary figures.

Public Holidays

2009: 1 January (New Year's Day), 9 February* (Makhabuja), 6 April (for Chakri Day), 13–15 April (Songkran Festival), 1 May (Labour Day), 5 May (Coronation Day), 8 May* (Visakhabuja), 1 July (Half Year Bank Holiday), 8 July (Khao Phansa, beginning of Buddhist Lent), 8 July* (Asalhabuja), 12 August (Queen's Birthday), 23 October (Chulalongkorn Day), 5 December (King's Birthday), 10 December (Constitution Day), 31 December (New Year's Eve).

2010: 1 January (New Year's Day), February/March* (Makhabuja), 6 April (Chakri Day), 13–15 April (Songkran Festival), 28 April (Visakhabuja), 1 May (Labour Day), 5 May* (Coronation Day), 1 July (Half Year Bank Holiday), July* (Khao Phansa, beginning of Buddhist Lent), July* (Asalhabuja), 12 August (Queen's Birthday), 23 October (Chulalongkorn Day), 5 December (King's Birthday), 10 December (Constitution Day), 31 December (New Year's Eve).

* Regulated by the Buddhist lunar calendar.

Weights and Measures

The metric system is in force, but a number of traditional measures are also used.

THAILAND

Statistical Survey

Source (unless otherwise stated): National Statistical Office, Thanon Larn Luang, Bangkok 10100; tel. (2) 281-0333; fax (2) 281-3815; e-mail onsoadm@nso.go.th; internet www.nso.go.th.

Area and Population

AREA, POPULATION AND DENSITY

Area (sq km)	513,120*
Population (census results)†	
1 April 1990	54,548,530
1 April 2000	
Males	29,844,870
Females	30,762,077
Total	60,606,947
Population (official estimates at mid-year)†	
2005	62,418,054
2006	62,828,706
2007	63,038,247
Density (per sq km) at mid-2007	122.9

* 198,117 sq miles.
† Excluding adjustment for underenumeration.

REGIONS
(estimates at mid-2007)

	Area (sq km)	Population ('000)	Density (per sq km)
Bangkok	1,568.7	5,716	3,643.9
Central Region	102,336.0	15,410	150.6
Northern Region	169,644.3	11,872	70.0
Northeastern Region	168,855.3	21,386	126.7
Southern Region	70,715.2	8,655	122.4
Total	513,119.5	63,038	122.9

PRINCIPAL TOWNS
(population at 2000 census)

Bangkok Metropolis*	6,320,174	Pak Kret	141,788
Samut Prakan	378,694	Si Racha	141,334
Nanthaburi	291,307	Khon Kaen	141,034
Udon Thani	220,493	Nakhon Pathom	120,657
Nakhon Ratchasima	204,391	Nakhon Si Thammarat	118,764
Hat Yai	185,557	Thanya Buri	113,818
Chon Buri	182,641	Surat Thani	111,276
Chiang Mai	167,776	Rayong	106,585
Phra Padaeng	166,828	Ubon Ratchathani	106,552
Lampang	147,812	Khlong Luang	103,282

* Formerly Bangkok and Thonburi.

Mid-2007 ('000, incl. suburbs, UN estimate): Bangkok 6,704 (Source: UN, *World Urbanization Prospects: The 2007 Revision*).

BIRTHS, MARRIAGES AND DEATHS*

	Registered live births		Registered marriages		Registered deaths	
	Number	Rate (per 1,000)	Number	Rate (per 1,000)	Number	Rate (per 1,000)
1998	897,495	14.7	324,262	5.3	317,793	5.2
1999	754,685	12.3	348,803	5.7	362,607	5.9
2000	773,009	12.5	339,443	5.4	365,741	5.9
2001	790,425	12.7	324,661	n.a.	369,493	6.0
2002	782,911	12.5	n.a.	n.a.	380,364	6.1
2003	742,183	11.8	328,356	n.a.	384,131	6.1
2004	813,069	13.0	365,721	n.a.	393,592	6.3
2005†	809,485	13.0	345,234	n.a.	395,374	6.4

* Registration is incomplete. According to UN estimates, the average annual rates in 1990–95 were: Births 18.8 per 1,000; Deaths 6.8 per 1,000; in 1995–2000: Births 16.5 per 1,000; Deaths 7.8 per 1,000; in 2000–05: Births 15.3 per 1,000; Deaths 8.5 per 1,000 (Source: UN, *World Population Prospects: The 2008 Revision*).
† Provisional.

Life expectancy (years at birth, WHO estimates): 72.0 (males 69.0; females 74.9) in 2006 (Source: WHO, *World Health Statistics*).

ECONOMICALLY ACTIVE POPULATION*
('000 persons aged 15 years and over, July–September of each year)

	2005	2006	2007
Agriculture, hunting and forestry	15,008	14,887	15,082
Fishing	441	428	410
Mining and quarrying	40	55	54
Manufacturing	5,350	5,307	5,593
Electricity, gas and water	107	99	105
Construction	1,853	2,039	1,939
Wholesale and retail trade; repair of motor vehicles, motorcycles and personal and household goods	5,297	5,402	5,525
Hotels and restaurants	2,300	2,215	2,303
Transport, storage and communications	1,076	1,053	1,027
Financial intermediation	340	350	350
Real estate, renting and business activities	652	659	717
Public administration and defence; compulsory social security	1,096	1,170	1,287
Education	1,122	1,080	1,085
Health and social work	611	603	647
Other community, social and personal service activities	719	710	718
Private households with employed persons	242	222	229
Extra-territorial organizations and bodies	2	0	1
Activities not adequately defined	48	66	51
Total employed	36,302	36,345	37,122
Unemployed	496	450	442
Total labour force	36,798	36,795	37,564

* Excluding the armed forces.
Source: ILO.

THAILAND

Health and Welfare

KEY INDICATORS

Total fertility rate (children per woman, 2006)	1.8
Under-5 mortality rate (per 1,000 live births, 2006)	8
HIV/AIDS (% of persons aged 15–49, 2007)	1.4
Physicians (per 1,000 head, 2000)	0.4
Hospital beds (per 1,000 head, 2000)	2.2
Health expenditure (2006): US $ per head (PPP)	346
Health expenditure (2006): % of GDP	3.5
Health expenditure (2006): public (% of total)	64.4
Access to water (% of persons, 2006)	98
Access to sanitation (% of persons, 2006)	96
Human Development Index (2006): ranking	81
Human Development Index (2006): value	0.786

For sources and definitions, see explanatory note on p. vi.

Agriculture

PRINCIPAL CROPS
('000 metric tons)

	2005	2006	2007
Rice, paddy	30,292	29,269	27,879*
Maize	3,943	3,740	3,619
Sorghum	95	53	57
Cassava (Manioc, Tapioca)	16,938	22,584	26,411
Sugar cane	49,586	47,658	64,366
Beans, dry	133	112	113
Soybeans (Soya beans)	221	215	218
Groundnuts, with shell*	114	117	114
Coconuts	1,871	1,815	1,705
Oil palm fruit	5,003	6,715	7,643
Cabbages and other brassicas†	265	265	265
Tomatoes†	270	270	270
Pumpkins, squash, gourds†	226	226	226
Cucumbers and gherkins†	222	222	222
Onions, dry	279	280†	280†
Garlic	107	81	74
Maize, green	273	305†	305†
Watermelons†	432	432	432
Bananas†	2,000	2,000	2,000
Oranges†	350	350	350
Tangerines, mandarins, clementines, satsumas†	670	670	670
Mangoes, mangosteens and guavas†	1,800	1,800	1,800
Pineapples	2,183	2,705	2,320
Papayas†	131	131	131
Tobacco, unmanufactured†	70	70	70
Natural rubber	2,977	3,071	3,122

* Unofficial figure.
† FAO estimate(s).

Aggregate production ('000 metric tons, may include official, semi-official or estimated data): Total cereals 34,508 in 2005, 33,201 in 2006, 31,702 in 2007; Total roots and tubers 17,191 in 2005, 22,842 in 2006, 26,676 in 2007; Total vegetables (incl. melons) 3,342 in 2005, 3,346 in 2006, 3,339 in 2007; Total fruits (excl. melons) 8,312 in 2005, 7,811 in 2006, 7,426 in 2007.

Source: FAO.

LIVESTOCK
('000 head, year ending September)

	2005	2006	2007
Horses	6	2	2*
Cattle	5,610	6,042	6,481
Buffaloes	1,771	1,763	1,744
Pigs	7,534	7,688	8,381
Sheep	42	51	52
Goats	338	324	310*
Chickens	187,371	203,201	209,105
Ducks	21,540	20,844	21,000
Geese and guinea fowl*	270	270	270

* FAO estimate(s).
Source: FAO.

LIVESTOCK PRODUCTS
('000 metric tons)

	2005	2006	2007
Cattle meat	248.4*	196.9	198.0
Buffalo meat*	62.5	62.5	61.7
Pig meat	668.9*	700.0	700.0
Chicken meat†	950.0	1,100.0	1,050.0
Duck meat*	85.0	85.0	85.0
Cows' milk	888.2	826.5	683.9
Hen eggs*	468.7	513.3	531.5
Other poultry eggs*	310	310	310

* FAO estimate(s).
† Unofficial figures.
Source: FAO.

Forestry

ROUNDWOOD REMOVALS
('000 cubic metres, excl. bark, FAO estimates)

	2005	2006	2007
Sawlogs, veneer logs and logs for sleepers	300	300	300
Pulpwood	2,900	2,900	2,900
Other industrial wood	5,500	5,500	5,500
Fuel wood	19,866	19,736	19,615
Total	28,566	28,436	28,315

Source: FAO.

SAWNWOOD PRODUCTION
('000 cubic metres, incl. railway sleepers)

	2000	2001	2002
Coniferous (softwood)	17	18	18*
Broadleaved (hardwood)	203	215	270
Total	220	233	288

* FAO estimate.
2003–07: Production assumed to be unchanged from 2002 (FAO estimates).
Source: FAO.

Fishing

('000 metric tons, live weight)

	2004	2005	2006
Capture	2,839.6	2,814.3	2,776.3
Bigeyes	136.6	121.2	118.3
Sardinellas	119.9	127.4	120.5
Anchovies, etc.	163.2	159.7	158.9
Indian mackerels	160.4	166.8	158.1
Aquaculture	1,260.0	1,304.2*	1,385.8*
Catfish (hybrid)	159.3	150.0*	146.0*
Whiteleg shrimp	251.7	374.5	490.0
Giant tiger prawn	106.9	26.1	10.2
Green mussel	261.7	270.7	272.9
Total catch	4,099.6	4,118.5*	4,162.1*

* FAO estimate.
Source: FAO.

THAILAND

Mining

(production in metric tons, unless otherwise indicated)

	2004	2005	2006
Lignite ('000 metric tons)	20,038	21,429	19,056
Crude petroleum ('000 barrels)	31,299	41,570	47,067
Natural gas—gross production (million cu m)	24,963	25,363	27,466
Iron ore—gross weight	135,580	230,946	264,289
Iron ore—metal content	68,000	116,000	132,000
Zinc ore—metal content*	43,400	30,572	32,100
Tin concentrates—metal content	586	158*	190*
Manganese ore—metal content*	2,180	42,400	480
Tungsten concentrates—metal content*	180	430	380
Tantalum—metal and oxide powder	317	150	230
Antimony ore—metal content	52	356*	1,409
Silver (kilograms)	10,700	14,100	11,400
Gold (kilograms)	4,500	4,400	3,500
Marble—dimension stone ('000 cu m)	236.6	267.8	547.6
Granite—dimension stone ('000 cu m*)	10.0	9.5	10.0
Granite—industrial ('000 metric tons)*	3,500	3,000	3,200
Limestone ('000 metric tons)*	133,196	130,584	136,583
Dolomite ('000 metric tons)	992.9	795.5	899.5
Calcite ('000 metric tons)	436.6	692.9	626.0
Silica sand ('000 metric tons)	587.7	718.3	861.8
Ball clay ('000 metric tons)	610.2	393.9	1,003.3
Kaolin—marketable production ('000 metric tons)	430.4	580.4	675.9
Phosphate rock, crude	2,580	3,020	900
Fluorspar—metallurgical grade ('000 metric tons)	2,375	295	3,240
Feldspar	1,001.1	1,149.7*	1,067.7
Barite	211.3	4.0	4.5
Perlite*	6,000	5,500	6,000
Gypsum ('000 metric tons)	7,619	7,113	8,355
Gemstones ('000 carats)	911	699	81

* Estimate(s).

Source: US Geological Survey.

Industry

SELECTED PRODUCTS

('000 metric tons, unless otherwise indicated)

	2006	2007	2008*
Raw sugar	5,719	7,344	8,195
Beer (million litres)	2,011	2,161	2,160
Spirits (million litres)	635	551	631
Synthetic fibre	725.4	674.6	592.7
Wood pulp	999.4	1,037.4	948.5
Petroleum products (million litres)	49,285	49,856	51,216
Cement	39,408	35,668	31,651
Galvanized iron sheets	297.7	247.2	207.5
Integrated circuits (million units)	13,954	14,334	13,758
Computer monitors ('000 units)	1,380	942	705
Computer keyboards ('000 units)	958	931	633
Hard disk drives ('000 units)	153,980	205,277	246,986
Printers ('000 units)	16,577	17,439	15,693

* Provisional.

Source: Bank of Thailand, Bangkok.

Finance

CURRENCY AND EXCHANGE RATES

Monetary Units
100 satangs = 1 baht.

Sterling, Dollar and Euro Equivalents (31 December 2008)
£1 sterling = 51.103 baht;
US $1 = 35.055 baht;
€1 = 48.786 baht;
1,000 baht = £19.57 = $28.53 = €20.50.

Average Exchange Rate (baht per US $)
2006   37.882
2007   34.523
2008   33.322

Note: Figures refer to the average mid-point rate of exchange available from commercial banks. In July 1997 the Bank of Thailand began operating a managed 'float' of the baht. In addition, a two-tier market was introduced, creating separate exchange rates for purchasers of baht in domestic markets and those who buy the currency overseas.

GOVERNMENT FINANCE

(central government transactions, non-cash basis, '000 million baht, year ending 30 September)

Summary of Balances

	2004/05	2005/06*	2006/07*
Revenue	1,498.7	1,576.4	1,659.4
Less Expense	1,166.1	1,265.5	1,502.2
Net operating balance	332.6	310.8	157.2
Less Net acquisition of non-financial assets	155.6	161.3	145.9
Net lending/borrowing	177.0	149.5	11.2

Revenue

	2004/05	2005/06*	2006/07*
Taxes	1,223.0	1,313.6	1,374.4
Taxes on income, profits and capital gains	491.8	576.7	614.9
Taxes on goods and services	601.1	629.4	659.7
Social contributions	73.3	74.0	79.8
Grants	1.9	1.7	1.7
Other revenue	200.5	187.1	203.5
Total	1,498.7	1,576.4	1,659.4

Expense/Outlays

Expense by economic type	2004/05	2005/06*	2006/07*
Compensation of employees	403.3	505.6	559.5
Use of goods and services	253.1	264.2	398.6
Consumption of fixed capital	34.5	35.4	38.5
Interest	90.8	112.8	93.3
Subsidies	88.9	26.8	33.6
Grants	173.0	190.9	205.1
Social benefits	93.5	113.1	170.6
Other expense	29.1	16.6	3.0
Total	1,166.1	1,265.5	1,502.2

THAILAND

Outlays by functions of government†	2004/05	2005/06*	2006/07*
General public services	220.7	340.0	304.7
Defence	83.5	89.7	42.9
Public order and safety	74.5	82.4	136.5
Economic affairs	397.3	286.2	398.6
Agriculture, forestry and fishing	71.8	71.2	109.0
Fuel and energy	73.5	17.2	31.8
Transport	69.0	56.6	55.6
Environmental protection	7.0	35.6	4.8
Housing and community amenities	28.6	38.8	10.6
Health	115.9	125.7	185.6
Recreation, culture and religion	9.1	16.6	14.6
Education	268.1	279.6	334.4
Pre-primary and primary	155.7	n.a.	n.a.
Secondary	23.7	n.a.	n.a.
Tertiary	42.5	n.a.	n.a.
Social protection	117.0	132.2	215.7
Total	1,321.7	1,426.8	1,648.2

* Preliminary figures.
† Including net acquisition of non-financial assets.

Source: IMF, *Government Finance Statistics Yearbook*.

INTERNATIONAL RESERVES
(US $ million at 31 December)

	2006	2007	2008
Gold*	1,693	2,234	2,347
IMF special drawing rights	1	—	131
Reserve position in IMF	143	111	213
Foreign exchange	65,147	85,100	108,317
Total	66,984	87,445	111,008

* Revalued annually on the basis of the London market price.

Source: IMF, *International Financial Statistics*.

MONEY SUPPLY
('000 million baht at 31 December)

	2005	2006	2007
Currency outside banks	603.4	621.6	685.8
Demand deposits at deposit money banks	256.2	254.9	275.5
Total money (incl. others)	863.0	880.2	965.2

Source: IMF, *International Financial Statistics*.

COST OF LIVING
(Consumer Price Index; base: 2007 = 100)

	2005	2006	2008
Food (incl. non-alcoholic beverages)	91.9	96.1	111.6
Tobacco and alcoholic beverages	90.7	98.5	102.9
Energy	84.9	97.7	108.0
Clothing (incl. footwear)	99.6	99.8	100.3
Housing and furnishing	97.9	99.9	96.9
All items (incl. others)	93.4	97.8	105.4

Source: Bank of Thailand.

NATIONAL ACCOUNTS
(million baht at current prices)

National Income and Product

	2005	2006	2007*
Compensation of employees	2,072,848	2,248,699	2,438,879
Operating surplus	3,324,676	3,714,294	4,088,374
Domestic factor incomes	5,397,524	5,962,993	6,527,253
Consumption of fixed capital	927,456	995,296	1,077,263
Gross domestic product (GDP) at factor cost	6,324,980	6,958,289	7,604,516
Indirect taxes	857,811	922,630	929,407
Less Subsidies	89,898	39,622	40,612
GDP in market prices	7,092,893	7,841,297	8,493,311
Net factor income from abroad	−344,014	−316,810	−325,793
Gross national product	6,748,879	7,524,487	8,167,518

Expenditure on the Gross Domestic Product

	2006	2007*	2008*
Government final consumption expenditure	927,575	1,037,571	1,083,829
Private final consumption expenditure	4,376,585	4,561,528	4,992,474
Changes in inventories	31,150	10,753	131,436
Gross fixed capital formation	2,197,221	2,247,174	2,486,616
Total domestic expenditure	7,532,531	7,857,026	8,694,355
Exports of goods and services	5,777,554	6,218,219	6,956,257
Less Imports of goods and services	5,503,772	5,544,488	6,705,464
Statistical discrepancy	34,984	−37,446	157,637
GDP in market prices	7,841,297	8,493,311	9,102,785
GDP at constant 1988 prices	4,059,645	4,259,633	4,369,481

Gross Domestic Product by Economic Activity

	2006	2007*	2008*
Agriculture, hunting and forestry	730,438	807,898	949,672
Fishing	105,338	106,028	104,236
Mining and quarrying	256,837	276,670	316,127
Manufacturing	2,750,367	3,023,454	3,272,584
Electricity, gas and water	238,889	248,119	261,339
Construction	231,899	246,622	256,922
Wholesale and retail trade; repair of motor vehicles, motorcycles and personal and household goods	1,122,655	1,192,687	1,231,114
Hotels and restaurants	386,062	416,592	441,870
Transport, storage and communications	569,875	622,080	633,928
Financial intermediation	286,220	311,488	355,157
Real estate, renting and business activities	208,757	215,397	212,856
Public administration and defence; compulsory social security	349,853	373,210	388,620
Education	316,690	360,152	376,051
Health and social work	150,010	163,849	168,461
Other community, social and personal service activities	128,669	119,853	124,169
Private households with employed persons	8,738	9,212	9,679
GDP in market prices	7,841,297	8,493,311	9,102,785

* Preliminary figures.

Source: National Economic and Social Development Board, Bangkok.

THAILAND

BALANCE OF PAYMENTS
(US $ million)

	2005	2006	2007
Exports of goods f.o.b.	109,369	127,929	150,026
Imports of goods f.o.b.	–105,981	–114,085	–124,479
Trade balance	3,388	13,844	25,547
Exports of services	20,163	24,822	30,357
Imports of services	–27,027	–33,015	–38,425
Balance on goods and services	–3,477	5,651	17,478
Other income received	3,640	4,659	6,772
Other income paid	–10,813	–11,502	–12,433
Balance on goods, services and income	–10,650	–1,193	11,817
Current transfers received	3,351	3,764	4,395
Current transfers paid	–348	–396	–457
Current balance	–7,647	2,175	15,755
Direct investment abroad	–501	–1,033	–2,156
Direct investment from abroad	8,055	9,004	9,498
Portfolio investment assets	–1,522	–2,025	–9,777
Portfolio investment liabilities	7,070	5,714	2,871
Financial derivatives assets	382	–270	—
Financial derivatives liabilities	–908	623	—
Other investment assets	–1,726	–10,005	–4,663
Other investment liabilities	232	3,641	1,211
Net errors and omissions	1,981	4,845	4,337
Overall balance	5,417	12,669	17,077

Source: IMF, *International Financial Statistics*.

External Trade

PRINCIPAL COMMODITIES
(distribution by SITC, '000 million baht)

Imports c.i.f.	2006	2007	2008
Food	157.6	170.5	228.0
Crude materials (inedible) except fuels	145.9	160.4	219.1
Mineral fuels, lubricants, etc.	972.0	899.5	1,238.3
Chemicals and related products	503.8	535.5	654.1
Basic manufactures	899.9	907.3	1,120.1
Machinery	1,821.7	1,764.0	1,887.7
Total (incl. others)	4,942.9	4,870.2	5,944.0

Exports f.o.b.	2006	2007	2008
Food	534.4	582.6	736.0
Crude materials (inedible) except fuels	289.7	288.7	309.4
Mineral fuels and lubricants	247.2	235.2	376.0
Chemicals and related products	394.6	419.3	459.6
Basic manufactures	620.0	676.7	734.9
Machinery	2,203.7	2,366.4	2,473.4
Miscellaneous manufactured articles	543.0	552.7	612.3
Total (incl. others)	4,937.4	5,242.0	5,853.6

Source: Bank of Thailand, Bangkok.

PRINCIPAL TRADING PARTNERS
('000 million baht)

Imports c.i.f.	2006	2007	2008
Australia	130.7	132.2	171.6
China, People's Republic	521.5	564.6	667.1
France	56.2	45.2	49.5
Germany	125.9	136.3	149.5
Hong Kong	59.2	50.1	64.9
India	62.0	71.9	86.9
Indonesia	131.9	138.6	179.8
Italy	57.2	47.4	53.6
Japan	985.8	988.0	1,112.2
Korea, Republic	196.7	184.2	227.3
Malaysia	325.3	299.9	322.1
Philippines	81.3	74.6	75.4
Russia	49.0	53.6	95.5
Singapore	218.1	218.7	235.3
Switzerland	50.0	51.9	131.5
Taiwan	196.0	199.8	206.2
United Arab Emirates	272.4	237.8	371.6
United Kingdom	50.5	52.7	60.1
USA	367.1	330.2	379.6
Total (incl. others)	4,942.9	4,870.2	5,944.0

Exports f.o.b.	2006	2007	2008
Australia	165.2	197.4	263.2
Belgium	54.6	57.3	55.8
Canada	47.2	47.0	47.1
China, People's Republic	446.0	510.3	532.3
France	54.2	56.8	62.1
Germany	88.6	99.0	105.3
Hong Kong	272.8	295.4	330.8
Indonesia	126.2	163.7	208.1
Italy	56.8	63.6	65.1
Japan	623.9	620.2	661.5
Korea, Republic	101.6	102.2	121.1
Malaysia	252.0	268.5	325.5
Netherlands	123.1	131.0	137.4
Philippines	97.8	99.9	115.2
Singapore	318.6	327.9	332.4
Switzerland	35.0	48.8	66.0
Taiwan	128.1	114.8	88.8
United Arab Emirates	56.1	75.9	92.2
United Kingdom	129.4	122.4	130.9
USA	740.7	662.0	667.7
Viet Nam	116.9	130.7	165.1
Total (incl. others)	4,937.4	5,242.0	5,853.6

Source: Bank of Thailand, Bangkok.

Transport

RAILWAYS
(year ending 30 September)

	2003/04	2004/05	2005/06
Passengers carried ('000)	50,873	49,671	48,867
Passenger-kilometres (million)	9,332	9,052	8,824
Freight carried ('000 metric tons)	13,796	12,817	12,566
Freight ton-kilometres (million)	4,085	3,621	3,508

ROAD TRAFFIC
('000 motor vehicles in use at 31 December)

	2005	2006
Passenger cars	3,396.5	3,312.9
Buses and trucks	766.0	848.8
Vans and pick-ups	4,752.4	4,173.6
Motorcycles	15,501.0	15,650.3
Total (incl. others)	25,266.3	24,807.3

THAILAND

SHIPPING

Merchant Fleet
(registered at 31 December)

	2005	2006	2007
Number of vessels	789	789	858
Total displacement ('000 grt)	3,025.3	2,822.7	2,846.9

Source: Lloyd's Register-Fairplay, *World Fleet Statistics*.

International Sea-borne Freight Traffic
(Ports of Bangkok and Laem Chabang, year ending 30 September)

	2004/05	2005/06	2006/07
Goods loaded ('000 metric tons)	21,456	22,401	24,883
Goods unloaded ('000 metric tons)	30,071	32,951	38,024
Vessels entered	7,640	8,975	n.a.

Source: Port Authority of Thailand.

CIVIL AVIATION
(traffic on scheduled services)

	2002	2003	2004
Kilometres flown (million)	194	204	223
Passengers carried ('000)	18,112	17,892	20,343
Passenger-km (million)	48,337	45,449	51,564
Total ton-km (million)	6,241	5,920	6,579

Sources: UN, *Statistical Yearbook*.

Tourism

FOREIGN TOURIST ARRIVALS BY COUNTRY OF RESIDENCE*

Country of origin	2004	2005	2006
Australia	396,040	421,594	538,490
China, People's Republic	779,070	761,904	1,033,305
France	250,995	260,704	319,910
Germany	438,238	436,552	507,942
Hong Kong	656,941	438,519	463,339
India	300,163	352,766	429,732
Japan	1,182,067	1,181,913	1,293,313
Korea, Republic	909,667	815,814	1,101,499
Malaysia	1,388,981	1,341,535	1,578,632
Singapore	732,180	795,322	818,162
Sweden	221,277	222,297	307,284
Taiwan	556,341	375,299	472,851
United Kingdom	628,679	680,978	745,525
USA	557,098	585,479	640,674
Total (incl. others)	11,737,413	11,567,341	13,821,802

* Includes Thai nationals resident abroad.

Receipts from tourism (US $ million, including passenger transport): 13,054 in 2004; 12,102 in 2005; 15,653 in 2006.

Source: World Tourism Organization.

Communications Media

	2005	2006	2007
Telephones ('000 main lines in use)	7,034.7	7,071.6	7,024.0
Mobile cellular telephones ('000 subscribers)	31,136.5	40,723.2	51,376.8
Internet users ('000)	9,909.0	11,413.0	13,416.0
Broadband subscribers ('000)	105.0	n.a.	913.0

Personal computers ('000 in use): 3,716 in 2004.

Radio receivers ('000 in use): 13,959 in 1997.

Television receivers ('000 in use): 18,400 in 2001.

Facsimile machines ('000 in use): 150 in 1997.

Book production (titles, excluding pamphlets): 8,142 in 1996.

Daily newspapers: 35 (with average circulation of 2,766,000 copies) in 1994; 35 (with average circulation of 2,700,000* copies) in 1995; 30 (with average circulation of 3,808,000 copies) in 1996.

Non-daily newspapers: 280 in 1995; 320 in 1996.
* Provisional.

Sources: International Telecommunication Union; UNESCO, *Statistical Yearbook*; UN, *Statistical Yearbook*.

Education

(2005, unless otherwise indicated)

	Institutions	Teachers	Students
Ministry of Education:			
Office of the Permanent Secretary	3,774	123,486	2,296,415
Office of the Basic Education Commission	32,340	420,965	8,697,983
Office of the Higher Education Commission	156	45,824	1,950,892
Office of Vocational Education Commission	408	16,731	615,548
Mahidol Wittayanusorn School	1	63	704
Mahamakut Buddhist University*	8	150	6,436
Mahachulalongkornrajavidyalaya University*	12	373	8,999
Bangkok Metropolitan Education Department	437	13,196	349,063
Royal Thai Police	192	2,082	29,985
Department of Local Administration	520	18,297	400,361
Ministry of Social Development and Human Security	3	38	407
Ministry of Public Health	39	2,971	17,750
Merchant Marine Training Centre	1	220	918
Civil Aviation Training Centre	1	37	1,052
National Bureau of Buddhism	404	3,188	51,414
Fine Arts Department	16	1,423	10,014
Office of Sports and Recreational Development	28	1,857	13,794
Armed Forces	11	1,400	7,476

* Figures for 2004.

Source: Ministry of Education.

Adult literacy rate (UNESCO estimates): 94.1% (males 95.9%; females 92.6%) in 2007 (Source: UNESCO Institute for Statistics).

Directory

The Constitution

A new Constitution, approved by referendum earlier in the month, took effect on 24 August 2007. Its provisions include the following:

GENERAL PROVISIONS

Thailand is one indivisible Kingdom, and sovereignty resides in the Thai people. The King as Head of State exercises power through the National Legislative Assembly, the Council of Ministers (Cabinet), the Courts and other institutions in accordance with the rule of law.

The human dignity, rights, liberty and equality of the people shall be protected. The Thai people, irrespective of their origin, sex or religion, shall enjoy equal protection under the Constitution. The Constitution is the supreme law of the State. When no provision of the Constitution is applicable to a case, it shall be decided in accordance with constitutional convention.

THE KING

The King shall be enthroned in a position of revered worship and shall not be violated or exposed to any sort of accusation or action. He

THAILAND

is a Buddhist and upholder of religions. He holds the position of Head of the Thai Armed Forces. He has the prerogative to create titles and confer decorations. He selects and appoints qualified persons to be the President of the Privy Council and not more than 18 Privy Councillors to constitute the Privy Council. The Privy Council has a duty to render such advice to the King on all matters pertaining to his functions as he may consult. Whenever the King is absent from the Kingdom or unable to perform his functions, he will appoint a Regent. For the purpose of maintaining national, public safety or national economic security, or of averting public calamity, the King may issue an Emergency Decree which shall have the force of an Act. The issuance of such Decree shall only be made when the Council of Ministers is of the opinion that it is unavoidable. The King has the prerogative to declare and lift martial law, and to declare war with the approval of the National Assembly.

RIGHTS, LIBERTIES AND DUTIES OF THE THAI PEOPLE

All persons are equal before the law and shall enjoy equal protection under the law. Men and women shall enjoy equal rights. Unjust discrimination against a person on the grounds of origin, race, language, sex, age, physical or health condition, personal status, economic or social standing, religious belief, education or constitutional political views shall not be permitted. A person shall enjoy the rights and liberty in his or her life and person. Torture, brutal acts or punishment by cruel or inhuman means shall not be permitted. A person shall enjoy the liberty of dwelling. A person shall enjoy the liberty of travelling and the liberty of making the choice of his or her residence within the Kingdom. A person's family rights, dignity, reputation or the right of privacy shall be protected. A person shall enjoy the liberty of communication by lawful means. A person shall enjoy full liberty to profess a religion, a religious sect or creed and observe religious precepts or exercise a form of worship in accordance with his or her belief. No person shall be inflicted with a criminal punishment unless he or she has committed an act which the law in force at the time of commission provides to be an offence and imposes punishment. A person shall have the right to an uncomplicated, convenient, quick and thorough access to justice procedure. A person shall enjoy the liberty to express his or her opinion, make speeches, write, print, publicize and make expression by other means. A person shall enjoy an equal right to receive basic education for the duration of not less than 12 years, which shall be provided by the State without charge. A person shall enjoy an equal right to receive standard public health service, and the indigent shall have the right to receive free medical treatment from public health centres of the State. A person shall have the right to gain access to public information in possession of a state agency, state enterprise or local government organization, unless the disclosure of the information shall affect the security of the State, public safety or interests of other persons. A person shall enjoy the liberty to assemble peacefully and without arms, to unite and form an association, a union, league, co-operative, farmers' group, private organization or other group. No person shall exercise the rights and liberties in the Constitution to overthrow the democratic form of government with the King as Head of State or acquire power to rule the country by any means that is not in accordance with the provisions of the Constitution. Every person shall have the duty to uphold the nation, religion, the King and the democratic form of government with the King as Head of State. Every person shall have the duty to exercise his or her right to vote in an election. Failure to vote will result in result in withdrawal of the right to vote as provided by law. Every person shall have the duty to defend the country, serve in the armed forces, pay taxes and duties, render assistance to the official services, receive education and training, uphold the national arts and culture, and knowledge, and conserve natural resources and environment as provided by law.

THE NATIONAL ASSEMBLY

The National Assembly consists of the House of Representatives and the Senate. It may meet jointly or separately. The President of the House of Representatives is President of the National Assembly. The President of the Senate is Vice-President of the National Assembly. A bill may be proposed only by the Council of Ministers, no fewer than 20 members of the House of Representatives, Courts of statutory agencies, or no fewer than 10,000 eligible voters who sign a petition to propose legislation. A bill approved by the National Assembly is presented by the Prime Minister to the King to be signed within 20 days from the date of receipt, and shall come into force upon its publication in the Government Gazette. If the King refuses his assent, the National Assembly must re-deliberate such bill. If the National Assembly resolves to reaffirm the bill with a two-thirds' majority, the Prime Minister shall present such bill to the King for signature once again. If the King does not sign and return the bill within 30 days, the Prime Minister shall cause the bill to be promulgated as an Act in the Government Gazette as if the King had signed it.

The House of Representatives consists of 480 members, 400 of whom are elected on a constituency basis and 80 of whom are elected on a party-list basis. A person seeking election to the House of Representatives must be of Thai nationality by birth, be not less than 25 years of age, and be a member of any and only one political party for a consecutive period of not less than 90 days, up to the date of applying for candidacy in an election. The term of the House of Representatives is four years from the election day. The King has the prerogative to dissolve the House of Representatives for new election of members of the House, and the day for the new general election must be fixed within 45 days of the promulgation of the Royal Decree. Members of the House may not renounce their party affiliation without resigning their seats. Members of the House of Representatives comprising no less than one-fifth of the existing members have the right to call for a general debate of no confidence in the Prime Minister. The said motion must propose a suitable replacement. For the motion of no confidence to be carried, it must have votes exceeding half the number of the existing members of the House. Members of the House of Representatives comprising not less than one-sixth of the total number have the right to submit a motion for a general debate of no confidence in an individual Minister.

The Senate consists of 150 members, one member from each province, and the remainder to be appointed by a selection committee consisting of the President of the Constitutional Court, the President of the Election Commission, the President of the Ombudsman, the President of the National Counter Corruption Commission, the President of the Office of Auditor General, the President of the National Human Rights Commission, a judge to be assigned by the general meeting of the Supreme Court of Justice and a judge to be assigned by the Supreme Administrative Court. The Selection Committee shall appoint persons proposed by different organizations, including academia, the public sector, the private sector, occupational groups and other groups. A person seeking election or appointment to the Senate must be of Thai nationality by birth, of not less than 40 years of age, have graduated with not lower than a Bachelor's degree or its equivalent, and must not be the descendants, spouse or ancestors of members of the House of Representatives or persons holding any position in a political party. Senators must not have been members of a political party or members of the House of Representatives for a period of at least five years prior to the date of application or nomination. The term of the Senate is six years from the election day. Upon the expiration of the term of the elected Senate, the King shall issue a Royal Decree calling for a new election of Senators, and the election must be fixed within 30 days.

THE COUNCIL OF MINISTERS

The King appoints the Prime Minister and not more than 35 other Ministers to constitute the Council of Ministers (Cabinet) having the duty to carry out the administration of state affairs on the principle of collective responsibility. The Prime Minister must be appointed by the House of Representatives and must receive the approval of more than half the total number of members of the House. The Prime Minister shall not serve in office for more than eight years. A Minister must be of Thai nationality by birth, of not less than 35 years of age and be a graduate with not lower than a Bachelor's degree or its equivalent.

The National Economic and Social Advisory Council has the duty to give advice and recommendations to the Council of Ministers on economic and social issues and relevant laws. A national economic and social development plan and other plans as provided by law must be approved by the National Economic and Social Development Council prior to their implementation.

THE COURTS

The trial and adjudication of cases are the powers of the courts, which must proceed in accordance with the Constitution and the law and in the name of the King. A judge is free to adjudicate correctly, justly and quickly in accordance with the Constitution and the law. Judges are removed and appointed by the King.

The Constitutional Court consists of the President and eight other judges to be appointed by the King upon advice from the Senate. The President and judges of the Constitutional Court shall hold office for nine years and only for one term.

There are three levels of the Courts of Justice; namely Courts of First Instance, Courts of Appeal and the Supreme Court of Justice.

Administrative Courts have the power to try and adjudicate cases of dispute between a state agency, state enterprise, local government organization and state official.

LOCAL GOVERNMENT

The State shall give autonomy to localities in accordance with the principle of self-government according to the will of the people in the locality. A local government shall have powers and duties to provide public services for the benefits of the local people. A local

THAILAND

government organization shall have a local assembly and a local administrative committee or local administrators. Members of the local assembly shall be elected. Members of the local administrative committee or local administrators shall be directly elected by the people or approved by the local assembly. Members of a local assembly, local administrative committee or local administrators shall hold office for four years. A member of a local administrative committee or local administrator shall not be a government official holding a permanent position or receiving a salary, or an official or employee of a state agency, state enterprise or local government organization.

AMENDMENT OF THE CONSTITUTION

A motion for amendment must be proposed either by the Council of Ministers or by not less than one-fifth of the total number of members of the House of Representatives or National Assembly, or not less than 50,000 eligible voters. A motion for amendment must be proposed in the form of a draft Constitution Amendment and the National Assembly shall consider it in three readings. Promulgation must be approved by the votes of more than half of the total number of members of both Houses.

The Government

HEAD OF STATE

King: HM King BHUMIBOL ADULYADEJ (King Rama IX—succeeded to the throne June 1946).

PRIVY COUNCIL

Members: Gen. (retd) PREM TINSULANONDA (President), Dr CHAOVANA NASYLVANTA, THANIN KRAIVICHIEN, Rear-Adm. M. L. USNI PRAMOJ, Air Vice-Marshal KAMTHON SINDHAVANANDA, Air Chief Marshal SIDDHI SAVETSILA, CHULANOPE SNIDVONGS, Gen. PICHITR KULLAVANIJAVA, AMPOL SENARONG, CHAMRAS KEMACHARU, M. R. THEPKAMOL DEVAKULA, Prof. KASEM WATANACHAI, PALAKORN SUWANNARAT, SAWAT WATTANAYAKORN, SANTI THAKARAL, Adm. CHUMPOL PACHUSANONDA, ANTANITHI DITSAMANAJ, Gen. SURAYUD CHULANONT, SUPACHAI PHOONGAM, CHANCHAI LIKHITCHITTA.

CABINET
(April 2009)

Prime Minister: ABHISIT VEJJAJIVA.
Deputy Prime Ministers: SUTHEP THUAGSUBAN, KORBSAK SABHAVASU, SANAN KAJORNPRASART.
Ministers in the Prime Minister's Office: SATIT WONGNONGTAEY, VIRACHAI VIRAMETEEKUL.
Minister of Defence: Gen. PRAWIT WONGSUWAN.
Minister of Finance: KORN CHATIKAVANIJ.
Minister of Foreign Affairs: KASIT PIROMYA.
Minister of the Interior: CHAOVARAT CHANWEERAKUL.
Minister of Information and Communications Technology: RANONGRUK SUWANCHAWEE.
Minister of Tourism and Sports: CHUMPOL SILAPA-ARCHA.
Minister of Commerce: PORNTHIVA NAKASAI.
Minister of Industry: CHARNCHAI CHAIRUNGRUENG.
Minister of Social Development and Human Security: ISSARA SOMCHAI.
Minister of Agriculture and Co-operatives: THEERA WONGSAMUT.
Minister of Transport: SOPHON SARAM.
Minister of Natural Resources and Environment: SUWIT KHUNKITTI.
Minister of Energy: WANNARAT CHARNNUKUL.
Minister of Justice: PIRAPAN SALIRATHAVIBHAGA.
Minister of Labour: PHAITHOON KAEOTHONG.
Minister of Culture: TEERA SLUKPETCH.
Minister of Science and Technology: KHUNYING KALAYA SOPHONPANICH.
Minister of Education: JURIN LAKSANAWISIT.
Minister of Public Health: WITTHAYA KAEWPARADAI.

MINISTRIES

Office of the Prime Minister: Government House, Thanon Nakhon Pathom, Bangkok 10300; tel. (2) 280-3526; fax (2) 282-8792; e-mail webmaster@opm.go.th; internet www.opm.go.th.

Ministry of Agriculture and Co-operatives: Thanon Ratchadamnoen Nok, Bangkok 10200; tel. (2) 281-5955; fax (2) 282-1425; e-mail webmaster@moac.go.th; internet www.moac.go.th.

Ministry of Commerce: 44/100 Thanon Nonthaburi 1, Amphur Muang, Nonthaburi, Bangkok 11000; tel. (2) 507-8000; fax (2) 507-7717; e-mail webmaster@moc.go.th; internet www.moc.go.th.

Ministry of Culture: Thanalongkorn Bldg, Thanon Boromrachanonnee, Bangplud, Bangkok 10700; tel. (2) 422-8888; e-mail webmaster@m-culture.go.th; internet www.m-culture.go.th.

Ministry of Defence: Thanon Sanamchai, Bangkok 10200; tel. (2) 222-1121; fax (2) 226-3117; internet www.mod.go.th.

Ministry of Education: Wang Chankasem, Thanon Ratchadamnoen Nok, Bangkok 10300; tel. (2) 281-9809; fax (2) 281-9241; e-mail website@emisc.moe.go.th; internet www.moe.go.th.

Ministry of Energy: 17 Kasatsuk Bridge, Thanon Rama I, Rong Mueng, Pathumwan, Bangkok 10330; tel. (2) 223-3344; fax (2) 222-3785; e-mail moen@energy.go.th; internet www.energy.go.th.

Ministry of Finance: Thanon Rama VI, Samsennai, Phaya Thai, Rajatevi, Bangkok 10400; tel. (2) 273-9021; fax (2) 273-9408; e-mail prinya@mof.go.th; internet www.mof.go.th.

Ministry of Foreign Affairs: Thanon Sri Ayudhya, Bangkok 10400; tel. (2) 643-5000; fax (2) 225-6155; e-mail information@mfa.go.th; internet www.mfa.go.th.

Ministry of Industry: 75/6 Thanon Rama VI, Ratchathewi, Bangkok 10400; tel. (2) 202-3000; fax (2) 202-3048; internet www.industry.go.th.

Ministry of Information and Communications Technology: Bangkok 10210; tel. (2) 238-5422; fax (2) 238-5423; e-mail pr@mict.go.th; internet www.mict.go.th.

Ministry of the Interior: Thanon Atsadang, Bangkok 10200; tel. (2) 222-1141; fax (2) 223-8851; e-mail webteam@moi.go.th; internet www.moi.go.th.

Ministry of Justice: Thanon Ratchadaphisek, Chatuchak, Bangkok 10900; tel. (2) 502-8051; fax (2) 502-8059; e-mail webmaster@moj.go.th; internet www.moj.go.th.

Ministry of Labour: Thanon Mitmaitri, Dindaeng, Huay Kwang, Bangkok 10400; tel. (2) 232-1421; fax (2) 246-1520; e-mail webmaster@mol.go.th; internet www.mol.go.th.

Ministry of Natural Resources and Environment: 92 Phaholyothin Soi 7, Samsen Nai, Bangkok 10400; tel. (2) 298-2754; fax (2) 298-2020; e-mail web@mnre.go.th; internet www.monre.go.th.

Ministry of Public Health: Thanon Tiwanon, Amphoe Muang, Nonthaburi 11000; tel. (2) 590-1000; fax (2) 591-8492; e-mail eng-webmaster@health.moph.go.th; internet www.moph.go.th.

Ministry of Science and Technology: Thanon Rama VI, Ratchathewi, Bangkok 10400; tel. (2) 246-0064; fax (2) 246-5146; internet www.most.go.th.

Ministry of Social Development and Human Security: Bangkok 10100; tel. (2) 659-6399; e-mail society@m-society.go.th; internet www.m-society.go.th.

Ministry of Tourism and Sports: Thanon Rama I, Pathumwan, Bangkok 10330; tel. (2) 283-1500; fax (2) 356-0746; e-mail webmaster@mots.go.th; internet www.mots.go.th.

Ministry of Transport: 38 Thanon Ratchadamnoen Nok, Khet Pom Prab Sattruphai, Bangkok 10100; tel. (2) 281-3871; fax (2) 283-3049; e-mail mot@mot.go.th; internet www.mot.go.th.

Legislature

RATHA SAPHA (NATIONAL ASSEMBLY)

Woothi Sapha (Senate)

The Senate consists of 150 members, of whom 76 members are elected to represent each of Thailand's 75 provinces and Bangkok, and the remainder are selected by a committee consisting primarily of judicial officials (see The Constitution). Senators thus selected are drawn from lists of nominees made by organizations in various sectors.

Elections to the Senate were held on 2 March 2008.

Speaker of the Senate: PRASOBSUK BOONDECH.

THAILAND

Sapha Poothaen Rassadorn (House of Representatives)
Speaker of the House of Representatives and President of the National Assembly: CHAI CHIDCHOB.

Election, 23 December 2007

Party	Seats
People's Power Party*	233
Democrat Party	164
Chart Thai*	34
Puea Pandin	24
Matchimathipataya*	11
Ruam Jai Thai Chart Pattana	9
Pracharaj	5
Total	**480†**

* Dissolved by the Constitutional Court on 2 December 2008.

† A total of 400 candidates were elected in multi-member constituencies and the remaining 80 through a party-list system. By-elections were held in 29 constituencies on 11 January 2009, following the dissolution in the previous month of the governing People's Power Party, Chart Thai and Matchimathipataya. The Democrat Party was reported to have won seven of the 29 seats contested, with a further 13 being secured by its allies, the newly established Chart Thai Pattana (10 seats) and Puea Pandin (three seats). Puea Thai won five seats and Pracharaj four.

Election Commission

Election Commission of Thailand (ECT): Srijullasup Bldg, 19th Floor, 44 Thanon Rama I, Pathumwan, Bangkok 10330; tel. (2) 613-7333; fax (2) 219-3411; e-mail dav@ect.go.th; internet www.ect.go.th; Chair. APHICHART SUKHATKHANON.

Political Organizations

Democrat Party (DP) (Prachatipat): 67 Thanon Setsiri, Samsen Nai, Phyathai, 10400 Bangkok; tel. (2) 270-0036; fax (2) 279-6086; e-mail admin@democrat.or.th; internet www.democrat.or.th; f. 1946; liberal; Leader ABHISIT VEJJAJIVA; Sec.-Gen. SUTHEP THUAGSUBAN.

Ekkaparb (Solidarity): 670/104 Soi Thepnimit, Thanon Jaransanitwong, Bangpaid, Bangkok 10700; tel. (2) 424-0291; fax (2) 424-8630; f. 1989; opposition merger by the Community Action Party, the Prachachon Party, the Progressive Party and Ruam Thai; Leader CHAIYOS SASOMSAP; Sec.-Gen. NEWIN CHIDCHOB.

Muan Chon (Mass Party): 630/182 Thanon Prapinklao, Bangkok 10700; tel. and fax (2) 424-0851; f. 1985; dissolved after defection of leader Capt. Chalerm Yoobamrung to New Aspiration Party (NAP); re-formed in 2002 following merger of NAP with Thai Rak Thai; Leader Gen. VORAVIT PIBOONSILP; Sec.-Gen. KAROON RAKSASUK.

Pracharaj (Royal People Party): 18/F, TPI Tower, 26/56 Thanon Chan Tat Mai, Tungmahamek, Sathorn, Bangkok 10120; f. 2006 by breakaway faction of Thai Rak Thai; Leader SNOH THIENTHONG; Sec.-Gen. CHIENGCHUANG KANLAYANAMITH.

Puea Pandin (For the Land): 1 Thanon Witthayu, Lumpini, Pathumwan, Bangkok 10330; tel. (2) 253-0428; e-mail pueapandin@gmail.com; internet www.ppd.or.th; f. 2007; Leader PRACHA PROMNOK; Sec.-Gen. WACHARA PHANCHET.

Puea Thai (For Thais): c/o House of Representatives, Bangkok; f. 2008; est. to accommodate mems of People's Power Party upon its dissolution by Constitutional Court in Dec. 2008; Leader YONGYUTH WICHAIDITH.

Ruam Jai Thai Chart Pattana (Thais United National Development): c/o House of Representatives, Bangkok; f. 2007; est. by merger of Chart Pattana and Thais United; merged in Jan. 2009 with Friends of Newin grouping (est. in 2008 by Newin Chidchob and other defectors from the People's Power Party); Leader WANNARAT CHARNNUKUL.

Other parties that contested the 2007 election included Farmer Network of Thailand, For our Homeland, Free Thai, Prachamati, Rak Muang Thai and Artist Party.

The People's Alliance for Democracy (PAD) was formed in early 2006 to oppose the Government of Thaksin Shinawatra. Compromising mainly monarchists, academics, businesspeople and military elements, the loose coalition was voluntarily dissolved following the removal of the Thaksin Government in the coup of September 2006. The PAD was re-established after the victory at the election of December 2007 of the Thaksin-affiliated People's Power Party and its allies. The large-scale demonstrations of PAD supporters were instrumental in the removal of the Government of Samak Sundarajev in September 2008.

Groupings in armed conflict with the Government include:

Barisan Revolusi Nasional (BRN) (National Revolutionary Front): Yala; f. 1963; was organized into three principal factions—the BRN Congress (its military wing); the BRN Co-ordinate (its political wing); and the BRN Uram (its religious wing)—in the 1980s; Muslim secessionists.

Bersatu (Council of the Muslim People of Pattani): Pattani; f. 1989; umbrella organization including the BRN and the PULO (see below); Pattani secessionists.

Gerakan Mujahideen Islami Pattani (GMIP): Pattani; f. 1986; dissolved in 1993 following internal disagreement, but re-formed in 1995; seeks the transformation of Pattani into an Islamic state; Leader KARIM KARUBANG.

Pattani United Liberation Organization (PULO): advocates secession of the five southern provinces (Satun, Narathiwat, Yala, Pattani and Songkhla); Pres. LUKMAN B. LIMA (acting).

Runda Kumpulan Kecil (RKK): Yala; f. 2005; splinter group of the BRN Congress; seeks the implementation of an independent Islamic state in Thailand's southern provinces; Leader USTAZ RORHING AHSONG.

Diplomatic Representation

EMBASSIES IN THAILAND

Argentina: 16th Floor, Suite 1601, Glas Haus Bldg, 1 Soi Sukhumvit 25, Klongtoey, Bangkok 10110; tel. (2) 259-0401; fax (2) 259-0402; e-mail embtail@mozart.inet.co.th; Ambassador FELIPE FRYDMAN.

Australia: 37 Thanon Sathorn Tai, Bangkok 10120; tel. (2) 344-6300; fax (2) 344-6593; e-mail austembassy.bangkok@dfat.gov.au; internet www.austembassy.or.th; Ambassador PAUL GRIGSON.

Austria: 14 Soi Nandha, off Thanon Sathorn Tai, Soi 1, Bangkok 10120; tel. (2) 303-6057; fax (2) 287-3925; e-mail bangkok-ob@bmeie.gv.at; Ambassador ARNO RIEDEL.

Bangladesh: 727 Soi Thonglor, Thanon Sukhumvit 55, Bangkok 10110; tel. (2) 185-1340; fax (2) 185-1361; e-mail bdoot@samart.co.th; Ambassador MUSTAFA KAMAL.

Belgium: 17th Floor, Sathorn City Tower, 175 Thanon Sathorn Tai, Tungmahamek, Sathorn, Bangkok 10120; tel. (2) 679-5454; fax (2) 679-5467; e-mail bangkok@diplobel.fed.be; internet www.diplomatie.be/bangkok; Ambassador RUDI VEESTRAETEN.

Bhutan: 375/1 Soi Ratchadanivej, Thanon Pracha-Uthit, Huay Kwang, Bangkok 10320; tel. (2) 274-4740; fax (2) 274-4743; e-mail bht_emb_bkk@yahoo.com; Ambassador SINGYE DORJI.

Brazil: 34th Floor, Lumpini Tower, 1168/101 Thanon Rama IV, Sathorn, Bangkok 10120; tel. (2) 679-8567; fax (2) 679-8569; e-mail info@brazilembassy.or.th; internet www.brazilembassy.or.th; Ambassador EDGARD TELLES RIBEIRO.

Brunei: 12 Soi Ekamai 2, Thanon Sukhumvit 63, Prakanong Nua, Wattana, Bangkok 10110; tel. (2) 714-7395; fax (2) 714-7383; Ambassador Pengiran Dato' Paduka Haji SHARIFUDDIN BIN Haji YUSSOF.

Bulgaria: 83/24 Soi Witthayu 1, Thanon Witthayu, Lumpini, Pathumwan, Bangkok 10330; tel. (2) 627-3872; fax (2) 627-3874; e-mail bulgemth@csloxinfo.com; Chargé d'affaires KAMEN VELICHKOV.

Cambodia: 518/4, Thanon Pracha Uthit, Ramkhamhaeng Soi 39, Wangtonglang, Bangkok 10310; tel. (2) 957-5851; fax (2) 957-5850; e-mail recbkk@cscoms.com; Ambassador YOU AY.

Canada: Abdulrahim Bldg, 15th Floor, 990 Thanon Rama IV, Bangrak, Bangkok 10500; tel. (2) 636-0540; fax (2) 636-0565; e-mail bngkk@international.gc.ca; internet geo.international.gc.ca/asia/bangkok; Ambassador DAVID SPROULE.

Chile: 83/17 Witthayu Place, Soi Witthayu 1, Thanon Witthayu, Lumpini, Pathumwan, Bangkok 10330; tel. (2) 251-9470; fax (2) 2251-9475; e-mail embajada@chile-thai.com; internet www.chile-thai.com; Ambassador JOAQUÍN MONTES.

China, People's Republic: 57 Thanon Ratchadaphisek, Bangkok 10310; tel. (2) 245-7043; fax (2) 246-8247; e-mail chinaemb_th@mfa.gov.cn; internet www.chinaembassy.or.th/eng; Ambassador GUAN MU.

Cuba: Mela Mansion Apartment 3C, 5 Soi Sukhumvit 27, Klongtoey Nua, Wattana, Bangkok 10110; tel. (2) 665-2803; fax (2) 661-6560; e-mail cubaemb1@loxinfo.co.th; internet embacuba.cubaminrex.cu/tailandiaing; Ambassador MARÍA LUISA FERNÁNDEZ.

Czech Republic: 71/6 Soi Ruamrudi 2, Thanon Ploenchit, Bangkok 10330; tel. (2) 255-3027; fax (2) 253-7637; e-mail bangkok@embassy.mzv.cz; internet www.mfa.cz/bangkok; Ambassador IVAN HOTĚK.

THAILAND

Denmark: 10 Soi Attakarn Prasit, Thanon Sathorn Tai, Bangkok 10120; tel. (2) 343-1100; fax (2) 213-1752; e-mail bkkamb@um.dk; internet www.ambbangkok.um.dk; Ambassador MICHAEL STERNBERG.

Egypt: 6 Las Colinas Bldg, 42nd Floor, Sukhumvit 21, Wattana, Bangkok 10110; tel. (2) 661-7184; fax (2) 262-0235; e-mail egyptemb@truemail.co.th; Ambassador MOHAMED ASHRAF MOHAMED KAMAL EL KHOLY.

Finland: Amarin Tower, 16th Floor, 500 Thanon Ploenchit, Bangkok 10330; tel. (2) 250-8801; fax (2) 250-8802; e-mail sanomat.ban@formin.fi; internet www.finland.or.th; Ambassador LARS ERIK BACKSTRÖM.

France: 35 Soi Rong Phasi Kao, Thanon Charoenkrung, Bangkok 10500; tel. (2) 657-5100; fax (2) 657-5111; e-mail ambassade@ambafrance-th.org; internet www.ambafrance-th.org; Ambassador LAURENT BILI.

Germany: 9 Thanon Sathorn Tai, Bangkok 10120; tel. (2) 287-9000; fax (2) 287-1776; e-mail info@german-embassy.or.th; internet www.bangkok.diplo.de; Ambassador Dr HANNS HEINRICH SCHUMACHER.

Greece: Unit 25/5-9, 9th Floor, BKI/YWCA Bldg, 25 Thanon Sathorn Tai, Bangkok 10120; tel. (2) 679-1462; fax (2) 679-1463; e-mail embgrbkk@ksc.th.com; Ambassador IOANNIS PAPADOPOULOS.

Holy See: 217/1 Thanon Sathorn Tai, Bangkok 10120 (Apostolic Nunciature); tel. (2) 212-5853; fax (2) 212-0932; e-mail nuntiusth@csloxinfo.com; Apostolic Nuncio Most Rev. SALVATORE PENNACCHIO (Titular Archbishop of Montemarano).

Hungary: Oak Tower, 20th Floor, President Park Condominium, 95 Sukhumvit Soi 24, Prakhanong, Bangkok 10110; tel. (2) 661-1150; fax (2) 661-1153; e-mail mission.bgk@kum.hu; internet www.mfa.gov.hu/emb/bangkok; Ambassador Dr ANDRAS BALOGH.

India: 46 Soi Prasarnmitr, 23 Thanon Sukhumvit, Bangkok 10110; tel. (2) 258-0300; fax (2) 258-4627; e-mail indiaemb@mozart.inet.co.th; internet indianembassy.gov.in/bangkok; Ambassador VIJAYA LATHA REDDY.

Indonesia: 600–602 Thanon Phetchaburi, Ratchathewi, Bangkok 10400; tel. (2) 252-3135; fax (2) 255-1267; e-mail kukbkk@ksc11.th.com; internet www.kbri-bangkok.com; Ambassador MOHAMMAD HATTA.

Iran: 215 Thanon Sukhumvit, Soi 49, Klongtan Nua, Wattana, Bangkok 10110; tel. (2) 390-0871; fax (2) 390-0867; e-mail info@iranembassy.or.th; internet www.iranembassy.or.th; Ambassador MOHSEN PAKAEIN (designate).

Israel: Ocean Tower II, 25th Floor, 75 Sukhumvit, Soi 19, Thanon Asoke, Bangkok 10110; tel. (2) 204-9200; fax (2) 204-9255; e-mail info@bangkok.mfa.gov.il; internet bangkok.mfa.gov.il; Ambassador YAEL RUBINSTEIN.

Italy: 399 Thanon Nang Linchee, Thungmahamek, Yannawa, Bangkok 10120; tel. (2) 285-4090; fax (2) 285-4793; e-mail ambasciata.bangkok@esteri.it; internet www.italian-embassy.org.ae/Ambasciata_Bangkok; Ambassador IGNAZIO DI PACE.

Kenya: 62 Thonglor Soi 5, Thanon Sukhumvit 55, Klongtan, Wattana, Bangkok 10110; tel. (2) 712-5721; fax (2) 712-5720; Ambassador RICHARD TITUS EKAI.

Korea, Democratic People's Republic: 14 Mooban Suanlaemthong 2, Thanon Pattanakarn, Suan Luang, Bangkok 10250; tel. (2) 319-2686; fax (2) 318-6333; Ambassador O YONG SON.

Korea, Republic: 23 Thanon Thiam-Ruammit, Huay Kwang, Bangkok 10320; tel. (2) 247-7537; fax (2) 247-7535; e-mail korea_emb_th@yahoo.co.kr; Ambassador HAN TAE-KYU.

Kuwait: 100/44 Sathorn Nakhon Tower, 24th Floor, Thanon Sathorn Nua, Bangrak, Bangkok 10500; tel. (2) 636-6600; fax (2) 636-7360; e-mail kwembasy@inet.co.th; Ambassador HAFEEZ MOHAMMED SALEM AL-AJMI.

Laos: 502/502/1–3 Soi Sahakarnpramoon, Thanon Pracha Uthit, Wangthonglang, Bangkok 10310; tel. (2) 539-6667; fax (2) 539-3827; e-mail sabaidee@bkklaoembassy.com; internet www.bkklaoembassy.com; Ambassador OUAN PHOMMACHACK.

Malaysia: 35 Thanon Sathorn Tai, Tungmahamek, Sathorn, Bangkok 10120; tel. (2) 679-2190; fax (2) 679-2208; e-mail malbangkok@kln.gov.my; internet www.kln.gov.my/mission/bangkok; Ambassador Dato' SHARAANI BIN IBRAHIM.

Mexico: 20/60–62 Thai Wah Tower I, 20th Floor, Thanon Sathorn Tai, Bangkok 10120; tel. (2) 285-0995; fax (2) 285-0667; e-mail mexthai@loxinfo.co.th; internet www.sre.gob.mx/tailandia; Ambassador LUIS ARTURO PUENTE ORTEGA.

Mongolia: 100/3, Soi Ekamai 22, Thanon Sukhumvit 63, Prakanong Nua, Wattana, Bangkok 10110; tel. (2) 381-1400; fax (2) 392-4199; e-mail mongemb@loxinfo.co.th; internet www.mongolmissionbkk.com; Ambassador DASHPUREV LUVSANDOO.

Morocco: Sathorn City Tower, 12th Floor, 175 Thanon Sathorn Tai, Sathorn, Bangkok 10120; tel. (2) 679-5604; fax (2) 2679-5603; e-mail sifambkk@samarts.com; internet www.moroccoembassybangkok.org; Ambassador EL HASSANE ZAHID.

Myanmar: 132 Thanon Sathorn Nua, Bangkok 10500; tel. (2) 233-2237; fax (2) 236-6898; Ambassador U YE WIN.

Nepal: 189 Soi 71, Thanon Sukhumvit, Prakanong, Bangkok 10110; tel. (2) 390-2280; fax (2) 381-2406; e-mail nepembkk@asiaaccess.net.th; Ambassador NAVIN PRAKASH JUNG SHAH.

Netherlands: 15 Soi Tonson, Thanon Ploenchit, Lumpini, Pathumwan, Bangkok 10330; tel. (2) 309-5200; fax (2) 309-5205; e-mail ban@minbuza.nl; internet www.mfa.nl/ban; Ambassador TJACO VAN DEN HOUT.

New Zealand: M Thai Tower, 14th Floor, All Seasons Place, 87 Thanon Witthayu, Lumpini, Pathumwan, Bangkok 10330; tel. (2) 254-2530; fax (2) 253-9045; e-mail nzembbkk@loxinfo.co.th; internet www.nzembassy.com/home.cfm?c=21; Ambassador BROOK BARRINGTON.

Nigeria: 412 Thanon Sukhumvit 71, Prakhanong, Wattana, Bangkok 10110; tel. (2) 711-3076; fax (2) 392-6398; e-mail info@embnigeriabkk.com; Ambassador UMARU A. SULAIMAN (designate).

Norway: UBC II Bldg, 18th Floor, 591 Thanon Sukhumvit, Soi 33, Bangkok 10110; tel. (2) 204-6500; fax (2) 262-0218; e-mail emb.bangkok@mfa.no; internet www.emb-norway.or.th; Ambassador MERETE FJELD BRATTESTED.

Oman: 82 Saeng Thong Thani Tower, 32nd Floor, Thanon Sathorn Nua, Bangkok 10500; tel. (2) 639-9380; fax (2) 639-9390; Ambassador HAFEEDH SALIM MOHAMED BA-OMAR.

Pakistan: 31 Soi Nana Nua, Thanon Sukhumvit, Bangkok 10110; tel. (2) 253-0288; fax (2) 253-0290; e-mail parepbkk@ji-net.com; Ambassador KHATEER HASSAN KHAN.

Panama: 1168/37 Lumpini Tower Bldg, 16th Floor, Tungmahamek, Sathorn, Bangkok 10120; tel. (2) 679-7988; fax (2) 679-7991; e-mail embajada@panathai.com; internet www.panathai.com; Ambassador DAVID GUARDIA VARELA.

Peru: Glas Haus Bldg, 16th Floor, 1 Soi Sukhumvit 25, Khet Wattana, Bangkok 10110; tel. (2) 260-6243; fax (2) 260-6244; e-mail peru@peruthai.or.th; internet www.peru.org.pe; Ambassador CARLOS MANUEL VELASCO MENDIOLA.

Philippines: 760 Thanon Sukhumvit, cnr Soi 30/1, Klongtan, Klongtoey, Bangkok 10110; tel. (2) 259-0139; fax (2) 259-2809; e-mail inquiry@philembassy-bangkok.net; internet www.philembassy-bangkok.net; Ambassador ANTONIO V. RODRIGUEZ.

Poland: 100/81-82, Vongvanij Bldg B, 25th Floor, Thanon Phra Ram IX, Huay Kwang, Bangkok 10310; tel. (2) 645-0367; fax (2) 645-0365; e-mail polemb@loxinfo.co.th; internet www.bangkok.polemb.net; Ambassador (vacant).

Portugal: 26 Bush Lane, Thanon Charoenkrung, Bangkok 10500; tel. (2) 234-2123; fax (2) 238-4275; e-mail portemb@loxinfo.co.th; Ambassador ANTÓNIO FELIX MACHADO DE FARIA E MAYA.

Qatar: Capital Tower, 14th Floor, All Seasons Place, 87/1 Thanon Witthayu, Lumpini, Pathumwan, Bangkok 10330; tel. (2) 660-1111; fax (2) 660-1122; e-mail info@qatarembassy.or.th; internet www.qatarembassy.or.th; Ambassador ABDALLA IBRAHIM ABDULRAHMAN AL-HAMAR.

Romania: 20/1 Soi Rajakhru, Phaholyothin Soi 5, Thanon Phaholyothin, Phayathai, Bangkok 10400; tel. (2) 617-1551; fax (2) 617-1113; e-mail romembnk@ksc.th.com; Ambassador RADU GABRIEL MATEESCU.

Russia: 78 Thanon Sap, Bangrak, Bangkok 10500; tel. (2) 234-9824; fax (2) 237-8488; e-mail rusembbangkok@rambler.ru; internet www.thailand.mid.ru; Ambassador YEVGENY V. AFANASIEV.

Saudi Arabia: 82 Saeng Song Thani Bldg, 23rd Floor, Thanon Sathorn Nua, Bangrak, Bangkok 10500; tel. (2) 639-2960; fax (2) 639-2950; Ambassador NABIL H. H. ASHRI.

Singapore: 129 Thanon Sathorn Tai, Bangkok 10120; tel. (2) 286-2111; fax (2) 286-6966; e-mail singemb_bkk@sgmfa.gov.sg; internet www.mfa.gov.sg/bangkok; Ambassador PETER CHAN.

Slovakia: 25/9-4, BKI/YWCA Bldg, 9th Floor, Thanon Sathorn Tai, Tungmahamek, Bangkok 10120; tel. (2) 677-3445; fax (2) 677-3447; e-mail slovakemb@actions.net; Ambassador VASIL PYTEL.

South Africa: M-Thai Tower, Floor 12A, All Seasons Place, 87 Thanon Witthayu, Pathumwan, Lumpini, Bangkok 10330; tel. (2) 250-9012; fax (2) 685-3500; e-mail dha@loxinfo.co.th; internet www.saembbangkok.com; Ambassador DOUGLAS HARVEY MONRO GIBSON.

Spain: Lake Rajada Office Complex, 23rd Floor, 193 Thanon Ratchadaphisek, Klongtoey, Bangkok 10110; tel. (2) 661-8284; fax (2) 661-9220; e-mail emb.bangkok@mae.es; internet www.mae.es/embajadas/bangkok/es/home; Ambassador JUAN MANUEL LÓPEZ NADAL.

Sri Lanka: Ocean Tower II, 13th Floor, 75/6–7 Sukhumvit, Soi 19, Bangkok 10110; tel. (2) 261-1934; fax (2) 261-1936; e-mail slemb@ksc.th.com; Ambassador JAYARATNA BANDA DISANAYAKA.

THAILAND

Sweden: First Pacific Place, 20th Floor, 140 Thanon Sukhumvit, Bangkok 10110; tel. (2) 263-7200; fax (2) 263-7260; e-mail ambassaden.bangkok@foreign.ministry.se; internet www.sweden abroad.com/bangkok; Ambassador LENNART LINNÉR.

Switzerland: 35 Thanon Witthayu, Lumpini, Pathumwan, Bangkok 10330; tel. (2) 253-0156; fax (2) 255-4481; e-mail ban.vertretung@eda.admin.ch; internet www.eda.admin.ch/bangkok_emb; Ambassador RODOLPHE S. IMHOOF.

Turkey: 61/1 Soi Chatsan, Thanon Suthisarn, Huay Kwang, Bangkok 10310; tel. (2) 274-7262; fax (2) 274-7261; e-mail turemb@cscoms.com; Ambassador CINAR ALDEMIR.

Ukraine: 33/F, CRC Tower, All Seasons Place, 87/2 Thanon Witthayu, Lumpini, Pathumwan, Bangkok 10330; tel. (2) 685-3216; fax (2) 685-3217; e-mail emb_th@mfa.gov.ua; internet www.mfa.gov.ua/thailand; Ambassador MARKIIAN CHUCHUK.

United Arab Emirates: 82 Saeng Thong Thani Bldg, 25th Floor, Thanon Sathorn Nua, Bangkok 10500; tel. (2) 639-9820; fax (2) 639-9818; Ambassador SALIM ISSA ALI AL-KATTAM AL-ZAABI.

United Kingdom: 14 Thanon Witthayu, Lumpini, Pathumwan, Bangkok 10330; tel. (2) 305-8333; fax (2) 255-8619; e-mail info.bangkok@fco.gov.uk; internet ukinthailand.fco.gov.uk; Ambassador QUINTON MARK QUAYLE.

USA: 95 Thanon Witthayu, Lumpini, Pathumwan, Bangkok 10330; tel. (2) 205-4000; fax (2) 254-1171; e-mail acsbkk@state.gov; internet bangkok.usembassy.gov; Ambassador ERIC G. JOHN.

Viet Nam: 83/1 Thanon Witthayu, Lumpini, Pathumwan, Bangkok 10330; tel. (2) 251-3551; fax (2) 251-7203; e-mail vnemb.th@mofa.gov.vn; internet www.vietnamembassy-thailand.org; Ambassador NGUYEN DUY HUNG.

Judicial System

SUPREME COURT

(Sarn Dika)

Thanon Ratchadamnoen Nai, Bangkok 10200; tel. (2) 221-3161; e-mail supremc@judiciary.go.th; internet www.supremecourt.or.th.

The final court of appeal in all civil, bankruptcy, labour, juvenile and criminal cases. Its quorum consists of three judges. However, the Court occasionally sits in plenary session to determine cases of exceptional importance or where there are reasons for reconsideration or overruling of its own precedents. The quorum, in such cases, is one-half of the total number of judges in the Supreme Court.

President (Chief Justice): WIRAT LIMWICHAI.

Vice-Presidents: PHICHIT KHAMFAENG, THEERARAT PHATTARANWAT, MONGKHOL THAPTHIENG, PANYA SUTHIBODI, WATTANCHAI CHOTICHUTRAKUL, RUNGROJ RUENRENGWONG.

COURT OF APPEALS

(Sarn Uthorn)

Thanon Ratchadaphisek, Chatuchak, Bangkok 10900; internet www.judiciary.go.th/appealc.

Appellate jurisdiction in all civil, bankruptcy, juvenile and criminal matters; appeals from all the Courts of First Instance throughout the country, except the Central Labour Court, come to this Court. Two judges form a quorum.

Chief Justice: KAIT CHATANIBAND.

Deputy Chief Justices: PORNCHAI SMATTAVET, CHATISAK THAMMASAKDI, SOMPOB CHOTIKAVANICH, SOMPHOL SATTAYA-APHITARN.

COURTS OF FIRST INSTANCE

Includes the categories of general courts (Civil Courts, Criminal Courts, Provincial Courts and Kwaeng Courts), juvenile and family courts, and specialized courts (Central Labour Court, Central Tax Court, Central Intellectual Property and International Trade Court, Central Bankruptcy Court).

Religion

Buddhism is the predominant religion, professed by more than 95% of Thailand's total population. About 4% of the population are Muslims, being ethnic Malays, mainly in the south. Most of the immigrant Chinese are Confucians. The Christians number about 427,000, mainly in Bangkok and northern Thailand. Brahmins, Hindus and Sikhs number about 85,000.

BUDDHISM

Sangha Supreme Council

The Religious Affairs Dept, Thanon Ratchadamnoen Nok, Bangkok 10300; tel. (2) 281-6080; fax (2) 281-5415.

Governing body of Thailand's 350,000 monks, nuns and novices.

Supreme Patriarch of Thailand: NYANASAMVARA SUVADDHANA.

The Buddhist Association of Thailand: 41 Thanon Phra Aditya, Bangkok 10200; tel. (2) 281-5693; fax (2) 281-9564; f. 1934; under royal patronage; 7,139 mems; Pres. NUTTAPASH INTUPUTI.

CHRISTIANITY

The Roman Catholic Church

For ecclesiastical purposes, Thailand comprises two archdioceses and eight dioceses. At 31 December 2006 there were an estimated 326,978 adherents in the country, representing about 0.5% of the population.

Catholic Bishops' Conference of Thailand

122/11 Soi Naksuwan, Thanon Nonsi, Yannawa, Bangkok 10120; tel. (2) 681-5365; fax (2) 681-5370; e-mail cbct_th@hotmail.com; f. 1969; Pres. Cardinal MICHAEL MICHAI KITBUNCHU (Archbishop of Bangkok).

Archbishop of Bangkok: Cardinal MICHAEL MICHAI KITBUNCHU, Assumption Cathedral, 51 Thanon Oriental, Charoenkrung 40, Bangrak, Bangkok 10500; tel. (2) 237-1031; fax (2) 237-1033; e-mail arcdibkk@loxinfo.co.th.

Archbishop of Tharé and Nonseng: Bishop LOUIS CHAMNIERN SANTISUKNIRAN, POB 6, Amphoe Muang, Sakon Nakhon 47000; tel. (42) 711-272; fax (42) 712-023.

The Anglican Communion

Thailand is within the jurisdiction of the Anglican Bishop of Singapore (q.v.).

Other Christian Churches

Baptist Church Foundation (Foreign Mission Board): 90 Soi 2, Thanon Sukhumvit, Bangkok 10110; tel. (2) 252-7078; Mission Admin. TOM WILLIAMS (POB 832, Bangkok 10501).

Church of Christ in Thailand: 328 Thanon Phayathai, Khet Phayathai, Bangkok 10400; tel. (2) 214-6001; fax (2) 214-6010; e-mail webmaster_cct@cct.or.th; internet www.cct.or.th; f. 1934; c. 100,000 communicants; Moderator Rev. Dr BOONRATNA BOAYEN; Gen. Sec. Rev. Dr SINT KIMHACHANDRA.

ISLAM

Office of the Chularajmontri: 100 Soi Prom Pak, Thanon Sukhumvit, Bangkok 10110; Sheikh Al-Islam (Chularajmontri) Haji SAWASDI SUMALAYASAK.

BAHÁ'Í FAITH

National Spiritual Assembly: 1415 Sriwara Soi 94, Wangthonglang, Bangkapi, Bangkok 10310; tel. (2) 530-7417; fax (2) 935-6515; e-mail nsa@bahai.or.th; internet www.thai-bahais.org; mems resident in 76 provinces.

The Press

DAILIES

Thai Language

Baan Muang: 1 Soi Pluem-Manee, Thanon Vibhavadi Rangsit, Bangkok 10900; tel. (2) 513-3101; fax (2) 513-3106; internet www.banmuang.co.th; f. 1972; Editor MANA PRAEBHAND; circ. 200,000.

Daily News: 1/4 Thanon Vibhavadi Rangsit, Laksi, Bangkok 10210; tel. (2) 561-1456; fax (2) 940-9875; internet www.dailynews.co.th; f. 1964; Editor PRACHA HETRAKUL; circ. 800,000.

Khao Sod (Fresh News): 12 Thanon Tethsaban Naruaman, Prachanivate 1, Chatuchak, Bangkok 10900; tel. (2) 580-0021; fax (2) 580-2301; e-mail matisale@matichon.co.th; internet www.matichon.co.th/khaosod; Editor-in-Chief KIATICHAI PONGPANICH; circ. 650,000.

Kom Chad Luek (Sharp, Clear, Deep): 44 Moo 10, Thanon Bangna Trad, Km 4.5, Bang Na, Bangkok 10260; tel. (2) 325-5555; fax (2) 317-2071; internet www.komchadluek.com; Editor ADISAL LIMPRUNGPATAKIT.

Krungthep Turakij Daily: Nation Multimedia Group Public Co Ltd, 44 Moo 10, Thanon Bangna Trad, Bang Na, Prakanong, Bangkok 10260; tel. (2) 317-0042; fax (2) 317-1489; e-mail kteditor@nationgroup.com; internet www.bangkokbiznews.com;

THAILAND

f. 1987; Publr and Group Editor SUTHICHAI YOON; Editor DUANGKAMOL CHOTANA; circ. 75,882.

Manager Daily: Baan Phra Atit, 102/1 Thanon Phra Atit, Phra Nakorn, Bangkok; internet www.manager.co.th; f. 1990; Editor KHUNTHONG LORSERIVANICH.

Matichon: 12 Thanon Tethsaban Naruaman, Prachanivate 1, Chatuchak, Bangkok 10900; tel. (2) 580-0021; fax (2) 580-2301; e-mail matisale@matichon.co.th; internet www.matichon.co.th; f. 1977; Man. Editor PRASONG LERTRATANAVISUTH; circ. 550,000.

Naew Na (Frontline): 96 Moo 3, Thanon Vibhavadi Rangsit, Talaat Bang Khen, Bangkok 10210; tel. (2) 973-4250; fax (2) 552-3800; e-mail naewna@naewna.com; internet www.naewna.com; Editor WANCHAI WONGMEECHAI; circ. 200,000.

Post Today: 136 Thanon Na Ranong, Sonthorn Kosa, Klongtoey, Bangkok 10110; tel. (2) 240-3700; fax (2) 671-3147; e-mail nhakranl@posttoday.com; internet www.posttoday.com; f. 2003; business news; Editor NA KAL LAOHAWILAI; circ. 100,000.

Siam Keela (Siam Sport): 66/26–29, Moo 12, Soi Ram Indra 40, Thanon Ram Indra, Klong Kum, Bueng Kum, Bangkok 10230; tel. (2) 508-8000; e-mail webmaster@siamsport.co.th; internet www.siamsport.co.th; f. 1973.

Siam Rath (Siam Nation): 12 Mansion 6, Thanon Ratchadamnoen, Bangkok 10200; tel. (2) 622-1810; fax (2) 224-1982; e-mail siamrath@siamrath.co.th; internet www.siamrath.co.th; f. 1950; Editor CHACHAWAN KHONGUDOM; circ. 120,000.

Thai Rath: 1 Thanon Vibhavadi Rangsit, Bangkok 10900; tel. (2) 272-1030; fax (2) 272-1324; e-mail feedback@thairath.co.th; internet www.thairath.co.th; f. 1948; Editor SORAWUT WACHARAPHOL; circ. 800,000.

Thai Post: 1852 Thanon Kasemrat, Klong Toei, Bangkok 10110; tel. (2) 240-2612; fax (2) 249-0295; internet www.thaipost.net; Editor ROJ NGAMMAEN.

Than Setakij (Economic Base): 222 Than Setakij Bldg, Thanon Vibhavadi Rangsit, Chatuchak, Bangkok 10900; tel. (2) 513-9896; e-mail webmaster@thannews.th.com; internet www.thannews.th.com.

English Language

Bangkok Post: Bangkok Post Bldg, 136 Soi Na Ranong, Klongtoey, Bangkok 10110; tel. (2) 240-3700; fax (2) 240-3666; e-mail edmger@bangkokpost.co.th; internet www.bangkokpost.net; f. 1946; morning; Editor-in-Chief PICHAI CHUENSUKSAWADI.

Business Day: Olympia Thai Tower, 22nd Floor, 444 Thanon Ratchadaphisek, Huay Kwang, Bangkok 10310; tel. (2) 512-3579; fax (2) 512-3565; e-mail info@bday.net; internet www.biz-day.com; f. 1994; business news; Man. Editor CHATCHAI YENBAMROONG.

The Nation: 44 Moo 10, Editorial Bldg, 6th Floor, Thanon Bangna Trad, Km 4.5, Bang Na, Phra Khanong, Bangkok 10260; tel. (2) 325-5555; fax (2) 751-4446; e-mail info@nationgroup.com; internet www.nationmultimedia.com; f. 1971; morning; Publr and Group Editor SUTHICHAI YOON; Editor TULSATHIT TAPTIM; circ. 55,000.

Chinese Language

Sing Sian Yit Pao Daily News: 267 Thanon Charoenkrung, Talad-Noi, Bangkok 10100; tel. (2) 222-6601; fax (2) 225-4663; e-mail info@singsian.com; internet www.singsian.com; f. 1950; Man. Dir NETRA RUTHAIYANONT; Editor TAWEE YODPETCH; circ. 70,000.

Tong Hua Daily News: 877/879 Thanon Charoenkrung, Talad-Noi, Bangkok 10100; tel. (2) 236-9172; fax (2) 238-5286; Editor CHART PAYONITHIKARN; circ. 85,000.

WEEKLIES
Thai Language

Bangkok Weekly: 533–539 Thanon Sri Ayudhya, Bangkok 10400; tel. (2) 245-2546; fax (2) 247-3410; Editor VICHIT ROJANAPRABHA.

Mathichon Weekly Review: 12 Thanon Tethsaban Naruaman, Prachanivate 1, Chatuchak, Bangkok 10900; tel. (2) 580-0021; fax (2) 580-2301; e-mail weekly@matichon.co.th; internet www.matichon.co.th/weekly; Editor RUANGCHAI SABNIRAND; circ. 300,000.

Siam Rath Weekly Review: 12 Mansion 6, Thanon Rajdamnern, Bangkok 10200; Editor PRACHUAB THONGURAI.

Sakul Thai: 58 Soi 36, Thanon Sukhumvit, Bangkok 10110; tel. (2) 258-5861; fax (2) 258-9130; internet www.sakulthai.com; Editor SANTI SONGSEMSAWAS.

English Language

Bangkok Post Weekly Review: U-Chuliang Bldg, 3rd Floor, 968 Thanon Phra Ram Si, Bangkok 10500; tel. (2) 233-8030; fax (2) 238-5430; f. 1989; Editor ANUSSORN THAVISIN; circ. 10,782.

FORTNIGHTLIES
Thai Language

Darathai: 9-9/1 Soi Sri Ak-Sorn, Thanon Chuapleung, Tungmahamek, Sathorn, Bangkok 10120; tel. (2) 249-1576; fax (2) 249-1575; f. 1954; television and entertainment; Editor USA BUKKAVESA; circ. 80,000.

Dichan: 1400 Thai Bldg, Thanon Phra Ram Si, Bangkok; tel. (2) 249-0351; fax (2) 249-9455; e-mail dichan@pacific.co.th; Man. Editor KHUNYING TIPYAVADI PRAMOJ NA AYUDHYA.

Praew: 65/101–103 Thanon Chaiyaphruk, Taling Chan, Bangkok; tel. (2) 422-9999; fax (2) 434-3555; e-mail chantana@amarin.co.th; internet www.praew.com; f. 1979; women and fashion; Editorial Dir SUPAWADEE KOMARADAT; Editor CHANTANA YUTDHANAPHUM; circ. 150,000.

MONTHLIES

Bangkok 30: 98/5–6 Thanon Phra Arthit, Bangkok 10200; tel. (2) 282-5467; fax (2) 280-1302; f. 1986; Thai; business; Publr SONCHAI LIMTHONGKUL; Editor BOONSIRI NAMBOONSRI; circ. 65,000.

Chao Krung: 12 Mansion 6, Thanon Rajdamnern, Bangkok 10200; Thai; Editor NOPPHORN BUNYARIT.

The Dharmachaksu (Dharma-vision): Foundation of Mahamakut Rajavidyalai, 241 Thanon Phra Sumeru, Bangkok 10200; tel. and fax (2) 629-1391; e-mail books@mahamakuta.inet.co.th; internet www.mahamakuta.inet.co.th; f. 1894; Thai; Buddhism and related subjects; Editor SAENG CHANDR-NGAM; circ. 5,000.

Grand Prix: 4/299 Moo 5, Soi Ladplakhao 66, Thanon Ladplakhao, Bangkhen, Bangkok 10220; tel. (2) 971-6450; fax (2) 971-6469; e-mail pinyo@grandprixgroup.com; internet www.grandprixgroup.com/gpi/maggrandprix/grandprix.asp; f. 1970; Editor PINYO SILPASARTDUMRONG; circ. 80,000.

The Investor: Pansak Bldg, 4th Floor, 138/1 Thanon Phetchaburi, Ratchathawi, Bangkok 10400; tel. (2) 282-8166; f. 1968; English language; business, industry, finance and economics; Editor TOS PATUMSEN; circ. 6,000.

Kasikorn: Dept of Agriculture, Catuchak, Bangkok 10900; tel. (2) 561-4677; fax (2) 579-5369; e-mail pannee@doa.go.th; internet www.doa.go.th; f. 1928; Thai; agriculture and agricultural research; Editor-in-Chief SOPIDA HE-MAKOM; Editor PANNEE WICHACHOO.

Look: 1/54 Thanon Sukhumvit 30, Pra Khanong, Bangkok 10110; tel. (2) 258-1265; Editor KANOKWAN MILINDAVANIJ.

Look East: 52/38 Soi Saladaeng 2, Silom Condominium, 12th Floor, Thanon Silom, Bangkok 10500; tel. (2) 235-6185; fax (2) 236-6764; f. 1969; English; Editor ASHA SEHGAL; circ. 30,000.

Metro Magazine: 109 Moo 8, 7th Floor, Srithepthai Bldg, Thanon Bangna Trad, Bang Na, Bangkok 10260; tel. (2) 746-7250; fax (2) 746-7266; e-mail mon@bkkmetro.com; internet www.bkkmetro.com; f. 1996; English language; lifestyle, events listings and consumer-oriented articles; Publr and Editor-in-Chief MUNINTRA SAENGSUVIMOL; circ. 35,000.

Motorcycle Magazine: 4/299 Moo 5, Soi Ladplakhao 66, Thanon Ladplakhao, Bangkhan, Bangkok 10220; tel. (2) 522-1731; fax (2) 522-1730; e-mail motorcycle@grandprixgroup.com; f. 1972; Publr PRACHIN EAMLAMNOW; circ. 70,000.

Saen Sanuk: 50 Soi Saeng Chan, Thanon Sukhumvit 42, Bangkok 10110; tel. (2) 392-0052; fax (2) 391-1486; English; travel and tourist attractions in Thailand; Editor SOMTAWIN KONGSAWATKIAT; circ. 85,000.

Sarakadee Magazine: 28-30 Soi Parinayok, Bangkok 10200; tel. (2) 281-6110; fax (2) 282-7003; e-mail admin@sarakadee.com; internet www.sarakadee.com; Thai; events, culture and nature.

Satawa Liang: 689 Thanon Wang Burapa, Bangkok; Thai; Editor THAMRONGSAK SRICHAND.

Villa Wina Magazine: Chalerm Ketr Theatre Bldg, 3rd Floor, Bangkok; Thai; Editor BHONGSAKDI PIAMLAP.

NEWS AGENCY

Thai News Agency (TNA): 63/1 Thanon Phra Rama 9, Huay Kwang, Bangkok 10320; operated by MCOT PLC, fmrly the Mass Communications Organization of Thailand; news service in Thai and English.

PRESS ASSOCIATIONS

Confederation of Thai Journalists: 299 Thanon Ratchasima, Dusit, Bangkok 10300; tel. (2) 668-9422; fax (2) 668-7505; internet www.ctj.in.th; Pres. CHATRI LIMCHAROON; Sec.-Gen. NATTAYA CHETCHOTIROS.

Press Association of Thailand: 299 Thanon Ratchasima, Dusit, Bangkok 10300; tel. (2) 537-3777; fax (2) 537-3888; e-mail

THAILAND

webmaster@thaipressasso.com; internet www.thaipressasso.com; f. 1941; Pres. MANIT LUEPRAPHAI.

Thai Journalists' Asscn: 538/1 Thanon Samsen, Dusit, Bangkok 10300; tel. (2) 668-9422; fax (2) 668-7505; e-mail reporter@inet.co.th; internet www.tja.or.th; Pres. ANANT NILMANON.

There are also regional press organizations and journalists' organizations.

Publishers

Advance Media: 1400 Rama IV Shopping Centre, Klongtoey, Bangkok 10110; tel. (2) 249-0358; Man. PRASERTSAK SIVASAHONG.

Amarin Printing and Publishing Public Co Ltd: 65/101–103 Moo 4 Thanon Chaiyaphruk, Taling Chan, Bangkok 10170; tel. (2) 422-9999; fax (2) 434-3555; e-mail info@amarin.co.th; internet www.amarin.com; f. 1976; general books and magazines; CEO METTA UTAKAPAN.

Bhannakij Trading: 34 Thanon Nakornsawan, Bangkok 10100; tel. (2) 282-5520; fax (2) 282-0076; Thai fiction, school textbooks; Man. SOMSAK TECHAKASHEM.

Chalermnit Publishing Co Ltd: 108 Thanon Sukhumvit, Soi 53, Bangkok 10110; tel. (2) 662-6264; fax (2) 662-6265; e-mail chalermnit@hotmail.com; internet www.chalermnit.com; f. 1937; dictionaries, history, literature, guides to Thai language, works on Thailand and South-East Asia; Man. Dir Dr PARICHART JUMSAI.

Prae Pittaya Ltd: POB 914, 716–718 Wangburabha, Bangkok 10200; tel. (2) 221-4283; fax (2) 222-1286; general Thai books; Man. CHIT PRAEPANICH.

Praphansarn: 674–676 Thanon Charansanitwong, Bang Yee Khan, Bang Plat, Bangkok 10700; tel. (2) 435-1671; fax (2) 434-6812; e-mail editor@praphansarn.com; internet www.praphansarn.com; f. 1961; Thai pocket books; Man. Dir SUPHOL TAECHATADA.

Ruamsarn (1977): 864 Wangburabha, Thanon Panurangsri, Bangkok 10200; tel. (2) 221-6483; fax (2) 222-2036; f. 1951; fiction and history; Man. PITI TAWEWATANASARN.

Silkworm Books: 6 Thanon Sukkasem, T. Suthep, Muang, Chiang Mai 50200; tel. (53) 226-161; fax (53) 226-643; e-mail info@silkwormbooks.com; internet www.silkwormbooks.com; f. 1991; South-East Asian studies; English language.

Suksapan Panit (Business Organization of Teachers' Institute): 128/1 Thanon Ratchasima, Bangkok 10300; tel. (2) 416-7403; internet www.suksapan.or.th; f. 1950; general, textbooks, children's, pocket books; Pres. PANOM KAW KAMNERD.

Thai Watana Panich: 905 Thanon Rama 3, Yannawa, Bangkok 10120; tel. (2) 683-3333; fax (2) 683-2000; e-mail webmaster@twp.co.th; internet www.twp.co.th; children's, school textbooks; Man. Dir INTIRA BUNNAG.

White Lotus Co Ltd: POB 1141, Bangkok 10501; tel. (3) 823-9883; fax (3) 823-9885; e-mail ande@loxinfo.co.th; internet whitelotusbooks.com; f. 1972; regional interests, incl. art and culture, history, sociology and natural history; Publr DIETHARD ANDE.

PUBLISHERS' ASSOCIATION

Publishers' and Booksellers' Association of Thailand (PUBAT): 83/159 Moo 6, Thanon Ngam Wong Wan, Thung Song Hong, Lak Si, Bangkok 10210; tel. (2) 954-9560; fax (2) 954-9565; e-mail info@pubat.or.th; internet www.pubat.or.th; f. 1960; organizes national book fairs and provides promotional opportunities for publishers; Pres. RITRUAN ARAMCHAROEN; Gen. Sec. SUCHADA SAHATKUL.

Broadcasting and Communications

TELECOMMUNICATIONS

National Telecommunications Commission (NTC): 87 Thanon Phaholyothin, Soi 8, Phayatai, Bangkok 10400; tel. (2) 271-3511; fax (2) 290-5240; e-mail prnews@ntc.or.th; internet www.ntc.or.th; f. 2004; responsible for regulation and administration of telecommunications industry; Chair. Gen. CHOOCHART PROMPRASITM; Sec.-Gen. SURANAN WONGVITHAYAKAMJORN.

Advanced Info Service Public Co Ltd: 414 Thanon Phaholyothin, Shinawatra Tower I, Phayathai, Bangkok 10400; tel. (2) 299-5000; fax (2) 299-5719; e-mail callcenter@ais.co.th; internet www.aisco.th; mobile telephone network operator providing 3G (third generation) cellular services; CEO VIKROM SRIPRATAKS; Chair. SOMPRASONG BOONYACHAI.

CAT Telecom Public Co Ltd: 99 Thanon Chaengwattana, Laksi, Bangkok 10210; tel. (2) 104-4649; fax (2) 104-4649; e-mail pr@cattelecom.com; internet www.cattelecom.com; f. 2003 following division of Communications Authority of Thailand (CAT); originally state-owned; telephone operator; privatized in 2004; Chair. SATHIT LIMPONGPAN.

Samart Corpn Public Co Ltd: 99/1 Moo 4, Software Park Bldg, 35th Floor, Thanon Chaengwattana, Klong Gluar, Pak-kred, Nonthaburi 11120; tel. (2) 502-6000; fax (2) 502-6043; e-mail nikhila@samartcorp.com; internet www.samartcorp.com; f. 1952; telecommunications installation and distribution; Hon. Chair. CHERDCHAI VILAILUCK; Chair. TONGCHAT HONGLADAROMP.

Thai Telephone and Telecommunication Public Co Ltd (TT&T): 252/30 Muang Thai Phatra Complex Tower 1, 24th Floor, Thanon Ratchadaphisek, Huay Kwang, Bangkok 10320; tel. (2) 693-2100; fax (2) 693-2124; e-mail ir@ttt.co.th; internet www.ttt.co.th; f. 1992; distributors of telecommunications equipment and services; Chair. SONGRIT KUSOMROSANANAN; Pres. PRACHUAB TANTINONDA.

Thailand Post Co Ltd: 111 Moo 3, Thanon Chaengwattana, Thung Song Hong, Laksi, Bangkok 10210; tel. (2) 831-3131; fax (2) 831-3514; e-mail contact@thailandpost.co.th; internet www.thailandpost.com; f. 2003; Chair. PHAWORN PANICHAPHAN; Man. Dir ORMSIN CHEEWAPRUEK.

TOT Public Co Ltd: 89/2 Moo 3, Thanon Chaengwattana, Thung Song Hong, Laksi, Bangkok 10210; tel. (2) 505-1000; e-mail prtot@tot.co.th; internet www.tot.co.th; f. 2002; state-owned; fmrly Telephone Organization of Thailand; name changed to TOT Corpn Public Co Ltd; name changed as above in 2005; telephone operator; de facto regulator; Chair. Prof. THEERAYUT BUNYASOPORN; Pres. WARUT SUWAKORN.

Total Access Communications Public Co Ltd: Chai Bldg, 19th Floor, 333/3 Moo 4, Thanon Vibhavadi Rangsit, Ladyao, Chatuchak, Bangkok 10900; tel. (2) 202-87000; fax (2) 202-8102; e-mail feedback@dtac.co.th; internet www.dtac.co.th; f. 1989; mobile telephone network operator; 41.46% owned by United Communication Industry Public Co Ltd; 29.94% owned by Telenor Asia Pte Ltd; Chair. BOONCHAI BENCHARONGKUL; CEO TORE JOHNSEN.

True Corpn PCL: 18 True Tower, Thanon Ratchadaphisek, Huay Kwang, Bangkok 10310; tel. (2) 643-1111; fax (2) 643-9669; internet www.truecorp.co.th/eng/index.jsp; f. 1990 under the name Telecomasia Corpn PCL; name changed as above in 2004; telecommunications services; Chair. DHANIN CHEARAVANONT; Pres. and CEO SUPACHAI CHEARAVANONT.

True Move: 18 True Tower, Thanon Ratchadaphisek, Huay Kwang, Bangkok 10310; tel. (2) 647-5000; internet www.truemove.com; f. 2002; fmrly TA Orange Co Ltd; name changed as above in 2005; mobile telephone network operator; Chief Exec. SUPACHAI CHEARAVANONT.

United Communication Industry Public Co Ltd (UCOM): 333/3 Chai Bldg, 18th Floor, Thanon Vibhavadi Rangsit, Ladyao, Chatuchak, Bangkok 10900; tel. (2) 202-8000; fax (2) 202-8929; e-mail ir.ucom@dtac.co.th; internet www.ucom.co.th; telecommunications service provider; Chair. SRIBHUMI SUKHANETR; Pres. and Chief Exec. BOONCHAI BENCHARONGKUL.

BROADCASTING

Regulatory Authority

Radio and Television Executive Committee (RTEC): Programme, Administration and Law Section, Division of RTEC Works, Government Public Relations Dept, Thanon Ratchadamnoen Klang, Phra Nakhon Region, Bangkok 10200; constituted under the Broadcasting and TV Rule 1975, the committee consists of 17 representatives from 14 government agencies and controls the administrative, legal, technical and programming aspects of broadcasting in Thailand; regulatory functions were assumed by the National Broadcasting Commission; Dir-Gen. BOWON TECHAINDRA.

Radio

Radio Thailand (RTH): National Broadcasting Services of Thailand, Government Public Relations Dept, Soi Aree Sampan, Thanon Phra Ram VI, Khet Phayathai, Bangkok 10400; tel. (2) 618-2323; fax (2) 618-2340; internet www.prd.go.th/mcic/radio.htm; f. 1930; govt-controlled; educational, entertainment, cultural and news programmes; operates 109 stations throughout Thailand; Dir of Radio Thailand PAITOON SRIRAWD.

Home Service: 12 stations in Bangkok and 97 affiliated stations in 50 provinces; operates three programmes; Dir CHAIVICHIT ATISAB.

External Services: f. 1928; in Thai, English, French, Vietnamese, Khmer, Japanese, Burmese, Lao, Malay, Chinese (Mandarin), German and Bahasa Indonesia; Dir AMPORN SAMOSORN.

Ministry of Education Broadcasting Service: Centre for Innovation and Technology, Ministry of Education, Bangkok; tel. (2) 246-0026; f. 1954; morning programmes for schools (Mon.–Fri.); after-

THAILAND

noon and evening programmes for general public (daily); Dir of Centre PISAN SIWAYABRAHM.

Pituksuntirad Radio Stations: stations at Bangkok, Nakorn Rachasima, Chiang Mai, Pitsanuloke and Songkla; programmes in Thai; Dir-Gen. PAITOON WAIJANYA.

Radio Saranrom: Thanon Ratchadamnoen, POB 2-131, Bangkok 10200; tel. (2) 224-4904; fax (2) 226-1825; internet www.mfa.go.th/web/151.php; f. 1968 as Voice of Free Asia; name changed as above in 1998; operated by the Ministry of Foreign Affairs; broadcasts in Thai; Dir of Broadcasting PAIBOON KUSKUL.

Television

Bangkok Broadcasting & TV Co Ltd (Channel 7): 998/1 Soi Sirimitr, Phaholyothin, Talad Mawchid, POB 456, Bangkok 10900; tel. (2) 272-0201; fax (2) 272-0010; e-mail prdept@ch7.com; internet www.ch7.com; commercial.

Bangkok Entertainment Co Ltd (Channel 3): 3199 Maleenont Tower, Thanon Phra Ram IV, Klong Ton, Klongtoey, Bangkok 10110; tel. (2) 204-3333; fax (2) 204-1384; e-mail internet@thaitv3.com; internet www.thaitv3.com; Programme Dir PRAVIT MALEENONT.

The Mass Communication Organization of Thailand (Modernine TV): 222 Thanon Asoke-Dindaeng, Bangkok 10300; tel. (2) 201-6000; fax (2) 245-1855; e-mail webmaster@mcot.net; internet www.mcot.net; f. 1952 as Thai Television Co Ltd; colour service; also operates radio stations and news agency; Dir-Gen. WASANT PAILEEKLEE.

National Broadcasting of Thailand (NBT): Public Relations Dept, Fortune Town Bldg, 26th Floor, Thanon Ratchadaphisek, Huay Kwang, Bangkok 10310; tel. and fax (2) 248-1601; internet www.prd.go.th/p_link/pr_tv.php; f. 1985; fmrly Channel 11; Dir-Gen. SURIN PLAENGPRASOPCHOK.

The Royal Thai Army Television HSA-TV (Channel 5): 210 Thanon Phaholyothin, Sanam Pao, Bangkok 10400; tel. (2) 227-0060; fax (2) 271-0930; e-mail webadmin@tv5.co.th; internet www.tv5.co.th; f. 1958; operates channels nation-wide; Dir-Gen. Maj.-Gen. KITTITAT PANECHAPHAN.

Thai Public Broadcasting Service: 1010 Shinwatra Tower III, Thanon Vibhavadi Rangsit, Chatuchak, Bangkok 10900; tel. (2) 791-1000; fax (2) 791-1010; e-mail webmaster@thaipbs.or.th; internet www.thaipbs.or.th; f. 2008; succeeded the former iTV.

Thai TV Global Network: c/o Royal Thai Army HSA-TV, 210 Thanon Phaholyothin, Sanam Pao, Bangkok 10400; tel. (2) 278-1697; fax (2) 615-2066; e-mail tgn@tv5.co.th; internet www.thaitvglobal.com; established with the co-operation of all stations; distributes selected news, information and entertainment programmes from domestic stations for transmission to 170 countries world-wide via six satellite networks; Chair. Maj.-Gen. SOONTHORN SOPHONSIRI.

Finance

(cap. = capital; p.u. = paid up; res = reserves; dep. = deposits; m. = million; brs = branches; amounts in baht)

BANKING

Central Bank

Bank of Thailand: 273 Thanon Samsen, Bangkhunprom, Bangkok 10200; tel. (2) 283-5353; fax (2) 280-0449; e-mail webmaster@bot.or.th; internet www.bot.or.th; f. 1942; bank of issue; cap. 20m., res 7,688.0m., dep. 419,905m. (Dec. 2006); Gov. TARISA WATANAGASE; 4 brs.

Commercial Banks

Bangkok Bank Public Co Ltd: 333 Thanon Silom, Bangrak, Bangkok 10500; tel. (2) 231-4333; fax (2) 231-4742; e-mail info@bangkokbank.com; internet www.bangkokbank.com; f. 1944; cap. 19,088.4m., res 195,424.2m., dep. 1,267.0m. (Dec. 2007); 49% foreign-owned; Chair. CHARTRI SOPHONPANICH; Pres. CHARTSIRI SOPHONPANICH; 656 local brs, 22 overseas brs.

Bank of Ayudhya Public Co Ltd: 1222 Thanon Rama III, Bang Phongphang, Yan Nawa, Bangkok 10120; tel. (2) 296-2000; fax (2) 683-1484; e-mail webmaster@krungsri.com; internet www.krungsri.com; f. 1945; cap. 29,408.1m., res 11,010.0m., dep. 583,480.5m. (Dec. 2006); Pres. TAN KONG KHOON; Chair. VERAPHAN TEEPSUWAN; 384 local brs, 3 overseas brs.

BankThai Public Co Ltd: 44 Thanon Sathorn Nua, Silom, Bangrak, Bangkok 10500; tel. (2) 638-8000; fax (2) 633-9026; e-mail webmaster@bankthai.co.th; internet www.bankthai.co.th; f. 1998; cap. 14,935m., res −3,601m., dep. 252,913m. (Dec. 2005); Chair. TAWEE BUTSUNTORN; Pres. SUBHAK SIRAWAKSA; 98 brs.

Kasikorn Bank Public Co Ltd: 1 Soi Kasikornthai, Thanon Ratburana, Bangkok 10140; tel. (2) 888-8000; fax (2) 888-8882; e-mail info@kasikornbank.com; internet www.kasikornbank.com; f. 1945; fmrly Thai Farmers Bank Public Co Ltd; name changed as above April 2003; cap. 23,882m., res 31,242m., dep. 809,845m. (Dec. 2007); 48.98% foreign-owned; Chair. BANYONG LAMSAM; CEO BANTHOON LAMSAM; Pres. Dr PRASARN TRAIRATVORAKUL; 508 local brs, 4 overseas brs.

Kiatnakin Bank Public Co Ltd: Amarin Tower, 12th Floor, 500 Thanon Ploenchit, Pathumwan, Bangkok 10330; tel. (2) 680-3333; fax (2) 256-9933; internet www.kiatnakinbank.com; f. 1971 under the name Kiatnakin Finance and Securities Co Ltd; name changed in 1999 to Kiatnakin Finance Public Co Ltd following separation of its finance and securities businesses; name changed as above in 2005; Chair. NAWAAPORN RYANSKUL; Pres. TAWATCHAI SUDTIKITPISAIN; 16 brs.

Krung Thai Bank Public Co Ltd (State Commercial Bank of Thailand): 35 Thanon Sukhumvit, Klongtoey, Bangkok 10110; tel. (2) 255-2222; fax (2) 255-9391; e-mail call@contactcenter.ktb.co.th; internet www.ktb.co.th; f. 1966; cap. 57,604.0m., res 8,627m., dep. 1,045,118.9m. (Dec. 2007); taken under the control of the central bank in 1998, pending transfer to private sector; merged with First Bangkok City Bank Public Co Ltd in 1999; Chair. SUPARUT KAWATKUL; Pres. APISAK TANTIVORAWONG; 719 local brs, 7 overseas brs.

Siam City Bank Public Co Ltd: 1101 Thanon Phetchaburi Tadmai, Bangkok 10400; tel. (2) 208-5000; fax (2) 253-1240; e-mail scibweb@scib.co.th; internet www.scib.co.th; f. 1941; cap. 21,128m., res 4,128m., dep. 362,187m. (Dec. 2006); taken under the control of the central bank in Feb. 1998; merged with Bangkok Metropolitan Bank Public Co Ltd in April 2002; Chair. SOMPOL KIATPHAIBOOL; Pres. and CEO CHAIWAT UTAIWAN; 387 local brs, 1 overseas br.

Siam Commercial Bank Public Co Ltd: 9 Thanon Ratchadaphisek, Ladyao, Chatuchak, Bangkok 10900; tel. (2) 544-1000; fax (2) 937-7754; e-mail investor.relations@scb.co.th; internet www.scb.co.th; f. 1906; cap. 33,991.9m., res 26,447.1m., dep. 816,206.4m. (Dec. 2006); Exec. Chair. Dr VICHIT SURAPHONGCHAI; Pres. and CEO KHUNYING JADA WATTANASIRITHAM; 477 local brs, 4 overseas brs.

Standard Chartered Bank (Thai) Public Co Ltd: 90 Thanon Sathorn Nua, Silom, Bangkok 10500; tel. (2) 724-4000; fax (2) 236-1968; internet www.standardchartered.co.th; f. 1933 as Wang Lee Bank Ltd, renamed 1985; cap. 11,386m., res 7,965m., dep. 102,022m. (July 2007); taken under the control of the central bank in July 1999, 75% share sold to Standard Chartered Bank (United Kingdom); name changed to Standard Chartered Nakornthon Bank PCL in 1999; name changed as above in 2005; Chair. KAIKHUSHRU SHIAVAX NORGALWALA; CEO MEE HAR FOO; 67 brs.

Thanachart Bank Public Co Ltd: 1st, 2nd, 14th and 15th Floors, Thonson Bldg, 900 Thanon Phoenchit, Lumpini, Pathumwan, Bangkok 10330; tel. (2) 655-9000; fax (2) 655-9001; e-mail nfs_rb@nfs.co.th; f. 2002; Man. Dir SUVARNAPHA SUVARNAPRATHIP.

TMB Bank Public Co Ltd: 3000 Thanon Phahon Yothin, Ladyao, Chatuchak, Bangkok 10900; tel. (2) 299-1111; fax (2) 273-7121; e-mail ir@tmbbank.com; internet www.tmbbank.com; f. 1957; fmrly known as Thai Military Bank Public Co Ltd; name changed as above 2005; merged with DBS Thai Danu Bank Public Co Ltd and Industrial Finance Corpn of Thailand Sept. 2004; cap. 435,287.3m., res −287,748.9m., dep. 499,083.4m. (Dec. 2007); Chair. SOMCHAINUK ENGTRAKUL; Pres. and CEO SUBHAK SIWARAKSA; 431 local brs, 3 overseas brs.

United Overseas Bank (Thai) Public Co Ltd (UOBT): 191 Thanon Sathorn Tai, Bangkok 10120; tel. (2) 343-3000; fax (2) 287-2973; e-mail webmaster@uob.co.th; internet www.uob.co.th; f. 1998 as the result of the merger of Laem Thong Bank Ltd with Radanasin Bank; name changed to UOB Radanasin Bank Public Co Ltd in Nov. 1999; name changed as above in 2005 following merger with Bank of Asia Public Co Ltd; cap. 82,170.6m., res −23,909.3m., dep. 170,446.1m. (Dec. 2007); Chair. WEE CHO YAW; Pres. and CEO WONG KIM CHOONG; 154 brs.

Development Banks

Bank for Agriculture and Agricultural Co-operatives (BAAC): 469 Thanon Nakorn Sawan, Dusit, Bangkok 10300; tel. (2) 280-0180; fax (2) 280-0442; e-mail train@baac.or.th; internet www.baac.or.th; f. 1966 to provide credit for agriculture; cap. and res 49,911m., dep. 431,401m. (March 2006); Exec. Chair. VARATHEP RATANAKORN; Pres. ENNOO SUESUWAN (acting); 491 brs.

Export-Import Bank of Thailand (EXIM THAILAND): EXIM Bldg, 1193 Thanon Phaholyothin, Phayathai, Bangkok 10400; tel. (2) 271-3700; fax (2) 271-3204; e-mail info@exim.go.th; internet www.exim.go.th; f. 1993; provides financial services to Thai exporters and Thai investors investing abroad; cap. 6,500m., res 2,159m., dep. 12,313m. (Dec. 2007); Chair. NARONGCHAI AKRASANEE; Pres. APICHAI BOONTHERAWARA; 10 brs.

THAILAND

Directory

Government Housing Bank: 63 Thanon Rama IX, Huay Kwang, Bangkok 10310; tel. (2) 645-9000; fax (2) 246-1789; e-mail crm@ghb.co.th; internet www.ghb.co.th; f. 1953 to provide housing finance; Chair. WISUDHI SRISUPHAN; Pres. KHAN PRACHUABMOH; 120 brs.

Small and Medium Enterprise Development Bank of Thailand: 9th Floor, Siripinyo Bldg, 475 Thanon Sri Ayudhaya, Rajtavee, Bangkok 10400; tel. (2) 201-3700; fax (2) 201-3723; e-mail sme@smebank.co.th; internet www.smebank.co.th; f. under above name in 2002; fmrly Small Industries Finance Office, which became Small Industrial Finance Co Ltd in 1991; Chair. PONGPANU SVETARUNDRA.

Savings Bank

Government Savings Bank: 470 Thanon Phaholyothin, Phayathai, Bangkok 10400; tel. (2) 299-8000; fax (2) 299-8490; e-mail news@gsb.or.th; internet www.gsb.or.th; f. 1913; cap. 0.1m., res 8,765m., dep. 538,823m. (Dec. 2005); Chair. SOMCHAINUK ENGTRAKUL; Dir-Gen. Dr CHARNCHAI MUSIGNISARKORN; 578 brs.

Bankers' Association

Thai Bankers' Association: Lake Rachada Office Complex, Bldg 2, 4th Floor, 195/5–7 Thanon Ratchadaphisek, Klongtoey, Bangkok 10110; tel. (2) 264-0883; fax (2) 264-0888; e-mail infodesk@tba.or.th; internet www.tba.or.th; f. 1958; Chair. APISAK TANTIVORAWONG.

STOCK EXCHANGE

Stock Exchange of Thailand (SET): The Stock Exchange of Thailand Bldg, 62 Thanon Ratchadaphisek, Klongtoey, Bangkok 10110; tel. (2) 229-2000; fax (2) 654-5649; e-mail infoproducts@set.or.th; internet www.set.or.th; f. 1975; 27 mems; Pres. PATAREEYA BENJAPOLCHAI; Chair. PAKORN MALAKUL NA AYUDHYA.

Securities and Exchange Commission: Diethelm Towers B, 10th/13th–16th Floors, 93/1 Thanon Witthayu, Pathumwan, Bangkok 10330; tel. (2) 695-9999; fax (2) 256-7711; e-mail info@sec.or.th; internet www.sec.or.th; f. 1992; supervises new share issues and trading in existing shares; chaired by Minister of Finance; Sec.-Gen. THIRACHAI PHUVANAT NARANUBULA.

INSURANCE

In March 1997 the Government granted licences to 12 life assurance companies and 16 general insurance companies, bringing the total number of life insurance companies to 25 and non-life insurance companies to 83.

Selected Insurance Companies

Aioi Bangkok Insurance Co Ltd: 22nd Floor, Bangkok Insurance/YMCA Bldg, 25 Thanon Sathorn Tai, Thungmahamek, Sathorn, Bangkok 10120; tel. (2) 620-8000; fax (2) 677-3978-9; e-mail center@aioibkkins.co.th; f. 1951; fmrly known as Wilson Insurance Co Ltd; fire, marine, motor car, general; CEO YOSHIHIKO FUKASAWA; Pres. NOPADOL SANTIPAKORN.

American International Assurance Co Ltd: American International Tower, 181 Thanon Surawongse, Bangkok 10500; tel. (2) 634-8888; fax (2) 236-6452; e-mail bkk.group@aig.com; internet www.aia.co.th; f. 1983; ordinary and group life, group and personal accident, credit, life; Exec. Vice-Pres. and Gen. Man. DHADOL BUNNAG.

Ayudhya Insurance Public Co Ltd: Ploenchit Tower, 7th Floor, Thanon Ploenchit, Pathumwan, Bangkok 10300; tel. (2) 263-0335; fax (2) 263-0589; e-mail info@ayud.co.th; internet www.ayud.co.th; non-life; Chair. VERAPHAN TEEPSUWAN; Pres. ROWAN D'ARCY.

Bangkok Insurance Public Co Ltd: Bangkok Insurance Bldg, 25 Thanon Sathorn Tai, Bangkok 10120; tel. (2) 285-8888; fax (2) 677-3737; e-mail corp.comm1@bki.co.th; internet www.bki.co.th; f. 1947; non-life; Chair. and Pres. CHAI SOPHONPANICH.

Bangkok Union Insurance Public Co Ltd: 175–177 Bangkok Union Insurance Bldg, Thanon Surawongse, Bangrak, Bangkok 10500; tel. (2) 233-6920; fax (2) 237-1856; e-mail underwrite@bui.co.th; internet www.bui.co.th; f. 1929; non-life; Chair. MANU LIEWPAIROT.

China Insurance Co (Siam) Ltd: 36/68–69, 20th Floor, PS Tower, Thanon Asoke, Sukhumvit 21, Bangkok 10110; tel. (2) 259-3718; fax (2) 259-1402; f. 1948; non-life; Chair. JAMES C. CHENG; Man. Dir FANG RONG-CHENG.

Indara Insurance Public Co Ltd: 364/29 Thanon Sri Ayudhya, Ratchathewi, Bangkok 10400; tel. (2) 247-9261; fax (2) 247-9260; e-mail contact@indara.co.th; internet www.indara.co.th; f. 1949; non-life; Chair. PRATIP WONGNIRUND; Man. Dir SUCHART TRISIRIWETAWATTANA.

Mittare Insurance Co Ltd: 295 Thanon Si Phraya, Bangrak, Bangkok 10500; tel. (2) 237-4646; fax (2) 236-1376; internet www.mittare.com; f. 1947; life, fire, marine, health, personal accident, automobile and general; fmrly Thai Prasit Insurance Co Ltd; Chair. SURACHAN CHANSRICHAWLA; Man. Dir SUKHATHEP CHANSRICHAWLA.

Navakij Insurance Public Co Ltd: 90/4-6, 100/50-55 Sathorn Nakorn Tower, Thanon Sathorn Nua, Silom, Bangrak, Bangkok 10500; tel. (2) 636-7900; fax (2) 636-7997; internet www.navakij.co.th; f. 1933; Pres. NIPHON TANGJEERAWONGSA.

Ocean Life Insurance Co Ltd: 170/74–83 Ocean Tower I Bldg, Thanon Ratchadaphisek, Klongtoey, Bangkok 10110; tel. (2) 261-2300; fax (2) 261-3344; e-mail info@oli.co.th; internet www.oli.co.th; f. 1949; life; Chair. KIRATI ASSAKUL; Man. Dir DAYANA BUNNAG.

Paiboon Insurance Co Ltd: Thai Life Insurance Bldg, 19th–20th Floors, 123 Thanon Ratchadaphisek, Bangkok 10310; tel. (2) 246-9635; fax (2) 246-9660; f. 1927; non-life; Chair. ANUTHRA ASSAWANONDA; Pres. VANICH CHAIYAWAN.

Prudential TS Life Assurance Public Co Ltd: Sengthong Thani Tower, 28th, 30th and 31st Floors, 82 Thanon Sathorn Nua, Bangkok 10500; tel. (2) 639-9500; fax (2) 639-9699; e-mail customer.service.ptsl@ibm.net; internet www.prudential.co.th; f. 1983; Chair. BURAPHA ATTHAKON; Man. Dir TED C. RIDGEWAY.

Siam Commercial New York Life Insurance Public Co Ltd: 4th Floor, SCB Bldg 1, 1060 Thanon Phetchaburi, SCB Chidlom, Ratchathewi, Bangkok 10400; tel. (2) 655-3000; fax (2) 256-1517; e-mail customerservice@scnyl.com; internet www.scnyl.com; f. 1976; life; Chair. and CEO KANNIKA CHALITAPHORN.

Southeast Insurance (2000) Co Ltd (Arkanay Prakan Pai Co Ltd): Southeast Insurance Bldg, 315G, 1–3 Thanon Silom, Bangrak, Bangkok 10500; tel. (2) 631-1331; internet www.seic2000.com; f. 1946; life and non-life; Chair. CHAYUT CHIRALERSPONG; Gen. Man. WICHAI INTARANUKULAKIJ.

Syn Mun Kong Insurance Public Co Ltd: 279 Thanon Srinakarin, Bangkapi, Bangkok 10240; tel. (2) 379-3140; fax (2) 731-6590; e-mail info@smk.co.th; internet www.smk.co.th; f. 1951; fire, marine, automobile and personal accident; Chair. RUENGWIT DUSADEESURAPOJ; Man. Dir RUENGDEJ DUSADEESURAPOJ.

Thai Health Insurance Co Ltd: 31st Floor, RS Tower, 121/89 Thanon Ratchadaphisek, Din-Daeng, Bangkok 10400; tel. (2) 642-3100; fax (2) 642-3130; e-mail info@thaihealth.co.th; internet www.thaihealth.co.th; f. 1979; Chair. APIRAK THAIPATANAGUL; Man. Dir VARANG SRETHBHAKDI.

Thai Insurance Public Co Ltd: 34/3 Soi Lang Suan, Thanon Ploenchit, Lumpini, Pathumwan, Bangkok 10330; tel. (2) 613-0100; fax (2) 652-2870; e-mail tic@thaiins.com; internet www.thaiins.com; f. 1938; non-life; Chair. KAVI ANSVANANDA.

Thai Life Insurance Co Ltd: 123 Thanon Ratchadaphisek, Din-Daeng, Bangkok 10400; tel. (2) 247-0247; fax (2) 246-9945; internet www.thailife.com; f. 1942; life; Chair. and CEO VANICH CHAIYAWAN.

ThaiSri Insurance Co Ltd: 126/2 Thanon Krunthonburi, Klongsam, Bangkok 10600; tel. (2) 878-7111; fax (2) 860-7365; e-mail info@thaisri.com; internet www.thaisri.com; f. 1997; personal accident, automobile, fire, marine; jt venture between Thai Metropole Insurance and Zurich Financial Services Group (Switzerland); Chair. SIRIN NIMMANAHAEMINDA; Pres. NATEE PANICHEWA.

Viriyah Insurance Co Ltd: RS Tower, 121/7 Thanon Ratchadaphisek, Din-Daeng, Bangkok 10320; tel. (2) 239-1000; fax (2) 641-3902; e-mail info@viriyah.co.th; internet www.viriyah.co.th; f. 1947; Chair. JARE CHUTHARATTANAKUL; Man. Dir SUVAPORN THONGTHEW.

Associations

General Insurance Association: 223 Soi Ruamrudee, Thanon Witthayu, Bangkok 10330; tel. (2) 256-6032; fax (2) 256-6039; e-mail general@thaigia.com; internet www.thaigia.com; Pres. JEERAPHAN ASAWATHANAKUL; Sec.-Gen. ANON VANGVASU; 67 mems.

Thai Life Assurance Association: 36/1 Soi Sapanku, Thanon Rama IV, Thungmahamek, Sathorn, Bangkok 10120; tel. (2) 287-4596; fax (2) 679-7100; e-mail tlaa@tlaa.org; internet www.tlaa.org; Pres. SARA LAMSAM; Sec.-Gen. PHERAPONG UNCHIT; 25 mems.

Trade and Industry

GOVERNMENT AGENCIES

Board of Investment (BOI): 555 Thanon Vibhavadi Rangsit, Chatuchak, Bangkok 10900; tel. (2) 537-8111; fax (2) 537-8177; e-mail head@boi.go.th; internet www.boi.go.th; f. 1958; formed to publicize investment potential and encourage economically and socially beneficial investments and also to provide investment information; chaired by the Prime Minister; Sec.-Gen. ATCHAKA SIBUNRUANG BRIMBLE.

Board of Trade of Thailand: 150/2 Thanon Rajbopit, Bangkok 10200; tel. (2) 622-1860; fax (2) 225-3372; internet www.thaiechamber.com; f. 1955; mems: chambers of commerce, trade asscns, state enterprises and co-operative societies (large and medium-sized companies have associate membership); Chair. AIVA TAULANANDA.

Financial Sector Restructuring Authority (FSRA): 130–132 Tower 3, Thanon Witthayu, Pathumwan, Bangkok 10330; tel. (2) 263-2620; fax (2) 650-9872; f. 1997 to oversee the restructuring of Thailand's financial system; Chair. KAMOL JUNTIMA; Sec.-Gen. MONTRI CHENVIDAYAKAM.

Forest Industry Organization: 76 Thanon Ratchadamnoen Nok, Bangkok 10100; tel. (2) 282-3243; fax (2) 282-5197; e-mail info@fio.co.th; internet www.fio.co.th; f. 1947; oversees all aspects of forestry and wood industries; Man. MANOONSAK TONTIWIWATTANA.

Office of the Cane and Sugar Board: Ministry of Industry, Thanon Phra Ram Hok, Bangkok 10400; tel. (2) 202-3291; fax (2) 202-3293; e-mail ocsb0601@ocsb.go.th; internet www.ocsb.go.th; Sec.-Gen. PRASERT TAPANEEYANGKUL.

Rubber Estate Organization: Nabon Station, Nakhon Si Thammarat Province 80220; tel. (75) 411554; e-mail reothai@reothai.co.th; internet www.reothai.co.th; Man. Dir CHAIROJ THAMMARATTANA (acting).

DEVELOPMENT AGENCIES

National Economic and Social Development Board: 962 Thanon Krung Kasem, Bangkok 10100; tel. (2) 282-8454; fax (2) 281-3938; e-mail mis@nesdb.go.th; internet www.nesdb.go.th; economic and social planning agency; Sec.-Gen. AMPON KITTI-AMPON.

Royal Developments Projects Board: Office of the Prime Minister, Government House, Thanon Nakhon Pathom, Bangkok 10300; tel. (2) 280-6193; e-mail webmaster@rdpb.go.th; internet www.rdpb.go.th; Sec.-Gen. SOMPOL PANMANEE.

CHAMBER OF COMMERCE

Thai Chamber of Commerce: 150 Thanon Rajbopit, Bangkok 10200; tel. (2) 622-1860; fax (2) 225-3372; e-mail tcc@thaiechamber.com; internet www.thaiechamber.com; f. 1946; 2,000 mems, 10 assoc. mems (1998); Chair. PHAIRUSH BURAPACHAISRI; Pres. VICHIEN TEJAPHAIBOON.

INDUSTRIAL AND TRADE ASSOCIATIONS

The Federation of Thai Industries: Queen Sirikit National Convention Center, Zone C, 4th Floor, 60 Thanon Ratchadaphisek Tadmai, Klongtoey, Bangkok 10110; tel. (2) 345-1000; fax (2) 345-1296; e-mail information@off.fti.or.th; internet www.fti.or.th; f. 1987; fmrly The Association of Thai Industries; 4,800 mems; Chair. SANTI WILATSAKDANON.

Mining Industry Council of Thailand: Soi 222/2, Thai Chamber of Commerce University, Thanon Vibhavadi Rangsit, Din-Daeng, Bangkok 10400; tel. (2) 275-7684; fax (2) 692-3321; e-mail miningthai@miningthai.org; internet www.miningthai.org; f. 1983; intermediary between govt organizations and private mining enterprises; Chair. YONGYOTH PETCHSUWAN; Sec.-Gen. ORANUCH RAMAKOMUT.

Rice Exporters' Association of Thailand: 37 Soi Ngamdupli, Thanon Phra Rama IV, Tungmahamek, Sathorn, Bangkok 10120; tel. (2) 287-2674; fax (2) 287-2678; e-mail contact@riceexporters.or.th; internet www.riceexporters.or.th; Pres. CHOOKIERT OPHASAWONG; Sec.-Gen. KORBSUK IEMSURI.

Sawmills Association: 101 Thanon Amnuaysongkhram, Dusit, Bangkok 10300; tel. (2) 243-4754; fax (2) 243-8629; e-mail info@thaisawmills.com; internet www.thaisawmills.com; Pres. SURASAK IEMDEENGAMLERT.

Thai Coffee Exporters Association: 1302–1306 Thanon Songwad, Samphanthawong, Bangkok 10100; tel. (2) 221-1264; fax (2) 225-1962; e-mail cofexpo@cscoms.com.

Thai Contractors' Association: 110 Thanon Witthayu, Bangkok 10330; tel. (2) 251-0697; fax (2) 255-3990; e-mail webmaster@tca.or.th; internet www.tca.or.th; f. 1928 under the name The Engineering Association of Siam; name changed to The Engineering Contractors Asscn in 1967 and as above in 1983; Pres. POLPAT KARNASUTA; Sec.-Gen. ANGSURAS AREEKUL.

Thai Diamond Manufacturers Association: 87/139–40, Modern Town Bldg, 18/F, Soi Ekamai 3, Thanon Sukhumvit 63, Klong Ton Nua, Wattana, Bangkok 10110; tel. (2) 390-0341; fax (2) 711-4039; e-mail odtcbkk@loxinfo.co.th; internet www.thaidiamonds.org; 11-mem. board; Pres. CHIRAKITTI TANGKATHAC.

Thai Food Processors' Association: Tower 1, Ocean Bldg, 9th Floor, 170/21–22 Thanon Ratchadaphisek Tadmai, Klongtoey, Bangkok 10110; tel. (2) 261-2684; fax (2) 261-2996; e-mail thaifood@thaifood.org; internet www.thaifood.org; Pres. VILAI KIATSRICHART.

Thai Lac Association: 57/1 Soi Saphantia, Thanon Sipraya, Mahapreuktaram, Bangrak, Bangkok 10500; tel. (2) 233-4583; fax (2) 633-2913.

Thai Maize and Produce Traders' Association: Sathorn Thani II Bldg, 11th Floor, 92/26–27 Thanon Sathorn Nua, Bangrak, Bangkok 10500; tel. (2) 234-4387; fax (2) 236-8413.

Thai Pharmaceutical Manufacturers Association: 188/107 Thanon Charan Sanit Wong, Banchanglaw, Bangkoknoi, Bangkok 10700; tel. (2) 863-5106; fax (2) 863-5108; e-mail tpma@asiaaccess.net.th; f. 1969; Pres. CHERNPORN TENGAMNUAY.

Thai Rice Mills Association: 81–81/1 Trok Rongnamkheng, 24 Thanon Charoenkrung, Talat Noi, Samphanthawong, Bangkok 10100; internet www.thairicemillers.com; tel. (2) 235-7863; fax (2) 234-7286; Pres. WATTANA RATTANAWONG.

Thai Rubber Association: 45–47 Thanon Chotivithayakun 3, Hat Yai, Songkhla 90110; tel. (74) 429-011; fax (74) 429-312; e-mail webmaster@thainr.com; internet www.thainr.com; f. 1951; est. as Thai Rubber Traders' Asscn; Pres. LUKCHAI KITTIPHOL.

Thai Silk Association: Textile Industry Division, Soi Trimitr, Thanon Rama IV, Klongtoey, Bangkok 10110; tel. (2) 712-4328; fax (2) 258-8769; e-mail thsilkas@thaitextile.org; internet www.thaitextile.org/tsa; f. 1962; Pres. SETR VANIJVONGSE.

Thai Sugar Manufacturing Association: 78 Keatnakin Bldg, Captain Bush Lane, Thanon Charoenkrung, Bangkok 10500; tel. (2) 233-5858; fax (2) 233-4156; e-mail tsma2000@cscoms.com; internet www.thaisugar.org.

Thai Sugar Producers' Association: 8th Floor, Thai Ruam Toon Bldg, 794 Thanon Krung Kasem, Pomprap, Bangkok 10100; tel. (2) 282-0990; fax (2) 281-0342.

Thai Tapioca Trade Association: Sathorn Thani II Bldg, 20th Floor, 92/58 Thanon Sathorn Nua, Silom, Bangkok 10500; tel. (2) 234-4724; fax (2) 236-6084; e-mail ttta@loxinfo.co.th; internet www.ttta-tapioca.org; f. 1963; Pres. CHEN WONGBOONSIN.

Thai Textile Manufacturing Association: 454–460 Thanon Sukhumvit, Klongton, Klongtoey, Bangkok 10110; tel. (2) 258-2023; fax (2) 260-1525; e-mail ttma@thaitextile.org; internet www.thaitextile.org/ttma; f. 1960; Pres. PHONGSAK ASSAKUL.

Union Textile Merchants' Association (Thai Textile Merchants' Association): 562 Espreme Bldg, 4th Floor, Thanon Rajchawong, Samphanthawong, Bangkok 10100; tel. (2) 622-6711; fax (2) 622-6714; e-mail tma@thaitextile.org; internet www.thaitextile.org/tma; Chair. THAVON TANTISIRIVIT.

UTILITIES
Electricity

Electricity Generating Authority of Thailand (EGAT): 53 Thanon Charan Sanit Wong, Bang Kruai, Nothaburi, Bangkok 11130; tel. (2) 436-0000; fax (2) 436-4723; e-mail webmaster@egat.co.th; internet www.egat.co.th; f. 1969; Gov. SOMBAT SANTIJAREE.

Electricity Generating Public Co Ltd (EGCO): EGCO Tower, 222 Moo 5, Thanon Vibhavadi Rangsit, Tungsonghong, Laksi, Bangkok 10210; tel. (2) 998-5999; fax (2) 955-0956; e-mail corp_com@egco.com; internet www.egco.com; a subsidiary of the Electricity Generating Authority of Thailand (EGAT); 59% transferred to the private sector in 1994–96; 14.9%-owned by China Light and Power Co (Hong Kong); Chair. PORNCHAI RUJIPRAPA; Pres. VINIT TANGNOI.

The Metropolitan Electricity Authority: 30 Soi Chidlom, Thanon Ploenchit, Lumpini, Pathumwan, Bangkok 10330; tel. (2) 254-9550; fax (2) 251-9586; internet www.mea.or.th; f. 1958; one of the two main power distribution agencies in Thailand; Gov. PORNTHAPE THUNYAPONGCHAI.

The Provincial Electricity Authority: 200 Thanon Ngam Wongwan, Chatuchak, Bangkok 10900; tel. (2) 589-0100; fax (2) 589-4850; e-mail webmaster@pea.co.th; internet www.pea.co.th; f. 1960; one of the two main power distribution agencies in Thailand; Gov. ADISORN KIERTICHOKWIWAT.

Water

Metropolitan Waterworks Authority: 400 Thanon Prachachuen, Laksi, Bangkok 10210; tel. (2) 504-0123; fax (2) 503-9493; e-mail mwa1125@mwa.co.th; internet www.mwa.co.th; f. 1967; state-owned; provides water supply systems in Bangkok; Gov. CHAROEN CHAIKITTISILPA.

Provincial Waterworks Authority: 72 Thanon Chaengwattana, Don Muang, Bangkok 10210; tel. (2) 551-1020; fax (2) 552-1547; e-mail pr@pwa.co.th; internet www.pwa.co.th; f. 1979; provides water supply systems except in Bangkok Metropolis; Gov. CHAVALIT SARUN; Chair. SURA-AT THONGNIRAMOL.

CO-OPERATIVES

In January 2002 there were 5,617 co-operatives, with a combined membership in excess of 8m. people. Of the total number of co-operatives, 64% were in agriculture, 24% in thrift and credit, 8% in the consumer market and 4% in services.

THAILAND

Directory

TRADE UNIONS

Confederation of Thai Labour (CTL): 25/20 Thanon Sukhumvit, Viphavill Village, Tambol Paknam, Amphur Muang, Samutprakarn, Bangkok 10270; tel. (2) 756-5346; fax (2) 323-1074; internet www.ctl.or.th; represents 44 labour unions; Pres. MANAS PHOSORN.

Labour Congress of Thailand (LCT): 420/393–394 Thippavan Village 1, Thanon Teparak, Samrong-Nua, Muang, Samutprakarn, Bangkok 10270; tel. and fax (2) 384-6789; e-mail lct_org@hotmail.com; f. 1978; represents 224 labour unions, four labour federations and approx. 140,000 mems; Pres. PRATNENG SAENGSANK; Gen. Sec. SAMAM THOMYA.

National Congress of Private Employees of Thailand (NPET): 142/6 Thanon Phrathoonam Phrakanong, Phrakanong, Klongtoey, Bangkok 10110; tel. and fax (2) 392-9955; represents 31 labour unions; Pres. BANJONG PORNPATTANANIKOM.

National Congress of Thai Labour (NCTL): 1614/876 Samutprakarn Community Housing Project, Sukhumvit Highway Km 30, Tai Baan, Muang, Samutprakarn, Bangkok 10280; tel. (2) 389-5134; fax (2) 385-8975; represents 171 unions; Pres. PANAS THAILUAN.

National Free Labour Union Congress (NFLUC): 277 Moo 3, Thanon Ratburana, Bangkok 10140; tel. (2) 427-6506; fax (2) 428-4543; represents 51 labour unions; Pres. ANUSSAKDI BOONYAPRANAI.

National Labour Congress (NLC): 586/248–250 Moo 2, Mooban City Village, Thanon Sukhumvit, Bang Phu Mai, Mueng, Samutprakarn, Bangkok 10280; tel. and fax (2) 709-9426; represents 41 labour unions; Pres. CHIN THAPPHLI.

Thai Trade Union Congress (TTUC): 420/393–394 Thippavan Village 1, Thanon Teparak, Tambol Samrong-nua, Amphur Muang, Samutprakarn, Bangkok 10270; tel. and fax (2) 384-0438; f. 1983; represents 172 unions; Pres. PANIT CHAROENPHAO.

Thailand Council of Industrial Labour (TCIL): 99 Moo 4, Thanon Sukhaphibarn 2, Khannayao, Bungkum, Bangkok; tel. (2) 517-0022; fax (2) 517-0628; represents 23 labour unions; Pres. TAVEE DEEYING.

Transport

RAILWAYS

Thailand has a railway network of 4,429 km, connecting Bangkok with Chiang Mai, Nong Khai, Ubon Ratchathani, Nam Tok and towns on the isthmus.

State Railway of Thailand: 1 Thanon Rong Muang, Rong Muang, Pathumwan, Bangkok 10330; tel. (2) 220-4567; fax (2) 225-3801; e-mail info@railway.co.th; internet www.railway.co.th; f. 1897; 4,429 km of track in 2007; responsible for licensing a 4,044-km passenger and freight rail system, above ground; Chair. SIWA SAENGMANEE; Gov. BANCHA KONGNAKORN (acting).

Bangkok Mass Transit System Public Co Ltd: 1000 Thanon Phahonyothin, Chom Phon, Chatuchak, Bangkok 10900; tel. (2) 617-7300; fax (2) 617-7133; e-mail nuduan@bts.co.th; internet www.bts.co.th; f. 1992; responsible for the construction and management of the Skytrain, a two-line, 23.5-km elevated rail system, under the supervision of the Bangkok Metropolitan Area, the initial stage of which was opened in December 1999; Chair. KASAME CHATIKAVANIJ; Exec. Chair. and CEO KEEREE KANJANAPAS.

Mass Rapid Transit Authority of Thailand (MRTA): 175 Thanon Rama IX, Huay Kwang, Bangkok 10320; tel. (2) 612-2444; fax (2) 612-2436; e-mail pr@mrta.co.th; internet www.mrta.co.th; a 20-km subway system was opened in Bangkok in July 2004; as part of the planned extension of the mass rapid transit system to 291 km, was charged with the construction of three new lines, totalling 91 km in length: 27-km Blue Line (Hua Lamphong–Bang Khae; Bang Sue–Tha Phra); 24-km Orange Line (Bang Kapi–Bang Bumru); and 40-km Purple Line (Bang Yai–Rat Burana); Chair. KRIENGSAK LOHACHALA; Sec.-Gen. PRAPAT CHONGSANGUAN.

ROADS

The total length of the road network was an estimated 180,053 km in 2006. A network of toll roads has been introduced in Bangkok in an attempt to alleviate the city's severe congestion problems.

Bangkok Mass Transit Authority (BMTA): 131 Thanon Thiam Ruammit, Huay Kwang, Bangkok 10310; tel. (2) 246-0973; fax (2) 247-2189; e-mail cnai.bmta@motc.go.th; internet www.bmta.co.th; controls Bangkok's urban transport system; Chair. ATHIKHOM TONLES; Dir and Sec. PINATE PUAPATANAKUL.

Department of Highways: Thanon Sri Ayudhya, Ratchathewi, Bangkok 10400; tel. (2) 245-9912; e-mail doh9999@doh.go.th; internet www.doh.go.th; Dir-Gen. SONGSAK PHAECHAROEN.

Department of Land Transport: 1032 Thanon Phaholyothin, Chatuchak, Bangkok 10900; tel. (2) 272-5671; fax (2) 272-5680; e-mail admin@dlt.go.th; internet www.dlt.go.th; Dir-Gen. VICHAN KUNAGULSAWAT.

Department of Rural Roads: 218/1, Thanon Phra Ram VI, Phayathai, Bangkok 10400; tel. (2) 299-4591; fax (2) 299-4606; e-mail webmaster@dor.go.th; internet www.dor.go.th; f. 2002; Dir-Gen. RAPHIN CHARUTUL.

Expressway and Rapid Transit Authority of Thailand (ETA): 2380 Thanon Phaholyothin, Senanikhom, Chatuchak, Bangkok 10900; tel. (2) 579-5380; e-mail webmasters@eta.co.th; internet www.eta.co.th; f. 1972; Dir-Gen. PHACHOEN PHAIROJSAK.

SHIPPING

There is an extensive network of canals, providing transport for bulk goods. The port of Bangkok is an important shipping junction for South-East Asia, and consists of 37 berths for conventional and container vessels.

Marine Department: 1278 Thanon Yotha, Talardnoi, Samphanthawong, Bangkok 10100; tel. (2) 233-1311; fax (2) 236-7148; e-mail marine@md.go.th; internet www.md.go.th; Dir-Gen. TAWALYARAT ONSIRA.

Port Authority of Thailand: 444 Thanon Tarua, Klongtoey, Bangkok 10110; tel. (2) 269-3000; fax (2) 249-0885; e-mail info@port.co.th; internet www.port.co.th; 18 berths at Bangkok Port, 12 berths at Laem Chabang Port; originally scheduled for transfer to private sector in 1999, but plans have been repeatedly delayed; Chair. CHALOR KOTCHARAT; Dir-Gen. SUNIDA SAKULRATTANA.

Principal Shipping Companies

Jutha Maritime Public Co Ltd: Mano Tower, 2nd Floor, 153 Soi 39, Thanon Sukhumvit, Bangkok 10110; tel. (2) 260-0050; fax (2) 259-9825; e-mail office@jutha.co.th; internet www.jutha.co.th; services between Thailand, Malaysia, Korea, Japan and Viet Nam; Chair. Rear-Adm. CHANO PHENJATI; Man. Dir CHANET PHENJATI.

Precious Shipping Public Co Ltd: Cathay House, 7th Floor, 8/30 Thanon Sathorn Nua, Bangrak, Bangkok 10500; tel. (2) 696-8800; fax (2) 633-8460; e-mail psl@preciousshipping.com; internet www.preciousshipping.com; Chair. Adm. AMNARD CHANDANAMATTHA; Man. Dir HASHIM KHALID MOINUDDIN.

Regional Container Lines Public Co Ltd: Panjathani Tower, 30th Floor, 127/35 Thanon Ratchadaphisek, Chongnonsee Yannawa, Bangkok 10120; tel. (2) 296-1096; fax (2) 296-1098; e-mail rclbkk@rclgroup.com; internet www.rclgroup.com; Chair. KUA PHEK LONG; Pres. SUMATE TANTHUWANIT.

Thai International Maritime Enterprises Ltd: Sarasin Bldg, 5th Floor, 14 Thanon Surasak, Bangkok 10500; tel. (2) 236-8835; services from Bangkok to Japan; Chair. and Man. Dir SUN SUNDISAMRIT.

Thai Maritime Navigation Co Ltd: Manorom Bldg, 15th Floor, 51 Thanon Rama IV, Klongtoey, Bangkok 10110; tel. (2) 672-8690; fax (2) 249-0108; e-mail tmn@tmn.co.th; internet www.tmn.co.th; f. 1940; state-owned; services from Bangkok to Japan, the USA, Europe and ASEAN countries; Chair. NIPHON CHAKSUDUL; Sec.-Gen. SUWAPHAT SUVANNAKIJBORIHAN.

Thai Mercantile Marine Ltd: 599/1 Thanon Chua Phloeng, Klongtoey, Bangkok 10110; tel. (2) 240-2582; fax (2) 249-5656; e-mail tmmbkk@asiaaccess.net.th; f. 1967; services between Japan and Thailand; Chair. SUTHAM TANPHAIBUL; Man. Dir TANAN TANPHAIBUL.

Thoresen Thai Agencies Public Co Ltd: 26/26–27 Orakarn Bldg, 8th Floor, Soi Chidlom, Thanon Ploenchit, Kwang Lumpinee, Khet Pathumwan, Bangkok 10330; tel. (2) 254-8437; fax (2) 655-5631; e-mail tta@thoresen.com; internet www.thoresen.com; shipowner, liner operator, shipping agent (in Thailand and Viet Nam), ship repairs, offshore and diving services; Chair. M. R. CHANDRAM S. CHANDRATAT; Man. Dir M. L. CHANDCHUTHA CHANDRATAT.

Unithai Group: 11th Floor, 25 Alma Link Bldg, Soi Chidlom, Thanon Ploenchit, Pathumwan, Bangkok 10330; tel. (2) 254-8400; fax (2) 254-8424; e-mail info@unithai.com; internet www.unithai.com; regular containerized/break-bulk services to Europe, Africa and Far East; also bulk shipping/chartering; Chair. SIVAVONG CHANGKASIRI; CEO NARONG BOONYASAQUAN.

CIVIL AVIATION

Bangkok, Chiang Mai, Chiang Rai, Hat Yai, Phuket and Surat Thani airports are of international standard. U-Tapao is an alternative airport. Suvarnabhumi International Airport, a new facility located south-east of Bangkok, opened in September 2006, with an eventual capacity of 45m. passengers a year. Bangkok's former international airport at Don Muang was subsequently reopened to domestic commercial flights.

Airports of Thailand Public Co Ltd (AOT): 333 Thanon Cherdwutagard, Don Muang, Bangkok 10210; tel. (2) 535-1111; fax (2) 531-

THAILAND

5559; e-mail aotpr@airportthai.co.th; internet www.airportthai.co.th; f. 1998; Chair. PIYAPAN CHAMPASUT.

Department of Civil Aviation: 71 Soi Ngarmduplee, Thanon Rama IV, Tung Mahamek, Sathorn District, Bangkok 10120; tel. (2) 287-0320; fax (2) 286-3373; e-mail dca@aviation.go.th; internet www.aviation.go.th; f. 1963; Dir-Gen. CHAISAK ANGKASUWAN.

Bangkok Airways: 99 Mu 14, Thanon Vibhavadi Rangsit, Chom Phon, Chatuchak, Bangkok 10900; tel. (2) 265-5678; fax (2) 265-5500; e-mail reservation@bangkokair.com; internet www.bangkokair.com; f. 1968 as Sahakol Air; name changed as above in 1989; privately owned; scheduled and charter passenger services to 20 regional and domestic destinations; Pres. PUTTIPONG PRASARTTONG-OSOTH; CEO Dr PRASERT PRASARTTONG-OSOTH.

Nok Air: 89 Thanon Vibhavadi Rangsit, Bangkok 10900; tel. (2) 513-0121; fax (2) 513-0203; e-mail public.info@thaiairways.co.th; internet www.nokair.com; f. 2004; 39%-owned by Thai Airways International Public Co Ltd; flights to six domestic destinations; CEO PATEE SARASIN.

One-Two-Go: 18 Thanon Ratchadaphisek, Klongtoey, Bangkok 10110; tel. (2) 229-4260; fax (2) 229-4278; e-mail info@orient-thai.com; internet www.fly12go.com; f. 2003; subsidiary of Orient Thai Airlines; low-cost domestic flights; Chair. UDOM TANTIPRASONGCHAI.

Orient Thai Airlines: 138/70 17th Floor, Jewellery Centre, Thanon Nares, Bangrak, Bangkok 10500; tel. (2) 229-4260; fax (2) 229-4278; e-mail info@orient-thai.com; internet www.orient-thai.com; f. 1993 as Orient Express Air; domestic and international flights; CEO and Man. Dir UDOM TANTIPRASONGCHAI.

PB Air: 17th Floor, UBC2 Bldg, 591 Sukhumvit 33, Watanna, Bangkok 10110; tel. (2) 261-0271; fax (2) 261-0229; e-mail admin@pbair.com; internet www.pbair.com; f. 1990; scheduled domestic passenger services; Exec. Chair. CHATRACHAI BUNYA-ANANTA; Chair. PIYA BHIROM BHAKDI.

Phuket Air: 1168/102, 34th Floor, Lumpini Tower Bldg, Thanon Rama IV, Thungmahamek, Bangkok 10120; tel. (62) 679-8999; fax (62) 285-6408; e-mail info@phuketairlines.com; internet www.phuketairlines.com; f. 1999; international charter services; Pres. VIKROM AISIRI.

SGA Airlines: 19/18-19 Royal City Ave Block A, Thanon Phra Ram 9, Bangkapi, Huay Kwang, Bangkok 10310; tel. (2) 641-4190; fax (2) 641-4807; internet www.sga.co.th; f. 2002; scheduled and chartered domestic services; Pres. JAIN CHARNNARONG.

SkyStar Airways: 18 SCB Park Plaza, 18th Floor, Tower 2, Thanon Ratchadaphisek, Chatuchak, Bangkok 10900; tel. (2) 716-1288; fax (2) 716-1287; e-mail info@skystarairways.com; internet www.skystarairways.com; f. 2005; scheduled and charter flights to the Republic of Korea; Pres. Gen. ARCHAVIN SVETASRENI.

Thai AirAsia Co Ltd: 89/170, 9/F, Juthamas Bldg, Thanon Vibhavadi Rangsit, Talad Bang Khen, Laksi, Bangkok; internet www.airasia.com; f. 2004; 50% owned by Asia Aviation, 49% owned by Air Asia Sdn Bhd (Malaysia); low-cost domestic flights; Chair. ARAK CHOLTANON; CEO TASSAPON BIJLEVELD.

Thai Airways International Public Co Ltd (THAI): 89 Thanon Vibhavadi Rangsit, Bangkok 10900; tel. (2) 545-1000; fax (2) 545-3322; e-mail public.info@thaiairways.co.th; internet www.thaiair.com; f. 1960; 51% owned by the Ministry of Finance; shares listed in July 1991, began trading in July 1992; merged with Thai Airways Co in 1988; domestic services from Bangkok to 20 cities; international services to over 50 destinations in Australasia, Europe, North America and Asia; Chair. SURACHAI TANSITPONG; Pres. Air Chief Marshal NARONGSAK SANGAPONG.

Tourism

Thailand is a popular tourist destination, noted for its temples, palaces, beaches and islands. In 2006 tourist arrivals rose to 13.8m., from 11.6m. in the previous year. Revenue from tourism (including passenger transport) was an estimated US $15,653m. in 2006.

Tourism Authority of Thailand (TAT): 1600 Thanon Phetchaburi Tat Mai, Makkasan, Ratchathewi, Bangkok 10400; tel. (2) 250-5500; fax (2) 250-5511; e-mail center@tat.or.th; internet www.tat.or.th; f. 1960; Gov. SIRI MANONAN.

TIMOR-LESTE
(EAST TIMOR)

Introductory Survey

Location, Climate, Language, Religion, Flag, Capital

The Democratic Republic of Timor-Leste, which is styled Timor Loro Sa'e (Timor of the rising sun) in the principal indigenous language, Tetum, occupies the eastern half of the island of Timor, which lies off the north coast of Western Australia. The western half of the island is Indonesian territory and constitutes part of the East Nusa Tenggara Province. In addition to the eastern half of Timor island, the territory also includes an enclave around Oecusse (Oekussi) Ambeno on the north-west coast of the island, and the islands of Ataúro (Pulo Cambing) and Jaco (Pulo Jako). Timor's climate is dominated by intense monsoon rain, succeeded by a pronounced dry season. The north coast of the island has a brief rainy season from December to February; the south coast a double rainy season from December to June, with a respite in March. The mountainous spine of the island has heavy rains that feed torrential floods. Tetum and Portuguese are the official languages. More than 30 languages are in use in Timor-Leste. The predominant religion is Christianity; 86% of the population were adherents of Roman Catholicism in 1997. Islam and animism are also practised. A national flag was officially adopted on 20 May 2002. The flag (proportions 1 by 2) displays a black triangle at the hoist (approximately one-third of the length of the flag) overlapping a yellow triangle (approximately one-half of the length of the flag) on a red background. The black triangle bears a five-pointed white star with one point aimed at the upper hoist corner. The capital is Dili.

Recent History

The Portuguese began trading in Timor in about 1520, principally for sandalwood, and they later established settlements and several ports on the island. They were forced to move to the north and east of the island by the Dutch, who had arrived in the early part of the 18th century and had established themselves at Kupana in the south-west. The division of the island between Portugal and the Netherlands was formalized in a treaty of 1859, although the boundaries were modified slightly in 1904. Portuguese Timor and Macao were administered as a single entity until 1896, when Portuguese Timor became a separate province. The eastern half remained a Portuguese overseas province when the Dutch recognized the western area as part of Indonesia in 1949.

The military coup in Portugal in April 1974 was followed by increased political activity in Portuguese Timor. In August 1975 the União Democrática Timorense (UDT—Timorese Democratic Union) demanded independence for Timor. The UDT allied with two other parties, the Associação Popular Democrática de Timor (APODETI—Popular Democratic Association of Timor) and the Klibur Oan Timor Asuwain (KOTA—Association of Timorese Heroes) against the alleged threat of a Communist regime being established by the Frente Revolucionária do Timor Leste Independente (Fretilin—Revolutionary Front for an Independent East Timor), and fighting broke out. The UDT forces were supported by the Indonesians. Gains on both sides were uneven, with Fretilin in control of Dili in mid-September. In the same month the Portuguese administration abandoned the capital and moved to the offshore island of Ataúro. A Portuguese attempt to arrange peace talks was rejected in October. The Indonesians intervened directly and by the beginning of December Indonesian troops controlled the capital. In November Portuguese-Indonesian peace talks in Rome were unsuccessful, and diplomatic relations were suspended after Indonesian military involvement. Two meetings of the UN Security Council voted for immediate withdrawal of Indonesian troops. Fretilin's unilateral declaration of independence in November was recognized in December by the People's Republic of China. In December the enclave of Oecusse (Oekussi) Ambeno in West Timor was declared part of Indonesian territory. In May 1976 the People's Representative Council of East Timor voted for integration with Indonesia. However, the UN did not recognize the composition of the Council as being representative, and by mid-1976 the Portuguese had not formally ceded the right to govern, although they had no remaining presence in the territory.

In July 1976 East Timor was declared the 27th province of Indonesia. Human rights organizations claimed that as many as 200,000 people, from a total population of 650,000, might have been killed by the Indonesian armed forces during the annexation. In February 1983 the UN Commission on Human Rights adopted a resolution affirming East Timor's right to independence and self-determination. In September, following a five-month cease-fire (during which government representatives negotiated with Fretilin), the armed forces launched a major new offensive. The rebels suffered a serious set-back in August 1985, when the Australian Government recognized Indonesia's incorporation of East Timor. In November 1988 Gen. Suharto, the President of Indonesia, visited East Timor, prior to announcing that travel restrictions (in force since the annexation in 1976) were to be withdrawn. The territory was opened to visitors in December. In October 1989 the Pope visited East Timor, as part of a tour of Indonesia, and made a plea to the Government to halt violations of human rights. In November 1990 the Government rejected proposals by the military commander of Fretilin, José Alexandre (subsequently known as Kay Rala and also as 'Xanana') Gusmão, for unconditional peace negotiations aimed at ending the armed struggle in East Timor.

In 1991 tension in East Timor increased prior to a proposed visit by a Portuguese parliamentary delegation. Some Timorese alleged that the armed forces had initiated a campaign of intimidation to discourage demonstrations during the Portuguese visit. The mission, which was to have taken place in November, was postponed, owing to Indonesia's objection to the inclusion of an Australian journalist who was a prominent critic of Indonesia's policies in East Timor. In November the armed forces fired on a peaceful demonstration (believed to have been originally organized to coincide with the Portuguese visit) at the funeral of a separatist sympathizer in Dili. The Indonesian Armed Forces (ABRI), which admitted killing 20 civilians, claimed that the attack had been provoked by armed Fretilin activists. Independent observers and human rights groups refuted this and estimated the number of deaths at between 100 and 180. There were also subsequent allegations of the summary execution of as many as 100 witnesses. Under intense international pressure, Suharto established a National Investigation Commission. However, the impartiality of the Commission was challenged on the grounds that it excluded non-governmental organizations, and Fretilin announced that it would boycott the investigation. Despite this, the Commission's findings received cautious foreign approbation, as they were mildly critical of ABRI and stated that 50 people had died, and 90 disappeared, in the massacre. The senior military officers in East Timor were replaced, and 14 members of the armed forces were tried by a military tribunal. The most severe penalty received by any of the soldiers involved was 18 months' imprisonment; this contrasted starkly with the sentences of convicted demonstrators, which ranged from five years' to life imprisonment.

In July 1992 Indonesia and Portugal agreed to resume discussions on East Timor under the auspices of the UN Secretary-General. In August the UN General Assembly adopted its first resolution condemning Indonesia's violations of fundamental human rights in East Timor. In September the appointment of Abílio Soares as Governor of East Timor provoked widespread criticism in the province; although Soares was a native of East Timor, he was a leading advocate of the Indonesian occupation. In October the US Congress suspended defence training aid to Indonesia, in protest at the killing of separatist demonstrators in November 1991. In October 1992, prior to the anniversary of the massacre, Amnesty International reported that hundreds of suspected supporters of independence had been arrested and tortured to prevent a commemorative demonstration.

In November 1992 Xanana Gusmão was arrested. He was subsequently taken to Jakarta, where he was to be tried in

February 1993 on charges of subversion and illegal possession of firearms. Two weeks after his capture, Gusmão publicly recanted his opposition to Indonesian rule in East Timor and advised Fretilin members to surrender. However, it transpired that he was co-operating with the authorities only in order to gain the opportunity to speak publicly at a later date. In May Gusmão was found guilty of rebellion, conspiracy, attempting to establish a separate state and illegal possession of weapons, and was condemned to life imprisonment. The sentence was commuted to 20 years by Suharto in August. During the same month it was announced that all government combat forces were to be withdrawn from East Timor, leaving only troops involved in development projects. In September, however, the acting leader of Fretilin, Konis Santana, declared that, contrary to announcements, the Indonesians were renewing their forces in East Timor and that killings and atrocities continued.

In December 1993 Xanana Gusmão managed to convey letters to the Portuguese Government and the International Commission of Jurists demanding an annulment of his trial, owing to the lack of impartiality of his defence lawyer. The Government subsequently banned Gusmão from receiving visitors. In January 1994 Indonesia announced to the UN Secretary-General's envoy that it would facilitate access to East Timor by human rights and UN organizations. In May, however, a privately organized human rights conference being held in the Philippines, entitled the Asia-Pacific Conference on East Timor, provoked diplomatic tension with the Indonesian Government, which had attempted to force the abandonment of the conference. The outcome of the conference was the establishment of an Asia-Pacific coalition on East Timor, which consisted mainly of non-governmental organizations active in the region.

In July 1994 the Indonesian authorities suppressed a demonstration in Dili, following weeks of increasing tension in the capital; at least three people were reportedly killed during the protest. In August it was reported that the armed forces had held talks with Xanana Gusmão, included in which was the discussion of the possibility of holding a referendum under the auspices of the UN to determine the future status of the disputed territory. The Indonesian Minister of Foreign Affairs, Ali Alatas, held discussions in October in New York, USA, with José Ramos Horta, the Secretary for International Relations of Fretilin, the first such talks to be officially recognized. At the beginning of November President Suharto agreed to hold talks with exiled East Timorese dissidents. However, the Government's increasingly conciliatory position on East Timor was reported largely to be a superficial attempt to improve the country's human rights image prior to the holding of the Asia-Pacific Economic Co-operation (APEC, see p. 185) summit meeting in Bogor, 60 km south of Jakarta, in mid-November.

In January 1995 Alatas, the Portuguese Minister of Foreign Affairs and the UN Secretary-General met in Geneva, Switzerland, for the fifth round of talks on East Timor. Agreement was reached to convene a meeting between separatist and pro-integrationist Timorese activists under the auspices of the UN, called the All-Inclusive Intra-East Timorese Dialogue (AETD). The AETD, which was held in June 1995, March 1996 and October 1997, failed to achieve any conclusive progress. The sixth and seventh rounds of talks between the Portuguese and Indonesian ministers responsible for foreign affairs took place in July 1995 and January 1996, again with little progress.

In September 1995 the worst rioting that year took place in protest against Indonesian Muslim immigrants, following an Indonesian prison official's alleged insult to Roman Catholicism. Mosques and Muslim businesses were burned, and some Muslims were forced to flee the island. Further riots erupted in October, in which rival groups of separatists and integrationists clashed on the streets. The Roman Catholic Apostolic Administrator in Dili, the Rt Rev. Carlos Filipe Ximenes Belo, persuaded the rioters to return home following an agreement with ABRI; however, the agreement was subsequently broken by the armed forces, who arrested more than 250 alleged rioters.

From September 1995 East Timorese activists began forcing entry into foreign embassies in Jakarta and appealing for political asylum. They were granted asylum by the Portuguese, who were still officially recognized by the UN as the administrative power in East Timor. The Indonesian Government permitted the asylum-seekers to leave, but denied that there was any persecution in East Timor. The culmination of the successful campaign was the storming in December of the Dutch and Russian embassies by 58 and 47 activists respectively. The demonstrators, some of whom were non-Timorese and belonged to a radical group called the People's Democratic Union, demanded unsuccessfully a meeting with the UN High Commissioner for Human Rights (UNHCHR, see p. 51), José Ayala Lasso, who was visiting Indonesia and who, following a brief visit to East Timor, confirmed the occurrence of severe violations of human rights in the province.

In February 1996 President Suharto and the Portuguese Prime Minister met in Bangkok, Thailand (the first meeting on the subject of East Timor by heads of government). During the negotiations Portugal offered to re-establish diplomatic links in return for the release of Xanana Gusmão and the guarantee of human rights in East Timor. International awareness of East Timor was heightened in October, when Bishop Belo and José Ramos Horta were jointly awarded the Nobel Prize for Peace. The Indonesian Government, displeased with the Nobel committee's choice, declared that there would be no change in its policy on East Timor. Four days after the announcement of the award, Suharto visited East Timor for the first time in eight years.

Following the announcement of the Nobel Peace Prize, Belo repeated demands that the Government conduct a referendum on the issue of autonomy for East Timor. In November 1996 he became involved in a controversy regarding an interview that he had given to a German periodical, *Der Spiegel*, which quoted several controversial remarks, allegedly made by Belo, about the treatment of the East Timorese people by the Indonesian Government and ABRI. Belo denied having made the remarks, but was requested to appear before a parliamentary commission in Jakarta to explain the matter. This controversy, and the temporary confiscation of Belo's passport by the Indonesian authorities (which threatened to prevent Belo's visit to Norway to receive the Nobel award), prompted five days of demonstrations in his support in Dili. The rallies were reportedly the largest since 1975, but were conducted peacefully.

The award of the Nobel Peace Prize to Ramos Horta proved even more controversial. The Governor of East Timor accused Ramos Horta of ordering the torture and killing of East Timorese people. Ramos Horta himself declared that the award should have been made to Xanana Gusmão and invited the Indonesian Government to enter into serious negotiations on the future of East Timor. Ramos Horta was banned from visiting the Philippines for the duration of an APEC summit meeting which took place there in late 1996; this ban was subsequently extended.

In November 1996 the Indonesian Government withdrew permission for foreign journalists to visit East Timor, where they had planned to attend a press conference conducted by Belo. In December Ramos Horta and Belo attended the Nobel Prize ceremony in Oslo, Norway. Riots in Dili (following a gathering of Belo's supporters to welcome him upon his return) resulted in the death of a member of ABRI; it was reported later in the month that at least one East Timorese citizen had been killed by the Indonesian authorities in a raid to capture those believed to be responsible for the soldier's death. (However, it was generally recognized by non-governmental organizations working in East Timor that the Indonesian authorities had become more lenient about allowing demonstrations in 1996.)

Following an increase in clashes between resistance forces and ABRI prior to the general election, in June 1997 a military commander of Fretilin, David Alex, was apprehended by the Indonesian armed forces. His subsequent death in custody was highly controversial; resistance groups rejected the official explanation that he had been fatally injured in a clash with security forces and claimed that he had been tortured to death. Guerrilla activity subsequently intensified and in September at least seven Indonesian soldiers were killed in a clash with resistance forces. Further fighting took place in November and December.

In November 1997 the Australia-East Timor Association released a report cataloguing human rights abuses perpetrated by members of the Indonesian armed forces against Timorese women; abuses cited in the report included enforced prostitution, rape and compulsory sterilization programmes. Also in November shots were fired when Indonesian troops stormed the campus of the University of East Timor in Dili, following a vigil held by students to commemorate the massacre in Dili in 1991. According to reports, at least one student was killed in the incident, a number of others were injured and many were arrested. Belo accused the Indonesian security forces of having used 'excessive force', and this was confirmed by a report made by the Indonesian National Commission on Human Rights in early December. Also in December the Commission demanded the abolition of the country's anti-subversion legislation. In the same month two Timorese were sentenced to death under the legislation for their part in an ambush of election security officials earlier in the year, prompting threats of increased guerrilla activities by separatist forces, and a further four were sentenced to 12 years' imprisonment for taking part in armed resistance operations. Meanwhile, Abílio Soares, who had been re-elected as Governor of East Timor in September, ordered the arrest of the leaders of the recently formed Movement for the Reconciliation and Unity of the People of East Timor (MRUPT), which he declared to be a proscribed movement.

In January 1998 it was announced that a Timorese resistance congress that was due to be held in Portugal in March was to be replaced by a national convention to ensure the participation of the UDT. The convention, held in April, unanimously approved the 'Magna Carta' of East Timor, a charter intended to provide the basis for the constitution of future self-determination within the territory, and ratified plans for the establishment of the Conselho Nacional de Resistência Timorense (National Council of Timorese Resistance), a body intended to give the Timorese resistance movement a single national structure and to bring together representatives of the defunct National Council of Maubere Resistance (CNRM), Fretilin and the UDT. Xanana Gusmão was appointed President of the new Conselho Nacional de Resistência Timorense, and Ramos Horta was named as Vice-President. In March 1998, meanwhile, Konis Santana, the acting military leader of Fretilin, died following an accident; Taur Matan Ruak was appointed as his successor.

The accession of B. J. Habibie to the Indonesian presidency in May 1998 raised hopes that independence for East Timor might be granted in the near future. However, while President Habibie publicly suggested that the territory might be given a new 'special' status within Indonesia and that troops might be withdrawn, there was no initial indication that the Government was contemplating independence for the territory. While a number of prominent political prisoners were released soon after Habibie replaced Suharto as President, Xanana Gusmão's 20-year sentence was reduced by a mere four months. Following the killing of an East Timorese youth by Indonesian soldiers in June, the Government renewed efforts to demonstrate its conciliatory position and, in late July, effected a much-publicized withdrawal of a limited number of troops from the territory. However, opposition groups subsequently claimed that fresh troops were being sent by the Indonesian Government to replace those leaving (a claim denied by Indonesian military leaders).

In August 1998 it was announced that Indonesia and Portugal had agreed to hold discussions on the possibility of 'wide-ranging' autonomy for East Timor, and in early November the UN was reported to be opening discussions with the two countries regarding a UN plan for extensive autonomy for the territory. Following an outbreak of severe violence in the Alas region of East Timor later that month, in which 82 people were reported to have been killed, Portugal suspended its involvement in the talks; however, in January 1999 it was announced that the talks were to resume. During his visit to East Timor in December 1998, UN special envoy Jamsheed Marker held talks with both Gusmão and Belo; in the same month, Gusmão reportedly advocated that the Timorese people should consider the UN's proposal for autonomy, but only as a transitional stage prior to the holding of a referendum (the possibility of which, in December, was still ruled out by the Indonesian Government).

In January 1999 the Australian Government announced a significant change in its policy on East Timor, stating that it intended actively to promote 'self-determination' in the territory (although the precise intended meaning of 'self-determination' remained unclear). Later in the same month, total independence for East Timor in the near future emerged as an apparent possibility when, in its boldest move to date to appease the East Timorese and the international community, the Indonesian Government suggested that a vote might be held in the national legislature, the Majelis Permusyawaratan Rakyat (MPR, People's Consultative Assembly), following the election to the House of Representatives (part of the MPR) scheduled for June, on the issue of Indonesia's granting independence to the territory. As a result of a request from the UN Secretary-General, Kofi Annan, the Government also announced that it was to allow Xanana Gusmão to serve the remainder of his 20-year prison sentence under house arrest in Jakarta. Following the Government's announcement regarding the possibility of independence for East Timor, a number of outbreaks of violence, attributed to supporters of the territory's integration with Indonesia, were reported to have occurred.

On 27 January 1999 the Indonesian Government unexpectedly announced that, if the East Timorese voted to reject Indonesia's proposals for autonomy, it would consider granting independence to the province. Although the Indonesian Government was initially opposed to a referendum on the issue of independence for East Timor, it signed an agreement with Portugal on 5 May, giving its assent to a process of 'popular consultation' taking the form of a UN-supervised poll to determine the future status of East Timor. (In an Australian television interview in November 2008 Habibie revealed that his decision to allow a referendum was due to heavy influence from the Australian Prime Minister, John Howard, who had written to Habibie suggesting that East Timor be given the opportunity to vote on independence.) The UN Mission in East Timor (UNAMET) was established by the UN Security Council in June to organize the poll in which the East Timorese could opt for a form of political autonomy or for independence. The 'popular consultation' was initially scheduled to be held on 8 August, and all East Timorese, including those living in exile, were to be allowed to participate in the ballot.

Following the announcement of the scheduled referendum, violence in the territory escalated. Anti-independence militia groups based within East Timor initiated a campaign of violence and intimidation in advance of the poll, which included summary killings, kidnappings, harassment and the forced recruitment of young East Timorese. The Indonesian military itself was discovered to be not only supporting but also recruiting, training and organizing many of the militias. Violence continued to escalate throughout the territory during April and May 1999. In one incident in April anti-independence militia members massacred 57 people in a churchyard in the town of Liquiça (Likisia); further massacres were reported to have occurred in other areas, including Dili. Also in April Xanana Gusmão (now under house arrest in Jakarta) responded to the increasing violence from anti-independence militias by reversing his previous position and urging guerrillas in Fretilin's military wing, the Forças Armadas Libertação Nacional de Timor Leste (Falintil), to resume their struggle. Although rival pro-independence and integrationist factions signed a peace accord in June supporting a cease-fire and disarmament in advance of the scheduled referendum, the violence continued unabated.

The escalating violence in the territory, together with logistical difficulties, led the UN to postpone the referendum to 21 August 1999 and then to 30 August. Although intimidation and violence by the militias continued, the referendum proceeded on 30 August. About 98.5% of those eligible to vote participated in the poll, which resulted in an overwhelming rejection, by 78.5% of voters, of the Indonesian Government's proposals for autonomy and in the endorsement of independence for East Timor. However, the announcement of the result of the referendum precipitated a rapid descent into anarchy. Pro-Jakarta militias embarked upon a campaign of murder and destruction in which hundreds of civilians were killed; as many as 500,000 (according to the UN) were forced to flee their homes, and many buildings were destroyed in arson attacks. While many of those who were displaced from their homes sought refuge in the hills, about one-half were estimated by the UN to have left the territory (a large number having entered West Timor), some involuntarily. In one incident during the campaign of extreme violence that followed the announcement of the result of the referendum, anti-independence militia members stormed the residence of Bishop Belo, evicting at gunpoint some 6,000 refugees who had sought shelter in the compound; the home of the bishop was burned down and dozens of East Timorese were reported to have been killed in the attack. Bishop Belo was evacuated to Australia, while Xanana Gusmão (who was released from house arrest in Jakarta by the Indonesian Government on 7 September) took refuge in the British embassy in Jakarta. Thousands of civilians besieged the UN compound in Dili, the premises of other international agencies, churches and police stations, seeking protection from the indiscriminate attacks of the militias. On 7 September martial law was declared in the territory, and a curfew was imposed. However, the violence continued unabated, and in mid-September, following international condemnation of the situation and intense diplomatic pressure, the Indonesian Government reversed its earlier opposition to a proposal by the Australian Government and agreed to permit the deployment of a multinational peace-keeping force. As the massacre of civilians continued, thousands of refugees were airlifted to safety in northern Australia, along with the remaining employees of the UN (many local staff members of UNAMET were among the victims of the violence); shortly after the UN withdrew its staff, anti-independence militia members set fire to the UN compound in Dili. Meanwhile, aid agencies warned that as many as 300,000 East Timorese people would starve if humanitarian assistance were not urgently provided.

The first contingent of several thousand UN peace-keeping troops, forming the International Force for East Timor (Interfet), was deployed in the territory on 20 September 1999. Led by Australia, which committed 4,500 troops, the force gradually restored order. A week later the Indonesian armed forces formally relinquished responsibility for security to the multinational force. At the end of October, after 24 years as an occupying force, the last Indonesian soldiers left East Timor. In late September Indonesia and Portugal reiterated their agreement for the transfer of authority in East Timor to the UN. On 19 October the result of the referendum was ratified by the MPR, thus permitting East Timor's accession to independence to proceed. Shortly thereafter, on 25 October, the UN Security Council established the UN Transitional Administration in East Timor (UNTAET—subsequently the UN Mission of Support in East Timor—UNMISET) as an integrated peace-keeping operation fully responsible for the administration of East Timor during its transition to independence. UNTAET, with an initial mandate until 31 January 2001, was to exercise all judicial and executive authority in East Timor, to undertake the establishment and training of a new police force, and to assume responsibility for the co-ordination and provision of humanitarian assistance and emergency rehabilitation; the transfer of command of military operations in the territory from Interfet to the UNTAET peace-keeping force was completed on 23 February 2000. Meanwhile, the UN also began a large-scale emergency humanitarian relief effort; however, many displaced and homeless East Timorese remained without access to adequate food supplies, shelter and basic health care facilities.

Following reports that in mid-October 1999 Indonesian troops and militias had entered the isolated East Timorese enclave of Oecusse (situated within West Timor) and allegedly massacred around 50 people, Interfet troops were deployed in Oecusse; most of the enclave's population of 57,000 were believed to have been removed to refugee camps in West Timor, and by early November only 10,000 of its citizens had been accounted for. Following his popularly acclaimed return to Dili in October, Xanana Gusmão met with the UNTAET Transitional Administrator, Sérgio Vieira de Mello, in November, and reportedly communicated the concerns of local East Timorese organizations that they were being marginalized by UNTAET officials. In late November he visited Jakarta in order to establish relations with the Indonesian Government, and in early December he visited Australia, where he met with representatives of the Australian Government to discuss the Timor Gap Treaty. (The Treaty, which had been concluded between Australia and Indonesia in 1991, provided a framework for petroleum and gas exploration in the maritime zone between Australia and East Timor and for the division of any resulting royalties between Australia and Indonesia. However, Indonesia ceased to be party to the original Treaty when it relinquished control of East Timor in October 1999, and the transitional administration in East Timor subsequently expressed a desire to renegotiate the terms of the Treaty, which the UN considered to have no legal standing, as Indonesian sovereignty over East Timor had never been recognized by the international body. In February 2000 a memorandum of understanding (MOU) relating to the Treaty was signed by the Australian Government and East Timor's UN administrators, temporarily maintaining the arrangement for the division of royalties (although between Australia and East Timor rather than Australia and Indonesia). East Timor received its first payment of royalties from Australia under the MOU in October 2000. In the same month, however, the formal renegotiation of the Treaty began, with East Timor requesting the redrawing of the boundaries covered by the Treaty and a larger share of petroleum and gas royalties. Following independence in May 2002 both countries formally signed the Treaty. However, owing to prolonged negotiations over the division of royalties, Australia did not ratify the agreement until March 2003.)

On 1 December 1999 José Ramos Horta returned to East Timor after 24 years of exile. Ramos Horta, who commanded much popular support, urged the East Timorese people to show forgiveness towards their former oppressors and called for reconciliation between Indonesia and East Timor. On 11 December Vieira de Mello convened the first meeting of the National Consultative Council (NCC) in Dili; the 15-member Council, comprising members of the Conselho Nacional de Resistência Timorense and other East Timorese political representatives as well as UNTAET officials, was established in late 1999 to advise UNTAET.

A number of mass graves containing the bodies of suspected victims of the violence perpetrated by the anti-independence militias both before and after the holding of the referendum in August 1999 were discovered in East Timor (including two in the Oecusse enclave) in late 1999 and early 2000. In December 1999 Sonia Picado Sotela, the Chair of the International Commission of Inquiry in East Timor, confirmed that the team of UN investigators had discovered evidence of 'systematic killing'.

In January 2000 a panel appointed by the Indonesian Government to investigate human rights abuses in East Timor delivered its report to the Indonesian Attorney-General. The panel reportedly named 24 individuals whom it recommended should be prosecuted for their alleged involvement in violations of human rights in the territory. One of those named was the former Minister of Defence and Security and Commander-in-Chief of the Indonesian armed forces, Gen. Wiranto, who had since been appointed Co-ordinating Minister for Political, Legal and Security Affairs in the Indonesian Government; also named were a number of senior military officers, as well as leaders of the pro-Jakarta militias responsible for the extreme violence perpetrated during the period following the referendum. However, pro-independence leaders in East Timor strongly criticized the report as inadequate. In the same month the International Commission of Inquiry in East Timor recommended that the UN establish an independent international body to investigate allegations of human rights violations in East Timor, and an international tribunal to deal with the cases of those accused by the investigators. In February the recently appointed President of Indonesia, Abdurrahman Wahid, visited East Timor and publicly apologized for the atrocities committed by the Indonesian armed forces during the Republic's occupation of the territory. Wahid reaffirmed the commitment of the Indonesian Government to the prosecution of any individuals implicated in the violation of human rights in East Timor. In the same month Wahid suspended Gen. Wiranto from the Indonesian Government. (Wiranto subsequently resigned in May.) The UN Secretary-General, Kofi Annan, made an official visit to East Timor in mid-February, during which he pledged that investigations into violations of human rights in the territory would be carried out.

In April 2000 UNTAET signed an agreement with the Indonesian Government regarding the extradition to East Timor of Indonesian citizens who were to be charged in connection with the violence of 1999. In July 2000 a team from the Indonesian Attorney-General's Office visited East Timor to investigate a limited number of cases of human rights violations. However, relations between East Timor and Indonesia remained tense, and the introduction in August 2000 (in the closing stages of the annual session of the country's principal legislative body, the MPR) of an amendment to Indonesia's Constitution providing for the exclusion of military personnel from retroactive prosecution prompted fears among many international observers that the possibility of the prosecution of members of the Indonesian military believed responsible for recent human rights abuses in East Timor would be placed in serious jeopardy (despite the suggestions of senior Indonesian legislators that the amendment would probably not apply to crimes such as genocide, war crimes and terrorism). In September the Indonesian Attorney-General's Office named 19 people whom it suspected of involvement in the violence of 1999. While human rights groups in both East Timor and Indonesia welcomed the publication of the list, which included the names of several former high-ranking members of the Indonesian armed forces, there was widespread disappointment that Gen. Wiranto was not among those named.

In June 2000 an agreement was reached between UNTAET and East Timorese leaders on the formation of a new transitional coalition Government, in which the two sides were to share political responsibility. The Cabinet of the new transitional Government, which was formally appointed in July, initially included four East Timorese cabinet ministers: João Carrascalão, President of the UDT and a Vice-President of the Conselho Nacional de Resistência Timorense, who was allocated responsibility for infrastructure; Mari Alkatiri, Secretary-General of Fretilin, who was appointed Minister for Economic Affairs;

Father Filomeno Jacob, who was appointed to oversee social affairs; and Ana Pessôa, who was placed in charge of internal administration. The new Cabinet also included four international representatives. Mariano Lopes da Cruz, an East Timorese national, was appointed as Inspector-General. It was reported that Xanana Gusmão, while holding no formal position in the new Government, was to be consulted on an informal basis by Sérgio Vieira de Mello (who was to retain ultimate control over the approval of any draft legislation proposed to the Cabinet) with respect to all political decisions. In October the Cabinet was expanded to nine members, with the appointment of José Ramos Horta as Minister of Foreign Affairs.

In mid-July 2000 UNTAET approved the establishment of a 'National Council' to advise the new Cabinet. The East Timorese National Council, the membership of which was expanded from 33 to 36 in October, consisted of a selection of East Timorese representatives from the political, religious and private sectors. The new National Council was inaugurated on 23 October and replaced the 15-member NCC. In the same month Xanana Gusmão was elected to lead the National Council.

In August 2000, meanwhile, Xanana Gusmão retired as the Military Commander of Falintil, in order to concentrate on his political role in the process of guiding East Timor towards full independence, relinquishing control of the guerrilla army to his deputy, Taur Matan Ruak. Initially, the future of Falintil appeared uncertain, and the refusal of the UN to allow the active involvement of the unit in attempts to combat incursions by Indonesian paramilitaries into East Timor led Gusmão to voice indirect criticism of the international organization in his resignation speech. In February 2001, however, a new East Timorese Defence Force (ETDF) was established, consisting of an initial 650 recruits drawn exclusively from the ranks of Falintil, which was itself to be dissolved. The former Military Commander of the guerrilla army, Taur Matan Ruak, was promoted to the rank of Brigadier-General and appointed to command the new force. Meanwhile, a fund was established to finance the support and retraining of an estimated 1,000 Falintil veterans who were to be demobilized. Training of the new Defence Force was to be conducted by Portugal and Australia; its role was described as that of 'policing', with the defence of the territory remaining the responsibility of UNTAET peace-keeping troops.

In December 2000 four of the five East Timorese members of the transitional Cabinet threatened to resign, reportedly in protest at their treatment by the UN. The ministers, who allegedly claimed that they were merely 'puppet ministers' in the new coalition Government, demanded further clarification of the legal status of the Cabinet and of their authority as individual cabinet ministers, and called for the establishment of a more clearly defined relationship between UNTAET and the Cabinet. Further complaints about UNTAET's treatment of East Timorese officials were voiced at a donors' conference for East Timor held in the same month, and press reports suggested the existence of a level of public resentment of the UN's presence in East Timor. However, in January 2001 Ramos Horta warned that any attempt to scale down the UN's presence in East Timor would destabilize the territory's progression towards independence. In late January 2001 the UN Security Council extended UNTAET's mandate (which had initially been scheduled to expire on 31 January 2001) until 31 January 2002. However, it was acknowledged that modifications of the mandate might be necessary to take into account developments in East Timor's progression towards full independence and, in January 2002, the mandate was extended until 20 May 2002, the date set for independence. From August 2000, meanwhile, in a move that allowed for greater formal East Timorese influence in the governing of the territory during the period preceding the territory's accession to full independence, a process commenced whereby the transitional Government began to be redefined as the East Timorese Transitional Administration (ETTA). Consisting of both UNTAET and East Timorese staff, ETTA was composed of the transitional Cabinet, the National Council and the judiciary. Final authority over ETTA rested with the Special Representative of the UN Secretary-General and Transitional Administrator, Sérgio Vieira de Mello.

In February 2001 legislation providing for an election to an 88-seat Constituent Assembly, to be conducted on 30 August, was approved. The single chamber was to comprise 75 deputies elected on a national basis, using proportional representation, and one elected delegate from each of East Timor's 13 districts, chosen on a 'first-past-the-post' basis. The members of the Constituent Assembly were to be responsible for the preparation and adoption of a constitution, which would require the endorsement of at least 60 members. Meanwhile, a National Constitutional Commission, comprising representatives of various groups, was to be established in order to facilitate consultation with the people of East Timor.

In March 2001 Xanana Gusmão tendered his resignation as Speaker of the National Council, having become disaffected by the stagnation of the political process. At the same time he announced that he would not stand for President in the forthcoming election for the post, despite commanding an overwhelming level of public support for his candidacy. In April UNTAET announced that José Ramos Horta would serve as Gusmão's replacement on the National Council, prompting his resignation as the Minister for Foreign Affairs (the two posts could not be held simultaneously). However, in the 9 April election for the post of Speaker, Manuel Carrascalão emerged victorious, defeating Ramos Horta, and criticized UNTAET for supporting his rival. Two weeks later José Ramos Horta resigned from the National Council and resumed his position in the transitional Cabinet. In June the Conselho Nacional de Resistência Timorense announced its dissolution, reportedly in order to enable the groups of which it was comprised to evolve into fully independent political parties, and, in August, Gusmão finally yielded to immense popular pressure and international encouragement and announced his intention to stand for the presidency in 2002.

On 30 August 2001 91.3% of the eligible populace turned out to vote in the country's first free parliamentary election. Fretilin secured 55 of the 88 seats available in the Constituent Assembly, commanding 57% of the votes cast. In second place, with seven seats, was the Partido Democrático (PD, Democratic Party). The Partido Social Democrata (PSD, Social Democrat Party) and the Associação Social-Democrata Timorense (ASDT, Timor Social Democratic Association) won six seats each. In September Sérgio Vieira de Mello swore in the members of the Constituent Assembly, and five days later the second transitional Government was appointed. Mari Alkatiri of Fretilin was appointed leader of the Cabinet and retained the economy portfolio. José Ramos Horta continued as Minister for Foreign Affairs. Of 20 available government positions, nine were allocated to Fretilin, two to the PD and the remaining nine to independents and various experts. In October the Constituent Assembly appointed a committee to oversee the drafting of the Constitution, taking into account the views of over 36,000 East Timorese summarized in reports presented by 13 Constitutional Commissions. In November 2001 the Assembly approved the structure of the draft Constitution.

In December 2000 UNTAET issued its first indictments for crimes committed against humanity in connection with the violence that had surrounded the referendum in 1999, charging 11 people (including an officer of the Indonesian special forces) with the murder of nine civilians in September 1999. In January 2001 an East Timor court sentenced a former pro-Jakarta militia member to 12 years' imprisonment for the murder of a village chief in September 1999, marking the first successful prosecution related to the violence of 1999. In September 2001 the UN filed 'extermination' charges against nine militiamen and two Indonesian soldiers accused of murdering 65 people two years previously. In October, in the first civil case of its kind, a US federal court awarded six East Timorese a total of US $66m. in damages after Indonesian Gen. Johny Lumintang was found to bear responsibility for human rights abuses. In December 2001 a UN tribunal took the first step in bringing those responsible for the atrocities committed in 1999 to justice. Of the 11 individuals indicted in December 2000, 10 were convicted of crimes against humanity and sentenced to prison terms of up to 33 years. However, the Jakarta authorities resisted the extradition of the indicted Indonesian Special Forces Officer to stand trial.

In February 2000, meanwhile, the Australian Government announced that all 470 East Timorese refugees remaining in Australia were expected to be returned to East Timor by the end of the month. Also in February, however, the UN expressed its concern that very few of the estimated 90,000 East Timorese refugees remaining in camps across the border in West Timor were returning to East Timor; it had earlier been reported that pro-Jakarta militias had been intimidating the refugees in West Timor and preventing them from returning home. In September the UN temporarily suspended its relief work among East Timorese refugees in West Timor, following the murder by pro-Jakarta militias of three UN aid workers in the territory earlier in the month. The murders prompted international criticism of the Indonesian Government for its failure to control the militia groups operating in West Timor. In November Ramos Horta alleged that estimates of the number of East Timorese refugees residing in West Timor (reported by some sources to be as high as 130,000) were being deliberately exaggerated by the Indonesian Government, and estimated the actual number of refugees to be no higher than 60,000–70,000. In December 2000 and January 2001, in an attempt to dispel the fears of refugees remaining in West Timor about the security situation in East Timor, UNTAET arranged for a number of groups of refugees to visit their homeland. The visits resulted in a number of refugees opting to return permanently to East Timor.

In June 2001 refugees from East Timor participated in a process of registration through which they were permitted to decide whether or not they wished to return to the newly independent state. Of the 113,791 refugees who took part, 98% wished to remain in Indonesia. However, it was thought that intimidation by pro-Indonesia militias might have influenced the result and that the survey did not necessarily reflect the participants' long-term intentions. In the same month the six men accused of the murder of the three UN aid workers in September 2000 were found guilty of violence against people and property rather than murder and given light sentences. The UN criticized the verdicts and pressed for a review.

Following the formal declaration of the election results, the families of former East Timorese militiamen began returning to their homeland in mid-September 2001. In October the Indonesian authorities announced the imminent halting of aid to an estimated 80,000 East Timorese who remained in refugee camps in West Timor and in November Gusmão visited West Timor in an effort to promote reconciliation and encourage thousands of the remaining refugees to return home.

In October 2001 the newly elected Constituent Assembly requested that the UN formally grant East Timor independence on 20 May 2002. Gusmão reluctantly lent his support to the request, although he commented that the choice of date was too politically partisan as it commemorated the 28th anniversary of the founding of the country's first political party. However, the UN Security Council endorsed the Assembly's request, and agreed to maintain a peace-keeping presence in the region for between six months and two years after the granting of independence.

On 22 March 2002 the Constituent Assembly finally promulgated East Timor's first Constitution, which was to become effective upon independence on 20 May of that year. The document provided for the adoption of Tetum and Portuguese as the country's official languages.

On 14 April 2002 East Timor held its first presidential election, which resulted in an overwhelming victory for Gusmão, who secured almost 83% of the votes cast. The only other candidate was Francisco Xavier do Amaral. Later in the same month Madalena Brites Boavida was sworn in as Minister of Finance and Planning in the second transitional Government, following the resignation of Fernando Borges.

On 20 May 2002 East Timor celebrated its formal accession to independence, upon which it became known officially as the Democratic Republic of Timor-Leste. The tenure of the UN interim administration was officially terminated and UNTAET was replaced by a smaller mission, UNMISET (see above), which was to remain in the country for two years to support administrative development and to assist in the maintenance of law and order, while downsizing its military presence as rapidly as possible. Xanana Gusmão was officially inaugurated as President and swore in the country's first Government. The National Parliament, as the Constituent Assembly had become, then held its inaugural session. Prime Minister Alkatiri stressed that the new Government would give priority to spending on health and education. The President of Indonesia, Megawati Sukarnoputri, attended the independence day celebrations, despite criticism from several members of the Indonesian legislature. On the following day Sérgio Vieira de Mello left the country; he was succeeded by Kamalesh Sharma, the head of UNMISET. Tension developed between Gusmão and Alkatiri after the latter was seen to have used Fretilin's parliamentary majority to secure the passage of a new Constitution that rendered Gusmão a largely symbolic head of state. The ill feeling persisted and in November 2002 Gusmão called for the resignation of one of Alkatiri's firmest allies, Rogério Lobato, Minister for Internal Administration. However, Gusmão eventually retreated from his position, following which relations between the President and the Prime Minister appeared to improve somewhat.

In July 2002 President Gusmão visited Indonesia on his first official trip abroad since assuming the presidency. In September Timor-Leste became the 191st member of the UN. In the same month the Indonesian Government announced that the remaining refugee camps in West Timor would be closed at the end of 2002 and, in November, Gusmão visited the province in an effort to encourage the estimated 30,000 refugees who remained there to return to their homeland. In the following month the Government declared a state of alert in the country following an outbreak of rioting in Dili during which two people were killed. The protests had begun when a police officer allegedly shot at a student participating in a peaceful demonstration outside the police headquarters in the city. The violence was the worst to have occurred in the country since independence. In January 2003 further violence ensued when a group of armed men attacked villages near the town of Atsabe in the Ermera district, resulting in the deaths of five people. In the following month a bus travelling to Dili was ambushed by a group of armed men; two people subsequently died. It was feared that the violence reflected the possible establishment of several militias and insurgent groups intent on undermining the stability of the new nation.

In March 2003 Prime Minister Alkatiri announced the appointment of Ana Pessôa to the newly created post of Deputy Prime Minister. The justice portfolio, formerly held by Pessôa, was allocated to her deputy, Domingos Sarmento. In the following month, owing to the apparent increase of violence in Timor-Leste in the preceding months, the UN Security Council announced that UNMISET would no longer follow its original downsizing plan (under which the phased withdrawal of UN troops from the country would have commenced in July 2003) and would instead implement an alternative two-phase plan. Under the new strategy, UNMISET would retain primary responsibility for national security until December 2003, maintaining its peace-keeping force at its existing level, before preparing to hand over full responsibility for national defence to Falintil-ETDF (see Defence) on 20 May 2004. In May 2003 the UN Security Council formally extended the mandate of UNMISET until 20 May 2004. In October 2003 the Timorese authorities assumed responsibility for the administration of border crossings in the country from the UN. However, in February 2004 UN Secretary-General Kofi Annan recommended that the mandate of UNMISET be extended, in a modified form and with a considerably reduced military presence, for a further six months following its expiry in May, in order to allow for consolidation of the progress that had been made in the country. In May 2004 the UN Security Council voted unanimously to renew UNMISET's mandate for an additional period of six months, extending the mission until 20 May 2005. In March 2005 Annan recommended that UNMISET be deployed for an additional year, extending the mandate until 20 May 2006, a suggestion that both the USA and Australia opposed, insisting that peace-keeping forces were no longer required in the country.

From mid-2002, at a specially created court in Jakarta (the Ad Hoc Indonesian Human Rights Tribunal on East Timor), the trials took place of 18 officers, government officials and militiamen believed to have participated in the violence that had surrounded the referendum for independence in 1999. In August 2002 Abílio Soares, the former Governor of East Timor, was found guilty of two charges of 'gross rights violations'; he was sentenced to a three-year prison term. The sentence was widely criticized for its apparent leniency. In the same month the former chief of police in East Timor, Timbul Silaen, was acquitted of charges of failing to control his subordinates; five other Indonesian police and army officers were also acquitted shortly afterwards. In November former Indonesian militia leader Eurico Guterres was sentenced to 10 years in prison, having been convicted of crimes against humanity. In the following month the former military chief of Dili, Lt-Col Soedjarwo, was sentenced to a five-year prison term for his role in the violence. In March 2003 the court sentenced Brig.-Gen. Noer Muis, a former army chief in East Timor, to five years in prison for crimes against humanity. In August Indonesian armed forces officer Maj.-Gen. Adam Damiri, the last and most senior official to be tried by the tribunal, was convicted of having failed to prevent atrocities in East Timor and sentenced to three years in prison. The court was subjected to widespread international criticism, owing to the fact that only six of those tried were convicted of the charges against them. In April 2004, following an appeal, the Indonesian Supreme Court upheld the conviction of Abílio Soares. However, in July the Jakarta High Court overruled the guilty verdicts of Lt-Col Soedjarwo, Brig.-Gen. Muis, Maj.-Gen. Damiri and Col Gultom (a former Dili police chief), and also halved the sentence of Eurico Guterres to five years. The decision meant that all of the police and military officials indicted by the Tribunal had been released, leaving only the two civilians (Soares and Guterres) serving sentences. The USA and the European Union (EU) denounced the acquittals as massive failings of justice. In November, moreover, Soares was cleared of the charges against him by Indonesia's Supreme Court, leaving only the conviction of Guterres standing. However, having reinstated his 10-year sentence in March 2006, the Supreme Court decided to rescind Guterres' conviction in April 2008, and he was released from prison.

In early 2003 a UN-sponsored Special Panel for Serious Crimes (SPSC) that had been established in Dili began to issue indictments for crimes against humanity against several military officials in relation to the violence surrounding the referendum in 1999, including the former chief of the Indonesian armed forces, Gen. Wiranto, who awaited prosecution for the first time. Wiranto denied the charges against him. However, the Indonesian Government stated that it would refuse to permit the extradition of those charged to face trial. In April 2003 the SPSC sentenced José Cardosa Fereira, an East Timorese militia leader, to a 12-year prison term following his conviction for crimes against humanity. In June Quelo Mauno, a former leader of a pro-Indonesia militia, was convicted of the murder of an independence supporter in Oecusse in 1999 and sentenced to seven years in prison. In the following month the Dili court found a further two former pro-Indonesia militia leaders guilty of crimes against humanity and, by February 2004, some 47 people had been convicted of crimes relating to the referendum period. Meanwhile, the total number of people indicted by the court had risen to approximately 350, many of whom were resident in Indonesia; the Indonesian Government continued to refuse to extradite those indicted to stand trial. In May 2004 the SPSC finally issued an arrest warrant for Wiranto, who had been nominated in the previous month as a candidate for Indonesia's presidential election, the first round of which was scheduled for July. Fearing a breach in relations with Indonesia, President Gusmão and the Prosecutor-General, Longuinhos Monteiro, both acted to distance themselves from the warrant, insisting that a good rapport with neighbouring countries should take precedence over court proceedings to hold people accountable for crimes committed during the emergence of their nation. In December 2004 Timor-Leste and Indonesia agreed to establish the joint Commission of Truth and Friendship (CTF) to investigate the killings carried out during the period of the Timorese vote for independence, and this was formally approved by their respective Governments in March 2005. However, the CTF was rapidly dismissed by the international community; none of the crimes committed during Indonesian occupation prior to 1999 was to be investigated, and the CTF process was not intended to lead to prosecution. Furthermore, offenders who co-operated 'fully in revealing the truth' were to be guaranteed impunity, irrespective of the nature of their crimes. In August 2005, despite the overwhelmingly negative response to the Commission, the 10-member panel was formally sworn in. Meanwhile, in February of that year the UN established the Commission of Experts, which was to review the judicial processes of the Ad Hoc Indonesian Human Rights Tribunal on East Timor, as well as the Serious Crimes Investigation Unit and the SPSC in Timor-Leste.

In February 2004, as sporadic outbreaks of violence, reportedly perpetrated by rebel militias based in rural areas, continued to occur in Timor-Leste, Cristiano da Costa, the leader of the Conselho Popular pela Defesa da República Democrática de Timor Leste (CPD-RDTL, Popular Council for the Defence of the Democratic Republic of East Timor), announced that his organization intended to challenge the legitimacy of the established Government in Timor-Leste following the planned withdrawal of UNMISET in May 2004. However, UNMISET's mandate was subsequently extended for an additional year, although its presence was reduced to a mere 604 officers, while responsibility for law and order in the capital and for external security was transferred to the Government in advance of the formal full transfer of power. It was feared that the methods employed by the Government to suppress insurgents might result in further instability in the country. The use of the police to suppress political opposition was a particular cause for concern. In July 2004 the National Union of Resistance Staff and Veterans held a rally in Dili, demanding a cabinet reorganization and the dismissal of the unpopular Rogério Lobato. Police officers were drafted in, and resorted to beatings and the use of tear gas to disperse the crowd; some witnesses also claimed that guns were fired. Dili was the scene of another disturbance in December of the same year, when a group of 20 armed soldiers attacked a police station, injuring two officers and causing damage to the premises. There were also numerous reported sightings of alleged ex-militia groups, especially within border areas. In January 2005, in an operation intended to verify the accuracy of one such reported sighting in the Bobonaro district, police encountered six armed men and, following the resultant exchange of gunfire, one of the group was arrested. Prime Minister Alkatiri was quick to assert that it should not be assumed that the men were necessarily acting at the behest of the Indonesian army.

In December 2004 the first local elections since Timorese independence were held in Bobonaro and in the enclave of Oecusse. In order to promote female participation, a minimum of three women were to be elected to each village council. There was a high turn-out, exceeding 90% in some areas, and voters were able to cast their ballots in a calm and orderly manner, free from intimidation. However, there were numerous logistical problems, including errors on the electoral roll, which prohibited some people from casting their vote and delayed the outcome of the elections from being determined. By October 2005 elections had been held in the remaining 11 districts. While local councils held extremely limited authority, the election results revealed a considerable decline in popular support for Fretilin. Timor-Leste's principal party still maintained a sizeable majority, but its share of the vote decreased to less than 50% in some regions, representing a marked decline from previous levels of support.

Meanwhile, on 20 May 2005 the mandate of UNMISET was officially concluded, and the last remaining UN troops were withdrawn from Timor-Leste in the following month. The UN Office in Timor-Leste (UNOTIL) was established to facilitate the transfer of complete power to the Timorese authorities; its mandate was due to be concluded on 19 May 2006.

In July 2005 Prime Minister Alkatiri effected a cabinet reorganization, providing for an enlarged government comprising 17 ministries, with 15 deputy ministers and 11 state secretaries. Four state secretary portfolios, including those of defence and of public works, were transformed into full ministries. Alkatiri relinquished the role of Minister of Development and assumed control of the natural resources, minerals and energy policy portfolio. Abel Ximenes was selected to be the new Minister of Development; Antoninho Bianco was appointed as the inaugural Minister of Defence; and Odete Victor became Minister for Public Works.

In early February 2006 an estimated 400 soldiers (approximately one-quarter of Timor-Leste's 1,600-strong army) staged a protest about living conditions in their barracks and about alleged discrimination against soldiers from western regions of the country; they claimed that army officers, who were predominantly from Timor-Leste's eastern regions, frequently passed over for promotion soldiers from western regions in favour of those from their own localities. Having deserted their duties, the protesting soldiers presented a petition to President Gusmão, who promised a government inquiry into their complaints and urged them to return to their barracks. However, the rebellion escalated in late February when more than 170 additional soldiers deserted their barracks. The military leadership issued an ultimatum, demanding that they return to duty or be dismissed; when they had failed to return by March, the Commander-in-Chief of the Army, Brig.-Gen.Taur Matan Ruak, sanctioned their dismissal. Ruak's action precipitated a series of large-scale protests, which escalated into violence at the end of April, when supporters of the dismissed soldiers clashed with the police. The demonstrations, said to involve gangs, developed into looting, the destruction of property and eventually ethnic violence between eastern and western Timorese, which had claimed at least 37 lives and caused the displacement of an estimated 100,000 people by the following month. Prime Minister Alkatiri was criticized over his Government's handling of the situation, and anti-Government sentiments were increasingly voiced among protesters, who demanded Alkatiri's resignation. The turmoil led to the resignation of the Minister for Development, Abel Ximenes, at the beginning of May. At a Fretilin congress in mid-May, José Luís Guterres, the Timorese ambassador to the USA and Permanent Representative to the UN, withdrew his leadership challenge against Alkatiri after it emerged that the vote was to be determined by a show of hands rather than a secret ballot. At the end of May, in response to a request from Alkatiri, Australia deployed troops to Timor-Leste as part of an international effort to restore stability; Malaysia and New Zealand also contributed troops, while Portugal dispatched a contingent of police officers. The Minister for Foreign Affairs and Co-operation, Ramos Horta, attributed the unrest in part to a 'failure of leadership'; it was reported that Ramos Horta had communicated with Maj. Alfredo Reinado, the leader of the protesting soldiers. President Gusmão subsequently acted to curb the violence by assuming emergency powers and control of the country's security from the Minister for Defence, Roque Rodrigues, and the Minister for Interior Affairs, Rogério Lobato, both of whom resigned. Gusmão later assigned their portfolios to Ramos Horta, who engaged in dialogue with leaders of the rebel troops. Alkatiri finally yielded to considerable pressure to resign from several quarters, including Gusmão and the protesters, at the end of June, following the resignation of Ramos Horta on the previous day. Ramos Horta was appointed Prime Minister, retaining the defence portfolio, in July, in advance of the swearing in of a new Cabinet comprising several ministers of the previous administration, including the Minister for Agriculture, Forestry and Fisheries, Estanislau Aleixo da Silva, as Deputy Prime Minister. Rui Maria de Araújo retained the health portfolio and was additionally promoted to the position of Deputy Prime Minister, while José Luís Guterres became Minister for Foreign Affairs and Co-operation. The new Government was to remain in power until parliamentary elections, scheduled for mid-2007, were held.

In an indication that the security situation had improved significantly, in July 2006 Australia began to reduce its deployment in Timor-Leste, although some 2,000 personnel were projected to remain; in September Malaysia withdrew its remaining forces. Maj. Reinado was apprehended at the end of July following the expiry of a weapons amnesty, but escaped from prison in August. In the same month UNOTIL was replaced by the UN Integrated Mission in Timor-Leste (UNMIT) for an initial period of six months. With an authorized strength of up to 1,608 police personnel and up to 34 military liaison and staff officers, supported by civilian staff, UNMIT aimed to maintain security and promote reconciliation and good governance. (UNMIT's mandate was later extended—see below.)

In October 2006 the UN Independent Special Commission of Inquiry for Timor-Leste released its report on the unrest: among other conclusions, it found that Rodrigues, Lobato and Ruak had unlawfully transferred weapons to civilians and that, although Alkatiri was not necessarily directly implicated in the transfer, he had failed to denounce it. The Commission consequently recommended further investigation into Alkatiri's involvement. The findings followed allegations that Alkatiri had formed a militia to consolidate his power base and to take action against opponents. Lobato's trial began in January 2007. In March he was found guilty of arming a group of civilians, led by Vicente da Conceição, a former Falintil guerrilla, and was sentenced to seven-and-a-half-years' imprisonment. (In October da Conceição was himself arrested and charged in connection with his role in the unrest.) Although stability had been largely restored, outbursts of violence continued, and the ongoing plight of refugees was highlighted by the Australian Minister of Defence, Dr Brendan Nelson, in November 2006; it was estimated that 70,000 internally displaced people remained in camps. Maj. Reinado continued to elude the security forces, despite the Government's attempts at negotiation, and at the beginning of March 2007 reports of an unsuccessful attempt to capture Reinado prompted protests in Dili.

In February 2007 Prime Minister Ramos Horta declared his candidacy for the forthcoming presidential election. In March President Gusmão indicated his desire to become Prime Minister and announced that he intended to join the Congresso Nacional da Reconstrução de Timor-Leste (CNRT—National Congress for the Reconstruction of Timor-Leste), a new political party, following the expiry of his presidential term. The first stage of the presidential election, held on 9 April, was contested by eight candidates. Francisco Guterres, the President of Fretilin, secured 27.9% of the votes cast, followed by Ramos Horta, who was favoured by Gusmão, with 21.8%, and Fernando de Araújo, President of the PD, with 19.2%. An official appeal against the results, lodged by three of the losing candidates, including de Araújo, on the grounds of alleged widespread manipulation of the vote and other serious irregularities, was dismissed. The National Electoral Commission had earlier rejected demands from five of the candidates for a recount of the votes.

As no candidate achieved the requisite overall majority, the two leading contenders proceeded to a second round of voting, which was conducted on 9 May 2007: Ramos Horta received 69.2% of the votes cast. Francisco Guterres duly conceded defeat, promising to support the new President for the sake of the country's development. Unlike the first round, which had been marred by widespread violence and intimidation, the second stage of polling was conducted peacefully with no reports of any serious irregularities. Turn-out was high in both the first and second rounds, at 81.8% and 81.0%, respectively. The election victory of Ramos Horta, who formally took office on 20 May, was attributed to the support of the five non-Fretilin candidates who had been defeated in the first round of voting. Shortly after the inauguration ceremony one man was killed and several others injured in clashes in Dili between supporters of rival political parties. Meanwhile, Estanislau Aleixo da Silva, hitherto the Deputy Prime Minister, assumed the role of Prime Minister in an interim capacity. Among the incoming President's priorities were plans for radical reform of the police force and judiciary. He also intended to address the issue of the nearly 600 so-called 'petitioner soldiers' who had abandoned their barracks in February 2006 in protest at low pay and discrimination (see above).

The legislative election held on 30 June 2007 was contested by 14 political organizations and alliances. The number of seats in the National Parliament was reduced from 88 to 65. International observers declared their satisfaction with the conduct of the polls, in which 80.5% of the electorate participated. The electoral campaign had been generally peaceful, with the notable exception of the killing of two CNRT supporters in early June and a few minor clashes between rival supporters. Fretilin remained the largest party in the legislature following the elections, winning 21 seats, although its share of the vote declined to 29% compared with 57% at the 2001 election. The CNRT came a close second, with 24% of the vote and 18 seats, while an alliance of the ASDT and the PSD took 11 seats and the PD eight. Fretilin's relatively poor performance was attributed to public disillusion with the pace of reform since independence.

As none of the parties had secured sufficient seats to govern alone, talks aimed at forming a coalition government ensued. On 6 July 2007 the CNRT, the ASDT-PSD alliance and the PD announced their intention to establish a coalition. However, Fretilin insisted on its right, as the largest parliamentary party, to participate in government, initially suggesting that it could form a minority administration and later proposing the creation of a 'government of national unity'. After weeks of deadlock, on 6 August Ramos Horta invited the CNRT-led coalition to form a government. The President's decision was denounced as unconstitutional by Fretilin and prompted violent protests by supporters of the party. Nevertheless, Gusmão was inaugurated as Prime Minister on 8 August; his new Cabinet included José Luís Guterres as Deputy Prime Minister. Gusmão pledged to improve security, to combat corruption and to facilitate the return to their homes of the thousands of refugees who remained in camps following their displacement during the unrest of April–May 2006. Meanwhile, Fernando de Araújo was elected Speaker of the National Parliament at its first session at the end of July.

President Ramos Horta held a meeting with Alfredo Reinado in mid-August 2007, under the mediation of the Swiss-based Centre for Humanitarian Dialogue. However, Reinado subsequently rejected attempts by the Timorese Government to initiate further talks aimed at achieving a negotiated settlement. In mid-November another leader of the 'petitioner soldiers', former Lt Gastão Salsinha, announced that the dismissed troops would not engage in dialogue with the Government until they were reinstated into the armed forces. A week later Reinado reiterated this demand for reintegration into the military, threatening to mount further attacks in Dili if the Government did not comply. He also demanded the withdrawal of foreign troops and judges from Timor-Leste. Four former soldiers were convicted of murder and sentenced to up to 12 years' imprisonment in late November for shooting dead eight unarmed police officers in April 2006. Reinado's trial on charges of murder, attempted murder and revolt commenced *in absentia* in early December 2007, after he refused to surrender to the authorities. None the less, the Government persisted in its efforts to maintain contact with the rebel soldiers.

The UN Secretary-General, Ban Ki-Moon, visited Timor-Leste in mid-December 2007, pledging continued UN assistance for the reform of the security forces and the judiciary. The process of gradually transferring authority from UNMIT to the national police commenced in early February 2008, when local officers assumed control of three police posts in Dili, although they were to remain under UN supervision.

On 11 February 2008 President Ramos Horta was shot by renegade soldiers in an attack on his residence in Dili, during which Reinado and another rebel were killed by presidential guards. Seriously injured, the President was evacuated to Darwin, Australia, for medical treatment. Prime Minister Gusmão, who had been targeted shortly afterwards in a separate assault reportedly led by Gastão Salsinha, but was unharmed, announced a 48-hour state of emergency in response to what he described as an attempted coup, imposing a night-time curfew in Dili and a ban on public gatherings and protests. Australia swiftly dispatched around 200 additional troops to Timor-Leste following the apparent assassination attempts, amid fears of renewed conflict, although no further violent incidents were reported in the days that followed. Speaker Fernando de Araújo replaced his deputy, Vicente Guterres, as acting President on 13 February after returning from overseas. On the same day arrest warrants were issued for several people suspected of involvement in the shootings, including Salsinha, and a 10-day extension of the state of emergency was approved by the National Parliament. Salsinha subsequently announced that he had assumed the leadership of the group of 'petitioner soldiers' and denied that they had attempted to murder Ramos Horta and Gusmão. Several days later Angelita Pires, reported to be Reinado's legal adviser and former partner, and alleged to have been with the rebel leader in the hours before the attacks, was arrested on suspicion of conspiracy, but was released on bail. Prime Minister Gusmão ordered the Timorese military and police forces temporarily to form a joint command to boost efforts to apprehend the perpetrators of the shootings. Meanwhile, the Prosecutor-General, Longuinhos Monteiro, stated that the authorities now believed that the rebels had intended to kidnap the President and Prime Minister rather than kill them. Three officers from the US Federal Bureau of Investigation were assisting Monteiro with his investigations.

The National Parliament voted to prolong the state of emergency for a further 30 days on 22 February 2008, and later that month UNMIT's mandate was extended for a further year. By late February most of the 'petitioner soldiers' had agreed to hold talks with the Government aimed at resolving their situation and were being held in a camp in Dili. In early March Amaro da Costa, a senior rebel leader, was the first of a number of suspects to surrender to the joint command that month, although several others, including Salsinha and Marcelo Caetano, whom Ramos Horta had apparently identified as the gunman who had shot him, remained at large. Having undergone a series of operations in Australia, on 17 April Ramos Horta returned to Dili, where he was welcomed by several thousand supporters, and resumed office immediately, urging Salsinha and his followers to surrender. Four former Timorese soldiers suspected of involvement in the shootings were detained in Indonesia and later extradited to Timor-Leste. In the week after Ramos Horta's return, the National Parliament agreed to his request to rescind the state of emergency, although in the district in which the rebels were believed to be in hiding it was extended for a further month, to 22 May. On 23 April Ramos Horta announced his intention to pardon former government minister Rogério Lobato (see above). The decision was widely seen as a tactic to encourage Salsinha and his followers to surrender, and was received with alarm by international groups. In late April, following several days of negotiations with security officials, Salsinha, Caetano and 10 other rebels surrendered, relinquishing their weapons at a formal ceremony in Dili attended by Ramos Horta and Deputy Prime Minister José Luís Guterres. It was hoped that an end to the insurrection would encourage the estimated 100,000 displaced people who remained in camps to return to their homes. Meanwhile, the Australian Government announced the withdrawal of the additional troops that had been deployed to Timor-Leste in February. None the less, some 750 troops from Australia and 170 from New Zealand remained in the country to support UNMIT in its efforts to maintain security.

In late May 2008, on the sixth anniversary of Timor-Leste's accession to independence, President Ramos Horta announced the names of 80 recipients of presidential pardons. Among the recipients was Joni Marques, former leader of the Alfa militia group, who in 2001 had been given a prison sentence of more than 33 years for an attack on a convoy in 1999 in which people, including nuns and priests, had been killed. Ramos Horta's intention to provide amnesty to Timorese perpetrators of violence during the 1999 and 2006 crises was demonstrated further when, in July 2008, he drafted legislation to give criminals the opportunity to avoid court by issuing a public apology, and which allowed for compensation of up to US $10,000 to be paid to the families of victims. International monitoring agencies, including the International Crisis Group, expressed concern at the President's actions, and suggested that such pardons might undermine the rule of law. The draft legislation had yet to be presented to Parliament in April 2009. In March of that year 28 people, including Australian citizen Angelita Pires, were formally charged with the attempted assassination of President Ramos Horta and Prime Minister Gusmão; Ramos Horta was reported to welcome the announcement of the charges and to be considering the granting of pardons. In the same month Timorese investigators and Australian forensic scientists discovered the remains of 16 people in unmarked graves on the outskirts of Dili, believed to be the bodies of protesters killed during the 1991 Dili massacre (see above).

Meanwhile, in late July 2008 the National Parliament approved the budget for 2008/09, which projected total expenditure of US $788m. This represented a rise of more than 120% in comparison with the previous year and followed a warning from the World Bank that Timor-Leste's increasing use of income from its petroleum revenues (see Economic Affairs) in such a manner was unsustainable. With global commodity prices having risen sharply in the first half of 2008, the Government intended to allocate much of the additional funding to increases in its subsidies for food and fuel, in order to ensure economic stability. An aid agency's report released on World Food Day, in mid-October, found that more than 70% of households surveyed were 'food insecure'. The organization calculated that some families were at risk of severe food shortages for up to five months of each year. However, the Government's plans to use the assets of the long-term petroleum fund to ease inflationary pressures were placed in jeopardy in November when, following a legal challenge from the opposition Fretilin, the Constitutional Court ruled that the Government's projected increase in budgetary expenditure was unconstitutional.

In February 2009 the UN Security Council voted to extend the mandate of UNMIT for a further 12 months. In late March the head of UNMIT, Atul Khare, announced that the mission was to begin the transfer of responsibility to the Timor-Leste police, stating that in the preceding months significant progress had been made towards the restoration of stability. Longuinhos Monteiro, hitherto the Prosecutor-General, was appointed to command the new police force. (He was replaced as Prosecutor-General by Ana Pessôa, the former Deputy Prime Minister, who had also served as Minister of Justice.) The transition was to commence in the eastern district of Lautem in May. However, UN troops were to remain in the area to monitor developments and to provide logistical support if necessary. Futhermore, at a meeting of the country's development partners in early April, Khare acknowledged that, while peace and security had been re-established to an extent during 2008, Timor-Leste still depended on significant, ongoing international aid in order to continue its long-term development. In the same month Prime Minister Gusmão appointed the former Governor of Dili and ex-leader of the PSD, Mário Carrascalão, to the new position of second Deputy Prime Minister. Carrascalão was charged with the task of auditing government departments to identify corruption and financial mismanagement. Later in that month a draft of the World Bank's annual report, obtained by an Australian newspaper, was alleged to have warned that poor decision-making and financial management by the Government, as well as ongoing corruption and the politicization of the security forces and civil service, were undermining Timor-Leste's development and jeopardizing political stability and peace.

In the conduct of its foreign affairs, Timor-Leste accorded high priority to the development of cordial relations with Indonesia. In June 2003 Prime Minister Alkatiri paid his first official visit to Indonesia, holding talks with President Megawati Sukarnoputri. However, despite an agreement between the two countries to co-operate in resolving outstanding border demarcation issues, in early 2004 Indonesia caused tensions by announcing that it planned to deploy security forces on the disputed islet of Sinai, located off Oecusse. The Government had previously protested when Indonesia had conducted military exercises on the islet in late 2003. In June 2004 the Timorese Minister for Foreign Affairs, José Ramos Horta, and his Indonesian counterpart,

Hassan Wirayuda, signed an agreement that resolved 90% of the border demarcation question. The remaining nine disputed land segments included territory in the Oecusse enclave; however, six of the nine segments were subsequently agreed upon in October, leaving merely three areas still to be resolved. A formal border agreement between the two countries was signed by the respective heads of state during a visit by Indonesian President Susilo Bambang Yudhoyono to Dili in April 2005. During his stay Yudhoyono paid his respects at the cemetery in which victims from the 1991 Dili massacre (see above) were buried. It was hoped that the visit would facilitate the forging of closer relations. In October, however, tensions arose between the two countries after clashes in the Oecusse enclave, allegedly involving gangs that were supported by Indonesian troops. Both the Timorese and the Indonesian Ministers of Foreign Affairs dismissed the violence as mere civilian land disputes arising from confusion over the delineation of the border. Relations were further sullied by a report published in January 2006 by the Commission for Reception, Truth and Reconciliation (a national body created in 2002, charged with investigating alleged human rights violations during Indonesia's occupation of Timor-Leste). The report documented a catalogue of abuses allegedly carried out by Indonesian security forces in Timor-Leste between April 1974 and October 1999, claiming that as many as 180,000 Timorese civilians had died as a result of the Indonesian army's alleged deliberate policy of starvation. Later that month a scheduled meeting between Presidents Gusmão and Yudhoyono was cancelled; no official reason was given for the decision, but it was widely perceived to be as a result of Yudhoyono's displeasure with the findings of the report. In February 2007 the CTF (Commission of Truth and Friendship—see above), jointly formed by Indonesia and Timor-Leste in 2004 to establish the truth about the events of 1999, held its first hearing. The CTF held five sessions of hearings between February and September 2007, before retiring to prepare its recommendations. Prominent figures who appeared before the Commission included Gen. Wiranto, Gusmão and Brig.-Gen. Ruak. In July the UN prohibited its officials from testifying, owing to the decision to grant amnesty to perpetrators of serious crimes, while human rights organizations continued to criticize the process, claiming that insufficient numbers of victims had been summoned to give evidence. Meanwhile, in early June, some two weeks after taking office as President of Timor-Leste, José Ramos Horta visited Indonesia. Ramos Horta and Indonesian President Yudhoyono reaffirmed their commitment to the CTF, extending its mandate by six months, and emphasized the importance of further improving bilateral relations. In July 2008 the CTF released its report, which found the Indonesian army responsible for the human rights crimes owing to its role in funding the pro-Indonesia militia groups that were the main perpetrators of the violence that occurred. Many international human rights organizations dismissed the report because its remit did not include the prosecution of individuals. The Presidents of Indonesia and Timor-Leste formally accepted the report's findings; however, President Yudhoyono stopped short of an official apology, instead expressing his 'deepest remorse'. In October President Ramos Horta urged the UN, which had boycotted the CTF, to end its ongoing investigation into the crimes committed during and after the 1999 independence vote, reportedly stating that maintaining strong relations with Indonesia was Timor-Leste's first priority.

In September 2007 President José Ramos Horta announced that he had established a task force to prepare for Timor-Leste's eventual accession to the Association of South East Asian Nations (ASEAN, see p. 194), with a view to securing membership within around five years.

Meanwhile, Timor-Leste's relations with Australia were strained by ongoing discussions relating to the Timor Sea Treaty. In November 2003 bilateral negotiations began concerning the demarcation of the maritime boundary between the two countries, an important issue owing to its ramifications for the allocation of revenues from petroleum and gas fields in the Timor Sea. Australia refused to recognize the boundary delineated by the UN Convention on the Law of the Sea. Prime Minister Alkatiri accused Australia of deliberately attempting to stall the negotiations, following its refusal to agree to the holding of monthly discussions in order to bring about a more rapid resolution to the boundary issues. Months of acrimonious dispute ensued, during which numerous aid agencies, including the British-based Oxfam, accused Australia of pushing Timor-Leste to the point of ruin; Oxfam declared that if a maritime boundary were established between the two countries under international law, 'most, if not all' of the petroleum reserves would be allocated to Timor-Leste. In September 2004 the two countries appeared finally to have agreed upon a revenue-sharing arrangement, which over a period of 30 years would afford Timor-Leste $A5,000m. in tax and royalty payments from the natural gas project in the Timor Sea. However, the negotiations again broke down, principally owing to the two countries' failure to agree on the contentious boundary issues. In February 2005 further acrimony ensued when the Australian Government agreed to a mid-point boundary with New Zealand but still refused to consider a similar arrangement with Timor-Leste, provoking widespread accusations of blatant hypocrisy. Instead, Australia proposed that the decision with Timor-Leste be deferred for up to 100 years while the major petroleum and gas deposits were exhausted, dismissing Timor-Leste's bid for a mid-point boundary as an 'ambit claim'. In November a deal was finally reached, with both countries agreeing to share equally the oil and gas revenues from the disputed region, which included the Greater Sunrise Project; a final decision on the contentious issue of the delineation of a maritime boundary was deferred for 50 years in order to allow petroleum and gas projects to proceed. The agreement was formally signed in the Australian city of Sydney in January 2006 and entered into force in February 2007, following ratification by Timor-Leste's National Parliament. Despite these tensions, the Australian Government remained a major source of financial assistance for Timor-Leste, and announced a $A240m. four-year aid programme in August. The new Prime Minister of Australia, Kevin Rudd, visited Dili soon after taking office in December, pledging continued support for Timor-Leste in the area of security. Timorese President Ramos Horta and Prime Minister Gusmão had both urged Rudd to maintain Australian troops in Timor-Leste until at least the end of 2008. Rudd returned to Timor-Leste shortly after the attacks on Ramos Horta and Gusmão in February 2008. Australia had dispatched additional troops to the country following the shootings (see above). In April Ramos Horta requested Australian assistance in investigating the source of a large sum of money that the President claimed had been deposited in an Australian bank account held jointly by Alfredo Reinado and his associate, Angelita Pires, as well as a series of telephone calls to Australia apparently made by Reinado. The Australian Minister for Foreign Affairs, Stephen Smith, subsequently rejected Timorese suggestions that Australia was delaying the investigation into the shooting, stating that telecommunications records had already been provided and urging the Timorese authorities to follow the appropriate procedures to gain access to financial records. In March 2009 the Prosecutor-General announced that Pires had been charged with conspiracy over the shooting of Ramos Horta and would stand trial in mid-2009.

In October 2008 the Australian Government recalled 100 troops, but reaffirmed its commitment to providing military support until political stability had been achieved. In December the Australian Governor-General, Quentin Bryce, visited Timor-Leste to meet with the President and Prime Minister, and in March 2009 Australian Minister for Defence Joel Fitzgibbon, during an official visit, opened an Australian-funded specialist military training centre.

Meanwhile, in 2008 Timor-Leste continued to strengthen its relations with the region. In October an agreement was signed to allow South Korea to import gas from Timor-Leste's Greater Sunrise fields by 2013, the first such energy accord to be concluded by Timor-Leste. In March 2009 Prime Minister Gusmão travelled to Japan for a meeting with his Japanese counterpart, Taro Aso. Gusmão's four-day visit included discussions with other government officials.

Government

In March 2002 the Constituent Assembly promulgated East Timor's first Constitution and, on 14 April, the territory held its first presidential election. The President serves a five-year term. Upon the territory's accession to independence in May of that year, the Constituent Assembly transformed itself into the National Parliament. (The number of seats in the National Parliament was reduced from 88 to 65 at the 2007 election.) In 2002 the UN Transitional Administration in East Timor (UNTAET) formally relinquished its responsibility for the administration of the country and was succeeded by the UN Mission of Support in East Timor (UNMISET), which remained in the country, in a supporting role, ultimately for three years. UNMISET was replaced in May 2005 by the UN Office in Timor-

TIMOR-LESTE

Leste (UNOTIL), which was superseded by the UN Integrated Mission in Timor-Leste (UNMIT) in August 2006.

Defence

Following the official completion of the mandate of the UN Mission of Support in East Timor (UNMISET), the last remaining UN peace-keeping troops withdrew from Timor-Leste in mid-2005. As assessed at November 2008, according to Western estimates, the East Timorese Defence Force (Falintil-ETDF) comprised 1,286 army personnel, including a naval element of 36.

Economic Affairs

In 2007, according to estimates by the World Bank, Timor-Leste's gross national income (GNI), measured at average 2005–07 prices, was US $1,604m., equivalent to $1,510 per head. During 2000–07, it was estimated, the population increased at an average annual rate of 4.5%, while gross domestic product (GDP) per head, in real terms, grew by 1.0% in 2000–07. Overall GDP grew, in real terms, at an average annual rate of 2.8% during 2000–07, according to IMF figures. According to the Asian Development Bank (ADB), GDP increased by 8.0% in 2007, and by 10.0% in 2008.

The agricultural sector, according to FAO, in mid-2005 engaged some 81% of the Timorese labour force. In 2006 the agricultural sector (including forestry and fishing) contributed an estimated 27.5% of non-oil GDP. Coffee is a significant export commodity. According to IMF estimates, revenue from coffee exports, which constituted some 75% of total non-oil export receipts in 2006, reached US $6m. Following an excellent harvest, the value of coffee exports reached an estimated US $11.6m. in 2008. The coffee sector remained extremely susceptible to climatic conditions, which, combined with poor irrigation systems, were primarily responsible for significant fluctuations in annual output. There are small plantations of coconut, cloves and cinnamon. Subsistence crops include rice, maize and cassava. A government decision to subsidize rice imports in 2008 was criticized by international financial institutions for depreciating the value of local rice crops, which was expected to lead to a substantial decrease in local production. Livestock raised includes cattle and water buffalo. There is some small-scale fishing, and the forestry sector may yield as yet undeveloped potential. According to ADB figures, the GDP of the agricultural sector increased, in real terms, at an average annual rate of 1.2% in 2002–07. Real growth in the sector's GDP was estimated by the ADB at 0.3% in 2006, but the sector contracted in 2007, by some 5.6%.

The industrial sector (including mining and quarrying, manufacturing, utilities and construction) contributed an estimated 13.9% of non-oil GDP in 2007. According to figures from the ADB, industrial GDP declined at an average annual rate of 0.3% in 2002–07. The industrial sector's GDP declining significantly in 2006, by 18.1%, but grew by 28.7% in 2007.

In the 1990s sizeable natural gas fields were discovered in and around the Timor Gap zone, and petroleum reserves in the region were estimated by some sources to total a potential 500m. barrels. Although detailed data for the contribution made to GDP by petroleum and gas activities were not available, the IMF estimated that these sectors generated incomes of US $342m. in 2005 and $492m. in 2006 (equivalent to 138% of the value of non-oil GDP in the latter year). The Timor Sea Arrangement, relating to the sharing of petroleum and gas royalties with Australia, was signed in 2002 (see Recent History). In 2003 a US company was granted permission to develop the Bayu-Undan liquefied natural gas (LNG) field in the Timor Sea. The mining sector, excluding petroleum and gas, was estimated to have contributed only 0.5% of GDP in 2007. In addition to offshore petroleum and gas, mineral resources include high-grade marble. According to the ADB, the GDP of the non-oil mining sector was estimated to have decreased at an average annual rate of 9.9% in 2002–07. However, the sector's GDP increased by 11.8% in 2007.

There is a small manufacturing sector, which is mainly concerned with the production of textiles, the bottling of water and coffee processing. In 2007 the manufacturing sector provided an estimated 2.3% of non-oil GDP. In May 2004 year one of the world's largest wet-processing coffee factories was opened in Estado, which, together with expanded production at the existing Maubisse factory, was expected to increase significantly Timor-Leste's annual coffee output. According to ADB figures, manufacturing GDP declined, in real terms, by 4.6% in 2002–07. The GDP of the manufacturing sector increased by 10.1% in 2007.

In 2002 the Government elected to transfer control of the national power authority, Electricidade de Timor-Leste (EDTL), to external management. Although the basic rehabilitation of the existing rural power infrastructure was largely complete by 2003, supplies of electricity subsequently remained intermittent. The country's total generating capacity stood at only 40 MW in 2008. In that year a major programme of electrification was announced, and it was envisaged that by the end of 2010 an additional 180 MW would be available following the construction of new power stations, which were to operate with imported oil.

The services sector (including UN contributions) was responsible for an estimated 58.7% of non-oil GDP in 2007. According to ADB figures, the services sector's GDP contracted at an average annual rate of 4.2% in 2002–07. The sector's GDP, in real terms, declined by 5.9% in 2006, but increased by 11.9% in 2007. In 2007 public administration and defence accounted for an estimated 24.8% of non-oil GDP. Tourism remained negligible, owing to a lack of basic infrastructure, as well as to prohibitively high air fares from Indonesia and Australia.

In 2007 Timor-Leste recorded a visible trade deficit of US $192m., while there was a surplus of $1,168m. on the current account of the balance of payments (largely owing to the allocation of oil and gas export revenues to the income and transfers accounts). Reliable data for exports of oil and gas were not available (see above), but these, together with coffee, constituted the most significant merchandise exports in 2008.

In 2008 the Ministry of Finance envisaged budgetary expenditure of US $319.2m. Total government revenue was projected to rise from $711.7m. in 2007 to $1,379.3m. in 2008. The ADB estimated the fiscal surplus to be the equivalent of 251.8% of GDP in 2008. The Government's subsequent budget was deemed unconstitutional (see Recent History). Australia is a major provider of development assistance, with emphasis on governance, law, training, security and public sector services. After significantly increasing its aid following the 2006 crisis, Australia's aid budget for Timor-Leste was projected at $A96.3m. in 2008/09. According to figures from the IMF, consumer prices increased by an average annual rate of 4.3% in 2000–08; the inflation rate reached 7.6% in 2008. In 2001 the rate of unemployment was estimated by the ADB at 5.3%. According to the census of 2004, those recorded as unemployed, or deterred from seeking work, accounted for one-half of Dili residents aged between 15 and 24 years.

Following independence in May 2002, Timor-Leste became a member of the Asian Development Bank (ADB, see p. 191), the Comunidade dos Países de Língua Portuguesa (Community of Portuguese-Speaking Countries, see p. 438) and the UN Economic and Social Commission for Asia and the Pacific (ESCAP, see p. 36). The country was also granted observer status at the Association of South East Asian Nations (ASEAN, see p. 194). Timor-Leste attended the third Summit of the African, Caribbean and Pacific group of states (ACP), held in Fiji in July 2002, as an observer.

Upon independence in 2002 Timor-Leste's first National Development Plan (NDP) was implemented. Its objectives, over an 18-year period, included the reduction of poverty and the introduction of a phased programme of development. External aid remained of vital importance to the Timorese economy. Timor-Leste's natural gas resources appeared to offer the greatest hopes of long-term economic self-sufficiency. The agreement signed by Timor-Leste and Australia in January 2006 regarding the allocation of revenue from the Greater Sunrise gas project (see Recent History) was a significant development. In June 2005 the Government approved the creation of a Petroleum Fund, which was to serve as a long-term repository for all petroleum revenues. Nearly all of the Government's own revenue in 2008 was derived from this fund, the value of which was reported to have more than doubled to reach US $4,200m. by the end of that year. Most of the assets were invested in US government securities. Timor-Leste benefited greatly from the strength of international oil prices that prevailed until mid-2008, and higher petroleum revenues permitted a consolidation of the country's fiscal position. Strong non-petroleum and non-UN growth were expected to continue in 2009, particularly following the renewal in February of the mandate of the UN mission in the country and the prospect of a further improvement in security. Agricultural production also rose in 2008, with rice production increasing by some 21%. None the less, the World Food Programme was reported to be supporting 30% of the Timorese population. The incidence of poverty was reported to have risen from 36% of the population in 2001 to 50% in 2007. Substantial increases in food and fuel costs were recorded in 2008, and the overall rate of inflation reached a high point of 10.6% in June of that year. However, inflationary pressures were expected to ease in 2009. A major challenge for the Government remained the provision of basic services, particularly in rural areas, and more than 50% of the capital budget for the period 2009–12 was to be allocated to the programme of electrification (see above).

Education

The education system was badly disrupted by the civil conflict of 1999. It was estimated that 75%–80% of primary and secondary schools were either partially or completely destroyed. However, a total of 240,000 students registered for the 2000/01 academic year, a much higher number than anticipated. In 2004/05 enrolment within primary education included 68% (males 70%, females 67%) of pupils in the relevant age-group. In the same year, enrolment within secondary education was equivalent to 53% (males 53%, females 53%) of pupils in the relevant age group. Literacy rates were reported to have reached only 41% by 1998, with lower rates recorded for women than for men, although this had increased moderately to 58.6% by 2004. In January 2001 the reopening of the university improved the country's tertiary education facilities, enabling the enrolment of 4,500 students on degree courses and 3,000 on bridging programmes. In 2001/02 enrolment in tertiary education was equivalent to 10% (males 9%, females 11%) of students in the relevant age group. Following Timor-Leste's accession to nationhood in May 2002, the Government accorded priority to the development of education. In June 2002 the Emergency Schools Readiness Project, funded by the Trust Fund for East Timor (TFET), was completed, having effected the renovation of 535 schools and 2,780 classrooms since August 2000. It was succeeded by the Fundamental School Quality Project, under which 65 primary schools were to be constructed during 2002/03. The budget of the Central Fund for East Timor (CFET) allocated an estimated US $17.1m. to the education sector in 2002/03, 24.2% of total expenditure.

Public Holidays

2009: 1 January (New Year's Day), 10 April (Good Friday), 1 May (Labour Day), 20 May (Independence Day), 15 August (Assumption), 30 August (Constitution Day), 20 September (Liberation Day), 1 November (All Saints' Day), 12 November (Santa Cruz Day), 8 December (Immaculate Conception), 25 December (Christmas Day).

2010: 1 January (New Year's Day), 2 April (Good Friday), 1 May (Labour Day), 20 May (Independence Day), 15 August (Assumption), 30 August (Constitution Day), 20 September (Liberation Day), 1 November (All Saints' Day), 12 November (Santa Cruz Day), 8 December (Immaculate Conception), 25 December (Christmas Day).

Weights and Measures

The metric system is in force.

Statistical Survey

Area and Population

AREA, POPULATION AND DENSITY

Area (sq km)	14,609*
Population (census results)	
31 October 1990	747,750
31 July 2004	
Males	467,757
Females	456,885
Total	924,642
Population (UN estimates at mid-year)†	
2006	1,029,000
2007	1,064,000
2008	1,098,000
Density (per sq km) at mid-2008	75.2

* 5,641 sq miles.
† Source: UN, *World Population Prospects: The 2008 Revision*.

PRINCIPAL TOWNS
(population at 2000)

Dili (capital)	48,200		Maliana	12,300
Dare	17,100		Ermera	12,000
Baucau	14,200			

Source: Stefan Helders, *World Gazetteer* (internet www.world-gazetteer.com).

Mid-2007 (incl. suburbs, UN estimate): Dili 159,000 (Source: UN, *World Urbanization Prospects: The 2007 Revision*).

BIRTHS AND DEATHS
(annual averages, UN estimates)

	1990–95	1995–2000	2000–05
Birth rate (per 1,000)	43.1	45.8	40.0
Death rate (per 1,000)	15.8	13.0	10.1

Source: UN, *World Population Prospects: The 2008 Revision*.

Life expectancy (years at birth, WHO estimates): 66.3 (males 63.8; females 69.1) in 2008 (Source: WHO, *World Health Statistics*).

Health and Welfare

KEY INDICATORS

Total fertility rate (children per woman, 2006)	6.7
Under-5 mortality rate (per 1,000 live births, 2006)	55
Physicians (per 1,000 head, 2004)	0.10
Health expenditure (2006): US $ per head	169
Health expenditure (2006): % of GDP	16.4
Health expenditure (2006): public (% of total)	88.8
Access to water (% of persons, 2006)	62
Access to sanitation (% of persons, 2006)	41
Human development index (2006): ranking	158
Human development index (2006): value	0.483

For sources and definitions, see explanatory note on p. vi.

Agriculture

PRINCIPAL CROPS
('000 metric tons, FAO estimates)

	2005	2006	2007
Maize	80.0	90.0	63.4
Cassava (Manioc)	48.0	47.5	49.7
Rice, paddy	60.0	65.0	41.4
Sweet potatoes	26.0	26.0	26.0
Beans, dry	4.5	4.5	4.5
Groundnuts, with shell	4.0	4.0	4.0
Coconuts	14.0	14.0	14.0
Bananas	2.0	2.0	2.0
Guavas, mangoes and mangosteens	3.0	3.0	3.0
Coffee, green	14.5	14.0	14.0

Aggregate production ('000 metric tons, may include official, semi-official or estimated data): Total cereals 140 in 2005, 155 in 2006, 105 in 2007; Total roots and tubers 120 in 2005, 118 in 2006, 111 in 2007; Total vegetables (incl. melons) 18 in 2005, 18 in 2006, 18 in 2007; Total fruits (excl. melons) 7 in 2005, 7 in 2006, 7 in 2007.

Source: FAO.

TIMOR-LESTE

LIVESTOCK
('000 head, FAO estimates)

	2004	2005	2006
Cattle	171	172	171
Buffaloes	108	110	110
Pigs	346	350	346
Horses	48	48	48
Goats	81	82	80
Sheep	25	26	25
Chickens	2,100	2,200	2,200

2007: Production assumed to be unchanged from 2006 (FAO estimates).

Source: FAO.

LIVESTOCK PRODUCTS
('000 metric tons, FAO estimates)

	2004	2005	2006
Cattle meat	1.3	1.4	1.1
Pig meat	10.1	10.2	10.1
Chicken meat	2.0	2.2	1.8
Hen eggs	2.0	2.2	1.8

Source: FAO.

Fishing

(metric tons, live weight, FAO estimates)

	2004	2005	2006
Total catch	350	350	350

Source: FAO.

Finance

CURRENCY AND EXCHANGE RATES (US currency is used)

Monetary Units
100 cents (centavos) = 1 United States dollar ($).

Sterling and Euro Equivalents (31 December 2008)
£1 sterling = US $1.4578;
€1 = $1.3917;
US $100 = £68.60 = €71.85.

BUDGET
(US $ million, calculated on cash basis)

Revenue	2004/05	2005/06	2006/07
Domestic revenue	36.9	33.9	40.5
Direct taxes	10.7	8.8	11.8
Indirect taxes	19.0	16.0	19.3
Non-tax revenues and other	7.1	9.1	9.3
Oil and gas revenues	265.6	481.8	993.1
Tax revenues	209.4	345.3	498.4
Royalties and interest	56.2	136.5	494.6
Grants	34.2	1.0	11.3
Total	**336.7**	**516.7**	**1,044.8**

Expenditure	2004/05	2005/06	2006/07
Recurrent expenditure	56.4	66.1	133.9
Salaries and wages	25.1	25.7	40.3
Goods and services	26.0	34.4	64.5
Transfers	—	—	11.8
Subsidies to agencies	5.3	6.0	17.4
Capital expenditure	2.8	15.6	20.8
Carried over from previous year	11.3	11.0	17.9
Total	**70.4**	**92.7**	**172.5**

Source: IMF, *Timor-Leste: Selected Issues and Statistical Appendix* (June 2008).

2007 (general government budget, US $ million, estimates): *Revenue*: Domestic revenue 14.4 (Direct taxes 4.1, Indirect taxes 5.0, Non-tax revenues and other 5.3); Oil and gas revenues 697.3 (Taxes and royalties 634.1, Petroleum fund interest 63.2); Total 711.7. *Expenditure*: Salaries and wages 19.1; Goods and services 57.5; Minor capital 3.0; Capital and development 0.1; Public transfer payments 12.1; Total 91.8.

2008 (general government budget, US $ million, estimates): *Revenue*: Domestic revenue 20.7 (Direct taxes 3.2, Indirect taxes 8.3, Non-tax revenues and other 9.2); Oil and gas revenues 1,358.6 (Taxes and royalties 1,249.7, Petroleum fund interest 108.7, Other petroleum revenue 0.2); Total 1,379.3. *Expenditure*: Salaries and wages 46.7; Goods and services 124.4; Minor capital 23.8; Capital and development 60.5; Public transfer payments 63.9; Total 319.2.

MONEY SUPPLY
(US $ million at 31 December)

	2005	2006	2007
Currency outside banks	1.790	1.811	2.273
Demand deposits	37.391	51.304	72.663
Total	**39.181**	**53.115**	**74.935**

Source: IMF, *International Financial Statistics*.

COST OF LIVING
(Consumer Price Index; base: 2000 = 100)

	2006	2007	2008
All items	116.3	128.2	139.9

Source: IMF, *International Financial Statistics*.

NATIONAL ACCOUNTS
(US $ million at current prices)

Expenditure on Non-oil Gross Domestic Product

	2005	2006	2007
Government final consumption expenditure	157.8	175.9	259.0
Private final consumption expenditure	329.5	301.6	352.2
Change in stocks	6.8	6.8	8.2
Gross fixed capital formation	61.9	61.0	103.0
Total domestic non-oil expenditure	**556.0**	**545.3**	**722.4**
Exports of goods and services	38.3	39.4	43.4
Less Imports of goods and services	262.5	258.0	370.3
Non-oil GDP in purchasers' values	**331.9**	**326.8**	**395.5**
Non-oil GDP at constant 2000 prices	**331.1**	**319.8**	**371.7**

TIMOR-LESTE

Non-oil Gross Domestic Product by Economic Activity

	2005	2006	2007
Agriculture, forestry and fishing	111.3	116.6	124.7
Mining and quarrying (non-oil)	2.9	1.9	2.2
Manufacturing	11.8	8.7	10.2
Electricity, gas and water	5.0	5.0	6.0
Construction	33.4	29.8	44.4
Wholesale and retail trade	24.9	25.4	31.0
Transport and communications	33.8	25.4	31.0
Finance, rents and business services	28.3	28.8	33.6
Public administration and defence	80.5	85.2	112.6
United Nations	18.0	25.6	57.7
Non-oil GDP in purchasers' values	349.9	352.5	453.3

Source: IMF, *Timor-Leste: Selected Issues and Statistical Appendix* (June 2008).

BALANCE OF PAYMENTS
(US $ million, estimates)

	2005	2006	2007
Exports of goods f.o.b.	9	9	8
Imports of goods f.o.b.	−125	−123	−200
Trade balance	−117	−114	−192
Services (net)	−159	−183	−324
Balance on goods and services	−275	−297	−516
Income (net)	365	647	1,330
Balance on goods, services and income	90	350	814
Current transfers (net)	185	181	354
Current balance	275	531	1,168
Capital transfers	55	56	42
Financial account (net)	−357	−656	−1,063
Overall balance	−29	−70	147

Source: IMF, *Timor-Leste: Selected Issues and Statistical Appendix* (June 2008).

External Trade

SELECTED COMMODITIES
(US $ '000)

Imports c.i.f	2004	2005
Cereals	8,111	4,690
Preparations of cereals, flour, starch or milk; pastry cooks' products	2,113	2,162
Beverages, spirits and vinegar	1,739	2,229
Mineral fuels, mineral oils and products of their distillation; bituminous substances; mineral waxes	36,757	35,136
Nuclear reactors, boilers, machinery and mechanical appliances; parts thereof	4,651	7,847
Vehicles, other than railway or tramway rolling stock, and parts thereof	14,735	7,018
Electrical machinery and equipment and parts thereof; sound recorders and reproducers; televisions, etc.	9,821	5,470
Pharmaceutical products	2,652	2,636
Iron or steel articles	1,391	2,629
Plastics and articles thereof	1,287	2,362
Total (incl. others)	113,489	101,619

Exports f.o.b (excl. oil and gas)	2004	2005
Coffee	6,899	7,630
Total (incl. others)	6,972	8,093

Re-exports (US $ '000): 98,682 in 2004. Note: the significance of re-exports may appear overstated owing to the inclusion of data connected with the outflow of foreign personnel and equipment as peace-keeping operations were scaled down.

2005 (US $ '000, revised figures): Total imports 109,109; Total domestic exports (excl. oil and gas) 8,086; Re-exports 35,364.

2006 (US $ '000): Total imports 100,803; Total domestic exports (excl. oil and gas) 8,445; Re-exports 52,241.

Source: Ministério do Plano e das Finanças, Dili.

PRINCIPAL TRADING PARTNERS
(US $ '000)

Imports c.i.f.	2004	2005
Australia	20,051	14,145
China, People's Republic	1,149	1,684
Indonesia	60,200	47,769
Japan	1,269	10,535
Korea, Republic	1	878
Malaysia	709	788
Portugal	1,686	1,656
Singapore	15,154	14,796
Thailand	1,306	1,122
Viet Nam	5,242	4,534
Total (incl. others)	113,489	101,619

Exports f.o.b. (excl. oil and gas)	2004	2005
Australia	511	445
Canada	—	44
Germany	441	1,672
Indonesia	1,277	406
Japan	80	100
New Zealand	48	24
Norway	71	71
Portugal	579	968
Singapore	158	91
Taiwan	93	196
Thailand	—	48
USA	3,551	3,978
Total (incl. others)	6,972	8,093

Source: Ministério do Plano e das Finanças, Dili.

SHIPPING

Merchant Fleet
(registered at 31 December)

	2005	2006	2007
Number of vessels	—	—	1
Total displacement ('000 grt)	—	—	1,134

Source: Lloyd's Register-Fairplay, *World Fleet Statistics*.

Tourism

TOURIST ARRIVALS
('000 foreign visitors, excl. Indonesians, at classified hotels*)

	1996	1997	1998
Total	0.8	1.0	0.3

* Arrivals at non-classified hotels: 204 in 1996; 245 in 1997; 41 in 1998.

Communications Media

	2005	2006	2007
Internet users	1,000	1,200	n.a.
Telephones ('000 main lines in use)	2.3	2.4	2.4
Mobile cellular telephones ('000 subscribers)	33.1	49.1	78.2

Daily newspapers: 2 in 2004.

Non-daily newspapers: 3 in 2004.

Source: UNESCO Institute for Statistics and International Telecommunication Union.

Education

(2004/05, unless otherwise indicated)

	Teachers	Students
Pre-primary	237	6,987
Primary	5,211	177,970
Lower Secondary	1,810	50,014
Upper Secondary	1,350	24,808
Tertiary*	123	6,349

*2001/02 estimates.

Source: UNESCO Institute for Statistics.

Adult literacy rate (UNESCO estimate): 58.6% in 2003 (Source: UN Development Programme, *Human Development Report*).

Directory

The Constitution

The Constitution of the Democratic Republic of East Timor was promulgated by the Constituent Assembly on 22 March 2002 and became effective on 20 May 2002, when the nation formalized its independence. (From this date the country elected to be known by its official name, the Democratic Republic of Timor-Leste.) The main provisions of the Constitution are summarized below:

FUNDAMENTAL PRINCIPLES

The Democratic Republic of East Timor is a democratic, sovereign, independent and unitary state. Its territory comprises the historically defined eastern part of Timor island, the enclave of Oecussi, the island of Ataúro and the islet of Jaco. Oecussi Ambeno and Ataúro shall receive special administrative and economic treatment.

The fundamental objectives of the State include the following: to safeguard national sovereignty; to guarantee fundamental rights and freedoms; to defend political democracy; to promote the building of a society based on social justice; and to guarantee the effective equality of opportunities between women and men.

Sovereignty is vested in the people. The people shall exercise political power through universal, free, equal, direct, secret and periodic suffrage and through other forms stated in the Constitution.

In matters of international relations, the Democratic Republic of East Timor shall establish relations of friendship and co-operation with all other peoples. It shall maintain privileged ties with countries whose official language is Portuguese.

The State shall recognize and respect the different religious denominations, which are free in their organization. Tetum and Portuguese shall be the official languages.

FUNDAMENTAL RIGHTS, DUTIES, LIBERTIES AND GUARANTEES

All citizens are equal before the law and no one shall be discriminated against on grounds of colour, race, marital status, gender, ethnic origin, language, social or economic status, political or ideological convictions, religion, education and physical or mental condition. Women and men shall have the same rights and duties in family, political, economic, social and cultural life. Rights, freedoms and safeguards are upheld by the State and include the following: the right to life; to personal freedom, security and integrity; to habeas corpus; to the inviolability of the home and of correspondence; to freedom of expression and conscience; to freedom of movement, assembly and association; and to participate in political life. Freedom of the press is guaranteed.

Rights and duties of citizens include the following: the right and the duty to work; the right to vote (at over 17 years of age); the right to petition; the right and duty to contribute towards the defence of sovereignty; the freedom to form trade unions and the right to strike; consumer rights; the right to private property; the duty to pay taxes; the right to health and medical care; the right to education and culture.

ORGANIZATION OF POLITICAL POWER

Political power lies with the people. The organs of sovereignty shall be the President of the Republic, the National Parliament, the Government and the Courts. They shall observe the principle of separation and interdependence of powers. There shall be free, direct, secret, personal and regular universal suffrage. No one shall hold political office for life.

PRESIDENT OF THE REPUBLIC

The President of the Republic is the Head of State and the Supreme Commander of the Defence Force. The President symbolizes and guarantees national independence and unity and the effective functioning of democratic institutions. The President of the Republic shall be elected by universal, free, direct, secret and personal suffrage. The candidate who receives more than one-half of the valid votes shall be elected President. Candidates shall be original citizens of the Democratic Republic of East Timor, at least 35 years of age, in possession of his/her full faculties and have been proposed by a minimum of 5,000 voters. The President shall hold office for five years. The President may not be re-elected for a third consecutive term of office.

The duties of the President include the following: to preside over the Supreme Council of Defence and Security and the Council of State; to set dates for elections; to convene extraordinary sessions of the National Parliament; to dissolve the National Parliament; to promulgate laws; to exercise the functions of the Supreme Commander of the Defence Force; to veto laws; to appoint and dismiss the Prime Minister and other government members; to apply to the Supreme Court of Justice; to submit relevant issues of national interest to a referendum; to declare a State of Emergency following the authorization of the National Parliament; to appoint and dismiss diplomatic representatives; to accredit foreign diplomatic representatives; to declare war and make peace with the prior approval of the National Parliament.

COUNCIL OF STATE

The Council of State is the political advisory body of the President of the Republic. It is presided over by the President of the Republic and comprises former Presidents of the Republic who were not removed from office, the Speaker of the National Parliament, the Prime Minister, five citizens elected by the National Parliament and five citizens nominated by the President of the Republic.

NATIONAL PARLIAMENT

The National Parliament represents all Timorese citizens, and shall have a minimum of 52 and a maximum of 65 members, elected by universal, free, direct, equal, secret and personal suffrage for a term of five years. The duties of the National Parliament include the following: to enact legislation; to confer legislative authority on the Government; to approve plans and the Budget and monitor their execution; to ratify international treaties and conventions; to approve revisions of the Constitution; to propose to the President of the Republic that issues of national interest be submitted to a referendum. The legislative term shall comprise five legislative sessions, and each legislative session shall have the duration of one year.

GOVERNMENT

The Government is the supreme organ of public administration and is responsible for the formulation and execution of general policy. It shall comprise the Prime Minister, the Ministers and the Secretaries of State, and may include one or more Deputy Prime Ministers and Deputy Ministers. The Council of Ministers shall comprise the Prime Minister, the Deputy Prime Ministers, if any, and the Ministers. It shall be convened and presided over by the Prime Minister. The Prime Minister shall be appointed by the President of the Republic. Other members of the Government shall be appointed by the President at the proposal of the Prime Minister. The Government shall be responsible to the President and the National Parliament. The Government's programme shall be submitted to the National Parliament for consideration within 30 days of the appointment of the Government.

JUDICIARY

The Courts are independent organs of sovereignty with competence to administer justice. There shall be the Supreme Court of Justice and other courts of law, the High Administrative, Tax and Audit Court, other administrative courts of first instance and military courts. There may also be maritime courts and courts of arbitration.

It is the duty of the Public Prosecutors to represent the State. The Office of the Prosecutor-General shall be the highest authority in public prosecution and shall be presided over by the Prosecutor-General, who is appointed and dismissed by the President of the Republic. The Prosecutor-General shall serve for a term of six years.

ECONOMIC AND FINANCIAL ORGANIZATION

The economic organization of East Timor shall be based on the co-existence of the public, private, co-operative and social sectors of ownership, and on the combination of community forms with free initiative and business management. The State shall promote national investment. The State Budget shall be prepared by the Government and approved by the National Parliament. Its execution shall be monitored by the High Administrative, Tax and Audit Court and by the National Parliament.

NATIONAL DEFENCE AND SECURITY

The East Timor defence force—Falintil-ETDF—is composed exclusively of national citizens and shall be responsible for the provision of military defence to the Democratic Republic of East Timor. There shall be a single system of organization for the whole national territory. Falintil-ETDF shall act as a guarantor of national independence, territorial integrity and the freedom and security of the population against any external threat or aggression. The police shall guarantee the internal security of the citizens.

The Superior Council for Defence and Security is the consultative organ of the President of the Republic on matters relating to defence and security. It shall be presided over by the President of the Republic and shall include a higher number of civilian than military entities.

GUARANTEE AND REVISION OF THE CONSTITUTION

Declaration of unconstitutionality may be requested by: the President of the Republic; the Speaker of the National Parliament; the Prosecutor-General; the Prime Minister; one-fifth of the Members of the National Parliament; the Ombudsman.

Changes to the Constitution shall be approved by a majority of two-thirds of Members of Parliament and the President shall not refuse to promulgate a revision statute.

FINAL AND TRANSITIONAL PROVISIONS

Confirmation, accession and ratification of bilateral and multilateral conventions, treaties, agreements or alliances that took place before the Constitution entered into force shall be decided by the respective bodies concerned; the Democratic Republic of East Timor shall not be bound by any treaty, agreement or alliance not thus ratified. Any acts or contracts concerning natural resources entered into prior to the entry into force of the Constitution and not subsequently confirmed by the competent bodies shall not be recognized.

Indonesian and English shall be working languages, together with the official languages, for as long as is deemed necessary.

Acts committed between 25 April 1974 and 31 December 1999 that can be considered to be crimes of humanity, of genocide or of war shall be liable to criminal proceedings within the national or international courts.

The Government

HEAD OF STATE

President: José Ramos Horta (took office 20 May 2007).

CABINET
(April 2009)

Prime Minister and Minister for Defence and Security: Kay Rala (Xanana) Gusmão.
Deputy Prime Ministers: José Luís Guterres, Mário Viegas Carrascalão.
Minister for State Administration: Arcângelo Leite Pinto.
Minister for Foreign Affairs: Zacarias Albano da Costa.
Minister for Justice: Maria Lúcia Lobato.
Minister for Health: Nélson Martins.
Minister for Planning and Finance: Maria Madalena Emília Pires.
Minister for Education, Culture, Youth and Sport: João Câncio Freitas.
Minister for Economy and Development: João Gonçalves.
Minister for Agriculture, Forestry and Fisheries: Mariano Sabino Lopes.
Minister for Social Solidarity: Paulo Assis Belo.
Minister for Tourism, Trade and Industry: Gil da Costa Alves.
Minister for Infrastructure: Pedro Lay.

MINISTRIES

Office of the President: Palácio das Cinzas, Kaikoli, Dili; tel. 3339011.
Office of the Prime Minister: Palácio do Governo, Av. Presidente Nicolau Lobato, Dili; tel. 7243559; fax 3339503; e-mail mail@primeministerandcabinet.gov.tp; internet www.pm.gov.tp.
Ministry of Agriculture, Forestry and Fisheries: Dili; e-mail agriculture@gov.east-timor.org; internet www.maf.gov.tl.
Ministry of Defence: Palácio do Governo 3, Edif. 4, Av. Presidente Nicolau Lobato, Dili; tel. 3310478; e-mail sed-tl@easttimor.minihub.org; internet www.timor-leste.gov.tl/mindef.
Ministry of Economy and Development: Dili.
Ministry of Education, Culture, Youth and Sport: Dili; e-mail education@gov.east-timor.org.
Ministry of Finance: Palácio do Governo, Edif. 5, Av. Presidente Nicolau Lobato, Dili; tel. 3339546; e-mail info@mof.gov.tl; internet www.mof.gov.tl.
Ministry of Foreign Affairs: Av. Praia dos Coqueiros, Marconi, Dili; tel. 3339600; fax 3339025; e-mail administration@mnec.gov-tl.net; internet www.mne.gov.tl.
Ministry of Health: Edif. dos Serviços Centrais do Ministério da Saúde, Rua de Caicoli, POB 374, Dili; tel. 3322467; fax 3325189; e-mail ministerforhealthtl@yahoo.com; internet www.minsau.gov.tl.
Ministry of Infrastructure: Fomento Bldg, Mandarin, Dili.
Ministry of Justice: Av. Jacinto Candido, Dili; tel. 3331160; e-mail mj@mj.gov.tl; internet www.mj.gov.tl.
Ministry of Natural Resources, Minerals and Energy Policy: Dili.
Ministry of Social Solidarity: Dili.
Ministry of State Administration and Territorial Management: Dili.
Ministry of Tourism, Trade and Industry: Dili.
Ministry of Transport, Communications and Public Works: Av. Bispo Medeiros, Dili; tel. 3339354; fax 3339350; e-mail info@mtcop.gov.tl; internet www.timor-leste.gov.tl/MTC.

President and Legislature

PRESIDENT

Presidential Election, First Ballot, 9 April 2007

Candidate	Votes	% of votes
Francisco Guterres (Fretilin)	112,666	27.89
José Ramos Horta (Independent)	88,102	21.81
Fernando de Araújo (PD)	77,459	19.18
Francisco Xavier do Amaral (ASDT)	58,125	14.39
Lucia Maria B. F. Lobato (PSD)	35,789	8.86
Manuel Tilman (KOTA)	16,534	4.09
Avelino Coelho da Silva (PST)	8,338	2.06
João Viegas Carrascalão (UDT)	6,928	1.72
Total	**403,941**	**100.00**

Presidential Election, Second Ballot, 9 May 2007

Candidate	Votes	%
José Ramos Horta	285,835	69.18
Francisco Guterres	127,342	30.82
Total	**413,177**	**100.00**

NATIONAL PARLIAMENT

A single-chamber Constituent Assembly was elected by popular vote on 30 August 2001. Its 88 members included 75 deputies elected

TIMOR-LESTE

under a national system of proportional representation and one representative from each of Timor-Leste's 13 districts, elected under a 'first-past-the-post' system. Upon independence on 20 May 2002 the Constituent Assembly became the National Parliament; it held its inaugural session on the same day. At the election of June 2007 the number of members was reduced from 88 to 65.

Speaker: FERNANDO DE ARAÚJO.

General Election, 30 June 2007

	Seats
Frente Revolucionária do Timor Leste Independente (Fretilin)	21
Congresso Nacional da Reconstrução de Timor-Leste	18
Associação Social-Democrata Timorense-Partido Social Democrata Timor Lorosae (ASDT-PSD)	11
Partido Democrático (PD)	8
Partido Unidade Nacional (PUN)	3
Aliança Democrática Klibur Oan Timor Asuwain-Partido do Povo de Timor (AD KOTA-PPT)	2
Partido Unidade Nacional Democrática da Resistência Timorense (UNDERTIM)	2
Total	**65**

Election Commission

National Electoral Commission (CNE): Av. Bispo Medeiros-Kintal, Dili; tel. 3310082; f. 2004; govt body; Chair. Dr FAUSTINO CARDOSO.

Political Organizations

Associação Popular Democrática de Timor Pro Referendo (Apodeti Pro Referendo) (Pro-Referendum Popular Democratic Association of Timor): c/o Frederico Almeida Santos Costa, CNRT Office, Balide, Dili; tel. 3324994; f. 1974; est. as Apodeti; adopted present name in Aug. 2000; fmrly supported autonomous integration with Indonesia; Pres. FREDERICO ALMEIDA SANTOS COSTA.

Associação Social-Democrata Timorense (ASDT) (Timor Social Democratic Association): Av. Direitos Humanos Lecidere, Dili; tel. 3983331; f. 2001; Pres. FRANCISCO XAVIER DO AMARAL.

Barisan Rakyat Timor Timur (BRTT) (East Timor People's Front): fmrly supported autonomous integration with Indonesia; Pres. FRANCISCO LOPES DA CRUZ.

Congresso Nacional da Reconstrução de Timor-Leste (CNRT) (National Congress for the Reconstruction of Timor-Leste): Rua Nu Laran, Bairro dos Grilos, Dili; tel. 7358696; internet www.cnrt-timor .org; f. 2007; Pres. KAY RALA 'XANANA' GUSMÃO.

Conselho Popular pela Defesa da República Democrática de Timor Leste (CPD-RDTL) (Popular Council for the Defence of the Democratic Republic of East Timor): opp. the Church, Balide, Dili; tel. 3481462; f. 1999; promotes adoption of 1975 Constitution of Democratic Republic of East Timor; Spokesperson CRISTIANO DA COSTA.

Frente Revolucionária do Timor Leste Independente (Fretilin) (Revolutionary Front for an Independent East Timor): Rua dos Mártires da Pátria, Dili; tel. 3321409; internet fretilin-rdtl.blogspot .com; f. 1974 to seek full independence for East Timor; entered into alliance with the UDT in 1986; Pres. FRANCISCO GUTERRES.

Klibur Oan Timor Asuwain (KOTA) (Association of Timorese Heroes): Rua dos Mártires da Pátria, Fatuhada, Dili; tel. 3324661; e-mail clementinoamaral@hotmail.com; f. 1974 as pro-integration party; supported independence with Timorese traditions; Pres. MANUEL TILMAN.

Movement for the Reconciliation and Unity of the People of East Timor (MRUPT): f. 1997; Chair. MANUEL VIEGAS CARRASCALÃO.

Partai Democratik Maubere (PDM) (Maubere Democratic Party): Blk B II, 16 Surikmas Lama Kraik, Fatumeta, Dili; tel. 3184508; e-mail pdm_party@hotmail.com; f. 2000; Pres. PAOLO PINTO.

Partai Liberal (PL) (Liberal Party): Talbessi Sentral, Dili; tel. 3786448; Pres. ARMANDO JOSÉ DOURADO DA SILVA.

Partido Democrata Cristão (PDC) (Christian Democrat Party): Former Escola Cartilha, Rua Quintal Kiik, Bairro Economico, Dili; tel. 3324683; e-mail arlindom@octa4.net.au; f. 2000; Pres. ANTÓNIO XIMENES.

Directory

Partido Democrático (PD) (Democratic Party): 1 Rua Democracia, Pantai Kelapa, Dili; tel. 3608421; e-mail flazama@hotmail.com; Pres. FERNANDO DE ARAÚJO.

Partido Nacionalista Timorense (PNT) (Nationalist Party of Timor): Dili; tel. 3323518; internet pnt-timor-leste.planetaclix.pt; Pres. Dr ABÍLIO ARAÚJO.

Partido do Povo de Timor (PPT) (Timorese People's Party): Dili; tel. 3568325; f. 2000; pro-integration; supported candidacy of Xanana Gusmão for presidency of East Timor; Pres. Dr JACOB XAVIER.

Partido Republika National Timor Leste (PARENTIL) (National Republic Party of East Timor): Perumnar Bairopite Bob Madey Ran, Fahan Jalam, Ailobu Laran RTK; tel. 3361393; Pres. FLAVIANO PEREIRA LOPEZ.

Partido Social Democrata Timor Lorosae (PSD) (Social Democrat Party of East Timor): Apartado 312, Correios de Dili, Dili; tel. 3357027; e-mail psdtimor@hotmail.com; f. 2000; Pres. ZACARIAS ALBANO DA COSTA.

Partido Socialista de Timor (PST) (Socialist Party of Timor): Rua Colegio das Madras, Balide, Dili; tel. 3560246; e-mail kaynaga@ hotmail.com; Marxist-Leninist Fretilin splinter group; Pres. AVELINO COELHO DA SILVA.

Partido Trabalhista Timorense (PTT) (Timor Labour Party): 2B Rua Travessa de Befonte, 2 Bairro Formosa, Dili; tel. 3322807; f. 1974; Pres. PAULO FREITAS DA SILVA.

Partido Unidade Nacional (PUN) (United National Party): c/o National Parliament, Dili; f. 2005; Pres. FERNANDA BORGES.

Partido Unidade Nacional Democrática da Resistência Timorense (UNDERTIM): c/o National Parliament, Dili; Pres. CORNELIO GAMA.

União Democrata-Cristão de Timor (UDC/PDC) (Christian Democratic Union of Timor): 62 Rua Almirante Américo Thomás, Mandarin, Dili; tel. 3325042; f. 1998; Pres. VINCENTE DA SILVA GUTERRES.

União Democrática Timorense (UDT) (Timorese Democratic Union): Palapagoa Rua da India, Dili; tel. 3881453; e-mail joaocarrascalao@email.msn.com; internet fitini.net/udttimor; f. 1974; allied itself with Fretilin in 1986; Pres. JOÃO CARRASCALÃO; Sec.-Gen. DOMINGOS OLIVEIRA.

Diplomatic Representation

EMBASSIES IN TIMOR-LESTE

Australia: Av. dos Mártires da Pátria, Dili; tel. 3322111; fax 3322247; e-mail austemb_dili@dfat.gov.au; internet www .easttimor.embassy.gov.au; Ambassador PETER HEYWARD.

Brazil: Av. Governador Serpa Rosa, POB 157, Farol, Dili; tel. 3324203; fax 3324620; e-mail esctimor@office.net.au; Ambassador EDSON MARINHO DUARTE MONTEIRO.

China, People's Republic: Av. Governador Serpa Rosa, Farol, Dili; tel. 3325168; fax 3325166; e-mail chinaemb_tp@mfa.gov.cn; Ambassador SU JIAN.

Indonesia: Farol, Palapaco, POB 207, Dili; tel. 3317107; fax 3312332; e-mail kukridil@hotmail.com; internet www.kbridili.org; Ambassador AHMED BEY SOFWAN.

Japan: Pertamina 6, Dili; tel. 3323131; fax 3323130; e-mail japrepet@yahoo.co.jp; Ambassador KENJI SHIMIZU.

Korea, Republic: Av. de Portugal, Motael, Dili; tel. 3321635; fax 3323636; e-mail koreadili@mofat.go.kr; Ambassador RYU JIN-KYU.

Malaysia: Rua Almirante Américo Thomás, Mandarin, Dili; tel. 3321804; fax 3321805; e-mail mwdili@mail.timortelecom.tp; internet www.kln.gov.my/perwakilan/dili; Ambassador NAZARUDIN BIN SALLEH.

New Zealand: Rua Alferes Duarte Arbiro, Lighthouse Area, Farol, Dili; fax 3324982; e-mail dili@mfat.gov.nz; Ambassador TIM MCIVOR.

Philippines: Rooms 8–10, Hotel Turismo, Rua Direitos Humanos, Bidau Lecidere, Dili; tel. 33310408; fax 3310407; e-mail dilipe@dfa .gov.ph; Ambassador FARITA A. AGUILUCHO-ONG.

Portugal: Edif. ACAIT, Av. Presidente Nicolau Lobato, Dili; tel. 3312533; fax 3312526; e-mail embaixada.portugal@embpor.tp; internet www.embpor.tp; Ambassador JOÃO RAMOS PINTO.

Thailand: Av. de Portugal, Motael, Dili; tel. 3310609; fax 3322179; e-mail thaidli@mfa.go.th; Ambassador WIWAT KUNTHONTHIEN.

USA: Av. de Portugal, Praia dos Coqueiros, Dili; tel. 3324684; fax 3313206; e-mail larsonta@state.gov; Ambassador HANS G. KLEMM.

Judicial System

Until independence was granted on 20 May 2002 all legislative and executive authority with respect to the administration of the judiciary in East Timor was vested in UNTAET. During the transitional period of administration a two-tier court structure was established, consisting of District Courts and a Court of Appeal. The Constitution, promulgated in March 2002, specified that Timor-Leste should have three categories of courts: the Supreme Court of Justice and other law courts; the High Administrative, Tax and Audit Court and other administrative courts of first instance; and military courts. The judiciary would be regulated by the Superior Council of the Judiciary, the function of which would be to oversee the judicial sector and, in particular, to control the appointment, promotion, discipline and dismissal of judges. The effectiveness of the newly established judicial system was severely impaired by Timor-Leste's lack of human and material resources. In July 2002 there were only 22 judges in Timor-Leste, none of whom possessed more than two years of legal experience. In July 2003 the Court of Appeal was reconstituted. However, in the same month a ruling by its President that Timor-Leste's law should be based on that of Portugal and not Indonesia (as was currently the case) threatened to have serious consequences for the legal system.

Court of Appeal: Dili; Pres. CLAUDIO XIMENES.

Office of the Prosecutor-General: Dili; Prosecutor-General ANA MARIA PESSÔA PEREIRA DA SILVA PINTO.

Religion

In 2004 it was estimated that about 93.5% of the total population were Roman Catholic.

CHRISTIANITY

The Roman Catholic Church

Timor-Leste comprises the dioceses of Dili and Baucau, directly responsible to the Holy See. In December 2006 there were an estimated 958,452 Roman Catholics.

Bishop of Baucau: Most Rev. BASILIO DO NASCIMENTO, Largo da Catedral, Baucau 88810; tel. 4121209; fax 4121380.

Bishop of Dili: Most Rev. ALBERTO RICARDO DA SILVA, Av. dos Direitos Humanos, Bidau Lecidere, CP 4, Dili 88010; tel. 3324850; fax 3321177.

Protestant Church

Igreja Protestante iha Timor Lorosa'e: Jl. Raya Comoro, POB 1186, Dili 88110; tel. and fax 3323128; f. 1988; est. as Gereja Kristen Timor Timur (GKTT); adopted present name 2000; Moderator Rev. FRANCISCO DE VASCONCELOS; 30,000 mems.

The Press

The Constitution promulgated in March 2002 guarantees freedom of the press in Timor-Leste.

Lalenok (Mirror): Rua Gov. Celestino da Silva, Farol, Dili; tel. 3321607; e-mail lalenok@hotmail.com; f. 2000; publ. by Kamelin Media Group; Tetum; 3 a week; Dir-Gen. and Chief Editor VIRGÍLIO DA SILVA GUTERRES; Editor JOSÉ MARIA POMPELA; circ. 300.

Lian Maubere: Dili; f. 1999; weekly.

The Official Gazette of East Timor: Dili; f. 1999 by UNTAET; forum for publication of all govt regulations and directives, acts of national organs or institutions of and other acts of public interest requiring general notification; published in English, Portuguese and Tetum, with translations in Bahasa Indonesia available on request.

Suara Timor Lorosae: 7 Av. Martinez da Patria, Dili; tel. 322823; fax 322821; e-mail redaksi@suaratimorlorosae.com; internet www.suaratimorlorosae.com; f. 2000; daily; Editor-in-Chief and Publr SALVADOR J. XIMENES SOARES.

Tais Timor: Dili; f. 2000; fmrly published by the Office of Communication and Public Information (OCPI) of the UN; Tetum, English, Portuguese and Bahasa Indonesia; every fortnight; distributed free of charge; circ. 75,000.

Timor Post: 6 Rua Dom Aleixo Corte-Real, Dili; f. 2000; managed by editors and staff of the fmr Suara Timor Timur; Bahasa Indonesia, Tetum, Portuguese and English; daily; Man. Editor OTELIO OTE; Chief Editor and Dir ADERITO HUGO DA COSTA; circ. 600.

PRESS ASSOCIATION

Sindicato dos Jornalistas de Timor-Leste (SJTL): Rua Dom Aleixo Corte-Real, Bebora, Dili; tel. 7248549; e-mail sjti@yahoo.com; f. 2001; Pres. RODOLFO DE SOUSA.

Timor Lorosae Journalists' Association (TLJA): Rua de Caicoli, Dili; tel. 3324047; fax 3327505; e-mail ajtl_tlja@hotmail.com; f. 1999; Co-ordinator OTELIO OTE; Pres. VIRGÍLIO DA SILVA GUTERRES.

Broadcasting and Communications

TELECOMMUNICATIONS

In July 2002 the Government granted a consortium led by Portugal Telecom a 15-year concession permitting it to establish and operate Timor-Leste's telecommunications systems. Under the terms of the concession the consortium agreed to provide every district in Timor-Leste with telecommunications services at the most inexpensive tariffs viable within 15 months. At the expiry of the concession in 2017 the telecommunications system was to be transferred to government control.

Timor-Leste Telecom (TT): Sala No. 7, Hotel Timor, Av. dos Mártires da Pátria, POB 135, Dili; tel. 3303000; fax 3303209; e-mail info@timortelecom.tp; internet www.timortelecom.tp; f. 2002; jt venture mainly operated by Portugal Telecom; provides telecommunications services in Timor-Leste; CEO JOSÉ BRANDÃO DE SOUSA; 114 employees.

BROADCASTING

Following independence UNMISET transferred control of public television and radio in Timor-Leste to the new Government. In 2003 a Public Broadcasting Service was established, controlled by an independent board of directors.

Radio

There are 18 radio stations operating in Timor-Leste, including community radio stations for each of the country's 13 districts. In addition to the public service, Ratio Timor-Leste, the Roman Catholic Church operates a radio station, Radio Kamanak, while a third populist station, Voz Esperança, broadcasts in Dili. A fourth radio station, Radio Falintil FM, also operates in Dili and, in October 2003, the Christian station Voice FM was established. In 2000 the US radio station, Voice of America, began broadcasting to Timor-Leste seven days a week in English, Portuguese and Bahasa Indonesia.

Radio Timor-Leste (RTL): Rua de Caicoli, Dili; tel. 3321826; e-mail radio@rttl.org; internet www.rttl.org; fmrly Radio UNTAET; name changed as above in 2002; broadcasts mainly in Bahasa Indonesia, but also in English, Portuguese and Tetum, to an estimated 90% of Timor-Leste's population; Man. PAULA RODRIGES.

Television

TV Timor-Leste (TVTL): Rua de Caicoli, Dili; tel. 3321825; e-mail tv@rttl.org; internet www.rttl.org; f. 2000; est. as Televisaun Timor Lorosa'e by UNTAET; adopted present name in May 2002; broadcasts in Tetum and Portuguese; Gen. Man. ANTONIO DIAZ.

Finance

(cap. = capital; res = reserves; dep. = deposits)

BANKING

In February 2001 the East Timor Central Payments Office was officially opened. This was succeeded in November of that year by the Banking and Payments Authority, which was intended to function as a precursor to a central bank.

Banking and Payments Authority (BPA): Av. Bispo Medeiros, POB 59, Dili; tel. 3313712; fax 3313713; e-mail info@bancocentral.tl; internet www.bancocentral.tl; inaugurated Nov. 2001; regulates and supervises Timor-Leste's financial system, formulates and implements payments system policies, provides banking services to Timor-Leste's administration and foreign official institutions, manages fiscal reserves; fmrly Central Payments Office; cap. US $18.2m., res $1.9m., dep. $117.9m. (March 2006); Chair. and Gen. Man. ABRAÃO F. DE VASCONSELOS; Dep. Gen. Mans MARIA JOSÉ DE JESUS SARMENTO, NUR AINI DJAFAR ALKATIRI.

Instituição de Micro Finanças de Timor-Leste (IMFTL): Av. Martires da Patria, Mandarin, Dili; tel. 3339186; fax 3310444; e-mail smspirito@hotmail.com; f. 2002; microfinance.

Foreign Banks

Australia and New Zealand Banking Group Ltd (ANZ) (Australia): Cnr Av. Presidente Nicolau Lobato and Rua Belarmino Lobo,

Bidau Lecidere, POB 264, Dili; tel. 3324800; fax 3324822; e-mail anzeasttimor@anz.com; internet www.anz.com/TimorLeste; retail and commercial banking services; Gen. Man. CHRIS DURMAN; Group CEO JOHN MCFARLANE.

Banco Nacional Ultramarino (Portugal): Edif. BNU, 12–13 Av. Presidente Nicolau Lobato, Dili; tel. 3323385; fax 3323678; e-mail cgd.timor@mail.timortelecom.tp; internet www.cgd.pt/english/international_network/timor.htm; Gen. Man. Dr CORREIA PINTO; 9 brs.

PT Bank Mandiri (Persero) (Indonesia): 12 Av. Presidente Nicolau Lobato, Colmera, Dili; tel. 3317777; fax 3317444; e-mail dili_timorleste@bankmandiri.co.id; internet www.bankmandiri.co.id; Group Chair. EDWIN GERUNGAN.

Trade and Industry

GOVERNMENT AGENCIES

Direcção Nacional de Petróleo e Gas: 1st Floor, Fomento Bldg, Mandarin, POB 171, Dili; tel. and fax 3317143; e-mail amandiogusmao@yahoo.com; internet www.timor-leste.gov.tl/EMRD; controlled by the Ministry of Natural Resources, Minerals and Energy Policy; Dir AMANDIO GUSMÃO SOARES.

National Petroleum Authority: 5 Av. de Portugal, POB 113, Farol, Dili; tel. 3324098; fax 3324082; e-mail dilioffice@timorseada.org; internet www.timorseada.org; f. 2008; responsible for management of government petroleum revenues; Pres. GUALDINO DO CARMO DA SILVA.

TradeInvest Timor-Leste: Memorial Hall, Av. Praia dos Coqueiros Farol, Dili 8000; tel. 3331084; fax 3331087; e-mail tradeinvest_tl@yahoo.com; internet www.timor-leste.gov.tl/TradeInvest; f. 2005; est. to encourage devt of entrepreneurship within Timor-Leste.

UTILITIES

As a result of the civil conflict in 1999, some 13–23 power stations were reported to require repairs ranging from moderate maintenance to almost complete rehabilitation. The rehabilitation of the power sector was funded largely by foreign donors. By July 2003 31 generators had been restored, supplying electricity to Dili, as well as to 12 districts and 33 subdistricts.

Electricidade de Timor-Leste (EDTL): EDTL Bldg, Rua Estrada de Balide, Caicoli, Dili; tel. 3339254; fax 7230095; e-mail virgiliofguterres@hotmail.com; govt dept; responsible for power generation, distribution and financial management of power sector in Timor-Leste; transferred to external management in 2002; Dir VIRGILIO GUTERRES.

CO-OPERATIVE

Cooperativa Café Timor (CCT): 16 Rua Barros Gomes, Dili; f. 2000 under the Timor Economic Rehabilitation and Development Project; produces, markets and distributes organic coffee; also provides information and advisory services for member farmers; Operational Dir SISTO MONIZ PIEDADE; 19,000 mems.

TRADE UNIONS

Konfederasaun Sindikatu Timor-Leste (KSTL) (Trade Union Confederation of Timor-Leste): Rua Sebastião da Costa, Colmera, Dili; f. 2001; represents nine unions, comprising approximately 4,700 workers within the press, teaching, nursing, and the construction, agricultural, maritime and transport sectors; Pres. JOSÉ DA CONCEIÇÃO DA COSTA.

Labour Advocacy Institute of East Timor (LAIFET): Rua Abílio Monteiro Palapaso, Dili; tel. 3317243; Dir DOMINGOS BAPTISTA DE ARAÚJO.

Serikat Buruh Socialis Timor (SBST) (Timor Socialist Workers' Union): Dili; controlled by Partido Socialista de Timor; Dir Dr LUCIANO DA SILVA.

Transport

ROADS

The road network in Timor-Leste is poorly designed and has suffered from long-term neglect. In December 1999 the World Bank reported that some 57% of the country's 1,414 km of paved roads were in poor or damaged condition. Many gravel roads are rough and potholed and are inaccessible to most vehicles. Some repair and maintenance work on the road network was carried out in 2005, using funding supplied by external donors.

SHIPPING

Timor-Leste's maritime infrastructure includes ports at Dili, Carabela and Com, smaller wharves at Oecusse (Oekussi) and Liquiça (Likisia), and slip-landing structures in Oecusse, Batugade and Suai. In November 2001, following its reconstruction, the management of the port at Dili was transferred to the Government. The port was expected to be a significant source of revenue.

Port Authority of Timor-Leste (APORTIL): 2 Rua Almirante Américo Thomás, Dili; f. 2003.

Principal Shipping Companies

Everise Freight Forwarding Inc: 2 Rua Belarmino Lobo, Dili; tel. 3324844; fax 3312856; e-mail everisedili@yahoo.com.

SDV Logistics (East Timor): Av. Presidente Nicolau Lobato, Bairro dos Grilos, POB 398, Dili; tel. 3322818; fax 3324077; e-mail dili@sdv.com; internet www.sdveasttimor.com; f. 1999; freight forwarder, shipping agent and customs broker; Man. Dir ERIC MANCINI.

CIVIL AVIATION

Timor-Leste has two international airports and eight grass runways. In June 2001 Dili Express Pte was the first Timor-based company to begin international flights, with a service to Singapore. In 2005 Timor-Leste's first national carrier, Kakoak Air, commenced operations. Air North and Austasia operate regular flights from Australia to Dili; the latter carrier (in collaboration with SilkAir) launched a direct flight between Singapore and Dili in August 2008.

Civil Aviation Division (CAD): Dili; tel. 3317110; fax 3317111; e-mail henriques_sabino@yahoo.com; internet www.timor-leste.gov.tl/CAA; arm of the Ministry of Transport, Communications and Public Works; responsible for overall planning, implementation and operation of aviation services in Timor-Leste; Dir JULIÃO X. CARLOS.

Kakoak Air: Dili; f. 2005; operates twice-weekly passenger service between Dili and Kupang, Indonesia; Gen. Dir JORGE SERANNO.

Tourism

The tourism sector remains undeveloped. The country's first national park was established in 2007. Nino Konis Santana National Park, which encompasses more than 123,600 ha, aims to protect a number of endangered species, including 25 endemic birds. The park also incorporates a marine area of 55,600 ha, which contains a globally important biodiversity of coral and reef fish.

Turismo de Timor-Leste: Apartado 194, Dili; tel. 3310371; fax 3339179; e-mail info@turismotimorleste.com; internet www.turismotimorleste.com; f. 2002; Dir MIGUEL LOBATO.

TOGO

Introductory Survey

Location, Climate, Language, Religion, Flag, Capital

The Togolese Republic lies in West Africa, forming a narrow strip stretching north from a coastline of about 50 km (30 miles) on the Gulf of Guinea. It is bordered by Ghana to the west, by Benin to the east, and by Burkina Faso to the north. The climate in the coastal area is hot and humid, with an average annual temperature of 27°C (81°F); rainfall in this zone averages 875 mm (34.4 ins) per year, and is heaviest during May–October. Precipitation in the central region is heaviest in May–June and in October, and in the north, where the average annual temperature is 30°C (86°F), there is a rainy season from July–September. The official languages are French, Kabiye and Ewe. About one-half of the population follows animist beliefs, while about 35% are Christians and 15% Muslims. The national flag (approximate proportions 3 by 5) has five equal horizontal stripes, alternately green and yellow, with a square red canton, containing a five-pointed white star, in the upper hoist. The capital is Lomé.

Recent History

Togoland, of which modern Togo was formerly a part, became a German colony in 1894. Shortly after the outbreak of the First World War, the colony was occupied by French and British forces. After the war, a League of Nations mandate divided Togoland into two administrative zones, with France controlling the larger eastern section, while the United Kingdom governed the west. The partition of Togoland split the homeland of the Ewe people, who inhabit the southern part of the territory, and this has been a continuing source of friction. After the Second World War, French and British Togoland became UN Trust Territories. In May 1956 a UN-supervised plebiscite in British Togoland produced, despite Ewe opposition, majority support for a merger with the neighbouring territory of the Gold Coast, then a British colony, in an independent state. The region accordingly became part of Ghana in the following year. In October 1956, in another plebiscite, French Togoland voted to become an autonomous republic, with internal self-government, within the French Community. Togo's foremost political parties at that time were the Comité de l'unité togolaise (usually known as the Unité togolaise—UT), led by Sylvanus Olympio, and the Parti togolais du progrès (PTP), led by Nicolas Grunitzky, Olympio's brother-in-law. In 1956 Grunitzky became Prime Minister in the first autonomous Government, but in April 1958 a UN-supervised election was won by the UT. Olympio became Prime Minister and led Togo to full independence on 27 April 1960.

At elections in April 1961 Olympio became Togo's first President, while the UT was elected (unopposed) to all 51 seats in the Assemblée nationale. At the same time a referendum approved a new Constitution. On 13 January 1963 the UT regime was overthrown by a military revolt, in which Olympio was killed. Grunitzky subsequently assumed the presidency on a provisional basis. A referendum in May approved another Constitution, confirmed Grunitzky as President and elected a new legislature from a single list of candidates, giving equal representation to the four main political parties.

President Grunitzky was deposed by a bloodless military coup, led by Lt-Col (later Gen.) Etienne (Gnassingbé) Eyadéma, the Army Chief of Staff, on 13 January 1967. Eyadéma, a member of the Kabiye ethnic group, who had taken a prominent part in the 1963 rising and was reputedly Olympio's assassin, assumed the office of President in April. Political parties were banned, and the President ruled by decree. In November 1969 a new ruling party, the Rassemblement du peuple togolais (RPT), was founded, led by Eyadéma.

In Togo's first elections for 16 years, held on 30 December 1979, Eyadéma (the sole candidate) was confirmed as President of the Republic for a seven-year term. At the same time a new Constitution was overwhelmingly endorsed, while the list of 67 candidates for a single-party Assemblée nationale was approved by 96% of votes cast. On 13 January 1980 Eyadéma proclaimed the 'Third Republic'. In December 1986 President Eyadéma was re-elected, unopposed, for a further seven-year term.

In December 1990 a new constitution was drafted, which envisaged, *inter alia*, a plurality of political parties. Meanwhile, several recently formed, unofficial opposition movements formed a co-ordinating organization, the Front des associations pour le renouveau (FAR), led by Yawovi Agboyibo, to campaign for the immediate introduction of a multi-party political system. Eyadéma subsequently agreed to implement a general amnesty for political dissidents and to permit the legalization of political organizations. Following instances of violent unrest in April 1991, Eyadéma, fearing a civil conflict between the Kabiye and Ewe ethnic groups (the Government and armed forces were composed overwhelmingly of members of the first group, while opposition groups for the most part represented the Ewe people), announced that a new constitution would be introduced within one year, and that multi-party legislative elections would be organized. At the end of the month it was announced that the FAR was to be disbanded. Agboyibo subsequently formed his own party, the Comité d'action pour le renouveau (CAR), which in May became one of 10 parties to enter into a Front de l'opposition démocratique (FOD, later renamed the Coalition de l'opposition démocratique—COD).

Following the organization of a general strike by the FOD, the Government agreed, in June 1991, that a 'national conference' would be held, with the power to choose a transitional Prime Minister and to establish a transitional legislative body. The conference opened in July, however, when it adopted resolutions suspending the Constitution, dissolving the Assemblée nationale and giving the conference sovereign power, government representatives withdrew. Subsequently the conference resolved to 'freeze' the assets of the RPT, to transfer most of the powers of the President to a Prime Minister, and to prevent Eyadéma from contesting future elections. In defiance of a decree issued by Eyadéma temporarily suspending proceedings, the conference elected a Prime Minister, Joseph Kokou Koffigoh (a senior lawyer and prominent human rights activist), announced the dissolution of the RPT and the formation of a transitional legislature, the Haut Conseil de la République (HCR). Eyadéma capitulated, signing a decree that proclaimed Koffigoh as transitional Prime Minister. In September Koffigoh formed a transitional Government, most of whose members had not previously held office: he himself assumed the defence portfolio.

In October 1991 members of the armed forces seized control of the national broadcasting station, demanding that full executive powers be restored to Eyadéma. They returned to barracks on Eyadéma's orders. Koffigoh confirmed that a constitutional referendum and elections would be held in 1992. In November 1991, following the adoption of legislation by the HCR confirming the dissolution of the RPT, troops seized the broadcasting headquarters and surrounded the Prime Minister's residence, demanding that Eyadéma nominate a new government and that the HCR be abolished. At least 20 people were killed in the fighting that ensued. In December troops captured Koffigoh during an attack on his residence, killing several of his guards. Koffigoh agreed to form a new government. At the end of December the reconvened HCR restored legal status to the RPT and announced the formation of a transitional 'Government of National Union', which comprised many of the members of the previous transitional administration, but also two close associates of Eyadéma.

In January 1992 an electoral schedule was announced; the constitutional referendum and local, legislative and presidential elections were to be held by June of that year. In May the attempted assassination of Gilchrist Olympio, the son of the former President, who was regarded as a potential presidential candidate, and the murder of another prominent member of the opposition provoked renewed unrest. In late May the Council of Ministers abandoned the electoral timetable. In July the HCR adopted the draft Constitution and an electoral code, and the constitutional referendum was scheduled for August, although it was subsequently postponed. Meanwhile, a report published by the International Federation of Human Rights concluded that members of the armed forces had been responsible for the attempted murder of Olympio, implicating Eyadéma's son, Capt. Ernest Gnassingbé (a military officer). Later in July Tavio Ayao Amorin, a member of the HCR regarded as a radical was shot and fatally wounded. In response, the recently formed

Collectif de l'opposition démocratique (COD-2), an alliance of some 25 political organizations and trade unions, called a general strike, which was widely observed. In August agreement was reached on opposition access to the state-controlled media, and on the extension until 31 December of the transition period. In late August the HCR restored to Eyadéma the power to preside over the Council of Ministers, and to represent Togo abroad; furthermore, his agreement would henceforth be necessary in the appointment of members of the Government.

The transitional Government was dissolved on 1 September 1992. Later that month a new transitional Government, led by Koffigoh, was appointed, including representatives of 10 parties; the most influential ministries were allocated to members of the RPT. On 27 September the new Constitution was approved in a referendum by 98.1% of the votes cast. At the end of the month, however, it was announced that the local, legislative and presidential elections were to be further postponed. In October eight opposition parties announced the formation of a 'Patriotic Front', to be led by the leader of the Union togolaise pour la démocratie (UTD), Edem Kodjo, and Agboyibo. In November Koffigoh dismissed two ministers (both adherents of the RPT) for their conduct during an attack on the HCR by members of the armed forces in October, but Eyadéma overruled this decision.

In January 1993 Eyadéma dissolved the Government, reappointing Koffigoh as Prime Minister, and stated that he would appoint a new government of national unity to organize elections. His action provoked protests by the opposition parties, who claimed that, according to the Constitution, the HCR should appoint a Prime Minister since the transition period had now expired. In the same month two ministers representing the French and German Governments visited Togo to offer mediation in the political crisis. During their visit at least 20 people were killed when police opened fire on anti-Government protesters. Thousands of Togolese subsequently fled from Lomé, many seeking refuge in Benin or Ghana. In February inter-Togolese discussions organized by the French and German Governments in France failed when the presidential delegation withdrew after one day. In that month the French, German and US Governments suspended their programmes of aid to Togo. A new Government, in which supporters of Eyadéma retained the principal posts, was formed in February. In March COD-2 member parties stated that they now regarded Koffigoh as an obstacle to democratization, and nominated a 'parallel' Prime Minister, Jean-Lucien Savi de Tové.

In April 1993 a new electoral schedule was announced, envisaging elections to the presidency and the legislature in July and August, respectively. The RPT designated Eyadéma as its presidential candidate. In May the COD-2 declared that it would boycott the elections, alleging that they would not be fairly conducted, and that opposition politicians had no guarantee of their safety. In July, however, the Togolese Government and the COD-2 signed an agreement establishing 25 August as the date for the first round of presidential voting. The agreement stipulated that the Togolese armed forces should be confined to barracks during the election period, and that international military observers should be present to confirm this, while international civilian observers should also be present for the election. An independent, nine-member Commission électorale nationale (CEN) was to be established, to include three members nominated by the opposition parties. Later in July the COD-2 nominated Kodjo as its presidential candidate; however, in the same month two other candidates—Agboyibo and Abou Djobo Boukari—were nominated by parties affiliated to the COD-2. Three candidates eventually contested the presidential election held on 25 August at which Eyadéma was reported to have obtained 96.49% of the votes cast. French election observers concluded that the poll had not been satisfactorily conducted; observers from the USA and Germany had withdrawn from Togo shortly before the elections took place.

In the legislative elections, finally held on 6 and 20 February 1994, some 347 candidates contested 81 seats. Despite the murder of an elected CAR representative after the first round, and violent incidents at polling stations during the second round, international observers expressed themselves satisfied with the conduct of the elections. The opposition won a narrow victory in the polls, with the CAR winning 36 seats and the UTD seven; the RPT obtained 35 seats and two other smaller pro-Eyadéma parties won three. During March Eyadéma consulted the main opposition parties on the formation of a new government. In late March the CAR and the UTD reached an agreement on the terms of their alliance and jointly proposed the candidacy of Agboyibo for Prime Minister. In March and April the Supreme Court declared the results of the legislative elections invalid in three constituencies (in which the CAR had won two seats and the UTD one) and ordered by-elections. In April Eyadéma nominated Kodjo as Prime Minister. The CAR subsequently declared that it would not participate in an administration formed by Kodjo. Kodjo took office on 25 April; his Government, formed in May, comprised eight members of the RPT and other pro-Eyadéma parties, three members of the UTD, and eight independents.

At the by-elections, conducted on 4 and 18 August 1996 in the presence of 22 international observers, the RPT won control of all three constituencies. Consequently, the RPT and its allies were able to command a majority in the legislature, thus precipitating the resignation of the Kodjo administration. On 20 August Eyadéma appointed Kwassi Klutse, hitherto Minister of Planning and Territorial Development, as Prime Minister, and the new Council of Ministers, appointed in late August, comprised almost exclusively supporters of Eyadéma. In November the Union pour la justice et la démocratie, which held two seats in the legislature, announced that it was officially to merge with the RPT, thus giving the RPT an overall majority, with 41 seats.

In September 1997 a new electoral code was approved, providing for a CEN comprising nine members, chaired by the President of the Court of Appeal and including four members appointed by the opposition. The CAR, however, boycotted the legislative session in protest at the Government's refusal to reveal the findings of a report by a mission of the European Union (EU, see p. 255) on the country's electoral process. Later that month opposition parties, led by the CAR and the Union des forces de changement (UFC), organized a demonstration in Lomé in protest at the new electoral law and condemned as fraudulent the Government's preparations for the forthcoming presidential election.

Shortly before the presidential election, which was held on 21 June 1998, the Government had refused to permit the presence of 500 national observers trained by the EU. The election proceeded amid accusations of electoral malpractice, and on the following day counting of votes was halted without explanation, reportedly when the early returns showed Eyadéma to be in second place. Four members of the CEN resigned the same day, alleging intimidation. The Minister of the Interior and Security, Gen. Seyi Memene, announced that he assumed responsibility for the ballot count, and that Eyadéma had been re-elected President with 52.1% of the valid votes cast. Gilchrist Olympio, who had contested the election from exile in Ghana, was officially stated to have won 34.1%. Following the announcement of the result, violent protests erupted throughout Lomé. The USA condemned the conduct of the election, and called on the Government to respect its own laws and electoral code, while the EU decided not to recognize the result, which was, none the less, confirmed by the Constitutional Court.

In September 1998 Klutse announced his new Council of Ministers. Despite Eyadéma's stated intention to form a government of national unity, no opposition figures were willing to be included. Among the few new appointments was Koffigoh, as Minister of State, responsible for Foreign Affairs and Co-operation. In November the Government survived a legislative vote of censure tabled by the CAR and the UTD.

Elections to the Assemblée nationale took place on 21 March 1999, contested only by the RPT and by two small parties loyal to Eyadéma, including Koffigoh's Coordination nationale des forces nouvelles, as well as by 12 independent candidates. (The principal opposition parties had boycotted the polling.) The Constitutional Court ruled that the RPT had won 77 seats, and that independent candidates had taken two seats. By-elections were to take place in two constituencies in which voting had been invalidated. (Both of these seats were subsequently won by the RPT.) Despite international criticism, Eyadéma rejected demands for fresh elections, declaring that the opposition had been afforded ample opportunity to participate. In April Klutse tendered his Government's resignation; in May Eugene Koffi Adogboli was appointed Prime Minister.

In May 1999 Amnesty International published a report detailing numerous abuses of human rights committed by Togolese security forces, alleging that hundreds of political opponents of Eyadéma had been killed following the 1998 presidential election. In late July 1999 Eyadéma (who rejected the validity of the report) urged the UN and the Organization of African Unity (OAU, now the African Union—AU, see p. 172) to assist in the establishment of an international commission of inquiry into the allegations; such a commission was established in June 2000.

Discussions between the Government and opposition began in Lomé in July 1999, with the assistance of four international facilitators, representing France, Germany, the EU and La Francophonie. Eyadéma's announcement that he would not stand for re-election in 2003 and that new legislative elections would be held, was widely credited with breaking the deadlock in negotiations, and, after the opposition had agreed to accept Eyadéma's victory in the presidential election, an accord was signed on 29 July 1999 by all the parties involved in negotiations. The accord made provision for the creation of an independent electoral body and for the creation of a code of conduct to regulate political activity.

The first meeting took place in August 1999 of the 24-member Comité paritaire de suivi (CPS) responsible for the implementation of the accord, composed of an equal number of opposition and pro-Eyadéma representatives, and also including intermediaries from the EU. Harry Octavianus Olympio, the Minister for the Promotion of Democracy and the Rule of Law (and a cousin of Gilchrist Olympio), was appointed to head the CPS. Despite the reservations of the UFC, a compromise agreement on announcing election results was reached in September, and in December agreement was reached on a revised electoral code, providing for the establishment of an independent electoral commission. In April 2000 Eyadéma obliged the Assemblée nationale to accept the new electoral code. The EU subsequently offered to provide financial support for the elections, which were scheduled to be held later in 2000. The 20 members of the new Commission électorale nationale indépendante (CENI) were named in June, and in July Arthème Ahoomey-Zounou of the Convergence patriotique panafricaine (CPP—formed in 1999 by the amalgamation of the UTD and three smaller parties, and headed by Edem Kodjo) was elected as president of the CENI.

In August 2000 Adogboli was overwhelmingly defeated in a legislative vote of no confidence; he therefore presented his resignation and that of his Government to Eyadéma. In late August Eyadéma appointed Agbéyomè Kodjo, hitherto the President of the Assemblée nationale, and regarded as a close ally of the President, as Prime Minister. A government reshuffle was effected in October. In January 2001 the CENI announced that the legislative elections would be held in two rounds, on 14 and 28 October 2001, and that the disputed electoral registers from the 1998 presidential election would be used in these polls.

In February 2002 the Assemblée nationale approved amendments to electoral legislation and to the remit and constitution of the CENI; notably, henceforth all candidates for legislative elections were required to have been continuously resident in Togo for six months prior to elections, with presidential candidates to have been resident for a continuous 12 months. The CENI was also to be reduced in size from 20 to 10 members, and decisions were to be taken by a two-thirds' majority, instead of the four-fifths' majority required hitherto; these amendments led to a further postponement of the elections, which had been scheduled to take place in March. These measures attracted international disapproval, notably prompting the EU to suspend aid intended to finance the legislative elections. In mid-February five opposition parties issued a joint communiqué accusing the Government of having broken the conditions of the accord signed in July 1999, and in early March 2002 they rejected an invitation by Kodjo to nominate representatives to the CENI. The Government consequently announced that no date for the legislative elections could be announced until a complete electoral commission had been formed. In late March 10 opposition parties, which had not been party to the accord signed in 1999 and were therefore excluded from the CPS, announced the formation of a Coordination des partis de l'opposition constructive, headed by Harry Octavianus Olympio, who had also assumed the leadership of the Rassemblement pour le soutien de la démocratie et du développement (RSDD). In mid-May 2002 a committee of seven judges (the Comité de sept magistrats—C-7), charged with monitoring the electoral process at the proposed legislative elections, was appointed. At the end of May the EU announced that it would not renew funding for the three facilitators it supported in Togo, in view of the continued lack of progress towards democracy.

In June 2002 Eyadéma dismissed Kodjo as Prime Minister and appointed Koffi Sama, the Secretary-General of the RPT, as Prime Minister; a new Government, which included several principal members of the former administration, was appointed in early July. Kodjo subsequently issued a statement criticizing the 'monarchic, despotic' regime of Eyadéma, and (in contrast to his former stated position) called for measures to ensure that Eyadéma would be unable to amend the Constitution to stand for a further term of office. The state prosecutor filed a suit against Kodjo on charges of disseminating false information and demeaning the honour of the President; Kodjo was expelled from the RPT and subsequently left Togo, taking up residence in France.

In early October 2002 the Assemblée nationale was dissolved, pending fresh elections on 27 October. In late October nine opposition parties that had declined to participate in the elections announced the formation of a new alliance, the Coalition des forces démocrates (CFD); members of the grouping included the CAR, the CPP and the UFC, in addition to a faction of 'renovators' within the RPT (which subsequently became the Pacte socialiste pour le renouveau—PSR, led by Maurice Dahuku Pere). Meanwhile, a group of 'constructive opposition' parties (including the RSDD), which were prepared to participate in the electoral process and form alliances with the RPT, formed the Coordination des partis politiques de l'opposition constructive (CPOC). The 81 seats of the Assemblée nationale were contested by 126 candidates, comprising 118 candidates nominated by 15 parties and eight independent candidates, although the RPT was the sole party to contest every seat. The RPT won 72 seats (in 46 of which they had been unopposed) and the RSDD three, while three other parties won a total of five seats, and one independent candidate was elected. The C-7, which now comprised six judges (following the resignation of one member of the committee on the day before the elections), estimated electoral turn-out at 67.4%, although the CFD claimed that only 10% of the electorate had voted. Eyadéma reappointed Sama as Prime Minister in mid-November; a new Government was formed in early December. All ministers were members of the RPT, with the exception of Harry Octavianus Olympio, who was appointed Minister responsible for Relations with Parliament.

In December 2002 the Assemblée nationale approved several constitutional amendments regarding the eligibility of presidential candidates. The restriction that had limited the President to serving two terms of office was to be removed, and the age of eligibility was to be reduced from 45 to 35 years. (It was widely believed that these measures were intended to permit Eyadéma to serve a further term of office, and also to permit the possible presidential candidacy of Eyadéma's son, Faure Gnassingbé.) Candidates were henceforth to be required to hold solely Togolese citizenship. In February 2003 the UFC, having opposed the constitutional amendments, announced its withdrawal from the CFD, after other parties within the grouping agreed to appoint representatives to the CENI prior to the holding of a presidential election later in the year. In late April Eyadéma confirmed that he was to seek re-election; however, in May the CENI rejected the candidacy of Gilchrist Olympio, who had recently returned to Togo. (This rejection was confirmed by the Constitutional Court later in the month.) By mid-May six opposition candidates (including four representatives of the constituent parties of the CFD) had emerged. Emmanuel Bob Akitani, the First Vice-President of the UFC, was announced as his party's candidate, following Olympio's debarment.

Eyadéma was returned to office in the presidential election held on 1 June 2003, receiving 57.8% of the votes cast. His nearest rival was Bob Akitani, with 33.7% of votes. Several of the defeated candidates declared that the election had been conducted fraudulently, although observers from the Economic Community of West African States (ECOWAS), the AU and the Conseil de l'Entente refuted these claims. Eyadéma was inaugurated for a further term of office on 20 June. Sama resigned as Prime Minister later in the month, but was reappointed as premier on 1 July, apparently with instructions from Eyadéma to form a government of national unity. However, most opposition parties reportedly declined representation in the administration, and the new Government, formed on 29 July, included only two representatives of the 'constructive opposition'. Faure Gnassingbé received his first ministerial posting, as Minister of Equipment, Mines, Posts and Telecommunications. In December Dama Dramani was elected as Secretary-General of the RPT, replacing Sama.

Talks between the EU and the Government on the conditions for a resumption of economic co-operation commenced in April 2004 in Brussels, Belgium; the government delegation, led by Sama, pledged to implement 22 measures such as introducing more transparent conditions for fair elections, revising the press code and guaranteeing political parties the freedom to conduct their activities without fear of harassment. Under pressure from the EU to strengthen democracy, President Eyadéma officially opened talks between the Government and opposition parties in May. In early June an EU mission charged with assessing Togo's progress in implementing democratic reforms held meetings with the Government, political and religious leaders and human rights organizations. In August the Assemblée nationale adopted amendments to the press code, notably abolishing prison sentences for offences such as defamation and repealing the powers of the Ministry of the Interior, Security and Decentralization to order the closure or seizure of newspapers.

In November 2004 the EU announced that it was to resume partial economic co-operation with Togo, in view of progress towards fulfilment of the 22 conditions established in April. It was emphasized, however, that the full resumption of development aid was dependent on the holding of free and fair elections within six months. In December Eyadéma announced that legislative elections would be held during the first half of 2005. In anticipation of the proposed elections, in January 2005 the Assemblée nationale adopted legislation introducing several amendments to the electoral code in accordance with the demands of the EU, notably strengthening the powers of the CENI and increasing its membership to 13, to include two representatives of civil society.

On 5 February 2005 Prime Minister Sama announced that President Eyadéma had died while being transported out of the country for medical treatment. The Togolese military closed the country's borders, thus preventing Natchaba, the President of the Assemblée nationale, who according to the Constitution was to assume the functions of head of state pending elections to be held within 60 days, from returning to Togo from a visit to Europe. Hours later it was announced that the Constitution had been suspended and that the armed forces had pledged their allegiance to Eyadéma's son, Faure Gnassingbé, as the new head of state. The following day an extraordinary session of the Assemblée nationale was convened, at which deputies voted to remove Natchaba from his post as President of the legislature and appoint Gnassingbé in his place. The Assemblée also approved a constitutional amendment authorizing an interim president to serve the remainder of the deceased predecessor's term, rather than arranging elections within 60 days (Eyadéma's term was due to expire in June 2008).

Gnassingbé was formally sworn in as President of Togo on 7 February 2005. The circumstances of his succession provoked domestic and international condemnation: the inauguration ceremony was boycotted by diplomats from Nigeria, the EU, the USA and the UN, while the AU and ECOWAS demanded that Gnassingbé stand down to allow fair and democratic elections to be held. Meanwhile, the Togolese opposition called a two-day strike for 8 and 9 February, in protest at the perceived *coup d'état*; however, the strike was only partially observed. Subsequent protests, concentrated in the Lomé suburb of Bè, reportedly a stronghold of opposition support, resulted in at least four deaths and several injuries from clashes with security forces, who allegedly used tear gas and live ammunition to disperse protesters.

Following intense diplomatic pressure from ECOWAS, and from Nigeria in particular, Gnassingbé announced on 18 February 2005 that elections would be held within 60 days—however, he declined to stand down before that time. Following this announcement, on 21 February the Assemblée nationale voted to reverse the constitutional amendments adopted on 6 February. Judging these concessions to be insufficient, ECOWAS imposed an arms embargo on Togo and travel restrictions on members of the Government, while the ambassadors of ECOWAS states were withdrawn from Lomé. The AU declared its support for the imposition of sanctions, while the USA announced that it would terminate all military assistance to Togo unless Gnassingbé stood down. On 25 February it was revealed that Gnassingbé had been appointed President of the RPT, and endorsed as the party's candidate in the forthcoming presidential election. Later that day, Gnassingbé announced that he was resigning from the post of President of the Assemblée nationale, and hence from the position of interim President, stating that he did not wish to compromise the transparency and fairness of the election. Abbas Bonfoh, Vice-President of the Assemblée nationale, became the acting head of state. The announcement was welcomed by ECOWAS, whose sanctions were immediately lifted; opposition groups, however, continued to demand that Natchaba (who returned to Togo in early March)

should assume the post of interim President, and sporadic protests continued, concentrated once more in Bè.

The date of the election was subsequently set for 24 April 2005; ECOWAS approved the date, although the opposition protested that it would be impossible to organize fair and transparent elections in such a brief period of time. (The EU also expressed doubts that fair elections could be held so promptly, and declined to send electoral observers.) Nevertheless, the radical opposition, which had grouped itself into a coalition of six parties (including, in addition to the four parties of the Front uni de l'opposition, the PSR and the UFC), subsequently announced that it would present a single candidate, Bob Akitani, to stand against Gnassingbé. Two members of the 'constructive opposition'—Harry Octavianus Olympio and the leader of the Parti du renouveau et de la rédemption, Nicolas Lawson—announced their candidacies; Gnassingbé's candidature was supported by five small parties of the 'constructive opposition' as well as by the RPT.

On 11 April 2005 a peaceful demonstration in the capital was reported to have been attended by several thousand supporters of the opposition, who protested against what was described as the 'repression' exercised by the authorities, and demanded that polling be postponed. On 16 April at least seven people were reported to have been killed, and some 150 injured, in clashes between supporters of the opposition and supporters of the youth wing of the RPT in Lomé. On 22 April Bonfoh dismissed the Minister of the Interior, Security and Decentralization, Maj. François Akila Esso Boko, after Boko had called for the presidential election to be postponed and for the appointment of a temporary premier from the opposition, citing the risk of civil war if the elections went ahead; following his dismissal, Esso Boko sought asylum in the German embassy in Lomé. On 23 April Lawson announced the withdrawal of his candidacy, in protest at Esso Boko's dismissal.

The Presidential elections were held, as scheduled, on 24 April 2005, amid ongoing tensions. Although widespread violence was not reported on polling day, the seizure of ballot boxes, following the closure of polls, in areas of Lomé in which the opposition was known to have considerable support, and in other areas of the interior, was reported. Preliminary results, issued by the CENI on 26 April, indicated that Gnassingbé had been elected as President by a significant majority. Although Gnassingbé announced that he envisaged the establishment of a government of national unity, the announcement of his victory precipitated widespread rioting, particularly in Lomé and in southern regions, with some reports suggesting that as many as 100 people had died in the violence. (According to official figures, 22 people were killed in the rioting.) Meanwhile, Gilchrist Olympio, who had returned to Togo in March, declared that Bob Akitini had been the legitimate winner of polling, claiming that the opposition candidate had received more than 70% of the votes cast. However, on 27 April ECOWAS observers issued a report on the elections, stating that the irregularities in the conduct of the election had not been such as to invalidate or draw into question the declared results. By early May more than 20,000 Togolese were reported to have fled the country for either Benin or Ghana. On 3 May the Constitutional Court announced the final results of the elections, which were not substantially different from the preliminary figures declared by the CENI; Gnassingbé was attributed 60.16% of the votes cast, compared with the 38.25% awarded to Bob Akitani; Lawson (despite the formal withdrawal of his candidacy) and Harry Octavianus Olympio each received around 1%. Some 63% of the electorate were reported to have voted. Gnassingbé was inaugurated as President on 4 May. Although the European Parliament adopted a resolution criticizing the conduct of the election, the election result was generally accepted by the international community.

On 19 May 2005 President Olusegun Obasanjo of Nigeria chaired a reconciliation summit in Abuja, the Nigerian capital, under the aegis of ECOWAS and the AU, which was attended by Gnassingbé, Gilchrist Olympio and other opposition leaders, as well as the Heads of State of Benin, Burkina Faso, Gabon, Ghana and Niger. (Bob Akitani was unable to participate owing to ill health.) The talks ended without agreement, however, as the radical opposition continued to reject the legitimacy of Gnassingbé's victory and demanded a full investigation of alleged election irregularities as a precondition for entering into any power-sharing arrangement. None the less, Gnassingbé subsequently held meetings with a number of opposition leaders to discuss the formation of what he termed a government of national unity. While the UFC upheld its refusal to participate in negotiations, most of the other opposition parties decided to join the talks. In late May the AU removed sanctions against Togo, declaring that it considered conditions in Togo to be constitutional. Meanwhile, refugees continued to flee Togo, amid reports that opposition supporters were being arrested or kidnapped by the security forces, and by late May 34,416 Togolese refugees (19,272 in Benin and 15,144 in Ghana) had been registered by the office of the UN High Commissioner for Refugees (UNHCR). It was estimated that a further 10,000 people had been internally displaced within Togo. Several thousand more people were reported to have fled Togo in subsequent months.

On 8 June 2005 Gnassingbé announced the appointment of former premier Edem Kodjo, regarded as a member of the moderate opposition, as Prime Minister. Negotiations between the President and five 'radical' opposition parties had been unsuccessful, as Gnassingbé refused to accede to several principal opposition demands, including the scheduling of fresh presidential elections and the transfer of some presidential powers to the Prime Minister. Later in June the formation of a 30-member Council of Ministers, dominated by the RPT, but also including several representatives of the opposition and of civil society, was announced. Notably, Tchessa Abi of the PSR, was appointed as Keeper of the Seals, Minister of Justice; the other five members of the six-party coalition refused to participate and later condemned Abi's acceptance of a ministerial position, deciding to expel the PSR from the coalition. (The Minister of Culture, Tourism and Leisure, Gabriel Sassouvi Dosseh-Anyroh was expelled from the UFC, following his acceptance of a post in the administration.) Zarifou Ayéva, the leader of the moderate opposition Parti pour la démocratie et le renouveau (which was absorbed into the RPT later in the year), was appointed as Minister of State, Minister of Foreign Affairs and African Integration, while an elder brother of the President, Kpatcha Gnassingbé, became Minister-delegate at the Presidency of the Republic, responsible for Defence and Veterans.

The return of the refugees was discussed by Gnassingbé and Gilchrist Olympio at a meeting in Rome, Italy, in July 2005, at which the two men also condemned violence and agreed that political prisoners arrested during the electoral process should be released. In late September Gnassingbé announced that the holding of legislative elections was to be expedited (although no date was specified), and that, in a measure intended to promote national unity, the country's first President, Sylvanius Olympio, was to be officially rehabilitated. In early November, as a further gesture of reconciliation, some 460 political prisoners were released from gaol in Lomé; the release of political prisoners was also expected to take place in other cities and regions.

In mid-March 2006 the Government announced, that, to encourage Togolese refugees to return to their country no legal proceedings were to be taken against opposition activists suspected of involvement in the unrest in 2005, excepting those involved in 'bloody crimes'; moreover, President Gnassingbé called for a formal resumption of the national dialogue between the authorities and the opposition. The inter-Togolese national dialogue, which had broken down following the death of Eyadéma, finally resumed in Lomé in April 2006, with the participation of six political parties (the CAR, the Convention démocratique des peuples africains—Branche Togolaise, the CPP, the Parti pour la démocratie et le renouveau, the RPT and the UFC), as well as two civil society organizations and the Government.

On 20 August 2006, following negotiations chaired by the President of Burkina Faso, Blaise Compaoré, the Government signed a comprehensive political accord with the main opposition parties in Lomé that provided for the establishment of a transitional government, which would include members of opposition parties. It also called for the re-establishment of the CENI, which would organize and supervise transparent and democratic elections. (In January 2007 the CENI was approved as the official decision-making body for national elections.) Agboyibo replaced Kodjo as Prime Minister in September 2006 and tasked with forming a government of national unity and organizing elections for 2007. He announced the formation of his new Council of Ministers later that month. In June 2007 the EU agreed to provide funding to support the forthcoming elections (initially scheduled to take place that month but subsequently postponed until August). Meanwhile, in March Adji Ayassour replaced Payadowa Boukpessi as Minister of Finance, the Budget and Privatization. The Minister of Youth and Sports, Richard Attipoé, was killed in a helicopter crash in Sierra Leone in June. His successor was not immediately appointed.

After further delays, legislative elections finally took place on 14 October 2007; the RPT secured 50 of the available 81 seats, the UFC took 27 seats and the CAR four. Voter turn-out was estimated at 95% and international observers declared the election to have been largely free and fair, despite allegations by opposition parties of procedural irregularities. In November Agboyibo, having completed his task of leading the country through legitimate legislative elections, submitted his resignation; Komlan Mally, hitherto Minister of Towns and Town Planning, was appointed Prime Minister in early December and named a new 21-member Council of Ministers, including Léopold Messan Gnininvi as Minister of State, Minister of Foreign Affairs and Regional Integration. Notable dismissals included that of Minister of Defence and Veterans Kpatcha Gnassingbé, the President's half-brother; responsibility for his portfolio was assumed by the presidency. The EU had announced in November its resumption of full co-operation with Togo and granted the country €123m. in development aid.

In April 2008 the UN Office of the High Commissioner for Human Rights initiated the process of establishing a truth and reconciliation commission to investigate the political violence which took place in 2005, following the death of former President Eyadéma. The first stage was to administer surveys to 30,000 people asking how such a commission should be designed; around 23,000 responses were received by September.

Mally resigned as Prime Minister on 5 September 2008, and two days later Gnassingbé appointed Gilbert Houngbo, who had previously served as the head of the UN Development Programme in Africa, as his replacement. Houngbo formed a new Council of Ministers later that month, in which Mally was appointed to the second most senior cabinet post, that of Minister of State, Minister of Health. There were a number of new additions to the Government, including Kofi Esaw, hitherto the Togoloese ambassador to Ethiopia, who was named Minister of Foreign Affairs and Regional Integration, replacing Gnininvi, who was appointed as Minister of State, Minister of Industry, Crafts and Technological Innovation. In October Agboyibo stood down as leader of the CAR, and was replaced by Dodji Apevon. In December the Government met to discuss a bill proposing the abolition of the death penalty.

Kpatcha Gnassingbé was arrested in mid-April 2009 and charged with attempting to overthrow the Government. He had unsuccessfully sought refuge at the US embassy in Lomé after a raid by security forces on his residence, that reportedly resulted in the deaths of two soldiers. In early May 10 civilians were arrested in connection with the coup attempt; 18 soldiers had by this time already been detained.

Relations with neighbouring Ghana have frequently become strained, as the common border with Togo has periodically been closed in an effort to combat smuggling and to curb political activity by exiles on both sides. In March 1993 and January 1994 the Togolese Government accused Ghana of supporting armed attacks on Eyadéma's residence, reflecting earlier accusations of Ghanaian involvement in unrest in Togo in early 1991. Full diplomatic relations between the two countries, suspended since 1982, were formally resumed in November 1994, and various joint commissions were subsequently reactivated. The newly elected President of Ghana, John Kufuor, visited Togo to mark the celebrations for Liberation Day on 13 January 2001, and a rapprochement in relations between the two countries was subsequently reported.

Relations with fellow ECOWAS members were jeopardized by the perceived *coup d'état* by which Gnassingbé assumed power following the death of his father Eyadéma (see above). Relations with Nigeria, in particular, were further compromised when the Togolese authorities refused to grant an aeroplane carrying the advance delegation of President Olusegun Obasanjo permission to land in Lomé. Nigeria withdrew its ambassador to Togo and imposed restrictions on visits of Togolese officials to Nigeria following the incident, anticipating the sanctions imposed by ECOWAS after Gnassingbé initially declined to stand down as interim President in advance of presidential elections. Following Gnassingbé's resignation on 25 February 2005, Nigeria and the other ECOWAS member states lifted their sanctions, returned their ambassadors to Lomé and resumed co-operation with Togo, approving the 24 April date for the presidential election and pledging to provide assistance to ensure the fairness and transparency of the poll. In February 2007 Benin, Nigeria and Togo signed a security agreement to promote stability and development within the three countries. An early warning system was to be established and the ECOWAS policy of free movement of goods and persons would be implemented.

In early 2009 Togo deployed 200 soldiers to assist peace-keeping operations with the UN Mission in the Central African Republic and Chad (MINURCAT); in April it was reported that a Togolese officer in Chad had been killed by a French Foreign Legion soldier serving with the EU bridging military operation in Eastern Chad and North Eastern Central African Republic.

Government

Under the terms of the Constitution that was approved in a national referendum on 27 September 1993, and subsequently modified, executive power is vested in the President of the Republic, who is directly elected, by universal adult suffrage, for a period of five years. The legislature is the unicameral Assemblée nationale, whose 81 members are also elected, by universal suffrage, for a five-year period. The Prime Minister is appointed by the President from among the majority in the legislature, and the Prime Minister, in consultation with the President, nominates other ministers. For administrative purposes, the country is divided into five regions. It is further divided into 30 prefectures and sub-prefectures.

Defence

As assessed at November 2008, Togo's armed forces officially numbered about 8,550 (army around 8,100, air force 250, navy 200). Paramilitary forces comprised a 750-strong gendarmerie. Military service is by selective conscription and lasts for two years. Togo receives assistance with training and equipment from France. The defence budget was estimated at 20,000m. francs CFA in 2007.

Economic Affairs

In 2007, according to estimates by the World Bank, Togo's gross national income (GNI), measured at average 2005–07 prices, was US $2,383m., equivalent to $360 per head (or $800 on an international purchasing-power parity basis). During 2000–07, it was estimated, the population increased at an average annual rate of 2.9%, while gross domestic product (GDP) per head declined by an average of 0.4% per year. Overall GDP increased, in real terms, at an average annual rate of 2.4% in 2000–07. Real GDP increased by 2.1% in 2007.

Agriculture (including forestry and fishing) contributed 40.9% of GDP in 2006; in the previous year 56.7% of the working population were employed in the sector. The principal cash crops are cotton (which contributed 8.9% of earnings from merchandise exports in 2007), coffee and cocoa. Togo has generally been self-sufficient in basic foodstuffs: the principal subsistence crops are cassava, yams, maize, sorghum and rice. Imports of livestock products and fish are necessary to satisfy domestic needs. According to the African Development Bank (AfDB), during 2000–07 agricultural GDP increased at an average annual rate of 3.0%; agricultural GDP increased by 3.5% in 2007.

Industry (including mining, manufacturing, construction and power) contributed 17.7% of GDP in 2006, and employed 10.1% of the working population in 1990. During 2000–07, according to the AfDB, industrial GDP increased by an average of 5.0% per year; industrial GDP increased by 2.5% in 2007.

Mining and quarrying contributed 2.9% of GDP in 2006. Togo has the world's richest reserves of first-grade calcium phosphates. Concerns regarding the high cadmium content of Togolese phosphate rock have prompted interest in the development of lower-grade carbon phosphates, which have a less significant cadmium content; exports of crude fertilizers and crude minerals provided 16.6% of earnings from merchandise exports in 2002. Limestone and marble are also exploited. There are, in addition, smaller deposits of iron ore, gold, diamonds, zinc, rutile and platinum. In 1998 marine exploration revealed petroleum and gas deposits within Togo's territorial waters. In October 2002 the Togolese Government, the Hunt Oil Co of the USA and Petronas Carigali of Malaysia signed a joint-venture oil-production agreement, providing for the first offshore drilling in Togolese territorial waters. The GDP of the mining sector was estimated to have declined at an average annual rate of 3.2% in 1991–95.

Manufacturing contributed 7.9% of GDP in 2006. About 6.6% of the labour force were employed in the sector in 1990. Major companies are engaged notably in agro-industrial activities, the processing of phosphates, steel-rolling and in the production of cement. An industrial 'free zone' was inaugurated in Lomé in 1990, with the aim of attracting investment by local and foreign interests by offering certain (notably fiscal) advantages in return for guarantees regarding export levels and employment; a second 'free zone' has since opened, and provision has been made for 'free zone' terms to apply to certain businesses operating outside the regions. According to the AfDB, manufacturing GDP increased by an average of 7.0% per year in 2000–07; manufacturing GDP increased by 6.5% in 2007.

Togo's dependence on imports of electrical energy from Ghana was reduced following the completion, in 1988, of a 65-MW hydroelectric installation (constructed in co-operation with Benin) at Nangbeto, on the Mono river. In early 2004 the Togolese and Beninois authorities announced that the Adjaralla hydroelectric installation, also on the Mono river, was to be modernized, and its production capacity increased markedly. In 2005 some 60.4% of electricity produced in Togo was generated from petroleum sources; the remaining 39.6% was generated from petroleum. In 2007 fuel imports constituted 27.0% of all merchandise imports by value. It was planned to connect the electricity grids of Togo and Benin, and to construct further power stations in both countries. A pipeline to supply natural gas from Nigeria to Togo (and also to Benin and Ghana) commenced operations in April 2007.

The services sector contributed 41.4% of GDP in 2006, and engaged 24.4% of the employed labour force in 1990. Lomé has been of considerable importance as an entrepôt for the foreign trade of land-locked countries of the region. However, political instability in the early 1990s and in 2005 resulted in the diversion of a large part of this activity to neighbouring Benin and undermined the tourism industry (previously an important source of foreign exchange). According to the AfDB, the GDP of the services sector declined by an average of 0.1% per year in 2000–07; however, services GDP increased by 0.4% in 2006 and by 1.1% in 2007.

In 2006 Togo recorded a visible trade deficit of US $464.4m., while there was an estimated deficit of $340.4m. on the current account of the balance of payments. In 2007 the principal source of imports was France (19.2%); other major suppliers were the People's Republic of China and the Netherlands. The principal market for exports in that year was Niger (which took 12.7% of Togo's exports); other significant purchasers were Benin, India, Burkina Faso, Mali and Ghana. The principal exports in 2007 were cement, iron and steel, crude fertilizers and cotton. The principal imports in that year were refined petroleum products, cement, medicinal and pharmaceutical products, textile yarn and fabrics, and cereals and cereal preparations.

Togo's estimated overall budget deficit for 2008 was 36,500m. francs CFA. Togo's total external debt was US $1,806m. at the end of 2006, of which $1,565m. was long-term public debt. In 2004 the cost of debt-servicing was equivalent to 1.6% of the value of exports of goods and services. Consumer prices increased by an annual average of 3.1% in 2000–08. Consumer prices increased by 8.7% in 2008.

Togo is a member of the Economic Community of West African States (see p. 243), of the West African organs of the Franc Zone (see p. 316), of the International Cocoa Organization (see p. 422), of the International Coffee Organization (see p. 422) and of the Conseil de l'Entente (see p. 425). Togo was admitted to the Islamic Development Bank (see p. 340) in 1998.

From the 1990s Togo's economy was adversely affected by a number of economic and political factors. A sharp and sustained decline in the output of phosphates, historically one of the major sources of export earnings, persistently low international prices for another principal export, cotton, and high international prices for petroleum imports, had a negative impact on the trade balance. The European Union (EU) suspended development aid to Togo in 1993, citing the lack of a functioning democratic system within the country, while further external sources of aid were withheld in the wake of alleged irregularities in the 1998 presidential election. Both the USA and the EU declared themselves dissatisfied with the conduct of the 2002 legislative polls, and much international aid remained suspended. The accession to the presidency of Faure Gnassingbé in early 2005, widely denounced as a coup, and the consequent unrest (leading more than 30,000 Togolese to flee the country), did little to encourage international economic assistance. However, following the holding of free and fair legislative elections in October 2007 the EU agreed to resume development aid. In April 2008 the IMF approved a Poverty Reduction and Growth Facility worth some US $108.4m., augmented by $29m. in September as the country suffered a series of misfortunes, including the surge in international prices for food and petroleum. Heavy flooding in mid-2008 resulted in the destruction of roads and bridges, severely disrupting transport and exports. GDP growth in that year was estimated at only 1.1%. The decline in demand for exports, and in prices for phosphates and cotton (precipitated by the global financial crisis) added to the country's difficulties. Meanwhile, in November, Togo qualified for debt relief under the IMF/World Bank initiative for heavily indebted poor countries initiative, which would lead to the eventual cancellation of much of the country's arrears. Challenges in the late 2000s remained the reduction of poverty (some 62% of the population were estimated to be living below the poverty line in 2006), improving transparency and accountability in the public sector, fostering a favourable business climate, and, more immediately, repairing the damage caused to infrastructure by recent flooding. The IMF forecast GDP growth of 1.8% in 2009.

Education

Primary education, which begins at six years of age and lasts for six years, is (in theory) compulsory. Secondary education, beginning at the age of 12, lasts for a further seven years, comprising a first cycle of four years and a second of three years. According to UNESCO estimates, in 2006/07 enrolment at primary schools included 77.2% of children in the relevant age-group (82.3% of boys; 72.2% of girls), while in 1999/2000 secondary enrolment was equivalent to 22.2% of the relevant age-group (boys 30.0%; girls 14.4%). Proficiency in the two national languages, Ewe and Kabiye, is compulsory. Mission schools are important, educating almost one-half of all pupils. In 2000/01 18,455 students were enrolled in institutions providing higher education. The Université du Lomé (formerly the University du Bénin) had about 14,000 students in the early 2000s, and scholarships to French universities are available. A second university opened in Kara, in the north of Togo, in early 2004. In 2002 spending on education represented 13.6% of total budgetary expenditure.

Public Holidays

2009: 1 January (New Year's Day), 13 January (Liberation Day, anniversary of the 1967 coup), 24 January (Day of Victory, anniversary of the failed attack at Sarakawa), 13 April (Easter Monday), 24 April (Day of Victory), 27 April (Independence Day), 1 May (Labour Day), 21 May (Ascension Day), 1 June (Whit Monday), 15 August (Assumption), 20 September* (Id al-Fitr, end of Ramadan), 23 September (anniversary of the failed attack on Lomé), 1 November (All Saints' Day), 27 November* (Tabaski, Feast of the Sacrifice), 25 December (Christmas).

2010: 1 January (New Year's Day), 13 January (Liberation Day, anniversary of the 1967 coup), 24 January (Day of Victory, anniversary of the failed attack at Sarakawa), 5 April (Easter Monday), 24 April (Day of Victory), 27 April (Independence Day), 1 May (Labour Day), 13 May (Ascension Day), 24 May (Whit Monday), 15 August (Assumption), 10 September* (Id al-Fitr, end of Ramadan), 23 September (anniversary of the failed attack on Lomé), 1 November (All Saints' Day), 16 November* (Tabaski, Feast of the Sacrifice), 25 December (Christmas).

* These holidays are dependent on the Islamic lunar calendar and may vary by one or two days from the dates given.

Weights and Measures

The metric system is in force.

Statistical Survey

Source (except where otherwise indicated): Direction de la Statistique, BP 118, Lomé; tel. 221-62-24; fax 221-27-75; e-mail dgscn_tg@yahoo.fr; internet www.stat-togo.org.

Area and Population

AREA, POPULATION AND DENSITY

Area (sq km)	56,600*
Population (census results)	
1 March–30 April 1970	1,997,109
22 November 1981	2,703,250
Population (UN estimates at mid-year)†	
2006	6,145,000
2007	6,300,000
2008	6,459,000
Density (per sq km) at mid-2008	114.1

* 21,853 sq miles.
† Source: UN, *World Population Prospects: The 2008 Revision*.

Ethnic Groups (percentage of total, 1995): Kabré 23.7; Ewe 21.9; Kabiyé 12.9; Watchi 10.1; Guin 6.0; Tem 6.0; Mobamba 4.9; Gourmantché 3.9; Lamba 3.2; Ncam 2.4; Fon 1.2; Adja 0.9; Others 2.9 (Source: La Francophonie).

ADMINISTRATIVE DIVISIONS
(2003, official estimates)

Region	Area (sq km)	Population ('000)	Density (per sq km)	Principal city
Centrale	13,317	478	35.9	Sokodé
Kara	11,738	647	55.1	Kara
Maritime	6,100	2,113	346.4	Lomé
Plateaux	16,975	1,142	67.3	Atakpamé
Savanes	8,470	590	69.7	Dapaoug
Total	**56,600**	**4,970**	**87.8**	

PRINCIPAL TOWNS
(2003, official estimates)

Lomé (capital)	839,000	Atakpamé	68,000
Golfe Urbain	355,000	Kpalimé	68,000
Sokodé	101,000	Dapaong	49,000
Kara	95,000	Tsevie	44,300

Mid-2007 (incl. suburbs, UN estimate): Lomé 1,452,000 (Source: UN, *World Urbanization Prospects: The 2007 Revision*).

BIRTHS AND DEATHS
(annual averages, UN estimates)

	1990–95	1995–2000	2000–05
Birth rate (per 1,000)	41.0	38.4	35.8
Death rate (per 1,000)	10.9	10.0	9.2

Source: UN, *World Population Prospects: The 2008 Revision*.

Life expectancy (years at birth, WHO estimates): 57 (males 55; females 60) in 2006 (Source: WHO, *World Health Statistics*).

TOGO

ECONOMICALLY ACTIVE POPULATION
(census of 22 November 1981)

	Males	Females	Total
Agriculture, hunting, forestry and fishing	324,870	254,491	579,361
Mining and quarrying	2,781	91	2,872
Manufacturing	29,307	25,065	54,372
Electricity, gas and water	2,107	96	2,203
Construction	20,847	301	21,148
Trade, restaurants and hotels	17,427	87,415	104,842
Transport, storage and communications	20,337	529	20,866
Financing, insurance, real estate and business services	1,650	413	2,063
Community, social and personal services	50,750	12,859	63,609
Activities not adequately defined	14,607	6,346	20,953
Total employed	484,683	387,606	872,289
Unemployed	21,666	7,588	29,254
Total labour force	506,349	395,194	901,543

Mid-2005 (estimates in '000): Agriculture, etc. 1,485; Total labour force 2,621 (Source: FAO).

Health and Welfare

KEY INDICATORS

Total fertility rate (children per woman, 2006)	5.0
Under-5 mortality rate (per 1,000 live births, 2006)	107
HIV/AIDS (% of persons aged 15–49, 2007)	3.3
Physicians (per 1,000 head, 2004)	0.04
Hospital beds (per 1,000 head, 2005)	0.9
Health expenditure (2006): US $ per head (PPP)	70
Health expenditure (2006): % of GDP	5.5
Health expenditure (2006): public (% of total)	27.8
Access to water (% of persons, 2006)	59
Access to sanitation (% of persons, 2006)	12
Human Development Index (2006): ranking	159
Human Development Index (2006): value	0.479

For sources and definitions, see explanatory note on p. vi.

Agriculture

PRINCIPAL CROPS
('000 metric tons)

	2005	2006	2007
Rice, paddy	72.9	76.3	74.2*
Maize	509.5	543.3	500.0*
Millet	42.2	43.7	45.0†
Sorghum	206.0	224.6	200.0*
Cassava (Manioc)	678.2	767.4	770.0†
Taro (Cocoyam)	12.9	13.4	14.0†
Yams	585.4	621.1	630.0†
Beans, dry	67.4	52.8	52.0†
Groundnuts, with shell	33.4	39.3	37.0*
Coconuts†	14.5	14.5	15.0
Oil palm fruit†	115	120	120
Seed cotton	172*	130†	84†
Bananas†	19	19	19
Oranges†	12.2	12.5	13.0
Coffee, green*	8.4	10.1	10.1
Cocoa beans*	59.0	73.0	70.0

* Unofficial figure(s).
† FAO estimate(s).

Aggregate production ('000 metric tons, may include official, semi-official or estimated data): Total cereals 833 in 2005, 889 in 2006, 820 in 2007; Total roots and tubers 1,280 in 2005, 1,405 in 2006, 1,417 in 2007; Total vegetables (incl. melons) 135 in 2005, 133 in 2006, 135 in 2007; Total fruits (excl. melons) 52 in 2005, 32 in 2006, 33 in 2007.

Source: FAO.

LIVESTOCK
('000 head, year ending September, FAO estimates)

	2005	2006	2007
Cattle	280	281	282
Sheep	1,850	1,900	1,950
Pigs	320	330	340
Goats	1,480	1,490	1,499
Horses	2	2	2
Chickens	9,000	10,000	11,100

Source: FAO.

LIVESTOCK PRODUCTS
('000 metric tons, FAO estimates)

	2005	2006	2007
Cattle meat	5.7	5.7	5.8
Sheep meat	4.1	4.2	4.3
Goat meat	3.7	3.8	3.8
Pig meat	4.0	5.1	5.2
Chicken meat	11.2	11.6	12.9
Game meat	4.5	4.5	4.6
Cows' milk	9.3	9.5	9.5
Hen eggs	6.4	7.3	8.1

Source: FAO.

Forestry

ROUNDWOOD REMOVALS
('000 cubic metres, excluding bark)

	2005	2006	2007
Sawlogs, veneer logs and logs for sleepers	86	86	86
Other industrial wood	80	80	80
Fuel wood	5,762	5,816	5,871
Total	5,928	5,982	6,037

Source: FAO.

Fishing

('000 metric tons, live weight)

	2004	2005	2006
Capture	28.0	27.7	24.9
Tilapias	3.5	3.5	3.5
Other freshwater fishes	1.5	1.5	1.5
West African ilisha	2.2	1.2	1.1
Bigeye grunt	1.5	0.8	0.8
Round sardinella	4.7	9.4	2.5
European anchovy	6.9	6.5	7.0
Atlantic bonito	1.4	1.2	0.8
Jack and horse mackerels	0.9	0.5	0.7
Jacks, crevalles	1.2	1.0	0.7
Other mackerels	2.0	n.a.	n.a.
Aquaculture	1.5*	1.5	3.0
Total catch	29.5	29.3	27.9

* FAO estimate.
Source: FAO.

Mining

('000 metric tons, estimates)

	2004	2005	2006
Limestone	2,400	2,400	2,400
Phosphate rock (gross weight)	1,115	1,350	1,650
Phosphate content	418	481	590

Source: US Geological Survey.

TOGO   Statistical Survey

Industry

SELECTED PRODUCTS
('000 metric tons, unless otherwise indicated)

	2003	2004	2005
Palm oil	7.0	7.0	7.0
Cement	800	800	800
Electric energy (million kWh)	293	184	187

Sources: FAO; US Geological Survey; UN, *Industrial Commodity Statistics Yearbook*.

Finance

CURRENCY AND EXCHANGE RATES

Monetary Units
100 centimes = 1 franc de la Communauté financière africaine (CFA).

Sterling, Dollar and Euro Equivalents (31 December 2008)
£1 sterling = 687.113 francs CFA;
US $1 = 471.335 francs CFA;
€1 = 655.957 francs CFA;
10,000 francs CFA = £14.55 = $21.22 = €15.24.

Average Exchange Rate (francs CFA per US $)
2006   522.89
2007   479.27
2008   447.81

Note: An exchange rate of 1 French franc = 50 francs CFA, established in 1948, remained in force until January 1994, when the CFA franc was devalued by 50%, with the exchange rate adjusted to 1 French franc = 100 francs CFA. This relationship to French currency remained in effect with the introduction of the euro on 1 January 1999. From that date, accordingly, a fixed exchange rate of €1 = 655.957 francs CFA has been in operation.

BUDGET
('000 million francs CFA)

Revenue*	2006	2007	2008†
Tax revenue	179.1	195.9	198.7
Direct tax revenue	46.9	n.a.	n.a.
Indirect tax revenue	132.3	n.a.	n.a.
Taxes on international trade	92.3	106.2	112.6
Other current revenue	16.8	7.4	11.0
Total	195.9	203.3	209.8

Expenditure‡	2006	2007	2008†
Current expenditure	214.3	222.4	205.9
Salaries and wages	59.3	64.3	73.2
Other operational expenses	9.6	n.a.	n.a.
Interest payments on public debt	0.5	n.a.	n.a.
External	10.0	n.a.	n.a.
Capital expenditure	41.6	24.1	63.4
Externally financed	18.2	10.1	36.0
Total‡	255.9	246.5	269.3

* Excluding grants received ('000 million francs CFA): 16.0 in 2006; 20.4 in 2007; 23.0 in 2008 (estimate).
† Estimates.
‡ Including lending minus repayments.

Source: IMF, *Togo: First Review Under the Three-Year Arrangement Under the Poverty Reduction and Growth Facility and Request for Modification of Performance Criteria and Augmentation of Access—Staff Report; Press Release on the Executive Board Discussion; and Statement by the Executive Director for Togo* (October 2008).

INTERNATIONAL RESERVES
(excluding gold, US $ million at 31 December)

	2005	2006	2007
IMF special drawing rights	—	0.1	0.1
Reserve position in IMF	0.5	0.5	0.5
Foreign exchange	194.1	373.9	437.5
Total	194.6	374.5	438.1

Source: IMF, *International Financial Statistics*.

MONEY SUPPLY
('000 million francs CFA at 31 December)

	2005	2006	2007
Currency outside banks	63.3	100.4	122.0
Demand deposits at deposit money banks	121.5	145.3	150.7
Total money (incl. others)	186.7	248.4	278.4

Source: IMF, *International Financial Statistics*.

COST OF LIVING
(Consumer Price Index for Lomé; base: 1996 = 100)

	2004	2005	2006
Food, beverages and tobacco	101.9	113.0	111.7
Clothing	114.9	116.0	115.3
Housing, water, electricity and gas	109.1	112.4	120.5
All items (incl. others)	115.3	123.1	125.8

Source: IMF, *Togo: Statistical Appendix* (June 2007).
All items (base: 2000 = 100): 116.3 in 2006; 117.4 in 2007; 127.6 in 2008. (Source: IMF, *International Financial Statistics*).

NATIONAL ACCOUNTS
('000 million francs CFA at current prices)
Expenditure on the Gross Domestic Product

	2004	2005	2006
Final consumption expenditure	1,063.4	1,168.7	1,234.7
Households Non-profit institutions serving households	958.8	1,028.5	1,094.0
General government	104.6	140.2	140.7
Gross capital formation	113.5	131.8	151.2
Gross fixed capital formation	125.1	126.6	151.2
Changes in inventories Acquisitions, *less* disposals, of valuables	−11.6	5.2	0.0
Total domestic expenditure	1,176.9	1,300.5	1,385.9
Exports of goods and services	421.1	448.4	468.9
Less Imports of goods and services	574.7	636.2	696.0
GDP at market prices	1,023.3	1,112.7	1,158.8
GDP at constant 2000 prices	966.5	978.5	998.1

2007 (US $ million at current prices): General government final consumption expenditure 268.96; Household final consumption expenditure 2,471.14; Gross capital formation 332.19; *Total domestic expenditure* 3,072.29; Exports of goods and services 1,030.54; Imports of goods and services −1,565.58; *GDP at market prices* 2,537.25 (Source: African Development Bank).

TOGO

Gross Domestic Product by Economic Activity

	2004	2005	2006
Agriculture, hunting, forestry and fishing	370.8	436.7	432.4
Mining and quarrying	29.9	33.0	31.0
Manufacturing	83.9	95.3	83.6
Electricity, gas and water	35.7	36.1	36.0
Construction	26.0	27.3	36.5
Trade, restaurants and hotels	126.8	124.2	156.4
Transport, storage and communications	57.9	56.8	69.1
Banking and insurance	21.6	23.1	24.6
Non-market services	103.4	99.1	98.7
Other services	77.1	80.6	89.2
Sub-total	933.1	1,012.3	1,057.4
Import duties and taxes	90.2	100.3	101.4
GDP in purchasers' values	1,023.3	1,112.7	1,158.8

Source: IMF, *Togo: Statistical Appendix* (June 2007).

BALANCE OF PAYMENTS
(US $ million)

	2004	2005	2006
Exports of goods f.o.b.	601.0	660.2	754.5
Imports of goods f.o.b.	−853.3	−1,172.4	−1,218.9
Trade balance	−252.3	−512.2	−464.4
Exports of services	150.0	176.8	216.0
Imports of services	−239.3	−278.5	−297.8
Balance on goods and services	−341.6	−613.9	−546.2
Other income received	39.1	44.2	47.7
Other income paid	−72.5	−78.7	−85.5
Balance on goods, services and income	−375.1	−648.4	−584.0
Current transfers received	206.8	229.3	284.6
Current transfers paid	−37.4	−41.5	−40.9
Current balance	−205.7	−460.7	−340.4
Capital account (net)	40.1	51.1	64.0
Direct investment abroad	12.6	14.9	14.4
Direct investment from abroad	57.3	77.0	77.3
Portfolio investment assets	−26.5	−26.2	2.0
Portfolio investment liabilities	26.2	28.7	60.6
Financial derivatives liabilities	—	0.5	—
Other investment assets	5.7	68.8	42.5
Other investment liabilities	216.6	123.7	217.3
Net errors and omissions	14.4	8.8	20.0
Overall balance	140.8	−113.5	157.8

Source: IMF, International Financial Statistics.

External Trade

PRINCIPAL COMMODITIES
(US $ million)

Imports c.i.f.	2004	2005	2007*
Food and live animals	53.2	62.1	83.6
Fish, crustaceans and molluscs and preparations thereof	4.9	8.6	7.8
Fish, fresh, chilled or frozen	4.0	7.5	5.9
Fish, frozen, excl. fillets	3.9	7.2	5.7
Cereals and cereal preparations	26.4	32.7	40.9
Wheat and meslin, unmilled	17.0	21.0	21.8
Mineral fuels, lubricants, etc.	128.2	171.8	212.8
Petroleum products, refined	127.1	170.4	210.3
Animal and vegetable oils, fats and waxes	14.2	10.5	7.6
Chemicals and related products	53.8	47.8	71.5
Medicinal and pharmaceutical products	24.0	30.4	48.6
Basic manufactures	142.8	136.2	190.2
Textile yarn, fabrics, made-up articles and related products	27.9	26.6	45.5
Cotton fabrics, woven†	11.5	12.6	24.1

Imports c.i.f.—continued	2004	2005	2007*
Other woven fabrics, 85% plus of cotton, bleached, etc., finished	10.2	10.5	17.3
Non-metallic mineral manufactures	46.5	44.3	74.5
Lime, cement and fabricated construction materials	41.3	39.1	66.4
Cement	39.5	37.3	63.7
Iron and steel	45.4	41.0	37.4
Iron and steel bars, rods, shapes and sections	25.4	23.3	18.2
Machinery and transport equipment	77.1	95.0	111.2
Telecommunications, sound recording and reproducing equipment	6.8	19.2	24.8
Telecommunication equipment, parts and accessories	3.5	16.4	20.9
Road vehicles	35.7	35.1	37.1
Passenger motor vehicles (excl. buses)	11.9	11.2	18.4
Miscellaneous manufactured articles	39.2	35.9	66.7
Total (incl. others)	557.8	592.6	787.1

Exports f.o.b.	2004	2005	2007*
Food and live animals	74.6	62.6	26.7
Cereals and cereal preparations	9.0	8.5	4.5
Coffee, tea, cocoa, spices, and manufactures thereof	28.1	24.8	9.1
Coffee, not roasted; coffee husks and skins	2.8	4.3	3.7
Crude materials, inedible, except fuels	112.7	70.1	61.7
Textile fibres and their waste‡	60.4	31.1	25.5
Cotton	59.6	30.0	25.0
Raw cotton, excl. linters, not carded or combed	49.0	26.6	25.0
Cotton, carded or combed	10.4	3.3	0.0
Crude fertilizers and crude minerals	48.3	35.9	31.4
Crude fertilizers and crude minerals (unground)	48.1	34.9	31.4
Basic manufactures	150.8	141.8	163.7
Non-metallic mineral manufactures	99.1	98.8	122.7
Cement	98.2	98.6	122.6
Iron and steel	41.3	32.4	35.1
Iron and steel bars, rods, shapes and sections	27.7	14.9	14.8
Machinery and transport equipment	5.1	6.8	1.5
Total (incl. others)	389.6	359.9	280.0

* Data for 2006 not available.
† Excluding narrow or special fabrics.
‡ Excluding wool tops and wastes in yarn.

Source: UN, *International Trade Statistics Yearbook*.

TOGO

PRINCIPAL TRADING PARTNERS
(US $ million)

Imports c.i.f.	2004	2005	2007*
Belgium	26.9	23.2	29.5
Benin	14.8	12.0	9.9
Brazil	14.0	16.1	15.5
Canada	7.4	9.6	10.0
China, People's Repub.	46.5	78.0	124.0
Côte d'Ivoire	33.8	38.3	20.6
France (incl. Monaco)	108.7	104.3	151.1
Germany	18.3	17.3	15.6
Ghana	9.8	8.0	28.4
Hong Kong	14.3	12.1	4.1
India	9.8	14.0	16.6
Indonesia	11.5	5.8	21.4
Italy	20.8	26.4	17.5
Japan	9.1	10.8	13.7
Netherlands	18.7	23.4	87.4
Nigeria	6.3	4.9	12.0
Saudi Arabia	15.0	4.7	0.5
Senegal	4.9	4.6	6.4
South Africa	8.0	11.2	23.6
Spain	16.0	25.0	16.5
Ukraine	12.4	7.6	8.8
United Kingdom	11.4	12.1	6.5
USA	13.5	6.9	33.4
Total (incl. others)	557.8	592.6	787.1

Exports f.o.b.	2004	2005	2007*
Australia	6.5	3.4	0.0
Belgium	10.5	3.2	2.3
Benin	47.5	41.6	30.5
Brazil	4.3	6.3	2.1
Burkina Faso	50.9	66.3	27.3
China, People's Repub.	17.3	7.9	5.1
Côte d'Ivoire	2.6	6.2	9.3
France (incl. Monaco)	15.5	5.0	1.7
Germany	2.0	7.5	0.8
Ghana	46.2	73.0	16.4
India	15.6	21.2	27.4
Indonesia	8.0	1.3	1.9
Italy	3.2	3.1	1.5
Mali	43.5	26.5	19.9
Morocco	3.0	6.5	1.4
Netherlands	15.4	3.9	1.4
New Zealand	7.5	3.1	1.8
Niger	13.1	10.8	35.6
Nigeria	7.3	14.7	0.7
Pakistan	3.5	4.8	0.0
Senegal	14.7	3.2	5.4
Thailand	3.7	1.4	6.5
USA	1.5	4.1	1.6
Total (incl. others)	389.6	359.9	280.0

* Data for 2006 not available.

Source: UN, *International Trade Statistics Yearbook*.

Transport

RAILWAYS
(traffic)

	1997	1998	1999
Passengers carried ('000)	152.0	35.0	4.4
Freight carried ('000 metric tons)	250	759	1,090
Passenger-km (million)	12.7	3.4	0.4
Freight ton-km (million)	28.8	70.6	92.4

Source: Société Nationale des Chemins de Fer du Togo, Lomé.

ROAD TRAFFIC
(motor vehicles registered at 31 December)

	1994	1995	1996*
Passenger cars	67,936	74,662	79,200
Buses and coaches	529	547	580
Goods vehicles	31,457	32,514	33,660
Tractors (road)	1,466	1,544	1,620
Motorcycles and scooters	39,019	52,902	59,000

* Estimates.

Source: IRF, *World Road Statistics*.

SHIPPING

Merchant Fleet
(registered at 31 December)

	2005	2006	2007
Number of vessels	27	26	28
Total displacement ('000 grt)	20.6	18.5	19.3

Source: Lloyd's Register-Fairplay, *World Fleet Statistics*.

International Sea-borne Freight Traffic
('000 metric tons)

Port Lomé	1997	1998	1999
Goods loaded	432.4	794.6	1,021.4
Goods unloaded	1,913.9	1,912.9	1,812.4

Source: Port Autonome de Lomé.

CIVIL AVIATION
(traffic on scheduled services)*

	1999	2000	2001
Kilometres flown (million)	3	3	1
Passengers carried ('000)	84	77	46
Passenger-km (million)	235	216	130
Total ton-km (million)	36	32	19

* Including an apportionment of the traffic of Air Afrique.

Source: UN, *Statistical Yearbook*.

Tourism

FOREIGN TOURIST ARRIVALS*

	2004	2005	2006
Belgium, Luxembourg and the Netherlands	1,024	3,517	1,073
Benin	7,434	5,909	6,495
Burkina Faso, Mali and Niger	8,132	8,069	6,408
Côte d'Ivoire	5,860	5,916	6,181
France	17,674	16,511	24,753
Germany	879	1,092	1,102
Ghana	2,161	1,880	2,438
Italy	960	674	857
Nigeria	3,572	3,356	3,598
United Kingdom	879	619	859
USA	2,097	2,141	2,703
Total (incl. others)	82,686	80,763	94,096

* Arrivals at hotels and similar establishments, by country of residence.

Receipts from tourism (US $ million, incl. passenger transport): 25 in 2004; 27 in 2005; 26 in 2006.

Source: World Tourism Organization.

TOGO

Communications Media

	2005	2006	2007
Telephones ('000 main lines in use)	62.8	82.1	99.5
Mobile cellular telephones ('000 subscribers)	443.6	708.0	1,190.4
Personal computers ('000 in use) .	185	n.a.	n.a.
Internet users ('000)	300	320	n.a.

Television receivers ('000 in use): 150 in 2000.

Radio receivers ('000 in use): 940 in 1997.

Facsimile machines ('000 in use): 17 in 1997.

Daily newspapers: 1 (average circulation 10,000 copies) in 1999; 1 (average circulation 10,000 copies) in 2000.

Book production (number of titles): 5 in 1998.

Sources: International Telecommunication Union; UNESCO, *Statistical Yearbook*, UNESCO Institute for Statistics; UN, *Statistical Yearbook*.

Education

(2006/07, unless otherwise indicated)

	Institutions*	Teachers	Males	Females	Total
Pre-primary .	319	888	11,225	11,334	22,559
Primary . .	4,701	26,103	547,622	473,995	1,021,617
Secondary . .	n.a.	11,029†	264,707‡	134,331‡	399,038‡
Tertiary . . .	n.a.	388*	15,336§	3,119§	18,455§

* 1999/2000.
† 2003/04.
‡ 2004/05.
§ 2000/01.

Source: UNESCO Institute for Statistics.

Adult literacy rate (UNESCO estimates): 53.2% (males 68.7%; females 38.5%) in 2000 (Source: UNESCO Institute for Statistics).

Directory

The Constitution

The Constitution that was approved in a national referendum on 27 September 1992, and subsequently amended, defines the rights, freedoms and obligations of Togolese citizens, and defines the separation of powers among the executive, legislative and judicial organs of state.

Executive power is vested in the President of the Republic, who is elected, by direct universal adult suffrage, with a five-year mandate. The legislature, the Assemblée nationale, is similarly elected for a period of five years, its 81 members being directly elected by universal suffrage. The President of the Republic appoints a Prime Minister who is able to command a majority in the legislature, and the Prime Minister, in consultation with the President, appoints other government ministers. A Constitutional Court is designated as the highest court of jurisdiction in constitutional matters.

Constitutional amendments, approved by the Assemblée nationale in late December 2002, removed the previous restriction limiting the President to serving two terms of office; reduced the minimum age for presidential candidates from 45 to 35 years; and required presidential candidates holding dual or multiple citizenships to renounce their non-Togolese nationality or nationalities.

An amendment authorizing an interim President to serve the remainder of a deceased predecessor's term was approved by the Assemblée nationale in February 2005; later that month, however, the amendment was reversed.

The Government

HEAD OF STATE

President: FAURE GNASSINGBÉ (inaugurated 4 May 2005).

COUNCIL OF MINISTERS
(May 2009)

Prime Minister: GILBERT HOUNGBO.
Minister of State, Minister of Health: KOMLAN MALLY.
Minister of State, Minister of Industry, Crafts and Technological Innovation: Prof. LÉOPOLD MESSAN GNININVI.
Minister of State, Minister of Territorial Administration, Decentralization and Local Communities, Spokesperson for the Government: PASCAL BODJONA.
Minister of State, Minister of Water, Sanitation and Village Hydraulics: Gen. ZACHARIE NANDJA.
Minister of Town Planning and Housing: ISSIFOU OKOULOU-KANTCHATI.
Minister of the Economy and Finance: ADJI AYASSOR.
Minister of Co-operation, Development and Land Settlement: GILBERT BAWARA.
Keeper of the Seals, Minister of Justice, responsible for Relations with the Institutions of the Republic: KOKOU TOZOUN.
Minister of Foreign Affairs and Regional Integration: KOFI ESAW.
Minister of Higher Education and Research: MESSAN ADIMADO ADUAYOM.
Minister of Security and Civil Protection: Col ATCHA TITIKPINA.
Minister of Primary and Secondary Education and Literacy: SAMBIANI SANKARDJA LARÉ.
Minister of Post, Telecommunications and Technological Innovations: KOKOUVI DOGBÉ.
Minister of Social Affairs, the Promotion of Women, the Protection of Children and the Elderly: MÉMOUNATOU IBRAHIMA.
Minister of Agriculture, Stockbreeding and Fisheries: KOSSI MESSAN EWOVOR.
Minister of Mines, Energy and Water: NOUPOKOU DAMMIPI.
Minister of Public Works and Transport: KOMLAN KADJE.
Minister of Labour and Social Security: OCTAVE NICOUÉ BROOHM.
Minister of the Environment and Forest Resources: KOSSIVI AYIKOE.
Minister of the Civil Service, Administrative Reform and Relations with the Institutions of the Republic: NINSAO GNOFAME.
Minister of Technical Education and Professional Training: HENRIETTE KUEVI AMEDJOGBE.
Minister of Tourism: BATIENNE KPABRE-SYLLI.
Minister of Communication and Culture: OULEGOH KEYEWA.
Minister of Human Rights, the Consolidation of Democracy and Civil Formation: YAKOUBOU KOUMADJO HAMADOU.
Minister of Sport and Leisure: PADUMHÈKOU TCHAOU.
Minister-delegate to the President, responsible for Trade and the Promotion of the Private Sector: GUY MADJÉ LORENZO.
Minister-delegate to the Prime Minister, responsible for Basic Development: VICTORINE SIDEMEHODOGBE.
Secretary-of-State to the Prime Minister, responsible for Youth and Youth Employment: NATHALIE MANZINEWÈ BITHO.
Secretary of State to the Minister Co-operation, Development and Land Settlement, responsible for Land Settlement: BANDIFOH OURO-AKONDO.

MINISTRIES

Office of the President: Palais Présidentiel, ave de la Marina, Lomé; tel. 221-27-01; fax 221-18-97; e-mail presidence@republicoftogo.com; internet www.republicoftogo.com.

Office of the Prime Minister: Palais de la Primature, BP 1161, Lomé; tel. 221-15-64; fax 221-37-53; internet www.gouvernement.tg.

Ministry of Agriculture, Stockbreeding and Fisheries: 5 ave de Duisburg, BP 385, Lomé; tel. 220-40-20; fax 220-44-99; internet ministereagriculture.com.

Ministry of the Civil Service, Administrative Reform and Relations with the Institutions of the Republic: angle ave de la

TOGO

Marina et rue Kpalimé, BP 372, Lomé; tel. 221-41-83; fax 222-56-85; internet fonctionpubliquetogo.com.

Ministry of Communication, Culture and Civic Training: BP 40, Lomé; tel. 221-29-30; fax 221-43-80; e-mail info@republicoftogo.com.

Ministry of Co-operation, Development and Land Settlement: Lomé; internet ministerecooperation.com.

Ministry of the Economy and Finance: CASEF, ave Sarakawa, BP 387, Lomé; tel. 221-00-37; fax 221-25-48; e-mail eco@republicoftogo.com; internet www.ministerefinances.com.

Ministry of the Environment, Tourism and Forest Resources: Lomé; tel. 221-56-58; fax 221-03-33; internet ministereenvironnement.com.

Ministry of Foreign Affairs and Regional Integration: pl. du Monument aux Morts, BP 900, Lomé; tel. 221-36-01; fax 221-39-74; e-mail diplo@republicoftogo.com.

Ministry of Health: rue Branly, BP 386, Lomé; tel. 221-35-24; fax 222-20-73; internet ministeresante.com.

Ministry of Higher Education and Research: rue Col de Roux, BP 12175, Lomé; tel. 222-09-83; fax 222-07-83; internet www.ministereeducation.org.

Ministry of Human Rights and Democracy: BP 1325, Lomé; tel. 222-60-63; fax 220-07-74; e-mail mdhdcab@yahoo.fr.

Ministry of Justice: ave de la Marina, rue Colonel de Roux, Lomé; tel. 221-26-53; fax 222-29-06; internet ministerejustice.com.

Ministry of Labour and Social Security: Lomé.

Ministry of Mines, Energy and Water: Lomé.

Ministry of Post, Telecommunication and Technological Innovations: ave de Sarakawa, BP 389, Lomé; tel. 223-14-00; fax 221-68-12; e-mail eco@republicoftogo.com; internet ministeretelecom.com.

Ministry of Primary and Secondary Education, Technical Education, Professional Training and Literacy: BP 398, Lomé; tel. 221-20-97; fax 221-89-34.

Ministry of Public Works, Transport, Town Planning and Housing: Lomé.

Ministry of Security and Civil Protection: rue Albert Sarraut, Lomé; tel. 222-57-12; fax 222-61-50; e-mail info@republicoftogo.com.

Ministry of Social Affairs, the Promotion of Women, the Protection of Children and the Elderly: Lomé.

Ministry of Territorial Administration, Decentralization and Local Communities: Lomé.

Ministry of Trade, Industry, Crafts and Small and Medium-sized Enterprises: 1 ave de Sarakawa, face au Monument aux Morts, BP 383, Lomé; tel. 221-20-25; fax 221-05-72; e-mail eco@republicoftogo.com.

Ministry of Youth, Sport and Leisure: BP 40, Lomé; tel. 221-22-47; fax 222-42-28.

President and Legislature

PRESIDENT

Presidential Election, 24 April 2005

Candidate	Votes	% of votes
Faure Gnassingbé (RPT)	1,323,622	60.16
Emmanuel Bob Akitani (UFC)	841,642	38.25
Nicolas Lawson (PRR)	22,979	1.04
Harry Octavianus Olympio (RSDD)	12,033	0.55
Total	**2,200,276**	**100.00**

LEGISLATURE

Assemblée nationale
Palais des Congrès, BP 327, Lomé; tel. 222-57-91; fax 222-11-68; e-mail assemblee.nationale@syfed.tg.refer.org.

President: El Hadj ABASS BONFOH.

General Election, 14 October 2007

Party	Votes	% of votes	Seats
Rassemblement du peuple togolais (RPT)	922,636	32.71	50
Union des forces de changement (UFC)	867,507	30.75	27
Comité d'action pour le renouveau (CAR)	192,218	6.81	4
Others	838,484	29.72	—
Total	**2,820,845**	**100.00**	**81**

Election Commission

Commission électorale nationale indépendante (CENI): 198 rue des Echis, BP 7005, Lomé; tel. 222-29-51; fax 222-39-61; e-mail info@cenitogo.tg; internet www.cenitogo.tg; 19 mems; Pres. TOZIM POTOPERE.

Political Organizations

In mid-2007 there were 68 registered political parties, of which the following were among the most influential:

Alliance démocratique pour la Patrie (ADP): Lomé; f. 2006; opposed to regime of Pres. Faure Gnassingbé; Leaders AGBEYOME KODJO, MAURICE DAHUKU PERE.

Coalition des forces démocrates (CFD): Lomé; f. Oct. 2002 by nine parties that boycotted legislative elections held in that month; opposed the administration of fmr Pres. Eyadéma; the UFC left the coalition in Feb. 2003; Chair. EDEM KODJO (acting).

Constituent parties and groupings include:

Convergence patriotique panafricaine (CPP): BP 12703, Lomé; tel. 221-58-43; f. 1999 by merger of the Parti d'action pour la démocratie (PAD), the Parti des démocrates pour l'unité (PDU), the Union pour la démocratie et la solidarité (UDS) and the Union togolaise pour la démocratie (UTD); did not participate in legislative elections in 2002; Pres. EDEM KODJO; First Vice-Pres. JEAN-LUCIEN SAVI DE TOVÉ.

Front uni de l'opposition (Le Front): Lomé; f. 2002; Co-ordinator Me YAWOVI AGBOYIBO.

Alliance des démocrates pour le développement intégral (ADDI): Lomé; tel. 221-47-90; Leader Dr NAGBANDJA KAMPATIBE.

Comité d'action pour le renouveau (CAR): 58 ave du 24 janvier, BP06, Lomé; tel. 222-05-66; fax 221-62-54; e-mail yagboyibo@bibway.com; moderately conservative; Leader Me YAWOVI AGBOYIBO; Sec.-Gen. DODJI APEVON; 251,349 mems (Dec. 1999).

Convention démocratique des peuples africains—Branche togolaise (CDPA—BT): 2 rue des Cheminots, BP 13963, Lomé; tel. and fax 225-38-46; e-mail cdpa-bt.cdpa-bt@orange.fr; internet www.cdpa-bt.net; f. 1991; socialist; Gen.-Sec. LÉOPOLD GNININVI; First Sec. Prof. EMMANUEL Y. GU-KONU.

Union pour la démocratie et la solidarité—Togo (UDS—Togo): 276 blvd Circulaire, BP 8580, Lomé; tel. 222-55-64; fax 221-81-95; e-mail uds-togo@wanadoo.fr; Leader ANTOINE FOLLY.

Pacte socialiste pour le renouveau (PSR): Lomé; f. 2003 by fmr 'renovationist' mems of RPT; Leader TCHESSA ABI.

Coordination des partis politiques de l'opposition constructive (CPOC): Lomé; f. 2002; alliance of 'constructive opposition' parties that favoured working with the regime of fmr Pres. Eyadéma

In mid-2003 members included:

Juvento—Mouvement de la jeunesse togolaise: Lomé; f. 2001; nationalist youth movement; Pres. ABALO FIRMIN.

Mouvement des croyants pour l'égalité et la paix (MOCEP): Lomé; Leader COMLANGAN MAWUTOÈ D'ALMEIDA.

Union pour la démocratie et le progrès social (UDPS): Lomé; Sec.-Gen. SEKODONA SEGO.

Coordination nationale des forces nouvelles (CFN): Lomé; f. 1993; centrist; Pres. Me JOSEPH KOKOU KOFFIGOH.

Parti démocratique togolais (PDT): Lomé; Leader M'BA KABASSÉMA.

Parti du renouveau et de la rédemption (PRR): Lomé; Pres. NICOLAS LAWSON.

Parti des travailleurs (PT): 49 ave de Calais, BP 13974, Nyékonakpoé, Lomé; tel. 913-65-54; socialist; Co-ordinating Sec. CLAUDE AMEGANVI.

Rassemblement du peuple togolais (RPT): pl. de l'Indépendance, BP 1208, Lomé; tel. 226-93-83; internet www.rpt.tg; e-mail rpttogo@yahoo.fr; f. 1969; sole legal party 1969–91; Pres. FAURE GNASSINGBÉ; Sec.-Gen. SOLITOKI ESSO.

Rassemblement pour le soutien de la démocratie et du développement (RSDD): Lomé; tel. 222-38-80; expelled from the CPOC (q.v.) in August 2003; Leader HARRY OCTAVIANUS OLYMPIO.

Union des forces de changement (UFC): 59 rue Koudadzé, Lom-Nava, BP 62168 Lomé; tel. and fax 221-33-32; e-mail contact-togo@ufctogo.com; internet www.ufctogo.com; f. 1992; social-democratic; First Vice-Pres. Emmanuel Bob Akitani contested presidential election in June 2003 under the designation Parti des forces de changement—Union des forces de changement; Pres. GILCHRIST OLYMPIO; First Vice-Pres. EMMANUEL BOB AKITANI; Sec.-Gen. JEAN-PIERRE FABRE.

Union des libéraux indépendants (ULI): f. 1993 to succeed Union des démocrates pour le renouveau; Leader KWAMI MENSAN JACQUES AMOUZOU.

Diplomatic Representation

EMBASSIES IN TOGO

China, People's Republic: 1381 rue de l'Entente, BP 2690, Lomé; tel. 222-38-56; fax 221-40-75; e-mail chinaemb_tg@mfa.gov.cn; Ambassador YANG MIN.

Congo, Democratic Republic: Lomé; tel. 221-51-55; Ambassador LOKOKA IKUKELE BOMOLO.

Egypt: 1163 rue de l'OCAM, BP 8, Lomé; tel. 221-24-43; fax 221-10-22; Ambassador ADEL MOSTAFA AHMED EL-SALASY.

France: 13 ave du Golfe, BP 337, Lomé; tel. 223-46-40; fax 223-46-01; e-mail Eric.BOSC@diplomatie.fr; internet www.ambafrance-tg.org; Ambassador DOMINIQUE RENAUX.

Gabon: Lomé; tel. 222-18-93; fax 222-18-92; Ambassador (vacant).

Germany: blvd de la République, BP 1175, Lomé; tel. 223-32-32; fax 223-32-46; e-mail amballtogo@cafe.tg; Ambassador ALEXANDER BECKMANN.

Ghana: 8 rue Paulin Eklou, Tokoin-Ouest, BP 92, Lomé; tel. 221-31-94; fax 221-77-36; e-mail ghmfa01@cafe.tg; Ambassador KENNETH ASARE BOSOMPEM.

Guinea: Lomé; tel. 221-74-98; fax 221-81-16.

Korea, Democratic People's Republic: Lomé; Ambassador KIM PYONG GI.

Libya: Cite OUA, BP 4872, Lomé; tel. 261-47-08; fax 261-47-10; Chargé d'affaires a.i. AHMED M. ABDULKAFI.

Nigeria: 311 blvd du 13 janvier, BP 1189, Lomé; tel. and fax 221-59-76; Ambassador BABA GANA ZANNA.

USA: rue Kouenou, angle rue 15 Beniglato, BP 852, Lomé; tel. 221-29-94; fax 221-79-52; e-mail RobertsonJJ2@state.gov; internet togo.usembassy.gov; Ambassador PATRICIA MCMAHON HAWKINS.

Judicial System

Justice is administered by the Constitutional Court, the Supreme Court, two Appeal Courts and the Tribunaux de première instance, which hear civil, commercial and criminal cases. There is a labour tribunal and a tribunal for children's rights. In addition, there are two exceptional courts, the Cour de sûreté de l'Etat, which judges crimes against internal and external state security, and the Tribunal spécial chargé de la répression des détournements de deniers publics, which deals with cases of misuse of public funds.

Constitutional Court: 32 ave Augustino de Souza, Lomé; tel. 221-72-98; fax 221-07-40; f. 1997; seven mems; Pres. ATSU KOFFI AMEGA.

Supreme Court: BP 906, Lomé; tel. 221-22-58; f. 1961; consists of three chambers (judicial, administrative and auditing); Chair. FESSOU LAWSON; Attorney-General KOUAMI AMADOS-DJOKO.

State Attorney: ATARA NDAKENA.

Religion

It is estimated that about 50% of the population follow traditional animist beliefs, some 35% are Christians and 15% are Muslims.

CHRISTIANITY

The Roman Catholic Church

Togo comprises one archdiocese and six dioceses. At 31 December 2006 there were an estimated 1,560,602 adherents in the country, representing about 24.5% of the total population.

Bishops' Conference

Conférence Episcopale du Togo, 561 rue Aniko Palako, BP 348, Lomé; tel. 221-22-72; fax 222-48-08.

Statutes approved 1979; Pres. Most Rev. AMBROISE KOTAMBA DJOLIBA (Archbishop of Sokodé).

Archbishop of Lomé: Most Rev. DENIS KOMIVI AMUZU-DZAKPAH, Archevêché, 561 rue Aniko Palako, BP 348, Lomé; tel. 221-22-72; fax 221-02-46; e-mail archlom@yahoo.cfr.

Protestant Churches

There are about 250 mission centres, with a personnel of some 250, affiliated to European and US societies and administered by a Conseil Synodal, presided over by a moderator.

Directorate of Protestant Churches: 1 rue Maréchal Foch, BP 378, Lomé; Moderator Pastor AWUME (acting).

Eglise Evangélique Presbytérienne du Togo: 1 rue Tokmake, BP 2, Lomé; tel. 221-46-69; fax 222-23-63; e-mail eeptbs@laposte.tg; internet www.eeptaction.org; Moderator Rev. EMANUEL AWANYOH.

Fédération des Evangéliques du Togo: Lomé; Co-ordinator HAPPY AZIADEKEY.

BAHÁ'Í FAITH

Assemblée spirituelle nationale: BP 1659, Lomé; tel. 221-21-99; e-mail asnbaha@yahoo.fr; Sec. ALLADOUM NGOMNA; 19,002 adherents (2006).

The Press

DAILY

Togo-Presse: BP 891, Lomé; tel. 221-53-95; fax 222-37-66; internet www.editogo.tg/presse.php; f. 1961; official govt publ; French, Kabiye and Ewe; political, economic and cultural; circ. 8,000.

PERIODICALS

L'Aurore: Lomé; tel. 222-65-41; fax 222-65-89; e-mail aurore37@caramail.com; weekly; independent; Editor-in-Chief ANKOU SALVADOR; circ. 2,500.

Carrefour: 596 rue Ablogame, BP 6125, Lomé; tel. 944-45-43; f. 1991; pro-opposition; weekly; Dir HOLONOU HOUKPATI; circ. 3,000 (2000).

Cité Magazine: 50 ave Pas de Souza, BP 6275, Lomé; tel. and fax 222-67-40; e-mail citemag@cafe.tg; internet www.cafe.tg/citemag; monthly; Editor-in-Chief GAËTAN K. GNATCHIKO.

Le Citoyen: Lomé; tel. 221-73-44; independent.

La Colombe: Lomé; f. 2001; weekly.

Le Combat du Peuple: 62 rue Blagogee, BP 4682, Lomé; tel. 904-53-83; fax 222-65-89; f. 1994; pro-opposition weekly; Editor LUCIEN DJOSSOU MESSAN; circ. 3,500 (2000).

Le Courrier du Golfe: rue de l'OCAM, angle rue Sotomarcy, BP 660, Lomé; tel. 221-67-92.

Crocodile: 299 rue Kuévidjin, no 27 Bé-Château, BP 60087, Lomé; tel. 221-38-21; fax 226-13-70; f. 1993; pro-opposition; weekly; Dir VIGNO KOFFI HOUNKANLY; Editor FRANCIS-PEDRO AMAZUN; circ. 3,500 (2000).

Le Débat: BP 8737, Lomé; tel. 222-42-84; f. 1991; 2 a month; Dir PROSPER ETEH.

La Dépêche: BP 20039, Lomé; tel. and fax 221-09-32; e-mail ladepeche@hotmail.com; f. 1993; 2 a week; Editor ESSO-WE APPOLINAIRE MÈWÈNAMÈSSÈ; circ. 3,000.

L'Etoile du matin: S/C Maison du journalisme, Casier no 50, Lomé; e-mail wielfridsewa18@hotmail.com; f. 2000; weekly; Dir WIELFRID SÉWA TCHOUKOULI.

Etudes Togolaises (Revue Togolaise des Sciences): Institut National de la Recherche Scientifique, BP 2240, Lomé; tel. 221-01-39; fax 221-21-59; e-mail inrs@tg.refer.org; f. 1965; 2 a year; scientific review, mainly anthropology.

L'Eveil du Peuple: Lomé; weekly; re-established in 2002, having ceased publication in 1999.

L'Evénement: 44–50 rue Douka, Kotokoucondji, BP 1800, Lomé; tel. 222-65-89; f. 1999; independent; weekly; Dir MENSAH KOUDJODJI; circ. 3,000 (2000).

TOGO

L'Exilé: Maison du journalisme, Casier no 28, Lomé; e-mail jexil@hotmail.com; f. 2000; weekly; independent; Editor HIPPOLYTE AGBOH.

Game su/Tev Fema: 125 ave de la Nouvelle Marché, BP 1247, Lomé; tel. 221-28-44; f. 1997; monthly; Ewe and Kabiye; govt publ. for the newly literate; circ. 3,000.

Hébdo-forum: 60 rue Tamakloe, BP 3681, Lomé; weekly.

Journal Officiel de la République du Togo (JORT): BP 891, Lomé; tel. 221-37-18; fax 222-14-89; govt acts, laws, decrees and decisions.

Kpakpa Désenchanté: BP 8917, Lomé; tel. 221-37-39; weekly; independent; satirical.

Kyrielle: BP 823, Lomé; tel. 948-13-69; fax 905-38-35; e-mail kyriellj@yahoo.fr; f. 1999; monthly; culture, sport; Dir CRÉDO TETTEH; circ. 3,000 (2000).

Libre Togovi: BP 81190, Lomé; tel. 904-43-36; e-mail libretogovi@mail.com; 2 a week; pro-democracy, opposed to Govt of fmr Pres. Eyadéma; distributed by the Comité presse et communication de la concertation nationale de la société civile.

La Matinée: Tokoin Nkafu, rue Kpoguédé, BP 30368, Lomé; tel. 226-69-02; f. 1999; monthly; Dir KASSÉRÉ PIERRE SABI.

Le Miroir du Peuple: 48 rue Defale, BP 81231, Lomé; tel. 946-60-24; e-mail nouveau90@hotmail.com; f. 1998; fmrly Le Nouveau Combat; weekly; independent; Dir ELIAS EDOH HOUNKANLY; circ. 1,000 (2000).

Motion d'Information: BP 1251, Lomé; tel. 910-81-15; fax 221-81-95; e-mail motion-info@wanadoo.fr; f. 1997; weekly; pro-opposition; Dir CARLOS KÉTOHOU.

Nouvel Echo: BP 3681, Lomé; tel. 947-72-40; f. 1997; pro-opposition; weekly; Dir ALPHONSE NEVAME KLU; Editor CLAUDE AMEGANVI.

Nouvel Eclat: Lomé; tel. 225-51-60; e-mail charlpass@hotmail.com; f. 2000; weekly; Dir CHARLES PASSOU; circ. 2,500 (2000).

Nouvel Horizon: Maison du journalisme, Casier no 38, BP 81213, Lomé; tel. 222-09-55; f. 2000; weekly; Dir DONNAS A. AMOZOUGAN; circ. 3,000 (2000).

La Nouvelle République: Lomé; tel. 945-55-43; e-mail nouvelle.republique@caramail.com; f. 1999; Dir WIELFRID SÉWA TCHOUKOULI; circ. 2,500 (2000).

La Parole: Lomé; tel. 221-55-90.

Politicos: Lomé; tel. 905-32-66; fax 226-13-70; e-mail politicos@hotmail.com; f. 1993; weekly; Dir GERMAIN ESSOHANAM POULI; circ. 1,500 (2000).

Le Regard: BP 81213, Lomé; tel. 904-09-09; fax 226-13-70; e-mail leregard13@caramail.com; f. 1996; weekly; pro-opposition; supports promotion of human rights; Editor ABASS DURMAN MIKAÏLA; circ. 3,000 (2000).

Le Reporter des Temps Nouveaux: Maison du journalisme, Casier no 22, BP 1800, Lomé; tel. and fax 226-18-22; e-mail lereporter39@hotmail.com; f. 1998; weekly; independent; political criticism and analysis; Dir. AUGUSTIN AMÉGAH; circ. 3,000 (2000).

Le Scorpion—Akéklé: S/C Maison du journalisme, BP 81213, Lomé; tel. 944-43-80; fax 226-13-70; e-mail lescorpion@webmails.com; f. 1998; opposition weekly; Dir DIDIER AGBLETO; circ. 3,500 (2000).

Le Secteur Privé: angle ave de la Présidence, BP 360, Lomé; tel. 221-70-65; fax 221-47-30; monthly; publ. by Chambre de Commerce et d'Industrie du Togo.

Le Soleil: Lomé; tel. 904-41-97; fax 904-89-10; e-mail lesoleil@francemail.com; f. 1999; weekly; Dir YVES LACLÉ; circ. 2,000 (2000).

Témoin de la Nation: Maison du journalisme, Casier no 48, BP 434, Lomé; tel. 221-24-92; f. 2000; weekly; Dir ELIAS EBOH.

Tingo Tingo: 44–50 rue Douka, Kotokoucondji, BP 80419, Lomé; tel. and fax 222-17-53; e-mail jtingo-tingo@yahoo.fr; f. 1996; weekly; independent; Editor AUGUSTIN ASIONBO; circ. 3,500 (2000).

Togo-Images: BP 4869, Lomé; tel. 221-56-80; f. 1962; monthly series of wall posters depicting recent political, economic and cultural events in Togo; publ. by govt information service; Dir AKOBI BEDOU; circ. 5,000.

Togo-Presse: BP 891, Lomé; tel. 221-53-95; fax 22-37-66; f. 1962; publ. by Govt in French, Ewe and Kabre; political, economic and cultural affairs; Dir WIYAO DADJA POUWI; circ. 5,000 (2000).

La Tribune du Peuple: BP 1756, Lomé; tel. 222-65-89; e-mail novapress.tg@assala.com; weekly; pro-opposition; Dir KODJO AFATSAO SILIADIN.

PRESS ASSOCIATION

Union des Journalistes Indépendants du Togo: BP 81213, Lomé; tel. 226-13-00; fax 221-38-21; e-mail maison-du-journalisme@ids.tg; also operates Maison de Presse; Sec.-Gen. GABRIEL AYITÉ BAGLO.

NEWS AGENCY

Agence Togolaise de Presse (ATOP): 35 rue des Medias, BP 891, Lomé; tel. 221-53-95; fax 222-37-66; e-mail atop.togo@gmail.com; internet www.atoptogo.info; f. 1975; Dir-Gen. SEEDEM ABASSA.

Publishers

Centre Togolais de Communication Evangélique—Editions Haho (CTCE—Editions Haho): 1 rue Sylvanus Olympio, BP 378, Lomé; tel. 221-45-82; fax 221-29-67; e-mail ctce_ctce@yahoo.fr; f. 1983; general literature, popular science, poetry, school textbooks, Christian interest; Dir TOMPY KUDZO NAKOU.

Editions Akpagnon: BP 3531, Lomé; tel. and fax 222-02-44; e-mail yedogbe@yahoo.fr; f. 1978; general literature and non-fiction; Man. Dir YVES-EMMANUEL DOGBÉ.

Editions de la Rose Bleue: BP 12452, Lomé; tel. 222-93-39; fax 222-96-69; e-mail dorkenoo_ephrem@yahoo.fr; general literature, poetry; Dir EPHREM SETH DORKENOO.

Les Nouvelles Editions Africaines du Togo (NEA-TOGO): 239 blvd du 13 janvier, BP 4862, Lomé; tel. and fax 222-10-19; e-mail neatogo@yahoo.fr; general fiction, non-fiction and textbooks; Dir-Gen. KOKOU A. KALIPE; Editorial Dir TCHOTCHO CHRISTIANE EKUE.

Les Presses de l'Université du Lomé: BP 1515, Lomé; tel. 225-48-44; fax 225-87-84.

Société Nationale des Editions du Togo (EDITOGO): BP 891, Lomé; tel. 221-61-06; f. 1961; govt-owned; general and educational; Pres. BIOSSEY KOKOU TOZOUN; Man. Dir WIYAO DADJA POUWI.

Broadcasting and Communications

TELECOMMUNICATIONS

Moov Togo: 225 blvd du 13 janvier, BP 14511 Lomé; tel. 220-13-20; fax 220-13-23; e-mail moovcontact@moov.tg; internet www.moov.tg; operates mobile cellular telecommunications in 80 localities; Dir-Gen. FRÉDÉRIC FERAILLE.

Togo Télécom: ave N. Grunitzky, BP 333, Lomé; tel. 221-44-01; fax 221-03-73; e-mail togotelecom@togotel.net.tg; internet www.togotel.net.tg; Dir-Gen. KOSSIVI PAUL AYIKOE.

> **Togo Cellulaire—Togocel:** Lomé; tel. 004-05-06; e-mail togocel@togocel.tg; internet www.togocel.tg; f. 2001; provides mobile cellular communications services to more than 70% of the territory of Togo.

BROADCASTING

Radio

Legislation providing for the liberalization of radio broadcasting was ratified in November 1990. However, no definitive licences for radio stations had been issued by mid-2002, when 11 private stations were, nevertheless, in operation.

Radiodiffusion du Togo (Internationale)—Radio Lomé: BP 434, Lomé; tel. 221-24-93; fax 221-24-92; e-mail radiolome@radiolome.tg; internet www.radiolome.tg; f. 1953; state-controlled; radio programmes in French, English and vernacular languages; Dir AMÉVI DABLA.

Radiodiffusion du Togo (Nationale): BP 21, Kara; tel. 660-60-60; f. 1974 as Radiodiffusion Kara (Togo); state-controlled; radio programmes in French and vernacular languages; Dir M'BA KPENOUGOU.

Radio Avenir: BP 20183, 76 blvd de la Kara, Doumassessé, Lomé; tel. 221-20-88; fax 221-03-01; f. 1998; broadcasts in French, English, Ewe and Kotokoli; Dir KPÉLE-KOFFI AHOOMEY-ZUNU.

Radio Carré Jeunes: BP 2550, Adidogomé, Lomé; tel. 225-77-44; e-mail carrejeunes@yahoo.fr; f. 1999; community radio stn; popular education, cultural information; broadcasts in French, Ewe, Kabyè and other local languages; Dir FOLY ALODÉ GLIDJITO AMAGLI.

Radio de l'Evangile-Jésus Vous Aime (JVA): Klikamé, Bretelle Atikoumé, BP 2313, Lomé; tel. 225-44-95; fax 225-92-81; e-mail radio.jva@fatad.org; f. 1995; owned by the West Africa Advanced School of Theology (Assemblies of God); Christian; education and development; broadcasts on FM frequencies in Lomé and Agou in French, English and 12 local languages; Dir Pastor DOUTI LALLEBILI FLINDJA.

Radio Galaxy: BP 20822, 253 rue 48, Doumassessé, Lomé; tel. and fax 221-63-18; e-mail radiogalaxy@yahoo.fr; f. 1996; broadcasts in French, English, Ewe and Kabyè; Dir PAUL S. TCHASSOUA.

Radio Kanal FM: Immeuble de CAMPOS, ave Champs de Course, BP 61554, Lomé; tel. 221-33-74; fax 220-19-68; e-mail kanalfm@cafe.tg; internet www.kanalfm.tg; f. 1997; broadcasts in French and Mina; independent; Dir MODESTE MESSAVUSSU-AKUE.

Radio Maria Togo: BP 30162, 155 de la rue 158, Hédzranawoé, Lomé; tel. 226-11-31; fax 226-35-00; e-mail info.tog@radiomaria.org; internet www.radiomaria.tg; f. 1997; Roman Catholic; broadcasts in French, English and six local languages; Dir NOËLIE ASSOGBAVI.

Radio Metropolys: 157 rue Missahoé, Tokoin Hôpital, derrière Pharmacie Ave Marie, Lomé; tel. 222-86-81; e-mail metropolys.lome@voila.fr; f. 2000; secular and apolitical broadcasts in French only; Dir NOËLIE ASSOGBAVI.

Radio Nana FM: BP 6035, Immeuble du Grand Marché du Lomé, Lomé; tel. 220-12-02; e-mail nanafm@woezon.com; f. 1999; broadcasts in French and Mina; community stn; political, economic and cultural information; Dir PETER DOGBÉ.

Radio Nostalgie: 14 ave de la Victoire, Quartier Tokoin-Hôpital, BP 13836, Lomé; tel. 222-25-41; fax 221-07-82; e-mail nostalgietogo@yahoo.fr; internet www.nostalgie.tg; f. 1995; broadcasts in French, Ewe and Mina; Pres. and Dir-Gen. FLAVIEN JOHNSON.

Radio Tropik FM: BP 2276, Quartier Wuiti, Lomé; tel. 226-11-11; e-mail tropikfm@nomade.fr; f. 1995; broadcasts in French, Kabyè and Tem; Dir BLAISE YAO AMEDODJI.

Radio Zion: BP 13853, Kpalimé, Lomé; tel. 441-09-15; f. 1999; religious; broadcasts in French, Ewe and Kabyè; Dir EMMANUEL KOUNOUGNA.

Television

Télévision Togolaise: BP 3286, Lomé; tel. 221-53-57; fax 221-57-86; e-mail televisiontogolaise@yahoo.fr; internet www.tvt.tg; f. 1973; state-controlled; three stations; programmes in French and vernacular languages; Dir KUESSAN YOVODEVI.

Broadcasting Association

Organisation Togolaise des Radios et Télévisions Indépendantes (ORTI): Lomé; tel. 221-33-74; e-mail kawokou@syfed.tg.refer.org; Pres. RAYMOND AWOKOU KOUKOU.

Finance

(cap. = capital; res = reserves; dep. = deposits; m. = million; br(s). = branch(es); amounts in francs CFA, unless otherwise indicated)

BANKING

Central Bank

Banque centrale des états de l'Afrique de l'ouest (BCEAO): rue Branly, BP 120, Lomé; tel. 221-25-12; fax 221-76-02; e-mail ocourrier@lome.bceao.int; internet www.bceao.int; HQ in Dakar, Senegal; f. 1962; bank of issue for the mem. states of the Union économique et monétaire ouest-africaine (UEMOA, comprising Benin, Burkina Faso, Côte d'Ivoire, Guinea-Bissau, Mali, Niger, Senegal and Togo); cap. and res 1,148,589m., total assets 5,099,908m. (Dec. 2005); Gov. PHILIPPE-HENRI DACOURY-TABLEY; Dir in Togo AYÉWANOU AGETOHO GBEASOR; br. at Kara.

Commercial Banks

Banque Internationale pour l'Afrique au Togo (BIA—Togo): 13 rue de Commerce, BP 346, Lomé; tel. 221-32-86; fax 221-10-19; e-mail bia-togo@cafe.tg; f. 1965; fmrly Meridien BIAO—Togo; 60.2% owned by Banque Belgolaise (Belgium); cap. and res 567m., total assets 51,793m. (Dec. 2003); Pres. VICTOR ALIPUI; Gen. Man. JEAN-PAUL LE CALM; 7 brs.

Banque Togolaise pour le Commerce et l'Industrie (BTCI): 169 blvd du 13 janvier, BP 363, Lomé; tel. 221-46-41; fax 221-32-65; e-mail btci@btci.tg; internet www.btci.tg; f. 1974; 23.8% by Groupe BNP Paribas (France) 24.8% owned by Société Financière pour les Pays d'Outre-mer (Switzerland); cap. 1,700m., res 1,706m., dep. 91,564m. (Dec. 2006); Pres. BARRY MOUSSA BARQUÉ; Dir-Gen. YAO PATRICE KANEKATOUA; 9 brs.

Ecobank Togo (EBT): 20 rue du Commerce, BP 3302, Lomé; tel. 221-72-14; fax 221-42-37; e-mail ecobanktg@ecobank.com; internet www.ecobank.com; f. 1988; 80.7% owned by Ecobank Transnational Inc (operating under the auspices of the Economic Community of West African States), 14.0% by Togolese private investors; cap. 2,000.0m., res 5,323.3m., dep. 78,071.6m. (Dec. 2006); Man. Dir SYLVIAN YAGNI-ANGATE; 3 brs.

Ecobank Transnational Inc: 2 ave Sylvanus Olympio, BP 3261, Lomé; tel. 221-03-03; fax 221-51-19; e-mail info@ecobank.com; internet www.ecobank.com; f. 1985; holding co for banking cos in Benin, Burkina Faso, Cameroon, Côte d'Ivoire, Ghana, Guinea, Liberia, Mali, Niger, Nigeria, Senegal and Togo, Ecobank Development Corpn and EIC Bourse; cap. and res US $105.5m., total assets $1,523.1m. (Dec. 2003); Pres. and Dir-Gen. PHILIP C. ASIODU.

Financial Bank Togo: BP 325, 11 ave du 24 janvier, Lomé; tel. 221-62-21; fax 221-62-25; e-mail info-tg@financial-bank.com; internet www.financial-bank.com; f. 2004; 85.3% owned by Financial BC SA Togo; cap. 1,500m., res −285m., dep. 8,869m. (Dec. 2006); Gen. Man. JEAN-PIERRE GALIBERT.

Société Interafricaine de Banque (SIAB): 14 rue de Commerce, BP 4874, Lomé; tel. 221-28-30; fax 221-58-29; e-mail info@siab-togo.com; internet www.siab-togo.com; f. 1975; fmrly Banque Arabe Libyenne-Togolaise du Commerce Extérieur; 86% owned by Libyan Arab Foreign Bank, 14% state-owned; cap. and res 181m., total assets 6,999m. (Dec. 2003); Pres. AYAWOVI DEMBA TIGNOKPA; CEO KHALIFA ACHOUR ETTALUA.

Union Togolaise de Banque (UTB): blvd Circulaire, BP 359, Lomé; tel. 221-64-11; fax 221-22-06; e-mail utbsg@cafe.tg; internet www.utb.tg; f. 1964; 100% state-owned; transfer to majority private ownership proposed; cap. and res −12.3m., total assets 49.0m. (Dec. 2003); Chair. ELOM K. DADZIE; Dir-Gen. ALEXIS LAMSEH LOOKY; 11 brs.

Development Banks

Banque Ouest-Africaine de Développement (BOAD): 68 ave de la Libération, BP 1172, Lomé; tel. 221-42-44; fax 221-72-69; e-mail boadsiege@boad.org; internet www.boad.org; f. 1973; promotes West African economic development and integration; cap. 682,100m., total assets 849,993m. (Dec. 2004); Interim Pres. ISSA COULIBALY.

Banque Togolaise de Développement (BTD): ave des Nîmes X, angle ave N. Grunitzky, BP 65, Lomé; tel. 221-36-41; fax 221-44-56; e-mail togo_devbank@bibway.com; f. 1966; 43% state-owned, 20% owned by BCEAO, 13% by BOAD; transfer to majority private ownership pending; cap. 3,065m., res 7,591m., dep. 34,514m. (Dec. 2006); Chair. and Pres. ESSO KANDJA; Gen. Man. ZAKARI DAROU-SALIM; 8 brs.

Société Nationale d'Investissement et Fonds Annexes (SNI & FA): 11 ave du 24 janvier, BP 2682, Lomé; tel. 221-62-21; fax 221-62-25; e-mail sni@ids.tg; f. 1971; 23% state-owned; cap. 2,600m., total assets 13,219m. (Dec. 2001); Pres. PALOUKI MASSINA; Dir-Gen. RICHARD K. ATTIPOE.

Savings Bank

Caisse d'Epargne du Togo (CET): 23 ave de Kléber Dadjo, Lomé; tel. 221-20-60; fax 221-85-83; e-mail cet@ids.tg; internet www.cet.tg; state-owned; privatization proposed; cap. and res 544m., total assets 27,988m. (Dec. 2006); Pres. DJOSSOU SEMONDJI.

Credit Institution

Société Togolaise de Crédit Automobile (STOCA): 3 rue du Mono, BP 899, Lomé; tel. 221-37-59; fax 221-08-28; e-mail stoca@ids.tg; f. 1962; 93.3% owned by SAFCA; cap. and res −112m., total assets 1,677m. (Dec. 2003); Pres. DIACK DIAWAR; Dir-Gen. DÉLALI AGBALE.

Bankers' Association

Association Professionnelle des Banques et Etablissements Financiers du Togo: Lomé; tel. 221-24-84; fax 221-85-83.

STOCK EXCHANGE

Bourse Régionale des Valeurs Mobilières (BRVM): BP 3263, Lomé; tel. 221-23-05; fax 221-23-41; e-mail brvm@brvm.org; internet www.brvm.org; f. 1998; national branch of BRVM (regional stock exchange based in Abidjan, Côte d'Ivoire, serving the member states of UEMOA); Man. in Togo NATHALIE BITHO ATCHOLI.

INSURANCE

Colina Togo: 10 rue du Commerce, BP 1349, Lomé; tel. 222-93-65; fax 221-73-58; e-mail togo@groupecolina.com; internet www.colina-sa.com; affiliated to Colina SA (Côte d'Ivoire); Dir-Gen. MARCUS LABAN.

Compagnie Commune de Réassurance des Etats Membres de la CICA (CICA—RE): 43, ave du 24 janvier, 07 BP 12410, Lomé; tel. 223-62-69; fax 261-35-94; e-mail cica-re@cica-re.com; internet www.cica-re.com; f. 1981; reinsurance co operating in 12 west and central African states; Pres. ALBERT PAMSY; Dir-Gen. N'GUESSAN JEAN BAPTISTE KOUAME.

Groupement Togolais d'Assurances (GTA): route d'Atakpamé, BP 3298, Lomé; tel. 225-60-75; fax 225-26-78; e-mail gta@laposte.tg; f. 1974; 62.9% state-owned; all classes of insurance and reinsurance; Pres. Minister of the Economy, Finance and Privatization; Man. Dir KOSSI NAMBEA.

Sicar Gras Savoye Togo: 140 blvd du 13 janvier, BP 2932, Lomé; tel. 221-35-38; fax 221-82-11; e-mail sicargs@sicargs.tg; internet www.grassavoye.com; affiliated to Gras Savoye (France); Dir GUY BIHANNIC.

UAT: Immeuble BICI, 169 blvd du 13 janvier, BP 495, Lomé; tel. 221-10-34; fax 221-87-24.

Trade and Industry

ECONOMIC AND SOCIAL COUNCIL

Conseil Economique et Social: Lomé; tel. 221-53-01; f. 1967; advisory body of 25 mems, comprising five trade unionists, five reps of industry and commerce, five reps of agriculture, five economists and sociologists, and five technologists; Pres. KOFFI GBODZIDI DJONDO.

GOVERNMENT AGENCIES

Direction Générale des Mines et de la Géologie: BP 356, Lomé; tel. 221-30-01; fax 221-31-93; organization and administration of mining in Togo; Dir-Gen. ANKOUME P. AREGBA.

EPZ Promotion Board: BP 3250, Lomé; tel. 253-53-53; fax 251-98-98; e-mail sazof@zonefranchetogo.tg; internet www.zonefranchetogo.tg; promotes the Export Processing Zone at Lomé internationally; Asst Dir-Gen. ATSOUVI YAWO SIKPA.

Société d'Administration des Zones Franches (SAZOF): BP 2748, Lomé; tel. 221-07-44; fax 221-43-05; administers and promotes free zones; Dir Gen. YAZAZ EGBARÉ.

Société Nationale de Commerce (SONACOM): 29 blvd Circulaire, BP 3009, Lomé; tel. 221-31-18; f. 1972; cap. 2,000m. francs CFA; importer of staple foods; Dir-Gen. JEAN LADOUX.

DEVELOPMENT ORGANIZATIONS

Agricultural development is under the supervision of five regional development authorities, the Sociétés régionales d'aménagement et de développement.

Agence Française de Développement (AFD): 437 ave de Sarakawa, BP 33, Lomé; tel. 221-04-98; fax 221-08-27; e-mail afdlome@groupe-afd.org; internet www.afd.fr; Country Dir YVES PICARD.

Association Française des Volontaires du Progrès (AFVP): BP 1511, Lomé; tel. 221-09-45; fax 221-85-04; e-mail afvp@togo-imet.com; internet www.afvp.org; f. 1965; Nat. Del. MARC LESCAUDRON.

Association Villages Entreprises: BP 23, Kpalimé; tel. and fax 441-00-62; e-mail averafp@hotmail.com; Dir KOMI AFELETE JULIEN NYUIADZI.

Office de Développement et d'Exploitation des Forêts (ODEF): 59 QAD rue de la Kozah, BP 334, Lomé; tel. 221-79-86; fax 221-34-91; e-mail kodefly@yahoo.fr; f. 1971; develops and manages forest resources; Man. Dir BADÉKÉNÉ K. KOMMONGOU.

Recherche, Appui et Formation aux Initiatives d'Autodéveloppement (RAFIA): BP 43, Dapaong; tel. 770-80-89; fax 770-82-37; f. 1992; Dir NOIGUE TAMBILA LENNE.

Service de Coopération et d'Action Culturelle: BP 91, Lomé; tel. 221-21-26; fax 221-21-28; e-mail scac-lome@tg.refer.org; administers bilateral aid from the French Ministry of Foreign Affairs; Dir HENRI-LUC THIBAULT.

Société d'Appui a la Filière Café-Cacao-Coton (SAFICC): Lomé; f. 1992; development of coffee, cocoa and cotton production.

CHAMBER OF COMMERCE

Chambre de Commerce et d'Industrie du Togo (CCIT): ave de la Présidence, angle ave Georges Pompidou, BP 360, Lomé; tel. 221-70-65; fax 221-47-30; e-mail ccit@ccit.tg; internet www.ccit.tg; f. 1921; Pres. JONATHAN FIAWOO; Sec.-Gen. DJAHLIN BROOHM (acting); br. at Kara.

EMPLOYERS' ORGANIZATIONS

Conseil National du Patronat: 55 ave N. Grunitzky, BP 12429, Lomé; tel. and fax 221-08-30; f. 1989; Pres. A. J. KOUDOYOR.

Groupement Interprofessionnel des Entreprises du Togo (GITO): BP 345, Lomé; Pres. CLARENCE OLYMPIO.

Syndicat des Commerçants Importateurs et Exportateurs du Togo (SCIMPEXTO): BP 1166, Lomé; tel. 222-59-86; Pres. C. SITTERLIN.

Syndicat des Entrepreneurs de Travaux Publics, Bâtiments et Mines du Togo: BP 12429, Lomé; tel. 221-19-06; fax 221-08-30; Pres. JOSÈPHE NAKU.

UTILITIES

Electricity

Communauté Electrique du Bénin: ave de la Kozah, BP 1368, Lomé; tel. 221-61-32; fax 221-37-64; e-mail dg@cebnet.org; f. 1968 as a jt venture between Togo and Benin to exploit the energy resources in the two countries; Chairs TCHAMDJA ANDJO, Z. MARIUS HOUNKPATIN; Man. DJIBRIL SALIFOU.

Togo Electricité: 426 ave du Golfe, BP 42, Lomé; tel. 221-27-43; fax 221-64-98; e-mail m.ducommun@ids.tg; internet www.togoelectricite.com; f. 2000 to replace Compagnie Energie Electrique du Togo; production, transportation and distribution of electricity; Man. Dir MARC DUCOMMUN-RICOUX.

Gas

Société Togolaise de Gaz SA (Togogaz): BP 1082, Lomé; tel. 221-44-31; fax 221-55-30; 71% privatization pending; Dir-Gen. JOËL POMPA.

Water

Société Togolaise des Eaux (STE): 53 ave de la Libération, BP 1301, Lomé; tel. 221-34-81; fax 221-46-13; f. 2003 to replace Régie Nationale des Eaux du Togo; production and distribution of drinking water.

TRADE UNIONS

Collectif des Syndicats Indépendants (CSI): Lomé; f. 1992 as coordinating org. for three trade union confederations.

Confédération Nationale des Travailleurs du Togo (CNTT): Bourse du Travail, BP 163, 160 blvd du 13 janvier, Lomé; tel. 222-02-55; fax 221-48-33; f. 1973; Sec.-Gen. DOUEVI TCHIVIAKOU; 35,000 mems (2007).

Confédération Syndicale des Travailleurs du Togo (CSTT): 14 rue Van Lare, BP 3058, Lomé; tel. 222-11-17; fax 222-44-41; e-mail cstt-tg@cstt-togo.org; f. 1949, dissolved 1972, re-established 1991; comprises 36 unions and 7 professional federations (Agro-Alimentation, Education, General Employees, Industry, Public Services, Transport, Woodwork and Construction); Sec.-Gen. BELIKI ADRIEN AKOUETE; 55,266 mems (2007).

Union Nationale des Syndicats Indépendants du Togo (UNSIT): Tokoin-Wuiti, BP 30082, Lomé; tel. 221-32-88; fax 221-95-66; e-mail unsit@netcom.tg; f. 1991; Sec.-Gen. NORBERT GBIKPI-BENISSAN; 17 affiliated unions; 8,061 mems (2007).

Transport

RAILWAYS

Société Nationale des Chemins de Fer du Togo (SNCT): BP 340, Lomé; tel. 221-43-01; fax 221-22-19; e-mail togorail@yahoo.com; f. 1900; owned by West African Cement (Wacem) since Jan. 2003; total length 519 km, incl. lines running inland from Lomé to Atakpamé and Blitta (276 km), Lomé to Tabligbo (77 km); a coastal line, running through Lomé and Aného, was closed to passenger traffic in 1987 (a service from Lomé to Kpalimé—119 km—has also been suspended); passengers carried (1999): 4,400 (compared with 628,200 in 1990); freight handled (2007): 631,798 metric tons; Gen. Man. M. M. REDDY.

ROADS

In 2000 there were an estimated 7,520 km of roads, of which 2,376 km were paved. The rehabilitation of the 675-km axis road that links the port of Lomé with Burkina Faso, and thus provides an important transport corridor for land-locked West African countries, was considered essential to Togo's economic competitiveness; in 1997 the World Bank provided a credit of US $50m. for the rehabilitation of a severely deteriorated 105-km section of the road between Atakpamé and Blitta. In 1998 Kuwait awarded Togo a loan of 6,000m. francs CFA francs to improve the Notse-Atakpamé highway. Other principal roads run from Lomé to the borders of Ghana, Nigeria and Benin.

Africa Route International (ARI—La Gazelle): Lomé; tel. 225-27-32; f. 1991 to succeed Société Nationale de Transports Routiers; Pres. and Man. Dir BAWA S. MANKOUBI.

SHIPPING

The major port, at Lomé, generally handles a substantial volume of transit trade for the land-locked countries of Mali, Niger and Burkina Faso, although political unrest in Togo, in the early 1990s, resulted in the diversion of much of this trade to neighbouring Benin. In 1995 the Banque ouest-africaine de développement approved a loan of 5,000m. francs CFA to help finance the rehabilitation of the infrastructure at Lomé port. The project aimed to re-establish Lomé as one of the principal transit ports on the west coast of Africa, and further upgrading of the port's facilities, including the computerization of port operations and the construction of a new container terminal, was implemented in the late 1990s, with private sector funding. By 1999 freight traffic had recovered to 2.8m. metric tons, compared

TOGO

with only 1.1m. tons in 1993. There is another port at Kpémé for the export of phosphates.

Port Autonome de Lomé: BP 1225, Lomé; tel. 227-47-42; fax 227-08-18; e-mail togoport@togoport.tg; internet www.togoport.tg; f. 1968; transferred to private management in Jan. 2002; Pres. ASSIBA AMOUSSOU-GUENOU; Man. Dir Adm. ADEGNON KODJO FOGAN; 1,600 employees (2003).

Conseil National des Chargeurs Togolais (CNCT): BP 2991, Lomé; tel. 223-71-00; fax 227-08-40; e-mail cnct@cnct.tg; internet www.cnct.tg; f. 1980; restructured 2001; Dir-Gen. TOÏ GNASSINGBÉ.

Ecomarine International (Togo): Immeuble Ecomarine, Zone Portuaire, BP 6014, Lomé; tel. 227-48-04; fax 227-48-06; e-mail ecomarine@ecomarineint.com; f. 2001 to develop container-handling facility at Lomé Port; operates maritime transport between Togo, Senegal and Angola; Chair. Alhaji BAMANGA TUKUR.

Société Ouest-Africaine d'Entreprises Maritimes Togo (SOAEM—Togo): Zone Industrielle Portuaire, BP 3285, Lomé; tel. 221-07-20; fax 221-34-17; f. 1959; forwarding agents, warehousing, sea and road freight transport; Pres. JEAN FABRY; Man. Dir JOHN M. AQUEREBURU.

Société Togolaise de Navigation Maritime (SOTONAM): pl. des Quatre Etoiles, rond-point du Port, BP 4086, Lomé; tel. 221-51-73; fax 227-69-38; state-owned; privatization pending; Man. PAKOUM KPEMA.

SOCOPAO—Togo: 18 rue du Commerce, BP 821, Lomé; tel. 221-55-88; fax 221-73-17; f. 1959; freight transport, shipping agents; Pres. GUY MIRABAUD; Man. Dir HENRI CHAULIER.

SORINCO—Marine: 110 rue de l'OCAM, BP 2806, Lomé; tel. 221-56-94; freight transport, forwarding agents, warehousing, etc.; Man. AHMED EDGAR COLLINGWOOD WILLIAMS.

Togolaise d'Affrètements et d'Agence de Lignes SA (TAAL): 21 blvd du Mono, BP 9089, Lomé; tel. 223-19-00; fax 221-06-09; e-mail taalsa@togo-imet.com; internet www.taal.tg; f. 1992; shipping agents, haulage management, crewing agency, forwarding agents; Pres. and Man. Dir LAURENT GBATI TAKASSI-KIKPA.

CIVIL AVIATION

There are international airports at Tokoin, near Lomé (Gnassingbé Eyadéma International Airport), and at Niamtougou. In addition, there are smaller airfields at Sokodé, Sansanné-Mango, Dapaong and Atakpamé.

Africa West Cargo: route de l'Aéroport, Zone Franche Aéroportuaire, BP 10019, Lomé; tel. 226-88-10; fax 226-17-49; e-mail info@africawestcargo.com; internet www.africawestcargo.com; f. 1997; air freight operator; CEO YANNICK ERBS.

Air Togo—Compagnie Aérienne Togolaise: Aéroport International de Lomé-Tokoin, BP 20393, Lomé; tel. 226-22-11; fax 226-22-30; e-mail airtogo@airtogo.net; internet www.airtogo.net; f. 1963; cap. 5m. francs CFA; scheduled internal services; Man. Dir AMADOU ISAAC ADE.

Société aéroportuaire de Lomé-Tokoin (SALT): Aéroport International de Lomé-Tokoin, BP 10112, Lomé; tel. 223-60-60; fax 226-88-95; e-mail salt@cafe.tg; Dir-Gen. Dr AKRIMA KOGOE.

Transtel Togo: Lomé; f. 2001; flights between Togo and France and Belgium; Gen. Man. M. MOROU.

Tourism

Togo's tourist industry declined precipitously in the wake of the political instability of the early 1990s; occupancy rates in the capital's hotels dropped from 33% in 1990 to 10% in 1993. The tourist industry did, however, recover in the late 1990s. Some 94,096 foreign tourist arrivals were reported in 2006. In that year receipts from tourism totalled US $26m.

Office National Togolais du Tourisme (ONTT): BP 1289, Lomé; tel. 221-43-13; fax 221-89-27; e-mail angelodjiss@yahoo.fr; internet www.togo-tourisme.com; f. 1963; Dir ANGELO DJISSODEY.

TONGA

Introductory Survey

Location, Climate, Language, Religion, Flag, Capital

The Kingdom of Tonga comprises about 170 islands in the south-western Pacific Ocean, about 650 km (400 miles) east of Fiji. The Tonga (or Friendly) Islands are divided into three main groups: Vava'u, Ha'apai and Tongatapu. Only 36 of the islands are permanently inhabited. The climate is mild (16°–21°C or 61°–71°F) for most of the year, though usually hotter (27°C or 81°F) in December and January. The languages are Tongan, which is a Polynesian language, and English. Tongans are predominantly Christians of the Wesleyan faith, although there are some Roman Catholics and Anglicans. The national flag (proportions 1 by 2) is red, with a rectangular white canton, containing a red cross, in the upper hoist. The capital is Nuku'alofa, on Tongatapu Island.

Recent History

The basis of the constitutional monarchy was established in the 19th century. The kingdom was neutral until 1900, when it became a British Protected State. The treaty establishing the Protectorate was revised in 1958 and 1967, giving Tonga increasing control over its affairs. Prince Tupouto'a Tungi, who had been Prime Minister since 1949, succeeded to the throne as King Taufa'ahau Tupou IV in December 1965 and appointed his brother, Prince Fatafehi Tu'ipelehake, as Prime Minister. Tonga achieved full independence, within the Commonwealth, on 4 June 1970.

Elections to the Legislative Assembly held in May 1981 resulted unexpectedly in the new Assembly becoming dominated by traditionalist conservatives. In March 1982 the Minister of Finance, Mahe Tupouniua, resigned at the King's request after refusing to grant him extrabudgetary travel funds. Further elections to the Legislative Assembly took place in May 1984. In September 1985 the King declared his support for the French Government's programme of testing nuclear weapons in the South Pacific, on the grounds that it was in the broader interests of the Western alliance. However, he upheld his former statement of opposition to the tests in French Polynesia.

Elections were held in February 1987 to the nine commoner seats in the Legislative Assembly; among the six newcomers to the legislature were reported to be some of the Government's harshest critics. In July 1988 the Supreme Court awarded 26,500 pa'anga in damages to 'Akilisi Pohiva, the editor of a local independent journal and an elected member of the Legislative Assembly, after the Government had been found guilty of unfairly dismissing him from his post in the Ministry of Education in 1985, because he had reported on controversial issues. The court ruling intensified opposition demands for the abolition of perceived feudal aspects within Tongan society.

In September 1989 the commoner members of the Legislative Assembly boycotted the Assembly, leaving it without a quorum, in protest at the absence of the Minister of Finance, whom they had wanted to question about the proceeds of the Government's sale of Tongan passports to foreign nationals, a process that had begun in 1983 as a means of acquiring revenue. Upon resuming their seats in the Assembly later in the month, the commoners introduced a motion demanding the reform of the Assembly to make it more accountable to the people. The motion proposed the creation of a more balanced legislature by increasing elected representation from nine to 15 seats and reducing noble representation to three seats (the Cabinet's 12 members also sit in the Assembly). In March 1990 a group of Tongan conservatives submitted an electoral petition, alleging bribery and corruption by Pohiva, the leader of the pro-reform commoners, and his colleagues, who had been re-elected by substantial majorities in the February general election. (In July 1988 the King had indicated his opposition to majority rule, claiming that the monarchical Government reacted more quickly to the needs of the people than the Government of a parliamentary democracy.)

In October 1990 Pohiva initiated a court case against the Government, claiming that its controversial sale of passports to foreign citizens was unconstitutional and illegal. The passports were sold mainly in Hong Kong, for as much as US $30,000 each, allowing the purchasers, in theory, to avoid travel restrictions imposed on Chinese passport-holders. However, in February 1991 a constitutional amendment to legalize the naturalization of the new passport-holders was adopted at an emergency session of the Legislative Assembly, and the case was therefore dismissed. In March a large demonstration was held in protest at the Government's actions, and a petition urging the King to invalidate the 426 passports in question and to dismiss the Minister of Police (who was responsible for their sale), was presented by prominent commoners and church leaders. In the following month the Government admitted that the former President of the Philippines, Ferdinand Marcos, and his family had been given Tongan passports as gifts, after his removal from power in 1986. The events that ensued from the sale of passports were widely viewed as indicative of the growing support for reform and for greater accountability in the government of the country. By 1996 most of the 6,600 passports sold under the scheme had expired.

In August 1991 the Prime Minister, Prince Fatafehi Tu'ipelehake, retired from office, owing to ill health (the Prince died in April 1999), and was succeeded by the King's cousin, Baron Vaea of Houma, who had previously held the position of Minister of Labour, Commerce and Industries.

Plans by campaigners for democratic reform to establish a formal political organization were realized in November 1992, when the Pro-Democracy Movement was founded. The group, led by Fr Seluini 'Akau'ola (a Roman Catholic priest), organized a constitutional convention in the same month, at which options for the introduction of democratic reform were discussed. However, the Government refused to recognize or to participate in the convention, prohibiting any publicity of the event and denying visas to invited speakers from abroad. Nevertheless, the pro-democracy reformists appeared to be attracting increased public support, and, at elections in February 1993, won six of the nine elective seats in the Legislative Assembly. Pohiva's position was undermined when, in December 1993 and February 1994, he lost two defamation cases in the Supreme Court, following the publication of allegations of fraudulent practice in his journal, *Kele'a*. In August 1994 Tonga's first political party was formed when the Pro-Democracy Movement (which had been recognized in 1992, the group having been formed in the early 1970s as the Human Rights and Democracy Movement in Tonga) launched its People's Party, under the chairmanship of a local businessman, Huliki Watab.

In May 1995 the Minister of Finance, Cecil Cocker, resigned from the Cabinet following allegations that he had sexually harassed three women while attending a regional conference in Auckland. Cocker received an official reprimand for his conduct from New Zealand's acting Prime Minister, Don McKinnon.

Elections took place on 24 January 1996, at which pro-democracy candidates retained six seats in the Legislative Assembly. In March three journalists, including the editor of *The Times of Tonga*, were arrested and imprisoned in connection with an article in the newspaper that criticized the newly appointed Minister of Police, Fire Services and Prisons, Clive Edwards, for unfavourable remarks that he had made regarding the People's Party. All three were subsequently released, but were found guilty in April under a law against angering a civil servant.

In July 1996 the Legislative Assembly voted to resume the sale of Tongan passports to Hong Kong Chinese, despite the controversy caused by the similar scheme operated in the early 1990s (see above). As many as 7,000 citizenships were to be made available for between 10,000 and 20,000 pa'anga, granting purchasers all the rights of Tongan nationality, except ownership of land.

In September 1996 a motion to impeach the Minister of Justice and Attorney-General, Tevita Topou, was proposed in the Legislative Assembly. The motion alleged that Topou had continued to receive his daily parliamentary allowance during an unauthorized absence from the Assembly. Moreover, the publication of details of the impeachment motion, which had been reported to *The Times of Tonga* by Pohiva, before it had been submitted to the Legislative Assembly, resulted in the imprisonment of Pohiva and of the newspaper's editor, Kalafi Moala, and also the deputy editor, Filakalafi Akau'ola, for contempt of parliament. The three were subsequently released, although in October Moala was found guilty on a further charge of contempt. In the same month the King closed the Assembly (which had been expected to sit until mid-November) until further notice. He denied that he had taken this decision in order to prevent further impeachment proceedings against Topou. Furthermore, in February 1997 the Speaker of the Legislative Assembly was found guilty of contempt of court for criticizing the Chief Justice's decision to release the three journalists imprisoned in September of the previous year. The Government rejected accusations made in early 1997 by journalists in Tonga and media organizations throughout the region that it was attempting to force the closure of *The Times of Tonga*, despite forbidding Moala (who was resident in New Zealand) to enter Tonga without written permission from the Government, banning all government-funded advertising in the publication and forbidding all government employees to give interviews to its journalists.

Parliament reopened in late May 1997. In June Akau'ola was arrested once again and charged with sedition for publishing a letter in *The Times of Tonga* that questioned government policy. However, in the same month the Government suffered a significant reverse when the Court of Appeal ruled that the imprisonment of Pohiva and the two journalists in late 1996 had been unlawful. In August the Prime Minister of New Zealand, Jim Bolger, paid an official visit to Tonga. Following the visit, Pohiva, who had unsuccessfully sought a meeting with Bolger, criticized New Zealand's relationship with Tonga, claiming that financial assistance from the country hindered democratic reform.

In September 1997, following a formal apology from Topou, the Legislative Assembly voted to abandon impeachment proceedings against him. In October Pohiva announced that he was helping to prepare a proposed draft Constitution for presentation to the Legislative Assembly; the document's principal recommendation was to be the direct election of all 30 members of the Assembly.

In March 1998 Fakafanua, a former Minister of Lands, Survey and Natural Resources, was arrested and remanded on bail in connection with charges of fraud, extortion and accepting bribes. He was released by the Supreme Court later in the month after he accused the police of unlawful imprisonment. One police officer was convicted of this charge in April, while five other men, including Edwards, were acquitted.

In mid-September 1998 the King closed the Legislative Assembly in response to a petition, signed by more than 1,000 people, that sought the removal from office of the Speaker, Eseta Fusitu'a. A parliamentary committee was forced to conduct an inquiry into the activities of Fusitu'a, who was accused of misappropriating public funds and of abusing his position. Pohiva and other pro-democracy activists commended the king for his decisive action in response to the petition. Draft legislation presented later that month, which proposed that in future the Legislative Assembly should appoint cabinet ministers (a responsibility hitherto reserved for the King), was regarded as further evidence of the increasing influence of the pro-democracy lobby in the political life of the country.

At the general election held on 11 March 1999 five members of the reformist Tonga Human Rights and Democracy Movement (formerly the Pro-Democracy Movement/People's Party) were returned to the Legislative Assembly, compared with six at the previous election. In April Veikune was appointed as Speaker and Chairman of the Legislative Assembly, replacing Eseta Fusitu'a, who had lost her seat at the general election. In late 1999 the former Minister for Lands, Survey and Natural Resources, Fakafanua, appeared in court on charges of forgery and bribery.

In January 2000 the King appointed his youngest son, Prince 'Ulukalala-Lavaka-Ata, as Prime Minister, replacing Baron Vaea who had in 1995 announced his desire to retire. It had been expected that Crown Prince Tupouto'a would take up the position, but his support for constitutional reform in Tonga (notably the abolition of life-time terms for the Prime Minister and ministers) contrasted with the King's more conservative approach. In March of that year a report published by the US State Department claimed that Tonga's system of Government, whereby the Legislative Assembly was not directly elected, was in breach of UN and Commonwealth human rights guide-lines. The report was welcomed by the leader of the Tonga Human Rights and Democracy Movement, 'Akilisi Pohiva, who reiterated the party's demands for greater democracy, set out in a draft constitution completed in late 1999.

In January 2001 the Prime Minister announced a reallocation of cabinet positions in which he assumed responsibility for the newly created telecommunications portfolio. In the same month claims in a newspaper report that members of the pro-democracy movement had been involved in a plot to assist an escape from prison, to seize weapons from the army and to assassinate a cabinet minister were vehemently denied by representatives of the group. Meanwhile, ongoing concerns for the freedom of the media in Tonga were renewed following the arrest of the deputy editor of *The Times of Tonga* on charges of criminal libel.

In February 2001 the Tonga Human Rights and Democracy Movement launched a public petition to amend Tonga's Nationality Act to allow Tongans who had taken up citizenship in other countries to retain their Tongan citizenship. Their stated objective in undertaking the petition was to acknowledge Tonga's dependence on remittances from Tongans living overseas.

In September 2000, meanwhile, protests took place in Nuku'alofa, prompted by concerns that Chinese immigrant businesses, encouraged by the Government to establish themselves in Tonga, were creating unfavourable economic conditions for Tongan enterprises. The Tonga Human Rights and Democracy Movement appealed to the Government to cease issuing work permits to foreign (predominantly Chinese) business people and to end the sale of Tongan passports. In order to protect this money from his ministers, who he feared would squander it on unsuitable public works projects should it enter Tonga, the King requested that the funds be placed in the Tonga Trust Fund, held in a Californian cheque account, at the San Francisco branch of the Bank of America. In June 1999 Jesse Bogdonoff, a Bank of America employee, successfully sought royal approval to invest the money in a company in Nevada called Millennium Asset Management, where Bogdonoff was named as the Fund's Advising Officer. Bogdonoff later claimed that he had made a profit of about US $11m., which so impressed the King that he appointed Bogdonoff as Court Jester. The balance of the Fund and the interest it had accrued (totalling some $40m.) was due to be returned to Tonga on 6 June 2001; instead the money appeared to have vanished, along with Millennium Asset Management, which had ceased to exist. In September Princess Pilolevu, acting as Regent in the absence of the King and the Crown Prince, dismissed Kinikinilau Tutoatasi Fakafanua, currently Minister of Education but who at the time of the incident had been Minister of Finance, along with the Deputy Prime Minister and Minister of Justice, Tevita Tupou, both of whom were trustees of the fund. She appointed the Minister of Police, Fire Services and Prisons, Clive Edwards, as Acting Deputy Prime Minister. Parliament created a committee to investigate the crime and tabled a motion to impeach Fakafanua and Tupou. There were no apparent reprisals, or legal action, against Bogdonoff, who claimed that he had been deliberately misled as to the value of the funds. In October the Acting Deputy Prime Minister denied that the Privy Council had directed the transfers from the Fund or that any ministers were implicated. He stressed that at least $2.1m. of the fund, invested in Tongan banks, was duly accounted for. However, in June 2002 the Government admitted that about $26m. had been lost as a result of Bogdonoff's actions and that legal proceedings had been initiated in the USA. It was announced in February 2003 that the case would be heard in December of that year; also in February the Legislative Assembly began impeachment proceedings against the ministers implicated in the matter. In February 2004 it was reported that the Government had agreed to settle out of court with Bogdonoff, who was to pay just $1m. in compensation to the Tongan authorities.

In January 2002 Pohiva published allegations that the King held a secret 'offshore' bank account containing US $350m., some of which was believed to be the proceeds of gold recovered from an 18th century shipwreck. He claimed to possess a letter written to the King from within the palace referring to the account. The Government dismissed the letter as a forgery. Nevertheless, Pohiva was briefly held in custody in February, while police searched the offices of the Tonga Human Rights and Democracy Movement and confiscated computer equipment, in an attempt to find the source material of the allegations. Later that month New Zealand's Minister of Foreign Affairs and Trade condemned Tonga as being endemically corrupt, implying that New Zealand's annual aid of $NZ6m. profited the élite rather than the Tongan people as a whole. In February the King admitted that he did possess an overseas account, with the Bank of Hawaii, but claimed that it contained the profits of vanilla sales from his own plantation. Nevertheless, Pohiva was formally charged with the use and publication of a forged document. In May 2002 he was acquitted of charges of sedition.

A general election was held on 6–7 March 2002, at which 52 candidates competed for the nine commoners' seats in the Legislative Assembly. The Tonga Human Rights and Democracy Movement won seven seats. In September, having repeatedly failed since 1998 to secure government approval for the group's registration under this name, the organization once again became known as the Human Rights and Democracy Movement in Tonga (HRDMT). However, in November 2005 the Government gave approval for a licence to be granted under the Incorporated Societies Act as Friendly Islands Human Rights and Democracy Movement Inc (FIHRDM Inc).

In July 2002 it was reported that Pohiva, Moala and Akau'ola were seeking damages from the Tongan Government for wrongful imprisonment, following their incarceration in 1996 on charges of contempt of parliament. Concerns for the freedom of the media re-emerged in February 2003 when the Government declared *The Times of Tonga*, the twice-weekly newspaper printed in New Zealand, to be a 'prohibited import', describing it as a foreign publication with a political agenda. The ban was challenged, and in April Tonga's Chief Justice, Gordon Ward, ruled that it was both illegal and unconstitutional. However, within hours of the ruling the Government ordered a new ban under different legislation. Ward overruled the ban in the following month, describing it as 'an ill-disguised attempt to restrict the freedom of the press', but on arrival from New Zealand 2,000 copies of the paper were seized by the Tongan customs authorities. Moreover, a few days later legislation was proposed that aimed to limit the power of the Supreme Court by excluding laws and ordinances approved by the Legislative Assembly and the Privy Council from judicial review. In early June the Supreme Court granted an injunction to *The Times of Tonga* ordering the Government to allow its distribution. The Government once again defied the order, stating that it would appeal. In mid-June the newspaper (which had been banned in Tonga since February) was finally allowed to go on sale within the country, after Gordon Ward had threatened each individual member of the Cabinet with contempt of court if they did not permit its distribution.

One of the most vocal critics of the affair was the King's nephew, Prince 'Uluvalu Tu'ipelehake, who in June 2003 expressed concern that the attempts to legislate against the freedom of the press and to restrict the right to seek judicial review would bring Tonga into disrepute. In mid-July it was reported that the Government had abandoned its proposals to limit the powers of the Supreme Court, as a result of strong opposition to the plans. However, later that month the Legislative Assembly approved the Media Operators' Bill, which introduced restrictions on the involvement of foreign nationals in Tonga's media. The legislation was widely viewed as a further attempt to ban *The Times of Tonga*, the editor of which resided in New Zealand. In early October Tonga's Roman Catholic bishop led a march by some 8,600 people to the government buildings in Nuku'alofa. The demonstration, which was the largest of its kind in Tonga's history, aimed to persuade the Government not to introduce any further restrictions on media freedom in the country. However, a few days later the Legislative Assembly voted in favour of a constitutional amendment allowing for greater control of the media, and shortly afterwards introduced the Newspaper Act, which gave the Government increased powers to regulate the content of newspapers in the country. It was reported that the legislation had been approved by 16 parliamentary votes to 11, with virtually all of the elected members voting against the proposals and virtually all of the appointed members voting in favour.

The introduction of legislation restricting media freedom in the country in late 2003 threatened to jeopardize Tonga's international relations, and in November the New Zealand Government announced that it was to review its relationship with Tonga. The Tongan Government summoned New Zealand's ambassador to the islands to register its displeasure. However, in January 2004 Prince 'Uluvalu Tu'ipelehake appealed to Australia's Minister for Foreign Affairs, Alexander Downer, to encourage political reform and to support attempts to increase democratic representation in Tonga.

In February 2004 the King of Tonga's second son, Ma'atu Fatafehi Alaivahamama'o Tuku'aho, died of a heart attack at 48 years of age. Some 6,000 people attended his funeral and the King and Queen announced that they would undertake a period of mourning lasting 100 nights.

Serious financial problems at the national carrier, Royal Tongan Airlines, culminated in April 2004 in the grounding and repossession of the company's passenger jet in Auckland, New Zealand, and the consequent suspension of all international flights. Domestic flights continued to be operated by the airline, but in the following month the entire company ceased all operations when its last remaining domestic aircraft broke down and it was announced that no funds were available to repair it. The failure of the airline caused considerable disquiet throughout Tonga, particularly among those involved in the islands' increasingly important tourist industry. At the opening session of the Legislative Assembly in late May seven of the nine elected representatives staged a boycott, demanding the resignation of the Prime Minister, who they claimed had allowed millions of pa'anga to be wasted during his tenure as chairman of the airline.

A legal challenge to the constitutional amendments governing media freedom, introduced by the Government in 2003, was begun in the Supreme Court in August 2004. Shortly before the legal hearing began the Prime Minister announced the dismissal of three cabinet ministers, including the Minister of Police, Fire Services and Prisons, Clive Edwards, who had been one of the principal proponents of the constitutional amendments. In November the Prime Minister announced that four new cabinet ministers would be appointed from among the elected members of the Legislative Assembly (two from the Nobles and two from the People's Representatives) following the elections in March 2005. The announcement, which represented a departure from the usual procedure whereby ministers were selected from outside parliament, was seen by many, including members of the pro-democracy movement, as a welcome concession towards democratic reform. However, Clive Edwards criticized the proposals, claiming that they were anti-democratic, as they required two members of the Legislative Assembly, elected by the people, to relinquish their seats in order to assume the new positions from which they could be dismissed at the discretion of the King.

Elections for the nine Nobles' seats took place on 16 March and for the nine commoners' seats on 17 March 2005. The latter were contested by a record number of 60 candidates. Two newly elected members from each group were appointed to positions in the Cabinet, and a by-election for the four vacated seats took place on 3–5 May. The Minister of Defence, 'Aloua Fetu'utolu Tupou, died suddenly in mid-April. One of the new representatives elected at the subsequent by-election was the former cabinet minister and member of the newly formed People's Democratic Party (PDP), Clive Edwards. The PDP had been launched in April by a breakaway group from the HRDMT, which had stated its intention to pursue political reform in a more aggressive manner. The new organization was registered in early July, despite fears that this might be deemed illegal, as no provision existed in the Constitution for the establishment of political parties.

In late May 2005 some 8,000 people marched to Tonga's Royal Palace in one of the largest demonstrations of its kind to take place in the country. The protesters presented a petition to the King expressing discontent at high electricity prices charged by the Shoreline Power Group and the excessive salaries reportedly paid to the company's executives. Demonstrators urged the Government to renationalize the generation and distribution of power supply in Tonga.

In July 2005 public servants voted to approve the first national strike in Tonga's history, following the Government's rejection of a request by the Public Service Association (PSA) to reconsider large disparities in salary increases awarded to public sector workers in the recent budget. Almost all of the country's teachers, numerous health care workers and employees from many other public services, initially totalling some 3,000 workers, joined the strike. Accusations of government attempts to restrict the PSA's access to the media were made when the power supply of a private television station was cut shortly before a statement by the PSA was due to be broadcast. During the third week of the strike some 10,000 people marched to the Royal Palace in support of the PSA. Striking public servants expressed the hope that the King might overrule the Cabinet, which had hitherto rejected their demands. Subsequent reports of vandalism against school property and government vehicles were received, and an attempt had apparently been made to burn down the house of a senior executive of the Shoreline Power Group. Moreover, an unoccupied house belonging to the King on the island of Tongatapu was destroyed by fire in an incident believed by some to be related to recent events in the country. A range of measures, including a new salary scale, subsequently proposed by the Government, was again rejected by the PSA. However, the strike ended in early September when the two sides signed an agreement allowing for salary increases of between 60% and 80%. More significantly, the agreement also provided for the establishment of a commission to review the country's Constitution and to examine possibilities for a more democratic form of government. This represented a major victory for the PSA, which had maintained throughout the dispute that the basic cause of its grievances lay in Tonga's political system. Shortly afterwards a further demonstration by more than 10,000 people took place, appealing to the King to dismiss the entire Government and to conduct a constitutional review within 12 months. Protesters also reiterated their demands for the re-nationalization of government assets, particularly power generation, but also Tonga's orbital satellite positions and its internet domain address. In October the King agreed to the establishment of a parliamentary committee to examine the issue of constitutional reform.

In February 2006, following the Cabinet's consideration of measures to permit a significant reduction in the number of public servants, the PSA threatened further strike action, stating that the Government's proposals breached the agreement signed in September 2005. Also in February 2006, Prime Minister 'Ulukalala-Lavaka-Ata resigned from office, relinquishing all his portfolios. People's Representative Dr Feleti (Fred) Sevele, a commoner and advocate of constitutional reform, was appointed acting Prime Minister. Sevele also assumed temporary responsibility for the Prince's other ministerial portfolios (including civil aviation, telecommunications, marine and ports). Prince 'Ulukalala had confronted increasing demands for his resignation, amid accusations of incompetence and inefficiency. In view of his pro-democracy stance, the appointment of Sevele was widely welcomed. He was expected to be influential in the establishment of democratic government in Tonga, partly owing to his close relationship with the progressive Crown Prince.

In March 2006 the proposals relating to the reduction in the number of government departments were hastily approved by the Cabinet in order to meet final deadlines for submission. It was agreed that most ministries would remain in place, although some were to merge, thereby reducing the existing 16 ministries to 14. Following his confirmation in the position of Prime Minister at the end of March, Dr Feleti Sevele retained responsibility for the portfolios of labour, commerce, industries, disaster relief and communications in a reallocation of cabinet portfolios in mid-May. Other changes included the replacement of Cecil Cocker as Deputy Prime Minister by Dr Viliami Tangi and the appointment of 'Alisi Taumoepeau, the country's first female minister, who became Attorney-General and Minister of Justice. During the course of his first official visit to New Zealand, Prime Minister Feleti Sevele confirmed that about one-quarter of posts in the civil service were to be abolished, as part of the Government's commitment to the reduction of budgetary expenditure. The National Committee for Political Reform (NCPR) was due to present its findings in August, but in July its Chairman, Prince 'Uluvalu Tu'ipelehake, was killed in a car accident in the USA.

On 11 September 2006, after a protracted illness, King Taufa'ahau Tupou IV died in New Zealand, prompting a month of national mourning. Among those present at the King's funeral were the New Zealand Prime Minister, Helen Clark, and Crown Prince Naruhito of Japan. Crown Prince Tupouto'a succeeded to the throne as King George Tupou V. Two new ministers were later appointed to the Cabinet: Afu'olo Matoto became Minister of Public Enterprises, while Lisiate 'Akolo was named Minister of Labour, Commerce and Small Industries. In October the NCPR's report on political reform, which had been submitted to King Tupou IV in late August, was discussed at length by members of the Legislative Assembly. The report envisaged a 26-member legislature, comprising 17 representatives elected by the people and nine representatives elected by nobles; the King would nominate a Prime Minister from the legislature, who would in turn select the cabinet from among the elected representatives. Prime Minister Sevele subsequently stated that the Cabinet had proposed the establishment of a new parliamentary tripartite committee composed of cabinet members and nobles' and people's representatives, which would deliberate on the political reform process and present its conclusions in the following year. As part of its 'roadmap for political reform' the Cabinet made the following recommendations: that the Legislative Assembly should comprise between 23 and 28 representatives, nine of whom would be nobles' representatives and 14 people's representatives, elected according to constituency; the Cabinet should comprise between 12 and 14 members, including two Governors, with at least two-thirds being elected representatives of the Legislative Assembly; the King should appoint two-thirds of the Cabinet on the advice of the Prime Minister and the remaining one-third independently; the Prime Minister should be an elected representative of the Legislative Assembly, appointed by the King on the advice of the Legislative Assembly, and with responsibility for portfolio assignment.

In mid-November 2006 demonstrations in Nuku'alofa against the slow pace of democratic reform developed into riots, with protesters engaging in widespread looting and destruction. According to reports, approximately 80% of the buildings in the business area of the city were burned down, and police later verified that at least six bodies had been found in the ruins. Responding to Sevele's appeal, security forces from Australia and New Zealand arrived to help restore stability. In the aftermath of the violence hundreds of people were arrested. Apparently in response to the unrest, it was announced that a new, modified programme of reform had been approved, envisaging a 30-member legislature made up of 21 people's representatives and nine nobles' representatives. The Prime Minister, it was agreed, would be elected by the legislature. It was revealed that King Tupou V had in fact endorsed the reforms in the previous month, but the final decision had been delayed pending the conclusions of the tripartite committee. Soon after, King Tupou V, in an address to the Legislative Assembly prior to its recess, highlighted the reconstruction efforts necessary after the 'shame' of the unrest, and reiterated the importance of democratic reform that was 'appropriate' for Tonga.

In early 2007 five pro-reform people's representatives, including Clive Edwards, were detained on charges that included sedition, in connection with their alleged involvement in the riots of November 2006. In September other charges against the representatives were abandoned; however, each representative still awaited the outcome of a charge of sedition. In early April 2009 the Supreme Court dismissed an application by the accused to have the indictment quashed and ordered that the trial proceed. Meanwhile, in March of that year a further five people's representatives were found not guilty of sedition in relation to the 2006 riots, and in May four men were cleared by a jury of the Supreme Court of charges relating to the destruction and damage of property in Nuku'alofa. Several others were convicted in February 2008 of various offences related to the riots, while the emergency measures proclaimed following the unrest remained in effect. In June 2007 the Minister of Agriculture, Forestry and Fisheries, Peauafi Haukinima, resigned; Prime Minister Sevele assumed responsibility for his portfolios in an acting capacity. Sevele also took charge of finance following the departure of Siosiua 'Utoikamanu in February 2008, but later transferred the portfolio to Afu'alo Matoto, who became Minister of Finance, National Planning, Public Enterprises and Information. From March Fineasi Funaki, the Minister of Tourism, was reportedly forfeiting three months' salary because of his appropriation of funds provided by the Chinese embassy. In June 2008 an independent anti-corruption commission was established to investigate alleged financial wrongdoing within the Government; however, the commission was reportedly criticized by pro-democracy people's representative 'Akilisi Pohiva, as it did not have the power to investigate the activities of the King. The formation of the Paati Langafonua Tu'uola (PLT), a new political organization, was announced by its president, Sione Fonua, in August 2007.

On 23 April 2008 29 nobles elected nine representatives to the Assembly, and on the following day elections were held to determine the nine commoners' seats. Approximately 48% of the electorate voted in the latter election, in which 71 candidates participated. Pro-democracy candidates, including several awaiting trial on sedition charges, secured a majority of the commoners' seats, indicating continuing popular support for the reform movement. Although the elections were described as the last to be held under the prevailing system (with constitutional changes expected to increase dramatically the proportions of democratically elected seats, as well as reducing the number of ministers nominated by the King, scheduled to be introduced in 2010) reformists urged the King to formalize the process at his forthcoming coronation. In early May the King named Tu'ilakepa as the new Speaker of the Assembly. This was followed in July by the approval of the Constitutional and Electoral Commission Act charged with determining the nature of the country's political reforms. The Commission was to be composed of five commissioners nominated by the Cabinet, Nobles, People's Representatives and Judicial Services Commission respectively. The new body was allocated the specific task of examining the type of reforms required in the country's political system, whereupon it was to report to the Government and Legislative Assembly.

In July 2008, in accordance with the new King's undertaking to relinquish his private business interests as soon as possible, the Tongan Government agreed to purchase the Shoreline Power Group. The Minister of Finance, National Planning, Public Enterprises and Information, Afu'alo Matoto, confirmed that the Government was to pay US $25m. for ownership of Shoreline, the country's only electric power generation facility, using funds derived from the sale of government shares in the Westpac Bank of Tonga. The King was also in the process of divesting himself of his interests in the telecommunications sector and elsewhere.

Shortly before his coronation in August 2008, King Tupou V announced that he was voluntarily surrendering certain powers in favour of the Prime Minister, although the King was to retain judicial powers granting him the right to commute prison sentences and to appoint judges. The King also reiterated his commitment to parliamentary reform, confirming the projected increase in the number of people's representatives to 17 and the intention to allow Parliament, rather than the monarch, to select the Prime Minister. The coronation ceremony itself took place between 30 July and 2 August 2008. The lavish event was attended by more than 1,400 guests, including many foreign dignitaries. After his coronation the King travelled to Tonga's outlying islands to attend further celebrations, which continued until 22 August. The emergency regulations imposed following the riots of November 2006 were extended on a monthly basis throughout 2008, in November prompting Clive Edwards to urge Australia and New Zealand to denounce the Government's actions. The state of emergency was extended for a further month in late April 2009. In May Prime Minister Sevele dismissed reported criticisms from Edwards that the process of political reform was being obstructed by the Government. Edwards allegedly claimed that the tabling of the Constitutional and Electoral Commission's first report had been delayed, thus ensuring that recommended changes would not be in place in time for the early elections that were scheduled for 2010.

A friendship treaty that Tonga signed with the USA in July 1988 provided for the safe transit within Tongan waters of US ships capable of carrying nuclear weapons. Tonga was virtually alone in the region in failing to condemn the French Government for its decision to resume nuclear-weapons tests in the South Pacific in mid-1995. However, in May 1996 it was announced that Tonga was finally to accede to the South Pacific Nuclear-Free Zone Treaty (see p. 394).

In September 1990 Tongasat, a Tongan telecommunications company founded earlier that year by Tongan citizens jointly with a US entrepreneur, laid claim to the last 16 satellite positions remaining in the earth's orbit that were suitable for trans-Pacific communications. Despite the protests of leading member nations of Intelsat (the international consortium responsible for most of the world's satellite services), the International Telecommunication Union (see p. 142), was obliged to approve the claim, and Tongasat was subsequently granted six positions. A dispute with Indonesia, concerning that country's use of satellite positions reserved by Tonga in 1990, was resolved by the signing of an agreement in December 1993. In May of the following year the two countries established diplomatic relations at ambassadorial level.

In November 1998 Tonga announced that it had decided to terminate its diplomatic links with Taiwan and to establish relations with the People's Republic of China. Tonga opened a consulate in China in May 2005. Several Chinese businesses were targeted in the Nuku'alofa riots of November 2006, prompting China to evacuate hundreds of its citizens. Tonga renewed a bilateral trade agreement with China in 2005, and an agreement on joint technical and economic co-operation was signed in May 2007. In March 2009 Japan opened its first embassy in Tonga, and the Tongan Government joined a growing number of Pacific countries, including Fiji and Samoa, to establish diplomatic relations with Cuba. Also in March, Tonga named its first High Commissioner to New Zealand: the High Commission was expected to open in Wellington by mid-2009.

In January 2002, in the Red Sea, Israeli commandos seized a ship that was allegedly transporting weapons to Palestinians. The ship was flying a Tongan 'flag of convenience' and had been registered in the Kingdom. The reformist politician 'Akilisi Pohiva criticized Tonga's policy of international ship registration, which generated income through sales of flags of convenience. (The issue of international shipping registration had never been debated in Parliament.) Following the seizure, the registration system was closed in June. However, in September another Tongan-registered ship was seized off the coast of Italy and its crew arrested on suspicion of plotting an al-Qa'ida-sponsored terrorist attack in Europe. Furthermore, it was reported in early October that the Greek businessman in charge of the Tongan International Registry of Ships, Pelopidas Papadopoulos, had absconded with the proceeds of the operation owed to the Tongan Government, totalling some US $0.3m.

In November 2008, following the success of a similar scheme in New Zealand, the Australian Government signed a memorandum of understanding with Tonga, Kiribati, Vanuatu and Papua New Guinea, whereby 2,500 Pacific islanders would be permitted to work in Australia, in the horticultural industry, on a seasonal basis. In February 2009 50 Tongans, the first of a projected 800 from the country, arrived in south-eastern Australia to begin work there.

Government

Tonga is a hereditary monarchy. The King is Head of State and Head of Government. He appoints, and presides over, the Privy Council which acts as the national Cabinet. Apart from the King, the Council includes 14 ministers (increased from 10 in 2005), appointed for life and led by the Prime Minister, and the Governors of Ha'apai and Vava'u. The unicameral Legislative Assembly comprises the King and 33 members: the Privy Council, nine hereditary nobles (chosen by their peers) and nine representatives elected by all adult Tongan citizens. Elected members hold office for three years. There are no official political parties, although opposition groupings continue to campaign for democratic reform. In July 2008 the King announced that he was to relinquish his absolute powers but retain control of judicial affairs.

Defence

Tonga has its own defence force, consisting of both regular and reserve units. Projected government expenditure on defence in the financial year 1999/2000 was 3.3m. pa'anga (5.0% of total budgetary expenditure); in the same year estimated expenditure on law and order was 4.6m. pa'anga (6.9% of total current expenditure).

Economic Affairs

In 2007, according to estimates by the World Bank, Tonga's gross national income (GNI), measured at average 2005–07 prices, was US $233m., equivalent to $2,320 per head (or $3,650 per head on an international purchasing-power parity basis). During 2000–07, it was estimated, the population increased at an average annual rate of 0.4%, while gross domestic product (GDP) per head increased, in real terms, by an average of 1.1% per year. Overall GDP increased, in real terms, at an average annual rate of 1.5% in 2000–07. GDP was estimated by the Asian Development Bank (ADB) to have contracted by 3.5% in 2007, before the economy grew by 1.2% in 2008.

Agriculture (including forestry and fishing) contributed 26.6% of GDP in 2007, and engaged about 32% of the employed labour force in 2005. According to the ADB, agricultural GDP increased at an average annual rate of 0.9% in 2000–07. The principal cash crops are coconuts, vanilla and squash (pumpkin), which normally form the major part of Tonga's exports. In 2007 squash accounted for 16.9% of export earnings. Vanilla acquired greater significance in the 1990s, but production subsequently declined, and vanilla beans accounted for only 1.7% of total export earnings in 2007. Yams, taro, sweet potatoes, watermelons, tomatoes, cassava, lemons and limes, oranges, groundnuts and breadfruit are also cultivated as food crops, while the islanders keep pigs, goats, poultry and cattle. The importance of the fishing industry increased from the 1990s. Exports of fish reached 11.3m. pa'anga in 2002, when they contributed 37.2% of total export earnings. The value of sales declined in subsequent years, and in 2007 fish accounted for 27.5% of export receipts. The ADB estimated that agricultural GDP increased by 1.6% in 2006 but declined by 0.9% in 2007.

Industry (including mining, manufacturing, construction and utilities) provided an estimated 12.1% of GDP in 2007 and engaged 26.4% of the employed labour force in 1996. According to the ADB, industrial GDP declined at an average annual rate of 0.7% in 2000–07. Compared with the previous year, industrial GDP was calculated by the ADB to have contracted by 2.1% in

2006 and by 5.9% in 2007. Manufacturing contributed an estimated 2.4% of GDP in 2007, and (with mining) employed 22.8% of the labour force in 1996. Output of food products and beverages dominates the manufacturing sector. Other manufacturing activities include the production of concrete blocks, small excavators, furniture, handicrafts, textiles, leather goods, sports equipment (including small boats), brewing and coconut oil. There is also a factory for processing sandalwood. The mining sector is undeveloped, as Tonga possesses no known mineral resources on land. In March 2009, however, it was announced that a company based in Australia was to explore in Tongan waters for undersea deposits of high-grade metals, such as copper, gold, zinc and silver.

In an attempt to reduce fuel imports, a 2-MW wave-energy power plant was constructed in the early 1990s and would, it was hoped, supply one-third of the islands' total electricity requirements when in full operation. A project to provide all the outer islands with solar power by 2000 was begun in 1996. Imports of mineral products accounted for 26.5% of total import costs in 2007.

Service industries contributed an estimated 61.3% of GDP in 2007 and engaged 39.5% of the employed labour force in 1996. According to ADB figures, the GDP of the services sector increased at an average annual rate of 3.2% in 2000–07. The ADB estimated that the GDP of the services sector expanded by 7.1% in 2006 and by 1.9% in 2007. Tourism makes a significant contribution to the economy. Tourism receipts increased from US $11m. in 2005 to $16m. in 2006. Visitor arrivals were reported to have risen from 46,040 in 2007 to 49,400 in 2008.

In 2007, according to the ADB, Tonga recorded a visible trade deficit of US $95m., and a deficit of $25m. on the current account of the balance of payments. The latter was equivalent to 10.8% of GDP in 2008. In 2007 the principal sources of imports were New Zealand (33.7%), Fiji (13.3%) and Australia (11.7%), while New Zealand and the USA were the principal markets for exports (purchasing 35.6% and 29.1% respectively). The principal exports in that year were foodstuffs. Squash, vanilla and fish are important export items. The principal imports were foodstuffs, mineral products, machinery and transport equipment and basic manufactures.

According to the ADB, in the financial year ending 30 June 2007 there was a budgetary deficit of 4.2m. pa'anga. The central government budgetary surplus, estimated at the equivalent of 2.0% of GDP, was recorded in 2008. Tonga's total external debt reached US $83m. in 2008, compared with $82m. in 2007. In 2007 the cost of debt-servicing was equivalent to 10.5% of the total revenue from exports of goods and services. In 2008/09 official development assistance from Australia was projected at $A19.3m., while aid from New Zealand in the same year amounted to $NZ12.0m. The annual rate of inflation averaged 8.8% in 2000–07. According to ADB figures, consumer prices increased by an average of 5.1% in 2007 and 9.9% in 2008. Some 5.5% of the labour force were unemployed in 2003, according to the ADB.

Tonga is a member of the Pacific Community (see p. 391), the Pacific Islands Forum (see p. 393), the Asian Development Bank (ADB, see p. 191) and the UN Economic and Social Commission for Asia and the Pacific (ESCAP, see p. 36). The country is a signatory of the Lomé Conventions and the successor Cotonou Agreement (see p. 311) with the European Union (EU). Tonga was formally admitted to the World Trade Organization (WTO, see p. 410) in July 2007.

The constraints on Tonga's economic development have included large-scale emigration and over-reliance on the agricultural sector, in particular sales of squash to the international market. The relatively low rate of growth recorded in 2006 was, in part, attributable to the decline in prices on the world market for Tonga's principal export product, squash; the squash industry subsequently remained depressed. Budgetary and inflationary pressures rose following the implementation of increases of 60%–80% in public sector salaries (see Recent History). In 2007 and 2008 these increases were expected to reach the equivalent of 11.0% and 7.8% respectively of GDP. However, the value of these pay increases was subsequently eroded by the rise in consumer prices. Further increases for civil servants were under consideration in 2009, with a view to stimulating consumption. Inflationary pressures were compounded in 2008 by the substantial increases in the costs of fuel and foodstuffs. The rate of inflation reached a high point of 12.6% in May 2008, but these pressures subsequently began to ease. Meanwhile, riots in the capital of Nuku'alofa in November 2006 (see Recent History) had an adverse impact on the economy. Reconstruction costs alone were estimated at more than 50m. pa'anga. With rebuilding work thus progressing, the economy grew modestly in 2008, following the contraction of the previous year. The construction sector thus performed well, expanding by 6.9% in 2008, not only as a result of the rebuilding work but also owing to the implementation of new tourism infrastructure projects. The tourism industry continued to expand, with visitor arrivals increasing in that year. However, the agricultural sector continued to perform poorly in 2008, the weakness attributable once again to low international prices for squash and vanilla. Remittances from Tongans resident overseas remained an important source of income. Such remittances were reported to have declined in real terms in 2007–08, however, and were expected to continue to do so in 2009, as the deterioration in global economic conditions reduced the availability of employment opportunities in countries such as the USA. In April 2009, following its previous provision of a grant of US $11.3m., the ADB announced that it was to grant further assistance, of $10m., to support Tonga in its attempts to address its economic problems. GDP was forecast by the ADB to contract by 2.0% in 2009. A report released by the IMF in May 2009 drew attention to the country's difficulties in containing the public debt, owing to the recent increases in government borrowing in order to finance reconstruction projects in Nuku'alofa.

Education

Free state education is compulsory for children between five and 14 years of age, while the Government and other Commonwealth countries offer scholarship schemes enabling students to go abroad for higher education. In 1999 there were 117 primary schools, with a total of 16,941 pupils in 2006. There were a total of 14,311 pupils in secondary education in 2006 and secondary schools numbered 69 in 1999. In 2000 enrolment at pre-primary schools included 22% of pupils from the relevant age-group. In 2005 enrolment at primary school level included 95.4% of children in the relevant age-group while in 2004 enrolment in secondary schools included 67.7% of children. There were also four technical and vocational colleges in 2001, with a total of 467 students, and one teacher-training college, with 288 students. In 1990 there were 230 Tongans studying overseas. Some degree courses are offered at the university division of 'Atenisi Institute. A new establishment offering higher education, the 'Unuaki 'o Tonga Royal Institute (UTRI), opened in 2004. Recurrent government expenditure on education in 1999/2000 was an estimated 10.9m. pa'anga (equivalent to 16.5% of total recurrent budgetary expenditure).

Public Holidays

2009: 1 January (New Year's Day), 10–13 April (Easter), 25 April (ANZAC Day), 4 June (Independence Day), 12 July (Birthday of the Heir to the Crown of Tonga), 1 August (Official Birthday of King Tupou V), 4 November (Tonga National Day), 4 December (Tupou I Day), 25–26 December (Christmas Day and Boxing Day).

2010: 1 January (New Year's Day), April (Easter), 25 April (ANZAC Day), 4 June (Independence Day), 12 July (Birthday of the Heir to the Crown of Tonga), 1 August (Official Birthday of King Tupou V), 4 November (Tonga National Day), 4 December (Tupou I Day), 25–26 December (Christmas Day and Boxing Day).

Weights and Measures

In 1980 Tonga adopted the metric system of weights and measures in place of the imperial system.

TONGA

Statistical Survey

Source (unless otherwise indicated): Tonga Government Department of Statistics, POB 149, Nuku'alofa; tel. (676) 23300; fax (676) 24303; e-mail dept@stats.gov.to; internet www.spc.int/prism/country/to/stats.

AREA AND POPULATION

Area: 748 sq km (289 sq miles).

Population: 97,784 at census of 30 November 1996; 101,991 (males 51,772, females 50,219) at census of 30 November 2006. *By Island Group* (2006 census, provisional): Tongatapu 71,260; Vava'u 15,485; Ha'apai 7,572; 'Eua 5,165; Niuas 1,652; Total 101,134. *Mid-2008* (estimate): 102,724 (Source: Secretariat of the Pacific Community).

Density (at mid-2008): 137.3 per sq km.

Principal Towns (population at 2006 census, provisional): Nuku'alofa (capital) 23,438; Neiafu 4,108; Haveluloto 3,384; Tofoa-Koloua 3,193; Vaini 3,076 (Source: Thomas Brinkhoff, *City Population*—internet www.citypopulation.de). *Mid-2007* (incl. suburbs, UN estimate): Nuku'alofa 25,000 (Source: UN, *World Urbanization Prospects: The 2007 Revision*).

Births, Marriages and Deaths (2006 unless otherwise indicated): Registered live births 2,945 (birth rate 28.9 per 1,000); Registered marriages (2003) 697 (marriage rate 6.9 per 1,000); Registered deaths 709 (death rate 7.0 per 1,000). Source: mainly UN, *Demographic Yearbook* and *Population and Vital Statistics Report*.

Life Expectancy (years at birth, WHO estimates): 71.0 (males 73.2; females 69.0) in 2006. Source: WHO, *World Health Statistics*.

Economically Active Population (persons aged 15 years and over, 1996): Agriculture, forestry and fishing 9,953; Mining and quarrying 43; Manufacturing 6,710; Electricity, gas and water 504; Construction 500; Trade, restaurants and hotels 2,506; Transport, storage and communications 1,209; Financing, insurance, real estate and business services 657; Public administration and defence 3,701; Education 1,721; Health and social work 510; Other community, social and personal services 1,320; Extra-territorial organizations 72; *Total employed* 29,406 (males 18,402, females 11,004); Unemployed 4,502 (males 3,293, females 1,209); *Total labour force* 33,908 (males 21,695, females 12,213). *Mid-2005* (estimates): Agriculture, etc. 12,000; Total labour force 38,000 (Source: FAO).

HEALTH AND WELFARE
Key Indicators

Total Fertility Rate (children per woman, 2006): 3.8.

Under-5 Mortality Rate (per 1,000 live births, 2006): 24.

Physicians (per 1,000 head, 2002): 0.3.

Hospital Beds (per 1,000 head, 2004): 2.9.

Health Expenditure (2006): US $ per head (PPP): 289.

Health Expenditure (2006): % of GDP: 5.4.

Health Expenditure (2006): public (% of total): 75.3.

Access to Sanitation (% of persons, 2004): 96.

Human Development Index (2006): ranking 85.

Human Development Index (2006): value 0.774.

For sources and definitions, see explanatory note on p. vi.

AGRICULTURE, ETC.

Principal Crops ('000 metric tons, 2007, FAO estimates): Sweet potatoes 6.8; Cassava 9.7; Taro 3.8; Yams 4.7; Other roots and tubers 2.2; Coconuts 58.5; Pumpkins, squash and gourds 21.0; Other vegetables and melons 6.4; Bananas 0.8; Plantains 3.3; Oranges 1.2; Lemons and limes 2.7.

Livestock ('000 head, year ending September 2007, FAO estimates): Pigs 81; Horses 12; Cattle 11; Goats 13; Chickens 330.

Livestock Products (metric tons, 2007, FAO estimates): Pig meat 1,550; Other meat 718; Hen eggs 30; Cows' milk 370.

Forestry ('000 cu m, 1999): *Roundwood Removals* (excl. bark): 2; *Sawnwood Production:* 2 (FAO estimate). *2000–07:* Annual output as in 1999 (FAO estimates).

Fishing (metric tons, live weight, 2006): Marine fishes 2,100 (Snappers and jobfishes 283; Albacore 414; Bigeye tuna 117; Yellowfin tuna 227); Marine crustaceans 350 (FAO estimate); Total catch (incl. others, FAO estimate) 2,500 (excl. aquatic plants 356).

Source: FAO.

INDUSTRY

Production (2007): Electric energy 46 million kWh. Source: Asian Development Bank.

FINANCE

Currency and Exchange Rates: 100 seniti (cents) = 1 pa'anga (Tongan dollar or $T). *Sterling, US Dollar and Euro Equivalents* (31 October 2008): £1 sterling = $T3.4597; US $1 = $T2.1390; €1 = $T2.7288; $T100 = £28.90 = US $46.75 = €36.65. *Average Exchange Rate* (pa'anga per US $): 1.9430 in 2005; 2.0259 in 2006; 1.9709 in 2007.

Budget ('000 pa'anga, year ending 30 June 2007): *Revenue:* Taxation 135,362; Non-tax revenue 18,007; Capital receipts 37; Total 153,405 (excl. grants received from abroad 12,635). *Expenditure:* Current expenditure 151,698; Capital expenditure 5,914; Total 157,611 (excl. net lending 1,036). Source: Asian Development Bank.

International Reserves (US $ million at 31 December 2008): IMF special drawing rights 0.74; Reserve position in the IMF 2.64; Foreign exchange 66.38; Total 69.75. Source: IMF, *International Financial Statistics*.

Money Supply ('000 pa'anga at 31 December 2007): Currency outside banks 22,466; Demand deposits at deposit money banks 65,188; Total money 87,654. Source: IMF, *International Financial Statistics*.

Cost of Living (Consumer Price Index, excl. rent; base: November 2002 = 100): All items 170.7 in 2006; 146.2 in 2007; 199.7 in 2008. Source: IMF, *International Financial Statistics*.

Gross Domestic Product (million pa'anga at constant 2000/01 prices, year ending 30 June): 295.6 in 2004/05; 308.5 in 2005/06; 307.7 in 2006/07. Source: Asian Development Bank.

Gross Domestic Product by Economic Activity (million pa'anga at current prices, year ending 30 June 2007, provisional): Agriculture, forestry and fishing 112.7; Mining and quarrying 1.6; Manufacturing 10.1; Electricity, gas and water 10.6; Construction 29.1; Trade, restaurants and hotels 60.8; Transport, storage and communications 23.6; Finance and real estate 49.8; Public administration 83.2; Other services 42.7; *Sub-total* 424.2; *Less* Imputed bank service charges 14.7; *Gross value added in basic prices* 409.5; Indirect taxes, less subsidies 96.0; GDP at market prices 505.7. Source: Asian Development Bank.

Balance of Payments (US $ '000, 2007): Exports of goods f.o.b. 8,689; Imports of goods f.o.b. –127,398; *Trade balance* –118,709; Exports of services 32,986; Imports of services –52,102; *Balance on goods and services* –137,825; Other income received 11,189; Other income paid –3,804; *Balance on goods, services and income* –130,441; Current transfers received 119,118; Current transfers paid –12,850; *Current balance* –24,172; Capital account (net) 18,254; Direct investment from abroad 27,352; Other investment assets 466; Other investment liabilities –5,992; Net errors and omissions –315; *Overall balance* 15,594. Source, IMF, *International Financial Statistics*.

EXTERNAL TRADE

Principal Commodities ('000 pa'anga, 2007): *Imports:* Animals and animal products 30,142; Vegetable products 8,745; Prepared foodstuffs 43,192; Mineral products 74,392; Chemical products 10,833; Wood and wood products 8,720; Wood pulp, paper and paperboard 8,741; Base metals and articles thereof 13,875; Machinery, mechanical appliances and electrical equipment 30,372; Transportation equipment 12,918; Miscellaneous manufactured articles 6,393; Works of art, collectors' pieces and antiques 15,099; Total (incl. others) 281,032. *Exports* (including re-exports): Animal and animal products 5,621; Vegetable products 8,598; Chemical products 744; Wood and wood products 437; Machinery, mechanical appliances and electrical equipment 537; Total (incl. others) 16,716.

Principal Trading Partners ('000 pa'anga, 2007): *Imports:* Australia 32,924; China, People's Republic 17,501; Fiji 37,372; Indonesia 4,208; Japan 7,320; New Zealand 94,766; Singapore 47,942; USA (incl. Hawaii) 28,545; Total (incl. others) 281,032. *Exports:* American Samoa 599; Australia 1,155; Japan 2,063; Korea, Republic 304; New Zealand 5,949; Samoa 757; Taiwan 353; USA (incl. Hawaii) 4,858; Total (incl. others) 16,716.

TRANSPORT

Road Traffic (registered motor vehicles, 2004): Passenger cars 6,580; Light goods vehicles 5,183; Heavy goods vehicles 2,698; Buses 114; Taxis 845; Total (incl. others) 16,748.

Shipping: *International Traffic* ('000 metric tons, 1998 unless otherwise indicated): Goods loaded 13.8; Goods unloaded 80.4. Vessels entered ('000 net registered tons) 1,950 in 1991 (Source: UN, *Statistical Yearbook*). *Merchant Fleet* (registered at 31 December 2007): Vessels 48; Total displacement ('000 grt) 66.7 (Source: Lloyd's Register-Fairplay, *World Fleet Statistics*).

Civil Aviation (traffic on scheduled services, 2004): Kilometres flown 1 million; Passengers carried 75,000; Passenger-km 19 million; Total ton-km 1 million. Source: UN, *Statistical Yearbook*.

TOURISM

Foreign Tourist Arrivals (excl. cruise-ship passengers): 41,208 in 2004; 41,862 in 2005; 39,451 in 2006.

Tourist Arrivals by Country (2006): Australia 8,710; Fiji 1,400; Germany 708; Japan 722; New Zealand 17,445; United Kingdom 970; USA 6,090; Total (incl. others) 39,451.

Tourism Receipts (US $ million, excl. passenger transport): 13 in 2004; 15 in 2005; 16 in 2006.

Source: World Tourism Organization.

COMMUNICATIONS MEDIA

Radio Receivers (1997): 61,000 in use.

Television Receivers (1997): 2,000 in use.

Telephones ('000 main lines, 2007): 21.0 in use.

Mobile Cellular Telephones (2007): 46,500 subscribers.

Personal Computers (2002): 2,000.

Internet Users (2007): 8,400.

Broadband Subscribers (2007): 800.

Facsimile Machines (1996): 250 in use.

Daily Newspapers (1996): 1; estimated circulation 7,000.

Non-daily Newspapers (2001): 2; estimated circulation 13,000.

Sources: UNESCO, *Statistical Yearbook*; UN, *Statistical Yearbook*; Audit Bureau of Circulations, Australia; and International Telecommunication Union.

EDUCATION

Primary (2006, unless otherwise indicated, provisional): 117 schools (1999); 760 teachers; 16,941 pupils.

General Secondary (2006, unless otherwise indicated, provisional): 39 schools (1999); 999 teachers; 14,311 pupils.

Technical and Vocational: 4 colleges (2001); 45 teachers (1990); 467 students (1999).

Teacher-training (1999, unless otherwise indicated): 1 college; 22 teachers (1994); 288 students.

Universities, etc. (1985): 17 teachers; 85 students.

Other Higher Education: 36 teachers (1980); 620 students (1985); in 1990 230 students were studying overseas on government scholarships.

Directory

The Constitution

The Constitution of Tonga is based on that granted in 1875 by King George Tupou I. It provides for a government consisting of the Sovereign; a Privy Council, which is appointed by the Sovereign and consists of the Sovereign and the Cabinet; the Cabinet, which consists of a Prime Minister, a Deputy Prime Minister, several other ministers (formerly eight but increased to 12 in 2005) and the Governors of Ha'apai and Vava'u; a Legislative Assembly and a Judiciary. Limited law-making power is vested in the Privy Council and any legislation passed by the Executive is subject to review by the Legislative Assembly. The unicameral Legislative Assembly comprises the King, the Cabinet, nine hereditary nobles (chosen by their peers) and nine representatives elected by all adult Tongan citizens. Elected members hold office for three years.

The Government

HEAD OF STATE

The Sovereign: HM King GEORGE TUPOU V (succeeded to the throne 11 September 2006).

CABINET
(April 2009)

Prime Minister and Minister of Foreign Affairs and Defence: Dr FELETI (FRED) SEVELE.

Deputy Prime Minister, Minister of Health and Acting Minister of Police: Dr VILIAMI TANGI.

Minister of Finance, National Planning, Public Enterprises and Information: AFU'ALO MATOTO.

Minister of Education, Women's Affairs and Culture: Dr TEVITA HALA PALEFAU.

Governor of Ha'apai: MALUPO.

Minister of Labour, Commerce and Industries: LISIATE 'AKOLO.

Minister of Information and Communication: 'ESETA FUSITU'A.

Minister of Lands, Survey, Natural Resources and Environment and Acting Governor of Vava'u: TUITA.

Minister of Training, Employment, Youth and Sports: TU'IVAKANO.

Minister of Works: NUKU.

Minister of Agriculture, Forestry and Fisheries: Prince TU'IPELEHAKE.

Attorney-General and Minister of Justice: MALIA VIVIENA 'ALISI NUMIA AFEAKI TAUMOEPEAU.

Minister of Civil Aviation, Marine and Ports: PAUL KARALUS.

Minister of Tourism: FINEASI FUNAKI.

GOVERNMENT MINISTRIES AND OFFICES

Office of the Prime Minister: POB 62, Taufa'ahau Rd, Kolofo'ou, Nuku'alofa; tel. 24644; fax 23888; e-mail pmomail@pmo.gov.to; internet www.pmo.gov.to.

Palace Office: Salote Rd, Kolofo'ou, Nuku'alofa; tel. 21000; fax 24102; internet www.palaceoffice.gov.to.

Ministry of Agriculture, Food, Forestry and Fisheries: Administration Office, Vuna Rd, Kolofo'ou, Nuku'alofa; tel. 23038; fax 23039; e-mail pvea@kalianet.to.

Ministry of Civil Aviation: POB 845, Salote Rd, Nuku'alofa; tel. 24144; fax 24145; e-mail info@mca.gov.to; internet www.mca.gov.to.

Ministry of Education: POB 61, Vuna Rd, Kolofo'ou, Nuku'alofa; tel. 23511; fax 23596; e-mail moe@kalianet.to.

Ministry of Finance and National Planning: Treasury Bldg, POB 87, Vuna Rd, Kolofo'ou, Nuku'alofa; tel. 23066; fax 21010; e-mail info@finance.gov.to; internet www.finance.gov.to.

Ministry of Foreign Affairs: National Reserve Bank Bldg, Salote Rd, Kolofo'ou, Nuku'alofa; tel. 23600; fax 23360; e-mail secfo@candw.to.

Ministry of Health: POB 59, Taufa'ahau Rd, Tofoa, Nuku'alofa; tel. 23200; fax 24921; internet www.health.gov.to.

Ministry of Internal Affairs: POB 110, Salote Rd, Fasi-moe-afi, Nuku'alofa; tel. 23688; fax 23880.

Ministry of Justice: POB 130, Railway Rd, Kolofo'ou, Nuku'alofa; tel. 21055; fax 23098; internet www.justice.gov.to.

Ministry of Labour, Commerce and Industries: POB 110, Nuku'alofa; tel. 23688; fax 23887; e-mail info@mlci.gov.to; internet www.mlci.gov.to.

Ministry of Lands, Survey and Natural Resources: POB 5, Vuna Rd, Kolofo'ou, Nuku'alofa; tel. 23611; fax 23216; internet www.lands.gov.to.

Ministry of Marine and Ports: POB 397, Vuna Rd, Ma'ufanga, Nuku'alofa; tel. 22555; fax 26234; e-mail marine@kalianet.to.

Ministry of Police, Fire Services and Prisons: Mauikisikisi Rd, Longolongo; tel. 23233; fax 23226.

Ministry of Public Enterprises and Information: Nuku'alofa; tel. 28144; fax 24598.

TONGA
Directory

Ministry of Works and Disaster Relief Activities: 'Alaivaha-mama'o Rd, Vaololoa, Nuku'alofa; tel. 23100; fax 25440; e-mail mowtonga@kalianet.to.

Legislative Assembly

The Legislative Assembly consists of the Speaker, the members of the Cabinet, nine nobles chosen by the 33 Nobles of Tonga, and nine representatives elected by all Tongans over 21 years of age. There are elections every three years, and the Assembly is required to meet at least once every year. The most recent election was held on 24 April 2008, when pro-democracy candidates won a majority of the nine seats.

Speaker and Chairman of the Legislative Assembly: Tu'ilakepa.

Political Organizations

Although the Constitution of Tonga does not provide for the official establishment of political parties, the following groups have been active:

Friendly Islands Human Rights and Democracy Movement Inc (FIHRDM Inc): POB 843, Nuku'alofa; tel. 25501; e-mail demo@kalianet.to; f. late 1970s; est. and recognized in 1992 as the Pro-Democracy Movement; application in 1998 for incorporation under new name of Tonga Human Rights and Democracy Movement refused by the Govt; reverted to the name of Human Rights and Democracy Movement in Tonga (HRDMT) in 2002; assumed present name in Nov. 2005; campaigns for democratic reform and increased parliamentary representation for the Tongan people; Sec. 'Akilisi Pohiva.

Kotoa Movement: f. 2001; campaigns in support of monarchy; Sec. Semisi Kailahi.

Paati Langafonua Tu'uloa (PLT): f. 2007; Pres. Sione Fonua.

People's Democratic Party: Nuku'alofa; f. 2005; breakaway group from HRDMT; Pres. Sione Teisina Fuko; Vice-Pres. Sione Tu'alau Mangisi; Sec. Semisi Tapueluelu.

Diplomatic Representation

EMBASSIES AND HIGH COMMISSIONS IN TONGA

Australia: Salote Rd, Private Bag 35, Nuku'alofa; tel. 23244; fax 23243; e-mail ahctonga@kalianet.to; internet www.tonga.embassy.gov.au; High Commissioner Bruce Hunt.

China, People's Republic: Vuna Rd, POB 877, Nuku'alofa; tel. 24554; fax 24595; e-mail chinaemb_to@mfa.gov.cn; Ambassador Fan Guijin.

Japan: 5th Floor, NRBT Bldg, POB 330, Nuku'alofa; tel. 22221; fax 27025; Ambassador Yasuo Takase.

New Zealand: cnr Taufa'ahau and Salote Rds, POB 830, Nuku'alofa; tel. 23122; fax 23487; e-mail nzhcnuk@kalianet.to; High Commissioner Christine Bogle.

Judicial System

There are eight Magistrates' Courts, the Land Court, the Supreme Court and the Court of Appeal.

Appeal from the Magistrates' Courts is to the Supreme Court, and from the Supreme Court and Land Court to the Court of Appeal (except in certain matters relating to hereditary estates, where appeal lies to the Privy Council). The Chief Justice and Puisne Judge are resident in Tonga and are judges of the Supreme Court and Land Court. The Court of Appeal is presided over by the Chief Justice and consists of three judges from other Commonwealth countries. In the Supreme Court the accused in criminal cases, and either party in civil suits, may elect trial by jury. In the Land Court the judge sits with a Tongan assessor. Proceedings in the Magistrates' Courts are in Tongan, and in the Supreme Court and Court of Appeal in Tongan and English.

Supreme Court

POB 11, Nuku'alofa; tel. 23599; fax 22380; e-mail cj_tonga@kalianet.to.

Chief Justice: Anthony Ford.

Puisne Judge: Robert Shuster.

Chief Registrar: Manakovi Pahulu.

Religion

The Tongans are almost all Christians, and about 36% of the population belong to Methodist (Wesleyan) communities. There are also significant numbers of Roman Catholics (15%) and Latter-day Saints (Mormons—15%). Anglicans (1%) and Seventh-day Adventists (5%) are also represented. Fourteen churches are represented in total.

CHRISTIANITY

Kosilio 'ae Ngaahi Siasi 'i Tonga (Tonga National Council of Churches): POB 1205, Nuku'alofa; tel. 23291; fax 27506; e-mail tncc@kalianet.to; f. 1973; three mem. churches (Free Wesleyan, Roman Catholic and Anglican); Chair. Rt Rev. Alifaleti Mone; Gen. Sec. Rev. Siketi Tonga.

The Anglican Communion

Tonga lies within the diocese of Polynesia, part of the Church of the Province of New Zealand. The Bishop of Polynesia is resident in Fiji.

Archdeacon of Tonga and Samoa: The Ven. Sam Koy, The Vicarage, POB 31, Nuku'alofa; tel. 22136.

The Roman Catholic Church

The diocese of Tonga, directly responsible to the Holy See, comprises Tonga and the New Zealand dependency of Niue. At 31 December 2006 there were an estimated 14,796 adherents in the diocese. The Bishop participates in the Catholic Bishops' Conference of the Pacific, based in Fiji.

Bishop of Tonga: Soane Patita Mafi, Toutaimana Catholic Centre, POB 1, Nuku'alofa; tel. 23822; fax 23854; e-mail cathbish@kalianet.to.

Other Churches

Church of Jesus Christ of Latter-day Saints (Mormon): Mission Centre, POB 58, Nuku'alofa; tel. 26007; fax 23763; 53,000 mems; Pres. Lynn C. McMurray.

Church of Tonga: Nuku'alofa; f. 1928; a branch of Methodism; 6,912 mems; Pres. Rev. Finau Katoanga.

Free Constitutional Church of Tonga: POB 23, Nuku'alofa; tel. 23896; fax 24458; f. 1885; 20,034 mems (2008); Pres. Rev. Semisi Fonua; brs in Australia, New Zealand and USA.

Free Wesleyan Church of Tonga (Koe Siasi Uesiliana Tau'ataina 'o Tonga): POB 57, Nuku'alofa; tel. 23522; fax 24020; e-mail fwc@kalianet.to; internet www.fwc.to; f. 1826; 36,500 mems; Pres. Rev. Dr 'Alifaleti Mone.

Tokaikolo Christian Fellowship: Nuku'alofa; f. 1978; breakaway group from Free Wesleyan Church; 5,000 mems.

BAHÁ'Í FAITH

National Spiritual Assembly: POB 133, Nuku'alofa; tel. 21568; fax 23120; e-mail nsatonga@patco.to; mems resident in 142 localities.

The Press

Eva, Your Guide to Tonga: POB 958, Nuku'alofa; tel. 25779; fax 24749; e-mail vapress@matangitonga.to; internet www.matangitonga.to; f. 1989; 4 a year; publication suspended under media restrictions in Jan. 2004; Editor Pesi Fonua; circ. 4,500.

Ko e Kele'a (Conch Shell): POB 1567, Nuku'alofa; tel. 25501; fax 26330; internet www.planet-tonga.com/tongatimes/kelea; f. 1986; monthly; activist-orientated publication, economic and political; Editor 'Akilisi Pohiva; circ. 3,500.

Lali: Nuku'alofa; f. 1994; monthly; English; national business magazine; Publr Kalafi Moala.

Lao and Hia: POB 2808, Nuku'alofa; tel. 14105; weekly; Tongan; legal newspaper; Editor Sione Hafoka.

Matangi Tonga: POB 958, Nuku'alofa; tel. 25779; fax 24749; e-mail vapress@matangitonga.to; internet www.matangitonga.to; f. 1986; monthly; national news magazine ceased publication following suspension of licence in Jan. 2004 and subsequently published solely on internet; Man. Editor Mary Fonua.

'Ofa ki Tonga: c/o Tokaikolo Fellowship, POB 2055, Nuku'alofa; tel. 24190; monthly; newspaper of Tokaikolo Christian Fellowship; Editor Rev. Liufau Vailea Saulala.

Taumu'a Lelei: POB 1, Nuku'alofa; tel. 27161; fax 23854; e-mail tmlcath@kalianet.to; f. 1931; monthly; Roman Catholic; Editor Dr Soane Lilo Foliaki.

The Times of Tonga/Koe Taimi'o Tonga: POB 880, Nuku'alofa; tel. 23177; fax 23292; e-mail times@kalianet.to; internet timesoftonga.com; f. 1989; twice-weekly; English edition covers Pacific and world news, Tongan edition concentrates on local news;

TONGA

Directory

licence suspended in Feb. 2004; Publr KALAFI MOALA; Editor MATENI TAPUELUELU; circ. 8,000.

Tohi Fanongonongo: POB 57, Nuku'alofa; tel. 26533; fax 24020; e-mail fwctf@kalianet.to; monthly; Wesleyan; Editor Rev. TEVITA PAUKAMEA TIUETI.

Tonga Chronicle/Kalonikali Tonga: POB 197, Nuku'alofa; tel. 23302; fax 23336; e-mail chroni@kalianet.to; internet www.netstorage.com/kami/tonga/news; f. 1964; govt-sponsored; weekly; Tongan and English; Man. 'ALIFELETI TU'IHALAMAKA; circ. 3,000.

Publisher

Vava'u Press Ltd: POB 958, Nuku'alofa; tel. 25779; fax 24749; e-mail vapress@matangitonga.to; internet www.matangitonga.to; f. 1980; books and magazines; Pres. PESI FONUA.

Broadcasting and Communications

TELECOMMUNICATIONS

Tonga Communications Corporation: Private Bag 4, Nuku'alofa; tel. 20000; fax 26701; internet www.tcc.to; f. 2000; responsible for domestic and international telecommunications services; Man. Dir STEPHEN TUSLER.

Digicel Tonga: Nuku'alofa; f. 2008; CEO TANYA MENZIES.

Tongasat—Friendly Islands Satellite Communications Ltd: POB 2921, Nuku'alofa; tel. 24160; fax 23322; e-mail info@tongasat.com; internet www.tongasat.com; 80% Tongan-owned; private co but co-operates with Govt in management and leasing of orbital satellite positions; Chair. Princess SALOTE MAFILE'O PILOLEVU TUITA; Man. Dir SEMISI PANUVE.

BROADCASTING

Radio

Tonga Broadcasting Commission: POB 36, Tungi Rd, Fasi-moe-afi, Nuku'alofa; tel. 23550; fax 28921; internet www.tonga-broadcasting.com; independent statutory board; commercially operated; manages two stations, A3Z Radio Tonga 1 and Radio Tonga 2, with programmes in Tongan and English; Gen. Man. ELENOA AMANAKI.

93FM: Pacific Partners Trust, POB 478, Nuku'alofa; tel. 23076; fax 24970; broadcasts in English, Tongan, German, Mandarin and Hindi.

A3V The Millennium Radio 2000: POB 838, Nuku'alofa; tel. 25891; fax 24195; e-mail a3v@tongatapu.net.to; broadcasts on FM; musical programmes; Gen. Man. SAM VEA.

Tonga News Association: Nuku'alofa; Pres. PESI FONUA.

Television

Oceania Broadcasting Inc started relaying US television programmes in 1991. The Tonga Broadcasting Commission launched the country's first television service in July 2000. The studios and broadcasting facilities are located near Nuku'alofa, providing local news and sport.

Oceania Broadcasting Network: POB 91, Nuku'alofa; tel. 23314; fax 23658; reportedly ceased operations in late 2006.

Television Tonga: Fasi-moe-afi, Nuku'alofa; f. 2000; 60% of programmes in English; 40% of programmes in Tongan; Man. KATALINA TOHI.

Tonfön TV: POB 895, Nuku'alofa; fax 23047; e-mail customerservice@tonfon.to; internet www.tonfon.to; part of Shoreline Group of cos; operates 5 channels.

Finance

(cap. = capital; res = reserves; dep. = deposits; m. = million; amounts in Tongan dollars)

BANKING

Central Bank

National Reserve Bank of Tonga: Private Bag 25, Nuku'alofa; tel. 24057; fax 24201; e-mail nrbt@reservebank.to; internet www.reservebank.to; f. 1989; assumed central bank functions of Bank of Tonga; issues currency; manages exchange rates and international reserves; cap. 2.0m., res 15.7m., dep. 75.4m. (June 2007); Gov. SIOSI MAFI; Chair. Crown Prince TUPOUTO'A LAVAKA.

Other Banks

Australia and New Zealand Banking Group Ltd: cnr of Salote and Railway Rds, POB 910, Nuku'alofa; tel. 24944; fax 23870; e-mail anztonga@anz.com; internet www.anz.com/Tonga; Gen. Man. PAUL PELZER.

MBf Bank Ltd: POB 3118, Nuku'alofa; tel. 24600; fax 24662; e-mail info@mbfbank.to; internet www.mbfbank.to; f. 1993; 93.35% owned by MBf Asia Capital Corpn Holdings Ltd, 4.75% owned hitherto by King George Tupou V, 0.95% owned by Tonga Investments Ltd, 0.95% owned by Tonga Co-operative Federation Society; Gen. Man. H. K. YEOH.

Tonga Development Bank: Fatafehi Rd, POB 126, Nuku'alofa; tel. 23333; fax 23775; e-mail tdevbank@tdb.to; internet www.tdb.to; f. 1977; to provide credit for developmental purposes, mainly in agriculture, fishery, tourism and housing; cap. 10.5m., res 9.9m. (Dec. 2007); Man. Dir SIMIONE SEFANAIA; 5 brs.

Westpac Bank of Tonga: POB 924, Nuku'alofa; tel. 23933; fax 25066; e-mail westpactonga@westpac.com.au; internet www.westpac.to; f. 1973 as Bank of Tonga; name changed as above in 2002; owned by Westpac Banking Corpn (Australia); cap. 3.0m., res 10.6m., dep. 137.1m. (Sept. 2006); Gen. Man. MISHKA TU'IFUA; 6 brs.

Trade and Industry

DEVELOPMENT ORGANIZATIONS

Tonga Investments Ltd: POB 27, Nuku'alofa; tel. 24388; fax 24313; f. 1992; to replace Commodities Board; govt-owned; manages five subsidiary companies; Chair. Baron VAEA OF HOUMA; Man. Dir ANTHONY WAYNE MADDEN.

Tonga Association of Small Businesses: Nuku'alofa; f. 1990; to cater for the needs of small businesses; Chair. SIMI SILAPELU.

CHAMBER OF COMMERCE

Tonga Chamber of Commerce and Industry: Tungi Arcade, POB 1704, Nuku'alofa; tel. 25168; fax 26039; e-mail chamber@kalianet.to; internet www.tongachamber.org; Pres. PAULA TAUMOEPEAU.

TRADE ASSOCIATIONS

Tonga Kava Council: Nuku'alofa; to promote the development of the industry both locally and abroad; Chair. TO'IMOANA TAKATAKA.

Tonga Squash Council: Nuku'alofa; promotes the development of the industry; introduced a quota system for exports in 2004; Pres. TSUTOMU NAKAO; Sec. STEVEN EDWARDS.

UTILITIES

Shoreline Power Group: POB 47, Taufa'ahau Rd, Kolofo'ou, Nuku'alofa; tel. 23311; fax 23632; provides electricity via diesel motor generation, took over operations from the Tonga Electric Power Board in 2004; purchased by Tongan Govt in 2008; CEO SOANE RAMANLAL.

Tonga Water Board: POB 92, Taufa'ahau Rd, Kolofo'ou, Nuku'alofa; tel. 23298; fax 23518; operates four urban water systems, serving about 25% of the population; Man. SAIMONE P. HELU.

CO-OPERATIVES

Tonga Co-operative Federation Society: Tungi Arcade, Nuku'alofa.

TRADE UNIONS

Association of Tongatapu Squash Pumpkin Growers: Nuku'alofa; f. 1998.

Public Service Association (PSA): Nuku'alofa; Pres. FINAU TUTONE; Gen. Sec. (vacant).

Tonga Nurses' Association and Friendly Islands Teachers' Association (TNA/FITA): POB 859, Nuku'alofa; tel. and fax 23972; e-mail fita@candw.to; Pres. FINAU TUTONE; Gen. Sec. TOKANKAMEA PULEIKU.

Transport

ROADS

Total road length was estimated at 680 km in 2000, of which some 27% were all-weather paved roads. Most of the network comprises fair-weather-only dirt or coral roads.

TONGA

SHIPPING

The chief ports are Nuku'alofa, on Tongatapu, and Neiafu, on Vava'u, with two smaller ports at Pangai and Niuatoputapu.

Shipping Corporation of Polynesia Ltd: Queen Salote Wharf, Vuna Rd, POB 453, Nuku'alofa; tel. 23853; fax 23250; e-mail info@olovaha.com; internet www.olovaha.com; govt-owned; regular inter-islands passenger and cargo services; Chair. 'ALISI TAUMOEPEAU; CEO JOHN JONESSE.

Uata Shipping Lines: 'Uliti Uata, POB 100, Nuku'alofa; tel. 23855; fax 23860.

Warner Pacific Line: POB 93, Nuku'alofa; tel. 21088; services to Samoa, American Samoa, Australia and New Zealand; Man. Dir MA'AKE FAKA'OSIFOLAU.

CIVIL AVIATION

Tonga is served by Fua'amotu International Airport, 22 km from Nuku'alofa, and airstrips at Vava'u, Ha'apai, Niuatoputapu, Niuafo'ou and 'Eua. In September 2006 it was announced that a government-owned agency, Tonga Airports Ltd (TAL), was to assume responsibility for the management of all airports with effect from January 2007. Domestic services are provided by Airlines Tonga, a joint venture between Air Fiji and Teta Tours (a Tongan travel company). Chathams Pacific, owned by Air Chathams of New Zealand, became Tonga's second carrier in April 2008. Air New Zealand provides a regular service to Australia and New Zealand and a regional carrier, Reef Air, operates between Tonga, Niue and Fiji. The New Zealand-based low-cost airline, Pacific Blue, commenced direct flights between Sydney and Tonga and between Auckland and Tonga in 2005.

Airlines Tonga: c/o Teta Tours, cnr of Railway St and Wellington St, Nuku'alofa; tel. 23690; fax 23238; e-mail tetatour@kalianet.to; internet www.airfiji.com.fj/pages.cfm/home/airlines-tonga.html; f. 2006; jt venture between Teta Tours of Tonga and Air Fiji Ltd; sole operator of domestic services in Tonga from Nov. 2006; Man SITAFOOTI 'AHO.

Chathams Pacific (The Friendly Islands Airline): POB 907, Nuku'alofa; tel. 28000; fax 23447; e-mail sales@chathamspacific.com; internet www.chathamspacific.com; f. 2008; owned by Air Chathams (New Zealand); Gen. Man. RUSSELL JENKINS.

Tourism

Tonga's attractions include scenic beauty and a pleasant climate. Visitor arrivals increased from an estimated 46,040 in 2007 to 49,400 in 2008. In 2006 revenue from the industry totalled US $16m. The majority of tourists were from New Zealand, the USA and Australia.

Tonga Tourist Association: POB 74, Nuku'alofa; tel. 23344; fax 23833; e-mail royale@kalianet.to; Pres. PAPILOA FOLIAKI; Sec. KOLOLIANA NAUFAHU.

Tonga Visitors' Bureau: Vuna Rd, POB 37, Nuku'alofa; tel. 25334; fax 23507; e-mail info@tvb.gov.to; internet www.tongaholiday.com; f. 1978; Dir VA'INGA PALU.

Tourism Tonga Inc: Nuku'alofa; f. 2009.

TRINIDAD AND TOBAGO

Introductory Survey

Location, Climate, Language, Religion, Flag, Capital

The Republic of Trinidad and Tobago consists of Trinidad, the southernmost of the Caribbean islands, and Tobago, which is 32 km (20 miles) to the north-east. Trinidad, which accounts for 94% of the total area, lies just off the north coast of Venezuela, on the South American mainland, while the country's nearest neighbour to the north is Grenada. The climate is tropical, with a dry season from January to May. Rainfall averages 1,561 mm (61.5 ins) per year. Annual average daytime temperatures range between 32°C (90°F) and 21°C (70°F). The official and main language is English, but French, Spanish, Hindi and Chinese are also spoken. In 2000 some 55% of the population were Christians, mainly Roman Catholics (30%) and Anglicans (25%), while 23% were Hindus and 6% Muslims. The national flag (proportions 3 by 5) is deep red, divided by a white-edged black diagonal stripe from upper hoist to lower fly. The capital is Port of Spain, on the island of Trinidad.

Recent History

Trinidad was first colonized by the Spanish in 1532, but was ceded to the British in 1802. Africans were transported to the island to work as slaves, but slavery was abolished in 1834. Shortage of labour led to the arrival of large numbers of Indian and Chinese immigrants, as indentured labourers, during the second half of the 19th century. In 1888 the island of Tobago, which had finally been ceded to the British in 1814, was joined with Trinidad as one political and administrative unit, and the territory remained a British colony until its independence on 31 August 1962.

Modern politics emerged in the 1930s with the formation of a trade union movement. The first political party, the People's National Movement (PNM), was founded in 1956 by Dr Eric Williams. It campaigned successfully at the elections to the Legislative Council in September 1956, and Williams became the colony's first Chief Minister in October. In 1958 the territory became a member of the newly established Federation of the West Indies, and in the following year achieved full internal self-government, with Williams as Premier. The Federation collapsed in 1961, however, following the secession of Jamaica and, subsequently, Trinidad and Tobago. After independence, in 1962, Williams was restyled Prime Minister, and the Governor became Governor-General. In 1967 Trinidad and Tobago became the first member of the Commonwealth (see p. 217) to join the Organization of American States (OAS, see p. 373).

In April 1970 the Government declared a state of emergency, following violent demonstrations, lasting several weeks, by supporters of 'Black Power', protesting against foreign influence in the country's economy and demanding solutions to the problem of unemployment, which was particularly severe among Trinidadians of African descent. On the day that the emergency was proclaimed, part of the Trinidad and Tobago Regiment (the country's army) mutinied. The mutiny collapsed after only three days, and some officers and soldiers who participated were subsequently imprisoned. At a general election in May 1971, the PNM won all 36 seats in the House of Representatives.

A new Constitution came into effect on 1 August 1976, whereby Trinidad and Tobago became a republic, within the Commonwealth. The first parliamentary elections of the republic were held in September, when the PNM won 24 of the 36 seats in the House of Representatives. The United Labour Front (ULF), a newly formed party led by trade unionists, won 10 seats, while the Democratic Action Congress (DAC) won the two Tobago seats. The former Governor-General, Ellis Clarke, was sworn in as the country's first President in December 1976. A parliamentary resolution in 1977 to grant Tobago self-rule resulted, after long resistance from the Government, in the formation in 1980 of a Tobago House of Assembly, giving the island limited autonomy. Tobago was granted full internal self-government in January 1987.

Williams died in March 1981, having consistently refused to nominate a successor. The President selected George Chambers, a deputy leader of the PNM and Minister of Agriculture, to assume the leadership on an interim basis. He was formally adopted as party leader in May and confirmed as Prime Minister. The PNM increased its majority in the House of Representatives in a general election in November. The ULF, the DAC and the Tapia House Movement, campaigning jointly as the Trinidad and Tobago National Alliance, succeeded in retaining only 10 seats. The newly formed Organization for National Reconstruction (ONR), led by a former PNM minister, Karl Hudson-Phillips, secured 22% of the total vote but no seats.

Co-operation between the four opposition parties increased, and, at local elections in August 1983, they successfully combined to inflict electoral defeat on the PNM. In August 1984 the National Alliance and the ONR established a common front, to be known as the National Alliance for Reconstruction (NAR). At elections to the Tobago House of Assembly in November 1984, the DAC achieved a convincing victory, reducing the PNM's representation to one seat. In September 1985 Arthur Napoleon Raymond (A. N. R.) Robinson, leader of the DAC and a former Deputy Prime Minister in the PNM Government, was elected leader of the NAR. In February 1986 the four parties merged to form one opposition party, still known as the NAR.

The stringent economic policies of the PNM Government undermined its public support and provoked labour unrest over wage restraint, notably in a bitter strike at Trinidad's petroleum refineries during May 1984. The next general election, held in December 1986, resulted in a decisive victory for the NAR. Robinson was appointed Prime Minister. Chambers was among those members of the PNM who lost their seats, and in January 1987 Patrick Manning, the former Minister of Energy, was appointed leader of the parliamentary opposition. In March Noor Mohammed Hassanali, formerly a senior judge, took office as President, following the retirement of Ellis Clarke.

The NAR experienced internal difficulties during 1987 and 1988. In June 1987 former members of the Tapia House Movement announced that they were to leave the NAR. In February 1988 more than 100 NAR members met to discuss the leadership of the alliance and the direction of its policies. Two cabinet ministers (including Basdeo Panday, the Minister of External Affairs) and one junior minister were subsequently dismissed from the Government. All three were former members of the ULF, which derived most of its support from the 'East' Indian community. Despite their accusations of racism against the NAR leadership, they were expelled from the party in October. In April 1989 Panday and the other dissidents announced the formation of a left-wing opposition party, the United National Congress (UNC). In July 1990 Panday was elected leader of the UNC at the party's first national assembly. In September President Hassanali confirmed Panday as the leader of the parliamentary opposition, replacing Manning. The UNC, with six seats in the House of Representatives, replaced the PNM, with only three seats, as the principal opposition party.

In July 1990 members of the Jamaat al Muslimeen, a small Muslim group led by Yasin Abu Bakr, attempted to seize power. The rebels destroyed the capital's police headquarters and took control of the parliament building and the state television station. Some 45 people were taken hostage, among them Robinson and several cabinet ministers. The rebels demanded Robinson's resignation, elections within 90 days and an amnesty for those taking part in the attempted coup. On 28 July a state of emergency was declared and a curfew was imposed: police preoccupation with the political crisis had resulted in widespread looting in the capital. On 31 July the Prime Minister, who had sustained gunshot wounds, was released from captivity by the rebels. On 1 August the attempted coup, in which some 30 people were killed and another 500 injured, ended after the rebels surrendered unconditionally. An amnesty pardoning them, signed by the President of the Senate, Joseph Emmanuel Carter, in his capacity as acting Head of State, was proclaimed invalid, on the grounds that it had been signed under duress. In mid-August Bakr and his followers were charged with treason, a capital offence.

In November 1991 the imprisoned Jamaat al Muslimeen rebels won an appeal to the Judicial Committee of the Privy Council in the United Kingdom (the final court of appeal for

Trinidad and Tobago), which ruled that the validity of the presidential pardon issued during the attempted coup in July 1990 should be determined before the rebels were brought to trial, and that an application for their release should be heard by the High Court of Trinidad and Tobago immediately. On 30 June 1992 the High Court ruled that the pardon was valid, and ordered the immediate release of the 114 defendants. The Government announced that it would pursue all legal means of appeal against the decision, which it deemed to be of great constitutional significance. In March 1993 delays in the payment of compensation to the rebels, for what the High Court ruled was their wrongful imprisonment, led Bakr to threaten 'action' against the Government. In October the Court of Appeal ruled to uphold the decision of the High Court. In October 1994 the Privy Council ruled to overturn the decisions of the High Court and the Court of Appeal, declaring the pardon invalid. As a result, the Jamaat al Muslimeen would be unable to claim compensation for wrongful imprisonment. However, it was also ruled that to rearrest the rebels and try them for offences committed during the insurrection would constitute an abuse of the legal process. However, the Jamaat al Muslimeen was subsequently awarded some TT $2.1m. in compensation for the destruction of its buildings following the coup attempt.

A general election, held in December 1991, resulted in a decisive victory for the PNM. The implementation of unpopular austerity measures was widely acknowledged as the main cause of the defeat of the NAR, and Robinson resigned as leader. A notable feature of the elections was the re-emergence of ethnic voting, with the vast majority of the votes divided between the Afro-Trinidadian-orientated PNM and the largely Indo-Trinidadian UNC, which secured 13 seats in the House of Representatives. Patrick Manning was sworn in as Prime Minister the day after the ballot. A promise made by the PNM in its election manifesto to settle a public sector claim for salaries and allowances withheld during the austerity programme of the outgoing NAR Government was honoured in the budget submitted to Parliament in January 1992. However, the Government's continued failure to effect a settlement led to escalating industrial unrest. In February 1993 several thousand public sector employees joined protests against the delay in payments and at the Government's plans to restructure inefficient state enterprises, involving some 2,600 redundancies. In early 1994 a government offer of a settlement of the public sector claim was rejected by the majority of employees. In mid-1995 the Government introduced a new plan to settle the claim, involving the issue of bonds with tax credits, which was accepted by the Trinidad and Tobago Unified Teachers' Association. However, industrial action resumed in September, when some 25,000 public sector employees observed a 24-hour strike in support of demands for a more favourable settlement. In March 1996, following a further 48-hour stoppage, agreement was finally reached on a settlement involving the issue, over a period of four years, of bonds worth TT $1,000m. Meanwhile, industrial unrest persisted in opposition to continuing government plans for the rationalization and privatization of unproductive public utilities.

The NAR retained control of the Tobago House of Assembly following elections in December 1992. In July 1993 the Government and the Tobago House of Assembly agreed to begin discussions concerning the upgrading of Tobago's constitutional status. Measures subsequently submitted for consideration by the legislature included the establishment of an executive council on Tobago and the appointment of an independent senator to represent the island.

Appeals for the restoration of capital punishment, prompted by growing public concern at the increasing rate of murder and violent crime in Trinidad and Tobago, gained considerable impetus in August 1993 following the murder of the country's Prison Commissioner. Warrants issued shortly afterwards for the execution of two convicted murderers were suspended following protests by human rights organization Amnesty International. In July 1994 Trinidad and Tobago conducted its first execution since 1979. However, the convicted murderer, Glen Ashby, was hanged only minutes before a facsimile transmission from the Privy Council in the United Kingdom was sent to the Court of Appeal in Trinidad granting a stay of execution. Reportedly, an undertaking had been given by the Attorney-General, Keith Sobion, that the execution would not be conducted until all applications for a stay had been exhausted. In July 1994 the Privy Council issued a conservatory order whereby, in the case of two men due to be heard by the Trinidad Court of Appeal, should their execution be ordered, it could not be conducted until the case had been heard by the Privy Council itself. This decision provoked protest from the Chief Justice of Trinidad and Tobago, who accused the Privy Council of pre-empting the Court of Appeal's exercise of its jurisdiction. Subsequently, the Government announced its intention to introduce legislation establishing the Court of Appeal as the final appeal court for criminal cases, pending regional agreement on a Caribbean appeal court. In March 1995 an international jurists' inquiry found that the execution of Ashby was illegal and that sufficient evidence existed to cite Sobion for contempt of court. However, the report was non-binding, and no action was taken.

In July 1995 the Speaker of the House of Representatives, Occah Seapaul, was accused by the Government of bringing her office into disrepute; an unsuccessful attempt by Seapaul to sue a former business partner, Victor Jattan, had led the court to question the veracity of her testimony. Seapaul refused to accede to demands for her resignation. Lacking the necessary two-thirds' majority in the legislature to unseat Seapaul, the Government introduced draft legislation to amend the Constitution in order to allow the removal of the Speaker by means of a simple majority. The proposal was approved by the Senate, but debate of the bill was obstructed in the House of Representatives by Seapaul, who adjourned the session and ordered the suspension of the leader of the House, Ken Valley, for six months, on a charge of contempt. In August acting President Joseph Emmanuel Carter declared a limited state of emergency in the capital, thus empowering the Government to place Seapaul under house arrest and facilitating the prompt approval in the House of Representatives of the constitutional amendment. The state of emergency was ended after four days, and Seapaul was released from detention, having agreed to vacate her position pending a High Court ruling on constitutional motions filed by her against the Government.

A general election was held in November 1995. The PNM and the UNC each secured 17 seats, while the NAR won the remaining two. Following discussions between the leader of the UNC, Basdeo Panday, and Robinson, who had resumed the leadership of the NAR in October, a coalition Government was established, with Panday as Prime Minister. The Cabinet included Robinson as Minister Extraordinaire and Adviser to the Cabinet, with special responsibility for Tobago. It was widely understood that the NAR's support for the UNC in forming the Government had been dependent on undertakings concerning the prompt upgrading of Tobago's constitutional status.

The NAR secured 10 of the 12 elective seats in elections to the Tobago House of Assembly in December 1996; the PNM obtained one seat, and the remaining seat was won by an independent candidate.

In mid-February 1997 Robinson was elected President to replace Noor Mohammed Hassanali on his retirement from the position in March. However, the appointment (by an electoral college comprising the members of the Senate and the House of Representatives) was, for the first time, contested: traditionally, all parties support the nominee of the Government for the presidency, which is a ceremonial position only. On this occasion, however, the PNM objected to the Government's nomination of Robinson, owing to his status as an active politician with party affiliation.

In March 1998 militia of the Jamaat al Muslimeen prevented employees of the Ministry of Works and Transport from establishing a barrier around land inhabited by the Jamaat al Muslimeen, in order to halt further expansion of settlements. Bakr denounced the Government for attempting to provoke a violent reaction from the militants. A fence was eventually constructed after Government employees resumed their task, under the protection of the police force. In December 1999 the Jamaat al Muslimeen repeated their warning that they would not permit building work to take place adjacent to their headquarters.

In January 2000 Hanraj Sumairsingh, a member of the UNC, was found murdered. It was subsequently reported that Sumairsingh had written to the Prime Minister several times regarding threats by the Minister of Local Government, Dhanraj Singh, following Sumairsingh's revelation of alleged corruption in the unemployment relief programme administered by Singh's ministry. In October Singh was dismissed from his government post and replaced by Carlos John. Singh was charged with the murder of Sumairsingh, but in October 2003 he was found not guilty of ordering the killing.

In October 1997 it was announced that the Government had approved a proposal by the Attorney-General to expedite executions of persons convicted of murder, whereby the Government would allow only 18 months for completion of a hearing before the UN Human Rights Committee (UNHRC) and the Inter-American Commission on Human Rights (IACHR), in the event of the Privy Council rejecting an appeal. The Government hoped, by imposing a time limit on the UNHRC and the IACHR, to complete the appeals process within the five years allowed by the Privy Council as the maximum length of time between sentencing and execution. In April 1998 the Government refused to grant leave for the hearing of appeals against the death penalty made by nine men convicted of murder (the so-called 'Chadee gang'). The nine subsequently appealed to the UNHRC. In May 1998 the Government announced that it was withdrawing from the UNHRC and the IACHR, as neither body had been able to guarantee to hear appeals within the 18 months requested by the Government. Many Caribbean states expressed their support for Trinidad and Tobago, although the opposition PNM criticized the withdrawals as damaging the islands' international reputation, while the Roman Catholic Church and Amnesty International also criticized the move on humanitarian grounds. In June 1998 the IACHR ordered Trinidad and Tobago not to execute five people whose cases it had been scheduled to review; however, the authorities announced that the IACHR no longer had any jurisdiction over the cases, and that the executions would be carried out.

In October 1998, in what was considered a landmark case, the Privy Council rejected the appeals of two convicted murderers, who had claimed that their constitutional rights had been infringed by the conditions in which they had been imprisoned. In January 1999, in a further landmark judgment, the Privy Council ruled that, even though Trinidad and Tobago had withdrawn from the IACHR, two convicted killers could not be executed while their appeals were being considered by the Commission, since the appeals had been made prior to the withdrawal. In April the Privy Council ordered the release of three prisoners who had spent almost four years awaiting execution.

In May 1999 the Privy Council rejected an appeal for clemency made by the nine members of the Chadee gang, who had claimed that they were being held in cruel and degrading conditions. However, the Privy Council granted a stay of execution on the grounds that the Court of Appeal in Trinidad and Tobago had been hurried into a decision by the Government, in order to allow time to consider the legality of hanging as a means of administering the death penalty. At the end of May the Privy Council ruled that Trinidad and Tobago could legally proceed with the nine executions, which, despite international protests, were carried out in early June.

In April 2000 the Government announced that it was to withdraw from the first optional protocol to the International Covenant on Civil and Political Rights, following a judgment from the UNHRC that Trinidad and Tobago could not continue to adhere to the resolution while differing on the subject of the death sentence. The announcement attracted widespread international condemnation. The Government, however, stated that the withdrawal was intended purely to prevent condemned murderers from addressing lengthy appeals to the UNHRC. The Government also announced the introduction of a constitutional amendment, which would allow executions to proceed before the IACHR and the UNHRC had ruled on the cases. On 14 February 2001, at a Caribbean Community and Common Market (CARICOM, see p. 206) summit in Barbados, the leaders of 11 Caribbean states signed an agreement to establish the Caribbean Court of Justice (CCJ). The Court was to replace the Privy Council as the final court of appeal, and was to be based in Trinidad and Tobago. The CCJ would be financed by a US $100m. trust fund raised by the Caribbean Development Bank. In February Parliament voted to accept the authority of the new Court to settle CARICOM matters. The Court was eventually inaugurated on 16 April 2005. However, owing to UNC opposition to adopting the appellate jurisdiction of the CCJ, the new Court was only to have jurisdiction over CARICOM matters.

At a general election in December 2000 the UNC secured 19 of the 36 seats in the House of Representatives, while the PNM won 16 seats and the NAR secured one. Panday was inaugurated as Prime Minister for the second time. At elections to the Tobago House of Assembly, held on 29 January 2001, the PNM secured eight of the 12 elective seats, ending the traditional domination of the House by the NAR, which obtained the remaining four seats.

The Government was beset by allegations of corruption in mid-2001 regarding the receipt of payments in exchange for supporting tenders for contracts with the state-owned oil company, Petrotin, and irregularities in the accounts of the North West Regional Health Authority (NWRHA). Minister of Communications and Information Technology Ralph Maraj threatened to resign if Panday did not act to curb corruption. Panday responded by relieving Maraj and Panday's party rival, Attorney-General Ramesh Maharaj, of some of their responsibilities. Maharaj, with Maraj and two other cabinet members, formed a faction within the UNC. This faction, which was known as Team Unity, subsequently gained control of the party's national executive. Despite attempts by Team Unity to prevent UNC constituent elections from taking place on 9 September, supporters of Panday were victorious in 30 of the 34 constituencies.

In October 2001 it was confirmed that Maharaj and the Minister of Food Production and Marine Resources, Trevor Sudama, had been dismissed from their government posts for their continued criticism of the Prime Minister. Maraj later also resigned from his position. The Government's legislative majority was effectively lost when the three ministers subsequently formed a coalition with the PNM and the NAR and obstructed attempts by Panday to approve the budget. Amid increasing pressure from the opposition for his resignation and threats of a vote of no confidence in his Government, on 10 October Panday asked President Robinson to dissolve Parliament in preparation for a general election, to be held on 10 December.

Meanwhile, in September 2001 an independently published report into the allegations of corruption at the NWRHA recommended the dismissal of four senior executives. In November Dr Tim Gopeesingh, the former Chairman of the NWRHA, admitted to charges of fraud in relation to a cheque for US $50,000 issued to Panday by Gopeesingh in his capacity as leader of UNC's Northwest Liaison Office, at the time of the 2000 elections. In December Panday and other government ministers were implicated in alleged instances of misconduct relating to contracts given to the US-owned power company Inncogen Ltd to supply electricity to four new factories in Trinidad, which had failed to be built.

In the general election of 10 December 2001 the UNC and the PNM secured an equal number (18) of seats in the House of Representatives. The two party leaders reached an agreement on political collaboration in government, although not a coalition arrangement, that would allow the President to appoint the Prime Minister and Speaker in the House of Representatives and to reform the electoral process. However, following the appointment of Manning as Prime Minister and PNM nominee Max Richards as Speaker of the House of Representatives, the UNC withdrew from the post-election agreement.

Panday's refusal to be sworn in as leader of the opposition and to agree to elect a Speaker in the House of Representatives (Richards had withdrawn from the position after his impartiality was questioned) prevented the convening of the new Parliament in early January 2002. Panday announced the UNC's intention to prevent Parliament from sitting for the next six months, thereby forcing Manning to call a new election, according to the provisions of the Constitution. Following concern expressed by the business community at the effect of the political impasse on the country's economy, at the end of January Manning and Panday met for discussions. However, neither these meetings, nor negotiations mediated by CARICOM leaders in February, provided a solution to the dispute. Later in February Manning agreed to put the UNC's proposals for an executive comprising equal numbers of PNM and UNC representatives to the PNM party council. The UNC accused the Prime Minister of deliberately delaying the process. In the following month controversy also arose over Robinson's continued occupation of the position of President. His tenure expired on 18 March, but, as the legislature had not been convened, Robinson obtained Manning's permission to remain in office. The first session of the new House of Representatives was reconvened in early April; however, owing to the failure of the two parties to elect a Speaker, proceedings were adjourned.

Meanwhile, in March 2002 Panday's former finance minister, Brian Kuei Tung, and several senior government officials and prominent businessmen were arrested on charges of fraud and misbehaviour in public office with regard to the construction of a new terminal at Piarco Airport. Manning ordered a Commission of Inquiry into the project. In July the Commission of Inquiry accused two more UNC members of Parliament of criminal activity. Former Minister of Works and Transport Carlos John was accused of ignoring tender procedures during his time in office and in the same month cocaine worth US $246,000 and two missiles were apparently found at the home of the former housing minister Sadiq Baksh. Panday was also questioned by the authorities regarding his failure to declare a joint bank account held with his wife in the United Kingdom, and in September he was officially charged with fraud. In April 2006 Panday was found guilty of failing fully to declare his income while Prime Minister. He was sentenced to two years' imprisonment.

A report by the Commission of Inquiry into the Elections and Boundaries Commission in June 2002 documented countless flaws in its practices and recommended that all its members should resign. However, its members failed to relinquish their posts, despite Manning's pledge to implement the recommended reforms. In July Manning announced that if Parliament failed to elect a Speaker by 31 October, further elections would be held. Manning made a final attempt to convene Parliament in August; however, the members again failed to elect a Speaker, some UNC representatives resorting deliberately to voting against their own candidate. Manning subsequently dissolved Parliament and announced that elections would take place on 7 October. In September a new political party, the Citizens' Alliance, was formed. It was led by a former PNM finance minister, Wendell Mottley, and aimed to prevent another tied election.

In elections held in October 2002 the PNM won 20 seats in the House of Representatives, while the UNC secured 16 seats. Manning again acceded to the office of Prime Minister, stating his intention to seek solutions to issues that divided the nation's political and racial communities. He appointed a new Cabinet, which included most of the members of the previous administration in their former positions. One of the new Government's first acts was the proposal of legislation aimed at preventing abduction and acts of terrorism, in addition to a planned increase in penalties for acts of corruption committed by holders of public office.

The Government's preferred candidate, Maxwell Richards, was elected President on 14 February 2003. In August the Government inaugurated a Committee on Race Relations to promote understanding and mutual respect among the various sectors of the population. In November Manning carried out a cabinet reorganization; notable among the reallocation of portfolios was the appointment of Howard Lee Chin, hitherto Minister of National Security, to the newly established tourism portfolio. The new ministry had been created in an attempt to increase growth in the sector.

Despite government efforts, in 2003 and 2004 there were increasing concerns over the continuing rise in crime rates, particularly kidnapping and murder. The number of kidnappings for ransom totalled 51 in 2004, compared with 27 in 2002, while the number of murders rose from 172 in 2002 to 260 in 2004. In June 2003 the Senate approved legislation imposing a minimum 25-year prison sentence on those convicted of kidnap. In the following year in an additional effort to address the rising levels of violent crime the Government initiated a joint military-police unit.

In a landmark ruling, in November 2003 the Privy Council ruled that Trinidad and Tobago's mandatory death sentence for convicted murderers was unconstitutional and inconsistent with the country's international obligations. The ruling followed an appeal brought by Balkissoon Roodal, who had been sentenced to death in July 1999. However, in July 2004 the Privy Council overturned its earlier ruling. A panel of nine judges, rather than the customary five, decreed that the Trinidadian Constitution did not allow outside intervention to abolish the mandatory death penalty. However, the judges further ruled that this would not apply to the estimated 100 prisoners who had benefited from the November judgment.

In October 2004 Manning announced that the Integrity Commission would investigate allegations that the Minister of Housing, Dr Keith Rowley, had used materials designated for a state hospital for a private sector project. However, the Prime Minister dismissed opposition demands that Rowley resign and in February 2008 the Commission ruled that it had found no evidence to pursue the allegations. All four members of the Commission were forced to resign in February 2009 after the courts ruled that they had acted illegally in their investigation, while Rowley was awarded substantial damages.

In April 2005 a parliamentary inquiry cleared Rowley of assaulting a UNC member of Parliament in the tearoom of the legislature in the previous September. However, the UNC criticized the inquiry and urged members not to sign the report exonerating Rowley. Two UNC members, Gillian Lucky and Fuad Khan, responded by declaring themselves to be independent members of Parliament. In April it was disclosed that an independent tribunal was to investigate allegations that Chief Justice Satnarine Sharma had sought to pervert the course of justice. The Attorney-General and the Director of Public Prosecutions claimed that Sharma had attempted to prevent a doctor being charged with the murder of his wife. Sharma subsequently filed for a judicial review of Manning's actions, claiming that the Prime Minister's recommendation for an investigation into the allegations was biased.

Despite continuing concerns about the rise in criminal activity and allegations of government corruption, at an election to the Tobago House of Assembly in January 2005 the governing PNM increased its majority from eight to 11 of the 12 seats, while the NAR, which had campaigned on a pro-devolution platform, secured just one legislative seat.

Allegations of political corruption persisted throughout 2005. In May corruption charges were filed against Panday, his wife, and the former UNC Minister of Works and Transport, Carlos John, in relation to the construction project at Piarco Airport. In November former Minister of Works and Transport Franklin Khan was charged with six counts of corruption, while in January 2006 Minister of Energy and Energy Industries Eric Williams was charged with accepting bribes from a potential contractor. Both Williams and Khan denied the charges. Seven charges of misconduct against Williams were dismissed in December 2007. The case against Khan was proceeding through the courts in mid-2009 although a majority of the charges were dropped in April of that year.

In July–October 2005 five bombs exploded in Port of Spain, injuring at least 30 people. The bombs were believed to be criminal, rather than terrorist, attacks; police suggested that they may have been planted to distract attention from drugs-related activities. Following the fourth explosion five people, including Yasin Abu Bakr, were arrested, but were subsequently released without being charged. The Jamaat al Muslimeen denied responsibility for the attacks. The authorities' perceived failure to find the perpetrators prompted widespread anger throughout the country. Mounting public pressure on the Government to curb the deterioration in law and order culminated on 22 October in a demonstration in the capital, attended by thousands of protesters.

In September 2005 Manning pledged to reduce unemployment, which, he claimed, was a major cause of the high crime rate. He also announced that he had invited the British Metropolitan Police Service and the USA's Federal Bureau of Investigation to establish specialist units in Trinidad and Tobago. (Some 39 police officers from the United Kingdom arrived in April 2006. They were expected to be incorporated into the Special Anti-Crime Unit for at least two years.) In October 2005 the Minister of National Security, Martin Joseph, admitted that the murder rate and the rate of detection were unacceptable and that the increase in drugs- and arms-trafficking was largely responsible for the rise in kidnappings and killings. The total number of murders in 2005 rose to 389, while the rate of detection declined from 44% in 2002 to 21% in mid-2005. Some 80% of murders were committed with illegal guns. The number of murders in 2006 stood at 368.

In November 2005 the Government announced a number of initiatives aimed at stemming the rise in violent crime. Proposed reforms to the police force increased Parliament's role in selecting members of the Police Service Commission and the Police Commissioner, while removing the Prime Minister's right to veto the appointment of the latter. The reforms also conferred on the Commissioner of Police greater powers of discipline and management. Another proposal was the establishment of a court expressly for hearing cases involving gun-related crime and kidnapping. Furthermore, legislation would prevent kidnappers and alleged perpetrators of more than three violent crimes from securing bail, and allow suspected kidnappers to be held for up to 60 days before being charged.

In November 2005 Yasin Abu Bakr was rearrested and charged with seditious speech, incitement and terrorism, after allegedly preaching a sermon that called for a war on affluent Muslims who refused to pay *zakat*, a tithe for the poor, to his organization. In February 2006 the Attorney-General sought high court authorization for the state to confiscate 12 properties from members of the Jamaat al Muslimeen in compensation for damage caused during the attempted coup in 1990.

TRINIDAD AND TOBAGO
Introductory Survey

In September 2006 Winston Dookeran announced his resignation as political leader of the UNC to launch a new political organization, to be known as Congress of the People (COP). Some 20,000 people attended the launch rally.

At a general election held on 5 November 2007 the PNM secured 45.9% of the votes cast and 26 seats in the enlarged 41-seat House of Assembly. The main opposition party, now known as the United National Congress—Alliance (UNC—A), won the remaining 15 seats and 29.8% of votes. Despite securing 22.6% of votes, the COP failed to secure a seat in the legislature. Some 66% of the registered electorate participated in the ballot. However, the PNM did not gain the two-thirds' parliamentary majority necessary in order to gain legislative approval for proposed constitutional reforms, including the creation of an executive president. Manning continued as Prime Minister but relinquished the finance portfolio, assigning it to Karen Nunez-Tesheira. He introduced 12 other new ministers, including Paula Gopee-Scoon as Minister of Foreign Affairs, and appointed Brigid Annisette-George as Attorney-General. Manning committed his administration to diversifying the economy, aiding growth in the commodities, information technology and tourism sectors, in order for Trinidad and Tobago to achieve Developed Nation status by 2020. He was also faced with the problem of increasing public concern over the level of crime; the number of murders in 2007 was subsequently recorded as the highest on record at 395. After the election defeat, Basdeo Panday replaced Kamla Persad-Bissessar as leader of the UNC—A. In February 2008 Maxwell Richards was re-elected unopposed for a second term as President.

In late April 2008 Manning dismissed Dr Keith Rowley as Minister of Trade and Industry, owing to his 'unacceptable behaviour' at a meeting of the Urban Development Corporation of Trinidad and Tobago. However, Rowley claimed that the action had been taken because of his suggestion of possible corruption in the Corporation's financial operations. He was replaced by Dr Lenny Saith, who was in turn replaced by Mariano Browne as Minister of Trade and Industry in a cabinet reorganization in the following year.

Elections to the Tobago House of Assembly were held in January 2009, at which the incumbent PNM obtained eight of the 12 seats, while the opposition Tobago Organisation of the People (TOP), formed in 2008, won four seats. Some 56% of eligible voters participated in the poll.

In January 2009 Manning announced plans for significant constitutional reforms, which included the establishment of an executive president as head of government and head of state, an expansion of the Senate (from 31 to 37 members) and a reorganization of the judiciary. The proposals were to undergo a two-year public consultation period before being debated by Parliament.

On 16 March 2009 Kamla Persad-Bissessar, an opposition member and former Attorney-General, filed a motion of no confidence against the Minister for Finance, Nunez-Tesheira, alleging that the latter had abused her position when she withdrew personal savings from CLICO Investment Bank, having been party to privileged information about the poor financial state of the organization.

The role of the Integrity Commission was questioned in May 2009 when some 10 days after their appointment by the President all five members resigned from the body, citing concerns over the internal organization of the group and public perceptions of its function.

In July 1991 Trinidad and Tobago ratified with Venezuela a joint declaration on maritime boundaries, under which Trinidad and Tobago's maritime boundary was to be extended from 200 nautical miles (370 km) to 350 nautical miles (648 km). Relations with Venezuela deteriorated in late 1996 and early 1997 owing to a series of incidents involving Trinidadian fishing vessels. In May 1997 a two-year fishing agreement was completed for approval by both Governments. However, tensions were revived later in the month after 15 Trinidadian fishermen were arrested by Venezuelan coast-guards. The Trinidadian Government referred the issue to the OAS and, in response, Venezuela briefly withdrew its ambassador from the country. A revised two-year treaty was endorsed in December, permitting an unlimited number of vessels from each country into a shared fishing area. A joint fisheries commission was also re-established. In August 2003 the two countries signed a memorandum of understanding on the joint exploitation of cross-border oil and gas fields. Negotiations recommenced in January 2006. The discussions stalled temporarily following Trinidad and Tobago's refusal to sign Venezuela's PetroCaribe energy accord, launched the previous year, which offered oil concessions and favourable financing terms to Caribbean nations. The accord was expected adversely to affect, at least initially, Trinidad and Tobago's energy sector. However, negotiations resumed in March, and in February 2007 an agreement was reached on the division of the cross-border Loran natural gas field, which apportioned some 75% of the gas to Venezuela.

In July 2000 talks were held to find a solution to the maritime border dispute between Trinidad and Barbados. Despite further talks being held over the next two years, little progress was made. In January 2004 the Prime Minister of Trinidad and Tobago indicated he would refer the matter to CARICOM. Bilateral relations deteriorated in February after several Barbadian fishermen were arrested in Trinidad and Tobago's waters; Barbados subsequently imposed economic sanctions on imports from Trinidad and Tobago, which they were later ordered to lift by CARICOM's Council for Trade and Economic Development. Meanwhile, in February Barbados announced plans to seek UN arbitration under the UN Convention on the Law of the Sea. Hearings on the boundary dispute commenced in October 2005, and in April 2006 a decision was handed down establishing a median line between the two exclusive economic zones. The Centre rejected Trinidad and Tobago's claim to a large area to the south-east of Barbados and instructed the two countries to negotiate a fishing agreement for a large disputed area to the north of Tobago, which would remain in Trinidad and Tobago's possession. Progress on the agreement stalled in mid-2008 pending a study by FAO, and, although the Prime Ministers of the two countries expressed their commitment to achieve a resolution, none had been reached by mid-2009.

Government

Legislative power is vested in the bicameral Parliament, consisting of the Senate, with 31 members, and the House of Representatives, with 41 members. Representatives are elected for a five-year term by universal adult suffrage. The President is a constitutional Head of State, chosen by an electoral college of members of both the Senate and the House of Representatives. Members of the Senate are nominated by the President in consultation with, and on the advice of, the Prime Minister and the Leader of the Opposition. The Cabinet has effective control of the Government and is responsible to Parliament. Tobago Island was granted its own House of Assembly in 1980 and given full internal self-government in January 1987. The Tobago House of Assembly has 15 members, of whom 12 are elected; the remaining three members are selected by the majority party.

Defence

As assessed at November 2008, the defence forces consisted of an army estimated at 3,000 men, and a coastguard of 1,063, with 25 patrol craft. Included in the coastguard is an air force of 50. The defence budget for 2007 was an estimated TT $350m. (US $55m.).

Economic Affairs

In 2007, according to estimates by the World Bank, Trinidad and Tobago's gross national income (GNI), measured at average 2005–07 prices, was US $18,795m., equivalent to US $14,100 per head (or US $22,490 on an international purchasing-power parity basis). During 2000–07, it was estimated, the population increased at an average annual rate of 0.4%, while gross domestic product (GDP) per head increased, in real terms, by an average of 8.3% per year. Overall GDP increased, in real terms, at an average annual rate of 8.7% in 2000–07; according to the World Bank, economic growth was 6.0% in 2007.

Agriculture (including forestry, hunting and fishing) contributed 0.4% of GDP in 2007, and employed 3.8% (excluding unclassified activities) of the working population in the same year. The principal cash crops are sugar cane, coffee, cocoa and citrus fruits. The fishing sector is small-scale, but is an important local source of food. During 2000–06, according to the World Bank, agricultural GDP declined by an average of 3.3% per year. The sector expanded by 9.7% in 2005, but contracted by 0.6% in 2006.

Industry (including mining and quarrying, manufacturing, construction and power) provided 57.1% of GDP in 2007, and employed 31.9% (excluding undefined activities) of the working population in the same year. During 2000–06, according to the World Bank, industrial GDP increased at an average annual rate of 12.9%. Industrial GDP increased by 18.1% in 2006.

The petroleum sector provided an estimated 42.9% of GDP in 2007. In that year the mining and quarrying sector (including petroleum production) employed some 3.9% of the working population (excluding activities undefined). The petroleum industry is the principal sector of Trinidad and Tobago's economy. According to the IMF, the GDP of the petroleum sector increased at an estimated annual average rate of 15.0% during 2001–05; the sector grew by 8.2% in 2005. Trinidad has the world's largest deposits of natural asphalt, and substantial reserves of natural gas. In 2006 Trinidad and Tobago was the world's second largest producer (after Chile) of methanol, a by-product of natural gas. Cement, limestone and sulphur are also mined.

Manufacturing contributed an estimated 5.5% of GDP in 2007 and employed 9.2% (excluding undefined activities) of the working population in the same year. During 2000–06 manufacturing GDP increased at an average annual rate of 9.6%. Manufacturing GDP increased by 11.8% in 2006.

Almost all of the country's energy is derived from natural gas (it provided 99.5% of total electricity production in 2005). Natural gas is also used as fuel for the country's two petroleum refineries and several manufacturing plants. Imports of fuel products comprised 33.5% of the value of merchandise imports in 2007. In the same year exports of gas accounted for an estimated 37.1% of total exports, while exports of petroleum and petroleum products accounted for an estimated 29.0%.

The services sector contributed an estimated 42.5% of GDP in 2007 and employed some 64.3% (excluding unclassified activities) of the working population in the same year. Tourism is a major source of foreign exchange; in 2006 receipts from tourism totalled US $357m. and some 457,434 foreign tourists visited the islands. However, there were fears that the increasing rates of violent crime would adversely affect tourism revenues. In February 2004 Prime Minister Manning announced a series of initiatives to promote leisure and 'eco-tourism' in Tobago and business tourism in Trinidad. According to the World Bank, the GDP of the services sector increased at an average annual rate of 5.3% in 2000–06. Sectoral GDP increased by 4.5% in 2006.

In 2007 Trinidad and Tobago recorded a visible trade surplus of US $5,721m., and there was a surplus of US $5,364m. on the current account of the balance of payments. In 2007 the principal source of imports was the USA (24.8%); other major suppliers were Canada and Venezuela. The USA was also the principal market for exports (56.4%) in that year; other significant purchasers were Jamaica and Barbados. The principal exports in 2007 were mineral fuels and lubricants (66.1%), chemicals (20.6%) and basic manufactures (5.1%). The principal imports were mineral fuels and lubricants (33.5%), machinery and transport equipment (25.0%) and basic manufactures (13.1%).

In 2007/08 there was an estimated budgetary surplus of TT $1,724.1m. At the end of 2004 Trinidad and Tobago's total external debt was US $2,652m., of which US $1,197m. was long-term public debt. In 2004 the cost of debt-servicing was equivalent to 5.4% of the value of exports of goods and services. The annual rate of inflation averaged 5.8% in 2000–07. Consumer prices increased by an estimated average of 12.0% in 2008. An estimated 5.5% of the labour force was unemployed in 2007.

Trinidad and Tobago is a member of the Caribbean Community and Common Market (CARICOM, see p. 206), the Inter-American Development Bank (IDB, see p. 318), the Latin American Economic System (SELA, see p. 427), and the Association of Caribbean States (ACS, see p. 424). In November 2005 a bilateral free trade agreement was signed with Costa Rica, enabling duty-free access to markets for more than 90% of goods. Trinidad and Tobago was one of the six founder members of CARICOM's Caribbean Single Market and Economy (CSME), which was inaugurated on 1 January 2006. It was anticipated that the CSME would facilitate the free movement of goods, services and labour throughout most of the CARICOM region. The CSME was scheduled to be fully operational by 31 December 2008.

The discovery of significant petroleum and natural gas deposits in the 1990s, combined with substantial foreign investment, meant that by the early 21st century the energy sector was a major contributor to Trinidad and Tobago's economy. The development of a major liquefied natural gas (LNG) plant at Point Fortin from 2001 would eventually make Trinidad and Tobago one of the world's leading suppliers of LNG. In September 2003 BP Energy Company of Trinidad and Tobago (formerly BP Amoco) announced the discovery of the country's largest ever natural gas deposit. Substantial foreign investment allowed increased industrialization, which, combined with high international fuel prices, contributed to rapid economic expansion and a substantial trade surplus between 2002–06. However, concerns about rising crime rates damaged investor confidence, increased security costs for businesses and threatened the tourism industry. Furthermore, there was concern over the standard of public services and infrastructure, as well as the increasing public sector debt. The economy has shown signs of diversifying, with the energy sector growing at a slower rate than the non-energy sector. This was predominantly due to expansion in manufacturing, finance and real estate as a result of continued construction growth. Increased investment in the non-energy sector as well rising food prices led to high rates of inflation in the mid-2000s, from 9.1% in 2006 to 7.6% in 2007 before increasing to 12.0% in 2008. GDP growth was 6.0% in 2007, slowing to 3.4% in 2008. In January 2009 it was announced that CL Financial Group, Trinidad's largest financial conglomerate, would receive government funding to continue its operations, thus confirming that the country's financial sector was not immune to the global credit crisis. Lower petroleum and natural gas prices and a slowdown in the construction sector contributed to a projection of zero GDP growth, according to the Governor of the Central Bank, in 2009.

Education

Primary and secondary education is provided free of charge. Attendance at school is officially compulsory for children between five and 12 years of age. Primary education begins at the age of five and lasts for seven years. Secondary education, beginning at 12 years of age, lasts for up to five years, comprising a first cycle of three years and a second of two years. Entrance to secondary schools is determined by the Common Entrance Examination. Many schools are administered jointly by the state and religious bodies. In 2005 enrolment at primary schools included 84.6% of children in the relevant age-group (males 84.7%; females 84.5%), while enrolment at secondary schools was equivalent to 65.1% of children in the relevant age-group (males 63.8%; females 66.5%). In 2000 the Government announced an education reform programme to improve access to, and levels of, education. A school-to-work apprenticeship programme was also to be established.

The Trinidad campus of the University of the West Indies (UWI), at St Augustine, offers undergraduate and postgraduate programmes. The UWI Institute of Business offers postgraduate courses, and develops programmes for local companies. Other institutions of higher education are the Eric Williams Medical Sciences complex, the Polytechnic Institute and the East Caribbean Farm Institute. The country has one teacher training college and three government-controlled technical institutes and vocational centres, including the Trinidad and Tobago Hotel School. In the late 1990s the Government established the Trinidad and Tobago Institute of Technology, and the College of Science, Technology and Applied Arts of Trinidad and Tobago. In March 2004 a Steering Committee was appointed to conduct a strategic review of tertiary education, and distance and lifelong learning, in an attempt to improve consistency within the tertiary sector and in relation to the education system as a whole. Budgeted expenditure on education by the central Government in 2009 was TT $7,121.6m., equivalent to some 14.4% of total government expenditure.

Public Holidays

2009: 1 January (New Year's Day), 30 March (Spiritual Baptist Shouters' Liberation Day), 10–13 April (Easter), 30 May (Indian Arrival Day), 11 June (Corpus Christi), 19 June (Labour Day), 1 August (Emancipation Day), 31 August (Independence Day), 20 September* (Id al-Fitr, end of Ramadan), 24 September (Republic Day), 17 October† (Diwali), 25–26 December (Christmas).

2010: 1 January (New Year's Day), 2–5 April (Easter), 30 March (for Spiritual Baptist Shouters' Liberation Day), 22 May (Corpus Christi), 30 May (Indian Arrival Day), 19 June (Labour Day), 1 August (Emancipation Day), 30 August (for Independence Day), 24 September (Republic Day), 10 September* (Id al-Fitr, end of Ramadan), 5 November† (Diwali), 25–26 December (Christmas).

* These holidays are dependent on the Islamic lunar calendar and may vary by one or two days from the dates given.

† Dependent on lunar sightings.

Weights and Measures

The metric system is replacing the imperial system of weights and measures.

TRINIDAD AND TOBAGO

Statistical Survey

Sources (unless otherwise stated): Central Statistical Office, National Statistics Bldg, 80 Independence Sq., POB 98, Port of Spain; tel. 623-6945; fax 625-3802; e-mail info@cso.gov.tt; internet www.cso.gov.tt; Central Bank of Trinidad and Tobago, POB 1250, Port of Spain; tel. 625-4835; fax 627-4696; e-mail info@central-bank.org.tt; internet www.central-bank.org.tt.

Area and Population

AREA, POPULATION AND DENSITY

Area (sq km)	5,128*
Population (census results)	
2 May 1990	1,213,733
15 May 2000	
Males	633,051
Females	629,315
Total	1,262,366
Population (official estimates at mid-year)	
2005	1,294,500
2006	1,297,900
2007	1,303,200
Density (per sq km) at mid-2007	254.1

* 1,980 sq miles. Of the total area, Trinidad is 4,828 sq km (1,864 sq miles) and Tobago 300 sq km (116 sq miles).

POPULATION BY ETHNIC GROUP
(1990 census*)

	Males	Females	Total	%
African	223,561	221,883	445,444	39.59
Chinese	2,317	1,997	4,314	0.38
'East' Indian	226,967	226,102	453,069	40.27
Lebanese	493	441	934	0.08
Mixed	100,842	106,716	207,558	18.45
White	3,483	3,771	7,254	0.64
Other	886	838	1,724	0.15
Unknown	2,385	2,446	4,831	0.43
Total	560,934	564,194	1,125,128	100.00

* Excludes some institutional population and members of unenumerated households, totalling 44,444.

ADMINISTRATIVE DIVISIONS
(population at 2000 census)

	Population	Capital
Trinidad	1,208,282	Port of Spain
Port of Spain (city, capital)	49,031	—
San Fernando (city)	55,419	—
Arima (borough)	32,278	Arima
Chaguanas (borough)	67,433	Chaguanas
Point Fortin (borough)	19,056	Point Fortin
Diego Martin	105,720	Petit Valley
San Juan/Laventille	157,295	Laventille
Tunapuna/Piarco	203,975	Tunapuna
Couva/Tabaquite/Talparo	162,779	Couva
Mayaro/Rio Claro	33,480	Rio Claro
Sangre Grande	64,343	Sangre Grande
Princes Town	91,947	Princes Town
Penal/Debe	83,609	Penal
Siparia	81,917	Siparia
Tobago	54,084	Scarborough

BIRTHS AND DEATHS
(annual averages, UN estimates)

	1990–95	1995–2000	2000–05
Birth rate (per 1,000)	18.2	15.1	14.5
Death rate (per 1,000)	6.9	7.2	7.9

Source: UN, *World Population Prospects: The 2008 Revision.*

Life expectancy (years at birth, WHO estimates): 68.9 (males 65.5; females 72.4) in 2006 (Source: WHO, *World Health Statistics*).

ECONOMICALLY ACTIVE POPULATION
('000 persons aged 15 years and over)

	2003	2004	2005
Agriculture, forestry, hunting and fishing	31.4	26.0	24.8
Mining and quarrying	16.9	20.1	20.4
Manufacturing	55.0	58.7	55.6
Electricity, gas and water	7.4	7.3	6.9
Construction	72.6	83.8	94.8
Wholesale and retail trade, restaurants and hotels	99.0	101.2	103.5
Transport, storage and communication	41.5	41.6	41.8
Finance, insurance, real estate and business services	45.0	46.3	45.0
Community, social and personal services	163.2	175.3	178.5
Other services	1.9	1.8	2.5
Total employed	534.1	562.2	574.0
Unemployed	62.4	51.1	49.7
Total labour force	596.6	613.3	623.7
Males	360.4	365.3	364.9
Females	236.1	248.0	258.8

Source: ILO.

2006 ('000 persons aged 15 and over): Agriculture 25.7; Petroleum and gas (incl. mining and quarrying) 20.4; Manufacturing 55.5; Construction (incl. utilities) 104.5; Transport, storage and communications 42.7; Wholesale and retail trade 106.6; Community, social and personal services 181.0; Finance, insurance and real estate 48.1; Not classified 1.6; *Total employed* 586.2; Unemployed 39.0; *Total labour force* 625.2.

2007 ('000 persons aged 15 and over): Agriculture 22.4; Petroleum and gas (incl. mining and quarrying) 23.2; Manufacturing 54.1; Construction (incl. utilities) 110.2; Transport, storage and communications 41.5; Wholesale and retail trade 108.3; Community, social and personal services 178.6; Finance, insurance and real estate 49.6; *Total employed* 587.9; Unemployed 34.5; *Total labour force* 622.4.

Health and Welfare

KEY INDICATORS

Total fertility rate (children per woman, 2006)	1.6
Under-5 mortality rate (per 1,000 live births, 2006)	38
HIV/AIDS (% of persons, aged 15–49, 2007)	1.5
Physicians (per 1,000 head, 1997)	0.79
Hospital beds (per 1,000 head, 2005)	2.6
Health expenditure (2006): US $ per head (PPP)	811
Health expenditure (2006): % of GDP	4.2
Health expenditure (2006): public (% of total)	54.1
Access to water (% of persons, 2006)	94
Human Development Index (2006): ranking	57
Human Development Index (2006): value	0.833

For sources and definitions, see explanatory note on p. vi.

TRINIDAD AND TOBAGO

Agriculture

PRINCIPAL CROPS
('000 metric tons)

	2005	2006*	2007*
Rice, paddy	2.1	2.3	2.5
Maize	3.1*	3.0	3.0
Taro (Cocoyam)	4.9*	4.9	4.9
Sugar cane	420.0	420.0	475.0
Pigeon peas	1.0	1.0	1.1
Coconuts*	18.0	18.0	18.0
Cabbages*	1.1	1.1	1.1
Lettuce*	1.5	1.5	1.5
Tomatoes	1.6	1.7	1.8
Pumpkins, squash and gourds	2.2	2.2	2.2
Cucumbers and gherkins*	2.0	2.0	2.1
Aubergines*	3.0	3.0	3.0
Watermelons*	1.2	1.2	1.5
Bananas*	7.0	7.0	7.0
Plantains*	4.7	4.7	5.0
Oranges*	5.3	5.3	5.3
Lemons and limes*	1.7	1.7	1.7
Grapefruit and pomelo*	2.8	2.8	2.8
Pineapples*	4.5	4.5	4.5
Coffee, green*	0.4	0.4	0.4
Cocoa beans*	1.4	1.4	1.4

* FAO estimate(s).

Aggregate production ('000 metric tons, may include official, semi-official or estimated data): Total cereals 5 in 2005, 5 in 2006, 5 in 2007; Total roots and tubers 9 in 2005, 9 in 2006, 10 in 2007; Total vegetables (incl. melons) 18 in 2005, 19 in 2006, 19 in 2007; Total fruits (excl. melons) 69 in 2005, 31 in 2006; 31 in 2007.

Source: FAO.

LIVESTOCK
('000 head year ending September, FAO estimates)

	2005	2006	2007
Horses	1.3	1.3	1.3
Asses	4.1	n.a.	n.a.
Cattle	29.0	29.0	30.0
Buffaloes	5.7	5.7	5.7
Pigs	43.0	43.0	45.0
Chickens	28,200	28,200	28,500
Sheep	3.4	3.4	3.5
Goats	59.3	59.3	60.0

Source: FAO.

LIVESTOCK PRODUCTS
('000 metric tons, FAO estimates)

	2005	2006	2007
Cattle meat	0.8	0.8	0.8
Pig meat	2.9	2.9	3.0
Chicken meat	57.6	57.6	60.0
Cows' milk	10.5	10.5	11.0
Hen eggs	3.8	3.8	3.9

Source: FAO.

Forestry

ROUNDWOOD REMOVALS
('000 cubic metres, excl. bark)

	2005	2006	2007
Sawlogs, veneer logs and logs for sleepers	65.0	65.0	65.0
Fuel wood*	34.5	34.1	33.8
Total	99.5	99.1	98.8

* FAO estimates.

Source: FAO.

SAWNWOOD PRODUCTION
('000 cubic metres, incl. railway sleepers)

	2004	2005	2006
Total (all broadleaved)	32	41	41

2007: Production assumed to be unchanged from 2006 (FAO estimates).

Source: FAO.

Fishing

('000 metric tons, live weight of capture)

	2004	2005	2006
Demersal percomorphs	2.4	3.8	1.9
Atlantic bonito	0.3	0.1	0.0
King mackerel	0.6	0.7	0.7
Serra Spanish mackerel	2.1	2.7	1.8
Frigate and bullet tunas	0.4	n.a.	n.a.
Tuna-like fishes	0.0	0.5	0.1
Sharks, rays, skates, etc.	1.3	2.2	0.8
Other marine fishes	1.5	2.3	1.4
Penaeus shrimps	0.6	0.7	0.8
Total catch (incl. others)	10.0	13.4	8.4

Source: FAO.

Mining

('000 barrels, unless otherwise indicated)

	2004	2005	2006
Crude petroleum	44,985	52,740	52,105
Natural gas liquids	10,687	9,889	11,215
Natural gas (million cu m)*	30,273	33,270	40,082

* Figures refer to the gross volume of output; marketed production (in million cu m) was: 29,456 in 2004; 31,348 in 2005; n.a. in 2006.

Source: US Geological Survey.

Industry

SELECTED PRODUCTS
('000 metric tons, unless otherwise indicated)

	2005	2006	2007
Raw sugar	33	35	25
Crude oil ('000 barrels)	52,740	52,105	43,807
Natural gas liquids ('000 barrels)	9,889	11,251	12,450
Fertilizers	5,915	5,817	5,902
Methanol	4,695	6,016	5,933
Cement	686	883	902
Iron (direct reduced)	2,055	2,072	2,063
Steel:			
billets	712	673	695
wire rods	472	486	510

Electric energy: (million kWh) 6,437 in 2003; 6,430 in 2004; 7,058 in 2005.
Source: UN, *Industrial Commodity Statistics Yearbook*.

TRINIDAD AND TOBAGO

Statistical Survey

Finance

CURRENCY AND EXCHANGE RATES

Monetary Units
100 cents = 1 Trinidad and Tobago dollar (TT $).

Sterling, US Dollar and Euro Equivalents (31 December 2008)
£1 sterling = TT $9.1650
US $1 = TT $6.2869;
€1 = TT $8.7495;
TT $100 = £10.91 = US $15.91 = €11.43.

Average Exchange Rate (TT $ per US $)
2006   6.3080
2007   6.3256
2008   6.2846

CENTRAL GOVERNMENT BUDGET
(TT $ million)

Revenue	2004/05	2005/06	2006/07
Energy sector	13,961.3	21,416.0	20,079.2
Corporation tax	10,805.6	17,614.8	16,206.2
Withholding tax (oil)	429.2	614.3	928.7
Royalties	1,228.5	1,679.3	1,681.0
Unemployment levy	820.4	1,311.3	1,111.0
Oil impost	42.7	65.9	63.9
Excise duties	634.8	130.4	88.4
Non-energy sector	15,677.4	17,490.9	19,955.6
Taxes	13,878.2	15,414.3	17,266.8
Taxes on income	8,141.2	7,922.5	8,888.1
Taxes on property	62.7	64.4	83.7
Taxes on goods and services	4,200.8	5,591.1	6,288.5
Value-added tax	2,962.5	4,184.2	4,829.0
Taxes on international trade	1,473.5	1,836.3	2,006.5
Non-tax revenue of non-oil sector	1,799.1	2,076.6	2,688.8
Capital revenue and grants	9.1	4.0	29.6
Total	29,647.9	38,910.9	40,064.4

Expenditure	2004/05	2005/06	2006/07
Current expenditure	21,842.4	26,582.6	29,984.0
Wages and salaries	5,309.2	5,455.6	6,221.3
Goods and services	3,170.1	3,843.2	4,283.8
Interest payments	2,541.5	2,453.3	2,698.1
Domestic	1,875.5	1,825.5	604.1
External	666.0	600.8	2,094.0
Transfers and subsidies	10,821.6	14,830.4	16,780.8
Households	2,601.2	4,341.2	8,455.9
Loans and grants to statutory boards and state enterprises	2,481.6	3,805.5	4,916.8
Capital expenditure and net lending	2,798.6	4,615.3	7,781.9
Total	24,641.0	31,197.9	37,765.9

2007/08 (TT $ million): *Revenue:* Energy sector 25,586.9; Non-energy sector 21,037.0; Total 46,623.9. *Expenditure:* Current expenditure 35,620.6; Capital expenditure and net lending 9,279.2; Total 44,899.8.

INTERNATIONAL RESERVES
(US $ million at 31 December)

	2006	2007	2008
Gold (national valuation)	39.0	51.2	52.9
IMF special drawing rights	3.0	0.9	1.1
Reserve position in IMF	51.8	35.4	61.1
Foreign exchange	6,514.7	6,657.4	9,380.4
Total	6,608.5	6,744.9	9,495.5

Source: IMF, *International Financial Statistics*.

MONEY SUPPLY
(TT $ million at 31 December)

	2005	2006	2007
Currency outside banks	2,425.4	2,654.4	3,182.8
Demand deposits at commercial banks	9,358.6	10,219.2	11,083.6
Total money (incl. others)	13,292.6	14,994.5	16,777.2

Source: IMF, *International Financial Statistics*.

COST OF LIVING
(Consumer Price Index; base: January 2003 = 100)

	2006	2007	2008
Food	185.4	217.6	274.0
Clothing	91.3	93.3	95.8
Transport	110.1	114.4	117.8
Housing and utilities	108.9	113.5	119.8
All items (incl. others)	122.3	132.0	147.9

NATIONAL ACCOUNTS
(TT $ million at current prices)

Expenditure on the Gross Domestic Product

	2005	2006	2007*
Government final consumption expenditure	11,707.0	13,121.5	15,221.6
Private final consumption expenditure	41,976.2	57,058.3	72,142.4
Gross capital formation	14,748.8	15,555.5	17,666.2
Total domestic expenditure	68,432.0	85,735.3	105,030.2
Exports of goods and services	66,224.5	79,417.6	76,089.7
Less Imports of goods and services	39,257.1	44,596.9	49,005.1
GDP in purchasers' values	95,399.4	120,556.0	132,114.8

*Provisional.

Gross Domestic Product by Economic Activity

	2005	2006	2007*
Agriculture, hunting, forestry and fishing	471.0	449.3	472.6
Petroleum	40,682.4	56,470.6	56,828.9
Manufacturing	5,936.4	6,427.8	7,317.1
Electricity and water	889.9	981.5	898.0
Construction and quarrying	7,278.7	8,224.2	10,653.2
Transport, storage and communication	6,347.6	6,831.5	8,281.6
Distribution	11,970.5	15,878.5	19,101.9
Finance, insurance and real estate	10,965.7	13,561.0	15,243.9
Government	6,675.3	7,458.4	8,818.5
Other services	4,143.5	4,474.9	4,924.6
Sub-total	95,361.0	120,757.7	132,540.3
Less Financial intermediation services indirectly measured	3,040.7	4,010.4	4,430.9
Value-added tax	3,079.1	3,808.7	4,005.4
GDP in purchaser's values	95,399.4	120,556.0	132,114.8

*Provisional.

TRINIDAD AND TOBAGO

BALANCE OF PAYMENTS
(US $ million)

	2005	2006	2007
Exports of goods f.o.b.	9,672	14,217	13,391
Imports of goods f.o.b.	−5,725	−6,517	−7,670
Trade balance	3,948	7,700	5,721
Exports of services	897	814	924
Imports of services	−541	−363	−377
Balance on goods and services	4,304	8,151	6,268
Other income received	84	262	267
Other paid	−844	−1,198	−1,231
Balance on goods, services and income	3,544	7,215	5,304
Current transfers received	102	105	121
Current transfers paid	−52	−49	−61
Current balance	3,594	7,271	5,364
Direct investment (net)	599	513	830
Portfolio investment assets	−258	−200	−272
Other investment (net)	−1,894	−5,679	−3,808
Net errors and omissions	−653	−808	−593
Overall balance	1,388	1,096	1,521

Source: IMF, *International Financial Statistics*.

External Trade

PRINCIPAL COMMODITIES
(TT $ million)

Imports c.i.f.	2005	2006	2007
Food and live animals	2,718.6	2,759.5	3,397.4
Beverages and tobacco	264.5	252.3	251.1
Crude materials except fuels	1,665.5	1,877.4	3,611.2
Mineral fuels and lubricants	12,482.6	14,329.7	16,187.6
Animal and vegetable oils and fats	112.8	132.8	184.6
Chemicals	2,632.9	3,321.1	3,663.0
Manufactured goods	4,502.3	5,025.6	6,328.8
Machinery and transport equipment	9,484.4	10,936.7	12,089.2
Miscellaneous manufactured articles	1,958.3	2,246.0	2,560.0
Total (incl. others)	35,869.1	40,934.2	48,329.5

Exports f.o.b.*	2005	2006	2007
Food and live animals	1,048.3	1,168.1	1,220.0
Beverages and tobacco	800.7	868.0	929.9
Crude materials except fuels	252.7	283.3	2,392.2
Mineral fuels and lubricants	42,503.2	68,025.7	55,757.0
Animal and vegetable oils and fats	49.3	15.2	14.3
Chemicals	11,518.3	13,337.5	17,407.3
Manufactured goods	2,984.0	4,152.6	4,308.8
Machinery and transport equipment	875.8	944.2	1,852.1
Miscellaneous manufactured articles	514.6	501.0	498.6
Miscellaneous transactions and commodities	1.8	2.2	3.1
Total	60,548.5	89,298.0	84,383.8

* Including ships' stores and bunkers.

PRINCIPAL TRADING PARTNERS
(TT $ million)

Imports c.i.f.	2005	2006	2007
Barbados	179.5	204.1	280.5
Canada	770.7	911.4	1,981.3
Central and South America*	10,236.5	11,040.0	12,695.8
Venezuela	2,164.6	1,755.0	1,887.3
European Free Trade Association (EFTA)	425.8	159.3	162.8
European Union (EU)†	1,989.8	3,241.1	4,353.0
Guyana	137.7	117.5	160.5
Jamaica	93.3	110.2	99.7
United Kingdom	1,417.6	1,072.8	1,342.8
USA	10,295.7	11,152.5	12,000.7
Total (incl. others)	35,869.1	40,934.2	48,329.5

Exports f.o.b.‡	2005	2006	2007
Barbados	2,542.0	2,915.2	1,782.6
Canada	654.3	1,076.0	854.5
Central and South America*	3,814.2	4,370.3	5,558.8
European Union (EU)†	602.2	8,357.2	8,560.3
Guyana	1,671.6	2,089.0	1,466.4
Jamaica	4,496.9	5,055.0	3,818.6
United Kingdom	460.8	759.3	1,348.2
USA	34,888.9	50,553.3	47,338.1
Total (incl. others)	59,861.5	88,275.5	83,897.4

* Excluding Belize, French Guiana, Guyana and Suriname.
† Excluding the United Kingdom, listed separately.
‡ Excluding ships' stores and bunkers.

Transport

ROAD TRAFFIC
(motor vehicles in use)

	1997	1998	1999
Passenger cars	194,300	213,400	229,400
Commercial vehicles	47,700	51,100	53,900

Source: UN, *Statistical Yearbook*.

Total number of registered vehicles: 292,908 in 1999; 316,163 in 2000; 331,595 in 2001 (provisional figure).

SHIPPING
Merchant Fleet
(registered at 31 December)

	2005	2006	2007
Number of vessels	102	104	111
Total displacement ('000 grt)	39.0	38.8	51.1

Source: Lloyd's Register-Fairplay, *World Fleet Statistics*.

International Sea-borne Freight Traffic
(estimates, '000 metric tons)

	1988	1989	1990
Goods loaded	7,736	7,992	9,622
Goods unloaded	4,076	4,091	10,961

Source: UN, *Monthly Bulletin of Statistics*.

1998: Port of Spain handled 3.3m. metric tons of cargo.

TRINIDAD AND TOBAGO

CIVIL AVIATION
(traffic on scheduled services)

	2002	2003	2004
Kilometres flown (million)	28	31	28
Passengers carried ('000)	1,269	1,084	1,132
Passenger-km (million)	2,875	2,671	3,013
Total ton-km (million)	295	276	314

Source: UN, *Statistical Yearbook*.

Tourism

FOREIGN TOURIST ARRIVALS

Country of origin	2004	2005	2006
Barbados	35,456	35,319	31,218
Canada	43,565	47,702	49,242
Germany	8,178	8,666	6,706
Grenada	19,575	19,501	14,814
Guyana	22,328	22,208	23,673
Saint Lucia	8,192	8,823	8,902
Saint Vincent and Grenadines	11,747	12,658	12,288
United Kingdom	66,090	63,523	58,612
USA	159,467	167,985	170,893
Venezuela	10,528	10,191	9,906
Total (incl. others)	442,596	463,191	457,434

Tourism receipts (US $ million, incl. passenger transport): 568 in 2004; 593 in 2005; 357 in 2006.

Source: World Tourism Organization.

Communications Media

	2005	2006	2007
Telephones ('000 main lines in use)	323.5	325.5	323.8
Mobile cellular telephones ('000 subscribers)	800.0	900.0	1,007.7
Internet users ('000)	163.0	288.0	430.8
Broadband subscribers ('000)	10.8	20.6	15.6

Radio receivers (1997, '000 in use): 680.
Facsimile machines (1998, number in use): 5,024.
Daily newspapers: 4 in 1997 (average circulation: 191,000 in 2001).
Non-daily newspapers: 5 in 1997 (average circulation 167,000 in 2001).
Television receivers ('000 in use): 449 in 2001.

Sources: International Telecommunication Union; UN, *Statistical Yearbook*; UNESCO, *Statistical Yearbook*.

Education

(2004/05, unless otherwise indicated)

	Institutions	Teachers	Males	Females	Total
Pre-primary	50*	2,186	15,673	14,805	30,478
Primary	480†	7,839	66,654	63,049	129,703
Secondary	101†	5,896	47,256	48,932	96,188
University and equivalent	3‡	1,800	7,515	9,405	16,920

* Government schools and assisted schools only, in 1992/93.
† 2001/02.
‡ 2003/04.

Source: UNESCO.

Adult literacy rate (UNESCO estimates): 98.7% (males 99.1%; females 98.3%) in 2007 (Source: UNESCO Institute for Statistics).

Directory

The Constitution

Trinidad and Tobago became a republic, within the Commonwealth, under a new Constitution on 1 August 1976. The Constitution provides for a President and a bicameral Parliament comprising a Senate and a House of Representatives. The President is elected by an Electoral College of members of both the Senate and the House of Representatives. The Senate consists of 31 members appointed by the President: 16 on the advice of the Prime Minister, six on the advice of the Leader of the Opposition and nine at the President's own discretion from among outstanding persons from economic, social or community organizations. The House of Representatives consists of 41 members who are elected by universal adult suffrage. The duration of a Parliament is five years. The Cabinet, presided over by the Prime Minister, is responsible for the general direction and control of the Government. It is collectively responsible to Parliament.

The Government

HEAD OF STATE

President: Prof. GEORGE MAXWELL RICHARDS (took office 17 March 2003; re-elected by vote of the Electoral College of the Parliament 11 February 2008).

THE CABINET
(April 2009)

Prime Minister: PATRICK MANNING.
Attorney-General: BRIGID ANNISETTE-GEORGE.
Minister of Agriculture, Land and Marine Resources: ARNOLD PIGGOTT.
Minister of Community Development, Culture and Gender Affairs: MARLENE MCDONALD.
Minister of Education: ESTHER LE GENDRE.
Minister of Energy and Energy Industries: CONRAD ENIL.
Minister of Finance: KAREN NUNEZ-TESHEIRA.
Minister of Foreign Affairs: PAULA GOPEE-SCOON.
Minister of Health: JERRY NARACE.
Minister of Information: NEIL PARSANLAL.
Minister of Labour and Small and Micro Enterprise Development: RENNIE DUMAS.
Minister of Legal Affairs: PETER TAYLOR.
Minister of Local Government: HAZEL ANNE MARIE MANNING.
Minister of National Security: MARTIN JOSEPH.
Minister of Planning, Housing and the Environment: Dr EMILY GAYNOR DICK-FORDE.
Minister of Public Administration: KENNEDY SWARATSINGH.
Minister of Public Utilities: MUSTAPHA ABDUL-HAMID.
Minister of Science, Technology and Tertiary Education: CHRISTINE KANGALOO.
Minister of Social Development: Dr AMERY BROWNE.
Minister of Sport and Youth Affairs: GARY HUNT.
Minister of Tourism: JOSEPH ROSS.
Minister of Trade and Industry and Minister in the Ministry of Finance: Dr MARIANO BROWNE.
Minister of Works and Transport: COLM IMBERT.
Minister in the Ministry of Finance: MARIANO BROWNE.
Minister in the Office of the Prime Minister: LENNY SAITH.

TRINIDAD AND TOBAGO

Minister of State in the Ministry of National Security: DONNA COX.
Minister of State in the Ministry of Planning, Housing and the Environment: TINA GRONLUND-NUNEZ.
Minister of State in the Ministry of Science, Technology and Tertiary Education: FITZGERALD JEFFREY.
Minister of State in the Ministry of Social Development: ALICIA HOSPEDALES.
Minister of State in the Ministry of Works and Transport: ROGER JOSEPH.
Minister of State in the Office of the Prime Minister: STANFORD CALLENDER.

MINISTRIES

Office of the President: President's House, Circular Rd, St Ann's, Port of Spain; tel. 624-1261; fax 625-7950; e-mail presoftt@carib-link.net.

Office of the Prime Minister: Whitehall, 29 Maraval Rd, Port of Spain; tel. 622-1625; fax 622-0055; e-mail permsec@opm.gov.tt; internet www.opm.gov.tt.

Ministry of Agriculture, Land and Marine Resources: St Clair Circle, St Clair, Port of Spain; tel. 622-1221; fax 622-8202; e-mail apdmalmr@trinidad.net; internet www.agriculture.gov.tt.

Ministry of the Attorney-General: Cabildo Chambers, 23–27 St Vincent St, Port of Spain; tel. 623-7010; fax 625-0470; e-mail ag@ag.gov.tt.

Ministry of Community Development, Culture and Gender Affairs: ALGICO Bldg, Jerningham Ave, Belmont, Port of Spain; tel. 625-3012; fax 625-3278; e-mail cdcga@tstt.net.tt; internet www.cdcga.gov.tt.

Ministry of Education: 18 Alexandra St, St Clair; tel. 622-2181; fax 622-4892; e-mail mined@tstt.net.tt; internet www.moe.gov.tt.

Ministry of Energy and Energy Industries: Level 9, Riverside Plaza, Cnr Besson and Piccadilly Sts, Port of Spain; tel. 623-6708; fax 623-0306; e-mail info@energy.gov.tt; internet www.energy.gov.tt.

Ministry of Finance: Level 8, Eric Williams Finance Bldg, Independence Sq., Port of Spain; tel. 627-9700; fax 627-5882; e-mail comm.finance@gov.tt; internet www.finance.gov.tt.

Ministry of Foreign Affairs: Knowsley Bldg, 1 Queen's Park West, Port of Spain; tel. 623-4116; fax 624-4220; e-mail press@foreign.gov.tt; internet www.foreign.gov.tt.

Ministry of Health: Cnr Park and Edwards Sts, Port of Spain; tel. 627-0012; fax 623-9528; e-mail sandra.jones@health.gov.tt; internet www.healthsectorreform.gov.tt.

Ministry of Information: Level 5, NALIS Bldg, Abercromby St, Port of Spain.

Ministry of Labour and Small and Micro Enterprise Development: Level 11, Riverside Plaza, Cnr Besson and Piccadilly Sts, Port of Spain; tel. 623-4241; fax 624-4091; e-mail rplan@tstt.net.tt; internet www.labour.gov.tt.

Ministry of Legal Affairs: Registration House, Huggins Bldg, South Quay, Port of Spain; tel. 623-7163; fax 625-9803; e-mail mlalr@tstt.net.tt.

Ministry of Local Government: Kent House, Maraval Rd, Port of Spain; tel. 622-1669; fax 622-4783; e-mail molg2@carib-link.net; internet www.localgov.gov.tt.

Ministry of National Security: Temple Court, 31–33 Abercromby St, Port of Spain; tel. 623-2441; fax 627-8044; e-mail info@mns.gov.tt; internet www.nationalsecurity.gov.tt.

Ministry of Planning, Housing and the Environment: NHA Bldg, 44–46 South Quay, Port of Spain; tel. 623-4663; fax 625-2793; e-mail info@housing.gov.tt; internet www.planning.gov.tt.

Ministry of Public Administration: Level 7, National Library Bldg, Cnr Hart and Abercromby Sts, Port of Spain; tel. 623-8578; fax 623-6027.

Ministry of Public Utilities: Sacred Heart Bldg, 16–18 Sackville St, Port of Spain; tel. 623-4853; fax 625-7003.

Ministry of Science, Technology and Tertiary Education: Level 3, Nahous Bldg, Cnr Agra and Patna Sts, St James; tel. 622-9922; fax 622-7640; e-mail stte@stte.gov.tt; internet www.stte.gov.tt.

Ministry of Social Development: Ansa McAl Bldg, 69 Independence Sq., Port of Spain; tel. and fax 627-4853; e-mail infor@msd.gov.tt; internet www.socialservices.gov.tt.

Ministry of Sport and Youth Affairs: ISSA Nicholas Bldg, Cnr Frederick and Duke Sts, Port of Spain; tel. 625-8874; fax 623-5006.

Ministry of Tourism: Clarence House, 127–129 Duke St, Port of Spain; tel. 624-1403; fax 625-3894; e-mail mintourism@tourism.gov.tt.

Ministry of Trade and Industry: Levels 11–17, Nicholas Tower, 63-65 Independence Sq., Port of Spain; tel. 623-2931; fax 627-8488; e-mail info@tradeind.gov.tt; internet www.tradeind.gov.tt.

Ministry of Works and Transport: Level 6, Administrative Bldg, Cnr Richmond and London Sts, Port of Spain; tel. 625-1225; fax 625-8070; internet www.mowt.gov.tt.

Legislature

PARLIAMENT

Senate

President: DANNY MONTANO.

House of Representatives

Speaker: BARENDRA SINANAN.
Election, 5 November 2007

Party	% of votes	Seats
People's National Movement	45.9	26
United National Congress—Alliance	29.8	15
Congress of the People	22.6	—
Total (incl. others)	100.0	41

TOBAGO HOUSE OF ASSEMBLY

The House is elected for a four-year term of office and consists of 12 elected members and three members selected by the majority party.

Chief Secretary: ORVILLE LONDON.
Election, 19 January 2009

Party	Seats
People's National Movement	8
Tobago Organisation of the People	4
Total	12

Election Commission

Elections and Boundaries Commission (EBC): Scott House, 134–138 Frederick St, Port of Spain; tel. 623-4622; fax 627-7881; Chair. Dr NORBERT MASSON.

Political Organizations

Congress of the People: 12 Pasea Main Rd, Tunapuna; tel. 662-1067; e-mail secretariat@coptnt.com; internet www.coptnt.com; f. 2006; Leader WINSTON DOOKERAN; Chair. ROY AUGUSTUS.

Democratic Action Congress: Scarborough; f. Jan. 2003 by faction of National Alliance for Reconstruction (q.v.); only active in Tobago; Leader HOCHOY CHARLES.

Democratic National Assembly (DNA): Port of Spain; f. 2006; Chair. DARA HEALY; Leader Dr KIRK MEIGHOO.

Democratic Party of Trinidad and Tobago (DPTT): Port of Spain; f. 2001; joined the United National Congress—Alliance (UNC—A) in July 2007; Chair. WAYNE RODRIGUES; Leader STEVE ALVAREZ.

National Alliance for Reconstruction (NAR): 71 Dundonald St, Port of Spain; tel. 627-6163; f. 1983 as a coalition of moderate opposition parties; reorganized as a single party in 1986; joined the United National Congress—Alliance (UNC—A) in July 2007; Leader CARSON CHARLES; Chair. CHRISTO GIFT.

National Democratic Party (NDP): Port of Spain; f. 2005; joined the United National Congress—Alliance (UNC—A) in July 2007; Leader MICHAEL SIMS.

National Transformation Movement (NTM): Port of Spain; f. 2006; Leader LLOYD ELCOCK.

People's National Movement (PNM): Balisier House, 1 Tranquility St, Port of Spain; tel. 625-1533; fax 627-3311; e-mail info@pnmtt.org; internet www.pnm.org.tt; f. 1956; moderate nationalist party; Leader PATRICK MANNING; Chair. FRANKLIN KHAN; Gen. Sec. MARTIN JOSEPH.

Tobago Organisation of the People (TOP): Tobago; f. 2007; only active in Tobago; Leader ASHWORTH JACK.

TRINIDAD AND TOBAGO

United National Congress—Alliance (UNC—A): Rienzi Complex, 78–81 Southern Main Rd, Couva; tel. 636-8145; e-mail info@unc.org.tt; internet www.unc.org.tt; f. 1989 as the United National Congress; formed an alliance with the Democratic Party of Trinidad and Tobago (DPTT), the National Alliance for Reconstruction (NAR) and the National Democratic Party (NDP) to contest the 2007 general election and adopted the above name; social democratic; Leader BASDEO PANDAY; CEO TIM GOPEESINGH.

Diplomatic Representation

EMBASSIES AND HIGH COMMISSIONS IN TRINIDAD AND TOBAGO

Argentina: TATIL Bldg, 4th Floor, 11 Maraval Rd, POB 162; Port of Spain; tel. 628-7557; fax 628-7544; e-mail etrin@mrecic.gov.ar; internet www.trinidadytobago.embajada-argentina.gov.ar; Ambassador JOSÉ LUIS VIGNOLO.

Brazil: 18 Sweet Briar Rd, St Clair, POB 382, Port of Spain; tel. 622-5779; fax 622-4323; e-mail brastt@wow.net.tt; internet www.brazilembtt.org; Ambassador LUIZ FERNANDO DE ATHAYDE.

Canada: Maple House, 3–3A Sweet Briar Rd, St Clair, POB 1246, Port of Spain; tel. 622-6232; fax 628-1830; e-mail pspan@international.gc.ca; internet www.portofspain.gc.ca; High Commissioner JOHN MUNDY (acting).

China, People's Republic: 39 Alexandra St, St Clair, Port of Spain; tel. 622-6976; fax 622-7613; e-mail tian@wow.net; internet tt.chineseembassy.org; Ambassador HUANG XING.

Cuba: Furness Bldg, 2nd Floor, 90 Independence Sq., Port of Spain; tel. 627-1306; fax 627-3515; e-mail embajador@tstt.net.tt; Ambassador SERGIO OLIVA GUERRA.

Dominican Republic: Suite 8, 1 Dere St, Queen's Park West, Port of Spain; tel. 624-7930; fax 623-7779; e-mail embdomtrinidadytobago@serex.gov.do; Ambassador JOSÉ MANUEL CASTILLO BETANCES.

El Salvador: 29 Long Circular Rd, St James, Port of Spain; tel. 628-4454; fax 622-8314; Ambassador CARLOS MAURICIO PINEDA.

France: TATIL Bldg, 6th Floor, 11 Maraval Rd, Port of Spain; tel. 622-7447; fax 628-2632; e-mail francett@wow.net; internet www.ambafrance-tt.org; Chargé d'affaires a.i. YVES DRILLET.

Germany: 7–9 Marli St, Newtown, POB 828, Port of Spain; tel. 628-1630; fax 628-5278; e-mail germanembassy@tstt.net.tt; internet www.port-of-spain.diplo.de; Ambassador Dr ERNST MARTENS.

Guatemala: Regents Towers, Apt 701, Westmoorings-by-the-Sea, Westmoorings; tel. 633-9506; fax 633-3809; e-mail embaguatt@tstt.net.tt; Ambassador ALEJANDRO VELA AQUINO.

Holy See: 11 Mary St, St Clair, POB 854, Port of Spain; tel. 622-5009; fax 628-5457; e-mail apnuntt@googlemail.com; Apostolic Nuncio Most Rev. THOMAS EDWARD GULLICKSON (Titular Archbishop of Bomarzo).

India: 6 Victoria Ave, POB 530, Port of Spain; tel. 627-7480; fax 627-6985; e-mail hcipos@tstt.net.tt; High Commissioner JAGJIT SINGH SAPRA.

Jamaica: 2 Newbold St, St Clair, Port of Spain; tel. 622-4995; fax 628-9043; e-mail jhctnt@tstt.net.tt; High Commissioner PETER BLACK.

Japan: 5 Hayes St, St Clair, POB 1039, Port of Spain; tel. 628-5991; fax 622-0858; e-mail embassyofjapan@tstt.net.tt; internet www.tt.emb-japan.go.jp; Ambassador KOICHIRO SEKI.

Korea, Republic: 60 Eagle Crescent, Fairways, Maraval, Port of Spain; tel. 622-9081; fax 627-6317; e-mail koremb.tt@gmail.com; Chargé d'affaires a.i. CHONG-ON WONG.

Mexico: 12 Hayes St, St Clair, Port of Spain; tel. 622-1422; fax 628-8488; e-mail info@mexico.tt; Ambassador RICARDO VILLANUEVA HALLAL.

Netherlands: Life of Barbados Bldg, 3rd Floor, 69–71 Edward St, POB 870, Port of Spain; tel. 625-1210; fax 625-1704; e-mail info@holland.tt; internet www.holland.tt; Ambassador H. P. P. M. HORBACH.

Nigeria: 3 Maxwell-Phillip St, St Clair, Port of Spain; tel. 622-4002; fax 622-7162; e-mail nigerianpos@tstt.net.tt; High Commissioner JOHN MUSA.

Panama: Suite 6, 1A Dere St, Port of Spain; tel. 623-3435; fax 623-3440; e-mail embapatt@wow.net; Ambassador GERARDO MALONEY.

South Africa: 2nd Floor, Victoria Park Suites, 14–17 Victoria Sq., Port of Spain; tel. 468-4245; fax 623-3067; e-mail betsie.erasmus@southafrica.org.tt; Chargé d'affaires a.i. ROY SETLHAPELO.

Suriname: TATIL Bldg, 5th Floor, 11 Maraval Rd, Port of Spain; tel. 628-0704; fax 628-0086; e-mail surinameembassy@tstt.net.tt; Ambassador FIDELIA GRAAND-GALON.

United Kingdom: 19 St Clair Circle, St Clair, POB 778, Port of Spain; tel. 622-2748; fax 622-4555; e-mail csbhc@tstt.net.tt; internet www.britishhighcommission.gov.uk/trinidadandtobago; High Commissioner ERIC JENKINSON.

USA: 15 Queen's Park West, POB 752, Port of Spain; tel. 622-6371; fax 625-5462; e-mail usispos@trinidad.net; internet trinidad.usembassy.gov; Ambassador Dr ROY L. AUSTIN.

Venezuela: 16 Victoria Ave, POB 1300, Port of Spain; tel. 627-9821; fax 624-2508; e-mail embaveneztt@tstt.net.tt; Chargé d'affaires a.i. JOSÉ SALVUCHY.

Judicial System

The Chief Justice, who has overall responsibility for the administration of justice in Trinidad and Tobago, is appointed by the President after consultation with the Prime Minister and the Leader of the Opposition. The President appoints and promotes judges on the advice of the Judicial and Legal Service Commission. The Judicial and Legal Service Commission, which comprises the Chief Justice as chairman, the chairman of the Public Service Commission, two former judges and a senior member of the bar, appoints all judicial and legal officers. The Judiciary comprises the higher judiciary (the Supreme Court) and the lower judiciary (the Magistracy). In February 2005 Parliament voted to accept the authority of the Caribbean Court of Justice (CCJ) to settle international trade disputes. The Court was formally inaugurated in Port of Spain on 16 April 2005.

Chief Justice: IVOR ARCHIE.

Supreme Court of Judicature: Knox St, Port of Spain; tel. 623-2417; fax 627-5477; e-mail ttlaw@wow.net; internet www.ttlawcourts.org; the Supreme Court consists of the High Court of Justice and the Court of Appeal. The Supreme Court is housed in three locations: Port of Spain, San Fernando and Tobago. There are 23 Supreme Court Puisne Judges, who sit in criminal, civil, and matrimonial divisions; Registrar EVELYN ANN PETERSEN.

Court of Appeal: The Court of Appeal hears appeals against decisions of the Magistracy and the High Court. Further appeals are directed to the Judicial Committee of the Privy Council of the United Kingdom, sometimes as of right and sometimes with leave of the Court. The Court of Appeal consists of the Chief Justice, who is President, and six other Justices of Appeal.

The Magistracy and High Court of Justice

The Magistracy and the High Court exercise original jurisdiction in civil and criminal matters. The High Court hears indictable criminal matters, family matters where the parties are married, and civil matters involving sums over the petty civil court limit. High Court judges are referred to as either Judges of the High Court or Puisne Judges. The Masters of the High Court, of which there are four, have the jurisdiction of judges in civil chamber courts. The Magistracy (in its petty civil division) deals with civil matters involving sums of less than TT $15,000. It exercises summary jurisdiction in criminal matters and hears preliminary inquiries in indictable matters. The Magistracy, which is divided into 13 districts, consists of a Chief Magistrate, a Deputy Chief Magistrate, 13 Senior Magistrates and 29 Magistrates.

Chief Magistrate: MELISSA ROBERTSON (acting), Magistrates' Court, St Vincent St, Port of Spain; tel. 625-2781.

Director of Public Prosecutions: CARLA BROWN-ANTOINE (acting).

Religion

In 2000 it was estimated that one-half the population practised Christianity, including Anglican (7.8%), Pentecostal (6.8%), Seventh-day Adventist (4%) and Presbyterian (3.3%), while some 22.5% of the population was Hindu, 5.8% Muslim and 5.4% Shouter Baptist.

CHRISTIANITY

Caribbean Conference of Churches: POB 876, Curepe; tel. 662-2979; fax 662-1303; e-mail cchq@tstt.net.tt; internet www.ccc-caribe.org; f. 1973; Pres. Rev. Dr LESLEY G. ANDERSON; Gen. Sec. GERARD A. J. GRANADO.

Christian Council of Trinidad and Tobago: Hayes Court, 21 Maraval Rd, Port of Spain; tel. 637-9329; f. 1967; church unity org. formed by the Roman Catholic, Anglican, Presbyterian, Methodist, African Methodist, Spiritual Baptist and Moravian Churches, the Church of Scotland and the Salvation Army, with the Ethiopian Orthodox Church and the Baptist Union as observers; Pres. The Rt Rev. CALVIN WENDELL BESS (Anglican Bishop of Trinidad and Tobago); Sec. GRACE STEELE.

TRINIDAD AND TOBAGO

The Anglican Communion

Anglicans are adherents of the Church in the Province of the West Indies, comprising eight dioceses. The Archbishop of the West Indies is the Bishop of Nassau and the Bahamas.

Bishop of Trinidad and Tobago: The Rt Rev. CALVIN WENDELL BESS, Hayes Court, 21 Maraval Rd, Port of Spain; tel. 622-7387; fax 628-1319; e-mail bessc@tstt.net.tt; internet www.trinidad.anglican.org.

Protestant Churches

Baptist Union of Trinidad and Tobago: 104 High St, Princes Town; tel. 655-2291; e-mail baptuni@tstt.net.tt; f. 1816; Pres. Rev. EDWIN H. LEWIS; Gen. Sec. Rev. JOHN S. C. BRAMBLE; 24 churches, 3,300 mems.

Presbyterian Church of Trinidad and Tobago: POB 187, Paradise Hill, San Fernando; tel. and fax 652-4829; e-mail pctt@tstt.net.tt; internet www.presbyterianchurchtt.org; f. 1868; Moderator Rt Rev. ELVIS ELAHIE; Gen. Sec. ALVIN SEEREERAM; 40,000 mems.

The Roman Catholic Church

For ecclesiastical purposes, Trinidad and Tobago comprises the single archdiocese of Port of Spain. At 31 December 2006 there were some 337,000 adherents in the country, representing about 26% of the total population.

Antilles Episcopal Conference: 9A Gray St, Port of Spain; tel. 622-2932; fax 628-3688; e-mail aec@carib-link.net; internet www.caholiccaribbean.org; f. 1975; 21 mems from the Caribbean and Central American regions; Pres. Most Rev. LAWRENCE ALOYSIUS BURKE (Archbishop of Kingston, Jamaica); Gen. Sec. Rev. GERARD E. FARFAN.

Archbishop of Port of Spain: EDWARD JOSEPH GILBERT, 27 Maraval Rd, Port of Spain; tel. 622-1103; fax 622-1165; e-mail abishop@carib-link.net.

HINDUISM

Hindu immigrants from India first arrived in Trinidad and Tobago in 1845. The vast majority of migrants, who were generally from Uttar Pradesh, were Vishnavite Hindus, who belonged to sects such as the Ramanandi, the Kabir and the Sieunaraini. The majority of Hindus currently subscribe to the doctrine of Sanathan Dharma, which evolved from Ramanandi teaching.

Arya Pratinidhi Sabha of Trinidad Inc (Arya Samaj): Seereeram Memorial Vedic School, Old Southern Main Rd, Montrose Village, Chaguanas; tel. 663-1721; e-mail president@trinidadaryasamaj.org; Pres. LAKHRAM VIJAY BACHAN.

Pandits' Parishad (Council of Pandits): Maha Sabha Headquarters, Eastern Main Rd, St Augustine; tel. 645-3240; works towards the co-ordination of temple activities and the standardization of ritual procedure; affiliated to the Maha Sabha; 200 mems.

Sanathan Dharma Maha Sabha of Trinidad and Tobago Inc: Maha Sabha Headquarters, Eastern Main Rd, St Augustine; tel. 645-3240; e-mail mahasabha@ttemail.com; f. 1952; Hindu pressure group and public org.; organizes the provision of Hindu education; Pres. Dr D. OMAH MAHARAJH; Sec. Gen. SATNARAYAN MAHARAJ.

The Press

DAILIES

Newsday: 23A Chacon St, Port of Spain; tel. 623-2459; fax 657-5008; internet www.newsday.co.tt; f. 1993; CEO and Editor-in-Chief THERESE MILLS; circ. 2,200,000.

Trinidad Guardian: 22 St Vincent St, POB 122, Port of Spain; tel. 623-8871; fax 625-5702; e-mail letters@ttol.co.tt; internet guardian.co.tt; f. 1917; morning; independent; Editor-in-Chief ANTHONY WILSON; circ. 52,617.

Trinidad and Tobago Express: 35 Independence Sq., Port of Spain; tel. 623-1711; fax 627-1451; e-mail express@trinidadexpress.com; internet www.trinidadexpress.com; f. 1967; morning; CEO KEN GORDON; Editor ALAN GEERE; circ. 55,000.

PERIODICALS

The Boca: Crews Inn Marina and Boatyard, Village Sq., Chaguaramas; tel. 634-2055; fax 634-2056; e-mail enquiry@boatersenterprise.com; internet www.theboca.com; monthly; magazine of the sailing and boating community; Man. Dir JACK DAUSEND.

The Bomb: Southern Main Rd, Curepe; tel. 645-2744; weekly; Publr SAT MAHARAJ.

Caribbean Beat Magazine: 6 Prospect Ave, Maraval, Port of Spain; tel. 622-3821; fax 628-0639; e-mail info@meppublishers.com; internet www.caribbean-beat.com; f. 1991; 6 a year; distributed by Caribbean Airlines; Publr JEREMY TAYLOR; Editor JUDY RAYMOND.

Catholic News: 31 Independence Sq., Port of Spain; tel. 623-6093; fax 623-9468; e-mail cathnews@trinidad.net; internet www.catholicnews-tt.net; f. 1892; weekly; Editor JUNE JOHNSTON; circ. 16,000.

Economic Bulletin: Eric Williams Plaza, Independence Sq., POB 1250, Port of Spain; tel. 625-4835; fax 627-4696; e-mail info@central-bank.org.tt; internet www.central-bank.org.tt; f. 1950; issued 3 times a year by the Central Bank; Information Man. KAREN CAMPBELL.

Energy Caribbean: 6 Prospect Ave, Maraval, Port of Spain; tel. 622-3821; fax 628-0639; e-mail dchin@meppublishers.com; internet www.meppublishers.com; f. 2002; bi-monthly; Editor DAVID RENWICK.

Showtime: Cnr 9th St and 9th Ave, Barataria; tel. 674-1692; fax 674-3228; circ. 30,000.

Sunday Express: 35 Independence Sq., Port of Spain; tel. 623-1711; fax 627-1451; e-mail express@trinidadexpress.com; internet www.trinidadexpress.com; f. 1967; circ. 51,405.

Sunday Guardian: 22 St Vincent St, POB 122, Port of Spain; tel. 623-8870; fax 625-7211; e-mail esunday@ttol.co.tt; internet www.guardian.co.tt; f. 1917; independent; morning; Editor-in-Chief DOMINIC KALIPERSAD; circ. 48,324.

Sunday Punch: Cnr 9th St and 9th Ave, Barataria; tel. 674-1692; fax 674-3228; internet www.tntmirror.com; weekly; Editor ANTHONY ALEXIS; circ. 40,000.

Tobago News: Milford Rd, Scarborough; tel. 639-5565; fax 625-4480; e-mail ccngroupc@tstt.net.tt; internet www.thetobagonews.com; f. 1985; weekly; Editor COMPTON DELPH.

Trinidad and Tobago Gazette: 2–4 Victoria Ave, Port of Spain; tel. 625-4139; weekly; official govt paper; circ. 3,300.

Trinidad and Tobago Mirror: Cnr 9th St and 9th Ave, Barataria; tel. 674-1692; fax 674-3228; internet www.tntmirror.com; 2 a week; Editors KEN ALI, KEITH SHEPHERD; circ. 35,000.

Tropical Agriculture: Faculty of Agriculture and Natural Sciences, University of the West Indies, St Augustine; tel. and fax 645-3640; e-mail tropicalagri@fans.uwi.tt; f. 1924; journal of the School of Agriculture (fmrly Imperial College of Tropical Agriculture); quarterly; Editor-in-Chief Prof. FRANK A. GUMBS.

Publishers

Caribbean Children's Press: 1A Lazare St, St James; tel. and fax 628-4248; f. 1987; educational publishers for primary schools.

Caribbean Educational Publishers: Gulf View Link Rd, La Romaine; tel. 657-9613; fax 652-5620; e-mail mbscep@tstt.net.tt; Pres. TEDDY MOHAMMED.

Charran Publishing House Ltd: Wrightson Road, POB 126, Port of Spain; tel. 625-9821; fax 623-6597; e-mail charran_pub@yahoo.com; internet www.charranpublishers.com; Man. Dir REGINALD CHARRAN.

Lexicon Trinidad Ltd: Lot 87, Frederick Settlement Industrial Estate, Caroni; tel. 662-1863; fax 663-0081; e-mail lexiconadmin@gmail.com; Dir KEN JAIKARANSINGH.

Morton Publishing: 97 Saddle Rd, Maraval; tel. 348-3777; fax 762-9923; e-mail morton@morton-pub.com; internet www.morton-pub.com; f. 1977; educational books; Pres. DOUG MORTON; Dir JULIE MORTON.

Royards Publishing Co: 7A Macoya Industrial Estate, Macoya; tel. 663-6002; fax 663-6316; e-mail royards@aol.com; internet www.royards.com; f. 1984; educational publishers; Dirs CLIFFORD NARINESINGH, DWIGHT NARINESINGH.

Trinidad Publishing Co Ltd: 22–24 St Vincent St, Port of Spain; tel. 623-8870; fax 625-7211; e-mail business@ttol.co.tt; internet guardian.co.tt; f. 1917; Man. Dir GRENFELL KISSOON.

Broadcasting and Communications

TELECOMMUNICATIONS

Regulatory Body

Telecommunications Authority of Trinidad and Tobago (TATT): Suites 3–5, BEN Court, 76 Boundary Rd, San Juan; tel. 675-8288; fax 674-1055; e-mail info@tatt.org.tt; internet www.tatt.org.tt; f. 2001 to oversee the liberalization of the telecommunications sector; Chair. Dr KHALID HASSANALI.

TRINIDAD AND TOBAGO

Major Companies

bmobile: 52 Jerningham Ave, Belmont; fax 625-5807; e-mail service@tstt.co.tt; internet www.bmobile.co.tt; f. 1991 as TSTT Cellnet; name changed as above 2006; 51% state-owned, 49% by Cable & Wireless (United Kingdom); mobile cellular telephone operator; Vice-Pres. GARY BARROW.

Columbus Communications Trinidad Ltd (CCTL): Port of Spain; fax 624-9584; e-mail residentialsales@columbustrinidad.com; internet www.flowtrinidad.com; f. 2005; digital cable television, internet and local telephone service providers; mobile cellular telephone licence granted in 2006; Pres. and CEO JOHN REID; 250 employees (2007).

Digicel Trinidad and Tobago: 11–13 Victoria Ave, Port of Spain; tel. 628-7000; fax 622-0887; e-mail tt.customer.care@digicelgroup.com; internet www.digiceltrinidadandtobago.com; owned by an Irish consortium; mobile cellular telephone licence granted in 2005; Chair. DENIS O'BRIEN; CEO NIALL DORRIAN.

One Caribbean Media Ltd (OCM): 35 Independence Sq., Port of Spain; tel. 623-1711; fax 625-5712; e-mail tjohnson@trinidadexpress.com; internet www.onecaribbeanmedia.net; f. 2006 by merger of Caribbean Communications Network (CCN) and The Nation Corpn (Barbados); Chair. Sir FRED GOLLOP; CEO TERRENCE FARRELL.

Open Telecom Ltd: 88 Edward St, Port of Spain; tel. 622-6736; e-mail sales@opentelecom.com; internet www.gillettegroup.com/opentelecom/index.htm; Chair. PETER GILLETTE.

Telecommunication Services of Trinidad and Tobago (TSTT) Ltd: 1 Edward St, POB 3, Port of Spain; tel. 625-4431; fax 627-0856; e-mail tsttceo@tstt.net.tt; internet www.tstt.co.tt; 51% state-owned, 49% by Cable & Wireless (United Kingdom); 51% privatization pending; CEO ROBERTO PEÓN.

BROADCASTING

Radio

Homeviewtnt.com: Port of Spain; e-mail customerservice@homeviewtnt.com; internet www.homeviewtnt.com; operates 6 commercial radio stations: Radio 90.5 FM; Sangeet 106 FM; 103 FM; Ebony 104 FM; Vibe CT105 FM; Radio Trinbago 94.7 FM.

Hott 93 FM: Cumulus Broadcasting Inc, 3A Queens Park West, Port of Spain; tel. 623-4688; fax 624-3234; e-mail studio@hott93.com.

Love 94.1 and Power 102 FM: 88–90 Abercromby St, Port of Spain; tel. 627-6937; fax 624-8223; e-mail 102@cablenett.net; internet www.power102fm.com; CEO O'BRIAN HAYNES; Man. SHARON PITT.

Music Radio 97 FM: Long Circular Rd, St James; tel. 622-9797; fax 624-3234.

Trinidad Broadcasting Co Ltd (Radio Trinidad, Radio Nine Five): Broadcasting House, 11B Maraval Rd, POB 716, Port of Spain; tel. 622-1151; fax 622-2380; commercial.

Trinidad Broadcasting Company (Radio Trinidad 730 AM, Rhythm Radio, Caribbean Tempo and WEFM 96.1 FM): 22 St Vincent St, Port of Spain; tel. 623-9202; fax 622-2380; f. 1947; commercial; four programmes; Man. Dir GRENFELL KISSOON.

Trinidad and Tobago Radio Network: 35 Independence Sq., Port of Spain; tel. 624-7078.

Television

TV6: 35 Express House, Independence Sq., Port of Spain; tel. 627-8806; fax 627-1451; e-mail tjohnson@trinidadexpress.com; internet www.onecaribbeanmedia.net; f. 1991; operates channels 6 and 18; owned by One Caribbean Media Ltd (OCM); Chair. Sir FRED GOLLOP; CEO CRAIG REYNALD.

Finance

(cap. = capital; dep. = deposits; res = reserves; m. = million; brs = branches; amounts in TT $)

BANKING

Central Bank

Central Bank of Trinidad and Tobago: Eric Williams Plaza, Brian Lara Promenade, POB 1250, Port of Spain; tel. 625-4835; fax 627-4696; e-mail info@central-bank.org.tt; internet www.central-bank.org.tt; f. 1964; cap. 100.0m., res 100.0m., dep. 29,044.2m. (Sept. 2006); Gov. EWART S. WILLIAMS.

Commercial Banks

Citibank (Trinidad and Tobago) Ltd: 12 Queen's Park East, POB 1249, Port of Spain; tel. 625-1046; fax 624-8131; internet www.citicorp.com; f. 1983; fmrly The United Bank of Trinidad and Tobago Ltd; name changed as above 1989; owned by Citicorp Merchant Bank Ltd; cap. 30.0m., res 14.7m., dep. 455.5m. (Dec. 1996); Chair. SURESH MAHARAJ; Country Man. STEVE BIDESHI; 2 brs.

Citicorp Merchant Bank Ltd: 12 Queen's Park East, POB 1249, Port of Spain; tel. 623-3344; fax 624-8131; cap. 57.1m., res 28.5m., dep. 473.6m. (Dec. 2002); owned by Citibank Overseas Investment Corpn; Chair. SURESH MAHARAJ; Man. Dir KAREN DARBASIE.

First Citizens Bank Ltd: 9 Queen's Park East, Port of Spain; tel. 624-3178; fax 627-4548; e-mail enquiries@simplyfirst.net; internet www.firstcitizenstt.com; f. 1993 following merger of National Commercial Bank of Trinidad and Tobago Ltd, Trinidad Co-operative Bank Ltd and Workers' Bank of Trinidad and Tobago; state-owned; cap. 340.0m., res 253.4m., dep. 8,472.1m. (Sept. 2006); Chair. SAMUEL A. MARTIN; CEO LARRY HOWAI; 22 brs.

RBTT Ltd: Royal Court, 19–21 Park St, POB 287, Port of Spain; tel. 623-1322; fax 625-3764; e-mail royalinfo@rbtt.co.tt; internet www.rbtt.com; f. 1972 as Royal Bank of Trinidad and Tobago to take over local brs of Royal Bank of Canada; present name adopted April 2002; bought by Royal Bank of Canada in 2007; cap. 404.0m., res 215.4m., dep. 10,083.1m. (March 2006); Chair. PETER J. JULY; CEO SURESH SOOKOO; 21 brs.

Republic Bank Ltd: 9–17 Park St, POB 1153, Port of Spain; tel. 623-1056; fax 624-1323; e-mail email@republictt.com; internet www.republictt.com; f. 1837 as Colonial Bank; became Barclays Bank in 1972; name changed as above 1981; merged with Bank of Commerce Trinidad and Tobago Ltd 1997; cap. 537.1m., res 951.8m., dep. 28,549.4m. (Sept. 2006); Chair. RONALD F. HARFORD; Man. Dir DAVID DULAL-WHITEWAY; 34 brs.

Republic Finance & Merchant Bank Ltd: 9–17 Park St, POB 1153, Port of Spain; tel. 623-1056; fax 624-1323; e-mail email@republictt.com; internet www.republictt.com; f. 1965; owned by Republic Bank Ltd (q.v.); cap. 30.0m., res 44.5m., dep. 1,836.5m. (Sept. 2004); Chair. RONALD F. HARFORD; Man. Dir CHERYL F. GREAVES.

Scotiabank Trinidad and Tobago Ltd: 56–58 Richmond St, POB 621, Port of Spain; tel. 625-3566; fax 627-5278; e-mail scotiamain@tstt.net.tt; internet www.scotiabankatt.com; cap. 267.6m., res 301.2m., dep. 9,588.4m. (Oct. 2007); Chair. ROBERT H. PITFIELD; Man. Dir RICHARD P. YOUNG; 23 brs.

Development Banks

Agricultural Development Bank of Trinidad and Tobago: 87 Henry St, POB 154, Port of Spain; tel. 623-6261; fax 624-3087; e-mail adbceo@tstt.net.tt; f. 1968; provides long-, medium- and short-term loans to farmers and the agri-business sector; Chair. NOEL GARCIA; CEO JACQUELINE RAWLINS.

DFL Caribbean: 10 Cipriani Blvd, POB 187, Port of Spain; tel. 623-4665; fax 624-3563; e-mail dfl@dflcaribbean.com; internet www.dflcaribbean.com; provides short- and long-term finance, and equity financing for projects in manufacturing, agro-processing, tourism, industrial and commercial enterprises; total assets US $84.2m. (Dec. 1998); Chair. AUDLEY WALKER; Man. Dir GERARD M. PEMBERTON.

Credit Unions

Co-operative Credit Union League of Trinidad and Tobago Ltd: 32–34 Maraval Rd, St Clair; tel. 645-6943; fax 645-3130; e-mail culeague@tstt.net.tt; internet www.ccultt.org; Pres. BRIAN MOORE; Chair. CALVIN MOSES.

STOCK EXCHANGE

Trinidad and Tobago Stock Exchange Ltd: Nicholas Tower, 10th Floor, 63–65 Independence Sq., Port of Spain; tel. 625-5107; fax 623-0089; e-mail ttstockx@tstt.net.tt; internet www.stockex.co.tt; f. 1981; 30 cos listed (2008); electronic depository system came into operation in 2003; Chair. ANDREW MCEACHRANE; CEO WAIN ITON.

INSURANCE

American Life and General Insurance Co (Trinidad and Tobago) Ltd: ALGICO Plaza, 91–93 St Vincent St, POB 943, Port of Spain; tel. 625-4425; fax 623-6218; e-mail algico@wow.net; Man. Dir GORDON DEANE.

Bankers Insurance Co of Trinidad and Tobago Ltd: 177 Tragarete Rd, Port of Spain; tel. 622-4613; fax 628-6808; e-mail bankersinsurance@hcu.co.tt; internet www.hinducreditunion.com; subsidiary of Hindu Credit Union.

Barbados Mutual Life Assurance Society: The Mutual Centre, 16 Queen's Park West, POB 356, Port of Spain; tel. 628-1636; Gen. Man. HUGH MAZELY.

Capital Insurance Ltd: 38–42 Cipero St, San Fernando; tel. 657-8077; fax 652-7306; f. 1958; motor and fire insurance; 10 brs and 9 agencies.

Colonial Fire & General Insurance Co Ltd (COLFIRE): e-mail info@colfire.com; internet www.colfire.com; f. 1995; mem. of C. L.

Financial Group; Chair. ROBERT NG CHOW; Man. Dir WILLARD P. HARRIS.

Colonial Life Insurance Co (Trinidad) Ltd (CLICO): Colonial Life Bldg, 29 St Vincent St, POB 443, Port of Spain; tel. 623-1421; fax 627-3821; e-mail info@clico.com; internet www.clico.com; f. 1936; Central Bank assumed control of CLICO in Jan. 2009; Chair. LAWRENCE A. DUPREY; CEO CLAUDIUS DACON.

CUNA Caribbean Insurance Society Ltd: 37 Wrightson Rd, POB 193, Port of Spain; tel. 623-7963; fax 623-6251; e-mail cunains@trinidad.net; internet www.cunacaribbean.com; f. 1991; marine aviation and transport; motor vehicle, personal accident, property; Gen. Man. ANTHONY HALL; 3 brs.

Furness Anchorage General Insurance Ltd: 11–13 Milling Ave, Sea Lots, POB 283, Port of Spain; tel. 623-0868; fax 625-1243; e-mail furness@wow.net; internet www.furnessgroup.com; f. 1979; general; Chair. IGNATIUS SEVEIRANO FERREIRA; Exec. Chair. WILLIAM A. FERREIRA.

GTM Fire Insurance Co Ltd: 95–97 Queen St, Port of Spain; tel. 623-1525; e-mail gtmis@tstt.net.tt.

Guardian General Insurance Ltd: Princes Court, Keate St, Port of Spain; tel. 623-4741; fax 623-4320; e-mail info@guardiangenerallimited.com; internet www.guardiangenerallimited.com; founded by merger of NEMWIL and Caribbean Home; Chair. HENRY PETER GANTEAUME; CEO RICHARD ESPINET.

Guardian Life of the Caribbean: 1 Guardian Dr., West Moorings, Port of Spain; tel. 625-5433; internet www.guardianlife.co.tt; Chair. ARTHUR LOK JACK; Pres. and CEO DOUGLAS CAMACHO.

Gulf Insurance Ltd: 1 Gray St, St Clair, Port of Spain; tel. 622-5878; fax 628-0272; e-mail info@gulfinsuranceltd.com; internet www.gulfinsuranceltd.com; f. 1974; general; Exec. Chair. GERRARD LEE-INNISS.

Maritime Financial Group: Maritime Centre, 10th Ave, POB 710, Barataria; tel. 674-0130; fax 638-6663; f. 1978; property and casualty; CEO JOHN SMITH.

Motor and General Insurance Co Ltd: 1–3 Havelock St, St Clair, Port of Spain; tel. 622-2637; fax 622-5345.

New India Assurance Co (T & T) Ltd: 22 St Vincent St, Port of Spain; tel. 623-1326; fax 625-0670; e-mail newindia@wow.net; tel. www.newindia.co.in.

Presidential Insurance Co Ltd: 54 Richmond St, Port of Spain; tel. 625-4788; e-mail pic101@tstt.net.tt.

Trinidad and Tobago Export Credit Insurance Co Ltd: 30 Queen's Park West, Port of Spain; tel. and fax 628-2762; e-mail eximbank@wow.net; internet www.eximbankt.com; state-owned; CEO BRIAN AWANG; Gen. Man. JOSEPHINE IBLE.

Trinidad and Tobago Insurance Ltd (TATIL): 11 Maraval Rd, POB 1004, Port of Spain; tel. 622-5351; fax 628-0035; e-mail info@tatil.co.tt; internet www.tatil.co.tt; acquired by ANSA McAL in 2004; Chair. JOHN JARDIM; CEO RELNA VIRE.

United Insurance Co: 30 O'Connor St, Woodbrook, Port of Spain; tel. 628-8343; fax 628-6575; e-mail trinidad@unitedinsure.com; internet unitedinsure.com; 95.0% owned by Barbados Shipping and Trading Co; Gen. Man. DENNIS BENISAR.

INSURANCE ORGANIZATIONS

Association of Trinidad and Tobago Insurance Companies: 28 Sackville St, Port of Spain; tel. 624-2817; fax 625-5132; e-mail jsc-attic@trinidad.net; internet www.attic.org.tt; Chair. INEZ SINANAN.

National Insurance Board: Cipriani Pl., 2A Cipriani Blvd, Port of Spain; tel. 625-2171-8; fax 627-1787; e-mail nib@nibtt.co.tt; internet www.nibtt.co.tt; f. 1971; statutory corporation; Chair. CALDER HART; Exec. Dir JEFFREY MCFARLANE.

Trade and Industry

GOVERNMENT AGENCIES

Cocoa and Coffee Industry Board: 27 Frederick St, POB 1, Port of Spain; tel. 625-0298; fax 627-4172; e-mail ccib@tstt.net.tt; f. 1962; marketing of coffee and cocoa beans, regulation of cocoa and coffee industry; Man. BARRY JOEFIELD.

Export-Import Bank of Trinidad and Tobago Ltd (EXIM-BANK): 30 Queen's Park West, Port of Spain; tel. 628-2762; fax 622-3545; e-mail eximbank@wow.net; internet www.eximbankt.com; Chair. CLARRY BENN; CEO BRIAN AWANG.

Trinidad and Tobago Forest Products Ltd (TANTEAK): Connector Rd, Carlsen Field, Chaguanas; tel. 665-0078; fax 665-6645; f. 1975; harvesting, processing and marketing of state plantation-grown teak and pine; privatization pending; Chair. RUSKIN PUNCH; Man. Dir CLARENCE BACCHUS.

DEVELOPMENT ORGANIZATIONS

National Energy Corporation of Trinidad and Tobago Ltd: PLIPDECO House, Orinoco Dr., POB 191, Point Lisas, Couva; tel. 636-4662; fax 679-2384; e-mail infocent@carib-link.net; internet www.ngc.co.tt; owned by the Nat. Gas Co of Trinidad and Tobago Ltd (q.v.); f. 1979; Chair. KENNETH BIRCHWOOD; Pres. FRANK LOOK KIN.

National Housing Authority: 44–46 South Quay, POB 555, Port of Spain; tel. 627-1703; fax 625-3963; e-mail info@housing.gov.tt; internet www.housing.gov.tt; f. 1962; Chair. ANDRE MONYEIL; CEO NOEL GARCIA.

Point Lisas Industrial Port Development Corporation Ltd (PLIPDECO): PLIPDECO House, Orinoco Dr., POB 191, Point Lisas, Couva; tel. 636-2201; fax 636-4008; e-mail plipdeco@plipdeco.com; internet www.plipdeco.com; f. 1966; privatized in the late 1990s; deep-water port handling general cargo, liquid and dry bulk, to serve adjacent industrial estate, which now includes iron and steel complex, methanol, ammonia, urea and related downstream industries; Chair. Commdr KAYAM MOHAMMED; Pres. ROGER TRABOULAY.

CHAMBERS OF COMMERCE

South Trinidad Chamber of Industry and Commerce: Suite 313, Cross Crossing Shopping Centre, Lady Hailes Ave, San Fernando; tel. 652-5613; fax 653-4983; e-mail execoffice@stcic.org; internet www.stcic.org; f. 1956; Pres. CHARLES PERCY; CEO Dr THACKWRAY DRIVER.

Trinidad and Tobago Chamber of Industry and Commerce (Inc): Chamber Bldg, Columbus Circle, Westmoorings, POB 499, Port of Spain; tel. 637-6966; fax 637-7425; e-mail chamber@chamber.org.tt; internet www.chamber.org.tt; f. 1891; Pres. IAN WELCH; CEO JOAN FERREIRA; 600 mems.

INDUSTRIAL AND TRADE ASSOCIATIONS

Agricultural Society of Trinidad and Tobago: 1st Floor, Henry St, Port of Spain; tel. 623-7797; fax 623-3087; e-mail agrisoc@tstt.net.tt.

Coconut Growers' Association (CGA) Ltd: Eastern Main Rd, POB 229, Laventille, Port of Spain; tel. 623-5207; fax 623-2359; e-mail cgaltd@tstt.net.tt; f. 1936; 354 mems; Exec. Chair. PHILIPPE AGOSTINI.

Co-operative Citrus Growers' Association of Trinidad and Tobago Ltd: Eastern Main Rd, POB 174, Laventille, Port of Spain; tel. 623-2255; fax 623-2487; e-mail ccga@wow.net; internet www.ccga.co.tt; f. 1932; Pres. FELIX CLARK; Gen. Man. KENNETH DEBIQUE; 437 mems.

Pan Trinbago Inc: Victoria Park Suites, 14–17 Park St, Port of Spain; tel. 623-4486; fax 625-6715; e-mail admin@pantrinbago.co.tt; internet www.pantrinbago.co.tt; f. 1971; official body for Trinidad and Tobago steelbands; Pres. PATRICK LOUIS ARNOLD; Sec. RICHARD FORTEAU.

Shipping Association of Trinidad and Tobago: 15 Scott Bushe St, Port of Spain; tel. 623-3355; fax 623-8540; e-mail gm@shipping.co.tt; internet www.shipping.co.tt; f. 1938; Pres. HAYDN JONES; Gen. Man. E. JOANNE EDWARDS-ALLEYNE.

Sugar Association of the Caribbean: Brechin Castle, Couva; tel. 636-2449; fax 636-2847; f. 1942; promotes and protects sugar industry in the Caribbean; Chair. IAN MCDONALD; Sec. A. MOHAMMED; 6 mem. asscns.

Trinidad and Tobago Contractors' Association: Morequito Ave, Valsayn Park, Valsayn; tel. 637-2967; fax 637-2963; e-mail ttcaservice@rave-tt.net; internet www.ttca.com; f. 1968; represents contractors and manufacturers and suppliers to the sector; Pres. MIKEY JOSEPH.

Trinidad and Tobago Manufacturers' Association: 1TTMA Bldg, 42 Tenth Ave, Barataria; tel. 675-8862; fax 675-9000; e-mail info@ttma.com; internet www.ttma.com; f. 1956; Pres. KAREN DE MONTBRUN; 260 mems.

EMPLOYERS' ORGANIZATION

Employers' Consultative Association of Trinidad and Tobago (ECA): 23 Chacon St, Port of Spain; tel. 625-4723; fax 625-4891; e-mail ecatt@tstt.net.tt; internet www.ecatt.org; f. 1959; Chair. CLARENCE RAMBHARAT; CEO LINDA BESSON; 500 mems.

STATE HYDROCARBONS COMPANIES

National Gas Co of Trinidad and Tobago Ltd (NGC): Orinoco Dr., Point Lisas Industrial Estate, POB 1127, Port of Spain; tel. 636-4662; fax 679-2384; e-mail ngc@ngc.co.tt; internet www.ngc.co.tt; f. 1975; purchases, sells, compresses, transmits and distributes natural gas to consumers; Chair. KEITH AWONG; Pres. S. ANDREW MCINTOSH.

Petroleum Co of Trinidad and Tobago Ltd (Petrotrin): Petrotrin Administration Bldg, Cnr Queen's Park West and Cipriani Blvd, Port of Spain; tel. 625-5240; fax 624-4661; e-mail kharnanan@petrotrin.com; internet www.petrotrin.com; f. 1993 following merger between Trinidad and Tobago Oil Co Ltd (Trintoc) and Trinidad and Tobago Petroleum Co Ltd (Trintopec); govt-owned; petroleum and gas exploration and production; operates refineries and a manufacturing complex, producing a variety of petroleum and petrochemical products; Chair. MALCOLM JONES; Pres. WAYNE BERTRAND; Gen. Man. KAIN LOOK YEE.

Petrotrin Trinmar Operations: Petrotrin Administration Bldg, Point Fortin; tel. 648-2127; fax 648-2519; f. 1962; owned by Petrotrin; marine petroleum and natural gas co; Gen. Man. ALLAN RUSSELL; 705 employees.

Trintomar Ltd: Petrotrin Administration Bldg, Pointe-à-Pierre; tel. 647-8861; fax 647-3193; e-mail lisle.ramyad@petrotrin.com; f. 1988; 80% owned by EOG Resources, 20% owned by NGC; develops offshore petroleum sector; Man. LISLE RAMYAD.

UTILITIES

Regulatory Authority

Regulated Industries Commission: 90 Independence Sq., Port of Spain; tel. 627-0821; fax 624-2027; e-mail ricoffice@ric.org.tt; internet www.ric.org.tt; Chair. DENNIS PANTIN; Exec. Dir HARJINDER S. ATWAL.

Electricity

Power Generation Co of Trinidad and Tobago (PowerGen): 6A Queen's Park West, Port of Spain; tel. 624-0383; fax 625-3759; 51% owned by Trinidad and Tobago Electricity Commission; 39% owned by Mirant (USA); 10% owned by BP; operates 3 generation plants in Point Lisas, Port of Spain and Penal; Gen. Man. GARTH CHATOOR.

Trinidad and Tobago Electricity Commission (T&TEC): 63 Frederick St, POB 121, Port of Spain; tel. 623-2611; fax 623-3759; e-mail ttecisd@trinidad.net; internet www.ttec.co.tt; state-owned electricity transmission and distribution co; Chair. DEVANAND RAMLAL; Gen. Man. INDARJIT SINGH (acting).

Trinity Power Ltd: Railway Rd, Dow Village, Couva; tel. 679-4542; fax 679-4463; e-mail gthompson@trinitypm.com; jt venture by Power Management Co (51.1%) and Centennial Energy; fmrly Inncogen Ltd; Gen. Man. CELIA LOUGHEIDE.

Gas

National Gas Co of Trinidad and Tobago Ltd: see State Hydrocarbons Companies.

Water

Water and Sewerage Authority (WASA): Farm Rd, St Joseph; tel. 662-9272; fax 652-1253; internet www.wasa.gov.tt; Chair. Dr ROLLIN BERTRAND; CEO ERROL GRIMES.

TRADE UNIONS

Federation of Independent Trade Unions and NGOs (FITUN): Paramount Bldg, 99A Circular Rd, San Fernando; tel. 652-2701; fax 652-7170; e-mail fitun_tt@yahoo.com; f. 2003; Pres. DAVID ABDULLAH; Gen. Sec. MORTON MITCHELL.

National Trade Union Centre (NATUC): 16 New St, Port of Spain; tel. 625-3023; fax 627-7588; e-mail natuc@carib-link.net; f. 1991 as umbrella org. unifying entire trade-union movt, incl. former Trinidad and Tobago Labour Congress and Council of Progressive Trade Unions; Pres. ROBERT GIUSEPPI; Gen. Sec. VINCENT CARBERA.

Principal Affiliates

Airline Superintendents' Association: c/o Data Centre Bldg, Piarco International Airport, Port of Spain; tel. 664-3401; fax 664-3303; Pres. JEFFERSON JOSEPH; Gen. Sec. THEO OLIVER.

All-Trinidad Sugar and General Workers' Trade Union (ATSGWTU): Rienzi Complex, Exchange Village, Southern Main Rd, Couva; tel. 636-2354; fax 636-3372; e-mail atsgwtu@tstt.net.tt; f. 1937; Pres. RUDRANATH INDARSINGH; Gen. Sec. SYLVESTER MARAJH; 2,000 mems.

Amalgamated Workers' Union: 16 New St, Port of Spain; tel. 627-6717; fax 627-8993; f. 1953; Pres.-Gen. CYRIL LOPEZ; Sec. FLAVIUS NURSE; c. 7,000 mems.

Association of Technical, Administrative and Supervisory Staff: Brechin Castle, Couva; Pres. Dr WALLY DES VIGNES; Gen. Sec. ISAAC BEEPATH.

Aviation, Communication and Allied Workers' Union: Aero Services Bldg, Orange Grove Rd, Tacarigua; tel. and fax 640-6518; f. 1982; Pres. CHRISTOPHER ABRAHAM; Gen. Sec. SIEUNARINE BALROOP.

Banking, Insurance and General Workers' Union: 85 Eight Street, Barataria, Port of Spain; tel. 675-9135; fax 675-4664; e-mail union@bigwu.org; internet www.bigwu.org; f. 1974 as Bank and General Workers' Union; name changed as above following merger with Bank Employees' Union in 2003; Pres. VINCENT CABRERA; Gen. Sec. TREVOR JOHNSON.

Communication, Transport and General Workers' Trade Union: Aero Services Credit Union Bldg, Orange Grove Rd, Tacarigua; tel. and fax 640-8785; e-mail cattu@tstt.net.tt; Pres. JAGDEO JAGROOP; Gen. Sec. RAYMOND SMALL.

Communication Workers' Union: 146 Henry St, Port of Spain; tel. 623-5588; fax 625-3308; e-mail cwutdad@tstt.net.tt; f. 1953; Pres. PATRICK HALL; Gen. Sec. LYLE TOWNSEND; c. 2,100 mems.

Contractors' and General Workers' Trade Union (CGWTU): 37 Rushworth St, San Fernando; tel. 657-8072; fax 657-6834; Pres. OWEN HINDS; Gen. Sec. AINSLEY MATTHEWS.

Customs and Excise Extra Guard Association: Nicholas Court, Abercromby St, Port of Spain; tel. 625-3311; Pres. ALEXANDER BABB; Gen. Sec. NATHAN HERBERT.

Fire Service Association (FSA): 127 Edward St, Port of Spain; tel. 627-6700; fax 627-6701; Vice-Pres. MICHAEL SPENCER; Sec. SHARON NICHOLSON-CHARLES (acting).

National General Workers' Union: c/o 143 Charlotte St, Port of Spain; tel. 623-0694; Pres. JIMMY SINGH; Gen. Sec. CHRISTOPHER ABRAHAM.

National Union of Domestic Employees (NUDE): 53 Wattley Circular Rd, Mount Pleasant Rd, Arima; tel. 667-5247; fax 664-0546; e-mail domestic@tstt.net.tt; f. 1982; Gen. Sec. IDA LE BLANC.

National Union of Government and Federated Workers: 145–147 Henry St, Port of Spain; tel. 623-4591; fax 625-7756; e-mail headoffice@nugfw.org.tt; internet nugfw.org.tt; f. 1937; Pres. Gen. ROBERT GUISEPPI; Gen. Sec. JACQUELINE JACK; c. 20,000 mems.

Oilfield Workers' Trade Union (OWTU): Paramount Bldg, 99A Circular Rd, San Fernando; tel. 652-2701; fax 652-7170; e-mail owtu@owtu.org; internet www.owtu.org; f. 1937; Pres. (vacant); Gen. Sec. WENDY JOY WHITE; 9,000 mems.

Public Services Association: 89–91 Abercromby St, POB 353, Port of Spain; tel. 623-7987; fax 627-2980; e-mail psa@tstt.net.tt; f. 1938; Pres. JENNIFER BAPTISTE-PRIMUS; Sec. KAREN FERREIRA; c. 15,000 mems.

Seamen and Waterfront Workers' Trade Union: 1D Wrightson Rd, Port of Spain; tel. 625-1351; fax 625-1182; e-mail swwtu@tstt.net.tt; f. 1937; Pres.-Gen. MICHAEL ANNISETTE; Sec.-Gen. ROSS ALEXANDER; c. 3,000 mems.

Steel Workers' Union of Trinidad and Tobago: c/o ISPAT, Point Lisas, Couva; tel. 679-4666; fax 679-4175; e-mail swutt@tstt.net.tt; Pres. LEX LOVELL; Gen. Sec. PHILIP SANCHO.

Transport and Industrial Workers' Union: 114 Eastern Main Rd, Laventille, Port of Spain; tel. 623-4943; fax 623-2361; e-mail tiwu@tstt.net.tt; f. 1962; Pres. ROLAND SUTHERLAND; Gen. Sec. JUDY CHARLES; c. 5,000 mems.

Trinidad and Tobago Airline Pilots' Association (TTALPA): 35A Brunton Rd, St James; tel. 628-6556; fax 628-2418; e-mail info@ttalpa.org; internet www.ttalpa.org; Chair. Capt. ANTHONY WIGHT; Man. CHRISTINE DAVIS.

Trinidad and Tobago Postal Workers' Union: c/o General Post Office, Wrightson Rd, POB 692, Port of Spain; tel. 625-2121; fax 642-4303; Pres. (vacant); Gen. Sec. EVERALD SAMUEL.

Trinidad and Tobago Unified Teachers' Association: Cnr Fowler and Southern Main Rd, Curepe; tel. 645-2134; fax 662-1813; e-mail ttuta@trinidad.net; Pres. CLYDE PERMELL; Gen. Sec. DAVID LEWIS.

Union of Commercial and Industrial Workers: TIWU Bldg, 114 Eastern Main Rd, POB 460, Port of Spain; tel. and fax 626-2285; f. 1951; Pres. KELVIN GONZALES; Gen. Sec. ROSALIE FRASER; c. 1,500 mems.

Transport

RAILWAYS

In 2005 the Ministry of Works and Transport announced plans to reintroduce a railway service, which had been discontinued in 1968. The design phase of the project began in 2008 and construction was expected to take 10–15 years, costing an estimated TT $15,000m. Services on the first section of railway line, connecting Port of Spain, St Joseph and Chaguanas, were expected to commence in 2009.

ROADS

In 1999 there were 8,320 km (5,170 miles) of roads in Trinidad and Tobago, of which 51.1% were paved. In 2005 the Ministry of Works and Transport announced plans to invest some TT $140m. in building a 40-km highway to connect Princes Town to Mayaro. In the same year the US Agency for International Development allocated US $3.2m. to fund the repair of roads damaged by 'Hurricane Ivan' in 2004.

Public Transport Service Corporation: Railway Bldgs, South Quay, POB 391, Port of Spain; tel. 623-2341; fax 625-6502; f. 1965; national bus services, operates a fleet of buses; CEO EDISON ISAAC.

SHIPPING

The chief ports are Port of Spain, Pointe-à-Pierre and Point Lisas in Trinidad and Scarborough in Tobago. Port of Spain handles 85% of all container traffic, and all international cruise arrivals. In 1998 Port of Spain handled 3.3m. metric tons of cargo. Port of Spain and Scarborough each have a deep-water wharf. Port of Spain possesses a dedicated container terminal, with two large overhead cranes. Plans were put in place in 2002 for an expansion of operations, through the purchase of an additional crane, the computerization of operations, and the deepening of the harbour (from 9.75 m to 12 m).

Caribbean Drydock Ltd: Port Chaguaramas, Western Main Rd, Chaguaramas; tel. 634-4226; fax 625-1215; ship repair, marine transport, barge and boat construction.

Point Lisas Industrial Port Development Corporation Ltd (PLIPDECO): see Trade and Industry—Development Organizations.

Port Authority of Trinidad and Tobago: Dock Rd, POB 549, Port of Spain; tel. 623-2901; fax 627-2666; e-mail vilmal@patnt.com; internet www.patnt.com; f. 1962; Chair. DEREK HUDSON; CEO CHRISTOPHER MENDEZ.

Shipping Association of Trinidad and Tobago: 15 Scott Bushe St, Port of Spain; tel. 623-3355; fax 623-8570; e-mail satt@wow.net; internet shipping.co.tt; Pres. HAYDN JONES; Gen. Man. JENNIFER GONZÁLEZ.

CIVIL AVIATION

Piarco International Airport is situated 25.7 km (16 miles) south-east of Port of Spain and is used by numerous airlines. The airport was expanded and a new terminal was constructed in 2001. Piarco remains the principal air transportation facility in Trinidad and Tobago. However, following extensive aerodrome development at Crown Point Airport (located 13 km from Scarborough) in 1992 the airport was opened to jet aircraft. It is now officially named Crown Point International Airport. There is a domestic service between Trinidad and Tobago.

Airports Authority of Trinidad and Tobago (AATT): Airport Administration Centre, Caroni North Bank Rd, Piarco; tel. 669-5311; fax 669-2319; e-mail aatt@tntairports.com; internet www.tntairports.com; administers Piarco and Crown Point International Airports; Chair. JOHN ECKSTEIN; Gen. Man. SANDRA PERKINS (acting).

Caribbean Airlines: Sunjet House, 30 Edward St, Port of Spain; tel. 625-7200; e-mail mail@caribbean-airlines.com; internet www.caribbean-airlines.com; f. 2007 as successor to BWIA (f. 1940); operates scheduled passenger and cargo services linking destinations in the Caribbean region, South America, North America and Europe; CEO PHILIP SAUNDERS; Chair. ARTHUR LOK JACK.

Tourism

The climate and coastline attract visitors to Trinidad and Tobago. The latter island is generally believed to be the more beautiful and is less developed. The annual pre-Lenten carnival is a major attraction. In 2006 there were 457,434 foreign visitors, excluding cruise ship passengers. Tourism receipts were estimated at US $357m. in 2006. In 2000 there were an estimated 104,061 cruise-ship passenger arrivals. However, this declined to 67,196 by 2005 before increasing to 85,677 in 2006. There were 3,815 hotel rooms in Trinidad and Tobago in 2008, of which 57.5% were on Tobago.

Tourism Development Co of Trinidad and Tobago (TDC): Maritime Centre, Level 1, 29 Tenth Ave, Barataria; tel. 675-7034; fax 675-7722; e-mail info@tdc.co.tt; internet www.tdc.co.tt; f. 1993 as Tourism and Industrial Devt Co of Trinidad and Tobago; restructured and renamed as above in 2005; Chair. DAVID LEWIS; Pres. ERNEST M. LITTLES.

Trinidad Hotels, Restaurants and Tourism Association (THRTA): c/o Trinidad & Tobago Hospitality and Tourism Institute, Airway Rd, Chaguaramas; tel. 634-1174; fax 634-1176; e-mail info@tnthotels.com; internet www.tnthotels.com; Pres. KEVIN KENNY; Exec. Dir GREER ASSAM.

Tobago Hotel and Tourism Association: Apt 1, Lambeau Credit Union Bldg, Auchenskeoch, Carnbee; tel. and fax 639-9543; e-mail tthtatob@tstt.net.tt; Pres. CAROL ANN BIRCHWOOD-JAMES.

TUNISIA

Introductory Survey

Location, Climate, Language, Religion, Flag, Capital

The Republic of Tunisia lies in north Africa, bordered by Algeria to the west and by Libya to the south-east. To the north and east, Tunisia has a coastline on the Mediterranean Sea. The climate is temperate on the coast, with winter rain, but hot and dry inland. Temperatures in Tunis are generally between 6°C (43°F) and 33°C (91°F). The country's highest recorded temperature is 55°C. Average annual rainfall is up to 1,500 mm in the north, but less than 200 mm in the southern desert. The official language is Arabic, and there is a small Berber Tamazight-speaking minority. French is widely used as a second language. Islam is the state religion, and almost all of the inhabitants are Muslims. There are small minorities of Christians and Jews. The national flag (proportions 2 by 3) is red, with a white disc, containing a red crescent moon and a five-pointed red star, in the centre. The capital is Tunis.

Recent History

Formerly a French protectorate, Tunisia was granted internal self-government by France in September 1955 and full independence on 20 March 1956. Five days later elections were held for a Constitutional Assembly, which met in April and appointed Habib Bourguiba as Prime Minister in a Government dominated by members of his Néo-Destour (New Constitution) Party. In July 1957 a republic was established, with Bourguiba as Head of State, and a new Constitution was promulgated in June 1959. At elections held in November Bourguiba was elected unopposed to the new office of President, and the Néo-Destour Party won all 90 seats in the new National Assembly.

By 1964 the Néo-Destour Party had become the only legal political organization and in November of that year it was renamed the Parti socialiste destourien (PSD). A moderate socialist economic programme was introduced, which began with the expropriation of foreign-owned lands. However, attempts to introduce agricultural collectivization in 1964–69, under the direction of Ahmad Ben Salah, Minister of Finance and Planning, were abandoned in September 1969 because of resistance from the rural population. Ben Salah was dismissed, arrested and subsequently sentenced to 10 years' hard labour. He escaped in 1973 and fled to Europe, from where he organized the radical Mouvement de l'unité populaire (MUP). In 1970 Hédi Nouira, hitherto Governor of the Banque Centrale de Tunisie, was appointed Prime Minister. He began to reverse Ben Salah's socialist economic policies, with the introduction of liberal economic reforms in the sectors of industry and agriculture.

Liberalization of the economy was not accompanied by political reform, and the extensive powers of Nouira and Bourguiba were increasingly challenged by younger PSD members in the early 1970s. However, at the 1974 PSD Congress, Bourguiba was elected President-for-Life of the PSD and Nouira was confirmed as Secretary-General. In March 1975, after approving the necessary amendments to the Constitution, the National Assembly elected Bourguiba President-for-Life of Tunisia. Political differences emerged concerning economic policy, and the previously loyal trade union movement, the Union Générale Tunisienne du Travail (UGTT), led by Habib Achour, began to assert its independence from the PSD. In January 1978, for the first time since independence, a 24-hour general strike took place, organized by the UGTT. In violent clashes between troops and strikers, at least 50 people were killed and many trade union leaders, including Achour, were arrested. Subsequently Achour was sentenced to 10 years' hard labour and a new Secretary-General of the UGTT, Tijani Abid, declared the willingness of trade unions to co-operate with the Government.

In April 1980 Nouira resigned, owing to ill health, and was succeeded as Prime Minister and Secretary-General of the PSD by Muhammad Mzali. Under Mzali, signs of greater political tolerance became apparent. The one-party system ended in mid-1981, when the Parti communiste tunisien (PCT), which had been proscribed in 1963, was granted legal status. The Government announced that any political group that gained more than 5% of the votes cast in the forthcoming legislative elections would also be officially recognized. Many of the UGTT leaders imprisoned after the 1978 disturbances were pardoned, and Achour was reappointed Secretary-General of the UGTT. At elections to the National Assembly in November 1981 the PSD and the UGTT formed an electoral alliance, the Front national, which received 94.6% of the total votes cast and won all 126 seats in the new Assembly.

In July 1986 Mzali was replaced as Prime Minister by Rachid Sfar (hitherto Minister of Finance), and was dismissed as Secretary-General of the PSD. Mzali subsequently fled to Algeria, and was sentenced *in absentia* to terms of imprisonment and hard labour for defamatory comments against Tunisian leaders and mismanagement of public funds. Elections to the National Assembly in November were boycotted by the opposition parties, with the result that the PSD, opposed only by 15 independent candidates, won all 125 seats.

During late 1987 President Bourguiba's behaviour became increasingly erratic. In October he revoked several of his recent appointments of leading state officials, and dismissed Sfar from the premiership. Zine al-Abidine Ben Ali was appointed Prime Minister and Secretary-General of the PSD; he retained the interior portfolio, which he had held since 1986. On 7 November 1987 seven doctors declared that President Bourguiba was unfit to govern, owing to senility and ill health. In accordance with the Constitution, Ben Ali was sworn in as President. Hédi Baccouche (previously Minister of Social Affairs) was appointed Prime Minister, and a new Council of Ministers was formed, which excluded several close associates of Bourguiba. Ben Ali announced plans to reform the Constitution and to permit greater political freedom. In the same month the Government permitted the publication of previously suspended opposition newspapers, and by early 1988 some 3,000 political and non-political detainees had been released. In February the PSD was renamed the Rassemblement constitutionnel démocratique (RCD), in order to reflect the new administration's commitment to democratic reform.

In April 1988 legislation was enacted by the National Assembly to institute a multi-party political system, and in July the Assembly approved a series of proposals to reform the Constitution. The office of President-for-Life was abolished, and the President was, henceforth, to be elected by universal suffrage every five years and limited to two consecutive terms of office. In the same month there was a significant reorganization of the Government, notably affecting ministers who had served under Bourguiba. In September two further opposition parties, the left-wing Rassemblement socialiste progressiste and the liberal Parti social pour le progrès (renamed the Parti social libéral—PSL—in 1993) were legalized. In November the Government claimed that there were no longer any political prisoners in Tunisia, a total of 8,000 people having been released during the first year of Ben Ali's regime.

Ben Ali was nominated as the sole candidate (supported by all the officially recognized parties) for the presidential election of 2 April 1989, and was duly elected President, receiving 99.3% of the votes cast. In legislative elections the RCD won all 141 seats in the National Assembly, with some 80% of the votes cast. The fundamentalist Hizb an-Nahdah or the Parti de la renaissance (whose candidates contested the election as independents, since the party was not officially recognized), won some 13% of the votes cast, but failed to win any seats under an electoral system that favoured the ruling party. In September Ben Ali dismissed Prime Minister Baccouche, following a disagreement concerning the Government's economic policy, and appointed Hamed Karoui, the former Minister of Justice, in his place.

In May 1990 the National Assembly approved a reformed electoral code, introducing a system of partial proportional representation for forthcoming municipal elections. The winning party was to receive 50% of the seats, while the remainder were to be distributed among all the parties, according to the number of votes received by each one. However, the six legal opposition parties boycotted the elections, held in June, arguing that they were neither free nor fair. Consequently, the RCD won control of all but one of the 245 municipal councils.

Ben Ali stated in December 1991 that changes to the electoral system, to be formulated in consultation with opposition parties, would be implemented during 1992, with the aim of ensuring greater representation at the national level for parties other than the RCD. In December 1992 Ben Ali announced a revision of the electoral code, to include the introduction of partial proportional representation at legislative elections scheduled for March 1994. However, this apparent willingness to co-operate with the legalized opposition was accompanied by further repression of the Islamist movement, with increased censorship of publications sympathetic to their cause, and the harassment of suspected activists.

In March 1992 the human rights organization Amnesty International published a report which detailed the arrests of some 8,000 suspected an-Nahdah members over an 18-month period, and cited 200 cases of the torture and ill-treatment of detainees. It also claimed that at least seven Islamists had died while in custody. The Government initially denied the allegations, but later conceded that some violations of human rights had occurred. In mid-March it was announced that human rights 'units' were to be established within the Ministries of Foreign Affairs, Justice and the Interior, although new restrictions were imposed on the activities of unofficial, quasi-political groups such as the Ligue tunisienne des droits de l'homme (LTDH). In the same month an amnesty was granted to more than 1,000 detainees. In July and August the trials were held in Tunis of 171 alleged members of an-Nahdah, and of 108 alleged members of the organization's military wing, who were all accused of conspiring to overthrow the Government; 46 of the defendants were sentenced to life imprisonment, 16, including Rachid Ghannouchi, the leader of an-Nahdah, *in absentia*. (In 1993 Ghannouchi was granted political asylum in the United Kingdom.) Prison sentences of between one and 24 years were imposed on the remainder. In October appeals on behalf of 265 of those convicted were rejected, and another 20 an-Nahdah sympathizers were reportedly arrested in police raids.

There were indications in 1993 of a revival of political activity, and in April a new political organization, the Mouvement du renouveau (MR—Ettajdid, now known as the Mouvement ettajdid), held its first Congress. In November Ben Ali announced that presidential and legislative elections were to take place in March 1994. His candidacy for the presidency was supported not only by the RCD, but also by most of the legal opposition parties. In January 1994 the National Assembly adopted reforms to the electoral code: thenceforth 19 of the 163 seats in the enlarged Assembly were to be allocated to opposition parties in proportion to their overall national vote. At the presidential election, which took place concurrently with the legislative elections on 20 March 1994, Ben Ali was re-elected President, receiving 99.9% of the votes cast. The RCD received 97.7% of the total votes cast in the legislative elections, securing all 144 seats that were contested under a simple majority system. Of the 19 seats reserved for opposition candidates, the Mouvement des démocrates socialistes (MDS) secured 10, the MR four, the Union démocratique unioniste (UDU) three and the Parti de l'unité populaire (PUP) two.

In October 1995 Muhammad Mouada, the MDS Secretary-General, was arrested and accused of having received money from an unnamed foreign country. The previous day Mouada had, in an open letter to the President, criticized the lack of political freedom in Tunisia; however, government officials denied any connection between the letter and Mouada's arrest. In late October the Tunisian authorities prevented Khemais Chamari, an MDS member of the National Assembly, from travelling to Malta to attend an international conference on human rights. In the following month Chamari's parliamentary immunity was withdrawn, in order to allow judicial charges (relating to Mouada's trial) to be brought against him. Meanwhile, in an apparently conciliatory gesture towards the opposition, Ben Ali pardoned the leader of the Parti communiste des ouvriers tunisiens (PCOT), Hamma Hammami, who had been imprisoned in April 1994, and his associate Muhammad Kilani, the former editor of the PCOT journal. (Nevertheless, Hammami apparently remained the object of official harassment, and in July 1999 he was given a nine-year prison sentence *in absentia* for belonging to an illegal organization. However, having commenced a hunger strike to protest against his subsequent imprisonment in 2002, Hammami was released on health grounds in September of that year.) Meanwhile, in February 1996 Mouada was sentenced to two years' imprisonment for 'illegal detention of currency'. Although a court of appeal subsequently reduced his term by one year, at the end of the month Mouada was sentenced to 11 years' imprisonment for maintaining links with and receiving money from Libya. In July Chamari was sentenced to five years' imprisonment for breaching security proceedings relating to Mouada's trial. Human rights organizations protested at the severity of the sentence and appealed to the Tunisian authorities to release all political detainees. In December Mouada and Chamari were released conditionally on humanitarian grounds.

In December 1996 Ben Ali announced plans to amend the electoral law, which, *inter alia*, would lower the minimum eligible age of candidates for the National Assembly (from 25 to 23 years) and increase the representation of legal opposition parties in the Assembly and in municipal councils. Political parties would not be permitted to be based on religion, language, race or region, nor to have foreign links. The scope of referendums was also to be widened. In December 1997 the Council of Ministers reached consensus on draft legislation to amend the electoral law.

In January 1999 draft legislation was presented to the National Assembly to introduce extraordinary provisions to the Constitution which would allow pluralism in the presidential election scheduled for that year. The amendments, which were approved in March, allowed for the leaders of all political parties to contest the presidency provided that they had held their current leadership position for at least five consecutive years, and that their party was represented by one or more deputies in the legislature. (Hitherto opposition parties had been unable to present candidates, owing to the requirement that they be supported by at least 30 deputies in the Assembly.) Despite the new provisions, only two leaders of opposition parties were eligible to contest the presidency, namely Abderrahmane Tlili (UDU) and Muhammad Belhadj Amor (PUP). Ben Ali had himself been re-elected Chairman of the RCD at a party congress in July 1998, when he had been formally nominated as the party's presidential candidate.

The first contested presidential election since independence was held on 24 October 1999. As expected, Ben Ali comprehensively defeated his two rivals, securing 99.5% of the vote. Voter participation was officially estimated at 91.4%. At concurrent elections to the National Assembly the RCD won all of the 148 seats contested under a simple majority system. Of the 34 seats reserved for opposition candidates, 13 were won by the MDS, the UDU and the PUP both took seven seats, the MR won five and the PSL two. Some 91.5% of the electorate voted, according to official sources. In November the President effected a major government reorganization: Hamed Karoui was replaced as Prime Minister by Muhammad Ghannouchi (previously Minister of International Co-operation and Foreign Investment) and Abdallah Kallel succeeded Ali Chaouch as Minister of the Interior. At municipal elections held in May 2000 the RCD won more than 94% of the 4,128 seats being contested, and maintained control over all local councils.

In June 2000 the President of the Conseil national pour les libertés en Tunisie (CNLT), Moncef Marzouki, visited London, United Kingdom, where he reportedly held talks with the leader of an-Nahdah, Rachid Ghannouchi, and proposed future co-operation between secular and Islamist factions of the Tunisian opposition. In December Marzouki received a one-year prison sentence, having been convicted of belonging to an illegal group and of disseminating false information. His sentence was suspended in September 2001 by the court of appeal, although his civil rights were not restored. In December, shortly after the ban on his leaving Tunisia had been revoked, Marzouki departed for France.

Meanwhile, in November 2000 President Ben Ali announced a number of initiatives aimed at furthering the democratization process and promoting human rights in Tunisia. The measures included: state compensation for detainees held in police custody without reasonable grounds; the transfer of responsibility for the prison system from the Ministry of the Interior to the Ministry of Justice; new legislation to improve conditions in prisons and to reduce censorship of the press; and an increase, by 50%, in government subsidies allocated for other political parties and their publications.

At the fifth congress of the LTDH, held in October 2000, a new executive board was elected, with Mokhtar Trifi, an outspoken critic of the Ben Ali regime, as President. Four former members of the board subsequently filed a suit against the new leadership, claiming that, owing to procedural irregularities, it was invalid, and in November a court imposed a moratorium on the activities of the LTDH. The Tunisian Government denied having ordered the ruling, but was strongly criticized by international and local human rights groups for its perceived role in the affair. Trial proceedings against the LTDH began in January 2001, and in the following month a judgment was issued that the results of the October congress should be invalidated. In March Trifi was charged with dissemination of false information and violation of the recent court ruling; however, in June the court of appeal ruled that the LTDH could resume its activities and ordered it to hold another congress within a year.

In March 2001 more than 250 human rights activists in Tunisia produced a petition that demanded wide-ranging democratic reforms in the country prior to the presidential and legislative elections scheduled for 2004. In the same month some 100 moderate figures in civil society signed a separate petition accusing Ben Ali of corruption and nepotism and denouncing his plans to amend the Constitution so as to permit him to seek a fourth term in office. In April an-Nahdah released a joint communiqué with Mouada's faction of the MDS, proposing the formation of an opposition coalition to unite Islamists and liberals against the Ben Ali regime. Later that month the President instructed the Ministry of the Interior to investigate all alleged abuses by the security forces against Tunisian citizens and to ensure that those found guilty were punished; however, the detention and imprisonment of several leading opponents of the regime continued. Meanwhile, in late April the National Assembly approved revisions to the press code under which the offence of 'defamation of public order' was abolished. The amendments also removed the threat of prison sentences for certain violations of the code. The changes were, however, condemned as inadequate by the Association des journalistes tunisiens.

The central committee of the ruling RCD announced in September 2001 that it would formally propose changes to the country's Constitution in order to enable Ben Ali to seek a fourth presidential term. In April 2002 members of the National Assembly overwhelmingly approved a constitutional reform bill, and at a referendum held on 26 May, according to official figures, the constitutional changes were approved by 99.5% of voters; the rate of voter participation was officially recorded at 95.6%. The amendments raised the age limit for presidential candidates from 70 to 75 years, and removed the limit on the number of terms that could be served by a President. In August 2003 the changes were promulgated and Ben Ali formally announced his intention to stand for a fourth term at elections scheduled for late 2004. Provision was also made for the creation of a second legislative chamber, to be called the Chamber of Advisers, for the establishment of a two-round presidential election system and for a number of measures that would improve civil liberties and public freedoms.

In April 2002 a tanker lorry exploded outside a synagogue on the island of Djerba, causing the deaths of 21 people, most of whom were German tourists. The driver of the lorry was among those killed. The Tunisian authorities initially claimed that the explosion had been an accident, but a spokesman for the Israeli Ministry of Foreign Affairs insisted that it was an anti-Semitic terrorist attack. The Tunisian authorities subsequently confirmed that the explosion had been a 'premeditated criminal act'. A number of Arabic newspapers immediately carried claims that the al-Qa'ida (Base) organization of Osama bin Laden—the principal suspect in the September 2001 attacks on New York and Washington, DC—was responsible. In June 2002 the Qatar-based satellite television station Al-Jazeera broadcast a statement by a spokesman for al-Qa'ida, asserting that the attack had been perpetrated in the name of al-Qa'ida in protest against Israel's recent military offensive against Palestinian-controlled areas of the West Bank. In November eight people were arrested in Lyon, France, in connection with the explosion, while in early 2003 several arrests took place in Spain, France and Saudi Arabia. In May 2007 two men were sentenced to five years' imprisonment each by a court in Madrid, Spain, for their role in the financing of the attack; in June the uncle of the lorry driver was sentenced to 20 years in gaol by a court in Tunis for helping to prepare the explosion. The trial of three men (including the principal suspect in the September 2001 attacks, Khalid Sheikh Muhammad) for their alleged involvement in the Djerba synagogue explosion began in France in early January 2009; two of the men were subsequently sentenced to prison sentences of 18 and 12 years. However, it was ordered that a ruling on Sheikh Muhammad, who was in US custody in Guantánamo Bay, Cuba, be postponed until he could appear before the court in person.

In January 2003 Ben Ali announced the merger of a number of ministries, reducing them in number from 29 to 25, in an attempt to improve efficiency in government operations. The most notable changes were the creation of a Ministry of Justice and Human Rights and of a Ministry of Employment. Ben Ali carried out a further minor reshuffle of the Council of Ministers in January 2004 and another limited reorganization of the Government took place in March. Muhammad Rachid Kechiche was appointed Minister of Finance in place of Munir Jeidan, who assumed Kechiche's previous post of Government Secretary-General in charge of Relations with the Chamber of Deputies and the Chamber of Advisers.

In July 2003 Abdallah Zouari, an Islamist journalist who had been released from detention in June 2002, having served an 11-year sentence for 'belonging to an illegal organization', was sentenced to four months' imprisonment for libel; in August 2003 Zouari received a further nine-month term for 'failing to obey an administrative order'. Between October and December Radhia Nasraoui, a prominent Tunisian human rights lawyer, undertook a hunger strike in protest against what she alleged was harassment by the authorities, claiming that she had been targeted because she had defended political prisoners and had accused the Government of using torture against opposition activists.

In the months prior to the 2004 presidential election, a group of opposition figures, including Moncef Marzouki, now the leader of the Congrès pour la République, urged President Ben Ali to step down and the Constitution to be amended so as to prevent the President from remaining in office indefinitely. Ben Ali responded by addressing members of the RCD in July 2004 and assuring them that the elections would be held 'within a context of transparency and the respect of law', while requesting that foreign observers be present at the elections. By mid-September four candidates had officially registered to run for President—namely Ben Ali, Muhammad Bouchiha of the PUP, Mounir Béji of the PSL and Muhammad Ali Halouani of the MR. The Parti démocrate progressiste (PDP) announced in mid-October that it was withdrawing its candidates for the legislative elections in protest at what it considered an illegitimate electoral process in which it was denied access to the media and faced serious delays in having its manifesto approved. The presidential election took place on 24 October; Ben Ali received 94.49% of the votes cast, while Bouchiha secured 3.78%, Halouani 0.95% and Béji 0.79%. Voter turn-out was officially estimated at 91.5%. At the legislative elections, which took place concurrently, the RCD won all of the 152 seats contested under a simple majority system, 25% of which would be occupied by women under new legislation, while of the 37 reserved for the opposition, the MDS won 14 seats, the PUP 11, the UDU seven, and the MR and PSL three and two seats, respectively. In November Ben Ali announced a major reshuffle of the Council of Ministers, appointing new Ministers of National Defence, of Foreign Affairs and of the Interior and Local Development, and creating new Ministries of Transport and of Environment and Land Planning.

A report published in July 2004 by the US-based Human Rights Watch criticized the Government's treatment of political prisoners, many of whom, it claimed, had spent several years in solitary confinement, and urged the Tunisian authorities to allow domestic and international monitors to inspect prison standards. In April 2004, meanwhile, eight young people were arrested and sentenced to between 19 and 26 years' imprisonment for using the internet to plan terrorist activities (although six subsequently had their sentences reduced to 13 years). In June the leader of the UDU, Abderrahmane Tlili, was imprisoned for nine years, after being convicted of abusing his position while he was head of the Office de l'Aviation Civile et des Aéroports. In November President Ben Ali pardoned 80 Islamist prisoners. A further 20 Islamist convicts were freed in July 2007 as part of an amnesty to mark the 50th anniversary of the Tunisian republic, including three former leaders of the banned an-Nahdah party.

At a meeting of the Central Committee of the RCD in February 2005, Ben Ali announced plans to create a national electoral observatory in time for the forthcoming municipal elections. Held on 8 May, the RCD won 4,098 of the 4,366 council seats contested at the municipal elections. In July elections were first held to the new Chamber of Advisers, as provided for by the constitutional amendments of 2002. The new second chamber was composed of 126 members, of whom 43 were indirectly elected by municipal councillors and parliamentary deputies (as representatives of the regions) and 42 by the main professional federations and trade unions; the remaining 41 members were appointed by the President. All 43 regional representatives elected were RCD candidates. The Chamber of Advisers held its inaugural session in October, and Abdullah Kallel was elected as Speaker; however, 14 seats remained vacant after the UGTT refused to elect its members to the new chamber. Meanwhile, in August Ben Ali effected a major reshuffle of the Council of Ministers: Abdelwahab Abdallah, a former principal adviser to the President, was appointed Minister of Foreign Affairs and Kamel Morjane received the defence portfolio. Ali Chaouch, the former interior minister, assumed the post of Minister of Social Affairs, Solidarity and Tunisians Abroad and was succeeded as Secretary-General of the RCD by Morjane's predecessor, Hédi M'henni. A further reorganization was announced by Ben Ali in September 2007, which included the appointment of Mondher Zenaïdi as Minister of Public Health and Sarra Kanoun Jarraya as Minister of Women's, Family, Children's and Elderly Affairs.

In September and October 2006 the Tunisian authorities increasingly began to take action against the wearing of the Islamic headscarf, following public comments by Ben Ali and other senior politicians that it was a 'sectarian' form of dress that was not native to the country. (President Bourguiba had introduced a ban on headscarves in schools and government offices in 1981.) Also in October 2006 Tunisia closed its embassy in Qatar in protest at an interview with Moncef Marzouki broadcast by Al-Jazeera, in which he spoke against the Government's human rights record and advocated a campaign of civil resistance. In January 2007 the Minister of the Interior and Local Development, Rafik Belhaj Kacem, confirmed that police had shot dead 14 members of a suspected militant Islamist organization and arrested a number of others in Soliman, near Tunis. Two members of the security forces were killed during the operation. Kacem reported that the group, which had been assembled by six militants who had entered the country from Algeria and which was suspected of having links to the Algerian Groupe salafiste pour la prédication et le combat (which in that month restyled itself as 'al-Qa'ida in the Islamic Maghreb—AQIM, see the chapter on Algeria), had been in possession of explosives and details of foreign embassies and diplomatic staff in Tunis. In January 2008 a court in Tunisia issued its judgment on the suspected militants: two of the defendants were handed down death penalties, eight were sentenced to life imprisonment, and a further 20 received prison terms ranging from five to 30 years. The LTDH subsequently issued a statement concluding that, while violence was unacceptable as a means of political expression, the proceedings had lacked the 'minimum conditions' necessary for a fair trial.

In September 2007 two leading members of the PDP went on a hunger strike to protest against legal efforts to evict the party and its official weekly newspaper, Al-Mawkif, from their premises for alleged violation of the lease agreement. PDP Secretary-General Maya Jribi and Al-Mawkif Managing Director Ahmed Néjib Chebbi ended their hunger strike a month later, when the owner of the party offices abandoned a lawsuit against the party and sanctioned a new lease agreement. The outcome was hailed by Jribi as a victory for the Tunisian people in their 'struggle for freedom'. None the less, it was reported in April 2008 that the distribution of Al-Mawkif was being prevented by the authorities, with some sources claiming that this apparent official censorship of the newspaper was linked to Chebbi's declared intention to contest the presidential election scheduled for 2009. Al-Mawkif's Editor-in-Chief and its Publications Director also went on a hunger strike later that month to protest against these alleged restrictions on the publication and distribution of the newspaper. However, they suspended their strike after two weeks following a return to normal patterns of distribution for Al-Mawkif.

Meanwhile, in November 2007 Ben Ali made a speech in front of a large audience in Radès to mark the 20th anniversary of his accession to power. The Tunisian President used the occasion to propose a reduction in the voting age, from 20 to 18 years, and an amendment of the electoral law to preclude any single party from holding more than 75% of seats in municipal councils. During the speech Ben Ali announced a range of measures designed to promote democracy and human rights in the country; these included increasing the level of funding allocated to opposition parties and their press. None the less, in May 2008 the recently founded Syndicat National des Journalistes Tunisiens (SNJT—which replaced the pro-Government Association des Journalistes Tunisiens) made renewed demands for a review of media regulations in line with international standards of press freedom. This followed the publication of an SNJT report which detailed the various alleged violations of journalists' rights that had occurred in the previous year. The SNJT repeated its demands in early February 2009, after the Government banned an edition of the daily newspaper At-Tariq al-Jadid that reproduced the transcript of a legal case. This, together with the forced closure of a Tunisian radio station a few days earlier, was considered to be further evidence of a significantly compromised level of media freedom in the country. Nevertheless, in a message sent by Ben Ali to the SNJT on the occasion of World Press Freedom Day in early May, the President pledged his commitment to granting 'due attention to the concerns and aspirations of the Tunisian media community'.

In late July 2008 President Ben Ali was unanimously re-elected by the RCD congress as Chairman of the party. He thereby effectively became the RCD candidate for the presidential election scheduled to take place in October 2009. Ben Ali's apparent intention to run for a fifth presidential term immediately began to provoke speculation regarding his intention to make himself President for Life (a designation abolished in 1988). Also at the congress, the President announced a series of modifications to the structure of the RCD, among them a reduction in the number of vice-chairmen from two to one, and efforts to recruit new, younger members to the party. At the end of August Ben Ali effected a reorganization of the Council of Ministers, appointing six new ministers. Notably, Slim Tletli, hitherto a presidential adviser, was appointed as Minister of Employment and Professional Integration of Youth, while Abdessalem Mansour, a former banking executive, assumed the post of Minister for Agriculture and Water Resources. Several new secretaries of state were also appointed.

As part of celebrations to mark the 21st anniversary of his accession to the presidency, on 7 November 2008 Ben Ali pardoned 21 imprisoned members of an-Nahdah (said to be the last remaining group of detainees from the banned party); a further 23 prisoners were also reported to have been pardoned. While human rights organizations generally responded with cautious optimism to the release of prisoners, they none the less expressed concerns regarding the infringement of liberties routinely encountered by political prisoners upon their release, and urged a wider amnesty for all detainees imprisoned for non-violent political convictions and practices.

In anticipation of the legislative and presidential elections due later in the year, in March 2009 the Chamber of Deputies adopted a series of amendments to the electoral code (first proposed by Ben Ali in November 2007—see above). The amendments, which were subsequently promulgated by the President in April 2009, were intended to promote greater plurality and ensure increased electoral transparency and participation. Notable among the new measures were an increase in the proportion of seats allocated to the opposition in the Chamber of Deputies from 20% to 25%, and the imposition of a 75% upper limit on the share of seats that could be obtained by any one list in the municipal councils (regardless of the number of votes obtained). The age of eligibility to vote was to be reduced from 20 years to 18.

Relations with the other countries of the Maghreb improved considerably in the 1980s. A meeting between President Bourguiba and President Ben Djedid Chadli of Algeria in March 1983 led to the drafting of the Maghreb Fraternity and Co-operation Treaty, which envisaged the eventual creation of a Greater Maghreb Union, and was signed by Mauritania in December. In January 1988 Tunisia and Algeria held further discussions on the establishment of a greater Arab Maghreb, and in April border restrictions between Tunisia and Libya were removed. In February 1989, at a meeting of North African heads of state in Morocco, a treaty was concluded that proclaimed the Union of the Arab Maghreb (Union du Maghreb arabe—UMA, see p. 429), comprising Algeria, Libya, Mauritania, Morocco and Tunisia. The treaty envisaged: the establishment of a council of heads of state; regular meetings of ministers responsible for foreign affairs; and, eventually, the free movement of goods, people, services and capital throughout the countries of the region.

In 1982 President Bourguiba permitted the Palestine Liberation Organization (PLO) to establish its headquarters near Tunis. In October 1985 Israeli aircraft attacked the PLO headquarters, causing the deaths of some 72 people, including 12 Tunisians. US support for the right of Israel to retaliate (the attack was a reprisal for the murder of three Israeli citizens in Cyprus) severely strained relations between Tunisia and the USA. In April 1988 Abu Jihad, the military commander of the

PLO, was assassinated at his home in Tunis. The Tunisian Government blamed Israel for the murder, and complained to the UN Security Council. The PLO transferred its offices to Gaza in mid-1994, following the signing of the PLO-Israeli Cairo Agreement on implementing Palestinian self-rule in the Gaza Strip and Jericho.

In January 1988 the Tunisian Government announced that diplomatic relations with Egypt, which had been severed in 1979, would be resumed. In March 1990 Ben Ali made the first visit to Cairo by a Tunisian President since 1965, and signed several agreements on bilateral co-operation. In September 1990 a majority of members of the League of Arab States (the Arab League, see p. 344) resolved to move the League's headquarters from Tunis (where it had been established 'temporarily' in 1979) to its original site in Cairo: the Tunisian Government protested at the decision.

Tunisia assumed the annual presidency of the UMA in January 1993. The Government made clear its determination to reactivate the process of Maghreb union, as well as dialogue with the European Community (now European Union—EU, see p. 255). In April 1994 the UMA ratified 11 agreements designed to improve co-operation and trade within the Maghreb. However, tensions between the UMA's member states subsequently undermined the activities of the Union. In March 1999 Ben Ali made his first official visit to Morocco, during which he pledged to strengthen relations with that country, and to revive the UMA. A summit meeting of ministers responsible for foreign affairs of the five UMA member states was arranged, and proceeded in the Algerian capital in March 2001. However, the meeting, which was to have made preparations for the first summit meeting of UMA heads of state since 1995, quickly broke down owing to disagreements between Moroccan and Algerian representatives. Following several further unsuccessful attempts to co-ordinate a summit meeting, in April 2008 celebrations were held in Tangier, Morocco, to mark the 50th anniversary of the summit at which the idea of a union of Arab Maghreb states was first proposed. The event ended with renewed calls for greater regional collaboration and a regalvanized UMA. A year later delegates responsible for foreign affairs from the UMA member states met in Tripoli, Libya, where they reiterated their commitment to improving political and economic co-operation among the countries of North Africa.

Relations with Algeria improved appreciably after the second round of Algerian elections, at which the fundamentalist Front islamique du salut (FIS) had been expected to secure victory, was suspended in January 1992, and Tunisia welcomed the appointment of Muhammad Boudiaf as Chairman of the High Council of State, as well as the suppression of the FIS. During a visit to Tunis in February 1993, Boudiaf's successor, Ali Kafi, exchanged letters with Ben Ali to ratify the official demarcation of the 1,000-km border between Tunisia and Algeria, which had been the subject of dispute since Algerian independence. In early 1995 six Tunisian border guards were killed in an attack perpetrated by Algerian Islamists in protest at the Tunisian authorities' alleged support for the Algerian security forces. Another serious incident occurred at the joint border in May 2000, when Tunisian security forces responded to an attack by Algerian Islamists; three of the Islamists were killed and two Tunisian soldiers wounded. The attack followed the signing of a bilateral customs agreement aimed at ending cross-border smuggling, considered by the Algerian Government to facilitate the activities of Islamist groups in Algeria. A number of bilateral agreements were signed during a visit to Algeria by Ben Ali in February 2002; most notably, the two countries pledged to formalize delineation of their maritime border.

In October 1994 Tunisia and Israel signalled the beginning of the normalization of bilateral relations with the announcement of plans to establish interests offices in the Belgian embassies in Tunis and Tel-Aviv. The offices opened in April and May 1996, respectively. Relations between the two countries were strained in early 1997, following Tunisia's criticism of Israel's alleged failure to implement agreements concluded with the PLO; although the two countries' respective interests offices remained open, Tunisia suspended the process of normalizing relations with Israel. The Tunisian Government installed a liaison office in the Gaza Strip in April 1995; a second office was planned for Jericho. In February 2000 a senior-level delegation from Tunisia visited Israel, where it was agreed, *inter alia*, that the two countries would establish a joint committee for advancing trade and tourism. However, in October, in response to the escalating Israeli–Palestinian crisis and what the Tunisian authorities deemed to be Israeli aggression, Tunisia announced that it had severed all diplomatic ties with Israel. In March 2004 Tunisia postponed a summit meeting of the Arab League, scheduled to be held in Tunis, citing differences among member states concerning an agenda for the talks (reportedly to include an appropriate Arab response to US pressure for political reform in the Middle East and to recent Israeli actions in the Palestinian territories). The summit eventually commenced in Tunis in May; however, conflicts over the summit's agenda remained and no agreement was reached on an Arab-Israeli peace initiative.

In June 1993 President Ben Ali, addressing the European Parliament in Strasbourg, advocated the establishment of a Euro-Maghreb Development Bank, which, by stimulating economic growth in North Africa, would alleviate illegal immigration into Europe. In July 1995 Tunisia concluded an association agreement with the EU, designed to foster closer commercial and political co-operation. Several Tunisian deputies demanded a suspension of the association agreement in June 2000, after EU member states, particularly France, criticized the Tunisian authorities' failure to protect human rights. Relations between France and Tunisia deteriorated further during 2001, when the French Government again criticized the growing use of violence against human rights activists and voiced its concern at gaol sentences imposed upon prominent opposition figures. Relations improved, however, during 2002–04 and, during a visit by President Jacques Chirac to Tunisia in December 2003, the two countries signed a number of co-operation agreements relating to tourism and bilateral social security arrangements. In November 2005 the EU made an official complaint to the Tunisian Government days before the UN-sponsored World Summit on the Information Society was scheduled to begin in Tunis. Tunisian security forces had prevented a group of international delegates, including the German ambassador to the UN and representatives of international human rights bodies, from entering the German cultural institute in the Tunisian capital. In April 2008 the French President, Nicolas Sarkozy, made his first state visit to Tunisia since taking office in May 2007. During the visit Sarkozy and Ben Ali supervised the signing of several agreements designed to increase civilian nuclear and aviation co-operation between the two countries. Ben Ali also expressed support for Sarkozy's proposed community of EU member states and countries bordering the Mediterranean Sea. When the Union for the Mediterranean (as it came to be known) was officially inaugurated at a summit meeting in the French capital in mid-July, President Ben Ali was among the many leaders of the 43 member nations to be in attendance. Meanwhile, in late 2008 it was reported that the EU was considering granting Tunisia 'advanced status' relations, in recognition of the strengthening economic, political and social partnership, as well as what it considered to be Tunisia's commitment to the implementation of social reforms.

In December 2003 the US Secretary of State, Colin Powell, visited Tunisia for talks with President Ben Ali and the Tunisian Minister of Foreign Affairs, Habib Ben Yahia. Powell praised the excellent relations between the two countries and Tunisia's contribution to the 'war on terror'; however, he urged the Tunisian Government to pursue further political and economic reforms. In February 2004 Ben Ali visited Washington, DC, where he met with the US President, George W. Bush, to discuss a number of trade-related issues. During the talks Bush also stressed that, while the USA applauded Tunisia's efforts to liberalize its society, it remained critical of the country's human rights record and the continued oppression of the Tunisian media. In June 2007 the Minister of Foreign Affairs, Abdelwahab Abdallah, met Vice-President Dick Cheney and Secretary of State Condoleezza Rice during an official visit to Washington; the US Administration reiterated its support for Tunisia and spoke positively of its leaders' commitment to implementing democratic reforms. Bilateral relations were further consolidated in September 2008, when Rice visited Tunisia as part of a tour of Maghreb states. She met with Ben Ali and held discussions with Tunisian officials on issues including counter-terrorism and domestic reform. In a statement to the press, Rice commended the progress that Tunisia had made in promoting women's rights, and urged the authorities to make every effort to ensure that the 2009 elections would be free and fair.

Government

Under the 1959 Constitution (with subsequent amendments), legislative power is held by the unicameral National Assembly, with 189 members who are elected by universal adult suffrage for a five-year term. (Of the 189 members, 152 are elected under a simple majority system, while 37 seats are reserved for the opposition, allotted according to the proportion of votes received nationally by each party. An amendment to the electoral code adopted in March 2009 provided for an increase in the share of seats reserved for opposition members to 25%, with effect from legislative elections due to take place in October of that year.) In 1988 a multi-party system was officially permitted by law. Executive power is held by the President, elected for five years by popular vote at the same time as the Assembly. The President, who is Head of State and Head of Government, appoints a Council of Ministers, led by a Prime Minister, which is responsible to him. For local administration the country is divided into 24 governorates.

Defence

As assessed at November 2008, total armed forces numbered an estimated 35,800 (including some 22,700 conscripts), consisting of an army of 27,000, a navy of about 4,800 and an air force of 4,000. Paramilitary forces included a 12,000-strong national guard. From 2003 women were required to complete military service. Officer-training is undertaken in the USA and France, as well as in Tunisia. The defence budget for 2007 totalled an estimated TD 625m.

Economic Affairs

In 2007, according to estimates by the World Bank, Tunisia's gross national income (GNI), measured at average 2005–07 prices, was US $32,820m., equivalent to $3,200 per head (or $7,130 per head on an international purchasing-power parity basis). During 2000–07, it was estimated, the population increased at an average annual rate of 1.0%, while gross domestic product (GDP) per head increased, in real terms, by an average of 3.8%. Overall GDP increased, in real terms, at an average annual rate of 4.9% per year in 2000–07; according to official estimates, it grew by 6.3% in 2007 and by 5.0% in 2008.

Agriculture (including forestry and fishing) contributed an estimated 10.2% of GDP in 2008 and employed 18.5% of the working population in 2007. The principal crops are wheat, barley, potatoes, olives, tomatoes and watermelons. However, Tunisia imports large quantities of cereals, dairy produce, meat and sugar. The country's main agricultural export is olive oil; olives, citrus fruit and dates are also grown for export. During 2000–07, according to the World Bank, agricultural GDP increased at an average annual rate of 2.6%. Agricultural GDP decreased by 1.3% in 2008, according to official estimates.

Industry (including mining, manufacturing, construction and power) contributed an estimated 36.3% of GDP in 2008 and engaged 32.5% of the employed labour force in 2007. According to the World Bank, industrial GDP increased by an average of 3.5% per year during 2000–07, and by an estimated 3.9% in 2008.

Mining (excluding hydrocarbons) contributed an estimated 1.2% of GDP in 2008. In 1994 mining (with gas, electricity and water) employed 1.6% of the working population. In 2007 the principal mineral export was petroleum (which accounted for 16.2% of total export earnings). Tunisia's proven published oil reserves at the end of 2007 were estimated at 600m. barrels, sufficient to maintain production (at 2007 levels—averaging an estimated 98,000 barrels per day) for 16.7 years. Iron, zinc, lead, barite, gypsum, phosphate, fluorspar and sea salt are also mined. In addition, Tunisia possesses large reserves of natural gas. The GDP of the mining sector (excluding hydrocarbons) decreased by 3.8% in 2008, according to official estimates.

Manufacturing (excluding hydrocarbons) contributed an estimated 19.6% of GDP in 2008, and employed 19.6% of the working population in 1994. Manufacturing is based on the processing of the country's principal agricultural and mineral products. Other important sectors include textiles, construction materials, machinery, chemicals, and paper and wood. In 2000–07, according to the World Bank, manufacturing GDP increased at an average annual rate of 3.5%. Manufacturing GDP grew by an estimated 5.3% in 2008.

Energy is derived principally from gas (which contributed 90.4% of total electricity output in 2005) and petroleum (8.2%), although Tunisia also has several hydroelectric plants. Imports of mineral fuels and lubricants comprised 12.8% of the value of total imports in 2007. In the mid-2000s the Tunisian electricity grid was interconnected with that of Libya.

The services sector accounted for an estimated 53.5% of GDP in 2008 and employed 49.0% of the working population in 2007. Tourism represents an important source of revenue: receipts from tourism in 2006 totalled US $2,999m., and there were 6.5m. tourist arrivals in the same year. The GDP of the services sector increased by an average of 6.0% per year in 2000–07, according to the World Bank. Growth in the sector's GDP was recorded at 6.6% in 2008, according to official estimates.

In 2007 Tunisia recorded a visible trade deficit of US $2,876m., and a deficit of $904m. on the current account of the balance of payments. In 2007 the principal sources of imports were France-including Monaco (accounting for 21.4% of the total), Italy (19.5%), Germany and Spain. The principal markets for Tunisian exports in that year were also France-including Monaco (taking 32.2%), Italy (23.3%), Germany and Spain. The member states of the European Union (EU, see p. 255) accounted for 80.5% of Tunisia's exports and 71.4% of its imports in 1999. Tunisia's principal exports in 2007 were miscellaneous manufactured articles, mineral fuels and lubricants, basic manufactures and chemicals and related products. The principal imports in that year were machinery and transport equipment, basic manufactures, mineral fuels and lubricants, and chemicals and related products.

In 2007 there was a preliminary budgetary deficit of TD 1,247m. (excluding receipts from privatization). The 2008 budget forecast a deficit of TD 1,248m. (excluding receipts from privatization). At the end of 2006 Tunisia's total external debt was US $18,480m., of which $15,144m. was long-term public debt. In that year the cost of debt-servicing was equivalent to 14.4% of the value of exports of goods and services. The average annual rate of inflation was 3.0% in 2000–07; consumer prices increased by 3.1% in 2007. A reported 14.1% of the labour force were unemployed in 2007, with university graduates accounting for some 60% of those without jobs.

Tunisia is a member of the Arab Fund for Economic and Social Development (AFESD, see p. 183), the Arab Monetary Fund (see p. 184) and the Union of the Arab Maghreb (Union du Maghreb arabe—UMA, see p. 429).

From the mid-1990s Tunisia experienced strong growth, low inflation and declining poverty as a result of its efforts to restructure and diversify the economy. As part of the Government's privatization programme, the sale of 33.5% of Banque du Sud was completed in November 2005, raising revenue of some US $80m. Under an ambitious programme to develop the tourism sector, it was aimed to increase the number of visitors to the country to 10m. by 2010. Meanwhile, the Tunisian economy continued to become more closely integrated with those of the EU member states, and in January 2008 all trade barriers between Tunisia and the EU were removed when the country formally entered into a free trade agreement. Unemployment remained a serious issue in Tunisia, with the level of joblessness particularly high among the country's youth. One of the principal aims of the Government's 11th development plan (for 2007–11), approved in July 2007, was the reduction of unemployment to 13.4% by 2011. Assessing the economy in mid-2008, the IMF projected growth of 5.8% in 2009. However, in the context of the global economic downturn, there was a risk that a decine in global prices of energy and mining commodities, important exports for Tunisia and contributors to strong growth in the mid-2000s, would result in a widening of the trade deficit in 2009. Furthermore, recession in Tunisia's largest European trading partners was likely to result in reduced demand for the country's exports and lower remittances from migrant workers.

Education

Education is compulsory in Tunisia for a period of nine years between the ages of six and 16. Primary education begins at six years of age and normally lasts for six years. Secondary education begins at the age of 12 and lasts for seven years, comprising a first cycle of three years and a second cycle of four years. In 2005/06, according to UNESCO estimates, the total enrolment at primary schools included 96.1% of the relevant age-group. Enrolment at secondary schools included 65.0% of the appropriate age-group in 2002/03. Arabic is the first language of instruction in primary and secondary schools, but French is also used. The University of Tunis was divided in 1988 to form separate institutions, one for the arts, the other for the sciences, and two new universities were opened in 1986, at Monastir and Sfax. In 2006/07 the number enrolled at the 178 higher educational establishments in Tunisia was equivalent to 326,185 full-time students. Public expenditure on education was equivalent to 18.2% of total government spending in 2001/02.

Public Holidays

2009: 1 January (New Year's Day), 20 March (Independence Day), 21 March (Youth Day), 9 April (Martyrs' Day), 1 May (Labour Day), 25 July (Republic Day), 13 August (Women's Day),

TUNISIA

20 September* (Aid es-Seghir—Id al-Fitr, end of Ramadan), 15 October (Evacuation of Bizerta), 7 November (accession of President Ben Ali), 27 November* (Aid el-Kebir—Id al-Adha, Feast of the Sacrifice).

2010: 1 January (New Year's Day), 20 March (Independence Day), 21 March (Youth Day), 9 April (Martyrs' Day), 1 May (Labour Day), 25 July (Republic Day), 13 August (Women's Day), 10 September* (Aid es-Seghir—Id al-Fitr, end of Ramadan), 15 October (Evacuation of Bizerta), 7 November (accession of President Ben Ali), 16 November* (Aid el-Kebir—Id al-Adha, Feast of the Sacrifice).

* These holidays are dependent on the Islamic lunar calendar and may differ by one or two days from the dates given.

Weights and Measures

The metric system is in force.

Statistical Survey

Source (unless otherwise stated): Institut National de la Statistique, Ministère du Développement Economique, 70 rue al-Cham, 1002 Tunis; tel. (71) 891-002; fax (71) 792-559; e-mail ins@e-mail.ati.tn; internet www.ins.nat.tn.

Area and Population

AREA, POPULATION AND DENSITY

Area (sq km)	
Land	154,530
Inland waters	9,080
Total	163,610*
Population (census results)	
20 April 1994	8,785,364
28 April 2004	
Males	4,965,435
Females	4,945,437
Total	9,910,872
Population (official estimate at 1 July)	
2006	10,128,100
2007	10,225,400
2008	10,326,600
Density (per sq km) at 1 July 2008	66.8†

* 63,170 sq miles.
† Land area only.

GOVERNORATES
(at 1 July 2008)

	Area (sq km)*	Population (estimates)	Density (per sq km)
Tunis	346	992,900	2,869.7
Ariana	498	473,100	950.0
Ben Arous	761	555,600	779.1
Manouba	1,060	358,600	338.3
Nabeul	2,788	733,400	263.1
Zaghouan	2,768	167,100	60.4
Bizerte	3,685	538,800	146.2
Béja	3,558	304,300	85.5
Jendouba	3,102	420,500	135.6
Le Kef	4,965	256,700	51.7
Siliana	4,631	233,200	50.4
Kairouan	6,712	553,800	82.5
Kasserine	8,066	424,900	52.7
Sidi Bouzid	6,994	405,900	58.0
Sousse	2,621	590,400	225.3
Monastir	1,019	494,900	485.7
Mahdia	2,966	389,900	131.5
Sfax	7,545	904,800	119.9
Gafsa	8,990	332,400	37.0
Tozeur	4,719	101,300	21.5
Kébili	22,084	147,800	6.7
Gabès	7,175	354,400	49.4
Médenine	8,588	447,300	52.1
Tataouine	38,889	144,600	3.7
Total	**163,610**	**10,326,600**	**63.1**

* Including inland water.

Note: Total for population may not be equal to the sum of components, owing to rounding.

PRINCIPAL TOWNS
(2004, census results)

Tunis (capital)	728,453	Ettadhamen	118,487
Sfax (Safaqis)	265,131	Kairouan (Qairawan)	117,930
Ariana	240,749	Gabès	116,323
Sousse	173,047	Bizerta (Bizerte)	114,371

Source: Thomas Brinkhoff, *City Population* (internet www.citypopulation.de).

Mid-2007 (incl. suburbs, UN estimate): Tunis 745,000 (Source: UN, *World Urbanization Prospects: The 2007 Revision*).

BIRTHS, MARRIAGES AND DEATHS

	Registered live births		Registered marriages		Registered deaths	
	Number	Rate (per 1,000)	Number	Rate (per 1,000)	Number	Rate (per 1,000)
1990	205,345	25.4	55,612	6.8	45,700	5.6
1991	207,455	25.2	59,010	7.1	46,500	5.6
1992	211,649	25.2	64,700	7.6	46,300	5.5
1993	207,786	24.1	54,120	6.3	49,400	5.7
1994	200,223	22.7	52,431	5.9	50,300	5.7
1995	186,416	20.8	53,726	6.0	52,000	5.8
1996	178,801	19.7	56,349	6.2	40,817	5.5
1997	173,757	18.9	57,861	6.3	42,426	5.6

Birth rate (per 1,000): 17.1 in 2005; 17.1 in 2006; 17.4 in 2007.

Death rate (per 1,000): 5.9 in 2005; 5.6 in 2006; 5.5 in 2007.

Life expectancy (years at birth, WHO estimates): 72 (males 70; females 75) in 2006 (Source: WHO, *World Health Statistics*).

EMPLOYMENT
('000 persons aged 15 years and over at 20 April 1994)

	Males	Females	Total
Agriculture, forestry and fishing	393.7	107.3	501.0
Manufacturing	244.7	211.0	455.7
Electricity, gas and water*	34.4	2.4	36.8
Construction	302.6	3.2	305.8
Trade, restaurants and hotels†	277.8	37.8	315.6
Community, social and personal services‡	503.9	163.2	667.1
Activities not adequately defined	28.6	10.0	38.6
Total employed	**1,785.7**	**534.9**	**2,320.6**

* Including mining and quarrying.
† Including financing, insurance, real estate and business services.
‡ Including transport, storage and communications.

Total labour force ('000 persons aged over 15 years): 3,506.2 in 2006; 3,593.2 in 2007; 3,677.7 in 2008.

TUNISIA

Health and Welfare

KEY INDICATORS

Total fertility rate (children per woman, 2006)	1.9
Under-5 mortality rate (per 1,000 live births, 2006)	23
HIV/AIDS (% of persons aged 15–49, 2007)	0.1
Physicians (per 1,000 head, 2004)	1.34
Hospital beds (per 1,000 head, 2004)	1.8
Health expenditure (2006): US $ per head (PPP)	488
Health expenditure (2006): % of GDP	5.3
Health expenditure (2006): public (% of total)	43.7
Access to water (% of persons, 2006)	94
Access to sanitation (% of persons, 2006)	85
Human Development Index (2006): ranking	95
Human Development Index (2006): value	0.762

For sources and definitions, see explanatory note on p. vi.

Agriculture

PRINCIPAL CROPS
('000 metric tons)

	2005	2006	2007
Wheat	1,627	1,251	1,443
Barley	465	354	535
Potatoes	310	365	350
Broad beans, horse beans, dry	45	40	67
Almonds, with shell	43	56	58
Olives	600	1,050	900
Artichokes	12	16	19
Tomatoes	960	855	1,000
Pumpkins, squash and gourds*	37	46	36
Cucumbers and gherkins*	37	37	37
Chillies and peppers, green	256	256	260*
Onions and shallots, green	138†	235	180
Onions, dry	117†	120	160
Peas, green	15*	15	15*
Carrots and turnips*	52	51	50
Watermelons	350	467	490
Oranges	101	127	141
Tangerines, mandarins, clementines and satsumas	33	35	35
Lemons and limes	28	27	31
Grapefruit and pomelos*	72	71	72
Apples	100	120	102
Pears	53	65	55
Apricots	26	28	24
Peaches and nectarines	108	110	101
Grapes	135	140	125
Figs	25	24	22
Dates	125	125	120*

* FAO estimate(s).
† Unofficial figure.

Aggregate production ('000 metric tons, may include official, semi-official or estimated data): Total cereals 2,136 in 2005, 1,646 in 2006, 2,020 in 2007; Total roots and tubers 310 in 2005, 365 in 2006, 350 in 2007; Total pulses 89 in 2005, 84 in 2006, 116 in 2007; Total vegetables (incl. melons) 2,248 in 2005, 2,370 in 2006, 2,504 in 2007; Total fruits (excl. melons) 1,066 in 2005, 1,050 in 2006, 1,003 in 2007.

Source: FAO.

LIVESTOCK
('000 head, year ending September)

	2005	2006	2007
Horses*	57	57	57
Asses*	230	n.a.	n.a.
Cattle	686	703	710
Camels*	231	231	230
Sheep	7,213	7,484	7,618
Goats	1,427	1,497	1,551
Chickens*	64,000	62,000	64,000
Turkeys*	4,400	4,000	5,000

* FAO estimates.
Source: FAO.

LIVESTOCK PRODUCTS
('000 metric tons)

	2005	2006	2007
Cattle meat	52.7	56.3	58.0*
Sheep meat	53.4	56.3	56.0*
Chicken meat	87.4	66.2	95.0*
Cows' milk	920.0	66.2	95.0
Sheep's milk*	17.9	17.2	17.2
Goats' milk*	12.2	12.2	12.2
Hen eggs*	80.0	74.0	82.0
Wool, greasy*	8.8	8.8	8.8

* FAO estimate(s).
Source: FAO.

Forestry

ROUNDWOOD REMOVALS
('000 cu m, excl. bark, FAO estimates)

	2005	2006	2007
Sawlogs, veneer logs and logs for sleepers	25	25	25
Pulpwood	75	75	75
Other industrial wood	118	118	118
Fuel wood	2,149	2,156	2,163
Total	2,367	2,374	2,381

Source: FAO.

SAWNWOOD PRODUCTION
('000 cu m, incl. sleepers)

	1992	1993	1994
Coniferous (softwood)	2.2	5.8	6.8
Broadleaved (hardwood)	4.0	13.6	13.6
Total	6.2	19.4	20.4

1995–2007: Production as in 1994 (FAO estimates).
Source: FAO.

Fishing

('000 metric tons, live weight)

	2004	2005	2006
Capture	111.5	109.2	111.3
Mullets	7.4	6.7	6.2
Common pandora	2.9	2.8	2.4
Sargo breams	0.4	0.4	0.3
Bogue	3.0	2.8	2.9
Jack and horse mackerels	7.0	5.5	7.8
Sardinellas	13.5	12.8	13.6
European pilchard	14.3	18.6	24.8
Chub mackerel	9.4	9.0	4.9
Common cuttlefish	6.0	6.2	6.4
Aquaculture	2.5	2.7	2.8
Total catch (incl. others)	114.1	111.8	114.1

Source: FAO.

TUNISIA

Mining

('000 metric tons, unless otherwise indicated)

	2004	2005	2006*
Crude petroleum ('000 barrels)	25,700	26,200	25,000
Natural gas (million cu m)	2,298	2,343	2,149
Iron ore: gross weight	256	206	214
Iron ore: metal content	134	108	112
Lead concentrates (metric tons)†	5,470	8,708	—
Zinc concentrates (metric tons)†	29,011	15,889	—
Phosphate rock‡	8,051	8,220	7,801
Barite (Barytes) (metric tons)	1,813	—	—
Salt (marine)	1,117	1,132	1,127
Gypsum (crude)§	108	113	120

* Preliminary figures.
† Figures refer to metal content of concentrates.
‡ Figures refer to gross weight. The estimated phosphoric acid content (in '000 metric tons) was: 1,241 in 2004; 1,217 in 2005; 1,181 in 2006 (preliminary).
§ Estimated production.

Source: US Geological Survey.

Industry

SELECTED PRODUCTS
('000 metric tons, unless otherwise indicated)

	2002	2003	2004
Superphosphates	796	875	868
Cement	6,022	6,038	6,662
Beer ('000 hectolitres)	1,100	997	n.a.
Wine ('000 hectolitres)	271	246	n.a.
Olive oil	30	70	n.a.
Flour	753	785	n.a.
Refined sugar	126	131	n.a.
Crude steel	200	86	70*
Quicklime	471	446	476
Motor gasoline ('000 barrels)	3,380	3,600	3,450
Kerosene ('000 barrels)	1,590	1,270	1,310
Diesel oil ('000 barrels)	3,500	3,780	3,220
Residual fuel oil ('000 barrels)	4,020	4,050	3,960
Electric energy (million kWh)	11,281	11,829	13,067

* Preliminary figure.

2005 ('000 metric tons unless otherwise indicated): Superphosphates 848; Cement 6,691; Crude steel 66; Quicklime 424; Motor gasoline ('000 barrels) 1,840; Kerosene ('000 barrels) 1,770; Diesel oil ('000 barrels) 3,600; Residual fuel oil ('000 barrels) 4,060.

2006 ('000 metric tons unless otherwise indicated): Superphosphates 792; Cement 6,932; Crude steel 68; Quicklime 401; Motor gasoline ('000 barrels) 1,540; Kerosene ('000 barrels) 1,050; Diesel oil ('000 barrels) 3,780; Residual fuel oil ('000 barrels) 4,020.

Sources: partly UN, *Industrial Commodity Statistics Yearbook*; US Geological Survey.

Finance

CURRENCY AND EXCHANGE RATES

Monetary Units
1,000 millimes = 1 Tunisian dinar (TD).

Sterling, Dollar and Euro Equivalents (31 December 2008)
£1 sterling = 1.910 dinars;
US $1 = 1.310 dinars;
€1 = 1.823 dinars;
100 Tunisian dinars = £52.37 = $76.34 = €54.86.

Average Exchange Rate (dinars per US $)
2006 1.3310
2007 1.2814
2008 1.2321

Statistical Survey

BUDGET
(million dinars)*

Revenue†	2006‡	2007‡	2008§
Tax revenue	8,470	9,518	10,378
Direct taxes	3,107	3,708	4,328
Trade taxes	490	514	510
Value-added tax (VAT)	2,466	2,660	2,937
Excise	1,255	1,362	1,423
Other taxes	1,153	1,274	1,180
Non-tax revenue	1,314	1,339	1,733
Capital revenue	6	5	3
Total	9,789	10,862	12,114

Expenditure‖	2006‡	2007‡	2008§
Current expenditure	8,317	9,166	10,506
Wages and salaries	4,901	5,297	5,794
Goods and services	744	789	877
Interest payments	1,130	1,182	1,240
Domestic	499	582	615
External	631	600	625
Transfers and subsidies	1,542	1,898	2,438
Non-allocated	—	—	157
Capital expenditure	2,539	2,677	3,047
Direct investment	1,412	1,413	1,545
Capital transfers and equity	1,127	1,264	1,344
Non-allocated	—	—	158
Total	10,856	11,843	13,553

* Figures refer to the consolidated accounts of the central Government, including administrative agencies and social security funds. The data exclude the operations of economic and social agencies with their own budgets.
† Excluding grants from abroad (million dinars): 48 in 2006 (preliminary); 38 in 2007 (preliminary); 120 in 2008 (projected). Also excluded are receipts from privatization (million dinars): 3,000 in 2006 (preliminary); 50 in 2007 (preliminary); 100 in 2008 (projected).
‡ Preliminary figures.
§ Projected figures.
‖ Excluding net lending (million dinars): 112 in 2006 (preliminary); 354 in 2007 (preliminary); 29 in 2008 (projected).

Source: IMF, *Tunisia: 2008 Article IV Consultation—Staff Report; Public Information Notice on the Executive Board Discussion; and Statement by the Executive Director for Tunisia* (October 2008).

CENTRAL BANK RESERVES
(US $ million at 31 December)

	2006	2007	2008
Gold (national valuation)	3.4	3.6	3.4
IMF special drawing rights	1.3	2.0	5.2
Reserve position in IMF	30.5	32.0	31.2
Foreign exchange	6,741.4	7,816.8	8,812.9
Total	6,776.6	7,854.4	8,852.7

Source: IMF, *International Financial Statistics*.

MONEY SUPPLY
(million dinars at 31 December)

	2006	2007	2008
Currency outside banks	3,873	4,099	4,400
Demand deposits at commercial banks	5,856	6,745	7,554
Total money (incl. others)	10,339	11,579	12,959

Source: IMF, *International Financial Statistics*.

COST OF LIVING
(Consumer Price Index; base: 2000 = 100)

	2005	2006	2007
Food	115.2	121.4	124.8
Electricity, gas and other fuels	125.3	134.4	139.7
Clothing	108.9	111.9	115.6
Rent	118.3	121.9	n.a.
All items (incl. others)	113.8	118.9	122.6

Source: ILO.

TUNISIA

Statistical Survey

NATIONAL ACCOUNTS
(million dinars at current prices, estimates)

Expenditure on the Gross Domestic Product

	2006	2007	2008
Government final consumption expenditure	6,195.7	6,608.9	7,231.4
Private final consumption expenditure	26,000.9	28,332.1	31,166.1
Gross fixed capital formation	9,690.5	10,965.4	12,790.0
Change in inventories	406.0	738.3	1,146.7
Total domestic expenditure	42,293.1	46,644.7	52,334.2
Exports of goods and services	21,006.4	25,407.6	32,089.7
Less Imports of goods and services	21,914.8	26,414.2	33,469.3
GDP in purchasers' values	41,384.7	45,638.1	50,954.6
GDP at constant 1990 prices	22,546.8	23,978.3	25,169.3

Gross Domestic Product by Economic Activity

	2006	2007	2008
Agriculture and fishing	4,595.4	4,720.0	4,884.3
Mining (excluding hydrocarbons)	238.5	262.2	554.9
Manufacturing (excluding hydrocarbons)	7,007.2	7,785.8	9,425.6
Hydrocarbons, electricity and water	2,895.5	4,021.9	4,743.8
Construction and public works	2,328.6	2,471.2	2,728.8
Transport and telecommunications	4,410.5	5,033.0	5,709.9
Hotels and restaurants	2,324.6	2,474.6	2,683.1
Trade, finance, etc.	9,043.8	9,863.1	10,950.3
Non-market services	5,520.5	5,958.8	6,407.4
Sub-total	38,364.6	42,590.6	48,088.1
Less Imputed bank service charges	1,117.0	1,241.0	1,435.5
Gross value added at factor cost	37,247.6	41,349.6	46,652.6
Indirect taxes, *less* subsidies	4,137.1	4,288.5	4,302.0
GDP in purchasers' values	41,384.7	45,638.1	50,954.6

BALANCE OF PAYMENTS
(US $ million)

	2005	2006	2007
Exports of goods f.o.b.	10,631	11,689	15,148
Imports of goods f.o.b.	−12,594	−14,202	−18,024
Trade balance	−1,963	−2,513	−2,876
Exports of services	4,021	4,295	4,909
Imports of services	−2,191	−2,454	−2,803
Balance on goods and services	−133	−673	−769
Other income received	316	367	563
Other income paid	−1,794	−1,756	−2,316
Balance on goods, services and income	−1,611	−2,062	−2,523
Current transfers received	1,340	1,470	1,650
Current transfers paid	−28	−27	−32
Current balance	−299	−619	−904
Capital account (net)	129	145	154
Direct investment abroad	−72	−71	−104
Direct investment from abroad	785	3,311	1,620
Portfolio investment liabilities	12	65	30
Other investment assets	17	19	−178
Other investment liabilities	394	−729	109
Net errors and omissions	−28	−38	−36
Overall balance	936	2,082	689

Source: IMF, *International Financial Statistics*.

External Trade

PRINCIPAL COMMODITIES
(US $ million)

Imports c.i.f.	2005	2006	2007
Food and live animals	829.9	906.9	1,529.0
Cereal and cereal preparations	378.5	407.7	941.7
Mineral fuels, lubricants, etc.	1,798.4	2,218.4	2,442.9
Petroleum and related products	1,530.6	1,861.8	1,990.7
Gas, natural and manufactured	264.7	353.5	449.1
Chemicals and related products	1,381.8	1,488.8	1,898.8
Plastics in primary forms	310.9	345.8	471.2
Basic manufactures	3,213.3	3,594.2	4,798.0
Textile yarn, fabrics and related products	1,613.6	1,593.9	1,997.5
Cotton fabrics, woven	823.9	766.1	959.0
Machinery and transport equipment	3,792.5	4,531.1	5,621.1
General industrial machinery and equipment	541.0	608.6	860.2
Electrical machinery, apparatus and appliances	1,056.9	1,339.5	1,568.7
Road vehicles	854.3	970.3	1,217.8
Miscellaneous manufactured articles	1,299.4	1,414.3	1,656.1
Total	13,174.3	15,007.3	19,099.4

Exports f.o.b.	2005	2006	2007
Food and live animals	538.4	524.8	687.4
Mineral fuels, lubricants, etc.	1,357.3	1,518.2	2,456.1
Petroleum and related products	1,357.2	1,518.1	2,455.8
Petroleum oils and oils obtained from bituminous materials, crude	1,092.1	1,175.4	2,056.3
Animal and vegetable oils	430.1	773.7	674.1
Chemicals and related products	987.6	1,054.3	1,425.7
Fertilizers	419.9	457.0	661.7
Basic manufactures	947.2	1,197.7	1,543.6
Machinery and transport equipment	2,011.5	2,398.9	2,910.5
Electrical machinery, apparatus and appliances	1,446.1	1,581.8	1,862.3
Miscellaneous manufactured articles	3,928.0	3,959.0	4,758.7
Articles of clothing and clothing accessories	3,124.3	3,018.1	3,571.1
Men's or boy's outerwear	986.7	879.9	1,023.1
Footwear	443.8	470.4	575.8
Total	10,493.6	11,694.4	15,165.4

Source: UN, *International Trade Statistics Yearbook*.

PRINCIPAL TRADING PARTNERS
(US $ million)*

Imports c.i.f.	2005	2006	2007
Algeria	135.4	194.8	299.8
Argentina	138.0	121.2	208.2
Belgium	346.3	342.0	478.1
Brazil	152.7	210.8	222.2
China, People's Republic	381.1	492.3	654.0
France (incl. Monaco)	3,029.3	3,391.7	4,082.2
Germany	1,085.3	1,182.0	1,512.7
Italy	2,757.4	2,901.3	3,724.2
Japan	213.0	250.1	289.6
Libya	510.0	726.4	646.3

TUNISIA

Imports c.i.f.—continued	2005	2006	2007
Netherlands	240.6	231.4	277.7
Russia	375.4	547.7	814.5
Spain	677.5	699.1	886.0
Sweden	100.7	151.8	144.8
Switzerland (incl. Liechtenstein)	142.8	171.1	163.2
Turkey	297.5	313.1	496.1
Ukraine	221.2	277.6	305.2
United Kingdom	288.0	256.3	357.2
USA	329.5	431.4	647.2
Total (incl. others)	13,174.3	15,007.3	19,099.4

Exports f.o.b.	2005	2006	2007
Algeria	182.9	188.1	287.0
Belgium	288.2	276.3	358.1
France (incl. Monaco)	3,453.8	3,776.9	4,877.6
Germany	885.4	917.2	1,247.5
India	97.7	131.1	141.0
Italy	2,514.4	2,583.4	3,531.0
Libya	472.7	620.7	697.5
Morocco	109.4	108.7	172.9
Netherlands	225.8	233.3	358.5
Spain	576.0	748.2	783.5
Switzerland (incl. Liechtenstein)	48.3	258.4	262.9
Turkey	106.7	121.3	180.8
United Kingdom	279.3	340.0	652.8
USA	95.5	262.7	167.2
Total (incl. others)	10,493.6	11,694.4	15,165.4

*Imports by country of production; exports by country of last destination.

Source: UN, *International Trade Statistics Yearbook*.

Transport

RAILWAYS
(traffic)

	2004	2005	2006
Passengers carried ('000)	36,320	36,791	37,814
Passenger-kilometres (million)	1,294	1,319	1,407
Freight carried ('000 metric tons)	11,001	10,799	10,979
Freight net ton-kilometres (million)	2,081	2,068	2,174

ROAD TRAFFIC
(estimates, motor vehicles in use at 31 December)

	2000	2001	2002
Passenger cars	516,525	552,897	585,194
Buses and coaches	11,143	11,973	12,181
Lorries and vans	240,421	253,760	266,499
Road tractors	8,307	9,165	9,605

Source: International Road Federation, *World Road Statistics*.

2004: Passenger cars 825,990; Buses and coaches 12,181; Lorries and vans 106,883; Motorcycles 6,057.

SHIPPING

Merchant Fleet
(vessels registered at 31 December)

	2005	2006	2007
Number of vessels	75	75	73
Total displacement ('000 grt)	169.3	168.1	140.2

Source: Lloyd's Register-Fairplay, *World Fleet Statistics*.

International Sea-borne Freight Traffic
('000 metric tons)

	2004	2005	2006
Goods loaded*	6,976	7,227	7,538
Goods unloaded	14,032	14,454	15,235

*Excluding Algerian crude petroleum loaded at La Skhirra.

CIVIL AVIATION
(traffic on scheduled services)

	2002	2003	2004
Kilometres flown (million)	24	25	28
Passengers carried ('000)	1,789	1,720	1,940
Passenger-km (million)	2,511	2,459	2,853
Total ton-km (million)	266	261	299

Source: UN, *Statistical Yearbook*.

Tourism

FOREIGN TOURIST ARRIVALS BY NATIONALITY
('000)

	2004	2005	2006
Algeria	914.1	930.7	945.3
Austria	84.4	86.4	92.0
Belgium	140.8	155.1	164.3
France	1,020.8	1,170.1	1,234.7
Germany	569.5	571.9	547.4
Italy	448.3	472.8	464.3
Libya	1,435.8	1,404.0	1,472.4
Switzerland	99.1	92.8	103.1
United Kingdom	300.8	327.5	350.7
Total (incl. others)	5,997.9	6,378.4	6,549.5

Receipts from tourism (US $ million, incl. passenger transport): 2,432 in 2004; 2,800 in 2005; 2,999 in 2006.

Source: World Tourism Organization.

Communications Media

	2005	2006	2007
Telephones ('000 main lines in use)	1,257.5	1,268.5	1,273.3
Mobile cellular telephones ('000 subscribers)	5,680.7	7,339.0	7,842.4
Personal computers ('000 in use)	568	n.a.	n.a.
Internet users ('000)	953.8	1,294.9	1,722.2
Broadband subscribers ('000)	17.6	45.5	114.2

Radio receivers ('000 in use): 2,060 in 1997.

Facsimile machines (number in use): 31,000 in 1997.

Book production (titles): 1,260 in 1999.

Daily newspapers: 7 (average circulation 180,000) in 2000; 10 in 2004.

Non-daily newspapers: 39 (average circulation 963,861) in 2001.

Periodicals (titles): 182 in 2000 (average circulation 525,000).

Television receivers ('000 in use): 1,900 in 2000.

Sources: UNESCO, *Statistical Yearbook*; UNESCO Institute for Statistics; UN, *Statistical Yearbook*; and International Telecommunication Union.

Education

(2007/08, unless otherwise indicated)

	Institutions	Teachers	Students
Primary (public)			
1st cycle	4,507	58,716	1,019,421
2nd cycle	1,750	36,063	569,649
Secondary (public)	485	35,323	499,936
Higher	190	18,608*	335,649*

*Full-time equivalent.

Adult literacy rate (UNESCO estimates): 77.7% (males 86.4%; females 69.0%) in 2007 (Source: UNESCO Institute for Statistics).

Directory

The Constitution

A new Constitution for the Republic of Tunisia was promulgated on 1 June 1959 and amended on 12 July 1988; further amendments were approved by national referendum on 26 May 2002. Its main provisions are summarized below:

NATIONAL ASSEMBLY

Legislative power is exercised by a bicameral parliament: the Chamber of Deputies and the Chamber of Advisers, which was established by the constitutional amendments approved in May 2002. Every citizen who has had Tunisian nationality for at least five years and who has attained 20 years of age has the right to vote. The Chamber of Deputies, which is elected (at the same time as the President) every five years, shall hold two sessions every year, each session lasting not more than three months. Additional meetings may be held at the demand of the President or of a majority of the deputies. The Chamber of Advisers currently consists of 126 members; while this number is revised every six years, it must never exceed two-thirds of the number of members of the Chamber of Deputies. One-third of the members of the Chamber of Advisers is composed of representatives of the main professional unions and federations, one-third by representatives of the 24 governorates (one or two from each governorate, depending on the size of its population), and the remainder are appointed by the President. The members of the Chamber of Advisers serve a six-year term; one-half of its members are replaced every three years.

HEAD OF STATE

The President of the Republic is both Head of State and Head of the Executive. He must be not less than 40 years of age and not more than 75 (not more than 70, prior to the May 2002 amendments). The President is elected by universal suffrage for a five-year term. The amendments approved in May 2002 removed restrictions on the renewal of the presidential mandate (previously, this was renewable twice consecutively). The President is also the Commander-in-Chief of the army and makes both civil and military appointments. The Government may be censured by the National Assembly, in which case the President may dismiss the Assembly and hold fresh elections. If censured by the new Assembly thus elected, the Government must resign. Should the presidency fall vacant for any reason before the end of a President's term of office, the President of the National Assembly shall take charge of affairs of the state for a period of 45 to 60 days. At the end of this period a presidential election shall be organized. The President of the National Assembly shall not be eligible as a presidential candidate.

COUNCIL OF STATE

Comprises two judicial bodies: an administrative body dealing with legal disputes between individuals and state or public bodies, and an audit office to verify the accounts of the state and submit reports.

ECONOMIC AND SOCIAL COUNCIL

Deals with economic and social planning and studies projects submitted by the National Assembly. Members are grouped in seven categories representing various sections of the community.

The Government

HEAD OF STATE

President: ZINE AL-ABIDINE BEN ALI (took office on 7 November 1987; elected 2 April 1989; re-elected 20 March 1994, 24 October 1999 and 24 October 2004).

COUNCIL OF MINISTERS
(April 2009)

Prime Minister: MUHAMMAD GHANNOUCHI.
Minister of State, Special Adviser to the President and Spokesman for the Presidency: ABDELAZIZ BEN DHIA.
Minister Director of the Presidential Office: AHMAD IYADH OUEDERNI.
Minister of Foreign Affairs: ABDELWAHAB ABDALLAH.
Minister of the Interior and Local Development: RAFIK BELHAJ KACEM.
Minister of National Defence: KAMEL MORJANE.
Minister of Justice and Human Rights: BÉCHIR TEKKARI.
Minister of Religious Affairs: BOUBAKER AL-AKHZOURI.
Minister of Women's, Family, Children's and Elderly Affairs: SARRA KANOUN JARRAYA.
Minister of Social Affairs, Solidarity and Tunisians Abroad: ALI CHAOUCH.
Minister of Education and Training: HATEM BEN SALEM.
Minister of the Environment and Sustainable Development: NADHIR HAMADA.
Minister of Culture and Heritage Preservation: ABDERRAOUF EL-BASTI.
Minister of Public Health: MONDHER ZENAÏDI.
Minister of Youth, Sports and Physical Education: SAMIR LABIDI.
Minister of Employment and Professional Integration of Youth: SLIM TLETLI.
Minister of Finance: MUHAMMAD RACHID KECHICHE.
Minister of Communication Technologies: HAJ KLAÏ.
Minister of Agriculture and Water Resources: ABDESSALEM MANSOUR.
Minister of Transport: ABDERRAHIM ZOUARI.
Minister of Tourism: KHELIL LAJIMI.
Minister of Trade and Handicrafts: RIDHA TOUITI.
Minister of Equipment, Housing and Territorial Development: SLAHEDDINE MALOUCHE.
Minister of Development and International Co-operation: MUHAMMAD NOURI JOUINI.
Minister of State Property and Land Affairs: RIDHA GRIRA.
Minister in charge of Communications and of Relations with the Chamber of Deputies and the Chamber of Councillors: RAFAÂ DEKHIL.
Minister of Higher Education, Scientific Research and Technology: LAZHAR BOUOUNI.
Minister of Industry, Energy and Small and Medium Enterprises: AFIF CHELBI.
Minister-delegate to the Prime Minister, in charge of Civil Service and Administrative Development: ZOUHAIR MDHAFFER.
Government Secretary-General: ABD AL-HAKIM BOURAOUI.

There are, in addition, 16 Secretaries of State. The Governor of the Central Bank also has full ministerial status.

MINISTRIES

Office of the President: Palais de Carthage, 2016 Carthage; internet www.carthage.tn.
Office of the Prime Minister: place du Gouvernement, La Kasbah, 1008 Tunis; tel. (71) 565-400; e-mail prm@ministeres.tn; internet www.ministeres.tn.
Ministry of Agriculture and Water Resources: 30 rue Alain Savary, 1002 Tunis; tel. (71) 786-833; e-mail mag@ministeres.tn.
Ministry of Communication Technologies: 3 bis rue d'Angleterre, 1000 Tunis; tel. and fax (71) 359-000; e-mail info@infocom.tn; internet www.infocom.tn.
Ministry of Culture and Heritage Preservation: 8 rue 2 Mars 1934, la Kasbah, 1006 Tunis; tel. (71) 563-006; fax (71) 563-816; e-mail minculture@email.ati.tn; internet www.culture.tn.
Ministry of Development and International Co-operation: place Ali Zouaoui, 1069 Tunis; tel. (71) 240-133; fax (71) 799-069; e-mail boc@mdci.gov.tn; internet www.investissement.tn.
Ministry of Education and Training: blvd Bab Benat, 1030 Tunis; tel. (71) 568-768; e-mail med@ministeres.tn; internet www.education.tn.
Ministry of Employment and Professional Integration of Youth: 10 ave Ouled Haffouz, 1006 Tunis; tel. (71) 792-432; fax (71) 794-615; e-mail webmaster@email.ati.tn; internet www.info-emploi.tn.
Ministry of the Environment and Sustainable Development: Centre Urbain Nord, Ariana, 2080 Tunis; tel. (70) 728-455; fax (70) 728-655; e-mail boc@mineat.gov.tn; internet www.environnement.nat.tn.
Ministry of Equipment, Housing and Territorial Development: 10 blvd Habib Chrita, Cité Jardin, 1002 Tunis; tel. (71) 842-244; fax (71) 780-397; e-mail meh@ministeres.tn.
Ministry of Finance: place du Gouvernement, La Kasbah, 1008 Tunis; tel. (71) 571-888; fax (71) 572-390; e-mail mfi@ministeres.tn; internet www.portail.finances.gov.tn.

TUNISIA

Ministry of Foreign Affairs: ave de la Ligue des états arabes, Tunis; tel. (71) 847-500; e-mail mae@ministeres.tn; internet www.diplomatie.gov.tn.

Ministry of Higher Education, Scientific Research and Technology: ave Ouled Haffouz, 1030 Tunis; tel. (71) 786-300; fax (71) 786-701; e-mail mes@mes.rnu.tn; internet www.mes.tn.

Ministry of Industry, Energy and Small and Medium Enterprises: Immeuble Beya, 40 rue 8011, Montplaisir, 1002 Tunis; tel. (71) 791-132; fax (71) 782-742; e-mail webmaster@industrie.gov.tn; internet www.industrie.gov.tn.

Ministry of the Interior and Local Development: ave Habib Bourguiba, 1000 Tunis; tel. (71) 333-000; fax (71) 340-888; e-mail mint@ministeres.tn.

Ministry of Justice and Human Rights: 31 ave Bab Benat, 1006 Tunis; tel. (71) 561-440; fax (71) 586-106; e-mail mju@ministeres.tn.

Ministry of National Defence: blvd Bab Menara, 1030 Tunis; tel. (71) 560-240; fax (71) 561-804; e-mail defnat@defense.tn; internet www.defense.tn.

Ministry of Public Health: Bab Saâdoun, 1006 Tunis; tel. (71) 560-545; fax (71) 567-100; e-mail msp@ministeres.tn; internet www.santetunisie.rns.tn.

Ministry of Religious Affairs: 176 ave Bab Benat, 1009 Tunis; tel. (71) 570-147; fax (71) 570-123; e-mail mar@ministeres.tn; internet www.affaires-religieuses.tn.

Ministry of Social Affairs, Solidarity and Tunisians Abroad: 25 ave Bab Benat, 1006 Tunis; tel. (71) 567-502; fax (71) 568-722; e-mail mas@ministeres.tn; internet www.social.tn.

Ministry of State Property and Land Affairs: 19 ave de Paris, 1000 Tunis; tel. (71) 341-644; fax (71) 342-410; e-mail mdeaf@ministeres.tn; internet www.cpf.gov.tn.

Ministry of Tourism: 1 ave Muhammad V, 1001 Tunis; tel. (71) 341-077; fax (71) 332-070; e-mail mta@ministeres.tn.

Ministry of Trade and Handicrafts: 37 ave Kheireddine Pacha, 1002 Tunis; tel. (71) 890-070; fax (71) 781-324; e-mail mcmr@ministeres.tn; internet www.commerce.gov.tn.

Ministry of Transport: blvd 7 Novembre 1987, 2035 Tunis; tel. (71) 772-110; e-mail mtr@ministeres.tn.

Ministry of Women's, Family, Children's and Elderly Affairs: 2 rue d'Alger, 1001 Tunis; tel. (71) 252-514; fax (71) 349-900; e-mail maffepa@email.ati.tn; internet www.femmes.tn.

Ministry of Youth, Sports and Physical Education: Avenue Med Ali Akid, Cité El Khadhra, 1003 Tunis; tel. (71) 841-433; fax (71) 800-267; e-mail Portail.sport@sport.tn; internet www.sport.tn.

President and Legislature

PRESIDENT

Presidential Election, 24 October 2004

Candidate	Votes	% of votes
Zine al-Abidine Ben Ali	4,204,292	94.49
Muhammad Bouchiha	167,986	3.78
Muhammad Ali Halouani	42,213	0.95
Mounir Béji	35,067	0.79
Total*	**4,449,558**	**100.00**

* Excluding 14,779 invalid votes.

LEGISLATURE

Majlis an-Nuab
(Chamber of Deputies)

President: FOUAD MEBAZAÂ.

Election, 24 October 2004

Party	Votes	% of votes	Seats
Rassemblement constitutionnel démocratique	3,678,645	87.62	152
Mouvement des démocrates socialistes	194,829	4.64	14
Parti de l'unité populaire	152,987	3.64	11
Union démocratique unioniste	92,708	2.21	7
Mouvement du renouveau	43,268	1.03	3
Parti social libéral	25,261	0.60	2
Others	10,473	0.25	0
Total*	**4,198,171**	**100.00**	**189†**

* Excluding 15,305 spoilt ballot papers.

† Under the terms of an amendment to the electoral code adopted by the National Assembly in 1998, 20% of the seats in the National Assembly (and thus 37 in the current legislature) were reserved for candidates of opposition parties. These were allotted according to the proportion of votes received nationally by each party.

Majlis al-Mustasharin
(Chamber of Advisers)

Speaker: ABDULLAH KALLEL.

Election, 3 July 2005

	Seats*
Representatives of the main professional unions and federations	42
Representatives of the governorates†	43
Appointed by the President‡	41
Total	**126**

* Members of the Chamber of Advisers serve a six-year term; one-half of its members are replaced every three years.
† One or two members are elected from each of the 24 governorates, depending on the size of its population.
‡ Appointed on 1 August 2005.

Political Organizations

Congrès pour la République: Tunis; e-mail cprtunisie@yahoo.fr; internet www.cprtunisie.net; f. 2001; Leader MONCEF MARZOUKI.

Forum démocratique pour le travail et les libertés (FDTL): Tunis; internet www.fdtl.org; f. 2002; Leader Dr MUSTAPHA BEN JAAFAR.

Mouvement des démocrates socialistes (MDS): Tunis; in favour of a pluralist political system; participated in 1981 election and was officially recognized in Nov. 1983; Political Bureau of 11 mems, National Council of 60 mems, normally elected by the party Congress; Sec.-Gen. ISMAIL BOULAHYA.

Mouvement ettajdid: 6 rue Métouia, 1000 Tunis; tel. (71) 256-400; fax (71) 240-981; internet ettajdid.org; f. 1993 as Mouvement du renouveau, successor to Parti communiste tunisien; legal; Sec.-Gen. AHMED BRAHIM; Pres. of Nat. Council MUHAMMAD ALI HALOUANI.

Mouvement de l'unité populaire (MUP): Tunis; supports radical reform; split into two factions, one led by Ahmed Ben Salah living in exile until 1988; the other became the Parti de l'unité populaire (see below); Co-ordinator BRAHIM HAYDER.

Parti démocrate progressiste (PDP): Tunis; e-mail admin@pdpinfo.org; internet www.pdpinfo.org; f. 1983 as Rassemblement socialiste progressiste; officially recognized in Sept. 1988; name changed as above in 2001; leftist; Sec.-Gen. MAYA JRIBI.

Parti de la renaissance—Hizb an-Nahdah: Tunis; e-mail nahdha@ezzeitouna.org; fmrly Mouvement de la tendance islamique (banned in 1981); Leader RACHID GHANOUCHI; Sec.-Gen. Sheikh ABD AL-FATHA MOUROU.

Parti communiste des ouvriers tunisiens (PCOT): Tunis; e-mail pcot@albadil.org; internet www.albadil.org; illegal; Leader HAMMA HAMMAMI.

Parti social libéral (PSL): 42 ave Hédi Chaker, 1002 Tunis; tel. and fax (71) 789-050; fax (71) 789-060; e-mail p.s.l@gnet.tn; internet www.psltunisie.org; f. 1988; officially recognized in Sept. 1988 as the Parti social pour le progrès; adopted present name in 1993; liberal; Pres. Dr MONDHER THABET.

Parti de l'unité populaire (PUP): 7 rue d'Autriche, 1002 Tunis; tel. (71) 289-678; fax (71) 796-031; internet www.elwahda.org.tn; split from MUP (see above); officially recognized in Nov. 1983; Leader MUHAMMAD BOUCHIHA.

Parti des verts pour le progrès (PVP): f. 2006; seeks to promote awareness of the environment; Sec.-Gen. MONGI KHAMASSI.

Rassemblement constitutionnel démocratique (RCD): ave Muhammad V, 1040, Tunis; e-mail contact@rcd.tn; internet www.rcd.tn; f. 1934 as the Néo-Destour Party, following a split in the Destour (Constitution) Party; renamed Parti socialiste destourien in 1964; adopted present name in Feb. 1988; moderate left-wing republican party, which achieved Tunisian independence; Political Bureau of nine mems, and a Cen. Cttee of 200, elected by the party Congress; Chair. ZINE AL-ABIDINE BEN ALI; Vice-Chair. MUHAMMAD GHANNOUCHI; Sec.-Gen. MUHAMMAD GHARIANI.

Union démocratique unioniste (UDU): Tunis; officially recognized in Nov. 1988; supports Arab unity; Sec.-Gen. AHMED INOUBLI.

TUNISIA   *Directory*

Diplomatic Representation
EMBASSIES IN TUNISIA

Algeria: 18 rue de Niger, 1002 Tunis; tel. (71) 783-166; fax (71) 788-804; Ambassador YOUSSEF YOUSSFI.

Argentina: 10 rue al-Hassan et Houssaine, BP 9, al-Menzah IV, 1002 Tunis; tel. (71) 231-222; fax (71) 750-058; e-mail embargentunez@gnet.tn; Ambassador JESÚS FERNANDO TABOADA.

Austria: 16 rue ibn Hamdiss, BP 23, al-Menzah, 1004 Tunis; tel. (71) 751-091; fax (71) 767-824; e-mail tunis-ob@bmeia.gv.at; Ambassador Dr JOHANN FRÖHLICH.

Bahrain: 72 rue Mouaouia ibn Soufiane, BP 79, al-Menzah VIII, 2019 Tunis; tel. (71) 750-865; fax (71) 766-549; e-mail tunis.mission@mofa.gov.bh; Ambassador Sheikh MUHAMMAD BIN ALI AL-KHALIFA.

Belgium: 47 rue du 1er juin, BP 24, 1002 Tunis; tel. (71) 781-655; fax (71) 792-797; e-mail tunis@diplobel.org; internet www.diplomatie.be/tunis; Ambassador THOMAS ANTOINE.

Brazil: 5 rue Sufétula, BP 83, 1002 Tunis; tel. (71) 893-569; fax (71) 846-995; e-mail brasemb.tunis@gnet.tn; internet www.ambassadedubresil.com; Ambassador ELIM S. DUTRA.

Bulgaria: 5 rue Ryhane, BP 6, Cité Mahragène, 1082 Tunis; tel. (71) 798-962; fax (71) 791-667; e-mail tunis@embassy.transat.bg; internet www.mfa.bg/tunis; Ambassador PETKO DOYKOV.

Canada: 3 rue du Sénégal, place d'Afrique, BP 31, Belvédère, 1002 Tunis; tel. (71) 104-000; fax (71) 104-190; e-mail tunis@international.gc.ca; internet www.dfait-maeci.gc.ca/tunisia; Ambassador BRUNO PICARD.

China, People's Republic: 22 rue Dr Burnet, 1002 Tunis; tel. (71) 780-064; fax (71) 792-631; e-mail ambassade.chine@ati.tn; Ambassador LI BEIFEN.

Congo, Democratic Republic: 11 rue Tertullien, Notre Dame, Tunis; tel. (71) 281-833; Ambassador MBOLADINGA KATAKO.

Côte d'Ivoire: 17 rue el-Mansoura, BP 21, Belvédère, 1002 Tunis; tel. (71) 755-911; fax (71) 755-901; e-mail acitn@ambaci-tunis.org; Ambassador YAPO ATCHAPO THOMAS.

Cuba: 1 rue Amilcar, al-Menzah VIII, 1004 Tunis; tel. (71) 767-235; fax (71) 755-922; e-mail embajador-tunez@topnet.tn; internet emba.cubaminrex.cu/tunezar; Ambassador GABRIEL TIEL CAPOTE.

Czech Republic: 98 rue de Palestine, BP 53, Belvédère, 1002 Tunis; tel. (71) 780-456; fax (71) 793-228; e-mail tunis@embassy.mzv.cz; internet www.mzv.cz/tunis; Ambassador JAROMÍR PŘÍVRATSKÝ.

Egypt: ave Muhammad V, Quartier Montplaisir, rue 8007, Tunis; tel. (71) 792-233; fax (71) 794-389; e-mail egyembassy.tunis@planet.tn; Ambassador AHMED CHAFIK ISMAIL ABDELMOTI.

Finland: Dar Nordique, rue du Lac Neuchâtel, Les Berges du Lac, 1053 Tunis; tel. (71) 861-777; fax (71) 961-080; e-mail sanomat.tun@formin.fi; internet www.finlandtunis.org; Ambassador LAURA REINILÄ.

France: 2 place de l'Indépendance, 1000 Tunis; tel. (71) 105-111; fax (71) 105-100; e-mail courier@ambassadefrance-tn.org; internet www.ambassadefrance-tn.org; Ambassador SERGE DEGALLAIX.

Germany: 1 rue al-Hamra, BP 35, Mutuelleville, 1002 Tunis-Mutuelleville; tel. (71) 786-455; fax (71) 788-242; e-mail reg1@tunis.diplo.de; internet www.tunis.diplo.de; Ambassador Dr HORST-WOLFRAM KERLL.

Greece: 6 rue Saint Fulgence, Notre Dame, 1082 Tunis; tel. (71) 288-411; fax (71) 789-518; e-mail gremb.tun@mfa.gr; Ambassador DIMITRIOS KARATIDIS.

Hungary: 12 rue Achtart, 1082 Nord Hilton, BP 572, Tunis; tel. (71) 780-544; fax (71) 781-264; e-mail huembtun@planet.tn; internet www.mfa.gov.hu/emb/tunis; Ambassador Dr PÁL PATAKI.

India: 4 place Didon, Notre Dame, 1002 Tunis; tel. (71) 787-819; fax (71) 783-394; e-mail embassy.india@email.ati.tn.

Indonesia: BP 63, al-Menzah, 1004 Tunis; tel. (71) 860-377; fax (71) 861-758; e-mail kbritun@gnet.tn; Ambassador HERTOMO REKSODIPUTRO.

Iran: 10 rue de Docteur Burnet, Belvédère, 1002 Tunis; tel. (71) 790-084; fax (71) 793-177; Ambassador MUHAMMAD TAGHI MOAYED.

Iraq: ave Tahar B. Achour, route X2 m 10, Mutuelleville, Tunis; tel. (71) 962-480; fax (71) 963-737; e-mail tunemb@iraqmofamail.net; Ambassador GHAZI TAHIR KHALID.

Italy: 37 rue Jamal Abdelnaceur, 1000 Tunis; tel. (71) 321-811; fax (71) 324-155; e-mail ambitalia.tunisi@esteri.it; internet www.ambtunisi.esteri.it; Ambassador ANTONIO D'ANDRIA.

Japan: 9 rue Apollo XI, BP 163, Cité Mahrajène, 1082 Tunis; tel. (71) 791-251; fax (71) 786-625; internet www.tn.emb-japan.go.jp; Ambassador SHIGERU ENDO.

Jordan: 10 Nahj ash-Shankiti, 1002 Tunis; tel. (71) 785-829; fax (71) 786-461; e-mail emb.jordan@planet.tn; Ambassador SAMIR MUSTAPHA KHALIFA.

Korea, Republic: 16 rue Caracalla, BP 297, Notre Dame, 1082 Tunis; tel. (71) 799-905; fax (71) 791-923; e-mail tunisie@mofat.go.kr; internet tun.mofat.go.kr; Ambassador SON SE-JOO.

Kuwait: 40 route Ariane, al-Menzah, Tunis; tel. (71) 754-811; fax (71) 767659; e-mail tunis@mofa.gov.kw; Ambassador ABD AL-HAMID AL-FAILAKAWI.

Lebanon: rue d'Ormia, 1053 Les Berges du Lac, Tunis; tel. (71) 960-420; fax (71) 960-001; e-mail ambassadeliban@planet.tn; Ambassador FARID ABBOUD.

Libya: 48 bis rue du 1er juin, Mutuelleville, 1002 Tunis; tel. (71) 780-866; fax (71) 795-338.

Mali: 117 ave Jugurtha Matuelleville, BP 54, Nouvelle Ariana, 1002 Tunis; tel. (71) 792-589; fax (71) 791453; e-mail ambamali@wanadoo.tn; Ambassador ARAFA M'BARAKOU ASKIA TOURÉ.

Mauritania: 17 rue Fatma Ennechi, BP 62, al-Menzah, Tunis; tel. (71) 234-935; Ambassador AHMED S. OULD SALECK.

Morocco: 39 ave du 1er juin, 1002 Tunis; tel. (71) 782-775; fax (71) 787-103; e-mail ambamaroc@sifamatunis.net; Ambassador NAJIB ZEROUALI EL-OUARITI.

Netherlands: 6–8 rue Meycen, BP 47, Belvédère, 1082 Tunis; tel. (71) 797-724; fax (71) 785-557; e-mail tun@minbuza.nl; internet www.hollandembassy-tunisia.com; Ambassador RITA DULCI RAHMAN.

Norway: BP 124, Les Berges du Lac, 1053 Tunis; tel. (71) 861-777; fax (71) 961-080; e-mail emb.tunis@mfa.no; Ambassador THORBJORN GAUSTADSAETHER.

Pakistan: 35 rue Ali Ayari, al-Menzah IX, Tunis; tel. (71) 871-330; fax (71) 871-410; e-mail pareptunis@yahoo.com; Ambassador FAIZ MUHAMMAD KHOSO.

Poland: 5 Impasse no. 1, rue de Cordoue, El Manar I, Tunis; tel. (71) 873-837; fax (71) 872-987; e-mail amb.pologne@wanadoo.tn; internet www.tunis.polemb.net; Ambassador KRZYSZTOF OLENDZKI.

Portugal: 2 rue Sufétula, Belvédère, 1002 Tunis; tel. (71) 893-981; fax (71) 791-008; e-mail ambport@hexabyte.tn; Ambassador MARIA RITA DA FRANCA SOUSA E FERRO LEVY GOMES.

Qatar: rue Alhadi Krai, Northern al-Omran Quarter, 1082 Tunis; tel. (71) 849-600; fax (71) 749-073; e-mail tunis@mofa.gov.qa; Ambassador SAAD BIN NASSER AL-HUMAIDI.

Romania: 18 ave d'Afrique, BP 57, al-Menzah V, 1004 Tunis; tel. (71) 766-926; fax (71) 767-695; e-mail amb.roumanie@planet.tn; internet www.ambassade-roumanie.intl.tn; Ambassador SORIN-MIHAIL TĂNĂSESCU.

Russia: 4 rue Bergamotes, BP 48, El Manar I, 2092 Tunis; tel. (71) 882-446; fax (71) 882-478; e-mail ambrustn@mail.ru; internet www.tunisie.mid.ru; Ambassador ANDREI POLYAKOV.

Saudi Arabia: blvd du 7 Novembre, Centre Urbain-Nord C, Mahrajène, 1080 Tunis; tel. (70) 728-666; fax (70) 728-440; Ambassador IBRAHIM AS-SAAD AL-BRAHIM.

Senegal: 122 ave de la Liberté, Belvédère, Tunis; tel. (71) 802-397; fax (71) 780-770; internet www.ambasenegal.intl.tn; Ambassador ABDOURAHMANE SOW.

Serbia: 4 rue de Libéria, Belvédère, 1002 Tunis; tel. (71) 783-057; fax (71) 796-482; e-mail amb.serbia@gnet.tn; Chargé d'affaires a.i. IVAN KANDIJAS.

Somalia: 6 rue Hadramout, Mutuelleville, Tunis; tel. (71) 289-505; Ambassador AHMAD ABDALLAH MUHAMMAD.

South Africa: 7 rue Achtart, Nord Hilton, 1082 Tunis; tel. (71) 800-311; fax (71) 796-742; e-mail sa@emb-safrica.intl.tn; internet www.southafrica.intl.tn; Ambassador LUCAS DON NGAKANE.

Spain: 22–24 ave Dr Ernest Conseil, Cité Jardin, 1002 Tunis; tel. (71) 782-217; fax (71) 786-267; e-mail emb.tunez@maec.es; Ambassador JUAN RAMÓN MARTINEZ SALAZAR.

Sudan: 37 rue d'Afrique, al-Menzah V, 1008 Tunis; tel. (71) 231-322; fax (71) 751-756; e-mail contact@soudanembassy-tn.com; internet www.sudanembassy-tn.com; Ambassador OMAR HAIDER ABU ZEID.

Switzerland: BP 56, Les Berges du Lac, 1053 Tunis; tel. (71) 962-997; fax (71) 965-796; e-mail tun.vertretung@eda.admin.ch; internet www.eda.admin.ch/tunis; Ambassador CHRISTIAN FAESSLER.

Syria: 119 Azzouz Ribai-Almanar 3, Tunis; tel. (71) 888-188; Ambassador Dr SAMI GLAIEL.

Turkey: 30 ave d'Afrique, BP 134, al-Menzah V, Tunis; tel. (71) 750-668; fax (71) 767-045; e-mail tunus.be@planet.tn; Ambassador HÜSEYIN NACI AKINCI.

Ukraine: 7 rue Saint Fulgence, Notre Dame, 1002 Tunis; tel. (71) 845-861; fax (71) 840-866; e-mail ambassade.ukraine@planet.tn; Ambassador VALERIY RYLACH.

United Arab Emirates: 9 rue Achtart, Nord Hilton, Belvédère, 1002 Tunis; tel. (71) 788-888; fax (71) 788-777; e-mail emirates.embassy@planet.tn; Ambassador MUHAMMAD HAMAD OMRANE.

United Kingdom: rue du Lac Windermere, Les Berges du Lac, 1053 Tunis; tel. (71) 108-700; fax (71) 108-749; e-mail TunisConsular

TUNISIA

.tunis@fco.gov.uk; internet ukintunisia.fco.gov.uk; Ambassador CHRISTOPHER PAUL O'CONNOR.

USA: Les Berges du Lac, 1053 Tunis; tel. (71) 107-000; fax (71) 107-090; e-mail tuniswebsitecontact@state.gov; internet tunis.usembassy.gov; Ambassador ROBERT F. GODEC.

Yemen: rue Mouaouia ibn Soufiane, al-Menzah VI, Tunis; tel. (71) 237-933; Ambassador HUSSEIN DHAIFULLAH AL-AWADHI.

Judicial System

The Cour de Cassation in Tunis has three civil and one criminal sections. There are three **Cours d'Appel** at Tunis, Sousse and Sfax, and 13 **Cours de Première Instance**, each having three chambers, except the **Cour de Première Instance** at Tunis, which has eight chambers. **Justices Cantonales** exist in 51 areas.

Religion

The Constitution of 1956 recognizes Islam as the state religion, with the introduction of certain reforms, such as the abolition of polygamy. An estimated 99% of the population are Muslims. Minority religions include Judaism (an estimated 1,500 adherents in 2008) and Christianity. The Christian population comprises Roman Catholics, Greek Orthodox, and French and English Protestants.

ISLAM

Grand Mufti of Tunisia: Sheikh KAMAL AD-DIN JA'EIT.

CHRISTIANITY

The Roman Catholic Church

There were an estimated 20,100 adherents in Tunisia in December 2006.

Bishop of Tunis: Most Rev. MAROUN ELIAS LAHHAM, Evêché, 4 rue d'Alger, 1000 Tunis; tel. (71) 335-831; fax (71) 335-832; e-mail eveche.tunisie@evechetunisie.org; internet www.diocesetunisie.org.

The Protestant Church

Reformed Church of Tunisia: 36 rue Charles de Gaulle, 1000 Tunis; tel. (71) 327-886; e-mail eglisereformee@yahoo.fr; f. 1880; c.220 mems; Pastor WILLIAM BROWN.

The Press

DAILIES

Al-Chourouk (Sunrise): 25 rue Jean Jaurès, BP 36619, Tunis; tel. (71) 331-000; fax (71) 253-024; e-mail directiongenerale@alchourouk.com; internet www.alchourouk.com; Arabic; Dir SLAHEDDINE AL-AMRI; Editor-in-Chief ABD AL-HAMID RIAHI; circ. 70,000.

Al-Horria: 8 rue de Rome, 1000 Tunis; tel. (71) 351-578; fax (71) 350-721; e-mail alhorria@email.ati.tn; internet www.alhorria.info.tn; Arabic; organ of the RCD; Dir and Editor-in-Chief MONGI ZEIDI; circ. 50,000.

La Presse de Tunisie: 6 rue Ali Bach-Hamba, 1000 Tunis; tel. (71) 341-066; fax (71) 349-720; e-mail contact@lapresse.tn; internet www.lapresse.tn; f. 1936; French; Pres. and Dir-Gen. MUHAMMAD GONTARA; circ. 40,000.

Le Quotidien: 25 rue Jean Jaurès, 1000 Tunis; tel. (71) 331-000; fax (71) 253-02; e-mail directiongenerale@lequotidien-tn.com; internet www.lequotidien-tn.com; f. 2001; French; Dir SLAHEDDINE AL-AMRI; Editor-in-Chief CHOUKRY BAKOUCHE; circ. 20,000.

Le Renouveau: 8 rue de Rome, 1000 Tunis; tel. (71) 352-058; fax (71) 352-927; e-mail lerenouveau@lerenouveau.com.tn; internet www.lerenouveau.com.tn; f. 1988; French; organ of the RCD; Dir and Editor-in-Chief NEJIB OUERGHI.

As-Sabah (The Morning): ave du 7 novembre 1987, BP 441, al-Menzah, 1004 Tunis; tel. (71) 238-222; fax (71) 232-761; e-mail redaction@assabah.com.tn; internet www.assabah.com.tn; f. 1951; Arabic; Dir MUSTAPHA AL-JABER; Editor-in-Chief NOUREDDINE ACHOUR; circ. 50,000.

As-Sahafa: 6 rue Ali Bach-Hamba, 1000 Tunis; tel. (71) 341-066; fax (71) 349-720; e-mail contact@essahafa.info.tn; internet www.essahafa.info.tn; f. 1936; Arabic; Dir SAHRAOUI GAMOUN.

Le Temps: ave 7 novembre 1987, BP 441, al-Menzah, 1004 Tunis; tel. (71) 238-222; fax (71) 232-761; e-mail redaction@letemps.com.tn; internet www.letemps.com.tn; f. 1975; French; Dir MUSTAPHA AL-JABER; Editor-in-Chief RAOUF KHALSI; circ. 42,000.

PERIODICALS

Afrique Economie: 16 rue de Rome, BP 61, 1015 Tunis; tel. (71) 347-441; fax (71) 353-172; e-mail iea@planet.tn; f. 1970; monthly; Dir MUHAMMAD ZERZERI.

Al-Akhbar (The News): 1 passage d'al-Houdaybiyah, 1000 Tunis; tel. (71) 344-100; fax (71) 355-079; internet www.akhbar.tn; f. 1984; weekly; Arabic; general; Dir MUHAMMAD BEN YOUSUF; circ. 75,000.

Journal Les Annonces: 6 rue de Sparte, BP 1343, Tunis; tel. (71) 350-177; fax (71) 347-184; e-mail nejib.azouz@planet.tn; internet www.elilane.com; f. 1978; 2 a week; French and Arabic; Dir MUHAMMAD NEJIB AZOUZ; circ. 170,000.

Al-Anouar at-Tounissia (Tunisian Lights): 25 rue ach-Cham, 5000 Tunis; tel. (71) 331-000; fax (71) 253-024; internet www.alanouar.com; Arabic; Dir SLAHEDDINE AL-AMRI; circ. 165,000.

L'Avenir: 26 rue Gamal Abd an-Nasser, BP 1200, Tunis; tel. (71) 258-941; f. 1980; weekly; organ of the Mouvement des démocrates socialistes (MDS).

Al-Bayan (The Manifesto): 61 rue Abderrazek, Chraîbi, 1001 Tunis; tel. (71) 339-633; fax (71) 338-533; e-mail darelbayane@gnet.tn; f. 1976; weekly; general; organ of the Union tunisienne de l'industrie, du commerce et de l'artisanat; Dir HÉDI DJILANI; circ. 100,000.

Al-Biladi (My Country): 15 rue 2 mars 1934, Tunis; f. 1974; Arabic; political and general weekly for Tunisian workers abroad; Dir HÉDI AL-GHALI; circ. 90,000.

Bulletin Mensuel de Statistiques: Institut National de la Statistique, 70 rue al-Cham, BP 265, 1080 Tunis; tel. (71) 891-002; fax (71) 792-559; e-mail ins@mdci.gov.tn; internet www.ins.nat.tn; monthly.

Conjoncture: 37 ave Kheireddine Pacha, 1002 Tunis; tel. (71) 891-826; fax (71) 200-706; e-mail conjoncture2003@yahoo.fr; f. 1974; monthly; economic and financial surveys; Dir HABIB BEDHIAFI; circ. 5,000.

Démocratie: Tunis; f. 1978; monthly; French; organ of the MDS; Dir HASSIB BEN AMMAR; circ. 5,000.

Dialogue: 15 rue 2 mars 1934, Tunis; tel. (71) 264-899; f. 1974; weekly; French; cultural and political organ of the RCD; Dir NACEUR BECHEKH; circ. 30,000.

L'Economiste Maghrébin: 3 rue el-Kewekibi, 1002 Tunis; tel. (71) 790-773; fax (71) 793-707; e-mail leconomiste@planet.tn; internet www.leconomiste.com.tn; f. 1990; bi-weekly; French; Dir HÉDI MÉCHRI; circ. 30,000.

Etudiant Tunisien: Tunis; f. 1953; French and Arabic; Chief Editor FAOUZI AOUAM.

Al-Fajr (Dawn): Tunis; f. 1990; weekly; Arabic; organ of the Parti de la renaissance—Hizb an-Nahdah.

El-Fallah: 8451 rue Alain Savary, al-Khadra, 1003 Tunis; tel. (71) 806-800; fax (71) 809-181; e-mail utap.tunis@email.ati.tn; internet www.utap.org.tn; weekly; organ of the Union tunisienne de l'agriculture et de la pêche (UTAP); Dir MABROUK BAHRI; Editor GHARBI HAMOUDA; circ. 7,000.

Al-Fikr (Thought): Tunis; f. 1955; monthly; Arabic; cultural review.

L'Hebdo Touristique: rue 8601, 40, Zone Industrielle, La Charguia 2, 2035 Tunis; tel. (71) 786-866; fax (71) 794-891; e-mail haddad.tijani@planet.tn; f. 1971; weekly; French; tourism; Dir TIJANI HADDAD; circ. 5,000.

IBLA: Institut des Belles Lettres Arabes, 12 rue Jemaâ el-Haoua, 1008 Tunis; tel. (71) 560-133; fax (71) 572-683; e-mail ibla@gnet.tn; internet www.iblatunis.org; f. 1937; 2 a year; French, Arabic and English; social and cultural review on Maghreb and Muslim-Arab affairs; Dir JEAN FONTAINE; circ. 800.

Al-Idhaa wa Talvaza (Radio and Television): 71 ave de la Liberté, Tunis; tel. (71) 782-700; fax (71) 796-691; e-mail revue@ertt.nat.tn; f. 1956; fortnightly; Arabic language broadcasting magazine; Dir MUSTAPHA KHAMMARI; Editor JAMEL KARMAOUI.

Irfane (Children): 6 rue Muhammad Ali, 1000 Tunis; tel. (71) 256-877; fax (71) 351-521; f. 1965; monthly; Arabic; Dir-Gen. RIDHA EL OUADI; circ. 100,000.

Jeunesse Magazine: 6 rue Muhammad Ali, 1000 Tunis; tel. (71) 256-877; fax (71) 351-521; f. 1980; monthly; Arabic; Dir-Gen. RIDHA EL OUADI; circ. 30,000.

Journal Officiel de la République Tunisienne: ave Farhat Hached, 2040 Radès; tel. (71) 299-914; fax (71) 297-234; f. 1860; the official gazette; French and Arabic editions publ. twice weekly by the Imprimerie Officielle (The State Press); Pres. and Dir-Gen. ROMDHANE BEN MIMOUN; circ. 20,000.

Al-Mawkif: 10 rue Eve Nohelle, 1001 Tunis; tel. (71) 332-271; fax (71) 332-194; e-mail mawkef_21@yahoo.fr; f. 1984; weekly; organ of the Parti démocrate progressiste; Dir AHMED NÉJIB CHEBBI; Editor-in-Chief RACHID KHECHANA.

Al-Maraa (The Woman): 56 blvd Bab Benat, 1006 Tunis; tel. (71) 567-845; fax (71) 567-131; e-mail unft@email.a.t.i.tn; f. 1961;

monthly; Arabic/French; political, economic and social affairs; issued by the Union nationale de la femme tunisienne; Pres. AZIZA HABIRA; circ. 10,000.

Al-Moussawar: 10 rue ach-Cham, Tunis; tel. (71) 289-000; fax (71) 289-357; internet www.almoussawar.com; weekly; circ. 75,000.

Mouwatinoun (Citizens): Tunis; internet www.fdtl.org; f. 2007; weekly; Arabic; organ of the Forum démocratique pour le travail et les libertés (FDTL).

Outrouhat: Tunis; monthly; scientific; Dir LOTFI BEN AÏSSA.

Réalités: 6–7 rue de Cameroun, 1002 Tunis; tel. (71) 788-313; fax (71) 787-160; e-mail redaction@realites.com.tn; internet www.realites.com.tn; f. 1979; weekly; French/Arabic; Dir TAÏEB ZAHAR; circ. 25,000.

At-Tariq al-Jadid (New Road): 6 rue Metouia, 1069 Tunis; tel. (71) 256-400; fax (71) 240-981; f. 1981; weekly; Arabic; organ of the Mouvement ettajdid; Dir MUHAMMAD HARMEL; Editor-in-Chief HICHAM SKIK.

Tounes el Khadra: 8451 rue Alain Savary, al-Khadra, 1003 Tunis; tel. (71) 806-800; fax (71) 809-181; e-mail utap.tunis@email.ati.tn; internet www.utap.org.tn; f. 1976; bi-monthly; agricultural, scientific and technical; organ of the UTAP; Dir MABROUK BAHRI; Editor GHARBI HAMOUDA; circ. 5,000.

Tunis Hebdo: 1 passage d'al-Houdaybiyah, 1000 Tunis; tel. (71) 344-100; fax (71) 355-079; e-mail tunishebdo@tunishebdo.com.tn; internet www.tunishebdo.com.tn; f. 1973; weekly; French; general and sport; Dir MUHAMMAD BEN YOUSUF; circ. 35,000.

Tunisia News: rue 8601, 40, Zone Industrielle, La Charguia 1, 2035 Tunis; tel. (71) 786-866; fax (71) 794-891; e-mail haddad.tijani@planet.tn; f. 1993; weekly; English; Dir TIJANI HADDAD; circ. 5,000.

NEWS AGENCY

Tunis Afrique Presse (TAP): 7 ave Slimane Ben Slimane, al-Manar, 2092 Tunis; tel. (71) 889-000; fax (71) 883-500; e-mail desk.inter@email.ati.tn; internet www.tap.info.tn; f. 1961; Arabic, French and English; offices in Algiers, Rabat, Paris and New York; daily news services; Chair. and Gen. Man. MUHAMMAD BEN EZZEDDINE.

Publishers

Ad-Dar al-Arabia Lil Kitab: 4 ave Mohieddine el-Klibi, al-Manar, BP 32, al-Manar 2, 2092 Tunis; tel. (71) 888-255; fax (71) 888-365; e-mail mal@gnet.tn; f. 1975; general literature, children's books, non-fiction; Dir-Gen. MUSTAPHA ATTIA.

Centre de Publications Universitaires: Campus Universitaire, BP 255, 1080 Tunis; tel. (71) 874-000; fax (71) 871-677; e-mail cpu@cpu.rnu.tn; internet www.mes.tn/cpu; educational books, journals.

Cérès Editions: 6 rue Alain Savary, Belvédère, 1002 Tunis; tel. (71) 280-505; fax (71) 287-216; e-mail info@ceres-editions.com; internet www.ceres-editions.com; f. 1964; social sciences, art books, literature, novels; Man. Editor KARIM BEN SMAIL.

Dar Cheraït: Centre Culturel et Touristique Dar Cheraït, Route Touristique, 2200 Tozeur; tel. (76) 452-100; fax (76) 452-329; e-mail darcherait@planet.tn; internet www.darcherait.com.tn.

Dar al-Kitab: 5 ave Bourguiba, 4000 Sousse; tel. (73) 25097; f. 1950; literature, children's books, legal studies, foreign books; Pres. TAÏEB KACEM; Dir FAYÇAL KACEM.

Dar as-Sabah: ave 7 Novembre 1987, BP 441, al-Menzah, 1004 Tunis; tel. (71) 717-222; fax (71) 232-761; f. 1951; 200 mems; publishes daily and weekly papers, including the dailies As-Sabah and Le Temps, which circulate throughout Tunisia, North Africa, France, Belgium, Luxembourg and Germany; Chair. MUHAMMAD SAKHER EL MATERI; Dir-Gen. MUSTAPHA AL-JABER.

Editions Apollonia: 4 rue Claude Bernard, 1002 Tunis; tel. (71) 786-381; fax (71) 799-190; e-mail sales@apollonia.com.tn; internet www.apollonia.com.tn; art, literature, essays, poetry.

Editions Bouslama: 15 ave de France, 1000 Tunis; tel. (71) 243-745; fax (71) 381-100; f. 1960; history, children's books; Man. Dir ALI BOUSLAMA.

Institut National de la Statistique: 70 rue al-Cham, BP 265, 1080 Tunis; tel. (71) 891-002; fax (71) 792-559; e-mail ins@mdci.gov.tn; internet www.ins.nat.tn; publishes a variety of annuals, periodicals and papers concerned with the economic policy and devt of Tunisia.

Librairie al-Manar: 60 ave Bab Djedid, BP 179, 1008 Tunis; tel. (71) 253-224; fax (71) 336-565; e-mail librairie.almanar@planet.tn; f. 1938; general, educational, Islam; Man. Dir HABIB M'HAMDI.

Société d'Arts Graphiques, d'Edition et de Presse (SAGEP): 15 rue 2 mars 1934, La Kasbah, 1000 Tunis; tel. (71) 564-988; fax (71) 569-736; f. 1974; prints and publishes daily papers, magazines, books, etc.; Dir-Gen. MAHMOUD MEFTAH.

Sud Editions: 79 rue de Palestine, 1002 Tunis; tel. (71) 785-179; fax (71) 848-664; e-mail sud.editions@planet.tn; f. 1976; Arab literature, art and art history, history, sociology, religion; Man. Dir MUHAMMAD MASMOUDI.

GOVERNMENT PUBLISHING HOUSE

Imprimerie Officielle de la République Tunisienne: 40 ave Farhat Hached, 2098 Radès; tel. (71) 434-211; fax (71) 434-234; e-mail iort@iort.gov.tn; internet www.iort.gov.tn; f. 1860; Pres. and Dir-Gen. HOSNI TOUMI.

Broadcasting and Communications

TELECOMMUNICATIONS

Société Tunisienne d'Entreprises des Télécommunications (SOTETEL): rue des Entrepreneurs, Zone Industrielle, BP 640, La Charguia 2, 1080 Tunis; tel. (71) 941-100; fax (71) 940-584; e-mail sotetel@email.ati.tn; internet www.sotetel.com.tn; f. 1981; transferred to private ownership in 1998; Dir-Gen. HÉDI FRIOUI.

Orascom Telecom Tunisia (Tunisiana): 11 rue 8607, Zone Industrielle, La Charguia 1, 2035 Tunis; tel. (22) 121-432; e-mail abdelaziz.djilani@tunisiana.com; internet www.tunisiana.com; f. 2002; Chair. and CEO NAGUIB SAWIRIS.

Tunisie Télécom: Cité Ennassim, ave du Japon, Montplaisir, 1073 Tunis; tel. (71) 901-717; fax (71) 900-777; e-mail actel.virtuelle@ttnet.tn; internet www.tunisietelecom.tn; 65% state-owned, 35% owned by Tecom-Dig (Dubai, United Arab Emirates); Pres. and Gen. Man. MUHAMMAD OUAILI.

BROADCASTING

Radio

Etablissement de la Radiodiffusion-Télévision Tunisienne (ERTT): 71 ave de la Liberté, 1002 Tunis; tel. (71) 847-300; fax (71) 781-058; e-mail info@radiotunis.com; internet www.radiotunis.com; govt service; broadcasts in Arabic, French, German, Italian, Spanish and English; radio stations at Gafsa, El-Kef, Monastir, Sfax, Tataouine and Tunis (three); television stations Tunis 7 and Canal 21; Pres. MUSTAPHA KHAMMARI.

Radio Mosaïque: Tunis; tel. (71) 287-246; e-mail dg@mosaiquefm.net; internet www.mosaiquefm.net; f. 2003; first privately owned radio station when launched in 2003; broadcasts in Arabic and French to Tunis and the north-east of the country; Dir-Gen. NOUREDDINE BOUTAR.

Television

Etablissement de la Radiodiffusion-Télévision Tunisienne: internet www.tunisie7.tn; see Radio.

Office National de la Télédiffusion (ONT) (National Broadcasting Corporation of Tunisia): Cite Ennasim, 1 Borjel, BP 399, 1080 Tunis; tel. (71) 801-177; fax (71) 781-927; e-mail ont@telediffusion.net.tn; internet www.telediffusion.net.tn; f. 1993.

Finance

(cap. = capital; dep. = deposits; res = reserves; m. = million; brs = branches; amounts in dinars unless otherwise stated)

BANKING

Central Bank

Banque Centrale de Tunisie (BCT): 25 rue Hédi Nouira, BP 777, 1080 Tunis; tel. (71) 340-588; fax (71) 354-214; e-mail boc@bct.gov.tn; internet www.bct.gov.tn; f. 1958; cap. 6.0m., res 81.6m., dep. 2,778.2m. (Dec. 2006); Gov. TAOUFIK BACCAR; 10 brs.

Commercial Banks

Amen Bank: ave Muhammad V, 1002 Tunis; tel. (71) 835-500; fax (71) 833-517; e-mail amenbank@amenbank.com.tn; internet www.amenbank.com.tn; f. 1967 as Crédit Foncier et Commercial de Tunisie; name changed as above in 1995; cap. 70.0m., res 134.6m., dep. 1,965.2m. (Dec. 2006); Chair. and Pres. RACHID BEN YEDDER; Gen. Man. AHMAD EL-KARM; 81 brs.

Arab Banking Corpn Tunisie: ABC Building, rue du Lac d'Annecy, Les Berges du Lac, 1053 Tunis; tel. (71) 861-861; fax (71) 860-921; e-mail abc.tunis@arabbanking.com; internet www.arabbanking.com; f. 2000; cap. 40m., res −25.2m., dep. 164.4m. (Dec. 2006); Chair. MUHAMMAD HUSSAIN LAYAS; Country Man. SADDEK EL-KABER; 4 brs.

Arab Tunisian Bank: 9 rue Hédi Nouira, POB 520, 1001 Tunis; tel. (71) 351-155; fax (71) 342-852; e-mail atbbank@atb.com.tn; internet www.atb.com.tn; f. 1982; 64.2% owned by Arab Bank PLC (Jordan); cap. 60m., res 100.4m., dep. 1,952.8m. (Dec. 2006); Pres. SAMAR EL-MOLLA; Dir-Gen. MUHAMMAD FERID BEN TANFOUS; 62 brs.

Attijari Bank: 95 ave de la Liberté, 1002 Tunis; tel. (71) 141-400; fax (71) 782-663; e-mail courrier@attijaribank.com.tn; internet www.attijaribank.com.tn; f. 1968 as Banque du Sud; present name adopted 2006; cap. 150.0m., res –49.6m., dep. 2,172.30m. (Dec. 2007); shareholders include Attijariwafa Bank, Morocco (37.11%) and Banco Santander, Spain (17.46%); Pres. MONCEF CHAFFAR; Dir-Gen. HASSAN BERTAL; 93 brs.

Banque de l'Habitat: 21 ave Kheireddine Pacha, BP 242, 1002 Tunis; tel. (71) 785-277; fax (71) 784-417; e-mail banquehabitat@bh.fin.tn; internet www.bh.com.tn; f. 1984; 32.62% govt-owned; cap. 75m., res 130.1m., dep. 2,615.3m. (Dec. 2005); Pres. and Chair. ABOU HAFS AMOR NAJÏ; 79 brs.

Banque Internationale Arabe de Tunisie (BIAT): 70–72 ave Habib Bourguiba, BP 520, 1080 Tunis; tel. (71) 340-733; fax (71) 346-454; e-mail correspondent.banking@biat.com.tn; internet www.biat.com.tn; f. 1976; cap. 170.0m., res 233.4m., dep. 4,141.3m. (Dec. 2007); Gen. Man SLAHEDDINE LADJIMI; 112 brs.

Banque Nationale Agricole: rue Hédi Nouira, 1001 Tunis; tel. (71) 831-000; fax (71) 832-807; e-mail bna@bna.com.tn; internet www.bna.com.tn; f. 1989 by merger of the Banque Nationale du Développement Agricole and the Banque Nationale de Tunisie; cap. 100.0m., res 249.5m., dep. 3,964.0m. (Dec. 2006); Pres. and Gen. Man. MONCEF DAKHLI; 147 brs.

Banque de Tunisie SA: 2 rue de Turquie, BP 289, 1001 Tunis; tel. (71) 332-188; fax (71) 349-401; e-mail finance@bt.com.tn; internet www.bt.com.tn; f. 1884; cap. 75.0m., res 224.9m., dep. 1,624.2m. (Dec. 2007); Pres. ALIA ABDALLAH; 83 agencies.

Banque Tuniso-Koweïtienne: 10 bis ave Muhammad V, BP 49, 1001 Tunis; tel. (71) 340-000; fax (71) 343-106; e-mail contact.btkd@planet.tn; internet www.btknet.com; f. 1981 as Banque Tuniso-Koweïtienne de Développement; present name adopted 2007; Chair. MOTLAQ MUBARAK AS-SANAA; Dir-Gen. ABDELGHAFFAR EZZEDDINE.

Société Tunisienne de Banque (STB): rue Hédi Nouira, BP 638, 1001 Tunis; tel. (71) 340-477; fax (71) 348-400; e-mail stb@stb.com.tn; internet www.stb.com.tn; f. 1957; 24.81% govt-owned; merged with Banque Nationale de Développement Touristique and Banque de Développement Economique de Tunisie in 2000; cap. 124.2m., res 293.8m., dep. 3,243.6m. (Dec. 2006); Pres. and Dir-Gen. LAROUSSI BAYOUDH; 117 brs.

Union Bancaire pour le Commerce et l'Industrie: 139 ave de la Liberté, Belvédère, 1002 Tunis; tel. (71) 842-000; fax (71) 346-737; e-mail saber.mensi@bnpparibas.com; internet www.ubcinet.net; f. 1961; cap. 50.0m., res 92,123m., dep. 1,164.7m. (Dec. 2006); affiliated to and 50% owned by BNP Paribas (France); Pres. and Gen. Man. SLAHEDDINE BOUGERRA; 87 brs.

Union Internationale de Banques SA: 65 ave Habib Bourguiba, BP 109, 1000 Tunis; tel. (71) 347-000; fax (71) 353-090; e-mail lilia.meddeb@uib.fin.tn; internet www.uib.com.tn; f. 1963 as a merging of Tunisian interests by the Société Franco-Tunisienne de Banque et de Crédit with Crédit Lyonnais (France) and other foreign banks, including Banca Commerciale Italiana; 52.3% owned by Société Générale (France); cap. 106.0m., res 59.68m., dep. 1,621.5m. (Dec. 2006); Pres. BERNARD DAVID; Gen. Man. KAMEL NAJI; 94 brs.

Merchant Banks

Banque d'Affaires de Tunisie (BAT): 32 rue Hédi Karray, 1082 Tunis; tel. (71) 703-175; fax (71) 703-604; e-mail bat@bat.com.tn; internet www.bat-tunisie.com; f. 1997; cap. 4.5m.; Gen. Man. HABIB KARAOUL.

International Maghreb Merchant Bank (IM Bank): Immeuble Maghrebia, Bloc B, 3ème étage, Les Berges du Lac, 2045 Tunis; tel. (71) 860-816; fax (71) 860-057; e-mail imbank@imbank.com.tn; internet www.imbank.com.tn; f. 1995; Pres. OLIVIER PASTRÉ; CEO KACEM BOUSNINA.

Development Banks

Banque de Tunisie et des Emirats (BTE): 5 bis blvd Muhammad Badra, 1002 Tunis; tel. (71) 112-000; fax (71) 783-756; e-mail imed.cherif@bte.com.tn; internet www.bte.com.tn; f. 1982 as Banque de Tunisie et des Emirats d'Investissement; name changed as above in 2005; cap. 90.0m., res 38.4m., dep. 53.6m. (Dec. 2006); Chair. SALAM RACHID AL-MOHANNADI; Gen. Man. CHEDLI AISSA.

Banque Tunisienne de Solidarité (BTS): 56 ave Muhammad V, 1002 Tunis; tel. (71) 844-040; fax (71) 845-537; e-mail bts@email.ati.tn; internet www.bts.com.tn; f. 1997; provides medium- and short-term finance for small-scale projects; cap. 40m.; Pres. NAÏJA AHMED; 25 brs.

Banque Tuniso-Libyenne: 25 ave Kheireddine Pacha, BP 102, Belvédère, 1002 Tunis; tel. (71) 781-500; fax (71) 782-818; f. 1983 as Banque Arabe Tuniso-Libyenne de Développement et de Commerce; name changed as above in 2005; promotes trade and devt projects between Tunisia and Libya, and provides funds for investment in poorer areas; cap. 70.0m., res 2.5m., dep. 123.5m. (Dec. 2005); Pres. and Man. Dir SAÏD M'RABET.

Société Tuniso-Séoudienne d'Investissement et de Développement (STUSID): 32 rue Hédi Karray, BP 20, 1082 Tunis; tel. (71) 718-233; fax (71) 719-233; e-mail commercial@stusid.com.tn; internet www.stusid.com.tn; f. 1981; provides long-term finance for devt projects; cap. 100.0m., res 84.4m., dep. 10.5m. (Dec. 2002); Chair. Dr ABD AL-AZIZ A. AN-NASRALLAH; Pres. and Dir-Gen. ABD AL-WAHEB NACHI.

'Offshore' Banks

Alubaf International Bank: 8007 rue Montplaisir, BP 51, Belvédère, 1002 Tunis; tel. (71) 783-500; fax (71) 793-905; e-mail alub.alubaf.com.tn; internet www,alubaf.com.tn; f. 1985; 100% owned by Libyan Arab Foreign Bank; cap. US $25.0m., res $6.8m., dep. $147.9m. (Dec. 2007); Chair. Dr AHMAD MNEISSI; Gen. Man. MUHAMMAD LAHMAR.

Beit Ettamwil Saudi Tounsi (BEST): 88 ave Hédi Chaker, 1002 Tunis; tel. (71) 790-000; fax (71) 780-235; e-mail bestbank@planet.tn; f. 1983; Islamic bank; Pres. Dr SALAH JEMIL MALAIKA.

North Africa International Bank: ave Kheireddine Pacha, BP 485, 1002 Tunis; tel. (71) 950-800; fax (71) 950-840; e-mail naib@naibank.com; internet www.naibbank.com; f. 1984; cap. US $30.0m., res $16.5m., dep. $129.8m. (Dec. 2004); Chair. and Gen. Man. GIUMA M. WAHEBA; 1 br.

Tunis International Bank: 18 ave des Etats-Unis d'Amérique, BP 81, 1002 Tunis; tel. (71) 782-411; fax (71) 782-223; e-mail tib1.tib@planet.tn; internet www.tib.com.tn; f. 1982; 86.6% owned by United Gulf Bank (Bahrain); cap. US $25.0m., res $25.9m., dep. $421.6m. (Dec. 2007); Chair. MASOUD J. HAYAT; Dep. Chair. and Man. Dir MUHAMMAD FEKIH; 3 brs.

STOCK EXCHANGE

Bourse des Valeurs Mobilières de Tunis (Bourse de Tunis): Tour Babel, Escalier E, Cité Montplaisir, 1073 Tunis; tel. (71) 780-288; fax (71) 789-189; e-mail info@bvmt.com.tn; internet www.bvmt.com.tn; f. 1969; Chair. YOUSUF KORTOBI; Dir-Gen. MUHAMMAD BICHIOU.

INSURANCE

BEST Reinsurance (BEST Re): Rue du Lac de Côme, Les Berges du lac, BP 484, 1080 Tunis; tel. (71) 860-355; fax (71) 861-011; e-mail general@bestre.com.tn; internet www.best-re.com; f. 1985; operates according to Islamic principles; cap. US $100m.; Dir-Gen. RIADH KARRAY.

Caisse Tunisienne d'Assurances Mutuelles Agricoles—Mutuelle Générale d'Assurances (CTAMA—MGA): 6 ave Habib Thameur, 1069 Tunis; tel. (71) 340-933; fax (71) 332-276; e-mail ctama@planet.tn; internet www.ctamamga.com; f. 1912; Pres. MOKTAR BELLAGHA; Dir-Gen. MEZRI JELIZI.

Cie d'Assurances Tous Risques et de Réassurance (ASTREE): 45 ave Kheireddine Pacha, BP 780, 1002 Tunis; tel. (71) 792-211; fax (71) 794-723; e-mail courrier@astree.com.tn; internet www.astree.com.tn; f. 1949; cap. 4m.; Pres. and Dir-Gen. MUHAMMAD HABIB BEN SAAD.

Cie Tunisienne pour l'Assurance du Commerce Extérieur (COTUNACE): ave Muhammad V, Montplaisir I, rue 8006, 1002 Tunis; tel. (71) 783-000; fax (71) 782-539; e-mail cotunace.ddc@planet.tn; internet www.cotunace.com.tn; f. 1984; cap. 5m.; 65 mem. cos; Pres. and Dir-Gen. MONCEF ZOUARI.

Société Tunisienne d'Assurance et de Réassurance (STAR): ave de Paris, Tunis; tel. (71) 340-866; fax (71) 340-835; e-mail star@star.com.tn; internet www.star.com.tn; f. 1958; Pres. and Dir-Gen. ABDELKRIM MERDASSI.

Tunis-Ré (Société Tunisienne de Réassurance): ave Muhammad V, Montplaisir 1, BP 29, 1073 Tunis; tel. (71) 844-011; fax (71) 787-573; e-mail tunisre@tunisre.com.tn; internet www.tunisre.com.tn; f. 1981; various kinds of reinsurance; cap. 35m. (2006); Chair. and Gen. Man. MUHAMMAD DKHILI.

Trade and Industry

GOVERNMENT AGENCIES

Centre de Promotion des Exportations (CEPEX): Centre Urbain, BP 225, 1080 Tunis; tel. (71) 234-200; fax (71) 237-325; e-mail info@cepex.nat.tn; internet www.cepex.nat.tn; f. 1973; state export promotion org.; Pres. and Dir-Gen. YOUSSEF NEJI.

Foreign Investment Promotion Agency (FIPA): rue Slaheddine al-Ammami, Centre Urbain Nord, 1004 Tunis; tel. (71) 752-540; fax (71) 231-400; e-mail boc.fipa@mdci.gov.tn; internet www.investintunisia.tn; f. 1995; Dir-Gen. Mongia Khemiri.

Office du Commerce de la Tunisie (OCT): 65 rue de Syrie, 1002 Tunis; tel. (71) 785-619; fax (71) 784-491; e-mail OCT@Email.ati.tn; f. 1962; Pres. and Dir-Gen. Slaheddine Makhlouf; Sec.-Gen. Mustapha Debbabi.

CHAMBERS OF COMMERCE AND INDUSTRY

Chambre de Commerce et d'Industrie de Tunis: 31 ave de Paris, 1000 Tunis; tel. (71) 247-322; fax (71) 354-744; e-mail ccitunis@planet.tn; internet www.ccitunis.org.tn; f. 1885; 30 mems; Pres. Mounir Mouakhar.

Chambre de Commerce et d'Industrie du Centre: rue Chadli Khaznadar, 4000 Sousse; tel. (73) 225-044; fax (73) 224-227; e-mail ccis.sousse@planet.tn; internet www.ccicentre.org.tn; f. 1895; 30 mems; Pres. Néjib Mellouli; Dir Faten Basly.

Chambre de Commerce et d'Industrie du Nord-Est: Tom Bereaux Bizerte Center, angle rues 1er mai, Med Ali, 7000 Bizerte; tel. (72) 431-044; fax (72) 431-922; e-mail ccine.biz@gnet.tn; internet www.ccibizerte.org.tn; f. 1902; 30 mems; Pres. Faouzi Ben Aissa; Dir Moufida Chakroun.

Chambre de Commerce et d'Industrie de Sfax: Rue du Lieutenant Hammadi Tej, BP 794, 3000 Sfax; tel. (74) 296-120; fax (74) 296-121; e-mail ccis@ccis.org.tn; internet www.ccis.org.tn; f. 1895; 35,000 mems; Pres. Abdessalem Ben Ayed; Dir Sofiene Sallemi.

INDUSTRIAL AND TRADE ASSOCIATIONS

Agence des Ports et des Installations de Pêches (APIP): Port de Pêche de La Goulette, BP 64, 2060 Tunis; tel. (71) 736-012; fax (71) 735-396; e-mail apip@apip.com.tn; internet www.apip.nat.tn; fishing ports authority; Pres. and Dir-Gen. Sghaïer Houcine.

Agence de Promotion de l'Industrie (API): 63 rue de Syrie, 1002 Tunis; tel. (71) 792-144; fax (71) 782-482; e-mail api@api.com.tn; internet www.tunisieindustrie.nat.tn; f. 1987 by merger; co-ordinates industrial policy, undertakes feasibility studies, organizes industrial training and establishes industrial zones; overseas offices in Belgium, France, Germany, Italy, the United Kingdom, Sweden and the USA; 24 regional offices; Gen. Man. Muhammad Ben Abdallah.

Centre Technique du Textile (CETTEX): ave des Industries, Zone Industrielle, Bir el-Kassaâ, BP 279, Ben Arous, 2013 Tunis; tel. (71) 381-133; fax (71) 382-558; e-mail cettex@cettex.com.tn; internet www.cettex.com.tn; f. 1991; responsible for the textile industry; Dir-Gen. Muhammad Néjib Karafi.

Cie des Phosphates de Gafsa (CPG): Cité Bayech, 2100 Gafsa; tel. (76) 226-022; fax (76) 224-132; e-mail cpg.gafsa@cpg.com.tn; internet www.gct.com.tn; f. 1897; production and marketing of phosphates; Pres. and Dir-Gen. Muhammad Ridha Ben Mosbah.

Entreprise Tunisienne d'Activités Pétrolières (ETAP): 27 ave Kheireddine Pacha, BP 83, 1073 Tunis; tel. (71) 782-288; fax (71) 786-141; e-mail dexprom@etap.com.tn; internet www.etap.com.tn; responsible for exploration and investment in hydrocarbons; Pres. and CEO Khaled Becheikh.

Office des Céréales: Ministry of Agriculture and Water Resources, 30 rue Alain Savary, 1002 Tunis; tel. (71) 780-550; fax (71) 794-152; e-mail office.cereales@email.ati.tn; f. 1962; responsible for the cereals industry; Chair. and Dir-Gen. Muhammad Fadhel Zerreli.

Office National des Mines: 24 rue 8601, BP 215, 1080 Tunis; tel. (71) 788-242; fax (71) 794-016; e-mail contact@onm.nat.tn; internet www.onm.nat.tn; f. 1963; mining of iron ores; research and study of mineral wealth; Dir-Gen. Abdelbaki Mansouri.

Office des Terres Domaniales (OTD): 60 rue Alain Savary, 1002 Tunis; tel. (71) 771-086; fax (71) 795-026; e-mail boc@otd.nat.tn; f. 1961; responsible for agricultural production and the management of state-owned lands; Pres. and Dir-Gen. Abdelhakim Khaldi.

UTILITIES

Electricity and Gas

Société Tunisienne de l'Electricité et du Gaz (STEG): 38 rue Kemal Atatürk, BP 190, 1080 Tunis; tel. (71) 341-311; fax (71) 349-981; e-mail dpsc@steg.com.tn; internet www.steg.com.tn; f. 1962; responsible for generation and distribution of electricity and for production of natural gas; Pres. and Dir-Gen. Othman Ben Arfa; 35 brs.

Water

Société Nationale d'Exploitation et de Distribution des Eaux (SONEDE): ave Slimane ben Slimane, el-Manar 2, 2092 Tunis; tel. (71) 887-000; fax (71) 871-000; e-mail sonede@sonede.com.tn; internet www.sonede.com.tn; f. 1968; production and supply of drinking water; Pres. and Dir-Gen. Muhammad Ali Khouaja.

TRADE AND OTHER UNIONS

Union Générale des Etudiants de Tunisie (UGET): 11 rue d'Espagne, Tunis; f. 1953; 600 mems; Pres. Mekki Fitouri.

Union Générale Tunisienne du Travail (UGTT): 29 place Muhammad Ali, 1000 Tunis; tel. (71) 332-400; fax (71) 354-114; e-mail ugtt.tunis@email.ati.tn; internet www.ugtt.org.tn; f. 1946 by Farhat Hached; affiliated to ITUC; 360,000 mems in 24 affiliated unions; 18-mem. exec. bureau; Sec.-Gen. Abdessalem Jerad.

Union Nationale de la Femme Tunisienne (UNFT): 56 blvd Bab Benat, 1008 Tunis; tel. (71) 560-178; fax (71) 567-131; e-mail unft@email.ati.tn; internet www.unft.org.tn; f. 1956; promotes the rights of women; 150,000 mems; 28 regional delegations, 199 professional training centres, 13 professional alliances; Pres. Aziza Hatira; Vice-Pres. Faïza Azouz; 23 brs abroad.

Union Tunisienne de l'Agriculture et de la Pêche (UTAP): rue 8451, ave Alain Savary, 1003 Tunis; tel. (71) 806-800; fax (71) 809-181; internet www.utap.org.tn; f. 1955 as Union Nationale des Agriculteurs Tunisiens (which supplanted the Union Générale des Agriculteurs Tunisiens, f. 1950); name changed as above in 1995; Pres. Mabrouk Bahri.

Union Tunisienne de l'Industrie, du Commerce et de l'Artisanat (UTICA): Cité Administrative, Lot 7, Cité El Khadhra, 1003 Tunis; tel. (71) 142-000; fax (71) 142-100; internet www.utica.org.tn; f. 1946; mems: 15 national federations and 170 syndical chambers at national levels; Pres. Hédi Djilani.

Transport

RAILWAYS

In 2006 the total length of railways was 2,157 km; 37.8m. passengers travelled by rail in Tunisia in that year. Plans for an expansion of the public transport system were in progress in the mid-2000s.

Société Nationale des Chemins de Fer Tunisiens (SNCFT): Gare de Tunis ville, pl. Barcelone, 1001 Tunis; tel. (71) 334-444; fax (71) 254-320; e-mail sncft@sncft.com.tn; internet www.sncft.com.tn; f. 1956; state org. controlling all Tunisian railways; Pres. and Dir-Gen. Abd al-Aziz Chabane.

Société des Transports de Tunis (TRANSTU): 1 ave Habib Bourgiba, BP 660, 1025 Tunis; tel. (71) 259-422; fax (71) 342-727; e-mail contact@snt.com.tn; internet www.snt.com.tn; f. 2003 following merger of the Société Nationale des Transports and the Société du Métro Léger de Tunis; operates 5 light train routes with 136 trains, and 206 local bus routes with 1,050 buses; also operates in the suburbs of Tunis-Goulette-Marsa, with 18 trains; plans approved in 2006 for expansion of the light rail system, with five new express lines; Pres. and Dir-Gen. Chedly Hajri.

ROADS

In 2004 there were 262 km of motorways, 4,080 km of main roads and 6,520 km of secondary roads. The total length of the road network was 19,232 km, of which 65.8% was paved.

Société Nationale de Transport Interurbain (SNTRI): ave Muhammad V, BP 40, Belvédère, 1002 Tunis; tel. (71) 784-433; fax (71) 791-621; e-mail marketing@sntri.com.tn; internet www.sntri.com.tn; f. 1981; Dir-Gen. Sassi Yahia.

Société des Transports de Tunis: see above.

There are 12 **Sociétés Régionales des Transports**, responsible for road transport, operating in different regions in Tunisia.

SHIPPING

Tunisia has seven major ports: Tunis-La Goulette, Radès, Bizerta, Sousse, Sfax, Gabès and Zarzis. There is a special petroleum port at La Skhirra. In April 2009 the Government invited bids for the construction of a new deep-water port at Enfidha.

Office de la Marine Marchande et des Ports: Bâtiment Administratif, Port de la Goulette, 2060 La Goulette; tel. (71) 735-300; fax (71) 735-812; e-mail ommp@ommp.nat.tn; internet www.ommp.nat.tn; maritime port administration; Pres. and Dir-Gen. Ali Labiedh.

Cie Générale Maritime: Résidence Alain Savary, Bloc D7, Apt 74, 1003 Tunis; tel. and fax (71) 860-430; e-mail logwan.girgen@gnet.tn; Chair. Elias Maherzi.

Cie Tunisienne de Navigation SA (CTN): 5 ave Dag Hammarskjöold, BP 40, 1001 Tunis; tel. (71) 341-777; fax (71) 345-736; e-mail cotunav@ctn.com.tn; internet www.ctn.com.tn; f. 1959; state-owned; brs at Bizerta, La Goulette, Sfax and Sousse; Pres. and Dir.-Gen. Ali Khalifa.

TUNISIA

Gabès Marine Tankers (GMT): Immeuble SETCAR, route de Sousse, km 13, 2034 Tunis; tel. (71) 454-644; fax (71) 450-350; e-mail gabesmarine@gmt.com.tn; internet www.setcar-group.com; f. 1994; part of the Setcar Group; Chair. FÉRID ABBÈS.

Gas Marine: Immeuble SETCAR, route de Sousse, km 13, 2034 ez-Zahra; tel. (71) 454-644; fax (71) 454-650; Chair. HAMMADI ABBÈS.

Hannibal Marine Tankers: 2ème Etage, Residence Lakeo, rue du Lac Michigan, Les Berges du Lac, 1053 Tunis; tel. (71) 960-037; fax (71) 960-243; e-mail hannibal.tankers@gnet.tn; Gen. Man. AMEUR MAHJOUB.

Société Tunisienne de Navigation Petrolière (PETRONAV): Residence Raoudha, Les Berges du Lac, 1053 Tunis; tel. (71) 861-965; fax (71) 861-780; Chair. HICHEM KHATTECH.

Société Nouvelle de Transport Kerkennah (SONOTRAK): 179 ave Muhammad Hédi Khefacha, Gare Maritime de Kerkenna, 3000 Sfax; tel. (74) 498-216; fax (74) 497-496; e-mail jabeur.m@planet.tn; internet kerkennah.free.fr/sonotrak/indexsonotrak.htm; Chair. TAOUFI JRAD.

Tunisian Shipping Agency: Zone Industrielle, Radès 2040, BP 166, Tunis; tel. (71) 448-379; fax (71) 448-410; e-mail tsa.rades@planet.tn; Chair. MUHAMMAD BEN SEDRINE.

CIVIL AVIATION

There are international airports at Tunis-Carthage, Sfax, Djerba, Monastir, Tabarka, Gafsa and Tozeur. Construction of a new airport at Enfidha, 100 km south of Tunis, commenced in March 2005 and was scheduled to be completed by October 2009.

Office de l'Aviation Civile et des Aéroports: BP 137 and 147, Aéroport International de Tunis-Carthage, 1080 Tunis; tel. (71) 755-000; fax (71) 755-133; e-mail relations.exterieures@oaca.nat.tn; internet www.oaca.nat.tn; f. 1970; civil aviation and airport authority; Pres. and Dir-Gen. MUHAMMAD CHERIF.

Nouvelair Tunisie: Zone Touristique Dkhila, 5065 Monastir; tel. (73) 520-600; fax (73) 520-650; e-mail info@nouvelair.com.tn; internet www.nouvelair.com; f. 1989 as Air Liberté Tunisie; name changed as above in 1996; Tunisian charter co; flights from Tunis, Djerba and Monastir airports to Scandinavia and other European countries; Chair. AZIZ MILAD; Gen. Man. KAMEL OUERGHEMNI.

Sevenair: 10 rue de l'Artisanat, La Charguia 11, Tunis; tel. (71) 942-323; fax (71) 942-272; e-mail info@sevenair.com.tn; internet www.sevenair.com.tn; f. 1992 as Tuninter; Tunisian charter co; Man. Dir ABD AL-KARIM OUERTANI.

TunisAir (Société Tunisienne de l'Air): blvd du 7 novembre 1987, 2035 Tunis; tel. (71) 700-100; fax (71) 700-897; e-mail Resaonline@tunisair.com.tn; internet www.tunisair.com; f. 1948; 45.2% govt-owned; 20% of assets privatized in 1995; flights to Africa, Europe and the Middle East; Pres. and Dir-Gen. NABIL CHETTAOUI.

Tunisavia (Société de Transports, Services et Travaux Aériens): blvd du leader Yasser Arafat, 2035 Tunis-Carthage International Airport, Tunis; tel. (71) 280-555; fax (71) 281-333; e-mail siege@tunisavia.com.tn; internet www.tunisavia.com.tn; f. 1974; helicopter and charter operator; Pres. AZIZ MILAD; Gen. Man MOHSEN NASRA.

Tourism

The main tourist attractions are the magnificent sandy beaches, Moorish architecture and remains of the Roman Empire. Tunisia contains the site of the ancient Phoenician city of Carthage. Tourism, a principal source of foreign exchange, has expanded rapidly, following extensive government investment in hotels, improved roads and other facilities. The number of hotel beds increased from 71,529 in 1980 to 188,600 in 1999. There were 6.5m. foreign tourist arrivals in 2006 (compared with 4.7m. in 1998), and receipts from tourism totalled US $2,999m. in 2006.

Office National du Tourisme Tunisien: 1 ave Muhammad V, 1001 Tunis; tel. (71) 341-077; fax (71) 350-997; e-mail ontt@email.ati.tn; internet www.bonjour-tunisie.com; f. 1958; Dir-Gen. KHALED CHEIKH.

TURKEY

Introductory Survey

Location, Climate, Language, Religion, Flag, Capital

The Republic of Turkey lies partly in south-eastern Europe and partly in western Asia. The European and Asian portions of the country (known, respectively, as Thrace and Anatolia) are separated by the Sea of Marmara, linking the Black Sea and the Aegean Sea. Turkey has an extensive coastline: on the Black Sea, to the north; on the Mediterranean Sea, to the south; and on the Aegean Sea, to the west. Most of Turkey lies in Asia, the vast Anatolian peninsula being bordered to the east by Armenia, Georgia, the Nakhichevan Autonomous Republic (part of Azerbaijan) and Iran, and to the south by Iraq and Syria. The smaller European part of the country is bordered to the west by Greece and Bulgaria. In the Asian interior the climate is one of great extremes, with hot dry summers and cold, snowy winters on the plateau. Temperatures in Ankara are generally between −4°C (25°F) and 30°C (86°F). On the Mediterranean coast it is more equable, with mild winters and warm summers. The principal language is Turkish, spoken by 90% of the population. About 7% speak Kurdish, mainly in the south-east. In 1928 the Arabic characters of the written Turkish language were superseded by Western-style script. Islam is the religion of 99% of the population. The national flag (proportions 2 by 3) is red, with a white crescent and a five-pointed white star to the left of centre. The capital is Ankara.

Recent History

Turkey was formerly a monarchy, ruled by a Sultan, with his capital in Constantinople (now İstanbul). At its zenith, the Turkish Empire, under the Osmanlı (Ottoman) dynasty, extended from the Persian (Arabian) Gulf to Morocco, including most Arab regions and south-eastern Europe. Following the dissolution of the Ottoman Empire after the First World War, political control of Turkey itself passed to the nationalist movement led by Mustafa Kemal, a distinguished army officer. On 23 April 1920, in defiance of the Sultan, a newly elected assembly established a provisional Government, led by Kemal, in Ankara, then a minor provincial town. Kemal's forces waged war against the Greek army in 1920–22, forcing the Greeks to evacuate Smyrna (İzmir) and eastern Thrace (the European portion of Turkey). The new regime abolished the sultanate in November 1922 and declared Turkey a republic, with Ankara as its capital and Kemal as its first President, on 29 October 1923. The Ottoman caliphate (the former monarch's position as Islamic religious leader) was abolished in March 1924.

Kemal remained President of Turkey, with extensive dictatorial powers, until his death in 1938. He pursued a radical programme of far-reaching reform and modernization, including the: secularization of the state (in 1928); abolition of Islamic courts and religious instruction in schools; emancipation of women (enfranchised in 1934); banning of polygamy; development of industry; introduction of a Latin alphabet; adoption of the Gregorian (in place of the Islamic) calendar; and encouragement of European culture and technology. Another Westernizing reform was the introduction of surnames in 1934: Kemal assumed the name Atatürk ('Father of the Turks'). His autocratic regime attempted, with considerable success, to replace the country's Islamic traditions by the principles of republicanism, nationalism, populism and state control.

Following Atatürk's death, his Cumhuriyet Halk Partisi (CHP—Republican People's Party), the only authorized political grouping, remained in power under his close associate, İsmet İnönü, who had been Prime Minister in 1923–24 and 1925–37. İnönü was President from 1938 to 1950, and maintained Turkey's neutrality during most of the Second World War (Turkey declared war on Germany in February 1945). After the war İnönü introduced some liberalization of the regime. The one-party system was ended in 1946, when opposition leaders, including Celâl Bayar and Adnan Menderes, registered the Demokratik Parti (DP—Democratic Party); numerous other parties were subsequently formed. The DP won Turkey's first free election in 1950, and ruled for the next decade. Bayar became President, with Menderes as Prime Minister.

In May 1960 the Government was overthrown by a military coup, led by Gen. Cemal Gürsel, who assumed the presidency, claiming that the DP regime had betrayed Atatürk's principle of secularism. A series of coalition governments, mostly led by İnönü, held office from November 1961 until October 1965, when an election was won by the conservative Adalet Partisi (Justice Party), led by Süleyman Demirel, which appealed to supporters of the former DP. The Demirel Government remained in power until March 1971, when escalating student and labour unrest caused the armed forces to demand its resignation. 'Guided democracy', under military supervision, continued until October 1973, with a succession of right-wing 'non-party' administrations, martial law and the rigorous suppression of all left-wing activities.

The return to civilian rule began in April 1973, when the Turkish Grand National Assembly (TGNA—the legislative body established in 1961) chose Adm. Fahri Korutürk as President, in preference to a candidate supported by the armed forces. Military participation in government was ended by an election in October 1973. No single party received sufficient support to form a government, and it was not until January 1974 when Bülent Ecevit, leader of the CHP (which had become a left-of-centre party), took office as Prime Minister, having negotiated a coalition with the Milli Selamet Partisi (MSP—National Salvation Party), a pro-Islamic right-wing group. Deteriorating relations with Greece were exacerbated by the Greek-backed coup in Cyprus (q.v.) in July 1974, when Turkey responded by dispatching troops, and occupying the northern part of the island, to protect the Turkish Cypriot population. Despite the failure of the coup, Turkish forces retained control of northern Cyprus, and the island remained effectively partitioned.

A long period of political instability was fostered by a succession of unsuccessful coalitions, headed by either Ecevit or Demirel, and prompted an escalation in political violence, mainly involving clashes between left-wing and right-wing groups. On 12 September 1980, as the violence neared the scale of a civil war, the armed forces, led by Gen. Kenan Evren, Chief of the General Staff, seized power in a bloodless coup; a five-member National Security Council (NSC) was formed, which appointed a mainly civilian Cabinet. Martial law was declared throughout the country. In December the NSC published a decree endowing the military regime with unlimited powers. During 1981–83 a campaign to eradicate all possible sources of political violence was undertaken. In April 1981 former politicians were banned from future political activity, and in October all political parties were disbanded.

The new Government succeeded in reducing the level of political violence in Turkey and in restoring law and order. However, that this had been achieved at the expense of respect for human rights caused concern among Western governments: Turkey was banned from the Parliamentary Assembly of the Council of Europe (see p. 236), aid from the European Community (EC, now European Union—EU, see p. 255) was suspended, and fellow members of NATO urged Turkey to return to democratic rule as soon as possible. In October 1981 a Consultative Assembly was established to draft a new constitution, which was approved by referendum in November 1982; objections were widely expressed that the President was to be accorded excessive powers while judicial powers and the rights of trade unions and the press were to be curtailed. An appended 'temporary article' installed Evren as President for a seven-year term.

In May 1983 the NSC revoked the ban on political organizations, permitting the formation of parties, subject to strict rules, in preparation for the first election to be held under the new Constitution. All the former political parties remained proscribed, and 723 former members of the TGNA and leading party officials were banned from political activity for up to 10 years. Followers of the former parties thus regrouped under new names and with new leaders. Of the 15 new parties, however, only three were allowed to take part in the election: the Milliyetçi Demokrasi Partisi (MDP—Nationalist Democracy Party) and the Halkçı Partisi (HP—Populist Party), both of which had the tacit support of the NSC, and the conservative Anavatan Partisi

(ANAVATAN—Motherland Party), led by Turgut Özal. In the November election ANAVATAN won 211 of the 400 seats in the unicameral legislature, and Özal was appointed Prime Minister in December. This result, which was followed by the holding of local government elections in March 1984, suggested a decisive rejection of military rule.

In November 1985 the HP and the Sosyal Demokrasi Partisi (Social Democratic Party), respectively the main opposition parties within and outside the National Assembly, merged to form the Sosyal Demokrat Halkçı Parti (SHP—Social Democratic Populist Party). However, the left-wing opposition was split as a result of the immediate formation of the Demokratik Sol Parti (DSP—Democratic Left Party), which drew support from the former CHP. The MDP voted to disband in May 1986.

At a national referendum in September 1987 a narrow majority approved the repeal of the ban on participation in political affairs, imposed on more than 200 politicians in 1981. This enabled Ecevit to assume the leadership of the DSP, while Demirel was elected as leader of the Doğru Yol Partisi (DYP—True Path Party). In a general election conducted in November 1987 ANAVATAN obtained 292 of the 450 seats in the enlarged TGNA, while the SHP won 99 seats and the DYP 59.

Özal succeeded Evren as President in November 1989, having secured the support of the simple majority required in a third round of voting by the TGNA in October. Yıldırım Akbulut, the Speaker of the TGNA and a former Minister of the Interior, was subsequently appointed Prime Minister. However, having been defeated by former Minister of Foreign Affairs Mesut Yılmaz in a contest for the ANAVATAN leadership in June 1991, Akbulut subsequently resigned as premier. In accordance with the Constitution, President Özal invited Yılmaz, the leader of the party's liberal faction, to head a new administration.

In a general election held on 20 October 1991 the DYP, under Demirel's leadership, received an estimated 27.3% of the votes cast, narrowly defeating ANAVATAN (with 23.9%) and the SHP (20.6%). Demirel formed a coalition administration with the SHP (who with the DYP accounted for 266 of the 450 newly elected deputies in the TGNA), with Erdal İnönü, the SHP leader, as deputy premier. The coalition outlined a programme for political and economic reform, and international observers were impressed by Demirel's apparent commitment to human rights. The implementation of amendments designed to discourage torture were, however, impeded by a lack of consensus within the Government, and the problems were exacerbated during 1992 by a succession of political defections from the SHP, which by September had reduced the representation of the coalition parties in the TGNA to 229. Although the DYP and the SHP performed well at municipal elections in June, the reactivation of the CHP in September (following a relaxation of guide-lines for the formation of political parties) threatened to undermine left-wing support for the Government.

At a special ANAVATAN party conference in December 1992, concern was expressed that right-wing extremism had become the dominant force behind the party leadership, prompting the emergence of a dissident, more conservative faction of the party. Subsequently some 70 deputies announced their intention to leave ANAVATAN in order to form a new party headed by President Özal. In April 1993, however, Özal died of heart failure. In May Süleyman Demirel was elected to the presidency, with a simple majority in a third round of voting by the TGNA. Minister of State Tansu Çiller was elected to the DYP party leadership in June and promptly assumed the premiership. Çiller (Turkey's first female Prime Minister) formed a new Cabinet, retaining the 12 SHP members of the previous Government but replacing 17 former DYP ministers, notably several Demirel loyalists. The Prime Minister's personal support was consolidated in December, when five DYP ministers were replaced.

The new administration was strained by a sharp escalation of violence on the part of the outlawed Partiya Karkeren Kurdistan (PKK—Kurdistan Workers' Party). Plans to extend cultural and educational rights to the Kurds were abandoned following strong opposition from Demirel, right-wing members of the DYP and military leaders, who, in October, effectively resisted a proposal to discuss the establishment of local autonomy for the Kurdish population in the south-east of the country.

In early 1994 Çiller's political standing was damaged by a devaluation of the Turkish lira, following a loss of confidence in the currency on the part of international credit agencies. The DYP performed unexpectedly well in municipal elections in March, however; Çiller was thus able to pursue her programme of economic austerity, although in July the Constitutional Court halted her accelerated privatization plans. In February 1995 a special conference of the SHP voted to merge with the CHP, consequently increasing the Government's parliamentary majority but forcing a renegotiation of the conditions of the coalition. Agreement was reached by Çiller and Hikmet Çetin, the CHP leader, in March, and an extensive reorganization of the Government was undertaken in order to accommodate the party. Çetin became Deputy Prime Minister and Minister of State; İsmet İnönü assumed the foreign affairs portfolio. In June the DYP obtained 39% of votes cast in municipal elections, a result that Çiller claimed to be a vindication of her personal standing as leader and of her Government's policies, in particular the pursuit of closer relations with the EU. However, efforts by the Prime Minister to extend democratic rights within the Constitution encountered considerable opposition, both from conservative elements within her own party and from the fundamentalist Islamist Refah Partisi (RP—Welfare Party). Certain constitutional reforms, including the removal of restrictions on political associations and trade unions, the lowering of the age of eligibility to vote from 21 to 18 years and the expansion of the TGNA by 100 parliamentary seats to 550, were finally approved in July. Yet Çiller failed to obtain sufficient support for the amendment of the 'anti-terrorism' legislation, which was expected to be crucial in securing the European Parliament's ratification of the EU-Turkish customs union (see below).

Deniz Baykal was elected leader of the CHP in September 1995. All CHP ministers subsequently resigned their cabinet positions, and ensuing coalition negotiations with Çiller failed as it became apparent that the political differences between the two leaders were insurmountable. Later in September Demirel was forced to accept the Prime Minister's resignation, but Çiller was immediately invited to form a new government. A significant obstacle to a new DYP-CHP agreement was removed when Çiller conceded the necessity of holding an early general election. A DYP-CHP Government, headed by Çiller, with Baykal as Deputy Prime Minister and Minister of Foreign Affairs, took office in November.

At the general election held in December 1995, the RP, which had campaigned to strengthen political and economic relations with other Islamic countries, to withdraw from NATO and the EU customs union, and to increase state involvement in the economy, secured the largest number of parliamentary seats (158), with 21.4% of the votes cast. The DYP won 135 seats, with 19.2% of the votes, while ANAVATAN took 132, with 19.7% of the votes. Since no party had an absolute majority, the two other parties securing parliamentary representation, the DSP and the CHP, were expected to have considerable political leverage in the new parliament. (Under the new electoral arrangements, eight other parties secured no seats in the legislature, having failed to reach the minimum requirement of 10% of support.) In January 1996 President Demirel invited RP leader Necmettin Erbakan to attempt to form a government. However, despite Erbakan's declared willingness to negotiate an agreement with any of the four main parties, no coalition partner could be found. Subsequent efforts by Çiller to form a government through an agreement with ANAVATAN also failed, and in February Demirel invited Mesut Yılmaz, of ANAVATAN, to establish a new administration. Following protracted negotiations, Yılmaz and Çiller reached a coalition agreement, which was signed and approved by Demirel in March; Çiller conceded the premiership to Yılmaz, under a rotating arrangement. The new Government secured a parliamentary vote of confidence, but was soon strained by tensions between the two leaders, and allegations of corruption against Çiller. In April and May ANAVATAN deputies failed to support Çiller, following votes in the TGNA to establish commissions to investigate her alleged illegal involvement in the sale of the TEDAŞ state electricity company and of a Turkish car manufacturer. Members of the DYP accused Yılmaz of further undermining Çiller's position by passing information to the media detailing evidence of the misappropriation of secret security funds under her premiership, in order to force her resignation before her scheduled assumption of the office of Prime Minister in 1997. Meanwhile, opposition parties questioned the credibility of the Government after the Constitutional Court annulled the March 1996 vote of confidence. At the end of May Çiller announced the withdrawal of her party's support for the Government and publicly called for Yılmaz's resignation. Political tensions were heightened in that month by an assassination attempt on President Demirel.

In June 1996, having won 34% of the votes cast in municipal elections, the RP renewed its demands for a general election and secured the DYP's support for a censure motion against the Government to be considered in the TGNA. This was withdrawn when Yılmaz announced the resignation of his Government, following the official publication of the Constitutional Court's ruling. Necmettin Erbakan was subsequently invited to form a government, and at the end of June the RP concluded an agreement with the DYP; Erbakan was to lead the new coalition administration, with Çiller assuming the deputy premiership and foreign affairs portfolio. The leaders asserted that the objective of the new Government was to secure political and economic stability, and they guaranteed that Turkey would adhere to its existing international and strategic agreements. Eight DYP deputies in the TGNA resigned from the party in protest at the coalition with the RP, and a further 15 DYP deputies failed to endorse the new administration in a parliamentary vote of confidence conducted in July. Although the Government secured a narrow majority, it was immediately confronted by local demonstrations and mounting international concern regarding several hundred left-wing prisoners who had initiated a hunger strike in May, in protest at their treatment and conditions of confinement. At the end of July, following the deaths of 12 protesters and widespread unrest within many prisons, the Government concluded an agreement with the prisoners to end their action in return for guarantees that included the transfer of 102 activists from a high-security prison in Anatolya and greater access to medical care.

The contradictions inherent in the new RP-DYP administration became evident in many aspects of government policy. In foreign affairs, the Government attempted to reassure its Western allies of its continued support. At the end of July 1996 the mandate for the use of Turkish airbases by allied forces engaged in 'Operation Provide Comfort' (see below) was extended, and in August a new military co-operation agreement was signed with Israel, expanding on an accord concluded in February. In addition, there was evidence of the military's asserting its authority by dismissing 13 officers in August on disciplinary charges relating to Islamist practices (50 officers had been dismissed on similar grounds in December 1995). At the same time, however, Prime Minister Erbakan embarked on a tour of Asian and Middle Eastern Muslim countries in order to strengthen bilateral relations and co-operation. In August Turkey and Iran finalized an economic agreement, shortly after legislation had been ratified in the USA that threatened punitive measures against countries undertaking investments in Iran. Censure motions brought against Erbakan's administration by three opposition parties were defeated in a single vote in the TGNA. In January 1997 the TGNA cleared Çiller of the final corruption charges against her. In the same month Hüsamettin Cindoruk, who had been expelled from the DYP in October 1995, established a new breakaway party, the Demokrat Türkiye Partisi (Democratic Turkey Party).

There were civil disturbances in February 1997, following an Islamist rally in the Sincan district of Ankara, at which Iran's ambassador to Turkey criticized Turkey's relations with Israel and its NATO allies and advocated the introduction of *Shari'a* law. At the same time pressure from the military and DYP members of the Government forced the RP to withdraw proposals to extend Muslim education and to allow religious garments to be worn by public workers. In late February the Government defeated a censure motion in the TGNA, proposed by the DSP and CHP in protest at the Government's alleged undermining of the secular state. At a meeting of the NSC held at the end of February, the military leadership presented an 18-point memorandum which set out to ensure the protection of Turkish secular state traditions, including greater supervision of Islamic financial and media operations, the removal of Islamists from public administration and closure of all unauthorized Islamic groupings; the military warned of punitive action if the proposals were not implemented. Political tension was defused when Erbakan, who had initially criticized the NSC for attempting to impose laws on the Government, signed a memorandum endorsing the NSC measures and declared that the leaders of all the main political parties were unanimous in their view that the Constitution must be upheld. The Council of Ministers agreed in March to implement the NSC proposals, but concern subsequently arose over the failure of the Government to act on the measures. Two dissident DYP government ministers resigned in protest at Erbakan's leadership, and demanded an early election on the grounds that their party leader, Çiller, had failed to restrain the Islamist tendencies of the RP. At a meeting of the NSC held in April, however, Erbakan agreed to pursue the military's demands, including restrictions on Islamic education. Although the Government defeated an opposition attempt in that month to pursue a censure motion in the TGNA, the political situation remained critical, and charges from the military, opposition parties and dissident members of the DYP that the Government was undermining the modern secular tradition were reinforced when the country's chief prosecutor initiated legal proceedings to ban the RP (on the grounds that the party had violated the Constitution). By June the coalition had lost its majority in the TGNA as a result of defections principally from the DYP. Erbakan announced that he would seek an early election, but the military continued to exert pressure on the Government, and the Prime Minister finally resigned. President Demirel asked the ANAVATAN leader, Mesut Yılmaz, to form a new administration, and a coalition with the DSP and the Democratic Turkey Party was inaugurated in July; the coalition controlled only a minority of seats in the TGNA, and was dependent on the support of the CHP. The tripartite Government pledged to improve law and order, implement previously proposed changes to the education system, and vigorously pursue EU membership. Defections from the DYP continued, and by the end of July its representation in the TGNA had been reduced from 135 to 93.

In August 1997 the TGNA approved legislation extending compulsory education from five to eight years. This was intended to raise the entry age to Islamic schools from 11 to 14, thus reducing attendance at such schools and lessening Islamic influence. The RP organized popular demonstrations in protest against the legislation (which constituted a principal demand of the military). A further 73 members of the armed forces were expelled, owing to suspected affiliation to Islamist organizations, while further public demonstrations were prompted by the military's insistence on the strict enforcement of the ban on wearing Islamic dress in public buildings, notably educational establishments. In early March 1998 the University of Istanbul temporarily annulled the ban and the Government stated that it would not be strictly enforced. In mid-March the Government survived its third censure motion, which was presented against the Minister for Education for his handling of the issue of Islamic dress. A few days later 20 members of a proscribed Islamist organization were arrested for inciting the demonstrations. At the end of the month the NSC criticized the Government for advocating a relaxation of the enforcement of anti-Islamic legislation; the Government subsequently proposed further measures to curb Islamist radicalism, and the universities announced their decision to enforce the dress code.

Meanwhile, Çiller's participation in the coalition with the RP and her opposition to a possible ban on the party had caused offence to the secular establishment, causing a deterioration in the previously good relations between Çiller and the armed forces. In March 1998 the Court of Appeals ruled that Çiller could not be prosecuted in connection with a particular allegation that she had misused government funds during her premiership, owing to the threat to national security interests. However, in April her loss of support in the TGNA led to a vote in favour of the commencement of an investigation into alleged irregularities in Çiller's accumulation of wealth between 1991 and 1996. In October 1997 Çiller's husband, Ozer Çiller, had been charged with forgery.

In January 1998 the Constitutional Court ordered the dissolution of the RP on the grounds that it was responsible for undermining the secular regime, and banned seven of its members, including Erbakan, from holding political office for five years. Many former RP deputies joined the Fazilet Partisi (FP—Virtue Party), which had been established in December 1997. By March 1998 the FP's representation in the TGNA had risen to 140 seats, making it the largest parliamentary party (ANAVATAN controlled 139 seats). In April the mayor of Istanbul, Reçep Tayyip Erdoğan, who was expected to assume the leadership of the FP, was sentenced to 10 months' imprisonment for inciting hatred; he was released pending an appeal. Erdoğan's conviction, the January ruling and the investigation of hundreds of public officials for their alleged support of Islamist organizations was widely criticized.

The stability of Yılmaz's minority Government was threatened by the demands of the CHP for an early general election. The CHP demonstrated its power in April 1998 by voting with the opposition in favour of an investigation into allegations of corruption against the Prime Minister. Following an agreement signed by Yılmaz and CHP leader Deniz Baykal, the Prime

Minister announced in June 1998 that he was to resign at the end of the year; he was to be succeeded by an interim government that would call early elections for April 1999.

In May 1998 Çiller's husband was found guilty of misleading a parliamentary commission; his sentence, of five months' imprisonment, was later commuted to a fine. In August 12 former RP politicians, including Erbakan and FP leader Recai Kutan, were charged with illegally diverting funds from the party prior to its dissolution. An investigation into Çiller's assets was begun in September. Further investigations were launched in that month into Çiller and the former Minister of Finance for financial irregularities, and the immunity of the former TGNA Speaker was revoked, to allow an investigation, at his request, into his conduct following corruption allegations. Meanwhile, the Court of Appeal upheld the prison sentence on the mayor of Istanbul. As a result of his conviction, Erdoğan was deprived of his position of mayor; he also resigned from the FP. In December new charges were filed against him for insulting the judiciary in a speech following his sentencing. In November 1998 corruption charges against Çiller were dismissed by a parliamentary commission, owing to insufficient evidence, while Erbakan was acquitted on charges of slandering the judiciary, and Minister of State Güneş Taner was removed from office following a parliamentary censure motion arising from corruption allegations. In December Ozer Çiller was acquitted on charges of falsifying documents.

The Government resigned in November 1998, after the TGNA approved a motion of no confidence submitted by the CHP in response to accusations of corruption against Yılmaz. In January 1999, following protracted political manoeuvring, Bülent Ecevit of the DSP formed a Government, comprising DSP and independent deputies, which was to hold office until the elections in April. Also in January a motion was filed for the dissolution of the pro-Kurdish nationalist Halkın Demokrasi Partisi (HADEP—People's Democracy Party), owing to its alleged links with the Kurdish separatist PKK (see below); however, in March the Constitutional Court ruled that HADEP was to be allowed to contest the elections.

In February 1999 the trial began of 79 alleged Islamists, including Erbakan. Hasan Celal Güzel, the leader of the Yeniden Doğuş Partisi (YDP—Rebirth Party), was sentenced to one year's imprisonment in that month for inciting hatred in a speech at a meeting in Kayseri province; he received a further one-year sentence in May for insulting the President, and was imprisoned for five months from December for incitement to vengeance and hostility. Meanwhile, the High Election Council ruled that former RP deputies would not be allowed to take part in the forthcoming elections as independent candidates.

Despite pressure to postpone the elections, voting proceeded as scheduled on 18 April 1999. No party secured an outright majority in the TGNA; the DSP won 136 of the 550 seats, and subsequently formed a coalition with the Milliyetçi Hareket Partisi (MHP—Nationalist Movement Party), which had won 129 seats, and ANAVATAN, with 86 seats. The remaining seats in the TGNA were won by the FP (111) and the DYP (85), with three seats won by independent candidates. HADEP performed strongly in the south-east, but failed to secure the 10% of the national vote necessary for a seat in the TGNA. The CHP leader, Deniz Baykal, resigned following the poor performance of his party. The new Government, led by Bülent Ecevit, won a parliamentary vote of confidence in June.

In August 1999 some 17,100 people were killed in an earthquake measuring 7.8 on the Richter scale, which struck near İzmit, in north-west Turkey. Both the Government and the armed forces were criticized for the lack of co-ordination and for the slowness of their response to the crisis. A second earthquake, measuring 7.2 on the Richter scale, resulted in a further 800 deaths in the same region in November. In that month Turkey enacted legislation to allow conscripts to pay to shorten their military service in order to raise funds for reconstruction after the earthquake.

Several articles of a political parties act relating to the closure of parties were approved in August 1999: no party would be permitted to reform, even under a different name, party officials would be prohibited from active politics for five years and would be forbidden from standing as candidates for the party, although they would be permitted to stand as independent candidates. In September the FP submitted its preliminary defence against the motion to ban it. In October the assets of Erbakan and nine other former RP officials were frozen as part of the continuing trial of a case brought by the Treasury demanding the repayment of aid given to the RP in 1997, as well as the repayment of allegedly unregistered party funds. In March 2000 Erbakan was sentenced to one year in prison and a lifetime ban from politics for provoking animosity and hatred in a speech made in 1994; his conviction was upheld by an appeals court in July. (In January 2001, however, his sentence was suspended, under penal legislation allowing conditional release for certain convictions. Moreover, in July 2006 the European Court of Human Rights—ECHR—ruled that Erbakan had not received a fair trial.) In December 1999, meanwhile, 300 people were detained following protests over the ban on wearing headscarves in universities; the Court of Appeals ruled that the prerogative to wear Islamic headscarves was not a democratic right.

In January 2000, following a lack of agreement within the TGNA on a suitable presidential candidate (Demirel's term of office was to end in May), Ecevit announced plans for a constitutional amendment that would allow Demirel to renew his term. Despite the agreement of the governing coalition for the proposal, a vote in the TGNA failed to achieve the necessary level of support for the amendment to be carried. In April the parties of the governing coalition agreed to nominate the Chairman of the Constitutional Court, Ahmet Necdet Sezer, as their joint candidate for the presidency; he was elected in a third round of voting.

In June 2000 the TGNA rejected a recommendation to indict former Prime Minister Mesut Yılmaz on corruption charges related to the sale of state-owned land. The rejection came after Yılmaz indicated that ANAVATAN could be forced to withdraw its support from the governing coalition, and thereby cause the collapse of the Government. In July, as part of a minor reorganization, Yılmaz joined the Government as Minister of State, also replacing Cumhur Ersümer, the Minister of Energy and Natural Resources, as Deputy Prime Minister. At HADEP's national conference in November Murat Bozlak was elected unopposed as leader, replacing Ahmet Turan Demir. Deniz Baykal was re-elected leader of the CHP in the same month.

Under the relative stability of the Ecevit Government, the Turkish economy appeared to be making significant improvements during 2000, with the implementation of structural reform measures. In November, however, a severe banking crisis was provoked by an investigation by the Banking and Supervision Agency into 10 failed banks. The investigation exposed the vulnerability of the banking sector and the lack of confidence of foreign investors in the Turkish economy, as a result of a widening current account deficit and delays to the structural reform programme. The IMF and the World Bank agreed to emergency loans in order to support the programme. In February 2001 a second economic crisis was precipitated following a dispute between the President and Prime Minister: Sezer had accused Ecevit of not responding adequately to allegations of government corruption. Opposition parties and the business community had demanded the dismissal of Deputy Prime Minister Hüsamettin Özkan, the Minister of Energy and Natural Resources, Cumhur Ersümer, and the Minister of Public Works, Koray Aydın, and the initiation of a parliamentary investigation into the affairs of Ersümer and Aydın. The precarious balance of power within the governing coalition was, however, thought to have dissuaded Ecevit from undertaking any action against the alleged corruption. Later in February Turkey, with the support of the IMF, abandoned its exchange rate controls and allowed the lira to float, while empowering the Central Bank to pursue a rigorous monetary policy to control inflation.

Following the crisis, in March 2001 Ecevit replaced the Minister of Finance, Reçep Onal, with Kemal Derviş, a senior economist at the World Bank, in an attempt to salvage Turkey's economic reforms and restore confidence in the financial markets. He also replaced the Governor of the Central Bank, Gazi Erçel, with Süreyya Serdegeçti. Following Derviş's appointment, the head of the Banking and Supervision Agency resigned. Derviş announced an emergency plan for economic stabilization, which included the restructuring of three state-owned banks under one supervisory board, and succeeded in securing the financial support of the IMF and the World Bank. Yet the political implications of the financial crisis continued to be felt in April, as anti-Government demonstrations involving tens of thousands of people degenerated into riots in Ankara and İzmir, which were dispersed by security forces. Ecevit, however, rejected demands for his Government to resign. Later in the month it was announced that 15 officials and business executives were to be tried on conspiracy and bribery charges, following a high-profile investigation into corruption in the state energy sector. The testimonies of the defendants resulted in the resignation of Ersümer, who was succeeded as head of the energy portfolio by Zeki Cakan of the ANAVATAN in early May.

In May 2001 the TGNA approved legislation designed to meet conditions demanded by the IMF before the latter was to release US $10,000m. in financial aid. A major condition was the privatization of Turkey's telecommunications sector, which was widely opposed by TGNA members. At the end of the month the Minister of State for Privatization, Yuksel Yalova, resigned, owing to disagreements within the Government over the liberalization of the tobacco industry stipulated by the IMF. Prime Minister Ecevit attempted to replace Yalova with the Minister of the Interior, Sadettin Tantan, but the latter refused the transfer and resigned from his cabinet and ANAVATAN posts in June, following disagreements with Mesut Yılmaz. Tantan was succeeded as Minister of the Interior by Rüştü Kazim Yücelen, hitherto State Minister in charge of human rights. In July the Minister of Communications, Enis Öksüz, resigned, owing to his opposition to the planned IMF-imposed reforms in the telecommunications sector. In September the Minister of Public Works and Housing, Koray Aydın, also resigned from his government post and from the TGNA, after corruption charges were brought against him with regard to his alleged receipt of funds from contracts relating to reconstruction in the aftermath of the 1999 earthquake damage.

In June 2001 the Constitutional Court banned the FP, on the grounds that it was essentially a continuation of the banned Islamist RP and was thus regarded as seeking to undermine the secular system. The Court expelled two FP members from the TGNA; however, it refrained from ordering the mass expulsions of the 100 remaining FP members from the legislature, who were allowed to remain in place as independents or join two planned successor parties. The ban was, nevertheless, opposed by most TGNA members, who were reportedly concerned that it would lead to more political instability. In July the ECHR upheld the Government's 1998 decision to ban the RP. In July 2001 former FP leader Recai Kutan established a new Islamist party, Saadet Partisi (SP—Felicity Party), incorporating about one-half of the former members of the FP (mainly from the conservative wing); the new party pledged to defend religious rights without challenging the secular state. It was believed that, as with the FP, Erbakan was the main force in the party. In August the remaining members of the FP joined the new reformist Islamist Adalet ve Kalkınma (AKP—Justice and Development Party), established by the former mayor of İstanbul, Recep Tayyip Erdoğan, and FP member Gül as an alternative to the SP. Shortly afterwards Erdoğan came under investigation for comments he had reportedly made in 1994 that allegedly insulted the Turkish state.

The TGNA in October 2001 overwhelmingly approved a number of constitutional amendments designed to facilitate Turkey's admission to the EU. The changes largely pertained to political freedoms and civil liberties, including minority rights (notably regarding the use of the Kurdish language); however, amendments to articles concerning the death penalty refrained from abolishing capital punishment outright. Significantly, the number of civilians on the powerful NSC would rise from five to nine, thereby lessening the power of the military (which would retain five members). Improved rights for women were approved in November.

In January 2002 the Constitutional Court imposed restrictions on the political activities of AKP leader Erdoğan, owing to his earlier allegedly seditious activities. The Court banned him from contesting the elections to the TGNA, and ordered his party to remove him from its leadership within six months. In March Ankara's Higher Criminal Court sentenced Erbakan to two years and four months in prison for embezzling party funds. (In December 2003 the Court of Appeals in Ankara upheld this sentence, although it was deferred for one year on medical grounds.)

In February 2002 the TGNA approved additional laws on freedom of thought and expression by means of a 'mini-reform' programme designed to satisfy EU standards. In subsequent weeks the ruling coalition experienced increasing disagreement over the possible execution of PKK leader Abdullah Öcalan, and on broadcasting and education in the Kurdish language, with the MHP taking an uncompromising stance on these issues in opposition to ANAVATAN. In July Prime Minister Ecevit was forced to call early elections to the TGNA for November, after several of his ministers and numerous DSP party legislators resigned, thereby denying the ruling coalition a majority in the TGNA. Earlier that month the MHP had publicly called for an early election. Notable resignations included those of Deputy Prime Minister and Minister of State Hüsamettin Özkan and Minister of Foreign Affairs İsmail Cem. Cem formed a new party, the Yeni Türkiye Partisi (YTP—New Turkey Party), with 62 defectors from the DSP, whose representation in the TGNA had fallen from 128 seats to 65 seats. Ecevit appointed DSP member Şükrü Sina Gürel as Deputy Prime Minister and Minister of State, and concurrently Minister of Foreign Affairs. In early August the Minister of Finance, Kemal Derviş, resigned, and subsequently agreed to co-operate with the CHP. At the end of the month the notably pro-EU and strongly secularist commander of the army's ground forces, Gen. Hilmi Özkök, was appointed to the powerful position of Chief of the General Staff for a four-year term.

In September 2002 the AKP, which was leading in opinion polls, underwent a reverse, when Turkey's highest election board confirmed the Constitutional Court's decision to ban Erdoğan from holding public office. Although he had publicly professed secular and pro-European views, Erdoğan retained the distrust of the secularist military and judiciary, and in October the chief prosecutor sought to obtain an outright ban on the AKP, although this was not implemented. Attempts by several political parties to delay the election also failed.

The elections to the TGNA, held on 3 November 2002, significantly transformed the Turkish political landscape. With voter participation of 79.0%, the AKP won 34.3% of the votes cast, securing 363 seats in the TGNA. Only one other party, the CHP, achieved the 10% of the vote required for representation in the TGNA, winning 19.4% of the votes cast and securing 178 seats. Following the election, President Sezer appointed AKP deputy leader Abdullah Gül as Prime Minister, since Erdoğan was ineligible for the position. (None the less, Erdoğan acted as de facto Prime Minister, exerting a strong influence on the new Government and making a number of official foreign visits.) The new Council of Ministers largely consisted of technocrats from the AKP. Three Deputy Prime Ministers were appointed, while Ali Babacan became Minister of State with responsibility for the Economy and Kemal Unakıtan acquired the finance portfolio. Mehmet Vecdi Gönül was appointed Minister of National Defence. Owing to the fact that AKP's representation in the TGNA was only four seats less than the two-thirds' majority needed to amend the Constitution, and the party commanded the support of several independents, in December the legislature approved constitutional reforms allowing Erdoğan to contest a forthcoming by-election. Initially vetoed by Sezer, these changes were subsequently re-endorsed by the TGNA, forcing the President to accept them.

In January 2003 Erdoğan was re-elected leader of the AKP and immediately announced plans to contest the by-election for the TGNA, membership of which would allow him to become Prime Minister. In February the electoral commission endorsed his candidacy, and Erdoğan was elected to the TGNA on 9 March. Two days later President Sezer appointed Erdoğan as Prime Minister. Erdoğan appointed a new Council of Ministers, which retained most ministers from the incumbent Government. Gül replaced Yalçınbayır as Deputy Prime Minister and also assumed the foreign affairs portfolio. In June the TGNA adopted a further series of human rights reforms, including additional legislation to permit education and broadcasting in Kurdish and other minority languages, and to amend the existing legal definition of terrorism, in order to qualify for accession negotiations with the EU. At the end of that month Sezer vetoed one of the amendments, under which peaceful advocacy of an independent Kurdish state would no longer be illegal. However, the TGNA utilized its power to overrule the veto by returning the legislation to the President without amendment. Further reforms approved by the TGNA (in accordance with EU requirements) in July included the reconstitution of the predominantly military NSC as an entirely advisory body and the offer of a qualified amnesty to supporters of KADEK (the Congress for Freedom and Democracy in Kurdistan—see below), with the specific exclusion of those believed to have committed acts of violence; these measures were formally approved by Sezer in August. In September a decision by the Court of the Appeals over the November 2002 elections confirming the disqualification of DEHAP (as HADEP had become reconstituted in March 2003—see below) for malpractice prompted concern that the results would be annulled, thereby ending the majority of the AKP. However, on 4 October 2003 the High Electoral Council upheld the election results. In the same month an independent parliamentary deputy joined the Liberal Demokratik Parti, which consequently secured one seat in the TGNA.

Some 25 people were killed and about 300 injured in suicide bombings outside two of İstanbul's largest synagogues on 15 November 2003. On 20 November a further two suicide bombs exploded outside the Hong Kong and Shanghai Banking Corporation and the British consulate in İstanbul, killing some 31 people (including the Consul-General) and injuring more than 450. Although several extremist Turkish Islamist groups, including the Great Eastern Islamic Raiders' Front (IBDA-C), claimed responsibility for the attacks, the involvement of the militant Islamist al-Qa'ida (Base) network led by Osama bin Laden was immediately suspected. Erdoğan condemned all acts of terrorism in a national statement, and demonstrations were staged in Turkey against the bombings, although popular sentiment also attributed blame to the US-led military action in Iraq. By the end of that month a total of 62 had been killed in the four bomb attacks, and 159 had been arrested on suspicion of involvement, of whom a number had been charged. The Turkish authorities announced that the bombings had been organized by a cell of Turkish nationals connected to al-Qa'ida, all of whom had been trained outside Turkey; one principal suspect was repatriated from Syria, while another was arrested on Turkey's south-eastern border with Iran.

Local government elections, which were held on 28 March 2004, resulted in a strong increase in support for the AKP, which secured 42% of the votes cast and 58 of the country's 81 provinces. The CHP, having become subject to internal factional divisions, won only 18% of the votes. In May, as part of the series of reforms intended to bring Turkey into conformity with EU human rights and democratic standards, the TGNA adopted draft constitutional amendments to: abolish the death penalty and anti-terrorist state security courts; guarantee equality for women; and establish full parliamentary control over the budget of the armed forces. The approval in that month of new education legislation, ending restrictions on university entrance for those trained in religious schools, was viewed with concern by defendants of Turkey's official secularism. Consequently, the Government's decision at the beginning of June, following a veto by President Sezer, to suspend the introduction of the legislation was generally welcomed. Security concerns shortly before a NATO summit, attended by US President George Bush, in June were heightened by further explosions in İstanbul, including a suicide bombing, in which four people were killed. In the same month Turkey's stated commitment to new human rights standards, in compliance with EU requirements, was demonstrated by the Supreme Court's decision to order the release of the four Kurdish former parliamentary deputies, who had been sentenced to 15 years' imprisonment in 1994 for supporting the PKK. Following their release, a court in July 2004 overturned their convictions and ordered retrials. The most celebrated of the four, Leyla Zana, after her release, urged the organization to reinstate the cease-fire ended by the organization in September 2003 (see below). In a further significant measure, the TGNA in July 2004 authorized the prosecution for corruption of former Prime Minister Mesut Yılmaz and three other former ministers. In August a further three bombs exploded at hotels in İstanbul, killing two people, and were again attributed by the authorities to Kurdish militants.

In January 2005, following the provisional offer by the EU in December 2004 to commence accession negotiations, Islamist party leaders criticized the conditions imposed and demanded that the Government organize a referendum on EU membership; protests were organized in İstanbul and in İzmit. In February 2005 the Chairman of the Human Rights Consultative Council tendered his resignation, citing continuing impediments posed by the Government (which had rejected a previous critical report of the Council over the stance on human rights). Turkey's new penal code, adopted as a precondition for the commencement of EU accession talks (see below), entered into force at the beginning of June, after a two-month postponement. Sezer subsequently vetoed an amendment reducing the penalties for anti-secular teaching in illegal religious schools. However, at the end of June the TGNA overruled the President's veto, which was supported by the ruling AKP.

The Government's announcement in late 2005 that the renowned Turkish writer, Orhan Pamuk, had been charged with denigrating the Turkish state, after he made a reference in an interview to a Swiss newspaper to the massacre of some 1.5m. Armenians by Turks between 1915 and 1923, prompted international criticism. Pamuk's trial began, amid nationalist protests, in December 2005 but was immediately adjourned, after the municipal court in İstanbul ruled that, under the terms of the unrevised penal code, the Ministry of Justice should decide whether or not it proceed. In January 2006 the charges against Pamuk were abandoned, after the Minister of Justice referred the case back to the court, which refused to uphold it. (It was reported, however, that some 60 journalists were on trial at that time on charges of insulting the Turkish state.) Pamuk was awarded the Nobel Prize for Literature in October. However, in January 2008 the Supreme Court of Appeals overturned the dismissal of the case against Pamuk, asserting that the charges were legitimate. Following a further appeal lodged by the municipal court, in May 2009 the Supreme Court of Appeals once again ruled that the case against the author was valid.

In February 2006 the trial began of five prominent journalists, including the editor of a principal Armenian newspaper, who had been charged with denigrating the judiciary, after criticizing a September 2005 court decision to prohibit a university conference in İstanbul on the massacre of Armenians in 1915–23. The murder of a prominent Armenian-Turkish journalist and human rights campaigner, Hrant Dink, in İstanbul in January 2007 provoked considerable outrage among the population. Eight suspects, some with close links to nationalist organizations, were arrested following Dink's killing, while several local police officers were suspended from duty for allegedly having failed to offer sufficient protection to the journalist after he had received death threats, or for apparently having shown support to the incarcerated principal suspect. A teenage youth suspected of having links with extreme right-wing nationalist organizations had reportedly confessed to Dink's murder. Trial proceedings against the alleged murderer, together with 17 other suspects, commenced in the Turkish capital in July.

Meanwhile, in February 2006 Erdoğan criticized the decision of the Council of State to refuse to allow the promotion of a teacher who had worn a headscarf on her way to work. In May an extremist Islamist lawyer angered at the ruling entered the Council of State building and assassinated a senior judge. Large demonstrations followed in Ankara, supported by the judiciary and the Chief of the General Staff, Gen. Hilmi Özkök; protesters demanded the protection of secularization in Turkey. (The Islamist lawyer was given two terms of life imprisonment by an Ankara court in February 2008, having been one of four defendants convicted of involvement in the murder.) In August Gen. Yaşar Büyükanıt succeeded Özkök as Chief of the General Staff. In April 2006, meanwhile, after controversially rejecting the Government's selected appointee to the post of Governor of the Central Bank, Sezer approved the nomination of Durmuş Yılmaz, a long-standing director of the bank; Yılmaz pledged commitment to the IMF-supported policy of monetary restraint. In the same month the trial of two Syrian nationals, including a suspected member of al-Qa'ida, was merged with that of 71 defendants charged with involvement in the bombings in İstanbul in November 2003. (In February 2007 seven people—six Turks and a Syrian—were sentenced to life imprisonment for their involvement in the attacks; 41 were given prison terms of between four and 18 years, while 26 were acquitted.) In March 2006 three people were killed when a bomb exploded near the Governor's office in the south-eastern town of Van, and in April a further bomb attack was staged at the offices of the AKP in İstanbul. A number of suspected al-Qa'ida militants were detained in south-eastern Turkey in January 2008, on suspicion of plotting large-scale attacks within the country.

In mid-April 2007, as the TGNA began preparations to elect a successor to President Sezer (whose term of office was to end on 16 May), some 300,000 people held a demonstration in Ankara to demand that Turkey remain a secular state. The protest was organized amid strong speculation that Prime Minister Erdoğan was intending to stand for the presidency; many feared that Erdoğan would pursue an Islamist agenda if he became President. In late April, however, the day before the deadline for the registration of candidates, the Prime Minister declared that the Minister of Foreign Affairs, Abdullah Gül, had been chosen as the ruling AKP's candidate. Gül immediately pledged to retain Turkey's secular status should he be elected to the presidency, although there was considerable scepticism about the likelihood of this since Gül's wife chooses to wear the Islamic headscarf. The initial round of voting in the TGNA was boycotted by the CHP and other opposition parties, who complained that they had not been consulted about Gül's application; they lodged an appeal with the Constitutional Court for the voting process to be cancelled. Since Gül secured only 357 out of 550 votes at the first round—10 fewer than the requisite number—it was announced at the end of the month that the Constitutional Court had annulled the initial vote. Prime Minister Erdoğan subsequently asked the legislature to approve proposals initiated by his party to endorse a constitutional amendment enabling the President henceforth to be directly elected for a five-year term and that a general election (scheduled for November) be brought forward to June in order to resolve the political crisis. The Higher Council of Elections ruled in May that an election should be held on 22 July. Meanwhile, the AKP's legislation was approved by the TGNA, but subsequently vetoed by President Sezer, initially in May 2007.

The AKP of Prime Minister Erdoğan obtained 46.7% of the votes and 341 seats at the legislative elections, on 22 July 2007, against the CHP's 20.9% and 112 seats. The MHP came third, with 14.3% and 71 seats; however, one of the party's elected representatives died on 26 July, resulting in one seat remaining vacant. Pro-Kurdish deputies entered the TGNA as independents—the first time that there had been Kurdish representation in the legislature for 13 years. In early August Köksal Toptan of the AKP was elected Speaker of the Assembly, in succession to Bülent Arınç. Shortly afterwards Abdullah Gül signalled his desire to remain a candidate for the presidency, and he was endorsed unanimously by his party. The first round of the presidential vote was held on 20 August; Gül failed to secure the required two-thirds' majority to be elected at this stage. However, by the third round of voting, on 28 August, at which a simple majority was required, Gül was chosen as Turkey's 11th President, securing 339 votes. At his inauguration the new President again pledged his commitment to secularism, pluralism and freedom of belief. A new Council of Ministers was approved by President Gül at the end of the month. Among the principal appointees were Ali Babacan as Minister of Foreign Affairs and Chief Negotiator of Turkey for European Union Affairs, and Dr Beşir Atalay as Minister of Internal Affairs. The new Government's programme, which won a vote of confidence in early September, included proposals to reform and modernize the Turkish Constitution, and measures aimed at increasing economic prosperity. Concerns were raised in mid-September when the Prime Minister recommended an amendment to the Constitution proposing to overturn the ban on women wearing the Islamic headscarf in Turkish universities. At the nation-wide referendum held on 21 October, a reported 68.95% of eligible voters approved the constitutional reforms regarding the direct election of future Turkish presidents. The serving term of a president was also reduced from seven to five years (renewable once), while that of TGNA deputies was reduced from five to four years.

In late January 2008 the AKP and the MHP together submitted a motion to the TGNA that would end the ban on the wearing of the Islamic headscarf by women at universities. The two constitutional amendments were passed into law by President Gül in late February, having received parliamentary approval. The development provoked anger among Turkish secularists, who protested against the decision in Ankara and elsewhere. Two secularist opposition parties, the CHP and the DSP, lodged an appeal with the Constitutional Court on the grounds that the legislation contravened the secular principles of Turkey's constitution. In mid-March an indictment was filed at the Constitutional Court by Abdurrahman Yalçınkaya, a prosecutor at the Court of Appeals, which presented detailed evidence of alleged 'anti-secular activities' of the AKP and called for the closure of the party and a five-year suspension from politics for 71 senior party officials, including the incumbent President and Prime Minister. The Court voted unanimously to hear the case against the ruling party. The AKP denied the anti-secular charges, and contended that banning the party would amount to overturning the democratic outcome of the legislative elections. In early June the Constitutional Court rescinded the recent legislation pertaining to the wearing of headscarves at universities, on the grounds that it was unconstitutional. However, the AKP narrowly avoided disbandment when the verdict was announced at the end of July. A minimum of seven votes from 11 judges was required to effect the closure of a political party: six voted to disband the party; four voted for a financial penalty, and one rejected the case. None the less, the Court found the party guilty of being a 'focal point of anti-secular activity', and ordered that its state funding be halved for a year.

Meanwhile, in early July 2008 four gunmen attacked the US Consulate in İstanbul. Three police officers and three militants were killed in the ensuing gun battle, while a fourth militant escaped. (No consular staff were reported to have been harmed in the attack.) Several suspects were arrested in connection with the incident in the following months, but reports that the militants were members of a terrorist cell with links to al-Qa'ida remained unconfirmed. Two bombs exploded in a busy suburban district of İstanbul in late July, killing 17 people and injuring as many as 150. Prime Minister Erdoğan blamed the attacks on the PKK, although the group denied any involvement.

Following the discovery of a hoard of munitions at a property belonging to a retired army officer in İstanbul in June 2007, an investigation was launched into the existence of a clandestine nationalist organization, known as Ergenekon, with alleged links to senior military, police, judicial and media figures. From early 2008 a series of high-profile arrests were made in connection with the investigation. In July 21 people, including two retired army generals, were detained. In August Gen. İlker Başbuğ succeeded Yaşar Büyükanıt as Chief of the General Staff. Başbuğ was replaced as Ground Forces Commander by Gen. Işık Koşaner who, in a speech in late August, denied allegations of links between the military and Ergenekon; he also reiterated the army's readiness to take action, if needed, to protect Turkey's secular Constitution. Trial proceedings against 86 suspected members of Ergenekon were initiated in October. Suspects were charged with various offences, which included belonging to a terrorist organization and plotting to overthrow the Government. According to the prosecution, the organization had plotted to foment disorder through a series of violent incidents, including high-profile assassinations, in order to undermine the Government and provoke a military coup. The organization was also indicted with responsibility for several violent incidents, previously attributed to Islamist militants, such as the murder of a judge at the Council of State in May 2006 (see above) and a bomb attack at the offices of *Cumhuriyet* newspaper, also in 2006. Among those that Ergenekon allegedly planned to assassinate were the President, the Prime Minister and the writer Orhan Pamuk. As many as 40 additional suspects, including three retired generals and a former police chief, were arrested in January 2009. In March charges against an additional 56 suspects were appended to the ongoing trial proceedings. Further arrests in April included those of employees of newspapers and universities. Later that month the Supreme Court of Appeals ordered that the trial relating to the Council of State attack of 2006 be merged with the Ergenekon trial. The proliferation of arrests during 2008 and early 2009 prompted some critics to accuse the Government of exploiting the case to discredit their political rivals.

Meanwhile, amid the ongoing tension between the Government and its secularist opponents, Erdoğan publicly declared that the forthcoming municipal elections, scheduled for 29 March 2009, would serve as a referendum on his leadership. The Prime Minister campaigned vigorously, appearing at large political rallies throughout Turkey and exhorting the electorate to reinforce his mandate to lead the country. The AKP won 38.8% of the votes cast, consolidating its position as Turkey's dominant political party. However, the result represented a reduction in the party's popularity when compared to the municipal elections of 2004 (at which it won 41.7% of the votes), and the legislative elections in 2007 (when it won 46.7%). Both the main opposition parties achieved gains in their share of the municipal vote: the CHP polled 23.1% and the MHP 16.1%. At least five people, including election candidates, were reportedly killed in violent clashes between supporters of rival candidates in towns in south-eastern Turkey during the election campaign.

A major reorganization of the Council of Ministers, involving 17 ministerial changes, was announced on in early May 2009. Ali Babacan, hitherto Minister of Foreign Affairs, was appointed Deputy Prime Minister and accorded responsibility for economic co-ordination; the foreign affairs portfolio was reassigned to Ahmet Davutoğlu, a foreign affairs adviser to the Prime Minister who had played a central role in Turkey's mediation of indirect peace talks between Israel and Syria during 2008 (see below). Other significant changes included the appointment of Mehmet Şimşek as Minister of Finance, and Sadullah Ergin as Minister of Justice.

Although Turkey was readmitted to the Parliamentary Assembly of the Council of Europe in May 1984, the Assembly continued to advocate the establishment of full democracy and political freedom in the country. In July 1987 all martial law decrees were repealed when martial law was replaced with a state of emergency in several provinces. The Government's signing, in January 1988, of UN and Council of Europe agreements denouncing torture, however, met with a cynical response from both the domestic and international media. Turkey's human rights record has continued to be a focus of international scrutiny.

In July 1999 the ECHR found Turkey guilty of 13 counts of violating rights of free speech and ordered it to pay some 110,000m. lira in damages. In August amnesty legislation was approved by the TGNA to ease the extreme overcrowding in Turkish prisons, with the release of some 26,500 prisoners (of a total prison population of 69,000) and the reduction in sentence for a further 32,000. Although the legislation was initially intended to encourage Kurdish rebels to surrender, it was subsequently altered so that prisoners serving sentences for terrorism would not benefit from the law. However, the bill received widespread criticism and was vetoed by President Demirel in September. Unrest broke out in that month in prisons across the country as a result of the poor conditions and overcrowding; 10 prisoners were killed and a number of guards were taken hostage. The Minister of Justice later announced that a special force was to be established to ensure prison security. In September some 100 people were arrested in İstanbul while trying to issue a press release on the prison incidents. Prison unrest continued, and in February 2000 a protocol was signed providing for the education of prison inmates.

The ECHR in December 1999 found Turkey guilty of breaking the European Convention on Human Rights by its closure of the pro-Kurdish Demokrasi Partisi (DEP—Democracy Party, see below) and ordered it to pay compensation of 70,000 French francs. It was also announced that a human rights consultation committee was to be established to provide information and to act on any complaints received. A report published by the Turkish Human Rights Foundation in June 2000 asserted that as many as 1m. people had been victims of torture over the preceding decade. The report criticized the fact that perpetrators of torture were not subjected to due investigation.

In November 2000 hundreds of political prisoners throughout Turkey (mainly members of left-wing organizations) embarked on a hunger strike, in protest against plans to transfer them to high-security prisons where they would be held in isolation cells. Following attempts to force-feed the prisoners, in violation of international medical ethics, confrontations ensued between the prisoners and the authorities. In December Turkish security forces raided some 20 prisons in an attempt to end the hunger strikes. The three-day action resulted in the deaths of 30 prisoners and two soldiers. After the authorities regained control of the prisons, over 1,000 prisoners were transferred to the isolation cells. There were widespread allegations, supported by human rights organizations Human Rights Watch and Amnesty International, that many prisoners had been subjected to torture both before and after their transfer to these cells, where many prisoners resumed their hunger strike. Also in December the TGNA approved legislation granting an amnesty to as many as 35,000 prisoners by reducing their sentences by 10 years; the legislation was, however, rejected by President Sezer on the grounds that it was divisive and would not serve the cause of justice. By the end of April the number of deaths resulting from the hunger strike had reached 20, with some 30 more seriously ill. The Government refused to open negotiations with the prisoners, although the Minister of Justice announced an initiative to improve prison inspections. In May EU officials warned that failure to resolve the issue could jeopardize Turkey's candidacy for the EU. During the remainder of 2001 many of the strikers were released or hospitalized; of these, some subsequently ended their strike. In November police stormed the houses of some of the released strikers in an attempt forcibly to end the strikes; four protesters reportedly died of self-immolation during the police operation. By January 2003 104 people had died as a result of the ongoing hunger strikes, but no compromise had been reached on the issue of prison accommodation.

Meanwhile, during 2001 the TGNA introduced new legislation, including constitutional amendments, designed to improve the country's human rights and civil liberties in preparation for eventual EU accession (see above). In March the Government had announced a new programme aimed at facilitating EU membership that entailed, *inter alia*, the eventual abolition of the death penalty and ending restrictions on freedom of expression, as well as improving the rights of minorities, but EU officials criticized the programme for its lack of specifics. Despite such plans, the TGNA approved a four-month extension of the state of emergency in the predominantly Kurdish south-east of the country, and in May the Turkish Radio and Television Supreme Council ordered the closure of 89 radio and television stations for broadcasting separatist and disruptive programmes. In October the TGNA approved wide-ranging constitutional amendments embracing improvements in civil liberties and human rights; further liberalizing reforms were approved in February 2002 (see above). Meanwhile, in November women were granted new rights, including equal status to men in several key areas.

In June 2002 the Government proposed additional reforms that abolished the death penalty and removed a ban on broadcasting and education in the Kurdish language. In August the TGNA formally abolished the death penalty in peacetime; in September, however, Amnesty International released a report alleging the widespread use of torture by police, citing testimony from more than 60 individuals during the first half of 2002. In October a court in İstanbul sentenced 10 police officers to prison terms ranging from five to 10 years for beating, torturing and sexually abusing 15 teenage suspects in 1995. The police officers had been acquitted on two previous occasions, resulting in strong condemnation by human rights groups. The officers launched an appeal against their verdict, but in April 2003 the Court of Appeals upheld the sentences. Following his appointment as Prime Minister in March, Erdoğan immediately pledged to bring about major improvements in Turkey's human rights record and to eliminate the use of torture. A series of reforms, approved by the TGNA in July (see above), included provisions for the prompt investigation of allegations of torture and for prohibiting the trial of civilians in military courts in peacetime. In May 2004 the TGNA approved a number of constitutional amendments, in accordance with EU requirements, which included the removal of references to the death penalty and the abolition of the country's system of State Security Courts (used to try dissidents). However, Turkey's perceived failure to maintain the pace of its reforms led, by November 2006, to the suspension of some parts of its accession negotiations (see below).

The Government's position on the Kurdish situation remained a major element of its human rights policy. In January 2002 the Government acted against a campaign to allow the Kurdish language to be taught in schools and universities by arresting hundreds of activists. In February an İstanbul court acquitted a publisher, Fatih Tas, for disseminating 'separatist' articles, written by US academic and linguist Noam Chomsky, which criticized US support for Turkish military operations aimed at suppressing Kurdish nationalism. Chomsky himself attended the trial in support of Tas. In March clashes between security forces and Kurds at a HADEP-organized Kurdish new year celebration in Mersin resulted in the deaths of two policemen and one demonstrator. The decision by the AKP Government in November to permit a maximum of 30 minutes per day of Kurdish language programmes on state television and a maximum of 45 minutes on state radio was greeted with disappointment by Kurdish groups, who had long sought unlimited broadcasting of Kurdish programmes on commercial and local radio and television stations. In March 2003 a ruling by Turkey's Constitutional Court banned HADEP from political activity on the grounds that it had been aiding the PKK (a charge denied by the party). Some 46 members of the party were also subjected to a five-year ban. Shortly afterwards HADEP became reconstituted as the Demokratik Halkın Partisi (DEHAP—Democratic People's Party).

A significant increase in outbreaks of urban terrorism in early 1990, together with a perceived increase in the influence of fundamentalist thought, led to widespread fears of a return to the extremist violence of the late 1970s. The increase in terrorist attacks by Islamist and left-wing groups, especially the Dev-Sol (Revolutionary Left), was exacerbated by the Government's stance in the Gulf crisis of 1990–91 (see below), and both factions unleashed a series of attacks against Western targets in Turkey, including US civilians, diplomatic missions and offices of several national airlines and banks in İstanbul and Ankara. The leader of Dev-Sol, Dursun Karatas, was detained in France in September 1994, and diplomatic efforts began to ensure his extradition. Two weeks later a former Minister of Justice, Mehmet Topaç, was shot dead by Dev-Sol members in Ankara. In August 1995 several bombs exploded in İstanbul (killing two civilians), at least one of which was reported to have been placed by a previously unknown Islamist group. In January 1996 a left-wing faction of Dev-Sol, Devrimci Halk Kurtuluş Partisi— Cephesi (DHKP—C, the Revolutionary People's Liberation Party—Front), claimed responsibility for the murder of two leading Turkish business executives in İstanbul. At the end of the year it was reported that Dev-Sol had been subsumed by the DHKP—C.

In January 2000 the Government launched a major operation against the fundamentalist guerrilla group Hezbollah (apparently sponsored by fundamentalist elements in Iran, but unrelated to the Lebanese group of the same name). An armed confrontation between police and Hezbollah members resulted in the death of its leader, Hüseyin Velioğlu, and the capture of two of his closest associates; information provided by these associates led to the discovery of the bodies of nine men, believed to have been abducted by the group in İstanbul. In early 2000 the operation succeeded in detaining some 690 suspected Hezbollah members and the bodies of more than 50 people, believed to have been victims of the group, were discovered. At that time the Government denied that it had tolerated the activities of Hezbollah, owing to its anti-PKK activities, and the office of the Chief of the General Staff strongly denied allegations of links between Hezbollah and the army. In February Çiller denied that the state had supplied weapons to Hezbollah during her time as Prime Minister, and in March two regional FP staff were arrested on suspicion of membership of Hezbollah. In October Turkish security forces captured Mehmet Sudan, Velioğlu's successor, and the Ministry of the Interior reported that since January some 1,600 people with ties to Hezbollah had been arrested.

In December 2000 two police officers were killed following an attack on a police bus in İstanbul. In January 2001 the DHKP—C claimed responsibility for a suicide bomb attack on a police building, which killed two people. In April Sahil Izzet Erdis, the leader of the outlawed IBDA—C, was sentenced to death on charges of seeking to overthrow the secular state. In September a suicide bomber, believed to be acting on behalf of the DHKP—C, killed two policemen and a foreign tourist in central İstanbul. In May 2002 the EU designated the DHKP—C as a terrorist organization. Security forces arrested several members of DHKP—C in two attempted military operations during November 2004. In June 2006 four members of the organization were arrested following the shooting of a police officer in İstanbul. In January 2007 a further five DHKP—C members (including Karatas) were detained by the Turkish authorities.

In 1984 the outlawed PKK, seeking the creation of a Kurdish national homeland in Turkey, launched a violent guerrilla campaign against the Turkish authorities in the south-eastern provinces. The Government responded by arresting suspected Kurdish leaders, sending in more security forces, establishing local militia groups and imposing martial law (and later states of emergency) in the troubled provinces. Violence continued to escalate, however, and in April and May 1990 clashes between rebel Kurds, security forces and civilians resulted in the deaths of 140 people. The conflict entered a new phase when, in August and October 1991, and March 1992 (in retaliation for continuing cross-border attacks on Turkish troops), government fighter planes conducted numerous sorties into northern Iraq in order to attack suspected PKK bases there. In the course of these raids many civilians and refugees (including Iraqi Kurds) were reportedly killed, prompting international observers and relief workers publicly to call into question the integrity of the exercises. The Iraqi Government lodged formal complaints with the UN, denouncing Turkish violations of Iraq's territorial integrity.

Violence in the south-eastern provinces, resulting from ethnic tension, persisted throughout 1992 and 1993, despite the stated commitment of the Demirel administration to foster new initiatives for improved relations with ethnic minorities. In late 1992 Turkish air and ground forces (in excess of 20,000 troops), conducted further attacks upon PKK bases inside northern Iraq, hoping to take advantage of losses inflicted on the Kurdish rebels by an offensive in October initiated by Iraqi Kurdish *peshmerga* forces, aimed at forcing the PKK from Iraq. Hopes that a negotiated resolution to the conflict might be achieved, following the unilateral declaration of a cease-fire by the PKK in March 1993, were frustrated by renewed fighting in May and an intensification of the conflict in June. The bombing of several coastal resorts and of tourist attractions in central İstanbul confirmed the PKK's intention to disrupt the country's economy and to attract international attention to the conflict. PKK activists and supporters also conducted protests and attacked Turkish property throughout Europe.

In November 1993 a 10,000-strong élite anti-terrorist force was created to counter the PKK forces, in addition to the estimated 150,000–200,000 troops already positioned in the area of conflict. In 1994 the security forces mounted a heavy offensive against the separatists, and again conducted air attacks on suspected PKK strongholds in south-eastern Turkey and in northern Iraq. Reports that an estimated 6,000 Kurds were forcibly displaced into northern Iraq as a result of the destruction of their villages by security forces were denied by the Minister of Foreign Affairs. In September security forces initiated an operation in the eastern Munzur mountains to destroy PKK stores and supply routes. In November a Kurdish proposal for a cease-fire, accompanied by international mediation, to achieve a peaceful settlement to the conflict was rejected by the Government, which emphasized the success of its anti-terrorist campaign.

On 20 March 1995 a massive offensive, involving 35,000 air and ground force troops, was initiated against PKK targets in northern Iraq. Turkish forces advanced some 40 km across the border, prompting protests from Iraq, as well as concern on the part of the USA and the EU that the military intervention should not be consolidated into a permanent occupation force. The Turkish Government insisted that the offensive was designed to destroy PKK base camps and to force the separatists from northern Iraq (where, it claimed, the PKK had taken advantage of a power vacuum in the region to become securely established). The UN assisted in the evacuation of several thousand Kurds from the northern Iraqi town of Zakho, amid reports of intimidation by the occupying Turkish troops. Under increasing international pressure, Turkey undertook a complete withdrawal of its troops by May. Official figures stated that 555 Kurdish separatists and 58 Turkish soldiers were killed as a result of the operation. Earlier, in April, the PKK had obtained permission to convene in the Netherlands, in an attempt to establish a Kurdish parliament-in-exile, prompting Turkey temporarily to recall its ambassador to the Netherlands. Fighting was again resumed in the south-east of the country in June, and in July a further week-long offensive was conducted against Kurdish bases in northern Iraq. In December the PKK leader, Abdullah Öcalan, announced a unilateral cease-fire on the part of his organization. By March 1996, having received no assurances of a cease-fire from the Turkish authorities, Öcalan advised tourists against visiting the country, warning of possible renewed attacks against major tourist sites. During April an estimated 400 PKK members were killed in the renewed military operation. In the following months PKK activists were frequently pursued into northern Iraq by Turkish ground and air forces, provoking protests from the Iraqi Government, and fighting in the south-eastern provinces escalated. In June five soldiers were killed in a suicide bomb attack in Tunceli, eastern Turkey. A further two suicide attacks, reportedly by PKK members, were perpetrated in October, killing 10 people. In response, Turkish security forces conducted air raids against PKK targets in northern Iraq, which continued into early 1997. An estimated 2,800 PKK activists were killed during 1996 as a result of the conflict, in addition to 532 members of the security forces and 145 civilians.

In May 1997 Turkey again launched a massive military offensive against the PKK in northern Iraq, involving the mobilization of 50,000 troops. Turkey claimed that the incursion was in response to an appeal by the Iraqi-based Kurdistan Democratic Party (KDP), which co-operated with the Turkish attack. The operation elicited rigorous condemnation from Iraq, Iran and Syria, but the response from members of NATO was muted. By June Turkish military officials claimed that the attack had achieved its objectives of destroying several PKK bases in northern Iraq and estimated that more than 3,000 PKK troops had been killed. A further offensive, launched in September, was speculated to be part of a Turkish plan to establish a security zone in northern Iraq to prevent cross-border attacks by the PKK. This assumption was apparently confirmed by the lifting of the state of emergency in three of the nine south-eastern provinces in October.

Despite PKK threats to extend the separatist struggle throughout Turkey if the Turkish Government refused to seek a political solution to the conflict, additional Turkish troops entered northern Iraq in February 1998. Further operations against the PKK took place in April, including the capture of a former PKK commander, Semdin Sakik. Sakik had surrendered to the DPK in March, following a disagreement with Öcalan, which fuelled speculation concerning internal dissent within the movement. In August the PKK declared a unilateral cease-fire; this was, however, rejected by the Government.

Relations with Syria, which had already deteriorated in July 1998 (owing to Syria's repeated claim to the Hatay region of Turkey), worsened in early October, after Turkey threatened the use of force if Syria did not expel Öcalan and close down terrorist training camps in both Syria and the Beka'a valley in Lebanon. It was reported that 10,000 Turkish troops had been deployed near the border; the Turkish ambassador to Syria was also recalled. Egypt and Iran both attempted to mediate in the dispute, and, following a meeting of Turkish and Syrian officials in late October, an agreement was signed under which Syria would not allow the PKK to operate on its territory; Öcalan was thus forced to leave the country, and he arrived in Italy in November. Turkey had already temporarily recalled its ambassador to Italy in October, after a meeting of the Kurdish parliament-in-exile was hosted there. Relations deteriorated further when Italy refused to extradite Öcalan to Turkey and Öcalan applied for asylum. Demonstrations were held in Turkey against Italy, and Italian goods were boycotted; Turkey also threatened to end diplomatic relations with Italy if Öcalan's asylum request was granted. However, in January 1999 Öcalan was reported to have left Italy after his application was turned down. In the following month he was captured at the Greek embassy in Kenya and returned to Turkey. Widespread Kurdish protests were held throughout Europe.

At the end of February 1999 Öcalan was formally charged, in the absence of defence counsel, and the first hearing was set for late March. PKK violence in protest at the trial continued in that month, and there were also threats of violence against tourists in Turkey. A series of bomb attacks in Istanbul were later attributed to a new Kurdish group, the Nationalist Kurdish Revenge Teams. In April a further operation was launched against the PKK, involving the deployment of some 15,000 Turkish troops in northern Iraq. Semdin Sakik, the former PKK commander who had been captured in March 1998, was sentenced to death in May 1999; his sentence was upheld by the Supreme Court in October. In June Öcalan was convicted on treason charges and sentenced to death; violent demonstrations were held in protest at his sentence. A third PKK leader, Cevat Soysal, was arrested in Moldova in July.

The PKK agreed to a cease-fire in early August 1999, at which time Öcalan announced that the PKK was prepared to surrender its arms in exchange for Kurdish rights; PKK fighters withdrew from Turkey at the end of the month. However, the Government insisted that the PKK cease hostilities entirely in order for Turkey to reassess the situation. Following a statement issued by Öcalan in September in which he urged PKK rebels to show their commitment to the end of hostilities by surrendering to Turkish forces, two eight-member PKK delegations travelled to Ankara where they were arrested and detained by the authorities.

In September 1999 the Kurdish parliament-in-exile convened in Brussels, where it voted to dissolve and to join the Kurdistan National Congress. Following the cease-fire the number of armed confrontations in the south-east had declined substantially and in October the Government reduced the number of checkpoints in the region. In November Öcalan's death sentence was upheld on appeal and the chief prosecutor rejected his application for a final appeal; his lawyers referred the case to the ECHR. A second trial against Öcalan, together with 101 other defendants, began in Ankara in December for a series of offences including extortion and murder allegedly carried out in the 1970s; the trial was adjourned until February 2000. In January 2000 the parties of the governing coalition announced that they had agreed to delay Öcalan's execution until a ruling had been given by the ECHR.

The PKK announced formally the end to its war against Turkey in February 2000, and stated that it would campaign for Kurdish rights within a framework of peace and democracy. In February three HADEP mayors were arrested and charged with aiding the PKK; they were released on bail, following protests both from within Turkey and internationally. Relations with the EU deteriorated further in February, when Turkey denied EU politicians permission to visit Öcalan in prison. At that time 18 people, including the HADEP leader, Ahmet Turan Demir, were sentenced to almost four years' imprisonment for organizing demonstrations in support of Öcalan. Despite the PKK's cease-fire declaration, Turkish troops continued to push into Kurdish strongholds throughout the year. In September at least 38 civilians were reported to have been killed, following sorties by Turkish fighter planes into northern Iraq targeting suspected PKK bases, and in early 2001 Turkish troops advanced into Kurdish northern Iraq in an attempt to suppress PKK activities. Some 2,500 PKK rebels were believed to be based along the Iran–Iraq border at this time.

In June 2000 there were reports of increased tension within the PKK leadership, with some members, including (according to some sources) Öcalan's brother, Osman, no longer acknowledging Abdullah Öcalan as leader of the organization. In September Selahattin Celik, a founder member of the PKK, formed a breakaway group, styling itself 'the Initiative', to continue the PKK's military campaign. However, Celik, who was based in Germany, lacked the resources and forces to wage a guerrilla war. The hearing of the appeal against Öcalan's death sentence began at the ECHR in November. Öcalan's appeal was based on the grounds that he had not received a fair trial in Turkey under the terms of the European Convention on Human Rights.

In April 2002 the PKK formally announced a change of name to the Congress for Freedom and Democracy in Kurdistan (KADEK), under the leadership of Öcalan, and asserted its wish to campaign peacefully for Kurdish rights. Although the movement had abandoned its initiative for an independent Kurdish state, the announcement was received with scepticism on the part of the Turkish Government. However, KADEK was not included in the EU's list of organizations designated as 'terrorist', and it was believed that its agenda had been designed to win support from the EU. In June the ECHR awarded compensation to 13 Kurdish former members of the TGNA who had been imprisoned by the Government in 1994 for supporting the PKK. In November 2002, in a sign that the Government had acknowledged the conversion of the PKK, the state of emergency that prevailed in the two remaining south-eastern provinces of Diyarbakır and Sirnak was finally ended.

In October 2002, meanwhile, the State Security Court officially commuted Öcalan's death sentence to life imprisonment, in accordance with the abolition of the death penalty in peacetime by the TGNA in August. The court's decision was controversial, since Öcalan was widely despised by the Turkish public for his armed insurrections during the 1980s and 1990s. In March 2003 the ECHR issued a non-binding ruling that Öcalan had not received a fair trial, and criticized Turkey for violating some of Öcalan's rights; however, the ECHR rejected accusations by Öcalan's lawyers of inhumane treatment and illegal detention. Turkey immediately appealed against the ECHR, fearing renewed pressure from the EU to hold a retrial if the ruling was upheld. Despite its success in defeating Kurdish separatism, the Government continued to fear the possible emergence of a Kurdish state in northern Iraq after the USA's war against Iraqi President Saddam Hussain's regime in March–April 2003 (see below). A partial amnesty offered to supporters of KADEK by the Government in July failed, apparently owing to the effective exclusion of the movement's leadership, with only eight members accepting the terms by the end of August. In September, following renewed attacks by the organization in eastern Turkey, KADEK formally ended the cease-fire declared in February 2000, accusing the authorities of failing to address demands for improved Kurdish rights and freedom of expression. In November 2003 KADEK was reconstituted as the Kongreya Gelê Kurdistanê (KONGRA-GEL—Kurdistan People's Congress), which, in January 2004, the US Administration added to its list of designated 'terrorist' organizations.

After revoking its cease-fire, KONGRA-GEL organized sporadic attacks during 2004. In July government troops launched an offensive against KONGRA-GEL positions at the border with Iraq. In November further clashes between security forces and KONGRA-GEL militants, in which six rebels were killed, were reported in south-eastern Turkey. In early 2005 security forces repelled an attack staged from northern Iraq by suspected KONGRA-GEL members, and also arrested two KONGRA-GEL militants who had been planning a bomb attack in Mersin. In April the KONGRA-GEL leadership announced that the organization was to revert to its original name, PKK (although it appeared that not all elements of the movement did so). In May the ECHR ruled that the trial of Öcalan had been unfair, on the grounds that he had not been tried by an independent tribunal (owing to the presence of a military judge on the panel); the Turkish Government indicated that a further trial would be conducted.

A series of bomb attacks in July and August 2005 were attributed to Kurdish militants (although the PKK denied responsibility), including one on a tourist bus in the Aegean Sea resort of Kuşadası, in which five people died, and another against an army unit in south-eastern Turkey. In September some 88 PKK supporters were arrested in İstanbul, after protesting at being prevented from attending a rally in support of Öcalan (who was said to have been placed in solitary confinement). Despite the PKK's extension until early October of a unilateral cease-fire, which it had declared in August, clashes between rebels and government forces continued in the east of the country. Later in October Kurdish protests erupted in the north-western town of Eskişehir, where the trial was in process of four security officers accused of killing two civilians, including a minor, while in pursuit of rebels. In November rioting erupted in the south-eastern town of Şemdinli, after three suspected perpetrators of a bomb attack apparently aimed against a PKK supporter, in which one person was killed, were discovered to be police intelligence agents. The Government subsequently pledged that an investigation would be conducted into the incident. Security forces continued to stage operations in eastern Turkey against members of the PKK and its re-emerged military wing, Hezên Parastina Gel (HPG—People's Defence Forces). In March 2006 some 50 suspected militants were detained after a security operation in central Turkey. Between 28 March and 1 April the funeral of four suspected PKK supporters in the south-eastern town of Viranşehir precipitated large-scale Kurdish rioting in the regional capital, Diyarbakır; some 12 people were killed in the disturbances. In April a series of bomb attacks in İstanbul resulted in three deaths, and in August the coastal resorts of Marmaris and Antalya were also targeted: a further three people were killed in the Antalya blast and in both bombings there were dozens of casualties, including many foreign nationals. Responsibility for the attacks was claimed by a group calling itself Teyrêbazên Azadiya Kurdistan (TAK—Kurdistan Freedom Falcons), which purported to be linked to the PKK. In September Erdoğan emphatically rejected a call from the imprisoned Öcalan for a cease-fire to be imposed by the organization on 1 October. Öcalan was reported to have demanded a retrial against his sentence in the following month. A suicide bomb attack carried out at a shopping centre in Ankara in May 2007 resulted in the deaths of six people. Turkish security officials claimed that the attack had been perpetrated by Kurdish extremists, although spokesmen for the PKK denied responsibility.

As many as 10,000 people took part in a demonstration in İstanbul in June 2008 to demand fresh initiatives to resolve the Kurdish conflict. In July 33 PKK fighters were reportedly killed in clashes with security forces in Şırnak province in south-eastern Turkey. Renewed clashes between Government forces and Kurdish rebels in the Iraq–Turkey border region in the latter half of 2008 (see below) led to increased tension between Kurds and the authorities throughout Turkey, and several bombings were attributed to Kurdish separatists. Erdoğan embarked on a tour of the mainly Kurdish south-eastern provinces in early November, calling for national unity and solidarity in the face of separatism and terrorism; his presence provoked violent demonstrations in several towns. Meanwhile, the Demokratik Toplum Partisi (Democratic Society Party—DTP), a pro-Kurdish political party formed in 2005 to replace DEHAP, was under threat of closure following a Constitutional Court indictment, first lodged in mid-2007, that accused the party of promoting separatism and supporting the PKK. (The court's verdict was still pending in May 2009.) In December former deputy Leyla Zana, previously imprisoned in 1994 for supporting the PKK (see above), was sentenced to 10 years' imprisonment on charges of disseminating PKK propaganda. In mid-February 2009 at least 50 people were arrested in various south-eastern towns as demonstrations marking the 10th anniversary of the imprisonment of Öcalan escalated into violent clashes with security forces. The DTP made performed strongly in south-eastern Turkey in the municipal elections in March, retaining control of local councils in Diyarbakır, Hakkari and Şırnak provinces, and gaining control of Van and Siirt at the expense of the AKP. In mid-April as many as 50 people were reportedly arrested in a security operation targeting alleged PKK supporters; among those detained were three senior members of the DTP.

Turkey has been a member of NATO since 1952, and is widely considered to have fulfilled a crucial role in NATO defence strategy in south-eastern Europe. During the 1990s Turkey's importance to its key ally, the USA, increased as its strategic location allowed it to co-operate with the USA in regional security issues. The Turkish Government responded positively to requests from the USA for logistical aid, following the forcible annexation of Kuwait by Iraq in August 1990, and complied with UN proposals for economic sanctions against Iraq by closing its border to all non-essential trade and, later, to traffic. In September Turkey and the USA extended an agreement to allow the USA access to more than 25 military establishments, in return for military and economic aid, that had been initially signed in 1980, and renewed in 1987. In January 1991 a resolution to extend the war powers of the Government and effectively endorse the unrestricted use of Turkish airbases by coalition forces was agreed by the TGNA. US aircraft subsequently embarked upon bombing missions into north-eastern Iraq from NATO bases inside south-eastern Turkey. In February and March the US Government announced substantial increases in military and economic aid to Turkey. In April an estimated 600,000 Kurds attempted to flee northern Iraq into Turkey. Following a massive international relief effort and the subsequent repatriation of the majority of refugees, the Turkish Government agreed to the deployment in south-east Turkey of a 3,000-strong multi-national 'rapid reaction force', which would respond to any further acts of aggression by Iraq against the Kurds in the newly created 'safe havens'. While all ground forces were withdrawn in October, the Turkish Government agreed to the continued use of its airbases by a small allied air-strike force to conduct patrols of northern Iraq under the mandate of 'Operation Provide Comfort'. The mandate was granted six-month extensions, despite increasing unease on the part of the Turkish authorities that the Kurdish enclave was providing a refuge for PKK separatists. Difficulties in Turkey's relations with the USA arose in 1994, following a decision by the US Congress to withhold some military and economic aid in order to encourage greater respect for human rights in the Turkish Government's treatment of Kurdish separatists.

In March 1996 the Turkish Government assured the TGNA that the mandate for the use of Turkish bases for allied aircraft engaged in 'Operation Provide Comfort' would be terminated, following the approval of a final three-month extension. In July, however, the new RP Prime Minister, Necmettin Erbakan, in spite of his earlier election pledge to conclude the arrangement, secured a final extension of the operation's mandate until the end of the year. In September the Turkish Government refused permission for the use of its airbases for a US military operation against Iraqi forces that had violated the Kurdish area in northern Iraq. Turkey amassed an estimated additional 20,000 troops along the border and revealed proposals to establish a temporary security zone in the region in order to stem any influx of refugees from Iraq and to prevent the PKK from exploiting the situation. The Government also undertook to relocate the military co-ordination centre of 'Operation Provide Comfort' from Zakho in northern Iraq to Silopi in south-eastern Turkey. ('Operation Provide Comfort' was superseded by the more limited aerial surveillance operation 'Northern Watch' in January 1997.) In October 1996 the Turkish Government was actively involved in negotiations between the conflicting Kurdish factions in northern Iraq to secure a peace agreement, not least in an attempt to end the power vacuum in that region which threatened Turkey's security. A second round of talks, following the conclusion of a preliminary agreement at the end of October, was initiated in November. During 1996 Turkey pursued diplomatic efforts to secure the reopening of the petroleum pipeline from Kirkuk in northern Iraq to Yumurtalik in Turkey, which had been closed since August 1990 as a result of UN-imposed economic sanctions. The pipeline was finally reactivated in December, in accordance with a UN agreement permitting the export of US $2,000m. of petroleum by Iraq over a six-month period, in order to fund the purchase of essential medical and other humanitarian supplies. As relations between Iraq and the UN deteriorated from the end of 1997, Turkey announced that it opposed the use of its Incirlik airbase for potential US-led strikes against Iraq and urged a peaceful solution to the crisis. Relations deteriorated further in late 1998, and Turkey again urged a diplomatic solution. Although Turkey was informed of the airstrikes against Iraq in December, in January 1999 it announced that Turkish airbases would not be used in any new operation against Iraq.

Following the suicide attacks on the USA in September 2001, perpetrated by Osama bin Laden's al-Qa'ida network, Turkey emerged as a crucial ally in the former's 'war on terror', immediately pledging its co-operation. In October the TGNA agreed in principle to send troops to Afghanistan and allow foreign forces to be stationed in Turkey, and in December US Secretary of State Colin Powell visited Turkey to discuss security and bilateral trade issues. (It was believed that, in return for assisting in the US-led campaign, Turkey would gain financial assistance from the USA and be able to persuade the Administration to pressure the EU into accepting Turkey's membership.) Meanwhile, hundreds of Turkish commandos were deployed in Uzbekistan in preparation for possible combat in Afghanistan, and 90 of these entered northern Afghanistan to train the opposition United

National Islamic Front for the Salvation of Afghanistan (the United Front—UF, or 'Northern Alliance'). Turkey had for some years had contacts with the UF's Gen. Abdulrashid Dostam, having given him asylum in the late 1990s. Turkey assumed command of the International Security Assistance Force (ISAF) in Afghanistan in June 2002, raising its troop presence in that country to 1,000. (Turkish command of the ISAF ended in February 2003, whereupon control of the force passed to Germany and the Netherlands.)

In 2002 Turkish leaders became increasingly concerned about the possibility that the USA would open a 'second front' in its military campaign to overthrow the regime of Saddam Hussain. In particular, the Government feared a break-up of the Iraqi state and the creation of a Kurdish state in northern Iraq that could be used to foster Kurdish nationalism in its own territory, and the possible mass exodus of Iraqi Kurds into Turkey. There were also concerns about the disruption to Turkish-Iraqi trade and economic co-operation that any US-led attack would bring. Ecevit's illness and the subsequent preparations for elections to the TGNA in November meant that no agreements between Turkey and the USA were reached over the latter's planned invasion of Iraq. Relations between the two countries were further complicated by the victory of the AKP in the elections, and overwhelming public opposition to war against Iraq. By January 2003 a number of senior US officials had visited Turkey to persuade the Government to accept the deployment of 62,000 US troops in the south-east of the country, and the use of the region as a staging post for a 'northern front' in the planned conflict. Following lengthy negotiations, the US Government offered a financial package of US $6,000m. in direct grants and an additional $20,000m. in loans and trade concessions in compensation for any economic losses incurred during the war; however, the Turkish authorities considered this sum to be insufficient. President Sezer warned in February that US forces could only be deployed in Turkey if the USA obtained a second UN resolution from the UN Security Council authorizing the use of force against Iraq.

On 1 March 2003 the TGNA rejected a motion allowing the USA to deploy troops in Turkey. (Although 264 members of the TGNA had voted in favour of the deployment, with 250 against, the motion was four votes short of a majority of deputies in attendance.) As many as 50 AKP legislators voted against the Government, underscoring the level of opposition to US plans for a military campaign to oust the Iraqi regime. On 20 March the TGNA voted only to allow the use of Turkish airspace for the conflict, but endorsed the deployment of Turkish troops in Iraq if considered necessary. The US-led coalition forces initiated attacks against the Iraqi regime on that day, and shortly thereafter abandoned attempts to negotiate the use of Turkish bases. The aid package was withdrawn following the TGNA vote, but in April the USA offered a new, reduced package totalling a loan of US $8,500m. in order to repair bilateral relations. The US Secretary of State, Colin Powell, visited Ankara at that time and secured Turkish permission for humanitarian aid and US logistical supplies to be delivered to US and coalition troops in Iraq via Turkish territory. In September the Turkish and US Governments signed an agreement approving the loan to compensate for the adverse effects of the March–April conflict in Iraq. In October a motion proposed by the Council of Ministers in favour of contributing peace-keeping troops to the US-led coalition in Iraq was endorsed by the TGNA. Following widespread protests in both Turkey and Iraq, however, Erdoğan announced that he would consider reversing this decision, and in November the planned deployment of Turkish forces in Iraq was cancelled.

Amid an intensification of PKK violence in south-eastern Turkey during 2006, the likelihood grew of a large-scale Turkish military incursion to attempt to defeat PKK rebels in northern Iraq. By July 2007, according to Hoshyar az-Zibari, the Iraqi Minister of Foreign Affairs, Turkish armed forces along the countries' mutual border amounted to some 140,000 personnel. In August, after a reported 12 Turkish soldiers had died during fighting with PKK militants in that month, Erdoğan and the Iraqi Prime Minister, Nuri al-Maliki, reached a memorandum of understanding aimed at ending the 'safe haven' of the PKK in northern Iraq. A further security co-operation pact was signed in late September, although the Iraqi Government refused Turkey's principal demand that its military be permitted to enter Iraqi territory in pursuit of Kurdish fighters. A large number of Turkish soldiers were reported to have been killed during clashes with the PKK in subsequent weeks. In October the TGNA endorsed a decision to allow Turkish military raids into northern Iraq, despite US President Bush and al-Maliki urging the Turkish leadership to show restraint. In November Bush pledged that the USA would increase its military co-operation with Turkey, in an apparent effort to dissuade the Turkish Government from launching a major incursion into Iraqi territory. Nevertheless, in December Turkish troops began an offensive against PKK bases in Iraq's northern region, in response to a series of cross-border raids by armed Kurdish separatists to carry out bomb attacks against Turkish soldiers in south-eastern Turkey. The Iraqi Government protested to its Turkish counterpart that it had not been consulted over the military action, while the President of the Kurdish Autonomous Region, Masoud Barzani, described Turkey's actions as a violation of Iraqi sovereignty. In late February 2008 it was initially reported that up to 10,000 Turkish troops had entered northern Iraq, in what appeared to be a much larger incursion than that of the previous December, and with the additional launching of air-strikes against PKK militant bases; however, it was reported at the end of February that only several hundred troops had participated in the military campaign. Nevertheless, dozens of PKK militants were killed in the week-long offensive, together with several Turkish soldiers. (The Turkish military claimed by this time to have killed at least 230 PKK fighters, and to have lost 27 of its soldiers; however, PKK sources alleged that around 90 Turkish soldiers had died in the recent incursion.)

Sporadic cross-border clashes between Turkish forces and PKK rebels continued throughout 2008. At least 45 PKK fighters were reportedly killed in air-strikes between March and June. Meanwhile, in an unofficial visit to Ankara in March, Iraq's Kurdish President, Jalal Talabani, pledged his commitment to curtailing the activities of the PKK in northern Iraq. Prime Minister Erdoğan visited Iraq in July, the first visit by a Turkish premier in some 18 years, holding talks with his Iraqi counterpart on strengthening economic and political ties; the Iraqi authorities also reiterated their support for Turkey's campaign against the PKK in northern Iraq. The military offensive against PKK positions in northern Iraq intensified following an attack on a Turkish army border camp in the Şemdinli district in early October, in which at least 15 soldiers were killed. In that month the TGNA voted to extend the Government's mandate to launch military operations against targets in northern Iraq. In January 2009 the establishment of a joint command centre to combat PKK operations in northern Iraq was announced, involving Turkish, Iraqi and US intelligence authorities. According to Turkish military sources 696 PKK rebels had been killed and 177 captured during the conflict in 2008, while 171 members of the security forces and 51 civilians were killed in that year. Despite a decrease in the intensity of the conflict at the beginning of 2009, renewed air-strikes were launched against PKK targets in northern Iraq from early February.

Meanwhile, in early October 2007 Turkey temporarily withdrew its ambassador to Washington, DC, in protest against the adoption by the foreign affairs committee of the US House of Representatives of a non-binding resolution describing as 'genocide' the killing of an estimated 1.5m. Armenians following the First World War (see above). In his first visit to a Muslim country since becoming US President, Barack Obama travelled to Turkey in early April 2009. In a speech to the TGNA he emphasized the importance of US-Turkish ties, and used the platform to address all Muslim nations, declaring that the USA was not 'at war with Islam'. He also urged the EU to admit Turkey as a full member. In a statement issued on Armenian Remembrance Day later that month, Obama described the killing of an estimated 1.5m. Armenians in 1915–23 as a 'great atrocity' but, crucially, refrained from using the term 'genocide', despite a pre-election pledge to do so. The Turkish Ministry of Foreign Affairs issued a statement that described some aspects of the President's statement as 'unacceptable', however, Obama's careful choice of words was widely believed to reflect his Administration's desire to expedite the normalization of Turkish-Armenian ties (see below).

Although Turkey and Greece are both members of NATO, long-standing disputes over sovereignty in the Aegean Sea and concerning Cyprus have strained relations between the two countries, and tension was exacerbated when Turkey granted recognition to the 'Turkish Republic of Northern Cyprus' ('TRNC'), proclaimed in November 1983 (see the chapter on Cyprus). In April 1988 the Greek Prime Minister, Andreas Papandreou, officially accepted Turkey's status as an associate of the EC by signing the Protocol of Adaptation (consequent on Greece's accession to the EC) to the EC-Turkey Association

Agreement, which the Greek Government had hitherto refused to do, and in June Turgut Özal became the first Turkish Prime Minister to visit Greece for 36 years. In February 1990 relations deteriorated again, following violent clashes between Christians and the Muslim minority in western Thrace, in Greece. Throughout the early 1990s Turkey and Greece maintained strong support for their respective communities in Cyprus during the ongoing, but frequently interrupted, negotiations to resolve the issue.

The issue of the demarcation of territorial waters in the Aegean re-emerged as a source of tension with Greece in 1994. Turkey insisted that it would retaliate against any expansion of territorial waters in the region, as provided for under the terms of the UN Convention on the Law of the Sea (UNCLOS), which entered into force in November. Military exercises in the region were undertaken by both Turkish and Greek naval vessels, and resumed in June 1995 following ratification of UNCLOS by the Greek Parliament. Bilateral relations, which remained strained during 1995 over the issue of the treatment of the Muslim minority in western Thrace, deteriorated sharply in early 1996, owing to a series of incidents in the Aegean in which both countries claimed sovereignty of Imia (Kardak), a small, uninhabited island. Turkey's claim was based on a concession granted by Italy prior to the 1947 settlement that awarded the main Dodecanese islands to Greece. The dispute was exploited by nationalist media in both countries; however, the threat of military action was averted in February 1996 when the two sides agreed to a petition of the US Government to withdraw naval vessels from the region and to pursue efforts to conclude a diplomatic solution. Differences remained on the means of achieving a settlement, with Greece proposing to take the dispute to international arbitration, an option endorsed by the EU Council of Ministers, and Turkey advocating bilateral negotiations. Throughout 1996 relations remained strained as a result of several minor confrontations between Greek and Turkish patrol vessels in the Aegean, persistent Greek allegations of violations of its airspace by Turkish aircraft and Turkish concern at the treatment of the ethnic population in western Thrace. From mid-1996 an escalation in intercommunal tension in Cyprus emphasized divisions between the two countries. Turkey remained committed in its support for the 'TRNC' authorities and resolved to respond with military action to the proposed deployment of an anti-aircraft missile system in the Greek Cypriot territory. A joint defence doctrine was agreed by the Turkish and 'TRNC' authorities in January 1997, and in March a co-operation accord, providing for some US $250m. in economic assistance to the 'TRNC', was ratified by the two sides.

In April 1997, following Greece's continued refusal to conduct bilateral discussions with Turkey over sovereignty rights in the Aegean, Turkey rejected proposals to refer the dispute over Imia (Kardak) to the International Court of Justice (ICJ). At the end of April the Greek and Turkish ministers responsible for foreign affairs held bilateral talks in Malta under EU auspices, during which it was agreed that each country would establish a committee of experts to help resolve bilateral disputes. The two committees were to be separate and independent and were to communicate through the EU. In July, at a NATO summit in Madrid, Spain, direct talks took place between Demirel and the Greek Prime Minister, Konstantinos Simitis. The so-called Madrid agreement was signed, in which both sides pledged to respect the other's sovereign rights and to renounce violence, and the threat of violence, in their dealings with each other. Later in July, following earlier statements from Turkey expressing the hope that Greece would revoke its veto on EU aid, Greece stated that the veto would not be removed unless Turkey agreed to international arbitration over the disputed islet of Imia (Kardak).

In July 1997 Turkey announced the formation of a joint committee to implement partial integration between Turkey and the 'TRNC', in response to the EU's agreement to commence accession talks with Cyprus. Turkey also declared in September that should the EU continue to conduct membership talks with the Greek Cypriot Government, then it would seek further integration with the 'TRNC'. Shortly afterwards Turkey banned all Greek Cypriot ships from entering Turkish ports. Following the involvement of Greece in Greek Cypriot military exercises in October, in November Turkish forces engaged in military manoeuvres in the 'TRNC'. However, Yılmaz and Simitis held a cordial meeting later in November and agreed to explore confidence-building measures. Yet relations continued to be strained by accusations of violations of airspace and territorial waters, made by both Greece and Turkey. The most serious incident occurred in October 1997 when Greece accused Turkey of harassing a plane carrying the Greek Minister of Defence. In January 1998 Turkey declared that a Greek plan to extend its territorial waters from six to 12 miles under UNCLOS was unacceptable, as were plans to open several Aegean islets for settlement. Turkey also protested to the UN that the proposed opening of an airbase at Paphos in southern Cyprus would destabilize the military situation on the island. In April Greece again vetoed the release of aid promised to Turkey under the Turkish-EU customs union.

Relations deteriorated in 1998 as a result of a purchase agreement between the Greek Cypriot Government and Russia for anti-aircraft missiles. Turkey maintained that their deployment would be a threat to its territory and in July announced that it planned to deploy missiles in the 'TRNC' if the missiles deal proceeded. In December, however, the Greek Cypriot Government announced that it would not be deploying the missiles in Cyprus and that they would be deployed on Crete, Greece. In January 1999 Turkey refused to pay compensation which had been awarded by the ECHR to a Greek Cypriot woman for land lost as a result of the Turkish occupation of northern Cyprus.

In early 1999 Greece denied Turkish accusations of Greek support for the PKK, although Öcalan was later captured at the Greek embassy in Kenya. In March Turkey alleged that Greece had unilaterally suspended 'confidence-building' talks on the dispute in the Aegean, and denied a claim that Turkish aircraft had violated Greek airspace. In August relations between the two countries improved markedly, following the Greek response to the earthquake that occurred in north-west Turkey at the end of that month. Greek rescue teams were among the first to arrive in Turkey, and Greece agreed to lift its veto on EU development loans and aid to Turkey; Turkey reciprocated the gesture by sending a rescue team to Greece following a smaller-scale earthquake in Athens in September. A joint business council announced that it was to resume its activities in that month, and the Turkish and Greek ministers responsible for foreign affairs met for discussions in Brussels. Train services linking Greece and Turkey were introduced in November. In January 2000 the Greek Minister of Foreign Affairs made the first official visit to Turkey by a Greek foreign minister for 38 years, during which it was agreed that direct talks would be held to reduce military tensions in the Aegean. In February his Turkish counterpart made an equally historic visit, becoming the first Turkish foreign minister to visit Greece in 40 years. In October, however, Greece withdrew from a joint NATO military exercise in the Aegean, after it accused Turkey of preventing Greek aircraft from flying over the disputed islands of Limnos and Ikaria. This followed a joint NATO military exercise with Greek and Turkish troops on a Greek beach in June, which had been considered to be a mark of considerable progress in Greek-Turkish relations. In February 2001 the Greek parliament decreed a 'Genocide Day' to commemorate the Turkish assault on the Greek community in eastern Turkey by Atatürk's forces in 1922. However, in April 2001 both Turkey and Greece announced major reductions in their weapons-procurement programmes, and in May Greece announced measures to improve the rights of its ethnic Turks (mainly in Thrace). In June the two countries discussed the possibility of allowing Turkish nationals to visit Greek islands in the Aegean for day trips without the need for visas, and the Minister of Foreign Affairs, İsmail Cem, received his Greek counterpart, Georgios Papandreou, to discuss friendship-building measures such as the demining of their mutual border and co-hosting the 2008 European Football Championship. In November 2001 Turkey and Greece signed an agreement that allowed Greece to repatriate illegal Turkish immigrants.

None the less, Cyprus continued to overshadow bilateral relations, and in May 2001 Cem warned that there would be 'no limits' to Turkey's response were Cyprus to be admitted to EU membership before a political settlement had been reached; in November Ecevit warned that Turkey could annex the 'TRNC' if this were to occur. In February 2002 the Turkish and Greek foreign ministers recommenced talks, following the resumption of negotiations between the Greek and Turkish Cypriot sides on the island. In mid-March Turkey and Greece discussed ongoing disputes over the Aegean Sea, including the control of the continental shelves and the resources beneath them. Later in the month the two Governments signed an agreement to build a 285-km natural gas pipeline from Ankara to Komotini, Greece, thereby allowing Iranian gas to flow to the EU via the existing

Tabriz–Ankara pipeline. In October Greece offered its support for the scheduling of EU accession negotiations with Turkey.

Following the elections to the TGNA in November 2002, Reçep Tayyip Erdoğan stated that a final peace agreement over Cyprus would accelerate Turkey's chances of joining the EU. Erdoğan, whose political priority was Turkey's EU membership, was increasingly in conflict with Turkish Cypriot leader Rauf Denktaş's unyielding stance on reaching a political solution. In January 2003 Erdoğan publicly criticized Denktaş and stated that he was in favour of a new policy for Cyprus, with a view to achieving a solution by 28 February 2003 in order to allow the 'TRNC' to join the EU in 2004 at the same time as the Greek part of the island. During late 2002 and early 2003 the Turkish- and Greek-Cypriot leaders had made significant progress towards reaching a final agreement, which would permit the entire island to accede to the EU on 1 May 2004. However, negotiations on the peace plan failed in March 2003 (see the chapter on Cyprus). Following further UN-sponsored discussions in New York, on 13 February 2004 agreement was reached on a reunification plan based on proposals drafted by the UN Secretary-General, Kofi Annan. The Greek Cypriot President, Tassos Papadopoulos, and Denktaş, resumed UN-sponsored negotiations in the Cypriot capital, Nicosia, on 19 February. Greece and Turkey joined the negotiations later in March; however, both Papadopoulos and Denktaş subsequently opposed a final resolution, which was to be submitted for approval by both the Greek- and Turkish-Cypriot communities at a referendum. On 24 April the reunification plan was endorsed by Turkish Cypriots by 64.9% of votes cast at the referendum, but rejected by Greek Cypriots by an overwhelming majority of 75.8% of the votes; consequently, only the Greek part of Cyprus was admitted to the EU on 1 May. EU officials subsequently announced measures to alleviate the economic sanctions in force against the 'TRNC'.

In April 2005 the Turkish Cypriot Prime Minister, Mehmet Ali Talat, who strongly supported reunification of the island and full participation in the EU, was elected to the 'TRNC' presidency, replacing Denktaş. In late January 2008 the Greek Prime Minister, Dr Konstantinos (Kostas) Karamanlis, undertook an official three-day visit to Turkey—the first such visit by a Greek premier since 1959. In February 2008 Papadopoulos was defeated at the first round of the Greek Cypriot presidential elections, and at the second round Demetris Christofias was elected to succeed him. It was strongly hoped that the election of Christofias, who became the EU's first communist head of state, would facilitate the procurement of a swift and lasting resolution to Cyprus's long-running division, and, therefore, prove advantageous to Turkish hopes of EU accession. In mid-March it was announced that Christofias was to meet with Talat in Nicosia in order to discuss the resumption of reunification talks. The announcement followed a meeting, held earlier in March, between the two leaders' aides, during which convergence was reported to have been reached on a number of disputed issues. At their discussions in Nicosia on 21 March, Christofias and Talat agreed to: open the Ledra Street crossing as a symbol of reconciliation between their two communities (this occurred on 3 April); establish a number of working groups and technical committees; and devise a precise agenda for UN-sponsored reunification negotiations to take place. A subsequent meeting between Christofias and Talat was scheduled for June.

Following the 1980 military coup, the EC-Turkish Association Council (which had been established in 1963) was suspended, together with all community aid to the country. Turkey was readmitted to associate membership of the EC in September 1986, but failed to gain access to the suspended EC aid or to extend the rights of the large number of Turkish workers in Europe. In April 1987 Turkey made a formal application to become a full member of the EC. In December 1989 the application was effectively rejected, at least until 1993, by the Commission of the European Communities. The Commission cited factors including Turkey's unsatisfactory human rights record, high rate of inflation, dependence upon the rural population and inadequate social security provisions as falling short of EC expectations. During informal discussions in 1993 representatives of the EC reiterated their concern at abuses of human rights in Turkey and the lack of progress in the political negotiations regarding Cyprus; however, they recognized the strategic importance of Turkey's role as a stable regional influence.

The Turkish Government began to implement measures to construct a customs union with the EU, which was to become effective on 1 January 1995. Human rights issues remained the main obstacle to securing an agreement, and in December 1994 the customs union was postponed on these grounds. In February 1995 Greece withdrew its veto on the customs union, having received assurance on the accession of Cyprus to the EU, and the agreement was signed in March; however, it was to be subject to ratification by the European Parliament. The Turkish Government subsequently pursued efforts to introduce new democratization legislation and to secure the support of European leaders for the customs union by extending guarantees on human rights and treatment of its Kurdish population. The final terms of the arrangement were agreed at a meeting of the EU-Turkish Association Council in October, and were approved by the European Parliament in December. The EU was expected to provide a total of ECU 1,800m. over a five-year period, in order to assist the implementation of the new trade regime and to alleviate any initial hardships resulting from the agreement. The customs union came into effect on 1 January 1996. Its implementation was, however, delayed, owing to Greek opposition to the release of ECU 375m. in aid, claiming that Turkish action in the Aegean was a violation of the agreement. In July Greece withdrew its opposition to Turkey's participation in an EU-Mediterranean assistance programme, although the block on funds from the customs union remained in effect. Throughout 1996 the Turkish Government criticized the EU for its failure to adhere to the terms of the economic agreement. In January 1997 Turkey warned that it would disrupt any expansion of NATO if the EU refused to consider the Turkish membership application. Previously, Turkey had prevented the use of NATO facilities by members of Western European Union, owing to Greek opposition to Turkey's full participation in the regional defence grouping.

Relations with the EU were tense in 1997 as the next group of EU applicants was selected. In December, following EU announcements that Turkey would not be invited to join the EU, but that it would be invited to a newly created EU Conference, which was to include both EU and non-EU states, Turkey stated that it would not attend such a conference and that it would also cease negotiations on Cyprus, human rights and the Aegean disputes. It further threatened to boycott EU goods and to withdraw its application to the EU if it was not included in a list of candidates by June. On 20 December Turkey announced a six-month freeze in relations with the EU. The EU later announced it was withholding all aid to Turkey for 1998, owing to the situation in the south-east of the country and its human rights problems. Turkey officially declined its invitation to the EU Conference in March 1998 and in May also declined to attend a scheduled meeting of the EU-Turkish Association Council. Relations with France deteriorated in May when the French National Assembly adopted a motion recognizing the Turkish 'genocide' against the Armenians in 1915–23; a number of bilateral military and commercial contracts were suspended as a result. However, in February 2000 the French Senate decided not to place the draft law recognizing the Armenian 'genocide' (approved by the National Assembly in 1998) on its agenda for discussion.

In October 1999 an EU report declared Turkey to be a suitable candidate to join that body, although Turkey stated that it would not accept any extraordinary conditions attached to such a candidacy, particularly with relation to Öcalan and the Kurdish problem. A number of EU members offerred their support to Turkey in late 1999, including Greece and Italy. In December Turkey was invited to attend the EU summit in Helsinki, Finland, and to accept formal status as a candidate for membership. The Government initially objected, owing to attached conditions concerning Cyprus and the Aegean dispute with Greece, but following a visit to Turkey by Javier Solana, the Secretary-General of the Council of the European Union, decided to accept. It announced at that time that it would seek an end to its territorial disputes with Greece by 2004, the deadline set by the EU for a review.

In August 2000 Turkey signed the International Covenant of Civil and Political Rights and the International Covenant on Economic, Social and Cultural Rights. This was described as a positive step by the EU in its progress to accession report on Turkey in November, although it pointed out that Turkey had not yet acceded to a number of other major human rights instruments, such as the abolition of the death penalty and the Convention on the Elimination of All Forms of Racial Discrimination. The report concluded that Turkey did not yet meet the Copenhagen criteria (which state that a country must have achieved 'stability of institutions guaranteeing democracy, the rule of law, human rights and respect for and protection of minorities'), thus making accession negotiations impossible, and described the overall human rights record in Turkey as worrying. It also stated that although Turkey had the basic features of a democratic system, it was slow to implement institutional reforms. Accession was also conditional on a satisfactory settlement of the Cyprus problem. This condition led to the Turkish withdrawal from the UN-sponsored proximity talks in protest. Prime Minister Ecevit accused the EU of 'deception' over Turkey's membership application, stating that it had reneged on a promise not to link Turkey's application to a resolution of the Cyprus problem and disputes with Greece over territorial rights in the Aegean Sea. A rewording of the Cyprus condition was later approved by Turkey; however, further tension was caused by Turkey's obstruction of an EU-NATO agreement enabling the EU's planned Rapid Reaction Force to use NATO assets, despite Turkey's offer to contribute up to 6,000 troops to the force.

Meanwhile, the Armenian 'genocide' question continued to provoke tension between Turkey and the international community. In April 2000 Turkey complained to Israel after the Israeli education minister stated that he believed school pupils should be taught of the 'genocide' of the Armenians; the minister was speaking at a meeting to mark the 85th anniversary of the massacre. In October the TGNA threatened not to renew the USA's mandate to use a Turkish airbase if the US Congress backed a draft resolution which referred to the killing of the 1.5m. Armenians by Turkey in 1915–23 as 'genocide'. Following intervention by President Bill Clinton, the House of Representatives agreed to withdraw the resolution. The European Parliament adopted a resolution in November that formally accused Turkey of genocide against Armenians in 1915 (at the same time it also called on Turkey to pull its forces out of the 'TRNC'). Turkey reacted angrily, with the FP proposing a legislative investigation 'with the aim of removing wrong and biased opinions'. Relations with France were, however, more seriously damaged in January 2001, after the French National Assembly unanimously voted to recognize the 1915–23 massacre of Armenians under the Ottoman Empire as 'genocide', against the wishes of the Government. In November 2000 the French Senate had already voted to recognize the massacre as genocide; none the less, the French Government attempted to reassure Turkey that bilateral relations remained intact. Following the National Assembly vote, however, Ecevit stated that the French action would damage relations and recalled Turkey's ambassador to France immediately after the vote for consultations. The Government further announced plans to erect a 'genocide' monument to the 1.5m. Algerians killed in the 1954–62 war of independence against the French.

Relations between Turkey and the EU received a setback in early May 2001 when the ECHR ruled that Turkey had grossly violated the human rights of thousands of Greek Cypriots during its invasion, and subsequent occupation of northern Cyprus since 1974. The court highlighted the failure of the Turkish Government to investigate the fate of missing Greek Cypriots, and their forcible eviction from the north and the subsequent confiscation of their property.

In late May 2001 Turkey nominally agreed to grant the EU's Rapid Reaction Force access to NATO assets for future operations. Although Turkey would be consulted on such matters, it would not have the same participation rights or veto powers as the existing 15 EU members. However, Turkish officials remained dissatisfied at the arrangements, having lobbied strongly for a greater influence in EU security planning. Turkey also feared that an upsurge of violence in Cyprus would necessitate the deployment of the Rapid Reaction Force on the island, placing the EU directly against itself, and had unsuccessfully sought guarantees against such an eventuality. In December Turkey finally reached agreement with the EU regarding the Rapid Reaction Force after months of British diplomacy.

In August 2001, meanwhile, the ECHR ruled that the Government's decision to ban the Islamist FP did not violate human rights laws. In October the TGNA passed constitutional amendments designed to facilitate EU membership but stopped short of abolishing the death penalty, a crucial EU demand. The issue of capital punishment placed the EU at odds with the ultra-nationalist MHP in the ruling coalition, which had pledged to exact the death penalty imposed on PKK leader Abdullah Öcalan. In August 2002 the EU welcomed the TGNA's vote to abolish the death penalty in peacetime, as part of a broader package of reforms, and, similarly, reacted positively to the commutation of Öcalan's death sentence to life imprisonment in October of that year (see above). The new AKP Government elected in November pledged to accelerate efforts to join the EU. However, in that month Valéry Giscard d'Estaing, the Chairman of the Convention on the Future of Europe, stated publicly that Turkey should never be allowed to join the EU, and that its accession would mean the 'end of the European Union'. Senior EU officials distanced themselves from the remarks, which were also dismissed by Erdoğan. At the EU summit in Copenhagen, Denmark, in December, EU leaders agreed to delay negotiations on Turkish membership until after December 2004, and to resume discussions then only if Turkey had fulfilled all the entry obligations. Several EU members, notably France and Germany, remained less enthusiastic about Turkish membership, citing its poor human rights record, which Turkey again pledged to improve. Erdoğan warned that continuing delays to negotiations and attempts to exclude Turkey from the EU could cause increased anti-Muslim sentiments against the organization.

A further complication to Turkish ambitions for EU membership emerged with the failure of a UN plan for the reunification of Cyprus in April 2004 (see above). The resultant accession of only Greek Cypriot Cyprus to the EU on 1 May presented complications for Turkey's EU aspirations, although the Greek Cypriot Government declared that it would not veto Turkey's membership application, provided that it met the standards stipulated by the EU. An official visit to Greece by Erdoğan in May—the first by a Turkish premier in 16 years—reflected the improvement in relations between the two countries. An EU summit in Brussels in June reaffirmed that a decision would be taken in December on whether Turkey had made sufficient progress on the EU's criteria for membership and that formal accession negotiations would be initiated if standards were considered to have been met. However, severe doubts about Turkey's qualifications had been presented in a European Parliament resolution, which had been adopted overwhelmingly in April, drawing attention to Turkey's continued use of torture, to the persecution of minorities and other contraventions.

Nevertheless, in October 2004 the European Commission announced its approval of Turkey's qualification for accession negotiations, on condition that reforms continued. In many EU member states, however, there was increasing popular opposition to the admission of Turkey, especially in Germany and France, where the opposition was believed to reflect concern over the accession of a predominantly Muslim country; some favoured an option that Turkey be offered 'privileged member' status, rather than full membership. On 17 December the EU extended a provisional invitation to Turkey to commence accession negotiations on 3 October 2005, subject to the Turkish Government's fulfilment of a number of criteria, including continued progress in political and economic reforms. Erdoğan accepted an EU requirement to sign a customs accord with member states by that date, but insisted that the protocol would not constitute official Turkish recognition of the authorities of Greek Cyprus; instead he agreed to a compromise arrangement, whereby Turkey made a commitment for future recognition. The British Prime Minister welcomed the agreement; however, both the French and Austrian Governments pledged to conduct national referendums on Turkish entry, while a demonstration in protest at Turkish membership was conducted in Italy. In June 2005 the German Bundestag (Federal Assembly) became the latest EU legislature to attract Turkish anger by condemning the Armenian 'genocide' and accusing the Turkish Government of failing to address the issue.

In July 2005, pending an EU decision on the opening of accession negotiations in October, the Turkish Government signed the requisite customs protocol with Cyprus and the other nine new EU member states, but appended a declaration reaffirming that the accord did not constitute official recognition of Greek Cyprus. In September EU member states adopted a draft declaration stating that Turkish recognition of Cyprus was necessary to the accession process, but without stipulating a date for this (thereby posing no obstacle to the beginning of negotiations). At the beginning of October intensive debate took place between EU member states to resolve the impasse over Austria's insistence that Turkey be offered the lesser option of 'privileged partnership' (to which the Turkish Government remained opposed), rather than full membership. Austria withdrew its veto to the admission of Turkey, after Croatia was unexpectedly declared eligible to enter into membership negotiations (see the chapter on Croatia). Turkey's accession negotiations with the EU were officially approved on 3 October, and opened on the following day.

In early November 2005 an EU report, while welcoming Turkey's economic performance (see Economic Affairs), criticized a lack of progress in political reforms, citing continued human rights violations, including torture, and the necessity for further judicial reforms. Furthermore, the subsequent reluctance of the Turkish authorities to open ports and airports to Greek Cypriot-registered traffic by the end of 2006, in adherence to the customs protocol and as a condition to progress in the accession negotiations, prompted criticism from EU officials and repeated threats from the Greek Cypriot Government to veto Turkey's membership. Nevertheless, EU ministers responsible for foreign affairs formally opened the first chapter of accession negotiations with Turkey in June. Attempts by the Finnish presidency of the EU to broker a deal under which the EU would take charge of the port of Famagusta in the 'TRNC' while the nearby town of Varosha would be returned to Greek Cypriot control were eventually abandoned in late November. Meanwhile, relations with France worsened in October 2006, when the French National Assembly endorsed a bill making it a crime to deny that Armenians suffered genocide at the hands of Turks in 1915–23; the vote was criticized by the EU. In the same month the EU advised Turkey that safeguarding freedom of expression in the country was to be regarded as a matter of urgency. During 2005–06 court proceedings were initiated against several prominent novelists who were accused of 'insulting Turkishness' under Article 301 of the penal code.

In late November 2006 the European Commission recommended the suspension of negotiations on eight of 35 chapters of the accession talks (these included trade, financial services and transport), a decision that was endorsed at the summit meeting of the European Council in early December. At the end of December Turkey pledged to implement a six-year 'roadmap' and reform programme and to continue implementing all the required judicial and military reforms, even in those areas where negotiations had been suspended. In March 2007 the EU resumed negotiations with Turkey on the accession chapter relating to enterprise and industry. However, in June, following the inauguration as French President of Nicolas Sarkozy in the previous month, France blocked the commencement of negotiations on the accession chapter relating to economic and monetary union, apparently in a further move to prevent Turkey's eventual accession to the EU. (French officials later asserted that they were not opposed to the commencement of further negotiating chapters with Turkey, but that they believed that all options, including that of 'preferential partnership', should be considered.) Later in June the EU did extend membership discussions with Turkey on two new, smaller chapters concerning financial controls and statistics. In November the European Commission urged the Turkish Government to accelerate its political and social reform process, citing the treatment of the minority Kurdish population and Article 301 as particular areas where further progress was required. Accession talks concerning health and consumer affairs, as well as inter-European transport links, were initiated in mid-December. The TGNA approved amendments to Article 301 at the end of April 2008, although critics of the Government countered that the changes were not as far-reaching as they had hoped. Under the newly revised legislation, it would become a crime to insult 'the Turkish nation' rather than 'Turkishness', while the maximum sentence for someone convicted of such a crime was to be shortened from three to two years.

In its latest progress report on Turkey's EU accession, published in November 2008, the European Commission expressed concern at the lack of progress on key reforms in Turkey, particularly regarding human rights and freedom of speech. The report concluded that recent amendments to Article 301, introduced in April, provided inadequate protection for freedom of speech. None the less, two new negotiating chapters, concerning free movement of capital, and information and media, commenced in December. Turkey created its first post within the Council of Ministers dedicated exclusively to EU negotiations in January 2009. Egemen Bağış, a former AKP Vice-Chairman in charge of Foreign Affairs, was appointed Minister of State and Chief Negotiator for EU Affairs, the responsibilities of which role had hitherto been undertaken by the Minister of Foreign Affairs. During a Franco-German summit in Berlin in May 2009, President Sarkozy and German Chancellor Angela Merkel reiterated their opposition to Turkey's full membership of the EU, repeating their preference for the negotiation of a 'privileged partnership' arrangement. Turkish officials again rejected this proposal and urged all European states to adhere to the ongoing accession process.

Following the formal dissolution of the USSR in December 1991, the Turkish Government sought to further its political, economic and cultural influence in the Caucasus and Central Asia, in particular with Azerbaijan, Kazakhstan, Kyrgyzstan, Turkmenistan and Uzbekistan, all of which share ethno-linguistic ties with Turkey. Following the outbreak of war between Armenia and Azerbaijan in 1991, Turkey blockaded Armenia and provided support to its 'Turkic' ally, Azerbaijan. In April 1992 Prime Minister Demirel undertook an official visit to several former Soviet republics, pledging aid of more than US $1,000m. in the form of credits for the purchase of Turkish goods and contracts. At the same time programmes broadcast by the Turkish national television company began to be relayed, by satellite, to the region. In June leaders of 11 nations, including Turkey, Greece, Albania and six former Soviet republics, established the Organization of the Black Sea Economic Co-operation (BSEC, see p. 380), and expressed their commitment to promoting greater co-operation with regard to transport, energy, information, communications and ecology. In October 1994 a meeting of the heads of state of Turkey, Azerbaijan, Turkmenistan, Uzbekistan, Kazakhstan and Kyrgyzstan took place in İstanbul, in an effort to develop and improve relations among the 'Turkic' republics. Summit meetings have subsequently been convened each year. In the late 1990s Turkey sought to encourage Western firms to build a new petroleum pipeline from Baku, Azerbaijan, to the Turkish port of Ceyhan, thereby allowing the transportation of petroleum from the Caspian Sea to the Mediterranean, via Azerbaijan and Georgia. Such a scheme would also increase Turkey's importance to the EU by making it the centre of the Transport Corridor Europe–Caucasus–Asia (TRACECA) project. Despite the cost of the pipeline, construction began in June 2002. In October 2000 President Sezer signed military co-operation pacts with Kyrgyzstan and Uzbekistan, allowing Turkey to train and equip their armed forces. In mid-2001 work began on a new natural gas pipeline from Dzhubga, Russia, to Samsun, Turkey, beneath the Black Sea, which would increase Turkey's dependency on Russian natural gas. During a significant visit to Turkey in December 2004 the Russian President, Vladimir Putin, signed co-operation agreements in the fields of trade, defence and finance.

In August 2008 Russian customs authorities took measures to impede the passage of imports from Turkey. (Russia is Turkey's largest trading partner, and the Russian measures threatened to inflict substantial losses on Turkey's export sector.) The action was believed to result from Turkey's permitting US naval vessels to use the Bosphorus to transport aid to Georgia after Russia's military action there (see the chapter on Georgia). In September it was reported that Turkey was imposing similar retaliatory restrictions on Russian imports, although the trade dispute appeared to have been resolved by the end of the month. In May 2009 Prime Minister Erdoğan visited Russia and held talks with his counterpart, Vladimir Putin, on energy co-operation and regional affairs. The premiers announced the extension of a contract for the supply of Russian natural gas to Turkey.

Diplomatic relations between Turkey and Armenia, which had been suspended since Turkey closed its border with Armenia in 1993, in response to Armenia's conflict with Azerbaijan, remained suspended in 2008. However, following the installation of Serge Sarkissian as President of Armenia in April of that year, there were renewed hopes of a rapprochement. President Gül accepted an invitation from President Sarkissian to attend the first football match between the national teams in the Armenian capital, Yerevan, on early September, and, in doing so, became the first Turkish head of state to visit Armenia. In July, meanwhile, officials of Turkey's Ministry of Foreign Affairs confirmed speculation that Turkish and Armenian delegations had met in Switzerland for informal discussions on bilateral relations. However, the Armenian 'genocide' question, remained a critical obstacle to the restoration of normal relations. Turkey's Minister of Foreign Affairs, Ali Babacan, held direct talks on bilateral relations with his Armenian counterpart in mid-April 2009 during a BSEC conference in Yerevan. Moreover, in late April the Ministry of Foreign Affairs announced that the Swiss-mediated negotiations had resulted in an agreement on a comprehensive framework for the normalization of bilateral ties.

In late 1995 a long-standing dispute with Syria and Iraq concerning the water supply from the Euphrates and Tigris rivers re-emerged as a major source of tension in Turkey's external relations. (Hostilities with Syria had already intensified during the year over that country's apparent support for the PKK, with the Turkish Government accusing Syria of supplying armaments to the separatist organization.) In December Syria issued a formal protest at the construction of a new hydroelectric dam on the Euphrates river (as part of the extensive southern Anatolia project—GAP) arguing that it would adversely affect the supply of water flowing into Syria. Further protests by Syria and Iraq that Turkey was storing their share of water from the two rivers and restricting flow, in contravention of previous agreements, resulted in a ruling, in March 1996, by the Council of the Arab League that the waters of the rivers should be shared equally between the three countries. In September 1997 President Demirel appealed for talks with Syria and Iraq on the use of the waters of the Euphrates. In August 1998, however, the Government refused to revive water talks with Syria and Iraq, citing issues that had first to be improved between the countries, primarily that of terrorism. Relations between Syria and Turkey improved during 1999 and in October officials from the two countries reportedly agreed to open a new border crossing. However, in January 2000 Turkey appealed to the USA not to remove Syria from its list of nations accused of sponsoring terrorism, until such time as all PKK bases had been removed from Syria, and ruled out any concessions on the water issue in order to aid talks between Israel and Syria. In March Turkey and Syria announced a new framework for bilateral relations and discussed the basic principles that would apply to them, although in that month Turkey warned against the use of a map, prepared by Syria for use at a trade fair, which showed the Turkish region of Hatay as Syrian territory. A major rapprochement materialized in early 2002 when Turkey signed an agreement with Syria allowing for joint military exercises. In early 2003 Turkey and Syria agreed to co-operate in bringing about a peaceful solution to the crisis over Iraq's alleged weapons of mass destruction and the US pursuit of regime change in Iraq. President Bashar al-Assad became the first Syrian Head of State to undertake an official visit to Turkey in January 2004.

In early 1996 Turkey signed a new military and intelligence co-operation agreement with Israel, which permitted the use of Turkish airbases and airspace for military training purposes. The pact stemmed from common concerns about Iran, Iraq and Syria, and received support from the USA, a strong ally of both Turkey and Israel. The Arab League denounced the agreement as 'an act of aggression'. Business deals quickly followed, especially those concerning the supply of Turkish water to Israel. However, the gradual improvement in Turkey's relations with its Arab neighbours from 2000 made the pact with Israel less significant, and, in response to the increasing violence between Israelis and Palestinians in the West Bank and Gaza, Prime Minister Ecevit in April 2002 accused Israel of 'genocide' against the Palestinians. None the less, in August Turkey signed an agreement with Israel according to which it would sell the latter 50m. cu m of water every year for the next 20 years. In May 2004 relations with Israel became further strained, when Prime Minister Erdoğan condemned an Israeli offensive in Gaza. In January 2005, however, the Turkish Deputy Prime Minister and Minister of Foreign Affairs made an official visit to Israel—the first by a Turkish politician since the AKP Government was elected in November 2002.

Turkey received praise for its role as host and mediator for indirect peace talks between Syria and Israel during 2008. The talks, several rounds of which took place in İstanbul in mid-2008, were believed to be making progress towards a possible settlement of Israel and Syria's territorial dispute over the Golan Heights. However, negotiations were suspended following the launch of Israel's military offensive against Islamic Resistance Movement (Hamas) targets in Gaza in late December (see the chapters on Israel and the Palestinian Autonomous Areas). Turkey, along with most other Muslim countries, voiced strong condemnation of Israel's actions. In late January 2009 there was an angry exchange between Erdoğan and Israeli President Shimon Peres during a debate on Gaza at the World Economic Forum in Davos, Switzerland. Erdoğan accused Israel of having committed crimes against humanity, and walked out when he was not afforded as much time to speak on the matter as the Israeli President. Nevertheless, a meeting between the foreign ministers of Israel and Turkey, which took place in Brussels in early March at the time of a NATO foreign ministers summit, signalled some improvement in relations. The ministers discussed bilateral ties and the importance of the Turkish-Israeli relationship for regional stability. In May President Gül indicated Turkey's readiness to resume its role as mediator in the stalled Syrian-Israeli peace talks.

In April 1996 the Turkish and Iranian authorities ordered the expulsion of diplomatic personnel following accusations of Iranian involvement in Islamist terrorist attacks committed in Turkey in the early 1990s. In August relations with Iran were strengthened by the conclusion of an agreement providing for the construction of a 320-km pipeline between the two countries and the export of substantial supplies of natural gas from Iran by 1999 (later revised to 1998). In December 1996 the Presidents of Turkey and Iran agreed to pursue greater economic and security co-operation. A trade agreement was concluded granting each other the status of most favoured nation. In February 1997 the Iranian ambassador to Turkey provoked a diplomatic crisis by advocating the introduction of Islamic law in Turkey. Criticism of the actions of the Turkish military by an Iranian consul-general later in that month resulted in both men being asked to leave the country. Iran responded by expelling two Turkish diplomats. However, both countries immediately undertook diplomatic initiatives to restore relations, and in March it was agreed that all bilateral agreements were to be pursued. Following negotiations, it was announced in September that full diplomatic relations were to be resumed.

In October 1998 Iran and Turkey established a committee to demarcate their joint border; they later signed a memorandum to increase customs co-operation at their main border crossing. In February 1999 the two countries agreed to implement measures aimed at more effective co-operation on border security. In June a meeting of the Turkish-Iranian border committee was held for the first time since 1994; a number of issues were discussed and it was agreed that the committee should meet every year. In July, however, the Turkish chargé d'affaires was twice summoned to the Iranian Ministry of Foreign Affairs following the alleged bombing of an Iranian border region by Turkey in which five people died, although Turkey claimed that its air force had bombed Kurdish targets in Iraq not Iran. In August a meeting of the Turkish-Iranian security commission ended with the signing of a memorandum of understanding in which the two countries agreed to combat illegal organizations within their respective territories. In October Turkey announced it would contribute to compensation for the Iranian bomb damage; a Turkish report into the incident concluded that Turkey had bombed Iraq not Iran, although some people with Iranian citizenship, living in northern Iraq, might have been affected. In October Iran's President Muhammad Khatami welcomed the improvement in ties with Turkey, although in that month Iran expressed concern about Turkey's co-operation with Israel. In December Turkey protested to Iran following the death of a soldier in a clash on the border. In January 2000 the Iranian and Turkish ministers responsible for foreign affairs held talks in Ankara and signed a memorandum of understanding to promote bilateral co-operation. During 2001 both countries sought to improve co-operation in combating drugs-trafficking and organized crime. However, rising tensions between Azerbaijan and Iran over claims to the Caspian Sea, Turkey's strong support for Azerbaijan, its continuing alliance with Israel, and competition for influence in the Caucasus and Central Asia, threatened to bring occasional tensions to the relationship. In early 2003 both Turkey and Iran were seeking to increase their influence in Iraq during the build-up of US military forces in the region, and after the subsequent collapse of the regime of Saddam Hussain, Turkey sought to develop ties with Iraq's ethnic Turkoman minority, with Iran favouring the majority Shi'a population.

Government

Under the Constitution approved by referendum in November 1982 (with subsequent amendments), legislative power is vested in the unicameral Turkish Grand National Assembly (TGNA), with 550 deputies, who are elected by universal adult suffrage for a five-year term. Executive power is vested in the President, to be elected by the TGNA for a seven-year term and empowered to appoint a Prime Minister and senior members of the judiciary, the Central Bank and broadcasting organizations; to dissolve the TGNA; and to declare a state of emergency entailing rule by decree. For administrative purposes, Turkey comprises 81 provinces and 2,074 municipalities.

Defence

Turkey joined the North Atlantic Treaty Organization (NATO) in 1952. Military service in the army lasts for 15 months. The total strength of the active armed forces, as assessed at November 2008, was 510,600 (including 359,500 conscripts), comprising an army of 402,000, a navy of 48,600 and an air force of 60,000. There was a gendarmerie numbering 150,000 and a coast guard of 3,250 (including 1,400 conscripts). Reserve forces totalled 378,700 in the armed forces and 50,000 in the gendarmerie. In April 2005 the Governments of Greece and Turkey announced military co-operation measures, including the establishment of direct communications between two air force bases, in an effort to ease tension concerning air space violations over the Aegean Sea. Increased military co-operation between Greece and Turkey was agreed in December 2007; the new measures included the formation of a joint military unit for multinational peace-keeping missions. Defence expenditure for 2008 was budgeted at some US $8,840m.

Economic Affairs

In 2007, according to estimates by the World Bank, Turkey's gross national income (GNI), measured at average 2005–07 prices, was US $592,850m., equivalent to $8,020 per head (or $12,350 per head on an international purchasing-power parity basis). During 2000–07, it was estimated, the population increased at an average annual rate of 1.3%, while gross domestic product (GDP) per head rose, in real terms, by an average of 3.5% per year. Overall GDP increased, in real terms, by an annual average of 4.9% in 2000–07. According to official figures, GDP increased by 4.7% in 2007, but the rate of growth declined to 1.1% in 2008.

Agriculture (including forestry and fishing) contributed 8.6% to GDP in 2008, and engaged 26.4% of the employed population in 2007. The country is self-sufficient in most basic foodstuffs. The principal agricultural exports are cotton, tobacco, wheat, fruit and nuts. Other important crops are barley, maize, sugar beet, potatoes and onions. The raising of sheep, goats, cattle and poultry is also an important economic activity. During 2000–08 agricultural GDP increased by an annual average of 0.8%; the agricultural sector grew by 4.1% in 2008.

Industry (including mining, manufacturing, construction and power) contributed 27.0% to GDP in 2008, and engaged 25.5% of the employed population in 2007. During 2000–08 industrial GDP increased by an annual average of 4.7%; however, the industrial sector contracted by 0.6% in 2008.

Mining contributed 1.5% to GDP in 2008, and engaged 0.6% of the employed population in 2007. Chromium, copper and borax are the major mineral exports. Coal, petroleum, natural gas, bauxite, iron ore, manganese and sulphur are also mined. The development and expansion of Turkey's gold-mining facilities was in progress in the mid-2000s. During 2000–08 mining GDP increased by an annual average of 2.4%; growth in the mining sector was reported at 5.4% in 2008.

Manufacturing contributed 17.9% to GDP in 2008, and employed 18.6% of the employed population in 2007. The most important branches, measured by gross value of output, are textiles, food-processing, petroleum refineries, iron and steel, and industrial chemicals. During 2000–08 manufacturing GDP increased by an annual average of 4.7%; growth in the manufacturing sector was 7.5% in 2008.

Energy is derived principally from thermal power plants. In 2005 45.3% of energy was derived from natural gas, 26.7% from coal, 24.4% from hydroelectric power and a further 3.4% from petroleum. The energy sector contributed 2.3% to GDP in 2008, and employed 0.5% of the employed population in 2007. Total domestic output of crude petroleum and natural gas accounts for some 12% of the country's hydrocarbon requirements. Imports of petroleum and its products comprised 13.4% of the value of total imports in 2008. A major development project for south-east Anatolia, scheduled for completion in 2010, was to increase Turkey's energy production by 70% and to irrigate 1.6m. ha of uncultivable or inadequately irrigated land, by constructing dams and hydroelectric plants on the Tigris and Euphrates rivers and their tributaries. In July 2006 the second largest petroleum pipeline in the world—transporting oil between Baku, Azerbaijan, and the Turkish terminal at Ceyhan, via Tbilisi, Georgia—was formally inaugurated. In 2005 a new 'blue stream' natural gas pipeline running between Russia and Turkey under the Black Sea was also opened. In early 2006 the Government confirmed that the country's first nuclear installation was to be constructed in the Black Sea province of Sinop, with its completion envisaged for 2012; two further nuclear power plants were scheduled to be built by 2015.

The services sector contributed 64.4% of GDP in 2008, and engaged 48.0% of the employed population in 2007. Tourism is one of Turkey's fastest growing sources of revenue. Total tourist arrivals increased to more than 23.3m. in 2007, according to provisional figures, and tourists generated some US $16,851m. in revenue in 2006. Remittances from Turkish workers abroad also make an important contribution to the economy, amounting to $2,835m. in 2001. During 2000–08 the GDP of the services sector increased by an annual average of 8.4%; growth in the sector was 2.6% in 2008.

In 2007 Turkey recorded a visible trade deficit of US $46,669m., and there was a deficit of $37,697m. on the current account of the balance of payments. In 2008 the principal source of imports (15.5% of the total) was Russia; other major suppliers were Germany, the People's Republic of China and the USA. Germany was the principal market for exports in that year (9.8% of the total); other important purchasers were the United Kingdom, the United Arab Emirates, Italy and Russia. Exports in 2008 were dominated by basic manufactures (mainly textiles), machinery and transport equipment, and clothing and accessories. In that year the principal imports were machinery and transport equipment, mineral fuels (particularly petroleum), basic manufactures and chemical products.

In 2006 there was an overall budgetary deficit of 3,995m. new Turkish liras. Turkey's external debt at the end of that year was US $207,854m., of which $67,214m. was long-term public debt. In that year the cost of debt-servicing was equivalent to 33.2% of the value of exports of goods and services. The annual rate of inflation averaged 21.6% in 2000–07. Consumer prices increased by 9.6% in 2006 and by 8.8% in 2007. In 2007 the rate of unemployment was 9.9%.

Turkey is a member of numerous international and regional organizations, including the Developing Eight (D-8, see p. 425), the Economic Co-operation Organization (ECO, see p. 249), and the Organization of the Black Sea Economic Co-operation (see p. 380). Turkey was accepted as a candidate for membership of the European Union (EU, see p. 255) in December 1999. (For details regarding Turkey's accession negotiations with the EU, see Recent History.)

Turkey's economy has been afflicted by persistently high rates of inflation, an expanding public sector deficit, ongoing political instability and a poor rate of tax collection. The country experienced a severe financial crisis in November 2000 and again in February 2001, resulting in soaring interest rates and an effective devaluation of the lira. The Turkish authorities have in recent years, and particularly since the election in late 2002 of the pro-European AKP, made the focus of economic planning the achievement of the levels of macroeconomic stability required for attaining membership of the EU. The Government's national development plan for 2007–13 had this as its principal aim. At the beginning of 2005 the Government established a new monetary unit, the new Turkish lira, as part of ongoing efforts to restrain inflation (the old currency remained in circulation until the end of the year). In May 2005 a three-year stand-by arrangement was approved with the IMF to support the Government's economic and financial programme. Following a period of strong GDP growth in the mid-2000s, a slowing in GDP growth in 2007 reflected in large part reduced agricultural output as a result of drought and the impact on exports of an increase over the year in the value of the Turkish lira, in conjunction with the impact of political uncertainty in the second quarter of the year (see Recent History). High international prices for food and fuels resulted in an increase in the rate of inflation in 2008. Furthermore, from the latter part of the year the impact of the global financial crisis resulted in a sharp decline in output, particularly in the manufacturing sector, notably causing a rapid increase in the rate of unemployment: according to official data, the rate of unemployment stood at 16.1% in February 2009. GDP growth in 2008 was substantially lower than in the mid-2000s, despite a recovery in the agricultural sector. Progress in early 2009 in ongoing discussions with the IMF for a new stand-by arrangement was impeded by the latter's concern at the deterioration in public finances: the Government expected to record a primary budget deficit equivalent to 0.5% of GDP in 2009, in contrast to substantial surpluses in 2000–07.

Education

Legislation took effect in 1997 to increase the duration of compulsory primary education from five to eight years, for children between six and 14 years of age. All state education up to University or Higher Institute levels is co-educational and provided free of charge. The number of primary schools, according to provisional figures, reached 34,093 in 2007/08, compared with 12,511 in 1950. Secondary education, which lasts for at least three years, may be undertaken in general high schools, open high schools or vocational and technical high schools. According to provisional figures, there were 3,830 general high schools in 2007/08. In 2005/06, according to UNESCO estimates, enrolment at primary schools included 91.4% of pupils in the relevant age group, while 68.7% of pupils in the appropriate age group

TURKEY

were enrolled at secondary schools. In 2005/06 almost 2.2m. students attended 1,306 higher education institutes. Government expenditure on education was budgeted at about YTL 21,355m in 2007.

Public Holidays

2009: 1 January (New Year's Day), 23 April (National Sovereignty and Children's Day), 1 May (Labour and Solidarity Day), 19 May (Commemoration of Atatürk, and Youth and Sports Day), 30 August (Victory Day), 20–22 September* (Şeker Bayram—End of Ramadan), 29 October (Republic Day), 27–30 November* (Kurban Bayram—Feast of the Sacrifice).

2010: 1 January (New Year's Day), 23 April (National Sovereignty and Children's Day), 1 May (Labour and Solidarity Day), 19 May (Commemoration of Atatürk, and Youth and Sports Day), 30 August (Victory Day), 10–13 September* (Şeker Bayram—End of Ramadan), 29 October (Republic Day), 16–19 November* (Kurban Bayram—Feast of the Sacrifice).

* These holidays are dependent on the Islamic lunar calendar and may vary by one or two days from the dates given.

Weights and Measures

The metric system is in force.

Statistical Survey

Sources (unless otherwise stated): T.C. Başbakanlık Türkiye İstatistik Kurumu (Turkish Statistical Institute), Necatibey Cad. 114, 06580-Yücetepe/Ankara; tel. (312) 400410; internet www.turkstat.gov.tr.

Area and Population

AREA, POPULATION AND DENSITY

Area (sq km)	
Land	769,604
Inland water	13,958
Total	783,562*

Population (periodic census results)
21 October 1990	56,473,035
22 October 2000	
Males	34,346,735
Females	33,457,192
Total	67,803,927

Population (annual census results at 31 December)†
2007	70,586,256
2008	71,517,100
Density (per sq km) at 31 December 2008	92.9‡

* 302,535 sq miles.
† In accordance with new methodology employing Address Based Population Registration System introduced in 2007.
‡ Land area only.

PROVINCES
(annual population census at 31 December 2008)

	Area (sq km)	Population	Density (per sq km)
Adana	14,046	2,026,319	144.3
Adıyaman	7,606	585,067	76.9
Afyon	14,719	697,365	47.4
Ağrı	11,499	532,180	46.3
Aksaray	7,966	370,598	46.5
Amasya	5,704	323,675	40.6
Ankara	25,402	4,548,939	179.1
Antalya	20,791	1,859,275	89.4
Ardahan	4,968	112,242	22.6
Artvin	7,367	166,584	22.6
Aydın	7,904	965,500	122.2
Balıkesir	14,473	1,130,276	78.1
Bartın	2,080	185,368	89.1
Batman	4,659	485,616	104.2
Bayburt	3,739	75,675	20.2
Bilecik	4,307	193,169	44.9
Bingöl	8,254	256,091	31.0
Bitlis	7,095	326,897	46.1
Bolu	8,323	268,882	32.3
Burdur	7,135	247,437	34.7
Bursa	10,886	2,507,963	230.4
Çanakkale	9,950	474,791	47.7
Çankırı	7,492	176,093	23.5
Çorum	12,796	545,444	42.6
Denizli	11,804	917,836	77.8
Diyarbakır	15,204	1,492,828	98.2
Düzce	2,593	328,611	126.7
Edirne	6,098	394,644	64.7
Elazığ	9,281	547,562	59.0
Erzincan	11,728	210,645	18.0
Erzurum	25,331	774,967	30.6
Eskişehir	13,902	741,739	53.4

—continued	Area (sq km)	Population	Density (per sq km)
Gaziantep	6,845	1,612,223	235.5
Giresun	6,832	421,766	61.7
Gümüşhane	6,437	131,367	20.4
Hakkari	7,179	258,590	36.0
Hatay	5,831	1,413,287	242.4
Iğdir	3,588	184,025	51.3
Isparta	8,871	407,463	45.9
İstanbul	5,315	12,697,164	2,388.9
İzmir	12,016	3,795,978	315.9
Kahramanmaraş	14,457	1,029,298	71.2
Karabük	4,109	216,248	52.6
Karaman	8,869	230,145	25.9
Kars	10,139	312,128	30.8
Kastamonu	13,158	360,424	27.4
Kayseri	17,109	1,184,386	69.2
Kırıkkale	4,570	279,325	61.1
Kırklareli	6,300	336,942	53.5
Kırşehir	6,530	222,735	34.1
Kilis	1,428	120,991	84.7
Kocaeli	3,625	1,490,358	411.1
Konya	40,814	1,969,868	48.3
Kütahya	12,014	565,884	47.1
Malatya	12,103	733,789	60.6
Manisa	13,229	1,316,750	99.5
Mardin	8,806	750,697	85.2
Mersin	15,512	1,602,908	103.3
Muğla	12,949	791,424	61.1
Muş	8,067	404,309	50.1
Nevşehir	5,392	281,699	52.2
Niğde	7,365	338,447	46.0
Ordu	5,952	719,278	120.8
Osmaniye	3,196	464,704	145.4
Rize	3,922	319,410	81.4
Sakarya	4,880	851,292	174.4
Samsun	9,364	1,233,677	131.7
Siirt	5,473	299,819	54.8
Sinop	5,817	200,791	34.5
Sivas	28,567	631,112	22.1
Şanlıurfa	19,336	1,574,224	81.4
Şırnak	7,152	429,287	60.0
Tekirdağ	6,342	770,772	121.5
Tokat	10,073	617,158	61.3
Trabzon	4,664	748,982	160.6
Tunceli	7,686	86,449	11.2
Uşak	5,363	334,111	62.3
Van	22,983	1,004,369	43.7
Yalova	850	197,412	232.2
Yozgat	14,074	484,206	34.4
Zonguldak	3,310	619,151	187.1
Total	**783,562**	**71,517,100**	**91.3**

TURKEY

PRINCIPAL TOWNS
(population at annual census of 31 December 2008)

İstanbul	12,569,041	Hatay		683,991
Ankara (capital)	4,395,888	Balıkesir		662,199
İzmir (Smyrna)	3,450,537	Eskişehir		653,663
Bursa	2,204,874	Sakarya		622,046
Adana	1,763,351	Denizli		620,193
Konya	1,423,546	Kahramanmaraş		598,471
Gaziantep	1,410,286	Aydın		556,700
Kocaeli	1,392,733	Tekirdağ		521,554
Antalya	1,273,940	Van		514,481
Mersin	1,229,431	Malatya		492,411
Diyarbakır	1,051,511	Erzurum		485,107
Kayseri	1,001,449	Mardin		422,537
Şanlıurfa	885,929	Sivas		405,769
Manisa	843,999	Trabzon		390,797
Samsun	776,385			

BIRTHS, MARRIAGES AND DEATHS

	Live births Number*	Rate (per 1,000)	Marriages Number	Rate (per 1,000)	Deaths Number*	Rate (per 1,000)
2002	1,362,000	19.6	519,044	7.5	429,000	6.2
2003	1,361,000	19.4	575,257	8.2	436,000	6.2
2004	1,360,000	19.1	625,635	8.8	443,000	6.2
2005	1,361,000	18.9	651,896	9.1	450,000	6.2
2006	1,362,000	18.7	650,233	8.9	456,000	6.3
2007	1,361,000	18.4	638,311	9.1	464,000	6.3

* Figures are projected estimates.

Recorded deaths (province and district centres only): 197,520 in 2005; 210,146 in 2006; 212,731 in 2007 (preliminary).

Life expectancy (years at birth, WHO estimates): 72.9 (males 70.6; females 75.2) in 2006 (Source: WHO, *World Health Statistics*).

ECONOMICALLY ACTIVE POPULATION*
(sample surveys, '000 persons aged 15 years and over)

	2005	2006	2007
Agriculture, hunting, forestry and fishing	6,493	6,088	5,601
Mining and quarrying	120	128	135
Manufacturing	4,084	4,186	3,949
Electricity, gas and water	80	93	100
Construction	1,173	1,267	1,224
Wholesale and retail trade; repair of motor vehicles, motorcycles and personal and household goods	3,611	3,729	3,500
Hotels and restaurants	949	1,001	989
Transport, storage and communications	1,133	1,163	1,123
Financial intermediation	238	238	235
Real estate, renting and business activities	638	772	773
Public administration and defence; compulsory social security	1,217	1,225	1,283
Education	906	907	856
Health and social work	530	591	546
Other services	874	942	875
Total employed	**22,046**	**22,330**	**21,189**
Unemployed	2,519	2,446	2,333
Total labour force	**24,565**	**24,776**	**23,522**
Males	18,213	18,297	17,363
Females	6,352	6,480	6,158

* Excluding armed forces.
Source: ILO.

WORKERS ABROAD

	2000	2001	2002
Turkish citizens working abroad (number)	1,170,226	1,178,412	1,200,725
Workers' remittances from abroad (US $ million)	4,560	2,786	1,936

Turkish citizens working abroad (number): 1,197,968 in 2003; 1,195,612 in 2004.

Sources: Undersecretariat of the Prime Ministry for Foreign Trade; Secretariat of the State Planning Organization.

Health and Welfare

KEY INDICATORS

Total fertility rate (children per woman, 2006)	2.2
Under-5 mortality rate (per 1,000 live births, 2006)	26
HIV/AIDS (% of persons aged 15–49, 2001)	<0.1
Physicians (per 1,000 head, 2006)	1.6
Hospital beds (per 1,000 head, 2005)	3
Health expenditure (2006): US $ per head (PPP)	645
Health expenditure (2006): % of GDP	5.6
Health expenditure (2006): public (% of total)	71.5
Access to water (% of persons, 2006)	97
Access to sanitation (% of persons, 2006)	88
Human Development Index (2006): ranking	76
Human Development Index (2006): value	0.798

For sources and definitions, see explanatory note on p. vi.

Agriculture

PRINCIPAL CROPS
('000 metric tons)

	2005	2006	2007
Wheat	21,500	20,010	17,678
Rice, paddy	600	696	685
Barley	9,500	9,551	7,423
Maize	4,200	3,811	3,875
Rye	270	271	264
Oats	270	209	202
Potatoes	4,090	4,397	4,281
Sugar beet	15,181	14,452	14,800
Beans, dry	210	196	174
Chick peas	600	552	524
Lentils	570	623	580
Walnuts	150	130	184
Hazelnuts, with shell	530	661	499
Olives	1,200	1,767	1,525
Sunflower seed	975	1,118	1,031
Cabbages and other brassicas	675	686	659
Lettuce and chicory	372	391	382
Spinach	238	242	225
Tomatoes	10,050	9,855	9,920
Cauliflowers and broccoli	126	152	156
Pumpkins, squash and gourds	368	365	347
Cucumbers and gherkins	1,745	1,800	1,876
Aubergines (Eggplants)	930	924	791
Chillies and peppers, green	1,829	1,842	1,091
Onions and shallots, green	200	201	201*
Onions, dry	2,070	1,765	1,779
Garlic	109	96	95
Beans, green	555	564	499
Carrots and turnips	390	402	405
Watermelons	3,970	3,805	3,445
Cantaloupes and other melons	1,766	1,770*	1,770*
Bananas	150	178	187
Oranges	1,445	1,536	1,472
Tangerines, mandarins, etc.	715	791	739
Lemons and limes	600	710	707
Grapefruit and pomelos	150	180	182
Apples	2,570	2,002	2,266
Pears	360	318	349
Quinces	100	106	122
Apricots	860	460	528

TURKEY

—continued

	2005	2006	2007
Sweet cherries	280	310	392
Sour cherries	140	121	174
Peaches and nectarines	510	553	558
Plums and sloes	220	214	225
Strawberries	200	211	239
Grapes	3,850	4,000	3,923
Figs	285	290	271
Tea	218	205	192
Anise, badian, fennel and coriander	24	20	20
Tobacco, unmanufactured	135	98	98*

* FAO estimate.

Aggregate production ('000 metric tons, may include official, semi-official or estimated data): Total cereals 36,354 in 2005, 34,637 in 2006, 30,212 in 2007; Total roots and tubers 4,090 in 2005, 4,397 in 2006, 4,281 in 2007; Total pulses 1,565 in 2005, 1,606 in 2006, 1,493 in 2007; Total vegetables (incl. melons) 26,288 in 2005, 25,736 in 2006, 24,454 in 2007; Total fruits (excl. melons) 12,636 in 2005, 12,035 in 2006, 12,390 in 2007.

Source: FAO.

LIVESTOCK
('000 head, year ending September)

	2005	2006	2007
Horses	212	208	204
Asses	452	423	368
Cattle	10,069	10,526	10,871
Buffaloes	104	105	101
Camels	1	1	1
Pigs	4	2	1
Sheep	25,201	25,304	25,400*
Goats	6,610	6,517	6,500*
Chickens	296,876	317,497	344,820
Ducks	770	656	525
Geese and guinea fowls	1,251	1,067	830
Turkeys	3,902	3,697	3,902

* FAO estimate.
Source: FAO.

LIVESTOCK PRODUCTS
('000 metric tons)

	2005	2006	2007*
Cattle meat	321.7	340.7	351.0
Buffalo meat	1.6	1.8	1.7
Sheep meat*	272	272	272
Goat meat*	43	45	45
Horse meat*	2.0	2.0	2.0
Chicken meat	936.7	917.7	900.0
Cows' milk	10,026.2	10,867.3	11,000.0
Buffalo milk	38.1	36.4	35.1
Sheep milk	789.9	790.0*	790.0
Goats' milk	253.8	252.0*	250.0
Hen eggs	753.3	733.3	744.0
Honey	82.3	83.8	87.0

* FAO estimate(s).
Source: FAO.

Forestry

ROUNDWOOD REMOVALS
('000 cubic metres, excl. bark)

	2005	2006	2007
Sawlogs, veneer logs and logs for sleepers	5,107	5,676	5,848
Pulpwood	4,403	4,747	5,323
Other industrial wood	1,692	1,830	1,848
Fuel wood	4,983	5,831	4,645
Total	16,185	18,084	17,664

Source: FAO.

SAWNWOOD PRODUCTION
('000 cubic metres, incl. railway sleepers)

	2005	2006	2007
Coniferous (softwood)	3,787	4,103	4,226
Broadleaved (hardwood)	2,658	2,368	2,373
Total	6,445	6,471	6,599

Source: FAO.

Fishing
('000 metric tons, live weight)

	2004	2005	2006
Capture	550.5	426.5	533.0
Blue whiting	4.4	4.1	3.5
Mullets	27.5	25.5	21.8
European anchovy	340.0	138.6	270.0
Bluefish	19.9	18.4	8.4
Mediterranean horse mackerel	18.1	13.5	14.1
Striped venus	16.9	10.8	48.3
Aquaculture*	94.7	119.8	129.1
Trout	45.1	49.3	57.7
Seabasses	26.3	37.5	38.4
Gilthead seabream	20.4	28.3	28.5
Total catch*	645.2	546.3	662.1

* FAO estimates.
Source: FAO.

Mining
('000 metric tons, unless otherwise indicated)

	2004	2005[1]	2006[1]
Hard coal	2,843	3,050	3,071
Lignite	43,754	55,626	61,006
Crude petroleum ('000 barrels)	16,270	16,500	13,600
Natural gas ('000 cu m)[2]	344,196	600,000	750,000
Iron ore: gross weight	4,120	4,598	3,251
Iron ore: metal content	2,200	2,450	1,730
Copper[1,3]	49.0	54.0	46.0
Bauxite[4]	365.8	475.3	771.2
Lead: mine output[3]	18.7	21.0	16.5
Lead: concentrates[1,3]	17.0	19.0	15.0
Chromium[5]	506.4	688.4	457.9
Silver (kilograms)[4,6]	73,000[1]	80,000	80,000
Gold (kilograms)[1,3,7]	4,500	5,000	4,500
Marble ('000 cu m)	669.0	800.0	1,200.0
Limestone[6]	30,963	35,000	40,000
Quartzite	2,961.9	3,200.0	3,400.0
Dolomite	2,109.4	2,200.0	2,500.0
Bentonite	850.0[1]	925.0	1,000.0
Kaolin	536.0	580.0	650.0
Silica sand[8]	1,188	1,200	1,200
Gypsum[6]	250.1	250.0	300.0
Magnesite: mine output	3,733.0	3,400.0	2,088.0
Feldspar: mine output	1,983.3	2,332.0	2,900.0
Borate minerals: mine output	2,878.9	3,478.8	3,955.6
Borate minerals: concentrates	1,588.0	1,824.6	1,818.9
Nitrogen[9]	329.4	330.0	100.0
Perlite: mine output	133.8	156.9	120.0
Pumice	1,036.0	1,000.0	930.0
Pyrites[8]	765.4	800.0	900.0
Sodium sulphate: concentrates	523.3	550.0	550.0

[1] Estimated production.
[2] Marketed production only.
[3] Figures refer to metal content of ores and concentrates.
[4] Figures refer to public sector production only. Data for private sector production are not available, but production is estimated to have been 30,000 metric tons in each year.
[5] Figures refer to gross weight of ores.
[6] Excluding production used for making cement.
[7] Figures include estimated output from the by-products of refining other base metals.
[8] Figures refer to gross weight of minerals.
[9] Nitrogen content of ammonia.

Source: US Geological Survey.

TURKEY

Industry

SELECTED PRODUCTS
('000 metric tons, unless otherwise indicated)

	2005	2006	2007*
Margarine	625.5	612.7	577.8
Refined sunflower seed oil	240.1	264.0	258.1
Flour	2,297.0	2,205.4	2,374.0
Sugar	1,927.9	1,805.5	1,666.1
Beer (million litres)	893.6	905.9	920.5
Raki (million litres)	44.1	37.8	38.1
Cigarettes (with filter)	104.2	128.3	119.6
Cotton yarn	458.8	532.0	542.9
Wool yarn	41.6	37.6	38.0
Products of the paper industry	553.0	600.2	622.8
Wood block flooring ('000 sq m)	3,371.5	5,182.8	4,930.6
Calf skins ('000 sq m)	580.6	490.1	544.8
Leather for clothing and gloves ('000 sq m)	287.4	506.3	385.7
Leather shoes ('000 pairs)	47,206.8	60,701.0	58,732.2
Crude steel	20,961.2	23,307.5	25,760.9
Pig-iron	178.4	122.0	264.8
Cement	41,100.3	47,906.4	49,552.6
Polyethylene	273.6	384.6	393.9
Propylene	140.8	198.7	240.5
Ammonia	370.6	111.5	—
Sulphuric acid	164.6	304.3	331.4
Ethylene	314.4	488.8	486.3
Motor oil	7,549.2	7,616.5	7,338.4
Motor gasoline	3,733.7	3,760.8	4,147.3
Naphthas	1,467.3	1,527.6	990.6
Jet fuel	1,997.0	2,119.4	2,557.7
Liquefied petroleum gas	767.5	800.7	761.2
Asphalt	1,763.6	2,225.3	2,291.0
Fuel oil (No. 6)	6,388.6	6,192.3	6,023.3
Kerosene	57.2	36.3	71.9
Composed fertilizers	1,599.5	1,272.6	1,379.7
Other fertilizers	1,623.3	1,723.0	1,534.7
Domestic refrigerators ('000)	5,098.9	6,222.7	6,161.5
Domestic washing machines ('000)	4,433.8	5,410.2	5,407.8
Ovens ('000)	4,540.9	5,646.0	5,769.7
Vacuum cleaners ('000)	1,206.7	1,487.8	1,575.9
Television receivers ('000, colour)	20,790.1	17,930.4	12,591.6
Tyres for automobiles ('000 units)	17,535.2	17,489.2	17,557.9
Tractors (number)	38,800	42,496	37,524
Passenger motor cars (number)	635,137	756,381	855,460
Pick-up trucks (number)	128,426	136,594	154,979
Buses and minibuses (number)	59,070	46,510	38,264
Electricity (million kWh)	161,956.2	n.a.	n.a.

* Preliminary.

Finance

CURRENCY AND EXCHANGE RATES

Monetary Units
100 kuruş = 1 new Turkish lira.

Sterling, Dollar and Euro Equivalents (28 November 2008)
£1 sterling = 2.402 new liras;
US $1 = 1.566 new liras;
€1 = 1.993 new liras;
100 new Turkish liras = £41.63 = US $63.85 = €50.17.

Average Exchange Rate (new Turkish liras per US $)
2005 1.3436
2006 1.4285
2007 1.3033

Note: A new currency, the new Turkish lira, equivalent to 1,000,000 of the former units, was introduced on 1 January 2005. Figures in this survey have been converted retrospectively to reflect this development.

CONSOLIDATED BUDGET
(million new Turkish liras)

Revenue	2001	2002	2003
General budget	50,890.5	74,603.7	98,558.7
Taxation	39,735.9	59,631.9	84,316.2
Taxes on income	15,647.6	19,343.2	25,716.0
Taxes on wealth	433.3	734.3	2,092.1
Taxes on goods and services	18,103.2	30,064.0	43,927.0
Taxes on foreign trade	5,551.1	9,487.2	12,578.7
Non-tax revenue	7,418.4	10,874.5	10,222.8
Special revenue and funds	3,736.2	4,097.3	4,019.8
Annexed budget revenues	652.5	988.6	1,691.7
Total	51,543.0	75,592.3	100,250.4

Expenditure	2001	2002	2003
Current expenditure	20,448.0	31,108.0	38,513.9
Personnel	15,211.9	23,089.2	30,209.5
Other current expenditure	5,236.1	8,018.8	8,304.4
Investment expenditure	4,149.6	6,891.8	7,179.7
Transfers	55,981.5	77,682.6	94,761.3
Interest payments	41,062.2	51,870.7	58,609.2
Domestic debt interest	37,494.3	46,807.0	52,718.9
Foreign debt interest	3,567.9	5,063.6	5,890.3
Transfers to state-owned economic enterprises	1,107.1	2,170.0	1,881.0
Tax rebates	2,918.2	5,665.8	8,335.9
Social security payments	5,112.0	11,205.0	15,922.0
Other transfers	5,268.8	6,746.1	9,973.2
Total	80,579.1	115,682.4	140,454.8

2004 (million new Turkish liras): Total revenue 121,869.9; Total expenditure 152,169.9.

2005 (million new Turkish liras): Total revenue 150,462.7; Total expenditure 158,579.4.

2006 (million new Turkish liras, central management budget): Total revenue 171,309.3; Total expenditure 175,304.0.

Source: Ministry of Finance, İstanbul.

INTERNATIONAL RESERVES
(US $ million at 31 December)

	2006	2007	2008
Gold (national valuation)	2,373	3,123	3,229
IMF special drawing rights	12	50	23
Reserve position in IMF	170	178	174
Foreign exchange	60,710	73,156	70,231
Total	63,265	76,507	73,657

Source: IMF, *International Financial Statistics*.

MONEY SUPPLY
(million new Turkish liras at 31 December)

	2005	2006	2007
Currency outside banks	17,774	23,881	24,357
Demand deposits at deposit money banks	45,178	43,235	50,280
Total money (incl. others)	63,040	67,218	74,737

Source: IMF, *International Financial Statistics*.

TURKEY

COST OF LIVING
(Consumer Price Index; base: 2003 = 100)

	2005	2006	2007
Food and non-alcoholic beverages	112.08	122.95	138.21
Alcoholic beverages and tobacco	135.18	163.54	179.77
Clothing and footwear	110.44	110.35	115.33
Housing, water, electricity, gas and other fuels	120.00	135.18	150.34
Household goods	113.64	120.01	129.13
Health	112.64	116.95	122.53
Transport	123.73	136.44	144.09
Communications	104.89	107.61	106.71
Recreation and culture	117.06	122.88	127.38
Education	135.16	145.65	156.14
Restaurants and hotels	133.49	152.08	169.10
Miscellaneous goods and services	117.71	137.05	144.66
All items	117.48	128.76	140.03

NATIONAL ACCOUNTS
(million new Turkish liras at current prices)

National Income and Product

	2004	2005	2006
Compensation of employees	113,261.8	129,713.7	151,230.9
Operating surplus	214,252.1	238,887.7	288,516.5
Domestic factor incomes	327,513.9	368,601.4	439,747.4
Consumption of fixed capital	30,169.0	31,715.4	35,967.5
Gross domestic product (GDP) at factor cost	357,682.9	400,316.8	475,714.9
Indirect taxes	73,633.0	87,909.9	101,870.4
Less Subsidies	804.4	1,024.3	1,263.0
GDP in purchasers' values	430,511.5	487,202.4	576,322.3
Factor income received from abroad	10,040.1	11,907.9	n.a.
Less Factor income paid abroad	11,619.2	12,709.2	n.a.
Gross national product (GNP)	428,932.3	486,401.0	n.a.
Less Consumption of fixed capital	30,169.0	31,715.4	n.a.
National income in market prices	398,763.4	454,685.7	n.a.

Expenditure on the Gross Domestic Product

	2006	2007	2008
Government final consumption expenditure	93,525.3	107,816.0	121,813.4
Private final consumption expenditure	534,849.2	597,721.8	662,155.4
Increase in stocks	−1,782.7	−2,964.2	16,924.0
Gross fixed capital formation	169,044.7	184,118.2	192,831.2
Total domestic expenditure	795,636.5	886,691.8	993,724.0
Exports of goods and services	171,926.9	188,224.8	227,353.1
Less Imports of goods and services	209,172.1	231,738.1	270,932.9
GDP in purchasers' values	758,390.8	843,178.4	950,144.3
GDP at constant 1998 prices	96,738.3	101,254.6	102,328.1

Gross Domestic Product by Economic Activity

	2006	2007	2008
Agriculture, forestry and fishing	62,662.8	64,331.7	73,748.5
Mining and quarrying	8,952.4	10,530.7	13,029.6
Manufacturing	130,393.1	141,853.3	153,085.2
Electricity, gas and water	13,452.1	16,117.9	19,511.9
Construction	35,849.3	41,013.3	44,792.4
Wholesale and retail trade	94,856.3	103,129.2	116,206.8
Hotels and restaurants	17,041.9	19,074.2	21,433.9
Transport, storage and communications	104,123.0	117,583.1	134,838.5
Financial institutions	21,860.6	27,392.5	33,070.3
Ownership of dwellings	74,467.2	91,070.1	106,383.6

—continued	2006	2007	2008
Real estate, renting and business activities	27,822.9	34,598.7	40,756.8
Public administration and defence; compulsory social security	29,620.6	32,998.0	36,342.3
Education	21,241.9	24,633.6	27,881.3
Health and social work	12,061.1	13,910.3	15,604.8
Other community, social and personal services	12,784.0	14,653.8	15,802.0
Private households with employed persons	1,229.1	1,494.2	1,707.5
Sub-total	668,418.3	754,384.5	854,195.2
Taxes, less subsidies	100,462.6	101,722.6	110,876.6
Less Financial intermediation services indirectly measured	10,490.1	12,928.7	14,927.5
GDP in purchasers' values	758,390.8	843,178.4	950,144.3

BALANCE OF PAYMENTS
(US $ million)

	2005	2006	2007
Exports of goods f.o.b.	78,365	93,611	115,356
Imports of goods f.o.b.	−111,353	−134,552	−162,025
Trade balance	−32,988	−40,941	−46,669
Exports of services	26,648	25,312	28,853
Imports of services	−11,376	−11,481	−14,974
Balance on goods and services	−17,716	−27,110	−32,790
Other income received	3,608	4,383	6,384
Other income paid	−9,483	−11,074	−13,527
Balance on goods, services and income	−23,591	−33,801	−39,933
Current transfers received	1,475	2,244	2,778
Current transfers paid	−21	−336	−542
Current balance	−22,137	−31,893	−37,697
Direct investment abroad	−1,064	−924	−2,106
Direct investment from abroad	10,031	19,989	22,195
Portfolio investment assets	−1,233	−4,029	−2,063
Portfolio investment liabilities	14,670	11,402	2,780
Other investment assets	259	−13,437	−4,852
Other investment liabilities	20,839	29,690	32,613
Net errors and omissions	1,811	−177	1,182
Overall balance	23,176	10,621	12,052

Source: IMF, *International Financial Statistics*.

TURKEY
Statistical Survey

External Trade

PRINCIPAL COMMODITIES
(distribution by SITC, US $ million, excl. military goods)

Imports c.i.f.	2006	2007	2008
Crude materials (inedible) except fuels	9,190.8	12,240.2	16,199.5
Metalliferous ores and metal scrap	4,602.6	6,390.1	9,865.7
Mineral fuels, lubricants, etc.	28,858.8	33,881.0	48,281.0
Petroleum, petroleum products, etc.	16,608.3	19,339.2	27,034.4
Chemicals and related products	18,407.5	22,104.8	25,541.5
Organic chemicals	3,434.0	3,792.9	4,168.6
Medicinal and pharmaceutical products	3,343.1	3,838.4	4,738.4
Plastics in primary forms	5,367.9	6,835.0	7,321.0
Basic manufactures	24,883.8	32,163.1	36,292.6
Textile yarn, fabrics, etc.	4,686.0	6,152.2	5,801.5
Iron and steel	8,140.7	11,341.0	15,031.4
Machinery and transport equipment	43,036.6	49,856.4	51,594.1
Power-generating machinery and equipment	3,960.3	5,067.4	6,236.3
Machinery specialized for particular industries	5,740.4	6,759.7	5,315.0
General industrial machinery, equipment and parts	5,619.9	6,970.5	7,899.7
Road vehicles	11,145.2	12,035.4	12,357.9
Miscellaneous manufactured articles	7,941.2	9,874.0	11,486.3
Non-monetary gold, unwrought or semi-manufactured	4,012.7	5,325.1	5,382.7
Total (incl. others)	139,576.2	170,057.2	201,960.3

Exports f.o.b.	2006	2007	2008
Food and live animals	6,594.5	7,821.5	9,147.4
Vegetables and fruit	4,260.9	4,901.5	5,300.8
Chemicals and related products	3,923.1	4,736.7	6,121.5
Basic manufactures	23,854.9	29,947.6	40,593.9
Textile yarn, fabrics, etc.	7,584.7	8,945.2	9,407.1
Non-metallic mineral manufactures	2,477.2	3,060.7	3,987.2
Iron and steel	7,239.3	9,562.2	16,841.5
Machinery and transport equipment	26,385.9	34,241.3	39,093.8
Road vehicles	11,730.3	15,701.0	17,961.1
Miscellaneous manufactured articles	16,745.8	20,009.3	20,796.9
Clothing and accessories (excl. footwear)	12,051.9	13,885.5	13,591.6
Total (incl. others)	85,534.7	107,213.7	131,965.7

PRINCIPAL TRADING PARTNERS
(US $ million, excl. military goods*)

Imports c.i.f. (excl. grants)	2006	2007	2008
Algeria	1,864.5	2,108.5	3,262.2
Austria	1,077.2	1,351.4	1,525.5
Belgium	2,476.9	2,868.7	3,150.7
China, People's Republic	9,669.1	13,234.1	15,658.2
France	7,240.0	7,849.7	9,022.0
Germany	14,768.2	17,540.0	18,686.6
India	1,579.4	2,299.7	2,457.9
Iran	5,626.6	6,613.8	8,199.7
Italy	8,663.5	9,967.8	11,011.5
Japan	3,216.7	3,703.4	4,026.8
Korea, Republic	3,556.3	4,369.9	4,091.1
Libya	2,297.4	399.7	336.3
Netherlands	2,160.1	2,655.0	3,056.3

Imports c.i.f. (excl. grants)—*continued*	2006	2007	2008
Romania	2,669.0	3,112.8	3,547.8
Russia	17,806.2	23,508.5	31,364.5
Saudi Arabia	2,252.1	2,440.0	3,322.4
Spain	3,832.6	4,342.8	4,548.2
Sweden	1,488.1	1,716.1	1,908.9
Switzerland	4,014.8	5,268.9	5,588.4
Ukraine	3,059.1	4,519.1	6,106.3
United Kingdom	5,137.6	5,477.1	5,324.0
USA	6,260.9	8,163.6	11,975.7
Total (incl. others)	139,576.2	170,057.2	201,960.3

Exports f.o.b.	2006	2007	2008
Algeria	1,020.7	1,231.7	1,613.5
Austria	709.9	844.0	990.8
Belgium	1,381.1	1,735.8	2,122.4
Bulgaria	1,568.0	2,060.2	2,149.2
China, People's Republic	693.0	1,039.5	1,437.2
Denmark	827.1	1,008.5	953.4
Egypt	709.4	902.7	1,425.7
France	4,604.3	5,974.2	6,615.1
Germany	9,686.2	11,993.1	12,948.8
Greece	1,602.6	2,262.7	2,430.0
Iran	1,066.9	1,387.4	2,029.0
Iraq	2,589.4	2,844.7	3,915.2
Israel	1,529.2	1,658.2	1,935.2
Italy	6,752.3	7,479.7	7,814.1
Netherlands	2,539.2	3,018.9	3,143.1
Poland	1,060.1	1,436.4	1,586.4
Romania	2,350.5	3,644.2	3,980.4
Russia	3,237.6	4,726.9	6,477.5
Saudi Arabia	982.2	1,486.9	2,197.4
Spain	3,720.5	4,579.6	4,043.7
United Arab Emirates	1,985.7	3,240.9	7,974.9
United Kingdom	6,814.3	8,626.5	8,160.8
USA	5,060.9	4,168.2	4,289.4
Total (incl. others)	85,534.7	107,213.7	131,965.7

* Imports by country of origin, exports by country of last consignment.

Transport

RAILWAYS
(traffic)

	2004	2005	2006
Passengers carried ('000)	76,756	76,306	77,414
Passenger-km (million)	5,237	5,036	5,277
Freight carried ('000 metric tons)*	17,708	18,945	19,745
Freight ton-km (million)	9,417	9,152	9,676

* Excluding parcels and departmental traffic.

ROAD TRAFFIC
(motor vehicles by use)

	2005	2006	2007
Passenger cars	5,772,745	6,140,992	6,472,156
Minibuses	338,539	357,523	372,601
Buses and coaches	163,390	175,949	189,128
Small trucks	1,475,057	1,695,624	1,890,459
Trucks	676,929	709,535	729,202
Motorcycles and mopeds	1,441,066	1,822,831	2,003,492
Special purpose vehicles	30,333	34,260	38,573

SHIPPING

Merchant Fleet
(registered at 31 December)

	2005	2006	2007
Number of vessels	1,156	1,184	1,252
Total displacement ('000 grt)	5,044.7	4,848.8	4,995.1

Source: Lloyd's Register-Fairplay, *World Fleet Statistics*.

TURKEY

International Sea-borne Traffic

	1999	2000	2001
Vessels entered (number)	23,097	25,199	20,431
Passengers disembarked (number)	482,715	600,948	590,454
Goods unloaded ('000 metric tons)*	71,453	79,337	68,342
Vessels cleared (number)	18,097	18,385	18,916
Passengers embarked (number)	484,244	593,493	599,474
Goods loaded ('000 metric tons)*	25,075	25,477	34,137

* Including timber.

CIVIL AVIATION
(scheduled services)

	2003	2004	2005
Domestic services:			
Kilometres flown ('000)	28,180	28,489	35,886
Number of passengers	4,991,517	5,805,291	7,151,491
Passenger-km ('000)	2,751,910	3,223,299	3,991,885
Freight handled (metric tons)	29,146	30,710	31,504
Total ton-km ('000)	275,681	321,118	392,055
International services:			
Kilometres flown ('000)	101,738	109,038	122,899
Number of passengers	4,802,897	5,617,506	6,486,320
Passenger-km ('000)	12,223,997	14,227,375	16,359,597
Freight handled (metric tons)	88,993	93,736	87,851
Total ton-km ('000)	1,617,729	1,849,177	2,104,407

Tourism

VISITOR ARRIVALS BY NATIONALITY
(provisional)

Country	2005	2006	2007
Austria	486,051	429,708	472,482
Azerbaijan	411,652	380,132	434,577
Belgium	485,758	451,426	542,712
Bulgaria	1,621,704	1,177,903	1,239,667
France	701,190	657,859	768,167
Georgia	367,339	549,328	630,979
Germany	4,240,122	3,762,469	4,149,805
Greece	548,784	412,819	447,950
Iran	957,245	865,942	1,058,206
Israel	393,805	362,501	511,435
Italy	401,852	402,573	514,803
Netherlands	1,253,885	997,466	1,057,403
Russia	1,864,682	1,853,442	2,465,336
Sweden	405,956	326,255	338,182
Ukraine	380,392	487,917	593,302
United Kingdom	1,757,843	1,678,845	1,916,130
USA	434,991	532,404	642,911
Total (incl. others)	21,124,886	19,819,833	23,340,911

Tourism receipts (million US $, excl. passenger transport, incl. expenditure of Turkish nationals residing abroad): 18,153.5 in 2005; 16,850.9 in 2006; n.a. in 2007.

Communications Media

	2005	2006	2007
Telephones ('000 main lines in use)	18,978.2	18,831.6	18,412.8
Mobile cellular telephones ('000 subscribers)	43,609.0	52,662.7	61,975.8
Internet users ('000)	11,204.3	13,150.0	n.a.
Broadband subscribers ('000)	1,589.8	2,773.7	4,346.1

Personal computers ('000 in use): 3,703 in 2004.
Radio receivers ('000 in use): 11,300 in 1997.
Television receivers ('000 in use): 21,152 in 2001.
Facsimile machines (number in use): 108,014 in 1997.
Book production (titles): 2,920 in 1999.
Daily newspapers (number): 588 in 2004.
Non-daily newspapers (number): 1,771 in 2004.

Sources: International Telecommunication Union; UNESCO Institute for Statistics; UN, *Statistical Yearbook*.

Education

(2007/08, unless otherwise indicated, provisional figures)

	Institutions	Teachers	Students
Pre-primary	22,506	25,901	701,762
Primary	34,093	445,452	10,870,570
Secondary:			
general	3,830	106,270	1,980,452
vocational and teacher training	4,450	84,771	1,264,870
Higher*	1,306	84,785	2,181,217

* Figures for 2005/06.

Adult literacy rate (UNESCO estimates): 88.7% (males 96.2%; females 81.2%) in 2007 (Source: UNESCO Institute for Statistics).

Directory

The Constitution

In October 1981 the National Security Council (NSC), which took power in September 1980, announced the formation of a Consultative Assembly to draft a new constitution, replacing that of 1961. The Assembly consisted of 40 members appointed directly by the NSC and 120 members chosen by the NSC from candidates put forward by the governors of the 67 provinces; all former politicians were excluded. The draft Constitution was approved by the Assembly in September 1982 and by a national referendum in November. Its main provisions are summarized below:

Legislative power is vested in the unicameral Grand National Assembly, which (following an amendment in July 1995) comprises 550 deputies. The election of deputies is by universal adult suffrage for a five-year term. Executive power is vested in the President, who is elected by the Grand National Assembly for a seven-year term and is empowered to: appoint a Prime Minister and senior members of the judiciary, the Central Bank and broadcasting organizations; dissolve the Assembly; and declare a state of emergency entailing rule by decree. Strict controls on the powers of trades unions, the press and political parties were also included. An appended 'temporary article' automatically installed the incumbent President of the NSC as Head of State for a seven-year term, assisted by a Presidential Council comprising members of the NSC.

In July 2003 the Grand National Assembly approved an amendment reducing the number of NSC members from 13 to six. The NSC

TURKEY

was henceforth to be a predominantly civilian advisory body, comprising the President, Prime Minister, Chief of General Staff, and Ministers of Foreign Affairs, National Defence and Internal Affairs. Amendments approved by the Assembly in May 2004 included guarantees of equal rights between men and women, the removal of references to capital punishment and the abolition of State Security Courts. (For details regarding further constitutional amendments, see Recent History.)

The Government

HEAD OF STATE

President: ABDULLAH GÜL (took office 28 August 2007).

COUNCIL OF MINISTERS
(May 2009)

Prime Minister: REÇEP TAYYIP ERDOĞAN.
Deputy Prime Ministers: BÜLENT ARINÇ, ALI BABACAN, CEMIL ÇIÇEK.
Minister of Foreign Affairs: Prof. Dr AHMET DAVUTOĞLU.
Minister of Justice: SADULLAH ERGIN.
Minister of National Defence: MEHMET VECDI GÖNÜL.
Minister of Internal Affairs: Dr BEŞIR ATALAY.
Minister of Finance: MEHMET ŞIMŞEK.
Minister of National Education: NIMET ÇUBUKÇU.
Minister of Public Works and Settlement: FARUK MUSTAFA DEMIR.
Minister of Health: Prof. Dr REÇEP AKDAĞ.
Minister of Transport: BINALI YILDIRIM.
Minister of Agriculture and Rural Affairs: Dr MEHMET MEHDI EKER.
Minister of Labour and Social Security: ÖMER DINÇER.
Minister of Industry and Trade: NIHAT ERGÜN.
Minister of Energy and Natural Resources: Dr TANER YILDIZ.
Minister of Culture and Tourism: ERTUĞRUL GÜNAY.
Minister of the Environment and Forestry: Prof. Dr VEYSEL EROĞLU.
Minister of State and Chief Negotiator of Turkey for European Union Affairs: EGEMEN BAĞIŞ.
Ministers of State: Prof. Dr MEHMET AYDIN, MEHMET ZAFER ÇAĞLAYAN, FARUK ÇELIK, SELMA ALIYE KAVAF, FARUK NAFIZ ÖZAK, HAYATI YAZICI, CEVDET YILMAZ.

MINISTRIES

President's Office: Cumhurbaşkanlığı Köşkü, 06689 Çankaya, Ankara; tel. (312) 4702308; fax (312) 4701316; e-mail cumhurbaskanligi@tccb.gov.tr; internet www.cankaya.gov.tr.
Prime Minister's Office: Başbakanlık, Bakanlıklar, Ankara; tel. (312) 4189056; fax (312) 4180476; e-mail bimer@basbakanlik.gov.tr; internet www.basbakanlik.gov.tr.
Deputy Prime Ministers' Office: Başbakan yard. ve Devlet Bakanı, Bakanlıklar, Ankara; tel. (312) 4191621; fax (312) 4191547.
Ministry of Agriculture and Rural Affairs: Tarım ve Köyişleri Bakanlığı, Kampüsü Eskişehir Yolu 9km Lodumlu, Ankara; tel. (312) 2873360; fax (312) 2863964; e-mail admin@tarim.gov.tr; internet www.tarim.gov.tr.
Ministry of Culture and Tourism: Kültür ve Turizm Bakanlığı, Atatürk Bul. 29, 06050 Opera, Ankara; tel. (312) 3090850; fax (312) 3124359; e-mail info@kulturturizm.gov.tr; internet www.kultur.gov.tr.
Ministry of Energy and Natural Resources: Enerji ve Tabii Kaynaklar Bakanlığı, İnönü Bul. 27, Bahçelievler, Ankara; tel. (312) 2126420; fax (312) 2156586; e-mail bilgi@enerji.gov.tr; internet www.enerji.gov.tr.
Ministry of the Environment and Forestry: Çevre ve Orman Bakanlığı, Söğütözü Cad. 14E, Ankara; tel. (312) 2075000; fax (312) 2150094; e-mail webmaster@cevreorman.gov.tr; internet www.cevreorman.gov.tr.
Ministry of Finance: Maliye Bakanlığı, Dikmen Cad., Ankara; tel. (312) 4250018; fax (312) 4250058; e-mail bshalk@maliye.gov.tr; internet www.maliye.gov.tr.
Ministry of Foreign Affairs: Dişişleri Bakanlığı, Dr Sadık Ahmet Cad. 12, 06100 Balgat, Ankara; tel. (312) 2921000; fax (312) 2873869; e-mail webmaster@mfa.gov.tr; internet www.mfa.gov.tr.
Ministry of Health: Sağlık Bakanlığı, Mithatpasa Cad. 3 Sihhiye, 06434 Ankara; tel. (312) 5852250; fax (312) 4339885; e-mail info@saglik.gov.tr; internet www.saglik.gov.tr.
Ministry of Industry and Trade: Sanayi ve Ticaret Bakanlığı, Eskişehir Yolu üzeri 7 km, Ankara; tel. (312) 2860365; fax (312) 2864005; e-mail webmaster@sanayi.gov.tr; internet www.sanayi.gov.tr.
Ministry of Internal Affairs: İçişleri Bakanlığı, Bakanlıklar, Ankara; tel. (312) 4257214; fax (312) 4181795; e-mail basin@icisleri.gov.tr; internet www.icisleri.gov.tr.
Ministry of Justice: Adalet Bakanlığı, 06659 Kizilay, Ankara; tel. (312) 4177770; fax (312) 4193370; e-mail info@adalet.gov.tr; internet www.adalet.gov.tr.
Ministry of Labour and Social Security: Çalışma ve Sosyal Güvenlik Bakanlığı, İnönü Bul. 42, 06100 Emek, Ankara; tel. (312) 2966000; fax (312) 4179765; tel. iletisim@csgb.gov.tr; internet www.csgb.gov.tr.
Ministry of National Defence: Milli Savunma Bakanlığı, 06100 Ankara; tel. (312) 4254596; fax (312) 4184737; internet www.msb.gov.tr.
Ministry of National Education: Milli Eğitim Bakanlığı, Atatürk Bul., Bakanlıklar, Ankara; tel. (312) 4191410; fax (312) 4177027; e-mail meb@meb.gov.tr; internet www.meb.gov.tr.
Ministry of Public Works and Settlement: Bayındırlık ve İskan Bakanlığı, Vekaletler Cad. 1, 06100 Ankara; tel. (312) 4186443; fax (312) 4251288; e-mail webadmin@bayindirlik.gov.tr; internet www.bayindirlik.gov.tr.
Ministry of Transport: Ulaştırma Bakanlığı, Hakkı Turayliç Cad. 5, 06338 Emek, Ankara; tel. (312) 2031116; fax (212) 2124930; e-mail okm@ubak.gov.tr; internet www.ubak.gov.tr.

Legislature

BÜYÜK MILLET MECLISI
(Grand National Assembly)

Speaker: KÖKSAL TOPTAN.

General Election, 22 July 2007

Party	Valid votes cast	% of valid votes	Seats
Adalet ve Kalkınma Partisi (AKP)	16,340,534	46.66	341
Cumhuriyet Halk Partisi (CHP)	7,300,234	20.85	112
Milliyetçi Hareket Partisi (MHP)	5,004,003	14.29	70
Independents	1,822,253	5.20	26
Demokrat Parti (DP)	1,895,807	5.41	0
Genç Parti (GP)	1,062,352	3.03	0
Saadet Partisi (SP)	817,843	2.34	0
Others	774,289	2.21	0
Total	**35,017,315***	**100.00**	**549†**

* Excluding 870,653 invalid votes.
† One of the elected representatives of the MHP died on 26 July 2007, thus one seat remained vacant.

Election Commission

Yüksek Seçim Kurulu (YSK) (High Electoral Board): Kızılırmak Cad. 9, 06640 Küçükesat, Ankara; tel. (312) 4191040; fax (312) 4195308; internet www.ysk.gov.tr/ysk/index.html; independent; Chair. MUHAMMER AYDIN.

Political Organizations

Political parties were banned from 1980–83. Legislation enacted in March 1986 stipulated that a party must have organizations in at least 45 provinces, and in two-thirds of the districts in each of these provinces, in order to take part in an election. A political party is recognized by the Government as a legitimate parliamentary group only if it has at least 20 deputies in the Grand National Assembly.

In mid-1992, following the adoption of less restrictive legislation concerning the formation of political parties, several new parties were established, and the left-wing CHP, dissolved in 1981, was reactivated.

Adalet ve Kalkınma Partisi (AKP) (Justice and Development Party): Söğütözü Cad. 6, Çankaya, Ankara; tel. (312) 2045000; fax (312) 2045020; internet www.akparti.org.tr; f. 2001; Islamist-orientated; Leader RECEP TAYYIP ERDOĞAN.

Anavatan Partisi (ANAVATAN) (Motherland Party): 13 Cad. 3, Balgat, Ankara; tel. (312) 2865000; fax (312) 2865019; e-mail anavatan@anavatan.org.tr; internet www.anavatan.org.tr; f. 1983;

supports freedom of thought and expression, of religion and of enterprise; Chair. ERKAN MUMCU.

Bağımsız Türkiye Partisi (BTP) (Independent Turkey Party): Bestekar Sok. 45 Kavaklıdere, Ankara; tel. (312) 4269146; fax (312) 4262908; e-mail btp@btp.org.tr; internet www.btp.org.tr; f. 2001; Chair. Prof. Dr HAYDAR BAŞ.

Büyük Birlik Partisi (BBP) (Great Unity Party): Tuna Cad. 28, Yenişehir, Ankara; tel. (312) 4340923; fax (312) 4355818; e-mail iletisim@bbp.org.tr; internet www.bbp.org.tr; f. 1993; Chair. (vacant).

Cumhuriyet Halk Partisi (CHP) (Republican People's Party): Anadolu Bul. 12 Söğütözü, Ankara; tel. and fax (312) 2074000; e-mail halklailiskiler@chp.org.tr; internet www.chp.org.tr; f. 1923 by Kemal Atatürk; dissolved in 1981 and reactivated in 1992; merged with Sosyal Demokrat Halkçı Parti (Social Democratic Populist Party) in Feb. 1995 and with the Yeni Türkiye Partisi in Oct. 2004; left-wing; Leader DENIZ BAYKAL; Sec.-Gen. TARHAN ERDEM.

Değisen Türkiye Partisi (DEPAR) (Changing Turkey Party): Aşağlı Öveçler 6, Cad. 78, Sok. 15/2, Dikmen, Ankara; tel. (312) 4794875; fax (312) 4795964; f. 1998; Chair. GÖKHAN ÇAPOĞLU.

Demokrasi ve Barış Partisi (DBP) (Democracy and Peace Party): Menekşe 1, Sok. 10-A/7, Kızılay, Ankara; tel. (312) 4173587; f. 1996; pro-Kurdish; Leader REFIK KARAKOÇ.

Demokrat Parti (DP) (Democratic Party): Akay Cad. 16, Kızılay, Ankara; tel. (312) 4441946; fax (312) 4168638; e-mail dp@dp.org.tr; internet www.dp.org.tr; f. 1983 as Doğru Yol Partisi (True Path Party); renamed as above in May 2007, amid planned merger with Anavatan Partisi (Motherland Party); however, merger subsequently failed; centre-right; Chair. HÜSAMETTIN CINDORUK.

Demokratik Sol Parti (DSP) (Democratic Left Party): Fevzi Çakmak Cad. 17, Ankara; tel. (312) 2124950; fax (312) 2124188; e-mail dsp@dsp.org.tr; internet www.dsp.org.tr; f. 1985, drawing support from mems of the fmr Republican People's Party; centre-left; Sec.-Gen. MASUM TÜRKER.

Demokratik Toplum Partisi (DTP) (Democratic Society Party): Barışmanço Cad. 32, Sok. 37 Balgat, Ankara; tel. (12) 2863200; fax (12) 2851819; internet www.dtp.org.tr; f. 2004 as Democratic Society Movement; registered as pol. party 2005; Pres. AHMET TÜRK.

Emek Partisi (EMEP) (Labour Party of Turkey): Kocamustafapaşa Cad., Turan Topal Sok., Findikoba Ishani 2/2, Fatih, İstanbul; tel. (212) 5884332; fax (212) 5884341; e-mail international@emep.org; internet www.emep.org; f. 1996; advocates scientific socialism; Pres. LEVENT TÜZEL.

Emekci Halk Partisi (EHP) (Working People's Party): f. Jan. 2004.

Genç Parti (GP) (Youth Party): İller Sok. 7, Mebusevleri, 06580 Tandoğan, Ankara; tel. (312) 2969700; fax (312) 2969757; internet www.gencpartiliyiz.com; f. 2002; populist, nationalist; Leader CEM UZAN.

Halkın Yükselişi Partisi (HYP) (People's Ascent Party): Filistin Sok. 30, Ankara; tel. (312) 4480621; fax (312) 4476968; e-mail hypgenelmerkez@hyp.org.tr; internet www.hyp.org.tr; f. 2005; advocates social democratic principles; Leader YAŞAR NURI ÖZTÜRK.

İşçi Partisi (IP) (Workers' Party): Toros Sok. 9, Sıhhıye, Ankara; tel. (312) 2318111; fax (312) 2292994; e-mail ip@ip.org.tr; internet www.ip.org.tr; f. 1992; Chair. DOĞU PERINÇEK.

Liberal Demokratik Parti (LDP) (Liberal Democratic Party): İstanbul; tel. (212) 2546860; fax (212) 2550291; e-mail ldp@liberal.tc; internet www.ldp.org.tr; f. 1994; Chair. CEM TOKER.

Millet Partisi (MP) (Nation Party): Atatürk Bul. 72/37, Kızılay, Ankara; tel. (312) 4194060; fax (312) 3127651; e-mail milletpartisi@hotmail.com; internet www.milletpartisi.org; f. 1992; Chair. AYKUT EDIBALI.

Milliyetçi Hareket Partisi (MHP) (Nationalist Action Party): Ceyhun Atif Kansu Cad. 128, Balgat, Ankara; tel. (312) 4725555; fax (312) 4731544; e-mail bilgi@mhp.org.tr; internet www.mhp.org.tr; f. 1983; fmrly the Democratic and Conservative Party; Leader DEVLET BAHÇELI; Sec.-Gen. FARUK BAL.

Özgürlük ve Dayanisma Partisi (ODP) (Freedom and Solidarity Party): GMK Bul. 87/18, Maltepe, Ankara; tel. (312) 2317232; fax 2320347; e-mail odp@odp.org.tr; internet www.odp.org.tr; f. 1996; Leader UFUK URAS.

Özgür Toplum Parti (OTP) (Free Society Party): f. June 2003; assoc. with Halkın Demokrasi Partisi; Leader AHMET TURAN DEMIR.

Saadet Partisi (SP) (Felicity Party): Ziyabey Cad. 2, Sok. 15, 06520 Balgat, Ankara; tel. (312) 2848800; fax (312) 2856246; e-mail info@saadet.org.tr; internet www.saadet.org.tr; f. 2001; replaced conservative wing of Islamist fundamentalist and free-market advocating Fazilet Partisi (Virtue Party), which was banned in that year; Chair. RECAI KUTAN.

Türkiye Komünist Partisi (TKP) (Communist Party of Turkey): Osmanağa Mahallesi Nüzhet Efendi Sok. 4, Kadıköy, İstanbul; tel. (216) 3455480; fax (216) 3461137; e-mail tkp@tkp.org.tr; internet www.tkp.org.tr; f. 1981 as the Party of Socialist Power; name changed as above in 2001; Gen. Sec. AYDEMIR GÜLER.

Yurt Partisi (Homeland Party): Necatibey Cad. 61/15, Kızılay, Ankara; tel. (312) 2325166; fax (312) 2324909; e-mail genelmerkez@yurtpartisi.org.tr; internet www.yurtpartisi.org.tr; f. 2002; nationalist and conservative party; Leader SAADETIN TANTAN.

The following proscribed organizations were engaged in an armed struggle against the Government:

Devrimci Halk Kurtuluş—Cephesi (DHKP—C) (Revolutionary People's Liberation Party—Front): e-mail dhkc@ozgurluk.org; left-wing faction of Dev-Sol; subsumed parent org. in 1996.

Partiya Karkeren Kurdistan (PKK) (Kurdistan Workers' Party): internet www.pkk.org; f. 1978; 57-member directorate; launched struggle for an independent Kurdistan in 1984; declared cease-fire 2000; renamed Congress for Freedom and Democracy in Kurdistan (KADEK) April 2002 and KONGRA-GEL Nov. 2003; return to fmr name, PKK, announced April 2005, following resumption of armed struggle; name KONGRA-GEL continued to be used by some elements; re-emerged military wing, Hezên Parastina Gel (HPG—People's Defence Forces); Chair. ZÜBEYIR AYDAR; Leader ABDULLAH ÖCALAN.

Diplomatic Representation

EMBASSIES IN TURKEY

Afghanistan: Cinnah Cad. 88, 06551 Çankaya, Ankara; tel. (312) 4422523; fax (312) 4422269; Ambassador MASOOD KHALILI.

Albania: Ebuziya Tevfik Sok. 17, Çankaya, Ankara; tel. (312) 4416103; fax (312) 4416109; e-mail embassy.ankara@mfa.gov.al; Ambassador ALTIN KODRA.

Algeria: Şehit Ersan Cad. 42, 06680 Çankaya, Ankara; tel. (312) 4687719; fax (312) 4687593; e-mail cezayirbe@yahoo.fr; Ambassador SMAÏL ALLAOUA.

Argentina: Uğar Mumcu Cad. 60/3, 06700 Gaziosmanpaşa, Ankara; tel. (312) 4462062; fax (312) 4462063; e-mail embargturquia@yahoo.com.ar; Ambassador SEBASTIÁN BRUGO MARCÓ.

Australia: Uğur Mumcu Cad. 88, 7th Floor, 06700 Gaziosmanpaşa, Ankara; tel. (312) 4599500; fax (312) 4464827; e-mail dima-ankara@dfat.gov.au; internet www.turkey.embassy.gov.au; Ambassador PETER LEO DOYLE.

Austria: Atatürk Bul. 189, Kavaklıdere, Ankara; tel. (312) 4190431; fax (312) 4189454; e-mail ankara-ob@bmeia.gv.at; Ambassador Dr HEIDEMARIA GÜRER.

Azerbaijan: Cemal Nadir Sok. 20 Celikler Apt, Çankaya, Ankara; tel. (312) 4412620; fax (312) 4412600; e-mail azer-tr@tr.net; Ambassador ZAKIR HASHIMOV.

Bangladesh: Cinnah Cad. 78/7–10, 06690 Çankaya, Ankara; tel. (312) 4392750; fax (312) 4422408; e-mail bdootankara@superonline.com; Ambassador Maj.-Gen. MUHAMMAD ISHTIAQ.

Belarus: Abidin Daver Sok. 17, 06550 Çankaya, Ankara; tel. (312) 4416769; fax (312) 4416674; e-mail turkey@belembassy.org; Ambassador NATALYA ZHYLEVICH.

Belgium: Mahatma Gandhi Cad. 55, Gaziosmanpaşa, Ankara; tel. (312) 4056166; fax (312) 4468251; e-mail ankara@diplobel.fed.be; internet www.diplomatie.be/ankara; Ambassador MARC VAN RYSELBERGHE.

Bosnia and Herzegovina: Turan Emeksiz Sok. 3/9, Park Evleri B Blok, Gaziosmanpaşa, Ankara; tel. (312) 4273602; fax (312) 4273604; e-mail bh_emb@kablonet.com.tr; Ambassador NADA JANKOVIĆ.

Brazil: Reşit Galip Cad., İlkadım Sok. 1, 06700 Gaziosmanpaşa, Ankara; tel. (312) 4481840; fax (312) 4481838; e-mail brasemb@brasembancara.org; internet www.brasembancara.org; Ambassador CESÁRIO MELANTONIO NETO.

Bulgaria: Atatürk Bul. 124, 06680 Kavaklıdere, Ankara; tel. (312) 4672071; fax (312) 4672574; e-mail bulankemb@ttnet.com; Ambassador BRANIMIR MLADENOV.

Canada: Cinnah Cad. 58, 06690 Çankaya, Ankara; tel. (312) 4092700; fax (312) 4092811; e-mail ankra@international.gc.ca; internet geo.international.gc.ca/canada-europa/turkey; Ambassador MARK BAILEY (designate).

Chile: Reşit Galip Cad., İrfanli Sok. 14/1–3, 06700 Gaziosmanpaşa, Ankara; tel. (312) 4473418; fax (312) 4474725; e-mail embassy@chile.org.tr; internet www.chile.org.tr; Ambassador FRANCISCO MARAMBIO.

China, People's Republic: Gölgeli Sok. 34, 06700 Gaziosmanpaşa, Ankara; tel. (312) 4360628; fax (312) 4464248; e-mail chinaemb_tr@

TURKEY

mfa.gov.cn; internet www.chinaembassy.org.tr; Ambassador SUN GUOXIANG.

Croatia: Kelebek Sok. 15/A, 06700 Gaziosmanpaşa, Ankara; tel. (312) 4469460; fax (312) 4464700; e-mail ankara@mvpei.hr; internet tr.mvp.hr; Ambassador GORDAN BAKOTA.

Cuba: Şölen Sok. 8, 06550 Çankaya, Ankara; tel. (312) 4428970; fax (312) 4414007; e-mail embacubatur@tr.net; Ambassador ERNESTO GÓMEZ ABASCAL.

Czech Republic: Kaptanpaşa Sok. 15, 06700 Gaziosmanpaşa, Ankara; tel. (312) 4056139; fax (312) 4463084; e-mail ankara@embassy.mzv.cz; internet www.mzv.cz/ankara; Ambassador EVA FILIPI.

Denmark: Mahatma Gandhi Cad. 74, 06700 Gaziosmanpaşa, Ankara; tel. (312) 4466141; fax (312) 4472498; e-mail ankamb@um.dk; internet www.ambankara.um.dk; Ambassador JESPER VAHR.

Egypt: Atatürk Bul. 126, 06680 Kavaklıdere, Ankara; tel. (312) 4261026; fax (312) 4270099; e-mail egankara@yahoo.com; Ambassador Dr ALAA ELDIN A. SHAWKY ELHADIDI.

Estonia: Gölgeli Sok. 16, 06700 Gaziosmanpaşa, Ankara; tel. (312) 4056970; fax (312) 4056976; e-mail embassy.ankara@mfa.ee; internet www.estemb.org.tr/embassy; Ambassador AIVO ORAV.

Ethiopia: Reşit Galip Cad., Gökçek Sok. 11, Ankara; tel. (312) 4360400; fax (312) 4481938; e-mail ethembank@ttnet.net.tr; Ambassador MULATU TESHOME WIRTU.

Finland: Kader Sok. 44, 06700 Gaziosmanpaşa, Ankara; tel. (312) 4261930; fax (312) 4680072; e-mail sanomat.ank@formin.fi; internet www.finland.org.tr; Ambassador KIRSTI ESKELINEN.

France: Paris Cad. 70, 06540 Kavaklıdere, Ankara; tel. (312) 4554545; fax (312) 4554527; e-mail ambaank@yahoo.fr; internet www.ambafrance-tr.org; Ambassador BERNARD EMIÉ.

Georgia: Kılıç Ali Sok. 12, Oran, Ankara; tel. (312) 4918030; fax (312) 4918032; e-mail ankara.emb@mfa.gov.ge; internet www.turkey.mfa.gov.ge; Ambassador TARIEL LEBANIDZE.

Germany: Atatürk Bul. 114, 06690 Kavaklıdere, Ankara; tel. (312) 4555100; fax (312) 4266959; e-mail infomail@germanembassyank.com; internet www.ankara.diplo.de; Ambassador Dr ECKART CUNTZ.

Greece: Zia ür-Rahman Cad. 9–11, 06670 Gaziosmanpaşa, Ankara; tel. (312) 4480873; fax (312) 4463191; e-mail gremb.ank@mfa.gr; Ambassador FOTIOS-JEAN XYDAS.

Holy See: Apostolic Nunciature, Birlik Mah. 3, Cad. 37, PK 33, 06552 Çankaya, Ankara; tel. (312) 4953514; fax (312) 4953540; e-mail vatican@tr.net; Apostolic Nuncio Most Rev. ANTONIO LUCIBELLO (Titular Archbishop of Thurio).

Hungary: Sancak Mah. Layoş, Koşut Cad. 2, Yıldız, Çankaya, Ankara; tel. (312) 4422273; fax (312) 4415049; e-mail mission.ank@kum.hu; internet www.mfa.gov.hu/kulkepviselet/TR/hu; Ambassador ISTVÁN SZABÓ.

India: H.E. Mr. R.S. Jassal Cinnah Cad. 77, 06680 Çankaya, Ankara; tel. (312) 4382195; fax (312) 4403429; e-mail chancery@indembassy.org.tr; internet www.indembassy.org.tr; Ambassador RAMINDER SINGH JASSAL.

Indonesia: Abdullah Cevdet Sok. 10, 06680 Çankaya, Ankara; tel. (312) 4382190; fax (312) 4382193; e-mail indoank@indoank.org; Ambassador AWANG BAHRIN.

Iran: Tahran Cad. 10, Kavaklıdere, Ankara; tel. (312) 4682821; fax (312) 4682823; e-mail iranembassy_ankara@hotmail.com; Ambassador BAHMAN HOSSEINPOUR.

Iraq: Turan Emeksiz Sok. 11, 06700 Gaziosmanpaşa, Ankara; tel. (312) 4687421; fax (312) 4684832; e-mail ankemb@iraqmofamail.net; Ambassador MUEZ AL-KHATIB (designate).

Ireland: Uğur Mumcu Cad. 88, MNG Binası B Blok Kat 3, Gaziosmanpaşa 06700 Ankara; tel. (312) 4466172; fax (312) 4468061; e-mail ankaraembassy@dfa.ie; Ambassador ANTHONY MANNIX.

Israel: Mahatma Gandhi Cad. 85, 06700 Gaziosmanpaşa, Ankara; tel. (312) 4597500; fax (312) 4597555; e-mail info@ankara.mfa.gov.il; internet ankara.mfa.gov.il; Ambassador GAVRIEL LEVY.

Italy: Atatürk Bul. 118, 06680 Kavaklıdere, Ankara; tel. (312) 4574200; fax (312) 4574280; e-mail ambasciata.ankara@esteri.it; internet www.italian-embassy.org.ae/Ambasciata_Ankara; Ambassador CARLO MARSILI.

Japan: Reşit Galip Cad. 81, 06692 Gaziosmanpaşa, Ankara; tel. (312) 4460500; fax (312) 4371812; e-mail culture@jpn-emb.org.tr; internet www.tr.emb-japan.go.jp; Ambassador NOBUAKI TANAKA.

Jordan: Dede Korkut Sok. 18 Mesnevi, 06690 Çankaya, Ankara; tel. (312) 4402054; fax (312) 4404327; e-mail jordembank@superonline.com; Ambassador FARIS SHAWKAT AL-MUFTI.

Kazakhstan: Kılıç Ali Sok. 6, Oran Sitesi, Çankaya, Ankara; tel. (312) 4919100; fax (312) 4904455; e-mail kazank@kazakhstan.org.tr; internet www.kazakhstan.org.tr; Ambassador BAGDAT AMREYEV.

Korea, Republic: Cinnah Cad., Alaçam Sok 5, 06690 Çankaya, Ankara; tel. (312) 4684822; fax (312) 4682279; e-mail turkey@mofat.go.kr; internet tur-ankara.mofat.go.kr; Ambassador KIM CHANG-YEOB.

.Kosovo: Hirfanli Sok. 14, Çankaya, Ankara; tel. (312) 4467054; fax (312) 4467055; e-mail embassy.turkey@ks-gov.net; Chargé d'affaires a.i. BEKIM SEJDIU.

Kuwait: Reşit Galip Cad. Kelebek Sok. 110, Gaziosmanpaşa, Ankara; tel. (312) 4450576; fax (312) 4466839; e-mail kuwait@ada.net.tr; Ambassador ABDULLAH ABD AL-AZIZ AD-DUWAIKH.

Kyrgyzstan: Turan Günes Bul. 15 Cad. 21, Yıldız Oran, Ankara; tel. (312) 4913508; fax (312) 4913513; e-mail kirgiz-o@tr.net; Ambassador MAMBETJUNUS ABYLOV.

Latvia: Reşit Galip Cad. 95, Çankaya, Ankara; tel. (312) 4056136; fax (312) 4056137; e-mail embassy.turkey@mfa.gov.lv; Ambassador IVARS PUNDURS.

Lebanon: Kızkulesi Sok. 44, Gaziosmanpaşa, 06700 Ankara; tel. (312) 4467487; fax (312) 4461023; e-mail lebembas@ttnet.net.tr; Chargé d'affaires WAJIB ABD AS-SAMAD.

Libya: Cinnah Cad. 60, 06690 Çankaya, Ankara; tel. (312) 4381110; fax (312) 4403862; e-mail ashaabiankara@hotmail.com; Chargé d'affaires a.i. MUHAMMAD ZENATI.

Lithuania: Mahatma Gandhi Cad. 17/8–9, 06700 Gaziosmanpaşa, Ankara; tel. (312) 4470766; fax (312) 4470663; e-mail amb.tr@urm.lt; internet tr.mfa.lt; Ambassador DARIUS PRANCKEVIČIUS.

Macedonia, former Yugoslav republic: Karaca Sok. 24/5–6, 06700 Gaziosmanpaşa, Ankara; tel. (312) 4399204; fax (312) 4399206; e-mail ankara@mfa.gov.mk; Ambassador MELPOMENI KORNETI.

Malaysia: Mahatma Gandhi Cad. 58, 06700 Gaziosmanpaşa, Ankara; tel. (312) 4463547; fax (312) 4464130; e-mail malankara@kln.gov.my; internet www.kln.gov.my/perwakilan/ankara; Ambassador Dato' SAIPUL ANWAR ABD AL-MUIN.

Mexico: Kırkpınar Sok. 8/6, 06540 Çankaya, Ankara; tel. (312) 4423033; fax (312) 4420221; e-mail mexico@embamextur.com; internet www.mexico.org.tr; Ambassador SALVADOR CAMPOS ICARDO.

Moldova: Kaptanpaşa Sok. 49, 06700 Gaziosmanpaşa, Ankara; tel. (312) 4465527; fax (312) 4465816; e-mail ankara@mfa.md; Ambassador MIHAIL BARBULAT.

Mongolia: Koza Sok. 109, 06700 Gaziosmanpaşa, Ankara; tel. (312) 4467977; fax (312) 4467791; e-mail mogolelc@yahoo.com; internet web.ttnet.net.tr/mogolelc; Ambassador OCHIRYN OCHIRJAV.

Morocco: Reşit Galip Cad., Rabat Sok. 11, 06700 Gaziosmanpaşa, Ankara; tel. (312) 4376020; fax (312) 4471405; e-mail sifamatr@tr.net; Ambassador MUHAMMAD LOTFI AOUAD.

Netherlands: Hollanda Cad. 3, 06550 Yıldız, Ankara; tel. (312) 4091800; fax (312) 4091898; e-mail ank@minbuza.nl; internet www.nl.org.tr; Ambassador P. M. KURPERSHOEK.

New Zealand: PK 162, İran Cad. 13/4, 06700 Kavaklıdere, Ankara; tel. (312) 4679054; fax (312) 4679013; e-mail nzembassyankara@ttmail.com; internet www.nzembassy.com/turkey; Ambassador HAMISH COOPER.

Nigeria: Uğur Mumcu Sok. 56, 06700 Gaziosmanpaşa, Ankara; tel. (312) 4481077; fax (312) 4481082; e-mail nigeriaembassyturkey@yahoo.co.uk; Ambassador AHMED A. M. MADORI.

Norway: Kirkpinar Sok. 18, 06540 Çankaya, Ankara; tel. (312) 4058010; fax (312) 4430544; e-mail emb.ankara@mfa.no; internet www.norway.org.tr; Ambassador CECILIE LANDSVERK.

Oman: Mahatma Gandhi Cad. 63, 06700 Gaziosmanpaşa, Ankara; tel. (312) 4470630; fax (312) 4470632; e-mail omanembassy@yahoo.com; Ambassador MUHAMMAD NASSER AL-WOHAIBI.

Pakistan: İran Cad. 37, 06700 Gaziosmanpaşa, Ankara; tel. (312) 4271410; fax (312) 4671023; e-mail parepankara@yahoo.com; internet www.pakembassyankara.com; Ambassador Lt-Gen. (retd) SYED IFTIKHAR HUSSAIN SHAH.

Philippines: Mahatma Gandhi Cad. 56, 06700 Gaziosmanpaşa, Ankara; tel. (312) 4465831; fax (312) 4465733; e-mail ankarape@dfa.gov.ph; Ambassador BAHNARIM A. GUINOMLA.

Poland: Atatürk Bul. 241, 06650 Kavaklıdere, Ankara; tel. (312) 4675619; fax (312) 4678963; e-mail polamb@superonline.com; internet www.polonya.org.tr; Chargé d'affaires a.i. KRZYSZTOF LEWANDOWSKI.

Portugal: Kuleli Sok. 26, 06700 Gaziosmanpaşa, Ankara; tel. (312) 4056028; fax (312) 4463670; e-mail embaixada@portugal.org.tr; Ambassador JOSÉ MANUEL DE CARVALHO LAMEIRAS.

Qatar: Bakü Sok. 6, Diplomatik Site, Oran, Ankara; tel. (312) 4907274; fax (312) 4906757; e-mail ankara@mofa.gov.qa; Ambassador ABD AR-RAZAK ABD AL-GHANI.

TURKEY

Romania: Bükreş Sok. 4, 06680 Çankaya, Ankara; tel. (312) 4271243; fax (312) 4271530; e-mail romania@attglobal.net; Chargé d'affaires a.i. PETRE STOICESCU.

Russia: Karyağdı Sok. 5, 06692 Çankaya, Ankara; tel. (312) 4392122; fax (312) 4383952; e-mail rus-ankara@yandex.ru; internet www.turkey.mid.ru; Ambassador VLADIMIR E. IVANOVSKII.

Saudi Arabia: Turan Emeksiz Sok. 6, 06700 Gaziosmanpaşa, Ankara; tel. (312) 4685540; fax (312) 4274886; e-mail tremb@mofa.gov.sa; Ambassador MUHAMMAD AL-HUSSAINI ASH-SHARIF.

Senegal: İran Cad. 47/5, Gaziosmanpaşa, Ankara; tel. (312) 4663086; fax (312) 4272213; Ambassador BABACAR CARLOS MBAYE.

Serbia: Paris Cad. 47, 06450 Kavaklıdere, Ankara; tel. (312) 4260236; fax (312) 4278345; e-mail embserank@tr.net; Ambassador VLADIMIR CURGUS (recalled Feb. 2008).

Slovakia: Atatürk Bul. 245, 06692 Kavaklıdere, Ankara; tel. (312) 4675075; fax (312) 4682689; e-mail emb.ankara@mzv.sk; Ambassador VLADIMÍR JAKABČÍN.

Slovenia: Kırlangıç Sok. 36, 06700 Gaziosmanpaşa, Ankara; tel. (312) 4054221; fax (312) 4260216; e-mail van@gov.si; Ambassador MITJA ŠTRUKELJ.

South Africa: Filistin Sok. 27, 06700 Gaziosmanpaşa, Ankara; tel. (312) 4464056; fax (312) 4466434; e-mail political@southafrica.org.tr; internet www.southafrica.org.tr; Ambassador TEBOGO JOSEPH SEOKOLO.

Spain: Abdullah Cevdet Sok. 8, 06680 Çankaya, Ankara; tel. (312) 4380392; fax (312) 4426991; e-mail emb.ankara@mae.es; Ambassador JOAN CLOS I MATHEU.

Sudan: Sancak Mah. 12 Cad. 16, 06550 Çankaya, Ankara; tel. (312) 4413885; fax (312) 4413886; e-mail ankara@mfa.gov.sd; Ambassador MUHAMMAD AL-HASSAN AHMED AL-HAJ.

Sweden: Katip Çelebi Sok. 7, 06692 Kavaklıdere, Ankara; tel. (312) 4554100; fax (312) 4554120; e-mail ambassaden.ankara@foreign.ministry.se; internet www.swedenabroad.com/ankara; Ambassador CHRISTER ASP.

Switzerland: Atatürk Bul. 247, 06692 Kavaklıdere, Ankara; tel. (312) 4573100; fax (312) 4671199; e-mail ank.vertretung@eda.admin.ch; internet www.eda.admin.ch/ankara; Ambassador RAIMUND KUNZ.

Syria: Abdullah Cevdet Sok. 7, 06680 Çankaya, Ankara; tel. (312) 4409657; fax (312) 4385609; Ambassador Dr NIDAL QABALAN.

Tajikistan: Ferit Recai Ertugrul Cad. 20, Oran, Ankara; tel. (312) 4911607; fax (312) 4911603; e-mail tajemb_turkey@inbox.ru; Ambassador SHUKHRAT M. SULTONOV.

Thailand: Çankaya Cad. Kader Sok. 45/3–4, 06700 Gaziosmanpaşa, Ankara; tel. (312) 4673059; fax (312) 4277284; Ambassador KANYA CHAIMAN.

Tunisia: Ferit Recai Ertugrul Cad 19, Oran Diplomatic Site, Ankara; tel. (312) 919635; fax (312) 4919634; e-mail at.ankara@superonline.com; Ambassador GHAZI JOMAA.

'Turkish Republic of Northern Cyprus': Rabat Sok. 20, 06700 Gaziosmanpaşa, Ankara; tel. (312) 4376031; fax (312) 4465238; e-mail kktcbe@superonline.com; Ambassador TAMER GAZIOĞLU.

Turkmenistan: Koza Sok. 28, 06700 Çankaya, Ankara; tel. (312) 4416122; fax (312) 4417125; e-mail tmankara@ttnet.net.tr; Ambassador MAKSAT DOVLETSAHEDOV.

Ukraine: Sancak Mahallesi 206 Sok. 17, 06550 Çankaya, Ankara; tel. (312) 4415499; fax (312) 4406815; e-mail emb_tr@mfa.gov.ua; internet www.mfa.gov.ua/turkey; Ambassador OLEKSANDR MISCHENKO.

United Arab Emirates: Turan Güneş Bul. 15, Cad. 290, Sok. 3, Sancak Mah., Çankaya, Ankara; tel. (312) 4901414; fax (312) 4912333; e-mail uaeemb@uaeemb.net; internet www.uaeemb.net; Ambassador KHALID KHALIFA AL-MUALLA.

United Kingdom: Şehit Ersan Cad. 46/A, 06680 Çankaya, Ankara; tel. (312) 4553344; fax (312) 4553351; e-mail britembinf@fco.gov.uk; internet ukinturkey.fco.gov.uk; Ambassador NICK BAIRD.

USA: Atatürk Bul. 110, 06100 Kavaklıdere, Ankara; tel. (312) 4555555; fax (312) 4670019; e-mail webmaster_ankara@state.gov; internet turkey.usembassy.gov; Ambassador JAMES F. JEFFREY.

Uzbekistan: Sancak Mah. 211 Sok. 3, 06550 Çankaya, Ankara; tel. (312) 4413871; fax (312) 4427058; e-mail embankara@post.mfa.uz; Ambassador ULFAT S. KADYROV.

Venezuela: Koza Sok. 91/3, 06700 Gaziosmanpaşa, Ankara; tel. (312) 4478131; fax (312) 4470711; e-mail mision-ankara@embavenez-turquia.com; Chargé d'affaires a.i. RAÚL JOSÉ BETANCOURT SEELAND.

Viet Nam: Çayhane Sok. 34, Gaziosmanpaşa, Ankara; tel. (312) 4468049; fax (312) 4465623; e-mail dsqvnturkey@yahoo.com; internet www.vietnamembassy-turkey.org; Ambassador NGUYEN SY XUNG.

Yemen: Fethiye Sok. 2, 06700 Gaziosmanpaşa, Ankara; tel. (312) 4462637; fax (312) 4461778; e-mail yemenemb@superonline.com; Ambassador NORIA ABDULLAH AL-HAMAMI.

Judicial System

Until the foundation of the Turkish Republic, a large part of the Turkish civil law—the laws affecting the family, inheritance, property, obligations, etc.—was based on the Koran, and this holy law was administered by special religious (*Shari'a*) courts. The legal reform of 1926 was not only a process of secularization, but also a radical change of the legal system. The Swiss Civil Code and the Code of Obligation, the Italian Penal Code and the Neuchâtel (Cantonal) Code of Civil Procedure were adopted and modified to fit Turkish customs and traditions.

According to current Turkish law, the power of the judiciary is exercised by judicial (criminal), military and administrative courts. These courts render their verdicts in the first instance, while superior courts examine the verdict for subsequent rulings.

SUPERIOR COURTS

Constitutional Court: Consists of 11 regular and four substitute members, appointed by the President. Reviews the constitutionality of laws, at the request of the President of the Republic, parliamentary groups of the governing party or of the main opposition party, or of one-fifth of the members of the National Assembly, and sits as a high council empowered to try senior members of state. The rulings of the Constitutional Court are final. Decisions of the Court are published immediately in the Official Gazette, and shall be binding on the legislative, executive and judicial organs of the state; Chief Justice HAŞIM KILIÇ.

Court of Appeals: The court of the last instance for reviewing the decisions and verdicts rendered by judicial courts. It has original and final jurisdiction in specific cases defined by law. Members are elected by the Supreme Council of Judges and Prosecutors; Chief Justice HASAN GERÇEKER.

Council of State: An administrative court of the first and last instance in matters not referred by law to other administrative courts, and an administrative court of the last instance in general. Hears and settles administrative disputes and expresses opinions on draft laws submitted by the Council of Ministers. Three-quarters of the members are appointed by the Supreme Council of Judges and Public Prosecutors, the remaining quarter is selected by the President of the Republic.

Military Court of Appeals: A court of the last instance to review decisions and verdicts rendered by military courts, and a court of first and last instance with jurisdiction over certain military persons, stipulated by law, with responsibility for the specific trials of these persons. Members are selected by the President of the Republic from nominations made by the Military Court of Appeals.

Supreme Military Administrative Court: A military court for the judicial control of administrative acts concerning military personnel. Members are selected by the President of the Republic from nominations made by the Court.

Court of Jurisdictional Disputes: Settles disputes among judicial, administrative and military courts arising from disagreements on jurisdictional matters and verdicts.

Court of Accounts: A court charged with the auditing of all accounts of revenue, expenditure and government property, which renders rulings related to transactions and accounts of authorized bodies on behalf of the National Assembly.

Supreme Council of Judges and Public Prosecutors: The President of the Council shall be the Minister of Justice, and the Under-Secretary to the Minister of Justice shall serve as an ex officio member of the Council. Three regular and three substitute members from the Court of Appeals, together with two regular and two substitute members of the Council of State, shall be appointed to the Supreme Council by the President of the Republic for a four-year term. Decides all personnel matters relating to judges and public prosecutors.

Public Prosecutor: The law shall make provision for the tenure of public prosecutors and attorneys of the Council of State and their functions. The Chief Prosecutor of the Republic, the Chief Attorney of the Council of State and the Chief Prosecutor of the Military Court of Appeals are subject to the provisions applicable to judges of higher courts.

Military Trial: Military trials are conducted by military and disciplinary courts. These courts are entitled to try the military offences of military personnel and those offences committed against military personnel or in military areas, or offences connected with military service and duties. Military courts may try non-military persons only for military offences prescribed by special laws.

TURKEY

Religion

ISLAM

More than 99% of the Turkish people are Muslims. However, Turkey is a secular state. Although Islam was stated to be the official religion in the Constitution of 1924, an amendment in 1928 removed this privilege. Since 1950 subsequent Governments have tried to re-establish links between religion and state affairs, but secularity was protected by the revolution of 1960, the 1980 military takeover and the 1982 Constitution.

Diyanet İşleri Başkanlığı (Presidency of Religious Affairs): Eski-şehir Yolu 9 km Çankaya, Ankara; tel. (312) 2957000; e-mail diyanet@diyanet.gov.tr; internet www.diyanet.gov.tr; Pres. Prof. Dr ALI BARDAKOĞLU.

CHRISTIANITY

The town of Antioch (now Antakya) was one of the earliest strong-holds of Christianity, and by the 4th century had become a patri-archal see. Formerly in Syria, the town was incorporated into Turkey in 1939. Constantinople (now İstanbul) was also a patriarchal see, and by the 6th century the Patriarch of Constantinople was recog-nized as the Ecumenical Patriarch in the East. Gradual estrange-ment from Rome developed, leading to the final breach between the Catholic West and the Orthodox East, usually assigned to the year 1054.

There are estimated to be about 100,000 Christians in Turkey.

The Orthodox Churches

Armenian Patriarchate: Ermeni Patrikliği, 34130 Kumkapı, İstanbul; tel. (212) 5170970; fax (212) 5164833; e-mail info@lraper.org; internet www.lraper.org; f. 1461; 100,000 adherents (incl. workers from Armenia—2007); Patriarch MESROB II.

Bulgarian Orthodox Church: Bulgar Ortodoks Kilisesi, Halâskâr Gazi Cad. 319, Şişli, İstanbul; Rev. Archimandrite GANCO ÇOBANOF.

Greek Orthodox Church: The Ecumenical Patriarchate (Rum Ortodoks Patrikhanesi), Sadrazam Ali Paşa Cad. 35, 34220 Fener-Haliç, İstanbul; tel. (212) 5255416; fax (212) 5316533; e-mail patriarchate@ec-patr.org; internet www.ec-patr.org; Archbishop of Constantinople (New Rome) and Ecumenical Patriarch BARTHOLO-MEW I.

The Roman Catholic Church

At 31 December 2006 there were an estimated 31,691 adherents in the country.

Bishops' Conference: Conferenza Episcopale di Turchia, Satırcı Sok 2, Harbiye, 34373 İstanbul; tel. (212) 2190089; fax (212) 2411543; f. 1987; Pres. Most Rev. RUGGERO FRANCESCHINI (Archbishop of İzmir).

Armenian Rite

Patriarchate of Cilicia: f. 1742; Patriarch NERSES BEDROS TAR-MOUNI XIX (resident in Beirut, Lebanon).

Archdiocese of İstanbul: Sakızağacı Cad. 31, PK 183, 80072 Beyoğlu, İstanbul; tel. (212) 2441258; fax (212) 2432364; f. 1928; Archbishop HOVHANNES TCHOLAKIAN.

Byzantine Rite

Apostolic Exarchate of İstanbul: Hamalbaşı Cad. 44, PK 259, 80070 Beyoğlu, İstanbul; tel. (212) 2440351; fax (212) 2411543; f. 1911; Apostolic Admin. LOUIS PELÂTRE (Titular Bishop of Sasima).

Bulgarian Catholic Church: Bulgar Katolik Kilisesi, Eski Par-makkapı Sok. 15, Galata, İstanbul.

Latin Rite

Metropolitan Archdiocese of İzmir: Church of St Polycarp, Necatibey Bul. 2, PK 267, 35210 İzmir; tel. (232) 4840531; fax (232) 4845358; e-mail curiaves@yahoo.it; f. 1818; Archbishop of İzmir Most Rev. RUGGERO FRANCESCHINI.

Apostolic Vicariate of Anatolia: Mithat Paşa Cad. 5, PK 75, 31200 Iskenderum; tel. (326) 6175916; fax (326) 6139291; e-mail curiaves@yahoo.it; f. 1990; Vicar Apostolic LUIGI PADOVESE (Titular Bishop of Monteverde).

Apostolic Vicariate of İstanbul: Papa Roncalli Sok. 83, 80230 Harbiye, İstanbul; tel. (212) 2480775; fax (212) 2411543; e-mail vapostolique@yahoo.fr; f. 1742; Vicar Apostolic LOUIS PELÂTRE (Titular Bishop of Sasima).

Maronite Rite

The Maronite Patriarch of Antioch, Cardinal Nasrallah Pierre Sfeir, is resident in Lebanon.

Melkite Rite

The Greek Melkite Patriarch of Antioch, Grégoire III Laham, is resident in Damascus, Syria.

Syrian Rite

The Syrian Catholic Patriarch of Antioch, Ignace Pierre VIII Abdel Ahad, is resident in Beirut, Lebanon.

Patriarchal Exarchate of Turkey: Sarayarkası Sok 15, PK 84, 34437 Ayazpaşa, İstanbul; tel. (212) 2432521; fax (212) 2490261; e-mail info@suryanikatolikkilisesi.com; f. 1908; Patriarchal Exarch Fr. YUSUF SAĞ.

The Anglican Communion

Within the Church of England, Turkey forms part of the diocese of Gibraltar in Europe. The Bishop is resident in the United Kingdom.

Anglican Chaplaincy in İstanbul: Christ Church, Serdar Ekram Sok. 82, Karaköy, İstanbul; tel. (212) 2515616; fax (212) 2435702; e-mail parson@tnn.net; internet www.anglicanistanbul.com; Chaplain Rev. Canon IAN SHERWOOD.

JUDAISM

There are estimated to be about 23,000 Jews in Turkey.

Jewish Community of Turkey: Türkiye Hahambaşılığı, Yemenici Sok 21, Beyoğlu, 34430 Tünel, İstanbul; tel. (212) 2938794; fax (212) 2441980; e-mail info@musevicemaati.com; internet www.musevicemaati.com; Chief Rabbi ISAK HALEVA.

The Press

Almost all İstanbul papers are also printed in Ankara and İzmir on the same day, and some in Adana. Among the most serious and influential papers are the dailies *Milliyet* and *Cumhuriyet*. The weekly *Gırgır* is noted for its political satire. The most popular dailies are the İstanbul papers *Sabah, Hürriyet, Milliyet* and *Zaman; Yeni Asır*, published in İzmir, is the best-selling quality daily of the Aegean region. There are numerous provincial newspapers with a limited circulation.

PRINCIPAL DAILIES

Adana

Yeni Adana: Abidinpaşa Cad. 70, 01010 Adana; tel. (322) 3599984; fax (322) 3593655; e-mail yeniadana@yeniadana.net; internet www.yeniadana.net; f. 1918; political; Propr ÇETIN REMZI YÜREĞIR; Chief Editor AHMET YAHŞI; circ. 2,000.

Ankara

Ankara Ticaret: Rüzgârlı Caddesi, Ibrahim Müteferrika Sok. 2/10, Ankara; tel. (312) 3112131; fax (312) 3116690; f. 1954; commercial; Chief Editor ZEKI OCAK; Gen. Man. ISTIKLAL YARADILIŞ; circ. 2,470.

Belde: Rüzgarlı Gayret Sok. 7/1, Ulus, Ankara; tel. (312) 3106820; f. 1968; Propr İLHAN İŞBILEN; circ. 3,399.

The New Anatolian: Şehit Ersan Cad. 4/15–16 Kavaklıdere, Ankara; tel. (312) 4674151; fax (312) 4674156; e-mail tna@thenewanatolian.com; internet www.thenewanatolian.com; English language; Founder İLHAN ÇEVIK; Editor-in-Chief METE BELOVACIKLI.

Tasvir: Rüzgarlı Plevne Sok. 14, Ulus, Ankara; tel. (312) 3101443; fax (312) 3122209; f. 1960; conservative; Editor ENDER YOKDAR; circ. 3,055.

Turkish Daily News: Sogutozu Mahallesi Dumlupinar Bul. 102, 06510 Çankaya, Ankara; tel. (312) 2070090; fax (312) 2070094; e-mail tdn@tdn.com.tr; internet www.turkishdailynews.com; f. 1961; English language; CEO NURI M. ÇOLAKOĞLU; Exec. Editor EYÜP CAN SAĞLIK; circ. 54,500.

Türkiye Ticaret Sicili: Karanfil Sok. 56, Bakanlıklar, Ankara; tel. (312) 4138000; fax (312) 4258173; e-mail ttsgmd@tobb.org.tr; internet www.ticaretsicil.gov.tr; f. 1957; commercial; Publr KEMAL CIRAK; Editor YALÇIN KAYA AYDOS.

Vakit: Ada 55, İstoç Bağcılar, İstanbul; tel. (212) 6592056; fax (212) 4474209; e-mail haber@vakit.com.tr; internet www.vakit.com.tr; f. 1978; Man. Editor AHMET KARAHASANOĞLU; circ. 3,384.

Yeni Tanin: Ankara; f. 1964; political; Propr BURHANETTIN GÖGEN; Man. Editor AHMET TEKEŞ; circ. 3,123.

Yirmidört Saat: Gazeteciler Cemiyeti Çevre Sok. 35, Çankaya, Ankara; tel. (312) 4271522; fax (312) 4682384; e-mail info@gazetecilercemiyeti.org.tr; internet www.gazetecilercemiyeti.org.tr; f. 1978; Propr NAZMI BILGIN.

TURKEY

Eskişehir

Istikbal: İstiklal Mah. Porsuk Bulvari Adalar Sok. 5, Eskişehir; tel. (222) 2201901; fax (222) 2201902; e-mail info@istikbalgazetesi.com; internet www.istikbalgazetesi.com; f. 1950; morning; Editor MURAT TAŞKIN.

Gaziantep

Olay (Event): Olay Medya Plaza, Topraklik, Gaziantep; tel. (342) 3228686; fax (342) 3228687; e-mail olay@olaymedya.com; internet www.olaymedya.com; f. 1992; Man. EROL MARAS.

İstanbul

Akşam: Davutpaşa Cad. 34, 34020 Zeytinburnu, İstanbul; tel. (212) 4493000; fax (212) 4819561; e-mail editor@aksam.com.tr; internet www.aksam.com.tr; Man. Dir SERDAR TURGUT.

Apoyevmatini: İstiklâl Cad., Suriye Pasajı 348, Beyoğlu, İstanbul; tel. (212) 2437635; f. 1925; Greek language; Publr EUSEVIA ADOSOGLOU; Editor MICHAEL VASSILIADIS; circ. 580.

Bugün: Medya Plaza Basın Ekspres Yolu, 34540 Güneşli, İstanbul; tel. (212) 5504850; fax (212) 5023340; e-mail bugun@bugun.com.tr; internet www.bugun.com.tr; f. 1989; Propr ONAY BILGIN; circ. 184,884.

Cumhuriyet (Republic): Prof. Nurettin Mazhar Öktel Sok. 2, 34381 Şişli, İstanbul; tel. (212) 3437274; fax (212) 3437264; e-mail posta@cumhuriyet.com.tr; internet www.cumhuriyet.com.tr; f. 1924; morning; liberal; Man. Editor HIKMET ÇETİNKAYA; circ. 75,000.

Dünya (World): Basınevi Balamir Sok. 7, İstanbul; tel. (216) 6811800; fax (216) 6803975; e-mail dunya@dunyagazetesi.com.tr; internet www.dunyagazetesi.com.tr; f. 1952; morning; economic; Editor-in-Chief OSMAN S. AROLAT; circ. 60,000.

Fotomaç: Medya Plaza, Basın Ekspres Yolu, 34540 Güneşli, İstanbul; tel. (212) 5504900; fax (212) 5028217; internet www.fotomac.com.tr; f. 1991; sport; Chief Officer İBRAHIM SETEN; circ. 250,000.

Günaydın-Tan: Alayköşkü, Cad. Eryilmaz Sok. 13, Cağaloğlu, İstanbul; tel. (212) 5120050; fax (212) 5260823; f. 1968; Editor-in-Chief SECKIN TURESAY.

Hürriyet: Babiali Cad. 15–17, Guneslikoy, 34540 Bakırköy, İstanbul; tel. (212) 5550050; fax (212) 5156705; e-mail editor@hurriyet.com.tr; internet www.hurriyet.com.tr; f. 1948; morning; independent political; Propr AYDIN DOĞAN; Chief Editor ERTUĞRUL ÖZKÖK; circ. 542,797.

Meydan (Nationalism): Yüzyıl Mahallesi, Mahmutbey Viyadüğü Altı, İkitelli, 34410 Cağaloğlu, İstanbul; tel. (212) 5056111; fax (212) 5056436; f. 1990; Propr REFIK ARAS; Editor UFUK GULDEMIR.

Milli Gazete: Cemal Ulusoy Cad. 38/A, 34620 Bahçelievler, İstanbul; tel. (212) 6971000; fax (212) 6931801; e-mail milli@milligazete.com.tr; internet www.milligazete.com.tr; f. 1973; pro-Islamist; right-wing; Editor-in-Chief EKREM KIZILTAŞ; circ. 51,000.

Milliyet: Doğan Medya Center, Bağcilar, 34204 İstanbul; tel. (212) 5056111; fax (212) 5056233; e-mail webadmin@milliyet.com.tr; internet www.milliyet.com.tr; f. 1950; morning; political; Editor-in-Chief DERYA SAZAK; circ. 630,000.

Nor Marmara: İstiklâl Cad., Solakzade Sok. 5, PK 507, İstanbul; tel. (212) 2444736; e-mail info@normarmara.com; internet www.normarmara.com; f. 1940; Armenian language; Propr and Editor-in-Chief ROBER HADDELER; Gen. Man. ARI HADDELER; circ. 2,200.

Sabah (Morning): Medya Plaza, Basın Ekspres Yolu, Günesli, İstanbul; tel. (212) 5504810; fax (212) 5028143; internet www.sabah.com.tr; assets seized by the state Savings Deposit Insurance Fund in April 2007; transfer to ownership of Turkuvaz Radyo Televizyon ve Gazetecilik AŞ (a subsidiary of Çalık Holding) was approved by the Fund in Feb. 2008, for completion by May; Editor-in-Chief ERGUN BABAHAN; circ. 550,000.

Tercüman: Davutpaşa Cad. 34, Zeytinbumu, İstanbul; tel. (212) 4493000; fax (212) 4819550; internet www.tercuman.com.tr; f. 1961; right-wing; Propr SEDAT COLAK; Chief Editor BÜLENT CAN; circ. 32,869.

Türkiye (Turkey): Ekim Cad. 29, 34197 Yenibosna, İstanbul; tel. (212) 4543000; fax (212) 4543100; e-mail info@tg.com.tr; internet www.turkiyegazetesi.com.tr; f. 1970; Dir of Publs NUH ALBAYRAK; circ. 450,000.

Yeni Nesil (New Generation): Sanayi Cad., Selvi Sok. 5, Yenibosna, Bakırköy, İstanbul; tel. (212) 5846261; fax (212) 5567289; f. 1970 as Yeni Asya; political; Editor-in-Chief UMIT SIMSEK.

Yeni Şafak: Yenidoğan Mah., Şenay Sok. 2, Kat 1, Bayrampaşa, İstanbul; tel. (212) 6122390; fax (212) 6121903; internet yenisafak.com.tr; Editor-in-Chief YUSUF ZIYA CÖMERT.

Yeniyüzyıl: Medya Plaza Basın Ekspres Yolu, 34540 Güneşli, İstanbul; tel. (212) 5028877; fax (212) 5028295; Editor KEREM ÇALISKAN.

Zaman (Time): Ahmet Taner Kislali Cad. 6, 34194 Yenibosna, İstanbul; tel. (212) 4541454; fax (212) 4548634; e-mail a.karakoca@zaman.com.tr; internet www.zaman.com.tr; f. 1962; morning; political, independent; CEO EKREM DUMANLI; Editor-in-Chief EKREM DUMANLI; circ. 741,251.

İzmir

Rapor: Gazi Osman Paşa Bul. 5, İzmir; tel. (232) 4254400; f. 1949; Owner DINÇ BILGIN; Man. Editor TANJU ATEŞER; circ. 9,000.

Ticaret Gazetesi: 1571 Sok. 16, 35110 Çınarlı, 35110 İzmir; tel. (232) 4619642; fax (232) 4619646; e-mail ticinfo@unimedya.net.tr; internet www.ticaretgazetesi.com; f. 1942; commercial news; Editor-in-Chief AHMET SÜKUTI TÜKEL; Man. Editor CEMAL M. TÜKEL; circ. 5,009.

Yeni Asır (New Century): Gaziosmanpaşa Bul. 5, 35260 Çankaya, İzmir; tel. (232) 4415000; fax (232) 4464222; e-mail yasir@yeniasir.com.tr; internet www.yeniasir.com.tr; f. 1895; political; Man. Editor AYDIN BILGIN; Editorial Dir HAMDI TÜRKMEN; circ. 60,000.

Konya

Yeni Konya: Şeref Şirin Mah. İstanbul Cad., Ay İşhanı 3/167, Karatay/Konya; tel. (332) 3507575; fax (332) 3509920; internet www.yenikonya.com.tr; f. 1945; political; Gen. Man. MUSTAFA TATLISU; Chief Editor ALI SAKAL; monthly circ. 1,657.

Yeni Meram: Konya; tel. (332) 3452424; e-mail yenimeram@yenimeram.com.tr; internet www.yenimeram.com.tr; f. 1949; political; Propr ÇETÝN REMZÝ YÜREÐYR; Chief Editor YALÇIN REMZÝ YÜREÐYR; monthly circ. 44,000.

WEEKLIES

Ankara

EBA Briefing: Bestekar Sok. 21/8, Kavaklıdere, Ankara; tel. (312) 4180628; fax (312) 4180432; f. 1975; publ. by Ekonomik Basın Ajansı (Economic Press Agency); political and economic survey; Publrs ORHAN TOLUN, YAVUZ TOLUN.

Ekonomi ve Politika: Kavaklıdere, Ankara; f. 1966; economic and political; Publr ZIYA TANSU.

Turkish Economic Gazette: Atatürk Bul. 149, Bakanlıklar, Ankara; tel. (312) 4177700.

Turkish Probe: Hülya Sok. 45, 06700 GOP, Ankara; tel. (312) 4475647; fax (312) 4468374; English language; Publr A. ILHAN ÇEVIK; Editor-in-Chief ILNUR ÇEVIK; circ. 2,500.

Türkiye İktisat Gazetesi: Karanfil Sok 56, 06582 Bakanlıklar, Ankara; tel. (312) 4184321; fax (312) 4183268; f. 1953; commercial; Chief Editor MEHMET SAĞLAM; circ. 11,500.

Antalya

Pulse: PK 7, Kemer, Antalya; tel. and fax (242) 8180105; e-mail uras@ada.net.tr; internet www.turkpulse.com; politics and business; English; publ. online; Publr VEDAT URAS.

İstanbul

Aktüel: Medya Plaza Basın Ekspres Yolu, 34540 Güneşli, İstanbul; tel. (212) 5504870; e-mail aktuel@birnumara.com.tr; internet aktuel.birnumara.com.tr; f. 1991; Gen. Man. GÜLAY GÖKTÜRK; Man. Editor ALEV ER.

Bayrak: Çatalçeşme Sok. 50/5, 34410 Cağaloğlu, İstanbul; tel. (212) 5275575; fax (212) 5268363; f. 1970; political; Editor MEHMET GÜNGÖR; circ. 10,000.

Elegans Magazine: Valikonağı Cad. Y.K.V. Binası K:5 D:3 34365 Nişantaşı, İstanbul; tel. (212) 2336506; fax (212) 2312878; e-mail elegans@elegans.com.tr; internet www.elegans.com.tr; f. 1985; social, economic and global issues; Publr ÖMER TAYFUN YUMAK.

Ekonomik Panaroma: Büyükdere Cad. Ali Kaya Sok. 8, 80720 Levent, İstanbul; tel. (212) 2696680; f. 1988; Gen. Man. AYDIN DEMIRER.

Ekonomist: Hürriyet Medya Towers, 34212 Güneşli, İstanbul; tel. (212) 4103256; fax (212) 4103255; e-mail ekonomist@doganburda.com; internet www.ekonomist.com.tr; f. 1991; CEO MEHMET Y. YILMAZ.

Gırgır: Alayköşkü Cad., Çağaloğlu, İstanbul; tel. (212) 2285000; satirical; Propr and Editor OĞUZ ARAL; circ. 500,000.

İstanbul Ticaret: İstanbul Chamber of Commerce, Ragip Gümüşpala Cad. 84, 34378, Eminönü, İstanbul; tel. (212) 5114150; fax (212) 5131565; f. 1958; commercial news; Publr MEHMET YILDIRIM.

Tempo: Hürriyet Medya Towers 34212 Güneşli, İstanbul; tel. (212) 4103282; fax (212) 4103311; e-mail tempo@doganburda.com; internet www.tempodergisi.com.tr; f. 1987; Editor NEVAL BATLAS.

TURKEY
Directory

Türk Dünyası Araştırmalar Dergisi: Hürgüç Gazetecilik AŞ Hürriyet Tesisleri, Güneşli, İstanbul; tel. (212) 5500081; Dir SEDAT SIMAVI; Gen. Man. MEHMET Y. YILMAZ.

PERIODICALS

Ankara

Azerbaycan Türk Kültür Dergisi: Vakıf İş Hanı 324, Anafartalar, Ankara; f. 1949; literary and cultural periodical of Azerbaijani Turks; Editor Dr AHMET YAŞAT.

Bayrak Dergisi: Bestckar Sok. 44/5, Kavaklıdere, Ankara; f. 1964; Publr and Editor HAMI KARTAY.

Bilim ve Teknik: Bilim ve Teknik Dergisi Tübitak, Atatürk Bul. 221, Kavaklıdere, 06100 Ankara; tel. (312) 4685300; fax (312) 4277489; e-mail bteknik@tubitak.gov.tr; internet www.tubitak.gov.tr; f. 1967; monthly; science; Propr Prof. NÜKET YETIS; Man. Editor GIGDEM ATAKUMAN.

Devlet Opera ve Balesi Genel Müdürlüğü: Ankara; tel. (312) 3241476; fax (312) 3107248; f. 1949; state opera and ballet; Gen. Dir. RENGIM GOKMEN.

Eğitim ve Bilim (Education and Science): Kızılırmak Cad. 8, Kocatepe, Ankara; tel. (312) 4180614; fax (312) 4175365; e-mail egitimvebilim@ted.org.tr; internet www.ted.org.tr; f. 1928; quarterly; publ. by the Turkish Educational Asscn; Editor Dr SELAHATTIN GELBAL.

Karınca: Türk Kooperatifçilik Kurumu, Mithatpaşa Cad. 38/A, 06420 Kızılay, Ankara; tel. (312) 4359899; fax (312) 4304292; f. 1934; monthly review publ. by the Turkish Co-operative Asscn; Editor Prof. Dr RASIH DEMIRCI; circ. 5,000.

Maden Tetkik Arama Genel Müdürlüğü: MTA Dergisi Editörlüğü, MTA Geological Research Dept, G Blok, 06520 Ankara; e-mail editorluk@mta.gov.tr; internet www.mta.gov.tr; f. 1935; 2 a year; publ. by General Directorate of Mineral Research and Exploration of Turkey; English edn *Bulletin of Mineral Research and Exploration* (2 a year); Gen. Dir MEHMET ÜZER; Editor-in-Chief Prof. Dr ERGUN GÖKTEN.

Mimarlık (Architecture): Konur Sok. 4/2, Kızılay, Ankara; tel. (312) 4173727; fax (312) 4180361; e-mail mimarlikdergisi@mimarlarodasi.org.tr; internet www.mimarlarodasi.org.tr; f. 1963; every 2 months; publ. by the Chamber of Architects of Turkey; Editor N. MÜGE CENGİZKAN; circ. 20,000.

Mühendis ve Makina: Sümer 2 Sok. 36/1A, 06640 Demirtepe, Ankara; tel. (312) 2313159; fax (312) 2313165; e-mail mmo@mmo.org.tr; internet www.mmo.org.tr/muhendismakina; f. 1957; engineering; monthly; publ. by the Chamber of Mechanical Engineers; Propr MEHMET SOĞANCI; Editor YÜKSEL KÖKEN; circ. 30,000.

Teknik ve Uygulama: Konur Sok. 4/4, 06442 Kızılay, Ankara; tel. (312) 4182374; f. 1986; engineering; every 2 months; publ. by the Chamber of Mechanical Engineers; Propr İSMET RIZA ÇEBI; Editor UĞUR DOĞAN; circ. 3,000.

Türk Arkeoloji ve Etnoğrafya Dergisi (General Directorate of Monuments and Museums): Kültür ve Turizm Bakanlığı, Kültür Varlıkları ve Müzeler Genel Müdürlüğü-II. Meclis Binası Ulus, 06100 Ankara; tel. (312) 3104960; fax (312) 3115085; e-mail kulturvarlikmuze@kulturturizm.gov.tr; internet www.kulturturizm.gov.tr; archaeological.

Türk Devlet Tiyatrosu: Devlet Tiyatrosu Genel Müdürlüğü Ulus, Ankara; tel. (312) 3244094; fax (312) 3126007; e-mail genelmudur@dtgm.gov.tr; internet www.devtiyatro.gov.tr; f. 1949; art, theatre.

Türk Dili: Türk Dil Kurumu, Atatürk Bul. 217, 06680 Kavaklıdere, Ankara; tel. (312) 4286100; fax (312) 4285288; e-mail tdili@tdk.gov.tr; internet www.tdk.gov.tr; f. 1951; monthly; Turkish literature and language; Editor Prof. Dr ŞÜKRÜ HALUK AKALIN.

Turkey—Economic News Digest: Karanfil Sok. 56, Ankara; f. 1960; Editor-in-Chief BEHZAT TANIR; Man. Editor SADIK BALKAN.

Türkiye Bankacılık: PK 121, Ankara; f. 1955; commercial; Publr MUSTAFA ATALAY.

Türkiye Bibliyografyası: Milli Kütüphane Başkanlığı, 06490 Bahçelievler, Ankara; tel. (312) 2126200; fax (312) 2230451; e-mail katalog@mkutup.gov.tr; internet www.mkutup.gov.tr; f. 1928; monthly; Turkish national bibliography; publ. by the Turkish National Library, Cataloguing and Classification Dept; Dir AHMET ÇELENKOĞLU.

Türkiye Makaleler Bibliyografyası (Bibliography of Articles in Turkish Periodicals): Milli Kütüphane Başkanlığı, 06490 Bahçelievler, Ankara; tel. (312) 2126200; fax (312) 2230451; e-mail bibliografya@mkutup.gov.tr; internet www.mkutup.gov.tr; f. 1952; monthly; Turkish articles, bibliography; publ. by the Turkish National Library, Bibliography Preparation Dept; Dir SEMA AKINCI.

İstanbul

Arkeoloji ve Sanat Dergisi (Archaeology and Art Magazine): Hayriye Cad. 3/4 Çorlu Apt., 34425 Beyoğlu, İstanbul; tel. (212) 2456838; fax (212) 2456877; e-mail info@arkeolojisanat.com; internet arkeolojisanat.com; f. 1978; bi-monthly; publ. by Archaeology and Art Publications; Publr and Editor NEZIH BAŞGELEN; English-Language Submissions Editor BRIAN JOHNSON.

Bankacılar: Nıspetıye Cad. Akmerkez, B3 Blok. Kat 13–14, 80630 Etiler, İstanbul; tel. (212) 2820973; fax (212) 2820946; publ. by the Banks' Asscn of Turkey; quarterly.

İstanbul Ticaret Odası Mecmuası: Gümüşpala Cad. 84, 34378 Eminönü, İstanbul; tel. (212) 5114150; fax (212) 5131565; f. 1884; quarterly; journal of the İstanbul Chamber of Commerce (ICOC); English; Editor-in-Chief CENGIZ ERSUN.

Musiki Mecmuası (Music Magazine): POB 336, Sem'i Bey Sok. 19/3, Yıldızbakkal, Kadıköy, İstanbul; tel. (216) 3306299; e-mail etemungor@hotmail.com; f. 1948; monthly; music and musicology; Editor ETEM RUHI ÜNGÖR.

Nûr (The Light): Nuruosmaniye Cad., Sorkun Han 28/2, 34410, Cağaloğlu, İstanbul; tel. (212) 5277607; fax (212) 5208231; e-mail sozler@ihlas.net.tr; internet www.sozler.com.tr; f. 1986; religion; Publr MEHMET NURI GÜLEÇ; Editor CEMAL UŞAK; circ. 10,000.

Pirelli Mecmuası: Büyükdere Cad. 117, Gayrettepe, İstanbul; tel. (212) 2663200; fax (212) 2520718; e-mail bilyay@ibm.net; f. 1964; monthly; Publr Türk-Pirelli Lastikleri AŞ; Editor UĞUR CANAL; circ. 24,500.

Ruh ve Madde Dergisi (Spirit and Matter): Ruh ve Madde Publications and Health Services Co, Hasnun Galip Sok., Pembe Çıkmazı 4, D 6/8, 80072 Beyoğlu, İstanbul; tel. (212) 2431814; fax (212) 2520718; e-mail info@ruhvemadde.com; internet www.ruhvemadde.com; f. 1959; organ of the Foundation for Spreading the Knowledge to Unify Humanity; Editor HALUK HACALOĞLU.

Sevgi Dünyası (World of Respect): Aydede Cad. 4/5, 80090 Taksimi, İstanbul; tel. (212) 2504242; fax (212) 2702252; e-mail editor@dostlik.org; internet www.dostluk.org; f. 1963; monthly; social, psychological and spiritual; Publr and Editor Dr REFET KAYSERILIOĞLU.

Turkey: Ihlas Holding Merkez Binası 29, Ekim Cad. 23, 34197 Yenibosna, İstanbul; tel. (212) 4542520; fax (212) 4542555; e-mail info@img.com.tr; internet www.img.com.tr/turkey; f. 1982; monthly; English language; economics; Editor MEHMET SÖZTUTAN; circ. 43,000.

Varlık Yayınları AŞ: Ayberk Ap. Piyerloti Cad. 7–9, Çemberlitaş, 34400 İstanbul; tel. (212) 5162004; fax (212) 5162005; e-mail varlik@varlik.com.tr; internet www.varlik.com.tr; f. 1933; monthly; literary; Editors FILIZ NAYIR DENIZTEKIN, ENVER ERCAN; circ. 4,000.

İzmir

İzmir Ticaret Odası Dergisi: Atatürk Cad. 126, 35210 İzmir; tel. (232) 4417777; fax (232) 4837853; f. 1927; every 2 months; publ. by Chamber of Commerce of İzmir; Sec.-Gen. Prof. Dr İLTER AKAT; Man. ÜMIT ALEMDAROĞLU.

NEWS AGENCIES

Anadolu Ajansı: Mustafa Kemal Bul. 128/C, Tandogan, Ankara; tel. (312) 2317000; fax (312) 2312174; e-mail aa1@anadoluajansi.com.tr; internet www.aa.com.tr; f. 1920; Chair. and Dir-Gen. HILMI BENGI.

ANKA Ajansı: Cinnah Cad. 11/5 Kavaklıdere, Ankara; tel. (312) 4682500; fax (312) 4268471; e-mail anka@ankaajansi.com; internet www.ankaajansi.com.tr; Dir-Gen. VELI ÖZDEMIR.

Bağımsız Basın Ajansı (BBA): Saglam Fikir Sok. 11, Esentepe, 80300 İstanbul; tel. (212) 2122936; fax (212) 2122940; e-mail bba@bba.tv; internet www.bba.tv; f. 1971; provides camera crewing, editing and satellite services in Turkey, the Balkans, the Middle East and the former Soviet republics to broadcasters world-wide.

Cihan News Agency: Cobancesme Mah. Kalender Sok. 16, 34590 Yenibosna, İstanbul; tel. (212) 5524057; fax (212) 4541456; e-mail newssales@cihan.com.tr; internet www.cihanmedia.com; f. 1992; part of Feza Media Corpn; Production Man. ZEKI SAATÇI.

Hürriyet Haber Ajansı: Hürriyet Medya Towers, Güneşli, 34544 İstanbul; tel. (212) 6770365; fax (212) 6770372; e-mail ucebeci@hurriyet.com.tr; f. 1963; Dir-Gen. UĞUR ÇEBECI.

İKA Haber Ajansı (Economic and Commercial News Agency): Atatürk Bul. 199/A-45, Kavaklıdere, Ankara; tel. (312) 1267327; f. 1954; Dir ZIYA TANSU.

Milha News Agency: Doğan Medya Center, Bağcılar, 34554 İstanbul; tel. (212) 5056111; fax (212) 5056233.

TEBA—Türk Ekonomik Basın Ajansı (Turkish Economic Press Agency): Süleyman Hacı Abdullahoğlu Cad. 5, D3 Balgat, Ankara; tel. (312) 2842006; fax (312) 2840638; e-mail teba@tebahaber.com.tr; internet www.tebahaber.com.tr; f. 1981; private economic news service; Propr ORHAN TOLUN; Editor YAVUZ TOLUN.

TURKEY

Ulusal Basın Ajansı (UBA): Meşrutiyet Cad. 5/10, Ankara; Man. Editor OĞUZ SEREN.

JOURNALISTS' ASSOCIATION

Türkiye Gazeteciler Cemiyeti: Türkocağı Cad. 1, Cağaloğlu, İstanbul; tel. (212) 5138300; fax (212) 5268046; e-mail tgc@tgc.org.tr; internet www.tgc.org.tr; f. 1946; Pres. ORHAN ERİNÇ; Sec. RIDVAN YELE.

Publishers

Altın Kitaplar Yayınevi Anonim ŞTİ: Celal Ferdi Gökçay Sok., Nebioğlu Han, Kat. 1, Cağaloğlu, İstanbul; tel. (212) 5268012; fax (212) 5268011; e-mail info@altinkitaplar.com.tr; internet www.altinkitaplar.com.tr; f. 1959; fiction, non-fiction, biography, children's books, encyclopaedias, dictionaries; Publrs FETHI UL, TURHAN BOZKURT; Chief Editor MÜRSIT UL.

Arkadas Co Ltd: Yuva Mah. 3702, Sok. 4, Yenimahalle, Ankara; tel. (312) 3946270; fax (312) 3946285; e-mail info@arkadas.com.tr; internet www.arkadas.com.tr; f. 1980; fiction, educational and reference books; Gen. Man. CUMHUR OZDEMIR.

Arkeoloji ve Sanat Yayınları (Archaeology and Art Publications): Hayriye Cad. 3/4 Çorlu Apt., 34425 Beyoğlu, İstanbul; tel. (212) 2930378; fax (212) 2456877; e-mail info@arkeolojisanat.com; internet www.arkeolojisanat.com; f. 1978; classical, Byzantine and Turkish studies, art and archaeology, numismatics and ethnography books; Publr NEZIH BASGELEN; Senior Editor BRIAN JOHNSON.

Bilgi Yayınevi: Meşrutiyet Cad. 46/A, Yenişehir, 06420 Ankara; tel. (312) 4318122; fax (312) 4317758; e-mail info@bilgiyayinevi.com.tr; internet www.bilgiyayinevi.com.tr.

Doğan Burda Derg: Hürriyet Medya Towers, 34212 Güneşli, İstanbul; tel. (212) 4103571; fax (212) 4103581; e-mail dalan@doganburda.com; internet www.doganburda.com; Gen. Man. MEHMET ALI YALÇINDAĞ.

IKI NOKTA (Research Press & Publications Industry & Trade Ltd): Eğitim M. Kasap İsmail S. Öğün İş Merkezi 5/2, 34722 Kadıköy, İstanbul; tel. (216) 3490141; fax (216) 3376756; e-mail info@ikinokta.com.tr; internet www.ikinokta.com; humanities; Pres. YÜCEL YAMAN.

Iletisim Yayınları: Binbirdirek Meydanı Sok., Iletisim Han 7/2, 34122 Cağaloğlu, İstanbul; tel. (212) 5162260; fax (212) 5161258; e-mail iletisim@iletisim.com.tr; internet www.iletisim.com.tr; f. 1984; fiction, non-fiction, encyclopaedias, reference; Gen. Man. NIHAT TUNA.

Inkilap Kitabevi: Çobançeşme Mah. Altay Sok. 8 Yenibosna, İstanbul; tel. (212) 4961111; fax (212) 4961112; e-mail posta@inkilap.com; internet www.inkilap.com; f. 1935; general reference and fiction; Man. Dir A. FIKRI; Dir of Foreign Rights S. DIKER.

Kabalci Yayınevi: Ankara Cad. 47, Cağaloğlu, İstanbul; tel. (212) 5226305; fax (212) 5268495; e-mail info@kabalci.com.tr; internet www.kabalci.com.tr; art, history, literature, social sciences; Pres. SABRI KABALCI.

Metis Yayınları: Ipek Sok. 5, 34433 Beyoğlu, İstanbul; tel. (212) 2454696; fax (212) 2454519; e-mail rights@metisbooks.com; internet www.metisbooks.com; f. 1982; fiction, literature, non-fiction, social sciences; Dir SEMIH SÖKMEN.

Nobel Medical Publishing: Millet Cad. 111 Çapa, İstanbul; tel. (212) 6328333; fax (212) 5870217; e-mail destek@nobeltip.com; internet kurumsal.nobeltip.com; f. 1974; medical books and journals; CEO RIFKI BIROĞLU; Dir ERSAL BINGÖL.

Nurdan Yayınları Sanayi ve Ticaret Ltd Sti; Prof. Kâzim Ismail Gürkan Cad. 13, Kati 1, 34410 Cağaloğlu, İstanbul; tel. (212) 5225504; fax (212) 5125186; e-mail nurdan@nurdan.com.tr; internet www.nurdan.com.tr; f. 1980; children's and educational; Dir NURDAN TÜZÜNER.

Parantez Yayınları AŞ: Istikal Cad. 212 Alt Kat 8, Beyoğlu, İstanbul; tel. and fax (212) 2528567; e-mail parantez@parantez.net; internet www.parantez.net; f. 1991; Publr METIN ZEYNIOĞLU.

Payel Yayınevi: Cağaloğlu Yokusu Evren han Kat 3/51, 34400 Cağaloğlu, İstanbul; tel. (212) 5284409; fax (212) 5124353; f. 1966; science, history, literature; Editor AHMET ÖZTÜRK.

Remzi Kitabevi AŞ: Akmerkez E3 Blok Kat. 14, Etiler, İstanbul; tel. (212) 2822080; fax (212) 2822090; e-mail post@remzi.com.tr; internet www.remzi.com.tr; f. 1927; general and educational; Dirs EROL ERDURAN, ÖMER ERDURAN, AHMET ERDURAN.

Seckin Yayınevi: Saglik Sok. 19B, 06410 Sihhiye, Ankara; tel. (312) 4353030; fax (312) 4355088; e-mail satis@seckin.com.tr; internet www.seckin.com.tr; f. 1959; accounting, computer science, economics, law; Dir KORAY SEÇKIN.

Türk Dil Kurumu (Turkish Language Institute): Atatürk Bul. 217, 06680 Kavaklıdere, Ankara; tel. (312) 4286100; fax (312) 4285288; e-mail bilgi@tdk.org.tr; internet tdk.gov.tr; f. 1932; non-fiction, research, language; Pres. Prof. Dr ŞÜKRÜ HALUK AKALIN.

Varlık Yayınları AŞ: Ayberk Ap. Piyerloti Cad. 7–9, Çemberlitaş, 34400 İstanbul; tel. (212) 5162004; fax (212) 5162005; e-mail varlik@varlik.com.tr; internet www.varlik.com.tr; f. 1933; fiction and non-fiction books, and cultural monthly review; Dirs FILIZ NAYIR DENIZTEKIN, OSMAN DENIZTEKIN.

GOVERNMENT PUBLISHING HOUSE

Ministry of Culture and Tourism: Directorate of Publications, Necatibey Cad. 55, 06440 Kızılay, Ankara; tel. (312) 2315450; fax (312) 2315036; e-mail yayimlar@kutuphanelergm.gov.tr; internet www.kultur.gov.tr; f. 1973; Dir ALI OSMAN GÜZEL.

PUBLISHERS' ASSOCIATION

Türkiye Yayıncılar Birliği Derneği (Publishers' Association of Turkey): Kazım Ismail Gürkan Cad. 12/3, Ortaklar Han, 34440 Cağaloğlu, İstanbul; tel. (212) 5125602; fax (212) 5117794; e-mail info@turkyaybir.org.tr; internet www.turkyaybir.org.tr; f. 1985; Pres. ÇETIN TÜZÜNER; Sec. METIN CELÂL ZEYNIOĞLU; 230 mems.

Broadcasting and Communications

TELECOMMUNICATIONS

Regulatory Authorities

Bilgi Teknolojileri ve İletişim Kurumu (Information and Communication Technologies Authority): Yeşilırmak Sok., 16 Demirtepe, 06430 Ankara; tel. (312) 2947400; fax (312) 2947145; e-mail info@tk.gov.tr; internet www.tk.gov.tr; f. 2000; Chair. Dr TAYFUN ACARER.

General Directorate of Communications: Hakkı Turayliç Cad. 5 Kat 7–8, Emek, Ankara; tel. (312) 2031000; fax (312) 2121775; e-mail soytas@ubak.opr.tr; internet www.ubak.gov.tr/tr/hgm; Dir-Gen. ALI ZOR.

Principal Operators

Turkcell: Mesrutiyet Cad. 71, 34430 Tepebaşi, İstanbul; tel. (212) 3131000; fax (212) 2925393; e-mail musteri.hizmetleri@turkcell.com.tr; internet www.turkcell.com.tr; provides mobile cellular services; 40.3% held by the Cukurova Group, 37.1% by Sonera Holding; 35.1m. subscribers at March 2008; Chair. MEHMET EMIN KARAMEHMET; CEO SÜREYYA CILIV.

Türksat AŞ: Konya Yolu 40 km, Gölbaşı, Ankara; tel. (312) 6153000; fax (312) 4995115; e-mail info@turksat.com.tr; internet www.turksat.com.tr.

Turk Telekom: İstanbul; tel. (212) 3493939; fax (212) 3529499; e-mail iletisim@turktelekom.com.tr; internet www.turktelekom.com.tr; 55% owned by Oger Telecoms Joint Venture Group; Chair. Dr PAUL DOANY.

BROADCASTING

Regulatory Authority

Radyo ve Televizyon Üst Kurulu (RTÜK) (Radio and Television Supreme Council): Bilkent Plaza B2 Blok, Bilkent, 06530 Ankara; tel. (312) 2975000; fax (312) 2661985; e-mail rtuk@rtuk.org.tr; internet www.rtuk.org.tr; f. 1994; responsible for assignment of channels, frequencies and bands, controls transmitting facilities of radio stations and TV networks, draws up regulations on related matters, monitors broadcasting and issues warnings in case of violation of the Broadcasting law; Pres. ZAHID AKMAN.

Radio

Türkiye Radyo ve Televizyon Kurumu (TRT) (Turkish Radio and Television Corpn): Turan Güneş Bul., 06450 Oran, Ankara; tel. (312) 4904300; fax (312) 4912817; e-mail aktifhat@trt.net.tr; internet www.trt.net.tr; f. 1964; controls Turkish radio and television services, incl. four national radio channels; Dir-Gen. İBRAHIM ŞAHIN; Head of Radio ÇETIN TEZCAN.

Voice of Turkey: PK 333, 06443 Yenişehir, Ankara; tel. (312) 4909800; fax (312) 4909845; e-mail tsr@trt.net.tr; internet www.trt.net.tr/wwwtrt/tsr.aspx; f. 1937; external service of the TRT; Head of External Service OSMAN DILEKCI.

There are also more than 50 local radio stations, an educational radio service for schools and a station run by the Turkish State Meteorological Service. The US forces have their own radio and television service.

TURKEY   Directory

Television

Türkiye Radyo ve Televizyon Kurumu (TRT): (Turkish Radio and Television Corpn): Oran Sitesi Turan Güneş Bul. A Block Kat 6, 06450 Oran, Ankara; tel. (212) 2597275; e-mail aktifhat@trt.net.tr; internet www.trt.net.tr; four national, one regional and two international channels in 2008; launched a new Kurdish-language channel in January 2009; Dir-Gen. İBRAHIM ŞAHIN; Head of Television NILGÜN ARTUN; Dir Ankara TV GÜRKAN ELÇI.

As of 2008 there were 23 national, 16 regional and 212 local terrestrial television broadcasters. There are also cable and satellite channels. Digitürk is the main satellite pay-TV platform, with 1.1m. subscribers in 2006.

Finance

(cap. = capital; res = reserves; dep. = deposits; m. = million; brs = branches; amounts in new Turkish liras unless otherwise indicated; note: figures have been converted retrospectively to reflect the introduction on 1 January 2005 of the new unit of currency, equivalent to 1,000,000 of the old Turkish lira)

The Central Bank of the Republic of Turkey (Türkiye Cumhuriyet Merkez Bankası AŞ) was founded in 1931, and constituted in its present form in 1970. The Central Bank is the bank of issue and is also responsible for the execution of monetary and credit policies, the regulation of the foreign and domestic value of the Turkish lira jointly with the Government, and the supervision of the credit system. In 1987 a decree was issued to bring the governorship of the Central Bank under direct government control. In 2001 the Central Bank was granted policy independence.

In June 1999 an independent supervisory body, the Regulatory and Supervisory Board for Banking, was established by law to monitor the financial sector. The treasury, the Ministry of Finance, the Central Bank, the state planning organization, the Capital Markets Board and the Banks' Association of Turkey were each to nominate one member to the Board for a six-year term. The Board was operational from mid-2000. Other legislation passed in June 1999 incorporated core principles of the Basle Committee on Banking Supervision relating to risk-based capital requirements, loan administration procedures, auditing practices and credit risk issues.

The largest of the private-sector Turkish banks is the Türkiye İş Bankası AŞ, which operates 918 branches in the country.

There are several credit institutions in Turkey, including the Türkiye Sınai Kalınma Bankası AŞ (Industrial Development Bank of Turkey), which was founded in 1950, with the assistance of the World Bank, to encourage private investment in industry by acting as underwriter in the issue of share capital.

There are numerous co-operative organizations, including agricultural co-operatives in rural areas. There are also a number of savings institutions.

In 1990 the Turkish Government announced plans to establish a structure for offshore banking. A decree issued in October of that year exempted foreign banks, operating in six designated free zones, from local banking obligations.

At the end of 1999 the number of banks operating in Turkey (excluding the Central Bank) totalled 81, of which seven were state owned. Following a number of liquidations, mergers and acquisitions in the banking system after 2000, the number of banks had been reduced to 48 by the end of 2004. By March 2008 this number had been further reduced, to 46. Of this total, 13 were development and investment banks; the number of state-owned banks had been reduced to three, with the control of Birleşik Fon Bankası AŞ (formerly Bayindirbank) passing to the Savings Deposit Insurance Fund. There were 11 private commercial banks and 18 foreign-owned banks.

BANKING

Regulatory Authority

Bancacılık Düzenleme ve Denetleme Kurumu (BDDK) (Banking Regulation and Supervisory Agency): Atatürk Bul. 191, 06680 Kavaklidere, Ankara; tel. (312) 4556500; fax (312) 4240879; e-mail bilgi@bddk.org.tr; internet www.bddk.org.tr; Chair. TEVFIK BILGIN.

Central Bank

Türkiye Cumhuriyet Merkez Bankası AŞ (Central Bank of the Republic of Turkey): Head Office, İstiklal Cad. 10 Uluş, 06100 Ankara; tel. (312) 3103646; fax (312) 3107434; e-mail iletisimbilgi@tcmb.gov.tr; internet www.tcmb.gov.tr; f. 1931; bank of issue; cap. 46.2m., res 779.5m., dep. 84,232.3m. (Dec. 2006); Gov. DURMUŞ YILMAZ; 21 brs.

State Banks

Türkiye Cumhuriyeti Ziraat Bankası (Agricultural Bank of the Turkish Republic): Doğanbey Mah., Atatürk Bul. 8, 06107 Uluş, Ankara; tel. (312) 5842000; fax (312) 5844053; e-mail zbmail@ziraatbank.com.tr; internet www.ziraat.com.tr; f. 1863; absorbed Türkiye Emlâk Bankası AŞ (Real Estate Bank of Turkey) in July 2001; cap. 2,221.9m., res 2,257.4m., dep. 60,620.8m. (Dec. 2006); Chair. Prof. Dr İLHAN ULUDAĞ; Gen. Man. CAN AKIN ÇAĞLAR; 1,177 brs in Turkey, 9 brs abroad.

Türkiye Halk Bankası AŞ: Esikişehir Yolu, 2 Cad. 63, Söğütözü, 06520 Ankara; tel. (312) 2892000; fax (312) 2893575; e-mail info@halkbank.com.tr; internet www.halkbank.com.tr; f. 1938; absorbed Türkiye Öğretmenler Bankası TAŞ in 1992; acquired 96 brs of Türkiye Emlak Bankası in 2001; merged with Pamukbank TAŞ in 2004; cap. 1,250.0m., res 1,666.3m., dep. 27,897.7m. (Dec. 2006); Chair. HASAN CEBECI; Gen. Man. HÜSEYIN AYDIN; 586 brs in Turkey, 2 brs abroad.

Türkiye Vakıflar Bankası TAO (Vakifbank) (Foundation Bank of Turkey): Camlik Cad. Cayir Cimen Sok. 2, 34330 1 Levent, İstanbul; tel. (212) 3167116; fax (212) 3167126; e-mail international@vakifbank.com.tr; internet www.vakifbank.com.tr; f. 1954; cap. 2,500.0m., res 1,219.0m., dep. 26,651.3m. (Dec. 2006); Chair. YUSUF BEYAZIT; Gen. Man. BILAL KARAMAN; 302 brs in Turkey, 1 br. abroad.

Principal Commercial Banks

Akbank TAŞ: Sabancı Center, 34330 4 Levent, 80745 İstanbul; tel. (212) 3855555; fax (212) 2697787; e-mail investor.relations@akbank.com; internet www.akbank.com; f. 1948; absorbed Ak Uluslararası Bankası AŞ in Sept. 2005; 20% owned by Citigroup; cap. 2,200.0m., res 3,302.3m., dep. 41,303.2m. (Dec. 2006); Chair. SUZAN SABANCI DINÇER; Pres. and CEO ZAFER KURTUL; 715 brs in Turkey, 2 brs abroad.

Alternatifbank AŞ: Cumhuriyet Cad. 22–24, Elmadağ, 34367 İstanbul; tel. (212) 3156500; fax (212) 2331500; e-mail kalite@abank.com.tr; internet www.abank.com.tr; f. 1991; 95.6% owned by Anadolu Group; cap. 224.3m., res –45.7m., dep. 1,162.5m. (Dec. 2006); Chair. TUNCAY ÖZILHAN; CEO MURAT ARIĞ; 42 brs.

ING Bank: Eski Büyükdere Cad., Ayazaga Köyyolu 6, Maslak, 34398 İstanbul; tel. and fax (212) 4440600; internet www.ingbank.com.tr; f. 1990; fmrly Oyak Bank; owned by ING Groep NV (Netherlands); cap. 1,074.1m., res 62.9m., dep. 9,716.3m. (Dec. 2007); Chair. JOHN T. MCCARTHY; Gen. Man. HAKAN EMINSOY; 365 brs in Turkey, 1 br. in Bahrain.

Şekerbank TAŞ: Büyükdere Cad. 171, Metrocity İş Merkezi, A-Blok 34330 1 Levent, İstanbul; tel. (212) 3440737; fax (212) 3197162; e-mail intdiv@sekerbank.com.tr; internet www.sekerbank.com.tr; f. 1953; cap. 125.0m., res 247.1m., dep. 3,446.2m. (Dec. 2006); 33.98% owned by TuranAlem Securities, Kazakhstan; Chair. HASAN BASRI GÖKTAN; Gen. Man. MERIÇ ULUŞAHIN; 203 brs.

Tekstilbank AŞ: Büyükdere Cad. 63, 34398 Maslak, İstanbul; tel. (212) 3355335; fax (212) 3281328; e-mail ir@tekstilbank.com.tr; internet www.tekstilbank.com.tr; f. 1986; cap. 300.0m., res 38.8m. dep. 1,792.1m. (Dec. 2006); 75.4% owned by GSD Holdings; Chair. and Gen. Man. ÇIM GÜZELAYDINLI; 60 brs.

Türk Ekonomi Bankası AŞ (TEB): Meclisi Mebusan Cad. 57, 34427 Fındıklı, İstanbul; tel. (212) 2512121; fax (212) 2525058; internet www.teb.com.tr; f. 1927; fmrly Kocaeli Bankası TAŞ; jt venture between Colakoğlu Group and BNP Paribas SA; dep. $6,014m.; total assets $10,019m. (Dec. 2007); Chair. YAVUZ CANEVI; CEO and Gen. Man. VAROL CIVIL; 275 brs.

Türkiye Garanti Bankası AŞ (Garantibank): Nispetiye Mah, Aytar Cad. 2, 34340 Levent Beşiktaş, İstanbul; tel. and fax (212) 3181818; fax (212) 3181888; e-mail mutlus@garanti.com.tr; internet www.garantibank.com; f. 1946; owned by Doğuş Group; cap. 2,100.0m., res 1,551.3m., dep. 39,335.4m. (Dec. 2006); Chair. FERIT FAIK ŞAHENK; Pres., CEO and Gen. Man. ERGUN ÖZEN; 487 brs in Turkey, 5 brs abroad.

Türkiye İş Bankası AŞ (İşbank): İş Kuleleri, 34330 Levent, İstanbul; tel. (212) 3160000; fax (212) 3160900; e-mail halkla.iliskiler@isbank.com.tr; internet www.isbank.com.tr; f. 1924; cap. 9,449m., res 3,100m., dep. 63,539m. (Dec. 2008); Chair. CANER ÇIMENBIÇER; CEO and Gen. Man. H. ERSIN ÖZINCE; 1035 brs in Turkey, 11 abroad.

Yapı ve Kredi Bankası AŞ: Yapı Kredi Plaza, Blok D, 80620 İstanbul; tel. (212) 3397000; fax (212) 3396000; internet www.ykb.com.tr; f. 1944; cap. 3,082.3m., res 83.9m., dep. 36,695.6m. (Dec. 2006); merged with Koçbank AŞ in 2006; CEO and Gen. Man. TAYFUN BAYAZIT; COO ALESSANDRO DECIO; 415 brs.

TURKEY

Development and Investment Banks

İller Bankasi Genel Müdürülügü: Atatürk Bul. 21, 06053 Opera, Ankara; tel. (312) 5087000; fax (312) 5087399; e-mail ilbank@ilbank.gov.tr; internet www.ilbank.gov.tr; CEO HIDAYET ATASOY; 19 brs.

Türkiye Kalkınma Bankası (Development Bank of Turkey): İzmir Cad. 35, 06440 Kızılay Ankara; tel. (312) 4179200; fax (312) 4183967; e-mail tkbhaberlesme@tkb.com.tr; internet www.tkb.com.tr; cap. 160.0m., res 221.5m., dep. 4.5m. (Dec. 2006); Chair. and Gen. Dir ABDULLAH ÇELIK.

Türkiye Sınai Kalkınma Bankası AŞ (Industrial Development Bank of Turkey): Meclisi Mebusan Cad. 81, Findikli, 34427 İstanbul; tel. (212) 3345050; fax (212) 3345234; e-mail info@tskb.com.tr; internet www.tskb.com; f. 1950; cap. 300.0m., res 182.1m., dep. 481.3m. (Dec. 2006); Chair. CAHIT KOCAÖMER; CEO and Pres. HALIL EROĞLU; 2 brs.

Savings Deposit Insurance Fund Bank

Birleşik Fon Bankasi AŞ: Büyükdere Cad. 143, 34394 Esentepe, İstanbul; tel. (212) 3401000; fax (212) 3473217; e-mail callcenter@fonbank.com.tr; internet www.fonbank.com.tr; fmrly Bayindirbank; name changed as above 2005; control passed to Savings Deposit Insurance Fund in 2001.

Banking Organization

Banks' Association of Turkey: Nıspetıye Cad. Akmerkez B3 Blok. Kat 13–14, 34340 Etiler, İstanbul; tel. (212) 2820973; fax (212) 2820946; e-mail gensek@tbb.org.tr; internet www.tbb.org.tr; f. 1958; Chair. ERSIN ÖZINCE; Sec.-Gen. Dr EKREM KESKIN.

STOCK EXCHANGE

İstanbul Menkul Kıymetler Borsası (İMKB): Resitpaşa Mah., Tuncay Artun Cad., 34467 Emirgan, İstanbul; tel. (212) 2982100; fax (212) 2982500; e-mail info@ise.org; internet www.ise.org; f. 1866; revived in 1986 after being dormant for about 60 years; 104 mems of stock market, 132 mems of bond and bills market (April 2008); Chair. and CEO HÜSEYIN ERKAN; Senior Vice-Chair. ARIL SEREN.

INSURANCE

AKSigorta: Meclis-i Mebusan Cad. 147 Fındıklı, 34427 İstanbul; tel. (212) 3934300; fax (212) 3343900; e-mail info@aksigorta.com.tr; internet www.aksigorta.com.tr; f. 1960; Chair. M. AKIN KOZANOĞLU; Gen. Man. I. RAGIP YERGIN.

Anadolu Sigorta TAŞ (Anadolu Insurance Co): Büyükdere Cad. İş Kuleleri Kule 2 Kat. 23–26 34330 4 Levent, İstanbul; tel. (212) 3500350; fax (212) 3500355; e-mail bilgi@anadolusigorta.com.tr; internet www.anadolusigorta.com.tr; f. 1925; Chair. BURHAN KARAGÖZ; CEO MUSTAFA ALI SU.

Ankara Sigorta TAŞ (Ankara Insurance Co): Bankalar Cad. 80, 34420 Karaköy, İstanbul; tel. (212) 2521010; fax (212) 3104649; internet www.ankarasigorta.com.tr; f. 1936; Chair. ÖZKAN ELGIN; Gen. Man. ŞABAN ÇAĞIRAN (acting).

AXA Sigorta AŞ: Meclis-i Mebusan Cad. Oyak İş Hanı 15, 34427 Salıpazarı, İstanbul; tel. (212) 3342424; fax (212) 2521515; e-mail iletisim@axasigorta.com.tr; internet www.axasigorta.com.tr; Chair.and CEO HAKKI CEMAL ERERDI; 10 brs.

Başak Groupama Sigorta AŞ: Eski Büyükdere Cad. 2, 34398 Maslak, İstanbul; tel. (212) 3676767; fax (212) 3676868; e-mail sigorta@basakgroupama.com.tr; internet www.basakgroupama.com.tr; Gen. Man. ENIS BASIM.

Ergoisviçre Sigorta AŞ: Kısıklı Cad. 30, Altunizade 34662, İstanbul; tel. (216) 5548100; fax (216) 4741387; e-mail ergoisvicre@ergoisvicre.com.tr; internet www.ergoisvicre.com.tr; f. 1926 as La Suisse Umum Sigorta, acquired by İsviçre in 1981; jt venture between Ergo and Isviçre in 2006; fire, accident, marine, engineering, agricultural; Chair. OKAN BALCI; Gen. Man. MURAT BALCI; 11 regional brs.

Eureko Sigorta: Büyükdere Cad., Nurol Plaza 71, 34398 Maslak İstanbul; tel. (212) 3931000; fax (212) 2854424; e-mail esmusterihizmetleri@eurekosigorta.com.tr; internet www.eurekosigorta.com.tr; f. 1989 as Garanti Sigorta; renamed as above in Oct. 2007; 80% owned by Eureko BV (Netherlands) and 20% by Türkiye Garanti Bankasi AŞ; Chair. ERGUN ÖZEN; CEO OKAN UTKUERI.

Fiba Sigorta AS: Rüzgalıbahçe Mah. Cumhuriyet Cad. Acarlar İş Merkezi 12 C Blok, 34805 Kavacık, Beykoz İstanbul; tel. (216) 5386000; fax (216) 5386290; e-mail info@fibasigorta.com.tr; internet www.fibasigorta.com.tr; Pres. YENER DINÇMEN.

Güneş Sigorota: Güneş Plaza, Büyükdere Cad. 110, 34394 Esentepe-Şişli, İstanbul; tel. (212) 4441957; fax (212) 3556464; e-mail gunes@gunessigorta.com.tr; internet www.gunessigorta.com.tr; f. 1957; Chair. BILAL KARAMAN; Gen. Man. MEHMET İLKER AVCI.

Güven Sigorta TAŞ: Bankalar Cad. 81, 34420 Karaköy, İstanbul; tel. (212) 3135555; fax (212) 2378085; e-mail info@guvensigorta.com.tr; internet www.guvensigorta.com.tr; f. 1924; owned by Turkish Agricultural Credit Co-operatives Central Union; all brs of insurance; Gen. Man. BÜLENT SOMUNCU.

Hür Sigorta AŞ: Büyükdere Cad., Hür Han 15/A, 80260 Şişli, İstanbul; tel. (212) 2322010; fax (212) 2463673; e-mail hursigorta@hursigorta.com.tr; internet www.hursigorta.com.tr; Chair. BÜLENT SEMILER; Gen. Man. GÜNER YALÇINER.

Işik Sigorta AŞ: Küçüksu Cad. Akçakoca Sok. 6 Kat 2, 34768 Ümraniye, İstanbul; tel. (216) 6337100; fax (216) 6318448; e-mail bilgi@isiksigorta.com.tr; internet www.isiksigorta.com; Chair. TAHSIN TEKOĞLU.

Koç Allianz Sigorta AŞ: Bağlarbaşı, Kısıklı Cad. 11, 34662 Altunizade, İstanbul; tel. (216) 5566666; fax (216) 5566777; e-mail info@kocallianz.com.tr; internet www.kocallianz.com.tr; f. 1923; 82.4% owned by Allianz; Chair. RAHMI M. KOÇ; CEO GEORGE D. SARTOREL.

Liberty Sigorta AŞ: Meclisi Mebusan Cad. 21, Karaköy, İstanbul; tel. (212) 2514035; fax (212) 2491046; e-mail halklailiskiler@libertysigorta.com.tr; internet www.libertysigorta.com.tr; f. 1954 as Şeker Sigorta AŞ; renamed as above in 2006; 90.43% owned by Liberty Mutual Group (USA); Gen. Man. Dr MUSTAFA AKAN.

Milli Reasürans TAŞ: Teşvikiye Cad. 35A–B, 34367 Teşvikiye, İstanbul; tel. (212) 2314730; fax (212) 2308608; e-mail info@millire.com; internet www.millire.com; f. 1929; premium income 838.2m., total assets 1,222.9m. (Dec. 2007); Chair. CANER ÇIMENBIÇER; Dir and Gen. Man. CAHIT NOMER.

Ray Sigorta: Haydar Aliyev Cad. 35, Tarabya 34457 Sarıyer, İstanbul; tel. (212) 3632500; fax (212) 2994849; e-mail info@raysigorta.com.tr; internet www.raysigorta.com.tr; f. 1958; Doğan Group is major shareholder.

Türkiye Genel Sigorta AŞ: Meclisi Mebusan Cad. 25, 34433 Salıpazarı, İstanbul; tel. (212) 3349000; fax (212) 3349019; e-mail genel@genelsigorta.com; internet www.genelsigorta.com; f. 1948; 80% owned by Mapfre Internacional (Spain); Chair. ANGEL ALONSO BATRES; Gen. Man. HULUSI TAŞKIRAN.

Yapi Kredi Sigorta AŞ: Yapi Kredi Plaza, A Blok, Büyükdere Cad., 34330 Levent, İstanbul; tel. (212) 3360606; fax (212) 3360808; e-mail yksigorta@yksigorta.com.tr; internet www.yksigorta.com.tr; f. 1944; Chair. TAYFUN BAYAZIT; Gen. Man. MURAT GÜVENEL.

Zurich Sigorta: Meclis-i Mebusan Cad. 47/6, 34427 Findikli, İstanbul; tel. (212) 3931600; fax (212) 2928761; e-mail info@zurichsigorta.com.tr; internet www.zurichsigorta.com.tr; fmrly TEB Sigorta; owned by Zurich Financial Services Group (Switzerland); Chair. ANNETTE ELIZABETH COURT; Gen. Man. ALI ERTUĞRUL BUL.

Trade and Industry

GOVERNMENT AGENCIES

Özelleştirme İdaresi Başkanlığı (OIB) (Privatization Administration): Ziya Gökalp Cad. 80, Kurtuluş Ankara; tel. (312) 4304560; fax (312) 4403271; e-mail info@oib.gov.tr; internet www.oib.gov.tr; co-ordinates privatization programme; Pres. METIN KILCI.

Rekabet Kurumu (Turkish Competition Authority): Bilkent Plaza B3 Blok PK, 06800 Bilkent, Ankara; tel. (312) 2914444; fax (312) 2667920; e-mail rek@rekabet.gov.tr; internet www.rekabet.gov.tr; f. 1997; prevents restriction of competition, oversees mergers and monitors state aid; Pres. and Chair. Prof. Dr NURETTIN KALDIRIMCI.

DEVELOPMENT ORGANIZATION

Turkish Atomic Energy Authority: Prime Minister's Office, Eskişehir Yolu 9km, 06530 Lodumlu, Ankara; tel. (312) 2958700; fax (312) 2878761; e-mail bilgi_taek@taek.gov.tr; internet www.taek.gov.tr; f. 1956; controls the development of peaceful uses of atomic energy; 11 mems; Pres. OKAY ÇAKIROĞLU; Vice-Pres. ALI ALAT.

CHAMBERS OF COMMERCE AND INDUSTRY

Union of Chambers and Commodity Exchanges of Turkey (UCCET) (Türkiye Odalar Borsalar Birliği—TOBB): Atatürk Bul. 149, 06640 Bakanlıklar, Ankara; tel. (312) 4138000; fax (312) 4183268; e-mail info@tobb.org.tr; internet www.tobb.org.tr; f. 1950; represents 364 chambers and commodity exchanges; Pres. RIFAT HISARCIKLIOĞLU.

Ankara Chamber of Commerce (Ankasa Tabip Odasi—ATO): Mithatpaşa Cad. 62/18 Kızılay, 06420 Ankara; tel. (312) 4188700; fax (312) 4187794; e-mail ato@ato.org.tr; internet www.ato.org.tr; Pres. GÜLRIZ ERSÖZ.

Ankara Chamber of Industry: Atatürk Bul. 193, Kavaklıdere, Ankara; tel. (312) 4171200; fax (312) 4175205; e-mail dim@aso.org.tr;

TURKEY
Directory

internet www.aso.org.tr; f. 1963; Chair. TARIK ARTUMAÇ; Dir M. NURETTIN ÖZDEBIR.

İstanbul Chamber of Commerce (ICOC): Reşadiye Cad. 34112 Eminönü, İstanbul; tel. (212) 4556000; fax (212) 5131565; e-mail ito@ito.org.tr; internet www.ito.org.tr; f. 1882; more than 300,000 mems; Pres. MURAT YALÇINTAŞ.

İstanbul Chamber of Industry: Meşrutiyet Cad. 62, 34430 Tepebaşı, İstanbul; tel. (212) 2522900; fax (212) 2495084; e-mail info@iso.org.tr; internet www.iso.org.tr; f. 1952; more than 12,500 mems (2006); Chair. C. TANIL KÜÇÜK; Gen. Sec. METE MELEKSOY.

İzmir Chamber of Commerce: Atatürk Cad. 126, 35210 İzmir; tel. (232) 4449292; fax (232) 4984698; e-mail info@izto.org.tr; internet www.izto.org.tr; f. 1885; Pres. EKREM DEMIRTAŞ; Sec.-Gen. ADNAN YILDIRIM.

EMPLOYERS' ASSOCIATIONS

Türk Sanayicileri ve İşadamları Derneği (TÜSİAD) (Turkish Industrialists' and Businessmen's Association): Meşrutiyet Cad. 74, 34420 Tepebaşı, İstanbul; tel. (212) 2495448; fax (212) 2933783; e-mail tusiad@tusiad.org; internet www.tusiad.org; f. 1971; 451 mems; Chair. ARZUHAN YALÇINDAĞ; Sec.-Gen. Dr HALUK R. TÜKEL.

Türkiye İşveren Sendikaları Konfederasyonu (TİSK) (Turkish Confederation of Employer Associations): Hoşdere Cad. Reşat Nuri Sok. 108, 06540 Çankaya, Ankara; tel. (312) 4397717; fax (312) 4397592; e-mail tisk@tisk.org.tr; internet www.tisk.org.tr; f. 1962; represents (on national level) 22 employers' asscns, with 8,300 affiliated enterprises; official representative in labour relations; Pres. TUĞRUL KUDATGOBILIK; Sec.-Gen. BÜLENT PIRLER.

UTILITIES

In November 2007 the Ministry of Finance stated that it intended to implement the delayed privatization of Turkey's electricity distribution grid in 2008.

Electricity

Elektrik Üretim Anonim Şirketi (EÜAŞ) (Electricity Generation Co Inc): İnönü Bul. 27, Bahçelievler, 06490 Ankara; tel. (312) 2126900; fax (312) 2130103; e-mail basinhalk@euas.gov.tr; internet www.euas.gov.tr; f. 2001, following devolution of responsibilities of fmr Elektrik Üretim-İletim AŞ into separate entities for generation, transmission and wholesale activities; responsible for electricity generation; Gen. Man. SEFER BÜTÜN.

Türkiye Elektrik Iletim Anonim Şirketi (TEIAŞ) (Turkish Electricity Transmission Company): İnönü Bul. 27, Bahçelievler, 06490 Ankara; tel. (312) 2038000; fax (312) 2138870; internet www.teias.gov.tr; f. 2001 (see EÜAŞ, above); responsible for electricity transmission; Chair. and Gen. Man. İLHAMI ÖZŞAHIN.

Water

General Directorate of State Hydraulic Works (DSI): İnönü Bul., Yücetepe, 06100 Ankara; tel. (312) 4178300; fax (312) 4182498; e-mail idarim@dsi.gov.tr; internet www.dsi.gov.tr; f. 1953; controlled by the Ministry of Energy and Natural Resources; responsible for the planning and devt of water resources; Dir-Gen. HAYDAR KOÇAKER.

TRADE UNIONS

Confederations

DİSK (Türkiye Devrimci İşçi Sendikaları Konfederasyonu) (Confederation of Progressive Trade Unions of Turkey): Cad. Abide-I Hürriyet 117, Kat. 5-6-7, Şişli, İstanbul; tel. (212) 2910005; fax (212) 2342075; e-mail disk@disk.org.tr; internet www.disk.org.tr; f. 1967; member of ITUC, European Trade Union Confed. and Trade Union Advisory Cttee; 26 affiliated unions; Pres. SÜLEYMAN ÇELEBI; Sec.-Gen. TAYFUN GÖRGÜN.

Türk-İş (Türkiye İşçi Sendikaları Konfederasyonu Genel Başkanlığı) (Confederation of Turkish Trade Unions): Bayındır Sok 10, 06410 Kizilay, Ankara; tel. (312) 4333125; fax (312) 4336809; e-mail turkis@turkis.org.tr; internet www.turkis.org.tr; f. 1952; mem. of ITUC, European Trade Union Confed. and OECD/Trade Union Advisory Cttee; 32 national unions and federations with 1.7m. mems; Gen. Man. MUSTAFA KUMLU.

Principal DİSK Trade Unions

BASS (Türkiye Devrimci Banka ve Sigorta İşçileri Sendikası) (Bank and Insurance Employees Unionı): Sumer 2 Sok. 29 Kat. 4, 06640 Kizilay, Ankara; tel. (312) 2325009; fax (212) 2316730; e-mail bass-w@tr.net; internet www.bass-sen.org.tr; Pres. TURGUT YILMAZ; 15,000 mems.

Basın-İş (Türkiye Basın, Yayın, Grafiker ve Ambalaj İşçileri Sendikası) (Press, Publishing, Graphical and Packing Workers): Necatibey Cad., Hanimeli Sok. 26/7, 06430 Sihhiye, Ankara; tel. (312) 2302908; fax (312) 2294315; e-mail basinis@basin-is.org; internet www.basin-is.org; f. 1963; Pres. YAKUP AKKAYA; Gen. Sec. ISMAIL HAKKI KÜTÜKÇÜ; 5,000 mems.

Birlesik Metal-İs (Birlesik Metal İşçileri Sendikası): Tünel Yolu Cad. 2, 34744 Bostancı, Kadıköy, İstanbul; tel. (216) 3808590; fax (216) 3736502; e-mail info@birlesikmetal.org; internet www.birlesikmetal.org; Pres. ADNAN SERDAROĞLU; Gen. Sec. SELÇUK GÖKTAŞ; 58,800 mems.

Demiryol-İş (Türkiye Demiryolu İşçileri Sendikası) (Railway Workers): Necatibey Cad., Sezenler Sok 5, 06430 Yenişehir, Ankara; tel. (312) 2318029; fax (312) 2318032; e-mail demiryolis@demiryolis.org.tr; internet www.demiryolis.org.tr; f. 1952; Pres. ERGÜN ATALAY; Gen. Sec. HÜSEYIN KAYA; 25,000 mems.

Dev. Sağlık-İş (Türkiye Devrimci Sağlık İşçileri Sendikası) (Union of Progressive Health Employees): Millet Cad., Sadi Çeşme Sok. Başak İş Merkezi 25 Kat. 1, Aksaray, İstanbul; tel. (212) 5337719; fax (212) 6315904; e-mail bilgi@devsaglikis.org.tr; internet www.devsaglikis.org.tr; f. 1974; Pres. ARZU ÇERKEZOĞLU; Gen. Sec. TUFAN SERTLEK; 4,396 mems.

Genel-İş (Türkiye Genel Hizmet İşçileri Sendikası) (Municipal Workers): Çankırı Cad. 28, Kat. 5–9, Ulus, Ankara; tel. (312) 3091547; fax (312) 3091046; e-mail bilgi@genel-is.org.tr; internet www.genel-is.org.tr; f. 1983; Pres. EROL EKICI; Gen. Sec. KANI BEKO; 50,000 mems.

Gıda-İş (Türkiye Gıda Sanayii İşçileri Sendikası): Molla Şeref Mah. Ali Yeşim Sok. 13 D/5 Fındıkzade-Fatih, İstanbul; tel. (212) 5233620; fax (212) 5233621; e-mail disk_gidais@mynet.com; Pres. CELAL OVAT; Gen. Sec. SEYIT ASLAN; 31,000 mems.

Koop-İş (Türkiye Kooperatif ve Büro İşçileri Sendikası) (Co-operative and Office Workers): Özveren Sok. 6, Maltepe, Ankara; tel. (312) 2320910; fax (312) 2295836; e-mail bilgi@koopis.org.tr; internet www.koopis.org.tr; f. 1964; Pres. EYÜP ALEMDAR; Gen. Sec. AHMET GÜVEN; 29,000 mems.

Lastik-İş (Türkiye Petrol, Kimya ve Lastik Sanayii İşçileri Sendikası): Bulgurlu Mah. Üçpınarlar Cad. Enver Sok. 1 Rıza Kuas Merkez Binası, 34696 Üsküdar, İstanbul; tel. (216) 3390400; fax (216) 3392313; e-mail lastik-is@lastik-is.org.tr; internet www.lastik-is.org.tr; Pres. ABDULLAH KARACAN; Gen. Sec. NURI SERIM; 18,000 mems.

Limter-İş (Liman, Tersane Gemi Yapım Onarım İşçileri Sendikası) (Harbour, Shipyard, Ship Building and Repairs): Evliya Çelebi Mah. Deniz Sok. 1 K2 D3, Tuzla, İstanbul; tel. (216) 4467545; fax (216) 4467546; e-mail limteris@gmail.com; f. 1947; Pres. CEM DINÇ; Gen. Sec. ZAFER TEKTAŞ; 7,000 mems.

Nakliyat-İş (Nakliye İşçileri Sendikası) (Transportation Workers): Kemalpaşa Mah., Atatürk Bul. Emlak Kredi Bankası Blokları 146 B Blok Kat. 4 Daire 16, Eminönü, İstanbul; tel. (212) 5142671; fax (212) 5142669; e-mail nakliyatis@ttnet.net.tr; Pres. ALI RIZA KÜÇÜKOSMANOĞLU; Gen. Sec. YURDAL ŞENOL.

OLEYIS (Otel, Lokanta, Eğlence Yerleri İşçileri Sendikası) (Hotel, Restaurant and Places of Entertainment Workers): Cumhuriyet Cad. 37/4 Beyoğlu, İstanbul; tel. (212) 2356393; fax (212) 3615139; f. 1947; Pres. KAMER AKTAŞ; Gen. Sec. MEHMET EMIN ÜNAL; 4,000 mems.

Sosyal-İş (Türkiye Sosyal Sigortalar, Eğitim, Büro, Ticaret Kooperatif Banka ve Güzel Sanatlar İşçileri Sendikası) (Banking, Insurance and Trading): Mithatpaşa Cad. 56/10 Kızılay, Ankara; tel. (312) 4301773; fax (312) 4323963; e-mail sosyal-is@sosyal-is.org.tr; internet www.sosyal-is.org.tr; Pres. ÖZCAN KESGEÇ; Gen. Sec. TAMER ATIŞ; 31,000 mems.

Tekstil İşçileri Sendikası: M. Nezihi Özmen Mah., Akçay Sok. 22 D2 Güngören, İstanbul; tel. (212) 6372900; fax (212) 6372909; e-mail esgudum@disktekstil.org; internet www.disktekstil.org; Pres. SÜLEYMAN ÇELEBI; Gen. Sec. MUHARREM KILIÇ; 45,000 mems.

Tümka-İş (Türkiye Tüm Kağıt Selüloz Sanayii İşçileri Sendikası): Kınalıtepe Sok. Simitaş 4, Blok 16 D15, Merter, İstanbul; tel. (212) 6776334; fax (212) 5390551; internet www.tumkais.org; Pres. KEMAL YILMAZ; Gen. Sec. İLHAN ÖZEL; 3,000 mems.

Other Principal Trade Unions

Denizciler (Türkiye Denizciler Sendikası) (Seamen): Rıhtım Cad. Denizciler Sok. 5 Tophane, Karaköy, İstanbul; tel. (212) 2929081; fax (212) 2933938; e-mail kul@cakakul.av.tr; internet www.turkiyedenizcilersendikasi.org.tr; f. 1959; Pres. TURHAN UZUN; Gen. Sec. ŞÜKRÜ AKARDAŞ; 4,272 mems.

Fındık-İş (Fiskobirlik İşçileri Sendikası) (Hazelnut producers): Giresun; Pres. AKÇIN KOÇ; Gen. Sec. ERSAIT ŞEN.

Hava-İş (Türkiye Sivil Havacılık Sendikası) (Civil Aviation): İncirli Cad., Volkan Apt, 68/1 Bakırköy, İstanbul; tel. (212) 6602095; fax (212) 5719051; Pres. ATILAY AYÇIN; Gen. Sec. MUSTAFA YAĞCI; 11,200 mems.

Liman-İş (Türkiye Liman ve Kara Tahmil İşçileri Sendikası) (Longshoremen): Necatibey Cad., Sezenler Sok. 4, Kat. 5, Sıhhıye,

Ankara; tel. (312) 2317418; fax (312) 2302484; e-mail liman-is@tr-net.net.tr; f. 1963; Pres. Raif Kiliç; Gen. Sec. Erding Çakir; 5,000 mems.

Şeker-İş (Türkiye Şeker Sanayii İşçileri Sendikası) (Sugar Industry): Karanfil Sok. 59, Bakanlıklar, Ankara; tel. (312) 4184273; fax (312) 4259258; e-mail info@sekeris.org.tr; internet www.sekeris.org.tr; f. 1952; Pres. İsa Gök; Gen. Sec. Fethi Tekin; 35,000 mems.

Tarım-İş (Türkiye Orman, Topraksu, Tarım ve Tarım Sanayii İşçileri Sendikası) (Forestry, Agriculture and Agricultural Industry Workers): Bankacı Sok. 10, 06700 Kocatepe, Ankara; tel. (312) 4190456; fax (312) 4193113; e-mail info@tarimis.org.tr; internet www.tarimis.org.tr; f. 1961; Pres. Bedrettin Kaykaç; Gen. Sec. Mustafa Çardakçı; 15,000 mems.

Tekgıda-İş (Türkiye Tütün, Müskirat Gıda ve Yardımcı İşçileri Sendikası) (Tobacco, Drink, Food and Allied Workers): 4 Levent Konaklar Sok., İstanbul; tel. (212) 2644996; fax (212) 2789534; e-mail bilgi@tekgida.org.tr; internet www.tekgida.org.tr; f. 1952; Pres. Mustafa Türkel; Gen. Sec. Mecit Amaç; 176,000 mems.

Teksif (Türkiye Tekstil, Örme ve Giyim Sanayii İşçileri Sendikası Genel Merkezi) (Textile, Knitting and Clothing Workers' Union of Turkey): Ziya Gökalp Cad. Aydoğmuş Sok. 1, 06600 Ankara; tel. (312) 4312170; fax (312) 4357826; e-mail teksif@oda.net.tr; internet www.teksif.org.tr; f. 1951; Pres. Nazmi Irgat; Gen. Sec. Mehmet Çakan; 60,000 mems.

Tez-Koop-İş (Türkiye, Ticaret, Kooperatif, Eğitim, Büro ve Güzel Sanatlar İşçileri Sendikası) (Commercial and Clerical Employees): Üç Yıldız Cad. 29, Subayevleri, Ayınlıkevler, 06130 Ankara; tel. (312) 3183979; fax (312) 3183988; e-mail sendika@tezkoopis.org; internet www.tezkoopis.org.tr; f. 1962; Pres. Gürsel Doğru; Gen. Sec. Sedat Ölmez; 30,000 mems.

Türk Harb-İş (Türkiye Harb Sanayii ve Yardımcı İşkolları İşçileri Sendikası) (Defence Industry and Allied Workers): İnkılap Sok. 20, Kızılay, Ankara; tel. (312) 4175097; fax (312) 4171364; internet www.harb-is.org.tr; f. 1956; Pres. Ahmet Kalfa; Gen. Sec. Salim Tilkici; 25,000 mems.

Türk-Metal (Türkiye Metal, Çelik, Mühimmat, Makina ve Metalden Mamul, Eşya ve Oto, Montaj ve Yardımcı İşçileri Sendikası) (Auto, Metal and Allied Workers): Kızılırmak Mah., Adalararası Sok. 3, Eskişehir Yolu 1 km, 06560 Söğütözü, Ankara; tel. (312) 2926400; fax (312) 2844018; e-mail bilgiislem@turkmetal.org.tr; internet www.turkmetal.org.tr; f. 1963; Pres. Mustafa Özbek; Gen. Sec. Muharrem Aslıyüce; 247,000 mems.

Yol-İş (Türkiye Yol, Yapı ve İnşaat İşçileri Sendikası) (Road, Construction and Building Workers): Sümer 1 Sok. 18, Kızıloy, Ankara; tel. (312) 2324687; fax (312) 2324810; e-mail yildirimkoc@yol-is.org.tr; internet www.yol-is.org.tr; f. 1963; Pres. Fikret Barin; Gen. Sec. Tevfik Ozcelik; 70,000 mems.

Transport

RAILWAYS

The total length of the railways in operation within the national frontiers was 10,984 km in 2005, of which 8,697 km were main lines, 2,336 km were electrified and 3,111 km were signalled. There are direct rail links with Bulgaria to Iran and Syria. Construction of a new line connecting Turkey with Georgia and Azerbaijan commenced in late 2007, with an anticipated completion date of 2009/10. İstanbul operates an 18-km light railway system, and opened its first metro line in September 2000. Both systems are being expanded. Ankara and İzmir both operate metro railways.

Türkiye Cumhuriyeti Devlet Demiryolları İşletmesi Genel Müdürlüğü (TCDD) (Turkish State Railways): Talatpaşa Bul., 06330 Gar, Ankara; tel. (312) 3090515; fax (312) 3123215; e-mail tcddapk@tcdd.gov.tr; internet www.tcdd.gov.tr; f. 1924; operates all railways and connecting ports (see below) of the State Railway Administration, which acquired the status of a state economic enterprise in 1953, and a state economic establishment in 1984; 470 main-line diesel locomotives, 74 main-line electric locomotives, 965 passenger coaches and 16,070 freight wagons; Chair. of Bd and Gen. Dir Süleyman Karaman.

ROADS

In January 2008 the total road network was estimated at 63,899 km of classified roads, of which 1,987 km were motorways, 31,333 km were highways and 30,579 km were secondary roads.

Bayındırlık ve İskan Bakanlığı, Karayolları Genel Müdürlüğü (KGM) (General Directorate of Highways): İnönü Bul., Yücetepe, 06100 Ankara; tel. (312) 4157000; fax (312) 4186996; e-mail info@kgm.gov.tr; internet www.kgm.gov.tr; f. 1950; Dir-Gen. Mehmet Cahit Turhan.

SHIPPING

At the end of 2007 Turkey's merchant fleet comprised 1,252 vessels and had an aggregate displacement of 4,995,134 grt.

General-purpose public ports are operated by two state economic enterprises. The ports of Bandırma, Derince, Haydarpaşa (İstanbul), İskenderun, İzmir and Samsun, all of which are connected to the railway network, are operated by Turkish State Railways (see above), while the smaller ports of Antalya, Giresun, Hopa, Tekirdağ and Trabzon are operated by the Turkish Maritime Organization. Control of the port of Mersin was transferred to the private sector in 2007 under a 36-year concession agreement. However, a similar arrangement involving the port of İzmir was suspended in March 2008.

Turkish Maritime Organization (TDI): Genel Müdürlüğü, Rıhtım Cad. Merkez Han 32, 34425 Karaköy, İstanbul; tel. (212) 2515000; fax (212) 2495391; e-mail tdibasin@tdi.gov.tr; internet www.tdi.com.tr; Gen. Man. Burhan Külünk.

Port of Bandırma: TCDD Liman İşletme Müdürlüğü, Bandırma; tel. (266) 7182000; fax (266) 7136011; e-mail bandirmaliman@tcdd.gov.tr; Port Man. Okkes Demirel; Harbour Master Rusen Okan.

Port of Derince: TCDD Liman İşletme Müdürlüğü, Derince; tel. (262) 2399021; e-mail derinceliman@tcdd.gov.tr; Port Man. Ali Arif Aytaç; Harbour Master Haydar Doğan.

Port of Haydarpaşa (İstanbul): TCDD Liman İşletme Müdürlüğü Haydarpaşa, İstanbul; tel. (216) 3488020; fax (216) 3451705; e-mail haydarpasaliman@tcdd.gov.tr; Port Man. Nedim Ozcan; Harbour Master İsmail Safaer.

Port of İskenderun: TCDD Liman İşletme Müdürlüğü, İskenderun; tel. (326) 6140044; fax (326) 6132424; e-mail iskenderunliman@tcdd.gov.tr; Port Man. Hilmi Sönmez; Harbour Master İshak Özdemir.

Port of İzmir: TCDD Liman İşletme Müdürlüğü, İzmir; tel. (232) 4631600; fax (232) 4632248; e-mail izmirliman@tcdd.gov.tr; Port Man. Güngör Erkaya; Harbour Master Mehmet Ongel.

Port of Mersin: Liman İşletmesi Yolcu, Mersin; tel. (324) 2390939; fax (324) 2390849; e-mail marketing@mersinport.com.tr; internet www.mersinport.com.tr; managed since 2007 by a consortium of PSA International (Singapore) and Akfen (Turkey) under a 36-year concession; Port Man. Peter Ong Kim Pong; Harbour Master Raci Tarhusoğlu.

Port of Samsun: TCDD Liman İşletme Müdürlüğü, Samsun; tel. (362) 2332293; fax (362) 4451626; e-mail samsunliman@tcdd.gov.tr; Port Man. Saffet Yamak; Harbour Master Capt. Arif H. Uzunoğlu.

Private Companies

Akmar Shipping Group: Küçükbakkalköy Mah. Cicek Sok. 4, Aksoy Plaza, 34750 Kadıköy, İstanbul; tel. (216) 5762666; fax (216) 5727195; e-mail info@akmar.com.tr; internet www.akmar.com.tr; f. 2004; Chair. Necdet Aksoy.

Deniz Nakliyatı TAŞ (Turkish Cargo Lines): Fahrettin Kerim Gökay Cad. Denizciler İş Merkezi No. 14, A Blok Kat. 1, Altunizade/Üsküdar, İstanbul; tel. (216) 4747400; fax (216) 4747430; e-mail tcl@tcl.com.tr; internet www.tcl.com.tr; f. 1955; bulk carriers; Gen. Man. Cemil Gücüyener; 2 large and 2 small handy bulk/ore carriers.

İstanbul Deniz Otobusleri Sanayi ve Ticaret AŞ: Kennedy Cad., Hizli Feribot Iskelesi Yenikapi, İstanbul; tel. (212) 4556900; fax (212) 5173958; e-mail info@ido.com.tr; internet www.ido.com.tr; f. 1987; ferry co; Chair. Huseyin Eren; Man. Dir Ahmet Paksoy; 88 vessels.

Kiran Group of Shipping Companies: Fahrettin Kerim Gorkay Cad. 18, Denizciler İş Merkezi B Blok Kat. 2, 34662 Altunizade, İstanbul; tel. (216) 5541400; fax (216) 5541414; e-mail kiran@kiran.com.tr; internet www.kiran.com.tr; f. 1959; Chair. Turgut Kiran; Man. Dir Tamer Kiran; 19 vessels.

Ozsay Seatransportation Co Inc: Güzelyalı, E-5 Üzeri 18, 34903 Pendik, İstanbul; tel. (216) 4933610; fax (216) 4930306; e-mail ozsay@tnn.net; internet www.ozsay.com; Pres. Recep Kalkavan; Man. Dir Omer Kalkavan; 10 vessels.

Pinat Gida Sanayi ve Ticaret AŞ: Pak Ismerkezi Prof. Dr Bulent Tarcan Sok 5/3, 80290 Gayrettepe, İstanbul; tel. (212) 2747533; fax (212) 2750317; e-mail pinat@pinat.com.tr; Pres. Engin Pak; Man. Dir Alpay Citak; 7 vessels.

Türkiye Denizcilik İşletmeleri Denizyolları İşletmesi Müdürlüğü (TDI): Meclisi Mebusan Cad. 18, 80040 Salıpazarı, İstanbul; tel. (212) 2521700; fax (212) 2515767; e-mail bilgiedinme@tdi.gov.tr; internet www.tdi.com.tr; ferry co; Chair. Erkan Arikan; Man. Dir Kadir Kurtoğlu; 5 vessels.

Vakif Deniz Finansal Kiralama AŞ: Rihtim Cad. 201 Tahir Han kat 6, PK 853, 80040 Karaköy, İstanbul; 73.8% by VakifBank; leasing services to the maritime transportation industry; 15 vessels.

Yardimci Shipping Group of Companies: Aydintepe Mah. Tersaneler Cad. 50 Sok 7, 81700 Tuzla, İstanbul; tel. (216) 4938000; fax (216) 4928080; e-mail info@yardimci.gen.tr; internet www.yardimci

.gen.tr; f. 1976; Chair. KEMAL YARDIMCI; Man. Dir HUSEYIN YARDIMCI; 6 vessels.

Shipping Associations

SS Gemi Armatörleri Motorlu Taşıyıcılar Kooperatifi (Turkish Shipowners' Asscn): Meclisı Mebusan Cad., Dursun Han, Kat. 7, No. 89, Salıpazarı İstanbul; tel. (212) 2510945; fax (212) 2492786; f. 1960; Pres. GÜNDÜZ KAPTANOĞLU; Man. Dir A. GÖKSU; 699 vessels.

Türk Armatörler Birliği (Turkish Shipowners' Union): Meclisı Mebusan Cad. Dursun Han, Kat. 7 No. 89, Salıpazarı, İstanbul; tel. (212) 2453022; fax (212) 2492786; f. 1972; 460 mems; Pres. ŞADAN KALKAVAN; Co-ordinator HAKAN ÜNSALER.

Vapur Donatanları ve Acenteleri Derneği (Turkish Shipowners' and Shipping Agents' Asscn): Kilic Ali Pasa Mah. Ilyas Celebi Sok. No. 23, 34433 Cihangir-Beyoğlu, İstanbul; tel. (212) 2443294; fax (212) 2432865; e-mail vapurd@vda.org.tr; internet www.vda.org.tr; f. 1902; world-wide agency service; Pres. RUHI DUMAN; Man. Dir NESLIHAN BAŞARSLAN.

CIVIL AVIATION

The management of Turkey's airports and provision of the air traffic service and its control in Turkish airspace is performed by the Devlet Hava Meydanları İşletmesi Genel Müdürlügü (General Directorate of State Airports Authority). Atatürk (İstanbul), Esenboğa (Ankara), Adnan Menderes (İzmir and Trabzon), Antalya, Adana, Trabzon, Milas–Bodrum, Süleyman Demirel and Nevşehir–Kapadokya airports are open for international and domestic flights, both regular and charter. Adıyaman, Ağrı, Ferit Melen, Gaziantep, Kahraman Maraş, Kars, Körfez, Mardin, Samsun–Çarşamba, Siirt, Tokat, Uşak and Şanlıurfa Aerodromes are open only for domestic flights.

Devlet Hava Meydanları İşletmesi Genel Müdürlügü (General Directorate of State Airports Authority): Konya Yolu Üzeri, 06330 Etiler, Ankara; tel. (312) 2126120; fax (312) 2123917; e-mail dhmi@dhmi.gov.tr; internet www.dhmi.gov.tr; f. 1984; Chair. of Bd and Dir-Gen. ORHAN BIRDAL.

Sivil Havacılık Genel Müdürlügü (Directorate General of Civil Aviation): Bosna Hersek Cad. 5 Emek, Ankara; tel. (312) 2036000; fax (312) 2124684; internet www.shgm.gov.tr; Gen. Man. ALI ARIDURU.

Atlasjet Havacilik AŞ (Alfa Airlines Inc): Yesilyurt Mah. Eski Halkali Yolu Alacati Evleri Yani 5/B, 34153 Florya, İstanbul; tel. (212) 6632000; fax (212) 6632751; internet www.atlasjet.com; f. 2001; passenger and cargo; 12 aircraft; Chair. TUNCAY DOĞANER; CEO ORHAN COŞKUN.

Fly Air (ESN): Cevizli Sok. 7 Senlikkoy Mah., 34153 Florya, İstanbul; tel. (212) 4243837; fax (212) 5149902; e-mail info@flyair.com.tr; internet www.flyair.com.tr; f. 2002; charter and scheduled flights, international and cargo; 13 aircraft.

Inter Airlines (Istanbul Airlines): Çağlayan Mah. 2004, Sok. 26, Barınaklar, Antalya; tel. (242) 3104400; fax (242) 3240928; e-mail info@interekspres.com; internet www.interekspres.com; f. 1999; charter flights to European destinations; Chair. ÖMER TOROSLUOĞLU; Gen. Man. ERCÜMENT FILIZ.

Onur Air Taşımacılık AŞ: Senlikköy Mah., Çatal Sok. 3, 34153 Florya, İstanbul; tel. (212) 6632300; fax (212) 6632319; e-mail info@onurair.com.tr; internet www.onurair.com.tr; f. 1992; regional and domestic passenger and cargo charter services; Chair. CANKUT BAGANA.

Pegasus Airlines: Basın Ekspres Yolu 2, Halkalı, İstanbul; tel. (212) 6977777; fax (212) 6939777; internet www.flypgs.com; f. 1990; charter services; 17 aircraft; Chair. ALI SABANCI; Gen. Man. SERTAÇ HAYBAT; 17 planes.

Sky Airlines: Güzeloba Mah. Ay 1 Sok. 1, 07230 Antalya; tel. (242) 3108800; fax (242) 3108808; e-mail info@skyairlines.net; internet www.skyairlines.net; f. 2000; regional passenger charter flights; seven aircraft; Chair. TALHA GÖRGÜLÜ; Gen. Man. TAHIR GÖRGÜLÜ.

Sonmez Hava Yolları: 9 km Yeni Yalova Yolu, PK 189, Bursa; tel. (224) 2610440; fax (224) 2610428; e-mail helikopter@sonmezholding.com.tr; internet www.sonmezholding.com.tr; f. 1984; scheduled flights and dedicated freight; Chair. ALI OSMAN SÖNMEZ.

SunExpress (Güneş Ekspres Havacilik AŞ): Mehmetçik Mah. Aspendos Bul. Aspendos İş Merkezi 63/1-2, 07300 Antalya; tel. (242) 3102626; fax (242) 3102650; e-mail travelcenter@sunexpress.com; internet www.sunexpress.com; f. 1990; charter and scheduled passenger and freight; serves European destinations; Man. Dir PAUL SCHWAIGER.

Türk Hava Yolları AO (THY) (Turkish Airlines Inc): Genel Müdürlük Binas, Atatürk Hava Limanı, 34830 Yeşilköy, İstanbul; tel. (212) 4636363; fax (212) 4652121; e-mail customer@thy.com; internet www.thy.com.tr; f. 1933; 49.12% state-owned; extensive internal network and scheduled and charter flights to destinations in the Middle East, Africa, the Far East, Central Asia, the USA and Europe; 102 aircraft; Chair. CANDAN KARLITEKIN; Gen. Man. TEMEL KOTIL.

Tourism

Visitors to Turkey are attracted by the climate, fine beaches and ancient monuments. With government investment, the country has rapidly become a leading holiday destination for European tourists (particularly from the United Kingdom and Germany). In 2007 the number of tourists increased to a provisional 23.3m. (compared with 7.5m. in 1999), while receipts from tourism reached US $16,851m. in 2006.

Ministry of Culture and Tourism: See The Government—Ministries; Dir-Gen. of Information MUSTAFA SYAHHAN; Dir-Gen. of Investments and Establishments KUDRET ASLAN.

TURKMENISTAN

Introductory Survey

Location, Climate, Language, Religion, Flag, Capital

Turkmenistan is situated in the south-west of Central Asia. It is bordered to the north by Uzbekistan, to the north-west by Kazakhstan, to the west by the Caspian Sea, to the south by Iran and to the south-east by Afghanistan. The climate is severely continental, with extremely hot summers and cold winters. The average temperature in January is −4°C (25°F), but winter temperatures can fall as low as −33°C (−27°F). In summer temperatures often reach 50°C (122°F) in the south-eastern Kara-Kum desert; the average temperature in July is 28°C (82°F). Precipitation is slight throughout much of the country: average annual rainfall ranges from only 80 mm (3.1 ins) in the north-west to about 300 mm (11.8 ins) in mountainous regions. Turkmen, a member of the Southern Turkic group, is the official language. Most of the population are Sunni Muslims. Islam in Turkmenistan has traditionally featured elements of Sufi mysticism and shamanism, and pilgrimages to local religious sites are reported to be common. The national flag (proportions 2 by 3) consists of a maroon stripe bearing a vertical design of five different carpet patterns above a wreath of olive branches on a green background, with five white, five-pointed stars framed by a narrow white crescent moon, in its upper dexter corner. The capital is Aşgabat.

Recent History

In 1877 Russia began a campaign against the Turkmen, which culminated in the battle of Gök Tepe in 1881, at which some 20,000 Turkmen are estimated to have been killed. In 1895 the Russian conquest was confirmed by agreement with the British; the international boundary thus established divided some Turkmen under Russian rule from others in the British sphere of influence. In 1917 the Bolsheviks attempted to take power in the region, but found limited local support. An anti-Bolshevik Russian Provisional Government of Transcaspia was formed, and a Turkmen Congress was also established. Soviet forces were sent to Aşgabat, and a Turkestan Autonomous Soviet Socialist Republic was declared on 30 April 1918. In July nationalists, aided by British forces, ousted the Bolshevik Government and established an independent Government in Aşgabat, protected by a British garrison. After the British withdrew, however, the Government was soon removed, and by 1920 Red Army troops were in control of Aşgabat. As part of the National Delimitation of Central Asia, the Turkmen Soviet Socialist Republic (SSR) was established on 27 October 1924. In May 1925 it became a constituent republic of the USSR. Political power in the republic became the preserve of the Communist Party of Turkmenistan (CPT).

The Soviet agricultural collectivization programme, which was begun in 1929 and entailed the forcible settlement of traditionally nomadic people in collective farms, provoked military resistance, and guerrilla warfare against Soviet power continued until 1936. In 1928 all Islamic institutions in Turkmenistan were closed, including schools, courts and mosques. In the early 1930s there was a campaign among the Turkmen intelligentsia for greater political autonomy, in response to which many intellectuals were imprisoned or executed. The scope of the purges widened in the late 1930s to include government and CPT officials. The immigration of Russians into the urban areas of Turkmenistan, from the 1920s, gradually diminished the proportion of Turkmen in leading posts in the republic. The development of extensive irrigation projects enabled rapid development of cotton-growing, particularly after 1945.

In the late 1980s Turkmenistan's role as a provider of raw materials (mainly natural gas and cotton) to more developed regions of the USSR provoked strong criticism of the relationship between republican and the all-Union authorities. The environmental and health hazards connected with intensive agriculture were also widely discussed in the republican media. However, the geographical remoteness of the republic inhibited its involvement in the political changes occurring in other Soviet republics. In the absence of any significant pro-democracy movement, the CPT dominated the republic's elections to the all-Union Congress of People's Deputies in the Soviet and Russian capital, Moscow, in early 1989. In September, however, Turkmen intellectuals formed Unity (Agzybirlik), a 'popular front' organization concerned with the status of Turkmen language and culture and environmental matters, which initially gained official registration but was banned in January 1990. Only the CPT and its approved organizations were permitted to participate in elections to the republican Supreme Soviet on 7 January. When the new Supreme Soviet convened, Saparmyrat Niyazov, the First Secretary of the CPT since 1985, was elected Chairman of the Supreme Soviet, the highest government office in the republic.

In May 1990 Turkmen officially became the state language, replacing Russian; Turkmenistan was the last of the Soviet republics to introduce such legislation. On 22 August the Turkmenistani Supreme Soviet adopted a declaration of sovereignty. On 27 October Niyazov was elected, by direct ballot, to the new post of executive President of Turkmenistan. He was unopposed in the election and reportedly received 98.3% of the votes cast. In late 1990 and early 1991 Turkmenistan participated in negotiations towards a new Union Treaty, which was to redefine the status of the republics within the structure of the USSR. The underdeveloped state of the economy, and the republic's dependence on the central Government for subsidies, ensured that the republic's leadership was one of the most enthusiastic proponents of the preservation of the USSR. At the all-Union referendum on the status of the USSR in March 1991, 95.7% of eligible voters in Turkmenistan approved the preservation of the USSR as a 'renewed federation', the highest proportion of any Soviet republic.

President Niyazov made no public announcements either opposing or supporting the attempted coup by conservative communist elements in Moscow of August 1991. However, opposition groups, including Unity, publicly opposed the coup, which led to the arrest of several of their leaders. Following the failure of the coup attempt, Niyazov remained in power and announced that the CPT would be retained as the ruling party; however, in December the CPT changed its name to the Democratic Party of Turkmenistan (DPT), with Niyazov as its Chairman. On 18 October Turkmenistan was among the signatories of the treaty establishing an economic community of eight republics. This was followed on 26 October by a national referendum, at which, according to the official results, 94.1% of the electorate voted for independence. On the following day the Turkmenistani Supreme Council adopted a law on independence. The name of the republic was changed from the Turkmen SSR to Turkmenistan. On 21 December Turkmenistan became a signatory, with 10 other republics, of the Alma-Ata (Almaty) Declaration, which formally established the Commonwealth of Independent States (CIS, see p. 225); this decision was subsequently ratified by the Turkmenistani Supreme Council.

The DPT and Niyazov came to dominate independent Turkmenistan, particularly in the Council of Ministers and the Supreme Council. Although Niyazov reportedly continued to enjoy widespread popular support, there was some criticism of his increasingly authoritarian style of leadership, which involved rigid control of the media and the restriction of opposition activity. The promotion of a presidential 'cult of personality' was reported to have prompted the resignation, in mid-1992, of the Minister of Foreign Affairs, Abdy Kuliyev. The new Constitution, adopted on 18 May, further enhanced presidential authority, making Niyazov Chairman of the Government (prime minister), as well as Head of State, and giving him certain legislative prerogatives. In June Niyazov was re-elected, unopposed, to the presidency, receiving a purported 99.5% of the votes cast in a direct ballot.

Other significant structural changes were introduced under the new Constitution. The Supreme Council was to be replaced as Turkmenistan's legislature by a 50-member Majlis (Assembly); however, until the expiry of its five-year term, the Supreme Soviet elected in 1990 (renamed as the Majlis) was to be retained as the republican legislature. The Khalk Maslakhaty (People's Council) was established as the 'supreme representative body of popular power'. The Khalk Maslakhaty was to act in a supervisory capacity, and would not diminish the authority of the

President or the Majlis; however, it was to debate and decide important political and economic issues, and would also be empowered to demand changes to the Constitution and to vote to express 'no confidence' in the President, if it found his actions to be at variance with the law. The Khalk Maslakhaty was to comprise the 50 deputies of the Majlis in addition to 50 elected and 10 appointed representatives from the electoral districts of Turkmenistan (the former were directly elected in November–December 1992); it was also to include other members of local government and prominent figures, including the members of the Government and the Chairman of the Supreme Court, and was to be headed by the President.

After the new Constitution was adopted, there were fears that the rights of Turkmenistan's ethnic minorities (the most numerous of which, Russians and Uzbeks, represented some 10% and 9%, respectively, of the total population in the early 1990s) were in jeopardy, as the document stipulated that only ethnic Turkmen would be eligible for employment in state enterprises. Moreover, the Russian language was to lose the status of 'language of inter-ethnic communication'. Although the population is predominantly Muslim, Turkmenistan's Constitution guaranteed state secularism, a principle that was strongly emphasized by President Niyazov.

The presidential personality cult was strengthened during 1993, with numerous institutions, streets and public buildings being named after Niyazov. Notably, the Caspian Sea port of Krasnovodsk was renamed Türkmenbaşi ('Head of the Turkmen', a recently introduced mode of address for Niyazov). In December the Majlis voted to extend Niyazov's term of office until 2002, on the grounds that the republic's political and economic stability depended on the realization of Niyazov's '10 Years of Prosperity' programme of gradual reforms. The extension of Niyazov's presidency was endorsed by a reported 99.99% of the electorate in a referendum held on 15 January 1994.

Elections to the new, 50-member Majlis were held in December 1994, officially with the participation of 99.8% of the registered electorate. It was reported that 49 of the 50 deputies had been elected unopposed. The Majlis convened later in the month; the overwhelming majority of the deputies were believed to be members of the DPT.

Despite the result of the referendum of January 1994, elements of opposition to Niyazov were believed to be active in Turkmenistan, as well as in exile in other republics of the CIS, in particular Russia, where Abdy Kuliyev led an opposition group known as the Turkmenistan Foundation. In June 1995 the Turkmenistani Supreme Court sentenced two opposition leaders to respective terms of 12 and 15 years' imprisonment in a labour colony, having found them guilty of involvement in an alleged plot to assassinate Niyazov. In July 1995 a protest rally took place in Aşgabat (reportedly the first to be held in Turkmenistan since independence), at which up to 1,000 demonstrators criticized Niyazov's leadership and the continuing economic hardships. In August, in what was interpreted as a response to the previous month's unrest, Niyazov dismissed 10 of Turkmenistan's 50 local etrap (district or raion) administrative leaders. In October the President also dismissed several senior members of the Council of Ministers.

In 1996 and 1997 Niyazov effected widespread dismissals of government officials, as well as local administrative leaders and members of the judiciary. In February 1998 the President revealed that he planned to amend the Constitution after the legislative elections of December 1999, devolving certain presidential powers to the Majlis and relinquishing the premiership (although in the event he retained the latter position). In April 1998 elections to the Khalk Maslakhaty were held, with the reported participation of 99.5% of the electorate.

Turkmenistan continued to attract the censure of international human rights organizations during the late 1990s. In April 1998 a delegation of the Organization for Security and Co-operation in Europe (OSCE, see p. 366) appealed to Niyazov to release eight political prisoners who had been detained since the demonstration of July 1995. Niyazov agreed to their release, following which he made his first official visit to the USA where he met President Bill Clinton. Niyazov's systematic purging of government and other officials continued in May 1998. An attempted military rebellion that occurred in western Turkmenistan in September was followed by the dismissal of the Minister of Defence, and the comprehensive reorganization of senior personnel of the armed forces and border troops.

The promotion of the presidential cult of personality appeared to intensify during 1998: in December a giant ceremonial arch, the 'Arch of Independence', surmounted by a revolving gold-plated statue of the President, was inaugurated in central Aşgabat, and Niyazov was unanimously re-elected Chairman of the DPT. In what was interpreted as an effort to counter growing international accusations of dictatorial methods, the President declared, in December, that the elections to the Majlis scheduled for late 1999 would be contested on a multi-party basis, and that the establishment of new political parties would be permitted in advance of the poll. In December the Khalk Maslakhaty voted to abolish the death penalty; Turkmenistan thus became the first Central Asian state to proscribe capital punishment.

Elections to the Majlis were conducted on 12 December 1999. According to official reports, some 99% of the registered electorate participated in the poll. In the event, the DPT was the only party represented and the OSCE declined an invitation to monitor the poll, claiming that there was little evidence of a genuinely democratic process. In late December the new Majlis approved an amendment to the Constitution whereby Niyazov's presidential term was extended indefinitely. Niyazov had made repeated claims that the success of democratic and economic reform would be dependent on the continuity of successive 10-year plans. Following the Majlis' endorsement of the amendment, Niyazov announced that the creation of opposition political parties would not be contemplated before 2010. These developments further aroused the concerns of the international community, and there was considerable outrage when, in March 2000, the leader of the unofficial popular opposition front, Unity, Nurberdi Nurmämmet, was sentenced to five years' imprisonment on charges of hooliganism and intent to murder, after he protested that the December 1999 amendment to the Constitution was undemocratic.

On 1 January 2000 Turkmenistan formally adopted a revised form of the Latin script, replacing the Cyrillic script that had been introduced for the Turkmen language in the 1920s. In July Niyazov issued an order declaring that, henceforth, knowledge of the Turkmen language would be a mandatory requirement for all government officials; heads of state organizations, ministries and higher-education institutions were given 30 days to learn the language or lose their positions. Furthermore, all candidates for leadership posts were to have their genealogies over the previous three generations verified.

In January and June 2000 President Niyazov dismissed a number of prominent government officials, including three Deputy Chairmen. Niyazov also instructed Turkmenistani citizens and government organizations to close any bank accounts held abroad, in order to curtail the outflow of capital from Turkmenistan. At the end of July the President dismissed Boris Shikhmuradov, the Minister of Foreign Affairs; he was replaced by Batyr Berdiyev. It was also announced that all officials, including government ministers, would henceforth be appointed for a six-month probation period.

In the early 2000s Niyazov oversaw the introduction of a number of policies intended to develop a strong Turkmen national identity, including the closure of the opera and ballet theatre in Aşgabat, which Niyazov denounced as 'alien' to Turkmen culture. A principal element of Niyazov's proposals to promote a Turkmen national culture was the publication of the *Ruhnama*, or national code of spiritual conduct, a volume purportedly written by the President. This text became a key element of the school curriculum, and was in effect elevated to the status of a holy text, with display of the volume required in mosques and citations from the work included in inscriptions in religious and public buildings, and with knowledge of the text, moreover, becoming a prerequisite for entry into various professions. (A second volume of the *Ruhnama* was published in September 2004.)

In July 2001 Berdiyev was dismissed as Minister of Foreign Affairs, and replaced by Rashid Merepov. In late October Shikhmuradov was dismissed as ambassador to the People's Republic of China. He fled to exile in Moscow from where, in early November, he issued a statement condemning Niyazov's rule. Meanwhile, it was reported that a warrant for Shikhmuradov's arrest on charges of the misappropriation of state property had been issued by the Prosecutor-General, Gurbanbibi Atajanova, along with a request for his extradition from Russia. Although Shikhmuradov denied the charges, Turkmenistani officials claimed that his actions were an attempt to avoid prosecution; it was also widely speculated that Shikhmuradov intended to replace Niyazov by means of a coup. In January 2002 he established the People's Democratic Movement of Turkmenistan, with the aim of deposing Niyazov. In early February Nurmukhammet Hanamov resigned as ambassador to Turkey in order to join the opposition movement. In mid-February a former Deputy Chairman, Khudayberdy Orazov, announced his support for the opposition-in-exile. The Turkmenistani authorities subsequently issued a request for the extradition of Khanamov and accused Orazov of embezzling state funds. Meanwhile, in March Niyazov dismissed a number of senior officials from the defence, intelligence and security services (including the Minister of Defence), whom he accused of plotting to remove him from power. In addition, the State Border Service was placed under the direct control of the President. A new Minister of Internal Affairs was appointed in May, and in the same month Seitbay Gandimov was dismissed as Deputy Chairman and Chairman of the Central Bank, following allegations of links to Orazov. A further cabinet reorganization followed in August. Government changes in September included the appointment of three new ministers and the creation of a Ministry of National Security, under Batyr Busakov, to replace the Committee for National Security. In late September the newly appointed Chairman of the Central Bank was dismissed, following the theft from the bank of US $41.5m. In the same month Niyazov announced the creation of so-called 'labour armies', comprising 20,000 men under the age of 35, which were to be drafted to work without remuneration on public projects; the term of service was to be two years, irrespective of previous army service. Further government changes took place in mid-November, and Ovezgeldy Atayev was elected Chairman of the Majlis.

On 25 November 2002 it was widely reported that an assassination attempt had been made against the presidential motorcade, as it travelled through Aşgabat. An emergency cabinet meeting was held, and Niyazov publicly accused former officials Shikhmuradov and Khanamov, among others, of an attempted coup. An official announcement the following day reported the arrest of 16 suspects, although international human rights organizations reported hundreds of detentions in subsequent days. Also on 25 November Shikhmuradov, who had clandestinely returned to Turkmenistan, was arrested in Aşgabat. Following a televised confession, a one-day trial at the Supreme Court on 30 December found Shikhmuradov guilty of the attempt on Niyazov's life, and he was sentenced to 25 years' imprisonment (subsequently increased to a life sentence by the Majlis). Orazov and Khanamov were also convicted *in absentia*, and former Minister of Foreign Affairs Batyr Berdiyev was detained and sentenced in early 2003 to 25 years' imprisonment for his alleged involvement in the assassination attempt; the opposition-in-exile subsequently indicated that Berdiyev may have died. Meanwhile, opposition leader Murad Esenov, in exile in Sweden, claimed that the assassination attempt had been staged as a pretext for the arrest of Shikhmuradov and other members of the opposition, and the OSCE, concerned at the circumstances surrounding Shikhmuradov's trial and confession, sent a fact-finding mission to Aşgabat. In late December the Uzbekistani ambassador to Turkmenistan (the embassy of which country had been searched, in violation of the Vienna Convention on Diplomatic Relations) was expelled from the country, having been accused of harbouring Shikhmuradov immediately after the attack (see below). In June 2003 Orazov reportedly stated that Shikhmuradov and his opposition allies had intended to stage a coup, but that they had no intention of killing Niyazov.

In February 2003 Niyazov issued decrees that temporarily reinstated the requirement for exit visas (which had been abolished in December 2001), and imposed severe restrictions on the exchange of Turkmenistani currency. (The requirement for exit visas was abolished again in March 2004.) The import of foreign periodicals was prohibited, and more severe restrictions were imposed on journalists. Meanwhile, on 6 April 2003 elections to the Khalk Maslakhaty and to district and village councils took place, with the participation of some 89.3% of the electorate. The OSCE, which had accused the authorities of widespread human rights abuses in a report issued in March, questioned the legitimacy of the electoral process.

On 15 August 2003 amendments to the Constitution elevated the Khalk Maslakhaty, which was henceforth to comprise 2,507 members, to the status of a 'permanently functioning supreme representative body of popular authority', and required it to remain in continuous session. The Khalk Maslakhaty was also accorded a number of legislative powers, which enabled it to adopt constitutional laws, thus effectively displacing the Majlis as the country's leading legislative body. Other changes to the Constitution forbade Turkmenistani citizens from holding dual nationality, superseding an agreement on dual nationality reached with Russia in December 1993 (see below).

Government changes in September 2003 included the appointment of Maj.-Gen. Agageldy Mamatgeldiyev as Minister of Defence. As part of further restructuring in November, two new Deputy Chairmen and a new Minister of National Security were appointed. Also in November a new law was approved, restricting the activities of religious groups by criminalizing any confession not registered with the Ministry of Justice (at that time the only state-registered faiths were Sunni Islam and Russian Orthodox Christianity). The formation of political parties on religious grounds was also prohibited. (These laws were revised in March 2004.) In the same month a new law came into force, which severely restricted the activities of non-governmental organizations, imposing fines, prison sentences and periods of 'corrective labour' for those convicted under the new guide-lines. In late November the UN General Assembly adopted a resolution (which was, notably, supported by Russia), expressing grave concerns over human rights violations in Turkmenistan. At the end of the month Niyazov pardoned more than 7,000 prisoners.

In December 2003 President Niyazov reorganized the state broadcasting organizations. Further government changes were made in January 2004, including the appointment of a new Minister of Petroleum, Natural Gas and Mineral Resources. In February Niyazov replaced 15,000 medical workers with army conscripts, in an attempt to reduce government expenditure on health care. In April the Minister of the Economy and Finance, the Minister of Education and the heads of two state-controlled banks were dismissed. In May Niyazov signed a decree prohibiting the use of child labour in the cotton industry. A further presidential decree, issued in June, invalidated all higher-education degrees received abroad; all teachers with such degrees were to be dismissed. Niyazov implemented further government changes in July. In August Geldymuhammet Ashirkulov was appointed Minister of Internal Affairs. (In December Ashirkulov was, in turn, replaced by Akmamed Rahmanov.) Meanwhile, in October Niyazov removed Enebai Atayeva as Deputy Chairman and Governor of the cotton-producing Ahal Velayat (Region). This dismissal reportedly reflected dissatisfaction with the nation-wide cotton harvest; the regional deputy governor and four heads of cotton-producing associations were also replaced. In the same month the UN General Assembly adopted a second resolution criticizing human rights violations in Turkmenistan; on this occasion, Russia abstained from voting, while Uzbekistan voted against the resolution, despite its explicit condemnation of discrimination by the Government of Turkmenistan against Russians, Uzbeks and other minority ethnic groups in the country.

Elections to the Majlis were conducted on 19 December 2004. According to official reports, 76.9% of the registered electorate participated in the poll, at which the DPT was the only party represented. (A second round of voting took place on 9 January 2005 in seven districts where candidates had failed to obtain the required 50% plus one of the votes cast.) In February 2005 Niyazov announced plans to close all hospitals outside Aşgabat, stating that the provision of hospitals outside the capital was unnecessary, particularly given the shortage of doctors. Niyazov also ordered the closure of rural libraries, asserting that the rural Turkmenistani population was largely illiterate and therefore made limited use of the existing facilities. The President imposed further restrictions in April, prohibiting the import and circulation of all foreign print media, and refusing to renew the licences of international shipping firms and express couriers. In June a report published by the London School of Hygiene and Tropical Medicine (United Kingdom) expressed concern at the 'systematic dismantling' of Turkmenistan's health care system; the report urged the international community to apply pressure on Turkmenistan to improve services.

Throughout 2005 and in the first months of 2006 President Niyazov frequently replaced state officials; many of those dismissed were accused of corruption or other abuses of office, and sentenced to long custodial terms. Notably, in late May 2005 the deputy prime minister for the Fuel and Energy Sector, Yolly Gurbanmuradov, was dismissed, having been accused of having abused his position for personal gain when he had served as head of the State Bank for Foreign Economic Activities in 1993–2001. In July 2005 it was reported that Gurbanmuradov had been sentenced to 25 years' imprisonment. Meanwhile, in May 2005 Niyazov dismissed the Chairman of the Central Bank, who was accused of corruption. Niyazov further reorganized the energy sector in August and September of that year. In mid-April 2006

Niyazov appointed Muhammetguly Ogshukov, previously First Deputy Prosecutor-General, to replace Atajanova as Prosecutor-General. Although Niyazov initially stated that Atajanova was to retire (having occupied the post since 1997), later in the month Atajanova admitted to charges made by Niyazov that she had taken bribes and stolen state property. In early May Niyazov declared invalid the presidential decree relieving her of her post in connection with her retirement, instead decreeing that she was relieved of her duties for having committed 'shameful' deeds and having damaging the title of the office of Prosecutor-General. In the same month work was completed on a palace made of ice, the construction of which had cost some US $21.5m., in Aşgabat. Elections to the 625 municipal councils (gengeşes) took place on 23 July.

On 21 December 2006 President Niyazov died, having suffered a heart attack. Under the terms of the Constitution, the role of acting President should have been assumed by Ovezgeldy Atayev, Chairman of the Majlis; however, Atayev was dismissed from his post shortly after Niyazov's death, when state prosecutors announced they would be investigating Atayev on criminal charges. Subsequently, the State Security Council appointed the Deputy Chairman of the Government and Minister of Health and the Medical Industry, Gurbanguly Berdymuhamedov, to act as President until presidential elections had been held. Meanwhile, Akja Nurberdiyeva succeeded Atayev as Chairman of the Majlis. Six candidates contested the presidential elections, which were held on 11 February 2007. As had widely been predicted, Berdymuhamedov won by an overwhelming majority, receiving 89.2% of the votes cast; the rate of participation by the electorate was officially recorded at 98.6%. Berdymuhamedov was inaugurated as President on 14 February. From mid-February the appointment of government ministers and other senior state officials was announced, including several ministers who had served under Niyazov. Among the principal appointments were those of Rashid Meredov as deputy premier and Minister of Foreign Affairs, Mamatgeldiyev as Minister of Defence and Murad Karryev as Minister of Justice; Muhammetgeldy Annaamanov was appointed Minister of Education, replacing Hydyr Saparliyev, who was promoted to the position of deputy premier. New appointments were also made to regional governorships and to the chairmanship of the Supreme Court and to the Office of the Prosecutor-General.

The most significant of President Berdymuhamedov's early decrees was the Code of Social Guarantees, signed into law on 19 March 2007, which restored pension rights that had been removed from an estimated 100,000 senior citizens in the previous year. On 31 March Berdymuhamedov was elected Chairman of the Khalk Maslakhaty. In a speech to the body, the President announced a programme of agricultural reforms and plans to extend public access to the internet, which hitherto had been severely restricted, in Turkmenistan. (The first public access point to the internet in the country had been opened in February in Aşgabat.) In April the Minister of Internal Affairs appointed in February was dismissed, reportedly for failing to address corruption within the ministry and an increase in drug abuse within the country, and was replaced by Khodjamyrat Annagurbanov. In July Berdymuhamedov effected a limited government reorganization and replaced a number of other senior officials. In early October Berdymuhamedov dismissed Minister of Internal Affairs Annagurbanov and the Minister of National Security, both of whom, according to an official announcement, were to be subject to criminal proceedings on undisclosed charges. Charymyrat Amanov was appointed to the Ministry of National Security, while Orazgeldy Amanmyradov received the internal affairs portfolio. In November Berdymuhamedov appointed a new Deputy Chairman of the Government, responsible for Trade and Textiles. On 9 December elections were conducted to councils in each of Turkmenistan's Velayats. In April 2008 Hojamyrat Geldimyradov, hitherto Minister of Finance, was appointed as Deputy Chairman of the Government, responsible for Economic Affairs, while the deputy premier responsible for Transport and Communications, Gurbannazar Ashyrov, was dismissed, having been subject to criticism for the conduct of his actions by the President; the Chairman of the Central Bank was also replaced. Later in April Berdymuhamedov established a special commission to revise the Constitution, and officially abolished the names of the months introduced by Niyazov (which had included various titles of Niyazov and his parents). In May it was announced that the gold revolving statue of Niyazov and the Arch of Independence constructed in 1998 were to be relocated to a less prominent location on the outskirts of the capital. On 21 July the text of a new draft constitution was announced, following the proposals of the constitutional commission. In August Deriyageldi Orazov, a former mayor of Aşgabat, was appointed Deputy Chairman, responsible for Construction.

On 26 September 2008 the new Constitution was approved at an extraordinary session of the Khalk Maslakhaty; it provided, *inter alia*, for the dissolution of the Khalk Maslakhaty, and the division of its powers between the President and the Majlis, which was to be enlarged to number 125 deputies. The President was henceforth to be responsible for appointing regional governors and mayors directly. Elections to the expanded 125-member Majlis were conducted on 14 December 2008, with a second round of voting following in one district on 28 December. A CIS observer mission stated that the poll had been conducted in accordance with the country's legislation and democratic standards. However, human rights groups and the OSCE, which had also dispatched a small monitoring mission to Turkmenistan, criticized the absence of democratic alternatives for the electorate. Opposition parties disputed the official voter participation figure of 93.8%, and claimed that participation amounted to only about 30% of the electorate. The new Majlis was convened on 9 January 2009; Akja Nurberdiyeva was re-elected its Chairman. It was reported that about 90% of the elected deputies were members of the DPT, while the remainder were independent candidates endorsed by the ruling party. Following the resignation of a deputy, a poll was repeated in one district on 8 February 2009.

In January 2009 Tuvakmammed Japarov, hitherto the head of the Supreme Control Chamber of Turkmenistan (a financial regulatory body created in 2007), was appointed Deputy Chairman of the Government, responsible for Economic Affairs, following the resignation of Geldimyradov on grounds of ill health. Berdymuhamedov also replaced a number of ministers, governors and senior managers of state concerns; these included the Minister of Energy and Industry and the Chairman of government petroleum agency Türkmenneft, apparently after investigations conducted by the Supreme Control Chamber and the Office of the Prosecutor-General revealed financial irregularities in the fuel and energy sector. Later that month Mamatgeldiyev (who was the remaining long-standing government member installed by Niyazov and widely regarded as Berdymuhamedov's adviser) also tendered his resignation as Minister of Defence, citing ill health; Yalym Berdiyev, hitherto Secretary of the State Security Council, was appointed to succeed him. In March the head of the presidential administration was replaced. In April Berdymuhamedov dismissed the Editor-in-Chief of the government newspaper *Türkmenistan*, who was believed to have controlled state publications under Niyazov.

One of the fundamental principles of Turkmenistan's foreign policy is that of 'permanent neutrality', a concept that is enshrined in the Constitution. The republic's neutral status was recognized by the UN General Assembly in December 1995, two months after Turkmenistan became the first of the former Soviet republics to join the Non-aligned Movement (see p. 439). The policy of neutrality has led Turkmenistan to adopt a somewhat equivocal attitude towards its membership of the CIS. President Niyazov consistently expressed opposition to centralized structures within the Commonwealth, preferring to regard it as a 'consultative body'. Moreover, the republic refused to sign a number of CIS agreements on closer political, military and economic integration, and at the beginning of September 2005 Niyazov confirmed that Turkmenistan intended to withdraw from full membership of the CIS, but would remain an associate member of the organization.

None the less, Turkmenistan's most important political ally and economic partner remains Russia, the leading CIS state. In December 1993 Turkmenistan became the first of the former Soviet republics to sign an agreement on dual citizenship with Russia; it was hoped that this would further strengthen bilateral relations, while helping to stem the exodus of ethnic Russians from the republic. However, at a meeting in Moscow in April 2003, Niyazov and President Vladimir Putin of Russia agreed to rescind the agreement. In the same month Niyazov decreed that the estimated 95,000 dual passport holders in Turkmenistan should renounce either their Russian or Turkmenistani citizenship within two months, prompting protests from the Russian Ministry of Foreign Affairs, which insisted that the new agreement was not meant to apply retroactively and, moreover, had not yet been ratified by Russia. In June the lower chamber of the Russian legislature, the Gosudarstvennaya Duma (State

Duma), adopted a resolution condemning Niyazov's unilateral revocation of dual citizenship. Nevertheless, in August the Khalk Maslakhaty adopted constitutional amendments forbidding Turkmenistani citizens from holding dual citizenship, and placing any dual citizens remaining in the country in breach of the law.

Meanwhile, Turkmenistan's natural gas exports were a persistent cause of friction between the two countries. Transport of natural gas from Turkmenistan was dependent on the use of the former Soviet pipeline system, which remained largely under Russian control. In 1993 Turkmenistan's access to European markets through this system was effectively curbed by Russia's decision to direct Turkmenistani gas exports to Ukraine and the South Caucasus. However, as a result of the recipient countries' delay in paying for their gas imports, Turkmenistan suspended all deliveries in 1993–95, a measure that in turn was severely detrimental to the Turkmenistani economy. Although gas exports to Ukraine and the South Caucasus were resumed in 1996, in 1997 Niyazov announced the dissolution of the Turkmenistani-Russian company Türkmenrosgaz (which held a monopoly on the sale and export of Turkmenistani gas) because the company was in severe debt. In response, the Russian Government denied Turkmenistan access to the regional pipeline system. In subsequent years, delivery of natural gas supplies to both Russia and Ukraine has been interrupted on numerous occasions, as a result of disputes over tariffs and payments.

In September 2006 President Niyazov declared that Russia and the People's Republic of China were priority customers for gas, while casting doubts on the prospects for the proposed trans-Caspian and trans-Afghanistan pipelines. Turkmenistan's success in convincing Russia to agree to a substantial price increase for gas in the same month underscored the latter's need to continue to exert control over Turkmenistani gas supplies, on which it was dependent in order to meet its own export commitments to Western Europe and elsewhere. Following Niyazov's death in December 2006, in May 2007 President Berdymuhamedov met Presidents Putin of Russia and Nursultan Nazarbayev of Kazakhstan in the port city of Türkmenbaşi, where an agreement was reached to export Turkmenistani gas to Russia by way of Kazakhstan; Russia accepted a 40% price increase for imports of Turkmenistani gas over the following year. In March 2009 Berdymuhamedov met Putin (who, following the expiry of his second term as President, had become Russian premier in 2008) during an official visit to Moscow; however, discussions failed to result in the signature of an agreement on a proposed pipeline across Turkmenistan. In early April 2009 the Turkmenistani Government accused the Russian state-controlled natural gas monopoly Gazprom of having caused an explosion on a natural gas pipeline in Turkmenistan (thereby disrupting the country's exports), by unexpectedly reducing the flow of imported gas; Russian energy officials claimed that the blast had resulted from negligence on the part of the Turkmenistani authorities and poor pipeline infrastructure. (The incident followed Russia's suspension of gas supplies to Europe in January, following a dispute with Ukraine over payment arrears.) Berdymuhamedov ordered that an investigation be conducted into the explosion, which had significantly strained relations between the two states; it was reported that Gazprom had halted gas imports from Turkmenistan. A visit to Aşgabat by a Russian delegation, led by Russian Deputy Chairman of the Government Igor Sechin, to meet Berdymuhamedov for consultations, failed to ease tensions. At an energy security conference, convened in Aşgabat later in April, Berdymuhamedov declared that Turkmenistan would seek to diversify the country's export partners for gas and that it intended to increase co-operation with Europe (thereby appearing to assert an energy policy independent of that of Russia).

Of the remaining CIS member states, Turkmenistan has concentrated on developing closer relations with the neighbouring Central Asian republics of Kazakhstan, Kyrgyzstan, Tajikistan and Uzbekistan. Turkmenistan remained neutral regarding the civil war in Tajikistan (q.v.), and it did not contribute troops to the joint CIS peace-keeping forces in the region, although it did host some of the Tajikistani peace negotiations. In July 2001 Turkmenistan and Kazakhstan signed a treaty demarcating their shared border. In September 2000 Turkmenistan and Uzbekistan had signed a treaty defining their 1,867 km-border, and, under President Niyazov's orders, a 1,700-km fence was installed along the border in 2001. Relations with Uzbekistan deteriorated sharply in late 2002, following the alleged coup attempt in Turkmenistan on 25 November (see above). In December the Uzbekistani embassy in Aşgabat was searched for evidence of complicity in the plot, and Uzbekistan's ambassador to Turkmenistan was subsequently declared *persona non grata*. The Uzbekistani authorities reacted with hostility, and troops from both countries were deployed along their common border. Stricter border controls were subsequently implemented. In mid-November 2004 President Niyazov and President Islam Karimov of Uzbekistan met for their first presidential summit in more than four years in Buxoro, Uzbekistan, where they signed three bilateral agreements, pledging friendship between the two countries, mutual trust, and co-operation; simplifying regulations concerning cross-border travel for residents of border zones; and agreeing on a framework for sharing regional water resources. The Presidents declared that all bilateral issues had been resolved, and in early December they celebrated the demarcation of the border between the two countries. A new Uzbekistani ambassador to Turkmenistan was appointed in January 2005.

The legal status of the Caspian Sea, and the ownership of the extensive deposits of petroleum and natural gas beneath it, provoked controversy from the mid-1990s between all five of the littoral states (Turkmenistan, Azerbaijan, Iran, Kazakhstan and Russia). At a special conference on the Sea's status, held in Aşgabat in November 1996, the Ministers of Foreign Affairs of all five countries established a working group to formulate the demarcation of national boundaries. Nevertheless, in early 1997 Turkmenistan and Azerbaijan were engaged in a dispute over the status of two Caspian oilfields (the Azeri and Çirağ fields—known as the Khazar and Kaverochkin fields in Turkmenistan), which were being developed by Azerbaijan and a consortium of international companies. The situation deteriorated in July 1997, when Azerbaijan announced its intention to develop, in conjunction with a consortium of Russian companies, a third oilfield, which both countries laid claim to, known as Kyapaz to the Azeris and as Serdar to the Turkmen. Although Russia subsequently withdrew from the project, Azerbaijan refused to abandon its claim to the field. Apparently in response, in September Turkmenistan launched its first international tender for petroleum and gas exploration in the Caspian Sea, and announced that it expected Azerbaijan to compensate it for developing the Azeri and Çirağ fields. The commercial exploitation of the latter field began in November. Although Kazakhstan and Russia signed an agreement in October 2000 defining the legal status of the Caspian Sea, the remaining littoral states made limited progress. In November 2003 representatives of the five littoral states, meeting in Tehran, Iran, signed a UN-sponsored framework Convention for the Protection of the Marine Environment of the Caspian Sea, which sought to alleviate environmental damage in the Caspian Sea region. In mid-January 2005 President Niyazov approved a proposal from a Canadian company, Buried Hill Energy and Petroleum, to develop the Serdar oilfield, prompting protests from Azerbaijan. In June 2008 President Berdymuhamedov and his Azerbaijani counterpart, meeting in St Petersburg, Russia, reached agreement on the reopening of the Turkmenistani embassy in the Azerbaijani capital, Baku, which had been closed since 2001, and announced the establishment of an intergovernmental commission on bilateral co-operation.

Iran plays the most important role in Turkmenistan's foreign relations outside the CIS. In 1992 a number of agreements on closer political, economic and cultural integration were signed, including an accord to construct a railway line between Iran and Turkmenistan. The line, which linked the Turkmenistani city of Tejen with the northern Iranian city of Mashad, was opened in May 1996, thus affording Turkmenistan access both to the Persian (Arabian) Gulf and to İstanbul, Turkey. Turkmenistan and Iran also signed an agreement on the construction of a 140-km gas pipeline between the Korpeje natural gas deposit in south-western Turkmenistan and the city of Kord Kuy in northern Iran. The pipeline was to be the first segment on a route that, it was envisaged, would eventually transport Turkmenistani gas via Iran to Turkey and thence to Western Europe. The inauguration of the pipeline in December 1997 opened the first alternative export route for Turkmenistan's natural gas, and thus promised greater economic independence for the republic from Russia.

In March 2003 work on a project, conceived in 1999, to construct an underwater trans-Caspian gas export pipeline to Turkey, via Azerbaijan and Georgia, was suspended indefinitely, owing to disagreement between Turkmenistan and Azerbaijan over the division of the pipeline's anticipated throughput. Mean-

TURKMENISTAN

while, in late April 2002 President Niyazov requested UN support for the construction of a proposed 1,680-km gas pipeline from Dauletabad in Turkmenistan to Fazilka, a village on the Pakistan–India border, via Afghanistan, led by the US company Unocal. In December an agreement was signed on the construction of the pipeline, which was expected to be able to carry some 708,000m. cu m of gas per year. The project was subject to prolonged delays, and in 2008 it was announced that construction of the pipeline, which was additionally to supply gas to India, would commence in 2010.

President Niyazov confirmed his country's neutrality in the civil war in Afghanistan by developing equal relations with the Taliban and their opponents, the United National Islamic Front for the Salvation of Afghanistan, commonly known as the United Front or the 'Northern Alliance', in the late 1990s. Turkmenistan was central in organizing peace negotiations between the Taliban and United Front in both July 1999 and December 2000. Niyazov maintained the country's neutrality following the large-scale suicide attacks in the USA in September 2001, which were attributed to the Saudi Arabian-born leader of the Islamist militant al-Qa'ida (Base) organization, Osama bin Laden, who had developed a close association with the Taliban. Nonetheless, Niyazov gave his consent to the use of Turkmenistan's ground and air transport 'corridors' for the delivery of humanitarian aid to Afghanistan during air-strikes against al-Qa'ida and its Taliban hosts; Niyazov refused US troops access to Turkmenistan's military bases, however, reaffirming the country's policy of non-interference.

In April 2006 Turkmenistan and the People's Republic of China signed an agreement to construct a natural gas pipeline from Turkmenistan to China; China was to purchase 30,000m. cu m of Turkmenistani gas per year for 30 years from 2009. In August 2007 the Turkmenistani Government awarded China rights to develop gas reserves in the east of the country for the project. Chinese President Hu Jintao made an official visit to Turkmenistan in August 2008; agreement was reached for closer energy co-operation, including a pledge to increase the annual flow of natural gas to China through the Turkmenistan–China gas pipeline under construction, from 30,000m. cu m to 40,000m. cu m. In January 2009 Turkmenistan indicated that the export of gas to China, scheduled to commence that year, was to be delayed.

Turkmenistan enjoys close relations with Turkey (which has been regarded as competing with Iran for political and economic influence in the region), not least owing to the Turkmens' ethnic and linguistic ties with the Turks. Turkmenistan is a member, with both Turkey and Iran (among others), of the Economic Co-operation Organization (ECO, see p. 249).

In September 2007 President Berdymuhamedov, addressing the UN General Assembly, announced that he planned to develop co-operation with the international community in all areas of activity; he and other members of the Turkmenistani Government also met with US officials to discuss reforms and private investment. At the end of February 2008 further discussions on energy co-operation were conducted during a visit to Aşgabat by a senior US official. In April, following a visit to Turkmenistan by the EU external relations commissioner, the Government pledged to supply 10,000m. cu m of gas per year for the EU's planned Nabucco pipeline project from 2009, together with the opportunity for investments in new fields. On 22 April 2009 the European Parliament approved the conclusion of an interim trade agreement with Turkmenistan, stating that this might be used to influence the authorities in strengthening the reform process. (The agreement, which had been advocated by the European Commission and the majority of EU member states, had previously been delayed by the European Parliament, owing to concern over the human rights situation in Turkmenistan.)

Government

Under the terms of the 1992 Constitution, the President of the Republic is directly elected, by universal adult suffrage, for five years, although in December 1993 the legislature voted to extend President Niyazov's mandate—due to expire in 1997—until 2002 (this was endorsed in a national referendum in January 1994). In December 1998 the Khalk Maslakhaty endorsed an amendment to the Constitution whereby Niyazov's mandate was extended indefinitely, and he remained in office until his death in December 2006. The President is both Head of State and Head of Government (Prime Minister in the Council of Ministers), holding executive power in conjunction with the Council of Ministers (which is appointed by the President), and is concurrently Supreme Commander of the Armed Forces. The supreme legislative body is the Majlis (Assembly), which is directly elected for a term of five years. Under a new Constitution, which was officially adopted on 26 September 2008, the Khalk Maslakhaty (People's Council, which had functioned as the country's supreme legislative body since 2003) was abolished, and its powers transferred to the President and the expanded 125-member Majlis. Turkmenistan is divided into five velayats (regions), which are subdivided into 50 etraps (districts) and 625 gengeşes (municipalities).

Defence

In mid-1992 Turkmenistan began the establishment of national armed forces, based upon the former Soviet military units still stationed in the republic; under an agreement with Russia, these forces were initially under joint Turkmenistani and Russian command. Since 1993 Turkmenistan has co-operated with Russia and Kazakhstan in the operation of the Caspian Sea Flotilla, another former Soviet force, based, under Russian command, at Astrakhan, Russia. In May 1994 Turkmenistan became the first Central Asian republic of the former USSR to join the North Atlantic Treaty Organization's 'Partnership for Peace' programme (see p. 353). However, one of the fundamental principles of Turkmenistan's foreign policy is that of 'permanent neutrality', which is enshrined in the Constitution. The republic's neutrality was recognized by the UN General Assembly in December 1995, two months after Turkmenistan became the first former Soviet republic to join the Non-aligned Movement (see p. 439). As assessed at November 2008, the armed forces numbered 22,000, comprising an army of 18,500, an air force of 3,000 and a navy (largely coastguard units) of 500. Military service lasts for 24 months. The budget for 2007 allocated US $209m. to defence.

Economic Affairs

In 2005, according to estimates by the World Bank, Turkmenistan's gross national income (GNI), measured at average 2003–05 prices, was US $4,350 per head on an international purchasing-power parity basis. During 2000–07, it was estimated, the population increased at an average annual rate of 1.4%. Gross domestic product (GDP) per head increased, in real terms, by an average of 8.3% per year in 1995–2005. Overall GDP increased, in real terms, at an average annual rate of 5.2% per year in 2000–06, according to the Asian Development Bank (ADB, see p. 191). GDP increased by 11.6% in 2007 and by 10.5% in 2008.

Agriculture contributed 20.3% of GDP in 2006, according to the ADB. The sector employed 31.5% of the total economically active population at mid-2005, according to FAO. Although the Kara-Kum desert covers some 80% of the country's territory, widespread irrigation has enabled rapid agricultural development; however, over-intensive cultivation of the principal crop, cotton, together with massive irrigation projects, have led to serious ecological damage. In 1996 cotton contributed an estimated 11.5% of GDP, although the Government planned to reduce cotton production in favour of food production by 2010. Other important crops include grain, vegetables and fruit (in particular grapes and melons), although the country remains heavily dependent on imports of foodstuffs. Livestock husbandry (including the production of astrakhan and karakul wools) plays a central role in the sector, and silkworms are bred. According to the ADB, agricultural GDP increased, in real terms, by an annual average of 2.3% in 2000–06. Real agricultural GDP increased by 6.5% in 2006.

Industry (including mining, manufacturing, construction and power) contributed 41.2% of GDP in 2006, according to the ADB. In 2004 13.8% of the employed labour force were engaged in the sector. During 2000–06 industrial GDP increased, in real terms, at an average annual rate of 3.9%. Real industrial GDP increased by 8.0% in 2006.

Turkmenistan is richly endowed with mineral resources, in particular natural gas and petroleum (recoverable reserves of which were estimated at some 2,670,000m. cu m and 600m. barrels, respectively, at the end of 2007). In 2007 Turkmenistan produced approximately 67,400m. cu m of gas, and production of petroleum averaged 198,000 barrels per day. A new power installation, constructed at a cost of US $120m. in the town of Daşoguz, commenced production in December 2007; it was expected to generate more than 1,500m. kWh of electricity per year. In addition, Turkmenistan has large deposits of iodine, bromine, sodium sulphate, clay, gypsum and different types of salt.

The manufacturing sector contributed 21.7% of GDP in 2004, according to the World Bank. The principal branches of manufacturing are the processing of mineral resources (predominantly petroleum and natural gas) and textiles (mainly cotton products). Petroleum is refined at three refineries, at Türkmenbaşi, Seidi and Türkmenabat. According to the World Bank, manufacturing GDP increased by 24.0% in 1998–2003. Sectoral growth was estimated at 25.6% in 2002 and 34.7% in 2003.

In 2004 an estimated 11,500m. kWh of electricity was produced domestically; of electricity produced in 1994, some 20% was reported to have been exported, while a proportion of the remainder was distributed free of charge to domestic users. (Some charges for domestic electricity use were introduced in 1996; however, the 2006 budget provided for free distribution.) In 2003 mineral fuels accounted for just 0.7% of the value of merchandise imports, according to ADB estimates.

The services sector provided 38.5% of GDP in 2006, according to the ADB. The sector employed some 33.6% of the working population in 2004. Services GDP increased, in real terms, at an average annual rate of 5.5% in 2000–06. Real services GDP increased by 10.9% in 2006.

According to the ADB, in 2007 Turkmenistan recorded a trade surplus of US $5,216.1m. and a surplus of $4,524.7m. on the current account of the balance of payments. In 2007 the principal source of imports (accounting for 14.3% of the total) was the United Arab Emirates; other major suppliers were Turkey, the People's Republic of China, Ukraine and Russia. The principal markets for exports were Ukraine (47.0%) and Iran. In 2003 the principal exports were basic manufactures. The principal imports in that year were machinery and transport equipment, basic manufactures, chemicals, miscellaneous manufactured articles, and food and live animals.

In 2006 Turkmenistan recorded an overall budgetary surplus of an estimated 5,843,000m. manats (equivalent to some 5.9% of GDP). At the end of 2006 total external debt was US $881m., of which $725m. was long-term public debt. The annual average inflation rate declined from 1,748% in 1994 to 24.2% in 1999. According to the ADB, inflation averaged 8.8% per year in 2000–07. Consumer prices increased by an annual average of 9.0% in 2007. In 2004 some 62,000 people were registered as unemployed (about 2.6% of the labour force); however, unofficial sources estimated the rate to be considerably higher.

Turkmenistan became a member of the IMF and the World Bank in 1992. It also joined the European Bank for Reconstruction and Development (EBRD, see p. 251) as a 'Country of Operations' and, with five other former Soviet republics, the Economic Co-operation Organization (ECO, see p. 249). Turkmenistan became a member of the Islamic Development Bank (IDB, see p. 340) in 1994, and it joined the ADB in 2000.

The disruptions in inter-republican trade that followed the dissolution of the USSR in December 1991 damaged Turkmenistan's industrial sector, which relied heavily on imported goods. Moreover, the failure, or delay, of many of Turkmenistan's trading partners in the Commonwealth of Independent States to pay for imports of natural gas (the mainstay of the republic's economy) resulted in huge arrears, and Turkmenistan was forced to suspend deliveries several times throughout the 1990s and early 2000s. The opening of a new gas pipeline to Iran in 1997 did, however, contribute to some revival in the economically crucial gas sector. In 2003 Turkmenistan concluded major agreements with both Russia and Ukraine to supply them with natural gas for 25 years. In December 2007 Turkmenistan signed an agreement for the construction of a new gas pipeline link to Russia via Kazakhstan, and negotiated a significant increase in the price paid by Russia for Turkmenistani gas. However, a dispute over the cause of an explosion on a natural gas pipeline in Turkmenistan strained relations in April 2009, reportedly prompting Russia to halt gas imports from Turkmenistan (see Recent History). A pipeline link with China had been expected to be completed in 2009; however, in January 2009 the Turkmenistani Government indicated that the export of gas to China was to be delayed. In an indication of its desire to diversify its export markets for gas, in April 2008 the Government agreed to supply gas for the European Union's planned Nabucco pipeline project. In April 2009, moreover, the European Parliament approved the conclusion of an interim trade agreement with Turkmenistan. Following the death of President Niyazov in 2006, there were signs that the country's new leadership intended to pursue significant reforms and greater international integration, economic stability having hitherto been hindered by an inefficient tax system and a poorly regulated banking sector, largely under state control, as well as a lack of structural reform or market liberalization. In 2008 the Government made some effort to develop the private sector and the non-hydrocarbons sector, removing limits on foreign exchange transactions and introducing measures to liberalize the financial sector, and at the beginning of 2009 the manat was redenominated. Further reforms aimed at attracting more foreign investment to the country included the adoption, in September 2008, of a new Constitution that protected private property rights and committed the country to the principles of the market economy. According to the ADB, strong growth was recorded during 2007–08, driven by energy exports and public investment, and by early 2009 the global economic downturn had yet to affect the country's economy significantly; real GDP growth of 10.0% was forecast for 2009.

Education

A state-funded education system was introduced under Soviet rule. Although some schools provided instruction in Russian, Uzbek and Kazakh, President Niyazov pledged to eradicate teaching in languages other than Turkmen. Following the death of Niyazov, in February 2007 the new President increased the period of primary and secondary education from nine to 10 years (effective from the beginning of the 2007/08 school year). In 1990 the total enrolment at higher schools was equivalent to 21.8% of the relevant age-group. The 1999 budget allocated 26.9% of total expenditure (1,048,700m. manats) to education. Free education at Turkmenistan's 16 universities was apparently abolished in 2003, while it was reported that the number of places for students in educational establishments had been sharply reduced since the mid-1990s.

Public Holidays

2009: 1 January (New Year's Day), 12 January (Memorial Day), 19 February (National Flag Day), 8 March (International Women's Day), 21 March (Novrus Bairam, Spring Holiday), 9 May (Victory Day), 18 May (Revival and Unity Day), 20 September* (Oraza Bairam—Id al-Fitr, end of Ramadan), 6 October (Remembrance Day), 27–28 October (Independence Day), 27 November* (Kurban Bairam—Id al-Adha, Feast of the Sacrifice), 12 December (Neutrality Day).

2010: 1 January (New Year's Day), 12 January (Memorial Day), 19 February (National Flag Day), 8 March (International Women's Day), 21 March (Novrus Bairam, Spring Holiday), 9 May (Victory Day), 18 May (Revival and Unity Day), 10 September* (Oraza Bairam—Id al-Fitr, end of Ramadan), 6 October (Remembrance Day), 27–28 October (Independence Day), 16 November* (Kurban Bairam—Id al-Adha, Feast of the Sacrifice), 12 December (Neutrality Day).

* These holidays are dependent on the Islamic calendar and may vary by one or two days from the dates given.

Weights and Measures

The metric system is in force.

TURKMENISTAN

Statistical Survey

Principal sources (unless otherwise stated): IMF, *Turkmenistan, Economic Review, Turkmenistan—Recent Economic Developments* (December 1999); World Bank, *Statistical Handbook: States of the Former USSR*.

Area and Population

AREA, POPULATION AND DENSITY

Area (sq km)	488,100*
Population (census results)	
12 January 1989	3,533,925
10 January 1995	
Males	2,225,331
Females	2,257,920
Total	4,483,251
Population (UN estimates at mid-year)†	
2006	4,911,000
2007	4,977,000
2008	5,044,000
Density (per sq km) at mid-2008	10.3

* 188,456 sq miles.
† Source: UN, *World Population Prospects: The 2008 Revision*; these estimates are substantially lower than those produced by the state statistics institute (see below).

Population (official estimate): 6,800,200 at 1 April 2006 (Source: National Institute of State Statistics and Information).

POPULATION BY ETHNIC GROUP
(official estimates at 1 January 1993)

	Number	%
Turkmen	3,118,000	73.3
Russian	419,000	9.8
Uzbek	382,000	9.0
Kazakh	87,000	2.0
Others	248,000	5.8
Total	4,254,000	100.0

Ethnic groups (percentage of total, at census of 1995): Turkmen 77.0; Uzbek 9.2; Russian 6.7; Kazakh 2.0; Others 5.1 (Source: US Embassy in Turkmenistan).

PRINCIPAL TOWNS
(estimated population at 1 January 1999)

Aşgabat (capital)	605,000	Türkmenbaşi‡	70,000
Türkmenabat*	203,000	Bayramaly	60,000
Daşoguz	165,000	Tejen	54,000
Mari	123,000	Serdar§	51,000
Balkanabat†	119,000		

* Formerly Charjew (Chardzhou).
† Formerly Nebit-Dag.
‡ Formerly Krasnovodsk.
§ Formerly Gyzylarbat (Kizyl-Arvat).

1 July 2002 (official estimate): Aşgabat 743,000.

Mid-2007 (incl. suburbs, UN estimate): Aşgabat 744,000 (Source: UN, *World Urbanization Prospects: The 2007 Revision*).

BIRTHS, MARRIAGES AND DEATHS

	Registered live births		Registered marriages		Registered deaths	
	Number	Rate (per 1,000)	Number	Rate (per 1,000)	Number	Rate (per 1,000)
1987	126,787	37.2	31,484	9.2	26,802	7.9
1988	125,887	36.0	33,008	9.4	27,317	7.8
1989	124,992	34.9	34,890	9.8	27,609	7.7

Registered deaths: 25,755 (death rate 7.0 per 1,000) in 1990; 27,403 (7.3 per 1,000) in 1991; 27,509 (6.8 per 1,000) in 1992; 31,171 (7.2 per 1,000) in 1993; 32,067 (7.3 per 1,000) in 1994.

1998 (provisional): Live births 98,461 (birth rate 20.3 per 1,000); Marriages 26,361 (marriage rate 5.4 per 1,000); Deaths 29,628 (death rate 6.1 per 1,000).

Source: UN, *Demographic Yearbook*.

Births (annual averages, UN estimates): Birth rate (per 1,000): 32.6 in 1990–95; 24.5 in 1995–2000; 23.3 in 2000–05 (Source: UN, *World Population Prospects: The 2008 Revision*).

Deaths (annual averages, UN estimates): Death rate (per 1,000): 8.6 in 1990–95; 7.7 in 1995–2000; 7.7 in 2000–05 (Source: UN, *World Population Prospects: The 2008 Revision*).

2007: Birth rate 21.9 per 1,000; death rate 8.3 per 1,000 (Source: UN, *Statistical Yearbook for Asia and the Pacific*).

Life expectancy (years at birth, WHO estimates): 63.1 (males 59.6; females 66.7) in 2006 (Source: WHO, *World Health Statistics*).

EMPLOYMENT
('000 persons at 31 December)

	1996	1997	1998*
Agriculture	769.8	778.8	890.5
Forestry	2.5	2.9	1.9
Industry†	172.0	188.1	226.8
Construction	136.2	122.8	108.2
Trade and catering	91.8	101.2	115.8
Transport and communications	77.7	77.9	90.7
Information-computing services	1.3	1.0	1.2
Housing and municipal services	50.2	46.8	48.3
Health care and social security	97.4	100.4	89.2
Education, culture and arts	183.8	185.9	190.5
Science, research and development	9.2	6.9	5.2
General administration	24.7	25.3	28.8
Finance and insurance	8.7	9.6	12.6
Other activities	41.5	28.3	29.0
Total	1,666.8	1,675.9	1,838.7

* Provisional.
† Comprising manufacturing (except printing and publishing), mining and quarrying, electricity, gas, water, logging and fishing.

2004 ('000 persons at 31 December, estimates): Employed 2,110 (Agriculture 1,017, Industry 291, Other 802); Unemployed 62; Total labour force (incl. those not registered) 2,389 (Source: Asian Development Bank, *Key Indicators of Developing Asian and Pacific Countries*).

Mid-2005 ('000 persons, estimates): Agriculture, etc. 716; Total (incl. others) 2,276 (Source: FAO).

TURKMENISTAN

Health and Welfare

KEY INDICATORS

Total fertility rate (children per woman, 2006)	2.6
Under-5 mortality rate (per 1,000 live births, 2006)	51
HIV/AIDS (% of persons aged 15–49, 2007)	<0.1
Physicians (per 1,000 head, 2006)	2.5
Hospital beds (per 1,000 head, 2006)	4.3
Health expenditure (2006): US $ per head (PPP)	259
Health expenditure (2006): % of GDP	4.8
Health expenditure (2006): public (% of total)	66.7
Access to water (% of persons, 2004)	71
Access to sanitation (% of persons, 2004)	62
Human Development Index (2006): ranking	108
Human Development Index (2006): value	0.728

For sources and definitions, see explanatory note on p. vi.

Agriculture

PRINCIPAL CROPS
('000 metric tons)

	2005	2006	2007*
Wheat	2,834†	3,260*	2,700
Rice, paddy	120†	135*	111
Barley	65†	78*	59
Potatoes*	160	175	159
Sugar beet*	230	235	234
Seed cotton	1,000†	700†	946
Cabbages and other brassicas	56†	58*	52
Tomatoes	278†	282*	256
Onions, dry	94†	96*	88
Carrots and turnips	58†	60*	54
Watermelons*	230	250	240
Grapes*	170	180	175
Apples*	40	43	40

* FAO estimate(s).
† Unofficial figure.

Aggregate production ('000 metric tons, may include official, semi-official or estimated data): Total cereals 3,035 in 2005, 3,489 in 2006, 2,886 in 2007; Total roots and tubers 160 in 2005, 175 in 2006, 159 in 2007; Total vegetables (incl. melons) 780 in 2005, 815 in 2006, 755 in 2007; Total fruits (excl. melons) 269 in 2005, 287 in 2006, 274 in 2007.

Source: FAO.

LIVESTOCK
('000 head at 1 January)

	2005	2006	2007
Horses*	16	17	16
Asses	25*	n.a.	n.a.
Camels*	40	41	40
Cattle	2,025	2,065†	1,948*
Pigs*	30	29	30
Sheep	14,267†	15,694*	15,500*
Goats	822†	904†	900*
Chickens*	7,000	7,500	7,000
Turkeys*	200	200	200

* FAO estimate(s).
† Unofficial figure.
Source: FAO.

LIVESTOCK PRODUCTS
('000 metric tons, FAO estimates)

	2005	2006	2007
Cattle meat	100	102	102
Sheep meat	90	93	90
Goat meat	7	7	6
Chicken meat	12	14	13
Cows' milk	1,140	1,197	1,333
Hen eggs	35	37	34
Honey	8	9	n.a.
Wool, greasy	20	20	20

Source: FAO.

Fishing

(metric tons, live weight)

	2003	2004	2005*
Capture	14,543	14,992	15,000
Azov sea sprat	14,276	14,674	14,680
Aquaculture	24	16	16
Total catch	14,567	15,008	15,016

* FAO estimates.

2006: Catch assumed to be unchanged from 2005 (FAO estimates).

Source: FAO.

Mining

('000 metric tons, unless otherwise indicated)

	2003	2004	2005
Crude petroleum*	10,000	10,100	9,500
Natural gas (million cu metres)*	55,100	54,600	58,800
Bentonite†	50	50	50
Salt (unrefined)†	215	215	215
Gypsum (crude)†	100	100	100

* Source: BP, *Statistical Review of World Energy*.
† Estimates from US Geological Survey.

2006 ('000 metric tons, unless otherwise indicated): Crude petroleum 9,200; Natural gas (million cu metres) 62,200 (Source: BP, *Statistical Review of World Energy*).

2007 ('000 metric tons, unless otherwise indicated): Crude petroleum 9,800; Natural gas (million cu metres) 67,400 (Source: BP, *Statistical Review of World Energy*).

TURKMENISTAN

Industry

SELECTED PRODUCTS
('000 metric tons, unless otherwise indicated)

	2000	2001	2002
Cottonseed oil	48	45	26
Wheat flour	544	561	537
Woven cotton fabrics (million sq metres)	34	61	78
Woven silk fabrics ('000 sq metres)	216	115	283
Blankets	14	7	10
Knotted wool carpets and rugs ('000 sq metres)	1,040	1,434	1,475
Footwear, excl. rubber ('000 pairs)	478	444	253
Nitric acid (100%)	192	151	212
Ammonia (nitrogen content)	117	99	130
Nitrogenous fertilizers (a)*	89	72	103
Phosphate fertilizers (b)*†	11	11	17
Soap	3.0	2.5	1.6
Motor spirit (petrol)	1,132	1,283	1,292
Gas-diesel (distillate fuel) oil	2,247	2,547	2,360
Residual fuel oils	1,536	1,586	1,640
Clay building bricks (million)	309	269	279
Quicklime	17	17	15
Cement	420	448	486
Electric energy (million kWh)	9,845	10,610	10,700

* Production in terms of (a) nitrogen or (b) phosphoric acid.
† Official figures.

Electric energy (million kWh): 10,800 in 2003; 11,920 in 2004; 12,820 in 2005.

Motor spirit (petrol) ('000 metric tons): 1,361 in 2003; 1,265 in 2004; 1,313 in 2005.

Gas-diesel (distillate fuel) oil ('000 metric tons): 2,478 in 2003; 2,511 in 2004; 2,606 in 2005.

Cement ('000 metric tons): 200 in 2003; 450 in 2004.

Source: mainly UN, *Industrial Commodity Statistics Yearbook*.

Woven woollen fabrics (million sq metres): 2.8 in 1996; 3.2 in 1997; 2.5 in 1998 (Source: UN, *Industrial Commodity Statistics Yearbook*).

Ethyl alcohol ('000 hectolitres): 2 in 1997; 1 in 1998; 1 in 1999 (Source: UN, *Industrial Commodity Statistics Yearbook*).

2003 ('000 metric tons, unless otherwise indicated, estimates): Wheat flour 503; Nitrogenous fertilizers 96 (Source: Asian Development Bank, *Key Indicators of Developing Asian and Pacific Countries*).

Finance

CURRENCY AND EXCHANGE RATES

Monetary Units
100 tenge = 1 Turkmen manat.

Sterling, Dollar and Euro Equivalents (28 November 2008)
£1 sterling = 21,853.8 manats;
US $1 = 14,250.0 manats;
€1 = 18,136.0 manats;
10,000 Turkmenistani manats = 0.46 = $0.70 = €0.55.

Note: The Turkmenistani manat was introduced on 1 November 1993, replacing the Russian (formerly Soviet) rouble at a rate of 1 manat = 500 roubles. Following the introduction of the Turkmenistani manat, a multiple exchange rate system was established. The foregoing information refers to the official rate of exchange. This rate was maintained at US $1 = 4,165 manats between May 1997 and April 1998. It was adjusted to $1 = 5,200 manats in April 1998. In addition to the official rate, there was a commercial bank rate of exchange until this market was closed in December 1998. There is also a 'parallel' market rate, which averaged $1 = 6,493 manats in 1998 and reached $1 = 14,200 manats at mid-1999.

BUDGET
('000 million manats)

Revenue*	1997	1998	1999†
State budget	2,067.3	1,867.5	2,382.3
Personal income tax	108.3	157.4	224.9
Profit tax	579.6	412.0	422.0
Value-added tax	797.9	714.9	946.3
Natural resources tax	231.2	43.1	201.1
Excise tax	92.4	221.3	377.8
Other receipts*	257.9	318.8	210.1
Pension and Social Security Fund	471.0	711.0	832.5
Medical Insurance Fund	32.7	8.2	0.0
Repayments on rescheduled gas debt	246.6	474.1	478.3
Total	**2,817.6**	**3,060.8**	**3,693.1**

Expenditure	1997	1998	1999‡
National economy	843.9	461.1	623.3
Agriculture	632.5	331.4	223.2
Transport and communications	121.1	63.4	190.0
Other	90.3	66.3	210.1
Socio-cultural services†	975.7	1,850.0	1,907.9
Education	435.3	919.2	1,048.7
Health	443.1	493.8	550.6
Communal services	9.1	337.9	188.6
Culture, recreation and other purposes	88.2	99.1	120.0
Defence§	440.2	435.8	582.0
Pension and Social Security Fund	387.8	511.5	605.9
Interest payments	72.1	11.1	18.0
Public administration and other purposes	94.3	153.4	157.2
Total	**2,814.0**	**3,422.8**	**3,894.3**

* Including grants received and road fund revenues.
† Approved budget.
‡ Excluding expenditure of the Pension and Social Security Fund.
§ Variable coverage, owing to changes in classification.

1997 ('000 million manats, revised figures): Revenue 2,761.5; Expenditure 2,781.8 (Source: Asian Development Bank).

1998 ('000 million manats, revised figures): Revenue 3,077.5; Expenditure 3,440.3 (Source: Asian Development Bank).

1999 ('000 million manats, revised figures): Revenue 3,895.4; Expenditure 3,890.3 (Source: Asian Development Bank).

2000 ('000 million manats): Revenue 6,034.1 (Tax revenue 5,909.0); Expenditure 6,121.0 (Current expenditure 5,831.0, Capital expenditure 290.0) (Source: Asian Development Bank).

2001 ('000 million manats): Revenue 7,824.0 (Tax revenue 7,783.0); Expenditure 7,605.0 (Current expenditure 7,223.0, Capital expenditure 382.0) (Source: Asian Development Bank).

2002 ('000 million manats): Revenue 8,243.1 (Current revenue 8,243.1, incl. Tax revenue 7,827.0); Expenditure 8,166.0 (Current expenditure 7,684.0, Capital expenditure 482.0) (Source: Asian Development Bank).

2003 ('000 million manats): Revenue 10,716.0 (Current revenue 10,716.0, incl. Tax revenue 10,222.0); Expenditure 11,497.0 (Current expenditure 10,811.0, Capital expenditure 686.0) (Source: Asian Development Bank).

2004 ('000 million manats): Revenue 14,262.4 (Current revenue 14,262.0, incl. Tax revenue 13,454.0); Expenditure 13,188.0 (Current expenditure 13,188.0, Capital expenditure 754.0) (Source: Asian Development Bank).

2005 ('000 million manats): Revenue 18,285.0 (Current revenue 18,285.0, incl. Tax revenue 17,629.0); Expenditure 17,565.0 (Current expenditure 16,703, Capital expenditure 862) (Source: Asian Development Bank).

2006 ('000 million manats): Revenue 22,474 (Current revenue 22,474, incl. Tax revenue 21,085); Expenditure 16,631 (Current expenditure 15,665, Capital expenditure 966) (Source: Asian Development Bank).

INTERNATIONAL RESERVES
(US $ million at 31 December)

	2003	2004	2005
Total	2,673.0	2,714.0	3,600.0

Source: Asian Development Bank, *Key Indicators of Developing Asian and Pacific Countries*.

TURKMENISTAN

MONEY SUPPLY
('000 million manats at 31 December)

	1996	1997	1998
Currency in circulation	270.2	407.7	1,040.2
Demand deposits at banks	130.0	423.4	259.8

Total money ('000 million manats at 31 December): 2,552 in 1999; 4,965 in 2000; 5,792 in 2001; 5,877 in 2002; 8,280 in 2003; 9,393 in 2004; 11,948 in 2005; 14,063 in 2006; 18,602 in 2007 (Source: Asian Development Bank)

COST OF LIVING
(Consumer Price Index; base: 2000 = 100)

	2005	2006	2007
All items	150.3	166.1	181.0

Source: Asian Development Bank.

NATIONAL ACCOUNTS
('000 million manats at current prices)

Expenditure on the Gross Domestic Product

	2004	2005	2006
Final consumption expenditure	47,899.4	46,450.9	67,003.3
Households	} 39,605.2	} 36,103.7	} 54,385.4
Non-profit institutions serving households			
General government	8,294.2	10,347.2	12,617.9
Gross capital formation	15,061.0	17,904.7	23,707.3
Total domestic expenditure	62,960.4	64,355.6	90,710.6
Exports of goods and services	40,241.8	50,856.9	62,772.4
Less Imports of goods and services	38,857.8	37,365.8	54,462.0
GDP in market prices	64,344.4	77,846.7	99,020.9

Gross Domestic Product by Economic Activity

	2004	2005	2006
Agriculture	12,086.4	15,267.3	18,984.0
Mining and quarrying			
Manufacturing	} 22,148.3	} 26,857.9	} 34,238.6
Electricity, gas and water			
Construction	2,593.5	3,667.2	4,230.6
Trade	2,850.3	3,263.0	4,214.1
Transport and communications	4,220.7	5,040.7	6,450.1
Finance			
Public administration	} 16,798.2	} 19,506.9	} 25,325.8
Other activities			
GDP at factor cost	60,697.4	73,603.0	93,443.2
Indirect taxes, less subsidies	3,647.1	4,243.7	5,577.6
GDP in purchasers' values	64,344.4	77,846.7	99,020.9

Source: Asian Development Bank.

BALANCE OF PAYMENTS
(US $ million)

	1996	1997	1998
Exports of goods f.o.b.	1,692.0	774.0	614.1
Imports of goods f.o.b.	−1,388.3	−1,005.0	−1,137.1
Trade balance	303.7	−230.9	−523.0
Services (net)	−323.4	−402.5	−471.0
Balance on goods and services	−19.7	−633.5	−994.0
Other income (net)	16.7	84.8	32.6
Balance on goods, services and income	−3.0	−548.7	−961.4
Current transfers (net)	4.8	−31.2	26.9
Current account	1.8	−579.9	−934.5
Direct investment	108.1	102.4	64.1
Trade credit (net)	60.8	−266.5	56.5
Other (net)	−211.6	1,035.9	749.7
Net errors and omissions	46.4	−71.4	33.9
Overall balance	5.4	220.6	−30.3

Current balance (US $ million): 876.9 in 2005; 3,347.2 in 2006; 4,524.7 in 2007 (Source: Asian Development Bank, *Key Indicators of Developing Asian and Pacific Countries*).

External Trade

PRINCIPAL COMMODITIES
(US $ million)

Imports c.i.f.	2001	2002	2003
Food and live animals	129.4	114.3	130.3
Beverages and tobacco	56.8	70.1	67.4
Mineral fuels, lubricants, etc.	39.1	25.7	17.7
Chemicals	178.6	210.8	271.2
Basic manufactures	448.7	394.2	487.7
Machinery and transport equipment	1,204.7	857.6	1,125.6
Miscellaneous manufactured articles	128.1	112.7	165.2
Total (incl. others)	2,348.8	2,119.4	2,450.0*

Exports f.o.b.	2001	2002	2003
Food and live animals	4.7	3.4	2.9
Beverages and tobacco	—	0.6	0.3
Mineral fuels, lubricants, etc.	123.7	83.8	152.4
Chemicals	7.0	28.4	55.0
Basic manufactures	141.6	150.6	169.6
Machinery and transport equipment	14.5	17.1	16.9
Miscellaneous manufactured articles	52.8	74.1	80.8
Total (incl. others)	2,620.2	2,855.6	3,320.0*

*Estimate.

2004 (US $ million): Total imports 3,148.4; Total exports 3,853.9.
2005 (US $ million): Total imports 2,947.0; Total exports 4,944.1.
2006 (US $ million): Total imports 2,557.7; Total exports 7,155.5.
2007 (US $ million): Total imports 3,716.8; Total exports 8,932.9.

Source: Asian Development Bank.

TURKMENISTAN

PRINCIPAL TRADING PARTNERS
(US $ million)

Imports	2005	2006	2007
Azerbaijan	300.9	10.5	12.5
China, People's Repub.	99.5	178.7	344.0
France	97.0	95.5	55.9
Germany	146.3	215.4	238.2
Iran	167.8	211.0	240.2
Russia	246.5	251.7	285.4
Turkey	198.7	309.5	372.9
Ukraine	205.9	254.4	303.7
United Arab Emirates	343.3	431.5	491.3
USA	260.9	124.1	203.2
Total (incl. others)	2,703.3	2,781.2	3,427.9

Exports	2005	2006	2007
Afghanistan	110.7	136.8	163.3
Armenia	103.2	127.6	152.2
Azerbaijan	220.9	335.5	400.4
Hungary	103.2	127.6	152.2
Iran	841.1	1,038.3	1,351.7
Italy	201.1	221.0	197.4
Turkey	145.9	172.9	360.8
Ukraine	2,434.6	3,009.0	3,591.5
United Arab Emirates	157.7	194.6	253.3
USA	132.5	73.6	213.0
Total (incl. others)	5,698.7	6,343.5	7,646.8

Note: Data reflect the IMF's direction of trade methodology, and, as a result, the totals may not be equal to those presented for trade in commodities.

Source: Asian Development Bank.

Transport

RAILWAYS
(traffic)

	1996	1997	1999*
Passenger journeys (million)	7.8	6.4	3.1
Passenger-km (million)	2,104	958	701
Freight transported (million metric tons)	15.9	18.5	17.2
Freight ton-km (million)	6,779	7,445	7,337

* Data for 1998 were not available.

Source: *Railway Directory*.

SHIPPING

Merchant Fleet
(registered at 31 December)

	2005	2006	2007
Number of vessels	45	53	53
Total displacement ('000 grt)	48.5	53.4	51.9

Source: Lloyd's Register-Fairplay, *World Fleet Statistics*.

CIVIL AVIATION
(estimated traffic on scheduled services)

	2002	2003	2004
Kilometres flown (million)	22	22	17
Passengers carried ('000)	1,407	1,412	1,612
Passenger-kilometres (million)	1,608	1,538	1,916
Total ton-kilometres (million)	156	150	182

Source: UN, *Statistical Yearbook*.

Tourism

FOREIGN VISITOR ARRIVALS*

Country of nationality	2003	2004	2005
France	298	636	683
Germany	466	1,191	1,028
Iran	5,623	9,341	7,173
Japan	269	770	428
Netherlands	84	324	453
Russia	115	318	13
USA	181	343	332
Total (incl. others)	8,214	14,799	11,611

* Arrivals of non-resident tourists at national borders.

Tourism receipts (US $ million): 66 in 1996; 74 in 1997; 192 in 1998.

Source: World Tourism Organization.

Communications Media

	2004	2005	2006
Telephones ('000 main lines in use)	376.1	398.1	n.a.
Mobile cellular telephones ('000 subscribers)	50.1	105.0	216.9
Internet users ('000)	36	48	65

2007: Internet users ('000) 70.

Television receivers ('000 in use): 880 in 2001.

Book production (including pamphlets): 450 titles (5,493,000 copies) in 1994.

Radio receivers ('000 in use): 1,225 in 1997.

Personal computers ('000 in use): 2 in 1999.

Sources: International Telecommunication Union; UNESCO, *Statistical Yearbook*.

Education

1990/91: 76,000 students at higher schools (Source: UNESCO, *Statistical Yearbook*).

Institutions (2005): Secondary schools 1,704; Secondary specialized schools 15; Higher schools (incl. universities) 16 (Source: Permanent Mission of Turkmenistan to the United Nations).

Students enrolled at universities (2003): 14,859 (Source: UNICEF).

Adult literacy rate (UNESCO estimates): 99.5% (males 99.7%; females 99.3%) in 2007 (Source: UNESCO Institute for Statistics).

Directory

The Constitution

The Constitution of Turkmenistan, which was adopted on 26 September 2008, replaced the Constitution of 1992. Its main provisions are as follows:

Turkmenistan is defined a democratic and secular state and a presidential republic. The basic human rights of the individual, including freedom of religion, are guaranteed. Minority ethnic groups are granted equality under the law. The Constitution enshrines the separation of powers, with the independence of the judiciary. Turkmen is the only official language. The state's transition to a market economy is provided for in the Constitution.

The President of the Republic is directly elected by universal adult suffrage for a five-year term. A President may hold office for a maximum of two terms. The President is not only Head of State, but also Chairman of the Government (Prime Minister in the Council of Ministers) and Supreme Commander-in-Chief of the National Armed Forces. The President must ratify all parliamentary legislation and in certain circumstances may legislate by decree. The President appoints the Council of Ministers, governors and other local officials, and the members of an electoral commission. The President establishes and heads a State Security Council. Supreme legislative power resides with the 125-member Majlis, a unicameral parliament that is directly elected for a five-year term. Regional, district and municipal councils are directly elected. Judicial power is exercised by the Supreme Court, the High Commercial Court, and military and other courts. Judges, who are independent, are appointed by the President for a term of five years.

The Government

HEAD OF STATE

President of the Republic: GURBANGULY BERDYMUHAMEDOV (elected 11 February 2007; inaugurated 14 February 2007).

COUNCIL OF MINISTERS
(April 2009)

Chairman of the Government: GURBANGULY BERDYMUHAMEDOV.
Deputy Chairman, responsible for Construction: DERIYAGELDI ORAZOV.
Deputy Chairman, responsible for Petroleum and Natural Gas: TACHBERDY TAGIYEV.
Deputy Chairman, responsible for Transport and Communications: NAZARGULY SHAGULYYEV.
Deputy Chairman, responsible for Economic Affairs: TUVAKMAMMED JAPAROV.
Deputy Chairman and Minister of Foreign Affairs: RASHID MEREDOV.
Deputy Chairman, responsible for Education, Science, Health, Culture, Sport, the Mass Media and Social Organizations: HYDYR SAPARLIYEV.
Deputy Chairman, responsible for the Textile Industry, Trade and the Chamber of Commerce and Industry: HOJAMUHAMMET MUHAMMEDOV.
Deputy Chairmen: MAISA YAZMUHAMMEDOV, MYRATGELDY AKMAMMEDOV.
Minister of National Security: CHARYMYRAT AMANOV.
Minister of Defence: YALYM BERDIYEV.
Minister of Justice: MURAD KARRYEV.
Minister of Internal Affairs: ORAZGELDY AMANMYRADOV.
Minister of Finance: ANNAMUHAMMET GOCHIYEV.
Minister of Social Security: BEKMYRAT SHAMYRADOV.
Minister of Construction: SHAMUHAMMET DURDYLYYEV.
Minister of Culture, Television and Radio: GULMYRAT MEREDOV.
Minister of Energy and Industry: YARMUKHAMMED ORAZGULYYEV.
Minister of Railways: ORAZBERDY HUDAIBERDIEV.
Minister of Communications: OVLIYAGULY JUMAGULYYEV.
Minister of Road Transport and Highways: GURBANMYRAT HANGULIYEV.
Minister of the Petroleum and Gas Industry and Mineral Resources: ANNAGULY DERYAYEV.
Minister of Trade and Foreign Economic Relations: NOKERGULY ATAGULYEV.
Minister of the Textile Industry: HOJAMYRAT METEKOV.
Minister of Health and the Medical Industry: ATA SERDAROV.
Minister of Education: MUHAMMETGELDY ANNAAMANOV.
Minister of Water Resources: ANNAGELDI YAZMYRADOV.
Minister of Agriculture: ESENMYRAT ORAZGELDIYEV.
Minister of the Economy and Development: BYASHIMMYRAT HOJAMAMMEDOV.
Minister of Environmental Protection: MAGTYMGULY AKMURADOV.

Note: The Chairmen of the three state concerns, Türkmennebit/Turkmenneft (Turkmen Oil), Türkmengaz/Turkmengaz (Turkmen Gas) and Türkmenhaky/Turkmenkover (Turkmen Carpets) have the status of State Ministers.

MINISTRIES

Office of the President and the Council of Ministers: 744000 Aşgabat, Presidential Palace; tel. (12) 35-45-34; fax (12) 35-51-12; internet www.turkmenistan.gov.tm.
Ministry of Agriculture: 744000 Aşgabat, ul. Azad 63; tel. (12) 35-66-91; fax (12) 35-01-18; e-mail minselhoz@online.tm.
Ministry of Communications: 744000 Aşgabat, ul. Gurungan 40; tel. (12) 35-21-52; fax (12) 35-05-95; e-mail mincom@telecom.tm.
Ministry of Construction: 744000 Aşgabat, ul. 2049; tel. (12) 51-23-59.
Ministry of Culture, Television and Radio: 744000 Aşgabat, ul. Pushkin 14; tel. (12) 35-30-61; fax (12) 35-35-60.
Ministry of Defence: 744000 Aşgabat, ul. Galkynyş 4; tel. (12) 35-22-59.
Ministry of the Economy and Development: Aşgabat.
Ministry of Education: 744000 Aşgabat, ul. Gurungan 2; tel. (12) 35-58-03; fax (12) 39-88-11.
Ministry of Energy and Industry: 744000 Aşgabat, ul. 2008 6; tel. (12) 35-38-70; fax (12) 39-06-82.
Ministry of Environmental Protection: 744000 Aşgabat, ul. 2035 102; tel. (12) 35-43-17; fax (12) 51-16-13; e-mail ministr@nature-tm.org.
Ministry of Finance: 744000 Aşgabat, ul. 2008 4; tel. (12) 51-05-63; fax (12) 51-18-23.
Ministry of Foreign Affairs: 744000 Aşgabat, pr. Magtymguly 83; tel. (12) 26-62-11; fax (12) 35-42-41; e-mail mfatm@online.tm.
Ministry of Health and the Medical Industry: 744000 Aşgabat, pr. Magtymguly 90; tel. (12) 35-60-47; fax (12) 35-50-32.
Ministry of Internal Affairs: 744000 Aşgabat, ul. Magtymguly 85; tel. (12) 35-59-23.
Ministry of Justice: 744000 Aşgabat, ul. 2022 86; tel. (12) 38-04-11.
Ministry of National Security: 744000 Aşgabat, pr. Magtymguly 91; fax (12) 51-07-55.
Ministry of the Petroleum Industry and Mineral Resources: 744000 Aşgabat, ul. Gurungan 28; tel. (12) 39-38-27; fax (12) 39-38-21; e-mail ministryoilgas@online.tm.
Ministry of Railways: 744000 Aşgabat, ul. S. Türkmenbaşi 9.
Ministry of Road Transport and Highways: 744000 Aşgabat, ul. 1916 141; tel. (12) 35-02-36; fax (12) 35-18-43; e-mail tcentr@online.tm.
Ministry of Social Security: 744007 Aşgabat, ul. 2003 3; tel. (12) 25-30-03.
Ministry of the Textile Industry: 744000 Aşgabat, ul. Annadurdiyeva 52; tel. (12) 51-03-03.
Ministry of Trade and Foreign Economic Relations: 744000 Aşgabat, ul. Gurungan 1; tel. (12) 35-10-47; fax (12) 35-73-24; e-mail mtfer@online.tm.
Ministry of Water Resources: 744000 Aşgabat, ul. 2005 1; tel. (12) 39-06-15; fax (12) 39-85-39.

President

Following the death of President Gen. SAPARMYRAT NIYAZOV on 21 December 2006, the hitherto Deputy Chairman of the Government and Minister of Health and the Medical Industry, GURBANGULY BERDYMUHAMEDOV, assumed the presidency in an acting capacity, before being elected President in an election held on 11 February 2007. BERDYMUHAMEDOV was elected by 89.2% of votes cast, with a participation rate of some 98.6% of registered voters, according to official results; he was inaugurated on 14 February.

TURKMENISTAN

Legislature

Majlis
(Assembly)

744000 Aşgabat, ul. Bitarap Türkmenistan 17; tel. (12) 35-31-25; fax (12) 35-31-47.

Chairman: AKJA NURBERDIYEVA.

The Majlis is directly elected for a term of five years. Elections to an expanded 125-member Majlis were conducted on 14 December 2008, with a second round of voting following in one district on 28 December. It was reported that about 90% of the elected deputies were members of the ruling Democratic Party of Turkmenistan, while the remainder were independent candidates endorsed by the party. Following the resignation of a deputy, a poll was repeated in one district on 8 February 2009.

Election Commission

Central Election Commission: Aşgabat; comprises a chairman, two vice-chairmen, a secretary and 12 mems, all appointed by the President of the Republic; Chair. MURAT KARIYEV; Sec. JEREN TAIMOVA.

Political Organizations

Democratic Party of Turkmenistan: 744014 Aşgabat, ul. Gurungan 28; tel. (12) 25-12-12; name changed from Communist Party of Turkmenistan in 1991; Chair. GURBANGULY BERDYMUHAMEDOV; Sec. ONJIK MUSAYEV.

Unity (Agzybirlik): 744000 Aşgabat; e-mail agzybirlik@hotmail.com; internet www.agzybirlik.com; f. 1989; unregistered popular front organization; Leader NURBERDI NURMÄMMET.

Turkmenistan is effectively a one-party state, with the Democratic Party of Turkmenistan (led by the President of the Republic) dominant in all areas of government. The President of the Republic is also the leader of the **National Revival Movement of Turkmenistan (Galknyş)**. There are, however, several unregistered opposition groups, such as **Unity (Agzybirlik)**. A **Social Democratic Party** was reportedly established in Aşgabat in August 1996, upon the merger of several small unofficial groups.

Other opposition elements are based in other republics of the Commonwealth of Independent States, in particular Russia. A leading opposition figure in exile is a former Minister of Foreign Affairs, ABDY KULIYEV, whose **United Democratic Opposition of Turkmenistan (ODOT)** is based in Moscow, Russia, while the **Movement for Democratic Reform**, founded in 1996, is based in Sweden. The **Fatherland (Watan)** movement is also based in Sweden (e-mail info@watan.ru; internet watan.ru) and comprises Turkmen and other Central Asian oppositionists. In January 2002 a former Minister of Foreign Affairs, BORIS SHIKHMURADOV, established the opposition **People's Democratic Movement of Turkmenistan** (PDMT; internet gundogar.org); however, he was imprisoned in December, having been convicted of orchestrating the attempted assassination of President Saparmyrat Nizayov in November. Another opposition leader accused of conspiring with Shikhmuradov was NURMUKHAMMET HANAMOV, founder of the **Republican Party of Turkmenistan** (RPT; internet tmrepublican.org; Co-Chair. NURMUKHAMMET HANAMOV, SAPAR YKLYMOV).

Opposition leaders met in Prague, Czech Republic, in September 2003 and announced the formation of the **Union of Democratic Forces of Turkmenistan (UDFT)**, comprising four main groups: the RPT; Fatherland; the ODOT; and the **Revival Social Political Movement**.

Diplomatic Representation

EMBASSIES IN TURKMENISTAN

Afghanistan: 744000 Aşgabat, Gerogly 14; tel. (12) 39-58-21; fax (12) 39-58-20; e-mail eira.tm@gmail.com; Ambassador (vacant).

Armenia: 744000 Aşgabat, Gerogly 14; tel. (12) 35-44-18; fax (12) 39-55-38; e-mail eat@online.tm; Ambassador VLADIMIR BADALIAN.

Azerbaijan: 744000 Aşgabat, M. Kosayev 44; tel. (12) 36-46-08; fax (12) 36-46-10; e-mail azsefir_ashg@online.tm; internet www.azembassyashg.com; Ambassador ELKHAN BAKHADUR OĞLU GUSEYINOV.

Belarus: 744000 Aşgabat, ul. Gorky 51; tel. (12) 33-11-83; fax (12) 33-11-85; e-mail turkmenistan@belembassy.org; Ambassador YURIY H. MALUMOV.

China, People's Republic: 744036 Aşgabat, Berzengi raion, ul. Archabil, Hotel 'Kuwwat'; tel. (12) 48-01-70; fax (12) 48-18-13; e-mail chinaemb_tkm@mfa.gov.cn; internet tm.china-embassy.org; Ambassador WU HONGBIN.

France: 744000 Aşgabat, ul. Esgerler 35; tel. (12) 36-35-50; fax (12) 36-36-40; e-mail cad.achgabat-amba@diplomatie.gouv.fr; Ambassador CHRISTIAN LECHERVY.

Georgia: 744000 Aşgabat, ul. Azadi 139A; tel. (12) 33-02-48; fax (12) 33-08-28; e-mail georgia@online.tm; internet www.turkmenistan.mfa.gov.ge; Ambassador IOSEB CHAKHVASHVILI.

Germany: 744000 Aşgabat, ul. Hydyr Derzhazhev, Hotel 'Ak Altin'; tel. (12) 36-35-15; fax (12) 36-35-22; e-mail info@aschgabat.diplo.de; Ambassador REINER MORELL.

Holy See: 744000 Aşgabat, Merkezi Poçta, POB 98; tel. (12) 39-11-40; fax (12) 35-36-83; e-mail aszomi@online.tm; internet www.catholic-turkmenistan.org; Apostolic Nuncio ANTONIO LUCIBELLO (Titular Archbishop of Thurio) (resident in Ankara, Turkey).

India: 744000 Aşgabat, ul. Yu. Emre 2/1, Imperial International Business Centre; tel. (12) 45-81-52; fax (12) 45-61-56; e-mail indembhoc@online.tm; Ambassador MOHAMMED AFZAL.

Iran: 744000 Aşgabat, ul. 2072 3; tel. (12) 35-02-37; fax (12) 35-05-65; e-mail isroiref@online.tm; Ambassador MOHAMMAD REZA FORQANI.

Japan: 744000 Aşgabat, ul. 1945 60, Paytagt Trading Centre; tel. (12) 47-70-82; fax (12) 47-70-83.

Kazakhstan: 744036 Aşgabat, ul. Garaşizlik 11/13; tel. (12) 48-04-68; fax (12) 48-04-75; e-mail emb@kaztm.info; Ambassador ASKHAT OAZBAY.

Korea, Democratic People's Republic: 744000 Aşgabat; Ambassador KIM YON CHJE.

Korea, Republic: 744000 Aşgabat, Berzengi 25; tel. (12) 48-97-61; fax (12) 48-97-60; Ambassador KIM CHONG-YUL.

Kyrgyzstan: 744000 Aşgabat, ul. Gerogly 85; tel. and fax (12) 35-55-06; e-mail kg@online.tm; internet kyrgtm.by.ru; Ambassador BORUBEK ASHIROV.

Libya: 744000 Aşgabat, ul. Azad 17A; tel. (12) 35-49-17; fax (12) 39-35-26; Chargé d'affaires a.i. RAGAB BEN KHAMADI.

Poland: 744005 Aşgabat, ul. Azadi 17A; tel. (12) 27-40-35; fax (12) 27-31-22; e-mail ambasada.aszchabad@gmail.com; internet www.aszchabad.polemb.net; Ambassador MACIEJ LANG.

Romania: 744000 Aşgabat, ul. Kusayeva 107; tel. (12) 34-76-55; fax (12) 34-76-20; e-mail ashabat@mae.ro; Chargé d'affaires a.i. CIOCAN LAURENŢIU.

Russia: 744005 Aşgabat, pr. S. Türkmenbaşi 11; tel. (12) 35-39-57; fax (12) 39-84-66; e-mail emb-rus@online.tm; internet www.turkmenistan.mid.ru; Ambassador IGOR A. BLATOV.

Saudi Arabia: 744000 Aşgabat, ul. Yu. Emre 2/1, Imperial International Business Centre; tel. (12) 45-49-63; fax (12) 45-49-70; e-mail tmemb@mofa.gov.sa; Ambassador ABD AL-AZIZ IBRAHIM AL-GHADEER.

Tajikistan: 744000 Aşgabat, ul. Gurungan 19; tel. (12) 35-56-96; fax (12) 39-31-74; e-mail tadjemb_tm@mail.ru; Ambassador KOZIDAVLAT KOIMDODOV.

Turkey: 744000 Aşgabat, ul. Şevçenko 9; tel. (12) 35-41-18; fax (12) 39-19-14; e-mail askabat.be@mfa.gov.tr; Ambassador HAKKI AKIL.

Ukraine: 744001 Aşgabat, ul. Azadi 49; tel. (12) 39-13-73; fax (12) 39-10-28; e-mail emb_tm@mfa.gov.ua; internet www.mfa.gov.ua/turkmenistan; Ambassador VIKTOR A. MAYKO.

United Arab Emirates: 744000 Aşgabat, Khalifa Centre, pr. S. Türkmenbaşi 124; tel. (12) 45-69-15; fax (12) 45-69-16; Ambassador HASSAN ABDULLAH AL-ADHAB.

United Kingdom: 744001 Aşgabat, Four Points Ak Altin Hotel, 3rd Floor, Office Bldg 301–308; tel. (12) 36-34-62; fax (12) 36-34-65; e-mail beasb@online.tm; internet ukinturkmenistan.fco.gov.uk; Ambassador PETER BUTCHER.

USA: 744000 Aşgabat, ul. Puşkin 9; tel. (12) 35-00-45; fax (12) 39-26-14; e-mail irc-ashgabat@iatp.edu.tm; internet turkmenistan.usembassy.gov; Chargé d'affaires a.i. RICHARD M. MILES.

Uzbekistan: 744006 Aşgabat, ul. Gerogly 50A; tel. (12) 33-10-55; fax (12) 34-23-37; Ambassador SHERZOD FAYZIYEV.

Judicial System

Chairman of the Supreme Court: YARANMURAT YAZMYRADOV.

Prosecutor-General: CHARY HOJAMYRADOV, 744000 Aşgabat, ul. Seidi; fax (12) 35-44-82.

Religion

The majority of the population are adherents of Islam. In June 1991 the Supreme Soviet of the Turkmen SSR adopted a Law on Freedom of Conscience and Religious Organizations. In April 1994 a council (gengeş) for religious affairs was established, within the office of the President; it was chaired by the qazi (supreme Islamic judge) of Turkmenistan, with the head of the Orthodox Church in Turkmenistan serving as Deputy Chairman. In November 2003 new legislation, replacing that of 1991, was approved, restricting the activities of religious groups, although registration requirements for religious communities were made more flexible by a presidential decree, issued in early 2004. Further legislation, approved in March of that year, reduced the membership threshold required for a group to register from 500 to five. Prior to these amendments, only Sunni Muslim and Russian Orthodox Christian groups had been permitted to register. By mid-2004 groups of Seventh-day Adventist and Baptist Christians, Hare Krishnas and Bahá'ís had also registered.

ISLAM

Turkmen are traditionally Sunni Muslims, but with elements of Sufism. Islam was severely persecuted by the Soviet regime from the late 1920s. Until July 1989 Aşgabat was the only Central Asian capital without a functioning mosque. The Muslims of Turkmenistan are officially under the jurisdiction of the Muslim Board of Central Asia, based in Tashkent, Uzbekistan, but, in practice, the Government permits little external influence in religious affairs. The Board is represented in Turkmenistan by a qazi, who is responsible for appointing Muslim clerics in all rural areas.

Qazi of Turkmenistan: ROVSHEN ALLABERDIYEV.

CHRISTIANITY

The Russian Orthodox Church (Moscow Patriarchate)

The Church in Turkmenistan comes under the jurisdiction of the Eparchy of Tashkent and Central Asia, headed by the Metropolitan of Tashkent and Central Asia, VLADIMIR (IKIM), based in Uzbekistan.

Roman Catholic Church

The Church is represented in Turkmenistan by a Mission, established in September 1997. There were an estimated 80 adherents at 31 December 2007.

Superior: Fr ANDRZEJ MADEJ, 744000 Aşgabat, ul. Gerogly 20A, POB 98; tel. (12) 39-11-40; fax (12) 35-36-83; e-mail amadej@oblaci.pl.

The Press

At 2008 23 newspapers and 17 periodicals were published in Turkmenistan. All publications listed below are in Turkmen, except where otherwise stated.

PRINCIPAL NEWSPAPERS

Adalat (Justice): 744005 Aşgabat, ul. 2033 1/4; tel. (12) 39-79-04; weekly; Editor-in-Chief DOVLET H. GURBANGELDIYEV; circ. 42,575.

Aşgabat/Ashkhabad: 744004 Aşgabat, ul. Galkynyş 20; tel. (12) 22-33-04; f. 1960; 3 a week; journal of the Union of Writers of Turkmenistan; popular; in Turkmen and Russian; Editor-in-Chief SAPARMYRAT GARAKHANOV; Deputy Editor-in-Chief ORAZ AKGAYEV; circ. 6,832.

Beyik Türkmenbaşiyn Nesli (Generation of Türkmenbaşi the Great): 744064 Aşgabat, ul. Galkynyş 20; tel. (12) 39-17-64; f. 1922; 3 a week; for young people; Editor ANNAGUL NARLIEVA; circ. 21,591.

Dogry ÿol (True Path): 744000 Aşgabat; internet www.dogryyol.com; in Russian; news of Turkmenistan and Central Asia; online only; pro-opposition.

Edebiyat we sungat (Literature and Art): 744004 Aşgabat, ul. Galkynyş 20; tel. (12) 35-30-34; f. 1958; weekly; Editor ANNAMYRAT POLADOV; circ. 19,111.

Esger (Soldier): 744004 Aşgabat, ul. 2038 29; tel. (12) 35-68-09; f. 1993; weekly; organ of the Council of Ministers; military newspaper; Editor-in-Chief AGAMYRAT GELDYEV; circ. 40,200.

Galkynyş (Revival): 744604 Aşgabat, ul. Galkynyş 20; tel. (12) 22-34-23; weekly; Editor-in-Chief KHUDAIBERDI DIVANGULIYEV; circ. 44,586.

Habarlar: 744004 Aşgabat, ul. Galkynyş 20; tel. (12) 46-84-70; weekly; in Russian and Turkmen; television and radio; business; advertisements; Editor-in-Chief R. BALABAN; circ. 3,596.

Mugallymlar gazeti (Teachers' Newspaper): 744004 Aşgabat, ul. G. Kuliyev 20; tel. (12) 35-09-66; f. 1952; 3 a week; organ of the Ministry of Education; Editor REJEPNUR GURBANNAZAROV; circ. 75,226.

Neitralnyi Turkmenistan (Neutral Turkmenistan): 744004 Aşgabat, ul. Galkynyş 20; tel. and fax (12) 39-42-76; e-mail nt@online.tm; internet www.tmpress.gov.tm; f. 1924; 6 a week; organ of the Majlis and the Council of Ministers; in Russian; Editor-in-Chief BEKDURDY AMANSARIYEV; circ. 30,091.

Novosti Turkmenistana (Turkmenistan News): 744000 Aşgabat, ul. Bitarap Turkmenistan 24A; tel. (12) 39-12-21; fax (12) 51-02-34; f. 1994; weekly; in Russian, English and Turkmen; publ. by Türkmen Dowlet Khabarlar Gullugy news agency; circ. 500.

Syyasy sokhbetdeş (Political Symposium): 744604 Aşgabat, ul. Galkynyş 20; tel. (12) 25-10-84; f. 1992; weekly; organ of the Democratic Party of Turkmenistan; Editor AKBIBI YUSUPOVA; circ. 14,500.

Turkmenistan: Zolotoi Vek (Turkmenistan: The Golden Age): 744000 Aşgabat; internet www.turkmenistan.gov.tm; online only; in Russian; publ. by Democratic Union of Journalists of Turkmenistan.

Türkmening yupekyoli (Turkmen Railwayman): 744007 Aşgabat, ul. Chary Nurymov 3; tel. (12) 35-06-52; f. 1936; weekly; organ of the Turkmenistan State Railways; covers transport and communications; Editor BAYRAM SAHEDOV; circ. 7,000.

Türkmenistan: 744004 Aşgabat, ul. Galkynyş 20; tel. (12) 39-14-55; f. 1920; 6 a week; organ of the Council of Ministers and the Majlis; Editor-in-Chief AMANMUHAMMET REJEPOV; circ. 25,591.

Türkmenistan—Altyn Asar/ Turkmenistan—Zolotoi Vek/ Turkmenistan—The Golden Age: 744004 Aşgabat, ul. Galkynyş 20; tel. (12) 38-61-18; e-mail nt@online.tm; internet turkmenistan.gov.tm/_tm; f. 2003; online only; publ. by Govt and President; in Turkmen, Russian and English.

Watan (Fatherland): 744604 Aşgabat, ul. Galkynyş 20; tel. (12) 22-34-56; f. 1925; 3 a week; Editor-in-Chief AMANMUHAMMET REPOW; circ. 25,419.

PRINCIPAL PERIODICALS

Monthly, unless otherwise indicated.

Diller duniesi (World of Languages): 744014 Aşgabat, ul. O. Kuliyeva 22; tel. (12) 29-15-41; f. 1972; 6 a year; publ. by the Ministry of Education; in Russian and Turkmen.

Diyar: 744604 Aşgabat, ul. Galkynyş 20; tel. (12) 35-53-97; f. 1992; foreign policy and international relations; publ. by the President of the Republic and the Council of Ministers; Editor-in-Chief ASHIRBERDY GURBANOV; circ. 12,881.

Finansovye vesti (Financial News): 744004 Aşgabat, ul. Galkynyş 20; tel. (12) 29-42-76; f. 1994; in Russian, English and Turkmen; publ. by the Ministry of Finance.

Garagum (Kara-Kum): 744005 Aşgabat, ul. Galkynyş 20; tel. (12) 35-11-15; f. 1928; literary; Editor SAPAR ORAYEV; circ. 2,546.

Guneş (The Sun): 744000 Aşgabat, ul. Galkynyş 20; tel. (12) 22-33-05; for children; Editor-in-Chief SHADURDY CHARYGYLLYEV; circ. 44,696.

Gurbansoltan Eje: 744604 Aşgabat, ul. Galkynyş 20; tel. (12) 22-33-09; f. 1931; fmrly *Ovadan* (Beautiful); for women; Editor AKBIBI YUSUBOVA; circ. 56,626.

Izvestiya Akademii Nauk Turkmenistana (Academy of Sciences of Turkmenistan News): 744000 Aşgabat, ul. Azad 59; f. 1946; 6 a year; in Russian and Turkmen.

Politicheskii sobesednik (Political Colloquium): 744604 Aşgabat, ul. Galkynyş 20; tel. (12) 25-10-84; f. 1937; in Russian; publ. by the Democratic Party of Turkmenistan; circ. 2,300.

Saglyk (Health): 744000 Aşgabat, ul. Kerbabayeva 39/57; tel. (12) 39-16-21; f. 1990; 6 a year; publ. by the Ministry of Health and the Medical Industry; Editor-in-Chief BAYRAMAMMED TACHMAMEDOV; circ. 35,071.

Türkmen dili khem edebiyati (Turkmen Language and Literature): 744000 Aşgabat; tel. (12) 41-88-03; f. 1991; 6 a year; publ. by the Ministry of Education.

Türkmen dunyasi: 744004 Aşgabat, ul. Azad 20; tel. (12) 47-81-18; organ of the Humanitarian Association of World Turkmen; Editor-in-Chief ANNABERDY AGABAYEV; circ. 11,956.

Türkmen medeniyeti (Turkmen Culture): 744007 Aşgabat, ul. O. Kuliyeva 21; tel. (12) 25-37-22; f. 1993; 2 a year; publ. by the Ministry of Culture, Television and Radio; Editor GELDYMYRAT NURMUKHAMMEDOV.

Türkmen sporty/Sport Turkmenistana (Turkmen Sport): 744004 Aşgabat, ul. Galkynyş 20; tel. (12) 22-33-72; weekly; in Turkmen and Russian; Editor-in-Chief VIKTOR MIHAYLOV; circ. 2,500.

Türkmenistanyn Lukmancykygy: 744004 Aşgabat, ul. A. Gulmammedov 4A; tel. (12) 35-25-40; every two months; health policy; Editor-in-Chief O. SERDAROV.

Türkmenistanyn oba khozhalygy (Agriculture of Turkmenistan): 744000 Aşgabat, ul. Azad 63; tel. (12) 35-19-38; f. 1929; Editor BYASHIM TALLYKOV; circ. 3,500.

Türkmenistanyng Mejlisining Maglumatlary (Bulletin of the Majlis of Turkmenistan): 744000 Aşgabat, ul. Garaşizlik 110; tel. (12) 35-50-39; fax (12) 35-31-47; e-mail mejlis@online.tm; f. 1960; 4 a year; in Russian and Turkmen.

Vozrozhdeniye (Rebirth): 744604 Aşgabat, ul. Galkynyş 20; tel. (12) 35-10-84; in Russian; political; Editor-in-Chief H. DIVANGULYEV; circ. 1,500.

NEWS AGENCY

Türkmen Dowlet Khabarlar Gullugy (Turkmen State News Service): 744000 Aşgabat, ul. Bitarap Turkmenistan 24A; tel. (12) 39-12-21; fax (12) 51-02-34; e-mail tpress@online.tm; f. 1967; Dir JEREN TAIMOVA.

Publishers

Magaryf Publishing House: 744000 Aşgabat; Dir N. ATAYEV.

Turkmenistan State Publishing Service: 744000 Aşgabat, ul. Galkynyş 20; tel. (12) 46-90-13; f. 1965; politics, science and fiction; Chair. ANNANUR CHARYYAROV.

Ylym Publishing House: 744000 Aşgabat, ul. Azad 59; tel. (12) 29-04-84; f. 1952; desert development, science; Dir N. I. FAIZULAYEVA.

Broadcasting and Communications

TELECOMMUNICATIONS

MTS Turkmenistan: Aşgabat, ul. 2038 56; tel. (12) 42-52-05; internet www.mts.tm; provides over 85% of mobile cellular telecommunications services in Turkmenistan; majority owned by Mobile TeleSystems (Russia); wireless internet services introduced in 2008; Pres. LEONID MELAMED.

Türkmentelekom: 744000 Aşgabat, ul. Asudalyk 36; tel. (12) 51-12-77; fax (12) 51-02-40; e-mail admin@telecom.tm; internet www.telecom.tm; f. 1993; Dir-Gen. ANNALY CH. BERDINOBATOV.

BROADCASTING

Turkmen State Information Agency (Türkmen Dovlet Habarlary): 744004 Aşgabat, ul. Gurungan; tel. (12) 39-12-21; fax (12) 51-02-34; e-mail tpress@online.tm; Head JEREN TAIMOVA.

Radio

Turkmen National Radio Co: 744000 Aşgabat, ul. Navoi 5; tel. (12) 39-25-20; Chair. MURAD ORAZOV.

  Char Tarapdan (From All Sides): tel. (12) 39-86-72; Dir BERDIMYRAT ABDYYEV.

  Miras (Heritage): tel. (12) 35-68-50; Dir GURBANDURDY REJEPOV.

  Watan (Fatherland): tel. (12) 51-12-96; Dir NURBERDI DADEBAYEV.

Television

Turkmen National Television Co: 744000 Aşgabat, ul. Navoi 5; tel. (12) 39-25-20; Chair. MURAD ORAZOV.

  Altyn Asyr (Golden Age): tel. (12) 39-85-06; Dir SHADURDY ALOVOV (acting).

  Miras (Heritage): tel. (12) 35-20-43; Dir BYAGUL CH. NURMURADOVA.

  Türkmenistan: tel. (12) 35-00-86; Dir MURAD A. ORAZOV.

  Yaşlyk (Youth): tel. (12) 35-00-86; Dir (vacant).

Finance

(cap. = capital; res = reserves; dep. = deposits; m. = million; brs = branches; amounts in Turkmen manats)

BANKING

In late 2002 there were 12 commercial banks operating in Turkmenistan. The state retains substantial interests and involvement in banking.

Central Bank

Central Bank of Turkmenistan: 744000 Aşgabat, ul. Bitarap Türkmenistan 36; tel. (12) 38-10-27; fax (12) 51-08-12; e-mail merkezb2@online.tm; f. 1991; central monetary authority, issuing bank and supervisory authority; Chair. GUVANCHMURAT B. GEOKLENOV; 5 brs.

Other Banks

Daihanbank: 744000 Aşgabat, ul. 2067 60; tel. and fax (12) 41-98-68; e-mail daybank@online.tm; f. 1989 as independent bank, Agroprombank, reorganized 1999; specializes in agricultural sector; Chair. of Bd TUMAR MAMMEDOV; 70 brs.

Garagum International Joint-Stock Bank: 744000 Aşgabat, ul. O. Kuliyeva 3; tel. (12) 35-22-01; fax (12) 35-38-54; f. 1993 as International Bank for Reconstruction, Development and Support of Entrepreneurship, name changed 2000; Chair. BEGENCH CHOPANOV.

Garaşyslyk Bank: 744000 Aşgabat, ul. Gerogly 30A; tel. (12) 35-48-75; fax (12) 39-01-24; e-mail garash@cbtm.net; f. 1999 following merger of Gas Bank and Aşgabat Bank; cap. US $5m. (Oct. 2003); Chair. (vacant); 5 brs.

Kreditbank: 744000 Aşgabat, pr. Magtymguly; tel. (12) 35-02-22; fax (12) 35-03-09; e-mail kreditbank@online.tm; f. 1995; fmrly Rossiiskii Kredit; Chair. BATYR BAYRIYEV.

President Bank: 744000 Aşgabat, ul. Gurungan 22; tel. (12) 35-79-43; fax (12) 51-08-12; e-mail presidentbank@cbtm.net; f. 2000; cap. US $60m.; Exec. Dir (vacant).

Savings Bank of Turkmenistan (Sberbank): 744000 Aşgabat, pr. Magtymguly 86; tel. (12) 35-46-71; fax (12) 35-40-04; f. 1923, reorganized 1989; wholly state-owned; Chair. BEGENCH BAYMUKHAMEDOV; 120 brs.

Senagatbank: 744013 Aşgabat, pr. S. Türkmenbaşi 42; tel. (12) 45-31-33; fax (12) 45-44-09; e-mail senagat@online.tm; f. 1989; cap. 31,200m., res 1,394m., dep. 32,547m. (Feb. 2005); Chair. EYEBERDI ATAYEV; 5 brs.

Turkmen Turkish Commercial Bank: 744000 Aşgabat, pr. Magtumguly 111/2, POB 15; tel. (12) 51-14-07; fax (12) 51-11-23; e-mail ttcb@online.tm; f. 1993, with 50% Turkish ownership; cap. 26,000.0m., res 2,220.8m., dep. 34,463.5m. (Dec. 2005); Chair. BATIR SAHATOV.

Türkmenbank—State Commercial Bank 'Türkmenistan': 744000 Aşgabat, ul. Gurungan 10A; tel. (12) 51-07-21; fax (12) 39-67-35; e-mail turkmenbank@ctbm.net; f. 1992; Chair. ATAMYRAT ATALYKOV.

Türkmenbaşi Bank: 744000 Aşgabat, ul. Annadurdiyeva 54; tel. (12) 51-24-50; fax (12) 51-11-11; e-mail mail@investbank.org; f. 1992 as Investbank, renamed in 2000; Chair. BELA KHODZHAMYRADOV; 23 brs.

Türkmenvnesheconombank—State Bank for Foreign Economic Affairs of Turkmenistan: 744000 Aşgabat, ul. Garaşizlik 32; tel. (12) 40-60-40; fax (12) 40-60-45; e-mail tveb@online.tm; internet ww.tfeb.gov.tm; f. 1992 as independent bank, from Soviet Vneshekonombank; wholly state-owned; cap. 344,064m., dep. 4,599,973m., total assets 5,059,082m. (Dec. 2006); Chair. RAHIMBERDI JEPBAROV (acting); 5 brs.

COMMODITY EXCHANGE

State Commodity and Raw Materials Exchange of Turkmenistan: 744000 Aşgabat, pr. Magtymguly 111; tel. (12) 35-43-21; fax (12) 51-03-04; e-mail info@exchange.gov.tm; internet www.exchange.gov.tm; f. 1994; Chair. YAGMYRGELDY MYRATLYEV.

Trade and Industry

GOVERNMENT AGENCIES

National Institute of State Statistics and Information on Turkmenistan (Türkmenmillihasabat): 744000 Aşgabat, ul. 2033 72; tel. (12) 39-42-65; fax (12) 35-43-79; e-mail staff@natstat.gov.tm; f. 1997; Dir KAKAMYRAT MOMMADOV.

State Agency for Foreign Investment (SAFI): 744000 Aşgabat, ul. Azad 53; tel. and fax (12) 35-04-16; e-mail saffi@online.tm; f. 1996; monitors and regulates all foreign investment in Turkmenistan; registers foreign cos in Turkmenistan; Dir (vacant).

DEVELOPMENT ORGANIZATION

Small and Medium Enterprise Development Agency (SMEDA): 744000 Aşgabat, ul. 2015 8; tel. (12) 34-42-59; fax (12) 34-51-49; e-mail smeda@cat.glasnet.ru; jt venture between Turkmen Govt and the European Union (EU); Dir SERDAR BABAYEV.

CHAMBER OF COMMERCE

Chamber of Commerce and Industry of Turkmenistan: 744000 Aşgabat, ul. 2037 17; tel. (12) 35-64-03; fax (12) 35-13-52; e-mail mission@online.tm; f. 1959; Chair. ARSLAN F. NEPESOV.

INDUSTRIAL AND TRADE ASSOCIATION

Union of Manufacturers and Entrepreneurs: Aşgabat, ul. Ostrovskogo 26; tel. (12) 34-66-69; Chair. ALEXANDER DADEYEV.

UTILITIES

Electricity

Kuvvat Turkmen State Energy Technology Corpn: 744000 Aşgabat, ul. 2008 6; tel. (12) 35-68-04; fax (12) 39-06-82; e-mail kuvvat@online.tm; state electrical power generation co and agency; Chair. YUSUP DAVYDOV.

STATE HYDROCARBONS COMPANIES

Türkmenbaşi Oil Refinery: 745000 Balkan Velayat, Türkmenbaşi, POB 5; tel. (00222) 7-45-45; fax (00222) 7-45-44; production and refining of petroleum; sales of petroleum and liquefied natural gas; Dir (vacant).

Türkmengaz: 744036 Aşgabat, ul. 1939 56; tel. (12) 40-32-00; fax (12) 40-32-54; e-mail annam@online.tm; f. 1996; govt agency responsible for natural gas operations, incl. development of system of extraction, processing of gas and gas concentrate, and gas transportation and sale; Chair. BAYMYRAT HOJAMUHAMMEDOV.

Türkmengeologiya: 744000 Aşgabat, ul. 2023 7/32; tel. (12) 35-13-46; fax (12) 35-50-15; govt agency responsible for natural gas and petroleum exploration; Chair. TORE YAGSHIMURAADOV.

Türkmenneft: 745100 Balkan Velayat, Balkanabat, pr. Magtymguly 49; tel. (00243) 2-19-45; govt agency responsible for petroleum operations and production; Chair. ORAZDURDY KHODZHAMURADOV; Gen. Dir KHAKIM IMAMOV.

Türkmenneftegazstroi: 744036 Aşgabat, ul. Arçabil 56; tel. (12) 40-35-01; fax (12) 40-35-01; e-mail tngg@online.tm; govt agency for construction projects in the hydrocarbons sector; Chair. GURBANBERDY ORAZMURADOV.

TRADE UNIONS

Federation of Trade Unions of Turkmenistan: 744000 Aşgabat, pr. S. Türkmenbaşi 13; tel. (12) 35-62-08; fax (12) 35-21-30; Chair. ENEBAY G. ATAYEVA.

Committee of Trade Unions of Ahal Velayat: 744000 Ahal Velayat, pos. Anau, Gyaver etrap; tel. 41-39-19; Dir A. TAGANOV.

Committee of Trade Unions of Daşoguz Velayat: 746311 Daşoguz Velayat, Niyazovsk, S. Türkmenbaşi shayoly 8; Dir SH. IGAMOV.

Transport

RAILWAYS

The main rail line in the country runs from Türkmenbaşi (formerly Krasnovodsk), on the Caspian Sea, in the west, via Aşgabat and Mari, to Türkmenabat (formerly Charjew) in the east. From Türkmenabat one line runs further east, to the other Central Asian countries of the former USSR, while another runs north-west, via Uzbekistan and Kazakhstan, to join the Russian rail network. In 2007 the total length of rail track in use in Turkmenistan was 2,523 km. A 203-km rail link from Türkmenabat to Atamarut was opened in 1999. In 1996 a rail link was established with Iran (on the route Tejen–Serakhs–Mashad), thus providing the possibility of rail travel and transportation between Turkmenistan and İstanbul, Turkey, as well as giving access to the Persian (Arabian) Gulf. A 540-km railway line, running south–north across the country from Aşgabat to Daşoguz, via Garagum, was completed in early 2006.

Turkmenistan State Railways (Türkmendemorjollari): 744007 Aşgabat, pr. S. Türkmenbaşi 7; tel. (12) 35-55-45; fax (12) 51-06-32; f. 1992; Pres. B. P. REDJEPOV.

ROADS

In 1999 there was an estimated total of 24,000 km of roads, of which some 19,500 km were hard-surfaced. In early 2008 construction was under way on a principal road of 1,200 km, which was to link Türkmenbaşi with the eastern town of Farap.

SHIPPING

Shipping services link Türkmenbaşi (formerly Krasnovodsk) with Baku (Bakı, Azerbaijan), Makhachkala (Dagestan, Russia) and the major Iranian ports on the Caspian Sea. The Amu Dar'ya river is an important inland waterway. From 2000 Türkmenbaşi port was undergoing an extensive process of modernization.

Shipowning Companies

Neftec: 745100 Balkan Velayat, Türkmenbaşi; tel. (2) 765-81; fax (2) 766-89.

Turkmen Maritime Steamship Co: 745100 Balkan Velayat, Türkmenbaşi, ul. Shagadama 8; tel. (2) 767-34.

Turkmen Shipping Co: 745100 Balkan Velayat, Türkmenbaşi, ul. Shagadama 8; tel. (2) 972-67; fax (2) 767-85.

Türkmenderyayollary: 746000 Lebap Velayat, Türkmenabat, ul. Gyamichiler 8; tel. (2) 223-12; fax (2) 23-46-88; f. 1992 as Turkmen River Shipping Co; renamed as above in 1998.

Türkmenneftflot: 745100 Balkan Velayat, Türkmenbaşi, POB 6; tel. (2) 762-62.

CIVIL AVIATION

Turkmenistan's international airport is at Aşgabat. In December 2007 it was announced that the National Civil Aviation Authority of Turkmenistan (Türkmenhovayollary) was to sign an agreement with the Turkish company Polimeks on the construction of an airport in Türkmenbaşi, at a cost of €125m.

National Civil Aviation Authority of Turkmenistan (Türkmenhovayollary): 744000 Aşgabat, ul. 2007 3A; tel. (12) 35-10-52; fax (12) 35-44-02; e-mail aviahead@online.tm; f. 1992; Dir-Gen. MERDAN AYAZOV.

Turkmenistan Airlines: 744000 Aşgabat, ul. Magtymguly 80; tel. (12) 35-10-52; fax (12) 35-44-02; f. 1992; domestic and international scheduled and charter passenger flights, incl. services to Europe, Central and South-East Asia, and the Middle East; three divisions: Ahal Air Co, Khazar Air Co and Lebap Air Co; Head GURBANYAZ TIRKISHOV.

Tourism

Although the tourism sector in Turkmenistan remains relatively undeveloped, owing, in part, to the vast expanse of the Kara-Kum desert (some 80% of the country's total area), the Government has made efforts to improve the standard of visitor accommodation (there are a number of new luxury hotels in Aşgabat) and to improve the capacity and efficiency of the capital's international airport. The scenic Kopet Dagh mountains, the Caspian Sea coast, the archaeological sites and mountain caves of Kugitang, and the hot subterranean mineral lake at Kov-Ata are among the country's natural attractions, while the ancient cities of Mari and Nisa—former capitals of the Seljuk and Parthian empires, respectively—are of considerable historical interest. In addition, Kunya-Urgench is an important site of Muslim pilgrimage. In 2005, according to the World Tourism Organization, there were 11,611 visitors from abroad; receipts from tourism totalled US $192m. in 1998.

State Committee for Tourism and Sport: 744000 Aşgabat, ul. Pushkin 17; tel. (12) 35-47-77; fax (12) 39-67-40; e-mail turkmentan@online.tm; internet www.tourism-sport.gov.tm; founded on the basis of the State Tourist Corpn Turkmensyyakhat; f. 2000; Chair. GURBANMAMMET ELYASOV.

TUVALU

Introductory Survey

Location, Climate, Language, Religion, Flag, Capital

Tuvalu is a scattered group of nine small atolls (five of which enclose sizeable lagoons), extending about 560 km (350 miles) from north to south, in the western Pacific Ocean. Its nearest neighbours are Fiji to the south, Kiribati to the north and Solomon Islands to the west. The climate is warm and pleasant, with a mean annual temperature of 30°C (86°F), and there is very little seasonal variation. The average annual rainfall is about 3,500 mm (140 ins), the wettest months being November to February. The inhabitants speak Tuvaluan and English. Almost all of them profess Christianity, and about 98% are Protestants. The national flag (proportions 1 by 2) is light blue with the United Kingdom flag as a rectangular canton in the upper hoist, occupying one-quarter of the area, and nine five-pointed yellow stars (arranged to symbolize a map of the archipelago) in the fly. The flag was reintroduced in February 1997 to replace a design, adopted in October 1995, omitting the British union flag. The capital is on Funafuti Atoll.

Recent History

Tuvalu was formerly known as the Ellice (or Lagoon) Islands. Between about 1850 and 1875 many of the islanders were captured by slave-traders and this, together with European diseases, reduced the population from about 20,000 to 3,000. In 1877 the United Kingdom established the Western Pacific High Commission (WPHC), with its headquarters in Fiji, and the Ellice Islands and other groups were placed under its jurisdiction. In 1892 a British protectorate was declared over the Ellice Islands, and the group was linked administratively with the Gilbert Islands to the north. In 1916 the United Kingdom annexed the protectorate, which was renamed the Gilbert and Ellice Islands Colony (GEIC). During the Japanese occupation of the Gilbert Islands in 1942–43, the administration of the GEIC was temporarily moved to Funafuti in the Ellice Islands. (For more details of the history of the GEIC, see the chapter on Kiribati.)

A series of advisory and legislative bodies prepared the GEIC for self-government. In May 1974 the last of these, the Legislative Council, was replaced by the House of Assembly, with 28 elected members (including eight Ellice Islanders) and three official members. A Chief Minister was elected by the House and chose between four and six other ministers, one of whom had to be from the Ellice Islands.

In January 1972 the appointment of a separate GEIC Governor, who assumed most of the functions previously exercised by the High Commissioner for the Western Pacific, increased the long-standing anxiety of the Ellice Islanders over their minority position as Polynesians in the colony, dominated by the Micronesians of the Gilbert Islands. In a referendum held in the Ellice Islands in August and September 1974, more than 90% of the voters favoured separate status for the group, and in October 1975 the Ellice Islands, under the old native name of Tuvalu ('eight standing together', which referred to the eight populated atolls), became a separate British dependency. The Deputy Governor of the GEIC took office as Her Majesty's Commissioner for Tuvalu. The eight Ellice representatives in the GEIC House of Assembly became the first elected members of the new Tuvalu House of Assembly. They elected one of their number, Toaripi Lauti, to be Chief Minister. Tuvalu was completely separated from the GEIC administration in January 1976. The remainder of the GEIC was renamed the Gilbert Islands and achieved independence, as Kiribati, in July 1979.

Tuvalu's first separate elections took place in August 1977, when the number of elective seats in the House of Assembly was increased to 12. An independence Constitution was finalized at a conference in London in February 1978. After five months of internal self-government, Tuvalu became independent on 1 October 1978, with Lauti as the first Prime Minister. The pre-independence House of Assembly was redesignated Parliament. In September 2000 Tuvalu was formally admitted to the UN.

In 1983 the USA formally renounced its claim, dating from 1856, to the four southernmost atolls. Following elections to Parliament in September 1981, Lauti was replaced as Prime Minister by Dr Tomasi (later Sir Tomasi) Puapua. Puapua was re-elected Prime Minister following subsequent elections in September 1985.

In February 1986 a nation-wide poll was conducted to establish public opinion as to whether Tuvalu should remain an independent constitutional monarchy, with the British monarch at its head, or become a republic. Only on one atoll did the community appear to be in favour of the adoption of republican status. In March Tupua (later Sir Tupua) Leupena, a former Speaker of Parliament, was appointed Governor-General, replacing Sir Penitala Teo, who had occupied the post since independence in 1978.

At a general election in September 1989 supporters of Puapua were reported to have been defeated in the election, and an opponent, Bikenibeu Paeniu (who had been appointed Minister of Community Services within the previous year), was elected Prime Minister. In October 1990 Toaripi Lauti succeeded Sir Tupua Leupena as Governor-General.

Legislation approved by Parliament in mid-1991, which sought to prohibit all new religions from the islands and to establish the Church of Tuvalu as the State Church, caused considerable controversy and extensive debate. A survey showed the population to be almost equally divided over the matter, although Paeniu firmly opposed the motion, describing it as incompatible with basic human rights.

In August 1991 the Government announced that it was to prepare a compensation claim against the United Kingdom for the allegedly poor condition of Tuvalu's economy and infrastructure at the time of the country's achievement of independence in 1979. Moreover, Tuvalu was to seek additional compensation for damage caused during the Second World War when the United Kingdom gave permission for the USA to build airstrips on the islands (some 40% of Funafuti was uninhabitable because of large pits created by US troops during the construction of an airstrip on the atoll). Relations with the United Kingdom deteriorated further in late 1992, when the British Government harshly criticized the financial policy of Paeniu's Government. Paeniu defended his Government's policies, and stated that continued delays in the approval of aid projects from the United Kingdom meant that Tuvalu would not be seeking further development funds from the British Government.

At a general election held in September 1993, three of the 12 incumbent members of Parliament lost their seats. However, at elections to the premiership held in the same month, Paeniu and Puapua received six votes each. When a second vote produced a similar result, the Governor-General dissolved Parliament, in accordance with the Constitution. Paeniu and his Cabinet remained in office until the holding of a further general election in November. At elections to the premiership in the following month Kamuta Latasi defeated Paeniu by seven votes to five. Puapua, who had agreed not to challenge Paeniu in the contest in favour of supporting Latasi, was elected Speaker of Parliament. In June 1994 Latasi removed the Governor-General, Toomu Malaefono Sione, from office, some seven months after he had been appointed to the position, and replaced him with Tulaga (later Sir Tulaga) Manuella. Latasi alleged that Paeniu's appointment of Sione had been politically motivated.

In December 1994, in what was widely regarded as a significant rejection of its political links with the United Kingdom, the Tuvaluan Parliament voted to remove the British union flag from the Tuvalu national flag. A new design was selected and the new flag was inaugurated in October 1995. Speculation that the British monarch would be removed as Head of State intensified during 1995, following the appointment of a committee to review the Constitution. The three-member committee was to examine the procedure surrounding the appointment and removal of the Governor-General, and, particularly, to consider the adoption of a republican system of government.

In late 1996 the Deputy Prime Minister, Otinielu Tausi, and the parliamentary Speaker, Dr Tomasi Puapua, both announced their decision to withdraw their support for Latasi's Government, thereby increasing the number of opposition members in Parliament from five to seven. This reversal appeared to be in response to increasing dissatisfaction among the population with Latasi. This had been perceived firstly with his unpopular initiative to replace the country's national flag, and was exacerbated by revelations that the leasing of Tuvalu's telephone code to a foreign company had resulted in the use of the islands' telephone system for personal services considered indecent by the majority of islanders. (It was announced by the Government in October 2000 that the lease was to be terminated by the end of the year.) Opponents of the Prime Minister submitted a parliamentary motion of no confidence in his Government in December, which was approved by seven votes to five. Paeniu subsequently defeated Latasi, by a similar margin, to become Prime Minister, and a new Cabinet was appointed. The new premier acted promptly to restore the country's original flag, by proposing a parliamentary motion in February 1997, which was approved by seven votes to five.

A total of 35 candidates contested a general election on 26 March 1998. The period prior to the election had been characterized by a series of bitter disputes between Paeniu and Latasi, in which both had made serious accusations of sexual and financial misconduct against the other. Five members of the previous Parliament were returned to office, although Latasi unexpectedly failed to secure re-election. Paeniu was subsequently re-elected Prime Minister by 10 votes to two. In June the new Government announced a series of development plans and proposals for constitutional reform, including the introduction of a code of conduct for political leaders and the creation of an ombudsman's office. Paeniu stated that his administration intended to consult widely with the population before any changes were implemented. Also in 1998 Puapua was appointed Governor-General, replacing Manuella.

On 13 April 1999 Paeniu lost a parliamentary vote of confidence and was forced to resign. Later in the month Ionatana Ionatana, hitherto the Minister of Health, Education, Culture, Women and Community Affairs, was elected by Parliament as the new Prime Minister. On his appointment Ionatana immediately effected a reorganization of the Cabinet.

Potentially the most significant new source of revenue for many years was established in September 1998 when the Government signed an agreement to lease the country's national internet suffix '.tv' to a Canadian information company. The company, which defeated several other business interests to secure the deal, was expected to market the internet address to international television companies. Although that arrangement subsequently failed, it was announced in February 2000 that a US $50m. deal on the sale of the '.tv' suffix had been concluded with a US company. The sale was expected to generate some $10m. annually in revenue. The funds generated from the sale enabled Tuvalu officially to join the UN, and participate in the 55th annual UN General Assembly Meeting, held in September 2000.

In early December 2000 Prime Minister Ionatana Ionatana died unexpectedly. The Deputy Prime Minister, Lagitupu Tuilimu was immediately appointed as interim Prime Minister, pending the election of a replacement. In late February 2001 Parliament elected as Prime Minister the Minister of Internal Affairs and Rural and Urban Development, Faimalaga Luka; he assumed responsibility for the additional portfolios of foreign affairs, finance and economic planning, and trade and commerce, and immediately named a new cabinet. A vote of no confidence was upheld against Luka in December 2001 while he was away in New Zealand, undergoing a medical examination. Koloa Talake, a former Minister of Finance, was elected Prime Minister in the same month, winning eight of the 15 votes cast (the number of parliamentary seats having been increased from 12 to 15). He appointed an entirely new Cabinet.

Talake announced in March 2002 that lawyers were preparing evidence for further legal action against the United Kingdom, seeking compensation for the alleged inequality of the division of assets between Tuvalu and Kiribati when the two nations had achieved independence in the late 1970s. Following the general election held on 25 July 2002, Saufatu Sopoanga, a former Minister of Finance, defeated Amasone Kilei, the opposition candidate, by eight votes to seven to become the new Prime Minister. Sopoanga subsequently announced his intention to hold a referendum on the adoption of a republican system of Government in Tuvalu.

In May 2003 two by-elections resulted in the loss of the Government's one-seat majority. The Government's subsequent refusal to convene Parliament (allegedly in order to evade a vote of no confidence) was strongly criticized by the opposition. The Government maintained that it would regain its majority with an imminent defection from the opposition and would then convene Parliament. In July, however, the situation remained unchanged and the opposition consequently sought a court order obliging Sopoanga to convene Parliament. The appointment, in early September, of Faimalaga Luka, hitherto Speaker and a member of Parliament, as the country's new Governor-General necessitated an additional by-election, which resulted in a further delay to Parliament's being convened. However, following the success of its candidate at the by-election, and (as anticipated) the defection of an opposition member, the Government regained its majority in mid-October. Parliament was finally convened in early November.

In April 2004 the Government announced that a team of officials was touring the outer islands to canvas opinion on the adoption of republican status for Tuvalu. If islanders indicated sufficient support for the proposal, a referendum would be held. In March 2005 the Prime Minister indicated that he expected the referendum to go ahead, stating that he had encountered widespread concern among Tuvaluans that the British Government was failing to meet its financial obligations to the islands.

In August 2004 the Prime Minister, Saufatu Sopoanga, was ousted by nine parliamentary votes to five in a vote of no confidence after a member of the Government crossed the floor to vote with the opposition and was joined by the Speaker. However, the election of a new Prime Minister was delayed by Sopoanga's decision to relinquish his seat, thus necessitating the organization of a by-election before Parliament could select a premier. Deputy Prime Minister Maatia Toafa assumed the role of acting Prime Minister in the interim. Sopoanga regained his seat in a by-election in early October, and on 11 October acting Prime Minister Maatia Toafa was elected to the premiership, defeating Sopoanga by eight votes to seven.

In April 2005 it was announced that Sio Patiale, a member of Parliament, was to resign on grounds of ill health. The consequent by-election was expected to be very significant, owing to the possibility that it might result in a majority for the opposition in Parliament. In the same month the Governor-General, Faimalaga Luka, resigned, having reached the maximum permitted age for the post of 65, and was replaced by Filiomea Telito. Luka died in August of that year. A further by-election in September, caused by the resignation of another member of Parliament, was won by a candidate who decided to support the Government, thus consolidating its majority.

In May 2005 the President of Taiwan visited three countries in the Pacific, including Tuvalu, in an attempt to improve diplomatic relations. During his brief visit, the Prime Minister signed a joint communiqué with his Tuvaluan counterpart.

Tuvalu's annual visitor arrival numbers were greatly increased by a meeting of ministers which the country hosted in Funanfuti in June 2005. Some 80 delegates from 14 Pacific island countries attended the meeting to discuss issues concerned with economic development in the region.

The legislative election held on 3 August 2006 resulted in major changes to the composition of Parliament, with the entry of eight new members. Maatia Toafa was the only cabinet member to retain a seat, and was subsequently replaced as Prime Minister by Apisai Ielemia in mid-August. Ielemia assumed additional responsibility for the foreign affairs portfolio, while Taavau Teii was appointed Deputy Prime Minister and Minister for Natural Resources. Other appointments to the new Government included Lotoala Metia as Minister of Finance, Economic Planning and Industries and Willie Telavi as Minister of Home Affairs and Rural Development.

On 30 April 2008 a referendum on Tuvalu's system of government was conducted. The level of participation was reportedly low, at approximately 21% of the electorate. The majority of voters rejected proposals for a republican system, with a president as head of state: according to reports, 1,260 voters (or 65%) out of a total of 1,939 preferred the retention of the existing system of constitutional monarchy.

In February 2009 Prime Minister Ielemia undertook a state visit to Taiwan and participated in discussions with Taiwanese President Ma Ying-jeou, following which the two leaders pledged their commitment to the development of bilateral relations. President Ma also expressed Taiwan's support for Tuvalu in addressing the problems arising from global warming (see below).

In 1989 a UN report on the 'greenhouse effect' (the heating of the earth's atmosphere) listed Tuvalu as one of the island groups which would completely disappear beneath the sea in the 21st century, unless drastic action were taken. At the UN World Climate Conference, held in Geneva in late 1990, Paeniu appealed for urgent action by developed nations to combat the environmental changes caused by the 'greenhouse effect', which were believed to include a 10-fold increase in cyclone frequency (from two in 1940 to 21 in 1990), an increase in salinity in ground water and a considerable decrease in the average annual rainfall. However, the Government remained critical of the inertia with which it considered certain countries had reacted to its appeal for assistance and reiterated the Tuvaluan people's fears of physical and cultural extinction. The subsequent Prime Minister, Kamuta Latasi, was similarly critical of the industrial world's apparent disregard for the plight of small island nations vulnerable to the effects of climate change, particularly when Tuvalu was struck by tidal waves in 1994 (believed to be the first experienced by the islands). The Government of Tuvalu was strongly critical of Australia's refusal to reduce its emission of pollutant gases (known to contribute to the 'greenhouse effect') at the Conference of the Parties to the UN Framework Convention on Climate Change (UNFCCC, see UN Environment Programme, see p. 65) in Kyoto, Japan, in late 1997. In August 2001 Tuvalu was one of six members of the Pacific Islands Forum to demand a meeting with US President George W. Bush to try to enlist his support for the Kyoto Protocol. Although the USA produced nearly one-third of the industrialized countries' carbon-dioxide emissions, it had repeatedly refused to adopt the Kyoto Protocol, which urged industrial nations to reduce carbon-dioxide emissions by 5.2% from 1990 levels by 2012. The Kyoto Protocol was finally ratified by Australia in December 2007.

The installation of a new sea-level monitoring station began in December 2001 as part of the South Pacific Sea Level and Climate Monitoring Project administered by the Australian aid agency, AusAID. In January 2002 it was reported that the Government had engaged a US law firm to prosecute the USA and other nations for failing to meet their commitments to the UNFCCC. In September 2003 Tuvalu's Prime Minister addressed the 58th session of the UN General Assembly in New York and appealed for collective action to mitigate the impact of climate change and rising sea-levels on the islands. He once again urged all industrialized nations, particularly the USA, to sign the Kyoto Protocol. The option of resettlement on neighbouring islands, including Fiji, was under consideration, but only as a last resort, and the Government was also considering the purchase of land in other countries for economic reasons, while declaring that this might be a useful long-term solution should the problems caused by climate change worsen. In December 2007 it was reported that water from wells was becoming increasingly unsuitable for consumption, while high tides were causing frequent flooding.

Tuvalu was subject to considerable international criticism in mid-2004 regarding its decision to join the International Whaling Commission (IWC, see p. 418). Environmental and animal welfare groups accused the Tuvaluan Government of accepting financial incentives from Japan in return for agreeing to use its vote to support a removal of the ban on commercial whaling at the commission's annual meeting in Italy in July 2004. In early 2006 the US ambassador to Tuvalu, Larry Dinger, received a petition from Greenpeace, the international environmentalist group, urging Tuvalu to cease voting with Japan at the IWC. In May of the same year, however, prior to the IWC's annual meeting in Japan, Tuvalu reiterated its stance. Tuvalu later denied that Japan had secured its vote at the meeting through its financing of infrastructure projects in Tuvalu after IWC delegates voted narrowly in favour of the resolution calling for a resumption of commercial whaling.

Government

Tuvalu is a constitutional monarchy. Executive authority is vested in the British sovereign, as Head of State, and is exercisable by her representative, the Governor-General, who is appointed on the recommendation of the Prime Minister and acts, in almost all cases, on the advice of the Cabinet. Legislative power is vested in the unicameral Parliament, with 15 members elected by universal adult suffrage for four years (subject to dissolution). The Cabinet is led by the Prime Minister, who is elected by and from the members of Parliament. On the Prime Minister's recommendation, other ministers are appointed by the Governor-General. The Cabinet is responsible to Parliament. Each of the inhabited atolls has its own elected Island Council, which is responsible for local government.

Economic Affairs

In 2007 the UN's Economic and Social Commission for Asia and the Pacific (ESCAP) estimated Tuvalu's gross domestic product (GDP) at current prices to be US $29.6m., equivalent to some $2,811 per head. During 2000–07, it was estimated, the population increased at an average annual rate of 0.5%. According to figures from ESCAP, overall GDP increased, in real terms, at an average annual rate of 5.3% in 2000–07. Compared with the previous year, GDP rose by 3.0% in 2007.

Agriculture (including fishing) is, with the exception of copra production, of a basic subsistence nature. According to ESCAP estimates the sector contributed some 16.6% of GDP in 2007; the GDP of the agricultural sector increased at an average annual rate of 2.0% in 2000–05. Compared with the previous year, agricultural GDP increased by 1.6% in 2007. In 2005, according to FAO, the sector engaged some 25% of the labour force. Coconuts (the source of copra) are the only cash crop. Pulaka, taro, papayas, the screw-pine (*Pandanus*) and bananas are cultivated as food crops and honey is produced. From the 1990s agriculture was increasingly affected by climate change and rising sea-levels. More frequent high tides caused flooding and damaged crops, particularly the important taro crop; such floods have also killed tree roots, which reduced the harvest of coconuts and other fruits. Livestock comprises pigs, poultry and goats. Fish and other sea products are staple constituents of the islanders' diet. The sale of fishing licences to foreign fleets is an important source of income and earned $A11.8m. in 2001 (compared with $A3.6m. in 1997), equivalent to 50.3% of current revenue. However, revenue from this source declined in subsequent years, owing to decreases in catches.

Industry (including mining, manufacturing, construction and utilities) accounted for 13.6% of GDP in 2007, according to ESCAP estimates. In 2000–05, according to the same source, industrial GDP expanded at an average annual rate of 5.9%. Compared with the previous year, the sector's GDP increased by 2.9% in 2007. Manufacturing is confined to the small-scale production of coconut-based products, soap and handicrafts. The manufacturing sector contributed some 3.7% of GDP in 2002.

Energy is derived principally from a power plant (fuelled by oil) and, on the outer islands, solar power. In 1989 mineral fuels accounted for almost 13% of total import costs. With financial assistance from the Japanese Government, construction work on the electricity station on Funafuti was proceeding in 2006/07.

The Government is an important employer (engaging 1,185 people in 2001, equivalent to about one-half of the labour force) and consequently the services sector makes a relatively large contribution to Tuvalu's economy (providing some 69.7% of GDP in 2007, according to ESCAP estimates). According to ESCAP estimates, the GDP of the services sector increased at an average annual rate of 5.0% in 2000–05. Compared with the previous year, the sector's GDP expanded by 2.6% in 2007. The islands' remote situation and lack of amenities have hindered the development of a tourist industry. Visitor arrivals were reported to total 1,130 in 2007, in comparison with 1,135 in 2006. An important source of revenue has been provided by remittances from Tuvaluans working abroad. Remittances from Tuvaluan seafarers employed on foreign vessels were estimated at $A4m. in 2006. In 2001 receipts from the leasing of the islands' internet domain address reached US $1.6m., while revenue from telecommunication licence fees totalled $0.31m.

Tuvalu recorded a visible trade deficit of US $28.6m. in 2003; in that year the cost of imports exceeded $24.0m., while export revenue totalled only $147,100. The principal source of imports in 2005 was Fiji (47.0%). The principal market for exports were Italy and Fiji. The principal imports in 2005 were mineral products, prepared foodstuffs, machinery, mechanical appliances and electrical equipment, and transport equipment.

According to ADB figures, the 2007 budget allowed for expenditure of $A23.7m., while revenue (including grants of $A3.6m.) totalled $A19.1m. (in comparison with $A28.6m. in 2006). None the less, with the support of the Consolidated Investment Fund (a depository of the Tuvalu Trust Fund—TTF), the budget deficit was reduced to $A4.6m. in 2007, equivalent to an estimated 14.3% of GDP. The TTF was established in 1987, with assistance from New Zealand, Australia and the United Kingdom, to generate funding, through overseas investment, for development projects. By September 2006 the assets of the TTF were estimated to total $A77m. In 2006 the TTF contributed more than $A11m. to the Consolidated Investment Fund. In 2008/09 New Zealand budgeted for bilateral assistance worth $NZ2.6m. Aid

TUVALU

from Australia was budgeted at $A6.2m. for the same year. Tuvalu has also received significant financial assistance from Taiwan since the establishment of diplomatic relations. Other donors have included Japan and the European Union. The annual rate of inflation averaged 2.8% in 2000–07. According to the ADB, the inflation rate increased from 2.2% in 2007 to 5.3% in 2008.

Tuvalu is a member of the Pacific Community (see p. 391), the Pacific Islands Forum (see p. 393) and the UN Economic and Social Commission for Asia and the Pacific (ESCAP, see p. 36). In 1993 the country was admitted to the Asian Development Bank (ADB, see p. 191).

The islands have continued to suffer from the increasing impact of climate change (see Recent History). In February 2005 high tides flooded homes, government buildings and the airport, also causing damage to agricultural produce. The country is also vulnerable to drought. Tuvalu's high dependence on imports has resulted in a persistent trade deficit. In February 2000 the sale of the '.tv' internet suffix (see Recent History) substantially increased the islands' income. Proceeds from the sale were used to develop the country's infrastructure. The Government of Apisai Ielemia, which took office in August 2006, hoped to reduce the disparities in living standards between Funafuti and the outer islands. In an effort to raise remittances from overseas workers, with external assistance the Tuvalu Maritime Training Institute was to be substantially upgraded and expanded. The Government's short-term development strategy has been formulated within a programme known as Te Kakeega II, eight strategic areas of focus being identified. However, the achievement of these aims was largely dependent upon the performance of the TTF. Revenue from the sale of fishing licences was becoming more vulnerable to the fluctuations in fish stocks caused by the increasing frequency of the climatic phenomena known as El Niño and La Niña. Income from fishing licence fees rose by 18.7% in 2008, while revenues from the '.tv' internet domain facility remained similar to those of the previous year. Income from grants was lower than anticipated in 2008. Although budget expenditure increased by almost 10% in 2008, capital spending remained at the same level as in the previous year, largely owing to the higher than expected costs of a medical treatment programme. The Government was also required to raise electricity subsidies, in order to offset the rising costs of fuel imports. The rate of inflation accelerated in 2008, reaching 13.4% in the third quarter of the year, thus highlighting Tuvalu's vulnerability to increases in fuel and transport costs. However, inflationary pressures were expected to be reduced in 2009. The ADB forecast GDP growth of 1.0% in 2009.

Education

Education is provided by the Government, and is compulsory between the ages of six and 15 years. In 2001 there were 10 primary schools, with a total of 2,067 pupils and 103 teachers in 2006. There were two secondary schools in 2006, with 52 teachers and 629 pupils in 2004. Enrolment in pre-primary level education in 2003/04 was equivalent to 99% of children from the relevant age-group while enrolment in primary schools was equivalent to 98.5% of children from the relevant age-group. In 2000/01 enrolment in secondary schools was equivalent to 84.4% of children from the relevant age-group. The only tertiary institution is the Tuvalu Maritime Training Institute at Amatuku on Funafuti. Further training or vocational courses are available in Fiji and Kiribati. The University of the South Pacific (based in Fiji) has an extension centre on Funafuti. A programme of major reforms in the education system in Tuvalu, begun in the early 1990s, resulted in the lengthening of primary schooling (from six to eight years) and a compulsory two years of secondary education, as well as the introduction of vocational, technical and commerce-related courses at the Maritime Training School. Adult literacy was estimated at 98% at the 1991 census. Total government expenditure on education in 2001 was equivalent to some 35% of total budgetary expenditure. The education sector received funding of US $10.5m. in 2005, as part of a joint grant provided by the New Zealand Government and the World Bank.

Public Holidays

2009: 1 January (New Year's Day), 13 March (Commonwealth Day), 10–13 April (Easter), 1 June (Queen's Official Birthday), 4 August (National Children's Day), 1–2 October (Tuvalu Day, anniversary of independence), 14 November (Prince of Wales's Birthday), 25 December (Christmas Day), 26 December (Boxing Day).

2010: 1 January (New Year's Day), 9 March (Commonwealth Day), 2–5 April (Easter), 7 June (Queen's Official Birthday), 4 August (National Children's Day), 1–2 October (Tuvalu Day, anniversary of independence), 14 November (Prince of Wales's Birthday), 25 December (Christmas Day), 26 December (Boxing Day).

Weights and Measures

The metric system has been introduced, but the imperial system is still employed.

Statistical Survey

Source (unless otherwise indicated): Central Statistics Division, Ministry of Finance and Economic Planning, Private Bag, Vaiaku, Funafuti; tel. 20107; fax 21210; e-mail statistics@tuvalu.tv; internet www.spc.int/prism/country/tv/stats/.

AREA AND POPULATION

Land Area: 25.6 sq km (9.9 sq miles).

Population: 9,043 at census of 17 November 1991; 9,561 (males 4,729, females 4,832) at census of 1 November 2002 (*By Atoll:* Funafuti 4,492; Vaitupu 1,591; Niutao 663; Nanumea 664; Nukufetau 586; Nanumaga 589; Nui 548; Nukulaelae 393; Niulakita 35). Mid-2008 (estimate): 9,729 (Source: Secretariat of the Pacific Community).

Density (at mid-2008): 380.0 per sq km.

Principal Towns (population at 2002 census): Alapi 1,024; Fakaifou 1,007; Senala 589; Teone 540; Vaiaku (capital) 516; Motufoua 506. Source: Thomas Brinkhoff, *City Population* (internet www.citypopulation.de).

Births and Deaths (2006): Registered live births 184; Registered deaths 31.

Life Expectancy (years at birth, WHO estimates): 64.5 (males 64.0; females 65.1) in 2006. Source: WHO, *World Health Statistics*.

Economically Active Population: In 1979 there were 936 people in paid employment, 50% of them in government service. In 1979 114 Tuvaluans were employed by the Nauru Phosphate Co, with a smaller number employed in Kiribati and about 255 on foreign ships. At the 1991 census the total economically active population (aged 15 years and over) stood at 2,383 (males 1,605, females 778). *Mid-2005* (estimates): Agriculture, etc. 1,000; Total labour force 4,000 (Source: FAO).

HEALTH AND WELFARE

Key Indicators

Total Fertility Rate (children per woman, 2006): 3.0.

Under-5 Mortality Rate (per 1,000 live births, 2006): 36.

Physicians (per 1,000 head, 2003): 0.9.

Hospital Beds (per 1,000 head, 2001): 5.6.

Health Expenditure (2006): US $ per head (PPP): 205.

Health Expenditure (2006): % of GDP: 11.4.

Health Expenditure (2006): public (% of total): 92.3.

Access to Sanitation (% of persons, 2004): 90.

For sources and definitions, see explanatory note on p. vi.

AGRICULTURE, ETC.

Principal Crops (metric tons, 2007, FAO estimates): Coconuts 1,700; Roots and tubers 150; Vegetables 540; Bananas 280.

Livestock ('000 head, year ending September 2007, FAO estimates): Pigs 13.6; Chickens 45; Ducks 15.

Livestock Products (metric tons, 2007, FAO estimates): Chicken meat 45; Pig meat 95; Hen eggs 22; Honey 3.

Fishing (metric tons, live weight, 2006, FAO estimates): Total catch 2,201 (Skipjack tuna 1,000; Yellowfin tuna 900).
Source: FAO.

FINANCE

Currency and Exchange Rates: Australian and Tuvaluan currencies are both in use. Australian currency: 100 cents = 1 Australian dollar ($A). *Sterling, US Dollar and Euro Equivalents* (31 December 2008): £1 sterling = $A2.1042; US $1 = $A1.4434; €1 = $A2.0088; $A100 = £47.52 = US $69.28 = €49.78. *Average Exchange Rate* ($A per US dollar): 1.3280 in 2006; 1.1951 in 2007; 1.1922 in 2008.

Budget ($A '000, 2007): Current revenue 15,526 (Revenue from taxation 6,327, Non-tax revenue 9,198); Expenditure 23,682. Source: Asian Development Bank.

Official Development Assistance (US $ million, 2002): Bilateral 11.2; Multilateral 0.5; Total 11.7 (all grants). *2006:* Total assistance 15.3. Source: UN, *Statistical Yearbook for Asia and the Pacific*.

Cost of Living (Consumer Price Index for Funafuti; base: July–Sept. 2003 = 100): All items 105.1 in 2005; 109.1 in 2006; 112.7 in 2007. Source: Asian Development Bank.

Gross Domestic Product (US $ million at constant 1990 prices): 17 in 2005; 17 in 2006; 17 in 2007.

Expenditure on the Gross Domestic Product (US $ million at current prices, 2007): Government final consumption expenditure 16; Private final consumption expenditure 27; Gross fixed capital formation 17; *Total domestic expenditure* 60; Exports of goods and services 4; *Less* Imports of goods and services 34; *GDP in purchasers' values* 30. Source: UN Statistics Division, National Accounts Main Aggregates Database.

Gross Domestic Product by Economic Activity (US $ million at current prices, 2007): Agriculture, hunting, forestry and fishing 5; Mining, manufacturing and utilities 3 (Manufacturing 1); Construction 1; Trade, restaurants and hotels 4; Transport, storage and communications 4; Other services 15; *Gross value added* 33; Net taxes on products –3 (obtained as residual); *GDP in purchasers' values* 30. Source: UN Statistics Division, National Accounts Main Aggregates Database.

Balance of Payments ($A '000, 2003): Exports of goods f.o.b. 444; Imports of goods f.o.b. –28,995; *Trade balance* –28,552; Exports of services and other income 7,403; Imports of services and other income –17,687; *Balance on goods, services and income* –38,836; Current transfers (net) 20,833; *Current balance* –18,003. Source: Asian Development Bank, *Key Indicators of Developing Asian and Pacific Countries*.

EXTERNAL TRADE

Principal Commodities ($A '000, 2005): *Imports:* Animals and animal products 1,473.8; Vegetable products 1,224.2; Prepared foodstuffs 2,385.1; Mineral products 3,661.2; Chemical products 734.5; Textiles and textile articles 759.2; Base metals and articles thereof 695.1; Machinery, mechanical appliances and electrical equipment 2,318.9; Transportation equipment 884.8; Total (incl. others) 16,908.0. *Exports:* Mineral products 5.9; Wood and wood products 10.0; Base metals and articles thereof 12.3; Machinery, mechanical appliances and electrical equipment 13.9; Transportation equipment 9.3; Instruments—measuring, musical 14.9; Total (incl. others) 80.0.

Principal Trading Partners (US $ million, 2005): *Imports*: Australia 3.49; China, People's Republic 6.99; Fiji 18.48; Japan 7.26; New Zealand 1.90; Total (incl. others) 39.36. *Exports*: Denmark 0.03; Fiji 0.19; Germany 0.04; Italy 0.53; Poland 0.02; Total (incl. others) 0.98.

Source: Asian Development Bank, *Key Indicators of Developing Asian and Pacific Countries*.

TRANSPORT

Shipping: *Merchant Fleet* (registered at 31 December 2007): Vessels 155; Total displacement ('000 grt) 857,338. Source: Lloyd's Register-Fairplay, *World Fleet Statistics*.

TOURISM

Tourist Arrivals: 1,290 in 2004; 1,085 in 2005; 1,135 in 2006.

Tourist Arrivals by Country of Residence (2006): Australia 136; Fiji 197; Japan 250; New Zealand 147; United Kingdom 55; USA 56; Total (incl. others) 1,135.

Source: World Tourism Organization.

COMMUNICATIONS MEDIA

Non-daily Newspapers (1996): 1; estimated circulation 300*.

Telephones (main lines, 2005): 900 in use†.

Mobile Cellular Telephones (subscribers, 2005): 1,300.

Internet Users (2005): 1,700.

Radio Receivers (1997): 4,000 in use*.

Facsimile Machines (1993): 10 in use‡.

* Source: UNESCO, *Statistical Yearbook*.
† Source: International Telecommunication Union.
‡ Source: UN, *Statistical Yearbook*.

EDUCATION

Pre-school (2005): 57 teachers; 647 pupils.

Primary (2001, unless otherwise indicated): 9 government schools, 1 private school; 103 teachers (2005); 2,010 pupils (2005).

General Secondary (2005): 2 government schools; 56 teachers; 593 pupils. A maritime school offers training for 60 merchant seamen per year, with vocational, technical and commerce-related courses. The University of the South Pacific has an extension centre in Funafuti offering diploma and vocational courses and the first two years of degree courses (the latter requiring completion in Suva, Fiji).

Directory

The Constitution

A new Constitution came into effect at independence on 1 October 1978. Its main provisions are as follows:

The Constitution states that Tuvalu is a democratic sovereign state and that the Constitution is the Supreme Law. It guarantees protection of all fundamental rights and freedoms and provides for the determination of citizenship.

The British sovereign is represented by the Governor-General, who must be a citizen of Tuvalu and is appointed on the recommendation of the Prime Minister. The Prime Minister is elected by Parliament, and up to four other ministers are appointed by the Governor-General from among the members of Parliament, after consultation with the Prime Minister. The Cabinet, which is directly responsible to Parliament, consists of the Prime Minister and the other ministers, whose functions are to advise the Governor-General upon the government of Tuvalu. The Attorney-General is the principal legal adviser to the Government. Parliament is composed of 15 members directly elected by universal adult suffrage for four years, subject to dissolution, and is presided over by the Speaker (who is elected by the members). The Constitution also provides for the operation of a Judiciary (see Judicial System) and for an independent Public Service. Under a revised Constitution that took effect on 1 October 1986, the Governor-General no longer has the authority to reject the advice of the Government.

The Government

HEAD OF STATE

Sovereign: HM Queen ELIZABETH II.

Governor-General: FILOIMEA TELITO (took office 15 April 2005).

CABINET
(April 2009)

Prime Minister and Minister of Foreign Affairs: APISAI IELEMIA.

Deputy Prime Minister and Minister of Natural Resources: TAAVAU TEII.

Minister of Finance, Economic Planning and Industries: LOTOALA METIA.

Minister of Works, Communications and Transport: TAUKELINA FINIKASO.

Minister of Home Affairs: WILLIE TELAVI.

Minister of Public Utilities and Industries: KAUSEA NATANO.

Minister of Education, Sports and Health: IAKOBA ITALELI.

TUVALU

MINISTRIES

Office of the Prime Minister: Private Mail Bag, Vaiaku, Funafuti; tel. 20101; fax 20820.

Ministry of Education, Sports and Culture: Vaiaku, Funafuti; tel. 20405; fax 20832.

Ministry of Finance and Economic Planning: PMB, Vaiaku, Funafuti; tel. 20202; fax 20210; e-mail secfin@tuvalu.tv.

Ministry of Foreign Affairs: Vaiaku, Funafuti; tel. 20102; fax 20820.

Ministry of Health: Vaiaku, Funafuti; tel. 20403; fax 20832.

Ministry of Home Affairs and Rural Development: Vaiaku, Funafuti; tel. 20172; fax 20821.

Ministry of Local Government, Women and Youth: Vaiaku, Funafuti.

Ministry of Natural Resources, Energy and Environment: Vaiaku, Funafuti; tel. 20827; fax 20826.

Ministry of Trade, Tourism and Commerce: PMB, Vaiaku, Funafuti; tel. 20182; fax 20829.

Ministry of Works, Communications and Transport: PMB, Vaiaku, Funafuti; tel. 20052; fax 20772; e-mail tuvmet@tuvalu.tv.

Legislature

PARLIAMENT

Parliament has 15 members, who hold office for a term of up to four years. A general election was held on 3 August 2006. There are no political parties.

Speaker: KAMUTA LATASI.

Diplomatic Representation

There are no embassies or high commissions in Tuvalu. The British High Commissioner in Fiji is also accredited as High Commissioner to Tuvalu. Other Ambassadors or High Commissioners accredited to Tuvalu include the Australian, New Zealand, US, French and Japanese Ambassadors in Fiji.

Judicial System

The Supreme Law is embodied in the Constitution. The High Court is the superior court of record, presided over by the Chief Justice, and has jurisdiction to consider appeals from judgments of the Magistrates' Courts and the Island Courts. Appeals from the High Court lie with the Court of Appeal in Fiji or, in the ultimate case, with the Judicial Committee of the Privy Council in the United Kingdom.

There are eight Island Courts with limited jurisdiction in criminal and civil cases.

High Court: Vaiaku, Funafuti; tel. 20837.

Chief Justice: VINCENT LUNABEK.

Attorney-General: ESE APINELU (acting).

Religion

CHRISTIANITY

Te Ekalesia Kelisiano Tuvalu (The Christian Church of Tuvalu): POB 2, Funafuti; tel. 20755; fax 20651; f. 1861; autonomous since 1968; derived from the Congregationalist foundation of the London Missionary Society; some 91% of the population are adherents; Pres. Rev. TOFIGA FALANI; Gen. Sec. Rev. KITIONA TAUSI.

Roman Catholic Church: Catholic Centre, POB 58, Funafuti; tel. and fax 20527; e-mail cathcent@tuvalu.tv; 131 adherents (31 Dec. 2006); Superior Fr CAMILLE DESROSIERS.

Other churches with adherents in Tuvalu include the Church of Jesus Christ of Latter-day Saints (Mormons), the Jehovah's Witnesses, the New Apostolic Church and the Seventh-day Adventists.

BAHÁ'Í FAITH

National Spiritual Assembly: POB 48, Funafuti; tel. 20860; mems resident in 8 localities.

The Press

Tuvalu Echoes: Broadcasting and Information Office, Vaiaku, Funafuti; tel. 20138; fax 20732; f. 1984; fortnightly; English; Editor MELAKI TAEPE; circ. 250.

Te Lama: Ekalesia Kelisiano Tuvalu, POB 2, Valuku, Funafuti; tel. and fax 20755; e-mail gs_ekt@yahoo.com; quarterly; religious; Pres. Rev. TOFIGA FALANI; Editor Rev. KITIONA TAUSI; circ. 1,000.

Broadcasting and Communications

TELECOMMUNICATIONS

Tuvalu Telecommunications Corporation: Vaiaku, Funafuti; tel. 20001; fax 20800; e-mail media@tuvalu.tv; f. 1994.

BROADCASTING

Tuvalu Media Corporation: PMB, Vaiaku, Funafuti; tel. 20731; fax 20732; e-mail media@tuvalu.tv; internet www.tuvalu-news.tv/tmc; f. 1999; govt-owned; Chief Broadcasting and Information Officer PUSINELLI LAAFAI.

Radio

Radio Tuvalu: Broadcasting and Information Office, PMB, Vaiaku, Funafuti; tel. 20138; fax 20732; f. 1975; daily broadcasts in Tuvaluan and English, 43 hours per week; Programme Producer RUBY S. ALEFAIO.

Finance

BANKS

Development Bank of Tuvalu: PMB 9, Vaiaku, Funafuti; tel. 20199; fax 20850; f. 1993; replaced the Business Development Advisory Bureau.

National Bank of Tuvalu: POB 13, Vaiaku, Funafuti; tel. 20803; fax 20802; e-mail nbt@tuvalu.tv; f. 1980; commercial bank; govt-owned; ($A '000) cap. 471.0, res 3,120.4, dep. 17,531.9 (Dec. 2005); Chair. AUNESE SIMATI; Gen. Man. SIOSE P. TEO; brs on all atolls.

Trade and Industry

GOVERNMENT AGENCIES

National Fishing Corporation of Tuvalu (NAFICOT): POB 93, Funafuti; tel. 20724; fax 20152; fishing vessel operators; seafood processing and marketing; agents for diesel engine spare parts, fishing supplies and marine electronics; Gen. Man. SEMU SOPOANGA TAAFAKI.

Tuvalu Philatelic Bureau: POB 24, Funafuti; tel. 20224; fax 20712; e-mail philatelic@tuvalu.tv.

CHAMBER OF COMMERCE

Tuvalu Chamber of Commerce: POB 27, Vaiaku, Funafuti; tel. 20917; fax 20646; e-mail tpasefika@hotmail.com; Chair. MATANILE IOSEFA; Sec. TEO PASEFIKA.

UTILITIES

Electricity

Tuvalu Electricity Corporation (TEC): POB 32, Vaiaku, Funafuti; tel. 20352; fax 20351; e-mail thomas@tuvalu.tv; Gen. Man. MAFALU LOTOLUA.

CO-OPERATIVES

Tuvalu Co-operative Society Ltd: POB 11, Funafuti; tel. 20747; fax 20748; e-mail mlaafai@tuvalu.tv; f. 1979; by amalgamation of the eight island socs; controls retail trade in the islands; Gen. Man. MONISE LAAFAI; Registrar AUNESE MAKOI.

Tuvalu Coconut Traders Co-operative: Contact TAAI KATALAKE.

TRADE UNION

Tuvalu Overseas Seamen's Union (TOSU): POB 99, Funafuti; tel. 20609; fax 20610; e-mail tosu@tuvalu.tv; f. 1988; Gen. Sec. TOMMY ALEFAIO.

Transport

ROADS
Funafuti has some impacted-coral roads totalling some 8 km in length; elsewhere, tracks exist.

SHIPPING
There is a deep-water lagoon at the point of entry, Funafuti, and ships are able to enter the lagoon at Nukufetau. Irregular shipping services connect Tuvalu with Fiji and elsewhere. The Government operates an inter-island vessel.

CIVIL AVIATION
In 1992 a new runway was constructed with aid from the European Union to replace the grass landing strip on Funafuti. Air Marshall Islands operates a three-weekly service between Funafuti, Nadi (Fiji) and Majuro (Marshall Islands). The Government of Tuvalu purchased a substantial shareholding (estimated at some US $2m.) in Air Fiji in 2001. Air Pacific commenced a twice-weekly service from Fiji in August 2008.

Tourism

In 2004 there was one hotel, with 16 rooms, on Funafuti and three guest houses. Visitor arrivals were estimated to total 1,130 in 2007. The majority of visitors are from Fiji, Australia, Japan and New Zealand.

Tuvalu Tourism Office: Ministry of Finance, Economic Planning and Industries, PMB, Funafuti; tel. 20408; fax 20210; e-mail lleneuoti@yahoo.com; internet www.timelesstuvalu.com; Tourism Officer LONO LENEUOTI.

UGANDA

Introductory Survey

Location, Climate, Language, Religion, Flag, Capital

The Republic of Uganda is a land-locked equatorial country in East Africa, bordered by Sudan to the north, the Democratic Republic of the Congo to the west, Kenya to the east and Rwanda, Tanzania and Lake Victoria to the south. The climate is tropical, with temperatures, moderated by the altitude of the country, varying between 15°C and 30°C. The official language is English and there are many local languages, the most important of which is Luganda. About 75% of the population follow Christian beliefs, while some 15% are Muslims. The national flag (proportions 2 by 3) has six horizontal stripes: black, gold, red, black, gold and red. In the centre is a white disc containing a crested crane. The capital is Kampala.

Recent History

Formerly a British protectorate, Uganda became an independent member of the Commonwealth on 9 October 1962. The Government was led by Dr Milton Obote, leader of the Uganda People's Congress (UPC) from 1960 and Prime Minister from April 1962. At independence the country comprised four regions, including the kingdom of Buganda, which had federal status. Exactly one year after independence Uganda became a republic, with Mutesa II, Kabaka (King) of Buganda, as first President. In February 1966 Obote led a successful coup against the Kabaka, and in April he became executive President. In September 1967 a new Constitution was introduced, establishing a unitary republic, and Buganda was brought under the control of the central Government. In 1969 all opposition parties were banned.

Obote was overthrown in January 1971 by the army, led by Maj.-Gen. (later Field Marshal) Idi Amin Dada, who assumed full executive powers and suspended political activity. Amin declared himself Head of State, took over legislative powers and suspended parts of the 1967 Constitution. In August 1972 Amin, proclaiming an 'economic war' to free Uganda from foreign domination, undertook a mass expulsion of non-citizen Asians (who comprised the majority of the resident Asian population), thereby incurring widespread international condemnation.

Amin's regime was characterized by the ruthless elimination of suspected opponents, mass flights of refugees to neighbouring countries and periodic purges of the army (which, in turn, perpetrated numerous atrocities). Relations within the East African Community (EAC), comprising Uganda, Kenya and Tanzania, deteriorated during the 1970s. In February 1976 Amin claimed that large areas of western Kenya were historically part of Uganda, and in November 1978 Uganda annexed the Kagera salient from Tanzania. In early 1979 an invasion force comprising Tanzanian troops and the Uganda National Liberation Army (UNLA) gained control of the southern region of Uganda. Amin's forces capitulated, and in April a Tanzanian assault force entered Kampala. The remaining pro-Amin troops were defeated in June. Amin fled initially to Libya and in 1980 took up permanent residence in Saudi Arabia. He remained in exile there until his death in August 2003.

A provisional Government, the National Executive Council (NEC), was established in April 1979 from the ranks of the Uganda National Liberation Front (UNLF, a coalition of 18 previously exiled groups), with Dr Yusuf Lule, a former vice-chancellor of Makerere University, as President. Lule was succeeded in June by Godfrey Binaisa (a former Attorney-General), who was, in turn, overthrown by the Military Commission of the UNLF in May 1980, after he had decided to allow only UNLF members to stand in parliamentary elections and attempted to reorganize the leadership of the UNLA. The elections, in December, were contested by four parties and won by the UPC, with Obote, who remained its leader, becoming President for the second time. The defeated parties complained of gross electoral malpractice by UPC supporters.

The Obote Government was subject to constant attack from guerrilla groups operating inside the country. Hundreds of Obote's opponents were detained, including Democratic Party (DP) members of the National Assembly. Following the withdrawal of Tanzanian troops in June 1981, there were reports from the West Nile Region of further atrocities by Ugandan soldiers. In January 1982 the Uganda Popular Front was formed to co-ordinate, from abroad, the activities of the main opposition groups in exile: the Uganda Freedom Movement (UFM), the Uganda National Rescue Front and the National Resistance Movement (NRM), led by Lule and his former Minister of Defence, Lt-Gen. Yoweri Museveni. The NRM had a military wing, the National Resistance Army (NRA), led by Museveni. Lule died in 1985, whereupon Museveni became sole leader of the NRM and NRA.

In July 1985 Obote was overthrown in a military coup, led by Brig. (later Lt-Gen.) Basilio Okello. (Obote was subsequently granted political asylum by Zambia.) A Military Council, headed by Lt-Gen. (later Gen.) Tito Okello, the Commander-in-Chief of the army, was established to govern the country, pending elections to be held one year later. In subsequent months groups that had been in opposition to Obote, with the exception of the NRA and the NRM (see below), reached agreement with the new administration and accepted positions on the Military Council. An amnesty was declared for exiles who had supported Amin.

In August 1985 the NRA, led by Museveni, entered into negotiations with the Government (under the auspices of President Daniel arap Moi of Kenya), while conducting a simultaneous military campaign to overthrow Okello. During the following two months the NRA gained control of large areas of the country and in January 1986 the NRA took control of Kampala by force and dissolved the Military Council. Okello fled to Sudan, and then to Tanzania. On 29 January Museveni was sworn in as President, and in February he announced the formation of a new Cabinet, comprising mainly members of the NRA and NRM, but also representatives of other political groups including the DP, the UPC, the UFM, the Federal Democratic Movement (FEDEMO), and three members of the previous administration. A National Resistance Council (NRC) was formed to act in place of a legislature for an indefinite period. All party political activity was banned in March, although political organizations were not proscribed. At a summit meeting in March the Heads of State of all the countries adjoining Uganda pledged their support for Museveni.

The most widespread source of disruption during 1987 was a rebellion that had arisen in northern and eastern Uganda in late 1986 by the cultish 'Holy Spirit' movement; between December 1986 and November 1987 some 5,000 ill-equipped 'Holy Spirit' fighters were reportedly killed in clashes with the NRA. By December 1987 the rebellion had been suppressed and its leader had escaped to Kenya. Surviving members of the movement, however, regrouped as the Lord's Resistance Army (LRA—see below).

In February 1989 the first national election since 1980 was held. The NRC, hitherto composed solely of presidential nominees, was expanded from 98 to 278 members, to include 210 elected representatives. While 20 ministerial posts were reserved for nominated members of the NRC, 50 were allocated to elected members. Also in February Museveni appointed a constitutional commission to assess public opinion on Uganda's political future and to draft a new constitution.

In October 1989 (despite opposition from the DP) the NRC approved draft legislation to prolong the Government's term of office by five years from January 1990 (when its mandate had been due to expire): the NRM justified seeking to extend its rule by claiming that it required further time in which to prepare a new constitution, organize elections, eliminate guerrilla activity, improve the judiciary, police force and civil service and rehabilitate the country's infrastructure. In March 1990 the NRM extended the national ban on party political activity (imposed in March 1986) for a further five years. In May 1991 Museveni formally invited all former resident Asians expelled at the time of the Amin regime to return, pledging the restitution of expropriated property.

In December 1992 the Constitutional Commission presented its draft Constitution to the Government. The draft was published in March 1993, and in the following month the NRC passed legislation authorizing the establishment of a Constituent Assembly (see below). In July the NRC adopted a constitutional amendment revoking the abolition of traditional rulers, as provided for under the 1967 Constitution. Restored traditional rulers would, however, have only ceremonial significance.

In January 1994 the Ugandan National Democratic Alliance and the Ugandan Federal Army agreed to suspend their armed struggle, under the provisions of a government amnesty, and in March the surrender of senior members of the Ruwenzunuru Kingdom Freedom Movement in the south-west signified the end of a conflict dating from independence. During January the Government took part in negotiations with the LRA. However, following the collapse of the discussions, the LRA intensified guerrilla activities in northern Uganda. From 1994 large numbers of security forces were deployed in the region, representing a considerable burden on national resources; they failed, however, to suppress the rebellion (see below).

At elections to the 288-member Constituent Assembly, which took place on 28 March 1994, more than 1,500 candidates contested the 214 elective seats. Although the elections were officially conducted on a non-party basis, NRM members were believed to have secured the majority of votes in the centre, west and south-west of the country, whereas UPC and DP members, who advocated an immediate return to multi-party politics, secured the most seats in the north and east. The Constituent Assembly, which also comprised nominated representatives of the armed forces, political parties, trade unions, and youth and disabled organizations, debated and amended the draft Constitution, finally enacting it in September 1995. The Constitution, under whose terms a national referendum on the future introduction of a multi-party political system took place in 2000 (see below), was promulgated in October 1995.

A presidential election took place in May 1996, at which Museveni was returned to office, winning 74.2% of the votes cast. The election was pronounced free and fair by international observers. Legislative elections took place in June at which the total membership of the NRC, redesignated the Parliament under the new Constitution, was reduced from 278 to 276, comprising 214 elected and 62 nominated representatives.

During 1993–98 the LRA was alleged to have killed as many as 10,000 people, while some 220,000 sought refuge in protected camps; economic activity in the region was devastated. The LRA's use of abducted children as soldiers (reportedly some 10,000 by early 1999) attracted widespread international condemnation. The Government strongly resisted pressure to resume negotiations with the LRA, prompting some speculation that Museveni (a southerner) might be prepared to profit from the disablement of opposition strongholds in the northern region. In May 1999, however, the Government appeared to modify its policy towards the LRA by offering it an amnesty and promising its leader, Joseph Kony, a cabinet post in the event of his being democratically elected. In the west, meanwhile, the Uganda People's Defence Forces (UPDF, as the NRA had been restyled) fought intermittently with two rebel groups: the Allied Democratic Front (ADF), mainly comprising Ugandan Islamic fundamentalist rebels, exiled Rwandan Hutu militiamen and former soldiers from Zaire (which became the Democratic Republic of the Congo—DRC—in May 1997), and the West Nile Bank Front (WNBF). Although WNBF activities subsided in mid-1997, following the killing of several hundred of its members by Sudanese rebels, the ADF mounted a persistent terror campaign from mid-1997 against western Ugandan targets, threatening tourism to the region and disrupting economic activity. In August 1999, confronted by escalating security problems on various fronts, the Government was reported to have recalled for military service some 10,000 demobilized troops, and in September the command structure of the UPDF was reorganized. In November the UPDF launched a new offensive against the ADF in the Ruwenzori region. In December the Parliament adopted legislation that extended (not without conditions, in some cases) an amnesty to all rebels in opposition to President Museveni. The ADF's response was apparently to intensify its struggle.

In July 1999 legislation was enacted providing for the proposed referendum on a multi-party political system to take place in 2000 as planned. However, most political parties announced that they would boycott the referendum on the grounds that it would be manipulated by the NRM for its own objectives. Ugandan political leaders had criticized the readiness of some Western donors (in particular those that formed the Referendum 2000 Group in December 1999) to support the referendum process, claiming that by so doing they were legitimizing the prevailing suspension of active political opposition. In February 2000 Uganda's Multi-Party National Referendum Committee appealed for a postponement of the referendum on the grounds that the Electoral Commission had not made funds available to some advocates of a return to political pluralism. In the same month the Referendum 2000 Group expressed concern at the Government's failure to implement measures on which it had made conditional its support of the referendum process. At the referendum, which proceeded on 29 June, 90.7% of participants voted in favour of retaining the existing 'no-party' political system. However, the result was effectively nullified by the Constitutional Court in 2004 (see below).

A presidential election was held on 12 March 2001. The election had been scheduled for 7 March, but was delayed to allow the Electoral Commission time to check and amend the electoral register after it was found to contain about 2.5m. more voters than there were citizens eligible to vote. At the election, which had a participation rate of 70%, Museveni was re-elected President, winning 69.3% of the votes cast. His main challenger, Kizza Besigye, won 27.8%.

Legislative elections were held on 26 June 2001, at which 50 parliamentarians, including 10 ministers, failed to secure re-election. The rate of voter participation was reported as being low. The total number of seats in Parliament was increased to 292 (comprising 214 elected and 78 nominated representatives), of which the NRM reportedly secured more than 70%. In July Museveni appointed a new Cabinet, which included the 10 ministers who had failed to retain their parliamentary seats in June. Notably, Amama Mbabazi was appointed as Minister of Defence, a portfolio hitherto held by Museveni.

In May 2002 Parliament approved the Political Parties and Organizations Act 2002, which severely curtailed the activities of political parties, while classifying the NRM as a 'political system' rather than a party. The Act also provided for the dissolution of all parties not registered by 17 January 2003. However, in March 2003 opposition leaders successfully challenged two clauses of the Act in the Constitutional Court, which ruled that the NRM was not a system, but a political party, and suspended the section of the Act that required parties to register, pending the outcome of a further petition against the Act. (The Attorney-General later clarified that parties would still be obliged to register, but not by a particular time.) The ruling allowed political parties to operate nationally for the first time in 17 years. The NRM became the first party to apply for registration, in June 2003. Meanwhile, in late May Museveni effected a cabinet reorganization, notably appointing Prof. Gilbert Bukenya as Vice-President, following the resignation of the incumbent, Dr Speciosa Kazibwe, and dismissing a number of ministers who had recently expressed opposition to a proposal to revoke the current two-term limit on the presidential mandate. This proposal was endorsed by the Cabinet in August. By April 2004 some 60 new political parties had emerged, although only 13 had applied for registration.

In June 2004 the Constitutional Court issued a ruling that annulled the Referendum (Political System) Act of 2000 and effectively nullified the June 2000 referendum at which a return to a multi-party system had been rejected. Thus, legislative elections, scheduled to be held concurrently with the presidential election in 2006, would be held under the new system—subject to approval at a referendum, which was to be held in July 2005 (see below). In November 2004 the Constitutional Court repealed legislation preventing political parties from contesting elections. The Court also rejected an appeal from opposition parties against mandatory registration and ruled that parties would have six months to register prior to the 2006 elections.

Meanwhile, it was reported in August 2004 that a new opposition party, the Forum for Democratic Change (FDC), had been formed by a merger of Reform Agenda, the Parliamentary Advocacy Forum and the National Democratic Forum. Several parliamentarians affiliated to the UPC had apparently joined the new party.

In February 2005 the Constitution (Amendment) Bill, which provided for a return to multi-party democracy, was presented to the Parliament. The Bill also contained a provision for the removal of the two-term limit on the presidency. Parliament approved the removal of the two-term limit on the presidency in June, and voted in favour of the holding of a national referendum on the restoration of multi-party democracy. At the referendum, which took place on 28 July, 92.5% of participants approved the motion. The rate of voter participation was low, however, at just 47%. The opposition had called for a boycott of the referendum.

In October 2005 Besigye returned from four years of self-imposed exile in South Africa in order to contest the presidential election as the FDC's candidate. (He had left Uganda following the presidential elections of 2001 claiming to fear for his safety.) Besigye was arrested in November 2005 and charged with rape and treason and later that month also appeared before a military tribunal on charges of terrorism and illegally possessing weapons. In January 2006 the High Court ruled that the military tribunal's authority to detain Besigye had expired and ordered his release; his trial was adjourned until after the election.

Meanwhile, in April 2005 it was reported that former President Obote was considering a return from exile in Zambia. However, the Ugandan Government stated that it had yet to receive a formal request from Obote for permission to re-enter Uganda, and that until it did so it would not declare its position on the issue. Obote died in October, still in exile. His body was returned to Uganda where he was accorded a state funeral. In mid-November President Museveni confirmed his intention to stand for a third term in office. He was subsequently elected unopposed as the NRM candidate.

At the presidential election, held on 23 February 2006, Museveni won 59.3% of the valid votes cast and was elected for a third term. Besigye was the only other candidate to mount a credible challenge, receiving 37.4% of the votes. While international observers did not condemn the process outright, they reported a number of serious flaws and concluded that a law passed in 1997 that effectively granted the NRM access to public funds for campaigning did not provide a fair basis for multi-party elections. (Parliamentary elections were held concurrently with the presidential election; according to preliminary results, the NRM secured 191 seats in the 319-member Parliament, while the FDC took 37 seats.)

In March 2006 Besigye was acquitted of rape. The military conceded that Besigye would not have to face a court martial while on trial for treason, but did not drop the charges against him and appealed against the ruling that the terrorism and weapons charges must be heard in the High Court. In April Besigye challenged the results of the presidential election in the Supreme Court. The Court unanimously decided that the Electoral Commission had not conducted the election in compliance with the Constitution and other relevant legislation. However, it further ruled (by four votes to three) that this had not substantially affected the final outcome of the election. Besigye's trial for treason commenced in April; he and his 22 co-defendants denied the charges. In late May Museveni unveiled his new Cabinet. Most notably, Gen. Ali Moses was replaced as First Deputy Prime Minister by Eriya Kategaya.

In March 2007 security agents raided the High Court and arrested six supporters of Besigye who had been granted bail. One lawyer was beaten unconscious during the heavily armed raid. In response, the judiciary commenced industrial action and only agreed to return to work after Museveni expressed regret for the incident one week later. Violence erupted on the streets of Kampala in April after protests against plans to allocate one-third of the Mabira forest to an Asian-owned sugar company turned hostile, forcing police to protect Asian businesses and a Hindu temple. An Asian man and two other people were killed. In October Besigye announced that he was to relinquish the presidency of the FDC in 2010, allowing sufficient time for a new leader to be selected ahead of the presidential elections scheduled for 2011. In February 2009, however, Besigye was re-elected as President of the FDC, and it was widely believed that he would once again challenge Museveni for the presidency in the forthcoming elections. The official candidate would be decided by FDC delegates in 2010.

In July 2008 it was reported that Museveni would stand for a fourth consecutive term as president in the elections scheduled for 2011; the President subsequently confirmed this on the condition that NRM delegates selected him as the preferred candidate. In February 2009 Museveni reshuffled his Cabinet, replacing the Minister of Finance, Planning and Economic Development, Ezra Suruma, with Sydda Bbumba, who had previously held the gender, labour and social services portfolio. There were several new additions to the Government, including Gabriel Opio, who was named as the new Minister of Gender and Social Affairs, while Hope Mwesigye became the Minister of Agriculture, Animal Industry and Fisheries. Other notable changes included the appointment of Museveni's wife, Janet Museveni, as Minister of State for the Karamoja region.

During 1987 Uganda's relations with neighbouring Kenya deteriorated, with the Museveni Government accusing the regime of President Moi of sheltering and supporting Ugandan rebels. When, in October, Uganda stationed troops at the two countries' common border, Kenya threatened to retaliate with force against any attempts by Ugandan military personnel to cross the frontier in pursuit of rebels. In December there were clashes between Kenyan and Ugandan security forces and the border was temporarily closed. In late December, following the intervention of the Organization of African Unity (now the African Union—AU, see p. 172), discussions between the Heads of State of the two countries led to a resumption of normal traffic across the border. However, several incursions into Kenya by Ugandan troops were subsequently reported. In November 1994 the Presidents of Uganda, Kenya and Tanzania met in Arusha, Tanzania, and established a permanent commission for co-operation between the three countries. In March 1996 Museveni, Moi and President Benjamin Mkapa of Tanzania, meeting in Nairobi, Kenya, formally inaugurated the Secretariat of the Permanent Tripartite Commission for East African Co-operation, which aimed to revive the EAC (see p. 425). A treaty for the re-establishment of the EAC, providing for the creation of a free trade area (with the eventual introduction of a single currency), for the development of infrastructure, tourism and agriculture within the Community and for the establishment of a regional legislature and court was ratified by the three Heads of State in November 1999. Museveni, Mkapa and President Mwai Kibaki of Kenya signed a protocol in March 2004 on the creation of a customs union, whereby most duties on goods within the EAC would be eliminated. The customs union was established on 1 January 2005.

During 1988 tension arose along Uganda's border with Zaire (now the DRC—see above), owing to a number of attacks by Zairean troops on NRA units; further border clashes occurred in 1992. In November 1996 Ugandan rebels were reportedly operating from within Zaire with the support of Zairean troops. In late 1996 and early 1997 the Ugandan authorities repeatedly denied allegations that Ugandan forces were occupying territory in eastern Zaire; however, it was widely reported that the Museveni Government supplied armaments and tactical support to Laurent-Désiré Kabila's Alliance des forces démocratiques pour la libération du Congo-Zaïre, which took power in Zaire in May 1997. The Museveni administration, however, subsequently withdrew its support from the new regime in the DRC, as President Kabila made no attempt to sever the ongoing supply of armaments to Ugandan guerrilla groups operating in the DRC–Uganda border region. In November 1998 the Museveni administration, in co-operation with the Rwandan Government, formed a joint military command. The Kabila regime accused Uganda and Rwanda of creating, with DRC rebels, a Tutsi-dominated alliance with expansionist ambitions; it was also alleged that the DRC's two eastern neighbours were illegally exploiting mineral interests in the area occupied by their forces. In July 1999 a comprehensive cease-fire agreement was concluded in Lusaka, Zambia, by the Heads of State of all the countries engaged militarily in the civil war in the DRC, including those of Angola, Namibia and Zimbabwe, who had supported the DRC Government. The cease-fire was to be monitored by a joint military commission, while a UN peace-keeping force was to be deployed on the withdrawal from the DRC of all foreign troops. However, the implementation of the Lusaka accord did not proceed smoothly. In mid-August tensions escalated into hostilities between Ugandan and Rwandan armed forces around the city of Kisangani, in the DRC. In May 2000 the DRC Government signed an agreement in which it consented to the deployment of 500 UN military observers and 5,000 support troops, the UN Mission in the Democratic Republic of the Congo (MONUC, see p. 88), to monitor the frequently violated cease-fire that had been inaugurated by the Lusaka accord. Almost immediately afterwards, however, hostilities erupted again between Ugandan and Rwandan troops in Kisangani. In mid-May Uganda and Rwanda withdrew their troops in Kisangani to prepare the way for its eventual cession to the control of MONUC. In December all parties in the conflict signed an agreement under which all forces would withdraw 15 km from positions of military engagement by January 2001, to allow UN peace-keepers to ensure the observance of the cease-fire. In January 2001 President Kabila was assassinated by one of his bodyguards; he was succeeded by his son, Joseph Kabila, who immediately engaged in international efforts to end the conflict. In mid-March the groups involved in the conflict, under the aegis of the UN Security Council, commenced the military disengagement of their forces. However, factions subsequently refused to proceed with the withdrawal from military positions until MONUC guaranteed security in the region. Following the publication of a UN report, in April, alleging that Burundi, Rwanda and Uganda were illegally exploiting the DRC's mineral reserves, Museveni announced that Uganda would withdraw its remaining troops from the DRC and pull out of the UN-sponsored Lusaka accord. In late 2001 Rwandan troops occupied positions in the eastern DRC that had been vacated by the UPDF in June of that year, prompting fears that clashes would again erupt between Rwandan and Ugandan forces. Despite the redeployment of Ugandan troops in the northeast of the DRC in January 2002, to prevent escalating fighting between the rebel factions from reaching the border with Uganda, negotiations between Uganda and Rwanda continued, with British mediation, and in April the two countries signed a peace agreement in Kigali. In September a peace accord was signed by Uganda and the DRC in Luanda, Angola, providing for the normalization of relations between the two countries and the complete withdrawal of Ugandan troops from the DRC. Uganda subsequently began the withdrawal of its troops, although the UN permitted some of them to remain near the north-eastern town of Bunia to assist with maintaining security. In March 2003 the Governments of Uganda and the DRC and local rebel groups signed a cease-fire agreement, although later that month the Rwandan Government threatened to resume military engagement in eastern DRC if the UN failed to secure the withdrawal of all Ugandan troops. In response to the continuing violence around Bunia, which was in contravention of the peace agreement, the UN Security Council issued a resolution calling for increased numbers of military and humanitarian observers to be stationed in the DRC under the MONUC mandate, and the immediate withdrawal of Ugandan troops. The Ugandan Government subsequently pledged to withdraw forces from the DRC, and all remaining Ugandan troops left the north-east of the country in May. In April 2005 the International Criminal Court (ICC, see p. 324), based in The Hague, Netherlands, began proceedings against Uganda following accusations by the DRC Government that Ugandan troops had violated human rights and massacred Congolese civilians while deployed in the country. The DRC also demanded reparations for destruction and looting allegedly carried out by the UPDF. The Ugandan Government denied the claims. In early September 2007 Uganda and the DRC agreed to the establishment of a joint force, supported by MONUC and tasked with removing LRA fighters from the DRC by December. However, later in September an incident was reported in which Ugandan troops were alleged to have opened fire on a passenger boat from the DRC, killing several people. A number of LRA soldiers were captured in October and a senior LRA official surrendered to UN peace-keepers. Four other high-ranking LRA members had previously been indicted by the ICC for crimes against humanity.

From the late 1980s Sudanese troops reportedly made repeated incursions into Ugandan territory in pursuit of Sudanese rebels. Relations between the two countries deteriorated seriously in 1994, when each Government accused the other of harbouring and supporting their respective outlawed guerrilla groups; in April 1995 Uganda severed diplomatic relations with Sudan. Relations between the two countries remained strained: in September 1996 and in February 1997 it was alleged that Sudanese aircraft had attacked northern Uganda, and in April, despite a continuing dialogue mediated by Iran and Libya, the Sudanese authorities claimed that their forces had killed several hundred Ugandan soldiers who had been assisting Sudanese rebels from within Sudanese territory. In February 1998 Uganda deployed troops along the Uganda–Sudan border, with the aim of preventing LRA rebels from taking captives over the frontier into Sudan. In December, in Kenya, the Presidents of Uganda and Sudan unexpectedly signed an accord that set out a comprehensive resolution of the two countries' differences. The Nairobi Agreement committed Uganda and Sudan to the renunciation of force as a means of settling disputes; to the disarmament and disbandment of terrorist groups and the cessation of support for rebel groups; to the repatriation of prisoners of war; and to the restoration of full diplomatic relations by the end of February 2000. Joint committees were to be established to oversee the implementation of the Agreement from January 2000. In September Uganda and Sudan agreed to disarm the LRA, which had been active throughout 2000, and to relocate it at least 1,000 km deeper within Sudanese territory. It was also agreed that the Governments of Uganda, Sudan, Libya and Egypt, in collaboration with the Carter Center, Canada, the UN Children's Fund and the office of the UN High Commissioner for Refugees (UNHCR), would set up a body to find and repatriate all children abducted from Sudan by rebel groups. Rebel attacks continued in northern Uganda, however, and in January 2001 President Museveni threatened to send troops to pursue rebel groups into Sudanese territory. Following a Libyan diplomatic initiative in that month, Sudan and Uganda agreed to restore diplomatic relations. In August the Ugandan embassy reopened in the Sudanese capital, Khartoum, and a chargé d'affaires was appointed; relations were upgraded to an ambassadorial level in April 2002. In August 2001 the Sudanese President, Lt-Gen. Omar Hassan Ahmad al-Bashir, announced that his Government would no longer provide support for the LRA, and in December bank accounts used by the LRA in London, United Kingdom, were frozen. Negotiations between Sudan and Uganda continued successfully throughout early 2002, with both countries remaining committed to implementing the Nairobi Agreement. In March it was announced that Sudan was to allow the UPDF to deploy forces within its borders in order to pursue operations against the LRA, and later that month the Ugandan Government announced that its troops had captured all four main bases in Sudan belonging to the LRA. In November the Sudanese authorities agreed to extend permission for Ugandan troops to remain on its territory for as long as Uganda deemed necessary.

In early 2003 Museveni agreed to a cease-fire and appointed a delegation to commence peace negotiations with the LRA, but these soon collapsed. The Government ordered 800,000 people in northern Uganda to enter refugee camps for their protection; however, the LRA continued to attack the camps. In October LRA attacks, which had begun to spread further south and east, intensified, and a counter-offensive by the UPDF in December had little success. Nevertheless, Museveni claimed in January 2004 that the LRA had been 'defeated decisively'. Also in January the ICC announced that it was to initiate plans for an investigation into the activities of the LRA, referred for consideration by the Court in the previous month by Museveni. In late February, in one of the worst attacks in recent years, the LRA massacred more than 200 civilians sheltering in a refugee camp near Lira, in northern Uganda. In the following weeks the UPDF launched assaults on two LRA groups in two villages near the camp, killing 16 rebels in one attack and five in the other. Thousands demonstrated in Lira against the Government's failure to protect civilians, and the protests rapidly became violent. The UPDF commenced a new offensive in southern Sudan, and in March killed more than 50 rebels entering Uganda from Sudan. Despite the UPDF's continued claims of imminent victory, the LRA attacks continued unabated. The Government introduced legislation in mid-2004 that allowed the prosecution by the ICC of Ugandans suspected of war crimes. In June it was reported that at least 12 high-ranking LRA commanders had taken advantage of an amnesty offered by the Government and surrendered; among them was Kony's personal secretary.

In November 2004 an LRA spokesman stated that the group no longer believed a military end to the conflict was possible, and that the LRA was thus willing to negotiate towards a peace accord. A cease-fire was agreed, although fighting continued outside the cease-fire zone. Delegations representing the Government and the LRA met in December in Kitgum, in northern Uganda, and Museveni subsequently extended the cease-fire until the end of December. Although there were indications at the end of December that the Government and LRA were close to agreeing a permanent truce, the LRA postponed the signing of a memorandum of understanding in order to continue internal consultations. Shortly afterwards a UPDF force was ambushed, for which Museveni blamed the LRA. The Government refused to extend the cease-fire, and UPDF troops re-occupied the cease-fire zone in order to prevent attacks on civilians. A cease-fire was agreed in February 2005, during which an amnesty was offered to LRA fighters who wished to surrender. Later that month Brig. Sam Kolo, the LRA's chief negotiator in the recent peace talks, escaped an attack by LRA combatants with the help of the UPDF, to whom he surrendered. The UPDF stated that Kolo's life was in danger following a dispute with the LRA's deputy leader, Vincent Otti. The Government's chief negotiator confirmed that Otti would take Kolo's place in any future negotiations. However, many observers regarded Kolo as one of the LRA's most rational commanders, and attributed to him the success of recent negotiations. In March, following a government request, the ICC agreed to delay issuing arrest warrants for LRA commanders after concerns were raised that they would be reluctant to negotiate if they feared arrest once peace had been established. The cease-fire agreed in February lapsed in March and fighting resumed. The UPDF began an offensive against LRA bases, while the LRA, in turn, attacked villages and resumed its abduction of children.

In September 2005 two groups of LRA fighters, one led by Otti, entered the DRC from southern Sudan. Representatives of the UN met for first time with the LRA and urged the group to disarm. The meeting was also attended by senior members of DRC military. In October the ICC issued arrest warrants for Kony, Otti and three other LRA commanders. Kony was indicted on 12 counts of crimes against humanity, including sexual enslavement, and 21 counts of war crimes. The UPDF claimed to have recently killed one of the five indicted LRA commanders. Shortly after the warrants were issued the LRA altered its tactics and began to attack humanitarian workers. In November it killed two UN mine clearance experts in southern Sudan. Later that month Otti offered to enter into peace negotiations, stating he was willing to be tried by the ICC, but added that the UPDF had also committed crimes during the conflict for which the Government should be tried. In April 2006 it was announced that refugee camps in the Lango and Teso sub-regions were to close (but not those in the Acholi sub-region). Also in that month the Ugandan Parliament approved legislation that enabled the Government to exclude Kony and others from the amnesty offered to the LRA.

In July 2006 peace talks between the LRA and the Government commenced in Juba, southern Sudan. On 26 August both sides agreed on a truce and a cease-fire came into force on 29 August. By September UNHCR estimated that more than 300,000 people had left displacement camps in recent months. However, it emerged in October that both the Ugandan army and the LRA had violated the terms of their truce, according to a report by a peace process monitoring team. The LRA rebels had pledged to assemble at two neutral points in southern Sudan by mid-September in return for an amnesty. In December President Museveni held direct talks with a member of the LRA for the first time when he spoke by satellite telephone with Otti. A cessation of hostilities agreement, signed by both sides, was also extended in the same month for a second time, until 28 February 2007. However, the LRA withdrew from the talks in January, citing security fears after al-Bashir apparently indicated that he sought to eradicate the LRA from Sudan. The issues of reconciliation and accountability also remained contentious. It was believed that the LRA would not sign a peace deal while warrants for the arrest of Kony and his commanders remained in place. Following a meeting between the UN Special Envoy for areas affected by the LRA, the former President of Mozambique, Joaquim Chissano, and Kony in mid-March, the LRA agreed to resume negotiations on condition that other African mediators join the talks along with Sudan. In mid-April the LRA signed a new cease-fire with the Government. Under the new agreement the LRA was granted six weeks in which to assemble its fighters at Ri-Kwangba near the border with the DRC. Peace talks resumed in Juba at the end of May. In November Kony appointed Okot Odhiambo as deputy leader of the LRA amid unconfirmed reports that Otti had been executed alongside his family and several commanders who remained loyal to him. Sources within the LRA insisted that Otti was still alive and that rumours of Otti's death were unfounded. Observers raised concerns that the LRA was taking a more radical stance, which could threaten the success of the peace talks. In January 2008 Otti's death was confirmed, although the cause of death remained unclear. A new cease-fire was agreed between the Government and the LRA in late January, ahead of peace talks which were to resume at the end of the month. Violence had largely subsided during the latest round of peace negotiations and refugees had begun to return home. Negotiations were ongoing in March to determine a timescale for demobilization, however, mediators were confident that they were close to agreeing a final peace deal to end the conflict.

In April 2008, however, peace talks collapsed when Kony failed to appear at a meeting between LRA and government negotiators, held on the border between Sudan and the DRC; Kony indicated that he was not ready to sign a full peace agreement until the ICC arrest warrant for him was lifted, and later dismissed his chief negotiator. In May a new court was established to deal specifically with human rights violations committed during the LRA insurgency in northern Uganda. The War Crimes Court was set up as a special division of the Uganda High Court, in what was widely regarded as an attempt to persuade the ICC to drop indictments against LRA commanders, following the recent breakdown in negotiations. (In March President Museveni had refused to hand over LRA leaders to stand trial at the ICC, stating that they should instead be tried by northern Uganda's traditional justice system.) In May a report by Human Rights Watch claimed that the LRA had taken advantage of the recent cease-fire to resume abduction and enslavement of civilians, including children, from neighbouring countries; Kony was believed to be rearming and preparing for a renewed conflict. In June military chiefs from the DRC, Uganda, southern Sudan and the MONUC command met in Kampala to discuss a military solution for dealing with the LRA and threatened to launch attacks on LRA positions in north-east DRC. In July the Sudanese Government ordered UPDF troops to withdraw from southern Sudan, claiming that they were responsible for recent attacks on civilians. In the following month Chissano reported that Kony had been in contact with him and was now willing to sign a final peace deal; however, this failed to materialize, and attacks on civilians in Sudan and the DRC continued. In late 2008 the situation deteriorated further after Kony once again failed to appear at a meeting having committing himself to a peace agreement, effectively ending any hope of a negotiated settlement. In December Ugandan, Sudanese and Congolese forces launched a joint offensive against LRA positions in northeast DRC. The LRA launched attacks on Congolese villages in response and massacred civilians; by March 2009 as many as 1,000 civilians were believed to have been killed in reprisal for the offensive. In March a senior LRA commander, Thomas Kwoyelo, was captured in eastern DRC, while later that month Ugandan troops began to withdraw from the country as the joint offensive came to an end.

During the late 1980s an estimated 250,000 Rwandan refugees were sheltering in Uganda. Relations with Rwanda deteriorated in October 1990, following the infiltration of northern Rwanda by an invasion force of some 4,000 Rwandan rebels who had been based in Uganda. In February 1991 a conference was held on the Rwandan security situation; an amnesty was agreed for all Rwandans who were exiled abroad, and the rebels were urged to observe a cease-fire. Nevertheless, the allegedly Uganda-based Rwandan rebels continued to operate in northern Rwanda during 1991–93. The victory in Rwanda of the Front patriotique rwandais (FPR) in mid-1994 brought about a significant change in bilateral relations; Maj.-Gen. Paul Kagame, Rwandan Vice-President and Minister of National Defence, had previously served in the Ugandan NRA, as had other members of the FPR administration. In August 1995 Museveni made an official visit to Rwanda, and both countries made commitments to enhance economic and social co-operation. In August 1998 Uganda and Rwanda jointly deployed troops in the DRC (see above). Relations between the two countries worsened again during their involvement in the hostilities in the DRC; there were frequent reports of fighting, especially around the town of Kisangani. However, this tension eased when both armies withdrew from Kisangani during May 2000 (see above), and in July Museveni and Kagame met to discuss relations between their respective countries. In January 2001 at least 15,000 Rwandan refugees, most of them Hutu, entered Uganda following an order in Tanzania to expel all non-citizens. A further 7,000 Rwandan refugees had entered Uganda through Tanzania by July. In July 2003 the Rwandan Government signed a tripartite agreement with the Ugandan authorities and UNHCR, providing for the voluntary repatriation of some 26,000 Rwandans resident in refugee camps in western Uganda. In February 2004 an improvement in diplomatic relations between Rwanda and Uganda (following progress in the situation in the DRC) was demonstrated by a bilateral agreement to strengthen co-operation in several fields. Relations with the DRC deteriorated in 2007 due to a dispute over the ownership of Rukwanzi island in Lake Albert, on the border between the two countries; tension had increased in the area following the recent discovery of oil in the Lake Albert basin. In August a British national working for a Canadian oil company was killed in a clash involving Congolese and Ugandan security forces, and in the following month Museveni and the DRC President, Joseph Kabila, held a meeting in which they agreed to carry out a joint demarcation of the border. None the less there were further violent incidents in late 2007, and in May 2008 Congolese troops occupied a disputed border area; Museveni and Kabila subsequently agreed to implement joint administration of Rukwanzi island. However, in September a spokesman for the UPDF claimed that a survey had been conducted which found the island was in Ugandan territory.

At the end of 2007, according to UNHCR, the number of refugees in Uganda totalled 228,959, including 162,063 from Sudan, 41,782 from the DRC and 17,846 from Rwanda.

Following a two-day summit in Nairobi in December 2006, the Presidents of Burundi, the DRC, Kenya, Zambia, Tanzania and

UGANDA

Uganda signed a regional security, stability and development treaty. Provisions included a development plan, estimated to cost in excess of US $2,000m. to be funded from contributions by member states and donors in conjunction with the African Development Bank. Measures to disarm remaining rebel groups, prevent arms trafficking and assist refugees were also included.

In March 2007 1,700 Ugandan peace-keepers were deployed in Somalia as part of the AU Mission in Somalia (AMISOM) to assist with the stabilization of that country; the deployment of an additional battalion of Ugandan troops in April 2009 brought the total strength of the AMISOM force to around 4,000.

Government

Following the January 1986 coup, power was vested in a broad-based interim Government, headed by an executive President. A National Resistance Council (NRC) was formed to legislate by decree. In addition, resistance committees were formed at local and district level. Political activity was suspended, although political parties were not banned. National elections were held in February 1989. Representatives were elected directly to local-level resistance committees; these elected representatives to district-level resistance committees, and these, in turn, elected representatives to the NRC. The NRC was expanded from 98 members, all nominated by the President, to 278 members, of whom 68 were nominated by the President and 210 were elected. In October 1989 the NRC approved legislation prolonging the Government's term of office by five years from January 1990, when its mandate had been due to expire. A new Constitution was enacted by an elected Constituent Assembly in September 1995 and came into force in the following month. The first direct presidential election was held in May 1996, and national legislative elections took place in the following month to a 276-member Parliament, as the NRC became—comprising 214 directly elected and 62 nominated members. Voting also took place in June for local councils (which replaced the resistance committees). Further local elections were held in November 1997 and January 2002. Under the terms of the new Constitution, a national referendum on the future introduction of a multi-party political system took place in June 2000, at which voters overwhelmingly endorsed the retention of the existing 'no-party' system (this was nullified by the Constitutional Court in 2004—see Recent History). Legislation to amend the Constitution in order to allow multi-party politics, and to remove the two-term limit on the presidency, was approved by the Parliament in early 2005 and by 92.5% of voters at a referendum held on 28 July 2005. Following legislative elections in June 2006, the number of seats in Parliament stood at 319, comprising 215 directly elected representatives and 104 nominated members, including 69 women.

Defence

As assessed at November 2008, the Uganda People's Defence Forces was estimated to number 45,000 men, including paramilitary forces (a border defence unit of about 600 men, a police air wing of about 800 men, about 400 marines and local defence units of about 3,000 men, with a further 7,000 reportedly under training). Defence was allocated an estimated 406,000m. shillings by the central Government in 2008. The Lord's Resistance Army was thought to have about 1,500 members, with about 600 in Uganda and the remainder in Sudan.

Economic Affairs

In 2007, according to estimates by the World Bank, Uganda's gross national income (GNI), measured at average 2005–07 prices, was US $10,469m., equivalent to $340 per head (or $920 per head on an international purchasing-power parity basis). During 2000–07, it was estimated, the population increased at an average annual rate of 3.3%, while gross domestic product (GDP) per head increased, in real terms, by an average of 2.3% per year. Overall GDP increased, in real terms, at an average annual rate of 5.7% in 2000–07; growth was 6.5% in 2007.

Agriculture (including hunting, forestry and fishing) contributed 22.2% of GDP in 2007 and engaged 68.7% of the employed labour force in 2003. The principal cash crops are coffee, tobacco, tea and cotton. Cassava, sweet potatoes, maize, sugar cane and cocoa are also cultivated, and the production of cut flowers is an important activity. Together, coffee, tea, cocoa and spices provided 25.2% of export earnings in 2007. The main subsistence crops are plantains, cassava, sweet potatoes, maize, millet, sorghum, beans, groundnuts and rice. In addition, livestock (chiefly cattle, goats, sheep and poultry) are reared, and freshwater fishing is an important rural activity. Agricultural GDP increased by an average of 4.4% per year in 2000–07, according to the World Bank; it increased by 4.8% in 2007.

Industry (including mining, manufacturing, construction and power) contributed 24.7% of GDP in 2007, and employed 7.8% of the working population in 2003. Industrial GDP increased at an average annual rate of 7.4% in 2000–07, according to the World Bank; it increased by 8.1% in 2007.

Mining has made a negligible contribution to GDP since the 1970s (0.3% in 2007) and in 2003 it employed just 0.3% of the working population. The Government aims to encourage renewed investment in the sector. Output of copper, formerly an important export, virtually ceased during the late 1970s. However, the state-owned Kilembe copper mine in western Uganda was transferred to private ownership and the first phase of preparations to reopen the mine was expected to be completed during 2005; the second phase was expected to take a further 10 months to complete. In 2006 Uganda Gold Mining Ltd (UGM) signed an agreement with Kilembe Mines Ltd transferring ownership of 70% of the Kilembe copper mine to UGM. That company was to complete a feasibility study for renewed copper exploitation by 2009. The production of cobalt from stockpiled copper pyrites commenced in 1999. Uganda is believed to possess the world's second largest deposit of gold, which began to be exploited again in the mid-1990s. Apatite and limestone are also mined. There are, in addition, reserves of iron ore, magnetite, tin, tungsten, beryllium, bismuth, asbestos, graphite, phosphate and tantalite.

Manufacturing contributed 7.5% of GDP in 2007 and in 2003 it employed 6.1% of the working population. The most important manufacturing activities are the processing of agricultural commodities, brewing, vehicle assembly and the production of textiles, cement, soap, fertilizers, paper products, metal products, shoes, paints, matches and batteries. Manufacturing GDP increased by an average of 5.2% per year in 2000–07, according to the World Bank. The sector's GDP increased by 5.0% in 2007.

Energy is derived principally from hydroelectric power, although Uganda generates only about two-thirds of national energy requirements. Significant investment has, however, been made in hydroelectric power projects in recent years. Imports of petroleum and petroleum products accounted for 18.5% of the value of Uganda's merchandise imports in 2007.

The services sector contributed 53.1% of GDP in 2007, and engaged 23.5% of the employed labour force in 2003. Trade is the most important aspect of the sector. Services GDP increased by an average of 8.1% per year in 2000–07, according to the World Bank. GDP in the sector increased by 9.0% in 2007.

In 2007 Uganda recorded a visible trade deficit of US $1,296.4m., and there was a deficit of $744.7m. on the current account of the balance of payments. In 2007 the principal sources of imports were Kenya (13.5%), United Arab Emirates (UAE), India, the People's Republic of China, Japan and South Africa. The UAE (13.3%), Sudan, Kenya, the DRC, Switzerland-Liechtenstein and Rwanda were the main markets for exports in that year. The Common Market for Eastern and Southern Africa (COMESA, see p. 215) and the European Union (EU, see p. 255) are important trading partners: in 2003 they took 28.3% and 17.7%, respectively, of total imports and provided 27.7% and 26.3%, respectively, of total exports. The principal exports in 2007 were coffee, fish and tobacco; the main imports in that year were petroleum products, road vehicles and medical and pharmaceutical products.

In the financial year ending 30 June 2008 Uganda's central government budgetary surplus was an estimated 285,000m. shillings. In the previous financial year Uganda had recorded a deficit of 459,000m., equivalent to 2.0% of GDP. Uganda's external debt totalled US $1,264m. at the end of 2006, of which $1,107m. was long-term public debt. In that year the cost of debt-servicing was equivalent to 4.8% of the value of exports of goods and services. The annual average rate of inflation was 5.9% in 2000–08; consumer prices increased by 12.1% in 2008.

Uganda is a member of the COMESA, the African Development Bank (see p. 170) and the East African Community (EAC, see p. 425).

Uganda is regarded as having an open, deregulated economy, with conditions favourable to investment. As such, the country has enjoyed good relations with international donors, and during 1998–2000 Uganda secured international aid and debt-relief, including assistance under the IMF's initiative for heavily indebted poor countries, to the value of US $1,500m. Following the conclusion of an IMF arrangement in 2005, the IMF announced that Uganda's economy had improved to the point where it no longer qualified for aid. However, in December 2006 it was announced that Uganda would still qualify for the IMF's Policy Support Instrument, a non-lending programme which aimed to support low-income countries through advice, monitoring and endorsement of the country's economic policies. Nevertheless, Uganda remains one of poorest nations in the world, and the country's economy faces two main challenges. Firstly, to sustain growth (which is still largely dependent on agricultural exports) at a sufficient level to enable the reduction of poverty, with income distributed more evenly throughout the country; and secondly to reduce its reliance on foreign aid, which finances around one-half of the country's expenditure. GDP growth in 2005–07 was hampered by prolonged drought and power shortages, and as a result of the power deficits in the previous two years, in August 2007 construction of a hydroelectric power station at Bujagali with financial assistance from the World Bank began. Construction of a further hydroelectric power station at Karuma was expected to commence in 2009. The country's agricultural exports were also hindered from 2003 by the coffee wilt disease which affects the Robusta coffee variety. Uganda is Africa's second biggest producer of Robusta coffee and it was estimated by the Uganda Coffee Development Authority that the disease was losing the country some $27m. a year in export revenue. Following several years of economic growth and low inflation, the global economic slowdown began to affect Uganda from mid-2008. High international food and fuel prices led to inflation of 14.0% in the year to March 2009 and the IMF predicted that export revenue and incoming foreign direct investment would also be negatively affected. It was feared that this would have a knock-on effect on infrastructure investment which Uganda still desperately needed. The IMF forecast GDP growth of 6.2% in 2009, down slightly from 7.1% in 2008.

Education

Education is not compulsory. Most schools are supported by the Government, although a small proportion are sponsored by missions. Traditionally all schools have charged fees. In 1997, however, the Government introduced an initiative known as Universal Primary Education (UPE), whereby free primary education was to be phased in for up to four children per family. Primary education begins at six years of age and lasts for seven years. Secondary education, beginning at the age of 13, lasts for a further six years, comprising a first cycle of four years and a second of two years. In 2002/03, according to UNESCO, enrolment at pre-primary level was 3% (for both boys and girls). In 2005/06, according to UNESCO, enrolment at pre-primary level included 1.8% (for both boys and girls) of children in the relevant age-group. In 2005/06 enrolment at secondary schools included 16.2% of children (males 16.9%; females 15.4%) in the relevant age-group, while in 2004/05 just 3.5% of those in the relevant age-group (males 4.3%; females 2.7%) were enrolled in tertiary education. In addition to Makerere University in Kampala there is a university of science and technology at Mbarara, and a small Islamic university is located at Mbale. In 2004 58,823 students were enrolled in university. In 2004 spending on education represented 18.3% of total budgetary expenditure.

Public Holidays

2009: 1 January (New Year's Day), 26 January (Liberation Day), 8 March (International Women's Day), 10–13 April (Easter), 1 May (Labour Day), 3 June (Martyrs' Day), 9 June (National Heroes' Day), 20 September* (Id al-Fitr, end of Ramadan), 9 October (Independence Day), 27 November* (Id al-Adha, Feast of the Sacrifice), 25 December (Christmas), 26 December (Boxing Day).

2010: 1 January (New Year's Day), 26 January (Liberation Day), 8 March (International Women's Day), 2–5 April (Easter), 1 May (Labour Day), 3 June (Martyrs' Day), 9 June (National Heroes' Day), 10 September* (Id al-Fitr, end of Ramadan), 9 October (Independence Day), 16 November* (Id al-Adha, Feast of the Sacrifice), 25 December (Christmas), 26 December (Boxing Day).

* These holidays are dependent on the Islamic lunar calendar and the exact dates may vary by one or two days from those given.

Weights and Measures

The metric system is in force.

Statistical Survey

Sources (unless otherwise stated): Uganda Bureau of Statistics, POB 13, Entebbe; tel. (41) 320165; fax (41) 320147; e-mail ubos@infocom.co.ug; internet www.ubos.org; Statistics Department, Ministry of Finance, Planning and Economic Development, POB 8147, Kampala.

Area and Population

AREA, POPULATION AND DENSITY

Area (sq km)	
Land	197,323
Inland water and swamp	44,228
Total	241,551*
Population (census results)	
12 January 1991	16,671,705
12 September 2002	
Males	11,929,803
Females	12,512,281
Total	24,442,084
Population (official estimates at mid-year)	
2006	27,356,900
2007	28,247,300
2008	29,592,600
Density (per sq km) at mid-2008	122.5

* 93,263 sq miles.

PRINCIPAL ETHNIC GROUPS
(at census of 12 September 2002)*

Acholi	1,145,357		Basoga	2,062,920
Baganda	4,126,370		Iteso	1,568,763
Bagisu	1,117,661		Langi	1,485,437
Bakiga	1,679,519		Lugbara	1,022,240
Banyakole	2,330,212			

* Ethnic groups numbering more than 1m. persons, excluding population enumerated in hotels.

DISTRICTS
(population, official estimates at mid-2004)

Central	7,015,300		Northern	5,812,700
Kalangala	41,400		Adjumani	225,100
Kampala	1,290,500		Apac	716,800
Kayunga	306,800		Arua	915,500
Kiboga	249,200		Gulu	491,000
Luwero	496,100		Kitgum	307,500
Masaka	777,300		Kotido	705,400
Mpigi	424,300		Lira	805,200
Mubende	742,400		Moroto	185,500
Mukono	845,800		Moyo	229,800
Nakasongola	129,200		Nakapiripirit	170,500
Rakai	485,700		Nebbi	453,500
Sembabule	190,700		Pader	315,300
Wakiso	1,035,800		Yumbe	291,500
Eastern	6,712,400		Western	6,761,500
Bugiri	464,800		Bundibugyoi	232,900
Busia	239,500		Bushenyi	746,400
Iganga	757,300		Hoima	380,000
Jinja	436,100		Kabale	479,400
Kaberamaido	130,600		Kabarole	368,300
Kamuli	753,200		Kamwenge	312,300
Kapchorwa	208,600		Kanungu	212,300
Katakwi	343,800		Kasese	568,600
Kumi	417,500		Kibaale	454,100
Mayuge	346,800		Kisoro	224,300
Mbale	760,800		Kyenjojo	405,700
Pallisa	552,200		Masindi	512,900
Sironko	305,700		Mbarara	1,142,500
Soroti	406,800		Ntungamo	400,000
Tororo	589,300		Rukungiri	322,000

UGANDA

PRINCIPAL TOWNS
(population according to provisional results of census of 12 September 2002)*

Kampala (capital)	1,208,544	Entebbe		57,518
Gulu	113,144	Kasese		53,446
Lira	89,971	Njeru		52,514
Jinja	86,520	Mukono		47,305
Mbale	70,437	Arua		45,883
Mbarara	69,208	Kabale		45,757
Masaka	61,300	Kitgum		42,929

* According to administrative divisions of 2002.

Mid-2007 ('000, incl. suburbs, UN estimate): Kampala 1,420 (Source: UN, *World Urbanization Prospects: The 2007 Revision*).

BIRTHS AND DEATHS
(annual averages, UN estimates)

	1990–95	1995–2000	2000–05
Birth rate (per 1,000)	49.4	48.3	47.4
Death rate (per 1,000)	17.3	17.3	15.2

Source: UN, *World Population Prospects: The 2008 Revision*.

2006: Birth rate 47.6 per 1,000; Death rate 13.8 per 1,000 (Source: African Development Bank).

2007: Birth rate 46.6 per 1,000; Death rate 13.4 per 1,000 (Source: African Development Bank).

Life expectancy (years at birth, WHO estimates): 49.6 (males 48.6; females 50.6) in 2006 (Source: WHO, *World Health Statistics*).

EMPLOYMENT
(persons aged 10 years and over, census of 12 September 2002)*

	Males	Females	Total
Agriculture, hunting and forestry	2,545,962	2,649,779	5,195,741
Fishing	102,043	16,743	118,786
Mining and quarrying	13,613	6,127	19,740
Manufacturing	108,653	45,594	154,247
Electricity, gas and water supply	12,860	1,509	14,369
Construction	105,769	2,939	108,708
Wholesale and retail trade, repair of motor vehicles, motorcycles and personal and household goods	191,191	143,145	334,336
Hotels and restaurants	23,741	64,099	87,840
Transport, storage and communications	119,437	5,798	125,235
Financial intermediation Real estate, renting and business activities	14,539	7,562	22,101
Public administration and defence, compulsory social security	146,319	27,278	173,597
Education	124,167	85,015	209,182
Health and social work	54,327	53,108	107,435
Other community, social and personal service activities	22,736	26,734	49,470
Private households with employed persons	14,019	19,115	33,134
Not classifiable by economic activity	120,219	76,167	196,386
Total employed	3,719,595	3,230,712	6,950,307

* Excluding population enumerated at hotels.

2003 ('000 persons aged 10 years and over): Agriculture, hunting and forestry 6,278.3; Fishing 83.3; Mining and quarrying 27.8; Manufacturing 564.9; Electricity, gas and water supply 9.3; Construction 120.4; Wholesale and retail trade, repair of motor vehicles, motorcycles and personal and household goods 1,074.2; Hotels and restaurants 240.8; Transport, storage and communications 175.9; Real estate, renting and business activities 37.0; Public administration and defence, compulsory social security 74.1; Education 240.8; Health and social work 74.1; Other community, social and personal service activities 148.2; Private households with employed persons 111.1; *Total employed* 9,260.0; Unemployed 346.0; *Total labour force* 9,606.0 (Source: ILO).

Health and Welfare

KEY INDICATORS

Total fertility rate (children per woman, 2006)	6.6
Under-5 mortality rate (per 1,000 live births, 2006)	134
HIV/AIDS (% of persons aged 15–49, 2007)	5.4
Physicians (per 1,000 head, 2004)	0.1
Hospital beds (per 1,000 head, 2006)	1.1
Health expenditure (2006): US $ per head (PPP)	143
Health expenditure (2006): % of GDP	7.2
Health expenditure (2006): public (% of total)	26.9
Access to water (% of persons, 2006)	64
Access to sanitation (% of persons, 2006)	33
Human Development Index (2006): ranking	156
Human Development Index (2006): value	0.493

For sources and definitions, see explanatory note on p. vi.

Agriculture

PRINCIPAL CROPS
('000 metric tons)

	2005	2006	2007
Rice, paddy	153	154	162
Maize	1,170	1,258	1,262
Millet	672	687	732
Sorghum	449	440	456
Potatoes	585	628	650
Sweet potatoes	2,604	2,628	2,602
Cassava (Manioc)	5,576	4,926	4,456
Sugar cane	2,150*	1,950†	2,000†
Beans, dry	478	424	435
Cow peas, dry	71	71	75
Pigeon peas	85	88	89
Soybeans	158	175	176
Groundnuts, with shell	159	154	165
Sesame seed	161	166	168
Seed cotton†	55	63	75
Onions, dry†	147	147	147
Bananas†	615	615	615
Plantains	9,045	9,054	9,231
Coffee, green	158	133	168
Tea	38	34	35†
Tobacco, unmanufactured	31	32†	33†

* Unofficial figure.
† FAO estimate(s).

Aggregate production ('000 metric tons, may include official, semi-official or estimated data): Total cereals 2,459 in 2005, 2,557 in 2006, 2,631 in 2007; Total roots and tubers 8,765 in 2005, 8,182 in 2006, 7,708 in 2007; Total vegetables (incl. melons) 556 in 2005, 556 in 2006, 556 in 2007; Total fruits (excl. melons) 9,713 in 2005, 9,671 in 2006, 9,848 in 2007.

Source: FAO.

LIVESTOCK
('000 head, year ending September)

	2005	2006	2007
Asses	18*	n.a.	n.a.
Cattle	6,770	6,973	7,182
Sheep	1,600	1,648	1,697
Goats	7,800	8,034	8,275
Pigs	2,000	2,000*	2,000*
Chickens	25,174	22,849	23,750

* FAO estimate.
Source: FAO.

UGANDA

LIVESTOCK PRODUCTS
('000 metric tons, FAO estimates)

	2005	2006	2007
Cattle meat	106	106	106
Sheep meat	6	6	6
Goat meat	29	29	29
Pig meat	98	60	60
Chicken meat	38	38	38
Cows' milk	735	760	795
Hen eggs	20	20	21

Source: FAO.

Forestry

ROUNDWOOD REMOVALS
('000 cubic metres, excl. bark, FAO estimates)

	2005	2006	2007
Sawlogs, veneer logs and logs for sleepers	1,055	1,055	1,055
Other industrial wood	2,120	2,120	2,120
Fuel wood	36,797	37,343	37,900
Total	39,972	40,518	41,075

Source: FAO.

SAWNWOOD PRODUCTION
('000 cubic metres, incl. railway sleepers)

	2005	2006	2007
Coniferous (softwood)	24	24	24
Broadleaved (hardwood)	101	93	93
Total	125	117	117

Source: FAO.

Fishing
('000 metric tons, live weight)

	2004	2005	2006
Capture	371.8	416.8	367.1
Cyprinids	22.9	25.7	22.7
Tilapias	138.8	155.6	137.0
African lungfishes	12.9	14.5	12.8
Characins	20.0	22.4	19.8
Nile perch	156.3	175.2	154.3
Aquaculture	5.5	10.8	32.4
Total catch	377.3	427.6	399.5

Note: Figures exclude aquatic animals, recorded by number rather than weight. The number of Nile crocodiles captured was: 600 in 2004; 300 in 2005; n.a. in 2006.

Source: FAO.

Mining
('000 metric tons, unless otherwise indicated)

	2005	2006	2007*
Cement (hydraulic)*	630.0	630.0	650.0
Tantalum and niobium (columbium) concentrates (kilograms)	273	275	275
Cobalt (metric tons)	638	689	698
Gold (kilograms)	46	22	20
Limestone	540.8	425.6	450.0
Salt (unrefined)*	2	2	2

* Estimates.

Source: US Geological Survey.

Industry

SELECTED PRODUCTS
('000 metric tons, unless otherwise indicated)

	2003	2004	2005
Soft drinks (million litres)	78.5	111.5	163.5
Sugar	139.5	189.5	182.9
Soap	101.3	93.4	127.6
Cement	507.1	559.0	692.7
Paint (million litres)	1.9	2.2	8.2
Edible oil and fat	56.0	58.1	43.3
Animal feed	20.9	19.6	17.3
Footwear (million pairs)	3.4	3.6	46.3
Wheat flour	42.2	25.7	20.3
Processed milk (million litres)	14.9	19.6	18.5
Cotton and rayon fabrics (million sq metres)	11.1	10.1	13.6
Clay bricks, tiles, etc.	33.3	15.4	36.2
Corrugated iron sheets	39.2	48.8	61.6

Source: Bank of Uganda.

Finance

CURRENCY AND EXCHANGE RATES

Monetary Units
100 cents = 1 new Uganda shilling.

Sterling, Dollar and Euro Equivalents (31 August 2008)
£1 sterling = 3,008.5 new Uganda shillings;
US $1 = 1,645.0 new Uganda shillings;
€1 = 2,423.9 new Uganda shillings;
10,000 new Uganda shillings = £3.32 = $6.08 = €4.13.

Average Exchange Rate (new Uganda shillings per US $)
2005 1,780.7
2006 1,831.5
2007 1,723.5

Note: Between December 1985 and May 1987 the official exchange rate was fixed at US $1 = 1,400 shillings. In May 1987 a new shilling, equivalent to 100 of the former units, was introduced. At the same time, the currency was devalued by 76.7%, with the exchange rate set at $1 = 60 new shillings. Further adjustments were implemented in subsequent years. Foreign exchange controls were mostly abolished in 1993.

BUDGET
('000 million new shillings, year ending 30 June)

Revenue	2004/05	2005/06	2006/07
Revenue	1,915	2,267	2,667
Grants	1,256	1,129	907
Total	3,170	3,395	3,574

Expenditure	2004/05	2005/06	2006/07
Recurrent expenditure	2,233	2,234	2,442
Wages and salaries	867	867	987
Non-wages	1,117	1,117	1,220
Interest payments	249	250	236
Development expenditure	1,238	1,770	1,339
External expenditure	720	819	625
Domestic expenditure	519	951	714
Net lending and investment	−29	−29	101
Statistical discrepancy	−164	−443	151
Total	3,278	3,532	4,033

2007/08 ('000 million new shillings, year ending 30 June): Total revenue 4,186 (incl. grants 996); Total expenditure 3,901.

Source: Bank of Uganda.

UGANDA

Statistical Survey

INTERNATIONAL RESERVES
(US $ million at 31 December)

	2006	2007	2008
IMF special drawing rights	0.1	0.3	0.2
Foreign exchange	1,801.8	2,559.5	2,300.4
Total	1,801.9	2,559.8	2,300.6

Source: IMF, *International Financial Statistics*.

MONEY SUPPLY
('000 million new shillings at 31 December)

	2004	2005	2006
Currency outside banks	588.61	710.22	885.87
Demand deposits at commercial banks	752.63	894.22	1,020.61
Total money	1,341.24	1,604.45	1,906.49

Source: IMF, *International Financial Statistics*.

COST OF LIVING
(Consumer Price Index for all urban households; base: 2000 = 100)

	2005	2006	2007
Food	126.1	139.1	142.8
Clothing	102.3	106.8	111.9
Rent, fuel and light	130.1	139.1	164.6
All items (incl. others)	124.1	133.3	141.4

2008: Food 171.1; All items (incl. others) 158.5.
Source: ILO.

NATIONAL ACCOUNTS
('000 million new shillings at current prices)

Expenditure on the Gross Domestic Product

	2005	2006	2007
Government final consumption expenditure	2,441	2,692	2,689
Private final consumption expenditure	13,387	16,142	18,745
Increase in stocks	42	53	62
Gross fixed capital formation	3,812	4,126	5,014
Total domestic expenditure	19,682	23,013	26,510
Exports of goods and services	2,717	3,003	3,767
Less Imports of goods and services	4,521	5,851	7,268
GDP in purchasers' values	17,878	20,166	23,009
GDP at constant 2002 prices	14,814	15,859	17,281

Gross Domestic Product by Economic Activity

	2005	2006	2007
Agriculture, hunting, forestry and fishing	4,284	4,553	4,826
Mining and quarrying	49	55	62
Manufacturing	1,226	1,394	1,620
Electricity, gas and water	662	783	1,063
Construction	2,156	2,256	2,608
Wholesale and retail trade	2,267	2,738	3,290
Hotels and restaurants	724	818	923
Transport, storage and communications	916	1,218	1,475
Financial intermediation	439	510	683
Business services and real estate	1,552	1,749	2,005
General government services	658	720	747
Education	1,227	1,419	1,563
Health	279	311	340
Other services	345	416	506
Sub-total	16,784	18,940	21,711
Less Financial intermediation services indirectly measured	274	330	408
Gross value added at basic prices	16,510	18,610	21,303
Net taxes on products	1,371	1,555	1,705
GDP at market prices	17,878	20,166	23,009

BALANCE OF PAYMENTS
(US $ million)

	2005	2006	2007
Exports of goods f.o.b.	1,017.0	1,187.6	1,686.2
Imports of goods f.o.b.	−1,745.6	−2,215.6	−2,982.5
Trade balance	−728.6	−1,027.9	−1,296.4
Exports of services	507.4	452.3	499.3
Imports of services	−777.1	−949.9	−1,178.0
Balance on goods and services	−998.2	−1,525.6	−1,975.1
Other income received	49.8	71.9	98.4
Other income paid	−298.9	−298.0	−377.2
Balance on goods, services and income	−1,247.2	−1,751.7	−2,253.9
Current transfers received	1,184.3	1,762.8	1,816.2
Current transfers paid	−350.9	−334.2	−307.0
Current balance	−413.9	−323.1	−744.7
Capital account (net)	—	3,428.1	—
Direct investment from abroad	379.8	393.2	484.0
Portfolio investment liabilities	−13.4	21.7	14.3
Other investment assets	−7.1	76.1	282.2
Other investment liabilities	134.4	137.1	547.9
Net errors and omissions	1.9	41.5	62.1
Overall balance	81.7	3,774.5	645.9

Source: IMF, *International Financial Statistics*.

External Trade

PRINCIPAL COMMODITIES
(distribution by SITC, US $ million)

Imports c.i.f.	2005	2006	2007
Food and live animals	212.1	233.7	277.6
Cereals and cereal preparations	141.2	156.8	158.8
Crude materials (inedible) except fuels	54.2	54.7	59.7
Mineral fuels, lubricants, etc.	348.5	539.6	654.0
Petroleum, petroleum products and related materials	343.2	526.6	645.6
Animal and vegetable oils, fats and waxes	73.7	89.7	125.1
Chemicals and related products	268.4	337.5	443.1
Medicinal and pharmaceutical products	85.7	123.1	175.8
Plastics in primary forms	62.6	70.6	96.1
Basic manufactures	362.8	430.3	570.9
Non-metallic mineral manufactures	537.2	662.8	955.0
Iron and steel	118.8	141.6	173.4
Machinery and transport equipment	537.2	662.8	955.0
Telecommunications and sound recording/reproducing apparatus	100.4	137.0	246.5
Electrical machinery, apparatus, etc.	20.9	7.1	18.8
Road vehicles (incl. air-cushion vehicles) and parts (excl. tyres, engines and electrical parts)	192.2	216.4	294.2
Miscellaneous manufactured articles	186.4	186.9	251.9
Total (incl. others)	2,054.1	2,557.3	3,493.4

UGANDA

Statistical Survey

Exports f.o.b.	2005	2006	2007
Food and live animals	419.3	462.0	572.0
Fish, crustaceans, molluscs and preparations thereof	139.9	140.7	117.7
Cereals and cereal preparations	31.0	36.7	43.1
Coffee, tea, cocoa, spices and manufactures	223.7	225.8	336.2
Beverages and tobacco	39.5	38.9	98.2
Tobacco and tobacco manufactures	32.3	27.7	67.3
Crude materials (inedible) except fuels	108.0	100.8	115.7
Textile fibres (not wool tops) and their wastes (not in yarn)	39.3	26.8	29.6
Crude animal and vegetable materials n.e.s.	39.8	41.1	50.2
Mineral fuels, lubricants and related materials	37.8	42.2	49.0
Petroleum, petroleum products and related materials	33.0	37.3	40.3
Basic manufactures	50.6	57.8	133.1
Iron and steel	29.7	31.3	63.1
Machinery and transport equipment	42.6	89.5	169.9
Miscellaneous manufactured articles	13.3	16.0	31.4
Gold, non-monetary (excl. gold ores and concentrates)	73.0	122.6	65.0
Total (incl. others)	812.8	962.2	1,336.7

Source: UN, *International Trade Statistics Yearbook*.

PRINCIPAL TRADING PARTNERS
(US $ million)

Imports c.i.f.	2005	2006	2007
Bahrain	20.8	85.8	61.7
Belgium	31.1	35.8	48.5
China, People's Repub.	109.2	138.3	274.3
France (incl. Monaco)	35.3	37.4	101.0
Germany	49.3	74.9	81.6
Hong Kong	16.5	20.5	40.1
India	131.8	209.0	345.0
Italy	49.2	33.1	44.7
Japan	146.6	174.5	233.0
Kenya	520.7	401.0	472.4
Malaysia	47.2	48.9	63.2
Netherlands	43.9	51.7	55.8
Saudi Arabia	22.8	52.3	47.4
Singapore	9.8	37.3	60.2
Sweden	22.6	31.9	98.7
South Africa	143.7	156.3	207.2
Tanzania	30.1	28.7	29.2
United Arab Emirates	136.7	325.3	420.5
United Kingdom	99.4	124.0	117.8
USA	78.1	89.7	101.9
Total (incl. others)	2,054.1	2,557.3	3,493.4

Exports f.o.b.	2005	2006	2007
Australia	4.0	7.2	2.4
Belgium	33.7	39.6	52.8
Burundi	20.8	20.6	42.7
Congo, Democratic Repub.	60.4	44.8	100.0
Congo, Republic	9.9	8.1	42.3
France (incl. Monaco)	39.6	38.4	32.7
Germany	33.8	41.9	65.1
Hong Kong	13.5	12.4	10.3
Italy	5.7	14.6	13.3
Japan	5.2	3.9	5.3
Kenya	72.4	88.0	118.2
Netherlands	85.4	61.9	66.6
Rwanda	36.1	30.5	83.3

Exports f.o.b.—*continued*	2005	2006	2007
Singapore	28.9	34.5	22.5
South Africa	9.8	10.9	10.7
Spain	18.0	19.3	26.6
Sudan	50.5	91.7	157.1
Switzerland-Liechtenstein	74.9	45.4	86.6
Tanzania	15.4	13.7	30.6
United Arab Emirates	84.3	186.3	177.9
United Kingdom	26.8	30.0	53.3
USA	16.4	14.2	19.6
Total (incl. others)	812.8	962.2	1,336.7

Transport

RAILWAYS
(traffic)

	1994	1995	1996
Passenger-km (million)	35	30	28
Freight ton-km (million)	208	236	187

Freight traffic ('000 ton-km): 212,616 in 2003; 229,439 in 2004; 185,559 in 2005.

ROAD TRAFFIC
(vehicles in use)

	2003	2004	2005
Passenger cars	56,837	59,786	65,472
Buses and coaches	20,572	23,443	28,436
Lorries and vans	64,650	70,215	71,887
Motorcycles	80,088	89,212	108,207

CIVIL AVIATION
(traffic on scheduled services)

	2002	2003	2004
Kilometres flown (million)	2	2	3
Passengers carried ('000)	41	40	46
Passenger-km (million)	237	237	272
Total ton-km (million)	42	44	50

Source: UN, *Statistical Yearbook*.

Tourism

FOREIGN TOURIST ARRIVALS

Country of residence	2004	2005	2006
India	9,366	10,691	11,829
Kenya	220,062	138,346	160,306
Rwanda	65,298	80,522	111,385
South Africa	n.a.	10,423	11,135
Tanzania	67,885	50,723	n.a.
United Kingdom	22,402	28,227	31,495
USA	18,898	21,968	28,120
Total (incl. others)	512,379	467,728	538,586

Tourism receipts (US $ million, incl. passenger transport): 257 in 2004; 383 in 2005; 356 in 2006 (Source: World Tourism Organization).

UGANDA

Communications Media

	2005	2006	2007
Telephones ('000 main lines in use)	87.5	108.1	162.3
Mobile cellular telephones ('000 subscribers)	1,315.3	2,008.8	4,195.3
Internet users ('000)	500	1,500	2,000
Broadband subscribers	800	1,200	1,900

Source: partly International Telecommunication Union.

Personal computers ('000 in use): 250 in 2005.

Television receivers ('000 in use, 2000): 610.

Radio receivers ('000 in use, 1997): 2,600.

Facsimile machines (number in use, year ending 30 June 1996): 3,000 (estimate).

Book production (titles, excl. pamphlets and govt publications, 1996): 288.

Daily newspapers: 2 titles (average circulation 40,000 copies) in 1996; 7 titles in 2004.

Sources: mainly UNESCO, *Statistical Yearbook*; UN, *Statistical Yearbook*; UNESCO Institute for Statistics.

Education

(2005/06, unless otherwise indicated)

	Institutions	Teachers	Students
Pre-primary	n.a.	1,664	69,340
Primary	n.a.	150,135	7,363,721
Secondary*	n.a.	36,336	760,337
Tertiary†	n.a.	4,168	88,360
Teacher training colleges‡	10	n.a.	16,170
Technical schools and institutes‡	25	n.a.	7,999
Universities‡	18	n.a.	58,823

* 2004/05.
† 2003/04.
‡ 2004.

Source: mainly UNESCO Institute for Statistics.

Adult literacy rate (UNESCO estimates): 73.6% (males 81.8%; females 65.5%) in 2007 (Source: UNESCO Institute for Statistics).

Directory

The Constitution

Following the military coup in July 1985, the 1967 Constitution was suspended, and all legislative and executive powers were vested in a Military Council, whose Chairman was Head of State. In January 1986 a further military coup established an executive Presidency, assisted by a Cabinet of Ministers and a legislative National Resistance Council (NRC). In September 1995 a Constituent Assembly (comprising 214 elected and 74 nominated members) enacted a draft Constitution. The new Constitution was promulgated on 8 October 1995. Under its terms, a national referendum on the introduction of a multi-party political system was to take place in 2000. The referendum produced an overwhelming vote in favour of retaining the existing 'no-party' system; however, the referendum was annulled by the Constitutional Court in 2004. A direct presidential election took place in May 1996, followed in June of that year by legislative elections to the Parliament. This body, comprising 214 elected members and 62 nominated members, replaced the NRC. At the general election of June 2001 the number of nominated members was increased to 78. Legislation outlining the transition to multi-party politics was passed by the Parliament on 28 June 2005 and approved by 92.5% of voters in a national referendum held on 28 July 2005. The legislation also removed the two-term limit on the presidency.

The Government

HEAD OF STATE

President: Gen. (retd) YOWERI KAGUTA MUSEVENI (took office 29 January 1986; elected 9 May 1996, re-elected 12 March 2001 and 23 February 2006).

Vice-President: Prof. GILBERT BALIBASEKA BUKENYA.

THE CABINET
(April 2009)

Prime Minister: Prof. APOLO NSIBAMBI.

First Deputy Prime Minister and Minister in Charge of East African Affairs: ERIYA KATEGAYA.

Second Deputy Prime Minister and Minister of Public Service: HENRY MUGANWA KAJURA.

Third Deputy Prime Minister and Minister of Internal Affairs: KIRUNDA KIVEJINJA.

Minister of Security: AMAMA MBABAZI.

Minister in Charge of the Presidency: BEATRICE WABUDEYA.

Minister in the Office of the Prime Minister, in charge of General Duties: JANAT MUKWAYA.

Minister of Agriculture, Animal Industry and Fisheries: HOPE MWESIGYE.

Minister of Defence: Dr CRISPUS KIYONGA.

Minister of Relief and Disaster Preparedness: TARSIS KABWEGYERE.

Minister of Education and Sports: GERALDINE BITAMAZIRE.

Minister of Energy and Minerals: HILLARY ONEK.

Minister of Information and National Guidance: KABAKUMBA L. MATSIKO.

Minister of Finance, Planning and Economic Development: SYDDA BBUMBA.

Minister of Works and Transport: JOHN NASASIRA.

Minister of Justice and Attorney-General: GERALD KIDDU MAKUBUYA.

Minister of Gender and Social Affairs: GABRIEL OPIO.

Minister of Trade and Industry: KAHINDA OTAFIIRE.

Minister of Water and Environment: MARIA MUTAGAMBA.

Minister of Lands, Housing and Urban Development: OMARA ATUBO.

Minister of Health: Dr STEPHEN MALLINGA.

Minister of Foreign Affairs: SAM KUTESA.

Minister of Information Communication Technology: AGGREY AWORI.

Minister of Local Government: ADOLF MWESIGYE.

Minister without Portfolio: DOROTHY HYUHA.

In addition to the Cabinet Ministers, there are 44 Ministers of State. The Chief Whip is also a member of the Cabinet.

MINISTRIES

Office of the President: Parliament Bldg, POB 7168, Kampala; tel. (41) 4258441; fax (41) 4256143; e-mail aak@statehouse.go.ug; internet www.statehouse.go.ug.

Office of the Prime Minister: POB 341, Kampala; tel. (41) 4236252; fax (41) 4341139; e-mail ps@opm.go.ug; internet www.opm.go.ug.

Ministry of Agriculture, Animal Industry and Fisheries: POB 102, Entebbe; tel. (41) 4320987; fax (41) 4321255; e-mail mosagr@hotmail.com; internet www.agriculture.go.ug.

Ministry of Defence: Bombo, POB 7069, Kampala; tel. (41) 4270331; fax (41) 4245911; e-mail spokesman@defenceuganda.mil.ug; internet www.defenceuganda.mil.ug.

Ministry of Relief and Disaster Preparedness: POB 341, Kampala; tel. (41) 4236967.

Ministry of Education and Sports: Embassy House and Development Bldg, Plot 9/11, Parliament Ave, POB 7063, Kampala; tel. (41) 4234451; fax (41) 42230437; e-mail pro@education.go.ug; internet www.education.go.ug.

Ministry of Energy and Mineral Development: Amber House, Kampala Rd, Kampala; tel. (41) 4311111; e-mail psmemd@energy.go.ug; internet www.energyandminerals.go.ug.

UGANDA

Ministry of Finance, Planning and Economic Development: Appollo Kaggwa Rd, Plot 2-12, POB 8147, Kampala; tel. (41) 4707000; fax (41) 4230163; e-mail webmaster@finance.go.ug; internet www.finance.go.ug.

Ministry of Foreign Affairs: Embassy House, POB 7048, Kampala; tel. (41) 4345661; fax (41) 4258722; e-mail info@mofa.go.ug; internet www.mofa.go.ug.

Ministry of Gender, Labour and Social Development: Plot 2, Lumumba Ave, Simbamanyo House, Kampala; tel. (41) 347854; fax (41) 256374; e-mail ps@mglsd.go.ug; internet www.mglsd.go.ug.

Ministry of Health: Plot 6, Lourdel Rd, Wandegeya, POB 7272, Kampala; tel. (41) 4340884; fax (41) 4340887; e-mail info@health.go.ug; internet www.health.go.ug.

Ministry of Information Communication Technology: NSSF House, Jinja Rd, Kampala; tel. (41) 4236262; fax (41) 4231314; internet www.ict.go.ug.

Ministry of Information and National Guidance: Kampala.

Ministry of Internal Affairs: Plot 75 Jinja Rd, POB 7191, Kampala; tel. (41) 4231059; fax (41) 4231063; e-mail info@mia.go.ug; internet www.mia.go.ug.

Ministry of Justice: Parliament Bldg, POB 7183, Kampala; tel. (41) 4230538; fax (41) 4254829; e-mail mojca@africaonline.co.ug; internet www.justice.go.ug.

Ministry of Lands, Housing and Urban Development: Kampala.

Ministry of Local Government: Uganda House, 8/10 Kampala Rd, POB 7037, Kampala; tel. (41) 4341224; fax (41) 4258127; e-mail info@molg.go.ug; internet www.molg.go.ug.

Ministry of Security: Kampala.

Ministry of Tourism, Trade and Industry: 6/8 Parliament Ave, POB 7103, Kampala; tel. (41) 4314000; fax (41) 4347286; e-mail mintrade@mtti.go.ug; internet www.mtti.go.ug.

Ministry of Water and Environment: POB 7096, Kampala; tel. (41) 4342931; e-mail mwle@mwle.go.ug; internet www.mwle.go.ug.

Ministry of Works and Transport: POB 10, Entebbe; tel. (42) 4320101; fax (42) 4320135; e-mail mowhc@utlonline.co.ug; internet www.miniworks.go.ug.

President and Legislature

PRESIDENT

Election, 23 February 2006

Candidate	Votes	% of votes
Gen. (Retd) Yoweri Kaguta Museveni (NRM)	4,078,677	59.28
Kizza Besigye (FDC)	2,570,572	37.36
John Ssebaana Kizito (DP)	109,055	1.59
Abed Bwanika (Ind.)	65,344	0.95
Miria Obote Kalule (UPC)	56,584	0.82
Total	**6,880,232**	**100.00**

PARLIAMENT

Speaker: EDWARD SSEKANDI.
Deputy Speaker: REBECCA KADAGA.

The National Resistance Movement, which took office in January 1986, established a National Resistance Council (NRC), initially comprising 80 nominated members, to act as a legislative body. National elections were held on 11–28 February 1989, at which 210 members of an expanded NRC were elected by members of district-level Resistance Committees (themselves elected by local-level Resistance Committees, who were directly elected by universal adult suffrage). The remaining 68 seats in the NRC were reserved for candidates nominated by the President (to include 34 women and representatives of youth organizations and trades unions). Political parties were not allowed to participate in the election campaign. In October 1989 the NRC approved legislation extending the Government's term of office by five years from January 1990, when its mandate was to expire. The Constituent Assembly (see Constitution) extended further the NRM's term of office in November 1994. Under the terms of the Constitution that was promulgated in October 1995, the NRC was restyled as the Ugandan Parliament. Legislative elections to the Parliament took place in June 1996 (again officially on a 'no-party' basis). The total membership of the Parliament was reduced from 278 to 276, comprising 214 elected and 62 nominated representatives. A national referendum on the future introduction of a multi-party political system was staged in June 2000, at which 90.7% of participants voted in favour of retaining the 'no-party' political system—the referendum was nullified in mid-2004 (see Recent History). Legislation was adopted by the Parliament in June 2005, and ratified by a national referendum on 28 July of that year, restoring multi-party politics and lifting the two-term limit on the presidency. Multi-party legislative elections were held on 23 February 2006, following which the number of seats in Parliament stood at 319, comprising 215 directly elected representatives, 69 nominated female representatives, 10 nominated representatives from the UPDF, five nominated representatives for young people, five nominated representatives for people with disabilities, five nominated representatives for workers and 10 ex officio members.

Election Commission

Electoral Commission: 53–56 Jinja Rd, POB 22678, Kampala; tel. (41) 4337500; fax (41) 4341907; e-mail info@ec.or.ug; internet www.ec.or.ug; f. 1997; independent; Chair. Dr BADRU M. KIGGUNDU.

Political Organizations

Political parties were ordered to suspend active operations, although not formally banned, in March 1986. At a referendum on the future restoration of a plural political system, which took place on 29 June 2000, the retention of the existing 'no-party' system was overwhelmingly endorsed by voters. However, the result was nullified by the Constitutional Court in mid-2004. Following a successful challenge to the Political Parties and Organisations Act 2002, political parties were permitted to resume their activities nationally from March 2003. Discussions on a proposed transition to multi-party politics commenced in 2004. By April of that year some 60 new political parties had emerged, but only 13 had sought registration. In mid-2005 legislation was passed allowing for a return to full multi-party democracy; the legislation was approved by 92.5% of voters in a national referendum held on 28 July 2005. By late 2007 36 parties had been officially registered.

Conservative Party (CP): POB 5145, Kampala; f. 1979; Leader KEN LUKYAMUZI.

Democratic Party (DP): City House, Plot 2/3 William St, POB 7098, Kampala; tel. and fax (41) 4252536; e-mail info@dpuganda.org; internet www.dpuganda.org; f. 1954; main support in southern Uganda; seeks a multi-party political system; Pres. JOHN SSEBAANA KIZITO; Vice-Pres. ZACHARY OLUM.

Forum for Democratic Change (FDC): FDC Villas, Entebbe Rd, Plot no. 109, Najjanankumbi, POB 26928, Kampala; tel. (41) 4267920; fax (41) 4267918; e-mail info@fdcuganda.org; internet www.fdcuganda.org; f. 2004 by a merger of the Reform Agenda, the Parliamentary Advocacy Forum and the National Democratic Forum; Leader KIZZA BESIGYE.

Forum for Integrity in Leadership (FIL): Plot 48B, Ntinda Rd, POB 7606, Kampala; Chair. EMMANUEL TUMUSIIME.

Justice Forum: POB 3999, Kampala; Leader MUHAMMAD KIBIRIGE MAYANJA.

Movement for Democratic Change (MDC): Balintuma Rd, Nakulabye, POB 70952, Kampala.

National Peasant Party (NPP): Plot 123, Katwe Rd, Sapoba House, POB 20692, Kampala.

National Resistance Movement (NRM): Plot 10, Kyadondo Rd, POB 7778, Kampala; tel. (41) 346295; e-mail info@nrm.ug; internet www.nrm.ug; f. as National Resistance Movement to oppose the UPC Govt 1980–85; also opposed the mil. Govt in power from July 1985 to Jan. 1986; its fmr mil. wing, the National Resistance Army (NRA), led by Lt-Gen. (later Gen. retd) Yoweri Kaguta Museveni, took power in Jan. 1986; name changed as above on registration in 2003; Chair. YOWERI MUSEVENI.

Uganda Patriotic Movement (UPM): POB 2083, Kampala; f. 1980; Sec.-Gen. JABERI SSALI.

Uganda People's Congress (UPC): Plot 8–10 Kampala Rd, Uganda House, POB 37047, Kampala; tel. and fax (41) 236748; e-mail upcsecretariat@upcparty.net; internet www.upcparty.net; f. 1960; socialist-based philosophy; mainly northern support; ruling party 1962–71 and 1980–85, sole legal political party 1969–71; Pres. MIRIA KALULE OBOTE; Sec.-Gen. PETER MUKIDI WALUBIRI.

The following organizations are in armed conflict with the Government:

Alliance of Democratic Forces (ADF): active since 1996 in south-eastern Uganda; combines Ugandan Islamic fundamentalist rebels, exiled Rwandan Hutus and guerrillas from the Democratic Republic of the Congo; Pres. Sheikh JAMIL MUKULU.

Lord's Resistance Army (LRA): f. 1987; claims to be conducting a Christian fundamentalist 'holy war' against the Govt; forces est. to number up to 1,500, operating mainly from bases in Sudan; Leader JOSEPH KONY; a breakaway faction (LRA—Democratic) is led by RONALD OTIM KOMAKECH.

Uganda National Rescue Front Part Two (UNRF II): based in Juba, Sudan; Leader ALI BAMUZE.

Uganda People's Freedom Movement (UPFM): based in Tororo and Kenya; f. 1994 by mems of the fmr Uganda People's Army; Leader PETER OTAI.

West Nile Bank Front (WNBF): operates in northern Uganda.

Diplomatic Representation

EMBASSIES AND HIGH COMMISSIONS IN UGANDA

Algeria: 14 Acacia Ave, Kololo, POB 4025, Kampala; tel. (41) 4232918; fax (41) 4341015; e-mail ambalgka@imul.com; Ambassador ABDELKADER AZIRIA.

Belgium: Rwenzori House, 3rd Floor, Plot 1, Lumumba Ave, POB 7043, Kampala; tel. (41) 4345559; fax (41) 4347212; e-mail kampala@diplobel.org; internet www.diplomatie.be/kampala; Ambassador JAN DE BRUYNE.

China, People's Republic: 37 Malcolm X Ave, Kololo, POB 4106, Kampala; tel. (41) 4259881; fax (41) 4235087; e-mail chinaemb_ug@mfa.gov.cn; internet ug.china-embassy.org; Ambassador SUN HEPING.

Congo, Democratic Republic: 20 Philip Rd, Kololo, POB 4972, Kampala; tel. (41) 4250099; fax (41) 4340140; Chargé d'affaires a.i. BISELELE WA MUTSHIPAYI.

Cuba: KAR Dr., 16 Lower Kololo Terrace, POB 9226, Kampala; tel. (41) 4233742; fax (41) 4233320; e-mail ecuba@africaonline.co.ug; Ambassador MARIANO L. BETANCOURT.

Denmark: Plot 3, Lumumba Ave, POB 11243, Kampala; tel. (31) 2263211; fax (31) 2264624; e-mail kmtamb@um.dk; internet www.ambkampala.um.dk; Ambassador NATHALIA FEINBERG.

Egypt: 33 Kololo Hill Dr., POB 4280, Kampala; tel. (41) 4254525; fax (41) 4232103; e-mail egyembug@utlonline.co.ug; Ambassador REDA ABDEL RAHMAN BEBARS.

Ethiopia: 3L Kitante Close, off Kira Rd, POB 7745, Kampala; tel. (41) 4348340; fax (41) 4341885; Ambassador Ato TERFA MENEGESHA.

France: 16 Lumumba Ave, Nakasero, POB 7212, Kampala; tel. (41) 4304500; fax (41) 4304520; e-mail ambafrance.kampala@diplomatie.gouv.fr; internet www.ambafrance-ug.org; Ambassador RENÉ FORCEVILLE.

Germany: 15 Philip Rd, Kololo, POB 7016, Kampala; tel. (41) 4501111; fax (41) 4501115; e-mail info@kampala.diplo.de; internet www.kampala.diplo.de; Ambassador REINHARD BUCHHOLZ.

Holy See: Chwa II Rd, Mbuya Hill, POB 7177, Kampala (Apostolic Nunciature); tel. (41) 4505619; fax (41) 4441774; e-mail nuntius@imul.com; Apostolic Nuncio PAUL TSCHANG IN-NAM.

India: 11 Kyaddondo Rd, Nakasero, POB 7040, Kampala; tel. (41) 4257368; fax (41) 4254943; e-mail hoc@hicomindkampala.org; High Commissioner NIRAJ SRIVASTAVA.

Iran: 9 Bandali Rise, Bugolobi, POB 24529, Kampala; tel. (41) 4441689; fax (41) 4443590; Ambassador ABOUTALEBI MORTEZA.

Ireland: 25 Yusuf Lule Rd, Nakasero, POB 7791, Kampala; tel. (41) 7713000; fax (41) 4344353; e-mail kampalaembassy@dfa.ie; Ambassador KEVIN KELLY.

Italy: 11 Lourdel Rd, Nakasero, POB 4646, Kampala; tel. (41) 4250442; fax (41) 4250448; e-mail segreteria.kampala@esteri.it; internet www.ambkampala.esteri.it; Ambassador PIETRO BALLERO.

Japan: Plot 8, Kyaddondo Rd, Nakasero, POB 23553, Kampala; tel. (41) 4349542; fax (41) 4349547; e-mail jembassy@jembassy.co.ug; Ambassador RYUUZI KIKUCHI.

Kenya: 41 Nakasero Rd, POB 5220, Kampala; tel. (41) 4458235; fax (41) 4458239; e-mail kenyahicom@africaonline.co.ug; High Commissioner JAPHETH R. GETUGI.

Korea, Democratic People's Republic: 10 Prince Charles Dr., Kololo, POB 5885, Kampala; tel. (41) 4546033; fax (41) 4450224; Ambassador PAK HYON JAE.

Libya: 26 Kololo Hill Dr., POB 6079, Kampala; tel. (41) 4344924; fax (41) 4344969; Sec. of People's Bureau ABDALLA ABDULMAULA BUJELDAIN.

Netherlands: Rwenzori Courts, 4th Floor, Plot 2, Nakasero Rd, POB 7728, Kampala; tel. (41) 2346000; fax (41) 2231861; e-mail kam@minbuza.nl; internet www.netherlandsembassyuganda.org; Ambassador JEROEN VERHEUL.

Nigeria: 33 Nakasero Rd, POB 4338, Kampala; tel. (41) 4433691; fax (41) 4432543; e-mail nighicom-sgu@africaonline.co.ug; High Commissioner CHUKUDI DIXON ORIKE.

Norway: 8A John Babiiha Ave, Kololo, POB 22770, Kampala; tel. (41) 4343621; fax (41) 4343936; e-mail emb.kampala@mfa.no; internet www.norway.go.ug; Ambassador BJØRG SCHONHOWD LEITE.

Russia: 28 Malcolm X Ave, Kololo, POB 7022, Kampala; tel. (41) 4433676; fax (41) 4345798; Ambassador VALERY I. UTKIN.

Rwanda: 2 Nakaima Rd, POB 2468, Kampala; tel. (41) 4344045; fax (41) 4458547; Ambassador IGNACE KAMALI KAREGESA.

Saudi Arabia: 3 Okurut Close, Kololo, POB 22558, Kampala; tel. (41) 4340614; fax (41) 4454017; Chargé d'affaires a.i. MAJED ABDULRAHMAN M. MARTHA AL-OTAIBI.

South Africa: Plot 15A, Nakasero Rd, POB 22667, Kampala; tel. (41) 4343543; fax (41) 4348216; e-mail kampala.sahc@foreign.gov.za; High Commissioner THANDUYISE HENRY CHILIZA.

Sweden: 24 Lumumba Ave, Nakasero, POB 22669, Kampala; tel. (41) 4340970; fax (41) 4340979; e-mail ambassaden.kampala@foreign.ministry.se; internet www.swedenabroad.com/kampala; Ambassador ANDERS JOHNSON.

Tanzania: 6 Kagera Rd, Nakasero, POB 5750, Kampala; tel. (41) 4456272; fax (41) 4343973; High Commissioner RAJAB H. GAMAHA.

United Kingdom: Plot 4, Windsor Loop Rd, POB 7070, Kampala; tel. (31) 2312000; fax (41) 4257304; e-mail bhcinfo@starcom.co.ug; internet ukinuganda.fco.gov.uk; High Commissioner MARTIN SHEARMAN.

USA: Plot 1577, Ggaba Rd, POB 7007, Kampala; tel. (41) 4259791; fax (41) 4259794; e-mail KampalaWebContact@state.gov; internet kampala.usembassy.gov; Ambassador STEVEN A. BROWNING.

Judicial System

Courts of Judicature: High Court Bldg, POB 7085, Kampala; tel. (41) 4233420; e-mail info@judicature.go.ug; internet www.judicature.go.ug.

The Supreme Court

Kabaka Anjagala Rd, Mengo.

Hears appeals from the Court of Appeal. Also acts as a Constitutional Court.

Chief Justice: BENJAMIN ODOKI.

Deputy Chief Justice: L. E. M. MUKASA-KIKONYOGO.

The Court of Appeal: 5 Parliament Ave, Kampala; hears appeals from the High Court; the Court of Appeal consists of the Deputy Chief Justice and no fewer than seven Justices of Appeal, the number thereof being prescribed by Parliament.

The High Court

POB 7085, Kampala; tel. (41) 4233422.

Has full criminal and civil jurisdiction and also serves as a Constitutional Court. The High Court consists of the Principal Judge and 27 Puisne Judges.

Principal Judge: JAMES OGOOLA.

Magistrates' Courts: These are established under the Magistrates' Courts Act of 1970 and exercise limited jurisdiction in criminal and civil matters. The country is divided into magisterial areas, presided over by a Chief Magistrate. Under the Chief Magistrate there are two categories of Magistrates. The Magistrates preside alone over their courts. Appeals from the first category of Magistrates' Court lie directly to the High Court, while appeals from the second categories of Magistrates' Court lie to the Chief Magistrate's Court, and from there to the High Court. There are 27 Chief Magistrates' Courts, 52 Magistrates' Grade I Courts and 428 Magistrates' Grade II Courts.

Religion

Christianity is the majority religion—its adherents constitute approximately 75% of the population. Muslims account for approximately 15% of the population. A variety of other religions, including traditional indigenous religions, several branches of Hinduism, the Bahá'í Faith and Judaism, are practised freely and, combined, make up approximately 10% of the population. There are few atheists in the country. In many areas, particularly in rural settings, some religions tend to be syncretistic: deeply held traditional indigenous beliefs are blended into or observed alongside the rites of recognized religions, particularly in areas that are predominantly Christian. Missionary groups of several denominations are present and active in the country, including the Pentecostal Church, the Baptist Church, the Episcopal Church/Church of Uganda, the Church of Christ and the Mormons.

UGANDA

CHRISTIANITY

The Roman Catholic and Anglican Churches claim approximately the same number of followers, accounting for approximately 90% of the country's professed Christians. The Seventh-day Adventist Church, the Church of Jesus Christ of Latter-day Saints (Mormons), the Orthodox Church, Jehovah's Witnesses, the Baptist Church, the Unification Church and the Pentecostal Church, among others, are also active.

The Anglican Communion

Anglicans are adherents of the Church of the Province of Uganda, comprising 29 dioceses. In 2002 there were about 8m. adherents.

Archbishop of Uganda and Bishop of Kampala: Most Rev. LIVINGSTONE MPALANYI-NKOYOYO, POB 14123, Kampala; tel. (41) 4270218; fax (41) 4251925; e-mail couab@uol.co.ug.

Greek Orthodox Church

Archbishop of East Africa: NICADEMUS OF IRINOUPOULIS (resident in Nairobi, Kenya); jurisidiction covers Kenya, Tanzania and Uganda.

The Roman Catholic Church

Uganda comprises four archdioceses and 15 dioceses. At 31 December 2006 there were an estimated 12,273,692 adherents (equivalent to some 42.8% of the total population).

Uganda Episcopal Conference

Uganda Catholic Secretariat, POB 2886, Kampala; tel. (41) 4510398; fax (41) 4510545.

f. 1974; Pres. Most Rev. MATTHIAS SSEKAMANYA (Archbishop of Lugazi).

Archbishop of Gulu: Most Rev. JOHN BAPTIST ODAMA, Archbishop's House, POB 200, Gulu; tel. (47) 4132026; e-mail metrog@africaonline.co.ug.

Archbishop of Kampala: CYPRIAN KIZITO LWANGA, Archbishop's House, POB 14125, Mengo, Kampala; tel. (41) 4270183; fax (41) 4345441; e-mail klarchdioc@utlonline.co.ug.

Archbishop of Mbarara: Most Rev. PAUL BAKYENGA, POB 150, Mbarara; tel. (485) 420052; fax (485) 421249; e-mail mbarchd@utlonline.co.ug.

Archbishop of Tororo: Most Rev. DENIS KIWANUKA LOTE, Archbishop's House, Plot 17 Boma Ave, POB 933, Mbale; tel. (45) 4433269; fax (45) 4433754; e-mail tororoad@africaonline.co.ug.

ISLAM

Muslims are mainly Sunni, although there are Shi'a followers of the Aga Khan among the Asian community.

The Uganda Muslim Supreme Council: POB 1146, Kampala; tel. (41) 4344499; fax (41) 4256500; Mufti of Uganda Sheikh SHABAN MUBAJJE; Chief Kadi and Pres. of Council HUSAYN RAJAB KAKOOZA.

BAHÁ'Í FAITH

National Spiritual Assembly: POB 2662, Kampala; tel. (31) 2262681; e-mail ugangabahai@gmail.com; mems resident in 2,721 localities.

JUDAISM

There is a small Jewish community, the Abayudaya, in central Uganda, with some 600 members and six synagogues.

The Press

DAILY AND OTHER NEWSPAPERS

The Citizen: Kampala; internet www.theugandacitizen.com; f. 2007; English.

The Economy: POB 6787, Kampala; weekly; English; Editor ROLAND KAKOOZA.

Financial Times: Plot 17/19, Station Rd, POB 31399, Kampala; tel. (41) 4245798; bi-weekly; English; Editor G. A. ONEGI OBEL.

Focus: POB 268, Kampala; tel. (41) 4235086; fax (41) 4242796; f. 1983; publ. by Islamic Information Service and Material Centre; 4 a week; English; Editor HAJJI KATENDE; circ. 12,000.

Guide: POB 5350, Kampala; tel. (41) 4233486; fax (41) 4268045; f. 1989; weekly; English; Editor-in-Chief A. A. KALIISA; circ. 30,000.

The Monitor: Plot 29–35, 8th St, POB 12141, Kampala; tel. (41) 4232367; fax (41) 4232369; e-mail editorial@monitor.co.ug; internet www.monitor.co.ug; f. 1992; daily; English; Man. Dir CONRAD NKUTU; Exec. Editor Dr PETER MWESIGE; circ. 22,000 (Mon.–Sat.), 24,000 (Sun.).

Mulengera: POB 6787, Kampala; weekly; Luganda; Editor ROLAND KAKOOZA.

Munnansi News Bulletin: POB 7098, Kampala; f. 1980; weekly; English; owned by the Democratic Party; Editor ANTHONY SGEKWEYAMA.

Munno: POB 4027, Kampala; f. 1911; daily; Luganda; publ. by the Roman Catholic Church; Editor ANTHONY SSEKWEYAMA; circ. 7,000.

New Vision: POB 9815, Kampala; tel. (41) 4337000; fax (41) 4232050; e-mail editorial@newvision.co.ug; internet www.newvision.co.ug; f. 1986; official govt newspaper; daily; English; Editor-in-chief ELS DE TERMMERMAN; circ. 34,000 (Mon.–Sat.), 42,000 (Sun.).

Bukedde: e-mail bukeddekussande@newvision.co.ug; daily; Luganda; Editor MAURICE SSEKWAUNGU; circ. 16,000.

Etop: e-mail etop@newvision.co.ug; weekly; vernacular; Editor KENNETH OLUKA; circ. 5,000.

Orumuri: tel. (485) 421265; internet www.orumuri.co.ug; weekly; vernacular; Editor JOSSY MUHANGI; circ. 11,000.

Rupiny: e-mail rupiny@newvision.co.ug; weekly; vernacular; Editor CHRIS BANYA; circ. 5,000.

Ngabo: POB 9362, Kampala; tel. (41) 4242637; f. 1979; daily; Luganda; Editor MAURICE SEKAWUNGU; circ. 7,000.

The Star: POB 9362, Kampala; tel. (41) 4242637; f. 1980; revived 1984; daily; English; Editor SAMUEL KATWERE; circ. 5,000.

Taifa Uganda Empya: POB 1986, Kampala; tel. (41) 4254652; f. 1953; daily; Luganda; Editor A. SEMBOGA; circ. 24,000.

Weekly Topic: POB 1725, Kampala; tel. (41) 4233834; weekly; English; Editor JOHN WASSWA; circ. 13,000.

PERIODICALS

Eastern Africa Journal of Rural Development: Dept of Agricultural Economics and Agribusiness, Makerere University, POB 7062, Kampala; tel. (77) 2616540; fax (41) 4530858; e-mail bkiiza@infocom.co.ug; annual; Editor BARNABAS KIIZA; circ. 800.

The Exposure: POB 3179, Kampala; tel. (41) 4267203; fax (41) 4259549; monthly; politics.

The Independent: Kampala; internet www.independent.co.ug; f. 2007; weekly; Editor ANDREW MWENDA.

Leadership: POB 2522, Kampala; tel. (41) 4422407; fax (41) 4421576; f. 1956; 11 a year; English; Roman Catholic; circ. 7,400; Editor Fr CARLOS RODRÍGUEZ.

Mkombozi: c/o Ministry of Defence, Republic House, POB 3798, Kampala; tel. (41) 4270331; f. 1982; military affairs; Editor A. OPOLOTT.

Musizi: POB 4027, Mengo, Kampala; f. 1955; monthly; Luganda; Roman Catholic; Editor F. GITTA; circ. 30,000.

Pearl of Africa: POB 7142, Kampala; monthly; govt publ.

Uganda Confidential: POB 5576, Kampala; tel. (41) 4250273; fax (41) 4255288; e-mail ucl@swiftuganda.com; internet www.swiftuganda.com/~confidential; f. 1990; monthly; Editor TEDDY SSEZI-CHEEYE.

NEWS AGENCY

Uganda News Agency (UNA): POB 7142, Kampala; tel. (41) 4232734; fax (41) 4342259; Dir CRISPUS MUNDUA (acting).

Publishers

Centenary Publishing House Ltd: POB 6246, Kampala; tel. (41) 4241599; fax (41) 4250427; f. 1977; religious (Anglican); Man. Dir Rev. SAM KAKIZA.

Fountain Publishers Ltd: POB 488, Kampala; tel. (41) 4259163; fax (41) 4251160; e-mail fountain@starcom.co.ug; internet www.fountainpublishers.co.ug; f. 1989; general, school textbooks, children's books, academic, scholarly; Man. Dir JAMES TUMUSIIME.

Longman Uganda Ltd: POB 3409, Kampala; tel. (41) 4242940; f. 1965; Man. Dir M. K. L. MUTYABA.

Uganda Printing and Publishing Corporation: POB 33, Entebbe; tel. (41) 4220639; fax (41) 4220530; f. 1993; Man. Dir P. A. BAKER.

Broadcasting and Communications

TELECOMMUNICATIONS

MTN Uganda Ltd: POB 24624, Kampala; tel. and fax (31) 2212333; e-mail mtn@mtn.co.ug; internet www.mtn.co.ug; f. 1998.

UGANDA   *Directory*

Uganda Communications Commission: Communications House, 12th Floor, 1 Colville St, POB 7376, Kampala; tel. (41) 4339000; fax (41) 4348832; e-mail ucc@ucc.co.ug; internet www.ucc.co.ug; f. 1998; regulatory body; Chair. Dr A. M. S. KATAHOIRE; Exec. Dir PATRICK MASAMBU.

Uganda Telecom Ltd (UTL): Rwenzori Courts, Plot 2/4A, Nakasero Rd, POB 7171, Kampala; tel. (41) 4333200; fax (41) 4345907; e-mail info@utlonline.co.ug; internet www.utl.co.ug; f. 1998; state-owned; privatization pending; Man. Dir ABDULBASET ELAZZABI.

Zain Uganda Ltd: Celtel House, 40 Wampewo Ave, Kololo, POB 6771, Kampala; tel. (75) 2230110; fax (41) 4230106; e-mail info.ug@zain.com; internet www.ug.zain.com; f. 1995; fmrly Celtel Uganda; Man. Dir YESSE OENGA.

BROADCASTING
Regulatory Body

Uganda Broadcasting Council (UBC): Broadcasting Council Secretariat, Worker's House, Northern wing, 6th Floor, Plot 1 Pilkington Rd, POB 27553, Kampala; tel. (41) 4251452; fax (41) 4250612; e-mail info@broadcastug.com; internet www.broadcastug.com; f. 1998; statutory body enacted by the Electronic Media Act of 2000; main functions include licensing and regulating radio and television stations, video and cinema operators and libraries for hiring out video recordings or cinema films; consists of 12 mems appointed by the Minister of Information Communication Technology; Chair. GODFREY MUTABAAZI; Dir-Gen. EDGAR TABAARO.

Radio

91.3 Capital FM: POB 7638, Kampala; tel. (41) 4235092; fax (41) 4344556; f. 1993; independent music station broadcasting from Kampala, Mbarara and Mbale; Chief Officers WILLIAM PIKE, PATRICK QUARCOO.

Central Broadcasting Service (CBS): POB 12760, Kampala; tel. (41) 4272963; fax (41) 4340031; f. 1996; independent station broadcasting in local languages and English to most of Uganda.

Radio One: POB 4589, Kampala; tel. (41) 4348211; fax (41) 4348311.

Radio Uganda: POB 7142, Kampala; tel. (41) 4257256; fax (41) 4256888; f. 1954; state-controlled; broadcasts in 24 languages, including English, Swahili and Ugandan vernacular languages; Commr for Broadcasting JACK TURYAMWIJUKA.

Sanyu Radio: Katto Plaza, Nkrumah Rd, Kampala; f. 1993; independent station broadcasting to Kampala and its environs.

Voice of Toro: POB 2203, Kampala.

Television

Sanyu Television: Naguru; f. 1994; independent station broadcasting to Kampala and its environs.

Uganda Television (UTV): POB 7142, Kampala; tel. (41) 4254461; f. 1962; state-controlled commercial service; programmes mainly in English, also in Swahili and Luganda; transmits over a radius of 320 km from Kampala; five relay stations are in operation, others are under construction; Controller of Programmes FAUSTIN MISANVU.

Finance

(cap. = capital; res = reserves; dep. = deposits; m. = million; brs = branches; amounts in new Uganda shillings, unless otherwise indicated)

BANKING
Central Bank

Bank of Uganda: 37–43 Kampala Rd, POB 7120, Kampala; tel. (41) 4258441; fax (41) 4230878; e-mail info@bou.or.ug; internet www.bou.or.ug; f. 1966; bank of issue; cap. 20,000m., res 149,276m., dep. 3,859,851m. (June 2007); Gov. EMMANUEL TUMUSIIME-MUTEBILE; Dep. Gov. DAVID G. OPIOKELLO (acting).

State Bank

Uganda Development Bank Ltd (UDBL): 15A Clement Hill Rd, Ruth Towers, POB 7210, Kampala; tel. (414) 355555; fax (414) 355556; e-mail info@udbl.co.ug; f. 1972; state-owned; reorg. 2001; privatization pending; cap. 11m. (Dec. 1993); CEO ANTHONY K. APPIAH.

Commercial Banks

Bank of Africa—Uganda Ltd: Plot 45 Jinja Rd, POB 2750, Kampala; tel. (41) 4302001; fax (41) 4230902; e-mail boa@boa-uganda.com; internet www.boa-uganda.com; f. 1986 as Allied Bank International (Uganda); name changed as above in 2005; 47.7% owned by Bank of Africa—Kenya, 21.9% by Aureos East Africa Fund, 19.8% by The Netherlands Development Finance Co, 10.6% by Central Holdings Ltd; cap. 4,001m., res 381m., dep. 67,950m. (Dec. 2006); Chair. JOHN CARRUTHERS; Man. Dir KWAME AHADZI; 5 brs.

Cairo International Bank: 30 Kampala Rd, POB 7052, Kampala; tel. (41) 4235666; fax (41) 4230130; e-mail cib@spacenetuganda.com; 44.4% owned by Banque du Caire, 36.1% owned by Kato Aromatics SAE, 6.5% each owned Bank of Egypt, Bank Misr and Bank of Alexandria; cap. 7,135m. (Dec. 2003); Chair. Dr IBRAHIM KAMEL; Man. Dir NABIL GHANEM.

Crane Bank Ltd: Crane Chambers, 38 Kampala Rd, POB 22572, Kampala; tel. (41) 4345345; fax (41) 4231578; e-mail cranebank@cranebanklimited.com; internet www.cranebanklimited.com; f. 1995; wholly owned by various private investors; cap. 5,000m., res 104m., dep. 172,741m. (Dec. 2006); Chair. SAMSON MUWANGUZI; Man. Dir A. R. KALAN.

DFCU Bank Ltd: Plot 2, Jinja Rd, POB 70, Kampala; tel. (41) 4256891; fax (41) 4231687; e-mail dfcubank@dfcugroup.com; internet www.dfcugroup.com; f. 1984 as Gold Trust Bank Ltd; current name adopted 2000; 60% owned by Commonwealth Development Corpn; total assets US $114.3m. (Dec. 2006); Chair. Dr WILLIAM KALEMA; Man. Dir COLIN MCCORMACK.

Diamond Trust Bank (Uganda) Ltd: Diamond Trust Bldg, Plot 17–19, Kampala Rd, POB 7155, Kampala; tel. (41) 4259331; fax (41) 4342286; e-mail info@dtbuganda.co.ug; internet www.dtbafrica.com; f. 1995; 40% owned by The Diamond Jubilee Investment Trust, 33.3% owned by Aga Khan Fund for Economic Development, 26.7% owned by Diamond Trust Bank Kenya Ltd; cap. 4,000m., res 253m., dep. 42,761m. (Dec. 2006); Chair. MAHMOOD MANJI; CEO VARGHESE THAMBI.

Mercantile Credit Bank Ltd: Plot 10, Old Port Bell Rd, POB 620, Kampala; tel. and fax (41) 4235967; e-mail mcb@afsat.com; cap. 1,000m. (Dec. 2003); Chair. PALLE MOELLER; Man. Dir NELSON LUGOLOBI.

National Bank of Commerce (Uganda) Ltd: Cargen House, Plot 13A, Parliament Ave, POB 23232, Kampala; tel. (41) 2347699; fax (41) 2347701; e-mail nbc@swiftuganda.com; cap. 4,631m. (Dec. 2003); Chair. AMOS NZEYI; Man. Dir G. BANGERA.

Nile Bank Ltd: Spear House, Plot 22, Jinja Rd, POB 2834, Kampala; tel. (41) 4346904; fax (41) 4257779; e-mail info@nilebank.co.ug; internet www.nilebank.co.ug; f. 1988; 15.88% owned by East African Development Bank, remainder owned by private investors; cap. 4,000m., res 889m., dep. 111,053m. (Dec. 2005); Chair. J. B. BYAMUGISHA; Man. Dir RICHARD P. BYARUGABA; 8 brs.

Orient Bank Ltd: Orient Plaza, Plot 6/6A, Kampala Rd, POB 3072, Kampala; tel. (41) 4236012; fax (41) 4236066; e-mail mail@orient-bank.com; internet www.orient-bank.com; f. 1993; cap. 5,000m., res 4,842m., dep. 108,263m. (Dec. 2006); Chair. MICHAEL COOK; CEO SHAMSHER KHEMANI; 6 brs.

Post Bank Uganda Ltd: Plot 11/13, Nkrumah Rd, POB 7189, Kampala; tel. (41) 4258551; fax (41) 4347107; e-mail postbank@imul.com; wholly state-owned; cap. 2,000m. (Dec. 2003); Chair. STEPHEN MWANJE.

Development Banks

Capital Finance Corpn Ltd: 4 Pilkington Rd, POB 21091, Kampala; tel. (41) 4345200; fax (41) 4258310; 70% owned by City Credit Bank Ltd; Chair. KEMAL LALANI; Man. Dir and CEO GHULAM HAIDER DAUDANI.

Centenary Rural Development Bank: 7 Entebbe Rd, POB 1892, Kampala; tel. (41) 4251276; fax (41) 4251273; e-mail info@centenarybank.co.ug; internet www.centenarybank.co.ug; cap. 4,110m. (Dec. 2003); Chair. Dr JOHN DDUMBA SSENTAMU; CEO HUNG LIHN.

Development Finance Co of Uganda Ltd: Rwenzori House, 1 Lumumba Ave, POB 2767, Kampala; tel. (41) 4231215; fax (41) 4259435; e-mail dfcu@dfcugroup.com; internet www.dfcugroup.com; owned by Commonwealth Devt Corpn (60%), Uganda Devt Corpn (18.5%) and International Finance Corpn (21.5%); cap. 3,978m. (Dec. 2003); Chair. WILLIAM S. KALEMA; Man. Dir C. MCCORMACK.

East African Development Bank (EADB): East African Development Bank Bldg, 4 Nile Ave, POB 7128, Kampala; tel. (41) 4230021; fax (41) 4259763; e-mail admin@eadb.org; internet www.eadb.org; f. 1967; Govts of Kenya and Tanzania 25.47% each; Govt of Uganda 23.02%; African Development Bank, Abidjan 11.33%; remaining 14.73% shared between various foreign banks and private investors; provides financial and tech. assistance to promote industrial development within Uganda, Kenya and Tanzania; regional offices in Nairobi and Dar es Salaam; cap. US $77.6m., res US $8.5m. (Dec. 2006); Chair. JOSEPH KINYUA.

Housing Finance Co Uganda Ltd: Investment House, 25 Kampala Rd, POB 1539, Kampala; tel. (41) 4341227; fax (41) 4341429; internet www.housingfinance.co.ug; 45% owned by Govt, 50% owned by National Social Security Fund, 5% owned by National Housing

UGANDA

Directory

and Construction Corpn; cap. 1,000m. (Dec. 2003); Chair. KEITH MUHAKANIZI; Man. Dir NICHOLAS OKWIR.

Foreign Banks

Bank of Baroda (Uganda) Ltd (India): 18 Kampala Rd, POB 7197, Kampala; tel. (41) 4233680; fax (41) 4230781; e-mail bobho@spacenet.co.ug; internet www.bankofbaroda.com; f. 1953; 80% owned by Bank of Baroda (India); cap. 4,000m., res 5,647m., dep. 126,995m. (Dec. 2004); Chair. J. K. CHANDER; Man. Dir K. K. SHUKLA; 6 brs.

Barclays Bank of Uganda Ltd (United Kingdom): POB 7101, Barclay House, Plot 4, Hannington Rd, Kampala; tel. (31) 4218300; fax (31) 4259467; e-mail barclays.uganda@barclays.com; internet www.barclays.com; f. 1969; wholly owned by Barclays Bank PLC (United Kingdom); cap. 4,000m., res 15,236m., dep. 328,553m. (Dec. 2005); Chair. GEORGE EGADU; Man. Dir NICK MBUVI; 4 brs.

Citibank (Uganda) Ltd (USA): Plot 4, Centre Court, Ternan Ave, Nakasero, POB 7505, Kampala; tel. (41) 4305500; fax (41) 4340624; internet www.citibank.com/eastafrica/uganda.htm; 99.9% owned by Citicorp Overseas Investment Corpn, 0.1% owned by Foremost Investment; cap. 21,285m. (Dec. 2003); Chair. Prof. J. M. L. SSEBUWUUFU; Man. Dir SHIRISH BHIDE.

Stanbic Bank Uganda Ltd (United Kingdom): Crested Towers, Short Tower, 17 Hannington Rd, POB 7131, Kampala; tel. (31) 4224111; fax (41) 4231116; e-mail ugandainfo@stanbic.com; internet www.stanbicbank.co.ug; f. 1906 as National Bank of India Uganda; adopted present name 1993; 80% owned by Stanbic Africa Holdings Ltd (United Kingdom); merged with Uganda Commercial Bank Ltd 2002; cap. 5,119m., res 52,432m., dep. 909,807m. (Dec. 2006); Chair. Dr MARTIN ALIKER; Man. Dir KITILI MBATHI; 2 brs.

Standard Chartered Bank Uganda Ltd (United Kingdom): 5 Speke Rd, POB 7111, Kampala; tel. (41) 44258211; fax (41) 44231473; e-mail scb.uganda@ug.standardchartered.com; internet www.standardchartered.com/ug; f. 1912; wholly owned by Standard Chartered Bank PLC; cap. 4,000m., res 22,806m., dep. 604,380m. (Dec. 2006); Chair. JAMES MULWANA; Man. Dir LAMIN MANJANG; 7 brs.

Tropical Africa Bank Ltd (Libya): Plot 27, Kampala Rd, POB 9485-7292, Kampala; tel. (41) 2341408; fax (41) 2232296; e-mail tabu10@calva.com; f. 1972; 50% govt-owned, 50% owned by Libyan Arab Foreign Bank; cap. 7,000m. (Dec. 2003); Chair. C. M. KASSAMI; Gen. Man. and CEO MOHAMED A. WAHRA.

STOCK EXCHANGE

Uganda Securities Exchange: Workers' House, 2nd Floor, Northern Wing, 1 Pilkington Rd, POB 23552, Kampala; tel. (41) 4343297; fax (41) 4343841; internet www.use.or.ug; f. 1997; Chair. GEOFFREY A. ONEGI-OBEL; Chief Exec. SIMON RUTEGA.

INSURANCE

East Africa General Insurance Co Ltd: Plot 14, Kampala Rd, POB 1392, Kampala; tel. (31) 22262221; fax (41) 4343234; e-mail vkrishna@eagen.co.ug; internet www.eagen.co.ug; f. 1949; public shareholding co; fire, life, motor, marine and accident; CEO VYASA KRISHNA.

National Insurance Corporation: Plot 3, Pilkington Rd, POB 7134, Kampala; tel. (41) 4258001; fax (41) 4259925; e-mail nic@nic.co.ug; internet www.nic.co.ug; f. 1964; 60% owned by IGI Plc, Nigeria, 40% state-owned; general and life; Man. Dir Dr SAMSON AKINWALE.

NICO Insurance (Uganda) Ltd: 3rd Floor Greenland Towers, Kampala Rd, Opposite Bank of Uganda, POB 24256, Kampala; tel. (31) 2264720; fax (31) 2264723; internet www.nicomw.com; subsidiary of NICO Holdings Ltd (based in Malawi); Man. Dir RONALD ZAKE.

Pan World Insurance Co Ltd: POB 7658, Kampala; tel. (41) 4341618; fax (41) 4341593; Gen. Man. GORDON SENTIBA.

Uganda American Insurance Co Ltd: POB 7077, Kampala; tel. and fax (41) 4533781; f. 1970; Man. Dir STAN MENSAH.

Uganda Co-operative Insurance Ltd: Plot 10, Bombo Rd, POB 6176, Kampala; tel. (41) 4241836; fax (41) 4258231; f. 1982; general; Chair. EPHRAIM KAKURU; Gen. Man. (vacant).

Trade and Industry

GOVERNMENT AGENCIES

Capital Markets Authority: 8th Floor, Jubilee Insurance Centre, 14 Parliament Ave, POB 24565, Kampala; tel. (41) 4342788; fax (41) 4342803; e-mail info@cmauganda.co.ug; internet www.cmauganda.co.ug; f. 1996 to develop, promote and regulate capital markets sector; CEO JAPHETH KATTO.

Enterprise Development Unit (EPD): Kampala; oversees privatization programme; Exec. Dir LEONARD MUGANWA.

Export and Import Licensing Division: POB 7000, Kampala; tel. (41) 4258795; f. 1987; advises importers and exporters and issues import and export licences; Prin. Commercial Officer JOHN MUHWEZI.

Uganda Advisory Board of Trade: POB 6877, Kampala; tel. (41) 4233311; f. 1974; issues trade licences and service for exporters.

Uganda Export Promotion Board: POB 5045, Kampala; tel. (41) 4230233; fax (41) 4259779; e-mail uepc@starcom.co.ug; internet www.ugandaexportsonline.com; f. 1983; provides market intelligence, organizes training, trade exhbns, etc.; Exec. Dir FLORENCE KATE.

Uganda Investment Authority: Investment Centre, TWED Plaza, Plot 22, Lumumba Ave, POB 7418, Kampala; tel. (41) 4301000; fax (41) 4342903; e-mail info@ugandainvest.com; internet www.ugandainvest.com; f. 1991; promotes foreign and local investment, assists investors, provides business information, issues investment licences; Exec. Dir Dr MAGGIE KIGOZI.

DEVELOPMENT ORGANIZATIONS

Agriculture and Livestock Development Fund: f. 1976; provides loans to farmers.

National Housing and Construction Corpn: Crested Towers, POB 659, Kampala; tel. (41) 4330002; fax (41) 4258708; e-mail sales@nhcc.co.ug; internet www.nhcc.co.ug; f. 1964; govt agent for building works; also develops residential housing; Chair. Dr COLIN SENTONGO; Gen. Man. M. S. KASEKENDE.

Uganda Industrial Development Corpn Ltd (ULDC): 9–11 Parliament Ave, POB 7042, Kampala; tel. (41) 4234381; fax (41) 4241588; f. 1952; Chair. SAM RUTEGA.

CHAMBER OF COMMERCE

Uganda National Chamber of Commerce and Industry: Plot 2, 1st Floor, Parliament Ave, Jumbo Plaza, POB 3809, Kampala; tel. (41) 4503024; fax (41) 4230310; e-mail info@chamberuganda.com; internet www.chamberuganda.com; Chair. OLIVE Z. KIGONGO.

INDUSTRIAL AND TRADE ASSOCIATIONS

CMB Ltd (Coffee Marketing Board): POB 7154, Kampala; tel. (41) 4254051; fax (41) 4230790; state-owned; privatization pending; purchases and exports coffee; Chair. Dr DDUMBA SSENTAMU; Man. Dir SAM KIGGUNDU.

Cotton Development Organization: POB 7018, Kampala; tel. (41) 4232968; fax (41) 4232975; Man. Dir JOLLY SABUNE.

Produce Marketing Board: POB 3705, Kampala; tel. (41) 4236238; Gen. Man. ESTHER KAMPAMPARA.

Uganda Coffee Development Authority (UCDA): Coffee House, Plot 35, Jinja Rd, POB 7267, Kampala; tel. (41) 4256940; fax (41) 4256994; e-mail ucdajc@ugandacoffee.org; internet www.ugandacoffee.org; f. 1991; enforces quality control and promotes coffee exports, maintains statistical data, advises Govt on local and world prices and trains processors and quality controllers; Man. Dir HENRY NGABIRANO.

Uganda Importers', Exporters' and Traders' Association: Kampala; tel. (41) 4343472.

Uganda Manufacturers' Association (UMA): Lugogo Show Grounds, POB 6966, Kampala; tel. (41) 4221034; fax (41) 4220285; e-mail information@uma.or.ug; internet www.uma.or.ug; promotes mfrs' interests; Chair. JAMES KALIBALA.

Uganda Tea Authority: POB 4161, Kampala; tel. (41) 4231003; state-owned; controls and co-ordinates activities of the tea industry; Gen. Man. MIRIA MARGARITA MUGABI.

EMPLOYERS' ORGANIZATION

Federation of Uganda Employers: Plot 60, Veron House, Ntinda, POB 3820, Kampala; tel. (41) 4220201; fax (41) 4286290; e-mail fue@infocom.co.ug; internet www.employers.co.ug; f. 1958; Chair. ALOYSIUS K. SSEMMANDA; Exec. Dir ROSEMARY N. SSENABULYA.

UTILITIES

Electricity

Electricity Regulatory Authority (ERA): ERA House, Plot 15 Shimon Rd, Nakasero, POB 10332, Kampala; tel. (41) 4341852; fax (41) 4341624; e-mail era@africaonline.co.ug; internet www.era.or.ug; f. 1999; CEO Eng. Dr F. B. SEBBOWA.

Uganda Electricity Board (UEB): POB 7059, Kampala; tel. (41) 4254071; fax (41) 4235119; f. 1948; privatization pending; Chair. J. E. N. KAGULE-MAGAMBO; 36 brs.

Water

National Water & Sewerage Corpn: Plot 39, Jinja Rd, POB 7053, Kampala; tel. (41) 4315100; fax (41) 4258299; e-mail info@nwsc.co

.ug; internet www.nwsc.co.ug; f. 1972; privatization pending; Man. Dir WILLIAM TSIMWA MUHAIRWE; 12 brs.

CO-OPERATIVES

In 2000 there were 6,313 co-operative societies, grouped in 34 unions. There is at least one co-operative union in each administrative district.

Uganda Co-operative Alliance: Plot 47/49, Nkurumah Rd, Kampala; tel. (41) 4258898; e-mail ucainfocen@uca.co.ug; internet www.uca.co.ug; co-ordinating body for co-operative unions, of which the following are among the most important:

Bugisu Co-operative Union Ltd: Palisa Rd, Private Bag, Mbale; tel. (45) 4233027; f. 1954; processors and exporters of Bugisu arabica coffee; 226 mem. socs; Gen. Man. WOMUTU.

East Mengo Growers' Co-operative Union Ltd: POB 7092, Kampala; tel. (41) 4270383; fax (41) 4243502; f. 1968; processors and exporters of coffee and cotton; 280 mem. socs; Chair. FRANCIS MUKAMA; Man. JOSEPH SSEMOGERERE.

Kakumiro Growers' Co-operative Union: POB 511, Kakumiro; processing of coffee and cotton; Sec. and Man. TIBIHWA-RUKEERA.

Kimeeme Livestock Co-operative Society: Mwanga II Rd, POB 6670, Kampala; f. 1984; farming and marketing of livestock; Chair. SAMUSI LUKIMA.

Lango Co-operative Union: POB 59, Lira; f. 1956; ginning and exporting of conventional and organic cotton produce; Chair. JOHNSON ENGOLE.

Masaka Co-operative Union Ltd: POB 284, Masaka; tel. (481) 420260; f. 1951; coffee, dairy farming, food processing, carpentry; 245 primary co-operative socs; Chair. J. M. KASOZI; Gen. Man. EDWARD C. SSERUUMA.

Nyakatonzi Growers Co-operative Union: Fort Portal Rd, POB 32, Kasese; tel. (483) 444370; fax (483) 444135; f. 1957; processors and exporters of coffee and cotton; Gen. Man. ADAM BWAMBALE.

South Bukedi Co-operative Union: 6 Busia Rd, POB 101, Tororo; tel. (45) 4244327; f. 1952; ginning and export of cotton lint; Gen. Man. MICHAEL O. OGUNDY.

South-west Nile Co-operative Union: POB 33, Pakwach, Nebbi; f. 1958; ginning and export of cotton; Gen. Man. PHILIP UPAKRWOTH.

Uganda Co-operative Savings and Credit Society: 62 Parliament Ave, POB 9452, Kampala; tel. (41) 4257410; f. 1973; Chair. PATRICK KAYONGO.

Uganda Co-operative Transport Union: 41 Bombo Rd, POB 5486, Kampala; tel. and fax (41) 4567506; e-mail uctultd@infocom.co.ug; f. 1971; general transport, imports of motor vehicles, vehicle repair and maintenance; Gen. Man. NUWAGIRA NABOTH MWEJUNE.

Wamala Growers' Co-operative Union Ltd: POB 99, Mityana; tel. (46) 4442036; e-mail kizitoherbert@yahoo.com; f. 1968; coffee and cotton growers, real estate agents, cattle ranchers, printers, mfrs of edible oils, bricks, tiles and clay products; 250 mem. socs; Gen. Man. HERBERT KIZITO.

West Mengo Growers' Co-operative Union Ltd: POB 7039, Kampala; tel. (41) 4567511; f. 1948; cotton growing and buying, coffee buying and processing, maize milling; 250 mem. socs; Chair. H. E. KATABALWA MIIRO.

West Nile Tobacco Co-operative Union: Wandi, POB 71, Arua; f. 1965; growing, curing and marketing of tobacco; Gen. Man. ANDAMAH BABWA.

TRADE UNION

National Organization of Trade Unions (NOTU): POB 2150, Kampala; tel. (41) 4256295; f. 1973; Chair. E. KATURAMU; Sec.-Gen. MATHIAS MUKASA; 89,500 mems (2007).

Transport

RAILWAYS

In 1997 there were 1,250 km of 1,000-mm-gauge track in operation. A programme to rehabilitate the railway network is under way.

Uganda Railways Corporation (URC): Nasser Rd, POB 7150, Kampala; tel. (41) 4254961; fax (41) 4344405; f. 1977 following the dissolution of East African Railways; management of operations assumed by Rift Valley Railways consortium in Nov. 2006; Man. Dir D. C. MURUNGI.

ROADS

Uganda's road network consists of approximately 10,000 km of national or trunk roads (of which some 2,200 km are bituminized, the rest being gravel), 25,000 km of district or feeder roads, 2,800 km of urban roads (comprising roads in Kampala City, the 13 municipal councils and the 50 town councils in the country) and 30,000 km of community roads. There are also private roads, some of which are open to the general travelling public. Road transport remains the dominant mode of transport in terms of scale of infrastructure and the volume of freight and passenger movement. The National (Trunk) Road Network carries 80% of Uganda's passenger and freight traffic and includes international routes linking Uganda to neighbouring countries and to the sea (via Kenya and Tanzania), and internal roads linking areas of high population and large administrative and commercial centres. It provides the only form of access to most rural communities. The Government is implementing a programme of continuous upgrading of key gravel roads to bitumen standard.

INLAND WATERWAYS

A rail wagon ferry service connecting Jinja with the Tanzanian port of Tanga, via Mwanza, was inaugurated in 1983, thus reducing Uganda's dependence on the Kenyan port of Mombasa. In 1986 the Uganda and Kenya Railways Corporations began the joint operation of Lake Victoria Marine Services, to ferry goods between the two countries via Lake Victoria.

CIVIL AVIATION

The international airport is at Entebbe, on Lake Victoria, some 40 km from Kampala. There are also several small airfields.

Civil Aviation Authority (CAA): POB 5536, Kampala; Passenger Terminal Bldg, 2nd floor, Entebbe International Airport; tel. (41) 4320516; fax (41) 4320571; e-mail info@caa.co.ug; internet www.caa.co.ug; Man. Dir AMBROSE AKANDONDA.

Principal Airlines

Air Uganda (AU): Kampala; f. 2007; services to Africa; CEO PETER DE WAAL.

Dairo Air Cargo Services: 24 Jinja Rd, POB 5480, Kampala; tel. (41) 4257731.

Eagle Air Ltd: Entebbe International Airport, POB 7392, Kampala; tel. (41) 4344292; fax (41) 4344501; e-mail eagle@swiftuganda.com; internet www.eagleuganda.com; f. 1994; domestic services, charter flights to neighbouring countries; Man. Dir Capt. ANTHONY RUBOMBORA.

Inter Air: Nile Ave, POB 22658, Kampala; tel. (41) 4255508.

Tourism

Uganda's principal attractions for tourists are the forests, lakes, mountains and wildlife and an equable climate. A programme to revive the tourist industry by building or improving hotels and creating new national parks began in the late 1980s. There were 538,586 tourist arrivals in 2006 (compared with 12,786 in 1983). Revenue from the sector in that year was estimated at US $356m., including revenue from the transport of passengers.

Uganda Tourist Board: Impala House, 13/15 Kimatti Ave, POB 7211, Kampala; tel. (41) 4342196; fax (41) 4342188; e-mail utb@visituganda.com; internet www.visituganda.com; Chair. PETER KAMYA; Gen. Man. IGNATIUS NAKISHERO.

UKRAINE

Introductory Survey

Location, Climate, Language, Religion, Flag, Capital

Ukraine is situated in east-central Europe. It is bordered by Poland, Slovakia, Hungary, Romania and Moldova to the west, by Belarus to the north, and by Russia to the north-east and east. To the south lie the Black Sea and the Sea of Azov. The climate is temperate, especially in the south. The north and north-west share many of the continental climatic features of Poland or Belarus. Average temperatures in Kyiv (Kiev) range from −6.1°C (21°F) in January to 20.4°C (69°F) in July, and average annual rainfall is 615 mm (24 ins). The official state language is Ukrainian, although Russian is widely spoken, except in the west. Most of the population are adherents of Orthodox Christianity, and there are many adherents of the Roman Catholic Church (mostly followers of Eastern rites), mostly in western regions. There are also a number of Protestant churches and small communities of Jews and Muslims, the latter principally comprising Crimean Tatars. The national flag (proportions 2 by 3) has two equal horizontal stripes, of pale blue over yellow. The capital is Kyiv.

Recent History

The original East Slavic state, Kyivan (Kievan) Rus, founded in the late 10th century, was based in what is now Ukraine ('the Borderlands'), and is claimed as the precursor of Russia, Belarus and Ukraine. Following the fall of the Rus principalities, in the 13th and 14th centuries, during the Mongol invasions, the Ukrainians (sometimes known as Little Russians or Ruthenians), mainly under Polish and Lithuanian rulers, developed distinctively from the other Eastern Slavs. Ukrainians first entered the Russian Empire in 1654, when a Cossack state east of the Dnipro (Dniepr) River, led by Hetman Bohdan Khmelnytsky, sought Russian protection from Polish invasion. In 1667 Ukraine was divided: the regions east of the Dnipro became part of Russia, while Western Ukraine was annexed by Poland. Russia gained more Ukrainian lands as a result of subsequent partitions of Poland (1793 and 1795) and, in the south, from the Ottoman Empire; the western regions were acquired by Austria.

When the Russian Empire collapsed, in 1917, Ukrainian nationalists set up a central Rada (council or soviet) in Kyiv and demanded autonomy from the Provisional Government in Petrograd (St Petersburg). After the Bolshevik coup, in November, the Rada proclaimed a Ukrainian People's Republic. In December the Bolsheviks established a rival Government in Kharkiv, and by February 1918 much of Ukraine was occupied by Soviet forces. In March, however, the Bolsheviks were forced to cede Ukraine to Germany, under the terms of the Treaty of Brest-Litovsk. Ukraine was the battleground for much of the fighting in the Civil War over the next two years, but in December 1920 a Ukrainian Soviet Socialist Republic (SSR) was established.

The Treaty of Rīga, which formally ended the Soviet–Polish War in 1921, assigned territories in western Ukraine to Poland, Czechoslovakia and Romania. Eastern and central lands formed the Ukrainian SSR, one of the founding members of the Union of Soviet Socialist Republics (USSR), in December 1922. The collectivization of agriculture from 1929 had severe consequences for the republic; at least 5m. Ukrainians were estimated to have died in a famine in 1933, which resulted from collectivization. In the 1930s advocates of the wider Ukrainian cultural or political autonomy were arrested, and by the late 1930s almost the entire Ukrainian cultural and political élite had been imprisoned, killed or exiled. Ukraine also suffered greatly during the Second World War, which resulted in an estimated 6m. deaths in the republic.

Soviet victory in the war, and the annexing of territories from Czechoslovakia, Poland and Romania resulted in the uniting of the western and eastern areas of Ukraine, and the republic gained representation, nominally separate from that of the USSR, at the UN. In 1954 Crimea (formerly part of Russia), the Tatar inhabitants of which had been deported *en masse* to Soviet Central Asia in 1944, was transferred to Ukrainian control.

During the 1960s there was an increase in covert opposition to the regime, manifested in the production of independent publications, known as *samvydav* (*samizdat*—self-publishing). In 1973 Petro Shelest, the First Secretary (leader) of the Communist Party of Ukraine (CPU) was dismissed and replaced by Vladimir Shcherbitsky, a loyal ally of the Soviet leader, Leonid Brezhnev.

The accession of the reformist Mikhail Gorbachev to the Soviet leadership, in 1985, had little initial effect in Ukraine. On 26 April 1986 a serious explosion occurred at the Chornobyl (Chernobyl) nuclear power station, in northern Ukraine. Only after unusually high levels of radiation were reported in other European countries did Soviet officials admit that large amounts of radioactivity had leaked into the atmosphere. Some 135,000 people were evacuated from a 50-km (30-mile) exclusion zone around Chornobyl (including large areas within neighbouring Belarus). Thirty-one people were killed in the initial explosion, but in 1996 it was reported that an estimated 2,500 deaths in Ukraine may have been caused by the accident, while a further 3.2m. people had been affected by the disaster, as a result of increased numbers of cancers and other related illnesses. Official secrecy surrounding the Chornobyl accident led to greater public support for opposition movements in Ukraine, such as the liberal nationalist Ukrainian People's Movement for Restructuring (Rukh), which was founded in 1988 by a group of prominent writers and intellectuals. Similarly, economic problems contributed to a growing militancy among mining communities in the Donbass region (around Donetsk, in eastern Ukraine), producing 11 strikes in the first three months of 1989, and the revival of hitherto 'underground' religious groups from 1988 resulted in the legalization of the Ukrainian (Byzantine rite) Catholic Church in December 1989.

Shcherbitsky was dismissed in September 1989; he was replaced by Volodymyr Ivashko. In local and republican elections, held on 4 March 1990, candidates supported by the Democratic Bloc, a coalition led by Rukh, won 108 of the 450 seats in the Verkhovna Rada (Supreme Council—republican legislature). Independents supported by the Bloc won about 60 seats, although an estimated 280 supported the CPU leadership. In June Ivashko was elected Chairman of the Verkhovna Rada (the highest state post in the Republic); he resigned later in the month as First Secretary of the CPU. On 16 July the Verkhovna Rada adopted a declaration of sovereignty. Later in the month Ivashko resigned as Chairman of the Verkhovna Rada, following his appointment as Deputy General Secretary of the Communist Party of the Soviet Union; he was replaced by Leonid Kravchuk, hitherto Second Secretary of the CPU. In October Vitold Fokin, a moderate reformist, succeeded Vitaliy Masol as Chairman of the Council of Ministers (Prime Minister).

The Government participated in negotiations on a new union treaty and signed the protocol to a draft treaty in March 1991. The Government also agreed to conduct the all-Union referendum on the future of the USSR (see the chapter on the Russian Federation), but appended a further question, asking if Ukraine's declaration of sovereignty should form the basis for participation in a renewed federation. Of the electorate, 84% participated in the referendum, 70% of whom approved Gorbachev's proposal to preserve the USSR as a 'renewed federation'. However, Ukraine's own question received greater support (80%), and an additional question in certain western regions, which asked voters if they supported a fully independent Ukraine, secured the support of 90% of those voting.

Following the attempted coup by conservative communists in Moscow, the Russian and Soviet capital, on 19 August 1991, the Verkhovna Rada, on 24 August, adopted a declaration of independence, pending confirmation by a referendum on 1 December, when direct presidential elections were also scheduled. The CPU was banned in late August. Kravchuk's support for Ukrainian independence ensured his election as President of the Republic on 1 December 1991, with 62% of the votes cast. In the referendum, some 90% of votes were cast in favour of independence (84% of the electorate participated), which thereby took effect. In early December an independent Ukrainian armed forces was established. In January 1992 a new interim currency coupon, which retained the Ukrainian name of the Soviet currency, the karbovanets, was introduced.

The Government was subject to intense criticism as inflation increased sharply in mid-1992, and resigned in September, having been conclusively defeated in a vote of no confidence. In October Leonid Kuchma, hitherto director-general of a missile factory in Dnipropetrovsk, was appointed Prime Minister, and a new Government was formed. Kuchma proposed a programme of economic reform, which was strongly opposed by left-wing groups, including the Socialist Party of Ukraine (SPU), which had been formed from elements of the CPU. As Ukraine began to experience 'hyperinflation', more than 2m. miners and factory workers, mainly in the Donbass region, joined a strike, in June 1993, demanding a referendum of confidence in the President and in the Verkhovna Rada. In September Kuchma again tendered his resignation, which was accepted by the legislature; Yufym Zvyahylsky was appointed as Prime Minister, in an acting capacity, although after several days President Kravchuk assumed direct control of the Government.

Elections to the new, 450-member Verkhovna Rada were held on 27 March 1994, with two subsequent rounds of voting in constituencies where candidates had failed to secure 50% of the votes cast. The CPU was permitted to contest the elections and won 86 seats, more than any other group, and, in alliance with the SPU and the Peasants' Party of Ukraine (PPU), formed the largest bloc in the Verkhovna Rada; 170 nominally independent candidates were elected. A notable political division between eastern (where left-wing parties obtained greater support) and western (where moderate nationalist parties won the greatest share of the votes) regions was evident in the election results. Further rounds of voting, held in late 1994 to fill the 112 vacant seats, failed to elect candidates in more than 50 seats. In May Oleksandr Moroz, the leader of the SPU, was elected Chairman of the Verkhovna Rada, which in June elected Masol as Prime Minister.

A presidential election held on 26 June 1994 was inconclusive, as no candidate secured the minimum 50% of the votes necessary for election. Kravchuk received the greatest share of votes cast, with 37.7%, followed by Kuchma, with 31.3%. In a second round of voting, held on 10 July, Kuchma was elected President, securing 52.1% of the votes. A continuing polarity in voting patterns was recorded between the east, where voters largely supported Kuchma, and the west, where Kravchuk secured a majority of votes cast. In March 1995 Masol resigned as Prime Minister and was replaced, in an acting capacity, by Yevhen Marchuk. In June the President and the Verkhovna Rada signed a Constitutional Agreement, granting the President additional powers until a new constitution was adopted, including the right to issue decrees with the force of legislation. Additionally, the President was to retain the prerogative to legislate economic reform until the expiry of his term in 1999.

In May 1996 Kuchma dismissed Marchuk as premier, appointing Pavlo Lazarenko in his place, and the new Constitution was adopted on 28 June. It confirmed the extensive new powers of appointment granted to the President in the interim Constitutional Agreement. In July the Cabinet of Ministers resigned; Lazarenko retained the premiership in the new Government. As unrest in the coal-mining industry continued, the Government commenced a structural reorganization of the sector, and in mid-July an agreement was reached with the trade unions to end an ongoing strike. The attempted assassination of Lazarenko, shortly after the signing of the agreement, was linked by some observers to his role in resolving the dispute. Lazarenko resigned in July 1997. In mid-July the legislature approved Valeriy Pustovoytenko as the new Prime Minister. In September the legislature approved a new electoral law, which provided for 225 seats in the 450-member Verkhovna Rada to be allocated by proportional representation on the basis of party lists, subject to a minimum threshold of 4% of the total votes cast, and for the remaining 225 to be elected from single-seat constituencies. Meanwhile, it was announced that Lazarenko was to be prosecuted on charges of embezzlement.

Some 30 parties and electoral blocs contested the legislative elections to the Verkhovna Rada, held on 29 March 1998, in which 70.8% of the electorate participated. The CPU obtained 123 seats, becoming the largest party in the legislature. Eight parties secured representation on the basis of party lists, and some 136 independent deputies were elected. Oleksandr Tkachenko, the leader of the PPU, was elected as legislative Chairman in July. Lazarenko was arrested in December as he attempted to enter Switzerland, and charged with money-laundering. In February 1999 the Verkhovna Rada endorsed a resolution allowing for Lazarenko to be charged, and shortly afterwards he was detained in the USA.

In the first round of voting in the presidential election, held on 31 October 1999, Kuchma won the largest proportion of the votes cast for any candidate, with 36.5%; his opponent in the second round was Petro Symonenko of the CPU, who had obtained 22.2% of the first round votes. The rate of participation was 70%. In early November Kuchma undertook a number of measures that were regarded as being intended to ensure his re-election in the second round, including the dismissal of governors of three oblasts (regions) in which Symonenko or the third-placed candidate, Moroz, had won the vote. In the second ballot, on 14 November, Kuchma retained the presidency, receiving some 57.7% of the votes cast; he was inaugurated on 30 November. The regional division in voting patterns evident in earlier presidential and parliamentary elections was not repeated. In December 1999 the Verkhovna Rada endorsed the nomination of Yushchenko (Governor of the National Bank of Ukraine—NBU—since 1993) as premier. Yushchenko's appointment precipitated discontent within left-wing factions in the legislature who, in January 2000, compelled the new centrist parliamentary majority led by Kravchuk to hold a separate session in an exhibition centre near the parliamentary building, where it voted unanimously to remove Tkachenko and his deputy from the chairmanship of the legislature. In February the majority faction elected Ivan Plyushch, an ally of Pustovoytenko, as legislative Chairman. After several days, deputies of the majority grouping gained entry to the parliamentary building, and normal activity resumed.

Meanwhile, a presidential decree, issued in January 2000, scheduled a referendum on proposed constitutional amendments for 16 April; more than 3m. signatures had reportedly been collected in favour of this proposal. Of the six questions initially intended to feature in the referendum, two were excluded from the plebiscite by the Constitutional Court. The four remaining questions—on the dissolution of the Verkhovna Rada should deputies fail to approve the state budget within three months of its submission; the reduction of the number of deputies from 450 to 300; the establishment of a bicameral legislature; and the placing of limitations on the immunity enjoyed by deputies—were approved by a majority of the 81% of the electorate that participated in the referendum. However, no proposal to implement these decisions ensued, and it thus appeared that the referendum had served primarily to increase the President's authority over the legislature.

In June 2000 Lazarenko was convicted, in absentia, of money-laundering by a court in Switzerland, and given an 18-month suspended prison sentence. In July the Deputy Prime Minister, responsible for Energy Issues, Yuliya Tymoshenko, a prominent instigator of reforms in the energy sector and the leader of the Fatherland party, was charged with corruption, as a result of investigations into her former ally, Lazarenko, in the USA.

In early November 2000 a decapitated corpse, believed to be that of an investigative journalist, Heorhiy Gongadze, missing since September, was discovered near Kyiv, by police. Gongadze, who had edited an online news site, Ukrainska Pravda (Ukrainian Truth), which had investigated incidents of high-level political corruption, had been a vocal critic of Kuchma; he had also made allegations of harassment by state officials. In late November Moroz released tape recordings in which what appeared to be the voices of Kuchma, the head of the presidential administration, Volodymyr Lytvyn, and the Minister of Internal Affairs, Yuriy Kravchenko, were discussing possible means of killing Gongadze. Controversy surrounded the authenticity of these, and other, recordings, which a former presidential security adviser, Maj. Mykola Melnychenko, had made over a period of several months, prior to fleeing Ukraine.

In January 2001 Kuchma dismissed Tymoshenko, as an investigation into her alleged involvement in tax evasion and the smuggling of Russian gas proceeded. In February further audio recordings were made public. After initially denying the authenticity of the recordings, Kuchma admitted that the recordings were of his voice, but stated that they had been edited in an attempt to incriminate him. Demonstrations in Kyiv to demand Kuchma's resignation continued for several weeks, of which Tymoshenko, leading a loose coalition of opposition movements, the National Salvation Forum (NSF), became the most prominent leader. In February, in an apparent concession to the demands of the protesters, Kuchma dismissed the head of the national security service, Gen. Leonid Derkach, and the head of the presidential bodyguard. In mid-February Tymoshenko was arrested on charges of tax evasion. In late February Gongadze's body was formally identified by the Prosecutor-General's office, and a murder inquiry was opened. In May Gongadze's death was officially attributed to a criminal attack, with no political motives, and it was announced that the investigation into his death was to be closed. Meanwhile, in March a demonstration by up to 18,000 anti-Kuchma protesters in Kyiv degenerated into violent clashes and was dispersed by police with tear gas; several prominent members of the extreme nationalist Ukrainian National Assembly-Ukrainian National Self-Defence Organization (UNA-UNSO) were arrested and charged with provoking unrest. In the same month Kuchma dismissed Kravchenko as Minister of Internal Affairs, replacing him with Yuriy Smirnov. At the end of March Tymoshenko was released from prison, and all charges against her were dismissed; in April the Supreme Court suspended Tymoshenko's re-arrest, although the charges against her remained under investigation.

In April 2001 the Verkhovna Rada approved a motion of no confidence in the Prime Minister and his Cabinet of Ministers, despite the economic growth that had been achieved during Yushchenko's premiership—the first growth recorded since independence. In May Anatoliy Kinakh, hitherto First Deputy Prime Minister, responsible for Economic Policy, was appointed to succeed Yushchenko as Prime Minister. In the second half of 2001 a number of electoral blocs were formed in preparation for the forthcoming legislative elections. In September Tymoshenko issued an appeal for other opposition groupings to join the NSF, but rejected the suggestion that the group unite with the Our Ukraine bloc of centrist and nationalist parties headed by Yushchenko; her supporters subsequently become known as the Yuliya Tymoshenko Bloc (YuTB). Meanwhile, supporters of Kuchma formed the For a United Ukraine (FUU) bloc, headed by Lytvyn, which incorporated five parties, including Kinakh's Party of Industrialists and Entrepreneurs of Ukraine, and the Party of the Regions (PR).

In February 2002 Ukrainian prosecutors charged Lazarenko, *in absentia*, with having ordered the murders of two parliamentary deputies in 1996 and 1998; in March 2002 the Government's director of arms exports, Valeriy Malev, was killed in an automobile collision. It subsequently emerged that several days before Malev's death Kuchma had been informed of the discovery of audio recordings made by Melnychenko, in which Kuchma and Malev were allegedly heard to discuss the sale of air-defence equipment to Iraq, in violation of UN sanctions.

In the legislative elections, held on 31 March 2002, Our Ukraine, which by this time comprised 10 moderate and nationalist parties, including two factions of Rukh, obtained both the largest share of the votes (23.6%) and the largest number of seats to be won by any party (112); FUU received the second largest number of seats (101), but only 11.8% of the votes cast. The CPU obtained 20.0% of the votes cast, but received only 66 seats. The Social-Democratic Party of Ukraine—United (SDPU—U) received 24 seats and 6.3% of the votes cast, the SPU 23 seats and 6.9% of the votes, and the YuTB 22 seats and 7.3% of the votes. A total of 93 independent candidates were elected. Opposition spokesmen alleged that incidents of electoral fraud had been perpetrated, and a report by observers from the Organization for Security and Co-operation in Europe (OSCE, see p. 366) indicated 'important flaws' in the organization of the elections. After the elections, Viktor Medvedchuk, the Chairman of the SDPU—U, was appointed to head the presidential administration, following the election of the incumbent, Lytvyn, as Chairman of the Verkhovna Rada.

In August 2002 Kuchma announced that a Constitutional Commission was to be formed to investigate the possibility of introducing constitutional reforms, with the intention of surmounting the executive–parliamentary tensions that had characterized much of Ukrainian politics since independence. In October a senior judge in Kyiv opened a criminal investigation into Kuchma, who was charged with violating 11 articles of the criminal code; the Supreme Court rejected an appeal by the Office of the Prosecutor-General declaring the case to be illegal. However, in November an ally of Kuchma, Vasyl Malyarenko, was elected as Chairman of the Supreme Court, replacing Vitaliy Boyko, and in late December the Court ruled that the investigation into Kuchma had indeed been opened illegally.

In mid-November 2002 Kuchma dismissed Kinakh as Prime Minister; he was replaced, on 16 November, by Viktor Yanukovych, latterly Governor of Donetsk Oblast. A new Government, in which several principal positions remained unchanged, was appointed later in the month. In early December a stable pro-presidential majority was finally established in the Verkhovna Rada.

In February 2003 Yushchenko issued a public statement, addressed to Kuchma, Yanukovych and Lytvyn, urging an end to what was described as 'political terror', including physical assaults against a number of political activists and the unsolved murders of several journalists. Later in the month anti-Kuchma demonstrations were held in several major cities. In mid-February the Verkhovna Rada rejected draft legislation on constitutional reform presented by deputies of the SDPU—U and the SPU, providing for the election of all 450 deputies by proportional representation on the basis of party lists; the draft, which was supported by deputies of Our Ukraine, the CPU and the YuTB, in addition to allies of the Government, was again rejected by the Verkhovna Rada in April. However, in March Kuchma submitted a draft on constitutional reform to the legislature, providing for the replacement of the unicameral legislature with a 300-seat State Assembly elected under a party list system and an 81-member House of the Regions; the parliament was to be granted the power to dismiss the Prime Minister, and the President the power to dissolve parliament. In April the two highest-ranking members of the Government were elected to senior positions in the PR: Yanukovych was elected as party Chairman and the First Deputy Prime Minister and Minister of Finance, Mykola Azarov, became the Chairman of the party's Political Council.

In June 2003 Lazarenko was released on bail in the USA (Lazarenko's trial, on charges of money-laundering, commenced in March 2004: In June of that year Lazarenko was convicted of money-laundering, fraud and extortion by a federal court in Los Angeles, CA, USA, and in August 2006 a US court sentenced Lazarenko to nine years' imprisonment.) In mid-June 2003 Kuchma submitted revised draft legislation on constitutional reform to the Verkhovna Rada; however, following the failure of the Verkhovna Rada to support either the constitutional amendments proposed by Kuchma or those presented by a group of opposition deputies, the President stated that he was prepared to co-operate with members of the legislative opposition. In September a new draft, prepared by members of the pro-presidential and CPU legislative factions (widely known as the Medvedchuk-Symonenko draft), was presented to the Verkhovna Rada; the draft envisaged the extension of the mandate of the existing legislature by one year, until 2007, when its replacement would be elected by a system of proportional representation. The draft also provided for the direct election, in 2004, of an interim President with reduced powers, until 2006, when a President would be elected by the Verkhovna Rada.

Meanwhile, in August 2003 Kuchma dismissed Smirnov as Minister of Internal Affairs; he was replaced by Mykola Bilokon. In September Anatoliy Zlenko retired as Minister of Foreign Affairs. He was replaced by Kostyantyn Hryshchenko, hitherto ambassador to the USA. In October Kuchma dismissed the Prosecutor-General, Svyatoslav Pyskun, nominating Hennadiy Vasilyev, hitherto the First Deputy Chairman of the Verkhovna Rada and a former Chief Prosecutor in Donetsk Oblast, as his replacement; the legislature approved the appointment in November. There were renewed concerns about the use of force to inhibit political debate, after Our Ukraine was prevented from holding a conference in Donetsk at the end of October. Reports stated that as many as 2,000 people had prevented members and supporters of the grouping from entering the building where the meeting was to have been held, and that material linking Yushchenko with Nazi symbols and ideology had been widely disseminated around the city. Our Ukraine, the YuTB and the SPU subsequently issued a statement accusing the Kuchma administration of dictatorial methods. In mid-November members of Our Ukraine were refused permission to hold a meeting in Sumy, and the electricity supply to the offices of a newspaper in the town was reportedly disconnected for the duration of a visit by Yushchenko. (In October Kuchma had ordered the Ministry of Internal Affairs and the State Security Service to investigate allegations made by Yushchenko that he was the target of an assassination plot.)

In late December 2003 the Verkhovna Rada provisionally approved the Medvedchuk-Symonenko draft on constitutional reform (however, the 274 votes cast in favour of the proposals, although sufficient to enable the bill to receive a second reading in the legislature, fell short of the 300 votes required for the approval of a constitutional amendment). The leadership of the Our Ukraine, YuTB and SPU factions did not support the proposals. On 30 December the Constitutional Court declared that Kuchma would be eligible to seek re-election upon the expiry of his term of office in October 2004, ruling that the constitutional provision that prevented the President from holding more than two consecutive mandates introduced during Kuchma's first term did not apply retroactively. On 3 February 2004 the Verkhovna Rada voted to amend the Medvedchuk-Symonenko draft on constitutional reform, removing those proposals pertaining to the election of the president by the legislature, which had attracted international criticism. This amendment, which was approved by 304 votes, was supported by the SPU, although Our Ukraine and the YuTB refused to participate in the voting. In March the Verkhovna Rada approved legislation, supported by the SPU and the CPU, introducing a proportional representation system for the election of all 450 parliamentary deputies; the percentage of the votes required for a party to obtain election was to be reduced from 4% to 3%. The vote was boycotted by the Our Ukraine and YuTB factions; the legislation was signed into law by Kuchma in early April. Also in March legislation was approved to modify the presidential election procedure, requiring candidates to submit the signatures of 500,000 eligible voters, rather than the 1m. required under legislation adopted in 1999. On 7 April the Verkhovna Rada failed to approve the competing proposals for reform embodied in the amended Medvedchuk-Symonenko draft. In accordance with the Constitution, the draft could not be reintroduced to the legislature for the period of one year.

Politics in 2004 were dominated by preparations for the presidential election. In April Yanukovych was named as the candidate for the pro-presidential bloc, while Yushchenko's candidacy was officially registered in August; 24 candidates registered to contest the poll. On 20 August two bombs exploded in a Kyiv market, and a further explosion occurred on 3 September; the authorities suggested that the explosions were connected to members of Our Ukraine, while the opposition claimed that the secret services had orchestrated the attacks in an attempt to discredit the opposition. In September Yushchenko was admitted to a clinic in Vienna, Austria, and subsequently emerged with his face severely scarred by lesions; it appeared that this resulted from his poisoning during a meal with senior members of the secret services, and Yushchenko himself accused the incumbent administration of seeking to murder him. Shortly before the first round of the election Yanukovych, in his capacity as Prime Minister, announced that the rate of state pensions was to be increased. In his capacity as presidential candidate, meanwhile, Yanukovych pledged to grant Russian the status of a joint official language and work towards permitting dual Ukrainian-Russian citizenship. Yushchenko, conversely, made it clear that he would, if elected, seek the closer integration of Ukraine into the European Union (EU, see p. 255) and the North Atlantic Treaty Organization (NATO, see p. 351).

After the first round of voting, held on 31 October 2004, no candidate secured a majority of votes cast. The Central Electoral Commission (CEC) published the final results of the poll on 10 November, awarding Yushchenko 39.9% of the votes cast, and Yanukovych 39.3%. Yushchenko and Yanukovych were, therefore, to proceed to a second round on 21 November. The CEC initially indicated that Yanukovych led by nearly 3% in the second round, with more than 99% of the votes counted, contradicting several exit polls endorsed by the opposition. Large-scale protests at the allegedly fraudulent conduct of the count, and in support of both Yushchenko and Tymoshenko, commenced in central Kyiv on 22 November, focused around the central Maidan Nezalezhnosti (Independence Square). The youth group Pora! (Enough!) played a principal role in the organization of the protests. The demonstrators established a tent settlement along Kyiv's main thoroughfare, and adopted the colour orange as a unifying symbol, leading what became known as the 'orange revolution'. Protests were almost entirely peaceful, with several hundred thousand people reportedly present at the height of the demonstrations. Meanwhile, a number of local administrations, including the city councils of Kyiv and Lviv, declared that they did not accept the results announced by the CEC and that they regarded Yushchenko as the legitimate Head of State, while demonstrations against the conduct of the election were reported across the country. The OSCE condemned the conduct of both rounds of voting. On 23 November Yushchenko took a symbolic oath of office in front of the Verkhovna Rada. On 24 November the CEC officially announced the preliminary results of the second round: Yanukovych was declared the winner, with 49.5% of the votes cast, while Yushchenko was deemed to have received 46.6%. Opposition protests persisted, however, with demands for a general strike the following day, and speeches and demonstrations continued in freezing conditions in central Kyiv, led by Yushchenko and Tymoshenko; protesters blockaded numerous government buildings. Smaller protests in favour of Yanukovych were also held, principally in eastern Ukraine, where the administrations of several oblasts (notably Donetsk and Luhansk) expressed their intention to hold referendums on autonomy or secession should Yushchenko be declared president.

Following an appeal to the Supreme Court regarding the conduct of the second round of voting, on 25 November 2004 the Court announced that it would suspend the publication of the election results until the opposition's complaints could be considered. A significant shift in the allegiances of the mass media was also observed, with staff at state-owned broadcasting outlets, which had hitherto been reported to demonstrate a clear pro-Yanukovych bias, announcing that they would begin 'full and impartial' coverage of the events surrounding the disputed vote. On 27 November the Verkhovna Rada voted to declare the 21 November ballot invalid and to express a lack of confidence in the CEC, while a subsequent motion of no confidence in Yanukovych's Government was passed on 1 December (these resolutions, however, carried no legal force, as they required the signature of President Kuchma to be binding). On 29 November it was reported that Serhiy Tihipko, hitherto the manager of Yanukovych's presidential campaign, had resigned from the position of Governor of the NBU, and considered his role within Yanukovych's campaign to have concluded. Meanwhile, Polish President Aleksander Kwaśniewski, Lithuanian President Valdas Adamkus and the EU High Representative for Common Foreign and Security Policy, Javier Solana Madariaga, arrived in Kyiv to attempt mediation between the two parties in the crisis. Yushchenko repeatedly stated that the only resolution that he considered acceptable was a repeat run of the second round of voting, a course of action described by Kuchma as lacking domestic or international precedent. On 3 December the Supreme Court ruled that the results of the second round of voting, as announced by the CEC on 24 November, were invalid, and ordered that a repeat election be conducted within three weeks.

Following extensive negotiations, on 8 December 2004 the Verkhovna Rada voted to support a series of amendments to the Constitution and electoral law, with some 420 deputies voting in favour of the proposals. The constitutional amendments incorporated several of the changes included in the Medvedchuk-Symonenko draft of amendments, among them the transfer of several powers of appointment from the President to the Prime Minister and the legislature. The amendments also provided for the expulsion from the legislature of any deputy who left the party or bloc on whose list he or she had been elected. Immediately after the vote, Kuchma signed the amendments into law, although they were not fully to take effect until after the legislative elections due to be held in March 2006. Kuchma also announced the dismissal of the Prosecutor-General, Hennadiy Vasilyev (who was replaced by his predecessor, Pyskun, after he won a court case declaring his dismissal in 2003 to be illegal), and approved a substantial reconstitution of the CEC. Yanukovych was granted leave from his position as Prime Minister in order to campaign for the repeated second round of voting; he was replaced in an acting capacity by Azarov. The repeat ballot was held on 26 December. Preliminary results suggested a victory for Yushchenko; however, Yanukovych lodged complaints against the conduct of the election with the CEC and, subsequently, the Supreme Court, thus causing the official publication of the results to be delayed until all legal means of protest had been exhausted. Meanwhile, on 27 December Minister of Transport and Communications Heorhiy Kirpa was found dead, as a result of multiple bullet wounds. Earlier in the month Yuriy Lyakh, Chairman of the Ukrainian Credit Bank, had been found dead in his office, from neck wounds apparently inflicted with a paper knife. Both cases were officially described as suicide, despite widespread speculation that both deaths had been political assassinations. On 31 December Yanukovych resigned as Prime Minister, and on 6 January 2005 Kuchma signed a decree dismissing the Cabinet of Ministers. On that date Yanukovych's complaints were rejected by the Supreme Court, and four days later Yushchenko was officially declared to have won the ballot of 26 December 2004, receiving 52.0% of the votes cast, compared with the 44.2% awarded to Yanukovych. A clear regional divide was evident in the results:

in 16 of the 27 primary administrative divisions of Ukraine, the most popular candidate in that region had obtained more than 75% of the votes cast; Yushchenko obtained such support in 12 administrative divisions, mainly in western and central Ukraine, including Kyiv City, while Yanukovych received similarly overwhelming majorities in four divisions: the eastern oblasts of Donetsk and Luhansk, the Autonomous Republic of Crimea, and in Sevastopol City. A final appeal, lodged by Yanukovych with the Supreme Court, was rejected on 20 January 2005, and Yushchenko was inaugurated as President on 23 January.

On 4 February 2005 the Verkhovna Rada voted to approve Yushchenko's nomination of Tymoshenko as Prime Minister and a new Cabinet of Ministers was announced, notably including Kinakh (who had announced his support for Yushchenko after the first round of voting) as First Deputy Prime Minister. Other ministerial appointments included Yuriy Lutsenko as Minister of Internal Affairs and Anatoliy Hrytsenko as Minister of Defence. Yushchenko also appointed many new regional governors, and named Petro Poroshenko, a prominent business executive, as Chairman of the National Security and Defence Council. Yanukovych, meanwhile, expressed his intention of leading a 'harsh opposition' to Yushchenko's administration. The new Government declared combating corruption to be a priority, and several privatizations conducted during Kuchma's presidency were targeted for investigation; the extent to which they should be investigated became a significant source of tension between the various parties and elements represented within the new administration. Similar tensions existed over other policy matters between the three main political groupings represented within the Government: nationalists and populists, associated chiefly with Tymoshenko; statist socialists linked with the SPU; and those elements regarded as more sympathetic to business interests, associated more closely with Yushchenko. The latter formed a new political party, People's Union Our Ukraine; Yushchenko was named as the Honorary Chairman of the party, Roman Bezsmertnyi (Yushchenko's electoral campaign manager and a Deputy Prime Minister) became the Chairman of the party's Council, and Yuriy Yekhanurov (a former First Deputy Prime Minister and Minister of the Economy, and the recently appointed Governor of Dnipropetrovsk Oblast) the Chairman of the party's Executive Committee.

Yushchenko also endorsed a reopening of the investigation into the death of Gongadze. On 4 March 2005 former Minister of Internal Affairs Kravchenko, who was alleged to be one of the officials who had discussed the killing of Gongadze on the audio recordings released in 2000, was found dead, reportedly as the result of suicide, shortly before he had been due to be questioned at the office of the Prosecutor-General. It was subsequently announced that four people were to be charged in connection with Gongadze's death. The trial of three men, all former police officers, commenced in January 2006; the fourth man, suspected of being Gongadze's killer, was believed to have fled Ukraine. (In March 2008 the three men were found guilty of murdering Gongadze, each receiving custodial sentences of 12–13 years, although the investigations failed to discover who had ordered the killing.)

Meanwhile, it soon became apparent that some of the new administration's policy decisions had been instrumental in reducing the hitherto strong rate of economic growth. Increases in social spending (introduced by both the new Government, and by the Yanukovych administration prior to the first round of voting in late 2004) led to heightened inflation. Moreover, Tymoshenko's decision, in April 2005, to maintain at existing levels the retail prices of petroleum (for which Ukraine was heavily dependent on Russia) resulted in several Russian companies limiting their supplies to Ukraine, purportedly in order to carry out repairs to pipelines, causing a severe shortfall relative to demand. Later in May Yushchenko issued a decree criticizing the Government's action in restraining prices as incompatible with the principles of market economics, and ordered that the limits imposed be rescinded as a matter of urgency. Meanwhile, interfactional disagreements in the Verkhovna Rada meant that several items of legislation, which had been intended to expedite Ukraine's application for membership of the World Trade Organization (WTO, see p. 410), were not approved by the legislature before the beginning of its summer recess.

The growing tensions between the constituent groupings that had supported the 'orange revolution' resulted in a series of resignations in early September 2005, amid accusations of corruption. On 1 September an adviser to Tymoshenko, Mykola Brodsky, alleged that elements close to Yushchenko were engaged in corrupt practices; one day later the Chief of the Presidential Staff, Oleksandr Zinchenko, announced his resignation, criticizing the corrupt actions of Poroshenko, in particular. On 8 September Mykola Tomenko announced his resignation as Deputy Prime Minister. Later the same day Yushchenko dismissed Tymoshenko and her Government, and also announced that Poroshenko had resigned from the National Security and Defence Council; he stated that the Government had been dismissed because it had failed to operate cohesively, having been undermined by factionalism and machinations. Tymoshenko subsequently criticized several close associates of Yushchenko, and stated that, as a result of her dismissal, the YuTB would effectively go into opposition and present its own list of candidates, separate from those of Our Ukraine, at the 2006 elections to the Verkhovna Rada.

The split between the YuTB and Our Ukraine was demonstrated on 20 September 2005, when the Verkhovna Rada narrowly failed to approve Yushchenko's nomination of Yekhanurov as Prime Minister. Consequently, in order to obtain support for Yekhanurov's nomination from the sizable PR faction within the legislature, Yushchenko and Yanukovych agreed a 10-point memorandum; among the controversial measures provided for by the document were an amnesty for all those involved in electoral fraud at the annulled second round of presidential voting in 2004, and an extension of the immunity from prosecution enjoyed by legislative deputies to members of regional and local councils. On 22 September Yekhanurov was confirmed as Prime Minister, having received 289 votes in favour of his nomination in the Verkhovna Rada, compared with the 223 votes obtained prior to the signature of the memorandum. Several ministers holding principal positions in the former administration retained their portfolios. New appointments included that of Arseniy Yatsenyuk as Minister of the Economy, and Stanislav Stashevskyi as First Deputy Prime Minister, replacing Kinakh, who became the Chairman of the National Security and Defence Council. The dismissal of Pyskun as Prosecutor-General, on 14 October, was a further significant personnel change; his replacement, in an acting capacity, was Serhiy Vynokurov, who subsequently announced that all criminal charges against Poroshenko had been abandoned. On 31 October the Verkhovna Rada approved the appointment of Oleksandr Medvedko as Prosecutor-General.

New arrangements for the purchase of natural gas (following a dispute with Russia—see below) were a source of considerable controversy within Ukraine and were instrumental in bringing about a vote of no confidence in the Government on 10 January 2006, which was approved by 250 votes to 50 against. (Tymoshenko stated that she would withdraw from the agreement on gas purchases in the event of her again becoming Prime Minister.) Although such a vote should, theoretically, have resulted in the Government's removal from office, the constitutional position at this time was obscure (the transfer of many of the powers of appointment from the President to the Prime Minister and the Chairman of the Verkhovna Rada, agreed in late 2004, had taken effect on 1 January 2006), and in the absence of a functioning Constitutional Court, President Yushchenko requested that the Yekhanurov administration remain in office until after the forthcoming legislative elections.

The legislative elections proceeded, as scheduled, on 26 March 2006, contested by 45 parties and blocs. The changes that had taken place in Ukrainian politics since the previous elections in 2002, and the introduction of a system of full proportional representation and the exclusion of nominally independent deputies, meant that the new Verkhovna Rada had a very different composition to the one that it replaced. The results of voting did, however, confirm the persistence of the division in support for parties between, on one hand, eastern and southern regions, and on the other hand, central and western regions. Yanukovych's PR became the largest party in the new legislature, with 32.1% of the total votes cast, receiving 186 seats. The YuTB was placed second, with 22.3% and 129 seats, while the Our Ukraine bloc (comprising several smaller, generally liberal or nationalist parties, in addition to Our Ukraine) obtained 14.0% and 81 seats, considerably less, in both percentage and seat terms, than the Our Ukraine electoral alliance of 2002 had received. Only two other groupings—the SPU, with 5.7% (33 seats), and the CPU, with 3.7% (21 seats)—surpassed the 3% quota required for representation. Although there were some suspicions of malpractice in the concurrent elections to the Crimean Supreme Council (see below), and some other minor flaws, the elections to the Verkhovna Rada were described by international monitors as free and fair. However, the formation of a coalition administration, required by the failure of any party of obtain a majority of seats, proved protracted. In late June it was announced that Our Ukraine, the YuTB and the SPU were to form a governing coalition supportive of Yushchenko, with Tymoshenko as premier. However, when the coalition declined to nominate Moroz of the SPU to the chairmanship of the Verkhovna Rada, that party announced its withdrawal from the coalition, which thereby ceased to hold a majority of legislative seats. The SPU subsequently announced that it would support a so-called 'anti-crisis coalition' headed by Yanukovych and the PR and also comprising the CPU and the SPU; these three parties controlled 240 of the 450 parliamentary seats. Subsequently, the anti-crisis coalition was also dissolved, and at the end of July, following protracted negotiations, a 'national unity coalition' was formed after Yushchenko and leaders of four of the five parliamentary parties signed a document titled the 'Universal of National Unity' that outlined various domestic and foreign policy aims. The remaining political faction, the YuTB, refused to sign the Universal and announced its intention to remain in opposition. The Universal was signed shortly before Yushchenko was constitutionally required either to submit a nomination for the premiership to a parliamentary vote of confidence or to dissolve parliament and call fresh elections (in the event that a government had not been formed).

Yushchenko decided against the dissolution of the Verkhovna Rada and accepted Yanukovych's nomination as Prime Minister, subject to Yanukovych's acceptance of the principles of the Universal, including the retention of Ukrainian as the sole official state language (outwith Crimea), the rejection of any restructuring of Ukraine on a federal basis, and the aspiration towards the eventual incorporation of Ukraine into European and Atlantic organizations (subject to approval on these matters in national referendums). On 4 August 2006 the Verkhovna Rada approved the nomination of Yanukovych as Prime Minister and the formation of a new Government, comprising representatives of the PR, Our Ukraine, the SPU and the CPU—the first Government in post-Soviet Ukraine to include members of the CPU. Our Ukraine did not enter officially into the coalition, although four members of the new Government belonged to the bloc, in addition to non-party allies of Yushchenko.

Despite the formation of a ruling coalition, tensions between President Yushchenko and Prime Minister Yanukovych were still evident, while the balance of powers between the President, Prime Minister and Verkhovna Rada, provided for by the amended Constitution, remained uncertain; in particular, several of Yanukovych's actions as Prime Minister appeared to overstep the responsibilities of that office. In September 2006 Yanukovych refused to sign several presidential decrees (which, in order to become valid, require the approval of the Prime Minister and Chairman of the Verkhovna Rada). In the same month Yanukovych expressed Ukraine's unpreparedness to enter into a closer relationship with NATO at a meeting of the Alliance in Brussels, Belgium (see below), despite such remarks being contrary both to the stated policy of Yushchenko (who, as President, was constitutionally responsible for foreign affairs) and to the terms of the Universal. Later in September the Verkhovna Rada voted to abolish a prohibition on parliamentary deputies switching party allegiance or becoming independent that had been introduced prior to the March legislative elections. At the end of the month Yanukovych demanded the dismissal of the governors of five eastern regions who were members of Our Ukraine, a demand which required presidential endorsement. In early October Our Ukraine announced its decision to withdraw its members from the Government and enter into the opposition; however, both Yushchenko and Yanukovych refused to accept the ministers' resignations.

On 15 November 2006 Minister of Foreign Affairs Borys Tarasyuk and Minister of Defence Anatoliy Hrytsenko (both of whom were strongly opposed to Yanukovych's intervention at NATO) had been due to present reports to the Verkhovna Rada, which had then been expected to vote to dismiss the two ministers, but these presentations (and the vote) were postponed for at least two weeks. However, on 1 December the Verkhovna Rada voted in favour of the dismissal of Tarasyuk and the Minister of Internal Affairs Lutsenko; Tarasyuk, who was, in the mean time, prevented from attending government meetings, subsequently had his dismissal overturned by a district court (on the grounds that his post was one answerable to the President, rather than to the Verkhovna Rada and the Government), although his dismissal was upheld by the appeals court in Kyiv in January 2007. Consequently, on 30 January Tarasyuk resigned from the Government.

There was continued instability within the governing coalition: on 20 March 2007 the Verkhovna Rada rejected Yushchenko's nomination of Volodymyr Ohryzko as Minister of Foreign Affairs. The legislature approved the appointment of Yatsenyuk to that position on the following day, as well as several other ministerial appointments. Later in the month a group of deputies hitherto loyal to Yushchenko, including Kinakh, announced that they would henceforth form part of the PR faction in the Verkhovna Rada. Frustrated at the inability to govern effectively, on 2 April Yushchenko issued a decree dissolving the Verkhovna Rada and scheduling pre-term parliamentary elections for 27 May. Yanukovych initially refused to accept the presidential decree and asked the Constitutional Court to rule on the constitutionality of the dissolution of parliament. Meanwhile, the Verkhovna Rada continued to meet, refusing to recognize the legitimacy of its dissolution. Supporters of Yanukovych staged demonstrations in Kyiv. (Subsequent reports appeared to confirm allegations that supporters of Yanukovych were being paid to travel to Kyiv and take part in demonstrations.) On 25 April Yushchenko announced that the parliamentary elections were to be delayed until 24 June. On 30 April the Verkhovna Rada approved a resolution calling for the concurrent holding of fresh presidential and legislative elections, to be held no later than December 2007 and subject to the introduction of a number of constitutional amendments. Yushchenko continued to insist, however, that the Constitution required any pre-term elections to be held no later than 60 days after the dissolution of the Verkhovna Rada. Meanwhile, the Constitutional Court had failed to issue any ruling on the legitimacy of the dissolution of the legislature within one month, as required; the acting Chairman of the Court, Ivan Dombrovsky, resigned in May, while several other judges of the Court were absent, resigned, or were dismissed, effectively rendering the Court unable to conduct its work. Meanwhile, it was reported on 4 May that Yushchenko and Yanukovych had agreed to fresh parliamentary elections being held later in the year, subject to the agreement of several constitutional amendments by the outgoing legislature; Yanukovych had abandoned demands for a presidential election to be held concurrently with the parliamentary polling.

On 1 June 2007 Yushchenko again dismissed Pyskun, who had been reappointed to the Office of Prosecutor-General in April, and replaced him, again, with Medvedko. On 5 June Yushchenko issued a further decree rescheduling legislative elections for 30 September, following a compromise arrangement, reached on 27 May, between Yushchenko, Yanukovych and Moroz. Our Ukraine and YuTB deputies subsequently withdrew from the Verkhovna Rada. In early July Our Ukraine formed an electoral alliance with the People's Self-Defence group of Lutsenko and several smaller parties, which became known as Our Ukraine-People's Self-defence bloc. Tymoshenko demanded that a national referendum to resolve the constitutional impasse be conducted to coincide with the elections, and began to organize a petition in support of the poll. However, the CEC ruled against the organization of an early constitutional referendum, on the grounds that it allowed insufficient time for preparation. In August the YuTB succeeded, after a legal appeal, in reversing a decision by the CEC to refuse to register it for the elections, on the grounds that it had submitted incomplete documentation. By the end of that month 21 political associations had registered with the CEC to contest the elections.

According to official results of the legislative elections on 30 September 2007, released by the CEC in mid-October, Yanukovych's PR won 34.4% of the votes and 175 seats, the YuTB 30.7% and 156 seats, the Our Ukraine-People's Self-defence bloc 14.2% and 72 seats, the CPU 5.4% and 27 seats, and the Lytvyn bloc 4.0% and 20 seats. The SPU, with 2.9% of the votes, narrowly failed to secure the minimum for parliamentary representation. Tymoshenko and the leader of the Our Ukraine-People's Self-defence bloc, Vyacheslav Kyrylenko, subsequently announced their intention to sign a coalition agreement, which would allow the two groupings a narrow parliamentary majority; Tymoshenko would be returned to the office of Prime Minister, while ministerial portfolios were to be divided equally between the two blocs. After Yushchenko urged co-operation with the PR, however, it was reported that Yanukovych's party had been offered deputy ministerial and other official posts in the new administration, prompting fears of further protracted coalition discussions. Although the elections were regarded by international observers to have met democratic standards, the official publication of the final results were delayed, pending the outcome of a legal challenge submitted by five small parties, including the SPU, based on alleged violations concerning the inclusion of Ukrainians resident abroad on voting lists. The Verkhovna Rada was convened on 23 November, when Yanukovych formally relinquished the presidency. Yatsenyuk was appointed Chairman of the Verkhovna Rada in 4 December. Following further protracted negotiations, the coalition agreement announced in October was finalized; on 18 December, after two failed attempts, Tymoshenko's nomination as Prime Minister was finally approved by 226 votes in the Verkhovna Rada. Her Government comprised 12 representatives of the YuTB and 11 of the Our Ukraine-People's Self-defence bloc; the new Minister of Foreign Affairs, Volodymyr Ohryzko, who, together with the Minister of Defence, had been nominated by the President in accordance with the Constitution, was independent.

In January 2008 it was reported that Lutsenko, who had been reappointed Minister of Internal Affairs, had assaulted the Mayor of Kyiv, Leonid Chernovetsky, following an altercation over allegedly corrupt agreements relating to the transfer of land ownership in the city. In March the Verkhovna Rada approved a resolution, supported by the YuTB, scheduling early mayoral elections in Kyiv, following a report by a government investigative commission on the activities of the Kyiv City authorities. Legislation under debate that strengthened presidential powers while reducing those of the Government was a subject of great controversy in the legislature, and served to exacerbate tensions between Tymoshenko and Yushchenko, who continued to criticize the Prime Minister's economic policies and accused her of encouraging corrupt practices in land auctions. Also in March a largely defunct political party, supportive of Yushchenko, United Centre, chaired by a strenuous opponent of Tymoshenko, Ihor Kril, was effectively re-established (Baloha was also a senior member of the party); Lutsenko also announced that his parliamentary People's Self-defence bloc would form the basis for a new party, and that it would not merge into Our Ukraine, as had previously been considered. In April the Constitutional Court ruled that the constitutional system could be amended by a national referendum (although the Verkhovna Rada would first be required to amend certain aspects of the existing Constitution). A protracted dispute between the President and the Government over the State Property Fund escalated in late April, when Yushchenko issued decrees in an effort to reverse a government decision to dismiss the head of the Fund, who had objected to privatization plans. Following continued denunciations of Tymoshenko by Yushchenko and his close associate, head of the presidential secretariat Viktor Baloha, in mid-May YuTB deputies blockaded the Verkhovna Rada, preventing Yushchenko from making his annual parliamentary address.

On 6 June 2008 the coalition of the YuTB and the Our Ukraine-People's Self-defence bloc lost its narrow parliamentary majority, after a deputy from each faction resigned. A parliamentary motion expressing no confidence in Tymoshenko's Government was defeated in early July. Following Russia's military action in Georgia in early August, a presidential aide accused Tymoshenko (who had refrained from criticizing Russia while Yushchenko had demonstrated strong support for President Mikheil Saakashvili—see below) of reaching a clandestine agreement with the Russia to support her in the next presidential election. On 1 September 2008 PR parliamentary faction leader Raisa Bohatyryova, who had been appointed National Security and Defence Council Secretary in December 2007, was expelled from the party, after refusing to endorse Yanukovych's support for the declared independence of the separatist regions of South Ossetia and Abkhazia from Georgia. On the following day Yushchenko announced the withdrawal of the Our Ukraine-People's Self-defence bloc from the ruling coalition, after the YuTB had supported the PR in voting for a parliamentary motion approving legislation that strengthened the powers of the Government, while reducing those of the President. On 16 September parliamentary Chairman Yatsenyuk officially declared that the governing coalition had failed and subsequently tendered his resignation; in the event that no new coalition was formed within 30 days, the President was required, under the Constitution, to schedule new elections. On 8 October Yushchenko officially dissolved the Verkhovna Rada and announced that further legislative elections would take place on 7 December. Following a legal challenge by Tymoshenko, he subsequently rejected a ruling by a regional court against his election decree and dismissed its judge. Later in October Yushchenko reconvened the Verkhovna Rada to debate financial austerity measures required for the disbursement of IMF assistance (following the onset of the international financial crisis—see Economic Affairs) and rescheduled the elections for 14 December. While legislation providing for the IMF-stipulated measures were approved by the Verkhovna Rada at the end of October, attempts to adopt legislation allocating funds to the organization of the elections failed. The Verkhovna Rada accepted Yatsenyuk's resignation on 12 November; Yushchenko announced that it would not be possible to organize legislative elections in 2008, as envisaged, in view of the financial difficulties. On 29 November Yushchenko was officially elected Chairman of Our Ukraine (having hitherto held the post in an honorary capacity).

On 9 December 2008 Lytvyn was elected as Chairman of the Verkhovna Rada (having held the post in 2002–06), prior to the formal signature of a further coalition agreement between Our Ukraine-People's Self-defence bloc, the YuTB and the Lytvyn bloc on 16 December. However, Kyrylenko withdrew from Our Ukraine-People's Self-defence bloc in protest at joining the new coalition and, together with a further 17 former members, subsequently formed a breakaway movement, known as For Ukraine (which held its inaugural meeting in February 2009). Yushchenko attributed responsibility for the increasing adverse effects on the economy, including a sharp decline in the value of the currency, to the Government, while Tymoshenko demanded that both the President and the Governor of the National Bank, Volodymyr Stelmakh, resign from office. Later in December 2008 the Verkhovna Rada adopted a motion expressing no confidence in Stelmakh. Following a further acrimonious dispute with Russia over natural gas payments in January 2009 (see below), Yushchenko also condemned a decision by Tymoshenko to request an emergency loan from the Russian Government. In early February Viktor Pynzenyk, who had expressed opposition to the Government's plan for economic recovery, tendered his resignation as Minister of Finance. In the same month the Ministry of Foreign Affairs threatened to expel the Russian ambassador in Ukraine (and former Russian premier), Viktor Chernomyrdin, following a newspaper interview in which he made a number of disparaging comments about the Ukrainian political leadership. In early March the Verkhovna Rada voted in favour of removing Ohryzko from the post of Minister of Foreign Affairs, on grounds of mismanagement of government policy; the motion also followed an ICJ ruling, issued in February, on a longstanding maritime territory dispute with Romania that awarded some 79% of the contested area to Romania.

At the beginning of April 2009 the Verkhovna Rada voted in favour of scheduling the presidential election for 25 October (rather than the date of 17 January 2010, at the end of the existing presidential term, favoured by Yushchenko, and as provided for by the Constitution). Yushchenko also proposed constitutional amendments for the creation of a second parliamentary chamber and an increase in presidential powers to allow him to veto certain government decisions. In early May, following a challenge by Yushchenko, the Constitutional Court overturned the proposed bringing forward of the election. Also in May 2009 Lutsenko offered his resignation from the post of Minister of Internal Affairs, at the request of Yushchenko, after he had been detained by police at the airport of Frankfurt, Germany, for allegedly intoxicated and violent behaviour; he denied the accusations and claimed that Baloha was responsible for a campaign against him. After parliamentary deputies belonging to the YuTB bloc opposed the acceptance of his resignation (which was likely to precipitate the collapse of the ruling coalition), the Verkhovna Rada voted in favour of a motion requesting his suspension for the duration of an investigation into the incident. Later that month Baloha submitted his resignation, accusing Yushchenko of failing to honour pledges he had made prior to his election, and also criticizing Tymoshenko.

Despite the political differences between the Ukrainian-speaking western regions and the Russian-speaking eastern regions that were evident during the 1990s and 2000s, only in the Crimean peninsula did any significant movement for re-unification with Russia emerge. (Speculation that several eastern and southern regions would hold referendums for autonomy in late 2004 appeared to be largely transient, and associated with the disputed presidential election, rather than representing any long-term political aspirations.) The situation was further complicated by the status of the Crimean Tatars, who had been forcibly deported to Soviet Central Asia in 1944, and who began to return to Crimea from late 1989. In a referendum held in

January 1991, residents of Crimea (which then had the status of an ordinary oblast) voted to restore it to the status of a nominally autonomous republic. The decision, although it had no legal basis, was ratified by the Verkhovna Rada. In June Crimean Tatars established 'parallel' institutions to those of the state, without any constitutional or legal status. The Kurultay (Assembly) was a popular assembly that was intended to convene once a year, the Qırımtatar Milly Meclisi (Crimean Tatar National Assembly) was to meet throughout the year, and a number of local assemblies were also established. In February 1992 the Crimean Supreme Council, the regional legislature, voted to transform the region into the Republic of Crimea, and in May declared Crimea an independent state, adopting a new Constitution. However, following threats from the Verkhovna Rada to impose an economic blockade and direct rule on Crimea, the independence declaration was rescinded. In June the Ukrainian Government confirmed Crimea's status as an autonomous republic within Ukraine, which was otherwise to remain a unitary state. (The city of Sevastopol was not, however, to form part of the autonomous republic.) Meanwhile, relations between the local leadership and Crimean Tatars, some 250,000 of whom had returned to Crimea by late 1992, deteriorated steadily, primarily as a result of disputes over the ownership of land and property, and the right to gain Ukrainian citizenship. In October a Tatar encampment was dispersed on the orders of the Crimean Government, and in response some 6,000 Tatars stormed the Crimean parliament building.

With the election of Yurii Meshkov as President of Crimea in January 1994, it appeared likely that the region would renew efforts towards sovereignty, as well as establish closer links with Russia. In response, the Verkhovna Rada approved constitutional amendments, according to which the Ukrainian President could nullify any measures taken by the Crimean authorities that he deemed to be illegal. In March a referendum was held in Crimea, simultaneously with the Ukrainian legislative elections; 70% of those voting in the referendum supported broader autonomous powers for Crimea. In May, following a vote by the Crimean parliament to restore the suspended Constitution of May 1992, the Ukrainian Government ordered the Crimean legislature to rescind its decision; the crisis appeared to have been defused by June 1994, when delegations from the Ukrainian and Crimean parliaments met in Simferopol, the Crimean capital, where it was agreed that Crimea would continue to be subject to Ukrainian law. In September the Crimean legislature voted to restrict the Crimean President's executive authority, in response to which Meshkov temporarily suspended parliament. Meanwhile, the Verkhovna Rada approved a constitutional amendment, permitting it to nullify any legislation adopted by the Crimean parliament that contravened the Ukrainian Constitution. In March 1995 the Ukrainian legislature voted to abolish both the Crimean Constitution of May 1992 and the Crimean presidency, and in April 1995 Kuchma imposed direct rule on Crimea.

In October 1995 the Crimean legislature approved a new Constitution. Before its final adoption by the Verkhovna Rada in December 1996, the Constitution underwent several amendments; notably, Ukrainian was recognized as the state language, although Russian was to be the language of all official correspondence of the autonomous republic. In February 1997, contrary to national law, which stipulates that the appointment of the Crimean Prime Minister is the prerogative of the Ukrainian President, the Crimean parliament arrogated to itself the power to appoint the regional Government. In April it appointed Anatolii Franchuk as the new Crimean premier, in place of Arkadii Demydenko. Kuchma suspended this resolution, declaring it to be a violation of the Ukrainian Constitution, but, following the approval of a second motion of no confidence in Demydenko, in June Kuchma consented to his dismissal. A new Council of Ministers headed by Franchuk was subsequently approved by the Crimean legislature. In October Kuchma exercised his veto over items of legislation approved by the Crimean Supreme Council—the adoption of Russian as the peninsula's official language of business communication, and the realignment of Crimea's time zone with that of Moscow—that were regarded as an assertion of the primacy of Crimea's links with Russia. Further conflict arose between the national Government and the Crimean legislature in February 1998, following the approval of legislation by the Verkhovna Rada, whereby all Ukrainian citizens were to be eligible to contest the seats in the Crimean legislature—hitherto, only citizens resident in Crimea had been eligible. In addition, the new legislation stated that elections to the Crimean parliament were to be held simultaneously with the elections to the Verkhovna Rada in March and not in September, as had previously been decided by the Crimean Supreme Council.

Elections to the Crimean legislature in March 1998 brought the issue of the status of the Crimean Tatars to the fore, when demonstrations were staged by Tatars appealing for the right to vote. The OSCE estimated that about one-half of the 165,000 Tatars resident in Crimea did not have Ukrainian citizenship and were, therefore, ineligible to vote. Leonid Grach, the leader of the CPU in Crimea, was elected Chairman of the new Crimean Supreme Council. In May a new Council of Ministers was appointed, with Sergei Kunitsyn as Chairman. In January 1999 a new Crimean Constitution came into effect, which granted the Crimean authorities the right to manage its own property and to pass a budget. Although citizenship had recently been granted to a number of Crimean Tatars, representatives of the group held a demonstration in May in Simferopol, demanding constitutional changes to ensure better representation and rights for Crimean Tatars and for the Crimean Tatar language to be recognized as a state language; subsequent protests culminated in a 20,000-strong demonstration in Simferopol in May 2000. In mid-July 2001 the Supreme Council dismissed Kunitsyn from the premiership for the third time. Although Kuchma had refused to recognize the previous dismissals, in late July Kuchma accepted Kunitsyn's removal from office, and expressed support for the new premier elected by the Crimean Supreme Council, Valerii Gorbatov of the Working Ukraine party.

As campaigning for the concurrent elections to the Verkhovna Rada and the Crimean Supreme Council, to be held on 31 March 2002, commenced, controversy was provoked at the end of February by the invalidation of Grach's candidacy for a seat in the Supreme Council, on technical grounds. Despite his disqualification, Grach's name appeared on ballot papers, and he was re-elected to the Supreme Council in defiance of the decision of the Crimean Court of Appeal. The elections to the Crimean Supreme Council demonstrated a sizeable shift in support away from the communists, towards centrists, whose grouping, known as the Kunitsyn Team, after its leader, won 39 of the 100 seats in the Council; a pro-communist electoral alliance, the Grach bloc, received 28 seats. Three other parties obtained representation, and 29 independent candidates were elected. In late April the Ukrainian Supreme Court approved Grach's appeal, thereby serving to legitimize his status as a deputy of the Crimean legislature. However, Grach was unsuccessful in his campaign for re-election as Chairman of the Crimean legislature, being defeated by a former Deputy Chairman, Boris Deich. The new parliament also voted for the dismissal of Gorbatov and the re-appointment of Kunitsyn as Prime Minister, and reformists loyal to Kunitsyn were successful in establishing a majority in the legislature. None the less, in the concurrent elections to the Verkhovna Rada, the CPU remained the most popular party on the peninsula. Notably, for the first time, Crimean Tatar deputies were elected to the Verkhovna Rada, within the Our Ukraine bloc. Russian nationalists only successfully attracted votes in the Crimean city of Sevastopol.

In early 2004 concern was expressed by ethnic Russians resident in Crimea that a measure, approved by the Crimean Government in 2000, which ordered foreign citizens resident in Crimea to pay higher rates for utilities and accommodation than those paid by Ukrainian citizens, was being applied to Russian citizens resident in the Republic. Meanwhile, an increase in ethnic tensions between Crimean Tatars and the Slavic inhabitants of the peninsula was reported in early 2004. Although it appeared that disputes over land were the principal source of tensions, some reports suggested that violence had been provoked by groups of Russian right-wing extremists and militant Cossack groups resident in neighbouring regions of Russia. In the first few months of the year, in advance of the 60th anniversary of the deportation of the Tatars from the peninsula, several clashes and violent incidents occurred, and in early April a petition, signed by over 35,000 Crimean Tatars, which alleged that the police force in Crimea were ignoring incidents of inter-ethnic violence against Tatars, was presented to President Kuchma. The continuing tension in Crimean society was reflected in the allegiances displayed in the presidential election of late 2004, when the peninsula's Russophone majority overwhelmingly supported Yanukovych, while the Crimean Tatar minority was reported to have voted principally for the victorious candidate, Yushchenko, in the hope that he would act to address their grievances regarding land distribution and greater ethnic autonomy. In late April 2005 Kunitsyn resigned as Prime Minister of Crimea, following his appointment as an adviser to President Yushchenko; the Crimean Supreme Council voted to approve Anatolii Matviyenko as his replacement. Matviyenko's appointment caused some controversy on the peninsula, both because he had never held any position of responsibility in Crimea and because of his affiliations with both Ukrainian nationalists and the YuTB, which did not enjoy significant support in the Republic. Matviyenko was subject to frequent criticism as Prime Minister, particularly for failing to resolve concerns about widespread corruption or the issue of land allocation to returning Crimean Tatars, and his premiership proved short-lived. Following the dismissal of Tymoshenko as Prime Minister of Ukraine, in early September, the Crimean Supreme Council voted to dismiss the republican Government; Matviyenko duly resigned on 20 September. On 23 September the Crimean Supreme Council approved the appointment of Anatolii Burdyugov, the leader of the Crimean branch of Yushchenko's People's Union Our Ukraine party, as Prime Minister, and a new Government was formed at the end of the month. In late February 2006 the Crimean legislature voted to hold a referendum on the proposed introduction of Russian as a state language within the peninsula; however, President Yushchenko stated that the referendum would be unconstitutional, and this ruling was subsequently confirmed by the CEC.

Elections to the Crimean Supreme Council, held concurrently with local elections and with those to the Verkhovna Rada on 26 March 2006, were marred by allegations of electoral fraud; moreover, one candidate was killed on polling day and, in early April, the body of a local councillor was found in unexplained circumstances, after his apparent abduction (however, police stated that the latter killing did not appear to have a political motive). At the end of March the President's Representative in Crimea, Volodomyr Kulich, announced that a commission comprising senior officials of several ministries and law-enforcement bodies was to be established to investigate the apparent electoral violations. Meanwhile, protesters outside the Crimean Parliament demanded that elections in districts where violations were found, be declared null and void. (No official results of the Crimean elections had been released by this time.) The national Prosecutor-General and Matviyenko (in his role as deputy head of the presidential secretariat, to which he had been appointed in November 2005) also became involved in the investigation of the alleged irregularities. The results of the elections were finally announced on 19 April. The For Yanukovych bloc (principally comprising the Party of the Regions) obtained the largest proportion of the votes cast, with 32.6%; it was awarded 44 of the 100 seats in the Supreme Council. The second-placed party was the pro-Russian Union party, with 7.6% of the votes and 10 seats. The Kunitsyn bloc obtained 10 seats, the CPU nine, the People's Movement of Ukraine-Rukh and the YuTB each obtained eight seats, the Nataliya Vitrenko People's Opposition bloc obtained seven seats, and the 'Ne Tak' Opposition bloc (which comprised several centrist parties associated with allies of former President Kuchma, most notably the SDPU—U) obtained four.

In late May 2006 the proposed staging of military exercises off the coast of Crimea, under the aegis of NATO and with the participation of the defence forces of 12 countries, were a focus for protests in the port of Feodosiya, in the east of Crimea, principally by Russian nationalists opposed to Ukrainian involvement with NATO. It was also reported that the local branches of the CPU and the PR supported the protests. Although similar exercises had taken place in the region on an annual basis since 1997, on each occasion, in accordance with the national Constitution, they had required the specific approval of the Verkhovna Rada. As the outgoing Verkhovna Rada had failed to vote to approve the exercises on three occasions, and the prolonged coalition negotiations following the elections to that body on 26 March had prevented the new legislature from convening, it became apparent that the forthcoming exercises had no legal standing. In early June the Crimean Supreme Council was reported to have voted to approve a statement declaring the peninsula a 'NATO-free territory'. (Some reports suggested, however, that this vote had not been taken within a formal parliamentary session, and, in any case, the statement had no constitutional meaning.) On 11 June some 200 US reserve troops began to leave Crimea, having been prevented from undertaking the construction work for which they had been contracted, and the proposed exercises were abandoned. Meanwhile, there were heightened ethnic tensions on the peninsula during 2006, mostly relating to questions of land ownership. In the first half of the year clashes broke out on several occasions in protest at the operations of a market located on a traditional Crimean Tatar burial site. (The market was moved to a new location later in the year.) In late December the Crimean branch of the CPU organized a 'people's referendum' on the peninsula (which was not, however, recognized as having any official status) on Ukraine's aspirations towards NATO membership. According to the results of the poll issued by the CPU, some 58% of eligible voters participated in the 'referendum', of whom almost 99% rejected the notion of Ukrainian accession to NATO.

Following the dissolution of the Verkhovna Rada and scheduling of pre-term elections for 30 September 2007, it was announced in July that Kunitsyn was again to head the pro-presidential coalition, reconstituted as Our Ukraine-People's Self-defence bloc, in Crimea. A number of electoral irregularities were reported in the Republic on 30 September; at the elections to the Verkhovna Rada, Yanukovych's PR secured some 61.0% of votes cast in the Republic, followed by the Our Ukraine-People's Self-defence bloc, with only 8.2%, the CPU, with 7.6%, and the YuTB, with about 6.9%. Following the elections, a temporary ban on demonstrations was ended by the Crimean authorities; in mid-October some 2,000 Crimean Tatars demonstrated in Simferopol to demand land for resettlement, and a further series of protests was planned.

Russia's military operation in Georgia in early August 2008, staged with the stated aim of seeking to protect those to whom it had recently granted citizenship in South Ossetia, and recognition of the separatist regimes in South Ossetia and Abkhazia on 26 August increased domestic and international fears of a similar conflict eventually breaking out in Crimea (particularly in view of Ukraine's aspirations towards eventual NATO membership). In early September the Ukrainian Government expressed concern that Russian passports had been issued to (ethnically Russian) residents of Crimea, and accused Russia of encouraging instability. The Ukrainian authorities formally protested to the Russian consulate in Sevastopol; however, the Representative of the President of Ukraine in Crimea, Leonid Zhunko, denied that a large-scale issuance of Russian passports had been conducted. On 17 September 2008 the Crimean legislature, the Supreme Council, approved an appeal to the Ukrainian Verkhovna Rada for the recognition of the independence of Abkhazia and South Ossetia, while pro-Russian groups demonstrated outside the parliamentary building in support of the separatist authorities in those territories.

Following the collapse of the USSR in 1991, the Ukrainian leadership was notably reluctant to sign any union agreement with the other former Soviet republics that might compromise its declaration of independence. It was this reluctance to enter into a renewed political union that led to the establishment of the Commonwealth of Independent States (CIS, see p. 225) by President Kravchuk, and the leaders of Russia and Belarus, on 8 December. Although relations with Russia, as Ukraine's major trading partner and a country with close ethnic, historic, cultural and familial links with Ukraine, remained generally good following independence, tensions existed between those who sought to renew closer relations with Russia and countries of 'Eurasia', and those who sought to emphasize Ukraine's independence and 'European' status. Ukraine agreed to a unified command for the strategic (principally nuclear-armed) forces of the former USSR, but began to establish its own conventional armed forces. In January 1994 a trilateral agreement on the removal of nuclear weapons from Ukraine was signed by Ukraine, Russia and the USA, and in November the Verkhovna Rada voted to ratify the Treaty on the Non-Proliferation of Nuclear Weapons (see p. 113). In December Kuchma formally signed the Treaty, and the Strategic Arms' Reduction Treaty (START) I entered into force. The transfer to Russia of Ukraine's nuclear weapons was completed by June 1996.

Throughout the 1990s Ukraine consistently refused to participate in organizations that it perceived as being dominated by Russia, although it became an associate member of the CIS Air Defence Agreement in 1995. In 1997 Ukraine initiated the establishment of the GUAM (Georgia-Ukraine-Azerbaijan-Moldova) grouping. In 2001 a permanent office of the grouping (known as GUUAM in 1999–2005, when Uzbekistan was also a member) was opened in Yalta, Crimea. In 2006, at a summit held in Kyiv, the grouping was formally inaugurated as a full international organization concerned with the promotion of democracy, energy security and strengthening relations; it was also redesignated as the Organization for Democracy and Economic Development—GUAM (see p. 440). As the Kuchma administration became increasingly isolated internationally in the early 2000s, particularly in response to allegations that it had illegally sold military equipment to the Iraqi regime of Saddam Hussain, Ukraine's relationship with Russia appeared to strengthen. In January 2003 Kuchma was elected as Chairman of the CIS, becoming the first non-Russian to hold that post. (He was, however, replaced by Russian President Vladimir Putin in 2004.) Later in 2003 proposals to form a 'single economic zone' with Belarus, Kazakhstan and Russia became increasingly popular, and were approved by the Verkhovna Rada in September, on the condition that participation did not contravene the Ukrainian Constitution, although interest in Ukraine's participation in such a zone waned following the election of Yushchenko as President in late 2004. In August 2005 Yushchenko and President Mikheil Saakashvili of Georgia, meeting in Borjomi, Georgia, signed the Borjomi Declaration, on the creation of a new Community of Democratic Choice, an alliance that intended to remove divisions and resolve conflicts in the Baltic, Black Sea and Caspian regions. The new, nine-country grouping was officially launched in December, at a meeting in Kyiv.

The principal controversy between Ukraine and Russia concerned ownership of the former Soviet Black Sea Fleet, based in Sevastopol, on the Crimean peninsula. Although both countries agreed in July 1992 to exercise joint control over the fleet for a transitional period of three years, in April 1995 the Russian parliament imposed a moratorium on plans to divide the fleet. Nevertheless, in June Russian President Boris Yeltsin and Kuchma agreed to the equal division of the fleet, with separate Ukrainian and Russian bases. The main Russian base was to be at Sevastopol, although the exact legal status of the city was left unresolved. Yeltsin and Kuchma signed an agreement on 31 May 1997, in accordance with which the Russian fleet was to lease three bays in Sevastopol for 20 years, while the Ukrainian fleet was to use the remainder. Upon expiry, the treaty could be renewed for five years, but would then be subject to renegotiation. A bilateral Treaty of Friendship, Co-operation and Partnership was also signed, in which, significantly, Russia for the first time recognized the sovereignty of Ukraine. Russia finally ratified the treaty in February 1999, and in June of that year and in March 2000 further agreements were signed between Russia and Ukraine pertaining to the fleet and the operations and services of jointly used facilities. In January 2003 a treaty delineating the land boundary between Russia and Ukraine (which remained largely unmarked and unregulated) was signed by Kuchma and President Vladimir Putin of Russia, although discussions on the status of the Sea of Azov, which lies between the two countries, remained unresolved. Work on the construction of a Russian dam in the Sea precipitated considerable controversy, and raised concerns that the territorial integrity of Ukraine was being violated. In December Presidents Kuchma and Putin signed an agreement on the use of the Sea of Azov, the entirety of which was defined as comprising the internal waters of both countries. Agreement was also reached on the maritime state boundary of Russia and Ukraine in the region.

The Ukrainian presidential election of 2004 caused considerable upheaval in diplomatic relations with Russia. During the course of the campaign, the Russian Government was accused by the Ukrainian opposition and external commentators of interference in favour of Yanukovych; notably, President Putin visited Ukraine before each round of voting to appear publicly with Yanukovych and Kuchma, and telephoned Yanukovych to congratulate him on his apparent victory after the second round before the official (and subsequently annulled) results had been announced. Some US $300m. were reported to have been donated to the Yanukovych campaign by the Russian authorities, and Putin described the demonstrations that resulted in the election being re-run as constitutionally illegitimate. Symbolically, and in accordance with promises made during his election campaign, President Yushchenko visited Moscow one day after his inauguration in January 2005, and emphasized the importance of maintaining co-operative relations with Russia. However, further diplomatic tension was caused by the appointment of Tymoshenko as Prime Minister in February, in part as a result of a warrant existing in Russia for her arrest on charges of the attempted bribery of Russian officials during her time as head of a Ukrainian natural gas trading company in the 1990s. In late 2005 the Russian state-controlled gas monopoly, Gazprom, issued demands that Ukraine pay market prices for the supply of natural gas, rather than the heavily subsidized rate (of $50 per 1,000 cu m) that it had paid hitherto. Following the failure of the Ukrainian authorities and Gazprom to reach agreement, on 1 January 2006 Gazprom suspended supplies to Ukraine, a measure that caused considerable hardship in Ukraine, as well as resulting in the loss of supplies to other European countries that received gas from pipelines traversing Ukraine. On 4 January supplies of natural gas to Ukraine were restored, after Ukraine agreed to pay $95 per 1,000 cu m for a mixture of Russian and Turkmenistani natural gas, which was to be supplied to Ukraine by a Swiss-registered company, RosUkrEnergo. This agreement was to be subject to renegotiation after six months.

The appointment of Yanukovych as Prime Minister in August 2006 facilitated an improvement in relations between Ukraine and Russia: on 15 August Yanukovych met Prime Minister Mikhail Fradkov of Russia at the Black Sea port of Sochi, and on 22 December President Putin visited Ukraine for the first time since Yushchenko's election. However, as a counterpoint to Ukraine's close economic ties with Russia, particularly with regard to gas supplies, in March 2007 Yushchenko and President Lech Kaczyński of Poland announced their intention to stage a summit in May, also involving Azerbaijan, Georgia and Kazakhstan, to discuss the extension of the Odesa–Brody pipeline as part of a wider initiative to reduce both Ukrainian and Polish reliance on Russian fuel imports. On 3 October Gazprom threatened again to suspend natural gas supplies to Ukraine, on the grounds that it was owed US $1,300m.; on 9 October, however, it was announced that a compromise agreement had been reached, whereby Ukraine was to repay $1,200m. by transferring gas from underground storage facilities in Ukraine to Gazprom for further export. Tymoshenko, who had recently returned to the office of Prime Minister, strenuously criticized an agreement reached between Russia and Ukraine, which retained the intermediary trading company in gas supplies to Ukraine, the Swiss-registered RosUkrEnergo. Meanwhile, Russia strongly criticized Ukraine's formal request for NATO membership (see below). Putin subsequently warned that, in the event that Ukraine joined NATO and agreed to the deployment on its territory of elements of the planned US national missile defence system, Russia would be prepared to target its missiles at Ukraine. In February 2008 Gazprom warned that it would reduce supplies to Ukraine, in response to debts incurred during the previous month; it was subsequently announced that Ukraine and Russia had reached a debt settlement, and also agreed to discontinue use of RosUkrEnergo as an intermediary. Later in February, however, Gazprom claimed that Ukraine had failed to sign the negotiated agreements. After further discussions, in April the Ukrainian Government announced that agreement had been reached on a new payment scheme; at the insistence of the Russian authorities, RosUkrEnergo was to remain the intermediary company, operating within Russia.

Following Russia's military operation against Georgia in early August 2008, Yushchenko, together with the Presidents of Estonia, Lithuania and Poland, and the Prime Minister of Latvia, visited Georgia in a demonstration of solidarity, where he attended a rally in support of President Saakashvili in Tbilisi, the Georgian capital. On 13 August Yushchenko issued a ruling, based on a resolution by the National Security and Defence Council, requiring Russia to request prior permission for movements of its Black Sea Fleet based at Sevastopol (after Russian vessels belonging to the Fleet participated in the conflict), and subsequently indicated that the Ukrainian authorities wished to increase the amount charged to Russia for the lease of the Black Sea naval base. Later in August he officially ended a bilateral agreement reached in 1992 (which had been abrogated by Russia in February) on Russian use of two Ukrainian radar stations, and offered to make them available to European nations.

In December 2008 a further dispute erupted with Russia, after Gazprom demanded some US $2,100m. owed by Ukraine for the non-payment of natural gas and incurred fines; although Ukrainian state utility Naftogaz Ukrainy announced at the end of that month that it was to pay $1,500m., continuing disagreement over the price Ukraine would pay for Russian gas and the level of transit fees to be paid by Gazprom during 2009 resulted in Russia's suspension of gas supplies to Ukraine on 1 January. After accusing Ukraine of abstracting gas intended for export to Europe flowing through Russian-owned pipelines in Ukraine, Russia also halted supplies to Europe by way of Ukraine on 7 January (resulting in severe disruptions to supplies to some 18 European countries during a period of extremely cold weather). Following intensive EU mediation and emergency discussions between Gazprom and Naftogaz, on 19 January Putin (as Russian premier) and Tymoshenko signed an agreement in Moscow

UKRAINE

whereby Ukraine would pay an average price for Russian gas in 2009 that would be 20% lower than that charged to European countries, while the transit price would remain unchanged (with both converging to market levels in 2010). Gas supplies to Europe by way of Ukraine were finally restored on 21 January. Following further discussions between Putin and Tymoshenko in Moscow at the end of April, it was agreed that Gazprom would not penalize Ukraine for failure to accept the contracted amount of gas in 2009 and would assist in payment of the transit fee to ensure supply, while Russia was invited to participate in an EU-supported programme to modernize Ukraine's gas transportation system (which had been announced in March).

Ukraine sought to counterbalance its close relations with Russia by a policy of engagement with Western nations and organizations, as part of what was termed a 'multi-vector' foreign policy. In 1994 Ukraine joined NATO's 'Partnership for Peace' (see p. 353) programme; a 'Charter on a Distinctive Relationship' was signed with the Organization in 1997, envisaging enhanced co-operation with the Alliance. In April 1999, in protest at NATO air-strikes against Yugoslavia (Serbia and Montenegro), the Verkhovna Rada voted to withdraw from the 'Partnership for Peace' programme; Ukraine rejoined the programme when the conflict ended in June.

Following pressure from the USA, in 1998 Ukraine cancelled an agreement to supply turbines to Bushehr nuclear power station in Iran. The USA, in return, pledged to allocate additional investment to the development of Ukraine's energy sector. In March 2000 the USA, one of the major aid donors to Ukraine in the mid-1990s, became concerned about allegations that Ukraine had misused IMF funds, and demanded a full audit of the central bank before any more assistance would be forthcoming. During a visit to Ukraine in June, US President Bill Clinton pledged aid towards the decommissioning of the Chornobyl reactor, which was closed in December. Relations with the USA deteriorated somewhat during 2002, following allegations that Ukraine, with the complicity of President Kuchma, had transferred military equipment to Iraq. In October a joint British-US inquiry failed to determine the veracity of the allegations, which the Ukrainian Government continued to deny. However, in March 2003, following the commencement of US-led military action in Iraq, Ukraine agreed to a request by the USA to dispatch an anti-nuclear, anti-biological and anti-chemical warfare unit, comprising 448 troops, to Kuwait. The Verkhovna Rada approved this measure in mid-March, although it also approved a motion condemning the US-led intervention. In June the Verkhovna Rada approved proposals to dispatch up to 1,800 troops to serve in the Polish-administered stabilization zone in southern Iraq; some 1,650 Ukrainian troops entered service in the zone from September. The participation of Ukrainian forces in Iraq appeared to lead to an improvement in relations with the USA, and in October Prime Minister Viktor Yanukovych visited Washington, DC, and met Vice-President Richard B. Cheney and Secretary of State Colin Powell. Yushchenko's inauguration as President was widely expected to lead to an improvement in US-Ukrainian relations, and the 'orange revolution' that had brought Yushchenko to power was generally regarded favourably in the USA. In early April 2005 Yushchenko visited the USA, meeting President George W. Bush and addressing the US Senate. Relations with the USA did not appear to be affected negatively by Yushchenko's approval, later that month, of a decree authorizing the withdrawal of Ukrainian peace-keeping troops from Iraq by the end of the year, as had been approved by the Verkhovna Rada in the previous year. In September 2007 the Ukraine authorities signed a US $505m. contract with a French company for the construction of a steel covering to protect the damaged concrete encasing the decommissioned Chornobyl nuclear reactor.

Ukraine signed a trade agreement with the EU in June 1995, and was formally admitted to the Council of Europe (see p. 236) in November. The Ukrainian leadership had long expressed an intention to pursue full membership of the EU; however, the failure to abolish capital punishment (which is prohibited by the conditions of membership of the organization) before March 2000 was a source of tension, as was the slow pace of political and economic reform and, in particular, concerns that President Kuchma may have been implicated in the murder of investigative journalist Heorhiy Gongadze in 2000. President Yushchenko, who was elected in late 2004, emphasized in his earliest diplomatic pronouncements that he regarded the integration of Ukraine into both the EU and NATO as fundamental goals of his presidency. However, the return of Yanukovych as Prime Minister in August 2006 delayed Ukraine's attempts to enter into a Membership Action Plan with NATO, which the USA was apparently eager to support. This trend was affirmed by remarks made by Yanukovych in September, at a meeting of NATO representatives in Brussels, Belgium, to the effect that Ukraine was not ready to join NATO. Yanukovych's remarks were disowned by Yushchenko and the Minister of Defence, Anatoliy Hrytsenko, and furthermore were regarded as a breach of both the Universal covenant and national Constitution (which states that the President is responsible for foreign policy). In 2007–08 Ukraine was due to complete a 10-year Partnership and Co-operation Agreement (PCA) with the EU. The PCA was then expected to be replaced by an Enhanced Agreement that would, however, not include a provision for future membership. Ukraine's membership application to the World Trade Organization (WTO, see p. 410), submitted in 1993, was formally approved on 5 February 2008, and was ratified by the legislature in April. Ukraine's accession to the WTO was expected to allow discussions on a free-trade agreement with the EU to proceed. In January 2008 the Ukraine Government formally requested a NATO Membership Action Plan (MAP), which was regarded as preparatory to membership. (Opposition parties, notably the PR and the CPU, strongly criticized Ukraine's request for NATO membership.) At a NATO summit meeting, which was convened in Bucharest, Romania, on 2 April, Ukraine and Georgia were not offered a MAP, although the Alliance made clear that it welcomed a closer relationship with both countries and would consider offering a MAP to each of them in due course; Russia's permanent representative to NATO had criticized US support for the aspirations towards NATO accession of those countries. Following Russia's military action in Georgia in early August, an EU summit meeting on Ukraine, which was conducted in Paris, France, on 9 September, resulted in an offer of an Association Agreement, providing for trade benefits and increased energy co-operation (although no pledge of Ukraine's future membership of the Union was issued); negotiations on visa-free entry to EU states for Ukrainian citizens began in late October.

Government

Executive power is vested in the President and the Prime Minister, and legislative power is the prerogative of the 450-member Verkhovna Rada (Supreme Council), which is directly elected for a four-year term. The President is elected by direct, popular vote for a five-year term. Prior to constitutional amendments agreed in late 2004, the President appointed the Prime Minister and the members of the Cabinet of Ministers. However, with effect from 2006 several presidential powers of appointment were transferred to the Prime Minister, who is elected by the Verkhovna Rada. The President retains the right to appoint certain principal ministers, and, in certain circumstances, to dissolve the legislature. Ukraine is a unitary state, divided for administrative purposes into 24 oblasts (regions), one autonomous republic (Crimea), and two metropolitan areas (Kyiv and Sevastopol). The Constitution guarantees local self-government to regions, cities, settlements and villages. Regional governors are appointed by the President.

Defence

In December 1991 the Verkhovna Rada adopted legislation establishing independent Ukrainian armed forces. As assessed at November 2008, there were 129,925 active personnel in the Ukrainian armed forces, including 70,753 ground forces, 45,240 in the air force, and 13,932 (including conscripts) in the navy. There were also paramilitary forces, comprising 45,000 in the Border Guard and an estimated 39,900 serving under the Ministry of Internal Affairs. In addition, some 9,500 were serving in civil defence troops. There were, additionally, some 1m. reserves. Military service is compulsory for males over 18 years of age, for a period of 12 months in the ground forces and air forces, and 18 months in the navy. The 2008 budget allocated an estimated 15,900m. hryvnyas to defence.

Economic Affairs

In 2007, according to the World Bank, Ukraine's gross national income (GNI), measured at average 2005–07 prices, was US $118,445m., equivalent to $2,550 per head (or $6,810 per head, on an international purchasing-power parity basis). During 2000–07 gross domestic product (GDP) per head increased, in real terms, at an average annual rate of 7.6% per year, while the population decreased by an average annual rate of 0.8%. Ukraine's GDP increased, in real terms, by an annual average rate of 7.6% in 2000–07. Real GDP increased by 7.3% in 2007.

Agriculture (including forestry and fishing) contributed 7.2% of GDP and provided 16.7% of employment in 2007. Ukraine has large areas of extremely fertile land, forming part of the 'black earth' belt, and the country is self-sufficient in almost all aspects of agricultural production. The principal crops are grain, potatoes, sugar beet and other vegetables. A programme to transfer state collective farms to private ownership was initiated in 1991, although by 1997 only 14% of land was managed by private farms, which in that year private farms contributed some 46% of total agricultural output. During 2000–07, according to the World Bank, agricultural GDP increased by an annual average of 2.8%, in real terms. In 2007 the GDP of the sector decreased by 0.8%.

Industry (including mining, manufacturing, construction and power) contributed an estimated 34.8% of GDP and provided 23.9% of employment in 2007. Heavy industry dominates the sector, particularly metal-working, mechanical engineering, chemicals and machinery products. According to the World Bank, industrial GDP increased by an average of 6.9% annually, in real terms, in 2000–07. Real industrial GDP increased by 8.8% in 2007.

In 2003 some 3.7% of the work-force were engaged in mining and quarrying; the sector contributed 4.8% of GDP in 2007. Ukraine has large deposits of coal (mainly in the huge Donbass coal basin) and high-grade iron ore, and there are also significant reserves of manganese, titanium, graphite, natural gas and petroleum. Production of coal declined by some 53% in 1989–95, and in 1996 the Government implemented a major reorganization of the coal-mining industry, including the closure of several loss-making mines.

The manufacturing sector provided 17.6% of employment in 2003 and contributed 21.8% of GDP in 2007. During 2000–07 real manufacturing GDP increased by an average annual rate of 9.9%. The GDP of the sector increased by 6.0% in 2007.

Ukraine is highly dependent on imports of energy products, of which Russia and Turkmenistan are the principal suppliers. Imports of mineral fuels comprised 29.7% of the value of total imports in 2008. Ukraine is also vitally important as an energy transit country, situated as it is between the mineral resource-rich countries of the former USSR and the developed economies of Europe. A pipeline from a new oil terminal at Odesa, on the Black Sea coast, to Brody, near the border with Poland, which was originally intended to carry petroleum from the Caspian Sea to central and western Europe, was completed in 2001; however, following Ukraine's failure to secure petroleum suppliers from the Caspian region, the pipeline entered operation in reverse direction, permitting Russian companies to pump their petroleum to the Black Sea for export. Two new nuclear reactors began energy production in 2004. In 2005 nuclear power accounted for 47.7% of Ukraine's electricity production; coal accounted for 26.7% and natural gas for 18.7%.

The services sector contributed 57.9% of GDP and engaged 59.4% of the employed labour force in 2007. During 2000–07 the real GDP of the sector increased by an average annual rate of 7.4%. The GDP of the sector increased by 9.2% in 2007. A significant event for the development of the tourist sector in Ukraine was the announcement, in April 2007, that the country was to co-host, with Poland, the 2012 football European Championship finals, although by mid-2009 doubts about the progress of various infrastructure projects in Ukraine meant that it appeared that the country was to play a less prominent role in the championship than had initially been envisaged.

In 2007 Ukraine recorded a trade deficit of US $10,572m., while there was a deficit of $5,272m. on the current account of the balance of payments. In 2007 the principal market for exports were Russia (accounting for 23.5% of total exports). Russia was also the principal source of imports in that year, providing 22.7% of all imports. Other significant suppliers of imports were Germany, Turkmenistan, the People's Republic of China and Poland. The principal exports in 2008 were base metals (some 41.2% of the total, comprising principally iron and steel), mineral products, chemical products, and machinery, mechanical and electrical equipment. The principal imports in that year were mineral products (which accounted for 29.7% of total imports), machinery, mechanical and electrical equipment, vegetable products, chemical products and vehicles and transportation equipment.

In 2007 a budgetary surplus of 11,099m. hryvnyas was recorded, equivalent to 1.5% of GDP. Ukraine's total external debt was US $49,887m. at the end of 2006, of which $9,538m. was long-term public debt. In that year the cost of debt-servicing was equivalent to 18.1% of the value of exports of goods and services. In 1996–2006 the average annual inflation rate was 12.4%. According to official figures, consumer prices increased by 16.6% in 2007 and by 22.3% in 2008. Some 6.4% of the labour force were unemployed in 2008.

Ukraine became a member of the IMF and the World Bank in 1992. It also joined the European Bank for Reconstruction and Development (EBRD, see p. 251) as a 'Country of Operations'. In June 1994 Ukraine signed an agreement of partnership and co-operation with the European Union (EU, see p. 255), which was ratified in 1998. An interim trade accord was signed with the EU in June 1995. Ukraine is a member of the Organization of the Black Sea Economic Co-operation (see p. 380), and acceded to the World Trade Organization (see p. 410) in 2008.

The economy showed significant signs of improvement from 2000, when GDP registered positive growth for the first time since the USSR's collapse. Although it had been anticipated that the administration of President Viktor Yushchenko (installed in January 2005) would implement economic reform and undertake extensive measures to combat corruption, in practice such efforts were frequently impeded by internal policy and personnel disputes. Ukraine's reliance on imported energy supplies, principally from Russia, and its economy's overdependence on steel exports, demonstrated the country's vulnerability to external shocks. These factors, along with a rapid growth in exposure to credit and increases in wage payments in the mid-2000s, were among the principal reasons that the country was one of those to be most severely affected by the international financial crisis from late 2008. In October of that year the IMF announced plans to lend some US $16,500m. to Ukraine under a two-year emergency stand-by arrangement to help restore financial stability, in particular with regard to the current account of the balance of payments and through the recapitalization of a number of banks. The loan was to be subject to the fulfilment of a number of budgetary and supervisory measures, including the achievement of a budget deficit in 2008 of no more than 1% of GDP, and of a balanced budget in 2009; notably, social expenditure was to increase in 2009. However, by April 2009 the continued economic downturn meant that, with the agreement of the IMF, the Government had issued a revised commitment to a budgetary deficit of no more than 4% of GDP for that year. Meanwhile, substantial increases in the payments demanded (by some 40% in 2007 alone) for the supply of Russian and Turkmenistani natural gas had a detrimental effect on the Ukrainian economy from 2006. Moreover, a dispute with the Russian state-controlled company Gazprom over the non-payment for gas supplies and associated fines, and over the rate of transit fees charged by Ukraine, resulted in the suspension of gas supplies to Ukraine (and thence onwards to some 18 European countries) for some 20 days in January 2009 (supplies had previously been suspended for similar reasons in January 2006, precipitating a vote of no confidence in the Ukrainian Government). It was subsequently agreed that the prices for both gas purchases charged to Ukraine by Gazprom, and the transit fees charged by Ukraine to Gazprom, would reach market levels in 2010. Meanwhile, it was reported in January 2009 that, on a year-on-year basis, GDP had declined by an annual rate of 20%, while the annual rate of inflation recorded in that month was 22.3%; the value of steel exports (the market price for which had dropped steeply) was reported to have declined by as much as one-third in the first quarter of 2009, compared with the same period in the previous year, although the depreciation of the national currency, the hryvyna, led to a slight upturn in exports in February of that year. By mid-May 2009 GDP was forecast to decline by more than 8% during that year.

Education

After Ukrainian was decreed the state language in 1990, policies were adopted to ensure that all pupils were granted the opportunity of tuition in Ukrainian. In 2001 there was also tuition in Russian, as well as in Romanian, Hungarian, Moldovan, Crimean Tatar and Polish. In the early 1990s there were significant changes to the curriculum, with a greater emphasis on Ukrainian history and literature. Some religious and private educational institutions were established in the early 1990s. Education is officially compulsory between seven and 15 years of age. Primary education begins at seven years of age and lasts for four years. Secondary education, beginning at 11, lasts for a maximum of seven years, comprising a first cycle of five years and a second of two years. In 2007/08 there were 15,300 pre-primary educational establishments in Ukraine (although 1,400 of these had their operations suspended), which provided for 1,137,000 students. In 2008/09 a total of 4,617,000 students attended 21,000 primary and general secondary institutions. An

UKRAINE

additional 454,400 students attended 1,022 vocational secondary educational institutions. In 2005/06 some 90% of children in the relevant age-group were enrolled in primary education, while enrolment at secondary level included 83.8% of children in the relevant age-group. In 2007/08 there were 2,813,800 students enrolled in higher education. Government expenditure on education in 2007 was 43,697m. hryvnyas (14.0% of total budgetary expenditure).

Public Holidays

2009: 1 January (New Year), 7 January (Orthodox Christmas), 8 March (International Women's Day), 20 April (Orthodox Easter Monday), 1 May (Labour Day), 9 May (Victory Day), 8 June (Pentecost Monday), 28 June (Constitution Day), 24 August (Independence Day).

2010: 1 January (New Year), 7 January (Orthodox Christmas), 8 March (International Women's Day), 5 April (Orthodox Easter Monday), 1 May (Labour Day), 9 May (Victory Day), 24 May (Pentecost Monday), 28 June (Constitution Day), 24 August (Independence Day).

Weights and Measures

The metric system is in force.

Statistical Survey

Principal source (unless otherwise stated): State Committee for Statistics, 01023 Kyiv, vul. Sh. Rustaveli 3; tel. (44) 226-20-21; fax (44) 235-37-39; e-mail info@ukrstat.gov.ua; internet www.ukrstat.gov.ua.

Area and Population

AREA, POPULATION AND DENSITY

Area (sq km)	603,700*
Population (census results)	
12 January 1989	51,706,742
5 December 2001	
Males	22,441,344
Females	26,015,758
Total	48,457,102
Population (official estimates at 1 January, rounded)	
2007	46,646,000
2008	46,372,700
2009	46,143,700
Density (per sq km) at 1 January 2009	76.4

* 233,090 sq miles.

POPULATION BY ETHNIC GROUP
(permanent inhabitants, census of 5 December 2001)

	'000	%
Ukrainian	37,541.7	78.13
Russian	8,334.1	17.34
Belarusian	275.8	0.57
Moldovan	258.6	0.54
Crimean Tatar	248.2	0.52
Others	1,393.9	2.90
Total	**48,052.3**	**100.00**

ADMINISTRATIVE DIVISIONS

	Area ('000 sq km)	Population (at 1 January 2009)*	Density (per sq km)
Regions			
Cherkasy	20.9	1,304,300	62.4
Chernihiv	31.9	1,121,300	35.2
Chernivtsi	8.1	904,100	111.6
Dnipropetrovsk	31.9	3,374,200	105.8
Donetsk	26.5	4,500,500	169.8
Ivano-Frankivsk	13.9	1,381,100	99.4
Kharkiv	31.4	2,782,400	88.6
Kherson	28.5	1,099,200	38.6
Khmelnytsky	20.6	1,341,400	65.1
Kirovohrad	24.6	1,027,000	41.8
Kyiv	28.1	1,727,800	61.5
Luhansk	26.7	2,331,800	87.3
Lviv	21.8	2,552,900	117.1
Mykolayiv	24.6	1,195,800	48.6
Odesa	33.3	2,392,200	71.8
Poltava	28.8	1,511,400	52.5
Rivne	20.1	1,151,000	57.3
Sumy	23.8	1,184,000	49.8
Ternopil	13.8	1,093,300	79.2
Transcarpathia	12.8	1,243,300	97.1
—continued	Area ('000 sq km)	Population (at 1 January 2009)*	Density (per sq km)
Vinnytsia	26.5	1,660,000	62.6
Volyn	20.2	1,036,200	51.3
Zaporizhzhya	27.2	1,821,300	67.0
Zhytomyr	29.9	1,294,200	43.3
Cities			
Kyiv	0.8	2,765,500	3,456.9
Sevastopol	0.9	380,100	422.3
Autonomous Republic			
Crimea	26.1	1,967,300	75.4
Total	**603.7**	**46,143,700**	**76.4**

* Official estimates, rounded.

PRINCIPAL TOWNS
(population at census of 5 December 2001, rounded figures)

Kyiv (Kiev, capital)	2,611,000	Poltava	318,000
Kharkiv	1,470,000	Chernihiv	305,000
Dnipropetrovsk	1,065,000	Cherkasy	295,000
Odesa	1,029,000	Sumy	293,000
Donetsk	1,016,000	Horlivka	292,000
Zaporizhzhya	815,000	Zhytomyr	284,000
Lviv	733,000	Dniprodzerzhynsk	256,000
Kryvyi Rih	669,000	Khmelnytsky	254,000
Mykolayiv	514,000	Kirovohrad	254,000
Mariupol*	492,000	Rivne	249,000
Luhansk†	463,000	Chernivtsi	241,000
Makiyivka	390,000	Kremenchuk	234,000
Vinnytsia	357,000	Ternopil	228,000
Simferopol	344,000	Ivano-Frankivsk	218,000
Sevastopol	342,000	Lutsk	209,000
Kherson	328,000	Bila Tserkva	200,000

* Known as Zhdanov from 1948 to 1989.
† Known as Voroshylovhrad from 1935 to 1958 and from 1970 to 1989.

BIRTHS, MARRIAGES AND DEATHS*

	Registered live births		Registered marriages		Registered deaths	
	Number	Rate (per 1,000)	Number	Rate (per 1,000)	Number	Rate (per 1,000)
2001	376,479	7.8	309,602	6.4	745,953	15.4
2002	390,687	8.1	317,228	6.6	754,911	15.7
2003	408,591	8.5	370,966	7.8	765,408	16.0
2004	427,259	9.0	278,230	5.9	761,263	16.0
2005	426,085	9.0	332,138	7.1	781,964	16.6
2006	460,368	9.8	354,959	7.6	758,093	16.2
2007	472,657	10.2	416,427	9.0	762,877	16.4
2008	510,588	11.0	321,992	7.0	754,462	16.3

* Rates for 1997–2000 are based on unrevised population estimates.

Life expectancy (years at birth, WHO estimates): 67.2 (males 61.5; females 73.1) in 2006 (Source: WHO, *World Health Statistics*).

UKRAINE

Statistical Survey

IMMIGRATION AND EMIGRATION

	2006	2007	2008
Immigrants	44,227	46,507	37,281
Emigrants	29,982	29,669	22,402

ECONOMICALLY ACTIVE POPULATION
(annual averages, '000 persons aged 15–70 years)

	2005	2006	2007
Agriculture, hunting, forestry and fishing	4,005.5	3,649.1	3,484.5
Mining and quarrying; manufacturing; electricity, gas and water supply	4,072.4	4,036.9	3,973.0
Construction	941.5	987.1	1,030.2
Wholesale and retail trade; repair of motor vehicles, motorcycles and personal and household goods; hotels and restaurants	4,175.2	4,406.9	4,564.4
Transport, storage and communications	1,400.5	1,428.8	1,451.9
Financial intermediation	247.9	286.0	344.4
Real estate, renting and business activities	966.6	1,041.9	1,134.7
Public administration and defence; compulsory social security	1,028.9	1,033.7	1,036.4
Education	1,668.2	1,690.5	1,693.7
Health and social work	1,356.6	1,356.7	1,359.0
Other community, social and personal service activities; private households with employed persons; extra-territorial organizations and bodies	816.7	812.8	832.5
Total employed	20,680.0	20,730.4	20,904.7
Total unemployed	1,600.8	1,515.0	1,417.6
Total labour force	22,280.8	22,245.4	22,322.3

Source: ILO.

2008 (annual averages, '000 persons aged 15–70 years): Total employed 20,972.3; Total unemployed 1,425.1; Total labour force 22,397.4.

Health and Welfare

KEY INDICATORS

Total fertility rate (children per woman, 2006)	1.2
Under-5 mortality rate (per 1,000 live births, 2006)	24
HIV/AIDS (% of persons aged 15–49, 2007)	1.6
Physicians (per 1,000 head, 2006)	3.1
Hospital beds (per 1,000 head, 2006)	8.7
Health expenditure (2006): US $ per head (PPP)	542
Health expenditure (2006): % of GDP	7.0
Health expenditure (2006): public (% of total)	55.0
Access to water (% of persons, 2006)	97
Access to sanitation (% of persons, 2006)	93
Human Development Index (2006): ranking	82
Human Development Index (2006): value	0.786

For sources and definitions, see explanatory note on p. vi.

Agriculture

PRINCIPAL CROPS
('000 metric tons)

	2005	2006	2007
Wheat	18,699.2	13,947.3	13,800.0*
Barley	8,975.1	11,341.2	6,000.0*
Maize	7,166.6	6,425.6	6,700.0*
Rye	1,054.2	583.6	550.0*
Oats	790.7	690.2	600.0*
Millet	140.6	123.5	75.0*
Buckwheat	274.7	229.2	160.0*
Potatoes	19,462.4	19,467.1	19,102.3
Sugar beet	15,467.8	22,420.7	16,978.0
Peas, dry	616.0	652.7	411.0
Sunflower seed	4,706.1	5,324.3	4,173.7
Cabbages and other brassicas	1,475.4	1,490.6	1,300.0†
Tomatoes	1,471.8	1,751.0	1,520.0†
Pumpkins, squash and gourds	585.4	553.8	480.0†
Cucumbers and gherkins	687.9	890.4	775.0†
Chillies and peppers, green	131.5	145.2	125.0†
Onions, dry	751.1	868.7	755.0†
Garlic	145.6	145.6	125.0†
Carrots and turnips	645.3	719.5	625.0†
Watermelons	256.4	562.8	490.0†
Apples	719.8	536.5	707.0†
Pears	177.3	81.4	107.2†
Apricots	94.2	28.0	36.9†
Sweet cherries	100.2	48.9	64.5†
Sour (Morello) cherries	181.8	95.6	126.0†
Plums and sloes	165.9	127.1	167.0†
Grapes	442.6	300.9	415.0†

* Official estimate.
† FAO estimate.

Aggregate production ('000 metric tons, may include official, semi-official or estimated data): Total cereals 37,258 in 2005, 33,511 in 2006, 28,035 in 2007; Total roots and tubers 19,462 in 2005, 19,467 in 2006, 19,102 in 2007; Total vegetables (incl. melons) 7,295 in 2005, 8,750 in 2006, 7,605 in 2007; Total fruits (excl. melons) 2,056 in 2005, 1,319 in 2006, 1,757 in 2007.

Source: FAO.

LIVESTOCK
('000 head at 1 January)

	2005	2006	2007
Horses	591	555	534
Cattle	6,903	6,514	6,175
Pigs	6,466	7,053	8,055
Sheep	875	872	923
Goats	879	757	693
Chickens	131,976	142,600	145,600
Ducks	8,393	8,900	9,700
Geese and guinea fowls	9,348	8,100	8,900
Turkeys	2,366	1,900	2,250

Source: FAO.

LIVESTOCK PRODUCTS
('000 metric tons)

	2005	2006	2007
Cattle meat	561.8	567.5	563.0
Pig meat	493.7	526.0	650.0
Chicken meat	496.6	589.1	670.0
Cows' milk	13,423.8	13,017.1	12,300.0
Sheep's milk	24.1	22.9	21.7*
Goats' milk	266.5	247.0	230.0*
Poultry eggs	756.3	825.7	789.7
Hen eggs	748.1	815.6	779.6
Honey	71.5	75.6	80.0*

* FAO estimate.

Source: FAO.

Forestry

ROUNDWOOD REMOVALS
('000 cubic metres, excl. bark)

	2005	2006	2007
Sawlogs, veneer logs and logs for sleepers	4,632	4,891	5,337
Pulpwood	953	1,000	1,059
Other industrial wood*	876	1,016	968
Fuel wood*	8,146	8,942	9,520
Total	14,606	15,849	16,884

* Unofficial figures.
Source: FAO.

SAWNWOOD PRODUCTION
('000 cubic metres, incl. railway sleepers)

	2005	2006	2007
Coniferous (softwood)	1,743	1,771	1,817
Broadleaved (hardwood)	673	614	708
Total	2,416	2,385	2,525

Source: FAO.

Fishing

('000 metric tons, live weight)

	2004	2005	2006
Capture	202.7	244.9	238.7
Azov sea sprat	8.5	14.6	11.7
Southern hake	1.0	n.a.	830.0
Blue grenadier	6.3	n.a.	7.5
Gobies	12.4	11.7	9.9
Snoek	7.4	n.a.	9.2
Sardinellas	3.8	5.0	12.9
European pilchard (sardine)	28.1	38.0	51.5
European sprat	30.9	35.7	21.3
European anchovy	9.4	6.9	7.0
Greenback horse mackerel	22.6	n.a.	20.6
Other jack and horse mackerels	3.6	0.8	4.4
Other mackerels	5.5	0.5	6.6
Antarctic krill	12.3	22.4	15.2
Wellington flying squid	20.1	n.a.	12.9
Aquaculture	26.2*	28.7	4.0
Common carp	14.8	16.2	0.1
Silver carp	7.0*	7.5	2.4
Total catch	229.0*	273.7	242.8

* FAO estimate.
Source: FAO.

Mining

('000 metric tons, unless otherwise indicated)

	2003	2004	2005
Hard (incl. coking) coal	63,866	62,100	58,000
Brown coal (incl. lignite)	950*	3,000	3,000
Crude petroleum	3,975	4,179	4,269
Natural gas (million cu m)	19,460	19,000	19,300
Iron ore: gross weight	62,497.6	65,540.0	68,569.6
Manganese ore*†	880	810	770
Ilmenite concentrate	421	370	370
Rutile concentrate	60	60	60
Zirconium concentrates*	35.0	35.0	35.0
Uranium concentrate (metric tons)†	800	800	800
Bentonite*	300	300	300
Kaolin	225	225	225
Potash salts (crude)*‡	60	50	65
Native sulphur*	142	136	135
Salt (unrefined)*	2,757	3,339	3,400
Graphite (metric tons)*	7,500	7,500	7,500
Peat*	1,000	1,000	1,000

* Estimated production.
† Figures refer to the metal content of ores and concentrates.
‡ Figures refer to potassium oxide content.

2006 ('000 metric tons, unless otherwise indicated): Coal 61,700; Crude petroleum 3,000; Natural gas (million cu m) 20,100; Iron ore: gross weight 74,000.

2007 ('000 metric tons, unless otherwise indicated): Coal 58,900; Crude petroleum 3,300; Natural gas (million cu m) 20,200; Iron ore: gross weight 77,900.

Source: US Geological Survey.

Industry

SELECTED PRODUCTS
('000 metric tons, unless otherwise indicated)

	2001	2002	2003
Margarine	167	170	123
Flour	2,686	2,724	2,540
Raw sugar*	1,947	1,621	2,486
Ethyl alcohol ('000 hectolitres)	2,643	2,840	2,546
Wine ('000 hectolitres)	1,425	2,081	2,045
Beer ('000 hectolitres)	13,059	15,000	17,012
Cigarettes (million)	69,731	81,088	96,776
Wool yarn: pure and mixed	3.7	3.5	3.0
Cotton yarn: pure and mixed	11.0	10.7	8.7
Flax yarn	1.3	0.8	0.2
Woven cotton fabrics (million sq metres)	46	57	27
Woven woollen fabrics (million sq metres)	7.4	7.0	6.5
Linen fabrics (million sq metres)	5.7	4.1	0.3
Footwear, excl. rubber ('000 pairs)	15,155	15,016	15,939
Hydrochloric acid	66.8	60.5	76.9
Sulphuric acid	1,040	935	1,131
Nitric acid	6	4	436
Phosphoric acid	30.9	18.5	31.3
Caustic soda (Sodium hydroxide)	134	133	160
Soda ash (Sodium carbonate)	651	679	656
Nitrogenous fertilizers (a)†	2,153	2,311	2,473
Phosphatic fertilizers (b)†	61	28	38
Potassic fertilizers (c)†	20	8	14
Rubber tyres ('000)‡	6,862	6,244	6,107
Rubber footwear ('000 pairs)	2,527	2,665	3,588
Clay building bricks (million)	1,382	1,462	1,563
Quicklime	4,367	4,456	4,962
Cement	5,786	4,456	4,962
Pig-iron	26,379	27,633	29,529
Crude steel: for castings	500	872	1,514
Crude steel: ingots	33,523	34,543	37,524

UKRAINE

—continued	2001	2002	2003
Tractors (number)§	3,640	2,980	4,531
Household refrigerators ('000)	509	583	340
Household washing machines ('000)	166	232	251
Radio receivers ('000)	26	33	21
Television receivers ('000)	148	159	415
Passenger motor cars ('000)	26	44	102
Buses and motor coaches (number)	2,474	2,102	2,655
Lorries (number)	6,747	2,343	1,265
Bicycles ('000)‖	109	245	281
Electric energy ('000 million kWh)	173	174	180

* Production from home-grown sugar beet.
† Production of fertilizers is in terms of (a) nitrogen; (b) phosphoric acid; or (c) potassium oxide.
‡ Tyres for road motor vehicles.
§ Tractors of 10 horse-power and over, excluding industrial tractors and road tractors for tractor-trailer combinations.
‖ Excluding children's bicycles.

Source: UN, *Industrial Commodity Statistics Yearbook*.

Raw sugar ('000 metric tons): 2,147 in 2004; 2,139 in 2005; 2,592 in 2006.

Sulphuric acid ('000 metric tons): 1,425 in 2004; 1,606 in 2005; 1,493 in 2006.

Caustic soda (Sodium hydroxide) ('000 metric tons): 210 in 2004; 209 in 2005; 183 in 2006; 172 in 2007.

Nitrogenous fertilizers (nitrogen content, '000 metric tons): 2,407 in 2004; 2,633 in 2005; 2,566 in 2006; 2,839 in 2007.

Rubber tyres ('000): 7,940 in 2004; 7,531 in 2005; 9,245 in 2006; 7,411 in 2007.

Cement ('000 metric tons): 10,600 in 2004; 12,200 in 2005; 13,700 in 2006; 15,000 in 2007.

Pig-iron ('000 metric tons): 31,000 in 2004; 30,700 in 2005; 32,900 in 2006; 35,600 in 2007.

Tractors (number): 5,806 in 2004; 5,543 in 2005; 3,703 in 2006; 5,282 in 2007.

Household refrigerators ('000): 581 in 2004; 711 in 2005; 731 in 2006; 824 in 2007.

Household washing machines ('000): 345 in 2004; 322 in 2005; 208 in 2006; 173 in 2007.

Television receivers ('000): 443 in 2004; 651 in 2005; 431 in 2006; 507 in 2007.

Passenger motor cars ('000): 174 in 2004; 192 in 2005; 267 in 2006; 380 in 2007.

Buses and motor coaches (number): 2,598 in 2004; 4,655 in 2005; 7,660 in 2006; 9,127 in 2007.

Electric energy ('000 million kWh): 182 in 2004; 186 in 2005; 193 in 2006; 196 in 2007.

Finance

CURRENCY AND EXCHANGE RATES

Monetary Units
100 kopiykas = 1 hryvnya.

Sterling, Dollar and Euro Equivalents (31 December 2008)
£1 sterling = 11.225 hryvnyas;
US $1 = 7.700 hryvnyas;
€1 = 10.716 hryvnyas;
100 hryvnyas = £8.91 = $12.99 = €9.33.

Average Exchange Rate (hryvnyas per US $)
2006   5.0500
2007   5.0500
2008   5.2672

Note: Following the dissolution of the USSR in December 1991, Russia and several other former Soviet republics retained the rouble (known as the karbovanets—KRB in Ukraine) as their monetary unit. In November 1992 this currency ceased to be legal tender in Ukraine, and was replaced (initially at par) by a currency coupon, also known as the karbovanets, or kupon, for a transitional period. Following the introduction of the transitional currency, Ukraine operated a system of multiple exchange rates, but in October 1994 the official and auction rates were merged. The unified exchange rate at 31 December 1995 was US $1 = 179,400 KRB. On 2 September 1996 Ukraine introduced a new currency, the hryvnya, at a rate of 100,000 KRB per hryvnya (1.750 hryvnyas per $).

GOVERNMENT FINANCE
(general government transactions, million hryvnyas)

Summary of Balances

	2005	2006	2007
Revenue	183,407	234,374	301,218
Less Expense	183,071	230,772	290,119
Net operating balance	336	3,603	11,099
Less Net acquisition of non-financial assets	6,225	9,112	12,903
Net lending/borrowing	–5,889	–5,510	–1,804

Revenue

	2005	2006	2007
Taxes	98,351	126,414	161,594
Taxes on income, profits and capital gains	42,328	50,448	70,915
Taxes on goods and services	46,592	65,713	77,575
Social contributions	55,460	70,413	93,467
Grants	199	163	118
Other revenue	29,397	37,385	46,039
Total	183,407	234,374	301,218

Expense/Outlays

Expense by economic type	2005	2006	2007
Compensation of employees	43,729	56,470	74,454
Use of goods and services	29,667	36,874	47,328
Interest	3,462	3,702	4,063
Subsidies	10,268	17,622	20,684
Grants	194	140	249
Social benefits	85,437	102,817	122,626
Other expense	10,315	13,148	20,715
Total	183,071	230,772	290,119

Outlays by functions of government*	2005	2006	2007
General public services	14,798	19,899	23,882
Defence	5,066	5,547	9,481
Public order and safety	10,210	12,701	16,357
Economic affairs	20,864	27,344	42,234
Environmental protection	890	1,541	2,052
Housing and community amenities	4,630	8,696	6,228
Health	16,805	20,954	28,220
Recreation, culture and religion	3,586	4,501	5,919
Education	26,374	33,274	43,697
Social protection	88,891	108,645	133,740
Total	192,112	243,102	311,810

* Including net acquisition of non-financial assets.

Source: IMF, *Government Finance Statistics Yearbook*.

INTERNATIONAL RESERVES
(US $ million at 31 December)

	2006	2007	2008
Gold (national valuation)	513.5	693.1	742.7
IMF special drawing rights	1.5	2.8	8.6
Foreign exchange	21,843.2	31,783.2	30,791.9
Total	22,358.2	32,479.1	31,543.2

Source: IMF, *International Financial Statistics*.

MONEY SUPPLY
(million hryvnyas at 31 December)

	2006	2007	2008
Currency outside banks	74,983.6	111,118.7	154,758.5
Demand deposits at banks	48,110.0	70,165.8	70,368.7
Total money (incl. others)	123,275.6	181,665.2	225,127.2

Source: IMF, *International Financial Statistics*.

UKRAINE

Statistical Survey

COST OF LIVING
(Consumer Price Index; base: previous year = 100)

	2005	2006	2007
Food and beverages	110.7	103.5	122.9
Other consumer goods	104.0	102.5	106.0
Services	115.8	149.4	112.0
All goods and services	110.3	111.6	116.6

2008: All goods and services 122.3.

NATIONAL ACCOUNTS
(million hryvnyas at current prices)

National Income and Product

	2005	2006	2007
Compensation of employees	216,600	268,631	351,936
Net operating surplus and mixed income	118,230	143,771	207,883
Domestic primary incomes	334,830	412,402	559,819
Consumption of fixed capital	50,545	58,265	73,071
Gross domestic product (GDP) at factor cost	385,375	470,667	632,890
Taxes on production and imports	62,777	82,377	101,230
Less Subsidies	6,700	8,891	13,389
GDP in market prices	441,452	544,153	720,731
Primary incomes received from abroad	3,822	6,684	18,410
Less Primary incomes paid abroad	8,863	15,378	21,735
Gross national income (GNI)	436,411	535,459	717,406
Less Consumption of fixed capital	50,545	58,265	73,071
Net national income	385,866	477,194	644,335
Current taxes and transfers from abroad	15,907	17,801	20,829
Less Current transfers paid abroad	1,077	1,374	2,437
Net national disposable income	400,696	493,621	662,727

Expenditure on the Gross Domestic Product

	2006	2007	2008
Final consumption expenditure	424,906	560,618	752,489
Households	319,383	422,837	576,565
Non-profit institutions serving households	5,173	5,843	7,638
General government	100,350	131,938	168,286
Gross capital formation	134,740	192,101	273,990
Gross fixed capital formation	133,874	195,179	258,176
Changes in inventories	655	-3,394	15,457
Acquisitions, less disposals, of valuables	211	316	357
Total domestic expenditure	559,646	752,719	1,026,479
Exports of goods and services	253,707	323,205	444,859
Less Imports of goods and services	269,200	362,979	521,474
GDP in market prices	544,153	712,945	949,864

Gross Domestic Product by Economic Activity

	2005	2006	2007
Agriculture, hunting, forestry and fishing	40,542	41,006	47,417
Mining and quarrying	17,939	22,064	31,695
Manufacturing	86,863	109,416	143,428
Electricity, gas and water supply	15,169	18,610	23,245
Construction	16,370	21,168	30,456
Wholesale and retail trade; repair of motor vehicles, motorcycles and personal goods	56,041	68,573	95,220
Transport, storage and communication	47,435	56,053	70,063
Education	20,882	26,243	32,905
Health and social work	13,965	17,722	22,542
Other economic activities	80,797	106,277	159,921
Sub-total	396,003	487,132	656,892
Less Financial intermediation services indirectly measured	7,402	13,009	22,098
Gross value added in basic prices	388,601	474,123	634,794
Taxes on products	54,183	71,618	88,212
Less Subsidies on products	1,332	1,588	2,275
GDP in market prices	441,452	544,153	720,731

BALANCE OF PAYMENTS
(US $ million)

	2005	2006	2007
Exports of goods f.o.b.	35,024	38,949	49,840
Imports of goods f.o.b.	-36,159	-44,143	-60,412
Trade balance	-1,135	-5,194	-10,572
Exports of services	9,354	11,290	14,161
Imports of services	-7,548	-9,164	-11,741
Balance on goods and services	671	-3,068	-8,152
Other income received	758	1,332	3,656
Other income paid	-1,743	-3,054	-4,315
Balance on goods, services and income	-314	-4,790	-8,811
Current transfers received	3,111	3,533	4,147
Current transfers paid	-266	-360	-608
Current balance	2,531	-1,617	-5,272
Capital account (net)	-65	3	3
Direct investment abroad	-275	133	-673
Direct investment from abroad	7,808	5,604	9,891
Portfolio investment assets	—	-3	-29
Portfolio investment liabilities	2,757	3,586	5,782
Other investment assets	-7,936	-15,424	-22,838
Other investment liabilities	5,749	10,189	22,994
Net errors and omissions	156	-62	-452
Overall balance	10,725	2,409	9,406

Source: IMF, *International Financial Statistics*.

UKRAINE   Statistical Survey

External Trade

PRINCIPAL COMMODITIES
(distribution by Harmonized System, US $ million)

Imports f.o.b.	2006	2007	2008
Prepared food, beverages, spirits, tobacco	1,654.7	2,090.9	2,679.2
Mineral products	13,506.2	17,280.4	25,441.5
Mineral fuels, oils, waxes and bituminous substances	12,711.6	15,984.2	22,832.1
Crude petroleum	4,403.6	4,553.5	4,513.7
Natural gas	4,769.4	6,572.6	9,438.8
Chemicals and related products	3,888.6	5,316.5	6,959.1
Pharmaceutical products	1,384.9	1,931.3	2,433.3
Plastics, rubbers, and articles thereof	2,527.7	3,412.9	4,476.8
Plastic and articles thereof	1,988.7	2,693.5	3,519.4
Textiles and textile articles	1,365.5	1,487.0	2,099.2
Base metals and articles thereof	3,327.3	4,742.7	6,390.0
Iron and steel	1,468.9	2,240.1	3,299.3
Machinery and mechanical appliances, electrical equipment and appliances, parts and accessories	7,873.4	10,571.7	13,378.6
Machinery and mechanical appliances, computers, etc.	5,191.4	7,436.6	9,570.3
Electrical machinery, equipment and parts, etc.	2,682.0	3,135.1	3,808.3
Vehicles, aircraft, vessels and associated transportation equipment	5,147.1	8,216.6	12,091.4
Vehicles other than railway or tramway rolling stock	4,898.3	7,770.8	11,370.3
Total (incl. others)	45,034.5	60,669.9	85,534.5

Exports f.o.b.	2006	2007	2008
Vegetable products	1,951.1	1,726.4	5,577.1
Cereals	1,354.2	763.7	3,703.8
Animal or vegetable fats and oils, etc.	971.4	1,718.0	1,945.8
Prepared food, beverages, spirits, tobacco	1,394.4	2,056.2	2,524.3
Mineral products	3,871.8	4,275.2	7,046.1
Ores, slag and ash	912.3	1,105.0	2,153.6
Mineral fuels, oils, waxes and bituminous substances	2,553.5	2,630.1	4,109.2
Chemicals and related products	3,387.3	4,047.2	5,045.4
Base metals and articles thereof	16,420.1	20,787.3	27,633.1
Iron and steel	13,051.2	16,743.8	22,991.9
Articles of iron and steel	2,361.6	2,912.5	3,534.6
Machinery and mechanical appliances, electrical equipment and appliances, parts and accessories	3,330.5	4,976.6	6,341.2
Machinery and mechanical appliances, computers, etc.	2,051.5	2,738.3	3,497.8
Electrical machinery, equipment and parts, etc.	1,279.0	2,238.2	2,843.4
Vehicles, aircraft, vessels and associated transportation equipment	2,081.1	3,304.7	4,324.1
Railway or tramway locomotives, rolling stock, track fixtures and fittings, signals, etc.	1,067.0	1,840.2	2,656.7
Total (incl. others)	38,367.7	49,248.1	67,002.5

PRINCIPAL TRADING PARTNERS
(US $ million)

Imports f.o.b.	2006	2007	2008
Austria	547.2	799.2	1,030.0
Belarus	1,255.2	1,444.8	2,809.6
China, People's Republic	2,310.2	3,307.1	5,601.5
Czech Republic	825.1	1,154.6	1,376.0
France (incl. Monaco)	989.8	1,330.0	1,682.5
Germany	4,267.6	5,830.0	7,165.2
Hungary	802.2	1,240.9	1,282.7
Italy	1,465.2	1,789.3	2,432.0
Japan	848.6	1,406.6	2,795.8
Kazakhstan	965.7	1,591.8	3,118.9
Korea, Republic	935.4	1,564.9	2,046.2
Netherlands	640.4	881.0	1,282.7
Poland	2,109.2	2,920.5	4,280.3
Romania	446.1	778.9	1,171.1
Russia	13,787.2	16,837.6	19,414.2
Sweden	565.0	610.3	696.2
Switzerland	283.2	429.8	1,171.6
Turkey	769.1	972.1	1,950.3
Turkmenistan	3,492.0	4,266.6	5,631.7
United Kingdom	620.6	886.4	1,375.8
USA	879.1	1,397.3	2,808.2
Uzbekistan	418.0	546.0	2,118.3
Total (incl. others)	45,034.5	60,669.9	85,534.4

Exports f.o.b.	2006	2007	2008
Algeria	466.7	440.0	345.0
Azerbaijan	422.0	631.2	910.6
Belarus	1,222.7	1,561.4	2,105.6
British Virgin Islands	480.9	610.8	862.0
Bulgaria	595.7	554.0	1,106.0
China, People's Republic	544.7	431.7	547.5
Czech Republic	341.6	429.0	670.8
Egypt	748.4	880.0	1,560.3
Germany	1,283.8	1,644.5	1,836.3
Hungary	946.1	1,235.1	1,367.1
India	850.1	744.1	1,005.6
Iran	318.3	509.5	859.2
Italy	2,500.4	2,675.2	2,911.7
Jordan	317.9	433.2	998.4
Kazakhstan	828.0	1,433.7	1,832.6
Moldova	671.2	911.3	1,178.1
Netherlands	710.7	765.7	1,118.0
Poland	1,344.5	1,636.9	2,338.3
Romania	625.9	628.6	670.8
Russia	8,650.7	12,668.3	15,739.1
Saudi Arabia	537.0	523.5	956.4
Slovakia	549.6	645.2	910.2
Spain	445.1	557.4	870.0
Switzerland	112.1	96.5	831.3
Syria	602.2	846.9	1,037.4
Turkey	2,390.0	3,650.0	4,633.4
United Arab Emirates	392.6	612.2	914.3
United Kingdom	388.2	324.9	640.6
USA	1,201.7	1,058.1	1,949.1
Total (incl. others)	38,367.7	49,248.1	67,002.5

Transport

RAILWAYS
(traffic)

	2006	2007	2008
Passengers carried ('000 journeys)	448,800	447,400	445,600
Freight carried ('000 metric tons)	476,800	512,500	498,800
Passenger-km (million)	53,400	53,400	53,225
Freight ton-km (million)	240,600	262,800	256,868

UKRAINE

ROAD TRAFFIC
(motor vehicles in use)

	1998	1999	2000
Passenger cars	4,877,787	5,210,774	5,250,129
Motorcycles and mopeds	2,609,201	2,432,787	2,251,505

2004: Passenger cars 5,445,830; Buses 175,945; Lorries and vans 917,427; Motorcycles 1,145,407.

Source: IRF, *World Road Statistics*.

INLAND WATERWAYS

	2006	2007	2008
Passengers carried ('000 journeys)	12,900	9,500	8,900
Freight carried ('000 metric tons)	16,877	18,543	14,522
Passenger-km (million)	100	200	123
Freight ton-km (million)	18,600	18,000	15,842

SHIPPING

Merchant Fleet
(registered at 31 December)

	2005	2006	2007
Number of vessels	658	655	655
Total displacement ('000 grt)	1,154.0	1,136.5	1,144.6

Source: Lloyd's Register-Fairplay, *World Fleet Statistics*.

International Sea-borne Freight Traffic
('000 metric tons)

	2006	2007	2008
Goods loaded	68,331.1	53,857.0	76,330.6
Goods unloaded	15,199.4	18,333.9	21,145.2

CIVIL AVIATION
(traffic on scheduled services)

	2006	2007	2008
Passengers carried ('000)	4,400	4,900	6,200
Passenger-kilometres (million)	8,600	9,500	10,777

Total ton-kilometres (million): 378.4 in 2008.

Kilometres flown (million): 38 in 2003 (Source: UN, *Statistical Yearbook*).

Tourism

TOURIST ARRIVALS

Country of residence	2006	2007	2008
Belarus	2,127,250	2,918,694	3,407,064
Hungary	1,159,711	1,251,724	1,033,376
Moldova	3,056,433	3,998,674	4,418,821
Poland	3,979,453	4,430,140	5,242,980
Romania	349,094	1,010,065	1,440,466
Russia	6,429,264	7,258,222	7,638,222
Slovakia	506,045	664,605	644,918
Total (incl. others)	18,935,775	23,122,157	25,449,078

Receipts from tourism (US $ million, incl. passenger transport): 2,931 in 2004; 3,542 in 2005; 4,018 in 2006. (Source: World Tourism Organization).

Communications Media

	2005	2006	2007
Book production (titles)	15,720	15,867	17,987
Newspapers (titles)	2,974	2,918	2,885
Magazines and other periodicals (titles)	2,182	2,301	2,420
Telephones ('000 main lines in use)	11,666.6	12,341.0	12,858.5
Mobile cellular telephones ('000 subscribers)	29,999.9	49,076.2	55,240.4
Internet users ('000)	8,000	9,000	10,000
Broadband subscribers ('000)	130	520	800

Radio receivers ('000 in use): 45,050 in 1997.

Television receivers ('000 in use): 23,000 in 2000.

Facsimile machines (number in use): 42,161 in 2000.

Personal computers: 1,810,000 in use in 2005.

Sources: mainly UNESCO, *Statistical Yearbook*; International Telecommunication Union.

2009 ('000 subscribers at 1 January): Mobile cellular telephones 55,694.5.

Education

(2008/09, unless otherwise indicated)

	Institutions	Teachers	Students
Pre-primary	15,300*†	191,500‡	1,137,000*
Primary *and* General secondary	21,000	524,000	4,617,000
Specialized secondary: vocational*	1,022	285,100	454,400
Higher	881	121,300‡	2,763,800

* 2007/08 figure(s).
† Including some 1,400 with activities suspended.
‡ 1993/94 figure.

Adult literacy rate (UNESCO estimates): 99.7% (males 99.8%; females 99.6%) in 2007 (Source: UNESCO Institute for Statistics).

Directory

Constitution

The Constitution of Ukraine, summarized below, was adopted at the Fifth Session of the Verkhovna Rada on 28 June 1996. It replaced the Soviet-era Constitution (Fundamental Law), originally approved on 12 April 1978, but amended several times after Ukraine gained independence in 1991, and entered into force the day of its adoption. On 8 December 2004, following the disputed (and subsequently annulled) second round of voting in the presidential election, the Verkhovna Rada approved a number of constitutional amendments, principally concerned with transferring a number of presidential powers, including the appointment of the majority of ministerial posts, to the Prime Minister and to the Verkhovna Rada. These amendments, which were signed into law on the same day by the outgoing President, took effect from 1 January 2006, excepting those pertaining to the Verkhovna Rada or Prime Minister, which entered into force in May 2006, following the assembly of a legislature after the general election held in March.

FUNDAMENTAL PRINCIPLES

Ukraine is a sovereign and independent, unitary and law-based state, in which power is exercised directly by the people through the bodies of state power and local self-government. The life, honour, dignity and health of the individual are recognized as the highest

UKRAINE

social value. The Constitution is the highest legal authority; the power of the State is divided between the legislative, the executive and the judicial branches. The state language is Ukrainian. The use and protection of Russian and other languages of national minorities, and the development of minorities' ethnic and cultural traditions is guaranteed. The State ensures protection of all forms of ownership rights and management, as well as the social orientation of the economy. The state symbols of Ukraine, its flag, coat of arms and anthem, are established.

THE RIGHTS, FREEDOMS AND DUTIES OF CITIZENS

The rights and freedoms of individuals are declared to be unalienable and inviolable regardless of race, sex, political or religious affiliation, wealth, social origin or other characteristics. Fundamental rights, such as the freedoms of speech and association and the right to private property, are guaranteed. Citizens have the right to engage in political activity and to own private property. All individuals are entitled to work and to join professional unions to protect their employment rights. The Constitution commits the State to the provision of health care, housing, social security and education. All citizens have the right to legal assistance. Obligations of the citizenry include military service and taxes. The age of enfranchisement for Ukrainian citizens is 18 years. Elections to organs of state authority are declared to be free and conducted on the basis of universal, equal and direct suffrage by secret ballot.

THE VERKHOVNA RADA

The Verkhovna Rada (Supreme Council) is the sole organ of legislative authority in Ukraine. It consists of 450 members, elected for a four-year term on the basis of proportional representation. The constitutional reforms approved in late 2004 prohibit deputies from leaving the party or bloc for whom they have been elected during the term of their elective mandate. Only Ukrainian citizens aged over 21 years, who have resided in Ukraine for the five previous years are eligible for election to parliament. The Verkhovna Rada is a permanently acting body, which elects its own Chairman and Deputy Chairmen.

The most important functions of the legislature include: the enactment of laws; the approval of the state budget and other state programmes; the scheduling of presidential elections; the removal (impeachment) of the President; the appointment of the Prime Minister; the declaration of war or conclusion of peace; the foreign deployment of troops; and consenting to international treaty obligations within the time limit prescribed by law. Within 15 days of a law adopted by the Verkhovna Rada being received by the President, the President shall officially promulgate it or return it for repeat consideration by parliament. If, during such consideration, the legislature readopts the law by a two-thirds' majority, the President is obliged to sign it and officially promulgate it within 10 days. The President of Ukraine may terminate the authority of the Verkhovna Rada if, within 30 days of a single, regular session, a plenary session cannot be convened, except within the last six months of the President's term of office.

THE PRESIDENT

The President of Ukraine is the Head of State, and is guarantor of state sovereignty and the territorial integrity of Ukraine. The President is directly elected for a period of five years. A presidential candidate must be aged over 35 years and a resident of the country for the 10 years prior to the election. The President may hold office for no more than two consecutive terms.

The President's main responsibilities include: the scheduling of elections and of referendums on constitutional amendments; the conclusion of international treaties; and the promulgation of laws. The President appoints certain senior members of the Cabinet of Ministers; the constitutional reforms agreed in late 2004 transferred responsibility for the appointment of the majority of Ministers to the Prime Minister.

The President is the Supreme Commander of the Armed Forces of Ukraine and chairs the National Security and Defence Council. The President may be removed from office by the Verkhovna Rada by impeachment, for reasons of state treason or another crime. The decision to remove the President must be approved by at least a three-quarters' majority in the Verkhovna Rada. In the event of the termination of the authority of the President, the Prime Minister executes the duties of the President until the election and entry into office of a new President.

THE CABINET OF MINISTERS

The principal organ of executive government is the Cabinet of Ministers, which is responsible before the President and accountable to the Verkhovna Rada. The Cabinet supervises the implementation of state policy and the state budget and the maintenance of law and order. The Cabinet of Ministers is headed by the Prime Minister. The duties of the Prime Minister include the submission of proposals to the President on the creation, reorganization and liquidation of ministries and other central bodies of executive authority. The Cabinet of Ministers must resign when a new President is elected, or in the event of the adoption of a vote of no confidence by the Verkhovna Rada.

JUDICIAL POWER

Justice in Ukraine is administered by the Constitutional Court and by courts of general jurisdiction. The Supreme Court of Ukraine is the highest judicial organ of general jurisdiction. Judges hold their position permanently, except for justices of the Constitutional Court and first judicial appointments, which are made by the President for a five-year term. Other judges, with the exception of justices of the Constitutional Court, are elected by the Verkhovna Rada. Judges must be at least 25 years of age, have a higher legal education and at least three years' work experience in the field of law, and have resided in Ukraine for no fewer than 10 years. The Procuracy of Ukraine is headed by the General Procurator, who is appointed with the consent of parliament and dismissed by the President. The term of office of the General Procurator is five years.

A Superior Justice Council, responsible for the submission of proposals regarding the appointment or dismissal of judges, functions in Ukraine. The Council consists of 20 members. The Chairman of the Supreme Court of Ukraine, the Minister of Justice, and the General Procurator are ex officio members of the Superior Justice Council.

LOCAL SELF-GOVERNMENT

The administrative and territorial division of Ukraine consists of the Autonomous Republic of Crimea, 24 provinces (oblasts), the cities of Kyiv and Sevastopol (which possess special status), districts (raions), cities, settlements and villages. Local self-government is the right of territorial communities. The principal organs of territorial communities are the district and provincial councils, which, with their chairmen, are directly elected for a term of four years. The chairmen of district and provincial councils are elected by the relevant council and head their executive structure. Provincial and district councils monitor the implementation of programmes of socio-economic and cultural development of the relevant provinces and districts, and adopt and monitor the implementation of district and provincial budgets, which are derived from the state budget.

THE AUTONOMOUS REPUBLIC OF CRIMEA

The Autonomous Republic of Crimea (which comprises the peninsula of Crimea, excluding the city of Sevastopol) is an inseparable, integral part of Ukraine. It has its own Constitution, which is adopted by the Supreme Council of the Autonomous Republic of Crimea (the representative organ of Crimea) and approved by the Verkhovna Rada. Legislation adopted by the Autonomous Republic's Supreme Council and the decisions of its Council of Ministers must not contravene the Constitution and laws of Ukraine. The Chairman of the Council of Ministers is appointed and dismissed by the Supreme Council of the Autonomous Republic of Crimea with the consent of the President of Ukraine. Justice in Crimea is administered by courts belonging to the single court system of Ukraine. An Office of the Representative of the President of Ukraine functions in Crimea.

The jurisdiction of the Autonomous Republic of Crimea includes: organizing and conducting local referendums; implementing the republican budget on the basis of the state policy of Ukraine; ensuring the function and development of the state and national languages and cultures; participating in the development and fulfilment of programmes for the return of deported peoples.

THE CONSTITUTIONAL COURT

The Constitutional Court consists of 18 justices, six of whom are appointed by the President, six by the Verkhovna Rada and six by the Assembly of Judges of Ukraine. Candidates must be citizens of Ukraine, who are at least 40 years of age and have resided in Ukraine for the previous 20 years. Justices of the Constitutional Court serve a term of nine years, with no right to reappointment. A Chairman is elected by a secret ballot of the members for a single three-year term.

The Constitutional Court provides binding interpretations of the Constitution. It rules on the constitutionality of: parliamentary legislation; acts of the President and the Cabinet of Ministers; the official interpretation of the Constitution of Ukraine; international agreements; and the impeachment of the President of Ukraine.

CONSTITUTIONAL AMENDMENTS AND THE ADOPTION OF A NEW CONSTITUTION

A draft law on amending the Constitution may be presented to the Verkhovna Rada by the President or at least one-third of the constitutional composition of the parliament. A draft law on amending the Constitution, which has been given preliminary approval by a majority of the constitutional composition of the Verkhovna Rada, is considered adopted if it receives the support of at least a two-thirds'

UKRAINE

parliamentary majority. In the case of its approval, it is confirmed by a nation-wide referendum designated by the President.

The Government

HEAD OF STATE

President: VIKTOR A. YUSHCHENKO (elected 26 December 2004; inaugurated 23 January 2005).

CABINET OF MINISTERS
(April 2009)

Prime Minister: YULIYA V. TYMOSHENKO.
First Deputy Prime Minister: OLEKSANDR V. TURCHYNOV.
Deputy Prime Minister: IVAN V. VASYUNYK.
Deputy Prime Minister: HRYHORIY M. NEMYRYA.
Minister of Education and Science: IVAN O. VAKARCHUK.
Minister of Transport and Communications: YOSYP V. VINSKY.
Minister of Culture and Tourism: VASYL V. VOVKUN.
Minister of the Economy: BOHDAN M. DANYLYSHYN.
Minister of Labour and Social Policy: LYUDMYLA L. DENISOVA.
Minister of Defence: YURIY I. YEKHANUROV.
Minister of the Protection of Health: VASYL M. KNYAZEVYCH.
Minister of Regional Development and Construction: VASYL S. KUYBIDA.
Minister of Housing and Communal Services: OLEKSIY YU. KUCHERENKO.
Minister of Internal Affairs: YURIY V. LUTSENKO.
Minister of Agrarian Policy: YURIY F. MELNYK.
Minister of Industrial Policy: VOLODYMYR S. NOVYTSKY.
Minister of Justice: MYKOLA V. ONISHCHUK.
Minister of Foreign Affairs: (vacant).
Minister of the Family, Youth and Sports: YURIY O. PAVLENKO.
Minister of Finance: (vacant).
Minister of the Coal Industry: VIKTOR I. POLTAVETS.
Minister of Fuel and Energy: YURIY V. PRODAN.
Minister of the Protection of the Environment: HEORHIY H. FILIPCHUK.
Minister for Emergency Situations and the Protection of the Population from the Consequences of the Chornobyl Catastrophe: VOLODYMYR M. SHANDRA.
Minister of the Cabinet of Ministers: PETRO M. KRUPKO.

MINISTRIES

Office of the President: 01220 Kyiv, vul. Bankova 11; tel. (44) 255-73-33; fax (44) 293-61-61; e-mail president@adm.gov.ua; internet www.president.gov.ua.

Office of the Cabinet of Ministers: 01008 Kyiv, vul. M. Hrushevskoho 12/2; tel. and fax (44) 254-05-84; e-mail web@kmu.gov.ua; internet www.kmu.gov.ua.

Ministry of Agrarian Policy: 01001 Kyiv, vul. Khreshchatik 24; tel. (44) 278-71-18; fax (44) 229-87-56; e-mail minister@minapk.kiev.ua; internet www.minagro.gov.ua.

Ministry of the Coal Industry: 01601 Kyiv, vul. Khmelnytskoho 4; tel. (44) 206-37-12; fax (44) 206-37-26; e-mail mvp@mvp.gov.ua; internet www.mvp.gov.ua.

Ministry of Culture and Tourism: 01030 Kyiv, vul. Ivana Franka 19; tel. (44) 235-23-78; fax (44) 235-32-57; e-mail minister@mincult.gov.ua; internet www.mincult.gov.ua.

Ministry of Defence: 01021 Kyiv, vul. M. Hrushevskoho 30/1; tel. (44) 253-11-56; fax (44) 226-20-15; internet www.mil.gov.ua.

Ministry of the Economy: 01008 Kyiv, vul. M. Hrushevskoho 12/2; tel. (44) 253-93-94; fax (44) 226-31-81; e-mail meconomy@me.gov.ua; internet www.me.kmu.gov.ua.

Ministry of Education and Science: 01135 Kyiv, pr. Peremohi 10; tel. (44) 486-25-21; fax (44) 274-10-49; e-mail press@mon.gov.ua; internet www.mon.gov.ua.

Ministry of Emergency Situations and the Protection of the Population from the Consequences of the Chornobyl Catastrophe: 01030 Kyiv, vul. O. Honchara 55A; tel. (44) 247-31-44; e-mail main@mns.gov.ua; internet www.mns.gov.ua.

Ministry of the Family, Youth and Sport: 01601 Kyiv, vul. Esplanadna 42; tel. (44) 289-12-64; fax (44) 289-12-94; internet www.kmu.gov.ua/sport/control.

Ministry of Finance: 01008 Kyiv, vul. M. Hrushevskoho 12/2; tel. (44) 206-59-44; fax (44) 425-90-26; e-mail infomf@minfin.gov.ua; internet www.minfin.gov.ua.

Ministry of Foreign Affairs: 01018 Kyiv, pl. Mykhailivska 1; tel. (44) 226-33-79; fax (44) 226-31-69; e-mail zsmfa@mfa.gov.ua; internet www.mfa.gov.ua.

Ministry of Fuel and Energy: 01601 Kyiv, vul. Khreshchatik 30; tel. (44) 206-38-00; fax (44) 462-05-61; e-mail kanc@mintop.energy.gov.ua; internet mpe.kmu.gov.ua.

Ministry of Housing and Communal Services: 03150 Kyiv, vul. Dymytrova 24; tel. (44) 287-23-84; fax (44) 289-01-66; e-mail minjkg@ukr.net; internet www.minjkg.gov.ua.

Ministry of Industrial Policy: 03035 Kyiv, vul. Surikova 3; tel. (44) 246-32-20; fax (44) 245-47-78; e-mail minister@industry.gov.ua; internet industry.kmu.gov.ua.

Ministry of Internal Affairs: 01024 Kyiv, vul. Ak. Bohomoltsya 10; tel. (44) 256-03-33; fax (44) 256-16-33; e-mail mail@centrmia.gov.ua; internet mvs.gov.ua.

Ministry of Justice: 01001 Kyiv, vul. Horodetskoho 13; tel. and fax (44) 228-37-23; e-mail themis@minjust.gov.ua; internet www.minjust.gov.ua.

Ministry of Labour and Social Policy: 01023 Kyiv, vul. Esplanadna 8/10; tel. (44) 226-24-45; fax (44) 289-00-98; e-mail info@mlsp.gov.ua; internet www.mlsp.gov.ua.

Ministry of the Protection of the Environment: 03035 Kyiv, vul. Uritskoho 35; tel. (44) 206-31-15; fax (44) 206-31-07; e-mail secr@menr.gov.ua; internet www.menr.gov.ua.

Ministry of the Protection of Health: 01021 Kyiv, vul. M. Hrushevskoho 7; tel. and fax (44) 293-24-39; fax (44) 25-36-975; e-mail moz@moz.gov.ua; internet www.moz.gov.ua.

Ministry of Regional Development and Construction: 01205 Kyiv, vul. V. Zhytomyrska 9; tel. (44) 226-22-08; fax (44) 226-20-97; e-mail mrb@minregionbud.gov.ua; internet www.minregionbud.gov.ua.

Ministry of Transport and Communications: 01135 Kyiv, pr. Peremohy 14; tel. (44) 235-97-70; fax (44) 216-72-06; e-mail com@mintrans.gov.ua; internet www.mintrans.gov.ua.

President

Presidential Election, First Ballot, 31 October 2004

Candidates	Votes	%
Viktor A. Yushchenko (Independent)	11,188,675	39.91
Viktor F. Yanukovych (Party of the Regions)	11,008,731	39.27
Oleksandr O. Moroz (Socialist Party of Ukraine)	1,632,098	5.82
Petro M. Symonenko (Communist Party of Ukraine)	1,396,135	4.98
Others	1,418,157	5.06
Against all candidates	556,962	1.99
Total*	28,035,184	100.00

* Including 834,426 invalid votes (2.98% of the total).

Second Ballot, 26 December 2004*

Candidates	Votes	%
Viktor A. Yushchenko (Independent)	15,115,712	51.99
Viktor F. Yanukovych (Party of the Regions)	12,848,528	44.20
Against all candidates	682,239	2.35
Total†	29,068,971	100.00

* The results of an initial second round of voting, conducted on 21 November 2004, in which the Central Electoral Commission had declared Yanukovych the winner, were annulled by the Supreme Court.
† Including 422,492 invalid votes (1.45% of the total).

Legislature

Verkhovna Rada
(Supreme Council)

01008 Kyiv, vul. M. Hrushevskoho 5; tel. (44) 255-21-15; fax (44) 253-32-17; e-mail umz@rada.gov.ua; internet www.rada.gov.ua.

Chairman: VOLODYMYR M. LYTVYN.

UKRAINE

General Election, 30 September 2007

Parties and blocs	Votes	%	Seats
Party of the Regions	8,013,895	34.37	175
Yuliya Tymoshenko bloc*	7,162,193	30.72	156
Our Ukraine-People's Self-defence bloc†	3,301,282	14.16	72
Communist Party of Ukraine	1,257,291	5.39	27
Lytvyn bloc‡	924,538	3.97	20
Socialist Party of Ukraine	668,234	2.87	—
Others	970,936	4.16	—
Total§	23,315,257	100.00	450

* Electoral bloc comprising Fatherland, the Reforms and Order Party and the Ukrainian Social Democratic Party.

† Electoral bloc comprising nine parties, including Our Ukraine People's Union, the 'Enough!' Civic Party, the People's Movement of Ukraine-Rukh, the Synod Ukrainian Republican Party and the Ukrainian People's Party.

‡ Electoral bloc comprising the People's Party and the Labour Party of Ukraine.

§ The total number of votes cast was 23,315,257, including 637,185 votes 'against all lists' (2.73% of the total) and 379,703 invalid votes (representing 1.63% of the total).

Election Commission

Central Electoral Commission of Ukraine (CEC) (Tsentralna vyborcha Komisiya Ukrainy): 01196 Kyiv, pl. L. Ukrainky 1; tel. (44) 286-84-62; e-mail post@cvk.gov.ua; internet www.cvk.gov.ua; Head VOLODYMYR SHAPOVAL.

Political Organizations

Since the 1990s Ukrainian politics has been characterized by frequent changes of formation and allegiance within and between various factions or blocs. At 1 February 2009 there were 162 political parties registered in Ukraine, of which the following were the most important:

Communist Party of Ukraine (CPU) (Komunistychna Partiya Ukrainy): 04070 Kyiv, vul. Borysohlibska 7; tel. (44) 425-54-87; e-mail press@kpu.net.ua; internet www.kpu.net.ua; banned 1991-93; advocates state control of economy and confederation with Russia; Sec. of Cen. Cttee PETRO M. SYMONENKO.

'Enough!' Civic Party (Hromadyanska Partiya 'Pora!'): 01025 Kyiv, vul. Desyatynna 1/3; tel. (44) 583-55-72; e-mail porapress@gmail.com; f. 2005 on the basis of the 'Yellow Pora' civil organization; supports expansion of democratic freedoms and greater integration with the West; contested 2006 legislative elections as mem. of the Enough!-Party of Reforms and Order civic bloc and 2007 legislative elections as mem. of the Our Ukraine-People's Self-defence bloc; Chair. of Political Council VLADYSLAV V. KASKIV.

Fatherland (Batkivshchyna): 01133 Kyiv, bulv. Lesi Ukrainky 26/916, POB 81; tel. (44) 286-65-42; fax (44) 285-69-07; e-mail sector@byti.org.ua; internet www.tymoshenko.com.ua; f. 1999; merged with Conservative Republican Party in 2002, and with Yabluko party in 2004; nationalist, populist, supportive of socially-orientated economics; contested 2006 and 2007 legislative elections as mem. of Yuliya Tymoshenko bloc; Chair. YULIYA V. TYMOSHENKO; 275,000 mems (2005).

Green Party of Ukraine (Partiya Zelenykh Ukrainy): 01030 Kyiv, vul. Chapayeva 2/16; tel. and fax (44) 278-26-63; e-mail sekretariat@greenparty.ua; internet www.greenparty.ua; f. 1990; Pres. VOLODYMYR O. KOSTERIN.

Our Ukraine People's Union (Our Ukraine) (Narodnyi Soyuz 'Nasha Ukraina') (Nasha Ukraina): 04070 Kyiv, vul. Borychiv Tik 22A; tel. (44) 206-60-97; e-mail tak@ua.org.ua; internet www.razom.org.ua; f. 2005 as People's Union Our Ukraine to support administration of Pres. Yushchenko; present name adopted 2007; contested 2006 legislative elections as mem. of the Our Ukraine bloc and 2007 legislative elections as mem. of Our Ukraine-People's Self-defence bloc; Chair. VIKTOR A. YUSHCHENKO; Chair. of Council VERA I. ULYANCHENKO.

Party of the Regions (PR) (Partiya Rehioniv): 01021 Kyiv, vul. Lypska 10; tel. (44) 594-95-01; fax (44) 594-74-32; e-mail partreg@ln.ua; internet www.partyofregions.org.ua; f. 1997 as the Workers' Solidarity Party of Regional Rebirth of Ukraine; present name adopted 2001; Chair. VIKTOR F. YANUKOVYCH.

People's Movement of Ukraine-Rukh (PMU-R) (Narodnyi Rukh Ukrainy): 01034 Kyiv, vul. O. Honchara 33; tel. (44) 246-47-67; fax (44) 531-30-42; e-mail org@nru.org.ua; internet www.nru.org.ua; f. 1989 as popular movement (Ukrainian People's Movement for Restructuring); registered as political party in 1993; contested 2006 legislative elections as mem. of Our Ukraine bloc and 2007 legislative elections as mem. of Our Ukraine-People's Self-defence bloc; national democratic party; Chair. BORYS I. TARASYUK.

People's Party (Narodna Partiya): 01034 Kyiv, vul. Reitarska 6 A; tel. (44) 270-61-86; fax (44) 270-65-91; e-mail info@narodna.org.ua; internet narodna.org.ua; f. 1996 as Agrarian Party of Ukraine; renamed People's Agrarian Party of Ukraine in 2004; present name adopted 2005; contested 2006 legislative elections as mem. of Lytvyn's People's bloc and 2007 legislative elections as mem. of Lytvyn bloc; centrist; Leader VOLODYMYR M. LYTVYN.

Progressive Socialist Party of Ukraine (Prohresyvna Sotsialistychna Partiya Ukrainy): 01011 Kyiv, vul. P. Mirnoho 27/51; tel. (44) 254-18-40; fax (44) 278-54-91; e-mail pspu@svitonline.com; internet www.vitrenko.org; f. 1996 by members of the Socialist Party of Ukraine; contested 2006 legislative elections as mem. of the Nataliya Vitrenko People's Opposition bloc; favours extension of Belarus-Russia Union to incorporate Ukraine; opposed to Ukraine seeking membership of NATO; Chair. NATALIYA M. VITRENKO.

Reforms and Order Party (Partiya 'Reformy i poryadok'): 01021 Kyiv, vul. Institutska 28; tel. (44) 536-91-26; fax (44) 536-91-27; e-mail ref_ord@i.com.ua; internet www.prp.org.ua; f. 1997 as Reforms and Order Party; changed name to Our Ukraine in mid-2004; in July 2005 the Ministry of Justice ruled that the party had acted unlawfully in adopting the name 'Our Ukraine', and the party reverted to its original name; contested 2006 legislative elections as part of the Enough!-Party of Reforms and Order civic bloc and 2007 legislative elections as part of the Yuliya Tymoshenko bloc; Chair. VIKTOR M. PYNZENYK.

Socialist Party of Ukraine (SPU) (Sotsialistychna Partiya Ukrainy): 02100 Kyiv, vul. Bazhova 12; tel. and fax (44) 296-68-27; e-mail international@spu.in.ua; internet www.spu.in.ua; f. 1991; formed as partial successor to the CPU; advocates democratic socialism; Leader and Gen. Sec. OLEKSANDR O. MOROZ.

Ukrainian People's Party (UPP) (Ukrainska Narodna Partiya): 01601 Kyiv, vul. Pushkinska 28A; tel. (44) 234-59-17; fax (44) 234-05-68; e-mail office@unp-ua.org; internet www.unp-ua.org; f. 1999 as breakaway faction of People's Movement of Ukraine-Rukh by fmr leader Vyacheslav Chornovil; fmrly Ukrainian People's Movement-Rukh; present name adopted 2003; contested 2006 legislative elections as mem. of Kostenko and Plyushch's Ukrainian People's bloc and 2007 legislative elections as mem. of Our Ukraine-People's Self-defence bloc; Chair. YURIY I. KOSTENKO.

Ukrainian Social Democratic Party (Ukrainska Sotsial-demokratychna Partiya): 03150 Kyiv, vul. Antonovycha 154; tel. (44) 595-55-00; fax (44) 495-64-62; e-mail kmpousdp@ukr.net; internet www.usdp.kiev.ua; f. 1998; contested 2007 legislative elections as mem. of the Yuliya Tymoshenko bloc; Leader YEVHEN V. KORNIYCHUK.

United Centre (Yedyny Tsentr): 04071 Kyiv, vul. Yaroslavska 56A; tel. (44) 207-44-77; fax (44) 207-44-72; e-mail press@edc.org.ua; internet www.edc.org.ua; f. 1999; fmrly Party of Private Property; supportive of Pres. Yushchenko; Chair. IHOR I. KRIL.

Diplomatic Representation

EMBASSIES IN UKRAINE

Afghanistan: 03069 Kyiv, vul. Yaslynska 9/7; tel. and fax (44) 275-58-93; e-mail afembkiev@yahoo.com; Ambassador MOHAMMED ASEF DELAWAR.

Algeria: 01901 Kyiv, vul. B. Khmelnytskoho 64; tel. (44) 486-70-79; fax (44) 486-70-08; e-mail ambalgkiev@bigmir.net; Ambassador MOKADDEM BAFDAL.

Argentina: 01901 Kyiv, vul. Fedorova 12; tel. (44) 490-25-16; fax (44) 238-69-22; e-mail eucra@mrecic.gov.ar; Ambassador LILA ROLDÁN VÁZQUEZ DE MOINE.

Armenia: 01901 Kyiv, vul. Volodymyrska 45; tel. (44) 234-90-05; fax (44) 235-43-55; e-mail despanut@visti.com; Ambassador ARMEN KHACHATRIAN.

Austria: 01030 Kyiv, vul. Ivana Franka 33; tel. (44) 277-27-90; fax (44) 230-23-52; e-mail kiew-ob@bmeia.gv.at; internet www.aussenministerium.at/kiew; Ambassador JOSEF MARKUS WUKETICH.

Azerbaijan: 04050 Kyiv, vul. Hlubochytska 24; tel. (44) 484-69-40; fax (44) 484-69-46; e-mail embass@faust.kiev.ua; internet www.azembassy.org.ua; Ambassador TALYAT MUSEIB OĞLU ALIYEV.

Belarus: 01030 Kyiv, vul. M. Kotsyubynskoho 3; tel. (44) 537-52-00; fax (44) 537-52-13; e-mail inbox@belembassy.org.ua; internet www.belembassy.org.ua; Ambassador VALENTYN V. VELICHKO.

Belgium: 01030 Kyiv, vul. Leontovicha 4; tel. (44) 238-26-00; fax (44) 238-26-01; e-mail ambabel@kiev.farlep.net; internet www.diplomatie.be/kiev; Ambassador MARC VINCK.

UKRAINE

Brazil: 01010 Kyiv, vul. Suvorova 14/12, POB 471; tel. (44) 280-63-01; fax (44) 280-95-68; e-mail kievbrem@brasil.kiev.ua; internet brasil.kiev.ua; Ambassador Renato Luiz Rodrigues Marques.

Bulgaria: 01023 Kyiv, vul. Hospitalna 1; tel. (44) 246-72-37; fax (44) 235-51-19; e-mail embuln@i.kiev.ua; internet www.mfa.bg/kyiv; Ambassador Dimitar Ts. Vladimirov.

Canada: 01901 Kyiv, vul. Yaroslaviv Val 31; tel. (44) 590-31-00; fax (44) 590-31-57; e-mail kyiv@international.gc.ca; internet www.kyiv.gc.ca; Ambassador Daniel Caron.

China, People's Republic: 01901 Kyiv, vul. M. Hrushevskoho 32; tel. (44) 253-13-29; fax (44) 253-73-71; internet ua.china-embassy.org; Ambassador Zhou Li.

Croatia: 01091 Kyiv, vul. Artema 51/50; tel. (44) 486-58-62; fax (44) 484-69-43; e-mail croemb.ukraine@mvpei.hr; internet ua.mvp.hr; Ambassador Željko Kirinčić.

Cuba: 01901 Kyiv, prov. Bekhterevskyi 5; tel. (44) 486-57-43; fax (44) 486-19-07; e-mail adriana@embcuba.com.ua; Ambassador Félix León Carballo.

Czech Republic: 01901 Kyiv, vul. Yaroslaviv Val 34a; tel. (44) 272-04-31; fax (44) 272-62-04; e-mail kiev@embassy.mzv.cz; internet www.mzv.cz/kiev; Ambassador Jaroslav Bašta.

Denmark: 01901 Kyiv, vul. B. Khmelnytskoho 56; tel. (44) 200-12-60; fax (44) 200-12-81; e-mail ievamb@um.dk; internet www.ambkyiv.um.dk; Ambassador Uffe Andersson Balslev.

Egypt: 01901 Kyiv, vul. Observatorna 19; tel. (44) 212-13-27; fax (44) 486-94-28; e-mail boustan@egypt-emb.kiev.ua; Ambassador Yaser Ateph.

Estonia: 01901 Kyiv, vul. Volodymyrska 61/11–37; tel. (44) 590-07-80; fax (44) 590-07-81; e-mail embassy.kiev@mfa.ee; internet www.estemb.kiev.ua; Ambassador Jaan Hein.

Finland: 01901 Kyiv, vul. Striletska 14; tel. (44) 278-70-49; fax (44) 278-20-32; e-mail sanomat.kio@formin.fi; internet www.finland.org.ua; Ambassador Christer Michelsson.

France: 01901 Kyiv, vul. Reitarska 39; tel. (44) 590-36-00; fax (44) 590-36-24; e-mail pressefr@carrier.kiev.ua; internet www.ambafrance-ua.org; Ambassador Jacques Faure.

Georgia: 04119 Kyiv, vul. Melnikova 83d; tel. (44) 451-43-53; fax (44) 451-43-56; e-mail kiev@georgia.com.ua; Ambassador Grigol Katamadze.

Germany: 01901 Kyiv, vul. B. Khmelnytskoho 25; tel. (44) 247-68-00; fax (44) 247-68-18; e-mail kanzlei@german-embassy.kiev.ua; internet kiew.diplo.de; Ambassador Dr Hans-Jürgen Heimsoeth.

Greece: 01901 Kyiv, vul. Panfilovtsiv 10; tel. (44) 254-54-71; fax (44) 254-39-98; e-mail greece@kiev.relc.com; internet www.greece.kiev.ua; Ambassador Dimitriou Charalambos.

Holy See: 01901 Kyiv, vul. Turhenyevska 40; tel. (44) 482-35-57; fax (44) 482-35-53; e-mail nuntius@visti.com; internet www.nuntiatura.kiev.ua; Apostolic Nuncio Most Rev. Ivan Jurkovič (Titular Archbishop of Corbavia).

Hungary: 01034 Kyiv, vul. Reitarska 33; tel. (44) 230-80-00; fax (44) 272-20-90; e-mail KEV@kum.hu; internet www.mfa.gov.hu/emb/kiev; Ambassador András Bársony.

India: 01901 Kyiv, vul. Teryokhina 4; tel. (44) 468-66-61; fax (44) 468-66-19; e-mail india@public.ua.net; internet www.indianembassy.org.ua; Ambassador Debabrata Saha.

Indonesia: 04107 Kyiv, vul. Nahirna 27b; tel. (44) 206-54-46; fax (44) 206-54-40; e-mail kbri@indo.ru.kiev.ua; internet www.kbri.kiev.ua; Ambassador Pindah Estuti Sunarto.

Iran: 01901 Kyiv, vul. Kruhlouniversytetska 12; tel. (44) 253-85-43; fax (44) 254-02-53; Ambassador Seyyed Mussa Kazemi.

Iraq: 01014 Kyiv, vul. Zvirynetska 35; tel. (44) 268-04-40; fax (44) 286-04-45; e-mail kefemb@iraqmofamail.com; Chargé d'affaires a.i. Khalid Jasim al-Shamari.

Israel: 01901 Kyiv, bulv. L. Ukrainky 34; tel. (44) 586-15-00; fax (44) 586-15-55; e-mail info@kiev.mfa.gov.il; internet ukraine.mfa.gov.il; Ambassador Zina Kalay-Kleitman.

Italy: 01901 Kyiv, vul. Yaroslaviv Val 32b; tel. (44) 230-31-00; fax (44) 230-31-03; e-mail ambasciata.kiev@esteri.it; internet www.ambkiev.esteri.it; Ambassador Petro Giovanni Donnici.

Japan: 01901 Kyiv, Muzeiniy prov. 4; tel. (44) 490-55-00; fax (44) 490-55-02; e-mail jpembua7f@sovamua.com; internet www.ua.emb-japan.go.jp; Ambassador Tadashi Idzava.

Kazakhstan: 01901 Kyiv, vul. Melnykova 26; tel. (44) 489-18-58; fax (44) 483-11-98; e-mail post@kazakh.kiev.ua; internet www.kazembassy.com.ua; Ambassador Amangeldy Zh. Zhumabayev.

Korea, Republic: 01034 Kyiv, vul. Volodymyrska 43; tel. (44) 246-37-59; fax (44) 246-37-57; e-mail korea@koremb.kiev.ua; internet ukr.mofat.go.kr; Ambassador Pak Ro-Byok.

Directory

Kuwait: 04210 Kyiv, vul. Obolonska nab. 19; tel. (44) 391-51-60; fax (44) 391-51-64; e-mail kuwait_embassy@ukr.net; Ambassador Hamood Youssef al-Roudhan.

Kyrgyzstan: 01901 Kyiv, vul. Artema 51/50; tel. and fax (44) 482-08-89; e-mail embassy.kg.kiev@silvercom.net; internet kyrgyzembassy.com.ua; Ambassador Erkin B. Mamkulov.

Latvia: 01010 Kyiv, vul. Sichnevoho Povstannya 6b; tel. (44) 490-70-30; fax (44) 490-70-35; e-mail embassy.ukraine@mfa.gov.lv; internet www.latemb.kiev.ua; Ambassador Atis Sjanits.

Lebanon: 01030 Kyiv, vul. Chapayeva 4/3; tel. (44) 234-15-91; fax (44) 234-15-65; e-mail lebembukr@foreigh.gov.lb; Ambassador Youssef Sadaka.

Libya: 04050 Kyiv, vul. Ovrutska 6; tel. (44) 238-60-70; fax (44) 238-60-68; Ambassador Feisal al-Shaari.

Lithuania: 01901 Kyiv, vul. Buslivska 21; tel. (44) 254-09-20; fax (44) 254-09-28; e-mail amb.ua@urm.lt; internet ua.mfa.lt; Ambassador Algirdas Kumža.

Macedonia, former Yugoslav republic: 03150 Kyiv, vul. I. Fedorova 12; tel. (44) 238-66-16; fax (44) 238-66-17; e-mail embmac@carrier.kiev.ua; Ambassador Ilija Isajlovski.

Malaysia: 01001 Kyiv, vul. Buslivksa 25; tel. (44) 286-89-40; fax (44) 286-89-42; e-mail malkiev@kln.gov.my; internet www.kln.gov.my/perwakilan/kiev; Ambassador Dato' Abdullah Sani bin Omar.

Mexico: 01004 Kyiv, vul. Krutyi uzviz 6/2; tel. (44) 251-29-44; fax (44) 251-29-33; e-mail embamexucrania@mexico.kiev.ua; internet www.mexico.kiev.ua; Ambassador Cesar Oscar Ocaranza Castañeda.

Moldova: 01010 Kyiv, vul. Sichnevoho Povstannya 6; tel. and fax (44) 280-77-21; e-mail kiev@mfa.md; Ambassador Sergiu Stati.

Morocco: 03680 Kyiv, pr. I. Fedorova 12; tel. (44) 284-33-26; fax (44) 568-58-84; e-mail morocco@kiev.farlep.net; Ambassador Abdeljalil Saubry.

Netherlands: 01901 Kyiv, Kontraktova pl. 7; tel. (44) 490-82-00; fax (44) 490-82-09; e-mail kie@minbuza.nl; internet www.netherlands-embassy.com.ua; Ambassador Ron Keller.

Nigeria: 01015 Kyiv, bulv. Panfiliovtsiv 36; tel. (44) 254-58-50; fax (44) 254-53-71; Ambassador Ibrahim Pada Kasaj.

Norway: 01901 Kyiv, vul. Striletska 15; tel. (44) 590-04-70; fax (44) 234-06-55; e-mail emb.kiev@mfa.no; internet www.norway.com.ua; Ambassador Olav Berstad.

Pakistan: 01015 Kyiv, pr. Panfilovtsiv 7; tel. (44) 280-25-77; fax (44) 254-45-30; e-mail parepkyiv@mail.kar.net; Ambassador Ghazanfar Ali Khan.

Peru: 01004 Kyiv, vul. Pushkinska 11/6; tel. (44) 278-28-39; fax (44) 279-26-56; e-mail peru@embaperu.kiev.ua; Ambassador Liliana de Olarte de Torres-Muga.

Poland: 01034 Kyiv, vul. Yaroslaviv Val 12; tel. (44) 230-07-00; fax (44) 270-63-36; e-mail ambasada@polska.com.ua; internet www.kijow.polemb.net; Ambassador Jacek Kluczkowski.

Portugal: 01901 Kyiv, vul. I. Fedorova 12; tel. (44) 287-58-61; fax (44) 230-26-25; e-mail geral@embport.kiev.ua; Ambassador Mário Jesus dos Santos.

Romania: 01030 Kyiv, vul. M. Kotsyubynskoho 8; tel. (44) 234-00-40; fax (44) 235-20-25; e-mail romania@iptelecom.net.ua; internet kiev.mae.ro; Ambassador Traian Laurențiu Hristea.

Russia: 03049 Kyiv, Povitroflotskyi pr. 27; tel. (44) 244-09-63; fax (44) 246-34-69; e-mail embrus@public.icyb.kiev.ua; internet www.embrus.org.ua; Ambassador Viktor S. Chernomyrdin.

Serbia: 04070 Kyiv, vul. Voloska 4; tel. (44) 425-60-60; fax (44) 425-60-47; e-mail ambars@ambars@adamant.net; Ambassador Goran Aleksić.

Slovakia: 01901 Kyiv, vul. Yaroslaviv Val 34; tel. (44) 272-03-10; fax (44) 272-32-71; e-mail embassy@kiev.mfa.sk; internet www.slovakia.kiev.ua; Ambassador Urban Rusnák.

Slovenia: 01030 Kyiv, vul. B. Khmelnytskoho 48; tel. (44) 585-23-31; fax 585-23-43; e-mail vki@gov.si; internet www.kijev.veleposlanistvo.si; Chargé d'affaires a.i. Boris Gole.

South Africa: 01004 Kyiv, vul. V. Vasylkivska 9/2, POB 7; tel. (44) 287-71-72; fax (44) 287-72-06; e-mail saemb@utel.net.ua; Ambassador Andries Venter.

Spain: 01901 Kyiv, vul. Khoriva 46; tel. (44) 492-73-20; fax (44) 492-73-27; e-mail embespua@mail.mae.es; Ambassador Luis Javier Gil Catalina.

Sweden: 01901 Kyiv, vul. Ivana Franka 34/33; tel. (44) 494-42-70; fax (44) 494-42-71; e-mail ambassaden.kiev@foreign.ministry.se; internet www.swedenabroad.com/kiev; Ambassador John-Christer Åhlander.

Switzerland: 01015 Kyiv, vul. Kozyatynska 12, POB 114; tel. (44) 281-61-28; fax (44) 280-14-48; e-mail kie.vertretung@eda.admin.ch; internet www.eda.admin.ch/kiev; Ambassador Georg Zubler.

UKRAINE

Syria: 03050 Kyiv, vul. Biloruska 5; tel. (44) 489-55-51; fax (44) 483-97-88; e-mail syrian-emb@ukr.net; Chargé d'affaires a.i. SULEIMAN ABUDIAB.

Turkey: 01901 Kyiv, vul. Arsenalna 18; tel. (44) 281-07-51; fax (44) 285-64-23; e-mail kievbe@binet.com.ua; Ambassador ŞERIF IŞCAN ERDOĞAN.

Turkmenistan: 01901 Kyiv, vul. Pushkinska 6; tel. (44) 279-34-49; fax (44) 279-30-34; e-mail ambturkm@ukrpack.net; Ambassador SERDAR S. MURADOV.

United Kingdom: 01025 Kyiv, vul. Desyatynna 9; tel. (44) 490-36-60; fax (44) 490-36-62; e-mail ukembinf@sovamua.com; internet ukinukraine.fco.gov.uk; Ambassador ROBERT LEIGH TURNER.

USA: 01901 Kyiv, vul. Yu. Kotsyubynskoho 10; tel. (44) 490-40-00; fax (44) 490-40-85; e-mail press@usembassy.kiev.ua; internet kiev.usembassy.gov; Ambassador WILLIAM B. TAYLOR, Jr.

Uzbekistan: 01901 Kyiv, vul. Volodymyrska 16; tel. (44) 501-50-00; fax 501-50-01; e-mail embassy@uzbekistan.org.ua; internet www.uzbekistan.org.ua; Ambassador ILHOM Y. HAYDAROV.

Viet Nam: 01011 Kyiv, vul. Tovarna 51A; tel. (44) 284-57-40; fax (44) 284-55-42; e-mail dsq@dsqvn.kiev.ua; Ambassador NGUYEN VAN THANEM.

Judicial System

Constitutional Court of Ukraine (Konstytutsiyniy sud Ukraini): 01033 Kyiv, vul. Zhylianska 14; tel. (44) 289-05-53; fax (44) 287-20-01; e-mail idep@ccu.gov.ua; internet www.ccu.gov.ua; f. 1996; Chair. ANDRIY A. STRYZHAK.

Supreme Court (Verkhovnyi sud Ukraini): 01024 Kyiv, vul. P. Orlyka 4; tel. (44) 253-63-08; internet www.scourt.gov.ua; Chair. VASYL V. OPONENKO; Chair. of Civil Chamber ANDRIY V. HNATENKO; Chair. of Criminal Chamber MYKOLA YE. KOROTKEVYCH; Chair. of Economic Chamber VALENTYN P. BARBARA; Chair. of Administrative Chamber VIKTOR V. KRYVENKO; Chair. of Military Judicial Commission OLEKSANDR F. VOLKOV.

Supreme Economic Court (Vyshyi hospodarskyi sud Ukraini): 01011 Kyiv, vul. Kopylenka 6; tel. (44) 536-05-00; fax (44) 536-18-18; e-mail kantselariya@vasu.arbitr.gov.ua; internet www.arbitr.gov.ua; f. 1991; Chair. SERHIY F. DEMCHENKO.

Office of the Prosecutor-General: 01011 Kyiv, vul. Riznytska 13/15; tel. (44) 226-20-27; fax (44) 280-28-51; e-mail ilrd@gp.gov.ua; internet www.gp.gov.ua; Prosecutor-General OLEKSANDR L. MEDVEDKO.

Religion

State Department for Ethnic and Religious Affairs (Derzhavnyi departament u spravakh natsionalnostei ta religii): 01025 Kyiv, vul. Volodymyrska 9; tel. (44) 278-17-18; e-mail mail@scnm.gov.ua; internet www.scnm.gov.ua; Chair. OLEKSANDR N. SAHAN.

CHRISTIANITY

The Eastern Orthodox Church

Eastern Orthodoxy is the principal religious affiliation in Ukraine. Until 1990 all legally constituted Orthodox church communities in Ukraine were part of the Ukrainian Exarchate of the Russian Orthodox Church (Moscow Patriarchate). In that year the Russian Orthodox Church in Ukraine was renamed the Ukrainian Orthodox Church (UOC), partly to counter the growing influence of the previously prohibited Ukrainian Autocephalous Orthodox Church (UAOC). A new ecclesiastical organization was formed in June 1992, when Filaret (Denisenko), the former Metropolitan of Kyiv, united with a faction of the UAOC to form the Kyiv Patriarchate. In July 1995 Filaret was elected as Patriarch, prompting some senior clergy to leave the church and join the UAOC. In the late 2000s the UOC (Moscow Patriarchate) remained the largest church organization in Ukraine.

Ukrainian Autocephalous Orthodox Church: 01001 Kyiv, vul. Tryokhsvyatytelska 8A; e-mail uapc-ptr@uapc-ptr.kiev.ua; internet www.uaoc.kiev.ua; f. 1921; forcibly incorporated into the Russian Orthodox Church (Moscow Patriarchate) in 1930; continued to operate clandestinely; formally revived in 1990; 1,219 parishes in 2009; Administrator Archbishop IHOR (ISICHENKO).

Ukrainian Orthodox Church (Kyiv Patriarchate): 01004 Kyiv, vul. Pushkinska 36; tel. (44) 234-10-96; fax (44) 234-30-55; e-mail patb@ukrpack.net; internet www.cerkva.info; f. 1992 by factions of the Ukrainian Orthodox Church (Moscow Patriarchate) and Ukrainian Autocephalous Orthodox Church; 4,221 parishes in 2009; Patriarch of Kyiv and all Rus-Ukraine FILARET (DENISENKO).

Directory

Ukrainian Orthodox Church (Moscow Patriarchate): 01015 Kyiv, vul. I. Mazepy 25/49; tel. (44) 255-12-04; fax (44) 254-53-01; e-mail mitropolia@svitonline.com; internet www.pravoslavye.org.ua; exarchate of the Russian Orthodox Church (Moscow Patriarchate); 11,738 parishes in 2009; Metropolitan of Kyiv and All-Ukraine VLADIMIR (SABODAN).

Russian Orthodox Old Belief (Old Ritual) Church (Russkaya Pravoslavnaya Staroobryadcheskaya Tserkov): 49017 Dnipropetrovsk, pr. K. Marksa 60/8; tel. (562) 52-17-75; internet www.staroobryad.narod.ru; f. 1652 by separation from the Moscow Patriarchate; divided into two main branches: the *popovtsi* (which have priests) and the *bezpopovtsi* (which reject the notion of ordained priests and the use of all sacraments, other than that of baptism). Both branches are further divided into various groupings. The largest group of *popovtsi* are those of the Belokrinitskii Concord; 56 parishes of the Belokrinitskii Concord in Ukraine in 2009, and 10 parishes of *bezpopovtsi* at that time; Bishop of Kyiv and all Ukraine SAVVAYIYE.

The Roman Catholic Church

Most Catholics in Ukraine are adherents of the Byzantine rites observed by the so-called 'Greek' Catholic Church, which is based principally in western Ukraine and Transcarpathia. Some controversy arose, in August 2005, when the seat of the head of the Byzantine-rite Church was relocated from Lviv to the Ukrainian capital, Kyiv. In 2009 there were 3,728 parishes of the Byzantine rites in Ukraine, 1,064 parishes of the Latin rite and 27 parishes of the Armenian rite. Ukraine comprises one archbishopric-major (of the Byzantine rite), three archdioceses (including one each for Catholics of the Latin, Byzantine and Armenian rites), one exarchate, and 15 dioceses (of which one is directly responsible to the Holy See). At 31 December 2006 there were an estimated 4,723,456 adherents (excluding adherents of the Armenian rite, for whom figures were not available), equivalent to some 8.6% of the population. Of that number, around 83% followed the Byzantine rites.

Byzantine Ukrainian Rite

Archbishop-Major of Kyiv and Halych: Cardinal LUBOMYR HUSAR, 01000 Kyiv, vul. Riznytska 11 B/28–29; tel. and fax (44) 254-56-10; e-mail arkyrparh-kv@voliacable.com; internet www.ugcc.org.ua; head of Ukrainian Greek Catholic Church; established in 1596 by the Union of Brest; forcibly integrated into the Russian Orthodox Church (Moscow Patriarchate) in 1946, but continued to function in an 'underground' capacity; relegalized in 1989; in 2005 the seat of the head of the Church was relocated from Lviv, in western Ukraine, to Kyiv.

Archbishop of Lviv: Most Rev. IHOR VOZNIAK, 79000 Lviv, pl. Sv. Yura 5; tel. and fax (32) 272-25-24; e-mail cerkvalviv@ugcc.org.ua.

Latin Rite

Archbishop of Lviv: Most Rev. MIECZYSŁAW MOKRZYCKI, 79011 Lviv, vul. Samchuka 14 A; tel. (32) 276-94-15; fax (32) 296-61-14; e-mail rka@lviv.farlep.net; internet www.rkc.lviv.ua.

Armenian Rite

Archbishop of Lviv: (vacant).

Protestant Churches

There were 9,069 Protestant communities registered in Ukraine in 2009.

All-Ukrainian Union of Associations of Evangelical Christians-Baptists: 01004 Kyiv, vul. L. Tolstoho 3B; tel. (44) 234-82-41; fax (44) 234-16-76; e-mail union@baptist.kiev.ua; 2,679 parishes in 2009, 134,757 adherents in 2006; affiliated to the Euro-Asiatic Federation of the Union of Evangelical Christians-Baptists; Pres. VYACHESLAV V. NESTERUK.

All-Ukrainian Union of Christians of the Evangelical Faith—Pentecostalists: 03115 Kyiv, vul. Oniskevycha 3; tel. (44) 452-21-40; fax (44) 424-25-80; internet uupc.org; 1,553 parishes in 2009; Pres. MYKHAILO S. PANOCHKO.

Embassy of the Blessed Kingdom of God for All Nations: 02152 Kyiv, vul. Tychchyny 18, Legkoatletleticheskiy manezh; tel. (44) 553-15-38; e-mail mail@godembassy.org; internet www.godembassy.org; f. 1994 as Word of Faith (Slovo Very); Pastor SUNDAY ADELAJA; 25,000 mems (2005).

Ukrainian Lutheran Church: 01004 Kyiv, vul. V. Vasylkivska 14/15; tel. (44) 235-77-21; fax (44) 234-08-00; e-mail vhorpynchuk@yahoo.com; internet www.ukrlc.org; 43 parishes in 2009; Leader of Church Bishop Dr VYACHESLAV HORPYNCHUK.

ISLAM

In 2009 there were 535 Islamic communities officially registered in Ukraine, of which 352 were members of the Religious Administration

UKRAINE

of Muslims of Crimea. An Islamic University was established in Donetsk in 1998.

All-Ukrainian Association of Muslim Social Organizations (Arraid): 04119 Kyiv, vul. Dekhtyarivska 25A; tel. (44) 490-99-00; fax (44) 490-99-22; e-mail office@arraid.org; internet www.arraid.org; f. 1997; brs in Dnipropetrovsk, Donetsk, Kharkiv, Luhansk, Lviv, Odesa, Simferopol, Vinnytsya and Zaporizhzhya; publishes periodical *Arraid (Pioneer)* in Arabic and Russian and educational material in Russian, Tatar and Ukrainian; undertakes charitable and educational work; Chair. ISMAIL KADI.

Religious Administration of Muslims of Crimea: 95000 Crimea, Simferopol, Kebir Çami Mosque; 352 communities in 2009; Mufti AJE NURALI ABLAIYEV.

Religious Administration of Muslims of Ukraine: 04071 Kyiv, vul. Lukyanovska; tel. (44) 465-18-77; fax (44) 456-17-70; e-mail islam@i.kiev.ua; internet www.islamyat.org; f. 1992; 72 communities in 2009; Mufti Sheikh AHMED TAMIM.

JUDAISM

In 2001 there were 103,600 Jews in Ukraine (according to census results), despite high levels of emigration from the 1970s. From 1989 there was a considerable revival in the activities of Jewish communities. In 2009 there were 295 Jewish religious communities registered in Ukraine (of which 124 were members of the Chabad-Lubavitch sect), compared with 12 synagogues in 1989.

All-Ukrainian Jewish Congress: 01023 Kyiv, vul. Mechnykova 14/1; tel. (44) 235-71-20; fax (44) 235-10-67; e-mail vek@i.kiev.ua; internet www.jewish.kiev.ua; f. 1997; affiliated to the Federation of Jewish Communities of the CIS and the Baltic states; unites 183 communities; Chief Rabbi of Ukraine AZRIEL CHAIKIN.

Jewish Confederation of Ukraine: 04071 Kyiv, vul. Shekavystka 29; tel. (44) 463-70-75; fax (44) 463-70-88; e-mail eku@jewukr.org; internet www.jewukr.org; f. 1999; Chief Rabbi of Kyiv and All Ukraine YAAKOV DOV BLEICH.

The Press

In 2006 there were a total of 2,918 newspapers and 2,301 periodicals published in Ukraine. In addition to newspapers published in Ukraine, several newspapers and magazines published in Russia have a large circulation in Ukraine.

The publications listed below are in Ukrainian, except where otherwise stated.

PRINCIPAL NEWSPAPERS

Demokratychna Ukraina (Democratic Ukraine): 03047 Kyiv, pr. Peremohy 50; tel. (44) 454-88-30; fax (44) 456-91-21; e-mail du@uct.ua; internet www.dua.com.ua; f. 1918; fmrly *Radyanska Ukraina* (Soviet Ukraine); 4 a week; Editor VITALIY ADAMENKO; circ. 62,400 (2005).

Den (The Day): 04212 Kyiv, vul. Marshala Tymoshenka 2L; tel. (44) 414-40-66; fax (44) 414-49-20; e-mail master@day.kiev.ua; internet www.day.kiev.ua; f. 1998; in Ukrainian and Russian; 5 a week; publ. by the Presa Ukrainy (Press of Ukraine) Publishing House; Editor-in-Chief LARYSA IVSHYNA.

Fakty i Kommentarii (Facts and Commentaries): 04116 Kyiv, vul. V. Vasylevskoy 27–29; tel. (44) 244-57-81; fax (44) 246-85-50; e-mail info@facts.kiev.ua; internet www.facts.kiev.ua; f. 1997; daily; politics, economics, sport, law, culture; in Russian; Chief Editor ALEKSANDR SHVETS.

Gazeta po-Kiyevski (Kyiv Newspaper): 04080 Kyiv, vul. Frunze 104A; tel. (44) 205-43-85; e-mail tsn@pk.kiev.ua; internet pk.kiev.ua; in Russian; 6 a week; Chief Editor SERGEI TIKHII.

Holos Ukrainy/Golos Ukrainy (Voice of Ukraine): 03047 Kyiv, vul. Nesterova 4; tel. (44) 441-88-11; fax (44) 224-72-54; e-mail mail@golos.com.ua; f. 1991; organ of the Verkhovna Rada; in Ukrainian and Russian; 5 a week; Editor SERHIY M. PRAVDENKO; circ. 150,000 (2002).

Kiyevskiye Vedomosti (Kyiv Gazette): 04086 Kyiv, vul. Olzhycha 29; tel. (44) 238-28-07; internet www.kv.com.ua; f. 1992; national daily; in Russian; also weekly edition (Fridays), in Ukrainian, *Kyivski Vidomosti*; Dir-Gen. VLADIMIR P. DERIKIT; Editor-in-Chief NIKOLAI V. ZAKREVSKII.

Kommersant-Ukraina (Businessman-Ukraine): 01011 Kyiv, vul. Rybalska 22; tel. (44) 497-37-20; internet www.kommersant.ua; f. 2005; owned by Kommersant Publishing House (Russia); in Russian; Dir-Gen. and Chief Editor ANDREI GOGOLEV.

Kyiv Post: 02140 Kyiv, pr. Bazhava 14A; tel. and fax (44) 496-45-63; e-mail editor@kyivpost.com; internet www.kyivpost.com; f. 1995; weekly; in English; Publr JED SUNDEN; Chief Editor BRIAN BONNER; circ. 22,000 (2007).

Literaturna Ukraina (Literary Ukraine): 01061 Kyiv, bulv. L. Ukrainky 20; tel. (44) 286-36-39; e-mail lit_ukraine@ukr.net; f. 1927; weekly; organ of Union of Writers of Ukraine; Editor PETRO PEREBYJNIS; circ. 7,150 (2007).

Molod Ukrainy (The Youth of Ukraine): 03047 Kyiv, pr. Peremohy 50; tel. (44) 454-83-83; fax (44) 235-31-52; e-mail mu@pressa.com.ua; f. 1925; 3 a week; Editor-in-Chief V. I. NIKIPYELOV; circ. 24,000 (2007).

Pravda Ukrainy (The Truth of Ukraine): 01032 Kyiv, vul. Starovokzalna 17; tel. (44) 270-62-16; e-mail vyasnopolska@pravda-ua.info; internet www.pravda-ua.info; f. 1938; weekly; in Russian; Editor-in-Chief VIKTORIYA YASNOPOLSKAYA; circ. 187,000.

Robitnycha Hazeta/Rabochaya Gazeta (Workers' Gazette): 03047 Kyiv, pr. Peremohy 50; tel. (44) 454-84-94; fax (44) 456-68-85; e-mail mail@rg.kiev.ua; internet www.rg.kiev.ua; f. 1957; 5 a week; publ. by the Cabinet of Ministers and Inter-regional Association of Manufacturers; Ukrainian and Russian edns; Dir-Gen. and Chief Editor ANATOLIY KRYVOLAPOV.

Silski Visti (Rural News): 03047 Kyiv, pr. Peremohy 50; tel. (44) 441-86-32; fax (44) 446-93-71; e-mail ssk@silvist.kiev.ua; internet www.silskivisti.kiev.ua; f. 1920; 3 a week; Chief Editor V. D. HRUZIN.

Ukraina Moloda (Ukraine The Young): 03047 Kyiv, pr. Peremohy 50; tel. and fax (44) 454-83-92; e-mail politika@umoloda.kiev.ua; internet www.umoloda.kiev.ua; f. 1991; 5 a week; independent; Editor MYKHAYLO DOROSHENKO; circ. 131,657 (2008).

Ukrainska Pravda (Ukrainian Truth): Kyiv; e-mail ukrpravda@gmail.com; internet www.pravda.com.ua; online only; in English, Russian and Ukrainian; Editor-in-Chief OLENA PRYTULA.

Ukrainske Slovo (The Ukrainian Word): 01010 Kyiv, vul. I. Mazepy 6; tel. (44) 280-70-59; fax (44) 280-62-65; e-mail ukrslovo@ukr.net; internet www.ukrslovo.com.ua; f. 1933; weekly; nationalist; Editor-in-Chief HRYHORIY KRYMCHUK.

Uryadoviy Kuryer (Official Courier): 01008 Kyiv, vul. Sadova 1; tel. (44) 253-12-95; fax (44) 253-39-50; e-mail letter@ukcc.com.ua; internet www.ukcc.com.ua; f. 1990; 5 a week; organ of the Cabinet of Ministers; Editor-in-Chief ALLA KOVTUR; circ. 83,000 (2008).

Vechirniy Kyiv (Evening Kyiv): 04136 Kyiv, vul. Marshala Hrechka 13; tel. (44) 434-61-09; fax (44) 443-96-09; internet www.vechirnij.kiev.ua; f. 1906; 5 a week; Editor-in-Chief OLEKSANDR BALABKO; circ. 45,000 (2005).

Vlada i Polityka/Vlast i Politika (Power and Politics): 01042 Kyiv, vul. P. Lumumby 4V/200; tel. (44) 201-01-28; fax (44) 201-01-29; e-mail vip@vipnews.com.ua; internet www.vipnews.com.ua; f. 2001; weekly; in Ukrainian and Russian; Dir-Gen. ANDRIY V. NAKONECHNYI; Editor-in-Chief YURIY L. UZDEMYR; circ. 22,000 (2002).

PRINCIPAL PERIODICALS

Avto-Tsentr (Autocentre): 03047 Kyiv, pr. Peremohy 50, POB 2; tel. (44) 206-56-01; fax (44) 458-44-04; e-mail info@autocentre.ua; internet www.autocentre.ua; f. 1997; weekly; motoring; in Russian; Editor-in-Chief SERGEI TARNAVSKII; circ. 200,000.

Barvinok (Periwinkle): 04119 Kyiv, vul. Dekhtyarivska 38–44; tel. (44) 213-99-13; fax (44) 211-04-36; e-mail barvinok@kievweb.com.ua; f. 1928; fortnightly; illustrated popular fiction for school-age children; in Ukrainian; Editor VASYL VORONOVYCH; circ. 40,000.

Berezil: 61002 Kharkiv, vul. Chernyshevskoho 59; tel. (57) 700-32-23; fax (57) 700-54-37; e-mail berezil@ukr.net; f. 1956; fmrly Prapor; monthly; journal of Union of Writers of Ukraine; fiction and socio-political articles; Editor-in-Chief VOLODYMYR NAUMENKO; circ. 5,000.

Delovaya Stolitsya (Capital City Business): 01135 Kyiv, vul. Pavlovska 29; tel. (44) 502-02-21; fax (44) 502-02-27; e-mail dsnews@dsnews.ua; internet www.dsnews.ua; f. 2001; weekly; in Russian; Editor-in-Chief INNA KOVTUN; circ. 67,500 (2008).

Dnipro (The Dnieper): 04119 Kyiv, vul. Dekhtyarivska 38–44; tel. (44) 446-11-42; f. 1927; 2 a month; novels, short stories, essays, poetry, social and political topics; Editor MYKOLA LUKIV.

Dzerkalo Tyzhnya/Zerkalo Nedyeli (Mirror of the Week): 03680 Kyiv, vul. Tverska 6; tel. (44) 536-02-44; fax (44) 269-74-52; e-mail info@mirror.kiev.ua; internet www.zerkalo-nedeli.com; weekly; politics, economics, the arts; Ukrainian and Russian edns; also English edition (online only); Editor-in-Chief VLADIMIR MOSTOVOI; circ. 30,000 (Russian edn), 12,000 (Ukrainian edn).

Dzvin (Bell): 79005 Lviv, vul. Kn. Romana 6; tel. (32) 272-36-20; f. 1940; monthly; journal of Union of Writers of Ukraine; fiction; Editor ROMAN FEDORIV; circ. 152,500.

Kompanyon (Companion): 01103 Kyiv, vul. Kykbydze 39; tel. (44) 494-25-01; fax (44) 494-25-05; e-mail komp@companion.ua; internet www.companion.ua; f. 1996; weekly; in Russian; economics, politics, business; Editor-in-Chief A. POHORELOV; circ. 25,000 (2004).

Kyiv: 01025 Kyiv, vul. Desyatinna 11; tel. (44) 229-02-80; f. 1983; monthly; journal of the Union of Writers of Ukraine and the Kyiv Writers' Organization; fiction; Editor-in-Chief PETRO M. PEREBYJNIS.

UKRAINE

Malyatko (Child): 04119 Kyiv, vul. Dekhtyarivska 38–44; tel. and fax (44) 483-98-91; e-mail malyatko_1@online.com.ua; f. 1960; monthly; illustrated; for pre-school children; Editor-in-Chief ZINAIDA LESHENKO; circ. 35,780 (2005).

Nataly: 02156 Kyiv, vul. Kyoto 25; tel. (44) 593-05-85; internet www.nataly.com.ua; monthly; women's interest; Editor-in-Chief ZHANNA LAVROVA; circ. 679,115 (2002).

Natsionalna Bezpeka i Oborona (National Security and Defence): 01034 Kyiv, vul. Volodymyrska 46, Olekander Razumkov Ukrainian Centre for Economic and Political Studies; tel. (44) 201-11-98; fax (44) 201-11-99; e-mail info@uceps.com.ua; internet www.uceps.com.ua; f. 2000; monthly; politics, economics, international relations; in Ukrainian and English; Pres. ANATOLIY GRYTSENKO.

Obrazotvorche Mistetstvo (Fine Arts): 04055 Kyiv, vul. Artema 1–5; tel. (44) 272-02-86; fax (44) 272-14-54; e-mail spilka@nbi.com.ua; f. 1933; 4 a year; publ. by the National Union of Artists of Ukraine; Editor-in-Chief OLEKSANDR FEDORUK; circ. 1,500 (2007).

Perets (Pepper): 03047 Kyiv, pr. Peremohy 50; tel. (44) 454-82-14; fax (44) 234-35-82; e-mail prudnyk@bigmir.net; f. 1922; monthly; publ. by the Presa Ukrainy Publishing House; satirical; Editor MYKHAYLO PRUDNYK; circ. 15,000 (2007).

Politychna Dumka/Politicheskaya Mysl/Political Thought: 01030 Kyiv, vul. Leontovycha 5; tel. and fax (44) 235-02-29; e-mail politdumka@bigmir.net; internet www.politdumka.kiev.ua; f. 1993; current affairs and political analysis; Ukrainian, Russian and English edns; Editor-in-Chief VOLODOMYR POLOKHALO.

Polityka i Chas/Politics and the Times: 02160 Kyiv, pr. Vozyednanya 15–17; tel. and fax (44) 550-31-44; e-mail times@uct.kiev.ua; f. 1994 to replace *Pid praporam Lenina* (Under the Banner of Lenin); monthly; organ of the Ministry of Foreign Affairs; international relations and foreign affairs; in Ukrainian (monthly) and English (quarterly); Editor-in-Chief LEONID BAIDAK; circ. 6,000 (2003).

Ukraina (Ukraine): 03047 Kyiv, pr. Peremohy 50; tel. and fax (44) 454-88-31; e-mail ukraina_mag@meta.ua; internet ukraina-magazine.com.ua; f. 1907; monthly; social, political and cultural life in Ukraine; illustrated; Editor-in-Chief IHOR PARYMSKY; circ. 40,000 (2007).

Ukrainskiy Teatr (Ukrainian Theatre): Kyiv; tel. (44) 228-24-74; f. 1936; 6 a year; journal of the Ministry of Art and Culture, and the Union of Theatrical Workers of Ukraine; Editor-in-Chief YURIY BOHDASHEVSKIY; circ. 4,100.

Vitchyzna (Fatherland): 01021 Kyiv, vul. M. Hrushevskoho 34; tel. (44) 253-28-51; f. 1933; 6 a year; Ukrainian prose and poetry; Editor OLEKSANDR HLUSHKO; circ. 50,100.

Vsesvit (The Whole World): 01021 Kyiv, vul. M. Hrushevskoho 34/1; tel. (44) 253-13-18; fax (44) 253-06-13; e-mail myk@vsesvit-review.kiev.ua; internet www.vsesvit-journal.com; f. 1925; monthly; foreign fiction, literary criticism and reviews of foreign literature and art; Exec. Editor OLEH MYKYTENKO; circ. 2,000–3,000 (2007).

Yeva (Eve): 04050 Kyiv, vul. Melnykova 12A/8; tel. (44) 568-59-53; fax (44) 568-58-96; e-mail info@evamag.com; f. 1998; 6 a year; fashion, design; Editor-in-Chief IRYNA B. DANYLEVSKA; circ. 10,000 (2002).

Yi (Ji): Lviv; e-mail info@ji.lviv.ua; internet www.ji-magazine.lviv.ua; f. 1989; independent; literature and literary criticism, culture, politics, philosophy; Chief Editor TARAS VOZNYAK.

Zhinka (Woman): 03047 Kyiv, pr. Peremohy 50; tel. and fax (44) 446-90-34; e-mail zhinka@cki.ipri.kiev.ua; f. 1920; monthly; publ. by Presa Ukrainy Publishing House; social and political subjects, fiction; for women; Editor LIDIYA MAZUR; circ. 250,000.

NEWS AGENCIES

Interfax-Ukraina (Interfax-Ukraine): 01034 Kyiv, vul. Reitarska 8/5 A; tel. (44) 464-04-65; fax (44) 464-05-69; e-mail news@interfax.kiev.ua; internet www.interfax.kiev.ua; f. 1992; Dir OLEKSANDR MARTYNENKO.

Respublika Ukrainian Independent Information Agency (UNIAR): 02005 Kyiv, vul. Mechnykova 14/1; tel. (44) 246-46-34; e-mail naboka@uniar.kiev.ua; internet www.uniar.com.ua; independent press agency; Dir S. NABOKA.

Ukrainian Independent Information and News Agency (UNIAN): 01001 Kyiv, vul. Khreshchatyk 4; tel. (44) 279-33-53; fax (44) 461-91-11; e-mail info@unian.net; internet www.unian.net; f. 1993; press agency and monitoring service; selected services are provided in Ukrainian, Russian and English; Gen. Dir OLEH I. NALIVAIKO; Editor-in-Chief OLEKSANDR A. KHARCHENKO.

Ukrainski Novyni Informatsyonnoye Ahentstvo (Ukrainian News Information Agency): 01033 Kyiv, vul. Volodymyrska 61/11/41; tel. (44) 494-31-60; fax (44) 494-31-67; e-mail office@ukranews.com; internet www.ukranews.com; f. 1993; economic and political news; in Ukrainian, Russian and English.

UkrInform–Ukrainian National Information Agency: 01001 Kyiv, vul. B. Khmelnytskoho 8/16B; tel. (44) 279-81-52; fax (44) 279-86-65; e-mail office@ukrinform.com; internet news.ukrinform.com.ua; f. 1918; Dir-Gen. VIKTOR CHAMARA.

Publishers

In 1996 there were 6,460 book titles (including pamphlets and brochures) published in Ukraine (total circulation 50.9m.). By 2006 the number of book titles published in Ukraine had increased to 15,867.

Donbas: 83015 Donetsk, vul. B. Khmelnytskoho 102; tel. (62) 304-01-56; fiction and criticism; in Ukrainian and Russian; Dir A. I. YEZHEL.

Folio: 61002 Kharkiv, vul. Chubarya 11; tel. (57) 700-42-29; fax (57) 715-64-92; e-mail trade@folio.com.ua; internet folio.com.ua; f. 1992; classic and contemporary fiction in Russian, Ukrainian and French; Gen. Man. OLEKSANDR V. KRASOVYTSKIY.

Kamenyar (Stonecrusher): 79000 Lviv, vul. Pidvalna 3; tel. and fax (32) 235-59-49; e-mail vyd_kamenyar@mail.lviv.ua; internet www.kamenyar.com.ua; f. 1939; state-owned; fiction and criticism; in Ukrainian and Polish; Dir DMYTRO I. SAPIGA.

Karpaty (The Carpathians): 88000 Transcarpathian obl., Uzhhorod, pl. Zhupanatska 3; tel. (312) 23-23-66; fiction and criticism; Dir V. V. BRASLAVETS.

Lybid (Swan): 01004 Kyiv, vul. Pushkinska 32; tel. and fax (44) 279-11-71; e-mail info@lybid.org.ua; internet www.lybid.org.ua; f. 1835; University of Kyiv press; Dir OLENA A. BOIKO.

Medytsyna Svitu (Medicines of the World): 79071 Lviv, vul. Kulparkivska 131; tel. (32) 263-34-65; fax (32) 297-80-49; e-mail msvitu@mail.lviv.ua; internet www.msvitu.lviv.ua; f. 1997; medical journals and books, history, art and religion; Dir ZINOVIY MATCHAK.

Molod (Youth): 04119 Kyiv, vul. Dekhtyarivska 38–44; tel. (44) 211-02-18; in Ukrainian; Dir OLHA I. POLONSKA.

Muzichna Ukraina (Musical Ukraine): 01034 Kyiv, vul. Pushkinska 32; tel. (44) 225-63-56; fax (44) 224-63-00; f. 1966; books on music; in Ukrainian; Dir ANATOLIY K. ANDRIYCHUK.

Mystetstvo: 01034 Kyiv, vul. Zolotovoritska 11; tel. (44) 235-53-92; fax (44) 279-05-64; e-mail mystetstvo@ukr.net; f. 1932; fine art criticism, theatre and screen art, tourism, Ukrainian culture; in Ukrainian, Russian, English, French and German; Dir NINA D. PRYBEHA.

Naukova Dumka (Scientific Thought): 01601 Kyiv, vul. Tereshchenkivska 3; tel. (44) 234-40-68; fax (44) 234-70-60; e-mail ndumka@i.kiev.ua; internet www.ndumka.kiev.ua; f. 1922; scientific books and periodicals; research monographs; Ukrainian literature; dictionaries and reference books; in Ukrainian, Russian and English; Dir IHOR R. ALEKSEYENKO.

Osvita (Education): 04053 Kyiv, vul. Yu. Kotsyubynski 5; tel. and fax (44) 486-54-44; e-mail osvita@kv.ukrtel.net; internet www.osvitapublish.com.ua; f. 1920; state-owned; educational books for schools of all levels; Dir-Gen. BORYS MAKSYMETS.

Prapor (Flag): 61002 Kharkiv, vul. Chubarya 11; tel. (57) 247-72-52; fax (57) 243-07-21; fmrly Berezil; general; in Ukrainian and Russian; Dir S. A. YEFYMENKO.

Prosvita (Enlightenment): 01032 Kyiv, bulv. Shevchenka 46; tel. (44) 234-15-86; fax (44) 234-95-23; e-mail office@prosvita.kiev.ua; internet www.prosvita.kiev.ua; f. 1990; textbooks for all levels of education from pre-school to higher education.

Sich (Camp): 49070 Dnipropetrovsk, pr. K. Marksa 60; tel. (562) 45-22-01; fax (562) 45-44-04; f. 1964; fiction, juvenile, socio-political, criticism; in Ukrainian, English, German, French and Russian; Dir YU. A. SKALOZUB.

Tavria: 95000 Crimea, Simferopol, vul. Gorkogo 5; tel. (652) 27-45-66; fax (652) 27-65-74; e-mail ingvi@ukr.net; fiction, criticism, folklore and geography; in Ukrainian, Russian and Crimean Tatar; Dir YU. YA. IVANICHENKO.

Tekhnika (Technology): 04053 Kyiv, vul. Observatorna 25; tel. (44) 212-10-90; f. 1930; industry and transport books, popular science, posters and booklets; in Ukrainian and Russian; Dir YURIY YU. KOSTRYTSYA.

Ukrainska Ensyklopedia im. M. P. Bazhana (Ukrainian M. P. Bazhan Encyclopedia): 01004 Kyiv, vul. Pushkinska 32 A; tel. (44) 235-11-08; encyclopedias, dictionaries and reference books; Dir MYKHAILO P. ZYABLYUK.

Ukrainskiy Pysmennyk (Ukrainian Writer): 01054 Kyiv, vul. O. Honchara 52; tel. and fax (44) 216-25-92; e-mail ukps@ln.ua; f. 1933; publishing house of the National Union of Writers of Ukraine; fiction; in Ukrainian; Dir OLEKSANDR A. SAVCHUK.

UKRAINE

Urozhai (Harvest): 03035 Kyiv, vul. Uritskoho 45; tel. (44) 245-09-95; f. 1925; books and journals about agriculture; Dir LILIYA A. PILKEVYCH.

Veselka (Rainbow): 04050 Kyiv, vul. Melnikova 63; tel. (44) 213-95-01; fax (44) 483-33-59; e-mail veskiev@iptelecom.net.ua; internet www.veselka-ua.com; f. 1934; books for pre-school and school-age children; in Ukrainian and foreign languages; Dir YAREMA P. HOYAN.

Zdorovya (Health): 01054 Kyiv, vul. Vorovskoho 32B; tel. (44) 216-89-08; books on medicine, physical fitness and sport; in Ukrainian; Dir VALERIY P. SYTNYK.

Znannya Ukrainy (Knowledge of Ukraine): 01034 Kyiv, vul. Striletska 28; tel. (44) 234-80-43; fax (44) 238-82-65; e-mail znannia@society.kiev.ua; internet www.znannia.com.ua; f. 1948; general non-fiction; Dir VOLODOMYR I. KARASOV.

Broadcasting and Communications

TELECOMMUNICATIONS

Regulatory Authority

State Committee for Communication and Information: 01001 Kyiv, vul. Khreshchatyk 22; tel. (44) 228-15-00; fax (44) 228-61-41; e-mail mailbox@stc.gov.ua; internet www.stc.gov.ua; Chair. IHOR V. KRAVETS.

Major Service Providers

Astelit: 03110 Kyiv, vul. Solomyanska 11 A; tel. (44) 233-31-31; internet www.life.com.ua; f. 2005; 51% owned by TurkCell (Turkey); provides mobile cellular telecommunications services under the brand name 'Life'.

Golden Telecom GSM: 01021 Kyiv, vul. Khreshchatyk 19 A; tel. (44) 490-00-90; fax (44) 490-00-70; e-mail info@goldentele.com; internet www.goldentele.com; mobile cellular telephone services; Gen. Man. YURIY BEZBORODIV.

KyivStar GSM: Kyiv, vul. I. Mazepy 24; tel. (44) 466-04-66; internet www.kyivstar.net; f. 1997; 54.2% owned by Telenor (Norway); provides mobile cellular telecommunications services under the brand names 'Ace & Base' and 'Djuice' in major cities and other regions across Ukraine; Pres. IHOR LITOVCHENKO; 15.1m. subscribers (May 2006).

MTS Ukraina: 01015 Kyiv, vul. Leiptsizka 15; fax (44) 230-02-56; e-mail slavik@umc.com.ua; internet www.umc.com.ua; f. 1991; fmrly Ukrainian Mobile Communications; present name adopted 2007; 100% owned by MTS (Russia); Gen. Man. ANDRIY DUBOVSKOV.

UkrTelecom: 01030 Kyiv, bulv. Shevchenka 18; tel. (44) 226-25-41; fax (44) 234-39-57; e-mail ukrtelecom@ukrtelecom.net; internet www.ukrtelecom.ua; f. 1993; national fixed telecommunications network operator; provides national and international telecommunications services; Chair. of Bd HEORHIY B. DZEKON.

BROADCASTING

Regulatory Authorities

National Council of Ukraine for Television and Radio Broadcasting: 01025 Kyiv, vul. Desyatynna 14; tel. (44) 278-68-32; fax (44) 228-75-75; e-mail shevch@ukr.net; internet www.nrada.gov.ua; f. 1994; monitoring and supervisory functions; issues broadcasting licences; Chair. VITALIY F. SHEVCHENKO.

State Committee for Television and Radio Broadcasting (Derzhavnyi komitet telebachennya i radiomovlennya Ukrainy): 01001 Kyiv, vul. Khreshchatyk 26/206; tel. (44) 239-63-89; internet comin.kmu.gov.ua; responsibilities include the supervision of 27 state-controlled television and radio companies; Chair. EDUARD PRUTNIK.

Radio

Hromadske (Community) Radio: 01025 Kyiv, vul. Volodymyrska 61/11/50; tel. (44) 494-40-14; information, news and discussion programmes.

National Radio Co of Ukraine-Ukrainian Radio (Natsionalna Radiokompaniya Ukrainy-Ukrainske Radio): 01001 Kyiv, vul. Khreshchatyk 26; tel. (44) 279-33-79; fax (44) 279-34-77; e-mail krutouz@nrcu.gov.ua; internet www.nrcu.gov.ua; state-owned; domestic broadcasts; also international broadcasts in English, German, Romanian and Ukrainian; Pres. VIKTOR I. NABRUSKO.

Several independent radio stations broadcast to the major cities of Ukraine.

Television

Ukrainian State Television and Radio Co (Derzhavna Teleradiomovna Kompaniya Ukrainy): 01001 Kyiv, vul. Khreshchatyk 26; tel. (44) 481-43-86; Chair. VITALIY DOKALENKO.

1+1: 01001 Kyiv, vul. Khreshchatyk 7/11; tel. and fax (44) 490-01-01; e-mail contact@1plus1.tv; internet www.1plus1.tv; f. 1995; independent; broadcasts for 24 hours daily to 95% of Ukrainian population; Chair. of Bd of Dirs OLEKSANDR YU. RODNYANSKY.

5 Kanal: 04176 Kyiv, vul. Elektrykiv 26; tel. (44) 239-16-86; internet 5.ua; terrestrial broadcasts to 14 cities, and cable and satellite broadcasts; 24-hour news broadcasts; Dir-Gen. IVAN ADAMCHUK.

Inter: 01601 Kyiv, vul. Dmitriyevska 30; tel. and fax (44) 490-67-65; e-mail pr@inter.ua; internet www.inter.kiev.ua; f. 1996.

Novy Kanal (New Channel): 04107 Kyiv, vul. Nahorna 24/1; tel. (44) 238-80-28; fax (44) 238-80-20; e-mail post@novy.tv; internet www.novy.tv; f. 1998; broadcasts in Ukrainian and Russian; Chair. OLEKSANDR M. TKACHENKO.

STB: 03113 Kyiv, vul. Shevtsova 1; tel. (44) 501-98-99; e-mail y@stb.ua; internet stb.ua; Chair. of Bd VOLODYMYR BORODYANSKY.

Finance

(cap. = capital; res = reserves; dep. = deposits; brs = branches; m. = million; amounts in hryvnyas, unless otherwise indicated)

BANKING

Central Bank

National Bank of Ukraine (Natsionalny Bank Ukrainy): 01601 Kyiv, vul. Institutska 9; tel. (44) 253-38-22; fax (44) 230-20-33; e-mail postmaster@bank.gov.ua; internet www.bank.gov.ua; f. 1991; cap. 10m., res 5,872m., dep. 36,480m. (Dec. 2006); Gov. VOLODYMYR S. STELMAKH.

Other State Banks

Republican Bank of Crimea: 95000 Crimea, Simferopol, ul. Gorkogo; tel. (652) 51-09-46; e-mail webmaster@rbc.crimea.ua.

UkrExImBank—State Export-Import Bank of Ukraine: 03150 Kyiv, vul. Horkoho 127; tel. (44) 247-80-70; fax (44) 247-80-82; e-mail bank@eximb.com; internet www.eximb.com; f. 1992; fmrly br. of USSR Vneshekonombank (External Trade Bank); cap. 1,631.6m., res 0.0m., dep. 15,833.2m., (Dec. 2006); Chair. of Bd VIKTOR V. KAPUSTIN; 30 brs.

Commercial Banks

Alfa-Bank (Ukraine): 01025 Kyiv, vul. Desyatinna 4/6; tel. (44) 490-46-00; fax (44) 490-46-01; e-mail mail@alfabank.kiev.ua; internet www.alfabank.com.ua; f. 1993; cap. US $272.6m., res $25.0m., dep. $1,552.2m. (Dec. 2007); Chair. ANDRIY VOLKOV.

Brokbiznesbank: 03057 Kyiv, pr. Peremohy 41; tel. (44) 206-29-83; fax (44) 459-67-80; e-mail bank@bankbb.com; internet www.bankbb.com; f. 1991; cap. 1,852.2m., res 217.8m., dep 9,427.3m. (Dec. 2007); Chair. of Council MYKOLA STRILA; Chair. of Bd SERHIY P. MISHTA; 235 brs.

Calyon Bank Ukraine: 01034 Kyiv, vul. Volodymyrska 23A; tel. (44) 490-14-01; fax (44) 490-14-02; e-mail ukr-general@ua.calyon.com; internet www.calyon.kiev.ua; f. 1993; 100% owned by Crédit Agricole (France); cap. 172m., res 96m., dep. 1,800m. (Dec. 2007); Pres. and Dir-Gen. JACQUES MOUNIER.

Donghorbank: 83086 Donetsk, vul. Artema 38; tel. (62) 332-73-03; fax (62) 332-73-24; e-mail pr_financing@dongorbank.com; internet www.dongorbank.com; f. 1992; cap. 304.4m., res 213.3m., dep. 3,969.8m. (Dec. 2007); Head of Management Bd VLADIMIR POPOVICH.

Finance and Credit Bank (Bank 'Financy ta Kredyt'): 04050 Kyiv, vul. Artema 60; tel. (44) 490-68-70; fax (44) 238-24-65; e-mail common@fc.kiev.ua; internet www.fc.kiev.ua; f. 1990; cap. 675.1m., dep. 6,111.7m., total assets 7,297.8m. (Dec. 2006); Chair. VLADIMIR H. KHLYVNYUK; 11 brs.

First Ukrainian International Bank/Pershyi Ukrainskyi Mizhnarodnyi Bank (FUIB): 83001 Donetsk, vul. Universitetska 2A; tel. (623) 32-45-03; fax (623) 32-47-00; e-mail corrbnk@fuib.com; internet www.fuib.com; f. 1991; cap. US $325.8m., res $78.8m., dep. $1,212.5m. (Dec. 2007); Chair. of Bd ALEKSANDRA G. VOROPAEVA.

Forum Bank (Bank Forum): 02100 Kyiv, bulv. Verkhovnoi Rady 7; tel. (44) 552-05-55; fax (44) 554-70-90; e-mail market@forum.com.ua; internet www.forum.com.ua; f. 1994; cap. 1,139.7m., res 68.4m., dep. 11,268.6m. (Dec. 2007); Chair. YAROSLAV V. KOLESNYK; 30 brs.

Indeks Bank: 01004 Kyiv, vul. Pushkinska 42/4; tel. (44) 581-07-76; fax (44) 581-07-76; e-mail liudmyla.leonova@indexbank.ua; internet www.indexbank.ua; f. 1993; 99.98% owned by Crédit Agricole

UKRAINE

Directory

(France); cap. 200.0m., res 37.4m., dep. 2,273.1m. (Dec. 2006); Chief Exec. and Chair. of Bd IGOR FRANTSKEVYCH.

Khreshchatyk Bank: 01001 Kyiv, vul. Khreshchatyk 8A; tel. and fax (44) 230-72-28; e-mail bank@xbank.com.ua; internet www.xcitybank.com.ua; f. 1993; present name adopted 1998; 23.7% owned by Kyiv City Administration; cap. US $109.0m., res $6.0m., dep. $890.1m. (Dec. 2007); Chair. of Bd DMYTRO M. GRYDZHYK; 160 brs.

Klyrynhovy Dom AB (Clearing House Joint-Stock Bank): 04070 Kyiv, vul. Borysohlibska 5A; tel. (44) 593-10-30; fax (44) 593-10-31; e-mail info@chls.kiev.ua; internet www.chls.kiev.ua; f. 1996; cap. 418.0m., dep. 1,722.2m., total assets 2,198.5m. (Dec. 2007); Chair. of Bd VIKTORIYA ANDREYIVSKA.

Kredobank: 79026 Lviv, vul. Sakharova 78; tel. (32) 297-23-20; fax (32) 297-08-37; e-mail office@kredobank.com.ua; internet www.kredobank.com.ua; f. 1990; present name adopted 2006; 98.2% owned by PKO Bank Polski SA (Poland); cap. 273.3m., dep. 2,954.5m., total assets 3,274.6m. (Dec. 2006); Pres. STEPAN I. KUBIV.

Kredytprombank: 01014 Kyiv, bulv. Druzhby Narodiv 38; tel. (44) 490-27-79; fax (44) 490-72-28; e-mail kpb@kreditprombank.com; internet www.kreditprombank.com; f. 1997; cap. 877.2m., res 78.4m., dep. 10,310.7m. (Dec. 2007); Chair. of Bd VIKTOR D. LEONIDOV.

Megabank: 61002 Kharkiv, vul. Artema 30; tel. (572) 14-33-63; fax (572) 47-20-78; e-mail mega@megabank.net; internet www.megabank.net; f. 1990; present name adopted 2001; cap. 250.1m., res 43.0m., dep. 1,592.7m. (Dec. 2007); Chair. of Supervisory Council VIKTOR G. SUBOTIN; Chair. of Bd OLENA ZHUKOVA; 8 brs.

Nadra Bank: 04053 Kyiv, vul. Artema 15; tel. (44) 459-37-00; fax (44) 288-00-22; e-mail pr@nadrabank.kiev.ua; internet www.nadra.com.ua; f. 1993; cap. US $83.7m., res $178.1m., dep. $3,147.3m. (Dec. 2007); Pres. and Chair. of Bd IGOR V. GILENKO; 691 brs and sub-brs.

OTP Bank: 01033 Kyiv, vul. Zhylyanska 43; tel. (44) 490-05-00; fax (44) 490-05-01; e-mail infobox.rbu@rbu-kiev.raiffeisen.at; internet www.rbua.com; f. 1998; present name adopted 2006; 100% owned by OTP Bank plc (Romania); cap. 540.0m., res 2.7m., dep. 10,009.3m. (Dec. 2006); Chair. of Bd DMITRI ZINKOV.

Pivdennyi Bank: 65059 Odesa, vul. Krasnova 6/1; tel. (482) 30-70-37; fax (482) 30-70-82; e-mail lds@pivdenny.odessa.ua; internet www.bank.com.ua; f. 1993; cap. 563.9m., res 99.6m., dep. 7,770.2m. (Dec. 2007); Chair. of Bd VADYM V. MOROKHOVSKIY; 16 brs.

PrivatBank: 49094 Dnipropetrovsk, nab. Peremohy 50; tel. (562) 39-05-11; fax (56) 778-54-74; e-mail privatbank@pbank.dp.ua; internet www.privatbank.ua; cap. 2,967m., res 856m., dep. 49.602m. (Dec. 2007); Chair. of Bd ALEKSANDR V. DUBILET; 51 brs.

Prominvestbank (Industrial-Investment Bank): 01001 Kyiv, prov. Shevchenka 12; tel. (44) 201-51-20; fax (44) 201-50-44; e-mail bank@pib.com.ua; internet www.pib.com.ua; f. 1922 as Stroibank, name changed 1992; cap. 200.2m., res 847.6m., dep. 22,151.6m. (Dec. 2007); Chair. VOLODYMYR P. MATVYENKO; 600 brs.

Raiffeisen Bank Aval: 01011 Kyiv, vul. Leskova 9; tel. (44) 490-88-01; fax (44) 490-87-55; e-mail info@aval.ua; internet www.aval.ua; f. 1992 as Aval Bank; present name adopted 2006; 95.7% owned by Raiffeisen International Bank Holding AG (Austria); cap. US $467.5m., res $375.0m., dep. $7,592.5m. (Dec. 2007); Pres. VOLODYMYR I. LAVRENCHUK; 1,400 brs and sub-brs.

Rodovid Bank: 04136 Kyiv, vul. Pivnichno-Syretska 1–3; tel. (44) 255-86-47; fax (44) 255-86-54; e-mail info@rodovidbank.com; internet www.rodovidbank.com; f. 1990; present name adopted 2004; cap. 435.0m., res 644.4m., dep. 8,623.0m. (Dec. 2007); Pres. SERHIY BUBKA; Chair. of Bd DENIS V. GORBUNENKO; 2 brs.

Sberbank Rossii (Ukraine): 01034 Kyiv, vul. Volodymyrska 46; tel. (44) 247-43-00; fax (44) 247-45-45; e-mail nrb@nrb-ukraine.com; internet www.nrb-ukraine.com; f. 2001; fmrly Bank NRB, present name adopted 2008; 100% owned by Sberbank—Savings Bank of the Russian Federation; cap. 75.6m., res 116.9m., dep. 1,522.9m. (Dec. 2007); Chair. of Bd VLADISLAV KRAVETS.

Swedbank: 01032 Kyiv, vul. Kominterna 30; tel. (44) 481-48-93; fax (44) 481-48-85; e-mail office@swedbank.ua; internet www.swedbank.ua; f. 1991; cap. US $147.2m., res $33.6m., dep. $1,750.0m. (Dec. 2007); Chair. of Bd SERHIY TIHIPKO.

Ukrgazbank: 01004 Kyiv, vul. Chervonoarmiyska 39; tel. (44) 594-11-63; fax (44) 239-28-44; e-mail office@ukrgasbank.com; internet www.ukrgasbank.com; f. 1993; cap. 512.8m., res 339.8m., dep. 8,903.1m. (Dec. 2007); Chair. VADYM P. LYASHKO.

Ukrprombank (Ukrainsky Promyslovy Bank): 01133 Kyiv, bulv. L. Ukrainky 26; tel. (44) 537-47-00; fax (44) 295-17-00; e-mail secretary@ukrprombank.kiev.ua; internet www.ukrprombank.com; f. 1989; cap. 842.0m., res 12.9m., dep. 5,562.6m. (Dec. 2006); Chair. OLEKSANDR SOLTUS.

UkrSibbank: 04070 Kyiv, vul. Andriyevksa 2/12; tel. (44) 230-48-88; fax (44) 230-48-98; e-mail office@ukrsibbank.com; internet www.ukrsibbank.com; f. 1990; commercial and investment banking, non-banking financial services; 51% owned by BNP Paribas SA (France); cap. 3,518.7m., res 5.3m., dep. 29,527.3m. (Dec. 2007); Chair. of Bd OLEKSANDR ADARYCH; 1,000 brs and sub-brs.

UkrSotsBank—Bank for Social Development: 03150 Kyiv, vul. Kovpaka 29; tel. (44) 230-32-24; fax (44) 230-32-23; e-mail info@ukrsotsbank.com; internet www.usb.com.ua; f. 1990; cap. 496.7m., res 387.6m., dep. 10,960m. (Dec. 2006); Chair. of Supervisory Council IHOR YUSHKO; Chair. of Bd BORIS TIMONKIN; over 500 brs.

VAB Bank-Vseukrainsky Aktsionerny Bank (All-Ukrainian Share Bank): 04119 Kyiv, vul. Zoolohichna 5; tel. (44) 481-33-47; fax (44) 481-33-49; e-mail fi@vab.ua; internet www.vab.ua; f. 1992; present name adopted 2007; cap. 191m., dep. 721m., total assets 1,221m. (2008); CEO PETER BARON; 170 brs.

VTB Bank: 01601 Kyiv, vul. Hoholevskaya 24; tel. (44) 486-04-90; e-mail post@mriya.com; internet www.vtb.com; f. 1992; cap. 163.6m., res −0.6m., dep. 2,232.4m. (Dec. 2006); Chair. of Bd VADIM PUSHKAROV; 20 brs.

Savings Bank

State Savings Bank of Ukraine—Oschadbank (Derzhavnyi Oshchadnyi Bank Ukrainy): 01023 Kyiv, vul. Hospitalna 12 G; tel. (44) 247-85-69; fax (44) 247-85-68; internet www.oschadnybank.com; f. 1991; cap. 878.5m., res 484.7m., dep. 7,400m. (2006); Chair. ANATOLIY GULEY; 6,300 brs.

Banking Association

Association of Ukrainian Banks (Asotsiatsiya Ukrainskykh Bankiv): 02002 Kyiv, vul. M. Raskova 15/703; tel. (44) 516-87-75; fax (44) 516-87-76; e-mail aub@carrier.kiev.ua; internet www.aub.com.ua; fmrly Commercial Bank Asscn; Pres. OLEKSANDR SUGONIAKO.

COMMODITY EXCHANGES

Carpathian Commodity Exchange: 78200 Ivano-Frankivsk obl., Kolomiya, vul. Vahylevycha 1, POB 210; tel. and fax (343) 32-19-61; f. 1996; Gen. Man. IVAN P. VATUTIN.

Crimea Universal Exchange: 95050 Crimea, Simferopol, vul. L. Chaikinoy 1/421; tel. (652) 22-04-32; fax (652) 22-12-73; f. 1923 as Simferopol Commodity Exchange; present name adopted 1991; Pres. NATALIYA S. SYUMAK.

Dnipro (Pridniprovska) Commodity Exchange: 49094 Dnipropetrovsk, vul. Nab. Peremohy 15A; tel. (562) 35-77-45; fax (56) 744-27-16; e-mail ptb@pce.dp.ua; originally founded 1908 as Katerinoslav Commodity Exchange; re-established with present name in 1991; brs in Dniprodzerzhynsk, Kryvyi Rih, Marhanets, Pavlohrad and Synelnykove; Gen. Man. VADYM F. KAMEKO.

Donetsk Commodity Exchange: 83086 Donetsk, vul. Pershotravnevska 12; tel. (62) 338-10-93; fax (62) 335-92-91; e-mail oltradex@pub.dn.ua; f. 1991; Gen. Man. PETRO O. VYSHNEVSKYI.

Kharkiv Commodity Exchange: 61003 Kharkiv, vul. Universytetska 5; tel. (572) 12-33-21; fax (572) 12-74-95; e-mail ss@htb.kharkov.ua; f. 1993; Pres. IHOR V. ZOTOV.

Kyiv Universal Exchange: 01103 Kyiv, Zaliznychne shose 57; tel. (44) 295-11-29; fax (44) 295-44-36; e-mail nva@iptelecom.net.ua; internet www.kue.kiev.ua; f. 1990; Pres. KONSTANTIN LAPUSHEN.

Odesa Commodity Exchange: 65114 Odesa, vul. Lyustdorfska doroha 140A; tel. (482) 61-89-92; fax (482) 47-72-84; e-mail yuri@oce.odessa.ua; f. 1796; re-established 1990; Gen. Man. MYKOLA O. NIKOLISHEN.

Ukrainian Universal Commodity Exchange: 03680 Kyiv, pr. Akadmika Hlushkova 1/6; tel. (44) 251-94-90; fax (44) 251-95-40; e-mail birga@uutb.kiev.ua; internet www.uutb.com.ua; f. 1991; Pres. OLEKSANDR M. BORKOVSKYI.

Zaporizhzhya Commodity Exchange 'Hileya': 69037 Zaporizhzhya, vul. 40 rokiv Radyanskoyi Ukrainy 41; tel. (612) 33-32-73; fax (612) 34-76-62; f. 1991; re-established 1996; Gen. Man. ANTON A. KHULAKHSIZ.

INSURANCE

State Insurance Companies

Crimean Insurance Co: 99011 Sevastopol, vul. Butakov 4; tel. (692) 55-30-28; fax (692) 54-23-00; e-mail ksk@ksk.in.ua; internet www.ksk.in.ua; f. 1993; Dir ISABELLA BILDER.

DASK UkrinMedStrakh: 01601 Kyiv, vul. O. Honshara 65; tel. (44) 216-30-21; fax (44) 216-96-92; e-mail ukrmed@ukrpack.com; f. 1999; provides compulsory medical insurance to foreigners and stateless persons temporarily resident in Ukraine.

Oranta Insurance Co: 01015 Kyiv, vul. Sichnevogo Povstannya 34B; tel. (44) 537-58-00; fax (44) 537-58-83; e-mail oranta@oranta.ua; internet www.oranta.ua; f. 1921; Chair. of Bd OLEG SPILKA.

Commercial Insurance Companies

AKB Garant Insurance Co: 03062 Kyiv, pr. Peremohy 67; tel. (44) 459-52-00; fax (44) 459-52-07; e-mail akb@garant.kiev.ua; internet www.garant.kiev.ua; f. 1994; general insurance services; Gen. Man. OLEKSANDR I. DYACHENKO.

Alkona Insurance Co: 03150 Kyiv, vul. Chervonoarmiyska 102; tel. and fax (44) 247-44-77; e-mail hdi@hdi.kiev.ua; internet www.hdi.kiev.ua; f. 1992; insurance and reinsurance.

ECCO Insurance Co: 01034 Kyiv, vul. Prorizna 4/23; tel. (44) 228-10-82; e-mail insurance@ecco-alpha.kiev.ua; internet www.ecco-insurance.at; f. 1991; affiliated to ECCO (Austria); life and non-life insurance.

EnergoPolis Insurance Co: 01033Kyiv, vul. Sh. Rustaveli 39–41; tel. (44) 244-02-36; fax (44) 244-05-94; e-mail office@enpolis.com.ua; internet www.enpolis.com.ua; Chair. of Bd and Dir-Gen. VIKTOR MYKOLAYCHUK.

Galinstrakh Insurance Co: 79012 Lviv, vul. Ak. Sakharova 34; tel. (32) 275-70-30; fax (32) 297-10-40; e-mail gis@is.lviv.ua; internet www.gis.com.ua; f. 1991; general insurance services; Chair. of Bd STEPHAN SOVINSKIY.

Ingo Ukraina Insurance Co: 01054 Kyiv, vul. Vorovskogo 33; tel. (44) 490-27-44; fax (44) 490-27-48; e-mail office@ingo.com.ua; internet www.ingo.com.ua; f. 1994; fmrly Ostra-Kyiv Insurance Co; re-insurance, medical, travel, property and cargo insurance; Chair. of Bd IHOR N. HORDYENKO.

Inter-Policy Insurance Co: 01033 Kyiv, vul. Volodymyrska 69; tel. (44) 287-70-96; fax (44) 289-74-45; e-mail office@inter-policy.com; internet www.inter-policy.com; f. 1993.

Kyiv Insurance Co: 04053 Kyiv, vul. Yu. Kotsubynskoho 20; tel. (44) 461-92-41; fax (44) 461-92-43; f. 1998.

Ostra Insurance Co: 65026 Odesa, vul. Pushkinska 13; tel. (48) 724-68-30; fax (48) 724-38-41; e-mail main@ostra.com.ua; internet www.ostra.com.ua; f. 1990; non-life; Chair. KHYRACH MAHDYEV.

PZU Ukraine Insurance Co: 04112 Kyiv, vul. Dehtyarivska 62; tel. (44) 238-62-38; fax (44) 581-04-55; e-mail mail@pzu.com.ua; internet www.pzu.com.ua; 100% owned by PZU (Poland); 4 subsidiary cos; life and non-life; Pres. IRENEUSZ WESOŁOWSKI.

QBE Ukraina Insurance: 04070 Kyiv, vul. Illinska 8; tel. (44) 537-53-90; fax (44) 537-53-99; e-mail insurance@qbe-ukraine.com; internet www.qbe-ukraine.com; f. 1998; affiliate of QBE Insurance (New Zealand).

Skide Insurance Co: 04050 Kyiv, vul. Hlybochytska 72; tel. (44) 417-40-04; fax (44) 228-40-33; e-mail skide@iptelecom.net.ua; f. 1991; Pres. VOLODYMYR BESARAB.

Sun Life Ukraine: 01032 Kyiv, vul. Starovokzalna 17; tel. (44) 235-20-02; fax (44) 235-89-17; e-mail office@sunlife.com.ua; internet www.sunlife.com.ua; f. 1993; life; Pres. ROSTYSLAV B. TALSKYI.

UkrGazPromPolis Insurance Co: 01034 Kyiv, vul. O. Honshara 41; tel. (44) 235-25-00; e-mail office@ugpp.com.ua; internet www.ugpp.com.ua; f. 1996; jointly owned by UkrGazProm, UkrGazProm-Bank and KyivTransGaz; Pres. KONSTANTYN O. YEFYMENKO.

Insurance Association

League of Insurance Organizations of Ukraine: 02660 Kyiv, vul. M. Roskovoyi 11; tel. and fax (44) 516-82-30; internet www.uainsur.com; f. 1992; non-profit asscn of insurance cos; Pres. ALEKSANDR FILONYUK.

Trade and Industry

GOVERNMENT AGENCY

State Property Fund of Ukraine (Fond Derzhavnoho Maina Ukrainy): 01133 Kyiv, vul. Kutuzova 18/9; tel. (44) 200-33-33; fax (44) 286-79-85; e-mail marketing@spfu.kiev.ua; internet www.spfu.gov.ua; Head DMYTRO M. PARFENENKO (acting).

NATIONAL CHAMBER OF COMMERCE

Ukrainian Chamber of Commerce and Industry (Torgovo-Promyslova Palata Ukrainy/Torgovo-Promyshlennaya Palata Ukrainy): 01601 Kyiv, vul. V. Zhytomyrska 33; tel. (44) 272-29-11; fax (44) 272-33-53; e-mail ucci@ucci.org.ua; internet www.ucci.org.ua; f. 1972; Pres. SERHIY P. SKRYPCHENKO; 27 regional brs with a total of c. 9,000 mems.

REGIONAL CHAMBERS OF COMMERCE

Chambers of Commerce are located in every administrative region of Ukraine, including the following:

Chamber of Commerce and Industry of Crimea: 95013 Crimea, Simferopol, ul. Sevastopolskaya 45; tel. (652) 24-86-38; fax (652) 49-33-45; e-mail cci@cci.crimea.ua; internet www.cci.crimea.ua; f. 1974; sub-brs in Armyansk, Dzhankoi, Feodosiya, Kerch, Yalta and Yevpatoriya; Pres. NEONILA M. GRACHEVA.

Dnipropetrovsk Chamber of Commerce: 49044 Dnipropetrovsk, vul. Shevchenka 4; tel. (562) 36-22-58; fax (562) 36-22-59; e-mail miv@dcci.dp.ua; internet www.dcci.dp.ua; brs at Kryvyi Rih and Dniprodzerzhynsk; Pres. VYTALIY H. ZHMURENKO.

Donetsk Chamber of Commerce: 83007 Donetsk, pr. Kyivsky 87; tel. (62) 387-80-00; fax (62) 387-80-01; e-mail info@dttp.donetsk.ua; internet www.cci.donbass.com; f. 1964; brs at Artemovsk, Horlivka, Kramatorsk, Makiyivka and Mariupol; Pres. GENNADII D. CHIZHIKOV.

Kharkiv Chamber of Commerce: 61037 Kharkiv, pr. Moskovksky 122; tel. (57) 714-96-90; fax (57) 738-64-79; e-mail info@kcci.kharkov.ua; internet www.kcci.kharkov.ua; Pres. VIKTOR I. LOBODA.

Kyiv Chamber of Commerce and Industry: 01504 Kyiv-54, vul. B. Khmelnytskoho 55; tel. (44) 246-83-01; fax (44) 246-99-66; e-mail info@kiev-chamber.org.ua; internet www.kiev-chamber.org.ua; Pres. MYKOLA V. ZASULSKIY.

Lviv Chamber of Commerce and Industry: 79011 Lviv, Stryiskiy park 14; tel. and fax (32) 276-46-11; e-mail lcci@cci.com.ua; internet www.lcci.com.ua; f. 1850; Pres. DMYTRO D. AFTANAS.

Odesa Chamber of Commerce and Industry: 65125 Odesa, vul. Bazarna 47; tel. (48) 38-04-82; fax (482) 49-63-07; e-mail orcci@orcci.odessa.ua; internet www.orcci.odessa.ua; f. 1924; brs at Illichivsk, Izmayil and Reni; Pres. SERHIY SHUVALOV.

Sevastopol Chamber of Commerce and Industry: 99011 Sevastopol, ul. B. Morskaya 34; tel. (692) 54-35-36; fax (692) 54-06-44; e-mail members@stpp.org.ua; internet www.stpp.org.ua; f. 1963; Pres. LYUDMILA I. VISHNYA.

Transcarpathian (Zakarpatska) Chamber of Commerce and Industry: 88015 Transcarpathian obl., Uzhhorod, vul. Hrushevskoho 62; tel. (312) 66-22-14; fax (312) 66-44-77; e-mail tpp@tpp.uzhgorod.ua; internet www.tpp.uzhgorod.ua; br. at Mukachevo; Pres. OTTO O. KOVCHAR.

Zaporizhzhya Chamber of Commerce: 69000 Zaporizhzhya, bulv. Tsentralnyi 4; tel. (612) 13-50-24; fax (612) 33-11-72; e-mail cci@cci.zp.ua; internet www.cci.zp.ua; brs at Berdyansk and Melitopol; Pres. VOLODOMYR I. SHAMYLOV.

EMPLOYERS' ORGANIZATION

Congress of Business Circles of Ukraine: 01061 Kyiv, vul. Prorizna 15; tel. (44) 228-64-81; fax (44) 229-52-84; Pres. VALERIY G. BABICH.

UTILITIES

Regulatory Bodies

National Electricity Regulatory Commission of Ukraine: 03057 Kyiv, vul. Smolenska 19; tel. (44) 241-90-01; fax (44) 241-90-47; e-mail box@nerc.gov.ua; f. 1994; promotion of competition and protection of consumer interests; Chair. YURIY PRODAN.

State Committee for Nuclear Regulation (Derzhanvnyi komitet yadernoho rehulyuvannya Ukrainy): 01011 Kyiv, vul. Arsenalna 9/11; tel. (44) 254-33-47; fax (44) 254-33-11; e-mail pr@hq.snrc.gov.ua; internet www.snrc.gov.ua; Chair. OLENA A. MYKOLAICHUK.

Electricity

EnergoAtom: 01032 Kyiv, vul. Vetrova 3; tel. (44) 281-48-83; e-mail pr@nae.atom.gov.ua; internet www.energoatom.kiev.ua; f. 1996; responsible for scientific and technical policy within the nuclear power industry; manages all five nuclear power producing installations in Ukraine; Pres. ANDRIY L. DERKACH.

Kyivenergo: 01001 Kyiv, pl. Ivana Franka 5; tel. (44) 201-58-67; fax (44) 239-47-06; e-mail pubrel@kievenergo.com.ua; internet www.kievenergo.com.ua; power generation and distribution; Chair. SERHIY M. TITENKO.

Zakhidenergo (West Energy): 79026 Lviv, vul. Kozelnytska 15; tel. (322) 39-07-10; fax (322) 39-07-17; e-mail kanc@gwce.energy.gov.ua; internet www.zakhidenergo.ua; f. 1995; power generation; Dir-Gen. PETRO I. OMELYANOVSKIY.

Gas

Naftogaz Ukrainy (Oil and Gas of Ukraine): 01001 Kyiv, vul. B. Khmelnytskoho 6B; tel. (44) 461-25-37; fax (44) 220-15-26; e-mail ngu@naftogaz.net; internet www.naftogaz.com; f. 1998; state-owned; production and distribution of gas and petroleum; storage of gas; gas- and condensate-processing; Chair. of Bd OLEH DUBYNA.

TRADE UNION FEDERATIONS

Confederation of Free Trade Unions of Ukraine (CFTUU) (Konfederatsiya Vilnykh Profspilok Ukrainy—KVPU): 03150 Kyiv,

UKRAINE

vul. V. Vasylkivska 54; tel. (44) 287-33-38; fax (44) 287-72-83; e-mail info@kvpu.org.ua; internet www.kvpu.org.ua; f. 1997; independent; Chair. MYKHAYLO YA. VOLYNETS.

Federation of Trade Unions of Ukraine (FTUU): 01012 Kyiv, Maidan Nezalezhnosti 2; tel. (44) 278-87-88; fax (44) 278-87-98; e-mail fpsu@fpsu.org.ua; internet www.fpsu.org.ua; f. 1990; fmr Ukrainian branch of General Confederation of Trade Unions of the USSR; affiliation of 46 trade union brs; Chair. VASYL KHARA.

Transport

RAILWAYS

In 2002 there were 22,078 km of railway track in use, of which more than 9,000 km were electrified. Lines link most towns and cities in the country, and with various major cities in other European countries.

State Railway Transport Administration—Ukrzaliznytsia: 03680 Kyiv, vul. Tverska 5; tel. (44) 223-00-10; fax (44) 258-80-11; e-mail ci@uz.gov.ua; internet www.uz.gov.ua; Dir-Gen. MYLHAILO KOSTYUK.

Ukrreftrans: 03049 Kyiv, vul. Furmanova 1/7; tel. (44) 245-47-22; e-mail sekretar@interntrans.com.ua; internet www.intertrans.com.ua; state-owned freight transportation service.

Dnipropetrovsk Metro: 49038 Dnipropetrovsk, vul. Kurchatova 8; tel. (562) 42-37-68; fax (56) 778-65-33; e-mail metrodp@ukr.net; internet gorod.dp.ua/metro/; f. 1995; one line with six stations; total length 8 km; total planned network of 74 km.

Kharkiv Metro: 61012 Kharkiv, vul. Engelsa 29; tel. (572) 12-59-83; fax (572) 23-21-41; e-mail metro@tender.kharkov.com; internet www.metro.kharkov.ua; f. 1975; three lines with 26 stations; total length 34 km; Gen. Man. LEONID A. ISAYEV.

Kyiv Metro: 03055 Kyiv, pr. Peremohy 35; tel. (44) 238-44-21; fax (44) 238-44-46; e-mail nto@metro.kiev.ua; internet www.metro.kiev.ua; f. 1960; three lines with 42 stations; Dir MYKOLA M. SHAVLOVSKIY.

ROADS

At 31 December 2002 there were 169,678 km of roads, of which 96.8% were paved.

INLAND WATERWAYS

The Dnipro (Dniepr—Dnieper) River, which links Kyiv, Cherkasy, Dnipropetrovsk and Zaporizhzhya with the Black Sea, is the most important route for river freight.

SHIPPING

The main ports are Yalta and Yevpatoriya in Crimea, and Odesa. In addition to long-distance international shipping lines, there are services to the Russian ports of Novorossiisk and Sochi, and Batumi and Sukhumi in Georgia. Although many passenger routes on the Black Sea ceased to operate in the 1990s, there are regular passenger services from Odesa to Haifa (Israel) and Istanbul (Turkey), and, in the summer months, between Odesa and Crimea. At December 2007 Ukraine's merchant fleet (655 vessels) had a total displacement of 1.1m. grt.

Port Authority

Odesa Commercial Sea Port: 65026 Odesa, pl. Mytna 1; tel. (48) 729-35-55; fax (48) 729-36-27; e-mail welcome@port.odessa.ua; internet www.port.odessa.ua; f. 1794; state-owned; cargo handling and storage, marine passenger terminal services; Gen. Man. MYKOLA P. PAVLYUK.

Shipping Companies

Azov Shipping Co: 87510 Donetsk obl., Mariupol, pr. Admirala Lunina 89; tel. (629) 31-15-00; fax (629) 31-12-25; e-mail admin@c2smtp.azsco.anet.donetsk.ua; f. 1871; Pres. SERHIY V. PRUSIKOV.

State Black Sea Shipping Co: 65026 Odesa, vul. Lanzheronovska 1; tel. (482) 25-21-60; fax (482) 60-57-33; Pres. BORIS SCHERBAK.

Ukrainian Danube Shipping Co: 68600 Odesa obl., Izmayil, vul. Chervonaflotska 28; tel. (4841) 2-55-50; fax (4841) 2-53-55; e-mail udp_t@udp.izmail.uptel.net; f. 1944; cargo and passenger services; Pres. PETR S. SUVOROV.

Ukrainian Shipping Co (UkrShip): 65014 Odesa, vul. Marazlyevska 8; tel. (48) 734-73-50; fax (48) 777-07-00; e-mail admin@ukrship.odessa.ua; f. 1996; Pres. A. SAVITSKIY.

Ukrrechflot Co: 04071 Kyiv, Nizhny val. 51; tel. and fax (44) 490-66-48; e-mail info@ukrrichflot.com.ua; f. 1992; jt-stock co; Dir-Gen. MIKHAILO CHUBAI.

Yugreftransflot: 99014 Crimea, Sevastopol, ul. Rybakov 5; tel. (692) 41-25-41; fax (692) 42-39-19; e-mail jsc@urtf.com; jt-stock co; Chair. VOLODYMYR ANDREYEV.

CIVIL AVIATION

The principal international airport is at Boryspil (Kyiv), but several other airports, including those at Dnipropetrovsk and Odesa, also service international flights.

AeroSvit Airlines: 01032 Kyiv, bulv. Shevchenko 58A; tel. (44) 246-50-70; fax (44) 246-50-46; e-mail av@aswt.kiev.ua; internet www.aerosvit.com; f. 1994; operates scheduled and charter passenger services to domestic and international destinations; Chief Exec. and Dir-Gen. GRYGORIY GURTOVOY.

ARP 410: 03151 Kyiv, Vozdukhoflotsky pr. 94; tel. (44) 246-26-64; fax (44) 243-40-33; e-mail arp410-cs@svitonline.com; f. 1999; domestic passenger and international cargo flights; Dir-Gen. ANATOLIY P. KUDRIN.

Donbassaero Airlines (Donbass-Vostochnye Aviyalinii Ukrainy—Donbassaero): 83021 Donetsk, vul. Vzlyotna 1, Donetsk International Airport; tel. (62) 388-51-03; fax (62) 332-00-55; e-mail info@donbass.aero; internet www.donbass.aero; f. 1933 as Donetsk State Airline; present name adopted 2007; passenger and cargo flights between Donetsk and domestic and international destinations; Dir-Gen. ALEKSANDR HRECHKO.

Khors Air Company: 01133 Kyiv, vul. L. Ukrainki 34; tel. (44) 294-94-11; fax (44) 573-86-72; e-mail aircargo@khors.com.ua; internet www.khors.com.ua; f. 1990; operates international, regional and domestic cargo and passenger services; Gen. Dir ANATOLIY VYSOCHANSKIY.

Ukraine International Airlines (Mizhnarodni Avialinyi Ukraini): 01054 Kyiv, ul. B. Khmelnytskogo 63A; tel. (44) 461-56-56; fax (44) 230-88-66; e-mail uia@ps.kiev.ua; internet www.ukraine-international.com; f. 1992; 61.6% state-owned, 22.5% owned jointly by SAir (Switzerland) and Austrian Airlines (Austria); operates domestic services, and international services to European and Middle Eastern destinations from Kyiv, Dnipropetrovsk, Kharkiv, Lviv, Odesa and Simferopol; Pres. VITALIY M. POTEMSKIY.

Tourism

The Black Sea coast of Ukraine has several popular resorts, including Odesa and Yalta. The Crimean peninsula is a popular tourist centre in both summer and winter, owing to its temperate climate. Kyiv, Lviv and Odesa have important historical attractions, and there are many archaeological monuments on the Black Sea coast, including the remains of ancient Greek and Ottoman settlements. However, the tourist industry remains relatively undeveloped. There were 25.5m. foreign tourist arrivals in Ukraine in 2008, compared with 18.9m. arrivals in 2006; receipts from tourism (including passenger transport) totalled US $4,018m. in 2006.

Ministry of Culture and Tourism: see The Government (Ministries).

Ministry of Health Resorts and Tourism of the Autonomous Republic of Crimea: 95005 Crimea, Simferopol, pr. Kirova 13; tel. (652) 54-46-68; fax (652) 25-94-38; e-mail tourism_crimea@ukr.net; internet www.tourism.crimea.ua; Minister ANDREW A. SUMTSOV.

State Tourism Administration of Ukraine (Derzhavna turystychna administratsiya Ukrainy): 01034 Kyiv, vul. Yaroslaviv val 36; tel. (44) 272-42-15; fax (44) 272-42-77; e-mail info@tourism.gov.ua; internet www.tourism.gov.ua; f. 1999; Chair. VALERIY I. TSYBUKH.

THE UNITED ARAB EMIRATES

Introductory Survey

Location, Climate, Language, Religion, Flag, Capital

The United Arab Emirates (UAE) lies in the east of the Arabian peninsula. It is bordered by Saudi Arabia to the west and south, and by Oman to the east. In the north the UAE has a short frontier with Qatar and a coastline of about 650 km on the southern shore of the Persian (Arabian) Gulf, separated by a detached portion of Omani territory from a small section of coast on the western shore of the Gulf of Oman. The climate is exceptionally hot in summer, with average maximum temperatures exceeding 40°C, and humidity is very high. Winter is mild, with temperatures ranging from 17°C to 20°C. Average annual rainfall is very low: between 100 mm and 200 mm. The official language is Arabic, spoken by almost all of the native population. Arabs are, however, outnumbered by non-Arab immigrants, mainly from India, Pakistan, Bangladesh and Iran. According to official census results, UAE nationals represented about 20% of the total population in 2005. Most of the inhabitants are Muslims, mainly of the Sunni sect. The national flag (proportions 1 by 2) has three equal horizontal stripes, of green, white and black, with a vertical red stripe at the hoist. The capital is Abu Dhabi.

Recent History

Prior to independence the UAE was Trucial Oman, also known as the Trucial States, and the component sheikhdoms of the territory were under British protection. Although from 1892 the United Kingdom assumed responsibility for the sheikhdoms' defence and external relations, they were otherwise autonomous and followed the traditional form of Arab monarchy, with each ruler having virtually absolute power over his subjects.

In 1952 the Trucial Council, comprising the rulers of the seven sheikhdoms, was established in order to encourage the adoption of common policies in administrative matters, possibly leading to a federation of the states. Petroleum, the basis of the area's modern prosperity, was first discovered in 1958, when deposits were located beneath the coastal waters of Abu Dhabi, the largest of the sheikhdoms. Onshore petroleum was found in Abu Dhabi in 1960, and commercial exploitation of petroleum began in 1962, providing the state with greatly increased revenue. However, Sheikh Shakhbut bin Sultan an-Nahyan, the Ruler of Abu Dhabi since 1928, failed to use the income from petroleum royalties to develop his domain. As a result, the ruling family deposed him in August 1966 and installed his younger brother, Sheikh Zayed bin Sultan. Under the rule of Sheikh Zayed, Abu Dhabi was transformed, with considerable income from the petroleum industry allocated for public works and the provision of welfare services. In 1966 petroleum was discovered in neighbouring Dubai (the second largest of the Trucial States), which also underwent a rapid development.

In January 1968 the United Kingdom announced its intention to withdraw British military forces from the area by 1971. In March 1968 the Trucial States joined nearby Bahrain and Qatar (which were also under British protection) in what was named the Federation of Arab Emirates. It was intended that the Federation should become fully independent, but the interests of Bahrain and Qatar proved to be incompatible with those of the smaller sheikhdoms, and both seceded from the Federation in August 1971 to become separate independent states. In July six of the Trucial States (Abu Dhabi, Dubai, Sharjah, Umm al-Qaiwain, Ajman and Fujairah) had agreed on a federal Constitution for achieving independence as the United Arab Emirates (UAE). The United Kingdom accordingly terminated its special treaty relationship with the States, and the UAE became independent on 2 December 1971. The remaining sheikhdom, Ras al-Khaimah, joined the UAE in February 1972. At independence Sheikh Zayed of Abu Dhabi took office as the first President of the UAE. Sheikh Rashid bin Said al-Maktoum, the Ruler of Dubai since 1958, became Vice-President, while his eldest son, Sheikh Maktoum bin Rashid al-Maktoum (Crown Prince of Dubai), became Prime Minister in the federal Council of Ministers. A 40-member consultative assembly, the Federal National Council (FNC), was also inaugurated.

In January 1972 the Ruler of Sharjah, Sheikh Khalid bin Muhammad al-Qasimi, was killed by rebels under the leadership of his cousin, Sheikh Saqr bin Sultan, who had been deposed as the sheikhdom's Ruler in June 1965. However, the rebels were defeated, and Sheikh Khalid was succeeded by his brother, Sheikh Sultan bin Muhammad al-Qasimi.

Sheikh Zayed, disappointed with progress towards centralization, reportedly announced in August 1976 that he was not prepared to accept another five-year term as President. In November, however, the highest federal authority, the Supreme Council of Rulers (comprising the Rulers of the seven emirates), re-elected him unanimously, following agreements granting the federal Government greater control over defence, intelligence services, immigration, public security and border control.

Owing to a dispute over a senior appointment in February 1978, the forces of Dubai and Ras al-Khaimah refused to accept orders from the Federal Defence Force. Although Ras al-Khaimah later reintegrated with the Federal Defence Force, Dubai's armed forces effectively remained a separate entity. In March 1979 a 10-point memorandum from the National Council, containing proposals for increased unity, was rejected by Dubai, which, together with Ras al-Khaimah, boycotted a meeting of the Supreme Council. In April Sheikh Maktoum resigned as Prime Minister; he was replaced by his father, Sheikh Rashid, who formed a new Council of Ministers in July, while retaining the post of Vice-President. Sheikh Ahmad bin Rashid al-Mu'alla, the Ruler of Umm al-Qaiwain (the smallest of the emirates) since 1929, died in February 1981, and was succeeded by his son, Rashid. Sheikh Rashid bin Humaid an-Nuaimi, the Ruler of Ajman since 1928, died in September 1981, and was succeeded by his son, Humaid.

The UAE was a founder member of the Co-operation Council for the Arab States of the Gulf (the Gulf Co-operation Council—GCC, see p. 229) in May 1981.

There was an attempted coup in Sharjah in June 1987, when Sheikh Abd al-Aziz, a brother of Sheikh Sultan, announced (in his brother's absence) the abdication of the Ruler, on the grounds that he had mismanaged the economy. The Supreme Council of Rulers intervened to endorse Sheikh Sultan's claim to be the legitimate Ruler of Sharjah, effectively restoring him to power. Sheikh Abd al-Aziz was given the title of Crown Prince and was granted a seat on the Supreme Council. In February 1990, however, Sheikh Sultan removed his brother from the post of Crown Prince and revoked his right to succeed him as Ruler. In July Sheikh Sultan appointed Sheikh Ahmad bin Muhammad al-Qasimi, the head of Sharjah's petroleum and mineral affairs office, as Deputy Ruler of Sharjah, although he was not given the title of Crown Prince.

The UAE became involved in a major international financial scandal in July 1991, when regulatory authorities in seven countries abruptly closed down the operations of the Bank of Credit and Commerce International (BCCI), in which the Abu Dhabi ruling family and agencies had held a controlling interest (77%) since April 1990. The termination of the bank's activities followed the disclosure of systematic, large-scale fraud by BCCI authorities prior to April 1990. By July 1991 BCCI's activities had been suspended in all 69 countries in which it had operated. At the conclusion of fraud trials in May 1994 all but one of the defendants were sentenced to terms of imprisonment ranging from three to 14 years. (In June 1995 a court of appeal overturned the guilty verdicts of two of those imprisoned.) New legislation was subsequently prepared to strengthen the role of the Central Bank and to enforce stricter regulation of the Emirates' financial sector.

Meanwhile, in October 1990, upon the death of his father, Sheikh Maktoum acceded to the positions of Ruler of Dubai and Vice-President and Prime Minister of the UAE. In January 1995 Sheikh Maktoum issued a decree naming Sheikh Muhammad bin Rashid al-Maktoum as Crown Prince, and Sheikh Hamdan bin Rashid al-Maktoum as Deputy Ruler of Dubai. In June 1996 legislation designed to make the provisional Constitution permanent was endorsed by the FNC, following its approval by the

Supreme Council of Rulers. At the same time Abu Dhabi was formally designated capital of the UAE.

In October 2003 Sheikh Zayed appointed Sheikh Hamdan bin Zayed an-Nayhan as a Deputy Prime Minister, in addition to his existing responsibilities as Minister of State for Foreign Affairs. In the following month Sheikh Zayed issued a decree installing Sheikh Muhammad bin Zayed an-Nahyan, the Chief of Staff of Federal Armed Forces, as Deputy Crown Prince of Abu Dhabi. Meanwhile, in June Sheikh Saqr bin Muhammad al-Qasimi, the ruler of Ras al-Khaimah, deposed his eldest son, Khalid, as Crown Prince and appointed a younger son, Sa'ud, in his place. Sheikh Khalid, a noted reformist, reportedly claimed that the decision had been influenced by his father's ill health. Tanks from the federal UAE armed forces arrived in Ras al-Khaimah city, apparently in an attempt to prevent supporters of Sheikh Khalid from demonstrating against the decision. Tension in the emirate quickly eased, however, after the departure of Sheikh Khalid to Oman. In January 2004 Sheikh Sa'ud ordered the release of 124 prisoners, including several of the protesters who had demonstrated against his appointment.

Sheikh Zayed died on 2 November 2004, following several years of ill health. His son, Sheikh Khalifa bin Zayed an-Nahyan, automatically succeeded him as Ruler of Abu Dhabi and was elected by the Supreme Council to the presidency the following day. The day before Sheikh Zayed's death a restructuring had been implemented of the Council of Ministers (the first such reorganization since 1997). The most significant changes were the appointment as Minister of Economy and Planning of Sheikha Lubna bint Khalid al-Qasimi, who became the first woman to hold a cabinet position in the UAE, and the combining of the petroleum and mineral resources ministry with the electricity and water portfolio to form a new Ministry of Energy, headed by Muhammad bin Dhaen al-Hamili. In December Sheikh Khalifa announced a similarly rare restructuring of the Abu Dhabi Executive Council, to be chaired by the new Crown Prince, Sheikh Muhammad, who also remained the Chief of Staff of Federal Armed Forces.

Sheikh Maktoum, who had reportedly suffered from heart problems, died suddenly in January 2006. He was immediately succeeded as Ruler of Dubai by his brother, Sheikh Muhammad bin Rashid al-Maktoum, who had been Dubai's Crown Prince since 1995. Sheikh Muhammad also replaced Sheikh Maktoum as Vice-President and Prime Minister of the UAE. His first Council of Ministers, approved by the President on 9 February, contained nine new ministers (including a second female minister) and several new portfolios; however, most of the key ministries remained unchanged. Sheikh Muhammad retained control of the Ministry of Defence, a position he has held since 1971.

In December 2005 Sheikh Khalifa announced tentative proposals to open one-half of the 40 seats in the FNC to indirect election via new national councils in each of the emirates. The President envisaged that this represented the first step towards wider participatory democracy and the federation's first general election. Officials indicated that the gradual democratization of the GCC states had created both external and internal pressure on the Government to adopt constitutional change. The partial elections to the FNC were held on 16, 18 and 20 December 2006: four members of the Council were elected from each of Abu Dhabi and Dubai, three each from Sharjah and Ras al-Khaimah, and two each from Fujairah, Umm al-Qaiwain and Ajman. The 20 seats were contested by 450 candidates, including 65 women. Just 6,689 selected UAE nationals (among them 1,189 women) were eligible to participate in the polls as members of the new electoral colleges (these had been chosen by the National Electoral Committee, established in August). The elected members included one woman, selected in Abu Dhabi. Overall voter turn-out in the seven emirates was reported to be 74.4%. The new FNC was inaugurated in February 2007. (Of its 20 appointed members, nine were women.) At the opening session, Abd al-Aziz Abdullah al-Ghurair was elected Speaker.

In February 2008 Sheikh Muhammad issued a decree appointing his son, Sheikh Hamdan bin Muhammad bin Rashid al-Maktoum, as Crown Prince of Dubai. The new Crown Prince and his younger brother, Sheikh Maktoum, were also named as Deputy Rulers of Dubai. (Sheikh Hamdan had been appointed Chairman of the Dubai Executive Council in September 2006.) The appointments were followed in the same month by a reorganization of the federal Council of Ministers. While the strategic portfolios of energy, foreign affairs and defence remained unchanged, other appointments were regarded as reflecting Sheikh Muhammad's policy priorities in further developing the business sector. Sheikha Lubna al-Qasimi was transferred from the post of Minister of Economy to the new position of Minister of Foreign Trade; she was replaced in her former role by Sultan bin Said al-Mansour, previously Minister of Governmental Sector Development; his ministry was also to take responsibility for industrial affairs. The appointment of Ghobash Said Ghobash, hitherto ambassador to the USA, as Minister of Labour was interpreted as a significant indicator that Sheikh Muhammad was seeking to address perceived international concerns regarding workers' rights in the UAE. Hadif Jowan adh-Dhahiri was appointed Minister of Justice, while Muhammad bin Abdullah al-Gargawi, the chief executive of Dubai Holding, who was regarded as a close associate of Sheikh Muhammad, was promoted to the position of Minister of Cabinet Affairs (having previously held the position of Minister of State). The new administration included four women. In March, following the amendment of pertinent legislation earlier in the year, the UAE's first female judge was appointed by the Ruler of Abu Dhabi.

Following the dissolution of the Ministry of Information and Culture in February 2006, a National Media Council (NMC) was established to act as the regulatory body for the UAE's media affairs (the remaining responsibilities of the Ministry of Information and Culture were transferred to a new Ministry of Culture, Youth and Community Development). In September 2007 Sheikh Muhammad issued a directive that was interpreted as instructing that journalists in the UAE would no longer be liable for imprisonment for libel. A new draft media law, formulated by the NMC, was adopted by the FNC in January 2009. The law stipulated that journalists could not be imprisoned for carrying out their duties, nor could they be forced to reveal the identity of confidential sources. However, journalists and media organizations would be liable to large fines and possible revocation of their licence if found guilty of publishing information deemed harmful to the state, untruthful, or damaging to the national economy. The law was expected to be ratified by the President by late 2009. A report on the new media law was published by the US-based Human Rights Watch in April 2009. While the report acknowledged that the new legislation represented progress on freedom of the press, it considered that the authorities were seeking to stifle legitimate criticism of the government and prevent accurate coverage of the difficult economic climate.

The UAE's record on human rights was reviewed under the UN Human Rights Council's Universal Periodic Review (UPR) process during 2008. A national report, outlining the Emirates' achievements and plans regarding human rights, with contributions from several Government ministries and domestic non-governmental organizations, was published in September. At a Council session in Geneva, Switzerland, in December, the UAE's Minister of State for Foreign Affairs announced that the UAE had agreed to adopt 36 recommendations on human rights made by other member states: these included proposals on human-trafficking, working conditions, freedom of the press and children's rights; 21 recommendations were rejected, including those on corporal and capital punishment, trade unions and women's rights; while a further 17 recommendations were reserved for further review. Of these last, nine had been rejected and eight either accepted or placed under consideration by the time of the final UPR session in March 2009, at which the Human Rights Council voted unanimously to endorse the UAE's national report. Nevertheless, the US Department of State's 2008 Human Rights Report on the UAE, published in February 2009, contained several negative observations on the human rights situation in the UAE, including its record on issues such as the mistreatment of prisoners, media censorship, people-trafficking and working conditions, as well as the allegation that a member of the royal family had tortured a foreign national because of a business dispute. The Ministry of Foreign Affairs issued a statement rejecting much of the criticism in the report, which, it claimed, contained 'generalities and unsubstantiated statements', and was the result of the application of a foreign value system to an Islamic state. In April a US television channel broadcast segments of a video recording which, it claimed, showed the alleged torture incident, and named the royal family member as Sheikh Issa bin Zayed an-Nayhan, a brother of Sheikh Khalifa.

A number of constitutional amendments were endorsed by the Supreme Council of Rulers in December 2008 and approved by the FNC in January 2009, including the extension of the FNC's legislative term from two to four years and an article prohibiting

FNC members from conducting business arrangements with government agencies during their legislative term.

Sheikh Rashid bin Ahmad al-Mu'alla, Ruler of Umm al-Qaiwain since 1981, died in January 2009. His son, Sheikh Saud bin Rashid al-Mu'alla, was immediately appointed to succeed him. Sheikh Rashid bin Saud bin Rashid al-Mu'alla was appointed Crown Prince.

Official figures published in late 2008 indicated that nonnationals made up made up more than 80% of the UAE's population and constituted over 90% of the work-force. (Some estimates put the proportion of Emirati employees in the private sector at less than 1%.) In February 2009 the Ministry of Labour announced new measures to protect the jobs of Emirati nationals.

In late 2008 and early 2009 the negative impact of the global economic downturn on the UAE's economy, particularly in the construction, property, financial services and tourism sectors, began to result in job losses, the cancellation of thousands of work permits for foreign workers, and the postponement or scaling down of numerous infrastructure projects. Dubai's highly service-based economy was considered to be paricularly vulnerable, and in February 2009 it was announced that the Central Bank of the UAE was to purchase some US $10,000m. of Dubai-issued bonds in order to enable Dubai to meet its debt-servicing obligations.

In May 2009 there was some uncertainty regarding the future of plans to create a GCC monetary union, with a common currency, by 2010, after the UAE announced that it was to withdraw from the project. The UAE's apparent abandonment of proposed monetary union arose from a recent decision of the GCC to locate key financial institutions, including the future central bank, in the Saudi Arabian capital, Riyadh, rather than in the UAE.

Conflict arose between the UAE and Iran in 1992 concerning the sovereignty of Abu Musa, an island situated between the states in the Persian (Arabian) Gulf. The island had been administered since 1991 under a joint agreement between Iran and Sharjah, in accordance with which an Iranian garrison was stationed on the island. In that year Iran had also seized the smaller neighbouring islands of Greater and Lesser Tunb. In April 1992 the Iranian garrison on Abu Musa was said to have seized civilian installations on the island. There were further allegations that Iranian officials were attempting to force expatriate workers employed by the UAE to leave the island, preventing the entry of other expatriates, and increasing the number of Iranian nationals there. However, in April 1993 all those who had been expelled from or refused entry to Abu Musa in 1992 were reportedly permitted to return. In October 1993 Sheikh Zayed announced the introduction of a federal law standardizing the limits of the UAE's territorial waters to 12 nautical miles (22.2 km) off shore, in response to a similar announcement by the Iranian authorities. In December 1994 the UAE announced its intention to refer the dispute to the International Court of Justice (ICJ) in The Hague, Netherlands, and in February 1995 it was alleged that Iran had deployed air defence systems on the islands. In November officials from the UAE and Iran, meeting in Qatar, failed to reach agreement on establishing an agenda for ministerial-level negotiations.

In March–April 1996 bilateral relations deteriorated further when Iran opened an airport on Abu Musa and a power station on Greater Tunb. In February 1999 the UAE protested at the construction by Iran of municipal facilities on Abu Musa and at recent Iranian military exercises near the disputed islands. Iran subsequently complained to the UN that, in disputing the location of its military exercises, the UAE was interfering in Iranian internal affairs. In November a tripartite committee, established by the GCC and comprising representatives of Oman, Qatar and Saudi Arabia, announced that it would continue efforts to facilitate a settlement. Sheikh Zayed boycotted a meeting of GCC leaders in Saudi Arabia, in protest at the lack of attention given to the dispute with Iran by the other GCC members at a time when they were increasingly moving towards improved relations with Iran. In December the UAE renewed its request for Iran to enter into direct negotiations or agree to international arbitration over the islands. In March 2000, following a statement by Iran that it would be prepared to negotiate over the islands, the UAE asserted that it would refer it to the GCC tripartite committee. No significant progress had been reached concerning a resolution of the territorial dispute by early 2009.

Commercial links between the two countries remained strong, meanwhile, with the UAE having particular importance as the largest supplier of imports to Iran. President Mahmoud Ahmadinejad of Iran made the first visit to the UAE by an Iranian head of state in May 2007. Prior to the visit, the UAE authorities released from custody 12 Iranian divers who had been detained earlier in the month in waters off Abu Musa. Sheikh Muhammad visited Iran in February 2008 (he was the most senior UAE official to visit the country since the Iranian Revolution in 1979. In an interview with the Dubai-based *Khaleej Times* in April 2008, Iran's ambassador to the UAE emphasized positive developments in bilateral co-operation, and indicated his country's preparedness to discuss and resolve issues through dialogue with the UAE. However, reports in August that Iran had established two maritime administrative offices on Abu Musa provoked strong condemnation from the UAE authorities and the GCC. None the less, an official visit to Tehran in late October by the UAE's Minister of Foreign Affairs, Sheikh Abdullah bin Zayed an-Nahyan, culminated in the signing of an agreement to establish a joint UAE-Iran commission to promote bilateral relations. While both countries were committed to the advancement of their political and economic ties, neither side showed any inclination to retreat from their stance on the disputed islands. In March 2009 a spokesman for Iran's Ministry of Foreign Affairs, in response to repeated GCC statements on the UAE's claims to sovereignty over the islands, described them as 'inseparable parts of Iran'. This duly provoked further condemnation from the UAE and the GCC, as well as renewed calls that the issue be referred to the ICJ.

Meanwhile, relations between the UAE and Saudi Arabia had also become strained by the UAE's trade negotiations with the USA (see below); Saudi Arabia considered that the GCC should negotiate any trade agreement as a single body. In December 2005 the relationship was weakened further in relation to a longstanding border dispute between the UAE and Saudi Arabia concerning the Shaybah oilfield in the Rub al-Khali desert region. The dispute was the principal focus of discussions between the UAE's President and the Saudi Minister of the Interior in June 2006.

In response to Iraq's occupation of Kuwait in August 1990, the UAE (which supported the US-led multinational effort against Iraq) announced that foreign armed forces opposing the Iraqi invasion would be provided with military facilities in the Emirates. By the mid-1990s, however, the UAE was among those states questioning the justification for the continued maintenance of international sanctions (imposed in 1990) against Iraq, in view of the resultant humanitarian consequences for the Iraqi population. Following the restoration of diplomatic ties with Iraq in 1998, the UAE's embassy in the Iraqi capital was reopened in April 2000. However, the Ruler of Fujairah was criticized in Iraq after a speech, at the UN Millennium Summit in New York in September, in which he called on Iraq to apply all pertinent UN Security Council resolutions, particularly those related to the issue of prisoners of war. Although Iraq's Minister of Trade visited Abu Dhabi in December, where he was received by Sheikh Zayed, the UAE lent its support to a declaration of the GCC annual summit meeting that urged Iraq to conform with UN resolutions: it was generally considered that the UAE had been compelled to endorse the declaration in return for GCC support in its territorial dispute with Iran. Addressing the Arab InterParliamentary Union in February 2001, Sheikh Zayed none the less urged Arab states to work jointly towards an end to the sanctions regime in force against Iraq. In November the UAE and Iraq signed a free trade agreement, which was ratified by Sheikh Zayed in May 2002. Following the kidnap of a member of its diplomatic staff in Iraq in May 2006, the UAE withdrew its chargé d'affaires from Baghdad. In June 2008, however, the UAE's Minister of Foreign Affairs visited Baghdad, becoming the first senior government official from a GCC country to do so since the US-led invasion of Iraq in 2003. This was followed, in July 2008, by the visit of Iraqi Prime Minister Nuri al-Maliki to Abu Dhabi, during which Sheikh Khalifa announced plans to reinstate full diplomatic relations and approved the cancellation of some US $7,000m. of Iraqi debt. A new UAE ambassador to Iraq, the first since 1990, took up his post in September.

The UAE severed diplomatic relations with the Taliban regime in Afghanistan in late September 2001, in response to the suicide attacks against New York and Washington, DC, on 11 September. Hitherto, the UAE had been one of only three states to maintain ties with the Taliban (the UAE's relations with the Taliban being at chargé d'affaires level). The Saudi Arabian-born

Osama bin Laden, whose al-Qa'ida (Base) organization was at that time based in Afghanistan, was the USA's principal suspect in having orchestrated the September 2001 attacks. After diplomatic relations were severed, the UAE's Minister of Foreign Affairs stated that the his Government had sought to persuade the Taliban to hand over bin Laden so that he might stand trial in an international court. In common with other GCC members, the UAE pledged support for the USA in its efforts to bring to justice the perpetrators of terrorism. None the less, the UAE emphasized that the success of the US-led 'coalition against terror' must be linked to a resumption of the Arab-Israeli peace process, and expressed concerns that military action should not target any Arab state. The UAE's banking sector came under international scrutiny after US investigators claimed to have evidence of transactions between banks in the UAE and the USA linking bin Laden with the suicide attacks. At the end of September the Emirates' Central Bank ordered that the assets in the UAE of 27 individuals and organizations accused by the USA of involvement in terrorism be frozen; in November the Central Bank reportedly ordered a freeze on the assets of a further 62 entities. Following the swift defeat of the Taliban regime in the US-led military offensive, which began in October, and the inauguration of a new Afghan interim administration in December 2001, the Afghan embassy in the UAE was reopened in February 2002; the opening of the UAE's embassy in Kabul was announced in March. In November the Central Bank tightened regulations on the informal money-transfer system known as *hawala*, after the practice was criticized by Western law enforcement agencies as an important element in the financing of terrorism.

At the summit meeting of the Council of the League of Arab States (the Arab League, see p. 344) convened in Beirut, Lebanon, in March 2002, the Minister of State for Foreign Affairs, Sheikh Hamdan bin Zayed an-Nahyan, declared the UAE to be opposed to any future US-led campaign to oust the regime of Saddam Hussain in Iraq as a potential second phase in the USA's declared 'war on terror'. The UAE continued to urge a diplomatic solution to the crisis, and promoted a plan for the Iraqi leader to go into exile in order to prevent a war to oust his regime; however, in March 2003 the UAE disregarded appeals by some members of the Arab League to refuse to provide facilities for military action in Iraq. At the commencement of the conflict later in that month some 3,000 US air force personnel and 72 combat aircraft were stationed in the UAE. Following the overthrow of Iraq's Baathist regime by the US-led coalition in early April and the subsequent announcement that US forces were to be withdrawn from Saudi Arabia, the USA stated that it would develop the adh-Dhafra airport in Abu Dhabi for use by its military aircraft. In the immediate aftermath of the ousting of the regime of Saddam Hussain, the UAE provided significant humanitarian aid to Iraq, and made clear its intention to participate in the reconstruction of the country. In early 2004 the UAE agreed to write off most of Iraq's US $3,800m. bilateral debt.

In July 2004 the UAE signed a Trade and Investment Framework Agreement with the USA—regarded as a preliminary step towards a bilateral free trade agreement. Free trade negotiations with the USA duly commenced in March 2005. However, the talks were postponed in March 2006, as a result of a disagreement between the two countries regarding the acquisition by the state-owned Dubai Ports World (DP World) of a British-based ports and ferries operator, P&O, whose holdings included six major US ports. DP World agreed to sell the six US ports after the House Appropriations Committee of the US House of Representatives, in opposition to the US executive, adopted an amendment that would prevent the operation of the US ports by DP World; it was considered a risk to US security that the ports should be held by UAE interests. DP World reached an agreement to sell the US ports to a US company in December of that year. Trade negotiations meanwhile resumed. In late 2007, however, the Office of the US Trade Representative announced that the two countries had agreed that they would be unable to conclude a free trade accord during the tenure of the incumbent US Administration; a new round of negotiations was expected to commence following the inauguration of a new US President in 2009. The USA indicated its expectation that further progress on issues of labour rights would be a prerequisite to an eventual agreement. In January 2008 US President George W. Bush delivered the key address of his first tour of the Middle East from Abu Dhabi. In April the UAE's Minister of Foreign Affairs, Sheikh Abdullah bin Zayed an-Nahyan, and the US Secretary of State, Condoleezza Rice, meeting in Bahrain in advance of a GCC-US summit, signed a memorandum of understanding governing co-operation in the peaceful use of nuclear energy. Prior to this agreement, the UAE (which had in January 2008 ratified the International Convention for the Suppression of Acts of Nuclear Terrorism) issued a policy document regarding plans for the potential development of nuclear energy for civilian use, including a commitment to forgo any domestic enrichment or reprocessing capability in exchange for the long-term supply of fuel from external sources. Military co-operation with the USA increased in December 2008 with the signing of a contract, worth over US $3,000m., for the provision of a US-made medium-range defensive missile system. This was followed, in mid-January 2009, by the signing of an agreement, subject to US congressional approval, on civilian nuclear co-operation, which brought the UAE a step closer to its ambition of developing the Gulf's first nuclear power network. Statements released by both parties expressed the hope that the UAE's nuclear energy programme would serve as a model for similar projects throughout the region.

Bilateral co-operation accords signed during the course of a visit to the UAE by President Nicolas Sarkozy of France in January 2008 included an arrangement whereby France would assist in the development of a civilian nuclear energy programme in the UAE. Agreement was also reached on the establishment by France of a permanent military base in Abu Dhabi, capable of accommodating some 500 armed forces personnel. A memorandum of understanding on co-operation in nuclear energy for civilian purposes was signed by the UAE and the United Kingdom in May.

Government

The highest federal authority is the Supreme Council of Rulers, comprising the hereditary rulers of the seven emirates, each of whom is virtually an absolute monarch in his own domain. Decisions of the Supreme Council require the approval of at least five members, including the rulers of both Abu Dhabi and Dubai. From its seven members, the Supreme Council elects a President and a Vice-President. The President appoints the Prime Minister and the federal Council of Ministers, responsible to the Supreme Council, to hold executive authority. The legislature is the Federal National Council (FNC), a consultative assembly that considers laws proposed by the Council of Ministers. The FNC comprises 40 members, of whom one-half are appointed by the emirates and the remainder are chosen by electoral colleges. A constitutional amendment extending the FNC's term from two to four years was endorsed by the Supreme Council of Rulers in December 2008 and approved by the FNC in January 2009. There are no political parties.

Defence

As assessed at November 2008, the armed forces totalled an estimated 51,000 men (of whom some 30% were thought to be expatriates): an army of 44,000, an air force of 4,500 and a navy of around 2,500. The Union Defence Force and the armed forces of Abu Dhabi, Dubai, Ras al-Khaimah and Sharjah were formally merged in 1976, although Dubai still maintains a degree of independence (as to a lesser extent do other emirates). Military service is voluntary. The defence budget for 2007 was estimated at AED 37,000m. Forces of the US Central Command, including 81 air force personnel (as assessed at November 2008), were also stationed in the UAE.

Economic Affairs

In 2004, according to estimates by the World Bank, the UAE's gross national income (GNI), measured at average 2002–04 prices, was US $103,461m., equivalent to $23,950 per head (or $23,990 on an international purchasing-power parity basis). During 2000–07, it was estimated, the population increased by an average annual rate of 4.3%. Gross domestic product (GDP) per head decreased, in real terms, by an average of 3.1% per year during 2000–05. Overall GDP increased, in real terms, by an average annual rate of 7.5% in 2000–07. According to UN figures, real GDP increased by 7.6% in 2007.

According to preliminary Central Bank figures, agriculture (including livestock and fishing) contributed 1.7% of GDP in 2007, and engaged 6.9% of the employed population in 2008. The principal crops are dates, tomatoes, aubergines, and pumpkins, squash and gourds. The UAE imports some 70% of food requirements. Some agricultural products are exported on a small scale. Livestock-rearing and fishing are also important. During 2000–07 agricultural GDP, according to UN data, increased, in real terms, at an average annual rate of 4.5%. The GDP of the sector increased by 7.4% in 2007.

Industry (including mining, manufacturing, construction and power) contributed 59.7% of GDP in 2007, according to preliminary Central Bank figures, and engaged 37.5% of the working population in 2008. During 2000–07, according to UN data, industrial GDP increased by an average of 6.4% per year. The GDP of the sector expanded by 6.9% in 2007.

Mining and quarrying contributed 38.2% of GDP in 2007, according to preliminary Central Bank data, and employed 1.4% of the working population in 2008. Petroleum production is the most important industry in the UAE, with balance of payments data as published by the IMF indicating that exports of crude petroleum and related products contributed 38.8% of total export revenues in 2007. At the end of 2007 the UAE's proven recoverable reserves of petroleum were 97,800m. barrels, representing 7.9% of world reserves. Production levels in 2007 averaged 2.92m. barrels per day (b/d). As a member of the Organization of the Petroleum Exporting Countries (OPEC, see p. 386), the UAE is subject to production quotas agreed by the Organization's Conference. The UAE has large natural gas reserves, estimated at 6,090,000m. cu m at the end of 2007 (3.4% of world reserves). Most petroleum and natural gas reserves are concentrated in Abu Dhabi. Dubai is the UAE's second largest producer of petroleum. Marble and sand are also quarried. According to IMF data, the GDP of the mining sector increased by 17.0% in 2006.

Manufacturing contributed 12.2% of GDP in 2007, according to preliminary Central Bank figures, and employed 12.7% of the working population in 2008. The major heavy industries in the UAE are related to hydrocarbons, and activities are concentrated in the Jebel Ali Free Zone (in Dubai) and the Jebel Dhanna-Ruwais industrial zone in Abu Dhabi. The most important products are liquefied petroleum gas, distillate fuel oils and jet fuels. There are two petroleum refineries in Abu Dhabi, and the emirate has 'downstream' interests abroad. The most important activities in the non-hydrocarbons manufacturing sector are aluminium, steel and chemicals. During 2000–07, according to UN data, manufacturing GDP increased at an average annual rate of 7.3%. UN figures indicated that the GDP of the sector increased by 8.7% in 2007.

Each of the emirates is responsible for its own energy production. Electric energy is generated largely by thermal power stations, utilizing the UAE's own hydrocarbons resources. In early 2008 the UAE signed an agreement with France regarding co-operation in the development of a civilian nuclear power programme; memoranda of understanding were subsequently also signed with the USA and the United Kingdom regarding civilian nuclear co-operation.

The services sector contributed 38.5% of GDP in 2007, according to preliminary Central Bank figures, and engaged 55.7% of the working population in 2008. The establishment of the Jebel Ali Free Zone in 1985 enhanced Dubai's reputation as a well-equipped entrepôt for regional trade, and significant growth in both re-exports and tourism has been recorded in recent years. The financial services and real estate sectors have also expanded rapidly as the UAE has pursued economic diversification. During 2000–07, according to UN data, the GDP of the services sector increased by an average of 9.3% per year. According to UN figures, the sector's GDP increased by 8.6% in 2007.

In 2007, according to preliminary Central Bank figures, the UAE recorded a visible trade surplus of AED 236,150m., and there was a surplus of AED 135,930m. on the current account of the balance of payments. In 2007 the principal source of imports was the People's Republic of China, which supplied 11.6% of total imports. Other important suppliers in that year were India, the USA, Japan and Germany. India was the principal market for non-petroleum exports in 2007, taking 22.3% of the total. The other member states of the Co-operation Council for the Arab States of the Gulf (the Gulf Co-operation Council—GCC, see p. 229) together took 12.3% of non-petroleum exports in that year. Largely through its re-export trade, the UAE is of particular importance as a supplier of goods to Iran. Excluding hydrocarbons and free trade exports, the principal exports in 2007 were base metals and articles of base metal, plastics, rubber and related articles, and prepared foodstuffs and beverages. The principal imports in that year were machinery and electrical equipment, pearls, precious or semi-precious stones and precious metals, and vehicles and other transport equipment.

Preliminary Central Bank figures for 2007 indicated a surplus of AED 69,024m. on the consolidated government budget, equivalent to 9.5% of GDP. Including oil and gas revenues from other government entities, the IMF put the overall surplus in that year at AED 166,400m. (equivalent to 25.2% of GDP). The federal budget, to which Abu Dhabi is the major contributor, represents about one-quarter of the country's total public expenditure, as the individual emirates have their own budgets for municipal expenditure and local projects. Annual inflation averaged 5.7% in 2000–07. Consumer prices increased by an annual average of 11.1% in 2007. Some 4% of the labour force were recorded as unemployed in 2008. More than 90% of the work-force are estimated to be non-UAE nationals.

In addition to its membership of OPEC (see p. 386) and the GCC (see p. 229), the UAE also belongs to the Organization of Arab Petroleum Exporting Countries (OAPEC, see p. 379) and the Arab Fund for Economic and Social Development (AFESD, see p. 183). The UAE, and Abu Dhabi in particular, is a major aid donor. Abu Dhabi disburses loans through the Abu Dhabi Fund for Development (ADFD). GCC member states established a unified regional customs tariff in January 2003, and agreed to create a single market and currency no later than January 2010. The economic convergence criteria for the monetary union were agreed at a GCC summit in Abu Dhabi in December 2005, and in January 2008 the GCC common market was launched. However, there was doubt regarding prospects for monetary union after the UAE announced in May 2009 that it was to withdraw from the project.

The sustained high level of international petroleum prices contributed substantially to very high rates of economic growth and strong fiscal and balance of payments surpluses in the UAE in 2003–07. None the less, successful efforts at diversification of economic activity, hitherto particularly in Abu Dhabi and Dubai, resulted in less reliance on the hydrocarbons sector than in many other petroleum-producing countries. Highly developed infrastructure and low import tariffs have enhanced the UAE's position as a centre for regional trade, with Central Bank figures indicating in 2007 that the rate of growth of re-exports was exceeding that of domestic exports. Meanwhile, the tourism, real estate and financial services sectors also grew rapidly, and the strong performance of the construction sector reflected the rapid expansion of infrastructure. Growth of the non-oil sector during 2003–07 averaged some 10% annually. Legislation was issued in late 2007 establishing a new federal body, the Emirates Investment Authority, with responsibility for making investments on behalf of the federal Government. In an assessment of the economy compiled in late 2008, the IMF projected overall GDP growth of 7.4% for that year, and non-oil growth of 8.6%. By the final quarter of the year the impact of the global economic downturn was particularly pronounced in Dubai, whose heavily service-based economic model, which had fuelled a boom in the construction sector, came under intense scrutiny. In March and September the Central Bank implemented measures to offset diminished liquidity arising from a rapid outflow of foreign deposits (which had hitherto contributed substantially to the availability of credit), and in October the federal Government announced a three-year guarantee of deposits and inter-bank lending. The federal Government intervened in late 2008 to merge two Dubai-based mortgage companies with an amalgamation of two of Abu Dhabi's banks in a new, majority state-owned Emirates Development Bank. In February 2009, furthermore, the Central Bank acquired US $10,000m. of a sovereign bond issue by the Government of Dubai (one half of the total issue), thereby allowing Dubai to meet its debt-servicing obligations for that year. Earlier in the same month the Government of Abu Dhabi made available some $4,300m. to five of its banks, in order to increase their capital and enhance lending capacity. Federal intervention in the economy was particularly notable in view of the traditional autonomy retained by each emirate in its economic affairs. In January 2009 a federal decree established a new council to co-ordinate pan-emirate and federal budgets and expenditure. A three-year strategic plan announced in November 2008 prioritized the industrial sector and stronger partnership with the private sector. Public spending was budgeted to increase in 2009 at federal and emirate level, with emphasis on the maintenance of infrastructure projects. Dubai, notably, was projected to incur its first fiscal deficit in 2009, as public spending was increased in an effort to stimulate the economy. By early 2009 several major construction projects had been deferred, temporarily easing pressure on power and water supply; however, it was considered critical to maintain programmes to expand capacity in utilities in order to address future demand. Job losses arising from deferred construction projects and reduced activity in services sectors such as tourism were considered likely to result in a decline in the non-national popula-

THE UNITED ARAB EMIRATES

tion, especially in Dubai, prompting some concern regarding possible future labour shortages.

Education

Primary education is compulsory, beginning at six years of age and lasting for six years. Secondary education, starting at the age of 12, also lasts for six years, comprising two equal cycles of three years. According to UNESCO estimates, enrolment at primary schools in 2006/07 included 90.9% of children in the relevant age group, while in 2005/06 79.0% of pupils in the appropriate age group were enrolled at secondary schools. Most of the teachers are from other Arab countries, notably Kuwait, Jordan and Egypt. The UAE has four state-run universities: two in Abu Dhabi (one of which, Zayed University, enrols female nationals only) and one each in Sharjah and Ajman. In addition there are numerous private universities and higher education institutions operating in the UAE. In 2008/09 16,372 students were enrolled at the UAE University at Al-Ain in Abu Dhabi, while more than 3,300 students were enrolled at Zayed University in 2007/08. Four higher colleges of technology (two for male and two for female students) opened in 1988; by 2008/09 there were higher colleges of technology in eight cities attended by over 16,000 students, all of whom were citizens of the UAE. In 2002/03 71,194 students were enrolled in university and other higher education. A branch of the Sorbonne University, based in Paris, France, opened in Abu Dhabi in October 2006, following an agreement signed earlier that year with the Ministry of Higher Education and Scientific Research. Many other students receive higher education abroad. Budgeted federal government expenditure by the Ministries of Education and of Higher Education and Scientific Research in the 2009/10 fiscal year totalled an estimated AED 9,706m. (23.0% of total expenditure by the central Government).

Public Holidays

2009: 1 January (New Year's Day), 9 March* (Mouloud, Birth of Muhammad), 19 July* (Leilat al-Meiraj, Ascension of Muhammad), 22 August* (first day of Ramadan), 20 September* (Id al-Fitr, end of Ramadan), 27 November* (Id al-Adha, Feast of the Sacrifice), 2 December (National Day), 18 December* (Muharram, Islamic New Year), 25 December (Christmas Day).

2010: 1 January (New Year's Day), 26 February* (Mouloud, Birth of Muhammad), 8 July* (Leilat al-Meiraj, Ascension of Muhammad), 11 August* (first day of Ramadan), 10 September* (Id al-Fitr, end of Ramadan), 16 November* (Id al-Adha, Feast of the Sacrifice), 2 December (National Day), 7 December* (Muharram, Islamic New Year), 25 December (Christmas Day).

* These holidays are dependent on the Islamic lunar calendar and may vary slightly from the dates given.

Weights and Measures

The imperial, metric and local systems are all in use.

Statistical Survey

Source (unless otherwise stated): Central Bank of the UAE, POB 854, Abu Dhabi; tel. (2) 6652220; fax (2) 6667494; e-mail uaecbadm@cbuae.gov.ae; internet www.centralbank.ae.

Area and Population

AREA, POPULATION AND DENSITY

Area (sq km)	77,700*
Population (census results)	
17 December 1995	2,411,041
6 December 2005	
UAE nationals	824,921
Males	418,057
Females	406,864
Non-UAE nationals	3,279,774†
Total	4,104,695
Population (official estimates at mid-year)	
2006	4,229,000
2007	4,488,000
2008	4,764,000
Density (per sq km) at mid-2008	61.3

* 30,000 sq miles.

† Including 335,615 non-national groups not enumerated on 6 December; the enumerated total of non-nationals was 2,944,159 (total enumerated population of UAE was 3,769,080).

POPULATION BY EMIRATE
(official estimates at mid-2008)

	Area (sq km)	Population ('000)	Density (per sq km)
Abu Dhabi	67,350	1,559	23.1
Dubai	3,900	1,593	408.5
Sharjah	2,600	946	363.8
Ajman	250	237	948.0
Ras al-Khaimah	1,700	231	135.9
Fujairah	1,150	145	126.1
Umm al-Qaiwain	750	53	70.7
Total	77,700	4,764	61.3

PRINCIPAL TOWNS
(estimated population at mid-2003)

Dubai	1,171,000	Ras al-Khaimah	102,000
Abu Dhabi (capital)	552,000	Fujairah	54,000
Sharjah	519,000	Umm Al-Quwain	38,000
Al-Ain	348,000	Khor-Fakkan	32,000
Ajman	225,000		

Mid-2006 (official estimate): Dubai 1,241,000 (Source: Statistics Centre, Municipality of Dubai, *Dubai in Figures*).

BIRTHS, MARRIAGES AND DEATHS

	Live births		Marriages*		Deaths	
	Number	Rate (per 1,000)	Number	Rate (per 1,000)	Number	Rate (per 1,000)
1996	47,050	18.9	6,275	2.5	4,785	1.9
1997	46,360	17.5	6,573	2.5	4,878	1.8
1998	48,136	17.0	6,920	2.4	5,033	1.8
1999	49,659	16.4	10,182	3.4	5,194	1.7
2000	53,686	16.5	8,965	2.8	5,396	1.7
2001	56,136	16.1	9,697	2.8	5,758	1.8
2002	58,070	15.5	11,285	3.0	5,994	1.6
2003	61,165	15.1	12,277	3.0	6,002	1.5

* Muslim marriages only.

Life expectancy (years at birth, WHO estimates): 77.8 (males 76.7; females 79.6) in 2006 (Source: WHO, *World Health Statistics*).

THE UNITED ARAB EMIRATES

EMPLOYMENT
(persons aged 15 years and over)

	2005	2006*	2007
Agriculture, hunting, forestry and fishing	193,044	209,066	225,499
Mining and quarrying	38,694	41,906	45,199
Oil and gas	33,200	35,956	38,783
Manufacturing	336,585	364,521	393,173
Electricity, gas and water supply	34,207	37,046	39,958
Construction	534,398	578,753	624,242
Wholesale and retail trade; repair of motor vehicles, motorcycles and personal and household goods	502,427	544,129	586,897
Hotels and restaurants	116,615	126,294	136,220
Transport, storage and communications	162,768	176,278	190,133
Financial intermediation	31,015	33,589	36,229
Real estate, renting and business activities	77,858	84,320	90,947
Public administration and defence; compulsory social security	286,105	309,851	334,207
Community, social and personal service activities	114,736	124,259	134,026
Private households with employed persons	222,506	240,975	259,916
Total employed	**2,650,958**	**2,870,987**	**3,096,646**

* Preliminary figures.
† Estimates.

2008 ('000 persons aged 15 years and over): Agriculture, hunting, forestry and fishing 233; Mining and quarrying 47 (Oil and gas 40); Manufacturing 431; Electricity, gas and water 39; Construction 757; Wholesale and retail trade; repair of motor vehicles, motorcycles and personal and household goods 643; Hotels and restaurants 146; Transport, storage and communications 204; Financial intermediation 42; Real estate, renting and business activities 97; Public administration and defence; compulsory social security 353; Community, social and personal service activities 142; Private households with employed persons 264; *Total employed* 3,397.

Health and Welfare

KEY INDICATORS

Total fertility rate (children per woman, 2006)	2.3
Under-5 mortality rate (per 1,000 live births, 2006)	8
HIV/AIDS (% of persons aged 15–49, 1994)	0.18
Physicians (per 1,000 head, 2004)	2.0
Hospital beds (per 1,000 head, 2005)	1.8
Health expenditure (2006): US $ per head (PPP)	673
Health expenditure (2006): % of GDP	2.6
Health expenditure (2006): public (% of total)	72.9
Human Development Index (2006): ranking	31
Human Development Index (2006): value	0.903

For sources and definitions, see explanatory note on p. vi.

Statistical Survey

Agriculture

PRINCIPAL CROPS
('000 metric tons, FAO estimates)

	2005	2006	2007
Potatoes	7.1	7.1	7.9
Cabbages	16.0	16.5	17.5
Lettuce	1.0	1.2	1.3
Spinach	0.9	1.0	1.2
Tomatoes	240.0	220.0	215.0
Cauliflowers and broccoli	13.0	10.8	11.5
Pumpkins, squash and gourds	21.5	20.0	20.0
Cucumbers and gherkins	26.5	16.2	17.2
Aubergines (Eggplants)	20.5	21.0	22.0
Chillies and peppers, green	6.0	5.5	5.6
Onions and shallots, green	16.0	16.5	16.5
Beans, green	1.2	1.1	1.2
Carrots and turnips	2.2	2.3	2.4
Watermelons	3.0	3.9	3.9
Cantaloupes and other melons	7.0	8.0	8.0
Lemons and limes	11.5	12.0	12.3
Mangoes, mangosteens and guavas	5.0	5.5	5.7
Dates	750.0	755.0	755.0

Aggregate production ('000 metric tons, may include official, semi-official or estimated data): Total vegetables (incl. melons) 476 in 2005; 479 in 2006; 483 in 2007; Total fruits (excl. melons) 778 in 2005; 778 in 2006; 779 in 2007.

Source: FAO.

LIVESTOCK
('000 head, year ending September, FAO estimates)

	2005	2006	2007
Cattle	117	120	125
Camels	250	255	260
Sheep	580	600	615
Goats	1,520	1,550	1,570
Chickens	16,500	15,000	15,500

Source: FAO.

LIVESTOCK PRODUCTS
('000 metric tons, FAO estimates)

	2005	2006	2007
Cattle meat	10.0	10.0	10.0
Camel meat	15.4	15.5	15.5
Sheep meat	12.6	14.0	14.0
Goat meat	16.0	15.5	15.5
Chicken meat	33.6	36.0	36.0
Cows' milk	12.0	12.0	12.0
Camels' milk	39.4	40.0	40.0
Sheep's milk	12.0	12.0	12.0
Goats' milk	35.5	36.0	36.0
Hen eggs	17.0	17.0	17.2

Source: FAO.

THE UNITED ARAB EMIRATES   Statistical Survey

Fishing

('000 metric tons, live weight of capture)

	2004	2005	2006*
Capture	90.0*	86.7	87.0
Groupers and seabasses	16.7*	14.5	14.5
Grunts and sweetlips	3.8*	3.7	3.7
Emperors (Scavengers)	20.2*	20.1	20.0
King soldier bream	5.9*	5.8	5.8
Sardinellas	4.7*	5.2	5.1
Stolephorus anchovies	4.1*	4.8	4.8
Narrow-barred Spanish mackerel	5.1	4.6	4.6
Jacks and crevalles	1.6*	1.6	1.6
Carangids	2.7*	2.2	2.2
Indian mackerel	3.1*	3.2	3.2
Aquaculture*	0.6	0.6	0.6
Total catch (incl. others)*	90.6	87.3	87.6

* FAO estimate(s).
Source: FAO.

Mining

(estimated production)

	2005	2006	2007
Crude petroleum (million metric tons)	129.0	139.0	135.9
Natural gas (million cu metres)*	47,000	47,400	49,200

* Excluding gas flared or recycled.
Source: BP, *Statistical Review of World Energy*.

Industry

SELECTED PRODUCTS
('000 barrels, unless otherwise indicated, estimates)

	2004	2005	2006
Cement ('000 metric tons)	9,000	9,800	9,800
Aluminium ('000 metric tons)	683	722	861
Motor spirit (petrol)	20,000	20,000	30,000
Kerosene	50,000	50,000	50,000
Gas-diesel (distillate fuel) oil	45,000	45,000	48,000
Residual fuel oils	20,000	20,000	19,000
Liquefied petroleum gas	88,000	n.a.	n.a.

Source: US Geological Survey.

Electric energy (million kWh): 49,450 in 2003; 52,417 in 2004; 60,698 in 2005 (Source: UN, *Industrial Commodity Statistics Yearbook*).

Finance

CURRENCY AND EXCHANGE RATES

Monetary Units
100 fils = 1 UAE dirham (AED).

Sterling, Dollar and Euro Equivalents (31 December 2008)
£1 sterling = 5.354 dirhams;
US $1 = 3.673 dirhams;
€1 = 5.111 dirhams;
100 UAE dirhams = £18.68 = $27.23 = €19.57.

Exchange Rate: The Central Bank's official rate was set at US $1 = 3.671 dirhams in November 1980. This remained in force until December 1997, when the rate was adjusted to $1 = 3.6725 dirhams.

BUDGET OF THE CONSOLIDATED GOVERNMENTS
(million UAE dirhams)

Revenue	2005	2006	2007*
Tax revenue	6,810	8,027	13,833
Custom revenue	3,852	4,461	8,020
Non-tax revenue	137,095	193,139	214,917
Revenue from petroleum and natural gas	111,377	164,775	176,265
Profit of joint stock corporations	4,624	9,478	6,613
Total	143,905	201,166	228,750

Expenditure	2005	2006	2007*
Current expenditure	84,255	103,907	121,314
Salaries and wages	16,654	17,693	21,265
Goods and services	24,383	26,177	35,420
Subsidies and transfers	18,916	30,806	29,692
Development expenditure	14,042	15,225	17,271
Loans and equity	6,133	6,845	21,141
Total	104,430	125,977	159,726

* Preliminary figures.

Consolidated government finances (consolidated accounts of the federal governments of Abu Dhabi, Dubai and Sharjah, '000 million UAE dirhams, 2007): *Revenue* (including IMF estimates of revenues from other government entities operating in the oil and gas sector): Total 333.4 (Hydrocarbons 234.5, Non-hydrocarbon 98.9). *Expenditure and grants:* Total 166.9 (Current 126.6, Development 17.3, Loans and equity 20.8, Foreign grants 2.3) (Source: IMF, *United Arab Emirates: 2008 Article IV Consultation—Staff Report; Staff Statement; and Public Information Notice on the Executive Board Discussion*—April 2009).

INTERNATIONAL RESERVES
(US $ million at 31 December, excluding gold)

	2005	2006	2007
IMF special drawing rights	9.6	12.2	13.7
Reserve position in IMF	133.0	93.3	63.2
Foreign exchange*	20,867.7	27,511.9	77,161.9
Total	21,010.3	27,617.4	77,238.8

* Figures exclude the Central Bank's foreign assets and accrued interest attributable to the governments of individual emirates.

Source: IMF, *International Financial Statistics*.

MONEY SUPPLY
(million UAE dirhams at 31 December)

	2005	2006	2007
Currency outside banks	17,522	21,837	25,941
Demand deposits at commercial banks	86,927	98,183	155,723
Total money	104,449	120,020	181,664

Source: IMF, *International Financial Statistics*.

THE UNITED ARAB EMIRATES

COST OF LIVING
(Consumer Price Index; base: 2000 = 100)

	2005	2006*	2007*
Food, beverages and tobacco	117.0	123.5	147.8
Clothing and footwear	114.8	119.2	127.6
Housing (incl. rent)	130.1	150.1	176.4
Furniture, etc.	110.5	113.2	122.3
Medical care and health services	123.4	127.5	134.4
Transport and communications	116.6	127.7	133.0
Recreation and education	121.7	124.6	128.3
All items (incl. others)	121.7	133.0	147.8

* Preliminary figures.

NATIONAL ACCOUNTS
(million UAE dirhams at current prices)

National Income and Product

	2002	2003	2004*
Compensation of employees	79,102	88,926	94,395
Operating surplus	157,785	193,950	242,972
Domestic factor incomes	236,887	282,876	337,367
Consumption of fixed capital	35,969	38,876	41,394
Gross domestic product (GDP) at factor cost	272,856	321,752	378,761
Indirect taxes, less subsidies	2,430	3,396	3,928
GDP in purchasers' values	275,286	325,148	382,689
Net factor income from abroad	−11,805	−16,261	−16,135
Gross national income	263,481	308,887	366,554
Less Consumption of fixed capital	35,969	38,876	41,394
National income in market prices	227,512	270,011	325,160
Less Net current transfers from abroad	1,050	1,000	1,500
National disposable income	226,462	269,011	323,660

* Preliminary figures.

Expenditure on the Gross Domestic Product

	2005	2006	2007*
Government final consumption expenditure	51,544	57,961	76,190
Private final consumption expenditure	242,176	271,793	319,867
Increase in stocks	5,724	6,663	7,435
Gross fixed capital formation	93,798	120,999	148,479
Total domestic expenditure	393,242	457,416	551,971
Exports of goods and services		534,666	664,345
Less Imports of goods and services	119,847	367,459	486,584
GDP in purchasers' values	513,089	624,623	729,732

* Preliminary figures.

Gross Domestic Product by Economic Activity

	2005	2006*	2007†
Agriculture, hunting, forestry and fishing	11,028	12,595	12,797
Mining and quarrying	174,114	239,115	282,633
Oil and gas	173,195	237,952	281,340
Manufacturing	61,194	75,555	90,530
Electricity and water	7,935	9,796	10,893
Construction	34,980	46,468	58,301
Wholesale and retail trade, and repairs	52,998	64,345	72,781
Restaurants and hotels	8,946	10,733	11,419
Transport, storage and communications	32,642	39,631	42,926
Financial institutions and insurance	28,426	36,705	40,919
Real estate and business services	35,920	47,455	55,490
Government services	34,735	40,153	49,266
Community, social and personal services	7,607	8,958	9,619
Private households with employed persons	2,382	2,702	2,798
Sub-total	492,908	634,204	740,377
Statistical discrepancy	−1	7	5
Less Imputed bank service charge	7,395	9,548	10,645
GDP in purchasers' values	485,513	624,623	729,732

* Preliminary figures.
† Estimates.

BALANCE OF PAYMENTS
('000 million UAE dirhams, preliminary estimates)

	2005	2006	2007
Exports of goods f.o.b.	430.74	534.67	664.35
Imports of goods f.o.b.	−273.58	−323.36	−428.19
Trade balance	157.15	211.30	236.15
Services (net)	−53.56	−66.23	−87.61
Income (net)	10.60	17.40	21.50
Balance on goods, services and income	114.19	162.47	170.05
Current transfers (net)	−24.70	−30.10	−34.11
Current balance	89.49	132.38	135.93
Capital and financial accounts (net)	−53.88	−58.99	41.52
Net errors and omissions	−26.11	−49.50	5.79
Overall balance	9.50	23.89	183.24

External Trade

PRINCIPAL COMMODITIES
(distribution by HS, million UAE dirhams)

Imports c.i.f.	2005	2006	2007
Vegetable products	8,304.5	9,041.2	12,563.1
Prepared foodstuffs, beverages, spirits and tobacco	7,057.2	7,895.6	8,412.9
Chemical products, etc.	12,729.6	15,754.7	21,485.5
Plastics, rubber and articles thereof	8,932.1	10,693.4	14,093.9
Textiles and textile articles	13,476.0	14,805.0	17,762.4
Pearls, precious or semi-precious stones, precious metals, etc.	50,693.6	52,475.3	76,902.9
Base metals and articles of base metal	22,924.6	32,689.5	46,459.6
Machinery and electrical equipment	57,443.7	66,439.9	88,859.3
Vehicles and other transport equipment	30,388.7	36,786.7	52,375.9
Total (incl. others)	242,421.9	284,453.2	387,807.8

THE UNITED ARAB EMIRATES

Statistical Survey

Exports f.o.b.*	2005	2006	2007
Vegetable products	503.0	298.2	235.2
Prepared foodstuffs, beverages, spirits and tobacco	2,035.1	2,576.7	2,952.9
Mineral products	817.8	1,060.1	1,919.3
Chemical products, etc.	879.2	997.7	1,133.4
Plastics, rubber and articles thereof	2,574.3	2,860.1	3,759.9
Textiles and textile articles	727.2	980.4	1,182.1
Stone, plaster, cement, ceramic and glassware	804.0	1,199.7	1,664.0
Base metals and articles of base metal	3,561.5	4,489.0	5,119.8
Machinery and electrical equipment	480.7	969.1	893.6
Vehicles and other transport equipment	146.4	709.3	598.6
Total (incl. others)†	14,650.9	23,180.8	33,070.2

*Excluding petroleum exports and excluding re-exports; re-exports amounted to 94,004.1m. dirhams in 2005, 91,163.0m. dirhams in 2006 and 120,954.1m. dirhams in 2007.
† Excluding free zone exports.

SELECTED MAJOR TRADING PARTNERS
(million UAE dirhams)

Imports	2005	2006	2007
Australia	3,663.0	5,245.5	9,869.7
Belgium/Netherlands/Luxembourg	7,532.0	9,603.8	11,411.2
Brazil	2,972.9	3,858.4	4,675.6
Canada	1,297.7	1,958.3	2,498.2
China, People's Republic	23,760.5	30,390.1	45,181.8
France (incl. Monaco)	8,540.9	8,681.5	11,270.5
GCC countries	10,536.5	16,887.9	17,688.0
Germany	16,344.2	20,970.9	26,232.7
India	31,685.4	30,426.3	45,018.1
Italy (incl. San Marino)	8,417.2	12,249.8	17,556.1
Japan	17,027.1	20,660.6	30,422.9
Korea, Republic	6,489.8	7,600.8	10,524.0
New Zealand	401.8	554.6	654.3
South Africa	2,355.2	1,779.9	4,649.4
United Kingdom	15,962.7	14,692.6	17,104.3
USA	18,514.7	23,222.6	31,084.6
Total (incl. others)	242,421.9	284,453.2	387,807.8

Exports*	2005	2006	2007
Australia	329.4	381.5	458.6
Belgium/Netherlands/Luxembourg	5,400.4	3,252.6	4,088.9
Brazil	20.7	36.9	143.2
Canada	90.2	117.1	171.9
GCC countries	16,225.8	13,051.6	18,881.6
Germany	1,612.7	888.7	908.0
India	19,588.6	17,354.6	34,382.6
New Zealand	108.1	135.4	179.6
United Kingdom	876.2	1,519.2	1,349.1
USA	2,224.3	2,140.2	2,180.3
Total (incl. others)	108,655.0	114,343.8	154,024.3

*Data for non-petroleum exports and all re-exports.

Transport

ROAD TRAFFIC
('000 registered motor vehicles in use)

	2000	2001	2002
Passenger cars (incl. taxis)	561.9	654.2	606.1
Trucks (incl. public)	83.3	66.2	66.2
Buses (incl. public)	14.7	13.3	16.0
Other	13.2	11.2	13.1

Total vehicles in use: 767 in 2002; 792 in 2003.

SHIPPING

Merchant Fleet
(registered at 31 December)

	2005	2006	2007
Number of vessels	406	417	446
Total displacement ('000 grt)	839.2	870.3	807.2

Source: Lloyd's Register-Fairplay, *World Fleet Statistics*.

International Sea-borne Shipping
(estimated freight traffic, '000 metric tons)

	1988	1989	1990
Goods loaded	63,380	72,896	88,153
Crude petroleum	54,159	63,387	78,927
Other cargo	9,221	9,509	9,226
Goods unloaded	8,973	8,960	9,595

Source: UN, *Monthly Bulletin of Statistics*.

CIVIL AVIATION
(traffic on scheduled services)*

	2002	2003	2004
Kilometres flown (million)	159	207	277
Passengers carried ('000)	9,667	11,610	14,314
Passenger-km (million)	33,125	41,504	54,703
Total ton-km (million)	5,261	6,760	8,979

*Figures include an apportionment (one-quarter) of the traffic of Gulf Air, a multinational airline with its headquarters in Bahrain.

Source: UN, *Statistical Yearbook*.

Tourism

FOREIGN TOURIST ARRIVALS*

Country	2002	2003	2004
Canada	95,878	55,297	57,718
Egypt	111,822	121,221	131,635
France	90,735	98,624	112,429
Germany	236,660	235,147	337,594
India	336,046	357,941	356,446
Iran	270,350	334,453	336,734
Jordan	73,140	76,553	76,308
Lebanon	74,225	83,137	90,409
Pakistan	154,711	183,724	173,152
Russia	267,655	324,484	340,716
United Kingdom	491,604	496,147	644,688
USA	123,112	175,116	192,948
Total (incl. others)†	5,445,367	5,871,023	6,195,006

*Figures refer to international arrivals at hotels and similar establishments.
† Total includes domestic tourists.

Receipts from tourism (US $ million, incl. passenger transport): 1,593 in 2004; 3,218 in 2005; 4,912 in 2006.

Source: World Tourism Organization.

THE UNITED ARAB EMIRATES

Communications Media

	2005	2006	2007
Telephones ('000 main lines in use)	1,236.9	1,309.7	1,385.5
Mobile cellular telephones ('000 subscribers)	4,534.1	5,519.3	7,594.5
Personal computers ('000 in use)	850	n.a.	n.a.
Internet users ('000)	1,321.7	1,708.5	2,300.0
Broadband subscribers ('000)	129.3	240.6	n.a.

Daily newspapers (titles): 9 in 2004.

Radio receivers ('000 in use): 820 in 1997.

Television receivers ('000 in use): 780 in 2001.

Facsimile machines ('000 in use): 50 in 1997.

Sources: partly UNESCO, *Statistical Yearbook*; UN, *Statistical Yearbook*; International Telecommunication Union.

Education

(Government schools only)

	2001/02	2002/03	2003/04
Institutions	740	744	755
Teachers*	27,616	27,954	27,855
Students			
Pre-primary	22,219	22,596	20,561
Primary	204,760	214,235	218,739
Secondary	65,195	65,202	64,618
Other schools	3,487	4,607	5,154

* Includes administrative and technical staff.

Adult literacy rate (UNESCO estimates): 90.4% (males 90.9%; females 89.2%) in 2007 (Source: UNESCO Institute for Statistics).

Directory

The Constitution

A provisional Constitution for the UAE took effect in December 1971. This laid the foundation for the federal structure of the Union of the seven emirates, previously known as the Trucial States.

The highest federal authority is the Supreme Council of Rulers, which comprises the Rulers of the seven emirates. It elects the President and Vice-President from among its members. The President appoints a Prime Minister and a Council of Ministers. Proposals submitted to the Council require the approval of at least five of the Rulers, including those of Abu Dhabi and Dubai. The legislature is the Federal National Council (FNC), a consultative assembly comprising 40 members, of whom one-half are appointed by the emirates and the remainder are chosen by electoral colleges for a two-year term. A constitutional amendment extending the FNC's term to four years was endorsed by the Supreme Council of Rulers in December 2008 and approved by the FNC in January 2009.

In July 1975 a committee was appointed to draft a permanent federal constitution, but the FNC decided in 1976 to extend the provisional document for five years. The provisional Constitution was extended for another five years in December 1981, and for further periods of five years in 1986 and 1991. In November 1976, however, the Supreme Council amended Article 142 of the provisional Constitution so that the authority to levy armed forces was placed exclusively under the control of the federal Government. Legislation designed to make the provisional Constitution permanent was endorsed by the FNC in June 1996, after it had been approved by the Supreme Council of Rulers.

The Government

HEAD OF STATE

President: Sheikh KHALIFA BIN ZAYED AN-NAHYAN (Ruler of Abu Dhabi, elected by the Supreme Council of Rulers as President of the UAE on 3 November 2004).

Vice-President: Sheikh MUHAMMAD BIN RASHID AL-MAKTOUM (Ruler of Dubai).

SUPREME COUNCIL OF RULERS
(with each Ruler's date of accession)

Ruler of Abu Dhabi: Sheikh KHALIFA BIN ZAYED AN-NAHYAN (2004).

Ruler of Dubai: Sheikh MUHAMMAD BIN RASHID AL-MAKTOUM (2006).

Ruler of Sharjah: Sheikh SULTAN BIN MUHAMMAD AL-QASIMI (1972).

Ruler of Ras al-Khaimah: Sheikh SAQR BIN MUHAMMAD AL-QASIMI (1948).

Ruler of Umm al-Qaiwain: Sheikh SAUD BIN RASHID AL-MU'ALLA (2009).

Ruler of Ajman: Sheikh HUMAID BIN RASHID AN-NUAIMI (1981).

Ruler of Fujairah: Sheikh HAMAD BIN MUHAMMAD ASH-SHARQI (1974).

COUNCIL OF MINISTERS
(May 2009)

Prime Minister and Minister of Defence: Sheikh MUHAMMAD BIN RASHID AL-MAKTOUM.

Deputy Prime Ministers: Sheikh SULTAN BIN ZAYED AN-NAHYAN, Sheikh HAMDAN BIN ZAYED AN-NAHYAN.

Deputy Prime Minister and Minister of the Interior: Lt-Gen. Sheikh SAIF BIN ZAYED AN-NAHYAN.

Deputy Prime Minister and Minister of Presidential Affairs: Sheikh MANSOUR BIN ZAYED AN-NAHYAN.

Minister of Finance: Sheikh HAMDAN BIN RASHID AL-MAKTOUM.

Minister of Foreign Affairs: Sheikh ABDULLAH BIN ZAYED AN-NAHYAN.

Minister of Higher Education and Scientific Research: Sheikh NAHYAN BIN MUBARAK AN-NAHYAN.

Minister of Public Works: Sheikh HAMDAN BIN MUBARAK AN-NAHYAN.

Minister of Economy: SULTAN BIN SAID AL-MANSOURI.

Minister of Foreign Trade: Sheikha LUBNA BINT KHALID AL-QASIMI.

Minister of Justice: Dr HADIF JOWAN ADH-DHAHIRI.

Minister of Energy: MUHAMMAD BIN DHAEN AL-HAMILI.

Minister of Labour: SAQR GHOBASH SAID GHOBASH.

Minister of Social Affairs: Dr MARIAM MUHAMMAD KHALFAN AR-ROUMI.

Minister of Education: HUMAID MUHAMMAD OBAID AL-QATTAMI.

Minister of Health: Dr HANIF HASSAN ALI.

Minister of the Environment and Water: Dr RASHID AHMAD AL-FAHD.

Minister of Culture, Youth and Community Development: ABD AR-RAHMAN MUHAMMAD AL-OWAIS.

Minister of Cabinet Affairs: MUHAMMAD BIN ABDULLAH AL-GARGAWI.

Minister of State for Financial Affairs: OBAID HUMAID AT-TAYER.

Minister of State for Foreign Affairs and for Federal National Council Affairs: Dr ANWAR MUHAMMAD GARGASH.

Ministers of State: REEM IBRAHIM AL-HASHEMI, Dr MAITHA SALIM ASH-SHAMSI.

FEDERAL MINISTRIES

Office of the Prime Minister: POB 12848, Dubai; tel. (4) 3534550; fax (4) 3530111; e-mail info@primeminister.ae; internet www.uaepm.ae.

Office of the Deputy Prime Minister: POB 831, Abu Dhabi; tel. (2) 4451000; fax (2) 4450066.

Ministry of Cabinet Affairs: POB 2350, Abu Dhabi; tel. (2) 6268100; fax (2) 6268033; e-mail info@moca.gov.ae; internet www.moca.gov.ae.

Ministry of Culture, Youth and Community Development: POB 17, Abu Dhabi; tel. (2) 4466145; fax (2) 4452504; e-mail mcycd@mcycd.gov.ae; internet www.mcycd.ae.

THE UNITED ARAB EMIRATES

Ministry of Defence: POB 46616, Abu Dhabi; tel. (4) 4461300; fax (4) 4463286; internet www.mod.gov.ae.

Ministry of Economy: POB 901, Abu Dhabi; tel. (2) 6265000; fax (2) 6260000; e-mail economy@economy.ae; internet www.economy.ae.

Ministry of Education: POB 295, Abu Dhabi; tel. (2) 6213800; fax (2) 6351164; e-mail moe@uae.gov.ae; internet www.moe.gov.ae.

Ministry of Energy: POB 59, Abu Dhabi; tel. (2) 6262288; fax (2) 6272291; e-mail pms@moenr.gov.ae; internet www.moenr.gov.ae.

Ministry of the Environment and Water: POB 213, Abu Dhabi; tel. (2) 4495100; fax (2) 4495150; e-mail info@moew.gov.ae; internet www.moew.gov.ae.

Ministry of Finance: POB 433, Abu Dhabi; tel. (2) 6726000; fax (2) 6768414; e-mail webmaster@mof.gov.ae; internet www.mof.gov.ae.

Ministry of Foreign Affairs: POB 1, Abu Dhabi; tel. (2) 4444488; fax (2) 4449200; e-mail mofa@mofa.gov.ae; internet www.mofa.gov.ae.

Ministry of Foreign Trade: Abu Dhabi; tel. (2) 4956000; fax (2) 4499164; e-mail info@moft.gov.ae; internet www.moft.gov.ae.

Ministry of Health: POB 848, Abu Dhabi; tel. (2) 6330000; fax (2) 6726000; e-mail info@moh.gov.ae; internet www.moh.gov.ae.

Ministry of Higher Education and Scientific Research: POB 45253, Abu Dhabi; tel. (2) 6428272; fax (2) 6428778; e-mail hkhalil@mohesr.ae; internet www.mohesr.ae.

Ministry of the Interior: POB 398, Abu Dhabi; tel. (2) 4414666; fax (2) 4414938; e-mail moi@moi.gov.ae; internet www.moi.gov.ae.

Ministry of Justice: POB 260, Abu Dhabi; tel. (2) 6814000; fax (2) 6810680; e-mail moj@uae.gov.ae.

Ministry of Labour: POB 809, Abu Dhabi; tel. (2) 4183888; fax (2) 6665889; e-mail minister@mol.gov.ae; internet www.mol.gov.ae.

Ministry of Presidential Affairs: Abu Dhabi; tel. (2) 6222221; fax (2) 6222228; e-mail webmaster@mopa.gov.ae; internet www.mopa.ae.

Ministry of Public Works: POB 878, Abu Dhabi; tel. (2) 6260606; fax (2) 6260026; e-mail webmaster@mpw.ae; internet www.mopw.gov.ae.

Ministry of Social Affairs: POB 809, Abu Dhabi; tel. (4) 2637777; fax (4) 2633525; e-mail info@msa.gov.ae; internet www.msa.gov.ae.

Ministry of State for Federal National Council Affairs: POB 130000, Abu Dhabi; tel. (2) 4041000; fax (2) 4041155; e-mail mfnca@mfnca.ae; internet www.mfnca.ae.

Ministry of State for Financial Affairs: POB 433, Abu Dhabi; tel. (2) 771133; fax (2) 793255.

Ministry of State for Foreign Affairs: POB 1, Abu Dhabi; tel. (2) 6660888; fax (2) 6652883.

Legislature

FEDERAL NATIONAL COUNCIL

Formed under the provisional Constitution, the Council is composed of 40 members from the various emirates (eight each from Abu Dhabi and Dubai, six each from Sharjah and Ras al-Khaimah, and four each from Ajman, Fujairah and Umm al-Qaiwain). Each emirate appoints its own representatives separately. The Council studies laws proposed by the Council of Ministers and can reject them or suggest amendments. In December 2005 Sheikh Khalifa announced that elections would be introduced to choose one-half of the members of the FNC, which would also be expanded and granted enhanced powers. In August 2006 a National Electoral Committee was established to preside over the elections, which were held during 16–20 December. A constitutional amendment extending the Council's term from two to four years was endorsed by the Supreme Council of Rulers in December 2008 and approved by the FNC in January 2009.

Speaker: ABD AL-AZIZ ABDULLAH AL-GHURAIR.

Diplomatic Representation

EMBASSIES IN THE UNITED ARAB EMIRATES

Afghanistan: POB 5687, Abu Dhabi; tel. (2) 6655560; fax (2) 6655576; Ambassador FARID ZEKRIA.

Algeria: POB 3070, Abu Dhabi; tel. (2) 448949; fax (2) 4470686; Ambassador HAMID CHEBIRA.

Argentina: POB 3325, Abu Dhabi; tel. (2) 4436838; fax (2) 4431392; e-mail info@argentinauae.ae; Ambassador RUBÉN EDUARDO CARO.

Australia: POB 32711, Al-Muhairy Centre, Level 14, Sheikh Zayed I St, Abu Dhabi; tel. (2) 6346100; fax (2) 6393525; e-mail abudhabi.embassy@dfat.gov.au; internet www.uae.embassy.gov.au; Ambassador JEREMY BRUER.

Austria: POB 35539, Al-Khazna Tower, 7th Floor, Najda St, Abu Dhabi; tel. (2) 6766611; fax (2) 6715551; e-mail abu-dhabi-ob@bmeia.gv.at; internet www.austrianembassy.ae; Ambassador Dr GERALD KRIECHBAUM.

Azerbaijan: POB 45766, Plot N-297, Villa Sector W/16, Al-Bateen Area, Abu Dhabi; tel. (2) 6662848; fax (2) 6663150; e-mail azembassy@emirates.net.ae; Ambassador ELKHAN MANOOF.

Bahrain: POB 3367, Abu Dhabi; tel. (2) 6657500; fax (2) 6674141; e-mail abudhabi.mission@mofa.gov.bh; Ambassador MUHAMMAD SAQR AL-MAAWDA.

Bangladesh: POB 2504, Villa 21, Delma St, Al-Rowdha, Abu Dhabi; tel. (2) 668375; fax (2) 667324; e-mail embassy@bdembassyuae.org; internet www.bdembassyuae.org; Ambassador MUHAMMAD NUZMUL QAWNAIN.

Belarus: POB 30337, Villa 434, 26th St, Ar-Rouda Area, Abu Dhabi; tel. (2) 4453399; fax (2) 4451131; e-mail belembas@emirates.net.ae; Ambassador ALEXANDER SIMISHKO.

Belgium: POB 3686, Al-Masood Tower, 6th Floor, Hamdan St, Abu Dhabi; tel. (2) 6319449; fax (2) 6319353; e-mail abudhabi@diplobel.fed.be; internet www.diplomatie.be/abudhabi; Ambassador ANICK VAN CALSTER.

Bosnia and Herzegovina: POB 43362, Abu Dhabi; tel. (2) 6444164; fax (2) 6443619; e-mail abhad@bhmc.ae; internet www.bhmc.ae; Ambassador RADOMIR KOSIĆ.

Brazil: POB 3027, St 5, Villa 3, Madinat Zayed, Abu Dhabi; tel. (2) 6320606; fax (2) 6327727; e-mail abubrem@emirates.net.ae; internet www.brazilembuae.ae; Ambassador RAUL CAMPOS DE CASTRO.

Brunei: POB 5836, Plot 8, Villa 1, St 27, E-33, Abu Dhabi; tel. (2) 4486999; fax (2) 4486333; e-mail abudhabi.uae@mfa.gov.bn; Ambassador Dato Paduka Haji ADNAN BIN Haji ZAINAL.

Canada: POB 6970, Abu Dhabi Trade Towers, West Tower, 9th and 10th Floors, Abu Dhabi; tel. (2) 6940300; fax (2) 6940399; e-mail abdbi@international.gc.ca; internet www.dfait-maeci.gc.ca/abudhabi; Ambassador SARA HRADECKY.

China, People's Republic: POB 2741, Plot 26, W-22, Abu Dhabi; tel. (2) 4434276; fax (2) 4436835; e-mail chinaemb_ae@mfa.gov.cn; internet ae.chineseembassy.org; Ambassador GAO YUNSHENG.

Czech Republic: POB 27009, City Bank Bldg, Corniche Plaza, Abu Dhabi; tel. (2) 6782800; fax (2) 6795716; e-mail abudhabi@embassy.mzv.cz; internet www.mzv.cz/abudhabi; Ambassador Dr VĚRA JEŘÁBKOVÁ.

Egypt: POB 4026, Abu Dhabi; tel. (2) 4445566; fax (2) 4449878; e-mail egemb_abudhabi@mfa.gov.eg; Ambassador MUHAMMAD SAID OBAID.

Eritrea: POB 2597, Abu Dhabi; tel. (2) 6331838; fax (2) 6346451; Ambassador OSMAN MUHAMMAD OMAR.

Finland: POB 3634, Al-Masood Tower, Hamdan St, Abu Dhabi; tel. (2) 6328927; fax (2) 6325063; e-mail sanomat.abo@formin.fi; internet www.finland.ae; Chargé d'affaires a.i. MATTI LASSILA.

France: POB 4014, Abu Dhabi; tel. (2) 4435100; fax (2) 4434158; e-mail ambafr@emirates.net.ae; internet www.ambafrance-eau.org; Ambassador ALAIN AZOUAOU.

The Gambia: Abu Dhabi; tel. (2) 6678030; Ambassador MAMBURY NJIE.

Germany: POB 2591, Abu Dhabi Mall, West Tower, 14th Floor, Abu Dhabi; tel. (2) 6446693; fax (2) 6446942; e-mail info@abu-dhabi.diplo.de; internet www.abu-dhabi.diplo.de; Ambassador KLAUS-PETER BRANDES.

Greece: POB 5483, Plot 141, Villa 1, E-48, Moroor, Abu Dhabi; tel. (2) 4492550; fax (2) 4492455; e-mail gremb.abd@mfa.gr; Ambassador DIONISIOS ZOIS.

Hungary: POB 44450, Abu Dhabi; tel. (2) 6766190; fax (2) 6766215; e-mail mission.abu@kum.hu; Ambassador JÁNOS GÖNCI.

India: POB 4090, Abu Dhabi; tel. (2) 4492700; fax (2) 4444685; e-mail indiauae@indembassyuae.org; internet www.indembassyuae.org; Ambassador TALMIZ AHMAD.

Indonesia: POB 7256, Abu Dhabi; tel. (2) 4454448; fax (2) 4455453; e-mail indoemb@emirates.net.ae; internet www.indoemb.org/kbri; Ambassador WAHID SUPRIYADI.

Iran: POB 4080, Abu Dhabi; tel. (2) 4447618; fax (2) 4448714; e-mail iranemb@eim.ae; internet www.iranembassy.org.ae; Ambassador HAMID REZA ASEFI.

Iraq: Manhal St, Haoudh 55, St 32, Abu Dhabi; tel. (2) 6655215; fax (2) 6655214; e-mail adbemb@iraqmofamail.net; Ambassador FARES UJAIL AL-YAWER.

Italy: POB 46752, Villa 438–439, St 26, Al-Manaseer Area, Abu Dhabi; tel. (2) 4435577; fax (2) 4434337; e-mail italianembassy.abudhabi@esteri.it; internet www.ambabudhabi.esteri.it; Ambassador PAOLO DIONISI.

THE UNITED ARAB EMIRATES

Japan: POB 2430, Abu Dhabi; tel. (2) 4435696; fax (2) 4434219; e-mail embjpn@japanembassyauh.com; internet www.uae.emb-japan.go.jp; Ambassador Tatsuo Watanabe.

Jordan: POB 4024, Abu Dhabi; tel. (2) 4447100; fax (2) 4449157; e-mail embjord1@emirates.net.ae; Ambassador Jamal Hamid ash-Shamaileh.

Kazakhstan: POB 39556, Al-Mushrif, W-52, Villa 61B, Abu Dhabi; tel. (2) 4476623; fax (2) 4476624; e-mail kazemb@emirates.net.ae; internet www.kazembemirates.net; Ambassador Askar A. Mussinov.

Kenya: POB 3854, Abu Dhabi; tel. (2) 6666300; fax (2) 6652827; e-mail kenyarep@emirates.net.ae; internet www.kenyaembassy.ae; Ambassador Bishar Abdi Rahman Hussein.

Korea, Republic: POB 3270, Abu Dhabi; tel. (2) 4435337; fax (2) 4435348; e-mail keauhlee@emirates.net.ae; Ambassador Chung Yong-Chil.

Kuwait: POB 926, Abu Dhabi; tel. (2) 4446888; fax (2) 4444990; e-mail abudhabi@mofa.gov.kw; Ambassador Faisal Abdullah Ibrahim al-Mishaan.

Lebanon: POB 4023, Abu Dhabi; tel. (2) 4492100; fax (2) 4493500; e-mail libanamb@emirates.net.ae; Ambassador Fauzi Youssef Fawaz.

Libya: POB 5739, Abu Dhabi; tel. (2) 4450030; fax (2) 4450033; e-mail sunnylib@eim.ae; Ambassador Muhammad al-Buaishi.

Malaysia: POB 3887, Abu Dhabi; tel. (2) 4482775; fax (2) 4482779; e-mail admin@malaysianembassy.ae; internet www.kln.gov.my/perwakilan/abudhabi; Ambassador Dato' Yahaya Abdul Jabar.

Mauritania: POB 2714, Abu Dhabi; tel. (2) 4462724; fax (2) 4465772; Ambassador Bebaha Ould Ibrahim Khalil.

Morocco: POB 4066, Abu Dhabi; tel. (2) 4433963; fax (2) 4433917; e-mail sifmabo@yahoo.com; internet www.moroccan-emb.ae; Ambassador Abdelkader az-Zaoui.

Nepal: POB 38282, Abu Dhabi; tel. (2) 6344385; fax (2) 6344469; e-mail nepemuae@emirates.net.ae; internet www.nepembassyuae.ae; Ambassador Arjun Bahdo.

Netherlands: POB 46560, Al-Masood Tower, 6th Floor, Suite 6, Abu Dhabi; tel. (2) 6321920; fax (2) 6313158; e-mail abu@minbuza.nl; internet www.netherlands.ae; Ambassador Gilles Arnout Beschoor Plug.

Nigeria: POB 110171, Abu Dhabi; tel. (2) 4431503; fax (2) 4431792; e-mail nigerabudhabi@yahoo.co.uk; Ambassador Alhaji Bashir Yoguda Gusau.

Norway: POB 47270, Abu Dhabi; tel. (2) 6211221; fax (2) 6213313; e-mail emb.abudhabi@mfa.no; internet www.norway.ae; Chargé d'affaires a.i. Åse Elin Bjerke.

Oman: POB 2517, Said bin Tahnon Sq., Al-Mushraf Area, Abu Dhabi; tel. (2) 4463333; fax (2) 4464633; e-mail omanemb@emirates.net.ae; Ambassador Sheikh Muhammad bin Abdullah al-Qatabi.

Pakistan: POB 846, Abu Dhabi; tel. (2) 4447800; fax (2) 4447172; e-mail pakisuae@emirates.net.ae; Ambassador Khurshid Ahmad Junejo.

Philippines: POB 3215, Plot 97, Villa 2, St 5, E-18/02, Abu Dhabi; tel. (2) 6415922; fax (2) 6412559; e-mail auhpe@emirates.net.ae; Ambassador Libran N. Cabactulan.

Poland: POB 2334, Abu Dhabi; tel. (2) 4465200; fax (2) 4462967; e-mail polonez@emirates.net.ae; internet www.plembassy.gov.ae; Ambassador Roman Chalaczkiewicz.

Qatar: POB 3503, 26th St, Al-Minaseer, Abu Dhabi; tel. (2) 4493300; fax (2) 4493311; e-mail abudhabi@mofa.gov.qa; Ambassador Abdullah M. al-Uthman.

Romania: 9 POB 70416, Abu Dhabi; tel. (2) 4459919; fax (2) 4461143; e-mail romaniae@emirates.net.ae; Ambassador Nikolai Goia.

Russia: POB 8211, Abu Dhabi; tel. (2) 6721797; fax (2) 6728713; e-mail ruconsl@emirates.net.ae; Ambassador Andriy Zakharov.

Saudi Arabia: POB 4057, Abu Dhabi; tel. (2) 4445700; fax (2) 4448491; e-mail aeemb@mofa.gov.sa; Ambassador Dr Abdullah bin Muammar.

Somalia: POB 4155, Abu Dhabi; tel. (2) 6669700; fax (2) 6651580; e-mail somen@emirates.net.ae; Ambassador Ahmed Mohammed Ajal.

South Africa: POB 29446, Abu Dhabi; tel. (2) 4473446; fax (2) 4473031; e-mail saemb@emirates.net.ae; internet www.southafrica.ae; Ambassador Yacoob Abba Omar.

Spain: POB 46474, Abu Dhabi; tel. (2) 6269544; fax (2) 6274978; e-mail emb.abudhabi@mae.es; Ambassador Manuel Piñeiro Souto.

Sri Lanka: POB 46534, Abu Dhabi; tel. (2) 6316444; fax (2) 6331661; e-mail lankemba@emirates.net.ae; Ambassador J. M. B Bandara.

Sudan: POB 4027, Abu Dhabi; tel. (2) 6666788; fax (2) 6654231; e-mail sudembll@emirates.net.ae; Ambassador Ahmed Ja'afer Ahmed Abdul Kareem.

Sweden: POB 31867, Abu Dhabi; tel. (2) 6210162; fax (2) 6394941; e-mail ambassaden.abudhabi@foreign.ministry.se; internet www.swedenabroad.com/abudhabi; Ambassador Bruno S. Beijer.

Switzerland: POB 46116, Abu Dhabi; tel. (2) 6274636; fax (2) 6269627; e-mail adh.vertretung@eda.admin.ch; internet www.eda.admin.ch/uae; Ambassador Wolfgang Amadeus Bruelhart.

Syria: POB 4011, Abu Dhabi; tel. (2) 4448768; fax (2) 4449387; Ambassador Dr Rustum az-Zobi.

Thailand: POB 47466, Abu Dhabi; tel. (2) 6421772; fax (2) 6421773; e-mail thaiauh@emirates.net.ae; internet www.thaiembassy.ae; Ambassador Karn Chiranond.

Tunisia: POB 4166, Abu Dhabi; tel. (2) 6811331; fax (2) 6812707; e-mail ambtunad@emirates.net.ae; Ambassador Muhammad as-Sediri.

Turkey: POB 3204, Abu Dhabi; tel. (2) 4454864; fax (2) 4452522; e-mail tcadbe@eim.ae; Ambassador Hakki Akil.

Ukraine: POB 45714, Abu Dhabi; tel. (2) 6327586; fax (2) 6327506; e-mail emb_ae@mfa.gov.ua; internet www.oae.mfa.gov.ua/oae; Ambassador Sergiy O. Pas'ko.

United Kingdom: POB 248, Abu Dhabi; tel. and fax (2) 6101100; fax (2) 6101586; e-mail information.abudhabi@fco.gov.uk; internet ukinuae.fco.gov.uk; Ambassador Edward Oakden.

USA: POB 4009, Abu Dhabi; tel. (2) 4142200; fax (2) 4142469; e-mail webmasterabudhabi@state.gov; internet abudhabi.usembassy.gov; Ambassador Richard G. Olson.

Yemen: POB 2095, Abu Dhabi; tel. (2) 4448457; fax (2) 4447978; e-mail yememb@emirates.net.ae; Ambassador Abdullah Hussain Muhammad ad-Defae'.

Judicial System

The 95th article of the Constitution of 1971 provided for the establishment of the Union Supreme Court and Union Primary Tribunals as the judicial organs of State.

The Union has exclusive legislative and executive jurisdiction over all matters that are concerned with the strengthening of the federation, such as foreign affairs, defence and Union armed forces, security, finance, communications, traffic control, education, currency, measures, standards and weights, matters relating to nationality and emigration, Union information, etc.

The late President Sheikh Zayed signed the law establishing the new federal courts on 9 June 1978. The new law effectively transferred local judicial authorities into the jurisdiction of the federal system.

Primary tribunals in Abu Dhabi, Sharjah, Ajman and Fujairah are now primary federal tribunals, and primary tribunals in other towns in those emirates have become circuits of the primary federal tribunals.

The primary federal tribunals may sit in any of the capitals of the four emirates and have jurisdiction on all administrative disputes between the Union and individuals, whether the Union is plaintiff or defendant. Civil disputes between Union and individuals will be heard by primary federal tribunals in the defendant's place of normal residence.

The law requires that all judges take a constitutional oath before the Minister of Justice and that the courts apply the rules of *Shari'a* (Islamic religious law) and that no judgment contradicts the *Shari'a*. All employees of the old judiciaries will be transferred to the federal authority without loss of salary or seniority.

In February 1994 President Sheikh Zayed ordered that an extensive range of crimes, including murder, theft and adultery, be tried in *Shari'a* courts rather than in civil courts.

Chief Shari'a Justice: Ahmad Abd al-Aziz al-Mubarak.

Religion

ISLAM

Most of the inhabitants are Muslims of the Sunni sect, while about 16% of Muslims are Shi'ites.

CHRISTIANITY

Roman Catholic Church

Apostolic Vicariate of Arabia: POB 54, Abu Dhabi; tel. (2) 4461895; fax (2) 4465177; e-mail vicapar@emirates.net.ae; internet www.stjosephsabudhabi.org; f. 1888; responsible for a territory covering most of the Arabian peninsula (including Saudi Arabia, the

UAE, Oman, Qatar, Bahrain and Yemen), containing an estimated 2,300,000 Catholics (31 December 2008); Vicar Apostolic Bishop PAUL HINDER (Vicar Apostolic of Arabia).

The Anglican Communion

Within the Episcopal Church in Jerusalem and the Middle East, the UAE forms part of the diocese of Cyprus and the Gulf. The Anglican congregations in the UAE are entirely expatriate. The Bishop in Cyprus and the Gulf resides in Cyprus, while the Archdeacon in the Gulf is resident in Bahrain.

Chaplain, St Andrew's Church: Rev. CLIVE WINDEBANK, St Andrew's Church, POB 262, Abu Dhabi; tel. (2) 4461631; fax (2) 4465869; e-mail standrew@emirates.net.ae; internet www.standrewauh.org.

The Press

The state regulator for the sector is the National Media Council, under the Chairmanship of Sheikh SAQR GHOBASH SAID GHOBASH (Minister of Labour).

ABU DHABI

Abu Dhabi Magazine: POB 662, Abu Dhabi; tel. (2) 6214000; fax (2) 6348954; f. 1969; Arabic, some articles in English; monthly; Editor ZUHAIR AL-QADI; circ. 18,000.

Abu Dhabi Official Gazette: POB 19, Abu Dhabi; tel. (2) 6688413; fax (2) 6669981; e-mail gazette@ecouncil.ae; f. 1965; Arabic; daily; official reports and papers.

Al-Ain Times: POB 15229, Al-Ain; tel. (3) 7671995; fax (3) 7671997; e-mail alaintimes@gmail.com; internet www.alaintimesuae.com; f. 2006; weekly; English and Arabic; publ. by Alpha Beta Publishers and Media Consultants; Chief Editor FADWA M. B. AL-MUGHARIBI.

Alrroya Aleqtisadiya (Economic Vision): POB 112494, Abu Dhabi; tel. (2) 6517777; fax (2) 6517772; internet www.alrroya.com; f. 2009; Arabic; business daily; publ. by Imedia LLC.

Adh-Dhafra: POB 4288, Abu Dhabi; tel. (2) 6328103; Arabic; weekly; independent; publ. by Dar al-Wahdah.

Emirates News: POB 791, Abu Dhabi; tel. (2) 4451446; fax (2) 4453662; e-mail emrtnews@emirates.net.ae; f. 1975; English; daily; publ. by Al-Ittihad Press, Publishing and Distribution Corpn; Chair. Sheikh ABDULLAH BIN ZAYED AN-NAHYAN; Man. Editor PETER HELLYER; circ. 21,150.

Hiya (She): POB 2488, Abu Dhabi; tel. (2) 4474121; Arabic; weekly for women; publ. by Dar al-Wahdah.

Al-Ittihad (Unity): POB 791, Abu Dhabi; tel. (2) 4455555; fax (2) 4455126; e-mail editor@alittihad.co.ae; internet www.alittihad.ae; f. 1972; Arabic; daily and weekly; publ. by Abu Dhabi Media Co; Man. Editor ALI ABU AR-RISH; circ. 58,000 daily, 60,000 weekly.

Majid: POB 791, Abu Dhabi; tel. (2) 4451804; fax (2) 4451455; e-mail majid-magazine@emi.co.ae; internet www.majid.ae; Arabic; f. 1979; weekly; children's magazine; publ. by Abu Dhabi Media Co; Man. Editor AHMAD OMAR; circ. 164,000.

The National: Abu Dhabi Media Company, 4th St, Sector 18, Zone 1, Abu Dhabi; tel. (2) 4144000; fax (2) 4144001; internet www.thenational.ae; f. 2008; English; daily; publ. Abu Dhabi Media Co; Man. Editor MARTIN NEWLAND.

Ar-Riyada wa-Shabab (Sport and Youth): POB 2710, Dubai; tel. (4) 4444400; fax (4) 4445973; Arabic; weekly; general interest.

UAE Press Service Daily News: POB 2035, Abu Dhabi; tel. (2) 4444292; f. 1973; English; daily; Editor RASHID AL-MAZROUI.

Al-Wahdah (Unity): POB 2488, Abu Dhabi; tel. (2) 4478400; fax (2) 4478937; f. 1973; daily; independent; Man. Editor RASHID AWEIDHA; Gen. Man. KHALIFA AL-MASHWI; circ. 20,000.

Zahrat al-Khaleej (Splendour of the Gulf): POB 791, Abu Dhabi; tel. (2) 4461600; fax (2) 4451653; e-mail abedrabbo@admedia.ae; f. 1979; Arabic; weekly; publ. by Abu Dhabi Media Co; women's magazine; Editor-in-Chief TALAL TOHME; circ. 10,000.

DUBAI

Al-Bayan (The Official Report): POB 2710, Dubai; tel. (4) 3444400; fax (4) 3447846; e-mail readers@albayan.ae; internet www.albayan.ae; f. 1980; Arabic; daily; publ. by Awraq Publishing, a subsidiary of Arab Media Group; CEO SAMI AL-QAMZI; Editor-in-Chief DA'EN SHAHIN; circ. 82,575.

Business 24/7: Arab Media Group, POB 500666, Dubai; tel. (4) 3062222; fax (4) 3407698; e-mail editor@business24-7.ae; internet www.business24-7.ae; f. 2007; English; business daily; publ. by Awraq Publishing, a subsidiary of Arab Media Group; Man. Editor MUSTAFA ALRAWI.

Emarat Al-Youm: POB 502012, Dubai; e-mail local@emaratalyoum; internet www.emaratalyoum.com; Arabic; daily; publ. by Awraq Publishing, a subsidiary of Arab Media Group; Editor SAMI AR-RIYAMI.

Emirates Woman: POB 2331, Dubai; tel. (4) 2824060; fax (4) 2827593; e-mail faye@motivate.co.ae; f. 1981; publ. by Motivate Publishing; English; monthly; fashion, health and beauty; Editor FAYE JAMES; circ. 20,324.

Gulf News: Sheikh Zayed Rd, POB 6519, Dubai; tel. (4) 3447100; fax (4) 3441627; e-mail editor@gulfnews.com; internet www.gulfnews.com; f. 1978; publ. by An-Nisr Publishing; English; daily; two weekly supplements, Junior News (Wed.), Gulf Weekly (Thur.); Editor-in-Chief ABD-AL HAMID AHMAD; circ. 103,000.

Al-Jundi (The Soldier): POB 2838, Dubai; tel. (4) 3532222; fax (4) 3744272; e-mail mod5@eim.ae; f. 1973; Arabic; monthly; military and cultural; Editor-in-Chief Brig. MUHAMMAD ALI ABDULLAH AL-EASSA; circ. 10,000.

Khaleej Times: POB 11243, Dubai; tel. (4) 3383535; fax (4) 3383345; e-mail ktimes@emirates.net.ae; internet www.khaleejtimes.com; f. 1978; a Galadari enterprise; English; daily; distributed throughout the region and in India, Pakistan and the United Kingdom; free weekly supplement, Weekend (Fri.); Publr and Editor-in-Chief MUHAMMAD A. R. GALADARI; Man. Dir QASSIM MUHAMMAD YOUSUF; circ. 70,000.

Al-Manara: Office 129, Bldg 10, Dubai Media City; tel. (4) 3901777; fax (4) 3904554; e-mail dar@almanaramagazine.ae; internet www.almanaramagazine.ae; Arabic; lifestyle; Editor WALID AS-SAADI.

Trade and Industry: POB 1457, Dubai; tel. (4) 2280000; fax (4) 2211646; e-mail dcciinfo@dcci.org; internet www.dubaichamber.ae; f. 1975; Arabic and English; monthly; publ. by Dubai Chamber of Commerce and Industry; circ. 26,000.

UAE Digest: POB 500595, Dubai; tel. (4) 3672245; fax (4) 3678613; e-mail info@sterlingp.ae; internet www.sterlingp.ae; English; monthly; publ. by Sterling Publications; current affairs; Man. Editor K. RAVEENDRAN.

Viva: POB 500024, Dubai; tel. (4) 2108000; fax (4) 2108080; e-mail vivaletters@itp.com; internet www.vivamagazine.ae; f. 2004; publ. by ITP; Editor MANDIE GOWER; circ. 23,000.

What's On: POB 2331, Dubai; tel. (4) 2824060; fax (4) 2827593; e-mail editor-wo@motivate.co.ae; internet www.whatsonlive.com; f. 1979; publ. by Motivate Publishing; English; monthly; Group Editor and Man. Partner IAN FAIRSERVICE; circ. 31,055.

Xpress: POB 6519, Dubai; tel. (4) 3447100; e-mail editor@alnisrmedia.com; internet www.xpress4me.com; f. 2007; English; weekly; publ. by An-Nisr Publishing; Editor NIRMALA JANSSEN.

RAS AL-KHAIMAH

Akhbar Ras al-Khaimah (Ras al-Khaimah News): POB 87, Ras al-Khaimah; Arabic; monthly; local news.

Al-Ghorfa: POB 87, Ras al-Khaimah; tel. (7) 2333511; fax (7) 2330233; f. 1970; Arabic and English; free monthly; publ. by Ras al-Khaimah Chamber of Commerce; Editor ZAKI H. SAQR.

Ras al-Khaimah Magazine: POB 200, Ras al-Khaimah; Arabic; monthly; commerce and trade; Chief Editor AHMAD AT-TADMORI.

SHARJAH

Al-Azman al-Arabia (Times of Arabia): POB 5823, Sharjah; tel. (6) 5356034.

The Gulf Today: POB 30, Sharjah; tel. (6) 5591919; fax (6) 5532737; e-mail nilofer@godubai.com; internet www.godubai.com/gulftoday; f. 1995; English; daily; circ. 38,000.

Al-Khaleej (The Gulf): POB 30, Sharjah; tel. (6) 5625304; fax (6) 5598547; e-mail kh_readers@alkhaleej.ae; internet www.alkhaleej.co.ae; f. 1970; Arabic; daily; political, independent; Editor GHASSAN TAHBOUB; circ. 82,750.

Sawt al-Khaleej (Voice of the Gulf): Sharjah; tel. (6) 5358003.

Ash-Sharooq (Sunrise): POB 30, Sharjah; tel. (6) 5598777; fax (6) 5599336; f. 1970; Arabic; weekly; general interest; Editor YOUSUF AL-HASSAN.

At-Tijarah (Commerce): Sharjah Chamber of Commerce and Industry, POB 580, Sharjah; tel. (6) 5116600; fax (6) 5681119; e-mail scci@sharjah.gov.ae; internet www.sharjah.gov.ae; f. 1970; Arabic/English; monthly magazine; circ. 50,000; annual trade directory; circ. 100,000.

NEWS AGENCY

Emirates News Agency (WAM): POB 3790, Abu Dhabi; tel. (2) 4454545; fax (2) 4044200; e-mail wamnews@eim.ae; internet www.wam.org.ae; f. 1977; operated by the Govt; Dir-Gen. IBRAHIM AL-ABED; Chief Editor JAMAL NASSER.

THE UNITED ARAB EMIRATES

Publishers

Abu Dhabi Media Co: 4th St, Sector 18, Zone 1, Abu Dhabi; tel. (2) 4144000; fax (2) 4144001; internet www.admedia.ae; f. 1999 as Emirates Media Inc., renamed as above 2007; diversified media co with operations in publishing, television, radio, digital media, distribution and printing; publ. The National and Al-Ittihad newspapers, Zahrat Al Khaleej and Majid magazines; Chair. MUHAMMAD KHALAF AL-MAZROUEI; CEO EDWARD BORGERDING.

All Prints: POB 857, Abu Dhabi; tel. (2) 6336999; fax (2) 6320844; e-mail allprints@allprints.co.ae; internet web.allprints.ae; f. 1968; publishing and distribution; Partners BUSHRA KHAYAT, TAHSEEN S. KHAYAT.

ITP: POB 500024, Dubai; tel. (4) 2108000; fax (4) 2108080; e-mail info@itp.com; internet www.itp.com; f. 1987; publishes more than 60 magazines including Ahlan!, Arabian Business, Timeout Dubai, Viva; CEO WALID AKAWI.

Motivate Publishing: POB 2331, Dubai; tel. (4) 2824060; fax (4) 2820428; e-mail motivate@motivate.ae; internet www.motivatepublishing.com; f. 1979; books and magazines; Man. Partner and Group Editor IAN FAIRSERVICE.

Sterling Publications: POB 500595, Dubai; tel. (4) 3672245; fax (4) 3678613; e-mail info@sterlingp.ae; internet www.sterlingp.ae; magazines including UAE Digest, Banking and Business Review, Ajman Today; Publr and Man. Dir SANKARA NARAYANAN; Man. Editor K. RAVEENDRAN.

Broadcasting and Communications

TELECOMMUNICATIONS

Telecommunications Regulatory Authority (TRA): POB 26662, Abu Dhabi; tel. (2) 6269999; fax (2) 6118229; e-mail info@tra.ae; internet www.tra.ae; f. 2004; Chair. MUHAMMAD BIN AHMAD AL-QAMZI; Dir-Gen. MUHAMMAD AL-GHANEM.

Emirates Integrated Telecommunications Co (du): POB 502666, Dubai; tel. (4) 3600000; fax (4) 3604440; e-mail talk-to-us@du.ae; internet www.du.ae; f. 2006; commenced operations under the brand name 'du' in Feb. 2007; 40% owned by the federal Govt, 20% by Mubadala Development Co, 40% by TECOM Investment and 20% by public shareholders; provides telecommunications services throughout the UAE; Chair. AHMAD BIN BYAT; CEO OSMAN SULTAN.

Emirates Telecommunications Corpn (Etisalat): POB 3838, Abu Dhabi; tel. (2) 6333111; fax (2) 6344432; e-mail prd@etisalat.co.ae; internet www.etisalat.co.ae; f. 1976; provides telecommunications services throughout the UAE; Chair. MUHAMMAD HASSAN OMRAN; CEO MUHAMMAD AL-QAMZI.

BROADCASTING

Radio

Abu Dhabi Radio: Abu Dhabi Media Co, 4th St, Sector 18, Zone 1, Abu Dhabi; tel. (2) 4144000; fax (2) 4144001; internet www.admedia.ae; f. 1969; broadcasts in Arabic over a wide area; also broadcasts in French, Bengali, Filipino and Urdu; affiliated channels include Emarat FM, Quran Kareem Radio, Sawt Al Musiqa; owned and operated by Abu Dhabi Media Company (fmrly Emirates Media Inc); Dir-Gen. ABD AL-WAHAB AR-RADWAN.

Arabian Radio Network: POB 502012, Dubai; tel. (4) 3912000; fax (4) 3912007; e-mail info@arnonline.com; internet www.arnonline.com; f. 2001; owned by Arab Media Group; operates nine stations; CEO ABDULLATIF AS-SAYEGH.

Capital Radio: POB 63, Abu Dhabi; tel. (2) 4451000; fax (2) 4451155; English-language FM music and news station, govt-operated; Station Man. AIDA HAMZA.

Ras al-Khaimah Broadcasting Station: POB 141, Ras al-Khaimah; tel. (7) 2851151; fax (7) 2353441; two transmitters broadcast in Arabic and Urdu; Dir Sheikh ABD AL-AZIZ BIN HUMAID.

Sharjah Radio and Television: POB 111, Sharjah; tel. (6) 5668888; fax (6) 5669999; e-mail admin@sharjahtv.net; internet www.sharjahtv.ae; Dir KHALID SAFAR.

Umm al-Qaiwain Broadcasting Station: POB 444, Umm al-Qaiwain; tel. (6) 7666044; fax (6) 7666055; e-mail uaqfm@emirates.net.ae; f. 1978; broadcasts music and news in Arabic, Malayalam, Sinhala and Urdu; Gen. Man. ALI JASSEM.

Television

Abu Dhabi Television: Abu Dhabi Media Company, 4th St, Sector 18, Zone 1, Abu Dhabi; tel. (2) 4144000; fax (2) 4144001; internet www.adtv.ae; f. 1969; relaunched in current form 2008; broadcasts entertainment and news programmes; affiliated channels include

Directory

Emirates Channel, Abu Dhabi Sports; owned by Abu Dhabi Media Company (fmrly Emirates Media Inc); Exec. Dir KARIM SARKIS.

Ajman Television: tel. (6) 7465000; fax (6) 7465135; e-mail public.relations@ajmantv.com; internet www.ajmantv.com; f. 1996; broadcasts in Arabic and English; Chair. ABDULLAH MUHAMMAD.

Arabian Television Network: Arab Media Group, POB 500666, Dubai; tel. (4) 3062222; fax (4) 3479965; e-mail info@arabmediagrouponline.com; internet www.arnonline.com; f. 2007; broadcasts own entertainment channels incl. SHOOFtv and Noor Dubai TV, also adapts int. brands for Arab market, such as MTV Arabia; owned by Arab Media Group; Gen. Man. MARYAM AL-FALASI.

Dubai Media Incorporated: POB 835, Dubai; tel. (4) 3369999; fax (4) 3360060; e-mail info@dmi.ae; internet www.dmi.gov.ae; f. 2004; channels include Dubai Television, Dubai One, Sama Dubai, Dubai Sports; state-owned; Chair. SHEIKH MAKTOUM BIN MUHAMMAD BIN RASHID AL-MAKTOUM; Man. Dir AHMAD ABDULLAH ASH-SHAIKH.

Sharjah Radio and Television: see Radio.

Finance

(cap. = capital; res = reserves; dep. = deposits; m. = million; brs = branches; amounts in dirhams, unless otherwise indicated)

BANKING

Central Bank

Central Bank of the United Arab Emirates: POB 854, Abu Dhabi; tel. (2) 6652220; fax (2) 6667494; e-mail admin@cbuae.gov.ae; internet www.centralbank.ae; f. 1973; acts as issuing authority for local currency; superseded UAE Currency Board in Dec. 1980; cap. 300.0m., res 1,260.0m., dep. 74,585.5m. (Dec. 2006); Chair. MUHAMMAD SHARIF FOULATHI; Gov. SULTAN BIN NASSER AS-SUWAIDI; 6 brs.

Principal Banks

Abu Dhabi Commercial Bank (ADCB): POB 939, Abu Dhabi; tel. (2) 6962222; fax (2) 6450384; e-mail info@adcb.com; internet www.adcb.com; f. 1985 by merger; 65% govt-owned, 35% owned by private investors; cap. 4,000m., res 5,315.5m., dep. 51,367.0m. (Dec. 2006); Chair. MUHAMMAD GHANIM AS-SUWAIDI; CEO ALA'A MUHAMMAD KHALIL ERAIQAT; 40 brs in the UAE, 2 in India.

Abu Dhabi Islamic Bank: POB 313, As-Sultan Tower, Baniyas St (Najda), Abu Dhabi; tel. (2) 6100600; fax (2) 6654340; e-mail adib@adib.co.ae; internet www.adib.ae; f. 1997; cap. 1,500.0m., res 3,046.1m., dep. 33,813.9m. (Dec. 2007); Chair. JAWAN AWAIDHA SUHAIL AL-KHAILI; Man. Dir KHAMIS BUHAROON.

Arab Emirates Investment Bank PJSC: POB 5503, Office 904, Twin Towers, Baniyas St, Deira, Dubai; tel. (4) 2222191; fax (4) 2274351; e-mail aeibank@emirates.net.ae; internet www.aeibank.com; f. 1976 as Arab Emirate Investment Bank Ltd; name changed as above in 2000; cap. 44.9m., res 131.9m., dep. 268.2m. (Dec. 2006); Chair. OMAR ABDULLAH AL-FUTTAIM; CEO KHALID SIFRI.

Bank of Sharjah Ltd: POB 1394, Sharjah; tel. (6) 5694411; fax (6) 5694422; e-mail bankshj@emirates.net.ae; internet www.bankofsharjah.com; f. 1973; cap. 1,250m., res 832.1m., dep. 4,858.1m. (Dec. 2006); Chair. AHMAD AN-NOMAN; Gen. Man. VAROUJ NERGUIZIAN; 2 brs.

Commercial Bank of Dubai PSC: POB 2668, Mankhool St, Dubai; tel. (4) 2121000; fax (4) 2121911; e-mail cbd-ho@cbd.ae; internet www.cbd.ae; f. 1969; 20% owned by Govt of Dubai; cap. 1,129.5m., res 3,450.7m., dep. 24,418.9m. (Dec. 2007); Chair. AHMAD HUMAID AT-TAYER; CEO PETER BALTUSSEN; 16 brs.

Commercial Bank International PSC: POB 4449, Ar-Riqah St, Dubai; tel. (4) 2275265; fax (4) 2279038; e-mail cbiho@emirates.net.ae; internet www.cbiuae.com; f. 1991; cap. 890.0m., res 192.8m., dep. 5,812.8m. (Dec. 2006); Chair. HAMAD ABDULLAH AL-MUTAWAA; CEO DOUWE J. OPPEDIJK; 9 brs.

Dubai Bank PJSC: POB 65555, Sheikh Zayed Rd, Dubai; e-mail info@dubaibank.ae; internet www.dubaibank.ae; tel. (4) 3328989; fax (4) 3290071; f. 2002 by Emaar Properties, a real estate developer; cap. 500.0m., res 40.3m., dep. 4,730.6m. (Dec. 2006); Chair. FADEL AL-ALI; CEO SALAAM ASH-SHAKSY.

Dubai Islamic Bank PJSC: POB 1080, Airport Rd, Deira, Dubai; tel. (4) 2953000; fax (4) 2954111; e-mail contactus@dib.ae; internet www.alislami.ae; f. 1975; cap. 2,800.0m., res 5,694.0m., dep. 52,382.4m. (Dec. 2006); Chair. Dr MUHAMMAD EBRAHIM ASH-SHAIBANI; Man. Dir KHALED AL-KAMDA; 44 brs.

Emirates Islamic Bank PJSC: POB 5547, Beniyas Rd, Deira, Dubai; tel. (4) 2287474; fax (4) 2272172; e-mail info@emiratesislamicbank.ae; internet www.emiratesislamicbank.ae; f. 1976 as Middle East Bank; became a Public Joint Stock Co (PJSC) in 1995; changed name as above in 2004; subsidiary (99.8% owned) of Emirates Bank Int.; cap. 747.5m., res 372.5m., dep. 14,067.3m. (Dec. 2007); Chair. SAYED MUHAMMAD RASHID ASH-SHARID; CEO IBRAHIM FAYEZ ASH-SHAMSI; 23 brs.

THE UNITED ARAB EMIRATES

Directory

Emirates NBD PJSC: POB 2923, Beniyas Rd, Deira, Dubai; tel. (4) 2256256; fax (4) 2227662; e-mail ibrahims@emiratesbank.com; internet www.emiratesnbd.com; f. 2007 by merger of Emirates Bank International PJSC with National Bank of Dubai PJSC; 56% owned by Govt of Dubai; total assets 254,000m. (Dec. 2007); Chair. AHMAD HUMAID AT-TAYER; CEO RICK PUDNER.

First Gulf Bank: POB 6316, Sheikh Zayed St, Abu Dhabi; tel. (2) 6816666; fax (2) 6814282; e-mail info@fgb.ae; internet www.fgb.ae; f. 1979; cap. 1,250.0m., res 6,491.8m., dep. 55,042.3m. (Dec. 2007); Chair. Sheikh MANSOUR BIN ZAYED AN-NAHYAN; CEO ABD AL-HAMID SAID; 5 brs.

Investbank PSC: POB 1885, Sharjah; tel. (6) 5693030; fax (6) 5694442; e-mail custserv@invest-bank.com; internet www.investbank.ae; f. 1975; cap. 1,000.0m., res 455.1m., dep. 6,104.7m. (Dec. 2007); Chair. Dr ABDULLAH OMRAN TARYAM; Gen. Man. SAMI R. FARHAT; 7 brs.

Mashreqbank PSC: POB 1250, Omer bin al-Khattab St, Deira, Dubai; tel. (4) 2223333; fax (4) 2226061; internet www.mashreqbank.com; f. 1967 as Bank of Oman; name changed as above in 1993; cap. 1,126.0m., res 1,419.4m., dep. 65,518.0m. (Dec. 2007); Chair. ABDULLAH BIN AHMAD AL-GHURAIR; CEO ABD AL-AZIZ ABDULLAH AL-GHURAIR; 36 brs in the UAE, 6 abroad.

Al-Masraf: POB 46733, ARBIFT Bldg, Hamdan St, Tourist Club Area, Abu Dhabi; tel. (2) 6721900; fax (2) 6777550; e-mail arbiftho@emirates.net.ae; internet www.arbift.com; f. 1976 as Arab Bank for Investment and Foreign Trade; renamed as above in 2007; jointly owned by the UAE Govt, the Libyan Arab Foreign Bank and the Banque Extérieure d'Algérie; cap. 460.0m., res 760.7m., dep. 5,155.5m. (Dec. 2006); Pres. and Chair. Dr ABD AL-HAFID M. ZLITNI; Gen. Man. IBRAHIM NASSER RASHID LOOTAH; 7 brs in the UAE.

National Bank of Abu Dhabi (NBAD): POB 4, Tariq ibn Ziad St, Abu Dhabi; tel. (2) 6111111; fax (2) 6275738; e-mail CustomerSupport@nbad.com; internet www.nbad.com; f. 1968; 73% owned by Abu Dhabi Investment Council, 3% by foreign institutions and the remainder by UAE citizens; cap. 1,224.1m., res 7,131.2m., dep. 82,816.6m. (Dec. 2006); Chair. NASSER AHMAD KHALIFA AS-SUWAIDI; CEO MICHAEL H. TOMALIN; 73 brs in the UAE, 29 abroad.

National Bank of Fujairah PSC: POB 2979, Dubai; tel. (4) 3971700; fax (4) 3973922; e-mail nbfho@nbf.ae; internet www.nbf.ae; f. 1982; owned jointly by Govt of Fujairah (36.78%), Govt of Dubai (9.78%), and UAE citizens and cos (51.25%); cap. 1,000.0m., res 486.6m., dep. 6,424.0m. (Dec. 2006); Chair. Sheikh SALEH BIN MUHAMMAD ASH-SHARQI; CEO STEVE MULLINS; 11 brs.

National Bank of Ras al-Khaimah PSC (RAKBANK): POB 5300, Rakbank Bldg, Oman St, al-Nakheel, Ras al-Khaimah; tel. (7) 2281127; fax (7) 2283238; e-mail nbrakho@emirates.net.ae; internet www.rakbank.ae; f. 1976; 52.75% owned by Govt of Ras al-Khaimah; cap. 536.3m., res 476.2m., dep. 7.366.3m. (Dec. 2006); Chair. Sheikh OMAR BIN SAQR AL-QASIMI; Gen. Man. GRAHAM HONEYBILL; 16 brs.

National Bank of Umm al-Qaiwain PSC: POB 800, Umm al-Qaiwain Private Properties Dept Bldg, King Faisal St, Umm al-Qaiwain; tel. (6) 7655225; fax (6) 7655440; e-mail nbuq@nbq.ae; internet www.nbq.ae; f. 1982; cap. 660.0m., res 554.8m., dep. 6,458.4m. (Dec. 2007); Chair. Sheikh SAUD BIN RASHID AL-MU'ALLA; Man. Dir and CEO Sheikh NASSER BIN RASHID AL-MU'ALLA; 16 brs.

Sharjah Islamic Bank: POB 4, Al-Borj Ave, Sharjah; tel. (6) 5115123; fax (6) 5681699; e-mail contact.center@sib.ae; internet www.sib.ae; f. 1976 as National Bank of Sharjah; name changed as above in 2005, reflecting the bank's conversion to *Shari'a*-compliant operations; commercial bank; cap. 1,100m., res 789.3m., dep. 4,506.1m. (Dec. 2006); Chair. Sheikh SULTAN BIN MUHAMMAD BIN SULTAN AL-QASSIMI; CEO MUHAMMAD AHMAD ABDULLAH; 13 brs.

Union National Bank: POB 3865, Salam St, Abu Dhabi; tel. (2) 6741600; fax (2) 6786080; e-mail feedback@unb.co.ae; internet www.unb.co.ae; f. 1983; fmrly Bank of Credit and Commerce (Emirates); cap. 1,562.5m., res 2,315.9m., dep. 41,019.2m. (Dec. 2007); Chair. Sheikh NAHYAN BIN MUBARAK AN-NAHYAN; CEO MUHAMMAD NASR ABDEEN; 26 brs in the UAE.

United Arab Bank: POB 25022, 6th Floor, HE Sheikh Abdullah bin Salem al-Qassimi Bldg, al-Qassimi St, Sharjah; tel. (6) 5733900; fax (6) 5733907; e-mail uarbae@emirates.net.ae; internet www.uab.ae; f. 1975; affiliated to Société Générale, France; 35% owned by Commercial Bank of Qatar; cap. 711.7m., res 570.4m., dep. 4,818.7m. (Dec. 2007); Chair. Sheikh FAISAL BIN SULTAN BIN SALEM AL-QASSIMI; CEO PAUL TROWBRIDGE; 9 brs.

Development Bank

Emirates Industrial Bank: POB 2722, 6th Floor, Arab Monetary Fund Bldg, Corniche Rd, Abu Dhabi; tel. (2) 6339700; fax (2) 6319191; e-mail projects_auh@emiratesindustrialbank.net; internet www.eib.ae; f. 1982; offers low-cost loans to enterprises with at least 51% local ownership; 51% state-owned; cap. 200m.; Chair. OBAID HUMAID AT-TAYER; Gen. Man. MUHAMMAD ABD AL-BAKI MUHAMMAD.

Bankers' Association

United Arab Emirates Bankers' Association: POB 44307, Abu Dhabi; tel. (2) 4467706; fax (2) 4463718; e-mail ebauae@emirates.net.ae; internet www.eba-ae.com; f. 1983; Chair. ABDULLAH AHMAD AL-GHURAIR (Chair., Mashreqbank PSC); Gen. Man. FATHI M. SKAIK.

STOCK EXCHANGES

Abu Dhabi Securities Exchange (ADX): POB 54500, Abu Dhabi; tel. (2) 6277777; fax (2) 6128728; e-mail info@adx.ae; internet www.adx.ae; f. 2000 as Abu Dhabi Securities Market, renamed as above 2008; Chair. NASSER AHMAD AS-SUWAIDI; Dir-Gen. TOM HEALY.

Dubai Financial Market (DFM): POB 9700, Dubai; tel. (4) 3055555; fax (4) 3314924; e-mail helpdesk@dfm.co.ae; internet www.dfm.co.ae; f. 2000; restructured to comply with *Shari'a* principles in 2006; 63 listed cos, seven bonds, 15 mutual funds (Sept. 2008); market capitalization AED 61,370m. (Feb. 2004); Chair. ESSA ABD AL-FATTAH KAZIM.

NASDAQ Dubai: POB 53536, Level 7, The Exchange Bldg, Gate District, Dubai International Financial Centre, Dubai; tel. (4) 3612222; fax (4) 3612130; e-mail corpcomm@nasdaqdubai.com; internet www.nasdaqdubai.com; f. 2005 as Dubai International Financial Exchange, renamed as above 2008; Chair. SOUD BA'ALAWY; CEO JEFF SINGER.

Regulatory Authority

Securities and Commodities Authority: POB 33733, Abu Dhabi; tel. (2) 6277888; fax (2) 6274600; e-mail contactus@sca.ae; internet sca-mo1.sca.ae; f. 2000; Chair. SULTAN BIN SAID AL-MANSOURI (Minister of Economy); CEO ABDULLAH SALEM AT-TURIFI.

INSURANCE

Abu Dhabi National Insurance Co (ADNIC): POB 839, Abu Dhabi; tel. (2) 6264000; fax (2) 6268600; e-mail adnic@adnic.ae; internet www.adnic.ae; f. 1972; subscribed 25% by the Govt of Abu Dhabi and 75% by UAE nationals; all classes of insurance; Chair. KHALIFA MUHAMMAD AL-KINDI.

Al-Ahlia Insurance Co: POB 128, Ras al-Khaimah; tel. (7) 2221479; e-mail farah@alahlia.com; internet www.alahli.com; f. 1977; Chair. HUSSAIN ALI SAJWANI; Gen. Man. YAHYA NOUR ED-DIN; 3 brs.

Al-Ain Ahlia Insurance Co: POB 3077, Abu Dhabi; tel. (2) 4459900; fax (2) 4456685; e-mail alainins@emirates.net.ae; internet www.alaininsurance.com; f. 1975; Chair. MUHAMMAD BIN J. R. AL-BADIE ADH-DHAHIRI; Gen. Man. MUHAMMAD MAZHAR HAMADEH; brs in Dubai, Sharjah, Tarif, Ghouifat and al-Ain.

Dubai Insurance Co PSC: POB 3027, Dubai; tel. (4) 2693030; fax (4) 2693727; e-mail dubins@emirates.net.ae; f. 1970; Chair. MAJID AL-FUTTAIM.

Sharjah Insurance Co: POB 792, Al Boorj Ave, Rolla, Sharjah; tel. (6) 5686690; fax (6) 5686545; internet www.shjins.com; e-mail sico@shjins.com; f. 1970; Chair. Sheikh MUHAMMAD BIN SAOUD AL-QASSIMI; Gen. Man. AHMED KHATER.

Union Insurance Co PSC: POB 1225, Ajman; tel. (6) 7466996; fax (6) 7466997; e-mail unins@emirates.net.ae; internet www.unioninsuranceuae.com; national insurance co of Ajman emirate; share capital 330m; Chair. ABDULLAH HUMAID AL-MAZROUI; Gen. Man. SAMER S. BUSHNAQ.

Trade and Industry

DEVELOPMENT ORGANIZATIONS

Abu Dhabi Development Finance Corpn: POB 814, Abu Dhabi; tel. (2) 6441000; fax (2) 6440800; e-mail opadfdmn@emirates.net.ae; provides finance to the private sector; Chair. Sheikh KHALIFA BIN ZAYED AN-NAHYAN; Dir-Gen. SAID KHALFAN MATAR AR-ROMAITHI.

Abu Dhabi Fund for Development (ADFD): POB 814, as-Salam St, Abu Dhabi; tel. (2) 6441000; fax (2) 6440800; e-mail ifo@adfd.ae; internet www.adfd.ae; f. 1971; offers economic aid to other Arab states and other developing countries in support of their development; cap. AED 4,000m.; Dir-Gen. SAID KHALFAN MATAR AR-ROMAITHI.

Abu Dhabi Investment Company (ADIC): POB 46309, Abu Dhabi; tel. (2) 6658100; fax (2) 6650575; e-mail info@adic.ae; internet www.adic.ae; f. 1977; investment and merchant banking activities in the UAE and abroad; 98% owned by the Abu Dhabi Investment Council and 2% by National Bank of Abu Dhabi; total assets AED 5,947m. (1997); Chair. KHALIFA M. AL-KINDI; CEO NAZEM FAWWAZ AL-KUDSI.

Abu Dhabi Investment Council (ADIC): POB 3600, Abu Dhabi; tel. (2) 4150000; fax (2) 4151000; f. 2006 as successor to Abu Dhabi

THE UNITED ARAB EMIRATES

Investment Authority (f. 1976); responsible for co-ordinating Abu Dhabi's investment policy; Chair. Sheikh KHALIFA BIN ZAYED AN-NAHYAN; 1 br. overseas.

Department of Economic Development Abu Dhabi: POB 12, Abu Dhabi; tel. (2) 6727200; fax (2) 6727749; e-mail ier@adeconomy.ae; internet www.adeconomy.ae; f. 1974; supervises Abu Dhabi's Economic Vision 2030 programme; Chair. NASSER AS-SOWAIDI; Under-Sec. MUHAMMAD OMAR ABDULLAH.

Dubai Holding: POB 66000, Dubai; tel. (4) 3622000; fax (4) 3622091; internet dubaiholding.com; f. 2004; supervises major industrial and infrastructure projects in Dubai; oversees activities of seven mem. cos including Dubai Properties Group, Jumeirah Group and Tatweer, as well as numerous subsidiaries; cap. AED 25,000m. (Oct. 2004); Chair. MUHAMMAD BIN ABDULLAH AL-GARGAWI; CEO AHMAD BIN BYAT.

General Holding Corpn (GHC): POB 4499, Abu Dhabi; tel. (2) 6144444; fax (2) 6312857; e-mail info@ghc.ae; internet www.ghc.ae; f. 1979 as General Industry Corpn; name changed as above 2004; responsible for the promotion of non-petroleum-related industry; Chair. Sheikh HAMAD BIN ZAYED AN-NAHYAN; Vice-Chair. NASSER AHMAD AS-SOWAIDI.

International Petroleum Investment Co (IPIC): POB 7528, Abu Dhabi; tel. (2) 6336555; fax (2) 6330111; e-mail administration@ipic.ae; internet www.ipic.ae; f. 1984; cap. US $200m.; state-owned venture to develop overseas investments in energy and energy-related projects; Chair. Sheikh MANSUR BIN ZAYED AN-NAHYAN; Man. Dir KHADEM ABDULLAH AL-QUBAISI.

CHAMBERS OF COMMERCE

Federation of UAE Chambers of Commerce and Industry: POB 3014, Abu Dhabi; tel. (2) 6214144; fax (2) 6339210; e-mail fcciauh@emirates.net.ae; internet www.fcci.gov.ae; POB 8886, Dubai; tel. (4) 2212977; fax (4) 2235498; e-mail fccidxb@emirates.net.ae; internet www.fcci-uae.com; f. 1976; seven mem. chambers; Chair. ABDULLAH RAHED AL-KHARJI; Sec.-Gen. ABDULLAH SULTAN ABDULLAH.

Abu Dhabi Chamber of Commerce and Industry: POB 662, Abu Dhabi; tel. (2) 6214000; fax (2) 6215867; e-mail services@adcci.gov.ae; internet www.abudhabichamber.ae; f. 1969; 45,000 mems; Pres. SALAH SALEM BIN OMAIR ASH-SHAMSI; Dir-Gen. MUHAMMAD RASHID AL-HAMELI.

Ajman Chamber of Commerce and Industry: POB 662, Ajman; tel. (6) 7422177; fax (6) 7471666; e-mail info@ajcci.gov.ae; internet www.ajcci.gov.ae; f. 1977; Chair. OBEID BIN ALI AL-MUHAIRI; Dir-Gen. MUHAMMAD AL-HAMRANI.

Dubai Chamber of Commerce and Industry: POB 1457, Dubai; tel. (4) 2280000; fax (4) 2211646; e-mail customercare@dubaichamber.ae; internet www.dubaichamber.ae; f. 1965; 108,000 mems (2007); Chair. ABD AR-RAHMAN SAIF AL-GHURAIR; Dir-Gen. HAMAD BUAIMIM.

Fujairah Chamber of Commerce, Industry and Agriculture: POB 738, Fujairah; tel. (9) 2222400; fax (9) 2221464; internet www.fujcci.ae; Pres. SAID ALI KHAMAS; Dir-Gen. MUHAMMAD KHALID AL-JASSEM.

Ras al-Khaimah Chamber of Commerce, Industry and Agriculture: POB 87, Ras al-Khaimah; tel. (7) 2333511; fax (7) 2330233; e-mail rcci@rakchamber.ae; internet www.rakchamber.ae; f. 1967; 17,840 mems (Dec. 2007); Chair. YOUSUF AL-NEAIMI; Dir-Gen. Dr ABD AL-RAHMAN ASH-SHAYEB AN-NAQPI.

Sharjah Chamber of Commerce and Industry: POB 580, Sharjah; tel. (6) 5116600; fax (6) 5681119; e-mail scci@sharjah.gov.ae; internet www.sharjah.gov.ae; f. 1970; 33,500 mems; Chair. AHMAD MUHAMMAD AL-MIDFA'A; Dir-Gen. SAID OBAID AL-JARWAN.

Umm al-Qaiwain Chamber of Commerce and Industry: POB 436, Umm al-Qaiwain; tel. (6) 7651111; fax (6) 7657056; e-mail uaqcci@emirates.net.ae; Pres. ABDULLAH RASHID AL-KHARJI; Man. Dir SHAKIR AZ-ZAYANI.

STATE HYDROCARBONS COMPANIES

Abu Dhabi

Supreme Petroleum Council: POB 898, Abu Dhabi; tel. (2) 602000; fax (2) 6023389; f. 1988; assumed authority and responsibility for the administration and supervision of all petroleum affairs in Abu Dhabi; Chair. Sheikh KHALIFA BIN ZAYED AN-NAHYAN; Sec.-Gen. YOUSUF BIN OMEIR BIN YOUSUF.

Abu Dhabi National Oil Co (ADNOC): POB 898, Abu Dhabi; tel. (2) 6020000; fax (2) 6023389; e-mail adnoc@adnoc.com; internet www.adnoc.ae; f. 1971; cap. AED 7,500m.; state company; deals in all phases of oil industry; owns two refineries: one on Umm an-Nar island and one at Ruwais; Habshan Gas Treatment Plant (scheduled for partial privatization); gas pipeline distribution network; a salt and chlorine plant; holds 60% participation in operations of ADMA-OPCO and ADCO, and 88% of ZADCO; has 100% control of Abu Dhabi National Oil Co for Oil Distribution (ADNOC-FOD), Abu Dhabi National Tanker Co (ADNATCO), National Drilling Co (NDC) and interests in numerous other companies, both in the UAE and overseas; ADNOC is operated by Supreme Petroleum Council, Chair. Sheikh KHALIFA BIN ZAYED AN-NAHYAN; CEO YOUSUF BIN OMEIR BIN YOUSUF.

Subsidiaries include:

Abu Dhabi Co for Onshore Oil Operations (ADCO): POB 270, Abu Dhabi; tel. (2) 6040000; fax (2) 6665523; e-mail webmaster@adco.ae; internet www.adco.ae; f. 1978; shareholders are ADNOC (60%), British Petroleum, Shell and Total (9.5% each), Exxon and Mobil (4.75% each) and Partex (2%); oil exploration, production and export operations from onshore oilfields; average production (1990): 1.2m. b/d; Chair. YOUSUF BIN OMEIR BIN YOUSUF; Gen. Man. ABD AL-MUNIM SAIF AL-KINDI.

Abu Dhabi Drilling Chemicals and Products Ltd (ADDCAP): POB 46121, Abu Dhabi; tel. (2) 6029000; fax (2) 6029010; e-mail addcap@emirates.net.ae; f. 1975; production of drilling chemicals and provision of marine services; wholly-owned subsidiary of ADNOC; Chair. YOUSUF BIN OMEIR BIN YOUSUF; Gen. Man. MAHFOUD A. DARBOUL ASH-SHEHHI.

Abu Dhabi Gas Industries Co (GASCO): POB 665, Abu Dhabi; tel. (2) 6030000; fax (2) 6037414; e-mail info@gasco.ae; internet www.gasco.ae; f. 1978; started production in 1981; recovers condensate and LPG from Asab, Bab and Bu Hasa fields for delivery to Ruwais natural gas liquids fractionation plant; capacity of 22,000 metric tons per day; ADNOC has a 68% share; Total, Shell Gas and Partex have a minority interest; Chair. YOUSUF OMEIR BIN YOUSUF; Gen. Man. MUHAMMAD SAHOO AS-SUWAIDI.

Abu Dhabi Gas Liquefaction Co (ADGAS): POB 3500, Abu Dhabi; tel. (2) 6061111; fax (2) 6065500; e-mail info@adgas.com; internet www.adgas.com; f. 1973; owned by ADNOC, 70%; Mitsui and Co, 15%; British Petroleum (BP), 10%; Total, 5%; operates LGSC and the LNG plant on Das Island which uses natural gas produced in association with oil from offshore fields and has a design capacity of approx. 2.3m. metric tons of LNG per year and 1.29m. tons of LPG per year; the liquefied gas is sold to the Tokyo Electric Power Co, Japan; Chair. A. N. AS-SUWEIDI; Gen. Man. SAIF AHMAD AL-GHAFLI.

Abu Dhabi Marine Operating Co (ADMA-OPCO): POB 303, Abu Dhabi; tel. (2) 6060000; fax (2) 6064888; e-mail webmaster@adma.ae; internet www.adma-opco.com; operates a concession 60% owned by ADNOC, 40% by Abu Dhabi Marine Areas Ltd (British Petroleum, Total and Japan Oil Development Co); f. 1977 as an operator for the concession; production (1984): 67,884,769 barrels (8,955,721 metric tons); Chair. YOUSUF BIN OMEIR BIN YOUSUF; Gen. Man. ALI R. AL-JARWAN.

Abu Dhabi Oil Refining Co (TAKREER): POB 3593, Abu Dhabi; tel. (2) 6027000; fax (2) 6027001; e-mail publicrelation@takreer.com; internet www.takreer.com; refining of crude oil; production of chlorine and related chemicals; Chair. YOUSUF BIN OMEIR BIN YOUSUF; Gen. Man. JASIM ALI AS-SAYEGH.

ADNOC Distribution: POB 4188, Abu Dhabi; tel. (2) 6771300; fax (2) 6722322; e-mail Information@adnoc-dist.ae; internet www.adnoc-dist.co.ae; 100% owned by ADNOC; distributes petroleum products in UAE and world-wide; Chair. YOUSUF BIN OMEIR BIN YOUSUF; Gen. Man. JAMAL JABER ADH-DHAREEF.

National Drilling Co (NDC): POB 4017, Abu Dhabi; tel. (2) 6776100; fax (2) 6779937; e-mail webmaster@ndc.ae; internet www.ndc.ae; drilling operations; Chair. ABDULLAH NASSER AS-SUWAIDI; Gen. Man. ABDALLAH SAEED AS-SUWAIDI.

National Petroleum Construction Co (NPCC): POB 2058, Abu Dhabi; tel. (2) 5549000; fax (2) 5549111; e-mail npccnet@eim.ae; internet www.npcc.ae; f. 1973; 'turnkey' construction and maintenance of offshore facilities for the petroleum and gas industries; cap. AED 100m.; Chair. HUSSAIN JASEM AN-NOWAIS; CEO AQEEL A. MADHI.

Ajman

Ajman National Oil Co (AJNOC): POB 410, Ajman; tel. (6) 7421218; f. 1983; 50% govt-owned, 50% held by Canadian and private Arab interests.

Dubai

DUGAS (Dubai Natural Gas Co Ltd): POB 4311, Dubai (Location: Jebel Ali); tel. (4) 8846000; fax (4) 8846118; wholly owned by Dubai authorities; Dep. Chair. and Dir SULTAN AHMAD BIN SULAYEM.

Dubai Petroleum Establishment: POB 2222, Dubai; tel. (4) 3846000; fax (4) 3846118; internet www.dubaipetroleum.ae; f. 1963 as Dubai Petroleum Co, renamed as above following restructure 2007; responsible for managing Dubai's offshore petroleum assets; Gen. Man. AL BOLEA; wholly owned by Dubai authorities.

Emarat: POB 9400, Dubai; tel. (4) 3434444; fax (4) 3433393; e-mail info@emarat.ae; internet www.emarat.ae; f. 1981 as Emirates General Petroleum Corpn, renamed as above 1996; wholly owned by Ministry of Finance and Industry; marketing and distribution of petroleum; Chair. MUHAMMAD BIN DHAEN AL-HAMILI; Gen. Man. JAMAL AL-MIDFA.

Emirates National Oil Co (ENOC): POB 6442, ENOC Complex, Sheikh Rashid Rd, Dubai; tel. (4) 3374400; fax (4) 3134702; e-mail webmaster@enoc.com; internet www.enoc.com; f. 1993; responsible for management of Dubai-owned cos in petroleum-marketing sector; Chief Exec. SAEED KHOORY.

Emirates Petroleum Products Co Pvt. Ltd (EPPCO): POB 5589, Dubai; tel. (4) 372131; fax (4) 3031605; e-mail f&e@eppcouae .com; internet www.eppcouae.com; f. 1980; jt venture between Govt of Dubai and Caltex Alkhaleej Marketing; sales of petroleum products, bunkering fuel and bitumen; Chair. Sheikh HAMDAN BIN RASHID AL-MAKTOUM.

Sedco-Houston Oil Group: POB 702, Dubai; tel. (4) 3224141; holds onshore concession of over 400,000 ha as well as the offshore concession fmrly held by Texas Pacific Oil; Pres. CARL F. THORNE.

Sharjah

A Supreme Petroleum Council was established in Sharjah in 1999; it was to assume the responsibilities of the Petroleum and Mineral Affairs Department.

Petroleum and Mineral Affairs Department: POB 188, Sharjah; tel. (6) 5541888; Dir ISMAIL A. WAHID.

Sharjah Liquefied Petroleum Gas Co (SHALCO): POB 787, Sharjah; tel. (6) 5286333; fax (6) 5286111; e-mail shalco@shalco.ae; f. 1984; gas processing; producer of liquified commercial propane and commercial butane; 100% owned by Sharjah authorities; Gen. Man. SALEH AL-ALI.

Umm al-Qaiwain

Petroleum and Mineral Affairs Department: POB 9, Umm al-Qaiwain; tel. (6) 7666034; Chair. Sheikh SULTAN BIN AHMAD AL-MU'ALLA.

UTILITIES

Abu Dhabi

Abu Dhabi Water and Electricity Authority (ADWEA): POB 6120, Abu Dhabi; tel. (2) 6943333; fax (2) 6943192; e-mail pr@adwea .gov.ae; internet www.adwea.gov.ae; f. 1999 to oversee the privatization of the water and electricity sectors; Chair. Sheikh DIAB BIN ZAYED AN-NAHYAN.

Abu Dhabi Distribution Co: POB 219, Abu Dhabi; tel. (2) 6423000; fax (2) 6426033; e-mail contactcentre@addc.ae; internet www.addc.ae; f. 1998; distribution of water and electricity; Chair. Shcikh DIAB BIN ZAYED AN-NAHYAN.

Abu Dhabi National Energy Co (TAQA): POB 55224, Abu Dhabi; tel. (2) 6943662; fax (2) 6422555; e-mail info@taqa.ae; internet www.taqa.ae; f. 2005; 51% owned by ADWEA; owns assets in power, water, petroleum and mineral sectors in the UAE and abroad; provides more than 85% of the water and electricity produced in Abu Dhabi; Chair. HAMAD AL-HURR AS-SUWAIDI; CEO PETER BARKER-HOMEK.

Abu Dhabi Transmission and Dispatch Co: POB 173, Abu Dhabi; tel. (2) 6414000; fax (2) 6426333; internet www.transco.ae; f. 1999; Chair. Dr ABDULLAH AS-SUWAIDI; Man. Dir DAVID COPESTAKE.

Abu Dhabi Water and Electricity Co (ADWEC): POB 51111, Abu Dhabi; tel. (2) 6943333; fax (2) 6425773; e-mail webmaster@ adwec.ae; internet www.adwec.ae; f. 1999; Chair. AHMAD SAIF AD-DARMAKI; Man. Dir GERHARDT GLEISSNER.

Al-Ain Distribution Co: POB 1065, al-Ain; tel. (3) 7636000; fax (3) 7629949; e-mail customercare@aadc.ae; internet www.aadc.ae; f. 1999; distribution of water and electricity; Chair. Sheikh DIAB BIN ZAYED AN-NAHYAN.

Bayounah Power Co: POB 33477, Abu Dhabi; tel. (2) 6731100; fax (2) 6730403; e-mail webmaster@adwea.gov.ae; internet www .bpc.ae; f. 1999; Chair. AHMAD HILAL AL-KUWAITI; Man. Dir ABD AL-JALEEL AL-KHOURY.

Al-Mirfa Power Co: POB 32277, Abu Dhabi; tel. (2) 8833044; fax (2) 8833011; e-mail info@ampc.ae; e-mail info@ampc.ae; internet www.ampc.ae; f. 1999 to control Mirfa and Madinat Zayed plants; capacity 300 MW electricity per day, 37m. gallons water per day; Chair. MUHAMMAD FOULAD; Gen. Man. PHILIP GRAHAM TILSON.

Emirates CMS Power Co: POB 47688, Abu Dhabi; tel. (2) 5067100; fax (2) 5067157; e-mail zelma.desouza@ecpc.ae; internet www.adwea.ae/priv/cms/; f. 1999; owns and operates the Taweelah A2 plant; Man. Dir BRIAN S. JACKSON.

Taweelah Asia Power Co (TAPCO): POB 32255, Abu Dhabi; tel. (2) 5627000; fax (2) 5627055; internet tapco.ae; subsidiary of Abu Dhabi National Energy Co; manages the Taweelah B water and power project; Exec. Man. Dir TOM SAMSON.

Dubai

Dubai Electricity and Water Authority (DEWA): POB 564, Dubai; tel. (4) 3244444; fax (4) 3248111; e-mail customercare@ dewa.gov.ae; internet www.dewa.gov.ae; CEO and Man. Dir SAID MUHAMMAD AHMAD AT-TAYER.

Northern Emirates (Ajman, Fujairah, Ras al-Khaimah and Umm al-Qaiwain)

Ministry of Energy: see Federal Ministries.

Sharjah

Sharjah Electricity and Water Authority (SEWA): Sharjah; tel. (2) 5288888; fax (2) 5288000; e-mail contactus@sewa.gov.ae; internet www.sewa.gov.ae; Chair. Sheikh SULTAN BIN MUHAMMAD AL-QASSIMI.

Transport

RAILWAYS

In mid-2005 Dubai Municipality awarded the construction contract for an urban light-railway system, provisionally known as Dubai Metro, to Mitsubishi Corpn of Japan. The first phase of the project was due to open in late 2009, and full operation of the four-line system was scheduled for 2015. Construction of a monorail linking the Palm Jumeirah development and the Atlantis station on the crescent began in 2006, under the title Palm Monorail. The Monorail, which cost over US $380m. to construct, began operating in May 2009. In February the Abu Dhabi authorities announced plans for the construction of a 130-km metro system, projected for completion by 2015. Plans for the construction of a federal railway network for passengers and freight, linking the seven emirates, gained final government approval in March. The 1,000-km network will be constructed in two phases, with the first phase, involving freight and industrial services, expected to take five years to complete. The establishment of a Union Railway Co, to own and operate the network, was also approved. It was anticipated that the federal network would eventually be linked to a planned railway for the member countries of the GCC.

ROADS

Roads are rapidly being developed in the UAE, and Abu Dhabi and Dubai are linked by a good road which is dual carriageway for most of its length. This road forms part of a west coast route from Shaam, at the UAE border with the northern enclave of Oman, through Dubai and Abu Dhabi to Tarif. An east coast route links Dibba with Muscat. Other roads include the Abu Dhabi–al-Ain highway and roads linking Sharjah and Ras al-Khaimah, and Sharjah and Dhaid. An underwater tunnel links Dubai Town and Deira by dual carriageway and pedestrian subway. Plans for the construction of a causeway between the UAE and Qatar were announced in December 2004; however, the project was subsequently delayed owing to objections from Saudi Arabia. An extensive development plan announced in July 2006, the Dubai Strategic Plan, was to allocate AED 44,000m. to road infrastructure up to 2020 and to include the construction of 500 km of new roads, more than 95 new interchanges, and upgrades of the emirate's existing road network. In addition, contracts for the construction of a 327-km Mafraq–Ghoueifat highway, linking the UAE with Qatar and Saudi Arabia were expected to be awarded in mid-2009. In 2004 there was a total paved-road network of 4,030 km.

SHIPPING

Dubai has been the main commercial centre in the Gulf for many years. Abu Dhabi has also become an important port since the opening of the first section of its artificial harbour, Port Zayed. Abu Dhabi's port capacity is to be greatly expanded with the construction of Khalifa Port and Industrial Zone; construction work on the offshore facility near Taweelah began in mid-2008. There are smaller ports in Sharjah, Fujairah, Ras al-Khaimah and Umm al-Qaiwain. Dubai possesses two docks capable of handling 500,000-ton tankers, seven repair berths and a third dock able to accommodate 1,000,000-ton tankers. The Dubai port of Mina Jebel Ali, which was to be expanded at a cost of some US $1,362m., has the largest manmade harbour in the world. Plans are under way to expand facilities at Sharjah's Khor Fakkan Port and Ras al-Khaimah's Mina Saqr Port. The first phase of the Mina Saqr project was completed in 2007, increasing the port's annual capacity to 350,000 20-ft equivalent units (TEUs); upon completion of the second phase, capacity would increase to 1.7m. TEUs per year.

THE UNITED ARAB EMIRATES

Abu Dhabi

Abu Dhabi Ports Company (ADPC): Mina Zayed, Abu Dhabi; tel. (2) 6952000; fax (2) 6952111; e-mail info@adpc.ae; internet www.adpc.ae; responsible for the devt and regulation of Abu Dhabi's ports and related industrial zones; Chair. Dr SULTAN AHMAD AL-JABER; CEO ALI SAEED AL-BADI.

Abu Dhabi Terminals: POB 422, Port Zayed, Abu Dhabi; tel. (2) 6730600; fax (2) 6731023; e-mail info@adterminals.ae; internet www.adterminals.ae; f. 2006; replaced Abu Dhabi Seaports Authority (f. 1972); administers Port Zayed, Musaffah port and Freeport; facilities at Port Zayed include 21 deep-water berths and five container gantry cranes of 40 metric tons capacity; cold storage 20,500 tons; handled a total of 390,087 TEUs in 2008; jt venture between ADPC and Mubadala; Chair. Sheikh SAID BIN ZAYED AN-NAHYAN; CEO MUHAMMAD AL-MANNAEI.

Abu Dhabi National Tanker Co (ADNATCO): POB 2977, 11th and 12th Floors Takreer Tower, Khalifa St, Abu Dhabi; tel. (2) 6028400; fax (2) 6028323; e-mail adnatco@adnatco.ae; internet www.adnatco.com; f. 1975; subsidiary co of ADNOC, operating owned and chartered tankships, and transporting crude petroleum, refined products and sulphur; Chair. NASSER AHMAD AS-SUWAIDI; Gen. Man. ALI OBAID AL-YABHOUNI.

Abu Dhabi Petroleum Ports Operating Co (IRSHAD): POB 61, Abu Dhabi; tel. (2) 6028000; fax (2) 6742094; e-mail info@irshad.ae; internet www.irshad.ae; f. 1979; manages Jebel Dhanna, Ruwais, Das Island, Umm an-Nar and Zirku Island SPM terminal, Mubarraz; operates fleet of 36 vessels; cap. AED 50m.; 60% owned by ADNOC, 40% by LAMNALCO Kuwait; Chair. YOUSUF BIN OMEIR BIN YOUSUF; Gen. Man. KHALIFA M. AL-GOBAISI.

National Marine Services Co (NMS): POB 7202, Abu Dhabi; tel. (2) 6339800; fax (2) 6211239; operate, charter and lease specialized offshore support vessels; cap. AED 25m.; owned 60% by ADNOC and 40% by Jackson Marine Corpn USA; Chair. SOHAIL FARES AL-MAZRUI; Gen. Man. Capt. HASSAN A. SHARIF.

Dubai

Dubai Ports World (DP World): POB 17000, 5th Floor, JAFZA 17, Dubai; tel. (4) 8811110; fax (4) 48811331; e-mail info@dpworld.com; internet www.dpworld.ae; f. 2005 by the merger of Dubai Ports Authority (f. 1991 by the merger of Mina Jebel Ali and Mina Rashid) and Dubai Ports International (f. 1999); subsidiary of state-controlled Dubai World; 23% sold via initial public offering Nov. 2007; storage areas and facilities for loading and discharge of vessels; operates ports of Mina Jebel Ali and Mina Rashid in Dubai, Port Zayed in Abu Dhabi, Fujairah Port and numerous other int. facilities; handled 42m. TEUs world-wide in 2006; CEO MUHAMMAD SHARAF; Sr Vice-Pres. and Man. Dir UAE Region MUHAMMAD AL-MUALLEM.

Drydocks World—Dubai: POB 8988, Dubai; tel. (4) 3450626; fax (4) 3450116; e-mail faxop@drydocks.gov.ae; internet www.drydocks.gov.ae; f. 1983; state-owned; dry-docking and repairs, tank cleaning, construction of vessels and floating docks, conversions, galvanizing, dredging, etc.; Man. Dir NAWAL AJUDHIANATH SAIGAL.

Sea Bridge Shipping: POB 8458, Dubai; tel. (4) 3379858; fax (4) 3372600; e-mail sbsops@sbshipping.com; internet www.sbshipping.com; shipping and freight agency; Chair. S. RAMAKRISHNAN; Man. Dir L. B. CULAS.

Vela International Marine: POB 26373, City Towers 2, Sheikh Zayed Rd, Dubai; tel. (4) 3123100; fax (4) 3310585; internet www.vela.ae; subsidiary of Saudi Arabian Oil Co; operates tankers; Pres. and CEO SALEH B. K'AKI.

Fujairah

Fujairah Port: POB 787, Fujairah; tel. (9) 2228800; fax (9) 2228811; e-mail info@fujairahport.ae; internet www.fujairahport.ae; f. 1982; operated by Dubai Ports World; offers facilities for handling container, general cargo and 'roll on, roll off' traffic; handled 565,723 TEUs in 1999; Chair. Sheikh SALEH BIN MUHAMMAD ASH-SHARQI; Gen. Man. Capt. MOUSA MURAD; Harbour Master Capt. TAMER MASOUD.

Ras al-Khaimah

Saqr Port Authority: POB 5130, Ras al-Khaimah; tel. (7) 2668444; fax (7) 2668533; e-mail info@saqrport.com; internet www.saqrport.com; port operators handling bulk cargoes, containers, general cargo and 'roll on, roll off' traffic; govt-owned; Chair. Sheikh SAQR BIN MUHAMMAD AL-QASIMI; CEO VEN GOVINDA.

Sharjah

Department of Seaports and Customs: POB 510, Sharjah; tel. (6) 5281327; fax (6) 5281425; e-mail shjports@eim.ae; internet www.sharjahports.ae; the authority administers Port Khalid, Hamriyah Port and Port Khor Fakkan and offers specialized facilities for container and 'roll on, roll off' traffic, reefer cargo and project and general cargo; in 2003 Port Khalid handled 145,482 TEUs of containerized shipping, and Port Khor Fakkan 1,444,451 TEUs; Port Khalid and Hamriyah Port together handled over 4m. metric tons of non-containerized cargo; Chair. (Ports and Customs) Sheikh KHALID BIN ABDULLAH AL-QASIMI; Dir-Gen. ISSA JUMA AL-MUTAWA.

Fal Shipping Co Ltd: POB 6600, Sharjah; tel. (6) 5286666; fax (6) 5280861; e-mail osman@faloil.co.ae; internet www.falgroup.com/htm/shipping.htm; operates a fleet of 21 tankships; Chair. ABDULLAH JUMA AS-SARI; Gen. Man. MUHAMMAD OSMAN FADUL.

Umm al-Qaiwain

Ahmed bin Rashid Port and Free Zone Authority: POB 279, Umm al-Qaiwain; tel. (6) 7655882; fax (6) 7651552; e-mail abrpaftz@emirates.net.ae; Pres. KHALID BIN RASHID AL-MU'ALLA; Gen. Man. MURTAZA K. MOOSAJEE.

CIVIL AVIATION

There are six international airports at Abu Dhabi, al-Ain (Abu Dhabi), Dubai (DIA), Fujairah and Ras al-Khaimah, and a smaller one at Sharjah, which forms part of Sharjah port, linking air, sea and overland transportation services. Owing to space constraints at DIA, construction work began in 2005 on a new airport, with an eventual capacity of 160m. passengers and 12m. metric tons of freight per year, at Jebel Ali (Dubai). The new airport, Al Maktoum International, part of the Dubai World Central commercial and residential infrastructure development, was expected to accommodate its first flights in mid-2010. Meanwhile, an expansion project at DIA, to increase annual capacity from 30m. to 75m. passengers, was scheduled for completion in 2011. As part of this project, a new third terminal began operating in late 2008 and plans for a fourth terminal, which would expand passenger capacity to 80m., were under discussion in early 2009. An expansion project at Abu Dhabi was expected to increase annual passenger capacity there to 20m. by 2010; a new runway and a new passenger terminal became operational during 2008. Plans to construct a new terminal at Sharjah International Airport, at a cost of US $354m., were announced in late 2008. In 1995 a total of 11.6m. passengers used the six UAE airports, 3.3m. of them passing through Abu Dhabi airports; in 2005 a record 23m. passengers used Dubai airport alone. Abu Dhabi withdrew from Gulf Air, which it had owned jointly with Bahrain and Oman (and previously with Qatar), in September 2005.

General Civil Aviation Authority: POB 6558, Abu Dhabi; tel. (2) 4447666; fax (2) 4054535; e-mail info@gcaa.ae; internet www.gcaa.ae; f. 1996; responsible for all aspects of civil aviation; Chair. SULTAN BIN SAID AL-MANSOURI (Minister of Economy); Dir-Gen. MUHAMMAD ABDULLAH AS-SALAMI.

Abu Dhabi Aviation: POB 2723, Abu Dhabi; tel. (2) 5758000; fax (2) 5757775; e-mail adava@abudhabiaviation.com; internet www.adaviation.com; f. 1976; domestic charter flights; Chair. Sheikh TAHNOON BIN ZAYED AN-NAHYAN; Gen. Man. MUHAMMAD IBRAHIM AL-MAZROUI.

Air Arabia: POB 132, Sharjah; tel. (6) 5088888; fax (6) 5580244; e-mail hraydan@airarabia.com; internet www.airarabia.com; f. 2003; owned by the Sharjah Govt; low-fare airline; serves 44 destinations across the Middle East, N Africa, S and Cen. Asia and Europe; handled 3.6m. passengers in 2008; Chair. Sheikh ABDULLAH BIN MUHAMMAD ATH-THANI; CEO ADEL ALI.

Emirates Airline: POB 686, Dubai; tel. (4) 2951111; fax (4) 2955817; e-mail corpcom@emiratesairline.com; internet www.emirates.com; f. 1985; owned by the Dubai Govt; operates services to over 100 destinations in 61 countries; carried 21.2m. passengers and 1.3m. metric tons of freight in 2007/08; Chair. and CEO Sheikh AHMAD BIN SAID AL-MAKTOUM; Exec. Vice-Chair. MAURICE FLANAGAN.

Etihad Airways: POB 35566, Abu Dhabi; tel. (2) 5058000; fax (2) 5058111; internet www.etihadairways.com; f. 2003; owned by the Abu Dhabi Govt; operates 37 aircraft serving 45 short- and long-haul destinations; carried 4.6m. passengers in 2007; Chair. Sheikh HAMAD BIN ZAYED AN-NAHYAN; CEO JAMES HOGAN.

Falcon Express Cargo Airlines (FECA): Dubai International Airport, POB 93722, Dubai; tel. (4) 2826886; fax (4) 2823125; e-mail admin@feca.bz; internet www.falcongroup.bz; f. 1995; dedicated courier freight.

RAK Airways: POB 31457, Ras al-Khaimah; tel. (7) 2075000; fax (7) 2447387; e-mail info@rakairways.com; internet www.rakairways.com; f. 2005; flights commenced 2007; owned by Govt of Ras al-Khaimah; operates from Ras al-Khaimah Int. Airport; Man. Dir Dr KHATER MASSAAD; CEO K. RAVINDRAN.

THE UNITED ARAB EMIRATES

Tourism

Tourism is an established industry in Dubai and Sharjah, and plans are being implemented to foster tourism in other emirates, notably in Abu Dhabi. In 2004 foreign visitors to the UAE totalled almost 6.2m., compared with 616,000 in 1990. Receipts from tourism totalled US $4,912m. in 2006.

Abu Dhabi Tourism Authority: POB 94000, Abu Dhabi; tel. (2) 4440444; fax (2) 4440400; e-mail contact@abudhabi.ae; internet www.exploreabudhabi.ae; f. 2004; Chair. Sheikh SULTAN BIN TAHNUN AN-NAHYAN; Dir-Gen. MUBARAK HAMAD AL-MUHEIRI.

Department of Tourism and Commerce Marketing: POB 594, Dubai; tel. (4) 2230000; fax (4) 2230022; e-mail info@dubaitourism.co.ae; internet www.dubaitourism.co.ae; f. 1997; 18 offices abroad; Chair. Sheikh MUHAMMAD BIN RASHID AL-MAKTOUM (Ruler of Dubai); Dir-Gen. KHALID A. BIN SULAYEM.

Fujairah Tourism Bureau: POB 829, Fujairah; tel. (9) 2231554; fax (9) 2231006; e-mail fujtourb@emirates.net.ae; internet fujairah-tourism.gov.ae; f. 1995; Chair. Sheikh SAID BIN SAID ASH-SHARQI; Dir WAHID BIN YOUSUF.

National Corporation for Tourism and Hotels (NCTH): POB 6942, Abu Dhabi; tel. (2) 4099999; fax (2) 4099990; e-mail ncth@emirates.net.ae; internet www.ncth.com; 20% owned by Govt of Abu Dhabi; Chair. HAMDAN BIN MUBARAK AN-NAYHAN.

Ras al-Khaimah Tourism Promotion Board: POB 31219, Ras Al Khaimah; tel. (7) 2445125; fax (7) 2447463; internet www.raktourism.com; f. 2006; Chair. Sheikh ABD AL-AZIZ BIN HUMAID AL-QASIMI; CEO Dr KHATER MASSAAD.

Sharjah Commerce and Tourism Development Authority: POB 26661, 9th Floor, Crescent Tower, Buheirah Corniche, Sharjah; tel. (6) 5566777; fax (6) 5563000; e-mail info@sharjah.org; internet www.sharjah-welcome.com; f. 1980; Dir.-Gen. MUHAMMAD ALI AN-NOMAN.

THE UNITED KINGDOM

Introductory Survey

Location, Climate, Language, Religion, Flag, Capital

The United Kingdom of Great Britain and Northern Ireland lies in north-western Europe, occupying the major portion of the British Isles. The country's only land boundary is with Ireland. Great Britain, consisting of one large island and a number of smaller ones, comprises England, Scotland to the north and Wales to the west. It is separated from the coast of western Europe by the English Channel to the south and by the North Sea to the east. The northern and western shores are washed by the Atlantic Ocean. Ireland lies to the west across the Irish Sea. Northern Ireland, which is a constitutionally distinct part of the United Kingdom, is situated in the north-east of Ireland and is composed of six of the nine counties in the Irish province of Ulster, with the rest of the island comprising the state of Ireland. The climate of the United Kingdom is generally temperate but variable. The average temperature is about 15°C (59°F) in summer and about 5°C (41°F) in winter. The annual average rainfall is 1,125 mm (44.3 ins). The official language is English, but Welsh is spoken by about one-fifth of the Welsh population. The Church of England is the established church in England. Other large Christian denominations are Roman Catholicism, Methodism, the United Reformed Church and the Baptists. The national flag (proportions 1 by 2), known as the Union Jack, is a superimposition of the red cross of Saint George of England, the white saltire of Saint Andrew of Scotland and the red saltire of Saint Patrick of Ireland, all on a blue background. The capital is London.

Recent History

At the end of the Second World War the United Kingdom still ruled a vast overseas empire, and successive British Governments, in response both to nationalist aspirations and world pressure, gradually granted independence to the colonies; almost all of these became members of the Commonwealth (see p. 217). Britain's dominance diminished over the Commonwealth, which became a free association of states, and by the end of the 1970s the country looked exclusively to the North Atlantic Treaty Organization (NATO, see p. 351) and to the European Community (EC, now European Union—EU, see p. 255) for its future security.

Following the general election of 1945, the Labour Party formed a Government under its Leader, Clement Attlee. The general election of 1951 was won by the Conservative Party, which subsequently formed a Government under Winston Churchill, the wartime Prime Minister. The Conservatives remained in power for 13 years, led successively by Churchill, Sir Anthony Eden (1955–57), Harold Macmillan (1957–63) and Sir Alec Douglas-Home (1963–64). The election of 1964 gave a small parliamentary majority to the Labour Party, led by Harold Wilson. The Labour Party was re-elected in 1966, but in 1970 a Conservative Government, under Edward Heath, was returned.

After the general election of February 1974 Wilson formed a minority Government; at a further election in October the Labour Party achieved a small majority in the House of Commons. Wilson resigned as Prime Minister in April 1976, and was succeeded by James Callaghan. His Labour Government immediately encountered a serious monetary crisis and, following a series of by-election defeats, became a minority Government again.

In the general election of May 1979 the Conservative Party won a parliamentary majority. A Government was formed under Margaret Thatcher, who became the United Kingdom's first female Prime Minister. Thatcherite policy proved controversial, owing to the austerity of certain economic measures and an accompanying increase in unemployment. New legislation restricted the power of the trade unions.

Michael Foot was elected Leader of the Labour Party in November 1980. The increasing prominence of extreme left-wing members caused serious rifts in the Labour Party, and in March 1981 four former ministers from the right wing of the party formed the Social Democratic Party (SDP). The SDP formed a political alliance with the Liberals later that year.

In April 1982 Argentine forces invaded the British dependency of the Falkland Islands (q.v.). The successful military campaign to recover the islands in June increased the Government's popularity, despite rising unemployment and strict monetary control of the economy. In the general election of June 1983 the Conservative Party increased its majority in the House of Commons to 146 seats. The Labour Party's parliamentary representation fell and Neil Kinnock subsequently replaced Foot as the Labour Leader.

At a general election in June 1987 the Conservative Party won an overall majority of 102 seats in the House of Commons. In March 1988 the SDP-Liberal Alliance formally merged as the Social and Liberal Democrats (later known as the Liberal Democrats), and in July Paddy Ashdown (of the former Liberal Party) was elected as party Leader.

In mid-1990 the introduction of a local tax, the community charge (or 'poll tax'), in conjunction with an economic recession, and the unpopularity of changes to the education system and of proposed reforms to the National Health Service (NHS), contributed to considerable national dissatisfaction with the Thatcher administration. The Government was also divided, chiefly over policy on integration with the EC. In November Sir Geoffrey Howe resigned as the Lord President of the Council, Leader of the House of Commons and Deputy Prime Minister, in protest against Thatcher's hostility towards economic and political union within the EC. Michael Heseltine (who had resigned as Secretary of State for Defence in 1986) announced that he would challenge Thatcher for the leadership of the Conservative Party. In the first ballot of the leadership election (conducted among Conservative Members of Parliament—MPs) Thatcher failed to achieve an outright victory and subsequently withdrew her candidacy. John Major, Chancellor of the Exchequer since October 1989, finally won the contest and was officially appointed Prime Minister in November 1990. (The community charge was replaced with a local 'council tax', based on property values, in April 1993.)

In a general election held in April 1992 the Conservative Party was re-elected with an overall, but substantially reduced, majority in the House of Commons. Economic recession continued and the Government's economic policies were criticized by political opponents and by industrial and business leaders. Divisions within the Conservative Party over the provisions of the Treaty on European Union (the Maastricht Treaty) were exacerbated by the United Kingdom's departure from the exchange rate mechanism (ERM) of the European Monetary System (see p. 296) in September. The Treaty was endorsed by the House of Lords, the non-elected upper chamber, in July 1993, despite fierce opposition from some Conservatives. However, in a vote to ratify the Treaty, by adopting a motion on its so-called 'social chapter', conducted in the House of Commons later in July, 'rebel' Conservatives joined the Opposition to defeat the motion. The Prime Minister introduced a confidence motion the following day, and speculation that Major would call a general election in the event of a defeat for the Government ensured the support of dissident MPs.

Following the Labour Party's fourth successive general election defeat, in April 1992, Kinnock announced his resignation as party Leader. In July John Smith was elected to replace him. Prior to his death, in May 1994, Smith reformed the relationship between the Labour Party and the trade unions, reducing the unions' influence over policy formulation and the election of party chiefs and parliamentary candidates. In July Tony Blair, Labour's parliamentary spokesman on home affairs, was elected Leader by the party's electoral college. Blair's initiative to abandon Labour's socialist commitment to common ownership of the means of production provoked a much-publicized reassessment of party ideology, and became a test of support for the new leadership. In April 1995 a special party conference endorsed a draft text to replace the relevant clause of the party's constitution.

By May 1995 the Government's majority in the House of Commons had been reduced to 10 members. In June Major announced his resignation as Leader of the Conservative Party, asserting that speculation regarding a challenge to his leadership was undermining both his authority as Prime Minister and that of the Government. The Secretary of State for Wales, John Redwood, resigned from the Cabinet in order to challenge Major as party Leader. In the ballot for the leadership, held in July, Major obtained 218 of the 329 votes of the parliamentary party (compared with Redwood's 89). By April 1996 the Government's majority in the House of Commons had declined to a single seat.

In March 1996 the imposition by the EU of a comprehensive trade ban on British beef products, in response to a major public health alert (see below), emboldened those Conservative MPs demanding a limitation in the country's convergence with the EU. In April Major committed a future Conservative administration to conducting a popular referendum on the country's participation in a European single currency. In June more than 70 Conservative MPs declared their support for a wider referendum on EU membership, demonstrating the increasing prominence of the so-called Eurosceptic faction of the party.

In December 1996 the Government officially lost its majority in the House of Commons when the Labour Party won a by-election for a previously Conservative-held seat. In February 1997 the Labour Party attempted to force a government defeat, in order to prompt a general election, by introducing a parliamentary censure motion against the Minister of Agriculture, Fisheries and Food, Douglas Hogg, for his administration of the bovine spongiform encephalopathy (BSE) crisis (see below). However, the Ulster Unionists upheld the Government's position by abstaining. By March the Conservatives' parliamentary minority had deepened, following a further Labour by-election victory and the defection of a Eurosceptic MP.

At a general election held on 1 May 1997 the Labour Party (now frequently referred to as New Labour, emphasizing the reforms undertaken under Blair's leadership) secured an overwhelming victory, winning 418 of the 659 parliamentary seats, with 44.3% of the votes cast in Britain. The Conservative Party won only 165 seats, with 31.5% of the vote. Moreover, for the first time in its history, the Conservative Party failed to win any parliamentary representation in Scotland or Wales. The Liberal Democrats increased their number of seats to 46, although with a slightly reduced share of the votes (17.2%, compared with 17.9% in 1992). Major immediately announced his resignation as Leader of the Conservative Party: William Hague, hitherto Secretary of State for Wales, was elected to the post (and thus as Leader of the Opposition) by Conservative MPs in June.

In the new Labour Government Gordon Brown, who had been prominent in the creation of New Labour, was named as Chancellor of the Exchequer and Robin Cook became the new Secretary of State for Foreign and Commonwealth Affairs, while the Labour Party's Deputy Leader, John Prescott, was appointed Deputy Prime Minister, assuming additional responsibility for the environment, transport and the regions. Peter Mandelson, one of Blair's closest advisers, and regarded as highly influential in the organization of Labour's election campaign, was appointed Minister without Portfolio, with responsibility for co-ordinating government policy (a non-Cabinet post). The new administration announced a series of radical policy proposals and government reforms, including an employment initiative, aimed initially at long-term unemployed 18–24 year olds, which was to be financed by a single taxation levy on the profits of privatized industries. Brown announced changes to the management and regulation of the economy and the financial sector (including a transfer of operational responsibility for monetary policy to the Bank of England), while Cook defined the Government's broad approach to foreign affairs, with greater emphasis on the country's role in international organizations and the incorporation of human rights concerns into foreign policy and trade decisions. A new Department for International Development was established, to assume the functions of the former Overseas Development Administration (previously under the authority of the Foreign and Commonwealth Office) at cabinet level. The Government's parliamentary programme included additional legislation intended to improve standards in education, the adoption of a national minimum wage, and constitutional reform.

In July 1997 the Government formally published its proposals for the establishment of devolved legislative authorities in Scotland and Wales. For Scotland a proposed new elected Parliament was envisaged as having powers to legislate on all domestic matters, including education, health, local government, law and order, and the possible mandate to vary taxes set by the United Kingdom Government. An executive level of government was to be headed by a First Minister. The 129 Members of the Scottish Parliament (MSPs) were to be elected every four years by a combined system of direct voting and a form of proportional representation. The National Assembly for Wales, like the Scottish body, was envisaged as assuming control of the annual block grant for the region from central government, and as undertaking responsibility for issues covered by the Welsh Office. The 60-member National Assembly was to be elected under the same system as in Scotland. In a referendum held in Scotland in September, 74.3% of those voting supported a new Parliament, while 63.5% approved its having tax-raising powers. The results, although representing only an estimated 44.7% and 38.1% of eligible voters, respectively, were considered by the Government as being an endorsement of its proposals. The referendum in Wales, held one week later, was less conclusive, with only 50.3% of participants (or some 25% of eligible voters) endorsing the National Assembly. None the less, the Government declared its intention to implement the majority decision. A political settlement on the future governance of Northern Ireland (see below), concluded in April 1998, provided for new constitutional arrangements regarding the status of Northern Ireland within the United Kingdom and for the establishment of a British-Irish Council.

In October 1998 the Leader of the Government in the House of Lords, Baroness Jay of Paddington, announced that legislation was to be introduced to remove the voting rights of hereditary peers, and that a Royal Commission was to be appointed to consider options for a definitive reform of the second chamber. Opposition from within the House of Lords was appeased in December when a compromise agreement was reached under which 92 hereditary peers were to retain their seats in an interim second chamber pending the definitive reform. Draft legislation for the abolition of hereditary peerages and the establishment of an interim chamber was published in January 1999. In October the upper chamber approved the House of Lords Bill, and in November it received royal assent. In January 2000 the Royal Commission published its proposals for the definitive reform of the upper house, recommending that the new chamber should comprise some 550 members, the majority of whom would be chosen by an independent commission, while a 'significant minority' (between 65 and 195) would be elected by regional proportional representation.

At elections to the new legislative authorities in Scotland and Wales, held in May 1999, the Labour Party, while securing the greatest number of seats, failed to gain an overall majority in either assembly. In Scotland the Labour Party obtained 56 of the total of 129 seats, while the SNP won 35 seats, the Conservative Party 18 seats, and the Liberal Democrats 17 seats; the remaining three seats were won by independent candidates. The Labour Party and the Liberal Democrats subsequently formed a coalition administration, headed by Labour's Donald Dewar as First Minister. In Wales the Labour Party secured 28 of the total of 60 seats, while Plaid Cymru obtained 17 seats, the Conservative Party nine and the Liberal Democrats six. Despite Labour's lack of an overall majority, in mid-May the Welsh First Minister, Alun Michael, opted to form a minority administration rather than a formal coalition. Powers were transferred to both the Scottish and the Welsh legislatures on 1 July 1999.

During 2000 there was considerable political upheaval in both Wales and Scotland. In February Rhodri Morgan succeeded Alun Michael as Welsh First Minister. Michael had resigned shortly before the National Assembly for Wales adopted a vote of no confidence in his leadership. In May the Leader of Plaid Cymru, Dafydd Wigley, resigned owing to ill health; he was replaced by Ieuan Wyn Jones in August. In October the ruling Labour Party entered into a coalition agreement with the Liberal Democrats, who obtained two portfolios, including that of Deputy First Minister, in the reorganized nine-member Welsh Cabinet. Meanwhile, in Scotland the unexpected resignation of Alex Salmond as Leader of the SNP in July precipitated a leadership contest in which John Swinney was elected as Salmond's successor. Following the death in October of Dewar, the Labour Party in Scotland elected Henry McLeish, the Minister for Enterprise and Lifelong Learning, to succeed him as their Leader. Later in that month McLeish was elected to succeed Dewar as First Minister.

In August 1999 the Liberal Democrats elected Charles Kennedy to succeed Ashdown as their Leader. In October Blair conducted a government reorganization in which Mandelson replaced Mo Mowlam as Secretary of State for Northern Ireland. Mandelson had been appointed President of the Board of Trade and Secretary of State for Trade and Industry in July 1998, but had resigned in December following allegations of financial impropriety. In January 2001 Mandelson resigned as Secretary of State for Northern Ireland after his initial denial of any direct involvement in an enquiry to the Home Office in June 1998, regarding the application for British citizenship of an Indian business executive, appeared to be false. Dr John Reid, hitherto Secretary of State for Scotland, was appointed to succeed Mandelson.

In February 2001 incidences of foot-and-mouth disease (FMD—a non-fatal yet highly contagious virus carried by cloven-hoofed animals) in south-east England prompted the European Commission to impose a temporary ban on the export of live animals, meat and dairy products from the United Kingdom. A continuing rise in the number of cases of FMD throughout the country, mounting pressure from agricultural interest groups and popular opposition to the timing of the polls led the Government to announce in April that emergency legislation would be introduced to provide for a five-week postponement of the local elections due to be held in May (the first time such legislation had been required during peacetime).

In early May 2001 Blair announced that a general election (as well as the postponed local elections) would be conducted on 7 June. The last case of FMD was identified in September and in January 2002 the Government announced that the United Kingdom was free of the disease. In February the European Commission agreed to lift remaining restrictions on the import and export of British meat, animal products and livestock. A report published by the National Audit Office in June 2002 confirmed that the losses to the British economy resulting from the FMD outbreak totalled some £5,000m. In July the report of an inquiry into the Government's handling of the crisis was published, which was highly critical of the Government's response to the outbreak, stating that FMD spread far wider than it should have as a result of inadequate contingency plans and the Government's slow response.

At the general election held on 7 June 2001 the Labour Party won a further comprehensive victory, securing 413 of the 659 parliamentary seats with 40.7% of the votes cast. The Conservative Party won 166 seats with 31.7% of the votes cast, while the Liberal Democrats increased their parliamentary representation to 53 seats, with 18.3% of the votes cast. The election, however, attracted the lowest rate of voter participation, 59.4%, since 1918. Following his party's poor performance, Hague announced his intention to resign the leadership of the Conservative Party; in September Iain Duncan Smith, hitherto the Conservative Party's parliamentary spokesman on defence, was elected to replace Hague. Meanwhile, in a major reorganization of the Cabinet, Jack Straw, hitherto Secretary of State for the Home Department, replaced Cook as Secretary of State for Foreign and Commonwealth Affairs and David Blunkett, formerly Secretary of State for Education, assumed Straw's portfolio. The Ministry of Agriculture, Fisheries and Food, which had been heavily criticized for its handling of the FMD outbreak, was replaced by the Department for the Environment, Food and Rural Affairs and a new Department for Work and Pensions was created. Furthermore, Blair removed the responsibility for transport, environment and the regions from the Deputy Prime Minister, Prescott, appointing Stephen Byers, previously Secretary of State for Trade and Industry, as head of the newly formed Department for Transport, Local Government and the Regions (DTLR).

Upon their release in November 2001, the Government's proposals for the reform of the House of Lords encountered fierce opposition from both Labour and opposition MPs concerning the number of directly elected members envisaged in the plans. The public consultation process on the proposals ended in January 2002. In May the Government effectively abandoned the recommendations, and in December a new joint committee of MPs and peers presented seven options for the future proportion of elected members in the House of Lords, ranging from a wholly elected chamber to a wholly appointed house. However, in February 2003 all seven options were rejected by MPs voting in the House of Commons.

In December 2001 a Labour MP defected to the Liberal Democrats, citing the Government's continued failure to improve public services and the decision to approve military action in Afghanistan (see below). Also in December anti-terrorism legislation was introduced in response to the events of 11 September in the USA (see below), which, most notably, provided for the detention of suspected international terrorists without trial if their deportation was not deemed possible.

However, in July 2002 the legislation was declared unlawful and in breach of the European Convention on Human Rights by the Special Immigration Appeals Committee (SIAC). In October the British Court of Appeal ruled against the July decision and in May 2003 Blunkett announced proposals that would allow police to hold terrorist suspects without charge for up to 14 days. In October the SIAC rejected appeals by 10 foreign nationals who had been detained indefinitely without trial.

In May 2002 Byers resigned as Secretary of State for Transport, Local Government and the Regions, having incurred criticism for his decision to place the heavily indebted rail infrastructure operating company, Railtrack, into administration in October 2001. (Byers had initially declared that he would not use public funds to compensate Railtrack shareholders, but the funding arrangements that he announced in March 2002 for the proposed successor company, Network Rail, were perceived as a reversal of this policy.) There followed a major reorganization of several government departments. The DTLR was abolished and a new Department for Transport was created, which was headed by Alistair Darling, hitherto Secretary of State for Work and Pensions.

In March 2003 Clare Short announced her intention to resign as Secretary of State for International Development if Blair approved British participation in the US-led campaign to oust the regime of Saddam Hussain in Iraq (see below) without a pertinent UN resolution. Following the failure to secure a second UN resolution authorizing military action in Iraq and the announcement that British troops would be deployed as part of the US-led coalition to remove Hussain, Cook resigned as Leader of the House of Commons, citing his unwillingness to accept collective responsibility for the decision to commit the United Kingdom to military action without international agreement or domestic support. Two ministers of state and a number of ministerial aides also resigned in protest at Blair's decision. Blair suffered another major reverse when 139 Labour MPs voted in favour of a motion stating that there was no moral justification for an attack on Iraq, although another motion endorsing his strategy was approved by 412 votes to 149. In April Blair appointed Reid to replace Cook. Short finally resigned from the Cabinet in May, accusing Blair of reneging on assurances he had made to her concerning the need for a UN mandate to establish a legitimate Iraqi government. She was succeeded by Baroness Amos of Brondesbury.

At elections to the Scottish and Welsh legislative authorities, held on 1 May 2003, the Labour Party again won the largest number of seats in both assemblies. In Wales Labour secured 30 of the 60 available seats, Plaid Cymru won 12 seats, the Conservatives 11, and the Liberal Democrats six; the remaining seat was taken by an independent candidate. Morgan subsequently appointed a new, all-Labour Cabinet. In Scotland the Labour Party obtained 50 of the total of 129 seats, while the SNP took 27, the Conservatives 18, the Liberal Democrats 17, the Scottish Green Party seven, and the Scottish Socialist Party six; the remaining four seats were won by independent candidates. In mid-May Jack McConnell, who had succeeded McLeish as Leader of the Labour Party in Scotland and First Minister in November 2001, announced a reorganized coalition administration, again comprising Labour and the Liberal Democrats.

In May 2003 Straw indicated that evidence that Iraq had possessed weapons of mass destruction might never be found, prompting allegations from a number of anti-war MPs that the perceived threat posed by that country had been exaggerated, and that the House of Commons had been misled. The British Broadcasting Corporation (BBC) came into conflict with the Government in the same month, when a BBC journalist alleged that a dossier published by the Government in September 2002 to explain the case for the removal of the Iraqi regime, had made exaggerated claims concerning Iraq's possession of chemical and biological weapons: he claimed that the Prime Minister's Director of Communications and Strategy, Alastair Campbell, was responsible for including misleading information in the dossier, against the wishes of the intelligence agencies. Blair denied the accusations and stated that the evidence had been compiled and approved by the Joint Intelligence Committee (JIC). In June 2003 it was announced that the parliamentary Foreign Affairs Select Committee (FASC) was to conduct an inquiry into whether the Government had provided accurate and complete information to Parliament in the period leading up to military action in Iraq, while the parliamentary Intelligence and Security Committee (ISC) was to investigate the role played by the intelligence agencies. In mid-June the ISC censured the Prime Minister's

Office for having published (in February) a second dossier which contained outdated material, but in September its report exonerated the Government of political interference in the assessment of secret intelligence. In July the FASC concluded that Campbell had not exerted improper influence on the drafting of the first dossier, but criticized his role in the production of the second, which had led Blair unwittingly to misinform Parliament that further intelligence existed on Iraq's alleged concealment of weapons of mass destruction. The BBC, however, while refusing to reveal its source, rejected Campbell's demand that it retract the story. Also in July the Ministry of Defence confirmed that Dr David Kelly, a senior adviser to the ministry, was the source of the BBC's information pertaining to Iraq's weapons. Later in that month Dr Kelly committed suicide. The Secretary of State for Defence, Geoff Hoon, denied responsibility for revealing Kelly's identity. Blair ordered an independent judicial inquiry, under Lord Hutton, into his death: its report, published in January 2004, concluded that there had been no duplicitous strategy on the part of the Government to reveal Dr Kelly's name to the media, but that the Ministry of Defence had erred by failing to inform Kelly that his name would be confirmed if journalists suggested it, and that its treatment of Kelly after his public exposure had been unsatisfactory. The report criticized the management and editorial systems of the BBC, whose Director-General, together with the Chairman of the Board of Governors, then resigned. In February 2004 Blair announced the establishment of a further inquiry, under Lord Butler of Brockwell, into the accuracy of the intelligence gathered on Iraqi weapons of mass destruction, which would examine any discrepancies between the information collected, evaluated and used by the Government before the conflict in Iraq and intelligence discovered by the Iraq Survey Group (see below) since the end of major combat operations in May 2003. In July 2004 Lord Butler published the findings from his inquiry, which revealed that intelligence surrounding the compilation of the first dossier was 'seriously flawed' and criticized the intelligence services for using unreliable sources of information within Iraq. It also disclosed that before the start of the war there was no proof that Iraq had any significant stocks of weapons of mass destruction. It also stressed that there was no evidence of 'deliberate distortion or culpable negligence' on the part of the JIC.

In June 2003, meanwhile, an extensive reorganization of the Cabinet included plans to effect major changes to the British legal and judicial system. Under the proposals the post of Lord Chancellor, which had been in existence for some 1,400 years, was to be abolished and a US-style supreme court was to replace the judicial function of the House of Lords as the United Kingdom's highest court of appeal. The Lord Chancellor's Office was replaced by a newly created Department for Constitutional Affairs, which also assumed responsibility for the abolished Scottish and Welsh Offices. Officials from those offices were located within the new department, although Darling assumed the position of Secretary of State for Scotland in addition to the transport portfolio, and Peter Hain, who replaced Reid as Leader of the House of Commons, retained the post of Secretary of State for Wales. Reid subsequently replaced Alan Milburn as Secretary of State for Health. Lord Falconer of Thoroton was appointed to head the Department for Constitutional Affairs, while also assuming temporarily the functions of the Lord Chancellor—although he would not sit as a judge—pending the full implementation of the reforms. Furthermore, an independent commission would assume responsibility for appointing judges. The decision to abolish such a historic position without prior consultation was heavily criticized by a number of MPs and Lords, and Blair was requested by the Speaker of the House of Commons to appear before the chamber to clarify the decisions and their repercussions. Consultation papers regarding the further reform of the House of Lords, which proposed the removal of the remaining 92 hereditary peers, the creation of a wholly appointed upper chamber with unchanged revising powers, the abolition of the position of Lord Chancellor and the creation of a supreme court, were published by the Government in September 2003. In March 2004 the House of Lords determined by 216 votes to 183 to refer the Constitutional Reform Bill to a Lords select committee for further scrutiny. The Government announced later in that month that it was postponing plans to abolish the remaining 92 hereditary peerages; it intended, however, to continue with plans to establish a supreme court and remove the post of Lord Chancellor. In July the clause providing for the removal of the Lord Chancellor was rejected by the House of Lords; the Government subsequently agreed only to modify the Lord Chancellor's role. In March 2005 an attempt by the Government to separate the Lord Chancellor's roles as supreme judge, Speaker of the House of Lords and government minister failed when a new amendment to the bill, proposing that the Lord Chancellor need not be a member of the House of Lords or a lawyer, was rejected by the upper house. However, the House of Lords subsequently voted by a majority of 12 to allow an MP who was not necessarily a lawyer to take on the role of Lord Chancellor, and the Constitutional Reform Bill received royal assent in late March. As part of the reform of the role of Lord Chancellor, in January 2006 the House of Lords formally agreed to elect a Speaker, the Lord Chancellor having hitherto traditionally presided over debates. In April the Constitutional Reform Act came into force, and the Lord Chief Justice of England and Wales, Lord Phillips of Worth Matravers, assumed control of the judiciary in England and Wales from the Lord Chancellor. The new Supreme Court was not scheduled to commence operations until October 2009.

In early October 2003 Blair effected a minor reshuffle of the Cabinet, following the death of the Leader of the House of Lords, Lord Williams of Mostyn. Baroness Amos was appointed to replace Lord Williams and Hilary Benn succeeded Amos as Secretary of State for International Development. In late October Duncan Smith announced his resignation as Leader of the Conservative Party after Conservative MPs approved a vote of no confidence in his leadership. He was replaced by Michael Howard, a former Secretary of State for the Home Department, who was elected Leader unopposed.

Dissent from within the Labour Party continued to threaten to undermine Blair's authority and in January 2004, in the most notable Labour revolt since Blair became Prime Minister, 72 Labour MPs voted against the Government's Higher Education Bill, which proposed to introduce repayable and variable university tuition fees from 2006. Only intense lobbying by a number of cabinet ministers secured the passage of the Bill—by five votes. On 10 June 2004, at elections to the European Parliament and at local elections, the Labour Party suffered significant losses. In the local elections Labour lost 464 seats and eight councils, leaving them with control of 39 councils, while the Conservatives gained 263 seats and 13 councils, increasing their total to 51 councils, and the Liberal Democrats suffered a net loss of two councils, leaving them with control of nine. In the European elections the Conservatives won 27 of the 78 seats allocated to the United Kingdom (compared with 36 in 1999) and Labour won 19 (a decline of 10 seats). The Liberal Democrats won 12 seats (compared with 10 in 1999), while the Eurosceptic UK Independence Party increased its representation in the European Parliament from three seats to 12. Electoral participation was registered at 38.2%, compared with 24% in 1999.

In November 2004 an inquiry was established to investigate accusations that the Secretary of State for the Home Department, David Blunkett, had expedited a visa application for the employee of his former lover. In early December the report of the inquiry revealed a 'chain of events' linking Blunkett to the dispatch of the application, although no evidence was uncovered of his direct intervention. Despite asserting his innocence of any deliberate wrongdoing, Blunkett resigned from the Cabinet. Charles Clarke, hitherto Secretary of State for Education and Skills, was appointed to replace him, while Ruth Kelly, the former Minister for the Cabinet Office, was allocated Clarke's role. Also in December the Law Lords ruled that the detention without trial under the 2001 Anti-Terrorism, Crime and Security Act of the remaining nine foreign suspects who could not be deported was discriminatory and in breach of their human rights, overturning an earlier ruling by SIAC. Clarke presented a new anti-terrorism bill to Parliament in February 2005 since the powers of detention under the 2001 Act were due to expire in March, as a result of the legal ruling. The new bill encountered strong criticism from human rights groups and was adopted by the House of Lords in mid-March, only after the Government had made significant amendments to it in response to its repeated rejection by the upper house.

At the general election on 5 May 2005 the Labour Party was re-elected for a third term, albeit with a substantially reduced majority, securing 356 of the 645 parliamentary seats contested, with 35.2% of the votes cast. The Conservative Party and the Liberal Democrats both increased their representation in the House of Commons, securing 197 seats (with 32.3% of the votes cast) and 62 seats (with 22.0%), respectively. Voting in one further constituency was postponed, owing to the death of a candidate. The rate of participation by eligible voters was 61.3%.

THE UNITED KINGDOM

The Labour Party's loss of popularity was attributed principally to a decline in personal support for Blair and the ongoing military action in Iraq. Following the election, Michael Howard announced his intention to step down as Leader of the Conservative Party. Blair commenced a major reorganization of ministerial portfolios on 6 May. David Blunkett returned to the Cabinet as Secretary of State for Work and Pensions, Reid was named as the new Secretary of State for Defence, replacing Hoon (who became Lord Privy Seal and Leader of the House of Commons), while Patricia Hewitt (hitherto Secretary of State for Trade and Industry and Minister for Women) took on Reid's former post as Secretary of State for Health. Alan Johnson, hitherto Secretary of State for Work and Pensions, was allocated the trade and industry portfolio, while David Miliband assumed the newly created post of Minister of Communities and Local Government.

On 7 July 2005 52 people were killed and more than 700 injured in four attacks—three on London Underground trains and one on a bus—perpetrated by suicide bombers in London. Of the four bombers, all of whom also died in the attacks, three were subsequently discovered to have been native British Muslims of Pakistani descent, while the fourth was a convert to Islam of Jamaican origin. In September Al-Jazeera, a Qatar-based television station, broadcast a videotaped communiqué, supplied to it by the militant Islamist al-Qa'ida (Base) organization, in which Mohammad Sidique Khan, who had been identified as one of the four 7 July bombers, cited the United Kingdom's participation in the invasion of Iraq in 2003 as one of the motivations for the attacks. In a separate part of the communiqué al-Qa'ida claimed responsibility for the attacks. On 21 July 2005 at least four further attempts to attack London Underground trains and a bus with bombs were unsuccessful owing to the failure of the bombs to explode. By the end of the month four men suspected of involvement in the 21 July attacks had been arrested in the United Kingdom. A fifth man was arrested a week later in the Italian capital, Rome, having fled to Italy following the attacks. Of the five initial detainees, all of whom were of African origin, two had obtained British citizenship in recent years, while a third had been granted indefinite leave to remain in the United Kingdom in 2000. In September 2005 Italy agreed to extradite the fifth suspect to the United Kingdom. In December a sixth man suspected of assisting in the failed attacks was extradited to the United Kingdom from Ethiopia, having been arrested in that country in the previous month. The trial of the six men on charges of conspiracy to murder commenced in January 2007. In July four of the defendants were found guilty and were each sentenced to life imprisonment. A retrial was expected to take place in the case of the two remaining defendants after the jury failed to reach a verdict. However, in November the two men each admitted lesser charges: one was convicted of conspiracy to cause explosions and the other of collecting information useful to a person committing or preparing an act of terrorism. The men were sentenced later that month, receiving prison terms of 33 years, and six years and nine months, respectively. In April 2009 three men were acquitted of charges of aiding the perpetrators of the 7 July bombings; two of the defendants were none the less convicted of the lesser charge of conspiring to attend terrorist training camps in Pakistan.

In April 2007 five British Muslims (who had been arrested in 2004) were convicted of conspiracy to cause explosions, having planned to detonate explosives made from fertilizer at a shopping centre, a night-club and gas installations. It was revealed during the trial that two men, who later perpetrated the suicide bombings in London on 7 July 2005, had been under surveillance by the security services in the course of the investigation, but had not been regarded as posing a serious threat. In September 2008 three men arrested in August 2006 in connection with an alleged plot to detonate improvised explosive devices aboard several transatlantic airliners were convicted of conspiring to commit murder. However, the Crown Prosecution Service announced its intention to seek a retrial of the three men after the jury failed to reach a verdict in relation to charges of conspiring to attack airliners; four other defendants were expected to be retried, following the failure of the jury to reach a verdict in relation to either charge. An eighth defendant was acquitted of all charges. The trial of the seven men and one other on charges of conspiracy to murder and conspiracy to attack airliners commenced at a court in London in February 2009.

The internal security service—known as MI5—was criticized for its failure to prevent the attacks of July 2005 and, in particular, for its decision, in June, to reduce its estimation of the threat to the United Kingdom from international terrorism to its lowest level since 11 September 2001. In response to the attacks, the Government published a new Terrorism Bill in September 2005. The draft legislation sought to establish new offences of preparing terrorist acts or assisting others to commit them; attendance at terrorist training facilities in any part of the world or providing such training; and 'direct or indirect encouragement' of terrorist acts and the release of communications that 'glorify, exalt or celebrate' acts of terrorism committed over the past 20 years. It was further proposed that the maximum period for which suspected terrorists could be detained without charge should be extended from 14 to 90 days. While a number of the bill's provisions were supported by both the Conservatives and the Liberal Democrats, representatives of those parties claimed that the Government had failed to justify the proposed extension of the maximum period of detention without charge to 90 days. Civil liberties organizations, meanwhile, claimed that such an extension would infringe suspects' human rights. In November the 90-day extension was emphatically rejected by the House of Commons. The rejection of the proposed legislation, which 49 Labour MPs had also refused to support, marked the first defeat that the Labour Government had suffered in the Commons since it assumed power in 1997. The defeat was followed by a vote in favour of extending the maximum permissible period of detention of terrorist suspects without charge to 28 days. In late March 2006 the House of Lords finally approved the Terrorism Bill; the Terrorism Act came into force in April.

Despite opposition from 25 Labour MPs, the Government's contentious Identity Cards Bill secured passage through the House of Commons in mid-October 2005. Later that month, however, the House of Lords adopted wide-ranging amendments to the Government's Racial and Religious Hatred Bill, with a view to guaranteeing freedom of speech in respect of religion. The proposed legislation was intended to afford to religious groups legal safeguards similar to those already enjoyed by ethnic groups. Also in late October the Government published a white paper in which it detailed proposals for the reform of the state school system. Strong opposition to the proposed reforms was expressed by elements within the Labour Party, who feared they would have a damaging effect on comprehensive secondary school education. In the same month the Secretary of State for Trade and Industry, Johnson, announced that he had concluded an agreement with public sector trade unions whereby a retirement age of 65 would apply for civil servants, nurses and teachers who joined those professions from April 2007, while the retirement age of those already so employed at April 2007 would remain fixed at 60. The reform was intended to reduce the Government's unfunded public sector pension deficit, which had been estimated at £400,000m.–£700,000m. In late November 2005 a government-appointed commission published recommendations on the longer-term reform of state pension arrangements, which included, notably, a proposal to increase the state pensionable age from 65 to 68 by 2050.

In early November 2005 David Blunkett resigned as Secretary of State for Work and Pensions after it transpired that aspects of his tenure of appointments by private companies, following his resignation from the Cabinet in December 2004 had contravened guidelines for former ministers accepting such positions within two years of relinquishing office. Blunkett was succeeded by John Hutton, previously Chancellor of the Duchy of Lancaster and Minister for the Cabinet Office. In December members of the Conservative Party elected David Cameron to be the new Leader of the party and, thus, of the Opposition. In January 2006, two days after he had issued a statement in which he admitted that he had received treatment for alcoholism, Charles Kennedy resigned as Leader of the Liberal Democrats. Sir Menzies Campbell, the Deputy Leader of the party under Kennedy, was elected as the Liberal Democrats' new Leader in March.

In December 2005 Blair dismissed calls that had been made by human rights organizations for a public inquiry into allegations that the United Kingdom's airspace and air transport facilities had been used in the transfer ('extraordinary rendition') of detainees, in particular terrorist suspects, by the US Central Intelligence Agency (CIA) to third countries where it was possible that they might be subjected to torture during interrogation. At a press conference in December Blair insisted that he had no evidence to suggest that anything illegal had occurred in connection with the so-called rendition flights. In January 2006, however, the *New Statesman* magazine published a Foreign and Commonwealth Office memorandum it had obtained in which it was stated that rendition flights were probably illegal under international law. The memorandum further stated that the Office's own investigations had discovered at least two instances of such flights across British airspace, but that there 'could be more'. In February the foreign affairs committee of the House of Commons stated in its annual report on human rights that the Government had been too slow to investigate allegations that as many as 200 rendition flights had crossed British airspace. According to the committee, the Government was obliged, under the UN Convention against Torture and Other Cruel, Inhuman or Degrading Treatment or Punishment, to investigate such allegations, together with other claims that the USA had established secret prisons in third countries for the purpose of interrogating detainees. Also in February Blair referred to the US camp for detained 'enemy combatants' at Guantánamo Bay, Cuba, as an anomaly that would eventually have to be addressed. On the previous day the High Court had granted three former residents of the United Kingdom who were detained at Guantánamo Bay permission to seek through the courts a petition by the British Government for their release, as it had already done in nine previous cases. In a statement to the House of Commons in February 2008, the Secretary of State for the Foreign and Commonwealth Office, David Miliband, admitted that a number of so-called rendition flights had in fact used facilities at Diego Garcia, in the Indian Ocean (the coral atoll was a British dependency, but had been leased by the USA for use as a military base since the 1960s). In October 2008 the case of Binyam Mohamed, an Ethiopian national resident in the United Kingdom who had been detained in Afghanistan by the US authorities in 2002, was referred to the Attorney-General by the Secretary of State for the Home Department. Mohamed alleged that members of the British intelligence services had colluded in his torture during a period of detention in Morocco, prior to being transferred to Guantánamo Bay in 2005; Miliband denied that the British authorities had been complicit in torture. Mohamed returned to Britain in February 2009, following his release from Guantánamo Bay, where all charges against him had been dropped. In March 2009 the Attorney-General, Baroness Scotland of Asthal, requested the Commissioner of the Metropolitan Police to investigate the allegations in relation to Mohamed. Although human rights groups and lawyers welcomed the investigation, they continued to demand a judicial inquiry to establish the full extent of British collusion in acts of torture.

In February 2006 the Government's Racial and Religious Hatred Bill received royal assent, following the rejection of two clauses of the bill by the House of Commons the previous month. Also in January the House of Lords introduced five amendments to the Government's Identity Cards Bill, including, notably, one that stipulated that the new cards should not become compulsory without new primary legislation. In February the House of Commons rejected one of the amendments introduced by the House of Lords that would have made identity cards wholly voluntary, while accepting the requirement for new primary legislation before the proposed identity cards could be made compulsory. Following a series of votes in which the House of Lords repeatedly rejected the Government's proposals, returning the bill to the Commons, in March both chambers accepted a compromise whereby all passport applicants would have their details placed on a national identity register from 2008, but could choose not to be issued an identity card until 2010. In November 2008 the Government began issuing identity cards to foreign nationals who applied to extend their leave to remain in the United Kingdom, while in early 2009 staff at London City and Manchester airports were required to carry identity cards. In May the Secretary of State for the Home Department, Jacqui Smith, announced that from late 2009 people living in the city of Manchester would be able to apply for an identity card, at an initial cost of £30; the cards were expected to become available nation-wide from 2012.

In March 2006, after the House of Lords Appointments Commission had expressed concern over a number of Labour nominations for peerages, it was revealed that four of the nominees had made unpublicized loans totalling at least £4.5m. to the Labour Party. A police investigation was subsequently launched into whether, effectively, the Labour Party had illegally sold 'titles of honour'. Although the police investigation was widened to examine the funding of both the Conservatives and the Liberal Democrats, the nominations called into question the Labour Party's commitment to transparency in political party funding, the reform of which it had begun after its election in 1997. Labour had in fact been under no legal obligation—as it would have been had they been donations—to declare the loans, but the fact that the party's treasurer, Jack Dromey, had been unaware of them strengthened the impression of duplicity. In July 2006 the Labour Party's principal fund-raiser, Lord Levy, was arrested in the course of the investigation, while during the year the Prime Minister was among about 90 others (including members of all three main political parties) who were interviewed by the police. However, in July 2007 the Crown Prosecution Service announced that no charges would be brought in relation to the allegations.

At local elections held on 4 May 2006 the Labour Party performed poorly, most notably in London, losing 319 seats and 17 councils, leaving them in overall control of 30 councils. The Conservative Party gained 316 seats and 11 councils, increasing their total to 68 councils. The Liberal Democrats failed to make any significant impact with net gains of two seats and one council, giving them control of 13 councils. On 5 May Blair effected a major reorganization of the Cabinet. Clarke was dismissed as Secretary of State for the Home Department, following criticism over the revelation in April that a number of foreign nationals convicted and imprisoned for crimes committed while living in Britain had not been considered for deportation following their release. Reid was appointed to the vacant position, and was replaced as Secretary of State for Defence by Des Browne. Margaret Beckett was appointed Secretary of State for Foreign and Commonwealth Affairs, succeeding Straw, who took the title of Lord Privy Seal and Leader of the House of Commons. Prescott remained as Deputy Prime Minister, although most of his policy responsibilities were allocated to a new Department for Communities and Local Government.

In December 2006 the Government attracted widespread criticism when the Attorney-General announced that a two-year investigation by the Serious Fraud Office into sales of military aircraft and equipment to Saudi Arabia by a British company, BAE Systems, had been abandoned in the interests of national security and foreign policy objectives in the Middle East. It had been alleged that BAE had provided millions of pounds in bribes to the Saudi royal family in order to secure sales contracts, in contravention of a law adopted in 2002. In March 2007 the Organisation for Economic Co-operation and Development (OECD, see p. 358) announced its intention to investigate whether the United Kingdom had contravened OECD's convention on combating bribery in international business transactions. In June the US Department of Justice instituted an inquiry into the allegations of corrupt payments by BAE Systems to secure Saudi arms contracts. Also in March the Government faced a rebellion among Labour MPs who were opposed to the renewal of the country's nuclear deterrent, and was obliged to rely on the support of opposition MPs in a vote on the construction of new Trident submarines carrying nuclear warheads.

New legislative proposals on the reform of the House of Lords, published in February 2007, suggested the abolition (over a transitional period) of all hereditary and life peerages and the reduction of the total membership of the upper house to 540, while MPs were to choose between a range of options on the proportion of members that would be elected and appointed. In a non-binding vote on these options, conducted in March, a majority of MPs favoured an upper house that would be entirely elected, while a smaller majority voted for one with 80% elected and 20% appointed members; in the House of Lords itself all the options were rejected and the house voted to retain a non-elected upper chamber.

At local and regional elections on 4 May 2007 the Labour Party incurred considerable losses. In Scotland the SNP gained 20 new seats, thus obtaining 47 of the 129 seats in the legislature, while Labour won 46, the Conservatives 17, the Liberal Democrats 16 and the Scottish Green Party two: the complexity of the voting procedure was blamed for the fact that about 7% of the ballot papers were declared invalid. On 16 May 2007 members of the Scottish Parliament elected the SNP Leader, Alex Salmond (who had regained that role in 2004), as First Minister, at the head of a minority SNP administration (with partial support from the Green members). In the election to the National Assembly for Wales Labour lost four seats, but remained the largest party in the legislature with 26 of the 60 seats, while Plaid Cymru won 15, the Conservative Party 12 and the Liberal Democrats six. Initial discussions between the outgoing First Minister, Labour's Rhodri Morgan, and the Leader of Plaid Cymru, Ieuan Wyn Jones, regarding the possible formation of a coalition ended in May without an agreement having been reached. However, in June Labour and Plaid Cymru finally agreed to form a coalition administration, with Morgan as First Minister and Wyn Jones as his Deputy.

In May 2007 a new Ministry of Justice, headed by the Lord Chancellor, Lord Falconer, was established to take over responsibility for prisons, probation services and sentencing from the Home Office. On 10 May Blair made the long-anticipated announcement that he would resign as Leader of the Labour Party, with effect from 27 June. As the sole candidate, Brown was confirmed as the new Leader of the Labour Party on 24 June. The election to the deputy leadership of the party, which took place on the same day, was closely contested by six candidates and was won in the fifth round of voting by the former Secretary of State for Social Security, Harriet Harman, who was also appointed party Chairman. Brown assumed the role of Prime Minister three days later, following Blair's resignation. At the end of June Brown announced an extensive reorganization of the Cabinet. Alistair Darling, previously the Secretary of State for Trade and Industry, replaced Brown as Chancellor of the Exchequer, while David Miliband was appointed Secretary of State for Foreign and Commonwealth Affairs. Straw was appointed Minister of Justice and Lord Chancellor for the transitional period and Jacqui Smith was named as Secretary of State for the Home Department. The Department for Education and Skills was divided to create two new departments: Children, Schools and Families and Innovation, Universities and Skills. The new portfolios were assumed by Ed Balls and John Denham, respectively. Harman was appointed Leader of the House of Commons, Lord Privy Seal and Minister for Women and Equality. Brown's appointments included five ministers who were not members of the Labour Party, as part of a strategy to create a government that extended beyond political affiliations to include talented experts from other fields.

The first week of Brown's premiership was marked by two failed bomb attacks, thought to have been perpetrated by Islamist terrorists. At the end of June 2007 two car bombs placed in central London failed to detonate, while a day later two men were arrested after driving a vehicle containing explosive materials into a terminal building at Glasgow Airport. (One of the men arrested in Glasgow died in August, having sustained severe injuries during the attack.) In July the Prime Minister announced a number of proposals for constitutional reform, including the transfer to Parliament of powers to approve military action overseas, which were further outlined in three consultation papers published in October.

High public approval ratings for Brown in the first months of his premiership led to speculation that he might call an early general election in late 2007. His popularity was in part due to his response to domestic crises, including the attempted terrorist attacks in London and Glasgow, extensive flooding in June and an outbreak of foot and mouth disease in August. This was compounded by his influence in securing a UN resolution at the end of July to send international troops to Darfur, Sudan, to help end the humanitarian crisis. However, following the announcement of new policy initiatives by the Conservative Party, including an increase in the threshold for inheritance tax and a levy on business executives with non-domicile status, who benefited from favourable income tax rules in the United Kingdom, Brown's standing in opinion polls declined. His political reputation was adversely affected by his belated confirmation in October that there would not be an early general election, and the Government suffered a further reverse with the admission in November that two compact discs containing the personal and banking details of 25m. individuals in the child benefit system had been lost by HM Revenue and Customs. Also in November the Labour Party was embroiled in a second funding scandal, when it was revealed that donations totalling £670,000 by a property developer, David Abrahams, were illegally channelled through third parties. The General-Secretary of the Labour Party, Peter Watt, submitted his resignation and Brown pledged to return the money. The Electoral Commission requested that the Metropolitan Police conduct an investigation into possible illegal party funding. However, in May 2009 the Crown Prosecution Service announced that no charges were to be brought in relation to Abrahams' donations.

In November 2007 the legislative reforms planned by the Government during the following 12 months were presented in the Queen's Speech. They included a further extension of counter-terrorism powers, restrictions on the entry requirements for migrant workers from countries outside of the European Economic Area (EEA—comprising the 27 member states of the EU, as well as Iceland, Liechtenstein and Norway) and reforms to the education system. The new Counter-Terrorism Bill, which was published in January 2008, contained provisions for the extension of the maximum period of pre-charge detention of terrorist suspects from 28 to 42 days in exceptional circumstances, subject to judicial and parliamentary approval. Although this was significantly shorter than the 56 days that had previously been under consideration, it provoked intense criticism from both opposition MPs and a number of Labour backbenchers. Meanwhile, in October 2007 Campbell unexpectedly announced his resignation as Leader of the Liberal Democrats, following criticism of his performance by some senior party members. He was replaced in mid-December by Nick Clegg.

In January 2008 the Secretary of State for Work and Pensions, Peter Hain (who concurrently held the post of Secretary of State for Wales), resigned following allegations of financial impropriety concerning donations to his campaign for election as Deputy Leader of the Labour Party. In a subsequent cabinet reorganization, James Purnell (hitherto Secretary of State for Culture, Media and Sport) was appointed to replace Hain. The Chief Secretary for the Treasury, Andy Burnham, assumed Purnell's portfolio, while Paul Murphy rejoined the Cabinet as Secretary of State for Wales.

In mid-February 2008 the Government announced the nationalization of a major commercial bank, Northern Rock, which had received emergency funds from the Bank of England in late 2007, owing to credit problems precipitated by the US mortgage crisis. Despite opposition from the Conservative Party, the Banking (Special Provisions) Bill was approved by the House of Commons on 20 February, by 293 votes to 167. The bill received royal assent on the following day.

Local elections on 1 May 2008 demonstrated the decline in popularity of the Government, which was exacerbated by public opposition to the abolition of the 10 pence starting rate of income tax in April 2008, which adversely affected those on low wages. At elections to 159 councils in England and Wales the Labour Party suffered significant losses, losing a total of 331 seats and nine councils. The Conservative Party performed well, gaining 294 seats and 12 councils, while the Liberal Democrats made a net gain of one council. In separate elections for the Mayor of London, the Conservative Party candidate, Boris Johnson, defeated the incumbent, Ken Livingstone of the Labour Party, winning 53.2% of the votes cast under a supplementary vote system. At a by-election in May for the vacant parliamentary seat of Crewe and Nantwich (which had been held by the previous, Labour Party MP since 1983) the Conservative Party candidate emerged victorious, winning by a large majority. At a separate by-election in Henley the following month, the Conservative Party candidate was returned with an increased majority, while the Labour Party candidate received fewer votes than the candidates of both the Green Party and the British National Party.

Despite widespread cross-party opposition, in June 2008 the Government's controversial Counter-Terrorism Bill, which contained provisions for the extension of the maximum period of detention for terrorist suspects from 28 to 42 days in exceptional circumstances, was narrowly approved by the House of Commons, with the support of members of the Democratic Unionist Party. The following day David Davis, the Conservative Party's spokesman on home affairs, unexpectedly announced his resignation from the Commons in order to prompt a by-election, citing his desire to focus attention on the perceived 'erosion of civil liberties in Britain'. He was immediately replaced as the Conservative Party's spokesman on home affairs. The Labour Party and the Liberal Democrats declined to field a candidate for the by-election, which took place in mid-July; Davis was re-elected by a large majority, with a turn-out of 34.5%. In October 2008 the House of Lords overwhelmingly rejected the proposals for an extension of the detention period for terrorist suspects, which were subsequently omitted from the Counter-Terrorism Bill; the bill was given royal assent in November.

Support for Brown's leadership within the parliamentary party declined further in July 2008, following the loss to the SNP of a by-election in Glasgow East, a constituency the Labour Party had won by a large majority at the general election of 2005. The by-election took place shortly after the resignation of Wendy Alexander as Leader of the Labour Party in Scotland at the end of June 2008. Alexander, regarded as a close associate of Brown, had been the subject of continued allegations of irregularities in the financing of her leadership campaign, which led to a one-day suspension from the Scottish Parliament imposed by the standards committee.

Media speculation regarding a potential leadership challenge, notably by David Miliband, extended until the Labour Party conference in September 2008, where Brown's speech was well-received. In early October, in a cabinet reorganization, Brown unexpectedly appointed Mandelson, who had served as the European Commissioner responsible for trade since 2004, to succeed John Hutton as Secretary of State for Business, Enterprise and Regulatory Reform. Hutton, in turn, was appointed as Secretary of State for Defence, in place of Des Browne. Geoff Hoon became Secretary of State for Transport, replacing Kelly, whose resignation had been made public in September. A new Department of Climate Change and Energy was created: Ed Miliband, previously Chancellor of the Duchy of Lancaster and Minister for the Cabinet Office, assumed responsibility for the new portfolio. Brown's political reputation was enhanced in late 2008 by his response to the global financial crisis, as he played a significant role in international efforts to co-ordinate measures to address the global economic downturn. In November the Labour Party won a by-election in Glenrothes, Scotland.

In December 2008 a senior Conservative Party MP, Damian Green, was arrested by police, following allegations that he had solicited the disclosure of information by a civil servant in the Home Office. The arrest provoked vehement criticism of both the Government and the House of Commons authorities after it was revealed that police officers had conducted a search of Green's parliamentary office without a warrant, which, it was claimed, undermined the principle of parliamentary privilege. Following calls for his resignation by several MPs on the grounds that he had failed in his duty to protect Parliament, the Speaker of the House of Commons, Michael Martin, was forced to issue a statement in which he denied having personally given permission for the search to be carried out. In April 2009 the Crown Prosecution Service announced that no charges were to be brought against Green in relation to the allegations.

The trials of two men arrested in June 2007 on suspicion of plotting to detonate explosive devices at locations in London and Glasgow (see above) began at a court in London in October 2008. At the trial's conclusion in December, one of the men, Bilal Abdulla, was convicted of conspiracy to murder and conspiracy to cause explosions, and was sentenced to 32 years' imprisonment. However, the other defendant, Muhammad Asha, was acquitted of all charges.

Meanwhile, from early 2008 the popularity of the Government and the wider reputation of parliamentarians were adversely affected by the publication of a series of media reports detailing expense claims submitted by MPs of both major parties, including some members of the Government. In January a former Conservative Party chief whip, Derek Conway, was suspended from the House of Commons for 10 days after an investigation by the parliamentary Standards and Privileges Committee found that he had made excessive payments to his two sons for work as parliamentary researchers. Conway denied any wrongdoing, but was subsequently expelled from the parliamentary Conservative Party. In May the High Court rejected an appeal by the Speaker of the Commons, Martin, against a decision by the Information Tribunal to allow the full disclosure of expense claims made by 14 prominent politicians, including Brown, Blair and Cameron, which had been requested by a group of journalists in 2005 under the Freedom of Information Act; the details of the expense claims were disclosed later that month. Further revelations in late 2008 and early 2009 regarding allowances for secondary residences implicated senior members of both the Labour Party and the Conservative Party and precipitated calls for a comprehensive reform of the system of parliamentary expenses. In March 2009 it was reported that the Secretary of State for the Home Department, Smith, had registered a house in London owned by her sister as her primary residence and claimed expense payments for the upkeep of her family home, situated in her constituency in Worcestershire. The following month Smith was forced to repay an expense payment she had received in April 2008, following revelations that her husband, whom she employed as a parliamentary assistant, had included charges for access to two adult films in the original claim.

Later in April 2009 Brown announced proposals for a reform of the expenses system, including the replacement of the current system of expenses by a standard daily allowance for attending Parliament. However, both the Conservative Party and the Liberal Democrats refused to support the proposal, which was subsequently withdrawn from reforms due to be considered by members of the Commons in early May. The reforms, which included new regulations requiring the submission of receipts for all items included in expense claims, as well as the publication of details regarding income earned by MPs from activities separate from their parliamentary role, were approved; however, no agreement was reached over a reform of second-home allowances, which were the subject of an ongoing inquiry by the independent public advisory body, the Committee on Standards in Public Life.

In mid-May 2009 MPs were subject to sustained criticism, following a series of reports published by a national newspaper, *The Daily Telegraph*, which detailed expense claims made by more than 100 MPs from the three main parties. Most notably, it was alleged that two Labour Party MPs had claimed money towards interest payments on mortgages which had already been paid off; the two MPs in question were subsequently suspended from the parliamentary Labour Party. Days later further allegations regarding second-homes allowance claims prompted the resignation of an Under-Secretary of State in the Ministry of Justice, Shahid Malik, pending an inquiry; Malik denied any impropriety. Meanwhile, a Conservative Party MP, Andrew Mackay, resigned as parliamentary adviser to the party leader, Cameron, following reports that he and his wife, also a Conservative Party MP, had each registered a different property as their primary residence, thus enabling them to claim second-home allowances for the upkeep of two separate properties. Later in May a substantial number of MPs from all three main parties, including the Liberal Democrat leader, Clegg, expressed support for a proposed motion of no confidence in Martin, who had been heavily criticized for his handling of events relating to the revelations regarding parliamentary expenses. The following day Martin announced his intention to resign both as Speaker of the Commons and as an MP in June.

At the end of January 2009 workers at an oil refinery in Lincolnshire began an unauthorized strike over allegations that an Italian company sub-contracted to undertake construction work at the refinery had discriminated against local workers by recruiting its staff directly from Italy and Portugal. The initial strike provoked several others during the following week at oil refineries, power stations and chemical plants across the United Kingdom. The Prime Minister criticized those leading the strikes, stating that unauthorized industrial action was 'not defensible', while the Secretary of State for Business, Enterprise and Regulatory Reform, Mandelson, denied that the company concerned had discriminated against local workers and insisted that the terms under which the Italian and Portuguese contractors had been employed conformed to EU regulations. Under an agreement negotiated with the unions, the strike action was abandoned in February after additional jobs were made available to British workers.

In April 2009 a meeting of the heads of state and of government of the Group of 20 leading industrialized and developing nations (G20, see p. 430) was held in London to discuss the global financial crisis. Questions were subsequently raised over the policing of the protests surrounding the meeting, following the death of a man in the financial district of London after he had been struck by a police officer. The Independent Police Complaints Commission launched investigations into the death and other allegations of police brutality, while an independent review of police tactics at public protests, including the controversial strategy of detaining protesters for hours behind police cordons, was undertaken at the request of the Metropolitan Police. Two parliamentary committees also heard evidence regarding police tactics at the protest.

In April 2009 one of Brown's senior advisers, Damian McBride, was forced to resign, following newspaper reports alleging that McBride had used an email account in the Prime Minister's Office to send messages to a Labour Party activist that contained false rumours of improprieties in the personal lives of a number of Conservative MPs for potential use on an internet site supportive of the Labour Party.

Later in April 2009 the announcement of the budget included a controversial proposal to increase the highest rate of income tax to 50%, despite the Labour Party's 2005 election manifesto commitment not to raise taxes during the ensuing Parliament, as well as measures to create jobs and assist business, including an incentive scheme to promote the purchase of new cars. Owing to the depth of the economic recession, the Chancellor of the Exchequer, Darling, announced that the Government would be forced to borrow record sums, resulting in a high fiscal deficit and level of public indebtedness. The Confederation of British Industry, as well as the Conservative Party and the Liberal Democrats, criticized the proposed time-scale for bringing public finances under control and questioned the forecasts for medium-term economic growth. These concerns were reiterated by a cross-party parliamentary committee the following month.

At the end of April 2009 the House of Commons approved a Liberal Democrat motion to allow veterans of the Brigade of Gurkhas who had retired from the British Army before 1997 the right to permanent residence in the United Kingdom, despite the Government's objections. The Government had introduced the right for Gurkhas who retired after 1997 to settle in the United Kingdom in 2004. The approval of the motion, which received the support of 28 Labour Party MPs, marked the first defeat the Government had suffered in the Commons since Brown assumed the premiership in June 2007. In May 2009 the Government announced that Gurkha veterans who had served for at least four years would be permitted to settle in the United Kingdom.

In 1920, faced with mounting popular support for independence in Ireland, where a guerrilla campaign was being waged by the clandestine Irish Republican Army (IRA), in an attempt to force British withdrawal, the British Government conceded to demands for Home Rule, but only to a limited extent, since this was strongly opposed by Protestants in the province of Ulster, who did not wish to become part of a Catholic-dominated all-Ireland state. The Government of Ireland Act (1920) thus provided for two parliaments in Ireland: one in Dublin, for 26 of the 32 counties of Ireland, which obtained dominion status as the Irish Free State, now Ireland (q.v.), in 1922, and one in Belfast, for the remaining six counties, which collectively became known as Northern Ireland and remained an integral part of the United Kingdom.

With the support of the Protestant majority in Northern Ireland, the Ulster Unionist Council (UUC), which had campaigned for the continuation of union with Great Britain, retained permanent control of the Belfast Parliament. Northern Ireland was governed by a one-party administration, with an all-unionist Cabinet headed by a provincial Prime Minister. The British monarch was represented by a Governor. Since Catholics were not only effectively excluded from political power, but also suffered discrimination in civil matters, a state of sectarian tension continued.

During the late 1960s an active civil rights movement emerged, which sought to end the Catholics' grievances by non-violent means. However, Protestant extremists viewed the movement as a republican threat, and resorted to violence against Catholic activists. The IRA was originally a small element in the civil rights movement, but, after increasingly serious disturbances, a breakaway group, calling itself the Provisional IRA, embarked on a campaign of violence with the aim of reuniting Ireland on its own terms. In April 1969 the Northern Ireland Government requested that British army units be assigned to protect important installations and in August the British and Northern Ireland Governments agreed that all security forces in the territory would be placed under British command. In March 1972, as a result of increased violence, the British Government assumed direct responsibility for law and order. Finding this unacceptable, the Northern Ireland Government resigned. The British Government prorogued the Northern Ireland Parliament and introduced direct rule from London, thus alienating many Protestants.

In 1973 new legislation abolished the office of Governor and the Northern Ireland Parliament, and provided for new constitutional arrangements. In June elections were conducted for a 78-member Northern Ireland Assembly, and an Executive was subsequently constituted from its members. An important part of this new 'power-sharing' arrangement was the establishment of a limited role for the Irish Government in Northern Ireland's affairs. Accordingly, in December, at Sunningdale (in southern England), the British and Irish Governments and the Northern Ireland Executive finalized an agreement to form a Council of Ireland (with members drawn from the Governments of Northern Ireland and Ireland), which would have a range of economic and cultural responsibilities in both parts of Ireland. However, the Sunningdale Agreement and the new devolved authority in Northern Ireland were rejected by many Protestants, and led, in 1974, to a general strike. A state of emergency was declared and the Executive was forced to resign. The Assembly was prorogued, and Northern Ireland returned to direct rule by the British Government. The collapse of the Sunningdale Agreement led to a rise in popularity of the more extreme Democratic Unionist Party (DUP—founded in 1971, and led by Rev. Dr Ian Paisley), which established itself as the main rival to the previously dominant Ulster Unionist Party (UUP—the 'official' Unionists).

Throughout the 1970s the Provisional IRA and the Irish National Liberation Army (INLA, which emerged in 1975) continued their terrorist attacks on both British military and civilian targets, while Protestant 'loyalist' paramilitary groups engaged in attacks on Roman Catholics.

Discussions between the Governments of the United Kingdom and Ireland in 1984–85 culminated in the signing of the Anglo-Irish Agreement in November 1985. The Agreement established the Intergovernmental Conference, through which British and Irish ministers were to meet regularly to discuss political, security, legal and cross-border matters relating to Northern Ireland. While giving the Irish Government a formal consultative role in Northern Ireland affairs, the Agreement recognized that the constitutional status of Northern Ireland remained unchanged and would not be altered without the consent of a majority of Northern Ireland's population. The Agreement had the support of the predominantly Catholic Social Democratic and Labour Party (SDLP), and was approved by the Irish and British Parliaments. However, it was strongly opposed by most unionist politicians, who organized mass demonstrations and violent protests against the Agreement. In June 1986 the Northern Ireland Assembly was dissolved.

The Provisional IRA's campaign of violence in Northern Ireland escalated during 1987, and in 1988 IRA members conducted a successful campaign against British military targets, particularly in Western Europe. Between late 1988 and early 1991 a series of terrorist attacks took place against British Army personnel and politicians in both Great Britain and in continental Europe.

In September 1989 the Irish Government demanded a review of the Ulster Defence Regiment (UDR), the main security force in Northern Ireland, following allegations that it had passed information to loyalist paramilitary groups, which had subsequently been used to target and murder members of the IRA. In May 1990 the allegations were confirmed. During the resulting prosecution of a member of the Ulster Defence Association (UDA) in January 1992, fresh evidence emerged of collusion between the security forces and loyalist paramilitary organizations, and details of events leading to the murder by the UDA in 1989 of a republican lawyer, Patrick Finucane, were revealed. In June 1999 a former British soldier, William Stobie, was charged with Finucane's murder. He subsequently claimed to have been working as a police informer at the time and to have warned them of the impending killing. Furthermore, it was revealed that Stobie had confessed to his involvement in the murder to the Royal Ulster Constabulary (RUC—the Northern Ireland police force) nine years earlier. In November 2001, however, Stobie was acquitted of any involvement in Finucane's murder, after it was ruled that, owing to medical reasons, the main prosecution witness was incapable of testifying. In August 2002, at the behest of the British Government, a former Canadian supreme court judge, Peter Cory, began investigating whether six cases where collusion between the security forces and paramilitary organizations had been alleged (including the Finucane murder) would be subject to public inquiries. Meanwhile, in December 2001 Stobie was assassinated by loyalist paramilitaries.

In April 2003 the interim results of an inquiry established in 1999, under the Commissioner of the Metropolitan Police Force, Sir John Stevens, were published. Stevens stated that he had found evidence of 'widespread collusion' between the security forces and loyalist paramilitaries in the murder of innocent civilians, and that the murders of Finucane and Adam Lambert, who had been killed by the UDA in 1987, could have been prevented. The report concluded that the RUC's investigation of Finucane's murder should have resulted in the early detection and arrest of his killers, and it was highly critical of the withholding of intelligence and evidence by the RUC and the British Army's Force Research Unit (FRU—a secret agency that recruited and controlled agents within loyalist and republican paramilitary organizations). Stevens also announced that a number of investigations remained ongoing and that 57 files had been sent to the Northern Ireland Director of Public Prosecutions. In May 2003 Kenneth Barrett, a senior member of the UDA, was arrested and charged with Finucane's murder. In June 2007 the Director of Public Prosecutions announced that no further prosecutions would be brought in the Finucane case.

In July 2003 the European Court of Human Rights in Strasbourg, France, ruled that the United Kingdom was guilty of a serious breach of the Human Rights Convention for failing to carry out an adequate investigation into Finucane's death. In March 2004 the Finucane family launched a court action against the British Government to force it to publish the Cory report and to set up a public inquiry into the murders of Patrick Finucane and three other people in the late 1990s. The report was published on 1 April 2004 and inquiries were immediately set up into the deaths of these people. However, a public investigation into Finucane's killing was delayed until Barrett's trial had been completed. In September Barrett was convicted of Finucane's murder, having pleaded guilty; he was sentenced to 22 years' imprisonment. In late September the Secretary of State for Northern Ireland, Paul Murphy, announced that an inquiry would be held under restrictions after the introduction of new legislation intended to address national security requirements. When the proposed bill on inquiries was announced in November, the Finucane family expressed concern that a large proportion of evidence in the case would have to be considered in private under its terms. The bill was also criticized by Cory and human rights organizations. Nevertheless, the Inquiries Act received royal assent in April 2005. The Finucane family continued to campaign for a public inquiry and to oppose any inquiry held under the terms of the Inquiries Act.

In January 1990, meanwhile, the British Government launched an initiative to convene meetings between representatives from the major political parties in Northern Ireland and the British and Irish Governments to discuss devolution in Northern Ireland and the future of its relations with Ireland. Sinn Féin (the political wing of the Provisional IRA) was to be excluded from the talks because of its refusal to denounce the IRA's campaign of violence. Bilateral discussions between the British Government and the DUP, the UUP, the SDLP and the Alliance Party eventually began in April 1991, and talks subsequently commenced between all the Northern Ireland parties and the Irish Government. The principal point of contention was the unionists' demand that Ireland hold a referendum on Articles 2 and 3 of its Constitution, which laid claim to the territory of Northern Ireland. The Irish Government, however, remained unwilling to make such a concession except as part of an overall settlement. In the absence of an agreement, the negotiations formally ended in November 1992, and the Anglo-Irish Conference resumed.

In August 1992 the British Government announced the proscription of the UDA under the Emergency Provisions Act, a measure that was widely regarded as long overdue in the light of the UDA's paramilitary activities from the early 1970s onwards (some committed under the name of Ulster Freedom Fighters—UFF). In late 1993 and early 1994 police in Great Britain made several large seizures of explosives, which the Government claimed to be evidence of improving anti-terrorist surveillance. During this period frequent discoveries of IRA devices and bomb alerts caused much disruption, especially to public transport services.

In October 1993 the British and Irish Prime Ministers, John Major and Albert Reynolds, issued a joint statement setting out the principles on which future negotiations were to be based. The statement emphasized the precondition that Sinn Féin permanently renounce violence before being admitted to the negotiations. In December Major and Reynolds made a joint declaration, known as the 'Downing Street Declaration', which provided a specific framework for a peace settlement. The initiative, which was widely supported by opposition parties in Britain and Ireland, referred to the possibility of a united Ireland and accepted the legitimacy of self-determination, while insisting on majority consent within Northern Ireland. The DUP, the UUP and Sinn Féin rejected the document, which effectively removed any confidence of achieving an imminent peace settlement. However, the British and Irish Governments reiterated their intention to pursue the peace process.

On 31 August 1994 the IRA announced 'a complete cessation of violence'. On 13 October the loyalist paramilitary groups declared a suspension of military activity, which was effectively to be linked to that of the IRA. Later that month Major announced new measures to restart the peace process, adopting the 'working assumption' that the IRA cease-fire was permanent. The first public meeting between Sinn Féin and government officials was held in December, marking the start of exploratory talks between the two sides. In February 1995 Major and the new Irish Prime Minister, John Bruton, presented a Framework Document, together with a separate British government paper on a new Northern Ireland Assembly. The Framework Document reaffirmed the principles of the Downing Street Declaration, and included provisions for the co-operation and involvement of both Governments in the peace settlement. In addition, the Document proposed the establishment of a cross-border body in which elected representatives of the Irish Parliament and a Northern Ireland Assembly might create and implement policy on issues agreed by the two Governments, in consultation with the Northern Ireland parties. The proposals for the Northern Ireland Assembly envisaged an elected authority with wide legislative and executive responsibility (except, initially, over taxation, and law and order), although it was to be monitored by a three-member elected panel. Both Governments emphasized that any final agreement about the proposals was to be subject to parliamentary approval and popular consent by means of a referendum.

Despite a positive Sinn Féin response to the Framework Document, the issue of decommissioning paramilitary weapons remained the major obstacle to peace negotiations. The Government repeatedly objected to Sinn Féin's linking of IRA decommissioning with the demilitarization of Northern Ireland. In May 1995, having agreed that these would be discussed as separate issues, the Secretary of State for Northern Ireland, Sir Patrick Mayhew, and the Sinn Féin President, Gerry Adams, met (the most senior-level encounter of the two sides in 20 years) at an investment conference for Northern Ireland, held in Washington, DC, USA. Further political dialogue was hindered by Sinn Féin's opposition to the British Government's insistence that decommissioning by paramilitary organizations be a precondition to conducting all-party negotiations.

In November 1995 the British and Irish Governments agreed to initiate preliminary talks (provisionally scheduled to commence in February 1996) with all the parties in Northern Ireland and to establish an international commission to assess the practicalities of the decommissioning of armaments and other aspects of the peace process. US President Bill Clinton endorsed this initiative during a visit later that month, and the commission, chaired by one of Clinton's advisers, George Mitchell, began meetings with all sides involved in the peace process in December. The final report of the international commission was issued in January 1996, and recommended proceeding with all-party talks on the condition that all sides endorse the eventual complete disarmament of paramilitary organizations, the renunciation of violence and the cessation of paramilitary 'punishment' attacks. According to the report, arms decommissioning was to be considered in parallel with the negotiations, while the eventual surrender of weaponry was to be conducted under international supervision, with those involved being free from prosecution. The report was generally supported by all sides.

In February 1996 the IRA abruptly terminated its cease-fire by exploding a large bomb in London. The organization blamed the British Government for the resumption of hostilities, citing its inflexible response to the Mitchell report. The security forces subsequently uncovered details of a revived bombing campaign in Great Britain. Bruton and Major declared that they would suspend all ministerial dialogue with Sinn Féin, but would intensify efforts to achieve a peaceful settlement. At the end of the month the leaders announced an initiative to pursue the peace process, incorporating nationalist and unionist demands. Consultations were to commence immediately on an electoral format to establish a forum for intersectoral dialogue prior to the initiation of comprehensive political negotiations, to be based on the 1995 Framework Document. In March the British Cabinet approved a 'hybrid' electoral system for the Northern Ireland forum, in an attempt to accommodate demands from all sides and to ensure a wide representation of the region's political groupings. Participants in the all-party negotiations were to be selected from among the 110 forum members. In the election, held on 30 May, the UUP secured 24% of the votes cast and the largest number of seats (30), while the DUP and the SDLP took 21 and 17 seats respectively. Sinn Féin's 15% share of the votes secured the party 17 seats. In addition, seven seats were won by the Alliance Party, three by the United Kingdom Unionist Party (UKUP) and two each by the Progressive Unionist Party (PUP), the Ulster Democratic Party (UDP), the Women's Coalition of Northern Ireland and representatives of Labour (a coalition of left-wing individuals and associations). The multi-party discussions, which commenced on 10 June, were undermined by Sinn Féin's exclusion, in the absence of a new IRA cease-fire declaration, and by unionist opposition to the appointment of Mitchell as Chairman, which they claimed was part of a nationalist agenda. Further political uncertainty followed an IRA bomb attack in Manchester in June.

In July 1996 political events in Northern Ireland were dominated by sectarian disputes regarding the organization of traditional Protestant marches. The peace process suffered a further reverse when the SDLP announced that it was to withdraw from the recently elected forum, owing to the British Government's management of the crisis to which the disputes gave rise.

In October 1996 the UUP and the SDLP agreed on a draft agenda, based on the provisions of the Mitchell report, to enable substantive multi-party talks to proceed without being dominated by the issue of weapons decommissioning. In November Sinn Féin revealed a set of proposals, formulated with the SDLP in order to bolster the peace process, which included the implementation by the British Government of confidence-building measures, such as the release of IRA prisoners, and a guarantee that Sinn Féin would be admitted to the talks in the event of a renewed IRA cease-fire. In response, Major defined the terms by which the party could join the talks, namely, a credible and lasting restoration of the IRA cease-fire and an end to all paramilitary training activities and punishment attacks. In January 1997 all-party talks resumed, but were suspended in March until after the general election in the United Kingdom, scheduled to be held in May. Prior to the poll the IRA undertook a co-ordinated programme of disruption in Great Britain, while sectarian tensions increased in Northern Ireland.

In the general election, held on 1 May 1997, the UUP secured 10 of the 18 seats available, with 32.7% of the votes cast in Northern Ireland. Sinn Féin regained a parliamentary mandate, winning two seats (with 16.1% of the votes). The SDLP won three seats, with 24.1% of the votes. The DUP lost two of its previously held seats, securing two seats (13.6%), and the UKUP won its first seat in a general election (1.6%).

The newly elected Labour Government generated renewed optimism that a peace settlement could be achieved. The Prime Minister, Tony Blair, proposed a timetable for the talks, and reiterated that he envisaged their conclusion no later than May 1998, when the results were to be put to a popular referendum. In June 1997 the British and Irish Governments announced a new initiative to accelerate the peace process, whereby the decommissioning of paramilitary weapons, together with other confidence-building measures, would be undertaken concurrently with political negotiations, in an attempt to facilitate Sinn Féin's participation in the process, and clarified that Sinn Féin would be eligible to join substantive negotiations six weeks after a new IRA cease-fire announcement.

In July 1997 the IRA announced a restoration of its cease-fire. A few days later the Irish and British Governments issued a joint statement that the all-party negotiations would commence on 15 September, with the participation of Sinn Féin. At the same time, however, the unionist parties rejected the measures for weapons decommissioning that had been formulated by the two Governments. At the end of August the new Secretary of State for Northern Ireland, Mo Mowlam, concluded that the restoration of the IRA cease-fire was 'unequivocal' and invited Sinn Féin to join the talks. Accordingly, in September Sinn Féin endorsed the so-called 'Mitchell principles', which committed participants to accepting the outcome of the peace process and renouncing violence as a means of punishment or resolving problems. The UUP, together with the DUP and UKUP, which had already declared their boycott of any discussions with Sinn Féin, and other loyalist representatives, failed to attend the opening session of the talks when they resumed in September, owing partly to a statement by the IRA that undermined Sinn Féin's endorsement of the Mitchell principles. The talks were further jeopardized by the explosion of a republican bomb in Co Armagh for which a proscribed dissident paramilitary faction, the Continuity Army Council, claimed responsibility. Nevertheless, the UUP rejoined the peace negotiations a few days later. In late September all eight parties to the talks signed a procedural agreement to pursue substantive negotiations. At the same time the Independent International Commission on Decommissioning (IICD) was inaugurated, under the chairmanship of the former head of the Canadian armed forces, Gen. John de Chastelain. The first meeting between a British Prime Minister and Sinn Féin leaders in more than 70 years took place at the talks in October, when Blair held private discussions with Adams and Martin McGuinness. In December the murder of the leader of the proscribed Loyalist Volunteer Force (LVF), Billy Wright, in the Maze Prison by INLA prisoners prompted an escalation of sectarian violence throughout Northern Ireland. In January 1998 Mowlam took the unprecedented action of meeting loyalist paramilitary prisoners within the Maze prison, which secured their continued endorsement of PUP and UDP participation in the peace discussions.

In January 1998 Blair and the Irish Prime Minister, Bertie Ahern, published a document outlining a framework for negotiations: this envisaged 'balanced constitutional change' by both Governments and proposed a devolved form of government within Northern Ireland. After intensive negotiations, on 10 April a settlement was announced. The Good Friday Agreement (or Belfast Agreement) envisaged radical reform of the political structures of Northern Ireland, its relations with Ireland, and its constitutional standing within the United Kingdom. The main provisions of the Agreement were as follows: the establishment of a 108-member elected Northern Ireland Assembly, with authority to legislate on all domestic matters currently administered by the Northern Ireland Office; an Executive Committee, to be elected by the Assembly and headed by a First Minister and Deputy First Minister; an obligation that the Assembly establish, within one year, a North/South Ministerial Council at which representatives of the Irish Government and the executive authority in Northern Ireland might consider issues of cross-border concern; regular meetings of representatives of the Irish Government with members of the British Parliament, the Northern Ireland Assembly and other regional assemblies of the United Kingdom, under a new British-Irish Council, with the objective of promoting co-operation, information exchange and agreement on issues of mutual interest; amendment of Articles 2 and 3 of the Irish Constitution; replacement of the 1985 Anglo-Irish Agreement with a new bilateral accord, incorporating a British-Irish Intergovernmental Council to oversee the Assembly and North/South Council; and a commitment by all parties to achieve the decommissioning of paramilitary weapons within two years. David Trimble, the Leader of the UUP, secured the critical support of his party for the settlement, although several dissident UUP politicians later joined the DUP and UKUP in their campaign to prevent an endorsement of the accord, and the Protestant Orange Order urged its members to oppose the Agreement. Sinn Féin approved the accord. Some 71.1% of voters in Northern Ireland and 94.4% of voters in Ireland approved the proposed peace settlement in referendums conducted on 22 May, securing its immediate future. Parties in Northern Ireland began almost immediately to prepare for the elections to the Northern Ireland Assembly, which were scheduled to be held on 25 June. Voting was to be conducted using the single transferable vote system of proportional representation, providing for six members to be elected from each of the 18 Westminster parliamentary constituencies, with a broad representation of political preferences.

In the elections to the Northern Ireland Assembly, conducted on 25 June 1998, the UUP won 28 of the 108 seats, while the SDLP took 24, despite having won the largest share of first-preference votes under the new voting system. Sinn Féin won 18 Assembly seats. Those opposed to the Good Friday Agreement secured a total of 28 seats, including 20 representatives of the DUP, five of the UKUP and three dissident UUP politicians. The remaining seats were won by the Alliance Party (six), the PUP (two) and the Women's Coalition (two). At the inaugural meeting of the Assembly, on 1 July, Trimble was elected as First Minister of the executive body, while Seamus Mallon of the SDLP was elected as Deputy First Minister. Sectarian violence soon threatened to disrupt the peace process following confrontations between the security forces and members of the Orange Order who, in defiance of the newly established Parades Commission, sought to march its traditional route along the predominantly Roman Catholic-inhabited Garvaghy Road in Portadown, Co Armagh, to the church at nearby Drumcree. However, following the deaths of three young Roman Catholics in a petrol bomb attack in Ballymoney, Co Antrim, in July the majority of the loyalists in Portadown abandoned their protest. In August the peace process again came under threat when 29 people in Omagh, Co Tyrone, were killed by an explosive device, planted by a dissident republican group, the Real IRA, representing the single largest toll of deaths in any incident since the onset of unrest associated with Northern Ireland. Later that month Ahern announced a series of anti-terrorism measures in an effort to facilitate convictions against terrorists based in Ireland. Similarly, Blair announced legislation, which was approved in September, including heightened powers to convict anyone conspiring within the United Kingdom to commit terrorist offences.

Progress in the peace process continued to be obstructed throughout late 1998 by a dispute between unionists and Sinn Féin concerning the decommissioning of paramilitary weapons, with Trimble insisting that the admittance of Sinn Féin representatives to the Executive Committee be conditional on progress in the demilitarization of the IRA. For its part, Sinn Féin insisted that the Good Friday Agreement did not specify when decommissioning should begin, only that it should be completed by May 2000. As a result of the dispute the deadline of 21 October 1998 for the formation of the Executive Committee and the North/South bodies was not met. In December agreement was finally reached on the responsibilities of the 10 government departments of the Executive Committee and of six North/South 'implementation' bodies. This was endorsed by the Northern Ireland Assembly in February 1999.

During 1999 the date for the devolution of powers to the new Northern Ireland institutions, envisaged as 10 March in the Good Friday Agreement, was postponed several times, and negotiations were halted in July when Trimble announced that the UUP would not participate in a devolved administration with Sinn Féin until some decommissioning had taken place. A review of the peace process, headed by George Mitchell, began in September. In that month the former Chairman of the Conservative Party, Chris Patten, who had been appointed in April 1998 to head an independent commission charged with conducting a review of policing in Northern Ireland, published his report. Recommended changes to the RUC included the establishment of an elected body of representatives, drawn from all sections of the community, to which the new force would be accountable, the active recruitment of Roman Catholic officers in order that the force should achieve a balanced representation, and a reduction in the number of serving officers from 13,500 to 7,500, subject to the successful conclusion of the peace process. The report provoked anger from unionists, who particularly objected to plans to change the force's name, oath and symbols. Sinn Féin, meanwhile, renewed its demand that the force be disbanded.

In November 1999 Mitchell concluded the review of the peace process, producing an agreement providing for the devolution of powers to the Executive Committee. The agreement followed a statement by the IRA that it would appoint a representative to enter discussions with the IICD. Trimble persuaded his party to approve the agreement. On 29 November the Northern Ireland Assembly convened to appoint the 10-member Executive Committee. On 2 December power was officially transferred from Westminster to the new Northern Ireland executive at Stormont Castle and, in accordance with the Good Friday Agreement, the Irish Government removed from the Irish Constitution its territorial claim over Northern Ireland. In mid-December the inaugural meeting was held of the North/South Ministerial Council. The British-Irish Council met for the first time later that month. In late December Peter Mandelson, the new Secretary of State for Northern Ireland, announced a review of security procedures in Northern Ireland and the withdrawal of some 2,000 troops from Northern Ireland, and in January 2000 he adopted the majority of the recommendations contained in the Patten report, provoking an angry response from unionists. In that month Adams dismissed the possibility of immediate IRA decommissioning, and a report by the IICD confirmed that there had been no disarmament. With the prospect of the collapse of the peace process, the British and Irish Governments engaged in intensive negotiations. On 1 February the IRA released a statement giving assurances that its cease-fire would not be broken and expressing support for the peace process. However, it failed to comply with an 11 February deadline to begin decommissioning, and legislation came into effect on that day suspending the new executive, legislative and co-operative institutions and returning Northern Ireland to direct rule. The IRA subsequently announced its withdrawal from discussions with the IICD. Adams refused to participate in any further review of the peace process until the suspended institutions had been restored.

Direct talks between the British and Irish Governments and the principal parties resumed in early May 2000, with the Government promising to restore the Northern Ireland institutions on 22 May and postpone the deadline for decommissioning until June 2001, subject to a commitment by the IRA on the arms issue. On 6 May the IRA responded by offering to 'initiate a process that will completely and verifiably put arms beyond use'. Under the offer a number of IRA arms depositories were to be regularly inspected by two independent international figures, Martti Ahtisaari, the former President of Finland, and Cyril Ramaphosa, a principal figure in the South African peace process. Trimble narrowly succeeded in securing the approval of the UUP of a return to power sharing, and on 30 May power was once again transferred from Westminster to the new Northern Ireland institutions. In accordance with their continued policy of attempting to impede the functioning of the Assembly, DUP ministers agreed to retake their places in the Assembly but announced their intention periodically to resign their posts in order to disrupt parliamentary business. In June the IRA allowed three arms depositories to be inspected by Ramaphosa and Ahtisaari and announced that it had also resumed contact with the IICD. The two inspectors affirmed that the arms they had seen were 'safely and adequately stored' and that they had installed devices at the depositories, which would enable them to detect if the weapons were subsequently tampered with.

In July 2000 the decision again to prohibit the Orange Order from marching along the Garvaghy Road in Portadown provoked renewed sectarian violence and numerous attacks on the security forces. Later in that month, under the terms of the Good Friday Agreement, the final group of 86 convicted terrorists was freed from prison in Northern Ireland. Their release was widely criticized as it had been conditionally linked to the commencement of IRA arms' decommissioning, which had yet to begin. In August Mandelson warned feuding loyalist paramilitary groups that they risked further delaying IRA decommissioning if they continued their retaliatory attacks. In an attempt to quell unrest, troops were once again deployed on the streets of Belfast, and John Adair, the Leader of the UFF, who was widely believed to be responsible for many of the incidents, was arrested and imprisoned; he had been released under the provisions of the Good Friday Agreement in September 1999. Nevertheless, revenge attacks continued throughout late 2000. In December, however, the feud was declared to be at an end by three of the four groups involved.

Meanwhile, in November 2000 the Northern Ireland Policing Bill received royal assent, and later in that month the House of Lords approved controversial legislation that would enable members of the Irish Parliament to stand for election to the Northern Ireland Assembly as well as to the British Parliament.

In March 2001 the IRA unexpectedly announced that it had re-established contact with the IICD. In an attempt further to disrupt the peace process, the Real IRA exploded two bombs outside the BBC's Television Centre building in London in March and April. The incident was widely condemned by all parties democratically involved in the peace process. The Real IRA had also been responsible for four previous attacks on Great Britain during 2000 and early 2001. In May 2001 the US Government designated the Real IRA as a foreign terrorist organization and froze its assets in the USA. In April 2003 five members of the Real IRA were sentenced to terms of imprisonment ranging from 16 to 22 years for their roles in the London bombings.

At the general election to the British Parliament held on 7 June 2001 the UUP won six seats (compared with 10 in 1997), with 26.8% of the votes cast in Northern Ireland. The DUP secured five seats, gaining three at the expense of the UUP, with 22.5% of the votes cast. Sinn Féin increased its parliamentary representation, winning four seats, with 21.7% of the votes, while the SDLP took only three seats, with 21.0% of the votes. The UUP suffered a further significant reverse at local elections held in Northern Ireland later in June, with Sinn Féin and the DUP making substantial gains at the UUP's expense.

Following Trimble's announcement of his intention to resign as First Minister on 1 July 2001 if the IRA had not commenced a process of decommissioning, Blair and Ahern held emergency talks with representatives from the UUP, Sinn Féin and the SDLP in June. On 1 July Trimble duly resigned. The administrative functions of the office of the First Minister were assumed on a caretaker basis by the Minister of Enterprise, Trade and Investment, Sir Reg Empey of the UUP. (Mallon's position of Deputy First Minister became vacant, although he continued to exercise the functions of his office.) Trimble's resignation triggered a six-week period at the end of which, barring the resolution of the impasse between the parties and the election of a First Minister and Deputy First Minister, new elections to the Assembly would have to be held. Later in July the IICD stated that the IRA had yet to decommission a single weapon, and had failed to outline how it intended to put its arms beyond use.

In early August 2001 the British and Irish Governments unveiled their joint 'Proposals for the Implementation of the Good Friday Agreement'. The proposals stipulated that while decommissioning was not a precondition of the Agreement, it remained indispensable to a political resolution and must be resolved in a manner 'acceptable to and verified by the IICD'. However, while Trimble stated that he would 'carefully consider' the proposals, he remained adamant that in the continued absence of IRA decommissioning of weapons there would be no progress. A few days later both the IICD and the IRA issued statements confirming that they had agreed upon a confidential decommissioning scheme, and de Chastelain announced that he was satisfied that the IRA had begun a process that would put arms 'completely and verifiably' beyond use. Trimble described the announcement as a 'step forward', but insisted that it was not sufficient for him to retract his resignation and demanded evidence of the destruction of weapons. Faced with the impending collapse of the Northern Ireland institutions, on 10 August the British Government suspended the Northern Ireland institutions for a 24-hour period. Under a legal loophole contained within the Good Friday Agreement, this decision allowed for a six-week extension to the previously imposed deadline for the election of a First Minister and Deputy. In response to the suspension, the IRA withdrew the offer to commence the process of decommissioning.

Also in August 2001 speculation that the RUC had ignored warnings of an imminent bomb attack in Omagh, prior to the atrocity in August 1998 (see above), prompted an inquiry by the Police Ombudsman for Northern Ireland, Nuala O'Loan, into the police force's investigation of the bombing. O'Loan's report, which was published in December 2001, stated that the RUC's Special Branch had failed to pass on two separate warnings from informants, and that a number of grave errors were made during the subsequent police investigation into the attack. In mid-August the British Government had announced revised policing proposals, which envisaged the equal division of recruitment to the police force between Protestants and Roman Catholics and allowed for the possibility of ex-paramilitary prisoners sitting on the 29 District Police Partnership Boards, providing they relinquished their support for terrorist organizations. Sinn Féin had rejected the proposals before their publication and insisted that they would refuse to nominate members to the new 19-member Northern Ireland Policing Board (NIPB), which would be responsible for overseeing the police. On 4 November the RUC was officially renamed the Police Service of Northern Ireland (PSNI), and three days later the NIPB held its inaugural meeting. The two vacant Sinn Féin seats on the board were allocated to the DUP and the UUP. In early February 2002 the Chairman of the NIPB issued a joint statement on behalf of the NIPB, O'Loan and the Chief Constable of the PSNI, Sir Ronnie Flanagan (who had been criticized in O'Loan's report), which recognized that 'on the basis of the information available the Omagh bombing could not have been prevented'. Later that month Flanagan announced his resignation. Meanwhile, in January Colm Murphy, the only person to have been charged in relation to the bomb attack, was sentenced to 14 years' imprisonment by the Special Criminal Court in Dublin for conspiracy to cause an explosion. In September Hugh Orde was appointed Chief Constable of the PSNI. In August 2003 the leader of the Real IRA, Kevin McKevitt, was sentenced to 20 years' imprisonment by the Special Criminal Court in Dublin for directing a terrorist organization. Investigations into the Omagh bombing continued in 2003 and 2004 and in March 2004 one of the five men being sued by the relatives of the Omagh victims in a civil court case was sentenced to three and a half years' imprisonment for membership of the Real IRA.

Meanwhile, on 22 September 2001 Dr John Reid, who had succeeded Mandelson as Secretary of State for Northern Ireland earlier in that year (see above), announced a further 24-hour suspension of the Assembly, thus granting the parties a further six weeks in which to overcome the continuing impasse. Trimble subsequently announced that the UUP would table a motion in the Assembly to exclude the two Sinn Féin ministers from the Executive, and that if, as was almost certain, the motion was defeated and there was still no progress on the decommissioning issue by the IRA, UUP ministers would begin to withdraw from the Executive, thus precipitating its collapse. Following continued sectarian clashes in late September (for which Reid held the UDA responsible) and the murder of a journalist in Co Armagh, for which the LVF claimed responsibility, the Secretary of State announced that the British Government no longer recognized the UDA/UFF and LVF cease-fires.

In October 2001 the UUP exclusion motion was duly defeated and the three UUP ministers and the two DUP ministers resigned. Later that month the IRA and the IICD issued separate statements, which affirmed that the IRA had taken the unprecedented step of putting a significant quantity of arms, ammunition and explosives beyond use. The announcement prevented the imminent collapse of the Northern Ireland institutions and was widely welcomed by all pro-Agreement parties. Trimble immediately announced that he would reappoint the three UUP ministers to the Executive and seek re-election to the post of First Minister. On 24 October the UUP ministers resumed their posts and on the following day the DUP resumed its two portfolios. Later in October Trimble received approval from the UUP Executive to resume his post as First Minister, with the SDLP Leader-elect, Mark Durkan, announcing his intention to stand for the position of Deputy First Minister. On 2 November, however, Trimble failed in his attempt to be re-elected as First Minister. Although he secured 70.6% of the total votes cast (including all 38 nationalist votes), two anti-Agreement members of the UUP voted against Trimble, thus preventing him from obtaining the constitutionally required majority of unionists in favour of his re-election. Following intensive negotiations, three members of the independent Alliance Party and one member of the Women's Coalition agreed to redesignate themselves temporarily as unionists, and on 6 November Trimble finally regained the post of First Minister. Durkan was returned as Deputy First Minister.

In December 2001 the British Government provoked considerable controversy when it announced that it had agreed to grant Sinn Féin MPs access to the facilities of the House of Commons and that they would receive their full parliamentary allowances and travel expenses, despite the fact that they still refused to take their seats in Parliament or participate in debates, and would not swear allegiance to the Queen. In January 2002 Sinn Féin MPs occupied offices in the House of Commons for the first time.

In mid-2002, despite the announcement in April that the IRA had put a further quantity of arms, ammunition and explosives beyond use, the fragility of the peace process was underscored by unprecedented levels of street violence in north and east Belfast. Adams' refusal to testify before a US investigation into alleged IRA links with left-wing rebels in Colombia, allied with allegations of IRA involvement in the theft of documents from PSNI Special Branch offices in Belfast in March 2002 and the discovery, in June, of an IRA intelligence database listing details of more than 200 judges, politicians and members of the security forces, provoked unionist demands that Sinn Féin ministers be removed from the power-sharing Executive and further 'crisis' meetings between the British and Irish Governments.

In July 2002 the IRA apologized for the deaths and injuries of 'non-combatants' caused as a result of its actions over the previous 30 years. The sincerity of the apology was questioned by Trimble, and senior unionists were sceptical that the IRA remained committed to the peace process in the light of continued sectarian violence in Belfast, for which the UUP maintained that the IRA was primarily responsible. Earlier in July, during talks between the British and Irish Governments and the pro-Agreement parties in Belfast, Trimble had implied that UUP ministers would resign from the Executive by the end of that month if the IRA did not clearly demonstrate its commitment to a 'full transition from violence to democracy'.

Violent sectarian disturbances continued in Belfast during August 2002. Early in that month the Real IRA was suspected to have been responsible for a bomb attack in which a Protestant man was killed—the first fatality caused by the organization since the Omagh bombing in August 1998—and in mid-August 2002 a Roman Catholic was murdered in an apparent revenge act for the earlier wounding of a young Protestant. The situation was exacerbated by the escalation of a feud between rival loyalist paramilitary groups, which resulted in a number of shootings, and unionists called for the establishment of an independent body to monitor the paramilitary cease-fires. Later in that month the ruling council of the UUP, the UUC, announced that it would withdraw the UUP's ministers from the Executive in January 2003 if the IRA and Sinn Féin had not demonstrated a complete transition to democracy and non-violence.

In early October 2002 Sinn Féin's offices at the Northern Ireland Assembly were raided by police, who, as part of a major investigation into intelligence-gathering by republicans, suspected that the IRA had infiltrated the Northern Ireland Office and gained access to large numbers of confidential documents. Among a number of people detained was Sinn Féin's Head of Administration, Denis Donaldson, who was charged with possession of documents likely to be of assistance to terrorist organizations. (In 2007 the case collapsed, when it emerged that Donaldson had acted as an informant for the British security services—see below.) Trimble accused Sinn Féin of a 'massive political conspiracy' and threatened to withdraw from the Executive unless the British Government proposed the expulsion of Sinn Féin from the Assembly. Emergency talks between the British and Irish Governments and the Northern

Ireland political leaders followed; however, Blair's demands for IRA concessions on the arms issue were not met. On 11 October the two DUP ministers resigned from the Executive, and on 14 October the Assembly was suspended and direct rule imposed. In a joint statement, Blair and Ahern announced that the devolved institutions would only be restored if Sinn Féin ended its link with paramilitary organizations and Blair subsequently called on the IRA to disband. Later that month the IRA announced the suspension of all contact with the IICD and claimed that the British Government was to blame for the current crisis, having failed to honour its commitments under the Good Friday Agreement.

In May 2003 Adams stated that the IRA leadership was determined 'that there will be no activities which will undermine in any way the peace process or the Good Friday Agreement'; however, Blair cited the refusal of the IRA to give him 'absolute clarity' that it had ceased all paramilitary activity as the reason for his decision again to postpone elections. Nevertheless, the British and Irish Governments published their Joint Declaration, which included plans to reduce the security forces from 14,500 to 5,000 by April 2005; to repeal anti-terrorist legislation specific to Northern Ireland; to establish an independent international monitoring body to assess any breaches of the Good Friday Agreement; to transfer policing and judicial powers to a devolved government; and provision that terrorists who had committed crimes for which they had not yet been convicted would have their cases heard at 'special judicial tribunals'. The Declaration also urged a full and permanent cessation of all paramilitary activity, including military attacks, intelligence gathering, weapons procurement and punishment attacks.

In June 2003 Trimble secured a narrow victory at an emergency meeting of the UUC over UUP MP Jeffrey Donaldson, who had attempted to persuade the party to support a motion to reject the Joint Declaration. Donaldson, Rev. Martin Smyth (the party's President) and David Burnside subsequently resigned the UUP Westminster whip, provoking further speculation about a split within the party. Days later the three dissident MPs were suspended from the party. In July the High Court in Belfast ruled that their suspension was 'unlawful, invalid and of no force or effect', and Trimble suffered a further reverse when more than 37% of the members of his constituency association expressed their lack of confidence in his leadership of the party. In September Trimble succeeded narrowly in passing a motion at the UUC which urged Donaldson, Smyth and Burnside to retake the party whip at Westminster; however, the three MPs insisted they would remain outside the parliamentary party and continue their opposition to the Joint Declaration.

Talks between the British and Irish Governments and the major Northern Ireland political parties continued during late 2003, and in September the four members of the International Monitoring Commission (IMC) were appointed. Trimble and Adams met with Ahern and Blair in London in mid-October, and it was revealed that elections to the Northern Ireland Assembly would take place on 26 November. However, later on the same day Trimble issued a statement in which he maintained that the acts of decommissioning of IRA weapons, witnessed by de Chastelain earlier that day, had lacked the transparency the UUP required to be convinced of the IRA's genuine desire to commit to a lasting peace. Trimble announced that the peace process would be put on hold pending the convening of the UUC, thus preventing the devolution of powers to the Northern Ireland institutions; however, both Blair and Ahern insisted that the elections would proceed on 26 November. The British Government acknowledged in late October that the devolved institutions would not be restored following the elections and that a review of the Good Friday Agreement would take place in early 2004, although Blair stressed that the fundamental principles of the Agreement were not a matter for negotiation. A statement issued by the IRA on 29 October maintained that it had honoured its commitments and that there would be no more acts of decommissioning until the UUP agreed to support the restoration of power sharing.

At the elections to the Northern Ireland Assembly, held on 26 November 2003, the DUP, which was opposed to the Good Friday Agreement, secured 30 of the 108 seats, thus becoming the largest party in the Assembly. The UUP won 27 seats, while Sinn Féin increased its parliamentary representation to 24 seats. The SDLP suffered a significant loss of support, winning just 18 seats. Of the remaining seats, six were won by the Alliance Party, while the PUP, the UKUP and an independent candidate each won one seat. The rate of voter participation was officially recorded at 63.1%. The election results increased the pressure on Trimble from anti-Agreement factions of the UUP, which again called for his resignation. Furthermore, the DUP demanded a full renegotiation of the Good Friday Agreement. However, both Ahern and Blair reiterated that the 'principles and values' of the Agreement would not be changed. In December an independent report into a series of car bombs detonated in Dublin and Monaghan, Ireland, in May 1974 in which 33 people were killed and some 300 were injured, concluded that there were 'grounds for suspecting' that British security forces had helped loyalist paramilitaries to carry out the atrocities. Families of the victims repeated their demands for a public inquiry into the incidents. Later in that month Jeffrey Donaldson resigned from the UUP; two other UUP deputies also left the party and in early January 2004 they confirmed that they would join the DUP. A few days later, however, Burnside and Smyth announced that they had retaken the UUP whip at Westminster.

In January 2004 the DUP Leader, Paisley, met Ahern at the Irish embassy in London, insisting that the DUP would not conduct face-to-face talks with Sinn Féin until the IRA had disbanded. The review of the Good Friday Agreement commenced in early February with Paisley setting out his party's own proposals for power sharing. While acknowledging that the proposals signalled progress on the part of the DUP, they were generally negatively received by Sinn Féin, which feared that they would lead to a return to unionist majority rule. In early March Trimble withdrew his party in protest at the alleged IRA involvement in the recent kidnapping of a dissident republican in Belfast. Later in that month Ahern and Blair met to hold talks with political groups and reiterated their commitment to the conclusion of a power-sharing agreement. In late March Trimble was re-elected as the Leader of the UUP. In April the IMC issued its first report, in which it detailed the levels of ongoing paramilitary activity by both loyalist and republican groups in Northern Ireland. The British Government subsequently announced that it would impose financial sanctions on Sinn Féin and the PUP.

The review of the Good Friday Agreement resumed at Leeds Castle in England in September 2004, having been put on hold for the European elections. As the talks began de Chastelain announced that the IRA would be prepared to decommission its weapons if a political deal were agreed upon; however, the talks ended with no agreement. In November the UDA indicated its intention to end violence and demilitarize following an announcement by the Secretary of State for Northern Ireland, Paul Murphy, that the UDA's February cease-fire would be officially recognized by the Government. On 17 November the British and Irish Governments passed their proposals for restoring the power-sharing executive to the DUP and Sinn Féin for consultation. One week later Paisley conferred with Blair and stated that the disarming of the IRA would only be an acceptable starting point for the power-sharing agreement if it was verified by photographic evidence. At the end of the month Adams met the PSNI Chief Constable, Orde, to discuss decommissioning, while Paisley met de Chastelain in Belfast to review the destruction of the IRA's weapons. On the following day Paisley issued an ultimatum to the IRA that if the peace accord were not restored in the current situation it would become an almost impossible task in the future, and also called for the IRA to repent of its past actions. Adams declared Paisley's comments to be offensive and stated that Sinn Féin would go no further in negotiations. On 8 December, despite being resigned to the collapse of the peace process, Blair and Ahern met in Belfast to reveal their final proposals to restore devolution. On the following day the IRA declared that photographic proof of decommissioning had never been an option and that although the IRA was committed to the peace process, it would not be subjected to a process of humiliation.

In December 2004 an estimated £26.5m. was stolen from the Belfast headquarters of Northern Bank. The PSNI immediately set up an investigation into the robbery and in January 2005 Orde stated that the IRA had been responsible for the robbery. In a report published in mid-February the IMC implicated not only the IRA but also Sinn Féin leaders (these accusations were vehemently denied by Adams). In early February Ahern and Blair warned the IRA that its failure to demilitarize was the only obstacle to an agreement on power sharing; on the following day the IRA withdrew its commitment to decommissioning. In March, responding to Sinn Féin's alleged involvement in the robbery of the Northern Bank, the British Parliament voted to withdraw from the party its entitlement to an allowance payable to Northern Irish political parties, and from Sinn Féin's four MPs their entitlement to personal parliamentary allowances. Early in April, in an initiative that aimed to break the deadlock over the restoration of devolution, Adams urged the IRA to embrace the political alternative to armed struggle that now existed. In May Sean Gerard Hoey, who had already been detained on charges of terrorism and membership of the Real IRA, was charged with the murder of the 29 people who had been killed in the Omagh bombing in 1998; his trial commenced in September 2006. In December 2007 Hoey was acquitted of all charges. At the trial's conclusion, the presiding judge expressed concerns over DNA evidence used by the prosecution and errors committed by the police force during its investigation into the bombings. Immediately following Hoey's acquittal, Orde defended the conduct of his officers, while acknowledging that it was highly unlikely that anyone would be convicted of perpetrating the bombing.

At the general election to the British Parliament held on 5 May 2005 the UUP recorded its worst electoral performance since the formation of Northern Ireland's first government in 1921, retaining only one of the five seats it had previously held, with 17.8% of the votes cast in Northern Ireland. The DUP secured nine seats, gaining four at the expense of the UUP, with 33.7% of the votes cast. Sinn Féin increased its parliamentary representation, winning five seats (compared with four in 2001), with 24.3% of the votes, while the representation of the SDLP, which took three seats with 17.5% of the votes, remained unchanged. Following the election, in which he had himself lost his seat, Trimble resigned as Leader of the UUP. (In June the UUP elected Empey as its new Leader.) In a major reorganization of ministerial portfolios on 6 May, Peter Hain replaced Paul Murphy as the Secretary of State for Northern Ireland. Hain's retention of the office—Secretary of State for Wales—that he had held in the outgoing Cabinet was criticized by the DUP, which claimed that the status of the Northern Ireland portfolio had thereby been diminished.

In May 2005, after he had held seemingly fruitless discussions with, separately, Sinn Féin and unionist leaders in London, Hain emphasized that progress in the peace process could only be achieved on the basis of the Good Friday Agreement. Paisley, however, described the Good Friday Agreement as 'dead', stating that progress would only be achieved through comprehensive, verifiable weapons decommissioning and the abandonment by the IRA of all criminal activities. Meanwhile, on 10 May the European Parliament adopted a resolution that accused members of the IRA of the murder of a Catholic man, Robert McCartney, in Belfast in January. Towards the end of the month a report by the IMC highlighted the IRA's continued military readiness and its recruitment and training campaign. In mid-June the House of Commons voted to extend for one year the withdrawal of parliamentary allowances from Sinn Féin and its MPs.

In July 2005 the IRA issued a communiqué in which it formally renounced its armed struggle and committed itself to the pursuit of its objectives, including the goal of a united Ireland, through peaceful means only. At the same time the IRA undertook to conclude the process of comprehensive, verifiable weapons decommissioning. Welcoming the IRA's communiqué in a joint statement, Blair and Ahern emphasized that the commitments it contained must be authenticated in action. Leading unionists, including Paisley and Empey, together with US President George W. Bush, responded to the IRA's announcement in a similar fashion. Unionist uncertainty over the good faith of the IRA's statement was reflected in the DUP's condemnation of the Government's decision to begin removing security facilities in South Armagh on the day after it had been issued. Hain's announcement, on 1 August, of a plan to reduce within two years the number of British army personnel in Northern Ireland by 50%, and to repeal anti-terrorism measures exclusive to Northern Ireland, likewise provoked condemnation by unionists. Loyalist violence that broke out that day in Belfast and continued sporadically throughout the month was attributed to a feud between the paramilitary Ulster Volunteer Force (UVF) and the LVF. On 10 September the most serious sectarian violence for 10 years erupted in Belfast and continued for three days, after the route of a march by the Orange Order was diverted away from a nationalist area in the west of the city. On 14 September, in view of incontrovertible evidence of the UVF's involvement in the unrest, Hain withdrew the United Kingdom's recognition of the UVF's 11-year cease-fire.

In late September 2005 the IRA formally declared in a communiqué that it had completed the process of weapons decommissioning. De Chastelain, who, together with two clergymen, one Catholic and one Protestant, had witnessed the decommissioning, announced at the same time that he was satisfied that the arms decommissioned represented the totality of the IRA's arsenal. Both Blair and Ahern welcomed the IRA's statement as a significant step towards peace and Hain stated that negotiations on the restoration of devolution should commence in early 2006. In early October 2005 the DUP presented Blair with a list of conditions that it insisted must be met to ensure that the unionist community received equal treatment with the IRA, and without whose fulfilment it would refuse to negotiate with Sinn Féin on power sharing. Unionists criticized a decision to restore to Sinn Féin from 1 November its entitlement to the allowance payable to Northern Ireland political parties, and condemned the Government's intention, announced by Hain in late October, to grant an amnesty to certain categories of suspects who remained at large, claiming that the Government had secretly offered the amnesty to the IRA as an inducement for it to abjure violence. At the end of October the LVF responded to weapons decommissioning by the IRA by disbanding all of its paramilitary units.

The DUP absented itself from talks held in mid-November 2005 between Hain, the Irish Minister for Foreign Affairs, Dermot Ahern, and representatives of Sinn Féin, including the party's chief negotiator, Martin McGuinness, who challenged Paisley to keep his word that he would share power with Sinn Féin after the IRA had decommissioned its arms. In early December, in a further response to the IRA's abandonment of its armed struggle, the Government announced that British military strength in Northern Ireland would be reduced to below 9,000 in the following month. In the same month the Public Prosecution Service retracted allegations that the IRA had infiltrated the Northern Ireland Office in 2002 (see above). After the former Sinn Féin official, Denis Donaldson, had confessed to having been an informer working for the British security services for some 20 years and been expelled from the party, Adams asserted that the allegations of infiltration had been part of an attempt by those within the security services who opposed Sinn Féin's participation in government to wreck the Northern Ireland Assembly. Later in December 2005, however, Hain dismissed calls for an inquiry into the affair.

In January 2006 Blair and the Irish Prime Minister, Bertie Ahern, announced that multi-party discussions would recommence on 6 February. In a report published days before the talks were due to begin the IMC alleged that the process of decommissioning IRA weapons had not been completed in September 2005, as the IRA had claimed and the IICD had verified. The IMC's report also accused some IRA members of organized criminal activity and asserted that the IRA continued to gather intelligence. At the same time, however, the IMC's report stated that the IRA no longer committed acts of terrorism. For its part, the IICD reaffirmed its claim that the IRA had completed the process of weapons decommissioning in September. At a conference of the DUP in early February Paisley described as a 'blatant lie' the claim that the IRA had completely disarmed and dismissed any question of sharing power with Sinn Féin before it did so. Despite these setbacks, multi-party talks seeking to restart the peace process were initiated on schedule on 6 February near Belfast.

In mid-February 2006 Hain presented to the House of Commons the Northern Ireland (Miscellaneous Provisions) Bill which, if adopted, would allow the Government to transfer responsibility for policing and justice to Northern Ireland politicians. The bill also provided for the organization of immediate elections to the Northern Ireland Assembly, in the event of political agreement being reached, rather than waiting until 2007 for such elections to be held. The body of Denis Donaldson was found in Co Donegal, Ireland, in April. Despite Sinn Féin's condemnation of the apparent murder and the IRA's claim that it had had 'no involvement whatsoever' in Donaldson's death, prominent unionists, including Paisley, blamed republicans for his death.

Two days after Donaldson's body had been discovered Blair and Ahern issued a major joint statement that sought to clarify the course that the renewed peace process should take in 2006. The two Prime Ministers stated their conviction that the IRA no longer represented a terrorist threat and that all parties should engage in political dialogue, and stated that their aim was to set out a practical framework and reasonable timescale for the restoration of devolution. The Northern Ireland Assembly was recalled on 15 May. The Assembly's primary responsibility was to elect a First Minister and a Deputy First Minister as soon as possible, to allocate ministerial portfolios, and to make other preparations for government. Once the Assembly had elected a First Minister and a Deputy First Minister on a cross-community basis and formed an Executive, power would automatically be devolved to the Assembly and at that point the British Government's power to suspend the Assembly would lapse definitively. In the event of the Assembly's being unable to elect First and Deputy First Ministers within the normal six-week period, Blair and Ahern stated that they would be prepared to allow a further period of 12 weeks after the summer recess for the formation of an Executive. However, if by 24 November the Assembly had failed to achieve this, the Prime Ministers' joint view was that no further purpose would be served by another election at that point or in May 2007. They would be obliged, therefore, to cancel salaries and allowances payable to members of the Assembly and to defer restoration of the Assembly and the Executive until a clear political willingness to exercise devolved power existed. Such a deferral would have immediate implications for the British and Irish Governments' joint stewardship of the peace process and detailed work was stated to have already begun on British-Irish partnership arrangements that would become necessary under such circumstances. In June 2006 a Preparation for Government Committee, comprising representatives of the principal parties, was established within the Assembly, to discuss the devolution of policing and justice and other key matters. Dissident republicans continued to use violent tactics, claiming responsibility for a number of arson attacks in August. In October the IMC confirmed that the IRA had dismantled its paramilitary structures and was no longer involved in organized crime; the report acknowledged, however, that dissident republican and loyalist factions and individuals were still engaged in violence and crime. In the same month discussions took place at St Andrews, in Scotland, between Blair, Ahern and the leaders of the principal Northern Ireland parties: the ensuing St Andrews Agreement established a schedule for the restoration of devolved government by March 2007 and the devolution of criminal justice and policing by 2008.

Following qualified approval of the St Andrews Agreement by Sinn Féin and the DUP, legislation giving effect to the accord was adopted by Parliament in late November 2006. The new law provided for the Northern Ireland Assembly to be redesignated as a transitional assembly and to be dissolved in January 2007, pending an election in March, after which parties would nominate assembly members to positions in a devolved executive, to take office on 26 March. In January Sinn Féin held a special party conference, at which delegates voted to support the PSNI and to take up the party's allocated places on the NIPB, thereby reversing the party's long-standing policy and removing the last obstacle to the process of devolution. In February the UDA (the principal loyalist paramilitary organization) announced that it would accept the participation of Sinn Féin in a future government, while in May the UVF announced that it had renounced paramilitary activity.

At the election to the Assembly, held on 7 March 2007, the DUP won 36 of the 108 seats, Sinn Féin 28, the UUP 18, the SDLP 16 and the Alliance Party seven. On 26 March Paisley and Adams committed themselves to forming a new power-sharing executive by 8 May, on which date Paisley was duly sworn in as First Minister and McGuinness as Deputy First Minister. The remaining 10 ministries were allocated using the so-called 'D'Hondt method', in proportion to the number of seats obtained by each party in the Assembly: the DUP four ministries, Sinn Féin three, the UUP two and the SDLP one. During 2007 relations between the two main parties within the Executive were cordial. In mid-July 2007 Paisley and McGuinness led a delegation of the Executive at a meeting of the North/South Ministerial Council in Armagh, the first such meeting since 2002 and the first to be attended by DUP ministers. In early December Paisley and McGuinness, along with members of the Executive, visited the USA. Meanwhile, in November 2007 the UDA announced the cessation of its paramilitary activity.

However, a series of disagreements between the DUP and Sinn Féin in early 2008 threatened to disrupt co-operation within the Executive. In January the Secretary of State for Northern Ireland, Shaun Woodward, was criticized by some senior members of the DUP after he indicated that the British Government envisaged the devolution of powers over the justice system and policing to the Executive by the end of 2008, in accordance with the provisions of the St Andrews Agreement. Paisley insisted that the IRA disband its army council, that arson attacks on Orange Order buildings cease and that financing measures be agreed by the Executive and the British Government before powers could be transferred. Adams, however, welcomed the proposals and accused the DUP of reneging on its commitment to the St Andrews Agreement. In March Adams and the Minister of Finance and Personnel, Peter Robinson of the DUP, held informal talks in an attempt to resolve disagreements between the parties following comments made by McGuinness and the DUP Minister for Enterprise, Trade and Investment, Nigel Dodds, which were deemed to be offensive. Earlier that month a cross-party Assembly committee had failed to reach an agreement over the devolution of powers, and by early May no further progress had been made.

In early March 2008 Paisley announced his intention to resign as leader of the DUP and, thus, as First Minister at the end of May. At a meeting of the party's executive committee the following month, Robinson was nominated to succeed Paisley as party leader. Paisley duly resigned from both posts and in June Robinson, having assumed the party leadership, was elected as First Minister by the Assembly. (McGuinness was concurrently re-elected as Deputy First Minister.) Five days later Robinson effected a reorganization of the Executive, reallocating the ministerial portfolios held by members of the DUP. The new deputy leader of the party, Nigel Dodds, succeeded Robinson as Minister of Finance and Personnel, and was in turn replaced as Minister of Enterprise, Trade and Investment by Arlene Foster. Sammy Wilson was appointed as Minister of the Environment, replacing Foster, while Gregory Campbell joined the Executive as Minister of Culture, Arts and Leisure.

However, from June 2008 a series of disagreements between the DUP and Sinn Féin, most notably regarding devolution, precipitated the latter's refusal to attend meetings of the Executive Committee. The British Prime Minister, visited Northern Ireland in September, affirming his support for further devolution and counselling the Northern Ireland parties to agree on a date for the transfer of powers. Nevertheless, days later a scheduled meeting of the Executive was cancelled, due to the refusal of Sinn Féin to participate. In mid-November, following the conclusion of protracted discussions between the two main parties, Robinson and McGuinness announced the details of an initial agreement outlining the process by which the transfer of powers over the justice system and policing to the Northern Ireland institutions could take place. Under the terms of the agreement, a temporary arrangement for the devolution of powers would be invoked, allowing the Assembly to elect by cross-community vote a single minister responsible for justice until May 2012, upon which date a permanent settlement would be enacted. The agreement also included the appointment of an independent Attorney-General for Northern Ireland (a role currently held by the Attorney-General for England and Wales). None the less, the parties failed to agree a timetable for devolution to take place.

In early 2009 a series of attacks against police officers and military personnel prompted concerns over the increased security threat from armed dissident republican groups. On 8 March two British soldiers were shot dead at a barracks in County Antrim, while two days later a police officer was killed in County Armagh; representatives of all the main parties condemned the killings, responsibility for which was claimed by two dissident republican groups, the Real IRA and the Continuity IRA. Later that month a prominent republican opponent of Sinn Féin's participation in the power-sharing arrangements, Colin Duffy, was charged with murder in relation to the deaths of the two soldiers. In April it was reported that McGuinness had received death threats from dissident republican groups, following a statement in which he accused the perpetrators of the killings in March of having 'betrayed' the republican movement. In early May the IMC published a report in which it stated that the threat from dissident republican paramilitaries remained 'serious'.

In November 1988 the European Court of Human Rights ruled in favour of four men who were protesting against being detained without charge in Northern Ireland for more than four days, under the Prevention of Terrorism Act (which allowed detention for up to seven days). In December the Government responded to the ruling by announcing a derogation from the European Convention for the Protection of Human Rights. In November 1991 the UN Committee Against Torture expressed concern over cases of alleged ill-treatment of terrorist suspects in detention and other abuses of human rights in Northern Ireland, which had been detailed in a report compiled by a prominent human rights organization, Amnesty International. In September 1995 the European Court of Human Rights unexpectedly overturned an earlier decision of the European Commission of Human Rights and ruled that the killing of three IRA activists in Gibraltar, in 1988, was in breach of Article 2 of the Convention, defining the 'right of life'. While clearing the Government of operating a 'shoot-to-kill' policy, the Court insisted that excessive and unlawful force had been used. In May 1997 the newly elected Labour Government announced that the European Convention was to be incorporated into United Kingdom law and applied in full in Northern Ireland and that the jurisdiction of British courts would be extended to cover the rights guaranteed in the Convention. The Human Rights Act received royal assent in November 1998 and came into force in October 2000. Meanwhile, in April 1998 a report of a special inquiry of the UN Human Rights Commission, initiated in October 1997, upheld complaints by human rights groups regarding the RUC's intimidation of lawyers defending terrorist suspects and the failure to extend adequate legal rights to those detained under emergency legislation. In particular, the report recommended a new inquiry into the allegations that the RUC failed to prevent the murder, by UDA activists, of the republican lawyer Patrick Finucane in Belfast in 1989 (see above). In May 2001 the European Court of Human Rights awarded compensation to the families of 10 IRA members killed by security forces in Northern Ireland during the 1980s and 1990s, after it agreed that the Government had breached Article 2 of the Convention. It also criticized the investigation into the shootings of eight of those 10 IRA members for its lack of independence.

A new official inquiry into the fatal shooting of 14 republican demonstrators by the security forces in Londonderry in January 1972, conducted by Lord Saville of Newdigate, began hearing evidence in March 2000. The destruction by the British army, prior to the inquiry, of rifles required as evidence prompted lawyers representing the families of the victims to accuse the Ministry of Defence of deliberately attempting to frustrate the process. In a significant development in November the lawyer acting for the 440 soldiers involved in the case accepted, in contrast to the findings of an original inquiry, that none of the civilians officially listed as killed or wounded in the incident had been armed. He did, however, maintain that a second list of at least 34 'untraced or unidentified casualties' who were never publicly acknowledged as injured in the incident could have included in their number gunmen who had fired on the soldiers. In May 2001 Martin McGuinness survived a motion of no confidence in the Northern Ireland Assembly, after he admitted in a written statement presented to the Saville inquiry that he was the IRA's adjutant (effectively second-in-command) in Londonderry in January 1972. McGuiness, however, denied that IRA gunmen had been involved in the exchanges of fire with security forces and rejected the claim of an eyewitness that he had fired the first shot. In January 2003 Sir Edward Heath, British Prime Minister in 1972, appeared before the inquiry and dismissed allegations that the shootings had been premeditated as 'absurd'. In November 2003 McGuinness appeared before the inquiry but refused to disclose the names of IRA members who had been with him in Londonderry on 'Bloody Sunday', despite being warned by Lord Saville that he could face further legal action. McGuinness insisted that the IRA had not conducted any military operations in Londonderry that day and that no IRA members had been killed or injured during the shootings. The inquiry concluded in November 2004 with the tribunal retiring to compile its report; the report was expected to be completed by the end of 2008. However, in November 2008 Lord Saville indicated that it would not be published until late 2009.

In June 2005 the Government published reports compiled, respectively, by the Council of Europe's Commissioner for Human Rights and the European Committee for the Prevention of Torture and Inhuman or Degrading Treatment or Punishment (CPT) that contained strong criticism of the United Kingdom's policies on terrorist suspects and those seeking political asylum in the country. Fault was found in particular with the Anti-Terrorism, Crime and Security Act (2001) because it enabled the Secretary of State for Home Affairs to subject suspects to control orders without trial. The report of the Commissioner also claimed that there were deficiencies in the procedures governing legal appeals by unsuccessful political asylum seekers against deportation. The Government strongly denied a claim by the CPT that detainees had been mistreated. Later in June 2005 human rights groups, with the support of opposition parties and some Labour MPs, sought to persuade the Government not to repatriate Zimbabwean asylum seekers whose applications had failed on the grounds that they risked mistreatment on their return to Zimbabwe. Also in June a report published by Amnesty International alleged that, by detaining them prior to deportation, the Government had infringed the human rights of as many as 25,000 failed applicants for political asylum in the United Kingdom in 2004. In July the Government announced that it had suspended its policy of deporting failed Zimbabwean applicants for political asylum pending a High Court's consideration of its legality. In October, in a 'test case', the Asylum and Immigration Tribunal ruled that an unsuccessful Zimbabwean applicant for political asylum could not be repatriated to Zimbabwe as he would be at risk of mistreatment there. On the following day, in response to the likelihood that British courts would uphold appeals by foreign nationals against deportation to countries where they risked persecution, the Government announced that it would seek to overrule a majority decision by the European Court of Human Rights in 1996 that national security interests could not take precedence over an individual's inalienable human rights.

The United Kingdom became a full member of the EC in January 1973. A referendum in 1975 endorsed British membership by a large majority. The first direct election of British representatives to the European Parliament took place in June 1979. During the 1980s the Thatcher Government demanded controls on spending by the EC, and particularly reform of the Common Agricultural Policy (CAP), and expressed scepticism regarding proposals for greater European economic unity, on the grounds that this was likely to entail a loss of national sovereignty. In October 1990, however, the United Kingdom joined the ERM. Following Major's assumption of the British premiership, relations with individual members of the EC (particularly Germany) improved, and the Government adopted a more pragmatic approach towards European developments. Nevertheless, the British Government agreed to the terms of the Maastricht Treaty only after substantial concessions had been granted for the United Kingdom. In particular, the United Kingdom's participation in the final stage of European Economic and Monetary Union (EMU), including the adoption of a single EC currency by 2000, was made optional.

British relations with the EU were adversely affected by concerns over the safety of beef from British cattle. In March 1996 a report by a government health advisory committee recognized a possible link between BSE, evident in cattle herds in all parts of the country, and a new strain of Creutzfeldt-Jakob disease (CJD), a degenerative disease affecting humans. The findings of the report provoked a serious crisis of consumer confidence within the United Kingdom and abroad, and several countries announced a ban on all imports of beef and related products from the United Kingdom. At the end of March comprehensive restrictions on the export from the United Kingdom of all live cattle, beef and derivatives were imposed by the European Commission. EU ministers of agriculture undertook to support the British Government in compensating farmers for any necessary slaughter of cattle herds, on condition that adequate measures were adopted to eradicate BSE.

The election, in May 1997, of the Labour Government generated expectations of a significant improvement of relations between the United Kingdom and the EU. The Blair administration immediately announced its intention to withdraw the country's option not to participate in the 'social chapter' of the Maastricht Treaty, and to promote completion of the internal economic market and enlargement of the EU. However, the new Government remained opposed to greater EU authority over national borders and immigration controls, and its demands for reform of the CAP. In June 1997 EU heads of state and of government signed the Treaty of Amsterdam, amending the Maastricht Treaty. The new agreement incorporated the social chapter, given the Labour Government's willingness to subscribe to the protocol, although it was not expected to be enforced in the United Kingdom until the new Treaty had been ratified by all members. The United Kingdom, together with Ireland, secured an exemption from obligations with regard to immigration, asylum and visa policies; however, Blair negotiated an option to participate in certain co-operative aspects of the border arrangements.

In July 1999 the European Commission formally ended the ban on British beef exports, with effect from 1 August, subject to the provision that all beef was de-boned and came from animals whose pedigree could be traced. However, despite the Commission's ruling, France announced that it would maintain its embargo on British beef pending a report by its own food safety agency on the advisability of ending restrictions. In October

2002, following a ruling by the European Court of Justice that the French embargo was illegal, the French Government removed the ban on British beef. (In November 2005 the British Department for Environment, Food and Rural Affairs lifted the ban on sales for human consumption of meat from cattle aged over 30 months, and in May 2006 the EU removed the remaining restrictions on the United Kingdom's foreign sales of live cattle and beef products.) Later in October 2002 relations between France and the United Kingdom were again strained following disagreements between Blair and the French President, Jacques Chirac, over EU agricultural policy reform. Bilateral relations deteriorated further after France invited the President of Zimbabwe, Robert Mugabe, to attend a summit of African leaders in Paris, despite the imposition earlier that year of sanctions prohibiting Mugabe and other Zimbabwean political leaders from travelling to EU countries. Relations between the United Kingdom and France were also strained by their differing views on the necessity of military action in Iraq (see below). In October 2003 Chirac visited London for talks with Blair, at which Chirac expressed his reservations over US-British policies in Iraq; however, they agreed to enhance co-operation to combat illegal immigration. In November 2004 Chirac again visited London to celebrate the 100th anniversary of the *entente cordiale* agreement, which had settled outstanding colonial disputes between the two countries. Following the election of Nicolas Sarkozy as President of France in May 2007, relations between the two countries improved. During an official state visit to the United Kingdom in March 2008, Sarkozy reiterated his intention to increase co-operation with the British Government over the construction of new nuclear energy plants, immigration and security.

In October 1997 the Chancellor of the Exchequer, Gordon Brown, attempted to clarify the Government's stance on the European single currency, following a period of intense speculation. He identified five key principles for participation in EMU, relating to its impact on the British economy and employment, and insisted that membership would have to be preceded by a sustained period of economic stability. In December Blair objected to a decision by other EU leaders to establish a new economic policy group, comprising representatives of countries adopting the single currency from 1 January 1999. None the less, the Government emphasized its commitment to the successful introduction of the euro (as the currency was designated). In May 1999 Blair expressed his intention to end what he termed Britain's 'ambivalence' towards the EU and to make the country a 'leading partner' in the bloc. Earlier in the year he had predicted that the relevant conditions for participation in EMU would be in place shortly after the next general election. In June 2003 Brown announced that four of the five key principles for deciding British participation in EMU had not yet been fulfilled. Nevertheless, he stated that the Government remained in favour of joining the single currency once the conditions were in place.

Despite his previously vehement stance opposing such a move, in April 2004 Blair announced plans to hold a referendum on the proposed new draft EU constitutional treaty. The draft had been prepared by a convention, headed by the former French President, Valéry Giscard d'Estaing, during 2002–03, and was finally approved by the leaders of the 25 member states of the EU in mid-June 2004. A bill was published in January 2005 to allow for a referendum on the treaty. In June, however, following the failure of the French and Dutch electorates to endorse the treaty in referendums, Straw announced that the Government would not proceed with a second reading of the bill in the House of Commons. At the same time Straw emphasized the Government's view that the treaty represented 'a sensible new set of rules for the enlarged EU'. In June 2007, at a summit meeting in Brussels, Belgium, EU leaders reached a preliminary agreement providing for a comprehensive reform treaty to replace the constitutional treaty rejected by French and Dutch voters. On 13 December the Reform Treaty (later known as the Treaty of Lisbon) was signed by EU heads of state and of government, including Brown, at a summit meeting in Lisbon, Portugal. A motion by the Conservative Party to ratify the treaty by national referendum was rejected by the House of Commons in March 2008. (Prior to the 2005 general election, all three main political parties had promised to ratify the constitutional treaty by means of a referendum.) The treaty was ratified by parliamentary vote in June 2008. In October the Conservative Party promised to conduct a national referendum on ratification of the Treaty of Lisbon, should it remain to enter into effect at the time of the next British general election.

Following Iraq's forcible annexation of Kuwait in August 1990, the British Government promptly supported the efforts of the USA in defending Saudi Arabia from potential Iraqi aggression and deployed some 42,000 personnel in the subsequent engagement in hostilities against Iraq, under the auspices of the UN. British troops also participated in subsequent humanitarian efforts to protect the Kurdish population within Iraq from persecution by the Iraqi armed forces. In January 1993 British fighter aircraft participated in US-led attacks on military targets in Iraq, launched in response to renewed Iraqi incursions into Kuwait and obstruction of a UN investigation into a suspected Iraqi nuclear weapons programme. In September 1996 the British Government gave political and logistical support to a series of air-strikes by the USA against targets in Iraq. In December 1998, following Iraq's refusal to co-operate with weapons inspections by the UN Special Commission (UNSCOM), the USA and the United Kingdom conducted a further series of air-strikes in an effort to 'degrade' Iraq's military capabilities. Further airborne attacks were conducted in early 1999 and mid-2000 in response to alleged violations by Iraq of the UN air exclusion zone. In February 2001 the United Kingdom and the USA were again involved in the bombardment of a number of targets in Iraq, in response to a reportedly increased threat to aircraft from those countries in the preceding weeks. The action was, however, condemned by several Western and Arab countries.

In March 2002 Blair faced opposition from within the Labour Party as speculation mounted about the possibility of further military action against Iraq. Blair indicated in July that he had 'tremendous concerns' about any possible military strikes on Iraq and subsequently announced his support for the UN Security Council's proposal that UN weapons inspectors be readmitted to Iraq. He did, however, stress in late August that the British Government was determined to deal with the threat posed by Iraq's possession of weapons of mass destruction. In early September, in response to mounting public opposition to possible military action in Iraq, Blair insisted that no decision on such action had yet been taken, but stated that he would publish a dossier outlining the 'real and unique threat' posed by the regime of the Iraqi President, Saddam Hussain, by the end of the month. Following a meeting with the US President, George W. Bush, Blair announced that the United Kingdom and the USA would attempt to secure a new UN Security Council resolution that would approve military action in Iraq, should that country fail to comply with UN weapons inspectors. Both British and US officials greeted with scepticism Iraq's declaration, made on 16 September, of its willingness to readmit weapons inspectors 'without conditions'; however, the People's Republic of China, France and Russia cautiously welcomed the move. In late September the British Government published the dossier outlining its case against the Iraqi regime and the perceived threat posed by that country's 'illicit weapons programmes' to the security of both the West and the Middle East (see above). However, it appeared that the United Kingdom and the USA were becoming increasingly isolated in their attempts to secure approval for the use of military force against Iraq. On 8 November, after a compromise had been reached between the five permanent members, the UN Security Council unanimously adopted Resolution 1441, which demanded, *inter alia*, that Iraq permit weapons inspectors from UNSCOM's replacement, the UN Monitoring, Verification and Inspection Commission (UNMOVIC), and the International Atomic Energy Agency (IAEA, see p. 113) unrestricted access to sites suspected of holding illegal weapons and required the Iraqi leadership to make a full declaration of its chemical, biological, nuclear and ballistic weapons, as well as related materials used in civilian industries, within 30 days. The resolution warned that this represented a 'final opportunity' for the Iraqi authorities to comply with their disarmament obligations under previous UN resolutions, affirming that Iraq would face 'serious consequences' in the event of non-compliance with the UN inspectors or of any 'false statements and omissions' in its weapons declaration. Later in November the Liberal Democrats' parliamentary motion proposing that no military action should be taken against Iraq without a fresh mandate from the UN and a vote in the House of Commons was defeated by 452 votes to 85; 32 Labour MPs voted in favour of the motion.

In mid-December 2002 the British Secretary of State for Foreign and Commonwealth Affairs, Jack Straw, denounced

Hussain's claims that he had destroyed all weapons of mass destruction as an 'obvious falsehood'. The USA also stated that Iraq was in 'material breach' of UN Resolution 1441 since it had failed to give a complete account of its weapons capabilities, citing in particular Iraq's failure to account for stocks of biological weapons such as anthrax. During January 2003 Blair, while asserting that conflict was not inevitable if Iraq complied with the UN's disarmament terms and insisting that UNMOVIC and the IAEA be granted sufficient time in order to complete their inspections, ordered large numbers of troops to the Persian (Arabian) Gulf region to join the increasing number of US forces already in position there. However, it also became apparent that month that disagreements over policy on Iraq within the Government, the Labour Party and Parliament as a whole were increasing, particularly following Blair's refusal in mid-January to guarantee that British troops would not be involved in a military campaign in Iraq should there be no UN resolution approving such action. On 27 January, 60 days after the resumption of UN weapons inspections in Iraq (as stipulated under Resolution 1441), the head of UNMOVIC, Hans Blix, and the Director-General of the IAEA, Muhammad el-Baradei, briefed the UN Security Council on the progress of inspections. El-Baradei stated that IAEA inspectors had found no evidence that Iraq had restarted its nuclear weapons programme, but requested more time for the organization to complete its research. Blix, for his part, claimed that there was no evidence that Iraq had destroyed known stocks of illegal chemical and long-range ballistic weapons, and announced that he was sceptical about Baghdad's willingness to disarm. Following the briefing, Straw declared Iraq to be in 'material breach' of Resolution 1441.

In January 2003, as the likelihood of a US-led military response to the crisis increased, the United Kingdom was one of eight European countries to sign a joint statement expressing support for the USA's stance on Iraq. The following month increasing British popular opposition to military action against Iraq precipitated nation-wide 'anti-war' demonstrations, including a march in London reportedly attended by some 1m. people. Blair continued with his efforts to secure a second UN Security Council resolution authorizing a US-led campaign in Iraq should inspectors from UNMOVIC continue to report Baghdad's non-compliance; however, on 26 February he suffered a damaging reverse when 122 Labour MPs supported an all-party motion in the House of Commons stating that the case for military action against Iraq was 'as yet unproven'. Earlier in February the USA had presented to the Security Council what it claimed to be overwhelming evidence of Iraq's possession of weapons of mass destruction, its attempts to conceal such weapons from the UN inspectorate and its links with international terrorism, including the al-Qa'ida network. Despite signs of progress being reported by Blix in mid-February in his report to the UN Security Council, on 24 February the United Kingdom, the USA and Spain presented a draft resolution to the Security Council effectively authorizing a US-led military campaign against Hussain's regime, in response to Iraq's failure to disarm peacefully. The resolution stated that a deadline of 17 March would be set, by which time Iraq should prove that it was disarming; however, no specific mention was made of consequent military action in the event of the deadline not being met by Iraq, apparently in an effort by the US-led coalition to persuade France, Russia and China not to exercise their right of veto. Officials from France, Russia and Germany responded to the draft resolution by presenting an alternative proposal involving an extended timetable of weapons inspections in order to avert a war. On 7 March Straw submitted an amended draft resolution to the Security Council which concluded that Iraq would have 'failed to take the final opportunity to disarm unless on or before 17 March the Council concludes that Iraq has demonstrated full, unconditional, immediate and active co-operation with its disarmament obligations under resolution 1441'. On 12 March Blair proposed six new conditions that Iraq must meet in order to prove that it was serious about disarmament: this was seen as an attempt at a compromise that might encourage wavering countries in the Security Council to support an amended resolution. The British proposals came a day after President Bush had rejected a suggested 45-day postponement of any decision to go to war by six countries that had the power to influence the Security Council vote, although Blair also indicated that British forces would participate in the anticipated US-led campaign in Iraq without the passing of a second UN resolution.

On 16 March 2003 Blair attended a summit meeting in the Azores, Portugal, along with President Bush and the Spanish Prime Minister, José María Aznar. The following day the United Kingdom, the USA and Spain withdrew their resolution from the UN, stating that they reserved the right to take their own action to ensure Iraqi disarmament. Later that day Bush issued an ultimatum giving Saddam Hussain and his two sons 48 hours to leave Baghdad or face military action. Shortly after the expiry of Bush's 48-hour deadline, on 19 March US and British armed forces launched a 'broad and concerted campaign' (code-named 'Operation Iraqi Freedom') to oust the regime of Saddam Hussain. US-led coalition forces crossed into Iraq from Kuwait and began a steady advance towards the capital. At the same time a campaign of massive air-strikes was launched against the key symbols of the Iraqi regime in and around Baghdad, including selected military bases, communications sites, government buildings and broadcasting headquarters. The US and British forces adopted a simultaneous campaign of issuing leaflets and broadcasting radio messages, in an effort to persuade Iraqi citizens to abandon their support for the incumbent regime: their declared intention was that Operation Iraqi Freedom would precipitate the disintegration of the regime 'from within'. British troops were principally engaged in securing towns in southern Iraq, including Iraq's second largest city, Basra, after the US-led coalition had seized control of the key southern port of Umm Qasr and the Al-Faw Peninsula. During the campaign Blair frequently stressed his desire that the UN should play a central role in the future of Iraq. Baghdad was captured by US forces on 9 April and, following the seizure by US troops of Saddam Hussain's birthplace and power base, Tikrit (to the north of Baghdad), on 14 April, the Iraqi regime appeared to have collapsed. Although the whereabouts of Saddam Hussain and his sons remained unknown, by late April a number of senior Iraqi officials had been captured and on 1 May President Bush officially declared an end to 'major combat operations' in Iraq. Hussain's sons Uday and Qusay were killed in July following an exchange of gunfire with US special forces in Mosul and Saddam Hussain was captured by US special forces on 14 December near Tikrit.

On 22 May 2003 the UN Security Council approved Resolution 1483, which recognized the US- and British-led Coalition Provisional Authority (CPA), headed by US diplomat L. Paul Bremer, III, as the legal occupying power in Iraq, and mandated the CPA to establish a temporary Iraqi governing authority. UN sanctions imposed on Iraq in 1990 were also lifted. However, it soon became clear that the arrest or elimination of the main figures of the old regime was not diminishing the level of armed resistance to coalition forces. In July 2003 the British Government formally assumed command of the multinational task force for south-eastern Iraq, with its headquarters in Basra, comprising some 16,000 troops, of whom 11,000 were British. In early September the British Government agreed to dispatch a further 1,200 troops to Iraq while placing another 1,800 soldiers on stand-by. In January 2004 Blair pledged that British troops would remain in Iraq for a minimum of a further two years and that there would be no reduction in the strength of British forces in the country until the transfer of power to a provisional Iraqi administration, scheduled for July that year.

Meanwhile, there appeared to be little sign of the chemical, biological and nuclear weapons which had been the *raison d'être* of the US-led campaign. In early October 2003 the Iraq Survey Group, a group of more than 1,000 experts established by the US-led coalition in May to investigate the presence of illegal weapons in Iraq, which had been given the task of locating supplies of these weapons, published its interim report. This indicated that while no such weapons themselves had been found, there was evidence of weapons-related programmes and of Iraqi attempts to gain nuclear technology on the international black market. In January 2004 the 400-member Joint Captured Material Exploitation Group, led by an Australian brigadier, was withdrawn from Iraq, leading to suggestions that the coalition had failed to locate conventional weapons or sites, such as missiles and launchers, that might be used in conjunction with banned weapons. In mid-September a draft report compiled by the Iraq Survey Group in Washington, DC, USA revealed that no weapons of mass destruction had been found in Iraq. Later that month at a Labour Party conference Blair apologized for the intelligence claim that Iraq possessed weapons of mass destruction; however, he refused to apologize for sending British troops to Iraq, stating that the removal of Saddam Hussain was sufficient justification.

On 28 June 2004, two days ahead of schedule, the USA formally transferred sovereignty to Iraq and the interim Prime Minister, Dr Ayad Allawi, and his cabinet ministers were sworn in. A further 400 British troops were sent to Iraq in preparation for the country's first multi-party elections for over 50 years, which took place on 30 January 2005. By the end of 2006 responsibility for two of the four provinces supervised by British forces had been transferred to the Iraqi security forces; responsibility for Maysan province was transferred in April 2007. In October the Prime Minister announced that some 1,000 troops were to be withdrawn from Iraq by December that year, upon the transfer of responsibility for Al-Basrah (Basra) province to the Iraqi security services and that further withdrawals would take place in early 2008, reducing the total number of troops to 2,500. In December control of Basra province was duly transferred and around 1,000 troops were withdrawn from the province accordingly. However, in April 2008 the Secretary of State for Defence, Des Browne, confirmed the postponement of further troop withdrawals, citing an increase in attacks on coalition and Iraqi forces by insurgents. During a visit to Iraq in December, the Prime Minister announced a timetable for the complete withdrawal of the 4,100 British troops who remained in Iraq. The withdrawal of British troops commenced at the end of March 2009, when responsibility for operations in the south of the country were transferred to US forces. On 30 April a special ceremony took place in Basra province to mark the end of the British mission in Iraq, one month earlier than planned.

The International Committee of the Red Cross voiced its concern over the treatment of Iraqi prisoners by coalition forces in a report published in February 2004. In May the Secretary of State for Defence, Geoff Hoon, admitted that British forces had taken part in incidents of assault in Iraq in the form of the forced hooding of detainees and stated that investigations were taking place into 33 incidents of alleged abuse. The Government encountered further criticism in early June when it was revealed that the Ministry of Defence was in fact investigating 75 claims of abuse. In June the House of Commons defence committee announced plans to form a cross-party parliamentary committee to investigate the role of British troops in Iraq, particularly following the transfer of power to Iraq at the end of the month. In mid-June it was announced that four British soldiers from the Royal Regiment of Fusiliers would be tried before a court martial on charges of assault and indecent assault following the emergence of personal photographs depicting incidents of abuse. They were tried in Osnabrück, Germany, in January 2005, convicted and sentenced to terms of imprisonment ranging from four months to two years. In July the Attorney-General announced that 11 British soldiers would appear before a court martial on charges, including unlawful killing, manslaughter and inhuman treatment of persons, that had been brought by the Army Prosecution Authority in connection with military operations in Iraq in 2003. In September 2005 the trial before a court martial began of four serving and three former members of the Parachute Regiment who were charged with murder and violent disorder in connection with a military operation in Iraq in 2003. All seven were acquitted in November 2005 on the grounds of insufficient evidence.

In early 1999 the United Kingdom was one of the principal participants in a NATO air offensive against the Federal Republic of Yugoslavia (now Serbia). The campaign, which began in March, was intended to end the atrocities committed by Serb forces against ethnic Albanians in the Serbian province of Kosovo (see the chapter on Serbia). Although NATO did not have a direct mandate from the UN Security Council for the offensive, it insisted that earlier UN resolutions provided ample justification for the use of force on humanitarian grounds. However, although NATO's stated targets were to be exclusively military, the campaign was widely criticized for the number of civilian casualties caused by NATO errors. It was also widely held that NATO was failing in its stated aim of averting a humanitarian disaster in Kosovo, because the air offensive had prompted Serbia to intensify its attacks on Kosovans, provoking a severe refugee crisis as hundreds of thousands of Kosovans attempted to flee the province. In March Blair announced the establishment of a cross-departmental group to respond to the refugee crisis, and pledged £10m. in aid. Following a visit to Kosovan refugee encampments in the former Yugoslav republic of Macedonia (FYRM) in May, Blair promised to increase aid to £40m. and announced that the United Kingdom would receive 1,000 refugees a week. The Government had earlier been criticized by its NATO partners for its reluctance to accept the refugees. As the military campaign developed Blair was perceived as the most determined of NATO's leaders in his effort to force the Yugoslav President, Slobodan Milošević, to accept the alliance's terms for a cessation of hostilities. In early June Milošević conceded to these demands, and by the end of that month Serb forces had withdrawn from Kosovo. British troops formed part of the force that entered the province to enforce the peace process. In November diplomatic relations between the two countries were restored.

The terrorist attacks on New York and Washington, DC, on 11 September 2001, for which the USA held the al-Qa'ida organization of Osama bin Laden responsible and in which 78 British citizens were killed, were denounced by Blair as an attack on the democratic world. The Prime Minister pledged that the United Kingdom would stand 'shoulder to shoulder' with the USA in its quest to bring the perpetrators of the attacks to justice and offered to provide military and diplomatic assistance to the US Administration. Blair, who by late October had held talks with more than 50 foreign heads of government, played a significant role in strengthening the international coalition against terrorism and obtaining support for military action against the Islamist Taliban regime in Afghanistan, which was suspected of harbouring senior al-Qa'ida figures, including bin Laden.

On 4 October 2001 the British Government released documents detailing evidence of al-Qa'ida's responsibility for the attacks on the USA, and three days later US and British armed forces commenced the aerial bombardment of suspected al-Qa'ida camps and strategic Taliban positions in Afghanistan. Blair stressed, however, that military strikes were part of a wider, lengthy campaign against terrorism involving diplomatic, economic and political action. In mid-October British military leaders agreed to deploy up to 1,000 ground troops in Afghanistan and the following month the Secretary of State for Defence, Geoff Hoon, confirmed that British troops were involved in ground operations in Afghanistan. In December it was announced that the United Kingdom had agreed to lead the International Security Assistance Force (ISAF), which was granted a six-month mandate by the UN to provide security in Kabul and its environs. ISAF was expected to comprise as many as 5,000 troops from 17 countries, some 2,000 of whom would be from the United Kingdom. The first British peace-keeping troops arrived in Afghanistan later in December. In March 2002 a separate force of 1,700 British combat troops was deployed in Afghanistan to assist US special forces with their pursuit of the remaining Taliban and al-Qa'ida fighters, and later that month Hoon stated that British troops would not be withdrawn from Afghanistan until the threat of al-Qa'ida and the Taliban had been eradicated. By the end of 2006 around 5,300 British troops remained stationed in Afghanistan, either participating in ISAF or assisting US special forces. In mid-2007 an additional 1,400 troops were deployed to Afghanistan. In June 2008 the Secretary of State for Defence, Des Browne, announced an increase in the number of British troops in Afghanistan, from 7,800 to 8,030, to take effect by mid-2009. The Prime Minister visited Afghanistan in late April 2009, where he announced a temporary increase in the size of the British contingent, to 9,000 troops, to take effect from August of that year. The contingent was expected to be reduced to 8,300 troops by 2010. By late April 2009 153 British military personnel had been killed in Afghanistan since 2001 (including 29 who died from non-combat injuries).

In November 1991 the United Kingdom and the USA demanded that Libya extradite for trial, either in the United Kingdom or the USA, two suspected intelligence agents who were alleged to be responsible for an explosion that destroyed a US passenger aircraft over Lockerbie, Scotland, in 1988. The United Kingdom subsequently supported the imposition, by the UN, of economic and political sanctions against Libya. In view of Libya's continued refusal to allow the suspects to be tried in Scotland, in August 1998 the United Kingdom and the USA conceded to a Libyan proposal, subsequently endorsed by the UN Security Council, that they be tried on neutral territory in the Netherlands. In March 1999 Libya finally agreed to the extradition of the suspects. The UN sanctions against Libya were subsequently suspended. The trial of Abd al-Baset Ali Muhammad al-Megrahi and Al-Amin Khalifa Fhimah, which was heard under Scottish law by a panel of Scottish judges in the presence of international observers, commenced in May 2000. At the end of January 2001 the judges announced that they had unanimously found al-Megrahi guilty of the murder of 270 people and sentenced him to life imprisonment. Fhimah was, however, acquitted, owing to lack of evidence of his involvement in the bombing, and freed to return to Libya. Despite mounting pressure from Arab League states, the British Secretary of State for Foreign and Commonwealth Affairs, Robin Cook, maintained that sanctions against Libya would not be permanently revoked until Libya accepted responsibility for the bombing and paid 'substantial' compensation. In March 2002, following an appeal that was unanimously rejected by the five judges, al-Megrahi was transferred to a prison in Scotland to begin his sentence; it was ruled in November 2003 that he would serve 27 years in prison before becoming eligible for parole. Also in March 2002 Libya appointed an ambassador to the United Kingdom for the first time in 17 years. In August 2002 a minister of the British Foreign and Commonwealth Office visited Libya for talks with Libyan leader Col Muammar al-Qaddafi, representing the first visit by a British government minister to Libya for some 20 years.

In March 2003 it was reported that, following negotiations in London, Libya had agreed to accept civil responsibility for the actions of its officials in the Lockerbie case and would pay compensation to the families of the victims, in stages, conditional upon the removal of UN and US sanctions. In August Libya informed the President of the UN Security Council that it accepted 'responsibility for the actions of its officials' in the Lockerbie bombing; agreed to pay compensation to the families of the victims; pledged co-operation in any further Lockerbie inquiry; and agreed to continue its co-operation in the 'war against terror' and to take practical measures to ensure that such co-operation was effective. Following the transfer of US $2,700m. in compensation to the International Bank of Settlements, the United Kingdom submitted a draft resolution to the Security Council requesting the formal lifting of UN sanctions against Libya. On 12 September 13 of the 15 members of the UN Security Council approved the lifting of the sanctions imposed against Libya; France and the USA abstained from the vote.

In December 2003 Blair announced that Libya had agreed to disclose and dismantle its programme to develop weapons of mass destruction and long-range ballistic missiles. The statement was the culmination of nine months of clandestine negotiations between Qaddafi and British and US diplomats during which the Libyan authorities had reportedly shown evidence of a 'well advanced' nuclear weapons programme, as well as the existence of large quantities of chemical weapons and bombs designed to carry poisonous gas. Libya also agreed to adhere to the Chemical Weapons Convention and to sign an additional protocol allowing the IAEA to carry out random inspections of its facilities. In February 2004 the first meeting between cabinet-level ministers of the United Kingdom and Libya for more than 20 years took place in London. In March Blair visited Tripoli and held talks with Qaddafi, after which the British Prime Minister stated that there was genuine hope for a 'new relationship', while Qaddafi insisted that he was willing to join the international 'war against terror'. It was also announced that British police officers would travel to Libya in April to continue investigations into the murder of a British police officer outside the Libyan People's Bureau in London in 1984. In September Qaddafi announced that Libya had dismantled its weapons of mass destruction programme and in December, with the unilateral sanctions imposed upon Libya by the USA having consequently been lifted, Libya paid the second instalment of its compensation to the families of those killed in the Lockerbie bombing. In May 2006 Libya was removed from the US list of states deemed to support international terrorism, the condition for the payment of the final instalment of compensation. In October 2005 a memorandum of understanding signed by Libya and the United Kingdom guaranteed that Libya would not subject to torture or execute any person who was repatriated to it from the United Kingdom. A further memorandum of understanding was signed by Qaddafi and Blair at the end of May 2007, which provided for negotiations on the transfer of prisoners, extradition and mutual assistance in criminal law. A final agreement was to be signed within 12 months.

In February 1990 diplomatic relations (severed in 1982) were restored between the United Kingdom and Argentina. While both countries continued to indicate that their respective claims to sovereignty over the Falkland Islands were not negotiable, political dialogue was able to proceed under a mutual arrangement to circumvent the issue of sovereignty. In September 1995 the two sides concluded an accord to allow exploration for offshore petroleum and gas deposits in the disputed waters around the Islands. A joint commission was to be established to supervise licensing and revenue-sharing. (The first licences were awarded in October 1996.) In October 1995 Major met with the Argentine President, Carlos Menem, at the UN headquarters in New York, USA (the first meeting at this level since the 1982 war). In October 1998 Menem made an official visit to the United Kingdom, the first by an Argentinian President in almost 40 years. In June 2000 relatives of the 323 Argentinians who were killed when a British submarine sank an Argentinian battleship during the Falklands conflict in 1982 announced their intention to take their claim for compensation from the British Government to the European Court of Human Rights. However, the claim was judged inadmissible in the following month, owing to the amount of time that had elapsed between the incident and the claim being lodged. In July 2001 Blair became the first serving British Prime Minister to visit Argentina.

The long-standing dispute with Spain over the sovereignty of Gibraltar has frequently strained relations between the two countries (see the chapters on Spain and Gibraltar). Dialogue between the United Kingdom and Spain over the future of Gibraltar resumed in July 2001 for the first time since 1998, and further discussions were held in Luxembourg in October 2001, although Gibraltar's Chief Minister, Peter Caruana, refused to attend either meeting. In November the British Government announced that it would be willing to consider joint sovereignty of the territory with Spain. This statement angered Caruana, who again boycotted talks between the British and Spanish Foreign Ministers, held in Barcelona, Spain, later that month at which the British and Spanish Governments concluded that they would reach an agreement on the future of the territory by mid-2002. In January 2002 Caruana agreed to attend discussions scheduled for the following month, on the condition that Gibraltar was granted equal status at the meeting and that Britain and Spain guaranteed that any proposal regarding British-Spanish joint sovereignty of the territory would be withdrawn if rejected at a referendum. Caruana's conditions were not met and he was again absent from talks held in early February. In March some 25,000 people protested in Gibraltar against the proposed power-sharing arrangement; nevertheless, both the Spanish and British Governments reiterated their determination to proceed with plans for a joint sovereignty agreement. However, in April, shortly before talks on the future of Gibraltar were scheduled to recommence, the Spanish Prime Minister stated that Spain would never cede its claim to sovereignty over the territory. In response to this announcement, Caruana insisted that if the British Government entered an agreement with Spain granting concessions over sovereignty, the Gibraltar Government would organize its own referendum, thus making it even more difficult for the British and Spanish Governments to secure popular approval for their proposals. In May Jack Straw, the British Secretary of State for Foreign and Commonwealth Affairs, visited Gibraltar and stated that he would not enter into an agreement with Spain that was not in the best interests of the citizens of Gibraltar. In July Straw confirmed that the United Kingdom was willing to share sovereignty of the territory with Spain, subject to approval by the residents of Gibraltar at a referendum, provoking angry protests in Gibraltar, and later in July Caruana announced that Gibraltar would conduct its own referendum on the sovereignty issue by the end of October. Both the Spanish and the British Governments condemned Caruana's decision to hold a referendum and stated that it would lack any validity. The Gibraltar referendum, held on 7 November, which explicitly asked if Gibraltarians approved 'of the principle that Britain and Spain should share sovereignty over Gibraltar' resulted in an overwhelming rejection of the Spanish and British proposals. Of those voting, 99.0% rejected shared sovereignty; the rate of voter participation was recorded at 87.9%. In June 2003 the British Government announced that talks with Spain regarding the possibility of sharing the sovereignty of Gibraltar had failed and suspended any further negotiations over the issue indefinitely. In December 2004 a tripartite meeting between the United Kingdom, Spain and Gibraltar was held in the United Kingdom, and it was subsequently announced that, henceforth, decisions on the territory's future must be agreed by all three parties. In March 2006 Straw sought to reassure Spain that, in the view of the British Government, Spanish rights over Gibraltar would not be affected by a proposed new constitution for the territory, despite the inclusion of references to the right to self-determination of Gibraltarians. In September agreements were signed by representatives of the three Governments allowing easier border crossings in and out of Gibraltar, direct commercial flights to Gibraltar from Spain, and improved telecommunications links. At a referendum held on 30 November 60.2% of those that voted approved the new Constitution; the rate of voter participation was 60.4%. The Constitution entered into force on 2 January 2007.

From the mid-2000s relations with Iran were strained. In May 2004 demonstrators in the Iranian capital, Tehran, demanded the closure of the British embassy in the city and the removal of the ambassador, in protest against British policy in Iraq, and threw petrol bombs at the building. Diplomatic relations deteriorated further in June when three British patrol crafts and eight Royal Navy personnel were captured on the Shatt al-Arab waterway by Iranian authorities who claimed the servicemen had entered Iranian territorial waters. After intense negotiations between British and Iranian diplomats, the men were released four days later and claimed that they had been forcibly escorted into Iranian waters. In October 2005 Blair warned Iran against supporting rebel factions in Iraq. The Iranian Government denied that it was doing so, and accused British forces stationed in Iraq of assisting Arab separatists responsible for recent bomb explosions in the Iranian city of Ahvaz. The United Kingdom, together with the USA and other Western governments, expressed suspicion during the early 2000s that Iran's programme of uranium enrichment was not, as Iran claimed, purely for peaceful purposes. In November 2004, after discussions with representatives of France, Germany and the United Kingdom, acting on behalf of the EU, Iran agreed to suspend its uranium enrichment programme, but in January 2006 it announced that it was resuming nuclear research and development. In December and again in March 2007 the UN Security Council imposed sanctions on Iran for refusing to comply with requests to desist from uranium enrichment. In April the Iranian navy arrested 15 British naval personnel whom it accused of intruding into Iranian territorial waters; they were released after almost two weeks in captivity.

Government

The United Kingdom is a constitutional monarchy. The Sovereign is the Head of State and the monarchy is hereditary. Parliament consists of the House of Commons and the House of Lords. The 646 members of the Commons are elected for a maximum of five years by direct suffrage by all citizens of 18 years and over, using single-member constituencies. The House of Lords is composed of hereditary Peers of the Realm and Life Peers and Peeresses created by the Sovereign for outstanding public service. Legislation may be initiated in either House but it usually originates in the Commons. Each bill has three readings in the Commons and it is then passed to the House of Lords who may return it to the Commons with amendments or suggestions. The House of Lords may delay, but cannot prevent, any bill from becoming law once it has been passed by the Commons. Executive power is held by the Cabinet, headed by the Prime Minister. The Cabinet is responsible to the House of Commons.

The Northern Ireland Act 1974 made the Secretary of State for Northern Ireland and his ministers answerable to Parliament at Westminster for the government of Northern Ireland, under a parliamentary order, renewable annually. In October 1982 a 78-member Northern Ireland Assembly was elected, in accordance with the Northern Ireland Act 1982: its role was primarily consultative, pending the devolution of executive power. The 1985 Anglo-Irish Agreement, signed by the Prime Ministers of the United Kingdom and of Ireland in November, left the constitutional status of Northern Ireland unaltered, but gave Ireland a consultative role in Northern Ireland affairs, through an Intergovernmental Conference. In June 1986 the British Government announced the dissolution of the Northern Ireland Assembly, four months before the end of its four-year term, following a boycott of meetings by some members, in protest at the Anglo-Irish Agreement. Elections to a new 108-member Assembly were held on 25 June 1998, as part of the multi-party agreement on the future governance of Northern Ireland, approved by a popular referendum in May. An Executive Committee, headed by a First Minister, was constituted from among the legislative members. Responsibility for all matters formerly implemented by the Northern Ireland Office was transferred to the devolved authority under new parliamentary legislation implemented in December 1999. The 1998 Agreement also provided for the establishment of a North/South Ministerial Council, to facilitate co-operation between the Irish Government and representatives of the Northern Ireland Executive on specific cross-border and all-island concerns, and of a British-Irish Council, comprising representatives of British and Irish Governments, members of the devolved authorities in Northern Ireland, Scotland and Wales, and representatives of the Isle of Man and the Channel Islands. The arrangements of the Anglo-Irish Agreement were replaced by a British-Irish Intergovernmental Conference, with responsibility to oversee the new political institutions. The new Northern Ireland institutions were suspended in February 2000, owing to a political impasse concerning the decommissioning of paramilitary weapons and Northern Ireland was returned to direct rule. On 30 May, following an agreement on the issue of decommissioning, power was once again transferred from Westminster to the new Northern Ireland institutions. The Northern Ireland Executive was suspended again on 14 October 2002 and Northern Ireland was returned to direct rule from Westminster, until the restoration of devolved government on 8 May 2007.

In 1999 devolved legislative authorities were established in Scotland and Wales. In Scotland a new elected Parliament, based in Edinburgh, was established with powers to legislate on all domestic matters (incl. education, health, local government and law and order) and with a mandate to vary taxes set by the Government of the United Kingdom by 3%. The Scottish Parliament has 129 members, elected every four years by a combined system of direct voting, on the basis of Westminster parliamentary constituencies, and a form of proportional representation, whereby additional members are elected from a party list on the basis of the larger constituencies used for elections to the European Parliament. The National Assembly for Wales, located in Cardiff, undertook responsibility for issues covered by the Welsh Office of the Government of the United Kingdom. The 60-member National Assembly was elected under the same system as in Scotland. Elections to the two assemblies took place simultaneously in May 1999 and the transfer of powers took place on 1 July. In mid-2008 a 16-member All Wales Convention was appointed to discuss the possible devolution of full legislative powers over domestic matters to the National Assembly for Wales.

Legislation providing for the abolition of all but 92 hereditary peers and the establishment of an interim second chamber pending a definitive reform of the House of Lords was passed in November 1999.

Defence

The United Kingdom is a member of the North Atlantic Treaty Organization (NATO, see p. 351) and maintains a regular army. The total strength of the armed forces in November 2008, including those enlisted outside Britain (3,520), was 160,280 (army 95,780, navy 30,880, air force 33,620). There was also a reserve force of 199,280. In November 2004 the European Union (EU, see p. 255) ministers responsible for defence agreed to create a number of 'battlegroups' (each comprising about 1,500 troops), which could be deployed at short notice to crisis areas around the world. The EU battlegroups, two of which were to be ready for deployment at any one time, following a rotational schedule, reached full operational capacity from 1 January 2007. The United Kingdom committed troops to two battlegroups (one comprising solely British troops and one in conjunction with the Netherlands). Military service is voluntary. The United Kingdom possesses its own nuclear weapons. Government-budgeted defence expenditure for 2008 totalled £34,050m.

Economic Affairs

In 2007, according to estimates by the World Bank, the United Kingdom's gross national income (GNI), measured at average 2005–07 prices, was US $2,608,513m., equivalent to $42,740 per head (or $33,800 per head on an international purchasing-power parity basis). During 2000–07, it was estimated, the population increased at an average annual rate of 0.5%, while gross domestic product (GDP) per head increased, in real terms, by an average of 2.1% per year over the same period. Overall GDP increased, in real terms, at an average annual rate of 2.6% in 2000–07. Real GDP increased by 3.0% in 2007, according to official figures.

Agriculture (including hunting, forestry and fishing) contributed 0.9% of GDP in 2006 and accounted for 1.4% of work-force jobs in December 2007. The principal crops include wheat, sugar beet, potatoes and barley. Livestock-rearing (particularly poultry and cattle) and animal products are important, as is fishing. The GDP of the agricultural sector increased, in real terms, by an average of 1.0% per year during 2000–07; it increased by 2.7% in 2006 before declining by 0.8% in 2007.

Industry (including mining, manufacturing, construction and power) contributed 22.9% of GDP in 2006 and accounted for 17.6% of work-force jobs in December 2007. Industrial GDP

THE UNITED KINGDOM

(excluding construction) decreased, in real terms, at an average annual rate of 0.4% during 2000–07; in 2007 (excluding construction) it increased by 0.4%.

Mining (including petroleum and gas extraction) contributed 2.3% of GDP in 2006 and engaged 0.8% of the employed labour force in 1990; together with the energy and water industries, the sector accounted for 0.6% of work-force jobs in December 2007. Natural gas, sand and gravel, limestone, crude petroleum, igneous rock and coal are the principal minerals produced. The GDP of the mining sector decreased, in real terms, at an average annual rate of 5.1% during 2000–07; the GDP of extractive industries decreased by 1.7% in 2007.

Manufacturing provided 12.6% of GDP in 2006 and accounted for 10.0% of work-force jobs in December 2007. The principal branches of manufacturing include transport equipment, food products, machinery, chemical products and metals and metal products. In real terms, the GDP of the manufacturing sector increased at an average annual rate of under 0.1% during 2000–07; manufacturing GDP increased by 0.7% in 2007.

Energy is derived principally from natural gas, petroleum and, to a lesser degree in recent years, coal. Of the United Kingdom's total consumption of energy in 2007, 48.1% was derived from petroleum, 31.2% was from natural gas, 17.9% from electricity (including nuclear power, hydroelectric power), 1.7% from solid fuels and 0.5% was from renewable and waste sources. At the end of 2008 19 nuclear power reactors were operating in the United Kingdom (a further 26 had been permanently shut down). In 2008 mineral fuels accounted for about 13.9% of the value of total merchandise imports. In mid-2003 plans were announced for the construction of three new offshore wind farms, which would provide sufficient energy to power 15% of British homes upon their completion. It was anticipated that they would supply some 5% of the United Kingdom's electric power by 2010.

Services accounted for 76.2% of GDP in 2006 and accounted for 81.0% of work-force jobs in December 2007. The United Kingdom is an important international centre for business and financial services. Financial intermediation and other business services (including renting and real estate) contributed 32.6% of GDP in 2006. Receipts from tourism totalled £15,960m. in 2007. Wholesale and retail trade (including the motor trade) and repairs (11.5% of GDP in 2006) and transport and communications (6.8% of GDP in 2006) are also major contributors to the economy. In real terms, the GDP of the services sector increased at an average annual rate of 3.3% during 2000–07; the sector's GDP increased by 3.7% in 2007.

In 2007 the United Kingdom recorded a visible trade deficit of £89,252m., and there was a deficit of £52,568m. on the current account of the balance of payments. In 2008 the principal source of imports (13.0%) was Germany, while the principal market for exports in that year was the USA (14.2%). Other major trading partners include the People's Republic of China, France, the Netherlands, Ireland and Belgium-Luxembourg. The principal imports in 2008 were petroleum and petroleum products, road vehicles and miscellaneous manufactured articles. Petroleum and petroleum products were also the leading export in that year, followed by road vehicles, pharmaceuticals and power generating equipment.

There was a budgetary deficit of £9,800m. in the financial year ending 31 March 2008. At the end of December 2008 general government debt was £750,300m. (equivalent to 52.0% of GDP). The annual rate of inflation, according to the retail price index, averaged 2.5% in 2000–08; retail prices increased by 4.0% in 2008, while consumer prices (excluding owner-occupier housing costs and council tax) increased by 3.6%. The rate of unemployment averaged 6.5% in November 2008–January 2009.

The United Kingdom is a member of the European Union (EU, see p. 255). It is also a member of the Organisation for Economic Co-operation and Development (OECD, see p. 358).

Following a period of recession in the early 1990s, the United Kingdom economy experienced a prolonged period of expansion, with sustained growth in GDP accompanied by a declining rate of unemployment and low rates of inflation. However, the worldwide economic slowdown in 2007/08 had an adverse effect on the economy of the United Kingdom. The shortage of credit in the global financial system, which originated in a crisis in the US low-income mortgage sector, caused substantial losses in the British financial sector, and led, notably, to the nationalization of a major commercial bank, Northern Rock, in February 2008. More drastic measures were implemented in October as it became clear that the lack of liquidity was threatening the existence of the banking system. The Government nationalized, in part, Royal Bank of Scotland, Lloyds TSB and HBOS with funding worth £37,000m. and £400,000m. was made available to the sector as a whole in order to guarantee liquidity. As the availability of credit contracted, house prices began to fall in 2008, following 12 consecutive years of price increases, consumer spending, both domestic and international, declined and the rate of mass redundancies in the financial services, retail and manufacturing sectors increased. In a bid to encourage spending, ease pressure on businesses and reduce mortgage repayments, the Bank of England cut interest rates to 3% (from 4.5%) in November. A further four cuts were implemented in quick succession and the rate stood at an historic low of 0.5% in April 2009. This policy was augmented by 'quantitative easing', in which the Bank of England increased the money supply by £75,000m. through the purchase of government and corporate bonds. According to the Office of National Statistics, the unemployment rate was 6.5% in January 2009, a rise from 5.2% the previous year. It was feared that the British economy would suffer a deeper and more prolonged recession than other major economies owing to the prominence of the financial services industry, which comprises one third of the country's GDP. By the end of 2008 public debt was equivalent to 52.0% of GDP. The economy was estimated to have grown by only 0.7% in 2008 and was forecast to contract by 3.8% in 2009.

Education

Education in the United Kingdom is compulsory for all children between the ages of five (four in Northern Ireland) and 16 and takes place in several stages: nursery (now part of the foundation stage in England), primary, secondary, further and higher education. Further education, the non-compulsory fourth stage, covers non-advanced education, which can be taken at both further (including tertiary) education colleges, higher education institutions and increasingly in secondary schools. Higher education, the fifth stage, is study beyond the General Certificate of Education (GCE) Advanced Level (A Level) and its equivalent, which, for most full-time students, takes place in higher education institutions. In November 2007 the Government announced plans to introduce an Education and Skills Bill, under which, most notably, the school-leaving age would be increased from 16 to 18 for pupils in England and Wales, by 2015.

Responsibility for education is substantially devolved: the Secretary of State for Children, Schools and Families is responsible, in principle, for all sectors of education in England, excluding further education, the responsibility for which rests with the Secretary of State for Innovation, Universities and Skills. From 2006 responsibility for all sectors of education in Wales was devolved to the Welsh Assembly Government. Since 1999 the Scottish Executive has had full responsibility for education in Scotland. Responsibility for education in Northern Ireland was devolved to the Northern Ireland Department of Education in May 2007, except for higher and further education, which are administered by the Northern Ireland Department for Employment and Learning. Assessment of the quality of schools is undertaken in England by the Office for Standards in Education (OFSTED), in Wales by Her Majesty's Chief Inspectorate For Education and Training in Wales, in Scotland by Her Majesty's Inspectorate of Education and in Northern Ireland by the Education and Training Inspectorate.

In recent years there has been a major expansion of pre-school education. Many children under the age of five attend state nursery schools or nursery schools attached to primary schools. Others may attend playgroups in the voluntary sector or privately run nurseries. In England and Wales many primary schools also operate an early admission policy where they admit children under the age of five into 'reception classes'. The primary stage covers three age ranges: nursery (under five), infant (five to seven or eight) and junior (up to 11 or 12), but in Scotland and Northern Ireland there is generally no distinction between infant and junior schools. Most public sector primary schools take both boys and girls in mixed classes.

Secondary education generally begins at the age of 11, although in England many areas have middle schools for children aged eight to 12 years or nine to 13 years. In most areas, the state-maintained system of comprehensive schools prevails. Pupils are admitted to such schools without reference to ability. Some localities, however, retain a system of grammar and secondary modern schools, to which admission is determined through a test of ability. (Selection by ability via the so-called '11 Plus' examination was to abolished in Northern Ireland, with effect from September 2009.) Specialist schools covering 10 areas (arts, business and enterprise, engineering, humanities, language, mathematics and computing, music, science, sports and technology) also operate in England. The Specialist Schools Programme helps schools, in partnership with private-sector sponsors and supported by additional government funding, to establish distinctive identities through their chosen specialisms and achieve their target to raise standards. Specialist schools have a special focus on their chosen subject area, but must meet the requirements of the National Curriculum and deliver a broad and balanced education to all pupils. Schools can also combine any two specialisms. In 2000 the Department for Education and Skills announced the introduction of Academies, which were to be mixed-ability schools, located mainly in disadvantaged urban areas. Academies were to be partially financed by private individual or institutional investors, faith groups or other organizations in the voluntary sector. By January 2009 there were 133 Academies in England. Special schools (day or boarding) are provided by local education authorities (LEAs) for certain children with special educational needs, although the vast majority are educated in ordinary schools. All children attending special schools are offered a curriculum designed to overcome their learning difficulties and to enable them to become self-reliant.

Examinations for the single-system General Certificate of Secondary Education (GCSE) may be taken (usually at the age of 16) in as many subjects as a candidate wishes. In 1989 the Government implemented legislation introduced under the Education Reform Act (1988), which provided for a National Curriculum and national testing of pupils aged seven, 11 and 14 years in state schools in England and Wales (Key Stages 1, 2 and 3, respectively). All state schools in England, Wales and Northern Ireland must conform to the national curriculums, which set out which subjects pupils should study, what they should be taught and what standards they should achieve. In Scotland the curriculum in state schools is not prescribed by statute, but the Secretary of State for Scotland issues national advice and guidance to schools and Scottish Local Authorities. The Qualifications and Curriculum Authority is the statutory body which advises the Government on all matters concerned with the curriculum and all aspects of school examinations and assessment in state schools in England. It is also responsible for vocational qualifications. Similar arrangements operate for Wales, Scotland and Northern Ireland. The A Level, generally taken at the age of 18, was introduced in the early 1950s, and serves as a qualification for entrance to higher education. Over the years there have been attempts to broaden the curriculum and experience of those taking A Levels (e.g. the Advanced Supplementary examination in 1989). In September 2000, however, a completely revised approach to the A Level was introduced, based entirely on a modular approach. Candidates are now able to take modules as they proceed through the course, rather than being examined in a single session at the end of the course. The new A Level qualification consists of two parts, the AS (Advanced Subsidiary), which can also be taken as a free-standing qualification, and A2. All students now take the AS and then, where appropriate, proceed to the more challenging A2 to complete their A level. From September 2008 pupils aged 14 years were able to undertake a Diploma, comprising up to three stages, lasting up to five years, in one of five vocational subject areas in place of GCSE and A Level examinations. In 1999/2000 National Qualifications (NQ) were introduced in Scotland. NQs include Standard Grades, Intermediate 1 and 2 and Higher Grades. Pupils study for the Scottish Certificate of Education (SCE)/NQ Standard Grade, approximately equivalent to GCSE, in their third (S3) and fourth (S4) years of secondary schooling (roughly ages 14 and 15), with courses taking two years to complete. Each subject has several elements, some of which are internally assessed in school, and Standard Grade courses are offered at three levels: Credit (grades 1–2), General (grades 3–4) and Foundation (grades 5–6). The Higher Grade requires one further year of study and, for the more able candidates, the range of subjects taken may be as wide as at Standard Grade, with as many as five or six subjects spanning both arts and science. Three or more Highers are regarded as being approximately the equivalent of two or more A Levels.

Since 1986 the National Council for Vocational Qualifications (NCVQ) has established a framework of National Vocational Qualifications (NVQ) in England, Wales and Northern Ireland. The framework is based on five defined levels of achievement, ranging from Level 1, broadly equating to foundation skills in semi-skilled occupations, to Level 5, equating to professional/senior management occupations. The competence-based system has also been extended in Scotland through a system of Scottish Vocational Qualifications (SVQ) along similar lines to the NVQs. The broader-based General National Vocational Qualification (GNVQ) was withdrawn from 2007 and was replaced by a range of alternative vocational qualifications, including the Edexcel or SQA National Certificate/Diploma, OCR Nationals, the General Certificate of Education (GCE—which replaced vocational A Levels in 2005) and GCSEs in applied subjects, all of which are usually studied at school or college. Its equivalent in Scotland, the General Scottish Vocational Qualification (GSVQ), was also discontinued.

Further and higher education may be pursued through vocational or academic courses, on a full-time, part-time or 'sandwich' basis. The decision to admit students is made by each institution according to its own entrance requirements. The term 'further education' may be used in a general sense to cover all non-advanced courses taken after the period of compulsory education, but more commonly it excludes those staying on at secondary school and those in higher education, i.e. courses in universities and colleges leading to qualifications above A Level, SQA Higher Grade, NVQ level three, and their equivalents. Since 1 April 1993 sixth-form colleges have been included in the further education sector.

Higher education is defined as courses that are of a standard that is higher than A Level, the SQA Higher Grade, NVQ Level 3 or the Edexcel (formerly BTEC) or SQA National Certificate/Diploma. Higher education students are most likely to be working towards one of the following qualifications. An Honours degree: the most common of these are Bachelor of Arts (BA Hons) and Bachelor of Science (BSc Hons). These are usually full-time three-year courses but can also be taken as longer part-time courses and may be available through distance learning. In Scotland, where students usually start a year earlier, a full-time first-degree generally takes four years for Honours and three years for the broad-based Ordinary degree. A Foundation degree: this is a new vocationally focused higher education qualification. It aims to increase the number of people qualified at higher technician and associate professional level (e.g. legal executives, engineering technicians, personnel officers, laboratory technicians, teaching assistants). Both full- and part-time courses are offered in a variety of work-related subjects and offer progression to a full Honours degree. A Higher National Diploma (HND) or Diploma of Higher Education (Dip HE): these take two years full-time, and there is the option of turning them into an Honours degree by studying for a further year. Some students go on to do postgraduate studies, usually leading to a Masters degree, such as a Master of Arts (MA), or Master of Science (MSc), or to a Doctorate (PhD). A Masters degree usually lasts one year full-time or two years part-time. A PhD usually lasts three years full-time or six years part-time.

In 2006/07 there were 124 universities (including the Open University), and 45 other higher education institutions offering courses of higher education in the United Kingdom. There is also one privately funded university, the University of Buckingham. The Open University, founded in 1969, and funded mainly by the Higher Education Funding Council for England, provides degree courses by means of printed texts, television broadcasts, audio-visual materials, correspondence tuition and, for some courses, short-term residential schools. No formal qualifications are required for entry to its courses. Some British universities and colleges also now offer study through distance learning, usually learning at home or work.

Educational establishments in the United Kingdom are administered and financed in several ways. Most schools are controlled by LEAs, which are part of the structure of local government, but some are 'assisted', receiving grants direct from central government sources and being controlled by governing bodies, which have a substantial degree of autonomy. Alongside the state system, there are independent schools, which do not receive grants from public funds but are financed by fees and endowments; many of these schools are administered by charitable trusts and church organizations.

The Learning and Skills Council (LSC) is responsible for funding the further education sector in England. The LSC is also responsible for funding provision for non-prescribed higher education in further education sector colleges and further education provided by LEA maintained and other institutions, referred to as 'external institutions'. Until 2006 the National Council for Education and Training for Wales (part of Education and Learning Wales—ELWa) largely funded further education provision made by further education institutions via a third party or sponsored arrangements. In 2006 the functions of ELWa were assumed by the Welsh Assembly Government, including the funding of higher education institutions in Wales. The Scottish Funding Council funds further education colleges in Scotland, while the Department for Employment and Learning funds further education colleges in Northern Ireland.

Government finance for publicly funded higher education institutions (to help meet the costs of teaching, research and related activities) is distributed by the Higher Education Funding Councils (HEFC) in England and Wales, the Scottish Funding Council, and the Department of Education in Northern Ireland. In addition, some designated higher education (mainly Higher National Diplomas/Higher National Certificates and Certificates of Higher Education) is also funded by these sources. The further education sources mentioned above fund the remainder.

Student loans are the main form of support for assistance with living costs for higher education students. The maximum loan in 2008/09 for full-time students was £6,475 (£6,480 for students from Wales). The amount of loan paid also depends on the student's and their family's income. Loans are repaid on the basis of income after the student has left their course, and only when the student's annual income exceeds £15,000. From September 2004 a full-time undergraduate would have to pay up to £1,150 towards the tuition fees for each year of the course. The level of the contribution is means-tested, although those on lower family incomes are entitled to free tuition. Since September 2006 universities in England have been entitled to set variable fees for individual courses, up to a maximum of £3,000, which will rise in line with inflation. However, any rise above the 2008/09 maximum contribution of £1,255 is subject to an access agreement in partnership with the Office for Fair Access. A full-time undergraduate at a publicly funded higher education institution whose course commenced in or after September 2006 was required to contribute up to £3,145 toward the tuition fees in 2008/09. However, for an undergraduate student whose course commenced before September 2006, the maximum contribution in 2008/09 was £1,255. Since the academic year 2000/01, eligible full-time Scottish-domiciled or EU students who are studying in Scotland no longer pay tuition fees. Other additional forms of student support include: dependant's allowances; young and mature student bursaries; hardship funds; disabled students' allowance and care leavers' grant; and the Maintenance Grant, which was introduced in September 2006.

Budgetary expenditure on education and training in 2007/08 totalled an estimated £78,800m., representing 14.1% of total current expenditure.

Public Holidays

2009: 1 January (New Year's Day), 2 January* (Scotland only), 17 March (St Patrick's Day, Northern Ireland only), 10 April* (Good Friday), 13 April† (Easter Monday), 4 May* (Early May Holiday), 25 May (Spring Holiday), 13 July (Battle of the Boyne, Northern Ireland only), 3 August* (Summer Bank Holiday, Scotland only), 31 August† (Late Summer Bank Holiday), 25 December (Christmas Day), 28 December* (Boxing Day).

2010: 1 January (New Year's Day), 2 January* (Scotland only), 17 March (St Patrick's Day, Northern Ireland only), 2 April (Good Friday), 5 April† (Easter Monday), 3 May* (Early May Bank Holiday), 31 May (Spring Bank Holiday), 12 July (Battle of the Boyne, Northern Ireland only), 2 August* (Summer Bank Holiday, Scotland only), 30 August† (Late Summer Bank Holiday), 25 December (Christmas Day), 26 December* (Boxing Day).

* Bank Holidays but not national holidays in Scotland.
† Excluding Scotland.

Weights and Measures

The metric system of weights and measures is now the primary system in force, although the imperial system is still used in limited areas.

Weight

1 pound (lb) = 16 ounces (oz) = 453.59 grams.
14 pounds = 1 stone = 6.35 kilograms.
112 pounds = 1 hundredweight (cwt) = 50.8 kilograms.
20 hundredweights = 1 ton = 1,016 kilograms.

Length

1 yard (yd) = 3 feet (ft) = 36 inches (ins) = 0.9144 metre.
1,760 yards = 1 mile = 1.609 kilometres.

Capacity

1 gallon = 4 quarts = 8 pints = 4.546 litres.

Statistical Survey

Source (unless otherwise stated): Office for National Statistics, 1 Drummond Gate, London SW1V 2QQ; internet www.statistics.gov.uk.

Statistics refer to the United Kingdom unless otherwise indicated.

Area and Population

AREA, POPULATION AND DENSITY

Land area (sq km)	242,495*
Population usually resident (census results)	
21 April 1991	56,466,700
29 April 2001	
Males	28,581,233
Females	30,207,961
Total	58,789,194
Population (official estimates at mid-year)	
2005	59,834,300
2006	60,587,300
2007	60,975,400
Density (per sq km) at mid-2007	251.5

* 93,628 sq miles.

DISTRIBUTION OF POPULATION
(at mid-2007, '000)

	Land area (sq km)	Population	Density (per sq km)
Great Britain	228,919	59,261.2	258.9
England	130,279	51,092.0	392.2
Wales	20,733	2,980.0	143.7
Scotland	77,907	5,144.2	66.0
Northern Ireland	13,576	1,759.1	129.6
Total	**242,495**	**60,975.4**	**251.5**

ADMINISTRATIVE AREAS
('000, population estimates at mid-2007)

England			
		Stoke-on-Trent	239
Greater London	7,557	Swindon	190
Metropolitan Counties:			
		Telford and Wrekin	162
Greater Manchester	2,562	Thurrock	150
Merseyside	1,350	Torbay	134
South Yorkshire	1,299	Warrington	195
Tyne and Wear	1,089	West Berkshire	151
		Windsor and	
West Midlands	2,604	Maidenhead	141
West Yorkshire	2,181	Wokingham	157

THE UNITED KINGDOM — Statistical Survey

Unitary Authorities:			
Bath and North-east Somerset	178	York	193
Blackburn with Darwen	141	*Non-Metropolitan Counties:*	
Blackpool	143	Bedfordshire	407
Bournemouth	163	Buckinghamshire	491
Bracknell Forest	114	Cambridgeshire	597
Brighton and Hove	254	Cheshire	689
Bristol	416	Cornwall/Isles of Scilly	532
Darlington	100	Cumbria	497
Derby	238	Derbyshire	758
East Riding of Yorkshire	333	Devon	750
Halton	120	Dorset	407
Hartlepool	91	Durham	505
Herefordshire	178	East Sussex	508
Isle of Wight	140	Essex	1,376
Kingston upon Hull	257	Gloucestershire	583
Leicester	293	Hampshire	1,277
Luton	189	Hertfordshire	1,066
Medway	252	Kent	1,395
Middlesbrough	139	Lancashire	1,168
Milton Keynes	228	Leicestershire	641
North Lincolnshire	159	Lincolnshire	693
North Somerset	205	Norfolk	841
North-east Lincolnshire	158	North Yorkshire	596
Nottingham	289	Northamptonshire	678
Peterborough	163	Northumberland	311
Plymouth	251	Nottinghamshire	772
Poole	138	Oxfordshire	636
Portsmouth	198	Shropshire	291
Reading	144	Somerset	523
Redcar and Cleveland	139	Staffordshire	826
Rutland	38	Suffolk	709
Slough	120	Surrey	1,098
South Gloucestershire	257	Warwickshire	527
Southampton	231	West Sussex	776
Southend-on-Sea	162	Wiltshire	453
Stockton-on-Tees	190	Worcestershire	555

Wales

Unitary Authorities:			
Blaenau Gwent	69	Isle of Anglesey	69
Bridgend	134	Merthyr Tydfil	56
Caerphilly	172	Monmouthshire	88
Cardiff	321	Neath Port Talbot	137
Carmarthenshire	180	Newport	140
Ceredigion	78	Pembrokeshire	118
Conwy	112	Powys	132
Denbighshire	97	Rhondda, Cynon, Taff	234
Flintshire	151	Swansea	228
Gwynedd	118	Torfaen	91
		Vale of Glamorgan	124
		Wrexham	132

Scotland

Unitary Authorities:			
Aberdeen City	209	Glasgow City	582
Aberdeenshire	239	Highland	217
Angus	110	Inverclyde	81
Argyll and Bute	91	Midlothian	80
Clackmannanshire	50	Moray	87
Comhairle nan Eilean Siar (Western Isles)	26	North Ayrshire	136
Dumfries and Galloway	148	North Lanarkshire	325
Dundee City	142	Orkney Islands	20
East Ayrshire	120	Perth and Kinross	142
East Dunbartonshire	105	Renfrewshire	170
East Lothian	94	Scottish Borders	111
East Renfrewshire	89	Shetland Islands	22
Edinburgh, City of	468	South Ayrshire	112
Falkirk	151	South Lanarkshire	310
Fife	361	Stirling	88
		West Dunbartonshire	91
		West Lothian	168

Northern Ireland

Unitary Authorities:			
Antrim	53	Derry	109
Ards	77	Down	69
Armagh	58	Dungannon	54
Ballymena	62	Fermanagh	61
Ballymoney	30	Larne	31
Banbridge	46	Limavady	34
Belfast	268	Lisburn	114
Carrickfergus	40	Magherafelt	43
Castlereagh	66	Moyle	17
Coleraine	57	Newry and Mourne	96
Cookstown	35	Newtownabbey	82
Craigavon	89	North Down	79
		Omagh	52
		Strabane	39

Sources: Office for National Statistics.

PRINCIPAL LOCALITIES*
('000, population estimates at mid-2007)

Greater London (capital)	7,557	Newcastle upon Tyne	272
Birmingham	1,010	Belfast	268
Leeds	761	Bolton	262
Glasgow City	582	Kingston upon Hull	257
Sheffield	530	South Gloucestershire	257
Bradford	497	Walsall	255
Edinburgh	468	Brighton and Hove	254
Manchester	458	Rotherham	253
Liverpool	436	Medway	252
Bristol	416	Plymouth	251
Kirklees	401	Aberdeenshire	239
Fife	361	Stoke-on-Trent	239
East Riding of Yorkshire	333	Derby	238
North Lanarkshire	325	Wolverhampton	236
Wakefield	322	Rhondda, Cynon, Taff	234
Cardiff	321	Southampton	231
South Lanarkshire	310	Milton Keynes	228
Wirral	310	Swansea	228
Coventry	308	Barnsley	225
Wigan	306	Oldham	220
Dudley	305	Salford	219
Leicester	293	Highland	217
Doncaster	291	Tameside	214
Nottingham	289	Trafford	213
Sandwell	288	Aberdeen City	206
Stockport	281	Rochdale	206
Sunderland	280	Solihull	204
Sefton	276		

* Local authority areas with populations greater than 200,000.

Sources: Office for National Statistics.

BIRTHS, MARRIAGES AND DEATHS*

	Registered live births		Registered marriages		Registered deaths	
	Number	Rate (per 1,000)	Number	Rate (per 1,000)	Number	Rate (per 1,000)
2000	697,029	11.6	305,912	5.2	610,579	10.4
2001	669,123	11.4	286,133	4.9	604,393	10.2
2002	668,777	11.3	293,021	4.9	608,045	10.2
2003	695,549	11.7	308,620	5.1	612,085	10.3
2004	715,996	12.0	313,550	5.2	583,082	9.7
2005	722,549	12.0	286,826	4.8	582,964	9.7
2006	748,563	12.4	275,137	4.5	572,224	9.4
2007	772,245	12.7	270,003	4.4	574,685	9.4

* In England and Wales, figures for births are tabulated by year of occurrence, while figures for Scotland and Northern Ireland are tabulated by year of registration. Births to non-resident mothers in Northern Ireland are excluded from the figures for the United Kingdom.

Sources: Office for National Statistics; General Register Office for Scotland; Northern Ireland Statistics and Research Agency.

Life expectancy (years at birth, WHO estimates): 79.2 (males 77.0; females 81.3) in 2006 (Source: WHO, *World Health Statistics*).

THE UNITED KINGDOM

IMMIGRATION AND EMIGRATION*

Immigrants
('000)

Origin†	2005	2006	2007
EU‡	182	205	222
Commonwealth countries	219	219	199
Australia, New Zealand, Canada	61	60	47
South Africa	29	21	17
India, Bangladesh, Sri Lanka	62	69	65
Pakistan	24	32	30
Caribbean	2	3	3
Other	41	34	37
Other territories	162	166	155
USA	25	23	23
Middle East	19	21	23
Total	563	591	577

Emigrants
('000)

Destination†	2005	2006	2007
EU‡	136	145	130
Commonwealth countries	128	147	127
Australia, New Zealand, Canada	86	100	83
South Africa	13	14	11
India, Bangladesh, Sri Lanka	9	14	14
Pakistan	7	2	5
Caribbean	2	2	1
Other	11	15	13
Other territories	95	106	82
USA	24	29	18
Middle East	11	16	11
Total	359	400	340

* Figures are compiled in accordance with the Total International Migration (TIM) methodology, which supplements International Passenger Survey (IPS) data (whereby small samples of detailed passenger numbers are extrapolated according to a weighting system) with estimates of migration between the UK and Ireland (agreed between the Irish Central Statistics Office and the UK Office for National Statistics), and with Home Office data on asylum seekers and their dependents. In addition, two adjustments are estimated to account for 'visitor switchers' (who stay longer than their stated intention) and 'migrant switchers' (who stay for less time than intended).
† Figures refer to the country of immigrants' last permanent residence or emigrants' intended future residence.
‡ Figures for all years show the EU as it was constituted at 31 December of year shown.

WORK-FORCE JOBS BY INDUSTRY
('000 at December)

	2005	2006	2007
Agriculture, hunting, forestry and fishing	453	454	451
Mining, energy and water	169	177	183
Manufacturing	3,319	3,224	3,172
Construction	2,149	2,215	2,208
Distribution, hotels and restaurants	7,078	7,014	7,117
Transport and communications	1,866	1,853	1,854
Banking, finance, insurance, etc.	6,364	6,503	6,651
Public administration, education and health*	7,892	7,967	7,991
Other services	1,962	2,004	1,992
Total	31,253	31,412	31,620
Males	16,671	16,748	16,789
Females	14,582	14,664	14,831

* Including public and private sectors.

Note: Since data correspond to jobs rather than employees, a single worker may be counted more than once; figures include armed forces personnel.

Economically active population (labour force survey, '000 persons aged 16 years and over, excl. armed forces, Nov. 2007–Jan. 2008): Total employed 29,457; Unemployed 1,608; Total labour force 31,065 (males 16,827, females 14,238).

Health and Welfare

KEY INDICATORS

Total fertility rate (children per woman, 2006)	1.8
Under-5 mortality rate (per 1,000 live births, 2006)	6
HIV/AIDS (% of persons aged 15–49, 2007)	0.2
Physicians (per 1,000 head, 2004)	2.3
Hospital beds (per 1,000 head, 2004)	3.9
Health expenditure (2006): US $ per head (PPP)	2,784
Health expenditure (2006): % of GDP	8.4
Health expenditure (2006): public (% of total)	87.4
Human Development Index (2006): ranking	21
Human Development Index (2006): value	0.942

For sources and definitions, see explanatory note on p. vi.

Agriculture

PRINCIPAL CROPS
('000 metric tons)

	2005	2006	2007
Wheat	14,863	14,747	13,362
Barley	5,495	5,239	5,149
Oats	532	728	740
Rye	40	43	38
Triticale (wheat-rye hybrid)	53	61	65
Potatoes	5,961	5,727	5,635
Sugar beet	8,687	7,150	6,500*
Rapeseed	1,902	1,890	2,108
Peas, dry	161	145	130*
Broad beans, dry	96†	150*	160*
Onions, dry	383.4	420.0*	355.0*
Mushrooms and truffles	74	68	72
Carrots and turnips	832.6	807.0	859.3
Cabbages and other brassicas	308.2	323.4	253.5
Cauliflower and broccoli	218.7	195.5	186.4
Peas, green	306.1	333.5	330.0*
Linseed	89	49	23
Lettuce and chicory	139.9	134.6	117.0*
Tomatoes	79.5	84.1	85.6
Cucumbers and gherkins	59.0	46.3	49.4
Apples	218.5	234.7	230.0*
Pears	23.8	29.1	30.0*
Strawberries	68.6	65.9	66.0*

* FAO estimate.
† Unofficial figure.

Aggregate production (may include official, semi-official or estimated data): Total cereals 20,998 in 2005, 20,832 in 2006, 19,369 in 2007; Total pulses 866 in 2005, 795 in 2006, 740 in 2007; Total roots and tubers 5,961 in 2005, 5,727 in 2006, 5,635 in 2007; Total vegetables (incl. melons) 2,709 in 2005, 2,925 in 2006, 2,801 in 2007; Total fruits (excl. melons) 365 in 2005, 367 in 2006, 364 in 2007.

Source: FAO.

LIVESTOCK
('000 head, year ending September)

	2005	2006	2007
Cattle	10,378	10,160	9,988
Sheep and lambs	35,253	34,722	33,582
Pigs	4,862	4,933	4,882
Chickens	160,509	148,929	157,265
Ducks and geese	2,790	3,451	2,520
Turkeys	6,935	6,123	3,832

Source: FAO.

THE UNITED KINGDOM

LIVESTOCK PRODUCTS
('000 metric tons, unless otherwise indicated)

	2005	2006	2007*
Cattle meat	762	847	850
Sheep meat	331	330	330
Pig meat	706	697	700
Chicken meat	1,333.8	1,288.8	1,300.0
Cows' milk	14,473	14,340	14,450
Hen eggs	609.0	594.0	590.0
Wool, greasy	60	60*	62

* FAO estimate(s).
Source: FAO.

Forestry

ROUNDWOOD REMOVALS
('000 cubic metres, excl. bark)

	2005	2006	2007
Sawlogs, veneer logs and logs for sleepers	5,003	5,313	5,715
Pulpwood	2,705	2,369	2,396
Other industrial wood	457	431	448
Fuel wood	317	317	459
Total	8,482	8,430	9,018

Source: FAO.

SAWNWOOD PRODUCTION
('000 cubic metres, incl. railway sleepers)

	2005	2006	2007
Coniferous (softwood)	2,716	2,862	3,100
Broadleaved (hardwood)	53	45	45
Total	2,770	2,907	3,145

Source: FAO.

Fishing
('000 metric tons, live weight)

	2004	2005	2006
Capture	653.4	669.9	623.8
Atlantic cod	21.2	20.0	20.8
Haddock	46.0	31.7	39.8
Blue whiting	59.8	126.1	82.1
Atlantic herring	96.3	130.8	109.6
Atlantic mackerel	174.7	126.6	115.7
Norway lobster	30.2	27.1	41.4
Common edible cockle	12.9	13.2	11.3
Aquaculture	207.2	172.8	171.8
Atlantic salmon	158.1	129.8	132.0
Total	860.6	842.7	795.7

Note: Figures exclude aquatic mammals, recorded by number rather than weight. The number of whales caught was: 467 in 2004; 2 in 2005; 54 in 2006.
Source: FAO.

Mining and Quarrying
('000 metric tons, unless otherwise indicated)

	2004	2005	2006*
Hard coal (incl. slurries)	25,096	20,498	18,588
Natural gas and petroleum:			
Methane—colliery	70	65	79,947
Methane—North Sea[1]	95,937	87,517	
Crude petroleum	87,516	72,121	69,665
Condensates and others[2]	7,858	7,543	6,913
Iron ore[3]	1*	0	0
China clay (sales)[4]	1,945	1,911	1,762
Ball clay (sales)	965	1,011	1,015
Fireclay[5]	402	395	400
Fuller's earth (sales)*[6]	28	6	—
Common clay and shale[5]	11,164	10,898	10,000
Slate[7]	901	928	900
Limestone[8]	81,641	77,596	90,000
Dolomite[8]	12,226	11,514	
Chalk[5]	7,997	7,105	7,000
Sandstone[9]	18,844	18,685	19,000
Common sand and gravel[10]	97,333	94,666	93,000
Igneous rock[11]	53,037	53,104	54,000
Gypsum	1,686	1,700*	1,700
Rock salt*	2,000	2,000	2,000
Salt from brine*	1,000	1,000	1,000
Salt in brine*[12]	2,800	2,800	2,800
Fluorspar*	50	61	60
Barytes	61	62	47
Talc	4	6	4
Potash[13]	912	732	716

* Estimate(s).
[1] 2005 figure refers to all methane.
[2] Includes ethane, propane and butane, in addition to condensates (pentane and hydrocarbons).
[3] Figures refer to gross weight. The estimated iron content is 55%.
[4] Dry weight.
[5] Excluding production in Northern Ireland.
[6] Estimates based on data from producing companies.
[7] Including waste used for constructional fill and powder and granules used in industry.
[8] Dolomite included with limestone for 2006.
[9] Including grit and conglomerate.
[10] Including marine-dredged sand and gravel for both home consumption and export.
[11] Excluding production in Northern Ireland and the Channel Islands.
[12] Used for purposes other than salt-making.
[13] Chloride (K_2O content).

Source: British Geological Survey.

Industry

SELECTED PRODUCTS
('000 metric tons, unless otherwise indicated)

	2004	2005	2006
Wheat flour	5,576	5,611	n.a.
Refined sugar[1]	1,390	1,300	n.a.
Margarine and other table spreads	431	n.a.	n.a.
Crude seed and nut oil[2]	747	n.a.	n.a.
Beer ('000 hectolitres)	57,459	56,255	53,763
Cigarettes ('000 million)	48.2	45.9	44.4
Butane and propane[3]	2,152	2,424	2,304
Petroleum naphtha[3]	3,168	3,019	2,734
Motor spirit (petrol)[3]	24,589	22,620	21,443
Aviation turbine fuel[3]	5,615	5,167	6,261
Burning oil[3]	3,613	3,325	3,374
Diesel fuel and gas oil[3]	28,647	28,486	26,038
Fuel oil[3]	11,308	10,155	11,280

THE UNITED KINGDOM

—continued	2004	2005	2006
Lubricating oils[3]	1,136	936	617
Petroleum bitumen (asphalt)[3]	2,196	1,912	1,749
Cement	11,405	11,216	11,469
Pig-iron[4]	10,180	10,189	10,696
Crude steel (usable)	13,766	13,239	13,905
Aluminium—(wrought remelt)	565.0	573.8	558.2
Refined lead—unwrought[5]	245.9	304.3	306.7
Passenger motor cars ('000)	1,646.8	1,595.7	1,442.1
Road goods vehicles ('000)	209.3	206.8	n.a.
Electric energy (million kWh)	393,867	398,372	398,327

[1] Production from home-grown sugar beet only.
[2] Including maize oil.
[3] Refinery production only (excluding supplies from other sources).
[4] Including blast-furnace ferro-alloys.
[5] Excluding hard lead.

2007: Beer ('000 hectolitres) 50,511; Cigarettes ('000 million) 42.0.

Finance

CURRENCY AND EXCHANGE RATES

Monetary Units
100 pence (pennies) = 1 pound sterling (£).

Dollar and Euro Equivalents (31 December 2008)
US $1 = 68.60 pence;
€1 = 95.47 pence;
£10 = $14.58 = €10.47.

Average Exchange Rate (pound sterling per US $)
2006   0.5435
2007   0.4998
2008   0.5412

BUDGET
(general government transactions, non-cash basis, year ending 31 March, £ '000 million)

Revenue

	2005/06	2006/07	2007/08
Inland revenue	277.0	298.0	319.1
Income tax (net)	130.5	143.4	147.4
Corporation tax	41.8	44.3	46.4
National insurance contributions	85.5	87.3	100.4
Customs and excise	120.7	125.9	132.1
Value added tax	72.9	77.4	80.6
Fuel duties	23.4	23.6	24.9
Business rates	19.8	21.0	21.4
Council tax	20.9	22.2	23.4
Other taxes and royalties	17.9	19.2	20.1
Interest and dividends	6.8	6.5	8.7
Gross operating surplus and rent	22.9	23.8	24.3
Other receipts and adjustments	0.2	2.9	−0.9
Total current revenue	**486.5**	**519.3**	**548.0**

Source: HM Treasury, *Public Sector Finances Databank* (March 2009).

Outlays

Outlays by function of government*	2005/06	2006/07	2007/08†
General public services	12.9	13.2	14.0
EU transactions	−0.6	−1.8	−1.6
International services	6.2	6.3	6.9
Public sector debt interest	26.8	28.6	31.2
Defence	30.9	32.2	33.8
Public order and safety	29.0	30.3	32.5
Enterprise and economic development	6.6	6.5	7.2
Science and technology	2.9	2.8	3.2
Employment policies	3.4	3.4	3.3
Agriculture, fisheries and forestry	5.6	5.1	5.3
Transport	17.0	20.1	21.3
Environment protection	8.4	9.2	10.0
Housing and community amenities	10.5	11.5	12.5
Health	89.7	94.5	102.6
Recreation, culture and religion	10.7	11.3	12.4
Education and training	69.6	72.8	78.8
Social protection	170.9	177.1	186.6
Unallocated expenditure	—	—	−0.9
Accounting adjustments	23.7	26.5	27.3
Less Public sector net investment	23.6	25.8	28.5
Total current expenditure‡	**500.7**	**523.9**	**557.8**

* Including net acquisition of non-financial assets.
† Estimates.
‡ Including depreciation.

Source: HM Treasury, *Public Expenditure Statistical Analyses* (April 2008).

OFFICIAL RESERVES
(US $ million at 31 December)*

	2006	2007	2008
Gold	6,341	8,344	8,628
IMF special drawing rights	396	360	448
Foreign currencies	40,990	44,315	40,487
Reserve position in IMF	1,414	1,099	2,350
Other reserve assets	4,074	3,060	−2,939
Total	**53,214**	**57,178**	**48,974**

* Reserves are revalued at 31 March each year.

Source: Bank of England.

MONEY SUPPLY
(£ million at 31 December)

	2005	2006	2007
Retail deposits and cash	922,687	996,671	1,073,021
Notes and coin in private sector	38,508	40,565	44,606
Bank deposits	709,941	768,053	817,865
Building society deposits	174,238	188,053	210,550
Wholesale deposits	405,633	500,888	600,716
Bank deposits	390,022	482,013	579,640
Building society deposits	15,612	18,875	21,075
Total broad money	**1,328,320**	**1,497,559**	**1,673,736**

Source: Bank of England.

THE UNITED KINGDOM

COST OF LIVING
(General Index of Retail Prices, annual averages; base: January 1987 = 100)

	2006	2007	2008
Food	157.1	164.3	179.5
Catering	245.6	253.6	264.2
Alcoholic drink	212.7	219.0	227.7
Tobacco	343.4	361.6	377.6
Housing	302.1	330.7	339.9
Fuel and light	199.1	213.2	253.6
Household goods	147.1	150.5	155.6
Household services	190.8	197.3	203.7
Clothing and footwear	94.5	93.7	90.3
Personal goods and services	209.1	215.2	222.3
Motoring expenditure	186.9	189.2	195.1
Fares and other travel costs	229.9	244.2	261.1
Leisure goods	92.2	89.8	87.2
Leisure services	266.8	275.6	287.2
All items	**198.1**	**206.6**	**214.8**

NATIONAL ACCOUNTS
(£ million at current prices)

National Income and Product

	2005	2006	2007
Compensation of employees	682,205	715,496	744,857
Gross operating surplus	344,209	368,310	403,540
Mixed income	74,858	78,908	83,628
Gross domestic product (GDP) at factor cost	**1,101,272**	**1,162,714**	**1,232,025**
Taxes on production and imports	162,288	171,453	180,262
Less Subsidies	11,055	12,307	12,079
Statistical discrepancy	—	—	834
GDP at market prices	**1,252,505**	**1,321,860**	**1,401,042**
Primary incomes received from abroad } Less Primary incomes paid abroad	21,020	8,821	6,818
Gross national income	**1,273,525**	**1,330,681**	**1,407,860**
Less Consumption of fixed capital	138,520	147,858	158,143
Net national income	**1,135,005**	**1,182,823**	**1,249,717**
Current transfers from abroad . } Less Current transfers paid abroad	−11,052	−10,657	−11,943
Net national disposable income	**1,123,953**	**1,172,166**	**1,237,774**

Expenditure on the Gross Domestic Product

	2005	2006	2007
Final consumption expenditure	1,079,305	1,132,537	1,190,314
Households	780,265	814,659	858,827
Non-profit institutions serving households	30,402	32,209	34,587
General government	268,638	285,669	296,900
Gross capital formation	215,914	232,527	257,513
Gross fixed capital formation	211,318	227,920	249,238
Changes in inventories	4,973	4,322	7,901
Acquisitions, less disposals, of valuables	−377	285	374
Total domestic expenditure	**1,295,219**	**1,365,064**	**1,447,827**
Exports of goods and services	331,028	376,384	368,337
Less Imports of goods and services	−373,742	−419,588	−415,817
Statistical discrepancy	—	—	695
GDP in purchasers' values	**1,252,505**	**1,321,860**	**1,401,042**
GDP at constant 2003 prices	**1,195,276**	**1,229,196**	**1,266,397**

Gross Domestic Product by Economic Activity

	2004	2005	2006
Agriculture, hunting, forestry and fishing	10,600	7,422	7,865
Mining and quarrying	22,560	27,669	32,202
Manufacturing	147,261	148,591	153,155
Electricity, gas and water supply	16,672	16,667	18,870
Construction	63,955	68,019	73,993
Wholesale and retail trade; repair of motor vehicles, motorcycles and personal and household goods	127,411	130,952	136,071
Hotels and restaurants	31,290	31,969	33,765
Transport, storage and communication	79,828	80,510	81,027
Financial intermediation	75,042	79,356	91,011
Real estate, renting and business activities	247,048	259,335	273,644
Public administration and defence	55,393	60,096	63,033
Education	61,814	66,186	69,345
Health and social work	74,417	78,497	81,883
Other community, social and personal services*	55,283	59,852	61,368
Gross value added at basic prices	**1,068,574**	**1,115,121**	**1,177,232**
Value added taxes on products	81,550	83,415	87,753
Other taxes on products	58,307	59,167	62,869
Less Subsidies on products	7,836	5,198	5,994
GDP in purchasers' values	**1,200,595**	**1,252,505**	**1,321,860**

* Including private households with employees, and extra-territorial organizations.

Note: Totals may not be equal to the sum of component parts, owing to rounding; deductions for financial intermediation services indirectly measured are assumed to have been made at sectoral origin.

BALANCE OF PAYMENTS
(£ million)

	2005	2006	2007
Exports of goods f.o.b.	211,608	243,635	220,703
Imports of goods f.o.b.	−280,197	−319,947	−309,955
Trade balance	**−68,589**	**−76,312**	**−89,252**
Exports of services	119,420	132,749	147,634
Imports of services	−93,545	−99,641	−105,862
Balance on goods and services	**−42,714**	**−43,204**	**−47,480**
Other income received	186,739	238,506	285,745
Other income paid	−164,867	−228,409	−277,139
Balance on goods, services and income	**−20,842**	**−33,107**	**−38,874**
Current transfers received	17,400	18,223	15,665
Current transfers paid	−29,249	−30,147	−29,359
Current balance	**−32,691**	**−45,031**	**−52,568**
Capital account (net)	1,503	975	2,641
Direct investment abroad	−44,005	−47,155	−130,335
Direct investment from abroad	97,845	80,539	111,343
Portfolio investment abroad	−151,039	−138,588	−96,957
Portfolio investment from abroad	132,718	152,609	175,172
Financial derivatives (net)	9,556	7,449	−19,001
Other investment abroad	−501,238	−395,720	−733,234
Other investment from abroad	487,400	382,315	734,033
Net errors and omissions	607	2,181	10,097
Overall balance	**656**	**−426**	**1,191**

THE UNITED KINGDOM

GROSS PUBLIC EXPENDITURE ON OVERSEAS AID
(£ million, year ending 31 March)

	2004/05	2005/06	2006/07
Total bilateral aid*	3,120.1	4,416.7	4,903.3
DFID† bilateral programmes	2,110.9	2,502.0	2,561.8
Poverty reduction budget support	347.0	473.1	461.0
Other financial aid	423.5	472.8	481.9
Technical co-operation	462.6	481.1	522.7
Grants and other aid in kind	530.4	628.3	692.1
Humanitarian assistance	332.3	406.0	336.5
DFID debt relief	14.9	40.8	67.6
Other bilateral programmes	1,009.2	1,914.8	2,341.5
CDC investments	238.3	172.8	278.8
Debt relief	627.4	1,588.4	1,866.6
Other‡	143.6	153.5	196.1
Total multilateral aid	1,904.7	2,005.6	2,337.6
European Community	1,224.1	1,193.8	1,125.4
World Bank Group	206.6	273.3	592.3
International Monetary Fund	1.8	23.7	0.0
Global Environmental Assistance	52.4	53.5	50.3
HIPC Trust Fund	42.1	11.1	18.7
Regional development banks	82.2	77.8	123.6
UN agencies	235.0	336.4	356.5
Other	60.5	36.1	70.8
Administrative costs	227.8	256.5	245.9
Total gross expenditure on aid	**5,252.5**	**6,678.8**	**7,486.8**

* Excluding official advances to CDC.
† Department for International Development (DFID).
‡ Mainly non-DFID debt relief.

Source: Department for International Development, *Statistics on International Development*.

External Trade

(Note: Figures include the Isle of Man and the Channel Islands)

PRINCIPAL COMMODITIES
(£ million)

Imports c.i.f.	2006	2007	2008
Food and live animals	19,814	21,324	25,306
Mineral fuels, lubricants, etc.	30,888	31,928	47,755
Petroleum, petroleum products, etc.	25,967	26,787	37,315
Chemicals and related products	31,727	34,645	37,770
Basic manufactures*	37,615	39,792	41,893
Machinery and transport equipment	139,828	117,726	120,856
Mechanical machinery and equipment	22,614	25,776	28,854
Electrical machinery, apparatus, etc.	75,087	46,006	47,628
Road vehicles and parts†	32,674	36,590	33,794
Other transport equipment	9,453	9,354	10,580
Miscellaneous manufactured articles	44,920	47,939	50,920
Clothing and footwear	14,546	14,969	16,066
Scientific and photographic apparatus	7,655	7,572	8,425
Total (incl. others)	319,947	310,612	343,964

Exports f.o.b.	2006	2007	2008
Food and live animals	6,770	7,374	8,726
Mineral fuels, lubricants, etc.	25,301	24,700	34,846
Petroleum, petroleum products, etc.	23,173	22,756	31,666
Chemicals and related products	37,179	38,891	43,877
Organic chemicals	8,009	7,601	8,391
Medicinal products	13,786	14,507	17,310
Basic manufactures*	27,664	29,378	32,557
Machinery and transport equipment	110,394	82,713	89,234
Mechanical machinery and equipment	28,245	28,969	32,232
Electrical machinery, apparatus, etc.	55,336	24,215	25,325
Road vehicles and parts†	19,334	21,114	22,551
Other transport equipment	7,479	8,415	9,126
Miscellaneous manufactured articles	25,974	26,695	28,453
Scientific and photographic apparatus	7,344	7,063	8,061
Total (incl. others)	243,635	220,858	251,088

* Sorted industrial diamonds, usually classified with natural abrasives (under 'crude materials'), are included with 'basic manufactures'.
† Excluding tyres, engines and electrical parts.

PRINCIPAL TRADING PARTNERS
(£ million)

Imports c.i.f.	2006	2007	2008
Austria	2,786	2,488	2,327
Belgium-Luxembourg	18,183	15,820	17,178
Canada	4,954	5,793	5,796
China, People's Republic	15,237	18,734	23,159
Denmark	6,439	3,444	3,905
Finland	3,118	2,619	2,777
France	26,376	21,896	23,154
Germany	42,660	44,565	44,636
Hong Kong	7,338	6,939	8,074
India	3,121	3,809	4,488
Ireland	10,770	11,338	12,286
Italy	12,775	13,316	13,891
Japan	7,857	7,885	8,531
Korea, Republic	3,069	3,073	3,509
Netherlands	22,275	23,079	25,715
Norway	14,453	14,316	21,650
Poland	3,622	3,695	4,330
Russia	5,740	5,248	6,923
Singapore	3,756	4,247	4,008
South Africa	3,904	3,060	4,734
Spain (excl. Canary Is)	12,144	10,489	10,745
Sweden	5,985	5,274	6,805
Switzerland	4,372	4,746	5,264
Turkey	3,946	4,632	4,885
USA	25,830	26,093	25,880
Total (incl. others)	319,947	310,612	343,964

THE UNITED KINGDOM

Exports f.o.b.	2006	2007	2008
Australia	2,488	2,630	3,122
Belgium-Luxembourg	15,082	12,122	13,266
Canada	3,894	3,291	3,282
China	3,264	3,860	5,117
Denmark	3,715	2,182	2,599
France	28,693	18,103	18,067
Germany	27,602	24,699	28,062
Hong Kong	2,864	2,726	3,702
India	2,693	2,968	4,164
Ireland	17,480	17,801	19,104
Italy	9,494	9,189	9,351
Japan	4,109	3,866	3,933
Netherlands	16,522	15,115	19,697
Norway	2,125	2,697	2,875
Poland	2,705	2,372	3,010
Russia	2,063	2,893	4,305
Spain (excl. Canary Is)	12,295	9,979	10,227
Sweden	5,246	4,904	5,194
Switzerland	4,189	3,808	4,701
USA	32,287	32,274	35,201
Total (incl. others)	243,635	220,858	251,088

Transport

RAILWAYS

	2004/05	2005/06	2006/07
Passenger journeys (million):			
Great Britain national railways	1,045	1,082	1,164
Northern Ireland railways	6.9	7.7	n.a.
Underground railways (London and Glasgow)	989	983	1,053
Light rail	172	177	192
Passenger-km (million):			
Great Britain national railways	41,762	43,211	46,497
Northern Ireland railways	225.2	240.5	n.a.
Underground railways (London and Glasgow)	7,649	7,628	7,989
Light rail	1,033	1,052	1,120
Freight carried (million metric tons)*	101	108	108
Freight ton-km ('000 million)*	20	22	22

* Great Britain only. Figures exclude parcels and materials for rail infrastructure.

Sources: Department for Transport (Great Britain); Department for Regional Development (Northern Ireland).

ROAD TRAFFIC
('000 licensed vehicles in Great Britain at 31 December)

	2004	2005	2006
Private motor cars	25,754	26,208	26,508
Motorcycles, scooters and mopeds	1,060	1,075	1,094
Light goods vehicles*	2,900	3,019	3,137
Heavy goods vehicles	434	433	446
Public passenger vehicles	100	103	107

* Goods vehicles less than 3,500 kg in weight.

Source: Department for Transport.

SHIPPING

Merchant Fleet
(registered at 31 December)

	2005	2006	2007
Number of vessels	1,563	1,598	1,637
Total displacement ('000 grt)	11,194.0	12,150.0	13,443.8

Source: Lloyd's Register-Fairplay, *World Fleet Statistics*.

International Sea-borne Freight Traffic
('000 metric tons)

	2004	2005	2006
Goods imported	342,425	354,391	365,112
Goods exported	230,645	230,529	218,627

Source: Department for Transport.

CIVIL AVIATION
(United Kingdom airlines)

	2005	2006	2007
All scheduled services:			
Aircraft stage flights (number)	1,016,354	1,037,729	1,052,799
Aircraft-km flown (million)	1,325	1,400	1,474
Passengers carried (million)	94	98	102
Passenger-km flown (million)	200,460	213,442	227,720
Total cargo carried (metric tons)	921,412	946,365	941,421
Total metric ton-km (million)	6,088	6,312	6,311
Freight metric ton-km (million)	5,998	6,213	6,199
Mail metric ton-km (million)	90	99	112
Domestic scheduled services:			
Aircraft stage flights (number)	394,069	399,438	383,591
Aircraft-km flown (million)	147	148	140
Passengers carried (million)	23	23	22
Passenger-km flown (million)	9,795	9,800	9,449
Total cargo carried (metric tons)	10,015	8,498	7,099
Total metric ton-km (million)	3	3	3
Freight metric ton-km (million)	3	2	2
Mail metric ton-km (million)	—	1	1
International scheduled services:			
Aircraft stage flights (number)	622,285	638,291	669,208
Aircraft-km flown (million)	1,178	1,251	1,333
Passengers carried (million)	71	75	80
Passenger-km flown (million)	190,666	203,642	218,271
Total cargo carried (metric tons)	911,398	937,868	934,323
Total metric ton-km (million)	6,085	6,482	6,308
Freight metric ton-km (million)	5,995	6,383	6,197
Mail metric ton-km (million)	90	99	111

Source: Civil Aviation Authority.

Tourism

FOREIGN VISITORS BY REGION OF ORIGIN
('000 unless otherwise indicated)

	2005	2006	2007
Europe	21,565	23,377	23,887
North America	4,234	4,764	4,403
Other countries	4,171	4,572	4,488
Total	29,970	32,713	32,778
Total expenditure (£ million)	14,248	16,002	15,960

Source: International Passenger Survey, Office for National Statistics, *Travel Trends*.

THE UNITED KINGDOM

VISITS BY COUNTRY OF PERMANENT RESIDENCE
('000)

	2005	2006	2007
Australia	919	956	941
Belgium	1,112	997	995
Canada	796	868	852
France	3,324	3,693	3,404
Germany	3,294	3,411	3,376
Ireland	2,806	2,909	2,970
Italy	1,186	1,477	1,615
Netherlands	1,720	1,791	1,823
Poland	1,041	1,326	1,294
Spain	1,786	1,981	2,227
Sweden	728	714	748
Switzerland	699	745	738
USA	3,438	3,896	4,403
Total (incl. others)	29,970	32,713	32,778

Source: International Passenger Survey, Office for National Statistics, *Travel Trends*.

Communications Media

	2005	2006	2007
Telephones ('000 main lines in use)	34,068.4	33,603.4	33,682.1
Mobile cellular telephones ('000 subscribers)	65,471.7	69,764.9	71,992.5
Internet users ('000)	32,200.0	37,800.0	40,200.0
Broadband subscribers ('000)	9,894.2	12,995.1	15,528.7

1996: Facsimile machines (number in use) 1,992,000.

1997: Radio receivers ('000 in use) 84,500.

1999: Book production (titles) 110,965.

2000: Daily newspapers 108 (average circulation 19,159,000); Non-daily newspapers 467 (average circulation 6,246,000).

Sources: UNESCO, *Statistical Yearbook*; UN, *Statistical Yearbook* and International Telecommunication Union.

Education

PRE-PRIMARY, PRIMARY AND SECONDARY EDUCATION

	2004/05	2005/06	2006/07
Schools	34,388	34,101	33,892
Public sector mainstream	29,998	29,711	29,470
Nursery	3,425	3,349[1]	3,326[1]
Primary	22,343	22,156	21,968
Secondary (incl. specialist)	4,230	4,206	4,176
Middle deemed secondary	260	250	248
Modern	124	115	113
Grammar	234	233	233
Technical	2	2	2
Comprehensive	3,427	3,424	3,398
Other	183	182	182
Non-maintained mainstream	2,476	2,493	2,542
Academies	17	27	46
Special schools	1,436	1,416	1,391
Maintained	1,329	1,311	1,285
Non-maintained	107	105	106
Pupil referral units	478	481	489
Teachers ('000):[2]	578.6	585.3	n.a.
Maintained nursery and primary schools	236.0	238.8[3]	n.a.
Maintained secondary schools	253.1	255.3[3]	n.a.
Non-maintained mainstream	67.8	68.8[3]	n.a.
All special schools	21.8	22.4[3]	n.a.
Full-time and part-time pupils ('000):	9,963.3	9,893.5	9,812.6
Maintained schools	9,305.3	9,229.1	9,136.1[3]
Nursery	141.9	150.8	157.1[3]
Primary	5,044.9	4,974.9	4,921.9[3]
Nursery classes	307.8	308.7	316.8[3]
Other classes	4,737.1	4,666.1	4,605.0[3]
Secondary	4,002.2	3,987.5	3,941.6[3]
Special schools	101.4	100.3	99.8[3]
Pupil referral units[4]	14.9	15.6	15.7[3]
Non-maintained schools	658.0	664.4	676.5[3]
Special schools	6.0	5.9	5.8[3]
Other	652.0	658.5	670.7[3]

[1] Excluding pre-school education centres not in partnership with a local authority.
[2] Qualified teachers only. Full-time teachers and the full-time equivalent of part-time teachers. Excluding Pupil Referral Unit teachers.
[3] Preliminary.
[4] England and Wales only; excluding pupils registered elsewhere.

Source: Department for Children, Schools and Families, London.

POST-COMPULSORY EDUCATION

	2004/05	2005/06	2006/07
Universities	119	123	124
Other higher education institutes	47	43	45
Further education institutes/colleges	480	476	459
Sixth-form colleges	102	102	96
Full-time teaching and research staff ('000)	170	171	n.a.
Students (incl. from overseas) taking higher education courses:			
full-time students ('000)	1,083.5	1,055.0	n.a.
part-time students ('000)	3,963.7	3,395.4	n.a.

Note: Figures for institutions include, but for teaching staff exclude, the Open University.

Source: Department for Children, Schools and Families, London.

THE UNITED KINGDOM

Directory

The Constitution

The United Kingdom is a constitutional monarchy. In the ninth century, when England was first united under a Saxon King, the monarchy was the only central power and the Constitution did not exist. Today, the Sovereign acts on the advice of her Ministers which she cannot, constitutionally, ignore; power, which has been at various times and in varying degrees in the hands of kings, feudal barons, ministers, councils and parliaments, or of particular groups or sections of society, is vested in the people as a whole, and the Sovereign is an essential part of the machinery of government which has gradually been devised to give expression to the popular will.

Both the powers of the Government and the functions of the Sovereign are determined by the Constitution, by the body of fundamental principles on which the State is governed and the methods, institutions and procedures which give them effect. But the United Kingdom has no written Constitution: there is no document, no one law or statute, to which reference can be made. The Constitution is an accumulation of convention, precedent and tradition which, although continually changing as the times change, is at any one moment binding and exact.

Some of the principles and many of the practices are secured by Statute, some are avowed by Declaration or Manifesto and many are incorporated in the Common Law. Magna Carta, in 1215, began the process by which the law of the land acquired a status of its own, independent of King and Parliament; the Bill of Rights of 1689 ended the long era of rivalry between Crown and Parliament and began the story of their co-operation; and the Reform Act of 1832 dramatically broadened the basis of representative government and prepared the way for further changes. The Constitution is, above all, based on usage. It has been modified to match changing customs and to meet successive situations. Any one Parliament could, if it chose, revise or repeal every law and disown every convention that has constitutional significance. It could destroy the whole fabric of political and social existence, including its own; because, according to the Constitution, Parliament, which represents the people, is supreme. The work of one Parliament is not binding on its successors, except in so far as changes must be made by constitutional means. Parliament cannot disobey the law, but it can change it.

It would be impossible to enumerate the principles which are extant in the British Constitution. In constitutional as in legal practice, the way has been to admit the general principle in quite practical terms related to specific practical problems: the Habeas Corpus Act, for example, which establishes the principle of no imprisonment without trial, makes no mention of the principle itself but lays down in most concrete terms the punishments that shall be inflicted on a judge, or other law officer, if he fails to issue the Writ (commanding the prisoner to be brought before the court) when applied for. The principles of the Constitution and constitutional practice are in fact inherent in the Common Law on the one hand and in the structure, functions and procedures of the various instruments of government on the other: of the Crown, of Parliament, of the Privy Council, of the Government and the Cabinet and of the government departments.

THE SOVEREIGN

The monarchy is hereditary, descending to the sons of the Sovereign in order of seniority or, if there are no sons, to the daughters.

The constitutional position of the Queen as head of the State, quite apart from her position as head of the Commonwealth, demands that she keep herself informed on all aspects of the life of her subjects, that she maintain absolute impartiality and that she should personally visit the different parts of her realm as often as it is possible for her to do so, but she has also quite specific functions, all exercised on ministerial advice: she summons, prorogues and dissolves Parliament; she must give Royal Assent to a Bill which has passed through both Houses of Parliament, before it becomes law; she is head of the judiciary (although the judiciary is now quite independent of the executive); she appoints all important state officials, including judges, officers of the forces and representatives abroad, and she confers honours and awards. Her formal consent is necessary before a Minister can take up office or a Cabinet be formed; and before a treaty may be concluded, war declared or peace made. These are some of the more essential functions. However, the Queen also has many residuary responsibilities, such as the guardianship of infants and persons of unsound mind, the creation of corporations, granting of printing rights for the Bible and Prayer Book and for state documents; and her signature and consent are necessary to many important state papers. Constitutional government cannot in fact be carried on without the Sovereign, so much so that provision has been made by Act of Parliament for the appointment of a Regent should the Sovereign be incapacitated or under age and for Counsellors of State to act in the temporary absence of the Queen.

PARLIAMENT

The Queen in Parliament—the House of Commons and the House of Lords—is the supreme legislative authority in the United Kingdom. Under the Parliament Act of 1911 the maximum life of one Parliament was fixed at five years: if, that is, Parliament has not meanwhile been dissolved for any other reason, such as the fall of the Government, then a general election is at the end of five years necessary by law. During its lifetime, the power of Parliament is theoretically absolute; it can make or unmake any law. In practice, of course, it must take account of the electorate. Parliament is prorogued at intervals during its life, which therefore consists of a number of sessions; by present custom, a session has normally 160 sitting days and is divided into five periods: from November (when the session is opened) until Christmas (about 30 days), from January till Easter (50), from Easter till Whitsun (30), from Whitsun until the end of July (40) and 10 days in October.

The House of Commons has 646 members, each elected for one geographical constituency. The Speaker, who is elected by the members immediately a new parliament meets, presides. Members of Parliament may be elected either at a general election or at a by-election (held in the event of the death, resignation or expulsion of the sitting member) and in either case hold their seats during the life of the existing parliament. All British subjects who are more than 18 years of age (and subjects of any Commonwealth country and of Ireland who are resident in the United Kingdom) have the vote unless legally barred (e.g. for insanity). Anyone who has the vote may stand as a candidate for election except clergymen of the Church of England, the established Churches of Scotland and Northern Ireland and the Roman Catholic Church, and certain officers of the Crown; civil servants must resign from the service if they wish to stand as a Member of Parliament.

There are over 700 members of the House of Lords, including 12 Lords of Appeal in Ordinary (appointed for life to carry out the judicial duties of the House); the two archbishops and the 24 senior diocesan bishops of the Church of England are also members. The House of Lords Act 1999 ended the right of hereditary peers to sit and vote in the House of Lords. An amendment to the Act provided for 92 of the existing hereditary peers to remain as members until the next stage of reform.

Members of Parliament whose views coincide form parties which agree in each case to support the policies put forward by their chosen leaders, and to present a common front on all important issues both in Parliament and to the electorate. This system evolved during the 17th and 18th centuries and is now essential to the working of the British Constitution. Under the party system, the Queen sends for the leader of the party which wins the majority of seats (although not necessarily of votes) at a general election and asks him or her to form a government. The party with the second largest number of seats forms the Opposition, which has quite specific functions. Members of other minority parties and independents may support the Government or Opposition as they choose. Each party has its own Whips, officials whose duty it is to arrange, (in consultation with the Whips of other parties), matters of procedure and organization; to ensure that members attend debates; and to muster for their party its maximum voting strength. In addition, each party has its own national and local organizations outside Parliament.

Parliamentary procedure, like the Constitution itself, is determined by rules, customs, forms and practices which have accumulated over many centuries. The Speaker is responsible for their application, and generally for controlling the course of business and debates in the house.

It is the duty of Parliament to make the laws which govern the life of the community, to appropriate the necessary funds for the various services of state and to criticize and control the Government. Parliament is also consulted before the ratification of certain international treaties and agreements.

Legislation may (with some exceptions) be initiated in either House and on either side of the House. In practice, most Public Bills are introduced into the House of Commons by the Government in power (the chief exceptions are Private Members' Bills) as the result of Cabinet decisions. Each Bill which is passed by the Commons at its third reading is sent to the House of Lords, who either accept it or return it to the Commons with suggested amendments. The Lords cannot in any instance prevent Bills passed by the Commons from becoming law: over Money Bills or Bills affecting the duration of Parliament they have no power at all, and by the Parliament Act of 1949 any other Bill passed by the Commons in two successive sessions may be presented for Royal Assent without the consent of the Lords, provided one year has elapsed between the date of the second reading in the Commons and the date of its final passing. In practice, the House of Lords is extremely unlikely to delay matters thus far, and its main function is to scrutinize the work of the

THE UNITED KINGDOM

Commons, to caution and suggest. Bills of a non-controversial kind are sometimes introduced initially in the House of Lords.

Northern Ireland

Following the prorogation of the Northern Ireland Parliament in 1972, responsibility for the Government of Northern Ireland rested with the Secretary of State for Northern Ireland. Direct rule continued until 1973, when the Northern Ireland Executive was established under the provisions of the Northern Ireland Constitution Act (1973). The Northern Ireland Executive assumed responsibility for the administration of Northern Ireland and was answerable to the Northern Ireland Assembly, elected in June 1973. The Executive collapsed in May 1974, and the Secretary of State resumed control of the Northern Ireland departments.

In October 1982 a new Northern Ireland Assembly was elected under the provisions of the Northern Ireland Act 1982. Under the Act, the Assembly was eventually to resume legislative and executive functions, provided that it produced proposals for the resumption of its powers, deemed to be acceptable to the people of Northern Ireland by Parliament. In June 1986 the Assembly was dissolved.

In November 1985 the Anglo-Irish Agreement was signed by the Prime Ministers of the United Kingdom and Ireland, leaving the status of Northern Ireland unaltered and confirming that the status of Northern Ireland would not be altered without the consent of a majority of its inhabitants. The Agreement provided for the establishment of an intergovernmental conference, through which the Government of Ireland was permitted to make proposals on matters relating to Northern Ireland affairs.

New constitutional arrangements for Northern Ireland were agreed by the leaders of Northern Ireland's political parties (with the exception of the Democratic Unionist Party and the United Kingdom Unionist Party) and by the British and Irish Governments in April 1998, and were approved in a popular referendum conducted in May. Accordingly, legislation was introduced into the United Kingdom Parliament to provide for the transfer of responsibility for the administration of Northern Ireland to an elected Assembly and Executive. A North/South Ministerial Council was established by the Assembly to undertake consideration of all-Ireland issues. Representatives of the Irish and British Governments, of the devolved authorities in Northern Ireland, Scotland and Wales and of the Channel Islands and Isle of Man were to convene under a British-Irish Council, to consider the development of the islands and formulate common policies, although with no legislative or administrative powers. A new bilateral agreement between the United Kingdom and Ireland subsumed the 1985 accord and established a new British-Irish Intergovernmental Conference. The new Northern Ireland institutions were suspended in February 2000, owing to a political impasse concerning the decommissioning of paramilitary weapons, and Northern Ireland was returned to direct rule. In May, following an agreement on the issue of decommissioning, power was once again transferred from Westminster to the new Northern Ireland institutions. The Northern Ireland Assembly and Executive were suspended again in October 2002 and Northern Ireland was returned to direct rule from Westminster. The Assembly was recalled on 15 May 2006. Elections to the Assembly took place on 7 March 2007 and the Assembly was recalled on 8 May.

Scotland and Wales

In 1999 devolved legislative authorities were established in Scotland and Wales. In Scotland a new elected Parliament, based in Edinburgh, was established with powers to legislate on all domestic matters (including education, health, local government and law and order) and with a mandate to vary taxes set by the Government of the United Kingdom by 3%. The Parliament has 129 members, elected every four years by a combined system of direct voting, on the basis of Westminster parliamentary constituencies, and a form of proportional representation, whereby additional members are elected from a party list on the basis of the larger constituencies used for elections to the European Parliament. The National Assembly for Wales, located in Cardiff, undertook responsibility for issues covered by the Wales Office of the Government of the United Kingdom. The 60-member National Assembly was elected under the same system as in Scotland. Elections to the two assemblies took place simultaneously in May 1999 and the transfer of powers took place on 1 July.

THE PRIVY COUNCIL

The power of the Privy Council has declined with the development of the Cabinet and its main function today is to give effect to decisions made elsewhere. There are at present over 500 Privy Counsellors, including Cabinet Ministers (who are automatically created Privy Counsellors), and people who have reached eminence in some branch of public affairs. Meetings are presided over by the Queen, and the responsible minister is the Lord President of the Council, an office which, since 1600, has always been held by a member of the party in power, who is usually also a leading member of the Cabinet. The Privy Council is responsible for making Orders in Council, of which there are two kinds: those made in virtue of the Royal prerogative, e.g. the ratification of treaties, and those which are authorized by Act of Parliament and are, in fact, a form of delegated legislation. It has also various advisory functions which cover such subjects as scientific, industrial, medical and agricultural research. An important organ of the Privy Council is the Judicial Committee.

HER MAJESTY'S GOVERNMENT

The Government is headed by the Prime Minister, who is also the leader of the party which holds the majority in the House of Commons. It includes ministers who are in charge of government departments and those who hold traditional offices which involve no special departmental duties; the Chancellor of the Exchequer and the Lord Chancellor, who are specially responsible for financial and economic and legal affairs, respectively; the law officers of the Crown (the Attorney-General and Solicitor-General and the Advocate-General for Scotland); the Ministers of State, who are usually appointed to assist Ministers in charge of departments; and Parliamentary Secretaries and Under-Secretaries.

The cabinet system developed during the 18th century from the informal meetings of Privy Counsellors who were also ministers, and who formed a committee of manageable size which could take decisions far more quickly and simply than larger bodies. The Cabinet today has between 15–25 members at the discretion of the Prime Minister—its main duty is to formulate policy for submission to Parliament.

The doctrine of ministerial responsibility has also evolved gradually, but was generally accepted by the middle of the 19th century. Each Minister must take full responsibility, particularly in Parliament, for the work of his own department; if his department fails over any important matter, he will be expected to resign. Ministers also assume collective responsibility for the work of the Government and for any advice which it may offer to the Crown.

The Government

HEAD OF STATE

Sovereign: Her Majesty Queen ELIZABETH II (succeeded to the throne 6 February 1952).

THE MINISTRY
(April 2009)

The Cabinet

Prime Minister, First Lord of the Treasury and Minister for the Civil Service: GORDON BROWN.

Chancellor of the Exchequer: ALISTAIR DARLING.

Secretary of State for Foreign and Commonwealth Affairs: DAVID MILIBAND.

Secretary of State for Justice and Lord Chancellor for the transitional period: JOHN (JACK) STRAW.

Secretary of State for the Home Department: JACQUELINE (JACQUI) SMITH.

Secretary of State for Health: ALAN JOHNSON.

Secretary of State for Business, Enterprise and Regulatory Reform: Lord MANDELSON.

Secretary of State for the Environment, Food and Rural Affairs: HILARY BENN.

Secretary of State for International Development: DOUGLAS ALEXANDER.

Secretary of State for Defence: JOHN HUTTON.

Leader of the House of Commons, Lord Privy Seal and Minister for Women and Equality: HARRIET HARMAN.

Secretary of State for Communities and Local Government: HAZEL BLEARS.

Secretary of State for Transport: GEOFFREY (GEOFF) HOON.

Secretary of State for Children, Schools and Families: EDWARD (ED) BALLS.

Secretary of State for Energy and Climate Change: EDWARD (ED) MILIBAND.

Secretary of State for Work and Pensions: JAMES PURNELL.

Secretary of State for Northern Ireland: SHAUN WOODWARD.

Leader of the House of Lords and Lord President of the Council: Baroness ROYALL OF BLAISDON.

Secretary of State for Culture, Media and Sport: ANDY BURNHAM.

Secretary of State for Innovation, Universities and Skills: JOHN DENHAM.

THE UNITED KINGDOM

Chief Secretary to the Treasury: YVETTE COOPER.
Secretary of State for Wales: PAUL MURPHY.
Secretary of State for Scotland: JIM MURPHY.

Also attending Cabinet

Chief Whip, Parliamentary Secretary to the Treasury and Minister for the North-East of England: NICK BROWN.
Chancellor of the Duchy of Lancaster and Minister for the Cabinet Office: LIAM BYRNE.
Minister of State for Housing, Department for Communities and Local Government: MARGARET BECKETT.
Minister of State for Employment and Welfare Reform, Department for Work and Pensions, and Minister for London: TONY MCNULTY.
Minister of State for Africa, Asia and the United Nations, Foreign and Commonwealth Office: Lord MALLOCH-BROWN.
Minister of State for Science and Innovation, Department for Innovation, Universities and Skills: Lord DRAYSON.

Attending Cabinet when respective ministerial responsibilities are discussed

Minister for the Olympics and Paymaster-General: TESSA JOWELL.
Attorney-General: Baroness SCOTLAND OF ASTHAL.
Minister of State for Europe, Foreign and Commonwealth Office: CAROLINE FLINT.
Minister of State for Children and Youth Justice, Department for Children, Schools and Families, and Minister for the North-West of England: BEVERLEY HUGHES.

Law Officers

Attorney-General: Baroness SCOTLAND OF ASTHAL.
Solicitor-General: VERA BAIRD.
Advocate-General for Scotland: Lord DAVIDSON OF GLEN CLOVA.

Ministers not in the Cabinet

Financial Secretary to the Treasury: STEPHEN TIMMS.
Economic Secretary to the Treasury: IAN PEARSON.
Exchequer Secretary to the Treasury: ANGELA EAGLE.
Financial Services Secretary to the Treasury: Lord MYNERS.
Minister of State, Foreign and Commonwealth Office: BILL RAMMELL.
Ministers of State, Ministry of Justice: MICHAEL WILLS, DAVID HANSON.
Minister of State for Security, Counter-terrorism, Crime and Policing, Home Office: VERNON COAKER.
Minister of State for Borders and Immigration, Home Office, and Minister of State, HM Treasury: PHIL WOOLAS.
Minister of State for the Armed Forces, Ministry of Defence: BOB AINSWORTH.
Minister of State for Public Health, Department of Health: DAWN PRIMAROLO.
Minister of State for Health Services, Department of Health, and Minister for the South-West of England: BEN BRADSHAW.
Minister of State for Care Services, Department of Health, and Minister for the East Midlands: PHIL HOPE.
Minister of State, Department for Business, Enterprise and Regulatory Reform: PAT MCFADDEN.
Minister of State, Department for Business, Enterprise and Regulatory Reform, and Minister of State, Department for International Development: GARETH THOMAS.
Minister of State for Trade and Investment, Department of Business, Enterprise and Regulatory Reform and Foreign and Commonwealth Office: Lord DAVIES OF ABERSOCH.
Minister of State for Farming and the Environment, Department for Environment, Food and Rural Affairs: JANE KENNEDY.
Minister of State for Sustainable Development and Energy Innovation, Department for Environment, Food and Rural Affairs and Department of Energy and Climate Change: Lord HUNT OF KINGS HEATH.
Minister of State for the Armed Forces, Ministry of Defence: BOB AINSWORTH.
Minister of State for Local Government, Department for Communities and Local Government: JOHN HEALEY.
Minister of State, Department for Transport: Lord ADONIS.
Minister of State for Schools and Learners, Department for Children, Schools and Families: JIM KNIGHT.
Minister of State, Department of Energy and Climate Change: MIKE O'BRIEN.
Minister of State for Pensions Reform, Department for Work and Pensions, and Minister for Yorkshire and the Humber: ROSIE WINTERTON.
Minister of State, Northern Ireland Office: PAUL GOGGINS.
Minister of State for Higher Education and Intellectual Property, Department for Innovation, Universities and Skills: DAVID LAMMY.
Minister for the East of England: BARBARA FOLLETT.
Minister for the South-East: JONATHAN SHAW.
Minister for the West Midlands: IAN AUSTIN.

MINISTRIES

Prime Minister's Office: 10 Downing St, London, SW1A 2AA; tel. (20) 7270-3000; fax (20) 7925-0918; internet www.number10.gov.uk.
Cabinet Office: 70 Whitehall, London, SW1A 2AS; tel. (20) 7276-1234; e-mail mst@cabinet-office.x.gsi.gov.uk; internet www.cabinet-office.gov.uk.
Department of Business, Enterprise and Regulatory Reform: 1 Victoria St, London, SW1H 0ET; tel. (20) 7215-5000; fax (20) 7215-0105; e-mail enquiries@berr.gsi.gov.uk; internet www.berr.gov.uk.
Department for Children, Schools and Families: Sanctuary Bldgs, Great Smith St, London, SW1P 3BT; tel. 0870-000-2288; fax (1928) 794248; e-mail info@dcsf.gsi.gov.uk; internet www.dcsf.gov.uk.
Department for Communities and Local Government: Eland House, Bressenden Place, London, SW1E 5DU; tel. (20) 7944-4400; fax (20) 7944-4101; e-mail contactus@communities.gov.uk; internet www.communities.gov.uk.
Department for Culture, Media and Sport: 2–4 Cockspur St, London SW1Y 5DH; tel. (20) 7211-6200; fax (20) 7211-6032; e-mail enquiries@culture.gov.uk; internet www.culture.gov.uk.
Ministry of Defence: Main Bldg, Whitehall, London, SW1A 2HB; tel. (20) 7218-9000; e-mail ministerial-correspondence@mod.uk; internet www.mod.uk.
Department of Energy and Climate Change: 3 Whitehall Place, London, SW1A 2HD; tel. (300) 060-4000; e-mail enquiries@decc.gsi.gov.uk; internet www.decc.gov.uk.
Department for Environment, Food and Rural Affairs: Nobel House, 17 Smith Sq., London, SW1P 3JR; tel. (20) 7238-6000; fax (20) 7238-6609; e-mail helpline@defra.gsi.gov.uk; internet www.defra.gov.uk.
Foreign and Commonwealth Office: King Charles St, London, SW1A 2AH; tel. (20) 7008-1500; internet www.fco.gov.uk.
Department of Health: Richmond House, 79 Whitehall, London, SW1A 2NS; tel. (20) 7210-4850; fax (20) 7210-5523; e-mail dhmail@dh.gsi.gov.uk; internet www.dh.gov.uk.
Home Office: 2 Marsham St, London, SW1P 4DF; tel. (20) 7035-4848; fax (20) 7035-4745; e-mail public.enquiries@homeoffice.gsi.gov.uk; internet www.homeoffice.gov.uk.
Department for Innovation, Universities and Skills: Kingsgate House, 66–74 Victoria St, London, SW1E 6SW; tel. (020) 7215-5555; e-mail info@dius.gsi.gov.uk; internet www.dius.gov.uk.
Department for International Development: 1 Palace St, London, SW1E 5HE; tel. (20) 7023-0000; fax (20) 7023-0019; e-mail enquiry@dfid.gov.uk; internet www.dfid.gov.uk.
Ministry of Justice: 102 Petty France, London, SW1H 9AJ; tel. (20) 3334-3555; fax (20) 3334-4455; e-mail general.queries@justice.gsi.gov.uk; internet www.justice.gov.uk.
Northern Ireland Office: 11 Millbank, London, SW1P 4PN; tel. (20) 7210-0260; fax (20) 7210-0213; e-mail info@nio.gov.uk; internet www.nio.gov.uk.
Scotland Office: Dover House, Whitehall, London, SW1A 2AU; tel. (20) 7270-6754; fax (20) 7270-6812; e-mail scotlandoffice.ministers@scotland.gsi.gov.uk; internet www.scotlandoffice.gov.uk.
Department for Transport: Great Minster House, 76 Marsham St, London, SW1P 4DR; tel. (20) 7944-8300; fax (20) 7944-9643; e-mail fax9643@dft.gsi.gov.uk; internet www.dft.gov.uk.
HM Treasury: 1 Horse Guards Rd, London, SW1A 2HQ; tel. (20) 7270-4558; fax (20) 7270-4861; e-mail public.enquiries@hm-treasury.gov.uk; internet www.hm-treasury.gov.uk.
Wales Office: Gwydyr House, Whitehall, London, SW1A 2ER; tel. (20) 7270-0534; fax (20) 7270-0578; e-mail wales.office@walesoffice.gsi.gov.uk; internet www.walesoffice.gov.uk.
Department for Work and Pensions: Caxton House, Tothill St, London, SW1H 9NA; tel. (20) 7340-4000; internet www.dwp.gov.uk.

THE UNITED KINGDOM

Legislature
PARLIAMENT

House of Commons

House of Commons Information Office, Norman Shaw North, London SW1A 2TT; tel. (20) 7219-4272; e-mail hcinfo@parliament.uk; internet www.parliament.uk.

Speaker: MICHAEL MARTIN (until 21 June 2009).
Chairman of Ways and Means and Deputy Speaker: Sir ALAN HASELHURST.
Leader of the House: HARRIET HARMAN.

General Election, 5 May 2005

	Votes	% of votes	Seats
Labour Party	9,556,183	35.2	356*
Conservative Party	8,772,598	32.3	198†
Liberal Democrats	5,982,045	22.0	62
Democratic Unionist Party	241,856	0.9	9
Scottish National Party	412,267	1.5	6
Sinn Féin	174,530	0.6	5
Plaid Cymru	174,838	0.6	3
Social Democratic and Labour Party	125,626	0.5	3
Ulster Unionist Party	127,314	0.5	1
Others	1,565,070	5.9	3
Total	**27,132,327**	**100.0**	**646†**

* Including the Speaker.
† Including the representative for the South Staffordshire constituency, for which the election was postponed until 24 June 2005, owing to the death of the Liberal Democrat candidate.

House of Lords
(May 2009)

Lord Speaker: Baroness HAYMAN.
Lord Chairman of Committees and Deputy Speaker: Lord BRABAZON OF TARA.
Leader of the House: Baroness ROYALL OF BLAISDON.

	Seats
Archbishops and Bishops	25
Life Peers under the Appellate Jurisdiction Act 1876	22
Life Peers under the Life Peerages Act 1958	598
Peers under the House of Lords Act 1999	92
Total	**737**

The Legislative Authorities and Executive Bodies of Northern Ireland, Scotland and Wales

New constitutional arrangements for Northern Ireland were agreed by the leaders of Northern Ireland's political parties (with the exception of the Democratic Unionist Party and the United Kingdom Unionist Party) and by the British and Irish Governments in April 1998, and were approved in a popular referendum conducted in May. Accordingly, legislation was introduced into the United Kingdom Parliament to provide for the transfer of responsibility for the administration of Northern Ireland to an elected Assembly and Executive. Elections to a new 108-member Assembly were held on 25 June 1998. An Executive Committee, headed by a First Minister, was constituted from among the legislative members. Responsibility for all matters formerly implemented by the Northern Ireland Office was transferred to the devolved authority under new parliamentary legislation implemented in December 1999. The new Northern Ireland institutions were suspended in February 2000, owing to a political impasse concerning the decommissioning of paramilitary weapons, and Northern Ireland was returned to direct rule. On 30 May, following an agreement on the issue of decommissioning, power was once again transferred from Westminster to the new Northern Ireland institutions. However, the Northern Ireland Executive was suspended again on 14 October 2002 and Northern Ireland was returned to direct rule. Following the signing by the main Northern Ireland political parties and the British and Irish Governments of the St Andrews Agreement in November 2006, elections to the Assembly were held on 7 March 2007. A power-sharing Executive Committee, headed by a First Minister, was again constituted and on 8 May power was transferred from Westminster to the Northern Ireland institutions.

In 1999 devolved legislative authorities were established for Scotland and Wales. An executive level of government, headed by a First Minister, was also established for each country. The Scottish Parliament assumed powers to legislate on all domestic matters, including education, health, local government and law and order. It also had a mandate to vary taxes set by the United Kingdom Government by 3%. The National Assembly for Wales (Cynulliad Cenedlaethol Cymru) assumed responsibility for issues covered by the Wales Office of the United Kingdom Government. Both assemblies were elected, for a term of four years, by a combined system of direct voting, on the basis of Westminster parliamentary constituencies, and a form of proportional representation, whereby additional members were elected from a party list on the basis of the larger constituencies used for election to the European Parliament. The transfer of powers to both the Scottish and the Welsh authorities took place on 1 July.

NORTHERN IRELAND

Legislature

Northern Ireland Assembly

Parliament Bldgs, Belfast, BT4 3XX; tel. (28) 9052-1333; fax (28) 9052-1961; e-mail info.office@niassembly.gov.uk; internet www.niassembly.gov.uk.

Presiding Officer: WILLIAM HAY.

Election, 7 March 2007

	First preference votes	% of first preference votes	Seats
Democratic Unionist Party	207,721	30.1	36
Sinn Féin	180,573	26.2	28
Ulster Unionist Party	103,145	14.9	18
Social Democratic and Labour Party	105,164	15.2	16
Alliance Party	36,139	5.2	7
Independents	21,993	2.8	1
Green Party	11,985	1.7	1
Progressive Unionist Party	3,822	0.6	1
Total (incl. others)	**690,313**	**100.0**	**108**

Executive Committee
(April 2009)

A power-sharing executive, comprising the Democratic Unionist Party (DUP), Sinn Féin (SF), the Ulster Unionist Party (UUP) and the Social Democratic and Labour Party (SDLP).

First Minister: PETER ROBINSON (DUP).
Deputy First Minister: MARTIN MCGUINNESS (SF).
Minister of Finance and Personnel: NIGEL DODDS (DUP).
Minister of Education: CAITRÍONA RUANE (SF).
Minister of Enterprise, Trade and Investment: ARLENE FOSTER (DUP).
Minister of Health, Social Services and Public Safety: MICHAEL MCGIMPSEY (UUP).
Minister for Social Development: MARGARET RITCHIE (SDLP).
Minister for Regional Development: CONOR MURPHY (SF).
Minister of the Environment: SAMMY WILSON (DUP).
Minister of Agriculture and Rural Development: MICHELLE GILDERNEW (SF).
Minister of Culture, Arts and Leisure: GREGORY CAMPBELL (DUP).
Minister for Employment and Learning: Sir REG EMPEY (UUP).

SCOTLAND

Legislature

Scottish Parliament

Edinburgh, EH99 1SP; tel. (131) 348-5000; fax (131) 348-5601; e-mail sp.info@scottish.parliament.uk; internet www.scottish.parliament.uk.

Presiding Officer: ALEX FERGUSSON.

THE UNITED KINGDOM

Election, 3 May 2007

	Total votes	%	Seats
Scottish National Party	1,297,628	33.1	47
Labour Party	1,259,642	32.1	46
Conservative Party	618,748	15.8	17
Liberal Democrats	556,903	14.2	16
Green Party	85,555	2.2	2
Others	104,023	2.7	1
Total	**3,922,499**	**100.0**	**129**

Cabinet
(April 2009)

First Minister: ALEX SALMOND.

Deputy First Minister and Cabinet Secretary for Health and Wellbeing: NICOLA STURGEON.

Cabinet Secretary for Finance and Sustainable Growth: JOHN SWINNEY.

Cabinet Secretary for Education and Lifelong Learning: FIONA HYSLOP.

Cabinet Secretary for Justice: KENNY MACASKILL.

Cabinet Secretary for Rural Affairs and the Environment: RICHARD LOCHHEAD.

Minister for Parliamentary Business: BRUCE CRAWFORD.

Minister for Culture, External Affairs and the Constitution: MICHAEL RUSSELL.

Minister for Public Health and Sport: SHONA ROBISON.

Minister for Housing and Communities: ALEX NEIL.

Minister for Enterprise, Energy and Tourism: JIM MATHER.

Minister for Transport, Infrastructure and Climate Change: STEWART STEVENSON.

Minister for Schools and Skills: KEITH BROWN.

Minister for Children and Early Years: ADAM INGRAM.

Minister for Community Safety: FERGUS EWING.

Minister for Environment: ROSEANNA CUNNINGHAM.

Lord Advocate: ELISH ANGIOLINI.

Solicitor-General: FRANK MULHOLLAND.

WALES

Legislature

National Assembly for Wales
(Cynulliad Cenedlaethol Cymru)
Cardiff Bay, Cardiff, CF99 1NA; tel. (800) 010-5500; internet www.assemblywales.org.

Presiding Officer: Lord ELIS-THOMAS.

Election, 3 May 2007

	Total votes	%	Seats
Labour Party	519,682	30.7	26
Plaid Cymru	423,878	25.0	15
Conservative Party	427,883	25.3	12
Liberal Democrats	258,950	15.3	6
Others	63,593	3.8	1
Total	**1,693,986**	**100.0**	**60**

Cabinet
(April 2009)

A coalition of the Labour Party and Plaid Cymru (PC).

First Minister: RHODRI MORGAN (Labour).

Deputy First Minister and Minister for the Economy and Transport: IEUAN WYN JONES (PC).

Minister for Finance and Public Service Delivery: ANDREW DAVIES (Labour).

Minister for Social Justice and Local Government: Dr BRIAN GIBBONS (Labour).

Minister for Children, Education, Lifelong Learning and Skills: JANE HUTT (Labour).

Minister for Rural Affairs: ELIN JONES (PC).

Minister for Health and Social Services: EDWINA HART (Labour).

Minister for Environment, Sustainability and Housing: JANE DAVIDSON (Labour).

Minister for Heritage: ALUN FFRED JONES (PC).

Counsel-General, Leader of the House, responsible for Assembly Business and Communications: CARWYN JONES (Labour).

Election Commission

The Electoral Commission: Trevelyan House, Great Peter St, London SW1P 2HW; tel. (20) 7271-0500; fax (20) 7271-0505; e-mail info@electoralcommission.org.uk; internet www.electoralcommission.gov.uk; f. 2000; independent; Chair. JENNY WATSON; Chief Exec. PETER WARDLE.

Political Organizations

Alliance Party: 88 University St, Belfast, BT7 1HE; tel. (28) 9032-4274; fax (28) 9033-3147; e-mail alliance@allianceparty.org; internet www.allianceparty.org; f. 1970; non-sectarian and non-doctrinaire party of the centre, attracting support from within both Catholic and Protestant sections of the community in Northern Ireland; 1,500 mems; Leader DAVID FORD.

British National Party: National Central Office, Admail 4148, London, EC1A 1UY; tel. (20) 7078-3286; e-mail enquiries@bnp.org.uk; internet www.bnp.org.uk; f. 1982 as a breakaway faction from the National Front; Chair. NICK GRIFFIN.

Communist Party of Britain: Ruskin House, 23 Coombe Rd, Croydon, CR0 1BD; tel. (20) 8686-1659; e-mail office@communist-party.org.uk; internet www.communist-party.org.uk; f. 1920; re-established 1988; Marxist-Leninist; Gen. Sec. ROBERT GRIFFITHS.

Conservative and Unionist Party: 30 Millbank, London, SW1P 4DP; tel. (20) 7222-9000; fax (20) 7222-1135; internet www.conservatives.com; f. 1870 as Conservative Central Office; aims to uphold the Crown and the Constitution; to build a sound economy based on freedom and enterprise; to encourage personal responsibility and a wider spread of ownership of property; to look after those most in need; to ensure respect for law and order; to improve educational standards and widen parents' choice; to strengthen Britain's defences, maintain its interests and increase its influence abroad; mem. of the International Democrat Union and the European Democrat Union; in the European Parliament part of the European People's Party-European Democrat Group; 320,000 mems (adherent on a local, rather than national, basis); Leader DAVID CAMERON; Chair. ERIC PICKLES.

Conservative Party in Northern Ireland: 70 Main St, Saintfield, Co Down, BT24 7AB; tel. (28) 9751-9025; e-mail office@conservativesni.org; internet www.conservativesni.org; party has no Assembly members, but is represented at council level; Chair. NEIL JOHNSTON.

Scottish Conservative Party: 83 Princes St, Edinburgh, EH2 2ER; tel. (131) 247-6890; fax (131) 247-6891; e-mail info@scottishconservatives.com; internet www.scottishconservatives.com; Chair. ANDREW FULTON; Leader ANNABEL GOLDIE.

Welsh Conservative Party: 4 Penlline Rd, Whitchurch, Cardiff, CF14 2XS; tel. (29) 2061-6031; fax (29) 2061-0544; e-mail ccowales@tory.org; internet www.welshconservatives.com; Chair. CATRIN EDWARDS; Assembly Leader NICK BOURNE.

Co-operative Party: 77 Weston St, London, SE1 3SD; tel. (20) 7367-4150; fax (20) 7407-4476; e-mail mail@party.coop; internet www.party.coop; f. 1917; under an Agreement with the Labour Party it is recognized as the political party representing the co-operative movement, and fields candidates, jointly with the Labour Party, who are Labour and Co-operative candidates at local and British parliamentary elections; promotes the principles of the co-operative movement; seeks to extend co-operative enterprise and cares for the interests of the consumer; individual mems in 200 brs; 47 societies are affiliated; Chair. GARETH THOMAS; Sec. PETER HUNT.

Democratic Unionist Party (DUP): 91 Dundela Ave, Belfast, BT4 3BU; tel. (28) 9052-1323; fax (28) 9052-1289; e-mail info@dup.org.uk; internet www.dup.org.uk; f. 1971; Leader PETER ROBINSON; Party Sec. MICHELLE MCILVEEN.

Green Party: 1A Waterlow Rd, London, N19 5NJ; tel. (20) 7272-4474; fax (20) 7272-6653; e-mail office@greenparty.org.uk; internet www.greenparty.org.uk; f. 1973 as People, adopted the name Ecology Party in 1975; present name adopted 1985; campaigns for the protection of the environment and the promotion of social justice; approx. 7,000 mems; Leader CAROLINE LUCAS; Chair. JAMES HUMPHREYS.

Labour Party: 39 Victoria St, London, SW1H 0HA; tel. (8705) 900200; fax (20) 7802-1234; e-mail info@new.labour.org.uk; internet www.labour.org.uk; f. 1900; a democratic socialist party affiliated to the Socialist International and the Party of European Socialists;

THE UNITED KINGDOM

aims to achieve a dynamic economy, serving the public interest, with a strong private sector and high quality public services; a just society, with full equality of opportunity; an open democracy, guaranteeing fundamental human rights and governmental accountability and a healthy environment; committed to co-operating with European institutions, the UN, the Commonwealth and other international bodies to secure peace, freedom, democracy, economic security and environmental protection for all; also committed to pursuing these aims with trade unions, co-operative societies, voluntary organizations, consumer groups and other representative bodies; Leader GORDON BROWN; Deputy Leader and Chair. HARRIET HARMAN; Gen. Sec. RAY COLLINS.

Scottish Labour: John Smith House, 145 West Regent St, Glasgow, G2 4RE; tel. (141) 572-6900; fax (131) 572-2566; e-mail scotland@new.labour.org.uk; internet www.scottishlabour.org.uk; Leader IAIN GRAY; Gen. Sec. COLIN SMYTH.

Welsh Labour: 1 Cathedral Rd, Cardiff, CF11 9HA; tel. (29) 2087-7700; internet www.welshlabour.org.uk; Leader RHODRI MORGAN.

Liberal Democrats: 4 Cowley St, London, SW1P 3NB; tel. (20) 7222-7999; fax (20) 7799-2170; e-mail info@libdems.org.uk; internet www.libdems.org.uk; f. 1988, following the merger of the Liberal Party (f. 1877) and the Social Democratic Party (f. 1981, disbanded 1990); c. 65,000 mems; Leader NICHOLAS (NICK) CLEGG; Pres. Baroness SCOTT OF NEEDHAM MARKET

Scottish Liberal Democrats: 4 Clifton Terrace, Edinburgh, EH12 5DR; tel. (131) 337-2314; fax (131) 337-3566; e-mail administration@scotlibdems.org.uk; internet www.scotlibdems.org.uk; Leader TAVISH SCOTT.

Welsh Liberal Democrats: 7 Blake Court, Schooner Way, Butetown, Cardiff, CF10 4DW; tel. (29) 2031-3400; fax (29) 2031-3401; e-mail enquiries@welshliberaldemocrats.org.uk; internet www.welshlibdems.org.uk; Leader KIRSTY WILLIAMS.

Plaid Cymru—Party of Wales: Tŷ Gwynfor, Marine Chambers, Anson Court, Atlantic Wharf, Cardiff, CF10 4AL; tel. (29) 2047-2272; fax (29) 2064-6001; e-mail post@plaidcymru.org; internet www.plaidcymru.org; f. 1925; promotes Welsh interests and seeks independence for Wales; formed a parliamentary alliance with the SNP in April 1986; 10,000 mems; Leader IEUAN WYN JONES; Pres. DAFYDD IWAN.

Progressive Unionist Party: 299 Newtownards Rd, Belfast, BT4 1AG; tel. (28) 9022-5040; fax (28) 9022-5041; e-mail movingforward@pup-ni.org.uk; internet www.pup-ni.org.uk; loyalist party in Northern Ireland; Leader DAWN PURVIS.

Respect: POB 64078, London, E1W 9BJ; tel. (7906) 241-772; e-mail admin@respectparty.org; internet www.therespectparty.net; f. 2004; has one member of the House of Commons and councillors in three local authorities; Chair. KAY PHILLIPS.

Scottish National Party (SNP): 107 McDonald Rd, Edinburgh, EH7 4NW; tel. (131) 525-8900; fax (131) 525-8901; e-mail snp.hq@snp.org; internet www.snp.org; f. 1934; advocates independence for Scotland as a member of the EU and Scottish control of national resources; Leader ALEX SALMOND.

Scottish Socialist Party: Suite 308, 93 Hope St, Glasgow, G2 6LD; tel. (141) 221-7470; e-mail ssp.glasgow@btconnect.com; internet www.scottishsocialistparty.org; f. 1998; Convener COLIN FOX.

Sinn Féin (We Ourselves): 53 Falls Rd, Belfast, BT12 4PD; tel. (28) 9022-3000; fax (28) 9022-3001; e-mail sfadmin@eircom.net; internet www.sinnfein.ie; f. 1905; seeks the reunification of Ireland and the establishment of a 32-county democratic socialist state; engages in community politics; Pres. GERRY ADAMS; Chair. DECLAN KEARNEY; Gen. Sec. DAWN DOYLE.

Social Democratic and Labour Party (SDLP): 121 Ormeau Rd, Belfast, BT7 1SH; tel. (28) 9024-7700; fax (28) 9023-6699; e-mail info@sdlp.ie; internet www.sdlp.ie; f. 1970; radical, left-of-centre principles with a view to the eventual reunification of Ireland by popular consent; Leader MARK DURKAN.

Socialist Labour Party: POB 112, Leigh, WN7 4WS; tel. and fax (870) 8503576; e-mail info@socialist-labour-party.org.uk; internet www.socialist-labour-party.org.uk; f. 1996; supports renationalization of industry, constitutional reform, withdrawal from the European Union; Leader ARTHUR SCARGILL; Pres. PAUL HARDMAN; Gen. Sec. IAN JOHNSON.

Socialist Party: POB 24697, London, E11 1YD; tel. (20) 8988-8777; e-mail info@socialistparty.org.uk; internet www.socialistparty.org.uk; f. 1991 as Militant Labour by fmr members of the Militant tendency (an extreme-left faction within the Labour Party); present name adopted 1997; registered with the Electoral Commission under the name Socialist Alternative; mem. of the Committee for a Workers' International (CWI); Gen. Sec. PETER TAAFFE.

Socialist Workers' Party (SWP): POB 42184, London, SW8 2WD; tel. (20) 7819-1170; fax (20) 7819-1179; e-mail enquiries@swp.org.uk; internet www.swp.org.uk; f. 1950; advocates workers' control through revolution, not reform; Nat. Sec. MARTIN SMITH.

Solidarity—Scotland's Socialist Movement: POB 7565, Glasgow, G42 2DN; e-mail info@solidarityscotland.org; internet www.solidarityscotland.org; f. 2006 by disaffected members of the Scottish Socialist Party; Leaders TOMMY SHERIDAN, ROSEMARY BYRNE.

Ulster Unionist Party: First Floor, 174 Albertbridge Rd, Belfast, BT5 4GS; tel. (28) 9046-3200; fax (28) 9045-6899; e-mail uup@uup.org; internet www.uup.org; f. 1905; governed Northern Ireland 1921–72; supports parity and equality for Northern Ireland within the United Kingdom; formed electoral alliance with the United Kingdom Conservative and Unionist Party in 2009; Leader Sir REG EMPEY.

UK Independence Party: POB 408, Newton Abbot, Devon, TQ12 9BG; tel. (1626) 831290; fax (1626) 831348; e-mail mail@ukip.org; internet www.ukip.org; f. 1993; advocates withdrawal from the European Union; 27,000 mems; Leader NIGEL FARAGE; Chair. PAUL NUTTALL.

Veritas: Office 404, 4th Floor, Albany House, 324–326 Regent St, London, W1B 3HH; tel. (870) 7606148; e-mail office@veritas-party.com; internet www.veritasparty.com; f. 2005; advocates withdrawal from the European Union; Leader THERESE MUCHEWICZ.

The following paramilitary organizations in Northern Ireland are proscribed: (nationalist) the Provisional Irish Republican Army (IRA), the Irish National Liberation Army, Cumann na mBan (women's section of the IRA), Fianna na hEireann (youth section of the IRA), the Continuity Army Council, Saor Eire and the Irish People's Liberation Organization; (loyalist) the Ulster Freedom Fighters, the Ulster Volunteer Force, the Red Hand Commando, the Ulster Defence Association (UDA), the Loyalist Volunteer Force (LVF), the Red Hand Defenders and the Orange Volunteers.

Diplomatic Representation

EMBASSIES AND HIGH COMMISSIONS IN THE UNITED KINGDOM

Afghanistan: 31 Prince's Gate, London, SW7 1QQ; tel. (20) 7589-8891; fax (20) 7584-4801; e-mail info@afghanistanembassy.org.uk; internet www.afghanistanembassy.org.uk; Chargé d'affaires a.i. Dr HAMEED HAAMI.

Albania: 2nd Floor, 24 Buckingham Gate, London, SW1E 6LB; tel. (20) 7828-8897; fax (20) 7828-8869; e-mail embassy.london@mfa.gov.al; internet www.albanianembassy.co.uk; Ambassador ZEF MAZI.

Algeria: 54 Holland Park, London, W11 3RS; tel. (20) 7221-7800; fax (20) 7221-0448; e-mail info@algerianembassy.org.uk; internet www.algerianembassy.org.uk; Ambassador MUHAMMAD SALAH DEMBRI.

Andorra: 63 Westover Rd, London, SW18 2RF; tel. (20) 8874-4806; fax (20) 8874-4902; Ambassador MARIA ROSA PICART DE FRANCIS.

Angola: 22 Dorset St, London, W1U 6QY; tel. (20) 7299-9850; fax (20) 7486-9397; e-mail embassy@angola.org.uk; internet www.angola.org.uk; Ambassador ANA MARIA TELES CARREIRA.

Antigua and Barbuda: 2nd Floor, 45 Crawford Pl., London, W1H 4LP; tel. (20) 7258-0070; fax (20) 7258-7486; e-mail enquiries@antigua-barbuda.com; internet www.antigua-barbuda.com; High Commr Dr CARL ROBERTS.

Argentina: 65 Brook St, London, W1K 4AH; tel. (20) 7318-1300; fax (20) 7318-1301; e-mail info@argentine-embassy-uk.org; internet www.argentine-embassy-uk.org; Chargé d'affaires a.i. ENRIQUE FERRER VIEYRA.

Armenia: 25A Cheniston Gdns, London, W8 6TG; tel. (20) 7938-5435; fax (20) 7938-2595; e-mail armemb@armenianembassyuk.com; internet www.armenianembassy.org.uk; Ambassador Dr VAHE GABRIELYAN.

Australia: Australia House, Strand, London, WC2B 4LA; tel. (20) 7379-4334; fax (20) 7240-5333; internet www.uk.embassy.gov.au; High Commr JOHN DAUTH.

Austria: 18 Belgrave Mews West, London, SW1X 8HU; tel. (20) 7344-3250; fax (20) 7344-0292; e-mail london-ob@bmeia.gv.at; internet www.bmeia.gv.at/london; Ambassador Dr GABRIELE MATZNER-HOLZER.

Azerbaijan: 4 Kensington Court, London, W8 5DL; tel. (20) 7938-3412; fax (20) 7937-1783; e-mail london@mission.mfa.gov.az; internet www.azembassy.org.uk; Ambassador FAKHRADDIN GURBANOV.

Bahamas: 10 Chesterfield St, London, W1J 5JL; tel. (20) 7408-4488; fax (20) 7499-9937; e-mail information@bahamashclondon.net; internet www.bahamashclondon.net; High Commr PAUL H. FARQUHARSON.

Bahrain: 30 Belgrave Sq., London, SW1X 8QB; tel. (20) 7201-9170; fax (20) 7201-9183; e-mail information@bahrainembassy.co.uk; internet www.bahrainembassy.co.uk; Ambassador Sheikh KHALIFA BIN ALI AL-KHALIFA.

THE UNITED KINGDOM

Directory

Bangladesh: 28 Queen's Gate, London, SW7 5JA; tel. (20) 7584-0081; fax (20) 7581-7477; e-mail bhclondon@btconnect.com; internet www.bhclondon.org.uk; High Commr ALLAMA SIDDIQI (acting).

Barbados: 1 Great Russell St, London, WC1B 3ND; tel. (20) 7631-4975; fax (20) 7323-6872; e-mail london@foreign.gov.bb; High Commr HUGH ANTHONY ARTHUR.

Belarus: 6 Kensington Court, London, W8 5DL; tel. (20) 7937-3288; fax (20) 7361-0005; e-mail uk@belembassy.org; internet www.uk.belembassy.org; Ambassador ALEKSANDR MIKHNEVICH.

Belgium: 17 Grosvenor Cres., London, SW1X 7EE; tel. (20) 7470-3700; fax (20) 7470-3795; e-mail london@diplobel.fed.be; internet www.diplomatie.be/london; Ambassador JEAN-MICHEL VERANNEMAN DE WATERVLIET.

Belize: 3rd Floor, 45 Crawford Pl., London, W1H 4LP; tel. (20) 7723-3603; fax (20) 7723-9637; e-mail bzhc-lon@btconnect.com; internet www.belizehighcommission.com; High Commr KAMELA PALMA.

Bolivia: 106 Eaton Sq., London, SW1W 9AD; tel. (20) 7235-4248; fax (20) 7235-1286; e-mail bolivianembassy@yahoo.co.uk; internet www.boembassy-london.com; Ambassador MARÍA BEATRIZ SOUVIRON CRESPO.

Bosnia and Herzegovina: 5–7 Lexham Gdns, London, W8 5JJ; tel. (20) 7373-0867; fax (20) 7373-0871; e-mail embassy@bhembassy.co.uk; internet www.bhembassy.co.uk; Ambassador JADRANKA NEGODIĆ.

Botswana: 6 Stratford Pl., London, W1C 1AY; tel. (20) 7499-0031; fax (20) 7495-8595; e-mail bohico@govbw.com; High Commr ROY BLACKBEARD.

Brazil: 32 Green St, London, W1K 7AT; tel. (20) 7399-9000; fax (20) 7399-9100; e-mail info@brazil.org.uk; internet www.brazil.org.uk; Ambassador CARLOS AUGUSTO REGO SANTOS-NEVES.

Brunei: 19–20 Belgrave Sq., London, SW1X 8PG; tel. (20) 7581-0521; fax (20) 7235-9717; e-mail bhcl@brunei-high-commission.co.uk; High Commr Pengiran Dato' MAIDIN HASHIM.

Bulgaria: 186–188 Queen's Gate, London, SW7 5HL; tel. (20) 7584-9400; fax (20) 7584-4948; e-mail ambass.office@bulgarianembassy.org.uk; internet www.bulgarianembassy-london.org; Ambassador Dr LACHEZAR NIKOLOV MATEV.

Cambodia: 64 Brondesbury Park, Willesden Green, London, NW6 7AT; tel. (20) 8451-7850; fax (20) 8451-7594; e-mail cambodianembassy@btconnect.com; internet www.cambodianembassy.org.uk; Ambassador HOR NAMBORA.

Cameroon: 84 Holland Park, London, W11 3SB; tel. (20) 7727-0771; fax (20) 7792-9353; High Commr NKWELLE EKANEY.

Canada: MacDonald House, 1 Grosvenor Sq., London, W1K 4AB; tel. (20) 7258-6600; fax (20) 7258-6533; e-mail ldn@international.gc.ca; internet www.london.gc.ca; High Commr JAMES R. WRIGHT.

Chile: 12 Devonshire St, London, W1G 7DS; tel. (20) 7580-6392; fax (20) 7436-5204; e-mail embachile@embachile.co.uk; internet www.echileuk.co.uk; Ambassador RAFAEL MORENO.

China, People's Republic: 49–51 Portland Pl., London, W1B 4JL; tel. (20) 7299-4049; fax (20) 7636-5578; e-mail press@chinese-embassy.org.uk; internet www.chinese-embassy.org.uk; Ambassador FU YING.

Colombia: 3 Hans Cres., London, SW1X 0LN; tel. (20) 7589-9177; fax (20) 7589-4718; e-mail mail@colombianembassy.co.uk; internet www.colombianembassy.co.uk; Ambassador NOEMÍ SANÍN POSADA.

Congo, Democratic Republic: 281 Gray's Inn Rd, London, WC1X 8QF; tel. (20) 7278-9825; fax (20) 7833-9967; Ambassador EUGÉNIE TSHIELA COMPTON.

Costa Rica: Flat 1, 14 Lancaster Gate, London, W2 3LH; tel. (20) 7706-8844; fax (20) 7706-8655; e-mail costarica@btconnect.com; Ambassador PILAR SABORÍO DE ROCAFORT.

Côte d'Ivoire: 2 Upper Belgrave St, London, SW1X 8BJ; tel. (20) 7235-6991; fax (20) 7259-5320; e-mail info@ambaci-uk.org; internet www.ambaci-uk.org; Ambassador PHILIPPE D. DJANGONÉ-BI.

Croatia: 21 Conway St, London, W1T 6BN; tel. (20) 7387-2022; fax (20) 7387-0310; e-mail croemb.london@mvpei.hr; internet uk.mfa.hr; Ambassador Dr IVICA TOMIĆ.

Cuba: 167 High Holborn, London, WC1V 6PA; tel. (20) 7240-2488; fax (20) 7836-2602; e-mail embacuba@cubaldn.com; internet www.cubaldn.com; Ambassador RENÉ JUAN MUJICA CANTELAR.

Cyprus: 13 St James' Sq., London, SW1Y 4LB; tel. (20) 7321-4100; fax (20) 7321-4164; e-mail cyphclondon@dial.pipex.com; internet www.mfa.gov.cy/highcomlondon; High Commr ALEXANDROS ZENON.

Czech Republic: 26 Kensington Palace Gdns, London, W8 4QY; tel. (20) 7243-1115; fax (20) 7727-9654; e-mail london@embassy.mzv.cz; internet www.mzv.cz/london; Chargé d'affaires a.i. MIROSLAV KOLATEK.

Denmark: 55 Sloane St, London, SW1X 9SR; tel. (20) 7333-0200; fax (20) 7333-0270; e-mail lonamb@um.dk; internet www.amblondon.um.dk; Ambassador BIRGER RIIS-JØRGENSEN.

Dominica: 1 Collingham Gdns, London, SW5 0HW; tel. (20) 7370-5194; fax (20) 7373-8743; e-mail dominicahighcom@btconnect.com; High Commr AGNES ADONIS (acting).

Dominican Republic: 139 Inverness Terrace, London, W2 6JF; tel. (9065) 508945; fax (20) 7727-3693; e-mail info@dominicanembassy.org.uk; internet www.dominicanembassy.org.uk; Ambassador ANIBAL DE CASTRO.

Ecuador: Flat 3B, 3 Hans Cres., Knightsbridge, London, SW1X 0LS; tel. (20) 7584-1367; fax (20) 7823-9701; e-mail eecugranbretania@mmrree.gov.ec; Ambassador EDUARDO CABEZAS MOLINA.

Egypt: 26 South St, London, W1K 1DW; tel. (20) 7499-3304; fax (20) 7491-1542; e-mail eg.emb_london@mfa.gov.eg; internet www.egyptianconsulate.co.uk; Ambassador HATEM SEIF EN-NASR.

El Salvador: 8 Dorset Sq., 1st and 2nd Floors, London, NW1 6PU; tel. (20) 7224-9800; fax (20) 7224-9878; e-mail elsalvador.embassy@gmail.com; internet embassy.el-salvador.org.uk; Ambassador Dr ROBERTO RICARDO AVILA AVILEZ.

Equatorial Guinea: 13 Park Pl., St. James's, London, SW1A 1LP; tel. (20) 7499-6867; fax (20) 7499-6782; internet www.embarege-londres.org; e-mail embarege-londres@embarege-londres.org; Ambassador AGUSTIN NZE NFUMU.

Eritrea: 96 White Lion St, London, N1 9PF; tel. (20) 7713-0096; fax (20) 7713-0161; e-mail paamba@erimbauk.com; Ambassador TESFAMICAEL GERAHTU OGBAGHIORGHIS.

Estonia: 16 Hyde Park Gate, London, SW7 5DG; tel. (20) 7589-3428; fax (20) 7589-3430; e-mail embassy.london@estonia.gov.uk; internet www.estonia.gov.uk; Ambassador Dr MARGUS LAIDRE.

Ethiopia: 17 Prince's Gate, London, SW7 1PZ; tel. (20) 7589-7212; fax (20) 7584-7054; e-mail info@ethioembassy.org.uk; internet www.ethioembassy.org.uk; Ambassador BERHANU KEBEDE.

Fiji: 34 Hyde Park Gate, London, SW7 5DN; tel. (20) 7584-3661; fax (20) 7584-2838; e-mail mail@fijihighcommission.org.uk; internet www.fijihighcommission.org.uk; High Commr PIO BOSCO TIKOISUVA.

Finland: 38 Chesham Pl., London, SW1X 8HW; tel. (20) 7838-6200; fax (20) 7235-3680; e-mail sanomat.lon@formin.fi; internet www.finemb.org.uk; Ambassador JAAKKO LAAJAVA.

France: 58 Knightsbridge, London, SW1X 7JT; tel. (20) 7073-1000; fax (20) 7073-1004; e-mail presse.londres-amba@diplomatie.gouv.fr; internet www.ambafrance-uk.org; Ambassador MAURICE GOURDAULT-MONTAGNE.

Gabon: 27 Elvaston Pl., London, SW7 5NL; tel. (20) 7823-9986; fax (20) 7584-0047; Ambassador OMER PIANKALI.

The Gambia: 57 Kensington Court, London, W8 5DG; tel. (20) 7937-6316; fax (20) 7937-9095; e-mail gambia@gamhighcom.wanadoo.co.uk; High Commr ELIZABETH YA ELI HARDING.

Georgia: 4 Russell Gdns, London, W14 8EZ; tel. (20) 7603-7799; fax (20) 7603-6682; e-mail georgia@geoemb.plus.com; internet www.geoemb.org.uk; Ambassador GIORGI BADRIDZE.

Germany: 23 Belgrave Sq., London, SW1X 8PZ; tel. (20) 7824-1300; fax (20) 7824-1449; e-mail info@london.diplo.de; internet www.london.diplo.de; Ambassador GEORG BOOMGAARDEN.

Ghana: 13 Belgrave Sq., London, SW1X 8PN; tel. (20) 7235-4142; fax (20) 7245-9552; e-mail information@ghanahighcommissionuk.com; internet www.ghanahighcommissionuk.com; High Commr ZED K. GRANT-ESSILFIE (acting).

Greece: 1A Holland Park, London, W11 3TP; tel. (20) 7229-3850; fax (20) 7229-7221; e-mail political@greekembassy.org.uk; internet www.greekembassy.org.uk; Ambassador VASSILIS-ACHILLEAS PISPINIS.

Grenada: The Chapel, Archel Rd, West Kensington, London, W14 9QH; tel. (20) 7385-4415; fax (20) 7381-4807; e-mail office@grenada-highcommission.co.uk; High Commr RUTH ROUSE.

Guatemala: 13 Fawcett St, London, SW10 9HN; tel. (20) 7351-3042; fax (20) 7376-5708; e-mail ambassador.gtm@btconnect.com; Ambassador ALFONSO MATTA FAHSEN.

Guinea: 258 Belsize Rd, London, NW6 4BT; tel. (20) 7316-1861; fax (20) 7316-1861; e-mail ambaguineeuk@yahoo.co.uk; Ambassador LANSANA KEÏTA.

Guyana: 3 Palace Court, Bayswater Rd, London, W2 4LP; tel. (20) 7229-7684; fax (20) 7727-9809; e-mail ghc.l@btconnect.com; internet www.guyanahc.com; High Commr LALESHWAR K. N. SINGH.

Holy See: 54 Parkside, London, SW19 5NE (Apostolic Nunciature); tel. (20) 8944-7189; fax (20) 8947-2494; e-mail nuntius@globalnet.co.uk; Apostolic Nuncio Most Rev. FAUSTINO SAINZ MUÑOZ (Titular Archbishop of Novaliciana).

Honduras: 115 Gloucester Pl., London, W1U 6JT; tel. (20) 7486-4880; fax (20) 7486-4550; e-mail hondurasuk@lineone.net; Ambassador IVÁN ROMERO-MARTÍNEZ.

Hungary: 35 Eaton Pl., London, SW1X 8BY; tel. (20) 7235-5218; fax (20) 7823-1348; e-mail office.lon@kum.hu; internet www.mfa.gov.hu/emb/london; Ambassador BORBÁLA CZAKÓ.

THE UNITED KINGDOM

Iceland: 2A Hans St, London, SW1X 0JE; tel. (20) 7259-3999; fax (20) 7245-9649; e-mail icemb.london@utn.stjr.is; internet www.iceland.org/uk; Ambassador Sverrir Haukur Gunnlaugsson.

India: India House, Aldwych, London, WC2B 4NA; tel. (20) 7836-8484; fax (20) 7836-4331; e-mail info@hcilondon.net; internet www.hcilondon.net; High Commr Shiv Shankar Mukherjee.

Indonesia: 38 Grosvenor Sq., London, W1X 2HW; tel. (20) 7499-7661; fax (20) 7491-4993; e-mail kbri@btconnect.com; internet www.indonesianembassy.org.uk; Ambassador Yuri Octavian Thamrin.

Iran: 16 Prince's Gate, London, SW7 1PT; tel. (20) 7225-3000; fax (20) 7589-4440; e-mail info@iran-embassy.org.uk; internet www.iran-embassy.org.uk; Ambassador Rasoul Movahedian Attar.

Iraq: 9 Holland Villas Rd, London, W14 8BP; tel. (20) 7602-8456; fax (20) 7371-1652; e-mail lonemb@iraqmofamail.net; internet www.iraqembassy.org.uk; Chargé d'affaires a.i. Abd al-Muhaimen al-Oraibi.

Ireland: 17 Grosvenor Pl., London, SW1X 7HR; tel. (20) 7235-2171; fax (20) 7245-6961; internet www.embassyofireland.co.uk; Ambassador Bobby McDonagh.

Israel: 2 Palace Green, Kensington, London, W8 4QB; tel. (20) 7957-9500; fax (20) 7957-9555; e-mail public3@london.mfa.gov.il; internet london.mfa.gov.il; Ambassador Ron Prosor.

Italy: 14 Three Kings Yard, London, W1K 4EH; tel. (20) 7312-2200; fax (20) 7312-2230; e-mail ambasciata.londra@esteri.it; internet www.amblondra.esteri.it; Ambassador Giancarlo Aragona.

Jamaica: 1–2 Prince Consort Rd, London, SW7 2BZ; tel. (20) 7823-9911; fax (20) 7589-5154; e-mail jamhigh@jhcuk.com; internet www.jhcuk.com; High Commr Burchell Anthony Whiteman.

Japan: 101–104 Piccadilly, London, W1J 7JT; tel. (20) 7465-6500; fax (20) 7491-9348; e-mail info@jpembassy.org.uk; internet www.uk.emb-japan.go.jp; Ambassador Shin Ebihara.

Jordan: 6 Upper Phillimore Gdns, London, W8 7HA; tel. (20) 7937-3685; fax (20) 7937-8795; e-mail info@jordanembassyuk.org; internet www.jordanembassyuk.org; Ambassador Dr Alia Bouran.

Kazakhstan: 33 Thurloe Sq., London, SW7 2SD; tel. (20) 7581-4646; fax (20) 7584-8481; e-mail london@kazakhstan-embassy.org.uk; internet www.kazakhstanembassy.org.uk; Ambassador Kairat Abusseitov.

Kenya: 45 Portland Pl., London, W1N 4AS; tel. (20) 7636-2371; fax (20) 7323-6717; e-mail knganga@kenyahighcommission.net; internet www.kenyahighcommission.net; High Commr Joseph Kirugumi Muchemi.

Korea, Democratic People's Republic: 73 Gunnersbury Ave, London, W5 4LP; tel. (20) 8992-4965; fax (20) 8992-2053; e-mail dprkrepmission@yahoo.co.uk; Ambassador Ja Song-Nam.

Korea, Republic: 60 Buckingham Gate, London, SW1E 6AJ; tel. (20) 7227-5500; fax (20) 7227-5503; internet www.koreanembassy.org.uk; Ambassador Yung-woo Chun.

Kosovo: 15 Stratton St, London, W1J 8LQ; tel. (20) 7659-6140; fax (20) 7659-6137; e-mail embassy.uk@ks-gov.net; Chargé d'affaires a.i. Dr Muhamet Hamiti.

Kuwait: 2 Albert Gate, London, SW1X 7JU; tel. (20) 7590-3400; fax (20) 7823-1712; e-mail kuwait@dircon.co.uk; internet www.kuwaitinfo.org.uk; Ambassador Khalid ad-Duwaisan.

Kyrgyzstan: Ascot House, 119 Crawford St, London, W1U 6BJ; tel. (20) 7935-1462; fax (20) 7935-7449; e-mail mail@kyrgyz-embassy.org.uk; internet www.kyrgyz-embassy.org.uk; Ambassador Dr Kuban Ilyasovich Mambetaliev.

Latvia: 45 Nottingham Pl., London, W1U 5LY; tel. (20) 7312-0040; fax (20) 7312-0042; e-mail embassy.uk@mfa.gov.lv; internet www.london.mfa.gov.lv; Ambassador Indulis Bērziņš.

Lebanon: 21 Palace Gardens Mews, London, W8 4RB; tel. (20) 7227-6696; fax (20) 7243-1699; e-mail emb.leb@btinternet.com; Ambassador Inaam Osseiran.

Lesotho: 7 Chesham Pl., London, SW1 8HN; tel. (20) 7235-5686; fax (20) 7235-5023; e-mail lhc@lesotholondon.org.uk; internet www.lesotholondon.org.uk; High Commr Prince Seeiso Bereng Seeiso.

Liberia: 23 Fitzroy Sq., London, W1 6EW; tel. (20) 7388-5489; fax (20) 7380-1593; e-mail liberianembassy@yahoo.co.uk; internet www.embassyofliberia.org.uk; Ambassador Wesley Momo Johnson.

Libya: 15 Knightsbridge, London, SW1X 7LY; tel. (20) 7201-8280; fax (20) 7245-0588; Chargé d'affaires Omar R. Jelban.

Lithuania: 84 Gloucester Pl., London, W1U 6AU; tel. (20) 7486-6401; fax (20) 7486-6403; e-mail amb.uk@urm.lt; internet uk.mfa.lt; Chargé d'affaires a.i. Janė Hanel.

Luxembourg: 27 Wilton Cres., London, SW1X 8SD; tel. (20) 7235-6961; fax (20) 7235-9734; e-mail londres.amb@mae.etat.lu; Ambassador Hubert Wurth.

Macedonia, former Yugoslav republic: Suites 2.1 and 2.2, 2nd Floor, Buckingham Court, Buckingham Gate, London, SW1E 6PE; tel. (20) 7976-0535; fax (20) 7976-0539; e-mail info@macedonianembassy.org.uk; internet www.macedonianembassy.org.uk; Ambassador Marija Efremova.

Madagascar: 8–10 Hallam St, London, W1W 6JE; tel. (20) 3008-4550; fax (20) 3008-4551; e-mail embamadlon@yahoo.co.uk; internet www.embassy-madagascar-uk.com; Chargé d'affaires Iary Berthine Ravaoarimanana.

Malawi: 70 Winnington Rd, London, N2 0TX; tel. (20) 8455-5624; fax (20) 3235-1066; e-mail malawihighcom@btconnect.com; internet www.malawihighcom.org.uk; High Commr Dr Francis Moto.

Malaysia: 45 Belgrave Sq., London, SW1X 8QT; tel. (20) 7235-8033; fax (20) 7235-5161; e-mail mwlon@btconnect.com; internet www.kln.gov.my/mission/london; High Commr Datuk Abd Aziz Mohammed.

Maldives: 22 Nottingham Pl., London, W1U 5NJ; tel. (20) 7224-2135; fax (20) 7224-2157; e-mail info@maldiveshighcommission.org; internet www.maldiveshighcommission.org; High Commr Dr Farahanaz Faisal.

Malta: Malta House, 36–38 Piccadilly, London, W1J 0LE; tel. (20) 7292-4800; fax (20) 7734-1831; e-mail maltahighcommission.london@gov.mt; High Commr Joseph Zammit Tabona.

Mauritius: 32–33 Elvaston Pl., London, SW7 5NW; tel. (20) 7581-0294; fax (20) 7823-8437; e-mail londonmhc@btinternet.com; High Commr Abhimanu Mahendra Kundasamy.

Mexico: 16 St George St, Hanover Sq., London, W1S 1FD; tel. (20) 7499-8586; fax (20) 7495-4035; e-mail mexuk@sre.gob.mx; internet www.sre.gob.mx/reinounido; Ambassador Juan José Bremer de Martino.

Moldova: 5 Dolphin Sq., Edensor Rd, London, W4 2ST; tel. (20) 8995-6818; fax (20) 8995-6927; e-mail londra@mfa.md; internet www.moldovanembassy.org.uk; Ambassador Natalia Solcan.

Mongolia: 7 Kensington Court, London, W8 5DL; tel. (20) 7937-0150; fax (20) 7937-1117; e-mail office@embassyofmongolia.co.uk; internet www.embassyofmongolia.co.uk; Ambassador Bulgaagiin Altangerel.

Montenegro: Trafalgar House, 5th Floor, 11–12 Waterloo Pl., London, SW1Y 4AU; tel. (20) 7863-8806; fax (20) 7863-8807; Ambassador Dragiša Burzan.

Morocco: 49 Queen's Gate Gdns, London, SW7 5NE; tel. (20) 7581-5001; fax (20) 7225-3862; e-mail ambalondres@maec.gov.ma; Ambassador Princess Chrifa Lalla Jamala Aloui.

Mozambique: 21 Fitzroy Sq., London, W1T 6EL; tel. (20) 7383-3800; fax (20) 7383-3801; e-mail sandra@mozambiquehc.co.uk; internet www.mozambiquehc.org.uk; High Commr António Gumende.

Myanmar: 19A Charles St, London, W1J 5DX; tel. (20) 7499-4340; fax (20) 7409-7043; e-mail melondon@btconnect.com; Ambassador U Nay Win.

Namibia: 6 Chandos St, London, W1G 9LU; tel. (20) 7636-6244; fax (20) 7637-5694; e-mail namibia.hicom@btconnect.com; High Commr George Mbanga Liswaniso.

Nepal: 12A Kensington Palace Gdns, London, W8 4QU; tel. (20) 7229-1594; fax (20) 7792-9861; e-mail eon@nepembassy.org.uk; internet www.nepembassy.org.uk; Chargé d'affaires a.i. Jhabindra P. Aryal.

Netherlands: 38 Hyde Park Gate, London, SW7 5DP; tel. (20) 7590-3200; fax (20) 7225-0947; e-mail london@netherlands-embassy.org.uk; internet www.netherlands-embassy.org.uk; Ambassador Pieter Willem (Pim) Waldeck.

New Zealand: New Zealand House, 80 Haymarket, London, SW1Y 4TQ; tel. (20) 7930-8422; fax (20) 7839-4580; e-mail aboutnz@newzealandhc.org.uk; internet www.nzembassy.com/uk; High Commr Derek William Leask.

Nicaragua: Suite 31, Vicarage House, 58–60 Kensington Church St, London, W8 4DB; tel. (20) 7938-2373; fax (20) 7937-0952; e-mail embanic1@yahoo.co.uk; Ambassador Piero Paolo Coen Ubilla.

Nigeria: Nigeria House, 9 Northumberland Ave, London, WC2N 5BX; tel. (20) 7839-1244; fax (20) 7839-8746; e-mail chancery@nigeriahc.org.uk; internet www.nigeriahc.org.uk; High Commr Dr Dalhatu Sarki Tafida.

Norway: 25 Belgrave Sq., London, SW1X 8QD; tel. (20) 7591-5500; fax (20) 7245-6993; e-mail emb.london@mfa.no; internet www.norway.org.uk; Ambassador Bjarne Lindstrøm.

Oman: 167 Queen's Gate, London, SW7 5HE; tel. (20) 7225-0001; fax (20) 7589-2505; Ambassador Hussain Ali Abdullatif.

Pakistan: 34–36 Lowndes Sq., London, SW1X 9JN; tel. (20) 7664-9200; fax (20) 7664-9224; e-mail pareplondon@supanet.com; internet www.pakmission-uk.gov.pk; High Commr Wajid Shamsul Hasan.

Panama: 40 Hertford St, London, W1J 7SH; tel. (20) 7493-4646; fax (20) 7493-4333; e-mail panama1@btconnect.com; Ambassador Liliana Fernándes.

THE UNITED KINGDOM

Directory

Papua New Guinea: 3rd Floor, 14 Waterloo Pl., London, SW1R 4AR; tel. (20) 7930-0922; fax (20) 7930-0828; internet www.pnghighcomm.org.uk; High Commr JEAN L. KEKEDO.

Paraguay: 3rd Floor, 344 Kensington High St, London, W14 8NS; tel. (20) 7610-4180; fax (20) 7371-4297; e-mail embapar@btconnect.com; internet www.paraguayembassy.co.uk; Chargé d'affaires JOSÉ EMILIO GOROSTIAGA-PEÑA.

Peru: 52 Sloane St, London, SW1X 9SP; tel. (20) 7235-1917; fax (20) 7235-4463; e-mail postmaster@peruembassy-uk.com; internet www.peruembassy-uk.com; Ambassador RICARDO V. LUNA MENDOZA.

Philippines: 6–8 Suffolk St, London, SW1Y 4HG; tel. (20) 7937-1800; fax (20) 7930-9787; e-mail embassy@philemb.co.uk; internet www.philemb.co.uk; Ambassador EDGARDO B. ESPIRITU.

Poland: 47 Portland Pl., London, W1B 1JH; tel. (870) 774-2700; fax (20) 7291-3575; e-mail polishembassy@polishembassy.org.uk; internet www.london.polemb.net; Ambassador BARBARA TUGE-ERECIŃSKA.

Portugal: 11 Belgrave Sq., London, SW1X 8PP; tel. (20) 7235-5331; fax (20) 7235-0739; e-mail london@portembassy.co.uk; Ambassador ANTÓNIO NUNES DE CARVALHO SANTANA CARLOS.

Qatar: 1 South Audley St, London, W1K 1NB; tel. (20) 7493-2200; fax (20) 7493-2661; Ambassador KHALID BIN RASHID BIN SALIM AL-HAMOUDI AL-MANSOURI.

Romania: Arundel House, 4 Palace Green, London, W8 4QD; tel. (20) 7937-9666; fax (20) 7937-8069; e-mail roemb@roemb.co.uk; internet londra.mae.ro; Ambassador ION JINGA.

Russia: 13 Kensington Palace Gdns, London, W8 4QX; tel. (20) 7229-6412; fax (20) 7727-8625; e-mail office@rusemblon.org; internet www.great-britain.mid.ru; Ambassador YURII V. FEDOTOV.

Rwanda: 120–122 Seymour Pl., London, W1H 1NR; tel. (20) 7724-9832; fax (20) 7724-8642; e-mail uk@ambarwanda.org.uk; internet www.ambarwanda.org.uk; Ambassador CLAVER GATETE.

Saint Christopher and Nevis: 2nd Floor, 10 Kensington Court, London, W8 5DL; tel. (20) 7937-9718; fax (20) 7937-7484; e-mail sknhighcomm@btconnect.com; High Commr JAMES E. WILLIAMS.

Saint Lucia: 1 Collingham Gdns, London, SW5 0HW; tel. (20) 7370-7123; fax (20) 7370-1905; e-mail hcslu@btconnect.com; High Commr ELDRIDGE STEPHENS.

Saint Vincent and the Grenadines: 10 Kensington Court, London, W8 5DL; tel. (20) 7565-2874; fax (20) 7937-6040; e-mail info@svghighcom.co.uk; High Commr CENIO E. LEWIS.

Saudi Arabia: 30 Charles St, London, W1J 5DZ; tel. (20) 7917-3000; fax (20) 7917-3330; e-mail ukemb@mofa.gov.sa; internet www.saudiembassy.org.uk; Ambassador Prince MUHAMMAD BIN NAWAF BIN ABDULAZIZ.

Senegal: 39 Marloes Rd, London, W8 6LA; tel. (20) 7937-7237; fax (20) 7938-2546; e-mail senegalembassy@hotmail.co.uk; internet www.senegalembassy.co.uk; Ambassador ABDOU SOURANG.

Serbia: 28 Belgrave Sq., London, SW1X 8QB; tel. (20) 7235-9049; fax (20) 7235-7092; e-mail london@serbianembassy.org.uk; internet www.serbianembassy.org.uk; Ambassador DEJAN POPOVIC.

Sierra Leone: 41 Eagle St, London, WC1R 4TL; tel. (20) 7404-0140; fax (20) 7430-9862; e-mail info@slhc-uk.org.uk; internet www.slhc-uk.org.uk; High Commr MELVIN H. CHALOBAH.

Singapore: 9 Wilton Cres., London, SW1X 8SP; tel. (20) 7235-8315; fax (20) 7245-6583; e-mail singhc_lon@sgmfa.gov.sg; internet www.mfa.gov.sg/london; High Commr MICHAEL ENG CHENG TEO.

Slovakia: 25 Kensington Palace Gdns, London, W8 4QY; tel. (20) 7313-6470; fax (20) 7313-6481; e-mail emb.london@mzv.sk; internet www.slovakembassy.co.uk; Ambassador JURAJ ZERVAN.

Slovenia: 10 Little College St, London, SW1P 3SH; tel. (20) 7222-5400; fax (20) 7222-5277; e-mail vlo@gov.si; internet london.embassy.si; Ambassador IZTOK JARC.

South Africa: South Africa House, Trafalgar Sq., London, WC2N 5DP; tel. (20) 7451-7299; fax (20) 7451-7284; e-mail webdesk@southafricahouse.com; internet www.southafricahouse.com; High Commr Dr LINDIWE MABUZA.

Spain: 39 Chesham Pl., London, SW1X 8SB; tel. (20) 7235-5555; fax (20) 7259-5392; e-mail embespuk@mail.mae.es; internet www.maec.es/embajadas/londres; Ambassador CARLOS MARÍA CASAJUANA PALET.

Sri Lanka: 13 Hyde Park Gdns, London, W2 2LU; tel. (20) 7262-1841; fax (20) 7262-7970; e-mail mail@slhc-london.co.uk; internet www.slhclondon.org; High Commr NIHAL JAYASINGHE.

Sudan: 3 Cleveland Row, St James's, London, SW1A 1DD; tel. (20) 7839-8080; fax (20) 7839-7560; e-mail admin@sudanembassy.co.uk; internet www.sudanembassy.co.uk; Ambassador OMAR MUHAMMAD AHMAD SIDDIG.

Swaziland: 20 Buckingham Gate, London, SW1E 6LB; tel. (20) 7630-6611; fax (20) 7630-6564; e-mail enquiries@swaziland.org.uk; High Commr HENRY ZEEMAN (acting).

Sweden: 11 Montagu Pl., London, W1H 2AL; tel. (20) 7917-6400; fax (20) 7724-4174; e-mail ambassaden.london@foreign.ministry.se; internet www.swedenabroad.com/london; Ambassador STAFFAN CARLSSON.

Switzerland: 16–18 Montagu Pl., London, W1H 2BQ; tel. (20) 7616-6000; fax (20) 7724-7001; e-mail swissembassy@lon.rep.admin.ch; internet www.swissembassy.org.uk; Ambassador ALEXIS P. LAUTENBERG.

Syria: 8 Belgrave Sq., London, SW1X 8PH; tel. (20) 7245-9012; fax (20) 7235-4621; e-mail info@syrianembassy.co.uk; internet www.syrianembassy.co.uk; Ambassador Dr SAMI KHIYAMI.

Tajikistan: Grove House, 27 Hammersmith Grove, London, W6 0NE; tel. (20) 8600-2520; fax (20) 8600-2501; e-mail info@tajembassy.org.uk; internet www.tajembassy.org.uk; Ambassador ERKIN S. KASYMOV.

Tanzania: 3 Stratford Pl., London, WIC 1AS; tel. (20) 7569-1470; fax (20) 7491-3710; e-mail hom@tanzania-online.gov.uk; internet www.tanzania-online.gov.uk; High Commr MWANAIDI S. MAAJAR.

Thailand: 29–30 Queen's Gate, London, SW7 5JB; tel. (20) 7589-2944; fax (20) 7823-7492; e-mail csinfo@thaiembassyuk.org.uk; internet www.thaiembassyuk.org.uk; Ambassador KITTI WASINONDH.

Tonga: 36 Molyneux St, London, W1H 5BQ; tel. (20) 7724-5828; fax (20) 7723-9074; e-mail snkioa@tongahighcom.co.uk; High Commr Dr SIONE NGONGO KIOA.

Trinidad and Tobago: 42 Belgrave Sq., London, SW1X 8NT; tel. (20) 7245-9351; fax (20) 7823-1065; e-mail tthc.info@btconnect.net; High Commr JOHN JEREMIE.

Tunisia: 29 Prince's Gate, London, SW7 1QG; tel. (20) 7584-8117; fax (20) 7584-3205; Ambassador HAMIDA MRABET LAÂBIDI.

Turkey: 43 Belgrave Sq., London, SW1X 8PA; tel. (20) 7393-0202; fax (20) 7393-0066; e-mail turkish.emb@btclick.com; internet www.turkishembassylondon.org; Ambassador MEHMET YIĞIT ALPOGAN.

Turkmenistan: 2nd Floor South, St George's House, 14–17 Wells St, London, W1P 3FP; tel. (20) 7255-1071; fax (20) 7323-9184; Ambassador YAZMURAD SERYAEV.

Uganda: Uganda House, 58/59 Trafalgar Sq., London, WC2N 5DX; tel. (20) 7839-5783; fax (20) 7839-8925; internet www.ugandahighcommission.co.uk; High Commr JOAN KAKIMA NYAKATUURA RWABYOMERE.

Ukraine: 60 Holland Park, London, W11 3SJ; tel. (20) 7727-6312; fax (20) 7792-1708; e-mail emb_gb@mfa.gov.ua; internet www.ukremb.org.uk; Ambassador IHOR KHARCHENKO.

United Arab Emirates: 30 Princes Gate, London, SW7 1PT; tel. (20) 7581-1281; fax (20) 7581-9616; e-mail information@uaeembassyuk.net; internet www.uaeembassyuk.net; Ambassador ABD AR-RAHMAN GHANIM AL-MUTAIWEE.

USA: 24–32 Grosvenor Sq., London, W1A 1AE; tel. (20) 7499-9000; internet london.usembassy.gov; Chargé d'affaires a.i. RICHARD LeBARON.

Uruguay: 125 Kensington High St, London, W8 5SF; tel. (20) 7937-4170; fax (20) 7376-0502; e-mail emburuguay@emburuguay.org.uk; Ambassador RICARDO VARELA.

Uzbekistan: 41 Holland Park, London, W11 2RP; tel. (20) 7229-7679; fax (20) 7229-7029; e-mail info@uzbekembassy.org; internet www.uzbekembassy.org; Ambassador OTABEK H. AKBAROV.

Venezuela: 1 Cromwell Rd, London, SW7 2HW; tel. (20) 7584-4206; fax (20) 7589-8887; e-mail info@venezlon.co.uk; internet www.venezlon.co.uk; Ambassador SAMUEL MONCADA.

Viet Nam: 12–14 Victoria Rd, London, W8 5RD; tel. (20) 7937-1912; fax (20) 7937-6108; e-mail embassy@vietnamembassy.org.uk; internet www.vietnamembassy.org.uk; Ambassador TRAN QUANG HOAN.

Yemen: 57 Cromwell Rd, London, SW7 2ED; tel. (20) 7584-6607; fax (20) 7589-3350; e-mail yemenembassy@btconnect.com; internet www.yemenembassy.org.uk; Ambassador MUHAMMAD TAHA MUSTAFA.

Zambia: Zambia House, 2 Palace Gate, London, W8 5NG; tel. (20) 7589-6655; fax (20) 7581-1353; e-mail immzhcl@btconnect.com; internet www.zhcl.org.uk; High Commr ANDERSON KASEBA CHIBWA.

Zimbabwe: Zimbabwe House, 429 Strand, London, WC2R 0QE; tel. (20) 7836-7755; fax (20) 7379-1167; e-mail zimlondon@yahoo.co.uk; Ambassador GABRIEL MHARADZE MACHINGA.

Judicial System

There are, historically, three sources of the law as administered in the law courts today: Statute Law, which is written law and consists mainly of Acts of Parliament; Common Law, which originated in ancient usage and has not been formally enacted; and Equity, which was the system evolved by the Lord Chancellor's court (Court of Chancery) to mitigate the strictness of some of the common law rules. The law of the European Community has now been added to these.

Scottish common and statute law differ in some respects from that current in the rest of the United Kingdom, owing to Scotland's retention of its own legal system under the Act of Union with England of 1707.

Three factors help to ensure a fair trial: the independence of judges, who, in the case of High Court Judges, are outside the control of the executive and can be removed from office only after an address from Parliament to the Sovereign (Circuit Judges can be removed by the Lord Chancellor); the participation of private citizens in all important criminal and some civil cases, in the form of a summoned jury of 12 persons, who judge, if necessary by a majority, the facts of a case, questions of law being decided by the judge; and the system of appeals to a higher court, including the Criminal and Civil Divisions of the Court of Appeal, and, thereafter, the House of Lords.

The Courts and Legal Services Act 1990 provided for radical change in the legal profession, including legislation permitting solicitors to appear in higher courts, and extensive reform of the civil courts, whereby the civil cases formerly heard in the High Court could be transferred to the county courts.

In June 2003 the Government announced its intention to create a new free-standing Supreme Court to take over the judicial functions of the House of Lords and the Judicial Committee of the Privy Council. The Supreme Court was established in March 2005, following the promulgation of the Constitutional Reform Act; the court was scheduled to commence operations on 1 October 2009.

MAGISTRATES' COURTS OR PETTY SESSIONS

The criminal courts of lowest jurisdiction are presided over by Justices of the Peace, who are unpaid lay people appointed by the Lord Chancellor. They have power to try all non-indictable offences, and some of the less serious indictable offences, if the defendant agrees. The trial of nearly all criminal offences begins in the magistrates' court. Approximately 95% of all criminal offences are dealt with solely by magistrates' courts. In the vast majority of committals for trial in the Crown Court magistrates are not required to consider evidence.

In London and in certain other large towns there are a small number of professional salaried magistrates, known as metropolitan stipendiary magistrates in London and as stipendiary magistrates in the provinces, who sit alone, whereas lay justices normally sit in threes when acting judicially.

Youth Courts, composed of specially trained justices selected by the justices of each petty sessional division (in London, by the Lord Chancellor), have power to try most charges against children aged under 18 years. The general public is excluded and there are restrictions on newspaper reports of the proceedings.

Magistrates also have power to grant, renew, transfer or remove or order the forfeiture of licences for the sale of alcoholic drinks, and to control the structural design of premises where alcohol is sold for consumption on the premises. They also control the licensing of betting shops, and grant bookmakers' permits.

COUNTY COURTS

A high proportion of civil actions are tried in these courts, which are presided over by a circuit judge, or, in some cases, a district judge, sitting alone. From 1 July 1991 county courts were granted unlimited jurisdiction.

THE CROWN COURT

The Crown Court came into being on 1 January 1972, under the Courts Act 1971, replacing Quarter Sessions and Assizes, to deal with serious criminal cases where trial by jury is required. The Crown Court sits at various centres throughout England and Wales. Court centres have been administratively divided into three tiers. The most serious offences are tried at first and second tier centres presided over by High Court Judges, Circuit Judges or Recorders. Circuit Judges or Recorders preside over third tier centres, where the less serious offences are tried. The Crown Court for the City of London is the Central Criminal Court (the Old Bailey).

HIGH COURT OF JUSTICE

Certain civil cases are heard in the three divisions of this court—Chancery, Queen's Bench and Family. The Chancery Division deals with litigation about property, patents, family trusts, companies, dissolution of partnerships and disputed estates. The Queen's Bench Division hears cases involving damage to property, personal injuries, etc. and also includes the Commercial and Admiralty Courts. The Family Division hears contested or complex divorce and separation cases and matters relating to children such as adoption, wardship or guardianship of minors.

Chancery Division

President: Sir ROBERT ANDREW MORRITT (Chancellor).

Judges: Sir WILLIAM ANTHONY BLACKBURNE, Sir NICHOLAS JOHN PATTEN, Sir PETER WINSTON SMITH, Sir KIM MARTIN JORDAN LEWISON, Sir DAVID ANTHONY STEWART RICHARDS, Sir GEORGE ANTHONY MANN, Sir NICHOLAS ROGER WARREN, Sir DAVID JAMES TYSON KITCHIN, Sir MICHAEL TOWNLEY FEATHERSTONE BRIGGS, Sir LAUNCELOT DINADIN JAMES HENDERSON, Sir PAUL HYACINTH MORGAN, Sir ALASTAIR HUBERT NORRIS, Sir GERALD EDWARD BARLING, Sir CHRISTOPHER DAVID LLOYD, Sir PHILIP JAMES SALES, Dame SONIA ROSEMARY SUSAN PROUDMAN, Sir RICHARD DAVID ARNOLD.

Queen's Bench Division

President: Sir ANTHONY TRISTRAM KENNETH MAY.

Judges: Sir STUART NEIL McKINNON, Sir ANDREW DAVID COLLINS, Sir ALEXANDER NEIL LOGIE BUTTERFIELD, Sir DAVID EADY, Sir DAVID HERBERT PENRY-DAVEY, Sir DAVID WILLIAM STEEL, Sir NICOLAS DUŠAN BRATZA (Judge of the European Court of Human Rights), Sir MICHAEL JOHN BURTON, Sir STEPHEN ROBERT SILBER, Dame ANNE JUDITH RAFFERTY, Sir RICHARD HENRY QUIXANO HENRIQUES, Sir STEPHEN MILES TOMLINSON, Sir ANDREW CHARLES SMITH, Sir CHRISTOPHER JOHN PITCHFORD, Sir DUNCAN BRIAN WALTER OUSELEY, Sir RICHARD GEORGE BRAMWELL McCOMBE, Sir RAYMOND EVAN JACK, Sir ROBERT MICHAEL OWEN, Sir COLIN CRICHTON MACKAY, Sir JOHN EDWARD MITTING, Sir DAVID RODERICK EVANS, Sir NIGEL ANTHONY LAMERT DAVIS, Sir PETER HENRY GROSS, Sir BRIAN RICHARD KEITH, Sir JEREMY LIONEL COOKE, Sir RICHARD ALAN FIELD, Sir COLMAN MAURICE TREACY, Sir PEREGRINE CHARLES HUGO SIMON, Sir ROGER JOHN ROYCE, Dame LAURA MARY COX, Sir ADRIAN BRUCE FULFORD, Sir JACK BEATSON, Sir MICHAEL GEORGE TUGENDHAT, Sir DAVID CLIVE CLARKE, Dame ELIZABETH GLOSTER, Sir DAVID MICHAEL BEAN, Sir ALAN FRASER WILKIE, Dame LINDA PENELOPE DOBBS, Sir HENRY EGAR GARFIELD HODGE, Sir PAUL JAMES WALKER, Sir DAVID CALVERT-SMITH, Sir CHRISTOPHER SIMON COURTENAY STEPHENSON CLARKE, Sir CHARLES PETER LAWFORD OPENSHAW, Dame CAROLINE JANE SWIFT, Sir BRIAN FREDERICK JAMES LANGSTAFF, Sir DAVID LLOYD JONES, Sir VIVIAN ARTHUR RAMSAY, Sir NICHOLAS EDWARD UNDERHILL, Sir STEPHEN JOHN IRWIN, Sir NIGEL JOHN MARTIN TEARE, Sir JOHN GRIFFITH WILLIAMS, Sir WYN LEWIS WILLIAMS, Sir TIMOTHY ROGER ALAN KING, Sir JOHN HENRY BOULTON SAUNDERS, Sir JULIAN MARTIN FLAUX, Sir NICHOLAS FELIX STADLEN, Sir ROBERT AKENHEAD, Sir DAVID ROBERT FOSKETT, Sir NICHOLAS JOHN GORROD BLAKE, Sir ROSS FREDERICK CRANSTON, Sir PETER DAVID WILLIAM COULSON, Sir DAVID MADDISON, Sir RICHARD OWEN PLENDER, Sir WILLIAM JAMES LYNTON BLAIR, Sir ALISTAIR GEOFFREY MACDUFF, Sir IAN DUNCAN BURNETT, Sir NIGEL HAMILTON SWEENEY, Dame ELIZABETH ANN SLADE, Sir NICHOLAS ARCHIBALD HAMBLEN, Sir GARY ROBERT HICKINBOTTOM, Sir TIMOTHY VICTOR HOLROYDE, Dame VICTORIA MADELINE SHARP, Sir ANDREW GEORGE LINDSAY NICOL.

Family Division

President: Sir MARK HOWARD POTTER.

Judges: Sir JAN PETER SINGER, Sir HUGH PETER DERWYN BENNETT, Sir EDWARD JAMES HOLMAN, Dame MARY CLAIRE HOGG, Sir ARTHUR WILLIAM HESSIN CHARLES, Sir DAVID RODERICK LESSITER BODEY, Dame JILL MARGARET BLACK, Sir JAMES LAWRENCE MUNBY, Sir PAUL JAMES DUKE COLERIDGE, Sir MARK HEDLEY, Dame ANNA EVELYN HAMILTON PAUFFLEY, Sir RODERIC LIONEL JAMES WOOD, Dame FLORENCE JACQUELENE BARON, Sir ERNEST NIGEL RYDER, Sir ANDREW EWART McFARLANE, Dame JULIA WENDY MACUR, Sir ANDREW JOHN GREGORY MOYLAN, Dame ELEANOR WARWICK KING, Dame JUDITH MARY FRANCES PARKER.

COURT OF APPEAL

An appeal lies in civil cases to this court from County Courts and the High Court of Justice and in criminal cases from the Crown Courts. The Master of the Rolls is the effective head of the court.

Ex Officio Judges

Lord Chief Justice of England and Wales: Lord JUDGE.

Master of the Rolls and Head of Civil Justice: Sir ANTHONY PETER CLARKE.

President of the Queen's Bench Division: Sir ANTHONY TRISTRAM KENNETH MAY.

President of the Family Division: Sir MARK HOWARD POTTER.

Chancellor of the High Court: Sir ROBERT ANDREW MORRITT.

Lords Justices of Appeal: Sir MALCOLM THOMAS PILL, Sir ALAN HYLTON WARD, Sir MATHEW ALEXANDER THORPE, Sir GEORGE MARK WALLER (Vice-President, Civil Division of the Court of Appeal), Sir JOHN FRANK MUMMERY, Sir JOHN GRANT McKENZIE LAWS, Sir STEPHEN JOHN SEDLEY, Sir BERNARD ANTHONY RIX, Dame MARY HOWARTH ARDEN, Sir DAVID WOLFE KEENE, Sir JOHN ANTHONY DYSON, Sir

THE UNITED KINGDOM

Andrew Centlivres Longmore, Sir Robert John Anderson Carnwath, Sir Thomas Scott Gillespie Baker, Dame Janet Hilary Smith, Sir Roger John Laugharne Thomas, Sir Robert Raphael Hayim (Robin) Jacob, Sir Nicholas Peter Rathbone Wall, Sir Maurice Ralph Kay, Sir Anthony Hooper, Sir Timothy Andrew Wigram Lloyd, Sir Martin James Moore-Bick (Deputy Head of Civil Justice), Sir Nicholas Allan Roy Wilson, Sir Alan George Moses, Sir Stephen Price Richards, Dame Heather Carol Hallett, Sir Anthony Phillip Gilson Hughes, Sir Brian Henry Leveson, Sir Roger Grenfell Toulson, Sir Colin Percy Farquharson Rimer, Sir Stanley Jeffrey Burnton, Sir Terrence Michael Elkan Barnet Etherton (Chairman of the Law Commission), Sir Rupert Michael Jackson, Sir John Bernard Goldring, Sir Richard Pearson Aikens, Sir Jeremy Mirth Sullivan, Sir Patrick Elias.

HOUSE OF LORDS

In civil and criminal cases this is the final court of appeal.

Senior Lord of Appeal in Ordinary: Lord Phillips of Worth Matravers.

Lords of Appeal in Ordinary: Lord Hope of Craighead, Lord Saville of Newdigate, Lord Scott of Foscote, Lord Rodger of Earlsferry, Lord Walker of Gestingthorpe, Lady Hale of Richmond, Lord Carswell, Lord Brown of Eaton-under-Heywood, Lord Mance, Lord Neuberger of Abbotsbury, Lord Collins of Mapesbury.

JUDICIAL COMMITTEE OF THE PRIVY COUNCIL

Final court of appeal for appeals from certain Commonwealth territories; also exercises domestic jurisdiction in ecclesiastical matters and appeals from disciplinary tribunals of certain professions.

Northern Irish Judicial System

The judicial system of Northern Ireland, so far as the Supreme Court is concerned, is a miniature of the English system, and is based on the Judicature (Northern Ireland) Act 1978. It consists, as in England, of the High Court, the Court of Appeal, and the Crown Court (which has jurisdiction in criminal matters). The jurisdiction of the Magistrates' Courts (Courts of Summary Jurisdiction) is exercised by a permanent judiciary of legally qualified resident magistrates.

COUNTY COURTS

The county court system corresponds to its English counterpart, but there is no system of pleadings, as is found in the English county court. There are also variations in jurisdiction levels. County court judges share with the judges of the High Court the exercise of the jurisdiction of the Crown Court.

HIGH COURT

The Lord Chief Justice of Northern Ireland: Sir Brian Kerr, Royal Courts of Justice, Chichester St, Belfast, BT1 3JF; tel. (28) 9023-5111; fax (28) 9031-3508; e-mail adminoffice@courtsni.gov.uk; internet www.courtsni.gov.uk.

Judges: Sir John Gillen, Sir Richard McLaughlin, Sir Ronald Weatherup, Sir Reginald Weir, Sir Charles Morgan, Sir Donnell Deeny, Sir Anthony Ronald Hart, Sir William Benjamin Synge Stephens, Sir Seamus Treacy, Sir Bernard McCloskey.

COURT OF APPEAL

President: The Lord Chief Justice of Northern Ireland

Judges: Sir Malachy Higgins, Sir Paul Frederick Girvan, Sir Anthony Campbell, Sir Patrick Coghlin.

Scottish Judicial System

CRIMINAL COURTS

Minor offences are dealt with in District courts.

Sheriff Court

Most criminal actions, including all but the most serious offences, are tried in this court. Each of the six sheriffdoms of Scotland has a Sheriff Principal and a number of Sheriffs, who hear the cases.

High Court of Justiciary

This is the supreme criminal court in Scotland: all the most serious cases are taken there. Appeal may be made to it from the Sheriff Court and from the District courts; there is, however, no further appeal to the House of Lords.

The 32 judges of this court are known as Lords Commissioners of Justiciary and are headed by the Lord Justice General and the Lord Justice Clerk. Apart from their criminal jurisdiction in this court, these judges are also judges of the Court of Session (see below) in civil cases. The Lord Justice General is also the President of the Court of Session.

High Court in Edinburgh: Lawnmarket, Edinburgh, EH1 2PE; tel. (131) 225-2595; fax (131) 240-6917; e-mail supreme.courts@scotcourts.gov.uk; internet www.scotcourts.gov.uk.

High Court in Glasgow: Saltmarket, Glasgow, G1 5JU; tel. (141) 552-3795; fax (141) 559-4519; e-mail supreme.courts@scotcourts.gov.uk; internet www.scotcourts.gov.uk.

CIVIL COURTS

Sheriff Court

This court hears civil as well as criminal cases, and in civil cases its jurisdiction is practically unlimited. It has concurrent jurisdiction with the Court of Session in divorce actions. Appeal may be made to the Court of Session or the Sheriff Principal.

Court of Session

This is the supreme civil court in Scotland. It has an Inner House and an Outer House.

The Inner House has two divisions of equal standing, each consisting of five judges (the quorum is three although due to pressure of business an extra division of three judges frequently sits) under the presidency of the Lord President and the Lord Justice Clerk respectively; it is mainly an appeal court, whence further appeal may be made to the House of Lords.

Court of Session: Parliament House, Parliament Sq., Edinburgh, EH1 1RQ; tel. (131) 225-2595; fax (131) 240-6755; e-mail supreme.courts@scotcourts.gov.uk; internet www.scotcourts.gov.uk.

First Division

Lord Justice General and President of the Court of Session: Lord Hamilton.

Judges: Lord Nimmo Smith, Lord Reed, Lord Kingarth, Lord Eassie.

Second Division

Lord Justice Clerk: Lord Gill.

Judges: Lord Osborne, Lord Wheatley, Lady Paton, Lord Caloway, Lord Clarke.

The Outer House deals with the major civil cases and divorce actions. The judges are those of the High Court of Justiciary, sitting in a civil capacity as judges of the Court of Session.

Judges: Lord Hardie, Lord Mackay of Drumadoon, Lord McEwan, Lord Menzies, Lord Drummond Young, Lord Emslie, Lady Smith, Lord Brodie, Lord Bracadale, Lady Dorrian, Lord Hodge, Lord MacPhail, Lord Glennie, Lord Kinclaven, Lord Turnbull, Lady Clark of Calton, Lord Brailsford, Lord Uist, Lord Malcolm, Lord Matthews, Lord Woolman, Lord Pentland, Lord Bannatyne, Lady Stacey.

Religion

CHRISTIANITY

Churches Together in Britain and Ireland: Bastille Court, 2 Paris Garden, London, SE1 8ND; tel. (20) 7654-7254; fax (20) 7654-7222; e-mail info@ctbi.org.uk; internet www.ctbi.org.uk; f. 1990 as successor to the British Council of Churches; co-ordinates the activities of its 38 member churches and liaises with ecumenical bodies in Britain and Ireland. Its work divisions include Church Life, Church and Society and International Affairs, Spirituality, Racial Justice, Mission and Inter-faith Relations. It provides a forum for joint decision-making and enables the churches to take action together; Gen. Sec. Rev. Canon Bob Fyffe.

Action of Churches Together in Scotland (ACTS): Inglewood House, Alloa, FK10 2HU; tel. (1259) 216980; fax (1259) 215964; e-mail ecumenical@acts-scotland.org; internet www.acts-scotland.org; aims to encourage and express unity of Christian Churches in Scotland; 9 mem. churches; Convener Rev. Mary Buchanan; Gen. Sec. Stephen Smyth.

Churches Together in England (CTE): 27 Tavistock Sq., London, WC1H 9HH; tel. (20) 7529-8131; fax (20) 7529-8134; e-mail office@cte.org.uk; internet www.churches-together.org.uk; f. 1990; 29 mem. bodies; Pres Most Rev. and Rt Hon. Dr Rowan Williams, Elizabeth Matear, Rt Rev. Nathan Hovhannisian, H.E. Cardinal Cormac Murphy-O'Connor; Gen. Sec. Rev. David Cornick.

THE UNITED KINGDOM

Churches Together in Wales (Cytûn): 58 Richmond Rd, Cardiff, CF24 3UR; tel. (29) 2046-4204; e-mail post@cytun.org.uk; internet www.cytun.org.uk; fmrly the Council of Churches for Wales; Chief Exec. Rev. ALED EDWARDS.

Irish Council of Churches: Inter-Church Centre, 48 Elmwood Ave, Belfast, BT9 6AZ; tel. (28) 9066-3145; fax (28) 9066-4160; e-mail info@irishchurches.org; internet www.irishchurches.org; f. 1922 (present name adopted 1966); 15 mem. churches; the organization of the churches in Ireland takes no account of the partition of the island into two separate political entities, with Ireland and Northern Ireland thus subject to a unified jurisdiction for ecclesiastical purposes; Pres. Rev. TONY DAVIDSON; Gen. Sec. MICHAEL EARLE.

The Anglican Communion

The Church of England

The Church of England is the Established Church, and as such acknowledges the authority of Parliament in matters in which secular authority is competent to exercise control. Queen Elizabeth I was declared 'supreme Governor on Earth' of the Church of England, and the Sovereign is consecrated to this office at coronation.

In England, there are two Provinces, Canterbury and York. The former contains 30, the latter 14, dioceses. Each Province has its ancient Convocations, the Upper and Lower House. By the Enabling Act the Constitution of the National Assembly of the Church of England ('Church Assembly') received statutory recognition in 1920, with power, subject to the control and authority of Parliament, of initiating legislation on all matters concerning the Church of England. Measures passed by the Assembly and approved by Parliament were submitted for the Royal Assent, having the force of Acts of Parliament.

In 1970, by the Synodical Government Measure (1969), the Church Assembly was reconstituted as the General Synod and was also given authority to exercise most of the functions of the Convocations. The House of Bishops consists of members of the Upper House of the Convocations (53 persons). The House of Clergy consists of the Lower Houses (a maximum of 259 persons). The House of Laity consists almost entirely of representatives of the dioceses elected by the deanery synods (a maximum of 258 persons).

In 2001 there were 1,372,000 people on the Church's electoral rolls. The Archbishops and the 24 senior Bishops sit in the House of Lords.

Archbishop of Canterbury, Primate of All England and Metropolitan: Most Rev. and Rt Hon. ROWAN WILLIAMS, Lambeth Palace, London, SE1 7JU; tel. (20) 7898-1200; fax (20) 7261-9836; internet www.archbishopofcanterbury.org.

Archbishop of York, Primate of England and Metropolitan: Most Rev. and Rt Hon. JOHN SENTAMU, Bishopthorpe Palace, Bishopthorpe, York, YO23 2GE; tel. (1904) 707021; fax (1904) 709204; e-mail office@archbishopofyork.org; internet www.archbishopofyork.org.

General Synod of the Church of England: Church House, Great Smith St, London, SW1P 3AZ; tel. (20) 7898-1000; fax (20) 7898-1369; e-mail synod@c-of-e.org.uk; internet www.cofe.anglican.org; 467 mems; Sec.-Gen. WILLIAM FITTALL.

The Church of Ireland

The See House, Cathedral Close, Armagh, BT61 7EE; tel. (28) 3752-7144; fax (28) 3752-7823; e-mail enquiries@ireland.anglican.org; internet www.ireland.anglican.org.

Ireland (including Northern Ireland) comprises two archdioceses and 10 dioceses; in 2006 there were 275,000 members of the Church of Ireland in Northern Ireland.

Archbishop of Armagh and Primate of All Ireland: Most Rev. ALAN HARPER, The See House, Cathedral Close, Armagh, BT61 7EE; tel. (28) 3752-7144; fax (28) 3752-7823; e-mail archbishop@armagh.anglican.org.

The Church in Wales

39 Cathedral Rd, Cardiff, CF11 9XF; tel. (29) 2034-8200; fax (29) 2038-7835; e-mail information@churchinwales.org.uk; internet www.churchinwales.org.uk.

The Province of Wales was created as a result of the Welsh Church Act of 1914, which took effect on 31 March 1920 and separated the four Welsh dioceses from the Province of Canterbury. It is divided into six dioceses served by 620 stipendiary clerics. The number of Easter communicants is approximately 75,000. The Church in Wales has an administrative governing body which is a legislative assembly composed of bishops, clergy and laity, and a representative body incorporated by Royal Charter, which holds and manages the property and central funds of the Church; Provincial Sec. JOHN SHIRLEY.

Archbishop of Wales: Most Rev. BARRY C. MORGAN, Llys Esgob, Cathedral Green, Llandaff, Cardiff, CF5 2YE; tel. (29) 2056-2400; fax (29) 2056-8410; e-mail archbishop@churchinwales.org.uk.

The Scottish Episcopal Church

21 Grosvenor Cres., Edinburgh, EH12 5EE; tel. (131) 225-6357; fax (131) 346-7247; e-mail office@scotland.anglican.org; internet www.scotland.anglican.org.

Formerly the Established Church of Scotland, was disestablished and disendowed in 1689; is in full communion with all branches of the Anglican Communion; seven dioceses: Aberdeen and Orkney, Argyll and The Isles, Brechin, Edinburgh, Glasgow and Galloway, Moray, Ross and Caithness, and St Andrews, Dunkeld and Dunblane. There is a Bishop in each diocese; one of them is elected by the other Bishops as the Primus; Churches, mission stations, etc. 310, clergy 402, communicants 29,810; Sec.-Gen. to the General Synod JOHN STUART.

Primus: Most Rev. IDRIS JONES (Bishop of Glasgow and Galloway), The Diocesan Centre, 5 St Vincent Pl., Glasgow, G1 2DH; tel. (141) 2215720; fax (141) 2217014; e-mail office@glasgow.anglican.org; internet www.glasgow.anglican.org.

The Roman Catholic Church

For ecclesiastical purposes Great Britain comprises seven archdioceses and 23 dioceses. There is also an apostolic exarchate for the Ukrainian Rite. Ireland (including Northern Ireland) comprises four archdioceses and 22 dioceses. The dioceses of Down and Connor and Dromore are completely in Northern Ireland, while the archdiocese of Armagh and the dioceses of Derry and Clogher are partly in Northern Ireland and partly in Ireland. At 31 December 2006 there were an estimated 4,097,772 adherents in England and Wales, of whom about 50,000 were of the Ukrainian Rite, and an estimated 702,890 adherents in Scotland. At the 2001 census 40.3% of the population of Northern Ireland gave their religion as Catholic or Roman Catholic.

Latin Rite

Bishops' Conference of England and Wales

39 Eccleston Sq., London, SW1V 1BX; tel. (20) 7630-8220; fax (20) 7901-4821; e-mail secretariat@cbcew.org.uk; internet www.catholic-ew.org.uk; President Most Rev. VINCENT NICHOLS (Archbishop of Westminster); Gen. Sec. Mgr ANDREW SUMMERSGILL.

Archbishop of Westminster: Most Rev. VINCENT NICHOLS, Archbishop's House, Westminster, London, SW1P 1QJ; tel. (20) 7798-9033; fax (20) 7798-9077; e-mail archbishop@rcdow.org.uk; internet www.rcdow.org.uk/archbishop.

Archbishop of Birmingham: (vacant), Archbishop's House, 8 Shadwell St, Queensway, Birmingham, B4 6EY; tel. (121) 236-9090; fax (121) 212-0171; e-mail archbishop@rc-birmingham.org; internet www.birminghamdiocese.org.uk.

Archbishop of Liverpool: Most Rev. PATRICK ALTHAM KELLY, Archbishop's House, Lowood, Carnatic Road, Mossley Hill, Liverpool, L18 8BY; tel. (151) 724-6398; fax (151) 724-6405; e-mail archbishop.liverpool@rcaolp.co.uk; internet www.archdiocese-of-liverpool.co.uk.

Archbishop of Southwark: Most Rev. KEVIN JOHN MCDONALD, Archbishop's House, 150 St George's Rd, Southwark, London, SE1 6HX; tel. (20) 7928-2495; fax (20) 7928-7833; e-mail secswk@rcsouthwark.co.uk; internet www.rcsouthwark.co.uk.

Archbishop of Cardiff: Most Rev. PETER SMITH, Archbishop's House, 41–43 Cathedral Rd, Cardiff, South Glamorgan, CF11 9HD; tel. (29) 2022-0411; fax (29) 2037-9036; e-mail arch@rcacd.org; internet www.rcacd.org.

Archbishop of Armagh and Primate of All Ireland: Cardinal SEÁN B. BRADY, Ara Coeli, Armagh, BT61 7QY; tel. (28) 3752-2045; fax (28) 3752-6182; e-mail admin@aracoeli.com; internet www.armagharchdiocese.org.

Bishops' Conference of Scotland

64 Aitken St, Airdrie, ML6 6LT; tel. (1236) 764061; fax (1236) 762489; e-mail gensec@bpsconfscot.com; internet www.bpsconfscot.com; President HE Cardinal KEITH MICHAEL PATRICK O'BRIEN (Archbishop of St Andrews and Edinburgh); Gen. Sec. Rev. PAUL M. CONROY.

Archbishop of St Andrews and Edinburgh: HE Cardinal KEITH MICHAEL PATRICK O'BRIEN, Archbishop's House, 42 Greenhill Gdns, Edinburgh, EH10 4BJ; tel. (131) 447-3337; fax (131) 447-0816; e-mail cardinal@staned.org.uk; internet www.archdiocese-edinburgh.com.

Archbishop of Glasgow: Most Rev. MARIO JOSEPH CONTI, Curial Offices, 196 Clyde St, Glasgow, G1 4JY; tel. (141) 226-5898; fax (141) 225-2600; e-mail info@rcag.org.uk; internet www.rcag.org.uk.

Ukrainian Rite

Apostolic Exarch: (vacant), Bishop's House, 22 Binney St, London, W1Y 1YN; tel. (20) 7629-1073; fax (20) 7355-3314; e-mail frben@catholic.org; internet www.cerkva.org.uk.

Protestant Churches

Association of Baptist Churches in Ireland: 19 Hillsborough Rd, Moira, Craigavon, County Armagh, BT67 0HG; tel. (28) 9261-9267; e-mail abc@thebaptistcentre.org; internet www.baptistireland.org; 111 churches; 93 ministers; 8,446 mems; Pres. Pastor DEREK BAXTER; Dir Pastor WILLIAM COLVILLE.

Baptist Union of Great Britain: Baptist House, POB 44, 129 Broadway, Didcot, Oxfordshire, OX11 8RT; tel. (1235) 517700; fax (1235) 517715; e-mail info@baptist.org.uk; internet www.baptist.org.uk; f. 1813; the Baptist form of church government is congregational; baptism by immersion of believers is practised; the churches are grouped in associations; mems (2006) 142,000; Gen. Sec. Rev. JONATHAN P. EDWARDS.

Church of Scotland: 121 George St, Edinburgh, EH2 4YN; tel. (131) 225-5722; fax (131) 220-3113; e-mail lturnbull@cofscotland.org.uk; internet www.churchofscotland.org.uk; the national Church of Scotland was reformed in 1560, and became Presbyterian in doctrine and constitution. In 1921 the Church of Scotland Act was passed, by which the articles declaring the full spiritual freedom of the Church are recognized as lawful. In 1925 the Church of Scotland (Property and Endowments) Act became law, and made over to the Church of Scotland places of worship, manses and endowments in absolute property, vesting the future control of them in Trustees. The union of the Church of Scotland and the United Free Church was effected in 1929; Moderator Rt Rev. DAVID LUNAN; Lord High Commr to the 2008 General Assembly GEORGE REID; 600,000 mems.

Elim Pentecostal Church: PO Box 38, Cheltenham, Glos, GL50 3HN; tel. (1242) 519904; fax (1242) 222279; e-mail info@elimhq.org.net; internet www.elim.org.uk; f. 1915; c. 580 churches and 60,000 adherents in Great Britain; Gen. Superintendent Rev. JOHN GLASS.

Free Church of Scotland: 15 North Bank St, The Mound, Edinburgh, EH1 2LS; tel. (131) 226-5286; fax (131) 220-0597; e-mail catherine@freechurchofscotland.org.uk; internet www.freechurch.org; f. 1843; 103 congregations; Principal Clerk of Assembly Rev. JAMES MACIVER.

Free Churches Group, Churches Together in England: 27 Tavistock Sq., London, WC1H 9HH; tel. (20) 7529-8131; fax (20) 7529-8134; e-mail office@cte.org.uk; internet www.churches-together.net; central body for the co-ordination of the work of the Free Churches throughout England and Wales; Moderator Cmmr ELIZABETH MATEAR; Exec. Sec. Rev. MARK FISHER.

Lutheran Council of Great Britain: 30 Thanet St, London, WC1H 9QH; tel. (20) 7554-2900; fax (20) 7383-3081; e-mail enquiries@lutheran.org.uk; internet www.lutheran.org.uk; Chair. Rev. JUHA RINTAMÄKI; Gen. Sec. Rev. THOMAS BRUCH.

Methodist Church: Methodist Church House, 25 Marylebone Rd, London, NW1 5JR; tel. (20) 7486-5502; fax (20) 7224-5228; e-mail enquiries@methodistchurch.org.uk; internet www.methodist.org.uk; f. 1739 by Rev. John Wesley, a priest of the Church of England; the governing body of the Church is the Annual Conference, which consists of ministers and lay representatives. The Church throughout Great Britain is divided into 33 Districts, and these hold their Synod Meetings in the autumn and the spring. The Districts are divided into Circuits, which hold regular Circuit Meetings, made up of representatives from the churches within the Circuit. There are also local Church Councils; 267,000 mems (2007); Pres. of the Methodist Conference (2008/09) Rev. STEPHEN POXON; Gen. Sec. of the Methodist Conference Rev. MARTYN ATKINS.

Methodist Church in Ireland: 1 Fountainville Ave, Belfast, BT9 6AN; tel. (28) 9032-4554; fax (28) 9023-9467; e-mail secretary@irishmethodist.org; internet www.irishmethodist.org; 220 churches; 303 ministers; 53,990 mems; Pres. Rev. AIAN W. FERGUSON; Sec. Rev. DONALD P. KER.

Moravian Church: 5 Muswell Hill, London, N10 3TJ; tel. (20) 8883-3409; fax (20) 8365-3371; e-mail office@moravian.org.uk; internet www.moravian.org.uk; f. 1457; Sec. Provincial Board JACKIE MORTEN.

Moravian Church in Ireland: 37 Deramore Park South, Malone Rd, Belfast, BT9 5JY; tel. (28) 9068-1554; e-mail derick.woods@btinternet.com; f. 1746; Chair. of Conf. DERICK WOODS.

Non-Subscribing Presbyterian Church of Ireland: 41A Rosemary St, Belfast, BT1 1QB; tel. and fax (28) 9032-5365; e-mail info@nspresbyterian.org; internet www.nspresbyterian.org; Moderator Rt. Rev. TOM BANHAM; Clerk Rev. NIGEL PLAYFAIR.

Presbyterian Church in Ireland: Church House, Fisherwick Pl., Belfast, BT1 6DW; tel. (28) 9032-2284; fax (28) 9041-7301; e-mail info@presbyterianireland.org; internet www.presbyterianireland.org; 549 churches; 381 ministers; 258,000 mems, 27,000 in 550 Sunday Schools; Moderator of the Gen. Assembly Rev. Dr DONALD PATTON; Clerk of Assembly and Gen. Sec. Rev. Dr DONALD WATTS.

Presbyterian Church of Wales: 81 Merthyr Rd, Whitchurch, Cardiff, CF14 1DD; tel. (29) 2062-7465; fax (29) 2061-6188; e-mail swyddfa.office@ebcpcw.org.uk; internet www.ebcpcw.org.uk; f. 1811; 832 churches, 77 full-time ministers, 34,819 mems (2005); Moderator of General Assembly Rev. JOHN OWEN; Gen. Sec. Rev. IFAN RH ROBERTS.

Salvation Army: 101 Newington Causeway, London, SE1 6BN; tel. (20) 7367-4500; fax (20) 7367-4728; e-mail info@salvationarmy.org.uk; internet www.salvationarmy.org.uk; f. 1865; Territorial Commdr JOHN MATEAR.

Union of Welsh Independents: Tŷ John Penri, 5 Axis Court, Riverside Business Park, Swansea Vale, Swansea, SA7 0AJ; tel. (1792) 795888; fax (1792) 795376; e-mail undeb@annibynwyr.org; internet www.annibynwyr.org; f. 1872; Pres. MARGARET JONES; Gen. Sec. Rev. Dr GERAINT TUDUR.

United Free Church of Scotland: 11 Newton Place, Glasgow, G3 7PR; tel. (141) 332-3435; fax (141) 333-1973; e-mail office@ufcos.org.uk; internet www.ufcos.org.uk; f. 1900; 64 congregations, 32 ministers and pastors, 4,000 mems; Moderator Rev. DAVID CARTLEDGE; Gen. Sec. Rev. JOHN O. FULTON.

United Reformed Church: United Reformed Church House, 86 Tavistock Pl., London, WC1H 9RT; tel. (20) 7916-2020; fax (20) 7916-2021; e-mail urc@urc.org.uk; internet www.urc.org.uk; f. 1972 by union of the Congregational Church in England and Wales and the Presbyterian Church of England; joined by the Churches of Christ 1981 and by the Scottish Congregational Church 2000; approx. 1,800 churches and 250,000 mems; Moderator Rev. Dr STEPHEN ORCHARD; Gen. Sec. Rev. Dr DAVID CORNICK.

Orthodox Churches

Council of Oriental Orthodox Churches: 34 Chertsey Rd, Church Sq., Shepperton, Middx, TW17 9LF; tel. and fax (1932) 232913; Sec. Deacon AZIZ M. A. NOUR.

Armenian Apostolic Church: POB 46207, London, W5 2YE; tel. (20) 7937-0152; fax (20) 7937-9049; e-mail info@accc.org.uk; internet www.accc.org.uk; Primate Bishop NATHAN HOVHANNISIAN.

Greek Orthodox Church (Archdiocese of Thyateira and Great Britain of the Oecumenical Patriarchate): Thyateira House, 5 Craven Hill, London, W2 3EN; tel. (20) 7723-4787; fax (20) 7224-9301; e-mail mail@thyateira.org.uk; internet www.thyateira.org.uk; f. 1922; Archbishop of Thyateira and Great Britain GREGORIOS; Chancellor Bishop ATHANASIOS OF TROPAEOU.

Russian Orthodox Patriarchal Church in Great Britain: Cathedral of the Assumption and All Saints, Ennismore Gdns, London, SW7 1NH; tel. (20) 7584-0096; fax (20) 7584-9864; e-mail sourozh@mail.ru; internet www.sourozh.org; Bishop ELISEY OF SOUROZH.

Serbian Orthodox Church: 131 Cob Lane, Bournville, Birmingham, B30 1QE; tel. (121) 458-5273; fax (121) 458-4986; Very Rev. MILENKO ZEBIĆ.

Other Christian Churches

First Church of Christ, Scientist: 8 Wright's Lane, Kensington, London, W8 6TA; tel. (20) 7937-3389; fax (20) 7937-3341; e-mail fccslon@tiscali.co.uk; internet www.ccs.org.uk; f. 1879; the Mother Church is the First Church of Christ, Scientist, in Boston, MA (USA); approx. 150 churches in Great Britain; District Man. for Great Britain and Ireland TONY LOBL.

Church of Jesus Christ of Latter-day Saints (Mormon): Press Office, 751 Warwick Rd, Solihull, West Midlands, B91 3DQ; tel. (121) 712-1202; fax (121) 712-1126; e-mail mclavertymw@ldschurch.org; internet www.lds.org.uk; f. 1830; c. 181,000 mems (2004); Area Pres. ELDER KENNETH JOHNSON.

General Assembly of Unitarian and Free Christian Churches: Essex Hall, 1–6 Essex St, London, WC2R 3HY; tel. (20) 7240-2384; fax (20) 7240-3089; e-mail info@unitarian.org.uk; internet www.unitarian.org.uk; f. 1928; Chief Exec. STEVE DICK.

Jehovah's Witnesses: Watch Tower House, The Ridgeway, London, NW7 1RN; tel. (20) 8906-2211; fax (20) 8371-0051; internet www.watchtower.org; f. 1900; there were an estimated 130,000 Jehovah's Witnesses in the UK in 2007.

The Religious Society of Friends (Quakers) in Britain: Friends House, 173 Euston Rd, London, NW1 2BJ; tel. (20) 7663-1000; fax (20) 7663-1001; e-mail enquiries@quaker.org.uk; internet www.quaker.org.uk; f. mid-17th century by George Fox; the Quakers have 15,800 mems and 8,400 'attenders' in Great Britain; Recording Clerk (Sec.) HELEN GRIFFITH.

Seventh-day Adventist Church Headquarters: Stanborough Park, Watford, Herts, WD25 9JZ; tel. (1923) 672251; fax (1923) 893212; e-mail info@adventist.org.uk; internet www.adventist.org.uk; f. 1863; there were an estimated 28,000 mems. in approx. 300 congregations across the UK and Ireland in late 2007; Communication Dir VICTOR HULBERT.

Spiritualists' National Union: Redwoods, Stansted Hall, Stansted Mountfitchet, Essex, CM24 8UD; tel. (845) 458-0768; fax (1279) 812034; e-mail snu@snu.org.uk; internet www.snu.org.uk;

f. 1891 (and inc. 1901); for the advancement of Spiritualism as a religion and a religious philosophy, it is a trust corporation officially recognized as the central and national body representing the Spiritualists of Great Britain; conducts the Arthur Findlay College of Psychic Science; c. 400 Spiritualist churches, societies and 20,000 individual mems; Pres. DUNCAN P. GASCOYNE; Gen. Sec. CHARLES S. COULSTON.

ISLAM

The Muslim community in the United Kingdom, which according to the 2001 census numbered 1.59m., consists mainly of people from the Indian sub-continent and their British-born descendants. The chief concentrations of Muslims are in London, the Midlands, South Wales, Lancashire and Yorkshire. There are more than 900 mosques in the United Kingdom; the oldest is the Shah Jehan Mosque in Woking, Surrey.

London Central Mosque Trust and Islamic Cultural Centre: 146 Park Rd, London, NW8 7RG; tel. (20) 7725-2213; fax (20) 7724-0493; e-mail info@iccuk.org; internet www.iccuk.org; Dir-Gen. Dr AHMAD AD-DUBAYAN.

Muslim Council of Britain: POB 57330, London, E1 2WJ; tel. (845) 2626786; fax (20) 7247-7079; e-mail admin@mcb.org.uk; internet www.mcb.org.uk; f. 1997; Sec.-Gen. Dr MUHAMMAD ABDUL BARI.

SIKHISM

According to the 2001 census, there were 336,000 Sikhs in the United Kingdom, who originally came from the Punjab region of the Indian sub-continent as well as from East Africa, although many are now British-born. Each gurdwara (temple) is independent, and there is no central national body.

Sikh Missionary Society, UK: 10 Featherstone Rd, Southall, Middx, UB2 5AA; tel. (20) 8574-1902; fax (20) 8574-1912; e-mail info@sikhmissionarysociety.org; internet www.sikhmissionarysociety.org; promotes Sikhism and acts as a resource centre for information and literature; Hon. Gen. Sec. SURINDER SINGH PUREWAL.

HINDUISM

According to the 2001 census, there were 559,000 Hindus in the United Kingdom, with their origins in India, East Africa and Sri Lanka, although many are now British by birth. Hindus in the United Kingdom are concentrated in London, the Midlands and Yorkshire.

JUDAISM

The Jewish community in the United Kingdom numbered 267,000, according to the 2001 census. There are about 350 synagogues in the United Kingdom.

Chief Rabbi of the United Hebrew Congregations of the Commonwealth: Rabbi Prof. Sir JONATHAN SACKS, Office of the Chief Rabbi, Alder House, 735 High Rd, London, N12 0US; tel. (20) 8343-6301; fax (20) 8343-6310; e-mail info@chiefrabbi.org; internet www.chiefrabbi.org.

Court of the Chief Rabbi (Beth Din): 735 High Rd, London, N12 0US; tel. (20) 8343-6270; fax (20) 8343-6257; e-mail info@bethdin.org.uk; Registrar D. FREI.

There is no comprehensive organization of synagogues covering the country as a whole. In London and the South-East there are the following major synagogue organizations:

Liberal Judaism: The Montagu Centre, 21 Maple St, London, W1T 4BE; tel. (20) 7580-1663; fax (20) 7631-9838; e-mail montagu@liberaljudaism.org; internet www.liberaljudaism.org; f. 1902; 9,300 mems, 31 affiliated synagogues, 3 assoc. communities; Chief Exec. Rabbi DANNY RICH.

Movement for Reform Judaism: The Sternberg Centre for Judaism, 80 East End Rd, Finchley, London, N3 2SY; tel. (020) 8349-5640; fax (20) 8349-5699; e-mail admin@reformjudaism.org.uk; internet www.reformjudaism.org.uk; Head Rabbi Dr TONY BAYFIELD.

Spanish and Portuguese Jews' Congregation: 2 Ashworth Rd, London, W9 1JY; tel. (20) 7289-2573; fax (20) 7289-2709; e-mail howardmiller@spsyn.org.uk; internet www.sandp.org; f. 1657; Pres. of the Bd of Elders ALFRED MAGNUS; Chief Exec. HOWARD MILLER.

Union of Orthodox Hebrew Congregations (UOHC): 140 Stamford Hill, London, N16 6QT; tel. (20) 8802-6226; fax (20) 8809-6590; e-mail ck@uohc.co.uk; f. 1926; over 100 affiliated synagogues in the United Kingdom and other Commonwealth countries; Gen. Sec. CHAYIM SCHNECK.

United Synagogue: Adler House, 735 High Rd, London, N12 0US; tel. (20) 8343-8989; fax (20) 8343-6262; internet www.theus.org.uk; f. 1870 by Act of Parliament; Pres. Dr SIMON HOCHHAUSER; Chief Exec. JEREMY JACOBS.

West London Synagogue of British Jews: 33 Seymour Pl., London, W1H 5AU; tel. (20) 7723-4404; fax (20) 7224-8258; e-mail admin@wls.org.uk; internet www.wls.org.uk; f. 1840; c. 4,000 mems; Senior Rabbi MARK L. WINER; Exec. Dir ALAN SHAPIRO.

BUDDHISM

According to the 2001 census, the Buddhist community in the United Kingdom numbered 152,000.

Buddhist Society: 58 Eccleston Sq., London, SW1V 1PH; tel. (20) 7834-5858; fax (20) 7976-5238; e-mail info@thebuddhistsociety.org; internet www.thebuddhistsociety.org; f. 1924; Registrar LOUISE MARCHANT.

BAHÁ'Í FAITH

National Spiritual Assembly of the Bahá'ís of the United Kingdom: 27 Rutland Gate, London, SW7 1PD; tel. (20) 7584-2566; fax (20) 7584-9402; e-mail nsa@bahai.org.uk; internet www.bahai.org.uk; f. 1923; Sec. Dr KISHAN MANOCHA; Chair. SHIRIN TAHZIB.

The Press

The United Kingdom has some of the highest circulation figures in the world for individual newspapers (*News of the World* and *The Sun* both 2.8m., and *Daily Mail* 2.1m. at April 2009). At 1 January 2004 there were more than 2,600 regional and local daily and weekly newspapers (including free titles) in the United Kingdom and the total weekly circulation of all newspapers was 136.4m.

There is no law which specifies the operations of the press but several items of legislation bear directly on press activities. Although exact reporting of legal proceedings appearing at the time of trial is protected from later charges of defamation, the freedom to report cases is subject to certain restrictions as defined in the Judicial Proceedings Act of 1926, in the Children's and Young Persons' Act of 1933 and in the Criminal Justice Act 1967. The strict laws of contempt of court and of libel somewhat limit the scope of the press. Journalists are subject to the former if they publish material liable to interfere with a matter which is *sub judice* but this law is qualified by the Administration of Justice Act of 1960 which declares an editor not guilty of contempt if, after taking reasonable care, he remained ignorant of the fact that proceedings were pending. The Scottish law of contempt is more severe than the English. Libel cases can involve the awarding of punitive damages against the press. The Defamation Act of 1952 lessened the possible repercussions of unintentional libel and made provision for the claim of fair comment by the defence.

The Official Secrets Act of 1911 prohibits the publication of secret information where this is judged not to be in the national interest. The Secretary of State for the Home Department is empowered to require a person with information about a violation of the Act to disclose his source. Journalists have no exemption here. The publication of morally objectionable and harmful material is treated in the Children's and Young Persons' (Harmful Publications) Act of 1955 and in the Obscene Publications Act.

Legislative measures have been taken to limit the excessive development of concentrations of newspaper ownership and the extent of the control by newspaper owners over other mass media such as the television. The Television Act of 1964 provided for intervention by the Postmaster-General or the Independent Broadcasting Authority where investments by newspaper owners in television companies are judged liable to lead to abuses. The Monopolies and Mergers Act of 1965 requires the written consent of the Department of Trade and Industry (now Department for Business, Enterprise and Regulatory Reform) for the transfer of daily or weekly papers with an aggregate average of over 500,000 copies per day of publication. The Department's decision is based on the conclusions of the Monopolies Commission to which, with the exception of cases of papers judged to be uneconomical and of papers with an average daily circulation of no more than 25,000 copies, all cases are referred for investigation.

The Press Complaints Commission, which replaced the Press Council in 1991, has an independent chairman and 16 members, drawn from the lay public and the press. It deals with complaints from the public and upholds an 18-point Code of Practice.

Among the most influential newspapers may be included: *The Times*, *The Guardian*, *The Independent*, *Daily Telegraph* and *Financial Times* (daily), *The Observer*, *The Independent on Sunday*, *The Sunday Times* and *Sunday Telegraph* (Sunday newspapers). Prominent among the popular press are: *Daily Express*, *Daily Mail*, *Daily Mirror* and *The Sun* (daily); *News of the World* and *Sunday Mirror* (Sunday newspapers).

No important newspaper is directly owned by a political party. The great rate of news consumption has fostered the growth of large national groups or chains of papers controlled by a single organization or individual. The largest of these chains are as follows:

Daily Mail and General Trust PLC: Northcliffe House, 2 Derry St, London, W8 5TT; tel. (20) 7938-6000; fax (20) 7938-4626; e-mail webmaster@dmgt.co.uk; internet www.dmgt.co.uk; controls through Associated Newspapers one national daily, *Daily Mail*, one national Sunday, *The Mail on Sunday*, two London dailies, *London Lite* and *Metro*; through Northcliffe Media controls 18 daily titles, 28 weekly titles and 50 free newspapers; Group Chair. Viscount ROTHERMERE; Group CEO MARTIN MORGAN.

Guardian Media Group PLC: 60 Farringdon Rd, London, EC1R 3GA; tel. (20) 7239-9711; fax (20) 7713-4709; internet www.gmgplc.co.uk; f. 1821; owned by the Scott Trust Ltd; subsidiary publishing cos include Guardian Newspapers Ltd (controls *The Guardian*, *The Observer*) and GMG Regional Media (controls *Manchester Evening News*); Chair. AMELIA FAWCETT; CEO CAROLYN MCCALL.

Independent News and Media (UK) Ltd: Independent House, 191 Marsh Wall, London, E14 9RS; tel. (20) 7005-2000; internet www.inmplc.com; British subsidiary of Ireland's Independent News & Media PLC; publishes one national daily, *The Independent*, and one national Sunday paper, *The Independent on Sunday*; also publishes *Belfast Telegraph* and *Sunday Life* in Northern Ireland; Group Chief Exec. GAVIN O'REILLY; Chief Exec., United Kingdom I. G. FALLON.

News International PLC: 1 Virginia St, London, E98 1XY; tel. (20) 7782-6000; fax (20) 7782-6097; internet www.newsint.co.uk; British subsidiary of USA's News Corporation; subsidiary cos: News Group Newspapers Ltd (controls *The Sun* and *News of the World*), Times Newspapers Ltd (controls *The Times* and *The Sunday Times*).

Trinity Mirror PLC: 1 Canada Sq., Canary Wharf, London, E14 5AP; tel. (20) 7293-3000; fax (20) 7293-3280; internet www.trinitymirror.com; f. 1999; by merger of Mirror Group Newspapers Ltd and Trinity International Holdings; controls a total of over 200 newspapers, including one national daily paper, *Daily Mirror*, two national Sunday papers, *The People*, *Sunday Mirror*, two Scottish national papers, *Daily Record* and *Sunday Mail*, and numerous regional and local papers; Chair. Sir IAN GIBSON; Chief Exec. SYLVIA (SLY) BAILEY.

United Business Media Ltd: Ludgate House, 245 Blackfriars Rd, London, SE1 9UY; tel. (20) 7921-5000; e-mail communications@ubmgroup.biz; internet www.ubmgroup.biz; f. 1996 by merger of United Newspapers and MAI group; international media and information group; three core business divisions—professional media, market research, news distribution; Chair. JOHN BOTTS; CEO DAVID LEVIN.

PRINCIPAL NATIONAL DAILIES
(average net circulation figures, in the United Kingdom only, as at April 2009, unless otherwise stated)

Daily Express: The Northern & Shell Bldg, 10 Lower Thames St, London, EC3R 6EN; tel. (871) 4341010; e-mail expressletters@express.co.uk; internet www.express.co.uk; f. 1900; Propr Northern and Shell Group; Editor PETER HILL; circ. 690,217.

Daily Mail: Northcliffe House, 2 Derry St, London, W8 5TT; tel. (20) 7938-6000; fax (20) 7937-4463; e-mail news@dailymail.co.uk; internet www.dailymail.co.uk; f. 1896; inc. *News Chronicle* (1960) and *Daily Sketch* (1971); Propr Associated Newspaper Holdings; Editor-in-Chief PAUL DACRE; Man. Dir GUY ZITTER; circ. 2,051,478.

Daily Mirror: 1 Canada Sq., Canary Wharf, London, E14 5AP; tel. (20) 7293-3000; fax (20) 7293-3280; e-mail mailbox@mirror.co.uk; internet www.mirror.co.uk; f. 1903; Propr Trinity Mirror PLC; Editor RICHARD WALLACE; circ. 1,218,460.

Daily Sport: 19 Gt Ancoats St, Manchester, M60 4BT; tel. (161) 236-4466; fax (161) 236-4535; internet www.dailysport.net; f. 1988; Propr Sport Media Group; Editor PAM MCVITIE; (Jan. 2009) circ. 72,592 (Mon.–Fri.); 47,551 (Sat.).

Daily Star: The Northern & Shell Bldg, 10 Lower Thames St, London, EC3R 6EN; tel. (8714) 341010; fax (20) 7922-7960; e-mail news@dailystar.co.uk; internet www.dailystar.co.uk; f. 1978; Propr Express Newspapers PLC; Editor DAWN NEESOM; circ. 287,609.

Daily Telegraph: 111 Buckingham Palace Rd, London, SW1W 0DT; tel. (20) 7931-2000; e-mail dtletters@telegraph.co.uk; internet www.telegraph.co.uk; *Daily Telegraph*, f. 1855, *Morning Post*, f. 1772; amalgamated 1937; Propr Press Acquisitions Ltd; Chief Exec. MURDOCH MACLENNAN; Editor WILLIAM LEWIS; circ. 778,273.

Financial Times: Number One Southwark Bridge, London, SE1 9HL; tel. (20) 7873-3000; fax (20) 7873-3076; internet www.ft.com; f. 1880; Propr Pearson PLC; CEO JOHN RIDDING; Editor LIONEL BARBER; circ. 118,043.

The Guardian: Kings Pl., 90 York Way, London, N1 9GU; and 164 Deansgate, Manchester, M3 3GG; tel. (20) 3353-2000; fax (20) 7837-2114; e-mail userhelp@guardian.co.uk; internet www.guardian.co.uk; tel. (161) 832-7200; fax (161) 832-5351; f. 1821; Propr Guardian Newspapers Ltd; Editor ALAN RUSBRIDGER; circ. 300,879.

The Independent: Independent House, 191 Marsh Wall, London, E14 9RS; tel. (20) 7005-2000; fax (20) 7005-2999; e-mail customerservices@independent.co.uk; internet www.independent.co.uk; f. 1986; Editor ROGER ALTON; circ. 157,777.

Racing Post: 1 Canada Sq., Canary Wharf, London, E14 5AP; tel. (20) 7293-3000; fax (20) 7293-3758; e-mail editor@racingpost.co.uk; internet www.racingpost.co.uk; f. 1986; covers national and international horse racing, greyhound racing, general sport and betting; Editor BRUCE MILLINGTON; circ. 57,751.

The Sun: 1 Virginia St, London, E98 1SN; tel. (20) 7782-4000; fax (20) 7782-4108; e-mail corporate.info@the-sun.co.uk; internet www.thesun.co.uk; f. 1921 as *Daily Herald*; present name since 1964; Propr News International PLC; Editor REBEKAH WADE; Man. Dir MIKE ANDERSON; circ. 2,822,917.

The Times: 1 Pennington St, London, E98 1TT; tel. (20) 7782-5000; fax (20) 7782-5046; internet www.timesonline.co.uk; f. 1785; Propr News International PLC; Editor JAMES HARDING; circ. 563,426.

LONDON DAILIES
(average net circulation figures as at April 2009, unless otherwise stated)

London Evening Standard: 2 Derry St, London, W8 5TT; tel. (20) 7938-6000; fax (20) 7937-2648; internet www.standard.co.uk; f. 1827; merged with *Evening News* 1980; Mon.–Fri.; evening; 75% stake acquired by Evening Standard Ltd in Jan. 2009; Editor GEORDIE GREIG; Man. Dir ANDREW MULLINS; circ. 263,312.

London Lite: Northcliffe House, 2 Derry St, London, W8 5TT; tel. (20) 7651-5450; internet www.thisislondon.co.uk; f. 2006; evening; distributed free of charge; Propr Associated Newspaper Holdings PLC; Editor TED YOUNG; circ. 400,387.

Metro: Northcliffe House, 2 Derry St, London, W8 5TT; tel. (20) 7651-5200; fax (20) 7806-8338; e-mail mail@ukmetro.co.uk; internet www.metro.co.uk; f. 1999; Mon.–Fri.; morning; distributed free of charge; also distributed in Bath, Birmingham, Brighton, Bristol, Cardiff, Derby, Edinburgh, Glasgow, Leeds, Leicester, Liverpool, Manchester, Newcastle, Nottingham and Sheffield; Propr Associated Newspaper Holdings PLC; Editor KENNY CAMPBELL; Man. Dir STEVE AUCKLAND; circ. 734,488 (London); 1,332,225 (total UK).

thelondonpaper: 1 Pennington St, London, E98 1XY; tel. (20) 7782-4835; e-mail laura.tait@newsint.co.uk; internet www.thelondonpaper.com; Mon.–Fri; evening; distributed free of charge; Propr News International; f. 2006; Editor STEFANO HATFIELD; circ. 500,759.

PRINCIPAL PROVINCIAL DAILIES
(average net circulation figures as at December 2008, unless otherwise stated)

Aberdeen

Evening Express: Aberdeen Journals Ltd, Lang Stracht, Mastrick, Aberdeen, AB15 6DF; tel. (1224) 690222; fax (1224) 699575; e-mail ee.news@ajl.co.uk; internet www.eveningexpress.co.uk; f. 1879; Editor DAMIAN BATES; circ. 52,029.

Press and Journal: Aberdeen Journals Ltd, Lang Stracht, Mastrick, Aberdeen, AB15 6DF; tel. (1224) 690222; fax (1224) 663575; e-mail pj.newsdesk@ajl.co.uk; internet www.pressandjournal.co.uk; f. 1747; morning; Editor DEREK TUCKER; circ. 78,121.

Belfast

Belfast Telegraph: 124–144 Royal Ave, Belfast, BT1 1EB; tel. (28) 9026-4000; fax (28) 9055-4506; e-mail newseditor@belfasttelegraph.co.uk; internet www.belfasttelegraph.co.uk; f. 1870; independent; evening; Proprs Independent News and Media PLC; Editor MARTIN LINDSAY; circ. 69,457.

Irish News: 113–117 Donegall St, Belfast, BT1 2GE; tel. (28) 9032-2226; fax (28) 9033-7505; e-mail newsdesk@irishnews.com; internet www.irishnews.com; f. 1855; Irish nationalist; morning; Editor NOEL DORAN; circ. 47,819.

News Letter: 2 Esky Drive, Carn Industrial Estate, Craigavon, BT63 5YY; tel. (28) 9089-7700; fax (28) 9066-9910; e-mail darwin.templeton@jpress.co.uk; internet www.newsletter.co.uk; f. 1737; unionist; morning; Editor DARWIN TEMPLETON; circ. 25,253.

Birmingham

Birmingham Mail: 6th Floor, Fort Dunlop, Fort Parkway, B24 9FF; tel. (121) 236-3366; fax (121) 233-0271; e-mail steve_dyson@birminghammail.net; internet www.birminghammail.net; f. 1870; evening; independent; Propr Trinity Mirror PLC; Editor STEVE DYSON; circ. 61,526.

Bradford

Telegraph & Argus: Hall Ings, Bradford, BD1 1JR; tel. (1274) 729511; fax (1274) 723634; e-mail newsdesk@bradford.newsquest.co.uk; internet www.telegraphandargus.co.uk; f. 1868; evening; Editor PERRY AUSTIN-CLARKE; circ. 34,042.

THE UNITED KINGDOM

Brighton

The Argus: Argus House, Crowhurst Rd, Hollingbury, Brighton, BN1 8AR; tel. (1273) 544544; fax (1273) 566114; e-mail editor@theargus.co.uk; internet www.theargus.co.uk; f. 1880; Propr Newsquest Media Group; Editor MICHAEL BEARD; circ. 30,070.

Bristol

Evening Post: Temple Way, Bristol, BS99 7HD; tel. (117) 934-3000; fax (117) 934-3575; e-mail epnews@bepp.co.uk; internet www.thisisbristol.co.uk; f. 1932; inc. the *Evening World*; Propr Northcliffe Newspapers; independent; Editor-in-Chief MIKE NORTON; circ. 46,522.

Western Daily Press: Temple Way, Bristol, BS99 7HD; tel. (117) 934-3000; fax (117) 934-3574; e-mail wdnews@bepp.co.uk; internet www.westerndailypress.co.uk; f. 1858; Propr Northcliffe Newspapers; morning; independent; Editor ANDY WRIGHT; circ. 38,211.

Cardiff

South Wales Echo: Six Park St, Cardiff, CF10 1XR; tel. (29) 2022-3333; fax (29) 2058-3624; e-mail mike.hill@mediawales.co.uk; internet www.walesonline.co.uk; f. 1884; Propr Trinity Mirror PLC; evening; independent; Editor MIKE HILL; circ. 41,550.

The Western Mail: Six Park St, Cardiff, CF10 1XR; tel. (29) 2022-3333; fax (29) 2058-3652; e-mail alan.edmunds@mediawales.co.uk; internet www.walesonline.co.uk; f. 1869; independent; Editor ALAN EDMUNDS; circ. 33,693.

Coventry

Coventry Telegraph: Corporation St, Coventry, CV1 1FP; tel. (24) 7663-3633; fax (24) 7655-0869; e-mail alan.kirby@coventrytelegraph.net; internet www.coventrytelegraph.net; f. 1891 as *Midland Daily Telegraph*; Propr Trinity Mirror PLC; independent; morning; Editor DAVID BROOKES; circ. 43,594.

Darlington

Northern Echo: POB 14, Priestgate, Darlington, Co Durham, DL1 1NF; tel. (1325) 505065; e-mail newsdesk@nne.co.uk; internet www.thenorthernecho.co.uk; f. 1869; morning; independent; Editor PETER BARRON; circ. 48,783.

Derby

Derby Evening Telegraph: Northcliffe House, Meadow Rd, Derby, DE1 2DW; tel. (1332) 291111; fax (1332) 253027; e-mail newsdesk@derbytelegraph.co.uk; internet www.thisisderbyshire.co.uk; f. 1932; inc. *Derby Daily Telegraph*, f. 1879, *Derby Daily Express*, f. 1884; Editor STEVE HALL; circ. 39,152.

Dundee

Courier and Advertiser: Albert Sq., Dundee, DD1 9QJ; tel. (1382) 223131; fax (1382) 225511; e-mail editor@thecourier.co.uk; internet www.thecourier.co.uk; f. 1810; morning; Editor WILLIAM HUTCHEON; circ. 69,414.

Edinburgh

Edinburgh Evening News: 108 Holyrood Rd, Edinburgh, EH8 8AS; tel. (131) 620-8703; fax (131) 620-8696; e-mail jmclellan@edinburghnews.com; internet www.edinburghnews.com; f. 1873; Propr Johnston Press PLC; Editor JOHN MCLELLAN; circ. 47,129.

The Scotsman: 108 Holyrood Rd, Edinburgh, EH8 8AS; tel. (131) 620-8620; fax (131) 620-8616; e-mail enquiries@scotsman.com; internet www.scotsman.com; f. 1817; morning; Propr Johnston Press PLC; Editor MIKE GILSON; circ. 48,135 (April 2009).

Glasgow

Daily Record: 1 Central Quay, Glasgow, G3 8DA; tel. (141) 309-3000; fax (141) 309-3340; internet www.dailyrecord.co.uk; f. 1895; morning; independent; Propr Trinity Mirror PLC; Editor-in-Chief BRUCE WADDELL; circ. 341,275 (April 2009).

Glasgow Evening Times: 200 Renfield St, Glasgow, G2 3Q3; tel. (141) 302-7000; fax (141) 302-6600; e-mail times@eveningtimes.co.uk; internet www.eveningtimes.co.uk; f. 1876; Propr Newsquest; Editor-in-Chief DONALD MARTIN; circ. 68,422.

The Herald: 200 Renfield St, Glasgow, G2 3QB; tel. (141) 302-7000; fax (141) 302-7171; e-mail news@theherald.co.uk; internet www.theherald.co.uk; f. 1783; morning; independent; Propr Newsquest; Editor-in-Chief DONALD MARTIN; circ. 58,704 (April 2009).

Scottish Daily Express: Citypoint Z, 25 Tyndrum St, Glasgow, G4 0JY; tel. (141) 332-4600; fax (141) 332-2555; e-mail scot.news@express.co.uk; internet www.express.co.uk/scottish; morning; regional edition of *Daily Express*; Propr Northern and Shell Group; Editor DAVID HAMILTON.

Grimsby

Grimsby Telegraph: 80 Cleethorpe Rd, Grimsby, DN31 3EH; tel. (1472) 360360; fax (1472) 372257; e-mail newsdesk@grimsbytelegraph.co.uk; internet www.thisisgrimsby.co.uk; f. 1898; evening; Editor MICHELLE LALOR; circ. 31,538.

Ipswich

East Anglian Daily Times: 30 Lower Brook St, Ipswich, IP4 1AN; tel. (1473) 230023; e-mail news@eadt.co.uk; internet www.eadt.co.uk; morning; Editor TERRY HUNT; circ. 32,208.

Kingston upon Hull

Hull Daily Mail: Blundell's Corner, Beverley Rd, Kingston upon Hull, HU3 1XS; tel. (1482) 327111; fax (1482) 584353; e-mail news@mailnewsmedia.co.uk; internet www.thisishullandeastriding.co.uk; f. 1885; evening; Editor JOHN MEEHAN; circ. 51,886.

Leeds

Yorkshire Evening Post: POB 168, Wellington St, Leeds, LS1 1RF; tel. (113) 243-2701; fax (113) 238-8536; e-mail eped@ypn.co.uk; internet www.yorkshireeveningpost.co.uk; f. 1890; Propr Johnston Press PLC; Editor PAUL NAPIER; circ. 49,064.

Yorkshire Post: POB 168, Wellington St, Leeds, LS1 1RF; tel. (113) 243-2701; fax (113) 244-3430; e-mail yp.newsdesk@ypn.co.uk; internet www.yorkshirepost.co.uk; f. 1754; morning; Propr Johnston Press PLC; Editor PETER CHARLTON; circ. 45,718.

Leicester

Leicester Mercury: St George St, Leicester, LE1 9FQ; tel. (116) 251-2512; fax (116) 253-0645; e-mail newsdesk@leicestermercury.co.uk; internet www.thisisleicestershire.co.uk; f. 1874; evening; Editor NICK CARTER; circ. 64,919.

Liverpool

Liverpool Echo: POB 48, Old Hall St, Liverpool, L69 3EB; tel. (151) 227-2000; fax (151) 472-2474; e-mail letters@liverpoolecho.co.uk; internet www.liverpoolecho.co.uk; f. 1879; evening; independent; Propr Trinity Mirror PLC; Editor ALASTAIR MACHRAY; circ. 97,779.

Manchester

Manchester Evening News: 1 Scott Pl., Hardman St, Manchester, M3 3RN; tel. (161) 832-7200; fax (161) 211-2034; e-mail newsdesk@men-news.co.uk; internet www.manchestereveningnews.co.uk; f. 1868; independent; Editor PAUL HORROCKS; circ. 153,724.

Middlesbrough

Evening Gazette: Borough Rd, Middlesbrough, TS1 3AZ; tel. (1642) 245401; fax (1642) 210565; e-mail darren.thwaites@eveninggazette.co.uk; internet www.gazettelive.co.uk; f. 1869; Propr Trinity Mirror PLC; Editor DARREN THWAITES; circ. 46,320.

Newcastle upon Tyne

Evening Chronicle: Groat Market, Newcastle upon Tyne, NE1 1ED; tel. (191) 232-7500; fax (191) 232-2256; e-mail ec.news@ncjmedia.co.uk; internet www.chroniclelive.co.uk; f. 1885; Propr Trinity Mirror PLC; Editor PAUL ROBERTSON; circ. 67,103.

The Journal: Groat Market, Newcastle upon Tyne, NE1 1ED; tel. (191) 232-7500; fax (191) 230-4144; e-mail jnl.newsdesk@ncjmedia.co.uk; internet www.journallive.co.uk; f. 1832; morning; Propr Trinity Mirror PLC; Editor BRIAN AITKEN; circ. 32,859.

Norwich

Eastern Daily Press: Prospect House, Rouen Rd, Norwich, NR1 1RE; tel. (1603) 628311; fax (1603) 623872; e-mail edp@archant.co.uk; internet www.edp24.co.uk; f. 1870; independent; Propr Archant Regional Ltd; Editor PETER FRANZEN; circ. 61,143.

Nottingham

Nottingham Evening Post: Castle Wharf House, Nottingham, NG1 7EU; tel. (115) 948-2000; fax (115) 964-4032; e-mail newsdesk@nottinghameveningpost.co.uk; internet www.thisisnottingham.co.uk; f. 1878; Editor MALCOLM PHEBY; circ. 51,526.

Plymouth

Western Morning News: 17 Brest Rd, Derriford Business Park, Plymouth, PL6 5AA; tel. (1752) 765500; fax (1752) 765535; e-mail wmnnewsdesk@westernmorningnews.co.uk; internet www.westernmorningnews.co.uk; f. 1860; Editor ALAN QUALTROUGH; circ. 37,819.

Portsmouth

The News: The News Centre, London Rd, Hilsea, Portsmouth, PO2 9SX; tel. (23) 9266-4488; e-mail newsdesk@thenews.co.uk; internet www.portsmouth.co.uk; f. 1877; evening; Editor MARK WALDRON; circ. 49,628.

Sheffield

The Star: York St, Sheffield, S1 1PU; tel. (114) 276-7676; fax (114) 272-5978; e-mail starnews@sheffieldnewspapers.co.uk; internet www.thestar.co.uk; f. 1887; evening; independent; Propr Johnston Press PLC; Editor ALAN POWELL; circ. 47,216.

Southampton

Southern Daily Echo: Newspaper House, Test Lane, Redbridge, Southampton, SO16 9JX; tel. (23) 8042-4777; fax (23) 8042-4545; e-mail newsdesk@dailyecho.co.uk; internet www.dailyecho.co.uk; f. 1888; Propr Newsquest; Editor IAN MURRAY; circ. 36,906.

Stoke-on-Trent

The Sentinel: Sentinel House, Etruria, Stoke-on-Trent, ST1 5SS; tel. (1782) 602525; fax (1782) 602616; e-mail newsdesk@thesentinel.co.uk; internet www.thisisthesentinel.co.uk; f. 1854; Editor-in-Chief MIKE SASSI; circ. 58,049.

Sunderland

Sunderland Echo: Echo House, Pennywell, Sunderland, Tyne and Wear, SR4 9ER; tel. (191) 501-5800; fax (191) 534-3807; e-mail echo.news@northeast-press.co.uk; internet www.sunderlandecho.com; f. 1873; evening; Editor ROB LAWSON; circ. 39,159.

Swansea

South Wales Evening Post: Adelaide St, Swansea, SA1 1QT; tel. (1792) 510000; fax (1792) 514197; e-mail postnews@swwmedia.co.uk; internet www.thisissouthwales.co.uk; f. 1930; Editor SPENCER FEENEY; circ. 47,875.

Telford

Shropshire Star: Waterloo Rd, Ketley, Telford, Shropshire, TF1 5HU; tel. (1952) 242424; fax (1952) 254605; e-mail newsroom@shropshirestar.co.uk; internet www.shropshirestar.com; f. 1964; evening; Propr Shropshire Newspapers Ltd; Editor SARAH-JANE SMITH; circ. 67,726.

Wolverhampton

Express and Star: 51–53 Queen St, Wolverhampton, West Midlands, WV1 1ES; tel. (1902) 313131; fax (1902) 710106; e-mail newsdesk@expressandstar.co.uk; internet www.expressandstar.co.uk; f. 1874; evening; Propr The Midland News Association Ltd; Editor ADRIAN FABER; circ. 130,216.

York

The Press: POB 29, 76–86 Walmgate, York, YO1 9YN; tel. (1904) 653051; fax (1904) 612853; e-mail newsdesk@ycp.co.uk; internet www.thepress.co.uk; morning; Editor KEVIN BOOTH; circ. 31,569.

PRINCIPAL WEEKLY NEWSPAPERS
(average net circulation figures as at April 2009, unless otherwise stated)

Asian Times: Ethnic Media Group, Whitechapel Technology Centre, Unit 2, 65 Whitechapel Rd, London, E1 1DU; tel. (20) 7650-2000; fax (20) 7650-2001; internet www.asiantimesonline.co.uk; Editor HAMANT VERMA; Man. Dir WAYNE BOWER.

Daily Star Sunday: Ludgate House, 245 Blackfriars Rd, London, SE1 9UX; tel. (20) 7928-8000; fax (20) 7633-0244; e-mail dailystarnewsdesk@dailystar.co.uk; internet www.dailystar.co.uk/sunday; f. 1978; Propr Express Newspapers PLC; Editor GARETH MORGAN; circ. 287,609.

The Independent on Sunday: Independent House, 191 Marsh Wall, London, E14 9RS; tel. (20) 7005-2000; fax (20) 7005-2627; internet www.independent.co.uk; f. 1990; Propr Independent Newspapers UK; Editor JOHN MULLIN; circ. 119,919.

The Mail on Sunday: Northcliffe House, 2 Derry St, London, W8 5TS; tel. (20) 7938-6000; fax (20) 7937-3829; internet www.mailonsunday.co.uk; f. 1982; Propr Associated Newspapers Ltd; Editor PETER WRIGHT; Man. Dir STEPHEN MIRON; circ. 1,876,015.

News of the World: 1 Virginia St, London, E1 9XR; tel. (20) 7782-1000; fax (20) 7583-9504; e-mail newsdesk@notw.co.uk; internet www.notw.co.uk; f. 1843; Propr News International; Sunday; Editor COLIN MYLER; Man. Dir MIKE ANDERSON; circ. 2,751,320.

The Observer: Kings Pl., 90 York Way, London, N1 9GU; tel. (20) 3353-2000; fax (20) 7713-4250; e-mail userhelp@guardian.co.uk; internet observer.guardian.co.uk; f. 1791; owned by Guardian Newspapers Ltd; Sunday; Editor JOHN MULHOLLAND; circ. 375,183.

The People: 1 Canada Sq., Canary Wharf, London, E14 5AP; tel. (20) 7293-3000; fax (20) 7293-3887; internet www.people.co.uk; f. 1881; Propr Trinity Mirror PLC; Editor LLOYD EMBLEY; circ. 533,531.

Scotland on Sunday: Barclay House, 108 Holyrood Rd, Edinburgh, EH8 8AS; tel. (131) 620-8620; fax (131) 620-8491; e-mail letters_sos@scotlandonsunday.com; internet scotlandonsunday.scotsman.com; f. 1988; Propr Johnston Press PLC; Editor LES SNOWDON; circ. 60,296.

Sunday Express: The Northern & Shell Bldg, 10 Lower Thames St, London, EC3R 6EN; tel. (871) 434-1010; fax (871) 520-7766; e-mail sunday.exletters@express.co.uk; internet www.express.co.uk; f. 1918; inc. *Sunday Despatch* 1961; independent; Propr Northern and Shell Group; Editor-in-Chief MARTIN TOWNSEND; circ. 597,083.

Sunday Herald: 200 Renfield St, Glasgow, G2 3QB; tel. (141) 302-7800; e-mail editor@sundayherald.com; internet www.sundayherald.com; f. 1999; Propr Newsquest Media Group; Editor RICHARD WALKER; circ. 40,298.

Sunday Life: 124–144 Royal Ave, Belfast, BT1 1EB; tel. (28) 9026-4300; fax (28) 9054-4507; e-mail writeback@belfasttelegraph.co.uk; internet www.sundaylife.co.uk; f. 1988; Editor MARTIN LINDSAY; circ. 63,528 (June–Dec. 2008).

Sunday Mail: 1 Central Quay, Glasgow, G3 8DA; tel. (141) 309-3000; fax (141) 242-3587; e-mail mailbox@sundaymail.co.uk; internet www.sundaymail.co.uk; Propr Trinity Mirror PLC; Editor ALLAN RENNIE; circ. 421,147.

Sunday Mercury: Weaman St, Birmingham, B4 6AZ; tel. (121) 234-5567; e-mail sundaymercury@mrn.co.uk; internet www.icbirmingham.co.uk; Propr Trinity Mirror PLC; f. 1918; Editor STEVE DYSON; circ. 54,375 (June–Dec. 2008).

Sunday Mirror: 1 Canada Sq., Canary Wharf, London, E14 5AP; tel. (20) 7293-3000; fax (20) 7822-3587; e-mail mailbox@mirror.co.uk; internet www.sundaymirror.co.uk; f. 1915; Propr Trinity Mirror PLC; independent; Editor TINA WEAVER; circ. 1,146,601.

The Sunday Post: 144 Port Dundas Rd, Glasgow, G4 OHZ; tel. (141) 332-9933; fax (141) 331-1595; e-mail mail@sundaypost.com; internet www.sundaypost.com; f. 1919; Propr D.C. Thomson & Co. Ltd; Editor DAVID POLLINGTON; circ. 356,724.

Sunday Sport: 19 Gt Ancoats St, Manchester, M60 4BT; tel. (161) 236-4466; fax (161) 236-4535; f. 1986; Propr Sport Media Group; Editor-in-Chief MURRAY MORSE; circ. 70,796 (Jan. 2009).

Sunday Sun: Groat Market, Newcastle upon Tyne, NE1 1ED; tel. (191) 201-6299; fax (191) 230-0238; e-mail colin.patterson@ncjmedia.co.uk; internet www.sundaysun.co.uk; f. 1919; Propr Trinity Mirror PLC; independent; north-east England; Editor COLIN PATTERSON; circ. 61,869 (June–Dec. 2008).

Sunday Telegraph: 111 Buckingham Palace Rd, London, SW1W 0DT; tel. (20) 7931-2000; e-mail stletters@telegraph.co.uk; internet www.telegraph.co.uk; f. 1961; Propr Press Acquisitions Ltd; Editor IAN MCGREGOR; circ. 559,090.

The Sunday Times: 1 Pennington St, London, E98 1ST; tel. (20) 7782-5000; fax (20) 7782-5658; internet www.sunday-times.co.uk; f. 1822; Propr News International; Editor JOHN WITHEROW; circ. 1,049,095.

Wales on Sunday: Media Wales Ltd, Six Park St, Cardiff, CF10 1XR; tel. (29) 2022-3333; e-mail tim.gordon@mediawales.co.uk; internet www.walesonline.co.uk; f. 1991; Editor TIM GORDON; circ. 35,955 (June–Dec. 2008).

SELECTED PERIODICALS
(circulation figures as at June 2008, unless otherwise stated)

Arts and Literature

Apollo: 22 Old Queen St, London, SW1H 9HP; tel. (20) 7961-0150; fax (20) 7961-0110; e-mail editorial@apollomag.com; internet www.apollo-magazine.com; f. 1925; owned by Press Holdings; monthly; fine and decorative art; Publr CELIA BAILEY; Editor MICHAEL HALL.

Architects' Journal: Greater London House, Hampstead Rd, London, NW1 7EJ; tel. (20) 7728-4574; fax (20) 7391-3435; e-mail kieran.long@emap.com; internet www.architectsjournal.co.uk; f. 1895; Thursday; Editor KIERAN LONG; circ. 13,491 (July 2005).

Architectural Review: Greater London House, Hampstead Rd, London, NW1 7EJ; tel. (20) 7728-4589; e-mail paul.finch@emap.com; internet www.arplus.com; f. 1896; monthly; Editor PAUL FINCH; circ. 18,544 (May 2007).

The Artist: Caxton House, 63–65 High St, Tenterden, Kent, TN30 6BD; tel. (1580) 763673; fax (1580) 765411; e-mail sally@tapc.co.uk; internet www.painters-online.co.uk; f. 1931; monthly; Editor SALLY BULGIN.

ArtReview: 1 Sekforde St, London, EC1R 0BE; tel. (20) 7107-2760; fax (20) 7107-2761; e-mail editorial@artreview.com; internet www.art-review.com; f. 1949; monthly; Editor REBECCA WILSON.

BBC Music Magazine: Origin Publishing Ltd, 14th Floor, Tower House, Fairfax St, Bristol, BS1 3BN; tel. (117) 927-9009; fax (117) 934-9008; e-mail music@bbcmagazinesbristol.com; internet www.bbcmusicmagazine.com; f. 1992; monthly; classical music; Editor OLIVER CONDY; circ. 47,104 (Dec. 2007).

The Bookseller: Endeavour House, 189 Shaftesbury Ave, London, WC2H 8TJ; tel. (20) 7420-6006; fax (20) 7420-6103; e-mail letters.to.editor@bookseller.co.uk; internet www.thebookseller.com; f. 1858; incorporates *Bent's Literary Advertiser* (f. 1802); Friday; Propr VNU Entertainment Media UK Ltd; Editor NEILL DENNY.

The Burlington Magazine: 14–16 Dukes Rd, London, WC1H 9SZ; tel. (20) 7388-1228; fax (20) 7388-1229; e-mail burlington@burlington.org.uk; internet www.burlington.org.uk; f. 1903; monthly; all forms of art, ancient and modern; Editor RICHARD SHONE.

Classical Music: Rhinegold Publishing Ltd, 241 Shaftesbury Ave, London, WC2H 8TF; tel. (20) 7333-1742; fax (20) 7333-1769; e-mail classical.music@rhinegold.co.uk; internet www.rhinegold.co.uk; f. 1976; fortnightly; Editor KEITH CLARKE; circ. 18,000 (July 2005).

Dancing Times: 45–47 Clerkenwell Green, London, EC1R 0EB; tel. (20) 7250-3006; fax (20) 7253-6679; e-mail dt@dancing-times.co.uk; internet www.dancing-times.co.uk; f. 1910; monthly; ballet and modern dance; Editor JONATHAN GRAY.

Empire: Endeavour House, Shaftesbury Ave, WC2H 8JG; tel. (20) 7182-8781; internet www.empireonline.co.uk; monthly; film; Editor MARK DINNING; circ. 187,202.

Film Review: Visual Imagination Ltd, 9 Blades Court, Deodar Rd, London, SW15 2NU; tel. (20) 8875-1520; fax (20) 8875-1588; e-mail filmreview@visimag.com; internet www.visimag.com/filmreview; f. 1955; monthly; Editor NIKKI BAUGHAN.

Folklore: The Folklore Society, c/o The Warburg Institute, Woburn Sq., London, WC1H 0AB; tel. (20) 7862-8564; e-mail enquiries@folklore-society.com; internet www.folklore-society.com; f. 1878; 3 a year; Editor Prof. PATRICIA LYSAGHT.

Gramophone: Teddington Studios, Broom Rd, Teddington, Middlesex, TW11 9BE; tel. (20) 8267-5336; fax (20) 8267-5844; e-mail gramophone@haymarket.com; internet www.gramophone.co.uk; f. 1923; monthly; Publr SIMON TEMLETT; Editor JAMES INVERNE; circ. 36,817 (Dec. 2007).

Granta: 12 Addison Ave, London, W11 4QR; tel. (20) 7605-1360; fax (20) 7704-0474; e-mail editorial@granta.com; internet www.granta.com; quarterly; Editor ALEX CLARK; circ. 80,000 (July 2005).

Index on Censorship: 6–8 Amwell St, London, EC1R 1UQ; tel. (20) 7278-2313; fax (20) 7278-1878; e-mail contact@indexoncensorship.org; internet www.indexoncensorship.org; f. 1972; four a year; concerned with freedom of expression throughout the world; Editor JO GLANVILLE.

Jazz Journal International: Jazz Journal Ltd, 3 & 3A Forest Rd, Loughton, Essex IG10 1DR; tel. (20) 8532-0456; fax (20) 8532-0440; f. 1948; monthly; Editor JANET COOK.

Language Learning Journal: Association for Language Learning, University of Leicester, University Rd, Leicester, LE1 7RH; tel. (116) 2297453; fax (116) 2297456; e-mail info@all-languages.org.uk; internet www.all-languages.org.uk; f. 1990; 2 a year; Editors Dr NORBERT PACHLER, Dr DOUGLAS ALLFORD.

mixmag: 90–92 Pentonville Rd, London, N1 9HS; tel. (20) 7078-8400; fax (20) 7833-9900; e-mail mixmag@mixmag.net; internet www.mixmag.net; f. 1983; publ. by Development Hell Ltd; monthly; dance music and club culture; Editor ANDREW HARRISON; circ. 34,073.

Mojo: Endeavour House, 189 Shaftesbury Ave, London, WC2H 8JG; tel. (20) 7436-1515; fax (20) 7182-8596; internet www.mojo4music.com; f. 1993; monthly; popular music; Editor PHIL ALEXANDER; circ. 106,367.

NME: IPC Media Ltd, The Blue Fin Bldg, 110 Southwark St, London, SE1 0SU; tel. (20) 3148-5000; fax (20) 3148-8107; e-mail conor_mcnicholas@ipcmedia.com; internet www.nme.com; f. 1952; Weds; popular music; Editor CONOR MCNICHOLAS; circ. 56,284.

Opera: 36 Black Lion Lane, London, W6 9BE; tel. (20) 8563-8893; fax (20) 8563-8635; e-mail editor@opera.co.uk; internet www.opera.co.uk; f. 1950; monthly; Editor JOHN ALLISON.

Poetry Review: 22 Betterton St, London, WC2H 9BX; tel. (20) 7420-9883; fax (20) 7240-4818; e-mail poetryreview@poetrysociety.co.uk; internet www.poetryreview.co.uk; f. 1909; quarterly; Editor FIONA SAMPSON; circ. 4,500.

Q Magazine: Endeavour House, 189 Shaftesbury Ave, London, WC2H 8JG; tel. (20) 7182-8000; fax (20) 7182-8547; internet www.q4music.com; f. 1986; monthly; music, general features; Editor PAUL REES; circ. 113,174.

Sight and Sound: British Film Institute, 21 Stephen St, London, W1T 1LN; tel. (20) 7255-1444; fax (20) 7436-2327; e-mail s&s@bfi.org.uk; internet www.bfi.org.uk/sightandsound; f. 1932; monthly; international film review; Editor NICK JAMES; circ. 20,283 (Dec. 2007).

The Stage: Stage House, 47 Bermondsey St, London, SE1 3XT; tel. (20) 7403-1818; fax (20) 7357-9287; e-mail editor@thestage.co.uk; internet www.thestage.co.uk; f. 1880; Thurs.; theatre, light entertainment, television, opera, dance; Man. Dir CAROLINE COMERFORD; circ. 34,000.

The Times Literary Supplement: Times House, 1 Pennington St, London, E98 1BS; tel. (20) 7782-5000; fax (20) 7782-4966; e-mail letters@the-tls.co.uk; internet www.the-tls.co.uk; f. 1902; Fri.; weekly journal of literary criticism; Editor Sir PETER STOTHARD; circ. 36,535.

Top of the Pops: Media Centre, 201 Wood Lane, London, W12 7TQ; tel. (020) 8433-1201; e-mail totp.magazine@bbc.co.uk; internet www.totpmag.com; monthly; popular music; Editor PETER HART; circ. 130,174.

Current Affairs and History

Antiquity: King's Manor, York, YO1 7EP; tel. and fax (1904) 433994; e-mail editor@antiquity.ac.uk; internet antiquity.ac.uk; f. 1927; quarterly; archaeology; Editor Prof. MARTIN CARVER.

The Big Issue: 1–5 Wandsworth Rd, London, SW8 2LN; tel. (20) 7526-3200; fax (20) 7526-3201; e-mail press@bigissue.com; internet www.bigissue.com; also offices based in Bristol, Cardiff, Glasgow, Manchester and the Midlands producing regional weekly editions; f. 1991; weekly; current affairs, social issues; Editor-in-Chief A. JOHN BIRD; total circ. 134,456.

Classical Quarterly: Journals Group, Cambridge University Press, The Edinburgh Bldg, Shaftesbury Rd, Cambridge, CB2 2RU; tel. (1223) 326070; fax (1223) 325150; e-mail journals@cambridge.org; internet journals.cambridge.org/jid_caq; f. 1906; 2 a year; language, literature, history and philosophy; Editors Dr RHIANNON ASH, Prof. JUDITH MOSSMAN.

Contemporary Review: POB 1242, Oxford, OX1 4FJ; tel. and fax (1865) 201529; e-mail editorial@contemporaryreview.co.uk; internet www.contemporaryreview.co.uk; f. 1866; quarterly; publ by Contemporary Review Co Ltd; politics, international affairs, social subjects, the arts; Editor Dr RICHARD MULLEN.

English Historical Review: Faculty of History, Old Boys' High School, George St, Oxford, OX1 2RL; e-mail ehr@history.ox.ac.uk; internet ehr.oxfordjournals.org; f. 1886; 6 a year; learned articles and book reviews; Editors G. W. BERNARD, MARTIN CONWAY.

The Historian: The Historical Association, 59A Kennington Park Rd, London, SE11 4JH; tel. (20) 7735-3901; fax (20) 7582-4989; e-mail enquiry@history.org.uk; internet www.history.org.uk; f. 1906; 4 a year; Editors Prof. BILL SPECK, IAN MASON; circ. 3,500 (July 2005).

History Today: 20 Old Compton St, London, W1D 4TW; tel. (20) 7534-8000; fax (20) 7534-8008; e-mail admin@historytoday.com; internet www.historytoday.com; f. 1951; monthly; illustrated general historical magazine; Editor PETER FURTADO; circ. 25,274 (Dec. 2007).

International Affairs: Royal Institute of International Affairs, Chatham House, 10 St James's Sq., London, SW1Y 4LE; tel. (20) 7957-5724; fax (20) 7957-5710; e-mail csoper@chathamhouse.org.uk; internet www.chathamhouse.org.uk; f. 1922; six per year; publ. by Wiley-Blackwell; original articles, and reviews of publications on international affairs; Editor CAROLINE SOPER.

Journal of Contemporary History: Unit 24A, The Bardfield Centre, Great Bardfield, Essex, CM7 4SL; tel. (1371) 811608; fax (870) 288-9730; e-mail office@jch.org.uk; internet www.jch.org.uk; f. 1966; quarterly; publ. by SAGE Publications Ltd; Editors RICHARD J. EVANS, STANLEY G. PAYNE.

London Gazette: POB 7923, London, SE1 5ZH; tel. (20) 7394-4517; fax (20) 7394-4572; e-mail london.gazette@tso.co.uk; internet www.londongazette.co.uk; f. 1665; 5 a week; the oldest continuously published newspaper in the UK; government journal of official, legal and public notices.

New Left Review: 6 Meard St, London, W1F 0EG; tel. (20) 7734-8830; fax (20) 7439-3869; e-mail mail@newleftreview.org; internet www.newleftreview.org; f. 1960; 6 a year; international politics, economics and culture; Editor SUSAN WATKINS.

New Statesman: 3rd Floor, 52 Grosvenor Gardens, London, SW1W 0AU; tel. (20) 7730-3444; fax (20) 7259-0181; e-mail info@newstatesman.co.uk; internet www.newstatesman.com; f. 1913; weekly; current affairs, politics and the arts; publ. by Progressive Media Group; Editor JASON COWLEY; circ. 26,208 (Dec. 2007).

People in Power: Cambridge International Reference on Current Affairs Ltd (CIRCA), 13–17 Sturton St, Cambridge, CB1 2SN; tel. (1223) 568017; fax (1223) 354643; e-mail pip@circaworld.com; internet www.peopleinpower.com; f. 1987; bi-monthly; current

THE UNITED KINGDOM

worldwide government listings; Man. Dir. ROGER EAST; Producer ROSEMARY PAYNE.

The Political Quarterly: Wiley-Blackwell, 9600 Garsington Rd, Oxford, OX4 2DQ; tel. (1865) 476303; fax (1865) 476770; internet www.wiley.com; f. 1930; Editors ANDREW GAMBLE, ANTHONY WRIGHT.

Private Eye: 6 Carlisle St, London, W1D 3BN; tel. (20) 7437-4017; fax (20) 7437-0705; e-mail strobes@private-eye.co.uk; internet www.private-eye.co.uk; f. 1961; fortnightly; satirical; Editor IAN HISLOP; circ. 205,231.

Prospect: 2 Bloomsbury Pl., London, WC1A 2QA; tel. (20) 7255-1281; fax (20) 7255-1279; e-mail editorial@prospect-magazine.co.uk; internet www.prospect-magazine.co.uk; f. 1995; monthly; political and cultural; Editor DAVID GOODHART; circ. 27,552.

Race & Class: The Institute of Race Relations, 2–6 Leeke St, London, WC1X 9HS; tel. (20) 7837-0041; fax (20) 7278-0623; e-mail info@irr.org.uk; internet www.irr.org.uk; f. 1959; quarterly; journal on racism, empire and globalization; Editors A. SIVANANDAN, HAZEL WATERS.

The Spectator: 22 Old Queen St, London, SW1H 9HP; tel. (20) 7961-0200; fax (20) 7961-0058; e-mail editor@spectator.co.uk; internet www.spectator.co.uk; f. 1828; Propr Press Holdings; Thurs.; independent political and literary review; Editor MATTHEW D'ANCONA; circ. 76,952.

Tribune: 9 Arkwright Rd, London, NW3 6AN; tel. (20) 7433-6410; fax (20) 7433-6419; e-mail mail@tribunemagazine.co.uk; internet www.tribuneweb.co.uk; f. 1937; Fri.; Labour's independent weekly; politics, current affairs, arts; Editor CHRIS MCLAUGHLIN.

Economics and Business

Accountancy Age: Incisive Media, 32–34 Broadwick St, London, W1A 2HG; tel. (20) 7316-9000; fax (20) 7316-9250; e-mail news@accountancyage.com; internet www.accountancyage.co.uk; f. 1969; weekly; Editor GAVIN HINKS; circ. 60,337 (June 2007).

The Banker: Number One Southwark Bridge, London, SE1 9HL; tel. (20) 7775-6359; e-mail stephen.timewell@ft.com; internet www.thebanker.com; f. 1926; monthly; monetary and economic policy, international and domestic banking and finance, banking technology, country surveys; Propr Pearson PLC; Editor-in-Chief STEPHEN TIMEWELL; circ. 28,771.

Campaign: Haymarket Marketing Publications Ltd, 174 Hammersmith Rd, London, W6 7JP; tel. (20) 8267-4656; fax (20) 8267-4915; e-mail campaign@haymarket.com; internet www.brandrepublic.com/campaign; f. 1968; advertising, marketing and media; Thurs.; Editor CLAIRE BEALE; circ. 10,012.

Crops: Farmers Weekly Group, 2nd Floor, Quadrant House, The Quadrant, Sutton, Surrey, SM2 5AS; tel. (20) 8652-4934; fax (20) 8652-8928; e-mail crops@rbi.co.uk; internet www.fwi.co.uk; f. 1984; fortnightly; publ. by Reed Business Information; Editor ROBERT HARRIS; circ. 14,792.

The Economic Journal: Wiley-Blackwell, 9600 Garsington Rd, Oxford, OX4 2QD; tel. (1865) 791100; fax (1865) 791347; e-mail rchandler@wiley.com; internet www.wiley.com; f. 1891; nine a year; Editors ANTONIO CICCONE, JÖRN-STEFFEN PISCHKE, STEVE MACHIN, ANDREW SCOTT, DAVID MYATT.

The Economist: 25 St James's St, London, SW1A 1HG; tel. (20) 7830-7000; fax (20) 7839-2968; e-mail letters@economist.com; internet www.economist.com; f. 1843; 50% owned by Pearson PLC, 50% by individual shareholders; Fri.; Editor JOHN MICKLETHWAIT; CEO ANDREW RASHBASS; circ. 182,539.

Euromoney: Nestor House, Playhouse Yard, London, EC4V 5EX; tel. (20) 7779-8888; fax (20) 7779-8653; e-mail hotline@euromoneyplc.com; internet www.euromoney.com; f. 1969; monthly; Editor CLIVE HORWOOD; circ. 25,368.

Farmers Weekly: Farmers Weekly Group, Quadrant House, 2nd Floor, The Quadrant, Sutton, Surrey, SM2 5AS; tel. (20) 8652-4911; fax (20) 8652-4005; e-mail farmers.weekly@rbi.co.uk; internet www.fwi.co.uk; f. 1934; Fri.; publ. by Reed Business Information; Editor JANE KING; circ. 68,897.

Investors Chronicle: Number One Southwark Bridge, London, SE1 9HL; tel. (20) 7382-3000; e-mail ic.cs@ft.com; internet www.investorschronicle.co.uk; f. as *Money Market Review* 1860; amalgamated with *Investors Chronicle* 1914; amalgamated with the *Stock Exchange Gazette* 1967; Fri.; independent financial and economic review; Editor OLIVER RALPH; circ. 31,919.

Management Today: 174 Hammersmith Rd, London, W6 7JP; tel. (20) 8267-4629; fax (20) 8267-4680; e-mail editorial@mtmagazine.co.uk; internet www.managementtoday.co.uk; f. 1966; monthly; Editor MATTHEW GWYTHER; circ. 100,002.

Education

Higher Education Quarterly: Wiley-Blackwell, 9600 Garsington Rd, Oxford, OX4 2DQ; tel. (1865) 776868; fax (1865) 714591; internet www.blackwellpublishing.com/hequ; f. 1946; Editor LEE HARVEY.

The Teacher: Hamilton House, Mabledon Pl., London, WC1H 9BD; tel. (20) 7380-4708; fax (20) 7387-8458; e-mail teacher@nut.org.uk; internet www.teachers.org.uk/theteacher; f. 1872; magazine of the NUT; news, comments and articles on all aspects of education; eight a year; Editor ELLIE CAMPBELL-BARR.

The Times Educational Supplement: 26 Red Lion Sq., London, WC1R 4HQ; tel. (20) 3194-3000; fax (20) 3194-3333; e-mail gerard.kelly@tsleducation.com; internet www.tes.co.uk; f. 1910; Fri.; Editor GERARD KELLY; circ. 57,714.

The Times Higher Education Supplement: 26 Red Lion Sq., London, WC1R 4HQ; tel. (20) 3194-3000; fax (20) 3194-3300; e-mail editor@thes.co.uk; internet www.thes.co.uk; f. 1971; Thurs.; Editor GERARD KELLY; circ. 21,140 (Dec. 2007).

Home, Fashion and General

Bella: H. Bauer Publishing Ltd, 1st Floor, 24–28 Oval Rd, London, NW1 7DT; tel. (20) 7241-8000; fax (20) 7241-8056; internet www.bauer.co.uk; f. 1987; Tuesday; fashion, beauty, health, cookery, handicrafts; Editor JULIA DAVIS; circ. 191,547.

Best: National Magazine Company, 72 Broadwick St, London, W1F 9EP; tel. (20) 7439-5000; fax (20) 7439-4580; e-mail best@acp-natmag.co.uk; internet www.natmags.co.uk; f. 1987; weekly; women's interest; Editor JANE ENNIS; circ. 301,437.

Chat: IPC Connect Ltd, The Blue Fin Bldg, 110 Southwark St, London, SE1 0SU; tel. (20) 3148-6153; fax (20) 3148-8111; e-mail ben_gelblum@ipcmedia.com; internet www.ipcmedia.com; weekly; women's interest; Editor GILLY SINCLAIR; circ. 489,682.

Company: National Magazine House, 72 Broadwick St, London, W1F 9EP; tel. (20) 7439-5000; fax (20) 7439-6886; e-mail company.mail@natmags.co.uk; internet www.natmags.co.uk; monthly; Editor CLAIRE IRVINE (acting); circ. 240,078.

Cosmopolitan: National Magazine House, 72 Broadwick St, London, W1F 9EP; tel. (20) 7439-5000; fax (20) 7439-5016; e-mail contact@natmags.co.uk; internet www.cosmopolitan.co.uk; f. 1972; monthly; women's interest; Editor LOUISE COURT; circ. 470,735.

Elle: 64 North Row, London, W1K 7LL; tel. (20) 7150-7000; fax (20) 7150-7001; e-mail lorraine.candy@hf-uk.com; internet www.hachettefilipacchiuk.co.uk; f. 1985; monthly; women's interest; Editor-in-Chief LORRAINE CANDY; circ. 203,471.

Esquire: National Magazine House, 72 Broadwick St, London, W1F 9EP; tel. (20) 7439-5000; fax (20) 7439-5675; e-mail info@esquire.co.uk; internet www.esquire.co.uk; f. 1991; monthly; men's interest; Editor JEREMY LANGMEAD; circ. 58,136.

Eve Magazine: 174 Hammersmith Rd, London, W6 7JP; tel. (20) 8267-5000; fax (20) 8267-8222; e-mail evemagazine@haymarket.com; internet www.evemagazine.co.uk; f. 2000; monthly; Editor NIC MCCARTHY; circ. 155,076.

FHM: Endeavour House, 189 Shaftesbury Ave, London, WC2H 8JG; tel. (20) 7436-1515; fax (20) 7182-8021; e-mail help@fhm.com; internet www.fhm.com; f. 1987; monthly; men's interest; Editor-in-Chief ANTHONY NOGUERA; circ. 280,392.

Glamour: Vogue House, Hanover Sq., London, W1S 1JU; tel. (20) 7499-9080; e-mail glamour-editorial@condenast.co.uk; internet www.glamour.com; f. 2001; monthly; women's interest; Editor JO ELVIN; circ. 551,351.

Good Housekeeping: National Magazine House, 72 Broadwick St, London, W1F 9EP; tel. (20) 7439-5000; fax (20) 7437-6886; e-mail contact@goodhousekeeping.co.uk; internet www.goodhousekeeping.co.uk; f. 1922; monthly; Editor-in-Chief LINDSAY NICHOLSON; circ. 430,930.

GQ: The Condé Nast Publications Ltd, Vogue House, Hanover Sq., London, W1S 1JU; tel. (20) 7499-9080; fax (20) 7495-1679; internet www.gq-magazine.co.uk; f. 1988; monthly; Editor DYLAN JONES; circ. 130,008.

Grazia: Endeavour House, 189 Shaftesbury Ave, London, WC2H 8JG; tel. (20) 7437-9011; e-mail feedback@graziamagazine.co.uk; internet www.graziamagazine.co.uk; f. 2005; weekly; Editor JANE BRUTON; circ. 227,102.

Harper's Bazaar: National Magazine House, 72 Broadwick St, London, W1F 9EP; tel. (20) 7439-5000; fax (20) 7437-6886; internet www.harpersbazaar.co.uk; f. 1929; Propr National Magazine Co Ltd; monthly; international fashion, beauty, general features; Editor LUCY YEOMANS; circ. 109,146.

Heat: Endeavour House, 189 Shaftesbury Ave, London, WC2H 8JG; tel. (20) 7437-9011; internet www.heatworld.com; f. 1999; Tues.; celebrity news, TV, radio, films; Editor JULIAN LINLEY; circ. 470,129.

THE UNITED KINGDOM

Hello!: Hello! Ltd, Wellington House, 69–71 Upper Ground, London, SE1 9PQ; tel. (20) 7667-8700; fax (20) 7667-8716; e-mail hello@hellomagazine.com; internet www.hellomagazine.com; Propr. Hola, SA (Spain); weekly; Publishing Dir CHARLOTTE STOCKTING; Editor KAY GODDARD; circ. 427,054.

Homes and Gardens: The Blue Fin Bldg, 110 Southwark St, London, SE1 0SU; tel. (20) 7261-6202; fax (20) 7261-6247; internet www.homesandgardens.com; f. 1919; monthly; Editor DEBORAH BARKER; circ. 143,900.

House & Garden: The Condé Nast Publications Ltd, Vogue House, Hanover Sq., London, W1S 1JU; tel. (20) 7499-9080; fax (20) 7629-2907; e-mail harriet.bindloss@condenast.co.uk; internet www.houseandgarden.co.uk; f. 1920; monthly; Editor SUSAN CREWE; circ. 142,511.

Ideal Home: IPC Media Ltd, The Blue Fin Bldg, 110 Southwark St, London, SE1 0SU; tel. (20) 3148-5000; e-mail ideal_home@ipcmedia.com; internet www.idealhomemagazine.co.uk; f. 1920; 11 a year; Editor ISOBEL MCKENZIE-PRICE; circ. 221,080.

InStyle: The Blue Fin Bldg, 110 Southwark St, London, SE1 0SU; tel. (20) 7261-4747; fax (20) 7261-6664; internet www.instylemagazine.co.uk; f. 2001; monthly; fashion, beauty; Editor TRISH HALPIN; circ. 180,879.

The Lady: 39–40 Bedford St, London, WC2E 9ER; tel. (20) 7379-4717; fax (20) 7497-2137; e-mail admin@lady.co.uk; internet www.lady.co.uk; f. 1885; Tues.; Editor ARLINE USDEN; circ. 29,095.

Loaded: IPC Media Ltd, The Blue Fin Bldg, 110 Southwark St, London, SE1 0SU; tel. (20) 3148-6751; e-mail jo_smalley@ipcmedia.com; internet www.loaded.co.uk; f. 1994; monthly; men's interest; Editor MARTIN DAUBNEY; circ. 95,371.

Marie Claire: IPC Media Ltd, The Blue Fin Bldg, 110 Southwark St, London, SE1 0SU; tel. (20) 3148-7664; e-mail marieclaire@ipcmedia.com; internet www.marieclaire.co.uk; f. 1988; monthly; women's interest; Man. Editor MARIE O'RIORDAN; circ. 316,765.

My Weekly: D. C. Thomson & Co Ltd, 80 Kingsway East, Dundee, DD4 8SL; tel. (1382) 223131; fax (1382) 452491; e-mail myweekly@dcthomson.co.uk; f. 1910; Thurs.; women's interest; Editor SALLY HAMPTON; circ. 155,087.

Now: The Blue Fin Bldg, 110 Southwark St, London, SE1 0SU; tel. (20) 3148-6373; fax (20) 3148-8110; internet www.nowmagazine.co.uk; weekly; celebrity news, TV, radio, films; Editor ABIGAIL BLACKBURN; circ. 447,094.

Nuts: The Blue Fin Bldg, 110 Southwark St, London, SE1 0SU; tel. (20) 7261-6174; e-mail nutsmagazine@ipcmedia.com; internet www.nutsmag.co.uk; f. 2004; weekly; Editor DOMINIC SMITH; circ. 250,061.

OK!: The Northern & Shell Bldg, 10 Lower Thames St, London, EC3R 6EN; tel. (871) 434-1010; e-mail editor@ok-magazine.com; internet www.ok-magazine.co.uk; weekly; Editor LISA BYRNE; circ. 607,048.

The People's Friend: D. C. Thomson & Co Ltd, 80 Kingsway East, Dundee, DD4 8SL; tel. (1382) 223131; fax (1382) 452491; e-mail peoplesfriend@dcthomson.co.uk; f. 1869; Weds; women's fiction, home, crafts, general; Editor ANGELA GILCHRIST; circ. 330,093.

Prima: 72 Broadwick St, London, W1F 9EP; tel. (20) 7439-5000; fax (20) 7312-4100; e-mail prima@natmags.co.uk; internet www.allaboutyou.com; f. 1986; monthly; Editor MAIRE FAHEY; circ. 282,544.

Reader's Digest: Reader's Digest Association Ltd, (British Edition) 11 Westferry Circus, Canary Wharf, London, E14 4HE; tel. (20) 7715-8000; fax (20) 7715-8716; e-mail theeditor@readersdigest.co.uk; internet www.readersdigest.co.uk; f. 1938; monthly; Editor SARAH SANDS; circ. 638,693.

The Scots Magazine: D. C. Thomson & Co. Ltd, 2 Albert Sq., Dundee, DD1 9QJ; tel. (1382) 223131; fax (1382) 322214; e-mail mail@scotsmagazine.com; internet www.scotsmagazine.com; f. 1739; monthly; Scottish interest; circ. 36,049.

She: 72 Broadwick St, London, W1F 9EP; tel. (20) 7439-5000; fax (20) 7437-6886; e-mail sian.rees@natmags.co.uk; internet www.natmags.co.uk; f. 1955; monthly; Editor SIÂN REES; circ. 173,377.

Take a Break: H. Bauer Publishing Ltd, 24–28 Oval Rd, London, NW1 7DT; tel. (20) 7241-8000; fax (20) 7241-8052; e-mail tab.features@bauer.co.uk; internet www.bauer.co.uk; f. 1990; Thurs.; Editor JOHN DALE; circ. 981,504.

Tatler: The Condé Nast Publications Ltd, Vogue House, Hanover Sq., London, W1S 1JU; tel. (20) 7499-9080; fax (20) 7409-0451; internet www.tatler.co.uk; f. 1709; monthly; Editor (vacant); circ. 90,128.

That's Life!: H. Bauer Publishing Ltd, 24–28 Oval Rd, London, NW1 7DT; tel. (20) 7241-8000; fax (20) 7241-8008; e-mail sales@tpc-london.com; internet www.bauer.co.uk; f. 1995; Thursday; Editor JO CHECKLEY; circ. 433,921.

Vanity Fair: The Condé Nast Publications Ltd, Vogue House, Hanover Sq., London, W1R 0AD; tel. (20) 7499-9080; fax (20) 7499-4415; internet www.vanityfair.co.uk; monthly; Editor HENRY PORTER; circ. 101,166.

Viz: Dennis Publishing Ltd, 30 Cleveland St, London, W1T 4JD; tel. (20) 7907-6000; fax (20) 7907-6020; e-mail viz@viz.co.uk; internet www.viz.co.uk; f. 1979; monthly; Editor SIMON DONALD; circ. 88,165 (Dec. 2007).

Vogue: The Condé Nast Publications Ltd, Vogue House, Hanover Sq., London, W1S 1JU; tel. (20) 7499-9080; fax (20) 7408-0559; internet www.vogue.co.uk; f. 1916; monthly; Editor ALEXANDRA SHULMAN; circ. 221,090.

The Voice: GV Media Group Ltd, Northern & Shell Tower, 6th Floor, 4 Selsdon Way, London, E14 9GL; tel. (20) 7510-0340; fax (20) 7510-0341; e-mail letters@gvmedia.co.uk; internet www.voice-online.co.uk; f. 1982; Monday; black interest; Editor STEVE POPE.

Wallpaper*: 7th Floor, The Blue Fin Bldg, 110 Southwark St, London, SE1 0SU; tel. (20) 3148-5000; fax (20) 3148-8119; e-mail marketing@wallpaper.com; internet www.wallpaper.com; f. 1996; monthly; Editor TONY CHAMBERS; circ. 108,050 (Dec. 2008).

Woman: The Blue Fin Bldg, 110 Southwark St, London, SE1 0SU; tel. (20) 3148-6491; e-mail woman@ipcmedia.com; internet www.ipcmedia.com/brands/woman; f. 1937; Tues.; Editor JACKIE HATTON; circ. 370,289.

Woman and Home: The Blue Fin Bldg, 110 Southwark St, London, SE1 0SU; tel. (20) 3148-7836; e-mail woman&home@ipcmedia.com; internet www.ipcmedia.com/brands/womanhome; f. 1926; monthly; Editor SUE JAMES; circ. 336,888.

Woman's Own: The Blue Fin Bldg, 110 Southwark St, London, SE1 0SU; tel. (20) 3148-6552; fax (20) 3148-8112; internet www.ipcmedia.com/brands/womansown; f. 1932; Tues.; Editor-in-Chief KAREN LIVERMORE; circ. 339,138.

Woman's Weekly: The Blue Fin Bldg, 110 Southwark St, London, SE1 0SU; tel. (20) 3148-6628; internet www.ipcmedia.com/brands/womansweekly; f. 1911; Weds; Editor DIANE KENWOOD; circ. 346,540.

Zoo: Mappin House, 4 Winsley St, London, W1W 8HF; tel. (20) 7182-8355; internet www.zootoday.com; f. 2004; weekly; Editor BEN TODD; circ. 161,331.

Law

Law Quarterly Review: 100 Avenue Rd, London, NW3 3PF; tel. (20) 7393-7000; fax (20) 7393-7010; internet www.sweetandmaxwell.co.uk; f. 1885; quarterly; Editor Prof. FRANCIS M. B. REYNOLDS.

Law Society's Gazette: 113 Chancery Lane, London, WC2A 1PL; tel. (20) 7242-1222; e-mail gazette-editorial@lawsociety.org.uk; internet www.lawgazette.co.uk; f. 1903; weekly; Editor-in-Chief PAUL ROGERSON; circ. 118,927.

The Lawyer: St Giles House, 50 Poland St, London, W1V 7AX; tel. (20) 7970-4614; fax (20) 7970-4640; e-mail catrin.griffiths@thelawyer.com; internet www.thelawyer.com; weekly; Editor CATRIN GRIFFITHS; circ. 31,571.

Leisure Interests and Sport

Autocar Magazine: Haymarket Consumer Media, Broom Rd, Teddington, Middx, TW11 9BE; tel. (20) 8267-5630; fax (20) 8267-5759; e-mail autocar@haynet.com; internet www.autocar.co.uk; f. 1895; Weds; Editor CHAS HALLETT; circ. 58,091.

Autosport: Haymarket Consumer Media, Broom Rd, Teddington, Middx, TW11 9BE; tel. (20) 8267-5118; e-mail rob.aherne@haymarket.com; internet www.autosport.com; f. 1950; Thurs.; covers all aspects of motor sport; Editor-in-Chief ANDY VAN DE BURGT; circ. 38,324 (Dec. 2007).

Car: Media House, Lynchwood Business Park, Lynchwood, Peterborough, PE2 6EA; tel. (1733) 468485; fax (1733) 468660; internet www.carmagazine.co.uk; f. 1962; monthly; Editor PHIL MCNAMARA; circ. 68,126.

Country Life: 9th Floor, The Blue Fin Bldg, 110 Southwark St, London, SE1 0SU; tel. (20) 3148-4445; fax (20) 3148-8129; e-mail milly_cumming@ipcmedia.com; internet www.countrylife.co.uk; f. 1897; Thurs.; Editor MARK HEDGES; circ. 40,821 (Dec. 2007).

The Countryman: The Water Mill, Broughton Hall, Skipton, BD23 3AG; tel. (1756) 701381; fax (1756) 701326; e-mail editorial@thecountryman.co.uk; internet www.thecountryman.co.uk; f. 1927; monthly; independent; Editor PAUL JACKSON; circ. 19,817 (Dec. 2007).

FourFourTwo: Haymarket Consumer Media, Broom Rd, Teddington, TW11 9BE; tel. (20) 8267-5848; fax (20) 8267-5354; e-mail martyn.jones@haymarket.com; internet www.fourfourtwo.com; f. 1994; monthly; football; Editor HUGH SLEIGHT; circ. 107,987.

BBC Gardeners' World Magazine: BBC Worldwide Ltd, Room AG193, 80 Wood Lane, London, W12 0TT; tel. (20) 8433-3959; fax (20) 8433-3986; e-mail gweditorial@bbc.co.uk; internet www.gardenersworld.com; f. 1991; monthly; Editor ADAM PASCO; circ. 303,623.

THE UNITED KINGDOM

Golf Monthly: The Blue Fin Bldg, 110 Southwark St, London, SE1 0SU; tel. (20) 7148-4530; e-mail golfmonthly@ipcmedia.com; internet www.golf-monthly.co.uk; f. 1911; monthly; Editor MICHAEL HARRIS; circ. 82,264.

BBC Good Food: BBC Worldwide Ltd, 80 Wood Lane, London, W12 0TT; tel. (20) 8433-1316; fax (20) 8433-1277; e-mail goodfoodrs@galleon.co.uk; internet www.bbcmagazines.com/goodfood; f. 1989; monthly; Editor GILLIAN CARTER; circ. 340,057.

Hi-Fi News: Leon House, 10th Floor, 233 High St, Croydon, Surrey, CR9 1HZ; tel. (20) 8726-8310; fax (20) 8726-8397; e-mail hi-finews@ipcmedia.com; internet www.hifinews.com; f. 1956; monthly; all aspects of high quality sound reproduction, record reviews; Editor PAUL MILLER; circ. 11,353.

Men's Health: 72 Broadwick St, London, W1F 9EP; tel. (20) 7339-4400; fax (20) 7339-4444; e-mail nicky.williams@natmag-rodale.co.uk; internet www.menshealth.co.uk; f. 1995; monthly; lifestyle, health, general features; Editor MORGAN REES; circ. 245,212.

Practical Photography: Media House, Lynchwood Business Park, Lynchwood, Peterborough, PE2 6EA; tel. (1733) 468546; fax (1733) 468387; e-mail practical.photography@bauerconsumer.co.uk; internet www.photoanswers.co.uk; monthly; Editor-in-Chief ANDREW JAMES; circ. 62,303 (2007).

Radio Times: BBC Worldwide Ltd, Media Centre, White City, 201 Wood Lane, London, W12 7TS; tel. 0870 608 4455; fax (20) 8433-3160; e-mail radio.times@bbc.com; internet www.radiotimes.com; f. 1923; weekly; programme guide to television and radio broadcasts; Editor GILL HUDSON; circ. 1,009,028.

Rugby World: The Blue Fin Bldg, 110 Southwark St, London, SE1 0SU; tel. (20) 3148-4702; e-mail paul_morgan@ipcmedia.com; internet www.rugbyworld.com; monthly; Editor PAUL MORGAN; circ. 48,381 (Dec. 2007).

Time Out: Time Out Magazine Ltd, Universal House, 251 Tottenham Court Rd, London, W1T 7AB; tel. (20) 7813-3000; fax (20) 7813-6001; e-mail net@timeout.co.uk; internet www.timeout.com; f. 1968; weekly; listings and reviews of events in London; Time Out Group also publishes city guides and specialized London guides; Editor (vacant); circ. 76,356.

TVTimes: The Blue Fin Bldg, 110 Southwark St, London, SE1 0SU; tel. (20) 3148-5570; e-mail tvtimes_letters@ipcmedia.com; internet www.ipcmedia.com/brands/tvtimes; f. 1955; features and listings of all television broadcasts; Editor IAN ABBOTT; circ. 336,929.

What Car?: Teddington Studios, Broom Rd, Teddington, Middx, TW11 9BE; tel. (20) 8267-5688; fax (20) 8267-5750; e-mail whatcar@haymarket.com; internet www.whatcar.com; f. 1973; 13 a year; Group Editor STEVE FOWLER; circ. 108,028.

What's On TV: The Blue Fin Bldg, 110 Southwark St, London, SE1 0SU; tel. (20) 3148-5928; e-mail wotv-postbag@ipcmedia.com; internet www.ipcmedia.com/brands/whatsontv; f. 1991; weekly; television programme guide and features; Editor COLIN TOUGH; circ. 1,346,815.

The Wisden Cricketer: Wisden Cricketer Publishing Ltd, 2nd Floor, 123 Buckingham Palace Rd, London, SW1W 9SL; tel. (20) 7705-4911; e-mail twc@wisdencricketer.com; internet wisdencricketer.com; f. 1921; monthly; Propr BSkyB Publications; Editor JOHN STERN; circ. 34,559 (Dec. 2007).

Zest: 72 Broadwick St, London, W1F 9EP; tel. (20) 7439-5000; fax (20) 7437-6886; e-mail contact@zest.co.uk; internet www.zest.co.uk; health, beauty, fitness and nutrition; Editor MANDIE GOWER; circ. 104,636.

Medicine, Science and Technology

Biochemical Journal: Portland Press Ltd, 3rd Floor, Eagle House, 16 Procter St, London, WC1V 6NX; tel. (20) 7280-4110; fax (20) 7280-4169; e-mail editorial@portlandpress.com; internet www.biochemj.org; f. 1906; 2 a month; publ. by Portland Press on behalf of the Biochemical Society; Chair. Editorial Board PETER SHEPHERD; Publr P. J. STARLEY.

British Journal of Psychiatry: 17 Belgrave Sq., London, SW1X 8PG; tel. (20) 7235-2351; fax (20) 7259-6507; e-mail bjp@rcpsych.ac.uk; internet bjp.rcpsych.org; monthly; original articles, reviews and correspondence; publ. by the Royal College of Psychiatrists; Editor PETER TYRER; circ. 14,100 (July 2005).

British Journal of Psychology: St Andrew's House, 48 Princess Rd East, Leicester, LE1 7DR; tel. (116) 254-9580; fax (116) 227-1314; e-mail journals@bps.org.uk; internet www.bpsjournals.co.uk; f. 1904; quarterly; publ. by the British Psychological Society; Editor Prof. PETER MITCHELL.

British Journal of Sociology: Wiley-Blackwell, 9600 Garsington Rd, Oxford, OX4 2DQ; tel. (1865) 776868; fax (1865) 714591; internet www.blackwellpublishing.com/bjos; f. 1950; quarterly; Editor RICHARD WRIGHT.

BMJ: BMA House, Tavistock Sq., London, WC1H 9JP; tel. (20) 7387-4499; fax (20) 7383-6418; e-mail editor@bmj.com; internet www.bmj.com; f. 1840; Sat.; 10 overseas editions; Editor Dr FIONA GODLEE; circ. 120,606.

Computer Weekly: Reed Business Information, Quadrant House, The Quadrant, Sutton, Surrey, SM2 5AS; tel. (20) 8652-8642; fax (20) 8652-8979; e-mail cwnews@rbi.co.uk; internet www.computerweekly.com; f. 1966; Tues.; Editor BRIAN McKENNA.

Computing: VNU Business Publications, VNU House, 32–34 Broadwick St, London, W1A 2HG; tel. (20) 7316-9000; fax (20) 7316-9160; e-mail computing@vnu.co.uk; internet www.computing.co.uk; f. 1973; Thursday; Editor BRYAN GLICK; circ. 115,000 (July 2005).

The Ecologist: Unit 102D, Lana House Studios, 116–118 Commercial St, London, E1 6NF; tel. (20) 7422-8100; fax (20) 7422-8101; e-mail editorial@theecologist.org; internet www.theecologist.org; f. 1970; to become internet-only publication from June 2009; all aspects of ecology, the environment, etc.; Editor PAT THOMAS.

Flight International: Reed Business Information, Quadrant House, The Quadrant, Sutton, Surrey, SM2 5AS; tel. (20) 8652-3842; fax (20) 8652-3840; e-mail flight.international@rbi.co.uk; internet www.flightinternational.com; f. 1909; Tuesday; Editor MURDO MORRISON.

Geographical Magazine: Circle Publishing, 1 Victoria Villas, Richmond, Surrey, TW9 2GW; tel. (20) 8332-2713; fax (20) 8332-9307; e-mail magazine@geographical.co.uk; internet www.geographical.co.uk; f. 1935; monthly; Editor GEORDIE TORR; circ. 21,684.

The Lancet: 32 Jamestown Rd, London, NW1 7BY; tel. (20) 7424-4910; fax (20) 7424-4911; e-mail editorial@lancet.com; internet www.thelancet.com; f. 1823; Sat.; medical; Editor Dr RICHARD HORTON.

Nature: Macmillan Magazines Ltd, 4 Crinan St, London, N1 9XW; tel. (20) 7833-4000; fax (20) 7843-4640; e-mail nature@nature.com; internet www.nature.com/nature; f. 1869; Thurs.; scientific; Editor-in-Chief Dr PHILIP CAMPBELL.

New Scientist: Lacon House, 84 Theobald's Rd, London, WC1X 8NS; tel. (20) 7611-1200; fax (20) 7611-1250; e-mail news@newscientist.com; internet cwww.newscientist.com; f. 1956; Thurs.; science and technology; Editor JEREMY WEBB; circ. 173,820 (worldwide).

Nursing Times: Emap Inform, Greater London House, Hampstead Rd, London, NW1 7EJ; tel. (20) 728-3702; fax (20) 7874-0505; e-mail nt@emap.com; internet www.nursingtimes.net; f. 1905; Tuesday; professional nursing journal; Editor RACHEL DOWNEY; circ. 35,754.

The Practitioner: Ludgate House, 245 Blackfriars Rd, London, SE1 9UY; tel. (20) 7921-8113; e-mail cchapman@cmpmedica.com; internet www.thepractitioner.co.uk; f. 1868; monthly; medical journal for General Practitioners; Editor CORINNE SHORT.

Religion and Philosophy

Catholic Herald: Herald House, 15 Lamb's Passage, Bunhill Row, London, EC1Y 8TQ; tel. (20) 7448-3602; fax (20) 7256-9728; e-mail editorial@catholicherald.co.uk; internet www.catholicherald.co.uk; f. 1888; Catholic weekly newspaper; Fri.; Editor LUKE COPPEN.

Church Times: 13–17 Long Lane, London, EC1A 9PN; tel. (20) 7776-1060; fax (20) 7776-1086; e-mail editor@churchtimes.co.uk; internet www.churchtimes.co.uk; f. 1863; Church of England and world-wide Anglican news; Fri.; Editor PAUL HANDLEY.

Jewish Chronicle: 25 Furnival St, London, EC4A 1JT; tel. (20) 7415-1500; fax (20) 7405-9040; e-mail editorial@thejc.com; internet www.thejc.com; f. 1841; Fri.; Editor DAVID ROWAN; circ. 32,875.

Methodist Recorder: 122 Golden Lane, London, EC1Y 0TL; tel. (20) 7251-8414; fax (20) 7251-8600; e-mail editorial@methodistrecorder.co.uk; internet www.methodistrecorder.co.uk; f. 1861; Thurs.; Man. Editor MOIRA SLEIGHT.

New Blackfriars: Blackfriars, Oxford, OX1 3LY; tel. (1865) 776868; fax (1865) 714591; e-mail fergus.kerr@english.op.org; internet www.wiley.com; f. 1920; 6 a year; religious and cultural; Editor Rev. FERGUS KERR.

Philosophy: Royal Institute of Philosophy, 14 Gordon Sq., London, WC1H 0AR; tel. (20) 7387-4130; e-mail j.garvey@royalinstitutephilosophy.org; internet www.royalinstitutephilosophy.org; f. 1925; quarterly; Editor ANTHONY O'HEAR.

The Universe: 1st Floor, St James's Bldgs, Oxford St, Manchester, M1 6FP; tel. (161) 236-8856; fax (161) 236-8530; e-mail newsdesk@totalcatholic.com; internet www.totalcatholic.com; f. 1860; Sun.; illustrated Catholic newspaper and review; publ. by Gabriel Communications Ltd; Editor JOSEPH KELLY.

Woman Alive: Christian Publishing and Outreach, Garcia Estate, Canterbury Rd, Worthing, West Sussex, BN13 1BW; tel. (1903)

THE UNITED KINGDOM

264556; e-mail womanalive@cpo.org.uk; internet www.womanalive.co.uk; f. 1982; monthly; Editor JACKIE STEAD.

PRESS ORGANIZATION

Press Complaints Commission: Halton House, 20–23 Holborn, London, EC1 2JD; tel. (20) 7831-0022; fax (20) 7831-0025; e-mail complaints@pcc.org.uk; internet www.pcc.org.uk; f. 1991 to replace the Press Council, following the report of the Committee on Privacy and Related Matters; an independent organization established by the newspaper and magazine industry through the Press Standards Board of Finance to deal with complaints from the public about the contents and conduct of newspapers and magazines; the Commission has an independent chairman and 16 members, drawn from the lay public (who are in the majority) and the press. It upholds a 16-point Code of Practice, agreed by a committee of editors representing the newspaper and magazine industry. It aims to ensure that the British press maintains the highest professional standards, having regard to generally established press freedoms; Chair. Sir CHRISTOPHER MEYER; Dir TIM TOULMIN.

NEWS AGENCIES

Press Association Ltd: 292 Vauxhall Bridge Rd, London, SW1V 1AE; tel. (870) 120-3200; fax (870) 120-3201; e-mail info@pa.press.net; internet www.pa.press.net; f. 1868; national news agency of the United Kingdom and Ireland; Exec. Chair PAUL POTTS; Man. Dir TONY WATSON; Editor JONATHAN GRUN.

Thomson Reuters: The Thomson Reuters Bldg, 30 The South Colonnade, Canary Wharf, London, E14 5EP; tel. (20) 7250-1122; fax (20) 7324-5400; e-mail editor@reuters.com; internet uk.reuters.com; f. 2008 by merger of Reuters Group PLC (f. 1851) and Thomson Corpn; world-wide news and information service to media and business clients in 57,900 organizations and media clients in 157 countries; Chair. DAVID THOMSON; CEO TOM GLOCER.

INSTITUTIONS

Chartered Institute of Journalists: 2 Dock Offices, Surrey Quays Rd, London, SE16 2XU; tel. (20) 7252-1187; fax (20) 7232-2302; e-mail memberservices@cioj.co.uk; internet www.cioj.co.uk; f. 1884; Pres. JOHN THORPE; Gen. Sec. DOMINIC COOPER.

The Journalists' Charity (Newspaper Press Fund): Dickens House, 35 Wathen Rd, Dorking, Surrey, RH4 1JY; tel. (1306) 887511; fax (1306) 888212; e-mail enquiries@journalistscharity.org.uk; internet www.journalistscharity.org.uk; f. 1864; charity for journalists and their dependants; Chair. ROBERT WARREN; Dir DAVID ILOTT.

Newspaper Publishers' Association (NPA): St Andrew's House, 8th Floor, 18-20 St Andrew St, London, EC4A 3AY; tel. (20) 7636-7014; fax (20) 7631-5119; f. 1906; comprises 8 national newspaper groups; Chair. TIM BROOKS; Dir DAVID NEWELL.

Newspaper Society (NS): St Andrew's House, 8th Floor, 18-20 St Andrew St, London, EC4A 3AY; tel. (20) 7632-7400; fax (20) 7632-7401; e-mail ns@newspapersoc.org.uk; internet www.newspapersoc.org.uk; f. 1836; represents the regional and local press; Pres. MICHAEL PELOSI; Dir DAVID NEWELL.

Periodical Publishers' Association Ltd: Queen's House, 28 Kingsway, London, WC2B 6JR; tel. (20) 7404-4166; fax (20) 7404-4167; e-mail info1@ppa.co.uk; internet www.ppa.co.uk; f. 1913; trade association for the British magazine industry; Chair. PETER PHIPPEN; Chief Exec. JONATHAN SHEPHARD; more than 350 mems.

Association of Publishing Agencies (APA): Queen's House, 3rd Floor, 55–56 Lincoln's Inn Fields, London, WC2A 3LJ; tel. (20) 7404-4166; fax (20) 7404-4167; e-mail info@apa.co.uk; internet www.apa.co.uk; f. 1993; trade association for the customer publishing industry; Chair. MARTIN MACCONNOL; CEO PATRICK FULLER.

UK Association of Online Publishers (AOP): Queen's House, 55–56 Lincoln's Inn Fields, London, WC2A 3LJ; tel. (20) 7404-4166; fax (20) 7404-4167; e-mail ruth.brownlee@ukaop.org.uk; internet www.ukaop.org.uk; f. 2002; represents the interests of online content providers; Chair. SIMON WALDMAN; Dir RUTH BROWNLEE.

Scottish Daily Newspaper Society: 21 Lansdowne Cres., Edinburgh, EH12 5EH; tel. (131) 535-1064; fax (131) 535-1063; e-mail info@sdns.org.uk; f. 1915; Dir JAMES B. RAEBURN.

Scottish Newspaper Publishers' Association: 48 Palmerston Pl., Edinburgh, EH12 5DE; tel. (131) 220-4353; fax (131) 220-4344; e-mail info@snpa.org.uk; internet www.snpa.org.uk; Dir SIMON M. L. FAIRCLOUGH.

See also under Employers' Organizations and Trade Unions.

Directory

Principal Publishers

Publishing firms in the United Kingdom are mainly located in London and many are members of large publishing groups, notably Random House, Reed Elsevier, the Pearson Group and Thomson Reuters. Fiction remains the largest category. The United Kingdom publishes more new titles every year than any other European country. In 2002 125,390 new titles were issued.

Anova Books Group Ltd: The Old Magistrates Court, 10 Southcombe St, London, W14 0RA; tel. (20) 7605-1400; fax (20) 7605-1401; e-mail info@anovabooks.com; internet www.anovabooks.com; f. 2005; fmrly Chrysalis Books; imprints: Batsford, Collins & Brown, Conway, National Trust Books, Paper Tiger, Pavilion, Portico, Robson, Salamander; Man. Dir POLLY POWELL; Chief Exec. ROBIN WOOD.

Asean Academic Press Ltd: POB 13945, London, E5 0XY; fax (20) 8533-5856; e-mail aapub@attglobal.net; internet www.aseanacademicpress.com; educational, technical, professional and scientific books on Asia.

Ashgate Publishing Ltd: Gower House, Croft Rd, Aldershot, Hants, GU11 3HR; tel. (1252) 331551; fax (1252) 368595; e-mail info@ashgatepublishing.com; internet www.ashgate.com; f. 1967; social sciences and humanities, art, business and public sector management books; imprints: Ashgate, Gower, Lund Humphries, Variorum; Chair. N. FARROW.

Atlantic Books: Ormond House, 26-27 Boswell St, London, WC1N 3JZ; tel. (20) 7269-1610; fax (20) 7430-0916; e-mail enquiries@groveatlantic.co.uk; internet www.atlantic-books.co.uk; f. 2000; subsidiary of Grove/Atlantic, Inc (USA); mem. of Independent Alliance; imprints: Guardian Books, Observer Books, Portobello Press; CEO and Publr TOBY MUNDY.

BBC Worldwide Ltd: Woodlands, 80 Wood Lane, London, W12 0TT; tel. (20) 8433-2000; fax (20) 8749-0538; e-mail bbcworldwide@bbc.co.uk; internet www.bbcworldwide.com; Chief Exec. JOHN SMITH.

Berlitz Publishing Co Ltd: 58 Borough High St, London, SE1 1XF; tel. (20) 7403-0284; fax (20) 7403-0290; e-mail publishing@berlitz.co.uk; internet www.berlitzpublishing.com; f. 1970; travel, languages, reference, leisure, children's books; owned by Apa Publications (Germany); Group Man. Dir JEREMY WESTWOOD.

A. & C. Black Publishers Ltd: 37 Soho Sq., London, W1D 3QZ; tel. (20) 7758-0200; fax (20) 7758-0222; e-mail enquiries@acblack.com; internet www.acblack.com; f. 1807; inc. Adlard Coles Nautical, Christopher Helm, Herbert Press, Pica Press, T & AD Poyser, Thomas Reed, Methuen Drama, Wisden; children's and educational books, music, arts and crafts, drama, reference, sport, theatre, travel, sailing, ornithology; owned by Bloomsbury Publishing PLC; Chair. NIGEL NEWTON; Editorial Dir JANET MURPHY.

Bloomsbury Publishing PLC: 36 Soho Sq., London, W1D 3QY; tel. (20) 7494-2111; fax (20) 7434-0151; e-mail csm@bloomsbury.com; internet www.bloomsbury.com; f. 1986; fiction, non-fiction and children's; Chair. JEREMY WILSON; CEO NIGEL NEWTON.

Bowker (UK) Ltd: 1st Floor, Medway House, Cantelupe Rd, East Grinstead, West Sussex, RH19 3BJ; tel. (1342) 310450; fax (1342) 310486; e-mail sales@bowker.co.uk; internet www.bowker.co.uk; owned by the Cambridge Information Group; business, general reference and bibliographic information; Man. Dir DOUG MCMILLAN.

Marion Boyars Publishers Ltd: 24 Lacy Rd, London, SW15 1NL; tel. (20) 8788-9522; fax (20) 8789-8122; e-mail catheryn@marionboyars.com; internet www.marionboyars.co.uk; f. 1975; fiction, plays, cinema, music, translations, literary criticism, sociology; Man. Dir CATHERYN KILGARRIFF.

Calder Publications Ltd: London House, 243-253 Lower Mortlake Rd, Richmond, Surrey, TW9 2LL; tel. (20) 8948-9550; fax (20) 8948-5599; e-mail info@oneworldclassics.com; internet www.calderpublications.com; f. 1950; acquired by Oneworld Publications in 2007; fiction, plays, music, opera, European classics, translations, general books, social science, politics; Calderbooks, Journal of Beckett Studies, English National Opera guides.

Cambridge University Press: The Edinburgh Bldg, Shaftesbury Rd, Cambridge, CB2 2RU; tel. (1223) 312393; fax (1223) 315052; e-mail information@cambridge.org; internet www.cambridge.org; f. 1534; academic and scientific monographs and textbooks, educational, English language teaching materials, microsoftware, Bibles, prayer books and academic journals; Chief Exec. STEPHEN R. R. BOURNE.

Canongate Books: 14 High St, Edinburgh, EH1 1TE; tel. (131) 557-5111; fax (131) 557-5211; e-mail info@canongate.co.uk; internet www.canongate.net; f. 1973; general, fiction, non-fiction; mem. of Independent Alliance; Chair. JAMIE BYNG.

Jonathan Cape Ltd: Random House, 20 Vauxhall Bridge Rd, London, SW1V 2SA; tel. (20) 7840-8563; fax (20) 7233-6117; e-mail enquiries@randomhouse.co.uk; internet www.randomhouse.co.uk; f. 1921; imprint of The Random House Group Ltd; general,

THE UNITED KINGDOM

biography, travel, belles-lettres, fiction, history, poetry; subsidiary imprint: The Bodley Head (biography, current affairs, humour); Publishing Dir DAN FRANKLIN.

Carlton Books: 20 Mortimer St, London W1T 3JW; tel. (20) 7612-0400; fax (20) 7612-0401; e-mail sales@carltonbooks.co.uk; internet www.carltonbooks.co.uk; f. 1992; Man. Dir JONATHAN GOODMAN.

Century: Random House, 20 Vauxhall Bridge Rd, London, SW1V 2SA; tel. (20) 7840-8554; fax (20) 7233-6127; e-mail enquiries@randomhouse.co.uk; internet www.randomhouse.co.uk; f. 1987; imprint of The Random House Group Ltd; general, biography, travel, current affairs, fiction, memoirs, music, philosophy; Man. Dir RICHARD CABLE.

Chatto and Windus: 20 Vauxhall Bridge Rd, London, SW1V 2SA; tel. (20) 7840-8540; fax (20) 7233-6117; internet www.randomhouse.co.uk; imprint of The Random House Group Ltd; general, academic, biography, memoirs, politics, history, literary criticism, current affairs, cultural studies and fiction; imprint: Hogarth Press; Dir ALISON SAMUEL.

Church House Publishing: Church House, Great Smith St, London, SW1P 3AZ; tel. (20) 7898-1451; fax (20) 7898-1449; e-mail publishing@c-of-e.org.uk; internet www.chpublishing.co.uk; Publ. Man. Dr THOMAS ALLAIN-CHAPMAN.

James Clarke and Co Ltd: POB 60, Cambridge, CB1 2NT; tel. (1223) 350865; fax (1223) 366951; e-mail publishing@jamesclarke.co.uk; internet www.jamesclarke.co.uk; f. 1859; academic and reference, history, philosophy, religion, theology; imprints: Acorn Editions, Lutterworth Press, Patrick Hardy Books; acquired James Nisbet & Co in 2008; Man. Dir ADRIAN BRINK.

CMP Information (CMPi): Riverbank House, Angel Lane, Tonbridge, Kent, TN9 1SE; tel. (1732) 364422; internet www.cmpi.biz; magazines and information services; CEO GARY HUGHES.

Collins Bartholomew: Westerhill Rd, Bishopbriggs, Glasgow, G64 2QT; tel. (141) 306-3752; fax (141) 306-3130; e-mail collinsbartholomew@harpercollins.co.uk; internet www.bartholomewmaps.com; f. 1826; cartographic division of HarperCollins Publishers; maps, atlases, bespoke mapping services and data; Exec. Dir SHEENA BARCLAY.

Conran Octopus: 2–4 Heron Quays, London, E14 4JP; tel. (20) 7531-8400; fax (20) 7531-8627; e-mail info@octopus-publishing.co.uk; internet www.octopusbooks.co.uk; illustrated reference books; imprint of Octopus Publishing Group Ltd; Publr LORRAINE DICKEY.

Constable and Robinson Ltd: 3 The Lanchesters, 162 Fulham Palace Rd, London, W6 9ER; tel. (20) 8741-3663; fax (20) 8748-7562; e-mail enquiries@constablerobinson.com; internet www.constablerobinson.com; biography and autobiography, general and military history, current affairs, psychology and self-help, health, popular science, and crime fiction; Man. Dir NICHOLAS ROBINSON.

Continuum International Publishing Group: The Tower Bldg, 11 York Rd, London, SE1 7NX; tel. (20) 7922-0880; fax (20) 7922-0881; e-mail rbairdsmith@continuumbooks.com; internet www.continuumbooks.com; f. 1994; popular culture, religion, humanities, social sciences, philosophy and education; imprints: Burns & Oates, Continuum, T&T Clark, Thoemmes Continuum, Hambledon Continuum and Network Continuum; Chair. PATRICK AUSTEN; CEO OLIVER GADSBY.

James Currey Publishers: 73 Botley Rd, Oxford, OX2 0BS; tel. (1865) 244111; fax (1865) 246454; e-mail editorial@jamescurrey.co.uk; internet www.jamescurrey.co.uk; African and world anthropology; Chair. JAMES CURREY; Man. Dir DOUGLAS H. JOHNSON.

Darton, Longman and Todd Ltd: 1 Spencer Court, 140–142 Wandsworth High St, London, SW18 4JJ; tel. (20) 8875-0155; fax (20) 8875-0133; e-mail info@darton-longman-todd.co.uk; internet www.darton-longman-todd.co.uk; f. 1959; theology, spirituality, religious biography and history, Bibles; Editorial Dir BRENDAN WALSH.

David & Charles Ltd: Brunel House, Forde Close, Newton Abbot, Devon, TQ12 4PU; tel. (870) 990-8222; fax (870) 442-2034; e-mail postmaster@davidandcharles.co.uk; internet www.davidandcharles.co.uk; f. 1960; owned by F+W Publications, Inc. (USA); general, trade and reference; Group Chair. and CEO DAVID NUSSBAUM.

André Deutsch Ltd: 20 Mortimer St, London, W1T 3JW; tel. (20) 7612-0400; fax (20) 7612-0401; e-mail enquiries@carltonbooks.co.uk; internet www.carltonbooks.co.uk; f. 1950; biography, memoirs, humour, art, politics, history, travel, sport; imprint of Carlton Books.

Dorling Kindersley PLC: 80 Strand, London, WC2R ORL; tel. (20) 7010-3000; fax (20) 7010-6060; internet www.dorlingkindersley-uk.co.uk; f. 1974; holding co Pearson PLC; illustrated reference books; CEO GARY JUNE.

Gerald Duckworth and Co Ltd: 1st Floor, East Wing, Greenhill House, 90–93 Cowcross St, London, EC1M 6BF; tel. (20) 7490-7300; fax (20) 7490-0080; e-mail info@duckworth-publishers.co.uk; internet www.ducknet.co.uk; f. 1898; trade, academic; Propr PETER MAYER.

Edinburgh University Press: 22 George Sq., Edinburgh, EH8 9LF; tel. (131) 650-4218; fax (131) 662-0053; e-mail timothy.wright@eup.ed.ac.uk; internet www.euppublishing.com; learned books and journals; Chair. IVON ASQUITH; Chief Exec. TIMOTHY WRIGHT.

Edward Elgar Publishing Ltd: The Lypiatts, 15 Lansdown Rd, Cheltenham, GL50 2JA; tel. (1242) 226934; fax (1242) 262111; e-mail info@e-elgar.co.uk; internet www.e-elgar.com; f. 1986; economics, law, business and management, public and social policy; Man. Dir E. ELGAR.

Elsevier Ltd: The Boulevard, Langford Lane, Kidlington, Oxford, OX5 1GB; tel. (1865) 843000; fax (1865) 843010; internet www.elsevier.com; f. 1958; academic and professional reference books; imprints: Academic Press, Architectural Press, Bailliere Tindall, Butterworth-Heinemann, Churchill Livingstone, Digital Press, Elsevier, Elsevier Advanced Technology, Focal Press, Gulf Professional, Made Simple Books, Morgan Kaufmann, Mosby, Newnes, North-Holland, Pergamon, Saunders; part of Reed Elsevier Group PLC; Man. Dir ANNA MOON.

Encyclopaedia Britannica UK Ltd: 2nd Floor, Unity Wharf, 13 Mill St, London, SE1 2BH; tel. (20) 7500-7800; fax (20) 7500-7878; e-mail enquiries@britannica.co.uk; internet www.britannica.co.uk; f. 1768; publs Encyclopaedia Britannica, Britannica Book of the Year, Great Books of the Western World, Britannica Learning Library, Britannica Almanac; Man. Dir IAN GRANT.

Euromonitor International: 60–61 Britton St, London, EC1M 5UX; tel. (20) 7251-8024; fax (20) 7608-3149; e-mail info@euromonitor.com; internet www.euromonitor.com; f. 1972; business and commercial reference; Chair. R. N. SENIOR; Man. Dir T. J. FENWICK.

Evans Publishing Group: 2A Portman Mansions, Chiltern St, London, W1U 6NR; tel. (20) 7487-0920; fax (20) 7487-0921; e-mail sales@evansbrothers.co.uk; internet www.evansbooks.co.uk; f. 1906; educational, children's, general and overseas books; Man. Dir S. T. PAWLEY; Publr SU SWALLOW.

Everyman's Library: Northburgh House, 10 Northburgh St, London, EC1V 0AT; tel. (20) 7566-6350; fax (20) 7490-3708; e-mail books@everyman.uk.com; internet www.randomhouse.co.uk/knopf/classics; f. 1906; publ. in United Kingdom by The Random House Group Ltd.

Faber and Faber Ltd: 3 Queen Sq., London, WC1N 3AU; tel. (20) 7465-0045; fax (20) 7465-0034; internet www.faber.co.uk; f. 1929; biography, autobiography, children's, film, drama, popular science, economics, fiction, history, music, poetry; mem. of Independent Alliance; Man. Dir STEPHEN PAGE.

The Folio Society Ltd: 44 Eagle St, London, WC1R 4FS; tel. (20) 7400-4200; fax (20) 7400-4242; internet www.foliosociety.com; f. 1947; fine illustrated editions of children's, fiction, food, gardening, history, biographies, poetry and travel books; Publishing Dir DAVID HAYDEN.

Footprint Handbooks Ltd: 6 Riverside Court, Lower Bristol Rd, Bath, BA2 3DZ; tel. (1225) 469141; fax (1225) 469461; e-mail discover@footprintbooks.com; internet www.footprintbooks.com; Dirs ANDY RIDDLE, PATRICK DAWSON.

W. Foulsham & Co Ltd: The Publishing House, Bennetts Close, Slough, Berks, SL1 5AP; tel. (1753) 526769; fax (1753) 535003; e-mail reception@foulsham.com; internet www.foulsham.com; f. 1819; finance, reference; Man. Dir BARRY BELASCO.

Fourth Estate: 77–85 Fulham Palace Rd, London, W6 8JB; tel. (20) 8741-4414; fax (20) 8307-4466; e-mail general@4thestate.co.uk; internet www.4thestate.co.uk; f. 1984; literature, humour, general reference, current affairs, literary and commercial fiction, cookery; imprint of HarperCollins Publishers; Pub. Dir NICHOLAS PEARSON.

Samuel French Ltd: 52 Fitzroy St, London, W1T 5JR; tel. (20) 7387-9373; fax (20) 7387-2161; e-mail theatre@samuelfrench-london.co.uk; internet www.samuelfrench-london.co.uk; f. 1830; drama; Chair. LEON F. EMBRY; Man. Dir VIVIEN GOODWIN.

Granta Books: 12 Addison Ave, London, W11 4QR; tel. (20) 7605-1360; fax (20) 7605-1361; e-mail publicity@granta.com; internet www.granta.com; fiction, political non-fiction; mem. of Independent Alliance; Editorial Dir GEORGE MILLER.

Gresham Books Ltd: 46 Victoria Rd, Summertown, Oxford OX2 7QD; tel. (1865) 513582; fax (1865) 512718; e-mail info@gresham-books.co.uk; internet www.gresham-books.co.uk; f. 1978; hymn books, school histories, music folders; Chief Exec. P. A. LEWIS.

Guinness World Records Ltd: 184-192 Drummond St, 3rd Floor, London, NW1 3HP; tel. (20) 7891-4567; fax (20) 7891-4501; internet www.guinnessworldrecords.com; f. 1954; acquired by Jim Pattison Group in 2008; music and general interest; Man. Dir ALISTAIR RICHARDS.

Hachette UK: 338 Euston Rd, London, NW1 3BH; tel. (20) 7873-6000; fax (20) 7873-6124; internet www.hachette.co.uk; f. 1993 as Hodder Headline; acquired by Hachette Livre (France) in 2004; present name adopted 2008; divisions: Hodder Education, John

Murray Ltd, Headline Publishing Group, Hodder and Stoughton Ltd, Hachette Children's Books, Orion, Octopus Publishing Group, Little, Brown Book Group, Chambers Harrap; Group Chief Exec. TIM HELY HUTCHINSON.

Robert Hale Ltd: Clerkenwell House, 45–47 Clerkenwell Green, London, EC1R 0HT; tel. (20) 7251-2661; fax (20) 7490-4958; e-mail enquire@halebooks.com; internet www.halebooks.com; f. 1936; memoirs, biography, travel, sport, fiction, belles-lettres, general non-fiction; Man. Dir JOHN HALE.

Hamlyn: 2–4 Heron Quays, London, E14 4JP; tel. (20) 7531-8400; fax (20) 7531-8650; e-mail info-ho@hamlyn.co.uk; internet www.hamlyn.co.uk; imprint of Octopus Publishing Group Ltd; cookery, DIY, gardening, sports, health, animals; Publishing Dir JANE BIRCH.

Harlequin Mills and Boon Ltd: Eton House, 18–24 Paradise Rd, Richmond, Surrey, TW9 1SR; tel. (20) 8288-2800; fax (20) 8288-2899; internet www.millsandboon.co.uk; f. 1908; romantic fiction; Man. Dir GUY HALLOWES.

HarperCollins Publishers Ltd: 77–85 Fulham Palace Rd, London, W6 8JB; tel. (20) 8307-4000; fax (20) 8307-4440; e-mail contact@harpercollins.co.uk; internet www.harpercollins.co.uk; f. 1819; owned by News International; fiction and non-fiction of all classes, including biographies, history, travel, nature, sport, art, children's, classics, atlases, reference, religion; imprints: Armada, Bartholomew, Collins, Collins Bibles, Collins Cartographic, Collins Classics, Collins Crime, Collins English Dictionaries, Collins Liturgical, Flamingo, Fontana, HarperCollins, HarperCollins Audio, HarperCollins Paperbacks, HarperCollins Science Fiction and Fantasy, Jets, Lions, Marshall Pickering, Nicholson, Times Books, Tolkien, Tracks, Young Lions; CEO and Publr VICTORIA BARNSLEY.

Harvill Secker: The Random House Group Ltd, 20 Vauxhall Bridge Rd, London, SW1V 2SA; tel. (20) 7840-8540; fax (20) 7233-6117; e-mail enquiries@randomhouse.co.uk; internet www.randomhouse.co.uk/harvillsecker; fiction, non-fiction, illustrated books; imprint of The Random House Group Ltd.

Haynes Publishing: Sparkford, Yeovil, Somerset, BA22 7JJ; tel. (1963) 440635; fax (1963) 440001; e-mail sales@haynes.co.uk; internet www.haynes.co.uk; f. 1960; transport, manuals etc.; Chair. J. H. HAYNES; CEO E. OAKLEY.

Headline Publishing Group: 338 Euston Rd, London, NW1 3BH; tel. (20) 7873-6000; fax (20) 7873-6124; e-mail headline.books@headline.co.uk; internet www.headline.co.uk; f. 1986; division of Hachette UK; fiction, autobiography, biography, food and wine, gardening, popular science, sport and TV tie-ins; Man. Dir MARTIN NEILD; CEO KATE WILSON.

Heinemann: Halley Court, Jordan Hill, Oxford, OX2 8EJ; tel. (1865) 311366; fax (1865) 310043; e-mail enquiries@pearson.com; internet www.heinemann.co.uk; imprint of Pearson Education; educational textbooks for UK and abroad; Man. Dir JOHN FALLON.

William Heinemann: Random House, 20 Vauxhall Bridge Rd, London, SW1V 2SA; tel. (20) 7840-8548; fax (20) 7233-6127; e-mail enquiries@randomhouse.co.uk; internet www.randomhouse.co.uk; arts, biography, fiction, history, science, travel; imprint of The Random House Group Ltd.

Hodder Education: 338 Euston Rd, London, NW1 3BH; tel. (20) 7873-6000; fax (20) 7873-6299; e-mail educationenquiries@hodder.co.uk; internet www.hoddereducation.co.uk; f. 1906; imprints: Hodder Arnold, Hodder Gibson, Hodder Murray and Teach Yourself; division of Hachette UK; Chief Exec. PHILIP WALTERS.

Hodder and Stoughton: 338 Euston Rd, London, NW1 3BH; tel. (20) 7873-6000; fax (20) 7873-6024; internet www.hodder.co.uk; f. 1868; division of Hachette UK; imprints: Mobius, Sceptre; general, biography, travel, fiction, current affairs; Man. Dir JAMIE HODDER-WILLIAMS.

Icon Books Ltd: Omnibus Business Centre, 39–41 North Rd, London, N7 9DP; tel. (20) 7697-9695; fax (1763) 208080; e-mail info@iconbooks.co.uk; internet www.iconbooks.co.uk; f. 1991; non-fiction; mem. of Independent Alliance; Man. Dir SIMON FLYNN.

Informa PLC: Mortimer House, 30–32 Mortimer St, London, W1W 7RE; tel. (20) 7017-5000; internet www.informa.com; journals and books; commercial, professional, academic and scientific, reference; Chair. DEREK MAPP; Chief Exec. PETER RIGBY.

IOP Publishing: Dirac House, Temple Back, Bristol, BS1 6BE; tel. (117) 929-7481; fax (117) 929-4318; e-mail info@iop.org; internet publishing.iop.org; f. 1874; scientific and technical publishers; Man. Dir J. R. COWHIG.

Jane's Information Group Ltd: Sentinel House, 163 Brighton Rd, Coulsdon, Surrey, CR5 2YH; tel. (20) 8700-3700; fax (20) 8763-1006; e-mail info.uk@janes.com; internet www.janes.com; owned by IHS, Inc (USA); intelligence and analysis on national and international defence, security and risk developments; Pres. and COO SCOTT KEY.

Jordan Publishing Ltd: 21 St Thomas St, Bristol, BS1 6JS; tel. (117) 923-0600; fax (117) 923-0486; e-mail achim.bosse@jordanpublishing.co.uk; internet www.jordanpublishing.co.uk; f. 1863; practical law books covering family law, litigation, company, property and private client law; Man. Dir CAROLINE VANDRIDGE-AMES.

Michael Joseph Ltd: 80 Strand, London, WC2R 0RL; tel. (20) 7010-3000; fax (20) 7010-6060; internet www.penguin.co.uk; f. 1936; general, fiction, non-fiction; division of Penguin; Publishing Dir LOUISE MOORE.

Richard Joseph Publishers Ltd: POB 15, Torrington, EX38 8ZJ; tel. (1805) 625750; fax (1805) 625376; e-mail info@sheppardsworld.co.uk; internet www.sheppardsworld.co.uk; f. 1990; reference and directories; publishes the weekly journal *Sheppard's Confidential*; Man. Dir RICHARD JOSEPH.

Kenyon-Deane: 10 Station Rd, Industrial Estate, Malvern, Worcs., WR13 6RN; tel. and fax (1684) 540154; e-mail simon@cressrelles.co.uk; internet www.cressrelles.co.uk; f. 1971; owned by Cressrelles Publishing Company Ltd; incorporates Kenyon House Press, H. F. W. Deane Ltd; plays and drama textbooks, specialists in all-women plays and plays for young people; Man. Dir LESLIE SMITH.

Kingfisher Publications PLC: New Penderel House, 283–288 High Holborn, London, WC1V 7HZ; tel. (20) 7903-9999; fax (20) 7242-4979; e-mail sales@kingfisherpub.com; internet www.kingfisherpub.com; children's books; imprints: Kingfisher; owned by Pan Macmillan Ltd; Man. Dir JOHN PICKETT.

Kogan Page Ltd: 120 Pentonville Rd, London, N1 9JN; tel. (20) 7278-0433; fax (20) 7837-6348; e-mail kpinfo@kogan-page.co.uk; internet www.kogan-page.co.uk; f. 1967; business, management, accountancy, textbooks, transport, careers, personal development, training, marketing, consumer, reference; Man. Dir HELEN KOGAN.

Lawrence and Wishart Ltd: 99A Wallis Rd, London, E9 5LN; tel. (20) 8533-2506; fax (20) 8533-7369; e-mail info@lwbooks.co.uk; internet www.lwbooks.co.uk; f. 1936; politics, history, feminism, race, economics, Marxist theory, cultural studies; Man. Editor SALLY DAVISON.

Letts Educational: 4 Grosvenor Pl., London, SW1X 7DL; tel. (20) 7096-2900; fax (20) 7096-2945; e-mail orders@lettsandlonsdale.co.uk; internet www.lettsandlonsdale.com; children's, educational, textbooks; Man. Dir ANDREW WARE.

LexisNexis Butterworths: Halsbury House, 35 Chancery Lane, London, WC2A 1EL; tel. (20) 7400-2500; fax (20) 7400-2842; internet www.lexisnexis.co.uk; f. 1818; part of Reed Elsevier PLC; law, tax, accountancy, banking books and journals; Group Man. Dir JOSH BOTTOMLEY.

Frances Lincoln: 4 Torriano Mews, Torriano Ave, London, NW5 2RZ; tel. (20) 7284-4009; fax (20) 7485-0490; e-mail reception@frances-lincoln.com; internet www.franceslincoln.com; f. 1977; illustrated non-fiction, children's fiction and non-fiction; Man. Dir JOHN NICOLL.

Little, Brown Book Group UK: 100 Victoria Embankment, London, EC4Y 0DY; tel. (20) 7911-8000; fax (20) 7911-8100; e-mail info@littlebrown.co.uk; internet www.littlebrown.co.uk; imprints: Abacus, Virago, Sphere, Orbit, Little Brown, Piatikus; division of Hachette UK; CEO and Publr URSULA MACKENZIE.

Liverpool University Press: 4 Cambridge St, Liverpool, L69 7ZU; tel. (151) 794-2233; fax (151) 794-2235; e-mail lup@liv.ac.uk; internet www.liverpool-unipress.co.uk; f. 1899; European and American literature, social, political, economic and ancient history, planning, hispanic studies, population studies, architecture, art, art history, cultural studies, science fiction criticism series; Dir ROBIN BLOXSIDGE.

Lonely Planet Publications: 2nd Floor, 186 City Rd, London, EC1V 2NT; tel. (20) 7106-2100; fax (20) 7106-2101; internet www.lonelyplanet.com; f. 1973; travel, languages; 75% share acquired by BBC Worldwide in 2007; Publr STEPHEN PALMER.

Lund Humphries: Wey Court East, Union Rd, Farnham, Surrey, GU9 7PT; tel. (1252) 331551; fax (1252) 344405; e-mail info@lundhumphries.com; internet www.lundhumphries.com; f. 1969; arts, graphic arts, design, architecture, photography, scholarly, Arabic language; Dir NIGEL FARROW.

McGraw-Hill Education: McGraw-Hill House, Shoppenhangers Rd, Maidenhead, Berks., SL6 2QL; tel. (1628) 502500; fax (1628) 770224; internet www.mcgraw-hill.co.uk; technical, scientific, computer studies, professional reference, general and medical books; Pres. HENRY HIRCHBERG.

Macmillan Education Ltd: Between Towns Rd, Oxford, OX4 3PP; tel. (1865) 405700; fax (1865) 405701; e-mail elt@macmillan.com; internet www.macmillaneducation.com; a division of Macmillan Publishers Ltd; English Language Teaching and educational books; Chair. CHRISTOPHER PATERSON; Man. Dir CHRIS HARRISON.

Manchester University Press: Oxford Rd, Manchester, M13 9NR; tel. (161) 275-2310; fax (161) 274-3346; e-mail d.rodgers@manchester.ac.uk; internet www.manchesteruniversitypress.co.uk; f. 1904; all branches of higher education, arts, science and social sciences; Chief Exec. DAVID RODGERS.

THE UNITED KINGDOM   *Directory*

Methuen Publishing Ltd: 8 Artillery Row, London, SW1P 1RZ; tel. (20) 7802-0018; fax (20) 7828-1244; e-mail info@methuen.co.uk; internet www.methuen.co.uk; f. 1889; literature, fiction, non-fiction, biography, sport, theatre, drama, humour, music; imprint: Politico's Publishing; Man. Dir PETER TUMMONS.

Mitchell Beazley: 2–4 Heron Quays, London, E14 4JP; tel. (20) 7531-8400; fax (20) 7531-8650; e-mail info@mitchell-beazley.co.uk; internet www.mitchell-beazley.co.uk; f. 1969; imprint of Octopus Publishing Group Ltd; Miller's antiques, arts and design, interiors and style, gardening, reference, wine and food; Publr DAVID LAMB.

John Murray Publishers: 338 Euston Rd, London, NW1 3BH; tel. (20) 7873-6000; fax (20) 7873-6446; internet www.hachette.co.uk; f. 1768; division of Hachette UK; biography, autobiography, memoir, history, travel, fiction, current affairs; Man. Dir ROLAND PHILIPPS.

Nelson Thornes Ltd: Delta Pl., 27 Bath Rd, Cheltenham, GL53 7TH; tel. (1242) 267100; fax (1242) 221914; e-mail cservices@nelsonthornes.com; internet www.nelsonthornes.com; educational; Man. Dir FRED GRAINGER.

Novello and Co Ltd: 14–15 Berners St, London, W1T 3LJ; tel. (20) 7612-7400; fax (20) 7612-7545; e-mail promotion@musicsales.co.uk; internet www.chesternovello.com; music; Man. Dir JAMES RUSHTON.

Octopus Publishing Group Ltd: 2–4 Heron Quays, London, E14 4JP; tel. (20) 7531-8400; fax (20) 7531-8650; e-mail info@octopus-publishing.co.uk; internet www.octopus-publishing.co.uk; division of Hachette UK; imprints: Bounty, Cassel Illustrated, Conran Octopus, Gaia Books, Godsfield Press, Hamlyn, Miller's, Mitchell Beazley, Philip's, Spruce; Chief Exec. ALISON GOFF.

Open University Press, McGraw-Hill Education: Shoppenhangers Rd, Maidenhead, SL6 2QL; tel. (1628) 502500; fax (1628) 770224; e-mail enquiries@openup.co.uk; internet www.openup.co.uk; academic, study skills, politics, sociology, psychology, education, higher education, media, film and cultural studies, health and social welfare, counselling and psychotherapy, management and public policy; Man. Dir SHONA MULLEN.

Orion Publishing Group: Orion House, 5 Upper St Martin's Lane, London, WC2H 9EA; tel. (20) 7240-3444; fax (20) 7240-4822; e-mail info@orionbooks.co.uk; internet www.orionbooks.co.uk; f. 1991; division of Hachette UK; imprints: Gollancz, Orion, Orion Children's, Phoenix, Weidenfeld & Nicolson; CEO PETER ROCHE.

Peter Owen Publishers: 73 Kenway Rd, London, SW5 0RE; tel. (20) 7373-5628; fax (20) 7373-6760; e-mail admin@peterowen.com; internet www.peterowen.com; f. 1951; general publishers of fiction, autobiography, biography, translations, history, the arts, etc.; Man. Dir PETER OWEN; Editorial Dir ANTONIA OWEN.

Oxford University Press: Gt Clarendon St, Oxford, OX2 6DP; tel. (1865) 556767; fax (1865) 556646; e-mail webenquiry.uk@oup.com; internet www.oup.com; f. c. 1478; Bibles, prayer books, the *Oxford English Dictionary*, the *Oxford Dictionary of National Biography* and many other dictionaries and books of reference, learned and general works from the humanities to the sciences, educational, electronic, music and children's books and audio-visual and English language teaching material; Sec. to the Delegates of the Press and Chief Exec. Dr HENRY REECE.

Palgrave Macmillan Ltd: Houndmills, Basingstoke, Hants., RG21 6XS; tel. (1256) 329242; fax (1256) 479476; e-mail palgrave@palgrave.com; internet www.palgrave.com; academic, professional, textbooks and journals; Man. Dir D. J. G. KNIGHT.

Pan Macmillan Ltd: 20 New Wharf Rd, London, N1 9RR; tel. (20) 7014-6000; fax (20) 7014-6001; e-mail books@macmillan.co.uk; internet www.panmacmillan.com; fiction and non-fiction, children's, general reference; imprints: Macmillan, Pan, Picador, Sidgwick & Jackson, Boxtree, Tor, Macmillan Children's Books, Campbell Books, Young Picador, Rodale; Chief Exec. RICHARD CHARKIN.

Pearson Education Ltd: Edinburgh Gate, Harlow, Essex, CM20 2JE; tel. (1279) 623623; fax (1279) 431059; e-mail enquiries@pearson.com; internet www.pearsoned.co.uk; Propr Pearson PLC; acquired Harcourt Education International in 2007; imprints include: Ginn, Heinemann, Longman, Payne-Gallway, Prentice Hall, Raintree, Rigby and Scott Prentice; CEO JOHN FALLON.

Pearson Publishing Group: Pearson Publishing Group, Chesterton Mill, French's Rd, Cambridge, CB4 3NP; tel. (1223) 350555; fax (1223) 356484; e-mail info@pearson.co.uk; internet www.pearson.co.uk; f. 1991; Chair. GEORGE PEARSON.

Penguin Books Ltd: 80 The Strand, London, WC2R 0RL; tel. (20) 7010-3000; fax (20) 7416-3099; e-mail editor@penguin.co.uk; internet www.penguin.co.uk; f. 1936; holding co Pearson PLC; paperback imprints: Penguin and Puffin; reprints and original works of fiction and non-fiction including travel, biography, science and social studies, reference books, handbooks, plays, poetry, classics and children's books; Penguin Group UK is made up of Penguin Press (Allen Lane, Reference, Penguin Classics and Penguin Modern Classics), Penguin General (imprints: Penguin, Hamish Hamilton, Michael Joseph, Viking, Fig Tree) and the children's division (imprints: Puffin, Ladybird, Warne); Chair. and Chief Exec. JOHN MAKINSON; CEO (UK) PETER FIELD.

Phaidon Press Ltd: Regent's Wharf, All Saints St, London, N1 9PA; tel. (20) 7843-1000; fax (20) 7843-1010; e-mail enquiries@phaidon.com; internet www.phaidon.com; art, architecture, children's, contemporary culture, cookery, design, decorative arts, fashion, photography and music, film, fine art; Chair. RICHARD SCHLAGMAN.

Philip's: 2–4 Heron Quays, London, E14 4JP; tel. (20) 7644-6940; fax (20) 7644-8464; e-mail philips@philips-maps.co.uk; internet www.philips-maps.co.uk; imprint of Octopus Publishing Group Ltd; maps, atlases, astronomy, encyclopaedias; Man. Dir JOHN GAISFORD.

Pluto Press: 345 Archway Rd, London, N6 5AA; tel. (20) 8348-2724; fax (20) 8348-9133; e-mail beech@plutobooks.com; internet www.plutobooks.com; academic, scholarly, current affairs and reference; Man. Dir ROGER VAN ZWANENBERG; Editorial Dir ANNE BEECH.

Profile Books Ltd: 3A Exmouth House, Pine St, Exmouth Market, London, EC1R 0JH; tel. (20) 7841-6300; fax (20) 7833-3969; e-mail info@profilebooks.co.uk; internet www.profilebooks.com; f. 1996; fiction, non-fiction; imprints: Economist Books, GreenProfile, Profile Business, Serpent's Tail; mem. of Independent Alliance; Man. Dir ANDREW FRANKLIN.

Proquest Information and Learning: The Quorum, Barnwell Rd, Cambridge, CB5 8SW; tel. (1223) 215512; fax (1223) 215514; e-mail marketing@proquest.co.uk; internet www.proquest.co.uk; f. 1973 as Chadwyck-Healey Ltd; changed name as above in 2001; academic; Chair. ALAN ALDWORTH; Gen. Man. STEVEN HALL.

Quercus Publishing PLC: 21 Bloomsbury Sq., London, WC1A 2NS; tel. (20) 7291-7200; e-mail publicity@quercusbooks.co.uk; internet www.quercusbooks.co.uk; f. 2004; fiction, non-fiction; mem. of Independent Alliance; CEO MARK EVANS.

The Random House Group Ltd: Random House, 20 Vauxhall Bridge Rd, London, SW1V 2SA; tel. (20) 7840-8400; fax (20) 7233-6115; e-mail enquiries@randomhouse.co.uk; internet www.randomhouse.co.uk; imprints: Arrow, Jonathan Cape, Cedar, Century, Chatto & Windus, Ebury Press, Everyman, Harvill Secker, William Heinemann, Hutchinson, Mainstream, Pimlico, Random House Children's Books, Rider, Vermilion, Vintage, Yellow Jersey; Chair. and CEO GAIL REBUCK.

Reader's Digest Association Ltd: 11 Westferry Circus, Canary Wharf, London, E14 4HE; tel. (20) 7715-8000; fax (20) 7715-8181; internet www.readersdigest.co.uk; various non-fiction, condensed and series fiction; Chair THOMAS RYDER; Man. Dir ANDREW LYNAM-SMITH.

Reed Business Information: Quadrant House, The Quadrant, Sutton, Surrey, SM2 5AS; tel. (20) 8652-3500; fax (20) 8652-8932; e-mail information@reedinfo.co.uk; internet www.reedbusiness.co.uk; f. 1866; business directories and online services; CEO KEITH JONES.

Reed Elsevier Group PLC: 1–3 Strand, London, WC2N 5JR; tel. (20) 7930-7077; fax (20) 7166-5799; internet www.reedelsevier.com; f. 1992; books, journals, magazines and electronic resources; divisions: science and medical, education, legal and business; Chair. JAN HOMMEN; Chief Exec. IAN SMITH.

Routledge: 2 Park Sq., Milton Park, Abingdon, Oxfordshire, OX14 4RN; tel. (20) 7017-6000; fax (20) 7017-6699; e-mail webmaster.books@tandf.co.uk; internet www.routledge.com; f. 1988; imprint of Taylor and Francis Group; professional, academic, reference; Man. Dir JEREMY NORTH.

SAGE Publications Ltd: 1 Oliver's Yard, 55 City Rd, London, EC1Y 1SP; tel. (20) 7324-8500; fax (20) 7324-8600; e-mail info@sagepub.co.uk; internet www.sagepub.co.uk; f. 1971; academic and professional social sciences, sciences and humanities; imprint: Sage Education; Man Dir STEPHEN BARR.

Schofield and Sims Ltd: Dogley Mill, Penistone Rd, Fenay Bridge, Huddersfield, West Yorks., HD8 0NQ; tel. (1484) 607080; fax (1484) 606815; e-mail post@schofieldandsims.co.uk; internet www.schofieldandsims.co.uk; f. 1901; educational; Chair. NICK PLATTS.

Scholastic Ltd: Villiers House, Clarendon Ave, Leamington Spa, Warwickshire, CV32 5PR; tel. (1926) 887799; fax (1926) 883331; internet www.scholastic.co.uk; f. 1964; direct marketing, educational and children's books; Group Man. Dir ALAN HURCOMBE (acting).

SCM-Canterbury Press Ltd: St Mary's Works, St Mary's Plain, Norwich, NR3 3BH; tel. (1603) 612914; fax (1603) 624483; e-mail admin@scm-canterburypress.co.uk; internet www.scm-canterburypress.co.uk; f. 1929; religious, theological; Group CEO ANDREW MOORE.

Scripture Union: 207–209 Queensway, Bletchley, Milton Keynes, Bucks, MK2 2EB; tel. (1908) 856000; fax (1908) 856111; e-mail info@scriptureunion.org.uk; internet www.scriptureunion.org.uk; f. 1867; Christian education and Bible reading guides; Chief Exec. KEITH CIVVAL.

THE UNITED KINGDOM

Short Books: 3A Exmouth House, Pine St, London, EC1R 0JH; tel. (20) 7833-9429; e-mail info@shortbooks.co.uk; internet www.shortbooks.co.uk; f. 2001; biography, fiction, non-fiction; mem. of Independent Alliance; Man. Dirs REBECCA NICOLSON, AUREA CARPENTER.

Simon and Schuster: Africa House, 64–78 Kingsway, London, WC2B 6AH; tel. (20) 7316-1900; fax (20) 7316-0331; e-mail enquiries@simonandschuster.co.uk; internet www.simonsays.co.uk; f. 1986; owned by CBS Corpn (USA); fiction, non-fiction, music, travel; imprints: Pocket Books, Touchstone, Scribner, Free Press; Man. Dir IAN S. CHAPMAN.

Society for Promoting Christian Knowledge: 36 Causton St, London, SW1P 4ST; tel. (20) 7592-3900; fax (20) 7592-3939; e-mail spck@spck.org.uk; internet www.spck.org.uk; f. 1698; religious; imprints: SPCK, Azure, Sheldon Press; Publishing Dir JOANNA MORIARTY.

Souvenir Press Ltd: 43 Great Russell St, London, WC1B 3PD; tel. (20) 7580-9307; fax (20) 7580-5064; e-mail souvenirpress@ukonline.co.uk; general; Man. Dir ERNEST HECHT.

The Stationery Office: St Crispins, Duke St, Norwich, NR3 1PD; tel. (1603) 622211; e-mail book.enquiries@tso.co.uk; internet www.tso.co.uk; f. 1786 as His Majesty's Stationery Office (govt publishing house); privatized in 1996; acquired by Williams Lea in 2007; business and publishing services; publishes *Hansard*, *Highway Code*, *British Pharmacopoeia*; Chief Exec. RICHARD DELL.

Sweet and Maxwell Ltd: 100 Avenue Rd, London, NW3 3PF; tel. (20) 7393-7000; fax (20) 7393-7010; e-mail customer.services@sweetandmaxwell.co.uk; internet www.sweetandmaxwell.co.uk; f. 1799; imprints: Stevens and Sons Ltd, W. Green, Round Hall, ESC Publishing, the European Law Centre; holding co Thomson Reuters; law books; Man. Dir PETER LAKE.

Taylor and Francis Group Ltd: 2 Park Sq., Milton Park, Abingdon, Oxfordshire, OX14 4RN; tel. (20) 7017-6000; fax (20) 7017-6699; e-mail info@tandf.co.uk; internet www.taylorandfrancisgroup.com; division of Informa PLC; imprints: Taylor and Francis, Routledge, Garland Science, CRC Press and Psychology Press; professional, academic, scientific, technical, reference; books and journals; Chief Exec. ROGER HORTON.

Thames and Hudson Ltd: 181A High Holborn, London, WC1V 7QX; tel. (20) 7845-5000; fax (20) 7845-5050; e-mail sales@thameshudson.co.uk; internet www.thamesandhudson.com; f. 1949; art, archaeology, history, etc.; Chair. THOMAS NEURATH; Man. Dir JAMIE CAMPLIN.

Thomson Reuters: The Quadrangle, 180 Wardour St, London, W1A 4YG; tel. (20) 7437-9787; e-mail general.info@thomsonreuters.com; internet www.thomsonreuters.com; f. 2008 by merger of Thomson Corpn and Reuters Group PLC (f. 1865); legal, financial; also owns Reuters news agency; Chair. DAVID THOMSON; CEO THOMAS H. GLOCER.

Transworld Publishers Ltd: 61–63 Uxbridge Rd, London, W5 5SA; tel. (20) 8579-2652; fax (20) 8579-5479; e-mail info@transworld-publishers.co.uk; internet www.booksattransworld.co.uk; imprints: Corgi, Bantam Books, Black Swan, Bantam Press, Doubleday, Expert Books, Eden Project Books, Channel 4 Books; all types of fiction and non-fiction; division of The Random House Group Ltd; Man. Dir LARRY FINLAY.

University of Wales Press: 10 Columbus Walk, Brigantine Pl., Cardiff, CF10 4UP; tel. (29) 2049-6899; fax (29) 2049-6108; e-mail post@uwp.co.uk; internet www.uwp.co.uk; f. 1922; academic and educational (Welsh and English); Dir ASHLEY DRAKE.

Usborne Publishing: Usborne House, 83–85 Saffron Hill, London, EC1N 8RT; tel. (20) 7430-2800; fax (20) 7430-1562; e-mail mail@usborne.co.uk; internet www.usborne.com; f. 1973; educational and children's publishing; Man. Dir T. P. USBORNE.

Virgin Books: 20 Vauxhall Bridge Rd, London, SW1V 2SA; tel. (20) 7840-8400; e-mail info@virgin-books.co.uk; internet www.virginbooks.com; 90% owned by The Random House Group Ltd; general, popular culture, film, music, humour, biography, fiction, non-fiction, erotica; imprints: Virgin, Black Lace and Nexus; Man. Dir JOHN SADLER.

Frederick Warne (Publishers) Ltd: 80 Strand, London, WC2R 0RL; tel. (20) 7010-3000; fax (20) 7010-6707; e-mail peterrabbit@penguin.co.uk; internet www.peterrabbit.com; f. 1865; a division of Penguin Books since 1983; classic illustrated children's books (including Beatrix Potter); Man. Dir SALLY FLOYER.

Wiley-Blackwell: 9600 Garsington Rd, Oxford, OX4 2DQ; tel. (1865) 776868; fax (1865) 714591; e-mail customerservices@oxon.blackwellpublishing.com; internet www.blackwellpublishing.com; f. 2001 as Blackwell Publishing Ltd, by merger of Blackwell Publishing and Blackwell Science; acquired by John Wiley & Sons, Inc. (USA) in 2007; academic, professional, business, medical and science books and journals; CEO ERIC A. SWANSON.

The Women's Press: 27 Goodge St, London, W1T 2LD; tel. (20) 7636-3992; fax (20) 7637-1866; e-mail david@the-womens-press.com; internet www.the-womens-press.com; f. 1978; feminist; Man. Dir CHARLOTTE GASCOIGNE.

Yale University Press: 47 Bedford Sq., London, WC1B 3DP; tel. (20) 7079-4900; fax (20) 7079-4901; e-mail sales@yaleup.co.uk; internet www.yalebooks.co.uk; f. 1973; the only US university press to operate a separate publishing co in Europe; Man. Dir ROBERT BALDOCK.

Zed Books Ltd: 7 Cynthia St, London, N1 9JF; tel. (20) 7837-0384; fax (20) 7833-3960; e-mail editorial@zedbooks.net; internet www.zedbooks.co.uk; f. 1977; academic, current affairs; Editors ELLEN MCKINLAY, TAMSINE O'RIORDAN.

PUBLISHERS' ORGANIZATIONS

Booktrust: Book House, 45 East Hill, London, SW18 2QZ; tel. (20) 8516-2977; fax (20) 8516-2978; e-mail query@booktrust.org.uk; internet www.booktrust.org.uk; non-profit-making organization funded by voluntary donations and membership fees; f. 1945; originally f. 1925 as The National Book Council to extend the use and enjoyment of books; renamed Book Trust 1986; publishes annotated book lists; postal book information service; administers book prizes, including the Orange Broadband Prize for Fiction and the John Llewellyn Rhys Prize; runs www.booktrusted.com, a website dedicated to children's books; Chair. ALISON MORRISON; Exec. Dir VIV BIRD.

The Publishers' Association: 29B Montague St, London, WC1B 5BW; tel. (20) 7691-9191; fax (20) 7691-9199; e-mail mail@publishers.org.uk; internet www.publishers.org.uk; f. 1896; represents book, journal and electronic publishers in the UK and seeks to promote the sales of British books; Pres. IAN HUDSON; Chief Exec. SIMON JUDEN; 127 mems.

Publishing Scotland: Scottish Book Centre, 137 Dundee St, Edinburgh, EH11 1BG; tel. (131) 228-6866; fax (131) 228-3220; e-mail enquiries@publishingscotland.org; internet www.publishingscotland.org; f. 1973 as Scottish Publishers' Assen; present name adopted 2007; assists member publishers in the promotion and marketing of their books; offers export services, seminars, events and training; Chief Exec. MARION SINCLAIR.

Broadcasting and Communications

REGULATORY AUTHORITY

Office of Communications (Ofcom): Riverside House, 2A Southwark Bridge Rd, London, SE1 9HA; tel. (20) 7981-3000; fax (20) 7981-3333; e-mail contact@ofcom.org.uk; internet www.ofcom.org.uk; f. 2003 to replace the Office of Telecommunications, the Broadcasting Standards Commission, the Radio Authority, the Radiocommunications Agency and the Independent Television Commission; the independent regulator for the British communications industries, with responsibilities across television, radio, telecommunications and wireless communications services; promotes choice, quality and value in electronic communications services, where appropriate, by encouraging competition between the providers of those services; ensures the most efficient use of the radiocommunications spectrum (the airwaves used for the transmission of all non-military wireless communications services); ensures that a wide range of electronic communications services, including broadband, is available across the United Kingdom; ensures that a wide range of television and radio programmes of high quality and wide appeal are broadcast; maintains plurality in the media by ensuring a sufficiently broad range of ownership; protects audiences against offensive or harmful material, unfairness or the infringement of privacy on television and radio; Chair. COLETTE BOWE; Chief Exec. ED RICHARDS.

TELECOMMUNICATIONS

Arqiva Ltd: Crawley Court, Winchester, Hampshire, SO21 2QA; tel. (1962) 823434; internet www.arqiva.com; f. 2008 by merger of Arqiva and National Grid Wireless; Chair. PETER SHORE; CEO TOM BENNIE.

British Telecommunications PLC: BT Centre, 81 Newgate St, London, EC1A 7AJ; tel. (20) 7356-5000; fax (20) 7356-6630; e-mail btgroup@bt.com; internet www.bt.com; wholly owned subsidiary of BT Group PLC; Chair. Sir MICHAEL RAKE; Chief Exec. IAN LIVINGSTON.

Cable and Wireless PLC: 26 Red Lion Sq., 3rd Floor, London, WC1R 4HQA; tel. (20) 7315-4000; internet www.cw.com; Chair. RICHARD LAPTHORNE; UK and International Chair. and Joint Group Man. Dir JOHN PLUTHERO; Joint Group Man. Dir TONY RICE.

Hutchison 3G UK Ltd (3): Star House, 20 Grenfell Rd, Maidenhead, Berkshire, SL6 1EH; tel. (8707) 330333; internet www.three.co

THE UNITED KINGDOM

.uk; f. 2003; mobile cellular telecommunications; owned by Hutchison Whampoa Ltd (Hong Kong); CEO KEVIN RUSSELL.

KCOM Group PLC: 37 Carr Lane, Hull, HU1 3RE; tel. (1482) 602100; fax (1482) 219289; e-mail corporate.communciations@kcom.com; internet www.kcom.com; f. 1904; fmrly Kingston Communications; Chair. MICHAEL ABRAHAMS; Chief Exec. MALCOLM FALLEN.

Orange: St James Court, Gt Park Rd, Almondsbury Park, Bradley Stoke, Bristol, BS32 4QJ; tel. (870) 376-8888; internet www.orange.co.uk; f. 1994; acquired by France Telecom in 2000; part of the Orange SA (France) group; Chief Exec. TOM ALEXANDER; Group Chair. DIDIER LOMBARD.

Telefónica O$_2$ UK: 260 Bath Rd, Slough, Berks, SL1 4DX; tel. (113) 2722000; e-mail feedback@o2.com; internet www.o2.co.uk; formerly BT Cellnet; demerged from BT Group in October 2002 as O$_2$; acquired by Telefónica, SA (Spain) in March 2006; CEO RONAN DUNNE.

THUS: 1–2 Berkeley Sq., 99 Berkeley St, Glasgow, G3 7HR; tel. (141) 567-1234; fax (141) 566-3035; e-mail thus.enquiries@thus.net; internet www.thus.net; f. 1994 as Scottish Power Telecommunications Holdings; demerged from ScottishPower and renamed THUS Group PLC 2002; acquired by Cable and Wireless 2008; offers fixed-line telecommunications services to business customers; also internet service provider; Chief Exec. JESPER LAURIDSEN.

Tiscali UK Ltd: 20 Broadwick St, London, W1F 8HT; tel. (20) 7087-2000; fax (20) 7087-2282; e-mail info@tiscali.com; internet www.tiscali.co.uk; f. 2001; provides fixed-line telecommunications, digital television services and broadband internet access; subsidiary of Tiscali SpA (Italy); CEO MARY TURNER.

T-Mobile (UK) Ltd: Hatfield Business Park, Hatfield, Herts, AL10 9BW; tel. (1707) 315000; internet www.t-mobile.co.uk; owned by Deutsche Telekom AG (Germany); fmrly One2One; CEO RICHARD MOAT (designate).

Virgin Media: Media House, Bartley Wood Business Park, Bartley Way, Hook, Reading, RG27 9UP; tel. (1256) 752000; fax (1256) 752100; internet www.virginmedia.com; f. 2007 by merger of NTL Inc and Virgin Mobile; Chair. JAMES F. MOONEY; CEO NEIL BURKETT.

Vodafone Group PLC: Vodafone House, The Connection, Newbury, Berks, RG14 2FN; tel. (1635) 33251; fax (1635) 676147; internet www.vodafone.com; Chair. Sir JOHN BOND; Group Chief Exec. VITTORIO COLAO.

BROADCASTING

British Broadcasting Corporation (BBC): Broadcasting House, Portland Pl., London, W1A 1AA; tel. (20) 7580-4468; fax (20) 7637-1630; internet www.bbc.co.uk; f. 1922; operates under Royal Charter; financed by the television licence fees; governed by BBC Trust, which replaced fmr Board of Governors in 2007; Chair. of BBC Trust Sir MICHAEL LYONS; Dir-Gen. MARK THOMPSON; Deputy Dir-Gen. MARK BYFORD; COO CAROLINE THOMSON; CEO of BBC Worldwide JOHN SMITH; Dir of Vision JANA BENNETT; Dir of Marketing, Communications and Audiences SHARON BAYLAY; Dir of BBC People LUCY ADAMS (from 1 June 2009); Dir of Audio and Music TIM DAVIE; Dir of Future Media and Technology ERIK HUGGERS.

Radio

British Broadcasting Corporation

BBC Radio provides a service of five national networks throughout the United Kingdom, 40 local radio stations in England and the Channel Islands, Radio Scotland, Radio Wales, Radio Cymru, broadcasting in Welsh, and Radio Ulster and Radio Foyle (in Northern Ireland); it also offers a number of specialist digital services; Dir of Audio and Music TIM DAVIE.

Radio 1: broadcasts 24 hours a day of contemporary music programmes; Controller ANDY PARFITT.

Radio 2: broadcasts popular music and culture; Controller BOB SHENNAN.

Radio 3: provides 24-hour broadcasts of classical music, drama, talks and documentaries; Controller ROGER WRIGHT.

Radio 4: broadcasts news and current affairs and also provides a wide range of features, drama and discussions; Controller MARK DAMAZER.

Radio Five Live: began broadcasting in March 1994, replacing Radio 5; provides a 24-hour service of news and sports programmes; also operates **Five Live Sports Extra**, a part-time digital network for sports events not broadcast elsewhere on BBC Radio; Controller ADRIAN VAN KLAVEREN.

6 Music: began broadcasting in 2002, digital station playing pop and rock music; Controller BOB SHENNAN.

1Xtra: began broadcasting in 2002; digital station playing contemporary urban music for a young audience; Controller ANDY PARFITT.

Asian Network: began broadcasting in 2002, digital station aimed at the Asian communities in the United Kingdom; Controller ANDY PARFITT.

BBC7: began broadcasting in 2002; digital radio station featuring archive material and original spoken-word programming; Controller MARK DAMAZER.

BBC World Service: Bush House, Strand, London, WC2B 4PH; tel. (20) 7240-3456; fax (20) 7557-1258; e-mail worldservice@bbc.co.uk; internet www.bbc.co.uk/worldservice; the World Service in English is broadcast for 24 hours daily and is directed to all areas of the world. In addition, there are special services, in 33 languages, to: the Far East (in Mandarin, Cantonese, Burmese, Indonesian, Thai and Vietnamese); the Indian sub-continent (in Bengali, Hindi, Nepali, Sinhala, Tamil and Urdu); the Caucasus and Central Asia (in Azeri, Kyrgyz and Uzbek); the Middle East and North Africa (in Arabic, Pashto, Farsi and Turkish); Africa (in Arabic, English, French, Hausa, Kinyarwanda/Kirundi, Portuguese, Somali and Swahili); and the Western Hemisphere (in Portuguese for Brazil and Spanish for Latin America). Services in the following languages are transmitted for listeners in Europe: Albanian, Macedonian, Romanian, Russian, Serbian, and Turkish; Dir PETER HORROCKS.

Independent Radio

Absolute Radio: 1 Golden Sq., London, W1F 9DJ; tel. (20) 7434-1215; fax (20) 7434-1197; internet www.absoluteradio.co.uk; began broadcasting April 1993 as Virgin Radio; present name adopted 2008; popular music; also operates two digital stations, **Absolute Classic Rock** and **Absolute Xtreme**; Propr TIML Radio Ltd; Chief Exec. DONNACH O'DRISCOLL.

Global Radio: 30 Leicester Sq., London, WC2H 7LA; tel. (20) 7766-6000; fax (20) 7766-6111; e-mail info@thisisglobal.com; internet www.thisisglobal.com; owns and operates radio stations across the United Kingdom, incl. 95.8 Capital FM, Choice FM, Classic FM, Galaxy, Gold, Heart, LBC and Xfm; Chair. CHARLES ALLEN; CEO STEPHEN MIRON.

Independent Radio News (IRN): 200 Gray's Inn Rd, 6th Floor, London, WC1X 8XZ; tel. (20) 7430-4090; fax (20) 7430-4092; e-mail news@irn.co.uk; internet www.irn.co.uk; f. 1973; produced by ITN Radio; news agency for the independent local radio network; Chair. TERRY SMITH; Man. Dir JOHN PERKINS.

The Local Radio Company PLC: 11 Duke St, High Wycombe, Buckinghamshire, HP13 6EE; tel. (1494) 688200; fax (1494) 688201; internet www.thelocalradiocompany.com; owns and operates 21 local radio licences across the United Kingdom; f. 2004 to purchase the entire share capital of Radio Investments Ltd; Chief Exec. RICHARD WHEATLY.

TalkSport UK: 18 Hatfields, London, SE1 8DJ; tel. (20) 7959-7800; fax (20) 7959-7808; internet www.talksport.net; began broadcasting February 1995 as Talk Radio UK; name changed as above January 2000; Propr UTV PLC; Man. Dir SCOTT TAUNTON.

Television

British Broadcasting Corporation

BBC Television: Television Centre, Wood Lane, London, W12 7RJ; tel. (20) 8743-8000; internet www.bbc.co.uk; operates two terrestrial services, BBC-1 and BBC-2, and six digital channels, BBC-3, BBC-4, CBeebies, CBBC, BBC News 24 and BBC Parliament; Dir of Vision JANA BENNETT.

BBC-1: internet www.bbc.co.uk/bbcone; provides a coverage of over 99% of the population of the United Kingdom. Colour service began in 1969; a breakfast-time television service began in 1983; Controller JAY HUNT.

BBC-2: internet www.bbc.co.uk/bbctwo; began broadcasting in 1964, and is available to 99% of the population. Colour service began in 1967; Controller JANICE HADLOW.

BBC-3: internet www.bbc.co.uk/bbcthree; digital entertainment channel; Controller DANNY COHEN.

BBC-4: internet www.bbc.co.uk/bbcfour; digital channel showing in-depth cultural programmes; Controller RICHARD KLEIN.

CBBC: internet www.bbc.co.uk/cbbc; digital service for children aged six to 13; Controller ANNE GILCHRIST.

CBeebies: internet www.bbc.co.uk/cbeebies; digital service aimed at under-fives; Controller MICHAEL CARRINGTON.

BBC News Channel: internet www.bbc.co.uk/news; 24-hour digital news service; Dir of News HELEN BOADEN; Controller KEVIN BAKHURST.

BBC Parliament: internet www.bbc.co.uk/parliament; provides coverage from the Houses of Parliament and the devolved Parliament and Assemblies in Scotland, Wales and Northern Ireland; Controller PETER KNOWLES.

THE UNITED KINGDOM

BBC Alba: c/o MG Alba, Seaforth Rd, Stornoway, Isle Of Lewis, HS1 2SD; tel. (1851) 705550; fax (1851) 706432; e-mail fios@mgalba.com; internet www.bbc.co.uk/alba; f. 2008 to provide radio and television programming in Scottish Gaelic; operates a free-to-air digital television channel, **BBC Alba**, and a radio station, **BBC Radio nan Gàidheal**; jtly managed by BBC and MG Alba (Gaelic Media Service); Chief Exec. DONALD CAMPBELL; Head of Content ALAN ESSLEMONT; Head of Service MARGARET MARY MURRAY.

Independent Television

In October 1991 the Independent Television Commission (ITC), in accordance with the provisions of the Broadcasting Act of 1990, awarded the 16 licences that constituted the renamed Channel 3 (ITV 1). The franchises were allocated by a system of competitive tendering, although the ITC was empowered to select a company presenting a lower bid in 'exceptional circumstances'. The new licences came into force on 1 January 1993, when Channel 4 (q.v.) also became an ITC licensee. By the end of 1995 the ITC had also issued 183 non-domestic satellite and licensable programme service licences. In October 1995 the ITC awarded the licence for the fifth terrestrial channel to Channel 5 Broadcasting; broadcasting commenced in March 1997. In June the ITC awarded the British Digital Broadcasting consortium (ONdigital, later renamed ITV Digital) three licences to operate digital terrestrial television (DTT) services in the United Kingdom. The first digital television services became available in the following year. However, following the collapse of ITV Digital in April 2002, the ITC withdrew the consortium's licences and in May it announced that they were to be re-tendered; in August one licence was awarded to the BBC and two to Crown Castle International (now Arqiva). DTV Services Ltd, a consortium of the BBC, Crown Castle International and BSkyB, subsequently announced its plans to launch Freeview, which would provide a wide range of free-to-view digital television channels. Freeview commenced broadcasting in late 2002. The ITC became part of Ofcom in late 2003. In early 2005 Ofcom published a provisional timetable outlining plans for the country to switch entirely from analogue to digital television region by region between 2008 and 2012. By the end of 2008 there were 9.5m. households in the United Kingdom receiving digital terrestrial television (Freeview).

Channel 4 Television: 124 Horseferry Rd, London, SW1P 2TX; tel. (20) 7306-8333; internet www.channel4.com; f. 1980; began broadcasting 1982; national television service; also operates 4 free-to-air digital channels: E4, Film4, More4 and 4Music; available across United Kingdom, except for parts of Wales served by S4C; due to become available across Wales in 2009; financed by advertising; in accordance with the Broadcasting Act (1990), Channel 4 became a public corporation and ITC licensee, responsible for selling its own advertising, from January 1993; Chair. LUKE JOHNSON; Chief Exec. ANDY DUNCAN; Dir of Television and Content KEVIN LYGO.

Five: 22 Long Acre, London, WC2E 9LY; tel. (8457) 050505; e-mail customerservices@five.tv; internet www.five.tv; awarded licence for fifth national terrestrial channel in October 1995; commenced broadcasting on 30 March 1997 as Channel 5; renamed as above in 2002; also operates 2 digital channels: Fiver and Five USA; owned by RTL Group (Luxembourg); Chair. DAVID ELSTEIN; Chair. and Chief Exec. DAWN AIREY; Dir of Programmes BEN GALE.

Freeview: DTV Services Ltd, Broadcast Centre, 27–29 Cursitor St, London, EC4A 1LT; tel. (8708) 809980; internet www.freeview.co.uk; f. 2002; a consortium of the BBC, Arqiva, ITV, Channel 4 and BSkyB providing Freeview, a digital service offering more than 40 television stations and additional interactive services; commenced transmission in late 2002; Man. Dir ILSE HOWLING.

Independent Television News Ltd (ITN): 200 Gray's Inn Rd, London, WC1X 8XZ; tel. (20) 7833-3000; fax (20) 7430-4305; internet www.itn.co.uk; f. 1955; ITV PLC holds a 40% stake, with Daily Mail and General Trust PLC, Thomson Reuters and United Business Media each holding a 20% stake; provides all national and international news programming for ITV 1 and the London region, plus news programming for Channel 4 and Independent Radio News (IRN); also operates the ITN Archive, ITN Factual, ITN On and ITN Source; became a profit-making company in 1993; Chief Exec. MARK WOOD.

ITV PLC: 200 Gray's Inn Rd, London, WC1V 8HF; tel. (20) 7620-1620; internet www.itvplc.com; f. 2004 following the merger of Carlton and Granada; owns all of the regional Channel 3 licences in England and Wales; Exec. Chair. MICHAEL GRADE.

Sianel Pedwar Cymru (S4C) (Channel Four Wales): Parc Tŷ Glas, Llanishen, Cardiff, CF14 5DU; tel. (29) 2074-7444; fax (29) 2075-4444; e-mail helo@s4c.co.uk; internet www.s4c.co.uk; f. 1980; commenced broadcasting in 1982; television service for Wales; due to become a wholly Welsh-language service in 2009; financed by UK Dept for Culture, Media and Sport and advertising revenue; Chair. JOHN WALTER JONES; Chief Exec. IONA JONES.

SMG PLC: Pacific Quay, Glasgow, G51 1PQ; tel. (141) 300-3300; e-mail communications@smg.plc.uk; internet www.smg.plc.uk; owns stv; Chair. RICHARD FINDLAY; Chief Exec. ROB WOODWARD.

Independent Television (ITV—Channel 3) Regional Licencees

Independent Television Association Ltd (ITV): ITV Network Centre, 200 Grays Inn Rd, London, WC1V 8HF; tel. (20) 7843-8000; fax (20) 7843-8158; e-mail info@itv.co.uk; internet www.itv.com; f. 1956; from 1992 the central co-ordinating body for Channel 3 (ITV 1); Dir of Television PETER FINCHAM.

GMTV: c/o London Television Centre, Upper Ground, London, SE1 9TT; tel. (20) 7827-7000; fax (20) 7827-7001; internet www.gm.tv; nationwide breakfast-time service; began broadcasting in January 1993 (replacing TV-am PLC); 75% owned by ITV PLC; Man. Dir PAUL CORLEY.

ITV Anglia: Anglia House, Norwich, NR1 3JG; tel. (1603) 615151; fax (1603) 631032; e-mail anglia@itvlocal.com; internet www.itvlocal.com/anglia; East of England; Propr ITV PLC; began broadcasting in 1959; Man. Dir NEIL THOMPSON.

ITV Border: Television Centre, Carlisle, CA1 3NT; tel. (1228) 525101; fax (1228) 541384; e-mail border@itvlocal.com; internet www.itvlocal.com/border; Borders and the Isle of Man; Propr ITV PLC; Chief Exec. PADDY MERRALL.

ITV Central: Gas St, Birmingham, B1 2JT; tel. (870) 600-6766; fax (844) 556-3820; e-mail central@itvlocal.com; internet www.itvlocal.com/central; East and West Midlands; Propr ITV PLC.

ITV Granada: Granada TV Centre, Quay St, Manchester, M60 9EA; tel. and fax (161) 832-7211; fax (161) 827-2180; e-mail granada@itvlocal.com; internet www.itvlocal.com/granada; north-west England; Propr ITV PLC; Man. Dir SUSAN WOODWARD.

ITV London: London Television Centre, Upper Ground, London, SE1 9LT; fax (20) 7261-8163; e-mail london@itvlocal.com; internet www.itvlocal.com/london; formed by a merger of Carlton and LWT in February 2004; Propr ITV PLC; Man. Dir CHRISTY SWORDS.

ITV Meridian: Solent Business Park, Whiteley, Hants, PO15 7PA; tel. and fax (1489) 442000; e-mail meridian@itvlocal.com; internet www.itvlocal.com; south and south-east England and Thames Valley; began broadcasting in January 1993; Propr ITV PLC; Man. Dir MARK SOUTHGATE.

ITV Tyne Tees: Television House, The Watermark, Gateshead, NE11 9SZ; tel. (844) 881-5000; e-mail tynetees@itvlocal.com; internet www.itvlocal.com/tynetees; f. 1959; north-east England; Propr ITV PLC; Regional Dir GRAEME THOMPSON.

ITV Wales: Television Centre, Culverhouse Cross, Cardiff, CF5 6XJ; tel. (844) 881-0100; fax (29) 2059-7183; e-mail wales@itvlocal.com; internet www.itvlocal.com/wales; fmrly HTV Wales; Propr ITV PLC; Man. Dir ELIS OWEN.

ITV West: The Television Centre, 470 Bath Rd, Bristol, BS4 3HG; tel. (844) 881-2345; fax (844) 881-2346; e-mail west@itvlocal.com; internet www.itvlocal.com/west; fmrly HTV West; Bristol, Gloucestershire, north Dorset, Somerset and Wiltshire; Propr ITV PLC; Man Dir MARK HASKELL.

ITV Westcountry: Language Science Park, Western Wood Way, Plymouth, PL7 5BQ; tel. and fax (844) 881-4900; e-mail westcountry@itvlocal.com; internet www.itvlocal.com/westcountry; Cornwall, Devon, Somerset and west Dorset; began broadcasting in January 1993; Propr ITV PLC; Man. Dir MARK HASKELL.

ITV Yorkshire: Television Centre, Kirkstall Rd, Leeds, LS3 1JS; tel. (113) 243-8283; fax (113) 243-3655; internet www.itvlocal.com/yorkshire; Propr ITV PLC; Man. Dir DAVID M. B. CROFT.

stv: Pacific Quay, Glasgow, G51 1PQ; tel. (141) 300-3000; fax (141) 300-3030; internet www.stv.tv; f. 1957; operates two services in central and northern Scotland; Propr SMG PLC; Man. Dir, SMG Television BOBBY HAIN.

UTV PLC: Havelock House, Ormeau Rd, Belfast, BT7 1EB; tel. (28) 9032-8122; fax (28) 9024-6695; e-mail info@utvplc.com; internet www.u.tv; started transmission 1959; Chair. JOHN B. MCGUCKIAN; Chief Exec. JOHN MCCANN; Man. Dir, Television MICHAEL WILSON.

Satellite and Cable Broadcasting

By the end of 2008 12.8m. households in the United Kingdom paid to subscribe to multi-channel satellite or cable television services. Of these, 8.9m. subscribed to digital satellite television with a further 3.4m. households subscribing to cable television (digital 3.3m.; analogue 100,000). Some 10.1m. households received free-to-view digital satellite television services. The major satellite and cable television companies are listed below.

BBC Worldwide Television: Media Centre, 201 Wood Lane, London, W12 7TQ; tel. (20) 8433-2000; fax (20) 8749-0538; internet www.bbcworldwide.com; began broadcasting in 1991; part of BBC Worldwide Ltd; broadcasts 24-hour news and information

('BBC World') and light entertainment programmes to Europe ('BBC Prime'); other news programmes broadcast to Africa, Asia (including a Japanese-language service to Japan), the Middle East, North America, Australia and New Zealand; Chief Exec. JOHN SMITH.

British Sky Broadcasting Group PLC (BSkyB): Grant Way, Isleworth, Middlesex, TW7 5QD; tel. (20) 7705-3000; fax (20) 7705-3030; internet www.sky.com; f. 1990 by merger of British Satellite Broadcasting (BSB) and Sky TV PLC (a subsidiary of News International); satellite broadcaster and programme provider; multi-channel digital television service SkyDigital (see below); Chair. JAMES MURDOCH; CEO JEREMY DARROCH.

SkyDigital: 6 Centaurs Business Park, Grant Way, Isleworth, Middlesex, TW7 5QD; tel. (20) 7705-3000; fax (20) 7705-3030; internet www.sky.com; owned by British Sky Broadcasting Group PLC; CEO JEREMY DARROCH.

Eurosport UK: 55 Drury Lane, London, WC2B 5SQ; tel. (20) 7468-7777; fax (20) 7468-0023; e-mail dorman@eurosport.com; internet www.eurosport.co.uk; began broadcasting in 1989; Man. Dir SIMON CRANE.

Freesat: POB 6296, London, W1A 3FF; tel. (845) 099-0990; e-mail info@freesat.co.uk; internet www.freesat.co.uk; f. 2007; commenced broadcasting in May 2008; free-to-air digital satellite service, offering more than 130 digital television and radio channels; jointly owned by the BBC and ITV PLC; Man. Dir EMMA SCOTT.

MTV Networks UK and Ireland: 17–29 Hawley Cres., London, NW1 8TT; tel. (20) 7284-7777; fax (20) 7284-7511; e-mail pressuk@mtvne.com; internet www.mtvnetworks.co.uk; began broadcasting in 1987; popular music; Man. Dir DAVID LYNN.

UKTV: 160 Great Portland St, London, W1W 5QA; tel. (20) 7299-6200; fax (20) 7299-6000; internet www.uktv.co.uk; began broadcasting 1992; 10 channels: Alibi, Blighty, Dave, Eden, G.O.L.D., Home, UKTV Food, UKTV Gardens, Watch and Yesterday; satellite, cable and DTT; co-owned by BBC Worldwide Ltd and Virgin Media; CEO DAVID ABRAHAM; Controller MATTHEW LITTLEFORD.

Finance

The United Kingdom's central bank is the Bank of England, which was established by Act of Parliament and Royal Charter in 1694 and nationalized under the Bank of England Act 1946. The Scottish and Northern Ireland banks issue their own notes but these are largely covered by holdings of Bank of England notes.

The Bank of England holds the main government accounts, acts as registrar of government stocks and as agent of the Government for a number of financial operations. It is also banker to a number of commercial banks. The London clearing banks maintain a substantial proportion of their total cash holdings in the form of balances at the Bank and these are used in the settlement of daily cheque and credit clearings. The Bank has traditionally been responsible for advising the Government on the formulation of monetary policy and for its subsequent execution. A new Bank of England Act, which accorded the Bank statutory operational independence for monetary policy, within agreed government economic targets, received Royal Assent in April 1998, and entered into force on 1 June. The Act provided for the establishment of a Monetary Policy Committee (MPC), with responsibility for analysing and formulating monetary policy within the framework of maintaining price stability and supporting the Government's economic policies. The Treasury was to reserve the right to direct the Bank with respect to monetary decisions in extreme circumstances. The MPC was to comprise the Governor of the Bank, the two newly-created Deputy-Governors, two other Bank officials and four members appointed by the Chancellor of the Exchequer. The Bank's Court of Directors was to review the MPC's procedures and produce an annual report, to be presented to Parliament, under new measures to promote greater accountability and transparency of the Bank's operations.

The commercial banks may be divided into two broad categories: clearing banks and other banks. Clearing banks play the main part in operating the money transmission system throughout the United Kingdom. The other banks comprise accepting houses (taking their name from their business of accepting bills of exchange for payment) and other British-owned banks, overseas-owned banks and consortium banks. As the use of bills of exchange has declined, all accepting houses have assumed the specialist financial services of merchant banks, which include the management of investment trusts, foreign currency trading and company mergers and acquisitions. Since the late 1980s several merchant banks have been incorporated into larger banking organizations to provide a full range of financial, including retail, banking services.

Consortium banks have been formed in the United Kingdom by groups of banks, mostly from overseas, but including some British clearing banks. Initially they were set up to afford shareholders access to the Eurocurrency markets. More recently consortia have been formed as a means of combining institutions from similar geographical areas, when a London operation would be uneconomic for individual banks. Consortium banks are important participants in the major inter-bank markets in sterling and currency deposits and certificates of deposit.

The discount houses are a specialized group of institutions peculiar to London. They raise the greater part of their funds from within the banking sector. These funds are borrowed by the houses at call or short notice (thereby providing the lending banks with a highly liquid interest-bearing investment) and are used to purchase correspondingly liquid assets—mainly Treasury and commercial bills, short-dated government stocks, certificates of deposit, local authority debt, etc. The discount houses are now more generally incorporated as part of the group of banks authorized by the Bank as listed money market institutions under the 1986 Financial Services Act. The United Kingdom's official reserves, comprising gold, convertible currencies and special drawing rights on the International Monetary Fund, are held in the Exchange Equalization Account operated since 1932 by the Bank of England as agent for the Treasury.

The London Gold Market engages in the trading, transporting, refining, melting, assaying and vaulting of gold. The unique feature of the London market is the 'fixing', which determines the price of gold on a twice-daily basis by matching orders from customers and markets throughout the world. In September 1996 the London Commodity Exchange merged with the London International Financial Futures and Options Exchange (LIFFE), which has since become unique as an exchange trading options on individual equities and on financial, agricultural, soft commodity and equity index products. LIFFE was acquired by the French-based Euronext security market in 2001.

The building society movement is important both as a medium of savings (the largest in the United Kingdom) and for the finance of house purchase in a country where more than two-thirds of dwellings are owner-occupied. The expansion of building societies into banking was a characteristic of the late 1980s. This trend was furthered in the 1990s with several large building societies converting to banks through public share offers or opting to merge with similar institutions or with retail banks in order to provide a comprehensive range of financial services. In 2001 there were 48 societies registered in the United Kingdom, compared with 190 in 1984. By March 2009 that number had increased to 53.

National Savings are administered by the Department for National Savings and the Trustee Savings Banks. Through the Department for National Savings the Government administers the National Savings Bank 'investment' and 'ordinary' accounts, National Savings certificates, Premium bonds and other securities, all aimed primarily at the small saver. The outlets for these services are some 14,500 post offices in the United Kingdom.

There are certain institutions set up to provide finance for specific purposes; the more important of these are the 3i Group PLC (which provides investment capital to companies which do not have ready access to capital markets) and the Agricultural Mortgage Corporation (loans against mortgages on agricultural property).

The main capital market is the London Stock Exchange, and since October 1986 the volume of business transacted has greatly expanded with the introduction of the Stock Exchange Automated Quotations system (SEAQ), an electronic trading system which allows off-floor trading. The process of automating trading was completed in October 1997 when the Stock Exchange Electronic Trading Service (Sets) became operational.

The United Kingdom has a highly developed insurance market, located primarily in London. Lloyd's, with its unique system of underwriting syndicates (of which there were 66 in September 2007) has an international reputation for marine and aviation insurance, and reinsurance, as well as a significant share of the British motor insurance market. Much of Lloyd's premium income comes from outside the United Kingdom through Lloyd's 176 accredited brokers. There are over 800 authorized insurance companies in the United Kingdom, dealing with life and general insurance, as well as international reinsurance.

BANKING
(cap. = capital; p.u. = paid up; auth. = authorized; m. = million; res = reserves; dep. = deposits; subs. = subscribed; brs = branches; amounts in pounds sterling)

The 1987 Banking Act replaced the Banking Act of 1979 under which a statutory framework for the supervision of the banking sector was established. The 1987 Act defines new criteria by which an institution can be authorized to accept deposits. The 1998 Banking Act, which replaced the 1987 Act, transferred the Bank's functions with regard to the supervision of banks to an independent Financial Services Authority.

Central Bank

Bank of England: Threadneedle St, London, EC2R 8AH; tel. (20) 7601-4444; fax (20) 7601-5460; e-mail enquiries@bankofengland.co.uk; internet www.bankofengland.co.uk; inc by Royal Charter in

THE UNITED KINGDOM

1694, and nationalized by Act of Parliament on 1 March 1946; amended by 1998 Bank of England Act (see above); the Government's banker and on its behalf manages the note issue and sets the official Bank rate; also the bankers' bank; mem. of the Cheque and Credit Clearing Company; cash centres at Leeds and Debden; agencies in Belfast, Birmingham, Bristol, Cambridge, Cardiff, Exeter, Glasgow, Greater London, Leeds, Liverpool, Manchester, Newcastle upon Tyne, Nottingham and Southampton; capital stock amounting to 14.6m. is held by the Treasury; cap. 15m., res 457m., dep. 68,867m. (Feb. 2008); Gov. MERVYN KING; Dep. Govs Sir JOHN GIEVE, CHARLES BEAN.

Principal Banks Incorporated in the United Kingdom

Abbey National PLC: Abbey National House, 2 Triton Sq., Regent's Pl., London, NW1 3AN; tel. (870) 607-6000; e-mail feedback@abbey.com; internet www.abbey.com; f. 1944 as Abbey National Building Society; current status assumed in 1989; owned by Banco Santander, SA (Spain); cap. 148m., res 1,857m., dep. 178,146m. (Dec. 2006); Chair. Lord BURNS; Chief Exec. ANTÓNIO HORTA-OSÓRIO; 793 brs.

Alliance & Leicester: Carlton Park, Narborough, Leicester, LE19 0AL; tel. (116) 201-1000; fax (116) 200-4040; internet www.alliance-leicester.co.uk; fmrly a building society; assumed banking status in 1997; broad-based financial services provider incl. business banking services through wholly-owned subsidiary, Girobank; acquired by Banco Santander, SA (Spain) in 2008; cap. 815m., res 85m., dep. 75,185m. (Dec. 2007); Chair. ALAN GILLESPIE; Chief Exec. DAVID BENNETT; 256 brs.

Barclays Bank PLC: 1 Churchill Place, London, E14 5HP; tel. (20) 7699-5000; fax (20) 7699-3463; internet group.barclays.com; inc. 1896; clearing bank; principal operating co of Barclays PLC (group holding co); cap. 1,651m., res 930m., dep. 1,157,800m. (Dec. 2007); Group Chair. MARCUS AGIUS; Chief Exec. JOHN VARLEY.

Clydesdale Bank PLC: 30 St Vincent Pl., Glasgow, G1 2HL; tel. (141) 248-7070; fax (141) 204-0828; internet www.cbonline.co.uk; f. 1838; wholly-owned by National Australia Bank Ltd; clearing bank; cap. 232m., res 594m., dep. 31,017m. (Dec. 2007); Chair. MALCOLM WILLIAMSON; Chief Exec. (Europe) LYNNE PEACOCK; 150 brs.

The Co-operative Bank PLC: POB 101, 1 Balloon St, Manchester, M60 4EP; tel. (161) 832-3456; fax (161) 829-4475; e-mail customerservice@co-operativebank.co.uk; internet www.co-operativebank.co.uk; f. 1872; clearing bank; merger with Britannia Building Society approved April 2009; cap. 55m., res – 14m., dep. 11,476m. (Jan. 2007); Chair. BOB BURLTON; Chief Exec. DAVID ANDERSON; 158 brs.

Coutts and Co: 440 Strand, London, WC2R 0QS; tel. (20) 7753-1000; fax (20) 7753-1050; internet www.coutts.com; f. 1692; private clearing bank and asset management; parent co Royal Bank Of Scotland Group PLC; Chair. DAVID DOUGLAS-HOME, Earl of Home; Chief Exec. SARAH DEAVES; 24 brs.

First Trust Bank: First Trust Centre, POB 123, 92 Ann St, Belfast, BT1 3AY; tel. (28) 9032-5599; fax (28) 9032-1754; internet www.firsttrustbank.co.uk; f. 1991 following merger of Northern Ireland operations of AIB Group, Ireland and TSB Northern Ireland; trading name of AIB Group (UK) PLC in Northern Ireland; Group Chair. (UK) DAVID PRITCHARD; Man. Dir TERRY McDAID; 57 brs.

HSBC Bank PLC: 8 Canada Sq., London, E14 5HQ; tel. (20) 7991-8888; internet www.hsbc.co.uk; f. 1836; from 1992 subsidiary of HSBC Holdings PLC; clearing bank; cap. 1,797m., res 15,278m., dep. 564,603m. (Dec. 2007); Chair. STEPHEN GREEN; Group Chief Exec. M. F. GEOGHEGAN; 1,700 brs.

Lloyds Banking Group PLC: 25 Gresham St, London, EC2V 7HN; tel. (20) 7626-1500; fax (20) 7356-2494; internet www.lloydsbankinggroup.com; f. 2009 by merger of Lloyds TSB Bank PLC and HBOS PLC; owns and operates Bank of Scotland, Cheltenham and Gloucester, Halifax and Lloyds TSB; 44.3% stake owned by UK Govt.; cap. 1,432m., res 1,238m., dep. 258,674m. (Dec. 2007); Chair. Sir VICTOR BLANK; Group Chief Exec. J. ERIC DANIELS.

National Westminster Bank PLC: 135 Bishopsgate, London, EC2M 3UR; tel. (20) 7726-1000; fax (20) 7375-5050; internet www.natwest.com; f. 1968; clearing bank; acquired by The Royal Bank of Scotland Group PLC in 2000; cap. 1,678m., res 9,110m., dep. 286,258m. (Dec. 2007); Group Chair. Sir PHILIP HAMPTON; Group Chief Exec. STEPHEN HESTER; 1,631 brs.

Northern Bank Limited: Donegall Sq. West, Belfast, BT1 6JS; tel. (28) 9004-5000; fax (28) 9089-3214; internet www.northernbank.co.uk; f. 1960; owned by Danske Bank Group; cap. 88m., res 20.7m., dep. 3,831.2m. (Dec. 2005); Chair. PETER STRAARUP; Chief Exec. DONALD PRICE; 94 brs.

Northern Rock PLC: Northern Rock House, Gosforth, Tyne and Wear, NE3 4PL; tel. (191) 285-7191; fax (191) 284-8470; internet www.northernrock.co.uk; taken under state ownership in Feb. 2008; cap. 124m., res 288m., dep. 104,165m. (Dec. 2007); Chair. RON SANDLER; Chief Exec. GARY HOFFMANN; 90 brs.

The Royal Bank of Scotland PLC: POB 1000, Gogaburn, Edinburgh, EH12 1HQ; tel. (131) 556-8555; fax (131) 557-6565; internet www.rbs.co.uk; f. 1985 as result of merger of Royal Bank of Scotland and Williams & Glyn's Bank. The Royal Bank of Scotland (est. by Royal Charter in 1727) merged with National Commercial Bank of Scotland in 1969. Williams & Glyn's Bank was result of merger of Glyn Mills & Co (est. 1753) and Williams Deacon's Bank (est. 1771); 57.9% stake acquired by UK Govt in Oct. 2008; cap. 2,530m., res 29,436m., dep. 1,600,673m. (Dec. 2007); Chair. Sir PHILIP HAMPTON; Group Chief Exec. STEPHEN HESTER; 639 brs.

Standard Chartered Bank: 1 Aldermanbury Sq., London, EC2V 7SB; tel. (20) 7280-7500; fax (20) 7280-7791; internet www.standardchartered.com; f. 1853; holding co Standard Chartered PLC; cap. US $705m., res $9,688m., dep. $273,297m. (Dec. 2007); Chair. JOHN PEACE (acting); Group Chief Exec. PETER SANDS; 570 brs.

Ulster Bank Ltd: 11–16 Donegall Sq. East, Belfast, BT1 5UB; tel. (28) 9027-6000; fax (28) 9027-5661; e-mail morrow@ulsterbank.com; internet www.ulsterbank.co.uk; f. 1836; mem. of Royal Bank of Scotland Group; cap. 717m., res 2,245m., dep. 40,841m. (Dec. 2006); Chair. SEAN DORGAN; Group Chief Exec. CORMAC McCARTHY; 214 brs.

Yorkshire Bank: 20 Merrion Way, Leeds, LS2 8NZ; tel. (113) 247-2000; fax (113) 242-0733; internet www.ybonline.co.uk; f. 1859; wholly owned by National Australia Bank Ltd; cap. 251.1m., res 91.4m., dep. 7,691.1m. (Sept. 2002); Chief Exec. (Europe) LYNNE PEACOCK; 260 brs.

Principal Merchant Banks

Ansbacher & Co: 2 London Bridge, London, SE1 9RA; tel. (20) 7089-4700; fax (20) 7089-4850; e-mail info@ansbacher.com; internet www.ansbacher.com; f. 1894; subsidiary of Qatar National Bank SAQ; cap. 59m., res 1m., dep. 471m. (Dec. 2007); Chair. and CEO HUGH TITCOMB.

Barclays Capital: 5 The North Colonnade, Canary Wharf, London, E14 4BB; tel. (20) 7623-2323; e-mail publisher@barclayscapital.com; internet www.barcap.com; investment banking division of Barclays PLC; Chief Exec. ROBERT E. DIAMOND, Jnr.

Brown, Shipley & Co Ltd: Founders Court, Lothbury, London, EC2R 7HE; tel. (20) 7606-9833; fax (20) 7282-3399; e-mail marketing@brownshipley.com; internet www.brownshipley.com; f. 1810; owned by KBC Group NV (Belgium); cap. issued 86.4m., dep. 573.7m. (Dec. 2001); Chair. STEPHEN BLANEY; Man. Dir IAN SACKFIELD.

Butterfield Bank (UK) Ltd (Butterfield Private Bank): 99 Gresham St, London, EC2V 7NG; tel. (20) 7776-6700; fax (20) 7776-6701; e-mail info@uk.butterfieldgroup.com; internet www.uk.butterfieldgroup.com; f. 1919; acquired by Bermuda's Bank of Butterfield 2004; cap. 17m., res 14m., dep. 917m. (Dec. 2007); Man. Dir GEORGE BOGUCKI.

Cater Allen Private Bank: Abbey House, 9 Nelson St, Bradford, BD1 5AN; tel. (114) 228-2407; e-mail info@caterallen.co.uk; internet www.caterallen.co.uk; f. 1981 by merger of Cater Ryder and Co Ltd (f. 1816) and Allen Harvey and Ross Ltd (f. 1888); part of Santander Private Banking UK; Chair. MALCOLM MILLINGTON; Man. Dir RICHARD J. DUNN.

Citibank International PLC: POB 242, Citigroup Centre, 33 Canada Sq., Canary Wharf, London, E14 5LB; tel. (20) 7500-5000; fax (20) 7500-1695; internet www.citibank.co.uk; f. 1972; cap. 1,506m., res 538m., dep. 25,430m. (Dec. 2006); Chair. and Chief Exec. WILLIAM J. MILLS.

Citigroup: 33 Canada Sq., Canary Wharf, London, E14 5LB; tel. (20) 7986-4000; internet www.citigroup.com; f. 2000 by merger of J. Henry Schroder & Co Ltd and Salomon Smith Barney; present name adopted 2001; Chair RICHARD PARSONS.

Close Brothers Ltd: 10 Crown Pl., London, EC2A 4FT; tel. (20) 7426-4000; fax (20) 7426-4044; e-mail enquiries@closebrothers.co.uk; internet www.closebrothers.co.uk; cap. 82m., res 241m., dep. 3,548m. (July 2007); Man. Dir STEPHEN HODGES.

DB UK Bank Limited: 23 Great Winchester St, London, EC2P 2AX; tel. (20) 7545-8000; fax (20) 7545-6155; internet www.db.com/unitedkingdom; f. 1838; as George Peabody & Co; renamed Morgan Grenfell & Co Ltd in 1910; present name adopted 2004; acquired by Deutsche Bank Group in 1989; cap. 385m., res 4.2m., dep. 7,279.2m. (Dec. 2004); Chair. S. J. DOBBIE; Chief Exec. D. G. PENFOLD; 1 br.

Dresdner Kleinwort: 30 Gresham St, London, EC2V 7PG; tel. (20) 7623-8000; fax (20) 7623-4069; internet www.dresdnerkleinwort.com; wholly owned subsidiary of Kleinwort Benson Group; ultimate holding co Dresdner Bank AG; share cap. 548.6m., res 67.5m., dep. 602.2m. (Dec. 2005); Chair. ALLAN C. D. YARROW.

Investec Bank (UK) Ltd: 2 Gresham St, London, EC2V 7QP; tel. (20) 7597-4000; fax (20) 7597-4472; internet www.investec.com; f. 1977 as Allied Arab Bank Ltd, name changed as above 1997; acquired Guinness Mahon & Co Ltd 1998; cap. 555m., res 51m., dep.

THE UNITED KINGDOM

10,131m. (March 2008); Chair. HUGH HERMAN; CEO BERNARD KANTOR.

Kaupthing Singer & Friedlander Ltd: 21 New St, Bishopsgate, London, EC2M 4HR; tel. (20) 3205-5000; fax (20) 3205-5001; e-mail ukmarketing@singers.co.uk; internet www.kaupthingsingers.co.uk; f. 1907; acquired by Kaupthing Banki hf (Iceland) in 2005; entered administration in Oct. 2008; cap. 202m., res 48m., dep. 4,764m. (Dec. 2007); COO BERNADETTE WILLOUGHBY; 4 brs.

N M Rothschild & Sons Limited: 1 King William St, London, EC4N 7AR; tel. (20) 7280-5000; fax (20) 7929-1643; internet www.nmrothschild.com; f. 1804; cap. 50m., res −2m., dep. 3,653m. (March 2007); Chair. Baron DAVID DE ROTHSCHILD; 4 brs.

UBS Limited (UBS Investment Bank): 100 Liverpool St, London, EC2M 2RH; tel. (20) 7567-8000; fax (20) 7568-4800; internet www.ubs.com/investmentbank; Group Chair. KASPER VILLIGER; CEO ALEX WILMOT-SITWELL, CARSTEN KENGETER.

Savings Organization

National Savings & Investments: 375 Kensington High St, London, W14 8SD; tel. (845) 9645-0000; e-mail pressoffice@nationalsavings.co.uk; internet www.nsandi.com; govt department and Executive Agency of the Chancellor of the Exchequer; money placed in National Savings and Investments is used by the Treasury to help cost-effectively manage the national debt and contribute towards the Government's financing needs; Chair. PAUL SPENCER (until 1 September 2009), MARTIN GRAY (from 1 September 2009); Chief Exec. JANE PLATT.

National Savings regional offices: Glasgow, G58 1SB; Durham, DH99 1NS; Blackpool, FY3 9ZW; Lytham St Annes, FY0 1YN; f. 1861; Chief Exec. PETER BAREAU.

Credit Institutions

ECI Ventures: 1st Floor, Brettenham House, Lancaster Pl., London, WC2E 7EN; tel. (20) 7606-1000; fax (20) 7240-5050; e-mail ecivmail@eciv.co.uk; internet www.eciv.co.uk; f. 1976; advises and manages ECI5 (£78m. UK Ltd Partnership), ECI6 (£100m. UK Ltd Partnership) and EC17 (£175m. UK Ltd Partnership) to provide equity capital, mainly for management buy-outs; Chair. Sir JOHN BANHAM.

Permira: 80 Pall Mall, London, SW1Y 5ES; tel. (20) 7632-1000; fax (20) 7930-3185; e-mail chris.davison@permira.com; internet www.permira.com; fmrly Schroder Ventures Europe; present name adopted 2001; advises 19 Permira Funds world-wide to provide equity capital for financial acquisitions, leveraged buy-outs and buy-ins, growth buy-outs, public-to-private transactions, 'turnarounds'; Chair. DAMON BUFFINI.

3i Group PLC: 16 Palace St, London, SW1E 5JD; tel. (20) 7928-3131; fax (20) 7928-0058; e-mail general_enquiries@3i.com; internet www.3i.com; f. 1945 as the Industrial and Commercial Finance Corpn Ltd by the English and Scottish clearing banks, renamed Finance for Industry PLC, renamed Investors in Industry Group PLC in 1983, and renamed as above in 1988; provides long-term and permanent financial advice; Chair. Baroness HOGG; Chief Exec. MICHAEL QUEEN.

Banking and Finance Organizations

Association of Foreign Banks (AFB): 1 Bengal Ct, London, EC3V 9DD; tel. (20) 7283-8300; fax (20) 7283-8302; e-mail secretariat@foreignbanks.org.uk; internet www.foreignbanks.org.uk; f. 1947; incorporated mems of the British Overseas and Commonwealth Banks' Association (f. 1917) in 1996; name changed as above in 2002; approx. 185 mem. banks; Chair. ROGER GIFFORD; Man. Dir JOHN TREADWELL.

Banking Code Standards Board: Level 12, City Tower, 40 Basinghall St, London, EC2V 5DE; tel. (845) 230-9694; fax (20) 7374-4414; e-mail helpline@bcsb.org.uk; internet www.bankingcode.org.uk; fmrly Independent Review Body; self-regulatory body which monitors and enforces Banking Code (for personal customers) and Business Banking Code; Chair. GERARD LEMOS; Chief Exec. ROBERT SKINNER.

British Bankers' Association (BBA): Pinners Hall, 105–108 Old Broad St, London, EC2N 1EX; tel. (20) 7216-8800; fax (20) 7216-8811; e-mail info@bba.org.uk; internet www.bba.org.uk; f. 1919; 225 mems; Chair. STEPHEN GREEN; Chief Exec. ANGELA KNIGHT.

Building Societies Association (BSA): 6th Floor, York House, 23 Kingsway, London, WC2B 6UJ; tel. (20) 7520-5900; fax (20) 7240-5290; e-mail web.master@bsa.org.uk; internet www.bsa.org.uk; represents building societies; Chair. JOHN GOODFELLOW; Dir-Gen. ADRIAN COLES.

The Chartered Institute of Bankers in Scotland: Drumsheugh House, 38B Drumsheugh Gardens, Edinburgh, EH3 7SW; tel. (131) 473-7777; fax (131) 473-7788; e-mail info@charteredbanker.com; internet www.charteredbanker.com; f. 1875; professional examinations, courses and publications; approx. 13,000 mems; Pres. MILLER MCLEAN; Chief Exec. SIMON THOMPSON.

London Investment Banking Association: 6 Frederick's Pl., London, EC2R 8BT; tel. (20) 7796-3606; fax (20) 7796-4345; e-mail liba@liba.org.uk; internet www.liba.org.uk; mems c. 55 British and foreign banks and securities houses; Chair. A. C. D. YARROW; Dir-Gen. JONATHAN TAYLOR.

London Money Market Association: 2 Gresham St, London, EC2V 7QP; tel. (20) 7597-4492; fax (20) 7597-4491; e-mail richard.vardy2@btinternet.com; internet www.lmma.org.uk; f. 1998; 22 mems include international banks, securities houses, building societies; Chair. IAN MAIR; Dep. Chair. R. J. VARDY, I. FOX.

STOCK EXCHANGE

The London Stock Exchange: 10 Paternoster Sq., London, EC4M 7LS; tel. (20) 7797-1000; fax (20) 7334-8916; e-mail enquiries@londonstockexchange.com; internet www.londonstockexchange.com; had its origins in the coffee houses of 17th-century London, when those wishing to invest or raise money bought and sold shares in joint-stock companies; formally constituted in 1802. By 1890 an association of stock exchanges had been formed. In 1965 a process of federation began which led to the amalgamation of all stock exchanges in the UK and Ireland in 1973. The Irish Stock Exchange officially ended its 200-year-old association with the London Stock Exchange in December 1995. In November 1986 the Exchange became a private limited company and member firms became shareholders of the Exchange with one vote each. In 1991, the 1875 Deed of Settlement was superseded as the Exchange's constitutional document by a Memorandum and Articles of Association. The governing council of the Exchange was replaced with a Board of Directors drawn from the Exchange's executive and from its customer and user base. In October 1996 an electronic quotation and trading system was introduced, which allowed for off-floor trading and direct global access to share price information. The old mandatory separation of the functions of brokers and jobbers and the system of fixed minimum commissions were then abolished. The Exchange regulates the operation of the marketplace as a Recognised Investment Exchange and also regulates listed companies as the United Kingdom's Competent Authority for Listing. The Official List is the Exchange's main market. In June 1995 an Alternative Investment Market (AIM) was established to accommodate smaller and expanding companies. In March 2000 the member institutions voted to end 199 years of mutual status and convert the London Stock Exchange into a public limited company. Its own shares were fully listed from July 2001. In October 2002 the London Stock Exchange opened a new derivatives trading platform, which would enable private investors to purchase covered warrants. The London Stock Exchange merged with its Italian counterpart, Borsa Italiana, in October 2007. In April 2009 there were 2,930 companies listed on the London Stock Exchange, including 1,151 UK-listed companies, 324 overseas-listed companies and 1,455 companies on AIM; Chair. CHRIS GIBSON-SMITH; Chief Exec. XAVIER ROLET.

SUPERVISORY BODIES

In May 1997 the Government announced its intention to establish a single statutory supervisory authority for the financial services sector. Accordingly, in November the then Securities and Investment Board was transformed into a new Financial Services Authority (FSA). From 1 June 1998, when the new Bank of England Act entered into force, the FSA incorporated the Board of Banking Supervision, which advises on supervision policy. The FSA also assumed responsibility for the supervision of insurance companies from the Department of Trade and Industry. On 1 December 2001 the FSA formally incorporated the activities of the existing regulatory bodies as well as the Building Societies Commission, the Registry of Friendly Societies and the Friendly Societies Commission, following the enactment of the 2000 Financial Services and Markets Act.

The Financial Ombudsman Service: South Quay Plaza, 183 Marsh Wall, London, E14 9SR; tel. (20) 7964-1000; fax (20) 7964-1001; e-mail complaint.info@financial-ombudsman.org.uk; internet www.financial-ombudsman.org.uk; f. 2001 to replace The Personal Investment Authority Ombudsman Bureau, The Insurance Ombudsman Bureau, The Office of the Banking Ombudsman, The Office of the Building Societies Ombudsman, The Office of the Investment Ombudsman, The Securities and Futures Authority Complaints Bureau, The Financial Services Authority Complaints Unit and The Personal Insurance Arbitration Service; Chair. Sir CHRISTOPHER KELLY; Chief Ombudsman WALTER MERRICKS.

Financial Services Authority (FSA): 25 The North Colonnade, Canary Wharf, London, E14 5HS; tel. (20) 7066-1000; fax (20) 7066-1099; e-mail consumerhelp@fsa.gov.uk; internet www.fsa.gov.uk; f. 1998 to undertake supervision, regulation and market surveillance of all areas of financial activity as defined under the 2000 Financial Services and Markets Act; single statutory regulator responsible for promoting orderly, efficient and fair markets, promoting public understanding of the financial system and reducing financial crime; Chair. Lord TURNER OF ECCHINSWELL; Chief Exec. HECTOR SANTS.

Securities & Investment Institute: 8 Eastcheap, London, EC3M 1AE; tel. (20) 7645-0600; fax (20) 7645-0601; e-mail info@sii.org.uk; internet www.sii.org.uk; f. 1992; aims to promote professional standards and ethics in the securities industry; Chair. SCOTT DOBBIE; Chief Exec. SIMON CULHANE.

INSURANCE

Lloyd's: 1 Lime St, London, EC3M 7HA; tel. (20) 7327-1000; fax (20) 7327-5229; e-mail enquiries@lloyds.com; internet www.lloyds.com; had its origins in the coffee house opened c. 1688 by Edward Lloyd and was incorporated by Act of Parliament (Lloyd's Acts 1871–1982); an international insurance market and Society of Underwriters, consisting of about 907 individual and (since January 1994) 1,155 corporate members grouped into syndicates who accept risks on the basis of unlimited and limited liability, respectively; business is effected through firms of accredited Lloyd's brokers who alone are permitted to place insurances either directly or by way of reinsurance, and some three-quarters of the annual premium income is from overseas business. Lloyd's accounts for approximately half of all international insurance premiums underwritten in the London market. The Lloyd's market is administered by the Corporation of Lloyd's through an 18-member Council, mostly elected by and from the underwriting membership. Lloyd's is regulated by the Financial Services Authority (FSA), under the Financial Services and Markets Act of 2000; capacity to accept insurance premiums of more than £16,300m. in 2008; 80 syndicates underwriting insurance in 2008, covering all classes of business from more than 200 countries and territories world-wide; Chair. Lord LEVENE; CEO RICHARD WARD.

Principal Insurance Companies

AEGON UK PLC: Edinburgh Park, Edinburgh, EH12 9SE; tel. (870) 600-0337; fax (131) 549-4188; e-mail louise.sutherland@aegon.co.uk; internet www.aegon.co.uk; f. 1831 as Scottish Equitable Life Assurance Society; restyled Scottish Equitable PLC in 1994; acquired by AEGON NV (Netherlands) in 1998 and present name adopted 1999; Chief Exec. OTTO THORESEN.

Allianz Insurance PLC: 57 Ladymead, Guildford, Surrey, GU1 1DB; tel. (1483) 568161; fax (1483) 300952; internet www.allianz.co.uk; part of the Allianz Group (Germany); f. 1905, fmrly Cornhill Insurance Co PLC; Chair. CLEMENT B. BOOTH; Chief Exec. ANDREW TORRANCE.

Aviva PLC: POB 420, St Helen's, 1 Undershaft, London, EC3P 3DQ; tel. (20) 7283-2000; e-mail aviva_info@aviva.com; internet www.aviva.com; formed by merger of Commercial Union and General Accident in 1998; merged with Norwich Union PLC in 2000; renamed as above in 2002; Chair. Lord SHARMAN OF REDLYNCH; Group Chief Exec. ANDREW MOSS.

AXA Insurance PLC: 1 Aldgate, London, EC3N 1RE; tel. (20) 7702-3109; fax (20) 7369-3909; e-mail customerservice@axa-insurance.co.uk; internet www.axa-insurance.co.uk; f. 1903; Chair. ANTHONY HAMILTON; CEO NICOLAS MOREAU.

The Co-operative Insurance: Miller St, Manchester, M60 0AL; tel. (161) 832-8686; fax (161) 837-4048; e-mail ibis@co-operativeinsurance.co.uk; internet www.co-operativeinsurance.co.uk; f. 1867; Chair. BOB BURLTON; Chief Exec. DAVID ANDERSON.

Direct Line Group: 3 Edridge Rd, Croydon, Surrey, CR9 1AG; tel. (20) 8686-3313; fax (20) 8681-0512; internet www.directline.com; wholly owned by The Royal Bank of Scotland; Man. Dir CHRIS MOAT.

Ecclesiastical Insurance Office PLC: Beaufort House, Brunswick Rd, Gloucester, GL1 1JZ; tel. (1452) 528533; fax (1452) 423557; e-mail information@eigmail.com; internet www.ecclesiastical.co.uk; f. 1887; Chair. NICHOLAS SEALY; Chief Exec. MICHAEL TRIPP.

Equitable Life Assurance Society: Walton St, Aylesbury, Buckinghamshire, HP21 7QW; tel. (845) 603-6771; fax (1296) 386383; e-mail enquiries@equitable.co.uk; internet www.equitable.co.uk; f. 1762; Chair. VANNI TREVES; Chief Exec. (vacant).

Friends Provident PLC: 100 Wood St, London, EC2V 7AN; tel. (870) 608-3678; fax (1306) 740150; e-mail customer.services@friendsprovident.co.uk; internet www.friendsprovident.co.uk; f. 1832; Exec. Chair. Sir ADRIAN A. MONTAGUE.

Legal and General Group PLC: Temple Court, 11 Queen Victoria St, London, EC4N 4TP; tel. (20) 7528-6200; fax (20) 7528-6222; internet www.legalandgeneral.com; f. 1836; Group CEO TIM BREEDON; Group Chair. ROB MARGETTS; Sec. DAVID BINDING.

Legal and General Insurance Ltd: Temple Court, 11 Queen Victoria St, London, EC4N 4TP; tel. (20) 7528-6200; fax (20) 7528-6222; f. 1946 as British Commonwealth Insurance Co; Chair. TIM BREEDON; Sec. JEAN WEBB.

Liverpool Victoria (LV): County Gates, Bournemouth, BH1 2NF; tel. (1202) 292333; fax (1202) 292253; internet www.lv.com; f. 1843; Chair. and Acting Chief Exec. DENNIS HOLT.

MGM Advantage: MGM House, Heene Rd, Worthing, Sussex, BN11 3AT; tel. (1903) 836067; fax (1903) 836004; e-mail customercentre@mgmadvantage.com; internet www.mgmadvantage.com; f. 1852; Chair. WILLIAM PROBY; CEO CHRIS EVANS.

The National Farmers Union Mutual Insurance Society Ltd: Tiddington Rd, Stratford upon Avon, Warwicks., CV37 7BJ; tel. (1789) 204211; fax (1789) 298992; internet www.nfumutual.co.uk; f. 1910; Chair. Sir DONALD CURRY; Group Chief Exec. IAN GEDEN.

Pearl: The Pearl Centre, Lynch Wood, Peterborough, Cambridgeshire, PE2 6FY; tel. (1733) 470470; fax (1733) 472300; e-mail customersupport@pearl.co.uk; internet www.pearl.co.uk; f. 1864; part of Pearl Group Limited; present name adopted Dec. 2003; Chair. JONATHAN EVANS.

Phoenix Life Ltd: 1 Wythall Green Way, Wythall Green, Birmingham, B47 6WG; tel. (845) 002-0036; internet www.phoenixlifegroup.co.uk; f. 2005 by a merger of Swiss Life UK and Royal & Sun Alliance UK life business; merged with Britannic Assurance PLC in 2007; subsidiary of Resolution PLC; Chair. DUNCAN FERGUSON; Group CEO PAUL THOMPSON.

The Prudential Assurance Co Ltd: 250 Euston Rd, London, NW1 2PQ; tel. (20) 7405-9222; fax (20) 7548-3465; e-mail media.relations@prudential.co.uk; internet www.prudential.co.uk; f. 1848; holding co: Prudential Corpn PLC; Group Chair. HARVEY MCGRATH; CEO MARK TUCKER.

Royal Liver Assurance Ltd: Royal Liver Bldg, Pier Head, Liverpool, L3 1HT; tel. (151) 236-1451; fax (151) 236-2122; internet www.royallivergroup.com; f. 1850; Chair. DAVID E. WOODS; Chief Exec. STEVE BURNETT.

The Royal London Mutual Insurance Society Ltd: 55 Gracechurch St, London, EC3V ORL; tel. (870) 850-6070; fax (1625) 605400; e-mail info@royal-london.co.uk; internet www.royal-london.co.uk; f. 1861; Chair. TIM MELVILLE-ROSS; CEO MIKE YARDLEY.

Scottish Life: POB 54, 19 St Andrew Sq., Edinburgh, EH2 1YE; tel. (131) 456-7777; fax (131) 456-7880; e-mail e-face@scottishlife.co.uk; internet www.scottishlife.co.uk; f. 1881; re-inc as a Mutual Company 1968; became part of Royal London Mutual Insurance Society in July 2001; Chief Exec. BRIAN DUFFIN.

RSA Insurance Group PLC: 9th Floor, 1 Plantation Place, 30 Fenchurch St, London, EC3M 3BD; tel. (20) 7111-7000; internet www.rsagroup.com; f. 1996 by merger of Royal Insurance Holdings PLC (f. 1845) and Sun Alliance Group PLC; present name adopted 2008; Chair. JOHN NAPIER; CEO ANDY HASTE.

Scottish Widows PLC: 15 Dalkeith Rd, Edinburgh, EH16 5BU; tel. (131) 655-6000; fax (131) 662-4053; e-mail cameron.walker@scottishwidows.co.uk; internet www.scottishwidows.co.uk; f. 1815 as Scottish Widows' Fund and Life Assurance Society; name changed as above March 2000 following acquisition by Lloyds TSB; mem. of Lloyds Banking Group; Chair. Lord LEITCH; Group Exec. Dir ARCHIE KANE.

Standard Life PLC: Standard Life House, 30 Lothian Rd, Edinburgh, EH1 2DH; tel. (131) 225-2552; e-mail customer_service@standardlife.com; internet www.standardlife.com; f. 1825; present name adopted 2006; assets under management £156,800m. (2009); Chair. GERRY GRIMSTONE; Group CEO Sir SANDY CROMBIE.

Swiss Re UK Ltd: 30 St Mary Axe, London, EC3A 8EP; tel. (20) 7933-3000; fax (20) 7933-5000; internet www.swissre.com; Chair. WALTER KIELHOLZ; CEO STEFAN LIPPE.

Wesleyan Assurance Society: Colmore Circus, Birmingham, B4 6AR; tel. (121) 335-3487; fax (121) 200-2971; internet www.wesleyan.co.uk; f. 1841; Chair. LOWRY D. MACLEAN; CEO CRAIG ERRINGTON.

Zurich Assurance Ltd: UK Life Centre, Station Rd, Swindon, SN1 1EL; tel. (1793) 511227; fax (1793) 506625; internet www.zurich.co.uk; f. 1872; Group Chair. MANFRED GENTZ; CEO JAMES SCHIRO.

Insurance Associations

Associated Scottish Life Offices: POB 25, Craigforth, Stirling, FK9 4UE; tel. (1786) 448844; fax (1786) 450427; constituted 1841 as an Association of General Managers of Scottish Offices transacting life assurance business; 7 full mems; Chair. GRAHAM POTTINGER; Dep. Chair. DAVID HENDERSON.

Association of British Insurers: 51 Gresham St, London, EC2V 7HQ; tel. (20) 7600-3333; fax (20) 7696-8999; e-mail info@abi.org.uk; internet www.abi.org.uk; f. 1985; principal trade association for insurance companies; protection, promotion, and advancement of the common interests of all classes of insurance business; c. 390 mems; Chair. ARCHIE KANE; Dir-Gen. STEPHEN HADDRILL.

British Insurance Brokers' Association (BIBA): 8th Floor, John Stow House, 18 Bevis Marks, London, EC3A 7JB; tel. (870) 950-1790; fax (20) 7626-9676; e-mail enquiries@biba.org.uk; internet www.biba

THE UNITED KINGDOM

.org.uk; f. 1977; Chair. DEREK THORNTON; Chief Exec. ERIC GALBRAITH.

Chartered Insurance Institute: 42–48 High Rd, South Woodford, London, E18 2JP; tel. (20) 8989-8464; fax (20) 8530-3052; e-mail customer.serv@cii.co.uk; internet www.cii.co.uk; f. 1897; inc 1912; approx. 90,000 mems; Pres. LORD HUNT OF WIRRAL; CEO Dr ALEXANDER SCOTT.

Fire Protection Association: London Rd, Moreton-in-Marsh, Gloucestershire, GL56 0RH; tel. (1608) 812500; fax (1608) 812501; e-mail fpa@thefpa.co.uk; internet www.thefpa.co.uk; f. 1946; Man. Dir JON O'NEILL.

Insurance Institute of London: 5th Floor, 20 Aldermanbury, London, EC2V 7HY; tel. (20) 7600-1343; fax (20) 7600-6857; e-mail iil.london@cii.co.uk; internet www.iilondon.co.uk; f. 1907; Pres. CHARLES PHILIPPS.

International Underwriting Association (IUA): London Underwriting Centre, 3 Minster Ct, Mincing Lane, London, EC3R 7DD; tel. (20) 7617-4444; fax (20) 7617-4440; e-mail info@iua.com; internet www.iua.co.uk; f. 1998; Chair. STEPHEN RILEY; Chief Exec. DAVE J. MATCHAM.

Associations of Actuaries

Faculty of Actuaries: 18 Dublin St, Edinburgh, EH1 3PP; tel. (131) 240-1300; fax (131) 240-1313; e-mail faculty@actuaries.org.uk; internet www.actuaries.org.uk; f. 1856; 1,275 Fellows, 13 Honorary Fellows; Pres. STEWART RITCHIE; Chief Exec. CAROLINE INSTANCE.

Institute of Actuaries: Staple Inn Hall, High Holborn, London, WC1V 7QJ; tel. (20) 7632-2100; fax (20) 7632-2111; e-mail institute@actuaries.org.uk; internet www.actuaries.org.uk; f. 1848; Royal Charter 1884; 16,287 mems (May 2008); Pres. NIGEL MASTERS; Chief Exec. CAROLINE INSTANCE.

Trade and Industry

GOVERNMENT AGENCIES

Advisory, Conciliation and Arbitration Service (Acas): Brandon House, 180 Borough High St, London, SE1 1LW; tel. (20) 7210-3613; fax (20) 7210-3615; internet www.acas.org.uk; f. 1975; an independent organization, under the direction of a council comprising employers, trade union representatives and independent members, appointed by the Secretary of State for Business, Enterprise and Regulatory Reform. The service aims to improve organizations and working life through good employment relations. Acas provides collective conciliation, arbitration, mediation, advisory, training and information services, and conciliates in individual employment rights issues; Chair. ED SWEENEY; Chief Exec. JOHN TAYLOR.

Central Arbitration Committee: 22nd Floor, Euston Tower, 286 Euston Rd, London, NW1 3JJ; tel. (20) 7904-2300; fax (20) 7904-2301; e-mail enquiries@cac.gov.uk; internet www.cac.gov.uk; f. 1976 as an independent body under the 1975 Employment Protection Act, in succession to Industrial Court/Industrial Arbitration Board; adjudicates on claims for statutory trade union recognition and de-recognition under the 1999 Employment Relations Act; determines disclosure of information complaints and considers applications and complaints received under the Information and Consultation of Employees Regulations 2004; considers applications in relation to the establishment and operation of European Works Councils, European Companies and European Co-operative Societies; Chair. Sir MICHAEL BURTON; Chief Exec. GRAEME CHARLES.

Charity Commission for England and Wales: Harmsworth House, 13–15 Bouverie St, London, EC4Y 8DP; tel. (845) 300-0218; fax (20) 7674-2300; e-mail enquiries@charitycommission.gsi.gov.uk; internet www.charitycommission.gov.uk; statutory organization responsible for the regulation of registered charities; Chief Exec. ANDREW HIND; Chair. SUZI LEATHER.

Competition Appeal Tribunal: Victoria House, Bloomsbury Pl., London, WC1A 2EB; tel. (20) 7979-7979; fax (20) 7979-7978; e-mail info@catribunal.org.uk; internet www.catribunal.org.uk; f. 2002; a specialist tribunal established to hear certain cases in the sphere of British competition and economic regulatory law; hears appeals against decisions of the Office of Fair Trading and the regulators in the telecommunications, electricity, gas, water, railways and air traffic services sectors under the Competition Act of 1998; reviews decisions of the Office of Fair Trading, the Competition Commission and the Secretary of State made pursuant to the merger control and market investigation provisions of the Enterprise Act of 2002; also has jurisdiction, under the Competition Act of 1998, to award damages in respect of infringements of EC or British competition law and, under the Communications Act of 2003, to hear appeals against decisions of Ofcom; headed by the President and a panel of Chairmen and 19 mems with backgrounds in law, economics, business, accountancy and regulation who sit with the President or a mem. of the panel of Chairmen to hear cases; Pres. Sir GERALD BARLING; Registrar CHARLES DHANOWA.

Competition Commission: Victoria House, Southampton Row, London, WC1B 4AD; tel. (20) 7271-0100; fax (20) 7271-0367; e-mail info@cc.gsi.gov.uk; internet www.competition-commission.org.uk; conducts in-depth inquiries into mergers, markets and the regulation of the major regulated industries; Chair. PETER FREEMAN; Chief Exec. DAVID SAUNDERS.

Competition Service: Victoria House, Bloomsbury Pl., London, WC1A 2EB; tel. (20) 7979-7979; fax (20) 7979-7978; e-mail info@catribunal.org.uk; internet www.catribunal.org.uk; f. 2003 under the Enterprise Act 2002; a corporate and executive non-departmental public body, whose purpose is to fund and provide support services to the Competition Appeal Tribunal; Dir of Operations JEREMY STRAKER.

Consumer Focus: 4th floor, Artillery House, Artillery Row, London, SW1P 1RT; tel. (20) 7799-7900; fax (20) 7799-7901; e-mail contact@consumerfocus.org.uk; internet www.consumerfocus.org.uk; f. 2008 by merger of Postwatch, energywatch and the National Consumer Council; Advocacy body for consumer rights; Chair. LARRY WHITTY.

Environment Agency: Rio House, Waterside Drive, Aztec West, Almondsbury, Bristol, BS32 4UD; tel. (8708) 506506; e-mail enquiries@environment-agency.gov.uk; internet www.environment-agency.gov.uk; f. 1996; incorporated former National Rivers Authority; Chair. of Board Lord SMITH; Chief Exec. PAUL LEINSTER.

Food Standards Agency: Aviation House, 125 Kingsway, London, WC2B 6NH; tel. (20) 7276-8000; fax (20) 7276-8004; e-mail helpline@foodstandards.gsi.gov.uk; internet www.food.gov.uk; f. 2000; Chair. Dame DEIRDRE HUTTON; Chief Exec. TIM SMITH.

Forestry Commission: Silvan House, 231 Corstorphine Rd, Edinburgh, EH12 7AT; tel. (131) 334-0303; fax (131) 334-3047; e-mail enquiries@forestry.gsi.gov.uk; internet www.forestry.gov.uk; government department responsible for protecting and expanding the forests and woodlands of England, Scotland and Wales and increasing their value to society and the environment; implements the Government's forestry policy within the framework of the Forestry Acts, administers the Woodland Grant Scheme, controls tree-felling through the issue of licences, administers plant health regulations to protect woodlands against tree-pests and diseases, and conducts research; responsible for the management of the national forests; Chair. Lord CLARK OF WINDERMERE; Dir-Gen. TIM ROLLINSON.

GLE oneLondon: New City Court, 20 St Thomas St, London, SE1 9RS; tel. (20) 7403-0300; fax (20) 7940-1742; e-mail info@gle.co.uk; internet www.gle.co.uk/onelondon; f. 2001 following merger between London Enterprise Agency and Greater London Enterprise; jointly owned by all 33 London borough councils; Man. Dir PETER THACKWRAY.

Health and Safety Executive: Caerphilly Business Park, Caerphilly, CF83 3GG; tel. (845) 345-0055; fax (845) 408-9566; e-mail hse.infoline@natbrit.com; internet www.hse.gov.uk; Chief Exec. GEOFFREY PODGER.

Learning and Skills Council: Cheylesmore House, Quinton Rd, Coventry, CV1 2WT; tel. (845) 019-4170; fax (24) 7682-3675; e-mail info@lsc.gov.uk; internet www.lsc.gov.uk; Chair. CHRIS BANKS; Chief Exec. GEOFF RUSSELL (acting).

National Audit Office: 151 Buckingham Palace Rd, London, SW1W 9SS; tel. (20) 7798-7000; fax (20) 7798-7894; e-mail enquiries@nao.gsi.gov.uk; internet www.nao.org.uk; audits the financial statements of all government departments and agencies, certain public bodies and international organizations; the Comptroller and Auditor-General is responsible for controlling receipts into, and issues from, the Consolidated and National Loans Funds and reports to Parliament on value for money issues or on important issues arising from the financial statements; Comptroller and Auditor-General TIM BURR.

Natural England: 1 East Parade, Sheffield, S1 2ET; tel. (114) 241-8920; fax (114) 241-8921; e-mail enquiries@naturalengland.org.uk; internet www.naturalengland.org.uk; f. 2006 by merger of English Nature, landscape, access and recreation sections of the Countryside Agency and the environmental land management functions of the Rural Development Service; advises Government and acts on issues relating to the conservation and enhancement of the environmental, economic and social well-being of the English countryside; Chair. Sir MARTIN DOUGHTY; Chief Exec. Dr HELEN PHILLIPS.

Office of Fair Trading: Fleetbank House, 2–6 Salisbury Sq., London, EC4Y 8JX; tel. (20) 7211-8000; fax (20) 7211-8800; e-mail enquiries@oft.gsi.gov.uk; internet www.oft.gov.uk; f. 1973; monitors consumer affairs, competition policy, consumer credit, estate agencies, etc.; Chair. PHILIP COLLINS; Chief Exec. JOHN FINGLETON.

Postal Services Commission (Postcomm): Hercules House, 6 Hercules Rd, London, SE1 7DB; tel. (20) 7593-2100; fax (20) 7593-

THE UNITED KINGDOM

2142; e-mail info@psc.gov.uk; internet www.psc.gov.uk; f. 2000 under the Postal Services Act of 2000 as an independent regulator for postal services in the UK; duties include ensuring the provision of a universal postal service, licensing postal operators, introducing competition into mail services, regulating Royal Mail and advising the Govt on the Post Office network; Chair. NIGEL STAPLETON; Chief Exec. TIM BROWN.

UK Statistics Authority: Statistics House, Tredegar Park, Newport, Gwent, NP10 8XG; tel. (0845) 604-1857; e-mail authority.enquiries@statistics.gov.uk; internet www.statisticsauthority.gov.uk; f. 2008; advises on the quality, quality assurance and priority-setting for National Statistics and on the procedures designed to deliver statistical integrity, to ensure National Statistics are trustworthy and responsive to public needs; Chair. Sir MICHAEL SCHOLAR; Chief Exec. KAREN DUNNELL.

United Kingdom Atomic Energy Authority (UKAEA): Harwell Science and Innovation Campus, Didcot, Oxfordshire, OX11 0RA; tel. (1235) 820220; fax (1235) 434452; internet www.ukaea.org.uk; f. 1954 to take responsibility for British research and development into all aspects of atomic energy; separated into AEA Technology, which operated as the Authority's commercial division, and UKAEA; AEA Technology transferred to the private sector in 1996. UKAEA's core task is to manage the decommissioning of reactors and other facilities used for the nuclear research and development programme. It also carries out fusion research. These activities are conducted at sites at Windscale (Cumbria), Dounreay (Caithness), Harwell and Culham (Oxfordshire) and Winfrith (Dorset); Chair. Lady BARBARA JUDGE; Chief Exec. NORMAN HARRISON.

DEVELOPMENT ORGANIZATIONS

Economic Research Institute of Northern Ireland (ERINI): Floral Buildings, 2–14 East Bridge St, Belfast, BT1 3NQ; tel. (28) 9072-7350; fax (28) 9031-9003; e-mail contact@erini.ac.uk; internet www.erini.ac.uk; f. 2004 to replace the Northern Ireland Economic Council (f. 1977); provides independent economic research, analysis and advice aimed at challenging and developing public policy-making and strategic thinking on issues facing Northern Ireland society; 15 mems representing trade union, employer and independent interests; Chair. JOHN BEATH; Dir VICTOR HEWITT.

Invest Northern Ireland (Invest NI): Bedford Sq., Bedford St, Belfast, BT1 7ES; tel. (28) 9023-9090; fax (28) 9043-6536; e-mail eo@investni.com; internet www.investni.com; f. 2002 to assume responsibility for the activities of the Industrial Development Board for Northern Ireland, the Local Enterprise Development Unit, the Industrial Research and Technology Unit, the Company Development Programme and the business support activities of the Northern Ireland Tourist Board; Invest NI is the main economic development agency in Northern Ireland and, sponsored by the Dept of Enterprise, Trade and Investment, aims to accelerate economic growth in Northern Ireland; Chair. STEPHEN KINGON; Chief Exec. LESLIE MORRISON.

London First: 1 Hobhouse Court, Suffolk St, London, SW1Y 4HH; tel. (20) 7665-1500; fax (20) 7665-1501; e-mail staff@london-first.co.uk; internet www.london-first.co.uk; promotes London as a business centre; Chair. DES GUNEWARDENA (acting); Pres. Lord SHEPPARD OF DIDGEMERE.

Overseas Development Institute: 111 Westminster Bridge Rd, London, SE1 7JD; tel. (20) 7922-0300; fax (20) 7922-0399; e-mail odi@odi.org.uk; internet www.odi.org.uk; f. 1960; independent policy unit on international development and humanitarian issues; Chair. Lord TURNER; Dir SIMON MAXWELL.

Scottish Enterprise: 5 Atlantic Quay, 150 Broomielaw, Glasgow, G2 8LU; tel. (141) 248-2700; fax (141) 221-3217; e-mail network.helpline@scotent.co.uk; internet www.scottish-enterprise.com; economic development agency for lowland Scotland; Chair. Sir JOHN WARD; Chief Exec. JACK PERRY.

CHAMBERS OF COMMERCE

British Chambers of Commerce (BCC): 65 Petty France, London, SW1H 9EU; tel. (20) 7654-5800; fax (20) 7654-5819; e-mail info@britishchambers.org.uk; internet www.britishchambers.org.uk; f. 1860; in January 1993 subsumed National Chamber of Trade (f. 1897); represents the new Approved Chamber Network in the United Kingdom (comprising 58 Chambers at June 2007); Pres. NEVILLE RAYNER; Dir-Gen. DAVID FROST.

International Chamber of Commerce (ICC) United Kingdom: 12 Grosvenor Pl., London, SW1X 7HH; tel. (20) 7838-9363; fax (20) 7235-5447; e-mail info@iccorg.co.uk; internet www.iccuk.net; f. 1920; British affiliate of the world business org.; Dir ANDREW HOPE.

London Chamber of Commerce and Industry: 33 Queen St, London, EC4R 1AP; tel. (20) 7248-4444; fax (20) 7489-0391; e-mail lc@londonchamber.co.uk; internet www.londonchamber.co.uk; Pres. STEPHEN GREENE; Chief Exec. JEFFREY ADAMS.

Directory

Northern Ireland Chamber of Commerce and Industry: Chamber of Commerce House, 22 Great Victoria St, Belfast, BT2 7BJ; tel. (28) 9024-4113; fax (28) 9024-7024; e-mail mail@northernirelandchamber.com; internet www.nicci.co.uk; f. 1783; Pres. BRO MCFERRAN; Chief Exec. ANN MCGREGOR; 4,000 mems.

INDUSTRIAL AND TRADE ASSOCIATIONS

Aluminium Federation: National Metalforming Centre, 47 Birmingham Rd, West Bromwich, B70 6PY; tel. (121) 601-6363; fax (870) 138-9714; e-mail alfed@alfed.org.uk; internet www.alfed.org.uk; f. 1962; Pres. HENRY DICKINSON; Sec.-Gen. WILL SAVAGE.

Association of the British Pharmaceutical Industry: 12 Whitehall, London, SW1A 2DY; tel. (20) 7930-3477; fax (20) 7747-1414; e-mail abpi@abpi.org.uk; internet www.abpi.org.uk; f. 1930; Pres. CHRIS BRINSMEAD; Dir-Gen. Dr RICHARD BARKER.

Association of Manufacturers of Domestic Appliances: Rapier House, 40–46 Lamb's Conduit St, London, WC1N 3NW; tel. (20) 7405-0666; fax (20) 7405-6609; e-mail info@amdea.org.uk; internet www.amdea.org.uk; f. 1969; 32 mem. cos; Chief Exec. DOUGLAS HERBISON.

BFM (British Furniture Manufacturers Association): Wycombe House, 9 Amersham Hill, High Wycombe, Bucks HP13 6NR; tel. (149) 4523-021; fax (149) 4474-270; e-mail info@bfm.org.uk; internet www.bfm.org.uk; merged in January 1993 with BFM Exhibitions and BFM Exports; Man. Dir ROGER MASON.

British Beer and Pub Association: Market Towers, 1 Nine Elms Lane, London, SW8 5NQ; tel. (20) 7627-9191; fax (20) 7627-9123; e-mail web@beerandpub.com; internet www.beerandpub.com; f. 1904; trade association for British brewing industry and multiple pub operators; Chair. MICHAEL TURNER; Chief Exec. DAVID LONG (acting).

British Cable Association: 3–30 Lingfield Rd, Wimbledon, SW19 4PU; tel. and fax (20) 8946-6978; e-mail peter.smeeth@btconnect.com; internet www.bcauk.org; f. 1903; fmrly British Cable Makers' Confederation; Sec.-Gen. PETER SMEETH.

British Cement Association: Riverside House, 4 Meadows Business Park, Station Approach, Blackwater, Camberley, Surrey, GU17 9AB; tel. (1276) 608700; fax (1276) 608701; e-mail info@bca.org.uk; internet www.bca.org.uk; Chair. CLIVE JAMES; Chief Exec. PAL CHANA.

British Ceramic Confederation: Federation House, Station Rd, Stoke-on-Trent, Staffs., ST4 2SA; tel. (1782) 744631; fax (1782) 744102; e-mail bcc@ceramfed.co.uk; internet www.ceramfed.co.uk; f. 1984; 125 mems; Chief Exec. KEVIN FARRELL.

British Clothing Industry Association (BCIA): 5 Portland Pl., London, W1B 1PW; tel. (20) 7636-7788; fax (20) 7636-7515; e-mail bcia@dial.pipex.com; f. 1980; Chair. PETER LUCAS; Dir JOHN R. WILSON.

British Electrotechnical and Allied Manufacturers' Association (BEAMA Ltd): Westminster Tower, 3 Albert Embankment, London, SE1 7SL; tel. (20) 7793-3000; fax (20) 7793-3003; e-mail info@beama.org.uk; internet www.beama.org.uk; f. 1905 as British Electrical and Allied Manufacturers' Association Ltd, present name from 2002; 460 mems; Pres. and Chair. RICHARD DICK; CEO DAVID DOSSETT.

British Exporters' Association: Broadway House, Tothill St, London, SW1H 9NQ; tel. (20) 7222-5419; fax (20) 7799-2468; e-mail hughbailey@bexa.co.uk; internet www.bexa.co.uk; Pres. Sir RICHARD NEEDHAM; Chair. RICHARD HILL; Dir HUGH BAILEY.

British Footwear Association: 3 Burystead Place, Wellingborough, Northants, NN8 1AH; tel. (1933) 229005; fax (1933) 225009; e-mail info@britfoot.com; internet www.britfoot.com; f. 1898; Exec. Officer ELAINE DAVIES.

British Glass: 9 Churchill Way, Chapeltown, Sheffield, S35 2PY; tel. (114) 290-1850; fax (114) 290-1851; e-mail info@britglass.co.uk; internet www.britglass.org.uk; over 100 mems; Dir-Gen. DAVID WORKMAN.

British Hospitality Association: Queen's House, 55/56 Lincoln's Inn Fields, London, WC2A 3BH; tel. (845) 880-7744; fax (20) 7404-7799; e-mail bha@bha.org.uk; internet www.bha.org.uk; f. 1907; Pres. Sir DAVID MICHELS; Chief Exec. ROBERT COTTON.

British Non-Ferrous Metals Federation: 5 Grovelands Business Centre, Boundary Way, Hemel Hempstead, HP2 7TE; tel. (1442) 275705; fax (1442) 275716; e-mail bnfmf@copperuk.org.uk; f. 1945; Dir DAVID PARKER.

The British Precast Concrete Federation Ltd: 60 Charles St, Leicester, LE1 1FB; tel. (116) 253-6161; fax (116) 251-4568; e-mail info@britishprecast.org; internet www.britishprecast.org; f. 1918; approx. 125 mems; Chief Exec. MARTIN A. CLARKE.

British Printing Industries Federation: Farringdon Point, 29–35 Farringdon Rd, London, EC1M 3JF; tel. (870) 240-4085; fax (20) 7405-7784; e-mail andrew.brown@bpif.org.uk; internet www

THE UNITED KINGDOM

.britishprint.com; f. 1900; 2,500 mems; Pres. MIKE TAYLOR; Chief Exec. MICHAEL JOHNSON.

British Rubber Manufacturers' Association: 6 Bath Pl., Rivington St, London, EC2A 3JE; tel. (20) 7457-5040; fax (20) 7972-9008; e-mail mail@brma.co.uk; internet www.brma.co.uk; f. 1968; Pres. JAMES RICKARD; Dir A. J. DORKEN.

The Carpet Foundation: MFC Complex, 60 New Rd, Kidderminster, Worcs., DY10 1AQ; tel. (1562) 755568; fax (1562) 865405; internet www.comebacktocarpet.com; 11 manufacturer and 1,100 retailer mems; Chair. JOHN DUNCAN; Chief Exec. MIKE HARDIMAN.

CBI: Centre Point, 103 New Oxford St, London, WC1A 1DU; tel. (20) 7379-7400; fax (20) 7240-1578; internet www.cbi.org.uk; f. 1965 as the Confederation of British Industry, name changed as above in 2001; acts as a national point of reference for all seeking views of industry and is recognized internationally as the representative organization of British industry and management; advises the Government on all aspects of policy affecting the interests of industry; has a direct corporate membership employing more than 4m., and a trade association membership representing more than 6m. of the workforce; Pres. MARTIN BROUGHTON (until 2 June 2009), HELEN ALEXANDER (from 2 June 2009); Dir-Gen. RICHARD LAMBERT.

Chemical Industries Association: King's Buildings, Smith Sq., London, SW1P 3JJ; tel. (20) 7834-3399; fax (20) 7834-4469; e-mail enquiries@cia.org.uk; internet www.cia.org.uk; Pres. ALISTAIR STEEL; Dir-Gen. JUDITH HACKITT.

Construction Confederation: 55 Tufton St, London, SW1P 3QL; tel. (870) 898-9090; fax (870) 898-9095; e-mail enquiries@thecc.org.uk; internet www.thecc.org.uk; f. 1878; 5,000 mems; Chair. JAMES WATES; Chief Exec. STEPHEN RATCLIFFE.

Dairy UK: 93 Baker St, London, W1U 6QQ; tel. (20) 7486-7244; fax (20) 7487-4734; e-mail info@dairyuk.org; internet www.dairyuk.org; f. 1933; Chair. MARK ALLEN; Dir-Gen. JIM BEGG.

Electrical Contractors' Association: ESCA House, 34 Palace Court, London, W2 4HY; tel. (20) 7313-4800; fax (20) 7221-7344; e-mail info@eca.co.uk; internet www.eca.co.uk; f. 1901; Pres. ALLAN LITTLER; Dir DAVID R. J. POLLOCK.

Energy Networks Association: 6th Floor, Dean Bradley House, 52 Horseferry Rd, London, SW1P 2AF; tel. (20) 7706-5100; e-mail info@energynetworks.org; internet 2008.energynetworks.org; f. 2003; represents British gas and electricity transmission and distribution licence holders; Chair. MARK MATHIESON; CEO DAVID SMITH.

Engineering Employers' Federation (EEF): Broadway House, Tothill St, London, SW1H 9NQ; tel. (20) 7222-7777; fax (20) 7222-2782; e-mail enquiries@eef-fed.org.uk; internet www.eef.org.uk; f. 1896; 6,000 mems through 14 associations; Pres. ALAN WOOD; CEO GILBERT TOPPIN.

Farmers' Union of Wales: Llys Amaeth, Plas Gogerddan, Aberystwyth, Ceredigion, SY23 3BT; tel. (1970) 820820; fax (1970) 820821; e-mail head.office@fuw.org.uk; internet www.fuw.org.uk; f. 1955; 14,000 mems; Pres. GARETH VAUGHAN.

Food and Drink Federation: 6 Catherine St, London, WC2B 5JJ; tel. (20) 7836-2460; fax (20) 7836-0580; e-mail generalenquiries@fdf.org.uk; internet www.fdf.org.uk; Dir-Gen. MELANIE LEECH.

Glass and Glazing Federation: 44–48 Borough High St, London, SE1 1XB; tel. (870) 042-4255; fax (870) 042-4266; e-mail info@ggf.org.uk; internet www.ggf.org.uk; f. 1977; trade organization for employers and cos in the flat glass, glazing, home improvement, plastic and window film industries; Chief Exec. NIGEL REES.

Institute of Export: Export House, Minerva Business Park, Lynch Wood, Peterborough, PE2 6FT; tel. (1733) 404400; fax (1733) 404444; e-mail institute@export.org.uk; internet www.export.org.uk; f. 1935; professional educational organization devoted to the development of British export trade and the interests of those associated with it; more than 6,000 mems; Pres. JAMES DAVIES; Chair. LESLEY BATCHELOR; Dir ANDY GIBSON.

Labour Relations Agency: 2-8 Gordon St, Belfast, BT1 2LG; tel. (28) 9032-1442; fax (28) 9033-0827; e-mail info@lra.org.uk; internet www.lra.org.uk; f. 1976; provides an impartial and confidential employment relations service to those engaged in industry, commerce and the public services in Northern Ireland; provides advice on good employment practices and assistance with the development and implementation of employment policies and procedures; also active in resolving disputes through its conciliation, mediation and arbitration services.

National Association of British and Irish Millers Ltd: 21 Arlington St, London, SW1A 1RN; tel. (20) 7493-2521; fax (20) 7493-6785; e-mail info@nabim.org.uk; internet www.nabim.org.uk; trade assoc. of the British flour milling industry; f. 1878; Dir-Gen. ALEXANDER WAUGH; Sec. NIGEL BENNETT.

National Farmers' Union: Agriculture House, Stoneleigh Park, Warwickshire CV8 2TZ; tel. (24) 7685-8500; fax (24) 7685-8501; e-mail nfu@nfu.org.uk; internet www.nfuonline.com; f. 1904 as Lincolnshire Farmers' Union, adopted present name in 1908; Pres. PETER KENDALL; Dir-Gen. RICHARD MACDONALD.

National Metal Trades Federation: Savoy Tower, 77 Renfrew St, Glasgow, G2 3BZ; tel. (141) 332-0826; fax (141) 332-5788; e-mail alex.shaw@nmtf.org.uk; Sec. ALEX SHAW.

Northern Ireland Hotels Federation: Midland Bldg, Whitla St, Belfast, BT15 1JP; tel. (28) 9035-1110; fax (28) 9035-1509; e-mail office@nihf.co.uk; internet www.nihf.co.uk; Pres. ISSAM HORSHI; Chief Exec. JANICE GAULT.

Northern Ireland Textiles and Apparel Asscn: 5C The Square, Hillsborough, BT26 6AG; tel. (28) 9268-9999; fax (28) 9268-9968; e-mail info@nita.co.uk; internet www.nita.co.uk; f. 1993; Dir LINDA MACHUGH; 30 mems.

Producers Alliance for Cinema and Television (PACT) Ltd: 2nd Floor, 1 Procter St, London, WC1V 6DW; tel. (20) 7067-4367; fax (20) 7067-4377; e-mail enquiries@pact.co.uk; internet www.pact.co.uk; film and TV producers; represents 1,000 companies; Chief Exec. JOHN MCVAY; Chair. CHARLES WACE.

Quarry Products Association: Gillingham House, 38–44 Gillingham St, London, SW1V 1HU; tel. (20) 7963-8000; fax (20) 7963-8001; e-mail info@qpa.org; internet www.qpa.org; fmrly British Ready Mixed Concrete Asscn, and the British Aggregate Construction Materials Industry Ltd; Chair LYNDA THOMPSON; Dir SIMON VAN DER BYL.

Scottish Building Federation: Crichton House, Crichton's Close, Edinburgh, EH8 8DT; tel. (131) 556-8866; fax (131) 558-5247; e-mail info@scottish-building.co.uk; internet www.scottish-building.co.uk; Pres. BILL IMLACH; Gen. Man. DOUGLAS FERGUS.

Scottish Enterprise—Textiles: Apex House, 99 Haymarket Terrace, Edinburgh, EH12 5DH; tel. (131) 313-6243; fax (131) 313-4231; internet www.scottish-textiles.co.uk; present name since 1991.

Sea Fish Industry Authority (Seafish): 18 Logie Mill, Logie Green Rd, Edinburgh, EH7 4HS; tel. (131) 558-3331; fax (131) 558-1442; e-mail seafish@seafish.co.uk; internet www.seafish.org; non-departmental public body sponsored by the four United Kingdom Government fisheries departments and funded by a levy on seafood; works with all sectors of the British seafood industry to satisfy consumers, raise standards, improve efficiency and secure a sustainable future; Chair. CHARLES HOWESON; Chief Exec. JOHN RUTHERFORD.

Society of British Aerospace Companies Ltd: Unit 7, Salamanca Sq, 9 Albert Embankment, London, SE1 7SP; tel. (20) 7091-4500; fax (20) 7091-4545; e-mail post@sbac.co.uk; internet www.sbac.co.uk; f. 1916; national trade association for the British aerospace, defence and security industry; Pres. ALLAN COOK; Dir-Gen. IAN HODDEN.

Society of Motor Manufacturers and Traders: Forbes House, Halkin St, London, SW1X 7DS; tel. (20) 7235-7000; fax (20) 7235-7112; e-mail membership@smmt.co.uk; internet www.smmt.co.uk; f. 1902; Pres. JOE GREENWELL; Chief Exec. PAUL EVERITT.

The Sugar Bureau: 6 Catherine St, London, WC2B 5JJ; tel. (20) 7379-6830; fax (20) 7836-4113; e-mail info@sugar-bureau.co.uk; internet www.sugar-bureau.co.uk; represents sugar companies in the UK, provides technical, educational and consumer information about sugar and health; Dir Dr ALISON BOYD.

Timber Trade Federation: Building Centre, 26 Store St, London, WC1E 7BT; tel. (20) 3205-0067; fax (20) 7291-5379; e-mail ttf@ttf.co.uk; internet www.ttf.co.uk; Chief Exec. JOHN WHITE.

Ulster Chemists' Asscn: 5 Annadale Ave, Belfast, BT7 3JH; tel. (28) 9069-0456; fax (28) 9069-0457; e-mail adrienne@uca.org.uk; internet www.uca.org.uk; f. 1901; promotion and protection of interests of community pharmacies in Northern Ireland; Pres. PAUL MCDONAGH.

Ulster Farmers' Union: Dunedin, 475 Antrim Rd, Belfast, BT15 3DA; tel. (28) 9037-0222; fax (28) 9037-1231; e-mail info@ufuhq.com; internet www.ufuni.org; f. 1918; Pres. GRAHAM FUREY; Chief Exec. CLARKE BLACK; 12,500 mems.

United Kingdom Petroleum Industry Association: Quality House, Quality Court, Chancery Lane, London, WC1A 1HP; tel. (20) 7269-7600; e-mail info@ukpia.com; internet www.ukpia.com; f. 1978; Pres. NICK THOMAS; Dir-Gen. CHRIS HUNT.

EMPLOYERS' ASSOCIATIONS

British Retail Consortium: 2nd Floor, 21 Dartmouth St, London, SW1H 9BP; tel. (20) 7854-8900; fax (20) 7854-8901; e-mail info@brc.org.uk; internet www.brc.org.uk; f. 1975; represents retailers; Chair. GEOFF MULCAHY; Dir-Gen. STEPHEN ROBERTSON.

Chartered Management Institute: Management House, Cottingham Rd, Corby, NN17 1TT; tel. (1536) 204222; fax (1536) 201651; e-mail enquiries@managers.org.uk; internet www.managers.org.uk; f. 1992 as the Institute of Management by amalgamation of British Institute of Management (f. 1947) and Institution of

THE UNITED KINGDOM

Industrial Managers (f. 1931); changed name as above in 2002; represents 81,000 individual mems and 450 corporate mems; Pres. Sir DAVID HOWARD; Chief Exec. RUTH SPELLMAN.

Federation of Small Businesses: Sir Frank Whittle Way, Blackpool Business Park, Blackpool, Lancashire FY4 2FE; tel. (1253) 336000; fax (1253) 348046; e-mail membership@fsb.org.uk; internet www.fsb.org.uk; f. 1974; represents the interests of British small businesses and the self-employed; 185,000 mems; Policy Chair. JOHN WRIGHT.

Institute of Directors: 116 Pall Mall, London, SW1Y 5ED; tel. (20) 7766-8888; fax (20) 7766-8833; e-mail enquiries@iod.com; internet www.iod.com; f. 1903; 53,000 mems; Chair. Dr NEVILLE BAIN; Dir-Gen. MILES TEMPLEMAN.

UTILITIES

Electricity and Gas

Regulatory Authorities

Northern Ireland Authority for Energy Regulation: Queens House, 10–18 Queens St, Belfast, BT1 6ED; tel. (28) 9031-1575; e-mail ofreg@nics.gov.uk; internet ofreg.nics.gov.uk; independent public body to regulate the electricity and natural gas industries in Northern Ireland; Chair. PETER MATTHEWS; Chief Exec. IAIN OSBOURNE.

Office of Gas and Electricity Markets (Ofgem): 9 Millbank, London, SW1P 3GE; tel. (20) 7901-7000; fax (20) 7901-7066; e-mail consumeraffairs@ofgem.gov.uk; internet www.ofgem.gov.uk; f. 1999 following merger of Offer and Ofgas; regulates the gas and electricity industries in England, Scotland and Wales and aims to promote the interests of all gas and electricity customers by promoting competition and regulating monopolies; Chair. Lord JOHN MOGG; Chief Exec. ALISTAIR BUCHANAN.

Principal Companies

British Energy: GSO Business Park, East Kilbride, G74 5PG; tel. (1355) 846000; fax (1355) 846001; e-mail john.mcnamara@british-energy.com; internet www.british-energy.com; production of electricity; operates 8 nuclear power stations and 1 coal-fired power station in the United Kingdom; acquired by EDF (France) Jan. 2009; sale of 20% stake to Centrica PLC pending; Chief Exec. BILL COLEY.

British Gas: Centrica PLC, Millstream, Maidenhead Rd, Windsor, Berkshire, SL4 5GD; tel. (845) 070-9010; e-mail house@britishgas.co.uk; internet www.britishgas.co.uk; part of Centrica Group; Chair. ROGER CARR; Man. Dir PHIL BENTLEY.

CE Electric UK: 98 Aketon Rd, Castleford, WF10 5DS; tel. (1977) 605934; fax (1977) 605944; internet www.ceelectricuk.com; subsidiary of MidAmerican Energy Holdings Co; delivers electricity to 3.6m. homes in the north-east of England, Yorkshire and Humberside; Dir J. M. FRANCE.

Central Networks: Herald Way, Pegasus Business Park, East Midlands Airport, Castle Donnington, DE74 2TU; tel. (800) 0963080; internet www.central-networks.co.uk; distribution of electricity; subsidiary of E.ON UK PLC; fmrly East Midlands Electricity PLC; merged with Midlands Electricity PLC in 2004 and name changed to above; Man. Dir JOHN CRACKETT.

EDF Energy: 40 Grosvenor Pl., London, SW1X 7GN; tel. (20) 7242-9050; e-mail info@edfenergy.com; internet www.edfenergy.com; producer and supplier of electricity and gas; Chair. PIERRE GADONNEIX; Chief Exec. VINCENT DE RIVAZ.

E.ON UK PLC: Westwood Way, Westwood Business Park, Coventry, CV4 8LG; tel. (24) 7642-4000; fax (24) 7642-5432; e-mail jonathan.smith@eon-uk.com; internet www.eon-uk.com; f. 2004; fmrly Powergen UK PLC; supplies, distributes and sells electricity; also retailer of gas; subsidiary of E.ON AG (Germany); Chair. Dr WULF H. BERNOTAT; Chief Exec. Dr PAUL GOLBY.

Green Energy (UK) PLC: 190 Strand, London, WC2 8JN; e-mail help@greenenergy.uk.com; internet www.greenenergy.uk.com; Chair. Sir PETER THOMPSON; CEO DOUGLAS STEWART.

National Grid PLC: 1–3 Strand, London, WC2N 5EH; tel. (20) 7004-3000; fax (20) 7004-3004; internet www.nationalgrid.com; Chair. Sir JOHN PARKER; CEO STEVE HOLLIDAY.

Northern Ireland Electricity PLC: 120 Malone Rd, Belfast, BT9 5HT; tel. (28) 9066-1100; e-mail customercontact@nie.co.uk; internet www.nie.co.uk; holding co Viridian Group; Chair. MIKE TOMS; Man. Dir LAURENCE MACKENZIE.

npower: Oak House, Bridgwater Rd, Warndon, Worcester, WR4 9FP; tel. (1793) 877777; fax (1793) 892525; internet www.npower.com; f. 1999 to combine the electricity and gas supply business of six companies; launched in 2000; retail arm of RWE npower PLC; CEO DAVID THRELFALL.

Phoenix Natural Gas Ltd: 197 Airport Rd West, Belfast, BT3 9ED; tel. (28) 9055-5555; fax (28) 9055-5500; e-mail info@phoenix-natural-gas.com; internet www.phoenix-natural-gas.com; f. 1997; CEO PETER DIXON.

RWE npower plc: Windmill Hill Business Park, Whitehill Way, Swindon, Wiltshire, SN5 6PB; tel. (1793) 877777; fax (1793) 893955; internet www.rwenpower.com; Group CEO ANDREW DUFF.

Scottish and Southern Energy PLC: Inveralmond House, 200 Dunkeld Rd, Perth, PH1 3AQ; tel. (1738) 456660; fax (1738) 455281; e-mail info@scottish-southern.co.uk; internet www.scottish-southern.co.uk; Chair. Sir ROBERT SMITH; CEO IAN MARCHANT.

Scottish Power PLC: Corporate Office, 1 Atlantic Quay, Glasgow, G2 8SP; tel. (141) 248-8200; fax (141) 248-8300; internet www.scottishpower.com; acquired by Iberdrola, SA (Spain) in 2007; Chair. JOSÉ IGNACIO SÁNCHEZ GALÁN; CEO NICK HORTER.

South Wales Electricity PLC: POB 7506, Perth, PH1 3QR; tel. (800) 052-5252; internet www.swalec.co.uk; part of Scottish and Southern Energy Group; CEO JOHN ROBINS.

Southern Electric: 55 Vastern Rd, Reading, Berks, RG1 8BU; internet www.southern-electric.co.uk; part of Scottish and Southern Energy Group; Group CEO IAN MARCHANT.

Water

Regulatory Authority

Water Services Regulation Authority (Ofwat): Centre City Tower, 7 Hill St, Birmingham, B5 4UA; tel. (121) 625-1300; fax (121) 625-1400; e-mail enquiries@ofwat.gsi.gov.uk; internet www.ofwat.gov.uk; independent economic regulator of the water and sewerage cos in England and Wales; ensures compliance with the functions specified in the Water Industry Act of 2003; Chair. PHILIP FLETCHER; Chief Exec. REGINA FINN.

Principal Companies

Anglian Water Services Ltd: POB 770, Lincoln, LN5 7WX; tel. (8457) 919155; fax (1480) 326981; internet www.anglianwater.co.uk; Chair. JONSON COX; CEO PETER SIMPSON.

Northern Ireland Water: Northland House, 3 Frederick St, Belfast, BT1 2NR; tel. (8457) 440088; e-mail waterline@niwater.com; internet www.niwater.com; Chief Exec. CHRIS MELLOR (acting).

Scottish Water: Castle House, 6 Castle Drive, Carnegie Campus, Dunfermline, KY11 8GG; tel. (845) 601 8855; e-mail customer.service@scottishwater.co.uk; internet www.scottishwater.co.uk; f. 2002; Chair. RONNIE MERCER; Chief Exec. RICHARD K. ACKROYD.

Severn Trent Water Ltd: 2297 Coventry Rd, Birmingham, B26 3PU; tel. (121) 722-4000; fax (121) 722-4800; internet www.stwater.co.uk; Chair. Sir JOHN EGAN; Chief Exec. TONY WRAY.

South East Water Ltd: Rocfort Rd, Snodland, Kent, ME6 5AH; tel. (845) 301-8045; e-mail contactcentre@southeastwater.co.uk; internet www.southeastwater.co.uk; merged with Mid Kent Water 2007; owned by Hastings Diversified Utilities Fund and the Utilities Trust of Australia; Chair. GORDON MAXWELL; Man. Dir PAUL BUTLER.

South Staffordshire Water PLC: POB 63, Walsall, WS2 7PJ; tel. (1922) 616239; internet www.south-staffs-water.co.uk; Exec. Chair. DAVID SANKEY; Man. Dir Dr JACK CARNELL.

South West Water Ltd: Peninsula House, Rydon Lane, Exeter, EX2 7HR; tel. (1392) 446688; fax (1392) 434966; internet www.southwestwater.co.uk; part of Pennon Group; Chair. KENNETH HARVEY; CEO CHRISTOPHER LOUGHLIN.

Southern Water PLC: POB 41, Worthing, West Sussex, BN13 3NZ; tel. (1903) 264444; fax (1903) 691435; e-mail customerservices@southernwater.co.uk; internet www.southernwater.co.uk; Chair. MIKE WELTON; CEO LES DAWSON.

Thames Water Utilities Ltd: POB 286, Swindon, SN38 2RA; tel. (845) 920-0888; internet www.thameswateruk.co.uk; acquired by Kemble Water Ltd in 2006; Chair. Sir PETER MASON; CEO DAVID OWENS.

Three Valleys Water PLC: POB 48, Bishops Rise, Hatfield, Herts, AL10 9HL; tel. (1707) 268111; fax (1707) 277188; internet www.3valleys.co.uk; Chair. Sir ALAN THOMAS; Man. Dir ANDREW SMITH.

United Utilities PLC: Dawson House, Great Sankey, Warrington, WA5 3LW; tel. (1925) 237000; fax (1925) 237073; internet www.uuplc.co.uk; Chair. Dr JOHN MCADAM; Chief Exec. PHILIP GREEN.

Welsh Water (Dwr Cymru Cyfyngedig): Pentwyn Rd, Nelson, Treharris, Mid Glamorgan, CF46 6LY; tel. (1443) 452300; fax (1443) 452809; e-mail enquiries@dwrcymru.com; internet www.dwrcymru.com; f. 1989; Chair. Lord BURNS; Man. Dir NIGEL ANNETT.

Wessex Water Services Ltd: Claverton Down Rd, Bath, BA2 7WW; tel. (1225) 526000; e-mail info@wessexwater.co.uk; internet www.wessexwater.co.uk; Propr YTL (Malaysia); Chair. and CEO COLIN SKELLETT.

THE UNITED KINGDOM   *Directory*

Yorkshire Water Services Ltd: POB 500, Bradford, BD6 2SZ; tel. (845) 124-2424; fax (1274) 372800; internet www.yorkshirewater.com; Chair. JOHN NAPIER; Man. Dir KEVIN WHITEMAN.

CO-OPERATIVE ORGANIZATIONS

Co-operatives UK: Holyoake House, Hanover St, Manchester, M60 0AS; tel. (161) 246-2900; fax (161) 831-7684; e-mail info@cooperatives-uk.coop; internet www.cooperatives-uk.coop; f. 1869; co-ordinates, informs and advises the 45 retail consumer co-operative societies and 700 worker co-operatives and employee-owned businesses; Chair. BEN REID; Society Sec. JOHN BUTLER; Chief Exec. Dame PAULINE GREEN.

Co-operative Group Ltd: New Century House, POB 53, Manchester, M60 4ES; tel. (161) 834-1212; fax (161) 834-4507; e-mail customer.relations@co-op.co.uk; internet www.co-operative.co.uk; f. 1863; merged with United Co-operatives in 2007; Chair. LEN WARDLE.

National Association of Co-operative Officials (NACO): 6A Clarendon Pl., Hyde, Cheshire, SK14 2QZ; tel. (161) 351-7900; fax (161) 366-6800; e-mail info@nacoco-op.org; internet www.naco.coop; f. 1918; Nat. Pres. KAREN FROGGATT.

TRADE UNIONS
Central Organizations

Trades Union Congress (TUC): Congress House, Great Russell St, London, WC1B 3LS; tel. (20) 7636-4030; fax (20) 7636-0632; e-mail info@tuc.org.uk; internet www.tuc.org.uk; f. 1868; a voluntary association of trade unions, the representatives of which meet annually to consider matters of common concern to their members. A General Council of 57 members is elected at the annual Congress to keep watch on all industrial movements, legislation affecting labour and all matters touching the interest of the trade union movement, with authority to promote common action on general questions and to assist trade unions in the work of organization. Through the General Council and its Executive Committee, the TUC campaigns on issues of concern to employees and provides services for affiliated unions. It also makes nominations to various bodies such as the Health and Safety Commission, the Equal Opportunities Commission and the Advisory, Conciliation and Arbitration Service Council. In 2008 60 unions, with a total membership of almost 6.5m., were affiliated to the TUC. The TUC is affiliated to the ITUC and the European Trade Union Confederation, and nominates the British Workers' Delegate to the International Labour Organization; Pres. SHEILA BEARCROFT; Gen. Sec. BRENDAN BARBER.

Irish Congress of Trade Unions (Northern Ireland Committee): 4–6 Donegall Street Pl., Belfast, BT1 2FN; tel. (28) 9024-7940; fax (28) 9024-6898; e-mail info@ictuni.org; internet www.ictuni.org; 36 affiliated unions in Northern Ireland, with a membership of 215,478 (2006); Gen. Sec. DAVID BEGG.

Scottish Trades Union Congress: 333 Woodlands Rd, Glasgow, G3 6NG; tel. (141) 337-8100; fax (141) 337-8101; e-mail info@stuc.org.uk; internet www.stuc.org.uk; f. 1897; 640,000 individual mems affiliated through 37 trade unions and 22 trades union councils (2009); Gen. Sec. GRAHAME SMITH.

Wales Trades Union Council: 1 Cathedral Rd, Cardiff; tel. (29) 2034-7010; fax (29) 2022-1940; e-mail wtuc@tuc.org.uk; internet www.wtuc.org.uk; f. 1973; Gen. Sec. MARTIN MANSFIELD.

Principal Trade Unions Affiliated to the TUC

Includes all affiliated unions whose membership is in excess of 10,000.

ACCORD: Simmons House, 46 Old Bath Rd, Charvil, Reading, Berks, RG10 9QR; tel. (118) 934-1808; fax (118) 932-0208; e-mail info@accordhq.org; internet www.accord-myunion.org; Gen. Sec. GED NICHOLS; 30,415 mems (2008).

Associated Society of Locomotive Engineers and Firemen (ASLEF): 9 Arkwright Rd, London, NW3 6AB; tel. (20) 7317-8600; fax (20) 7794-6406; e-mail info@aslef.org.uk; internet www.aslef.org.uk; f. 1880; Gen. Sec. KEITH NORMAN; 18,033 mems (2008).

Association of Teachers and Lecturers (ATL): 7 Northumberland St, London WC2N 5RD; tel. (20) 7930-6441; fax (20) 7930-1359; e-mail info@atl.org.uk; internet www.atl.org.uk; f. 1978; Pres. ANDY BALLARD; Gen. Sec. Dr MARY BOUSTED; 120,534 mems.

Bakers, Food and Allied Workers' Union (BFAWU): Stanborough House, Great North Rd, Stanborough, Welwyn Garden City, Herts., AL8 7TA; tel. (1707) 260150; fax (1707) 261570; e-mail info@bfawu.org; internet www.bfawu.org; f. 1861; Pres. RONNIE DRAPER; Gen. Sec. JOSEPH MARINO; 28,426 mems.

Broadcasting, Entertainment, Cinematograph and Theatre Union (BECTU): 373–377 Clapham Rd, London, SW9 9BT; tel. (20) 7346-0900; fax (20) 7346-0901; e-mail info@bectu.org.uk; internet www.bectu.org.uk; f. 1991 as a result of merger between Asscn of Cinematograph, Television and Allied Technicians (f. 1933) and the Broadcasting and Entertainment Trades Alliance (f. 1984); Pres. TONY LENNON; Gen. Sec. GERRY MORRISSEY; 26,210 mems (2008).

Chartered Society of Physiotherapy (CSP): 14 Bedford Row, London, WC1R 4ED; tel. (20) 7306-6666; fax (20) 7306-6611; e-mail enquiries@csp.org.uk; internet www.csp.org.uk; f. 1894; Pres. Baroness FINLAY OF LLANDAFF; Chief Exec. PHIL GRAY; 35,050 mems (2008).

Communications Workers' Union (CWU): 150 The Broadway, Wimbledon, London, SW19 1RX; tel. (20) 8971-7200; fax (20) 8971-7300; e-mail info@cwu.org; internet www.cwu.org; f. 1995 by merger of the National Communications Union and the Union of Communication Workers; Pres. DAVIE BOWMAN; Gen. Sec. BILLY HAYES; 236,679 mems.

Community: Swinton House, 324 Gray's Inn Rd, London, WC1X 8DD; tel. (20) 7239-1200; fax (20) 7278-8378; e-mail info@community-tu.org; internet www.community-tu.org; f. 2004 by the merger of the Iron and Steel Trades Confed. and the National Union of Knitwear, Footwear and Apparel Trades; Gen. Sec. MICHAEL J. LEAHY; 67,488 mems (2008).

Connect: 30 St George's Rd, Wimbledon, London, SW19 4BD; tel. (20) 8971-6000; fax (20) 8971-6002; e-mail union@connectuk.org; internet www.connectuk.org; trade union for professionals in the communications industry; fmrly Society of Telecom Executives, name changed as above in 2000; Pres. DENISE MCGUIRE; Gen. Sec. ADRIAN ASKEW; 19,472 mems (2009).

Educational Institute of Scotland (EIS): 46 Moray Pl., Edinburgh, EH3 6BH; tel. (131) 225-6244; fax (131) 220-3151; e-mail enquiries@eis.org.uk; internet www.eis.org.uk; f. 1847; professional and trade union org. for teachers and lecturers in schools, colleges and universities; Pres. DAVID DREVER; Gen. Sec. RONALD A. SMITH; 59,539 mems (2008).

Equity: Guild House, Upper St Martin's Lane, London, WC2H 9EG; tel. (20) 7379-6000; fax (20) 7379-7001; e-mail info@equity.org.uk; internet www.equity.org.uk; represents artists and performers; Pres. HARRY LANDIS; Gen. Sec. CHRISTINE PAYNE; 35,527 mems (2008).

FDA: 8 Leake St, London, SE1 7NN; tel. (20) 7401-5555; fax (20) 7401-5550; e-mail info@fda.org.uk; internet www.fda.org.uk; f. 1919; public sector managers and professionals; Pres. DAVID WATTS; Gen. Sec. JONATHAN BAUME; 18,566 mems.

Fire Brigades Union (FBU): Bradley House, 68 Coombe Rd, Kingston upon Thames, Surrey, KT2 7AE; tel. (20) 8541-1765; fax (20) 8546-5187; e-mail office@fbu.org.uk; internet www.fbu.org.uk; f. 1918; Pres. MICK SHAW; Gen. Sec. MATT WRACK; 47,071 mems.

GMB—Britain's General Union: 22–24 Worple Rd, Wimbledon, London, SW19 4DD; tel. (20) 8947-3131; fax (20) 8944-6552; e-mail info@gmb.org.uk; internet www.gmb.org.uk; f. 1982; Pres. MARY TURNER; Gen. Sec. PAUL KENNY; 590,125 mems (2008).

Musicians' Union (MU): 60–62 Clapham Rd, London, SW9 0JJ; tel. (20) 7582-5566; fax (20) 7582-9805; e-mail info@musiciansunion.org.uk; internet www.musiciansunion.org.uk; f. 1893; Gen. Sec. JOHN F. SMITH; 32,674 mems (2008).

National Association of Schoolmasters Union of Women Teachers (NASUWT): Hillscourt Education Centre, Rose Hill, Rednal, Birmingham, B45 8RS; tel. (121) 453-6150; fax (121) 457-6208; e-mail nasuwt@mail.nasuwt.org.uk; internet www.nasuwt.org.uk; f. 1919; merged with UWT 1976; Pres. JOHN MAYES; Gen. Sec. CHRIS KEATES; 265,202 mems (2008).

National Union of Journalists (NUJ): Headland House, 308-312 Gray's Inn Rd, London, WC1X 8DP; tel. (20) 7278-7916; fax (20) 7837-8143; e-mail info@nuj.org.uk; internet www.nuj.org.uk; f. 1907; Pres. CHRIS MORLEY; Gen. Sec. JEREMY DEAR; 32,409 mems (2008).

National Union of Rail, Maritime and Transport Workers (RMT): 39 Chalton Rd, London, NW1 1JD; tel. (20) 7387-4771; fax (20) 7387-4123; e-mail info@rmt.org.uk; internet www.rmt.org.uk; f. 1990 through merger of National Union of Railwaymen (f. 1872) and National Union of Seamen (f. 1887); Pres. JOHN LEACH; Gen. Sec. BOB CROW; 75,906 mems (2008).

National Union of Teachers (NUT): Hamilton House, Mabledon Pl., London, WC1H 9BD; tel. (20) 7388-6191; fax (20) 7387-8458; internet www.teachers.org.uk; Pres. MARTIN REED; Gen. Sec. CHRISTINE BLOWER (acting); 366,657 mems (2008).

Nationwide Group Staff Union (NGSU): Middleton Farmhouse, 37 Main Rd, Middleton Cheney, Banbury, OX17 2QT; tel. (1295) 710767; fax (1295) 712580; e-mail ngsu@ngsu.org.uk; internet www.ngsu.org.uk; Gen. Sec. TIM POIL; 13,892 mems (2008).

Nautilus UK: Oceanair House, 750–760 High Rd, Leytonstone, London, E11 3BB; tel. (20) 8989-6677; fax (20) 8530-1015; e-mail enquiries@nautilus.org; internet www.nautilusuk.org; f. 1936; fmrly the National Union of Marine, Aviation and Shipping Transport Officers; present name adopted 2006; Sec. BRIAN ORRELL; 16,274 mems (2008).

THE UNITED KINGDOM

Prison Officers' Association (POA): Cronin House, 245 Church St, London, N9 9HW; tel. (20) 8803-0255; fax (20) 8803-1761; internet www.poauk.org.uk; f. 1939; Chair. COLIN MOSES; Gen. Sec. BRIAN CATON; 36,172 mems (2008).

Prospect: New Prospect House, 8 Leake St, London, SE1 7NN; tel. (20) 7902-6600; fax (20) 7902-6667; e-mail enquiries@prospect.org.uk; internet www.prospect.org.uk; f. 1919 as the Institution of Professionals, Managers and Specialists; name changed as above in 2001; Pres. CATHARINE DONALDSON; Gen. Sec. PAUL NOON; 102,702 mems (2008).

Public and Commercial Services Union (PCS): 160 Falcon Rd, London, SW11 2LN; tel. (20) 7924-2727; fax (20) 7924-1847; internet www.pcs.org.uk; f. 1998 by merger of Civil and Public Services Asscn (f. 1903) and Public Services, Tax and Commerce Union (f. 1996); Pres. JANICE GODRICH; Gen. Sec. MARK SERWOTKA; 300,000 mems.

Society of Radiographers (SoR): 207 Providence Sq., Mill St, London, SE1 2EW; tel. (20) 7740-7200; fax (20) 7740-7204; e-mail info@sor.org; internet www.sor.org; f. 1920; Pres. ZENA MITTON; Chief Exec. RICHARD EVANS; 18,595 mems.

Transport Salaried Staffs' Association (TSSA): Walkden House, 10 Melton St, London, NW1 2EJ; tel. (20) 7387-2101; fax (20) 7383-0656; internet www.tssa.org.uk; f. 1897; Pres. ANDY BAIN; Gen. Sec. GERRY DOHERTY; 29,102 mems (2008).

Union of Construction, Allied Trades and Technicians (UCATT): UCATT House, 177 Abbeville Rd, Clapham, London, SW4 9RL; tel. (20) 7622-2442; fax (20) 7720-4081; e-mail info@ucatt.org.uk; internet www.ucatt.info; f. 1971; Pres. JOHN THOMPSON; Gen. Sec. ALAN RITCHIE; 129,065 mems (2008).

Union of Shop, Distributive and Allied Workers (USDAW): 188 Wilmslow Rd, Manchester, M14 6LJ; tel. (161) 224-2804; fax (161) 257-2566; e-mail enquiries@usdaw.org.uk; internet www.usdaw.org.uk; Pres. JEFF BROOME; Gen. Sec. JOHN HANNETT; 356,046 mems (2008).

UNISON: 1 Mabledon Pl., London, WC1H 9AJ; tel. (845) 355-0845; fax (20) 7551-1101; e-mail direct@unison.co.uk; internet www.unison.org.uk; f. 1993 through merger of Confederation of Health Service Employees (COHSE—f. 1910), National and Local Government Officers Asscn (NALGO—f. 1905) and National Union of Public Employees (NUPE—f. 1888); Pres. SUE HIGHTON; Gen. Sec. DAVE PRENTIS; 1,343,000 mems (2008).

Unite—The Union: 35 King St, London, WC2E 8JG; tel. (20) 7420-8900; fax (20) 7420-8998; e-mail simon.dubbins@amicustheunion.org; internet www.unitetheunion.com; f. 2007 by merger of Amicus and Transport and General Workers' Union; Joint Gen. Secs DEREK SIMPSON, TONY WOODLEY; 1,952,510 mems (2008).

United Road Transport Union (URTU): Almond House, Oak Green, Stanley Green Business Park, Cheadle Hulme, SK8 6QL; tel. (800) 526639; fax (161) 861-0976; e-mail info@urtu.com; internet www.urtu.com; f. 1890 as United Carters' Asscn; present name adopted 1964; Gen. Sec. ROBERT MONKS; 16,800 mems.

University and College Union (UCU): Carlow St, London, NW1 7LH; tel. (20) 7756-2500; fax (20) 7756-2501; e-mail hq@ucu.org.uk; internet www.ucu.org.uk; f. 2006 by merger of the Association of University Teachers and NATFHE—The University & College Lecturers' Union; Pres. SASHA CALLAGHAN; Gen. Sec. SALLY HUNT; 117,028 mems (2008).

Unions not affiliated to the TUC

Irish National Teachers' Organization (INTO): 23 College Gardens, Belfast, BT9 6BS (headquarters in Dublin); tel. (28) 9038-1455; fax (28) 9066-2803; e-mail infoni@into.ie; internet www.into.ie; f. 1868; affiliated to the Irish Congress of Trade Unions (Northern Ireland Committee); Northern Sec. FRANK BUNTING; 6,149 mems (Dec. 2006).

National Farmers' Union (NFU): see Industrial and Trade Associations.

Northern Ireland Public Service Alliance: Harkin House, 54 Wellington Park, Belfast, BT9 6DP; tel. (28) 9066-1831; fax (28) 9066-5847; e-mail info@nipsa.org.uk; internet www.nipsa.org.uk; affiliated to the Irish Congress of Trade Unions; Pres. (2008/09) BRIAN MOORE; Gen. Sec. JOHN COREY; 44,500 mems.

Services Industrial Professional Technical Union (SIPTU): 3 Antrim Rd, Belfast, BT15 2BE; tel. (28) 9031-4000; fax (28) 9031-4044; e-mail belfast@siptu.ie; internet www.siptu.ie; affiliated to the Irish Congress of Trade Unions (Northern Ireland Committee); Regional Sec. JOE CUNNINGHAM; 7,000 members.

Ulster Teachers' Union: 94 Malone Rd, Belfast, BT9 5HP; tel. (28) 9066-2216; fax (28) 9068-3296; e-mail office@utu.edu; internet www.utu.edu; f. 1919; affiliated to the Irish Congress of Trade Unions (Northern Ireland Committee); Pres. MELANIE HOUSTON; Gen. Sec. AVRIL HALL-CALLAGHAN; 6,700 mems (Dec. 2006).

Union of Democratic Mineworkers (UDM): The Miners' Offices, Berry Hill Lane, Mansfield, Nottinghamshire, NG18 4JU; tel. (1623) 626094; fax (1623) 642300; e-mail enquiries@udmoffices.co.uk; internet www.unionofdemocraticmineworkers.co.uk; f. 1986; Pres. and Gen. Sec. NEIL GREATREX; c. 1,500 mems.

National Federations

Confederation of Shipbuilding and Engineering Unions: 5th Floor, 35 King St, London, WC2E 8JG; tel. (20) 7420-8988; fax (20) 7420-1488; 750,000 mems in 7 affiliated trade unions; Gen. Sec. JOHN WALL.

Federation of Entertainment Unions: 1 Highfield, Twyford, Hampshire, SO21 1QR; tel. and fax (1962) 713134; e-mail harris.s@btconnect.com; f. 1990; 6 affiliated unions; Sec. STEVE HARRIS.

General Federation of Trade Unions (GFTU): Central House, Upper Woburn Pl., London, WC1H OHY; tel. (20) 7387-2578; fax (20) 7383-0820; e-mail gftuhq@gftu.org.uk; internet www.gftu.org.uk; f. 1899; represents specialist unions; Pres. DOUG NICHOLLS; Gen. Sec. MIKE BRADLEY; 34 affiliated unions with total membership of 225,687 (Dec. 2006).

Transport

RAILWAYS

The Railways Act 1993, providing for a process of rail privatization, received royal assent in November 1993. A separate, government-owned company, Railtrack, was set up on 1 April 1994 to take responsibility for infrastructure (track, signals and stations) and levy charges on train operators for track access. As a result of the 1993 Railways Act, 25 Train Operating Units (TOUs) came into being on 1 April 1994. The Director of Passenger Rail Franchises was responsible for awarding franchises for the 25 TOUs as early as practicable and was to monitor the franchises to ensure compliance with the agreed contracts. The first passenger train franchises were awarded in 1995, and two TOUs were transferred to private operators in 1996; the final TOU transferred to the private sector the following year. Railtrack was transferred to the private sector in 1996. In October 2001 the Government placed the heavily-indebted Railtrack in administration. Railtrack remained in administration until October 2002, when Network Rail, a 'not-for-profit' government-supported company, completed a takeover.

In February 1986 the Treaty of Canterbury was signed between the Governments of France and the United Kingdom, providing the constitutional basis for the construction of a tunnel between the two countries under the English Channel. The Channel Tunnel opened in May 1994, at an estimated cost of £4,700m., and comprises a fixed link of two rail tunnels and one service tunnel. Of the total length of 31 miles (50 km), 24 miles (38 km) are under the seabed. The rail services provider, Eurostar UK, moved all London operations from Waterloo International to St Pancras station in 2007.

DfT Rail and National Networks: Department for Transport, Great Minster House, 76 Marsham St, London SW1P 4DR; tel. (20) 7944-8300; fax (20) 7944-9643; e-mail rail@dft.gsi.gov.uk; internet www.dft.gov.uk/pgr/rail; f. 2005; strategic and financial responsibility for the railways, assumed many functions of the Strategic Rail Authority (SRA), which was dissolved in August 2005 following a national rail review in July 2004; Dir-Gen. MIKE MITCHELL.

Office of Rail Regulation: 1 Kemble St, London, WC2B 4AN; tel. (20) 7282-2000; fax (20) 7282-2040; e-mail rail.library@orr.gsi.gov.uk; internet www.rail-reg.gov.uk; f. 2004; Chair. CHRIS BOLT.

Network Rail Ltd: Kings Pl., 90 York Way, London, N1 9AG; tel. (20) 3356-9595; fax (20) 3356-9245; internet www.networkrail.co.uk; f. 2002 as a 'not-for-profit' company by train operators, rail unions and passenger groups to take over responsibility for running the UK rail network from Railtrack PLC; Chair. IAN MCALLISTER; Chief Exec. IAIN COUCHER.

Northern Ireland Railways Co Ltd: Central Station, East Bridge St, Belfast, BT1 3PB; tel. (28) 9089-9400; fax (28) 9089-9401; internet www.nirailways.co.uk; f. 1967; subsidiary of Northern Ireland Transport Holding Co (see under Roads) and part of the Translink rail and bus network; operates rail services for passenger traffic over 342 km and for freight traffic over 268 km of railway track; a high-speed passenger service between Belfast and Dublin, launched in co-operation with Irish Rail, began operations in 1997; Chief Exec. CATHERINE MASON; Gen. Man., Rail Services MALACHY MCGREEVY.

Channel Tunnel Rail Link

Eurotunnel Group: UK Terminal, Ashford Rd, Folkestone, Kent, CT18 8XX; tel. (1303) 282222; fax (1303) 850360; e-mail press@eurotunnel.com; internet www.eurotunnel.com; f. 1986; Anglo-French consortium contracted to design, finance and construct the Channel Tunnel under a concession granted for a period up to 2052

THE UNITED KINGDOM

(later extended to 2086); receives finance exclusively from the private sector; operates a service of road vehicle 'shuttle' trains and passenger and freight trains through the Channel Tunnel; Chair. and Chief Exec. JACQUES GOUNON.

Eurostar UK Ltd/Eurostar Group: Times House, Bravingtons Walk, Regent Quarter, London, N1 9AW; tel. (20) 7902-3658; e-mail press.office@eurostar.co.uk; internet www.eurostar.com; commenced international high-speed passenger rail services in 1994; provides services from London, and Ebbsfleet and Ashford (both in Kent), direct to Paris, Brussels, Lille, Calais-Frethun, Disneyland Paris, Avignon and Bourg St Maurice; Chair. GUILLAUME PEPY; CEO RICHARD BROWN.

Associations

Railway Industry Association: 22 Headfort Pl., London, SW1X 7RY; tel. (20) 7201-0777; fax (20) 7235-5777; e-mail ria@riagb.org.uk; internet www.riagb.org.uk; f. 1875; represents UK-based railway suppliers, with a free sourcing service for products and services; Chair. TONY KING; Dir-Gen. JEREMY CANDFIELD; 141 mems.

Association of Train Operating Companies: 3rd Floor, 40 Bernard St, London, WC1N 1BY; tel. (20) 7841-8000; e-mail atocnews@atoc.org; internet www.atoc.org; f. 1994; Chair. MIKE ALEXANDER; Dir-Gen. MICHAEL ROBERTS.

ROADS

Total road length in Great Britain in 2006 was 398,351 km (247,523 miles), of which 3,556 km (2,210 miles) was motorway. In 2005 there were 24,930 km (15,491 miles) of roads of all classes in Northern Ireland, including some 110 km (68 miles) of motorway.

Highways Agency: 123 Buckingham Palace Rd, London, SW1W 9HA; tel. and fax (8459) 556575; e-mail ha_info@highways.gsi.gov.uk; internet www.highways.gov.uk; executive agency of the Department for Transport; responsible for maintaining, operating and improving the motorway and trunk road network in England; Chief Exec. GRAHAM DALTON.

Northern Ireland Transport Holding Co: Chamber of Commerce House, 22 Great Victoria St, Belfast, BT2 7LX; tel. (28) 9024-3456; fax (28) 9033-3845; internet www.translink.co.uk/nithco.asp; publicly owned; owns Metro, Northern Ireland Railways Co Ltd and Ulsterbus, all part of the Translink rail and bus network; Chair. VERONICA PALMER; Chief Exec. CATHERINE MASON.

Ulsterbus Ltd: Milewater Rd, Belfast, BT3 9BG; Central Station, Belfast, BT1 3PB; tel. (28) 9089-9400; fax (28) 9035-1474; internet www.translink.co.uk/atulsterbus.asp; responsible for almost all bus transport in Northern Ireland, except Belfast city; services into Ireland; assoc. co Flexibus Ltd (minibus contract hire); Chief Exec. CATHERINE MASON; Gen. Man., Bus Services FRANK CLEGG (acting).

METROPOLITAN TRANSPORT

Docklands Light Railway: POB 154, Castor Lane, London, E14 0DS; tel. (20) 7363-9700; fax (20) 7363-9532; e-mail cservice@dlr.co.uk; internet www.dlr.co.uk; opened 1987; in 1992 responsibility was transferred from London Transport to the London Docklands Development Corpn; in 1998 the Railway was again transferred to the Dept for Environment, Transport and the Regions and in July 2000 the Railway became part of Transport for London; franchised to a private co, Docklands Railway Management (now Serco Docklands), in 1997; comprises a 40-station system bounded by Bank, Tower Gateway, Woolwich Arsenal, Beckton, Stratford and Lewisham; construction of an extension from Canning Town to Stratford International due to be completed in July 2010; Dir JONATHAN FOX.

Metro: Milewater Rd, Belfast, BT3 9BG; tel. (28) 9035-1201; fax (28) 9035-1474; internet www.translink.co.uk/metro.asp; responsible for operating municipal transport in the City of Belfast; subsidiary of Northern Ireland Transport Holding Co (see under Roads); Chief Exec. CATHERINE MASON.

Metrolink: Metrolink House, Queens Rd, Manchester, M8 0RY; tel. (161) 205-2000; e-mail customerservices@metrolink.co.uk; internet www.metrolink.co.uk; opened 1992; owned by the Greater Manchester Passenger Transport Executive (GMPTE); operated by Serco Metrolink; 37-station hybrid tram and rail network in Greater Manchester, bounded by Altrincham, Bury, Eccles and Manchester Piccadilly; construction of 4 new lines expected to be completed in 2012; Dir PHILIP PURDY.

Transport for London (TfL): Windsor House, 42–50 Victoria St, London, SW1H 0TL; tel. (20) 7941-4500; fax (20) 7649-9121; e-mail enquire@tfl.gov.uk; internet www.tfl.gov.uk; f. 2000; executive arm of Greater London Authority (GLA), responsible for activities of former London Transport; Chair. BORIS JOHNSON (Mayor of London); Commr PETER HENDY.

London Underground: 55 Broadway, London, SW1H 0BD; tel. (20) 7222-5600; internet www.tfl.gov.uk/tube; f. 1985; however, underground railway network dates back to 1863; responsible for providing and securing the services of underground rail in Greater London; Man. Dir RICHARD PARRY (acting).

SPT Subway: Consort House, 12 West George St, Glasgow, G2 1HN; tel. (141) 332-6811; e-mail enquiry@spt.co.uk; internet www.spt.co.uk/subway; f. opened 1896; electrified in 1923; owned and operated by Strathclyde Partnership for Transport (SPT); 10-km, 15-station underground rail network in central Glasgow; Dir, Subway Operations DAVID WALLACE.

Tyne and Wear Metro: Nexus House, St James' Blvd, Newcastle upon Tyne, NE1 4AX; tel. (191) 203-3333; fax (191) 203-3180; e-mail metro.communications@nexus.org.uk; internet www.tyneandwearmetro.co.uk; opened 1980; 77.5-km, 60-station light rail network serving Newcastle, Gateshead, North Tyneside, South Tyneside and Sunderland; owned and operated by Tyne and Wear Passenger Transport Executive (Nexus); Dir-Gen. BERNARD GARNER.

INLAND WATERWAYS

There are some 3,541 km (2,200 miles) of inland waterways in Great Britain under the control of British Waterways, varying from the river navigations and wide waterways accommodating commercial craft to canals taking small holiday craft.

British Waterways: 6 Clarendon Rd, Watford, Hertfordshire, WD17 1DA; tel. (1923) 201120; fax (1923) 201400; e-mail enquiries.hq@britishwaterways.co.uk; internet www.britishwaterways.co.uk; f. 1963; Chair. TONY HALES; Chief Exec. ROBIN EVANS.

SHIPPING

There are more than 400 ports in the United Kingdom, of which Grimsby and Immingham, the Tees and Hartlepool ports, London (Tilbury), Southampton, Milford Haven, Liverpool, the Forth ports, Felixstowe, Dover and Sullom Voe are the largest (in terms of the tonnage of goods traffic handled). Twenty-one ports, including Grimsby and Immingham, Hull, Southampton and five ports in South Wales, are owned and administered by Associated British Ports. The majority of the other large ports are owned and operated by public trusts, including London, which is administered by the Port of London Authority, and Belfast, administered by the Belfast Harbour Commissioners. Under the Ports Act (1991), trust ports were permitted to become private, commercial enterprises. By mid-1995 five major trust ports, including the Port of London Authority and the Medway Ports Authority, had been transferred to the private sector. In May 1998 the Government announced that the port of Belfast was to be transferred to the private sector. Sullom Voe, Bristol and a number of smaller ports are under the control of local authorities, and there are more than 100 ports owned and administered by statutory or private companies; of these, Liverpool (owned by Mersey Docks and Harbour Co), Felixstowe and Manchester are the largest.

Britain is linked to the rest of Europe by an extensive passenger and vehicle ship ferry service. There are regular freight services from Belfast, Larne and Warrenpoint, in Northern Ireland, to ports in Great Britain and Europe; passenger services operate daily between Northern Ireland and Great Britain.

Associated British Ports (ABP): 150 Holborn, London, EC1N 2LR; tel. (20) 7430-1177; fax (20) 7430-1384; e-mail pr@abports.co.uk; internet www.abports.co.uk; f. 1983; controls 21 UK ports; Chair. CHRIS CLARK; Chief Exec. PETER JONES.

The Baltic Exchange Ltd: 38 St Mary Axe, London, EC3A 8BH; tel. (20) 7623-5501; fax (20) 7369-1622; e-mail enquiries@balticexchange.co.uk; internet www.balticexchange.com; world market for chartering ships, charters aircraft, buys and sells ships and aircraft; Chair. MICHAEL DRAYTON; Chief Exec. JEREMY PENN.

British Ports Association (BPA): 4th Floor, Carthusian Court, 12 Carthusian St, London, EC1M 6EZ; tel. (20) 7260-1780; fax (20) 7260-1784; e-mail info@britishports.org.uk; internet www.britishports.org.uk; promotes and protects the general interests of port authorities, comments on proposed legislation and policy matters; Dir DAVID WHITEHEAD.

Port of London Authority: London River House, Royal Pier Rd, Gravesend, Kent, DA12 2BG; tel. (1474) 562200; fax (1474) 562281; internet www.portoflondon.co.uk; Chair. SIMON SHERRARD; Chief Exec. RICHARD EVERITT.

Principal Shipping Companies

Bibby Line Ltd: 105 Duke St, Liverpool, L1 5JQ; tel. (151) 708-8000; fax (151) 794-1000; e-mail enquiries@bibbyline.co.uk; internet www.bibbyline.co.uk; f. 1807; operates chemical carriers and shallow water accommodation units; Chair. S. P. SHERRARD; Man. Dir CY GREEN.

Boyd Line: The Orangery, Hesslewood Country Office Park, Ferriby Rd, Hessle, HU13 0LH; tel. (1482) 324024; fax (1482) 323737; e-mail jon.carden@boydline.co.uk; internet www.boydline.co.uk; vessel owners and managers; Man. Dir JONATHAN CARDEN; 2 vessels.

THE UNITED KINGDOM

BP Shipping Ltd: Chertsey Rd, Sunbury on Thames, Middlesex, TW16 7LN; tel. (1932) 771652; internet www.bpshipping.co.uk; f. 1915; division of BP PLC; Group Vice-Pres. and Chief Exec. DAVID BALDRY; 56 vessels.

CalMac Ferries Ltd: The Ferry Terminal, Gourock, Renfrewshire, PA19 1QP; tel. (1475) 650100; fax (1475) 637607; e-mail info@calmac.co.uk; internet www.calmac.co.uk; holding co owned by Scottish Govt.; extensive car and passenger services on Firth of Clyde, to Western Isles of Scotland and a service between Ballycastle, in Northern Ireland, and Rathlin Island; 31 ro-ro vessels; Chair. PETER TIMMS; Man. Dir LAWRIE SINCLAIR.

Clipper Marine Services Ltd: Brunswick House, 8–13 Brunswick Pl., Southampton, SO15 2AP; tel. (23) 8063-9777; fax (23) 8063-9888; e-mail cmsukmgt@clipper-group.com; internet www.clipper-group.com; f. 1899 as Crescent Marine Services; Gen. Man. JULIAN FOLKER.

Coastal Container Line Ltd: Coastal House, Victoria Terminal 3, West Bank Rd, Belfast, BT3 9JL; tel. (28) 9037-3200; fax (28) 9037-1333; internet www.coastalcontainer.co.uk; container services from Belfast and Dublin to Cardiff and Liverpool; Operations Dir JOHN FORRESTER.

James Fisher & Sons PLC: Fisher House, POB 4, Barrow-in-Furness, Cumbria, LA14 1HR; tel. (1229) 615400; fax (1229) 836761; e-mail b.reception@james-fisher.co.uk; internet www.james-fisher.co.uk; f. 1847; provider of marine services operating in all sectors; also supplier of engineering services to the nuclear energy industry; Exec. Chair. TIMOTHY C. HARRIS; CEO NICHOLAS P. HENRY.

Fyffes Group Ltd: Houndmills Rd, Houndmills Industrial Estate, Basingstoke, Hampshire, RG21 6XL; tel. (1256) 383200; fax (1256) 383259; e-mail info@fyffes.com; internet www.fyffes.com; f. 1901.

Geest Line: 3700 Parkway, Whiteley, Fareham, PO15 7AL; tel. (1489) 873575; fax (1489) 873562; e-mail quotes@geestline.com; internet www.geestline.com; container cargo transportation between the UK and the Caribbean; Man. Dir BILL SALMOND.

Goulandris Brothers (Chartering) Ltd: 34A Queen Anne's Gate, London, SW1H 9AB; tel. (20) 7222-5244; fax (20) 7222-6817; e-mail chartering@goulanbros.co.uk; internet www.goulanbros.co.uk; f. 1968; ship chartering and brokerage; Man. Dir BASIL GOULANDRIS.

Heyn Shipping Solutions: 1 Corry Pl., Belfast Harbour, Belfast, BT3 9AH; tel. (28) 9035-0035; fax (28) 9035-0011; e-mail info@heyn.co.uk; internet www.heyn.co.uk; liner and port agency; Man. Dir DAVID CLARKE.

Holbud Ship Management Ltd: Hydery House, 66 Leman St, London, E1 8EU; tel. (20) 7488-4901; fax (20) 7265-0654; ship agents; Dir B. D. SABARWAL.

Norfolkline Irish Sea Ferries: 12 Quays Terminal, Tower Rd, Birkenhead, Wirral, CH41 1FE; tel. (151) 906-2700; fax (151) 906-2718; internet www.norfolkline.com; fmrly Norse Merchant Ferries; owned by Norfolk Line BV (Netherlands); ro-ro freight, car and passenger services from Birkenhead–Belfast and Dublin, and Dover–Dunkirk (France).

OSG Ship Management (UK) Ltd: Moreau House, 116 Brompton Rd, London, SW3 1JJ; tel. (20) 7591-6660; fax (870) 607-9546; internet www.osg.com; bulk carriers, parcels tankers, conventional tankers; transportation of crude petroleum, petroleum products and liquified natural gas; Man. Dir Capt. IAN T. BLACKLEY.

P & O Ferries: Channel House, Channel View Rd, Dover, Kent, CT17 9TJ; tel. (1304) 863000; fax (1304) 863223; e-mail customer.services@poferries.com; internet www.poferries.com; car and passenger services across the English Channel and North Sea; subsidiary of DP World (Dubai, UAE); parent co of P&O Irish Sea Ferries; frmly P&O Stena Line; CEO HELEN DEEBLE.

Shell International Trading and Shipping Co Ltd: Shell Centre, York Rd, London, SE1 7NA; tel. (20) 7934-1234; e-mail shelltradingcommunications@shell.com; internet www.shell.com/shipping; world-wide operations trading and transporting crude petroleum and supplying petroleum products; incorporates Shell Tankers (UK) Ltd.

Stena Line Ltd: Stena House, Station Approach, Holyhead, Anglesey, LL65 1DQ; tel. (8705) 707070; e-mail info.uk@stenaline.com; internet www.stenaline.com; parent co Stena AB (Sweden); services from Great Britain to Northern Ireland, Ireland and the Netherlands; Group CEO GUNNAR BLOMDAHL; Area Dir, Irish Sea MICHAEL MCGRATH.

Stephenson Clarke Shipping Ltd: Eldon Court, Percy St, Newcastle upon Tyne, NE99 1TD; tel. (191) 232-2184; fax (191) 261-1156; e-mail all@scsbulk.co.uk; internet www.scsbulk.com; f. 1730; ship operators, agency and management services; Man. Dir TREVOR KINGSLEY-SMITH.

Andrew Weir & Co Ltd: Dexter House, 2 Royal Mint Court, London, EC3N 4XX; tel. (20) 7575-6000; fax (20) 7481-4784; e-mail aws@aws.co.uk; internet www.aws.co.uk; f. 1885; shipowners, ship managers; Man Dir STEVE CORKHILL.

Shipping Associations

Chamber of Shipping Ltd: Carthusian Court, 12 Carthusian St, London, EC1M 6EZ; tel. (20) 7600-1534; fax (20) 7726-2080; e-mail postmaster@british-shipping.org; internet www.british-shipping.org; Pres. MARTIN WATSON; Dir-Gen. MARK BROWNRIGG.

Passenger Shipping Association Ltd (PSA): 1st Floor, 41–42 Eastcastle St, London W1W 8DU; tel. (20) 7436-2449; fax (20) 7636-9206; e-mail h.tapping@psa-psara.org; internet www.the-psa.co.uk; fmrly Ocean Travel Development (f. 1958); 50 mems; Chair. LARS OLSSON; Dir WILLIAM GIBBONS.

CIVIL AVIATION

In addition to many international air services into and out of the country, an internal air network operates from more than 20 main commercial airports.

The principal airports are Heathrow and Gatwick serving London, and Manchester, Birmingham and Glasgow, which in 2007 handled 67.9m., 35.2m., 21.9m., 9.1m. and 8.7m. passengers, respectively. In March 1991 a new development was opened at Stansted, including a new terminal, cargo centre and rail link to central London. In 2007 Stansted handled 23.8m. passengers. A new £30m. London City Airport opened in 1987, providing domestic and international flights to and from city centres, mainly for business travellers. In 2008 London City Airport handled 3.3m. passengers. In March 2008 a fifth terminal building opened at Heathrow, increasing capacity at the airport to some 90m. passengers a year.

BAA PLC: 130 Wilton Rd, London, SW1V 1LQ; tel. (20) 7834-9449; fax (20) 7932-6699; e-mail baamediacentre@baa.com; internet www.baa.com; f. 1966 as British Airports Authority; privatized in 1987; propr of Heathrow, Stansted, Gatwick, Southampton, Glasgow, Aberdeen and Edinburgh airports; Chair. Sir NIGEL RUDD; CEO COLIN MATTHEWS.

Civil Aviation Authority (CAA): CAA House, 45–59 Kingsway, London, WC2B 6TE; tel. (20) 7379-7311; e-mail infoservices@caa.co.uk; internet www.caa.co.uk; f. 1972; public service enterprise and a regulatory body responsible for economic and safety regulation of civil aviation; advises Govt on aviation issues; conducts economic and scientific research; produces statistical data; regulates British airspace; represents consumer interests and manages airspace users' needs; Chair. Sir ROY MCNULTY.

NATS Ltd: Corporate and Technical Centre, 4000 Parkway, Whiteley, Fareham, Hants, PO15 7FL; tel. (1489) 616001; fax (1489) 615734; internet www.nats.co.uk; f. 1960 as National Air Traffic Control Services; name changed as above in 1972 when the org. became part of the CAA (q.v.); public-private partnership between the Airline Group (a consortium of British Airways, BMI, easyJet, Monarch, MyTravel, Thomsonfly and Virgin Atlantic), BAA PLC, NATS employees and the British Govt; provides air traffic control services over the UK and North Atlantic, at 15 British airports and at Gibraltar Airport. It operates and maintains a nation-wide communications, surveillance and navigation network; Chair. JOHN DEVANEY; CEO PAUL BARRON.

Principal Private Airlines

Air Southwest: Plymouth City Airport, Crownhill, Plymouth, PL6 8BW; tel. (870) 043-4553; e-mail other-queries@airsouthwest.com; internet www.airsouthwest.com; f. 2003; scheduled flights from Plymouth, Newquay and Bristol to destinations in the UK, France and Ireland; owned by Sutton Harbour Group; Group Man. Dir NIGEL GODEFROY.

British Airways PLC: Waterside, POB 365, Harmondsworth, Middlesex, UB7 0GB; tel. (845) 779-9977; internet www.britishairways.com; f. 1972; operates extensive domestic, European and world-wide services, scheduled services to more than 250 destinations in 99 countries; Chair. MARTIN BROUGHTON; Chief Exec. WILLIE WALSH.

bmi: Donington Hall, Castle Donington, Derby, DE74 2SB; tel. (1332) 854000; fax (1332) 854662; internet www.flybmi.com; f. 1938 as Air Schools Ltd; name changed to British Midland Airways Ltd in 1964 and as above in 2002; acquisition of 80% stake by Deutsche Lufthansa AG (Germany) pending; scheduled services to over 40 destinations world-wide; cargo and charter flights; Chair. Sir MICHAEL BISHOP; CEO NIGEL TURNER.

bmibaby: Donington Hall, Castle Donington, Derby, DE74 2SB; tel. (1332) 854000; internet www.bmibaby.com; f. 2002; low-cost passenger services to 30 European destinations; Man. Dir CRAWFORD RIX.

easyJet PLC: Hangar 89, London Luton Airport, Luton, Bedfordshire, LU2 9LS; tel. (1582) 445566; fax (1582) 443355; internet www.easyjet.co.uk; f. 1995; low-cost scheduled domestic and European passenger services from 15 UK airports; Chair. Sir COLIN CHANDLER (until 30 June 2009), Sir DAVID MICHELS (from 1 July 2009); Chief Exec. ANDREW HARRISON.

THE UNITED KINGDOM

First Choice Airways: Commonwealth House, Chicago Ave, Manchester Airport, M90 3DP; tel. (161) 489-0321; fax (161) 908-2275; e-mail eteam@firstchoice.co.uk; internet www.firstchoice.co.uk/flights; f. 1987 as air2000; present name adopted 2004; scheduled services from 26 airports in the United Kingdom to 80 destinations world-wide; subsidiary of TUI Travel PLC; Man. Dir, UK and Ireland DERMOT BLASTLAND.

Flybe: Jack Walker House, Exeter International Airport, Exeter, EX5 2HL; tel. (1392) 366669; fax (1392) 366151; e-mail corporate@flybe.com; internet www.flybe.com; f. 1979 as Jersey European Airways; name changed as above 2002; acquired BA Connect in 2007; independent regional airline providing low-cost domestic and European services; Chair. and CEO JIM FRENCH.

flyglobespan: Atlantic House, 38 Gardners Cres., Edinburgh, EH3 8DQ; tel. (870) 556-1522; internet www.flyglobespan.com; f. 2003; low-cost scheduled lights to 23 destinations world-wide, operating from nine UK airports; Chair. TOM DALRYMPLE.

Loganair Ltd: St Andrews Drive, Glasgow Airport, Abbotsinch, Paisley, Renfrewshire, PA3 2TG; tel. (141) 848-7594; fax (141) 887-6020; internet www.loganair.co.uk; f. 1962; signed franchise agreement with Flybe in 2008; Scottish domestic services and flights to Belfast, Birmingham, Londonderry and the Isle of Man; Chair. SCOTT GRIER; Chief Exec. PETER TIERNEY.

Monarch Airlines: Prospect House, Prospect Way, London Luton Airport, Luton, Bedfordshire, LU2 9NU; tel. (1582) 400000; fax (1582) 411000; internet www.flymonarch.com; f. 1967; scheduled and charter services to the Mediterranean; CEO PETER BROWN.

Thomsonfly: London Luton Airport, Luton, Bedfordshire, LU2 9ND; tel. (870) 190-0737; e-mail lynn.houghton@thomson.co.uk; internet www.thomsonfly.com; f. 2004; propr TUI AG (Germany); operates scheduled services from 20 UK airports to 80 destinations world-wide; Man. Dir COLIN MITCHELL.

Virgin Atlantic Airways: Manor Royal, Crawley, West Sussex, RH10 2NU; tel. (1293) 562345; fax (1293) 561721; internet www.virgin-atlantic.com; f. 1984; operates services to destinations in the USA, Africa, the Caribbean and the Far East; Chair. Sir RICHARD BRANSON; Chief Exec. STEVE RIDGWAY.

Tourism

In 2007 there were 32.8m. arrivals by foreign visitors to the United Kingdom; receipts from tourism totalled £15,960m. in that year.

Northern Ireland Tourist Board: St Anne's Court, 59 North St, Belfast, BT1 1NB; tel. (28) 9023-1221; fax (28) 9024-0960; e-mail info@nitb.com; internet www.discovernorthernireland.com; Chair. HOWARD HASTINGS; Chief Exec. ALAN CLARKE.

VisitBritain: Thames Tower, Black's Rd, London, W6 9EL; tel. (20) 8846-9000; fax (20) 8563-0302; e-mail corporatepr@visitbritain.org; internet www.visitbritain.com; markets Great Britain overseas; Chair. CHRISTOPHER RODRIGUES; CEO SANDIE DAWE.

VisitEngland: Thames Tower, Black's Rd, London, W6 9EL; tel. (20) 8846-9000; fax (20) 8563-0302; internet www.visitengland.com; f. 2009; promotes tourism in England to domestic visitors; Chair. Lady COBHAM; CEO JAMES BERRESFORD.

Visit London: 6th Floor, 2 More London Riverside, London, SE1 2RR; tel. (20) 7234-5800; fax (20) 7378-6525; e-mail enquiries@visitlondon.com; internet www.visitlondon.com; f. 1963; promotes London to leisure and business visitors; Chair. TAMARA INGRAM; Interim CEO SALLY CHATTERJEE.

VisitScotland: Ocean Point One, 94 Ocean Drive, Leith, Edinburgh, EH6 6JH; tel. (131) 472-2207; e-mail info@visitscotland.com; internet www.visitscotland.com; Chair. PETER LEDERER; Chief Exec. PHILIP RIDDLE.

Visit Wales: Brunel House, 2 Fitzalan Rd, Cardiff, CF24 0UY; tel. (845) 010-3300; fax (29) 2048-5031; e-mail info@visitwales.co.uk; internet www.visitwales.co.uk; Dir, Tourism and Marketing JONATHAN JONES.

UNITED KINGDOM CROWN DEPENDENCIES

The Channel Islands and the Isle of Man lie off shore from the United Kingdom but are not integral parts of the country. They are dependencies of the British Crown and have considerable self-government in internal affairs.

THE CHANNEL ISLANDS

The Channel Islands lie off the north-west coast of France to the west of Normandy, in the English Channel (la Manche). The bailiwicks of the Channel Islands (Guernsey and its dependencies, and Jersey) are the remnants of the Duchy of Normandy, which was in permanent union with the English (now British) Crown from 1106. They do not, however, form part of the United Kingdom. The islands have their own legislative assemblies and legal and administrative systems, their laws depending for their validity on Orders made by the Queen in Council. Her Majesty's Government in the United Kingdom is responsible for the defence and international relations of the islands, and the Crown is ultimately responsible for their good government. The bailiwicks do not form part of the European Union.

Guernsey

Introduction

The civil flag of Guernsey is white, bearing a red cross of St George, with a yellow couped cross superimposed on the cross. The capital is St Peter Port. English is the language in common use, but the Norman *patois* is spoken in some rural parishes. Dependencies of Guernsey are Alderney, Brecqhou, Herm, Jethou, Lihou and Sark. In addition to the British public holidays, Guernsey celebrates 9 May (Liberation Day).

Statistical Survey

including Herm and Jethou

Source (unless otherwise stated): Policy and Research Unit, Sir Charles Frossard House, La Charroterie, St Peter Port, Guernsey, GY1 1FH; tel. (1481) 717012; fax (1481) 717157; internet www.gov.gg.

AREA AND POPULATION

Area: 63.4 sq km (24.4 sq miles).

Population: 59,807 (males 29,138, females 30,669) at census of 29 April 2001. *2007* (estimate): 61,811.

Density (2007): 974.9 per sq km.

Parishes (2001 census): St Peter Port 16,488; Vale 9,573; Castel 8,975; St Sampson 8,592; St Martin 6,267; St Saviour 2,696; St Andrew 2,409; St Pierre du Bois 2,188; Forest 1,549; Torteval 973; Herm 95; Jethou 2; Total 59,807.

Births and Deaths (2007): Live births 645; Deaths 513. Source: UN, *Population and Vital Statistics Report*.

Economically Active Population (at 31 December 2008): Horticulture and other primary 534; Manufacturing 757; Construction 3,230; Utilities 412; Transport and storage 983; Information and communication 1,050; Hostelry 1,949; Wholesale, retail and repairs 4,577; Finance 6,991; Real estate activities 216; Professional, business, scientific and technical activities 1,852; Administrative and support service activities 1,359; Public administration 5,456; Education 465; Human health, social and charitable work activities 1,532; Arts, entertainment and recreation 384; Other services 723; *Total employed* 32,470 (males 17,644, females 14,826); Unemployed 325; Total labour force 32,795.

AGRICULTURE

The principal crops are flowers, much of which are grown under glass. About 16.3 sq km (6.2 sq miles) are cultivated.

FINANCE

Currency and Exchange Rates: 100 pence = 1 pound sterling (£). *Dollar and Euro Equivalents* (31 December 2008): US $1 = 68.60 pence; €1 = 95.47 pence; £10 = $14.58 = €10.47.

Note: Guernsey is in monetary union with the United Kingdom. It has its own coins and notes but United Kingdom coins and notes are also legal tender.

Budget (£ million, 2007): General revenue income 365; General revenue expenditure 294.

Cost of Living: (Retail Price Index at mid-year; base: 31 December 1999 = 100) All items 128.1 in 2006; 134.1 in 2007; 141.5 in 2008.

Gross Domestic Product by Economic Activity (£ '000, 2007, provisional): Horticulture 11,974; Other primary 11,267; Manufacturing 41,120; Construction 131,430; Utilities 12,467; Transport 33,098; Hostelry 48,232; Wholesale 34,608; Retail 118,022; Recreation 14,514; Information 41,766; Financial services 527,537; Legal, business and personal services 232,997; Health, education and public administration 231,808; Non-profit 6,711; *Total factor incomes* 1,497,551; *Less* Pensions 34,206; Other income 193,650; *Less* Adjustment to profit account 1,405; *Total* 1,655,590.

EXTERNAL TRADE

Principal Commodities: *Imports* (1999): Petroleum and oil 168,026,000 litres. *Exports* (1998, £ million): Light industry 47.0; Total flowers 34.0; Total vegetables 5.0.

TRANSPORT

Road Traffic (vehicles registered, 2006): Private vehicles 40,504; Commercial vehicles 7,733; Motorcycles 5,793.

Shipping (2006): Passenger movements 342,075.

Civil Aviation (2006): Passenger movements 869,076.

TOURISM

Number of Visitors (2006): 220,000.

COMMUNICATIONS MEDIA

Telephones (2004): 55,100 main lines in use.

Mobile Cellular Telephones (2004): 43,800.

Internet Users (2004): 36,000.

Source: International Telecommunication Union.

EDUCATION

Primary (2008): 4,674 pupils.

Secondary (2008): 4,359 pupils.

Directory

The Constitution

The Lieutenant-Governor and Commander-in-Chief of Guernsey is the personal representative of the Sovereign and the channel of communication between the Crown and the insular Government. He is appointed by the Crown. He is entitled to sit and speak in the Assembly of the States, but not to vote.

The Bailiff is appointed by the Crown and is President both of the Assembly of the States (the insular legislature), where he has a casting vote, and of the Royal Court of Guernsey.

The government of the island is conducted by a Policy Council, 10 departments and five 'specialist' committees. The Chief Minister may nominate a Deputy Chief Minister and Ministers for each of the 10 departments. Ministers and committee chairmen are elected by the members of the States of Deliberation.

The States of Deliberation is composed of the following members:

(a) The Bailiff, who is President ex officio.

(b) HM Procureur (Attorney-General) and HM Comptroller (Solicitor-General) Law Officers of the Crown, who are appointed by the Crown. They are entitled to sit in the States and to speak, but not to vote.

(c) The 45 People's Deputies elected by popular franchise.

(d) The two Alderney Representatives elected by the States of Alderney.

Projets de Loi (Permanent Laws) require the sanction of Her Majesty in Council.

The function of the States of Election is to elect persons to the office of Jurat. It is composed of the following members:

(a) The Bailiff (President ex officio).

(b) The 12 Jurats or 'Jures-Justiciers'.

(c) The 10 Rectors of the Parishes.

(d) HM Procureur and HM Comptroller.

(e) The 45 People's Deputies.

(f) The 34 Douzaine Representatives.

Meetings of the States and of the Royal Court, formerly conducted in French, are now conducted in English, but the proceedings in both are begun and ended in French.

The Government

Lieutenant-Governor and Commander-in-Chief of the Bailiwick of Guernsey: Sir FABIAN MALBON.

Secretary and ADC to the Lieutenant-Governor: Col R. H. GRAHAM.

Bailiff of Guernsey: GEOFFREY ROBERT ROWLAND.

Deputy Bailiff: RICHARD JOHN COLLAS.

HM Procureur (Attorney-General): JOHN NIKOLAS VAN LEUVEN.

HM Comptroller (Solicitor-General): HOWARD EDWARD ROBERTS.

Chief Executive of the States: MIKE BROWN.

POLICY COUNCIL
(April 2009)

Chief Minister: LYNDON TROTT.

Deputy Chief Minister and Minister of Public Services: BERNARD FLOUQUET.

Minister of the Treasury and Resources: CHARLES PARKINSON.

Minister of the Home Department: GEOFF MAHY.

Minister of Education: CAROL STEERE.

Minister of Health and Social Services: HUNTER ADAM.

Minister of Housing: DAVID JONES.

Minister of Commerce and Employment: CARLA MCNULTY BAUER.

Minister of Social Security: MARK DOREY.

Minister of the Environment: PETER SIRETT.

Minister of Culture and Leisure: MIKE O'HARA.

Judicial System

Justice is administered in Guernsey by the Royal Court, which consists of the Bailiff and the 12 Jurats. The Royal Court also deals with a wide variety of non-contentious matters. A Stipendiary Magistrate deals with minor civil and criminal cases. The Guernsey Court of Appeal deals with appeals from the Royal Court.

Religion

CHRISTIANITY

The Church of England

The Church of England in Guernsey is the established church. The Deanery includes the islands of Alderney, Sark, Herm and Jethou; it forms part of the diocese of Winchester.

Dean of Guernsey: Very Rev. Canon K. PAUL MELLOR, The Deanery, Cornet St, St Peter Port, GY1 1BZ; tel. (1481) 720036; e-mail paul@townchurch.org.gg.

The Roman Catholic Church

The diocese of Portsmouth includes the Channel Islands and part of southern England. In Guernsey there are three Roman Catholic churches, of which the senior is St Joseph and St Mary, Cordier Hill, St Peter Port.

Catholic Dean of Guernsey: Fr MICHAEL HORE, Ampthill House, Cordier Hill, St Peter Port, GY1 1JH; tel. (1481) 720196; fax (1481) 711247; e-mail sjoss.guernsey@virgin.net; internet catholic.org.gg.

Other Christian Churches

The Presbyterian Church and the Church of Scotland are represented by St Andrew's Church, The Grange, St Peter Port. The Baptist, Congregational, Elim and Methodist Churches are also represented in the island.

The Press

Guernsey Press and Star: The Guernsey Press Co, POB 57, Braye Rd, Vale, GY1 3BW; tel. (1481) 240240; fax (1481) 240235; e-mail newsroom@guernsey-press.com; internet www.guernsey-press.com; f. 1897; daily; independent; Editor RICHARD DIGARD; circ. 15,780 (Dec. 2008).

Guernsey Weekly Press: The Guernsey Press Co, POB 57, Braye Rd, Vale, GY1 3BW; tel. (1481) 240240; fax (1481) 240235; e-mail editorial@thisisguernsey.com; internet www.thisisguernsey.com; f. 1902; Thursday; independent; Editor RICHARD DIGARD.

Publishers

Toucan Press: The White Cottage, route de Carteret, Castel, GY5 7YG; tel. (1481) 257017; f. 1850; history, Thomas Hardy, Channel Islands; Man. Dir G. STEVENS COX.

Broadcasting and Communications

TELECOMMUNICATIONS

Cable and Wireless Guernsey Ltd: POB 3, Telecoms House, Upland Rd, St Peter Port, GY1 3AB; tel. (1481) 700700; fax (1481) 724640; e-mail contact@surecw.com; internet www.surecw.com/guernsey; operates under brand name Sure; fixed-line and mobile telecommunications services, as well as broadband internet services; Chief Exec. GEOFFREY HOUSTON.

Wave Telecom: 24 High St, St Peter Port, GY1 2JU; tel. (1481) 818181; internet www.wavetelecom.com; f. 2002; subsidiary of Jersey Telecom; offers fixed-line and mobile telecommunications services; Man. Dir TIM RINGSDORE.

BROADCASTING

Radio

BBC: Radio and Television (see United Kingdom).

BBC Radio Guernsey: Television House, Bulwer Ave, St Sampson, GY2 4LA; tel. (1481) 200600; fax (1481) 200361; e-mail radio.guernsey@bbc.co.uk; internet www.bbc.co.uk/guernsey; f. 1982; Man. Editor DAVID MARTIN.

Island FM: 12 Westerbrook, St Sampson, GY2 4QQ; tel. (1481) 242000; fax (1481) 241120; e-mail studio@islandfm.guernsey.net; internet www.islandfm.com; Programme Controller GARY BURGESS.

Television

Channel Television: Television House, Bulwer Ave, St Sampson, GY2 4LA; tel. (1481) 241888; fax (1481) 241889; e-mail broadcast.gsy@channeltv.co.uk; internet www.channelonline.tv; Exec. Chair. MICHAEL DESMOND.

(See also under Jersey.)

Finance

(cap. = capital; res = reserves; dep. = deposits; brs = branches; amounts in pounds sterling, unless otherwise indicated.)

Guernsey Financial Services Commission: POB 128, La Plaiderie Chambers, La Plaiderie, St Peter Port, GY1 3HQ; tel. (1481) 712706; fax (1481) 712010; e-mail info@gfsc.gg; internet www.gfsc.gg; f. 1988; regulates banking, investment, insurance and fiduciary activities; Dir-Gen. PETER NEVILLE.

BANKING

At December 2008 total bank deposits in Guernsey were £157,009m. in 48 financial institutions.

Adam and Company International Ltd: POB 402, Royal Bank Pl., 1 Glategny Esplanade, St Peter Port, GY1 3GB; tel. (1481) 715055; fax (1481) 726919; e-mail john.judge@adambank.com; internet www.adambank.com; f. 1990; cap. 0.5m., res 0.5m., dep. 150m. (Dec. 2006); Chair. D. J. CATHIE; Man. Dir J. JUDGE.

Bank Sarasin (CI) Ltd: POB 348, Park Court, Park St, St Peter Port, GY1 3UY; tel. (1481) 725147; fax (1481) 725157; e-mail ken.gibbs@sarasin.gg; internet www.sarasin.co.uk; Man. Dir KEN A. GIBBS.

Butterfield Bank (Guernsey) Ltd: POB 25, Regency Court, Glategny Esplanade, St Peter Port, GY1 3AP; tel. (1481) 711521; fax (1481) 714533; e-mail info@butterfield.gg; internet www.butterfieldbank.gg; f. 1989; subsidiary of Bank of N. T. Butterfield & Son Ltd (Bermuda); cap. 39m., res 2m., dep. 1,104m. (Dec. 2007); Man. Dir ROBERT MOORE.

Close Bank Guernsey Ltd: POB 116, Trafalgar Court, Admiral Park, St Peter Port, GY1 3EZ; tel. (1481) 726014; fax (1481) 727645; e-mail bankinggsy@closewm.com; internet www.closewm.com; f. 1965 as Rea Brothers (Guernsey) Ltd; present name adopted 1999; cap. 1m., dep. 386m. (July 2007); Chair. ANDREW HENTON; Man. Dir PHIL O'SHEA.

Crédit Suisse (Guernsey) Ltd: POB 368, Helvetia Court, South Esplanade, St Peter Port, GY1 3JY; tel. (1481) 719000; fax (1481) 724676; e-mail csguernsey.info@credit-suisse.com; internet www.credit-suisse.com/guernsey; f. 1986; cap. US $6m., res $260m., dep. $6,220m. (Dec. 2007); CEO R. MCGREGOR.

EFG Private Bank (Channel Islands) Ltd: POB 603, EFG House, St Julian's Ave, St Peter Port, GY1 4NN; tel. (1481) 723432; fax (1481) 723488; internet www.efggroup.com; f. 1992 as The Private Bank & Trust Co (Guernsey) Ltd; present name adopted 1997; cap. 5m., res 33m., dep. 819m. (Dec. 2006); Man. Dir D. G. GARDNER.

SG Hambros Bank (Channel Islands) Ltd: POB 6, Hambro House, St Julian's Ave, St Peter Port, GY1 3AE; tel. (1481) 726521; fax (1481) 727139; e-mail channelislands@sghambros.com; internet www.sghambros.com; f. 1967; formerly SG Hambros Bank and Trust (Guernsey) Ltd; name changed in 2005 following merger with SG Hambros Bank and Trust (Jersey) Ltd; merchant bankers; cap. 4.5m., res 129.3m., dep. 1,696.5m. (Dec. 2005); Chair. WARWICK J. NEWBURY; Chief Exec. RICHARD A. OLLIVER.

HSBC Private Bank (CI) Ltd: HSBC Private Bank Bldg, Park Pl., Park St, St Peter Port, GY1 1EE; tel. (1481) 710901; fax (1481) 711824; internet www.hsbcprivatebank.com; f. 1985; present name adopted 2008, following merger with HSBC Private Bank (Jersey) Ltd; cap. US $22m., res $463m., dep. $4,874m. (Dec. 2007); CEO GARY MILLER.

Investec Bank (Channel Islands) Ltd: POB 188, La Vieille Cour, St Peter Port, GY1 3LP; tel. (1481) 723506; fax (1481) 741147; e-mail enquiries@investec-ci.com; internet www.investec.com; f. 1977 as Guinness Mahon Guernsey Ltd; present name adopted 1999; cap. 15m., res 61m., dep. 1,721m. (March 2006); Chair. A. TAPNACK; Gen. Man. MORT MIRGHAVAMEDDIN.

Lloyds TSB Offshore Ltd Private Banking Office: POB 136, Sarnia House, Le Truchot, St Peter Port, GY1 4EN; tel. (1481) 708000; fax (1481) 727416; e-mail pvtbankingg@lloydstsb-offshore.com; internet www.privatebanking.lloydstsb-offshore.com; Head of Sales and Relationships GARY BROWNBRIDGE.

Rothschild Bank International Ltd: POB 58, St Julian's Court, St Julian's Ave, St Peter Port; tel. (1481) 713713; fax (1481) 727705; e-mail private.banking@rothschild.co.uk; internet www.rothschild.gg; f. 1967; present name adopted 2007; subsidiary of N. M. Rothschild & Sons Ltd, London; cap. 5m., res 0.1m., dep. 1,168m. (March 2007); Chair. CHRISTOPHER COLEMAN; Man. Dir PETER ROSE.

Royal Bank of Canada (Channel Islands) Ltd: POB 48, Canada Court, St Peter Port, GY1 3BQ; tel. (1481) 744000; fax (1481) 744001; e-mail infogpb@rbc.com; internet www.rbcprivatebanking.com; f. 1973; subsidiary of Royal Bank of Canada; cap. 5m., res 310m., dep. 6,711m. (Oct. 2007); Chair. M. J. LAGOPOULOS; Man. Dir C. C. BLAMPIED.

Schroders (CI) Ltd: POB 334, Regency Court, Glategny Esplanade, St Peter Port, GY1 3UF; tel. (1481) 703700; fax (1481) 703600; internet www.schroders.com/ci; f. 1992; cap. 0.5m., res 5m., dep. 829m. (Dec. 2006); Chair. P. MALLINCKROFT.

Banking Organization

Association of Guernsey Banks: c/o Kleinwort Benson (CI) Ltd, POB 44, Dorey Court, Admiral Park, St Peter Port, GY1 3BG; fax (1481) 724266; e-mail jim.gilligan@kbci.com; internet www.agb.org.gg; f. 1988; 49 mems; Chair. JIM GILLIGAN.

STOCK EXCHANGE

Channel Islands Stock Exchange (CISX): 1 Lefebvre St, St Peter Port, GY1 4PJ; tel. (1481) 713831; e-mail info@cisx.com; internet www.cisx.com; 50 cos listed; Chief Exec. TAMARA MENTESHVILI.

INSURANCE

At 31 March 2009 there were 372 international insurers and 23 domestic insurers operating in Guernsey.

Generali Worldwide Insurance Co Ltd: POB 613, Generali House, Hirzel St, St Peter Port, GY1 4PA; tel. (1481) 715400; fax (1481) 715390; e-mail enquiries@generali-guernsey.com; internet www.generali-gw.com; Chair. CHRISTOPHER SPENCER; CEO GAVIN TRADELIUS.

Heritage Group: POB 225, Heritage Hall, Le Marchant St, St Peter Port, GY1 4HY; tel. (1481) 716000; fax (1481) 712357; e-mail info@heritage.co.gg; internet www.heritage.co.gg; CEO RICHARD TEE.

Insurance Corpn of the Channel Islands Ltd: POB 160, Dixcart House, Sir William Pl., St Peter Port, GY1 4EY; tel. (1481) 707551; e-mail icci@insurancecorporation.com; internet www.insurancecorporation.com; mem. of the RSA Insurance Group; Man. Dir PETER GALLAGHER.

Islands' Insurance Brokers Ltd: Lancaster Court, Forest Lane, St Peter Port, GY1 1WJ; tel. (1481) 710731; fax (1481) 712223; e-mail insure@islandsinsurance.gg; internet www.islands-insurance.com; f. 1978; insurance broker; owned by National Farmers' Union Mutual Insurance Society Ltd; Dir PETER ROWE.

Trade and Industry

CHAMBER OF COMMERCE

Guernsey Chamber of Commerce: Suite 3, 16 Glategny Esplanade, St Peter Port, GY1 1WN; tel. (1481) 727483; fax (1481) 710755; e-mail office@guernseychamber.com; internet www.guernseychamber.com; f. 1808; Pres. PAUL LUXON; Dir BARRY CASH.

UTILITIES

Electricity

Guernsey Electricity: POB 4, Electricity House, Northside, Vale, GY1 3AD; tel. (1481) 200700; fax (1481) 246942; e-mail admin@electricity.gg; internet www.electricity.gg; Chair. KEN GREGSON; Man. Dir IAN WATSON.

Gas

Guernsey Gas: The Energy Centre, Admiral Park, St Peter Port, GY1 2BB; tel. (1481) 724811; internet www.gsygas.com; Dir PAUL GARLICK.

Water

Guernsey Water: POB 30, South Esplanade, St Peter Port, GY1 3AS; tel. (1481) 724552; fax (1481) 715094; internet www.water.gg; fmrly States of Guernsey Waterboard; name changed as above 2004; Dir of Water Services ANDREW REDHEAD.

Transport

SHIPPING

Alderney Shipping Co Ltd: POB 77, White Rock, St Peter Port, GY1 4BN; tel. (1481) 724810; fax (1481) 712081; e-mail annika@aldshp.co.uk; internet www.aldshp.co.uk.

Condor Ltd: 3rd Floor, La Plaiderie House, La Plaiderie, St Peter Port, GY1 1WD; tel. (1481) 729666; fax (1481) 712555; internet www.condorferries.co.uk; f. 1964; regular passenger service operating between the Channel Islands and St Malo (France), and between the Channel Islands and Poole, Weymouth and Portsmouth; Man. Dir ROBERT PROVAN; Gen. Man. NICK DOBBS.

Condorferries Freight: 3rd Floor, La Plaiderie House, La Plaiderie, St Peter Port, GY1 1WD; tel. (1481) 728620; fax (1481) 728521; e-mail jeff.vidamour@condorferries.co.uk; internet www.condorferries.co.uk; regular ro-ro freight services between Portsmouth, Guernsey, Jersey and St Malo (France); Freight Dir JEFF VIDAMOUR.

Herm Seaway Express: Albert Pier, St Peter Port; tel. (1481) 724161; fax (1481) 700226; Contact Peter Wilcox.

Isle of Sark Shipping Co Ltd: White Rock, St Peter Port, GY1 2LN; tel. (1481) 724059; fax (1481) 713999; e-mail info@sarkshipping.info; internet www.sarkshipping.info; operates daily services between Guernsey and Sark.

Trident Charter Co Ltd: Woodville, Les Dicqs, Vale, GY6 8JW; tel. (1481) 245253; fax (1481) 700226; e-mail peterwilcox@cw.gsy.net; Man. Peter Wilcox.

CIVIL AVIATION

Aurigny Air Services Ltd: States Airport, La Planque Lane, Forest, GY8 0DT; tel. (1481) 266444; fax (1481) 266446; e-mail customerrelations@aurigny.com; internet www.aurigny.com; f. 1968; scheduled passenger services from Guernsey to Alderney, Jersey, Bristol, East Midlands, London Gatwick, London Stansted, Manchester, Southampton and Dinard (France); freight services, tour operation, ambulance charters and third party handling; owned by the States of Guernsey; Man. Dir Malcolm Hart.

Blue Islands: Century House, 12 Victoria St, St Anne, Alderney, GY9 3UF; tel. (1481) 711321; fax (1481) 735235; e-mail enquiries@blueislands.com; internet www.blueislands.com; f. 1999 as Le Cocqs Air Link; name changed as above in 2006; scheduled passenger flights between Alderney, Guernsey and Jersey, and to Southampton, the Isle of Man, Geneva and Zürich (both Switzerland); Chair. Derek Coates; Man. Dir Paul Sabin.

Tourism

A total of 220,000 tourists visited Guernsey during 2006.

VisitGuernsey: POB 459, Raymond Falla House, Longue Rue, St Martin, GY1 6AF; tel. (1481) 234567; fax (1481) 238755; e-mail enquiries@visitguernsey.com; internet www.visitguernsey.com; Dir, Marketing and Tourism Chris Elliott.

Islands of the Bailiwick of Guernsey

Alderney

The area of Alderney is 7.9 sq km (3.1 sq miles) and at the 2001 census the population was 2,294. The principal town is St Anne's.

The President, who is elected for a four-year term, is the civic head of Alderney and has precedence on the island over all persons except the Lieutenant-Governor of Guernsey, and the Bailiff of Guernsey or his representative. He presides over meetings of the States of Alderney, which are responsible for the administration of the island with the exception of policing, public health and education, which are administered by the States of Guernsey. The States consist of 10 members who hold office for four years and are elected by universal suffrage of residents.

President of the States: Sir Norman Browse.

Chief Executive of the States: David Jeremiah.

Greffier: Sarah Kelly.

States of Alderney: POB 1, Alderney, GY9 3AA; tel. (1481) 822811; fax (1481) 822436; e-mail states@alderney.net; internet www.alderney.gov.gg.

Brecqhou and Lihou

Brecqhou (measuring 1.2 km by 0.5 km) is a dependency of Sark. Lihou (area 0.2 sq km) is, for administrative purposes, part of Guernsey.

Herm

Herm is held on a 100-year lease from the States of Guernsey by Wood of Herm Island Ltd, with a duty to preserve the island's outstanding natural beauty and peacefulness. Farming and tourism are the chief sources of income. The island has an area of 2.0 sq km (0.8 sq miles). At the 2001 census the population of Herm was 95.

Herm Island Administration Office: Herm Island, Guernsey, GY1 3HR; tel. (1481) 722377; fax (1481) 700334; e-mail admin@herm-island.com; internet www.herm-island.com; Admin. Dir Andrew Bailey.

Jethou

Jethou has an area of 0.2 sq km (0.07 sq miles) and is leased by the Crown to a tenant who has no official functions. At the 2001 census the population of Jethou was two.

Sark

The area of the island is 5.5 sq km (2.1 sq miles) and at the 2001 census the population was 589. No motor vehicles are permitted apart from a small number of tractors. In summer a daily boat service runs between Guernsey and Sark, and in winter a limited service is provided. There are two harbours on the island.

The Seigneur of Sark is the hereditary civic head of the island and thereby entitled to certain privileges. The Seigneur is a member of the Chief Pleas of Sark, the island's parliament, and has a suspensory veto on its ordinances. The Seigneur has the right, subject to the approval of the Lieutenant-Governor of Guernsey, to appoint the Seneschal of Sark, who is President of the Chief Pleas and Chairman of the Seneschal's Court, which is the local Court of Justice.

In March 2006 the Chief Pleas voted in favour of reducing the number of its members from 52 (comprising the owners of the island's 40 tenements—known as tenants—and 12 elected 'deputies of the people') to 28, of whom 14 were to be tenants and the remaining 14 residents. Under the reformed system the members of the Chief Pleas would be elected by universal suffrage of residents. An official opinion poll on the composition of the Chief Pleas was conducted between mid-August and early September. Some 56.0% of the valid votes cast (234 of a total of 418) supported open elections for all 28 seats in the Chief Pleas, while 44.0% of voters favoured the option of reserving 12 of the 28 seats specifically for residents and eight for tenants. A participation rate of 89.5% was recorded for the opinion poll, which was subsequently approved by the Chief Pleas. In February 2008 the Chief Pleas ratified the reform law, which would allow for the introduction of an elected chamber. The Privy Council of the United Kingdom approved the proposed changes in April and elections for a fully elected, 28-member Chief Pleas duly took place in December.

Seigneur of Sark: John Michael Beaumont.

Seneschal: Lt-Col Reginald J. Guille.

Greffier: Trevor J. Hamon.

Sark Committee Office: La Chasse Marette, GY9 0SF; tel. (1481) 832118; fax (1481) 833086; e-mail seigneur@sark.gov.gg; internet www.sark.info.

Sark Tourism: Harbour Hill, Sark, GY9 0SB; tel. (1481) 832345; fax (1481) 832483; e-mail contact@sark.info; internet www.sark.info.

JERSEY

Introduction

Jersey, the largest of the Channel Islands, is situated to the southeast of Guernsey, from which it is separated by 27 km (17 miles) of sea. The official language of Jersey is English (since 1960), although French is still used in the courts. The state and civil flag is white with a red saltire and coat of arms bearing three yellow lions and surmounted by a yellow crown. The capital is St Helier. In addition to the British public holidays, Jersey celebrates 9 May (Liberation Day).

Statistical Survey

Source (unless otherwise stated): States of Jersey Statistics Department, Cyril Le Marquand House, POB 140, JE4 8QT; tel. (1534) 440426; fax (1534) 440409; e-mail statistics@gov.je; internet www.gov.je/statistics.

AREA AND POPULATION

Area: 118.2 sq km (45.6 sq miles).

Population (census of 11 March 2001): 87,186 (males 42,484, females 44,702). *2007* (official estimate at 31 December): 90,800.

Density (at 31 December 2007): 768.2 per sq km.

Principal Towns (2001): St Helier 28,310; St Saviour 12,491; St Brelade 10,134; St Clement 8,196.

Births and Deaths (2007): Live births 1,030 (11.3 per 1,000); Deaths 707 (7.8 per 1,000).

Economically Active Population (at December 2007, rounded estimates): Agriculture and fishing 1,560; Manufacturing 1,510; Electricity, gas and water 520; Construction and quarrying 5,090; Wholesale and retail 8,590; Hotels, restaurants etc. 4,560; Transport, storage and communication 2,660; Financial services 13,090; Miscellaneous business activities (incl. computers) 3,840; Public administration 6,630; Education, health and other services 4,980; *Total employed* 53,040; Unemployed 320; *Total labour force* 53,360. Note: Totals may not be equal to the sum of components, owing to rounding.

AGRICULTURE, ETC.

Principal Crops: Some 56.5% of total land area was classified as agricultural in 2006. The principal crops are potatoes, cauliflowers and tomatoes. Dairy and cattle farming are important activities.

Fishing ('000 metric tons, 2007): Capture 1,710 (Wet fish 118, Brown crab 412, Lobster 155, Spider crab 106, Scallops 372, Whelk 545, Others 2); Aquaculture 791 (Oysters 737, Scallops 4, Mussels 50); *Total catch* 2,501.

FINANCE

Currency and Exchange Rates: 100 pence = 1 pound sterling (£). *Dollar and Euro Equivalents* (31 December 2008): US $1 = 68.60 pence; €1 = 95.47 pence; £10 = $14.58 = €10.47.

Note: Jersey is in monetary union with the United Kingdom. It has its own coins and notes but United Kingdom coins and notes are also legal tender.

Budget (£ million, 2007): Net consolidated fund income 667 (Tax 430); Consolidated fund expenditure 622 (Gross departmental expenditure 583, Capital servicing 39).

Money Supply (currency in circulation, £ million at 31 December 2006): Notes 69.6; Coins 6.4; *Total* 75.9.

Cost of Living (Retail Price Index at June; base June 2000 = 100, all items): 126.2 in 2006; 131.6 in 2007; 139.0 in 2008.

Gross National Income (£ million, 2007, preliminary): 3,740.

Gross Value Added by Economic Activity (£ million at current prices, 2007, preliminary): Agriculture 53; Manufacturing 53; Electricity, gas and water 36; Construction 212; Wholesale and retail trade 259; Hotels, restaurants and bars 119; Transport, storage and communications 157; Finance 2,177; Other business activities 746; Public administration 276; *Total* 4,089.

TRANSPORT

Road Traffic (vehicles registered at 31 December 2001): Motor cars 71,059; Motorcycles 5,676; Mopeds 2,200; Buses and minibuses 691; Tractors 2,369; Vans 7,562; Trucks 3,617; Total (incl. others) 94,538. *2008* (vehicles registered at 31 December): Total 111,861.

Shipping (2008): Passenger movements 728,000; Containerized freight ('000 metric tons handled) 334.

Civil Aviation (2005): Aircraft movements 70,012; Total passengers carried 1,483,477 (Arrivals 741,969, Departures 741,508). *2008:* Total passenger arrivals 800,454 (from UK 679,228).

TOURISM

Tourist Arrivals (2004): *Holiday and Leisure Visitors* (staying in paid accommodation): 377,820 (UK mainland 301,460; Other Channel Islands 14,900; France 29,380; Germany 10,060); *Total Arrivals*: 731,310. *2007:* Total visitor arrivals 739,280 (number staying in paid accommodation 375,860); Total revenues £234m.

COMMUNICATIONS MEDIA

Telephones (2006, estimate): 71,500 main lines in use.

Mobile Cellular Telephones (2006, estimate): 102,000.

Internet Users (2004): 27,000.

Source: partly International Telecommunication Union.

EDUCATION

Pupils (2008): Primary 6,980 (state schools 5,629, private 1,351); Secondary 6,328 (state schools 5,191, private 1,137).

Directory

The Constitution

The Lieutenant-Governor and Commander-in-Chief of Jersey is the personal representative of the Sovereign, the Commander of the Armed Forces of the Crown, and the channel of communication between the Crown and the insular Government. He is appointed by the Crown, and is entitled to sit and speak in the Assembly of the States of Jersey, but not to vote. He has a veto on certain forms of legislation.

The Bailiff is appointed by the Crown, and is President both of the Assembly of the States (the insular legislature) and the Royal Court of Jersey. In the States, he has a right of dissent and a casting vote.

The Deputy Bailiff is appointed by the Crown and, when authorized by the Bailiff to do so, he may discharge any function appertaining to the office of Bailiff.

The government of the island is conducted by a Council of Ministers, which consists of a Chief Minister and nine other ministers. The Chief Minister is elected by the States and nominates the other ministers, subject to the approval of the States. The States consist of 12 Senators (elected for six years, six retiring every third year), 12 Connétables (triennial), and 29 Deputies (triennial). They are elected by universal suffrage. The Dean of Jersey, the Attorney-General and Solicitor-General are appointed by the Crown and are entitled to sit and speak in the States, but not to vote. Permanent laws passed by the States require the sanction of Her Majesty in Council, but Triennial Regulations do not.

The Government

Lieutenant-Governor and Commander-in-Chief of Jersey: Lt-Gen. ANDREW RIDGEWAY.

Secretary and Aide-de-Campe to the Lieutenant-Governor: Lt-Col A. J. C. WOODROW.

Bailiff: Sir PHILIP MARTIN BAILHACHE.

Deputy Bailiff: MICHAEL CAMERON ST JOHN BIRT.

Dean of Jersey: Very Rev. ROBERT FREDERICK KEY.

Attorney-General: WILLIAM JAMES BAILHACHE.

Solicitor-General: TIMOTHY JOHN LE COCQ.

Greffier of the States: MICHAEL NELSON DE LA HAYE.

COUNCIL OF MINISTERS
(April 2009)

Chief Minister: TERENCE (TERRY) LE SUEUR.
Minister for the Treasury and Resources: PHILIP OZOUF.
Minister for Home Affairs: IAN LE MARQUAND.
Minister for Education, Sport and Culture: JAMES REED.
Minister for Health and Social Services: ANNE PRYKE.

UNITED KINGDOM CROWN DEPENDENCIES

The Channel Islands (Jersey)

Minister for Social Security: IAN GORST.
Minister for Economic Development: ALAN MACLEAN.
Minister for Transport and Technical Services: MICHAEL (MIKE) JACKSON.
Minister for Housing: TERENCE (TERRY) LE MAIN.
Minister for Planning and the Environment: FREDERICK (FREDDIE) COHEN.

Judicial System

Justice is administered in Jersey by the Royal Court, which consists of the Bailiff or Deputy Bailiff and 12 Jurats elected by an Electoral College. There is a Court of Appeal, which consists of the Bailiff (or Deputy Bailiff) and two Judges, selected from a panel appointed by the Crown. A final appeal lies to the Privy Council in certain cases.

A Stipendiary Magistrate deals with minor civil and criminal cases. He also acts as an Examining Magistrate in some criminal matters.

Religion

CHRISTIANITY

The Church of England

The Church of England is the established church. The Deanery of Jersey is an Ecclesiastical Peculiar, governed by its own canons, the Dean being the Ordinary of the Island; it is attached to the diocese of Winchester for episcopal purposes.

Dean of Jersey: Very Rev. ROBERT FREDERICK KEY, The Deanery, David Place, St Helier, JE2 4TE; tel. (1534) 720001; fax (1534) 617488; e-mail deanofjersey@jerseymail.co.uk.

The Roman Catholic Church

The diocese of Portsmouth includes the Channel Islands and part of southern England. The Episcopal Vicar for the Channel Islands resides at St Peter Port, Guernsey. In Jersey there are 12 Roman Catholic churches, including St Mary and St Peter's, Wellington Rd, St Helier (English), and St Thomas's, Val Plaisant, St Helier (French).

Catholic Dean of Jersey: Fr NICHOLAS FRANCE, 17 Val Plaisant, St Helier, JE2 4TA; tel. (1534) 720235; fax (1534) 607991; internet www.catholicchurchjersey.com.

Other Christian Churches

The Baptist, Congregational New Church, Methodist and Presbyterian churches are also represented.

The Press

Jersey Evening Post: Guiton House, Five Oaks, St Saviour, JE4 8XQ; tel. (1534) 611611; fax (1534) 611622; e-mail editorial@jerseyeveningpost.com; internet www.jerseyeveningpost.com; f. 1890; independent; Propr The Guiton Group; Editor CHRIS BRIGHT; circ. 20,070 (Dec. 2008).

Jersey Weekly Post: POB 582, Guiton House, Five Oaks, St Saviour, JE4 8XQ; tel. (1534) 611611; fax (1534) 611622; e-mail editorial@jerseyeveningpost.com; internet www.thisisjersey.com; Thursday; Propr The Guiton Group; Editor CHRIS BRIGHT; circ. 1,200.

Publishers

Ashton & Denton Publishing Co (CI) Ltd: 3 Burlington House, St Saviour's Rd, St Helier, JE2 4LA; tel. (1534) 735461; fax (1534) 875805; e-mail asden@supanet.com; f. 1957; local history, holiday guides, financial; Man. Dir A. MACKENZIE.

Barnes Publishing Ltd: 18 Great Union Rd, St Helier, JE2 3YA; tel. (1534) 618166; fax (1534) 607029; e-mail ian@barnespublishing.com; internet barnespublishing.com; f. 1992 as Apache Publishing; present name adopted 1998; Man. Dir IAN BARNES.

Broadcasting and Communications

TELECOMMUNICATIONS

Cable and Wireless Jersey: King St, St Helier, JE2 4WE; tel. (1534) 888291; fax (1534) 888292; e-mail hello@surecw.com; internet www.surecw.com/jersey; offers mobile cellular telecommunications under brand name *Sure Mobile*; Chief Exec., Sure Jersey GRAHAM HUGHES.

Jersey Airtel Ltd (Airtel Vodafone): 26 Queen St, St Helier, JE2 4WD; internet www.airtel-vodafone.com; f. 2007; mobile cellular telecommunications; owned by Bharti-Airtel Ltd (India); Chief Exec. DAVID WATSON.

Jersey Telecom: POB 53, No. 1 The Forum, Grenville St, St Helier, JE4 8PB; tel. (1534) 882882; fax (1534) 882883; e-mail enquiries@jerseytelecom.com; internet www.jerseytelecom.com; Chair. JOHN HENWOOD; CEO BOB LAWRENCE.

BROADCASTING

Radio

BBC: Radio and Television (see United Kingdom).

BBC Jersey: 18 and 21 Parade Rd, St Helier, JE2 3PL; tel. (1534) 870000; e-mail jersey@bbc.co.uk; internet www.bbc.co.uk/jersey; f. 1982; broadcasts 78 hours a week; Editor DENZIL DUDLEY.

Channel 103 FM: 6 Tunnell St, St Helier, JE2 4LU; tel. (1534) 888103; fax (1534) 877177; e-mail admin@channel103.com; internet www.channel103.com; f. 1992; Man Dir LINDA BURNHAM.

Television

Channel Television: Television Centre, St Helier, JE1 3ZD; tel. (1534) 816816; fax (1534) 816777; e-mail broadcast@channeltv.co.uk; internet www.channelonline.tv; f. 1962; daily transmissions; Exec. Chair. MICHAEL DESMOND.

Programmes are also received from the BBC, Channel 4 and Five in the United Kingdom and also from France.

Finance

Jersey Financial Services Commission: POB 267, 14–18 Castle St, St Helier, JE4 8TP; tel. (1534) 822000; fax (1534) 822001; e-mail info@jerseyfsc.org; internet www.jerseyfsc.org; f. 1998; financial services regulator; Dir-Gen. JOHN HARRIS.

BANKING

(cap. = capital; auth. = authorized; res = reserves; dep. = deposits; m. = million; br./brs = branch(es); amounts in pounds sterling, unless otherwise indicated)

In 2008 total bank deposits in Jersey were £206,080m. in 47 institutions.

Banks

ABN AMRO Private Banking: POB 255, 7 Castle St, St Helier, JE4 8TB; tel. (1534) 604000; fax (1534) 759041; e-mail pbclients@uk.abnamro.com; internet www.abnamroprivatebanking.com/jersey; f. 1997; Head of Private Banking PATRICK CROWLEY.

AIB Bank (CI) Ltd: POB 468, AIB House, 25 Esplanade, St Helier, JE1 2AB; tel. (1534) 883000; fax (1534) 883112; e-mail one@aib.je; internet www.aib.je; f. 1981; cap. 10.0m., dep. 2,268m. (Dec. 2007); Man. Dir D. J. MOYNIHAN.

Ansbacher (Channel Islands) Ltd: POB 393, 7–11 Britannia Pl., Bath St, St Helier, JE4 8US; tel. (1534) 504504; fax (1534) 504575; e-mail info@ansbacher.co.je; internet www.ansbacher.com/channelislands.html; f. 1984 as Westpac Banking Corpn (Jersey) Ltd; acquired by Henry Ansbacher Group in 1995; cap. 3m., res 9m., dep. 276m. (Dec. 2006); Man. Dir MARK BRIGHT.

Bank Leumi (Jersey) Ltd: POB 510, 27 Hill St, St Helier, JE4 5TR; tel. (1534) 702525; fax (1534) 617446; e-mail dlieberman@leumijersey.com; internet www.bankleumi.co.uk; f. 1993; cap. 10m., res 4m., dep. 192m. (Dec. 2006).

Bank of Scotland International Ltd: Halifax House, 31–33 New St, St Helier, JE4 8YW; tel. (1534) 613500; fax (1534) 759280; e-mail enquiry@bankofscotlandint.co.uk; internet www.bankofscotland-international.com; cap. 15.0m., dep. 822.8m. (Feb. 2001); f. 1986; Man. Dir GRAEME HALL.

Banque Transatlantique (Jersey) Ltd: POB 206, 47–49 La Motte St, St Helier, JE4 0XR; tel. (1534) 881471; fax (1534) 881473; e-mail btjersey@psilink.co.je; internet www.transat.tm.fr; Dir MARTIN HIBBS.

BHF-Bank (Jersey) Ltd: 6 Wests Centre, St Helier, JE2 4ST; tel. (1534) 879044; fax (1534) 879246; f. 1981; cap. €4.0m., res €16.5m., dep. €1,200.0m. (Dec. 2006); Man. JOHN M. ALCOCK.

Citibank (Channel Islands) Ltd: POB 104, 38 The Esplanade, St Helier, JE4 8ZT; tel. (1534) 608005; fax (1534) 608190; internet www.citibank.com/privatebank/index.htm; f. 1969; cap. US $0.9m., res $7.6m., dep. $216.4m. (Dec. 2005); Chair. PHILIP HOOPER.

Deutsche Bank International Ltd: POB 727, St Paul's Gate, New St, St Helier, JE4 8ZB; tel. (1534) 889900; fax (1534) 889911; internet www.dboffshore.com; f. 1972; cap. 15m., res 203m., dep. 4,803m. (Dec. 2007); CEO MARK HIRST.

Dexia Private Bank Jersey Ltd: POB 12, 2–6 Church St, St Helier, JE4 9NE; tel. (1534) 834400; fax (1534) 834411; e-mail dexiapbjsy@localdial.com; internet www.dexia-privatebank.je; f. 1996; Man. Dir DAVID G. SMITH.

Fairbairn Private Bank Ltd: Fairbairn House, 31 The Esplanade, St Helier, JE1 1FB; tel. (1534) 887889; fax (1534) 509725; e-mail jer@fairbairnpb.com; internet www.fairbairnpb.com; f. 1994 as Flemings (Jersey) Ltd, name changed as above in 2004; cap. 0.4m., res 11m., dep. 821m. (Dec. 2006); Man. Dir G. J. HORTON.

SG Hambros Bank (Channel Islands) Ltd: POB 78, SG Hambros House, 18 The Esplanade, St Helier, JE4 8PR; tel. (1534) 815555; fax (1534) 815640; e-mail channelislands@sghambros.com; internet www.sghambros.com; f. 1967 as Hambros (Jersey) Ltd; previously SG Hambros Bank and Trust (Jersey) Ltd; name changed in 2005 following merger with SG Hambros Bank and Trust (Guernsey) Ltd; subsidiary of SG Hambros Bank and Trust Ltd, London; cap. 4.5m., res 129.3m., dep. 1,696.5m. (Dec. 2005); Chair. WARWICK J. NEWBURY; Man. Dir RICHARD A. OLLIVER.

HSBC Bank International Ltd: HSBC House, St Helier, JE1 1HS; tel. (1534) 616000; fax (1534) 616001; e-mail offshore@hsbc.com; internet www.offshore.hsbc.com; f. 1967 as Midland Bank Finance Corpn (Jersey) Ltd; cap. 1m., res. 34m, dep. 5,939m. (Dec. 2006); Chief Exec. MARTIN DAVID SPURLING.

HSBC Bank Middle East Ltd: POB 315, HSBC House, The Esplanade, St Helier, JE4 8UB; tel. (1534) 606512; fax (1534) 606149; e-mail chris.keirle@hsbc.com; internet www.middleeast.hsbc.com; cap. US $431m., res $60m., dep. $32,729m. (Dec. 2007); Chair. DAVID HOWARD HODGKINSON.

ING Bank (Jersey) Ltd: 3rd Floor, Forum House, Grenville St, St Helier, JE2 4UF; tel. (1534) 880888; fax (1534) 880777; internet www.ing.je; f. 1988; name changed as above in 2003; Man. Dir PAUL VAN NESTE.

Kleinwort Benson (Channel Islands) Ltd: POB 76, Kleinwort Benson House, Wests Centre, St Helier, JE4 8PQ; tel. (1534) 613000; fax (1534) 613141; internet www.kleinwortbenson.com; f. 1962; mem. of the Dresdner Bank Group; cap. 5m., res 20m., dep. 2,182m. (Dec. 2006); Man. Dir MARTIN ANGUS TAYLOR.

Lloyds TSB Offshore Ltd: POB 160, 25 New St, St Helier, JE4 8ZU; tel. (1534) 854144; fax (1534) 503215; e-mail jerseyoffc@lloydstsb-offshore.com; internet www.lloydstsb-offshore.com; part of Lloyds TSB banking group; cap. 208m., res 187m., dep. 7,441m. (Dec. 2007); Chair. DAVID J. S. OLDFIELD.

JPMorgan Chase Bank: POB 127, JPMorgan House, Grenville St, St Helier, JE4 8QH; tel. (1534) 626262; fax (1534) 626301; Gen. Man. L. C. WORTHAM.

JP Morgan Trust Co (Jersey): POB 127, JPMorgan House, Grenville St, St Helier; tel. (1534) 626262; fax (1534) 626300; Chair. T. TODMAN; Man. Dir L. C. WORTHAM.

RBS Coutts Channel Islands: POB 6, 23–25 Broad St, St Helier, JE4 8ND; tel. (1534) 282345; internet www.rbscoutts.com.

The Royal Bank of Scotland International Ltd: POB 64, 71 Bath St, St Helier, JE4 8PJ; tel. (1534) 285200; fax (1534) 285222; internet www.rbsint.com; f. 1966; cap. 86.5m., res 686.3m., dep. 14,216.7m. (Dec. 2002); Chief Exec. IAN HENDERSON.

Standard Bank Jersey Ltd: POB 583, Standard Bank House, 47–49 La Motte St, St Helier, JE4 8XR; tel. (1534) 881188; fax (1534) 881199; e-mail sboff@standardbank.com; internet www.standardbank.com/wealth; f. 1977 as Brown Shipley (Jersey); present name adopted 2000; cap. 10m., res 1m., dep. 1,082m. (Dec. 2007); Chair. R. A. G. LEITH; CEO IAN GIBSON.

Standard Chartered (Jersey) Ltd: 15 Castle St, St Helier, JE4 8PT; tel. (1534) 704000; fax (1534) 704600; internet www.standardchartered.com/je; f. 1966 as Julian S. Hodge Bank (Jersey) Ltd; present name adopted 2004; cap. 7m., res 302m., dep. 4,553m. (Dec. 2006); CEO ALISON MACFADYEN.

INSURANCE

Jersey Mutual Insurance Soc.: 74 Halkett Pl., St Helier, JE1 1BT; tel. (1534) 734246; fax (1534) 733381; e-mail info@jerseymutual.com; internet www.jerseymutual.com; f. 1869; general and household; Pres. R. LE CORNU; Sec. R. A. JEANNE.

Trade and Industry

CHAMBER OF COMMERCE

Jersey Chamber of Commerce: Chamber House, 25 Pier Rd, St Helier, JE1 4HF; tel. (1534) 724536; fax (1534) 734942; e-mail admin@jerseychamber.com; internet www.jerseychamber.com; f. 1768; Pres. CLIVE SPEARS; Head, Marketing and Operations CATHERINE HARGREAVES; 600 mems.

Utilities

Electricity

Jersey Electricity Co Ltd: POB 45, Queen's Rd, St Helier, JE4 8NY; tel. (1534) 505460; fax (1534) 505565; e-mail jec@jec.co.uk; internet www.jec.co.uk; f. 1924; Chair. GEOFFREY GRIME; CEO CHRIS AMBLER.

Gas

Jersey Gas Co Ltd: POB 169, Thomas Edge House, Tunnell St, St Helier, JE4 8RE; tel. (1534) 755500; fax (1534) 769822; e-mail jerseygas@jsy-gas.com; internet www.jsygas.com; Man. Dir PAUL GARLICK.

Water

Jersey New Waterworks Co Ltd (Jersey Water): Mulcaster House, Westmount Rd, St Helier, JE1 1DG; tel. (1534) 707300; fax (1534) 707400; e-mail info@jerseywater.je; internet www.jerseywater.je; 73.9% stake owned by States of Jersey; Chair. DAVID NORMAN; Man. Dir HOWARD SNOWDEN.

Transport

SHIPPING

The harbour of St Helier has 1,400 m of cargo working quays, with 10 berths in dredged portion (2.29 m) and eight drying berths.

Condor Jersey Ltd: Elizabeth Terminal and Albert Quay, St Helier; tel. (1534) 607080; fax (1534) 280767; e-mail reservations@condorferries.co.uk; internet www.condorferries.co.uk; head office in Guernsey; daily services to mainland Britain; also regular services to Guernsey and St Malo (France); Gen. Man. NICK DOBBS.

CIVIL AVIATION

The States of Jersey Airport is at St Peter, Jersey.

Tourism

In 2007 Jersey recorded some 739,280 tourist arrivals; 375,860 visitors stayed in paid accommodation. Tourist expenditure in that year was £234m.

Jersey Tourism: Liberation Sq., St Helier, JE1 1BB; tel. (1534) 448800; fax (1534) 448898; e-mail info@jersey.com; internet www.jersey.com; Dir DAVID DE CARTERET.

THE ISLE OF MAN

Introduction

The Isle of Man lies in the Irish Sea between the Cumbrian coast of England and Northern Ireland. It is a dependency of the Crown and does not form part of the United Kingdom. It has its own legislative assembly and legal and administrative systems, its laws depending for their validity on Orders made by the Queen in Council. Her Majesty's Government in the United Kingdom is responsible for the defence and international relations of the island, and the Crown is ultimately responsible for its good government. However, control of direct taxation is exercised by the Manx Government and, although most rates of indirect taxation are the same on the island as in the United Kingdom, there is some divergence of rates. The capital is Douglas. In addition to the British public holidays, the Isle of Man also celebrates Senior Race Day of the annual Isle of Man Tourist Trophy (TT) Races (which, in 2009, falls on 12 June) and Tynwald Day (6 July).

Statistical Survey

Source: Isle of Man Government Offices, Bucks Rd, Douglas; tel. (1624) 685711; internet www.gov.im.

AREA AND POPULATION

Area: 572 sq km (221 sq miles).

Population (census, 23–24 April 2006): 80,058 (males 39,523, females 40,535).

Density (at 2006 census): 140.0 per sq km.

Principal Localities (2006 census): Douglas (capital) 26,218; Onchan 9,172; Ramsey 7,309; Peel 4,280; Port Erin 3,575; Braddan 3,151; Castletown 3,109.

Births and Deaths (2005): Live births 901 (birth rate 11.3 per 1,000); Deaths 775 (death rate 10.5 per 1,000). *2007:* Live births 919; Deaths 789.

Economically Active Population (2006 census): Agriculture, etc. 642; Manufacturing 2,248; Construction 3,374; Electricity, gas and water 603; Transport and communication 3,171; Wholesale and retail trade 4,550; Entertainment, catering and tourist accommodation 2,259; Banking and finance 7,010; Real estate and renting 1,072; Other professional, business and scientific services 3,741; Education 2,805; Medical and health services 3,316; Public administration 2,898; Other services 3,075; Activities not adequately defined 19; *Total employed* 40,783 (males 22,020, females 18,763); Unemployed 1,010 (males 634, females 376); *Total labour force* 41,793 (males 22,654, females 19,139).

AGRICULTURE, ETC.

Crops (area in acres, 2006): Cereals and potatoes 11,807; Grass 64,616; Rough grazing 27,101.

Livestock (2006): Cattle 29,654; Sheep 136,751; Pigs 601; Poultry 20,169.

Fishing (2006 unless otherwise indicated): *Amount Landed* (metric tons): Scallops 1,522; Queen scallops 1,133 (2005); *Value of Landings:* Scallops £1.5m.; Queen scallops £0.8m.; Total first-hand sale value of all landings: £3.1m.

FINANCE

Currency and Exchange Rates: 100 pence = 1 pound sterling (£). *Dollar and Euro Equivalents* (31 December 2008): US $1 = 68.60 pence; €1 = 95.47 pence; £10 = $14.58 = €10.47.

Note: The Isle of Man is in monetary union with the United Kingdom. It has its own coins and notes, but United Kingdom coins and notes are also legal tender.

Budget: (£ million, 2009/2010, estimates): *Total Revenue* 572.3 (Customs and excise 398.6; Income and other taxes 160.5); *Total Expenditure* 541.2 (Health and social security 246.8).

Cost of Living: (Retail Price Index at September; base: January 2000 = 100) All items 120.2 in 2005; 124.1 in 2006; 128.9 in 2007.

Gross Domestic Product (GDP) (£ million at constant 2005/06 factor cost): 1,467.6 in 2003/04; 1,543.3 in 2004/05; 1,634.1.

GDP by Economic Activity (£ million at current factor cost, 2005/06): Agriculture, hunting, forestry and fishing 19.2; Mining and quarrying 8.7; Manufacturing 126.9; Electricity, gas and water supply 32.2; Construction 134.1; Wholesale and retail trade, repair of motor vehicles, motorcycles and personal and household goods 135.6; Transport and communications 110.4; Catering and entertainment and tourist accommodation 52.6; Financial services, real estate, renting and business activities 670.7; Other professional, educational, scientific and medical service activities 402.4; Public administration 85.0; Other services 71.7; *Sub-total* 1,849.4; Ownership of dwellings, less adjustments –215.2; *Total* 1,634.1.

TRANSPORT

Road Traffic (registered vehicles, 2001): Private 45,195; Engineering 385; Goods 4,489; Agricultural 931; Hackney 790; Public service 146; Motorcycles, scooters and tricycles 4,519.

Shipping (2005/06, unless otherwise indicated): Passengers handled 598,108; Registered merchant vessels 316; Other registered vessels 613; Total displacement ('000 grt, 2006) 9,192.

Civil Aviation: Passengers handled 789,155 (2006); Freight carried 4,594 metric tons (2003).

TOURISM

Tourist Arrivals (2007): Staying visitors 247,810; Day visitors 3,380; Business travellers 72,947.

COMMUNICATIONS MEDIA

Telephone Connections (2001): Fixed 56,000; Mobile 32,000.

Television Licences (2000): 28,601.

EDUCATION

State Primary (2007/08): 35 schools, 6,683 students.
State Secondary (2007/08): 5 schools, 4,799 students.
College (2005/06): 1 college, 7,606 students.

There are, in addition, two private schools.

Directory

The Constitution

The Head of State of the Isle of Man is the British monarch as the Lord of Mann. The Lieutenant-Governor, who is the Crown's personal representative on the island, is appointed by the Head of State for a five-year term. The legislature is Tynwald, comprising two branches, the Legislative Council and the House of Keys, sitting together as one body, but voting separately on all questions except in certain eventualities. The House of Keys, the lower chamber, has 24 members, who represent single member and multi-member constituencies and are elected by adult suffrage for five years. Eight of the 11 members of the Legislative Council are elected by the House of Keys. The remainder are ex officio members: the Lord Bishop of Sodor and Man, the Attorney-General and the President of Tynwald, who is elected by all the members of Tynwald.

The Government

HEAD OF STATE

Lord of Mann: HM Queen ELIZABETH II.
Lieutenant-Governor: Sir PAUL HADDACKS.

COUNCIL OF MINISTERS
(April 2009)

Chief Minister: ANTHONY (TONY) BROWN.
Minister of Agriculture, Fisheries and Forestry: PHIL GAWNE.
Minister of Education: ANNE CRAINE.
Minister of Health and Social Security: EDDIE TEARE.
Minister of Home Affairs: ADRIAN EARNSHAW.
Minister of Local Government and the Environment: JOHN SHIMMIN.
Minister of Tourism and Leisure: MARTYN QUAYLE.
Minister of Trade and Industry: DAVID CRETNEY.
Minister of Transport: DAVID ANDERSON.
Minister of the Treasury: ALLAN BELL.

The Isle of Man

GOVERNMENT OFFICES

Isle of Man Government: Government Office, Bucks Rd, Douglas, IM1 3PN; tel. (1624) 6856711; fax (1624) 685710; e-mail enquiries.cso@gov.im; internet www.gov.im.

Department of Agriculture, Fisheries and Forestry: Rose House, 51–59 Circular Rd, Douglas, IM1 1AZ; tel. (1624) 685835; fax (1624) 685851; e-mail daff@gov.im; internet www.gov.im/daff.

Department of Education: St George's Court, Upper Church St, Douglas, IM1 2SG; tel. (1624) 685820; fax (1624) 685834; e-mail admin@doe.gov.im; internet www.gov.im/education.

Department of Health and Social Security: Markwell House, Market St, Douglas, IM1 2RZ; tel. (1624) 685656; e-mail minister@dhss.gov.im; internet www.gov.im/dhss.

Department of Home Affairs: Homefield, 88 Woodbourne Rd, Douglas, IM2 3AP; tel. (1624) 694300; fax (1624) 621298; e-mail generalenquiries.dha@gov.im; internet www.gov.im/dha.

Department of Local Government and Environment: Murray House, Mount Havelock, Douglas, IM1 2SF; tel. (1624) 685954; e-mail ceo.dlge@gov.im; internet www.gov.im/dlge.

Department of Tourism and Leisure: St Andrew's House, Douglas, IM1 2PX; tel. (1624) 686801; e-mail tourism@gov.im; internet www.gov.im/tourism.

Department of Trade and Industry: Hamilton House, Peel Rd, Douglas, IM1 5EP; tel. (1624) 682354; fax (1624) 682355; e-mail dti@gov.im; internet www.gov.im/dti.

Department of Transport: Sea Terminal, Douglas, IM1 2RF; tel. (1624) 686600; e-mail enquiries@dot.gov.im.

Department of the Treasury: Government Office, Bucks Rd, Douglas; tel. (1624) 685586; e-mail treasuryadmin@gov.im; internet www.gov.im/treasury.

External Relations Division: Government Office, Bucks Rd, Douglas, IM1 3PN; tel. (1624) 685703; fax (1624) 685710; e-mail enquiries.cso@gov.im; internet www.gov.im/cso/externalrelations.

Legislature

TYNWALD

President: NOEL QUAYLE CRINGLE.
Deputy President: STEPHEN CHARLES RODAN.

Legislative Council (Upper House)

President of the Council: NOEL QUAYLE CRINGLE.
Lord Bishop of Sodor and Man: Rt Rev. ROBERT M. E. PATERSON.
Attorney-General: WILLIAM JOHN HOWARTH CORLETT.
Members appointed by the House of Keys: GEORGE HENRY WAFT, EDWARD ALAN CROWE, EDWARD GEORGE LOWEY, CLARE MARGARET CHRISTIAN, DAVID ALEXANDER CALLISTER, DUDLEY MICHAEL WILLIAM BUTT, ALEXANDER FRANK DOWNIE, JUAN RICHARD TURNER.
Clerk: JONATHAN KING.

House of Keys (Lower House)

Speaker: STEPHEN CHARLES RODAN.
Clerk of Tynwald, Secretary of the House and Counsel to the Speaker: ROGER IAN SEXTON PHILLIPS.

The House of Keys consists of 24 members, elected by adult suffrage for five years—eight for Douglas, three for Onchan, two for Ramsey, one each for Peel and Castletown, and nine for rural districts. The last general election took place on 23 November 2006. Most members of the House of Keys are elected as independents. However, a small number are affiliated to political parties.

Political Organizations

Liberal Vannin: White Cot, King Edward's Rd, Onchan; tel. (1624) 853352; fax (1624) 852977; e-mail office@liberalvannin.org; internet www.liberalvannin.org; f. 2006; Chair. NIGEL MALPASS; Leader PETER KARRAN.

Manx Labour Party: f. 1918.

Mec Vannin: internet www.mecvannin.im; f. 1962; advocates the establishment of the Isle of Man as a sovereign republic; Pres. BERNARD MOFFATT; Chair. MARK KERMODE.

Judicial System

The Isle of Man is, for legal purposes, an autonomous sovereign country under the British Crown, with its own legislature and its own independent judiciary administering its own common or customary and statute law. The law of the Isle of Man is, in most essential matters, the same as the law of England and general principles of equity administered by the English Courts are followed by the Courts of the Isle of Man unless they conflict with established local precedents. Her Majesty's High Court of Justice of the Isle of Man is based upon the English system but modified and simplified to meet local conditions. Justices of the Peace are appointed by the Lord Chancellor of Great Britain usually on the nomination of the Lieutenant-Governor. The Deemsters (see below), the High Bailiff, the Mayor of Douglas, and the Chairmen of the Town and Village Commissioners are all ex-officio Justices of the Peace. The Manx Court of Appeal consists of the Deemsters and the Judge of Appeal.

First Deemster and Clerk of the Rolls: J.M. KERRUÍSH.
Second Deemster: D.C. DOYLE.
Judge of Appeal: G. F. TATTERSALL.

Religion

CHRISTIANITY

The Church of England

The Isle of Man forms the diocese of Sodor and Man, comprising 28 parishes. The parish church of St German at Peel was designated a cathedral in 1980.

Lord Bishop of Sodor and Man: Rt Rev. ROBERT M. E. PATERSON, Bishop's House, The Falls, Tromode Road, Douglas, IM4 4PZ; tel. (1624) 622108; fax (1624) 672890; e-mail bishop-sodor@iommail.net; internet www.gumbley.net/diocese.htm.

Roman Catholic Church

The deanery of the Isle of Man is part of the archdiocese of Liverpool. There are six Catholic churches on the island.

Dean of the Isle of Man: Very Rev. Canon BRENDAN ALGER, St Mary of the Isle, Hill St, Douglas, IM1 3EG; tel. (1624) 675509; fax (1624) 674359; e-mail bjpalger@yahoo.co.uk.

Other Churches

There are also congregations of the following denominations: Baptist, Bethel Non-Denominational, Christadelphian, Congregational, Greek Orthodox, Independent Methodist, Methodist, Presbyterian, Elim Pentecostal, United Reformed, and Religious Society of Friends (Quakers); also Christian Science, Jehovah's Witnesses and the Church of Jesus Christ of Latter-day Saints.

There are small Bahá'í, Jewish and Muslim communities on the island.

The Press

Isle of Man Courier: Publishing House, Peel Rd, Douglas, IM1 5PZ; tel. (1624) 695695; fax (1624) 661041; e-mail john.sherrocks@newsiom.co.im; internet www.iomonline.co.im; f. 1884; weekly; Editor RICHARD BUTT; circ. 36,932 (Dec. 2008).

Isle of Man Examiner: Publishing House, Peel Rd, Douglas, IM1 5PZ; tel. (1624) 695695; fax (1624) 661041; e-mail john.sherrocks@newsiom.co.im; internet www.iomonline.co.im; f. 1880; weekly; Editor RICHARD BUTT; circ. 12,356 (Dec. 2008).

The Manx Independent: Publishing House, Peel Rd, Douglas, IM1 5PZ; tel. (1624) 695695; fax (1624) 661041; e-mail john.sherrocks@newsiom.co.im; internet www.iomonline.co.im; f. 1987; Friday; Editor RICHARD BUTT; circ. 11,429 (Dec. 2008).

Manx Tails Magazine: Media House, Cronkbourne, Douglas, IM4 4SB; tel. (1624) 696560; fax (1624) 625623; e-mail mail@manninmedia.co.im; internet www.manninmedia.co.im/tails.html; f. 1982 as in-flight magazine of Manx Airlines; launched as an all-island publication in 2002; monthly; distributed free of charge; Editor SIMON RICHARDSON; circ. 36,400.

Sea Breezes Magazine: Media House, Cronkbourne, Douglas, IM4 4SB; tel. (1624) 696573; fax (1624) 661655; e-mail sb.enquiries@seabreezes.co.im; internet www.seabreezes.co.im; f. 1919; Editor Capt. ANDREW C. DOUGLAS.

Publishers

Amulree Publications: Lossan y Twoaie, Glen Rd, Laxey, IM4 7AN; tel. (1624) 862238; e-mail amulree@mcb.net; internet www.mcb.net/amulree; Propr BILL SNELLING.

Electrochemical Publications Ltd: Asahi House, 10 Church Rd, Port Erin, IM9 6AQ; tel. (1624) 834941; fax (1624) 835400; e-mail sales@elchempub.com; internet www.elchempub.com; Man. Dir WILLIAM GOLDIE.

Lily Publications Ltd: POB 33, Ramsey, IM99 4LP; tel. (1624) 898446; fax (1624) 898449; e-mail sales@lilypublications.co.uk; internet www.lilypublications.co.uk; f. 1991; Man. Dir MILES COWSILL.

Mannin Media Group Ltd: Media House, Cronkbourne, Douglas, IM4 4SB; tel. (1624) 696565; fax (1624) 625623; e-mail mail@manninmedia.co.im; internet www.manninmedia.co.im; Chief Exec. STEVEN BROWN.

The Manx Experience: Sunnybank Ave, Birch Hill, Onchan, IM3 3BW; tel. (1624) 627727; fax (1624) 663627; e-mail mail@manxexperience.co.uk; Man. Dirs GWYNNETH BROWN, COLIN BROWN.

Pines Press: The Pines, Ballelin, Maughold, Ramsey, IM7 1HJ; tel. (1624) 862030; f. 1987; Dir B. CLYNE.

Keith Uren Publishing: 12 Manor Lane, Farmhill, Braddan, IM2 2NX; tel. and fax (1624) 611100; e-mail portfolio@manxe.net; magazines.

Vathek Publishing Ltd: Bridge House, Dalby, IM5 3BP; tel. (1624) 844056; fax (1624) 845043; e-mail mlw@vathek.com; internet www.vathek.com; legal journals; Man. Dir MAIRWEN LLOYD-WILLIAMS.

Broadcasting and Communications

Isle of Man Communications Commission: Salisbury House, Victoria St, Douglas, IM1 2LW; tel. (1624) 677022; fax (1624) 626499; e-mail margaret.king@cc.gov.im; internet www.gov.im/government/boards/cc.xml; appointed by the Isle of Man Govt to represent the island's interests in all matters of telecommunications, radio and television; Chair. ADRIAN EARNSHAW (Minister of Home Affairs); Dir CARMEL MCLAUGHLIN.

TELECOMMUNICATIONS

Manx Telecom Ltd: Isle of Man Business Park, Cooil Rd, Braddan, IM99 1HX; POB 100, Douglas, IM99 1HX; tel. (1624) 624624; fax (1624) 636011; e-mail mail@manx-telecom.com; internet www.manx-telecom.com; subsidiary of Telefónica O2 UK PLC; Man. Dir CHRIS HALL.

BROADCASTING
Radio and Television

BBC: Radio and Television (see United Kingdom).

Energy FM: 100 Market St, Douglas, IM1 2PH; tel. (1624) 611936; fax (1624) 664699; internet www.energyfm.net; f. 2001.

ITV Border: Television (see United Kingdom).

Manx Radio: POB 1368, Douglas, IM99 1SW; tel. (1624) 682600; fax (1624) 682604; e-mail postbox@manxradio.com; internet www.manxradio.com; commercial station operated (by agreement with the Isle of Man Government) by Radio Manx Ltd; Chair. DAVID NORTH; Man. Dir ANTHONY PUGH.

3FM: 45 Victoria St, Douglas, IM1 3RS; tel. (1624) 616333; fax (1624) 614333; internet www.three.fm; music.

The Isle of Man also receives television programmes from Channel 4 and Five.

Finance

Isle of Man Government Financial Supervision Commission: POB 58, Finch Hill House, Bucks Rd, Douglas, IM99 1DT; tel. (1624) 689300; fax (1624) 689399; e-mail fsc@gov.im; internet www.fsc.gov.im; responsible for the licensing, authorization and supervision of banks, building societies, investment businesses, collective investment schemes and fiduciary service providers; also responsible for the Companies Registry; Chair. ROSEMARY PENN; Chief Exec. JOHN ASPDEN.

Treasury: Government Office, Bucks Rd, Douglas, IM1 3PU; tel. (1624) 685586; fax (1624) 685662; e-mail treasuryadmin@gov.im; internet www.gov.im/treasury; Minister ALLAN BELL; Chief Financial Officer P. M. SHIMMIN.

BANKING

(cap. = capital; res = reserves; dep. = deposits; m. = million; brs = branches; amounts in pounds sterling)

At 31 December 2008 total bank deposits in the Isle of Man amounted to some £57,290m., and there were 40 licensed banks and building societies. The Financial Supervision Commission may allow a major bank to establish a presence on the island on a managed bank basis, by awarding an 'offshore' banking licence.

AIB Bank (CI) Ltd: POB 186, 10 Finch Rd, Douglas, IM1 2PT; tel. (1624) 639639; fax (1624) 639636; e-mail one@aib.im; internet www.aib.im; f. 1977; cap. 10m., dep. 2,268m. (Dec. 2007); Man. Dir CHRISTOPHER HOWLAND.

Alliance & Leicester International Ltd: POB 226, 19–21 Prospect Hill, Douglas, IM99 1RY; tel. (1624) 663566; fax (1624) 663577; internet www.alil.co.im; owned by Banco Santander, SA (Spain); Man. Dir SIMON HULL.

Anglo Irish Bank Corpn (IOM) PLC: Jubilee Bldgs, Victoria St, Douglas, IM1 2SH; tel. (1624) 698000; fax (1624) 698001; e-mail enquiries@angloirishbank.co.im; internet www.angloirishbank.co.im; Man. Dir DAVID MACGREGOR.

Bank of Ireland (IOM) Ltd: POB 246, Christian Rd, Douglas, IM99 1XF; tel. (1624) 644222; fax (1624) 644298; e-mail info@boioffshore.com; internet www.boioffshore.com; f. 1981; cap. 5m., res 0.06m., dep. 2,656m. (March 2007); Chair. J. L. M. QUINN; Man. Dir MICHAEL MCKAY.

Barclays Private Bank and Trust (Isle of Man) Ltd: POB 48, Queen Victoria House, Victoria St, Douglas, IM99 1DF; tel. (1624) 682828; fax (1624) 620905; internet www.barclays.co.uk/privatebank; Man. Dir ALAN R. PATRICK.

Barclays Private Clients International Ltd: POB 213, Eagle Court, 25 Circular Rd, Douglas, IM99 1RH; tel. (1624) 684000; fax (1624) 684321; international banking services; Man. Dir T. PARKES; 6 brs.

Britannia International Ltd: POB 231, Britannia House, Athol St, Douglas, IM99 1SD; tel. (1624) 681100; fax (1624) 681105; e-mail enquiries@britanniainternational.com; internet www.britanniainternational.com; 'offshore' subsidiary of Britannia Building Society; Man. Dir MARK BERESFORD.

Cayman National Bank and Trust Co (Isle of Man) Ltd: 4–8 Hope St, Douglas, IM1 1AQ; tel. (1624) 646900; fax (1624) 662192; e-mail banking@cnciom.com; internet www.cnciom.com; f. 1985; subsidiary of Cayman National Corpn, Cayman Islands; cap. 4m., dep. 25m (Sep. 2007); Man. Dir IAN BANCROFT.

Celtic Bank Ltd: POB 114, Celtic House, Victoria St, Douglas, IM99 1JW; tel. (1624) 622856; fax (1624) 620926; f. 1977; issued cap. 6.8m., res 9m., dep. 476m. (March 2008); Chair. RICHARD G. DANIELSON; Chief Exec. SIMON YOUNG.

Close Bank (Isle of Man) Ltd: POB 203, St George's Court, Upper Church St, Douglas, IM99 1RB; tel. (1624) 643200; fax (1624) 622039; e-mail infoiom@closepb.com; internet www.closepb.com; f. 1976 as Rea Brothers (Isle of Man) Ltd; present name adopted 1999; merchant bank; cap. 5m., dep. 309m. (July 2007); Man. Dir ANDREW HENTON.

Conister Trust Ltd: Conister House, 16–18 Finch Rd, Douglas, IM1 2PT; tel. (1624) 694694; fax (1624) 624278; e-mail info@conistertrust.com; internet www.conistertrust.com; f. 1935; specializes in asset finance; cap. 7m., dep. 53m. (Dec. 2005); Chair. PETER HAMMONDS; CEO JERRY LINEHAN; 1 br.

Duncan Lawrie (IOM) Ltd: 14–15 Mount Havelock, Douglas, IM1 2QG; tel. (1624) 620770; fax (1624) 676315; e-mail iom@duncanlawrie.com; internet www.duncanlawrie.com; cap. 6m., dep. 165m. (Dec. 2008); Chair. P. J. FIELD; Man. Dir ALAN M. MOLLOY.

Fairbairn Private Bank (IOM) Ltd: St Mary's Court, 20 Hill St, Douglas, IM1 1EU; tel. (1624) 645000; fax (1624) 627218; e-mail iom@fairbairnpb.com; internet www.fairbairnpb.com; f. 1987 as Robert Fleming (IOM) Ltd; present name adopted 2004; cap. 5m., res 2m., dep. 486m. (Dec. 2006); Chair. H. ASKARI; Man. Dir G. J. HORTON.

Habib European Bank Ltd: 14 Athol St, Douglas, IM1 1JA; tel. (1624) 622554; fax (1624) 627135; e-mail habibbank@manx.net; internet www.habibbank.com; f. 1982; subsidiary of Habib Bank AG (Switzerland); cap. 5m., dep. 76m. (Dec. 2007); Gen. Man. A. SHAIKH.

Kaupthing Singer & Friedlander (Isle of Man) Ltd: POB 197, Samuel Harris House, 5–11 St George's St, Douglas, IM99 1SN; tel. (1624) 699222; fax (1624) 699200; e-mail international@kaupthing.com; internet www.kaupthing.co.im; f. 1971; banking licence suspended in Oct. 2008; cap. 5m., res 32m., dep. 349m. (Dec. 2006); Chair. A. DOHERTY; Man. Dir A. A. DOHERTY.

Nationwide International Ltd: POB 217, 5–11 St George's St, Douglas, IM99 1RN; tel. (1624) 696000; fax (1624) 696001; internet www.nationwideinternational.com; f. 1990; Chair. MATTHEW CARTER; Man. Dir CARL GANDY.

Standard Bank Isle of Man Ltd: Standard Bank House, 1 Circular Rd, Douglas, IM1 1SB; tel. (1624) 643643; fax (1624) 643800; e-mail sbiom@standardbank.com; internet www.sboff.com; f. 1972 as Standard Chartered Bank (Isle of Man) Ltd; present name adopted 1995; cap. 5m., res 12m., dep. 952m. (Dec. 2007); Man. Dir J. COYLE.

Zurich Bank International Ltd: POB 422, Lord St, Douglas, IM99 3AF; tel. (1624) 671666; fax (1624) 627526; e-mail relationship.banking@zurich.com; internet www.zurichbankinternational.com; f. 1983 as Dunbar International Ltd; present name adopted 2003; Chair. RICHARD DESMOND; Man. Dir GRAHAM SHEWARD.

'Offshore' Banks

Bank of Scotland International Ltd: POB 19, Evergreen House, 43 Circular Rd, Douglas, IM99 1AT; tel. (1624) 613500; fax (1624) 759280; e-mail enquiry@bankofscotlandint.com; internet www.bankofscotland-international.com; f. 1976; part of Lloyds Banking Group (United Kingdom); Chair. PETER JACKSON.

Bradford & Bingley International Ltd: 30 Ridgeway St, Douglas, IM1 1TA; tel. (1624) 695000; fax (1624) 695001; e-mail enquiries@bbi.co.im; internet www.bbi.co.im; f. 1989; subsidiary of Abbey National PLC; cap. and res 266m. (Dec. 2006); Man. Dir JOHN SHEATH.

Isle of Man Bank Ltd: POB 13, 2 Athol St, Douglas IM99 1AN; tel. (1624) 637000; fax (1624) 624686; internet www.iombank.com; f. 1865; cap. 8m., res 129m., dep. 1,547m. (Dec. 2007); bankers to Isle of Man Govt; mem. of the Royal Bank of Scotland Group; Chair. JAMES MORRIS; 11 brs.

RBS Coutts Isle of Man: POB 59, Royal Bank House, 2 Victoria St, Douglas, IM99 INJ; tel. (1624) 632222; fax (1624) 620988; e-mail info@rbscoutts.com; internet www.rbscoutts.com.

The Royal Bank of Scotland International Ltd: POB 151, Royal Bank House, 2 Victoria St, Douglas, IM99 1NJ; tel. (1624) 646464; fax (1624) 646497; e-mail marketingiom@rbsint.com; internet www.rbsinternational.com; Chief Exec. IAN HENDERSON.

Restricted Banks

Irish Permanent International: 12–14 Ridgeway St, Douglas, IM1 1EN; tel. (1624) 641641; fax (1624) 676795; e-mail info@irishpermanentintl.com; internet www.irishpermanentintl.com; Man. Dir PHILIP MURRAY.

Merrill Lynch Bank and Trust Co (Cayman) Ltd: Belgravia House, 34–44 Circular Rd, Douglas, IM1 1QW; tel. (1624) 688600; fax (1624) 688601; Man. N. ORDERS.

INSURANCE

There were 179 authorized insurance companies in the Isle of Man at 31 December 2007, including:

Canada Life International Ltd: St Mary's, The Parade, Castletown, IM9 1RJ; tel. (1624) 820200; fax (1624) 820201; e-mail customer.support@canadalifeint.com; internet www.canadalifeint.com; f. 1987; Man. Dir TONY PARRY.

Castletown Insurance Services Ltd: Compton House, Parliament Sq., Castletown, IM9 1LA; tel. (1624) 827710; fax (1624) 827709; e-mail rdrinkwater@castletowninsurance.com; internet www.castletowninsurance.com; f. 1998; Jt Man. Dirs CHRISTINE CROWTHER, RICHARD DRINKWATER.

CMI Insurance Co Ltd: Clerical Medical House, Victoria Rd, Douglas, IM99 1LT; tel. (1624) 638888; fax (1624) 625900; e-mail iom.policyadministration1@clericalmedical.com; part of Lloyds Banking Group (United Kingdom).

Friends Provident International Ltd: Royal Court, Castletown, IM9 1RA; tel. (1624) 821212; fax (1624) 824405; e-mail servicedesk@fpiom.com; internet www.fpinternational.com; Man. Dir PAUL QUIRK.

Hansard International Ltd: POB 192, Harbour Court, Lord St, Douglas, IM99 1QL; tel. (1624) 688000; fax (1624) 688008; e-mail enquiries@hansard.com; internet www.hansard.com; Exec. Chair. Dr LEONARD S. POLONSKY.

Isle of Man Assurance Ltd: IOMA House, Hope St, Douglas, IM1 1AP; tel. (1624) 681200; fax (1624) 681391; e-mail info@ioma.co.im; internet www.ioma.co.im; Chair. ROBIN BIGLAND; Man. Dir NIGEL WOOD.

Royal Insurance Service Co (IOM) Ltd: Jubilee Bldgs, 1 Victoria St, Douglas, IM99 1BF; tel. (1624) 645947; fax (1624) 620934; Man. DAVID STACEY.

Royal London 360°: Royal London House, Isle of Man Business Park, Cooil Rd, Douglas, IM2 2SP; tel. (1624) 681681; fax (1624) 677336; e-mail csc@royallondon360.com; internet www.royallondon360.com; f. 2008 by merger of Scottish Life International Insurance Co Ltd and Scottish Provident International Life Assurance Ltd; subsidiary of Royal London Mutual Insurance Society Ltd.

Royal Skandia Life Assurance Ltd: POB 159, Skandia House, King Edward Rd, Onchan, IM99 1NU; tel. (1624) 655555; fax (1624) 611715; e-mail support@royalskandia.com; internet www.royalskandia.com.

Tower Insurance Co Ltd: POB 27, Jubilee Bldgs, 1 Victoria St, Douglas, IM99 1BF; tel. (1624) 673446; fax (1624) 663864; e-mail tower.insurance@uk.royalsun.com; internet www.towerinsurance.co.im; subsidiary of RSA Insurance Group PLC (United Kingdom); Dir DAVID STACEY.

Zurich International Life Ltd: 43–51 Athol St, Douglas, IM99 1EF; tel. (1624) 662266; fax (1624) 662038; e-mail client.services@zurich.com; internet www.zurichintlife.com.

Supervisory Authority

Insurance and Pensions Authority: 4th Floor, HSBC House, Ridgeway St, Douglas, IM1 1ER; tel. (1624) 646000; fax (1624) 646001; e-mail ipa@gov.im; internet www.gov.im/ipa; Chief Exec. DAVID VICK.

Trade and Industry

CHAMBER OF COMMERCE

Isle of Man Chamber of Commerce: 17 Drinkwater St, Douglas, IM1 1PP; tel. (1624) 674941; fax (1624) 663367; e-mail enquiries@iomchamber.org.im; internet www.iomchamber.org.im; 400 mems; Pres. STUART MCCUDDEN; Chair. JOHN HOLLIS; Chief Exec. BARBARA O'HANLON.

UTILITIES

Electricity

Manx Electricity Authority: POB 177, Douglas, IM99 1PS; tel. (1624) 687687; fax (1624) 687612; e-mail mea@gov.im; internet www.gov.im/mea; Chair. QUINTIN GILL; Chief Exec. ASHTON LEWIS.

Gas

Manx Gas Ltd: Murdoch House, South Quay, Douglas, IM1 5PA; tel. (1624) 644444; fax (1624) 626528; e-mail info@manxgas.co.im; internet www.manxgas.co.im; f. 1999 by merger of Douglas Gas and Calor Manx Gas; Man. Dir ALAN BATES.

Water

Isle of Man Water Authority: Drill Hall, Tromode Rd, Douglas, IM2 5PA; tel. (1624) 695949; fax (1624) 695956; e-mail water@gov.im; internet www.gov.im/water; Chair. DAVID CANNAN; Chief Exec. JOHN SMITH.

TRADE UNIONS

In 1991 the Trade Union Act was approved by Tynwald, providing for the registration of trade unions. Although trade unions had been active previously on the Isle of Man, they had not received legal recognition.

Manx Fish Producers' Organization Ltd: Heritage Centre, The Quay, Peel, IM5 1TA; tel. (1624) 842144; fax (1624) 844395; e-mail manx.fa@lineone.net; Chair. MICHAEL MOORE.

Manx National Farmers' Union: Agriculture House, Ballafletcher Farm Rd, Tromode, IM4 4QE; tel. (1624) 662204; e-mail gensec@manx-nfu.org; internet www.manx-nfu.org; Pres. HOWARD QUAYLE; Gen. Sec. BELINDA LEACH.

Unite: 25 Fort St, Douglas, IM2 2LJ; tel. (1624) 621156; fax (1624) 673115; e-mail michael.hewer@unitetheunion.com; Regional Industrial Organizer MICK HEWER.

Transport

RAILWAYS

Isle of Man Transport: Transport Headquarters, Banks Circus, Douglas, IM1 5PT; tel. (1624) 662525; fax (1624) 663637; e-mail info@busandrail.dtl.gov.im; internet www.iombusandrail.info; 29 km (18 miles) of electric track; also 25 km (16 miles) of steam railway track, and Snaefell Mountain Railway (7 km of electric track); 85 buses; Head of Rail Services JOHN KENNAUGH; Head of Bus Services DAVE KINRADE.

ROADS

There are over 805 km (500 miles) of roads on the Isle of Man.

Dept of Transport: Sea Terminal, Douglas, IM1 2RF; tel. (1624) 686600; fax (1624) 686617; e-mail enquiries@dot.gov.im; internet www.gov.im/transport; Chief Exec. IAN THOMPSON.

SHIPPING

Döhle (IOM) Ltd: Fort Anne, Douglas, IM1 5PD; tel. (1624) 649649; e-mail info@doehle-iom.com; internet www.doehle-iom.com; fmrly Midocean Maritime Ltd; present name adopted 2001; part of Peter Döhle Group (Germany); ship management; Chair. JÖRG VANSELOW; COO CLIFF DAVIES.

Isle of Man Steam Packet Co Ltd: Imperial Bldgs, Douglas, IM1 2BY; tel. (1624) 645645; fax (1624) 645609; internet www.steam-packet.com; f. 1830; daily services operate all the year round between Douglas and Heysham and Liverpool; during the summer there are frequent services between the island and Dublin and Belfast; Chair. ROBERT QUAYLE; Chief Exec. MARK WOODWARD; fleet of 1 passenger/car ferry, 1 ro-ro passenger/freight ferry and 2 Seacat Fastcraft.

Mezeron Ltd: East Quay, Ramsey, IM8 1BG; tel. (1624) 812302; fax (1624) 815613; e-mail info@mezeron.com; internet www.mezeron.com; f. 1983; cargo services; acquired by Döhle (IOM) Ltd in 2008; Operations Dir NORMAN LEECE.

Ramsey Steamship Co Ltd: 8 Auckland Terrace, Parliament St, Ramsey, IM8 1AF; tel. (1624) 816202; fax (1624) 816206; e-mail tony@ramsey-steamship.com; internet www.ramsey-steamship.com; f. 1913; cargo services; Man. Dir A. G. KENNISH.

Tufton Oceanic Investments Ltd: 2nd Floor, St George's Court, Upper Church St, Douglas, IM1 1EE; tel. (1624) 663616; fax (1624) 663918; e-mail tufton@tuftonoceanic.com; internet www.tuftonoceanic.com; Chair. TAKIS KLERIDES; Man. Dir CATO BRAHDE.

CIVIL AVIATION

Island Aviation and Travel Ltd: Ronaldsway Airport, Ballasalla, IM9 2AS; tel. (1624) 824300; fax (1624) 824946; e-mail enquiries@iaat.co.uk; internet www.iaat.co.uk; provides executive charters to world-wide destinations, runs air-ambulance services, aircraft management, handling; Man. Dir JOHN CRITCHLEY.

Manx2 Ltd: Ronaldsway Airport, Ballasalla, IM9 2AS; tel. (1624) 822111; e-mail customer.services@manx2.com; internet www.manx2.com; scheduled passenger flights to Belfast City and Belfast International, Blackpool, East Midlands, Gloucestershire, Jersey and Leeds/Bradford; Chair. NOEL HAYES; Gen. Man. DYLAN EVANS.

Tourism

In 2007 a total of 247,810 tourists stayed at least one night on the Isle of Man.

Dept of Tourism and Leisure, Tourism Division: St Andrew's House, Douglas, IM1 2PX; tel. (1624) 686801; fax (1624) 686800; e-mail tourism@gov.im; internet www.visitisleofman.com; responsibilities of tourist board, also operates modern and vintage transport systems, a Victorian theatre and an indoor and outdoor sport and leisure complex; f. 1896; Dir of Tourism GEOFF LE PAGE.

UNITED KINGDOM OVERSEAS TERRITORIES

From February 1998 the British Dependent Territories were referred to as the United Kingdom Overseas Territories, following the announcement of the interim findings of a British government review of the United Kingdom's relations with the Overseas Territories. In March 1999 draft legislation confirming this change was published by the British Government: under the proposed legislation, the citizens of Overseas Territories would be granted the rights, already enjoyed by the citizens of Gibraltar and the Falkland Islands, to British citizenship and of residence in the United Kingdom. These entitlements were not reciprocal, and British citizens would not enjoy the same rights with regard to the Overseas Territories. The British Overseas Territories Act entered effect in May 2002. The British Government meanwhile announced its determination to ensure that legislation in the Overseas Territories adhered to British and European Union standards, particularly in the areas of financial regulation and human rights.

ANGUILLA

Introductory Survey

Location, Climate, Language, Religion, Flag, Capital

Anguilla, a coralline island, is the most northerly of the Leeward Islands, lying 113 km (70 miles) to the north-west of Saint Christopher (St Kitts) and 8 km (5 miles) to the north of St Maarten/St Martin. Also included in the territory are the island of Sombrero, 48 km (30 miles) north of Anguilla, and several other uninhabited small islands. The climate is sub-tropical, the heat and humidity being tempered by the trade winds. Temperatures average 27°C (80°F) and mean annual rainfall is 914 mm (36 ins), the wettest months being September to December. English is the official language. Many Christian churches are represented, the principal denominations being the Anglican and Methodist Churches. The flag (proportions 3 by 5 on land, 1 by 2 at sea) has a dark blue field with the Union flag in the upper hoist corner and, in the centre of the fly, a white shield bearing three orange circling dolphins above a light blue base. The capital is The Valley.

Recent History

Anguilla, previously inhabited by Arawaks and Caribs, was a British colony from 1650 until 1967. From 1825 the island became increasingly associated with Saint Christopher (St Kitts) for administrative purposes (also see chapter on Saint Christopher and Nevis). The inhabitants of Anguilla petitioned for separate status in 1875 and 1958. In February 1967, however, St Christopher-Nevis-Anguilla assumed the status of a State in Association with the United Kingdom, as did four other former British colonies in the Eastern Caribbean. These Associated States became independent internally, while the British Government retained responsibility for external affairs and defence.

In May 1967 the Anguillans, under the leadership of Ronald Webster, a local businessman and head of the only political party, the People's Progressive Party (PPP), repudiated government from Saint Christopher. After attempts to repair the breach between Saint Christopher and Anguilla had failed, British security forces were deployed in Anguilla in March 1969 to install a British Commissioner. Members of London's Metropolitan Police Force remained on the island until the Anguilla Police Force was established in 1972. In July 1971 the British Parliament approved the Anguilla Act, one clause of which stipulated that, should Saint Christopher-Nevis-Anguilla decide to end its associated status, Anguilla could be separated from the other islands. In August the British Government's Anguilla Administration Order 1971 determined that the British Commissioner would continue to be responsible for the direct administration of the island, with the co-operation of a local elected council. The terms of this Order were superseded by the introduction of a new Constitution in February 1976. Anguilla formally separated from Saint Christopher-Nevis-Anguilla on 19 December 1980, assuming the status of British Dependent Territory. In accordance with the terms of the British Government's Anguilla Constitution Order of 1982, a new Constitution came into operation in Anguilla on 1 April 1982.

Legislative elections were held in March 1976, and Webster was appointed Chief Minister. In February 1977, following his defeat on a motion of confidence, he was replaced by Emile Gumbs as Chief Minister and as leader of the PPP (renamed the Anguilla National Alliance—ANA—in 1980). Webster was returned to power, to lead the recently formed Anguilla United Party (AUP), at a general election in May 1980. The dismissal of the Minister of Agriculture in May 1981 led to serious divisions within the Government, and the resignation in sympathy of another minister precipitated the collapse of Webster's administration. Webster subsequently formed a new political party, the Anguilla People's Party (APP), which won five of the seven seats in a general election in June. An early general election in March 1984 resulted in a conclusive defeat for the APP, including the loss of Webster's own seat. Gumbs became Chief Minister, and pursued a policy of revitalizing the island's economy, mainly through tourism and attracting foreign investment. Webster resigned from the leadership of the APP, which was renamed the Anguilla Democratic Party (ADP).

The majority of the population expressed no desire for independence, but the new Government appealed for wider powers for the Executive Council, and for more aid and investment from the United Kingdom in the island's economy and infrastructure. In October 1985 the Governor appointed a committee to review the Constitution, in response to an earlier unanimous request from the House of Assembly for modifications, particularly concerning the status of women and of persons born overseas of Anguillan parents. The amendments, which provided for the appointment of a Deputy Governor and designated international financial affairs (the 'offshore' banking sector) as the Governor's responsibility, came into effect in May 1990.

Gumbs remained Chief Minister following a general election in February 1989. The ANA won only three seats in the House of Assembly but was supported by the independent member, Osbourne Fleming, who retained his cabinet portfolio. The ADP secured one seat and the revived AUP won two.

In May 1991 the British Government abolished capital punishment for the crime of murder in Anguilla (as well as in several other British Dependent Territories).

A general election in March 1994 failed to produce a clear majority for any one party, and a coalition was subsequently formed by the ADP and the AUP, which had each won two seats and, respectively, secured 31% and 11% of total votes cast. The ANA, under the leadership of Eric Reid, won two seats with 36% of the vote, while the remaining seat was secured by Fleming. The AUP leader, Hubert Hughes, was subsequently appointed Chief Minister, replacing Sir Emile Gumbs (as he had become). On becoming Chief Minister, Hughes immediately stated that he might seek Anguilla's independence from the United Kingdom.

In October 1995 the island suffered severe damage from 'Hurricane Luis'. Destruction of buildings and infrastructure, as well as damage to the agricultural sector, was estimated to be worth some EC $72m. Hughes was highly critical of the British Government's response to the hurricane, which he alleged was inadequate. In May 1997 Robert Harris, hitherto Deputy Governor, assumed office as Governor.

The announcement by the British Government in January 1997 that it was considering the extension of its powers in the Dependent Territories of the Caribbean attracted further criticism from Hughes. The proposed reintroduction of reserve powers, whereby the Governor (with the consent of the British Government) can amend, veto or introduce legislation without the agreement of the local legislature, provoked accusations from Hughes that the United Kingdom hoped to create a situation in which territories would be forced to seek independence. The British Government, however, maintained that the initiative had been prompted largely by a desire to secure Anguilla's financial services sector from exploitation by criminal organizations, particularly drugs-traffickers (which had remained a problem, owing to the territory's bank secrecy laws).

In September 1997 Hughes publicly denounced Robert Harris for being oblivious to his country's needs, and, furthermore, made allegations of corruption within the Civil Service Association (CSA). The CSA denied the claim and immediately requested a public apology. Meanwhile Osbourne Fleming pressed for Hughes' resignation, claiming that the remarks were unjustified and jeopardized public and investor confidence in the Government.

In May 1998 Hughes announced that public consultations would be undertaken on a proposal to reform Anguilla's constitutional status in the hope that a reformed Constitution could be in place before the general election, scheduled for March 1999. Hughes criticized the current Constitution for vesting executive authority in the Governor rather than in locally elected ministers. Hughes ruled out any prospect of creating a Senate on the grounds of the cost involved. In September 1998, however, the British Government announced that its Overseas Dependencies were to be renamed United Kingdom Overseas Territories. In March 1999 the British Government issued a policy document confirming the change of name, and guaranteeing citizens of Overseas Dependencies the right to British citizenship. The proposals also included the requirement that the Constitutions of Overseas Territories should be revised in order to conform to British and international standards. The process of revision of the Anguillan Constitution began in September 1999.

Following the general election of 4 March 1999 the composition of the legislature remained unaltered. The AUP-ADP coalition therefore kept control of the House of Assembly, and the four members of the Executive Council retained their portfolios.

In May 1999 the two ADP ministers threatened to withdraw from the coalition Government, accusing Hughes of excluding them from the decision-making process, and in June the ADP leader, Victor Banks, resigned his post as Minister of Finance and Economic Development, and withdrew from the ruling coalition. The other ADP minister, Edison Baird, refused, however, to resign his post, and was subsequently expelled from the party. Although Banks' resignation deprived the AUP-ADP coalition of its majority in the House of Assembly, Hughes announced that he did not intend to resign his position. Banks and the three members of the opposition ANA therefore withdrew from the House, demanding that fresh elections be held. Lacking the necessary quorum in the legislature, the Government was unable to implement policy or to introduce a budget for 1999/2000.

In January 2000 legal proceedings begun by Hughes, in an attempt to compel the Speaker to convene the House of Assembly, were rejected by the High Court. Hughes therefore announced that he would hold legislative elections in March 2000. At the elections, held on 3 March, the ANA won three seats, the AUP two, and the ADP one, while Edison Baird was elected as an independent. The ANA and the ADP, which had formed an electoral alliance, known as the Anguilla United Front, prior to the elections, therefore gained control of the House of Assembly. The leader of the ANA, Osbourne Fleming, was subsequently appointed the Chief Minister of an Executive Council that included two other ANA ministers, while Victor Banks was again appointed Minister of Finance, Economic Development, Investment and Commerce.

In February 2000 the Governor, Robert Harris, departed the island. Harris, who had reportedly been extremely frustrated by the island's political crisis, suggested that he had found it very difficult to work closely with the Government of Anguilla. Peter Johnstone replaced Harris as Governor, who, in turn, was replaced by Alan Huckle in May 2004.

Following Anguilla's inclusion on an Organisation for Economic Co-operation and Development (OECD, see p. 358) blacklist of tax havens in 2000, the Government introduced a number of articles of legislation to combat money-laundering on the island, including the establishment of a 'Money Laundering Reporting Authority'. OECD removed Anguilla from the list in March 2002, declaring that the Government had made sufficient commitments to improve transparency and effective exchange of information on tax matters by the end of 2005. In late 2002, however, the burgeoning financial sector faced further disruption when the United Kingdom, under pressure from the European Union (EU, see p. 255), as part of its effort to investigate tax evasion, demanded that Anguilla disclose the identities and account details of Europeans holding private savings accounts on the island. Anguilla, along with some other British Overseas Territories facing similar demands, claimed it was being treated unfairly compared with more powerful European countries, such as Switzerland and Luxembourg. In February 2004 a new financial regulatory body, the Anguilla Financial Services Commission, commenced operations. The Commission replaced the Financial Services Department of the Ministry of Finance and represented a further commitment to transparency within the sector. In April 2009 Anguilla was included on OECD's so-called 'grey list' of territories that had committed to improving transparency in the financial sector but had not yet substantially implemented such change.

In June 2001 the Government officially approved the draft of its National Telecommunications Policy, which would liberalize the sector. Although the legislation still needed to pass through parliament, in April 2003 Cable & Wireless, the country's sole telecommunications provider, signed an agreement with the Government to open the market for competition. The opposition argued that a single operator was more suitable in a country as small as Anguilla, where economies of scale were not achievable. It was argued that the proposed legislation could lead to a reduction in investment and consequent job losses.

In August 2003 the Government sold 6m. shares at US $1 each in the Anguilla Electricity Company, a profit-making public utility, in order to raise funds for the US $20m. expansion and reconstruction of Wallblake Airport. The proceeds of the sale were to go towards lengthening the airport's runway in order to accommodate larger aircraft. The AUP leader Hubert Hughes criticized the sale as unnecessary and questioned the transparency of the process.

In May 2004 Edison Baird replaced Hubert Hughes as Leader of the Opposition after Albert Hughes resigned from the AUP and transferred his support to Baird. Baird later formed a new political party, the Anguilla National Strategic Alliance (ANSA), in advance of the general election, which was constitutionally due by June 2005.

At the general election, which was held on 21 February 2005, the Anguilla United Front (the AUF, comprising the ANA and the ADP) secured four seats and 38.9% of the votes cast; the remaining three seats were shared by the Anguilla United Movement (as the AUP had been renamed, with one seat and 19.4% of the votes) and the ANSA (two seats and 19.2% of the ballot). The remaining 23% of the votes were shared between independent candidates and the Anguilla Progressive Party. Turn-out was 74.6%—considerably higher than expected. Analysts were also surprised by the scale of the AUF's victory; a closer contest had been expected, but the alliance campaigned strongly on the success of its infrastructural improvements, particularly the expansion of Wallblake Airport, during its previous administration. Fleming announced a new Executive Council on 22 February. The only change was the replacement as Minister of Education, Health, Social Development and Lands of Eric Reid, who retired and did not contest the election. Evans Rogers succeeded him.

In December 2005 the Government announced its intention to establish a new Constitutional and Electoral Reform Commission, to build on the work done by the previous electoral commission in 2001–04 in ascertaining the views of the people of Anguilla. The Commission began work in February 2006; key issues to be addressed were the fundamental rights and freedoms outlined in the Constitution, the powers of the Governor and the size of the House of Assembly. A report detailing the Commission's recommendations was submitted to the Governor in August, but elicited no publicly acknowledged response until March 2007, a delay which provoked anti-Government criticism—albeit limited and peaceful—from Anguillans. A public announcement by the Office of the Chief Minister in that month indicated that the Government was to receive a delegation from the British Foreign and Commonwealth Office (FCO) in July to facilitate discussions towards constitutional reform. This necessitated a preliminary review of the Commission's recommendations, together with public consultations, prior to the FCO representatives' arrival. The first in an extensive series of such reviews was convened in early March and attended by parliamentary representatives and the Chairman of the Constitutional and Electoral Reform Commission. While several sections of the extant Constitution were regarded by the Commission as still relevant and adequate, areas identified as problematic and in most urgent need of amendment included the administration of justice—particularly to reflect the abolition of the death penalty—transparency in judicial proceedings, enforcement of constitutional rights, and the appointment of the island Governor and deputies.

In addition, concern had been expressed that the existing number of ministers in the Executive Council (or 'Cabinet', in accordance with the Commission's proposals) was insufficient for the dispatch of governmental responsibilities and should be increased, but that the ratio of ministers to non-ministerial representatives in the House of Assembly should not exceed 50%; it was proposed that members of the Council be increased from three to five ministers, in addition to the Chief Minister (or 'Premier' under the recommendations). The Cabinet would comprise these six members, each awarded a vote, together with the Deputy Governor and the Attorney-General, who would remain without voting authority. The Premier would replace the Governor as chairman of the Cabinet, although the latter would retain the right to be informed by, consult and advise the Cabinet. Further, it was suggested that the size of the Assembly be increased from seven elected members to 13. (Should it be concluded that seven ministers be appointed in addition to the Chief Minister, the Assembly should grow to 15 members in order to accommodate the recommended majority of non-ministerial members.) An expanded Assembly, it was suggested, would also obviate the need for a Parliamentary Secretary. It was also proposed that, in the event of a motion of 'no confidence' being brought in the Assembly, there would be recourse to the pre-1982 Constitution, whereby the Governor would exercise discretion as to whether to call a general election. Such a motion might be upheld by a simple majority vote, as opposed to the existing two-thirds' majority requirement. An existing provision, reportedly not yet exercised, affording the Governor alternative powers to force legislation through the House of Assembly was considered a threat to democracy and the Commission urged for its repeal; similarly, the rescision of powers previously vested in the Secretary of State to disallow legislation passed by the Governor was advised, on the basis that such a provision was no longer required.

The Commission also proposed extensive electoral reform: *inter alia*, the institution of an independent Boundaries Commission was

UNITED KINGDOM OVERSEAS TERRITORIES

Anguilla

put forward, as was thorough revision of the Election Act. The abolition of the Judicial Services Commission and establishment of a Judicial and Legal Services Commission as its successor, endowed with powers to influence the Governor's judicial appointments, was also suggested and constituted a measure more consistent with other Caribbean states under the jurisdiction of the Eastern Caribbean Supreme Court. The embedding of the Financial Services Commission and its regulatory authority within the constitution was also promulgated in order to enhance supervision of the financial services industry in Anguilla.

Interpreted broadly, the Commission's recommendations sought to advance Anguilla's ambitions towards greater self-determination and the democratic, inclusive administration of its own affairs, gradually reducing the influence of the Government of the United Kingdom—upon whose unilateral authority so many of its existing constitutional statutes were premised. The institution of independent public service and advisory bodies was intended to equip a future government with the appropriate consultative resources to generate more comprehensive and effective legislative proposals for the advancement of Anguilla and the protection of its people.

Alan Huckle was succeeded by Andrew George as Governor in July 2006. The country's first indigenous Deputy Governor, lawyer Stanley Everton Reid, was sworn in later that month.

Andrew George retired as Governor in March 2009. He was replaced by Alistair Harrison in the following month.

In May 2002 the British Overseas Territories Act, having received royal assent in the United Kingdom in February, came into force and granted British citizenship to the people of its Overseas Territories, including Anguilla. Under the new law Anguillans would be able to hold British passports and work in the United Kingdom and anywhere else in the EU.

The proposed visit by a five-member delegation from the FCO to discuss constitutional reform, scheduled to take place between 23 and 27 July 2007, was postponed—only days in advance—by the Anguillan Government in order that further public consultations might be conducted. The Government confirmed, however, that it would be seeking 'full internal self-government' for Anguilla, and at the end of April 2008 it announced the commencement of work on a draft constitution. The proposed document was scheduled for completion in mid-2009, after which consultations between representatives of the Governments of Anguilla and the United Kingdom were to begin.

In July 2005 the Governments of Anguilla and the British Virgin Islands announced the formal establishment of the maritime boundary between the two territories. The boundary had been agreed in 2002 following discussions facilitated by the British Government. Co-operation between British Virgin Islands customs officials and their Anguillan counterparts enabled the recovery of a substantial quantity of drugs from a container vessel impounded in Anguilla in July 2006; the haul, comprising over 140 packages of compressed cannabis with an estimated street value of over US $1,500 per pound, was thought to be the largest ever seized on the island and an indication of the success of joint law enforcement initiatives in the region.

Government

The Constitution vests executive power in a Governor, appointed by the British monarch. The Governor is responsible for external affairs, international financial affairs, defence and internal security. In most other matters the Governor acts on the advice of the Executive Council, led by the Chief Minister. Legislative power is held by the House of Assembly, comprising 11 members: two ex officio, two nominated by the Governor, and seven elected for five years by universal adult suffrage. The Executive Council is responsible to the House. A review of the Constitution was ongoing in 2009.

Economic Affairs

In 2006 the gross national income (GNI) of Anguilla, measured at current prices, was EC $594.75m., equivalent to EC $42,837 per head. During 2000–08, it was estimated, the population increased at an average annual rate of 3.9%, while gross domestic product (GDP) per head increased, in real terms, by an average of 4.0% per year during 1998–2006. Overall GDP increased, in real terms, at an average annual rate of 9.0% in 2000–08; growth was 11.6% in 2008.

Agriculture (including crops, livestock and fishing) contributed 1.5% of GDP in 2008 and agriculture, fishing and mining engaged 3.3% of the employed labour force in 2002. Smallholders grow vegetables and fruit for domestic consumption; the principal crops are pigeon peas, sweet potatoes and maize. Livestock-rearing traditionally supplies significant export earnings, but the principal productive sector is the fishing industry (which is also a major employer). Real agricultural GDP increased by an annual average of 5.2% during 2000–08, although growth was an estimated 6.2% in 2008.

Industry (including mining, manufacturing, construction and power), which accounted for 34.1% of GDP in 2008 and (not including the small mining sector) engaged 18.8% of the employed labour force in 2001, is traditionally based on salt production and shipbuilding. Real industrial GDP increased by an annual average of 23.7% in 2000–08; the sector expanded by 30.2% in 2006 and by 12.7% in 2008.

The mining and quarrying sector, contributed 2.3% of GDP in 2008 and engaged only 0.2% of the working population in 1992. Anguilla's principal mineral product is salt. Mining GDP increased by an annual average of 27.2% during 2000–08; growth was 17.5% in 2008.

The manufacturing sector, accounting for 2.4% of employment in 2003 and for only 2.0% of GDP in 2008, consists almost entirely of boat-building and fisheries processing. Real manufacturing GDP increased by an annual average of 25.9% in 2000–08. Sectoral GDP increased by 8.1% in 2008.

The construction industry, which engaged 14.9% of the employed labour force in 2001, accounted for 25.8% of GDP in 2008. GDP in the construction sector increased at an annual average of 10.4% during 2000–08, in real terms; the sector expanded by 14.0% in 2008. Imported hydrocarbon fuels meet most energy needs.

The services sector accounted for 64.4% of GDP in 2008 and engaged 77.9% of the employed labour force in 2001. Tourism is increasingly the dominant industry of the economy, and is a catalyst for growth in other areas. The hotel and restaurant sector is the largest contributor to GDP, accounting for 17.4% of GDP in 2008. The hotel and restaurant sector decreased by 12.0% in 2008. In 2007 tourism expenditure totalled EC $311.9m. The USA provided 26.9% of visitors (including excursionists) in 2007. The opening of Anguilla's first championship-standard golf course in late 2006 was expected further to contribute to tourism revenues. The 'offshore' financial institutions are also important contributors to the GDP of the service industry, with the banking and insurance sector contributing 11.8% of GDP in 2008. The real GDP of the services sector increased at an annual average of 8.1% in 2000–08; growth was 7.3% in 2008.

In 2007 Anguilla recorded a merchandise trade deficit of EC $266.6m., and a deficit on the current account of the balance of payments of EC $254.8m. The trade deficit was partly offset by receipts from the 'invisibles' sector: tourism, financial services, remittances from Anguillans abroad and official assistance. The principal sources of imports are the USA, Puerto Rico and the Netherlands Antilles. The principal markets for exports are the USA and St Maarten. The main commodity exports are lobsters, fish, livestock and salt. Imports, upon which Anguilla is highly dependent, consist of foodstuffs, construction materials, manufactures, machinery and transport equipment.

In 2007, according to preliminary figures from the Eastern Caribbean Central Bank (ECCB, see p. 430), a budgetary deficit of EC $19.0m. was recorded (equivalent to 2.4% of GDP). Anguilla's external public debt totalled an estimated US $5,073.1m. in March 2008. Consumer prices increased by an annual average of 4.2% in 2000–07; the average annual rate of inflation increased by 5.2% in 2007. Some 7.8% of the labour force were unemployed in July 2002.

In April 1987 Anguilla became the eighth member of the ECCB and in 2001 joined the regional stock exchange, the Eastern Caribbean Securities Exchange (based in Saint Christopher and Nevis), established in the same year. The territory is also a member of the Organisation of Eastern Caribbean States (OECS, see p. 440) and an associate member of the Association of Caribbean States (ACS, see p. 424) and the Economic Community for Latin America and the Caribbean (ECLAC, see p. 40). As a dependency of the United Kingdom, Anguilla has the status of Overseas Territory in association with the EU (see p. 255). In 1999 Anguilla was granted associate membership of the Caribbean Community and Common Market (CARICOM, see p. 206).

The island has developed its limited resources in recent years. Both tourism and the international financial sector have apparently benefited from the perceived stability of dependent status. Construction is also an important industry, fuelled by the tourism sector. However, Anguilla remains particularly vulnerable to adverse climatic conditions. This was demonstrated in October 1995, when 'Hurricane Luis' devastated the island, and again in November 1999, when damage caused by 'Hurricane Lenny' forced the temporary closure of the island's two largest tourist resorts. The Government of Osbourne Fleming, which took office in 2000, committed itself to increased expenditure and state investment in tourism, financial services and fisheries. The Government also hoped to establish the island as a centre for information technology and electronic commerce, and to raise revenue from the sale and leasing of internet domain names. In February 2005 the Financial Services Commission introduced procedures, under the Anguilla Mutual Funds Act 2004, to allow the formation of mutual and hedge funds within 24 hours; it was hoped the new provisions would provide a further boost to the financial sector. The territory's reputation for stability was put at risk in 2008 after the United Kingdom's parliamentary Foreign Affairs Committee reported that Anguillan ministers had been accused of accepting bribes for development contracts. Anguilla was also included on an Organisation for Economic Co-operation and Development (see p. 358) list of territories in April 2009 that had yet substantially to implement moves towards transparency in the financial sector. Tourism remains the most important sector of the economy, although the impact of the global financial crisis has increased competition in the region and resulted in a declining market. The Caribbean Tourism Organization reported that Anguilla suffered the largest reduction in visitor arrivals in the first quarter of 2009, with a, 18.8% contraction. Economic growth was expected to be 5.9% in 2009 (compared with 6.2% in 2008). However, the threat of further reductions in the important tourism sector, concomitant with reduced foreign investment in financial services, meant growth could be significantly lower.

Education
Education is free and compulsory between the ages of five and 16 years. Primary education begins at five years of age and lasts for six years. Secondary education, beginning at 11 years of age, lasts for a further six years. There are six government primary schools and one government secondary school. In 2005/06 enrolment at primary schools included 91.6% of children in the relevant age-group, while enrolment at secondary schools for 2004/05 included 80.8% of pupils in the relevant age-group. A 'comprehensive' secondary school education system was introduced in September 1986. Post-secondary education is undertaken abroad. According to the 2005 budget address, recurrent government expenditure on education in 2000–04 averaged 13.8% of total recurrent expenditure, the second largest government expenditure in a single sector after health.

Public Holidays
2009: 1 January (New Year's Day), 10 April (Good Friday), 13 April (Easter Monday), 1 May (Labour Day), 30 May (Anguilla Day), 1 June (Whit Monday), 15 June (Queen's Official Birthday), 3 August (August Monday), 6 August (August Thursday), 7 August (Constitution Day), 19 December (Separation Day), 25–26 December (Christmas).
2010: 1 January (New Year's Day), 2 April (Good Friday), 5 April (Easter Monday), 1 May (Labour Day), 24 May (Whit Monday), 30 May (Anguilla Day), 14 June (Queen's Official Birthday—provisional), 3 August (August Monday), 6 August (August Thursday), 7 August (Constitution Day), 19 December (Separation Day), 25–26 December (Christmas).

Weights and Measures
The metric system has been adopted, although imperial weights and measures are also used.

Statistical Survey

Source (unless otherwise stated): Government of Anguilla, The Secretariat, The Valley; tel. 497-2451; fax 497-3389; e-mail stats@gov.ai; internet gov.ai/statistics.

AREA AND POPULATION

Area (sq km): 96 (Anguilla 91, Sombrero 5).

Population: 11,561 (males 5,705, females 5,856) at census of 9 May 2001. *Mid-2008:* 15,258 (Source: Eastern Caribbean Central Bank).

Density (at mid-2008): 158.9 per sq km.

Principal Towns (population at 2001 census): South Hill 1,495; North Side 1,195; The Valley (capital) 1,169; Stoney Ground 1,133. *Mid-2003* (UN estimate, incl. suburbs): The Valley 1,380 (Source: UN, *World Urbanization Prospects: The 2003 Revision*).

Births, Marriages and Deaths (2006 unless otherwise indicated): Registered live births 183 (birth rate 12.8 per 1,000); Registered marriages 75 (marriage rate 6.1 per 1,000) in 2003; Registered deaths 59 (death rate 4.1 per 1,000). *2008* Birth rate 13.1 per 1,000; Death rate 4.4 per 1,000. Sources: UN, *Population and Vital Statistics Report*; Pan American Health Organization.

Life Expectancy (years at birth): 80.5 (males 78.0; females 80.5) in 2008 (Source: Pan American Health Organization).

Economically Active Population (persons aged 15 years and over, census of 9 May 2001): Agriculture, fishing and mining 183; Manufacturing 135; Electricity, gas and water 81; Construction 830; Trade 556; Restaurants and hotels 1,587; Transport, storage and communications 379; Finance, insurance, real estate and business services 433; Public administration, social security 662; Education, health and social work 383; Other community, social and personal services 164; Private households with employed persons 164; Activities not stated 871; *Total employed* 5,644 (males 3,014, females 2,630); Unemployed 406 (males 208, females 198); *Total labour force* 6,050 (males 3,222, females 2,828). *July 2002:* Total employed 5,496 (males 3,009, females 2,487); Unemployed 465 (males 204, females 261); Total labour force 5,961 (Source: ILO).

HEALTH AND WELFARE

Total Fertility Rate (children per woman, 2008): 1.8.
Under-5 Mortality Rate (per 1,000 live births, 1997): 34.0.
Physicians (per 1,000 head, 2003): 1.2.
Hospital Beds (per 1,000 head, 2007): 2.2.
Health Expenditure (% of GDP, 2004): 4.3.
Access to Water (% of persons, 2004): 60.
Access to Sanitation (% of persons, 2004): 99.

Sources: Caribbean Development Bank, *Social and Economic Indicators 2004* and Pan American Health Organization.

For definitions, see explanatory note on p. vi.

AGRICULTURE, ETC.

Fishing (metric tons, live weight, 2006, FAO estimates): Marine fishes 180, Caribbean spiny lobster 60, Stromboid conchs 10; Total catch 250. Source: FAO.

INDUSTRY

Electric Energy ('000 kWh): 62,069 in 2004; 72,041 in 2005; 80,110 in 2006. Source: Eastern Caribbean Central Bank.

FINANCE

Currency and Exchange Rates: 100 cents = 1 Eastern Caribbean dollar (EC $). *Sterling, US Dollar and Euro Equivalents* (31 December 2008): £1 sterling = EC $3.936; US $1 = EC $2.700; €1 = EC $3.758; EC $100 = £25.41 = US $37.04 = €26.61. *Exchange Rate:* Fixed at US $1 = EC $2.70 since July 1976.

Budget (EC $ million, 2007): *Revenue:* Tax revenue 164.3 (Taxes on domestic goods and services 66.3, Taxes on international trade and transactions 97.3, Taxes on property 0.7); Non-tax revenue 46.1; Total 210.4. *Expenditure:* Current expenditure 170.4 (Personal emoluments 68.5, Other goods and services 53.7, Transfers and subsidies 13.0, Interest payments 7.1); Capital expenditure 59.0; Total 229.4. Source: Eastern Caribbean Central Bank, *Annual Economic and Financial Review 2007*.

Cost of Living (Consumer Price Index; base: 2000 = 100): All items 115.9 in 2005; 125.6 in 2006; 132.1 in 2007. Source: IMF, *International Financial Statistics*.

Gross Domestic Product (EC $ million at constant 1990 prices): 290.13 in 2006; 351.05 in 2007; 360.44 in 2008. Source: Eastern Caribbean Central Bank.

Expenditure on the Gross Domestic Product (EC $ million at current prices, 2008): Government final consumption expenditure 136.48; Private final consumption expenditure 965.81; Gross fixed capital formation 467.56; *Total domestic expenditure* 1,569.85; Export of goods and services 470.34; *Less* Import of goods and services 1,253.85; *GDP in purchasers' values* 786.35. Source: Eastern Caribbean Central Bank.

Gross Domestic Product by Economic Activity (EC $ million at current prices, 2008): Agriculture (including crops, livestock and fishing) 9.65; Mining and quarrying 14.74; Manufacturing 13.06; Electricity and water 26.27; Construction 168.13; Wholesale and retail 37.75; Hotels and restaurants 113.07; Transport and Communications 85.08; Banks and insurance 76.63; Real estate and housing 10.53; Government services 86.64; Other services 9.48; *Sub-total* 651.03; *Less* Financial intermediation services indirectly measured 44.64; *Gross value added in basic prices* 606.39; Taxes, less subsidies, on products 179.95; *GDP in purchasers' values* 786.35. Source: Eastern Caribbean Central Bank.

Balance of Payments (EC $ million, 2007): Export of goods f.o.b. 13.7; Imports of goods f.o.b. –280.3; *Trade balance* –266.6; Exports of services 138.1; Imports of services –130.6; *Balance on goods and services* –259.1; Other income received 17.0; Other income paid –7.8; *Balance on goods, services and income* –249.8; Current transfers received 11.4; Current transfers paid –16.4; *Current balance* –254.8; Capital account (net) 13.4; Direct investment from abroad 217.1; Portfolio investment liabilities 3.8; Other investment assets 54.6; Other investment liabilities –29.5; Net errors and omissions –1.5; *Overall balance* 3.0. Source: IMF, *International Financial Statistics*.

EXTERNAL TRADE

Principal Commodities (EC $ million, 2005): *Imports:* Food and live animals 57.4; Beverages and tobacco 25.1; Mineral fuels, lubricants, etc. 34.6; Chemicals and related products 22.7; Basic manufactures 61.9; Machinery and transport equipment 101.6; Miscellaneous manufactured articles 36.4; Total (incl. others) 350.6. *Exports* (incl. re-exports): Food and live animals 13.9; Beverages and tobacco 7.5; Basic manufactures 1.5; Machinery and transport equipment 14.8; Miscellaneous manufactured articles 1.9; Total (incl. others) 39.8.

Principal Trading Partners (EC $ million, 2005): *Imports:* Barbados 3.7; Guadeloupe 7.3; Guyana 6.6; Netherlands Antilles 22.3; Puerto Rico 27.4; Trinidad and Tobago 29.8; United Kingdom 16.1; USA 177.6; US Virgin Islands 5.6; Total (incl. others) 350.6. *Exports* (incl. re-exports): British Virgin Islands 1.7; Guadeloupe 0.8; Guyana 4.8; Netherlands Antilles 9.9; Saint Lucia 2.1; United Kingdom 10.7; USA 3.7; Total (incl. others) 39.8.

TRANSPORT

Road Traffic (motor vehicles licensed, 2003): Private cars 3,198; Hired cars 830; Buses/trucks/jeeps/pickups 2,002; Motorcycles 53; Tractors 5; Heavy equipment 168; Other 7.

Shipping: *Merchant Fleet* (registered at 31 December 2007): 4; Total displacement 805 grt. Source: Lloyd's Register-Fairplay, *World Fleet Statistics*.

TOURISM

Visitor Arrivals: 143,186 (stop-overs 62,084, excursionists 81,102) in 2005; 167,245 (stop-overs 72,962, excursionists 94,283) in 2006; 168,039 (stop-overs 76,207, excursionists 91,832) in 2007. Source: Eastern Caribbean Central Bank, *Annual Economic and Financial Review 2007*.

Visitor Arrivals by Country of Residence (2007): Canada 2,198; Caribbean 15,344; Germany 555; Italy 1,866; United Kingdom 4,480; USA 45,119; Total (incl. others) 168,039.

Tourism Receipts (EC $ million): 231.9 in 2005; 289.9 in 2006; 311.9 in 2007. Source: Eastern Caribbean Central Bank, *Annual Economic and Financial Review 2007*.

COMMUNICATIONS MEDIA

Radio Receivers (1997): 3,000 in use.

Television Receivers (1999): 1,000 in use.

Telephones (2002): 5,796 main lines in use.

Facsimile Machines (1993): 190 in use.

Mobile Cellular Telephones (2000): 15,000 subscribers.

Internet Connections (2002): 1,391.

Sources: partly UN, *Statistical Yearbook*; International Telecommunication Union.

EDUCATION

Pre-primary (2006/07 unless otherwise indicated): 11 schools (2003); 41 teachers (males 1, females 40); 468 pupils (males 237, females 231).

Primary (2006/07 unless otherwise indicated): 8 schools (2003); 89 teachers (males 6, females 83); 1,512 pupils (males 772, females 740).

General Secondary (2006/07 unless otherwise indicated): 1 school (2002/03); 97 teachers (males 30, females 67); 998 pupils (males 483, females 515).

Tertiary (2006/07): 20 teachers (males 10, females 10); 47 students (8 males, 39 females).

Adult Literacy Rate (UNESCO estimates): 95.4% (males 95.1%; females 95.7%) in 1995. Source: UNESCO, *Statistical Yearbook*.

Directory

The Constitution

The Constitution, established in 1976, accorded Anguilla the status of a British Dependent Territory. It formally became a separate dependency on 19 December 1980, and is administered under the Anguilla Constitution Orders of 1982 and 1990. British Dependent Territories were referred to as United Kingdom Overseas Territories from February 1998 and draft legislation confirming this change and granting citizens rights to full British citizenship and residence in the United Kingdom was published in March 1999. The British Overseas Territories Act entered into effect in May 2002. The British Government proposals also included the requirement that the Constitutions of Overseas Territories should be revised in order to conform to British and international standards. The process of revision of the Anguillan Constitution began in September 1999.

The British monarch is represented locally by a Governor, who presides over the Executive Council and the House of Assembly. The Governor is responsible for defence, external affairs (including international financial affairs), internal security (including the police), the public service, the judiciary and the audit. The Governor appoints a Deputy Governor. On matters relating to internal security, the public service and the appointment of an acting governor or deputy governor, the Governor is required to consult the Chief Minister. The Executive Council consists of the Chief Minister and not more than three other ministers (appointed by the Governor from the elected members of the legislative House of Assembly) and two *ex officio* members (the Deputy Governor and the Attorney-General). The House of Assembly is elected for a maximum term of five years by universal adult suffrage and consists of seven elected members, two *ex officio* members (the Deputy Governor and the Attorney-General) and two nominated members who are appointed by the Governor, one upon the advice of the Chief Minister, and one after consultations with the Chief Minister and the Leader of the Opposition. The House elects a Speaker and a Deputy Speaker.

The Governor may order the dissolution of the House of Assembly if a resolution of 'no confidence' is passed in the Government, and elections must be held within two months of the dissolution.

The Constitution provides for an Anguilla Belonger Commission, which determines cases of whether a person can be 'regarded as belonging to Anguilla' (i.e. having 'belonger' status). A belonger is someone of Anguillan birth or parentage, someone who has married a belonger, or someone who is a citizen of the United Kingdom Overseas Territories from Anguilla (by birth, parentage, adoption or naturalization). The Commission may grant belonger status to those who have been domiciled and ordinarily resident in Anguilla for not less than 15 years.

The Government

Governor: ALISTAIR HARRISON (took office 21 April 2009).

EXECUTIVE COUNCIL
(April 2009)

Chief Minister and Minister of Home Affairs, Natural Resources, Lands and Physical Planning: OSBOURNE FLEMING (AUF).

Minister of Finance, Economic Development, Investment and Tourism: VICTOR F. BANKS (AUF).

Minister of Social Development: EVANS MCNEIL ROGERS (AUF).

Minister of Infrastructure, Communications, Utilities, Housing, Agriculture and Fisheries: KENNETH HARRIGAN (AUF).

Attorney-General: WILHELM C. BOURNE.

Deputy Governor: STANLEY EVERTON REID.

Parliamentary Secretary with responsibility for Water, Agriculture and Fisheries: ALBERT HUGHES.

MINISTRIES

Office of the Governor: Government House, POB 60, The Valley; tel. 497-2622; fax 497-3314; e-mail governorsoffice@gov.ai.

Office of the Chief Minister: The Secretariat, POB 60, The Valley; tel. 497-2518; fax 497-3389; e-mail chief-minister@gov.ai.

All ministries are based in The Valley, mostly at the Secretariat (tel. 497-2451; internet www.gov.ai).

Legislature

HOUSE OF ASSEMBLY

Speaker: DAVID CARTY.
Clerk to House of Assembly: ADELLA RICHARDSON.
Election, 21 February 2005

Party	% of votes	Seats
Anguilla United Front (AUF)	38.9	4
Anguilla United Movement (AUM)	19.4	1
Anguilla National Strategic Alliance (ANSA)	19.2	2
Anguilla Progressive Party (APP)	9.5	—
Total (incl. others)	100.0	7

There are also two ex officio members and two nominated members.

Political Organizations

Anguilla National Strategic Alliance (ANSA): The Valley; Leader EDISON BAIRD.

UNITED KINGDOM OVERSEAS TERRITORIES

Anguilla

Anguilla Progressive Party (APP): The Valley; Leader ROY ROGERS.

Anguilla United Front (AUF): The Valley; internet www.unitedfront.ai; f. 2000; Leader OSBOURNE FLEMING; alliance comprising:

Anguilla Democratic Party (ADP): The Valley; f. 1981 as Anguilla People's Party; name changed 1984; reconstituted 2009; Chair. LEROY ROGERS.

Anguilla National Alliance: The Valley; f. 1980 by reconstitution of People's Progressive Party; Leader OSBOURNE FLEMING.

Anguilla United Movement (AUM): The Valley; f. 1979; revived 1984; previously known as the Anguilla United Party—AUP; conservative; Leader HUBERT B. HUGHES.

Judicial System

Justice is administered by the High Court, Court of Appeal and Magistrates' Courts. One of the 16 puisne judges of the Eastern Caribbean Supreme Court's High Court division, concurrently accredited to Montserrat, arbitrates in sittings of the High Court.

Puisne Judge: JANICE MESADIS GEORGE-CREQUE.

Religion

CHRISTIANITY

The Anglican Communion

Anglicans in Anguilla are adherents of the Church in the Province of the West Indies, comprising nine dioceses. Anguilla forms part of the diocese of the North Eastern Caribbean and Aruba.

Bishop of the North Eastern Caribbean and Aruba: Rt Rev. LEROY ERROL BROOKS, St Mary's Rectory, POB 180, The Valley; tel. 497-2235; fax 497-8555; e-mail brookx@anguilla.net.com.

The Roman Catholic Church

The diocese of St John's-Basseterre, suffragan to the archdiocese of Castries (Saint Lucia), includes Anguilla, Antigua and Barbuda, the British Virgin Islands, Montserrat and Saint Christopher and Nevis. The Bishop resides in St John's, Antigua.

Roman Catholic Church: St Gerard's, POB 47, The Valley; tel. 497-2405; e-mail stgerards@caribcable.com; internet www.stgerards-anguilla.org.

Protestant Churches

Methodist Church: POB 5, The Valley; tel. 497-2612; fax 497-8460; e-mail methodism@anguillanet.com; Supt Minister Rev. Dr H. CLIFTON NILES.

The Seventh-day Adventist, Baptist, Church of God, Pentecostal, Apostolic Faith and Jehovah's Witnesses Churches and sects are also represented.

The Press

Anguilla Life Magazine: POB 1622, The Valley; tel. 497-3080; fax 497-4196; e-mail anguillalife@anguillanet.com; 3 a year; Publr and Editor CLAIRE DEVENER; circ. 10,000.

The Anguillian Newspaper: POB 98, The Valley; tel. 497-3823; fax 497-8706; e-mail theanguillian@anguillanet.com; internet www.anguillian.com; weekly; Editor A. NAT HODGE.

The Light: Sandy Hill, POB 1373, The Valley; tel. 497-5641; fax 497-5641; e-mail thelight@anguillanet.com; internet www.thelightanguilla.com; f. 1993; owned by Hodgeco Publishing Inc; weekly; newspaper; Editor GEORGE C. HODGE.

Official Gazette: The Valley; tel. 497-5081; monthly; govt newssheet.

What We Do in Anguilla: Sandy Hill, POB 1373, The Valley; tel. 497-5641; fax 497-5795; e-mail thelight@anguillanet.com; f. 1987; monthly; tourism; Editor GEORGE C. HODGE; circ. 50,000.

Broadcasting and Communications

TELECOMMUNICATIONS

LIME: POB 77, The Valley; internet www.time4lime.com; fmrly Cable & Wireless (Anguilla) Ltd; name changed as above 2008; contact centres in Jamaica and Saint Lucia; CEO RICHARD DODD.

Wireless Ventures (Anguilla) Ltd: Babrow Bldg, The Valley; tel. 498-7500; fax 498-7510; e-mail customercareanguilla@digicelgroup.com; owned by Digicel Ltd (Bermuda); fmrly AT&T Wireless.

BROADCASTING

Radio

Caribbean Beacon Radio: Long Rd, POB 690, The Valley; Head Office: POB 7008, Columbus, GA 31908, USA; tel. 497-4340; fax 497-4311; f. 1981; privately owned and operated; religious and commercial; broadcasts 24 hours daily; Pres. Dr GENE SCOTT; CEO B. MONSELL HAZELL.

Heart Beat Radio: POB 5045, The Valley, AI 2640; tel. 498-3354; fax 497-5995; e-mail info@hbr1075.com; internet hbr1075.com; f. 2001; commercial; music and news programmes.

Klass 92.9 FM: POB 339, The Valley; tel. 497-3791; e-mail request@klass929.com; internet www.klass929.com; f. 2006; commercial; Owner ABNER BROOKS, Jr.

Kool FM: North Side, The Valley; tel. 497-0103; fax 497-0104; e-mail kool@koolfm103.com; internet www.koolfm103.com; commercial; Man. ASHLEY BROOKS.

Radio Anguilla: Dept of Information and Broadcasting, Secretariat, POB 225, The Valley; tel. 497-2218; fax 497-5432; e-mail radioaxa@anguillanet.com; internet www.radioaxa.com; f. 1969; owned and operated by the Govt of Anguilla since 1976; 250,000 listeners throughout the north-eastern Caribbean; broadcasts 17 hours daily; Dir of Information and Broadcasting KENNETH HODGE; News Editor WYCLIFFE RICHARDSON.

ZJF FM: The Valley; tel. 497-3157; f. 1989; commercial.

Television

Anguilla Television: terrestrial channels 3 and 9; 24-hour local and international English language programming.

Caribbean Cable Communications (Anguilla): Edwin Wallace Rey Dr., POB 336, The Valley; tel. 497-3600; fax 497-3602; e-mail customersupport@caribcable.com; internet www.caribcable.com; also broadcasts to Nevis; Pres. LEE BERTMAN.

Finance

(cap. = capital; res = reserves; dep. = deposits; m. = million; amounts in EC dollars)

CENTRAL BANK

Eastern Caribbean Central Bank: Fairplay Commercial Complex, POB 1385, The Valley; tel. 497-5050; fax 497-5150; e-mail eccbaxa@anguillanet.com; internet www.eccb-centralbank.org; HQ in Basseterre, Saint Christopher and Nevis; bank of issue and central monetary authority for Anguilla, Antigua and Barbuda, Dominica, Grenada, Montserrat, Saint Christopher and Nevis, Saint Lucia and Saint Vincent and the Grenadines; Gov. Sir K. DWIGHT VENNER; Country Man. MARILYN BARTLETT-RICHARDSON.

COMMERCIAL BANKS

Caribbean Commercial Bank (Anguilla) Ltd: POB 23, The Valley; tel. 497-3917; fax 497-3570; e-mail service@ccb.ai; internet www.ccb.ai; f. 1976; Chair. OSBOURNE B. FLEMING; Man. Dir STARRY WEBSTER-BENJAMIN.

FirstCaribbean International Bank Ltd: POB 140, The Valley; tel. 497-2301; fax 497-2980; e-mail care@firstcaribbeanbank.com; internet www.firstcaribbeanbank.com; f. 2002 following merger of Caribbean operations of Barclays Bank PLC and CIBC; Exec. Chair. MICHAEL MANSOOR; CEO JOHN D. ORR.

National Bank of Anguilla Ltd (NBA): POB 44, The Valley; tel. 497-2101; fax 497-3310; e-mail nbabankl@anguillanet.com; internet www.nba.ai; f. 1985; 5% owned by Govt of Anguilla; cap. 30.7m., res 20.2m., dep. 829.2m. (March 2007); CEO E. VALENTINE BANKS.

Scotiabank Anguilla Ltd: Fairplay Commercial Centre, POB 250, The Valley; tel. 497-3333; fax 497-3344; e-mail bns.anguilla@scotiabank.com; internet www.scotiabank.com; Man. Dir KERWIN BAPTISTE.

There are 'offshore' foreign banks based on the island, but most are not authorized to operate in Anguilla. There is a financial complex known as the Caribbean Commercial Centre in The Valley.

TRUST COMPANIES

Barwys Trust Anguilla Ltd: Caribbean Suite, The Valley; tel. 497-2189; fax 497-5007; e-mail info@barwys.com; internet www.barwys.com; Man. JOSEPH BRICE.

Codan Trust Co (Anguilla) Ltd: NBA Corporate Bldg, Caribbean Suite, POB 147, The Valley; tel. 498-4126; fax 498-8423; e-mail anguilla@conyersdillandpearman.com; internet conyersdillandpearman.com; subsidiary of Conyers, Dill and Pearman, Bermuda; Man. GARETH THOMAS.

First Anguilla Trust Co Ltd: Mitchell House, POB 174, The Valley, AI 2640; tel. and fax 498-8800; e-mail information@

firstanguilla.com; internet www.firstanguilla.com; owned by Webster Dyrud Mitchell; f. 1995; Dir PAM WEBSTER.

Fortis Intertrust (Anguilla) Ltd: National Bank Corporate Bldg, Airport Rd, POB 1388, The Valley; tel. 497-2189; fax 497-5007; e-mail anneke.soedhoe@fortisintertrust.com; internet www.fortisintertrust.com; Gen. Man. ANNEKE SOEDHOE.

GenevaTrust: National Bank Corporate Bldg, Caribbean Suite, Airport Rd, The Valley; tel. 870-3178; fax 870-3949; e-mail geneva@genevatrust.com; internet www.genevatrust.com; f. 2005 as the GenevaTrust Corporation; subsidiary of Geneva Assurance Ltd; CEO NADINE DE KOKER.

Global Trustees (Anguilla) Ltd: 201 The Rogers Office Bldg, Edwin Wallace Rey Dr., George Hill; tel. 498-5858; fax 497-5504; e-mail anguilla@gcsl.info; internet www.gcsl.info; fmrly Hansa Bank and Trust Co; Man. Dir CARLYLE K. ROGERS.

Harney Westwood & Riegels (Anguilla) (HWR Services (Anguilla) Ltd): Harlaw Chambers, POB 1026, The Valley; tel. 498-5000; fax 498-5001; e-mail anguilla@harneys.com; internet www.harneys.com; Man. KIMBERLY FLEMING.

Lutea (Anguilla) Ltd: Caribbean Suite, POB 1533, The Valley; tel. 498-0340; fax 498-0341; e-mail acharles@lutea.com; internet www.lutea.com; owned by the Lutea Group of Cos, administered in Jersey; Man. AINE CHARLES.

Mossack Fonseca & Co (British Anguilla) Ltd: Quantum Bldg, Suite 29, Caribbean Commercial Centre, The Valley; tel. 498-7777; fax 497-3727; e-mail anguilla@mossfon.com; internet www.mossfon.com; Man. SHERMA BAPTISTE.

Sinel Trust (Anguilla) Ltd: Sinel Chambers, POB 1269, The Valley; tel. 497-3311; fax 497-5659; e-mail arichardson@sineltrust.com; CEO ALEX RICHARDSON.

REGULATORY AUTHORITY

Anguilla Financial Services Commission: The Secretariat, POB 1575, The Valley; tel. 497-5881; fax 497-5872; e-mail info@fsc.org.ai; internet www.fsc.org.ai; f. 2004 to replace the Financial Services Dept of the Ministry of Finance, Economic Development, Investment, Tourism and Commerce; Chair. DENNIS CROSS.

STOCK EXCHANGE

Eastern Caribbean Securities Exchange: based in Basseterre, Saint Christopher and Nevis; tel. (869) 466-7192; fax (869) 465-3798; e-mail info@ecseonline.com; internet www.ecseonline.com; f. 2001; regional securities market designed to facilitate the buying and selling of financial products for the eight member territories—Anguilla, Antigua and Barbuda, Dominica, Grenada, Montserrat, Saint Christopher and Nevis, Saint Lucia and Saint Vincent and the Grenadines; Chair. Sir K. DWIGHT VENNER; Gen. Man. and CEO TREVOR E. BLAKE.

INSURANCE

A-Affordable Insurance Services Inc: Old Factory Plaza, POB 6, The Valley; tel. 497-5757; fax 497-2122.

British American Insurance Co Ltd: Herbert's Commercial Centre, POB 148, The Valley; tel. 497-2653; fax 497-5933; e-mail britam@anguillenet.com.

Caribbean Alliance Insurance Co Ltd: POB 1377, The Valley; tel. 497-3525; fax 497-3526.

D-3 Enterprises Ltd: Caribbean Commercial Complex, POB 1377, The Valley; tel. 497-3525; fax 497-3526; e-mail d-3ent@anguillanet.com; internet www.d-3enterprises.com; Man. Dir CLEMENT RUAN.

Gulf Insurance Ltd: c/o Ferry Boat Inn, POB 189, Blowing Point; tel. 497-6613; fax 497-6713; internet www.gulfinsuranceltd.com; Contact MARJORIE MCCLEAN.

Malliouhana-Anico Insurance Co Ltd (MAICO): Herbert's Commercial Centre, POB 492, The Valley; tel. 497-3712; fax 497-3710; e-mail maico@anguillanet.com; Man. MONICA HODGE.

National Caribbean Insurance Co Ltd: Herbert's Commercial Centre, POB 323, The Valley; tel. 497-2865; fax 497-3783.

National General Insurance Co N.V. (NAGICO): c/o Fairplay Management Services, POB 79, The Valley; tel. 497-2976; fax 497-3303; e-mail fairplay@anguillanet.com; internet www.nagico.com.

Nem West Indies Insurance Ltd (Nemwil): Old Factory Plaza, POB 6, The Valley; tel. 497-5757; fax 497-2122.

Trade and Industry

DEVELOPMENT ORGANIZATION

Anguilla Development Board: POB 285, Wallblake Rd, The Valley; tel. 497-3690; fax 497-2959.

CHAMBER OF COMMERCE

Anguilla Chamber of Commerce and Industry: POB 321, The Valley; tel. and fax 497-2839; e-mail acoci@caribcable.com; internet www.anguillachamber.com; Pres. JOHN BENJAMIN; Exec. Dir CALVIN BARTLETT.

INDUSTRIAL AND TRADE ASSOCIATION

Anguilla Financial Services Association (AFSA): POB 1071, The Valley; tel. 498-4224; fax 498-4220; e-mail info@anguillafinance.com; internet www.anguillafinance.com; Pres. JOHN D. K. LAWRENCE.

UTILITIES

Electricity

Anguilla Electricity Co Ltd: POB 400, The Valley; tel. 497-5200; fax 497-5440; e-mail info@anglec.com; internet www.anglec.com; f. 1991; operates a power-station and 12 generators; Chair. RODNEY REY; Gen. Man. THOMAS HODGE.

Transport

ROADS

Anguilla has 140 km (87 miles) of roads, of which 100 km are tarred.

SHIPPING

The principal port of entry is Sandy Ground on Road Bay. There is a daily ferry service between Blowing Point and Marigot (St Martin). The first phase of the Anguilla ports Development Project commenced in July 2006 with the development of Road Bay; upon completion in October, extensive work began at Blowing Point to create three new piers, two of which were to be devoted to ferry and passenger services. Construction of the new facilities was completed in 2007.

Link Ferries: Little Harbour; tel. 497-2231; fax 497-3290; e-mail fbconnor@anguillanet.com; internet www.link.ai; f. 1992; daily services to Julianna International Airport (St Martin) and charter services to neighbouring islands and offshore quays; Owner FRANKLYN CONNOR.

CIVIL AVIATION

Wallblake Airport, 3.2 km (2 miles) from The Valley, has a bitumen-surfaced runway with a length of 1,100 m (3,600 ft). In 1996 Anguilla signed an agreement with the Government of Aruba providing for the construction of a new jet airport on the north coast of the island, with finance of some US $30m. from the Aruba Investment Bank. Reconstruction and expansion of Wallblake Airport was completed in late 2004. Most of the cost of the EC $49.2m. project was allocated to the extension of the runway to accommodate mid-range aircraft. LIAT and Winair regional airlines also operate from Wallblake airport.

American Eagle: POB 659, Wallblake Airport; tel. 497-3131; fax 497-3502; regional partner co of American Airlines; operates scheduled flights from Puerto Rico 3 times a day (December to April) and once daily (May to November).

Anguilla Air Services: POB 559, Wallblake Airport; tel. 498-5922; fax 498-5921; e-mail info@anguillaairservices.com; internet www.anguillaairservices.com; f. Dec. 2006; operates passenger and cargo charter flights from Anguilla to neighbouring islands; Man. Dir CARL THOMAS.

Trans Anguilla Airways (2000) Ltd (TAA): POB 1329, Wallblake Airport; tel. 497-8690; fax 497-8689; e-mail transang@anguillanet.com; internet www.transanguilla.com; f. 1996; air charter service in the Eastern Caribbean; Chair. JOSHUA GUMBS.

Tourism

Anguilla's sandy beaches and unspoilt natural beauty attract tourists and also day visitors from neighbouring St Martin/St Maarten. In November 1999 'Hurricane Lenny' badly affected Anguilla, forcing the temporary closure of the island's two largest hotels. Tourism receipts totalled an estimated EC $311.9m. in 2007, and there were 746 hotel rooms on the island in 2005. Visitor arrivals totalled an estimated 168,039 in 2007, of which 27% were from the USA, 9% were from other Caribbean countries, while most of the remainder were from the United Kingdom, Canada, Italy and Germany.

Anguilla Hotel and Tourism Association: Coronation Ave, POB 1020, The Valley; tel. 497-2944; fax 497-3091; e-mail ahta@anguillanet.com; internet www.ahta.ai; f. 1981; Exec. Dir TRUDY NIXON.

Anguilla Tourist Board: Coronation Ave, POB 1388, The Valley, AI 2640; tel. 497-2759; fax 497-2710; e-mail atbtour@anguillanet.com; internet www.anguilla-vacation.com; Dir AMELIA VANTERPOOL-KUBISCH.

BERMUDA

Introductory Survey

Location, Climate, Language, Religion, Flag, Capital

The Bermudas or Somers Islands are an isolated archipelago, comprising about 138 islands, in the Atlantic Ocean, about 917 km (570 miles) off the coast of South Carolina, USA. Bridges and causeways link seven of the islands to form the principal mainland. The climate is mild and humid. Temperatures are generally between 8°C (46°F) and 32°C (90°F), with an average annual rainfall of 1,470 mm (58 ins). The official language is English, but there is a small community of Portuguese speakers. Most of the inhabitants profess Christianity, and numerous denominations are represented, the principal one being the Anglican Church. The flag (proportions 1 by 2) is the British 'Red Ensign' (this usage being unique among the British colonies), with, in the fly, the colony's badge: a seated red lion holding a shield (with a gold baroque border), which depicts the wreck off Bermuda of the ship of the first settlers. The capital is Hamilton.

Recent History

Bermuda was first settled by the British in 1609. It has had a representative assembly since 1620 (and thus claims one of the oldest parliaments in the world), and became a British crown colony in 1684. Bermuda was granted internal self-government by the Constitution introduced in 1968, although the British Government retains responsibility in certain matters. Various amendments to the 1968 Constitution were made in 1973, the most important being the establishment of the Governor's Council, through which the Governor exercises responsibility for external affairs, defence, internal security and the police. In 1974 the Government Leader was restyled Premier and the Executive Council became the Cabinet.

The first general election under the new Constitution, which took place in May 1968 against a background of rioting and racial tension (some 60% of the population are of African origin, the rest mostly of European extraction), was won by the United Bermuda Party (UBP), a moderate, multi-racial party whose policies were based on racial co-operation and continued support for dependent status. The underlying racial tensions were emphasized in 1972 and 1973 by shooting incidents which resulted in the deaths of the Governor, the Commissioner of Police and three others. In December 1977 the Governor's assassin and another convicted murderer were executed, and further rioting and arson ensued. A state of emergency was declared, and British troops were flown to Bermuda to restore order.

At the general election of May 1976, the UBP was returned to power with a decreased majority, winning 26 of the 40 seats in the House of Assembly. The remaining seats were won by the mainly black, left-wing Progressive Labour Party (PLP), which campaigned for independence. In August 1977 Sir John Sharpe, Premier and leader of the UBP since December 1975, resigned both posts and was succeeded by David Gibbons, the Minister of Finance.

In February 1978 a Royal Commission was established to investigate the causes of racial violence, and in August the Commission published a report which suggested the redrawing of constituency boundaries to improve the PLP's prospects for winning seats. Despite this, the UBP won the December 1980 election. Gibbons resigned as Premier and UBP leader in January 1982 and was succeeded by John Swan, the Minister of Home Affairs. At a general election in February 1983, the UBP increased its majority in the House of Assembly. Internal divisions within the PLP led to the expulsion from the party of four PLP members of the House of Assembly. These members, after sitting as independents, formed a new centre party, the National Liberal Party (NLP), in August 1985. In October Swan called an early general election, hoping to take advantage of the divided opposition. The UBP was decisively returned to power, securing 31 of the 40 seats in the House of Assembly, while the PLP retained only seven seats and the NLP won two. Following a general election in February 1989, the UBP remained in power, but with a reduced representation in the House of Assembly. By contrast, the PLP increased its representation.

Constitutional amendments introduced in 1979 included provision for closer consultation between the Premier and the Leader of the Opposition on the appointment of members of the Public Service Commission and the Boundaries Commission, and on the appointment of the Chief Justice. The 1978 Royal Commission recommended early independence for Bermuda, but the majority of the population at that time seemed to oppose such a policy. Swan had declared himself in favour of eventual independence for the colony, but only with the support of the Bermudian people.

In August 1992 Lord Waddington (former leader of the British House of Lords) replaced Sir Desmond Langley as Governor. Waddington remained in office until June 1997, when he was succeeded by Thorold Masefield.

At a general election in October 1993 (the first to be held since the voting age was lowered from 21 to 18 years in 1990), the UBP was returned to power, winning 22 seats in the House of Assembly, while the PLP secured 18. In February 1994 legislation providing for the organization of a referendum on independence for Bermuda was narrowly approved in the House of Assembly. The debate on independence was believed to have intensified as a result of the announcement in late 1993 that British and US forces would close their facilities and withdraw permanently from the island by April 1995 and September 1995, respectively. The PLP, which advocates independence for Bermuda, consistently opposed the organization of a referendum on the subject, believing that the independence issue should be determined by a general election. In May 1994 a PLP legislative motion to reject a proposed government inquiry into the possibilities for independence was narrowly approved, effectively halting further progress towards a referendum. However, the debate continued, and in October a government delegation travelled to London for official discussions on the subject. Further legislation regarding the proposed referendum was narrowly approved in March 1995, and it was subsequently announced that a vote would be held in August. The PLP encouraged its supporters to boycott the poll, which required not only a majority of votes, but also the approval of 40% of eligible voters in order to achieve a pro-independence result.

The referendum, which was delayed briefly owing to the passage of 'Hurricane Felix', took place on 16 August 1995. Some 59% of eligible voters participated in the poll (a relatively low level for Bermuda), of which 74% registered their opposition to independence from the United Kingdom, and 26% expressed their support for independence. The following day Swan resigned as Premier and as leader of the UBP. Factions within the governing party were perceived to have become considerably polarized during the independence debate, which had resulted in the division of opinion along racial lines. The Minister of Finance, Dr David Saul (who had remained neutral on the independence issue), was subsequently elected leader of the UBP, and Saul was therefore sworn in as Premier on 25 August. Saul stated that his principal objectives were to re-establish a climate of political stability (thus reassuring the international business community), to encourage the continued development of the financial services and tourism sectors and to reunite the UBP. However, under Saul's leadership divisions within the party appeared to deepen.

In an attempt to restore a measure of unity within the UBP, Saul announced a reallocation of cabinet portfolios in January 1997. In the reorganization three of the five party members who had supported a motion of censure against Saul in June of the previous year were appointed to positions in the Cabinet. In March, however, Saul announced his resignation as Premier, as a member of the House of Assembly and as the leader of the party. He was replaced by Pamela Gordon, who was elected to the party leadership (and thus as Premier) unopposed.

In May 1998 Gordon effected a major reorganization of the Cabinet with the expressed aim of making the Government 'more efficient and effective'. Elections to the House of Assembly took place in November. The PLP won its first ever majority in the House of Assembly, taking 26 seats, while the UBP obtained 14 seats. On 10 November a new Cabinet was appointed and party leader Jennifer Smith was sworn in as Bermuda's first PLP Premier. In her subsequent public address she sought to reassure the international business community that her Government would seek to enhance Bermuda's attractiveness as an international business centre, and that she would resist any attempts to alter the island's tax status. Smith further promised that, although independence for Bermuda remained a stated aim of her party, no immediate moves towards independence were planned.

In February 1999 Smith met members of the Organisation for Economic Co-operation and Development (OECD, see p. 358) to reassure them that Bermuda was determined to improve regulation of the 'offshore' financial services sector. In March the British Government published draft legislation redesignating its Dependencies as United Kingdom Overseas Territories, and guaranteeing their citizens' rights to a British passport and to residence in the United Kingdom. The document also stated, however, that the Overseas Territories would be obliged to reform their legislation to ensure compliance with European standards on human rights and on financial regulation. In October it was announced that in accordance with the proposed reforms, corporal and capital punishment were to be removed from the statute book.

A report by the Financial Action Task Force on Money Laundering (see p. 430) concluded in June 2000 that Bermuda appeared 'to have effective regulations and supervision' in place in its financial services sector. In the same month the Government agreed to co-operate with OECD in an international effort to reduce tax evasion, promising to end within five years the 'harmful' practices that had given the island a reputation as a tax haven. Measures included a pledge to exchange information about tax in Bermuda with other nations, the introduction of legislation for companies to audit accounts and for these to be made available to the Bermudian authorities, and in the opening up of previously sheltered sectors of the economy to international companies. The Government had, however, pledged to maintain its existing tax system, which included no income tax. In December the members of the House of Assembly agreed, for the first time, to declare their assets and financial interests.

In October 2000 the opposition UBP boycotted the opening of parliament in protest at government plans to reduce the number of seats in the House of Assembly. Pamela Gordon claimed that there had not been adequate public consultation on the matter. Premier Smith had rejected calls for a constitutional conference or a referendum on the proposals, which included replacing the two-member constituencies with single-member ones, although she did announce that the Government would hold a public meeting to discuss the issue. The PLP believed that the existing system was weighted in favour of the UBP, which was considered the party of the white population. The UBP claimed that changes made without proper consultation and a referendum would mean a move towards a 'black dictatorship'. In December the House of Assembly approved a motion requesting the British Government to approve the establishment of a boundaries commission, which would recommend the size of the island's constituencies. Any changes would be subject to ratification by the United Kingdom's Foreign and Commonwealth Office (FCO). In January 2001 the UBP submitted an 8,500-signature petition to the British Government, demanding a constitutional conference or referendum before any changes were made. Gordon also claimed that some Bermudians had refused to sign the petition fearing recriminations. The FCO, however, stated that a constitutional conference was unnecessary, and in April it began consultations over the proposed changes. The commission recommended reducing the number of seats in the House of Assembly by four, to 36. In addition, whereas deputies had previously been elected from 20 two-member constituencies, under the proposed scheme each member of parliament would be elected by a separate constituency. The FCO approved the changes before the July 2003 general election.

In October 2001 Gordon resigned as leader of the UBP. The party elected Grant Gibbons as her successor. In November Sir John Vereker succeeded Sir Thorold Masefield as Governor of Bermuda.

In May 2002 the British Overseas Territories Act, having received royal assent in the United Kingdom in February, came into force and granted British citizenship to the people of its Overseas Territories, including Bermuda. Under the new law Bermudians would be able to hold British passports and work in the United Kingdom and anywhere else in the European Union (see p. 255).

In mid-2002 the issue of financial transparency and corporate governance in Bermuda re-emerged following the disastrous collapse of the US energy concern Enron and several other multinationals in late 2001 and early 2002. The indictment on tax-evasion charges of Dennis Kozlowski, the former CEO of Tyco International Ltd, a manufacturer of electronic security systems with a nominal headquarters on the island, fuelled a growing campaign in the US media and the US Congress against the perceived lack of financial regulation and scrutiny in Bermuda. The Corporate Patriot Enforcement Act of 2005, approved by the US Congress in that year, sought to discourage US corporations to relocate their headquarters from the USA to offshore sites such as Bermuda, by making them still liable to pay tax in the USA.

At an election to the smaller 36-seat House of Assembly in July 2003, the PLP retained its parliamentary majority, securing 22 seats, but its share of the popular vote was reduced to 52% (compared with 48% for the UBP). Smith resigned as Premier following pressure from 11 'rebel' PLP MPs after it emerged that she had retained her seat, in what was regarded as a 'safe' PLP constituency, by just eight votes. She was replaced by the erstwhile Minister of Works and Engineering, William Alexander Scott. Scott's first Cabinet, announced a few days after the elections, consisted of 12 members, despite the PLP's pre-election pledge to reduce the size of the executive to eight in order to reduce costs.

In December 2004 Scott announced that a Bermuda Independence Commission would be established in order to foment debate regarding the island's future. This Commission was duly established in January 2005 and in November it submitted its report; however, its findings were criticized for being biased, as they failed to include contributions from the UBP, including only the ruling PLP's submission. In an attempt to quell the criticism, Scott declared that discussions would take place in 2006 regarding the future status of Bermuda. However, public opinion remained strongly in favour of maintaining links with the United Kingdom: according to opinion polls in June 2006, only 20% of the public supported independence, while a significant 65% opposed complete secession from the United Kingdom. In March both the UN and the British Government indicated their support for a referendum on the issue; however, Scott maintained that the question of independence should be decided at the next general election, which was constitutionally due by 2008. The issue of independence created political tension between the population's black majority, from which the PLP drew much of its support, and the white minority.

Scott's premiership was abruptly curtailed on 27 October 2006 after he was defeated in a PLP leadership contest; party delegates voted for former Minister of Transport and Tourism and Deputy Premier Ewart Brown to succeed the incumbent Premier. Demonstrating his intention to compete for the party leadership, Brown had resigned from his ministerial responsibilities earlier in the month; he was formally inaugurated as party leader on 30 October, resuming the portfolio for Transport and Tourism and announcing limited changes to the Government's composition. The most notable of these was the creation of a ministerial post for matters of social rehabilitation, to be occupied by erstwhile Minister of Community Affairs and Sports Dale Butler, whose newly vacated portfolio was assumed by Wayne Perinchief. Paula Ann Cox, the Minister of Finance, assumed the additional role of Deputy Premier. Brown emphasized the fundamental importance of a responsive social welfare framework to the future prosperity of Bermuda, pledging to invest substantially in the country's care system and confirming his commitment to addressing disruptive racial tensions among the island's communities. The latter concern proved of particular pertinence to the opposition UBP, embroiled as it was in an internal racial discrimination controversy which, in January 2007, precipitated the resignations of House of Assembly member Jamahl Simmons and party Chairwoman Gwyneth Rawlins. Both alleged serious charges of racial discrimination against factions within the party. Simmons claimed that a white élite within the UBP was attempting to remove him from his seat; the departure of two black party members only exacerbated public scepticism about the party's professed allegiance to an integrated Bermudian society. Calls for the resignation of leader Wayne Furbert ensued, with senior members asserting that intra-party schisms and dissension arising from the racism dispute threatened to undermine the UBP's political power.

The unauthorized disclosure, from a source within the Bermuda police, of documents implicating the Premier and a number of other high-ranking government officials in a corruption scandal, served to compromise relations with the United Kingdom in May 2007. Brown maintained that a previous inquiry, in 2004, into the alleged dubious arrangement between government personnel (including himself) and the state-owned Bermuda Housing Corporation—whereby considerable public funds were appropriated for private enrichment—had discharged him of any misconduct. Moreover, he blamed Governor Vereker for failing to ensure the documents' safe custody, and thereby allowing the information to enter the public realm.

On 12 December 2007 Richard Gozney was inaugurated as Governor of Bermuda. At a general election held on 18 December, the PLP secured a third consecutive term in office with 52.5% of the votes cast, while the UBP won 47.3% of the ballot. The parties' representation in the legislature remained as at the 2003 election: 22 seats for the PLP and 14 seats for the UBP. Brown was duly sworn in as Premier two days later, and his new Cabinet included the reappointment of Nelson Bascome as Minister of Health. (Bascome had resigned from the post in February amid a criminal investigation into his business practices during his tenure as Minister of Health and Family Services (in the late 1990s); he had been charged with two counts of theft and one of corruption in June, although the case was rejected in October 2007.) Allegations of corruption and issues of race featured prominently in the election campaign, with PLP candidates employing inflammatory rhetoric to suggest that the UBP, if elected, would install a regime oppressive to the black population. After failing to win the constituency seat he contested, Michael Dunkley was replaced as leader of the UBP by Kim Swan, who had been the party's leader in the Senate for six years.

Following increased drugs-smuggling and immigration violations by Jamaican nationals, in January 2003 it was announced that Jamaican visitors to Bermuda would henceforth require visas. In February 2005 a Supreme Court judge ruled as unlawful the Government's policy of deferring the right to apply for parole for prisoners convicted of drugs-smuggling until they had served one-half of their sentence. Prisoners convicted of non-drugs, non-sexual or non-violent offences were allowed to apply for parole after serving one-third of their sentence. In July the Misuse of Drugs Amendment Act introduced legislation allowing courts to fine those convicted of drugs offences up to US $1m. and to impose prison sentences of between 10 years and life. Despite the designation of a dedicated cabinet minister and employment of an eminent British police officer as Assistant Commissioner specializing in drugs crime prevention, drugs-related violent crime escalated during 2006. Police authorities had valued Bermuda's drugs trade at an estimated US $200m. by August of that year.

Concerns about the regulation of Bermuda's burgeoning financial services industry also intensified in 2006, with increased incidences of money-laundering and embezzlement. The arrest in Bermuda of Dutch businessman and oil magnate, John Deuss, in October of that year attracted considerable local and international media interest; Deuss was compelled to resign as Chairman and Chief Executive Officer of Bermuda Commercial Bank (BCB) following allegations of money-laundering, among other illegal practices, and extradited to the Netherlands. It had transpired in September that the principal shareholder in BCB, First Curaçao International Bank, was being investigated by Dutch and Caribbean regulators in relation to similar charges of financial malpractice. Despite these troubling developments, the House of Assembly ratified the Investment Funds Act 2006 in December, designed to facilitate the registration and license of investment funds in the territory by eliminating 'unnecessary' administrative protocols and to encourage further expansion in a sector already attractive to international fund operators. Bermuda's financial sector was criticized in February 2007 for its resistance to regulatory mechanisms and reluctance to engage in transparency exercises. Shortly after his election in November 2008 US President Barack Obama reiterated his determination to secure more stringent regulations in a number of tax havens, including Bermuda. In April 2009 OECD included Bermuda on its 'grey list' of tax havens which have committed to but not implemented an internationally agreed standard of transparency measures.

Government

Bermuda is a crown colony of the United Kingdom, with a wide measure of internal self-government. An appointed Governor, responsible for external affairs, defence and internal security, represents the British monarch. The bicameral legislature comprises the Senate (11 nominated members) and the House of Assembly, with 36 members representing separate constituencies elected for five years by universal adult suffrage. The Governor appoints the majority leader in the House as Premier, and the latter nominates other ministers. The Cabinet is responsible to the legislature. For the purposes of local government, the island has long been divided into nine parishes (originally known as 'tribes', except for the 'public land' of St George's, the capital until 1815). The town of St George's and the city of Hamilton constitute the two municipalities of the territory.

Defence

The local defence force is the Bermuda Regiment, with a strength of some 630 men and women in 1999. The Regiment employs selective conscription.

Economic Affairs

In 1997, according to estimates by the World Bank, Bermuda's gross national income (GNI), measured at average 1995–97 prices, was US $2,128m. During 2000–07, it was estimated, the population increased at an average annual rate of 0.4%, while overall gross domestic product (GDP) increased, in real terms, at an average annual rate of 4.4% in 2002–07; growth was estimated at 4.6% in 2007.

Agriculture (including fishing, mining and quarrying) engaged only 1.8% of the employed labour force in 2008 and contributed 0.7% of GDP in 2007. The principal crops were potatoes, carrots, bananas, vegetables and melons. Flowers (notably lilies) are grown for export. Other vegetables and fruit are also grown, but Bermuda remains very dependent upon food imports, which, with beverages and tobacco, accounted for 11.9% of total imports in 2007. Livestock-rearing includes cattle and goats (both mainly for dairy purposes), pigs and poultry. There is a small fishing industry, mainly for domestic consumption. In 2002–07 agricultural GDP increased by an annual average of 5.2%; the sector grew by 3.8% in 2007.

Industry (including manufacturing, construction, quarrying and public utilities) contributed 8.1% of GDP in 2007 and engaged an estimated 12.4% of the employed labour force in 2008. The main activities include ship repairs, boat-building and the manufacture of paints and pharmaceuticals. The principal industrial sector is construction (in which an estimated 9.1% of the total labour force were engaged in 2008). Most of Bermuda's water is provided by privately collected rainfall. Energy requirements are met mainly by the import of mineral fuels (fuels accounted for 9.2% of total imports in 2007). An explosion at Bermuda's only power plant in July 2005 reduced electricity production to just 85 MW from its full capacity of 165 MW. The cost of repairing the damage was estimated at B $10m. Industrial GDP increased by an average of 2.0% per year in 2002–07; the sector contracted by 2.3% in 2007.

Bermuda is overwhelmingly a service economy, with service industries contributing an estimated 91.1% of GDP in 2007 and engaging 85.8% of the employed labour force in 2008. In the latter year, 12.3% of the employed labour force worked in restaurants and hotels, but tourism is estimated to account for some 60% of all employment, directly and indirectly. The total number of tourists, particularly of cruise-ship passengers, is strictly controlled, in order to maintain Bermuda's environment and its market for wealthier visitors. Most tourists come from the USA (some 75.7% of total arrivals by air in 2005). In 2008 some 577,839 tourists visited Bermuda, a decline of 12.4% on the previous year's figure. In September 2003 the impact of 'Hurricane Fabian' led to the cancellation of several cruise-ship visits and the temporary closure of the international airport to commercial aircraft. In addition, two leading hotels suffered extensive damage. Largely as a consequence of the hurricane, tourism revenue declined to B $342.5m. in 2003, from B $378.8m. the previous year, before recovering slightly to B $353.7m. in 2004. In 2002–07 the GDP of the services sector increased by an annual average of 5.5%; services GDP increased by 6.0% in 2007.

There is a significant commercial and 'offshore' financial sector, and in 2000 Bermuda was the world's third largest insurance market, having doubled in size during the 1990s. In late 2001 the industry came under huge pressure from claims made in connection to the September terrorist attacks in the USA, although increased demand for insurance and reinsurance services led to a number of new companies being formed at the same time. It was estimated that, in 1995, the entire financial sector contributed more than one-third of foreign exchange earnings. An estimated 31.1% of the employed labour force were engaged directly in the finance, insurance, real estate and business sectors in 2008. International business was estimated to account for 25.9% of GDP in 2007. In 2008 the number of companies registered in Bermuda totalled 15,186. The GDP of the international business sector increased by an annual average of 11.2% in 2002–07; the sector increased by 16.6% in 2007. Another important source of income is the 'free-flag' registration of shipping, giving Bermuda one of the largest fleets in the world. In 1999 Bermuda passed the Electronic Transactions Act, designed to create an infrastructure to support the country's burgeoning 'e-commerce' sector, which was intended to become Bermuda's third major service industry, alongside financial services and tourism.

Bermuda is almost entirely dependent upon imports, has very few commodity exports and, therefore, consistently records a large visible trade deficit (B $1,068m. in 2006). Receipts from the service industries normally ensure a surplus on the current account of the balance of payments (recorded at $901m. in 2006). The USA is the principal source of imports (providing 72.2% of total imports in 2007) and the principal market for exports. Other important trading partners include the United Kingdom, Canada and France. The main exports are rum, flowers, medicinal and pharmaceutical products and the re-export of petroleum products. The principal imports are machinery and food, beverages and tobacco.

In 2008/09 there was an estimated budgetary surplus of some B $53.6m. (excluding debt and sinking fund contributions). The average annual rate of inflation was 3.3% in 2000–08. The rate averaged 4.8% in 2008. In February 2001 government figures indicated that unemployment had fallen for the first time since 1993.

Bermuda, the oldest colony of the United Kingdom, has the status of Overseas Territory in association with the European Union (see p. 255) and has also been granted Designated Territory status by the British Government (this allows Bermudian-based funds and unit trusts access to the British market). Bermuda's financial services also benefit from a special tax treaty with the USA. A similar agreement was signed in November 2005 with Australia, in which both parties would share tax information on a specific subject under investigation or audit. In 2000 Bermuda joined the Caribbean Tourism Organization. In July 2003 Bermuda became an associate member of the Caribbean Community and Common Market (CARICOM, see p. 206).

Bermudians enjoy a high standard of living, although there is considerable inequality in the distribution of wealth. There is also local disquiet at the cost of property. The PLP Government that took office in 2003 stated that addressing these issues was a key objective of their administration. The Government borrowed B $85m. to underpin the 2004/05 budget, which was mostly intended for expenditure on social projects, such as housing for the homeless and health services. Proximity to the USA and the parity of the US and Bermuda dollars help both tourism and financial industries, and Bermuda's status as a United Kingdom Overseas Territory remains a perceived contributor to political stability and financial integrity. The territory's insurance industry has experienced a period of rapid expansion and remains the most important component of the financial sector. Following a decline in the tourism sector in 2001, partly owing to the repercussions of the terrorist attacks on the USA in September, the Bermuda Alliance for Tourism launched a rebranding of Bermuda as a luxury destination, in order to attract higher-spending visitors. Against expectations, however, tourism expenditures continued to decline, in part owing to 'Hurricane Fabian', which caused several million Bermudian dollars-worth of damage in late 2003. Concerns were also raised over how much further the international business sector could expand without putting excessive strain on the local infrastructure. Furthermore, commentators regarded the islands' continuing heavy dependence on the tourism and 'offshore' finance sectors as potentially risky; in particular, discussion of changes to Bermuda's tax exemption laws resulted in several International Business Companies indicating their intentions to move to other regimes if financial conditions were to deteriorate. Bermuda was estimated to have the highest rate of GDP per head of anywhere in the world in 2007, at US $64,255. This was forecast to rise further, to $67,927 during 2008. However, with tourist arrivals from the important US market expected to decline owing to a contraction in that country's economy, and a decline in global hedge fund finance

UNITED KINGDOM OVERSEAS TERRITORIES

(which had supported Bermudian economic growth in recent years), the expansion of the economy was estimated to have reached only 2.5% in 2008. The ongoing impact of the global financial crisis meant that growth was forecast to remain at the same level in 2009. In the longer term, potential changes to the tax system have motivated numerous US businesses to relocate, subsequently reducing foreign investment and future growth potential.

Education

There is free compulsory education in government schools between the ages of five and 16 years, and a number of scholarships are awarded for higher education and teacher training. There are also seven private secondary schools which charge fees. In 2005/06 enrolment at secondary level institutions was equivalent to 84.5% of children in the relevant age-groups. The Bermuda College, founded in 1972, accepts students over the age of 16, and is the only post-secondary educational institution. Extramural degree courses are available through Queen's University, Canada, and Indiana and Maryland Universities, USA. A major programme to upgrade the education system, involving the establishment of five new primary and two secondary schools, was implemented between 1996 and 2002.

Public Holidays

2009: 1 January (New Year's Day), 10 April (Good Friday), 25 May (Bermuda Day), 30 July (Cup Match), 31 July (Somers' Day), 7 September (Labour Day), 13 October (Heroes' Day), 11 November (Remembrance Day), 25–28 December (Christmas).

2010: 1 January (New Year's Day), 2 April (Good Friday), 24 May (Bermuda Day), 29 July (Cup Match), 30 July (Somers' Day), 6 September (Labour Day), 13 October (Heroes' Day), 11 November (Remembrance Day), 25–27 December (Christmas).

Weights and Measures

The metric system has been widely adopted but imperial and US weights and measures are both used in certain fields.

Statistical Survey

Source: Dept of Statistics, POB HM 3015, Hamilton HM MX; tel. 297-7761; fax 295-8390; e-mail statistics@gov.bm; internet www.gov.bm.

AREA AND POPULATION

Area: 53.3 sq km (20.59 sq miles).

Population (civilian, non-institutional): 58,460 at census of 20 May 1991; 62,059 (males 29,802, females 32,257) at census of 20 May 2000. *Mid-2008* (estimate): 67,000 (Source: Pan American Health Organization).

Density (mid-2008): 1,257.0 per sq km.

Principal Towns (population at 1991 census): St George's 1,648; Hamilton (capital) 1,100.

Births, Marriages and Deaths (2002): Live births 830 (birth rate 13.4 per 1,000); Marriage rate 15.1 per 1,000; Deaths 404 (death rate 6.5 per 1,000). *2007:* Birth rate 11.3; Death rate 7.8 (Source: Pan American Health Organization).

Life Expectancy (years at birth, 2008): 78.3 (males 76.2; females 80.5). Source: Pan American Health Organization.

Employment (excluding unpaid family workers, 2008, preliminary data): Agriculture, forestry, fishing, mining and quarrying 718; Manufacturing 915; Electricity, gas and water 412; Construction 3,644; Wholesale and retail trade 4,708; Hotels and restaurants 4,938; Transport and communications 2,601; Financial intermediation 2,891; Real estate 623; Business activities 4,259; Public administration 4,223; Education, health and social services 3,287; Other community, social and personal services 2,148; International business activity 4,701; *Total employed* 40,068.

HEALTH AND WELFARE

Physicians (per 1,000 head, 2005): 2.1.

Hospital Beds (per 1,000 head, 2007): 5.0.

Health Expenditure (% of GDP, 2004): 4.3.

Health Expenditure (public, % of total, 1995): 53.2.

Source: partly Pan American Health Organization.

For other sources and definitions, see explanatory note on p. vi.

Bermuda

AGRICULTURE, ETC.

Principal Crops (metric tons, 2007, FAO estimates): Potatoes 1,100; Carrots and turnips 370; Vegetables and melons 2,935; Bananas 330.

Livestock (2007, FAO estimates): Cattle 600; Horses 900; Pigs 600.

Livestock Products (metric tons, 2007, FAO estimates): Cows' milk 1,350; Hen eggs 280.

Fishing (metric tons, live weight, 2006): Groupers 54; Snappers and jobfishes 33; Wahoo 86; Yellowfin tuna 31; Carangids 53; Caribbean spiny lobster 32; Total catch (incl. others) 380.

Source: FAO.

INDUSTRY

Electric Energy (production, million kWh): 664 in 2003; 661 in 2004; 665 in 2005. Source: UN, *Industrial Commodity Statistics Yearbook*.

FINANCE

Currency and Exchange Rates: 100 cents = 1 Bermuda dollar (B $). Sterling, US Dollar and Euro Equivalents (31 December 2008): £1 sterling = B $1.458; US $1 = B $1.000; €1 = B $1.392; B $100 = £68.60 = US $100.00 = €71.85. *Exchange Rate:* The Bermuda dollar is at par with the US dollar. Note: US and Canadian currencies are also accepted.

Budget (B $ million, 2008/09): Total current account revenue 985.3; Total current account expenditure 931.7. Note: Figures exclude interest on debt (21.5), sinking fund contribution (8.6), surplus available for capital expenditure (23.4) and capital expenditure (154.9).

Cost of Living (Consumer Price Index; base: 2000 = 100): All items 119.5 in 2006; 124.1 in 2007; 130.0 in 2008. Source: ILO.

Gross Domestic Product (US $ million at constant 1996 prices): 3,769.4 in 2005; 3,977.9 in 2006; 4,162.4 in 2007.

Expenditure on the Gross Domestic Product (B $ million at current prices, 2007, estimates): Government final consumption expenditure 748; Private final consumption expenditure 2,679; Gross fixed capital formation 1,343; Change in inventories 41; *Total domestic expenditure* 4,811; Exports of goods and services 2,469; *Less* Imports of goods and services 1,761; Statistical discrepancy 62; *GDP in purchasers' values* 5,581. Source: UN Statistics Division, National Accounts Main Aggregates Database.

Gross Domestic Product by Economic Activity (B $ million at current prices, 2007): Agriculture, forestry and fishing 45.0; Manufacturing 85.0; Electricity, gas and water 92.5; Construction and quarrying 322.5; Wholesale and retail trade and repair services 424.0; Restaurants and hotels 316.0; Transport and communications 322.4; Financial intermediation 823.0; Real estate and renting activities 821.7; Business activities 550.8; Public administration 285.7; Education, health and social work 353.8; Other community, social and personal services 113.7; International business activity 1,593.0; *Sub-total* 6,149.2; *Less* Imputed bank service charges 543.5; Indirect taxes, less subsidies 249.7; *GDP in purchasers' values* 5,855.4.

Balance of Payments (B $ million, 2006, estimates): Exports of goods f.o.b. 26; Imports of goods f.o.b. –1,094; *Trade Balance* –1,068; Exports of services 1,477; Imports of services –914; *Balance on goods and services* –505; Other income received 1,742; Other income paid –331; *Balance on goods, services and income* 906; Current transfers (net) –5; *Current balance* 901; Direct investment (net) –313; Portfolio investment (net) 407; Other investments (net) 1,339; Reserve assets (net) –10; *Overall balance* 2,324.

EXTERNAL TRADE

Principal Commodities (US $ million): *Imports* (2007): Food and live animals 135.2; Beverages and tobacco 55.0; Mineral fuels and lubricants 103.7 (Petroleum and petroleum products 100.9); Chemicals and related products 80.4 (Medicinal and pharmaceutical products 36.0); Basic manufactures 135.3; Machinery and transport equipment 270.3; Total (incl. others) 1,133.1. *Exports* (2003): Total 57.0.

Principal Trading Partners (US $ million, 2007): *Imports:* Canada 82.7; Caribbean countries 7.2; United Kingdom 26.8; USA 818.5; Total (incl. others) 1,133.1. *Exports* (1995): France 7.5; United Kingdom 3.9; USA 31.3; Total (incl. others) 62.9. *2003:* Total exports 57.

Source: partly UN, *International Trade Statistics Yearbook*.

UNITED KINGDOM OVERSEAS TERRITORIES

Bermuda

TRANSPORT

Road Traffic (vehicles in use, 2005): Private cars 21,978; Motorcycles 19,087; Buses, taxis and limousines 815; Trucks and tank wagons 4,058; Other 1,177; *Total* 47,115.

Shipping: *Ship Arrivals* (2004): Cruise ships 161; Cargo ships 186; Oil and gas tankers 21. *Merchant Fleet* (registered at 31 December 2007): 152; Total displacement 9,169,928 grt (Source: Lloyd's Register-Fairplay, *World Fleet Statistics*). *International Freight Traffic* ('000 metric tons, 1990): Goods loaded 130; Goods unloaded 470 (Source: UN, *Monthly Bulletin of Statistics*).

Civil Aviation (1999): Aircraft arrivals 6,024; Passengers 354,026; Air cargo 4,761,444 kg; Air mail 422,897 kg.

TOURISM

Visitor Arrivals: 635,272 (arrivals by air 298,973, cruise-ship passengers 336,299) in 2006; 659,572 (arrivals by air 305,548, cruise-ship passengers 354,024) in 2007; 577,839 (arrivals by air 291,431, cruise-ship passengers 286,408) in 2008.

Tourism Receipts (US $ million, incl. passenger transport): 426 in 2004; 429 in 2005; 508 in 2006. Source: World Tourism Organization.

COMMUNICATIONS MEDIA

Radio Receivers (1997): 82,000 in use.

Television Receivers (1999): 70,000 in use.

Telephones (2007): 57,700 main lines in use.

Mobile Cellular Telephones (2006): 60,100 subscribers.

Personal Computers (2002): 34,000 in use.

Internet Users (2007): 48,000.

Broadband Subscribers (2006): 23,600.

Daily Newspapers (2000): 1 (estimated circulation 17,700).

Non-daily Newspapers (2000): 2 (estimated circulation 11,600).

Sources: mainly UNESCO, *Statistical Yearbook*; UN, *Statistical Yearbook*; International Telecommunication Union.

EDUCATION

Pre-primary (1999, unless otherwise indicated): 12 schools (2006); 191 teachers; 429 pupils.

Primary: 17 (and 5 middle) schools (2006); 567 teachers (2005/06); 4,678 pupils (2005/06) (Source: partly UNESCO Institute for Statistics).

Senior (1999): 18 schools; 399 teachers; 2,335 pupils*.

Higher (2002): 1 institution; 544 students.

*Including six private schools.

2004: Local student enrolment 10,594 (government schools including pre-school 6,370, private schools excluding pre-school 3,512, Bermuda college 712); Teachers 1,310.

Adult Literacy Rate (UNESCO estimates): 99% (males 98%; females 99%) in 1998 (Source: UNESCO, *Statistical Yearbook*).

Directory

The Constitution

The Constitution, introduced on 8 June 1968 and amended in 1973 and 1979, contains provisions relating to the protection of fundamental rights and freedoms of the individual; the powers and duties of the Governor; the composition, powers and procedure of the Legislature; the Cabinet; the judiciary; the public service and finance.

The British monarch is represented by an appointed Governor, who retains responsibility for external affairs, defence, internal security and the police.

The Legislature consists of the monarch, the Senate and the House of Assembly. Three members of the Senate are appointed at the Governor's discretion, five on the advice of the Government leader and three on the advice of the Opposition leader. The Senate elects a President and Vice-President. The House of Assembly, consisting of 36 members elected under universal adult franchise, elects a Speaker and a Deputy Speaker, and sits for a five-year term.

The Cabinet consists of the Premier and at least six other members of the Legislature. The Governor appoints the majority leader in the House of Assembly as Premier, who in turn nominates the other members of the Cabinet. They are assigned responsibilities for government departments and other business and, in some cases, are assisted by Permanent Cabinet Secretaries.

The Cabinet is presided over by the Premier. The Governor's Council enables the Governor to consult with the Premier and two other members of the Cabinet nominated by the Premier on matters for which the Governor has responsibility. The Secretary to the Cabinet, who heads the public service, acts as secretary to the Governor's Council.

Voters must be British subjects aged 18 years or over (lowered from 21 years in 1990), and, if not possessing Bermudian status, must have been registered as electors on 1 May 1976. Candidates for election must qualify as electors, and must possess Bermudian status.

Under the British Overseas Territories Act, which entered into effect in May 2002, Bermudian citizens have the right to United Kingdom citizenship and the right of abode in the United Kingdom. British citizens do not enjoy reciprocal rights.

The Government

Governor and Commander-in-Chief: Sir RICHARD GOZNEY (took office 12 December 2007).

Deputy Governor: MARK ANDREW CAPES.

CABINET
(April 2009)

Premier and Minister of Tourism and Transport: Dr EWART FREDERICK BROWN.

Deputy Premier, Minister of Finance and Economic Development: PAULA A. COX.

Minister of Health: NELSON BASCOME.

Minister of the Environment and Sports: GLENN BLAKENEY.

Minister of Education: ELVIN JAMES.

Minister of Labour, Home Affairs and Housing: DAVID BURCH.

Minister of Energy, Telecommunications and E-Commerce: TERRY LISTER.

Minister of Works and Engineering: DERRICK BURGESS.

Minister of Culture and Social Rehabilitation: DALE D. BUTLER.

Attorney-General and Minister of Justice: Sen. KIM WILSON.

MINISTRIES

Office of the Governor: Government House, 11 Langton Hill, Pembroke HM 13; tel. 292-3600; fax 292-6831; e-mail depgov@ibl.bm; internet www.gov.bm.

Office of the Premier: Cabinet Office, Cabinet Bldg, 105 Front St, Hamilton HM 12; tel. 292-5501; fax 292-0304; e-mail premier@gov.bm; internet www.gov.bm.

Ministry of Culture and Social Rehabilitation: Melbourne House, Suite 304, 11 Parliament St, POB HM 788, Hamilton HM CX; tel. 296-1574; fax 295-2066; internet www.gov.bm.

Ministry of Education: Dundonald Pl., 14 Dundonald St, POB HM 1185, Hamilton HM EX; tel. 278-3300; fax 278-3348; internet www.moe.bm.

Ministry of Energy, Telecommunications and E-Commerce: F. B. Perry Bldg, 2nd Floor, 40 Church St, Hamilton HM 12; tel. 292-4595; fax 295-1462; e-mail gtelecom@gov.bm; internet www.mtec.bm.

Ministry of the Environment and Sports: Government Administration Bldg, 30 Parliament St, Hamilton HM 12; tel. 297-7590; internet www.gov.bm.

Ministry of Finance: Government Administration Bldg, 30 Parliament St, Hamilton HM 12; tel. 295-5151; fax 295-5727.

Ministry of Health: Continental Bldg, 25 Church St, Hamilton HM 12; tel. 278-4900; fax 292-2622; e-mail wjones@gov.bm; internet www.health.gov.bm.

Ministry of Justice and Attorney-General's Chambers: 1st Floor, Global House, 43 Church St, Hamilton HM 12; tel. 292-2463; fax 292-3608; e-mail agc@gov.bm.

Ministry of Labour, Home Affairs and Housing: Government Administration Bldg, 1st Floor, 30 Parliament St, Hamilton HM 12; tel. 297-7819; internet www.gov.bm.

Ministry of Tourism and Transport: Global House, 43 Church St, Hamilton HM 12; tel. 295-3130; fax 295-1013; e-mail clwhitter@gov.bm; internet www.gov.bm.

Ministry of Works and Engineering: General Post Office Bldg, 3rd Floor, 56 Church St, POB HM 525, Hamilton HM 12; tel. 297-

7699; fax 295-0170; e-mail nfox@bdagov.bm; internet www.wae.gov.bm.

Legislature

SENATE

President: CAROL ANN MARIE BASSETT.
Vice-President: Dr IDWAL WYN (WALWYN) HUGHES.
There are 11 nominated members.

HOUSE OF ASSEMBLY

Speaker: STANLEY W. LOWE.
Deputy Speaker: Dr JENNIFER M. SMITH.
Clerk to the Legislature: SHERNETTE WOLFE; tel. 292-7408; fax 292-2006; e-mail smwolffe@gov.bm.
General Election, 18 December 2007

Party	% of votes	Seats
Progressive Labour Party	52.5	22
United Bermuda Party	47.3	14
Total (incl. others)	100.0	36

Political Organizations

Progressive Labour Party (PLP): Alaska Hall, 16 Court St, POB 1367, Hamilton HM 17; tel. 292-2264; fax 295-7890; e-mail info@plp.bm; internet www.plp.bm; f. 1963; advocates the 'Bermudianization' of the economy, more equitable taxation, a more developed system of welfare and preparation for independence; Leader Dr EWART FREDERICK BROWN; Chair. DAVID BURT.

United Bermuda Party (UBP): Central Office, 3rd Floor, Bermudiana Arcade, 27 Queen St, Hamilton HM 11; tel. 295-0729; fax 292-7195; e-mail info@ubp.bm; internet www.ubp.bm; f. 1964; policy of participatory democracy, supporting system of free enterprise; Leader KIM SWAN; Chair. MICHAEL FAHY.

Judicial System

Chief Justice: RICHARD GROUND.
President of the Court of Appeal: EDWARD ZACCA.
Registrar of Supreme Court and Court of Appeal: MICHAEL J. MELLO.
Director of Public Prosecutions: RORY FIELD.

The Court of Appeal was established in 1964, with powers and jurisdiction of equivalent courts in other parts of the Commonwealth. The Supreme Court has jurisdiction over all serious criminal matters and has unlimited civil jurisdiction. The Court also hears civil and criminal appeals from the Magistrates' Courts. The three Magistrates' Courts have jurisdiction over all petty offences, and have a limited civil jurisdiction.

Religion

CHRISTIANITY

In 2000 it was estimated that 23% of the population were members of the Anglican Communion, 15% were Roman Catholics, 11% were African Methodist Episcopalians, 7% were Seventh-day Adventists and 4% were Wesleyan Methodists. The Presbyterian Church, the Baptist Church and the Pentecostal Church are also active in Bermuda.

The Anglican Communion

The Anglican Church of Bermuda consists of a single, extra-provincial diocese, directly under the metropolitan jurisdiction of the Archbishop of Canterbury, the Primate of All England. There are about 23,000 Anglicans and Episcopalians in Bermuda.

Bishop of Bermuda: Rt Rev. PATRICK WHITE, Bishop's Lodge, 18 Ferrar's Lane, Pembroke HM 08, POB HM 769, Hamilton HM CX; tel. 292-6987; fax 292-5421; internet www.anglican.bm.

The Roman Catholic Church

Bermuda forms a single diocese, suffragan to the archdiocese of Kingston in Jamaica. At 31 December 2006 there were an estimated 9,275 adherents in the territory. The Bishop participates in the Antilles Episcopal Conference (currently based in Port of Spain, Trinidad and Tobago).

Bishop of Hamilton in Bermuda: ROBERT JOSEPH KURTZ, 2 Astwood Rd, POB HM 1191, Hamilton HM EX; tel. 232-4414; fax 232-4447; e-mail rjkurtz@northrock.bm.

Protestant Churches

Baptist Church: Emmanuel Baptist Church, 35 Dundonald St, Hamilton HM 10; tel. 295-6555; fax 296-4491; Pastor RONALD K. SMITH.

Wesley Methodist Church: 41 Church St, Hamilton HM 12; tel. 292-0418; fax 295-9460; e-mail info@wesley.bm; internet www.wesley.bm; Rev. (vacant).

The Press

Bermuda Magazine: POB HM 283, Hamilton HM HX; tel. 295-0695; fax 295-8616; e-mail cbarclay@ibl.bm; f. 1990; quarterly; Editor-in-Chief CHARLES BARCLAY.

The Bermuda Sun: 19 Elliott St, POB HM 1241, Hamilton HM FX; tel. 295-3902; fax 292-5597; e-mail feedback@bermudasun.bm; internet www.bermudasun.bm; f. 1964; 2 a week; official govt gazette; Publr RANDY FRENCH; Editor TONY MCWILLIAM; circ. 12,500.

The Bermudian: 13 Addendum Lane, Pitt's Bay Rd, Pembroke HM 07; POB HM 283, Hamilton HM AX; tel. 232-7041; fax 232-7042; e-mail info@thebermudian.com; internet www.thebermudian.com; f. 1930; monthly; pictorial and lifestyle magazine; Editor TINA STEVENSON; circ. 7,500.

Bermudian Business Online: POB HM 283, Hamilton HM AX; tel. 232-7041; fax 232-7042; e-mail info@thebermudian.com; internet www.bermudianbusiness.com; f. 1996; publ. by The Bermudian Publishing Co Ltd; Publr TINA STEVENSON; circ. 2,500.

The Mid-Ocean News: 2 Par-la-Ville Rd, POB HM 1025, Hamilton HM DX; tel. 295-5881; fax 295-1513; e-mail thodgson@midoceannews.bm; internet www.midoceannews.bm; f. 1911; weekly with TV Guide; sister publication of The Royal Gazette; Editor TIM HODGSON; Man. Dir KEITH JENSEN; circ. 14,500.

Preview Bermuda: 19 Elliott St, POB HM 3273, Hamilton HM PX; tel. 292-4155; fax 292-4156; e-mail info@previewbermuda.com; internet www.previewbermuda.com; monthly magazine; caters to tourists and visitors to Bermuda; Publr JACKIE STEVENSON; circ. 15,000 per month.

The Royal Gazette: 2 Par-la-Ville Rd, POB HM 1025, Hamilton HM DX; tel. 295-5881; fax 292-2498; e-mail letters@royalgazette.bm; internet www.theroyalgazette.com; f. 1828; morning daily; incorporates The Colonist and Daily News (f. 1866); Editor WILLIAM J. ZUILL; Man. Dir KEITH JENSEN; circ. 17,500.

TV Week: 2 Par-la-Ville Rd, Hamilton HM 08; tel. 295-5881.

The Worker's Voice: 49 Union Sq., Hamilton HM 12; tel. 292-0044; fax 295-7992; e-mail biu@ibl.bm; fortnightly; organ of the Bermuda Industrial Union; Editor Dr B. B. BALL.

Publisher

Bermudian Publishing Co Ltd: POB HM 283, Hamilton HM AX; tel. 232-7041; fax 232-7042; e-mail info@thebermudian.com; internet www.thebermudian.com; social sciences, sociology, sports; Editor (vacant).

Broadcasting and Communications

TELECOMMUNICATIONS

Bermuda Digital Communications: 22 Reid St, Hamilton HM 11; tel. 296-4010; fax 296-4020; e-mail info@bdc.bm; internet www.bdc.bm; f. 1998; mobile cellular telephone operator; Chair. and CEO KURT EVE.

Bermuda Telephone Co (BTC): 30 Victoria St, POB 1021, Hamilton HM DX; tel. 295-1001; fax 295-1192; e-mail customersupport@btc.bm; internet www.btc.bm; f. 1987; Pres. and CEO FRANCIS R. MUSSENDEN.

Cable & Wireless (Bermuda) Ltd: 1 Middle Rd, Smith's FL 03, POB HM 151, Hamilton HM AX; tel. 497-7000; fax 297-7159; e-mail helpdesk@bda.cwplc.com; internet www.cw.com/bermuda; new fibre-optic submarine cable, 'Gemini Bermuda', to replace satellite dish in October 2007 as facilitator of Cable & Wireless' global communications services; CEO EDDIE SAINTS.

Digicel Bermuda: Washington Mall, 22 Church St, Phase II, POB 896, Hamilton HM 11; tel. 500-5000; fax 295-3235; e-mail info.bermuda@digicelgroup.com; internet www.digicelbermuda.com; f. 2005; Country Man. WAYNE MICHAEL CAINES.

TeleBermuda International Ltd (TBI): Bermuda Monetary House, 2nd Floor, 43 Victoria St, Hamilton HM 12; POB HM 3043, Hamilton HM NX; tel. 296-9000; fax 296-9010; e-mail save@

telebermuda.com; internet www.telebermuda.com; f. 1997; a division of GlobeNet Communications, provides an international service; owns a fibre-optic network connecting Bermuda and the USA; Pres. and CEO GREGORY SWAN.

BROADCASTING
Radio

Bermuda Broadcasting Co: POB HM 452, Hamilton HM BX; tel. 295-2828; fax 295-4282; e-mail zbmzfb@bermudabroadcasting.com; f. 1982 as merger of ZBM (f. 1943) and ZFB (f. 1962); operates 4 radio stations; Man. Dir ULRIC P. (RICK) RICHARDSON; Comptroller MALCOLM R. FLETCHER.

DeFontes Broadcasting Co Ltd (VSB): POB HM 1450, Hamilton HM FX; tel. 292-0050; fax 295-1658; e-mail mbishop@vsbbermuda.com; internet www.vsbbermuda.com; f. 1981 as St George's Broadcasting Co; commercial; 4 radio stations; Pres. KENNETH DEFONTES; Station Man. MIKE BISHOP.

Television

Bermuda Broadcasting Co: see Radio; operates 2 TV stations (Channels 7 and 9).

Bermuda Cablevision Ltd: 19 Laffan St, POB 1642, Hamilton HM GX; tel. 292-5544; fax 295-3023; e-mail info@cablevision.bm; internet www.cablevision.bm; f. 1988; 180 channels; Pres. DAVID LINES; Gen. Man. TERRY ROBERSON.

DeFontes Broadcasting Co Ltd (VSB): see Radio; operates 1 TV station.

Finance
(cap. = capital; res = reserves; dep. = deposits; m. = million; brs = branches; amounts in Bermuda dollars)

BANKING
Central Bank

Bermuda Monetary Authority: BMA House, 43 Victoria St, Hamilton HM 12; tel. 295-5278; fax 292-7471; e-mail info@bma.bm; internet www.bma.bm; f. 1969; central issuing and monetary authority; cap. 20.0m., res 18.7m., total assets 165.3m. (Dec. 2006); Chair. ALAN F. RICHARDSON; CEO MATTHEW ELDERFIELD.

Commercial Banks

Bank of Bermuda Ltd: 6 Front St, POB HM 1020, Hamilton HM DX; tel. 299-5613; fax 299-6559; e-mail kim.l.wheddon@bob.hsbc.com; internet www.bankofbermuda.bm; f. 1889; 100% acquired by HSBC Asia Holdings BV (Netherlands) in Feb. 2004; cap. 29.0m., res 390.4m., dep. 10,165.2m. (Dec. 2002); CEO PHILIP BUTTERFIELD; COO MICHAEL COLLINS; 6 brs.

Bank of N. T. Butterfield & Son Ltd: 65 Front St, POB HM 195, Hamilton HM 12; tel. 295-1111; fax 292-4365; e-mail contact@bntb.bm; internet www.bankofbutterfield.com; f. 1858; inc. 1904; cap. 29.9m., res 442.8m., dep. 10,042.8m. (Dec. 2006); Chair. ROBERT MULDERIG; Pres. and CEO ALAN R. THOMPSON; 5 brs.

Bermuda Commercial Bank Ltd: Bermuda Commercial Bank Bldg, 19 Par-la-Ville Rd, POB 1748, Hamilton HM GX; tel. 295-5678; fax 295-8091; e-mail enquiries@bcb.bm; internet www.bermuda-bcb.com; f. 1969; cap. 10.5m., res 11.3m., dep. 555.5m. (Dec. 2007); COO HORST E. FINKBEINER, II; Chief Financial Officer GREG REID.

STOCK EXCHANGE

Bermuda Stock Exchange: 3rd Floor, Washington Mall, Church St, Hamilton HM FX; tel. 292-7212; fax 292-7619; e-mail info@bsx.com; internet www.bsx.com; f. 1971; 427 listed equities, funds, debt issues and depositary programmes; Chair. DAVID BROWN; Pres. and CEO GREG WOJCIECHOWSKI.

INSURANCE

Bermuda had a total of some 1,600 registered insurance companies in 2002, the majority of which are subsidiaries of foreign insurance companies, or owned by foreign industrial or financial concerns. Many of them have offices on the island.

Insurance Information Office: Cedarpark Centre, 48 Cedar Ave, POB HM 2911, Hamilton HM LX; tel. 292-9829; fax 295-3532; e-mail biminfo@bii.bm; internet www.bermuda-insurance.org; division of the Bermuda Insurance Development Council; Dir DAVID FOX.

Major Companies

ACE Bermuda: ACE Global HQ, 17 Woodbourne Ave, POB HM 1015, Hamilton HM DX; tel. 295-5200; fax 298-9620; e-mail info@acebermuda.com; internet www.acebermuda.com; total revenue $14,154m. (Dec. 2007); Pres. and CEO G. REES FLETCHER; Chair. EVAN G. GREENBERG; Regional Exec. ALLISON TOWLSON.

Argus Insurance Co Ltd: Argus Insurance Bldg, 12 Wesley St, POB HM 1064, Hamilton HM EX; tel. 295-2021; fax 292-6763; e-mail insurance@argus.bm; internet www.argus.bm; Pres. and CEO GERALD D. E. SIMONS; Chair. JAMES A. C. KING.

Bermuda Insurance Development Council (IDC): c/o Bermuda Insurance Institute, The Cedar Parkade Bldg, 48 Cedar Ave, POB HM 2911, Hamilton HM LX; tel. 292-9829; fax 296-3840; e-mail fox@bii.bm; internet www.bermuda-insurance.org; Chair. ROGER GILLETT.

Bermuda Insurance Management Association (BIMA): POB HM 1752, Hamilton HM GX; tel. 295-4864; fax 292-7375; manages over 1,200 insurance and reinsurance cos; liaises with govt and other financial orgs with regard to insurance industry issues; Pres. PHILIP BARNES.

Paumanock Insurance Co Ltd: POB HM 2267, Hamilton HM JX; tel. 292-2404; fax 292-2648.

X. L. Insurance Co Ltd: 1 Bermudiana Rd, Hamilton HM 11; tel. 292-8515; fax 292-5226; e-mail info@xl.bm; internet www.xlinsurance.com; CEO MICHAEL S. MCGAVICK.

Trade and Industry
GOVERNMENT AGENCY

Bermuda Registrar of Companies: Government Administration Bldg, 30 Parliament St, Hamilton HM HX; tel. 297-7530; fax 292-6640; e-mail jfsmith@gov.bm; internet www.roc.gov.bm; Registrar of Companies STEPHEN LOWE.

DEVELOPMENT ORGANIZATION

Bermuda Small Business Development Corpn: POB HM 637, Hamilton HM CX; tel. 292-5570; fax 295-1600; e-mail bdasmallbusiness@gov.bm; internet www.bsbdc.bm; f. 1980; funded jtly by the Govt and private banks; guarantees loans to small businesses; Gen. Man. MICHELLE KHALDUN.

CHAMBER OF COMMERCE

Bermuda Chamber of Commerce: 1 Point Pleasant Rd, POB HM 655, Hamilton HM CX; tel. 295-4201; fax 292-5779; e-mail info@bermudacommerce.com; internet www.bermudacommerce.com; f. 1907; Pres. PHILIP BARNETT; Exec. Vice-Pres. DIANE GORDON; 750 mems.

INDUSTRIAL AND TRADE ASSOCIATION

Bermuda International Business Association (BIBA): Cedar House, Ground Floor, 20 Victoria St, Hamilton HM 12; tel. 292-0632; fax 292-1797; e-mail info@biba.org; internet www.biba.org; Chair. VICKI COELHO; CEO CHERYL PACKWOOD.

EMPLOYERS' ASSOCIATIONS

Bermuda Employers' Council: Reid House, Ground Floor, 31 Church St, Hamilton HM 12; tel. 295-5070; fax 295-1966; e-mail twarner@bec.bm; internet www.bec.bm; f. 1960; advisory body on employment and labour relations; Pres. WILLIAM DESILVA; Exec. Dir MARTIN LAW; 420 mems.

Construction Association of Bermuda: POB HM 238, Hamilton HM AX; tel. 292-0633; fax 292-0564; e-mail administrator@constructionassociationofbermuda.com; internet www.constructionbermuda.com; f. 1968; Pres. ALEX M. DECOUTO; 90 mems.

Hotel Employers of Bermuda: c/o Bermuda Hotel Asscn, 'Carmel', 61 King St, Hamilton HM 19; tel. 295-2127; fax 292-6671; e-mail johnh@ibl.bm; f. 1968; Pres. FRANK STOCEK; CEO JOHN HARVEY; 8 mems.

UTILITY

BELCO Holdings Ltd: 27 Serpentine Rd, POB HM 1026, Hamilton HM DX; tel. 295-5111; fax 292-8975; e-mail info@belco.bhl.bm; internet www.belcoholdings.bm; f. 1906; holding co for Bermuda Electric Light Co Ltd, and Bermuda Gas and Utility Co Ltd; Chair. J. MICHAEL COLLIER; Pres. and CEO A. L. VINCENT INGHAM.

TRADE UNIONS

In 2007 trade union membership was estimated at approximately 9,140. There are nine registered trade unions, eight of which profess membership of the Bermuda Trades Union Congress.

Bermuda Industrial Union: 49 Union Sq., Hamilton HM 12; tel. 292-0044; fax 295-7992; e-mail biu@biu.bm; f. 1946; Pres. CHRIS FURBERT; Gen. Sec. HELENA BURGESS; 5,202 mems.

UNITED KINGDOM OVERSEAS TERRITORIES

Bermuda Trades Union Congress (BTUC): POB 2080, Hamilton HM HX; tel. 292-6515; fax 292-0697; e-mail mcharles@but.bm; Pres. ANTHONY WOLFFE; Gen. Sec. MICHAEL CHARLES; principal mems of the BTUC include:

Bermuda Federation of Musicians and Variety Artists: Reid St, POB HM 6, Hamilton HM AX; tel. 291-0138; Sec.-Gen. LLOYD H. L. SIMMONS; 318 mems.

Bermuda Public Services Union: POB HM 763, Hamilton HM CX; tel. 292-6985; fax 292-1149; e-mail osimmons@bpsu.bm; internet www.bpsu.bm; re-formed 1961; Pres. ARMELL L. THOMAS; Gen. Sec. EDWARD G. BALL, Jr; 3,454 mems.

Bermuda Union of Teachers: POB HM 726, Hamilton HM CX; tel. 292-6515; fax 292-0697; e-mail butunion@ibl.bm; internet www.but.bm; f. 1919; Pres. LISA TROTT; Gen. Sec. MICHAEL A. CHARLES; 700 mems.

Transport

ROADS

There are some 225 km (140 miles) of public highways and 222 km of private roads, with almost 6 km reserved for cyclists and pedestrians. Each household is permitted only one passenger vehicle, and visitors may only hire mopeds, to limit traffic congestion.

SHIPPING

The chief port of Bermuda is Hamilton, with a secondary port at St George's. Both are used by freight and cruise ships. There is also a 'free' port, Freeport, on Ireland Island. In 2000 it was proposed to enlarge Hamilton docks in order to accommodate larger cruise ships. There remained, however, fears that such an enlargement would place excessive strain on the island's environment and infrastructure. Bermuda is a free-flag nation, and at December 2007 the shipping register comprised 152 vessels, totalling 9,169,928 grt.

Department of Marine and Ports Services: POB HM 180, Hamilton HM AX; tel. 295-6575; fax 295-5523; e-mail marineports@bolagov.bm; Dir of Marine and Ports Services FRANCIS RICHARDSON; Deputy Dir and Harbour Master MICHAEL DOLDING.

Department of Maritime Administration: Magnolia Pl., 2nd Floor, 45 Victoria St, POB HM 1628, Hamilton HM GX; tel. 295-7251; fax 295-3718; e-mail maradros@gov.bm; Chief Surveyor DUNCAN CURRIE; Registrar of Shipping ANGELIQUE BURGESS.

Principal Shipping Companies

B & H Ocean Carriers Ltd: Par-la-Ville Pl., 3rd Floor, 14 Par-la-Ville Rd, POB HM 2257, Hamilton HM JX; tel. 295-6875; fax 295-6796; e-mail info@bhcousa.com; internet www.bhocean.com; f. 1987; Chair. MICHAEL S. HUDNER.

Benor Tankers Ltd: Cedar House, 41 Cedar Ave, Hamilton HM 12; Pres. CARL-ERIK HAAVALDSEN; Chair. HARRY RUTTEN.

Bermuda Forwarders Ltd: 2 Mills Creek Park, POB HM 511, Hamilton HM CX; tel. 292-4600; fax 292-1859; e-mail info@bermudaforwarders.com; internet www.bermudaforwarders.com; international import and export handlers; Pres. TOBY KEMPE.

Bermuda Shipping Ltd: Waverley Bldg, 35 Church St, Hamilton HM 12; tel. 296-9798; fax 295-4556; e-mail meyershipping@ibl.bm; internet www.meyer.bm; f. 1867; CEO J. HENRY HAYWARD.

BEST Shipping: 6 Addendum Lane South, POB HM 335, Hamilton HM BX; tel. 292-8080; fax 295-1713; e-mail dsousa@best.bm; internet www.best.bm; f. 1987 as Bermuda Export Sea Transfer Ltd; sea and air freight services; Pres. and Man. Dir DAVID SOUSA.

Container Ship Management Ltd: 14 Par-la-Ville Rd, POB HM 2266, Hamilton HM JX; tel. 295-1624; fax 295-3781; e-mail csm@csm.bm; internet www.bcl.bm/csm; Pres. GEOFFREY FRITH.

Dorchester Atlantic Marine Limited Partnership: Richmond House, 12 Par-la-Ville Rd, POB HM 2089, Hamilton HM HX; tel. 295-0614; fax 292-1549; e-mail contact@dorchesteratlantic.com; internet www.dorchesteratlantic.com; f. 1970; fmrly Atlantic Marine Limited Partnership; Man. Dir JENS ALERS.

Gearbulk Holding Ltd: Par-la-Ville Pl., 14 Par-la-Ville Rd, Hamilton HM JX; tel. 295-2184; fax 295-2234; internet www.gearbulk.com; f. 1968; Pres. ARTHUR E. M. JONES.

Golden Ocean Management: Par-la-Ville Pl., 14 Par-la-Ville Rd, POB HM 1593, Hamilton HM 08; tel. 295-6935; fax 295-3494; internet www.goldenocean.no; Chair. and Pres. JOHN FREDRIKSON.

Norwegian Cruise Line: 3rd Floor, Reid House, Church St, POB 1564, Hamilton; internet www.ncl.com; Chair. EINAR KLOSTER.

Shell Bermuda (Overseas) Ltd: Shell House, Ferry Reach, POB 2, St George's 1.

Unicool Ltd: POB HM 1179, Hamilton HM EX; tel. 295-2244; fax 292-8666; Pres. MATS JANSSON.

Worldwide Shipping Ltd: 22 Church St, Suite 412, POB HM 1862, Hamilton HM 11; tel. 295-3770; fax 295-3801.

CIVIL AVIATION

The former US Naval Air Station (the only airfield) was returned to the Government of Bermuda in September 1995, following the closure of the base and the withdrawal of US forces from the islands. Bermuda does not have its own airline. From May 2006 the island was served by the low-cost US airline JetBlue, in addition to other British, Canadian and US airlines.

Department of Civil Aviation: POB GE 218, St George's GE BX; tel. 293-1640; fax 293-2417; e-mail info@dca.gov.bm; internet www.dca.gov.bm; responsible for all civil aviation matters; Dir of Civil Aviation THOMAS DUNSTAN.

Bermuda International Airport: 3 Cahow Way, St George's GE CX; tel. 293-2470; e-mail dao@gov.bm; internet www.bermudaairport.com; Gen. Man. AARON ADDERLEY.

Tourism

Tourism is the principal industry of Bermuda and is government-sponsored. The great attractions of the islands are the climate, scenery, and facilities for outdoor entertainment of all types. In 2007 a total of 659,572 tourists (including 354,024 cruise-ship passengers) visited Bermuda. In 2006 the industry earned an estimated US $508m. In 2006 there were 56 licensed hotels, 2,824 rooms and 5,698 beds; government projections were for 65 licensed hotels, 4,229 rooms and 8,870 beds to be available by the end of 2009.

Bermuda Department of Tourism: Global House, 43 Church St; tel. 292-0023; fax 292-7537; e-mail webmaster@bermudatourism.com; internet www.bermudatourism.com; Dir of Tourism BILLY GRIFFITH.

Bermuda Hotel Association: 'Carmel', 61 King St, Hamilton HM 19; tel. 295-2127; fax 292-6671; e-mail johnh@ibl.bm; internet www.experiencebermuda.com; Chair. MICHAEL WINFIELD; Exec. Dir JOHN HARVEY; 37 mem. hotels.

THE BRITISH ANTARCTIC TERRITORY

The British Antarctic Territory lies within the Antarctic Treaty area (i.e. south of latitude 60° S). The Territory, created by an Order in Council which came into force on 3 March 1962, consists of all islands and territories south of latitude 60° S, between longitudes 20° W and 80° W, and includes the South Orkney Islands, the South Shetland Islands, the Antarctic Peninsula and areas south and east of the Weddell Sea. With the island of South Georgia and the South Sandwich Islands (now forming a separate territory, q.v.), this area had been constituted by the United Kingdom as the Falkland Islands Dependencies in 1908. The flag of the British Antarctic Territory (proportions 1 by 2) has a white field bearing the union flag of the United Kingdom in the canton and, in the centre of the fly half of the flag, the arms of the territory, which consists of a white shield with three wavy blue horizontal lines at the top overlapped by a red triangle, apex downwards, bearing a brown and yellow torch with red-bordered yellow flames framed by golden rays, the shield supported by a golden lion and a black and white penguin with a yellow throat, both supporters surmounted by a scroll of yellow and light blue with a red reverse and the red inscription 'Research and Discovery'; above the shield, a helmet of grey, light blue and white supporting a torse, alternately of white and light blue, is depicted below a sailing ship of black flying the British Blue Ensign at the gaff. The Territory has its own legal system and postal administration, and is financially self-sufficient owing to revenue derived from income tax and the sale of postage stamps.

Area: Land covers about 1,709,400 sq km (660,003 sq miles).

Population: There is no permanent population, but scientists and support personnel staff the British Antarctic Survey stations. *2005/06:* Summer 200 (Rothera 148, Halley 37, Signy 15); Winter 37.

Commissioner, Head of Overseas Territories Directorate: COLIN ROBERTS, Overseas Territories Directorate, Foreign and Commonwealth Office, King Charles St, London, SW1A 2AH, United Kingdom; tel. (20) 7008-2743; internet www.fco.gov.uk.

Administrator: ROB BOWMAN, Polar Regions Unit, Overseas Territories Directorate, Foreign and Commonwealth Office, King Charles St, London, SW1A 2AH, United Kingdom; tel. (20) 7008-2617; fax (20) 7008-2086.

British Antarctic Survey: High Cross, Madingley Rd, Cambridge, CB3 0ET, United Kingdom; tel. (1223) 221400; fax (1223) 362616; e-mail basweb@bas.ac.uk; internet www.antarctica.ac.uk; f. 1962 to replace Falkland Islands Dependencies Surveyresponsible for almost all British scientific activities in Antarctica; operates two ice-strengthened ocean-going vessels (RRS *Ernest Shackleton* and RRS *James Clark Ross*), four de Havilland Twin Otter and one Dash-7 aircraft; Total Budget £61.4m. in 2007/08; Dir Prof. NICHOLAS OWENS.

RESEARCH STATIONS

	Latitude	Longitude
Halley	75° 35′ S	26° 34′ W
Rothera	67° 34′ S	68° 08′ W
Signy (summer only)	60° 43′ S	45° 36′ W

THE BRITISH INDIAN OCEAN TERRITORY (BIOT)

The British Indian Ocean Territory (BIOT) was formed in November 1965, through the amalgamation of the former Seychelles islands of Aldabra, Desroches and Farquhar with the Chagos Archipelago, a group of islands 1,930 km north-east of Mauritius, previously administered by the Governor of Mauritius. Aldabra, Desroches and Farquhar were ceded to Seychelles when that country was granted independence in June 1976. Since then BIOT has comprised only the Chagos Archipelago, including the coral atoll Diego Garcia, with a total land area of 60 sq km (23 sq miles), together with a surrounding area of some 54,400 sq km (21,000 sq miles) of ocean.

BIOT was established to meet British and US defence requirements in the Indian Ocean. Following the purchase of the islands by the British Crown in 1967, the coconut plantations (production of copra was previously the principal economic function of the islands) ceased to operate and the inhabitants were offered the choice of resettlement in Mauritius or in Seychelles. The majority (which numbered about 1,200) went to Mauritius, the resettlement taking place during 1969–73, prior to the construction of the military facility. Mauritius subsequently campaigned for the immediate return of the Territory, and received support from the Organization of African Unity (now the African Union) and from India. A protracted dispute with the United Kingdom over compensation for those displaced ended in 1982 when the British Government agreed to an *ex-gratia* payment of £4m. In July 2000 a judicial review of the validity of the Immigration Ordinance of 1971, under which the islanders were removed from BIOT, and which continued to prevent them from resettling in the Territory, was instigated. Meanwhile, in March 1999 it was disclosed that the displaced islanders and their families, then estimated to number up to 4,000, were not to be included in the offer of full British citizenship with the right of abode in the United Kingdom, that was to be extended to residents of other United Kingdom Overseas Territories by legislation pending in the British Parliament.

In November 2000 the British High Court ruled that the Chagos islanders (Ilois) had been illegally evicted from the Chagos Archipelago, and quashed Section 4 of the 1971 Ordinance, which prevented the return of the Ilois to BIOT. During the case it transpired that the British Government had received a subsidy of US $11m. on the purchase of Polaris submarines in the 1960s from the USA, in return for the lease of Diego Garcia for the US military. Furthermore, the Government had apparently termed the Ilois 'contract workers' in order to persuade the UN that the islanders were not an indigenous population with democratic rights. However, memorandums of the Foreign and Commonwealth Office revealed government knowledge of some of the Ilois living in the Chagos Archipelago for two generations. The British Secretary of State for Foreign and Commonwealth Affairs declined an appeal, thereby granting the islanders an immediate right to return to BIOT. Despite this, a new ordinance, issued in January 2001, allowed the residents to return to any of the islands in the Archipelago, except Diego Garcia, easing US fears of a population near its military base. The British Overseas Territories Act came into effect in May 2002, allowing the displaced islanders to apply for British citizenship. At that time the British Government was also examining the feasibility of a return to the Chagos Archipelago for the islanders, who continued to seek compensation. In October 2003 the High Court ruled that although the islanders could claim to have been ill-treated, the British Government had not known at the time that its actions were unlawful and their claims for compensation were dismissed. Many of the islanders subsequently moved to the United Kingdom.

In December 2000 the Ilois announced their intention to sue the US Government for US $6,000m. in compensation. The hearing of the case, in which the Ilois alleged genocide, torture and forced relocation, opened in December 2001. In mid-2002 the Chagos islanders initiated legal action against the recruitment consultancy that supplies civilian employees for the US naval base on Diego Garcia, alleging that the company had discriminated against them when appointing staff to the base; the consultancy was the first of 12 entities that the islanders intended to sue in the USA. (In April 2006 the US Federal Court of Appeals of the District of Columbia ruled that it had no authority to order compensation to those evicted in order to make way for the establishment of a US military base on Diego Garcia.)

In June 2004 the British Government issued two decrees explicitly stating the country's control of immigration services within the archipelago and banning the Ilois from returning. Nevertheless, in November the Chagossian group reached agreement for some 100 people to travel to Diego Garcia for the purpose of visiting the graves of relatives. In early April 2006 102 Chagossians commenced a visit to the archipelago. On 11 May the British High Court ruled that the exclusion of the islanders from their territory was irrational and unlawful. The British Government commenced proceedings to overturn the May ruling at the Court of Appeal in February 2007; however, in May that court confirmed that the residents of the Chagos Archipelago had been unlawfully removed and upheld the displaced islanders' immediate right to return. In November the House of Lords granted the British Government the right to appeal against the Court of Appeal's decision, on the condition that the Chagossian's costs were met by the British Government. The appeal was heard in mid-2008 and in November the House of Lords ruled in favour of the British Government, thus denying the Chagossians the right to return, and citing as its main reason the fact that the United Kingdom would have been obliged to meet the costs of economic, social and educational advancement of the residents. The ruling also stated that fair compensation had been agreed and paid, and that the British Government had no further obligations towards the Chagossians. Having exhausted the appeals process in the United Kingdom, the Chagossians announced that they would take their case to the European Court of Human Rights. It was estimated that only approximately 500 of the 2,000 deported during the 1960s and 1970s were still alive.

A 1966 agreement between the United Kingdom and the USA provided for BIOT to be used by both countries over an initial period of 50 years, with the option of extending this for a further 20 years. The United Kingdom undertook to cede the Chagos Archipelago to Mauritius when it was no longer required for defence purposes. Originally the US military presence was limited to a communications centre on Diego Garcia. In 1972, however, construction of a naval support facility was begun, apparently in response to the expansion of the Soviet maritime presence in the Indian Ocean. Diego Garcia has frequently been used as a base for US aircraft, carrying out air strikes on Iraq and Afghanistan. In March–April 2003 the base was used to launch bombing raids on Iraq in the US-led military campaign to oust the regime of Saddam Hussain. In February 2008 the British Secretary of State for the Foreign and Commonwealth Office admitted that, contrary to previous government statements, a number of so-called rendition flights (the transfer of detainees, in particular terrorist suspects, by the US Central Intelligence Agency to third countries where it was possible that they might be subjected to torture during interrogation) had used facilities at Diego Garcia.

In December 2000, following the British High Court's ruling, Mauritius again staked its claim for sovereignty over the Chagos Archipelago. In April 2004 Paul Bérenger, the recently installed Prime Minister of Mauritius, renewed the campaign to reclaim sovereignty after specialists in international law advised him that the decree by which the United Kingdom separated the Chagos Archipelago from Mauritius was illegal. An attempt was made to block the Mauritian Government from pursuing the case at the International Court of Justice on the basis of a long-standing ruling, whereby members of the Commonwealth could not take the United Kingdom to court; in July the ruling was extended to former members of the Commonwealth, in order to prevent Mauritius from circumventing the obstacle by withdrawing from that organization. Mauritius announced that it would pursue the matter at the General Assembly of the UN.

The civil administration of BIOT is the responsibility of a non-resident commissioner in the Foreign and Commonwealth Office in

UNITED KINGDOM OVERSEAS TERRITORIES

London, United Kingdom, represented on Diego Garcia by a Royal Navy commander and a small British naval presence. A chief justice, a senior magistrate and a principal legal adviser (who performs the functions of an attorney-general) are resident in the United Kingdom.

Land Area: about 60 sq km.

Population: There are no permanent inhabitants. In November 2004 there were about 4,000 US and British military personnel and civilian support staff stationed in the Territory.**Currency:** The official currency is the pound sterling, but the US dollar is also accepted.

Commissioner: COLIN ROBERTSHead of Overseas Territories Dept, Foreign and Commonwealth Office, King Charles St, London SW1A 2AH, United Kingdom; tel. (20) 7008-2890.

Administrator: JOANNE YEADONOverseas Territories Dept, Foreign and Commonwealth Office, King Charles St, London SW1A 2AH, United Kingdom; tel. (20) 7008-2890.

Commissioner's Representative: Commdr NEIL HINCH, RN, Diego Garcia, c/o BFPO Ships.

THE BRITISH VIRGIN ISLANDS

Introductory Survey

Location, Climate, Language, Religion, Flag, Capital

The British Virgin Islands consist of more than 60 islands and cays, of which only 16 are inhabited. The islands, most of which are mountainous and of volcanic origin (the only exception of any size is the coralline island of Anegada), lie at the northern end of the Leeward Islands, about 100 km (62 miles) to the east of Puerto Rico and adjoining the United States Virgin Islands. The climate is subtropical but extremes of heat are relieved by the trade winds. The average annual rainfall is 1,000 mm (39 ins). The official language is English. Most of the inhabitants profess Christianity. The flag is the British 'Blue Ensign', with the territory's badge (a green shield, with a white-clad virgin and 12 oil lamps, above a scroll bearing the motto 'vigilate') in the fly. The capital, Road Town, is situated on the island of Tortola.

Recent History

Previously peopled by Caribs, and named by the navigator Christopher Colombus after St Ursula and her 11,000 fellow-martyrs, the islands were settled by buccaneers and the Dutch, but were finally annexed by the British in 1672. In 1872 they became part of the British colony of the Leeward Islands, which was administered under a federal system. The federation was dissolved in July 1956, but the Governor of the Leeward Islands continued to administer the British Virgin Islands until 1960, when an appointed Administrator (restyled Governor in 1971) assumed direct responsibility. Unlike the other Leeward Islands, the British Virgin Islands did not join the Federation of the West Indies (1958–62), preferring to develop its links with the US Virgin Islands.

A new Constitution was introduced in April 1967, when H. Lavity Stoutt became the islands' first Chief Minister. He was later replaced by Willard Wheatley. At an election in September 1975 Stoutt's Virgin Islands Party (VIP) and the United Party (UP) each won three of the seven elective seats on the Legislative Council. Wheatley, sitting as an independent member, held the balance of power and he continued in office, with Stoutt as Deputy Chief Minister.

An amended Constitution took effect in June 1977, giving more extensive internal self-government; some electoral changes were also made (see Constitution). In the first election to the enlarged Legislative Council to take place under the new Constitution, in November 1979, independent candidates won five of the nine elective seats, with the VIP winning the remainder. Stoutt secured enough support to be reinstated as Chief Minister. In the November 1983 election the VIP and the UP each secured four seats. The one successful independent candidate, Cyril Romney, became Chief Minister and formed a coalition Government with members of the UP.

In August 1986 the Governor dissolved the Legislative Council six days before a scheduled council debate on a motion of no confidence against Romney (who had allegedly been involved with a company under investigation by the British police and the US Department of Justice's Drug Enforcement Administration). At a general election in the following month the VIP won five of the nine elective seats, with the UP and independent candidates (including Romney) taking two seats each. Stoutt was appointed Chief Minister.

The Deputy Chief Minister, Omar Hodge, was dismissed from the Executive Council in March 1988, following an official inquiry into allegations of financial malpractice (he continued to protest his innocence, and won a libel suit in January 1990). Hodge was replaced by Ralph O'Neal, formerly leader of the UP, who joined the VIP.

At a general election in November 1990 the VIP increased its majority, while the UP lost both its seats. Stoutt retained the post of Chief Minister.

The principal concern of the Stoutt administration in the early 1990s was the trade in, and increasing local use of, illicit drugs. In late 1990 the Stoutt administration introduced legislation to impose more stringent regulations governing the 'offshore' financial sector, while plans to review immigration policy were under discussion, in an attempt to reduce the number of illegal immigrants entering the territory. Both areas had previously been considered to be insufficiently protected from exploitation by traffickers seeking to introduce illicit drugs into the islands or to divert funds from their sale through the financial sector.

In August 1993 the British Government appointed three commissioners to review the territory's Constitution at the request of the Legislative Council. Proposed changes included the introduction of direct elections for the position of Chief Minister, the enlargement of the Legislative Council and the adoption of a bill of rights. The British Government's decision in early 1994 to accept the commission's proposal to enlarge the Legislative Council to 13 seats (by the creation of four seats representing the territory 'at large') was strongly criticized by Stoutt. His opposition to the changes intensified in July, when he failed to obtain a deferral of the decision in order that the Legislative Council could debate the issue. Discussions on various recommendations in the review continued in 1995 and 1996.

At elections to the newly enlarged legislature on 20 February 1995 the VIP won six seats, the UP and the Concerned Citizens' Movement (CCM—formerly IPM) each secured two seats and independent candidates won the remaining three seats. One of the successful independents, Alvin Christopher, subsequently gave his support to the VIP, thus providing the party with the majority required to form a Government, again headed by Stoutt. However, in May the Deputy Chief Minister, Ralph O'Neal, was appointed Chief Minister, following the sudden death of Stoutt.

In July 1996 the Governor, David Mackilligin, recommended that there should be a public debate on the continued use of judicial corporal punishment in the territory (the British Virgin Islands being the only British Dependent Territory in which the practice remained in force). The issue was raised owing to concern that, as a signatory to the European Convention on Human Rights, the United Kingdom was potentially in violation of the accord every time that a sentence of corporal punishment was passed in the islands.

In March 1999 the Government of the United Kingdom published draft legislation pertaining to its relationship with its Overseas Dependencies, which were to be renamed United Kingdom Overseas Territories (and had been referred to as such since February 1998). The legislation proposed the extension of British citizenship to the citizens of Overseas Territories, although it also required its Overseas Territories to amend their legislation on human rights and on the regulation of the financial services sector to meet international standards. In July the British Government appointed a consultant, Alan Hoole, a former Governor of Anguilla, to review the Constitution of the British Virgin Islands. In September Hoole proposed several changes to the Constitution, including the introduction of more frequent meetings of the Legislative Council and the removal of the Governor's powers to veto legislation. Under the terms of the proposed changes, the Governor was also to be obliged to consult with the Executive Council before implementing policy in his areas of special responsibility (foreign affairs, the civil service and defence). It was also suggested that members of the Legislative Council and senior civil servants should be obliged to declare their interests. In August the Governor outlined the Government's legislative programme. The main aim of the proposed legislation was to ensure that the regulation of the financial services sector conformed to international standards. Savage, who also announced the introduction of a comprehensive review of the education system, stated that the drafting of the proposed amendments to the Constitution would continue throughout the year.

Elections to the Legislative Council took place on 17 May 1999. The VIP retained control of the legislature, increasing its representation to seven seats. The recently founded National Democratic Party (NDP) took five seats, while the CCM retained one seat. The UP and several independent candidates also contested the elections. O'Neal subsequently re-appointed the members of the previous Executive Council.

In September 2000 the Legislative Council passed legislation abolishing judicial corporal punishment on the British Virgin Islands, in keeping with the United Kingdom's acceptance of the European Convention of Human Rights. In November the Legislative Council voted in favour of making 7 March, the birth date of H. Lavity Stoutt, a public holiday; this was to replace, from 2002, the public holiday of 14 November, the birthday of the Prince of Wales.

The Organisation for Economic Co-operation and Development (see p. 358) announced in April 2002 that the British Virgin Islands had made sufficient commitments to improve the transparency of its tax and regulatory systems to be removed from an updated list of 'unco-operative' tax havens, first published in 2000. Also in April, a tax information exchange agreement, designed to reduce the potential for abuse of the tax system, was signed with the USA. In the same month, the financial secretary, L. Allen Wheatley, was arrested in connection with the mishandling of government contracts relating to the Beef Island Airport development project, and in May the Government survived a motion of no confidence brought against it in connection with the airport development project. In November 2002 some of the charges against Wheatley were dropped after the prosecution was unable to provide sufficient evidence of fraud or breach of trust; however, the presiding magistrate determined there was enough evidence for Wheatley to answer related charges of theft and corruption. The trial of Wheatley and four other men began in November 2003; four of the five defendants pleaded guilty to approving an airport telecommunications contract based on inflated prices that cost the Government some US $450,000. In January 2004 Wheatley was sentenced to nine months in gaol; in return for the guilty pleas, prosecutors withdrew theft charges, which carried much harsher jail terms. (Wheatley had already been sentenced to five years' imprisonment on separate corruption charges in February 2003.)

In late 2002 the recovering financial sector faced further disruption when the United Kingdom, under pressure from a European Union (EU, see p. 255) investigation into tax evasion, demanded that the British Virgin Islands disclose the identities and account details of Europeans holding private savings accounts on the islands. The British Virgin Islands, along with some other British Overseas Territories facing similar demands, claimed it was being treated unfairly compared with more powerful European countries, such as Switzerland and Luxembourg. In January 2005 the Business Companies Act came into force, which eliminated the distinction between laws governing local and 'offshore' businesses. Further reform to the tax system also took place.

In May 2002 the British Overseas Territories Act, having received royal assent in the United Kingdom in February, came into force and granted British citizenship to the people of its Overseas Territories, including the British Virgin Islands. Under the new law British Virgin Islanders would be able to hold British passports and work in the United Kingdom and anywhere else in the EU.

In October 2002 Tom Macan succeeded Frank Savage as Governor. A general election was held on 16 June 2003. The NDP secured eight seats compared with the VIP's five after a campaign that was dominated by the issues of alleged corruption, management of public sector capital projects, and relations with the United Kingdom. Orlando Smith became the new Chief Minister.

Following the scandal over the Beef Island Airport development scheme, and in an attempt to hold public offices more accountable for their expenditure and renew public trust in the executive, in late September 2003 the new Government passed an Audit Act. A commission for constitutional review was appointed in April 2004, which was to consider, *inter alia*, the criteria for qualification for residency status, the reserve powers of the Governor, the duties of the Attorney-General and the introduction of an article relating to human rights into the Constitution. A Constitutional Review Report was released in 2005, based on the commission's findings. Among the suggestions included in the report were the reform of the legal system (including the introduction of legal aid), and a move towards a cabinet system of government, with the title of Chief Minister changing to Premier. The possibility of renaming the Legislative Council a Parliament was also examined. A first round of negotiations to discuss the proposed constitutional reform, between representatives of the British Government and the Chief Minister, was held in Barbados in March 2006. Negotiations continued throughout 2006, with subsequent rounds of discussions in June and October. These were augmented by two public consultations in September to obtain contributions towards a proposed Fundamental Rights Chapter within the new constitution. A fourth and final forum, conducted in London, United Kingdom, on 26–28 February 2007, sought to examine the provisions of a draft constitution document prepared by the Constitutional Review Commission and conclude debate upon the proposed new statutes. The British Foreign and Commonwealth Office Minister with responsibility for Overseas Territories, Lord David Triesman, endorsed the successful completion of negotiations, announcing the formulation of a new constitution for the territory that would simultaneously afford greater autonomy to the country while maintaining harmonious relations with the United Kingdom;

Chief Minister Smith expressed his satisfaction that '95 per cent' of the Review Commission's stated objectives for constitutional reform had been achieved.

The principal features of the proposed constitution included the institution of a cabinet system of government (whereby the Executive Council would be renamed 'the Cabinet'), within which the Premier (formerly Chief Minister) would command influence in the determination of the cabinet agenda, previously the subject of the Governor's sole arbitration, and a Cabinet Secretary would be appointed to set the Cabinet's agenda; the establishment of a National Security Council—to be comprised of the Governor, the Premier, a named government minister, the Attorney-General and the Commissioner of Police—conferring matters of internal security and policing of the islands from the sole remit of the British Government to that of the British Virgin Islands also, and upon whose recommendations the Governor would be obliged to act; the institution of an Office for Public Prosecutions; a reduction in the Governor's powers of veto; the inclusion of a Fundamental Rights Chapter to ensure the promotion and protection of citizens' human rights and freedoms; and provision for the creation of a sixth government ministry to accommodate the requirements of the territory's expanding population. The United Kingdom would retain some residual authority in order to regulate the development of the British Virgin Islands, embracing issues such as the observation of international standards in relation to the burgeoning financial services sector and the islands' natural disaster preparedness. Chief Minister Smith announced his Government's intention, at the end of March, to launch a constitutional education programme following finalization of the new constitution. After being approved by the United Kingdom Privy Council on 14 June, the Virgin Islands Constitutional Order 2007 became effective on 15 June, subsequent to the dissolution of the Legislative Council.

In February 2005 the Legislative Council approved the Firearms Amendment Act designed to reduce levels of gun crime committed with illegal weapons. New proposed legislation regarding the liberalization of the telecommunications sector was under discussion in Parliament in early 2006; however, the bill was subsequently withdrawn after disagreement over which members should vote. At the following parliamentary sitting, at the beginning of May, the bill was again presented for debate, but members voted for it to be removed from the order paper for a second time. The Minister for Communications and Works, J. Alvin Christopher, failed to vote in favour of withdrawing the proposed legislation, instead abstaining along with members of the opposition. The following week Christopher was dismissed from his government post; he was replaced by Elmore Stoutt.

Proposals for the liberalization of the telecommunications sector continued to feature in parliamentary discussion during 2006 and, in October, some tangible progress was made towards ending the 'three-way monopoly' within the territory's communications and broadcasting market, with the establishment of a Telecommunications Regulatory Commission (TRC). The authority, a statutory body affiliated to the Ministry of Communications and Works, was instituted under the Telecommunications Act 2006, which was ratified in June and effected on 24 October of that year. It was proposed that three or four operators would be awarded licences for the provision of a comprehensive range of telecommunications services and, in March 2007, the sole mobile provider in the British Virgin Islands, Cable & Wireless, signed an Interconnection Agreement memorandum of understanding with CCT Global Communications (operating locally as CCT Boatphone). In April the Government announced that it was inviting unitary licence applications—permitting operation in all sectors of the telecommunications market for 15 years—from only the three current providers. A fourth company, Digicel, initiated court proceedings against the TRC in respect of the restriction after its licence application was rejected. The High Court ruled in favour of Digicel, which was granted a licence to operate mobile services in December 2007. Digicel launched its mobile service in November 2008, providing coverage to 98% of the population.

On 18 April 2006 David Pearey was sworn in as Governor in succession to Tom Macan.

In an effort to enhance immigration monitoring in the British Virgin Islands, the Government implemented a new visa regime in April 2007 requiring that Jamaican nationals without residency or 'belonger' status obtain a visa to enter the territory; the passport office had commenced issuing of visas on 1 March, since which time over 850 such documents had been granted to Jamaicans. The measure followed the apprehension, during a border security initiative in February, of 49 illegal immigrants originating from Haiti and the Dominican Republic. In February 2009 it was announced that a fair knowledge of the territory was to be a requirement before any subject would be granted 'belonger' status.

The VIP achieved a convincing victory at a general election held on 20 August 2007, securing 10 seats while the NDP won two. An independent candidate won the remaining seat in the renamed legislature, the House of Assembly. The leader of the VIP, Ralph O'Neal, became the British Virgin Islands' first Premier, the title accorded to him under the terms of the new Constitution. O'Neal assumed responsibilities for the portfolios of finance and tourism, and Dancia Penn Sallah became the Deputy Premier and Minister of Health and Social Development. The new Premier also appointed Andrew Fahie as Minister of Education and Culture, Julian Fraser as Minister of Communications and Works, and Omar Hodge as Minister of Natural Resources and Labour. On assuming office, O'Neal pledged to address the increase in serious crime by reviewing levels of funding for the police force and the customs and immigration departments, and to enact a period of fiscal transparency and responsibility, particularly with regard to construction projects, owing to a predicted budget deficit of US $13m. for 2007.

Despite the ongoing global economic crisis, in April 2009 the House of Assembly approved a record budget of US $279.8m. Premier and Minister of Finance Ralph O'Neal envisaged expenditure of some $253.5m., with an estimated surplus of $26.1m.

It was announced in April 2009 that the Eastern Caribbean Supreme Court (ECSC) was to establish a new division of the court, based on Tortola, to preside over all stages of litigation concerning major domestic, international or cross-border commercial claims. Tortola had been chosen as the location for this new body because of its important role in the region's 'offshore' financial sector and because a number of multi-million dollar cases had been brought by commercial interests in the territory in recent years. Justice Edward Alexander Banner was sworn in on 30 March to preside over the new court, which was expected to come into effect in June 2009.

Government

Under the provisions of the 2007 Constitution, the Governor is appointed by the British monarch and is responsible for external affairs, defence and internal security, terms and conditions of service of public officers, and the administration of the Courts. The Governor also fulfils the role of Presiding Officer at meetings of the Cabinet, which comprises the Premier and five other members. The House of Assembly comprises 15 members: a Speaker, one ex officio member, and 13 members elected by universal adult suffrage.

Defence

The United Kingdom is responsible for the defence of the islands. In September 1999 it was announced that Royal Air Force patrols were to be undertaken from the islands in order to intercept drugs-traffickers. Central government expenditure on defence totalled US $0.4m. in 1997.

Economic Affairs

In 2007, according to UN estimates, the British Virgin Islands' gross domestic product (GDP) was US $1,156m., equivalent to some $51,273 per head. The population doubled during 1984–94, to 17,903, primarily owing to a large influx of immigrants from other Caribbean Islands, the United Kingdom and the USA. During 1995–2005, according to the Caribbean Development Bank (CDB), it was estimated, the population increased at an average annual rate of 3.1%, while GDP increased, in real terms, by 4.2% per year during 2000–07. Estimated growth was 1.3% in 2007.

Agriculture (including forestry and fishing) contributed 1.0% of GDP in 2007, and engaged 0.5% of the employed labour force in 2005. The islands produce fruit and vegetables for domestic consumption or export to the US Virgin Islands, and some sugar cane (for the production of rum). Food imports accounted for 18.9% of total import costs in 1997. The fishing industry caters for local consumption and export, and provides a sporting activity for tourists, although the Government has been looking to develop deep-sea fishing commercially for domestic and export markets.

Industry (including mining, manufacturing, construction and public utilities) accounted for 10.5% of GDP in 2007 and engaged 11.4% of the employed labour force in 2005. The mining sector is negligible, consisting of the extraction of materials for the construction industry and of some salt. Manufacturing, which provided 3.0% of GDP in 2007, consists mainly of light industry; there is one rum distillery, two factories for the production of ice, some plants producing concrete blocks and other construction materials, small boat manufacture and various cottage industries. Construction activity accounted for 5.7% of GDP in 2007. Most energy requirements must be imported (mineral fuels accounted for an estimated 8.5% of total imports in 1997).

Services, primarily tourism and financial services, constitute the principal economic sector of the British Virgin Islands, contributing 88.5% of GDP in 2007, and accounting for 88.1% of employment in 2005. The tourism industry earned some US $437m. in 2005, and employed about one-third of the working population, directly or indirectly. The British Virgin Islands is the largest 'bareboat' chartering centre in the Caribbean, and approximately 60% of stop-over visitors stay aboard yachts. Nevertheless, in 2002 the restaurants and hotels sector contributed 13.5% of GDP. The number of stop-over visitors reached 337,134 in 2005 (most of whom were from the USA), an 11.0% increase on the previous year's total; the ratio of tourists to local population is therefore higher than at any other Caribbean destination. Work to renovate Beef Island airport and to lengthen its runway was completed in mid-2004 was expected to provide a boost to tourism revenue in the second half of the decade.

Financial services expanded rapidly as a result of legislative measures adopted in 1984, and in 2004 the 'offshore' sector contributed over one-half of direct government revenue (some US $110m.). There were a cumulative total of 544,000 International Business Company (IBC) registrations in the islands in 1984–2004. By 2009 the number of companies registered was estimated at more than 700,000. The islands have also recorded significant growth in the establishment of mutual funds and of insurance companies. In January 2002 the Government created the Financial Services Commission, an independent regulatory authority for the sector, in order to meet international demands for a clear separation between the Government and financial services regulation.

In 2003, according to the CDB, the British Virgin Islands recorded a trade deficit of US $158.1m. The trade deficit is normally offset by receipts from tourism, development aid, remittances from islanders working abroad (many in the US Virgin Islands) and, increasingly, from the 'offshore' financial sector. The principal sources of imports (most of the islands' requirements must be imported) are the USA (which provided 56.9% of imports in 1997), Trinidad and Tobago, Antigua and Barbuda, and also the United Kingdom. The principal markets for the limited amount of exports are the US Virgin Islands and the USA and Puerto Rico; rum is exported to the USA. Machinery and transport equipment are the principal imports (accounting for 28.3% of total imports in 1997), and fruit and vegetables, rum, sand and gravel are the main exports.

The budget for the 2004 financial year recorded revenue at US $204.7m. against recurrent and capital expenditure of $214.2m. In 1996/97 there was a surplus of $56m. on the current account of the balance of payments. British budgetary support ceased in 1977, but the United Kingdom grants assistance for capital development. In 2004 total external debt was calculated to be $44.1m. In 1998 the territory received $1.2m. in development assistance. Central Government debt to GDP ratio was estimated at 10.0% in the same year. The average annual rate of inflation was 3.1% in 1995–2005; consumer prices increased by an average 0.7% in 2004 and by 2.3% in 2005. The rate of unemployment was estimated to be 3.5% in 2005.

The British Virgin Islands became an associate member of the Caribbean Community and Common Market (CARICOM, see p. 206) in 1991; it is a member of CARICOM's CDB (see p. 211) and an associate member of the Organisation of Eastern Caribbean States (OECS, see p. 440). In economic affairs the territory has close affiliations with the neighbouring US Virgin Islands, and uses US currency. As a dependency of the United Kingdom, the islands have the status of Overseas Territory in association with the European Union (EU, see p. 255).

The economy of the British Virgin Islands is largely dominated by tourism and by the provision of international financial services. The 'offshore' financial sector, which developed rapidly in the last two decades of the 20th century, is an important source of employment and the single most important source of government revenue. International attempts, notably by the Organisation for Economic Co-operation and Development (OECD, see p. 358), to encourage the reform of 'offshore' financial centres are therefore of great concern to the British Virgin Islands, particularly as IBCs, which are not taxed and which are not obliged to disclose their directors or shareholders, have been singled out for particular criticism. Despite the rise of the financial sector, tourism remains the most important sector of the economy, as the construction and retail sectors, among others, are to a certain extent dependent on its performance. The Government has expressed a desire to achieve greater diversification of the economy, in order to reduce reliance on tourism and financial services, both of which remained vulnerable to external pressures. Although the aftermath of the September 2001 terrorist attacks in the USA adversely affected tourism revenues in 2002, the economy performed strongly in 2003. In 2004 legislation was approved eliminating the distinction between 'onshore' and 'offshore' taxation regimes, in order to bring the economic structure of the Virgin Islands into conformity with EU and OECD requirements; a transitional period ended in January 2007. GDP growth of 1.5% was forecast for 2009, compared with an estimated 6.4% in 2008. Tourism declined by 0.5% in the first half of 2008 and the contraction was expected to accelerate as islands in the region were obliged to compete for a larger share of a declining market. The British Virgin Islands Tourism Board launched incentives in 2008 encouraging US travel agents to promote travel to the islands. A longer term threat to the economy was posed by the increasing scrutiny of the 'offshore' financial industry. Shortly after his election in November 2008 US President Barack Obama reiterated his determination to secure more stringent regulations in a number of tax havens, including the British Virgin Islands.

Education

Primary education is free, universal and compulsory between the ages of five and 11. Secondary education is also free and lasts from 12 to 16 years of age. In 2005/06 enrolment at primary schools included 94.7% of children in the relevant age-group; in 2004/05 enrolment at secondary schools included 88.2% of students in the relevant age category. Higher education is available at the University of the Virgin Islands (St Thomas, US Virgin Islands) and elsewhere in the Caribbean, in North America and in the United Kingdom. Central government expenditure on education in 1997 was US $17.1m.

Public Holidays
2009: 1 January (New Year's Day), 2 March (H. Lavity Stoutt's Birthday), 9 March (Commonwealth Day), 10 April (Good Friday), 13 April (Easter Monday), 1 June (Whit Monday), 13 June (Queen's Official Birthday), 29 June (Territory Day), 3–5 August (Festival Monday, Tuesday and Wednesday), 21 October (Saint Ursula's Day), 25–26 December (Christmas).
2010: 1 January (New Year's Day), 1 March (H. Lavity Stoutt's Birthday), 8 March (Commonwealth Day), 2 April (Good Friday), 5 April (Easter Monday), 24 May (Whit Monday), 12 June (Queen's Official Birthday), 2 July (Territory Day), 2–4 August (Festival Monday, Tuesday and Wednesday), 22 October (Saint Ursula's Day), 25–27 December (Christmas).

Weights and Measures
The imperial system is used.

Statistical Survey

Source: Development Planning Unit, Central Administrative Complex, Road Town, Tortola VG1110; tel. 494-3701; fax 494-3947; e-mail dpu@dpu.org; internet dpu.gov.vg.

AREA AND POPULATION

Area: 153 sq km (59 sq miles). *Principal Islands* (sq km): Tortola 54.4; Anegada 38.8; Virgin Gorda 21.4; Jost Van Dyke 9.1.

Population: 16,644 at census of 12 May 1991; 20,647 (males 10,627, females 10,020) at census of 21 May 2001 (Source: UN, *Demographic Yearbook*); 25,800 (estimate) at mid-2005; *By Island* (1980): Tortola 9,119; Virgin Gorda 1,412; Anegada 164; Jost Van Dyke 134; Other islands 156; (1991) Tortola 13,568 (Source: partly Caribbean Development Bank, *Social and Economic Indicators*).

Density (mid-2005): 168.6 per sq km.

Principal Town: Road Town (capital), population 13,000 (UN estimate, incl. suburbs, mid-2005). Source: UN, *World Urbanization Prospects: The 2005 Revision*.

Births, Marriages and Deaths (registrations, 2004): 316 live births (birth rate 14.7 per 1,000); 426 marriages (marriage rate 19.6 per 1,000); 120 deaths (death rate 5.5 per 1,000). *2008:* Crude birth rate 14.8 per 1,000; Crude death rate 4.5 per 1,000. Sources: Caribbean Development Bank, *Social and Economic Indicators*; Pan American Health Organization.

Life Expectancy (years at birth, estimates): 77.1 (males 75.9; females 78.3) in 2008. Source: Pan American Health Organization.

Employment (2005): Agriculture, hunting and forestry 78; Fishing 14; Mining and quarrying 37; Manufacturing 404; Electricity, gas and water supply 145; Construction 1,260; Wholesale and retail trade 1,624; Hotels and restaurants 2,573; Transport, storage and communications 454; Financial intermediation 797; Real estate, renting and business activities 1,307; Public administration and social security 5,142; Education 1,119; Health and social work 141; Other community, social and personal service activities 724; Private households with employed persons 404; Not classifiable by economic activity 9; Total 16,232.

HEALTH AND WELFARE

Physicians (per 1,000 head, 1999): 1.15.
Hospital Beds (per 1,000 head, 2006): 1.9.
Health Expenditure (% of GDP, 1995): 3.9. *2003* (public expenditure only): 3.1.
Health Expenditure (public, % of total, 1995): 36.5.
Source: Pan American Health Organization.
For definitions, see explanatory note on p. vi.

AGRICULTURE, ETC.

Livestock ('000 head, 2007, FAO estimates): Cattle 2.4; Sheep 6.1; Goats 10.0; Pigs 1.5.

Fishing (metric tons, live weight, 2006, FAO estimates): Snappers 370; Boxfishes 35; Jacks and crevalles 25; Caribbean spiny lobster 50; Marine fishes 800; Total catch (incl. others) 1,300.
Source: FAO.

INDUSTRY

Electric Energy (production, million kWh): 45 in 2003; 45 in 2004; 45 in 2005. Source: UN, *Industrial Commodity Statistics Yearbook*.

FINANCE

Currency and Exchange Rate: United States currency is used: 100 cents = 1 US dollar ($). *Sterling and Euro Equivalents* (31 December 2008): £1 sterling = US $1.458; €1 = US $1.392; US $100 = £68.60 = €71.85.

Budget (US $ million, 2004): *Revenue:* Tax revenue 72.6 (Import duties 24.2, Income and property tax 41.7, Passenger and hotel tax 6.7); Non-tax revenue 132.1 (Financial services sector 109.8); Total recurrent revenue 204.7. *Expenditure:* Recurrent expenditure 180.4 (Goods and services 62.9; Wages and salaries 83.6; Subsidies and transfers 32.9); Capital expenditure 33.8; Total expenditure 214.2.

Cost of Living (Consumer Price Index; base: 1995 = 100): All items 131.8 in 2003; 132.7 in 2004; 135.7 in 2005.

Gross Domestic Product (US $ million at constant 1990 prices): 919 in 2005; 1,000 in 2006; 1,095 in 2007. Source: UN Statistics Division, National Accounts Main Aggregates Database.

Expenditure on the Gross Domestic Product (US $ million at current prices, 2007): Government final consumption expenditure 108; Private final consumption expenditure 433; Gross fixed capital formation 278; Changes in inventories –17; *Total domestic expenditure* 802; Exports of goods and services 1,253; *Less* Imports of goods and services 899; *GDP in purchasers' values* 1,156. Source: UN Statistics Division, National Accounts Main Aggregates Database.

Gross Domestic Product by Economic Activity (rounded figures in current prices, US $ million, 1999): Agriculture, hunting and forestry 4.1; Fishing 5.4; Mining and quarrying 0.4; Manufacturing 27.0; Electricity, gas and water 11.1; Construction 49.0; Wholesale and retail trade 90.0; Hotels and restaurants 98.0; Transport, storage and communications 79.0; Financial intermediation 43.0; Real estate, renting and business services 188.0; Public administration 35.0; Education 13.6; Health and social work 9.5; Other community, social and personal services 15.8; Private households with employed persons 6.0; *Sub-total* 674.0; *Less* Imputed bank service charges 35.0; Indirect taxes, less subsidies 23.0; *GDP in purchasers' values* 662.0. Source: UN, *National Accounts Statistics*. *2007* (US $ million): Agriculture, hunting, forestry and fishing 12; Mining, manufacturing and utilities 59 (Manufacturing 35); Construction 66; Wholesale, retail trade, restaurants and hotels 324; Transport, storage and communication 134; Other activities 593; Total gross value added 1,188; Net taxes on products –32 (figure obtained as residual); GDP in purchasers' values 1,156 (Source: UN Statistics Division, National Accounts Main Aggregates Database).

EXTERNAL TRADE

Principal Commodities ($ '000): *Imports c.i.f.* (1997): Food and live animals 31,515; Beverages and tobacco 8,797; Crude materials (inedible) except fuels 1,168; Mineral fuels, lubricants, etc. 9,847; Chemicals 8,816; Basic manufactures 31,715; Machinery and transport equipment 47,019; Total (incl. others) 116,379. *Exports f.o.b.* (1996): Food and live animals 368; Beverages and tobacco 3,967; Crude materials (inedible) except fuels 1,334; Total (incl. others) 5,862. *2001* (exports, $ million) Animals 0.1; Fresh fish 0.7; Gravel and sand 1.4; Rum 3.6; Total 28.13.

Principal Trading Partners ($ '000): *Imports c.i.f.* (1997): Antigua and Barbuda 1,807; Trinidad and Tobago 2,555; United Kingdom 406; USA 94,651; Total (incl. others) 166,379. *Exports f.o.b.* (1996): USA and Puerto Rico 1,077; US Virgin Islands 2,001; Total (incl. others) 5,862. *1999:* Imports 208,419; Exports 2,081.

Source: mainly UN, *International Trade Statistics Yearbook*.

TRANSPORT

Road Traffic (motor vehicles registered and licensed, 2005): 13,392 (Private vehicles 9,201, Commercial vehicles 2,102, Rental vehicles 1,196, Taxis 483, Government 275, Motorcycles 135).

Shipping: *International Freight Traffic* ('000 metric tons, 2002): Goods unloaded 145.6. *Cargo Ship Arrivals* (2002): 2,027. *Merchant Fleet* (vessels registered, at 31 December 2007): 12; Total displacement 16,165 grt (Sources: British Virgin Islands Port Authority; Lloyd's Register-Fairplay, *World Fleet Statistics*).

Civil Aviation (passenger arrivals): 153,391 in 2003; 220,239 in 2004 (estimate); 220,116 in 2005 (estimate).

TOURISM

Visitor Arrivals ('000): 317.8 stop-over visitors, 300.4 cruise ship passengers in 2003; 303.8 stop-over visitors, 466.6 cruise ship passengers in 2004; 337.1 stop-over visitors, 449.2 cruise ship passengers in 2005.

Tourism Revenue (US $ million, incl. passenger transport): 342 in 2003; 393 in 2004; 437 in 2005. Source: World Tourism Organization.

COMMUNICATIONS MEDIA

Radio Receivers (1997): 9,000 in use.
Television Receivers (1999): 4,000 in use.
Telephones (2002): 12,000 main lines in use.
Facsimile Machines (1996): 1,200 in use.
Non-daily Newspapers (1996): 2 (estimated circulation 4,000).
Sources: UNESCO, *Statistical Yearbook*; UN, *Statistical Yearbook*.

EDUCATION

Pre-primary: 5 schools (1994/95); 45 teachers (2005/06); 653 pupils (2004/05).
Primary: 20 schools (1993/94); 194 teachers (2005/06); 2,923 pupils (2005/06).
Secondary: 4 schools (1988); 203 teachers (2005/06); 1,959 pupils (2005/06).
Tertiary (2004/05): 110 teachers; 1,200 pupils.
Sources: UNESCO Institute for Statistics; Caribbean Development Bank, *Social and Economic Indicators*.

Directory

The Constitution

The British Virgin Islands have had a representative assembly since 1774. Following a United Kingdom Government invitation in 2001 for its Overseas Territories to institute programs of constitutional reform, a new Constitution for the British Virgin Islands was finalized in May 2007 and formally ratified by the Privy Council of the United Kingdom in June. The Virgin Islands Constitutional Order 2007 became effective (largely—see below) from 15 June and represented the first comprehensive revision of the Territory's constitution since that which had precipitated the 1977 Constitution, which it replaced. Under the terms of the 2007 Constitution, the Governor is responsible for defence and internal security (including the police force), external affairs, terms and conditions of service of public officers, and the administration of the Courts. The Governor also possesses reserved legislative powers in respect of legislation necessary in the interests of his special responsibilities and fulfils the role of Presiding Officer at meetings of the Cabinet (formerly the 'Executive Council'). The Cabinet comprises the Premier (formerly 'Chief Minister'), one ex officio member (the Attorney-General), and four other ministers (appointed by the Governor on the advice of the Premier); a Cabinet Secretary sets the Cabinet's agenda under consultation with the Premier. The House of Assembly (formerly 'Legislative Council') consists of a Speaker, chosen from among the elected members of—or those eligible for election to—the Assembly, one ex officio member (the Attorney-General) and 13 elected members (nine members from one-member electoral districts and four members representing the territory 'at large').

The new Constitution also makes provision for the formation of a sixth government ministry, while a National Security Council, comprised of the Governor, Premier, Attorney-General, Commissioner of Police and a named government minister, advises the Governor upon matters of internal security and policing of the territory. A Fundamental Rights Chapter, ensuring the protection of citizens' human rights and freedoms, is also in effect. By mid-2009 a Public Service Commission and Judicial and Legal Services Commission had been instituted, while preparations for a Human Rights Commission were ongoing.

The division of the islands into nine electoral districts, instead of seven, came into effect at the November 1979 general election. The four 'at large' seats were introduced at the February 1995 general election. The minimum voting age was lowered from 21 years to 18 years.

Under the British Overseas Territories Act, which entered into effect in May 2002, British Virgin Islanders have the right to United Kingdom citizenship and the right of abode in the United Kingdom. British citizens do not enjoy reciprocal rights.

The Government

Governor: DAVID PEAREY (assumed office 18 April 2006).
Deputy Governor: INEZ ARCHIBALD.

CABINET
(April 2009)

Premier and Minister of Finance and Tourism: RALPH TELFORD O'NEAL.
Deputy Premier and Minister of Health and Social Development: DANCIA PENN SALLAH.
Minister of Natural Resources and Labour: OMAR HODGE.
Minister of Education and Culture: ANDREW FAHIE.
Minister of Communications and Works: JULIAN FRASER.
Attorney-General: KATHLEEN QUARTEY AYENSU.

MINISTRIES

Office of the Governor: 1 Government House Dr., POB 702, Road Town, Tortola VG1110; tel. 494-2345; fax 494-5790; e-mail bvigovernor@gov.vg; internet www.bvi.gov.vg.

Office of the Deputy Governor: Central Administration Bldg, West Wing, 33 Admin Dr., Road Town, Tortola VG1110; tel. 494-3701; fax 494-6481; e-mail webmaster@dgo.gov.vg; internet www.dgo.gov.vg.

Office of the Premier: 33 Admin Dr., Wickham's Cay 1, Road Town, Tortola VG1110; tel. 468-3701; fax 468-4435; e-mail premieroffice@gov.vg; internet www.bvigazette.org.

Ministry of Communications and Works: 33 Admin Dr., Wickham's Cay 1, Road Town, Tortola VG1110; tel. 468-0629; fax 494-3873; e-mail mcw@mail.bvi.org.

Ministry of Education and Culture: 33 Admin Dr., Wickham's Cay 1, Road Town, Tortola VG1110; tel. 468-0632; fax 494-5421; e-mail bvimecgov@hotmail.com.

Ministry of Finance and Economic Development: Central Administration Bldg, West Atrium, 2nd Floor, Road Town, Tortola VG1110; tel. 494-3701; fax 494-6180; e-mail finance@gov.vg; internet www.finance.gov.vg.

Ministry of Health and Welfare: West Atrium, Central Administration Bldg, Road Town, Tortola VG1110; tel. 494-3701; fax 494-5018; e-mail min.health@bvigovvernment.org.

Ministry of Natural Resources and Labour: 33 Administration Dr., Wickham's Cay 1, Road Town, Tortola VG1110; tel. 468-3701; e-mail nrl@gov.vg.

HOUSE OF ASSEMBLY

Speaker: ROY HARRIGAN.
Clerk: (vacant); tel. 468-6908.
General Election, 20 August 2007

Party	% of vote	Seats
Virgin Islands Party	45.2	10
National Democratic Party	39.6	2
Independent	15.2	1
Total	100.0	13

Political Organizations

Concerned Citizens' Movement (CCM): Road Town, Tortola VG1110; f. 1994 as successor to Independent People's Movt; Leader ETHLYN SMITH.

National Democratic Party (NDP): Road Town, Tortola VG1110; f. 1998; Chair. RUSSELL HARRIGAN; Leader ORLANDO SMITH.

United Party (UP): POB 3068, Road Town, Tortola VG1110; tel. 495-2656; fax 494-1808; e-mail liberatebvi@msn.com; f. 1967; Chair. CONRAD MADURO; Pres. HENRY KETTLE.

Virgin Islands Party (VIP): Road Town, Tortola VG1110; e-mail info@viparty.com; internet www.viparty.com; Chair. RALPH T. O'NEAL.

Judicial System

Justice is administered by the Eastern Caribbean Supreme Court (ECSC), based in Saint Lucia, which consists of two divisions: the High Court of Justice and the Court of Appeal. There are two resident High Court Judges. A visiting Court of Appeal, comprised of the Chief Justice and two Judges of Appeal, sits twice a year in the British Virgin Islands. There is also a Magistrates' Court, which hears prescribed civil and criminal cases. The final Court of Appeal is the Privy Council in the United Kingdom. Under the terms of the 2007 Constitution, a Judicial and Legal Services Commission, chaired by the Chief Justice, was established to counsel the Governor in matters relating to judicial appointments and regulation of the territory's legal system. In April 2009 the ECSC announced the establishment of a new division of the court, based on Tortola, to preside over all stages of litigation concerning major domestic, international or cross-border commercial claims. Justice Edward Alexander Banner was to preside over the new Commercial Court, which was expected to become operational in June 2009.

Resident Judges: INDRA HARIPRASHAD-CHARLES, RITA JOSEPH-OLIVETTI.

Magistrate: VALERIE STEPHENS.

Registrar: PAULA AJARIE.

Magistrate's Office: Magistrates Court, POB 140, Road Town, Tortola VG1110; tel. 494-3460; fax 494-2499; e-mail magistrate@vigilate.org.

Religion

CHRISTIANITY

The Roman Catholic Church

The diocese of St John's-Basseterre, suffragan to the archdiocese of Castries (Saint Lucia), includes Anguilla, Antigua and Barbuda, the British Virgin Islands, Montserrat and Saint Christopher and Nevis. The Bishop is resident in St John's, Antigua. In 2006 it was estimated that 11.4% of the population were Roman Catholic.

The Anglican Communion

The British and US Virgin Islands form a single, missionary diocese of the Episcopal Church of the United States of America. The Bishop of the Virgin Islands is resident on St Thomas in the US Virgin Islands. In 2005 it was estimated that 16.7% of the population were Anglican.

Protestant Churches

Various Protestant denominations are represented, principally the Methodist Church (an estimated 32.9% of the population in 2005). Others include the Seventh-day Adventist (6.3%), Church of God (9.2%) and Baptist Churches (4.7%).

The Press

The BVI Beacon: 10 Russell Hill Rd, POB 3030, Road Town, Tortola VG1110; tel. 494-3434; fax 494-6267; e-mail bvibeacn@surfbvi.com; internet www.bvibeacon.com; f. 1984; Thursdays; covers local and international news; also operates from the US Virgin Islands; Editor LINNELL M. ABBOTT; circ. 3,400.

The BVI StandPoint: Wickhams Cay, POB 4311, Road Town, Tortola VG1110; tel. 494-8106; fax 494-8647; e-mail editorial@vistandpoint.com; internet www.vistandpoint.com; fmrly BVI PennySaver, adopted current name in 2001; Tuesdays and Fridays; covers local and international news; Publr ELTON CALLWOOD; Editor CARMILITA JAMIESON; circ. 18,000.

The Island Sun: 112 Main St, POB 21, Road Town, Tortola VG1110; tel. 494-2476; fax 494-5854; e-mail issun@candwbvi.net; internet islandsun.com; f. 1962; Fridays; publ. by Sun Enterprises (BVI) Ltd; Editor VERNON W. PICKERING; circ. 3,000.

The Welcome (The British Virgin Islands Welcome Tourist Guide): POB 133, Road Town, Tortola; tel. 494-2413; fax 494-4413; e-mail jim@bviwelcome.com; internet www.bviwelcome.com; f. 1971; every 2 months; general, tourist information; Publr and Editor CLAUDIA COLLI; annual circ. 176,000.

Publishers

Caribbean Publishing Co (BVI) Ltd: POB 3403, Road Town, Tortola VG1110; tel. 494-2060; fax 494-3060; e-mail bvi-sales@caribpub.com; Gen. Man. MICHAEL ARNOLD.

Island Publishing Services Ltd: POB 133, Road Town, Tortola VG1110; tel. 494-2413; fax 494-4413; e-mail info@bviwelcome.com; publishes *The Welcome (The British Virgin Islands Welcome Tourist Guide)* (q.v.), *BVI Restaurant and Food Guide* (annual), *The Limin' Times* (weekly entertainment guide), and *The British Virgin Islands Cruise Ship Visitors' Guide*.

Broadcasting and Communications

TELECOMMUNICATIONS

A Telecommunications Regulatory Commission was established under the Telecommunications Act 2006 in October to facilitate the liberalization of the telecommunications sector, which had commenced earlier that year. In April 2007 a Telecommunications Liberalization Act was ratified by the Government; the legislation prepared the market for the addition of further operators after a period of three years until which time the market would be restricted to the existing three service providers. However, the market was subsequently opened to applications from alternative operators after Digicel pursued a successful lawsuit against the restriction: the first unitary licences were issued in June 2007, and Digicel was granted a mobile licence in December.

Regulatory Bodies

Telecommunications Regulatory Commission: Road Town, POB 4401, Tortola; tel. 468-9677; internet www.bvitrc.info; f. Oct. 2006; regulatory body; Chair. COLLIN SCATLIFFE; CEO DAVID IVERSON.

Telephone Services Management Unit: Central Administration Bldg, Road Town, Tortola VG1110; tel. 494-4728; fax 494-6551; e-mail tsmu@bvigovernment.org; govt agency.

Principal Companies

Caribbean Cellular Telephone (CCT Boatphone): Geneva Pl., Road Town, Tortola VG1110; tel. 494-5639; internet www.cctwireless.com; mobile cellular telephone operator.

Digicel: POB 4168, Road Town, Tortola; tel. 494-2048; fax 494-0111; e-mail angela.burns@digicelgroup.com; internet www.digicelbvi.com; granted licence to operate mobile cellular telephone network in British Virgin Islands in Dec. 2007; CEO ALAN BATES.

LIME: Cutlass Bldg, Wickhams Cay 1, POB 440, Road Town, Tortola VG1110; tel. 494-4444; fax 494-2506; e-mail support@candwbvi.net; internet www.time4lime.com; f. 1967 as Cable & Wireless (WI) Ltd; name changed as above 2008; Country Man. VANCE LEWIS.

BROADCASTING

Radio

Virgin Islands Broadcasting Ltd—Radio ZBVI: Baughers Bay, POB 78, Road Town, Tortola VG1110; tel. 494-2250; fax 494-1139; e-mail zbvi@caribsurf.com; internet www.zbvi.vi; f. 1965; commercial; Gen. Man. HARVEY HERBERT; Operations Man. SANDRA POTTER WARRICAN.

Television

BVI Cable TV: Fishlock Rd, POB 694, Road Town, Tortola VG1110; tel. 494-3205; fax 494-2952; operated by Innovative Communication Corporation, based in the US Virgin Islands; programmes from US Virgin Islands and Puerto Rico; secured a licence to compete in the newly liberalized telecommunications market in June 2007; 53 channels; Gen. Man. LUANNE HODGE.

Television West Indies Ltd (ZBTV): Broadcast Peak, Chawell, POB 34, Tortola VG1110; tel. 494-3332; commercial.

Finance

BANKING

Regulatory Authority

Financial Services Commission: Pasea Estate, POB 418, Road Town, Tortola VG1110; tel. 494-1324; fax 494-5016; e-mail commissioner@bvifsc.vg; internet www.bvifsc.vg; f. 2002; independent financial services regulator; Chair. ROBIN GAUL; Man. Dir and CEO ROBERT MATHAVIOUS.

Commercial Banks

Ansbacher (BVI) Ltd: International Trust Bldg, POB 659, Road Town, Tortola VG1110; tel. 494-3215; fax 494-3216.

Banco Popular de Puerto Rico: POB 67, Road Town, Tortola VG1110; tel. 494-2117; fax 494-5294; e-mail internet@bppr.com; internet www.bancopopular.com; Pres. and CEO RICHARD L. CARRIÓN; Man. SANDRA SCATLIFFE.

Bank of East Asia (BVI) Ltd: East Asia Chambers, POB 901, Road Town, Tortola VG1110; tel. 495-5588; fax 495-5088; internet www.hkbea.com; Gen. Man. PATRICK ANDREW NICHOLAS.

Bank of Nova Scotia (Canada): Wickhams Cay 1, POB 434, Road Town, Tortola VG1110; tel. 494-2526; fax 494-4657; e-mail joycelyn.murraine@scotiabank.com; internet www.bvi.scotiabank.com; f. 1967; Man. Dir JOYCELYN MURRAINE.

UNITED KINGDOM OVERSEAS TERRITORIES

The British Virgin Islands

Citco Fund Services (BVI) Ltd: Citco Bldg, Wickhams Cay, POB 662, Road Town, Tortola VG1110; tel. 494-2218; fax 494-3917; e-mail bvi-fund@citco.com; internet www.citco.com; f. 1978; Man. NICOLA GILLESPIE.

DISA Bank (BVI) Ltd: POB 985, Road Town, Tortola VG1110; tel. 494-4977; fax 494-4980; Man. ROSA RESTREPO.

First Bank Virgin Islands: Road Town Business Centre, Wickham's Cay 1, Road Town, Tortola VG1110; tel. 494-2662; fax 494-3863; internet www.firstbankvi.com; f. 1994 as a commercial bank in Puerto Rico; Man. ROBERT HIRST.

FirstCaribbean International Bank Ltd: Wickhams Cay 1, POB 70, Road Town, Tortola VG1110; tel. 494-2171; fax 494-4315; e-mail barcbvi@surfbvi.com; internet www.firstcaribbeanbank.com; f. 2003 following merger of Caribbean operations of Barclays Bank PLC and CIBC; Barclays relinquished its stake in June 2006; CEO JOHN D. ORR; Man. MICHAEL SPENCER.

HSBC Guyerzeller Bank (BVI) Ltd: POB 3162, Road Town, Tortola VG1110; tel. 494-5414; fax 494-5417; e-mail rhbvi@surfbvi.com; Dir KENNETH W. MORGAN.

Rathbone Bank (BVI) Ltd: POB 986, Road Town, Tortola VG1110; tel. 494-6544; fax 494-6532; e-mail rathbone@surfbvi.com; Man. Dir CORNEL BAPTISTE.

VP Bank (BVI) Ltd: Sir Francis Drake's Highway, POB 3463, Road Town, Tortola VG1110; tel. 494-1100; fax 494-1199; e-mail vpbank@surfbvi.com; internet www.vpbank.vg; Man. Dir Dr PETER REICHENSTEIN.

Development Bank

Development Bank of the British Virgin Islands: New Social Security Bldg, Wickhams Cay 1, POB 275, Road Town, Tortola VG1110; tel. 494-3737; fax 494-3119; e-mail vanterpooldbvi@candwbvi.net; state-owned; Chair. MEADE MALONE.

TRUST COMPANIES

Abacus Trust and Management Services Ltd: 333 Waterfront Dr., Road Town, Tortola VG1110; tel. 494-4388; fax 494-3088; e-mail info@mwmabacus.com; internet www.mwmabacus.com; f. 1994; Man. MEADE MALONE.

Aleman, Cordero, Galindo and Lee Trust (BVI) Ltd: POB 3175, Road Town, Tortola VG1110; tel. 494-4666; fax 494-4679; e-mail alcogalbvi@alcogal.com; Man. GABRIELLA CONTE.

AMS Trustees Ltd: Sea Meadow House, POB 116, Road Town, Tortola VG1110; tel. 494-3399; fax 494-3041; internet www.amsbvi.com; subsidiary of the AMS Group (British Virgin Islands); Man. (vacant).

Belmont Trust Ltd: Belmont Chambers, Tropic Isle Bldg, Nibbs St, POB 3443, Road Town, Tortola VG1110; tel. 494-5800; fax 494-2545; e-mail info@belmontbvi.net; internet www.belmontbvi.com; Man. ANDREA DOUGLAS.

CCP Financial Consultants Ltd: Ellen Skelton Bldg, Fishers Lane, POB 681, Road Town, Tortola VG1110; tel. 494-6777; fax 494-6787; e-mail ccp@surfbvi.com; internet www.ccpbvi.com; Man. JOSEPH ROBERTS.

Citco BVI Ltd: Wickhams Cay, POB 662, Road Town, Tortola VG1110; tel. 494-2217; fax 494-3917; e-mail bvi-trust@citco.com; internet www.citco.com; Man. NICOLA GILLESPIE.

HSBC International Trustee (BVI) Ltd: Woodbourne Hall, POB 916, Road Town, Tortola VG1110; tel. 494-5414; fax 494-5417; e-mail kenneth.morgan@htvg.vg; Dir KENNETH MORGAN.

Hunte & Co Services Ltd: Omar Hodge Bldg, 3rd Floor, Wickhams Cay I, POB 3504, Road Town, Tortola; tel. 495-0232; fax 495-0229; internet www.hunteandco.com; Office Man. DEBORAH BLANFORD.

Maples Finance BVI Ltd: Sea Meadow House, POB 173, Road Town, Tortola VG1110; tel. 494-3384; fax 494-4643; e-mail bviinfo@maplesandcalder.com; internet www.maplesandcalder.com; Man. ROBERT MCINTYRE.

Midocean Management and Trust Services (BVI) Ltd: POB 805, Road Town, Tortola VG1110; tel. 494-4567; fax 494-4568; e-mail midocean@maitlandbvi.com; Man. ELIZABETH WILKINSON.

Moore Stephens International Services (BVI) Ltd: Palm Grove House, Wickhams Cay I, POB 3186, Road Town, Tortola VG1110; tel. 494-3503; fax 494-3592; e-mail moorestephens@moorestephensbvi.com; internet www.moorestephens.com; Man. SELINA O'NEAL.

TMF (BVI) Ltd: POB 964, Road Town, Tortola VG11900; tel. 494-4997; fax 494-4999; e-mail bvi@tmf-group.com; internet www.tmf-group.com; Man. GRAHAM COOK.

Totalserve Trust Company Ltd: 197 Main St, POB 3540, Road Town, Tortola VG1110; tel. 494-6900; fax 494-6990; e-mail bvi@totalservecy.com; internet www.totalservecy.com; Man. DENESHAR MEADE.

Tricor Services (BVI) Ltd: POB 3340, Road Town, Tortola VG1110; tel. 494-6004; fax 494-6404; e-mail info@bvi.tricorservices.com; Man. PATRICK A. NICHOLAS.

Trident Trust Company (BVI) Ltd: Trident Chambers, Wickhams Cay, POB 146, Road Town, Tortola VG1110; tel. 494-2434; fax 494-3754; e-mail bvi@tridenttrust.com; internet www.tridenttrust.com; Man. BARRY R. GOODMAN.

At the beginning of 2007 there were some 2,600 active mutual and hedge funds registered with the British Virgin Islands International Finance Centre.

INSURANCE

Albion Insurance Management Ltd: POB 4623, Road Town, Tortola VG1110; tel. 494-9670; fax 495-9690; e-mail gtaylor@albionbvi.com; internet www.albionbvi.com; Man. GREGORY TAYLOR.

ALTA Insurance Management (BVI) Ltd: POB 4623, Road Town, Tortola VG1110; tel. 494-9670; fax 494-9690; e-mail gtaylor@altaholdings.com; internet www.altaholdings.com; Man. GREGORY TAYLOR.

AMS Insurance Management Services Ltd: Sea Meadow House, POB 116, Road Town, Tortola VG1110; tel. 494-4078; fax 494-8589; e-mail dlloyd@amsbvi.com; internet www.amsbvi.com; Man. DEREK LLOYD.

Belmont Insurance Management Ltd: POB 3443, Road Town, Tortola VG1110; tel. 494-5800; fax 494-2545; e-mail info@belmontbvi.com; internet www.belmontbvi.com; Man. SIMON OWEN.

Caledonian Insurance Services (BVI) Ltd: POB 4428, Road Town, Tortola VG1110; tel. 494-4111; fax 494-4222; e-mail insurance@caledonian.com; internet www.caledonian.com; Dir HARRY THOMPSON.

Captiva Global Ltd: POB 4428, Road Town, Tortola VG1110; tel. 494-4111; fax 494-4222; e-mail info@captiva.vg; internet www.captiva.vg; Man. Dir HARRY J. THOMPSON.

Caribbean Insurers Ltd (CIL): Mirage Bldg, POB 129, Road Town, Tortola VG1110; tel. 494-2728; fax 494-4393; e-mail info@caribbins.com; internet www.caribbeaninsurers.com; f. 1973; part of the Caribbean Insurers Group; Chair. and CEO JOHN WILLIAMS.

Euro-American Insurance Management Ltd: Euro American Bldg, R. G. Hodge Plaza, Wickham's Cay I, POB 3161, Road Town, Tortola VG1110; tel. 494-4692; fax 494-4695; e-mail eamsbvi@surfbvi.com; internet www.eamsonline.com; Man. Dir KAY REDDY.

Hunte & Co Insurance Management Services Ltd: POB 3504, Road Town, Tortola VG1110; tel. 495-0232; fax 495-0229; internet www.hunteandco.com; Man. ROSINA ANN-MARIE KNIGHT.

HWR Insurance Management Services Ltd (Harneys Insurance): POB 71, Road Town, Tortola VG1110; tel. 494-2233; fax 494-3547; e-mail insurance@harneys.com; internet www.harneys.com; Man. Dir DAVID SPYER.

Marine Insurance Office (BVI) Ltd (MIO): POB 874, Road Town, Tortola VG1110; tel. 494-3795; fax 494-4540; e-mail marinein@surfbvi.com; f. 1985; Man. WESLEY WOOLHOUSE.

Osiris Insurance Management Ltd: POB 2221, Road Town, Tortola VG1110; tel. 494-9820; fax 494-6934; e-mail osiristrust@surfbvi.com; internet osiristrust.com; Man. HARRY THOMPSON.

Trident Insurance Management (BVI) Ltd: POB 146, Road Town, Tortola VG1110; tel. 494-4078; fax 494-2519; e-mail trident@surfbvi.com; Man. DEREK LLOYD.

TSA Insurance Management Ltd: POB 3443, Road Town, Tortola VG1110; tel. 494-5800; fax 494-6563; e-mail jwilliams@surfbvi.com; Man. JOHN WILLIAMS.

USA Risk Group (BVI) Inc: POB 3140, Road Town, Tortola VG1110; tel. 494-4111; fax 494-4222; e-mail sgrayston@vim.usarisk.com; internet www.usarisk.com; Man. STUART H. GRAYSTON.

Several US and other foreign companies have agents in the British Virgin Islands. In 2006 57 new 'captive' insurers were registered by the British Virgin Islands International Financial Centre, increasing the total such registered to more than 400.

Trade and Industry

GOVERNMENT AGENCY

Trade and Investment Promotion Department: Central Administration Bldg, 33 Administration Dr., Road Town, Tortola VG1110; tel. 494-3701; fax 494-5676; e-mail trade@bvigovernment.org.

CHAMBER OF COMMERCE

British Virgin Islands Chamber of Commerce and Hotel Association: Tropic Aisle Bldg, Wickhams Cay 1, POB 376, Road Town, Tortola VG1110; tel. 494-3514; fax 494-6179; e-mail info@

bviccha.org; internet www.bviccha.org; f. 1986; Exec. Dir JOANNE ALLEN; Pres. (Business and Commerce) FRANKA PICKERING; Pres. (Hotels and Tourism) ROMNEY PENN; 250 mems.

UTILITIES

Electricity

British Virgin Islands Electricity Corpn (BVIEC): Long Bush, POB 268, Road Town, Tortola VG1110; tel. 494-3911; fax 494-4291; e-mail bviecgm@bvielectricity.com; internet www.bvielectricity.com; f. 1979; privatization pending; Chair. MARGARET PENN.

Water

Water and Sewerage Dept: POB 130, Baughers Bay, Road Town, Tortola VG1110; tel. 468-3416; fax 494-6746; e-mail water@surfbvi.com.

Transport

ROADS

In 2002 there were 132 km (82 miles) of access roads, 77 km of primary roads, 37 km of secondary roads and 90 km of tertiary roads. In 2005 13,392 vehicles were licensed, 9,201 of which were private vehicles.

Public Works Department: Baughers Bay, Tortola; tel. 494-2722; fax 494-4740; e-mail pwd@bvigovernment.org; responsible for road maintenance.

SHIPPING

There are two direct steamship services, one from the United Kingdom and one from the USA. Motor launches maintain daily mail and passenger services with St Thomas and St John, US Virgin Islands. A new cruise ship pier, built at a cost of US $6.9m. with assistance from the Caribbean Development Bank, was opened in Road Town in 1994 and was later expanded. Further expansion work was due to be completed in December 2008.

British Virgin Islands Ports Authority: Port Purcell, POB 4, Road Town, Tortola VG1110; tel. 494-3435; fax 494-2642; e-mail bviports@candwbvi.net; internet www.bviports.org; f. 1991; Chair. CARL DAWSON; Man. Dir VICTOR O'NEAL.

Tropical Shipping: Port Purcell Seaport, Island Shipping and Trading, POB 250, Road Town, Tortola VG1110; tel. 494-2674; fax 494-3505; e-mail lmoses@tropical.com; internet www.tropical.com; Man. LEROY MOSES.

CIVIL AVIATION

Terrance B. Lettsome (formerly Beef Island) Airport, about 16 km (10 miles) from Road Town, has a runway with a length of 1,500 m (4,921 ft). A new US $65m. airport terminal was opened at the airport in March 2002. Captain Auguste George Airport on Anegada has been designated an international point of entry and was resurfaced in the late 1990s. In June 2008 the Government signed an agreement with Halcrow Group Ltd of the United Kingdom to develop the airport on Virgin Gorda, including an extension to the runway to allow larger aircraft to land.

Director of Civil Aviation: DENNISTON FRAZER, Terrance B. Lettsome International Airport, Suite 217–19, Beef Island; tel. 468-6492; fax 468-6493; e-mail aviation@bvigovernment.org.

Tourism

The main attraction of the islands is their tranquillity and clear waters, which provide excellent facilities for sailing, fishing, diving and other water sports. In 2004 there were an estimated 1,370 hotel rooms. There are also many charter yachts offering overnight accommodation. There were some 358,056 stop-over visitors and 575,211 cruise ship passengers in 2007. The majority of tourists are from the USA. Receipts from tourism totalled some US $437m. in 2005.

British Virgin Islands Chamber of Commerce and Hotel Association: see Chamber of Commerce.

British Virgin Islands Tourist Board: 2nd Floor, AKARA Bldg, DeCastro St, Road Town, Tortola VG1110; tel. 494-3134; fax 494-3866; e-mail info@bvitourism.com; internet www.bvitourism.com; Chair. TERRY WALWYN.

THE CAYMAN ISLANDS

Introductory Survey

Location, Climate, Language, Religion, Flag, Capital

The Cayman Islands lie about 290 km (180 miles) west-north-west of Jamaica and consist of three main islands: Grand Cayman and, to the north-east, Little Cayman and Cayman Brac. The climate is tropical but is tempered by the trade winds, with a cool season between November and March, when temperatures average 24°C (75°F). The rainy season lasts from May until October. Mean annual rainfall is 1,524 mm (60 ins). The official language is English. Many Christian churches are represented. The flag is the British 'Blue Ensign', with the islands' coat of arms (a golden lion on a red background above three stars in green, representing the three main islands, superimposed on wavy lines of blue and white, the shield surmounted by a torse of white and blue bearing a yellow pineapple behind a green turtle, and with the motto 'He hath founded it upon the seas' on a scroll beneath) on a white roundel in the fly. The capital is George Town, on the island of Grand Cayman.

Recent History

The Cayman Islands came under acknowledged British rule in 1670 and were settled mainly from Jamaica and by privateers and buccaneers. The islands of Little Cayman and Cayman Brac were permanently settled only in 1833, and until 1877 there was no administrative connection between them and Grand Cayman. A representative assembly first sat in 1832. The islands formed a dependency of Jamaica until 1959, and the Governor of Jamaica held responsibility for the Cayman Islands until Jamaican independence in 1962, when a separate administrator was appointed (the title was changed to that of Governor in 1971). The 1959 Constitution was revised in 1972, 1992 and 1994.

For many years there have been no formal political parties on the islands, despite the emergence of a nascent party political system during the 1960s with the formation, in 1961, of the National Democratic Party (NDP), as part of a campaign for self-government. The Christian Democratic Party was formed as a conservative opposition. Both parties disappeared within a few years despite the electoral success of the NDP, largely owing to the system of gubernatorial nomination to the Executive Council. In the 1970s elections for the 12 elective seats in the Legislative Assembly came to be contested by 'teams' of candidates, as well as by independents. Two such teams were formed, Progress and Dignity (the more conservative) and Unity, but all candidates were committed to augmenting the economic success of the Caymans, and favoured continued dependent status. There are no plans for independence, and the majority of the population wish to maintain the islands' links with the United Kingdom.

At elections in November 1980 the Unity team, led by Jim Bodden, took eight of the 12 seats. In the November 1984 elections opposition independents won nine seats, aided by public disquiet at the rapid growth of the immigrant work-force, and the implications of the recent US challenges to the Cayman Islands' bank secrecy laws. In 1987 the Legislative Assembly successfully sought stricter regulations of status and residency for those able to participate in elections, in an attempt to protect the political rights of native Caymanians (in view of the very large immigrant population). At a general election in November 1988 seven of the existing members were returned, and five new members were elected. Prior to the election the teams had regrouped into more informal coalitions, indicating the primacy of personal over 'party' affiliations.

In July 1990 the Legislative Assembly approved proposals to review the Constitution, and in January 1991 the British Government sent two commissioners to the territory to discuss possible amendments. The implementation of most recommendations, including the appointment of a Chief Minister, was postponed pending a general election to be held in 1992. One of the amendments, however, which involved increasing the number of elective seats in the Legislative Assembly to 15, was adopted in March 1992. The proposed reforms had prompted the formation, in mid-1991, of the territory's first political organization since the 1960s, the Progressive Democratic Party (PDP). During 1992 the organization developed into a coalition and was renamed the National Team. At the general election in November 1992 National Team members secured 12 of the elective seats in the newly enlarged Legislative Assembly, while independent candidates won the remaining three. In November of that year James Ryan was appointed Chief Secretary, following the retirement of Lemuel Hurlston. The new Government opted to revoke the provisions in the Constitution for a Chief

Minister; however, in 1994 it introduced a ministerial system and created a fifth ministerial portfolio.

At a general election in November 1996 the governing National Team remained in power, although with a reduced majority, winning nine seats in the Legislative Assembly. Two new groupings, the Democratic Alliance and Team Cayman (which had formed in opposition to the Government's alleged mismanagement of the public debt and of Cayman Airways) secured two seats and one seat, respectively. Independent candidates won three seats.

In November 1997 the Minister of Community Development, Sport, Youth Affairs and Culture, McKeeva Bush, was dismissed from his post after it was alleged that a bank of which he was a director had authorized fraudulent loans totalling some US $1.1m. Bush (who denied any knowledge of the alleged corruption) was replaced by Julianna O'Connor Connolly, the first female minister on the island.

In March 1999 the Government of the United Kingdom published draft legislation pertaining to its relationship with its Overseas Dependencies, which were to be renamed United Kingdom Overseas Territories (and had been referred to as such since February 1998). The legislation proposed the extension of British citizenship to the citizens of Overseas Territories, although it also required the Territories to amend their legislation on human rights and on the regulation of the financial services sector to meet international standards. The Cayman Islands were praised for the introduction in 1998 of laws on tax evasion, and for strengthening the regulatory powers of the Monetary Authority, although concern was expressed that homosexuality remained a criminal offence in the islands. The issue of the legal status of homosexuality in the Cayman Islands had been highlighted in January 1998 by the authorities' refusal to permit a stop-over by a US cruise liner whose 900 passengers were homosexual men.

In late April 1999 representatives of the European Union (EU, see p. 255) held meetings with the overseas territories of member states to discuss proposed reforms of legislation relating to the financial services sector. The Cayman Islands delegation defended the islands' standards of regulation, arguing that the islands had implemented some of the strictest laws in the world against money-laundering, and that proposals to abolish the Cayman Islands' laws on banking secrecy would place the islands at a disadvantage, compared with the financial centres of Switzerland and Luxembourg. In early June the Cayman Islands announced that it was to seek certification under the UN's Offshore Initiative, and that consequently a UN agency, the Global Programme against Money Laundering, was to undertake a review of the islands' financial systems and regulations.

In August 1999 a US citizen, John Matthewson, was sentenced to five years' probation by a US court on charges of money-laundering in the Cayman Islands. Matthewson had reportedly escaped a prison sentence by revealing to US investigators the extent of his activities in the Cayman Islands and the extent to which the islands' financial system benefited those seeking to evade US taxation. The US Government subsequently charged several of Matthewson's clients with tax evasion, and it was widely believed that the case had seriously damaged the islands' reputation both for secrecy and as a reputable financial centre. However, the island authorities claimed that the Royal Cayman Islands Police had co-operated fully with the US investigators, and also observed that in 1998 the islands' policy of co-operation with US investigators in their efforts to prevent money-laundering had been singled out for praise in the US *International Narcotics Control Strategy Report*.

Drugs-related crime continued to be a serious problem in the 1990s, when an estimated 75% of all thefts and burglaries in the islands were attributed, directly or indirectly, to the drugs trade. The Mutual Legal Assistance Treaty (signed in 1986, and ratified by the US Senate in 1990) between the Cayman Islands and the USA provides for the mutual exchange of information for use in combating crime (particularly drugs-trafficking and the diversion of funds gained illegally from the drugs trade). Further legislation relating to the abuse of the financial sector by criminal organizations was approved in November 1996. In October 2005 the Government introduced longer sentences for possession of illegal firearms or bullet-proof vests. Offenders would be sentenced to a minimum of 10 years in prison and fined CI $100,000.

In a general election held on 8 November 2000 the governing National Team suffered a heavy defeat, losing six of its nine seats, including that held by Truman Bodden, the Leader of Government Business. The newly elected Legislative Assembly appointed Kurt Tibbetts of the Democratic Alliance as Leader of Government Business.

In an unprecedented development in November 2001, several members of the Legislative Assembly, dissatisfied with the Government's leadership during the economic slowdown, formed the United Democratic Party (UDP). McKeeva Bush, the leader of the new party and Deputy Leader of Government Business and Minister of Tourism, Environment and Transport, claimed that at least 10 members of the 15-member Assembly were UDP supporters. Subsequently, the passing of a motion of no confidence against the Leader of Government Business resulted in Tibbetts and Edna Moyle, the Minister of Community Development, Women's Affairs, Youth and Sport, leaving the Executive Council. Bush became the new Leader of Government Business, while two other legislators, Gilbert McLean and Frank McField, both members of the UDP, joined the Cabinet. In May 2002, at the UDP's inaugural convention, Bush was formally elected leader of the party. In the same month it was announced that the five opposition members of the legislative assembly had formed a new political party, the People's Progressive Movement (PPM), led by Tibbetts.

In March 2002 the three-member Constitutional Review Commission, appointed by the Governor in May 2001, submitted a new draft constitution. The proposed document had to be debated by the Legislative Assembly and then approved by the British Parliament before being formally adopted. The draft constitution included the creation of the office of Chief Minister, proposed a full ministerial government, and incorporated a bill of rights. The opposition demanded a referendum on the recommendations, on the grounds that the UDP had rejected several of the proposals, despite strong public support for the changes, but Bush forwarded the proposals to the British Foreign and Commonwealth Office (FCO), via the Governor's office. In December Bush and the leader of the opposition, Tibbetts, travelled to the United Kingdom in order to review the proposed constitution with FCO officials. Consensus, however, proved impossible to achieve. While the PPM called for a public referendum on issue, the UDP announced in February 2004 that it would not participate in the constitutional review process before the next election. These were originally scheduled to be held in November 2004, but were postponed, owing to the damage caused by 'Hurricane Ivan' in September 2004 (see below). In March 2006 an FCO delegation visited the Cayman Islands for informal discussions aimed at restarting the process of constitutional reform.

In May 2002 the British Overseas Territories Act, having received royal assent in the United Kingdom in February, came into force and granted British citizenship to the people of its Overseas Territories, including the Cayman Islands. Under the new law Caymanians would be able to hold British passports and work in the United Kingdom and elsewhere in the EU. Also in May, the Cayman Islands became an associate member of the Caribbean Community and Common Market (CARICOM, see p. 206). In the same month Bruce Dinwiddy succeeded Peter Smith as Governor.

In January 2003 Bush accused the United Kingdom of undermining the course of Cayman Islands' justice, after a routine money-laundering case was dismissed amid allegations of espionage and obstruction of justice by British intelligence agents. The trial collapsed after it was alleged that the Director of the Cayman Islands Financial Reporting Unit (and a key witness in the trial) had passed information about the case to an unnamed agency of the British Government, understood to be the Secret Intelligence Service (MI6). It was claimed that MI6 wished to protect the names of its sources within the Caribbean 'offshore' banking community. Bush demanded the British Government pay for the failed trial, estimated to cost some US $5m., and for any negative repercussions the affair might have for the reputation of the islands' banking sector. The United Kingdom, however, refused to compensate the Cayman Islands and maintained that although its intelligence agencies might have helped in the investigation, they had never interfered in the case. In March the Attorney-General, David Ballantyne, resigned amid accusations that he was aware that British intelligence agents were working covertly in the Cayman Islands; Samuel W. Bulgin, the erstwhile Solicitor-General, was appointed as Ballantyne's permanent successor in July.

The opposition PPM won a resounding victory at the general election of 11 May 2005, securing nine of the 15 legislative seats. The ruling UDP won only five seats, with the remaining seat going to an independent. The outgoing UDP Government had been criticized for its handling of the aftermath of 'Hurricane Ivan', which had caused an estimated CI $2,800m. of damage in September 2004, and also for its decision, in the same month, to grant 'belonger' status to some 3,000 people, a move interpreted by many as an attempt to increase the party's electoral support. The Leader of Government Business, Kurt Tibbetts, pledged to hold a referendum on increased autonomy for the islands. In November he announced a Freedom of Information Bill, to be debated in the Legislative Assembly, prior to a public consultation exercise. The proposed legislation was intended to promote government transparency and accountability, thus increasing constitutional democracy, and in January 2007 revisions to a draft version of the document were under discussion pending submission to the Cabinet for approval in March. However, anticipated consideration of the amendments to the bill was postponed beyond the fourth governmental convention of the 2006/07 fiscal year, conducted on 23 March; the logistics of implementing the necessary personnel training for the introduction of a dedicated Freedom of Information office and creation of an Information Commissioner role, with the equivalent governmental rank of the Auditor-General, was cited as the principal delaying factor. The legislation was finally approved at the end of August and in the following month the Freedom of Information Unit was officially opened. Following preparation time for the administration of requests for information to the relevant government departments, the law finally became effective on 5 January 2009. By April some 259 requests for data had been submitted to the Freedom of Information Unit.

In November 2005 Stuart Jack succeeded Bruce Dinwiddy as Governor. Governor Jack indicated in January 2007 that a general election would not be called before May 2009, and might be postponed until November of that year to allow the elected government sufficient opportunity to prepare for the June deadline by which the next budget should be announced. The opposition UDP, however, contended that an election was constitutionally due by November 2008, the previous ballot having been postponed from the corresponding month in 2004 owing to disruption caused by 'Hurricane Ivan'. The election was eventually scheduled for 20 May 2009.

In mid-February 2007 the Government announced the establishment of a Constitutional Review Secretariat to initiate renewed efforts towards constitutional reform in the territory from March. The mandate of the government-administered body, to be presided over by Cabinet Secretary Orrett Connor, was stated as promoting public awareness, disseminating information and expediting the public consultation process through education and the institution of an effective communication framework. Formal embarkation upon constitutional modernization—facilitated by the counsel of a British constitutional lawyer, Professor Jeffrey Jowell—was expected to commence once the Secretariat became fully operational, entailing a national referendum and negotiations with the United Kingdom in the advanced stages. In January 2008 the Government launched a series of public consultations ahead of a referendum scheduled to be held in May. The FCO affirmed in early April that the new Constitution must include a bill of rights and, in response, the Government postponed the referendum to allow a longer period of public deliberation. Discussions resumed in January 2009, and on 6 April it was announced that the referendum would be held on 20 May, at the same time as the legislative election. The Legislative Assembly was suspended on 23 March in anticipation of the ballot.

It was announced in April 2009 that Governor Jack would leave office in November; he was to be succeeded by Duncan Taylor from January 2010.

The US Senate Finance Committee reported in June 2007 that it had identified more than 14,000 registered companies purportedly maintaining headquarters at a single address in the Cayman Islands, and subsequently commissioned an inquiry into the anomaly by the Government Accountability Office. It was estimated that evasion of US tax obligations by such entities—achieved by establishing 'offshore' subsidiaries on the islands—had resulted in a US $100,000m. shortfall in tax-based revenue and precipitated a growing sentiment of hostilities between the two nations' respective regulatory authorities. The inquiry reported its findings in July 2008: it concluded that although the Cayman Islands adhered to international financial standards, the use of the islands by US citizens (5% of companies registered at the address were entirely US-owned and a further 40%–50% had a US billing address) was often indicative of illegal tax activities. The collapse in 2008 of several Cayman Island-based hedge funds, exacerbating the global financial crisis, caused increased attention to be focused on the territory's financial institutions. US President Barack Obama announced in May 2009 that he intended to implement stringent new laws governing tax havens, and called for more transparency from the 'offshore' sector, sentiments echoed by the British Prime Minister Gordon Brown.

In January 2008 Governor Jack ordered a Commission of Enquiry into civil service guide-lines. The Commission was deemed necessary following the unauthorized publication of government documents by then Permanent Secretary of Tourism Charles Clifford in 2004 after his resignation from the civil service. Clifford had been accused of leaking the files in order to benefit his party, the PPM, ahead of the 2005 general election. He was subsequently appointed Minister of Tourism. In March 2008 the Commission recommended several legislative changes to prevent recurrence of the disclosures, including the introduction of a one-year hiatus between resignation of civil servants and their eligibility for public office; although in August the Cabinet agreed to adopt several of the Commission's proposals, it rejected this recommendation.

Government

Under the revised Constitution of 1994, the Governor, who is appointed by the British monarch, is responsible for external affairs, defence, internal security and the public service. The Governor is Chairman of the Cabinet, comprising three members appointed by the Governor and five members elected by the Legislative Assembly. The Legislative Assembly comprises three official members and 15 members elected by universal adult suffrage for a period of four years. A constitutional review was under way in 2009.

Defence

The United Kingdom is responsible for the defence of the Cayman Islands.

Economic Affairs

In 2007, according to official estimates, the Cayman Islands' gross domestic product (GDP) was CI $2,140.8m., equivalent to some $40,242 per head. During 2000–07, according to official estimates, the population increased at an average annual rate of 4.3%, while GDP increased, in real terms, by 2.6% per year during 2000–07; growth was 2.2% in 2007.

Agriculture (which engaged only 1.9% of the employed labour force in 2007 and accounted for 0.4% of value added in the same year) is limited by infertile soil, low rainfall and high labour costs. The principal crops are citrus fruits and bananas, and some other produce for local consumption. Flowers (particularly orchids) are produced for export. Livestock-rearing consists of beef cattle, poultry (mainly for eggs) and pigs. The traditional activity of turtle-hunting has virtually disappeared; the turtle farm (the only commercial one in the world) now produces mainly for domestic consumption (and serves as a research centre), following the imposition of US restrictions on the trade in turtle products in 1979. Fishing is mainly for lobster and shrimp.

Industry, engaging 20.0% of the employed labour force and, according to the UN, accounting for 14.7% of value added in 2007, consists mainly of construction and related manufacturing, some food-processing and tourism-related light industries. The construction sector contributed 9.6% of value added in 2007, while manufacturing activities accounted for only about 1.9% of the total in that year. Energy requirements are satisfied by the import of petroleum products and gas (11.7% of total imports in 2007).

Service industries dominate the Caymanian economy, accounting for 78.2% of employment (excluding unclassified activities) in 2007 and contributing 83.3% of value added in the same year. The tourism industry is the principal economic activity, and in 1991 accounted for 22.9% of GDP and employed, directly and indirectly, some 50% of the working population. The industry earned an estimated US $353.0m. in 2005, compared to $519.0m. the year previous. Most visitors are from the USA (79.6% of tourist arrivals in 2007). The Cayman Islands is one of the largest 'offshore' financial centres in the world; during the 2007/08 fiscal year there were 279 banks and trust companies and 10,291 mutual funds on the islands, according to the Cayman Islands Monetary Authority. In 2007 the financial services sector engaged 9.7% of the working population, and in 1999 contributed about 36.0% of GDP.

In 2007 the Cayman Islands recorded a trade deficit of CI $860.3m. Receipts from tourism and the financial sector, remittances and capital inflows normally offset the trade deficit. The principal source of imports is the USA (which provided some 74.6% of total imports in 2007), which is also one of the principal markets for exports (34.6% in 1994). Other major trading partners in 2007 included the Netherlands Antilles (8.4% of total imports). The principal imports in 2007 were miscellaneous manufactured articles (45.5%), petroleum products and gas (11.7%), machinery and transport equipment (11.5%) and basic manufactures (8.6%).

An estimated government budget surplus of CI $39.0m. was recorded in 2007. In 1998 official development assistance totalled US $0.2m. At the end of 1999 the public debt stood at US $114.8m. The average annual rate of inflation was 2.9% in 2000–08; consumer prices increased by an annual average of 4.1% in 2008. According to official census figures, only 61% of the resident population of the islands were Caymanian in 2005 (compared with 79% in 1980). Some 3.8% of the labour force were unemployed in 2007.

The United Kingdom is responsible for the external affairs of the Cayman Islands, and the dependency has the status of Overseas Territory in association with the European Union (EU, see p. 255). The Cayman Islands gained associate member status in Caribbean Community and Common Market (CARICOM, see p. 206) in 2002; the territory is also a member of CARICOM's Caribbean Development Bank (CDB, see p. 211).

Both the principal economic sectors, 'offshore' finance and tourism, benefit from the Cayman Islands' political stability, good infrastructure and extensive development. Tourism continued to expand in the 2000s, although the Government attempted to limit tourist numbers in order to minimize damage to the environment, particularly the coral reef, and to preserve the islands' reputation as a destination for visitors of above-average wealth. The sector, nevertheless, was adversely affected by the damage caused by 'Hurricane Ivan' in September 2004. The financial sector, which benefits from an absence of taxation and of foreign exchange regulations, recorded consistently high levels of growth during the 1990s, and provided an estimated 30% of GDP in 1998. The banking sector was reckoned to be the world's fifth largest in 2000, owing to the absence of direct taxation, lenient regulation and strict confidentiality laws. By 2008 the jurisdiction dominated the hedge fund sector; by July some 10,037 hedge funds were registered in the islands. The Cayman

Islands have a policy of openly confronting the issues of financial transparency and of money-laundering, and an information exchange treaty with the USA was ratified in 1990. However, despite the efforts of the authorities, the vulnerability of the islands' financial services sector to exploitation by criminal organizations continued to cause concern. In June 2000 the Cayman Islands were included on a list of harmful tax regimes compiled by an agency of the Organisation for Economic Co-operation and Development (OECD, see p. 358) and were urged to make legislative changes, introducing greater legal and administrative transparency. The Government pledged to adopt international standards of legal and administrative transparency by 2005, and in 2001, following stricter regulation of the private banking sector, the Cayman Islands were removed from the blacklist. However, in April 2009 the Cayman Islands was included in OECD's so-called 'grey list' of territories that had committed to improving financial transparency, but had yet substantially to implement reform. In late 2002 the financial sector faced disruption when the United Kingdom, under pressure from an EU investigation into tax evasion, demanded that the Cayman Islands disclose the identities and account details of Europeans holding private savings accounts on the islands. The Cayman Islands, along with some other British Overseas Territories facing similar demands, claimed it was being treated unfairly, and refused to make any concessions. Nevertheless, the Legislative Assembly, after the British Government pledged to safeguard the territory's interests, voted to accept British/EU demands by 1 January 2005. The Government also faced increased pressure to reform the financial sector in 2009 from the incoming Administration of US President Barack Obama; while a senator, Obama co-sponsored legislation which aimed to recoup the estimated US $100,000m. in revenues lost to 'offshore' tax jurisdictions such as the Cayman Islands. Tourist arrivals declined by 10.1% in September 2008, compared with the same month in 2007, while the situation was expected to worsen in 2009, owing to the ongoing global economic downturn. Cruise-ship numbers continued to fall, partly owing to increased airline services to the islands, although this was not enough to prevent a net loss in tourism figures. With North America and Europe accounting for 93% of total air arrivals in 2008, the recession in those regions has been detrimental to the Cayman Islands. Nevertheless, GDP growth was forecast at 3.1% for 2008 and at 3.0% for 2009.

Education

Schooling is compulsory for children between the ages of five and 15 years. It is provided free in 10 government-run primary schools, and there are also three state secondary schools, as well as six church-sponsored schools (five of which offer secondary as well as primary education). Primary education, from five years of age, lasts for six years; in 2004/05 enrolment at primary schools included an estimated 81.1% of pupils in the relevant age-group. Secondary education lasts for seven years and enrolment at secondary-level institutions in 2004/05 included an estimated 95.6% of students in the relevant age-group. Some CI $100m. was allocated for education in the 2006/07 budget.

Public Holidays

2009: 1 January (New Year's Day), 26 January (National Heroes' Day), 25 February (Ash Wednesday), 10 April (Good Friday), 13 April (Easter Monday), 18 May (Discovery Day), 20 May (Election Day), 15 June (Queen's Official Birthday), 6 July (Constitution Day), 9 November (Remembrance Day), 25–28 December (Christmas).
2010: 1 January (New Year's Day), 25 January (National Heroes' Day), 17 February (Ash Wednesday), 2 April (Good Friday), 5 April (Easter Monday), 17 May (Discovery Day), 14 June (Queen's Official Birthday), 5 July (Constitution Day), 15 November (Remembrance Day), 25–28 December (Christmas),

Weights and Measures

The imperial system is in use.

Statistical Survey

Sources: Government Information Services, Cricket Sq., Elgin Ave, George Town, Grand Cayman; tel. 949-8092; fax 949-5936; The Information Centre, Economic and Statistics Office, Government Administration Bldg, Grand Cayman; tel. 949-0940; fax 949-8782; e-mail infostats@gov.ky; internet www.eso.ky.

AREA AND POPULATION

Area: 262 sq km (102 sq miles). The main island of Grand Cayman is about 197 sq km (76 sq miles), about one-half of which is swamp. Cayman Brac is 39 sq km (15 sq miles); Little Cayman is 26 sq km (11 sq miles).

Population: 39,410 (males 19,311, females 20,099) at census of 10 October 1999 (Grand Cayman 37,473, Cayman Brac 1,822, Little Cayman 115). 2007 (estimated population at 31 December): 53,886.
Density (31 December 2007): 205.7 per sq km.
Principal Towns (population at 1999 census): George Town (capital) 20,626; West Bay 8,243; Bodden Town 5,764. *Mid-2007* (UN estimate, incl. suburbs): George Town 28,000 (Source: partly UN, *World Urbanization Prospects: The 2007 Revision*).
Births, Marriages and Deaths (2007): Live births 744 (birth rate 14.0 per 1,000); Marriages 482 (marriage rate 9.1 per 1,000); Deaths 160 (death rate 3.0 per 1,000).
Life Expectancy (years at birth, 2008): 80.3 (males 77.7; females 83.0). Source: Pan American Health Organization.
Economically Active Population (sample survey, persons aged 15 years and over, October–November 2007): Agriculture and fishing 639; Manufacturing 658; Mining and quarrying 46; Construction 5,646; Electricity, gas and water supply 504; Wholesale and retail trade 3,619; Restaurants and hotels 3,499; Transport, post and telecommunication 2,004; Financial services 3,332; Public administration 2,509; Education, health and social work 2,833; Other community, social and personal service activities 2,008; Private households with employed persons 2,786; Business services 4,200; Extra-territorial organizations and bodies (calculated as residual) 18; Not classifiable by economic activity 780; *Total employed* 35,081; Unemployed 1,395; *Total labour force* 36,476 (Caymanian 18,465, non-Caymanian 18,011).

HEALTH AND WELFARE

Physicians (per 1,000 head, 2005): 1.4.
Health Expenditure: % of GDP (1997): 4.2.
Health Expenditure: public (% of total, 1997): 53.2.
Source: mainly Pan American Health Organization.

For definitions, see explanatory note on p. vi.

AGRICULTURE, ETC.

Livestock ('000 head, 2007, FAO estimates): Cattle 1.3; Goats 0.3; Pigs 0.4; Chickens 6.
Fishing (metric tons, live weight, 2006): Total catch 125 (all marine fishes).
Source: FAO.

INDUSTRY

Electric Energy (production, million kWh): 463.2 in 2005; 535.7 in 2006; 584.4 in 2007.

FINANCE

Currency and Exchange Rates: 100 cents = 1 Cayman Islands dollar (CI $). *Sterling, US Dollar and Euro Equivalents* (31 December 2008): £1 sterling = CI $1.215; US $1 = 83.3 CI cents; €1 = 86.2 CI cents; CI $100 = £82.32 = US $120.00 = €86.23. *Exchange rate:* Fixed at CI $1 = US $1.20.
Budget (CI $ million, 2007): *Revenue:* Taxes on international trade and transactions 178.6; Taxes on other domestic goods and services 223.2; Taxes on property 37.2; Other tax revenue 9.0; Non-coercive revenue 65.0 (Sales of goods and services 58.4); Total 513.0. *Expenditure:* Current expenditure 435.5 (Personnel costs 213.5, Supplies and consumable goods 101.0, Subsidies 88.1, Transfer payments 23.2, Interest payments 9.6); Extraordinary expenses 3.2; Other executive expenses 7.4; Capital expenditure and net lending 105.9; Total 552.0.
Cost of Living (Consumer Price Index; base: September 1994 = 100): All items 143.5 in 2006; 147.7 in 2007; 153.7 in 2008.
Gross Domestic Product (CI $ million at constant 1986 prices): 910.0 in 2005; 951.9 in 2006; 973.3 in 2007.
Gross Domestic Product by Economic Activity (CI $ million in current prices, 1991): Primary industries 5; Manufacturing 9; Electricity, gas and water 19; Construction 54; Trade, restaurants and hotels 138; Transport, storage and communications 65; Finance, insurance, real estate and business services 210; Community, social and personal services 42; Government services 63; Statistical discrepancy 1; *Sub-total* 606; Import duties less imputed bank service charge 11; *GDP in purchasers' values* 617. *2007* (CI $ million): Agriculture, hunting, forestry and fishing 8; Mining, manufacturing and utilities 113 (Manufacturing 37); Construction 209; Wholesale, retail trade, restaurants and hotels 507; Transport, storage and communication 237; Other activities 1,078; Total gross value added 2,152; Net taxes on products 36 (figure obtained as residual); GDP in pur-

chasers' values 2,188 (Source: UN Statistics Division, National Accounts Main Aggregates Database).

EXTERNAL TRADE

Principal Commodities (CI $ million, 2007): *Imports c.i.f.:* Food and live animals 61.0; Beverages and tobacco 46.8; Petroleum products and gas 102.9; Chemicals and related products 27.5; Basic manufactures 75.6; Machinery and transport equipment 101.8; Miscellaneous manufactured articles 401.6; Total (incl. others) 881.8. *Exports f.o.b.:* Total 21.5.

Principal Trading Partners (CI $ million): *Imports c.i.f.* (2007): Japan 7.3; Netherlands Antilles 74.0; United Kingdom 5.5; USA 657.6; Total (incl. others) 881.8. *Exports f.o.b.* (1994): USA 0.9; Total 2.6. *2007:* Total 21.5.

TRANSPORT

Road Traffic ('000 motor vehicles in use, 2002): Passenger cars 23.8; Commercial vehicles 6.4.

Shipping: *International Freight Traffic* ('000 metric tons): Goods loaded 735 (1990); Goods unloaded 239,138 (2000). *Cargo Vessels* (1995): Vessels 15, Calls at port 266. *Merchant Fleet* (vessels registered at 31 December 2007): 141; Total displacement 2,870,517 grt. (Source: Lloyd's Register-Fairplay, *World Fleet Statistics*).

TOURISM

Visitor Arrivals ('000): 1,966.8 (arrivals by air 167.8, cruise ship passengers 1,799.0) in 2005; 2,197.4 (arrivals by air 267.3, cruise ship passengers 1,930.1) in 2006; 2,007.2 (arrivals by air 291.5, cruise ship passengers 1,715.7) in 2007.

Stay-over Arrivals by Place of Origin ('000, 2007): Canada 17.4; Europe 20.4; USA 231.9; Total (incl. others) 291.5. Source: Cayman Islands Tourism Department, George Town.

Tourism Receipts (US $ million, incl. passenger transport): 523 in 2004; 356 in 2005; 509 in 2006. Source: World Tourism Organization.

COMMUNICATIONS MEDIA

Radio Receivers: 36,000 in use in 1997.

Television Receivers: 23,239 in use in 1999.

Telephones: 32,967 main lines in use in 2003.

Facsimile Machines: 116 in use in 1993.

Mobile Cellular Telephones (subscribers): 33,800 in 2004.

Fixed and Mobile Telecommunication Lines (number in service): 110,656 in 2005.

Internet Users: 22,000 in 2007.

Daily Newspapers: 2 (circulation 15,400) in 2004.

EDUCATION
(30 September 2006)

Institutions: Government 18; Private 11; Total 29.

Enrolment: *Government:* Pre-primary 41; Primary 2,339; Middle 1,171; Secondary 948; Total 4,499. *Private:* Pre-primary 292; Primary 1,253; Middle 558; Secondary 415; Total 2,518.

Directory

The Constitution

The Constitution of 1959 was revised in 1972, 1992 and 1994. Under its terms, the Governor, who is appointed for four years, is responsible for defence and internal security, external affairs, and the public service. The Cabinet (known as the Executive Council until 2003) comprises the Chairman (the Governor), the Chief Secretary, the Financial Secretary, the Attorney-General, the Cabinet Secretary (all four of whom are appointed by the Governor) and five other Ministers elected by the Legislative Assembly from their own number. The Governor assigns ministerial portfolios to the elected members of the Cabinet. There are 15 elected members of the Legislative Assembly (elected by direct, universal adult suffrage for a term of four years) and three official members appointed by the Governor. The Speaker presides over the Assembly. The United Kingdom retains full control over foreign affairs. In May 2001 the Governor appointed a Constitutional Review Commission to make recommendations on changes to the Cayman Islands' political structure and processes. A government-administered Constitutional Review Secretariat was established in March 2007 to resume evaluation of the Cayman Islands' Constitution following the disruption to previous efforts caused by 'Hurricane Ivan'.

The Government

Governor: STUART JACK (assumed office November 2005).
Governor-designate: DUNCAN TAYLOR (to take office January 2010).

CABINET
(April 2009)

Chairman: STUART JACK (The Governor).
Chief Secretary and Minister of Internal and External Affairs*: GEORGE A. MCCARTHY.
Attorney-General and Minister of Legal Affairs*: SAMUEL W. BULGIN.
Financial Secretary*: KENNETH JEFFERSON.
Cabinet Secretary*: ORRETT CONNOR.
Leader of Government Business and Minister for District Administration, Planning, Agriculture and Housing: D. KURT TIBBETTS.
Minister of Health and Human Services: ANTHONY S. EDEN.
Minister of Education, Training, Employment, Youth, Sports and Culture: ALDEN MCNEE MCLAUGHLIN.
Minister of Communications, Works and Infrastructure: V. ARDEN MCLEAN.
Minister of Tourism, Environment, Investment and Commerce: CHARLES CLIFFORD.

A District Commissioner, Ernie Scott, represents the Governor on Cayman Brac and Little Cayman.
* Appointed by the Governor.

LEGISLATIVE ASSEMBLY

Legislative Assembly: 33 Fort St, POB 890, George Town, Grand Cayman; tel. 949-4236; fax 949-9514; e-mail wendy.lauer@gov.ky; internet www.legislativeassembly.ky; Clerk WENDY LAUER.

Members: The Chief Secretary, the Financial Secretary, the Attorney-General, and 15 elected members. The most recent election to the Assembly was on 11 May 2005. In February 1991 a Speaker was elected to preside over the Assembly (despite provision for such a post in the Constitution, the functions of the Speaker had hitherto been assumed by the Governor).

Speaker: EDNA MOYLE.
Leader of Government Business: D. KURT TIBBETTS.

GOVERNMENT OFFICES

Office of the Governor: AALL Bldg, 4th Floor, North Church St, George Town, Grand Cayman; tel. 244-2401; fax 945-4131; e-mail staffoff@candw.ky; internet www.gov.ky.

All official government offices and ministries are located in the Government Administration Bldg, Elgin Ave, George Town, Grand Cayman.

Election Commission

Elections Office: Smith Road Profession Centre, 150 Smith Rd, 2nd Floor, George Town, Grand Cayman; tel. 949-8047; fax 949-0631; e-mail electionsoffice@candw.ky; internet www.electionsoffice.ky; Supervisor of Elections KEARNEY SIDNEY GOMEZ.

Political Organizations

People's Progressive Movement (PPM): POB 10526 APO, Grand Cayman; tel. 945-1776; f. 2002; Leader D. KURT TIBBETTS; Chair. ANTONY DUCKWORTH.

United Democratic Party (UDP): Edge Plaza, Unit 3, 6 Ashgo St, POB 10009, Grand Cayman; e-mail info@udp.ky; internet www.udp.ky; tel. 943-3338; fax 943-3339; f. 2001; Leader W. MCKEEVA BUSH; Chair. BILLY REID.

Judicial System

There is a Grand Court of the Islands (with Supreme Court status), a Summary Court, a Youth Court and a Coroner's Court. The Grand Court has jurisdiction in all civil matters, admiralty matters, and in trials on indictment. Appeals lie to the Court of Appeal of the Cayman Islands and beyond that to the Privy Council in the United Kingdom.

The Summary Courts deal with criminal and civil matters (up to a certain limit defined by law) and appeals lie to the Grand Court.
Chief Justice: ANTHONY SMELLIE.
President of the Court of Appeal: EDWARD ZACCA.
Solicitor-General: CHERYLL RICHARDS.
Clerk of the Courts of the Islands: VALDIS FOLDATS, Court's Office, Edward St, George Town, Grand Cayman KY1-1106; tel. 949-4296; fax 949-9856; e-mail valdis.foldats@gov.ky.

Religion

CHRISTIANITY

The oldest established denominations are (on Grand Cayman) the United Church of Jamaica and Grand Cayman (Presbyterian), and (on Cayman Brac) the Baptist Church. Anglicans are adherents of the Church in the Province of the West Indies (Grand Cayman forms part of the diocese of Jamaica). Within the Roman Catholic Church, the Cayman Islands forms part of the archdiocese of Kingston in Jamaica. Other denominations include the Church of God, Church of God (Full Gospel), Church of Christ, Seventh-day Adventist, Wesleyan Holiness, Jehovah's Witnesses, Church of the Latter Day Saints, Bahá'í and Church of God (Universal). In 1999 there were an estimated 90 churches in the Cayman Islands, including seven churches on Cayman Brac, and a Baptist Church on Little Cayman.

The Press

Cayman Islands Journal: The Compass Centre, Shedden Rd, POB 1365, George Town, Grand Cayman; tel. 949-5111; fax 949-7675; internet caymanianthejournal.cay.newsmemory.com; publ. by the Cayman Free Press; monthly; broadsheet business newspaper; Publr BRIAN UZZELL.

Cayman Net News: 85 North Sound Rd, Alissta Towers, POB 10707, Grand Cayman; tel. 946-6060; fax 949-0679; e-mail news@caymannetnews.com; internet www.caymannetnews.com; internet news service; publishes weekly newspaper (f. 2006); Publr and Editor-in-Chief DESMOND SEALES.

Caymanian Compass: The Compass Centre, Shedden Rd, POB 1365, George Town, Grand Cayman; tel. 949-5111; fax 949-7675; internet www.caycompass.com; f. 1965; publ. by the Cayman Free Press; 5 a week; Publr BRIAN UZZELL; circ. 10,000.

The Chamber: POB 1000, George Town, Grand Cayman; tel. 949-8090; fax 949-0220; e-mail info@caymanchamber.ky; internet www.caymanchamber.ky; f. 1965; monthly; newsletter of the Cayman Islands Chamber of Commerce; Editor WIL PINEAU; circ. 5,000.

Christian Lifestyle: GKF Bldg, Godfrey Nixon Way, POB 1217, Grand Cayman KY1 1108; tel. 926-2507; fax 947-2228; e-mail info@cstylemagazine.com; internet www.cstylemagazine.com; f. 2008; publ. every 2 months; Editor KAREN CHIN.

Gazette: Gazette Office, Government Information Service, Cayman Islands Government, Cricket Sq., Elgin Ave, Grand Cayman; tel. 949-8092; fax 949-5936; e-mail caymangazette@gov.ky; internet www.gazettes.gov.ky; official newspaper of the govt; publ. fortnightly on Monday; Editor-in-Chief PATRICIA EBANKS.

Key to Cayman: The Compass Centre, Shedden Rd, POB 1365 George Town, Grand Cayman KY1 1108; tel. 949-5111; fax 949-7675; e-mail info@cfp.ky; internet www.caymanfreepress.com; 2 a year; free tourist magazine; publ. by the Cayman Free Press; Cayman Free Press also publs bi-weekly *Caymanian Compass* newspaper and accompanying supplements, *Cayman Islands Journal*, *Cayman Islands Yearbook & Business Directory*, *Cayman Islands Map*, and *Inside Out*, a home and living magazine.

The New Caymanian: Grand Cayman; tel. 949-7414; fax 949-0036; weekly; Publr and Editor-in-Chief PETER JACKSON.

Publishers

Caribbean Publishing Co (Cayman) Ltd: 1 Paddington Pl., Suite 306, North Sound Way, POB 688, George Town, Grand Cayman; tel. 949-7027; fax 949-8366; internet www.caribbeanwhitepages.com; f. 1978.

Cayman Free Press Ltd: The Compass Centre, Shedden Rd, POB 1365, George Town, Grand Cayman; tel. 949-5111; fax 949-7675; e-mail info@cfp.ky; internet www.caymanfreepress.com; f. 1965.

Government Information Service: Gazette Office, Cayman Islands Govt, Cricket Sq., Elgin Ave, Grand Cayman; tel. 949-8092; fax 949-5936; e-mail caymangazette@gov.ky; internet www.gazettes.gov.ky; publr of official govt releases, *Gazette*.

Progressive Publications Ltd: Economy Printers Bldg, POB 764, George Town, Grand Cayman; tel. 949-5780; fax 949-7674.

Tower Marketing and Publishing: tel. 946-6000; fax 946-6001; e-mail info@tower.com.ky; internet www.tower.com.ky.

Broadcasting and Communications

REGULATORY AUTHORITY

Information and Communications Technology Authority (ICTA): Alissta Towers, 3rd Floor, 85 North Sound Rd, POB 2502, Grand Cayman KY1 1104; tel. 946-4282; fax 945-8284; e-mail info@icta.ky; internet www.icta.ky; f. 2002; responsible for the regulation and licensing of telecommunications, broadcasting, and all forms of radio which includes ship, aircraft, mobile and amateur radio and the management of the Cayman Islands internet domain; Chair. SAMUEL JACKSON; Man. Dir DAVID ARCHBOLD.

TELECOMMUNICATIONS

Digicel Cayman: Cayman Financial Centre, 36A Roys Dr., POB 700, George Town, Grand Cayman; tel. 623-3444; fax 623-3329; e-mail Care-cayman.customercare@digicelgroup.com; internet www.digicelcayman.com; f. 2003; owned by an Irish consortium; acquired the operations of Cingular Wireless (fmrly those of AT&T Wireless) in the country in 2005 (www.cingular.ky); CEO DENIS O'BRIEN.

LIME: Anderson Sq. Bldg, Anderson Sq., Sheddon Rd, POB 293, George Town, Grand Cayman; tel. 949-7800; fax 949-7962; e-mail cs@candw.ky; internet www.time4lime.com; f. 1966 as Cable & Wireless (Cayman Islands) Ltd; name changed as above 2008; Cable & Wireless' monopoly over the telecommunications market ended in 2004; Country Man. ANTHONY RITCH.

TeleCayman: Cayman Corporate Centre, 4th Floor, POB 704 GT, Grand Cayman; tel. 769-1000; fax 769-0999; e-mail customer@telecayman.com; internet www.telecayman.com; f. 2003; provides telephone and internet services; Senior Vice-Pres. GILBERT CHALIFOUX.

WestTel Ltd: Governors Sq., West Bay Rd, POB 31117, Grand Cayman; tel. 745-5555; fax 743-5554; e-mail support@westtel.ky; internet www.westtel.ky; f. 2003; provides telephone and internet services; independent affiliate of WestStar TV Ltd cable television co; Chief Technical Officer MICHAEL EDENHOLM.

BROADCASTING

Radio

Radio Cayman: Elgin Ave, POB 1110 GT, George Town, Grand Cayman, KY1-1102; tel. 949-7799; fax 949-6536; e-mail rcnews@gov.ky; internet www.radiocayman.gov.ky; started full-time broadcasting 1976; govt-owned commercial radio station; service in English; operates Radio Cayman One and Breeze FM; Dir NORMA MCFIELD.

Radio Heaven 97 FM: GKF Industrial Park, Godfrey Nixon Way, POB 31481 SMB, George Town, Grand Cayman; tel. 949-2797; fax 949-2707; e-mail contact@heaven97.com; internet www.heaven97.com; f. 1997; owned by Christian Communications Association; Christian broadcasting, music and news; commercial station.

Radio ICCI-FM: International College of the Cayman Islands, POB 136, Grand Cayman KY1-1501; tel. 947-1100; fax 947-1210; e-mail icci@icci.edu.ky; internet www.icci.edu.ky; f. 1973; radio station of the International College of the Cayman Islands; educational and cultural; Pres. Dr ELSA M. CUMMINGS.

Radio Vibe: Rankin's Plaza, 21 Eclipse Dr., POB 10734, Grand Cayman KY1-1007; tel. 949-8243; fax 946-9867; e-mail info@vibefm.ky; internet www.vibefm-cayman.com; operated by Paramount Media Services, in addition to Spin FM; Man. KENNY RANKINE.

Radio Z99.9 FM: 256 Crewe Rd, Suite 201, Crighton Bldg, POB 30110, Grand Cayman KY1-1201; tel. 945-1166; fax 945-1006; e-mail info@z99.ky; internet www.z99.ky; owned by Hurley's Entertainment Corpn Ltd; Man. Dir RANDY MERREN.

Television

Cayman Adventist Television Network (CATN/TV): POB 515, Grand Cayman KY1-1106; tel. 949-2739; e-mail mission@candw.ky; internet www.tagnet.org/cayman/tv.html; f. 1996; local and international programmes, mainly religious; Pres. JEFFREY THOMPSON.

Cayman Christian TV Ltd: POB 964, Grand Cayman KY1-1102; relays Christian broadcasting from the Trinity Broadcasting Network (USA); Vice-Pres. FRED RUTTY.

CITN Cayman 27: 45 Eclipse Way, POB 30563, Grand Cayman KY1-1203; tel. 745-0207; fax 749-1002; e-mail hlofters@weststartv.com; internet www.cayman27.com.ky; f. 1992 as Cayman International Television Network; 24 hrs daily; local and international news and US entertainment; 10-channel cable service of international programmes by subscription; Station Man. RICK ALPERT.

Weststar TV Ltd: 45 Eclipse Way, POB 31117, Grand Cayman KY1-1205; tel. 745-5555; e-mail info@weststartv.com; internet www

UNITED KINGDOM OVERSEAS TERRITORIES

.weststartv.com; f. 1993; operates wireless cable television service; affiliated to WestTel Ltd; Operations Man. RICHARD CORBIN.

Finance

(cap. = capital; res = reserves; dep. = deposits; m. = million; brs = branches)

Banking facilities are provided by commercial banks. The islands have become an important centre for 'offshore' companies and trusts. At July 2007 there were some 73,000 companies registered in the Cayman Islands. At the end of March 2008 there were 347 licensed banks and trusts and a total of 9,018 registered mutual funds. The islands were well-known as a tax haven because of the absence of any form of direct taxation. In mid-June 2006 assets held by banks registered in the Cayman Islands totalled US $1,413,000m.

Cayman Islands Monetary Authority (CIMA): 80E Shedden Rd, Elizabethan Sq., POB 10052 APO, George Town, Grand Cayman KY1 1001; tel. 949-7089; fax 945-2532; e-mail cima@cimoney.com.ky; internet www.cimoney.com.ky; f. 1997; responsible for managing the territory's currency and reserves and for regulating the financial services sector; cap. CI $8.1m., res CI $8.8m., dep. CI $54.8m. (Dec. 2004); Chair. CARLYLE MCLAUGHLIN, Jr; Man. Dir CINDY SCOTLAND.

PRINCIPAL BANKS AND TRUST COMPANIES

AALL Trust and Banking Corpn Ltd: AALL Bldg, POB 1166, George Town, Grand Cayman; tel. 949-5588; fax 945-5772; internet www.aall.com; Chair. ERIK MONSEN; Man. Dir KEVIN DOYLE.

Appleby Trust (Cayman) Ltd: Clifton House, 75 Fort St, POB 190, Grand Cayman KY1-1104; tel. 949-4900; fax 949-4901; e-mail cayman@applebyglobal.com; internet www.applebyglobal.com; f. 2006 following acquisition of business interests of Ansbacher (Cayman) Ltd; offices in Bermuda; Man. Dir JOHN FLETCHER.

Atlantic Security Bank: POB 10340, George Town 1097, Grand Cayman; internet www.asbnet.com; f. 1981 as Banco de Crédito del Peru International, name changed as above 1986; Chair. DIONISIO ROMERO; Pres. CARLOS MUÑOZ.

Julius Baer Bank and Trust Co Ltd: Windward Bldg 3, Regatta Office Park, Seven Mile Beach, POB 1100, George Town, Grand Cayman; tel. 949-7212; fax 949-0993; internet www.juliusbaer.ch; f. 1974; 100% owned by Julius Baer Holding Ltd (Switzerland); Man. Dir CHARLES FARRINGTON.

Banco Português do Atlântico: POB 30124, Grand Cayman; tel. 949-8322; fax 949-7743; e-mail bcpjvic@candw.ky; Gen. Man. HELENA SOARES CARNEIRO.

Banco Safra (Cayman Islands) Ltd: c/o Bank of Nova Scotia, POB 501, George Town, Grand Cayman; tel. 949-2001; fax 949-7097; f. 1993; cap. US $60.0m., res US $124.5m., dep. US $726.1m. (Dec. 2003).

BANIF-Banco Internaçional do Funchal (Cayman) Ltd: Genesis Bldg, 3rd Floor, POB 32338 SMB, George Town, Grand Cayman; tel. 945-8060; fax 945-8069; e-mail banifcay@candw.ky; internet www.banif.pt; Chair. and CEO Dr JOAQUIM FILIPE MARQUES DOS SANTOS; Gen. Man. VALDEMAR B. LOPES.

Bank of America Trust and Banking Corpn (Cayman) Ltd: BankAmerica Bldg, Fort St, POB 1092, George Town, Grand Cayman; tel. 949-7888; fax 949-7883; f. 1999; Man. Dir CHARLES FARRINGTON.

Bank of Bermuda (Cayman) Ltd: British American Tower, 3rd Floor, POB 513, George Town, Grand Cayman; tel. 949-9898; fax 949-7959; internet www.bankofbermuda.bm; f. 1968 as a trust; converted to a bank in 1988; total assets US $1,041m. (July 2001); Chair. HENRY B. SMITH; Man. Dir ALLEN BERNARDO.

Bank of Nova Scotia: 6 Cardinal Ave, POB 689, George Town, Grand Cayman; tel. 949-7666; fax 949-0020; e-mail scotiaci@candw.ky; internet www.scotiabank.com; also runs trust company; Man. Dir FARRIED SULLIMAN.

Bermuda Trust (Cayman) Ltd: 5th Floor, Bermuda House, POB 513, George Town, Grand Cayman; tel. 949-9898; fax 949-7959; internet www.bankofbermuda.bm; f. 1968 as Arawak Trust Co; became subsidiary of Bank of Bermuda in 1988; bank and trust services; Chair. JOHN CAMPBELL; Man. Dir KENNETH GIBBS.

BFC Bank (Cayman) Ltd: Trafalgar Pl., POB 1765, George Town, Grand Cayman; tel. 949-8748; fax 949-8749; e-mail bfc@candw.ky; f. 1985; FC Financière de la Cité, Geneva, 99.9%; cap. US $0.8m., res US $3.7m., dep. US $33.5m. (March 2001); Chair. SIMON C. TAY; Resident Man. CHERRYLEE BUSH.

Butterfield Bank (Cayman) Ltd: Butterfield House, 68 Fort St, POB 705, George Town, Grand Cayman; tel. 949-7055; fax 949-7761; e-mail info@butterfieldbank.ky; internet www.ky.butterfieldgroup.com; f. 1967; name changed as above in 2004, fmrly Bank of Butterfield International (Cayman) Ltd; subsidiary of Bank of N. T. Butterfield & Son Ltd, Bermuda; cap. US $16.5m., res US $0.05m.,

The Cayman Islands

dep. US $2,182.3m. (June 2004); Chair. ALAN THOMPSON; Man. Dir CONOR J. O'DEA; 3 brs.

Caledonian Bank and Trust Ltd: Caledonian House, 69 Dr Roy's Dr., POB 1043, George Town, Grand Cayman KY1-1102; tel. 949-0050; fax 949-8062; e-mail info@caledonian.com; internet www.caledonian.com; f. 1970; Chair. WILLIAM S. WALKER; Man. Dir DAVID S. SARGISON.

Cayman National Bank Ltd: Cayman National Bank Bldg, 4th Floor, 200 Elgin Ave, POB 1097, George Town, Grand Cayman; tel. 949-4655; fax 949-7506; e-mail cnb@caymannational.com; internet www.caymannational.com; f. 1974; subsidiary of Cayman National Corpn; cap. CI $2.4m., res CI $41.4m., dep. CI $466.0m. (Sept. 2002); Chair. BENSON O. EBANKS; Pres. STUART DACK; 6 brs.

CITCO Bank and Trust Co Ltd: Regatta Office Park, West Bay Rd, POB 31105 SMB, Grand Cayman; tel. 945-3838; fax 945-3888; e-mail cayman-bank@citco.com; internet www.citco.com.

Deutsche Bank (Cayman) Ltd: Boundary Hall, Cricket Sq., 171 Elgin Ave, POB 1984, George Town, Grand Cayman; tel. 949-8244; fax 949-8178; e-mail dmg-cay@candw.ky; internet www.dboffshore.com; f. 1983 as Morgan Grenfell (Cayman) Ltd; name changed to Deutsche Morgan Grenfell (Cayman) Ltd in 1996; name changed as above in 1998; cap. US $5.0m., res US $20.3m., dep. US $129.3m. (Dec. 1998); Chair. MARK HIRST; Regional Head JANET HISLOP.

Deutsche Bank International Trust Co (Cayman) Ltd: POB 1984, George Town, Grand Cayman; tel. 949-8244; fax 949-7866; f. 1999; Regional Man. TIM GODBER.

Deutsche Girozentrale Overseas Ltd: POB 694, George Town, Grand Cayman; tel. 914-9483; fax 949-0626; Man. Dir RAINER MACH.

Fidelity Bank (Cayman) Ltd: POB 914, George Town, Grand Cayman KY1 1103; tel. 949-7822; fax 949-6064; e-mail bank@fidelitycayman.com; internet www.fidelitycayman.com; f. 1979; Pres. and CEO BRETT HILL.

FirstCaribbean International Bank Ltd: POB 68, George Town, Grand Cayman; tel. 949-7300; fax 815-2292; internet www.firstcaribbeanbank.com; f. 2002 following merger of Caribbean operations of Barclays Bank PLC and CIBC; Barclays relinquished its stake to CIBC in June 2006; Exec. Chair. MICHAEL MANSOOR; CEO JOHN D. ORR; Cayman Islands Contact MARK MCINTYRE.

Fortis Bank (Cayman) Ltd: Grand Pavilion Commercial Centre, West Bay Rd, POB 2003, George Town, Grand Cayman; tel. 949-7942; fax 949-8340; e-mail phil.brown@ky.fortisbank.com; internet www.fortis.com; f. 1984 as Pierson, Heldring & Pierson (Cayman) Ltd; name changed to Mees Pierson (Cayman) Ltd in 1993; present name adopted in June 2000; Man. Dir ROGER HANSON.

HSBC Financial Services (Cayman) Ltd: Strathvale House, 2nd Floor, 90 North Church St, POB 1109, George Town, Grand Cayman; tel. 949-7755; fax 949-7634; e-mail hfsc.info@ky.hsbc.com; internet www.hsbc.ky; f. 1982; Dirs TOM CLARK, DAVID A. WHITEFIELD.

IBJ Whitehall Bank and Trust Co: West Wind Bldg, POB 1040, George Town, Grand Cayman; tel. 949-2849; fax 949-5409; Man. ROGER HEALY.

Intesa Bank Overseas Ltd: c/o Coutts (Cayman) Ltd, Coutts House, West Bay Rd, POB 705, George Town, Grand Cayman; tel. 945-4777; fax 945-4799; f. 1994 as Ambroveneto International Bank; name changed as above in March 1999; cap. US $10.0m., total assets US $1,339.8m. (Dec. 1999); Chair. FRANCESCO DE VECCHI; Man. Dirs RICHARD AUSTIN, ANDREW GALLOWAY.

LGT Bank in Liechtenstein (Cayman) Ltd: UBS House, 227 Elgin Ave, POB 852, George Town, Grand Cayman; tel. 949-7676; fax 949-8512; e-mail lgt.cayman@lgt.com; internet www.lgt-bank-in-liechtenstein.com.

Mercury Bank and Trust Ltd: POB 2424, George Town, Grand Cayman; tel. 949-0800; fax 949-0295; Man. VOLKER MERGENTHALER.

Merrill Lynch Bank and Trust Co (Cayman) Ltd: POB 1164, George Town, Grand Cayman; tel. 949-8206; fax 949-8895; internet www.ml.com.

RBS Coutts (Cayman) Ltd: Coutts House, 1446 West Bay Rd, POB 707, George Town, Grand Cayman KY1-1107; tel. 945-4777; fax 945-4799; internet www.rbscoutts.com; f. 1967; fmrly NatWest International Trust Corpn (Cayman) Ltd; 100% owned by Royal Bank of Scotland International (Holdings) Ltd (Jersey); Man. Dir DAVID NEUSCHAFFER.

Royal Bank of Canada: 24 Shedden Rd, POB 245, Grand Cayman; tel. 949-4600; fax 949-7396; internet www.royalbank.com; Man. HARRY C. CHISHOLM.

Royal Bank of Canada Trust Co (Cayman) Ltd: 24 Shedden Rd, POB 1586 GT, Grand Cayman; tel. 949-9107; fax 949-5777; internet www.rbcprivatebanking.com/cayman-islands.html; Man. Dir DEANNA BIDWELL.

Scotiabank and Trust (Cayman) Ltd: Scotia Centre, 6 Cardinal Ave, POB 501 GT, George Town, Grand Cayman; tel. 949-2001; fax 949-7097; e-mail cayman@scotiatrust.com; internet www.cayman

.scotiabank.com; fmrly Bank of Novia Scotia Trust Company (Cayman) Ltd; present name adopted Dec. 2003; Man. Dir FARRIED SULLIMAN.

UBS Fund Services (Cayman Islands) Ltd: UBS House, 227 Elgin Ave, POB 852, George Town, Grand Cayman, KY1-1103; tel. 914-1060; fax 914-4060; internet www.ubs.com/cayman-funds; Man. Dir DARREN STAINROD.

Development Bank

Cayman Islands Development Bank: Cayman Financial Centre, 36B Dr Roy's Dr., POB 1271 GT, George Town, Grand Cayman; tel. 949-7511; fax 949-6168; e-mail angela.miller@gov.ky; f. 2002; replaced the Housing Devt Corpn and the Agricultural and Industrial Devt Bd; under the jurisdiction of the Ministry of Tourism, Environment, Investment and Commerce; Devt Finance Institution Gen. Man. RALPH LEWIS.

Banking Association

Cayman Islands Bankers' Association: Macdonald Sq., Fort St, POB 676, George Town, Grand Cayman; tel. 949-0330; fax 945-1448; e-mail ciba@candw.ky; Pres. TIMOTHY GODBER; 86 full mems, 250 assoc. mems.

STOCK EXCHANGE

Cayman Islands Stock Exchange (CSX): 4th Floor, Elizabethan Sq., POB 2408, George Town, Grand Cayman; tel. 945-6060; fax 945-6061; e-mail csx@csx.com.ky; internet www.csx.com.ky; f. 1996; 1,477 cos listed (July 2007); CEO VALIA THEODORAKI.

INSURANCE

Several foreign companies have agents in the islands. A total of 951 insurance companies were registered at the end of December 2008. In particular, the islands are a leading international market for health insurance. Local companies include the following:

British Caymanian Insurance Agency Ltd: Elizabethan Sq., POB 74 GT, Grand Cayman KY1-1002; tel. 949-8699; fax 949-8411; e-mail gderry@candw.ky; Man. DERRY GRAHAM.

Cayman National Insurance Brokers Ltd: POB 10042, George Town, Grand Cayman KY1-1001; tel. 949-0111; fax 949-8163; e-mail cnib@caymannational.com; internet www.caymannational.com; part of the Cayman National Corpn; Gen. Man. MARY MELLIN.

Cayman Insurance Centre: POB 10056, Cayman Business Park; tel. 814-7230; e-mail trisha.anthony@cic.com.ky; internet www.cic.com.ky; Pres. LINDA CHAPMAN-KEY.

Cayman Islands National Insurance Co (CINICO): Phase 3, 1st Floor, Elizabethan Sq., POB 512 GT, Grand Cayman KY1-1106; tel. 949-8101; fax 949-8226; e-mail debanks@cinico.ky; internet www.cinico.ky; CEO and Pres. GORDON ROWELL.

Insurance Company of the West Indies (Cayman) Ltd (ICWI): 93 Hospital Rd, POB 461, Grand Cayman KY1-1106; tel. 949-6970; fax 949-6929; e-mail icwi@candw.ky; internet www.icwi.net; subsidiary of Insurance Company of the West Indies, Jamaica; Man. HEATHER LANIGAN.

Island Heritage Insurance Co Ltd: 802 West Bay Rd, Grand Pavilion Centre, POB 2501, Grand Cayman KY1-1104; tel. 949-7280; fax 945-6765; e-mail info@islandheritage.com.ky; internet www.island-heritage.com; property insurance; Chair. CONOR O'DEA.

Sagicor Life of the Cayman Islands Ltd: 198 North Church St, POB 1087, George Town, Grand Cayman KY1-1102; tel. 949-8211; fax 949-8262; e-mail customerservice@sagicor.com; internet www.sagicor.com; f. 2004 by merger between Global Life and Capital Life; Country Man. CLAUDETTE SAINT-REID.

Trade and Industry

GOVERNMENT AGENCY

Cayman Islands Investment Bureau: Cayman Corporate Centre, 1st Floor, Hospital Rd, POB 10087 APO, Grand Cayman KY1-1001; tel. 945-0943; fax 945-0941; e-mail info@investcayman.gov.ky; internet www.investcayman.ky; f. 2003; Exec. Dir Dr DAX BASDEO.

CHAMBER OF COMMERCE

Cayman Islands Chamber of Commerce: Macdonald Sq., 2nd Floor, Fort St, POB 1000, George Town, Grand Cayman KY1 1102; tel. 949-8090; fax 949-0220; e-mail info@caymanchamber.ky; internet www.caymanchamber.ky; f. 1965; Pres. EDDIE THOMPSON; CEO WIL PINEAU; 594 corporate mems and 78 associates.

TRADE ASSOCIATION

Cayman Islands Financial Services Association (CIFSA): POB 11048, Grand Cayman; tel. 946-6000; fax 946-6001; e-mail info@caymanfinances.com; internet www.caymanfinances.com; f. 2003; Dir EDUARDO D'ANGELO P. SILVA.

EMPLOYERS' ORGANIZATION

Labour Office: 4th Floor, Tower Bldg, Grand Cayman; tel. 949-0941; fax 949-6057; Dir DALE M. BANKS.

UTILITIES

Electricity

Electricity Regulatory Authority: Grand Pavilion, Suite 2, West Bay Rd, POB 10189, Grand Cayman KY1-1002; tel. 949-8372; fax 947-9598; e-mail general@caymanera.com; internet caymanera.com; f. 2005; Chair. KENDAL RYAN; Man. Dir PHILIP THOMAS.

Caribbean Utilities Co Ltd (CUC): Corporate HQ & Plant, North Sound Rd, POB 38, George Town, Grand Cayman; tel. 949-5200; fax 949-4621; e-mail service@cuc.ky; internet www.cuc-cayman.com; Pres. and CEO J. F. RICHARD HEW; Chair. DAVID RITCH.

Cayman Brac Power and Light Co Ltd (CBP&L): Stake Bay Point, POB 95, Stake Bay, Cayman Brac; tel. 948-2224; fax 948-2204; Gen. Man. JONATHAN TIBBETTS.

Water

Cayman Islands Water Authority: 13G Red Gate Rd, POB 1104 GT, George Town, Grand Cayman, KY1-1102; tel. 949-2837; fax 949-0094; e-mail info@waterauthority.ky; internet www.waterauthority.ky; Dir Dr GELIA FREDERICK-VAN GENDEREN; Chair. (vacant).

Consolidated Water Co Ltd (CWCO): Windward 3, 4th Floor, Regatta Business Park, POB 1114, George Town, KY1-1102 Grand Cayman; tel. 945-4277; fax 949-2957; e-mail info@cwco.com; internet ir.cwco.com; f. 1973; Pres. and CEO FREDERICK W. MCTAGGART; Dir and Chair. JEFFREY M. PARKER.

Transport

ROADS

There are some 406 km (252 miles) of motorable roads, of which 304 km are surfaced with tarmac. The road network connects all districts on Grand Cayman and Cayman Brac (which has 76 km of motorable road), and there are 43 km of motorable road on Little Cayman (of which about 18 km are paved). According to the 2009 budget address, US $5.3m. was to be allocated for ongoing improvements to the islands' road network.

SHIPPING

George Town is the principal port and a new port facility was opened in July 1977. Cruise liners, container ships and smaller cargo vessels ply between the Cayman Islands, Florida, Jamaica and Costa Rica. There is no cruise ship dock in the Cayman Islands. Ships anchor off George Town and ferry passengers ashore to the North or South Dock Terminals in George Town. The number of cruise ship passengers is limited to 6,000 per day. The port of Cayman Brac is Creek; there are limited facilities on Little Cayman. In December 2007 the shipping register comprised 141 vessels, with combined displacement totalling 2,870,517 grt.

Maritime Authority of Cayman Islands (MACI): Kirk House, 3rd Floor, 22 Albert Panton St, George Town, Grand Cayman; tel. 949-8831; fax 949-8849; e-mail cisac@cishipping.com; internet www.cishipping.com; f. 2005; wholly govt-owned; legal entity responsible for: enforcement of international maritime laws and conventions; implementation of maritime safety and security, Cayman Islands marine environment laws; formation of national maritime policy; representation and protection of national maritime interests at international forums; also undertakes vessel and mortgage registration, advisory and marine survey and audit services fmrly administered by CISR; Chair. SHARON E. ROULSTONE; CEO A. JOEL WALTON.

Port Authority of the Cayman Islands: Harbour Dr., POB 1358 GT, George Town, Grand Cayman, KY1-1108; tel. 949-2055; fax 949-5820; e-mail support@caymanport.com; internet www.caymanport.com; Port Dir PAUL HURLSTON.

Principal Shipping Companies

Cayman Islands Shipping Registry: Kirk House, 3rd Floor, 22 Albert Panton St, POB 2256, George Town, Grand Cayman KY1-1107; tel. 949-8831; fax 949-8849; e-mail cisrky@cishipping.com; internet www.cishipping.com; f. 1993; dept of Maritime Authority of Cayman Islands (MACI); Dir A. JOEL WALTON.

Seaboard Marine (Cayman): Mirco Commercial Centre, 2nd Floor, Industrial Park, POB 1372, George Town, Grand Cayman KY1-1108; tel. 949-4977; fax 949-8402; e-mail info@seaboardcayman.com; internet www.seaboardcayman.com; Man. Dir ROBERT FOSTER.

UNITED KINGDOM OVERSEAS TERRITORIES

Thompson Shipping Co Ltd: Cayman Shipping Centre, 2nd Floor, 432 Eastern Ave, POB 188, George Town, Grand Cayman KY1-1004; tel. 949-8044; fax 949-8349; e-mail info@thompsonshipping.com; internet www.thompsonshipping.com; f. 1977.

CIVIL AVIATION

There are two international airports in the Territory: Owen Roberts International Airport, 3.5 km (2 miles) from George Town, and Gerrard Smith International Airport on Cayman Brac. Both are capable of handling jet-engined aircraft. Edward Bodden Airport on Little Cayman can cater for light aircraft. Several scheduled carriers serve the islands.

Civil Aviation Authority of the Cayman Islands: Unit 4, Cayman Grand Harbour, POB 10277 APO, George Town, Grand Cayman; tel. 949-7811; fax 949-0761; e-mail civil.aviation@caacayman.com; internet www.caacayman.com; f. 1987; Dir-Gen. RICHARD SMITH; Chair. SHERIDAN BROOKS-HURST.

Cayman Airways Ltd: 91 Owen Roberts Dr., POB 10092 APO, Grand Cayman KY1 1001; tel. 949-8200; fax 949-7607; e-mail customerrelations@caymanairways.net; internet www.caymanairways.com; f. 1968; wholly govt-owned since 1977; operates local services and scheduled flights to Jamaica, Honduras and the USA; CEO GILLES FILIATREAULT (acting); CEO OLSON ANDERSON (designate).

Island Air: Airport Rd, POB 2433, George Town, Grand Cayman; tel. 949-5252; fax 949-7044; e-mail iair@candw.ky; internet islandair.ky; f. 1991; operates daily scheduled services between Grand Cayman, Cayman Brac and Little Cayman.

Tourism

The Cayman Islands are a major tourist destination, the majority of visitors coming from North America. The tourism industry was badly affected by the damage caused by 'Hurricane Ivan' in September 2004, severely reducing available accommodation and a major reconstruction effort was undertaken in 2005. The beaches and opportunities for diving in the offshore reefs form the main attraction for most tourists. In 2007 there were an estimated 4,484 hotel rooms. In 2008 there were 302,879 arrivals by air (compared with 291,503 in 2007) and some 1,553,053 cruise visitors (compared with 1,715,666 in 2007). The USA remained the core market for stay-over visitors to the islands (79.6% in 2007). In 2006 the tourism industry earned an estimated US $509.0m.

Cayman Islands Department of Tourism: Cricket Sq., POB 67, George Town, Grand Cayman KY1-1102; tel. 949-0623; fax 949-4053; internet www.caymanislands.ky; f. 1965; Dir SHOMARI SCOTT (acting).

Cayman Islands Tourism Association (CITA): Largatos Bldg, 73 Lawrence Blvd, POB 31086 SMB, Grand Cayman; tel. and fax 949-8522; e-mail info@cita.ky; internet www.cita.ky; f. 2001 as a result of the amalgamation of the Cayman Tourism Alliance and the Cayman Islands Hotel and Condominium Assn; Pres. KARIE BERGSTROM; Exec. Dir KEN THOMPSON.

Sister Islands Tourism Association (SITA): POB 187, Cayman Brac KY2-2101; tel. and fax 948-1345; e-mail sita@candw.ky; internet www.sisterislands.com; Pres. PETER HILLENBRAND (acting).

THE FALKLAND ISLANDS

Introductory Survey

Location, Climate, Language, Religion, Flag, Capital

The Falkland Islands, comprising two large islands and about 200 smaller ones, are in the south-western Atlantic Ocean, about 770 km (480 miles) north-east of Cape Horn, South America. The climate is generally cool, with strong winds (mainly westerly) throughout the year. The mean annual temperature is 6°C (42°F), while average annual rainfall is 635 mm (25 ins). The language is English. Most of the inhabitants profess Christianity, with several denominations represented. The flag is the British 'Blue Ensign', with the territory's coat of arms (a shield showing a white and violet ram standing in green grass, on a blue background, above a sailing ship bearing red crosses on its pennants and five six-pointed stars on its central sail, on three white horizontal wavy lines, with the motto 'Desire the Right' on a scroll beneath) on a white disc in the centre of the flag. The capital is Stanley, on East Falkland Island.

Recent History

The first recorded landing on the islands was made from a British ship in 1690, when the group was named after Viscount Falkland, then Treasurer of the Royal Navy. French sailors named the islands 'Les Malouines' (after their home port of Saint-Malo), from which the Spanish name 'Islas Malvinas' is derived. A French settlement was established in 1764 on the island of East Falkland, but in 1767 France relinquished its rights to the territory to Spain, which then ruled the adjacent regions of South America. Meanwhile, a British expedition annexed West Falkland in 1765, and a garrison was established. The British settlement, formed in 1765–66, was recognized by Spain in 1771 but withdrawn in 1774. The Spanish garrison was withdrawn in 1811.

When the United Provinces of the River Plate (now Argentina) gained independence from Spain in 1816, the Falkland Islands had no permanent inhabitants, although they provided temporary bases for sealing and whaling activities by British and US vessels. In 1820 an Argentine ship was sent to the islands to proclaim Argentine sovereignty as successor to Spain. An Argentine settlement was founded in 1826 but most of its occupants were expelled by a US warship in 1831. The remaining Argentines were ejected by a British expedition in 1832, and British sovereignty was established in 1833.

The islands became a Crown Colony of the United Kingdom, administered by a British-appointed Governor. However, Argentina did not relinquish its claim, and negotiations to resolve the dispute began in 1966 at the instigation of the UN. The inhabitants of the islands, nearly all British by descent, consistently expressed their desire to remain under British sovereignty.

After routine talks between delegations of the British and Argentine Governments in New York in February 1982, the Argentine foreign ministry announced that it would seek other means to resolve the dispute. Rumours of a possible invasion had begun in the Argentine press in January, and Argentina's military regime took advantage of a British protest at the presence of a group of Argentine scrap merchants, who had made an unauthorized landing on South Georgia in March and had raised an Argentine flag, to invade the Falkland Islands on 2 April. A small contingent of British marines was overwhelmed, the British Governor, Rex (later Sir Rex) Hunt, was expelled and an Argentine military governorship was established. The USA and the UN attempted (unsuccessfully) to mediate, in an effort to prevent military escalation. British forces, which had been dispatched to the islands immediately after the Argentine invasion, recaptured South Georgia on 25 April. The Argentine forces on the Falklands formally surrendered on 14 June, after a conflict in the course of which about 750 Argentine, 255 British and three Falklanders' lives were lost.

The Governor returned to the islands as Civil Commissioner on 25 June 1982, and the United Kingdom established a 'protection zone' around the islands, extending 150 nautical miles (278 km) off shore, as well as a garrison of about 4,000 troops. The British Government began an investigation into the possibilities of developing the islands' economy, and in November agreed to grant the Falkland Islanders full British citizenship. In November 1983 the post of Chief Executive of the Falkland Islands Government was created, in combination with the executive vice-chairmanship of the newly formed Falkland Islands Development Corporation. The Civil Commissioner, Sir Rex Hunt, retired in September 1985, whereupon a new Governor was appointed.

The issue of the sovereignty of the Falkland Islands remained a major impediment to the normalization of relations between Argentina and the United Kingdom. The Argentine Government refused to agree to a formal declaration that hostilities were ended until the United Kingdom agreed to participate in negotiations over sovereignty, while the United Kingdom refused to negotiate until Argentina had formally ended hostilities.

Following the return to civilian rule in Argentina in December 1983, the newly elected President, Dr Raúl Alfonsín, stated his Government's desire to seek a negotiated settlement to the dispute over the Falkland Islands. In October 1984 the Argentine Government removed restrictions on British companies and interests in Argentina as a possible prelude to resuming negotiations.

The British Government's refusal to discuss the issue of sovereignty, and its insistence on the paramountcy of the Falkland Islanders' wishes, were reflected in the new Constitution for the Falklands (approved by the islands' Legislative Council in January 1985), which guaranteed the islanders' right to self-determination.

The number of British troops stationed on the islands was reduced, following the opening, in mid-1985, of a new military airport at Mount Pleasant, about 30 km south-west of Stanley, enabling rapid reinforcement of the garrison, if necessary. In July the British

Government ended its ban on Argentine imports, which had been in force since 1982. In October elections took place on the Falklands for a new Legislative Council. In the same month, South Georgia and the South Sandwich Islands ceased to be dependencies of the Falkland Islands, although the Governor of the Falkland Islands was to be (ex officio) Commissioner for the territory.

In 1986 parliamentary delegations from the United Kingdom and Argentina conducted exploratory talks. However, the British Government remained intransigent on the issue of the sovereignty of the islands. In early 1986 Argentina's continued claim to the naval 'protection zone' was manifested in attacks on foreign fishing vessels by Argentine gunboats. In October the United Kingdom unilaterally declared a fisheries conservation and management zone extending 150 nautical miles (278 km) around the islands, with effect from February 1987, to prevent the over-fishing of the waters. The imposition of this zone, whose radius coincided with that of the naval protection zone, was condemned by the majority of UN members, as was the United Kingdom's rejection, in November 1986, of an offer by Argentina to declare a formal end to hostilities in exchange for the abolition of the protection zone. The resignation, in June 1989, of three members of the Legislative Council, in protest against a proposed agricultural grants scheme, prompted the dissolution of the legislative body. In the ensuing parliamentary elections in October, eight independent candidates, all of whom vigorously opposed renewing links, at any level, with Argentina, defeated 10 other candidates to take all the elective seats.

The successful independent candidates in elections to the eight elective seats of the Legislative Council in October 1993 and October 1997 expressed their reluctance to develop closer contacts with Argentina and their determination not to enter into negotiations with that country regarding the islands' sovereignty.

On 22 November 2001 a general election took place to elect members to a new Legislative Council. Of the eight elected, only three members had not served on the Legislative Council before. In a concurrent referendum the electorate voted against changing the two-constituency system (the Stanley constituency and the Camp constituency) to a single constituency for legislative elections.

A general election was held on 17 November 2005 in which eight independent candidates, of whom five were new members, were elected to the Legislative Council.

Beginning in 1982 the UN General Assembly voted annually, by an overwhelming majority, in favour of the resumption of negotiations between Argentina and the United Kingdom. The British Government consistently declined to engage in such dialogue. However, relations between Argentina and the United Kingdom improved, following the election, in May 1989, of a new Argentine President, Carlos Saúl Menem, who initially indicated that his country would be willing to suspend temporarily its demand that the issue of the sovereignty of the Falkland Islands be discussed, in the interests of the restoration of full diplomatic and commercial relations with the United Kingdom. In October a meeting of British and Argentine representatives, which took place in Madrid, Spain, culminated in the formal cessation of all hostilities, and the re-establishment of diplomatic relations at consular level. Restrictions on Argentine merchant vessels with regard to the naval protection zone around the Falkland Islands were also eased. In the following month, however, the United Kingdom announced that it was to increase the extent of its territorial waters around the islands from three to 12 nautical miles, in spite of protests from the Argentine authorities. In February 1990 Argentina and the United Kingdom conducted further negotiations in Madrid, as a result of which the two countries re-established full diplomatic relations. It was also announced that the naval protection zone around the Falkland Islands was to be modified in March, and that mutually agreed military procedures, which would ensure the security of the region, would take effect. In mid-1993 the further reduction of military restrictions around the islands was announced by both Governments.

Following successful negotiations between Argentina and the United Kingdom in Madrid in November 1990, an agreement regarding the protection and conservation of the South Atlantic fishing area was announced, whereby a temporary ban on fishing was to be extended, from late December, to an area incorporating an additional 50-mile (93-km) semicircular region to the east of the islands, beyond the existing 150-mile fishing zone. (The agreement was renewed in December 1991 and 1992.) The two sides also agreed to establish a South Atlantic Fisheries Commission, which was to meet at least twice in every year that the ban remained in place, in order to discuss fishing activity and conservation in the region. Throughout 1990 the Falkland Islands Government had appealed to the British Government to exercise its legal right under international law to extend the fisheries conservation and management zone, claiming that over-fishing of the previously well-stocked waters just beyond the 150-mile limit by vessels from Taiwan and the Republic of Korea (ignoring previously agreed voluntary restraints on fishing in the area) had seriously depleted stocks and posed a threat to the islands' lucrative squid-fishing industry.

In May 1993 the British Government announced that it would extend from 12 to 200 nautical miles its territorial jurisdiction in the waters surrounding South Georgia and the South Sandwich Islands. In December the Argentine Government indicated its acceptance of the United Kingdom's proposed extension of fishing rights around the Falkland Islands from 150 to 200 miles, in order to allow the islanders to fulfil an annual squid-fishing quota of 150,000 metric tons (effective from January 1994). The Argentine quota was agreed at 220,000 tons (compared with an estimated catch of 130,000 tons in 1992). In August 1994 the British Government unilaterally decided to extend its fisheries conservation zone north of the islands, thereby annexing a small but lucrative fishing ground (not previously protected by British or Argentine legislation) that was being plundered by foreign fishing vessels. In January 1997 the United Kingdom and Argentina agreed to resume negotiations on a long-term fisheries agreement that would include the disputed waters around the islands. Following the release of a Joint Declaration between the two Governments on 14 July 1999, both Governments agreed to co-operate to combat illegal fishing in the South West Atlantic and to ensure the sustainability of fish stocks in the region.

In November 1991 the Governments of both Argentina and the United Kingdom claimed rights of exploration and exploitation of the sea-bed and the subsoil of the continental shelf around the Falkland Islands (which were believed to be rich in petroleum reserves). In April 1992 the Falkland Islands Government invited tenders for seismic reports of the region. In December 1993 the British Geological Survey reported that preliminary seismic investigations indicated deposits in excess of those located in British North Sea oilfields. A bilateral agreement on petroleum and gas exploration in an area of 18,000 sq km, south-west of the islands, was concluded in New York, USA, in September 1994. A joint hydrocarbons commission would regulate licensing in the area, examining bids from Anglo-Argentine joint ventures (in which case taxes would be levied on operators by the respective Governments) or by third countries (from which royalties on revenues would be exacted by the Falkland Islands Government at a rate expected to approach 9%). The successful conclusion of the agreement appeared to dissipate Argentine objections, voiced earlier in the year, to the Falkland Islands' unilateral offer of rights to drill in 19 areas (comprising 44,000 sq km not covered by the Anglo-Argentine agreement) to the north and south of the islands. Licences to explore for hydrocarbons were awarded to five international consortia in October 1996. The possibility that commercial quantities of petroleum might be discovered prompted renewed discussion as to the amount of any future royalties exacted by the Falkland Islands Government that should be returned to the Government of the United Kingdom. In early 1997 the British Government indicated that it expected to benefit considerably from any such royalties, while the Falkland Islands administration proposed that some of the revenue could be used to finance the islands' defence expenditure (currently funded by the United Kingdom). Meanwhile, the Argentine Government claimed that it should be entitled to benefit from the discovery of petroleum in the region: draft legislation presented to Congress provided for the imposition of sanctions on petroleum companies and fishing vessels operating in Falkland Islands waters without Argentine authorization, in addition to the levying of 3% royalties from the sale of petroleum discovered in the area.

In late 1996 the Argentine Government suggested, for the first time, that it might consider shared sovereignty of the Falkland Islands with the United Kingdom. The proposal was firmly rejected by the British Government and by the Falkland Islanders, who reiterated their commitment to persuading the UN Special Political and Decolonization Committee to adopt a clause granting the islanders the right to self-determination.

In May 1999 formal negotiations between the Falkland Islands and Argentina took place in the United Kingdom. Issues under discussion included co-operation in fishing and petroleum exploration, Argentine access to the islands and the resumption of air links with mainland South America. (In March Chile had ended its country's regular air services to the islands in protest at the British Government's continued detention of the former Chilean President, Gen. Augusto Pinochet; Uruguay subsequently agreed not to establish an air link with the islands unless flights were routed via the Argentine capital.) The sovereignty of the Falkland Islands was not scheduled for discussion. Four of the islands' councillors also attended the three days of talks, thereby occasioning the first direct talks between Falkland Islanders and the Argentine Government. The dialogue continued in July in New York and London. On 14 July a joint Argentine-British declaration was issued that eliminated the restrictions on travel by Argentine citizens to the Falkland Islands and re-established airline services by the Chilean carrier LanChile between South America and the Falkland Islands (with a stop-over in Argentina). It was also agreed to increase bilateral co-operation between Argentina and the Falkland Islands on combating illegal fishing and conservation of fish stocks. Symbolic gestures included allowing the construction of a monument to the Argentine war dead at their cemetery on the islands (permission was finally granted in

March 2002), while in return the Argentine Government would cease to use the Spanish names given to Falklands locations during the 1982 occupation. The agreement did not affect claims to sovereignty. Even so, the round of talks provoked demonstrations by an estimated 500 people on the Falkland Islands. The protests resumed on 16 October when the first flights carrying Argentine visitors arrived in the Falklands. In July 2000 the Anglo-Argentine dialogue on joint petroleum and gas exploration was suspended by mutual agreement for an indefinite period of time.

On 3 December 2002 Howard Pearce succeeded Donald Lamont as Governor of the Falkland Islands and Commissioner of South Georgia and the Sandwich Islands. In March 2003 Chris Simpkins became the new Chief Executive; he replaced Michael Blanch, who had reached the end of his three-year contract.

In May 2003 the new Argentine President, Néstor Carlos Kirchner, promised in his inaugural speech to maintain his country's claim to the Falkland Islands; he reiterated that commitment in January 2005, and once more appealed for the resumption of bilateral negotiations. In November 2003 Argentina began to demand that the increasingly frequent air charter services flying from the Falkland Islands to Chile obtain permission to use Argentine airspace. The decision was intended to exert pressure on the British Government into reversing its policy of not allowing Argentine airlines to fly to the Falkland Islands. The services were suspended in January 2004 after the British Government lodged objections to the Argentine demands; the situation seemed likely to damage the territory's burgeoning tourism trade. In March a British proposal for the resumption of direct charter flights from Argentina to the Falkland Islands was rejected by the Kirchner Government, which continued to demand that an Argentine carrier be authorized to benefit from the increased passenger traffic between the Falkland Islands and mainland South America. A reference to the islands was included in a draft of the constitutional treaty of the European Union, to which Argentina strongly objected. At a meeting of the UN's Special Committee on Decolonization, held in mid-2005, the Falkland Islands appealed for the right to self-determination; the Committee requested that the Governments of Argentina and the United Kingdom resume negotiations.

Alan Huckle succeeded Howard Pearce as Governor of the Falkland Islands in August 2006. Melanie Chilton, Principal Crown Counsel, succeeded David Lang as Attorney-General on 1 November following the latter's retirement. However, Chilton resigned in the following month, citing family health reasons, and on 1 September 2007 David Pickup, former Director-General of Her Majesty's Revenue and Customs, assumed the role. In January 2008 Dr Tim Thorogood replaced Chris Simpkins as Chief Executive.

A constitutional review process was initiated by the British Government's Department of Overseas Territories in 1997, with the aim of according greater self-governance to the islands. A number of changes to the administration of the territory were proposed; a Constitutional Select Committee was convened on 2 February 2007 to complete the review discussions, and final proposals were submitted to the British Foreign and Commonwealth Office (FCO) for deliberation in June. Most notable among the amendments proposed were the insertion of the citizens' right to self-determination within the main body of the Constitution, the updating of provisions in accordance with the United Kingdom's obligations under the European Convention on Human Rights, and clarification of the Governor's and Chief Executive's roles as head of the Public Service and head of the Civil Service, respectively. Proposals for the establishment of a Complaints Commissioner and a Public Accounts Committee, the consolidation of electoral districts into a single constituency and the determination of the extent of self-government to be exercised by the territory were designated as matters requiring further consultation with the FCO before being written into statute. Officials from the FCO held two rounds of talks with the Constitutional Select Committee in December 2007 and February 2008 to discuss the draft new constitution. Following further public consultation, the new Constitution came into force on 1 January 2009. It asserted the islanders' right to self-determination and contained amendments to the rules under which British citizens would be eligible for Falklands Islands status, as well as provisions for a Public Accounts Committee and a Complaints Commissioner to improve transparency in the territory. It also provided further clarification of the division of powers between the Executive Council and the Governor, stating that the Governor must abide by the advice of the Executive Council on domestic policies, though not in matters of external affairs, defence and the administration of justice.

In January 2009 the Speaker of the Falkland Islands Legislative Council, Darwin Lewis Clifton, was found guilty of market abuse in his capacity as director of Desire, an oil and gas exploration company, and fined £59,000. He was replaced as Speaker in February by Keith Biles.

In enforcing the statutes of the Ottawa Convention, adopted under the Landmines Act 1998, the United Kingdom was required to identify and eliminate all mine devices within its territory and overseas jurisdictions within 10 years of the Convention's enactment. The resultant deadline for the destruction of all anti-personnel landmines in the Falkland Islands was established as March 2009. Of the 127 minefields laid by Argentine forces in 1982, 101 remained by February 2007; the minefields were enclosed by cordons and there had been no reported civilian fatalities from mine explosions since the end of the conflict. An assessment of the feasibility of eliminating the remaining landmines was conducted in October 2007 and revealed that the process would be technically possible but was expected to require a considerable amount of funding. At a meeting of Ottawa Convention signatories in Geneva, Switzerland, in November 2008, the United Kingdom requested a 10-year extension to the March 2009 deadline, a proposal that was accepted with the proviso that research into modern methods of mine-clearing be undertaken.

The Argentine Government formed a Congressional Observatory in June 2006 with the express function of actively reclaiming the Falkland Islands, which it continued to refer to as Argentine territory. In January 2007 the Argentine Minister of Foreign Affairs, International Trade and Worship, Jorge Taiana, had sought to enlist the support of the UN Secretary-General, Ban Ki-Moon, asserting that the United Kingdom had seized the archipelago by illegal means. President Kirchner maintained that the islanders possessed no right to self-determination, contending that the present population displaced indigenous Argentine residents upon settlement in 1833 with the intention of establishing a British colonial state, a claim strenuously refuted by the United Kingdom. In February Argentina rejected an invitation by the British Government to participate in joint commemorative celebrations to mark the 25th anniversary of the conflict's end. A joint hydrocarbon exploratory contract between Argentina and the United Kingdom was abandoned in the following month; the Argentine Government accused the British of pursuing a 'unilateral' approach to oil exploration initiatives and averred that there would be no further developments on the matter until the United Kingdom had agreed to resume negotiations over the islands' sovereignty. The original agreement, signed by former Argentine President Carlos Saúl Menem in 1995, followed the restoration of diplomatic relations between the two countries in 1990 and had been regarded as Argentine acknowledgment of the United Kingdom's claim to the sea floor surrounding the Falkland Islands. In April 2007 the Kirchner administration reiterated its claim to the territory and enjoined the British Government to cede to international demands to engage in dialogue over the future of the islands. The United Kingdom stated that it would not consider amendments to the governance or affiliations of the Falkland Islands unless and until a request to this effect was registered by the populace; it was asserted that no such request had been expressed by the islanders and, further, that they opposed Argentina's territorial offensive.

New legislation approved by the Argentine legislature on 11 April 2007 effectively required fishing companies wishing to operate in the maritime exclusion zone surrounding the islands to choose between Argentine or British authorities when making permit applications, and included restrictions against fishing in Argentine jurisdictional waters where a permit issued by the corresponding issuing authority was not held. A recent decision by the Falkland Islands authorities to begin issuing 25-year licences—as opposed to the one-year permits issued previously—had provoked protest from Argentina, which claimed its territorial rights had been disregarded.

The Argentine Government continued to seek a favourable resolution with regard to its claims of sovereignty over the Falkland Islands throughout 2007 and early 2008. During her inauguration speech in December 2007, the new President of Argentina, Cristina Fernández de Kirchner, stated that she was not prepared to make concessions in those claims, and her Government once again urged the United Kingdom to relaunch the negotiations process. However, in October 2007 the British Government announced its intention to submit a claim to the UN Commission on the Limits of the Continental Shelf for Atlantic seabed territory around the Falkland Islands. Argentine foreign minister Taiana insisted that his Government would challenge any such claim made by the United Kingdom. Furthermore, tensions between the two countries were exacerbated in early May 2008 when Taiana accused the British Government of 'illegitimately' issuing licences for hydrocarbon exploration and extraction activities in an area north of the Falkland Islands, part of the Argentine continental shelf. The British Government refused to concede to any of the claims made by its Argentine counterpart and maintained that it held sovereignty over the disputed area. On 24 April 2009 Argentina lodged a hostile claim before the UN Commission to some 1.7m. sq km (660,000 sq miles) of seabed surrounding the territory, as well as an area north of Antarctica, ahead of a 13 May deadline for demarcating possession of extended continental shelves. This was formally countered by the United Kingdom, which presented its own claim to the disputed region on 11 May. As a result, both claims were frozen, preventing either country from exploiting the areas beyond 200 nautical miles from its respective coastline.

Government

Administration is conducted by the appointed Governor (who is the personal representative of the British monarch), aided by the Executive Council, comprising two ex-officio members and three members elected by the Legislative Council. The Legislative Council is composed of two ex-officio members and eight elected members. Voting is by universal adult suffrage.

Defence

According to official sources, in May 2008 there were approximately 1,200 British troops stationed on the islands (450 army, 650 air force and 100 navy). The total cost of the conflict in 1982 and of building and maintaining a garrison for four years was estimated at £2,560m. The current annual cost of maintaining the garrison is approximately £65m. Total expenditure in 1999/2000 was £71.1m. The cost of maintaining British military personnel in the territory was £143.3m. in 2005/06. There is a Falkland Islands Defence Force, composed of islanders.

Economic Affairs

According to government estimates, gross domestic product (GDP) was some £70m. in 2001, with GDP per head of £24,030 and annual growth of an estimated 2%. Gross national income was estimated to have increased from £5m. in 1980 to more than £50m. in 2000.

Most of the agricultural land on the Falkland Islands is devoted to the rearing of sheep. However, the land is poor and more than four acres are required to support one animal. In the late 1990s annual exports of wool were valued at some £3.5m. Declining international wool prices encouraged agricultural diversification, such as the pursuit of organic farming, the breeding of cashmere goats and also the development of meat production (an abattoir was constructed to meet European Union standards, incurring expenditure of £372,332 in 2002 and a further £678,371 in 2003). Some vegetables are produced (notably in a hydroponic market garden), and there are small dairy herds (672 dairy cows in 2006/07). From 1987, when a licensing system was introduced for foreign vessels fishing within a 150-nautical-mile conservation and management zone (see Recent History), the economy was diversified and the islands' annual income increased considerably. Although revenue from the sale of licences declined in the 1990s following the Argentine Government's commencement of the sale of fishing licences in 1993, licences (and transshipments) totalled £22.9m. in 2001/02, equivalent to 51.5% of total budget revenue in that year. The revenue funds social provisions and economic development programmes. In the late 1980s about one-third of the world's total catch of *illex* and *loligo* squid was derived from this fishing zone. However, over-fishing in the area surrounding the conservation zone had a detrimental effect on stocks of fish in the islands' waters, and frequently the Government has been obliged to call an early halt to the exploitation of both squid types, as it did in both 2004 and 2005. The 2006 season for *illex* squid fishing began in mid-February, and by the end of March approximately 40 licences had been sold. Revenues from fishing licences and transshipment increased to approximately £16.1m. in 2005/06, approximately 37% of total revenues in that fiscal year.

Manufacturing activity on the islands reflects the predominance of the agricultural sector: a wool mill on West Falkland produces yarns for machine knitting, hand knitting and weaving. Several small companies in the Falklands produce garments for local and export sales. Some fish-processing also takes place on East Falkland.

The Falkland Islands are heavily dependent on imports of all fuels, except peat; households primarily depend on kerosene and diesel for heating purposes. Wind power is used in many remote locations to offset this dependence and reduce pollution of the atmosphere. The Falkland Islands Government licensed five consortia to explore for hydrocarbons in waters north of the islands in 1996. These companies, including Shell, Amerada Hess and LASMO, drilled six exploration wells in 1998. Five of the six wells had minor traces of hydrocarbons present, but no commercial quantities of petroleum were found in the initial phase of drilling. A British prospecting company has been granted an exploration licence to search for minerals on the islands. Mineral sands including garnet and rutile were being appraised, while more valuable minerals such as gold were being sought. In July 2002 the Falkland Islands Government granted 10 petroleum exploration licences to the Falklands Hydrocarbon Consortium (comprising Global Petroleum Ltd, Hardman Resources Ltd and Falkland Islands Holdings) for an area covering 57,700 sq km to the south of the islands. Activity was renewed in both the minerals and hydrocarbons sectors in 2005.

The Falkland Islands Development Corporation oversees the islands' economic development on behalf of the Government. Since the 1980s the Government has sought to promote the development of the tourism sector. Tourism, and in particular 'eco-tourism', was developing rapidly in the 2000s, and the number of visitors staying on the Falklands Islands had grown to some 3,000 a year, while around 40,000 tourists a year sailed through Stanley harbour on their way to Antarctica and sub-Antarctic islands such as South Georgia. The sale of postage stamps and coins represents a significant source of income; the value of sales of the former was £296,229 in 1996/97, while the value of sales of the latter totalled £49,351 in 1995/96.

In 2000 the islands recorded an estimated trade surplus of £28,041,897. Fish, most of which is purchased by the United Kingdom, Spain and Chile, is the islands' most significant export. The principal imports are fuel, provisions, alcoholic beverages, building materials and clothing. In 2001 the Government brought 100 reindeer from the South Georgia Islands (with the aim of increasing the number to 10,000 over the following 20 years) in order to export venison to Scandinavia and Chile.

The budget for the financial year 2005/06 provided for revenue of £43.5m. and expenditure of £43.9m. The islands are generally self-sufficient in all areas of the economy (although expenditures associated with defence are the responsibility of the British Government). The annual rate of inflation averaged 2.5% in 1995–2003; consumer prices increased by 0.7% in 2002 and by 1.2% in 2003. There is a significant shortage of local labour on the islands.

Since 1982 the economy of the Falkland Islands has enjoyed a period of strong and sustained growth, partly owing to substantial investment by the British Government during the 1980s, but primarily as a result of the introduction of the fisheries licensing scheme in 1987. It was anticipated that royalties derived from the sale of licences for the exploration and exploitation of hydrocarbons would strengthen the economy further. The services sector expanded rapidly during the late 1990s, while the importance of the agricultural sector decreased, not least because of its reliance on direct and indirect subsidies. A government development plan emphasized agricultural diversification and the promotion of tourism as its main economic aims; it also sought to develop services and to encourage the growth of activities related to the fishing industry (such as freezer plants and mussel farms). During 2008 seismic surveys conducted in the waters around the Falkland Islands suggested the area could yield as much as 18,000m. barrels of petroleum, although the sovereignty of the islands and their surrounding waters continue to be an obstacle to actual exploration. The authorities in Argentina had previously prohibited all oil companies working in that country from any involvement in oil exploration around the Falkland Islands. Meanwhile, a progress report on economic developments during 2004–07 was released in March 2008 and focused on successes in increasing the profitability of small businesses (an increase of 155% was reported between 2001 and 2006), growth in the number of tourist arrivals (39% growth in the number of long-stay tourists between 2003/04 and 2006/07) and achievements in maintaining lower than average rates of unemployment (3.7% in 2006). However, the review accepted that target GDP growth of 3% had not been achieved (largely as a result of disappointing revenues from the fishery sector) and that the proportion of GDP represented by government spending had only been reduced by 2% (to 42%) and not by the 5% originally predicted. (A medium-term financial plan, also launched in early 2008, sought to reduce annual expenditure by £0.5m. and increase revenue by the same amount each year during the next four years.) At the same time a new social and economic development programme for 2008–12 was published which identified the need to reduce over-reliance on the public sector and to increase, through the encouragement of entrepreneurs, the economic contribution of the private sector, in order to help achieve target GDP growth of 5% over the four-year period in question.

Education

Education is compulsory, and is provided free of charge, for children between the ages of five and 16 years. Facilities are available for further study beyond the statutory school-leaving age. In 2003 203 pupils were instructed by 18 teachers at the primary school in Stanley, while 160 pupils received instruction from 18 teachers at the secondary school in the capital; further facilities existed in rural districts, with six peripatetic teachers visiting younger children for two out of every six weeks (older children boarded in a hostel in Stanley). Total expenditure on education and training was estimated at £3.5m. for 2001/02.

Public Holidays

2009: 1 January (New Year's Day), 10 April (Good Friday), 21 April (HM the Queen's Birthday), 15 June (for Liberation Day), 5 October (Spring Holiday), 8 December (Anniversary of the Battle of the Falkland Islands in 1914), 25–29 December (Christmas).

2010: 1 January (New Year's Day), 2 April (Good Friday), 21 April (HM the Queen's Birthday), 14 June (Liberation Day), 4 October (Spring Holiday), 8 December (Anniversary of the Battle of the Falkland Islands in 1914), 25–29 December (Christmas).

Weights and Measures

Both the imperial and metric systems are in general use.

Statistical Survey

Source (unless otherwise stated): The Treasury of the Falkland Islands Government, Stanley, FIQQ 1ZZ; tel. 27143; fax 27144; internet www.falklands.gov.fk.

AREA AND POPULATION

Area: approx. 12,173 sq km (4,700 sq miles): East Falkland and adjacent islands 6,760 sq km (2,610 sq miles); West Falkland and adjacent islands 5,413 sq km (2,090 sq miles).

Population: 2,478 at census of 8 October 2006. Note: Figure excludes military personnel and civilians based at Mount Pleasant military base and the 84 residents absent on the night of the census.

Density (2006 census): 0.20 per sq km.

Principal Town (2006 census): Stanley (capital), population 2,115.

Births and Deaths (2000): Live births 27; Deaths 6.

Economically Active Population (persons aged 15 years and over, 2001 census): 2,475 (males 1,370, females 1,105).

AGRICULTURE, ETC.

Livestock (2007, official figures at 31 May): Sheep 530,009; Cattle 6,251; Goats 502; Reindeer 124; Horses 644; Poultry 3,419.

Livestock Products (metric tons, 2007, FAO estimates): Cattle meat 150; Sheep meat 800; Cows' milk 1,600; Wool, greasy 2,400. Source: FAO.

Fishing ('000 metric tons, live weight of capture, 2006): Southern blue whiting 1.8; Argentine hake 5.6; Patagonian grenadier 6.1; Patagonian squid 40.3; Argentine shortfin squid 5.4; Total catch (incl. others) 75.3. Source: FAO.

FINANCE

Currency and Exchange Rates: 100 pence (pennies) = 1 Falkland Islands pound (FI £). *Sterling, Dollar and Euro Equivalents* (31 December 2008): £1 sterling = FI £1.00; US $1 = 68.60 pence; €1 = 95.47 pence; FI £100 = £100.00 sterling = $145.78 = €104.75. *Average Exchange Rate* (FI £ per US dollar): 0.5345 in 2006; 0.4998 in 2007; 0.5412 in 2008. Note: The Falkland Islands pound is at par with the pound sterling.

Budget (FI £ million, 2005/06): *Revenue:* Sales and services 14.6; Fishing licences and transshipment 16.1; Investment income 4.9; Taxes and duties 7.9; Total 43.5. *Expenditure:* Operating expenditure 36.2 (Public works 8.1, Fisheries 6.6, Health care 5.3, Education 5.0, Aviation 2.0, Police and justice 1.3, Agriculture 1.1, Central administration 3.8, Other 3.0); Capital expenditure 7.7; Total 43.9.

Cost of Living (Consumer Price Index for Stanley; base: 2000 = 100): All items 101.3 in 2001; 102.0 in 2002; 103.2 in 2003. Source: ILO.

EXTERNAL TRADE

2000 (estimates): Total imports £18,958,103; Total exports £47,000,000. Fish is the principal export. Trade is mainly with the United Kingdom, Spain and Chile.

TRANSPORT

Shipping: *Merchant Fleet* (at 31 December 2007): Vessels 29; Displacement 51,016 grt. Source: Lloyd's Register-Fairplay, *World Fleet Statistics*.

Road Traffic: 3,065 vehicles in use in 1995.

TOURISM

Day Visitors (country of origin of cruise-ship excursionists, 2006/07 season): Canada 4,862; United Kingdom 6,736; USA 21,298; Total (incl. others) 51,282. *2007/08:* Total 62,200 (Source: Falkland Islands Tourist Board).

EDUCATION

2003 (Stanley): *Primary:* Teachers 18; Pupils 203. *Secondary:* Teachers 18; Pupils 160.

Directory

The Constitution

The present Constitution of the Falkland Islands came into force on 1 January 2009 (replacing that of 1985). The Governor, who is the personal representative of the British monarch, is advised by the Executive Council, comprising six members: the Governor (presiding), three elected members of the Legislative Council, and two ex officio members, the Chief Executive and the Director of Finance of the Falkland Islands Government, who are non-voting. The Legislative Council is composed of eight elected members and the same two (non-voting) ex officio members. One of the principal features of the Constitution is the reference in the preamble to the islanders' right to self-determination. The separate post of Chief Executive (responsible to the Governor) was created in 1983. The electoral principle was introduced, on the basis of universal adult suffrage, in 1949. The minimum voting age was lowered from 21 years to 18 years in 1977.

The Government

(April 2009)

Governor: ALAN HUCKLE (took office 25 August 2006).
Chief Executive of the Falkland Islands Government: Dr TIM THOROGOOD.
Government Secretary: PETER T. KING.
Director of Finance: KEITH PADGETT.
Attorney-General: DAVID PICKUP.
Commander, British Forces South Atlantic Islands: Brig. NICK DAVIS.

EXECUTIVE COUNCIL

The Council consists of six members (see Constitution, above).

LEGISLATIVE COUNCIL

Comprises the Governor, two ex-officio (non-voting) members and eight elected members.

GOVERNMENT OFFICES

Office of the Governor: Government House, Stanley, FIQQ 1ZZ; tel. 27433; fax 27434; e-mail gov.house@horizon.co.fk.

General Office: Legislature Dept, Gilbert House, Stanley, FIQQ 1ZZ; tel. 27455; e-mail clerkofcouncils@sec.gov.fk; internet www.falklands.gov.fk.

London Office: Falkland Islands Government Office, Falkland House, 14 Broadway, London, SW1H 0BH, United Kingdom; tel. (20) 7222-2542; fax (20) 7222-2375; e-mail representative@falklands.gov.fk; internet www.falklands.gov.fk; f. 1983.

Judicial System

The judicial system of the Falkland Islands is administered by the Supreme Court (presided over by the non-resident Chief Justice), the Magistrate's Court (presided over by the Senior Magistrate) and the Court of Summary Jurisdiction. The Court of Appeal for the Territory sits in England and appeals therefrom may be heard by the Judicial Committee of the Privy Council.

Chief Justice of the Supreme Court: CHRISTOPHER GARDNER, QC.
Judge of the Supreme Court and Senior Magistrate: JOHN TREVASKIS (acting).
Registrar to the Supreme Court and Courts Administrator: CHERILYN KING, Town Hall, Ross Rd, Stanley, FIQQ 1ZZ; tel. 27271; fax 27270.

FALKLAND ISLANDS COURT OF APPEAL

President: Judge BRIAN APPLEBY.
Registrar: MICHAEL J. ELKS.

Religion

CHRISTIANITY

The Anglican Communion, the Roman Catholic Church and the United Free Church predominate. Also represented are the Evangelist Church, Jehovah's Witnesses, the Lutheran Church, Seventh-day Adventists and the Bahá'í faith.

UNITED KINGDOM OVERSEAS TERRITORIES

The Anglican Communion

The Archbishop of Canterbury, the Primate of All England, exercises episcopal jurisdiction over the Falkland Islands and South Georgia.

Rector: Rev. Dr RICHARD HINES, The Deanery, Christ Church Cathedral, Stanley, FIQQ 1ZZ; tel. 21100; fax 21842; e-mail deanery@horizon.co.fk.

The Roman Catholic Church

Prefect Apostolic of the Falkland Islands: MICHAEL BERNARD MCPARTLAND, St Mary's Presbytery, 12 Ross Rd, Stanley, FIQQ 1ZZ; tel. 21204; fax 22242; e-mail stmarys@horizon.co.fk; internet www.southatlanticrcchurch.com; f. 1764; 300 adherents (2006).

The Press

The Falkland Islands Gazette: Cable Cottage, POB 587, Stanley, FIQQ 1ZZ; tel. 28460; fax 27276; e-mail bsteen@sec.gov.fk; internet www.falklands.gov.fk; govt publ.

Falkland Islands News Network: POB 141, Stanley, FIQQ 1ZZ; tel. and fax 21182; e-mail finn@horizon.co.fk; internet www.falklandnews.com; relays news daily online and via fax as FINN(COM) Service; Man. JUAN BROCK; publishes:

  Teaberry Express: Stanley, FIQQ 1ZZ; tel. 21182; weekly.

Penguin News: Ross Rd, Stanley, FIQQ 1ZZ; tel. 22709; fax 22238; e-mail pnews@horizon.co.fk; internet www.penguin-news.com; f. 1979; weekly; independent newspaper; Man. Editor JENNY COCKWELL; circ. 1,550.

Broadcasting and Communications

TELECOMMUNICATIONS

In 1989 Cable & Wireless PLC installed a £5.4m. digital telecommunications network covering the entire Falkland Islands. The Government contributed to the cost of the new system, which provides international services as well as a new domestic network. Further work to improve the domestic telephone system was completed in the late 1990s at a cost of £3.3m. The first mobile telephone network was introduced in 2005 and a broadband internet service in 2006.

Cable & Wireless South Atlantic Ltd: Ross Rd, POB 584, Stanley, FIQQ 1ZZ; tel. 20820; fax 20801; e-mail info@cwfi.co.fk; internet www.cwfi.co.fk; f. 1989; exclusive provider of national and international telecommunications services in the Falkland Islands under a licence issued by the Falkland Islands Govt; CEO AARON RICHARDSON.

BROADCASTING

Radio

Falkland Islands Radio Service: Broadcasting Studios, John St, Stanley, FIQQ 1ZZ; tel. 27277; fax 27279; e-mail cbishop@firs.co.fk; internet www.firs.co.fk; f. 1929; fmrly Falklands Islands Broadcasting Station; 24-hour service, financed by local Govt in association with SSVC of London, United Kingdom; broadcasts in English; Station Man. CORINA GOSS; Programme Controller LIZ ELLIOT.

British Forces Broadcasting Service (BFBS): BFBS Falkland Islands, Mount Pleasant, BFPO 655; tel. 32179; fax 32193; e-mail bfbsfalklands@bfbs.com; internet www.bfbs.com/falklands; 24-hour satellite service from the United Kingdom; Station Man. CHRIS PEARSON; Sr Engineer ADRIAN ALMOND.

Television

British Forces Broadcasting Service (BFBS): BFBS Falkland Islands, Mount Pleasant, BFPO 655; tel. 32179; fax 32193; internet www.bfbs.com/falklands; daily four-hour transmissions of taped broadcasts from BBC and ITV of London, United Kingdom; Sr Engineer COLIN MCDONALD.

KTV: 16 Ross Rd West, Stanley, FIQQ 1ZZ; tel. 22349; fax 21049; e-mail kmzb@horizon.co.fk; internet www.ktv.co.fk; satellite television broadcasting services; Man. MARIO ZUVIC BULIC.

Finance

BANK

Standard Chartered Bank: Ross Rd, POB 597, Stanley, FIQQ 1ZZ; tel. 22220; fax 22219; e-mail bank.info@fk.standardchartered.com; internet www.standardchartered.com/fk; branch opened in 1983; Man. RINO DONOSEPOETRO.

The Falkland Islands

INSURANCE

The British Commercial Union, Royal Insurance and Norman Tremellen companies maintain agencies in Stanley.

Consultancy Services Falklands Ltd: 44 John St, Stanley, FIQQ 1ZZ; tel. 22666; fax 22639; e-mail consultancy@horizon.co.uk; Man. ALISON BAKER.

Trade and Industry

DEVELOPMENT ORGANIZATION

Falkland Islands Development Corporation (FIDC): Shackleton House, West Hillside, Stanley, FIQQ 1ZZ; tel. 27211; fax 27210; e-mail develop@fidc.co.fk; internet www.fidc.co.fk; f. 1983; provides loans and grants; encourages private sector investment, inward investment and technology transfer; Gen. Man. (vacant).

CHAMBER OF COMMERCE

Chamber of Commerce: POB 378, Stanley, FIQQ 1ZZ; tel. 22264; fax 22265; e-mail commerce@horizon.co.fk; internet www.falklandislandschamberofcommerce.com; f. 1993; promotes private industry; operates DHL courier service; runs an employment agency; Pres. ROGER SPINK; 87 mems.

TRADING COMPANIES

Falkland Islands Co Ltd (FIC): Crozier Pl., Stanley, FIQQ 1ZZ; tel. 27600; fax 27603; e-mail fic@horizon.co.fk; internet www.the-falkland-islands-co.com; f. 1851; part of Falkland Islands Holding PLC; the largest trading co; retailing, wholesaling, shipping, insurance and Land Rover sales and servicing; operates as agent for Lloyd's of London and general shipping concerns; travel services; wharf owners and operators; Dir and Gen. Man. ROGER KENNETH SPINK.

Falkland Islands Meat Co: Sand Bay, East Falklands, FIQQ 1ZZ; tel. 27013; fax 27113; e-mail info@falklandmeat.co.fk; internet www.falklands-meat.com; exporters of lamb and mutton meat; Gen. Man. JOHN FERGUSON.

Falkland Oil and Gas Ltd (FOGL): 56 John St, Stanley, F1QQ 1ZZ; e-mail info@fogl.co.uk; internet www.fogl.co.uk; f. 2004; shareholders include Falkland Islands Holdings PLC (16%), Global Petroleum (14%) and RAB Capital PLC (33%); operates an offshore petroleum exploration programme with 8 licences covering 65,354 sq km; Chair. RICHARD LIDDELL; CEO TIM BUSHELL.

EMPLOYERS' ASSOCIATION

Sheep Owners' Association: Coast Ridge Farm, Fox Bay, FIQQ 1ZZ; tel. 42094; fax 42084; e-mail n.knight.coastridge@horizon.co.fk; f. 1967; asscn for sheep station owners; limited liability private co; Company Sec. N. KNIGHT.

TRADE UNION

Falkland Islands General Employees Union: Ross Rd, Stanley, FIQQ 1ZZ; tel. 21151; e-mail geu@horizon.co.fk; f. 1943; Chair. GAVIN SHORT; 100 mems.

CO-OPERATIVE SOCIETY

Stanley Co-operative Society: Stanley, FIQQ 1ZZ; tel. 21215; f. 1952; open to all members of the public; Man. NORMA THOM.

Transport

RAILWAYS

There are no railways on the islands.

ROADS

There are 29 km (18 miles) of paved road in and around Stanley. There are 54 km of all-weather road linking Stanley and the Mount Pleasant airport (some of which has been surfaced with a bitumen substance), and a further 37 km of road as far as Goose Green. There are 300 km of arterial roads in the North Camp on East Falkland linking settlements, and a further 197 km of road on West Falkland. Where roads have still not been built, settlements are linked by tracks, which are passable by all-terrain motor vehicle or motorcycle except in the most severe weather conditions.

SHIPPING

There is a ship on charter to the Falkland Islands Co Ltd which makes the round trip to the United Kingdom four or five times a year, carrying cargo. A floating deep-water jetty was completed in 1984. The British Ministry of Defence charters ships, which sail for the Falkland Islands once every three weeks. There are irregular cargo services between the islands and southern Chile and Uruguay. The

UNITED KINGDOM OVERSEAS TERRITORIES

Falkland Islands Development Corpn commissioned a port development plan in February 2007 for the upgrade of existing facilities to reflect growth in containerized traffic and cruise ship arrivals, and to accommodate proposed further oil exploration in territorial waters.

The Falkland Islands merchant fleet numbered 29 vessels, with a total displacement of 51,016 grt, at December 2007; the majority of vessels registered are deep-sea fishing vessels.

Stanley Port Authority: c/o Dept of Fisheries, POB 598, Stanley, FIQQ 1ZZ; tel. 27260; fax 27265; e-mail jclark@fisheries.gov.fk; Marine Officer and Harbour Master JON CLARK.

Private Companies

Byron Marine Ltd: 3 H Jones Rd, Stanley, FIQQ 1ZZ; tel. 22245; fax 22246; e-mail info@byronmarine.co.fk; internet www.byronmarine.co.fk; f. 1992; additional activites include oil exploration support services, deep-sea fishing and property; contracted managers of the Falkland Islands Government Port Facility; island-wide pilotage services; vessel agent; Man. Dir LEWIS CLIFTON.

Darwin Shipping Ltd: Stanley, FIQQ 1ZZ; tel. 27629; fax 27603; e-mail darwin@horizon.co.fk; internet www.the-falkland-islands-co.com; subsidiary of the Falkland Islands Co Ltd (q.v.); Man. ANDY WATSON.

Falkland Islands Co Ltd (FIC): see Trade and Industry—Trading Companies.

Seaview Ltd: 37 Fitzroy Rd, POB 215, Stanley, FIQQ 1ZZ; tel. 22669; fax 22670; e-mail seaview.agent@horizon.co.fk; internet www.fis.com/polar; operates subsidiary co, Polar Ltd (f. 1989); Man. Dir DICK SAWLE; Operations Man. ALEX REID.

Sulivan Shipping Services Ltd: Davis St, POB 159, Stanley, FIQQ 1ZZ; tel. 22626; fax 22625; e-mail sulivan@horizon.co.fk; internet www.sulivanshipping.com; f. 1987; provides port-agency and ground-handling services; Operations Man. MIGS COFRÉ.

CIVIL AVIATION

There are airports at Stanley and Mount Pleasant; the latter has a runway of 2,590 m (8,497 ft), and is capable of receiving wide-bodied jet aircraft. The British Royal Air Force operates two weekly flights from the United Kingdom. The Chilean carrier LAN Airlines (formerly LanChile) operates weekly return flights from Punta Arenas. An 'air bridge', operated by charter carriers subcontracted to the British Ministry of Defence, provides a link via Ascension Island between the Falkland Islands and the United Kingdom.

Falkland Islands Government Air Service (FIGAS): Stanley Airport, Stanley, FIQQ 1ZZ; tel. 27219; fax 27309; e-mail sminto@figas.gov.fk; f. 1948 to provide social, medical and postal services between the settlements and Stanley; aerial surveillance for Dept of Fisheries since 1990; operates five nine-seater aircraft to over 35 landing strips across the islands; Gen. Man. SHAUN MINTO.

Tourism

During the 2007/08 season some 62,200 day visitors from cruise ships visited the islands. US citizens constitute the primary visitor group. Wildlife photography, bird-watching and hiking are popular tourist activities. The Falkland Islands Development Corpn (FIDC) plans to develop the sector in collaboration with the Government and tourism operators in the territory. In 2005 the FIDC introduced a funding programme for the upgrade of tourism accommodation facilities that continued into the 2006/07 season.

Falkland Islands Tourist Board: POB 618, Stanley, FIQQ 1ZZ; tel. 22215; fax 27020; e-mail info@visitorfalklands.com; internet www.falklandislands.com; Gen. Man. JAKE DOWNING.

GIBRALTAR

Introductory Survey

Location, Climate, Language, Religion, Flag

The City of Gibraltar lies in southern Europe. The territory consists of a narrow peninsula of approximately 4.8 km (3 miles) in length, running southwards from the south-west coast of Spain, to which it is connected by an isthmus. About 8 km (5 miles) across the bay, to the west, lies the Spanish port of Algeciras, while 32 km (20 miles) to the south, across the Strait of Gibraltar, is Morocco. The Mediterranean Sea lies to the east. The climate is temperate, and snow or frost are extremely rare. The mean minimum and maximum temperatures during the winter are 13°C (55°F) and 18°C (65°F), respectively, and during the summer they are 13°C (55°F) and 29°C (85°F), respectively; the average annual rainfall is 890 mm (35 ins). The official language is English, although most of the population is bilingual in English and Spanish. More than three-quarters of the population are Roman Catholic. The flag (proportions 1 by 2) bears the arms of Gibraltar (a red castle with a pendant golden key) on a background, the upper two-thirds of which are white and the lower one-third red.

Recent History

Since the Second World War, this Overseas Territory has achieved considerable social and economic progress, through intensive development of its social and economic infrastructure, and by the expansion of commerce and the encouragement of tourism. Gibraltar has exercised control over most internal matters since 1969.

The Spanish Government lays claim to Gibraltar as a part of its territory, while the United Kingdom maintains that the Treaty of Utrecht (1713) granted sovereignty over Gibraltar to the United Kingdom in perpetuity (with the stipulation that, if the United Kingdom relinquished the colony, it would be returned to Spain). In 1963 the Spanish Government began a campaign, through the UN, for the cession of Gibraltar to Spain. It also imposed restrictions against Gibraltar, culminating in the closure of the frontier in 1969, the withdrawal of the Spanish labour force, and the severing of transport and communication links with Spain.

Following a referendum held in the territory in 1967, in which the overwhelming majority voted in favour of retaining British sovereignty, a new Constitution, promulgated in 1969, contained a provision that the British Government undertook never to enter into arrangements whereby the people of Gibraltar would pass under the sovereignty of another state against their freely and democratically expressed wishes. Gibraltar joined the European Community (EC, now European Union—EU, see p. 255) with the United Kingdom in 1973.

By 1977, a more flexible attitude by Spain towards Gibraltar became apparent. At talks held between Spanish and British ministers in November representatives of the Gibraltar Government were included for the first time as part of the British delegation. Further negotiations took place in 1979 and 1980. In October 1980 the British Parliament granted Gibraltarians the right to retain full British citizenship. Negotiations for the reopening of the frontier continued in 1982, but a change of attitudes in both countries, following the war between the United Kingdom and Argentina over the sovereignty of the Falkland Islands (q.v.), resulted in an indefinite postponement. In December Spain reopened the border to pedestrians of Spanish nationality and to British subjects resident in Gibraltar.

At the general election held in January 1984 the Gibraltar Labour Party—Association for the Advancement of Civil Rights (GLP—AACR), led by Sir Joshua Hassan, retained a majority of one seat in the House of Assembly. The Gibraltar Socialist Labour Party (GSLP), led by Joe Bossano, secured the remaining seven seats, replacing the Democratic Party of British Gibraltar as the opposition party in the House of Assembly. (Under the terms of the Constitution, the party with the largest share of the vote obtained a maximum of eight seats in the House of Assembly.)

In November 1984 the British and Spanish Governments agreed to provide equal rights for Spaniards in Gibraltar and for Gibraltarians in Spain; to allow free movement for all traffic between Gibraltar and Spain; and to conduct negotiations on the future of the territory, including (for the first time) discussions on sovereignty. Border restrictions were finally ended in February 1985, and negotiations took place between the British and Spanish Governments to improve cross-border co-operation, especially in tourism and civil aviation. In December, however, Spanish proposals for an interim settlement of the territory's future were rejected by the British Government as unacceptable since they implied the eventual automatic cession of Gibraltar to Spain. Subsequent discussions concerning principally Spain's demands for access to the Gibraltar airport (which the Spanish Government claimed was situated on land not covered by the terms of the Treaty of Utrecht) were inconclusive, owing to the Gibraltar Government's insistence that the airport remain exclusively under the control of the British and Gibraltar authorities. In December 1987 negotiators concluded an agreement that recommended increased co-operation between Spain and Gibraltar in the area of transport, in particular the joint administration of Gibraltar's airport. It was announced that Gibraltar's inclusion in an EC directive concerning air transport regulation was subject to the Gibraltar Government's approval of the British-Spanish agreement. However, the House of Assembly rejected the agreement, on the grounds that it would represent an infringement of British sovereignty, and voted unanimously to contest Gibraltar's exclusion from the EC directive.

At a general election held in March 1988, the GSLP received 58.2% of the votes cast, obtaining eight seats in the House of Assembly, and the GLP—AACR received 29.3% of the vote, securing seven seats. Bossano became Chief Minister, at the head of Gibraltar's first socialist Government. Bossano announced that he would not participate in British-Spanish negotiations concerning Gibraltar, on the grounds that the territory's sovereignty was not a matter for negotiation between Spain and the United Kingdom, and that the December 1987 agreement would, in his view, result in the absorption of Gibraltar into Spain.

In January 1989, in an unprecedented gesture of co-operation between Gibraltar and Spain, Bossano met the mayor of La Línea, the Spanish town bordering Gibraltar, and offered to assist in financing an economic revival in the region. In February 1990 the British and Spanish Governments agreed to contest a legal action that was to be brought by Gibraltar in the European Court of Justice against Gibraltar's exclusion from measures adopted to liberalize European air transport, which prevented the territory from expanding its air links with Europe. The decision to contest the action was considered to be a further attempt by the United Kingdom to persuade Gibraltar to co-operate with Spain. In March 1991 the United Kingdom withdrew the majority of British army personnel from Gibraltar, although the Royal Navy and Royal Air Force detachments remained.

In May 1991 the Spanish Prime Minister made an official visit to the United Kingdom, and was reported to have proposed a plan for joint sovereignty over Gibraltar, whereby the dependency would become effectively autonomous, with the British and Spanish monarchs as joint heads of state. Although it represented a significant concession by the Spanish Government, the plan was rejected by the Gibraltar Government. At the EC summit meeting held at Maastricht, Netherlands, in December, Spain continued to refuse to recognize Gibraltar's status as part of the EC, and remained determined to exclude it from the External Frontiers Convention (EFC), which was designed to strengthen common controls on entry into countries belonging to the EC. The continued failure to reach an agreement, particularly concerning the administration of Gibraltar airport, prevented the ratification of the EFC.

At a general election held in January 1992 the GSLP retained eight seats in the House of Assembly, and Bossano was returned for a second term as Chief Minister. The Gibraltar Social Democrats (GSD), which supported Gibraltar's participation in British-Spanish negotiations, secured the remaining seven seats. In February 1992, prior to discussions with British ministers in London, Bossano announced that Gibraltar was to attempt to obtain a revision of the 1969 Constitution, with the aim of achieving self-determination within four years. The British Government, however, stated that it would not consider granting independence to Gibraltar, unless the Spanish Government was prepared to accept the agreement, and excluded the possibility of formal negotiations on the issue.

In January 1993 Gibraltarians lodged a formal protest after increasingly stringent monitoring of vehicles by Spanish customs officials resulted in severe delays at the frontier. In March an official meeting between the foreign ministers of the United Kingdom and Spain achieved little progress; it was agreed, however, that contacts between British and Spanish officials were to be maintained. In early 1994 Bossano accused the British Government of subordinating the interests of Gibraltar to the promotion of harmonious relations with Spain, and demanded a renegotiation of the 1987 airport agreement on the grounds that its provisions had subsequently become redundant and contrary to EU law.

In late 1994 Spain alleged that insufficient action was being taken by Gibraltar to curtail the smuggling of tobacco from Gibraltar to Spain and of illegal narcotics between Morocco and Spain by Gibraltar-based speedboats. The imposition in October of stringent border inspections by Spain prompted a protest by the British Government. These border checks were eased following assurances that measures were being taken against those involved in smuggling. Spain reimposed frontier controls in March 1995, precipitating further criticism by the British Government. In July 1996 the Gibraltar authorities extended offences of money-laundering, hitherto applicable solely to proceeds from drugs-trafficking, to those from all crimes.

In July 1995, following the confiscation of more than 60 speedboats, alleged to be used in the transport of contraband, the Spanish Government eased frontier controls. The seizures provoked two days of riots and looting in Gibraltar, followed by a peaceful mass demonstration organized by Gibraltar business interests and trade unions in support of the continuing implementation of anti-smuggling measures. Although the British and Spanish Governments jointly agreed in September that the anti-smuggling measures were proving effective, the death of a Spanish civil guard in pursuit of smugglers in April 1996 led to the renewal of border controls by Spain.

Campaign debates in advance of legislative elections in May 1996 focused on Gibraltar's external relations. Bossano and the GSLP proposed that the territory's status be replaced before the year 2000 by a form of 'free association' with the United Kingdom, while the GSD declared as its aims the achievement of improved relations with both Spain and the United Kingdom and the modernization of Gibraltar's Constitution. The election attracted an unusually high turn-out (87.7% of eligible voters), and resulted in the GSD receiving 48% of the vote and the maximum of eight seats in the House of Assembly; the GSD leader, Peter Caruana, became Chief Minister. The GSLP received 39% of the vote and the Gibraltar National Party obtained 13%.

In November 1996 the Spanish Government lodged a complaint with the EU Commission over a private visit to Gibraltar by the EU Commissioner responsible for Immigration and Home and Judicial Affairs to view the operation of Spanish border controls. In the same month Chief Minister Caruana renewed his demand that Gibraltar be accorded equal status with the United Kingdom in future negotiations concerning the territory's interests. In January 1997 Caruana refused to attend discussions on Gibraltar, held in Madrid, Spain, between the United Kingdom and Spain, on the grounds that Gibraltar would not be granted power of veto. A suggestion by Spain that sovereignty over Gibraltar be shared between Spain and the United Kingdom for a 100-year period, with full control then passing to Spain, was rejected by the British Government.

In October 1997 Caruana informed the Decolonization Committee of the UN General Assembly that he was to seek from the British Government an extensive review of the territory's 1969 Constitution. It was to be proposed that Gibraltar would obtain additional autonomy in the conduct of its affairs while remaining in a close political and constitutional relationship with the United Kingdom, similar to that held by the Crown Dependencies of the Channel Islands and the Isle of Man (q.v.). During 1997 new tensions arose between the United Kingdom and Spanish Governments over the long-standing refusal by Spain to permit military aircraft from the United Kingdom and the North Atlantic Treaty Organization (NATO, see p. 351) to cross Spanish airspace on their approach to Gibraltar airport. In July the British Government indicated that it would oppose the full incorporation of Spain into NATO unless the ban was lifted. An indication by Spain of its willingness to open its airspace to these flights in return for joint military control of the airport was strongly opposed by Caruana and rejected by the British Government. In July 1998 Spain reversed its long-standing refusal to participate in NATO manoeuvres that were based in, or passed through, Gibraltar. In that month the Spanish Government unsuccessfully requested the British Government to consider a revived proposal for the shared sovereignty of Gibraltar for a period of 50 years, to be followed by the territory's full integration into Spain.

In November 1998 complaints by the Gibraltar Government arose over the conduct of Spanish fishing vessels in the Bay of Gibraltar, which were stated to be operating in violation of the territory's nature protection ordinance. In January 1999 a Spanish trawler was impounded by the Gibraltar authorities, and Spain began to intensify delays in road traffic crossing the frontier. An agreement reached in February between the Gibraltar authorities and the Spanish fishermen was not recognized by the Spanish Government.

At the general election held in February 2000 the GSD secured 58.7% of the vote, against 40.8% obtained by an electoral coalition of the GSLP and the Gibraltar Liberal Party (GLP). Caruana was reconfirmed as Chief Minister, and the GSD retained its eight seats in the House of Assembly. The rate of participation was again high, at 83.6%.

Extended negotiations between the Spanish and British Governments were concluded in April 2000 with a compromise agreement whereby Spain was to recognize the validity of Gibraltar identity cards and of the territory's financial institutions, provided that the 'competent authority' responsible for their supervision was the United Kingdom rather than the Gibraltar Government. It was also agreed that the British authorities would provide a facility, based in London, through which the Spanish and Gibraltar authorities could have indirect communication. An incidental effect of the agreement was to terminate the long-standing refusal by Spain to adopt any legislation by the EU that might have required it to deal directly with Gibraltar's police or financial regulatory authorities.

In March 2001 the Gibraltar political parties reached an agreement to request the previously proposed reforms to the 1969 Constitution, allowing self-determination, and to hold a referendum on decolonization. However, the move was condemned by Spain as a breach of the Treaty of Utrecht. In July 2001 the British and Spanish Governments renewed discussions on Gibraltar's future status for the first time since 1998. In response, the Gibraltarian legislature requested that a UN decolonization mission visit the territory. At a subsequent meeting in October, the British Secretary of State for Foreign and Commonwealth Affairs, Jack Straw, and his Spanish counterpart, Josep Piqué i Camps, agreed to work towards achieving a settlement on the issue by December 2002 (this was later modified to September 2002). Amid public criticism of proposals of joint British-Spanish sovereignty, Caruana rebuffed an invitation to attend the next round of negotiations, claiming that he would not be accorded equal status in the discussions. The Chief Minister also stated that the territory would not accept any change in sovereignty, the sharing of responsibility for its external affairs between Spain and the United Kingdom, nor Spanish military presence.

At the negotiations in November 2001, Piqué announced that Spain was prepared to increase the number of telephone lines available to Gibraltar from 35,000 to 100,000 and provide greater access to the Spanish health care system. However, the issue of the right of the citizens of Gibraltar to vote on the terms of an agreement regarding the future status of the territory remained a point of contention between Spain and the United Kingdom. At the end of the month the British Government announced that Gibraltarians would be given the right to vote in elections to the European Parliament, but ruled out the possibility of the territory's further integration into the United Kingdom. In an open letter published in the local press, Piqué attempted to allay Gibraltarians' fears of the implications of Spanish rule and urged Caruana to attend the negotiations. The following month, however, most of the territory's 300,000 citizens took part in a public demonstration against the proposals. Following further public protests in March 2002, EU leaders agreed to a joint British-Spanish request for a grant of £37m. to fund the development of Gibraltar's port, infrastructure and airport. Caruana rejected the proposals and threatened to organize a referendum.

Shortly before negotiations on the sovereignty issue were due to resume in May 2002, the Spanish Prime Minister, José María Aznar, asserted that Spain would never withdraw its territorial claim to Gibraltar. During a subsequent visit, Straw's efforts to persuade Gibraltar of the benefits of joint sovereignty, and to reassure its residents that any such agreement would be subject to approval by referendum, were met with scepticism. Also in May, the Overseas Territories Act, having received royal assent in the United Kingdom in February, came into force, granting British citizenship rights to the people of its Overseas Territories, including Gibraltar. Under the new law Gibraltarians would be able to hold British passports and work in the United Kingdom and other EU countries.

Negotiations between the Spanish and British Governments progressed in mid-2002, although discussions stalled over Spain's claims to eventual sovereignty rather than permanent co-sovereignty and its refusal to allow British control over the military base. In response, Caruana called a referendum for November 2002. Talks recommenced in September, but with no certain deadline. The referendum, held on 7 November, in which 87.9% of the electorate voted, demonstrated overwhelming (98.97%) opinion against joint sovereignty with Spain; it was, however, not recognized, by either Spain or the United Kingdom. Relations deteriorated later that month when the Spanish Minister of Foreign Affairs claimed that Gibraltar was partly responsible for the sinking of the oil tanker *Prestige* off the coast of Galicia in Spain, as Gibraltarian maritime officials had allegedly failed properly to examine the vessel when it had docked near the territory in June. The British Government, however, refuted these accusations. In January 2003 Caruana proposed constitutional reforms that would establish a decolonized status for the enclave but maintain its links with the United Kingdom. In June Denis MacShane, the British Minister of State for Europe, admitted the plan for joint sovereignty was practically unenforceable given the almost unanimous opposition of Gibraltar's population.

At a general election held on 28 November 2003 the GSD secured 51.5% of the vote, a significant decrease from the 2000 election, against 39.7% secured by the GSLP-GLP coalition. (79.2% of the electorate pariticpated.) The balance of seats in the House of Assembly, however, remained unchanged, with the GSD holding eight seats and the opposition seven seats. Caruana remained as Chief Minister.

For the purposes of the 2004 elections to the European Parliament, in late 2003 the British Parliament adopted legislation incorporating Gibraltar into the South-West region of the United Kingdom; for the first time, Gibraltarians were thus eligible to vote in European elections. Approximately 58% of the Gibaltarian electorate participated in the elections. In July 2005 the European Court of Justice heard a complaint submitted by the Spanish Government, which insisted that Gibraltarians were ineligible to vote in European elections; the case was rejected in June 2006.

In February 2004 three Gibraltarian soldiers from the Royal Gibraltar Regiment were charged with attempting to smuggle a large amount of hashish into Spain. The allegations were a considerable embarrassment to the Gibraltarian authorities, which had repeatedly denied claims that the territory was extensively used as a conduit for illegal drugs-trafficking. Celebrations by the Government and the people of Gibraltar to commemorate 300 years of British rule, held in mid-2004, and attended by the British Secretary of State for Defence, Geoff Hoon, were criticised by the Spanish authorities.

In October 2004 Straw and his recently appointed Spanish counterpart, Miguel Ángel Moratinos, held discussions in Madrid, at which they addressed the issue of the future format for talks on Gibraltar, which were to include Gibraltarian representation for the first time. Talks involving the three parties took place in the United Kingdom in December further to define this new forum, and in February 2005 the first official trilateral session took place in Málaga, Spain. As a result, a number of Technical Working Groups were established to focus on the most significant issues: the airport, border control, nuclear submarines, telecommunications and pensions. Following several further rounds of discussions, in September 2006 Caruana, Moratinos and the British Minister of State for Europe, Hoon, signed a series of agreements in Córdoba, Spain: allowing for the operation of flights from Spain and the rest of Europe to Gibraltar; increasing the number of telephone lines to the territory; addressing the issue of outstanding pension payments to Spaniards formerly employed in Gibraltar; and easing border restrictions. Moratinos also stated that the Spanish Government had received written assurances from the United Kingdom that nuclear submarines would no longer be docked in Gibraltar. The question of sovereignty was not addressed.

Meanwhile, following lengthy negotiations between the United Kingdom and Gibraltar, it was announced in March 2006 that agreement had been reached on the main provisions of a new draft constitution for the territory. The British authorities stressed that the proposals did not diminish British sovereignty over Gibraltar, which would remain a United Kingdom Overseas Territory. The preamble to the new constitution also made clear that the British Government would never enter into arrangements under which the people of Gibraltar would pass under the sovereignty of another state against their freely and democratically expressed wishes. The draft constitution confirmed that the people of Gibraltar had the right of self-determination (according to the provisions of the UN Charter); this right was not constrained by the Treaty of Utrecht, except in so far as Spain would have the right of refusal should Britain ever renounce sovereignty. Thus, Gibraltarian independence would be an option only with Spanish consent. The remainder of the text introduced substantial reforms. The main elements included limiting the responsibilities of the Governor to the areas of external affairs, defence, internal security and public services, thereby reversing the existing practice and giving Gibraltar much greater control over its internal affairs. The House of Assembly was to be restyled the Gibraltar Parliament and would be allowed to determine its own size. The Governor's powers to withhold assent to legislation passed by the Gibraltarian authorities would be streamlined and his power to disallow proposed new laws would be removed (although his mandate to make Orders in Council would be retained). New commissions were to be created to deal with appointments to the judiciary and to public services, and a new Police Authority for Gibraltar was to be established. In a referendum held on 30 November 2006 the Constitution was approved by 60.2% of valid votes, with 37.8% votes against and 1.7% blank ballots, with a participation rate of 60.4%. The new Constitution entered into force on 2 January 2007 (except for those provisions relating to the Parliament, which would take effect following legislative elections). Meanwhile, in September 2006 Lt-Gen. Sir Robert Fulton took office as Governor and Commander-in-Chief.

In February 2007 Caruana created two new ministries, the Ministry of Finance and the Ministry of Justice. The Chief Minister, who already had responsibility for financial affairs, formally became Minister of Finance and also assumed ministerial responsibility for justice, which had been the preserve of the unelected Attorney-General under the previous constitution. The approval of legislation, in July, that provided for transfer of the post of head of the judiciary from the Chief Justice to the President of the Court of Appeal, as provided for by the new Constitution, provoked some controversy. The Chief Justice, Derek Schofield, made known his opposition to the reform, stating that it threatened the independence of the judiciary. Schofield was suspended from office in mid-September, following accusations of misconduct. In March 2008 a tribunal of three retired senior British judges was requested to consider the accusations. In December the tribunal issued its final report, which recommended that Schofield be removed from office. The case was subsequently referred to the Privy Council of the United Kingdom for further consideration; the Council was expected to announce its findings in June 2009.

Meanwhile, on 7 September 2007 Caruana dissolved the House of Assembly and called elections to the new Gibraltar Parliament for 11 October. Following the elections, the GSD remained the largest party in the legislature, holding 10 of the 17 seats, having obtained 49.3% of the votes cast; 81.4% of the electorate voted. The only other grouping to obtain representation was the GSLP-GLP alliance, with seven seats and 45.5% of the votes cast. Caruana reassumed office as Chief Minister and Minister of Finance, but appointed a Minister of Justice, Daniel Feetham, to undertake the duties formerly the domain of the Attorney-General. Joe J. Holliday was appointed as Deputy Chief Minister and Minister for Enterprise, Development and Technology, while Yvette Del Agua became Minister for Health and Civil Protection. Jaime Netto and Luis Montiel joined the Government, assuming the portfolios of Family, Youth and Community Affairs and Employment, Labour and Industrial Relations, respectively. Upon his inauguration, Caruana made a speech to Parliament in which he described the new constitutional arrangements as having 'placed Gibraltar and the United Kingdom in a constitutional relationship with each other that is modern and non-colonial in nature', and pledged to explore the possibility of implementing further democratic reforms. In April 2008 Caruana effected a minor reorganization of government responsibilities: Holliday assumed responsibility for transport policy, while ceding the tourism brief to the Minister of the Environment, Ernest Britto.

Government

Gibraltar is a United Kingdom Overseas Territory. Executive authority is vested in the British Sovereign and is exercised by the Council of Ministers, presided over by the Chief Minister, except in areas reserved to the Governor. These are defined by the 2006 Constitution as external affairs, defence, internal security and public offices. The Gibraltar Parliament comprises the Speaker (who is elected by, but not from, the Parliament) and 17 members who are elected for a four-year term.

Defence

There is a local defence force, the Royal Gibraltar Regiment, which, following the abolition of conscription, was reorganized as a predominantly volunteer reserve unit; as assessed at November 2008, it comprised 175 members. British army personnel stationed in Gibraltar numbered 95 and there were about 70 Royal Air Force personnel. There is one Royal Navy base located in Gibraltar.

Economic Affairs

In 2005/06 Gibraltar's gross domestic product (GDP), measured at current prices, was £655.9m., equivalent to £20,591 per head. Gibraltar's population totalled some 28,231 at the census of May 2001; in 2007 it was estimated at 29,257.

Gibraltar lacks agricultural land and natural resources, and the territory is dependent on imports of foodstuffs and fuels. Foodstuffs were estimated to account for 6% of total imports (excluding petroleum products) in 2004.

The industrial sector (including manufacturing, construction and power) employed 16.2% of the working population at October 2007.

Manufacturing employed 2.1% of the working population at October 2007. The most important sectors are shipbuilding and ship-repairs, and small-scale domestic manufacturing (mainly bottling, coffee-processing, pottery and handicrafts).

Gibraltar is dependent on imported petroleum for its energy supplies. Mineral fuels (excluding petroleum products) accounted for about 55% of the value of total imports in 2004.

Tourism and banking make a significant contribution to the economy. In 2007 revenue from tourism was estimated at G£230.6m. Visitor arrivals by air in 2007 totalled some 159,666, according to official figures. The number of visitor arrivals via the land frontier also reached a record high in 2007; 9,430,102 people crossed into Gibraltar during that year. Many cross-border day visitors come to the country with the purpose of shopping. At October 2007 the financial sector employed about 9.6% of the working population. Several Spanish banks have established offices in Gibraltar, encouraging the growth of the territory as an 'offshore' banking centre, while the absence of taxes for non-residents has also encouraged the use of Gibraltar as a financial centre. By March 2009 there were 19 banks and 63 licensed insurance companies operating in Gibraltar. In November 2002, however, the European Commission ruled that Gibraltar's tax-free status was illegal and ordered Gibraltar to end its system of granting tax exemption to companies, which was unique in the European Union (EU, see p. 255). In March 2005 the Commission ruled that Gibraltar could extend the tax-exempt status of 8,464 companies registered in the territory until December 2010. In the intervening period the Gibraltar Government was to introduce a new taxation structure.

In 2007 Gibraltar recorded a visible trade deficit of £273.9m. The principal sources of imports in that year (excluding petroleum products) were the United Kingdom (accounting for 27.4% of the total) and Spain (26.1%). The principal imports in 2004 were mineral fuels and manufactured goods. The principal re-exports in that year were petroleum products, manufactured goods and wines, spirits, malt and tobacco.

In the year 2007/08 there was a forecast budgetary surplus of £15.1m. The annual rate of inflation averaged 2.2% during 2000–08. The rate averaged 2.5% in 2008. Less than 5.0% of the labour force was unemployed in 2004.

Gibraltar joined the European Community (now EU, see p. 255) with the United Kingdom in 1973.

The Gibraltar economy is based on revenue from the British defence forces, tourism, shipping, and banking and finance. In 1988 the Gibraltar Government declared its aim to develop the territory as an 'offshore' financial centre, to stimulate private investment, and to promote the tourism sector. A project to build a new financial and administrative centre on land reclaimed from the sea commenced in 1990, and in the same year a Financial Services Commission was appointed to regulate financial activities in Gibraltar. Following the reduction in British military personnel in Gibraltar in the early 1990s, revenue from the British defence forces (which had accounted for some 60% of the economy in 1985) declined sharply. In 1994 British defence forces contributed only 10% to total government revenue. After 1999 there was a significant increase in gambling outlets in Gibraltar, as leading operations transferred from the United Kingdom. By September 2008 the Government had issued 21 new licences. In early 2008 it was announced that a new casino and bingo development would be built in Gibraltar, at a cost of around £6m. Construction work on the project began later that year and the casino opened in January 2009. The three main sectors of the economy in the mid-2000s were financial services, tourism and shipping, and manufacturing. Gibraltar was allocated €8m. in EU Structural Funds to enhance competitiveness and employment covering the period 2007–13. In 2007 the Government announced its intention to reduce the corporate tax rate to 10% by 2010, compared with 35% in 2007; in the budget for that year an initial cut of 2% was introduced. In July 2008 the Government implemented a further reduction of 6%. The budget for 2008 also introduced cuts in personal income tax, most notably reducing the higher threshold from 40% to 38%. In December the European Court of Justice upheld Gibraltar's autonomy from the United Kingdom with regard to fiscal policy, rejecting a complaint submitted by the European Commission, which claimed that the proposal to reduce the rate of corporate tax constituted 'illegal state aid'. In a list published in May 2009, the Organisation for Economic Co-operation and Development continued to define Gibraltar as a 'tax haven', noting that it had committed to internationally agreed tax standards in 2002, but had not yet substantially implemented them; an agreement with the USA over the exchange of information regarding taxation, signed in March 2008, remained the only such document agreed by the Gibraltarian authorities.

Education

Education is compulsory between the ages of five and 15 years, and is provided free in government schools. The language of instruction is English. There are four nursery schools, 11 primary schools (of which one is private), one Service school (administered by the Ministry of Defence for the children of military personnel) and two secondary comprehensive schools—one for boys and one for girls. Scholarships for students in higher education are provided by both government and private sources. There is also one college providing technical and vocational training, and a special school for handicapped children. Government expenditure on education, employment and training in 2007/08 was forecast at G£23.2m. (equivalent to 10.7% of total spending).

Public Holidays

2009: 1 January (New Year's Day), 9 March (Commonwealth Day), 10 April (Good Friday), 13 April (Easter Monday), 4 May (May Day), 25 May (Spring Bank Holiday), 15 June (Queen's Official Birthday), 31 August (Late Summer Bank Holiday), 10 September (Gibraltar National Holiday), 25–26 December (Christmas).

2010: 1 January (New Year's Day), 8 March (Commonwealth Day), 2 April (Good Friday), 5 April (Easter Monday), 3 May (May Day), 31 May (Spring Bank Holiday), 14 June (Queen's Official Birthday), 30 August (Late Summer Bank Holiday), 10 September (Gibraltar National Holiday), 25–26 December (Christmas).

Weights and Measures

Imperial weights and measures are in use, but the metric system is gradually being introduced.

Statistical Survey

Source (unless otherwise indicated): Statistics Office, 99 Harbours Walk, The New Harbours, Gibraltar; tel. 20075515; fax 20051160; e-mail gibstats@gibtelecom.net; internet www.gibraltar.gov.gi .

AREA AND POPULATION

Area: 6.5 sq km (2.5 sq miles).

Population (excl. armed forces): 27,495 (males 13,644, females 13,851) at census of 12 November 2001 (Gibraltarians 22,882, Other British 2,627, Non-British 1,986). *2007* (official figure): 29,257 (Gibraltarians 23,616, Other British 3,223, Non-British 2,418).

Density (2007): 4,501.1 per sq km.

Births, Marriages and Deaths (2007, excl. armed forces): Live births 400 (birth rate 13.7 per 1,000); Marriages 929 (residents 132) (marriage rate for residents 4.5 per 1,000); Deaths 202 (death rate 6.9 per 1,000).

Life Expectancy (years at birth at census of 2001): Males 78.5; Females 83.3.

Employment (October 2007): Manufacturing 411 (Shipbuilding 203); Construction 2,486; Electricity, gas and water 295; Wholesale and retail trade, and repair of goods 2,816; Restaurants and hotels 1,071; Transport, storage and communications 1,123; Financial intermediation 1,889; Real estate, renting and business activities 2,453; Public administration and defence 2,252; Education 858; Health and social work 1,561; Other community, social and personal services 2,481; Total 19,696 (males 11,622, females 8,074). Figures cover only non-agricultural activities, excluding mining and quarrying.

INDUSTRY

Electric Energy (2007): 154.6m. kWh.

FINANCE

Currency and Exchange Rates: 100 pence (pennies) = 1 Gibraltar pound (G£). *Sterling, Dollar and Euro Equivalents* (31 December 2008): £1 sterling = G£1.0000; US $1 = 68.60 pence; €1 = 95.47 pence; G£10 = £10.00 sterling = $14.58 = €10.47. *Average Exchange Rate* (G£ per US dollar): 0.5435 in 2006; 0.4998 in 2007; 0.5412 in 2008. Note: The Gibraltar pound is at par with sterling.

Budget (G£ '000, year ending 31 March 2008, forecasts): *Recurrent Revenue:* Taxes 126,000; Duties 51,576; Gambling fees 9,665; Rates 15,544; Departmental fees and receipts 18,228; Government earnings 10,178; Total 231,191. *Recurrent Expenditure:* Education, employment and training 23,211; Heritage, culture, youth and sport 3,700; Housing 9,079; Environment and tourism 20,976; Social and civic affairs 20,572; Trade, industry, communications and transport 26,960; Health and civil protection 31,663; Administration 8,668; Finance 13,274; Law officers 535; Justice 21,814; Immigration and civil status 2,265; House of Assembly 1,256; Office of Principal Auditor 628; Consolidated fund charges 30,486; Contribution to social insurance funds 1,000; Total 216,087.

Cost of Living (Retail Price Index at January; base: April 1998 = 100): 114.8 in 2006; 117.8 in 2007; 120.8 in 2008.

Gross National Product (G£ million, at factor cost): 497.59 in 2003/04; 551.50 in 2004/05; 593.08 in 2005/06.

Gross Domestic Product (G£ million, at factor cost): 560.06 in 2003/04; 599.18 in 2004/05; 655.88 in 2005/06.

EXTERNAL TRADE

Imports c.i.f. (G£ million, excluding petroleum products): 303.0 in 2005; 366.4 in 2006; 425.7 in 2007.

Exports f.o.b. (G£ million, excluding petroleum products): 110.0 in 2005; 130.9 in 2006; 151.8 in 2007.

Principal Trading Partners (G£ '000, 2007, excluding petroleum products): *Imports:* United Kingdom 116,519; Spain 111,277; Denmark 3,495; Netherlands 6,272; USA 5,617; Japan 4,776; Total (incl. others) 425,741. Note: Figures for exports are not available.

TRANSPORT

Road Traffic (licences current at 31 December 2007): Private vehicles 14,599; Commercial vehicles 1,345; Motorcycles 7,655.

Shipping (merchant vessels, 2007): Tonnage entered ('000 grt) 282,108; Vessels entered 9,618.

Civil Aviation (2007): Passenger arrivals ('000) 179.7; Passenger departures ('000) 181.6; Freight loaded 63 metric tons; Freight unloaded 333 metric tons. Figures exclude military passengers and freight.

TOURISM

Visitor Arrivals ('000): 7,790.8 in 2005; 8,185.1 in 2006; 9,430.1 in 2007.

Tourism Receipts (G£ million): 209.77 in 2005; 210.50 in 2006; 230.58 in 2007.

COMMUNICATIONS MEDIA

Radio Receivers (1997): 37,000 in use (Source: UNESCO, *Statistical Yearbook*).

Television Licences (2005): 5,965.

Daily Newspapers (1999): 1.

Telephone Stations (2004): 34,476.

Facsimile Machines (1997): 322 in use (Source: UN, *Statistical Yearbook*).

Mobile Cellular Telephones (2000): 5,558 subscribers (Source: International Telecommunication Union).

Internet Connections (31 March 2007): 7,853.

EDUCATION

Primary (state schools, 2007, unless otherwise indicated): 11 schools (1999), 2,937 pupils.

Secondary (state schools, 2007, unless otherwise indicated): 2 schools (1999), 2,095 pupils.

Total Teaching Staff at Primary and Secondary Schools (state schools, 2007): 334.

Technical and Vocational (1999): 1 college, 201 full-time students.

Directory

The Constitution

Gibraltar is a United Kingdom Overseas Territory. Executive authority is vested in the British monarch and is exercisable by the elected Gibraltar Government, except in the specified areas of the Governor's responsibilities; the Governor is the representative of the British monarch. Relations with the British Government are maintained through the Foreign and Commonwealth Office.

Following the referendum of 10 September 1967 (in which the people of Gibraltar voted in favour of retaining British sovereignty), a new Constitution was introduced on 11 August 1969, containing a code of human rights and providing for its enforcement by the Supreme Court of Gibraltar. Following a referendum held on 30 November 2006, this Constitution was revoked in favour of a new one, effective from 2 January 2007. The text regarding human rights was further updated, among other developments enumerated below. Gibraltar controls the majority of its domestic affairs, while the United Kingdom is responsible for matters of external affairs, defence and internal security. The other main provisions are as follows:

BRITISH SOVEREIGNTY

The Preamble to the Gibraltar Constitution Order contains assurances that Gibraltar will remain part of the dominions of the British Crown (unless these provisions are amended by further legislation adopted by the British Parliament), and that the United Kingdom will never enter into arrangements under which the people of Gibraltar would pass under the sovereignty of another State against their freely and democratically expressed wishes.

THE GOVERNOR AND COMMANDER-IN-CHIEF

As a representative of the British monarch, the Governor and Commander-in-Chief is responsible for matters which directly relate to external affairs, defence and internal security (including certain police matters), and such functions in relation to appointments to public offices and related matters as are conferred on him by the Constitution. Any matter which falls outside these special responsibilities is the responsibility of the Council of Ministers. The Governor is also head of the executive and administers Gibraltar, acting generally on the advice of the Council of Ministers. In exceptional circumstances, the Governor has special powers to refuse any advice from the Council of Ministers which, in the Governor's opinion, may not be in the interests of maintaining financial and economic stability. The Governor's formal assent, on behalf of the Crown, is required for all legislation. In some cases, the prior concurrence of the Crown, conveyed through the Secretary of State for Foreign and Commonwealth Affairs, is also required.

GOVERNMENT

The Government is defined as the Council of Ministers together with the British monarch, who is represented in Gibraltar by the Governor. The Council of Ministers comprises the Chief Minister and between four and 10 other ministers appointed from the elected members of the Assembly by the Governor, in consultation with the Chief Minister. (If the number of elected members of parliament exceeds 17, then the number of ministers should equate to one-half of the total, not exceeding 15.) Ministers are collectively responsible to the Parliament. The Government is presided over by the Chief Minister; individual ministers may be given responsibility for specific business. A Minister of Finance holds responsibility for public finances (as opposed to the previous, unelected Financial and Development Secretary). Parliament is to scrutinize and approve all public expenditure, not just expenditure incurred through the Consolidated

UNITED KINGDOM OVERSEAS TERRITORIES

Fund. Heads of Departments and other government officials appear before it when required.

THE GIBRALTAR PARLIAMENT

Under the 2006 Constitution the former House of Assembly received the status of Parliament and the legislation it produces became 'Acts' rather than 'Ordinances', and the right of British Ministers to disallow such legislation was revoked. Parliament comprises the Speaker and at least 17 elected members. The Principal Auditor, the Ombudsman and the Clerk to the Parliament must be officers of Parliament. The Speaker, who cannot be an elected member of Parliament, is chosen by Parliament.

The normal term of Parliament is four years. Elections are open to all adult British subjects and citizens of Ireland who have been ordinarily resident in Gibraltar for a continuous period of six months prior to the date for registration as an elector. The minimum voting age is 18 years. Each elector may vote for a maximum of 10 candidates and up to 10 candidates from each party may stand for election.

The elected members of Parliament elect and appoint the Mayor, who carries out ceremonial and representational functions on behalf of the City of Gibraltar.

APPOINTMENTS TO THE PUBLIC SERVICE

From 2007 a Judicial Appointments Commission (under the Chairmanship of the President of the Court of Appeal) and a Specified Appointments Commission (dealing with the most senior office holders) were instituted, in addition to the already existing Public Service Commission. The Governor makes all appointments and dismissals but must accept and implement the advice he receives from these Commissions, except under exceptional circumstances, and may not act at his own discretion.

The Government

Governor and Commander-in-Chief: Lt-Gen. Sir ROBERT FULTON (took office 27 September 2006).

COUNCIL OF MINISTERS
(April 2009)

Chief Minister and Minister of Finance: PETER CARUANA.
Deputy Chief Minister and Minister for Enterprise, Development, Technology and Transport: JOE J. HOLLIDAY.
Minister of Justice: DANIEL FEETHAM.
Minister for Education and Training: CLIVE BELTRAN.
Minister for Health and Civil Protection: YVETTE DEL AGUA.
Minister for Housing: FABIAN VINET.
Minister for Employment, Labour and Industrial Relations: LUIS MONTIEL.
Minister for Family, Youth and Community Affairs: JAMES (JAIME) NETTO.
Minister for the Environment and Tourism: ERNEST BRITTO.
Minister of Culture, Heritage, Sport and Leisure: EDWIN REYES.

MINISTRIES

Office of the Governor: The Convent, Main St; tel. 20045440; fax 20047823; e-mail enquiry.gibraltar@fco.gov.uk.
Office of the Chief Minister: 6 Convent Pl.; tel. 20070071; fax 20076396; internet www.gibraltar.gov.gi/chief_minister/chief_minister_index.htm.
Ministry of Culture, Heritage, Sport and Leisure: 310 Main St; tel. 20041687; fax 20052589; e-mail minculture@gibtelecom.net.
Ministry of Education and Training: 23 Queensway; tel. 20077486; fax 20071564; e-mail info.det@gibraltar.gov.gi.
Ministry of Employment, Labour and Industrial Relations: Unit 76/77, Harbours Walk, New Harbours; tel. 20040408; fax 20073981; e-mail employment.service@gibraltar.gov.gi.
Ministry of Enterprise, Development, Technology and Transport: Suite 771, Europort; tel. 20052052; fax 2004677; e-mail info.medt@gibraltar.gov.gi.
Ministry of the Environment and Tourism: Joshua Hassan House, Secretary's Lane; tel. 20059800; fax 20076223; e-mail ministry@env.gov.gi.
Ministry of Family, Youth and Community Affairs: 14 Governor's Parade; tel. 20044070; e-mail kerenza.baker@gibraltar.gov.gi.
Ministry of Finance: 6 Convent Pl.; tel. 20070071; fax 20076396; e-mail financeministry@gibtelecom.net.
Ministry of Health and Civil Protection: Gibraltar Health Authority, 17 Johnstone's Passage; e-mail info@gha.gi.
Ministry of Housing: City Hall, John Mackintosh Sq.; tel. 20075603; fax 20052947; e-mail gibhouse@gibtelecom.net.
Ministry of Justice: 6 Convent Pl.; tel. 20059267; fax 20059271; e-mail moj@gibraltar.gov.gi.

Legislature

Gibraltar Parliament

156 Main St; tel. 20078420; fax 20042849; e-mail parliament@gibtelecom.net; internet www.gibraltar.gov.gi.

Speaker: HARESH K. BUDHRANI.

General Election, 11 October 2007

Party	Votes*	% of votes	Seats
Gibraltar Social Democrats	76,334	49.3	10
Gibraltar Socialist Labour Party	} 70,397	45.5	7
Gibraltar Liberal Party			
Progressive Democratic Party	5,799	3.7	—
New Gibraltar Democracy	1,210	0.8	—
Independent	1,003	0.6	—
Total	**154,743**	**100.0**	**17**

*Each voter was permitted to vote for a maximum of 10 candidates. The total number of ballots cast was 16,004.

Political Organizations

All political organizations in Gibraltar advocate self-determination for the territory.

Gibraltar Liberal Party (GLP): 95 Irish Town; tel. and fax 20076959; e-mail info@liberal.gi; internet www.liberal.gi; f. 1991 as the Gibraltar National Party; Leader Dr JOSEPH GARCÍA; Sec.-Gen. STEVEN LINARES.

Gibraltar Social Democrats (GSD): College Lane; tel. and fax 20044105; e-mail info@gsd.gi; internet www.gsd.gi; f. 1989; holds a majority of seats in the House of Assembly; absorbed the Gibraltar Labour Party in 2005; Leader PETER CARUANA; Gen. Sec. LAURA V. CORREA.

Gibraltar Socialist Labour Party (GSLP): Suite 16, Block 3, Watergardens; tel. 20050700; fax 20078983; e-mail hqgslp@gibtelecom.net; internet www.gslp.gi; f. 1976; Leader JOSEPH (JOE) BOSSANO.

New Gibraltar Democracy (NGD): f. 2005; Christian democratic; Leader CHARLES GOMEZ.

Progressive Democratic Party (PDP): POB 1373; tel. and fax 20049000; e-mail info@pdp.gi; internet www.pdp.gi; f. 2006; Leader KEITH AZOPARDI.

Judicial System

The 2006 Constitution provides for the protection of the fundamental rights and freedoms of the individual and the maintenance of a Supreme Court with unlimited jurisdiction to hear and determine any civil or criminal proceedings under any law. The Courts of Law of Gibraltar comprise a Court of Appeal, the Supreme Court and the Magistrates' Court.

The substantive law of Gibraltar is contained in Orders in Council which apply to Gibraltar, enactments of the Parliament of the United Kingdom which apply to or have been extended or applied to Gibraltar, locally enacted acts and subsidiary legislation, and common law and the rules of equity from time to time in force in the England so far as they may be applicable and subject to all necessary modification.

Court of Appeal

277 Main St.

holds three sessions each year; The Justices of Appeal are drawn from the English Court of Appeal.

President: Sir MURRAY STUART-SMITH.
Justices of Appeal: Sir PAUL KENNEDY, Sir PHILIP OTTON, Sir WILLIAM ALDOUS.

Supreme Court

277 Main St.

includes the office of Admiralty Marshal.

Chief Justice: ANTHONY E. DUDLEY (acting).
Justice: CHARLES JOHN PITTO (acting).

UNITED KINGDOM OVERSEAS TERRITORIES

Magistrates' Court

Stipendiary Magistrate: KAREN PRESCOTT (acting).

Religion

At the 2001 census 78.1% of the population were Roman Catholic, 7.0% Church of England, 4.0% Muslim, 2.1% Jewish and 1.8% Hindu.

CHRISTIANITY

The Roman Catholic Church

Gibraltar forms a single diocese, directly responsible to the Holy See. At 31 December 2006 there were an estimated 21,470 adherents in the territory (78.1% of the total population).

Bishop of Gibraltar: Rt Rev. CHARLES CARUANA, 215 Main St; e-mail epis.carroca@gibnynex.gi; internet www.catholicdiocese.gi; tel. 20076688; fax 20043112.

The Church of England

The diocese of Gibraltar in Europe, founded in 1980, has jurisdiction over the whole of continental Europe, Turkey and Morocco.

Bishop of Gibraltar in Europe: Rt Rev. GEOFFREY ROWELL, Bishop's Lodge, Church Rd, Worth, RH10 7RT, United Kingdom; tel. (1293) 883051; fax (1293) 884479; e-mail bishop@dioceseineurope.org.uk; internet europe.anglican.org.

Dean of the Cathedral of the Holy Trinity: Very Rev. JOHN PADDOCK, The Deanery, Bomb House Lane; tel. 20078377; fax 20078463; e-mail deangib@gibnet.gi; internet www.gibconnect.com/~holytrinity.

Other Christian Churches

Church of Scotland: St Andrew's Manse, 29 Scud Hill; tel. and fax 20077040; e-mail scotskirk@gibraltar.gi; internet www.scotskirkgibraltar.com; f. 1800; Minister (vacant); 50 mems.

Methodist Church: Wesley House, 297 Main St; tel. and fax 20040870; e-mail minister@methodist.org.gi; internet www.methodist.org.gi; Minister Rev. FIDEL PATRON; f. 1769; 80 mems.

ISLAM

A mosque to serve the Islamic community in Gibraltar and financed by the Government of Saudi Arabia was constructed in the late 1990s.

JUDAISM

Jewish Community: Managing Board, 91 Irish Town; tel. 20072606; fax 20040487; e-mail mbjc@gibtelecom.net; Pres. H. J. M. LEVY; Admin. Sec. S. LEVY; 600 mems.

The Press

Gibraltar Chronicle: 2 Library Gdns; tel. 20078589; fax 20079927; e-mail letters@chronicle.gi; internet www.chronicle.gi; f. 1801; daily (except Sun.); English; Man. Editor DOMINIQUE SEARLE; circ. 6,000.

Gibraltar Gazette: Ministry of Justice, Legislation Support Unit, Treasury Bldg, 23 John Mackintosh Sq.; tel. 20051246; fax 20041822; f. 1949; weekly; publ. by *Gibraltar Chronicle*; official notices; circ. 375.

Gibraltar Magazine: PMB 6377, POB 561, Irish Town; tel. and fax 20077748; e-mail gibmag@gibnet.gi; internet www.thegibraltarmagazine.com; f. 1995; monthly; English; business and leisure; Editor ANDREA MORTON.

Insight: tel. 40913; e-mail advert@insight-gibraltar.com; internet www.insight-gibraltar.com; f. 1992; print and internet magazine; circ. 6,000.

Panorama: 75–77 Irish Town; tel. 79797; fax 74664; e-mail contacts@panorama.gi; internet www.panorama.gi; f. 1975; weekly, Mon.; English; news and features; Editor JOE GARCÍA; circ. 4,000.

The New People: Suite No. 6/608, ICom House, 1–5 Irish Town; tel. 54374000; e-mail thenewpeople@gibtelecom.net; internet www.thenewpeople.net; f. 1996; weekly; English with Spanish section; Editor JUAN CARLOS PÉREZ; circ. 1,000.

Vox: Unit 91, Harbours Walk, New Harbours, POB 306; tel. 20077414; fax 20072531; e-mail editor@vox.gi; internet www.vox.gi; f. 1955; weekly; independent; in English and Spanish; Editor DEREK MCGRAIL; circ. 1,800.

Gibraltar

Broadcasting and Communications

TELECOMMUNICATIONS

Gibraltar Regulatory Authority (GRA): Suite 603, Europort; tel. 20074636; fax 20072166; e-mail info@gra.gi; internet www.gra.gi; f. 2000; statutory body responsible for the regulation of the radio spectrum, data protection and gambling; Chief Exec. PAUL CANESSA.

Gibtelecom: Suite 942, Europort; tel. 20052200; fax 20071673; e-mail info@gibtele.com; internet www.gibtele.com; f. 1990; jointly owned by Govt and Telekom Slovenije (Slovenia); operates local and international telephone and telecommunications services; provides a range of digital, satellite, mobile and internet services; Chair. JOE J. HOLLIDAY (Minister of Enterprise, Development, Technology and Transport); CEO TIM BRISTOW.

Sapphire Networks: Suite 303, Eurotowers, POB 797; tel. 20047200; fax 20047272; e-mail info@sapphire.gi; internet www.sapphire.gi; f. 2005; internet service provider.

BROADCASTING

Gibraltar Broadcasting Corporation (GBC): Broadcasting House, 18 South Barrack Rd; tel. 20079760; fax 20078673; e-mail gbc@gibraltar.gi; internet www.gbc.gi; f. 1963; responsible for television and radio broadcasting; Gen. Man. S. NEISH.

Radio

GBC—Radio (Radio Gibraltar): 24 hours daily in English and Spanish, including commercial broadcasting. In addition to local programmes, the BBC World Service programme is relayed.

Television

GBC—TV: operates in English for 24 hours daily; GBC and relayed BBC programmes are transmitted.

Finance

(cap. = capital; res = reserves; dep. = deposits; m. = million; brs = branches; amounts in G£)

BANKING

In March 2009 there were 19 banks operating in Gibraltar.

Regulatory Authority

Financial Services Commission: POB 940, Suite 943, Europort; tel. 20040283; fax 20040282; e-mail info@fsc.gi; internet www.fsc.gi; f. 1989; regulates the activities of the financial sector; CEO MARCUS KILLICK.

Banks

BBVA Privanza International (Gibraltar) Ltd: 260–262 Main St, POB 488; tel. 20079420; fax 20073870; e-mail bbvpring@gibnet.gi; Man. TONINO LETO.

Barclays Private Clients International (Gibraltar) Ltd: Regal House, 3 Queensway, POB 187; tel. 20052378; fax 20079987; e-mail gibraltar@barclays.co.uk; Chief Man. DOUGLAS REYES.

Credit Suisse (Gibraltar) Ltd: 1st Floor, Neptune House, Marina Bay, POB 556; tel. 20078399; fax 20076027; e-mail csg.mail@credit-suisse.com; f. 1987; Chair. M. SALZMANN; Man. Dir THOMAS WESTH OLSEN.

EFG Bank (Gibraltar) Ltd: Eurolife Bldg, 1 Corral Rd, POB 561; tel. 20040117; fax 20040110; e-mail atlaco@gibnet.gi; formerly Banco Atlántico (Gibraltar) Ltd; Man. EMILIO MARTÍNEZ PRIEGO.

SG Hambros Bank (Gibraltar) Ltd: Hambro House, 32 Line Wall Rd, POB 375; tel. 20002000; fax 20079037; e-mail gibraltar@sghambros.com; internet www.sghambros.com; f. 1981; acquired ABN AMRO Private Banking in 2008; owned by Société Générale (France); cap. 1.5m., res 10.2m., dep. 245.0m. (June 2005); Chair. WARWICK J. NEWBURY; Man. Dir EMMA PEREZ.

Jyske Bank (Gibraltar) Ltd: 76 Main St, POB 143; tel. 20072782; fax 20072732; e-mail jyskebank@jyskebank.ltd.gi; internet www.jbpb.com; f. 1855 as Galliano (A. L.) Bankers; in 1988 name changed as above; cap. 26.5m., res 0.9m., dep. 1,788.4m. (Dec. 2004); Chair. JENS LAURITZEN; Man. Dir TIM MARSHALL.

Lloyds TSB Bank PLC: 323 Main St, POB 482; tel. 20077373; fax 20070023; internet www.lloydstsb.gi; Man. ALBERT DOUGLAS LANGSTON.

Lombard Odier Darier Hentsch Private Bank Ltd: Suite 921, Europort, POB 407; tel. 20073350; fax 20073475; e-mail william.jardim@lombardodier.com.

NatWest Offshore Ltd: NatWest House, 57/63 Line Wall Rd, POB 707; tel. 20077737; fax 20074557; e-mail natwestgib@gibnynex.gi;

internet www.natwestoffshore.com; f. 1988; Chief Man. PETE YEOMAN.

Royal Bank of Scotland (Gibraltar) Ltd: 1 Corral Rd, POB 766; tel. 20073200; fax 20070152; e-mail marvincartwright@rbsint.com; internet www.rbsint.com.

Turicum Private Bank Ltd: Turicum House, 315 Main St, POB 619; tel. 20044144; fax 20044145; e-mail info@turicumprivatebank.com; internet www.turicumprivatebank.com; f. 1993; cap. and res €5.0m., dep. €15.7m. (Dec. 2003); Chair. Dr RAYMOND BISANG; Chief Exec. URS HÜNI.

Savings Bank

Gibraltar Savings Bank: Treasury Dept, Treasury Bldg, 23 John Mackintosh Sq.; tel. 20048396; fax 20077147; e-mail treasury@gibtelecom.net; dep. 242.2m. (March 2007); Dir C. VICTORY.

Association

Gibraltar Bankers' Association (GBA): POB 380; tel. 20073200; fax 20070152; e-mail langham@mercuryin.es; internet www.gba.gi; f. 1982; Pres. KERRY BLIGHT; 17 mem. banks.

INSURANCE

There were 63 licensed insurance companies operating in Gibraltar in March 2009.

BMI Insurance Services Limited: Unit 7, Portland House, Glacis Rd, POB 469; tel. 20051010; internet www.bmigroup.gi.

Capurro Insurance and Investments Ltd: 20 Line Wall Rd, POB 130; tel. 20040850; fax 20040851; e-mail info@capurroinsurance.com; internet www.capurroinsurance.com.

Castiel Winser Insurance and Financial Consultants: Natwest House, 57/63 Line Wall Rd, POB 464; tel. 20077723; fax 20079257; e-mail financialservices@castielwinser.com; f. 1985; Man. Dir SYDNEY ATTIAS.

Eurolife Assurance (International) Ltd: Eurolife Bldg, 1 Corral Rd, POB 233; tel. 20073495; fax 20073120; e-mail eurolife@gibnet.gi; Man. A. SMITH.

Eurolinx (Gibraltar) Ltd: Suites 21–22, Victoria House, 26 Main St, POB 671; tel. 20040240; fax 20040241; e-mail eurolinx@sapphirenet.gi; internet www.eurolinx.gi; f. 1990; Dir ALAN JOSEPH MONTEGRIFFO.

Gibro Insurance Services Ltd: Gibro House, 4 Giros Passage, POB 693; tel. 20043777; fax 20043538; e-mail gibroins@gibtelecom.net.

Middle Sea Insurance PLC: Suite 1A, 143 Main St, POB 502; tel. 20076434.

Norwich Union International Insurance Ltd: Regal House, 3 Queensway, POB 45; tel. 20079520; fax 20070942; e-mail nugib@gibnet.gi; f. 1984; cap. 1,6m.; CEO. ERIC D. CHALONER; Chair. PAUL L. SAVIGNON.

Ophir Insurance Services Ltd: 123 Main St, POB 914; tel. 20073871; fax 20050411; e-mail ophir@gibtelecom.net.

Association

Gibraltar Insurance Association: c/o POB 371, 2nd Floor, 85 Main St; tel. 20045578; fax 20045579; f. 1995; Pres. PENNY HUDSON.

Trade and Industry

GOVERNMENT AGENCY

Finance Centre Dept: Suite 761, Europort; tel. 20050011; fax 20051818; e-mail info@financecentre.gov.gi; f. 1997; part of Ministry of Finance; advises on financial services policy; marketing and promotion of financial services; liaison between regulator and private sector.

CHAMBER OF COMMERCE

Gibraltar Chamber of Commerce: Watergate House, 2–6 Casemates Sq., POB 29; tel. 20078376; fax 20078403; e-mail info@gibraltarchamberofcommerce.com; internet www.gibraltarchamberofcommerce.com; f. 1882; Pres. NICHOLAS RUSSO; 300 mems.

EMPLOYERS' ORGANIZATIONS

Gibraltar Federation of Small Businesses: GFSB House, POB 211, 112 Irish Town; tel. 20047722; fax 20047733; e-mail gfsb@gfsb.gi; internet www.gfsb.gi; f. 1996; Chair. CHARLES SERRUYA.

Gibraltar Hotel Association: c/o Caleta Hotel; tel. 20076501; fax 20071050; e-mail caleta@gibnynex.gi; internet www.caletahotel.com; f. 1960; Chair. FRANCO OSTUNI; seven mems.

Gibraltar Licensed Victuallers' Association: c/o Watergate Restaurant, Queensway Quay; tel. 20074195; f. 1976; Chair. MICHAEL OTON; 120 mems.

Gibraltar Motor Traders' Association: POB 167; tel. 20079004; f. 1961; Gen. Sec. G. BASSADONE; six mems.

Hindu Merchants' Association: POB 357; tel. 20079000; fax 20071966; e-mail vikram.nagrani@hassans.gi; f. 1964; Pres. VIKRAM NAGRANI; 575 mems.

PRINCIPAL TRADE UNIONS

Gibraltar Taxi Association: 19 Waterport Wharf; tel. 20070052; fax 20076986; e-mail gibtaxiass@gibtelecom.net; internet www.gibtaxi.com; f. 1957; Pres. CLIVE ZAMMIT; 100 mems.

Gibraltar Trades Council: 7 Hargraves Ramp, POB 279; tel. 20076930; fax 20079646; e-mail prospect.ggca@gibtelecom.net; comprises unions representing 70% of the working population; affiliated to the United Kingdom Trades Union Congress; Sec. MICHAEL J. A. TAMPIN; Pres. JOSEPH J. CORTES.

Affiliated unions:

Gibraltar General and Clerical Association (GGCA): 7 Hargrave's Ramp, POB 279; tel. 20076930; fax 20079646; e-mail prospect.ggca@gibtelecom.net; internet www.prospectbranches.org.uk/gibraltar; f. 1947; Pres. JOSÉ LUIS GARCÍA; Nat. Sec. MICHAEL J. A. TAMPIN; 1,205 mems (2009).

NASUWT (Gibraltar): 98 Harbours Walk, New Harbours; tel. 20076308; fax 77608; e-mail gtateachers@gibtelecom.net; f. 1962; fmrly known as the Gibraltar Teachers' Association; Pres. JOSEPH J. CORTES; 350 mems.

Unite (United Kingdom) (Gibraltar District): tel. 20074185; fax 20071596; f. 1924; Dist. Officer CHARLES SISARELLO; 4,239 mems.

UTILITIES
Electricity

Gibraltar Electricity Authority: Gibelec House, North Mole Rd; tel. 20048908; fax 20077408; e-mail enquiries@gibelec.gi; internet www.gibelec.gi; govt-owned; generation, distribution and supply of electricity.

Water

AquaGib Ltd: Suite 10B, Leanse Pl., 50 Town Range; tel. 20040880; fax 20040881; e-mail main.office@aquagib.gi; internet www.aquagib.gi; fmrly known as Lyonnais des Eaux (Gibraltar) Ltd; present name adopted 2003; 66.67% owned by Northumbrian Water Group (United Kingdom), 33.33% govt-owned; Man. Dir P. LATIN.

Transport

There are no railways in Gibraltar. There is a total road length of 53.1 km, including 12.9 km of highways and 6.8 km of footpaths.

ROADS

Ministry of Enterprise, Development, Technology and Transport: see Ministries.

SHIPPING

The Strait of Gibraltar is a principal ocean route between the Mediterranean and Black Sea areas and the rest of the world.

Gibraltar is used by many long-distance liners, and has dry dock facilities and a commercial ship-repair yard. Tax concessions are available to ship-owners who register their ships in Gibraltar.

Gibraltar Maritime Administration: Watergate House, 2/8 Casemate Sq.; tel. 20047771; fax 20047770; e-mail maritadmin@gibtelecom.net; internet www.gibmaritime.com; Administrator ALAN CUBBIN.

Gibraltar Port Authority: Port Office, North Mole; tel. 20077254; fax 20051513; e-mail ceo.gpa@gibtelecom.net; internet www.gibraltarport.com; CEO Capt. PETER W. HALL.

Cammell Laird (Gibraltar) Ltd: Main Wharf Rd, The Dockyard, POB 858; tel. 20059400; fax 20044404; e-mail mail@lairds.gi; internet www.lairds.gi; drydock facilities and general ship repairing; CEO JOSEPH CORVELLI.

M. H. Bland & Co Ltd: Cloister Bldg, Market Lane, POB 554; tel. 20079478; fax 20071608; internet www.mhbland.com; f. 1810; ship agents, stevedoring, warehousing; also operates cable-car service to peak of the Rock of Gibraltar; Chair. JOHN A. GAGGERO.

Association

Gibraltar Shipping Association: c/o Inchcape Shipping Services, POB 194; tel. 20046315; fax 20046316; e-mail mark.porral@iss-shipping.com; f. 1957; Sec. P. L. IMOSSI; 11 mems.

UNITED KINGDOM OVERSEAS TERRITORIES   *Montserrat*

CIVIL AVIATION

The airport is at North Front, on the isthmus, 2.5 km from the city centre. An agreement reached in September 2006 by Gibraltar, the United Kingdom and Spain allowed for the operation of flights from Spain and the rest of Europe to Gibraltar. Hitherto Spain had blocked direct air links between Gibraltar and European countries other than the United Kingdom. Commercial flights between Gibraltar and Spain began in December 2006. In accordance with the 2006 agreement, plans were announced in 2007 for a new airport terminal straddling the border between Gibraltar and Spain.

Gibraltar Civil Aviation Advisory Board: Air Terminal, Winston Churchill Ave; tel. 20073026; fax 20073925; e-mail info@gibraltar-airport.com; Sec. JOHN GONÇALVES.

Tourism

Gibraltar's tourist attractions include its climate, beaches and a variety of amenities. Following the reopening of the border with Spain in February 1985, the resumption of traffic by day-visitors contributed to the expansion of the tourist industry. In 2007 visitor arrivals numbered some 9.43m. (by sea: 292,675; air: 159,666; and land: 8,977,761), while revenue from tourism totalled G£230.58m.

Gibraltar Tourist Board: Duke of Kent House, Cathedral Sq.; tel. 20074950; fax 20074943; e-mail tourism@gibraltar.gi; internet www.gibraltar.gov.gi; CEO NICHOLAS GUERRERO.

MONTSERRAT

Introductory Survey

Location, Climate, Language, Religion, Flag, Capital

Montserrat is one of the Leeward Islands in the West Indies. A mountainous, volcanic island, it lies about 55 km (35 miles) north of Basse-Terre, Guadeloupe, and about 43 km south west of Antigua. The climate is generally warm, with a mean maximum temperature of 30°C (86°F) and a mean minimum of 23°C (73°F), but the island is fanned by sea breezes for most of the year. The average annual rainfall is about 1,475 mm (58 ins), although there is more rain in the central and western areas. English is the official language. Many Christian churches are represented, but the principal denominations are the Anglican, Roman Catholic and Methodist Churches. The flag is the British 'Blue Ensign', with the island's badge (a shield depicting a woman dressed in green holding a harp and a cross) on a white roundel in the fly. The capital is Plymouth.

Recent History

Montserrat was first settled by the British (initially Roman Catholic exiles) in 1632, by which time the few original Carib inhabitants had disappeared. It formed part of the federal colony of the Leeward Islands from 1871 until 1956, when the federation was dissolved and the presidency of Montserrat became a separate colony. Montserrat participated in the short-lived Federation of the West Indies (1958–62) and, from 1960, the island had its own Administrator (the title was changed to that of Governor in 1971). The Constitution (see below) came into force in 1960.

The first priority of successive legislatures has been to improve infrastructure and maintain a healthy economy. Between 1952 and 1970 William Bramble dominated island politics. His son, Austin Bramble, leader of the Progressive Democratic Party (PDP), opposed and succeeded him as Chief Minister. In November 1978 the People's Liberation Movement (PLM) won all seven elective seats in the Legislative Council, and the PLM's leader, John Osborne, became Chief Minister. In the general election of February 1983 the PLM was returned to government with five seats. The remainder were won by the PDP, whose commitment to development projects, agriculture and education complemented those of the PLM.

Attempts to form an opposition alliance between the PDP and the National Development Party (NDP—formed by business interests and former members of the PDP) were unsuccessful. Against a divided opposition, the PLM won four of the seven elective seats in the Legislative Council at an early general election in August 1987. The NDP won two seats, and the PDP one (Bramble lost his seat and announced his retirement from politics). Osborne was returned to office as Chief Minister.

Osborne was an advocate of independence from the United Kingdom, despite the apparent lack of popular support for this policy. A referendum on the issue was planned for 1990, but the devastation caused by 'Hurricane Hugo' in September 1989 meant that any plans for independence were postponed. Furthermore, the Osborne Government and the British authorities were embarrassed by controversy surrounding the hitherto lucrative 'offshore' financial sector. In early 1989 the Governor's office announced that the British police were investigating serious allegations against certain banks (involving the processing of illegal funds from a variety of criminal activities). Registration was suspended, several people were charged with criminal offences and, at the end of 1989, most banking licences were revoked. The Montserrat Government agreed to introduce recommended provisions for the regulation of the financial services industry, but Osborne objected strongly to a proposed amendment to the Constitution which transferred responsibility for the sector from the Chief Minister to the Governor. Agreement was subsequently reached, however, when Osborne acknowledged that 'offshore' finance was part of the British Government's responsibility for external affairs.

In late 1990 a dispute arose between the Chief Minister and his deputy, Benjamin Chalmers, who was reported to have accused Osborne of dishonesty in his relations with the Executive Council. Allegations of corruption continued in 1991, and in June an inquiry was undertaken by the British police to investigate the possible involvement of members of the Executive Council in the 1989 banking scandal, as well as in fraudulent land transfers.

The resignation of Chalmers in September 1991, following a further dispute with Osborne, resulted in the loss of the Government's majority in the Legislative Council. This prompted an early election in the following month, when the National Progressive Party (NPP), formed only two months prior to the election, secured a majority of seats. The NPP leader, Reuben Meade, became Chief Minister.

In December 1991 the Legislative Council approved legislation allowing the re-establishment of a comprehensive 'offshore' financial centre. Despite considerably improved regulation, more than 90% of the island's 'offshore' and commercial banks were again closed, following further investigations by British inspectors in mid-1992.

The eruption of Chances Peak volcano in July 1995, which had been dormant for more than 100 years, caused severe disruption to the island and threatened to devastate Plymouth and surrounding areas in southern Montserrat. In late August the threat of a more serious eruption prompted the evacuation of some 5,000 people to the north of the island, and the declaration by the Government of a state of emergency and a night curfew. As volcanic activity subsided in September, evacuated islanders returned to Plymouth and villages near the volcano. However, by December the area was again deemed to be unsafe, and 4,000 people were evacuated for a period of several weeks. The Governor and Chief Minister secured an agreement from the British Government for the provision of assistance with evacuation and rehabilitation programmes. A third evacuation took place in April 1996, following another series of eruptions, and it was announced that some 5,000 evacuees living in 'safe areas' would remain there at least until the end of the year. In that month the British Government announced that Montserratians would be granted residency and the right to work in the United Kingdom for up to two years. In August the British Government announced that it was to provide assistance worth £25m. to finance housing construction projects, infrastructure development, the provision of temporary health and education facilities and other public services in the northern 'safe areas' of the island. By the end of 1996 it was estimated that some 5,000 islanders had left the territory since the onset of volcanic activity in mid-1995.

In September 1996 the Government announced that the general election would take place, despite the continued disruption in the territory. The Deputy Chief Minister, Noel Tuitt, resigned from his post and from the NPP later that month, stating that he was disillusioned with Meade's leadership. Disagreement over the Government's management of the volcano crisis and its handling of aid funds led to the proposal, by an opposition member in October, of a motion of no confidence in the Chief Minister. Meade, however, avoided a vote on the motion by dissolving the Legislative Council.

No party won an overall majority at the election on 11 November 1996. The NPP secured only one seat (won by Meade). The recently formed People's Progressive Alliance (PPA), led by John Osborne, won two seats, as did both the Movement for National Reconstruction (MNR), led by Austin Bramble, and independent candidates. A four-member coalition cabinet (which included Meade, but did not include either PPA member) was subsequently formed under the leadership of Bertrand Osborne, who was sworn in as Chief Minister on 13 November.

UNITED KINGDOM OVERSEAS TERRITORIES

Montserrat

In June 1997 the scale of volcanic activity on the island increased dramatically with the eruption of the Soufrière Hills volcano, which left some two-thirds of the island uninhabitable, destroyed the capital and resulted in 19 deaths. Islanders were evacuated to 'safe areas' in the north of the country. The British Government released emergency aid to finance the construction of emergency shelters for evacuees, and for repairs to temporary hospital facilities. In July it was announced that a package of options for Montserratians was being formulated, which would offer islanders resettlement grants and assisted passage either to other islands within the Caribbean or to the United Kingdom. The 'safe area' in the north was to be developed for those wishing to remain on the island. By the end of July the population of Montserrat was estimated to have declined to 5,800; in the month since the eruption of the Soufrière Hills volcano some 800 islanders had moved to Antigua, bringing the total number who had moved there since the onset of volcanic activity in 1995 to some 3,000. Many more had resettled on other Caribbean islands or in the United Kingdom.

On 21 August 1997 Bertrand Osborne resigned as Chief Minister following four days of public demonstrations in protest at his handling of the volcano crisis, in particular at uncertainty surrounding the future of the islanders and at poor conditions in emergency shelters. On the same day the British Government announced the financial details of its voluntary evacuation scheme for those wishing to leave Montserrat. The offer, which comprised a relocation grant of £2,400 for adults and £600 for minors, in addition to travel costs, provoked an angry response from islanders, who protested that the grants were severely inadequate. Osborne's successor as Chief Minister, David Brandt, an independent member of the Legislative Council, criticized the British Government's offer while also accusing the Government of attempting to depopulate Montserrat by showing insufficient commitment to the redevelopment of the island. The British Secretary of State for International Development, Clare Short, denied that the United Kingdom was encouraging people to leave Montserrat. However, accusations made by Short, to the effect that the island's leaders were making unreasonable demands, caused considerable offence to the island Government and the controversy was assuaged only when the British Secretary of State for Foreign and Commonwealth Affairs, Robin Cook, announced the formation of a special inter-departmental committee charged with co-ordinating assistance to Montserrat. At the end of August George Foulkes, the Under-Secretary of State for International Development, visited the island for discussions with the Montserrat Government, during which he announced a five-year sustainable development plan for the north of the island, to include finance for new housing, social services and improved infrastructure. In September Tony Abbott was inaugurated as Governor of Montserrat, replacing Frank Savage.

In January 1998 Brandt renewed his accusations that the British Government was attempting to depopulate Montserrat by delaying the release of development funds. Prompted by these accusations, in February Cook made a formal visit to Montserrat; it was subsequently announced that the United Kingdom would provide further finance of £4.8m. for housing on the island. The new funding brought the total amount committed by the British Government in 1995–98, since the beginning of the volcano crisis, to £59m.

In May 1998 the British Government announced that all citizens of Montserrat, except those already resident in other countries, would be entitled to settle in the United Kingdom. The estimated 3,500 refugees already in the United Kingdom on temporary visas were to be allowed to apply for permanent residency. In early July the Soufrière Hills volcano erupted again, covering much of the island in ash, and postponing plans to re-open parts of Plymouth to residents. In August part of the central zone of Montserrat was re-opened, following operations to remove ash and debris.

In January 1999 an inquest into the 19 deaths during the eruptions found that in nine cases the British Government was in part to blame for the deaths. The jury criticized the public shelters provided, where conditions were described as 'deplorable', and the Government's failure to provide farming land in the 'safe area', which had led to some farmers choosing to risk their lives rather than abandon their farms. The Department for International Development denied culpability for the deaths, and announced that it was to spend a further £75m. on a three-year redevelopment programme in the north of the island.

In February 1999 studies were published confirming that the volcanic ash covering much of Montserrat contained significant amounts of silica, the cause of the lung disease silicosis. It was suggested that the threat to health from long-term exposure to the ash might further limit the number of areas of the island suitable for redevelopment. In July a bulletin from the Montserrat Volcano Observatory noted that there were no signs of decline in residual volcanic activity, warning that it would take decades for the lava still present to cool to ambient temperatures. Further explosions of ash and minor eruptions of lava continued throughout the rest of the year.

In September 1999 public consultations took place to discuss government proposals to establish a new capital at Little Bay, in the north-west of the island. The new town would take an estimated 10 years to construct. Progress on the project was finally achieved with the establishment of the Montserrat Development Corporation in 2007, whose mandate included the advancement of plans for the construction of the new capital, and the issuing of a contract to a local company to develop the infrastructure. Also in September 1999 the British Government announced further assistance for the construction of housing and expressed support for Government plans to establish Montserrat as a centre for international financial services. In March 2000 the dome of lava, which had been covering the Soufrière Hills volcano, collapsed, producing lava flows and mudslides in the west of the island, and covering much of the 'safe zone' with ash.

In May 2000 an advisory commission on electoral reform recommended the replacement of the constituency system, which was deemed redundant following the abandonment of much of the island, by a nine-member single constituency. It was intended that the new system would be in place prior to the general election, scheduled for late 2001.

In July 2001 there was a further partial collapse of the dome of lava covering the Soufrière Hills volanco. Hot ash and volcanic pebbles affected the communities of Salem and Olveston, and ash clouds severely disrupted air travel in the north-eastern Caribbean. In the following month Montserrat signed up to a British mortgage assistance programme, which would provide housing subsidies and loans to residents who had been made homeless as a result of volcanic activity. Many residents were still paying mortgages on homes in an off-limits zone of the island as well as paying rent for new accommodation.

In February 2001 Chief Minister Brandt's coalition Government collapsed, following the resignations of two members who accused Brandt of making decisions, in particular about a proposed new airport, without consulting other ministers. Their resignations forced Brandt to dissolve the Executive Council and announce that an early general election would be held on 2 April, under the new system of the nine-member single constituency (see above). At the election former Chief Minister John Osborne's newly formed New People's Liberation Movement (NPLM) won seven of the nine seats, while the NPP secured the remaining two seats. Osborne was sworn in as Chief Minister on 5 April.

In May 2001 Anthony Longrigg was inaugurated as Governor of Montserrat, replacing Tony Abbott.

In February 2002 the Organisation of Eastern Caribbean States (OECS, see p. 440) countries, including Montserrat, agreed to allow nationals of member states to travel freely within the OECS area and to remain in a foreign territory within the area for up to six months. In May the British Overseas Territories Act, having received royal assent in the United Kingdom in February, came into force and granted British citizenship to the people of its 14 Overseas Territories, including Montserrat. Under the new law Montserratians would be able to hold British passports and work in the United Kingdom and anywhere else in the European Union. In October 2003 the British Government formally backed plans for Montserrat to particpate fully in the Caribbean Single Market and Economy (CSME) proposed by the Caribbean Community and Common Market (CARICOM, see p. 206), of which Montserrat was a founder member. (As a United Kingdom Overseas Territory, Montserrat required prior approval from the British Government before undertaking international commitments.) The CSME came into force at the beginning of 2006, although Montserrat was not a founding member.

A massive volcanic eruption, reported to be the largest since 1995, occurred on 12 July 2003, causing infrastructural damage, and the destruction of numerous buildings in Salem, which was on the edge of the 'safe zone'. Further minor eruptions occurred in April 2005 and May 2006.

In May 2004 Deborah Barnes-Jones took over as Governor from Anthony Longrigg.

In the general election of 31 May 2006 no party won an overall majority. The Movement for Change and Prosperity (MCAP) secured the largest representation, with four seats, followed by the NPLM with three seats. The Montserrat Democratic Party (MDP) won one seat, as did former Chief Minister David Brandt, again standing as an independent. Lowell Lewis of the MDP assembled a coalition Government comprising the three NPLM representatives (including former Chief Minister John Osborne) and Brandt. The new Government was sworn in on 2 June, although allegations of corruption and mismanagement levelled against candidates from both the former government and opposition had overshadowed the election process and doubts were expressed about the new administration's compositional stability.

Concerns emerged in November 2006 relating to the ongoing constitutional revision process, which had been under negotiation with the Government of the United Kingdom since 1997. A series of Legislative Council debates examining a report of the Constitutional

Review Commission, first submitted in 2002, and negotiations with Ian Hendry of the British Constitutional Review Team, provoked an angry response from some members of the Chief Minister's Constitutional Advisory Committee. They alleged that Montserrat's increased reliance upon budgetary assistance from the United Kingdom—necessitated by volcanic disruption—was being exploited as a 'coercive tool' in the reform process. While the United Kingdom had encouraged Montserrat to express its preferences and recommendations towards the drafting of a new constitution, it was emphasized that ultimate authority would reside with the British Government, eliciting accusations that only a token democracy was being offered, disregarding Montserratian public consultations. Requests for a system of 'free association', permitting self-determination from the United Kingdom—drafting its own constitution without recourse to the administering nation, but retaining links with that country—and the appointment of an indigenous Deputy Governor who would assume some of the responsibilities of the British Governor in Montserrat, were similarly declined. That other former British colonial territories, including Bermuda, had been granted associated statehood instigated a consultation of the former Saint Christopher and Nevis-United Kingdom Associated Statehood Constitution as a template for Montserrat's submission to the British Constitutional Review Team. However, it was advised that any recommendations found not to concur with the United Kingdom's objective of securing the removal of Montserrat from the UN's Special Committee on Decolonization's list of prospective colonies would be rejected. Chief Minister Lewis stated in early 2008 that further meetings to discuss the constitutional reform process would not be conducted until the end of that year.

Also in November 2006 Montserrat became a signatory to the UN Convention Against Corruption during the eighth meeting of the Overseas Territories Consultative Council hosted in London, United Kingdom, by the British Overseas Territories Minister, Lord Triesman.

Peter Waterworth succeeded Deborah Barnes-Jones as Governor of Montserrat in July 2007.

In July 2007 the exclusion zone around the Soufrière Hills volcanic dome, which had been expanded to include settlements bordering Belham Valley to the north following recent volcanic activity, was reduced to its extent at the start of the year. In July 2008 the dome again partially collapsed, leading to the temporary evacuation of nearby residents.

Lewis disbanded the coalition Government on 21 February 2008 and formed a new political alliance with the MCAP. Minister of Communications and Works Idabelle Meade and Minister of Agriculture, Lands, Housing and the Environment Margaret Dyer-Howe, both members of the NPLM, were replaced by MCAP members Charles Kirnon and Reuben Meade, respectively. Lewis also announced that John Osborne, Minister of Education, Health and Community Services, would be replaced by a member of the MCAP by 31 March, giving the new coalition Government a majority in the Legislative Council, with six seats. Osborne's ministerial responsibilities were, accordingly, assigned to Roselyn Cassell-Sealy.

Reuben Meade and two former members of the Legislative Council expressed dissatisfaction in late March 2008 with the reformed electoral system during a public meeting to discuss proposed constitutional changes. They acknowledged that the voting tendencies of most residents of Montserrat were to respond to party personalities rather than to vote for the party itself, and that this was precluded by the present system. Meade proposed the adoption of a system in which four constituencies would be represented by two members, while the Chief Minister would be elected at large. He claimed that the implementation of such measures would aid community development and the rebuilding of the country.

In October 2008 opposition leader David Brandt filed a motion of no confidence against Chief Minister Lewis as a result of his perceived mismanagement of the island's economic affairs. Lewis avoided the motion by relinquishing the portfolios for finance and economic development to fellow minister Reuben Meade.

Following a Cuban Government-sponsored diplomatic excursion to Havana by Chief Minister Lowell in January 2007, Montserrat and Cuba pledged to strengthen bilateral relations, particularly in consideration of the burgeoning threat posed by the Soufrière Hills volcanic dome, which had been expanding consistently in the preceding months.

In July 2008 the Jamaican Prime Minister, Bruce Golding, visited Montserrat and signed a memorandum of understanding between the two countries. This pledged Jamaican support in areas such as cultural enhancement, tourism, economic development, education and health.

Government

Under the provisions of the 1960 Constitution and subsequent legislation, the Governor is appointed by the British monarch and is responsible for defence, external affairs and internal security. The Governor is President of the seven-member Executive Council. The Legislative Council comprises 12 members: a Speaker, two official members, two nominated and seven elected by universal adult suffrage. A constitutional review was begun in 2002 and was continuing in 2009.

Economic Affairs

In 2008 Montserrat's gross domestic product (GDP) at market prices was an estimated EC $131.90m., equivalent to approximately EC $26,706 per head. In 2000–08 real GDP decreased by an annual average of 1.4%; GDP increased by 2.9% in 2007 and by 11.8% in 2008.

Agriculture (including forestry and fishing) contributed an estimated 1.0% of GDP in 2008, and engaged 6.6% of the employed labour force in 1992. The sector was almost destroyed by the volcanic eruptions of 1997, which caused an 81.3% decline in agricultural production, and a return to subsistence farming. The sector's GDP contracted by a further 33.3% in 1998, in real terms, but increased by 7.6% in 1999 and by a massive 46.5% in 2000. A contraction of 17.3% in agricultural GDP in 2001 was followed, in 2002, by a 38.4% recovery. However, no growth was recorded in the sector in 2003, and the sector contracted by 17.8% in 2004, largely owing to a further eruption of the Soufrière Hills volcano in July 2003 that destroyed some 95% of that year's food crop. Prior to the volcanic eruption the principal crops grown were white potatoes, onions, rice and sea-island cotton. Cattle, goats, sheep and poultry were also farmed. Montserrat's fisheries are under-exploited, owing to the absence of a sheltered harbour. The agriculture sector grew by 8.2% in 2008.

Industry (including mining, manufacturing, construction and public utilities) contributed some 18.3% to GDP in 2008, and engaged some 30.9% of the employed labour force in 1987. Mining and quarrying contributed 2.7% of GDP in 2008. Manufacturing contributed 0.7% of GDP in 2008, engaged 5.6% of the employed labour force (together with mining) in 1992, and accounted for about 70% of exports in the early 1990s. Many industrial sites were destroyed in 1997, causing a decline in real manufacturing GDP of 45.2% in that year and of 85.0% in 1998. In 1999 the sector's GDP grew by 10.6%, but growth averaged just 0.4% annually in 2000–08. Light industries comprise the processing of agricultural produce (also cotton and tropical fruits), as well as spring-water bottling and the manufacture of garments and plastic bags. The assembly of electrical components, which accounted for 69% of export earnings in 1993, ceased in 1998, following further volcanic activity. In May 2006 the Government signed a 25-year contract with a British plastics recycling company to supply volcanic ash, to be used in the blending of recycled plastics. Exports of digital data-processing machines comprised 16.7% of total exports in 2003.

Construction contributed an estimated 8.6% of GDP in 2008 and employed 17.5% of the working population in 1988. The sector enjoyed growth in the early 1990s, owing to reconstruction programmes in response to the devastation caused by 'Hurricane Hugo' in 1989. Activity in the sector declined in the mid-1990s, before increasing in the middle of the decade, as a result of further reconstruction work following the volcanic eruptions. In 2000, however, real construction GDP fell by 35.8%. It continued to decrease, by 7.7%, in 2001, before increasing by 40.9% in 2002, although there was another contraction, of 2.9%, in 2003. The trend was reversed yet again in 2004, with the sector increasing by an estimated 2.4%, although it has performed poorly since then. The sector declined at an average annual rate of 12.9% between 2005 and 2008. Energy requirements are dependent upon the import of mineral fuels (29.1% of total imports in 2007).

It is hoped to re-establish Montserrat as a data-processing centre, and as a centre for financial services, which previously provided an important source of government revenue. The tourism sector, which in 2007 contributed a provisional EC $20.1m. in receipts, remains important to the island, and it is hoped to establish Montserrat as a centre for environmental tourism, with the volcano itself as the premier attraction. The GDP of the hotel and restaurant sector increased by an annual average of 6.8% between 2000–08. The sector grew by 4.2% in 2008. The real GDP of the services sector increased by an annual average of 1.9% during 2000–08, declining by 6.5% in 2007 before recording growth of 0.9% in 2008. Services contributed 80.7% of GDP in 2008.

In 2008 Montserrat recorded an estimated trade deficit of EC $66.5m. Earnings from the services sector, mainly tourism receipts and net transfers (in particular, the remittances from Montserratians abroad and the income of foreign retired people), generally offset persistent trade deficits. There was an estimated deficit on the current account of the balance of payments of EC $34.2m. in 2008. The principal trading partner is the USA (providing 43.2% of imports and receiving 3.7% of exports in 2007). Other trading partners of importance include Anguilla, Trinidad and Tobago, Saint Christopher and Nevis, the United Kingdom and Antigua and Barbuda. The export of rice and of electrical components, previously the most important of the island's few exports, ceased in 1998 following further volcanic activity. However, export receipts increased to some US $2.7m. by 2008. Food, beverage and tobacco imports constituted 17.2% of total imports in 2008; the principal imports were mineral fuels and lubricants, machinery and transport equipment and basic manufactures.

In 2007 there was a budgetary deficit of EC $8.0m (including grants of $76.0m.). The capital budget is funded almost entirely by overseas aid, notably from the United Kingdom and Canada. The United Kingdom initially provided aid worth £14.5m. for 1995–98 (additional assistance for emergency housing and other services necessitated by continued volcanic activity had brought this total to £59m. by the end of 1998). In 1999 official development assistance totalled US $65.6m., with British budgetary assistance of £75m. being made available for the three-year reconstruction programme agreed in January 1999. A £55m. programme for 2001–04 was followed by a further three-year £40m. programme extending to 2007. The aid programme for 2006 was valued at £14m., of which £10.2m. was a grant to cover the recurrent budget deficit. Montserrat's total external public debt was estimated at EC $11.2m. in 2007, according to figures from the Eastern Caribbean Central Bank (ECCB). Consumer prices increased by 3.1% in 2008. The Caribbean Development Bank (see p. 211) estimated the unemployment rate to stand at some 13% of the labour force in 2001.

Montserrat is a member of the ECCB, the Caribbean Community and Common Market (CARICOM, see p. 206), the Organisation of Eastern Caribbean States (OECS, see p. 440) and, as a dependency of the United Kingdom, has the status of Overseas Territory in association with the European Union (EU, see p. 255). The territory is also a member of the regional stock exchange, the Eastern Caribbean Securities Exchange (based in Saint Christopher and Nevis), established in 2001.

The eruption of the Soufrière Hills volcano in June 1997, and subsequent volcanic activity, rendered the southern two-thirds of Montserrat, including the capital, Plymouth, uninhabitable. Much of the country's infrastructure, including the main port and airport, was destroyed, and the island's agricultural heartland was devastated. The implications for the island's principal industry, tourism, were extremely severe. In August the British Government announced a five-year reconstruction programme for the development of the 'safe areas' in the north of the island. However, by mid-February 1998 the population of Montserrat had declined to just 2,850 (the population was an estimated 11,581 in 1994), owing to the lack of employment prospects and to poor living conditions. Of the remaining work-force, some 25% were employed by the Government or statutory bodies. The population was enumerated at 4,482 in the census of May 2001, and it was hoped that a reduction in volcanic activity would encourage Montserratians resident abroad to return home, thereby stimulating the economy. By 2008, however, the population was estimated to have reached just 4,939. It was anticipated that the ongoing reconstruction efforts and the development of the island as a centre for environmental tourism would stimulate short-term economic growth, while in the long term it was hoped to re-establish Montserrat as a centre for international financial services. At the end of 2003 some 22 International Business Companies and two banks were registered in the Territory. In mid-2008 Montserrat was named as one of the Caribbean economies at risk from illegal financial practice owing to a dearth of qualified investigators within the financial system. Although an estimated 150 people were working in the financial sector in Montserrat, only one employee was believed to be capable of investigating fraudulent behaviour. However, Montserrat's economic prospects depended entirely on the activity of the volcano, and although reconstruction work was in progress, other areas of the economy were likely to remain at extremely low levels of output for some years. The tourism sector was expected to suffer in 2009 as a result of the recession in the USA and United Kingdom. However, in early 2009 a new airline, Montserrat Airways, announced it would be running a service out of Montserrat starting mid-year. The service was to be partly funded by the Montserrat Tourist Board in order to stimulate economic growth, particularly in the tourism sector.

Education

Education, beginning at five years of age, is compulsory up to the age of 14. In 1993 there were 11 primary schools, including 10 government schools. Secondary education begins at 12 years of age, and comprises a first cycle of five years and a second, two-year cycle. In 1999 there were 11 nursery schools, two primary schools and one secondary school. sThere was also an extra-mural department of the University of the West Indies in Plymouth. In 2005/06 enrolment in primary education included 99.1% of pupils in the relevant age-group, while in 2003/04 the comparable enrolment ratio at secondary schools was 95.8%. In 2002 the European Union (EU) and the United Kingdom contributed a total of EC $6m. to the construction of a further education college, the Montserrat Community College, which was completed in late 2003. Three 'offshore' medical schools were licensed in 2003. The Ministry of Education was allocated a total of EC $8.3m. in the 2008 budget.

Public Holidays

2009: 1 January (New Year's Day), 17 March (St Patrick's Day), 10 April (Good Friday), 13 April (Easter Monday), 4 May (Labour Day), 1 June (Whit Monday), 13 June (Queen's Official Birthday), 3 August (August Monday), 23 November (Liberation Day), 25–26 December (Christmas), 31 December (Festival Day).

2010: 1 January (New Year's Day), 17 March (St Patrick's Day), 2 April (Good Friday), 5 April (Easter Monday), 3 May (Labour Day), 24 May (Whit Monday), 7 June (Queen's Official Birthday), 2 August (August Monday), 23 November (Liberation Day), 25–26 December (Christmas), 31 December (Festival Day).

Weights and Measures

The imperial system is in use but the metric system is being introduced.

Statistical Survey

Sources (unless otherwise stated): Government Information Service, Media Centre, Chief Minister's Office, Old Towne; tel. 491-2702; fax 491-2711; Eastern Caribbean Central Bank, POB 89, Basseterre, Saint Christopher; internet www.eccb-centralbank.org; OECS Economic Affairs Secretariat, *Statistical Digest*.

AREA AND POPULATION

Area: 102 sq km (39.5 sq miles).

Population: 10,639 (males 5,290, females 5,349) at census of 12 May 1991; 4,491 at census of 12 May 2001 (Source: UN, *Population and Vital Statistics Report*). 2008 (estimate at mid-year): 4,939.

Density (mid-2008): 48.4 per sq km.

Principal Towns: Plymouth, the former capital, was abandoned in 1997. Brades is the interim capital.

Births and Deaths (1999): 45 live births (birth rate 9.4 per 1,000); 59 deaths (death rate 12.4 per 1,000) (Source: UN, *Population and Vital Statistics Report*). 2003: Crude birth rate 9.6 per 1,000; Crude death rate 12.3 per 1,000 (Source: Caribbean Development Bank, *Social and Economic Indicators*). 2007: Crude birth rate 17.5 per 1,000; Crude death rate 7.0 per 1,000 (Source: Pan American Health Organization).

Life Expectancy (years at birth, estimates): 79.2 (males 76.98; females 81.5) in 2008. Source: Pan American Health Organization.

Employment (1992): Agriculture, forestry and fishing 298; Mining and manufacturing 254; Electricity, gas and water 68; Wholesale and retail trade 1,666; Restaurants and hotels 234; Transport and communication 417; Finance, insurance and business services 242; Public defence 390; Other community, social and personal services 952; Total 4,521 (Source: *The Commonwealth Yearbook*). 1998 (estimate): Total labour force 1,500.

HEALTH AND WELFARE

Physicians (per 1,000 head, 1999): 0.18.

Hospital Beds (per 1,000 head, 2007): 3.0.

Health Expenditure (public, % of GDP, 2000): 7.7.

Health Expenditure (public, % of total, 1995): 67.0.

Source: Pan American Health Organization.

For sources and definitions, see explanatory note on p. vi.

AGRICULTURE, ETC.

Principal Crops (metric tons, 2007, FAO estimates): Vegetables 495; Fruit (excl. melons) 395.

Livestock ('000 head, 2007, FAO estimates): Cattle 9.8; Sheep 4.8; Goats 7.1; Pigs 1.2.

Livestock Products ('000 metric tons, 2007, FAO estimates): Cattle meat 0.8; Cows' milk 2.3.

Fishing (metric tons, live weight, 2006, FAO estimate): Total catch 50 (all marine fishes).

Source: FAO.

INDUSTRY

Electric Energy (million kWh): 11.4 in 2006; 11.6 in 2007; 11.7 in 2008.

UNITED KINGDOM OVERSEAS TERRITORIES   *Montserrat*

FINANCE

Currency and Exchange Rates: 100 cents = 1 East Caribbean dollar (EC $). *Sterling, US Dollar and Euro Equivalents* (31 December 2008): £1 sterling = EC $3.936; US $1 = EC $2.700; €1 = EC $3.758; EC $100 = £25.41 = US $37.04 = €26.61. *Exchange Rate:* Fixed at US $1 = EC $2.70 since July 1976.

Budget (EC $ million, 2007): *Revenue:* Revenue from taxation 31.6 (Taxes on income and profits 14.4, Taxes on property 1.4, Taxes on domestic goods and services 3.4, Taxes on international trade and transactions 12.4); Non-tax revenue 4.2; Total 35.8 (excl. grants 76.0). *Expenditure:* Current expenditure 93.2 (Personal emoluments 37.9, Goods and services 30.8, Interest payments 1.0, Transfers and subsidies 23.5); Capital expenditure 26.6; Total 119.8.

International Reserves (US $ million at 31 December 2008): Foreign exchange 11.67. Source: IMF, *International Financial Statistics*.

Money Supply (EC $ million at 31 December 2007): Currency outside banks 15.07; Demand deposits at deposit money banks 33.24; Total money 48.32. Source: IMF, *International Financial Statistics*.

Cost of Living (Consumer Price Index; base: previous year = 100): All items 99.2 in 2003; 104.3 in 2004; 101.76 in 2005. Source: partly Caribbean Development Bank, *Social and Economic Indicators*.

Gross Domestic Product (EC $ million at constant 1990 prices): 67.35 in 2006; 69.30 in 2007; 77.47 in 2008.

Expenditure on the Gross Domestic Product (EC $ million at current prices, 2008): Government final consumption expenditure 80.67; Private final consumption expenditure 90.33; Gross fixed capital formation 37.63; *Total domestic expenditure* 208.63; Export of goods and services 47.89; *Less* Imports of goods and services 124.63; *GDP at market prices* 131.89.

Gross Domestic Product by Economic Activity (EC $ million at current prices, 2008): Agriculture, forestry and fishing 1.23; Mining and quarrying 3.38; Manufacturing 0.84; Electricity and water 7.98; Construction 10.85; Wholesale and retail trade 5.31; Restaurants and hotels 1.36; Transport 9.41; Communications 3.92; Banks and insurance 11.68; Real estate and housing 15.73; Government services 45.17; Other services 9.06; *Sub-total* 125.92; *Less* Financial intermediation services indirectly measured 10.74; *Gross value added at basic prices* 115.18; Taxes, less subsidies, on products 16.72; *GDP at market prices* 131.90.

Balance of Payments (EC $ million, 2008): Goods (net) −66.46; Services (net) −14.51; *Balance on goods and services* −80.97; Income (net) −10.85; *Balance on goods, services and income* −91.82; Current transfers (net) 57.59; *Current balance* −34.24; Capital account (net) 15.23; Direct investment (net) 5.15; Portfolio investment (net) 0.16; Public sector long-term investment −1.02; Commercial banks −9.25; Other investment assets −7.57; Other investment liabilities 32.00; Net errors and omissions 0.04; *Overall balance* 0.50.

EXTERNAL TRADE

Principal Commodities (US $ million, 2007): *Imports c.i.f.:* Food and live animals 3.9; Beverages and tobacco 1.2; Crude materials (inedible) except fuels 0.5; Mineral fuels, lubricants, etc. 8.6; Chemicals 1.6; Manufactured goods 4.2; Machinery and transport equipment 7.2; Miscellaneous manufactured articles 2.1; Total (incl. others) 29.6. *Exports f.o.b.:* Crude materials (inedible) except fuels 1.9; Machinery and transport equipment 0.3; Miscellaneous manufactured articles 0.3; Total (incl. others) 2.7.

Principal Trading Partners (US $ million, 2007): *Imports c.i.f.:* Barbados 0.3; Canada 0.4; China, People's Repub. 0.2; Jamaica 0.2; Japan 1.3; Netherlands 0.2; Trinidad and Tobago 10.0; United Kingdom 2.0; USA 12.8; Total (incl. others) 29.6. *Exports f.o.b.:* Anguilla 1.2; Antigua and Barbuda 0.2; St. Christopher and Nevis 0.8; United Kingdom 0.2; USA 0.1; Total (incl. others) 2.7.

Source: UN, *International Trade Statistics Yearbook*.

TOURISM

Tourist Arrivals (2007, provisional figures): Stay-over arrivals 7,746 (USA 2,109, Canada 388, United Kingdom 2,190, Caribbean 2,796, Others 263); Excursionists 968; Cruise-ship passengers 273; Total visitor arrivals (incl. others) 10,450. *2008* (rounded figure): Total 8,520.

Tourism Receipts (EC $ million): 24.3 in 2005; 20.9 in 2006; 20.1 in 2007 (provisional figure).

TRANSPORT

Road Traffic (vehicles in use, 1990): Passenger cars 1,823; Goods vehicles 54; Public service vehicles 4; Motorcycles 21; Miscellaneous 806.

Shipping: ('000 metric tons, 1990): *International Freight Traffic:* Goods loaded 6; Goods unloaded 49. Source: UN, *Monthly Bulletin of Statistics*.

Civil Aviation (1985): Aircraft arrivals 4,422; passengers 25,380; air cargo 132.4 metric tons.

COMMUNICATIONS MEDIA

Radio Receivers (1997): 7,000 in use.

Television Receivers (1999): 3,000 in use.

Telephones (2000): 2,811 main lines in use.

Mobile Cellular Telephones (2000): 489 subscribers.

Non-daily Newspapers (1996): 2 (estimated circulation 3,000).

Sources: UNESCO, *Statistical Yearbook*; International Telecommunication Union.

EDUCATION

Pre-primary: 11 schools (1999); 11 teachers (2005/06); 122 pupils (2005/06).

Primary: 2 schools (1999); 30 teachers (2005/06); 508 pupils (2005/06).

Secondary: 1 school (1999); 27 teachers (2005/06); 328 pupils (2005/06).

Sources: UNESCO, *Statistical Yearbook*; UNESCO Institute for Statistics.

Directory

The eruption in June 1997 of the Soufrière Hills volcano, and subsequent volcanic activity, rendered some two-thirds of Montserrat uninhabitable and destroyed the capital, Plymouth. Islanders were evacuated to a 'safe zone' in the north of the island.

The Constitution

The present Constitution came into force on 19 December 1989 and made few amendments to the constitutional order established in 1960. The Constitution now guarantees the fundamental rights and freedoms of the individual and grants the Territory the right of self-determination. Montserrat is governed by a Governor and has its own Executive and Legislative Councils. The Governor retains responsibility for defence, external affairs (including international financial affairs) and internal security. The Executive Council consists of the Governor as President, the Chief Minister and three other Ministers, the Attorney-General and the Financial Secretary. The Legislative Council consists of the Speaker (chosen from outside the Council), nine elected, two official and two nominated members. Owing to the disruption caused by evacuation from the south of the island, both the 2001 and 2006 general elections were conducted according to a new 'at large' voting system, without constituencies, but still choosing nine members of the legislature. A constitutional review process was ongoing in early 2009.

The Government

Governor: PETER ANDREW WATERWORTH (took office in July 2007).

EXECUTIVE COUNCIL
(April 2009)

President: PETER ANDREW WATERWORTH (The Governor).
Official Members:
Attorney-General: JAMES WOOD.
Financial Secretary: JOHN SKERRIT.
Chief Minister: Dr LOWELL LEWIS.
Minister of Agriculture, Lands, Housing and the Environment, and of Finance and Economic Development: REUBEN T. MEADE.
Minister of Communications and Works: CHARLES KIRNON.
Minister of Education, Labour, Health and Community Services: ROSELYN CASSELL-SEALY.
Clerk to the Executive Council: JUDITH JEFFERS.

UNITED KINGDOM OVERSEAS TERRITORIES

MINISTRIES

Office of the Governor: Farara Plaza, Brades; tel. 491-2688; fax 491-8867; e-mail govoffice.montserrat@fco.gov.uk; internet www.gov.ms/index/governor.htm.

Office of the Chief Minister: Govt HQ, POB 292, Brades; tel. 491-3378; fax 491-6780; e-mail ocm@gov.ms; internet www.gov.ms/index/chief_minister.htm.

Ministry of Agriculture, Lands, Housing and the Environment: Govt HQ, POB 272, Brades; tel. 491-2546; fax 491-9275; e-mail malhe@gov.ms; internet www.malhe.gov.ms.

Ministry of Communications and Works: Woodlands; tel. 491-2521; fax 491-3475; e-mail mcw@gov.ms; internet www.gov.ms/commsworks.

Ministry of Education, Health, Community Services and Labour: Govt HQ, POB 103, Brades; tel. 491-2541; fax 491-6941; e-mail deped@gov.ms; internet www.mehcs.gov.ms.

Ministry of Finance and Economic Development: Govt HQ, POB 292, Brades; tel. 491-2777; fax 491-2367; e-mail minfin@gov.ms; internet www.finance.gov.ms.

LEGISLATIVE COUNCIL

Speaker: Dr JOSEPH MEADE.

Election, 31 May 2006

Party	Seats
Movement for Change and Prosperity	4
New People's Liberation Movement	3
Montserrat Democratic Party	1
Independent	1
Total	9

There are also two ex officio members (the Attorney-General and the Financial Secretary) and two nominated members.

Political Organizations

Montserrat Democratic Party (MDP): c/o Kelsick & Kelsick, Woodlands Main Rd, POB 185, Brades; tel. 491-2102; e-mail kelkel@candw.ms; internet www.mdp.ms; Leader Dr LOWELL LEWIS; Chair. JEAN KELSICK.

Movement for Change and Prosperity (MCAP): POB 419, Brades; e-mail mail@mcap.ms; internet www.mcap.ms; f. 2005 by fmr mems of the National Progressive Party (NPP); Leader ROSELYN CASSELL-SEALY; Chair. RANDOLPH RILEY.

New People's Liberation Movement (NPLM): f. 1997 as successor party to People's Progressive Alliance and the Movement for National Reconstruction (MNR); opposition party; Leader JOHN OSBORNE; Chair. IDABELLE MEADE.

Judicial System

Justice is administered by the Eastern Caribbean Supreme Court (based in Saint Lucia—comprised of the Court of Appeal and the High Court), the Court of Summary Jurisdiction and the Magistrate's Court. A revised edition of the Laws of Montserrat came into force on 15 April 2005, following five years of preparation by a Law Revision Committee.

Puisne Judge (Montserrat Circuit): JANICE MESADIS GEORGE-CREQUE (concurrently accredited to Anguilla).

Magistrate: CLIFTON WARNER, Govt HQ, Brades; tel. 491-4056; fax 491-8866; e-mail magoff@gov.ms.

Registrar: AMILA DALEY, Govt HQ, Brades; tel. 491-3827; fax 491-4687.

Religion

CHRISTIANITY

The Montserrat Christian Council: St Peter's, POB 227; tel. 491-4864; fax 491-2139; Chair. Rev. B. RUTH ALLEN.

The Anglican Communion

Anglicans are adherents of the Church in the Province of the West Indies, comprising eight dioceses. Montserrat forms part of the diocese of the North Eastern Caribbean and Aruba. The Bishop is resident in The Valley, Anguilla.

The Roman Catholic Church

Montserrat forms part of the diocese of St John's-Basseterre, suffragan to the archdiocese of Castries (Saint Lucia). The Bishop is resident in St John's, Antigua and Barbuda.

Other Christian Churches

There are Baptist, Methodist, Pentecostal and Seventh-day Adventist churches and other places of worship on the island.

The Press

Montserrat Newsletter: Farara Plaza, Unit 8, Brades; tel. 491-2688; fax 491-8867; e-mail richard.aspin@fco.gov.uk; f. 1998; govt information publ; Publicity Officer RICHARD ASPIN.

The Montserrat Reporter: POB 306, Davy Hill; tel. 491-4715; fax 491-2430; e-mail editor@themontserratreporter.com; internet www.themontserratreporter.com; weekly on Fridays; circ. 2,000; Editor BENNETTE ROACH.

Broadcasting and Communications

TELECOMMUNICATIONS

Cable & Wireless (West Indies) Ltd: POB 219, Sweeney's; tel. 491-1000; fax 491-3599; e-mail venus.george@cwni.cwplc.com; internet www.cwmontserrat.com.

BROADCASTING

Prior to the volcanic eruption of June 1997 there were three radio stations operating in Montserrat. Television services can also be obtained from Saint Christopher and Nevis, Puerto Rico and from Antigua and Barbuda (ABS).

Radio

Gem Radio Network: POB 488, Barzey's; tel. 491-5728; fax 491-5729; f. 1984; commercial; Station Man. KEVIN LEWIS; Man. Dir KENNETH LEE.

Radio Antilles: POB 35/930; tel. 491-2755; fax 491-2724; f. 1963; in 1989 the Govt of Montserrat, on behalf of the OECS, acquired the station; has one of the most powerful transmitters in the region; commercial; regional; broadcasts in English and French; Chair. Dr H. FELLHAUER; Man. Dir KRISTIAN KNAACK; Gen. Man. KEITH GREAVES.

Radio Montserrat (ZJB): POB 51, Sweeney's; tel. 491-2885; fax 491-9250; e-mail queentest@gov.ms; internet www.zjb.gov.ms; f. 1952; first broadcast 1957; govt station; CEO LOWELL MASON.

Television

Cable Television of Montserrat Ltd: POB 447, Olveston; tel. 491-2507; fax 491-3081; Man. SYLVIA WHITE.

People's Television (PTV): POB 82, Brades; tel. 491-5110; Man. DENZIL EDGECOMBE.

Finance

The Eastern Caribbean Central Bank, based in Saint Christopher and Nevis, is the central issuing and monetary authority for Montserrat.

Eastern Caribbean Central Bank—Montserrat Office: 2 Farara Plaza, POB 484, Brades; tel. 491-6877; fax 491-6878; e-mail eccbmni@candw.ms; internet www.eccb-centralbank.org; Resident Rep. CHARLES T. JOHN.

Financial Services Commission: Phoenix House, POB 188, Brades; tel. 491-6887; fax 491-9888; e-mail fscmrat@candw.ms; internet fscmontserrat.org; f. 2002; the Commission consists of the Commissioner and three other mems appointed by the Governor; Chair. JOHN LAWRENCE.

BANKING

Bank of Montserrat Ltd: Hilltop, POB 10, St Peters; tel. 491-3843; fax 491-3163; e-mail bom@candw.ag; Man. ANTON DOLDRON.

Montserrat Building Society: POB 101, Brades Main Rd, Brades; tel. 491-2391; fax 491-6127; e-mail mbsl@candw.ms.

St Patrick's Co-operative Credit Union Ltd: POB 337, Brades; tel. 491-3666; fax 491-6566; e-mail monndf@candw.ms; Exec. Dir ROSELYN CASSELL-SEALY.

STOCK EXCHANGE

Eastern Caribbean Securities Exchange: based in Basseterre, Saint Christopher and Nevis; tel. (869) 466-7192; fax (869) 465-3798; e-mail info@ecseonline.com; internet www.ecseonline.com; f. 2001; regional securities market designed to facilitate the buying and selling of financial products for the eight member territories—Anguilla, Antigua and Barbuda, Dominica, Grenada, Montserrat, Saint Christopher and Nevis, Saint Lucia and Saint Vincent and the Grenadines; Chair. Sir K. DWIGHT VENNER; Gen. Man. and CEO TREVOR E. BLAKE.

INSURANCE

British American Insurance Co Ltd: POB 77, St Peter's; tel. 491-2361; fax 491-9361.

Insurance Services (Montserrat) Ltd: POB 185, Brades; tel. 491-2103; fax 491-6013; e-mail ismcall@candw.ag; Gen. Man. STEPHEN FRANCOIS.

NAGICO: Ryan Investments, Brades; tel. 491-3403; fax 491-7307; e-mail talicj@yahoo.com.

N. E. M. (West Indies) Insurance Ltd (NEMWIL): POB 287, Brades; tel. 491-3813; fax 491-3815.

United Insurance Co Ltd: Jacquie Ryan Enterprises Ltd, POB 425, Brades; tel. 491-2055; fax 491-3257; e-mail united@candw.ms; CEO JACQUIE RYAN.

Trade and Industry

GOVERNMENT AGENCY

Montserrat Economic Development Unit: Govt HQ, POB 292, Brades; tel. 491-2066; fax 491-4632; e-mail devunit@gov.ms; internet www.devunit.gov.ms.

CHAMBER OF COMMERCE

Montserrat Chamber of Commerce and Industry (MCCI): Vue Pointe Hotel, Old Towne, POB 384, Brades; tel. 491-3640; fax 491-6602; e-mail chamber@candw.ms; refounded 1971; 31 company mems, 26 individual mems; Pres. KENNY CASSELL; Sec.-Treas. ROSELYN CASSELL-SEALY.

UTILITIES

Electricity and Water

Montserrat Utilities Ltd (MUL): POB 16, St John's; tel. 491-2441; fax 491-3143; e-mail mul@mul.ms; internet www.mul.ms; f. 2008 by merger of Montserrat Electricity Services Ltd and Montserrat Water Authority; domestic electricity generation and supply; domestic water supply; Man. Dir LYNDELL GREER; Man. of Water and Sewerage EMILE DUBERRY.

Gas

Grant Enterprises and Trading: POB 350, Brades; tel. 491-9654; fax 491-4854; e-mail granten@candw.ms; domestic gas supplies.

TRADE UNIONS

Montserrat Allied Workers' Union (MAWU): POB 245, Dagenham, Plymouth; tel. 491-5049; fax 491-6145; e-mail bramblehl@candw.ag; f. 1973; private-sector employees; Pres. CHARLES RYAN; Gen. Sec. HYLROY BRAMBLE; 1,000 mems.

Montserrat Civil Service Association: POB 468, Plymouth; tel. 491-6797; fax 491-5655; e-mail lewisp@gov.ms; Pres. PAUL LEWIS.

Montserrat Seamen's and Waterfront Workers' Union: tel. 491-6335; fax 491-6335; f. 1980; Sec.-Gen. CHEDMOND BROWNE; 100 mems.

Montserrat Union of Teachers: POB 460, Plymouth; tel. 491-4382; fax 491-5779; f. 1978; Pres. HERMAN FRANCIS; Gen. Sec. HYACINTH BRAMBLE-BROWNE; 46 mems.

Transport

The eruption in June 1997 of the Soufrière Hills volcano, and subsequent volcanic activity, destroyed much of the infrastructure in the southern two-thirds of the island, including the country's principal port and airport facilities, as well as the road network.

ROADS

Prior to the volcanic eruption of June 1997 Montserrat had an extensive and well-constructed road network. There were 203 km (126 miles) of good surfaced main roads, 24 km of secondary unsurfaced roads and 42 km of rough tracks. Government expenditure on road rehabilitation works in 2006 amounted to more than US $3m., while a further US $0.5m. was allocated to the maintenance budget of the Public Works Department for surfacing of the secondary road network. The 2007 budget allocated funds of over US $5m. for continued road and infrastructure improvements, particularly in areas to become more densely populated through housing developments carried out under the Emergency Resettlement Strategy. A five-year roads development project proposal, to cost $20m., was also submitted to the British Department for International Development in that year.

SHIPPING

The principal port at Plymouth was destroyed by the volcanic activity of June 1997. An emergency jetty was constructed at Little Bay in the north of the island. Regular transshipment steamship services are provided by Harrison Line and Nedlloyd Line. The Bermuth Line and the West Indies Shipping Service link Montserrat with Miami, USA, and with neighbouring territories. Local protest followed the discontinuation of a ferry service with Antigua, which occurred at the end of July 2005, as a result of the inauguration of the new airport facilities. Owing to the dramatic impact its suspension had upon tourist arrivals, however, the ferry was reinstated in December 2008.

Port Authority of Montserrat: Little Bay, POB 383, Plymouth; tel. 491-2791; fax 491-8063; e-mail monpa@candw.ms; Man. SHAWN O'GARRO.

Montserrat Shipping Services: POB 46, Carr's Bay; tel. 491-3614; fax 491-3617.

CIVIL AVIATION

The main airport, Blackburne at Trants, 13 km (8 miles) from Plymouth, was destroyed by the volcanic activity of June 1997. A helicopter port at Gerald's in the north of the island was completed in 2000. A new, temporary international airport at Gerald's, financed at a cost of EC $51.95m. by the European Union and the British Department for International Development, was completed in 2005; a new terminal building was opened in February and the airport officially opened in July, to be serviced by Windward Islands Airways International (WINAIR). In the longer term, the Government intended to construct a permanent international airport at Thatch Valley. Montserrat is linked to Antigua by a helicopter service, which operates three times a day. The island is also a shareholder in the regional airline, LIAT (based in Antigua and Barbuda), which acquired its troubled rival, Caribbean Star Airlines, in October 2007. In July 2008, upon termination of WINAIR's contract, LIAT and Carib Aviation (also based in Antigua and Barbuda) entered into an agreement to operate scheduled flights into and out of the airport at Gerald's, renamed the John A. Osborne Airport in the same month.

Montserrat Airways Ltd: Plymouth; tel. 491-5342; charter services; subsidiary of Love Air, United Kingdom; Man. Dir NIGEL HARRIS.

Tourism

Since the 1997 volcanic activity, Montserrat has been marketed as an eco-tourism destination. Known as the 'Emerald Isle of the Caribbean', Montserrat is noted for its Irish connections, and for its range of flora and fauna. In 2007 there were 7,746 stay-over tourist arrivals. In that year some 36% of tourist arrivals were from Caribbean countries, 28% from the United Kingdom, 27% from the USA and 5% from Canada. In addition there were 968 excursionists and 273 cruise ship passengers. A large proportion of visitors are estimated to be Montserrat nationals residing overseas. The sector experienced a downturn in 2005 and 2006, partly attributed to increased volcanic activity on the island, when total visitor arrivals were reported as 12,996 and 9,500, respectively. A decline in the number of excursionists making day-trips to the island in these years (falling to 1,509 in 2006) was blamed on the discontinuation of the ferry service between Montserrat and Antigua, and transport links continued to pose a challenge to the sector. Following widespread protests the ferry was reinstated in December 2008. According to provisional figures, tourism earnings totalled EC $20.1m. in 2007.

Montserrat Tourist Board: 7 Farara Plaza, POB 7, Brades; tel. 491-2230; fax 491-7430; e-mail info@montserrattourism.ms; internet www.visitmontserrat.com; f. 1993; Chair. JOHN PONTEEN; Dir of Tourism ERNESTINE CASSELL.

THE PITCAIRN ISLANDS

Introductory Survey

Location, Climate, Language, Religion, Capital

The Pitcairn Islands consist of Pitcairn Island and three uninhabited islands, Henderson, Ducie and Oeno. Pitcairn, situated in the Pacific Ocean about midway between Panama and New Zealand, has an area of 4.5 sq km (1.75 sq miles) and had a population of 53 permanent residents at the end of 2008. Mean monthly temperatures range from 19°C (66°F) in August to 24°C (75°F) in February, and average annual rainfall is 2,000 mm. The official language is English, but most of the islanders use Pitcairnese or Pitkern, a dialect based on 18th-century seafarers' English and Tahitian. The islanders are adherents of the Seventh-day Adventist Church. The chief settlement is Adamstown on Pitcairn Island.

Recent History

Discovered in 1767 and first settled by mutineers of HMS Bounty in 1790, Pitcairn officially became a British settlement in 1887. In 1893 a parliamentary form of government was adopted, and in 1898 responsibility for administration was assumed by the High Commissioner for the Western Pacific. Pitcairn came under the jurisdiction of the Governor of Fiji in 1952, and, from 1970 onwards, of the British High Commissioner in New Zealand acting as Governor, in consultation with an Island Council, presided over by the Island Magistrate (who is elected triennially) and comprising one ex-officio member (the Island Secretary), five elected and three nominated members.

In 1987 the British High Commissioner in Fiji, acting on behalf of Pitcairn, the United Kingdom's last remaining dependency in the South Pacific, joined representatives of the USA, France, New Zealand and six South Pacific island states in signing the South Pacific Regional Environment Protection Convention, the main aim of which is to prevent the dumping of nuclear waste in the region.

In 1989 uninhabited Henderson Island was included on the UNESCO 'World Heritage List'. The island, 168 km (104 miles) east-north-east of Pitcairn, was to be preserved as a bird sanctuary. There are five species of bird unique to the island: the flightless rail or Henderson chicken, the green Henderson fruit dove, the Henderson crake, the Henderson warbler and the Henderson lorikeet. However, concern was expressed in 1994 following claims by scientists studying the island that its unique flora and fauna were threatened by the accidental introduction of foreign plant species by visitors and by an increase in the rat population.

Following some structural changes in the local government of Pitcairn, Steve Christian was elected to the position of Mayor in December 1999, presiding over the Island Council (a role previously fulfilled by the Island Magistrate).

In early 2000 British detectives began an investigation into an alleged rape case on the island. The British team was joined by the New Zealand police force in early 2001, when the case was widened to include 15 alleged sexual assaults, amid reports claiming that sexual abuse, particularly of children, was commonplace on the island. The trial, which was expected to take place in Auckland, New Zealand, would represent the first significant criminal case on Pitcairn since a murder trial in 1897. In November 2000 Auckland's Crown Solicitor, Simon Moore, was appointed Pitcairn's first Public Prosecutor, with the task of deciding whether to bring charges against 20 Pitcairn Islanders. His decision was delayed by the fact that many of the complainants now lived in New Zealand and by the logistical problems of a trial that could potentially involve the entire populace. However, in April 2003 a judicial delegation of eight people visited Pitcairn and nine men on the island were charged with a total of 64 offences, some of which dated back about 40 years. Many islanders expressed serious concern that their community would not be able to manage if the men (who constituted virtually the entire male workforce) were extradited to New Zealand to stand trial. In early June a further four men, all now resident in New Zealand, were charged with a total of 32 offences, including 10 charges of rape, which were alleged to have taken place on Pitcairn between five and 40 years previously. In April 2004 the Supreme Court of Pitcairn (sitting for only the second time in its history, at a special session in Auckland) rejected the accused men's application to be tried on Pitcairn, reiterating that they should stand trial in New Zealand. However, in late June Pitcairn's Court of Appeal (sitting for the first time in its history) overruled this decision and stated that, despite the logistical problems involved, the trial would be conducted on Pitcairn. Meanwhile, lawyers for the accused men argued that the trial should be abandoned as the islanders were all descendants of the Bounty mutineers, who had renounced all allegiance to the British Crown. Their claims that Pitcairn Islanders were not subject to British jurisdiction appeared to be supported by historical documents discovered in London. Moreover, a group of women from Pitcairn issued a public statement claiming that sexual relations between men and girls below the British legal age of consent were commonplace on the island, and not considered to be a criminal offence by either party or by the community as a whole. However, in late September 2004 the trial of seven of the defendants began in converted school premises on Pitcairn. Some 25 lawyers, police officers and journalists travelled to the island, and witnesses in New Zealand gave evidence via live satellite video link. The trial concluded in late October. Six of the seven defendants were found guilty of many of the 51 charges against them. One islander was acquitted of the charges against him. Among those convicted was the Mayor of Pitcairn, Steve Christian, who was found guilty of five counts of rape.

The convicted men, four of whom were given prison sentences of between two and six years while two received non-custodial sentences, began a legal challenge against their convictions in February 2005. Their defence was based on a previous claim that Pitcairn Islanders were not subject to British jurisdiction. In May their appeal was rejected by the Pitcairn Supreme Court, sitting in Auckland, New Zealand. In 2006 the men took their appeal to the United Kingdom's highest court, the Privy Council, arguing that they were not British subjects and that English law did not apply on Pitcairn. In October the judges rejected their appeal, declaring that Pitcairn had been ruled by the Crown as a British possession for more than 100 years, and was thus unable to reject a law affirming it as such. Furthermore, the judges decided that there was absolutely no doubt that the laws on sexual offences applied to the six men. The convicted men helped to build a new prison. Seven New Zealand prison officers were dispatched to staff the new facility.

In 2008 there were continued fears that the serious rift created in the island community by the repercussions of the trial might contribute to an eventual decline in the viability of Pitcairn. In October the Foreign and Commonwealth Office announced that the victims of sexual abuse would be eligible to apply for compensation. The compensation paid would be comparable to amounts awarded in similar cases in the United Kingdom. The closing date for the submission of applications for compensation was 31 March 2009.

At elections to the Island Council in December 2004 five new Council members were elected and Jay Warren, the only defendant to be acquitted in the recent trials, was elected as the island's Mayor. In April 2006 George Fergusson, the newly appointed British High Commissioner to New Zealand, replaced Richard Fell as Governor of Pitcairn, Henderson, Ducie and Oeno Islands. Michael Warren was elected Mayor in December 2007, defeating the incumbent, Jay Warren, and one other candidate; he was re-elected in December 2008.

In early 2007 a retired British police sergeant was recruited by the Foreign and Commonwealth Office on a 12-month contract to police the island.

The British Overseas Territories Act, which took effect in May 2002, granted citizenship rights in the United Kingdom to residents of the Overseas Territories, including Pitcairn. The legislation also entitled Pitcairn Islanders to hold British passports and to work in the United Kingdom and elsewhere in the European Union.

Economic Affairs

The economy has traditionally been based on subsistence gardening, fishing, handicrafts and the sale of postage stamps. Attempts to increase revenue from the island's agricultural output by producing dried fruits (notably bananas, mangoes and pineapples) began in 1999. Diversification of this sector to include production of jam, dried fish and coffee was subsequently under consideration. In early 1999 the Pitcairn Island police and customs office requested that no honey or beeswax be sent to the Territory in order to protect from disease the island's growing honey industry, which was being developed as a source of foreign exchange. Pitcairn honey, which was pronounced to be 'exceptionally pure' by the New Zealand Ministry of Agriculture, began to be exported, largely through internet sales, in late 1999. A new stamp was issued to commemorate the launch of the industry.

A reafforestation scheme, begun in 1963, concentrated on the planting of miro trees, which provide a rosewood suitable for handicrafts. An exclusive economic zone (EEZ) extending 370 km (200 nautical miles) off shore was designated in 1980 and officially declared in 1992. In 1987 the Governor of the islands signed a one-year fishing agreement with Japan, whereby the Japan Tuna Fisheries Co-operative Association was granted a licence to operate vessels within Pitcairn's EEZ. The agreement was subsequently renewed, but lapsed in 1990.

In early 1992 it was reported that significant mineral deposits, formed by underwater volcanoes, had been discovered within the islands' EEZ. The minerals, which were believed to include manganese, iron, copper, zinc, silver and gold, could (if exploited) dramatically affect the Territory's economy.

Development projects have been focused on harbour improvements, power supplies, telecommunications and road-building. A new health clinic was established, with British finance, in 1996.

Major improvements to the jetty and slipway at Bounty Bay and to the Hill of Difficulty road, which leads to the landing area, were carried out in 2005.

Pitcairn's first radio-telephone link was established in 1985, and a new telecommunications unit was installed in 1992. It was hoped that Pitcairn might find an additional source of revenue through the sale of website addresses in early 2000 when the island won a legal victory to gain control of its internet domain name suffix '.pn'. In 2008 television services became available for the first time, and the telephone system was upgraded to give islanders constant internet access. In March of that year, however, an international software security company reported that in per caput terms Pitcairn had become one of the world's worst offenders with regard to the relaying of unsolicited e-mails.

A steady decline in the population, owing mainly to emigration to New Zealand, has been a major problem. In March 2001 a New Zealand company expressed an interest in acquiring development rights on Pitcairn with the intention of establishing fishing and tourism projects. In May 2002 the company's director reportedly announced that the development would begin within the next 12 months, describing plans for a lodge on Pitcairn and for a floating hotel off Oeno Island. However, the British High Commission in Wellington emphasized that any such developments remained subject to the approval of the Pitcairn Island Council, but that the company was welcome to submit proposals.

In August 2004 the British Government announced the provision of US $6.5m. in emergency assistance for the Territory in order to avert a financial crisis. The aid programme included a grant (partly financed by the European Union) to fund improvements to the road between Bounty Bay and Adamstown, which were carried out in mid-2005. In 2006 the British Government provided £1.9m. for a project to repair local infrastructure. Plans for infrastructural development included the building of a breakwater at Bounty Bay. It was hoped that the project, jointly funded by the British Government and the European Development Fund, would make the island more accessible to passenger and cargo ships. Proposals for the use of wind power as an alternative energy source were also discussed.

New Zealand currency is used. There is no taxation (except for small licensing fees on guns and vehicles), and government revenue has been derived mainly from philatelic sales (one-half of current revenue in 1992/93), and from interest earned on investments. In 1998/99 revenue totalled $NZ492,000 and expenditure $NZ667,000. In the early 2000s revenue was estimated to total about $NZ415,000 annually. Capital assistance worth an average of £100,000 annually is received from the United Kingdom. In 2008 exports from Pitcairn to New Zealand were worth $NZ45,437, while imports from that country cost $NZ791,352. Exports to Australia totalled $A21,000 in 2000/01, while imports from Australia, consisting mainly of food, totalled $A7,000 in that year. Pitcairn's imports from the USA totalled US $3.9m. in 2008, while exports to the USA were worth US $477,000.

Hopes have been expressed that the development of the tourism sector might provide some impetus to economic growth in the near future. In particular, Pitcairn's potential for ecotourism has been considered as a possible source of revenue. Other initiatives included the improvement of cruise-ship berthing facilities, which was also under discussion in 2008. In 2005 a museum was constructed on the island to house some of Pitcairn's historical artefacts, including the *Bounty* cannon, which had been raised from Bounty Bay several years previously.

Education

Education is free and compulsory between the age of five and 15 years. Pupils attend the island's school from infant to secondary level. Secondary level students participate in correspondence courses. Students wishing to follow secondary or higher education in New Zealand are eligible for scholarships.

Public Holidays

2009: 1 January (New Year's Day), 23 January (Bounty Day), 10–13 April (Easter), 1 June (Queen's Birthday), 25 December (Christmas Day).

2010: 1 January (New Year's Day), 23 January (Bounty Day), 2–5 April (Easter), 7 June (Queen's Birthday), 25 December (Christmas Day).

Weights and Measures

The metric system is in force.

Statistical Survey

Source: Office of the Governor of Pitcairn, Henderson, Ducie and Oeno Islands, c/o British Consulate-General, Pitcairn Islands Administration, Private Box 105-696, Auckland, New Zealand; tel. (9) 366-0186; fax (9) 366-0187; e-mail pitcairn@iconz.co.nz.

AREA AND POPULATION

Area: 35.5 sq km. *By Island*: Pitcairn 4.35 sq km; Henderson 30.0 sq km; Oeno is less than 1 sq km and Ducie is smaller.

Population: 66 at census of 31 December 1991. *31 December 2008* (permanent residents only, annual census): 53.

Density (Pitcairn only, 31 December 2008): 12.2 per sq km.

Employment (able-bodied men, 2002): 9.

FINANCE

Currency and Exchange Rates: 100 cents = 1 Pitcairn dollar. The Pitcairn dollar is at par with the New Zealand dollar ($NZ). New Zealand currency is usually used.

Budget ($NZ, 1998/99): Revenue 492,000; Expenditure 667,000.

EXTERNAL TRADE

Trade with New Zealand ($NZ '000): *Imports:* 231.7 in 2006; 1,077.5 in 2007; 791.4 in 2008. *Exports:* 48.6 in 2006; 36.2 in 2007; 45.4 in 2008.

Trade with the USA (US $ '000): *Imports:* 1,365 in 2006; 1,895 in 2007; 3,879 in 2008. *Exports:* 105 in 2006; 89 in 2007; 477 in 2008.

TRANSPORT

Road Traffic (motor vehicles, 2002): Passenger vehicles 29 (two-wheeled 1, three-wheeled 6, four-wheeled 23); Tractors 3; Bulldozer 1; Digger 1.

Shipping: *Local Vessels* (communally-owned open surf boats, 2000): 3. *International Shipping Arrivals* (visits by passing vessels, 1996): Ships 51; Yachts 30.

COMMUNICATIONS

Telephones (2002): a party-line service with 15 telephones in use; 2 public telephones; 2 digital telephones. Most homes also have VHF radio.

Directory

THE CONSTITUTION AND GOVERNMENT

Pitcairn is a British settlement under the British Settlements Act 1887, although the islanders reckon their recognition as a colony from 1838, when a British naval captain instituted a Constitution with universal adult suffrage and a code of law. That system served as the basis of the 1904 reformed Constitution and the wider reforms of 1940, effected by Order in Council. The Constitution of 1940 provides for a Governor of Pitcairn, Henderson, Ducie and Oeno Islands (who, since 1970, is concurrently the British High Commissioner in New Zealand), representing the British monarch. A Mayor is elected every three years to preside over the Island Council. The Local Government Ordinance 1964 constituted an Island Council of 10 members: in addition to the Mayor, five members are elected annually; three are nominated for terms of one year (the Governor appoints two of these members at his own discretion); and the Island Secretary is an ex-officio member. In addition to the Island Council there is an Island Magistrate who presides over the Magistrate's Court of Pitcairn, and is appointed by the Governor. Liaison between the Governor and the Island Council is conducted by a Commissioner, usually based in the Office of the British Consulate-General in Auckland, New Zealand.

Customary land tenure provides for a system of family ownership (based upon the original division of land in the 18th century). Alienation to foreigners is not forbidden by law, but in practice this is difficult. There is no taxation, and public works are performed by the community.

Governor of Pitcairn, Henderson, Ducie and Oeno Islands: GEORGE FERGUSSON (British High Commissioner in New Zealand—took office April 2006).

Office of the Governor of Pitcairn, Henderson, Ducie and Oeno Islands: c/o British High Commission, 44 Hill St, POB 1812, Wellington, New Zealand; tel. (4) 924-2888; fax (4) 473-4982; e-mail ppa.mailbox@fco.gov.uk; Gov. GEORGE FERGUSSON; Deputy Gov. GINNY SILVA; Commissioner LESLIE JAQUES.

Pitcairn Islands Office: Private Box 105-696, Auckland, New Zealand; tel. (9) 366-0186; fax (9) 366-0187; e-mail admin@pitcairn.gov.pn; internet www.government.pn.

UNITED KINGDOM OVERSEAS TERRITORIES

Island Council
(April 2009)

Mayor: MICHAEL WARREN.
Island Secretary (ex officio): HEATHER MENZIES.
Government Treasurer: NADINE CHRISTIAN.
Island Auditor: MIKE LUPTON.

Other Members: BRENDA CHRISTIAN, DAVE BROWN, JACQUI CHRISTIAN, TURI GRIFFITHS, SIMON YOUNG (Governor's Appointee).
Elections to the Island Council take place each December. Meetings are held at the Court House in Adamstown.
Office of the Island Secretary: The Square, Adamstown.

JUDICIAL SYSTEM
Chief Justice: CHARLES BLACKIE.
Island Magistrate: SIMON YOUNG.
Public Prosecutor: SIMON MOORE.
Public Defender: PAUL DACRE.

RELIGION
Christianity
Since 1887 many of the islanders have been adherents of the Seventh-day Adventist Church.
Pastor: JOHN O'MALLEY, SDA Church, The Square, POB 24, Adamstown; fax 872-7620/9763.

THE PRESS
Pitcairn Miscellany: e-mail admin@miscellany.pn; internet www.miscellany.pn; monthly four-page mimeographed news sheet; f. 1959; edited by the Education Officer; circulation 1,400 in 2002; Editor P. FOLEY.

FINANCE, TRADE AND INDUSTRY
There are no formal banking facilities. A co-operative trading store was established in 1967. Industry consists of handicrafts, and the production of honey and dried fruit.

TRANSPORT
Roads
There are approximately 14 km (9 miles) of dirt road suitable for two-, three- and four-wheeled vehicles. In 2002 Pitcairn had one conventional motor cycle, six three-wheelers and 22 four-wheeled motor cycles, one four-wheel-drive motor car, three tractors, a five-ton digger and a bulldozer; traditional wheelbarrows are used occasionally. In 1995 a total of £79,000 was received from individual donors for work to improve the road leading to the jetty at Bounty Bay. Work to concrete the road, known as the Hill of Difficulty, was completed in mid-2006.

Shipping
No passenger ships have called regularly since 1968, and sea communications are restricted to cargo vessels operating between New Zealand and Panama, which make scheduled calls at Pitcairn three times a year, as well as a number of unscheduled calls. A shipping route between French Polynesia and Pitcairn was opened in 2006. There are also occasional visits by private yachts. The number of cruise ships calling at Pitcairn increased in the late 1990s, and 10 such vessels visited the island in 2000 (compared with just two or three annually in previous years). Two cruise ships called at Pitcairn in April 2005 before stopping at Oeno Island for the tourists to witness a solar eclipse near the island. Bounty Bay, near Adamstown, is the only possible landing site, and there are no docking facilities; in mid-2007 plans to build a breakwater at Bounty Bay were announced. In 1993 the jetty derrick was refitted with an hydraulic system. The islanders have three aluminium open surf boats. Major work to repair the slipway and jetty was carried out by the islanders in mid-2005.

SAINT HELENA AND DEPENDENCIES

Saint Helena

Introduction

Saint Helena lies in the South Atlantic Ocean, about 1,930 km (1,200 miles) from the south-west coast of Africa. Governed by the British East India Co from 1673, the island was brought under the direct control of the British Crown in 1834. At general elections held in September 1976, the Saint Helena Progressive Party, advocating the retention of close economic links with the United Kingdom, won 11 of the 12 elective seats in the Legislative Council. This policy has been advocated by almost all members of the Legislative Council brought to office at subsequent general elections (normally held every four years) up to and including that held in August 2005.

In October 1981 a commission was established by the Governor to review the island's constitutional arrangements. The commission reported in 1983 that it was unable to identify any proposal for constitutional change that would command the support of the majority of the islanders. In 1988, however, a formal Constitution was introduced to replace the Order in Council and Royal Instructions under which Saint Helena had been governed since 1967. The Constitution entered into force on 1 January 1989.

Owing to the limited range of economic activity on the island (see below), Saint Helena is dependent on development and budgetary aid from the United Kingdom. Since 1981, when the United Kingdom adopted the British Nationality Act, which effectively removed the islanders' traditional right of residence in Britain, opportunities for overseas employment have been limited to contract work, principally in Ascension and the Falkland Islands. In 1992 an informal 'commission on citizenship' was established by a number of islanders to examine Saint Helena's constitutional relationship with the United Kingdom, with special reference to the legal validity of the 1981 legislation as applied to Saint Helena. In April 1997 the commission obtained a legal opinion from a former Attorney-General of Saint Helena to the effect that the application of the Act to the population of Saint Helena was in contravention of the Royal Charter establishing British sovereignty in 1673. The commission indicated that it intended to pursue the matter further. In July 1997 private legislation was introduced in the British Parliament to extend full British nationality to 'persons having connections with' Saint Helena. In the following month the British Government indicated that it was considering arrangements under which islanders would be granted employment and residence rights in the United Kingdom. In February 1998, following a conference held in London of representatives of the British Dependent Territories, it was announced that a review was to take place of the future constitutional status of these territories, and of means whereby their economies might be strengthened. It was subsequently agreed that the operation of the 1981 legislation in relation to Saint Helena would also be reviewed. As an immediate measure to ameliorate the isolation of Saint Helena, the British Government conceded permission for civilian air landing rights on Ascension Island, which, with the contemplated construction of a small airstrip on Saint Helena, could facilitate the future development of the island as a tourist destination. In March 1999 the British Government published draft legislation proposing that full British nationality, including the right of abode in the United Kingdom, was to be restored to the population of Saint Helena and its dependencies, under the reorganization of the British Dependent Territories as the United Kingdom Overseas Territories. However, this had still not been implemented by July 2000, when the citizens took their case to the UN Committee on Decolonization, seeking British passports, a new constitution and administration as a Crown dependency rather than as a colony. In May 2002 the British Overseas Territories Act, which granted British citizenship to the people of the Overseas Territories, including Saint Helena and dependencies, came into effect, having received royal assent in February. Under the new legislation these citizens acquired the right to hold a British passport and to work in the United Kingdom, but not the other benefits of citizenship (such as reduced fees for education). The Act restored those rights removed by the British Nationality Act of 1981. In September 2002 an independent constitutional adviser visited Saint

UNITED KINGDOM OVERSEAS TERRITORIES — *Saint Helena and Dependencies*

Helena and consulted extensively with the island's residents on the options for future constitutional development. A consultative poll on the draft for a new constitution, which, *inter alia*, proposed the creation of a ministerial form of government, took place on 25 May 2005. The draft document was rejected by 52.6% of voters. Concern was expressed at the low rate of voter participation, recorded at 43% of registered voters. Nevertheless, it was indicated that elements of the rejected constitution were expected to be adopted, including a change to the number of constituencies on Saint Helena. The British Government subsequently stated that it wished to identify any possible improvements to the existing Constitution in conjunction with the new Executive Council, which took office following the elections held on 31 August 2005. In April 2008 Governor Gurr issued a consultation paper regarding a new draft constitution for Saint Helena and its dependencies. He stated that he wished to submit the draft to the Legislative Council before the general election scheduled for July 2009.

On 4 February 2002 a referendum was held by the Government in Saint Helena, Ascension Island, the Falkland Islands and on RMS *Saint Helena* on future access to the island; 71.6% of votes cast were in favour of the construction of an airport (28.4% opting for a shipping alternative). Plans for the airport and associated commercial developments were cancelled in February 2003, on the grounds of unprofitability and environmental concerns; however, following protests by islanders, in April the Executive Council invited tenders for the construction of the airport. In late January 2006 the Airport Development Bill was presented to the Legislative Council for approval and the following month it was announced that three consortia had pre-qualified to contest for the contract to construct the airport. The project was expected to cost some £40m., of which the British Government was reported to have agreed to contribute some £26.3m., approximately equal to the cost of replacing the mail ship in 2010. The airport, to be located on the eastern coast of the island, was scheduled to be fully functional by 2012. Construction was to begin in 2008. It was hoped that the airport would bring strong benefits to the local economy, particularly through the development of tourism. However, as a result of the global recession and the subsequent change in the United Kingdom's economic climate, the British Department for International Development (DfID) announced in December that the project would be postponed.

In May 2008 it was reported that the United Kingdom Government had registered claims with the UN Commission for the Limits of the Continental Shelf to extend its territorial waters surrounding Saint Helena, Ascension Island and Tristan da Cunha. It was hoped that these areas of sea-bed could be secured with the possibility of drilling for petroleum, gas and mineral resources in future years.

The economy of Saint Helena is heavily reliant on British aid. In 2006/07 the assistance totalled £14.76m. and consisted of direct budgetary aid (£6.9m.), an annual subsidy for the operation of the RMS *St Helena* (£3.1m.) and support for bilateral development assistance. Budget revenue totalled £21.30m. in 2006/07, and expenditure in that year was £16.96m. DfID granted Saint Helena an additional £4m. for expenditure in 2009/10, while in February 2009 the European Development Fund proposed the allocation of €16.6m. to Saint Helena and its dependencies. According to official estimates, Saint Helena's gross national product (GNP) totalled £15.6m. in 2005/06. Gross domestic product (GDP) was estimated to have decreased, in real terms, by an annual average of 1.6% during 1999/2000–2005/06; a decline of 10.1%, in real terms, was recorded for 2005/06. The population declined by an annual average of 3.2% during 1999/2000–2005/06, and, largely as a result of this, per-capita GDP increased, in real terms, by an annual average of 1.9% over the same period. The annual rate of inflation averaged 3.8% in 2000–07, and the rate, influenced to a large extent by the prevailing rates in its two most important trading partners, South Africa and the United Kingdom, has remained between 3% and 5% in recent years. In 2004 the rate of unemployment (including community work scheme placements) was estimated at 7.6%.

Saint Helena's persistently high rate of unemployment has resulted in widespread reliance on welfare benefit payments and a concurrent decline in living standards for the majority of the population (although an increase in economic migration in recent years has done much to alleviate this situation). Evidence of underlying social discontent emerged in April 1997, when minor public disorders broke out in Jamestown following the refusal of the Governor (who exercises full executive and legislative authority in Saint Helena) to accept the nomination of a prominent critic of government policy to the post of Director of the Department of Social Welfare. Two members of the Executive Council (which acts in an advisory capacity) resigned in protest at the action of the Governor, who subsequently announced that elections to the Legislative Council were to take place in July. Following the elections, held on 9 July, the Governor agreed to the nomination as Chairman of the Education Committee of the candidate he had previously refused to nominate to the Social Welfare Directorate. The newly elected Legislative Council became the first in which members were to receive a fixed salary to serve on a full-time basis, relinquishing any other employment during their term of office.

At the 1998 census 10.2% of the employed labour force were engaged in agriculture and fishing, 19.7% in industry (predominantly construction), 65.6% in services and 4.5% in unspecified activities. Employment in the public sector was estimated to be at 55% of the working population in 2004. In 2000 exports of fish (which, apart from a small quantity of coffee, is the only commodity exported) totalled 43.1 metric tons (compared with 27.2 tons in 1985) and export earnings from this source amounted to £113,000. Improvements in vessel capacity have helped increase fish exports in recent years. An increase in overseas philatelic sales has also generated significant revenues (£80,000 in 2006/07), as has a fledgling tourist industry (£426,000 in 2005/06). Timber production is being developed, with sales amounting to 390 cu m in 1999. However, a large proportion of the labour force (approximately 1,000) must seek employment overseas, principally on Ascension and the Falkland Islands. In March 2001 551 Saint Helenians were working on Ascension, and in December 1999 371 were working on the Falkland Islands; according to the British Foreign and Commonwealth Office, approximately 1,700 members of the work-force were employed offshore at the beginning of 2005.

Saint Helena is of interest to naturalists for its rare flora and fauna. The island has about 40 species of flora that are unique to Saint Helena.

Statistical Survey

Source (unless otherwise indicated): Development and Economic Planning Dept, Government of Saint Helena, Saint Helena Island, STHL 1ZZ; tel. 2777; fax 2830; e-mail depd@helanta.sh.

AREA AND POPULATION

Area: 122 sq km (47 sq miles).

Population: 5,644 at census of 22 February 1987; 5,157 (males 2,612, females 2,545) at census of 8 March 1998; 4,255 (males 2,166, females 2,089) at census of 10 February 2008 (Source: UN, *Population and Vital Statistics Report*).

Density (at 2008 census): 34.9 per sq km.

Principal Town (UN estimate, incl. suburbs): Jamestown (capital), population 1,787 in mid-2003 (Source: UN, *World Urbanization Prospects: The 2003 Revision*).

Births and Deaths (2006): Registered live births 35; Registered deaths 52. *2005:* Crude birth rate 8.4 per 1,000; Crude death rate 9.7 per 1,000.

Economically Active Population (1998 census): Agriculture, hunting and related activities 187; Fishing 20; Manufacturing 87; Electricity, gas and water 48; Construction 267; Wholesale and retail trade 344; Hotels and restaurants 24; Transport, storage and communications 181; Financial intermediation 17; Real estate, renting and business activities 7; Public administration and defence 293; Education 187; Health and social work 196; Other community services 87; Private household 74; Extra-territorial organizations 11; *Total employed* 2,037 (males 1,146; females 891); Unemployed 449 (males 290; females 159); *Total labour force* 2,486 (males 1,436, females 1,050). *2004:* Employed 1,813; Unemployed (incl. community work scheme) 150; Total labour force 1,963. *Mid-2005* (estimates): Agriculture, etc. 1,000; Total labour force 3,000 (Source: FAO).

AGRICULTURE, ETC.

Livestock (2006 livestock census): Cattle 865; Sheep 1,007; Pigs 654; Goats 630; Donkeys 110; Poultry 7,505 (Source: FAO).

Fishing (metric tons, live weight, including Ascension and Tristan da Cunha, 2006): Skipjack tuna 88; Yellowfin tuna 363; Tristan da Cunha rock lobster 464; Total catch (incl. others) 1,120. Figures include catches of rock lobster from Tristan da Cunha during the 12 months ending 30 April of the year stated. (Source: FAO*World Urbanization Prospects: The 2003 Revision*).

FINANCE

Currency and Exchange Rate: 100 pence (pennies) = 1 Saint Helena pound (£). *Sterling, Dollar and Euro Equivalents* (31 December 2008): £1 sterling = Saint Helena £1; US $1 = 68.60 pence; €1 = 95.47 pence; £10 = $14.58 = €10.47. *Average Exchange Rate* (£ per US dollar): 0.5435 in 2006; 0.4998 in 2007; 0.5412 in 2008. Note: The Saint Helena pound is at par with the pound sterling.

UNITED KINGDOM OVERSEAS TERRITORIES

Budget (2006/07): *Revenue:* £21.30m. (United Kingdom assistance £14.76m., Local revenue £6.5m.); *Expenditure:* £16.96m.

Gross Domestic Product (£ '000 at constant 2002 prices): 11,869 in 2003/04; 12,466 in 2004/05; 11,210 in 2005/06.

Money Supply (£ '000, 2006/07): Currency in circulation 3,618 (excl. commemorative coins valued at 514) (Source: ILO).

Cost of Living (Consumer Price Index; base: 2000 = 100): 115.8 in 2005; 120.8 in 2006; 126.4 in 2007 (Source: ILO).

EXTERNAL TRADE

Principal Commodities: *Imports* (1994/95, £ '000): Total 5,076 (Food and live animals 27.9%; Beverages and tobacco 8.5%; Mineral fuels, lubricants, etc. 8.5%; Chemicals and related materials 11.4%; Basic manufactures 12.7%; Machinery and transport equipment 11.7%; Miscellaneous manufactured articles 13.0%; Other commodities and transactions 3.3%); *Exports* (2000): Fish £113,000; Coffee n.a. Trade is mainly with the United Kingdom and South Africa. *2005/06:* Imports f.o.b. £7.8m.; Exports £0.3m.

TRANSPORT

Road Traffic (2005): 1,916 licensed vehicles.

Shipping: *Vessels Entered* (1999): 214. *Merchant Fleet* (31 December 2007): 3 vessels; Total displacement 3,657 grt (Source: Lloyd's Register-Fairplay, *World Fleet Statistics*).

COMMUNICATIONS MEDIA

Radio Receivers ('000 in use, 1997): 3 (Source: UNESCO, *Statistical Yearbook*).

Television Subscribers (April 2007): 1,161.

Telephones (main lines in use, April 2007): 2,283.

EDUCATION

Primary (2006/07): 2 schools; 14 teachers; 115 pupils.
Amalgamated School (2006/07): 1 school; 15 teachers; 116 pupils.
Intermediate (2006/07): 2 schools; 17 teachers; 119 pupils.
Secondary (2006/07): 1 school; 42 teachers; 324 pupils.

Directory

The Constitution

The Saint Helena Constitution Order 1988, which entered into force on 1 January 1989, replaced the Order in Council and Royal Instructions of 1 January 1967. Executive and legislative authority is reserved to the British Crown, but is ordinarily exercised by others in accordance with provisions of the Constitution. The Constitution provides for the office of Governor and Commander-in-Chief of Saint Helena and its dependencies (Ascension Island and Tristan da Cunha). The Legislative Council for Saint Helena consists of the Speaker, three ex officio members (the Chief Secretary, the Financial Secretary and the Attorney-General) and 12 elected members; the Executive Council is presided over by the Governor and consists of the above ex officio members and five of the elected members of the Legislative Council. The elected members of the legislature choose from among themselves those who will also be members of the Executive Council. Although a member of both the Legislative Council and the Executive Council, the Attorney-General does not vote on either. Members of the legislature provide the Chairmen and a majority of the members of the various Council Committees. Executive and legislative functions for the dependencies are exercised by the Governor (although an advisory Island Council was inaugurated on Ascension in November 2002).

The Government

(April 2009)

Governor and Commander-in-Chief: ANDREW GURR.
Chief Secretary: ANDREW WELLS.
Financial Secretary: VIRGINIA GRACE.
Chairmen of Council Committees:
Agriculture and Natural Resources: STEDSON GRAHAM FRANCIS.
Education: ERIC WILLIAM BENJAMIN.
Employment and Social Security: BRIAN WILLIAM ISAAC.

Saint Helena and Dependencies

Public Health and Social Services: WILLIAM ERIC DRABBLE.
Public Works and Services: BERNICE ALICIA OLSSON.
Speaker of the Legislative Council: ERIC GEORGE.
Business Finance Manager: CHERIE DILLON.

GOVERNMENT OFFICES

Office of the Governor: The Castle, Jamestown, STHL 1ZZ; tel. 2555; fax 2598; e-mail pagovernor@sainthelena.gov.sh; internet www.sainthelena.gov.sh.

Office of the Chief Secretary: The Castle, Jamestown, STHL 1ZZ; tel. 2555; fax 2598; e-mail ocs@helanta.sh.

Political Organizations

There are no political parties in Saint Helena. Elections to the Legislative Council, the latest of which took place in August 2005, are conducted on a non-partisan basis.

Judicial System

The legal system is derived from English common law and statutes. There are four Courts on Saint Helena: the Supreme Court, the Magistrate's Court, the Small Debts Court and the Juvenile Court. Provision exists for the Saint Helena Court of Appeal, which can sit in Jamestown or London.

Chief Justice: CHARLES W. EKINS.
Attorney-General: KEN BADDON.
Sheriff: G. P. MUSK.

Religion

The majority of the population belongs to the Anglican Communion.

CHRISTIANITY

The Anglican Communion

Anglicans are adherents of the Anglican Church of Southern Africa (formerly the Church of the Province of Southern Africa). The Metropolitan of the Province is the Archbishop of Cape Town, South Africa. St Helena forms a single diocese.

Bishop of Saint Helena: Rt Rev. JOHN SALT, Bishopsholme, POB 62, Saint Helena, STHL 1ZZ; tel. and fax 4471; e-mail bishop@helanta.sh; diocese f. 1859; has jurisdiction over the islands of Saint Helena and Ascension.

The Roman Catholic Church

The Church is represented in Saint Helena, Ascension and Tristan da Cunha by a Mission, established in August 1986. There were an estimated 87 adherents in the islands at 31 December 2000.

Superior: Rev. Fr MICHAEL MCPARTLAND (also Prefect Apostolic of the Falkland Islands); normally visits Tristan da Cunha once a year and Ascension Island two or three times a year; Rev. Fr MICHAEL DAVID GRIFFITHS, Sacred Heart Church, Jamestown, STHL 1ZZ; tel. and fax 2535.

Other Christian Churches

The Salvation Army, Seventh-day Adventists, Baptists, New Apostolics and Jehovah's Witnesses are active on the island.

BAHÁ'Í FAITH

There is a small Bahá'í community on the island.

The Press

St Helena Herald: Saint Helena News Media Board, Broadway House, Jamestown, STHL 1ZZ; tel. 2612; fax 2802; e-mail sthelena.herald@cwimail.sh; internet www.news.co.sh; f. 1986; govt-sponsored, independent; weekly; Chief Exec. VERNON QUICKFALL; circ. 1,600.

The St Helena Independent: St Helena Media Productions Ltd, 2nd Floor, Association Hall, Main St, Jamestown, STHL 1ZZ; tel. 2660; e-mail independent@cwimail.sh; internet www.saint.fm; f. 2005; independent; weekly.

Broadcasting and Communications

TELECOMMUNICATIONS

Cable & Wireless (St Helena) PLC: POB 2, Bishops Rooms, Jamestown, STHL 1ZZ; tel. 2155; fax 2206; e-mail webmaster@helanta.sh; internet www.cw.com/sthelena; f. 1899; provides national and international telecommunications.

BROADCASTING

Cable & Wireless PLC: The Moon, Jamestown, STHL 1ZZ; tel. 2200; f. 1995; provides a three-channel television service 24 hours daily from five satellite channels.

Saint FM: Association Hall, Main St, Jamestown, STHL 1ZZ; tel. 2660; e-mail fm@helanta.sh; internet www.saint.fm; f. 2004; independent FM radio station; also broadcasts on Ascension Island, Falkland Islands and Tristan da Cunha; Dir MIKE OLSSON.

Radio St Helena: Saint Helena Information Office, Broadway House, Jamestown, STHL 1ZZ; tel. 4669; fax 4542; e-mail radio.sthelena@helanta.sh; internet www.sthelena.se/radiosth.htm; independent service; providing broadcasts for 24 hours per day; local programming and relays of British Broadcasting Corporation World Service programmes; Station Man. TONY LEO.

Finance

BANK

Bank of Saint Helena: Post Office Bldg, Main St, Jamestown, STHL 1ZZ; tel. 2390; fax 2553; e-mail info@sthelenabank.com; internet www.sainthelenabank.com; f. 2004; replaced the Government Savings Bank; total assets £32,992,274 (31 March 2007); 1 br. on Ascension; Chair. LYN THOMAS; Man. Dir ROSEMARY BARGO.

INSURANCE

Solomon & Co PLC: Jamestown, STHL 1ZZ; tel. 2682; fax 2755; e-mail insurance@solomons.co.sh; internet www.solomons-sthelena.com; Solomon & Co operated an insurance agency on behalf of Royal SunAlliance Insurance Group during 1933–2002, until the latter co withdrew its interest from Saint Helena; negotiations for the foundation of a mutual insurance company on the island commenced in 2004; CEO TONY GREEN.

Trade and Industry

GOVERNMENT AGENCY

St Helena Development Agency: 2 Main St, POB 117, Jamestown, STHL 1ZZ; tel. 2920; fax 2166; e-mail enquiries@shda.co.sh; internet www.shda.helanta.sh; f. 1995; Chair. GEORGE STEVENS; Man. Dir LINDA HOUSTON.

CHAMBER OF COMMERCE

St Helena Chamber of Commerce: Jamestown, STHL 1ZZ; tel. 2258; fax 2598; internet www.chamber.co.sh.

CO-OPERATIVE

St Helena Growers' Co-operative Society: Jamestown, STHL 1ZZ; tel. and fax 2511; vegetable marketing; also suppliers of agricultural tools, seeds and animal feeding products; 108 mems (1999); Chair. STEDSON FRANCIS; Sec. PETER W. THORPE.

Transport

There are no railways in Saint Helena.

ROADS

In 2002 there were 118 km of bitumen-sealed roads, and a further 20 km of earth roads, which can be used by motor vehicles only in dry weather. All roads have steep gradients and sharp bends.

SHIPPING

St Helena Line Ltd: Andrew Weir Shipping, Dexter House, 2 Royal Mint Court, London, EC3N 4XX, United Kingdom; tel. (20) 7265-0808; fax (20) 7481-4784; internet www.aws.co.uk; internet www.rms-st-helena.com; five-year govt contract renewed in August 2006; service subsidized by the British Govt by £1.5m. annually; operates two-monthly passenger/cargo services by the RMS *St Helena* to and from the United Kingdom and Cape Town, South Africa, calling at the Canary Islands, Ascension Island and Vigo, Spain, and once a year at Tristan da Cunha; also operates programme of shuttle services between Saint Helena and Ascension Island and the St Helena Liner Shipping Service; Chair. GARRY HOPCROFT.

Tourism

Although Saint Helena possesses flora and fauna of considerable interest to naturalists, as well as the house (now an important museum) in which the French Emperor Napoleon I spent his final years in exile, the remoteness of the island, which is a two-day sea voyage from Ascension Island, has inhibited the development of tourism. The construction of an airport on Saint Helena, which was scheduled to be fully operational by 2012, should greatly increase the island's accessibility to the limited number of visitors that can currently be accommodated. A total of 8,968 tourists visited Saint Helena in 1997. There are three hotels and a range of self-catering facilities.

St Helena Tourist Office: The Canister, Main St, Jamestown, STHL 1ZZ; tel. 2158; fax 2159; e-mail enquiries@tourism.gov.sh; internet www.sthelenatourism.com; f. 1998; provides general information about the island; Dir PAMELA YOUNG.

Ascension

The island of Ascension lies in the South Atlantic Ocean, 1,131 km (703 miles) north-west of Saint Helena, of which it is a dependency. Discovered by Portuguese navigators in 1501, the island is a semi-barren, rocky peak of purely volcanic origin. Britain took possession of Ascension in 1815, in connection with Napoleon's detention on Saint Helena. The island is famous for green turtles, and is also a breeding ground for the sooty tern. Under an agreement with the British Government, US forces occupy Wideawake Airfield, which is used as a tracking station for guided missiles. Ascension has no indigenous population, being inhabited by British and US military personnel, *émigré* workers and government administrative staff from Saint Helena. There are also a number of expatriate civilian personnel of Merlin Communications International (MCI), which operates the British Broadcasting Corporation (BBC) Overseas World Service Atlantic relay station, Cable and Wireless PLC, which provides international communications services and operates the 'Ariane' satellite tracking station of the European Space Agency, and staff providing the island's common services. The island is an important communications centre. Ascension does not raise its own finance; the costs of administering the island are borne collectively by the user organizations, supplemented by income from philatelic sales. The island is developing a modest eco-tourism sector. Some revenue, which is remitted to the Saint Helena administration, is derived from fishing licences (estimated to be around £1m. in 1999). Facilities on Ascension underwent rapid development in 1982 to serve as a major staging post for British vessels and aircraft on their way to the Falkland Islands (q.v.), and the island has continued to provide a key link in British supply lines to the South Atlantic. On 31 March 2001 the joint venture between the BBC and Cable and Wireless to provide public services to the island was dissolved. The Ascension Island Government took over responsibility for health and education, the Ascension Island Works and Services Agency, a statutory body, was established to maintain transport and infrastructure, and any remaining services were taken over by the new Ascension Island Commercial Services Ltd (AICS) company. AICS was jointly owned by the Ascension Islands Government, the BBC and Cable and Wireless and had the declared aim of privatizing the new enterprises by April 2002. This development was regarded as reorientating public-service provision towards the demands of the resident population rather than the needs of those organizations using the island. The privatization process was ongoing in 2008.

Dissent developed among the resident population in June 2002, following the decision of the Foreign and Commonwealth Office to impose taxes for the first time on the island (including income tax, property tax and tax on alcohol and tobacco). The primary objection of the population was that this was 'taxation without representation', as the islanders do not possess the right to vote, to own property or even to live on the island. The Governor responded with plans to introduce a democratically elected council that would have a purely advisory function and no decision-making powers, claiming that the islanders initially needed to acquire experience of governance. On 22–23 August a vote on the democratic options took place on the island, with 95% of the votes cast being in favour of an Island Council, rather than an Inter-Island Council plus Island Council structure; 50% of those eligible to vote did so. The Council was to be chaired by the Administrator, on behalf of the Governor, and was to comprise seven elected members, the Attorney-General, the Director of Finance and one or two appointed members. Elections for councillors took place in October, and the Island Council was inaugurated in the following month. A joint consultative council was also to be established, with representatives from both Ascension and Saint Helena, in order to develop policy relating to economic development and tourism common to both islands.

The British Government subsequently stated its intention to enact legislation granting the islanders right of abode and the right to own property. However, following a visit to the island by a delegation of British officials in November 2005, it was announced that the proposed reforms would not be carried out. The British Government cited its reluctance fundamentally to change the nature of the territory and also maintained that granting such rights would impose greater financial liabilities on British taxpayers and would bring an unacceptable level of risk to the United Kingdom. In January 2006 The Island Council announced that it intended to seek clarification regarding the legality of the British Government's decision and reiterated its commitment to securing the islanders' right to abode and the right to purchase property.

In May 2007 the Island Council was suspended and the Ascension Island Advisory Group was established to provide advice to the Administrator on certain policy issues. The suspension was expected to remain in place until May 2008, after which elections would be held. It was anticipated that the Advisory Group would meet on a monthly basis, to be supplemented by informal meetings as necessary. Consultation papers were to be issued to encourage the people of Ascension to participate in the decision-making process. In October elections were held and a new Island Council was sworn in later that month. Meanwhile, in May it was reported that the United Kingdom Government had submitted a claim to the UN Commission for the Limits of the Continental Shelf regarding the extension of its territorial waters around Ascension Island (see Saint Helena Recent History).

As of early 2004 Ascension Island had a balanced fiscal budget, although with minimal reserves. Government expenditure funds one school, one hospital (offering limited services), police and judicial services; these services are provided without charge to local taxpayers. The Saint Helena-based firm Solomons has a primary role in the incipient private sector and a sports-fishing industry was in the process of being established. In early 2009 the European Development Fund was considering awarding a grant of some €16.6m. to Saint Helena and its dependencies for infrastructure and economic development projects, including a road improvement initiative for Ascension Island.

Area: 88 sq km (34 sq miles).

Population: There are no indigenous inhabitants, but some 1,100 personnel and employees and their families are permanently resident (mostly nationals of Saint Helena, with some 200 UK nationals and 150 US nationals).

Budget: (2003/04, £ million, year ending 31 March, estimates): Revenue 4.3; Expenditure 4.0 (Recurrent expenditure 3.3, Capital expenditure 0.7). *2008/09* (Consolidated Fund, £ million, year ending 31 March): Revenue 6.17.

Government: The Governor of Saint Helena, in his capacity as Governor of Ascension Island, is represented by an Administrator. Two advisory groups, one comprising senior managers of resident organizations, and one comprising their employees' representatives, assist the Administrator, who also has professional financial and technical advisers. In November 2002 an advisory Island Council, chaired by the Administrator and comprising seven elected members, the Attorney-General, the Director of Finance and two appointed members, was inaugurated.

Administrator: ROSS DENNYThe Residency, Georgetown Ascension, ASCN 1ZZ; tel. 7000; fax 6152; e-mail aigenquiries@ascension.gov.ac; internet www.ascension-island.gov.ac.

Magistrate: (vacant).

Justices of the Peace: G. F. THOMAS, A. FOWLER, J. PETERS, C. PARKER-YON.

Religion: Ascension forms part of the Anglican diocese of Saint Helena, which normally provides a resident chaplain who is also available to minister to members of other denominations. There is a Roman Catholic chapel served by visiting priests, as well as a small mosque.

Transport: *Road vehicles* (1998): 830. *Shipping* (1998): ships entered and cleared 105. The St Helena Line Ltd (q.v.) serves the island with a two-monthly passenger/cargo service between Cardiff, in the United Kingdom, and Cape Town, in South Africa. A vessel under charter to the British Ministry of Defence visits the island monthly on its United Kingdom–Falkland Islands service. A US freighter from Cape Canaveral calls at three-month intervals. *Air services*: A twice-weekly Royal Air Force Tristar service between the United Kingdom and the Falkland Islands transits Ascension Island both southbound and northbound. There is a weekly US Air Force military service linking the Patrick Air Force Base in Florida with Ascension Island, via Antigua and Barbuda.

Tourism: Small-scale eco-tourism is encouraged, although accommodation on the island is limited and all visits require written permission from the Administrator. Access is available by twice-weekly flights operated from the United Kingdom by the Royal Air Force (see above), and by the RMS *St Helena* (see Saint Helena—Shipping).

Tristan da Cunha

The island of Tristan da Cunha lies in the South Atlantic Ocean, 2,800 km (1,740 miles) west of Cape Town, South Africa. It comes under the jurisdiction of Saint Helena, 2,300 km (1,430 miles) to the north-east. Also in the group are Inaccessible Island, 37 km (23 miles) west of Tristan; the three Nightingale Islands, 37 km (23 miles) south; and Gough Island (Diego Alvarez), 425 km (264 miles) south. Tristan da Cunha was discovered in 1506, but remained uninhabited until occupied by US whalers during 1790–1811. The British Navy took possession of the island in 1817. Tristan's population was evacuated in 1961, after volcanic eruptions, but was resettled in 1963. The island's major source of revenue derives from a royalty for a crayfishing concession, supplemented by income from the sale of postage stamps and other philatelic items, and handicrafts. The fishing industry and the administration employ all of the working population. Some 20 power boats operating from the island land their catches to a fish-freezing factory built by the Atlantic Islands Development Corpn, whose fishing concession was transferred in January 1997 to a new holder, Premier Fishing (Pty) Ltd, of Cape Town, and later to another South African company, Ovenstone (Pty) Ltd. In February 2008 a fire destroyed the factory, along with the island's power plant; a new factory was due to be completed in mid-2009. The island's harbour was also renovated in 2008, in a project paid for by the British Department for International Development (DfID), and undertaken with the help of Royal Engineers from the United Kingdom. Budget estimates for 2005/06 projected a deficit of £147,507. Development aid from the United Kingdom ceased in 1980; since then the island has financed its own projects. In April 2008, prompted by concerns surrounding the island's dwindling capital reserves, Administrator David Morley warned that the island could be bankrupt within four years unless economic austerity measures were implemented immediately. Chief among these proposals was the introduction, with effect from 1 June 2008, of an incremental system of income tax (with a maximum rate of 13%). In June 2001 a hurricane in the main settlement of Edinburgh of the Seven Seas destroyed the hospital, community centre and numerous homes, and also killed many cattle; the satellite phone link was lost and the island was without electricity for one week, although no serious injuries were sustained. DfID granted a £75,000 emergency aid package in response to the disaster. However, the cost of repairs surpassed that figure considerably. Furthermore, the problem of poaching in the island's waters resulted in much of Tristan da Cunha's limited resources being used to fund fishing patrols rather than swiftly restoring the damaged infrastructure. It was reported in May 2008 that the United Kingdom Government had registered a claim with the UN Commission for the Limits of the Continental Shelf to extend its territorial waters around Tristan da Cunha (see Saint Helena Recent History).

Area: Tristan da Cunha 98 sq km (38 sq miles); Inaccessible Island 10 sq km (4 sq miles); Nightingale Islands 2 sq km (³⁄₄ sq mile); Gough Island 91 sq km (35 sq miles).

Population: (February 2009): 264 permanent residents on Tristan; there is a small weather station on Gough Island, staffed, under agreement, by personnel employed by the South African Government.

Fishing: Catch (metric tons, year ending 30 April): Tristan da Cunha rock lobster 377 in 2004; 373 in 2005; 464 in 2006. Source: FAO.

Budget: (2005/06, estimates): Revenue £711,320; Expenditure £858,827 (with excess expenditure financed from capital reserves of £1.2m.).

UNITED KINGDOM OVERSEAS TERRITORIES

Government: The Administrator, representing the Governor of Saint Helena, is assisted by an Island Council of eight elected members (of whom at least one must be a woman) and three appointed members, which has advisory powers in legislative and executive functions. The member receiving the largest number of votes at elections to the Council is appointed Chief Islander. The Council's advisory functions in executive matters are performed through 11 committees of the Council dealing with the separate branches of administration. Elections are held every three years. The last elections were held in March 2007.

Administrator: DAVID MORLEY, The Administrator's Office, Edinburgh of the Seven Seas, Tristan da Cunha, TDCU 1ZZ; tel. (satellite) 874-1445434; fax (satellite) 874-1445435; e-mail admin@tristandc.com; internet www.tristandc.com/administator.php.

Legal System: The Administrator is also the Magistrate and Coroner.

Religion: Adherents of the Anglican church predominate on Tristan da Cunha, which is within the Church of the Province of Southern Africa, and is under the jurisdiction of the Archbishop of Cape Town, South Africa. There is also a small number of Roman Catholics.

Transport: The St Helena Line Ltd (q.v.), the MV *Hanseatic*, and MS *Explorer* and the SA *Agulhas* each visit the island once each year, and two lobster concession vessels each make three visits annually, remaining for between two and three months. Occasional cruise ships also visit the island. There is no airfield.

Tourism: Permission from the Administrator and the Island Council is required for visits to Tristan da Cunha. Facilities for tourism are limited, although some accommodation is available in island homes.

SOUTH GEORGIA AND THE SOUTH SANDWICH ISLANDS

South Georgia, an island of 3,592 sq km (1,387 sq miles), lies in the South Atlantic Ocean, about 1,300 km (800 miles) east-south-east of the Falkland Islands. The South Sandwich Islands, which have an area of 311 sq km, lie about 750 km south-east of South Georgia.

The United Kingdom annexed South Georgia and the South Sandwich Islands in 1775. With a segment of the Antarctic mainland and other nearby islands (now the British Antarctic Territory), they were constituted as the Falkland Islands Dependencies in 1908. Argentina made formal claim to South Georgia in 1927, and to the South Sandwich Islands in 1948. In 1955 the United Kingdom unilaterally submitted the dispute over sovereignty to the International Court of Justice (based in the Netherlands), which decided not to hear the application in view of Argentina's refusal to submit to the Court's jurisdiction. South Georgia was the site of a British Antarctic Survey base (staffed by 22 scientists and support personnel) until it was invaded in April 1982 by Argentine forces, who occupied the island until its recapture by British forces three weeks later. The South Sandwich Islands were uninhabited until the occupation of Southern Thule in December 1976 by about 50 Argentines, reported to be scientists. Argentine personnel remained until removed by British forces in June 1982.

In mid-1989 it was reported that the British Government was considering the imposition of a conservation zone extending to 200 nautical miles (370 km) around South Georgia, similar to that which surrounds the Falkland Islands, in an attempt to prevent the threatened extinction of certain types of marine life.

Under the provisions of the South Georgia and South Sandwich Islands Order of 1985, the islands ceased to be governed as dependencies of the Falkland Islands on 3 October 1985. The Governor of the Falkland Islands is, *ex officio*, Commissioner for the territory.

In May 1993, in response to the Argentine Government's decision to commence the sale of fishing licences for the region's waters, the British Government announced an extension, from 12 to 200 nautical miles, of its territorial jurisdiction in the waters surrounding the islands, in order to conserve crucial fishing stocks.

In September 1998 the British Government announced that it would withdraw its military detachment from South Georgia in 2000, while it would increase its scientific presence on the island with the installation of a permanent team from the British Antarctic Survey to investigate the fisheries around the island for possible exploitation.

The small military detachment finally withdrew in March 2001. The British garrison stationed in the Falkland Islands would remain responsible for the security of South Georgia and the South Sandwich Islands. In August 2006 Alan Huckle succeeded Howard Pearce as Governor of the Falkland Islands and Commissioner of South Georgia and the South Sandwich Islands. During a restructuring of the South Georgia Government in May 2007, Assistant Commissioner and Director of Fisheries Harriet Hall was appointed to the newly created role of Chief Executive Officer; Hall assumed office in July, while retaining her responsibilities as Director of Fisheries.

Increased volcanic activity on Montagu Island, in the South Sandwich Islands, previously thought to be dormant, had been monitored closely by the British Antarctic Survey since 2001. In late 2005 Mount Belinda erupted, adding some 50 acres to the island's land area in just one month. The island is largely ice-covered and the eruption allowed scientists the rare opportunity to make direct observations of volcanic activity under ice sheets.

Budget revenue for 2007 amounted to £4.7m., while expenditure totalled £5.8m. The main sources of revenue are the sale of fishing licences, incomes from visitor landing charges, investment income, and philatelic and commemorative coin sales.

At the close of the 2007/08 cruise ship season on 31 March 2008, South Georgia had recorded a total of 64 ship calls and some 8,000 passengers to the island. Greater numbers of visitors to this inhospitable territory—coupled with a growing recognition of the climate change phenomenon—prompted the Government to review its existing biosecurity policy in an effort to prevent the introduction, or translocation, of potentially destructive species of flora and fauna to the island. Furthermore, a major legislative review was begun in early 2008, as a result of which the Government expected to implement changes to legislation governing tourism and visitor management.

The British Antarctic Survey maintains two research stations on South Georgia, at King Edward Point (winter personnel 9, summer personnel 12 in 2007/08) and Bird Island (winter personnel 4, summer personnel 10 in 2007/08).

Commissioner: ALAN HUCKLE (took office on 25 August 2006).

Assistant Commissioner and Director of Fisheries: Dr MARTIN COLLINS (Stanley, Falkland Islands).

THE TURKS AND CAICOS ISLANDS

Introductory Survey

Location, Climate, Language, Religion, Flag, Capital

The Turks and Caicos Islands consist of more than 30 low-lying islands forming the south-eastern end of the Bahamas chain of islands, and lying about 145 km (90 miles) north of Haiti. Eight islands are inhabited: Grand Turk and Salt Cay (both in the smaller Turks group to the east of the Caicos), South Caicos, Middle (Grand) Caicos, North Caicos, Providenciales (Provo), Pine Cay and Parrot Cay. The climate is warm throughout the year but tempered by constant trade winds. The average annual temperature is 27°C (82°F) and rainfall ranges from 530 mm (21 ins) in the eastern islands to 1,000 mm (40 ins) in the west. The official language is English, though some Creole is spoken by Haitian immigrants. Many Christian churches are represented, the largest denomination being the Baptist Union (25.5% of the population at the census of May 1990). The flag is the British 'Blue Ensign', with the shield from the islands' coat of arms, bearing a shell, a lobster and a cactus, in the fly. The capital is Cockburn Town, on Grand Turk island.

Recent History

The Turks and Caicos Islands were first settled by Amerindian peoples. The islands were then inhabited by privateers, and were settled from Bermuda and by exiled 'Loyalists' from the former

British colonies in North America. A Jamaican dependency from 1874 to 1959, the Turks and Caicos Islands became a separate colony in 1962, following Jamaican independence. After an administrative association with the Bahamas, the islands received their own Governor in 1972. The first elections under the present Constitution took place in 1976, and were won by the pro-independence People's Democratic Movement (PDM). In 1980 an agreement was made with the United Kingdom whereby, if the governing PDM won the 1980 elections, the islands would receive independence and a payment of £12m. However, lacking the leadership of J. A. G. S. McCartney, the Chief Minister (who had been killed in an aircraft accident in May 1980), the PDM lost the election in November to the Progressive National Party (PNP), which is committed to continued dependent status. At a subsequent general election, in May 1984, the PNP, led by the Chief Minister, Norman Saunders, won eight of the 11 elective seats.

In March 1985 the Chief Minister, the Minister for Development and Commerce and a PNP member of the Legislative Council were arrested in Miami, Florida, USA, on charges involving illicit drugs and violations of the US Travel Act. All three men were subsequently convicted and imprisoned (with Saunders receiving an eight-year sentence). Saunders resigned and was replaced as Chief Minister by Nathaniel Francis, hitherto the Minister of Public Works and Utilities.

In July 1986 a commission of inquiry into allegations of arson and administrative malpractice following the destruction by fire of a government building in December 1985 concluded that Francis and two of his ministers were unfit for ministerial office; all three ministers subsequently resigned. Two members of the PDM were also deemed to be unfit for public office. In the same month the Governor dissolved the Government, and the Executive Council was replaced by an interim advisory council, comprising the Governor and four members of the former Executive Council. A constitutional commission was appointed in September to review the future administration of the islands.

A general election, preceding the return to ministerial rule, took place in March 1988, following the British Government's acceptance of the principal recommendations of the constitutional commission in the previous year. Under a new multi-member system of representation (see Constitution, below), the PDM won 11 of the 13 seats on the Legislative Council, and the PNP won the remaining two. Oswald O. Skippings, the leader of the PDM, was appointed Chief Minister. The new Constitution strengthened the reserve powers of the Governor, but otherwise the form of government was similar to the provisions of the 1976 Constitution.

In April 1991 a general election took place, at which the PNP secured eight seats, defeating the PDM (which won the remaining five). Skippings was replaced as Chief Minister by C. Washington Misick, the leader of the PNP.

At a general election in January 1995 the PDM secured eight seats, while the PNP won four. Derek Taylor, leader of the PDM, was appointed Chief Minister.

A serious dispute arose between the Legislative Council and the Governor in August 1995, following the latter's decision to reappoint Kipling Douglas to the position of Chief Justice. Taylor, who claimed that Douglas did not enjoy the confidence of his Government, described the decision as provocative and disrespectful. Relations deteriorated in subsequent months, and in February 1996 a petition requesting the immediate removal of the Governor, signed by all members of the Government and opposition, was presented to the British Foreign and Commonwealth Office (FCO). A delegation of politicians from the territory travelled to the United Kingdom to reinforce the views of the Legislative Council, which were believed to be shared by a majority of islanders. In the following month, however, their demands were rejected by the British Government, which deployed a frigate in the islands' waters and ordered 100 police officers to prepare for immediate transfer to the territory in the event of civil disturbance. A climate of animosity between the Governor and the islanders persisted during 1996, and in September Bourke departed from the territory, without formal ceremony, following the expiry of his term of office. He was replaced by John Kelly.

At a general election held on 4 March 1999 the PDM increased its representation in the Legislative Council to nine seats. The PNP won the other four seats.

In June 2000 the Turks and Caicos Islands were included on a list of territories regarded as operating harmful tax regimes. The Organisation for Economic Co-operation and Development (OECD, see p. 358), which compiled the list, urged the Government to make legislative changes, in order to introduce greater legal and administrative transparency to prevent companies using the country's tax system for money-laundering or tax-evasion purposes. OECD removed the Turks and Caicos Islands from the list in March 2002, declaring that the Government had made sufficient commitments to improve transparency and effective exchange of information on tax matters by the end of 2005. In late 2002, however, the recovering financial sector faced further disruption when the United Kingdom, under pressure from a European Union (EU, see p. 255) investigation into tax evasion, demanded that the Turks and Caicos Islands disclose the identities and account details of Europeans holding private savings accounts on the islands. The Turks and Caicos Islands, along with some other British Overseas Territories facing similar demands, claimed it was being treated unfairly, but pledged to introduce the necessary legislation to implement the EU's Savings Tax Directive in 2004, provided it was granted the same allowances as powerful European countries, such as Switzerland and Luxembourg.

In April 2002 the Governor established a Constitutional Modernisation Review Body to discuss changes to the islands' Constitution. This all-party panel presented a report in September. Discussions on a new constitution took place in 2004 between representatives of the Turks and Caicos Islands and British Governments. Following further negotiations between government ministers in October 2005, it was agreed that a draft text of a modernized constitution would be drawn up by the FCO. This proposed document would be subject to approval by both the PDM and the PNP, after which a public consultation period would be held. Adoption of the amendments would be subject to approval by the Legislative Council.

In May 2002 the British Overseas Territories Act, having received royal assent in the United Kingdom in February, came into force and granted British citizenship rights to the people of its Overseas Territories, including the Turks and Caicos Islands. Under the new law, Turks and Caicos Islanders would be able to hold British passports and work in the United Kingdom and anywhere else in the EU. In March 2005 a delegation from the Turks and Caicos Islands made an official visit to the Bahamas in a bid to forge closer ties between the two Governments.

In October 2002 capital punishment for treason and piracy, the only remaining capital crime in the United Kingdom Overseas Territories, was abolished in the Turks and Caicos Islands. In December Jim Poston replaced Mervyn Jones as Governor.

At a general election in April 2003 the PDM won seven of the 13 seats in the Legislative Council. The PNP took the remaining six seats, but challenged the results in two of the more closely fought constituencies. By-elections were held in the two constituencies in August after evidence emerged of bribery and irregularities in voter registration lists; the PNP secured victory in both ballots and therefore wrested overall control of the Legislative Council from the PDM. Misick replaced Taylor as Chief Minister on 15 August.

In July 2005 James Poston was succeeded by Richard Tauwhare as Governor.

In spite of ongoing discussions regarding a new constitution, in April 2006 the Chief Minister met with members of the UN's Special Committee on Decolonization to discuss options for self-determination. Three directions were outlined: independence; independence by free association; or independence by way of integration. However, it was not clear how many islanders wanted independence, and the opposition questioned Misick's motives behind the talks. Misick subsequently issued a statement indicating that the PNP would not pursue independence during the constitutional discussions, nor would the matter feature as an objective of their electoral campaign ahead of the general election, scheduled for February 2007. A public consultation was conducted over a draft constitution, formulated pursuant to an agreement upon greater self-government for the territory, between United Kingdom and island representatives in October 2005, and approved by the Legislative Council on 28 June 2006. Following final submission to the FCO and endorsement by Queen Elizabeth II, the Council decreed the Turks and Caicos Constitutional Order 2006, adopting the new Constitution on 19 July. The Constitution was finally enacted on 9 August, when Chief Minister Misick and Deputy Chief Minister Floyd Hall were inaugurated as Premier and Deputy Premier, respectively. The new administrative regime instituted a new office of Deputy Governor, to which former Chief Secretary Mahala Wynns was appointed; the assignment complied with a new constitutional requirement that the position be occupied by a 'belonger' of the Turks and Caicos Islands. Notable amendments under the new Constitution included the investiture of a unicameral parliament, which would replace and enlarge upon the former Legislative Council. The new House of Assembly would comprise 21 members, 15 of whom were to be elected for a four-year term and four of whom were to be nominated from the Cabinet (formerly the Executive Council). The new legislature would also include the Attorney-General (an ex officio member) and the Speaker. The Cabinet would consist of the Premier, one ex officio member (the Attorney-General), and six ministers—to be appointed by the Governor from the elected House of Assembly—and would be presided over by the Governor. An Electoral District Boundaries 2006 Bill, in accordance with a provision within the new Constitution for the revision of electoral boundaries upon the recommendations of a dedicated commission, was approved by the legislature, affording the creation of two new constituencies to reflect the two additional elected members of the House of Assembly. The legislation was ratified by the House of Assembly in January 2007, creating two new electoral districts on the island of Providenciales.

A general election was held on 9 February 2007. The PNP were returned to office for a second term, winning 13 of the 15 seats in the

House of Assembly. The PDM secured the remaining two seats. Misick was reappointed Premier. The ballot followed a bitterly fought election campaign, in which the PDM made allegations of corruption against the ruling party.

In July 2007 it was alleged that the Premier had assaulted an opposition member of Parliament, Arthur Robinson, in response to criticism of Misick's despatch of his governmental responsibilities. It was claimed that Misick spent a significant proportion of time away from the islands, provoking PDM accusations that he had become an 'absentee premier'. The leader of the PDM, Floyd Seymour, subsequently demanded Misick's resignation. The Premier refused to yield to pressure to stand down when, in early April 2008, allegations of sexual assault surfaced against him by a US citizen who had been visiting the islands.

Governor Richard Tauwhare left office in July 2008; he was replaced by Gordon Wetherell, who was sworn in on 5 August.

In December 2008 Misick avoided a debate on a motion of 'no confidence' submitted by the PDM as a result of a dispute over parliamentary procedure. Parliament was subsequently prorogued by Governor Wetherell, to be reconvened in April 2009. Later in December Lillian Boyce, Minister of Health and Human Services, along with eight other members of the ruling PNP, drafted a letter to Governor Wetherell requesting that Misick resign, citing a loss of confidence from legislators. Boyce was sacked by Misick in January 2009 and replaced by Royal Robinson.

Deputy Premier Floyd Hall resigned on 13 February 2009, citing the legislative stalemate caused by the ongoing suspension of Parliament. Galmore 'Galmo' Williams, the Minister for Home Affairs, had resigned the previous day. Following the resignations Misick announced a reorganization of his Cabinet, in which the most notable appointment was that of former Minister of Health and Human Services, Boyce, who returned as Deputy Premier and Minister for Home Affairs only a month after her dismissal. Misick also announced that he would resign as Premier by the end of March, and that he would not be seeking re-election as leader of the PNP. At a special PNP convention held on 28 February, Galmo Williams was elected to succeed Misick. Misick stood down on 23 March, at which point Williams was sworn in as Premier. Williams promptly announced the formation of a new Cabinet.

In late March 2008, meanwhile, the United Kingdom's House of Commons Foreign Affairs Committee had expressed concern at allegations of corruption and poor governance on the Turks and Caicos Islands. As a result, in July Governor Tauwhare appointed a Commission of Inquiry to investigate the allegations. In late February 2009 Sir Robin Auld issued the Commission of Inquiry's interim report, which referred to a 'high probability of systemic corruption' and contained 24 recommendations, including the partial or full suspension of the Constitution and direct rule of the islands by the United Kingdom, acting through the Governor, with the advice of an Advisory Executive Council. The report was released by the Governor on 16 March; in April it was announced that the final report, which had been expected at the end of that month, would be delayed until 31 May.

Relations with Haiti were severely damaged in early May 2007 when a vessel carrying an estimated 160 Haitian migrants capsized in Turks and Caicos jurisdictional waters during an interception operation by the islands' coastguard. It was reported that 61 of those originally on board had died, while more than 20 migrants remained unaccounted for. Survivors alleged that a police vessel, ostensibly part of the rescue mission, had rammed the overburdened vessel twice prior to its capsize, claims that were vehemently denied by the Turks and Caicos authorities. However, suspicion remained that a 'deliberate criminal action' had been committed. In late February 2008 newspaper reports claimed that more than 1,000 Haitian nationals had landed on the islands since the beginning of the year, most of whom had been repatriated.

Government

Under the provisions of the 2006 Constitution (amending the 1988 revision of the 1976 Constitution), executive power is vested in the Governor, appointed by the British monarch. The Governor is responsible for external affairs, internal security, defence, international financial services and the appointment of public officers; other matters are resolved by the Governor upon the advice of the Cabinet. The Governor is President of the Cabinet, which comprises nine members: one ex officio (the Attorney-General), the Premier, and six appointed by the Governor from among the elected members of the House of Assembly. The House of Assembly comprises the Speaker, four nominated members, the ex officio member of the Cabinet and 15 members elected by universal adult suffrage.

Economic Affairs

In 2007, according to official estimates, the Turks and Caicos Islands' gross domestic product (GDP) was a preliminary US $829m., equivalent to some $23,768 per head. During 2000–07, it was estimated, the population increased at an average annual rate of 9.5%. GDP increased, in real terms, by 10.0% per year in 2003–07; growth in 2007 was 11.2%.

Agriculture is not practised on any significant scale in the Turks Islands or on South Caicos (the most populous island of the territory). None the less, the sector contributed a preliminary 1.0% to GDP in 2007. The other islands of the Caicos group grow some beans, maize and a few fruits and vegetables. There is some livestock-rearing, but the islands' principal natural resource is fisheries, which accounts for almost all commodity exports, the principal species caught being the spiny lobster (an estimated 417 metric tons in 2006) and the conch (an estimated 5,589 tons in that year). Conchs were being developed commercially (on the largest conch farm in the world) in 2007, and there was potential for larger-scale fishing. Exports of lobster and conch earned US $3.4m. in 1995, which constituted an increase of more than 14% compared with the previous year's earnings. Fish, crustaceans and molluscs contributed 34.4% to total export earnings in 2007.

Industrial activity consists mainly of construction (especially for the tourism industry) and fish-processing. The sector contributed a preliminary 22.9% to GDP in 2007. The islands possess plentiful supplies of aragonite. Imports of mineral fuels are needed to satisfy energy requirements.

The principal economic sector is the service industry, which in 2007 contributed an estimated 76.2% to GDP. This is dominated by tourism, which is concentrated on the island of Providenciales. The market is for wealthier visitors, mostly from the USA. Tourist arrivals increased from approximately 117,600 in 1999 to 165,400 in 2001 and this level was maintained with figures of 155,600 in 2002 and 163,600 in 2003. Tourism arrivals continued to rise, reaching 264,887 in 2007, while tourism receipts were US $355.1m. in 2005. The depreciation in value of the US dollar, the official currency of the Turks and Caicos, in 2003–04, prompted an increase in non-US visitors to the islands. In January 2004 it was announced that a new $35m. cruise-ship terminal would be constructed in Grand Turk, enabling, for the first time, large passenger liners to stop in the territory. The terminal was inaugurated in February 2006. An 'offshore' financial sector was encouraged in the 1980s, and new regulatory legislation was ratified at the end of 1989. In 2000 there were some 8,000 overseas companies registered in the islands.

In 2003 the Turks and Caicos Islands recorded a trade deficit of US $160.9m. (exports were 5.7% of the value of imports). This deficit is normally offset by receipts from tourism, aid from the United Kingdom and revenue from the 'offshore' financial sector. The USA is the principal trading partner, but some trade is conducted with the United Kingdom and with neighbouring nations.

According to figures from the Caribbean Development Bank (CDB), there was an overall budget deficit of US $7.9m. in 2003. In the Government's 2007/08 budget plan, there was an overall budgetary deficit of $33.4m. The islands received a total of $8.2m. in British development assistance in 1999/2000. The total external public debt was $20.0m. in 2003. The rate of inflation, which stood at about 4% in 1995, is dependent upon the movement of prices in the USA, the islands' principal trading partner. Unemployment increased to an estimated 10% in the late 1990s. A large number of Turks and Caicos 'belongers' have emigrated, many to the Bahamas, especially in search of skilled labour (there is no tertiary education in the territory). In July 2000 the CDB announced a loan to the Government of some $4m. to assist the Turks and Caicos Investment Agency.

The Turks and Caicos Islands, as a dependency of the United Kingdom, have the status of Overseas Territory in association with the European Union (EU, see p. 255). The islands are also a member of the CDB (see p. 211) and an associate member of the Caribbean Community and Common Market (CARICOM, see p. 206). The territory became an associate member of the Association of Caribbean States (ACS, see p. 424) in April 2006.

The economy and the population of the Turks and Caicos Islands were estimated to have doubled in size during the 1990s, making the islands one of the region's most dynamic economies. The remarkable economic growth experienced by the islands was chiefly owing to the increasing significance of the tourism and international financial services sectors, both of which benefited from the perceived stability of United Kingdom Overseas Territory status. The 'offshore' financial sector successfully rehabilitated its international reputation through the introduction, in 2002, of a supervisory body, the Financial Services Commission, and the implementation of more stringent regulatory legislation based on the maxim of 'privacy not secrecy'. In early 2004 the financial sector faced further regulatory disruption when the islands came under pressure to implement the EU's Savings Tax Directive (see Recent History). Economic growth in the islands—driven more by inward investment than by domestic production—remained highly dependent on external factors, and international proposals to force comprehensive reforms of 'offshore' financial services centres were, therefore, of particular concern. Although tourism grew steadily in the late 1990s, fears were expressed that the islands were in danger of becoming overdeveloped, and that their reputation as an unspoilt tourist location could be undermined. A further source of disquiet has been the exclusion of many inhabitants from the benefits of economic growth, as newly created jobs were often taken by low-wage migrant workers or by highly skilled expatriates. The tourism industry was expected to suffer following the introduction of new US legislation in January 2007, which required all passengers travelling between the Caribbean and the USA to hold valid passports, while it was anticipated that arrivals would decline in the latter part of 2008 and in 2009 following the onset of the global financial crisis, which particularly affected the USA. Furthermore, the recommendation made in early 2009 in the interim report of the Commission of Inquiry (see Recent History) that the powers of the premier, his cabinet and parliament be suspended (as systemic corruption was suspected) did not augur well for economic progress. Meanwhile, following the destruction caused by 'Hurricane Ike' in late 2008 (the Government estimated that 80% of homes had been damaged) the Caribbean Catastrophe Risk Insurance Facility offered US $6.3m. of aid for reconstruction. Real GDP was forecast to contract by 2.0% in 2009.

Education

Primary education, beginning at seven years of age and lasting seven years, is compulsory, and is provided free of charge in government schools. Secondary education, from the age of 14, lasts for five years, and is also free. In 1997 there were 21 primary schools, and in 1990 one private secondary school and four government secondary schools. In 2004/05 enrolment at primary schools included 78.0% of pupils in the relevant age-group, while enrolment at secondary schools included 70.2% of children in the appropriate age-group. In 1997 the Caribbean Development Bank approved a loan of just under US $4m. to fund the establishment of a permanent campus for the Turks and Caicos Community College.

Public Holidays

2009: 1 January (New Year's Day), 12 March (Commonwealth Day), 10 April (Good Friday), 13 April (Easter Monday), 25 May (National Heroes' Day), 8 June (Queen's Official Birthday), 3 August (Emancipation Day), 25 September (National Youth Day), 12 October (Columbus Day), 24 October (International Human Rights Day), 25–28 December (Christmas).

2010: 1 January (New Year's Day), 12 March (Commonwealth Day), 2 April (Good Friday), 5 April (Easter Monday), 26 May (National Heroes' Day), 7 June (Queen's Official Birthday), 2 August (Emancipation Day), 27 September (National Youth Day), 11 October (Columbus Day), 24 October (International Human Rights Day), 25–27 December (Christmas).

Weights and Measures

The imperial system is in use.

Statistical Survey

Source: Department of Economic Planning and Statistics, Ministry of Finance, South Base, Grand Turk; tel. 946-2801; fax 946-2557; e-mail info@depstc.org; internet www.depstc.org.

AREA AND POPULATION

Area: 948 sq km (366 sq miles). Note: Area includes low water level for all islands, but excludes area to high water mark.

Population: 7,413 at census of 12 May 1980; 11,465 at census of 31 May 1990; 19,886 (males 9,897, females 9,989) at census of 20 August 2001; *2008* (estimate): 36,605. *By Island* (2006, estimates): Grand Turk 5,718; South Caicos 1,118; Middle Caicos 307; North Caicos 1,537; Salt Cay 114; Parrot Cay 60; Providenciales 24,348.

Density (2008 estimate): 38.6 per sq km.

Principal Towns: Cockburn Town (capital, on Grand Turk), population 2,500 (1987 estimate); Cockburn Harbour (South Caicos), population 1,000. *Mid-2003* (UN estimate, incl. suburbs): Grand Turk 5,680 (Source: UN, *World Urbanization Prospects: The 2003 Revision*).

Births, Marriages and Deaths (2007 unless otherwise indicated): Live births 517 (birth rate 14.7 per 1,000); Marriages 468 (marriage rate 19.2 per 1,000 in 2006); Deaths 114 (death rate 3.3 per 1,000).

Life Expectancy (years at birth, 2008): 75.2 (males 72.9; females 77.6). Source: Pan American Health Organization.

Economically Active Population (2005): Agriculture and fishing 247; Mining and quarrying 56; Manufacturing 202; Utilities 269; Construction 2,402; Wholesale and retail trade 1,298; Hotels and restaurants 2,935; Transport, storage and communications 650; Financial intermediation 496; Real estate, renting and business services 1,607; Public administration 2,310; Education, health and social work 496; Other community, social and personal services 971; Private household employment 1,608; Activities not adequately defined 1,895; *Total employed* 17,442; Unemployed 1,524; *Total labour force* 18,966. *2006* (preliminary): Total employed 18,195; Unemployed 1,464; Total labour force 19,659.

HEALTH AND WELFARE

Total Fertility Rate (children per woman, 2008): 3.0.
Under-5 Mortality Rate (per 1,000 live births, 1997): 22.0.
Hospital Beds (per 1,000 head, 2007): 1.4.
Physicians (per 1,000 head, 2001): 7.3.
Health Expenditure (public, % of total, 2004): 12.6.
Health Expenditure (US $ per head, 2004): 741.2.
Access to Sanitation (% of persons, 2004): 96.
Source: partly Pan American Health Organization.

For other sources and definitions see explanatory note on p. vi.

AGRICULTURE, ETC.

Fishing (metric tons, live weight, 2006): Capture 6,018 (Caribbean spiny lobster 417, Stromboid conchs 5,589); Aquaculture 4; *Total catch* 6,022. Figures exclude aquatic plants and mammals.
Source: FAO.

INDUSTRY

Electric Energy (production, million kWh): 10 in 1999–2005.
Source: UN, *Industrial Commodity Statistics Yearbook*.

FINANCE

Currency and Exchange Rate: United States currency is used: 100 cents = 1 US dollar ($). Sterling and Euro Equivalents (31 December 2008): £1 sterling = US $1.4578; €1 = US $1.3917; $100 = £68.60 = €71.85.

Budget (US $ million, 2007/08): Total revenue and grants 280.31 (Current revenue 206.79, Capital revenue and grants 73.52); Total expenditure 313.73 (Current expenditure 235.85, Capital expenditure 77.89).

Gross Domestic Product (US $ million at constant 2000 prices): 481.9 in 2005; 568.1 in 2006; 632.0 in 2007 (preliminary).

Expenditure on the Gross Domestic Product (US $ million, 2007, preliminary): Government final consumption expenditure 143.0; Private final consumption expenditure 458.3; Gross capital formation 392.6; *Total domestic expenditure* 993.9; Exports of goods and services 522.6; *Less* Imports of goods and services 687.9; *GDP in market prices* 828.6.

Gross Domestic Product by Economic Activity (US $ million, 2007, preliminary): Agriculture and fishing 7.5; Mining and quarrying 10.0; Manufacturing 13.4; Utilities 26.4; Construction 125.5; Wholesale and retail trade 31.4; Hotels and restaurants 222.1; Transport, storage and communications 61.4; Financial intermediation 88.2; Real estate, renting and business activities 59.7; Public administration, defence and social security 61.8; Education 22.0; Health and social work 18.1; Other community, social and personal services 19.4; *Sub-total* 766.9; *Less* Financial intermediation services indirectly measured 59.3; *Gross value added in basic prices* 707.6; Taxes, less subsidies, on products 121.0; *GDP in market prices* 828.6.

Balance of Payments (US $ million, 2002): Exports of goods f.o.b. 8.7; Imports of goods f.o.b. −177.5; *Trade balance* −168.8; Exports of services 163.1; Imports of services −81.8; *Balance on goods and services* −87.5. Source: Caribbean Development Bank, *Social and Economic Indicators*.

EXTERNAL TRADE

Principal Commodities (US $ million, 2007): *Imports:* Food and live animals 58.8; Beverages and tobacco 16.6; Crude materials (inedible) except fuels 17.6; Mineral fuels, lubricants, etc. 48.4; Chemicals and related products 28.6; Basic manufactures 106.6; Machinery and transport equipment 154.6; Miscellaneous manufactured articles 130.2; Total (incl. others) 580.6. *Exports:* Food and live animals 5.7; Machinery and transport equipment 5.0; Miscellaneous manufactured articles 2.5; Total exports 16.3.

Principal Trading Partners (US $ million, 2007): Imports c.i.f.: Bahamas 2.5; USA 577.4; Total (incl. others) 580.6. Exports f.o.b.: USA 16.2; Total (incl. others) 16.3.

TRANSPORT

Road Traffic (1984): 1,563 registered motor vehicles.

Shipping: *International Freight Traffic* (estimates in '000 metric tons, 1990): Goods loaded 135; Goods unloaded 149. *Merchant Fleet* (vessels registered at 31 December 2007): 5; Total displacement 975 grt. Sources: UN, *Monthly Bulletin of Statistics*; Lloyd's Register-Fairplay, *World Fleet Statistics*.

TOURISM

Tourist Arrivals ('000): 176.1 (of which USA 123.3) in 2005; 248.3 (of which USA 169.7) in 2006; 264.9 in 2007.

Tourism Receipts (US $ million, estimates): 275.6 in 2003; 317.9 in 2004; 355.1 in 2005.

Source: Caribbean Development Bank, *Social and Economic Indicators*.

COMMUNICATIONS MEDIA

Radio Receivers (1997): 8,000 in use.

Telephones (2000, estimate): 6,000 main lines in use.

Facsimile Machines (1992): 200 in use.

Non-daily Newspapers (1996): 1 (estimated circulation 5,000).

Sources: UNESCO, *Statistical Yearbook*; UN, *Statistical Yearbook*.

EDUCATION

Pre-primary (2004/05, unless otherwise indicated): 21 schools (1996/97); 87 teachers (estimate); 1,083 pupils.

Primary (2004/05, unless otherwise indicated): 10 government schools (2005); 148 teachers; 2,220 pupils.

General Secondary (2004/05, unless otherwise indicated): 4 government schools (2005); 174 teachers (estimate); 1,558 pupils.

Vocational Education (2004/05, estimates): 12 teachers; 128 pupils.

Adult Literacy Rate (UNESCO estimates): 99% (males 99%; females 98%) in 1998.

Sources: partly UNESCO Institute for Statistics; Caribbean Development Bank, *Social and Economic Indicators*.

Directory

The Constitution

The Order in Council of July 1986 enabled the Governor to suspend the ministerial form of government, for which the Constitution of 1976 made provision. Ministerial government was restored in March 1988, following amendments to the Constitution, recommended by a constitutional commission. A further revision to the Constitution, whereby the islands acquired greater self-government, was passed by a resolution of the Legislative Council on 28 June 2006 and formally adopted on 19 July. The Turks and Caicos Islands Constitution Order 2006 became effective from 9 August.

The revised Constitution of 2006 provides for a Cabinet (formerly the Executive Council) and a House of Assembly (formerly the Legislative Council). Executive authority is vested in the British monarch and is exercised by the Governor (the monarch's appointed representative), who also holds responsibility for external affairs, internal security, defence, the appointment of any person to any public office and the suspension and termination of appointment of any public officer.

The Cabinet comprises: one ex officio member (the Attorney-General); the Premier (formerly the Chief Minister—appointed by the Governor) who is, in the judgement of the Governor, the leader of the political party represented in the House of Assembly that commands the support of a majority of the elected members of the House; and six other ministers from among the elected or nominated members of the House of Assembly, appointed by the Governor on the advice of the Premier. The Cabinet is presided over by the Governor.

The House of Assembly consists of the Speaker, the ex officio member of the Cabinet, 15 members elected by residents aged 18 and over, and four nominated members (appointed by the Governor, two on the advice of the Premier, one on the advice of the Leader of the Opposition and one at the Governor's discretion).

Provision was also included under the revised Constitution for the establishment of an Advisory National Security Council, mandated to advise the Governor on matters relating to defence and internal security, external affairs, and international financial services regulation. The Council would also make recommendations for the dispatch of the Governor's responsibilities in the event of a public emergency.

For the purposes of elections to the enlarged House of Assembly, an Electoral District Boundaries (Amendment) Bill was ratified on 8 January 2007, dividing the islands into 15 electoral districts. In 1988 and 1991 a multiple voting system was used, whereby three districts elected three members each, while the remaining five districts each elected two members. However, from the 1995 election a single-member constituency system was used.

The Government

Governor: GORDON WETHERELL (sworn in 5 August 2008).
Deputy Governor: MAHALA WYNNS.

CABINET
(April 2009)

President: GORDON WETHERELL (The Governor).

Premier and Minister of Development and District Administration: GALMORE 'GALMO' WILLIAMS.

Deputy Premier and Minister of Finance and Health: ROYAL ROBINSON.

Minister of Housing, Works, Public Safety and Telecommunications: SAMUEL BEEN.

Minister of Home Affairs and Human Services: KAREN DELANCY.

Minister of Education, Youth and Sports: AMANDA MISSICK.

Minister of Tourism and Airports Authority: WAYNE GARLAND.

Minister of Natural and Coastal Resources: GREGORY LIGHTBOURNE.

Ex Officio Member: Attorney-General: KURT DE FREITES.

GOVERNMENT OFFICES

Office of the Governor: Govt House, Grand Turk; tel. 946-2308; fax 946-2903; e-mail govhouse@tciway.tc.

Office of the Premier: Govt Sq., Grand Turk; tel. 946-2801; fax 946-2777.

Office of the Deputy Governor: South Base, Grand Turk; tel. 946-2702; fax 946-2886; e-mail cso@gov.tc.

Office of the Permanent Secretary: Finance Dept, Premier's Office, Govt Bldgs, Front St, Grand Turk; tel. 946-1115; fax 946-2777.

Attorney-General's Chambers: South Base, Grand Turk; tel. 946-2096; fax 946-2588; e-mail attorneygeneral@tciway.tc; internet www.lawsconsolidated.tc.

HOUSE OF ASSEMBLY

Speaker: CLAYTON GREEN.
Clerk to the Councils: RUTH BLACKMAN.

Election, 9 February 2007

Party	Seats
Progressive National Party (PNP)	13
People's Democratic Movement (PDM)	2
Total	**15**

There is one ex officio member (the Attorney-General), four appointed members, and a Speaker (assisted by a Deputy Speaker).

Political Organizations

People's Democratic Movement (PDM): POB 38, Grand Turk; favours internal self-govt and eventual independence; Chair. SHARLENE ROBINSON; Leader FLOYD SEYMOUR.

Progressive National Party (PNP): Providenciales; tel. 941-4663; fax 946-3673; e-mail pnp@tciway.tc; supports full internal self-govt; Chair. DONHUE GARDINER; Leader GALMORE 'GALMO' WILLIAMS.

United Democratic Party (UDP): Grand Turk; f. 1993; Leader WENDAL SWANN.

Judicial System

Justice is administered by the Supreme Court of the islands, presided over by the Chief Justice. There is a Chief Magistrate resident on Grand Turk, who also acts as Judge of the Supreme Court. There are also three Deputy Magistrates.

The Court of Appeal held its first sitting in February 1995. Previously the islands had shared a court of appeal in Nassau, Bahamas. In certain cases, appeals are made to the Judicial Committee of the Privy Council (based in the United Kingdom).

Judicial Department
Grand Turk; tel. 946-2114; fax 946-2720.
Chief Justice: CHRISTOPHER GARDNER.
Supreme Court Judge: (Providenciales) RICHARD WILLIAMS.
Chief Magistrate: (Providenciales) JOAN JOYNER.

Religion

CHRISTIANITY

The Anglican Communion

Within the Church in the Province of the West Indies, the territory forms part of the diocese of Nassau and the Bahamas. The Bishop is resident in Nassau. According to census results, there were 1,465 adherents in 1990.

Anglican Church: St Mary's Church, Front St, Grand Turk; tel. 946-2289; internet bahamas.anglican.org; Archbishop Rev. LAISH Z. BOYD.

The Roman Catholic Church

The Bishop of Nassau, Bahamas (suffragan to the archdiocese of Kingston in Jamaica), has jurisdiction in the Turks and Caicos Islands as Superior of the Mission to the Territory (founded in June 1984).

Roman Catholic Mission: Leeward Highway, POB 340, Providenciales; tel. and fax 941-5136; e-mail info_rcm@catholic.tc; internet www.catholic.tc; churches on Grand Turk, South and North Caicos, and on Providenciales; 132 adherents in 1990 (according to census results); Chancellor Fr PETER BALDACCHINO.

Other Christian Churches

Baptist Union of the Turks and Caicos Islands: South Caicos; tel. 946-3220; 3,153 adherents in 1990 (according to census results); Gen. Sec. Rev. GOLDSTONE WILLIAMS.

Jehovah's Witnesses: Kingdom Hall, Intersection of Turtle Cove and Bridge Rd, POB 400, Providenciales; tel. 941-5583.

Methodist Church: The Ridge, Grand Turk; tel. 946-2115; 1,238 adherents in 1990 (according to census results).

New Testament Church of God: POB N-1708, Orea Alley, Grand Turk; tel. 324-2582; fax 324-7891; e-mail info@churchofgodbtci.org; internet www.churchofgodbtci.org.

Seventh-day Adventists: Grand Turk; tel. 946-2065; Pastor PETER KERR.

The Press

Times of the Islands Magazine: Southwind Plaza, POB 234, Providenciales; tel. and fax 946-4788; e-mail timespub@tciway.tc; internet www.timespub.tc; f. 1988; quarterly; circ. 10,000; Editor KATHY BORSUK.

Turks and Caicos Free Press: Market Pl., POB 179, Providenciales; tel. 941-5615; fax 941-3402; e-mail freepress@tciway.tc; internet tcfreepress.com; f. 1991; Vox-Global Télématique; weekly; circ. 3,000; Editor Dr GILBERT MORRIS; Man. BARBARA SMITH.

Turks & Caicos Islands Real Estate Association Real Estate Magazine: Southwind Plaza, POB 234, Providenciales; tel. and fax 946-4788; e-mail timespub@tciway.tc; internet www.timespub.tc; 3 a year; circ. 15,000; Editor KATHY BORSUK.

Turks and Caicos Sun: Airport Plaza, Suite 5, POB 439, Providenciales; tel. 946-8542; fax 946-3281; e-mail turksandcaicossun@express.tc; internet www.suntci.com; f. 2005; publ. by Island Publishing Co Ltd; weekly; Publr and Editor-in-Chief HAYDEN BOYCE.

Turks and Caicos Weekly News: Leeward Highway, Cheshire House, POB 52, Providenciales; tel. 946-4664; fax 946-4661; e-mail tcnews@tciway.tc; internet www.tcweeklynews.com; Editor W. BLYTHE DUNCANSON.

Where, When, How: The Saltmills, Unit 6, POB 192, Providenciales; tel. 946-4815; fax 941-3497; e-mail info@wwhtci.com; internet www.wherewhenhow.com; f. 1994; bi-monthly; travel magazine; Co-Editor CHARLES ZDENEK; Co-Editor BRENDA ZDENEK; circ. 70,000 a year.

Broadcasting and Communications

TELECOMMUNICATIONS

Telecommunication Commission: Business Solutions Bldg, Leeward Hwy, Providenciales; tel. 946-1900; fax 946-1119; e-mail sales@tcitelecom.com; internet www.tcitelecom.com; f. 2004; regulates telecommunications; Telecommunications Officer JOHN WILLIAMS.

Digicel: Graceway House, Unit 207, Leeward Hwy, Providenciales; tel. 941-7600; fax 941-7601; e-mail tcicustomercare@digicelgroup.com; internet www.digiceltci.com; owned by an Irish consortium; granted licence in 2006 to provide mobile telecommunications services in Turks and Caicos; Chair. DENIS O'BRIEN.

LIME: Leeward Hwy, POB 78, Providenciales; tel. 946-2200; fax 946-4409; e-mail cwtci@tciway.tc; internet www.cw.tc; f. 1973; monopoly ended in Jan. 2006; fmrly Cable & Wireless (Turks and Caicos) Ltd; name changed as above 2008; CEO RICHARD DODD.

Radio

Power 92.5 FM: Providenciales; e-mail kenny@power925fm.com; internet www.power925fm.com.

Radio Providenciales: Leeward Hwy, POB 32, Providenciales; tel. 946-4496; fax 946-4108; commercial.

Radio Turks and Caicos (RTC): POB 69, Grand Turk; tel. 946-2010; fax 946-1600; e-mail teamrtc@rtc107fm.com; internet www.rtc107fm.com; govt-owned; commercial; broadcasts 105 hrs weekly; Man. LYNETTE SMITH.

Radio Visión Cristiana Internacional: North End, South Caicos; tel. 946-6601; fax 946-6600; e-mail radiovision@tciway.tc; internet www.radiovision.net; commercial; Man. WENDELL SEYMOUR.

Television

Television programmes are available from a cable network, and broadcasts from the Bahamas can be received in the islands.

TCI New Media Network: Leeward Hwy, Providenciales; e-mail news@tcinewmedianetwork.tc; internet tcinewmedianetwork.tc; f. 2008; govt-owned; Gen. Man. AVA-DAYNE KERR.

Turks and Caicos Television: Pond St, POB 80, Grand Turk; tel. 946-1530; fax 946-2896.

WIV Cable TV: Tower Raza, Leeward Hwy, POB 679, Providenciales; tel. 946-4273; fax 946-4790.

Finance

(cap. = capital; res = reserves; dep. = deposits; br(s). = branch(es); amounts in US $ unless otherwise indicated)

REGULATORY AUTHORITY

Financial Services Commission (FSC): Harry E. Francis Bldg, Pond St, POB 173, Grand Turk; tel. 946-2791; fax 946-2821; e-mail fsc@tciway.tc; f. 2002; regulates local and 'offshore' financial services sector; Man. Dir NEVILLE CADOGAN.

BANKING

Belize Bank: The Centre Mews, POB 270, Providenciales; tel. 941-5028; fax 941-5029; e-mail belizebank@tciway.tc; internet www.belizebank.com; Man. Dir ANDREW ASHCROFT.

Bordier International Bank and Trust Ltd: Caribbean Pl., Leeward Hwy, POB 5, Providenciales; tel. 946-4535; fax 946-4540; e-mail enquiries@bibt.com; internet www.bibt.com; Chair. FRANÇOIS BOHN; Man. ELISE HARTSHORN.

FirstCaribbean International Bank (Bahamas) Ltd: Leeward Hwy, POB 698, Providenciales; tel. 946-2831; fax 946-2695; e-mail care@firstcaribbeanbank.com; internet www.firstcaribbeanbank.com; f. 2002 following merger of Caribbean operations of Barclays Bank PLC and CIBC; Barclays relinquished its stake to CIBC in June 2006; Exec. Chair. MICHAEL MANSOOR; CEO JOHN D. ORR.

Scotiabank (Canada): Cherokee Rd, POB 15, Providenciales; tel. 946-4750; fax 946-4755; e-mail bns.turkscaicos@scotiabank.com; Man. Dir DAVID TAIT; br. on Grand Turk.

Turks and Caicos Banking Co Ltd: Duke St North, Cockburn Town, POB 123, Grand Turk; tel. 946-2368; fax 946-2365; e-mail services@tcbc.tc; internet www.turksandcaicos-banking.com; f. 1980; cap. 2.7m., dep. 9.7m.; Man. Dir ANTON FAESSLER; COO STEFAN O. STOTZ.

TRUST COMPANIES

Berkshire Trust Co Ltd: Caribbean Pl., POB 657, Providenciales; tel. 946-4324; fax 946-4354; e-mail berkshire.trust@tciway.tc; internet www.berkshire.tc; Pres. GORDON WILLIAMSON.

Chartered Trust Co: Town Centre Bldg, Mezzanine Floor, Butterfield Sq., POB 125, Providenciales; tel. 946-4881; fax 946-4041; e-mail reception@chartered-tci.com; internet www.chartered-tci.com; Man. Dir PETER A. SAVORY.

Meridian Trust Co Ltd: Caribbean Pl., Leeward Hwy, POB 599, Providenciales; tel. 941-3082; fax 941-3223; e-mail mtcl@tciway.tc; internet www.meridiantrust.tc; Man. Dir KEITH BURANT.

M & S Trust Co Ltd: Butterfield Sq., POB 260, Providenciales; tel. 946-4650; fax 946-4663; e-mail mslaw@tciway.tc; internet www

.mslaw.tc/trusts.htm; Man. Dir Timothy P. O'Sullivan; Man. Steve Ross.

Temple Trust Co Ltd: 228 Leeward Hwy, Providenciales; tel. 946-5740; fax 946-5739; e-mail info@templefinancialgroup.com; internet www.templefinancialgroup.com; f. 1985; CEO David C. Knipe.

INSURANCE

Turks and Caicos Islands National Insurance Board: Misick's Bldg, POB 250, Grand Turk; tel. 946-1048; fax 946-1362; e-mail nib@tciway.tc; internet www.nib.tc; 4 brs.

Turks and Caicos Association of Insurance Managers (TC-AIM): Southwinds Pl., Unit 6, Leeward Hwy, Providenciales; tel. 946-4987; fax 946-4621; internet turksandcaicos.tc/aim; f. 2000 as Association of Insurance Managers; name changed as above in 2003 when registered as a non-profit asscn; protects interests of domestic and 'offshore' insurance cos in the islands; Pres. Gary Brough; Treas. Ross Blumentritt.

Several foreign (mainly US and British) companies have offices in the Turks and Caicos Islands. More than 2,000 insurance companies were registered at the end of 2002.

Trade and Industry

GOVERNMENT AGENCIES

Financial Services Commission (FSC): see Finance.

General Trading Company (Turks and Caicos) Ltd: PMBI, Cockburn Town, Grand Turk; tel. 946-2464; fax 946-2799; shipping agents, importers, air freight handlers; wholesale distributor of petroleum products, wines and spirits.

Turks Islands Importers Ltd (TIMCO): Front St, POB 72, Grand Turk; tel. 946-2480; fax 946-2481; f. 1952; agents for Lloyds of London, importers and distributors of food, beer, liquor, building materials, hardware and appliances; Dir Hubert Magnus.

DEVELOPMENT ORGANIZATION

Turks and Caicos Islands Investment Agency (TC Invest): Hon. Headley Durham Bldg, Church Folly, POB 105, Grand Turk; tel. 946-2058; fax 946-1464; e-mail tcinvest@tciway.tc; internet www.tcinvest.tc; f. 1974 as Devt Bd of the Turks and Caicos Islands; statutory body; devt finance for private sector; promotion and management of internal investment; Chair. Lillian Misick; Pres. and CEO Colin R. Heartwell.

CHAMBERS OF COMMERCE

Grand Turk Chamber of Commerce: POB 148, Grand Turk; tel. 946-2324; fax 946-2504; e-mail tcimall@tciway.tc; internet www.tcimall.tc/grandturk/index.htm; f. 1974; 57 mem. cos; Pres. and Exec. Dir Glennevans Clarke; Hon. Sec. Sherlin Williams.

North Caicos Chamber of Commerce: tel. 231-1232; Pres. Franklyn Robinson; Sec. Llewyn Handfield.

Providenciales Chamber of Commerce: POB 361, Providenciales; tel. 242-6418; fax 946-4582; e-mail info@provochamber.com; internet www.provochamber.com; 131 mems (2006); Pres. and Treas. Tina Fenimore; Vice-Pres. Allan Hutchison.

UTILITIES

Electricity and Gas

Atlantic (Fortis Turks and Caicos) Ltd: New Airport Rd, Airport Area, South Caicos; tel. and fax 946-3201; Fortis Inc (Bermuda) completed its acquisition of 100% shares in the co in August 2006; sole provider of electricity in South Caicos; Pres. and CEO Eddinton Powell.

Provo Power Company (PPC) Ltd: Town Centre Mall, POB 132, Providenciales; tel. 946-4313; fax 946-4532; internet www.provopowercompany.com; Fortis Energy (Bermuda) completed its acquisition of 100% shares in the co, together with those of its sister co Atlantic Equipment and Power (Turks and Caicos) Ltd, in August 2006; cos referred to collectively as Fortis Turks and Caicos; sole supplier of electricity to Providenciales, North Caicos and Middle Caicos; Pres. and CEO Eddinton Powell.

Turks and Caicos Utilities Ltd: Pond St, POB 80, Grand Turk; tel. 946-2402; fax 946-2896; e-mail ewiggins@wrbenterprises.com.

Water

Provo Water Co: Grace Bay Rd, POB 39, Providenciales; tel. and fax 946-5205; e-mail provowater@tciway.tc.

Turks and Caicos Water Co: Provo Golf Clubhouse, Grace Bay Rd, POB 124, Providenciales; tel. 946-5126; fax 946-5127.

TRADE UNION

Turks and Caicos Service Workers Union: POB 369, Blue Mountain, Providenciales; tel. 3360; fax 8516; Pres. E. Conrad Howell.

Transport

ROADS

There are 121 km (75 miles) of roads in the islands, of which 24 km, on Grand Turk, South Caicos and Providenciales, are surfaced with tarmac. A causeway linking the North and Middle Caicos islands was completed in late 2007.

SHIPPING

There are regular freight services from Miami, Florida, USA. The main sea ports are Grand Turk, Providenciales, Salt Cay and Cockburn Harbour on South Caicos. A new US $40m. cruise ship terminal in Grand Turk, which would enable large passenger liners to stop in the territory, opened in February 2006.

Cargo Express Shipping Service Ltd: South Dock Rd, Providenciales; tel. 941-5006; fax 941-5062.

Seacair Ltd: Churchill Bldg, Front St, POB 170, Grand Turk; tel. 946-2591; fax 946-2226.

Tropical Shipping: c/o Cargo Express Services Ltd, South Dock Rd, Providenciales; tel. 941-5006; fax 941-5062; e-mail nbeen@tropical.com; internet www.tropical.com; Pres. Rick Murrell.

CIVIL AVIATION

There are international airfields on Grand Turk, South Caicos, North Caicos and Providenciales, the last being the most important; there are also landing strips on Middle Caicos, Pine Cay, Parrot Cay and Salt Cay. An expansion project at Providenciales airport was underway in 2008 and included a new terminal building and the lengthening of the runway in order for the airport to accommodate transatlantic flights.

Civil Aviation Authority: Hibiscus Sq., POB 168, Grand Turk; tel. 946-1607; fax 946-1659; e-mail cad@tciway.tc; Man. Dir Thomas Swann.

Air Turks and Caicos (2003) Ltd: 1 InterIsland Plaza, Old Airport Rd, POB 191, Providenciales; tel. 946-4181; fax 946-4040; e-mail fly@airtc.com; internet www.airturksandcaicos.com; also operates *SkyKing Ltd*.

Caicos Caribbean Airlines: South Caicos; tel. 946-3283; fax 946-3377; freight to Miami (FL, USA).

Cairsea Services Ltd: Old Airport Rd, POB 138, Providenciales; tel. 946-4205; fax 946-4504; e-mail info@cairsea.com; internet www.cairsea.com; Man. Dir Rodney Thompson.

Global Airways Ltd: POB 359, Providenciales; tel. 941-3222; fax 946-7290; e-mail global@tciway.tc; internet www.globalairways.tc; operates inter-island connections and Caribbean charter flights; Man. Dir Lindsey Gardiner.

Turks Air Ltd: Providenciales; tel. 946-4504; fax 946-4504; e-mail turksair@earthlink.net; twice-weekly cargo service to and from Miami (USA); Grand Turk Local Agent Cris Newton.

Turks and Caicos Airways Ltd: Providenciales International Airport, POB 114, Providenciales; tel. 946-4255; fax 946-4438; f. 1976 as Air Turks and Caicos; privatized 1983; scheduled daily inter-island service to each of the Caicos Islands, charter flights; Chair. Albray Butterfield; Dir-Gen. C. Moser.

Tourism

The islands' main tourist attractions are the numerous unspoilt beaches, and the opportunities for diving. Salt Cay has been designated a World Heritage site by UNESCO. Hotel accommodation is available on Grand Turk, Salt Cay, South Caicos, Parrot Cay, Pine Cay and Providenciales. In 2007 there were some 264,887 tourist arrivals. In 2006 some 68.3% of tourists were from the USA. In 2003 there were 2,473 hotel rooms (some 80% of which were on Providenciales). Revenue from the sector in 2005 totalled an estimated US $355.1m.

Turks and Caicos Hotel and Tourism Association: POB 251, Ports of Call, Providenciales; tel. 941-5787; fax 946-4001; e-mail tchta@tciway.tc; internet www.turksandcaicoshta.com; fmrly Turks and Caicos Hotel Asscn; over 90 mem. orgs; Pres. Butch Clare; CEO Caesar Campbell.

Turks and Caicos Islands Tourist Board: Front St, POB 128, Grand Turk; tel. 946-2321; fax 946-2733; e-mail provo@turksandcaicostourism.com; internet www.turksandcaicostourism.com; f. 1970; br. in Providenciales; Dir Lindsey Musgrove.

THE UNITED STATES OF AMERICA

Introductory Survey

Location, Climate, Language, Religion, Flag, Capital

The United States of America comprises mainly the North American continent between Canada and Mexico. Alaska, to the north-west of Canada, and Hawaii, in the central Pacific Ocean, are two of the 50 States of the USA. There is considerable climatic variation, with mean annual average temperatures ranging from 29°C (77°F) in Florida to −13.3°C (10°F) in Alaska. Average annual rainfall ranges from 1,831 mm (72.1 ins) in Arkansas to 191 mm (7.5 ins) in Nevada. Much of Texas, New Mexico, Arizona, Nevada and Utah is desert. The official language is English, although there are significant Spanish-speaking minorities. Christianity is the predominant religion. The national flag (proportions 10 by 19) has 13 alternating stripes (seven red and six white) with a dark blue rectangular canton, containing 50 white five-pointed stars, in the upper hoist. The capital is Washington, DC.

Recent History

Concern at the spread of communist influence in Asia dominated US foreign policy during the 1960s and early 1970s. From 1961, until their termination in 1973 by President Richard Nixon, US military operations against communist forces in South Viet Nam led to considerable political division within the USA and were widely criticized internationally. Following a series of scandals involving Nixon and senior administration officials in allegations of corruption and obstruction of justice, known as the 'Watergate' affair, Nixon resigned in August 1974 and was replaced by the Vice-President, Gerald Ford. In November 1976 Jimmy Carter, a Democrat, was elected President. Efforts by the new Administration to resolve tensions in the Middle East culminated in the signing in 1979 of a peace treaty between Egypt and Israel. In 1978 the USA severed formal links with Taiwan and established diplomatic relations with the People's Republic of China. Domestically, economic recession and inflation preoccupied the Carter Administration, and the President's management of the economy was a decisive factor in his defeat by the Republican candidate, Ronald Reagan, in the 1980 presidential election. Although economic recession and high unemployment persisted in the early period of the new Administration, the Republicans retained their previous level of congressional representation in the November 1982 elections. With the resumption of economic growth in 1983, and its strong resurgence through 1984, unemployment and inflation fell, and in November Reagan was re-elected for a further four-year term, securing the largest majority of electoral votes in US history.

In foreign affairs, the Reagan Administration generally pursued a firmly anti-communist line, notably in its active support of right-wing regimes in Latin America, where the US military occupation of Grenada in November 1983 attracted considerable international criticism, and in Africa and the Middle East. Generally friendly relations were, however, maintained with the People's Republic of China. The change of leadership in the USSR in November 1982 was followed by a period of deterioration in contacts between the two countries. Formal disarmament negotiations were renewed following the assumption of leadership in the USSR by Mikhail Gorbachev in 1985. However, US–Soviet relations were overshadowed by Reagan's pursuit of his Strategic Defense Initiative (SDI). Initiated in 1983, this advanced-technology research programme aimed to create a space-based system of defences against nuclear attack. The Reagan Government consistently refused to negotiate the termination of SDI, which was viewed by the USSR as a potential source of arms escalation and a first step in the militarization of space. US–Soviet relations experienced further strain following Soviet military intervention in Afghanistan in 1979.

During the Reagan period the USA adopted a forceful stance (generally welcomed by other Western governments) on international terrorism. However, in 1985 a ban on trade with Libya, which Reagan alleged to be promoting terrorist activity, received little support from other Western countries. In April 1986, following a terrorist attack on US military personnel in West Berlin, Reagan ordered the selective bombing of government offices and military installations in Tripoli and Benghazi, Libya. Direct US military involvement in the Middle East, which had been minimized since its withdrawal in 1984 from peace-keeping operations in Lebanon, was reactivated in July 1987, when Reagan agreed to a request by Kuwait to provide military protection for its petroleum tankers in the Persian (Arabian) Gulf, following attacks on them by Iran. Subsequent incidents in the Gulf brought the USA and Iran into armed confrontations. In April 1988 the USA was a signatory, with the USSR, Afghanistan and Pakistan, to an agreement for the phased withdrawal of Soviet troops from Afghanistan, which was completed in February 1989.

In November 1986 the USA abandoned the weapon deployment limits set by the 1979 Strategic Arms Limitation Treaty (SALT II), which, although never ratified by Congress, had been informally observed by both the USA and the USSR. In March 1987, however, the US Government responded favourably to an indication by the USSR of its willingness to expedite an agreement to eliminate medium-range nuclear missiles from Europe by 1992. Bilateral discussions in 1986 and 1987 resulted in ratification, in 1988, of an Intermediate Nuclear Forces treaty, the first to terminate an entire class of offensive nuclear weapon. The two leaders also agreed to pursue negotiations towards a new Strategic Arms Reduction Treaty (START) to reduce long-range nuclear weaponry by up to 50%. The further advancement of SDI, meanwhile, had become increasingly conjectural: the US Congress proved reluctant to allocate its high funding requirements, and during 1988 and 1989 expressed doubts about the feasibility of the project's goals. The USSR, while maintaining its objections to SDI, agreed in 1990 to exclude it from the ambit of negotiations on START. In July 1991 the USA and USSR signed START, providing for a 30% reduction in long-range nuclear weapons over a seven-year period.

In November 1986 details began to emerge of covert foreign policy operations by senior members of the Reagan Administration in relation to US contacts with the Government of Iran. The ensuing scandal, known as the 'Irangate' or 'Iran-Contra' affair, developed into a major political embarrassment for the President. Subsequent investigations by an independent commission, and by the US Congress, concluded that secret arms sales had been made to the Iranian Government, in return for an undertaking by Iran to help to secure the release of US hostages held by pro-Iranian Islamist groups in Lebanon, and that Reagan had been misled by officials of the security services into authorizing the arms transactions, and bypassing the required congressional consultative procedures. The report also upheld allegations that funds derived from the arms sales had been secretly diverted into bank accounts held by the Nicaraguan Contra rebels. Reagan, who accepted full personal responsibility for the 'Iran-Contra' affair, was exonerated of any deliberate attempt to misrepresent his role in the events. The closing months of Reagan's presidency were clouded by further political scandals involving senior presidential appointees.

At the November 1988 presidential election, Reagan was succeeded by his Vice-President, George Bush, although the Senate and House of Representatives both retained Democratic majorities. The initial months of the Bush Administration were dominated by concern over the formulation of effective measures to contain the federal budget deficit, and over the future course of arms reduction negotiations with the USSR. In June 1989, following an agreement to resume START discussions, President Bush proposed the initiation of new negotiations aimed at achieving substantial reductions in North Atlantic Treaty Organization (NATO) and Warsaw Pact countries' conventional ground forces in Europe. In September the USA and USSR finalized agreements on the monitoring of chemical weapons and procedures for the verification of limits on strategic forces and nuclear tests. A summit meeting between Bush and Gorbachev followed at Valletta, Malta, in December, which marked the opening of a new era in US–Soviet relations. Under discussion were the prospects for new agreements by the mid-1990s for reductions of 50% in nuclear strategic arms, together with substantial reductions in the size of conventional forces based in Europe.

The withdrawal by the USSR in late 1989 and early 1990 from the exercise of direct political influence on the internal affairs of the countries of Eastern Europe was accompanied by a further improvement in US–Soviet relations, and by the implementation of programmes of US economic aid for several of the former Soviet 'client' states. In September 1990 the USA and USSR, with France and the United Kingdom (the other powers that occupied Germany at the end of the Second World War), formally agreed terms for the unification of the two post-war German states, which took effect in the following month. In July the USA, together with the world's six largest industrial democracies, agreed to provide the USSR with economic and technical assistance in undertaking a change-over to a market economy. In the same month a summit meeting of NATO members proposed that the USSR and the other members of the Warsaw Pact alliance join in a formal declaration that the two military groupings were no longer adversaries and would refrain from the threat or use of force. This initiative was followed in November by the signing in Paris, France, by members of NATO and the Warsaw Pact, of a Treaty on Conventional Armed Forces in Europe (CFE), which provided for bilateral limits to be placed on the number of non-nuclear weapons sited between the Atlantic Ocean and the Ural Mountains. Immediately following the signing of the CFE Treaty, Presidents Bush and Gorbachev were present at a meeting of the Conference on Security and Co-operation in Europe (CSCE, now the Organization for Security and Co-operation in Europe—OSCE, see p. 366), at which the USA, the USSR and 32 other countries signed a charter declaring the end of the post-war era of confrontation and division in Europe.

In December 1989, following the failure of an internal coup attempt that received non-military US support, the USA carried out an armed invasion of Panama and subsequently installed an elected government. US troops were withdrawn in February 1990. In Nicaragua the defeat of the Sandinista Government in a general election in February 1990 was followed by the resumption of cordial relations with the US Government.

Following the invasion of Kuwait by Iraqi forces on 2 August 1990, and the subsequent annexation of that country by Iraq, the US Government assumed a leading international role in the implementation of political, economic and military measures to bring about an Iraqi withdrawal. The imposition of mandatory economic sanctions against Iraq by the UN Security Council on 6 August was quickly followed by 'Operation Desert Shield', in which US combat troops and aircraft were dispatched to Saudi Arabia, at that country's request, to secure its borders against a possible attack by Iraq. An offer, subsequently repeated, by President Saddam Hussain of Iraq to link withdrawal from Kuwait with a resolution of other outstanding Middle East problems, was rejected, and in late August the UN Security Council endorsed the use of military action to enforce its economic sanctions. Despite intense diplomatic activity, in which the USSR was prominent, the crisis deepened. In early September Presidents Bush and Gorbachev jointly demanded an Iraqi withdrawal, although the USSR expressed reluctance to support military operations by the UN. In late September the UN Security Council intensified its economic measures against Iraq. However, the ineffectiveness both of economic sanctions and of diplomatic negotiation had become evident by late November, and the USSR gave its assent to the use of force against Iraq, although it did not participate in the multinational force that was now arrayed in the Gulf region and included, under US command, air, sea and ground forces from the United Kingdom, France, Italy, Egypt, Morocco, Kuwait and the other Arab Gulf states. Jordan, which was active throughout the crisis in seeking to promote a negotiated settlement, was perceived by the US Government as sympathetic to Iraq, and US financial aid programmes to that country were suspended.

On 29 November 1990 the UN Security Council authorized the use of 'all necessary means' to force Iraq to withdraw from Kuwait, unless it did so by 15 January 1991. By early January 1991 the USA had established a considerable military presence in the Gulf region, and on 17 January 'Operation Desert Storm' was launched, with massive air and missile attacks against Iraqi positions, both in Iraq and Kuwait. In the course of the conflict, more than 110,000 attacking air missions were flown over Kuwait and Iraq by multinational air forces, while naval support operations were conducted from the Gulf. In the following weeks severe damage was inflicted on Iraqi military and economic targets, while counter-attacks by its air force, and attempts to draw Israel into the conflict by launching missile attacks on population centres, proved ineffective. A ground offensive by the multinational force was launched on 23–24 February, and Iraqi positions were quickly overrun. Hostilities were suspended on 28 February. The Government of Iraq accepted cease-fire terms on 3 March, leaving the multinational forces in control of Kuwait, together with an area of southern Iraq, comprising about 15% of that country's total national territory. Troop withdrawals from the occupied area of Iraq commenced in March, with the remaining US troops evacuated in early May, to be replaced by a UN peace-keeping force.

Following the termination of hostilities, in which 148 US troops died in combat, internal rebellions broke out within Iraq by groups opposed to President Saddam Hussain. The severity with which these were suppressed, particularly in the northern region among the Kurdish ethnic group, and the subsequent flight of refugees into neighbouring areas of Turkey and Iran, prompted large-scale international relief operations. The US Government was widely criticized for its refusal to support the anti-Government insurgents and to take action to depose Saddam Hussain. In May 1991 the USA began airlifting troops to northern Iraq to establish 'safe' enclaves, to which Kurdish refugees were encouraged to return. The US military continued to monitor events in these Kurdish areas from operational bases in Turkey and other strategic points in the region. In September 1996 the USA launched missile strikes from naval vessels in the Gulf at military targets in Iraq, in retaliation for attacks by Iraqi forces against Kurds in northern Iraq.

In the period following the Gulf War the US Government actively pursued initiatives to convene a regional conference, with joint and Soviet sponsorship, to seek a permanent solution to the wider problems of the Middle East. In August 1991 the US Secretary of State, James Baker, obtained the agreement of Egypt, Israel, Jordan, Lebanon and Syria to take part in such a conference, the opening session of which was convened in October. Successive negotiations failed to make any substantive progress, and traditionally close relations between Israel and the USA subsequently came under strain, following pressure by the US Government on Israel to suspend the construction of Jewish settlements in occupied territories, pending the eventual outcome of the peace negotiations.

In December 1991, following the replacement of the USSR by the Commonwealth of Independent States (CIS) comprising 11 of the former Soviet republics, the independence of each republic was recognized by the USA. In January 1992 a meeting was held between President Bush and President Boris Yeltsin of Russia, the dominant republic within the CIS. President Bush expressed concern that effective measures should be taken by the Russian Government to ensure that the nuclear weapons and related technical expertise of the former USSR did not become available to countries not in possession of nuclear weapons capability, or to nations in the Middle East or to the Democratic People's Republic of Korea (DPRK—North Korea). At a subsequent meeting held in February, the Russian leader assured President Bush that immediate safeguards were in force, and that all short-range nuclear warheads would be moved into Russia from sites in other CIS republics by July 1992. President Yeltsin also proposed that the USA and Russia should share in the joint future development of the SDI project (see above), and further reductions in nuclear arsenals were agreed by the two leaders. At a summit meeting held between Presidents Bush and Yeltsin in June 1992 in Washington, DC, agreement was reached on further substantial reductions in nuclear arms, under which, by 2003, total holdings of nuclear warheads would be reduced to less than one-half of the quotas contained in START.

In its relations with the former communist countries in Europe, the USA augmented its commitment to the CSCE with economic support, and promoted the membership of former members of the Warsaw Pact in the North Atlantic Co-operation Council, an offshoot of NATO. Contacts were also revived between the USA and Viet Nam, and in May 1992 there was a partial relaxation of a trade embargo in force since 1975. Relations with Iraq remained tense following the discovery, made in November 1991 by UN representatives, that President Saddam Hussain's regime was seeking to conceal its continuing development of nuclear weapons capability.

Following the conclusion of the Gulf War in early 1991, Bush's political popularity fell sharply, amid growing public perception that the Government was assigning greater priority to foreign affairs than to addressing the problems of the US economy, which had been in recession since early 1989. In April 1992 serious rioting broke out in Los Angeles and spread briefly to several other cities. The underlying causes of the disorders were widely ascribed to the worsening economic and social plight of the impoverished urban black minority.

The 1992 presidential election campaign, in which Bush was opposed by Bill Clinton, a Democratic state governor, and Ross Perot, a populist independent, was dominated by social and economic issues. Bush's record of economic management, particularly in relation to the persistence of federal budget deficits, provided the major line of attack by the opposing candidates. Voter turn-out, at 55%, was the highest at any presidential election since 1968, and gave a decisive majority, of 43% to 37%, to Clinton. Perot, whose campaign had concentrated on the question of federal deficit spending, obtained almost 19% of the popular vote.

Foreign affairs dominated the final months of the Bush Administration. In July 1992 contention arose between the Government of Iraq and the UN over the rights of UN observers to inspect Iraqi nuclear facilities, and in the following month the US Government sought to limit internal military operations by the Iraqi Government by imposing an air exclusion zone south of latitude 32°N. This was followed, in January 1993, by US participation in selective bombings of Iraqi missile sites. In December 1992 relations with the People's Republic of China, which had been strained since 1989 by the Chinese Government's persistent suppression of political dissent, were revived by the removal of a US embargo on sales of military equipment. In the same month President Bush launched 'Operation Restore Hope', under which 24,000 US troops were sent to Somalia, as part of an international force under US command, to protect shipments of food aid and to assist in the restoration of civil order.

Shortly before the transfer of the presidency to Bill Clinton in January 1993, Presidents Bush and Yeltsin met in Moscow to sign a second Nuclear Arms Reduction Treaty (START II), which provided for the elimination by 2003 of almost 75% of all US and CIS-held nuclear warheads. Clinton announced the termination of SDI, although there was subsequent discussion within the USA of its possible reactivation (see below). Although ratified by the US Senate in 1993, START II remained unratified by the Russian legislature until April 2000. However, arrangements agreed in late 1997 by the US and Russian Governments had extended by five years the period allowed for the elimination of Russia's long-range nuclear missiles.

The initial preoccupation of the Clinton Administration was the formulation of an economic recovery plan, to be phased over a five-year period, to reduce the federal budget deficit by means of increased taxation and economies in the cost of government, rather than by reduced levels of federal spending. Military expenditure was a particular area in which economies were proposed, while additional spending was planned for infrastructural projects and measures to stimulate economic activity. A major restructuring of the US health care system was also planned, and a commission to formulate proposals was placed under the chairmanship of President Clinton's wife, Hillary. Certain aspects of the economic recovery plan, particularly those relating to higher income tax and a new energy tax, encountered initial opposition in the Democrat-controlled Congress, but were eventually approved, in a modified form, by the House of Representatives in May 1993. Approval by the Senate, following further amendments, took place in June. By mid-1993, however, the President's initial popularity had fallen sharply, owing in part to perceptions of indecisiveness by Clinton in formulating effective policies. There was also widespread criticism of the competence of some of his advisers and appointees.

By mid-1993 the crisis in former Yugoslavia had assumed increased importance as a foreign policy issue, leading to disagreements between the USA and the Western European powers, which opposed US proposals to launch direct air strikes against military positions held by Bosnian Serbs. The US Administration, while avoiding any direct military commitment, gave its support, through NATO, to peace-keeping operations in Bosnia and Herzegovina. Clinton was unsuccessful, however, in efforts to secure the removal of the international embargo on arms sales to the Bosnian Muslims. In June 1994 the US Government endorsed proposals by the European Union (EU) countries for the tripartite partition of Bosnia and Herzegovina.

The Clinton Administration made renewed efforts to restore to power Fr Jean-Bertrand Aristide, the first democratically elected President of Haiti, who had taken refuge in the USA following his overthrow by a military junta in 1991. An economic embargo imposed by the Organization of American States (OAS, see p. 373), together with implied threats of military intervention by the US Government, had failed to displace the military regime, and conditions within Haiti had led large numbers of refugees to seek asylum in the USA, many of whom were forcibly repatriated by the US authorities. In June 1994, following the imposition in the previous month of international sanctions against Haiti by the UN Security Council, Clinton announced the suspension of all commercial and financial transactions with Haiti. In September, following a diplomatic mission led by former President Carter, a UN-sponsored multinational force, composed almost entirely of US troops, arrived in Haiti with the agreement of the military junta, which relinquished power in October. US troops were withdrawn from the UN force in March 1995. In January 2004 the Administration of George W. Bush (2001–09) condemned attacks on thousands of demonstrators protesting against the Aristide Government. In March, in the face of growing violence and under international pressure, Aristide resigned and went into exile, although he claimed that he had been unconstitutionally removed from office by the USA. Several hundred US marines were deployed in Haiti in March–June 2004 as the vanguard of a multinational UN Stabilization Mission in Haiti to disarm rebel forces and stabilize the country.

During 1993 the Clinton Administration continued to foster efforts to promote a general resolution of tensions in the Middle East. With US assistance, but as a direct result of secret diplomatic mediation by Norway, the Palestine Liberation Organization (PLO) and the Government of Israel signed an agreement providing for Palestinian self-government in the Occupied Territories and for mutual recognition by Israel and the PLO. In January 1994, following a meeting held in Geneva, Switzerland, between Clinton and President Hafiz al-Assad of Syria, negotiations were initiated for a settlement between Israel and Syria.

Political and economic contacts with Russia continued on a cordial level, with the two countries adopting a co-operative stance in many areas of foreign policy. In February 1994 the US Government lifted the remaining sanctions on trade with Viet Nam (see above) and in the following July the USA established full diplomatic relations with that country. Little progress, however, was made in the resolution of the persistently adverse US balance of trade with Japan, despite an agreement between the two countries in July 1993 to implement measures to reduce the trade deficit.

The prevention of nuclear proliferation, which remained a prime objective of US foreign policy, led in 1993 and early 1994 to a serious confrontation between the USA and North Korea. In March 1993 the DPRK, which is a signatory of the Nuclear Non-Proliferation Treaty (NPT) and is subject, by virtue of its membership of the International Atomic Energy Agency (IAEA, see p. 113), to the monitoring of its nuclear installations, refused to grant the IAEA inspectorate full access to its nuclear power facility. It cited as its reasons the existence of joint military exercises between the Republic of Korea (South Korea) and the USA and 'unjust acts' by the IAEA. The US Government stated that it had reason to suspect that the DPRK had been diverting nuclear plant material for the development of atomic weapons. In July Clinton visited South Korea, and warned the DPRK that any use of nuclear weapons by them would be met with military force. Despite increasing international pressure, and attempts at mediation by the UN, the DPRK repeatedly asserted its refusal to comply with the Treaty's inspection requirements. The crisis steadily worsened during early 1994, and in June the US Government, after seeking unsuccessfully to offer the DPRK economic aid, investment and diplomatic recognition, began to seek support for the imposition of UN economic sanctions. Later in the same month, following a visit to the DPRK by former President Carter (acting as an unofficial representative of the Government), the DPRK agreed to a temporary suspension of its nuclear programme, pending formal discussions with the US Government. These meetings were convened in July. Negotiations aimed at improving relations between the USA and the DPRK, and at fostering a political settlement between the DPRK and South Korea, were pursued throughout both Clinton Administrations. In March 1999 the US and DPRK Governments agreed on terms whereby US officials would receive unrestricted access to inspect DPRK nuclear facilities.

The collapse of Clinton's plans for health care reform following congressional opposition in 1994, together with increasing public concern about the domestic economy and the effectiveness of Clinton's policies on social issues (notably in the areas of welfare expenditure, law enforcement and the protection of traditional

THE UNITED STATES OF AMERICA

social values), led to a sharp rise in support for the conservative doctrines of politicians representing the right wing of the Republican Party. At congressional elections in November 1994, the Republicans gained control both of the Senate (for the first time since 1986) and the House of Representatives (which had been controlled by the Democrats since 1954). As a result, in 1995 serious divisions began to emerge between President Clinton and Congress. In June tensions arose over proposals to achieve a balanced federal budget. Negotiations proved inconclusive, and in November Clinton, in an effort to resolve the deadlock, refused to renew the temporary funding arrangements, causing an eight-day shutdown of all non-essential operations of the federal government. Agreement on the 1995/96 budget was eventually reached in April 1996, although disagreements on the timetable for, and the method of achieving, a balanced budget remained unresolved.

In the presidential election that was held in November 1996, Clinton decisively secured a second term in office, obtaining 49% of the popular vote. Robert Dole, the Republican nominee, obtained 41% of the votes, while Ross Perot, who was nominated by the Reform Party, an organization founded by him to seek radical reductions in federal government spending, attracted 8%. The Republicans retained control of the Senate and House of Representatives.

Following his inauguration in January 1997, Clinton declared the enhancement of educational standards to be a primary aim of his second term. Proposals were also announced to achieve further reductions in welfare dependency, by providing tax credits and other incentives to employers. Financial savings were to be achieved by further reductions in defence expenditure, and by the implementation of additional cuts in spending on health care for the elderly. Clinton reiterated his intention, however, of seeking improved provisions for insured health care, and of achieving a balanced federal budget by 2002. Agreement between Clinton and the Republican congressional leadership on the general terms of these budgetary measures was reached in May 1997.

In foreign affairs, the Clinton Administration continued to support economic reform in Russia and the successor states of the former USSR, with particular emphasis on fostering the changeover from defence to consumer production. Prior to the cease-fire declared in August 1996, the US Government expressed disapproval of the scale of Russian military operations in Chechnya, and in May 1995 the Clinton Administration was refused Russian co-operation in its ban on US trade and investment in Iran, in retaliation for that country's alleged involvement in international terrorism. Concerns expressed by Russia at the proposed enlargement of NATO were addressed at a summit meeting of Presidents Yeltsin and Clinton in Helsinki, Finland, in March 1997. (See the chapter on Russia for details of the subsequent agreement between NATO and Russia.)

The reluctance of the Clinton Administration to participate directly in UN military operations in Bosnia and Herzegovina was modified in June 1995 with a statement by Clinton that US ground troops would be sent to Bosnia and Herzegovina in 'emergency' circumstances on a 'limited basis' if required to assist in the redeployment of existing UN forces, or to participate in monitoring an eventual peace settlement. In November, following US-sponsored negotiations held in Dayton, Ohio, a peace agreement was reached by the opposing sides. As part of its implementation, the US Government agreed to contribute 20,000 troops to a multinational supervisory force of 60,000 troops under the command of NATO. The USA committed about 8,500 troops in an extended NATO peace-keeping operation in Bosnia and Herzegovina until mid-1998 and about 1,000 soldiers served as part of NATO's Stabilization Force until December 2004. A small contingent of US troops remained in Bosnia and Herzegovina in 2009.

Relations with the People's Republic of China pursued an uneven course under the Clinton Administration, owing to disagreements over trade matters and criticism by the USA of alleged abuses by the Chinese Government of human rights. Relations between the two countries declined sharply in February 1996, following US protests over Chinese military operations near Taiwan. Relations between the two countries were enhanced in October 1997 by a state visit to the USA by President Jiang Zemin, following which the US Government revoked a ban, in force since 1989, on the export of US nuclear technology to China. China, together with Russia and the USA, refused in December 1997 to sign an international treaty—the Ottawa Convention—banning the manufacture and use of anti-personnel land-mines; the US Government based its objection to the arrangements on its requirement for land-mines to protect its troops stationed in the Republic of Korea. (Following a two and a half year review of land-mine policy, in February 2004 the Bush Administration announced that it would not sign the treaty and would continue to use, indefinitely, 'non-persistent' land-mines that would self-destruct or self-deactivate after a certain period of time.) Following the settlement in 1999 of a dispute over infringements of US copyright and other intellectual property rights, Chinese enhanced trading privileges were granted permanent status in 2000, opening the way for the People's Republic of China to join the World Trade Organization (WTO, see p. 410).

Successive US Governments remained unwilling to restore relations with Cuba. Relations between the two countries deteriorated in March 1996, after two civilian aircraft carrying Cuban exiles protesting against the Government of Fidel Castro were shot down by the Cuban air force over international waters. In response, Clinton acceded to congressional demands to strengthen the US commercial and economic embargo that has been in force since 1962. Under the new measure, the Cuban Liberty and Solidarity (Helms-Burton) Act, the USA was to penalize foreign investors whose business in any way involved property in Cuba that was confiscated from US citizens following the 1959 revolution. In July a number of Canadian, Mexican and Italian companies were informed that sanctions were to be imposed on them under the Helms-Burton legislation, barring their senior executives and certain shareholders from visiting the USA. In response to intense international pressure, Clinton declared a temporary moratorium on certain provisions of the Helms-Burton Act, and in April 1997 the US Government and the EU, which had protested the measure, announced that a compromise had been agreed, subject to the abandonment by the US Government of certain sections of the Act. The moratorium on Title III of the Act was subsequently extended at six-monthly intervals and remained in operation in 2009. In late 2001 the USA lifted temporarily the trade embargo against Cuba to allow the purchase of food and medicines necessary for the reconstruction and aid effort following the devastation caused by 'Hurricane Michelle'. In April 2004 a motion, supported by the USA, condemning Cuba for human rights violations, was approved by the UN General Assembly; similar US-backed motions had been passed by the UN in 2002 and 2003. In April 2005 a milder, US-proposed motion requesting that the mandate of the UN's Special Rapporteur on Human Rights in Cuba be extended was approved by the General Assembly. In July Secretary of State Condoleezza Rice appointed Caleb McCarry Cuba Transition Co-ordinator, a position created at the behest of a special panel charged with directing the US Government's actions 'in support of a free Cuba' and hastening the end to President Castro's premiership. Bilateral relations deteriorated further in 2007 following the release from a US prison of Luis Posada Carriles, who was wanted in Cuba on terrorism charges. The Cuban Government accused the Bush Administration of hypocrisy in its so-called 'war on terror' (see below). The Government of Barack Obama (2009–) announced plans to relax certain sanctions against Cuba, including travel restrictions on Cuban-American citizens and limits on remittances, as well as allowing US telecommunications companies greater access to the Cuban market.

In December 1994 President Clinton proposed the formation, by 2006, of a Free Trade Area of the Americas (FTAA), comprising 34 countries of the Western hemisphere, although excluding Cuba. Negotiations were scheduled to conclude by January 2005, but stalled in November 2004 and had not yet recommenced by mid-2009. Meanwhile, however, the Venezuelan President, Lt-Col (retd) Hugo Chávez Frías, had commenced implementation of an alternative free trade initiative for the Americas, the Bolivarian Alternative for the Americas (Alternativa Bolivariana para las Américas—ALBA), in direct challenge to the moribund FTAA. Relations between the Bush and Chávez Governments deteriorated markedly in the 2000s, and in September 2008 the Venezuelan President suspended diplomatic relations with the USA in solidarity with the Bolivian Government of Evo Morales. Morales had expelled the US ambassador, accusing him of fomenting opposition dissent in Bolivia. The new Secretary of State, Hillary Clinton, intimated in mid-2009 that the Obama Government wanted to improve relations with the left-wing administrations in Bolivia and Venezuela, beginning with the resumption of diplomatic relations.

In January 2000 the Clinton Administration announced an aid package for the Andean region worth US $1,300m., the largest ever aid programme for Latin America. The main portion of the programme, which became known as the 'Plan Colombia', was to provide some $860m. to Colombia, three-quarters of which was allocated to the security forces in that country, to aid with the ongoing war against drugs-trafficking. The size of the military component of the Plan caused controversy internationally, as did the proposed aerial destruction of crops in the region. The Bush Administration implemented an Andean Counterdrug Initiative in 2001 to complement Plan Colombia, the focus of which was on improving social and economic conditions in the region. Nevertheless, the objective remained the same: to reduce significantly the flow of drugs from the Andean region into the USA. The incoming Obama Administration made no cuts to the funding of Plan Colombia, which totalled $660m. in 2009.

During his second term as President, Clinton was confronted by a number of other allegations, which he consistently denied, of perjury and obstruction of justice arising from accusations of sexual harassment, dating from prior to 1992 and extending throughout his presidency. These matters, which related to Clinton's period as a state official in Arkansas, were brought within the ambit of a congressionally mandated independent counsel, Kenneth Starr, who began in 1994 to examine the legal ramifications of the 'Whitewater' affair (President Clinton and his wife were accused of financial irregularities in their alleged involvement in a savings bank and property development company that collapsed in 1989, during Clinton's tenure as Governor of Arkansas). In January 1998 Starr was authorized by the Attorney-General to investigate whether a sexual relationship alleged by a former White House intern, Monica Lewinsky, had taken place with the President in 1995. Clinton vehemently denied any improper conduct with Lewinsky; however, in August 1998, following an offer of immunity from prosecution by Starr to Lewinsky, the President admitted that an inappropriate relationship had taken place with Lewinsky, although he had at no time sought to obstruct legal processes. Starr's report to Congress alleged that Clinton had committed 11 offences of perjury and obstruction of justice, constituting grounds for his removal from office. No evidence, however, was offered of wrongdoing by Clinton in relation to the 'Whitewater' affair. In October the House of Representatives voted to commence an impeachment inquiry against the President, but in February 1999 the Senate acquitted Clinton on the first and second articles of impeachment. A subsequent attempt in the Senate to obtain a vote of censure on Clinton was unsuccessful.

In August 1998 bomb attacks on US embassy buildings in Nairobi, Kenya, and Dar es Salaam, Tanzania, claimed 258 lives, and were followed by US air missile attacks on a factory site in Khartoum, Sudan (which was alleged to be a manufactory of chemicals for use in toxic gases), and on targets in Afghanistan, which were stated by the US Government to be operational centres for Osama bin Laden, a fugitive Saudi Arabian-born Islamist activist whom the USA believed to be responsible for past assaults on US forces and facilities in Somalia, Yemen and Saudi Arabia. Bin Laden was also held responsible for terrorist operations within the USA, including the 1993 bombing of the World Trade Center in New York. In October 2001 four associates of bin Laden were sentenced to life imprisonment by a US court for their involvement in the bomb attacks in Nairobi and Dar es Salaam.

In December 1998, following the termination by Iraq of international weapons inspections in its territory, the USA and the United Kingdom conducted a series of missile raids on Iraqi military sites. In March 1999 the US Government initiated and led, under NATO auspices, a sustained campaign of missile raids on military and related installations in Serbia and Montenegro, in support of international demands that the President of the Federal Republic of Yugoslavia, Slobodan Milošević, desist from the mass expulsion of members of the ethnic Albanian population of the Serbian province of Kosovo. NATO air attacks on Belgrade during May resulted in the accidental bombing by US aircraft of the diplomatic mission in the Yugoslav capital of the People's Republic of China, which, despite a subsequent apology and the payment of compensation by the US Government, led to a period of strained relations between the two countries. Following the military withdrawal of Serbian forces from Kosovo in June, US forces took a leading role in subsequent UN peace-keeping operations in the region.

Throughout Clinton's presidency the USA continued to pursue an active role in efforts to secure the settlement of conflicts in the Middle East (with particular reference to matters at issue between Israel, Syria and Lebanon) and in December 1999, under Clinton's auspices, the first substantive negotiations since 1996 between the Governments of Israel and Syria took place in Washington, DC. In March 2000 the US Government sought to move towards a rapprochement with Iran with the announcement that it was to ease some of the trade sanctions against Iran that had been in force since 1979.

In January 1999 the Clinton Administration indicated that it was considering an allocation of US $7,000m. over a three-year period from 2000 for new research into the SDI programme (see above), which had been initiated by President Reagan in 1983 and on which an estimated $55,000m. had been spent prior to its termination by Clinton in 1995. Under the new proposals, which attracted considerable congressional support from Republicans, the original concept of a space-based missile defence system was to be replaced by a network of ground- or sea-based interceptor rockets with the capability of destroying intercontinental ballistic missiles either accidentally launched or fired by a hostile power. This modification of the SDI, which was redesignated as the National Missile Defence (NMD) system, would require the agreement of Russia to amend prior anti-nuclear treaties. In May 2000 the USA, together with the United Kingdom, France, Russia and the People's Republic of China, announced a commitment to global nuclear disarmament, although no timetable was set out for the eventual elimination of stockpiles of these weapons. In early September 2001, in return for China's acceptance of the NMD, the USA pledged to keep China informed of its development and agreed to recognize that the Chinese might, in the future, want to resume nuclear weapons testing. The USA also urged China not to transfer ballistic missile technology to countries that the USA considered to be 'rogue states' (deemed by the Department of State to be those countries with the capabilities to use weapons of mass destruction without adherence to traditional international conventions).

A presidential election was held on 7 November 2000. Vice-President Al Gore was the Democratic Party candidate, while George W. Bush, the Governor of Texas and a son of former President Bush, was the Republican Party's nominee. Following voting, it emerged that the possession of an overall majority in the presidential Electoral College would depend on the 25 college mandates from the state of Florida, where the result of the ballot was in dispute. The state was initially declared in favour of Governor Bush, pending the result of a mandatory automated recount of the votes; however, the Democrats challenged the declaration (and the state government's refusal to permit the ballots to be recounted by electoral staff following the automated recount) in the Florida Supreme Court, claiming that a significant number of votes in certain counties had been incorrectly registered by the automated counting system. The Court ruled that the ballots in the counties concerned should be recounted by electoral staff and allowed an additional 12 days for this process to be completed. The US Supreme Court disallowed this ruling, however, and returned the matter to the Florida Supreme Court for further consideration. Only one county completed its 'manual' recount and the result remained in Governor Bush's favour (by 537 votes). The Democrats began further legal action, claiming that the importance of recounting all disputed ballots transcended time limits. The Florida Supreme Court upheld the appeal and ordered the recounting of some 45,000 disputed ballots. The Republicans challenged the verdict, claiming that no provision for such 'manual' recounts was made in the electoral legislation. The US Supreme Court upheld the Republican appeal, by a margin of five judges to four. With all legal options exhausted, and with the Florida legislature having voted to endorse a list of Republican electors irrespective of the outcome of further legal action, Vice-President Gore conceded defeat in Florida (and thereby nationally) on 13 December. Final results subsequently indicated that Vice-President Gore obtained 48.4% of the valid votes cast, compared with 47.9% obtained by Governor Bush. Thus, the latter became the first contender since 1876 to win a majority in the Electoral College while losing the national popular ballot.

President Bush's first Cabinet contained several individuals who had served in his father's Administration, as well as one member of Clinton's Cabinet. His Administration immediately suspended the implementation of a number of environmental regulations issued by Clinton shortly before his departure from office. The Administration's first budget, presented in February 2001, included provisions for reductions in levels of personal taxation. Environmental campaigners (who had expressed reservations over President Bush's attitude to environmental issues) and numerous foreign governments and international organizations strongly criticized the new President in March when his Administration withdrew support for the ratification process of the Kyoto Protocol on climate change agreed at the third Conference of the Parties to the Framework Convention on Climate Change in December 1997 (see UN Environment Programme, see p. 65), claiming it would be detrimental to US economic interests. In February 2002 Bush proposed voluntary, less far-reaching, measures to reduce emissions of 'greenhouse gases'. A government report on energy policy in May 2001, which included a proposal to introduce legislation authorizing exploratory drilling for oil in the Arctic National Wildlife Refuge in Alaska (ANWR), also prompted criticism from the environmental lobby. In August the House of Representatives voted in favour of the proposal by a narrow majority; however, the proposed legislation was rejected by the Senate in April 2002. The Administration subsequently introduced a provision to allow drilling to start in 2004, whereby federal revenue would be raised from the sale of leases to petroleum companies, but in March 2003 Congress removed the provision. In August the Government proposed further controversial amendments to regulations governing carbon emissions; under the new legislation, energy companies would no longer be required to install anti-pollution measures when upgrading equipment. The announcement prompted criticism from environmental groups, and legal contests against the proposals were immediately begun in 13 states. In March–April 2005 Congress narrowly approved a proposal to begin drilling in the ANWR. However, in its final version, the relevant legislation was part of a wider budget reconciliation bill that was only approved by both houses in late December once the ANWR provision had been removed. In what appeared to be a repetition of the previous year's events, in March 2006 the Senate narrowly approved legislation that would permit the opening of parts of the ANWR to drilling; however, the outcome was again contingent on congressional approval of another budget reconciliation bill. Government proposals for the inclusion of the ANWR in the USA's Strategic Petroleum Reserve were presented in March 2007 as a means of expediting the long-debated exploitation of the Refuge for its oil wealth. Conversely, proposed legislation to designate the coastal region of the ANWR as a wilderness area to be permanently exempted from oil exploration was introduced, by independent Senator Joseph Lieberman, to the Senate Natural Resources Committee for discussion in November, but was rejected before reaching the wider Senate. Despite ratification of minor amendments to existing ANWR legislation during that year, and the President's reiteration in April 2008 of the Refuge's potential as a resource for bolstering the Strategic Petroleum Reserve—with regard to the effects of escalating international oil prices upon the domestic economy—the existing restrictions were still in place in early 2009. The incoming President, Barack Obama, was strongly opposed to any future exploration of the ANWR. According to the US Geological Survey, recoverable oil reserves in the ANWR were estimated at 10,400m. barrels of oil in 2005; during that period the USA was consuming 20m. barrels per day.

President Bush's strong personal support for the NMD programme caused further concern both within the USA and abroad. In November 2001, following a summit meeting in Washington, DC, President Bush and Russian President Vladimir Putin both pledged to reduce their nation's nuclear arsenals by approximately two-thirds over the following decade; a formal agreement was signed in May 2002. In June the USA formally withdrew from the Anti-Ballistic Missile Treaty (ABM), signed with the USSR in 1972, claiming that its adherence prevented the development of the NMD. President Bush emphasized that the USA's withdrawal from the ABM would not undermine US–Russian relations. Putin described the withdrawal as a mistake, but insisted it would not damage Russian security. In December 2001 the USA received fierce criticism from EU member states after forcing the collapse of an international conference convened to reinforce the terms of the Biological and Toxic Weapons Convention, signed in 1972; the USA opposed plans that would have allowed international inspectors to monitor its military and industrial facilities. The USA attracted further international criticism by its refusal to sign up to the terms of the International Criminal Court (ICC), established to try war criminals, which was inaugurated at The Hague, Netherlands, in March 2003. The USA defended its position by claiming that members of its military could be put on trial on political grounds, and, in response, in the same month, Congress approved the American Service Member and Citizen Protection Act, which would enable the USA to free, by force if necessary, any member of its military arrested by the ICC. In mid-June the UN Security Council granted US forces exemption from prosecution by the ICC for one year. Early in the following month the USA reduced military aid to some 35 countries that refused to sign agreements that would give US citizens immunity from prosecution. In March 2006 Secretary of State Condoleezza Rice acknowledged that the retraction of such aid to Latin American countries had disadvantaged the USA's regional security strategy, while in July legislation was introduced into the House of Representatives by Democrats proposing a repeal of military assistance prohibitions against signatories to the ICC. By the following month some 101 Bilateral Immunity Agreements had been signed, exempting certain such US citizens from referral to the ICC. The deterioration of the crisis in Darfur, Sudan (see chapter on Sudan), later that year prompted appeals that the US Administration endorse the jurisdiction of the ICC in prosecuting Sudanese leaders, indicating the USA's recognition of the Court's importance in administering international justice. Following allegations of abuse and torture of Iraqi prisoners by US soldiers (see below), in June 2004 the USA withdrew a proposed resolution at the UN Security Council to give US personnel immunity from prosecution at the ICC.

On 11 September 2001 four commercial passenger aircraft were hijacked shortly after take-off from Boston, New York and Washington, DC. The two aircraft originating in Boston, both bound for Los Angeles, were diverted to New York and each was flown into one of the two towers of the World Trade Center, both of which subsequently collapsed. The third aircraft was flown into the Pentagon building (the headquarters of the Department of Defense) in Washington, DC, and the fourth aircraft, also apparently heading for Washington, DC, crashed in farmland near Pittsburgh, Pennsylvania. The death toll was eventually put at 2,752, including 266 passengers and crew (including the hijackers) on the four aircraft, 190 at the Pentagon, and the remainder in New York, principally those unable to escape from the towers before they collapsed, and members of the emergency services. On 13 September the Secretary of State, Gen. Colin Powell, identified Osama bin Laden (see above) and his al-Qa'ida (Base) organization, a network of fundamentalist Islamist militants, as responsible for the attacks. However, bin Laden, who was believed to be in Afghanistan, where he was harboured by the extremist Islamist Taliban regime, had already denied accusations that he had ordered the hijackings, although he expressed his approval of the attacks. In late 2002 an independent bipartisan inquiry, the National Commission on Terrorist Attacks Upon the United States, was established to investigate the circumstances surrounding the attacks (see below). In early March 2003 security forces in Rawalpindi, Pakistan, arrested the Kuwaiti-born Khalid Sheikh Mohammed, accused of being the operational planner behind the attacks, and released him into US custody for interrogation. In late March 2006, in a court in Virginia, Moroccan-born Zacarias Moussaoui pleaded guilty to charges of conspiracy to commit acts of terrorism, in relation to the attacks. Moussaoui had pleaded guilty to conspiracy charges in July 2002, but subsequently retracted his plea. In early May 2006 he was sentenced to life imprisonment without parole. In March 2007 Khalid Sheikh Mohammed, regarded as one of the principal agents of al-Qa'ida's operations, was tried by military commission, along with two other alleged key al-Qa'ida operatives. The US Department of Defense released a partial transcript of Sheikh Mohammed's trial at the detention centre in Guantánamo Bay, Cuba (see below), in which the suspect claimed involvement in 31 separate international terrorism plots and attacks, including orchestration of the 1993 and 2001 attacks on the World Trade Center, the beheading of US journalist Daniel Pearl in 2002 and numerous assassination attempts against international political leaders. However, speculation that such admissions had been obtained under duress, or torture, tarnished any belief in the international community that justice had been achieved and provoked further criticism of the interrogation methods employed at Guantánamo Bay. Charges brought by the US Government in February 2008 against six prisoners being held in Guantánamo Bay, including Khalid Sheikh Mohammed, elicited similar censure. The charges, for which military prosecutors were to seek the death penalty, related to the detainees' alleged involvement in the 2001 attacks and included conspiracy, murder, attacking civilians, destruction of property and terrorism.

In the immediate wake of the attacks on New York and Washington, DC, President Bush declared that those responsible should be captured 'dead or alive'. Both houses of Congress unanimously approved emergency anti-terrorism legislation, which made provision for increased military spending and US $20,000m. for reconstruction in New York, and adopted a resolution authorizing the President to use 'all necessary and appropriate force' against those who organized the attacks. Congress also approved the so-called 'Patriot Act' (Uniting and Strengthening America by Providing the Appropriate Tools Required to Intercept and Obstruct Terrorism—PATRIOT—Act of 2001), which was signed into law in late October 2001, giving wide-ranging powers to the Government to investigate citizens and non-citizens alike. The Act was viewed by critics as a threat to civil liberties. (The Patriot Act was scheduled to expire at the end of 2005, but was temporarily extended by Congress until February 2006. A continuance of the law, the USA Patriot Act Improvement and Reauthorization Act of 2005, was signed into law by the President in March 2006.) The Government began to form an international coalition against terrorism, for which most Western Governments pledged their support. NATO invoked Article Five of the NATO Charter (which states that an attack on a member state is an attack on all 19 members), which required members to assist the USA, according to judgement and resources; the Governments of the United Kingdom, France and Germany, among others, offered military and financial assistance. The Taliban regime in Afghanistan denied involvement in the terrorist attacks, and warned that it would retaliate if attacked. On 17 September 2001 the USA issued an ultimatum to the Taliban, via Pakistan (the only state with diplomatic links to the regime), to surrender bin Laden or face an imminent military assault. Several weeks of intense diplomatic activity ensued, during which time international support for the USA's so-called global 'war on terror' increased, and the US Government was apparently able to gather further evidence of the al-Qa'ida network's involvement in the attacks. The Taliban reportedly asked to see evidence of bin Laden's involvement in the attacks, a request rejected by the USA. In the meantime, US military forces increased their presence in the region around Afghanistan. Pakistan and Uzbekistan agreed to grant the US-led forces access to their airbases for emergency operations and Russia allowed access to its airspace for humanitarian missions. Saudi Arabia, although it refused to allow the USA to use its military bases, granted access to its airspace.

On 2 October 2001 NATO declared that it had received evidence from the USA that confirmed bin Laden's responsibility for the terrorist attacks. On 7 October US and British armed forces commenced military operations ('Operation Enduring Freedom') against Taliban military targets and suspected al-Qa'ida training camps in Afghanistan. In addition to military strikes, aircraft released food and medicine parcels to Afghan civilians; leaflets were also dropped offering protection and a reward in return for information on the whereabouts of al-Qa'ida leaders. On 14 October a senior Taliban official offered to surrender bin Laden to a third country in return for a cessation of US bombing, if the USA provided evidence of his involvement in the terrorist attacks, an offer the USA rejected. The US-led forces co-ordinated operations with the military wing of the exiled Afghan Government, the United National Islamic Front for the Salvation of Afghanistan (UIFSA—also known as the Northern Alliance). During November the latter made substantial territorial gains in northern and western Afghanistan, including the Afghan capital, Kabul, and Mazar-i-Sharif, a strategically important town in the north. In late November US ground forces were deployed for the first time, near the southern city of Kandahar, in an attempt to locate bin Laden. Kandahar fell to the US-led forces in early December, leaving only localized areas of Taliban resistance; US forces subsequently intensified their search for bin Laden, who was believed to be in the Tora Bora caves near Jalalabad, in the east of the country. US-led ground forces were still deployed in Afghanistan in May 2002, attempting to overcome a small number of Taliban and al-Qa'ida members who had not surrendered; bin Laden remained at large. The USA refused, however, to deploy peace-keeping troops in Afghanistan to support the interim administration of Hamid Karzai, which had replaced the Taliban regime in early December 2001, although it released previously withheld assets to his Government, and pledged financial aid to rebuild the country's infrastructure. In January 2002 the Bush Government pledged some US $296.8m. in funds for the reconstruction of Afghanistan.

In January 2002 the US military began transferring members of the Taliban and al-Qa'ida, who had been captured in battle, to the US naval base in Guantánamo Bay in Cuba. Initially, the USA refused to grant the detainees (numbering almost 300) prisoner-of-war status under the Geneva Convention of 1949 (which guaranteed trial by court martial or a civilian court, as opposed to a military tribunal), prompting criticism from its coalition partners, which intensified following the publication of photographs showing prisoners shackled and blindfolded. In February, following pressure from the British and French Governments, President Bush accorded partial protection of the Convention to captured Taliban fighters (he stopped short of full protection, however, claiming that the soldiers were members of an irregular militia); al-Qa'ida captives were offered no protection, as they were considered to be terrorists with no allegiance to any specific state or government. President Bush also abandoned an earlier demand to make the final judgment on a detainee's guilt or innocence. In late June the Supreme Court ruled that, while the President as Commander-in-Chief had the power to detain enemy combatants, they were entitled to legal representation in a US federal court. The following day the first three prisoners from Guantánamo Bay appeared before a military tribunal.

In July 2004 the National Commission on Terrorist Attacks Upon the United States delivered its final report into intelligence failures in the months preceding the attacks of 11 September 2001. It did not lay the blame on either the Clinton or Bush Governments, but asserted that both Administrations had failed to realize the immediacy of the threat posed by the al-Qa'ida network. The report highlighted opportunities to uncover the plot that had been overlooked by both the Central Intelligence Agency (CIA) and the Federal Bureau of Investigation (FBI). However, it did not conclude that the attacks could have been prevented. It also found that, while Osama bin Laden had approved Khalid Sheikh Mohammed's plan in 1999, there was no evidence to link al-Qa'ida with Saddam Hussain (see below). The report recommended, *inter alia*: the creation of a national director of intelligence with overall responsibility for all of the intelligence services; the formation of a national counter-terrorism centre to co-ordinate intelligence-gathering; a reduction in the number of congressional intelligence oversight committees; the establishment of an international network of intelligence-sharing; and the implementation of a national policy to address the threat of militant Islamism. On 17 December 2004, following its approval earlier in the month by both houses of Congress, President Bush enacted the Intelligence Reform and Terrorism Act, which drew on some of the recommendations of the Commission's report. The legislation was designed to restructure the security services and provided for a cabinet-level Director of National Intelligence, to be responsible for co-ordinating the activities of 15 different agencies, including the CIA and the FBI. In April 2005 Bush's nominee to the new post, the erstwhile US ambassador to Iraq, John D. Negroponte, was confirmed by the Senate. An internal investigation by the CIA into intelligence failings, concluded in January of that year, was particularly critical of its former director, George Tenet, who had resigned in June 2004.

In November 2005 it was reported that US intelligence services maintained a network of secret prisons—referred to as 'black sites'—in locations that included eastern EU countries. It was further alleged that terrorist suspects were taken from these prisons to countries where torture was tolerated, in a practice known as 'extraordinary rendition'. The following month Secretary of State Condoleezza Rice acknowledged the existence of rendition but denied any toleration of the torture of suspects. However, in January 2005 it had been revealed that, three years previously, the chief legal counsel to the President, Alberto Gonzales (who was appointed Attorney-General in January 2005), had issued a memorandum stating that the USA was not bound by the Geneva Conventions in its treatment of prisoners captured in Afghanistan. In another memorandum ordered by Gonzales in August 2002, it was proposed that CIA officers and other non-military personnel be exempted from a presidential directive for the humane treatment of prisoners. In February 2006 the UN Commission on Human Rights published a report that concluded that the methods used by the US military to interrogate prisoners at Guantánamo Bay amounted to torture, and appealed to the US Government to close the base and try the remaining detainees before courts on the US mainland. A military report to the Senate's armed forces committee in July found that treatment of the prisoners did not constitute torture, but that it was, however, abusive and degrading. In December President Bush approved an amendment to ban the 'cruel, inhuman and degrading' treatment of prisoners, although he appended a presidential signing statement to the effect that the President's authority superseded the new legislation. Department of State officials were summoned to appear before the UN Committee Against Torture in Geneva, Switzerland, in early May to answer enquiries relating to the alleged use of torture employed in extraordinary rendition. The Department of State delegation contended that it had sought assurances that detainees conveyed under this system would not be subjected to torture in their destination country and that US definitions of torture did not infringe those set out in the 1987 Convention. The UN concluded that interrogation methods involving 'waterboarding' (simulated drowning), sexual humiliation and the use of menacing dogs were unacceptable and should be eliminated. It also ruled that the detention of prisoners without charge for extended periods, the use of extraordinary rendition and reports of concealed prisons were issues of grave concern, and it urged that the detention centre at Guantánamo Bay be closed.

In late June 2006 the US Supreme Court ruled that military tribunals established for the trial of prisoners at Guantánamo Bay contravened the US uniform code of military justice and Geneva Conventions. The Court rejected the Bush Administration's contention that the President's authority as Commander-in-Chief, and the resolution of Congress approved following the 11 September terrorist attacks, sanctioned the institution of such military tribunals. However, the Department of Defense issued a memorandum in July declaring that all prisoners at Guantánamo Bay and other US military detention centres world-wide would be protected under Article III of the Geneva Conventions, assuring humane treatment of and basic judicial defence for those facing trial. The announcement corrected previous assertions that the Military Commissions Act precluded invocation of Geneva Conventions articles. The Military Commissions Act of 2006, intended to 'bring to justice' terrorists and other unlawful enemy combatants by means of thorough, fair trials administered by military commissions, was approved by Congress in late September and signed into law by President Bush in the following month. In March 2007 an Australian, David Hicks—a convert to Islam—became the first detainee to be granted trial by such a commission at Guantánamo Bay and the first convicted of a terrorism offence since the camp's inauguration in 2002. An appeal by the legal representatives of approximately 60 Guantánamo detainees (facing similar military tribunals), contending that the prisoners had a constitutional right to contest their imprisonment in a US federal court, was rejected, by two votes to one, in the US Court of Appeal in February 2007. The Court's ruling stated that non-citizens without property or residency in the USA were not entitled to US constitutional rights; the dissenting judge maintained that such a ruling contravened the principle of habeas corpus. However, in June 2008 the Supreme Court issued a ruling that all detainees at Guantánamo Bay were entitled to challenge their detention through the US civilian courts. The decision did not bring to an end the military tribunals, which continued throughout 2008; however, in November a US court ruled that five Algerian detainees should be released from the prison camp after they successfully challenged their right to a civilian trial.

Alleged use of 'harsh interrogation' techniques, including waterboarding, caused controversy in late 2007 when a report by the *New York Times*, published in October, claimed that the US Department of Justice had privately authorized their use by the CIA against terrorist suspects in 2005 while asserting that such methods did not contravene anti-torture legislation then before Congress. Later in the same month the Director of the CIA, Gen. Michael Hayden, defended the Agency's interrogation practices and use of extraordinary rendition as a lawful and indispensable means of obtaining information from suspects. However, on 6 December 2007—when an agreement was also reached by Congress negotiators on the terms of legislation to prohibit the use of 'harsh interrogation' techniques by the CIA—Hayden revealed that film tapes documenting the use of such procedures on two al-Qa'ida members in 2002 had been destroyed in November 2005, ostensibly to protect the identities of the CIA interrogators. Critics accused the Agency of destroying evidence that might provoke further allegations of torture in relation to their practices. A former CIA officer subsequently attested that waterboarding was used in the interrogation of Abu Zubaydah, the first high-ranking al-Qa'ida member to be captured after the terrorist attacks of 11 September 2001, and that he now considered the practice to constitute torture. In early January 2008 a criminal investigation was launched by Attorney-General Michael B. Mukasey, and in February Hayden, for the first time, admitted the use of waterboarding on three al-Qa'ida detainees, including Khalid Sheikh Mohammed. He declared, however, that the method had not been used in the previous five years and that he had banned its use in 2006. Further, he did not rule out its future employment and admitted he was unsure of its legality under current laws. In early March 2008 President Bush vetoed the legislation restricting 'harsh interrogation' techniques already approved by the House of Representatives in December 2007 and by the Senate in February 2008, claiming that such 'specialized interrogation procedures' were of proven effectiveness and, while not practised by the military, should remain available to the CIA.

Upon taking office in January 2009, President Barack Obama immediately instituted a 120-day hiatus on the military tribunals at Guantánamo Bay to allow for a thorough review of the situation. He also reiterated his pledge to close the prison camp within a year. The new President had already diverged significantly from the previous Administration by claiming that waterboarding constituted torture and by admitting the existence of secret CIA prisons. He also ordered that the CIA cease the torture of detainees. His decision was widely praised, although the presidential order stopped short of halting the CIA's right to use extraordinary rendition.

In his State of the Union address in January 2002, President Bush described Iran, Iraq and the DPRK as forming an 'axis of evil' that supported international terrorism and sought to develop weapons of mass destruction, and hinted that the USA was considering pre-emptive strikes against them. US allies warned against attacking states unless firm evidence of a link to terrorism could be found. In February Bush faced protests on a visit to South Korea, and members of South Korean President Kim Dae-Jung's ruling party accused Bush of damaging the so-called 'sunshine policy' of reconciliation with North Korea. In the same month Secretary of State Colin Powell made specific mention of removing Saddam Hussain from power in Iraq. In January it was announced that US troops were to be sent to the Philippines to fight against the Abu Sayyaf guerrilla group, which was believed to have links with the al-Qa'ida network. In May the 'axis of evil' was extended to include Cuba, Libya and Syria. The Bush Administration accused Cuba of maintaining a biological warfare programme and offering weapons technology to 'rogue states', and claimed that Libya and Syria had violated international weapons treaties. In December the Iranian Government denied US allegations of evidence of the secret manufacture of nuclear weapons. In mid-September 2003 the USA supported an IAEA resolution establishing a deadline of the end of October for Iran to disclose full details of its nuclear programme and provide evidence that it was not developing nuclear weapons. In mid-December Libya agreed to disclose and dismantle its programme to develop weapons of mass destruction and long-range ballistic missiles, following nine months of secret negotiations between the Libyan leader, Col Muammar al-Qaddafi, and US and British diplomats. In January 2004 a US delegation visited Libya to discuss the weapons-dismantling process. As a result, in February the USA ended the restrictions on its citizens travelling to Libya, in place since 1981, and in late June diplomatic relations were officially re-established between the two countries for the first time in 23 years; however, Libya was not removed from the US list of state sponsors of terrorism until May 2006. (In September 2008 Condoleezza Rice became the first US Secretary of State in 50 years to visit Libya.) In February 2005, in protest at what it believed to be Syria's role in the assassination of the Prime Minister of Lebanon, Rafiq Hariri, the USA removed its ambassador to Syria for consultations, and later demanded that all Syrian troops withdraw from Lebanon. (US–Syrian tensions were partly alleviated in September 2006 when an attempted attack on the US embassy in Damascus was foiled by the Syrian authorities.) In March 2005, for the first time, the USA agreed with France, Germany and the United Kingdom to offer Iran economic benefits if that country pledged to end its nuclear programme. However, in April 2006 the Iranian President, Mahmoud Ahmadinejad, announced that Iran had successfully achieved the enrichment of uranium for civilian purposes. The Iranian Government claimed that the enriched uranium was not weapons-grade, but was, rather, to be used as nuclear fuel. Early in May a draft UN resolution was promulgated, under which France, Germany, the United Kingdom and the USA again urged Iran to arrest its nuclear enrichment programme and to abandon construction of a heavy-water reactor by the end of August, or face economic sanctions. In return for compliance, a portfolio of incentives was offered, including the provision of light-water nuclear reactors for electricity generation. President Ahmadinejad issued an ambiguous letter in response, denouncing US foreign policy, but failing to confirm or reject the resolution's demands. In August, however, Iran's Supreme Leader, Ayatollah Ali Khamenei, declared that the country's nuclear programme would continue, and at the end of that month the heavy-water plant became operational.

A resolution was approved by the UN Security Council on 23 December 2006 imposing sanctions against Iran, which prevented the import or export of materials and technology associated with uranium enrichment enterprises and 'froze' the financial assets of 12 Iranians and 10 institutions associated with the country's nuclear development programme. Nevertheless, in January 2007 Iran announced that production of nuclear fuel for industrial purposes was to commence imminently and declared its intention to enhance economic and military co-operation with Iraq. US suspicions that the Iranian Government was supplying Iraqi Shi'ite militants with ammunition and weapons appeared substantiated in February when US military officials in the Iraqi capital reported the seizure of explosives components manufactured in Iran; however, the Chairman of the Joint Chiefs of Staff, Gen. Peter Pace, later acknowledged that links between the bomb materials and the Iranian administration could not be unequivocally proven. Furthermore, the National Intelligence Estimate, published in December 2007 and compiled using information supplied by the USA's 16 intelligence agencies, reported with 'high confidence' that Iran had ceased its nuclear weapons programme in 2003 and had not recommenced such activities by mid-2007, although it continued to enrich uranium.

In January 2002, following an escalation in the ongoing conflict in the Middle East, the USA brokered talks towards securing a cease-fire agreement between Israel and Palestine. In March the Israeli Prime Minister, Ariel Sharon, agreed to redeploy some Israeli troops from Palestinian areas. The following month Secretary of State Colin Powell visited Israel and held separate talks with Sharon and with Palestinian President Yasser Arafat in his besieged headquarters, in an attempt to bring an end to the crisis. However, the mission failed to bring about a cease-fire or the withdrawal of Israeli forces from Palestinian areas. At the end of April 2003 President Bush presented both the Israeli and Palestinian Prime Ministers with an internationally sponsored 'roadmap' for peace, envisaging the phased creation of a sovereign Palestinian state. However, despite acceptance of the plan, Israel continued work on the construction of a 'security fence' in the disputed West Bank region, begun in mid-2002. In July 2003 the US Administration threatened to withhold almost US $10,000m. in essential loan guarantees unless construction of the fence ceased. Following approval by the Israeli Government of a further phase of construction, in late November the US Congress cut $290m. from a total $1,400m. in loan guarantees to Israel as a penalty for the continuing expansion of Jewish settlements in the West Bank and Gaza. At a meeting between Bush and Sharon in Crawford, Texas, in April 2005, the President gave his support to Israel's planned withdrawal from the Gaza Strip, but criticized the continued expansion of Jewish settlements in the West Bank. In April 2006 the EU and USA suspended financial aid provisions to the Palestinian Authority, under the leadership of the militant Hamas movement, in response to its continued refusal to recognize the state of Israel. The inauguration of a Fatah and Hamas coalition Government in Palestine in March 2007, while representing a significant advance towards reconciliation, did not herald any immediate improvement in US–Palestinian relations. However, at a Middle East peace conference held in Annapolis, Maryland, in November, Israeli Prime Minister Ehud Olmert and Palestinian President Mahmoud Abbas agreed mutually to a deadline of December 2008 for the formulation of a peace settlement; however, no such agreement had been reached by April 2009. Bush demonstrated his continued commitment to the process in his final year in office by travelling to Israel and the West Bank in January 2008, his first visit to the area since becoming President. The US Administration's failure to demand an immediate end to the Israeli military offensive against the radical Hezbollah movement in southern Lebanon that began in July 2006 also strained US–Lebanese relations. Instead, the Bush Administration appealed for joint Lebanese–Israeli negotiations to bring about a long-lasting cease-fire.

In December 2001 Enron Corporation, the largest energy company in the USA, filed for bankruptcy. This was the largest ever bankruptcy in US history, with the immediate loss of 4,000 jobs. It subsequently emerged that Enron's accounts had been falsified over several years. Furthermore, it was revealed that Enron had donated more than US $500,000 to Bush's presidential campaign, and that Vice-President Dick Cheney had met senior Enron executives on several occasions in 2001 while drafting the proposed national energy plan. It was also reported that senior members of the Bush Administration had refused requests from Enron for financial assistance in 2001. An investigation into the bankruptcy was begun by the Department of Justice in early 2002. The firm was found guilty of obstructing justice in June, although the ruling was overturned by the Supreme Court in May 2005. Then, in June 2002 WorldCom, Inc, the second largest long-distance telecommunications company in the USA, revealed that it too had manipulated its accounts to show figures for cash flow and profits that were higher than in reality; the disclosure prompted the Securities and Exchange Commission to announce that the regulation of listed companies and subsequent penalties would become more stringent. WorldCom's Chief Executive, Bernie Ebbers, was arrested in early March 2004 and charged with fraud. Both Enron and WorldCom filed for Chapter 11 bankruptcy protection and continued to trade. In April WorldCom, now part of a restructured MCI, Inc, left Chapter 11 protection following a restatement of its accounts. Ebbers was found guilty of nine criminal charges in March 2005 and, in July, sentenced to 25 years in prison. In May 2006 Enron's founder, Kenneth Lay, and its former CEO, Jeffrey Skilling, were convicted of fraud, conspiracy and insider trading; Lay was found guilty on 10 separate counts, but died from a heart attack in July before sentence could be passed. Skilling was sentenced to 24 years' imprisonment; additionally, the liquidation of Skilling's assets, totalling $60m., was ordered, with $45m. of that sum to be transferred to a restitution fund for victims of the company's bankruptcy.

At mid-term elections held in November 2002, the Republicans assumed control of the Senate and increased their majority in the House of Representatives. Following his party's electoral success, in January 2003 President Bush announced a series of tax reductions worth US $726,000m. over 10 years. The 2004 budget, presented in the following month, included further requests for extensions to tax allowances. However, in March the proposals were vetoed by Congress, which was concerned over increased homeland security expenditure and the cost of the military operation in Iraq (see below). Eventually, in May Congress approved, by one vote, amended legislation that introduced tax cuts of some $350,000m. over the next decade. In early November Congress approved a presidential request for an additional $87,000m. in funding for reconstruction efforts in Iraq and Afghanistan. Also in November Congress enacted legislation extending Medicare (federal health care for the elderly) benefits to cover the cost of most prescription drugs.

In January 2004 the US-Visit programme was implemented, requiring that all visa-holders entering the USA were electronically fingerprinted and photographed on arrival. By January 2005 the programme had been extended to 50 land border crossings and was scheduled to reach a further 115 by the end of that year. In April 2006 some 500,000 people in Los Angeles participated in a march in protest at restrictive new immigration legislation; other protest marches took place in Phoenix, Denver and Milwaukee. The legislation, approved by the House of Representatives in the previous December, made illegal immigration a criminal offence, and approved the construction of a 1,130-km (700 miles) fence on the US–Mexican border. In early April the Senate failed to reach a compromise agreement on the proposed law that would provide 'non-immigrant visas' to some 11m. undocumented workers. The concession had the support of President Bush, but not of the Republican Party, which enjoyed a majority in the Senate. A 'day without immigrants' was declared on 1 May, on which thousands of immigrant workers held a one-day strike as a demonstration of their collective value to the US economy. The Senate ratified immigration legislation at the end of that month authorizing the establishment of a guest worker programme. Provisions were also made for immigrants to attain citizenship, subject to the satisfaction of certain criteria. The 2005 immigration control law had to be reconciled with this new legislation in order for it to become law, although several senior members of the House, in response, had indicated their opposition to any measures in the proposed legislation that might constitute an amnesty for illegal immigrants. By January 2007 it was estimated that there were 11m. illegal immigrants in the USA. In that month a study paper was submitted by the Congressional Research Service to the Department of Homeland Security cautioning that the cost of constructing and maintaining the proposed US–Mexican border security fence could reach US $49,000m. The report renewed debate as to the potential effectiveness of such a barrier; a similar measure implemented in the San Diego region had merely transferred immigrant incursions further along the border to southern Arizona, where security was less strictly enforced. During a visit to Mexico in March, President Bush was addressed by the Mexican President, Felipe Calderón Hinojosa, who reiterated his opposition to the proposed security fence. Nevertheless, by January 2009 some 962 km (601 miles) of the fence had been erected, with completion of the project scheduled for later that year.

Meanwhile, in August 2006 the federal Government implemented 'Operation Jump Start', an immigration control initiative effected in the southern border regions, including Arizona, Texas, California and New Mexico. The initiative entailed the deployment of 6,000 National Guard personnel in support of the Border Patrol, and succeeded in curtailing the illegal border crossings by an estimated 30% by early 2007. The Border Patrol had been expanded from approximately 9,000 operatives in 2001 to almost 13,000 by April 2007. Congressional debate towards devising a comprehensive reform of US immigration policy intensified in early March 2007, with Senate Majority Leader Harry Reid indicating that legislation to, *inter alia*, reinforce border security and offer a programme of 'earned citizenship' to illegal immigrants resident in the USA, would be approved by the Senate before the August recess. However, such approval was not secured and in August 2007 Secretary of Homeland Security Michael Chertoff and Secretary of Commerce Carlos Gutierrez instead outlined a series of measures that could be effected under existing laws. These included addressing border security by deploying additional personnel and an enhanced infrastructure, policing the employment of illegal workers by rendering employers accountable for their recruitment practices, streamlining current guest worker programmes, and facilitating the assimilation of 'newcomers'.

Presidential and legislative elections were held on 2 November 2004. The elections were notable for being the first in which unregulated, or so-called 'soft money', donations to the electoral campaigns of political parties from individuals, businesses and unions were banned. These funds were ostensibly intended only for general activities, but had often been used to support the campaigns of particular candidates. In the presidential ballot, President Bush was returned for a second term of office, taking some 51% of the popular vote. John Kerry, the Democratic challenger, conceded defeat before the final result was confirmed. In the concurrent legislative elections, the Republicans also increased their majority in both houses of Congress. The President was sworn in on 20 January 2005. His new Cabinet included Condoleezza Rice, hitherto Assistant to the President for National Security Affairs, as Secretary of State, and Alberto Gonzales, the President's former chief legal counsel, as Attorney-General. In early February Bush presented a 2006 budget plan to Congress, which proposed reductions in funding to 12 out of 23 government agencies. Spending cuts targeted subsidies to farmers, health care payments to the poor and military veterans, as well as education and environment programmes. The budget did not include the cost of a proposed restructuring of the social security system nor the additional cost of military operations overseas: to this last end, in early May a presidential request for a further US $82,000m., principally towards continued military involvement in Afghanistan and Iraq, was approved by Congress.

In late August 2005 'Hurricane Katrina' caused extensive damage to the Gulf coast states of Louisiana, Mississippi and Alabama. Louisiana was the worst affected state: an estimated 80% of the city of New Orleans was flooded. On 2 September President Bush declared a state of emergency in 13 states to release some US $10,500m. in emergency funding; on the same day Congress approved legislation for emergency aid amounting to $51,800m. Damage to infrastructure was blamed for delays in delivering relief to those affected by the hurricane: the first relief convoys took four days to arrive in New Orleans. The US Government appealed to the EU, NATO and the UN for crisis assistance. On 6 September the mayor of New Orleans ordered the evacuation of the entire city, some 480,000 people; however, an estimated 10,000 people, who were either unable or unwilling to move, remained in the city. More than 38,000 members of the National Guard were deployed in affected areas; 7,000 were deployed in New Orleans itself with orders to shoot to kill looters. They were joined by 8,500 soldiers on active duty. Meanwhile, the Government released oil supplies from the Strategic Petroleum Reserve to counter the disruption caused to the region's energy supply network, which accounted for almost one-third of domestic oil production. The impact of another hurricane, 'Hurricane Rita', along the Gulf coast at the end of September, further affected relief efforts. By May 2006 the official death toll as a result of 'Hurricane Katrina' was 1,836; a further 705 people remained missing.

The federal Government came under much criticism for its perceived slow reaction to 'Hurricane Katrina': on 9 September 2005 Michael Brown, the Director of the Federal Emergency Management Agency (FEMA), responsible for co-ordinating the relief effort, was relieved of his duties at the head of the recovery operation in Louisiana. Less than a week later, Brown resigned as FEMA Director. A report by the Government Accountability Office (GAO), published in February 2006, criticized government at all levels for its failure adequately to respond to the emergency. It found that relief efforts had been hampered by the absence of a clear chain of command, and compounded by insufficient planning and preparation; it also identified examples of waste and fraud in the appropriation of relief and reconstruction funds. Meanwhile, President Bush appealed to Congress for a further US $19,600m. towards reconstruction along the Gulf coast, particularly the strengthening of the protective levees around New Orleans. President Bush acknowledged that the management of reconstruction and relief efforts in the wake of 'Hurricane Katrina' had been inadequate, and reiterated this sentiment in August when it had emerged that of the $110,000m. designated by Congress to the cause, only $44,000m. had been disseminated.

The Republican Party faced a series of corruption scandals throughout 2005 and 2006. In September 2005 the Republican Majority Leader in the House of Representatives, Tom DeLay, was indicted on charges of having illegally financed Republican candidates in the 2002 election campaign. In October I. 'Scooter' Lewis Libby, chief of staff to Vice-President Dick Cheney, was indicted on charges that included obstruction of justice and perjury during an investigation into the leaking of the identity of CIA agent Valerie Plame in mid-2003. It was held that Plame's identity had deliberately been made public as a reprisal against her husband and former US Ambassador to Iraq, Senator Joseph Wilson, who had publicly accused the Administration of making selective use of intelligence to justify the invasion of Iraq in 2003. The Libby trial commenced in January 2007, although neither Libby nor Vice-President Cheney, also implicated in the scandal, testified. A number of other high-profile political figures became embroiled in proceedings, however, including Karl Rove, the President's political strategist—who was later acquitted of any charges—and President Bush himself. In March Libby was convicted of four out of five charges of perjury, and in June was sentenced to 30 months in prison. In the following month President Bush commuted Libby's sentence to a two-year probation period and a US $250,000 fine after describing the original sentence as 'excessive'.

In March 2006 lobbyist Jack Abramoff was sentenced to 70 months' imprisonment after pleading guilty to charges that included conspiracy to bribe public officials, fraud and tax evasion. The enactment of legislation banning members of Congress from accepting donations from lobbyists and extending regulation of designated revenue projects was approved by the Senate at the end of that month, while a similar, although less far-reaching, law was narrowly approved by the House of Representatives in early May. However, further casualties of the affair were to occur during the course of the year. David Safavian, head of federal procurement policy at the Office of Management and Budget, was convicted of perjury and obstruction in the Abramoff investigation in June; he was sentenced to 18 months' imprisonment. Another Republican to contribute to the catalogue of corruption within the party ranks was Congressman Mark Foley, who resigned his seat in September following allegations of inappropriate and sexual correspondence with former junior congressional employees.

In 2007 the federal budget proposed reductions in spending on social, health and welfare programmes, while appealing for existing tax cuts to be made permanent. There were increases in expenditure on defence and homeland security. However, the budget was criticized for omitting projected expenditure on reconstruction efforts in Iraq and Afghanistan after 2007 and reconstruction in New Orleans following 'Hurricane Katrina'. The budget also included projected revenue from leasing drilling rights in the ANWR (see above), despite the fact that the required legislation had yet to be approved by Congress. The Senate ratified a US $108,900m. emergency spending bill in May. In the same month legislation representing almost $70,000m. in tax reduction, encompassing cuts on stock dividends and capital gains until 2010, was enacted by the Senate. The law had been criticized as favouring affluent families at the expense of the poor.

At mid-term elections in November 2006, the Democrats secured control of both chambers of Congress. The Republican electoral defeat was regarded as indicative of citizens' loss of confidence in Bush's presidency, principally owing to the lack of progress in Iraq and escalating violence in Afghanistan, but also in regard to domestic policy, namely the perceived inadequacy of the federal Government's response to 'Hurricane Katrina', immigration policy, the erratic nature of economic recovery and the numerous cases of corruption within Republican ranks. Immediately following the elections, the Secretary of Defense, Donald Rumsfeld, ceded to demands for his resignation, citing the need for a 'fresh perspective' on the ongoing conflict in Iraq. Robert M. Gates, a former CIA Director, succeeded him. Rumsfeld had provoked criticism over strategic policy in Iraq, and had attracted international opprobrium for his apparent approval of 'harsh interrogation' techniques—widely regarded as a euphemism for torture (see above)—in the examination of terrorism suspects. In its first month in office, in January 2007, the new lower house approved proposals to increase federal funding for embryonic stem cell research; both chambers had previously approved the legislation, but it had been vetoed by President Bush in July 2006.

Further controversy involving the Republican Administration emerged in early 2007 after it was revealed that eight US state attorneys had been summarily dismissed under the direction of Attorney-General Alberto Gonzales. It was alleged that the dismissals, seven of which were effected in December 2006, resulted from the attorneys' failure sufficiently to pursue accusations of voting irregularities against Democratic candidates in the November 2006 elections. White House e-mails and documents released in the course of the ensuing investigation corroborated claims that the dismissals were politically motivated; Gonzales' Chief of Staff, D. Kyle Sampson, Karl Rove (then the President's Deputy Chief of Staff), and the then presidential counsel, Harriet Miers, were implicated by the revelations. It was also suggested that Sampson had advocated exploitation of a provision of the recently renewed Patriot Act (see above) that would enable the Attorney-General to effect new appointments to the vacancies created, thereby obviating the need for Senate approval. Miers had resigned from office on 4 January 2007, while Sampson tendered his resignation on 12 March. Gonzales testified before the Senate Judiciary Committee on 20 April when inconsistencies between his various statements regarding his knowledge of, and motivation for, the dismissals were scrutinized and found seriously to undermine his integrity as an impartial arbiter of justice. By May an earlier state attorney dismissal had emerged, dating from January 2006, suggesting that the dismissals had commenced five months earlier than previously thought. On 16 May 2007 Deputy Attorney-General Paul J. McNulty became the fourth senior Department of Justice official to resign in connection with the controversy, and on 17 September Gonzales finally stood down from office while maintaining that he had committed no wrongdoing. Karl Rove had relinquished his position as Deputy Chief of Staff in August 2007, citing personal reasons. Michael B. Mukasey was confirmed by the Senate as the new Attorney-General in early November, despite concerns from some Democrat senators arising from his failure explicitly to classify waterboarding as torture, his previous description of the technique as 'repugnant' notwithstanding.

There were a number of further resignations by key personnel in the Bush Administration in 2007 and 2008. Al Hubbard announced his departure from the National Economic Council, of which he was the Director, in November 2007, at a time when the economy of the USA was becoming increasingly unstable. Undersecretary of State for Public Diplomacy Karen Hughes, who was charged with improving the international perception of the USA, left her position in December. Hughes was the third adviser to President Bush to vacate office in six months, following Counselor to the President Dan Bartlett, in July, and Rove in August. Housing and Urban Development Secretary Alphonso Jackson resigned on 18 April 2008 amid an ongoing FBI investigation into allegations of favouritism in awarding housing contracts and as the US housing market continued to deteriorate, with house prices falling and repossession rates rising. The crisis in the housing market moved Congress to approve legislation in mid-2008: the Housing and Economic Recovery Act provided for emergency funding for federal mortgage institutions and was intended to restore confidence in the sector.

In response to the heightened international concern over global warming and the depletion of energy resources, President Bush signed the Energy Independence and Security Act in December 2007, increasing fuel-efficiency standards for passenger vehicles and stipulating that biofuels should account for 36,000m. gallons of motor fuel by 2022 in order reduce the USA's dependence on imported petroleum. In his State of the Union address, delivered in January 2008, Bush delineated policy consolidation measures to be enacted during his final term in office, and reaffirmed his commitment to combating climate change with initiatives including the establishment of a US $3,000m. international clean technology fund. He also urged Congress to approve a $150,000m. economic stimulus plan and to ensure that tax relief measures were made permanent, conceding that economic growth in the USA was slowing. Modest domestic policy plans focused on improving educational standards and broadening access to education, specifically through a $300m. scholarship scheme for pupils from low-income households.

Details emerged in March 2008 of a federal investigation into a prostitution ring that implicated the Democrat Governor of New York, Eliot Spitzer. Spitzer had campaigned for office on an anti-corruption mandate and tendered his resignation on 12 March after the Republican Minority Leader of the State Assembly, James Tedisco, threatened to initiate impeachment proceedings.

In September 2002 the Bush Administration attempted to address the new threats faced by the USA internationally and outlined the policies necessary to meet these challenges by issuing a National Security Strategy for the United States. In the same month the Republicans submitted a draft resolution to Congress, which would authorize President Bush to use 'any means necessary' to enforce existing UN resolutions against the regime of Saddam Hussain in Iraq and to defend US national interests by depriving Iraq of weapons of mass destruction. It was the first tangible evidence that the Administration was willing to deploy unilateral military action if the UN Security Council did not approve a new resolution authorizing military action against the Iraqi regime. The resolution was approved in October by both houses of Congress, with the provision that the Administration should first exhaust all available channels at the UN and other diplomatic means. As a result of US-led pressure, in November the UN Security Council passed unanimously Resolution 1441, which obliged Iraq, *inter alia*, to declare all weapons of mass destruction within 30 days, to comply with the UN Monitoring, Verification and Inspection Commission (UNMOVIC—the UN weapons inspectors, and successor to the UN Special Commission—UNSCOM), to allow UNMOVIC to resume its work within 45 days (UNSCOM had been expelled from Iraq in 1998), and to allow inspectors unrestricted access within Iraq, including Saddam Hussain's palaces. Later that month UNMOVIC resumed its operations and reported that the Iraqi Government was prepared to comply with Resolution 1441. In December Iraq presented its report on weapons of mass destruction to UNMOVIC; however, US officials declared Iraq to be in 'material breach' of Resolution 1441, for failing to comply with the demand for an accurate and complete account of its weapons programmes, and for resubmitting information that it had previously given to the UN. Following this development, the US and British Governments drew up a timetable to allow UNMOVIC to carry out intensified searches in early 2003, with the threat of military action against Saddam's regime for non-compliance.

In January 2003 some 70,000 US servicemen and -women joined the 60,000 troops already stationed in the Persian (Arabian) Gulf, and military exercises intensified. The French and German Governments expressed their opposition to any eventual conflict and called for a resolution to the problem by diplomatic means. In response, President Bush stated that the USA would lead a 'coalition of the willing' if support was withheld by other UN Security Council members and its traditional allies. The Administration took an increasingly uncompromising stance; the Secretary of Defense, Donald Rumsfeld, described France and Germany as 'old Europe' (as opposed to other more pro-US states in Southern and Eastern Europe), and the Secretary of State, Colin Powell, excluded the possibility of extending the time allocated to inspectors to find prohibited weapons in Iraq. However, Rumsfeld had also suggested the possibility of granting senior Iraqi leaders amnesty and avoiding conflict if they chose exile in a third country. In late January UNMOVIC reported that it had discovered substances and missiles that could be in contravention of UN resolutions. In February the USA, together with the United Kingdom, intensified its efforts to secure a second UN resolution that would authorize military intervention in Iraq; on 5 February Powell presented evidence of, *inter alia*, the alleged existence of weapons of mass destruction in Iraq, and possible links between Saddam Hussain's regime and al-Qa'ida. However, in mid-February UNMOVIC reported greater co-operation on the part of the Iraqi Government and that it had thus far failed to find any weapons of mass destruction. (On 13 February Saddam Hussain issued a presidential decree prohibiting weapons of mass destruction, although some al-Samoud missiles were found with a greater range than permitted under UN resolutions.) On 24 February the USA, with the United Kingdom and Spain, presented a draft resolution, reiterating that Iraq had been warned it would face serious consequences if it failed to disarm, and that it had failed to comply with Resolution 1441. In an effort to win the support of the 10 non-permanent members of the UN Security Council, the draft resolution contained no ultimatum to Iraq or explicit threat of attack. A few days later, however, President Bush insisted that only full disarmament could prevent war. In early March diplomatic efforts to resolve the crisis showed signs of breaking down when Russia and then France declared that they would employ their veto on any resolution leading to conflict, while the UN Secretary-General, Kofi Annan, questioned the legitimacy of a conflict in Iraq without UN approval. Nevertheless, Powell stated that the USA could go to war without a second UN resolution. UNMOVIC, meanwhile, reported that Iraq had destroyed part of its stock of al-Samoud missiles. An amended version of the draft for a second resolution was issued in mid-March and a deadline of 17 March given for Iraq to demonstrate full compliance with Resolution 1441. On 16 March President Bush, the British Prime Minister, Tony Blair, and the Spanish premier, José María Aznar, held an emergency summit in the Azores, Portugal, at the end of which the three leaders issued an ultimatum giving Saddam Hussain and his two sons 48 hours to leave Iraq or face invasion. The following day the USA, the United Kingdom and Spain decided not to seek a second UN resolution and condemned France for obstructing diplomatic efforts to reach a peaceful outcome. The President of France, Jacques Chirac, responded by criticizing the USA and the United Kingdom for making an 'unjustified' decision to resort to war, and for gravely undermining the UN. The USA announced that some 30 countries had expressed support for its 'coalition of the willing', although only the United Kingdom, Australia, the Czech Republic and Slovakia provided troops.

Shortly after the expiry of President Bush's 48-hour deadline, on 19 March 2003 US and British armed forces launched 'Operation Iraqi Freedom' to oust the regime of Saddam Hussain. A first wave of air-strikes against targets in the southern suburbs of the Iraqi capital, Baghdad, apparently aimed at leading members of the Iraqi regime (including the President himself), failed to achieve their target. Soon afterwards British and US forces crossed into Iraq from Kuwait and generally made a swift advance towards the capital. At the same time, a concerted campaign of massive air-strikes was launched by US-led forces against the key symbols of the Iraqi regime in and around Baghdad, including selected military bases, communications sites, government buildings and broadcasting headquarters. Government and military sites in other prominent Iraqi cities were targeted by the US-led coalition in subsequent days. The US and British forces adopted a simultaneous campaign of issuing leaflets and broadcasting radio messages, in an attempt to persuade Iraqi citizens to abandon their support for Saddam Hussain: their declared intention was that 'Operation Iraqi Freedom' would precipitate the disintegration of the regime 'from within'. Some criticism was made within the US Administration of senior military officials for underestimating the determination of the Iraqi forces. However, by 9 April US forces reached the centre of Baghdad and on 1 May the conflict was officially declared over: Iraq did not formally offer its surrender. In mid-April US Gen. (retd) Jay Garner, Director of the USA's Office of Reconstruction and Humanitarian Assistance in Iraq (ORHA), was appointed Civil Administrator in Iraq, with the intention of overseeing the peaceful transition to civilian rule by Iraqi nationals. An Iraq Survey Group was established to investigate the presence of illegal weapons in the country. In early May a US diplomat, L. Paul Bremer, succeeded Garner as Civil Administrator in Iraq. In late July US special forces killed Saddam Hussain's sons, Uday and Qusay, in Mosul, and on 13 December US special forces captured Saddam Hussain himself, in the village of Ad-Dawr near his birthplace, Tikrit: he was accorded prisoner-of-war status and held in US custody, pending his trial by a court to be convened by the Iraqi Governing Council. Legal custody of Saddam Hussain was transferred to the new Iraqi Interim Government in late June 2004, but he remained under US guard. The former Iraqi President's trial began in Baghdad in mid-October 2005, and on 30 December 2006 Saddam Hussain was executed by hanging, following the rejection of his appeal against the death sentence imposed by the Supreme Iraqi Criminal Tribunal on 5 November.

In July 2003 the US Administration admitted that claims, made in January, that the regime of Saddam Hussain had attempted to procure uranium from several African countries as part of its nuclear programme were 'possibly inaccurate'. The claims had formed part of the argument for declaring war on Iraq. In October the Iraq Survey Group published its first report; the report stated that although no weapons of mass destruction had been found thus far, there was evidence of weapons-related programmes. However, in January 2004 David Kay, the head of the Iraq Survey Group, resigned, stating that he did not believe that any stockpiles of weapons of mass destruction ever existed. Kay proposed the establishment of an independent inquiry into US intelligence on Iraqi weapons capability. The Survey Group left Iraq in January 2005. In an interim report to Congress in October 2004, Kay's successor, Charles Duelfer, concluded that Saddam Hussain had destroyed his stocks of weapons of mass destruction 10 years previously. In a report at the end of March 2005 the Survey Group was critical of the restructuring proposed at the CIA and FBI. It also criticized the agencies' failure to provide accurate information on the state of unconventional weapons in Iraq and highlighted weaknesses in their capacity accurately to report on nuclear programmes in Iran and the DPRK in particular. In July 2004 a Senate intelligence committee concluded that the CIA had provided the Bush Administration with flawed intelligence before the invasion of Iraq. At that time the Secretary of Energy, Spencer Abraham, announced that US officials had removed 1.77 metric tons of enriched uranium from Iraq in the previous month.

In late April 2004 photographs were published of US soldiers allegedly abusing prisoners at the Abu Ghraib prison near Baghdad. As further evidence of maltreatment continued to emerge, in early May the Department of Defense revealed that in September 2003 investigations had begun into some 20 cases of the deaths or alleged torture of prisoners in US custody in Iraq; however, the military denied that there was any evidence of systematic maltreatment of detainees. President Bush publicly condemned the abuse of prisoners. The first prosecution of one of the soldiers involved began in the USA in mid-June 2004. In August an internal military investigation directly implicated 27 soldiers in abuse at Abu Ghraib. In the same month an independent civilian panel confirmed 66 out of some 300 reported cases of prisoner abuse in US-run prisons in Iraq, Afghanistan and at Guantánamo Bay (see above). However, it did not find any systematic policy of abuse or instructions from senior military or government officials. In March 2005 it was announced that the USA was to hand over control of the prison to the Iraqi authorities. At that time in Iraq there were an estimated 10,000 prisoners at one British-run and three US-run prisons, including Abu Ghraib.

In late June 2004 L. Paul Bremer officially handed over sovereignty to the Interim Government of Iraq. The event took place in secret two days ahead of schedule, amid fears of terrorist attacks. Full diplomatic relations were restored. In the previous month the US Army had extended the period of duty of thousands of serving troops. In June the Army announced plans to call up 5,600 retired and discharged soldiers to compensate for a lack of trained specialists. As part of the Disabled Soldier Support System, it also hoped to retain soldiers who had been wounded; in December it was estimated that 900 out of 9,300 soldiers injured in Iraq would be eligible for the programme. In January 2005 the Department of Defense revealed that it planned to make cuts of US $60,000m. over the following six years and fundamentally to restructure the armed forces, diverting funds from costly weapons systems to manpower. At that time the cost of the military operation in Iraq had already exceeded $200,000m. In mid-July 2006 Muthanna became the first of Iraq's 18 provinces to be transferred from military control to the full responsibility of the Iraqi Government and signalled a measure of progress in the efforts to achieve stability. Despite fears of an escalation in sectarian violence, in early September authority over the Iraqi armed forces was formally conferred upon the Government of Iraq by the US-led coalition.

The Administration came under increasing pressure from 2005 to announce a timetable for the withdrawal of US troops from Iraq; however, President Bush remained adamant that a timetable for the withdrawal of troops would not be sought; the assertion was reflected in June 2006 by the Republican-controlled House of Representatives' rejection of a Democrat-sponsored resolution for such a schedule. The House also upheld a non-binding covenant supporting the conflict as integral to the global 'war on terror'. The Senate echoed this sentiment, dismissing by 93 votes to six plans to withdraw most combat troops by the end of the year. Nevertheless, concerns about the misuse of allocated reconstruction funding in Iraq, which precipitated the cancellation of contracts with US companies Parsons, Halliburton and Bechtel during 2006, provoked demands for an inquiry into the incidence of fraud and money-squandering during the execution of infrastructural projects. In June the Senate rejected such a resolution, although the Special Inspector General for Iraq Reconstruction (SIGIR) was, as of 30 April that year, pursuing 72 separate investigations into alleged fraudulence and profiteering by firms involved in the rebuilding efforts. In late July the results of an audit into the practices of the United States Agency for International Development concluded that an accounting scheme had been employed to conceal overspending on reconstruction ventures in Iraq. The disclosure in November by *The New York Times* that President Bush had endorsed a military authorization bill in October, which included a provision for the disbanding of the Office of the SIGIR, precipitated outrage among Democrats who regarded the measure as an executive attempt to conceal the Administration's mismanagement of reconstruction funds.

The bipartisan Iraq Study Group (ISG) was established in March 2006 to conduct an assessment of the situation in Iraq and generate proposals for a revised US strategy towards resolution of the conflict. The ISG submitted its report to Congress in early December, declaring the climate in Iraq to be 'grave and deteriorating', and cautioning that stability and democracy, as opposed to 'victory', should constitute the emphasis of future US military, diplomatic and political initiatives. The report delineated 79 recommendations for consideration by the President in formulating a new strategy for Iraq.

Despite the deployment of 15,600 US troops to Baghdad, the US military conceded in mid-October 2006 that its efforts to secure the Iraqi capital had been unsuccessful, and the UN reported that the number of US and Iraqi fatalities was unremittingly high. In November the head of US Central Command and leader of US forces in the Middle East, Gen. John Abizaid, advised that additional US troops were required to train the Iraqi military forces. He also opposed the suggestion of imposing a timetable for the withdrawal of US combat personnel. President Bush and his Iraqi counterpart, Nouri al-Maliki, pledged their intention for the expeditious transfer of responsibility from military to Iraqi government authority, with President al-Maliki expressing his ambition for Iraqi forces to have secured full control of the country by June 2007, although no definite timetable was advanced.

Bush announced his new strategy for Iraq in January 2007 entitled 'A New Way Forward'; its proposals included the deployment of a further 21,500 troops in Iraq. The new strategy was summarized as one that required greater commitment from the Iraqi Government to quell sectarian violence and establish democracy in the country through the attainment of a series of 'benchmarks', in return for US military reinforcements to assist in achieving the security and stability that would enable the Iraqi leaders to resume full responsibility for the territory. Bush cautioned that a withdrawal of US forces before this was accomplished would leave Iraq vulnerable to a 'contagion of violence' engulfing the whole region. A bipartisan 'special advisory council on the war on terror' was to be established to promote the image of a US Government united against terrorism. Expansion of the country's military capabilities was also requested, with the President asking Congress to authorize an increase of 92,000 personnel in the Army and Marine Corps over the next five years. Furthermore, establishment of a voluntary Civilian Reserve Corps was also suggested; this would augment the existing military reserve and ensure sufficient protection for the country in times of conflict. The decision to expand US participation in what was increasingly regarded as a civil war met with strenuous opposition from Democrats and ignited intense debate in Congress in the succeeding weeks. The Senate Foreign Relations Committee adopted a resolution against the deployment of further troops, but Congress failed to achieve unified opposition to the President's proposals—despite the House voting for a non-binding House Concurrent resolution to such effect—when a filibuster in the Senate on 17 February prevented voting on the resolution. Dispatch of US reinforcements began in February. The US Administration indicated its willingness to participate in negotiations with neighbouring Iran and Syria towards resolving the crisis in Iraq, as had been recommended by the ISG report. Members of the UN Security Council, diplomats from all six of Iraq's neighbouring countries, representatives from three international organizations, and US delegates attended a conference convened by Iraqi leaders in early March to discuss strategies for ending the violence in Iraq.

President Bush's proposed budget for 2008, presented in February 2007, incorporated a request for supplemental funding of US $93,400m. in 2008, and $141,000m. in 2009, to augment the Department of Defense's operations in the ongoing 'war on terror'. In March the House of Representatives voted in favour of emergency spending legislation that would provide $124,000m. for the funding of military operations in Iraq and Afghanistan over the next six months; however, attached to the provision was a timetable for the withdrawal, by 1 September 2008, of combat troops not devoted to security or training functions in Iraq. The Senate subsequently proposed a similar bill allowing $122,000m. in emergency funding and stipulating withdrawal of US troops by an earlier deadline of 31 March 2008; the legislation was narrowly approved. Both versions of the legislation, in harmony with the President's stated new strategy, recommended that 'benchmarks' be reached by the Iraqi Government in order to guarantee continued US support. A final version received congressional approval in late April. However, in early May the President vetoed the law, stating that setting a timetable for troop withdrawal would undermine military efforts and foster further insurgency in Iraq. In mid-May President Bush appointed Lt-Gen. Douglas Lute as deputy national security adviser to oversee developments in Iraq and Afghanistan and to mediate between the various state departments involved in war policy negotiations.

At a joint hearing of the House of Congress armed services and foreign affairs committees in September 2007, Gen. David Petraeus, the leader of US forces in Iraq, testified that the objectives of the 'surge' in troop numbers—30,000 extra US troops were dispatched to Iraq between February and June—were largely being met. He claimed that the tactic had reduced sectarian violence, and that in Anbar province in particular Sunni militias were now supporting US forces rather than presenting a hostile resistance. However, he acknowledged the ongoing difficulties of the situation and warned that a premature reduction in troop levels would have 'devastating consequences'. Petraeus advised that the US military presence could be scaled down in December 2007 and still further in July 2008, to the 2006 level of 130,000 troops. President Bush subsequently announced that 5,700 troops would be withdrawn from Iraq by the end of 2007 and a total of 21,500 by July 2008, in accordance with Petraeus's recommendations. Bush declined to give a timetable for a full withdrawal of troops, leading Democrats to criticize the scope of the plans. In February 2008 the President's 2009 federal budget presentation to Congress included a proposed 7.5% increase in spending on defence from 2008, to US $515,000m. An additional $70,000m. was allocated to fund the conflicts in Iraq and Afghanistan between the start of the fiscal year in October and January 2009, when the incoming president was due to take office. In a speech on 19 March 2008 in recognition of the fifth anniversary of the invasion of Iraq, Bush hailed the success of the 'surge' tactic amid criticism over the rising cost of the war. Estimates in this respect differed widely, with the non-partisan Congressional Budget Office placing the figure at $600,000m., while economist Joseph Stiglitz calculated that the total cost of the war for the USA alone would be $3,000,000m. Democrat consternation was further incited in April when Gen. Petraeus advocated a suspension in troop withdrawals after July in order to undertake a 45-day period of reassessment, as a result of which the President ordered an indefinite suspension to the exit, leaving a US force of around 140,000 combat personnel in the country from August. Petraeus was replaced as leader of US forces in Iraq by Gen. Raymond T. Odierno in September.

THE UNITED STATES OF AMERICA

By the end of April 2009 total losses of US military personnel in Iraq had reached at least 4,200, while estimates of total Iraqi fatalities were a matter of dispute, ranging from 90,000 to as many as 600,000. In February President Obama reiterated his electoral pledge to withdraw all US combat troops from Iraq by the end of August 2010; some 35,000 military personnel would remain in Iraq until 2011 to train and equip the Iraqi army and police. At the same time, the new President confirmed that a further 17,000 US troops would be deployed in Afghanistan. At the end of March Obama confirmed his Administration's shift in policy towards combating insurgency in Afghanistan and neighbouring Pakistan by announcing that a further 4,000 troops were to be dispatched to the region to support the Afghan army and police force there. The shift towards counterinsurgency tactics—a break from the US Army's traditional doctrine—continued in the following month after Secretary of Defense Robert M. Gates announced that he had requested the resignation of a senior US general in Afghanistan, Gen. David D. McKiernan, less than a year after his appointment. He was to be replaced by Lt-Gen. Stanley A. McChrystal, a veteran Special Operations commander.

Presidential and congressional elections were held on 4 November 2008. The Democratic representative was Illinois senator Barack Obama, the party's first African-American presidential nominee. Obama had been selected as the Democratic Party's representative in early June after a long campaign, defeating New York senator Hillary Clinton. Joseph Biden, the Delaware senator, was Obama's vice-presidential nominee. John McCain was the Republican Party's candidate, while the Governor of Alaska, Sarah Palin, was selected to be his running mate. In the event, Obama secured a clear victory, winning 52.9% of the valid votes cast and 365 electoral college votes, compared with McCain's 45.7% and 173 electoral college votes. The Democrats also performed well in the concurrently held congressional elections. The party increased its majority in the House of Representatives to 256 seats, and to at least 56 seats in the Senate (where elections to renew one-third of the seats were held), although it lacked the 60-member so-called 'super majority' in the latter. The result of the senate election in Minnesota was delayed owing to the closeness of the result. Following a lengthy legal process, the Democratic candidate, Al Franken, was declared the victor by a panel of state judges in mid-March 2009, only for the Republican incumbent, Norm Coleman, to file an appeal with the Minnesota Supreme Court, which was scheduled to hear the case in June. In April 2009 the Democrats' representation in the upper house was increased to 57 after Arlen Specter of Pennsylvania announced his defection from the Republican Party to the Democratic Party.

The search for a candidate to replace Barack Obama in the Senate became the focus of increased media attention in late 2008, after it was alleged that the Governor of Illinois, Rod Blagojevich, had attempted to 'sell' the vacant seat to the highest bidder. Blagojevich was arrested on federal corruption charges in December 2008 and subsequently impeached and removed from office on 29 January 2009. He was replaced by Lieutenant-Governor Patrick J. Quinn, III. Blagojevich's nomination for the Senate, Roland Burris, was initially barred from taking his seat owing to his connections with the disgraced Governor, but was eventually sworn in on 15 January. In the following month Burris admitted that he had been approached to fundraise for Blagojevich.

Obama was sworn in as President on 20 January 2009. His Cabinet included several high-profile appointments. Hillary Clinton, his rival in the Democratic primaries, was named Secretary of State, while Robert M. Gates, Secretary of Defense in the previous Bush Administration, was reappointed to the post. Timothy F. Geithner was installed as Secretary of the Treasury, and Gary F. Locke was appointed Secretary of Commerce. Obama's first choice for that post, Bill Richardson, had been forced to withdraw in December 2008 owing to an ongoing investigation into financial irregularities. A second nominee, Republican Judd Gregg, also withdrew his candidacy in mid-February 2009 after disagreements over economic policy. The President's candidate to take over the health and human services portfolio, former Senate majority leader Tom Daschle, also had retired from the nomination process at the end of January owing to tax discrepancies. Kathleen Sebelius was confirmed as Secretary of Health and Human Services at the end of April.

One of the first priorities of the new Administration was to gain congressional approval for a US $787,000m. economic stimulus programme aimed at alleviating the impact of the economic slowdown (see Economic Affairs). The series of measures, which included tax cuts, funding for infrastructural projects, the introduction of a cap on executive salaries, and several protectionist moves, was approved by Congress in mid-February 2009 and signed into law several days later. President Obama also announced a further $50,000m. in aid for homeowners struggling to meet mortgage payments.

Relations with the DPRK were severely strained in late 2002 when it emerged that the DPRK Government had resumed its nuclear energy programme, effectively breaking the accord signed with the USA in 1994. In October the DPRK demanded a treaty of non-aggression with the USA and asserted its right to possess nuclear weapons. In the following month the USA, the Republic of Korea, Japan and the EU suspended their supply of petroleum to the DPRK until its Government promised to terminate its nuclear weapons programme, although the DPRK denied it operated such a programme. However, in December it announced operations would resume at the Yongbyon nuclear plant, which was capable of producing weapons-grade plutonium. The USA considered that economic sanctions would be an effective means of containing North Korea, although this led to a more uncompromising stance from the DPRK, which said it would consider UN sanctions an 'act of war', and subsequently withdrew from the NPT in January 2003. In mid-July the DPRK claimed that it had made enough plutonium to produce six nuclear bombs. In late August six-party negotiations opened in the Chinese capital, Beijing, between the USA, the DPRK, the People's Republic of China, South Korea, Japan and Russia; however, little progress was achieved. In October President Bush announced that the USA would be prepared to offer security assurances to the DPRK in exchange for verifiable dismantling of any weapons programmes. In January 2004 a group of US nuclear scientists visited the Yongbyon plant, in an unofficial capacity, and announced that they had been shown plutonium but had seen no proof of a nuclear bomb. In February a further round of six-party talks took place in Beijing, but no significant resolutions were reached. Talks in June ended unsuccessfully and in February 2005 the DPRK admitted for the first time that it possessed nuclear weapons. Talks eventually resumed in August and the following month it appeared that a breakthrough had been made when the DPRK agreed in principle to end its weapons development programme in exchange for a civilian light-water reactor. However, the DPRK refused to begin dismantling its nuclear programme until it had received the reactor; the USA took the opposite position. Meanwhile, the US Administration alleged that the Banco Asia Delta in Macao, People's Republic of China, was laundering money on behalf of the DPRK Government and imposed a ban on transactions with the bank. The following month US authorities froze the assets of eight North Korean companies, which were accused of supporting the DPRK weapons programme. In October the US Department of Justice charged the DPRK with having forged millions of dollars worth of counterfeit US $100 bills—so-called 'Supernotes'—since 1989. The DPRK Government insisted that six-party negotiations would not resume until the economic sanctions against it were lifted. In October 2006, after the DPRK conducted its first nuclear test, the USA entered into further talks and in mid-February 2007 significant progress appeared to have been made when the Government of the DPRK agreed to effect the disarmament programme agreed upon in 2005. The process was to begin with the closure of the nuclear reactor in Yongbyon within 60 days, but progress once again stalled when the DPRK missed a deadline at the end of 2007 at which it was due to give a full account of its nuclear activities. The DPRK eventually declared its nuclear activities in June 2008, and in October the country was removed from the US Department of State's list of 'state sponsors of terrorism'. Nevertheless, six-party talks again broke down in December over verification of the disarmament programme, prompting the USA to suspend aid to the country.

In March 2006 an agreement was reached between President Bush and India's premier, Manmohan Singh, during discussions in New Delhi, India, under the terms of which India would be permitted to purchase nuclear fuel and technology from the USA in return for the separation of its military and civilian nuclear programmes and consent for UN inspection of its civilian nuclear facilities. US assistance for the advancement of India's nuclear programme, together with those of Pakistan and Israel, had previously been denied under US law as the three were not signatories of the NPT; the new agreement, if approved by Congress, would necessitate the amendment of the US Atomic

THE UNITED STATES OF AMERICA

Energy Act of 1954, although in effectively bypassing the NPT it was argued that the legislation would undermine these international safeguards. Ongoing objections from the Communist Party of India, contending that the agreement would facilitate the exertion of undue US influence over the country's foreign and nuclear policy, presented further obstruction to approval of the agreement, which, indeed, remained outstanding in early 2009.

An escalation in the conflict between Arab *Janjaweed* militia and ethnic groups in the Darfur region of Sudan, which had been ongoing since 2003, prompted protests in Washington, DC, and 18 other US cities in April 2006 to demand that the US Administration intervene to alleviate the humanitarian crisis there. In early May the Darfur Peace Agreement—negotiated by the US Deputy Secretary of State, Robert B. Zoellick, African Union representatives and other foreign officials working in Nigeria—was signed between the Sudanese Government and a faction of the Sudan Liberation Army. On 13 October President Bush signed the Darfur Peace and Accountability Act of 2006 into law, imposing sanctions against those responsible for genocide, crimes against humanity and war crimes, supporting strategies to defend civilians and humanitarian exercises, and promoting peace initiatives in Darfur. The legislation was augmented by an executive order—forbidding transactions with, and receipt of property of, the Sudanese Government—which came into effect simultaneously. The order, while specifically prohibiting transactions relating to the oil and petrochemical industries of Sudan, made provision for limited trade to continue with non-governmental concerns in other regions of Sudan. In mid-April 2007 President Bush announced further sanctions to be imposed against Sudan, including restrictions against 29 companies owned or operated by the Sudanese Government and three individuals accused of instigating violence in Darfur. Implementation of the measures was postponed, however, following an appeal from UN Secretary-General Ban Ki-Moon requesting that more time be allowed to negotiate a diplomatic solution. According to the US Department of State, by September 2006 the USA had contributed over US $1,000m. in humanitarian aid—including $400m. over the preceding 12 months for emergency food assistance—to the Sudanese people; the President's State of the Union address to Congress in January 2007 indicated that the US Government would continue to provide assistance to the people of Sudan while enjoining the international community to redouble its efforts in alleviating the crisis.

Government

The USA is a federal republic. Each of the 50 constituent states and the District of Columbia exercises a measure of internal self-government. Defence, foreign affairs, coinage, posts, the higher levels of justice, and internal security are the responsibility of the federal Government. The President is head of the executive and is elected for a four-year term by a college of representatives elected directly from each state. The President appoints the other members of the executive, subject to the consent of the Senate. The Congress is the seat of legislative power and consists of the Senate (100 members) and the House of Representatives (435 members). Two senators are chosen by direct election in each state, to serve a six-year term, and one-third of the membership is renewable every two years. Representatives are elected by direct and universal suffrage for a two-year term. The number of representatives of each state in Congress is determined by the size of the state's population. Ultimate judicial power is vested in the Supreme Court, which has the power to disallow legislation and to overturn executive actions that it deems unconstitutional.

Defence

As assessed at November 2008, US armed forces totalled 1,539,587: army 632,245, air force 340,530, navy 339,453 and 186,661 marine corps; there was also a Coast Guard numbering 40,698 (not including civilians). At the same time active reservists totalled 979,378. Military conscription ended in 1973. The Strategic Air Command and Polaris nuclear submarines are equipped with nuclear weapons. The USA is a member of the North Atlantic Treaty Organization (NATO) alliance. Estimated federal defence expenditure for 2008 totalled US $616,097m. (some 20.7% of total federal budgetary expenditure).

Economic Affairs

In 2007, according to estimates by the World Bank, the USA's gross national income (GNI), measured at average 2005–07 prices, was US $13,886,472m., equivalent to $46,040 per head (or $45,850 on an international purchasing-power parity basis).

Introductory Survey

During 2000–07, it was estimated, the population increased at an average annual rate of 1.0%, while gross domestic product (GDP) per head increased, in real terms, by an average of 1.5% per year. During the same period, according to official estimates, overall GDP increased, in real terms, at an average annual rate of 2.3%; GDP grew by 2.0% in 2007 and by 1.1% in 2008.

Agriculture (including forestry, fishing and hunting) contributed 1.1% of GDP in 2008 and engaged 1.4% of the employed civilian population in 2007. The principal crops are hay, potatoes, sugar beet and citrus fruit, which, together with cereals, cotton and tobacco, are important export crops. In recent years the production and export of soybeans has also become significant. The principal livestock are cattle, pigs and poultry. Food and live animals provided 6.6% of total exports in 2008. The GDP of the sector increased, in real terms, by an average of 3.2% per year in 2000–07. Real agricultural GDP increased by 6.9%, in real terms, in 2007, but declined by 0.5% in 2008.

Industry (including mining, manufacturing, construction and utilities) provided 20.0% of GDP in 2008 and engaged 20.6% of the employed civilian population in 2007. Industrial GDP increased, in real terms, at an average annual rate of 0.8% in 2000–07. The sector's GDP increased, in real terms, by 0.1% in 2007, but declined by 2.7% in 2008.

Mining and quarrying contributed 2.3% of GDP in 2008 and engaged 0.5% of the employed civilian population in 2007. The USA has significant mineral deposits, specifically of petroleum, natural gas, coal (with 242,721m. metric tons at the end of 2007, the USA had the largest proven recoverable reserves of coal in the world), copper, iron, silver and uranium. At the end of 2007 the USA's proven recoverable reserves of petroleum were 29,400m. barrels, equivalent to 2.4% of the world's proven oil reserves, and sufficient to sustain production at 2007 levels for almost 12 years. Crude petroleum production averaged 6.9m. barrels per day (b/d) in 2007. The USA's proven recoverable reserves of natural gas were estimated at 5,980,000m. cu m at the end of 2007, and production in that year totalled 545,900m. cu m (second only to Russia). Crude materials (excluding fuels) accounted for 5.9% of total exports in 2008; mineral fuels accounted for a further 5.9% of exports in that year. In real terms, the GDP of the sector decreased at an average annual rate of 1.2% during 2000–07. Real mining GDP rose by just under 0.1% in 2007, but fell by 0.8% in 2008.

Manufacturing contributed 11.5% of GDP in 2008 and the sector engaged 11.2% of the employed civilian population in 2007. In 2007 the principal branches of manufacturing (measured by value of output) were chemical products (15.4% of total manufacturing value added), motor vehicles and transport equipment (12.0%), food, beverages and tobacco products (10.8%), computer and electronic equipment (9.0%), fabricated metal products (8.7%) and machinery (7.8%). Manufacturing GDP increased, in real terms, by an average of 1.8% per year in 2000–07. Sectoral GDP for manufacturing increased by 2.9%, in real terms, in 2007, but declined by 2.7% in 2008.

According to the US Energy Information Administration (EIA), the USA is the world's largest producer, consumer and net importer of energy. Energy is derived principally from domestic and imported hydrocarbons. The EIA estimated that in 2007 75.4% of total electricity production was provided by fossil fuels (coal 32.7%, natural gas 27.6% and petroleum 15.1%), 11.7% was provided by nuclear power, and some 9.5% was derived from renewable sources. In 2008 fuel imports amounted to 23.2% (petroleum and petroleum products 21.1%) of total merchandise import costs.

Services (including government services) provided 78.9% of GDP in 2008 and engaged 78.0% of the employed civilian population in 2007. The combined GDP of all service sectors rose, in real terms, at an average rate of 4.0% per year during 2000–07. Of non-government services sub-sectors, the contribution of real estate, rental and leasing was most significant in 2008 (contributing 14.4% of the total value of non-government services). Services GDP increased, in real terms, by 8.2% in 2008.

In 2007 the USA recorded a visible trade deficit of US $815,300m. (excluding military transactions), and there was a deficit of $731,200m. on the current account of the balance of payments. In 2008 the People's Republic of China was the principal provider of imports (supplying 16.1% of the total), followed closely by Canada (16.0%). Other important supplier nations included Mexico, Japan and Germany. Canada was the principal export market in 2008, accounting for 20.1% of the total value of exports. Mexico was the USA's second largest export market in that year, taking 11.7% of the value of US exports, followed by the People's Republic of China, Japan and Germany. In 2008 machinery and transport equipment constituted the most significant category of both imports (accounting for 34.3% of the total value of imports) and exports (42.8% of the total).

A federal budget deficit of US $160,701m. was recorded for the financial year ending 30 September 2007, an amount equivalent to 1.2% of GDP in 2007. The deficit was reported to have increased to $458,555m. in 2008 (3.2% of GDP). The annual rate of inflation averaged 2.7% in 2000–07. The annual average rate was 3.8% in 2008. The rate of unemployment averaged 4.6% in 2007.

The USA is a member of the Organisation for Economic Co-operation and Development (OECD, see p. 358), the North American Free Trade Agreement (NAFTA, see p. 350) and the World Trade Organization (WTO, see p. 410). Agreement on a free trade accord, to be known as the Central American Free Trade Agreement (CAFTA), between the USA and Guatemala, Costa Rica, El Salvador, Honduras and Nicaragua was signed in May 2004 in Washington, DC. The Agreement, which was restyled DR-CAFTA following the inclusion of the Dominican Republic later that year, was ratified by Congress in late July 2005 and signed by President Bush early in the following month. DR-CAFTA came into effect in El Salvador, Honduras, Nicaragua and Guatemala in 2006, and in the Dominican Republic in 2007. Discussions to establish a Free Trade Area of the Americas, first proposed in 1995, stalled in late 2004, and (although it was agreed in mid-2006 to resume talks) no progress had been made by mid-2009.

The US economy grew throughout the 1990s and early 2000s, fuelled by robust consumer consumption. However, the country suffered an economic shock in late 2006 when the sub-prime mortgage crisis emerged: after house prices began to collapse in that year, many individuals were left unable to refinance mortgages as interest rates rose, leading to unprecedented levels of repossessions. The crisis had the effect of creating a nation-wide, and eventually global, 'credit crunch' as banks and mortgage lenders cut back on giving credit to customers and each other. In late April 2008 the Bush Administration distributed tax rebates totalling more than US $1,000m. to some 117m. homes in an attempt to encourage spending and boost growth; legislation approved in late July allowing for emergency aid to be given to federal mortgage institutions was also intended to restore confidence. However, the financial crisis intensified dramatically after the collapse of Lehman Brothers, an investment bank, and other financial ventures in September, which led to fears of a complete breakdown of the financial sector. A government-backed rescue plan for the banks, valued at $700,000m., was initially rejected by the House of Representatives, which led to the value of stocks and shares plummeting around the world, but it was subsequently approved in October. Real GDP growth slowed to 2.0% in 2007, down from 2.8% in 2006, and, while low, remained positive overall in 2008 at 1.1%; however, negative growth rates were recorded in the last two quarters of that year, which confirmed that the USA had entered recession. As both domestic and international demand for US goods and services decreased, the unemployment rate rose sharply, from 5.1% in March 2008 to 8.5% in March 2009. Following the inauguration of President Barack Obama in January 2009, Congress approved a $787,000m. fiscal stimulus package in February, which included tax cuts for low-and middle-income households, as well as large-scale government spending. In the same month the President announced his draft budget for 2010, worth $3,600,000m., which included measures to expand health care coverage and increase expenditure on education. In 2007 the budget deficit was equivalent to 1.2% of GDP, but this increased to 3.2% in 2008 and was forecast to rise significantly, to 12.9%, in 2009.

Education

Education is primarily the responsibility of state and local governments, but some federal funds are available to help meet special needs at primary, secondary and higher education levels. Public education is free in every state from elementary school through high school. The period of compulsory education varies among states, but most states require attendance between the ages of seven and 16 years. In 2007 there were an estimated 34.6m. pupils enrolled in public primary schools and 15.1m. in public secondary schools. Private school enrolment was approximately 4.7m. at primary level and about 1.4m. at secondary level. In 2004 there were 4,216 two-year and four-year universities and colleges, with a total enrolment of an estimated 18.2m. students in 2007. Federal government expenditure on education (including training and employment programmes) totalled US $88.3m. in 2009. Spending on education by state and local government in 2005/06 was $727,967m. (29.0% of total public expenditure).

Public Holidays*

2009: 1 January (New Year's Day), 19 January (Martin Luther King Day), 16 February (Presidents' Day), 25 May (Memorial Day), 3 July (for Independence Day), 7 September (Labor Day), 12 October (Columbus Day), 11 November (Veterans' Day), 26 November (Thanksgiving Day), 25 December (Christmas Day).

2010: 1 January (New Year's Day), 18 January (Martin Luther King Day), 15 February (Presidents' Day), 31 May (Memorial Day), 5 July (for Independence Day), 6 September (Labor Day), 11 October (Columbus Day), 11 November (Veterans' Day), 25 November (Thanksgiving Day), 24 December (for Christmas Day).

*Federal legal public holidays are designated by presidential proclamation or congressional enactment, but need not be observed in individual states, which have legal jurisdiction over their public holidays.

Weights and Measures

With certain exceptions, the imperial system is in force. One US billion equals 1,000 million; one US cwt equals 100 lb; long ton equals 2,240 lb; short ton equals 2,000 lb. A policy of gradual voluntary conversion to the metric system is being encouraged.

THE UNITED STATES OF AMERICA

Statistical Survey

Source (unless otherwise stated): Statistical Information Office, Population Division, Bureau of the Census, US Dept of Commerce, Washington, DC 20233-0001; internet www.census.gov.

Area and Population

AREA, POPULATION AND DENSITY

Area (sq km)	
Land	9,161,923
Water*	664,706
Total	9,826,630†
Population (census results)‡	
1 April 1990	248,709,873
1 April 2000	
Males	138,053,563
Females	143,368,343
Total	281,421,906
Population (official estimates at mid-year)§	
2006	298,362,973
2007	301,290,332
2008	304,059,724
Density (per sq km) at mid-2008‖	33.2

* Comprises Great Lakes, and inland, territorial, and coastal waters.
† 3,794,083 sq miles.
‡ Excluding adjustment for underenumeration; the adjusted total was 281,424,602.
§ Estimates of the resident population, based on adjusted 2000 census results.
‖ Land area only.

RACES
(2000 census)

	Number	%
White	211,460,626	75.14
Black	34,658,190	12.32
Asian	10,242,998	3.64
American Indian and Alaska Native	2,475,956	0.88
Native Hawaiian and Pacific Islander	398,835	0.14
Others*	22,185,301	7.88
Total	281,421,906	100.00

* Includes those of two or more races.

Hispanic or Latino population (all races): 35,305,818 (12.6%).

STATES
(population at census of 1 April 2000*)

State	Land area (sq km)	Residents ('000)	Density (per sq km)	Capital
Alabama	131,426	4,447	33.8	Montgomery
Alaska	1,481,347	627	0.4	Juneau
Arizona	294,312	5,131	17.4	Phoenix
Arkansas	134,856	2,673	19.8	Little Rock
California	403,933	33,872	83.9	Sacramento
Colorado	268,627	4,301	16.0	Denver
Connecticut	12,548	3,406	271.4	Hartford
Delaware	5,060	784	154.9	Dover
District of Columbia	159	572	3,596.7	Washington
Florida	139,670	15,982	114.4	Tallahassee
Georgia	149,976	8,186	54.6	Atlanta
Hawaii	16,635	1,212	72.9	Honolulu
Idaho	214,314	1,294	6.0	Boise
Illinois	143,961	12,419	86.3	Springfield
Indiana	92,895	6,080	65.5	Indianapolis
Iowa	144,701	2,926	20.2	Des Moines
Kansas	211,900	2,688	12.7	Topeka
Kentucky	102,896	4,042	39.3	Frankfort
Louisiana	112,825	4,469	39.6	Baton Rouge
Maine	79,931	1,275	16.0	Augusta
Maryland	25,314	5,296	209.2	Annapolis
Massachusetts	20,306	6,349	312.7	Boston
Michigan	147,121	9,938	67.5	Lansing
Minnesota	206,189	4,919	23.9	St Paul
Mississippi	121,488	2,845	23.4	Jackson
Missouri	178,414	5,595	31.4	Jefferson City
Montana	376,979	902	2.4	Helena

State—continued	Land area (sq km)	Residents ('000)	Density (per sq km)	Capital
Nebraska	199,099	1,711	8.6	Lincoln
Nevada	284,448	1,998	7.0	Carson City
New Hampshire	23,227	1,236	53.2	Concord
New Jersey	19,211	8,414	438.0	Trenton
New Mexico	314,309	1,819	5.8	Santa Fe
New York	122,283	18,976	155.2	Albany
North Carolina	126,161	8,049	63.8	Raleigh
North Dakota	178,647	642	3.6	Bismarck
Ohio	106,056	11,353	107.0	Columbus
Oklahoma	177,847	3,451	19.4	Oklahoma City
Oregon	248,631	3,421	13.8	Salem
Pennsylvania	116,074	12,281	105.8	Harrisburg
Rhode Island	2,706	1,048	387.2	Providence
South Carolina	77,983	4,012	51.4	Columbia
South Dakota	196,540	755	3.8	Pierre
Tennessee	106,752	5,689	53.3	Nashville
Texas	678,051	20,852	30.8	Austin
Utah	212,751	2,233	10.5	Salt Lake City
Vermont	23,956	609	25.4	Montpelier
Virginia	102,548	7,079	69.0	Richmond
Washington	172,348	5,894	34.2	Olympia
West Virginia	62,361	1,808	29.0	Charleston
Wisconsin	140,663	5,364	38.1	Madison
Wyoming	251,489	494	2.0	Cheyenne
Total	9,161,923	281,422	30.7	

* Includes armed forces residing in each State.

Note: Totals may not be equal to sum of components, owing to rounding.

PRINCIPAL TOWNS
(population at census of 1 April 2000)

New York	8,008,278	Oklahoma City	506,132
Los Angeles	3,694,820	Tucson	486,699
Chicago	2,896,016	New Orleans	484,674
Houston	1,953,631	Las Vegas	478,434
Philadelphia	1,517,550	Cleveland	478,403
Phoenix	1,321,045	Long Beach, CA	461,522
San Diego	1,223,400	Albuquerque	448,607
Dallas	1,188,580	Kansas City, MO	441,545
San Antonio	1,114,646	Fresno	427,652
Detroit	951,270	Virginia Beach, VA	425,257
San Jose	894,943	Atlanta	416,474
Indianapolis	791,926	Sacramento	407,018
San Francisco	776,733	Oakland	399,484
Jacksonville	735,617	Mesa City, AZ	396,375
Columbus, OH	711,470	Tulsa	393,049
Austin	656,562	Omaha	390,007
Baltimore	651,154	Minneapolis	382,618
Memphis	650,100	Honolulu	371,657
Milwaukee	596,974	Colorado Springs	360,980
Boston	589,141	St Louis	348,189
Washington, DC (capital)	572,059	Wichita	344,284
Nashville-Davidson	569,891	Santa Ana, CA	337,977
El Paso	563,662	Pittsburgh	334,563
Seattle	563,374	Arlington, TX	332,969
Denver	554,636	Cincinnati	331,285
Charlotte	540,828	Anaheim	328,014
Fort Worth	534,694	Toledo, OH	313,619
Portland, OR	529,121	Tampa	303,447

THE UNITED STATES OF AMERICA

BIRTHS, MARRIAGES, DEATHS

	Registered live births Number ('000)	Rate (per 1,000)	Registered marriages Number ('000)	Rate (per 1,000)	Registered deaths Number ('000)	Rate (per 1,000)
2000	4,059	14.4	2,329	8.3	2,403	8.5
2001	4,026	14.1	2,345	8.2	2,416	8.5
2002	4,022	13.9	2,254	7.8	2,443	8.5
2003	4,090	14.1	2,245	7.7	2,448	8.4
2004	4,112	14.0	2,279	7.8	2,398	8.2
2005	4,143	14.0	2,249	7.6	2,448	8.3
2006*	4,269	14.2	2,193†	7.4†	2,416	8.1
2007*	4,315	14.3	2,205†	7.3†	2,415	8.0

* Provisional figures.
† Data for Louisiana were not available.

Source: National Center for Health Statistics, US Department of Health and Human Services.

Life expectancy (years at birth, WHO estimates): 78.0 (males 75.5; females 80.4) in 2006 (Source: WHO, *World Health Statistics*).

IMMIGRATION
(year ending 30 September)

Country of birth	2005/06	2006/07	2007/08
Europe	164,244	120,821	119,138
Bosnia-Herzegovina	3,789	1,569	1,491
Poland	17,051	10,355	8,354
Russia	13,159	9,426	11,695
Ukraine	17,140	11,001	10,813
United Kingdom	17,207	14,545	14,348
Asia	422,284	383,508	383,608
Bangladesh	14,644	12,074	11,753
China, People's Republic	87,307	76,655	80,271
India	61,369	65,353	63,352
Iran	13,947	10,460	13,852
Korea, Republic	24,386	22,405	26,666
Pakistan	17,418	13,492	19,719
Philippines	74,606	72,596	54,030
Taiwan	8,086	8,990	9,073
Thailand	11,749	8,751	6,637
Viet Nam	30,691	28,691	31,497
Africa	117,422	94,711	105,915
Egypt	10,500	9,267	8,712
Ethiopia	16,152	12,786	12,917
Nigeria	13,459	12,448	12,475
Somalia	9,462	6,251	10,745
North America, Central America and the Caribbean	414,075	339,355	393,253
Canada	18,207	15,495	15,109
Mexico	173,749	148,640	189,989
Caribbean			
Cuba	45,614	29,104	49,500
Dominican Republic	38,068	28,024	31,879
Haiti	22,226	30,405	26,007
Jamaica	24,976	19,375	18,477
Central America			
El Salvador	31,782	21,127	19,659
Guatemala	24,133	17,908	16,182
South America	137,986	106,525	98,555
Brazil	17,903	14,295	12,195
Colombia	43,144	33,187	30,213
Ecuador	17,489	12,248	11,663
Peru	21,718	17,699	15,184
Venezuela	11,341	10,692	10,514
Total (incl. others and unknown)	1,266,129	1,052,415	1,107,126

Source: US Department of Homeland Security, *Yearbook of Immigration Statistics*.

Statistical Survey

ECONOMICALLY ACTIVE POPULATION
(annual averages, civilian labour force, '000 persons aged 16 years and over)

	2005	2006	2007
Agriculture, hunting, forestry and fishing	2,197	2,206	2,095
Mining and quarrying	624	687	736
Manufacturing	16,253	16,377	16,302
Electricity, gas and water	1,176	1,186	1,193
Construction	11,197	11,749	11,856
Wholesale and retail trade; repair of motor vehicles, motorcycles and personal and household goods	21,404	21,328	20,937
Hotels and restaurants	9,306	9,474	9,582
Transport, storage and communications	6,184	6,269	6,457
Financial intermediation	7,035	7,254	7,306
Real estate, renting and business activities	17,461	18,105	18,802
Public administration and defence; compulsory social security	6,530	6,524	6,746
Education	12,264	12,522	12,828
Health and social work	16,910	17,416	17,834
Other services	13,187	13,332	13,371
Total employed	141,730	144,427	146,047
Unemployed	7,591	7,001	7,078
Total labour force	149,320	151,428	153,124
Males	80,033	81,255	82,136
Females	69,288	70,172	70,988

Source: ILO.

Health and Welfare

KEY INDICATORS

Total fertility rate (children per woman, 2006)	2.1
Under-5 mortality rate (per 1,000 live births, 2006)	8
HIV/AIDS (% of persons aged 15–49, 2007)	0.6
Physicians (per 1,000 head, 2000)	2.56
Hospital beds (per 1,000 head, 2005)	3.2
Health expenditure (2006): US $ per head (PPP)	6,714.0
Health expenditure (2006): % of GDP	15.3
Health expenditure (2006): public (% of total)	45.8
Human Development Index (2006): ranking	15
Human Development Index (2006): value	0.950

For sources and definitions, see explanatory note on p. vi.

Agriculture

PRINCIPAL CROPS
('000 metric tons)

	2005	2006	2007
Wheat	57,280	49,316	53,603
Rice, paddy	10,125	8,788	8,956
Barley	4,613	3,923	4,612
Maize	282,311	267,598	332,092
Oats	1,667	1,359	1,330
Sorghum	9,981	7,050	12,827
Potatoes	19,229	19,713	17,654
Sweet potatoes	714	746	837
Sugar cane	24,137	27,033	27,751
Sugar beet	24,887	30,631	31,912
Beans, dry	1,235	1,100	1,151
Soybeans (Soya beans)	83,368	87,670	70,707
Groundnuts, with shell	2,209	1,576	1,697
Sunflower seed	1,823	972	1,318
Rapeseed	718	633	660
Cabbages and other brassicas	1,101	1,165	1,171
Lettuce	4,607	4,339	5,106
Tomatoes	10,983	11,298	11,500*
Cucumbers and gherkins	930	908	920*
Onions, dry	3,334	3,250	3,602
Peas, green	859	865*	875*

THE UNITED STATES OF AMERICA

—continued

	2005	2006	2007
String beans	995	1,002	1,050*
Carrots and turnips	1,637	1,583	1,600*
Maize, green	4,106	4,013	4,050*
Watermelons	1,742	1,908	1,944
Cantaloupes and other melons	1,179	1,126	1,150*
Oranges	8,393	8,166	7,357
Tangerines, mandarins, etc.	304	378	328
Lemons and limes	789	855	722
Grapefruit and pomelos	924	1,118	1,580
Apples	4,409	4,569	4,238
Pears	747	763	799
Peaches and nectarines	1,075	916	1,009
Plums	432	645	675*
Strawberries	1,053	1,090	1,115*
Grapes	7,088	5,757	6,105
Tobacco, unmanufactured	290	330	353

* FAO estimate.

Aggregate production (may include official, semi-official or estimated data): Total cereals 366,544 in 2005, 338,513 in 2006, 414,066 in 2007; Total fruits (excl. melons) 27,019 in 2005, 25,445 in 2006, 24,962 in 2007; Total oilcrops 18,119 in 2005, 18,138 in 2006, 15,110 in 2007; Total roots and tubers 19,944 in 2005, 20,460 in 2006, 18,493 in 2007; Total vegetables (incl. melons) 35,841 in 2005, 36,688 in 2006, 38,075 in 2007.

Source: FAO.

LIVESTOCK
('000 head at 1 January)

	2005	2006	2007
Cattle	95,438	96,702	97,003
Pigs	60,975	61,449	61,860
Sheep	6,135	6,230	6,165
Horses	9,200	9,500*	9,500*
Chickens (million)*	2,035	2,050	2,050
Turkeys (million)	252	262	272

* FAO estimate(s).

Source: FAO.

LIVESTOCK PRODUCTS
('000 metric tons)

	2005	2006	2007
Cattle meat	11,243	11,910	12,044
Sheep meat	85	84	83
Pig meat	9,383	9,550	9,953
Chicken meat	15,869	15,870	16,000*
Cows' milk	80,254	82,463	84,189
Hen eggs	5,330	5,360	5,308

* FAO estimate.

Source: FAO.

Forestry

ROUNDWOOD REMOVALS
('000 cubic metres)

	2005	2006	2007
Sawlogs and veneer logs	253,636	242,259	223,448
Pulp wood	160,815	160,813	160,662
Other industrial wood	9,005	9,062	9,203
Fuel wood	43,891	44,914	50,690
Total	467,347	457,048	444,003

Source: FAO.

SAWNWOOD PRODUCTION
('000 cubic metres)

	2005	2006	2007
Coniferous	69,187	65,549	58,755
Broadleaved	27,833*	27,355	25,608
Total	97,020*	92,903	84,363

* Unofficial figure.

Source: FAO.

Fishing

('000 metric tons, live weight)

	2004	2005	2006
Capture	4,959.8	4,893.0	4,859.9
Humpback salmon	135.2	224.4	100.6
Pacific cod	266.1	248.9	235.3
Walleye pollock	1,519.9	1,547.4	1,542.6
North Pacific hake	215.2	258.3	258.8
Atlantic menhaden	215.2	194.2	183.9
Gulf menhaden	464.1	369.9	407.7
American sea scallop	243.5	214.2	223.0
Atlantic surf clam	149.5	143.2	145.0
Aquaculture	606.5	492.4	465.1*
Channel catfish	286.0	275.8	256.8
Total catch	5,566.4	5,385.3	5,324.9*

* FAO estimate.

Note: Figures exclude aquatic plants (metric tons): 35,339 in 2004; 68,065 in 2005; 6,238 in 2006, and sponges (metric tons): 253.5 in 2004; 234.7 in 2005; 133.6 in 2006. Also excluded are aquatic mammals (recorded by number rather than weight); the number of whales and dolphins caught was: 427 in 2004; 283 in 2005; 40 in 2006. The number of seals and sea lions caught was: 2,038 in 2004; 1,914 in 2005; n.a. in 2006. The number of American alligators caught was: 368,409 in 2004; 356,398 in 2005; 421,220 in 2006.

Source: FAO.

Mining

('000 metric tons, unless otherwise indicated)

	2005	2006	2007[1]
Crude petroleum (million barrels)[2]	1,890	1,862	1,848
Natural gas (million cubic feet)[2,3]	18,927	19,410	20,019
Coal (million short tons)[2,4]	1,132	1,163	1,146
Iron ore[5]	54,329	52,706	52,489
Copper[6]	1,210	1,210	1,280
Lead[6]	143	153	123
Zinc[6]	748	725[7]	n.a.
Molybdenum (metric tons)[6]	58,000[7]	59,700	57,000
Silver (metric tons)[6]	1,230	1,140[7]	1,260
Uranium ('000 pounds)[2,8]	2,689	4,122[7]	n.a.
Gold (metric tons)[6]	256	252[7]	238
Platinum group metals (kilograms):[6]			
Platinum	3,920	4,000[7]	n.a.
Palladium	13,300	13,600[7]	n.a.
Lime	20,000	21,000[7]	20,200
Sand and gravel (million metric tons):			
Construction	1,270	1,320[7]	1,230
Industrial	30,600[7]	28,800	30,000
Stone, crushed (million metric tons)	1,700	1,770[7]	1,600

THE UNITED STATES OF AMERICA

—continued	2005	2006	2007[1]
Bentonite	4,710	4,940[7]	4,820
Fuller's Earth	2,730	2,540[7]	2,660
Kaolin	7,800	7,470[7]	7,110
Phosphate rock[3]	36,100	30,100[7]	29,700
Potash (a)[3,9]	1,200	1,100[7]	1,100
Soda ash	11,000	11,000[7]	11,100
Diatomite	653	799[7]	687
Boron (b)[9]	612	n.a.	n.a.
Salt	45,000[7]	40,600	45,400
Bromine (c)[9]	226	243[7]	n.a.

[1] Preliminary (incl. estimates).
[2] Source: Energy Information Administration, US Department of Energy.
[3] Figures refer to marketable production.
[4] 1 short ton = 0.907185 metric tons.
[5] Figures refer to the gross weight of usable ore.
[6] Figures refer to metal content of ores and concentrates.
[7] Estimate.
[8] Figures refer to gross weight of uranium oxide ore.
[9] Figures refer to the content of (a) K_2O, (b) B_2O_3 or (c) bromine contained in minerals and compounds.

Source (unless otherwise indicated): US Geological Survey.

Industry

PRINCIPAL MANUFACTURES
(value of shipments in $ '000 million)

	2005	2006
Food	532.4	537.8
Beverages and tobacco products	124.1	124.7
Wood products	112.1	112.4
Paper	161.9	170.4
Printing and related activities	96.9	99.7
Petroleum and coal products	475.8	549.0
Chemicals	610.9	657.7
Plastics and rubber products	200.3	211.3
Non-metallic mineral products	114.8	126.0
Primary metal industries	203.3	232.6
Fabricated metal products	289.4	317.2
Machinery	302.7	326.4
Computers and electronic products	372.9	390.8
Electrical equipment, appliances and components	112.0	120.0
Transportation equipment	690.7	698.3
Total (incl. others)	4,742.1	5,020.0

Source: Bureau of the Census, US Department of Commerce, *Annual Survey of Manufactures*.

Finance

CURRENCY AND EXCHANGE RATES

Monetary Units
100 cents = 1 United States dollar ($).

Sterling and Euro Equivalents (31 December 2008)
£1 sterling = US $1.459;
€1 = $1.392;
US $100 = £68.60 = €71.85.

FEDERAL BUDGET
($ million, year ending 30 September)*

Revenue	2007	2008†	2009†
Individual income taxes	1,163.5	1,219.7	1,259.0
Corporation income taxes	370.2	345.3	339.2
Social insurance taxes and contributions	869.6	910.1	949.4
Excise taxes	65.1	68.8	68.9
Estate and gift taxes	26.0	26.8	26.3
Customs duties and fees	26.0	29.2	29.1
Miscellaneous receipts	47.8	46.3	47.9
Allowance for economic growth package	—	−125.0	−20.0
Total	2,568.2	2,521.2	2,699.9

Expenditure	2007	2008†	2009†
National defence	552.6	607.3	675.1
International affairs	28.5	34.8	38.0
General science, space research and technology	25.6	27.6	29.2
Energy	−0.9	3.0	3.1
Natural resources and environment	31.8	35.5	35.5
Agriculture	17.7	21.0	19.1
Commerce and housing credit	0.5	7.4	4.2
Transportation	72.9	80.3	83.9
Community and regional development	29.6	27.6	23.3
Education, training, employment and social services	91.7	93.4	88.3
Health	266.4	284.5	299.4
Medicare	375.4	396.3	413.3
Income security	366.0	388.4	401.7
Social security	586.2	615.3	649.3
Veterans' benefits and services	72.8	86.6	91.9
Administration of justice	41.2	46.2	51.1
General government	17.5	19.8	21.5
Allowances	—	—	−0.5
Net interest	237.1	243.9	260.2
Undistributed offsetting receipts	−82.2	−87.7	−80.4
Total	2,730.2	2,931.2	3,107.4

* Including social security and postal service receipts and expenditures, which are extrabudgetary.
† Estimates published in February 2009.

Sources: Office of Management and Budget, Executive Office of the President; Financial Management Service, US Department of the Treasury.

THE UNITED STATES OF AMERICA

Statistical Survey

STATE AND LOCAL GOVERNMENT FINANCES
($ million, fiscal years*)

Revenue	2003/04	2004/05	2005/06
From federal government	423,112	438,432	452,233
From state and local governments	2,011,043	2,090,479	2,284,309
General revenue from own sources	1,464,285	1,588,292	1,733,785
Taxes	1,010,546	1,099,200	1,195,254
Property	317,941	335,981	359,109
Sales and gross receipts	361,027	384,383	412,114
Individual income	215,215	242,273	268,599
Corporation income	33,716	43,138	52,931
Other	82,647	93,425	102,500
Charges and miscellaneous	453,740	489,093	538,531
Utility and liquor stores	114,931	119,607	131,642
Insurance trust revenue	431,827	382,580	418,881
Employee retirement	365,318	316,576	352,521
Unemployment compensation	38,362	35,367	36,989
Other	28,147	30,637	29,372
Total	**2,434,155**	**2,528,912**	**2,736,542**

Expenditure	2003/04	2004/05	2005/06
General expenditure	1,903,915	2,012,422	2,121,946
Education	655,182	689,057	727,967
Elementary and secondary	451,942	473,406	500,528
Institutions of higher education	172,650	182,146	191,758
Other	30,590	33,505	35,681
Libraries	9,289	9,797	10,497
Public welfare	335,977	362,932	370,325
Hospitals	96,570	103,404	110,455
Health	64,373	66,971	71,110
Social insurance administration	4,364	4,340	4,614
Veterans' services	1,504	1,183	992
Highways	117,215	124,602	135,412
Other transportations	23,855	23,267	24,050
Police	70,088	74,727	79,066
Fire protection	28,991	31,439	34,167
Correction	56,326	59,151	62,667
Protective inspection	11,494	12,890	13,655
Natural resources	23,250	25,057	25,482
Parks and recreation	30,498	31,941	34,769
Housing and community development	37,236	39,969	41,980
Sewerage	34,930	36,599	39,220
Solid waste management	20,362	21,469	22,679
Financial administration	34,675	36,519	37,441
Judicial and legal services	33,054	34,991	36,823
General public buildings	11,336	11,858	12,103
Other government administration	21,002	22,945	24,968
Interest on general debt	81,812	81,119	85,660
Other and unallocable	100,533	106,195	115,844
Utility and liquor stores	160,262	160,682	174,679
Insurance trust expenditure	197,842	195,588	203,958
Unemployment compensation	43,278	29,849	28,097
Employee retirement	137,659	145,796	156,180
Other	16,905	19,943	19,681
Total†	**2,266,647**	**2,373,309**	**2,507,086**

* Figures refer to the fiscal year of individual state governments, normally ending 30 June, or, in the case of the following exceptions, ending on some date within the previous 12 months: the state government of Texas and Texas school districts (31 August); the state governments of Alabama and Michigan, all local governments in the District of Columbia, and Alabama school districts (30 September); all state and local governments of New York (31 March).
† Including intergovernmental expenditure ($ million): 4,627 in 2003/04; 4,617 in 2004/05; 6,504 in 2005/06.

Source: Governments Division, Bureau of the Census, US Department of Commerce, *Survey of Government Finances*.

INTERNATIONAL RESERVES
($ '000 million at 31 December)

	2006	2007	2008
Gold (national valuation)	11.04	11.04	11.04
IMF special drawing rights	8.87	9.48	9.34
Reserve position in IMF	5.04	4.24	7.68
Foreign exchange	40.94	45.80	49.58
Total	**65.89**	**70.56**	**77.64**

Source: IMF, *International Financial Statistics*.

CURRENCY AND COIN IN CIRCULATION*
($ million at end of June)

	2006	2007	2008
Total	797,131.3	812,760.5	826,313.9

* Currency outside Treasury and Federal Reserve banks, including currency held by commercial banks.

Source: Financial Management Service, US Department of the Treasury.

COST OF LIVING
(Consumer Price Index for all urban consumers, average of monthly figures. Base: 1982–84 = 100, unless otherwise indicated)

	2006	2007	2008
Food and beverages	195.7	203.3	214.2
Housing	203.2	209.6	216.3
Clothing	119.5	119.0	118.9
Transport	180.9	184.7	195.5
Medical care	336.2	351.1	364.1
Recreation*	110.9	111.4	113.3
Education and communication*	116.8	119.6	123.6
Other goods and services	321.7	333.3	345.4
All items	**201.6**	**207.3**	**215.3**

* Base: December 1997 = 100.

Source: Bureau of Labor Statistics, US Department of Labor.

NATIONAL ACCOUNTS
($ '000 million at current prices)

National Income and Product

	2006	2007	2008
Compensation of employees	7,440.4	7,819.4	8,062.3
Operating surplus	3,350.6	3,386.0	3,251.1
Domestic factor incomes	**10,791.0**	**11,205.4**	**11,313.4**
Consumption of fixed capital	1,623.9	1,720.5	1,832.3
Statistical discrepancy	−163.0	−81.4	135.8
Gross domestic product (GDP) at factor cost	**12,251.9**	**12,844.5**	**13,281.5**
Taxes on production and imports	976.2	1,015.5	1,033.8
Less Subsidies on production and imports	49.7	52.3	50.7
GDP in purchasers' values	**13,178.4**	**13,807.5**	**14,264.6**
Factor income received from abroad	725.4	861.7	798.3
Less Factor income paid abroad	647.1	759.3	665.1
Gross national product (GNP)	**13,256.7**	**13,909.9**	**14,397.8**
Less Consumption of fixed capital	1,623.9	1,720.5	1,832.3
Net national product	**11,632.8**	**12,189.4**	**12,565.5**
Statistical discrepancy	163.0	81.4	−135.8
National income in market prices	**11,795.8**	**12,270.8**	**12,429.7**

THE UNITED STATES OF AMERICA

Expenditure on Gross Domestic Product

	2006	2007	2008
Government final consumption expenditure	2,081.5	2,212.0	2,386.4
Private final consumption expenditure	9,207.2	9,710.2	10,057.9
Increase in stocks	49.3	−3.6	−47.0
Gross fixed investment	2,597.8	2,596.8	2,536.5
Total domestic expenditure	13,935.8	14,515.4	14,933.8
Exports of goods and services	1,480.8	1,662.4	1,859.4
Less Imports of goods and services	2,238.1	2,370.2	2,528.6
GDP in purchasers' values	13,178.4	13,807.5	14,264.6
GDP at chained 2000 prices	11,294.8	11,523.9	11,652.0

Gross Domestic Product by Economic Activity*

	2006	2007	2008
Private industries	11,529.3	12,064.6	12,424.6
Agriculture, forestry, fishing and hunting	121.6	167.9	157.7
Agriculture	91.1	137.3	n.a.
Forestry, fishing and related activities	30.5	30.7	n.a.
Mining	262.4	275.0	325.3
Electricity, gas and water	272.7	281.4	306.0
Construction	646.0	610.8	581.5
Manufacturing	1,577.4	1,616.8	1,637.7
Wholesale trade	773.2	805.3	818.8
Retail trade	866.5	892.5	885.5
Transport and storage	387.4	407.2	414.9
Information	559.6	586.3	622.0
Finance and insurance	1,060.9	1,091.4	1,064.9
Real estate and rental and leasing	1,624.8	1,719.8	1,783.5
Professional and business services	1,566.4	1,694.1	1,805.8
Professional, scientific and technical services	930.6	1,007.8	1,095.6
Management of companies and enterprises	246.9	271.3	283.8
Administrative and waste management services	388.9	415.1	426.5
Education	121.1	129.5	138.3
Health care and social assistance	904.8	957.4	1,019.7
Arts, entertainment and recreation	126.9	133.8	140.1
Hotels and restaurants	358.0	379.5	396.2
Other private services	299.5	315.6	326.8
Government	1,649.1	1,742.9	1,840.0
Federal	527.6	554.0	586.6
General government	460.1	484.2	n.a.
Government enterprises	67.4	69.8	n.a.
State and local	1,121.5	1,188.9	1,253.4
General government	1,037.2	1,099.0	n.a.
Government enterprises	84.3	89.9	n.a.
GDP in purchasers' values	13,178.4	13,807.5	14,264.6

* Distribution is based on the 1997 North American Industry Classification System (NAICS), which differs from ISIC.

Source: Bureau of Economic Analysis, US Department of Commerce.

BALANCE OF PAYMENTS
($ '000 million)

	2005	2006	2007
Exports of goods f.o.b.	898.5	1,026.9	1,152.6
Imports of goods f.o.b.	−1,681.8	−1,861.4	−1,967.9
Trade balance	−783.4	−834.6	−815.3
Exports of services	385.3	430.2	493.2
Imports of services	−313.5	−348.9	−378.1
Balance on goods and services	−711.6	−753.3	−700.3
Other income received	535.3	685.2	817.8
Other income paid	−462.9	−628.0	−736.0
Balance on goods, services and income	−639.2	−696.1	−618.5
Current transfers received	19.0	25.2	22.3
Current transfers paid	−108.8	−117.2	−135.0
Current balance	−729.0	−788.1	−731.2
—continued	2005	2006	2007
Capital account (net)	−4.0	−3.9	−1.8
Direct investment abroad	−36.2	−241.3	−333.3
Direct investment from abroad	112.6	242.0	237.5
Portfolio investment assets	−257.5	−499.0	−294.6
Portfolio investment liabilities	832.0	1,126.9	1,145.1
Financial derivatives liabilities	—	29.7	6.5
Other investment assets	−267.0	−513.9	−661.9
Other investment liabilities	302.7	692.3	675.0
Net errors and omissions	32.3	−47.1	−41.3
Overall balance	−14.1	−2.4	0.1

Source: IMF, *International Financial Statistics*.

FOREIGN AID
($ million, year ending 30 September)

	2003/04*	2004/05*	2005/06†
Multilateral assistance	1,464.7	1,702.8	1,797.2
Bilateral assistance	15,554.7	31,546.9	14,364.0
Military assistance	6,285.4	4,848.3	5,151.2

* Appropriated.
† Requested.

Source: US Agency for International Development.

External Trade

The customs territory of the USA includes Puerto Rico and the US Virgin Islands. Figures exclude trade with other US possessions.

PRINCIPAL COMMODITIES
(distribution by SITC, $ million)

Imports	2006	2007	2008
Food and live animals	56,093.5	60,879.2	66,183.5
Mineral fuels, lubricants, etc.	333,486.3	360,910.2	486,922.1
Petroleum, petroleum products, etc.	294,361.7	322,876.2	443,892.2
Chemicals and related products	142,775.8	155,358.6	176,825.3
Basic manufactures	223,109.3	227,224.7	231,669.3
Machinery and transport equipment	709,833.7	738,714.8	721,240.1
General industrial machinery, equipment and parts	59,677.0	63,938.8	66,793.3
Office machines and automatic data-processing machines	106,487.9	101,785.9	96,512.6
Telecommunications and sound equipment	115,294.5	129,802.5	133,223.3
Other electrical machinery, apparatus, etc.	109,742.7	113,622.6	112,674.5
Motor vehicles	211,708.3	210,650.4	190,896.5
Miscellaneous manufactured articles	276,409.8	293,818.7	290,009.0
Clothing and accessories (excl. footwear)	79,149.8	81,187.7	78,893.5
Total (incl. others)	1,853,938.5	1,956,961.8	2,100,141.2

THE UNITED STATES OF AMERICA

Exports	2006	2007	2008
Food and live animals	54,255.2	68,250.4	85,803.7
Crude materials (inedible) except fuels	50,149.3	62,432.3	76,543.4
Mineral fuels, lubricants, etc.	34,881.1	41,957.0	76,533.2
Chemicals and related products	138,578.4	158,189.8	179,137.1
Basic manufactures	103,488.2	112,545.6	124,969.7
Machinery and transport equipment	494,452.5	536,409.3	556,627.1
Power-generating machinery and equipment	46,638.8	53,082.2	58,059.5
Machinery specialized for particular industries	40,029.5	51,399.9	55,404.9
General industrial machinery, equipment and parts	47,075.1	51,877.8	58,949.0
Office machines and automatic data-processing machines	49,143.8	46,192.1	46,059.0
Telecommunication equipment, parts and accessories	34,562.0	38,584.9	41,219.8
Other electrical machinery, apparatus, etc.	106,767.7	104,793.7	105,807.5
Motor vehicles	89,347.2	102,812.1	106,295.4
Transport equipment	71,998.7	81,670.0	78,078.2
Miscellaneous manufactured articles	115,960.6	127,064.2	134,096.8
Professional, scientific and controlling instruments, etc.	43,805.7	47,606.3	50,362.9
Total (incl. others)	1,036,634.7	1,162,479.3	1,300,135.7

Source: Office of Trade and Industry Information (OTII), Manufacturing and Services, International Trade Administration, US Department of Commerce.

PRINCIPAL TRADING PARTNERS
($ million)

Imports	2006	2007	2008
Brazil	26,388.5	25,636.0	30,459.0
Canada	303,416.3	313,110.9	335,555.3
China, People's Republic	287,772.8	321,507.8	337,789.8
France (incl. Monaco)	37,148.6	41,589.0	43,997.1
Germany	89,072.8	94,364.5	97,552.9
India	21,826.3	24,024.4	25,761.9
Ireland	28,640.0	30,346.5	31,567.8
Israel	19,149.9	20,812.0	22,333.7
Italy	32,652.2	35,041.8	36,143.4
Japan	148,091.2	145,463.6	139,248.2
Korea, Republic	45,829.6	47,566.3	48,076.0
Malaysia	36,532.5	32,790.0	30,739.7
Mexico	198,258.6	210,799.0	215,914.9
Nigeria	27,916.4	32,770.2	38,068.2
Russia	19,783.5	19,360.2	26,775.0
Saudi Arabia	31,688.9	35,626.4	54,786.2
Taiwan	38,214.8	38,301.9	36,327.1
Thailand	22,471.5	22,752.9	23,547.7
United Kingdom	53,437.1	56,892.9	58,619.2
Venezuela	37,165.0	39,896.7	51,401.2
Total (incl. others)	1,855,119.3	1,953,698.8	2,100,141.2

Exports	2006	2007	2008
Australia	17,781.8	19,205.1	22,456.8
Belgium	21,347.2	25,291.9	19,026.4
Brazil	19,227.5	24,628.4	32,910.1
Canada	230,256.8	248,437.2	260,914.4
China, People's Republic	55,224.2	65,238.3	71,457.1
France (incl. Monaco)	24,217.2	27,407.1	29,186.9
Germany	41,319.5	49,652.0	54,732.3
Hong Kong	17,778.6	20,120.5	21,633.4
India	10,091.1	17,592.5	18,666.5
Israel	10,964.4	13,018.9	14,486.5
Italy	12,566.7	14,141.3	15,478.6
Japan	59,649.2	62,665.0	66,579.2

Exports—continued	2006	2007	2008
Korea, Republic	32,455.5	34,703.0	34,807.4
Malaysia	12,550.1	11,679.8	12,963.0
Mexico	134,167.1	136,541.3	151,538.6
Netherlands	31,101.8	32,986.0	40,223.1
Singapore	24,683.2	26,284.5	28,809.7
Switzerland	14,376.0	17,039.6	22,023.3
Taiwan	23,023.3	26,358.5	25,279.4
United Arab Emirates	11,921.4	11,609.4	15,748.8
United Kingdom	45,393.0	50,296.2	53,775.1
Total (incl. others)	1,037,143.0	1,162,708.3	1,300,135.7

Source: Office of Trade and Industry Information (OTII), Manufacturing and Services, International Trade Administration, US Department of Commerce.

Transport

RAILWAYS
(revenue traffic on class I railroads only)

	2002	2003	2004
Passengers carried ('000)*	23,269	24,595	25,215
Passenger-miles (million)*	5,314	5,680	5,511
Freight carried (million short tons)	2,207	2,240	2,398
Freight ton-miles ('000 million)	1,507	1,551	1,663

* AMTRAK passenger traffic only.

Source: Association of American Railroads, Washington, DC.

ROAD TRAFFIC
('000 motor vehicles registered at 31 December)

	2005	2006	2007
Passenger cars	136,568	135,400	135,933
Buses and coaches	807	822	834
Lorries (trucks) and vans	103,819	107,944	110,497
Motorcycles	6,227	6,679	7,138

Source: Federal Highway Administration.

INLAND WATERWAYS
(freight carried, million short tons)

	2005	2006	2007
Lake waterways	96.2	96.9	95.6
Coastal waterways	213.7	201.8	205.8
Internal waterways*	624.0	627.6	621.9
Total†	1,028.9	1,023.5	1,021.5

* Internal refers to freight moved solely within US boundaries, excluding traffic on the Great Lakes system. Figures also exclude waterway improvement materials and fish.
† Totals include intra-port and intra-territorial traffic.

Source: Waterborne Commerce Statistics Center, US Army Corps of Engineers.

THE UNITED STATES OF AMERICA

OCEAN SHIPPING
Sea-going Merchant Vessels

	2001	2002	2003
Number:			
passenger	11	13	11
container	90	91	87
roll-on/roll-off	60	60	64
bulk	15	17	20
tanker	142	130	110
other*	136	132	124
Total	454	443	416
Capacity ('000 dwt):			
passenger	99	104	90
container	3,058	3,201	3,309
roll-on/roll-off	1,260	1,273	1,411
bulk	604	706	837
tanker	8,447	7,532	5,828
other*	2,362	2,162	1,818
Total	15,830	14,978	13,294

* Includes breakbulk, partial container, refrigerated cargo, barge carrier and specialized cargo vessels.

Source: Maritime Administration, US Department of Transportation.

Vessels Entered and Cleared in Foreign Trade in all Ports

	1998	1999	2000
Entered:			
number	61,417	58,374	60,064
displacement ('000 net tons)	619,071	621,204	672,834
Cleared:			
number	60,711	56,599	57,864
displacement ('000 net tons)	630,816	618,990	670,855

Source: Maritime Administration, US Department of Transportation.

CIVIL AVIATION
(US airlines, revenue traffic on scheduled services)

	2003	2004	2005*
Number of departures ('000)	10,839	11,398	11,475
Domestic traffic:			
Passengers enplaned ('000)	592,412	640,683	670,152
Passenger-miles (million)	500,271	551,935	579,661
Freight ton-miles (million)†	12,342	12,756	12,634
Mail ton-miles (million)†	880	819	719
International traffic:			
Passengers enplaned ('000)	53,863	62,222	68,273
Passenger-miles (million)	156,638	181,743	199,326
Freight ton-miles (million)†	13,021	13,926	14,178
Mail ton-miles (million)†	492	477	476

* Provisional figures.
† Short tons (1 short ton = 0.907185 metric tons).

Source: Air Transport Association of America.

Tourism

FOREIGN VISITOR ARRIVALS
(by country of residence, '000)

	2006	2007	2008*
Australia	603	670	690
Canada	15,992	17,760	18,925
France	790	998	1,244
Germany	1,386	1,524	1,782
Italy	533	634	779
Japan	3,673	3,531	3,250
Korea, Republic	758	806	759
Mexico	13,317	14,327	13,763
United Kingdom	4,176	4,498	4,565
Total (incl. others)	50,977	55,979	58,029

* Preliminary.

Tourism receipts (incl. passenger transport, $ million): 107,756 in 2006; 122,298 in 2007; 142,107 in 2008 (preliminary).

Source: Office of Travel and Tourism Industries, International Trade Administration, US Department of Commerce.

Communications Media

	2005	2006	2007
Telephones ('000 main lines in use)	175,160.9	167,459.9	163,170.4
Mobile cellular telephones ('000 subscribers)	213,000	241,800	255,396
Internet users ('000)	197,800	210,200	220,000
Broadband subscribers ('000)	48,089.8	60,522.0	65,616.4

Personal computers ('000 in use): 223,810 in 2004.

Television receivers ('000 in use): 267,000 in 2001.

Radio receivers ('000 in use): 570,000 in 1996 (estimate).

Facsimile machines ('000 in use): 21,000 in 1997 (estimate).

Books published (number of titles): 96,080 in 2000.

Daily newspapers (2001): 1,468 titles with average circulation of 55,600.

Sources: International Telecommunication Union; UN, *Statistical Yearbook*.

Education

ENROLMENT
('000 students at September of each year, projections)

	2005	2006	2007
Public:			
elementary	34,205	34,221	34,589
secondary	14,908	15,078	15,055
higher	13,022	13,180	13,491
Private:			
elementary	4,723	4,711	4,681
secondary	1,350	1,384	1,385
higher	4,466	4,579	4,757

Total elementary and secondary school teaching staff (projected estimates, '000): 3,593 (public 3,143, private 450) in 2005; 3,632 (public 3,180, private 452) in 2006; 3,663 (public 3,204, private 459) in 2007.

Total higher education teaching staff (projected estimates): 1,290 (public 841, private 449) in 2005; 1,322 (public 854, private 468) in 2006; 1,371 (public 877, private 494) in 2007.

Source: National Center for Education Statistics, US Department of Education.

Directory

The Constitution
Adopted 4 March 1789.

PREAMBLE

We, the people of the United States, in order to form a more perfect Union, establish justice, insure domestic tranquility, provide for the common defence, promote the general welfare, and secure the blessings of liberty to ourselves and our posterity, do ordain and establish this Constitution for the United States of America.

ARTICLE I

Section 1

All legislative powers herein granted shall be vested in a Congress of the United States, which shall consist of a Senate and House of Representatives.

Section 2

1. The House of Representatives shall be composed of members chosen every second year by the people of the several States and the electors in each State shall have the qualifications requisite for electors of the most numerous branch of the State Legislature.

2. No person shall be a Representative who shall not have attained to the age of 25 years and been seven years a citizen of the United States and who shall not, when elected, be an inhabitant of that State in which he shall be chosen.

3. Representatives and direct taxes shall be apportioned among the several States, which may be included within this Union according to their respective numbers, which shall be determined by adding to the whole number of free persons, including those bound to service for a term of years, and excluding Indians not taxed, three-fifths of all other persons. The actual enumeration shall be made within three years after the first meeting of the Congress of the United States, and within every subsequent term of 10 years, in such manner as they shall by law direct. The number of Representatives shall not exceed one for every 30,000, but each State shall have at least one Representative; and until such enumeration shall be made, the State of New Hampshire shall be entitled to choose 3; Massachusetts 8; Rhode Island and Providence Plantations 1; Connecticut 5; New York 6; New Jersey 4; Pennsylvania 8; Delaware 1; Maryland 6; Virginia 10; North Carolina 5; South Carolina 5; and Georgia 3.*

4. When vacancies happen in the representation from any State, the Executive Authority thereof shall issue writs of election to fill such vacancies.

5. The House of Representatives shall choose their Speaker and other officers and shall have the sole power of impeachment.

* See Amendment XIV.

Section 3

1. The Senate of the United States shall be composed of two Senators from each State, chosen by the Legislature thereof, for six years; and each Senator shall have one vote.

2. Immediately after they shall be assembled in consequence of the first election, they shall be divided as equally as may be into three classes. The seats of the Senators of the first class shall be vacated at the expiration of the second year, of the second class at the expiration of the fourth year, and of the third class at the expiration of the sixth year, so that one-third may be chosen every second year, and if vacancies happen by resignation or otherwise, during the recess of the Legislature or of any State, the Executive therefore may make temporary appointment until the next meeting of the Legislature, which shall then fill such vacancies.

3. No person shall be a Senator who shall not have attained to the age of 30 years, and been nine years a citizen of the United States, and who shall not, when elected, be an inhabitant of that State for which he shall be chosen.

4. The Vice-President of the United States shall be President of the Senate, but shall have no vote unless they be equally divided.

5. The Senate shall choose their other officers, and also a President *pro tempore*, in the absence of the Vice-President, or when he shall exercise the office of the President of the United States.

6. The Senate shall have the sole power to try all impeachments. When sitting for that purpose, they shall be on oath or affirmation. When the President of the United States is tried, the Chief Justice shall preside; and no person shall be convicted without the concurrence of two-thirds of the members present.

7. Judgment of case of impeachment shall not extend further than to removal from office, and disqualification to hold and enjoy any office of honour, trust, or profit under the United States; but the party convicted shall nevertheless be liable and subject to indictment, trial, judgment, and punishment, according to law.

Section 4

1. The times, places and manner of holding elections for Senators and Representatives shall be prescribed in each State by the Legislature thereof; but the Congress may at any time by law make or alter such regulations, except as to places of choosing Senators.

2. The Congress shall assemble at least once in every year, and such meeting shall be on the first Monday in December, unless they shall by law appoint a different day.

Section 5

1. Each House shall be the judge of the elections, returns, and qualifications of its own members, and a majority of each shall constitute a quorum to do business; but a smaller number may adjourn from day to day, and may be authorized to compel the attendance of absent members in such manner and under such penalties as each House may provide.

2. Each House may determine the rules of its proceedings, punish its members for disorderly behaviour, and, with the concurrence of two-thirds, expel a member.

3. Each House shall keep a journal of its proceedings, and from time to time publish the same, excepting such parts as may in their judgment require secrecy; and the yeas and nays of the members of either House on any question shall, at the desire of one-fifth of those present, be entered on the journal.

4. Neither House, during the session of Congress shall, without the consent of the other, adjourn for more than three days, nor to any other place than that in which the two Houses shall be sitting.

Section 6

1. The Senators and Representatives shall receive a compensation for their services to be ascertained by law, and paid out of the Treasury of the United States. They shall in all cases, except treason, felony, and breach of the peace, be privileged from arrest during their attendance at the session of their respective Houses, and in going to and returning from the same; and for any speech or debate in either House they shall not be questioned in any other place.

2. No Senator or Representative shall, during the time for which he was elected, be appointed to any civil office under the authority of the United States which shall have been created, or the emoluments whereof shall have been increased during such time; and no person holding any office under the United States shall be a member of either House during his continuance in office.

Section 7

1. All bills for raising revenue shall originate in the House of Representatives, but the Senate may propose or concur with amendments, as on other bills.

2. Every bill which shall have passed the House of Representatives and the Senate shall, before it becomes a law, be presented to the President of the United States; if he approve, he shall sign it, but if not he shall return it, with his objections to that House in which it shall have originated, who shall enter the objections at large on their journal and proceed to reconsider it. If after such reconsideration two-thirds of that House shall agree to pass the bill, it shall be sent, together with the objections, to the other House, by which it shall likewise be reconsidered; and if approved by two-thirds of that House it shall become a law. But in such cases the votes of both Houses shall be determined by yeas and nays, and the names of the persons voting for and against the bill be entered on the journal of each House, respectively. If any bill shall not be returned by the President within 10 days (Sundays excepted) after it shall have been presented to him, the same shall be a law in like manner as if he had signed it, unless the Congress by their adjournment prevent its return; in which case it shall not be a law.

3. Every order, resolution, or vote to which the concurrence of the Senate and House of Representatives may be necessary (except on a question of adjournment) shall be presented to the President of the United States, and before the same shall take effect shall be approved by him, or being disapproved by him shall be repassed by two-thirds of the Senate and the House of Representatives, according to the rules and limitations prescribed in the case of a bill.

Section 8

1. The Congress shall have power
To lay and collect taxes, duties, imposts, and excises, to pay the debts and provide for the common defense and general welfare of the United States; but all duties, imposts, and excises shall be uniform throughout the United States.

2. To borrow money on the credit of the United States.

3. To regulate commerce with foreign nations; and among the several States and with the Indian tribes.

THE UNITED STATES OF AMERICA

4. To establish a uniform rule of naturalization and uniform laws on the subject of bankruptcies throughout the United States.

5. To coin money, regulate the value thereof, and of foreign coin, and fix the standard of weights and measures.

6. To provide for the punishment of counterfeiting the securities and current coin of the United States.

7. To establish post-offices and post-roads.

8. To promote the progress of science and useful arts by securing for limited times to authors and inventors the exclusive rights to their respective writings and discoveries.

9. To constitute tribunals inferior to the Supreme Court.

10. To define and punish piracies and felonies committed on the high seas, and offences against the law of nations.

11. To declare war, grant letters of marque and reprisal, and make rules concerning captures on land and water.

12. To raise and support armies, but no appropriation of money to that use shall be for a longer term than two years.

13. To provide and maintain a navy.

14. To make rules for the government and regulation of the land and naval forces.

15. To provide for calling forth the militia to execute the laws of the Union, suppress insurrections, and repel invasions.

16. To provide for organizing, arming and disciplining the militia, and for governing such part of them as may be employed in the service of the United States, reserving to the States respectively the appointment of the officers, and the authority of training the militia according to the discipline prescribed by Congress.

17. To exercise exclusive legislation in all cases whatsoever over such district (not exceeding 10 miles square) as may, by cession of particular States and the acceptance of Congress, become the seat of Government of the United States and to exercise like authority over all places purchased by the consent of the Legislature of the State in which the same shall be, for the erection of forts, magazines, arsenals, dry-docks, and other needful buildings.

18. To make all laws which shall be necessary and proper for carrying into execution the foregoing powers and all other powers vested by this Constitution in the Government of the United States, or in any department or officer thereof.

Section 9

1. The migration or importation of such persons as any of the States now existing shall think proper to admit shall not be prohibited by the Congress prior to the year 1808, but a tax or duty may be imposed on such importations, not exceeding 10 dollars for each person.

2. The privilege of the writ of habeas corpus shall not be suspended, unless when in cases of rebellion or invasion the public safety may require it.

3. No bill or attainder or *ex post facto* law shall be passed.

4. No capitation or other direct tax shall be laid, unless in proportion to the census or enumeration hereinbefore directed to be taken.

5. No tax or duty shall be laid on articles exported from any State.

6. No preference shall be given by any regulation of commerce or revenue to the ports of one State over those of another, nor shall vessels bound to or from one State be obliged to enter, clear, or pay duties to another.

7. No money shall be drawn from the Treasury but in consequence of appropriations made by law; and a regular statement and account of the receipts and expenditures of all public money shall be published from time to time.

8. No title of nobility shall be granted by the United States. And no person holding any office of profit or trust under them shall, without the consent of the Congress, accept of any present, emolument, office, or title of any kind whatever from any king, prince, or foreign state.

Section 10

1. No State shall enter into any treaty, alliance or confederation, grant letters of marque and reprisal, coin money, emit bills of credit, make anything but gold and silver coin a tender in payment of debts, pass any bill of attainder, *ex post facto* law, or law impairing the obligation of contracts, or grant any title of nobility.

2. No State shall, without the consent of the Congress, lay any impost or duties on imports or exports, except what may be absolutely necessary for executing its inspection laws, and the net produce of all duties and imposts, laid by any State on imports or exports, shall be for the use of the Treasury of the United States; and all such laws shall be subject to the revision and control of the Congress.

3. No State shall, without the consent of Congress, lay any duty of tonnage, keep troops or ships of war in time of peace, enter into agreement or compact with another State, or with a foreign power, or engage in war, unless actually invaded, or in such imminent danger as will not admit of delay.

ARTICLE II

Section 1

1. The Executive power shall be vested in a President of the United States of America. He shall hold his office during the term of four years, and, together with the Vice-President chosen for the same term, be elected as follows:

2. Each State shall appoint, in such manner as the Legislature thereof may direct, a number of electors equal to the whole number of Senators and Representatives to which the State may be entitled in the Congress; but no Senator or Representative or person holding an office of trust or profit under the United States shall be appointed an elector.

3. The electors shall meet in their respective States and vote by ballot for two persons, of whom one at least shall not be an inhabitant of the same State with themselves. And they shall make a list of all the persons voted for, and of the number of votes for each, which list they shall sign and certify and transmit, sealed, to the seat of the Government of the United States, directed to the President of the Senate. The President of the Senate shall, in the presence of the Senate and House of Representatives, open all the certificates, and the votes shall then be counted. The person having the greatest number of votes shall be the President, if such number be a majority of the whole number of electors appointed, and if there be more than one who have such a majority, and have an equal number of votes, then the House of Representatives shall immediately choose by ballot one of them for President; and if no person have a majority, then from the five highest on the list the said House shall in like manner choose the President. But in choosing the President, the vote shall be taken by States, the representation from each State having one vote. A quorum, for this purpose, shall consist of a member or members from two-thirds of the States, and a majority of all the States shall be necessary to a choice. In every case, after the choice of the President, the person having the greatest number of votes of the electors shall be the Vice-President. But if there should remain two or more who have equal votes, the Senate shall choose from them by ballot the Vice-President.*

4. The Congress may determine the time of choosing the electors and the day on which they shall give their votes, which day shall be the same throughout the United States.

5. No person except a natural born citizen, or a citizen of the United States, at the time of the adoption of the Constitution, shall be eligible to the office of President; neither shall any person be eligible to that office who shall not have attained to the age of 35 years and been 14 years a resident within the United States.

6. In case of the removal of the President from office, or of his death, resignation, or inability to discharge the powers and duties of the said office, the same shall devolve on the Vice-President, and the Congress may by law provide for the case of removal, death, resignation, or inability, both of the President and Vice-President, declaring what officer shall then act as President, and such officer shall act accordingly until the disability be removed or a President shall be elected.†

7. The President shall, at stated times, receive for his services a compensation, which shall neither be increased nor diminished during the period for which he shall have been elected, and he shall not receive within that period any other emolument from the United States, or any of them.

8. Before he enter on the execution of his office he shall take the following oath or affirmation:

'I do solemnly swear (or affirm) that I will faithfully execute the office of President of the United States, and will, to the best of my ability, preserve, protect, and defend the Constitution of the United States.'

* This clause is superseded by Amendment XII.
† This clause is amended by Amendments XX and XXV.

Section 2

1. The President shall be Commander-in-Chief of the Army and Navy of the United States, and of the militia of the several States when called into the actual service of the United States; he may require the opinion, in writing, of the principal officer in each of the executive departments upon any subject relating to the duties of their respective offices, and he shall have the power to grant reprieves and pardons for offences against the United States except in cases of impeachment.

2. He shall have power by and with the advice and consent of the Senate to make treaties, provided two-thirds of the Senators present concur; and he shall nominate and by and with the advice and consent of the Senate shall appoint ambassadors, other public ministers and consuls, judges of the Supreme Court, and all other officers of the United States whose appointments are not herein otherwise provided for, and which shall be established by law; but the Congress may by law vest the appointment of such inferior officers as they think proper in the President alone, in the courts of law, or in the heads of departments.

3. The President shall have power to fill up all vacancies that may happen during the recess of the Senate by granting commissions, which shall expire at the end of their next session.

Section 3

He shall from time to time give to the Congress information of the state of the Union, and recommend to their consideration such measures as he shall judge necessary and expedient; he may, on extraordinary occasions, convene both Houses, or either of them, and in case of disagreement between them with respect to the time of adjournment, he may adjourn them to such time as he shall think proper; he shall receive ambassadors and other public ministers; he shall take care that the laws be faithfully executed, and shall commission all the officers of the United States.

Section 4

The President, Vice-President, and all civil officers of the United States shall be removed from office on impeachment for conviction of treason, bribery or other high crimes and misdemeanours.

ARTICLE III

Section 1

The judicial power of the United States shall be vested in one Supreme Court, and in such inferior courts as the Congress may from time to time ordain and establish. The judges, both of the Supreme and inferior courts, shall hold their offices during good behaviour, and shall at stated times receive for their services a compensation, which shall not be diminished during their continuance in office.

Section 2

1. The judicial power shall extend to all cases in law and equity arising under this Constitution, the laws of the United States, and treaties made, or which shall be made, under their authority; to all cases affecting ambassadors, other public ministers and consuls; to all cases of admiralty and maritime jurisdiction; to controversies to which the United States shall be a party; to controversies between two or more States, between a State and citizens of another State, between citizens of different States, between citizens of the same State claiming lands under grants of different States, and between a State, or the citizens thereof, and foreign States, citizens, or subjects.

2. In all cases affecting ambassadors, other public ministers, and consuls, and those in which a State shall be party, the Supreme Court shall have original jurisdiction. In all the other cases before mentioned, the Supreme Court shall have appellate jurisdiction both as to law and fact, with such exceptions and under such regulations as the Congress shall make.

3. The trial of all crimes, except in cases of impeachment, shall be by jury, and such trials shall be held in the State where the said crimes shall have been committed; but when not committed within any State the trial shall be at such place or places as the Congress may by law have directed.

Section 3

1. Treason against the United States shall consist only in levying war against them, or in adhering to their enemies, giving them aid and comfort. No person shall be convicted of treason unless on the testimony of two witnesses to the same overt act, or on confession in open court.

2. The Congress shall have power to declare the punishment of treason, but no attainder of treason shall work corruption of blood, or forfeiture except during the life of the person attained.

ARTICLE IV

Section 1

Full faith and credit shall be given in each State to the public acts, records, and judicial proceedings of every other State. And the Congress may by general laws prescribe the manner in which such acts, records, and proceedings shall be proved, and the effect thereof.

Section 2

1. The citizens of each State shall be entitled to all privileges and immunities of citizens in the several States.

2. A person charged in any State with treason, felony, or other crime, who shall flee from justice, and be found in another State, shall, on demand of the Executive authority of the State from which he fled, be delivered up, to be removed to the State having jurisdiction of the crime.

3. No person held to service or labour in one State, under the laws thereof, escaping into another shall in consequence of any law or regulation therein, be discharged from such service or labour, but shall be delivered up on claim of the party to whom such service or labour may be due.

Section 3

1. New States may be admitted by the Congress into this Union; but no new State shall be formed or erected within the jurisdiction of any other State, nor any State be formed by the junction of two or more States, or parts of States, without the consent of the Legislatures of the States concerned, as well as of the Congress.

2. The Congress shall have the power to dispose of and make all needful rules and regulations respecting the territory or other property belonging to the United States; and nothing in this Constitution shall be so construed as to prejudice any claims of the United States, or of any particular State.

Section 4

The United States shall guarantee to every State in this Union a Republican form of government, and shall protect each of them against invasion, and on application of the Legislature, or of the Executive (when the Legislature cannot be convened) against domestic violence.

ARTICLE V

The Congress, whenever two-thirds of both Houses shall deem it necessary, shall propose amendments to this Constitution, or, on the application of the Legislature of two-thirds of the several States, shall call a convention for proposing amendments, which in either case, shall be valid to all intents and purposes, as part of this Constitution, when ratified by the Legislature of three-fourths of the several States, or by conventions in three-fourths thereof, as the one or the other mode of ratification may be proposed by the Congress, provided that no amendment which may be made prior to the year 1808 shall in any manner affect the first and fourth clauses in the Ninth Section of the First Article; and that no State, without its consent, shall be deprived of its equal suffrage in the Senate.

ARTICLE VI

1. All debts contracted and engagements entered into before the adoption of this Constitution shall be as valid against the United States under this Constitution as under the Confederation.

2. This Constitution and the laws of the United States which shall be made in pursuance thereof and all treaties made, or which shall be made, under the authority of the United States, shall be the supreme law of the land, and the judges in every State shall be bound thereby, anything in the Constitution or laws of any State to the contrary notwithstanding.

3. The Senators and Representatives before mentioned, and the members of the several State Legislatures, and all executives and judicial officers, both of the United States and of the several States, shall be bound by oath or affirmation to support this Constitution; but no religious test shall ever be required as a qualification to any office or public trust under the United States.

ARTICLE VII

The ratification of the Conventions of nine States shall be sufficient for the establishment of this Constitution between the States so ratifying the same.

Amendments to the Constitution

Ten Original Amendments, in force 15 December 1791:

AMENDMENT I

Congress shall make no law respecting an establishment of religion, or prohibiting the free exercise thereof; or abridging the freedom of speech or of the Press; or the right of the people peaceably to assemble and to petition the Government for a redress of grievances.

AMENDMENT II

A well-regulated militia being necessary to the security of a free State, the right of the people to keep and bear arms shall not be infringed.

AMENDMENT III

No soldier shall, in time of peace, be quartered in any house without the consent of the owner, nor in time of war but in a manner to be prescribed by law.

AMENDMENT IV

The right of the people to be secure in their persons, houses, papers, and effects, against unreasonable searches and seizures, shall not be violated, and no warrants shall issue but upon probable cause, supported by oath or affirmation, and particularly describing the place to be searched, and the persons or things to be seized.

AMENDMENT V

No person shall be held to answer for a capital or other infamous crime unless on a presentment or indictment of a Grand Jury, except in cases arising in the land or naval forces, or in the militia, when in actual service, in time of war or public danger; nor shall any person be subject for the same offense to be twice put in jeopardy of life or limb; nor shall be compelled in any criminal case to be a witness against himself, nor be deprived of life, liberty, or property, without due process of law; nor shall private property be taken for public use without just compensation.

AMENDMENT VI

In all criminal prosecutions, the accused shall enjoy the right to a speedy and public trial, by an impartial jury of the State and district wherein the crime shall have been committed, which districts shall have been previously ascertained by law, and to be informed of the nature and cause of the accusation; to be confronted with the witnesses against him; to have compulsory process for obtaining witnesses in his favour, and to have the assistance of counsel for his defense.

AMENDMENT VII

In suits at common law, where the value in controversy shall exceed 20 dollars, the right of trial by jury shall be preserved, and no fact tried by a jury shall be otherwise re-examined in any court of the United States than according to the rules of the common law.

AMENDMENT VIII

Excessive bail shall not be required, nor excessive fines imposed, nor cruel and unusual punishments inflicted.

AMENDMENT IX

The enumeration in the Constitution of certain rights shall not be construed to deny or disparage others retained by the people.

AMENDMENT X

The powers not delegated to the United States by the Constitution, nor prohibited by it to the States, are reserved to the States respectively, or to the people.

Subsequent Amendments:

AMENDMENT XI
(became part of the Constitution February 1795)

The judicial power of the United States shall not be construed to extend to any suit in law or equity, commenced or prosecuted against one of the United States, by citizens of another State, or by citizens or subjects of any foreign State.

AMENDMENT XII
(ratified June 1804)

The Electors shall meet in their respective States, and vote by ballot for President and Vice-President, one of whom at least shall not be an inhabitant of the same State with themselves; they shall name in their ballots the person voted for as President, and in distinct ballots the person voted for as Vice-President; and they shall make distinct list of all persons voted for as President, and of all persons voted for as Vice-President, and of the number of votes for each, which list they shall sign and certify, and transmit, sealed, to the seat of the Government of the United States, directed to the President of the Senate; the President of the Senate shall, in the presence of the Senate and House of Representatives, open all the certificates and the votes shall then be counted; the person having the greatest number of votes for President shall be the President, if such number be a majority of the whole number of Electors appointed; and if no person have such majority, then from the persons having the highest number, not exceeding three, on the list of those voted for as President, the House of Representatives shall choose immediately, by ballot, the President. But in choosing the President, the votes shall be taken by States, the representation from each State having one vote; a quorum for this purpose shall consist of a member or members from two-thirds of the States, and a majority of all the States shall be necessary to a choice. And if the House of Representatives shall not choose a President, whenever the right of choice shall devolve upon them, before the fourth day of March next following, then the Vice-President shall act as President, as in the case of the death or other constitutional disability of the President. The person having the greatest number of votes as Vice-President shall be the Vice-President if such number be a majority of the whole number of Electors appointed, and if no person have a majority, then, from the two highest numbers on the list the Senate shall choose the Vice-President; a quorum for the purpose shall consist of two-thirds of the whole number of Senators, and a majority of the whole number shall be necessary to a choice. But no person constitutionally ineligible to the office of President shall be eligible to that of Vice-President of the United States.

AMENDMENT XIII
(ratified December 1865)

1. Neither slavery nor involuntary servitude, except as a punishment for crime whereof the party shall have been duly convicted, shall exist within the United States, or any place subject to their jurisdiction.

2. Congress shall have the power to enforce this article by appropriate legislation.

AMENDMENT XIV
(ratified July 1868)

1. All persons born or naturalized in the United States, and subject to the jurisdiction thereof, are citizens of the United States and of the State wherein they reside. No State shall make or enforce any law which shall abridge the privileges or immunities of citizens of the United States, nor shall any State deprive any person of life, liberty, or property without due process of law, nor deny to any person within its jurisdiction the equal protection of the laws.

2. Representatives shall be apportioned among the several States according to their respective numbers, counting the whole number of persons in each State excluding Indians not taxed. But when the right to vote at any election for the choice of Electors for President and Vice-President of the United States, Representatives in Congress, the executive and judicial officers of a State, or the members of the Legislature thereof, is denied to any of the male inhabitants of such State, being 21 years of age, and citizens of the United States, or in any way abridged, except for participation in rebellion, or other crime, the basis of representation therein shall be reduced in the proportion which the number of such male citizens shall bear to the whole number of male citizens 21 years of age in such State.

3. No person shall be a Senator or Representative in Congress, or Elector of President and Vice-President or hold any office, civil or military, under the United States, or under any State, who, having previously taken an oath as member of Congress or as an officer of the United States, or as a member of any State Legislature, or as an executive or judicial officer of any State, to support the Constitution of the United States, shall have engaged in insurrection or rebellion against the same, or given aid and comfort to the enemies thereof. But Congress may, by vote of two-thirds of each House, remove such disability.

4. The validity of the public debt of the United States, authorized by law, including debts incurred for payment of pensions and bounties for services in suppressing insurrection and rebellion, shall not be questioned. But neither the United States nor any State shall assume or pay any debt or obligation incurred in aid of insurrection or rebellion against the United States, or any claim for the loss or emancipation of any slave; but all such debts, obligations, and claims shall be held illegal and void.

5. The Congress shall have power to enforce by appropriate legislation the provisions of this article.

AMENDMENT XV
(ratified March 1870)

1. The right of the citizens of the United States to vote shall not be denied or abridged by the United States or by any State on account of race, colour, or previous condition of servitude.

2. The Congress shall have power to enforce the provisions of this article by appropriate legislation.

AMENDMENT XVI
(ratified February 1913)

The Congress shall have power to lay and collect taxes on incomes, from whatever sources derived, without apportionment among the several States, and without regard to any census or enumeration.

AMENDMENT XVII
(ratified May 1913)

1. The Senate of the United States shall be composed of two Senators from each State, elected by the people thereof, for six years; and each Senator shall have one vote. The electors in each State shall have the qualifications requisite for electors of the most numerous branch of the State Legislature.

2. When vacancies happen in the representation of any State in the Senate, the executive authority of such State shall issue writs of election to fill such vacancies: provided that the Legislature of any State may empower the Executive thereof to make temporary appointment until the people fill the vacancies by election as the Legislature may direct.

3. This amendment shall not be so construed as to affect the election or term of any Senator chosen before it becomes valid as part of the Constitution.

AMENDMENT XVIII
(ratified January 1919*)

1. After one year from the ratification of this article the manufacture, sale, or transportation of intoxicating liquors within, the importation

thereof into, or the exportation thereof from the United States, and all territory subject to the jurisdiction thereof, for beverage purposes is hereby prohibited.

2. The Congress and the several States shall have concurrent power to enforce this article by appropriate legislation.

3. This article shall be inoperative unless it shall have been ratified as an amendment to the Constitution by the Legislatures of the several States, as provided in the Constitution, within seven years from the date of the submission hereof to the States by the Congress.
* Repealed by Amendment XXI.

AMENDMENT XIX
(ratified August 1920)

1. The right of citizens of the United States to vote shall not be denied or abridged by the United States or by any State on account of sex.

2. Congress shall have power by appropriate legislation to enforce the provisions of this article.

AMENDMENT XX
(ratified January 1933)

Section 1
The terms of the President and Vice-President shall end at noon on the 20th day of January, and the terms of Senators and Representatives at noon on the third day of January, of the years in which such terms would have ended if this article had not been ratified; and the terms of their successors shall then begin.

Section 2
The Congress shall assemble at least once in every year, and such meetings shall begin at noon on the third day of January, unless they shall by law appoint a different day.

Section 3
If, at the time fixed for the beginning of the term of the President, the President elect shall have died, the Vice-President elect shall become President. If a President shall not have been chosen before the time fixed for the beginning of his term, or if the President elect shall have failed to qualify, then the Vice-President elect shall act as President until a President shall have qualified; and the Congress may by law provide for the case wherein neither a President elect nor a Vice-President elect shall have qualified, declaring who shall then act as President, or the manner in which one who is to act shall be selected, and such person shall act accordingly until a President or Vice-President shall have qualified.

Section 4
The Congress may by law provide for the case of the death of any of the persons from whom the House of Representatives may choose a President whenever the right of choice shall have devolved upon them, and for the case of the death of any of the persons from whom the Senate may choose a Vice-President whenever the right of choice shall have devolved upon them.

Section 5
Sections 1 and 2 shall take effect on the 15th day of October following the ratification of this article.

Section 6
This article shall be inoperative unless it shall have been ratified as an amendment to the Constitution by the legislature of three-fourths of the several States within seven years from the date of its submission.

AMENDMENT XXI
(ratified December 1933)

Section 1
The 18th article of amendment to the Constitution of the United States is hereby repealed.

Section 2
The transportation or importation into any State, Territory or Possession of the United States for delivery or use therein of intoxicating liquors, in violation of the laws thereof, is hereby prohibited.

Section 3
This article shall be inoperative unless it shall have been ratified as an amendment to the Constitution by conventions in the several States, as provided in the Constitution, within seven years from the date of the submission hereof to the States by the Congress.

AMENDMENT XXII
(ratified February 1951)

No person shall be elected to the office of President more than twice, and no person who has held the office of President, or acted as President, for more than two years of a term to which some other person was elected President shall be elected to the office of President more than once. But this article shall not apply to any person holding the office of President when this Article was proposed by Congress, and shall not prevent any person who may be holding the office of President, or acting as President, during the term within which this Article becomes operative from holding the office of President or acting as President during the remainder of such term.

AMENDMENT XXIII
(ratified March 1961)

Section 1
The District constituting the seat of Government of the United States shall appoint in such manner as the Congress may direct:

A number of electors of President and Vice-President equal to the whole number of Senators and Representatives in Congress to which the District would be entitled if it were a State, but in no event more than the least populous State; they shall be in addition to those appointed by the States, but they shall be considered, for the purposes of the election of President and Vice-President, to be electors appointed by a State; and they shall meet in the District and perform such duties as provided by the 12th article of amendment.

Section 2
The Congress shall have power to enforce this article by appropriate legislation.

AMENDMENT XXIV
(ratified January 1964)

Section 1
The right of citizens of the United States to vote in any primary or other election for President or Vice-President, for electors for President or Vice-President, or for Senator or Representative in Congress, shall not be denied or abridged by the United States or any State by reason of failure to pay any poll tax or other tax.

Section 2
The Congress shall have power to enforce this article by appropriate legislation.

AMENDMENT XXV
(ratified February 1967)

Section 1
In the case of the removal of the President from office or of his death or resignation, the Vice-President shall become President.

Section 2
Whenever there is a vacancy in the office of the Vice-President, the President shall nominate a Vice-President who shall take office upon confirmation by a majority vote of both Houses of Congress.

Section 3
Whenever the President transmits to the President *pro tempore* of the Senate and the Speaker of the House of Representatives his written declaration that he is unable to discharge the powers and duties of his office, and until he transmits to them a written declaration to the contrary, such powers and duties shall be discharged by the Vice-President as Acting President.

Section 4
Whenever the Vice-President and a majority of either the principal officers of the executive departments or of such other body as Congress may by law provide, transmit to the President *pro tempore* of the Senate and the Speaker of the House of Representatives their written declaration that the President is unable to discharge the powers and duties of his office, the Vice-President shall immediately assume the powers and duties of the office as Acting President.

Thereafter, when the President transmits to the President *pro tempore* of the Senate and the Speaker of the House of Representatives his written declaration that no inability exists, he shall resume the powers and duties of his office unless the Vice-President and a majority of either the principal officers of the executive department or of such other body as Congress may by law provide, transmit within four days to the President *pro tempore* of the Senate and the Speaker of the House of Representatives their written declaration that the President is unable to discharge the powers and duties of his office. Thereupon Congress shall decide the issue, assembling within 48 hours for that purpose if not in session. If the Congress, within 21 days after receipt of the latter written declaration, or, if Congress is not in session, within 21 days after Congress is required to assemble, determines by two-thirds vote of both Houses that the President is unable to discharge the powers and duties of his office, the Vice-President shall continue to discharge the same as Acting President; otherwise, the President shall resume the powers and duties of his office.

AMENDMENT XXVI
(ratified July 1971)

Section 1
The right of citizens of the United States, who are 18 years of age or older, to vote shall not be denied or abridged by the United States or by any State on account of age.

Section 2
The Congress shall have power to enforce this article by appropriate legislation.

AMENDMENT XXVII
(ratified May 1992)

No law, varying the compensation for the services of the Senators and Representatives, shall take effect, until an election of Representatives shall have intervened.

By Article IV, Section 3 of the Constitution, implemented by vote of Congress and referendum in the territory concerned, Alaska was admitted into the United States on 3 January 1959, and Hawaii on 21 August 1959.

The Executive

HEAD OF STATE

President: BARACK HUSSEIN OBAMA (took office 20 January 2009).
Vice-President: JOSEPH R. BIDEN, Jr.

THE CABINET
(April 2009)

Secretary of State: HILLARY RODHAM CLINTON.
Secretary of the Treasury: TIMOTHY F. GEITHNER.
Secretary of Defense: ROBERT M. GATES.
Attorney-General: ERIC H. HOLDER, Jr.
Secretary of the Interior: KENNETH L. SALAZAR.
Secretary of Agriculture: THOMAS J. VILSACK.
Secretary of Commerce: GARY LOCKE.
Secretary of Labor: HILDA L. SOLIS.
Secretary of Health and Human Services: KATHLEEN SEBELIUS.
Secretary of Housing and Urban Development: SHAUN L. S. DONOVAN.
Secretary of Transportation: RAYMOND L. LAHOOD.
Secretary of Energy: STEVEN CHU.
Secretary of Education: ARNE DUNCAN.
Secretary of Veterans Affairs: Gen. (retd) ERIC K. SHINSEKI.
Secretary of Homeland Security: JANET NAPOLITANO.

Officials with Cabinet Rank

Vice-President: JOSEPH R. BIDEN, Jr.
Chief of Staff to the President: RAHM I. EMANUEL.
Chair of the Council of Economic Advisers: CHRISTINA ROMER.
Director of the Office of Management and Budget: PETER R. ORSZAG.
US Trade Representative: RONALD KIRK.
Administrator of the Environmental Protection Agency: LISA P. JACKSON.
Director of the Office of National Drug Control Policy: R. GIL KERLIKOWSKE.
Director of National Intelligence: Adm. (retd) DENNIS BLAIR.

GOVERNMENT DEPARTMENTS

Department of Agriculture: 1400 Independence Ave, SW, Washington, DC 20250; tel. (202) 720-5539; fax (202) 720-9997; e-mail ann.hamilton@usda.gov; internet www.usda.gov; f. 1889.

Department of Commerce: 1401 Constitution Ave, NW, Washington, DC 20230; tel. (202) 482-2000; e-mail cgutierrez@doc.gov; internet www.commerce.gov; f. 1913.

Department of Defense: 1400 Defense Pentagon, Washington, DC 20301; tel. (703) 428-0711; fax (703) 428-1982; internet www.defenselink.mil; f. 1947.

Department of Education: 400 Maryland Ave, SW, Washington, DC 20202; tel. (202) 401-2000; fax (202) 401-0596; internet www.ed.gov; f. 1979.

Department of Energy: Forrestal Bldg, 1000 Independence Ave, SW, Washington, DC 20585; tel. (202) 586-5000; fax (202) 586-4403; e-mail the.secretary@hq.doe.gov; internet www.energy.gov; f. 1977.

Department of Health and Human Services: 200 Independence Ave, SW, Washington, DC 20201; tel. (202) 619-0257; internet www.os.dhhs.gov; f. 1980.

Department of Homeland Security: 1600 Pennsylvania Ave, NW, Washington, DC 20528; tel. (202) 282-8000; e-mail john.minnick@dhs.gov; internet www.dhs.gov; f. 2002.

Department of Housing and Urban Development: 451 Seventh St, SW, Washington, DC 20410; tel. (202) 708-1112; fax (202) 708-0299; internet www.hud.gov; f. 1965.

Department of the Interior: 1849 C St, NW, Washington, DC 20240; tel. (202) 208-3100; fax (202) 208-5048; internet www.doi.gov; f. 1849.

Department of Justice: 950 Pennsylvania Ave, NW, Washington, DC 20530-0001; tel. (202) 514-2000; fax (202) 307-6777; e-mail askdoj@usdoj.gov; internet www.usdoj.gov; f. 1870; incl. the Office of the Attorney-Gen.

Department of Labor: Frances Perkins Bldg, 200 Constitution Ave, NW, Washington, DC 20210; tel. (202) 693-6000; fax (202) 693-6111; internet www.dol.gov; f. 1913.

Department of State: 2201 C St, NW, Washington, DC 20520; tel. (202) 647-4000; fax (202) 647-6738; internet www.state.gov; f. 1789.

Department of Transportation: 1200 New Jersey Ave, SE, Washington, DC 20590; tel. (202) 366-4000; fax (202) 366-7202; e-mail dot.comments@dot.gov; internet www.dot.gov; f. 1967.

Department of the Treasury: 1500 Pennsylvania Ave, NW, Washington, DC 20220; tel. (202) 622-2000; fax (202) 622-6415; internet www.ustreas.gov; f. 1789.

Department of Veterans Affairs: 810 Vermont Ave, NW, Washington, DC 20420; tel. (202) 273-6000; internet www.va.gov; f. 1989.

EXECUTIVE OFFICE OF THE PRESIDENT

The White House Office: 1600 Pennsylvania Ave, NW, Washington, DC 20500; tel. (202) 456-1414; fax (202) 456-2461; e-mail vice_president@whitehouse.gov; internet www.whitehouse.gov; co-ordinates activities relating to the President's immediate office; Chief of Staff to the Pres. RAHM EMANUEL.

Central Intelligence Agency: Office of Public Affairs, Washington, DC 20505; tel. (703) 482-0623; fax (703) 482-1739; internet www.cia.gov; f. 1947; Dir LEON E. PANETTA.

Council of Economic Advisers: Eisenhower Executive Office Bldg, 17th St and Pennsylvania Ave, NW, Washington, DC 20502; tel. (202) 395-5042; fax (202) 395-6958; internet www.whitehouse.gov/cea; f. 1946; Chair. CHRISTINA D. ROMER.

Council on Environmental Quality: 722 Jackson Pl., Washington, DC 20503; tel. (202) 395-5750; fax (202) 456-6546; internet www.whitehouse.gov/ceq; f. 1969; Chair. NANCY SUTLEY.

National Security Council: Eisenhower Executive Office Bldg, 17th St and Pennsylvania Ave, NW, Washington, DC 20504; tel. (202) 456-9371; internet www.whitehouse.gov/nsc; f. 1947; Asst to the Pres. for Nat. Security Affairs Gen. (retd) JAMES L. JONES, Jr.

Office of Administration: Eisenhower Executive Office Bldg, 17th St and Pennsylvania Ave, NW, Washington, DC 20503; tel. (202) 395-7235; fax (202) 456-6512; internet www.whitehouse.gov/oa; f. 1977; Dir BRADLEY KILEY.

Office of Faith-Based and Neighborhood Partnerships: The White House, 1600 Pennsylvania Ave, NW, Washington, DC 20502; f. 2001 as Office of Faith-Based and Community Initiatives; Dir JOSH DUBOIS.

Office of Management and Budget: 725 17th St and Pennsylvania Ave, NW, Washington, DC 20503; tel. (202) 395-3080; fax (202) 395-3888; internet www.whitehouse.gov/omb; Dir PETER R. ORSZAG.

Office of National AIDS Policy: The White House, Rm 464 EEOB, Washington, DC 20502; tel. (202) 456-7320; fax (202) 456-7315; internet www.whitehouse.gov/onap/aids.html; Dir (vacant).

Office of National Drug Control Policy: POB 6000, Rockville, MD 20849-6000; tel. (202) 395-6700; fax (301) 519-5212; internet www.whitehousedrugpolicy.gov; f. 1988; Dir R. GIL KERLIKOWSKE.

Office of Policy Development: Executive Office of the President, 1600 Pennsylvania Ave, NW, Washington, DC 20500; tel. (202) 456-6515; fax (202) 456-2878; internet www.whitehouse.gov/dpc; f. 1970; composed of the Domestic Policy Council (f. 1993) and the Nat. Economic Council; Asst to the Pres. for Domestic Policy and Dir of the Domestic Policy Council MELODY BARNES; Asst to the Pres. for

THE UNITED STATES OF AMERICA

Economic Policy and Dir of the Nat. Economic Council LAWRENCE SUMMERS.

Office of Science and Technology Policy: 725 17th St, Rm 5228, NW, Washington, DC, 20502; tel. (202) 456-7116; fax (202) 456-6021; e-mail info@ostp.gov; internet www.ostp.gov; f. 1976; Dir JOHN HOLDREN.

Office of the United States Trade Representative: Winder Bldg, 600 17th St, NW, Washington, DC 20508; tel. (202) 395-3230; fax (202) 395-4549; e-mail contactustr@ustr.eop.gov; internet www.ustr.gov; f. 1963; US Trade Rep. RONALD KIRK.

United States Mission to the United Nations: 799 United Nations Plaza, New York, NY 10017; tel. (212) 415-4404; fax (212) 415-4303; e-mail usa@un.int; internet www.un.int/usa; US Ambassador to the United Nations Dr SUSAN RICE.

USA Freedom Corps: 1600 Pennsylvania Ave, NW, Washington, DC 20500; e-mail info@usafreedomcorps.gov; internet www.usafreedomcorps.gov; f. 2002; Dir (vacant).

White House Military Office: Executive Office of the President, 1600 Pennsylvania Ave, NW, Washington, DC 20500; internet www.whitehouse.gov/whmo; areas of responsibility incl. Camp David (f. 1942) and Air Force One (f. 1962); Dir LOUIS CALDERA.

President and Legislature

PRESIDENT

Election, 4 November 2008

	Popular votes	% of Popular votes	Electoral College votes
Barack Obama (Democrat)	69,456,897	52.92	365
John McCain (Republican)	59,934,814	45.66	173
Others*	1,865,617	1.42	—
Total	131,257,328	100.00	538

*Including write-in candidates, etc.

CONGRESS

Senate
(April 2009)

The Senate comprises 100 members. Senators' terms are for six years, one-third of the Senate being elected every two years.

President of the Senate: Vice-President JOSEPH R. BIDEN, Jr.
President Pro Tempore: ROBERT C. BYRD.
Democrats: 57 seats.
Republicans: 40 seats.
Independents: 2 seats.
Vacant: 1 seat.
Majority Leader: HARRY M. REID.
Minority Leader: MITCH MCCONNELL.

Members
(With political party and year in which term expires—on 3 January in all cases.)

Alabama		
Jeff Sessions	Rep.	2015
Richard C. Shelby	Rep.	2011
Alaska		
Mark Begich	Dem.	2015
Lisa Murkowski	Rep.	2011
Arizona		
Jon Kyl	Rep.	2013
John McCain	Rep.	2011
Arkansas		
Mark L. Pryor	Dem.	2015
Blanche L. Lincoln	Dem.	2011
California		
Dianne Feinstein	Dem.	2013
Barbara Boxer	Dem.	2011
Colorado		
Mark Udall	Dem.	2015
Michael F. Bennett	Dem.	2011
Connecticut		
Joe I. Lieberman	Ind.	2013
Chris J. Dodd	Dem.	2011
Delaware		
Thomas Carper	Dem.	2011
Ted Kaufman	Dem.	2011
Florida		
Bill Nelson	Dem.	2013
Mel Martinez	Rep.	2011
Georgia		
Saxby Chambliss	Rep.	2015
Johnny Isakson	Rep.	2011
Hawaii		
Daniel K. Akaka	Dem.	2013
Daniel K. Inouye	Dem.	2011
Idaho		
James Risch	Rep.	2015
Michael Crapo	Rep.	2011
Illinois		
Richard J. Durbin	Dem.	2015
Roland W. Burris	Dem.	2011
Indiana		
Richard G. Lugar	Rep.	2013
Evan Bayh	Dem.	2011
Iowa		
Tom Harkin	Dem.	2015
Chuck Grassley	Rep.	2011
Kansas		
Pat Roberts	Rep.	2015
Sam Brownback	Rep.	2011
Kentucky		
Mitch McConnell	Rep.	2015
Jim Bunning	Rep.	2011
Louisiana		
Mary L. Landrieu	Dem.	2015
David Vitter	Rep.	2011
Maine		
Olympia J. Snowe	Rep.	2013
Susan M. Collins	Rep.	2015
Maryland		
Ben L. Cardin	Dem.	2013
Barbara A. Mikulski	Dem.	2011
Massachusetts		
Edward M. Kennedy	Dem.	2013
John F. Kerry	Dem.	2015
Michigan		
Debbie Stabenow	Dem.	2013
Carl Levin	Dem.	2015
Minnesota		
Amy Klobuchar	Dem.	2013
Vacant	—	2015
Mississippi		
Roger Wicker	Rep.	2013
Thad Cochran	Rep.	2015
Missouri		
Claire McCaskill	Rep.	2013
Christopher S. (Kit) Bond	Rep.	2011
Montana		
Jon Tester	Rep.	2013
Max Baucus	Dem.	2015
Nebraska		
E. Benjamin Nelson	Dem.	2013
Mike Johanns	Dem.	2015
Nevada		
John E. Ensign	Rep.	2013
Harry M. Reid	Dem.	2011
New Hampshire		
Jeanne Shaheen	Dem.	2015
Judd Gregg	Rep.	2011
New Jersey		
Robert Menéndez	Dem.	2013
Frank R. Lautenberg	Dem.	2015
New Mexico		
Jeff Bingaman	Dem.	2013
Robert Udall	Dem.	2015
New York		
Kirsten E. Gillibrand	Dem.	2011
Charles E. Schumer	Dem.	2011

THE UNITED STATES OF AMERICA

North Carolina
Kay Hagan	Dem.	2015
Richard Burr	Rep.	2011

North Dakota
Kent Conrad	Dem.	2013
Byron L. Dorgan	Dem.	2011

Ohio
Sherrod Brown	Dem.	2013
George V. Voinovich	Rep.	2011

Oklahoma
James M. Inhofe	Rep.	2015
Tom Coburn	Rep.	2011

Oregon
Jeff Merkley	Dem.	2015
Ronald L. Wyden	Dem.	2011

Pennsylvania
Robert P. Casey, Jr	Dem.	2013
Arlen Specter	Dem.	2011

Rhode Island
Sheldon Whitehouse, II	Dem.	2013
Jack Reed	Dem.	2015

South Carolina
Lindsey Graham	Rep.	2015
Jim DeMint	Rep.	2011

South Dakota
Tim Johnson	Dem.	2015
John Thune	Rep.	2011

Tennessee
Robert P. Corker	Rep.	2013
Lamar Alexander	Rep.	2015

Texas
Kay Bailey Hutchison	Rep.	2013
John Cornyn	Rep.	2015

Utah
Orrin G. Hatch	Rep.	2013
Bob F. Bennett	Rep.	2011

Vermont
Bernard Sanders	Ind.	2013
Patrick J. Leahy	Dem.	2011

Virginia
James H. Webb, Jr	Dem.	2013
Mark R. Warner	Dem.	2015

Washington
Maria Cantwell	Dem.	2013
Patty Murray	Dem.	2011

West Virginia
Robert C. Byrd	Dem.	2013
John D. (Jay) Rockefeller, IV	Dem.	2015

Wisconsin
Herb Kohl	Dem.	2013
Russell D. Feingold	Dem.	2011

Wyoming
Dr John Barrasso	Rep.	2013
Mike B. Enzi	Rep.	2015

House of Representatives
(April 2009)

A new House of Representatives, comprising 435 members, is elected every two years.

Speaker: NANCY PELOSI.

Democrats: 256 seats.

Republicans: 178 seats.

Vacant: 1 seat.

Majority Leader: STENY H. HOYER.

Minority Leader: JOHN BOEHNER.

Election Commission

Federal Election Commission: 999 E St, NW, Washington, DC 20463; tel. (202) 694-1100; fax (202) 219-3880; e-mail webmaster@fec.gov; internet www.fec.gov; f. 1975; independent; Chair. STEPHEN T. WALTHER.

Independent Agencies

Advisory Council on Historic Preservation: 1100 Pennsylvania Ave, NW, Suite 803, Old Post Office Bldg, Washington, DC 20004; tel. (202) 606-8503; fax (202) 606-8647; e-mail achp@achp.gov; internet www.achp.gov; f. 1966; Exec. Dir JOHN M. FOWLER.

African Development Foundation: 1400 I St, NW, Suite 1000, Washington, DC 20005-2248; tel. (202) 673-3916; fax (202) 673-3810; e-mail info@adf.gov; internet www.adf.gov; Pres. and CEO LLOYD O. PIERSON.

American Battle Monuments Commission: Courthouse Plaza II, Suite 500, 2300 Clarendon Blvd, Arlington, VA 22201-3367; tel. (703) 696-6900; fax (703) 696-6666; e-mail info@abmc.gov; internet www.abmc.gov; f. 1923; Sec. and CEO Brig.-Gen. (retd) JOHN W. NICHOLSON; Exec. Dir Brig.-Gen. (retd) WILLIAM J. LESZCZYNSKI, Jr.

Appalachian Regional Commission: 1666 Connecticut Ave, NW, Washington, DC 20009-1068; tel. (202) 884-7700; fax (202) 884-7682; e-mail info@arc.gov; internet www.arc.gov; f. 1965; Fed. Co-Chair. ANNE B. POPE; Alt. Fed. Co-Chair. (vacant).

Commission on Civil Rights: 624 Ninth St, NW, Washington, DC 20425; tel. (202) 376-7700; fax (202) 376-8116; e-mail publications@usccr.gov; internet www.usccr.gov; f. 1957; Chair. GERALD A. REYNOLDS; Staff Dir MARTIN DANNENFELSER.

Commission of Fine Arts: National Bldg Museum, Suite 312, 401 F St, NW, Washington, DC 20001-2728; tel. (202) 504-2200; fax (202) 504-2195; e-mail staff@cfa.gov; internet www.cfa.gov; f. 1910; Chair. EARL A. POWELL, III.

Commodity Futures Trading Commission (CFTC): 3 Lafayette Centre, 1155 21st St, NW, Washington, DC 20581; tel. (202) 418-5000; fax (202) 418-5521; e-mail oea@cftc.gov; internet www.cftc.gov; f. 1974; Chair. MICHAEL DUNN (acting).

Corporation for National and Community Service (CNS): 1201 New York Ave, NW, Washington, DC 20525; tel. (202) 606-5000; fax (202) 565-2799; e-mail info@cns.gov; internet www.nationalservice.gov; Chair. ALLAN D. SOLOMONT; CEO DAVID EISNER; Inspector-Gen. GERALD WALPIN.

Defense Nuclear Facilities Safety Board: 625 Indiana Ave, Suite 700, NW, Washington, DC 20004-2901; tel. (202) 694-7000; fax (202) 208-6518; e-mail mailbox@dnfsb.gov; internet www.dnfsb.gov; f. 1988; Chair. Dr A. J. EGGENBERGER.

Environmental Protection Agency: Ariel Rios Bldg, 1200 Pennsylvania Ave, NW, Washington, DC 20460; tel. (202) 272-0167; internet www.epa.gov; f. 1970; Admin. LISA JACKSON.

Equal Employment Opportunity Commission: 1801 L St, NW, POB 7033, Washington, DC 20507; tel. (202) 663-4900; fax (202) 663-4494; e-mail info@ask.eeoc.gov; internet www.eeoc.gov; f. 1965; Chair. STUART J. ISHIMARU (acting); Commissioner NAOMI J. EARP.

Export-Import Bank of the United States (Ex-Im Bank): see Finance—Banking.

Farm Credit Administration (FCA): 1501 Farm Credit Dr., McLean, VA 22102-5090; tel. (703) 883-4000; fax (703) 790-3260; e-mail info-line@fca.gov; internet www.fca.gov; f. 1933; Chair. and CEO LELAND A. STROM.

Federal Communications Commission (FCC): see Broadcasting and Communications.

Federal Deposit Insurance Corporation (FDIC): 550 17th St, NW, Washington, DC 20429; tel. (202) 736-0000; e-mail publicinfo@fdic.gov; internet www.fdic.gov; f. 1933; Chair. SHEILA C. BAIR; Dir THOMAS J. CURRY.

Federal Election Commission: see Election Commission.

Federal Emergency Management Agency: Federal Center Plaza, 500 C St, SW, Washington, DC 20472; tel. (202) 646-2500; fax (202) 646-2531; internet www.fema.gov; f. 1979; part of the Dept of Homeland Security; Admin. WILLIAM CRAIG FUGATE (acting).

Federal Home Mortgage Corporation (Freddie Mac): 8200 Jones Branch Dr., MS 200, McLean, VA 22102; tel. (703) 903-2000; internet www.freddiemac.com; f. 1970; CEO JOHN A. KOSKINEN (acting).

Federal Housing Finance Board: 1625 I St, NW, 4th Floor, Washington, DC 20006-4001; tel. (202) 408-2500; fax (202) 408-1435; e-mail fhfb@fhfb.gov; internet www.fhfb.gov; Chair. RONALD A. ROSENFELD.

Federal Labor Relations Authority (FLRA): 1400 K St, 4th Floor, NW, Washington, DC 20005; tel. (202) 218-7945; fax (202) 482-6635; e-mail jcrumpacker@flra.gov; internet www.flra.gov; f. 1978; Chair. CAROL WALLER POPE (acting).

Federal Maritime Commission: see Transport—Ocean Shipping.

Federal Mediation and Conciliation Service: 2100 K St, NW, Washington, DC 20427; tel. (202) 606-8100; fax (202) 606-4251; internet www.fmcs.gov; f. 1947; Dir SCOT L. BECKENBAUGH (acting).

THE UNITED STATES OF AMERICA   *Directory*

Federal National Mortgage Association (Fannie Mae): 3900 Wisconsin Ave, NW, Washington, DC 20016-2892; tel. (202) 752-7000; internet www.fanniemae.com; f. 1938; Pres. MICHAEL J. WILLIAMS.

Federal Reserve System: see Finance—Banking.

Federal Retirement Thrift Investment Board (FRTIB): 1250 H St, NW, Washington, DC 20005; tel. (202) 942-1600; fax (202) 942-1676; internet www.frtib.gov; f. 1986; Chair. ANDREW M. SAUL; Exec. Dir GREGORY T. LONG.

Federal Trade Commission: 600 Pennsylvania Ave, NW, Washington, DC 20580; tel. (202) 326-2222; fax (202) 326-2396; internet www.ftc.gov; f. 1914; Chair. JON LEIBOWITZ.

General Services Administration: 1800 F St, NW, Washington, DC 20405; tel. (202) 501-1231; fax (202) 501-1489; internet www.gsa.gov; f. 1949; Admin. PAUL F. PROUTY (acting).

Inter-American Foundation: 901 North Stuart St, 10th Floor, Arlington, VA 22203; tel. (703) 306-4319; fax (703) 306-4365; e-mail info@iaf.gov; internet www.iaf.gov; f. 1969; provides grants to non-governmental and community-based orgs in Latin America and the Caribbean; Chair. ROGER W. WALLACE.

Medicare Payment Advisory Commission (MedPAC): 601 New Jersey Ave, NW, Suite 9000, Washington, DC 2001; tel. (202) 220-3700; fax (202) 220-3759; e-mail webmaster@medpac.gov; internet www.medpac.gov; Chair. GLENN M. HACKBARTH.

Merit Systems Protection Board: 1615 M St, NW, Washington, DC 20419; tel. (202) 653-7200; fax (202) 653-7130; e-mail mspb@mspb.gov; internet www.mspb.gov; f. 1979; Chair. NEIL A. G. MCPHIE.

National Aeronautics and Space Administration (NASA): 300 E St, SW, Washington, DC 20546; tel. (202) 358-0000; fax (202) 358-3251; e-mail info-center@hq.nasa.gov; internet www.nasa.gov; f. 1958; Admin. CHRISTOPHER SCOLESE (acting).

National Archives and Records Administration: 8601 Adelphi Rd, College Park, MD 20740-6001; tel. (301) 837-1600; fax (301) 837-3218; internet www.archives.gov; f. 1934; Archivist of the United States ADRIENNE C. THOMAS (acting).

National Capital Planning Commission: 401 Ninth St, NW, Suite 500, Washington, DC 20004; tel. (202) 482-7200; fax (202) 482-7272; e-mail info@ncpc.gov; internet www.ncpc.gov; f. 1924; Chair. JOHN V. COGBILL, III.

National Commission on Libraries and Information Science: 1800 M St, NW, Suite 350, North Tower, Washington, DC 20036-5841; tel. (202) 606-9200; fax (202) 606-9203; e-mail info@nclis.gov; internet www.nclis.gov; f. 1970; Chair. C. BETH FITZSIMMONS.

National Council on Disability: 1331 F St, NW, Suite 850, Washington, DC 20004-1107; tel. (202) 272-2004; fax (202) 272-2022; e-mail ncd@ncd.gov; internet www.ncd.gov; f. 1978; Chair. JOHN R. VAUGHN.

National Credit Union Administration: 1775 Duke St, Alexandria, VA 22314-3428; tel. (703) 518-6330; fax (703) 518-6409; e-mail pacamail@ncua.gov; internet www.ncua.gov; f. 1970; Chair. MICHAEL E. FRYZEL.

National Endowment for the Arts: 1100 Pennsylvania Ave, NW, Washington, DC 20506-0001; tel. (202) 682-5400; fax (202) 682-5611; e-mail webmgr@arts.endow.gov; internet www.arts.gov; f. 1965; Chair. PATRICE WALKER POWELL (acting).

National Endowment for the Humanities: 1100 Pennsylvania Ave, NW, Rm 503, Washington, DC 20506; tel. (202) 606-8310; e-mail info@neh.gov; internet www.neh.gov; f. 1965; Chair. CAROLE M. WATSON.

National Labor Relations Board: 1099 14th St, NW, Washington, DC 20570-0001; tel. (202) 273-1991; fax (202) 273-1789; internet www.nlrb.gov; f. 1935; Chair. WILMA B. LIEBMAN.

National Mediation Board (NMB): 1301 K St, NW, Suite 250 East, Washington, DC 20005-7011; tel. (202) 692-5010; fax (202) 523-5080; internet www.nmb.gov; f. 1934; Chair. READ VAN DE WATER.

National Science Foundation (NSF): 4201 Wilson Blvd, Arlington, VA 22230; tel. (703) 292-5111; e-mail info@nsf.gov; internet www.nsf.gov; f. 1950; supports basic scientific and engineering research and education; Dir Dr ARDEN L. BEMENT, Jr.

National Transportation Safety Board: see Transport.

Nuclear Regulatory Commission (NRC): Office of Public Affairs, Washington, DC 20555; tel. (301) 415-8200; e-mail opa@nrc.gov; internet www.nrc.gov; Chair. DALE E. KLEIN.

Occupational Safety and Health Review Commission (OSHRC): 1120 20th St, 9th Floor, NW, Washington, DC 20036-3457; tel. (202) 606-5398; fax (202) 606-5052; internet www.oshrc.gov; f. 1970; Chair. THOMASINA V. ROGERS (acting).

Office of Government Ethics: 1201 New York Ave, NW, Suite 500, Washington, DC 20005-3917; tel. (202) 482-9300; fax (202) 482-9237; e-mail contactoge@oge.gov; internet www.usoge.gov; f. 1978; Dir ROBERT I. CUSICK.

Office of Personnel Management (OPM): Theodore Roosevelt Federal Bldg, 1900 E St, NW, Washington, DC 20415; tel. (202) 606-1800; fax (202) 606-2573; e-mail general@opm.gov; internet www.opm.gov; f. 1979; Dir JOHN BERRY.

Office of Special Counsel: 1730 M St, NW, Suite 300, Washington, DC 20036-4505; tel. (202) 254-3600; fax (202) 653-5151; e-mail adr@osc.gov; internet www.osc.gov; Special Counsel SCOTT J. BLOCH.

Peace Corps: Paul D. Coverdell Peace Corps HQ, 1111 20th St, NW, Washington, DC 20526; tel. (202) 692-2100; fax (202) 692-2101; e-mail webmaster@peacecorps.gov; internet www.peacecorps.gov; f. 1961; Dir RONALD A. TSCHETTER.

Pension Benefit Guaranty Corporation: 1200 K St, NW, Suite 12201, Washington, DC 20005-4026; tel. (202) 326-4010; fax (202) 326-4016; e-mail webmaster@pbgc.gov; internet www.pbgc.gov; f. 1974; Dir VINCENT A. SNOWBARGER.

Postal Rate Commission: 901 New York Ave, NW, Suite 200, NW, Washington, DC 20268-0001; tel. (202) 789-6800; fax (202) 789-6886; e-mail prc-webmaster@prc.gov; internet www.prc.gov; f. 1970; Chair. DAN G. BLAIR.

Railroad Retirement Board: 844 North Rush St, Chicago, IL 60611-2092; tel. (312) 751-4777; fax (312) 751-7154; e-mail opa@rrb.gov; internet www.rrb.gov; f. 1935; Chair. MICHAEL S. SCHWARTZ.

Securities and Exchange Commission: Station Pl., 100 F St, NE, Washington, DC 20549; tel. (202) 942-8088; fax (202) 942-9646; e-mail help@sec.gov; internet www.sec.gov; f. 1935; Chair. MARY SHAPIRO.

Selective Service System: 1515 Wilson Blvd, Arlington, VA 22209-2425; tel. (703) 605-4100; fax (703) 605-4106; e-mail information@sss.gov; internet www.sss.gov; f. 1940; Dir WILLIAM A. CHATFIELD.

Small Business Administration: 409 Third St, SW, Washington, DC 20416; tel. (202) 205-6650; fax (202) 205-6802; internet www.sba.gov; f. 1953; Admin. KAREN GORDON MILLS.

Smithsonian Institution: 1000 Jefferson Dr., SW, Washington, DC 20560-0001; tel. (202) 633-1000; e-mail info@si.edu; internet www.si.edu; f. 1846; Sec. G. WAYNE CLOUGH.

Social Security Administration: Office of Public Inquiries, Windsor Park Bldg, 6401 Security Blvd, Baltimore, MD 21235-0001; tel. (410) 965-3120; fax (410) 966-1463; internet www.ssa.gov; Commr MICHAEL J. ASTRUE.

Tennessee Valley Authority: 400 West Summit Hill Dr., Knoxville, TN 37902-1499; tel. (865) 632-2101; e-mail tvainfo@tva.gov; internet www.tva.gov; f. 1933; CEO and Pres. TOM KILGORE.

United States Agency for International Development (USAID): Ronald Reagan Bldg, 1300 Pennsylvania Ave, NW, Washington, DC 20523-0016; tel. (202) 712-4810; fax (202) 216-3524; e-mail pinquiries@usaid.gov; internet www.usaid.gov; f. 1961; Admin. ALONZO FULGHAM (acting).

United States Consumer Product Safety Commission: 4330 East-West Hwy, Bethesda, MD 20814-4408; tel. (301) 504-7923; fax (301) 504-0124; e-mail info@cpsc.gov; internet www.cpsc.gov; f. 1972; Chair. NANCY NORD (acting); Commr THOMAS H. MOORE; Exec. Dir PATSY SEMPLE.

United States International Trade Commission: 500 E St, SW, Washington, DC 20436; tel. (202) 205-2000; fax (202) 205-2798; e-mail webmaster@usitc.gov; internet www.usitc.gov; f. 1916; Chair. SHARA L. ARANOFF.

United States Postal Service: 475 L'Enfant Plaza, SW, Washington, DC 20260-0010; tel. (202) 268-2000; fax (202) 268-4860; internet www.usps.com; f. 1970; Postmaster-Gen. and CEO JOHN (JACK) E. POTTER.

United States Trade and Development Agency (USTDA): 1000 Wilson Blvd, Suite 1600, Arlington, VA 22209-3901; tel. (703) 875-4357; fax (703) 875-4009; e-mail info@ustda.gov; internet www.ustda.gov; f. 1961; Dir LEOCADIA L. ZAK (acting).

State Governments
(with expiration date of Governors' current term of office; legislatures at April 2009)

Alabama: Governor BOB RILEY (Rep.—Jan. 2011); Senate: Dem. 19, Rep. 13, Vacant 3; House: Dem. 62, Rep. 43.

Alaska: Governor SARAH PALIN (Rep.—Jan. 2011); Senate: Dem. 10, Rep. 10; House: Dem. 18, Rep. 22.

Arizona: Governor JAN BREWER (Rep.—Jan. 2011); Senate: Dem. 12, Rep. 18; House: Dem. 25, Rep. 35.

Arkansas: Governor MIKE BEEBE (Dem.—Jan. 2011); Senate: Dem. 27, Rep. 8; House: Dem. 71, Rep. 28, Green 1.

California: Governor ARNOLD SCHWARZENEGGER (Rep.—Jan. 2011); Senate: Dem. 26, Rep. 14; Assembly: Dem. 51, Rep. 29.

THE UNITED STATES OF AMERICA   *Directory*

Colorado: Governor WILLIAM RITTER, Jr (Dem.—Jan. 2011); Senate: Dem. 21, Rep. 14; House: Dem. 38, Rep. 27.

Connecticut: Governor M. JODI RELL (Rep.—Jan. 2011); Senate: Dem. 24, Rep. 12; House: Dem. 114, Rep. 37.

Delaware: Governor JACK MARKELL (Dem.—Jan. 2013); Senate: Dem. 16, Rep. 5; House: Dem. 24, Rep. 17.

Florida: Governor CHARLIE CRIST (Rep.—Jan. 2011); Senate: Dem. 14, Rep. 26; House: Dem. 44, Rep. 76.

Georgia: Governor GEORGE (SONNY) PERDUE (Rep.—Jan. 2011); Senate: Dem. 22, Rep. 34; House: Dem. 75, Rep. 105.

Hawaii: Governor LINDA LINGLE (Rep.—Jan. 2011); Senate: Dem. 23, Rep. 2; House: Dem. 45, Rep. 6.

Idaho: Governor C. L. (BUTCH) OTTER (Rep.—Jan. 2011); Senate: Dem. 7, Rep. 28; House: Dem. 18, Rep. 52.

Illinois: Governor PATRICK J. QUINN, III (Dem.—Jan. 2011); Senate: Dem. 37, Rep. 22; House: Dem. 70, Rep. 48.

Indiana: Governor MITCHELL DANIELS (Rep.—Jan. 2013); Senate: Dem. 17, Rep. 33; House: Dem. 52, Rep. 48.

Iowa: Governor CHESTER (CHET) CULVER (Dem.—Jan. 2011); Senate: Dem. 32, Rep. 18; House: Dem. 56, Rep. 44.

Kansas: Governor KATHLEEN SEBELIUS (Dem.—Jan. 2011); Senate: Dem. 9, Rep. 31; House: Dem. 48, Rep. 77.

Kentucky: Governor STEVE BESHEAR (Dem.—Jan. 2012); Senate: Dem. 15, Rep. 22, Ind. 1; House: Dem. 65, Rep. 35.

Louisiana: Governor BOBBY JINDAL (Rep.—Jan. 2012); Senate: Dem. 22, Rep. 15, Vacant 2; House: Dem. 52, Rep. 50, Ind. 3.

Maine: Governor JOHN E. BALDACCI, Jr (Dem.—Jan. 2011); Senate: Dem. 20, Rep. 15; House: Dem. 96, Rep. 54, Ind. 1.

Maryland: Governor MARTIN O'MALLEY, Jr (Dem.—Jan. 2011); Senate: Dem. 33, Rep. 14; House: Dem. 104, Rep. 36, Ind. 1.

Massachusetts: Governor DEVAL L. PATRICK (Dem.—Jan. 2011); Senate: Dem. 35, Rep. 5; House: Dem. 143, Rep. 16, Ind. 1.

Michigan: Governor JENNIFER M. GRANHOLM (Dem.—Jan. 2011); Senate: Dem. 17, Rep. 21; House: Dem. 67, Rep. 43.

Minnesota: Governor TIM PAWLENTY (Rep.—Jan. 2011); Senate: Dem. 46, Rep. 21; House: Dem. 87, Rep. 47.

Mississippi: Governor HALEY BARBOUR (Rep.—Jan. 2012); Senate: Dem. 27, Rep. 25; House: Dem. 74, Rep. 48.

Missouri: Governor JEREMIAH W. (JAY) NIXON (Dem.—Jan. 2013); Senate: Dem. 11, Rep. 23; House: Dem. 74, Rep. 89.

Montana: Governor BRIAN SCHWEITZER (Dem.—Jan. 2013); Senate: Dem. 27, Rep. 23; House: Dem. 50, Rep. 50.

Nebraska: Governor DAVE HEINEMAN (Rep.—Jan. 2011); Legislature: unicameral body comprising 49 members elected on a non-partisan ballot and classed as senators.

Nevada: Governor JAMES A. GIBBONS (Rep.—Jan. 2011); Senate: Dem. 12, Rep. 9; Assembly: Dem. 28, Rep. 14.

New Hampshire: Governor JOHN LYNCH (Rep.—Jan. 2011); Senate: Dem. 14, Rep. 10; House: Dem. 225, Rep. 175.

New Jersey: Governor JON S. CORZINE (Dem.—Jan. 2010); Senate: Dem. 23, Rep. 17; Assembly: Dem. 48, Rep. 32.

New Mexico: Governor WILLIAM B. RICHARDSON (Dem.—Jan. 2011); Senate: Dem. 27, Rep. 15; House: Dem. 45, Rep. 25.

New York: Governor DAVID A. PATERSON (Dem.—Jan. 2011); Senate: Dem. 32, Rep. 30; Assembly: Dem. 109, Rep. 41.

North Carolina: Governor BEVERLY (BEV) PERDUE (Dem.—Jan. 2013); Senate: Dem. 30, Rep. 20; House: Dem. 68, Rep. 52.

North Dakota: Governor JOHN HOEVEN (Rep.—Jan. 2013); Senate: Dem. 21, Rep. 26; House: Dem. 36, Rep. 58.

Ohio: Governor TED STRICKLAND (Dem.—Jan. 2011); Senate: Dem. 12, Rep. 21; House: Dem. 53, Rep. 46.

Oklahoma: Governor BRAD HENRY (Dem.—Jan. 2011); Senate: Dem. 22, Rep. 26; House: Dem. 40, Rep. 61.

Oregon: Governor THEODORE R. (TED) KULONGOSKI (Dem.—Jan. 2011); Senate: Dem. 18, Rep. 12; House: Dem. 36, Rep. 24.

Pennsylvania: Governor EDWARD G. RENDELL (Dem.—Jan. 2011); Senate: Dem. 21, Rep. 29; House: Dem. 104, Rep. 99.

Rhode Island: Governor DONALD L. CARCIERI (Rep.—Jan. 2011); Senate: Dem. 33, Rep. 4, Ind. 1; House: Dem. 69, Rep. 6.

South Carolina: Governor MARSHALL C. (MARK) SANFORD (Rep.—Jan. 2011); Senate: Dem. 19, Rep. 27; House: Dem. 53, Rep. 71.

South Dakota: Governor M. MICHAEL ROUNDS (Rep.—Jan. 2011); Senate: Dem. 14, Rep. 20, Ind. 1; House: Dem. 24, Rep. 46.

Tennessee: Governor PHIL BREDESEN (Dem.—Jan. 2011); Senate: Dem. 14, Rep. 19; House: Dem. 49, Rep. 50.

Texas: Governor RICK PERRY (Rep.—Jan. 2011); Senate: Dem. 12, Rep. 19; House: Dem. 74, Rep. 76.

Utah: Governor JON HUNTSMAN, Jr (Rep.—Jan. 2013); Senate: Dem. 8, Rep. 21; House: Dem. 22, Rep. 53.

Vermont: Governor JAMES H. DOUGLAS (Rep.—Jan. 2011); Senate: Dem. 23, Rep. 7; House: Dem. 95, Rep. 48, Ind. 7.

Virginia: Governor TIMOTHY M. KAINE (Dem.—Jan. 2010); Senate: Dem. 21, Rep. 19; House: Dem. 45, Rep. 53, Ind. 2.

Washington: Governor CHRISTINE O. GREGOIRE (Dem.—Jan. 2013); Senate: Dem. 31, Rep. 18; House: Dem. 64, Rep. 34.

West Virginia: Governor JOE MANCHIN, III (Dem.—Jan. 2013); Senate: Dem. 28, Rep. 6; House: Dem. 79, Rep. 21.

Wisconsin: Governor JAMES E. DOYLE (Dem.—Jan. 2011); Senate: Dem. 18, Rep. 15; Assembly: Dem. 52, Rep. 46.

Wyoming: Governor DAVE FREUDENTAHL (Dem.—Jan. 2011); Senate: Dem. 7, Rep. 23; House: Dem. 18, Rep. 41.

Political Organizations

Communist Party USA (CPUSA): 235 West 23rd St, 7th Floor, New York, NY 10011; tel. (212) 989-4994; fax (212) 229-1713; e-mail cpusa@cpusa.org; internet www.cpusa.org; f. 1919; mems in all 50 states, organized in over 40 states; Nat. Chair. SAM WEBB; Exec. Vice-Chair. JARVIS TYNER.

Democratic National Committee: 430 South Capitol St, SE, Washington, DC 20003; tel. (202) 863-8000; fax (202) 863-8174; internet www.democrats.org; f. 1848; Nat. Chair. TIMOTHY M. KAINE; Sec. ALICE TRAVIS GERMOND; Treas. ANDREW TOBIAS.

The Green Party of the United States: POB 57065, Washington, DC 20037; tel. (202) 319-7191; fax (202) 319-7193; e-mail info@gp.org; internet www.gp.org; f. 2001; Sec. HOLLY HART; Treas. JODY GRAGE.

Libertarian Party: 2600 Virginia Ave, NW, Suite 200, Washington, DC 20037; tel. (202) 333-0008; fax (202) 333-0072; e-mail info@lp.org; internet www.lp.org; f. 1971; advocates individual freedom, smaller govt and fewer taxes; Exec. Dir ROBERT KRAUS (acting).

Prohibition National Committee: POB 2635, Denver, CO 80201; tel. (303) 237-4947; e-mail umalcohol@aol.com; internet www.prohibition.org; f. 1869; opposes the manufacture and sale of alcoholic drinks; opposes abortion, drug abuse and euthanasia; Nat. Chair. GENE AMONDSON; Nat. Sec. PAUL B. SCOTT.

La Raza Unida Party (Partido Nacional La Raza Unida): 483 Fifth St, POB 13, San Fernando, CA 91340; tel. (818) 365-6534; e-mail pnlrunm@yahoo.com; internet larazaunida.tripod.com; f. 1970; aims to achieve self-determination and greater govt representation for Latinos through electoral processes; four state groups, 100 local groups; Nat. Chair. XENARO G. AYALA.

Republican National Committee: 310 First St, SE, Washington, DC 20003; tel. (202) 863-8500; fax (202) 863-8820; e-mail info@gop.com; internet www.rnc.org; f. 1854; Chair., Nat. Cttee MICHAEL STEELE; Co-Chair. JO ANN DAVIDSON.

Social Democrats, USA: POB 5307, Johnston, PA 15904; tel. (814) 410-2542; e-mail info@socialdemocratsusa.org; internet www.socialdemocratsusa.org; f. 1972 following split from the Socialist Party of America (f. 1901); Exec. Dir GABRIEL MCCLOSKEY-ROSS; Nat. Chair. RICHARD D'LOSS.

Socialist Labor Party: POB 218, Mountain View, CA 94042-0218; e-mail socialists@slp.org; internet www.slp.org; f. 1876 as the Workingmen's Party; present name adopted in 1877; advocates collective ownership and democratic control of all industries and services through industrial unions; Nat. Sec. ROBERT BILLS.

Socialist Party USA: A. J. Muste Bldg, 339 Lafayette St, Suite 303, New York, NY 10012; tel. and fax (212) 982-4586; e-mail natsec@socialistparty-usa.org; internet socialistparty-usa.org; f. 1972 following split from the Socialist Party of America (f. 1901); Co-Chairs. ANDREA PASON, JERRY LEVY; Nat. Sec. GREG PASON; 1,800 mems.

Socialist Workers Party: 306 West 37th St, 10th Floor, New York, NY 10018; tel. (212) 736-2540; fax (212) 244-4274; e-mail swpno@mac.com; f. 1938; communist; Nat. Sec. JACK BARNES.

Diplomatic Representation

EMBASSIES IN THE USA

Afghanistan: 2341 Wyoming Ave, NW, Washington, DC 20008; tel. 483-6410; fax 483-6488; e-mail info@embassyofafghanistan.org; internet www.embassyofafghanistan.org; Ambassador SAID TAYEB JAWAD.

Albania: 2100 S St, NW, Washington, DC 20008; tel. (202) 223-4942; fax (202) 628-7342; e-mail info@albanianembassy.org; internet www.albanianembassy.org; Ambassador ALEKSANDER SALLABANDA.

THE UNITED STATES OF AMERICA

Algeria: 2118 Kalorama Rd, NW, Washington, DC 20008; tel. (202) 265-2800; fax (202) 667-2174; e-mail ambalg2004@yahoo.com; internet www.algeria-us.org; Ambassador ABDALLAH BAALI.

Andorra: 2 United Nations Plaza, 25th Floor, New York, NY 10017; tel. (212) 750-8064; fax (212) 750-6630; Ambassador CARLES FONT-ROSSELL.

Angola: 2108 16th St, NW, Washington, DC 20009; tel. (202) 785-1156; fax (202) 822-9049; e-mail angola@angola.org; internet www.angola.org; Ambassador JOSEFINA PERPÉTUA PITRA DIAKITÉ.

Antigua and Barbuda: 3216 New Mexico Ave, NW, Washington, DC 20016; tel. (202) 362-5122; fax (202) 362-5225; e-mail embantbar@aol.com; Ambassador DEBORAH MAE LOVELL.

Argentina: 1600 New Hampshire Ave, NW, Washington, DC 20009; tel. (202) 238-6401; fax (202) 332-3171; internet www.embassyofargentina.us; Ambassador HÉCTOR MARCOS TIMERMAN.

Armenia: 2225 R St, NW, Washington, DC 20008; tel. (202) 319-1976; fax (202) 319-2982; e-mail armecon@speakeasy.net; internet www.armeniaemb.org; Ambassador TATOUL MARKARIAN.

Australia: 1601 Massachusetts Ave, NW, Washington, DC 20036-2273; tel. (202) 797-3000; fax (202) 797-3168; internet www.austemb.org; Ambassador DENNIS RICHARDSON.

Austria: 3524 International Court, NW, Washington, DC 20008-3022; tel. (202) 895-6700; fax (202) 895-6750; e-mail obwas@sysnet.net; internet www.austria.org; Chargé d'affaires a.i. ANDREAS RIECKEN.

Azerbaijan: 2741 34th St, NW, Washington, DC 20008; tel. (202) 337-3500; fax (202) 337-5911; e-mail azerbaijan@azembassy.com; internet www.azembassy.com; Ambassador YASHAR ALIYEV.

Bahamas: 2220 Massachusetts Ave, NW, Washington, DC 20008; tel. (202) 319-2660; fax (202) 319-2668; e-mail bahemb@aol.com; Ambassador CORNELIUS A. SMITH.

Bahrain: 3502 International Dr., NW, Washington, DC 20008; tel. (202) 342-1111; fax (202) 362-2192; e-mail info@bahrainembassy.org; internet www.bahrainembassy.org; Ambassador HOUDA ERZA EBRAHIM NONOO.

Bangladesh: 3510 International Dr., NW, Washington, DC 20008; tel. (202) 244-0183; fax (202) 244-2771; e-mail info@bangladoot.org; internet www.bangladoot.org; Ambassador M. HUMAYUN KABIR.

Barbados: 2144 Wyoming Ave, NW, Washington, DC 20008; tel. (202) 939-9200; fax (202) 332-7467; e-mail washington@foreign.gov.bb; Ambassador JOHN BEALE.

Belarus: 1619 New Hampshire Ave, NW, Washington, DC 20009; tel. (202) 986-1604; fax (202) 986-1805; e-mail usa@belarusembassy.org; internet www.belarusembassy.org; Ambassador MIKHAIL KHVOSTOV.

Belgium: 3330 Garfield St, NW, Washington, DC 20008; tel. (202) 333-6900; fax (202) 333-3079; e-mail washington@diplobel.org; internet www.diplobel.us; Ambassador DOMINICUS STRUYE DE SWIELANDE.

Belize: 2535 Massachusetts Ave, NW, Washington, DC 20008; tel. (202) 332-9636; fax (202) 332-6888; e-mail chancery@embassyofbelize.org; internet www.embassyofbelize.org; Ambassador NESTOR MENDEZ.

Benin: 2124 Kalorama Rd, NW, Washington, DC 20008; tel. (202) 232-6656; fax (202) 265-1996; Ambassador SÈGBÉ CYRILLE OGUIN.

Bolivia: 3014 Massachusetts Ave, NW, Washington, DC 20008; tel. (202) 483-4410; fax (202) 328-3712; e-mail webmaster@bolivia-usa.org; internet www.bolivia-usa.org; Chargé d'affaires a.i. ERIKA DUEÑAS.

Bosnia and Herzegovina: 2109 E St, NW, Washington, DC 20037; tel. (202) 337-1500; fax (202) 337-1502; e-mail info@bhembassy.org; internet www.bhembassy.org; Chargé d'affaires a.i. SVETOZAR MILETIĆ.

Botswana: 1531-1533 New Hampshire Ave, NW, Washington, DC 20036; tel. (202) 244-4990; fax (202) 244-4164; e-mail cratsiripe@gov.bw; internet www.botswanaembassy.org; Ambassador LAPOLOGANG CAESAR LEKOA.

Brazil: 3006 Massachusetts Ave, NW, Washington, DC 20008; tel. (202) 238-2700; fax (202) 238-2827; e-mail webmaster@brasilemb.org; internet www.brasilemb.org; Ambassador ANTONIO PATRIOTA.

Brunei: 3520 International Court, NW, Washington, DC 20008; tel. (202) 237-1838; fax (202) 885-0560; e-mail info@bruneiembassy.org; internet www.bruneiembassy.org; Chargé d'affaires a.i. ANGELA SHIM.

Bulgaria: 1621 22nd St, NW, Washington, DC 20008; tel. (202) 387-0174; fax (202) 234-7973; e-mail office@bulgaria-embassy.org; internet www.bulgaria-embassy.org; Ambassador LATECHEZAR PETKOV.

Burkina Faso: 2340 Massachusetts Ave, NW, Washington, DC 20008; tel. (202) 332-5577; fax (202) 667-1882; e-mail ambawdc@verizon.net; internet www.burkinaembassy-usa.org; Ambassador PARMANGA ERNEST YONLI.

Burundi: 2233 Wisconsin Ave, NW, Suite 212, Washington, DC 20007; tel. (202) 342-2574; fax (202) 342-2575; e-mail burundiembassy@erols.com; internet www.burundiembassy-usa.org; Ambassador CELESTIN NIYONGABO.

Cambodia: 4530 16th St, NW, Washington, DC 20011; tel. (202) 726-7742; fax (202) 726-8381; e-mail mail@embassyofcambodia.org; internet www.embassyofcambodia.org; Ambassador HEM HENG.

Cameroon: 2349 Massachusetts Ave, NW, Washington, DC 20008; tel. (202) 265-8790; fax (202) 387-3826; e-mail cdm@ambacam-usa.org; internet www.ambacam-usa.org; Ambassador JOSEPH FOE-ATANGANA.

Canada: 501 Pennsylvania Ave, NW, Washington, DC 20001; tel. (202) 682-1740; fax (202) 682-7701; e-mail canada@canadianembassy.org; internet www.canadianembassy.org; Ambassador MICHAEL WILSON.

Cape Verde: 3415 Massachusetts Ave, NW, Washington, DC 20007; tel. (202) 965-6820; fax (202) 965-1207; e-mail ambacvus@sysnet.net; internet www.virtualcapeverde.net; Ambassador JOSE BRITO.

Central African Republic: 1618 22nd St, NW, Washington, DC 20008; tel. (202) 483-7800; fax (202) 332-9893; e-mail car@ambarca.org; Ambassador EMMANUEL TOUABOY.

Chad: 2002 R St, NW, Washington, DC 20009; tel. (202) 462-4009; fax (202) 265-1937; e-mail info@chadembassy.org; internet www.chadembassy.org; Ambassador HASSABALLAH AHMAT SOUBIANE.

Chile: 1732 Massachusetts Ave, NW, Washington, DC 20036; tel. (202) 785-1746; fax (202) 887-5579; e-mail embassy@embassyofchile.org; internet www.chile-usa.org; Ambassador MARIANO FERNÁNDEZ AMUNATEGUI.

China, People's Republic: 2300 Connecticut Ave, NW, Washington, DC 20008; tel. (202) 558-0032; fax (202) 232-7855; e-mail chinaembassy_us@fmprc.gov.cn; internet www.china-embassy.org; Ambassador ZHOU WENZHONG.

Colombia: 2118 Leroy Pl., NW, Washington, DC 20008; tel. (202) 387-8338; fax (202) 232-8643; e-mail enwas@colombiaemb.org; internet www.colombiaemb.org; Ambassador CAROLINA BARCO ISAKSON.

Comoros: 336 East 45th St, 2nd Floor, New York, NY 10017; tel. (212) 750-1637; e-mail comun@undp.org; Ambassador MOHAMED TOIHIRI.

Congo, Democratic Republic: 1800 New Hampshire Ave, NW, Washington, DC 20009; tel. (202) 234-7690; fax (202) 237-0748; Ambassador FAIDA MITIFU.

Congo, Republic: 4891 Colorado Ave, NW, Washington, DC 20011; tel. (202) 726-5500; fax (202) 726-1860; e-mail info@embassyofcongo.org; internet www.embassyofcongo.org; Ambassador SERGE MOMBOULI.

Costa Rica: 2114 S St, NW, Washington, DC 20008; tel. (202) 234-2945; fax (202) 265-4795; e-mail embassy@costarica-embassy.org; internet www.costarica-embassy.org; Chargé d'affaires a.i. LAURA DACHNER.

Côte d'Ivoire: 3421 Massachusetts Ave, NW, Washington, DC 20007; tel. (202) 797-0300; fax (202) 462-9444; Ambassador CHARLES KOFFI.

Croatia: 2343 Massachusetts Ave, NW, Washington, DC 20008-2803; tel. (202) 588-5899; fax (202) 588-8936; e-mail public@croatiaemb.org; Ambassador KOLINDA GRABAR-KITAROVIĆ.

Cuba: 'Interests section' in the Embassy of Switzerland, 2630 16th St, NW, Washington, DC 20009; tel. (202) 797-8518; fax (202) 797-8521; e-mail consulcuba@sicuw.org; internet www.eda.admin.ch/eda/en/home/reps/nameri/vusa/wasemb/wacuba.html; Counsellor JORGE ALBERTO BOLAÑOS SUÁREZ.

Cyprus: 2211 R St, NW, Washington, DC 20008; tel. (202) 462-5772; fax (202) 483-6710; e-mail cypembwash@earthlink.net; internet www.cyprusembassy.net; Ambassador ANDREAS KAKOURIS.

Czech Republic: 3900 Spring of Freedom St, NW, Washington, DC 20008; tel. (202) 274-9100; fax (202) 966-8540; e-mail washington@embassy.mzv.cz; internet www.mzv.cz/washington; Ambassador PETR KOLAR.

Denmark: 3200 Whitehaven St, NW, Washington, DC 20008-3616; tel. (202) 234-4300; fax (202) 328-1470; e-mail wasamb@um.dk; internet www.ambwashington.um.dk; Ambassador FRIIS ARNE PETERSEN.

Djibouti: 1156 15th St, NW, Suite 515, Washington, DC 20005; tel. (202) 331-0270; fax (202) 331-0302; Ambassador ROBLÉ OLHAYE.

Dominica: 3216 New Mexico Ave, NW, Washington, DC 20016; tel. (202) 364-6781; fax (202) 364-6791; e-mail embdomdc@aol.com; Chargé d'affaires a.i. JUDITH ANN ROLLE.

Dominican Republic: 1715 22nd St, NW, Washington, DC 20008; tel. (202) 332-6280; fax (202) 265-8057; e-mail embassy@us.serex.gov

THE UNITED STATES OF AMERICA

.do; internet www.domrep.org; Chargé d'affaires a.i. WELLINGTON BENSOSME.

Ecuador: 2535 15th St, NW, Washington, DC 20009; tel. (202) 234-7200; fax (202) 667-3482; e-mail embassy@ecuador.org; internet www.ecuador.org; Ambassador LUIS BENIGNO GALLEGOS CHIRIBOGA.

Egypt: 3521 International Court, NW, Washington, DC 20008; tel. (202) 895-5400; fax (202) 244-4319; e-mail Embassy@egyptembassy.net; internet www.egyptembassy.net; Ambassador SAMEH SHOUKRY.

El Salvador: 1400 16th St, NW, Suite 100, Washington, DC 20036; tel. (202) 265-9671; fax (202) 232-3763; e-mail correo@elsalvador.org; internet www.elsalvador.org; Ambassador RENÉ ANTONIO LEÓN RODRÍGUEZ.

Equatorial Guinea: 2020 16th St, NW, Washington, DC 20009; tel. (202) 518-5700; fax (202) 518-5252; Ambassador PURIFICACIÓN ANGUE ONDO.

Eritrea: 1708 New Hampshire Ave, NW, Washington, DC 20009; tel. (202) 319-1991; fax (202) 319-1304; Ambassador GHIRMAI GHEBREMARIAM.

Estonia: 2131 Massachusetts Ave, NW, Washington, DC 20008; tel. (202) 588-0101; fax (202) 588-0108; e-mail info@estemb.org; internet www.estemb.org; Ambassador VÄINO REINART.

Ethiopia: 3506 International Dr., NW, Washington, DC 20008; tel. (202) 364-1200; fax (202) 587-0195; e-mail info@ethiopianembassy.org; internet www.ethiopianembassy.org; Ambassador SAMUEL ASSEFA.

Fiji: 2000 M St, NW, Suite 710, Washington, DC 20036; tel. (202) 466-8320; fax (202) 466-8325; e-mail info@fijiembassydc.com; internet www.fijiembassy.org; Ambassador WINSTON THOMPSON.

Finland: 3301 Massachusetts Ave, NW, Washington, DC 20008; tel. (202) 298-5800; fax (202) 298-6030; e-mail sanomat.was@formin.fi; internet www.finland.org; Ambassador PEKKA LINTU.

France: 4101 Reservoir Rd, NW, Washington, DC 20007; tel. (202) 944-6166; fax (202) 944-6072; e-mail info@ambafrance-us.org; internet www.ambafrance-us.org; Ambassador PIERRE VIMONT.

Gabon: 2034 20th St, NW, Suite 200, Washington, DC 20009; tel. (202) 797-1000; fax (202) 332-0668; Ambassador CARLOS BOUNGOU.

The Gambia: 1155 15th St, NW, Suite 1000, Washington, DC 20005-2076; tel. (202) 785-1399; fax (202) 785-1430; e-mail info@gambiaembassy.us; internet www.gambiaembassy.us; Ambassador NENEH MACDOULL-GAYE.

Georgia: 1101 15th St, NW, Suite 602, Washington, DC 20005; tel. (202) 387-2390; fax (202) 387-0864; e-mail embgeorgiausa@yahoo.com; internet www.use.mfa.gov.ge; Ambassador-designate BATU KURELIA.

Germany: 4645 Reservoir Rd, NW, Washington, DC 20007-1998; tel. (202) 298-4000; fax (202) 298-4249; internet www.germany.info; Ambassador KLAUS SCHARIOTH.

Ghana: 3512 International Dr., NW, Washington, DC 20008; tel. (202) 686-4520; fax (202) 686-4527; e-mail info@ghanaembassy.org; internet www.ghana-embassy.org; Chargé d'affaires a.i. ADOLPHUS K. ARTHUR.

Greece: 2217 Massachusetts Ave, NW, Washington, DC 20008; tel. (202) 939-1300; fax (202) 939-1324; e-mail greece@greekembassy.org; internet www.greekembassy.org; Ambassador ALEXANDROS P. MALLIAS.

Grenada: 1701 New Hampshire Ave, NW, Washington, DC 20009; tel. (202) 265-2561; fax (202) 265-2468; internet www.grenadaembassyusa.org; Chargé d'affaires a.i. PATRICIA CLARKE.

Guatemala: 2220 R St, NW, Washington, DC 20008; tel. (202) 745-4952; fax (202) 745-1908; e-mail info@guatemala-embassy.org; internet www.guatemala-embassy.org; Ambassador FRANCISCO VILLAGRÁN DE LEÓN.

Guinea: 2112 Leroy Pl., NW, Washington, DC 20008; tel. (202) 483-9420; fax (202) 483-8688; Ambassador (vacant).

Guinea-Bissau: POB 33813, Washington, DC 20033-3813; tel. and fax (301) 947-3958; Ambassador (vacant).

Guyana: 2490 Tracy Pl., NW, Washington, DC 20008; tel. (202) 265-6900; fax (202) 232-1297; e-mail guyanaembassydc@verizon.net; internet www.guyanaembassyusa.com; Ambassador BAYNEY RAM KARRAN.

Haiti: 2311 Massachusetts Ave, Washington, DC 20008; tel. (202) 332-4090; fax (202) 745-7215; e-mail embassy@haiti.org; internet www.haiti.org; Ambassador RAYMOND A. JOSEPH.

Holy See: 3339 Massachusetts Ave, NW, Washington, DC 20008; tel. (202) 333-7121; fax (202) 337-4036; e-mail nuntiususa@nuntiususa.org; Apostolic Nuncio Most Rev. PIETRO SAMBI (Titular Archbishop of Bellicastrum).

Honduras: 3007 Tilden St, NW, Suite 4-M, Washington, DC 20008; tel. (202) 966-7702; fax (202) 966-9751; e-mail embassy@hondurasemb.org; internet www.hondurasemb.org; Ambassador ROBERTO FLORES BERMUDEZ.

Hungary: 3910 Shoemaker St, NW, Washington, DC 20008; tel. (202) 362-6730; fax (202) 966-8135; e-mail informacio.was@kum.hu; internet www.huembwas.org; Ambassador Dr FERENC SOMOGYI.

Iceland: 1156 15th St, NW, Suite 1200, Washington, DC 20005-1704; tel. (202) 265-6653; fax (202) 265-6656; e-mail icemb.wash@utn.stjr.is; internet www.iceland.org/us; Ambassador HJALMAR HANNESSON.

India: 2107 Massachusetts Ave, NW, Washington, DC 20008; tel. (202) 939-7000; fax (202) 265-4351; e-mail information@indiagov.org; internet www.indianembassy.org; Chargé d'affaires a.i. ARUN SING.

Indonesia: 2020 Massachusetts Ave, NW, Washington, DC 20036-1084; tel. (202) 775-5200; fax (202) 775-5256; e-mail information@embassyofindonesia.org; internet www.embassyofindonesia.org; Ambassador SUDJADNAN PARNOHADININGRAT.

Iran: 'Interests section' in the Embassy of Pakistan, 2209 Wisconsin Ave, NW, Washington, DC 20007; tel. (202) 965-4990; fax (202) 965-1073; e-mail requests@daftar.org; internet www.daftar.org; Dir ALI JAZINI.

Iraq: 1801 P St, Washington, DC 20036; tel. (202) 483-7500; fax (202) 462-5066; e-mail admin@iraqiembassy.us; internet www.iraqiembassy.us; Ambassador SAMIR SHAKIR MAHMOOD AS-SUMAIDAIE.

Ireland: 2234 Massachusetts Ave, NW, Washington, DC 20008; tel. (202) 462-3939; fax (202) 232-5993; e-mail embirlus@aol.com; internet www.irelandemb.org; Ambassador MICHAEL COLLINS.

Israel: 3514 International Dr., NW, Washington, DC 20008; tel. (202) 364-5590; fax (202) 364-5566; e-mail ask@israelemb.org; internet www.israelemb.org; Ambassador SALLAI MERIDOR.

Italy: 3000 Whitehaven St, NW, Washington, DC 20008; tel. (202) 612-4400; fax (202) 518-2151; e-mail stampa@itwash.org; internet www.ambwashingtondc.esteri.it; Ambassador GIOVANNI CASTELLANETA.

Jamaica: 1520 New Hampshire Ave, NW, Washington, DC 20006; tel. (202) 452-0660; fax (202) 452-0081; e-mail info@emjamusa.org; internet www.jamaicaembassy.org; Ambassador ANTHONY JOHNSON.

Japan: 2520 Massachusetts Ave, NW, Washington, DC 20008-2869; tel. (202) 238-6700; fax (202) 238-2187; e-mail jicc@embjapan.org; internet www.us.emb-japan.go.jp; Ambassador ICHIRO FUJISAKI.

Jordan: 3504 International Dr., NW, Washington, DC 20008; tel. (202) 966-2664; fax (202) 966-3110; e-mail hkjembassydc@jordanembassyus.org; internet www.jordanembassyus.org; Ambassador HRH Prince ZEID RA'AD AL-HUSSEIN.

Kazakhstan: 1401 16th St, NW, Washington, DC 20036; tel. (202) 232-5488; fax (202) 232-5845; e-mail zakh.embusa@verizon.net; internet www.kazakhembus.com; Ambassador ERLAN A. IDRISSOV.

Kenya: 2249 R St, NW, Washington, DC 20008; tel. (202) 387-6101; fax (202) 462-3829; e-mail information@kenyaembassy.com; internet www.kenyaembassy.com; Ambassador PETER N. RATENG'OGINGA OGEGO.

Korea, Republic: KORUS House, 2370 Massachusetts Ave, NW, Washington, DC 20008; tel. (202) 939-5600; fax (202) 797-0595; e-mail webmaster@dynamic-korea.com; internet www.koreaembassyusa.org; Chargé d'affaires a.i. KYOU-HYUN KIM.

Kosovo: Presidential Plaza, 900 19th St, Suite 400, Washington, DC 20006; tel. (202) 380-3581; fax (202) 380-3628; e-mail embassy.usa@ks-gov.net; Ambassador AVNI SPAHIU.

Kuwait: 2940 Tilden St, NW, Washington, DC 20008; tel. (202) 966-0702; fax (202) 966-0517; e-mail kio@kuwait-info.org; internet www.kuwait-info.org; Ambassador Sheikh JABER AL-AHMED AL-SABAH.

Kyrgyzstan: 2360 Massachusetts Ave, NW, Washington, DC 20008; tel. (202) 449-9822; fax (202) 386 7550; e-mail consul@kgembassy.org; internet www.kgembassy.org; Ambassador ZAMIRA BEKSULTANOVNA SYDYKOVA.

Laos: 2222 S St, NW, Washington, DC 20008; tel. (202) 332-6416; fax (202) 332-4923; e-mail laoemb@verizon.net; internet www.laoembassy.com; Ambassador PHIANE PHILAKONE.

Latvia: 2306 Massachusetts Ave, NW, Washington, DC 20008; tel. (202) 328-2840; fax (202) 328-2860; e-mail embassy.usa@mfa.gov.lv; internet www.latvia-usa.org; Ambassador ANDREJS PILDEGOVICS.

Lebanon: 2560 28th St, NW, Washington, DC 20008; tel. (202) 939-6300; fax (202) 939-6324; e-mail info@lebanonembassyus.org; internet www.lebanonembassyus.org; Ambassador ANTOINE CHEDID.

Lesotho: 2511 Massachusetts Ave, NW, Washington, DC 20008; tel. (202) 797-5533; fax (202) 234-6815; e-mail lesothoembassy@verizon.net; internet www.lesothoemb-usa.gov.ls; Ambassador DAVID MOHLOMI RANTEKOA.

Liberia: 5201 16th St, Washington, DC 20011; tel. (202) 723-0437; fax (202) 723-0436; e-mail info@liberiaemb.org; internet www.embassyofliberia.org; Ambassador MILTON NATHANIEL BARNES.

THE UNITED STATES OF AMERICA

Libya: Liaison Office, 2600 Virginia Ave, NW, Suite 705, Washington, DC 20037; tel. (202) 944-9601; fax (202) 944-9606; e-mail libya@libyanbureau-dc.org; Chief of Office ALI SULEIMAN AUJALI.

Liechtenstein: 888 17th St, NW, Suite 1250, Washington, DC 20006; tel. (202) 331-0590; fax (202) 331-3221; e-mail tamara.brunhart@was.rep.llv.li; internet www.liechtenstein.li; Ambassador CLAUDIA FRITSCHE.

Lithuania: 4590 MacArthur Blvd, NW, Washington, DC 20007; tel. (202) 234-5860; fax (202) 328-0466; e-mail info@ltembassyus.org; internet www.ltembassyus.org; Ambassador AUDRIUS BRUZGA.

Luxembourg: 2200 Massachusetts Ave, NW, Washington, DC 20008; tel. (202) 265-4171; fax (202) 328-8270; e-mail washington.info@mae.etat.lu; internet washington.mae.lu; Ambassador JEAN-PAUL SENNINGER.

Macedonia: 2129 Wyoming Ave, NW, Washington, DC 20008; tel. (202) 667-0501; fax (202) 667-2131; e-mail usoffice@macedonianembassy.org; internet www.macedonianembassy.org; Ambassador Dr ZORAN JOLEVSKI.

Madagascar: 2374 Massachusetts Ave, NW, Washington, DC 20008; tel. (202) 265-3034; fax (202) 483-7603; e-mail malagasy.embassy@org; internet www.kln.gov.my/perwakilan/washington; Ambassador JOCELYN RADIFERA.

Malawi: 1029 Vermont Ave, NW, Suite 1000, Washington, DC 20005; tel. (202) 721-0270; fax (202) 721-0288; e-mail malawidc@aol.com; internet www.malawiembassy-dc.org; Ambassador HAWA NDILOWE.

Malaysia: 3516 International Court, NW, Washington, DC 20008; tel. (202) 572-9700; fax (202) 572-9882; e-mail mwalsh@kln.gov.my; Chargé d'affaires a.i. ILANGO KARUPPANNAN.

Maldives: 800 Second Ave, Suite 400E, New York, NY 10017; tel. (212) 599-6195; fax (212) 661-6405; e-mail info@maldivesembassy.us; internet www.maldivesembassy.us; Chargé d'affaires a.i. AHMED KHALEEL.

Mali: 2130 R St, NW, Washington, DC 20008; tel. (202) 332-2249; fax (202) 332-6603; e-mail info@maliembassy.us; internet www.maliembassy.us; Ambassador ABDOULAYE DIOP.

Malta: 2017 Connecticut Ave, NW, Washington, DC 20008; tel. (202) 462-3611; fax (202) 387-5470; e-mail maltaembassy.washington@gov.mt; internet www.foreign.gov.mt; Ambassador MARK MICELI-FARRUGIA.

Marshall Islands: 2433 Massachusetts Ave, NW, Washington, DC 20008; tel. (202) 234-5414; fax (202) 232-3236; e-mail info@rmiembassyus.org; internet www.rmiembassyus.org; Ambassador BENJAMIN GRAHAM.

Mauritania: 2129 Leroy Pl., NW, Washington, DC 20008; tel. (202) 232-5700; fax (202) 319-2623; e-mail info@mauritaniembassy-usa.org; Ambassador IBRAHIMA DIA.

Mauritius: 4301 Connecticut Ave, NW, Suite 441, Washington, DC 20008; tel. (202) 244-1491; fax (202) 966-0983; e-mail mauritius.embassy@prodigy.net; Ambassador KEERTEECOOMAR RUHEE.

Mexico: 1911 Pennsylvania Ave, NW, Washington, DC 20006; tel. (202) 728-1600; fax (202) 234-1698; e-mail mexembusa@sre.gob.mx; internet www.sre.gob.mx/eua; Ambassador ARTURO SARUKHAN CASAMITJANA.

Micronesia: 1725 N St, NW, Washington, DC 20036; tel. (202) 223-4383; fax (202) 223-4391; e-mail firstsecretary@fsmembassydc.org; internet www.fsmembassydc.org; Ambassador YOSIWO P. GEORGE.

Moldova: 2101 S St, NW, Washington, DC 20008; tel. (202) 667-1130; fax (202) 667-1204; e-mail washington@mfa.md; internet www.embassyrm.org; Ambassador NICOLAE CHIRTOACA.

Monaco: 2314 Wyoming Ave, NW, Washington, DC 20008; tel. (202) 234-1530; Ambassador GILLES ALEXANDRE NOGHES.

Mongolia: 2833 M St, NW, Washington, DC 20007; tel. (202) 333-7117; fax (202) 298-9227; e-mail esyam@mongolianembassy.us; internet www.mongolianembassy.us; Ambassador KHASBAZAR BEKHBAT.

Montenegro: 1610 New Hampshire Ave, NW, Washington, DC 20009; tel. (202) 234 6108; fax (202) 234 6109; Ambassador MIODRAG VLAHOVIĆ.

Morocco: 1601 21st St, NW, Washington, DC 20009; tel. (202) 462-7980; fax (202) 265-0161; Ambassador AZIZ MEKOUAR.

Mozambique: 1525 New Hampshire Ave, NW, Washington, DC 20036; tel. (202) 293-7146; fax (202) 835-9245; e-mail embamoc@aol.com; internet www.embamoc-usa.org; Ambassador ARMANDO ALEXANDRE PANGUENE.

Myanmar: 2300 S St, NW, Washington, DC 20008; tel. (202) 332-9044; fax (202) 332-9046; e-mail thuriya@aol.com; Chargé d'affaires a.i. LWIN MYINT.

Namibia: 1605 New Hampshire Ave, NW, Washington, DC 20009; tel. (202) 986-0540; fax (202) 986-0443; e-mail info@namibiaembassyusa.org; internet www.namibianembassyusa.org; Ambassador PATRICK NANDAGO.

Nauru: 800 Second Ave, New York, NY 10017; tel. (212) 937-0074; fax (212) 937-0079; Ambassador MARLENE MOSES.

Nepal: 2131 Leroy Pl., NW, Washington, DC 20008; tel. (202) 667-4550; fax (202) 667-5534; e-mail info@nepalembassyusa.org; internet www.nepalembassyusa.org; Ambassador SURESH CHANDRA CHALISE.

Netherlands: 4200 Linnean Ave, NW, Washington, DC 20008; tel. (202) 244-5300; fax (202) 362-3430; e-mail was@minbuza.nl; internet www.netherlands-embassy.org; Ambassador REGINA (RENÉE) JONES-BOS.

New Zealand: 37 Observatory Circle, NW, Washington, DC 20008; tel. (202) 328-4800; fax (202) 667-5227; e-mail info@nzemb.org; internet www.nzembassy.com; Ambassador ROY FERGUSON.

Nicaragua: 1627 New Hampshire Ave, NW, Washington, DC 20009; tel. (202) 387-4371; fax (202) 939-6545; e-mail nicaraguan.embassy@embanic.org; Chargé d'affaires a.i. ALCIDES MONTIEL.

Niger: 2204 R St, NW, Washington, DC 20008; tel. (202) 483-4224; fax (202) 483-3169; e-mail ambassadeniger@hotmail.com; internet www.nigerembassyusa.org; Ambassador AMINATA DJIBRILLA MAIGA TOURÉ.

Nigeria: 3519 International Court, NW, Washington, DC 20008; tel. (202) 986-8400; fax (202) 362-6541; e-mail babalola@nigeriaembassyusa.org; internet www.nigeriaembassyusa.org; Chargé d'affaires a.i. BABA GANA WIKIL.

Norway: 2720 34th St, NW, Washington, DC 20008; tel. (202) 333-6000; fax (202) 337-0870; e-mail emb.washington@mfa.no; internet www.norway.org; Ambassador WEGGER CHRISTIAN STRØMMEN.

Oman: 2535 Belmont Rd, NW, Washington, DC 20008; tel. (202) 387-1980; fax (202) 745-4933; Ambassador HUNAINA SULTAN AHMED AL-MUGHAIRY.

Pakistan: 3517 International Court, NW, Washington, DC 20008; tel. (202) 939-6200; fax (202) 387-0484; e-mail info@embassyofpakistan.org; internet www.embassyofpakistan.org; Ambassador HUSAIN HAQQANI.

Palau: 1700 Pennsylvania Ave, NW, Suite 400, Washington, DC 20006; tel. (202) 452-6814; fax (202) 452-6281; e-mail info@palauembassy.com; internet www.palauembassy.com; Ambassador HERSEY KYOTA.

Panama: 2862 McGill Terrace, NW, Washington, DC 20008; tel. (202) 483-1407; fax (202) 483-8413; e-mail info@embassyofpanama.org; internet www.embassyofpanama.org; Ambassador FEDERICO A. HUMBERT ARIAS.

Papua New Guinea: 1779 Massachusetts Ave, NW, Suite 805, Washington, DC 20036; tel. (202) 745-3680; fax (202) 745-3679; e-mail info@pngembassy.org; internet www.pngembassy.org; Ambassador EVAN JEREMY PAKI.

Paraguay: 2400 Massachusetts Ave, NW, Washington, DC 20008; tel. (202) 483-6960; fax (202) 234-4508; Ambassador JAMES SPALDING HELLMERS.

Peru: 1700 Massachusetts Ave, NW, Washington, DC 20036; tel. (202) 833-9860; fax (202) 659-8124; e-mail webadmin@embassyofperu.us; internet www.peruvianembassy.us; Ambassador FELIPE ORTIZ DE ZEVALLOS MADUEÑO.

Philippines: 1600 Massachusetts Ave, NW, Washington, DC 20036-2274; tel. (202) 467-9300; fax (202) 467-9417; e-mail info@philippineembassy-usa.org; internet www.philippineembassy-usa.org; Ambassador WILLY C. GAA.

Poland: 2640 16th St, NW, Washington, DC 20009; tel. (202) 234-3800; fax (202) 328-6271; e-mail polemb.info@earthlink.net; internet www.polandembassy.org; Ambassador ROBERT KUPIECKI.

Portugal: 2125 Kalorama Rd, NW, Washington, DC 20008; tel. (202) 328-8610; fax (202) 462-3726; internet www.portugalemb.org; Ambassador JOÃO DE VALLERA.

Qatar: 2555 M St, NW, Washington, DC 20037-1305; tel. (202) 274-1600; fax (202) 237-0061; e-mail info@qatarembassy.net; internet www.qatarembassy.net; Ambassador ALI BIN FAHAD AL-HAJRI.

Romania: 1607 23rd St, NW, Washington, DC 20008; tel. (202) 232-4846; fax (202) 232-4748; e-mail info@roembus.org; internet www.roembus.org; Ambassador ADRIAN COSMIN VIERITA.

Russia: 2650 Wisconsin Ave, NW, Washington, DC 20007; tel. (202) 298-5700; fax (202) 298-5735; e-mail russianembassy@mindspring.com; internet www.russianembassy.org; Ambassador SERGEY I. KISLYAK.

Rwanda: 1714 New Hampshire Ave, NW, Washington, DC 20009; tel. (202) 232-2882; fax (202) 232-4544; e-mail rwandaembassy@rwandaembassy.org; internet www.rwandaembassy.org; Ambassador JAMES KIMONYO.

THE UNITED STATES OF AMERICA

Saint Christopher and Nevis: 3216 New Mexico Ave, NW, Washington, DC 20016; tel. (202) 686-2636; fax (202) 686-5740; e-mail info@stkittsnevis.org; Ambassador (vacant).

Saint Lucia: OECS Bldg, 3216 New Mexico Ave, NW, Washington, DC 20016; tel. (202) 364-6792; fax (202) 364-6723; e-mail eofsaintlu@aol.com; Ambassador MICHAEL LOUIS.

Saint Vincent and the Grenadines: 3216 New Mexico Ave, NW, Washington, DC 20016; tel. (202) 364-6730; fax (202) 364-6736; e-mail mail@embvsg.com; internet www.embvsg.com; Ambassador LA CELIA PRINCE.

Samoa: 800 Second Ave, Suite 400J, New York, NY 10017; tel. (212) 599-6196; fax (212) 599-0797; e-mail samoa@un.int; Ambassador ALI'IOAIGA FETURI ELISAIA.

São Tomé and Príncipe: 400 Park Ave, 7th floor, New York, NY 10022; tel. (212) 317-0580; e-mail stp@un.int; Ambassador OVIDIO MANUEL BARBOSA PEQUENO.

Saudi Arabia: 601 New Hampshire Ave, NW, Washington, DC 20037; tel. (202) 342-3800; fax (202) 944-5983; e-mail info@saudiembassy.net; internet www.saudiembassy.net; Ambassador ADEL DIN AHMED AL-JUBEIR.

Senegal: 2112 Wyoming Ave, NW, Washington, DC 20008; tel. (202) 234-0540; fax (202) 332-6315; Ambassador Dr AMADOU LAMINE BA.

Serbia: 2134 Kalorama Rd, NW, Washington, DC 20008; tel. (202) 332-0333; fax (202) 332-3933; e-mail info@serbiaembusa.org; internet www.serbiaembusa.org; Ambassador Dr IVAN VUJAČIĆ.

Seychelles: 800 Second Ave, Suite 900C, New York, NY 10017; tel. (212) 687-9766; fax (212) 972-1786; Ambassador RONALD JEAN JUMEAU.

Sierra Leone: 1701 19th St, NW, Washington, DC 20009; tel. (202) 939-9261; fax (202) 483-1793; Ambassador BOCKARI KORTU STEVENS.

Singapore: 3501 International Pl., NW, Washington, DC 20008; tel. (202) 537-3100; fax (202) 537-0876; e-mail singemb_was@sgmfa.gov.sg; internet www.mfa.gov.sg/washington; Ambassador HENG CHEE CHAN.

Slovakia: 3523 International Court, NW, Suite 210, Washington, DC 20008; tel. (202) 237-1054; fax (202) 237-6438; e-mail information@slovakembassy-us.org; internet www.slovakembassy-us.org; Ambassador PETER BURIAN.

Slovenia: 2410 California St, NW, Washington, DC 20008; tel. (201) 667-5363; fax (202) 667-4563; e-mail vwa@gov.si; internet www.embassy.si/washington; Ambassador ROMAN KIRN.

Solomon Islands: 800 Second Ave, Suite 400L, New York, NY 10017; tel. (212) 599-6192; fax (212) 661-8925; e-mail simny@solomons.com; Ambassador COLIN D. BECK.

South Africa: 3051 Massachusetts Ave, NW, Washington, DC 20008; tel. (202) 232-4400; fax (202) 265-1607; e-mail info@saembassy.org; internet www.saembassy.org; Ambassador BARBARA MASEKELA.

Spain: 2375 Pennsylvania Ave, NW, Washington, DC 20037; tel. (202) 452-0100; fax (202) 833-5670; e-mail embespus@mail.mae.us; internet www.spainemb.org; Ambassador JORGE DEZCALLAR DE MAZARREDO.

Sri Lanka: 2148 Wyoming Ave, NW, Washington, DC 20008; tel. (202) 483-4025; fax (202) 232-7181; e-mail slembassy@usa.org; internet www.slembassyusa.org; Ambassador JALIYA WICKRAMASURIYA.

Sudan: 2210 Massachusetts Ave, NW, Washington, DC 20008; tel. (202) 338-8565; fax (202) 667-2406; e-mail info@sudanembassy.org; internet www.sudanembassy.org; Chargé d'affaires a.i. AKEC KHOC ACIEW KHOC.

Suriname: 4301 Connecticut Ave, NW, Suite 460, Washington, DC 20008; tel. (202) 244-7488; fax (202) 244-5878; e-mail esuriname@covad.net; internet www.surinameembassy.org; Ambassador JACQUES R. C. KROSS.

Swaziland: 1712 New Hampshire Ave, NW, Washington, DC 20009; tel. (202) 234-5002; fax (202) 234-8254; e-mail swaziland@compuserve.com; Ambassador EPHRAIM MANDLENKOSI M. HLOPHE.

Sweden: 2900 K St, NW, Washington, DC 20007; tel. (202) 467-2600; fax (202) 467-2699; e-mail ambassaden.washington@foreign.ministry.se; internet www.swedenabroad.com/washington; Ambassador JONAS HAFSTRÖM.

Switzerland: 2900 Cathedral Ave, NW, Washington, DC 20008; tel. (202) 745-7900; fax (202) 387-2564; e-mail was.vertretung@eda.admin.ch; internet www.swissemb.org; Ambassador URS JOHANN ZISWILER.

Syria: 2215 Wyoming Ave, NW, Washington, DC 20008; tel. (202) 232-6313; fax (202) 234-9548; e-mail info@syrembassy.net; internet www.syrianembassy.us; Ambassador IMAD MOUSTAPHA.

Tajikistan: 1005 New Hampshire Ave, NW, Washington, DC 20037; tel. (202) 223-6090; fax (202) 223-6091; e-mail tajikistan@verizon.net; internet www.tjus.org; Ambassador ABDUJABBOR SHIRINOV.

Tanzania: 2139 R St, NW, Washington, DC 20008; tel. (202) 939-6125; fax (202) 797-7408; e-mail ubalozi@tanzaniaembassy-us.org; internet www.tanzaniaembassy-us.org; Ambassador OMBENI SEFUE.

Thailand: 1024 Wisconsin Ave, NW, Washington, DC 20007; tel. (202) 944-3600; fax (202) 944-3611; e-mail info@thaiembdc.org; internet www.thaiembdc.org; Chargé d'affaires a.i. DAMRONG KRAIKRUAN.

Timor-Leste: 3415 Massachusetts Ave, NW, Washington, DC 20008; tel. (202) 965-1515; fax (202) 965-1517; e-mail embtlus@earthlink.net; Chargé d'affaires a.i. JORGE CAMEO.

Togo: 2208 Massachusetts Ave, NW, Washington, DC 20008; tel. (202) 234-4212; fax (202) 232-3190; Chargé d'affaires a.i. T. H. LOREMPO LANDJERGUE.

Tonga: 250 East 51st St, New York, NY 10022; tel. (917) 369-1025; fax (917) 369-1024; Ambassador FEKITAMOELOA ʻUTOIKAMANU.

Trinidad and Tobago: 1708 Massachusetts Ave, NW, Washington, DC 20036; tel. (202) 467-6490; fax (202) 785-3130; e-mail info@ttembwash.com; internet www.bordeglobal.com/ttembassy; Ambassador GLENDA MOREAN-PHILLIP.

Tunisia: 1515 Massachusetts Ave, NW, Washington, DC 20005; tel. (202) 862-1850; fax (202) 862-1858; Ambassador HABIB MANSOUR.

Turkey: 2525 Massachusetts Ave, NW, Washington, DC 20008; tel. (202) 612-6700; fax (202) 612-6744; e-mail contact@turkishembassy.org; internet www.turkishembassy.org; Ambassador NABI ŞENSOY.

Turkmenistan: 2207 Massachusetts Ave, NW, Washington, DC 20008; tel. (202) 588-1500; fax (202) 588-0697; e-mail turkmen@mindspring.com; internet www.turkmenistanembassy.org; Ambassador MERET BAIRAMOVICH ORAZOV.

Uganda: 5911 16th St, NW, Washington, DC 20011; tel. (202) 726-7100; fax (202) 726-1727; e-mail info@ugandaembassyus.org; internet www.ugandaembassy.com; Ambassador PEREZI KARUKUBIRO KAMUNANWIRE.

Ukraine: 3350 M St, NW, Washington, DC 20007; tel. (202) 333-0606; fax (202) 333-0817; e-mail mail@ukremb.com; internet www.ukraineinfo.us; Ambassador OLEH SHAMSHUR.

United Arab Emirates: 3422 International Court, NW, Washington, DC 20008; tel. (202) 243-2400; fax (202) 243-2432; e-mail info@uaeembassy-usa.org; internet www.uae-embassy.org; Ambassador YOUSEF AL OTAIBA.

United Kingdom: 3100 Massachusetts Ave, NW, Washington, DC 20008; tel. (202) 588-7800; fax (202) 588-7870; e-mail washi@fco.gov.uk; internet www.britainusa.com; Ambassador Sir NIGEL SHEINWALD.

Uruguay: 1913 Eye St, NW, Washington, DC 20006; tel. (202) 331-1313; fax (202) 331-8142; e-mail uruwashi@uruwashi.org; internet www.uruwashi.org; Ambassador CARLOS A. GIANELLI DEROIS.

Uzbekistan: 1746 Massachusetts Ave, NW, Washington, DC 20036; tel. (202) 887-5300; fax (202) 293-6804; e-mail info@uzbekistan.org; internet www.uzbekistan.org; Ambassador ABDULAZIZ KOMILOV.

Venezuela: 1099 30th St, NW, Washington, DC 20007; tel. (202) 342-2214; fax (202) 342-6820; e-mail apaiva@embavenez-us.org; internet www.embavenez-us.org; Chargé d'affaires a.i. ANGELO SANTOS.

Viet Nam: 1233 20th St, NW, Suite 400, Washington, DC 20036; tel. (202) 861-0737; fax (202) 861-0917; e-mail info@vietnamembassy.us; internet www.vietnamembassy-usa.org; Ambassador LE CONG PHUNG.

Yemen: 2319 Wyoming Ave, NW, Washington, DC 20008; tel. (202) 965-4760; fax (202) 337-2017; e-mail information@yemenembassy.org; internet www.yemenembassy.org; Ambassador ABDULWAHAB ABDULLA AL-HAJJRI.

Zambia: 2419 Massachusetts Ave, NW, Washington, DC 20008; tel. (202) 265-9717; fax (202) 332-0826; e-mail info@zambiainfo.org; internet www.zambiaembassy.org; Ambassador Dr INONGE MBIKUSITA LEWANIKA.

Zimbabwe: 1608 New Hampshire Ave, NW, Washington, DC 20009; tel. (202) 332-7100; fax (202) 483-9326; e-mail info@zimbabwe-embassy.us; Ambassador MACHIVENYIKA TOBIAS MAPURANGA.

Judicial System

Each state has a judicial system structured similarly to the Federal system, with a Supreme Court and subsidiary courts, to deal with cases arising under State Law. These courts have jurisdiction in most criminal and civil actions. Each state has its own bar association of lawyers and its own legal code.

THE UNITED STATES OF AMERICA

Supreme Court of the United States

Supreme Court Bldg, 1 First St, NE, Washington, DC 20543; tel. (202) 479-3211; fax (202) 479-2971; internet www.supremecourtus.gov.

The Supreme Court is the only Federal Court established by the Constitution. It is the highest court in the nation, comprising a Chief Justice and eight Associate Justices. Appointments, which are for life or until voluntary retirement, are made by the President, subject to confirmation by the US Senate.

Chief Justice: JOHN G. ROBERTS, Jr (appointed 2005).

Associate Justices: JOHN PAUL STEVENS (1975), ANTONIN SCALIA (1986), ANTHONY M. KENNEDY (1988), DAVID H. SOUTER (1990), CLARENCE THOMAS (1991), RUTH BADER GINSBURG (1993), STEPHEN G. BREYER (1994), SAMUEL A. ALITO, Jr (2006).

US Courts of Appeal

Administrative Office of the US Courts, Washington, DC 20544; tel. (202) 502-2600; internet www.uscourts.gov.

The USA is divided into 12 judicial circuits, in each of which there is one Court of Appeals. The Court of Appeals for the Federal Circuit has nation-wide specialized jurisdiction.

Federal Courts hear cases involving federal law, cases involving participants from more than one state, cases involving crimes committed in more than one state, and civil or corporate cases that cross state lines. Federal District Courts, of which there are 94, are the courts of first instance for most federal suits.

Federal Circuit: PAUL R. MICHEL (Chief Judge), PAULINE NEWMAN, HALDANE ROBERT MAYER, ALAN D. LOURIE, RANDALL R. RADER, ALVIN A. SCHALL, WILLIAM CURTIS BRYSON, ARTHUR J. GAJARSA, RICHARD LINN, TIMOTHY B. DYK, SHARON PROST, KIMBERLEY MOORE.

District of Columbia Circuit: DAVID B. SENTELLE (Chief Judge), DOUGLAS H. GINSBURG, KAREN LECRAFT HENDERSON, A. RAYMOND RANDOLPH, JUDITH W. ROGERS, DAVID S. TATEL, MERRICK B. GARLAND, JANICE ROGERS BROWN, THOMAS B. GRIFFITH, BRETT M. KAVANAUGH.

First Circuit (Maine, Massachusetts, New Hampshire, Rhode Island, Puerto Rico): SANDRA L. LYNCH (Chief Judge), JUAN R. TORRUELLA, MICHAEL BOUDIN, KERMIT V. LIPEZ, JEFFREY R. HOWARD.

Second Circuit (Connecticut, New York, Vermont): DENNIS JACOBS (Chief Judge), GUIDO CALABRESI, JOSÉ A. CABRANES, ROSEMARY S. POOLER, ROBERT D. SACK, SONIA SOTOMAYOR, ROBERT A. KATZMANN, BARRINGTON D. PARKER, REENA RAGGI, RICHARD C. WESLEY, PETER W. HALL, DEBRA ANN LIVINGSTON.

Third Circuit (Delaware, New Jersey, Pennsylvania, Virgin Islands): ANTHONY J. SCIRICA (Chief Judge), DOLORES K. SLOVITER, THEODORE A. MCKEE, MARJORIE O. RENDELL, MARYANNE TRUMP BARRY, THOMAS L. AMBRO, JULIO M. FUENTES, D. BROOKS SMITH, D. MICHAEL FISHER, MICHAEL A. CHAGARES, KENT A. JORDAN, THOMAS M. HARDIMAN.

Fourth Circuit (Maryland, North Carolina, South Carolina, Virginia, West Virginia): KAREN J. WILLIAMS (Chief Judge), J. HARVIE WILKINSON, III, PAUL V. NIEMEYER, M. BLANE MICHAEL, DIANA GRIBBON MOTZ, WILLIAM B. TRAXLER, Jr, ROBERT B. KING, ROGER L. GREGORY, DENNIS W. SHEDD, ALLYSON K. DUNCAN, G. STEVEN AGEE.

Fifth Circuit (Louisiana, Mississippi, Texas): EDITH H. JONES (Chief Judge), CAROLYN DINEEN KING, E. GRADY JOLLY, W. EUGENE DAVIS, JERRY E. SMITH, JACQUES L. WIENER, Jr, RHESA H. BARKSDALE, EMILIO M. GARZA, FORTUNATO P. BENAVIDES, CARL E. STEWART, JAMES L. DENNIS, EDITH BROWN CLEMENT, EDWARD C. PRADO, PRISCILLA R. OWEN, JENNIFER W. ELROD, LESLIE SOUTHWICK, CATHARINA HAYNES.

Sixth Circuit (Kentucky, Michigan, Ohio, Tennessee): DANNY J. BOGGS (Chief Judge), BOYCE F. MARTIN, Jr, ALICE M. BATCHELDER, KAREN NELSON MOORE, RANSEY GUY COLE, Jr, ERIC L. CLAY, RONALD LEE GILMAN, JULIA SMITH GIBBONS, JOHN M. ROGERS, JEFFREY S. SUTTON, DEBORAH L. COOK, DAVID W. MCKEAGUE, RICHARD ALLEN GRIFFIN, RAYMOND M. KETHLEDGE, HELENE N. WHITE.

Seventh Circuit (Illinois, Indiana, Wisconsin): FRANK H. EASTERBROOK (Chief Judge), WILLIAM J. BAUER, RICHARD D. CUDAHY, RICHARD A. POSNER, JOHN L. COFFEY, JOEL M. FLAUM, KENNETH F. RIPPLE, DANIEL A. MANION, MICHAEL S. KANNE, ILANA DIAMOND ROVNER, DIANE P. WOOD, TERENCE T. EVANS, ANN CLAIRE WILLIAMS, DIANE S. SYKES, JOHN D. TINDER, DAVID HAMILTON.

Eighth Circuit (Arkansas, Iowa, Minnesota, Missouri, Nebraska, North Dakota, South Dakota): JAMES B. LOKEN (Chief Judge), ROGER L. WOLLMAN, DIANA E. MURPHY, KERMIT E. BYE, WILLIAM J. RILEY, MICHAEL J. MELLOY, LAVENSKI R. SMITH, STEVEN M. COLLOTON, RAYMOND W. GRUENDER, DUANE BENTON, BOBBY E. SHEPHERD.

Ninth Circuit (Alaska, Arizona, California, Guam, Hawaii, Idaho, Montana, Nevada, Northern Mariana Islands, Oregon, Washington): ALEX KOZINSKI (Chief Judge), MARY M. SCHROEDER, HARRY PREGERSON, STEPHEN REINHARDT, DIARMUID F. O'SCANNLAIN, PAMELA ANN RYMER, ANDREW J. KLEINFELD, MICHAEL DALY HAWKINS, SIDNEY R. THOMAS, BARRY G. SILVERMAN, SUSAN P. GRABER, M. MARGARET MCKEOWN, KIM MCLANE WARDLAW, WILLIAM A. FLETCHER, RAYMOND C. FISHER, RONALD M. GOULD, RICHARD A. PAEZ, MARSHA S. BERZON, RICHARD C. TALLMAN, JOHNNIE B. RAWLINSON, RICHARD R. CLIFTON, JAY S. BYBEE, CONSUELO M. CALLAHAN, CARLOS T. BEA, MILAN D. SMITH, Jr, SANDRA S. IKUTA, N. RANDY SMITH.

Tenth Circuit (Colorado, Kansas, New Mexico, Oklahoma, Utah, Wyoming): ROBERT H. HENRY (Chief Judge), DEANELL REECE TACHA, PAUL J. KELLY, MARY BECK BRISCOE, CARLOS F. LUCERO, MICHAEL R. MURPHY, HARRIS L. HARTZ, TERRENCE L. O'BRIEN, MICHAEL W. MCCONNELL, TIMOTHY M. TYMKOVICH, NEIL M. GORSUCH, JEROME A. HOLMES.

Eleventh Circuit (Alabama, Florida, Georgia): J. L. EDMONDSON (Chief Judge), GERALD B. TJOFLAT, R. LANIER ANDERSON, STANLEY F. BIRCH, Jr, JOEL F. DUBINA, SUSAN H. BLACK, EDWARD E. CARNES, ROSEMARY BARKETT, FRANK M. HULL, STANLEY MARCUS, CHARLES R. WILSON, WILLIAM H. PRYOR, Jr.

United States Court of Federal Claims

717 Madison Pl., NW, Washington, DC 20005; tel. (202) 357-6400; internet www.uscfc.uscourts.gov.

Judges: EDWARD J. DAMICH (Chief Judge), CHRISTINE ODELL COOK MILLER, MARIAN BLANK HORN, FRANCIS M. ALLEGRA, LAWRENCE M. BASKIR, LYNN J. BUSH, NANCY B. FIRESTONE, LAWRENCE J. BLOCK, MARY ELLEN COSTER WILLIAMS, CHARLES F. LETTOW, SUSAN G. BRADEN, VICTOR J. WOLSKI, GEORGE W. MILLER, THOMAS C. WHEELER, MARGARET M. SWEENEY.

US Court of International Trade

1 Federal Plaza, New York, NY 10278-0001; tel. (212) 264-2800; fax (212) 264-1085; internet www.cit.uscourts.gov.

Judges: JANE A. RESTANI (Chief Judge), GREGORY W. CARMAN, DONALD C. POGUE, EVAN J. WALLACH, JUDITH M. BARZILAY, DELISSA A. RIDGWAY, RICHARD K. EATON, TIMOTHY C. STANCEU, LEO M. GORDON.

United States Tax Court

400 Second St, NW, Washington, DC 20217; tel. (202) 521-0700; internet www.ustaxcourt.gov.

Judges: JOHN O. COLVIN (Chief Judge), MARY ANN COHEN, MAURICE B. FOLEY, JOSEPH H. GALE, JOSEPH R. GOEKE, DAVID GUSTAFSON, HARRY A. HAINES, JAMES S. HALPERN, MARK V. HOLMES, DIANE L. KROUPA, L. PAIGE MARVEL, RICHARD T. MORRISON, ELIZABETH C. PARIS, MICHAEL B. THORNTON, JUAN F. VASQUEZ, THOMAS B. WELLS, ROBERT A. WHERRY, Jr.

Religion

Christianity is the predominant religion. The largest single denomination is the Roman Catholic Church. Other major groups in terms of membership are the Baptist, Methodist, Lutheran and Orthodox churches. Numerous other beliefs are represented, the largest in terms of adherents being Judaism, Islam and Buddhism.

CHRISTIANITY

National Council of the Churches of Christ in the USA: 475 Riverside Dr., Suite 880, New York, NY 10115-0050; tel. (212) 870-2025; fax (212) 870-3112; e-mail webmaster@ncccusa.org; internet www.ncccusa.org; f. 1950; an ecumenical org. of 35 Protestant and Orthodox denominations, representing 100,000 congregations of c. 45m. mems; Pres. VICKAN AYKAZIAN; Gen. Sec. Rev. Dr MICHAEL KINNAMON.

The Anglican Communion

The Episcopal Church in the USA: 815 Second Ave, New York, NY 10017-4564; tel. (212) 716-6273; fax (212) 697-5892; e-mail pboffice@episcopalchurch.org; internet www.iamepiscopalian.org; f. 1607; mem. of the Worldwide Anglican Communion and World Council of Churches; 7,200 parishes and missions; 2.4m. mems (2008); Presiding Bishop Most Rev. KATHARINE JEFFERTS SCHORI; Exec. Officer and Sec. Rev. Dr GREGORY S. STRAUB.

The Baptist Church

Members (1998 estimate): 33.1m., in 15 bodies, of which the following have the greatest number of members:

American Baptist Association: 4605 North State Line Ave, Texarkana, TX 75503-2928; tel. (903) 792-2783; fax (903) 792-8128; e-mail bssc@abaptist.org; internet www.abaptist.org; f. 1905; 1,867 churches; 280,973 mems (2000); Pres. Dr NEAL CLARK.

American Baptist Churches in the USA (ABCUSA): POB 851, Valley Forge, PA 19482-0851; 588 North Gulph Rd, King of Prussia, PA 19406; tel. (610) 768-2000; fax (610) 768-2275; e-mail cathy.brubaker@abc-usa.org; internet www.abc-usa.org; f. 1907; mem. of the World Council of Churches; 5,538 churches (2009); 1.5m. mems

THE UNITED STATES OF AMERICA

(2008); Pres. Rev. Mary Armacost Hulst; Gen. Sec. Rev. Dr A. Roy Medley.

Conservative Baptist Association of America: 3686 Stagecoach Rd, Unit F, Longmont, CO 80504-5660; tel. (720) 283-3030; fax (303) 772-5690; e-mail info@cbamerica.org; internet www.cbamerica.org; f. 1947; 1,200 churches; 200,000 mems; Nat. Exec. Dir Rev. Stephen LeBar.

General Association of Regular Baptist Churches: 1300 North Meacham Rd, Schaumburg, IL 60173-4806; tel. (888) 588-1600; fax (847) 843-3757; internet www.garbc.org; 1,330 churches; 245,636 mems (2000); Nat. Rep. Rev. John Greening.

National Baptist Convention, USA: 1700 Baptist World Center Dr., Nashville, TN 37207; tel. (615) 228-6292; fax (615) 262-3917; e-mail president@nationalbaptist.com; internet www.nationalbaptist.com; f. 1880; mem. of the World Council of Churches; 2,500 churches; 7.5m. mems; Pres. Dr William J. Shaw; Gen. Sec. Dr Harry Blake.

Southern Baptist Convention: 901 Commerce St, Nashville, TN 37203-3629; tel. (615) 244-2355; fax (615) 742-8919; e-mail cpmissions@sbc.net; internet www.sbc.net; f. 1845; 42,972 churches; 16.4m. mems (2003); Pres. Exec. Cttee Dr Morris H. Chapman.

The Lutheran Church

Members (1998 estimate): 8.3m., in 10 bodies, of which the following have the greatest number of members:

Evangelical Lutheran Church in America: 8765 West Higgins Rd, Chicago, IL 60631; tel. (773) 380-2700; fax (773) 380-1465; e-mail info@elca.org; internet www.elca.org; f. 1988; mem. of the World Council of Churches; 10,448 churches; 4.7m. mems (2007); Presiding Bishop Rev. Mark Stephen Hanson; Sec. David D. Swartling.

Lutheran Church—Missouri Synod: 1333 South Kirkwood Rd, St Louis, MO 63122-7295; tel. (314) 965-9000; fax (314) 996-1016; e-mail infocenter@lcms.org; internet www.lcms.org; f. 1847; 6,150 churches; 2.5m. mems (2007); Pres. Dr Gerald B. Kieschnick; Sec. Dr Raymond Hartwig.

The Methodist Church

Members (1998 estimate): 13.4m. in eight bodies, of which the following have the greatest number of members:

African Methodist Episcopal Church: 500 Eighth Ave South, Nashville, TN 37203; tel. (615) 254-0911; fax (615) 254-0912; e-mail cio@ame-church.com; internet www.ame-church.com; f. 1816; mem. of the Churches Uniting in Christ and World Council of Churches; 4,174 churches; 2.5m. mems (1999); Sr Bishop John Bryant; Gen. Sec. Dr Clement W. Fugh.

African Methodist Episcopal Zion Church: 3225 Sugar Creek Rd, POB 32843, Charlotte, NC 28269; tel. (704) 599-4630; e-mail admin@amez.org; internet www.amez.org; f. 1796; mem. of the Churches Uniting in Christ; 3,236 churches; 1.4m. mems (2003); Gen. Sec. Rev. Dr W. Robert Johnson, III.

United Methodist Church: POB 320, Nashville, TN 37202; e-mail umc@umcom.org; internet www.umc.org; f. 1968; mem. of the Churches Uniting in Christ and World Council of Churches; 34,892 churches; 8.2m. mems (2003); President of Council of Bishops Bishop Gregory Palmer; Exec. Sec. Ernest S. Lyght.

The Orthodox Churches

Members (2000 estimate): 5.8m. in 12 bodies, of which the following have the greatest number of members:

Antiochian Orthodox Christian Archdiocese of North America (Greek Orthodox Patriarchate of Antioch and all the East): 358 Mountain Rd, POB 5238, Englewood, NJ 07631-3798; tel. (201) 871-1355; fax (201) 871-7954; e-mail archdiocese@antiochian.org; internet www.antiochian.org; f. 1895; mem. of the World Council of Churches; 210 churches; 82,374 mems (2000); Primate Metropolitan Philip (Saliba); Auxiliaries Bishop Antoun (Khouri), Bishop Basil (Essey), Bishop Joseph (Zehlaoui), Bishop Alexander (Mufarrij), Bishop Mark (Maymon), Bishop Thomas (Joseph).

Armenian Apostolic Church of America: *Eastern Prelacy:* 138 East 39th St, New York, NY 10016; tel. (212) 689-7810; fax (212) 689-7168; e-mail email@armenianprelacy.org; internet www.armenianprelacy.org; *Western Prelacy:* 6252 Honolulu Ave, Suite 100, La Crescenta, CA 91214; tel. (818) 248-7737; fax (818) 248-7745; e-mail prelacy@aol.com; f. 1887; mem. of the World Council of Churches; 38 churches; 23,200 mems (2000); Prelate (Eastern Prelacy) Archbishop Oshagan Choloyan; Prelate (Western Prelacy) Archbishop Moushegh Mardirosian.

Armenian Church of America: *Eastern Diocese:*, 630 Second Ave, New York, NY 10016; tel. (212) 686-0710; fax (212) 686-0245; e-mail primate@armenianchurch.net; internet www.armenianchurch.net; *Western Diocese:*, 3325 North Glenoaks Blvd, Burbank, CA 91504; tel. (818) 558-7474; fax (818) 558-6333; e-mail info@armenianchurchwd.com; internet www.armenianchurchwd.com; f. 1889; mem. of the World Council of Churches; 89 churches; 45,800 mems (2000); Primate (Eastern Diocese) Archbishop Khajag Barsamian; Primate (Western Diocese) Archbishop Hovnan Derderian.

Greek Orthodox Archdiocese of America: 8–10 East 79th St, New York, NY 10021-0191; tel. (212) 570-3500; fax (212) 774-0251; e-mail archdiocese@goarch.org; internet www.goarch.org; f. 1921 as Greek Orthodox Archdiocese of North and South America; mem. of the World Council of Churches; 540 churches; 1.5m. mems (2008); Primate Archbishop Dimitrios; Chancellor Bishop Savas (of Troas).

Orthodox Church in America: POB 675, Syosset, NY 11791; tel. (516) 922-0550; fax (516) 922-0954; e-mail info@oca.org; internet www.oca.org; f. 1794; fmrly Russian Orthodox Greek Catholic Church of North America; mem. of the World Council of Churches; 456 churches; 115,000 mems (2000); Primate Metropolitan Herman; Chancellor Archpriest Alexander Garklavs.

The Albanian, Bulgarian, Coptic, Romanian, Russian, Serbian, Syrian and Ukrainian Orthodox Churches are also represented.

The Presbyterian Church

Members (1998 estimate): 4.1m. in nine bodies, of which the following have the greatest number of members:

Presbyterian Church in America: 1700 North Brown Rd, Lawrenceville, GA 30043-8143; tel. (678) 825-1000; fax (678) 825-1001; e-mail ac@pcanet.org; internet www.pcanet.org; f. 1973; 1,600 churches; 300,000 mems; Moderator E. J. Nusbaum; Stated Clerk Dr L. Roy Taylor.

Presbyterian Church (USA): 100 Witherspoon St, Louisville, KY 40202-1396; tel. (502) 569-5000; fax (502) 569-8080; e-mail presbytel@pcusa.org; internet www.pcusa.org; f. 1983; mem. of the Churches Uniting in Christ and World Council of Churches; 11,100 churches; 2.4m. mems (2007); Stated Clerk Gradye Parsons; Moderator Bruce Reyes-Chow; Exec. Dir Linda Valentine.

The Roman Catholic Church

At December 2006 there were 194 dioceses and eparchies, with some 66.6m. mems, equivalent to 22% of the population.

United States Conference of Catholic Bishops: 3211 Fourth St, NE, Washington, DC 20017-1194; tel. (202) 541-3000; fax (202) 541-3322; internet www.usccb.org; f. 2001 by merger of the Nat. Conference of Catholic Bishops (f. 1966) and US Catholic Conference (f. 1966); Pres. Cardinal Francis George (Archbishop of Chicago); Gen. Sec. Mgr David Malloy.

Archbishops

Anchorage: Roger L. Schwietz.
Atlanta: Wilton D. Gregory.
Baltimore: Edwin F. O'Brien.
Boston: Séan Patrick O'Malley.
Chicago: Cardinal Francis E. George.
Cincinnati: Daniel E. Pilarczyk.
Denver: Charles J. Chaput.
Detroit: Allen Henry Vigneron.
Dubuque: Jerome G. Hanus.
Galveston-Houston: Cardinal Daniel N. DiNardo.
Hartford: Henry J. Mansell.
Indianapolis: Daniel M. Buechlein.
Kansas City in Kansas: Joseph F. Nauman.
Los Angeles: Cardinal Roger M. Mahony.
Louisville: Joseph E. Kurtz.
Miami: John C. Favalora.
Milwaukee: (vacant).
Mobile: Thomas John Rodi.
Newark: John Joseph Myers.
New Orleans: Alfred C. Hughes.
New York: Timothy M. Dolan.
Oklahoma City: Eusebius J. Beltran.
Omaha: Elden F. Curtiss.
Philadelphia: Cardinal Justin F. Rigali, Stefan Soroka (Ukrainian, Byzantine Rite).
Pittsburgh: Basil Myron Schott.
Portland in Oregon: John G. Vlazny.
Saint Louis: (vacant).
Saint Paul and Minneapolis: John Clayton Nienstedt.
San Antonio: José H. Gómez.
San Francisco: George H. Niederauer.

THE UNITED STATES OF AMERICA

Santa Fe: Michael J. Sheehan.
Seattle: Alexander J. Brunett.
Washington: Donald W. Wuerl.

Other Christian Churches

Assemblies of God: 1445 North Boonville Ave, Springfield, MO 65802-1894; tel. (417) 862-5554; fax (417) 863-6614; e-mail asstsup@ag.org; internet www.ag.org; f. 1914; 2.8m. mems in 12,311 churches in USA (2006); Gen. Supt George O. Wood; Gen. Sec. James T. Bradford.

Christian Church (Disciples of Christ) in the USA and Canada: 130 East Washington St, POB 1986, Indianapolis, IN 46206-1986; tel. (317) 635-3100; fax (317) 635-3700; e-mail news@cm.disciples.org; internet www.disciples.org; f. 1804; 3,754 congregations (2008); 691,160 mems (2008); mem. of the Churches Uniting in Christ and World Council of Churches; Gen. Minister and Pres. Rev. Dr Sharon E. Watkins.

Christian Reformed Church in North America: 2850 Kalamazoo Ave, SE, Grand Rapids, MI 49560; tel. (616) 224-0832; fax (616) 224-5895; e-mail crcna@crcna.org; internet www.crcna.org; f. 1857; Calvinist; 1,023 churches; 266,000 mems (USA and Canada); Exec. Dir Rev. Gerard L. Dykstra.

Church of Christ: POB 472, Independence, MO 64051; tel. (816) 833-3995; fax (816) 833-0210; e-mail cofctl@sbcglobal; internet www.churchofchrist-tl.org; f. 1830; Sec. Council of Apostles Gen. Church Sec. Harvey E. Seibel.

Church of Christ, Scientist: 210 Massachusetts Ave, Boston, MA 02115; tel. (617) 450-2000; fax (617) 450-3554; e-mail info@churchofchristscientist.org; internet www.tfccs.com; f. 1879; 2,400 congregations world-wide; Pres. Mark Swinney; Man. Philip G. Davis.

Church of God in Christ: Mason Temple, 939 Mason St, Memphis, TN 38126; e-mail laity@cogic.org; internet www.cogic.org; f. 1907; 15,300 churches; 5.5m. mems (1991); Presiding Bishop Charles Edward Blake, Sr.

Church of Jesus Christ of Latter-day Saints (Mormon): 47 East South Temple St, Salt Lake City, UT 84150-0001; tel. (801) 240-1000; fax (801) 240-2033; internet www.lds.org; f. 1830; 12,112 wards and brs (congregations) in USA; 5.5m. mems in USA (2003); Pres. Thomas S. Monson.

Church of the Nazarene: 6401 The Paseo, Kansas City, MO 64131; tel. (913) 577-0500; fax (913) 577-0858; e-mail gensec@nazarene.org; internet www.nazarene.org; f. 1908; 22,807 congregations; 1.8m. mems (2008); Gen. Sec. David P. Wilson.

Friends United Meeting: 101 Quaker Hill Dr., Richmond, IN 47374-1980; tel. (765) 962-7573; fax (765) 966-1293; e-mail info@fum.org; internet www.fum.org; f. 1902; Quaker; mem. of the World Council of Churches; 44,000 mems (USA and Canada); Gen. Sec. Sylvia Graves.

Mariavite Old Catholic Church—Province of North America: 2803 10th St, Wyandotte, MI 48192-4994; tel. and fax (734) 281-3082; e-mail mariaviteocc@hotmail.com; f. 1930; 158 churches; 357,100 mems; Prime Bishop Most Rev. Archbishop Dr Robert R. J. M. Zaborowski.

Reformed Church in America: 475 Riverside Dr., New York, NY 10115-0001; tel. (212) 870-3071; fax (212) 870-2499; e-mail questions@rca.org; internet www.rca.org; f. 1628; Calvinist; mem. of the World Council of Churches; 935 churches; 329,437 mems; Gen. Sec. Rev. Wesley Granberg-Michaelson.

Seventh-day Adventists: 12501 Old Columbia Pike, Silver Spring, MD 20904-6600; tel. (301) 680-6400; fax (301) 680-6464; e-mail info@nad.adventist.org; internet www.nadadventist.org; f. 1863; 5,026 churches; c. 1m. mems (USA and Canada); Pres. Don Schneider; Sec. G. Alexander Bryant.

United Church of Christ: 700 Prospect Ave, Cleveland, OH 44115; tel. (216) 736-2100; fax (216) 736-2103; e-mail guessb@ucc.org; internet www.ucc.org; f. 1957; mem. of the Churches Uniting in Christ and World Council of Churches; 5,633 churches; 1.2m. mems; Gen. Minister and Pres. Rev. John H. Thomas.

United Pentecostal Church International: 8855 Dunn Rd, Hazelwood, MO 63042-2211; tel. (314) 837-7300; fax (314) 837-7304; e-mail info@upci.org; internet www.upci.org; f. 1945 by merger of the Pentecostal Church, Inc, and Pentecostal Assemblies of Jesus Christ; 4,358 churches (USA and Canada); c. 600,000 mems; Gen. Supt Rev. Kenneth N. Haney; Gen. Sec. Jerry Jones.

BAHÁ'Í FAITH

National Spiritual Assembly of Bahá'ís of the United States: External Affairs Office, 1320 19th St, NW, Suite 701, Washington, DC 20036-1610; tel. (202) 833-8990; fax (202) 833-8988; e-mail bahai-info@usbnc.org; internet www.bahai.us; f. 1844 in Persia (Iran); Chair. Jacqueline Left Hand Bull Delahunt; Sec.-Gen. Kenneth E. Bowers.

BUDDHISM

At mid-2000 there were an estimated 2.5m. Buddhists in the USA.

Association of American Buddhists: 301 West 45th St, New York, NY 10036; tel. (212) 489-1075; e-mail iwanttoknow@buddhismonline.us; internet www.buddhismonline.us; f. 1980; 15 regional groups; Pres. Ven. Dr Kevin R. O'Neil.

Buddhist Churches of America: 1710 Octavia St, San Francisco, CA 94109-4341; tel. (415) 776-5600; fax (415) 771-6293; e-mail bcahq@pacbell.net; internet buddhistchurchesofamerica.org; f. 1899; Hongwanji-ha Jodo Shinshu denomination; c. 230,000 mems; Presiding Bishop Socho Koshin Ogui; Exec. Dir Henry Shibata.

HINDUISM

At mid-2000 there were an estimated 1.0m. Hindus in the USA.

Ramakrishna-Vivekananda Center: 17 East 94th St, New York, NY 10128; tel. (212) 534-9445; fax (212) 828-1618; e-mail rvcnewyork@worldnet.att.net; internet www.ramakrishna.org; f. 1933; teachings based on the system of Vedanta; Minister and Spiritual Leader Swami Yuktatmananda; Dir Barry Zelikovsky.

ISLAM

At mid-2000 there were an estimated 4.1m. Muslims in the USA, of whom some 40% were African-American.

Council of Masajid of United States (CMUS): 45 Lilac St, Edison, NJ 08817; tel. (732) 985-3304; fax (732) 572-0486; e-mail dawud10@optonline.net; f. 1978; educational agency representing 650 local groups; Pres. Dawud Assad.

Federation of Islamic Associations in the US and Canada: 25351 Five Mile and Aubery Rd, Redford Township, MI 48239; tel. (313) 534-3295; fax (313) 534-1474; f. 1951; co-ordinating agency for 45 affiliated orgs; Gen. Sec. Nihad Hamed.

Islamic Center of New York: 1711 Third Ave, New York, NY 10029-7303; tel. (212) 722-5234; fax (212) 722-5936; internet www.icnyu.org; f. 1966; Dir Ziyad Monayain.

Islamic Mission of America: 143 State St, Brooklyn, NY 11201; tel. (718) 875-6607; f. 1948; maintains an educational and training institute; 15,000 mems; Chair. Mohamed Kabbaj; Dir Hajj D. A. Haroon.

JUDAISM

In 2004 there were an estimated 6.5m. Jews in North America.

American Jewish Congress: 825 Third Ave, Suite 18, New York, NY 10022; tel. (212) 879-4500; fax (212) 758-1633; e-mail contact@ajcongress.org; internet www.ajcongress.org; f. 1918; 50,000 mems; Chair. Jack Rosen; Pres. Richard S. Gordon.

Central Conference of American Rabbis: 355 Lexington Ave, New York, NY 10017; tel. (212) 972-3636; fax (212) 692-0819; e-mail info@ccarnet.org; internet www.ccarnet.org; f. 1889; organized rabbinate of Reform Judaism; 1,840 mems; Pres. Peter S. Knobel.

The Rabbinical Assembly: 3080 Broadway, New York, NY 10027-4650; tel. (212) 280-6000; fax (212) 749-9166; e-mail info@rabbinicalassembly.org; internet www.rabbinicalassembly.org; f. 1901; 1,550 mems; Pres. Rabbi Alvin K. Berkun; Sec. Rabbi William Gershon.

Union of Orthodox Jewish Congregations of America: 11 Broadway, New York, NY 10004; tel. (212) 563-4000; fax (212) 564-9058; e-mail info@ou.org; internet www.ou.org; f. 1898; 1,000 affiliated congregations representing c. 1.0m. mems; Chair. Harvey Blitz; Pres. Steven J. Savitsky.

Union for Reform Judaism: 633 Third Ave, New York, NY 10017-6778; tel. (212) 650-4000; fax (212) 650-4169; e-mail urj@urj.org; internet urj.org; f. 1873 as the Union of American Hebrew Congregations; present name adopted 2003; more than 900 affiliated congregations representing c. 1.5m. mems; Pres. Rabbi Eric H. Yoffie; Sr Vice-Pres. Rabbi Daniel Freelander.

United Synagogue of Conservative Judaism: 820 Second Ave, New York, NY 10017-4504; tel. (212) 533-7800; e-mail info@uscj.org; internet www.uscj.org; f. 1913; c. 700 affiliated congregations in North America representing c. 1.5m. mems; Pres. Dr Raymond Goldstein; Exec. Vice-Pres. Rabbi Jerome Epstein.

SIKHISM

At mid-2000 there were an estimated 234,000 Sikhs in the USA.

International Sikh Organization: 1901 Pennsylvania Ave, NW, Washington, DC 20006; Pres. Dr Gurmit Singh Aulakh.

THE UNITED STATES OF AMERICA

The Press

The USA publishes more newspapers and periodicals than any other country. Most dailies give a greater emphasis to local news because of the strong interest in local and regional affairs and the decentralized structure of many government services. These factors, together with the distribution problem inherent in the size of the country, are responsible for the lack of national newspapers. In 2007 the Newspaper Association of America (NAA) estimated that some 48.4% of the adult population read a daily newspaper.

Most influential and highly respected among the few newspapers with a national readership are *USA Today*, the *New York Times*, the *Washington Post*, *Los Angeles Times* and *The Wall Street Journal* (the financial and news daily with editions in New York City, California, Illinois and Texas, and a European and an Asian edition).

In 2008, according to the Audit Bureau of Circulations, 53 daily newspapers had circulations of over 250,000 copies. Among the largest of these, in order of daily circulation in 2008, were *USA Today*, *The Wall Street Journal*, *The New York Times*, *Los Angeles Times*, *Chicago Tribune*, *The Washington Post*, *New York Daily News*, *The New York Post*, *The Houston Chronicle* and *The Philadelphia Inquirer*.

In 2007, according to the NAA, there were 1,422 daily newspapers, with a total circulation of 50.7m. copies per day. The Sunday edition is an important and distinctive feature of US newspaper publishing; many Sunday newspapers run to over 300 pages. In 2007 there were 907 Sunday newspapers, with a total circulation of about 51.2m. In 2005 there were 6,659 weekly newspapers.

The famous tradition of press freedom in the USA is grounded in the First Amendment to the Constitution, which declares that 'Congress shall make no law. . . abridging the freedom of speech or of the Press. . .', and confirmed in the legislations of many states, which prohibit any kind of legal restriction on the dissemination of news.

Legislation affecting the Press is both state and federal. A source of controversy between the Press and the courts has been the threat of the encroachment by judicial decrees on the area of courtroom and criminal trial coverage. In 1972 the Supreme Court ruled that journalists were not entitled to refuse to give evidence before grand juries on information they have received confidentially. Since then the frequent issuing of subpoenas to journalists and the gaoling of several reporters for refusing to disclose sources has led to many 'shield' bills being put before Congress and state legislatures demanding immunity for journalists from both federal and state jurisdiction.

In recent years, increased production costs have subjected the industry to considerable economic strain, resulting in mergers and take-overs, a great decline in competition between dailies in the same city, and the appearance of inter-city dailies catering for two or more adjoining centres. A consequence of these trends has been the steady growth of newspaper groups or chains.

The following are among the principal daily newspaper groups:

Advance Publications, Inc: 950 Fingerboard Rd, Staten Island, NY; tel. (212) 286-2860; fax (718) 981-1456; internet www.advance.net; Chair. SAMUEL I. (SI) NEWHOUSE, Jr; Pres. DONALD E. NEWHOUSE; interests in cable television and internet news websites; owns Condé Nast Publications, Parade Publications, Fairchild Publications and American City Business Journals, among others.

American Community Newspapers: 14875 Landmark Blvd, Suite 110, Dallas, TX 75254; tel. (972) 628-4080; fax (972) 801-3496; e-mail gcarr@acnpapers.com; internet www.americancommunitynewspapers.com; CEO GENE M. CARR; 100 publs, incl. the Sun Newspapers group, and four speciality publs; combined circ. c. 1.4m.

Block Communications, Inc (BCI): 6450 Monroe St, Sylvania, OH 43560; tel. (419) 724-6212; e-mail info@blockcommunications.com; internet www.blockcommunications.com; f. 1900; Chair. WILLIAM BLOCK, Jr; Man. Dir ALLAN BLOCK; 2 daily newspapers, *The Pittsburgh Post-Gazette* and *The Toledo Blade*; also owns 2 cable cos, 5 television stations and a telephone co; interests in security, cable construction and advertising.

The Copley Press, Inc: 7776 Ivanhoe Ave, La Jolla, CA 92037; tel. (858) 454-0411; fax (858) 729-7629; internet www.copleynewspapers.com; f. 1928; Chair., Pres. and CEO DAVID C. COPLEY; 9 daily newspapers, incl. *The San Diego Union-Tribune*, 8 weekly newspapers and 1 bi-weekly newspaper; owns the Copley News Service syndicate (f. 1955).

Cox Newspapers, Inc: 6205 Peachtree Dunwoody Rd, Atlanta, GA 30328; tel. (678) 645-0000; e-mail christopher.caneles@coxinc.com; internet www.coxnews.com; f. 1898; Pres. SANDY SCHWARTZ; 17 daily newspapers, incl. *The Atlanta Journal-Constitution*, and 26 weekly newspapers; combined weekday circ. 1.2m., combined Sun. circ. 1.6m.

Dow Jones & Co Inc: 1 World Financial Center, 200 Liberty St, New York, NY 10281; tel. (212) 416-2000; fax (212) 416-3478; internet www.dowjones.com; f. 1882; acquired by News Corporation in December 2007; CEO LES HINTON; publs incl. *The Wall Street Journal*, the weekly financial magazine *Barron's* and the monthly *Far Eastern Economic Review*; also incl. the community newspaper subsidiary

Ottaway Newspapers, Inc (ONI): POB 401, Campbell Hall, NY 10916; tel. (845) 294-8181; e-mail dwaterman@ottaway.com; internet www.ottaway.com; f. 1936; merged with Dow Jones in 1970; Exec. Chair. PATRICK J. PURCELL; 8 daily and 15 weekly newspapers; over 20 other publs; daily print circ. 282,000, Sun. circ. 316,000 (Oct. 2008).

Freedom Communications, Inc: 17666 Fitch, Irvine, CA 92614-6022; tel. (949) 253-2300; fax (949) 474-7675; e-mail info@link.freedom.com; internet www.freedom.com; Chair. THOMAS W. BASSETT; CEO SCOTT N. FLANDERS; 33 daily newspapers, incl. *The Orange County Register*, and 77 weekly publs; combined weekday circ. c. 1m.; owns 8 television stations.

Gannett Co Inc: 7950 Jones Branch Dr., McLean, VA 22107; tel. (703) 854-6000; fax (703) 854-2046; e-mail gcishare@gannett.com; internet www.gannett.com; f. 1906; Chair., Pres. and CEO CRAIG A. DUBOW; 85 daily newspapers, incl. *USA Today*, *Detroit Free Press* and *The Arizona Republic*, c. 900 non-daily publs; combined weekday circ. 7.2m. (of which c. 2.3m. *USA Today*); owns 23 television stations broadcasting to 20m. households; owns and operates Newsquest Media Group (United Kingdom).

Hearst Corpn: Hearst Tower, 12th Floor, 300 West 57th St, New York, NY 10019; tel. (212) 649-4190; fax (212) 649-2108; e-mail hearstnewspapers@hearst.com; internet www.hearstcorp.com; acquired Prime Time, Inc (publr, San Antonio region) in late 2006; Chair. GEORGE R. HEARST, Jr; Vice-Chair. and CEO FRANK A. BENNACK, Jr; 16 daily newspapers, incl. the *Houston Chronicle* and *San Francisco Chronicle*, and 7 weekly newspapers; 18 monthly magazines incl. *Good Housekeeping*, *Cosmopolitan*, *O, The Oprah Magazine* and *Redbook*; owns or operates 26 television stations broadcasting to 18% of the US market; interests in radio broadcasting, cable networks, interactive media and business information publishing.

Lee Enterprises: 201 North Harrison St, Davenport, IA 52801-1939; tel. (563) 383-2100; e-mail information@lee.net; internet www.lee.net; f. 1890; Chair., Pres. and CEO MARY E. JUNCK; 49 daily newspapers (jt interest in further 4 dailies) and more than 300 weekly newspapers and speciality publs; combined weekday circ. 1.6m., combined Sunday circ. 1.9m.; interests in publishing and purchasing and distribution of raw materials.

The McClatchy Co: 2100 Q St, Sacramento, CA 95816-6899; tel. (916) 321-1855; fax (916) 321-1869; e-mail contact@mcclatchy.com; internet www.mcclatchy.com; acquired Knight Ridder in 2006; established 10 foreign news bureaux in that year; sold largest daily *Star Tribune* to Avista Capital Partners (New York) in early 2007; Chair., Pres. and CEO GARY B. PRUITT; 31 daily newspapers, incl. the *Miami Herald*, and community newspapers.

Media General, Inc: 333 East Franklin St, Richmond, VA 23219; tel. (804) 649-6000; e-mail etucker@mediageneral.com; internet www.mediageneral.com; Chair. J. STEWART BRYAN, III; Pres. and CEO MARSHALL N. MORTON; 24 daily newspapers, incl. *The Tampa Tribune*, *Richmond Times-Dispatch* and *Winston-Salem Journal*, as well as c. 275 weekly newspapers and other publs; owns 19 network-affiliated television stations.

MediaNews Group: 101 Colfax Ave, Suite 1100, Denver, CO 80202; tel. (303) 954-6360; fax (303) 954-6320; e-mail contact@medianewsgroup.com; internet www.medianewsgroup.com; Vice-Chair. and CEO WILLIAM DEAN SINGLETON; Pres. JOSEPH J. LODOVIC, IV; 54 daily newspapers, incl. *The Denver Post*; combined weekday circ. 2.4m., combined Sun. circ. 2.7m.; owns a television station in Anchorage, AK, and radio stations in Texas.

New York Times Co: 620 Eighth Ave, New York, NY 10018; tel. (212) 556-1234; internet www.nytco.com; Chair. ARTHUR SULZBERGER, Jr; Pres. and CEO JANET L. ROBINSON; 18 daily newspapers incl. *The New York Times*, *The International Herald Tribune* and *The Boston Globe*; owns one radio station and c. 50 internet websites; sold Broadcast Media Group to Oak Hill Capital Partners in May 2007.

E. W. Scripps Co: 312 Walnut St, 2800 Scripps Center, Cincinnati, OH 45202; POB 5380, Cincinnati, OH 45201; tel. (513) 977-3000; fax (513) 977-3721; e-mail corpcomm@scripps.com; internet www.scripps.com; Pres. and CEO RICHARD A. BOEHNE; 18 daily newspapers and 8 community newspapers; owns the Scripps Howard News Service syndicate, 10 television stations, and 6 cable and satellite programming networks.

Tribune Publishing: 435 North Michigan Ave, Chicago, IL 60611; tel. (312) 222-9100; fax (312) 222-4760; e-mail corp.info@tribune.com; internet www.tribune.com; f. 1847; subsidiary of Tribune Co; merged with the Times Mirror Co in 2000; Tribune Co acquired by private investor in Dec. 2007; Chair., Pres. and CEO SAMUEL ZELL; 8 daily newspapers incl. the *Chicago Tribune*, the *Los Angeles Times*,

THE UNITED STATES OF AMERICA

the *Baltimore Sun* and the Spanish-language newspaper *Hoy*; over 130 other publs; combined weekday circ. 2.3m., combined Sun. circ. 3.4m.; operates 20 television stations.

PRINCIPAL DAILY AND SUNDAY NEWSPAPERS

Alabama

Birmingham News: 2201 Fourth Ave North, POB 2553, Birmingham, AL 35203; tel. (205) 325-4444; fax (205) 325-3278; internet www.bhamnews.com; f. 1888; Publr Victor H. Hanson, III; Editor Thomas Scarritt; circ. Mon. to Fri. 140,438, Sat. 140,747, Sun. 170,151.

Huntsville Times: 2317 South Memorial Parkway, Huntsville, AL 35801-5623; tel. (256) 532-4000; fax (256) 532-4213; e-mail kevin.wendt@htimes.com; internet www.htimes.com; f. 1910; Publr Bob Ludwig; Editor Kevin Wendt; circ. Mon. to Fri. 53,194, Sat. 50,981, Sun. 71,786.

Montgomery Advertiser: 425 Molton St, Montgomery, AL 36104; tel. (334) 262-1611; fax (334) 261-1521; e-mail editor@montgomeryadvertiser.com; internet www.montgomeryadvertiser.com; f. 1829 as The Planter's Gazette; Publr Scott M. Brown; Exec. Editor Wanda S. Lloyd; circ. Mon. to Fri. 45,060, Sat. 43,556, Sun. 50,983.

Press-Register: 304 Government St, POB 2488, Mobile, AL 36652-2488; tel. (251) 219-5454; fax (334) 434-8662; e-mail cindy@al.com; internet www.press-register.com; f. 1813; CEO Cindy Martin; Editor-in-Chief Ken Booth; circ. Mon. to Fri. 99,433, Sat. 90,724, Sun. 112,761.

Alaska

Anchorage Daily News: POB 149001, Anchorage, AK 99514-9001; tel. (907) 257-4305; fax (907) 257-4544; e-mail newsroom@adn.com; internet www.adn.com; f. 1946; Pres. and Publr Patrick Doyle; Senior Vice-Pres. and Editor Pat Dougherty; circ. Mon. to Fri. 62,893, Sat. 61,733, Sun. 69,893.

Arizona

Arizona Daily Star: 4850 South Park Ave, POB 26807, Tucson, AZ 85726-6807; tel. (520) 573-4215; fax (520) 573-4200; e-mail jhumenik@azstarnet.com; internet www.azstarnet.com; f. 1877; Publr and Editor John M. Humenik; Exec. Editor Bobbie Jo Buel-Carter; circ. Mon. to Fri. 113,373, Sat. 104,584, Sun. 164,033.

Arizona Republic: 200 East Van Buren St, Phoenix, AZ 85004; tel. (602) 444-8000; fax (800) 699-0732; e-mail comments@azcentral.com; internet www.azcentral.com/arizonarepublic; f. 1890; Vice-Pres. and Exec. Editor Randy Lovely; circ. Mon. to Fri. 413,332, Sat. 422,466, Sun. 515,523.

Arkansas

Democrat-Gazette: 121 East Capitol Ave, POB 2221, Little Rock, AR 72203; tel. (501) 378-3400; fax (501) 372-4765; e-mail ffellone@arkansasonline.com; internet www2.arkansasonline.com; f. 1819; morning; Publr Walter E. Hussman, Jr; Exec. Editor Griffin Smith; circ. Mon. to Fri. 182,212, Sat. 179,749, Sun. 274,494.

California

Bakersfield Californian: 1707 Eye St, Bakersfield, CA 93301; tel. (805) 395-7500; fax (805) 395-7519; internet www.bakersfield.com; f. 1866; Publr and Chair. Virginia F. Moorhouse; Exec. Editor Mike Jenner; circ. Mon. to Fri. 59,433, Sat. 60,719, Sun. 68,825.

Daily Breeze: Copley Los Angeles Newspapers, 5215 Torrance Blvd, Torrance, CA 90503; tel. (310) 540-5511; fax (310) 540-6272; e-mail newsroom@dailybreeze.com; internet www.dailybreeze.com; f. 1894; Mon. to Sat. evening, Sun. morning; Publr Mark Ficcara; Exec. Editor Philip Sanfield; circ. Mon. to Fri. 65,590, Sat. 67,184, Sun. 66,318.

Daily News: 21860 Burbank Blvd, Suite 200, Woodland Hills, POB 4200, CA 91367; tel. (818) 713-3000; fax (818) 713-0058; e-mail feedback@dailynews.com; internet www.dailynews.com; f. 1911; publ. by Los Angeles Newspaper Group; morning; Publr Edward R. Moss; Editor Carolina Garcia; circ. Mon. to Fri. 137,344, Sat. 136,361, Sun. 145,164.

Fresno Bee: 1626 E St, Fresno, CA 93786; tel. (559) 441-6111; fax (559) 441-6499; e-mail blumbye@fresnobee.com; internet www.fresnobee.com; f. 1922; Publr and Pres. William H. Fleet; Exec. Editor Betsy Lumbye; circ. Mon. to Fri. 150,344, Sat. 144,056, Sun. 171,039.

Investor's Business Daily: 12655 Beatrice St, Los Angeles, CA 90066; tel. (310) 448-6700; fax (310) 577-7301; e-mail ibdnews@investors.com; internet www.investors.com; f. 1984; morning; Publr W. Scott O'Neill; Editor-in-Chief Wesley F. Mann; circ. Mon. to Fri. 161,421.

Los Angeles Times: 202 West First St, Los Angeles, CA 90012; tel. (213) 237-5000; fax (213) 237-7679; e-mail nancy.sullivan@latimes.com; internet www.latimes.com; f. 1881; Publr and CEO Eddy W. Hartenstein; Editor Russ Stanton; circ. Mon. to Fri. 773,884, Sat. 860,722, Sun. 1,101,981.

Modesto Bee: 1325 H St, POB 3928, Modesto, CA 95352; tel. (209) 578-2000; fax (209) 578-2207; e-mail mrandazzo@modbee.com; internet www.modbee.com; f. 1884; Publr and Pres. Eric Johnston; Vice-Pres. and Editor Mark Vasché; circ. Mon. to Fri. 78,001, Sat. 83,576, Sun. 81,952.

Oakland Tribune: 7677 Oakport St, Oakland, CA 94621; tel. (510) 208-6300; fax (510) 208-6477; e-mail mreynolds@bayareanewsgroup.com; internet www.oaklandtribune.com; f. 1874; Editor Martin Reynolds; circ. Mon. to Fri. 96,535, Sat. 84,916, Sun. 91,343.

Orange County Register: 625 North Grand Ave, POB 11626, Santa Ana, CA 92701-4347; tel. (877) 627-7009; fax (714) 796-3681; e-mail customerservice@ocregister.com; internet www.ocregister.com; Pres. and Publr Terry Horne; Editor Ken Brusic; circ. Mon. to Fri. 250,724, Sat. 275,919, Sun. 311,982.

Press Democrat: 427 Mendocino Ave, POB 569, Santa Rosa, CA 95402; tel. (707) 546-2020; fax (707) 521-5330; e-mail catherine.barratt@pressdemocrat.com; internet www.pressdemocrat.com; f. 1857; Publr Bruce W. Kyse; Exec. Editor Catherine Barnett; circ. Mon. to Fri. 78,022, Sat. 77,887, Sun. 78,505.

Press Enterprise: 3450 14th St, POB 792, Riverside, CA 92501; tel. (951) 368-9403; fax (951) 368-9022; e-mail mdevarenne@pe.com; internet www.pe.com; f. 1878; publ. by Belo Corpn; morning; Publr Ronald R. Redfern; Editor Maria De Varenne; circ. Mon. to Fri. 164,189, Sat. 163,089, Sun. 172,730.

Press-Telegram: 300 Oceangate, Long Beach, CA 90844-0001; tel. (562) 435-1161; fax (562) 499-1277; e-mail rich.archbold@presstelegram.com; internet www.presstelegram.com; Publr Mark Ficarra; Exec. Editor Rich Archbold; circ. Mon. to Fri. 85,595, Sat. 83,772, Sun. 85,191.

Sacramento Bee: 2100 Q St, POB 15779, Sacramento, CA 95826; tel. (916) 321-1000; fax (916) 321-1100; e-mail cdell@sacbee.com; internet www.sacbee.com; f. 1857; Pres. and Publr Cheryl Dell; Snr Vice-Pres. and Editor Melanie Sill; circ. Mon. to Fri. 268,755, Sat. 276,776, Sun. 307,480.

San Bernardino County Sun: 4030 North Georgia Blvd, San Bernardino, CA 92407; tel. (909) 889-9666; fax (909) 381-8741; e-mail nancy.kay@sbsun.com; internet www.sbsun.com; f. 1894; part of Los Angeles Media Group; Publr Fred Hamilton; Exec. Editor Frank Pine; circ. Mon. to Fri. 54,315, Sat. 52,580, Sun. 54,315.

San Diego Union-Tribune: 350 Camino de la Reina, San Diego, CA 92108; tel. (619) 299-3131; fax (619) 293-1896; e-mail letters@uniontrib.com; internet www.signonsandiego.com; f. 1868; Editor Jeff Rose; circ. Mon. to Fri. 288,669, Sat. 327,694, Sun. 355,537.

San Francisco Chronicle: 901 Mission St, San Francisco, CA 94103; tel. (415) 777-1111; fax (415) 896-1107; e-mail letters@sfchronicle.com; internet www.sfgate.com; f. 1865; subsidiary of Hearst Communications; Publr and Pres. Frank J. Vega; Exec. Vice-Pres. and Editor Philip Bronstein; circ. Mon. to Fri. 370,345, Sat. 386,113, Sun. 424,603.

San Francisco Examiner: 450 Mission, San Francisco, CA 94105; tel. (415) 359-2600; fax (415) 359-2766; e-mail sfeditor@examiner.com; internet www.sfexaminer.com; f. 1887; Publr John Wilcox; Exec. Editor James Pimentel; circ. Mon. to Fri. 70,000, Sat. 90,000.

San Jose Mercury News: 750 Ridder Park Dr., San Jose, CA 95190-0001; tel. (408) 920-5000; fax (408) 288-8060; e-mail jfensterwald@mercurynews.com; internet www.mercurynews.com; f. 1851; owned by MediaNews Group; Pres. and Publr Mac Tully; Editor and Vice-Pres. David J. Butler; circ. Mon. to Fri. 234,772, Sat. 203,203, Sun. 251,851.

Stockton Record: 530 East Market St, POB 900, Stockton, CA 95201; tel. (209) 943-6568; fax (209) 547-8186; e-mail newsroom@recordnet.com; internet www.recordnet.com; f. 1895; publ. by Ottaway Newspapers, Inc; Publr Roger Coover; Editor Mike Klocke; circ. Mon. to Fri. 57,486, Sat. 55,578, Sun. 62,585.

Colorado

Denver Post: 101 West Colfax Ave, Denver, CO 80202; tel. (303) 954-1010; fax (303) 820-1369; e-mail gmoore@denverpost.com; internet www.denverpost.com; f. 1892; Publr William Dean Singleton; Editor Gregory Moore; circ. Mon. to Fri. 225,193, Sun. 600,026.

The Gazette: 30 South Prospect, Colorado Springs, CO 80903; tel. (719) 632-5511; fax (719) 636-0202; e-mail liz.cobb@gazette.com; internet www.gazette.com; f. 1872; Pres. and Publr Steve Pope; Editor Jeff Thomas; circ. Mon. to Fri. 93,859, Sat. 98,461, Sun. 109,603.

THE UNITED STATES OF AMERICA   *Directory*

Connecticut

Connecticut Post: 410 State St, Bridgeport, CT 06604-4501; tel. (203) 333-0161; fax (203) 366-8158; e-mail edit@ctpost.com; internet www.connpost.com; f. 1883; Pres. and Publr JOHN J. DEAUGUSTINE; Editor TOM BADEN; circ. Mon. to Fri. 76,014, Sat. 58,627, Sun. 85,032.

Hartford Courant: 285 Broad St, Hartford, CT 06115; tel. (860) 241-6200; fax (860) 520-3176; e-mail nmeyer@courant.com; internet www.courant.com; f. 1764; Publr and CEO RICHARD GRAZIANO; Editor CLIFFORD TEUTSCH; circ. Mon. to Fri. 168,158, Sat. 151,938, Sun. 237,933.

New Haven Register: 40 Sargent Dr., New Haven, CT 06511; tel. (203) 789-5200; fax (203) 865-7894; e-mail mbrackenbury@nhregister.com; internet www.nhregister.com; f. 1812; Publr EDWARD CONDRA; Editor JACK KRAMER; circ. Mon. to Fri. 72,613, Sat. 58,289, Sun. 80,279.

Waterbury Republican-American: American-Republican, Inc, 389 Meadow St, POB 2090, Waterbury, CT 06722-2090; tel. (203) 574-3636; fax (203) 596-9277; e-mail ghanisek@rep-am.com; internet www.rep-am.com; f. 1844; morning; Publr WILLIAM J. PAPE, II; Exec. Editor JONATHAN F. KELLOGG; circ. Mon. to Fri. 50,903, Sat. 48,142, Sun. 57,385.

Delaware

News Journal: POB 15505, Wilmington, DE 19850; tel. (302) 324-2500; fax (302) 856-3919; e-mail newsroom@newsjournal.com; internet www.delawareonline.com; f. 1871; Publr CURTIS W. RIDDLE; Exec. Editor DAVID LEDFORD; circ. Mon. to Fri. 110,171, Sat. 102,698, Sun. 125,244.

District of Columbia

Washington Post: 1150 15th St, NW, Washington, DC 20071; tel. (202) 334-6000; fax (202) 334-5693; internet www.washingtonpost.com; f. 1877; Chair. BOISFEUILLET JONES; Publr KATHARINE WEYMOUTH; Exec. Editor MARCUS BRAUCHLI, Jr; Man. Editors ELIZABETH SPAYD, RAJU NARISETTI; circ. Mon. to Fri. 673,180, Sat. 612,905, Sun. 890,163.

Washington Times: 3600 New York Ave, NE, Washington, DC 20002-1947; tel. (202) 636-3000; fax (202) 832-2982; internet www.washingtontimes.com; f. 1982; Editor-in-Chief WESLEY PRUDEN; Exec. Editor JOHN SOLOMON; circ. Mon. to Fri. 93,763, Sat. 76,701, Sun. 37,680.

Florida

Daytona Beach News-Journal: 901 Sixth St, Daytona Beach, FL 32117; tel. (386) 252-1511; internet www.news-journalonline.com; f. 1904; morning; Publr, CEO and Pres. GEORGIA M. KANEY; Editor DON LINDLEY; circ. Mon. to Fri. 99,627, Sat. 103,909, Sun. 116,700.

Diario Las Américas: 2900 NW 39th St, Miami, FL 33142; tel. (305) 633-3341; fax (305) 635-7668; internet www.diariolasamericas.com; f. 1953; Spanish; Publr and Editor HORACIO AGUIRRE; circ. Mon. to Sat. 66,000, Sun. 70,000 (2007).

Florida Times-Union: 1 Riverside Ave, Jacksonville, FL 32202; POB 1949, Jacksonville, FL 322311; tel. (904) 359-4111; fax (904) 359-4478; e-mail rich.ray@jacksonville.com; internet jacksonville.com; f. 1864; Publr JIM CURROW; Editor FRANK DENTON; circ. Mon. to Fri. 144,391, Sat. 159,969, Sun. 201,352.

Florida Today: Cape Publs, Inc, POB 419000, Melbourne, FL 32941-9000; tel. (321) 242-3500; fax (321) 242-6601; internet www.floridatoday.com; f. 1966; morning; Publr and Pres. MARK MIKOLAJCZYK; Exec. Editor BOB STOVER; circ. Mon. to Fri. 79,499, Sat. 78,077, Sun. 93,604.

Ledger: POB 408, Lakeland, FL 33802; tel. (863) 802-7000; fax (863) 802-7900; e-mail skip.perez@theledger.com; internet www.theledger.com; f. 1924; morning; Publr JEROME FERSON; Exec. Editor SKIP PEREZ; circ. Mon. to Fri. 65,948, Sat. 65,750, Sun. 83,860.

Miami Herald: 1 Herald Plaza, Miami, FL 33132-1693; tel. (305) 350-2111; fax (305) 376-5287; e-mail dwilson@miamiherald.com; internet www.miamiherald.com; f. 1910; Publr and Pres. DAVID LANDSBERG; Exec. Editor ANDERS GYLLENHAAL; circ. Mon. to Fri. 240,223, Sat. 261,156, Sun. 311,245.

News-Press: 2442 Dr Martin Luther King Jr Blvd, Fort Myers, FL 33901-3987; tel. (941) 335-0200; fax (941) 335-0265; e-mail response@news-press.com; internet www.news-press.com; f. 1884; morning; Publr CAROL HUDLER; Sr Man. Editor CINDY MCCURRY-ROSS; circ. Mon. to Fri. 92,340, Sat. 92,362, Sun. 111,516.

Orlando Sentinel: 633 North Orange Ave, Orlando, FL 32801; tel. (407) 420-5000; fax (407) 420-5350; e-mail editor@orlandosentinel.com; internet www.orlandosentinel.com; f. 1876; morning; Publr HOWARD GREENBERG (acting); Editor CHARLOTTE HALL; circ. Mon. to Fri. 227,593, Sat. 226,375, Sun. 303,399.

Palm Beach Post: 2751 South Dixie Hwy, West Palm Beach, FL 33405; tel. (561) 820-4100; fax (561) 820-4407; internet www.palmbeachpost.com; f. 1916; Publr ALEX TAYLOR; Man. Editor BILL ROSE; Editor JOHN BARTOSEK; circ. Mon. to Fri. 164,474, Sat. 163,087, Sun. 195,608.

Pensacola News Journal: 101 East Romana St, Pensacola, FL 32502; POB 12710, Pensacola, FL 32591; tel. (850) 435-8600; fax (850) 435-8633; e-mail news@pnj.com; internet www.pnj.com; f. 1889; Publr KEVIN DOYLE; Exec. Editor RICHARD A. SCHNEIDER; circ. Mon. to Fri. 57,089, Sat. 55,330, Sun. 68,962.

Sarasota Herald-Tribune: 1741 Main St, Sarasota, FL 34236; tel. (941) 953-7755; fax (941) 957-5276; internet www.heraldtribune.com; f. 1925; Publr DIANE MCFARLIN; Exec. Editor MIKE CONNELLY; circ. Mon. to Fri. 114,904, Sat. 110,747, Sun. 125,644.

St Petersburg Times: 490 First Ave South, POB 1121, St Petersburg, FL 33701; tel. (727) 893-8111; fax (727) 893-8675; e-mail local@sptimes.com; internet www.tampabay.com; f. 1884; division of Poynter Institute for Media Studies; Chair., Editor and CEO PAUL TASH; circ. Mon. to Fri. 316,007, Sat. 329,646, Sun. 432,779.

Sun-Sentinel: 200 East Las Olas Blvd, Fort Lauderdale, FL 33301-2293; tel. (954) 356-4000; fax (954) 356-4559; internet www.sun-sentinel.com; f. 1960; Publr HOWARD GREENBERG; Editor JEFF GLICK; circ. Mon. to Fri. 218,286, Sat. 226,375, Sun. 303,399.

Tampa Tribune: 200 Parker St, Tampa, FL 33606; POB 191, Tampa, FL 33601; tel. (813) 259-8225; fax (813) 254-4952; e-mail lomoto@tbo.com; internet www.tbo.com; f. 1893; morning; Publr and Pres. DENISE E. PALMER; Editor JANET COATS; circ. Mon. to Fri. 220,522, Sat. 220,109.

Georgia

Atlanta Journal-Constitution: 72 Marietta St, POB 4689, Atlanta, GA 30302-4689; tel. (404) 526-5151; fax (404) 526-5746; e-mail insideajc@ajc.com; internet www.ajc.com; f. 1950; Sun. morning; Publr DOUG FRANKLIN; Editor JULIA WALLACE; circ. Mon. to Fri. 326,907, Sat. 329,765, Sun. 497,149.

Augusta Chronicle: 725 Broad St, POB 1928, Augusta, GA 30903-1928; tel. (706) 724-0851; fax (706) 722-5746; internet chronicle.augusta.com; f. 1785; Morris Communications Co, LLC; Publr WILLIAM S. MORRIS, III; Pres. DONALD W. BAILEY; circ. Mon. to Fri. 73,561, Sat. 72,650, Sun. 92,418.

Macon Telegraph: 120 Broadway, Macon, GA 31201; POB 4167, Macon, GA 31208; tel. (478) 744-4200; fax (478) 744-4663; e-mail letters@macontel.com; internet www.macon.com; f. 1826; Publr GEORGE MCCANLESS; Exec. Editor SHERRIE MARSHALL; circ. Mon. to Fri. 56,510, Sat. 54,075, Sun. 70,438.

Savannah Morning News: 1375 Chatham Parkway, Savannah, GA 31401; POB 1088, Savannah, GA 31402-1088; tel. (912) 236-9511; fax (912) 234-6522; internet www.savannahnow.com; f. 1850; Publr MICHAEL C. TRAYNOR; Exec. Editor SUSAN CATRON, Jr; circ. Mon. to Fri. 51,456, Sat. 49,030, Sun. 64,308.

Hawaii

Honolulu Advertiser: The News Bldg, 605 Kapi'olani Blvd, POB 3110, Honolulu, HI 96802; tel. (808) 525-8090; fax (808) 535-8037; e-mail hawaii@honoluluadvertiser.com; internet www.honoluluadvertiser.com; f. 1856; Pres. and Publr LEE P. WEBBER; Editor MARK PLATTE; circ. Mon. to Fri. 140,331, Sat. 149,069, Sun. 150,276.

Honolulu Star-Bulletin: Restaurant Row, 7 Waterfront Plaza, Suite 210, 500 Ala Moana, Honolulu, HI 96813; tel. (808) 529-4747; fax (808) 529-4750; e-mail mrovner@starbulletin.com; internet www.starbulletin.com; f. 1882; Pres. DENNIS FRANCIS; Editor FRANK BRIDGEWATER; circ. c. 66,000 (2003).

Idaho

Idaho Statesman: 1200 North Curtis Rd, POB 40, Boise, ID 83707; tel. (208) 377-6200; fax (208) 377-6449; e-mail vgowler@idahostatesman.com; internet www.idahostatesman.com; f. 1864; Publr MI-AI PARRISH; Editor and Vice-Pres. VICKI S. GOWLER; circ. Mon. to Fri. 61,927, Sat. 66,222, Sun. 81,939.

Illinois

Chicago Sun-Times: 350 North Orleans St, 10th Floor, Chicago, IL 60654; tel. (312) 321-3000; fax (312) 321-3084; e-mail aherrmann@suntimes.com; internet www.suntimes.com; f. 1948; Publr JOHN BARRON; Editor-in-Chief DONALD HAYNER; circ. Mon. to Fri. 312,274, Sat. 225,383, Sun. 247,469.

Chicago Tribune: 435 North Michigan Ave, Chicago, IL 60611-4041; tel. (312) 222-3232; fax (312) 222-4674; internet www.chicagotribune.com; f. 1847; publ. by Chicago Tribune Co; two sister newspapers: *RedEye* and *Hoy Chicago*; Publr BOB GREMILLION (acting); Editor GERALD KERN; circ. Mon. to Fri. 566,827, Sat. 473,849, Sun. 940,620.

THE UNITED STATES OF AMERICA

Daily Herald: POB 280, Arlington Heights, IL 60006; tel. (847) 427-4300; fax (847) 427-4608; e-mail jbaumann@dailyherald.com; internet www.dailyherald.com; f. 1872; owned by Paddock Publications Inc; Publr and Chair. DANIEL E. BAUMANN; Senior Vice-Pres. and Editor JOHN LAMPINEN; circ. Mon. to Fri. 143,152, Sat. 134,585, Sun. 141,091.

Journal Star: 1 News Plaza, Peoria, IL 61643; tel. (309) 686-3000; fax (309) 686-3296; e-mail kmauser@pjstar.com; internet www.pjstar.com; f. 1855; Publr KEN MAUSER; Man. Editor JOHN PLEVKA; circ. Mon. to Fri. 65,320, Sat. 70,255, Sun. 80,394.

Pantagraph: 301 West Washington St, POB 2907, Bloomington, IL 61702-2907; tel. (309) 829-9000; fax (309) 829-9104; e-mail bwinterland@pantagraph.com; internet www.pantagraph.com; f. 1837; Publr RICHARD JOHNSTON; Man. Editor JULIE GERKE; circ. Mon. to Fri. 47,764, Sat. 43,704, Sun. 50,081.

Rockford Register Star: 99 East State St, Rockford, IL 61104; tel. (815) 987-1200; fax (815) 987-1365; internet www.rrstar.com; f. 1888; acquired by GateHouse Media from Gannett Co in 2007; Publr SCOTT BOWERS; Gen. Man. TOM LASLEY; circ. Mon. to Fri. 55,913, Sat. 54,416, Sun. 69,693.

State Journal-Register: 1 Copley Plaza, POB 219, Springfield, IL 62705-0219; tel. (217) 788-1300; fax (217) 788-1551; e-mail sjr@sj-r.com; internet www.sj-r.com; f. 1831; Publr SCOTT BOWERS; Exec. Editor JON BROADBOOKS; circ. Mon. to Fri. 49,839, Sat. 49,108, Sun. 58,272.

Indiana

Evansville Courier and Press: 300 Walnut St, POB 268, Evansville, IN 47713; tel. (812) 424-7711; fax (812) 422-8196; e-mail courierpress@evansville.net; internet www.courierpress.com; f. 1845; Publr and Pres. JACK PATE; Man. Editor LINDA NEGRO; circ. Mon. to Fri. 68,220, Sat. 65,597, Sun. 86,201.

Indianapolis Star: POB 145, Indianapolis, IN 46206-0145; tel. (317) 444-8005; fax (317) 633-1038; internet www.indystar.com; Publr and Pres. MICHAEL G. KANE; Editor DENNIS R. RYERSON; circ. Mon. to Fri. 255,303, Sat. 217,991, Sun. 324,349.

Journal-Gazette: 600 West Main St, Fort Wayne, IN 46802; tel. (260) 461-8831; fax (219) 461-8648; e-mail pbeber@jg.net; internet www.journalgazette.net; f. 1863; publ. by Fort Wayne Newspapers; Publr JULIE INSKEEP; Editor CRAIG KLUGMAN; circ. Mon. to Fri. 64,304, Sat. 86,020, Sun. 111,485.

News-Sentinel: 600 West Main St, POB 100, Fort Wayne, IN 46802; tel. (260) 461-8324; fax (260) 461-8817; e-mail nsnews@news-sentinel.com; internet www.news-sentinel.com; f. 1833; publ. by Fort Wayne Newspapers; Publr MICHAEL J. CHRISTMAN; Editor LEO MORRIS; circ. Mon. to Fri. 24,196, Sat. 24,053.

Post-Tribune: 1433 East 83rd Ave, Merrillville, IN 46410; tel. (219) 648-3100; fax (219) 648-3249; internet www.post-trib.com; f. 1907; Publr LISA TATINA; Exec. Editor PAULETTE HADDIX; circ. Mon. to Fri. 60,325, Sat. 57,120, Sun. 61,118.

South Bend Tribune: 225 West Colfax Ave, South Bend, IN 46626; tel. (574) 235-6161; fax (574) 236-1765; e-mail sfunk@sbtinfo.com; internet www.southbendtribune.com; f. 1872; Publr and Editor DAVID C. RAY; circ. Mon. to Fri. 66,886, Sat. 76,046, Sun. 89,802.

The Times: 601 45th Ave, Munster, IN 46321; tel. (219) 933-3223; fax (219) 933-9249; e-mail dasher@nwitimes.com; internet www.thetimesonline.com; f. 1906; morning; Publr BILL MASTERSON, Jr; Exec. Editor WILLIAM NANGLE; circ. Mon. to Fri. 85,195, Sat. 82,481, Sun. 92,347.

Iowa

Cedar Rapids Gazette: 500 Third Ave, SE, Cedar Rapids, IA 52401; tel. (319) 398-8211; fax (319) 398-5846; e-mail steve.buttry@gazcomm.com; internet www.gazetteonline.com; f. 1883; Publr DAVE STOREY; Man. Editor DAN GEISER; circ. Mon. to Fri. 57,945, Sat. 65,373, Sun. 71,521.

Des Moines Register: 715 Locust St, POB 957, Des Moines, IA 50306-0957; tel. (515) 284-8000; fax (515) 268-2504; e-mail letters@dmreg.com; internet www.desmoinesregister.com; f. 1849; Pres. and Publr LAURA HOLLINGSWORTH; Editor CAROLYN WASHBURN; circ. Mon. to Fri. 138,519, Sat. 138,585, Sun. 222,122.

Quad-City Times: 500 East Third St, POB 3828, Davenport, IA 52801; tel. (563) 383-2200; fax (563) 383-2223; internet www.qctimes.com; f. 1855; division of Lee Enterprises, Inc.; Publr JULIE BECHTEL; Editor STEVE THOMAS; circ. Mon. to Fri. 51,890, Sat. 54,968, Sun. 67,753.

Sioux City Journal: 515 Pavonia St, Sioux City, IA 51102; tel. (712) 293-4250; fax (712) 279-5059; internet www.siouxcityjournal.com; f. 1864; subsidiary of Lee Enterprises, Inc.; Publr RON PETERSON; Editor CYNTHIA DONOVAN; circ. Mon. to Fri. 41,096, Sat. 40,235, Sun. 42,354.

Kansas

Topeka Capital-Journal: 616 SE Jefferson St, Topeka, KS 66607; tel. (785) 295-1111; fax (785) 295-1230; e-mail pete.goering@cjonline.com; internet www.cjonline.com; f. 1879; Publr MARK NUSBAUM; Editor (vacant); circ. Mon. to Fri. 44,864, Sat. 45,238, Sun. 53,180.

Wichita Eagle: 825 East Douglas Ave, POB 820, Wichita, KS 67201; tel. (316) 268-6000; fax (316) 268-6438; e-mail wenews@wichitaeagle.com; internet www.kansas.com; f. 1872; Publr PAM SIDDALL; Editor SHERRY CHISENHALL, Jr; circ. Mon. to Fri. 82,912, Sat. 94,486, Sun. 130,333.

Kentucky

Courier-Journal: 525 West Broadway, Louisville, KY 40201-7431; POB 740031, Louisville, KY 40201; tel. (502) 582-4011; fax (502) 582-4200; e-mail publisher@courier-journal.com; internet www.courier-journal.com; f. 1868; Publr and Pres. ARNOLD GARSON; Editor BENNIE L. IVORY; circ. Mon. to Fri. 215,328, Sat. 197,516, Sun. 258,778.

Lexington Herald-Leader: 100 Midland Ave, Lexington, KY 40508-1999; tel. (859) 231-3475; e-mail tisaac@herald-leader.com; internet www.kentucky.com; f. 1860; Pres. and Publr TIM KELLY; Interim Editor PETER BANIAK; circ. Mon. to Fri. 109,624, Sat. 109,495, Sun. 135,250.

Louisiana

Advocate: POB 588, Baton Rouge, LA 70821-0588; tel. (225) 383-1111; fax (225) 388-0371; internet www.2theadvocate.com; f. 1904; morning; Publr DOUGLAS L. MANSHIP; Man. Editor MILFORD FRYER; circ. Mon. to Fri. 97,912, Sat. 101,085, Sun. 121,677.

The Times: 222 Luke St, POB 30222, Shreveport, LA 71130; tel. (318) 459-3200; e-mail pzanmill@gannett.com; internet www.shreveporttimes.com; f. 1872; Publr PETE ZANMILLER; Man. Editor ROB RICHARDSON; circ. Mon. to Fri. 52,267, Sat. 50,635, Sun. 62,753.

Times-Picayune: 3800 Howard Ave, New Orleans, LA 70125-1429; tel. (504) 826-3279; fax (504) 826-3700; e-mail pkovacs@timespicayune.com; internet www.nola.com/t-p; f. 1880; Publr ASHTON PHELPS, Jr; Editor JIM AMOSS; circ. Mon. to Fri. 179,834, Sat. 176,709, Sun. 199,647.

Maine

Bangor Daily News: 491 Main St, POB 1329, Bangor, ME 04401; tel. (207) 990-8000; fax (207) 941-9476; e-mail bdnnews@bangordailynews.net; internet www.bangordailynews.com; f. 1834; Publr RICHARD J. WARREN; Exec. Editor A. MARK WOODWARD; circ. Mon. to Fri. 55,627, Sat. and Sun. 63,299.

Maine Sunday Telegram: 390 Congress St, POB 1460, Portland, ME 04104; tel. (207) 822-4076; fax (207) 879-1042; e-mail info@mainetoday.com; internet www.mainetoday.com; f. 1887; Publr (vacant); Man. Editor JEANNINE GUTTMAN; circ. 99,116.

Portland Press Herald: 390 Congress St, POB 1460, Portland, ME 04101-5009; tel. (207) 791-6650; fax (207) 791-6931; e-mail herald@portland.com; internet pressherald.mainetoday.com; f. 1862; Publr (vacant); Editor and Vice-Pres. JEANNINE A. GUTTMAN; circ. Mon. to Fri. 64,938, Sat. 62,284.

Maryland

Baltimore Sun: 501 North Calvert St, POB 1377, Baltimore, MD 21278; tel. (410) 332-6000; fax (410) 752-6049; e-mail publiceditor@baltsun.com; internet www.baltimoresun.com; f. 1837; Publr, Pres. and CEO TIMOTHY E. RYAN; Editor and Sr Vice-Pres. TIM FRANKLIN; circ. Mon. to Fri. 232,360, Sat. 210,901, Sun. 372,970.

Massachusetts

Boston Globe: 135 Morrissey Blvd, POB 55819, Boston, MA 02205-5819; tel. (617) 929-2000; fax (617) 929-3192; e-mail letters@globe.com; internet bostonglobe.com; f. 1872; Publr STEVE AINSLEY; Editor MARTIN D. BARON; circ. Mon. to Fri. 350,605, Sat. 330,547, Sun. 525,959.

Boston Herald: 1 Herald Sq., Boston, MA 02118; tel. (617) 426-3000; fax (617) 426-1896; e-mail letterstotheeditor@bostonherald.com; internet www.bostonherald.com; f. 1825; Publr PATRICK PURCELL; Man. Editor KEVIN CONVEY; circ. Mon. to Fri. 182,350, Sat. 143,282, Sun. 105,629.

Christian Science Monitor: 1 Norway St, Boston, MA 02115-3195; tel. (617) 450-7929; internet www.csmonitor.com; f. 1908; publ. by The First Church of Christ, Scientist; Editor JOHN YEMMA; circ. Mon. to Fri. 56,083.

Lowell Sun: 491 Dutton St, Lowell, MA 01853; tel. (978) 458-7100; fax (978) 970-4600; e-mail moneil@lowellsun.com; internet www.lowellsun.com; f. 1878; Mon. to Fri. evening, Sat. and Sun. morning;

THE UNITED STATES OF AMERICA

Publr and Pres. MARK O'NEIL; Editor JAMES CAMPANINI; circ. Mon. to Fri. 44,439, Sat. 40,205, Sun. 50,245.

Patriot Ledger: 400 Crown Colony Dr., POB 699159, Quincy, MA 02269-9159; tel. (617) 786-7200; fax (617) 786-7393; e-mail delivery@ledger.com; internet www.patriotledger.com; f. 1837; mem. of the South of Boston Media Group; Mon. to Fri. evening, weekend; Publr KIRK A. DAVIS; Editor CHAZY DOWALIBY; circ. Mon. to Fri. 51,105, Sat. and Sun. 60,953.

The Republican: 1860 Main St, Springfield, MA 01101; tel. (413) 788-1000; fax (413) 788-1301; e-mail csimison@repub.com; internet www.repub.com; f. 1824; fmrly Sunday Republican, merged with Union-News in 2003; Publr and CEO LARRY A. MCDERMOTT; Exec. Editor WAYNE E. PHANEUF; circ. Mon. to Fri. 83,897, Sat. 74,880, Sun. 119,021.

Worcester Telegram & Gazette: 20 Franklin St, POB 15012, Worcester, MA 01615-0012; tel. (508) 793-9100; fax (508) 793-9313; e-mail kparent@telegram.com; internet www.telegram.com; f. 1866; Publr BRUCE GAULTNEY; Editor HARRY T. WHITIN; circ. Mon. to Fri. 81,437, Sat. 87,586.

Michigan

Detroit Free Press: 615 West Lafayette Blvd, Detroit, MI 48226; tel. (313) 222-6400; fax (313) 222-5981; internet www.freep.com; f. 1831; subsidiary of the Gannett Corpn, Inc; Mon. to Fri. morning, Sat. and Sun.; Publr DAVID HUNKE; Vice-Pres. and Editor PAUL ANGER; circ. Mon. to Fri. 308,944, Sat. 288,231, Sun. 606,374.

The Detroit News: 615 West Lafayette Blvd, Detroit, MI 48226-3197; tel. (313) 222-2300; fax (313) 222-2335; e-mail jon.wolman@detnews.com; internet www.detnews.com; f. 1873; Publr and Editor JONATHAN WOLMAN; circ. Mon. to Fri. 188,171, Sat. 172,357.

Flint Journal: 200 East First St, Flint, MI 48502-1925; tel. (810) 766-6100; fax (810) 767-7518; e-mail fj@flintjournal.com; internet www.mlive.com/flintjournal; f. 1876; Mon. to Fri. evening, Sat. and Sun. morning; Publr DAVID C. SHARP; Editor TONY DEARING; circ. Mon. to Fri. 76,288, Sat. 76,109, Sun. 91,017.

Grand Rapids Press: 155 Michigan St, NW, Grand Rapids, MI 49503-2302; tel. (616) 222-5818; e-mail dgaydou@grpress.com; internet www.mslive.com/grpress; f. 1890; Publr DAN GAYDOU; Editor MICHAEL S. LLOYD; circ. Mon. to Fri. 128,930, Sat. 155,480, Sun. 177,026.

Kalamazoo Gazette: 401 South Burdick St, Kalamazoo, MI 49007; tel. (269) 345-3511; fax (269) 345-0583; e-mail jstephanak@kalamazoogazette.com; internet www.mlive.com/kgazette; f. 1883; Publr JAMES STEPHANAK; Editor REBECCA PIERCE; circ. Mon. to Fri. 49,127, Sat. 58,499, Sun. 22,470.

Lansing State Journal: 120 East Lenawee St, Lansing, MI 48919-0001; tel. (517) 377-1000; fax (517) 377-1298; e-mail publisher@lsj.com; internet www.lansingstatejournal.com; f. 1855; Pres. and Publr BRIAN PRIESTER; Exec. Editor MICHAEL HIRTEN; circ. Mon. to Fri. 58,948, Sat. 62,539, Sun. 76,887.

Oakland Press: 48 West Huron St, POB 436009, Pontiac, MI 48343; tel. (248) 332-8181; fax (248) 332-8294; e-mail glenn.gilbert@oakpress.com; internet www.theoaklandpress.com; f. 1843; Publr and Pres. KEVIN HAEZEBROECK; Exec. Editor GLENN GILBERT; circ. Mon. to Fri. 66,422, Sat. 66,525, Sun. 76,937.

Saginaw News: 203 South Washington Ave, Saginaw, MI 48607; tel. (989) 776-9764; e-mail pchaffee@thesaginawnews.com; internet www.mlive.com/saginawnews; f. 1859; Mon. to Fri. evening, Sat. and Sun. morning; Publr and Editor PAUL CHAFFEE; circ. Mon. to Fri. 39,143, Sat. 39,738, Sun. 48,839.

Minnesota

Duluth News Tribune: 424 West First St, Duluth, MN 55802; tel. (218) 723-5281; fax (218) 720-4120; e-mail news@duluthnews.com; internet www.duluthnewstribune.com; f. 1869; morning; Publr STEVEN MCLISTER; Exec. Editor ROB KARWATH; circ. Mon. to Fri. 40,305, Sat. 40,082, Sun. 62,468 (2007).

Star Tribune: 425 Portland Ave South, Minneapolis, MN 55488; tel. (612) 673-4000; fax (612) 673-4359; e-mail readerrep@startribune.com; internet www.startribune.com; f. 1920; Publr CHRIS HARTE; Editor and Sr Vice-Pres. NANCY BARNES; circ. Mon. to Fri. 322,362, Sat. 350,392, Sun. 534,750.

St Paul Pioneer Press: 345 Cedar St, St Paul, MN 55101; tel. (651) 222-1111; fax (651) 228-5500; e-mail infodesk@pioneerpress.com; internet www.twincities.com; f. 1849; Publr GUY L. GILMORE; Snr Editor THOM FLADUNG; circ. Mon. to Fri. 191,768, Sat. 190,864, Sun. 252,055.

Mississippi

Clarion-Ledger: 201 South Congress St, Jackson, MS 39201; tel. (601) 961-7000; fax (601) 961-7211; e-mail publisher@clarionledger.com; internet www.clarionledger.com; f. 1954; Publr and Pres. LARRY WHITAKER; Exec. Editor RONNIE AGNEW; circ. Mon. to Fri. 82,695, Sat. 82,709, Sun. 95,180.

Missouri

Kansas City Star: 1729 Grand Blvd, Kansas City, MO 64108; tel. (816) 234-4741; fax (816) 234-4467; e-mail mfannin@kcstar.com; internet www.kansascity.com; f. 1880; Publr MARK ZIEMAN; Editor MIKE FANNIN; circ. Mon. to Fri. 252,785, Sat. 255,889, Sun. 345,332.

News-Leader: 651 Boonville Ave, Springfield, MO 65806; tel. (417) 836-1100; fax (417) 837-1381; e-mail rbates@news-leader.com; internet www.news-leader.com; f. 1933; morning; Publr THOMAS A. BOOKSTAVER; Exec. Editor DON WYATT; circ. Mon. to Fri. 58,576, Sat. 58,716, Sun. 83,104.

St Louis Post-Dispatch: 900 North Tucker Blvd, St Louis, MO 63101; tel. (314) 657-7300; fax (314) 340-3050; e-mail generalmanager@stltoday.com; internet www.stltoday.com; f. 1878; Pres. and Publr KEVIN MOWBRAY; Editor ARNIE ROBBINS; circ. Mon. to Fri. 255,057, Sat. 253,947, Sun. 414,564.

Montana

Billings Gazette: POB 36300, Billings, MT 59107; tel. (406) 657-1200; fax (406) 657-1208; e-mail mgulledge@billingsgazette.com; internet billingsgazette.net; f. 1885; Publr MIKE GULLEDGE; Editor STEVE PROSINSKI; circ. Mon. to Fri. 45,530, Sat. 46,062, Sun. 50,940.

Nebraska

Lincoln Journal Star: Journal Star Printing Co, 926 P St, POB 81609, Lincoln, NE 68508; tel. (402) 475-4200; fax (402) 473-7291; e-mail jmaher@journalstar.com; internet journalstar.com; f. 1867; morning; Publr JOHN F. MAHER; Editor MICHAEL NELSON; circ. Mon. to Fri. 78,350, Sat. 69,345, Sun. 82,266.

Omaha World-Herald: 1334 Douglas St, Omaha, NE 68102-1122; tel. (402) 444-1000; fax (402) 345-0183; e-mail mike.reilly@owh.com; internet www.omaha.com; f. 1885; CEO and Publr TERRY KROEGER; Exec. Editor MIKE REILLY; circ. Mon. to Fri. 178,545, Sat. 168,427, Sun. 219,795.

Nevada

Las Vegas Review-Journal: 1111 West Bonanza Rd, POB 70, Las Vegas, NV 89125; tel. (702) 383-0211; fax (702) 383-4676; e-mail afleming@reviewjournal.com; internet www.lvrj.com; f. 1908; Publr SHERMAN R. FREDERICK; Editor THOMAS MITCHELL; circ. Mon. to Fri. 174,341, Sat. 171,181, Sun. 199,602.

Reno Gazette-Journal: POB 22000, Reno, NV 89520-2000; tel. (775) 788-6200; fax (775) 788-6458; e-mail rgjfeedback@rgj.com; internet www.rgj.com; f. 1870; Publr TED POWER; Exec. Editor BERYL LOVE; circ. Mon. to Fri. 57,423, Sat. 55,565, Sun. 66,465.

New Hampshire

New Hampshire Union Leader, New Hampshire Sunday News: Union Leader Corpn, 100 William Loeb Dr., POB 9555, Manchester, NH 03108-9555; tel. (603) 668-4321; fax (603) 668-0382; e-mail publisher@unionleader.com; internet www.unionleader.com; f. 1863 (New Hampshire Union Leader); f. 1946 (New Hampshire Sunday News); Pres. and Publr JOSEPH W. MCQUAID; Editorial Vice-Pres. CHARLES PERKINS, III; circ. Mon. to Fri. 51,782, Sat. 49,900, Sun. 67,226.

New Jersey

Asbury Park Press: 3601 Hwy 66, POB 1550, Neptune, NJ 07754-1550; tel. (732) 922-6000; fax (732) 918-4818; e-mail garys@app.com; internet www.app.com; f. 1879; Publr and Pres. THOMAS M. DONOVAN; Exec. Editor HOLLIS TOWNES; circ. Mon. to Fri. 140,882, Sat. 143,071, Sun. 184,095.

Courier-News: 1201 Route 22 West, Bridgewater, NJ 08807-0600; tel. (908) 722-8800; fax (908) 707-3252; e-mail couriernews@c-n.com; internet www.mycentraljersey.com; f. 1884; Publr and Pres. WILLIAM C. HIDLAY; Man. Editor PAUL GRZELLA; circ. Mon. to Fri. 31,370, Sat. 26,867, Sun. 30,940.

Courier-Post: 301 Cuthbert Blvd, POB 5300, Cherry Hill, NJ 08034; tel. (856) 663-3600; fax (856) 663-2831; e-mail thearon@courierpostonline.com; internet www.courierpostonline.com; f. 1875; Pres. and Publr WALT T. LAFFERTY; Exec. Editor EVERETT J. MITCHELL, II; circ. Mon. to Fri. 66,617, Sat. 70,461, Sun. 78,706.

Home News Tribune: 35 Kennedy Blvd, East Brunswick, NJ 08816; tel. (732) 246-5500; fax (732) 565-7208; e-mail hntmetro@thnt.com; internet www.mycentraljersey.com; f. 1879; Publr and Pres. WILLIAM C. HIDLAY; Exec. Editor PAUL GRZELLA; circ. Mon. to Fri. 49,076, Sat. 46,414, Sun. 54,170.

Jersey Journal: 30 Journal Sq., Jersey City, NJ 07306; tel. (201) 653-1000; fax (201) 217-2455; e-mail jjletters@jjournal.com; internet

THE UNITED STATES OF AMERICA — Directory

www.thejerseyjournal.com; f. 1867; Publr KENDRICK ROSS; Editor JUDITH A. LOCORRIERE; circ. Mon. to Fri. 24,940, Sat. 24,934.

The Record: 150 River St, Hackensack, NJ 07601-7172; tel. (201) 646-4000; fax (201) 646-4135; e-mail scandale@northjersey.com; internet www.northjersey.com; f. 1895; Chair. MALCOLM A. BORG; Editor and Vice-Pres. FRANK SCANDALE; circ. Mon. to Fri. 163,329, Sat. 165,916, Sun. 195,525.

Star-Ledger: 1 Star-Ledger Plaza, Newark, NJ 07102; tel. (973) 392-4121; e-mail jdennan@starledger.com; internet www.nj.com/starledger; f. 1917; Publr GEORGE ARWADY; Editor JIM WILLSE; circ. Mon. to Fri. 345,130, Sat. 281,901, Sun. 500,382.

The Times: 500 Perry St, POB 847, Trenton, NJ 08605; tel. (609) 989-5454; fax (609) 394-2819; e-mail letters@njtimes.com; internet www.nj.com/times; f. 1882; Publr RICHARD BILOTTI; Exec. Editor BRIAN S. MALONE; circ. Mon. to Fri. 54,745, Sat. 51,943, Sun. 56,449.

Trentonian: 600 Perry St, Trenton, NJ 08602; tel. (609) 989-7800; fax (609) 393-6072; e-mail editor@trentonian.com; internet www.trentonian.com; f. 1946; Publr WILLIAM T. (BILL) MURRAY; Editor AARON NOBEL; circ. Mon. to Fri. 39,449, Sat. 32,613, Sun. 26,496.

New Mexico

Albuquerque Journal: Albuquerque Publishing Co, 7777 Jefferson St NE, Albuquerque, NM 87109; tel. (505) 823-3800; e-mail jangel@abqjournal.com; internet www.abqjournal.com; f. 1880; Publr T. H. LANG; Editor KENT WALZ; circ. Mon. to Fri. 102,902, Sat. 107,887, Sun. 137,623.

New York

Albany Times Union: Times Union, News Plaza, POB 15000, Albany, NY 12212; tel. (518) 454-5694; fax (518) 454-5628; e-mail mbartoszek@timesunion.com; internet www.timesunion.com; f. 1856; Publr GEORGE HEARST, III; Exec. Editor REX SMITH; circ. Mon. to Fri. 89,256, Sat. 78,535, Sun. 141,064.

Buffalo News: 1 News Plaza, POB 100, Buffalo, NY 14240; tel. (716) 856-5555; fax (716) 856-5150; internet www.buffalonews.com; f. 1880; Publr STANFORD LIPSEY; Editor MARGARET M. SULLIVAN; circ. Mon. to Fri. 178,365, Sat. 181,570, Sun. 260,445.

Daily Gazette: 2345 Maxon Rd, Schenectady, NY 12308; POB 1090, Schenectady, NY 12301-1090; tel. (518) 374-4141; fax (518) 395-3089; e-mail gazette@dailygazette.com; internet www.dailygazette.com; f. 1894; Publr and Editor JOHN E. N. HUME, III; Editor JUDITH PATRICK; circ. Mon. to Fri. 47,277, Sat. 46,807, Sun. 46,356.

Democrat and Chronicle: 55 Exchange Blvd, Rochester, NY 14614-2001; tel. (585) 258-2220; fax (585) 258-3027; e-mail azoibi@gannett.com; internet www.democratandchronicle.com; f. 1833; Publr ALI M. ZOIBI; Editor KAREN MAGNUSON; circ. Mon. to Fri. 145,913, Sat. 163,585, Sun. 199,533.

Newsday: 235 Pinelawn Rd, Melville, NY 11747; tel. (631) 843-2000; fax (516) 843-2953; e-mail editor@newsday.com; internet www.newsday.com; f. 1940; Publr TIMOTHY P. KNIGHT; Editor JOHN MANCINI; circ. Mon. to Fri. 379,613, Sat. 339,389, Sun. 441,728.

Post-Standard: Clinton Sq., POB 4915, Syracuse, NY 13221; tel. (315) 470-0011; fax (315) 470-3081; e-mail mconnor@syracuse.com; internet post-standard.com; f. 1829; Editor and Publr STEPHEN A. ROGERS; Exec. Editor MICHAEL J. CONNOR; circ. Mon. to Fri. 110,061, Sat. 107,508, Sun. 158,529.

Press & Sun-Bulletin: 4421 Vestal Parkway East, Vestal, NY 13850; tel. (607) 798-1234; fax (607) 352-2645; internet www.pressconnects.com; f. 1985; Publr SHERMAN M. BODNER; Exec. Editor CALVIN STOVALL; circ. Mon. to Fri. 48,306, Sat. 47,564, Sun. 60,482.

Times Herald-Record ('The Record'): 40 Mulberry St, POB 2046, Middletown, NY 10940; tel. (914) 341-1100; fax (914) 343-2170; e-mail dosenenko@th-record.com; internet www.recordonline.com; f. 1956; Publr JOE VANDERHOOF; Exec. Editor DEREK OSENENKO; circ. Mon. to Fri. 75,745, Sat. 71,429, Sun. 81,794.

New York City

New York Daily News: 450 West 33rd St, New York, NY 10001; tel. (212) 210-2100; fax (212) 682-4953; internet www.nydailynews.com; f. 1919; Publr MORTIMER B. ZUCKERMAN; circ. Mon. to Fri. 703,137, Sat. 473,019, Sun. 704,157.

New York Post: 1211 Ave of the Americas, New York, NY 10036-8790; tel. (212) 930-8000; fax (212) 930-8540; e-mail aaquilina@nypost.com; internet www.nypost.com; f. 1801; Publr RUPERT MURDOCH; Editor-in-Chief COL ALLAN; circ. Mon. to Fri. 702,488, Sat. 433,956, Sun. 401,315.

New York Sun: 105 Chambers St, 2nd Floor, New York, NY 10007; tel. (212) 406-2000; fax (212) 571-9836; e-mail admin@nysun.net; internet www.nysun.com; f. 2002; Publr RONALD WEINTRAUB; Editor and Pres. SETH LIPSKY; circ. Mon. to Fri. 132,199 (2006).

New York Times: 620 Eighth Ave, New York, NY 10018; tel. (212) 556-1234; e-mail public@nytimes.com; internet www.nytimes.com; f. 1851; Chair. and Publr ARTHUR OCHS SULZBERGER, Jr; Pres. and Gen. Man. SCOTT H. HEEKIN-CANEDY; Exec. Editor BILL KELLER; circ. Mon. to Fri. 1,077,256, Sat. 994,044, Sun. 1,476,400.

Staten Island Advance: 950 Fingerboard Rd, Staten Island, New York, NY 10305; tel. (718) 981-1234; fax (718) 981-5679; e-mail silverstein@siadvance.com; internet www.statenislandadvance.com; f. 1886; Mon. to Sat. evening, Sun. morning; Publr CAROLINE DIAMOND HARRISON; Editor BRIAN J. LALINE; circ. Mon. to Fri. 56,875, Sat. 52,736, Sun. 69,311.

The Wall Street Journal: 200 Liberty St, New York, NY 10281; tel. (212) 416-2000; internet www.wsj.com; f. 1889; publ. by Dow Jones & Co Inc; morning; Chair. M. PETER MCPHERSON; CEO LES HINTON; Man. Editor ROBERT THOMSON; circ. Mon. to Fri. 2,062,312, Sat. 1,968,413.

North Carolina

Charlotte Observer: 600 South Tryon St, POB 32188-28232, Charlotte, NC 28202-1842; tel. (704) 358-5000; fax (704) 358-5036; e-mail charlottefeedback@charlotteobserver.com; internet www.charlotteobserver.com; f. 1886; Publr and Pres. ANN CAULKINS; Editor RICK THAMES; circ. Mon. to Fri. 210,616, Sat. 228,117, Sun. 264,170.

Citizen-Times: 14 Ohenry Ave, POB 2090, Asheville, NC 28802; tel. (828) 232-5934; fax (828) 251-0585; e-mail pfernandez@citizen-times.com; internet www.citizen-times.com; f. 1870; morning; Publr and Pres. RANDY HAMMER; Exec. Editor PHIL FERNANDEZ; circ. Mon. to Fri. 50,160, Sat. 44,436, Sun. 55,991.

Fayetteville Observer-Times: Fayetteville Publishing Co, 458 Whitfield St, POB 849, Fayetteville, NC 28302; tel. (910) 323-4848; fax (919) 486-3531; e-mail cbwell@fayobserver.com; internet www.fayobserver.com; f. 1816; morning; Publr CHARLES BROADWELL; Exec. Editor MIKE ARNHOLT; circ. Mon. to Fri. 61,875, Sat. 61,033, Sun. 65,595.

Greensboro News and Record: 200 East Market St, POB 20848, Greensboro, NC 27420-0848; tel. (336) 373-7000; fax (336) 373-7067; e-mail jrobinson@news-record.com; internet www.news-record.com; f. 1905; Publr and Pres. ROBIN SAUL; Exec. Editor JOHN ROBINSON; circ. Mon. to Fri. 84,339, Sat. 82,522, Sun. 101,409.

News and Observer: 215 South McDowell St, POB 191, Raleigh, NC 27602; tel. (919) 829-4500; fax (919) 829-4872; internet www.newsobserver.com; f. 1872; Publr ORAGE QUARLES, III; Exec. Editor JOHN DRESCHER; circ. Mon. to Fri. 176,083, Sat. 170,527, Sun. 211,245.

Winston-Salem Journal: 418 North Marshall St, POB 3159, Winston-Salem, NC 27102-3159; tel. (336) 727-7211; fax (336) 727-4071; e-mail mhall@journalnow.com; internet www.journalnow.com; Publr and Pres. MICHAEL MILLER; Exec. Editor CARL CROTHERS; circ. Mon. to Fri. 81,930, Sat. 85,915, Sun. 92,360.

North Dakota

The Forum: 101 Fifth St North, Box 2020, Fargo, ND 58107; tel. (701) 235-7311; fax (701) 241-5406; internet www.in-forum.com; f. 1878; Publr WILLIAM C. MARCIL; Editor MATT VON PINNON; circ. Mon. to Fri. 48,303, Sat. 54,023, Sun. 58,277.

Ohio

Akron Beacon Journal: 44 East Exchange St, POB 640, Akron, OH 44308; tel. (330) 996-3000; fax (330) 996-3033; internet www.ohio.com; f. 1839; Publr ANDREA MATHEWSON; Editor BRUCE WINGES; circ. Mon. to Fri. 122,373, Sat. 147,325, Sun. 157,713.

Canton Repository: 500 Market Ave South, Canton, OH 44711-2112; tel. (330) 580-8300; fax (330) 454-5610; e-mail newsroom@cantonrep.com; internet www.cantonrep.com; f. 1815; Publr KEVIN KAMPMAN; Editor JEFF GAUGER; circ. Mon. to Fri. 65,789, Sat. 67,236, Sun. 78,066.

Cincinnati Enquirer: 312 Elm St, Cincinnati, OH 45202; tel. (513) 768-8000; fax (513) 768-8340; e-mail mperry@enquirer.com; internet www.cincinnati.com; f. 1841; Publr and Pres. MARGARET E. BUCHANAN; Editor TOM CALLINAN; circ. Mon. to Fri. 212,369, Sat. 212,019, Sun. 279,825.

Cleveland Plain Dealer: 1801 Superior Ave East, Cleveland, OH 44114-2198; tel. (216) 999-4800; fax (216) 999-6354; e-mail tegger@plaind.com; internet www.plaindealer.com; f. 1842; Pres. and Publr TERRENCE C. Z. EGGER; Editor SUSAN GOLDBERG; circ. Mon. to Fri. 330,280, Sat. 310,320, Sun. 428,090.

Columbus Dispatch: 34 South Third St, Columbus, OH 43215; tel. (614) 461-5000; fax (614) 461-7580; e-mail letters@dispatch.com; internet www.dispatch.com; f. 1871; Pres. MICHAEL FIORILE; Editor BEN MARRISON; circ. Mon. to Fri. 199,524, Sat. 257,776, Sun. 334,422.

Dayton Daily News: 1611 South Main St, Dayton, OH 45409; tel. (937) 222-5700; fax (937) 225-2489; e-mail kriley@coxohio.com;

THE UNITED STATES OF AMERICA

internet www.daytondailynews.com; Publr MICHAEL JOSEPH; Editor KEVIN RILEY; circ. Mon. to Fri. 160,690, Sat. 108,477, Sun. 157,833.

News-Herald: 7085 Mentor Ave, Willoughby, OH 44094; tel. (440) 951-0000; fax (440) 951-0917; e-mail lkessel@news-herald.com; internet www.news-herald.com; f. 1880; Mon. to Sat. evening, Sun. morning; Publr STEVE ROSZCZYK; Exec. Editor TRICIA AMBROSE; circ. Mon. to Fri. 36,948, Sat. 37,383, Sun. 44,322.

Toledo Blade: 541 North Superior St, Toledo, OH 43660-1000; tel. (419) 724-6000; fax (419) 245-6191; e-mail luannsharp@theblade.com; internet www.toledoblade.com; f. 1835; Co-Publrs JOHN ROBINSON BLOCK, DIANA E. BLOCK; Exec. Editor RON ROYHAB; circ. Mon. to Fri. 119,901, Sat. 116,342, Sun. 147,141.

The Vindicator: 107 Vindicator Sq., POB 780, Youngstown, OH 44501-0780; tel. (330) 747-1471; fax (330) 747-6712; e-mail bjagnow@vindy.com; internet www.vindy.com; Publr BETTY H. BROWN JAGNOW; Gen. Man. MARK BROWN; circ. Mon. to Fri. 56,412, Sat. 59,082, Sun. 75,257.

Oklahoma

Daily Oklahoman: 9000 North Broadway, POB 25125, Oklahoma City, OK 73125; tel. (405) 475-3311; fax (405) 475-3183; internet www.newsok.com; f. 1894; Publr DAVID THOMPSON; Exec. Editor SUE HALE; circ. Mon. to Fri. 210,771, Sat. 183,122, Sun. 262,150.

Tulsa World: 315 South Boulder Ave, POB 1770, Tulsa, OK 74103; tel. (918) 581-8300; fax (918) 581-8353; e-mail letters@tulsaworld.com; internet www.tulsaworld.com; f. 1906; Publr ROBERT E. LORTON, III; Exec. Editor JOE WORLEY; circ. Mon. to Fri. 112,968, Sat. 125,200, Sun. 160,052.

Oregon

The Oregonian: 1320 SW Broadway, Portland, OR 97201-3469; tel. (503) 221-8150; fax (503) 294-4193; e-mail s.rowe@news.oregonian.com; internet www.oregonian.com; f. 1850; Publr FRED A. STICKEL; Editor SANDY ROWE; circ. Mon. to Fri. 304,399, Sat. 280,930, Sun. 361,988.

The Register-Guard: POB 10188, Eugene, OR 97440-2188; tel. (541) 485-1234; fax (541) 683-7631; e-mail tbaker@guardnet.com; internet www.registerguard.com; f. 1867; Publr and Editor TONY BAKER; circ. Mon. to Fri. 67,400, Sat. 72,278, Sun. 70,193.

Statesman Journal: 280 Church St, NE, POB 13009, Salem, OR 97309-3009; tel. (509) 399-6611; fax (503) 399-6706; e-mail newsroom@statesmanjournal.com; internet www.statesmanjournal.com; f. 1851; Publr and Pres. STEVE SILBERMAN; Exec. Editor BILL CHURCH; circ. Mon. to Fri. 47,131, Sat. 47,481, Sun. 53,101.

Pennsylvania

Bucks County Courier Times: 8400 Route 13, Levittown, PA 19057-5198; tel. (215) 949-4000; fax (215) 949-4114; e-mail pwalker@phillyburbs.com; internet www.phillyburbs.com; f. 1910; owned by Calkins Media Inc; Publr DALE LARSON; Exec. Editor PATRICIA S. WALKER; circ. Mon. to Fri. 60,233, Sat. 55,673, Sun. 63,571.

Call Chronicle: POB 1260, Allentown, PA 18105; tel. (610) 820-6500; fax (610) 820-6693; f. 1921; Sun.; Publr GARY K. SHORTS; Exec. Editor LAWRENCE H. HYMANS; circ. 189,000.

The Morning Call: 101 North Sixth St, POB 1260, Allentown, PA 18105; tel. (610) 820-6553; fax (610) 820-6693; e-mail marie.herb@mcall.com; internet www.mcall.com; Publr TIMOTHY R. KENNEDY; Editor ARDITH HILLIARD; circ. Mon. to Fri. 108,797, Sat. 113,178, Sun. 140,789.

Patriot-News: 812 Market St, Harrisburg, PA 17105; tel. (717) 255-8100; fax (717) 255-8456; internet www.patriot-news.com; f. 1854; Publr JOHN KIRKPATRICK; Exec. Editor DAVID NEWHOUSE; circ. 102,467 (morning), 154,021 (Sunday).

Philadelphia Daily News: 400 North Broad St, POB 7788, Philadelphia, PA 19130; tel. (215) 854-5900; fax (215) 854-5910; e-mail dailynews.opinion@phillynews.com; internet www.philly.com; f. 1925; Publr MARK J. FRISBY; Man. Editor MICHAEL DAYS; circ. Mon. to Fri. 107,269, Sat. 70,066.

Philadelphia Inquirer: 400 North Broad St, POB 8623, Philadelphia, PA 19101; tel. (215) 854-2000; fax (215) 854-4974; e-mail mleary@phillynews.com; internet www.philly.com/inquirer; f. 1829; Publr BRIAN TIERNEY; Editor WILLIAM K. MARIMOW; circ. Mon. to Fri. 334,150, Sat. 328,117, Sun. 630,665.

Pittsburg Post-Gazette: 34 Blvd of the Allies, Pittsburgh, PA 15222; tel. (412) 263-1100; fax (412) 391-8452; e-mail ssmith@post-gazette.com; internet www.post-gazette.com; f. 1786; Publrs WILLIAM BLOCK, Jr, JOHN ROBINSON BLOCK; Exec. Editor DAVID M. SHRIBMAN, Jr; circ. Mon. to Fri. 214,374, Sat. 198,096, Sun. 331,053.

Sunday News: Lancaster Newspapers, Inc, 8 West King St, POB 1328, Lancaster, PA 17608; tel. (717) 291-8811; fax (717) 399-6506; e-mail madams@lnpnews.com; internet www.lancasteronline.com/lol_pages/paper/sundaynews; f. 1923; Editor MARV ADAMS; circ. 100,060 (2007).

Tribune-Democrat: 425 Locust St, POB 340, Johnstown, PA 15907-0340; tel. (814) 532-5050; fax (814) 539-1409; e-mail cminemyer@tribdem.com; internet www.tribune-democrat.com; f. 1853; morning; Publr ROBIN QUILLON; Editor CHIP MINEMYER; circ. Mon. to Fri. 37,673, Sat. 37,857, Sun. 41,430.

Rhode Island

Providence Journal: 75 Fountain St, Providence, RI 02902-0050; tel. (401) 277-7000; fax (401) 277-7346; e-mail sareson@projo.com; internet www.projo.com; f. 1829; publ. by Belo Corpn; Publr HOWARD G. SUTTON; Exec. Editor JOEL P. RAWSON; circ. Mon. to Fri. 139,055, Sat. 177,824, Sun. 192,849.

South Carolina

Greenville News: 305 South Main St, POB 1688, Greenville, SC 29601-2605; tel. (864) 298-4100; fax (864) 298-4805; e-mail letters@greenvillenews.com; internet www.greenvilleonline.com; f. 1874; Publr STEVEN BRANDT; Editor JOHN S. PITTMAN; circ. Mon. to Fri. 81,010, Sat. 77,529, Sun. 108,568.

The Post and Courier: 134 Columbus St, Charleston, SC 29403-4800; tel. (843) 577-7111; fax (843) 937-5579; e-mail publiceditor@postandcourier.com; internet www.charleston.net; f. 1803; Publr LARRY W. TARLETON, Jr; Exec. Editor BILL HAWKINS; circ. Mon. to Fri. 100,400, Sat. 94,716, Sun. 110,289.

The State: 1401 Shop Rd, POB 1333, Columbia, SC 29202; tel. (803) 771-8380; fax (803) 771-8430; e-mail stateeditor@thestate.com; internet www.thestate.com; f. 1891; Publr HENRY HAITZ, III; Exec. Editor MARK LETT; circ. Mon. to Fri. 101,010, Sat. 106,822, Sun. 128,564.

South Dakota

Argus Leader: 200 South Minnesota Ave, POB 5034, Sioux Falls, SD 57117-5034; tel. (605) 331-2200; fax (605) 331-2294; e-mail jzimmerm@argusleader.com; internet www.argusleader.com; f. 1881; Publr RANDELL BECK; Exec. Editor MARICARROL KUETER; circ. Mon. to Fri. 48,960, Sat. 45,210, Sun. 65,709.

Tennessee

Chattanooga Times-Free Press: 400 East 11th St, Chattanooga, TN 37403; tel. (423) 756-6900; fax (423) 757-6383; e-mail tgriscom@timesfreepress.com; internet www.timesfreepress.com; f. 1888; Publr and Exec. Editor TOM GRISCOM; circ. Mon. to Fri. 71,716, Sat. 83,272, Sun. 95,039.

The Commercial Appeal: 495 Union Ave, Memphis, TN 38103; tel. (901) 529-2211; fax (901) 529-2522; internet www.commercialappeal.com; f. 1841; Pres. and Publr JOSEPH PEPE; Editor CHRIS PECK; circ. Mon. to Sat. 149,165, Sun. 190,828.

Knoxville News-Sentinel: 2332 News Sentinel Dr., Knoxville, TN 37921-5731; tel. (865) 523-3131; fax (865) 342-8650; internet www.knoxnews.com; f. 1886; Publr BRUCE HARTMANN; Editor JACK McELROY; circ. Mon. to Fri. 117,262, Sat. 124,493, Sun. 147.939.

The Tennessean: 1100 Broadway St, Nashville, TN 37203; tel. (615) 259-8800; fax (615) 259-8093; e-mail publisher@tennessean.com; internet www.tennessean.com; f. 1812; Publr ELLEN LEIFELD; Editor MARK SILVERMAN; circ. Mon. to Fri. 161,131, Sat. 168,881, Sun. 219,044.

Texas

Austin American-Statesman: 305 South Congress Ave, Austin, TX 78704; POB 670, Austin, TX 78767; tel. (512) 445-3500; fax (512) 445-3679; internet www.statesman.com; f. 1871; Publr MICHAEL VIVIO; Editor FRED ZIPP; circ. Mon. to Fri. 170,209, Sat. 167,278, Sun. 206,505.

Beaumont Enterprise: 380 Main St, POB 3071, Beaumont, TX 77701-2183; tel. (409) 833-3311; fax (409) 838-2857; e-mail tkelly@hearstnp.com; internet www.beaumontenterprise.com; f. 1880; Publr JOHN E. NEWHOUSE, II; Editor TIM KELLY; circ. Mon. to Fri. 45,684, Sat. 44,720, Sun. 51,342.

Corpus Christi Caller-Times: 820 North Lower Broadway, POB 9136, Corpus Christi, TX 78469; tel. (361) 884-2011; fax (361) 886-3732; internet www.caller.com; f. 1883; Publr PATRICK J. BIRMINGHAM; Editor LIBBY AVERYT; circ. Mon. to Fri. 53,368, Sat. 57,135, Sun. 73,746.

Dallas Morning News: 508 Young St, Dallas, TX 75202; tel. (214) 977-8222; fax (214) 977-8319; internet www.dallasnews.com; f. 1885; publ. by Belo Corpn; Publr JAMES M. MORONEY, III; Editor ROBERT W. MONG, Jr; circ. Mon. to Fri. 368,313, Sat. 362,834, Sun. 520,215.

El Paso Times: Times Plaza, El Paso, TX 79901-1470; tel. (915) 546-6104; fax (915) 546-6415; internet www.elpasotimes.com; f. 1881;

THE UNITED STATES OF AMERICA

Publr Ray M. Stafford; Editor (vacant); circ. Mon. to Fri. 72,027, Sat. 70,809, Sun. 82,927.

Fort Worth Star-Telegram: 400 West 7th St, Fort Worth, TX 76102; tel. (817) 390-7400; fax (817) 390-7789; e-mail newsroom@star-telegram.com; internet www.star-telegram.com; f. 1909; Publr Gary Wortel; Exec. Editor Jim Witt; circ. Mon. to Fri. 207,045, Sat. 209,384, Sun. 289,974.

Houston Chronicle: 801 Texas Ave, Houston, TX 77002; tel. (713) 362-7171; fax (713) 362-3575; e-mail online@chron.com; internet www.chron.com; f. 1901; Publr Jack Sweeney; Editor Jeff Cohen; circ. Mon. to Fri. 494,131, Sat. 482,152, Sun. 632,797.

Lubbock Avalanche-Journal: 710 Ave J, POB 491, Lubbock, TX 79401-1808; tel. (806) 762-8844; fax (806) 744-9603; e-mail terry.greenberg@lubbockonline.com; internet www.lubbockonline.com; f. 1900; Publr Stephen A. Beasley; Editor Terry Greenberg; circ. Mon. to Fri. 49,094, Sat. 47,068, Sun. 55,484.

San Antonio Express-News: 301 Ave E, San Antonio, TX 78205; tel. (210) 250-3000; fax (210) 250-3105; e-mail rrivard@express-news.net; internet www.mysanantonio.com; f. 1864; Publr Thomas A. Stephenson; Editor Robert Rivard; circ. Mon. to Fri. 225,447, Sat. 220,575, Sun. 315,959.

Utah

Deseret Morning News: 30 East 100 South, POB 1257, Salt Lake City, UT 84110; tel. (801) 236-6000; fax (801) 237-2121; e-mail rhall@desnews.com; internet www.deseretnews.com; f. 1850; Publr Jim M. Wall; Editor Joseph A. Cannon; circ. Mon. to Fri. 73,817, Sat. 74,126, Sun. 75,022.

Salt Lake Tribune: 90 South 400 West, Suite 700, Salt Lake City, UT 84101; tel. (801) 237-8782; fax (801) 257-8525; e-mail fitz@sltrib.com; internet www.sltrib.com; f. 1871; Man. Editor Tim Fitzpatrick; circ. Mon. to Fri. 121,699, Sat. 116,912, Sun. 143,296.

Standard-Examiner: 332 Standard Way, POB 12790, Ogden, UT 84412-2790; tel. (801) 625-4200; fax (801) 625-4508; e-mail ahowell@standard.net; internet www.standard.net; f. 1888; Publr Lee Carter; Exec. Editor Andy Howell; circ. Mon. to Fri. 61,696, Sat. 60,496, Sun. 64,439.

Vermont

Burlington Free Press: 191 College St, POB 10, Burlington, VT 05402-0010; tel. (802) 863-3441; fax (802) 660-1802; e-mail bhart@bfp.burlingtonfreepress.com; internet www.burlingtonfreepress.com; f. 1827; Publr Brad Robertson; Exec. Editor Mike Townsend; circ. Mon. to Fri. 41,901, Sat. 39,248, Sun. 47,566.

Virginia

Daily Press: 7505 Warwick Blvd, Newport News, VA 23607; tel. (757) 247-4600; fax (757) 245-8618; e-mail mccormick@aol.com; internet www.dailypress.com; f. 1896; Publr Digby A. Solomon; Editor Ernest C. Gates; circ. Mon. to Fri. 81,241, Sat. 89,114, Sun. 103,308.

Richmond Times-Dispatch: 300 East Franklin St, POB 85333, Richmond, VA 23219; tel. (804) 649-6000; e-mail letters@timesdispatch.com; internet www.timesdispatch.com; f. 1850; Publr Thomas A. Silvestri; Exec. Editor Glenn Proctor; circ. Mon. to Fri. 186,441, Sat. 184,175, Sun. 214,971.

Roanoke Times: 201 West Campbell Ave, POB 2491, Roanoke, VA 24010-2491; tel. (540) 981-3340; fax (540) 981-3346; internet www.roanoke.com; Publr Debbie Meade; Editor Carole Tarrant; circ. Mon. to Fri. 88,927, Sat. 88,822, Sun. 100,120.

USA Today: 7950 Jones Branch Dr., McLean, VA 22108-0605; tel. (703) 276-3400; internet www.usatoday.com; f. 1982; Pres. and Publr Craig A. Moon; Editor Kenneth Paulson; circ. Mon. to Fri. 2,284,219.

Virginian-Pilot: 150 West Brambleton Ave, POB 449, Norfolk, VA 23501-0449; tel. (757) 446-2000; fax (757) 446-2051; e-mail letters@pilotonline.com; internet thevirginianpilot.com; f. 1876; Publr Bruce Bradley; Man. Editor Maria Carillo; circ. Mon. to Fri. 175,005, Sat. 183,434, Sun. 200,012.

Washington

The Herald: 1213 California St, Everett, WA 98201; POB 930, Everett, WA 98206; tel. (425) 339-3435; fax (425) 339-3049; e-mail funk@herald.net; internet www.heraldnet.com; f. 1891; Publr Allen B. Funk; Exec. Editor Neal Pattison; circ. Mon. to Fri. 50,272, Sat. 47,987, Sun. 53,946.

News Tribune: 1950 South State St, POB 11000, Tacoma, WA 98411; tel. (253) 597-8742; fax (253) 597-8451; e-mail karen.peterson@thenewstribune.com; internet www.thenewstribune.com; f. 1883; Pres. and Publr David A. Zeeck; Exec. Editor Karen Peterson; circ. Mon. to Fri. 111,778, Sat. 107,286, Sun. 125,955.

Seattle Times: 1120 John St, POB 70, Seattle, WA 98111-0070; tel. (206) 464-2111; fax (206) 464-2261; e-mail pfoote@seattletimes.com; internet seattletimes.nwsource.com; f. 1896; Publr Frank A. Blethen; Exec. Editor David Boardman; circ. Mon. to Fri. 220,863, Sat. 196,377.

Spokesman-Review: 999 West Riverside, POB 2160, Spokane, WA 99210; tel. (509) 459-5000; fax (509) 459-3815; e-mail editor@spokesman.com; internet www.spokesman.com; f. 1883; Publr William Stacey Cowles; Editor (vacant); circ. Mon. to Fri. 89,779, Sat. 101,310, Sun. 113,081.

West Virginia

Charleston Daily Mail: 1001 Virginia St East, Charleston, WV 25301-2835; tel. (304) 348-5140; fax (304) 348-4847; e-mail dmnews@dailymail.com; internet www.dailymail.com; f. 1973; evening; Publr and Editor Nanya Friend; Man. Editor Bob Kelly; circ. Mon. to Fri. 21,723.

Wisconsin

Green Bay Press-Gazette: 435 East Walnut St, POB 23430, Green Bay, WI 54305-3430; tel. (920) 435-4411; fax (920) 431-8499; e-mail jdye@greenbaypressgazette.com; internet www.greenbaypressgazette.com; f. 1915; bought by Gannett Co in 1980; Publr William T. Nusbaum; Exec. Editor John Dye; circ. Mon. to Fri. 53,600, Sat. 61,853, Sun. 16,894.

Milwaukee Journal Sentinel: 333 West State St, POB 371, Milwaukee, WI 53201; tel. (414) 224-2919; fax (414) 224-2047; e-mail gstanley@journalsentinel.com; internet www.jsonline.com; f. 1837; Publr Elizabeth 'Betsy' Brenner; Editor Martin Kaiser; circ. Mon. to Fri. 217,755, Sat. 208,586, Sun. 384,539.

Post-Crescent: 306 West Washington St, POB 59, Appleton, WI 54911; tel. (920) 733-4411; fax (920) 733-1983; e-mail gmagno@postcrescent.com; internet www.postcrescent.com; f. 1920; Mon. to Sat. evening, Sun. morning; Publr Genia Lovett; Exec. Editor Dan Flannery; circ. Mon. to Fri. 51,509, Sat. 57,923, Sun. 67,070.

Wisconsin State Journal: 1901 Fish Hatchery Rd, POB 8058, Madison, WI 53713; tel. (608) 252-6100; fax (608) 252-6119; e-mail wsjcity@madison.com; internet www.madison.com/wsj; f. 1839; Publr William K. Johnston; Sr Editor David Dombrowski; circ. Mon. to Fri. 87,930, Sat. 92,260, Sun. 138,276.

Wyoming

Star-Tribune: 170 Star Lane, POB 80, Casper, WY 82602; tel. (307) 266-0500; fax (307) 266-0568; e-mail nathan.bekke@trib.com; internet www.trib.com; f. 1891; Publr Nathan Bekke; Editor Chad Baldwin; circ. Mon. to Fri. 28,312, Sat. 28,216, Sun. 29,860.

SELECTED PERIODICALS

AARP The Magazine: 601 E St, NW, Washington, DC 20049; tel. (202) 434-2560; e-mail aarpmagazine@aarp.org; internet www.aarpmagazine.org; f. 1958 following merger of *My Generation* and *Modern Maturity*; publ. of the American Assen of Retired Persons; 6 a year; general interest for the over-50s; Group Publr, Vice-Pres. and Publr Jim Fishman; Editor-in-Chief Hugh Delahanty; Editor Nancy Graham (acting); circ. 23,893,285; AARP also publishes *AARP Bulletin* (11 a year, circ. 24,248,164) and *AARP Segunda Juventud* (quarterly, in Spanish and English).

Allure: 4 Times Sq., New York, NY 10036; tel. (212) 286-2860; fax (212) 286-4654; internet www.allure.com; f. 1991; publ. by Condé Nast Publs Inc; monthly; women's fashion and wellbeing; Vice-Pres. and Publr Agnes Chapski; Editor-in-Chief Linda Wells; circ. 1,091,147.

American Heritage: 90 Fifth Ave, New York, NY 10011-8882; tel. (212) 367-3100; fax (212) 367-3149; e-mail mail@americanheritage.com; internet www.americanheritage.com; f. 1954; 8 a year; US history; Publr Frank Rosa; Editor Richard F. Snow; circ. 318,571; American Heritage also publishes *American Heritage of Inventions and Technology* and quarterly African-American history and culture magazine *American Legacy*.

The American Legion Magazine: 700 North Pennsylvania St, POB 1055, Indianapolis, IN 46206-1055; tel. (317) 630-1298; fax (317) 630-1223; e-mail magazine@legion.org; internet www.legion.org; f. 1919; publ. of The American Legion; monthly; Editor Jeff Stoffer; circ. 2,515,624.

American Rifleman: NRA Publications, 11250 Waples Mill Rd, Fairfax, VA 22030; tel. (703) 267-1329; e-mail publications@nrahq.org; internet www.nrapublications.org; f. 1885; official journal of the Nat. Rifle Assen; monthly; Editor-in-Chief Mark A. Keefe, IV; circ. 1,394,573.

American Teacher: 555 New Jersey Ave, NW, Washington, DC 20001-2079; tel. (202) 879-4400; fax (202) 783-2014; e-mail mailbox@

THE UNITED STATES OF AMERICA   Directory

aft.org; internet www.aft.org; f. 1916; 8 a year; Editor ROGER GLASS; circ. 800,000.

Architectural Digest: Condé Nast Publications Inc, 6300 Wilshire Blvd, Los Angeles, CA 90048; tel. (213) 965-3700; fax (213) 965-4975; internet www.architecturaldigest.com; f. 1920; monthly; Vice-Pres. and Publr GIULIO CAPUA; Editor-in-Chief PAIGE RENSE; circ. 850,502.

Arthritis Today: 1330 West Peachtree St, NW, Suite 100, Atlanta, GA 30309; tel. (404) 965-7635; e-mail atmail@arthritis.org; internet www.arthritis.org/resources/arthritistoday; f. 1987; publ. by the Arthritis Foundation; 6 a year; health and lifestyle magazine for sufferers of arthritis; Publr CINDY MCDANIEL; Editor-in-Chief MARCY O'KOON MOSS; circ. 721,367.

Barron's: 200 Liberty St, 9th Floor, New York, NY 10281; tel. (212) 416-2000; e-mail editors@barrons.com; internet www.barrons.com; f. 1921; publ. by Dow Jones & Co, Inc; Dow Jones & Co, Inc acquired by News Corpn in 2008; weekly; business and finance; Pres. and Editor EDWIN A. FINN, Jr; circ. 308,116.

Better Homes and Gardens: 1716 Locust St, Des Moines, IA 50309-3023; tel. (515) 284-3000; fax (515) 284-3684; internet www.bhg.com; f. 1922; monthly; Vice-Pres. and Publr JAMES T. CARR; Editor-in-Chief GAYLE BUTLER; Exec. Editor KITTY MORGAN; circ. 7,651,178.

Bon Appétit: 6300 Wilshire Blvd, 10th Floor, Los Angeles, CA 90048; tel. (323) 965-3600; fax (323) 930-2369; internet www.bonappetit.com; f. 1955; monthly; Vice-Pres. and Publr PAUL JOWDY; Editor-in-Chief BARBARA FAIRCHILD; circ. 1,371,495.

Boys' Life: 1325 West Walnut Hill Lane, POB 152079, Irving, TX 75015-2079; tel. (972) 580-2263; fax (972) 580-2079; e-mail boyslifemagazine@netbsa.org; internet www.boyslife.org; f. 1911; publ. by Boy Scouts of America; monthly; Publr J. WARREN YOUNG; Editor J. D. OWEN; circ. 1,183,133.

BusinessWeek: 1221 Ave of the Americas, 43rd Floor, New York, NY 10120; tel. (212) 512-2511; e-mail lou_tosto@businessweek.com; internet www.businessweek.com; f. 1929; publ. by BusinessWeek Group, a subsidiary of The McGraw-Hill Cos, Inc; weekly; business, finance and technology; Editor-in-Chief STEPHEN J. ADLER; circ. 925,226.

Car and Driver: 1585 Eisenhower Pl., Ann Arbor, MI 48108; tel. (734) 971-3600; fax (734) 971-9188; e-mail editors@caranddriver.com; internet www.caranddriver.com; f. 1956; publ. by Hachette Filipacchi Media US, Inc; Publr ROBERT G. HOUGHTLIN, III; Editor-in-Chief CSABA CSERE; circ. 1,303,077.

Catholic Digest: 1 Montauk Ave, Suite 200, New London, CT 06320-4967; tel. (800) 321-0411; fax (860) 572-0788; e-mail connors@catholicdigest.com; internet www.catholicdigest.com; f. 1936; monthly; Publr KATHLEEN STAUFFER; Editor DAN CONNORS; circ. 283,548.

Child: 375 Lexington Ave, 9th Floor, New York, NY 10017-5514; tel. (212) 499-2000; fax (212) 499-2038; e-mail mailcenter@child.com; internet www.child.com; f. 1986; 10 a year; Publr RICHARD BERENSON; Editor-in-Chief MIRIAM AROND; circ. 1,020,000.

Condé Nast Traveler: 4 Times Sq., 14th Floor, New York, NY 10036-6561; tel. (212) 286-2860; fax (212) 286-2094; e-mail beth_lusko@condenast.com; internet www.concierge.com/cntraveler; f. 1954; monthly; Publr LISA HENRIQUES HUGHES; Editor-in-Chief KLARA GLOWCZEWSKA; circ. 820,217.

Congressional Digest: Congressional Digest Corpn, POB 240, Boyds, MD 20841-0240; tel. (301) 634-3113; fax (240) 599-7679; e-mail info@congressionaldigest.com; internet www.congressionaldigest.com; f. 1921; monthly; Publr PAGE B. ROBINSON THOMAS.

Consumer Reports: 101 Truman Ave, Yonkers, NY 10703-1057; tel. (914) 378-2000; fax (914) 378-2900; e-mail pressroom@consumer.org; internet www.consumerreports.org; f. 1936; monthly; Editor-in-Chief KIM KLEMAN; Man. Editor ROBERT TIERNAN; circ. 4,000,000.

Consumers Digest: Consumers Digest Communications, 520 Lake Cook Rd, Suite 500, Deerfield, IL 60015; tel. (847) 607-3000; e-mail postmaster@consumersdigest.com; internet www.consumersdigest.com; f. 1959; 6 a year; Publr RANDY WEBER; circ. 1,200,000.

Cosmopolitan: 300 West 57th St, New York, NY 10019-3299; tel. (212) 649-3570; e-mail cosmo@hearst.com; internet www.cosmopolitan.com; f. 1886; women's interest; Publr DONNA KALAJIAN LAGANI; Editor-in-Chief KATE WHITE; circ. 2,937,861.

Country Home: 1716 Locust St, Des Moines, IA 50309; tel. (515) 284-2015; e-mail countryhome@meredith.com; internet www.countryhome.com; f. 1979; publ. by Meredith Corpn; 10 a year; lifestyle; Publr ANTHONY IMPERATO; Editor-in-Chief CAROL SHEEHAN; circ. 1,271,782.

Country Living: 300 West 57th St, New York, NY 10019-3788; tel. (212) 649-3500; e-mail countryliving@hearst.com; internet www.countryliving.com; f. 1978; monthly; Publr STEVEN GRUNE; Editor-in-Chief NANCY MERNIT SORIANO; circ. 1,625,836.

Discover: 90 Fifth Ave, New York, NY 10011; tel. (212) 624-4800; fax (212) 624-4813; e-mail bhostetter@discover.com; internet www.discovermagazine.com; f. 1980; publ. by Discover Media LLC; science and technology; Publr WILLIAM C. HOSTETTER; Exec. Editor COREY S. POWELL; circ. 717,122.

Ebony: Johnson Publishing, 820 South Michigan Ave, Chicago, IL 60605-2191; tel. (312) 322-9200; fax (312) 322-0039; internet www.ebonyjet.com/ebony; f. 1945; monthly; African-American general interest; Publr KENARD GIBBS; Editorial Dir BRYAN MONROE; circ. 1,450,416.

Elks Magazine: 425 West Diversey Pkwy, Chicago, IL 60614-6196; tel. (773) 755-4740; fax (773) 755-4792; e-mail elksmag@elks.org; internet www.elks.org/elksmag; f. 1922; 10 a year; publ. by the Benevolent and Protective Order of Elks of the United States of America; Editor CHERYL T. STACHURA; circ. 960,000.

Elle: 1633 Broadway, 44th Floor, New York, NY 10019; tel. (212) 767-5800; fax (212) 767-5980; internet www.elle.com; f. 1985; publ. by Hachette Filipacchi Media US, Inc; monthly; women's fashion; Sr Vice-Pres. and Group Publishing Dir CAROL SMITH; Editor-in-Chief ROBERTA MYERS; circ. 1,082,278.

Endless Vacation: 360 Lexington Ave, 19th Floor, New York, NY 10017; tel. (212) 481-3452; fax (212) 213-1287; e-mail barbara.peck@storyworldwide.com; internet www.endlessvacation.com; f. 1975; publ. by Resort Condominiums Int.; 5 a year; Publr BRIAN BRUNO; Editor BARBARA PECK; circ. 1,814,218.

Entertainment Weekly: 1675 Broadway, 30th Floor, New York, NY 10019; tel. (212) 522-5600; fax (212) 522-4482; e-mail letters@ew.com; internet www.ew.com; f. 1990; Publr SCOTT DONATON; Man. Editor RICK TETZELI; circ. 1,813,411.

ESPN The Magazine: 19 East 34th St, New York, NY 10016; tel. (212) 515-1000; fax (212) 515-1275; e-mail ms_support@espn.go.com; internet espn.go.com/magazine; f. 1998; fortnightly; subsidiary of Walt Disney DIS; men's sports and lifestyle; Editor-in-Chief GARY HOENIG; circ. 2,047,969.

Esquire: 300 West 57th St, New York, NY 10019-3797; tel. (212) 649-4020; fax (212) 649-4303; e-mail esquire@hearst.com; internet www.esquire.com; f. 1933; monthly; Vice-Pres. and Publr KEVIN O'MALLEY; Editor-in-Chief DAVID GRANGER; circ. 726,358.

Essence: 135 West 50th St, 4th Floor, New York, NY 10020; tel. (212) 642-0600; fax (212) 921-5173; e-mail info@essence.com; internet www.essence.com; f. 1970; monthly; African-American general interest; Editor-in-Chief ANGELA BURT-MURRAY; circ. 1,051,130.

Family Circle: 375 Lexington Ave, 9th Floor, New York, NY 10017-5514; tel. (212) 499-2000; fax (212) 499-6740; e-mail support@familycircle.com; internet www.familycircle.com; f. 1932; publ. by Meredith Corpn; every 3 weeks; Editor-in-Chief LINDA FEARS; circ. 3,896,088.

FamilyFun: 244 Main St, Northampton, MA 01060; tel. (212) 633-4485; e-mail ellen.antoville@disney.com; internet familyfun.go.com; f. 1991; publ. by Disney Publishing Worldwide; monthly; general interest for families with young children; Editor ANN HALLOCK; circ. 1,834,166.

Family Handyman (Home Service Publications): 2915 Commers Dr., Suite 700, Eagan, MN 55121; tel. (651) 454-9200; fax (651) 994-2250; e-mail fheditor@readersdigest.com; internet www.rd.com/familyhandyman; f. 1951; publ. by Reader's Digest Assen, Inc; 10 a year; Editor-in-Chief KEN COLLIER; circ. 1,162,273.

Fast Company: 7 World Trade Center, New York, NY 10007-2195; tel. (212) 389-5300; fax (212) 389-5496; e-mail loop@fastcompany.com; internet www.fastcompany.com; f. 1995; monthly; acquired by Mansueto Ventures LLC in 2005; global business practice; Publr HAROLD BOLLING; Editor-in-Chief ROBERT SAFIAN; circ. 742,316.

FHM: 110 Fifth Ave, New York, NY 10011; tel. (212) 201-6702; fax (212) 201-6965; e-mail andrew.ormson@emapmetrousa.com; internet www.fhmus.com; f. 2000; publ. by Emap Metro LLC; monthly; men's lifestyle, entertainment and fashion; Exec. Publr and Pres. DANA FIELDS; Editor-in-Chief SCOTT GRAMLING; circ. 1,250,275 (2006).

Field & Stream: 2 Park Ave, New York, NY 10016-5601; tel. (212) 779-5000; fax (212) 779-5114; e-mail fsletters@time4.com; internet www.fieldandstream.com; f. 1895; publ. by Bonnier Corpn; 11 a year; Publr ERIC ZINCZENKO; Editor ANTHONY LICATA; circ. 1,530,786.

Fitness: 375 Lexington Ave, New York, NY 10017; tel. (212) 499-2000; internet www.fitnessmagazine.com; f. 1992; acquired by Meredith Corpn in 2005; women's health and fitness; Publr LEE SLATTERY; Editor-in-Chief BETTY WONG; circ. 1,574,067.

Food & Wine: 1120 Ave of the Americas, New York, NY 10036; tel. (212) 382-5600; fax (212) 382-5879; e-mail christina.r.grdovic@aexp.com; internet www.foodandwine.com; f. 1978; publ. by American Express Publishing Corpn; monthly; Publr CHRISTINA R. GRDOVIC; Editor-in-Chief DANA COWIN; circ. 958,348.

THE UNITED STATES OF AMERICA

Forbes: 60 Fifth Ave, New York, NY 10011-8802; tel. (212) 620-2200; fax (212) 620-1875; e-mail readers@forbes.com; internet www.forbes.com; f. 1917; fortnightly; Pres. and Editor-in-Chief STEVE FORBES; Publr RICHARD KARLGAARD; Editor WILLIAM BALDWIN; circ. 926,899.

Fortune: 1271 Ave of the Americas, New York, NY 10020; tel. (212) 522-1212; fax (212) 522-0810; e-mail letters@fortune.com; internet www.fortune.com; f. 1930; Man. Editor ANDREW SERWER; circ. 866,859.

Game Informer: 724 North First St, 4th Floor, Minneapolis, MN 55401; tel. (612) 486-6100; fax (612) 486-6101; e-mail andy@gameinformer.com; internet www.gameinformer.com; f. 1991; owned by Sunrise Publs; monthly; computer gaming; Publr CATHY PRESTON; Editor-in-Chief ANDY MCNAMARA; circ. 3,498,935.

Glamour: 4 Times Sq., 16th Floor, New York, NY 10036; tel. (212) 286-2860; fax (212) 286-8336; e-mail letters@glamour.com; internet us.glamour.com; f. 1939; publ. by Condé Nast Publs Inc; monthly; Publr WILLIAM WACKERMANN; Editor-in-Chief CYNTHIA LEIVE; circ. 2,354,973.

Golf Digest: 20 Westport Rd, POB 850, Wilton, CT 06897; tel. (800) 438-0491; fax (203) 761-5135; e-mail editor@golfdigest.com; internet www.golfdigest.com; f. 1950; publ. by Condé Nast Publs Inc; monthly; Vice-Pres. and Publr THOMAS J. BAIR; Editor-in-Chief JERRY TARDE; circ. 1,647,048.

Golf Magazine: 2 Park Ave, New York, NY 10016-5601; tel. (212) 779-5000; fax (212) 779-5588; e-mail golfletters@golfonline.com; internet www.golfonline.com; f. 1959; publ. by Time Inc; monthly; Publr CHARLIE KAMMERER; Editor DAVID CLARKE; circ. 1,411,237.

Good Housekeeping: 300 West 57th St, New York, NY 10019-5288; tel. (212) 649-2000; fax (212) 265-3307; e-mail ghkletters@hearst.com; internet www.goodhousekeeping.com; f. 1885; monthly; Publr PATRICIA HAEGELE; Editor-in-Chief ROSEMARY ELLIS; circ. 4,668,818.

Gourmet: 4 Times Sq., 9th Floor, New York, NY 10036; tel. (212) 286-8050; fax (212) 286-2932; internet www.epicurious.com/gourmet; f. 1941; sister publ. of *Bon Appétit*, under parent publ. *Epicurious*; owned by CondéNet, online affiliate of Condé Nast Publs Inc; monthly; Vice-Pres. and Publr NANCY BERGER CARDONE; Editor RUTH REICHL; circ. 983,836.

GQ: 4 Times Sq., New York, NY 10036; tel. (212) 286-6410; fax (212) 286-7969; internet us.gq.com; f. 1957; publ. by Condé Nast Publs Inc; monthly; men's lifestyle; Vice-Pres. and Publr PETER HUNSINGER; Editor-in-Chief JIM NELSON; circ. 915,173.

Guideposts: 39 Seminary Hill Rd, Carmel, NY 10512; tel. (212) 929-1300; fax (212) 929-9574; e-mail gpeditors@guideposts.org; internet www.guidepostsmag.com; f. 1945; monthly; other publs incl. *Positive Thinking Magazine* (10 a year, circ. 335,000), *Angels on Earth* (6 a year, circ. 600,000) and *Guideposts Sweet 16* (6 a year); personal and spiritual development; Publr JANINE SCOLPINO; Editor-in-Chief EDWARD GRINNAN; circ. 2,213,354.

HANDY: 12301 Whitewater Dr., Minnetonka, MN 55343; tel. (952) 988-7294; fax (952) 988-7486; e-mail lokrend@namginc.com; internet www.handymanclub.com; f. 1993; publ. by North American Media Group Inc; official publ. of the Handyman Club of America; 6 a year; home improvement; Publr TOM SWEENEY; Editor LARRY OKREND; circ. 874,097.

Harper's Bazaar: 300 West 57th St, New York, NY 10019-3799; tel. (212) 903-5000; fax (212) 262-7101; e-mail bazaar@hearst.com; internet www.harpersbazaar.com; monthly; Publr VALERIE SALEMBIER; Editor-in-Chief GLENDA BAILEY; circ. 716,850.

Health: 2100 Lakeshore Dr., Birmingham, AL 35209; tel. (205) 445-6476; fax (205) 445-5123; e-mail health@timeinc.com; internet www.health.com; f. 1987; publ. by Southern Progress Corpn, a subsidiary of Time Inc; 10 a year; women's health and wellbeing; Publr and Vice-Pres. RENEE TULENKO; Editor-in-Chief ELLEN KUNES; circ. 1,383,173.

Highlights for Children: 803 Church St, Honesdale, PA 18431; tel. (570) 253-1080; fax (570) 251-7847; internet www.highlights.com; f. 1946; monthly; Editor-in-Chief CHRISTINE FRENCH CLARK; circ. 1,800,000 (2007).

Home: 1633 Broadway, 44th Floor, New York, NY 10019; tel. (212) 767-5518; e-mail homeeditor@hfnm.com; internet www.homemag.com; f. 1981; publ. by Hachette Filipacchi Media US Inc; 10 a year; home improvement and decoration; Vice-Pres. and Publr JOHN H. GRANT; Vice-Pres. and Editor-in-Chief DONNA SAPOLIN; circ. 828,630.

Hot Rod Magazine: 6420 Wilshire Blvd, Los Angeles, CA 90048-5515; tel. (332) 782-2000; fax (323) 782-2223; e-mail hotrod@primedia.com; internet www.hotrod.com; f. 1948; monthly; Sr Vice-Pres. and Group Publr DOUG EVANS; Editor-in-Chief DAVID FREIBURGER; circ. 675,535.

House and Garden: 750 Third Ave, 3rd Floor, New York, NY 10017; tel. (212) 630-2260; fax (212) 630-3280; internet www.houseandgarden.com; f. 1901; publ. by Condé Nast Publs Inc; monthly; Vice-Pres. and Publr JOSEPH LAGANI; Editor-in-Chief DOMINIQUE BROWNING; circ. 976,443.

House Beautiful: 300 West 57th St, 24th Floor, New York, NY 10019-5970; tel. (212) 903-5206; internet www.housebeautiful.com; f. 1896; monthly; Publr KATE KELLY SMITH; Editor-in-Chief STEPHEN DRUCKER; circ. 844,258.

Inc.: 7 World Trade Center, New York, NY 10007-2195; tel. (212) 389-5300; fax (212) 389-5393; e-mail mail@inc.com; internet www.inc.com; f. 1987; acquired by Mansueto Ventures LLC in 2005; monthly; small business resources and advice; Publr JOHN TEBEAU; Editor-in-Chief JANE BERENTSON; circ. 724,110.

In Style: 1271 Ave of the Americas, New York, NY 10020; tel. (212) 522-1212; internet www.instyle.com; f. 1994; publ. by Time Inc; celebrity, women's lifestyle and fashion; Man. Editor CHARLA LAWHON; circ. 1,827,644.

In Touch Weekly: 270 Sylvan Ave, Englewood Cliffs, NJ 07632; tel. (201) 569-6699; fax (201) 569-3584; e-mail contactintouch@intouchweekly.com; internet www.intouchweekly.com; f. 2002; publ. by Bauer Publishing USA; weekly; celebrity and entertainment; Publr MARK OLTARSH; Editor-in-Chief RICHARD SPENCER; circ. 955,719.

Jane: 750 Third Ave, New York, NY 10017; tel. (212) 630-4192; e-mail carlos_lamadrid@condenast.com; internet www.janemag.com; f. 1992; publ. by Condé Nast Publications; monthly; women's lifestyle; Vice-Pres. and Publr CARLOS LAMADRID; Editor-in-Chief BRANDON HOLLEY; circ. 706,561 (2005).

Jet: Johnson Publishing, 820 South Michigan Ave, Chicago, IL 60605-2191; tel. (312) 322-9200; fax (312) 322-0951; internet www.ebonyjet.com; f. 1951; weekly; African-American general interest; Man. Editor MALCOLM R. WEST; circ. 929,538.

Junior Scholastic: 557 Broadway, New York, NY 10012; tel. (212) 343-6100; fax (212) 343-6333; e-mail junior@scholastic.com; f. 1937; 18 a year; Editor LEE BAIER; circ. 615,000.

Kiplinger's Personal Finance: 1729 H St, NW, Washington, DC 20006-3904; tel. (202) 887-6400; fax (202) 331-8637; e-mail magazine@kiplinger.com; internet www.kiplinger.com; f. 1947; monthly; Editor FRED FRAILEY; circ. 831,306.

Ladies' Home Journal: 125 Park Ave, New York, NY 10017-5599; tel. (212) 557-6600; fax (212) 455-1010; e-mail lhj@meredith.com; internet www.lhj.com; f. 1883; monthly; Publr JULIE PINKWATER; Editor-in-Chief SALLY LEE; circ. 3,844,222.

The Lion: 300 22nd St, Oak Brook, IL 60523-8842; tel. (630) 571-5466; fax (630) 571-1685; e-mail magazine@lionsclubs.org; f. 1918; 11 a year; business and professional; Editor ROBERT KLEINFELDER; circ. 403,473.

Lucky: 4 Times Sq., 6th Floor, New York, NY 10036; tel. (212) 286-2860; fax (212) 286-4986; internet www.luckymag.com; f. 2000; publ. by Condé Nast Publs Inc; monthly; fashion and shopping; Vice-Pres. and Publr GINA SANDERS; Editor-in-Chief KIM FRANCE; circ. 1,156,306.

Marie Claire: 1790 Broadway, 3rd Floor, New York, NY 10019; tel. (212) 649-5000; fax (212) 501-5050; e-mail marieclairepromo@hearst.com; internet www.marieclaire.com; f. 1994; monthly; Publr SUSAN D. PLAGEMANN; Editor-in-Chief JOANNA COLES; circ. 979,529.

Martha Stewart Living: 11 West 42nd St, 25th Floor, New York, NY 10036; tel. (212) 827-8000; fax (212) 827-8204; e-mail msteuer@marthastewart.com; internet www.marthastewart.com; f. 1991; publ. by Martha Stewart Living Omnimedia, Inc; monthly; lifestyle and general interest; Group Publr SALLY PRESTON; Editor-in-Chief MICHAEL BOODRO; circ. 2,037,630; other publs incl. *Everyday Food* (f. 2003, circ. 982,589).

Maxim: 1040 Ave of the Americas, New York, NY 10018; tel. (212) 302-2626; fax (212) 302-2631; e-mail editors@maximmag.com; internet www.maximonline.com; f. 1997; publ. by Alpha Media Group; monthly; men's lifestyle and general interest; Editorial Dir JAMES KAMINSKY; circ. 2,535,884.

MediZine Healthy Living: 500 Fifth Ave, Suite 1900, New York, NY 10110; tel. (212) 695-2223; fax (212) 695-2936; e-mail requestinfo@medizine.com; internet www.medizine.com; f. 1994; quarterly; health and wellbeing; other publs incl. *Remedy* (f. 1995, circ. 2,400,000); *Diabetes Focus* (f. 2003, circ. 1,500,000); Editorial Dir DIANE UMANSKY; circ. 3,650,000.

Men's Fitness: 1 Park Ave, 10th Floor, New York, NY 10016; tel. (212) 545-4800; fax (212) 685-9644; e-mail jkimmel@amilink.com; internet www.mensfitness.com; f. 1985; publ. by AMI/Weider Publs; 10 a year; men's health, fitness and lifestyle; Publr MARC RICHARDS; Editor-in-Chief ROY S. JOHNSON; circ. 716,626.

Men's Health: 733 Third Ave, 15th Floor, New York, NY 10017; tel. (212) 573-0555; e-mail jon.hammond@rodale.com; internet www.menshealth.com; f. 1988; men's health and general interest; 10 a year; publ. by Rodale Inc; Vice-Pres. and Publr JACK ESSIG; Editor-in-Chief DAVID ZINCZENKO; circ. 1,816,671.

Men's Journal Magazine: 1290 Ave of the Americas, New York, NY 10104-0298; tel. and fax (212) 484-3429; e-mail vincent.krsulich@

THE UNITED STATES OF AMERICA

mensjournal.com; internet www.mensjournal.com; f. 1992; publ. by Wenner Media, Inc; monthly; men's general interest and active lifestyle; Publr Francis X. Farrell; Editor Brad Wieners; circ. 700,000.

Metropolitan Home: 1633 Broadway, 44th Floor, New York, NY 10019-6741; tel. (212) 767-5522; fax (212) 767-5636; e-mail metletters@hfnm.com; internet www.methome.com; f. 1981; publ. by Hachette Filipacchi Media US Inc; 10 a year; interior design and architecture; Publr Deborah Burns; Editor-in-Chief Donna Warner; circ. 563,417.

Midwest Living: 1716 Locust St, Des Moines, IA 50309; tel. (515) 284-3000; fax (515) 284-2700; e-mail brian.kightlinger@meredith.com; internet www.midwestliving.com; f. 1987; publ. by Meredith Corpn; 6 a year; lifestyle with focus on US Midwest; Publr Brian Kightlinger; Editor-in-Chief Greg Philby; circ. 955,750.

Money: Time & Life Bldg, Rockefeller Center, New York, NY 10020; tel. (212) 522-1210; fax (212) 522-0970; e-mail managing_editor@moneymail.com; internet money.cnn.com; f. 1972; monthly; Publr John Donnelly; Man. Editor Eric Schurenberg; circ. 1,956,109.

More: 125 Park Ave, New York, NY 10017-5529; tel. (212) 557-6600; fax (212) 455-1244; internet www.more.com; f. 1998; publ. by Meredith Corpn; 10 a year; women's lifestyle; Publr Brenda Saget Darling; Editor-in-Chief Lesley Jane Seymour; circ. 1,266,980.

Motor Trend: 6420 Wilshire Blvd, Los Angeles, CA 90048-5515; tel. (323) 782-2220; internet www.motortrend.com; f. 1949; publ. by Primedia, Inc; monthly; Publr Ira Gabriel; Editor-in-Chief Angus MacKenzie; circ. 1,112,574.

National Enquirer: 600 South East Coast Ave, Lantana, FL 33462-0001; tel. (561) 586-1111; fax (561) 540-1010; e-mail letters@nationalenquirer.com; internet www.nationalenquirer.com; f. 1926; publ. by American Media Inc; weekly; Publr David Jackson; Editor David Perel; circ. 956,095.

National Geographic Magazine: 1145 17th St, NW, Washington, DC 20036; tel. (212) 610-5500; fax (202) 775-6141; e-mail ngm@nationalgeographic.com; internet ngm.nationalgeographic.com; f. 1888; monthly; Pres. and CEO John Fahey; Editor-in-Chief Chris Johns; circ. 5,061,047.

National News: American Legion Auxiliary, 777 North Meridian St, 3rd Floor, Indianapolis, IN 46260; tel. (317) 569-4500; fax (317) 569-4502; e-mail nnpr@legion-aux.org; internet www.legion-aux.org; publ. of the American Legion Auxiliary (ALA); quarterly; Editor Stephanie L. Holloway; circ. 754,932 (June 2007).

The New Yorker: 4 Times Sq., New York, NY 10036-7448; tel. (212) 286-5400; fax (212) 286-4168; e-mail themail@newyorker.com; internet www.newyorker.com; f. 1925; weekly; Publr Drew Schutte; Editor David Remnick; circ. 1,043,931.

Newsweek: Newsweek Bldg, 251 West 57th St, New York, NY 10019-1894; tel. (212) 445-4000; fax (212) 445-5068; e-mail editors@newsweek.com; internet www.newsweek.com; f. 1933; weekly; Publr Patrick Hagerty; Editor John Meacham; circ. 2,737,450.

Nick Jr. Family Magazine: 1515 Broadway, 32nd Floor, New York, NY 10036; tel. (212) 654-6198; fax (212) 846-1907; e-mail nickjreditors@nick.com; internet www.nickjr.com; f. 1999; subsidiary of Viacom Int. Inc; monthly; parenting; Editor-in-Chief Freddi Greenberg; circ. 431,136.

North American Hunter: 12301 Whitewater Dr., Minnetonka, MN 55343; tel. (320) 846-6090; fax (320) 846-6092; e-mail rsundberg@namginc.com; internet www.huntingclub.com; f. 1979; publ. by North American Media Group Inc; 8 a year; official publ. of the North American Hunting Club; hunting and conservation; Publr Rich Sundberg; Editor Gordy Krahn; circ. 767,892.

O, The Oprah Magazine: 300 West 57th St, New York, NY 10019-5915; tel. (212) 903-5366; fax (212) 903-5388; e-mail omail@hearst.com; internet www.oprah.com/omagazine; f. 2001; monthly; Vice-Pres. and Publr Jill Seelig; Editor-in-Chief Susan K. Reed; circ. 2,394,303.

Organic Gardening: 400 South 10th St, Emmaus, PA 18098; tel. (610) 967-7111; fax (610) 967-8963; e-mail og@rodale.com; internet www.organicgardening.com; f. 1942; publ. by Rodale, Inc; 6 a year; Publr Chris Lambiase; Editor-in-Chief Scott Meyer; circ. 247,194.

Outdoor Life: 2 Park Ave, 10th Floor, New York, NY 10016-5601; tel. (212) 779-5316; fax (212) 779-5118; e-mail amanda.mcnally@bonniercorp.com; internet www.outdoorlife.com; f. 1898; publ. by Bonnier Corpn; 10 a year; Editor-in-Chief Todd W. Smith; Exec. Editor John Snow; circ. 949,183.

Outside: 400 Market St, Santa Fe, NM 87501; tel. (505) 989-7100; fax (505) 989-4700; e-mail letters@outsidemag.com; internet outside.away.com; f. 1976 as Mariah; publ. by Mariah Media Inc; monthly; adventure travel and outdoor recreation; Chair. and Editor-in-Chief Lawrence J. Burke; Vice-Pres. and Publr Scott Parmelee; circ. 694,244.

Parenting: 2 Park Ave, New York, NY 10016; tel. (212) 779-5000; internet www.parenting.com; f. 1987; publ. by Bonnier Corpn; monthly; other publs incl. *Babytalk* (f. 1935, circ. 2,000,000); Editor-in-Chief Susan Kane; Publr Greg Schumann; circ. 2,013,268.

Parents' Magazine: 375 Lexington Ave, 10th Floor, New York, NY 10017-5514; tel. (212) 878-8700; fax (212) 986-2656; e-mail support@parents.com; internet www.parents.com; f. 1926; monthly; Publr Diane Newman; Editor-in-Chief Dana Points; circ. 2,086,768.

PC Magazine: 28 East 28th St, New York, NY 10016; tel. (212) 503-5100; fax (212) 503-5000; e-mail stephanie_chang@ziffdavis.com; internet www.pcmag.com; f. 1981; publ. by Ziff Davis Media Inc; fortnightly; personal computer industry; Editor-in-Chief Lance Ulanoff; circ. 645,886.

PC World: PC World Communications, 501 Second St, San Francisco, CA 94107; tel. (415) 243-0500; fax (415) 442-1891; e-mail pcwletters@pcworld.com; internet www.pcworld.com; f. 1982; publ. by PC World Communications, Inc, a subsidiary of International Data Group; monthly; computer technology; Snr Vice-Pres. and Publr Michael Carroll; Editor Ed Albro; circ. 618,520.

People: Time and Life Bldg, 28th Floor, Rockefeller Center, 1271 Ave of the Americas, New York, NY 10020; tel. (212) 522-3347; fax (212) 522-0883; e-mail edit@people.com; internet www.people.com; f. 1974; publ. by Time Inc; weekly; celebrity and entertainment; Group Pres. Paul Caine; Man. Editor Larry Hackett; circ. 3,803,217.

Playboy: 680 North Lake Shore Dr., Chicago, IL 60611-4402; tel. (312) 751-8000; fax (312) 751-2818; e-mail edit@playboy.com; internet www.playboy.com/magazine-toc.html; f. 1953; monthly; men's interest; Publr Louis Mohn; Editor-in-Chief Hugh M. Hefner; circ. 2,700,653.

Popular Mechanics: 300 West 57th St, New York, NY 10019-5899; tel. (212) 649-2000; e-mail popularmechanics@hearst.com; internet www.popularmechanics.com; f. 1902; monthly; Publr William Congdon; Editor-in-Chief James B. Meigs; circ. 1,239,827.

Popular Science: 2 Park Ave, 9th Floor, New York, NY 10016; tel. (212) 779-5000; fax (212) 779-5108; e-mail letters@popsci.com; internet www.popsci.com; f. 1872; publ. by Bonnier Corpn; monthly; Publr Gregg R. Hano; Editor Mark Jannot; circ. 1,350,562.

Prevention: 400 South 10th St, Emmaus, PA 18098; tel. (610) 967-8045; fax (610) 967-9198; e-mail prevention@rodale.com; internet www.prevention.com; f. 1950; monthly; Vice-Pres. and Editor-in-Chief Liz Vaccariello; circ. 3,331,080.

Progressive Farmer: Lakeshore Park Plaza, 2204 Lakeshore Dr., Birmingham, AL 35209; tel. (205) 414-4700; fax (205) 414-4705; e-mail jodle@progressivefarmer.com; internet www.progressivefarmer.com; f. 1886; monthly; Publr Adrian Blake; Editor Jack Odle; circ. 675,000.

Reader's Digest: Reader's Digest Rd, Pleasantville, NY 10570-7000; tel. (914) 238-1000; fax (914) 238-4559; internet www.rd.com; f. 1922; monthly; Editor-in-Chief Peggy Northrop; circ. 8,445,916.

Real Simple: Time and Life Bldg, 1271 Ave of the Americas, Suite 41–46B, New York, NY 10020; tel. (212) 522-1212; fax (212) 467-1396; internet www.realsimple.com; f. 2000; publ. by Time Inc; monthly, plus two special issues; women's lifestyle and general interest; Publr Kevin White; Man. Editor Kristin van Ogtrop; circ. 2,026,466.

Redbook: 224 West 57th St, 6th Floor, New York, NY 10019-3796; tel. (212) 649-3450; fax (212) 581-8114; e-mail redbook@hearst.com; internet www.redbookmag.com; f. 1903; monthly; Vice-Pres. and Publr Mary E. Morgan; Editor-in-Chief Stacy Morrison; circ. 2,227,957.

ESPN RISE Magazine: SchoolSports, Inc, 971 Commonwealth Ave, Boston, MA 02215-1305; tel. (617) 779-9000; fax (617) 779-9100; e-mail feedback@risemag.com; internet www.risemag.com; f. 1997 as *SchoolSports Magazine*; acquired by ESPN in 2007; 9 a year; 25 regional edns distributed to c. 6,500 schools; sports and teenage active lifestyle; Editor-in-Chief Jonathan Segal; circ. 912,506.

Road & Track: 1499 Monrovia Ave, Newport Beach, CA 92663-2752; tel. (949) 720-5300; fax (949) 631-2757; e-mail rtletters@hfmus.com; internet www.roadandtrack.com; f. 1947; monthly; Publr John C. Driscoll, Jr; Editor-in-Chief Matt DeLorenzo; circ. 703,056.

Rolling Stone: 1290 Ave of the Americas, 2nd Floor, New York, NY 10104-0298; tel. (212) 484-1616; fax (212) 484-3429; e-mail feedback@rollingstone.com; internet www.rollingstone.com; f. 1967; fortnightly; Publr Jann S. Wenner; Man. Editor Will Dana; circ. 1,453,385.

Scholastic Parent & Child: 557 Broadway, New York, NY 10012; tel. (212) 343-6100; e-mail news@scholastic.com; internet teacher.scholastic.com/products/classmags/parent_child.htm; f. 1995; publ. by Scholastic Inc; 8 a year; Publr Risa Crandall; Editor-in-Chief Stephanie Izarek; circ. 1,347,780.

THE UNITED STATES OF AMERICA

Scientific American: 415 Madison Ave, New York, NY 10017-1179; tel. (212) 451-8200; fax (212) 754-1138; e-mail editors@sciam.com; internet www.sciam.com; f. 1845; monthly; Vice-Pres. and Publr BRUCE BRANDFON; Exec. Editor MARIETTE DICHRISTINA; circ. 637,794.

Scouting Magazine: 1325 West Walnut Hill Lane, POB 152079, Irving, TX 75015-2079; tel. (972) 580-2000; fax (972) 580-2079; e-mail scole@netbsa.org; internet www.scoutingmagazine.org; f. 1913; publ. by Boy Scouts of America; 6 a year; Publr J. WARREN YOUNG; Editor-in-Chief J. D. OWEN; Man. Editor SCOTT DANIELS; circ. 1,020,594.

SELF Magazine: 4 Times Sq., 5th Floor, New York, NY 10036; tel. (212) 286-2860; fax (212) 286-6174; e-mail comments@self.com; internet www.self.com; f. 1979; publ. by Condé Nast Publs Inc; monthly; Vice-Pres. and Publr KIMBERLY ANDERSON KELLEHER; Editor-in-Chief LUCY DANZIGER; circ. 1,495,033.

Seventeen: 300 West 57th St, New York, NY 10019-1798; tel. (212) 649-2000; e-mail mail@seventeen.com; internet www.seventeen.com; f. 1944; publ. by Hearst Corpn; monthly; Publr JAYNE JAMISON; Editor-in-Chief ANN SHOKET; circ. 2,024,147.

Shape: 1 Park Ave, 10th Floor, New York, NY 10016; tel. (212) 545-4800; fax (212) 252-1131; internet www.shape.com; f. 1981; publ. by American Media, Inc; women's health and fitness; Publr SABINE FELDMANN; Editor-in-Chief VALERIE LATONA; circ. 1,703,421.

Sierra: 85 Second St, 2nd Floor, San Francisco, CA 94105; tel. (415) 977-5572; fax (415) 977-5794; e-mail sierra.mail@sierraclub.org; internet www.sierraclub.org/sierra; f. 1893; official publ. of the Sierra Club; 6 a year; nature and ecology; Editor-in-Chief BOB SIPCHEN; circ. 612,221.

SmartMoney: 1755 Broadway, 2nd Floor, New York, NY 10019; tel. (212) 765-7323; e-mail editors@smartmoney.com; internet www.smartmoney.com; f. 1992; jt venture of Dow Jones & Co, Inc and Hearst Corpn; Publr BILL SHAW; Editor-in-Chief JONATHAN DAHL; circ. 826,822.

Smithsonian Magazine: 420 Lexington Ave, Suite 2335, New York, NY 10170; tel. (212) 916-1300; fax (212) 986-4259; e-mail bianchik@si.edu; internet www.smithsonianmag.com; f. 1970; monthly; Publr KERRY BIANCHI; Editor CAREY WINFREY; circ. 2,035,769.

Southern Living: 2100 Lakeshore Dr., Birmingham, AL 35209-6721; tel. (205) 877-6000; fax (205) 445-7523; internet www.southernliving.com; f. 1966; monthly; Vice-Pres. and Editor-in-Chief ELEANOR GRIFFIN; circ. 2,802,444.

Sporting News: 475 Park Ave South, 27th Floor, New York, NY 10016; tel. (646) 424-2227; fax (646) 424-2232; e-mail ebaker@sportingnews.com; internet www.sportingnews.com; f. 1886; acquired by American City Business Journals, Inc in 2006; weekly; Publr ED BAKER; Editor JOHN D. RAWLINGS; circ. 715,521.

Sports Illustrated: 1271 Ave of the Americas, 33rd Floor, New York, NY 10020-1339; tel. (212) 522-1212; fax (212) 522-0475; internet sportsillustrated.cnn.com; f. 1954; weekly; Editor TERRY MCDONNELL; circ. 3,260,964.

Star: 1 Park Ave, 3rd Floor, New York, NY 10016; tel. (212) 743-6523; fax (212) 532-0940; e-mail djackson@starmagazine.com; internet www.starmagazine.com; f. 1974; weekly; Vice-Pres. and Publr DAVID JACKSON; Editor-in-Chief CANDACE TRUNZO; circ. 1,320,963.

Sunset Magazine: 80 Willow Rd, Menlo Park, CA 94025-3691; tel. (650) 321-3600; fax (650) 327-5737; internet www.sunset.com; f. 1898; monthly; travel, home, garden, food and drink; Snr Vice-Pres. and Publr KEVIN LYNCH; Editor-in-Chief KATIE TAMONY; circ. 1,233,742.

TENNIS: 79 Madison Ave, 8th Floor, New York, NY 10016; tel. (212) 636-2700; fax (212) 636-2720; e-mail jwilliams@tennismagazine.com; internet www.tennis.com; f. 1965; acquired by Miller Publishing Group LLC in 1997; 10 a year; tennis, travel and lifestyle; Publr JEFF WILLIAMS; Editor-in-Chief JAMES MARTIN; circ. 604,177.

This Old House: 135 West 50th St, 10th Floor, New York, NY 10020; tel. (212) 522-9465; fax (212) 522-9435; e-mail toh_letters@thisoldhouse.com; internet www.thisoldhouse.com; f. 1995; publ. by Time Inc; 10 a year; home improvement; Editor J. SCOTT OMELIANUK; circ. 969,333.

Time: Time and Life Bldg, Rockefeller Center, 1271 Ave of the Americas, New York, NY 10020-1393; tel. (212) 522-1212; fax (212) 522-0023; e-mail letters@time.com; internet www.time.com; f. 1923; weekly; Pres. and Publr EDWARD R. MCCARRICK; Man. Editor RICHARD STENGEL; circ. 3,389,166.

Traditional Home: 125 Park Ave, New York, NY 10017; tel. (212) 557-6600; fax (212) 551-6914; e-mail traditionalhome@meredith.com; internet www.traditionalhome.com; f. 1978; publ. by Meredith Corpn; 8 a year; Publr DEBRA BRANDT; Editor-in-Chief ANN OMVIG MAINE; circ. 972,928.

Travel & Leisure: 1120 Ave of the Americas, 10th Floor, New York, NY 10036-6770; tel. (212) 382-5600; fax (212) 768-1568; e-mail tlquery@amexpub.com; internet www.travelandleisure.com; f. 1971; monthly; Editor-in-Chief NANCY NOVOGROD; circ. 975,505.

TV Guide: 11 West 42nd St, New York, NY 10036; tel. (212) 852-7500; fax (212) 852-7323; internet www.tvguide.com; f. 1953; weekly; Snr Vice-Pres. and Publr PETE HAEFFNER; Editor-in-Chief DEBRA BIRNBAUM; circ. 3,274,187.

US News & World Report: 1050 Thomas Jefferson St, NW, Washington, DC 20007-3837; tel. (202) 955-2000; fax (202) 955-2685; e-mail letters@usnews.com; internet www.usnews.com; f. 1933; weekly; Publr KERRY F. DYER; Chair. and Editor-in-Chief MORTIMER B. ZUCKERMAN; Editor BRIAN KELLY; circ. 1,828,293.

US Weekly: 1290 Ave of the Americas, 2nd Floor, New York, NY 10104-0298; tel. (212) 484-1616; fax (212) 484-4242; e-mail letters@usmagazine.com; internet www.usmagazine.com; f. 1977; weekly; Publr VICTORIA LASDON ROSE; Editor-in-Chief JANICE MIN; circ. 1,905,014.

Vanity Fair: 4 Times Sq., 7th Floor, New York, NY 10036; tel. (212) 286-2860; fax (212) 286-7036; e-mail vfmail@vf.com; internet www.vanityfair.com; f. 1983; publ. by Condé Nast Publs Inc; monthly; Publr EDWARD MENICHESCHI; Editor-in-Chief GRAYDON CARTER; circ. 1,144,001.

VFW Magazine: 406 West 34th St, Kansas City, MO 64111-2736; tel. (816) 756-3390; fax (816) 968-1169; e-mail info@vfw.org; internet www.vfw.org; f. 1912; 11 a year; Editor RICHARD K. KOLB; circ. 1,546,196.

VIA: 150 Van Ness Ave, San Francisco, CA 94102-5208; tel. (415) 565-2451; fax (415) 863-4726; e-mail viamail@csaa.com; internet www.viamagazine.com; f. 1917; publ. by the California State Automobile Asscn; 6 a year; motoring; Editor BRUCE ANDERSON; circ. 2,836,029.

VIBE: 215 Lexington Ave, New York, NY 10016; tel. (212) 448-7300; fax (212) 448-7400; internet www.vibe.com; f. 1993; acquired by Keith Glen Media from VIBE/Spin Ventures in 2006; monthly; urban music and culture; also publ. *VIBE Vixen* (quarterly, circ. 340,000); Publr LEN BURNETT; Editor-in-Chief DANYEL SMITH; circ. 863,283.

Vogue: 4 Times Sq., 12th Floor, New York, NY 10036; tel. (212) 286-2810; fax (212) 286-8593; e-mail voguemail@aol.com; internet www.style.com/vogue; f. 1892; monthly; also publ. *Men's Vogue* (10 a year, circ. 368,898) and *Teen Vogue* (10 a year, circ. 1,017,125); Snr Vice-Pres. and Publishing Dir THOMAS A. FLORIO; Editor ANNA WINTOUR; circ. 1,224,131.

Weight Watchers Magazine: 747 Third Ave, 24th Floor, New York, NY 10017; tel. (212) 370-0644; fax (212) 687-4398; f. 1968; monthly; Publr ANDREW AMILL; Editor KATE GREER; circ. 1,309,931.

WHERE: c/o Morris Visitor Publications, 699 Broad St, Suite 500, Augusta, GA 30901; tel. (800) 680-4035; internet wheretraveler.com; f. 1936; monthly; int. visitor information; 23 regional edns; Group Publr PETER BLACKWELL; Editorial Dir MARQ DE VILLIERS; circ. 1,120,373.

Woman's Day: 1633 Broadway, 42nd Floor, New York, NY 10019; tel. (212) 767-6418; e-mail womansday@hfmus.com; internet www.womansday.com; f. 1931; owned by Hachette Filipacchi; 17 a year; women's general interest; Vice-Pres. and Publr CARLOS LAMADRID; Editor-in-Chief JANE CHESNUTT; circ. 3,876,483.

Woman's World: Bauer Publishing, 270 Sylvan Ave, Englewood Cliffs, NJ 07632; tel. (201) 569-6699; fax (201) 569-5303; e-mail gregslattery@baueradsales.com; f. 1981; publ. by Bauer Publishing USA; weekly; women's general interest; other publs incl. *First* (circ. 1,377,895), *J-14* (circ. 440,857) and *Life & Style Weekly* (circ. 528,294); Publr GREG SLATTERY; Editor-in-Chief STEPHANIE SAIBLE; circ. 1,387,414.

Working Mother: 60 East 42nd St, 27th Floor, New York, NY 10165-0001; tel. (212) 351-6400; fax (212) 351-6483; e-mail editors@workingmother.com; internet www.workingmother.com; f. 1978; publ. by Working Mother Media, Inc; lifestyle magazine with focus on working mothers; Pres. and Publr JOAN SHERIDAN LABARGE; Editor-in-Chief SUZANNE RISS; circ. 831,150.

NEWS AGENCIES

Associated Press (AP): 450 West 33rd St, New York, NY 10001; tel. (212) 621-1500; fax (212) 621-1679; e-mail info@ap.org; internet www.ap.org; f. 1848; Pres. and CEO TOM CURLEY; c. 1,700 newspaper mems in the USA, 6,000 broadcast mems and over 8,500 subscribers abroad.

Bloomberg News: 731 Lexington Ave, New York, NY 10022; tel. (212) 318-2000; fax (212) 893-5999; internet www.bloomberg.com; f. 1981; Editor-in-Chief MATTHEW WINKLER.

Dow Jones Newswires: Harborside Financial Center, 600 Plaza II, Jersey City, NJ 07311-3992; tel. (201) 938-5400; fax (201) 938-5600; e-mail newswires@dowjones.com; internet www.djnewswires.com; parent co, Dow Jones & Company; acquired by News Corpn in 2008; Snr Vice-Pres. and Man. Editor NEAL LIPSCHUTZ.

THE UNITED STATES OF AMERICA

Jewish Telegraphic Agency, Inc (JTA): 330 Seventh Ave, 17th Floor, New York, NY 10001; tel. (212) 643-1890; fax (212) 643-8498; e-mail info@jta.org; internet www.jta.org; f. 1917; world-wide coverage of Jewish news; offices in Washington, DC, and Jerusalem, Israel; Pres. DANIEL J. KRIFCHER; Exec. Editor and Publr MARK J. JOFFE.

Religion News Service: 1101 Connecticut Ave, NW, Suite 350, Washington, DC 20036; tel. (202) 463-8777; fax (202) 463-0033; e-mail info@religionnews.com; internet www.religionnews.com; Editor KEVIN ECKSTROM.

United Media (UM): 200 Madison Ave, 4th Floor, New York, NY 10016; tel. (212) 293-8500; fax (212) 293-8505; e-mail pdixon@unitedmedia.com; internet www.unitedmedialicensing.com; f. 1978; licensing and syndication of news features; Pres. and CEO DOUGLAS R. STERN.

United Press International (UPI): 1133 19th St, NW, Washington, DC 20036; tel. (202) 898-8000; fax (202) 898-8048; e-mail editorforms@upi.com; internet www.upi.com; f. 1907; Chair. and Pres. CHUNG HWAN KWAK; serves c. 1,000 newspaper clients worldwide.

NATIONAL ASSOCIATIONS

American Business Media: 675 Third Ave, Suite 415, New York, NY 10017-5704; tel. (212) 661-6360; fax (212) 370-0736; e-mail info@abmmail.com; internet www.americanbusinessmedia.com; f. 1906; Pres. and CEO GORDON T. HUGHES, II; 350 mem. cos, 124 assoc. mems.

American Society of Magazine Editors (ASME): 810 Seventh Ave, 24th Floor, New York, NY 100192; tel. (212) 872-3700; fax (212) 906-0128; e-mail asme@magazine.org; internet asme.magazine.org; Chief Exec. SID HOLT; Exec. Dir MARLENE KAHAN; 850 mems.

Audit Bureau of Circulations (ABC): 900 North Meacham Rd, Schaumburg, IL 60173-4968; tel. (847) 605-0909; fax (847) 605-0483; e-mail kammi.altig@accessabc.com; internet www.accessabc.com; f. 1914; Chair. MERLE K. DAVIDSON; Pres. and Man. Dir MICHAEL J. LAVERY; over 4,000 mems.

Council of Literary Magazines and Presses (CLMP): 154 Christopher St, Suite 3C, New York, NY 10014-9110; tel. (212) 741-9110; fax (212) 741-9112; e-mail info@clmp.org; internet www.clmp.org; f. 1967; provides services to non-commercial US literary magazines and presses; Exec. Dir JEFFREY LEPENDORF; 347 mems.

Magazine Publishers of America (MPA): 810 Seventh Ave, 24th Floor, New York, NY 100192; tel. (212) 872-3700; fax (212) 888-4217; e-mail mpa@magazine.org; internet www.magazine.org; f. 1919; Pres. and CEO NINA B. LINK; 200 mem. cos and 90 assoc. mems.

National Newspaper Association: 134 Neff Annex, POB 7540, Columbia, MO 65205-7540; tel. (573) 882-5800; fax (573) 884-5490; e-mail info@nna.org; internet www.nna.org; f. 1885 as National Editorial Association; present name adopted 1964; Pres. JOHN W. STEVENSON; Exec. Dir BRIAN STEFFENS; over 2,700 mems.

Newspaper Association of America: 4401 Wilson Blvd, Suite 900, Arlington, VA 22203-1867; tel. (571) 366-1000; fax (571) 366-1195; internet www.naa.org; f. 1992; Chair. BO JONES; Pres. and CEO JOHN STURM; more than 2,000 mems in USA and Canada accounting for over 87% of US daily newspaper circulation.

The Newspaper Guild: 501 Third St, NW, Washington, DC 20001-2797; tel. (202) 434-7177; fax (202) 434-1472; e-mail guild@cwa-union.org; internet www.newsguild.org; f. 1933; journalists' org., organ of the Communications Workers of America trade union; Pres. BERNARD J. LUNZER; over 34,000 mems in the USA, Puerto Rico and Canada.

Periodical & Book Association of America Inc: 481 Eighth Ave, Suite 826, New York, NY 10001; tel. (212) 563-6502; fax (212) 563-4098; e-mail lscott@pbaa.net; internet www.pbaa.net; Pres. JOE GALLO; Exec. Dir LISA W. SCOTT; 110 mems.

Publishers

Abaris Books: 64 Wall St, Norwalk, CT 06850; tel. (203) 838-8625; fax (203) 857-0730; e-mail abaris@abarisbooks.com; internet www.abarisbooks.com; f. 1973; division of Opal Publishing Corpn; scholarly, fine art reference, philosophy; Publr ANTHONY S. KAUFMANN; Gen. Man. J. C. WEST.

Abbeville Press, Inc: 137 Varick St, New York, NY 10013; tel. (212) 366-5585; fax (212) 366-6966; e-mail abbeville@abbeville.com; internet www.abbeville.com; f. 1977; fine arts and illustrated books; Pres. and Publr ROBERT E. ABRAMS.

Abingdon Press: 201 Eighth Ave South, POB 801, Nashville, TN 37202-0801; tel. (615) 749-6290; fax (615) 749-6512; e-mail publicity@abingdonpress.com; internet www.abingdonpress.com; an imprint of The United Methodist Publishing House (f. 1789); religious; Vice-Pres. TAMMY GAINES.

Harry N. Abrams, Inc (HNA): 115 West 18th St, New York, NY 10011; tel. (212) 206-7715; fax (212) 519-1210; internet www.hnabooks.com; f. 1949; acquired by Times Mirror Co in 1966; imprints incl. Abrams Books (art, photography, design, architecture), Stewart, Tabori & Chang (f. 1981, cooking, design, gardening, crafts, pets, health, sports, and popular culture) and Amulet Books (f. 2004, youth fiction and non-fiction); owned by Groupe de la Martinière, France; Pres. and CEO MICHAEL JACOBS.

AFB Press: 11 Penn Plaza, Suite 300, New York, NY 10001; tel. (212) 502-7651; fax (212) 502-7774; e-mail press@afb.net; internet www.afb.org/store; publishing arm of the American Foundation for the Blind; books, journals, videos, and electronic materials on visual impairment for professionals, researchers and blind or visually impaired individuals and their families; Pres. and CEO CARL R. AUGUSTO; Dir and Editor-in-Chief NATALIE HILZEN.

Alfred Publishing Co, Inc: POB 10003, Van Nuys, CA 91410-0003; tel. (818) 892-2492; fax (818) 891-4875; e-mail customerservice@alfred.com; internet www.alfred.com; f. 1922; educational music, methods and texts; Pres. MORTY MANUS; CEO STEVEN MANUS.

Andrews McMeel Publishing: c/o Simon & Schuster, Inc, 100 Front St, Riverside, NJ 08075; tel. (816) 932-6700; fax (816) 932-6706; e-mail licensing@amuniversal.com; internet www.andrewsmcmeel.com; f. 1970; humour, general trade; Pres. and CEO HUGH T. ANDREWS.

Augsburg Fortress, Publishers: 100 South Fifth St, POB 1209, Minneapolis, MN 55440; tel. (612) 330-3300; fax (612) 330-3455; e-mail info@augsburgfortress.org; internet www.augsburgfortress.org; f. 1890; publishing arm of the Evangelical Lutheran Church in America; religious (evangelical Lutheran) non-fiction; Pres. and CEO BETH LEWIS.

August House Inc, Publishers: 3500 Piedmont Rd, NE Suite 310, Atlanta, GA 30305; tel. (404) 442-4420; fax (404) 442-4435; e-mail ahinfo@augusthouse.com; internet www.augusthouse.com; f. 1979; Southern regional, history, humour and folklore; CEO STEVE FLOYD.

B&H Publishing Group: 127 Ninth Ave North, Nashville, TN 37234-0143; tel. (615) 251-5614; fax (615) 251-2701; e-mail miriam.evans@bhpublishinggroup.com; internet www.bhpublishinggroup.com; f. 1891; fmrly Broadman & Holman Publrs; present name adopted in 2006; religious (Protestant), fiction, non-fiction, reference and juvenile; Pres. KENNETH H. STEPHENS; Publr DAVID SHEPHERD.

Baker Publishing Group: 6030 East Fulton Rd, Ada, MI 49301; tel. (616) 676-9185; fax (616) 676-9573; e-mail media@bakerbooks.com; internet www.bakerpublishinggroup.com; f. 1939; imprints incl. Brazos Press (Protestant and evangelical, Roman Catholic and Eastern Orthodox), Chosen Books (f. 1971, evangelical and charismatic Christian non-fiction), and Revell (Christian fiction and non-fiction); Pres. DWIGHT BAKER.

Ballantine Publishing Group: 1745 Broadway, New York, NY 10019; tel. (212) 572-2713; fax (212) 572-4912; e-mail bfi@randomhouse.com; internet www.randomhouse.com/rhpg; f. 1952; division of Random House Inc; fiction, non-fiction, reprints; Pres. GINA CENTRELLO.

Barnes and Noble Books: POB 111, Lyndhurst, NJ 07071; tel. (800) 422-7717; fax (212) 352-3660; e-mail customerservice@bn.com; internet www.barnesandnoble.com; f. 1873; division of Rowman & Littlefield Publrs, Inc; educational and general; Chair. LEONARD RIGGIO; CEO STEPHEN RIGGIO.

Barron's Educational Series, Inc: 250 Wireless Blvd, Hauppauge, NY 11788; tel. (631) 434-3311; fax (631) 434-3723; e-mail fbrown@barronseduc.com; internet www.barronseduc.com; f. 1945; general non-fiction, educational and juvenile; Chair. and CEO MANUEL H. BARRON; Pres. and Publr ELLEN SIBLEY.

Beacon Press: 25 Beacon St, Boston, MA 02108; tel. (617) 742-2110; fax (617) 723-3097; e-mail lriviere@beacon.org; internet www.beacon.org; f. 1854; dept of the Unitarian Universalist Asscn; world affairs, religion and general non-fiction; Dir HELENE ATWAN.

R. R. Bowker LLC: 630 Central Ave, New Providence, NJ 07974; tel. (888) 269-5372; fax (888) 286-1090; e-mail info@bowker.com; internet www.bowker.com; f. 1872; reference and bibliography; Pres. and CEO ANNIE CALLANAN.

Branden Books, Inc: POB 812094, Wellesley, MA 02482; tel. (781) 734-2046; fax (781) 790-1056; e-mail branden@brandenbooks.com; internet www.brandenbooks.com; f. 1909; art, music, classics, fiction and non-fiction; Pres. ROBERT CASO; Editor and Treas. ADOLPH CASO.

George Braziller, Inc: 171 Madison Ave, New York, NY 10016; tel. (212) 889-0909; fax (212) 689-5405; e-mail info@georgebraziller.com; internet www.georgebraziller.com; f. 1955; art, fiction and non-fiction; Publr GEORGE BRAZILLER.

Brookings Institution Press: 1775 Massachusetts Ave, NW, Washington, DC 20036-2103; tel. (202) 797-6000; fax (202) 536-

THE UNITED STATES OF AMERICA

3623; e-mail bibooks@brookings.edu; internet www.brookings.edu; f. 1927; economics, govt, foreign policy; Dir ROBERT L. FAHERTY.

Cambridge University Press: 32 Ave of the Americas, New York, NY 10013-2473; tel. (212) 924-3900; fax (212) 691-3239; e-mail information@cup.org; internet www.cambridge.org/us; scholarly; CEO STEPHEN BOURNE; Pres. RICHARD ZIEMACKI.

Catholic University of America Press: 620 Michigan Ave, NE, Washington, DC 20064; tel. (202) 319-5052; fax (202) 319-4985; e-mail cua-press@cua.edu; internet cuapress.cua.edu; f. 1939; scholarly; Dir DAVID J. MCGONAGLE.

Caxton Press: 312 Main St, Caldwell, ID 83605; tel. (208) 647-6465; fax (208) 459-7450; e-mail sgipson@caxtonpress.com; internet www.caxtonpress.com; f. 1903; Western Americana; Vice-Pres. and Publr SCOTT GIPSON.

Columbia University Press: 61 West 62nd St, New York, NY 10023; tel. (212) 459-0600; fax (212) 459-3678; e-mail cup_publicity@columbia.edu; internet www.columbia.edu/cu/cup; f. 1893; trade, educational, scientific and reference; Pres. and Dir JAMES D. JORDAN.

Concordia Publishing House (CPH): 3558 South Jefferson Ave, St Louis, MO 63118-3968; tel. (800) 325-3040; fax (800) 490-9889; e-mail order@cph.org; internet www.cph.org; f. 1869; publishing arm of the Lutheran Church-Missouri Synod; religious (Lutheran) children's books, devotionals and curriculum music; Pres. and CEO BRUCE G. KINTZ.

Cornell University Press: Sage House, 512 East State St, POB 250, Ithaca, NY 14850; tel. (607) 257-2338; fax (607) 277-2374; e-mail cupressinfo@cornell.edu; internet www.cornellpress.cornell.edu; f. 1869; scholarly, non-fiction; Dir JOHN G. ACKERMAN.

CQ Press: 2300 N St, NW, Suite 800, Washington, DC 20037; tel. (202) 729-1800; fax (202) 729-1418; e-mail lwallace@cqpress.com; internet www.cqpress.com; f. 1945; fmrly Congressional Quarterly Books; division of SAGE Publications; business, education and govt; directories; Pres. and Publr JOHN A. JENKINS.

Creative Co: 123 South Broad St, POB 227, Mankato, MN 56001; tel. (507) 388-6273; fax (507) 388-2746; f. 1932; juvenile; Pres. TOM PETERSON.

F. A. Davis Co: 1915 Arch St, Philadelphia, PA 19103; tel. (215) 568-2270; fax (215) 568-5065; e-mail info@fadavis.com; internet www.fadavis.com; f. 1879; medical, nursing and allied health textbooks; Pres. ROBERT H. CRAVEN, Jr.

Dover Publications, Inc: 31 East Second St, Mineola, NY 11501; tel. (516) 294-6953; fax (516) 742-5049; internet www.doverpublications.com; f. 1941; trade, reprints, scientific, classics, language, arts and crafts; Pres. PAUL NEGRI.

Dufour Editions, Inc: POB 7, Chester Springs, PA 19425-0007; tel. (610) 458-5005; fax (610) 458-7103; e-mail info@dufoureditions.com; internet www.dufoureditions.com; f. 1949; literature, political science, humanities, music and history; Pres. CHRISTOPHER MAY.

Duke University Press: POB 90660, Duke University, Durham, NC 27708-0660; tel. (888) 651-0122; fax (888) 651-0124; e-mail bpublicity@dukeupress.edu; internet www.dukeupress.edu; f. 1921; scholarly; Exec. Editor J. REYNOLDS SMITH.

Duquesne University Press: 600 Forbes Ave, Pittsburgh, PA 15282; tel. (412) 396-6610; fax (412) 396-5984; e-mail wadsworth@duq.edu; internet www.dupress.duq.edu; f. 1927; scholarly; Dir SUSAN WADSWORTH-BOOTH; Production Editor KATHY MEYER.

Ediciones Universal: 3090 South West Eighth St, Miami, FL 33135; tel. (305) 642-3234; fax (305) 642-7978; e-mail ediciones@ediciones.com; internet www.ediciones.com; f. 1965; Spanish language fiction and non-fiction; Man. JUAN MANUEL SALVAT.

Elsevier: 11830 Westline Industrial Dr., St Louis, MO 63146; tel. (314) 453-7010; fax (314) 453-7095; e-mail usbkinfo@elsevier.com; internet www.elsevier.com; f. 1962; division of Reed Elsevier Group PLC; health sciences imprints incl. Butterworth-Heinemann (f. 1975, technology, medicine and management), Churchill Livingstone (f. 1972, medicine), Hanley & Belfus (f. 1984, medical textbooks and reference materials), Mosby (f. 1906, textbooks and reference materials on medicine, nursing, allied health and veterinary medicine), and W. B. Saunders Co (f. 1888, medicine); science and technology imprints incl. Academic Press (science, technology and business), Architectural Press (architecture), Focal Press (media technology), and Morgan Kaufmann (f. 1984, computing); CEO ERIK ENGSTROM.

Encyclopaedia Britannica, Inc: 331 North LaSalle Street, Chicago, IL 60610; tel. (800) 621-3900; fax (800) 344-9624; e-mail international@eb.com; internet www.eb.com; f. 1768; encyclopaedias, atlases, dictionaries; CEO JORGE CAUZ.

Facts On File Inc: 132 West 31st St, 17th Floor, New York, NY 10001; tel. (212) 896-4269; fax (917) 339-0323; e-mail lkatz@factsonfile.com; internet www.factsonfile.com; f. 1941; acquired by Veronis Suhler Stevenson in 2005; imprints incl. Ferguson Publishing (f. 1907, children's reference); non-fiction, reference and electronic databases; Publr MARK MCDONNELL.

Farrar, Straus and Giroux, Inc (FSG): 18 West 18th St, New York, NY 10011; tel. (212) 741-6900; fax (212) 633-9385; e-mail fsg.publicity@fsgbooks.com; internet us.macmillan.com/fsg.aspx; f. 1946; acquired by Holtzbrinck Publrs, LLC in 1994; imprints incl. Hill and Wang (f. 1956), Faber and Faber, Inc, and North Point Press; literature, international fiction, history, current affairs and science; Chair. ROGER W. STRAUS; Pres. JONATHAN GALASSI.

Fordham University Press: University Box L, Bronx, NY 10458-5172; tel. (718) 817-4795; fax (718) 817-4785; e-mail bkaobrien@fordham.edu; internet www.fordhampress.com; f. 1907; scholarly; Editorial Dir HELEN TARTAR.

W. H. Freeman & Co, Publishers: 41 Madison Ave, 37th Floor, New York, NY 10010; tel. (212) 576-9400; fax (212) 689-2383; e-mail international@whfreeman.com; internet www.whfreeman.com; f. 1946; part of Holtzbrinck Publrs, LLC; textbooks; Pres. ELIZABETH WIDDICOMBE.

Samuel French, Inc: 45 West 25th St, New York, NY 10010; tel. (212) 206-8990; fax (212) 206-1429; e-mail info@samuelfrench.com; internet www.samuelfrench.com; f. 1830; plays; Man. Dir CHARLES R. VAN NOSTRAND.

Gale Cengage Learning: 27500 Drake Rd, Farmington Hills, MI 48331-3535; tel. (248) 669-4253; fax (248) 669-8064; e-mail lindsay.brown@cengage.com; internet gale.cengage.com; f. 1954; division of Cengage Learning; reference; Pres. GORDON T. MACOMBER.

Garland Science Publishing, Inc: 270 Madison Ave, New York, NY 10016; tel. (917) 351-7100; fax (212) 947-3027; e-mail info@garland.com; internet www.garlandscience.com; f. 1969; part of the Taylor & Francis Group; biology and chemistry textbooks; Vice-Pres. DENISE SCHANCK.

Genealogical Publishing Co: 3600 Clipper Mill Rd, Suite 260, Baltimore, MD 21211; tel. (410) 837-8271; fax (410) 752-8492; e-mail info@genealogical.com; internet www.genealogical.com; f. 1959; genealogy, immigration studies, heraldry and local history; Editor-in-Chief MICHAEL TEPPER.

The K. S. Giniger Co, Inc: 250 West 57th St, Suite 2602, New York, NY 10107; tel. (212) 570-7499; fax (212) 369-6692; f. 1965; general non-fiction; Pres. KENNETH S. GINIGER.

Greenwood Publishing Group, Inc: 88 Post Rd West, POB 5007, Westport, CT 06881; tel. (203) 226-3571; fax (203) 222-1502; e-mail webmaster@greenwood.com; internet www.greenwood.com; f. 1967; division of Reed Elsevier Group PLC; comprises Greenwood Press (reference), Heinemann (f. 1978, educational, teaching, professional development), Praeger Publrs (f. 1949, academic and general-interest non-fiction) and Libraries Unlimited (educational and reference); business reference and non-fiction; Pres. WAYNE SMITH.

Grove/Atlantic, Inc: 841 Broadway, New York, NY 10003-4793; tel. (212) 614-7850; fax (212) 614-7886; e-mail info@groveatlantic.com; internet www.groveatlantic.com; f. 1993 by merger of Grove Press and Atlantic Monthly Press (f. 1917); fiction, non-fiction, biography, history, social science, poetry; Pres. MORGAN ENTREKIN.

Hammond World Atlas Corpn: American Map-Langenscheidt Publishing Group, 15 Tyger River Dr., Duncan, SC 29334; tel. (864) 486-8289; fax (864) 486-0214; e-mail customerservice@americanmap.com; internet www.hammondmap.com; f. 1900; division of American Map-Langenscheidt Publishing Group; maps, atlases, cartography; Chair. and CEO STUART DOLGINS.

Harcourt Inc: 6277 Sea Harbor Dr., Orlando, FL 32887; tel. (407) 345-2000; fax (407) 352-3445; internet www.harcourt.com; f. 1919; division of Reed Elsevier Group PLC; fiction, textbooks, general; Pres. and CEO JAMES LEVY.

Harlequin Enterprises Ltd: 233 Broadway, New York, NY 10279; tel. (212) 553-4200; fax (212) 227-8969; e-mail public_relations@harlequin.ca; internet www.eharlequin.com; f. 1979; Harlequin Enterprises, Canada; imprints incl. Harlequin and Silhouette Books; women's fiction, adventure, mystery reprints; Pres. and Publr DONNA HAYES.

HarperCollins Publishers: 10 East 53rd St, New York, NY 10022; tel. (212) 207-7000; fax (212) 207-7759; internet www.harpercollins.com; f. 1817; subsidiary of News Corpn; imprints incl. Avon (f. 1941, romantic fiction), Collins (general reference), Rayo (Latino culture) and William Morrow (f. 1926, fiction and non-fiction); fiction, non-fiction, religious, children's, medical, general; Pres. and CEO BRIAN MURRAY.

Harvard University Press: 79 Garden St, Cambridge, MA 02138; tel. (617) 495-2600; fax (401) 531-2801; e-mail contact_hup@harvard.edu; internet www.hup.harvard.edu; f. 1913; classics, fine arts, philosophy, science, medicine, law, literature, political science, religion, history and govt; Dir WILLIAM P. SISLER.

Hastings House/Daytrips Publishers: POB 908, Winter Park, FL 32790-0908; tel. (407) 339-3600; fax (407) 339-5900; e-mail

THE UNITED STATES OF AMERICA

hastings_daytrips@earthlink.net; internet www.hastingshousebooks.com; f. 1936; travel; Publr PETER LEERS.

Holiday House, Inc: 425 Madison Ave, New York, NY 10017; tel. (212) 688-0085; fax (212) 421-6134; e-mail info@holidayhouse.com; internet www.holidayhouse.com; f. 1935; juvenile; Pres. JOHN H. BRIGGS, Jr.

Holloway House Book Publishing Co: 8060 Melrose Ave, Los Angeles, CA 90046-7082; tel. (323) 653-8060; fax (323) 655-9452; e-mail info@psiemail.com; internet www.hollowayhousebooks.com; f. 1960; black experience and American Indian literature, gambling, fiction, non-fiction; CEO BENTLEY MORRISS.

Holmes & Meier Publishers, Inc: POB 943, Teaneck, NJ 07666; tel. (201) 833-2270; fax (201) 833-2272; e-mail info@holmesandmeier.com; internet www.holmesandmeier.com; f. 1969; imprints incl. Africana Publishing Co (f. 1969); history, political science, area studies, Africana, Judaica, foreign literature in translation, college texts and scholarly; Publr MIRIAM H. HOLMES.

Hoover Institution Press: 434 Galvez Mall, Stanford University, Stanford, CA 94305-6010; tel. (650) 723-1754; fax (650) 723-1687; e-mail horaney@hoover.stanford.edu; internet www.hoover.org; f. 1962; scholarly; Assoc. Dir JEFFREY BLISS.

Houghton Mifflin Co: 222 Berkeley St, Boston, MA 02116; tel. (617) 351-5000; fax (617) 351-3604; e-mail trade_generalinterest@hmco.com; internet www.hmco.com; f. 1832; owned by Houghton Mifflin Riverdeep PLC, Ireland; general and educational; Chair. and CEO ANTHONY LUCKI; Pres. and COO GERALD HUGHES.

Indiana University Press: 601 North Morton St, Bloomington, IN 47404-3797; tel. (812) 855-8817; fax (812) 855-7931; e-mail iupress@indiana.edu; internet www.iupress.indiana.edu; f. 1950; trade and scholarly non-fiction; Dir JANET RABINOWITCH.

International Universities Press, Inc: 59 Boston Post Rd, Madison, CT 06443; tel. (203) 245-4000; fax (203) 245-0775; e-mail info@iup.com; internet www.iup.com; f. 1943; publrs of PsychoSocial Press; psychology, psychiatry, medicine, social sciences and journals; Exec. Vice-Pres. Dr MARGARET EMERY.

Islamic Books/Tahrike Tarsile Qur'ān, Inc: POB 731115, Elmhurst, NY 11373-0115; tel. (718) 446-6472; fax (718) 446-4370; e-mail read@koranusa.org; internet www.koranusa.org; f. 1978; Koran and Islamic religious texts; Pres. AUN ALI KHALFAN.

Jewish Publication Society: 2100 Arch St, 2nd Floor, Philadelphia, PA 19103; tel. (215) 832-0608; fax (215) 568-2017; e-mail jewishbook@jewishpub.org; internet www.jewishpub.org; f. 1888; Judaica; CEO and Editor-in-Chief Dr ELLEN FRANKEL.

Johns Hopkins University Press: 2715 North Charles St, Baltimore, MD 21218-4319; tel. (410) 516-6900; fax (410) 516-6998; e-mail rr@press.jhu.edu; internet www.press.jhu.edu; f. 1878; social and physical sciences, humanities, health sciences, economics, literary criticism, history; Dir KATHLEEN KEANE.

Kendall/Hunt Publishing Co: 4050 Westmark Dr., POB 1840, Dubuque, IA 52004-1840; tel. (563) 589-1000; fax (563) 589-1046; e-mail orders@kendallhunt.com; internet www.kendallhunt.com; f. 1944; business and educational; CEO MARK FALB.

Krieger Publishing Co: 1725 Krieger Dr., Malabar, FL 32950; tel. (321) 724-9542; fax (321) 951-3671; e-mail info@krieger-pubishing.com; internet www.krieger-publishing.com; f. 1970; space technology, adult education, history and natural sciences; Pres. DONALD E. KRIEGER.

Loyola Press: 3441 North Ashland Ave, Chicago, IL 60657; tel. (773) 281-1818; fax (773) 281-0885; e-mail lane@loyolapress.com; internet www.loyolapress.com; f. 1912; owned by the Society of Jesus, Chicago Province; religious (Roman Catholic) education and language, religious trade and arts; Pres. GEORGE A. LANE.

McGraw-Hill Companies, Inc: POB 182604, Columbus, OH 43272; tel. (877) 833-5524; fax (614) 759-3749; e-mail customer.service@mcgraw-hill.com; internet www.mcgraw-hill.com; f. 1888; information texts and services for business, industry, govt and the general public; Chair. and CEO HAROLD MCGRAW, III.

Merriam-Webster Inc: 47 Federal St, POB 281, Springfield, MA 01102; tel. (413) 734-3134; fax (413) 731-5979; e-mail jwithgott@merriam-webster.com; internet www.merriam-webster.com; f. 1831; subsidiary of Encyclopaedia Britannica, Inc; dictionaries, reference; Pres. and Publr JOHN M. MORSE.

Michigan State University Press: Manly Miles Bldg, Suite 25, 1405 South Harrison Rd, East Lansing, MI 48823-5245; tel. (517) 355-9543; fax (517) 432-2611; e-mail msupress@msu.edu; internet msupress.msu.edu; f. 1947; scholarly; Dir GABRIEL DOTTO.

The MIT Press: 55 Hayward St, Cambridge, MA 02142; tel. (617) 253-5646; fax (617) 258-6779; internet mitpress.mit.edu; f. 1932; computer sciences, architecture, design, linguistics, economics, philosophy, general science, neuroscience, cognitive science and engineering; Dir ELLEN W. FARAN.

Moody Publishers: 820 North LaSalle Blvd, Chicago, IL 60610; tel. (312) 329-2101; fax (312) 329-4157; e-mail pressinfo@moody.edu; internet www.moodypublishers.org; f. 1894; publishing division of Moody Bible Institute (f. 1886); religious; Vice-Pres., Publications GREG THORNTON.

William Morrow & Co Inc: 10 East 53rd St, New York, NY 10022; tel. (212) 207-7000; fax (212) 207-7633; internet www.harpercollins.com; f. 1926; division of HarperCollins; fiction, non-fiction, juvenile; Pres. and CEO JANE FRIEDMAN.

National Academy Press (NAP): 500 Fifth St, NW, POB 285, Washington, DC 20055; tel. (202) 334-3180; fax (202) 334-2793; e-mail bkline@nas.edu; internet www.nap.edu; f. 1863; division of Nat. Academy of Sciences; scientific and technical reports, abstracts, bibliographies, catalogues; Dir BARBARA KLINE POPE.

National Learning Corpn: 212 Michael Dr., Syosset, NY 11791; tel. (516) 921-8888; fax (516) 921-8743; e-mail info@passbooks.com; internet www.passbooks.com; f. 1967; professional and vocational study guides; Pres. MICHAEL P. RUDMAN.

New Directions Publishing Corpn: 80 Eighth Ave, New York, NY 10011; tel. (212) 255-0230; fax (212) 255-0231; e-mail editorial@ndbooks.com; internet www.ndpublishing.com; f. 1936; modern literature, poetry and criticism; Pres. and Publr PEGGY L. FOX.

New York University Press: 838 Broadway, 3rd Floor, New York, NY 10003-4812; tel. (212) 998-2575; fax (212) 995-3833; e-mail information@nyupress.org; internet www.nyupress.org; f. 1916; scholarly and non-fiction; Dir STEVE MAIKOWSKI.

Northwestern University Press: 629 Noyes St, Evanston, IL 60208; tel. (847) 491-2046; fax (847) 491-8150; e-mail nupress@northwestern.edu; internet www.nupress.northwestern.edu; f. 1958; scholarly and trade; Dir DONNA SHEAR.

W. W. Norton & Co Inc: 500 Fifth Ave, New York, NY 10110; tel. (212) 354-5500; fax (212) 869-0856; e-mail srothbard@wwnorton.com; internet www.wwnorton.com; f. 1924; college textbooks, paperbacks, fiction and non-fiction; CEO STEPHEN KING; Pres. DRAKE MCFEELY.

NOVA Publications: 7342 Lee Hwy, No. 201, Falls Church, VA 22046; tel. and fax (703) 280-5383; e-mail novapublic@aol.com; internet www.members.aol.com/novapublic/index.htm; f. 1993; military history, political science, Russian and Middle Eastern studies; Publr ARNOLD C. DUPUY.

Oceana Publications Inc: 75 Main St, Dobbs Ferry, NY 10522-1632; tel. (914) 693-8100; fax (914) 693-0402; e-mail editorial@oceanalaw.com; internet www.oceanalaw.com; f. 1948; international law and trade; division of Oxford University Press, Inc; Pres. DAVID R. COHEN.

The Ohio State University Press: 180 Pressey Hall, 1070 Carmack Rd, Columbus, OH 43210-1002; tel. (614) 292-6930; fax (614) 292-2065; e-mail info@osupress.org; internet www.ohiostatepress.org; f. 1957; scholarly; Dir MALCOLM LITCHFIELD.

Ohio University Press: 19 Circle Dr., The Ridges, Athens, OH 45701; tel. (740) 593-1154; fax (740) 593-4536; e-mail cunningh@ohio.edu; internet www.ohiou.edu/oupress; f. 1964; scholarly and regional studies; Dir DAVID SANDERS.

Open Court Publishing Co: 70 East Lake St, Suite 300, Chicago, IL 60601; tel. (312) 701-1720; fax (312) 701-1728; internet www.opencourtbooks.com; f. 1887; philosophy and general non-fiction; Pres. and Publr ANDRE CARUS.

Orbis Books: Walsh Bldg, POB 308, Maryknoll, NY 10545-0308; tel. (914) 941-7590; fax (914) 945-0670; e-mail orbisbooks@maryknoll.org; internet www.orbisbooks.com; f. 1970; theology, religion and social concerns; Publr ROBERT ELLSBERG.

Oxford University Press, Inc: 198 Madison Ave, New York, NY 10016; tel. (212) 726-6000; fax (212) 726-6446; e-mail custserv.us@oup.com; internet www.oup.com/us; f. 1896; non-fiction, trade, religious, reference, college textbooks, medical and music; Pres. TIM BARTON.

Paladin Press: Gunbarrel Tech Center, 7077 Winchester Circle, Boulder, CO 80301; tel. (303) 443-7250; fax (303) 442-8741; e-mail service@paladin-press.com; internet www.paladin-press.com; f. 1970; imprints incl. Sycamore Island Books and Flying Machines Press; military science and history; Chair. and Pres. PEDER C. LUND.

Paragon House: 1925 Oakcrest Ave, Suite 7, St Paul, MN 55113-2619; tel. (651) 644-3087; fax (651) 644-0997; e-mail paragon@paragonhouse.com; internet www.paragonhouse.com; f. 1982; academic non-fiction, university texts, reference; Exec. Dir GORDON L. ANDERSON.

Pearson Education: 1 Lake St, Upper Saddle River, NJ 07458; tel. (201) 922-0579; e-mail communications@pearsoned.com; internet www.pearsoned.com; imprints incl. Addison-Wesley, Allyn & Bacon, FT Prentice Hall, Scotts Foreman, Benjamins Cummings and Longman; educational; CEO JOHN FALLON.

THE UNITED STATES OF AMERICA

Penguin Group (USA) Inc: 375 Hudson St, New York, NY 10014; tel. (212) 366-2000; fax (212) 366-2666; internet us.penguingroup.com; f. 1996 by merger between Penguin Books USA and the Putnam Berkley Group; imprints incl. Ace Books (f. 1953, science fiction), Avery (f. 1976, health, self-help, diet, and fitness), Alpha (f. 1991, general reference), Berkley (f. 1955, mass-market and trade paperback), Dutton (f. 1852, fiction and non-fiction), Gotham (f. 2001, non-fiction), HP Books (automotive, photography, gardening, health and child care), Hudson Street Press (f. 2003, hardcover non-fiction), Jeremy P. Tarcher (f. 1976, non-fiction), NAL (f. 1948, paperback fiction), Penguin (f. 1936, paperback), Plume (f. 1970, paperback), Portfolio (f. 2001, business), Putnam (f. 1838, fiction and non-fiction), Riverhead (f. 1994, fiction), Sentinel (f. 2003, conservative), and Viking (f. 1925, fiction and non-fiction); CEO DAVID SHANKS; Pres. SUSAN PETERSEN KENNEDY.

Pennsylvania State University Press: University Support Bldg I, Suite C, 820 North University Dr., University Park, PA 16802; tel. (814) 865-1327; fax (814) 863-1408; e-mail info@psupress.org; internet www.psupress.org; f. 1956; scholarly non-fiction; Dir SANFORD G. 'SANDY' THATCHER.

Presbyterian Publishing Corpn (PPC): 100 Witherspoon St, Louisville, KY 40202-1396; tel. (502) 569-5081; fax (502) 569-5113; e-mail publicity@wjkbooks.com; internet www.ppcbooks.com; f. 1938; publishing arm of the Presbyterian Church (USA); imprints incl. Geneva Press (religious trade) and Westminster John Knox Press (f. 1938, non-denominational Christian, modern religious and scholarly); Pres. and Publr DAVIS PERKINS.

Princeton University Press: 41 William St, Princeton, NJ 08540; tel. (609) 258-4900; fax (609) 258-6305; e-mail webmaster@press.princeton.edu; internet press.princeton.edu; f. 1905; scholarly; Dir PETER J. DOUGHERTY; Editor-in-Chief BRIGITTA VAN RHEINBERG.

Quite Specific Media Group Ltd: 7373 Pyramid Pl., Hollywood, CA 90046; tel. (323) 851-5797; fax (323) 851-5798; e-mail info@quitespecificmedia.com; internet www.quitespecificmedia.com; f. 1967; costume, design, fashion and performing arts; Publr RALPH PINE.

Rand McNally: 8255 North Central Park Ave, Skokie, IL 60076; tel. (800) 934-3479; fax (847) 329-6361; e-mail kconkey@reynoldsgroup.com; internet www.randmcnally.com; f. 1856; maps, atlases, travel guides and educational; Pres. and CEO ROBERT APATOFF.

Random House Publishing Group: 1745 Broadway, New York, NY 10019; tel. (212) 782-9000; fax (212) 572-8026; internet www.randomhouse.com; f. 2003 by merger of the Random House Trade Group and Ballantine Books Group; imprints incl. Random House Inc (f. 1925, originals, reprints, paperbacks, juvenile, series, textbooks), Ballantine Books (f. 1952, hardcover, trade and mass-market paperback), Del Rey (f. 1977, science fiction and fantasy), Modern Library (f. 1925, non-fiction and history), One World (f. 1991, multicultural), Presidio Press (military history), and Villard (f. 1983, general fiction and non-fiction); Chair. and CEO MARKUS DOHLE.

Reader's Digest Association: Reader's Digest Rd, Pleasantville, NY 10570-7000; tel. (914) 238-1000; fax (914) 238-4559; internet www.rd.com; reference and non-fiction; Pres. and CEO MARY BERNER.

Rizzoli International Publications: 300 Park Ave South, New York, NY 10010-5399; tel. (212) 387-3400; fax (212) 387-3535; e-mail tkayiatos@rizzoliusa.com; internet www.rizzoliusa.com; f. 1975; division of RCS Media Group (Italy); fine arts, performing arts, architecture; Pres. and CEO MARCO AUSENDA; Vice-Pres. and Publr CHARLES MIERS.

Routledge: 270 Madison Ave, New York, NY 10016-0602; tel. (212) 216-7800; fax (212) 563-2269; e-mail info@taylorandfrancis.com; internet www.routledge.com; f. 1977; imprint of Taylor & Francis Group (q.v.); scholarly, professional, trade, humanities, social sciences.

Rutgers University Press: 100 Joyce Kilmer Ave, Piscataway, NJ 08854; tel. (732) 445-7762; fax (732) 445-7039; e-mail jwi@rutgers.edu; internet rutgerspress.rutgers.edu; f. 1936; trade, scholarly and regional; Dir MARLIE WASSERMAN.

William H. Sadlier Inc: 9 Pine St, New York, NY 10005; tel. (212) 227-2120; fax (212) 267-8696; e-mail wsd@sadlier.com; internet www.sadlier.com; f. 1832; textbooks; Pres. WILLIAM SADLIER DINGER.

St Martin's Press Inc: 175 Fifth Ave, New York, NY 10010; tel. (212) 674-5151; fax (212) 420-9314; e-mail webmaster@stmartins.com; internet www.stmartins.com; f. 1952; part of Holtzbrinck Publrs, LLC; general, scholarly, college textbooks, trade and mass-market; Pres. JOHN SARGENT.

Scarecrow Press, Inc: 4501 Forbes Blvd, Suite 200, Lanham, MD 20706; tel. (301) 459-3366; fax (301) 429-5748; e-mail custserv@rowman.com; internet www.scarecrowpress.com; f. 1950; subsidiary of Rowman & Littlefield, Inc; music, film, theatre, reference, textbooks, library and information science; Publr and Editorial Dir EDWARD KURDYLA.

Scholastic, Inc: 555 Broadway, New York, NY 10012; tel. (212) 343-6100; fax (212) 343-6930; e-mail customerservice@scholastic.com; internet www.scholastic.com; f. 1920; children's periodicals, textbooks, educational materials; Chair., Pres. and CEO M. RICHARD ROBINSON.

Simon & Schuster, Inc: 1230 Ave of the Americas, New York, NY 10020; tel. (212) 698-7000; fax (212) 698-7007; internet www.simonsays.com; f. 1924; part of the CBS Group; trade, juvenile, reference, educational, business and professional; imprints include Aladdin Paperbacks (juvenile fiction), Free Press (politics, history, religion, business, fiction), Howard Books (f. 1969, religion, gift books), Pocket Books (f. 1939, fiction), and Scribner (f. 1846, fiction); Pres. and CEO CAROLYN REIDY.

Peter Smith Publisher, Inc: 5 Lexington Ave, Magnolia, MA 01930; tel. (978) 525-3562; fax (978) 525-3674; reprints; Pres. MARY ANN LASH.

Smithsonian Institution Press: 750 Ninth St, NW, Suite 4300, Washington, DC 20560-0950; tel. (202) 275-2243; fax (202) 275-2243; e-mail info@sipress.si.edu; internet www.sipress.si.edu; f. 1848; scholarly and general interest, American studies and culture, anthropology, archaeology, natural science and museum studies; Dir DON FEHR.

Southern Illinois University Press: 1915 University Press Dr., Carbondale, IL 62901-4323; 1915 University Press Dr., SIUC Mail Code 6806, Carbondale, IL 62902-6806; tel. (618) 453-2281; fax (618) 453-1221; e-mail ladkins@siu.edu; internet www.siu.edu/~siupress; f. 1953; scholarly non-fiction; Dir ARTHUR M. (LAIN) ADKINS.

Springer: 233 Spring St, New York, NY 10013; tel. (212) 460-1500; fax (212) 460-1575; e-mail service-ny@springer.com; internet www.springer.com; f. 1964; part of Springer Science+Business Media; scientific, technical and medical; CEO DERK HAANK.

Stanford University Press: 1450 Page Mill Rd, Palo Alto, CA 94304; tel. (650) 723-9434; fax (650) 725-3457; e-mail info@www.sup.org; internet www.sup.org; f. 1925; Dir GEOFFREY BURN.

State University of New York Press: 194 Washington Ave, Suite 305, Albany, NY 12210-2384; tel. (518) 472-5000; fax (518) 472-5038; e-mail info@sunypress.edu; internet www.sunypress.edu; f. 1966; scholarly and general interest; Exec. Dir GARY DUNHAM.

Sterling Publishing Co, Inc: 387 Park Ave South, New York, NY 10016; tel. (212) 532-7160; fax (212) 213-2495; e-mail publicity@sterlingpub.com; internet www.sterlingpub.com; f. 1949; subsidiary of Barnes and Noble, Inc; imprints incl. Lark Books and Hearst; non-fiction and illustrated; Chair. BURTON H. HOBSON.

Syracuse University Press: Suite 110, 621 Skytop Rd, Syracuse, NY 13244-5290; tel. (315) 443-5534; fax (315) 443-5545; e-mail supress@syr.edu; internet www.syracuseuniversitypress.syr.edu; f. 1943; scholarly; Dir ALICE RANDAL PFEIFFER.

Taplinger Publishing Co Inc: POB 175, Marlboro, NJ 07746; tel. (305) 256-7880; fax (305) 256-7816; e-mail taplingerpub@yahoo.com; f. 1955; general fiction and non-fiction; Pres. LOUIS STRICK.

Taylor & Francis Group: 270 Madison Ave, New York, NY 10016; tel. (212) 216-7800; fax (212) 564-7854; e-mail info@taylorandfrancis.com; internet www.taylorandfrancis.com; f. 1972; division of Informa PLC; imprints incl. CRC Press (f. 1913, reference, science, engineering and medicine), Garland Science Publishing (f. 1969, molecular biology, immunology and protein science textbooks), Routledge (q.v.), and Taylor & Francis Books (f. 1972, academic, science and reference); Pres. EMMETT DAGES.

Charles C. Thomas, Publisher: 2600 South First St, Springfield, IL 62794-9265; tel. (217) 789-8980; fax (217) 789-9130; e-mail books@ccthomas.com; internet www.ccthomas.com; f. 1927; textbooks and reference on education, medicine, psychology and criminology; Pres. MICHAEL P. THOMAS.

Time Life, Inc: POB 4002011, Des Moines, IA 50340-2011; f. 1961; general non-fiction; Pres. and CEO JIM NELSON.

Tuttle Publishing: Airport Business Park, 364 Innovation Dr., North Clarendon, VT 05759-9436; tel. (802) 773-8930; fax (802) 773-6993; e-mail info@tuttlepublishing.com; internet periplupublishinggroup.com/tuttle; f. 1948; part of the Periplus Publishing Group; the Far East, particularly Japan, languages, art, crafts, martial arts, culture, juvenile, cookery; Publishing Dir EDWARD WALTERS.

United Nations Publications: United Nations Plaza, Room DC2-0853, New York, NY 10017; tel. (212) 963-8302; fax (212) 963-3489; e-mail publications@un.org; internet unp.un.org; f. 1946; world and national economies, international trade, social questions, human rights and international law; Chief of Section CHRISTOPHER WOODTHORPE.

University of Alabama Press: POB 870380, Tuscaloosa, AL 35487; tel. (205) 348-5180; fax (205) 348-9201; e-mail sgriffit@uapress.ua.edu; internet www.uapress.ua.edu; f. 1945; scholarly; Dir DANIEL J. J. ROSS.

THE UNITED STATES OF AMERICA

University of Alaska Press: POB 756240, Fairbanks, AK 99775-6240; tel. (907) 474-5831; fax (907) 474-5502; e-mail fypress@uaf.edu; internet www.uaf.edu/uapress; f. 1967; scholarly regional non-fiction, history, anthropology of the circumpolar north; Chair. of Editorial Bd PATRICIA H. PARTNOW.

University of Arizona Press: 355 South Euclid Ave, Suite 103, Tucson, AZ 85719; tel. (520) 621-1441; fax (520) 621-8899; e-mail uapress@uapress.arizona.edu; internet www.uapress.arizona.edu; f. 1959; scholarly, popular, regional and non-fiction; Dir CHRISTINE SZUTER.

University of Arkansas Press: McIlroy House, 105 N McIlroy Ave, Fayetteville, AR 72701; tel. (479) 575-3246; fax (479) 575-6044; e-mail cmoss@uark.edu; internet www.uapress.com; f. 1980; humanities, literature, regional studies, natural history, Middle Eastern studies, poetry, civil rights studies and American history; Dir LARRY MALLEY.

University of California Press: 2120 Berkeley Way, Berkeley, CA 94704-1012; tel. (510) 642-4247; fax (510) 643-7127; e-mail askucp@ucpress.edu; internet www.ucpress.edu; f. 1893; academic and scholarly; Dir LYNNE WITHEY.

University of Chicago Press: 1427 East 60th St, Chicago, IL 60637; tel. (773) 702-7700; fax (773) 702-9756; e-mail publicity@press.uchicago.edu; internet www.press.uchicago.edu; f. 1891; scholarly and general; Dir PAULA BARKER DUFFY.

University of Georgia Press: 330 Research Dr., Athens, GA 30602-4901; tel. (706) 369-6148; fax (706) 369-6131; e-mail books@ugapress.uga.edu; internet www.ugapress.org; f. 1938; academic, scholarly, poetry, fiction, non-fiction and literary trade; Dir NICOLE MITCHELL.

University of Hawaii Press: 2840 Kolowalu St, Honolulu, HI 96822; tel. (808) 956-8255; fax (808) 988-6052; e-mail uhpbooks@hawaii.edu; internet www.uhpress.hawaii.edu; f. 1947; Asian, Pacific and Hawaiian studies; Dir WILLIAM H. HAMILTON.

University of Idaho Press: 200 South Almon St, Moscow, ID 83844-4416; tel. (208) 885-3300; fax (208) 885-3301; e-mail uipress@uidaho.edu; f. 1972; scholarly, regional studies; Dir IVAR NELSON.

University of Illinois Press: 1325 South Oak St, Champaign, IL 61820; tel. (217) 333-0950; fax (217) 244-8082; e-mail uipress@uillinois.edu; internet www.press.uillinois.edu; f. 1918; scholarly and trade; Dir WILLIS REGIER.

University of Massachusetts Press: POB 429, Amherst, MA 01004-0429; tel. (413) 545-2217; fax (413) 545-1226; e-mail info@umpress.umass.edu; internet www.umass.edu/umpress; f. 1963; scholarly; Dir BRUCE G. WILCOX.

University of Michigan Press: 839 Greene St, Ann Arbor, MI 48104-3209; tel. (734) 764-4388; fax (734) 615-1540; e-mail dshafer@umich.edu; internet www.press.umich.edu; f. 1930; academic, textbooks and paperbacks; Dir PHILIP POCHODA.

University of Minnesota Press: 111 Third Ave South, Suite 290, Minneapolis, MN 55401-5250; tel. (612) 627-1970; fax (612) 627-1980; e-mail ump@umn.edu; internet www.upress.umn.edu; f. 1925; scholarly and general; Dir DOUGLAS M. ARMATO.

University of Missouri Press: 2910 LeMone Blvd, Columbia, MO 65201; tel. (573) 882-7641; fax (573) 884-4498; e-mail upress@umsystem.edu; internet press.umsystem.edu; f. 1958; scholarly; Dir BEVERLY JARRETT.

University of Nebraska Press: 1111 Lincoln Mall, Lincoln, NE 68588-0630; tel. (402) 472-3581; fax (402) 472-6214; e-mail pressmail@unl.edu; internet www.nebraskapress.unl.edu; f. 1941; scholarly and general; Dir LADETTE RANDOLPH.

University of New Mexico Press: 1312 Basehart SE, Suite 200s, Albuquerque, NM 87106; tel. (505) 277-2346; fax (505) 277-7141; e-mail unmpress@unm.edu; internet www.unmpress.com; f. 1929; scholarly and regional studies; Dir LUTHER WILSON.

University of North Carolina Press: 116 South Boundary St, Chapel Hill, NC 27514-3808; tel. (919) 966-3561; fax (919) 966-3829; e-mail uncpress@unc.edu; internet www.uncpress.unc.edu; f. 1922; biography, regional and scholarly; Dir KATE D. TORREY.

University of Notre Dame Press: 310 Flanner Hall, Notre Dame, IN 46556; tel. (574) 631-6346; fax (574) 631-8148; e-mail undpress.1@nd.edu; internet www.undpress.nd.edu; f. 1949; humanities and social sciences; Dir BARBARA J. HANRAHAN.

University of Oklahoma Press: 2800 Venture Dr., Norman, OK 73069-8216; tel. (405) 325-2000; fax (405) 325-4000; internet www.oupress.com; f. 1928; scholarly; Editor-in-Chief CHARLES E. RANKIN; Dir B. BYRON PRICE.

University of Pennsylvania Press: 3905 Spruce St, Philadelphia, PA 19104-4112; tel. (215) 898-6261; fax (215) 898-0404; e-mail custserv@pobox.upenn.edu; internet www.upenn.edu/pennpress; f. 1890; scholarly; Dir ERIC HALPERN.

University of Pittsburgh Press: Eureka Bldg, 3400 Forbes Ave, 5th Floor, Pittsburgh, PA 15260; tel. (412) 383-2456; fax (412) 383-2466; e-mail press@pitt.edu; internet www.upress.pitt.edu; f. 1936; scholarly; Dir CYNTHIA MILLER.

University of South Carolina Press: 1600 Hampton St, 5th Floor, Columbia, SC 29208; tel. (803) 777-5243; fax (800) 868-0740; e-mail lfogle@gwm.sc.edu; internet www.sc.edu/uscpress; scholarly and regional studies; Dir CURTIS L. CLARK.

University of Tennessee Press: Conference Center Bldg, 600 Henley St, Suite 110, Knoxville, TN 37996-4108; tel. (865) 974-3321; fax (865) 974-3724; e-mail custserv@utk.edu; internet www.utpress.org; f. 1940; scholarly, regional, and literary fiction; Dir JENNIFER M. SILER.

University of Texas Press: POB 7819, Austin, TX 78713-7819; tel. (512) 471-7233; fax (512) 232-7178; e-mail utpress@uts.cc.utexas.edu; internet www.utexas.edu/utpress; f. 1950; general, scholarly non-fiction; Dir JOANNA HITCHCOCK.

University of Utah Press: J. Willard Marriott Library, Suite 5400, 295 South 1500 East, Salt Lake City, UT 84112-0860; tel. (801) 585-9786; fax (801) 581-3365; e-mail peter.delafosse@utah.edu; internet www.uofupress.com; f. 1949; scholarly, regional and Middle East studies; Dir GLENDA COTTER (acting).

University of Virginia Press: POB 400318, Charlottesville, VA 22904-4318; tel. (434) 924-3469; fax (434) 982-2655; internet www.upress.virginia.edu; f. 1963; scholarly non-fiction, literature, history, Victorian, African and Afro-American studies; Dir PENELOPE KAISERLIAN.

University of Washington Press: POB 50096, Seattle, WA 98145-5096; tel. (206) 543-4050; fax (206) 543-3932; e-mail hfscustserv@press.jhu.edu; internet www.washington.edu/uwpress; f. 1920; general, scholarly, non-fiction and reprints; Dir PAT SODEN.

University of Wisconsin Press: 1930 Monroe St, 3rd Floor, Madison, WI 53711-2059; tel. (608) 263-1110; fax (608) 263-1120; e-mail uwiscpress@uwpress.wisc.edu; internet www.wisc.edu/wisconsinpress; f. 1936; scholarly and trade; Interim Dir SHEILA LEARY.

University Press of America, Inc: 4501 Forbes Blvd, Suite 200, Lanham, MD 20706; tel. (301) 459-3366; fax (301) 429-5749; internet www.univpress.com; f. 1975; scholarly; Vice-Pres. and Dir JUDITH ROTHMAN.

University Press of Florida: 15 North West 15th St, Gainesville, FL 32611-2079; tel. (352) 392-1351; fax (352) 392-7302; internet www.upf.com; f. 1945; general, scholarly, regional; Dir MEREDITH MORRIS-BABB.

University Press of Kansas: 2502 Westbrooke Circle, Lawrence, KS 66045; tel. (785) 864-4155; fax (785) 864-4586; e-mail upress@ku.edu; internet www.kansaspress.ku.edu; f. 1946; scholarly; Dir FRED M. WOODWARD.

University Press of Kentucky: 663 South Limestone St, Lexington, KY 40508-4008; tel. (606) 257-8400; fax (606) 323-1873; internet www.kentuckypress.com; f. 1943; non-fiction, scholarly and regional; Dir STEPHEN M. WRINN.

University Press of Mississippi: 3825 Ridgewood Rd, Jackson, MS 39211; tel. (601) 432-6205; fax (601) 432-6217; e-mail press@ihl.state.ms.us; internet www.upress.state.ms.us; f. 1970; scholarly, non-fiction and regional; Dir LEILA SALISBURY.

University Press of New England: 1 Court St, Lebanon, NH 03766; tel. (603) 448-1533; fax (603) 448-7006; e-mail upneweb@dartmouth.edu; internet www.upne.com; f. 1970; scholarly; Dir MICHAEL P. BURTON.

Vanderbilt University Press: POB 1813, Nashville, TN 37235; tel. (615) 322-3585; fax (615) 343-8823; e-mail vupress@vanderbilt.edu; internet www.vanderbiltuniversitypress.com; f. 1940; scholarly and trade; Dir MICHAEL AMES.

Wayne State University Press: 4809 Woodward Ave, Detroit, MI 48201; tel. (313) 577-6120; fax (313) 577-6131; e-mail jane.hoehner@wayne.edu; internet wsupress.wayne.edu; f. 1941; scholarly; Dir JANE HOEHNER.

Westview Press: 2465 Central Ave, Boulder, CO 80301; tel. and fax (720) 406-7336; e-mail westview.press@perseusbooks.com; internet www.perseusbooksgroup.com/westview; social sciences, humanities and science textbooks; f. 1975; part of the Perseus Books Group; Publr MARCUS BOGGS.

Wiley—Blackwell: 111 River St, Hoboken, NJ 07030-5774; tel. (201) 748-6000; fax (201) 748-6088; e-mail info@wiley.com; internet www.wiley.com; f. 1807; fmrly John Wiley and Sons, Inc; name changed as above in 2007; higher education, scientific, technical, medical, professional and trade; Chair. PETER B. WILEY; Pres. and CEO WILLIAM J. PESCE.

H. W. Wilson Co: 950 University Ave, Bronx, NY 10452; tel. (718) 588-8400; fax (718) 590-1617; e-mail esutter@hwwilson.com;

internet www.hwwilson.com; f. 1898; reference and indices; Pres. and CEO HAROLD REGAN.

Wolters Kluwer Health: 161 West Washington St, Suite 1100, Conshohocken, PA 19428; tel. (610) 234-4511; e-mail robert.dekker@wolterskluwer.com; internet www.wkhealth.com; division of Wolters Kluwer; medical and scientific reference; imprints incl. Lippincott, Williams & Wilkins (f. 1792, dentistry, science, human and veterinary medicine); Pres. and CEO JEFFERY McCAULLEY.

Yale University Press: POB 209040, New Haven, CT 06520-9040; tel. (203) 432-0960; fax (203) 432-0948; e-mail ivan.lett@yale.edu; internet yalepress.yale.edu/yup; f. 1908; scholarly; Dir JOHN DONATICH.

GOVERNMENT PUBLISHING HOUSE

Government Printing Office: 732 North Capitol St, NW, Washington, DC 20401; tel. (202) 512-0000; fax (202) 512-2104; e-mail contactcenter@gpo.gov; internet www.gpo.gov; Public Printer and CEO ROBERT C. TAPELLA.

ORGANIZATIONS AND ASSOCIATIONS

American Booksellers' Association (ABA): 200 White Plains Rd, Tarrytown, NY 10591; tel. (914) 591-2665; fax (914) 591-2724; e-mail avin@bookweb.org; internet www.bookweb.org; f. 1900; 2,500 mems; Pres. GAYLE SHANKS; CEO AVIN MARK DOMNITZ.

American Medical Publishers' Association (AMPA): 308 East Lancaster Ave, Suite 110, Wynnewood, PA 19096; tel. (610) 642-2810; fax (610) 642-0628; e-mail info@ampaonline.org; internet www.ampaonline.org; f. 1960; 75 mems; Exec. Dirs ROBIN B. BARTLETT, CHRISTINE BOYLAN.

Association of American University Presses, Inc: 71 West 23rd St, New York, NY 10010; tel. (212) 989-1010; fax (212) 989-0275; e-mail info@aaupnet.org; internet www.aaupnet.org; f. 1937; 125 mems; Exec. Dir PETER J. GIVLER.

The Children's Book Council, Inc: 12 West 37th St, 2nd Floor, New York, NY 10018-7480; tel. (212) 966-1990; fax (212) 966-2073; internet www.cbcbooks.org; f. 1945; 75 mems; Chair. SUZANNE MURPHY.

Florida Publishers Association, Inc: POB 430, Highland City, FL 33846-0430; tel. and fax (836) 647-5951; e-mail fpabooks@aol.com; internet www.flbookpub.org; f. 1983; fmrly Nat. Asscn of Independent Publrs; 150 mems; Exec. Dir BETSY WRIGHT-LAMPE.

Independent Book Publishers' Association (IBPA): 627 Aviation Way, Manhattan Beach, CA 90266; tel. (310) 372-2732; fax (310) 374-3342; e-mail info@ibpa-online.org; internet www.ibpa-online.org; f. 1983 as Publishers' Marketing Asscn; over 4,000 mem. publrs; Pres. FLORRIE BINFORD KICHLER; Exec. Dir TERRY NATHAN.

Independent Publishers Group: 814 North Franklin St, Chicago, IL 60610; tel. (312) 337-0747; fax (312) 337-5985; e-mail frontdesk@ipgbook.com; internet www.ipgbook.com; f. 1971; Pres. MARK SUCHOMEL; CEO CURT MATTHEWS.

Music Publishers' Association of the US: 243 Fifth Ave, Suite 236, New York, NY 10016; tel. (212) 327-4044; e-mail admin@mpa.org; internet www.mpa.org; f. 1895; 600 mems; Pres. LAUREN KEISER.

Publishers Group West (PGW): 1700 Fourth St, Berkeley, CA 94710; tel. (510) 528-1444; fax (510) 528-3444; e-mail info@pgw.com; internet www.pgw.com; f. 1976; subsidiary of Publishers Group Worldwide; Vice-Pres. International Sales CHITRA BOPADIKAR.

Small Press Distribution: 1341 Seventh St, Berkeley, CA 94710-1409; tel. (510) 524-1668; fax (510) 524-0852; e-mail spd@spdbooks.org; internet www.spdbooks.org; f. 1969; distributes exclusively independently published literature; Exec. Dir JEFFREY LEPENDORF.

Small Publishers Association of North America (SPAN): 1618 West Colorado Ave, Colorado Springs, CO 80904; tel. (719) 475-1726; fax (719) 471-2182; e-mail span@spannet.org; internet www.spannet.org; f. 1996 to promote the profile and interests of independent publrs and authors; Exec. Dir SCOTT FLORA; over 1,000 mems.

Broadcasting and Communications

Federal Communications Commission (FCC): 445 12th St, SW, Washington, DC 20554; tel. (202) 418-0200; fax (202) 418-0232; e-mail fccinfo@fcc.gov; internet www.fcc.gov; f. 1934; regulates inter-state and foreign communications by radio, television, wire and cable; Chair. MICHAEL J. COPPS (acting).

TELECOMMUNICATIONS

Principal Telecommunications Networks

Alltel Corpn (ALLTEL): Bldg 4, 3rd Floor, 1 Allied Dr., Little Rock, AR 72202-2099; tel. (501) 905-6078; e-mail dale.ingram@alltel.com; internet www.alltel.com; f. 1943 as Allied Telephone; current name adopted when merged with Mid-Continent in 1983; acquired by jt venture of TPG Capital and Goldman Sachs in May 2007; plans announced in June 2008 by Verizon Wireless, a jt venture of Verizon Communications and Vodafone Group PLC (United Kingdom), to acquire Alltel Corpn; mobile-only service operated from 2006; serves 13m. customers in 35 states; Pres. and CEO SCOTT FORD; c. 12m. subscribers.

AT&T, Inc (American Telegraph and Telephone): 175 East Houston St, San Antonio, TX 78205; tel. (212) 387-5400; fax (212) 226-4935; internet www.att.com; f. 1885; bought by SBC Communications in Jan. 2005, merger completed and present name adopted in Nov. 2005; merged with the BellSouth Corpn in Dec. 2006, and acquired full ownership of Cingular Wireless; 100m. customers; Chair. and CEO RANDALL L. STEPHENSON.

Comcast Corpn: 1500 Market St, Philadelphia, PA 19102; internet www.comcast.com; tel. (215) 286-7408; e-mail corporate_communications@comcast.com; f. 1963; acquired AT&T Broadband in 2002; acquired part of Adelphia Communications in 2006; 24.1m. cable subscribers in 39 states and the District of Columbia, 12.4m. internet customers, 3.5m. cable telephone subscribers; Chair. and CEO BRIAN L. ROBERTS; Exec. Vice-Pres. DAVID L. COHEN.

Frontier Communications: 3 High Ridge Park, Stamford, CT 06905-1390; tel. (203) 614-5600; fax (203) 614-4602; e-mail citizens@czn.com; internet www.czn.com; f. 1935; 3m. access lines in 24 states; fmrly Citizens Communications Co; acquisition of Commonwealth Telephone Enterprises completed in March 2007; Pres. and CEO MAGGIE WILDEROTTER; Exec. Vice-Pres. and COO DANIEL MCCARTHY.

Qwest Communications International, Inc: 1801 California St, Denver, CO 80202; tel. (303) 992-1400; fax (303) 896-8515; e-mail qnews@qwest.com; internet www.qwest.com; telephone and internet provider to 21.8m. customers in the USA; acquired US West in 2000; Chair. and CEO EDWARD A. MUELLER; Exec. Vice-Pres. of Operations ROBERT TREGEMBA.

SES AMERICOM: 4 Research Way, Princeton, NJ 08540-6684; tel. (609) 987-4000; fax (609) 987-4517; e-mail info.americom@ses-americom.com; f. 1975; fmrly GE American Communications, Inc; Pres. and CEO ROBERT BEDNAREK.

Verizon Communications: 140 West St, New York, NY 10007; tel. (800) 621-9900; internet www.verizon.com; f. 2000 by merger of Bell Atlantic Corpn and GTE Corpn; divisions include Verizon Business, fmrly MCI, Inc; 228,600 employees; Chair. and CEO IVAN G. SEIDENBERG; Pres. and COO DENNIS G. STRIGL.

Associations

United States Telecom Association (USTelecom): 607 14th St, NW, Suite 400, Washington, DC 20005; tel. (202) 326-7300; fax (202) 326-7333; e-mail pkrebs@ustelecom.org; internet www.ustelecom.org; Pres. and CEO WALTER B. MCCORMICK, Jr; Chair. RON B. MCCUE.

UTC—Utilities Telecom Council: 1901 Pennsylvania Ave, NW, Washington, DC 20006; tel. (202) 872-0030; fax (202) 872-1331; e-mail utc@utc.org; internet www.utc.org; f. 1948; name changed from United Telecom Council in 2007; non-profit asscn representing telecommunications and information interests of public utilities, natural gas pipelines and other infrastructure cos and their strategic business partners; Pres. and CEO BILL MORONEY.

BROADCASTING

The USA constitutes the world's biggest market for communications and broadcasting systems. The USA has the highest ratio of radio and television receivers per head of population of any country in the world. In 2004 radio sets were in use in 99% of homes and in 2007 there were an estimated 311m. television receivers in use. There were 6,635 cable systems in operation in the same year, serving an estimated 64.9m. subscribers. In 2008 78.7% of households with television receivers used video cassette recorders.

Radio

In 2004 there were 10,987 licensed commercial AM and FM radio stations operating in the USA. In 2004 the average US household had 8.0 radio sets in use.

Principal Domestic Networks

CBS RADIO: CBS RADIO, 1515 Broadway, New York, NY 10036; tel. (212) 846-3939; internet www.cbsradio.com; f. 1928; fmrly Infinity Broadcasting; division of CBS Corpn; owns CBS Radio Network serving more than 1,500 radio stations; operates 144 radio stations; Pres. and CEO DAN MASON.

Citadel Media Networks: 13725 Montfort Dr., Dallas, TX 75240; tel. (972) 991-9200; fax (214) 991-1071; e-mail omar.thompson@citcomm.com; internet www.citadelmedianetworks.com; f. 1944; fmrly ABC Radio Networks; name changed as above in 2009; fmrly

THE UNITED STATES OF AMERICA

Directory

wholly owned subsidiary of The Walt Disney Company; ABC Radio Business, as a spin-off concern of The Walt Disney Co, merged with a wholly owned subsidiary of Citadel Broadcasting Corpn in June 2007; 4,500 affiliated radio stations broadcasting five full service line networks; Pres. JAMES ROBINSON.

Clear Channel Radio: 200 East Basse Rd, San Antonio, TX 78209; tel. (210) 822-2828; e-mail lisacdollinger@clearchannel.com; internet www.clearchannel.com/radio; c. 1,000 radio stations; Pres. and Chief Financial Officer RANDALL MAYS; CEO MARK MAYS.

National Public Radio (NPR): 635 Massachusetts Ave, NW, Washington, DC 20001; tel. (202) 513-2300; fax (202) 513-3329; e-mail achristopher@npr.org; internet www.npr.org; f. 1970; private non-profit corpn providing programmes and support facilities to over 800 mem. stations nation-wide; also operates a global programme distribution service by radio, cable and satellite; Chair. ANTOINE W. VAN AGTMAEL; Pres. and CEO VIVIAN SCHILLER.

Westwood One Inc: 40 West 57th St, 5th Floor, New York, NY 10019; tel. (212) 641-2000; e-mail david_hillman@westwoodone.com; internet www.westwoodone.com; f. 1934; managed by CBS Radio, Inc, fmrly Infinity Broadcasting; subsidiary of Viacom, Inc; largest domestic outsource provider of traffic-reporting services, broadcasting to 7,700 radio stations; produces and distributes national news, sports, talk, music and special event programmes, in addition to local news, sports, weather and other information programming; operates BLAISE, CBS, CNN Max, Navigator, NBC, NeXt, Source Max and WONE radio networks; CFO ROD SHERWOOD.

Principal External Radio Services

American Forces Radio and Television Service/American Forces Network (AFRTS/AFN-BC): Defense Media Center (DMC), AFN Broadcast Center, 23755 Z St, Riverside, CA 92518; tel. (951) 413-2319; fax (951) 413-2227; e-mail larry.sichter@dma .mil; internet www.myafn.net; f. 1942; operated by Dept of Defense; provides encrypted US radio and TV programming in English exclusively to US military and Dept of Defense civilian personnel in 177 countries, US territories and aboard US Navy ships; Exec. Dir JEFFREY WHITE (DMC); Dir MELVIN RUSSELL (AFRTS).

RFE/RL (Radio Free Europe/Radio Liberty): 1201 Connecticut Ave, NW, Suite 1100, Washington, DC 20036; tel. (202) 457-6900; fax (202) 457-6992; e-mail jensend@rferl.org; internet www.rferl.org; f. 1950; private, non-profit corpn financed by the federal Govt; broadcasts from Prague, Czech Republic, to Eastern and South-Eastern Europe, Russia, the Caucasus, the Middle East, Central and South-West Asia; c. 1,000 hours weekly in 28 languages; Chair. JAMES K. GLASSMAN; Pres. JEFFREY GEDMIN.

Voice of America: 330 Independence Ave, SW, Washington, DC 20237; tel. (202) 203-4959; fax (202) 203-4960; e-mail askvoa@voanews.com; internet www.voanews.com; f. 1942; govt-funded; broadcasts c. 1,000 hours weekly in 45 languages to all areas of the world via radio, television and the internet; Dir DANFORTH W. AUSTIN.

Television

In 2007 commercial television stations numbered 1,364. The average US household had 2.8 television sets in use in 2007.

All analogue broadcasting was to cease by 12 June 2009.

Principal Networks

ABC, Inc (American Broadcasting Co, Inc): 500 South Buena Vista St, Burbank, CA 91521-4551; tel. (818) 460-7477; e-mail netaudr@abc.com; internet abc.go.com; f. 1953; subsidiary of the Walt Disney Co since 1996; 10 owned and 226 affiliated stations; production through Touchstone Television, and Disney television content distribution through Buena Vista Television; Pres., ABC-owned Television Stations WALTER C. LISS; Pres., Disney-ABC TV Group ANNE SWEENEY.

C-SPAN (Cable-Satellite Public Affairs Network): 400 North Capitol St, Suite 650, Washington, DC 20001; tel. (202) 737-3220; e-mail viewer@c-span.org; internet www.c-span.org; f. 1979; private, non-profit public service; earns its operating revenues through licence fees paid by cable and satellite systems offering the network to their customers; Chair. and CEO BRIAN LAMB; Co-Pres SUSAN SWAIN, ROBERT KENNEDY.

CBS Television Network (Columbia Broadcasting System Television Network): 51 West 52nd St, New York, NY 10019-6188; tel. (212) 975-4321; internet www.cbs.com; f. 1928; subsidiary of CBS Corpn; serves more than 200 affiliated stations; parent CBS Corpn subsidiary, CBS Television Stations Group, operates 39 stations, incl. 21 CBS, 11 The CW, 3 MyNetworkTV and 4 independents; CBS Corpn Pres. and CEO LESLIE MOONVES; Chair. SUMNER REDSTONE.

CNN (Cable News Network): 1 CNN Center, POB 105366, Atlanta, GA 30348; tel. (404) 827-1700; fax (404) 827-1099; e-mail public .information@turner.com; internet www.cnn.com; subsidiary of Time Warner; Pres. JONATHAN KLEIN; Pres., CNN News Group JIM WALTON.

FOX Broadcasting Co: 10201 West Pico Blvd, Los Angeles, CA 90035; tel. (310) 369-3553; e-mail scott.grogin@fox.com; internet www.fox.com ; f. 1986; subsidiary of News Corpn; more than 900 cable affiliations; Pres. KEVIN REILLY; Chair. PETER LIGUORI.

NBC Universal Television Stations: 30 Rockefeller Plaza, New York, NY 10112; tel. (212) 664-4444; fax (212) 664-5830; internet www.nbcuni.com; f. 1926; subsidiary of NBC Universal; 27 owned and over 200 affiliated stations; Pres. and CEO, NBC Universal JEFF ZUCKER.

PBS (Public Broadcasting Service): 2100 Crystal Dr., Arlington, VA 22202; tel. (703) 739-5000; fax (703) 739-0775; e-mail viewer@pbs .org; internet www.pbs.org; f. 1969; non-profit-making; financed by private subscriptions and federal govt funds; owned and operated by the 355 public US television stations; Pres. and CEO PAULA KERGER; COO WAYNE GODWIN.

Time Warner Cable, Inc (TWC): 290 Harbor Dr., Stamford, CT 06902-6732; tel. (203) 364-8203; fax (203) 328-0690; internet www .timewarnercable.com; cable television system serving c. 14.7m. subscribers in 33 states; acquired part of Adelphia Communications in 2005; 84% owned by Time Warner; Pres. and CEO GLENN A. BRITT; Chair. DON LOGAN.

Univision Network: 9405 North West 41st St, Miami, FL 33178-2301; tel. (305) 471-3900; fax (305) 471-4065; internet www.univision .com ; subsidiary of Univision Communications, Inc; acquired by Broadcasting Media Partners Inc, a group of private equity investors, in March 2007; Spanish-language television network; Pres. JOE UVA.

Associations

National Association of Broadcasters (NAB): 1771 N St, NW, Washington, DC 20036; tel. (202) 429-5300; fax (202) 429-4199; e-mail nab@nab.org; internet www.nab.org; f. 1922; trade asscn of radio and TV stations and networks; 8,300 mems; Chair. JOHN L. (JACK) SANDER; Pres. and CEO DAVID K. REHR.

National Cable and Telecommunications Association (NCTA): 25 Massachusetts Ave, NW, Suite 100, Washington, DC 20001-1413; tel. (202) 222-2300; e-mail webmaster@ncta.com; internet www.ncta.com; f. 1952 as Nat. Cable Television Asscn; represents cable operators for over 90% of customers and over 200 cable program networks; internet and digital telephone service provider; c. 3,100 mems; Pres. and CEO KYLE MCSLARROW.

Finance

BANKING

Commercial Banking System

The US banking system is the largest and, in many respects, the most comprehensive and sophisticated in the world. Banking has, however, been largely subject to state rather than federal jurisdiction, and this has created a structure very different from that in other advanced industrial countries. In general, no bank may open branches or acquire subsidiaries in states other than that in which it is based, although in June 1985 the US Supreme Court ruled that federal legislation prohibiting interstate banks does not preclude state governments from permitting regional interstate banking. A number of such mergers have followed, although some states continue to restrict banks to a single branch, or to operating only in certain counties of the state. Federal anti-trust laws also limit mergers of banks within a state. The effect of these measures has been to preserve the independence of a relatively large number of banks. However, the influence of these banks has been increasingly challenged by the formation of several groupings of regional banks. Federal legislation permitting the operation of interstate branch banking networks and the provision of non-banking financial services was enacted in November 1999. In October 2003 the Bank of America announced the acquisition of FleetBoston Financial Corporation, in an agreement that was to create the second largest banking company in the world. In 2008 the restructured Bank of America operated more than 6,100 branch offices, and controlled total deposits of more than US $882,997m. The merger in 2004 of JP Morgan Chase & Co and Bank One Corporation established the second largest bank in the USA, with 2,798 branches and total assets in December 2006 of $1,019,497m.

Following the failure of a number of banks in the late 1980s, the Federal Deposit Insurance Corporation, a government-sponsored body that insures deposits in banks and acts as receiver for national and state banks that have been placed in receivership, was obliged to provide assistance for a large number of institutions. Many banks, meanwhile, have expanded their 'fee income' activities (such as sales of mutual fund investments) to offset declines in customer borrowing, particularly from the industrial and commercial sectors.

THE UNITED STATES OF AMERICA

In 2008 the banking industry came under severe strain following the sharp contraction in world-wide credit markets and the declared bankruptcy, in September, of the financial services firm Lehman Brothers. The Emergency Economic Stabilization Act of 2008, approved by Congress in October, provided some US $700,000m. of rescue aid to the US Treasury to redistribute in the markets. In the same month the Government subsequently announced that it would purchase equity stakes in nine of the largest financial institutions, at a cost of around $250,000m.

The possession of bank accounts and the use of banking facilities are perhaps more widespread among all regions and social groups in the USA than in any other country. This has influenced the formulation of monetary theory and policy, as bank credit has become a more important factor than currency supply in the regulation of the economy. The use of current accounts and credit cards is so common that many authorities claim that the USA can be regarded as, effectively, a cashless society.

Bank Holding Companies

Since 1956 bank holding companies, corporations that control one or more banks in the USA, have become significant elements in the banking system. The proportion of banks owned by holding companies increased from 62% in 1984 to 76% in 2000. In 2004 there were some 5,151 bank holding companies, of which 12% had financial holding company status.

Banking Activities Overseas

From the mid-1960s, the leading banks rapidly expanded their overseas interests. At the end of 1960 there were only eight US banks operating foreign branches, mostly in Latin America and the Far East. The main factors behind this expansion were the geographical limitations imposed by law at home; the rapid expansion of US business interests abroad; the faster economic growth of certain foreign markets; and, finally, the profitability of the 'Eurodollar' capital markets. The expansion in the overseas activities of US banks reached a high point in 1984. Subsequently declining levels of profitability in this area have resulted in the closure of some overseas offices, although the aggregate total of assets held has continued to rise.

In 1981 the Federal Reserve Board sanctioned the establishment of domestic International Banking Facilities (IBF), permitting commercial banks within the US (including US branches and agencies of foreign banks) to transact certain types of foreign deposit and loan business free of reserve requirements and, in most cases, state income tax liability.

Federal Reserve System: 20th St and Constitution Ave, NW, Washington, DC 20551; tel. (202) 452-3000; fax (202) 452-3819; internet www.federalreserve.gov.

The Federal Reserve System, founded in 1913, comprises the Board of Governors, the Federal Open Market Committee, the Federal Advisory Council, the Consumer Advisory Council, the Thrift Institutions Advisory Council, the 25 branches of the 12 Federal Reserve Banks, together with all member banks.

The Board of Governors is composed of seven members appointed by the President of the United States with the advice and consent of the Senate.

The Reserve Banks are empowered to issue Federal Reserve notes fully secured by the following assets, alone or in any combination: (i) Gold certificates; (ii) US Government and agency securities; (iii) other eligible assets as described by statute; and (iv) Special Drawing Rights certificates. The Reserve Banks may discount paper for depository institutions and make properly secured advances to depository institutions. Federal Reserve Banks were established by Congress as the operating arms of the nation's central banking system. Many of the services performed by this network for depository institutions and for the Government are similar to services performed by banks and thrifts for business customers and individuals. Reserve Banks hold the cash reserves of depository institutions and make loans to them. They move currency and coin into and out of circulation, and collect and process millions of cheques each day. They provide banking services for the Treasury, issue and redeem government securities on behalf of the Treasury, and act in other ways as fiscal agent for the US Government. The Banks also take part in the primary responsibility of the Federal Reserve System, the setting of monetary policy, through participation on the Federal Open Market Committee.

The Comptroller of the Currency (see below) has primary supervisory authority over all federally chartered banks, and the banking supervisors of the States have similar jurisdiction over banks organized under State laws. State member banks are examined by the Federal Reserve.

In March 2004 some 2,900 commercial banks were members of the Federal Reserve System.

Board of Governors

Chairman: BEN S. BERNANKE.
Vice-Chairman: DONALD L. KOHN.
Governors: ELIZABETH A. DUKE, DANIEL K. TARULLO, KEVIN M. WARSH.
Secretary of the Board: JENNIFER J. JOHNSON.

Federal Reserve Banks

	Chairman	President
Boston	Lisa M. Lynch	Eric S. Rosengren
New York	Stephen Friedman	William C. Dudley
Philadelphia	William F. Hecht	Charles I. Plosser
Cleveland	Tanny B. Crane	Sandra Pianalto
Richmond	Lemuel E. Lewis	Jeffrey M. Lacker
Atlanta	D. Scott Davis	Dennis P. Lockhart
Chicago	John A. Canning, Jr	Charles L. Evans
St Louis	Stephen H. Lipsten	James B. Bullard
Minneapolis	James J. Hynes	Gary H. Stern
Kansas City	Lu M. Cordova	Thomas M. Hoenig
Dallas	James T. Hackett	Richard W. Fisher
San Francisco	T. Gary Rogers	Janet L. Yellen

Comptroller of the Currency

Independence Sq., 250 E St, SW, Washington, DC 20219; tel. (202) 874-5000; e-mail Jesse.Stiller@occ.treas.gov; internet www.occ.treas.gov.

The Comptroller of the Currency has supervisory control over all federally chartered banks (see Federal Reserve System).

Comptroller: JOHN C. DUGAN.

Principal Commercial Banks

(cap. = total capital and reserves; dep. = deposits; m. = million; amounts in US dollars)

In general, only banks with a minimum of $2,000m. deposits are listed. In states where no such bank exists, that with the largest deposits is listed.

Alabama

AmSouth Bank NA: 1900 Fifth Ave North, POB 11007, Birmingham, AL 35288; tel. (205) 801-0359; fax (205) 326-5015; internet www.amsouth.com; f. 1873; cap. 0.01m., dep. 45,924.0m. (Dec. 2005); Chair., Pres. and CEO C. DOWD RITTER.

Regions Bank: 417 North 20th St, POB 10247, Birmingham, AL 35202-0247; tel. (205) 326-7697; fax (205) 326-7779; internet www.regionsbank.com; f. 1928; cap. 0.1m., dep. 111,630.3m. (Dec. 2007); Pres. and CEO C. DOWD RITTER.

California

Bank of the West: 180 Montgomery St, San Francisco, CA 94104; tel. (415) 765-4800; fax (415) 434-3470; internet www.bankofthewest.com; f. 1874; cap. 0.005m., dep. 51,869.7m. (Dec. 2007); Chair. and CEO DON J. MCGRATH; 663 brs.

California Bank and Trust: 11622 El Camino Real, Suite 200, San Diego, CA 92130; tel. (858) 793-7400; fax (858) 793-7438; e-mail info@calbanktrust.com; internet www.calbanktrust.com; f. 1998; cap. 3.2m., dep. 8,709.2m. (Dec. 2007); Chair. and CEO DAVID BLACKFORD.

City National Bank: 400 Roxbury Dr. North, Beverly Hills, CA 90210; tel. (310) 888-6000; fax (310) 888-6045; e-mail contact@cnb.com; internet www.cnb.com; f. 1954; cap. 90.0m., dep. 13,518.5m. (Dec. 2007); Chair. and CEO RUSSELL GOLDSMITH; Pres. CHRISTOPHER J. WARMUTH; 45 brs.

Union Bank of California NA: 400 California St, 1st Floor, San Francisco, CA 94104; tel. (415) 765-3434; fax (415) 765-3507; e-mail Investor.Relations@uboc.com; internet www.uboc.com; f. 1996; cap. 604.6m., dep. 35,067.0m. (Dec. 2002); Pres. and CEO MASAAKI TANAKA; 323 brs.

Connecticut

Citizens Bank, Connecticut: 237 Main St, Middletown, CT 06457; tel. (860) 638-4411; fax (860) 638-4444; e-mail intbank@citizensbank.com; internet www.citizensbank.com; f. 1996; a division of RBS Citizens NA since 2007; dep. 4,205.8m., total assets 4,617.0m. (Dec. 2006); Chair., Pres. and CEO RICHARD M. BARRY; 48 brs.

Florida

Northern Trust NA: 700 Brickell Ave, Miami, FL 33131; tel. (305) 372-1000; fax (305) 789-1106; internet www.northerntrust.com; f. 1982; cap. 34.1m., dep. 9,608.5m. (Dec. 2007); Chair., Pres. and CEO WILLIAM L. MORRISON.

THE UNITED STATES OF AMERICA

Ocean Bank: 780 Northwest 42nd Ave, Miami, POB 441140, FL 33126; tel. (305) 442-2660; fax (305) 444-8153; e-mail obmail@oceanbank.com; internet www.oceanbank.com; f. 1982; cap. 8.5m., dep. 4,912.0m. (Dec. 2007); Pres. and CEO A. ALFONSO MACEDO; 23 brs.

Georgia

SunTrust Bank: 25 Park Pl., POB 4418, Atlanta, GA 30302; tel. (404) 588-7785; fax (404) 302-4782; internet www.suntrust.com; f. 1891; assumed all SunTrust Banks 2000; cap. 21.6m., dep. 147,282.57m. (Dec. 2007); Chair. and CEO JAMES M. WELLS, III.

Hawaii

Bank of Hawaii: 111 South King St, Honolulu, HI 96813; tel. (888) 643-3888; fax (808) 537-8440; e-mail info@boh.com; internet www.boh.com; f. 1897; cap. 14.9m., dep. 9,148.3m. (Dec. 2007); Chair., Pres. and CEO ALLAN R. LANDON.

First Hawaiian Bank: 999 Bishop St, Honolulu, HI 96813; tel. (808) 525-7000; fax (808) 525-8182; e-mail bfarias@fhb.com; internet www.fhb.com; f. 1858; cap. 16.2m., dep. 9,884.4m. (Dec. 2007); Chair. WALTER A. DODS, Jr; Pres. and CEO DONALD G. HORNER.

Illinois

First Midwest Bank: 300 Park Blvd, Suite 400, Itasca, IL 60143; internet www.firstmidwest.com; cap. 40.0m., dep. 7,128.1m. (Dec. 2007); Chair. and CEO JOHN O'MEARA; 103 brs.

Harris National Association: 111 West Monroe St, 12th Floor, Chicago, IL 60603; tel. (312) 845-2028; fax (312) 845-2199; internet www.harrisbank.com; f. 1882 as N. W. Harris & Co; present name adopted 2005; cap. 155.1m., dep. 36,359.5m. (Dec. 2007); Pres. and CEO WILLIAM DOWNE.

Northern Trust Co: 50 South LaSalle St, Chicago, IL 60675; tel. (312) 630-6000; fax (312) 444-5244; internet www.northerntrust.com; f. 1889; cap. 3.6m., dep. 51,765.6m. (Dec. 2007); Chair. and CEO WILLIAM A. OSBORN.

Kentucky

First Capital Bank of Kentucky: 293 N. Hubbards Lane, Louisville, KY 40207; tel. (502) 895-5040; e-mail localroots@fcbok.com; internet www.fcbok.com; f. 1996; total assets 319.6m. (Dec. 2007); Chair., Pres. and CEO H. DAVID HALE.

Louisiana

Whitney National Bank: 228 St Charles Ave, New Orleans, LA 70130; tel. (504) 586-7562; fax (504) 586-7412; e-mail lgarza@whitneybank.com; internet www.whitneybank.com; f. 1883; cap. 3,358.0m., dep. 9,624.6m. (Dec. 2007); Chair. and CEO JOHN C. HOPE, III; 130 brs.

Maryland

Provident Bank of Maryland: 114 East Lexington St, Baltimore, MD 21202-1725; tel. (410) 281-7000; fax (410) 277-2768; internet www.provbank.com; f. 1951; cap. 30.0m., dep. 5,675.6m. (Dec. 2007); Chair. and CEO PETER MARTIN.

Massachusetts

Citizens Bank, Massachusetts: 28 State St, Boston, MA 02109; tel. (617) 725-5500; fax (617) 725-5877; e-mail intbank@citizensbank.com; internet www.citizensbank.com; f. 1825; a division of RBS Citizens NA since 2007; dep. 30,403.2m., total assets 35,276.0m. (Dec. 2006); Chair., Pres. and CEO ROBERT E. SMYTH.

Michigan

Citizens Bank: 328 South Saginaw St, Flint, MI 48502; tel. (313) 766-7500; fax (313) 768-6948; internet www.citizensonline.com; f. 1871; cap. 29.2m., dep. 11,265.41m. (Dec. 2007); Chair., Pres. and CEO WILLIAM R. HARTMAN.

Comerica Bank: Comerica Tower, Detroit Center, 500 Woodward Ave, Detroit, MI 48226; tel. (313) 222-3300; fax (313) 961-7349; e-mail info@comerica.com; internet www.comerica.com; f. 1849; cap. 378.5m., dep. 53,217.6m. (Dec. 2007); Chair., Pres. and CEO RALPH W. BABB, Jr.

Fifth Third Bank: 111 Lyon NW, Grand Rapids, MI 49503; tel. (616) 771-5000; fax (616) 774-1119; internet www.53.com; f. 1853; cap. 16.4m., dep. 46,150.0m. (Dec. 2007); Chair. GEORGE A. SCHAEFER, Jr; 361 brs.

Minnesota

US Bank NA: 800 Nicollet Mall, Minneapolis, MN 55402; tel. (612) 303-0799; fax (612) 973-0838; e-mail international.banking@usbank.com; internet www.usbank.com; f. 1853; fmrly Firstar Bank NA, present name adopted in Aug. 2001; cap. 18.2m., dep. 194,839.3m. (Dec. 2007); Chair., CEO and Pres. RICHARD K. DAVIS; 2,498 brs.

Mississippi

Trustmark National Bank: 248 East Capitol St, POB 291, Jackson, MS 39201; tel. (601) 354-5863; fax (601) 949-2387; e-mail Trustmark@custhelp.com; internet www.trustmark.com; f. 1889; cap. 13.4m., dep. 7,686.8m. (Dec. 2007); Chair. and CEO RICHARD G. HICKSON.

Missouri

Commerce Bank NA: 1000 Walnut St, POB 13686, Kansas City, MO 64106; tel. (816) 234-2000; fax (816) 234-2799; e-mail mymoney@commercebank.com; internet www.commercebank.com; f. 1865; cap. 10.2m., dep. 13,206.0m. (Dec. 2007); Chair. and CEO DAVID W. KEMPER.

Montana

First Interstate Bank of Montana NA: 2 Main St, POB 7130, Kalispell, MT 59904; tel. (406) 752-5001; internet www.firstinterstatebank.com; f. 1891; dep. 4,008.0m., total assets 5,091.2m. (Dec. 2007); Chair. THOMAS W. SCOTT; Pres.and CEO LYLE R. KNIGHT.

Nebraska

First National Bank of Omaha: 1620 Dodge St, Omaha, NE 68102; tel. (402) 341-0500; fax (402) 633-3554; e-mail firstnational@fnni.com; internet www.firstnational.com; f. 1857; cap. 5.3m., dep. 7,935.6m. (Dec. 2007); Chair. BRUCE R. LAURITZEN; 31 brs.

New Hampshire

Citizens Bank, New Hampshire: 875 Elm St, Manchester, NH 03101; tel. (603) 634-7418; fax (603) 634-7481; e-mail intbank@citizensbank.com; internet www.citizensbank.com; f. 1853; a division of RBS Citizens NA since 2007; cap. 0.8m., dep. 9,250.3m. (Dec. 2006); Pres. CATHLEEN SCHMIDT; 76 brs.

New York

American Express Bank Ltd: American Express Tower, 23rd Floor, 200 Vesey St, New York, NY 10285-2300; tel. (212) 640-5000; fax (212) 693-1721; internet www.americanexpress.com; f. 1919; cap. 121.0m., dep. 12,992.0m. (Dec. 2006); Chair. and CEO KENNETH I. CHENAULT.

Bank of New York Mellon: 1 Wall St, New York, NY 10286; tel. (212) 495-1784; fax (212) 495-1398; e-mail comments@bankofny.com; internet www.bankofny.com; f. 1784; re-named as above after merger of Bank of New York Co and Mellon Financial Corpn in 2007; cap. 1,135.3m., dep. 68,630.0m. (Dec. 2006); Chair. and CEO ROBERT P. KELLY; Pres. GERALD L. HASSELL.

Bank of Tokyo–Mitsubishi UFJ, Ltd: 1251 Ave of the Americas, New York, NY 10020-1104; tel. (212) 782-4000; fax (212) 782-6415; internet www.btmna.com; f. 1955; cap. 132.9m., dep. 3,202.1m. (Dec. 2007); Chair. NAOTAKA OBATA; Pres. KATSUNORI NAGAYASU.

Citibank NA: 399 Park Ave, New York, NY 10043; tel. (212) 559-1000; fax (212) 223-2681; internet www.citibank.com; f. 1812; cap. 751.0m., dep. 1,072,013.0m. (Dec. 2007); Chair., Pres. and CEO WILLIAM R. RHODES.

Deutsche Bank Trust Company Americas: 60 Wall St, New York, NY 10005; tel. (212) 250-2500; fax (212) 250-4429; internet www.db.com; f. 1903; fmrly Bankers' Trust Co, present name adopted April 2002; cap. 3,627.0m., dep. 23,509.0m. (Dec. 2006); Chair. and CEO JOSEF ACKERMAN.

HSBC Bank USA NA: POB 2013, Buffalo, NY 14240; fax (716) 841-5391; internet www.banking.us.hsbc.com; f. 1999 following acquisition of Marine Midland Bank by Hongkong & Shanghai Banking Corpn; acquired Republic National Bank of New York in 2000; cap. 2.0m., dep. 164,636.3m. (Dec. 2007); Chair. MICHAEL F. GEOGHEGAN; Pres. and CEO PAUL LAWRENCE.

JP Morgan Chase: 270 Park Ave, New York, NY 10017; tel. (212) 270-6000; internet www.jpmorganchase.com; f. 1982 as Chase Manhattan Bank USA; present name adopted 2005; cap. 1,785.0m., dep. 1,125,220.0m. (Dec. 2007); Chair. and CEO JAMED DIMON.

M&T Bank Corpn: 1 M & T Plaza, Buffalo, NY 14203-2399; tel. (716) 842-4200; fax (716) 842-5021; internet www.mtb.com; f. 1856; Mfrs' and Traders' Trust Co; cap. 6,485m., dep. 41,266m. (Dec. 2007); Chair. and CEO ROBERT G. WILMERS; 736 brs.

Trustco Bank: 1 Sarnowski Dr., Glenville, NY 12302; tel. (518) 377-3311; fax (518) 381-3668; internet www.trustcobank.com; cap. 29.4m. (Dec. 2002), dep. 3,020.3m. (Dec. 2007); Pres. and CEO ROBERT A. MCCORMICK.

THE UNITED STATES OF AMERICA

United States Trust Co: 114 West 47th St, New York, NY 10036; tel. (212) 852-1000; fax (212) 995-5642; e-mail info@trust.com; internet www.ustrust.com; f. 1853; cap. 15.0m., dep. 9,585.5m. (Dec. 2006); Chair. and CEO JEFFREY S. MAURER.

North Carolina

Bank of America NA: Bank of America Corporate Center, 100 North Tryon St, Charlotte, NC 28255; tel. (704) 386-5000; fax (704) 386-0981; internet www.bankamerica.com; f. 1904; cap. 2,878.9m., dep. 1,144,832.5m. (Dec. 2007); Chair. and CEO KENNETH D. LEWIS.

Wachovia Bank NA: 301 South College St, Suite 4000, Charlotte, NC 28288-0013; tel. (704) 374-1246; internet www.wachovia.com; f. 1866; merged with Wells Fargo Bank in 2008; cap. 455.0m., dep. 544,178.0m. (Dec. 2007); Chair. and Acting CEO LANTY L. SMITH.

Ohio

FirstMerit Bank NA: 3 Cascade Plaza, Akron, OH 44308; tel. (330) 996-6300; fax (330) 384-7008; e-mail customerservice@firstmerit.com; internet www.firstmerit.com; cap. 57.6m., dep. 9,199.9m. (Dec. 2007); Chair. and CEO PAUL G. GREIG.

Huntington National Bank: 41 South High St, Columbus, OH 43287; tel. (614) 480-4685; fax (614) 331-5900; e-mail international@huntington.com; internet www.huntington.com; f. 1866; cap. 40.0m., dep. 45,854.4m. (Dec. 2007); Chair. and CEO STEVEN D. STEINOUR.

KeyBank NA: 127 Public Sq., Cleveland, OH 44114; tel. (216) 689-3000; fax (216) 689-3683; e-mail Investor_relations@keybank.com; internet www.key.com; f. 1849; cap. 50.0m., dep. 79,964.6m. (Dec. 2007); Chair. and CEO HENRY L. MEYER, III.

National City Bank: 1900 East Ninth St, POB 94750, Cleveland, OH 44114-3484; tel. (216) 575-2000; fax (216) 575-9263; internet www.nationalcity.com; f. 1845; acquired by PNC in 2008; cap. 7.3m., dep. 118,055.2m. (Dec. 2007); Chair., Pres. and CEO PETER E. RASKIND; c. 1,300 brs.

Oklahoma

Bank of Oklahoma NA: Bank of Oklahoma Tower, POB 2300, Tulsa, OK 74192; tel. (918) 588-6829; fax (918) 588-6026; internet www.bankofoklahoma.com; f. 1933; cap. 52.9m., dep. 13,089.6m. (Dec. 2007); Chair. GEORGE B. KAISER; Pres. and CEO STANLEY A. LYBARGER; 56 brs.

Pennsylvania

PNC Bank, NA: 1 PNC Plaza, 249 Fifth Ave, Pittsburgh, PA 15222-2707; tel. (412) 762-2000; fax (412) 762-5022; internet www.pnc.com; f. 1959; cap. 740.1m., dep. 103,780.3m. (Dec. 2007); Chair. and CEO JAMES E. ROHR; Pres. JOSEPH C. GUYAUX; 854 brs.

Rhode Island

Citizens Bank, Rhode Island: 1 Citizens Plaza, Providence, RI 02903; tel. (401) 454-2441; fax (401) 455-5859; e-mail intbank@citizensbank.com; internet www.citizensbank.com; f. 1996; cap. 1.0m., dep. 12,272.2m. (Dec. 2006); Chair., Pres. and CEO JOSEPH J. MARCAURELE; 78 brs.

South Carolina

Carolina First Bank: 102 South Main St, POB 1029, Greenville, SC 29602; tel. (864) 255-7900; fax (864) 239-6401; e-mail customerassistance@carolinafirst.com; internet www.carolinafirst.com; cap. 7.9m., dep. 11,853.3m. (Dec. 2007); part of The South Financial Group; Chair. and CEO H. LYNN HARTON; Pres. SCOTT M. FRIERSON.

South Dakota

Citibank (South Dakota) NA: 701 East 60th St, North, POB 6000, Sioux Falls, SD 57117; tel. (605) 331-2626; internet www.citibank.com; f. 1981; cap. 0.04m., dep. 4,768.1m. (Dec. 2005); Gen. Sec. DAVID L. ZIMBECK; Pres. KENDALL E. STORK.

Wells Fargo Bank NA: 101 North Phillips Ave, Sioux Falls, SD 57117; tel. (605) 575-7300; fax (605) 575-4815; e-mail ipb@wellsfargo.com; internet www.wellsfargo.com; f. 1960 as Wells Fargo Bank American Trust Co; fmrly Norwest Bank South Dakota NA, present name adopted in 2004; cap. 520.0m., dep. 399,104.0m. (Dec. 2007); Pres. and CEO JOHN G. STUMPF; 3,000 brs.

Tennessee

First Tennessee Bank NA: 165 Madison Ave, 9th Floor, POB 84, Memphis, TN 38101-0084; tel. (901) 523-4420; fax (901) 523-4438; internet www.firsttennessee.com; f. 1864; subsidiary of First Horizon National Corporation; cap. 367.3m., dep. 31,333.5m. (Dec. 2007); Chair. MICHAEL D. ROSE; Pres.and CEO BRYAN JORDAN; 183 brs.

Texas

Frost National Bank: 100 West Houston St, POB 1600, San Antonio, TX 78296; tel. (210) 220-4011; e-mail frostbank@frostbank.com; internet www.frostbank.com; f. 1899; cap. 8.5m., dep. 11,704.5m. (Dec. 2007); Pres. PAT FROST; Chair. and CEO RICHARD W. EVANS.

Virginia

Chevy Chase Bank, FSB: 7926 Jones Branch Dr., McLean, VA 22101; internet www.chevychasebank.com; f. 1955; total assets 15,106.6m. (Sept. 2007); Pres. ROBERT D. BROEKSMIT, II.

Co-operative Bank

CoBank: 5500 South Quebec St, Greenwood Village, CO 80111; tel. (303) 740-4000; fax (303) 740-4366; e-mail webmaster@cobank.com ; internet www.cobank.com; f. 1933; provides loan finance and domestic and international banking services for agricultural and farmer-owned co-operatives; cap. 1,791.4m. (Dec. 2007); Chair. EVERETT DOBRINSKI; Pres. and CEO ROBERT B. ENGEL.

Trade Bank

Export-Import Bank of the United States (Ex-Im Bank): 811 Vermont Ave, NW, Washington, DC 20571; tel. (202) 565-3946; fax (202) 565-3380; e-mail info@exim.gov; internet www.exim.gov; f. 1934; independent agency since 1945; cap. subscribed by the US Treasury; finances and facilitates US external trade, guarantees payment to US foreign traders and banks, extends credit to foreign governmental and private concerns; cap. 1,000.0m. (Sept. 2007); Chair. and Pres. JAMES H. (JIM) LAMBRIGHT.

BANKING ASSOCIATIONS

There is a State Bankers Association in each state.

American Bankers Association: 1120 Connecticut Ave, NW, Washington, DC 20036; tel. (202) 663-5000; fax (202) 828-4547; e-mail custserv@aba.com; internet www.aba.com; f. 1875; Pres. and CEO EDWARD (ED) YINGLING; Chair. ARTHUR R. CONNELLY.

Bank Administration Institute (BAI): 115 South LaSalle St, Suite 3300, Chicago, IL 60603-3801; tel. (312) 683-2464; fax (312) 683-2373; e-mail info@bai.org; internet www.bai.org; f. 1924; Chair. TIMOTHY P. MOEN; Pres. and CEO DEBORAH L. BIANUCCI.

Bankers' Association for Finance and Trade: 1120 Connecticut Ave, NW, 3rd Floor, Washington, DC 20036; tel. (202) 663-7575; fax (202) 663-5538; e-mail baft@aba.com; internet www.baft.org; f. 1921; affiliated to the American Bankers Asscn; Chair. CHARLES H. SILVERMAN; Pres. DONNA K. ALEXANDER.

Independent Community Bankers of America: 1615 L St, NW, Suite 900, Washington, DC 20036; tel. (202) 659-8111; e-mail info@icba.org; internet www.icba.org; f. 1930; Pres. and CEO CAMDEN R. FINE; 5,000 banks.

Mortgage Bankers Association of America: 1919 Pennsylvania Ave, Washington, DC 20006; tel. (202) 557-2700; e-mail info@mbaa.org; internet mortgagebankers.org; f. 1914; Chair. DAVID G. KITTLE; Pres. and CEO JOHN COURSON; 2,700 mems.

PRINCIPAL STOCK EXCHANGES

Boston Stock Exchange Inc: 100 Franklin St, Boston, MA 02110; tel. (617) 235-2000; internet www.bostonstock.com; f. 1834; Chair. and CEO MICHAEL J. CURRAN; 119 mems.

Chicago Stock Exchange: 1 Financial Pl., 440 South LaSalle St, Chicago, IL 60605; tel. (312) 663-2222; e-mail info@chx.com; internet www.chx.com; f. 1882; Chair. MICHAEL H. KERR; CEO DAVID A. HERRON; 445 mems.

Nasdaq Stock Market Inc: 1 Liberty Plaza, 165 Broadway, New York, NY 10006; tel. (212) 401-8700; internet www.nasdaq.com; f. 1998 by the American Stock Exchange and the Nat. Asscn of Securities Dealers (NASD); incorporated the Boston Stock Exchange in 2008; world-wide electronic trading market; CEO ROBERT GREIFELD; Pres. MAGNUS BÖCKER.

National Stock Exchange SM (NSX): 440 South LaSalle St, Suite 2600, Chicago, IL 60605; tel. (312) 786-8803; fax (312) 939-7239; internet www.nsx.com; f. 1885; fmrly Cincinnati Stock Exchange, name changed as above in Nov. 2003; Chair. JAMES M. ANDERSON; CEO JOSEPH S. RIZZELLO.

New York Stock Exchange Euronext (NYSE Euronext): 11 Wall St, New York, NY 10005; tel. (212) 656-3000; fax (212) 656-5549; e-mail mmedina@nyx.com; internet www.nyse.com; f. 1792; incorporated the American Stock Exchange in 2009; Chair. JAN MICHIEL HESSELS; CEO DUNCAN L. NIEDERAUER; 2,800 mems.

Philadelphia Stock Exchange (NASDAQ OMX PHLX): Stock Exchange Bldg, 1900 Market St, Philadelphia, PA 19103-3584; tel. (215) 496-5000; fax (215) 496-5460; e-mail info@phlx.com; internet

THE UNITED STATES OF AMERICA

www.phlx.com; f. 1790; acquired by NASDAQ OMX Group, Inc in 2008; Pres. THOMAS A. WITTMAN; CEO CHRISTOPHER R. CONCANNON; 505 mems.

INSURANCE
Principal Companies

Acacia Life Insurance Co: 7315 Wisconsin Ave, Bethesda, MD 20814-3202; tel. (301) 280-1000; fax (310) 280-1161; internet www .unificompanies.com; f. 1869; part of UNIFI Mutual Holding Co; life and health; Chair. BARBARA KRUMSIEK.

Allstate Corpn: 2775 Sanders Rd, Northbrook, IL 60062-6127; tel. (708) 402-5000; fax (708) 402-2351; e-mail directors@allstate.com; internet www.allstate.com; f. 1931; property and casualty, life, fire, indemnity; Pres. and CEO THOMAS J. WILSON.

American Family Insurance Group: 6000 American Pkwy, Madison, WI 53783-0001; tel. (608) 249-2111; internet www .amfam.com; f. 1927; life and annuities through subsidiary, American Family Life Insurance Co; property and casualty through eight other subsidiaries; Chair. and CEO DAVID R. ANDERSON; Pres. and COO JACK SALZWEDEL.

American Family Life Assurance Co of Columbus (AFLAC): 1932 Wynnton Rd, Columbus, GA 31999; tel. (706) 323-3431; e-mail news@aflac.com; internet www.aflac.com; f. 1955; life and health; Chair. and CEO DANIEL P. AMOS; Pres. KRISS CLONINGER, III.

American General Life and Accident Insurance Co: American General Center, MC 338N, Nashville, TN 37250; internet www .americangeneral.com; f. 1900; wholly owned subsidiary of American International Group, Inc (AIG); Pres. and CEO MATT WINTER.

American National Insurance Co: 1 Moody Plaza, Galveston, TX 77550-7999; tel. (409) 763-4661; internet www.anico.com; f. 1905; operating in 50 states, the District of Columbia, Puerto Rico and American Samoa; life and health, annuities, property and casualty, credit insurance and pension plan services; Chair., Pres. and CEO ROBERT L. MOODY.

American United Life Insurance Co: 1 American Sq., POB 368, Indianapolis, IN 46206-0368; tel. (317) 285-1877; internet www.aul .com; f. 1877; part of OneAmerica Financial Partners, Inc; owned by American United Mutual Insurance Holding Company (AUMIHC); life and health, annuities; Pres. and CEO DAYTON H. MOLENDORP.

Americo Life Insurance: POB 410288, Kansas City, MO 64141-0288; e-mail contactamerico@americo.com; internet www.americo .com; f. 1909; Pres. and CEO GARY L. MULLER.

Ameritas Life Insurance Corpn: 5900 O St, POB 81889, Lincoln, NE 68501-1889; fax (402) 467-7335; internet www.unificompanies .com; part of UNIFI Mutual Holding Co; life and health; Chair., Pres. and CEO JOANN M. MARTIN.

Assurant: 1 Chase Manhattan Plaza, New York, NY 10005; tel. (212) 859-7000; internet www.assurant.com; life and health; Chair. JOHN MICHAEL PALMS; Pres. and CEO ROBERT B. POLLOCK.

Auto-Owners Insurance Group: 6101 Anacapri Blvd, Lansing, MI 48917; tel. (517) 323-1200; fax (517) 323-8796; internet www .auto-owners.com; f. 1916; property and casualty through Auto-Owners Insurance Co and four other subsidiaries; life through Auto-Owners Life Insurance Co; CEO R. L. LOOYENGA.

Aviva USA: 699 Walnut St, Des Moines, IA 50309; tel. (515) 362-3600; fax (515) 557-2625; internet www.amerus.com; f. 1896 as AmerUS group; life and health, annuities; subsidiaries: AmerUS Annuity Group (Topeka, KS), AmerUS Life Insurance Co (Des Moines, IA), Bankers Life Insurance Co of New York (Woodbury, NY), Indianapolis Life Insurance Co (Indianapolis, IN); acquired by Aviva PLC in 2006; Chair., Pres. and CEO THOMAS C. GODLASKY.

AXA-Equitable, Inc: 1290 Ave of the Americas, New York, NY; tel. (212) 554-1234; fax (212) 262-9019; internet www.axa-equitable .com; f. 1859; subsidiary of AXA Financial, Inc; life and health, annuities; Chair. and CEO HENRI DE CASTRIES.

Baltimore Life Insurance Co: 10075 Red Run Blvd, Owings Mills, MD 21117-4871; tel. (410) 581-6600; fax (410) 581-6601; e-mail info@ baltlife.com; internet www.baltlife.com; f. 1882; life and health; Chair., Pres. and CEO L. JOHN PEARSON.

W. R. Berkley Corpn: 475 Steamboat Rd, Greenwich, CT 06830; tel. (203) 629-3040; fax (203) 629-3073; e-mail khorvath@wrberkley.com; internet www.wrbc.com; f. 1967; property and casualty through subsidiaries, divided into five business sectors: regional, reinsurance, specialty, alternative markets and international; Chair. and CEO WILLIAM R. BERKLEY.

Berkshire Hathaway, Inc: 1440 Kiewit Plaza, Omaha, NE 68131; tel. (402) 346-1400; internet www.berkshirehathaway.com; general insurance through Berkshire Hathaway Group; life insurance through subsidiary, Medical Protective, in Fort Wayne, IN; Chair. and CEO WARREN E. BUFFETT.

CIGNA Group Insurance: 2 Liberty Pl., 31st Floor, 1601 Chestnut St, Philadelphia, PA 19192; tel. (215) 761-4555; fax (215) 761-5588;

Directory

internet www.cigna.com; f. 1982; part of CIGNA Corpn; life and health; Chair. and CEO H. EDWARD HANWAY.

CNA Insurance: 333 South Wabash, Chicago, IL 60604; tel. (312) 822-5000; e-mail cna_help@cna.com; internet www.cna.com; part of Loews Corpn; property and casualty; Chair. and CEO THOMAS F. MOTAMED.

Combined Insurance Co of America (CICA): 1000 North Milwaukee Ave, Glenview, IL 60025; tel. (847) 953-2025; fax (847) 953-8070; internet www.combinedinsurance.com; f. 1949; life and health; operates as Combined Life Insurance Co of New York in NY; Chair. and CEO DOUGLAS R. WENDT.

Conseco, Inc: 11825 North Pennsylvania St, Carmel, IN 46032; tel. (317) 817-6100; internet www.conseco.com; f. 1979; life and health; subsidiaries: Conseco Life Insurance Co (IN), Conseco Insurance Co (IL), Conseco Variable Insurance Co (TX), Conseco Health Insurance Co (AZ), Conseco Senior Health Insurance Co (PA), Bankers Life & Casualty Co (Chicago, IL); Chair. R. GLENN HILLIARD; CEO C. JAMES PRIEUR.

Continental Casualty Co: CNA Plaza, 333 South Wabash Ave, Chicago, IL 60685-0001; tel. (312) 822-5000; fax (312) 822-6419; f. 1897; principal subsidiary of CNA; Chair. and CEO DENNIS H. CHOOKASZIAN.

The Continental Insurance Co: 180 Maiden Lane, New York, NY 10038-4925; tel. (212) 440-3000; fax (212) 440-3857; f. 1853; Chair. and CEO J. P. MASCOTTE.

Erie Insurance Group: 100 Erie Insurance Pl., Erie, PA 16530-0001; tel. (814) 870-2000; fax (814) 870-3126; e-mail mark .dombrowski@erieinsurance.com; internet www.erieinsurance.com; f. 1925; vehicle, home, commercial and life through network of independent agents; Pres. and CEO TERRENCE W. CAVANAUGH, Jr.

Farmers Insurance Group of Cos: 4680 Wilshire Blvd, Los Angeles, CA 90010-3807; tel. (213) 930-3200; fax (213) 932-3101; internet www.farmers.com; f. 1928; part of Farmers Group, Inc; owned by Zurich Financial Services; vehicle, home and life; operates in 41 states; subsidiaries: Farmers Insurance Exchange, Truck Insurance Exchange, Fire Insurance Exchange, Farmers New World Life Insurance Co (Mercer Island, WA); acquired Foremost Insurance Co (MI) in 2000; CEO PAUL N. HOPKINS.

Federal Insurance Co: POB 1615, Warren, NJ 07061; tel. (908) 903-2000; internet www.chubb.com; CEO JOHN D. FINNEGAN.

Fidelity National Financial (FNF): 601 Riverside Ave, Jacksonville, FL 32204; tel. (888) 934-3354; internet www.fnf.com; principal subsidiaries: Fidelity National Title Group and Fidelity National Property and Casualty Insurance Group; Chair. WILLIAM P. FOLEY, II; CEO AL STINSON.

First American Corpn: 1 First American Way, Santa Ana, CA 92707; tel. (714) 250-3000; e-mail corporate.communications@ firstam.com; internet www.firstam.com; f. 1889; Chair. and CEO PARKER S. KENNEDY.

General American Life Insurance Co: 700 Market St, POB 396, St Louis, MO 63166; tel. (314) 444-0605; fax (314) 444-0510; internet www.metlife.com; f. 1933; wholly owned subsidiary of MetLife, Inc; Chair., Pres. and CEO KEVIN EICHNER.

Genworth Financial, Inc: 6620 West Broad St, Richmond, VA 23230; tel. (888) 436-9678; e-mail contactus@genworth.com; internet www.genworth.com; f. 1871 as The Life Insurance Co of Virginia; life, long-term care, annuities; Chair., Pres. and CEO MICHAEL D. FRAIZER.

Guarantee Life Co: 8801 Indian Hills Dr., Omaha, NE 68114-4066; tel. (402) 390-7300; fax (402) 390-7577; f. 1901; Sr Vice-Pres. RANDY BIGGERSTAFF.

The Guardian Life Insurance Co of America: 7 Hannover Sq., New York, NY 10004; tel. (212) 598-8000; fax (212) 353-7034; internet www.guardianlife.com; f. 1860; life and health through 12 subsidiaries and affiliates; Pres. and CEO DENNIS J. MANNING.

Hanover Insurance Group, Inc: 440 Lincoln St, Worcester, MA 01653-0002; tel. (508) 855-1000; fax (508) 853-6332; e-mail abanek@ hanover.com; internet www.hanover.com; f. 1852; fmrly operated as Allmerica Financial Life Insurance and Annuity Co, name changed as above in 2005; property and casualty; operates as The Hanover Insurance Co, and as Citizens Insurance Co of America in MI; Chair. MICHAEL P. ANGELINI; Pres. and CEO FREDERICK H. EPPINGER.

Hartford Financial Services Group, Inc: Hartford Plaza, 690 Asylum Ave, Hartford, CT 06115; tel. (860) 547-5000; internet www .thehartford.com; f. 1810; vehicle, home, life, flood, property and casualty, group benefits, group reinsurance; Chair. and CEO RAMANI AYER; Pres. and COO THOMAS M. MARRA.

Integon General Insurance Corpn: 500 West Fifth St, Winston-Salem, NC 27102-3199; tel. (910) 770-2000; fax (910) 770-2122; f. 1920; part of GMAC Insurance Holdings, Inc since 1997.

John Hancock Life Insurance Co: POB 111, Boston, MA 02117; tel. (617) 572-6000; fax (617) 572-4539; e-mail investor_relations@

manulife.com; internet www.johnhancock.com; f. 1862; owned by Manulife (Canada); Pres. and CEO JOHN D. DESPREZ, III.

Kansas City Life Insurance Co: 3520 Broadway, Kansas City, MO 64141-6139; tel. (816) 753-7000; internet www.kclife.com; f. 1895; life and health; operates in 48 states and the District of Columbia; subsidiaries: Old American Insurance Co, Sunset Life Insurance Co of America; Chair., Pres. and CEO R. PHILIP BIXBY.

Liberty Mutual Group, Inc: 175 Berkeley St, Boston, MA 02116; tel. (617) 357-9500; fax (617) 350-7648; internet www.libertymutual.com; subsidiaries: Liberty Life Assurance Co of Boston, Liberty Mutual Insurance Co, Liberty Mutual Fire Insurance Co and Employers Insurance Co of Wasusau; Chair., Pres. and CEO EDMUND F. KELLY.

Lincoln National Life Insurance Co: 350 Church St, Hartford, CT 06103; tel. (877) 275-5462; e-mail personalservicecenter@lfg.com; internet www.lfg.com; f. 1905; part of Lincoln National Corpn; life and health; Chair. J. PATRICK BARRETT; Pres. and CEO DENNIS R. GLASS.

Manhattan Insurance Group: 10700 NW Freeway, Houston, TX 77092; tel. (860) 298-9343; fax (877) 626-4281; e-mail cs@manhattanlife.com; f. 1850; comprises Manhattan Life, Central United Life and Family Life Insurance; Chair. and CEO DAVID W. HARRIS.

Massachusetts Mutual Life Insurance Co (MassMutual): 1295 State St, Springfield, MA 01111-0001; tel. (413) 788-8411; fax (413) 744-6005; internet www.massmutual.com; f. 1851; part of MassMutual Financial Group; mutual life and health; Chair., Pres. and CEO STUART H. REESE.

Metropolitan Life Insurance Co (MetLife): 1 Madison Ave, New York, NY 10010-3681; tel. (212) 578-2211; fax (212) 689-1980; internet www.metlife.com; f. 1863; life and health; Chair., Pres. and CEO C. ROBERT HENRIKSON.

Minnesota Life Insurance Co: 400 Robert St North, St Paul, MN 55101; tel. (651) 665-3500; fax (651) 665-4488; internet www.minnesotamutual.com; f. 1880; affiliated to Securian Financial Group, Inc; life and health; Chair., Pres. and CEO ROBERT L. SENKLER.

Monarch Life Insurance Co: 1 Monarch Pl., Springfield, MA 01144-1001; tel. (413) 784-2000; fax (413) 784-6271; f. 1901; CEO ROGER T. SERVISON.

Mutual of Omaha Insurance Co: Mutual of Omaha Plaza, Omaha, NE 68175; tel. (402) 342-7600; internet mutualofomaha.com; f. 1909; life and health; operating in 50 states, the District of Columbia, the US Virgin Is, Puerto Rico and Guam; Chair. and CEO DANIEL P. NEARY; Pres. W. GARY GATES.

Nationwide Mutual Insurance Co: 1 Nationwide Plaza, Columbus, OH 43215-2220; tel. (614) 249-7111; e-mail casej6@nationwide.com; internet www.nationwide.com; f. 1925; property and casualty through 18 subsidiaries; life and retirement savings through 25 subsidiaries; also asset management and strategic investment; CEO JERRY JURGENSEN; Chair. and COO MARK THRESHER.

New York Life Insurance Co: 51 Madison Ave, New York, NY 10010-1603; tel. (212) 576-7000; fax (212) 576-6794; e-mail infonyl@e-mail.com; internet www.newyorklife.com; f. 1845; life and health; Chair. SEYMOUR (SY) STERNBERG; Pres.and CEO TED MATHAS.

The Northwestern Mutual Life Insurance Co: 720 East Wisconsin Ave, Milwaukee, WI 53202-4797; tel. (414) 271-1444; internet www.nmfn.com; f. 1857; mutual life and health; Pres. and CEO EDWARD J. ZORE.

Old Line Life Insurance Co of America: POB 401, Milwaukee, WI 53201; tel. (414) 271-2820; fax (414) 283-5556; f. 1910; Pres. and CEO JAMES A. GRIFFIN.

Pacific Life Insurance Co: 700 Newport Center Dr., Newport Beach, CA 92660-6397; tel. (949) 219-3011; fax (949) 219-7614; e-mail info@pacificlife.com; internet www.pacificlife.com; f. 1868; life, annuities and mutual funds; Chair., Pres. and CEO JAMES T. MORRIS; CFO KHANH T. TRAN.

Penn Mutual Life Insurance Co: 600 Dresher Rd, Horsham, PA 19044; tel. (215) 956-8000; fax (215) 956-7508; internet www.pennmutual.com; f. 1847; Chair., Pres. and CEO ROBERT E. CHAPPELL.

Phoenix Life Insurance Co: 1 American Row, POB 5056, Hartford, CT 06102-5056; tel. (860) 403-5000; e-mail webmaster@phoenixwm.com; internet www.phoenixwm.com; f. 1851; life and health, annuities; operating in all states, the District of Columbia, Puerto Rico, the US Virgin Is and Canada; Chair., Pres. and CEO DONA DAVIS YOUNG.

Pioneer Mutual Life Insurance Co: 101 North 10th St, Fargo, ND 58108; tel. (701) 297-5700; internet www.oneamerica.com; part of OneAmerica Financial Partners, Inc, owned by American United Mutual Insurance Holding Co (AUMIHC); life and health, annuities; Pres. and CEO DAYTON H. MOLENDORP.

Principal Financial Group, Inc: 711 High St, Des Moines, IA 50392; tel. (515) 247-5111; fax (515) 235-5491; internet www.principal.com; life and health; Chair. RICHARD L. KEYSER; Pres. and CEO LARRY D. ZIMPLEMAN.

The Progressive Group: 6300 Wilson Mills Rd, Mayfield Village, OH 44143; tel. (440) 461-5000; internet www.progressive.com; f. 1937; part of The Progressive Corpn; Chair. PETER B. LEWIS; Pres. and CEO GLENN M. RENWICK.

Protective Life Insurance Co: 2801 Hwy 280 South, Birmingham, AL 35223-2488; tel. (205) 879-9230; fax (205) 268-1000; internet www.protective.com; f. 1907; part of Protective Life Insurance Corpn; life and health; Chair., Pres. and CEO JOHN D. JOHNS.

The Prudential Insurance Co of America: 751 Broad St, Newark, NJ 07102-3714; tel. (973) 802-6000; fax (973) 802-7277; e-mail investor.relations@prudential.com; internet www.prudential.com; f. 1875; life and health; Chair. and CEO JOHN R. STRANGFELD.

QBE Insurance Group: Wall Street Plaza, 88 Pine Street, New York, NY 10005; tel. (212) 422-1212; fax (212) 422-1313; internet www.qbeusa.com; CEO VINCE MCLENAGHAN.

SAFECO Corpn: Safeco Plaza, 4333 Brooklyn Ave, NE, Seattle, WA 98185-0001; tel. (206) 545-5000; fax (206) 548-7117; internet www.safeco.com; f. 1929; part of Liberty Mutual Group since 2008; subsidiaries: SAFECO Property and Casualty Insurance Cos, SAFECO Surety; Pres. MICHAEL HUGHES.

Security Mutual Life Insurance Co of New York: 100 Court St, POB 1625, Binghamton, New York, NY 13902-1625; tel. (607) 723-3551; e-mail hpalmer@smlny.com; internet www.smlny.com; f. 1886; life and health, annuities; operating in all states; Chair., Pres. and CEO BRUCE W. BOYEA.

Southwestern Life Insurance Co: POB 2699, Dallas, TX 752221; tel. (214) 954-7111; fax (214) 954-7717; f. 1903; subsidiary of Southwestern Life Corpn.

StanCorp Financial Group: POB 711, Portland, OR 97207; tel. (503) 248-2700; fax (503) 321-7757; e-mail info@standard.com; internet www.standard.com; f. 1906; includes the Standard Insurance Company and Standard Life Insurance Company of New York; disability, group disability, group life, group dental, annuities; Chair. and CEO ERIC E. PARSONS; Pres. and COO GREG NESS.

State Farm Insurance: 1 State Farm Plaza, Bloomington, IL 61710-0001; tel. (309) 766-2311; fax (309) 766-6169; internet www.statefarm.com; f. 1929; vehicle, fire, life and health insurance; Chair. and CEO EDWARD B. RUST, Jr.

State Life Insurance Co: 1 American Sq., POB 368, Indianapolis, IN 46206-0368; tel. (317) 681-5300; fax (317) 681-5492; internet www.oneamerica.com; f. 1894; part of OneAmerica Financial Partners, Inc, owned by American United Mutual Insurance Holding Company (AUMIHC); life and health, annuities; Chair. DAYTON H. MOLENDORP; Pres. RICHARD MERRILL.

Teachers Insurance and Annuity Association-College Retirement Equities Fund (TIAA-CREF): 730 Third Ave, New York, NY 10017-3206; internet www.tiaa-cref.org; mutual life and health; Pres. and CEO ROGER W. FERGUSON, Jr.

Thrivent Financial for Lutherans: 4321 North Ballard Rd, Appleton, WI 54919-0001; tel. (920) 734-5721; e-mail mail@thrivent.com; internet www.thrivent.com; life and health; Chair., Pres. and CEO BRUCE J. NICHOLSON.

Torchmark Corpn: 3700 South Stonebridge Dr., POB 8080, McKinney, TX 75070-8080; tel. (972) 569-4000; e-mail tmkir@torchmarkcorp.com; internet www.torchmarkcorp.com; life and health; principal subsidiaries: American Income Life Insurance Co (Waco, TX), First United American Life Insurance Co (Syracuse, NY), Globe Life And Accident Insurance Co (Oklahoma City, OK), Liberty National Life Insurance Co (Birmingham, AL), United American Insurance Co (McKinney, TX), United Investors Life Insurance Co (Birmingham, AL); Chair. and CEO MARK S. MCANDREW.

Transamerica Corpn: 1150 South Olive St, Los Angeles, CA 90015-2290; tel. (213) 741-7629; fax (213) 742-5280; internet www.transamerica.com; f. 1906; part of AEGON Insurance Group; life and health, annuities, reinsurance; subsidiaries: Transamerica Occidental Life Insurance Co, Transamerica Life Insurance Co, Transamerica Financial Life Insurance Co; Pres. RON WAGLEY; Chair. FRANK HERRINGER.

The Travelers Companies, Inc: 385 Washington St, Saint Paul, MN 55102; tel. (615) 310-7911; fax (860) 277-1970; internet www.travelers.com; f. 2004 as St Paul Travelers by merger of St Paul Coes and Travelers Property and Casualty Corpn; adopted current name in 2007; Chair. and CEO JAY S. FISHMAN.

Union Central Life Insurance Co: 1876 Waycross Rd, POB 40888, Cincinnati, OH 45240; tel. (513) 595-2200; fax (513) 595-2559; internet www.unioncentral.com; f. 1867; part of UNIFI Mutual Holding Co; life and health; Chair. JOHN H. JACOBS.

THE UNITED STATES OF AMERICA

Unitrin, Inc: 1 East Wacker Dr., Chicago, IL 60601; tel. (312) 661-4600; e-mail mediarelations@unitrin.com; internet www.unitrin.com; life and health through Unitrin Life & Health Insurance Group (five subsidiaries); property and casualty through Unitrin Property & Casualty Insurance Group (19 subsidiaries); two further subsidiaries and five affiliated cos; Chair. RICHARD C. VIE; Pres. and CEO DONALD G. SOUTHWELL.

Unum Group: 1 Fountain Sq., Chattanooga, TN 37402; tel. (432) 294-1011; e-mail tawhite@unum.com; internet www.unumprovident.com; f. 1848; life and health; subsidiaries: Colonial Life Accident and Insurance Co, Paul Revere Life Insurance Co, Provident Life and Accident Insurance Co, Provident Life and Casualty Insurance Co, First Unum Insurance Co and Unum Life Insurance Co of America; Pres. and CEO KEVIN MCCARTHY.

USAA: 9800 Fredericksburg Rd, San Antonio, TX 78288; internet www.usaa.com; f. 1922; property and casualty through seven subsidiaries: United Service Automobile Asscn, USAA Casualty Insurance Co, USAA General Indemnity Co, Garrison Property and Casualty Insurance Co, USAA County Mutual Insurance Co, USAA Texas Lloyd's Co and USAA Ltd; life and annuities through two subsidiaries: USAA Life Insurance Co and USAA Life Insurance Company of New York (Highland Falls, NY); Pres. and CEO JOSUE (JOE) ROBLES, Jr.

Washington National Corporation: 300 Tower Pkwy, Lincolnshire, IL 60069; tel. (847) 793-3000; fax (847) 793-3737; f. 1911; Chair. and CEO ROBERT PATIN.

Western & Southern Financial Group: 400 Broadway, Mail Station 90, Cincinnati, OH 45202; tel. (866) 832-7719; fax (513) 629-1220; internet www.westernsouthern.com; f. 1888; operating in 44 states; life and health; subsidiaries: Western & Southern Life Insurance Co, Western-Southern Life Assurance Co, Columbus Life Insurance Co, Integrity Life Insurance Co, Lafayette Life Insurance Co; Chair., Pres. and CEO JOHN F. BARRETT.

Zenith Insurance Co: 21255 Califa St, Woodland Hills, CA 91367; tel. (818) 713-1000; fax (818) 592-0480; e-mail dfreeman@thezenith.com; internet www.thezenith.com; specializes in workers' compensation; subsidiary: ZNAT Insurance Co; Chair. and Pres. STANLEY R. ZAX.

INSURANCE ORGANIZATIONS

American Council of Life Insurance (ACLI): 101 Constitution Ave, NW, Washington, DC 20001-2133; tel. (202) 624-2000; fax (202) 624-2319; e-mail Media@acli.com; internet www.acli.com; f. 1976; 400 mem. cos; Pres. and CEO FRANK KEATING, Jr.

American Institute of Marine Underwriters (AIMU): 14 Wall St, 21st Floor, New York, NY 10005-2145; tel. (212) 233-0550; fax (212) 227-5102; e-mail aimu@aimu.org; internet www.aimu.org; f. 1898; 105 mems; Chair. DENNIS C. MARVIN; Pres. JAMES M. CRAIG.

American Insurance Association (AIA): 1130 Connecticut Ave, NW, Suite 1000, Washington, DC 20036; tel. (202) 828-7100; fax (202) 293-1219; e-mail info@aiadc.org; internet www.aiadc.org; f. 1964; 300 mems; Pres. and CEO LEIGH ANN PUSEY.

Casualty Actuarial Society: 4350 North Fairfax Dr., Suite 250, Arlington, VA 22203; tel. (703) 276-3100; fax (703) 276-3108; e-mail office@casact.org; internet www.casact.org; f. 1914; 4,400 mems; Pres. JOHN J. KOLLAR.

LIMRA International: 300 Day Hill Rd, Windsor, CT 06095; tel. (860) 688-3358; fax (860) 298-9555; e-mail customer.service@limra.com; internet www.limra.com; f. 1916; research and consultancy services for insurance cos; Chair. JAMES W. WEAKLEY; Pres. and CEO ROBERT A. KERZNER; 850 mems.

LOMA (Life Office Management Association): 2300 Windy Ridge Pkwy, Suite 600, Atlanta, GA 30339-8443; tel. (770) 951-1770; fax (770) 984-6417; e-mail askloma@loma.org; internet www.loma.org; f. 1924; 1,200 mem. cos; Pres. ROBERT A. KERZNER.

National Association of Health Underwriters (NAHU): 2000 North 14th St, Suite 450, Arlington, VA 22201; tel. (703) 276-0220; fax (703) 841-7797; e-mail info@nahu.org; internet www.nahu.org; CEO JANET TRAUTWEIN.

National Association of Life Underwriters: 2901 Telestar Court, Falls Church, VA 22042-1205; tel. (703) 770-8100; e-mail membersupport@naifa.org; internet www.naifa.org; 108,000 mems; CEO JOHN J. HEALY.

National Association of Mutual Insurance Cos (NAMIC): 3601 Vincennes Rd, POB 68700, Indianapolis, IN 46268-0700; tel. (317) 875-5250; fax (317) 879-8408; e-mail service@namic.org; internet www.namic.org; f. 1895; 1,400 mems; Pres. and CEO CHARLES M. CHAMNESS.

Reinsurance Association of America: 1301 Pennsylvania Ave, NW, Suite 900, Washington, DC 20004; tel. (202) 638-3690; fax (202) 638-0936; e-mail infobox@reinsurance.org; internet www.reinsurance.org; f. 1969; 35 mems; Pres. FRANKLIN W. NUTTER.

Directory

Trade and Industry

CHAMBER OF COMMERCE

US Chamber of Commerce: 1615 H St, NW, Washington, DC 20062-2000; tel. (202) 659-6000; fax (202) 463-5836; internet www.uschamber.com; f. 1912; mems: c. 3m. cos; over 100 US chambers of commerce in 91 countries; Pres. and CEO THOMAS J. DONOHUE; Chair. DONALD J. SHEPARD.

EMPLOYERS' ORGANIZATIONS

Chemicals

American Chemistry Council (ACC): 1300 Wilson Blvd, Arlington, VA 22209; tel. (703) 741-5000; fax (703) 741-6000; e-mail helpline@americanchemistry.com; internet www.americanchemistry.com; f. 1872; incl. the Plastics Division and Chlorine Chemistry Division; 136 mems; Pres. and CEO CAL DOOLEY; Sec. DELL PERELMAN.

American Pharmacists Association (APhA): 1100 15th St, NW, Suite 400, Washington, DC 20005-1707; tel. (202) 628-4410; fax (202) 783-2351; e-mail scorbitt@aphanet.org; internet www.pharmacist.com; f. 1852; over 60,000 mems; Pres. TIMOTHY L. TUCKER; Exec. Vice-Pres. and CEO JOHN A. GANS.

American Plastics Council (APC): 1300 Wilson Blvd, Arlington, VA 22209; tel. (703) 741-5000; fax (703) 741-6093; internet www.americanplasticscouncil.org; affiliate of the American Chemistry Council; 13 mem. cos and 1 affiliated trade asscn; Pres. RODNEY W. LOWMAN.

Consumer Specialty Products Association (CSPA): 900 17th St, NW, Suite 300, Washington, DC 20006; tel. (202) 872-8110; fax (202) 872-8114; e-mail info@cspa.org; internet www.cspa.org; f. 1914; fmrly Chemical Specialities Manufacturers Asscn; over 250 mems; Pres. CHRISTOPHER CATHCART.

Drug, Chemical and Associated Technologies Association, Inc (DCAT): 1 Washington Blvd, Suite 7, Robbinsville, NJ 08691; tel. (609) 448-1000; fax (609) 448-1944; e-mail info@dcat.org; internet www.dcat.org; f. 1890; fmrly Drug, Chemical and Allied Trades Asscn; name changed as above in 2003; 350 mems; Exec. Dir MARGARET M. TIMONY.

The Fertilizer Institute: Union Center Plaza, 820 First St, NE, Suite 430, Washington, DC 20002; tel. (202) 962-0490; fax (202) 962-0577; e-mail webmaster@tfi.org; internet www.tfi.org; f. 1883; 300 mem. orgs; Pres. FORD B. WEST.

National Community Pharmacists Association (NCPA): 100 Daingerfield Rd, Alexandria, VA 22314; tel. (703) 683-8200; fax (703) 683-3619; e-mail info@ncpanet.org; internet www.ncpanet.org; f. 1898; fmrly Nat. Asscn of Retail Druggists; 25,000 mems; Pres. HOLLY W. HENRY; Chair., Exec. Committee ROBERT GREENWOOD.

Pharmaceutical Research & Manufacturers of America (PhRMA): 950 F St, NW, Suite 900, Washington, DC 20004; tel. (202) 835-3400; fax (202) 835-3414; internet www.phrma.org; f. 1958; 67 mems; Pres. WILLIAM TAUZIN.

Soap and Detergent Association (SDA): 1500 K St, NW, Suite 300, Washington, DC, 20005; tel. (202) 347-2900; fax (202) 347-4110; e-mail info@cleaning101.com; internet www.cleaning101.com; f. 1926; c. 100 mems; Pres. and CEO ERNIE ROSENBERG.

Synthetic Organic Chemical Manufacturers' Association (SOCMA): 1850 M St, NW, Suite 700, Washington, DC 20036-5810; tel. (202) 721-4100; fax (202) 296-8120; e-mail info@socma.com; internet www.socma.com; f. 1921; 275 mem. cos; Chair. CHARLES HINNANT.

Construction
(see also Electricity, and Engineering and Machinery)

American Institute of Constructors (AIC): POB 26334, Alexandria, VA 22314; tel. (703) 683-4999; fax (703) 683-5480; e-mail admin@aicnet.org; internet www.aicnet.org; f. 1971; 1,600 mems; Pres. MARK GIORGI.

Associated Builders and Contractors, Inc (ABC): 4250 North Fairfax Dr., 9th Floor, Arlington, VA 22203-1607; tel. (703) 812-2000; e-mail gotquestions@abc.org; internet www.abc.org; f. 1950; 24,000 mems; Pres. and CEO M. KIRK PICKEREL.

Associated General Contractors of America (AGC) (AGC of America): 2300 Wilson Blvd, Suite 400, Arlington, VA 22201; tel. (703) 548-3118; fax (703) 548-3119; e-mail info@agc.org; internet www.agc.org; f. 1918; 33,000 mems; Pres. J. DOUG PRUITT; CEO STEPHEN E. SANDHERR.

Associated Specialty Contractors, Inc (ASC): 3 Bethesda Metro Center, Suite 1100, Bethesda, MD 20814-5372; tel. (301) 657-3110; fax (301) 215-4500; e-mail dgw@necanet.org; internet www.assoc-spec-con.org; f. 1955; 9 mem. asscns; Pres. DANIEL G. WALTER.

THE UNITED STATES OF AMERICA

Building Stone Institute (BSI): 551 Tollgate Rd, Suite C, Elgin, IL 60123; tel. (847) 695-0170; fax (847) 695-0174; e-mail barb@buildingstoneinstitute.org; internet www.buildingstoneinstitute.org; f. 1919; 400 mems; Pres. DOUG BACHLI; Sec. THOMAS SCHLOUGH.

Construction Specifications Institute (CSI): 99 Canal Center Plaza, Suite 300, Alexandria, VA 22314-1588; tel. (703) 684-0300; fax (703) 684-8436; e-mail csi@csinet.org; internet www.csinet.org; f. 1948; over 16,000 mems; Pres. GILMAN K. M. HU; Exec. Dir and CEO WALTER T. MARLOWE.

Mechanical Contractors Association of America, Inc (MCAA): 1385 Piccard Dr., Rockville, MD 20850-4340; tel. (301) 869-5800; fax (301) 990-9690; e-mail mcaainfo@mcaa.org; internet www.mcaa.org; f. 1889; 2,500 mems; Exec. Vice-Pres. and CEO JOHN R. GENTILLE.

National Association of Home Builders of the US (NAHB): 1201 15th St, NW, Washington, DC 20005; tel. (202) 266-8200; fax (202) 266-8400; internet www.nahb.org; f. 1942; 800 mem. asscns, 220,000 mems; Pres. and CEO GERALD M. HOWARD; Chair. JOE ROBSON.

National Association of Plumbing-Heating-Cooling Contractors (PHCC): 180 South Washington St, POB 6808, Falls Church, VA 22046; tel. (703) 237-8100; fax (703) 237-7442; e-mail naphcc@naphcc.org; internet www.phccweb.org; f. 1883; 4,000 mems; Pres. JOE SCHMITT; Pres.-Elect SKIP PFEFFER.

National Ready Mixed Concrete Association (NRMCA): 900 Spring St, Silver Spring, MD 20910; tel. (301) 587-1400; fax (301) 585-4219; e-mail info@nrmca.org; internet www.nrmca.org; f. 1930; 1,000 mems; Chair. HENRY BATTEN; Pres. ROBERT GARBINI.

National Tile Contractors Association (NTCA): POB 13629, Jackson, MS 39236; tel. (601) 939-2071; fax (601) 932-6117; internet www.tile-assn.com; f. 1947; Exec. Dir BART BETTIGA.

Tile Council of North America Inc (TCNA): 100 Clemson Research Blvd, Anderson, SC 29625; tel. (864) 646-8453; fax (864) 646-2821; e-mail info@tileusa.com; internet www.tileusa.com; f. 1945 as Tile Council of America; adopted current name in 2003; 130 mems; Exec. Dir ERIC ASTRACHAN.

US Green Building Council (USGBC): 1015 18th St, NW, Suite 508, Washington, DC 20036; tel. (202) 828-7422; fax (202) 828-5110; e-mail info@usgbc.org; internet www.usgbc.org; over 6,400 mem. orgs; Pres. and CEO S. RICHARD FEDRIZZI; Chair. GAIL VITTORI.

Electricity
(see also Construction, Electronics and Technology, Engineering and Machinery, and Trade and Industry—Utilities)

Edison Electric Institute (EEI): 701 Pennsylvania Ave, NW, Washington, DC 20004-2696; tel. (202) 508-5000; e-mail feedback@eei.org; internet www.eei.org; f. 1933; mems: 190 investor-owned electric utility cos, more than 65 int. affiliates; mems generate 70% of electricity produced by US utilities; Chair. DAVID M. RATCLIFFE.

National Association of Electrical Distributors (NAED): 1181 Corporate Lake Dr., St Louis, MO 63132; tel. (314) 991-9000; fax (314) 991-3060; e-mail info@naed.org; internet www.naed.org; f. 1908; 2,900 mems; Pres. and CEO TOM NABER.

National Electrical Contractors Association (NECA): 3 Bethesda Metro Center, Suite 1100, Bethesda, MD 20814-5372; tel. (301) 657-3110; fax (301) 215-4500; internet www.necanet.org; f. 1901; 4,200 mems; Pres. REX FERRY; CEO JOHN M. GRAU.

National Electrical Manufacturers Association (NEMA): 1300 North 17th St, Suite 1752, Rosslyn, VA 22209; tel. (703) 841-3200; fax (703) 841-5900; e-mail webmaster@nema.org; internet www.nema.org; f. 1926; 430 mem. cos; Pres.and CEO EVAN R. GADDIS.

Electronics and Technology

AeA: 5201 Great America Pkwy, Suite 400, Santa Clara, CA 95054; tel. (408) 987-4200; fax (408) 987-4298; e-mail csc@aeanet.org; internet www.aeanet.org; f. 1943; fmrly American Electronics Asscn; 2,500 mem. cos; Pres. and CEO PETER J. BONI.

Electronic Industries Alliance: 2500 Wilson Blvd, Arlington, VA 22201-3834; tel. (703) 907-7500; fax (703) 907-7501; internet www.eia.org; f. 1924; 1,300 mem. cos; Pres. MATHEW FLANIGAN (acting).

Institute of Electrical and Electronics Engineers, Inc (IEEE): 445 Hoes Lane, Piscataway, NJ 08854-4141; tel. (732) 981-0060; fax (732) 981-1721; e-mail staff-director@ieee.org; internet www.ieee.org; f. 1963; more than 375,000 mems world-wide; Pres. and CEO Dr JOHN R. VIG; Pres.-elect PEDRO RAY.

IPC (Association Connecting Electronics Industries): 3000 Lakeside Dr., Suite 309, Bannockburn, IL 60015; tel. (847) 615-7100; fax (847) 615-7105; e-mail mcgude@ipc.org; internet www.ipc.org; f. 1957; Chair. NILESH S. NAIK; Pres. and CEO DENNY MCGUIRK.

Telecommunications Industry Association (TIA): 2500 Wilson Blvd, Suite 300, Arlington, VA 22201; tel. (703) 907-7700; fax (703) 907-7727; e-mail tia@tiaonline.org; internet www.tiaonline.org; f. 1988; Pres. GRANT E. SEIFFERT.

Engineering and Machinery
(see also Electricity and Construction)

Air-Conditioning, Heating and Refrigeration Institute (AHRI): 2111 Wilson Blvd, Suite 500, Arlington, VA 22201; tel. (703) 524-8800; fax (703) 528-3816; e-mail ahri@ahrinet.org; internet www.ahrinet.org; f. 2007 by merger of the Air-Conditioning and Refrigeration Institute (ARI) and the Gas Appliance Mfrs Asscn (GAMA); 220 mems; Chair. KEITH COURSIN; CEO JACK KLIMP.

American Council of Engineering Companies (ACEC): 1015 15th St, NW, 8th Floor, Washington, DC 20005-2605; tel. (202) 347-7474; fax (202) 898-0068; e-mail acec@acec.org; internet www.acec.org; f. 1905; 5,700 mem. cos; Chair. JOHN F. HENNESSY, III; Pres. and CEO DAVID A. RAYMOND.

American Institute of Chemical Engineers (AIChE): 3 Park Ave, New York, NY 10016-5991; tel. (203) 702-7660; fax (203) 775-5177; e-mail fiob@aiche.org; internet www.aiche.org; f. 1908; over 46,000 mems world-wide; Pres. H. SCOTT FOGLER; Pres.-Elect HENRY T. 'HANK' KOHLBRAND.

American Institute of Mining, Metallurgical and Petroleum Engineers, Inc: 8307 Shaffer Pkwy, Littleton, CO 80127-4012; tel. (303) 948-4255; fax (303) 948-4260; e-mail aime@aimehq.org; internet www.aimehq.org; f. 1871; five constituent socs representing 100,000 mems; Pres. MICHAEL KARMIS; Exec. Dir J. RICK ROLATER.

American Society of Civil Engineers (ASCE): 1801 Alexander Bell Dr., Reston, VA 20191-4400; tel. (703) 295-6300; fax (703) 295-6222; e-mail webmaster@asce.org; internet www.asce.org; f. 1852; over 133,000 mems; Pres. D. WAYNE KLOTZ; Pres.-Elect BLAINE D. LEONARD.

American Society of Heating, Refrigerating and Air-Conditioning Engineers (ASHRAE): 1791 Tullie Circle, NE, Atlanta, GA 30329; tel. (404) 636-8400; fax (404) 321-5478; e-mail ashrae@ashrae.org; internet www.ashrae.org; f. 1894; 55,000 mems; Pres. WILLIAM HARRISON.

American Society of Naval Engineers, Inc: 1452 Duke St, Alexandria, VA 22314-3458; tel. (703) 836-6727; fax (703) 836-7491; e-mail asnehq@navalengineers.org; internet www.navalengineers.org; f. 1888; 6,000 mems; Exec. Dir Capt. (retd) DENNIS K. KRUSE.

Association of Coastal Engineers (ACE): c/o Patricia Ehrman, 2770 North West 43rd St, Suite B, Applied Technology and Management Inc, Gainesville, FL 32606; e-mail hugo@coastharborenq.com; internet www.coastalengineers.org; f. 1999; Pres. JOHN RAMSEY.

Association of Home Appliance Manufacturers (AHAM): 1111 19th St, NW, Suite 402, Washington, DC 20036; tel. (202) 872-5955; fax (202) 872-9354; e-mail info@aham.org; internet www.aham.org; f. 1915; Pres. JERRY G. RYDER.

AMT (The Association for Manufacturing Technology): 7901 Westpark Dr., McLean, VA 22102-4206; tel. (703) 893-2900; fax (703) 893-1151; e-mail amt@amtonline.org; internet www.amtonline.org; f. 1902; 370 mems; Pres. DOUGLAS K. WOODS.

Manufacturers Alliance/MAPI, Inc: 1600 Wilson Blvd, Suite 1100, Arlington, VA 22209-2411; tel. (703) 841-9000; fax (703) 841-9514; e-mail info@mapi.net; internet www.mapi.net; f. 1933; 500 mem. cos; Pres. and CEO THOMAS J. DUESTERBERG.

Petroleum Equipment Institute (PEI): POB 2380, Tulsa, OK 74101-2380; tel. (918) 494-9696; fax (918) 491-9895; e-mail info@pei.org; internet www.pei.org; f. 1951; over 1,600 mems world-wide; Pres. BLAIR SHWEDO.

SAE International (Society of Automotive Engineers): 400 Commonwealth Dr., Warrendale, PA 15096-0001; tel. (724) 776-4841; fax (724) 776-0790; e-mail customerservice@sae.org; internet www.sae.org; f. 1905; over 90,000 mems world-wide; Pres. JAMES E. SMITH.

Society of Naval Architects and Marine Engineers (SNAME): 601 Pavonia Ave, Suite 400, Jersey City, NJ 07306-2907; tel. (201) 798-4800; fax (201) 798-4975; e-mail ccali-poutre@sname.org; internet www.sname.org; f. 1893; over 10,000 mems; Pres. R. KEITH MICHEL; Exec. Dir PHILIP B. KIMBALL.

United Engineering Foundation (UEF): POB 70, Mount Vernon, VA 22121-0070; tel. (973) 244-2328; fax (973) 882-5155; e-mail engfnd@aol.com; internet www.uefoundation.org; f. 1914; umbrella org. of engineering socs, incl. ASME International, the Institute of Electrical and Electronics Engineers and the American Institute of Chemical Engineers; Pres. ARTHUR W. WINSTON; Exec. Dir Dr DAVID L. BELDEN.

Food

American Bakers Association (ABA): 1350 I St, NW, Suite 700, Washington, DC 20005-3300; tel. (202) 789-0300; fax (202) 898-1164; e-mail info@americanbakers.org; internet www.americanbakers.org; f. 1897; Pres. and CEO ROBB MACKIE.

THE UNITED STATES OF AMERICA

American Beverage Association (ABA): 1101 16th St, NW, Washington, DC 20036-4803; tel. (202) 463-6732; fax (202) 659-5349; e-mail info@ameribev.org; internet www.ameribev.org; f. 1919; fmrly Nat. Soft Drink Asscn; 1,700 mems; Pres. and CEO SUSAN K. NEELY.

American Council for Food Safety and Quality: 710 Striker Ave, Sacramento, CA 95834; tel. (916) 561-5900; fax (916) 561-5910; e-mail merlej@dfaofca.com; internet www.dfaofca.com; f. 1908; agricultural asscn (dried fruit and tree nuts); 51 mems; Pres. and CEO MERLE JACOBS.

American Farm Bureau Federation (FB): 600 Maryland Ave, SW, Suite 1000W, Washington, DC 20024; tel. (202) 406-3600; fax (202) 406-3602; e-mail webmaster@fb.org; internet www.fb.org; f. 1919; 50 mem. states and Puerto Rico; Pres. BOB STALLMAN; Exec. Vice-Pres. RICHARD NEWPHER.

American Meat Institute: 1150 Connecticut Ave, NW, 12th Floor, Washington, DC 20036; tel. (202) 587-4200; fax (202) 587-4300; e-mail webmaster@meatami.com; internet www.meatami.com; f. 1906; 1,100 mems; Pres. DAVID MINIAT.

Commodity Markets Council (CMC): 1300 L St, NW, Suite 1020, Washington, DC 20005; tel. (202) 842-0400; fax (202) 789-7223; e-mail mwalter@cmcmarkets.org; internet www.cmcmarkets.org; f. 1930 as the National Grain Trade Council; reformed as two separate entities, CMC and the Transportation, Elevator and Grain Merchants Asscn, in 2006; 40 mems; Chair. THOMAS J. ERICKSON; Pres. MICHAEL WALTER.

> **Transportation, Elevator, & Grain Merchants Association (TEGMA):** POB 26426, Kansas City, MO 64196; tel. (816) 628-1231; fax (816) 628-1905; e-mail bob.petersen@tegma.org; internet www.tegma.org; f. 2006 following the dissolution of the National Grain Trade Council; promotes efficiency, competitiveness and safety of handling and transportation of North American grain and grain products; 30 mems; Chair. MIKE MANDL; Pres. BOB PETERSEN.

Distilled Spirits Council of the US, Inc (DISCUS): 1250 Eye St, NW, Suite 400, Washington, DC 20005; tel. (202) 628-3544; internet www.discus.org; f. 1973; 12 active mems and 23 affiliates; Pres. and CEO Dr PETER H. CRESSY.

Food Marketing Institute (FMI): 2345 Crystal Dr., Suite 800, Arlington, VA 22202; tel. (202) 452-8444; fax (202) 429-4519; e-mail fmi@fmi.org; internet www.fmi.org; f. 1977; 1,500 mems; Pres. and CEO TIMOTHY M. HAMMONDS.

Foodservice Sales and Marketing Association (FSMA): 9192 Red Branch Rd, Suite 200, Columbia, MD 21045; tel. (410) 715-6672; fax (410) 997-9387; e-mail info@fsmaonline.com; internet www.fsmaonline.com; f. 2003; Pres. and CEO RICK ABRAHAM.

Grocery Manufacturers of America, Inc (GMA): 1350 I St, NW, Suite 300, Washington, DC 20005; tel. (202) 639-5900; fax (202) 639-5932; e-mail info@gmaonline.org; internet www.gmaonline.org; f. 1908; over 185 mems; Pres. and CEO C. MANLY MOLPUS (acting).

International Foodservice Distributors Association (IFDA): 1410 Spring Hill Rd, Suite 210, McLean, VA 22102; tel. (703) 532-9400; fax (703) 538-4673; internet www.ifdaonline.org; f. 1906; over 140 mems; Pres. and CEO MARK ALLEN.

National Association of Wheat Growers (NAWG): 412 Second St, NE, Suite 300, Washington, DC 20002-4993; tel. (202) 547-7800; fax (202) 546-2638; e-mail wheatworld@wheatworld.org; internet www.wheatworld.org; f. 1950; 20 affiliated mem. states; CEO DAREN COPPOCK.

National Beer Wholesalers Association (NBWA): 1101 King St, Suite 600, Alexandria, VA 22314-2944; tel. (703) 683-4300; fax (703) 683-8965; e-mail info@nbwa.org; internet www.nbwa.org; f. 1938; 2,750 mem. distributor cos; Pres. CRAIG A. PURSER.

National Cattlemen's Beef Association (NCBA): 9110 East Nichols Ave, Suite 300, Centennial, CO 80112; tel. (303) 694-0305; fax (303) 694-7372; e-mail terry.stokes@ymail.com; internet www.beefusa.org; f. 1898; 33,000 mems, plus 44 cattle asscns and 50 breed and industry asscns; Pres. ANDY GROSETA; CEO TERRY L. STOKES.

National Confectioners Association of the US (NCA): 8320 Old Courthouse Rd, Suite 300, Vienna, VA 22182; tel. (703) 790-5750; fax (703) 790-5752; e-mail info@candyusa.com; internet www.candyusa.com; f. 1884; includes Chocolate Mfrs Asscn; 340 mems; Pres. LAWRENCE T. GRAHAM.

National Dairy Council (NDC): 10255 West Higgins Rd, Suite 900, Rosemount, IL 60018; tel. (847) 803-2000; fax (847) 803-2077; e-mail ndc@dairyinformation.com; internet www.nationaldairycouncil.org; f. 1915; 600 mems.

National Farmers (NFO): 528 Billy Sunday Rd, Ames, IA 50010; tel. (800) 247-2110; e-mail info@nfo.org; internet www.nfo.org; f. 1955; c. 35,000 mems; Pres. PAUL OLSON.

National Farmers Union (NFU): 5619 DTC Pkwy, Suite 300, Greenwood Village, CO 80011-3136; tel. (303) 337-5500; fax (303) 771-1770; e-mail dave.frederickson@nfu.org; internet www.nfu.org; f. 1902; 250,000 mems; Pres. TOM BUIS.

National Frozen and Refrigerated Foods Association (NFRA): 4755 Linglestown Rd, Suite 300, POB 6069, Harrisburg, PA 17112; tel. (717) 657-8601; fax (717) 657-9862; e-mail info@nfraweb.org; internet www.nfraweb.org; f. 1945; over 400 mem. cos; Pres. and CEO NEVIN B. MONTGOMERY.

National Grocers Association (NGA): 1005 North Glebe Rd, Suite 250, Arlington, VA 22201-5758; tel. (703) 516-0700; fax (703) 516-0115; e-mail info@nationalgrocers.org; internet www.nationalgrocers.org; f. 1982; 3,000 mems; Pres. and CEO THOMAS K. ZAUCHA.

National Meat Association (NMA): NMA East: 1400 16th St, NW, Suite 400, Washington, DC 20036; tel. (202) 667-2108; NMA West: 1970 Broadway, Suite 825, Oakland, CA 94612; tel. (510) 763-1533; fax (510) 763-6186; e-mail staff@nmaonline.org; internet www.nmaonline.org; f. 1946; over 600 mems; Chair. JIM MAXEY.

North American Millers' Association (NAMA): 600 Maryland Ave, SW, Suite 825 West, Washington, DC 20024; tel. (202) 484-2200; fax (202) 488-7416; e-mail generalinfo@namamillers.org; internet www.namamillers.org; f. 1998; 48 mems and 28 assoc. mems; Chair. RICK L. SCHWEIN; Pres. BETSY FAGA.

United Fresh Fruit & Vegetable Association: 1901 Pennsylvania Ave, NW, Suite 1100, Washington, DC 20006; tel. (202) 303-3400; fax (202) 303-3433; e-mail united@unitedfresh.org; internet www.unitedfresh.org; f. 1904; 1,300 mems; Pres. and CEO THOMAS E. STENZEL.

US Dairy Export Council (USDEC): 2101 Wilson Blvd, Suite 400, Arlington, VA 22201-3061; tel. (703) 528-3049; fax (703) 528-3705; e-mail info@usdec.org; internet www.usdec.org; f. 1995; 86 mems; Pres. THOMAS M. SUBER.

Wine and Spirits Wholesalers of America, Inc (WSWA): 805 15th St, NW, Suite 430, Washington, DC 20005; tel. (202) 371-9792; fax (202) 789-2405; e-mail katrina@wswa.org; internet www.wswa.org; f. 1943; c. 450 mem. cos; Pres. and CEO CRAIG WOLF.

Iron and Steel

American Hardware Manufacturers Association (AHMA): 801 North Plaza Dr., Schaumburg, IL 60173-4977; tel. (847) 605-1025; fax (847) 605-1030; e-mail info@ahma.org; internet www.ahma.org; f. 1901; 500 mems; Pres. and CEO TIMOTHY S. FARRELL; Vice-Chair. WILLIAM P. FARRELL.

American Institute of Steel Construction (AISC): 1 East Wacker Dr., Suite 700, Chicago, IL 60601-1802; tel. (312) 670-2400; fax (312) 670-5403; internet www.aisc.org; f. 1921; Pres. ROGER E. FERCH.

American Iron and Steel Institute (AISI): 1140 Connecticut Ave, NW, Suite 705, Washington, DC 20036; tel. (202) 452-7100; e-mail webmaster@steel.org; internet www.steel.org; f. 1908; 32 mem. cos and 125 assoc. and affiliated mems; Chair. KEITH E. BUSSE; Pres. and CEO THOMAS J. GIBSON.

Steel Founders' Society of America (SFSA): 780 McArdle Dr., Unit G, Crystal Lake, IL 60014; tel. (815) 455-8240; fax (815) 455-8241; e-mail monroe@sfsa.org; internet www.sfsa.org; f. 1902; 80 mems; Exec. Vice-Pres. RAYMOND W. MONROE.

Steel Manufacturers Association (SMA): 1150 Connecticut Ave, NW, Suite 715, Washington, DC 20036; tel. (202) 296-1515; fax (202) 296-2506; e-mail stuart@steelnet.org; internet www.steelnet.org; 39 North American mem. cos and six mem. cos world-wide, as well as 107 assoc. mem. cos; Pres. THOMAS A. DANJCZEK.

Leather
(see also Textiles)

Leather Apparel Association (LAA): 19 West 21st St, Suite 403, New York, NY 10010; tel. (212) 727-1210; fax (212) 727-1218; e-mail info@leatherassociation.com; internet www.leatherassociation.com; f. 1990; over 100 mems; Pres. MORRIS GOLDFARB.

Leather Industries of America (LIA): 3050 K St, NW, Suite 400, Washington, DC 20007; tel. (202) 342-8497; fax (202) 342-8583; e-mail info@leatherusa.com; internet www.leatherusa.com; f. 1917; 64 mems; Pres. JOHN WITTENBORN.

Travel Goods Association (TGA): 5 Vaughn Dr., Suite 105, Princeton, NJ 08540; tel. (609) 720-1200; fax (609) 720-0620; e-mail info@travel-goods.org; internet www.travel-goods.org; f. 1938; 400 mems; Pres. MICHELE MARINI PITTENGER.

Lumber
(see also Paper)

American Forest and Paper Association (AF&PA): 1111 19th St, NW, Suite 800, Washington, DC 20036; tel. (202) 463-2700; fax (202) 463-2771; e-mail info@afandpa.org; internet www.afandpa.org; f. 1993; over 250 mems and trade asscns; Pres. W. HENSON MOORE.

THE UNITED STATES OF AMERICA   *Directory*

APA–The Engineered Wood Association: 7011 South 19th St, Tacoma, WA 98466-5333; tel. (253) 565-6600; fax (253) 565-7265; e-mail help@apawood.org; internet www.apawood.org; f. 1933 as Douglas Fir Plywood Asscn; later became American Plywood Asscn; adopted current name 1994; 109 mems; Pres. DENNIS HARDMAN.

Forest Resources Association Inc: 600 Jefferson Plaza, Suite 350, Rockville, MD 20852-1150; tel. (301) 838-9385; fax (301) 838-9481; e-mail rlewis@forestresources.org; internet www.forestresources.org; f. 1934; 1,300 mems; Pres. R. LEWIS.

National Lumber and Building Material Dealers Association (NLBMDA): 2025 M Street, NW, Suite 800, Washington, DC 20036-3309; tel. (202) 367-1169; fax (202) 367-2169; e-mail info@dealer.org; internet www.dealer.org; f. 1915; 20 mem. orgs, representing 8,000 cos; Pres. and CEO MICHAEL O'BRIEN.

National Wooden Pallet and Container Association (NWPCA): 1421 Prince St, Suite 340, Alexandria, VA 22314-2805; tel. (703) 519-6104; fax (703) 519-4720; e-mail bscholnick@palletcentral.com; internet www.palletcentral.com; f. 1946; Pres. and CEO BRUCE N. SCHOLNICK.

North American Wholesale Lumber Association (NAWLA): 3601 Algonquin Rd, Suite 400, Rolling Meadows, IL 60008; tel. (847) 870-7470; fax (847) 870-0201; e-mail info@lumber.org; internet www.lumber.org; f. 1893; over 650 mems; Pres. and CEO NICHOLAS R. KENT.

Southern Forest Products Association: 2900 Indiana Ave, Kenner, LA 70065-4605; tel. (504) 443-4464; fax (504) 443-6612; e-mail mail@spfa.org; internet www.sfpa.org; f. 1915; c. 160 mem. orgs; Pres. DIGGES MORGAN.

Western Wood Products Association (WWPA): Yeon Bldg, 522 South West Fifth Ave, Suite 500, Portland, OR 97204-2122; tel. (503) 224-3930; fax (503) 224-3934; e-mail info@wwpa.org; internet www.wwpa.org; f. 1964; c. 65 mem. orgs; Pres. and CEO MICHAEL R. O'HALLORAN.

Wood Products Manufacturers Association (WPMA): 175 State Rd East, POB 761, Westminster, MA 01473-0761; tel. (978) 874-5445; fax (978) 874-9946; e-mail woodprod@wpma.org; internet www.wpma.org; f. 1929; 664 mems; Pres. MAGGIE BRIGHAM; Exec. Dir PHILIP A. BIBEAU.

Metals and Mining
(see also Iron and Steel)

Aluminum Association, Inc: 1525 Wilson Blvd, Suite 600, Arlington, VA 22209; tel. (703) 358-2960; fax (703) 358-2961; e-mail lwilson@aluminum.org; internet www.aluminum.org; f. 1933; 82 mems; Pres. J. STEPHEN LARKIN.

American Zinc Association (AZA): 2025 M St, NW, Suite 800, Washington, DC 20036; tel. (202) 367-1151; fax (202) 367-2232; e-mail zincinfo@zinc.org; internet www.zinc.org; f. 1990; 10 regular mems, 14 affiliates; Exec. Dir GEORGE VARY.

ASM International: 9639 Kinsman Rd, Materials Park, OH 44073-0002; tel. (440) 338-5151; fax (440) 338-4634; e-mail customerservice@asminternational.org; internet asmcommunity.asminternational.org; f. 1913; fmrly the American Society for Materials; 40,000 mems world-wide; Man. Dir STANLEY C. THEOBALD.

Copper and Brass Fabricators Council, Inc: 3050 K St, NW, Suite 400, Washington, DC 20007; tel. (202) 833-8575; fax (202) 342-8451; e-mail copbrass@kelleydrye.com; f. 1964; 20 mem. cos; Pres. and Gen. Counsel DAVID A. HARTQUIST.

Copper Development Association, Inc (CDA): 260 Madison Ave, New York, NY 10016; tel. (212) 251-7200; fax (212) 251-7234; e-mail questions@cda.copper.org; internet www.copper.org; f. 1962; 65 mems; Pres. and CEO ANDREW G. KIRETA, Sr.

Fabricators and Manufacturers Association, International (FMA): 833 Featherstone Rd, Rockford, IL 61107; tel. (815) 399-8775; fax (815) 484-7701; e-mail info@fmanet.org; internet www.fmanet.org; f. 1970; 2,100 mems; Pres. and CEO GERALD M. SHANKEL.

Manufacturing Jewelers and Suppliers of America, Inc (MJSA): 45 Royal Little Dr., Providence, RI 02904; tel. (401) 274-3840; fax (401) 274-0265; e-mail info@mjsa.org; internet www.mjsa.org; f. 1903; 1,800 mems; Chair. ALAN BELL; COO JAMES K. MCCARTY.

Metal Powder Industries Federation (MPIF): 105 College Rd East, 1st Floor, Princeton, NJ 08540-6692; tel. (609) 452-7700; fax (609) 987-8523; e-mail info@mpif.org; internet www.mpif.org; f. 1944; 6 feds of 300 corp. mems; Exec. Dir and CEO C. JAMES TROMBINO.

Mining and Metallurgical Society of America (MMSA): POB 810, Boulder, CO 80306-0810; tel. (303) 444-6032; e-mail contactmmsa@mmsa.net; internet www.mmsa.net; f. 1908; 340 mems; Exec. Dir BETTY L. GIBBS; Pres. ROBERT V. WASHNOCK.

National Mining Association (NMA): 101 Constitution Ave, NW, Suite 500 East, Washington, DC 20001-2133; tel. (202) 463-2600; fax (202) 463-2666; e-mail craulston@nma.org; internet www.nma.org; f. 1995; over 325 mem. cos; Pres. and CEO HAROLD P. QUINN.

Northwest Mining Association (NWMA): 10 North Post St, Suite 220, Spokane, WA 99201; tel. (509) 624-1158; fax (509) 623-1241; e-mail nwma_info@nwma.org; internet www.nwma.org; f. 1895; 1,800 mems; Exec. Dir LAURA E. SKAER.

The Silver Institute: 1200 G St, NW, Suite 800, Washington, DC 20005; tel. (202) 835-0185; fax (202) 835-0155; e-mail info@silverinstitute.org; internet www.silverinstitute.org; f. 1971; 30 mems; Pres. ROBERT QUARTERMAN; Exec. Dir MICHAEL DIRIENZO.

Paper
(see also Lumber)

Association of Independent Corrugated Converters (AICC): 113 South West St, POB 25708, Alexandria, VA 22313; tel. (703) 836-2422; fax (703) 836-2795; e-mail info@aiccbox.org; internet www.aiccbox.org; mems: 603 box-makers, 480 associates; Chair. JERRY FRISEN; Pres. A. STEPHEN YOUNG.

North American Packaging Association (NAPA): 113 South West St, 3rd Floor, Alexandria, VA 22314; tel. (703) 684-2212; fax (703) 683-6920; e-mail info@paperbox.org; internet www.paperbox.org; f. 2006 by merger of National Paper Box Asscn and Canadian Paperboard Packaging Asscn; Pres. SCOTT MILLER.

NPTA Alliance: 401 North Michigan Ave, Chicago, IL 60611-4267; tel. (312) 321-4092; fax (312) 673-6736; e-mail newell@gonpta.com; internet www.gonpta.com; f. 1903; fmrly Nat. Paper Trade Asscn, Inc; restructured Sept. 2007 to operate under management of SmithBucklin Corpn; 2,000 mems; Chair. THOMAS G. KADIEN; CEO NEWELL HOLT.

Paperboard Packaging Council (PPC): 1350 Main St, Suite 1508, Springfield, MA 01103-1628; tel. (413) 686-9191; fax (413) 747-7777; e-mail paperboardpackaging@ppcnet.org; internet www.ppcnet.org; f. 1967; Pres. BEN MARKENS.

Petroleum and Fuel

American Association of Petroleum Geologists (AAPG): 125 West 15th St, POB 979, Tulsa, OK 74101-0979; tel. (918) 584-2555; fax (918) 560-2694; e-mail postmaster@aapg.org; internet www.aapg.org; f. 1917; 30,000 mems world-wide; Exec. Dir RICHARD D. FRITZ.

American Association of Petroleum Landmen (AAPL): 4100 Fossil Creek Blvd, Fort Worth, TX 76137-2791; tel. (817) 847-7700; fax (817) 847-7704; e-mail aapl@landman.org; internet www.landman.org; f. 1955; 7,000 mems and 43 affiliated asscns; Pres. MARSHALL E. LOCHAUSEN.

American Petroleum Institute (API): 1220 L St, NW, Washington, DC 20005-4070; tel. (202) 682-8000; e-mail mediacenter@api.org; internet www.api.org; f. 1919; 400 corporate mems; Pres. and CEO JACK GERARD; Vice-Pres. and Dir JIM CRAIG.

Association of Diesel Specialists (ADS): 10 Laboratory Dr., POB 13966, Research Triangle Park, NC 27709-3966; tel. (919) 406-8804; fax (919) 406-1306; e-mail info@diesel.org; internet www.diesel.org; more than 700 corp. and individual mems; Exec. Dir DAVID FEHLING.

Coal Exporters' Association of the US, Inc: 1130 17th St, NW, Washington, DC 20036; tel. (202) 463-2666; fax (202) 833-9636; e-mail eschlecht@nma.org; f. 1945; 35 mems; Exec. Dir MOYA PHELLEPS.

Independent Petroleum Association of America (IPAA): 1201 15th St, NW, Suite 300, Washington, DC 20005; tel. (202) 857-4722; fax (202) 857-4799; e-mail webmaster@ipaa.org; internet www.ipaa.org; f. 1929; 6,000 mems; Pres. BARRY RUSSELL.

National Ocean Industries Association (NOIA): 1120 G St, NW, Suite 900, Washington, DC 20005; tel. (202) 347-6900; fax (202) 347-8650; e-mail mkearns@noia.org; internet www.noia.org; f. 1972; over 300 mem. cos; Pres. TOM FRY.

National Petrochemical and Refiners' Association (NPRA): 1667 K St, NW, Suite 700, Washington, DC 20006; tel. (202) 457-0480; fax (202) 457-0486; e-mail info@npra.org; internet www.npradc.org; f. 1902; over 450 mems; Pres. CHARLES T. DREVNA.

Petroleum Marketers Association of America (PMAA): 1901 North Fort Myer Dr., Suite 500, Arlington, VA 22209-1604; tel. (703) 351-8000; fax (703) 351-9160; e-mail info@pmaa.org; internet www.pmaa.org; 45 mem. asscns; Pres. DANIEL F. GILLIGAN.

Western States Petroleum Association (WSPA): 1415 L St, Suite 600, Sacramento, CA 95814; tel. (916) 498-7750; fax (916) 444-5745; internet www.wspa.org; f. 1907; 30 mem. cos; Pres. JOSEPH SPARANO.

Printing and Publishing
(see also Publishers)

Association for the Suppliers of Printing, Publishing and Converting Technologies (NPES): 1899 Preston White Dr., Reston, VA 22091-4367; tel. (703) 264-7200; fax (703) 620-0994;

THE UNITED STATES OF AMERICA   *Directory*

e-mail npes@npes.org; internet www.npes.org; f. 1933; over 400 mem. cos; Pres. RALPH J. NAPPI.

Binding Industries Association International (BIA): 200 Deer Run Rd, Sewickley, PA 15143-2600; tel. (412) 259-1806; fax (412) 259-1800; e-mail jgoldstein@piagatf.org; internet www.bindingindustries.com; f. 1955; 90 mems; Exec. Dir JUSTIN GOLDSTEIN.

National Association for Printing Leadership (NAPL): 75 West Century Rd, Paramus, NJ 07652-1408; tel. (201) 634-9600; e-mail information@napl.org; internet www.napl.org; f. 1933; 150 assoc. mems; Pres. and CEO JOSEPH P. TRUNCALE.

National Association of Printing Ink Manufacturers (NAPIM): 581 Main St, 5th Floor, Woodbridge, NJ 07095; tel. (732) 855-1525; fax (732) 855-1838; e-mail napim@napim.org; internet www.napim.org; f. 1917; Exec. Dir JAMES E. COLEMAN.

Printing Industries of America, Inc/Graphic Arts Information Network (PIA/GATF): 200 Deer Run Rd, Sewickley, PA 15143; tel. (412) 741-6861; fax (412) 741-2311; e-mail gain@piagatf.org; internet www.gain.net; f. 1887 (PIA), 1924 (GATF); consolidated operations in 1999; 12,000 mems; Chair. JANET GREEN; Pres. and CEO MICHAEL MAKIN.

Public Utilities
(see also Trade and Industry—Utilities)

American Public Power Association (APPA): 1875 Connecticut Ave, NW, Suite 1200, Washington, DC 20009-5715; tel. (202) 467-2900; fax (202) 467-2910; e-mail mrufe@appanet.org; internet www.appanet.org; f. 1940; over 2,000 mem. utilities; Chair. MAUDE GRANTHAM-RICHARDS.

American Public Works Association (APWA): 2345 Grand Blvd, Suite 700, Kansas City, MO 64108-2625; tel. (816) 472-6100; fax (816) 472-1610; e-mail apwa@apwa.net; internet www.apwa.net; f. 1937; 29,000 mems; Exec. Dir PETER B. KING.

Rubber

Rubber Manufacturers Association (RMA): 1400 K St, NW, Suite 900, Washington, DC 20005-2043; tel. (202) 682-4800; e-mail info@rma.org; internet www.rma.org; f. 1915; over 100 mem. cos; Pres. and CEO CHARLES A. CANNON.

Stone, Clay and Glass Products

Glass Association of North America (GANA): 2945 South West Wanamaker Dr., Suite A, Topeka, KS 66614-5321; tel. (785) 271-0208; fax (785) 271-0166; e-mail gana@glasswebsite.com; internet www.glasswebsite.com; f. 1994; 208 mems; Exec. Vice-Pres. WILLIAM M. YANEK.

National Glass Association (NGA): 8200 Greensboro Dr., Suite 302, McLean, VA 22102-3881; tel. (703) 342-5642; fax (703) 442-0630; e-mail administration@glass.org; internet www.glass.org; f. 1948; c. 4,000 mem. cos; Pres. and CEO PHILIP J. JAMES.

National Stone, Sand and Gravel Association (NSSGA): 1605 King St, Alexandria, VA 22314; tel. (703) 525-8788; e-mail info@nssga.org; internet www.nssga.org; f. 2000 by merger of Nat. Aggregates Asscn and Nat. Stone Asscn; 950 mems; Pres. and CEO JENNIFER JOY WILSON.

Textiles

American Apparel and Footwear Association (AAFA): 1601 North Kent St, Suite 1200, Arlington, VA 22209; tel. (703) 524-1864; fax (703) 522-6741; e-mail mrust@apparelandfootwear.org; internet www.apparelandfootwear.org; f. 2000 following merger of American Apparel and Manufacturers Asscn and Footwear Industries of America; Pres. and CEO KEVIN M. BURKE.

American Fiber Manufacturers Association, Inc (AFMA): 1530 Wilson Blvd, NW, Suite 690, Arlington, VA 22209; tel. (703) 875-0432; fax (703) 875-0907; e-mail afma@afma.org; internet www.fibersource.com; f. 1933; 34 mems; Pres. PAUL T. O'DAY.

Apparel Retailers of America: 325 Seventh St, Suite 1000, NW, Washington, DC 20004-2801; tel. (202) 347-1932; fax (202) 457-0386; f. 1916; 1,200 mems; Exec. Dir DOUGLAS W. WIEGAND.

National Council of Textile Organizations (NCTO): 910 17th St, NW, Suite 1020, Washington, DC 20006; tel. (202) 822-8028; fax (202) 822-8029; e-mail info@ncto.org; internet www.ncto.org; f. 2004; Pres. CASS JOHNSON.

National Textile Association (NTA): 6 Beacon St, Suite 1125, Boston, MA 02108-3812; tel. (617) 542-8220; fax (617) 542-2199; e-mail info@nationaltextile.org; internet www.nationaltextile.org; f. 1854; fmrly Northern Textile Asscn and Knitted Textile Asscn; adopted current name in 2002; over 200 mems; Pres. KARL SPILHAUS.

Tobacco

Tobacco Associates, Inc: 8452 Holly Leaf Dr., McLean, VA 22102-2225; tel. (703) 821-1255; fax (703) 821-1511; e-mail taw@tobaccoassociatesinc.org; internet www.tobaccoassociatesinc.org; f. 1947; Pres. KIRK WAYNE.

Tobacco Merchants Association of the United States (TMA): POB 8019, Princeton, NJ 08543-8019; tel. (609) 275-4900; fax (609) 275-8379; e-mail tma@tma.org; internet www.tma.org; f. 1915; 170 mems; Pres. FARRELL DELMAN.

Transport

Aerospace Industries Association of America, Inc (AIA): 1000 Wilson Blvd, Suite 1700, Arlington, VA 22209-3928; tel. (703) 358-1000; fax (703) 358-1012; e-mail matt.grimison@aia-aerospace.org; internet www.aia-aerospace.org; f. 1919; 107 mems and 183 assoc. mems; Pres. and CEO MARION C. BLAKEY.

Air Transport Association of America, Inc: see Civil Aviation—Associations.

Alliance of Automobile Manufacturers (Auto Alliance): 1401 Eye St, NW, Suite 900, Washington, DC 20005; tel. (202) 326-5500; fax (202) 326-5598; internet www.autoalliance.org; f. 1999; asscn of 10 car and light truck mfrs; Pres. and CEO DAVE MCCURDY.

American Bureau of Shipping: see Ocean Shipping—Associations.

American Bus Association (ABA): 700 13th St, NW, Suite 575, Washington, DC 20005-5923; tel. (202) 842-1645; fax (202) 842-0850; e-mail abainfo@buses.org; internet www.buses.org; f. 1926; c. 3,250 mems; Pres. and CEO PETER J. PANTUSO.

American International Automobile Dealers' Association (AIADA): 211 North Union St, Suite 300, Alexandria, VA 22314; tel. (703) 519-7800; fax (703) 519-7810; e-mail goaiada@aiada.org; internet www.aiada.org; f. 1970; 11,000 mems; Pres. CODY LUSK.

American Public Transportation Association (APTA): 1666 K St, NW, Suite 1100, Washington, DC 20006; tel. (202) 496-4800; fax (202) 496-4321; e-mail info@apta.com; internet www.apta.com; f. 1882; 1,600 mems; Pres. WILLIAM W. MILLAR.

American Railway Engineering and Maintenance-of-Way Association (AREMA): 10003 Derekwood Lane, Suite 210, MD 20706; tel. (301) 459-3200; fax (301) 459-8077; e-mail fcramer@arema.org; internet www.arema.org; f. 1997; Exec. Dir and CEO Dr CHARLES EMELY.

American Short Line and Regional Railroad Association: see Railways—Associations.

American Trucking Associations (ATA): 2200 Mill Rd, Alexandria, VA 22314-4654; tel. (703) 838-1700; e-mail atamembership@trucking.org; internet www.truckline.com; f. 1933; 3,000 mems; Pres. and CEO WILLIAM GRAVES.

Association of American Railroads: see Railways—Associations.

Chamber of Shipping of America (CSA): see Ocean Shipping—Associations.

National Automobile Dealers Association (NADA): 8400 Westpark Dr., McLean, VA 22102-3522; tel. (703) 821-7000; e-mail nadainfo@nada.org; internet www.nada.org; f. 1917; over 19,700 mems; Pres. PHILLIP D. BRADY.

Owner/Operator Independent Drivers' Association (OOIDA): 1 North West OOIDA Dr., Grain Valley, MO 64029; tel. (816) 229-5791; e-mail webmaster@ooida.com; internet www.ooida.com; f. 1973; over 150,000 mems; Pres. JIM JOHNSTON.

Shipbuilders Council of America (SCA): 1455 F St, NW, Suite 225, Washington, DC 20005; tel. (202) 347-5462; fax (202) 347-5464; e-mail ibennitt@dc.bjllp.com; internet www.shipbuilders.org; f. 1921; absorbed the American Waterways Shipyard Conference (f. 1976) in 1999; 36 mem. cos and 25 affiliate mems; Pres. MATTHEW PAXTON.

Miscellaneous

American Advertising Federation (AAF): 1101 Vermont Ave, NW, Suite 500, Washington, DC 20005-6306; tel. (202) 898-0089; fax (202) 898-0159; e-mail aaf@aaf.org; internet www.aaf.org; f. 1967; 50,000 mems, 130 corp. mems; Pres. and CEO WALLACE S. SNYDER.

American Association of Exporters and Importers (AAEI): 1050 17th St, NW, Suite 810, Washington, DC 20036; tel. (202) 857-8009; fax (202) 857-7843; e-mail hq@aaei.org; internet www.aaei.org; f. 1921; 1,200 mems; Pres. and CEO HALLOCK NORTHCOTT.

American Marketing Association (AMA): 311 South Wacker Dr., Suite 5800, Chicago, IL 60606; tel. (312) 542-9000; fax (312) 542-9001; e-mail info@ama.org; internet www.marketingpower.com; f. 1937; 38,000 mems; Chair. TOM KINNEAR; CEO DENNIS L. DUNLAP.

American Society of Association Executives (ASAE): ASAE and the Center for Association Leadership, 1575 I St, NW, Washington, DC 20005-1103; tel. (202) 626-2798; fax (202) 371-8825; e-mail pr@asaecenter.org; internet www.asaecenter.org; f. 1920; over 22,000 mems; Pres.and CEO JOHN H. GRAHAM.

Association of Equipment Manufacturers (AEM): 6737 West Washington St, Suite 2400, Milwaukee, WI 53214-5647; tel. (414)

272-0943; fax (414) 272-1170; internet www.aem.org; f. 2002; Pres. DENNIS SLATER.

Consumer Healthcare Products Association (CHPA): 900 19th St, NW, Suite 700, Washington, DC 20006; tel. (202) 429-9260; fax (202) 223-6835; e-mail efunderburk@chpa-info.org; internet www.chpa-info.org; f. 1881; 170 mem. and assoc. mem. cos; Pres. LYNDA A. SUYDAM.

Institute for Supply Management (ISM): 2055 East Centennial Circle, POB 22160, Tempe, AZ 85285-2160; tel. (408) 752-6276; fax (408) 752-7890; e-mail pnovak@ism.ws; internet www.ism.ws; f. 1915; 40,000 mems; CEO PAUL NOVAK.

Motion Picture Association of America, Inc (MPAA): 1600 Eye St, NW, Washington, DC 20006; tel. (202) 293-1966; fax (202) 296-7410; internet www.mpaa.org; f. 1922; Chair. and CEO DAN GLICKMAN.

National Association of Manufacturers (NAM): 1331 Pennsylvania Ave, NW, Suite 600, Washington, DC 20004-1790; tel. (202) 637-3000; fax (202) 637-3182; e-mail manufacturing@nam.org; internet www.nam.org; f. 1895; 14,000 mems; Pres. and CEO JOHN ENGLER.

National Association of Realtors (NAR): 430 North Michigan Ave, Suite 500, Chicago, IL 60611-4087; fax (312) 329-8960; e-mail infocentral@realtors.org; internet www.realtor.org; f. 1908; 1.3m. mems; Pres. RICHARD F. GAYLORD.

National Center for Manufacturing Sciences (NCMS): 3025 Boardwalk, Ann Arbor, MI 48108-3230; tel. (734) 995-0300; fax (734) 995-1150; internet www.ncms.org; f. 1986; Pres. and CEO RICHARD B. JARMAN.

National Cooperative Business Association (NCBA): 1401 New York Ave, NW, Suite 1100, Washington, DC 20005-2160; tel. (202) 638-6222; fax (202) 638-1374; e-mail ncba@ncba.coop; internet www.ncba.org; f. 1916; 450 mems; Pres. and CEO PAUL HAZEN.

National Retail Federation (NRF): 325 Seventh St, NW, Suite 1100, Washington, DC 20004-2802; tel. (202) 783-7941; fax (202) 737-2849; e-mail mullint@nrf.com; internet www.nrf.com; f. 1911; merged with American Retail Federation in 1990 and incorporated Apparel Retailers of America in 1995; mems: more than 100 state, nat. and trade orgs; Chair. MYRON E. ULLMAN, III; Pres. and CEO TRACY MULLIN.

Personal Care Products Council: 1101 17th St, NW, Suite 300, Washington, DC 20036-4702; tel. (202) 331-1770; fax (202) 331-1969; internet www.personalcarecouncil.org; f. 1894; fmrly Cosmetic, Toiletry and Fragrance Asscn (CTFA); adopted current name 2007; 600 mem. cos; Pres. and CEO PAMELA G. BAILEY.

Society of Manufacturing Engineers (SME): 1 SME Dr., Dearborn, MI 48121; tel. (313) 271-1500; fax (313) 425-3401; e-mail service@sme.org; internet www.sme.org; f. 1932; Exec. Dir MARK TOMLINSON.

UTILITIES
Electricity

American Electric Power (AEP): 1 Riverside Plaza, Columbus, OH 43215-2372; tel. (614) 716-1000; e-mail jsloat@aep.com; internet www.aep.com; f. 1906 as the American Gas and Electricity Co; present name adopted 1958; electricity supplier to Arkansas, Indiana, Kentucky, Louisiana, Michigan, Ohio, Oklahoma, Tennessee, Texas, Virginia and West Virginia; Pres., Chair. and CEO MICHAEL G. MORRIS.

American Public Power Association: 2301 M St, NW, 3rd Floor, Washington, DC 20037-1484; tel. (202) 467-2900; fax (202) 467-2910; e-mail mrufe@appanet.org; internet www.appanet.org; f. 1940; asscn of local publicly owned electric utilities; c. 2,000 mems; Chair. MAUDE GRANTHAM-RICHARDS; CEO MARK CRISSOM.

Association of Edison Illuminating Cos: 600 North 18th St, POB 2641, Birmingham, AL 35291-0992; tel. (205) 257-2530; fax (205) 257-2540; e-mail aeicdir@bellsouth.net; internet www.aeic.org; f. 1885; mems comprise 78 investor-owned public utilities; Pres. RICHARD R. GRIGG; Exec. Dir EARL B. PARSONS, Jr.

Edison Electric Institute: 701 Pennsylvania Ave, NW, Washington, DC 2004-2696; tel. (202) 508-5000; fax (202) 508-5759; internet www.eei.org; f. 1933; mems comprise 184 investor-owned electric utility cos in the USA and 63 foreign mems; Chair. JAMES E. ROGERS; Pres. THOMAS R. KUHN.

Energy Telecommunications and Electrical Association (ENTELEC): 5005 West Royal Lane, Suite 190, Irving, TX 75063; tel. (888) 503-8700; fax (972) 915-6040; e-mail blaine@entelec.org; internet www.entelec.org; f. 1928 as the Petroleum Industry Electrical Asscn; changed name as above in 1978; 170 mems; Pres. GREG VAUGHN; Exec. Man. BLAINE SISKE.

National Rural Electric Co-operative Association: 4301 Wilson Blvd, Arlington, VA 22203; tel. (703) 907-5500; e-mail patrick.lavigne@nreca.coop; internet www.nreca.org; f. 1942; operates rural electric co-operative systems and public power distribution in 47 states; 900 mems; CEO GLENN ENGLISH.

Gas

American Gas Association (AGA): 400 North Capitol St, NW, Suite 400, Washington, DC 20001; tel. (202) 824-7000; fax (202) 824-7115; e-mail ccussimanio@aga.org; internet www.aga.org; f. 1918; represents 197 local utility cos; Pres. and CEO DAVID N. PARKER.

American Public Gas Association (APGA): 201 Massachusetts Ave, NE, Suite C-4, Washington, DC 20002; tel. (202) 464-2742; fax (202) 464-0246; e-mail mhager@apga.org; internet www.apga.org; f. 1961; promotes efficiency among public gas systems; 650 mems; Pres. and CEO BERT KALISCH.

Gas Technology Institute: 1700 South Mount Prospect Rd, Des Plaines, IL 60018; tel. (847) 768-0500; fax (847) 768-0501; e-mail businessdevelopmentinfo@gastechnology.org; internet www.gastechnology.org; f. 1976; fmrly Gas Research Institute; 175 mems; Chair. and CEO MARY JANE MCCARTNEY.

Natural Gas Supply Association: 805 15th St, NW, Suite 510, Washington, DC 20005-2207; tel. (202) 326-9300; fax (202) 326-9330; internet www.ngsa.org; f. 1967; monitors legislation and economic issues affecting natural-gas producers; Pres. R. SKIP HORVATH.

Water

American Water Works Association: 6666 West Quincy Ave, Denver, CO 80235-3098; tel. (303) 794-7711; fax (303) 347-0804; e-mail custsvc@awwa.org; internet www.awwa.org; f. 1881; 57,000 mems; Pres. MICHAEL J. LEONARD; Exec. Dir GARY J. ZIMMERMAN.

American Water Works Association Research Foundation (AwwaRF): 6666 West Quincy Ave, Denver, CO 80235-3098; tel. (303) 347-6100; fax (303) 730-0851; e-mail info@awwarf.org; internet www.awwarf.org; f. 1966; Chair. DAVID RAGER.

Association of Metropolitan Water Agencies: 1620 I St, NW, Suite 500, Washington, DC 20006; tel. (202) 331-2820; fax (202) 785-1845; e-mail vandehei@amwa.net; internet www.amwa.net; f. 1981; 63 mems; Pres. BRIAN RAMALEY; Exec. Dir DIANE VANDE HEI.

National Association of Water Companies: 1725 K St, NW, Suite 200, Washington, DC 20006; tel. (202) 833-8383; fax (202) 331-7442; e-mail peter@nawc.com; internet www.nawc.org; f. 1895; privately and commercially owned water cos; 161 mems; Pres. DIAN C. TAYLOR; Exec. Dir PETER L. COOK.

National Rural Water Association: 2915 South 13th St, Duncan, OK 73533; tel. (580) 252-0629; fax (580) 255-4476; e-mail info@nrwa.org; internet www.nrwa.org; Pres. RODNEY TART; Exec. Man. ROB JOHNSON.

TRADE UNIONS

In 2005 there were approximately 15.7m. union members in the USA, representing 12.5% of the civilian labour force.

Many trade unions based in the USA have members throughout North America. Approximately 30% of Canada's trade union members belong to unions having headquarters in the USA.

American Federation of Labor and Congress of Industrial Organizations (AFL-CIO): 815 16th St, NW, Washington, DC 20006; tel. (202) 637-5000; fax (202) 637-5058; internet www.aflcio.org; f. 1955; Pres. JOHN J. SWEENEY; Sec.-Treas. RICHARD L. TRUMKA; 56 affiliated unions with total membership of 10.5m. (2008).

AFL-CIO Affiliates
(with 50,000 members and over)

Amalgamated Transit Union: 5025 Wisconsin Ave, NW, Washington, DC 20016; tel. (202) 537-1645; fax (202) 244-7824; e-mail dispatch@atu.org; internet www.atu.org; f. 1892; Int. Pres. WARREN S. GEORGE; Int. Sec.-Treas. OSCAR OWENS; 160,000 mems (2007).

American Federation of Government Employees: 80 F St, NW, Washington, DC 20001; tel. (202) 639-6419; fax (202) 639-6441; e-mail communications@afge.org; internet www.afge.org; f. 1932; Nat. Pres. JOHN GAGE; 600,000 mems.

American Federation of Musicians of the United States and Canada: Paramount Bldg, Suite 600, 1501 Broadway, New York, NY 10036; tel. (212) 869-1330; fax (212) 764-6134; e-mail naglieri@afm.org; internet www.afm.org; f. 1896; Pres. THOMAS F. LEE; Sec.-Treas. SAM FOLIO; 90,000 mems.

American Federation of State, County and Municipal Employees: 1625 L St, NW, Washington, DC 20036-5687; tel. (202) 429-1000; fax (202) 429-1293; internet www.afscme.org; f. 1936; Pres. GERALD W. MCENTEE; Sec.-Treas. WILLIAM LUCY; 1.4m. mems.

American Federation of Teachers (AFT-AFL-CIO): 555 New Jersey Ave, NW, Washington, DC 20001; tel. (202) 879-4400; fax

THE UNITED STATES OF AMERICA

(202) 879-4556; internet www.aft.org; f. 1916; Pres. RANDI WEINGARTEN; Sec.-Treas. ANTONIA CORTESE; 1.4m. mems (2008).

American Federation of Television and Radio Artists: 260 Madison Ave, 7th Floor, New York, NY 10016-2401; tel. (212) 532-0800; fax (212) 545-1238; e-mail nyfilm@ios.com; internet www.aftra.com; f. 1937; Pres. BOB EDWARDS (acting); more than 70,000 mems (2007).

American Postal Workers Union: 1300 L St, NW, Washington, DC 20005; tel. (202) 842-4200; fax (202) 842-4297; internet www.apwu.org; f. 1971; Pres. WILLIAM BURRUS; Sec.-Treas. TERRY STAPLETON; more than 330,000 mems (2007).

Associated Actors and Artistes of America: 165 46th St West, New York, NY 10036; tel. (212) 869-0358; fax (212) 869-1746; f. 1919; Pres. THEODORE BIKEL; 7 nat. unions representing 125,000 mems.

Bakery, Confectionery, Tobacco Workers' and Grain Millers International Union: 10401 Connecticut Ave, Kensington, MD 20895; tel. (301) 933-8600; fax (301) 946-8452; internet www.bctgm.org; f. 1886; Int. Pres. FRANK HURT; Sec.-Treas. DAVID B. DURKEE; 120,000 mems (2006).

Communications Workers of America: 501 Third St, NW, Washington, DC 20001; tel. (202) 434-1100; fax (202) 434-1279; internet www.cwa-union.org; f. 1939; Pres. LARRY COHEN; Sec.-Treas. JEFFREY A. RECHENBACH; 740,000 mems (2006).

Glass Molders, Pottery, Plastics & Allied Workers International Union (AFL-CIO, CLC): 608 East Baltimore Pike, POB 607, Media, PA 19063-0607; tel. (610) 565-5051; fax (610) 565-0983; e-mail gmpiu@gmpiu.org; internet www.gmpiu.org; f. 1842; Pres. JOHN P. RYAN; Sec.-Treas. BRUCE R. SMITH; 51,000 mems.

Graphic Communications Conference (GCC): 1900 L St, NW, Washington, DC 20036; tel. (202) 462-1400; fax (202) 721-0600; e-mail webmessenger@gciu.org; internet www.gciu.org; f. 2005; Pres. GEORGE TEDESCHI; Sec.-Treas. ROBERT LACEY (acting); 125,000 mems (2003).

International Alliance of Theatrical Stage Employees, Moving Picture Technicians, Artists and Allied Crafts of the US, its Territories and Canada (IATSE): 1430 Broadway, 20th Floor, New York, NY 10018; tel. (212) 730-1770; fax (212) 730-7809; e-mail webmaster@iatse-intl.org; internet www.iatse-intl.org; f. 1893; Int. Pres. MATTHEW D. LOEB; Gen. Sec.-Treas. JAMES B. WOOD; 110,000 mems.

International Association of Bridge, Structural, Ornamental and Reinforcing Iron Workers: 1750 New York Ave, NW, Suite 400, Washington, DC 20006; tel. (202) 383-4800; fax (202) 638-4856; e-mail iwmagazine@iwintl.org; internet www.ironworkers.org; f. 1896; Gen. Pres. JOSEPH J. HUNT; Gen. Sec. WALTER W. WISE; 120,000 mems.

International Association of Fire Fighters: 1750 New York Ave, NW, Washington, DC 20006-5395; tel. (202) 737-8484; fax (202) 737-8418; internet www.iaff.org; f. 1918; Gen. Pres. HAROLD SCHAITBERGER; Sec.-Treas. VINCENT J. BOLLON; 290,000 mems.

International Association of Machinists and Aerospace Workers (IAM): 9000 Machinists Pl., Upper Marlboro, MD 20772-2687; tel. (301) 967-4500; fax (301) 967-4588; e-mail websteward@goiam.org; internet www.iamaw.org; f. 1888; Int. Pres. R. THOMAS BUFFENBARGER; Gen. Sec.-Treas. WARREN L. MART; 730,000 mems (2006).

International Brotherhood of Boilermakers, Iron Ship Builders, Blacksmiths, Forgers and Helpers: 753 State Ave, Suite 570, Kansas City, KS 66101; tel. (913) 371-2640; fax (913) 281-8101; e-mail tracy.buck@boilermakers.org; internet www.boilermakers.org; f. 1880; Int. Pres. NEWTON B. JONES; Int. Sec.-Treas. WILLIAM T. CREEDEN; 100,000 mems.

International Brotherhood of Electrical Workers: 900 Seventh St, NW, Washington, DC 20001; tel. (202) 833-7000; fax (202) 728-7676; e-mail glenn_perusek@ibew.org; internet www.ibew.org; f. 1891; Pres. EDWIN D. HILL; Sec.-Treas. LINDELL K. LEE; 750,000 mems.

International Longshoremen's Association: 17 Battery Pl., Suite 930, New York, NY 10004; tel. (212) 425-1200; fax (212) 425-2928; e-mail jmcnamara@ilaunion.org; internet www.ilaunion.org; f. 1892; Pres. RICHARD P. HUGHES, Jr; Sec.-Treas. ROBERT E. GLEASON; 65,000 mems.

International Union of Bricklayers and Allied Craftworkers: 620 F Street, NW, Washington, DC 20001; tel. (202) 783-3788; fax (202) 393-0219; e-mail askbac@bacweb.org; internet www.bacweb.org; f. 1865; Pres. JOHN J. FLYNN; Sec.-Treas. JAMES BOLAND; 100,000 mems (1999).

International Union of Operating Engineers: 1125 17th St, NW, Washington, DC 20036; tel. (202) 429-9100; fax (202) 778-2616; f. 1896; Gen. Pres. VINCENT J. GIBLIN; Gen. Sec.-Treas. CHRISTOPHER HANLEY; 400,000 mems (2006).

International Union of Painters and Allied Trades: 1750 New York Ave, NW, Washington, DC 20006; tel. (202) 637-0700; f. 1887; Gen. Pres. MICHAEL E. MONROE; Sec.-Treas. JAMES A. WILLIAMS.

International Union of Police Associations: 1549 Ringling Blvd, Suite 600, Sarasota, FL 34236; tel. (941) 487-2560; fax (941) 487-2570; e-mail iupa@iupa.org; internet www.iupa.org; Pres. SAMUEL A. CABRAL; Sec.-Treas. TIMOTHY A. SCOTT; 80,400 mems (2002).

Marine Engineers' Beneficial Association (MEBA): 444 North Capitol St, NW, Suite 800, Washington, DC 20001; tel. (202) 638-5355; fax (202) 638-5369; e-mail mebahq@d1meba.org; internet www.d1meba.org; f. 1875; Pres. DON KEEFE; Sec.-Treas. BILL VAN LOO; 50,000 mems.

National Association of Letter Carriers (NALC): 100 Indiana Ave, NW, Washington, DC 20001-2144; tel. (202) 393-4695; fax (202) 737-1540; e-mail nalcinf@nalc.org; internet www.nalc.org; f. 1889; Pres. WILLIAM H. YOUNG; Sec.-Treas. JANE E. BROENDEL; 300,058 mems (2006).

Office and Professional Employees International Union: 265 West 14th St, Suite 610, New York, NY 10011; tel. (212) 675-3210; fax (212) 727-3466; internet www.opeiu.org; f. 1945; Int. Pres. MICHAEL GOODWIN; Sec.-Treas. NANCY WOHLFORTH; 125,000 mems.

Retail, Wholesale and Department Store Union (RWDSU): 30 East 29th St, New York, NY 10016; tel. (212) 684-5300; fax (212) 779-2809; internet www.rwdsu.org; f. 1937; Pres. STUART APPELBAUM; Sec.-Treas. JACK WURM; 100,000 mems (1997).

Screen Actors Guild: 5757 Wilshire Blvd, Los Angeles, CA 90036-3600; tel. (323) 954-1600; fax (323) 549-6656; internet www.sag.org; f. 1933; Pres. ALAN ROSENBERG; Sec.-Treas. CONNIE STEVENS; 120,000 mems (Feb. 2006).

Seafarers International Union of North America: 5201 Auth Way, Camp Springs, MD 20746; tel. (301) 899-0675; fax (301) 899-7355; e-mail webmaster@seafarers.org; internet www.seafarers.org; f. 1938; Pres. MICHAEL SACCO; Sec.-Treas. DAVID W. HEINDEL; 80,000 mems.

Sheet Metal Workers' International Association: 1750 New York Ave, NW, Washington, DC 20006; tel. (202) 783-5880; fax (202) 662-0894; e-mail info@smwia.org; internet www.smwia.org; f. 1888; Gen. Pres. MICHAEL J. SULLIVAN; Gen. Sec.-Treas. JOSEPH J. NIGRO; 150,000 mems (1999).

Transport Workers' Union of America (TWU): 1700 Broadway, 2nd Floor, New York, NY 10019; e-mail mailbox@twu.org; internet www.twu.org; f. 1934; Int. Pres. JAMES C. LITTLE; Sec.-Treas. JOSEPH C. GORDON; 135,000 mems.

Transportation-Communications International Union: 3 Research Pl., Rockville, MD 20850; tel. (301) 948-4910; fax (301) 948-1369; internet www.goiam.org/tcunion.cfm; f. 1899; affiliated with IAM in 2005, with full merger scheduled before 2012; Pres. ROBERT A. SCARDELLETTI; Sec.-Treas. DANNY L. BIGGS; 46,576 mems (2005).

United Association of Journeymen and Apprentices of the Plumbing and Pipe Fitting Industry of the United States and Canada: 901 Massachusetts Ave, NW, Washington, DC 20001; tel. (202) 628-5823; fax (202) 628-5024; internet www.ua.org; f. 1889; Pres. WILLIAM P. HITE; Sec.-Treas. PATRICK PERNO; 304,000 mems (1999).

United Automobile, Aerospace and Agricultural Implement Workers of America (UAW): Solidarity House, 8000 East Jefferson Ave, Detroit, MI 48214; tel. (313) 926-5000; fax (313) 823-6016; internet www.uaw.org; f. 1935; Pres. RON GETTELFINGER; Sec.-Treas. ELIZABETH BUNN; 640,000 active mems (2006).

United Food and Commercial Workers International Union: 1775 K St, NW, Washington, DC 20006; tel. (202) 223-3111; internet www.ufcw.org; f. 1979; Int. Pres. JOSEPH T. HANSEN; Int. Sec.-Treas. ANTHONY M. PERRONE; 1.3m. mems.

United Mine Workers of America (UMWA): 8315 Lee Highway, Fairfax, VA 22031; tel. (703) 208-7200; internet www.umwa.org; f. 1890; Int. Pres. CECIL E. ROBERTS; Sec.-Treas. DANIEL J. KANE; 130,000 mems (1999).

United Steel, Paper and Forestry, Rubber, Manufacturing, Energy, Allied Industrial and Service Workers International Union (USW) (United Steelworkers): 5 Gateway Center, Pittsburgh, PA 15222; tel. (412) 562-2400; fax (412) 562-2445; e-mail webmaster@usw.org; internet www.usw.org; f. 1936; incorporated PACE International Union in 2005 and Independent Steelworkers Union in 2007; announced agreement in July 2008 to merge with Unite (United Kingdom) to create Workers Uniting; represents workers in the USA, Canada and the Caribbean; Int. Pres. LEO W. GERARD; Sec.-Treas. JAMES D. ENGLISH; 850,000 mems (2007).

United Transportation Union (UTU): 14600 Detroit Ave, Cleveland, OH 44107-4250; tel. (216) 228-9400; fax (216) 228-5755; e-mail pr@utu.org; internet www.utu.org; f. 1969; formed strategic alliance

THE UNITED STATES OF AMERICA

with USW in July 2006; Pres. MALCOLM B. FUTHEY; Gen. Sec. and Treas. KIM N. THOMPSON; 125,000 mems.

Utility Workers Union of America, AFL-CIO: 815 16th St, NW, Washington, DC 20006; tel. (202) 974-8200; fax (202) 974-8201; e-mail rfarley@aflcio.org; internet www.uwua.net; f. 1945; Pres. D. MICHAEL LANGFORD; Sec.-Treas. GARY M. RUFFNER; 50,000 mems (2009).

Independent Unions
(with 50,000 members and over)

American Nurses Association: 8515 Georgia Ave, Suite 400, Silver Spring, MD 20910; tel. (301) 628-5000; fax (301) 628-5001; e-mail ana@ana.org; internet www.nursingworld.org; f. 1896; Pres. REBECCA M. PATTON; 54 constituent mem. state asscns comprising 2.9m. mems.

Change to Win: 1900 L St, NW, Suite 900, Washington, DC 20036; tel. (202) 721-0660; fax (202) 721-0661; e-mail info@changetowin.org; internet www.changetowin.org; f. 2005 following split in the AFL-CIO; Int. Pres. JOSEPH HANSEN; Sec.-Treas. EDGAR ROMNEY.

Affiliates with 50,000 mems and over include:

International Brotherhood of Teamsters: 25 Louisiana Ave, NW, Washington, DC 20001; tel. (202) 624-6800; fax (202) 624-6918; internet www.teamster.org; f. 1903; withdrew from AFL-CIO in 2005; Pres. JAMES P. HOFFA; Gen. Sec.-Treas. C. THOMAS KEEGEL; 1.4m. mems.

Laborers' International Union of North America: 905 16th St, NW, Washington, DC 20006; tel. (202) 737-8320; fax (202) 737-2754; e-mail rgreer@liuna.org; internet www.liuna.org; f. 1903; Pres. TERENCE M. O'SULLIVAN; Gen. Sec.-Treas. ARMAND E. SABATONI; 820,000 mems (2003).

Service Employees' International Union (SEIU): 1313 L St, NW, Washington, DC 20005; tel. (202) 898-3200; fax (202) 898-3304; internet www.seiu.org; f. 1921; withdrew from AFL-CIO in 2005; Pres. ANDREW L. STERN; Sec.-Treas. ANNA BURGER; c. 2m. mems.

UNITE HERE: 275 Seventh Ave, New York, NY 10001-6708; tel. (212) 265-7000; e-mail esharfstein@unitehere.org; internet www.unitehere.org; f. 2004 by merger of the Union of Needletrades, Industrial and Textile Employees (UNITE—f. 1995) and Hotel Employees and Restaurant Employees Int. Union (HERE—f. 1891); Gen. Pres. BRUCE S. RAYNOR; Pres. (Hospitality Industries) JOHN W. WILHELM; c. 450,000 mems.

United Brotherhood of Carpenters and Joiners of America: 101 Constitution Ave, NW, Washington, DC 20001; tel. (202) 546-6206; fax (202) 543-5724; internet www.carpenters.org; f. 1881; withdrew from AFL-CIO in 2001; Pres. DOUGLAS J. MCCARRON; Sec.-Treas. ANDRIS J. SILINS; 520,000 mems (2006).

United Food and Commercial Workers International Union: 1775 K St, NW, Washington, DC 20006; tel. (202) 223-3111; internet www.ufcw.org; f. 1979; Int. Pres. JOSEPH T. HANSEN; Int. Sec.-Treas. ANTHONY M. PERRONE; 1.3m. mems.

Fraternal Order of Police: 701 Marriott Dr., Nashville, TN 37214; tel. (615) 399-0900; fax (615) 399-0400; e-mail pyoes@fop.net; internet www.fop.net; Nat. Pres. CHUCK CANTERBURY; Nat. Sec. PATRICK YOES; 325,000 mems.

International Longshore and Warehouse Union: 1188 Franklin St, 4th Floor, San Francisco, CA 94109-6800; tel. (415) 775-0533; fax (415) 775-1302; e-mail info@ilwu.org; internet www.ilwu.org; f. 1937; Pres. ROBERT MCELLRATH; Sec.-Treas. WILLIAM ADAMS; 59,500 mems (2006).

National Education Association of the United States: 1201 16th St, NW, Washington, DC 20036-3290; tel. (202) 833-4000; fax (202) 822-7974; internet www.nea.org; f. 1857; Pres. DENNIS VAN ROEKEL; Sec.-Treas. REBECCA PRINGLE; 3.2m. mems.

National Federation of Federal Employees: 805 15th St, NW, Suite 500, Washington, DC 20005; tel. (202) 216-4420; fax (202) 898-1861; e-mail guest@nffe.org; internet www.nffe.org; f. 1917; Pres. RICHARD N. BROWN; Sec.-Treas. JOHN M. PAOLINO; 120,000 mems (1999).

National Rural Letter Carriers' Association: 1630 Duke St, 4th Floor, Alexandria, VA 22314-3465; tel. (703) 684-5545; fax (703) 548-8735; internet www.nrlca.org; f. 1903; Pres. DON CANTRIEL; Sec.-Treas. CLIFFORD D. DAILING; 98,000 mems (1999).

National Treasury Employees Union: 1750 H St, NW, Washington, DC 20006; tel. (202) 572-5500; fax (202) 572-5644; internet www.nteu.org; f. 1938; Nat. Pres. COLLEEN M. KELLEY; 150,000 mems.

Transport

Federal Transit Administration: East Bldg, 1200 New Jersey Ave, SE, Washington, DC 20590; tel. (202) 366-4043; e-mail fta.adaassistance@dot.gov; internet www.fta.dot.gov; Exec. Dir MATTHEW WELBES.

National Transportation Safety Board: 490 L'Enfant Plaza, SW, Washington, DC 20594; tel. (202) 314-6000; internet www.ntsb.gov; f. 1967; seeks to ensure that all types of transportation in the USA are conducted safely; carries out studies and accident investigations; Chair. MARK V. ROSENKER (acting).

Surface Transportation Board: Mercury Bldg, 1925 K St, NW, Washington, DC 20423-0001; tel. (202) 245-0245; fax (202) 565-9016; internet www.stb.dot.gov; f. 1995 to succeed Interstate Commerce Commission; exercises regulatory authority over domestic surface common carriers; jurisdiction extends over rail, inland waterways and motorized traffic; Chair. FRANCIS P. MULVEY (acting).

Transportation Security Administration (TSA): 601 South 12th St, Arlington, VA 22202-4220; tel. (866) 289-9673; e-mail tsa-contactcenter@dhs.gov; internet www.tsa.gov; f. 2001 to ensure the security of the country's transport system against possible terrorist attacks; 50,000 employees; Admin. GALE ROSSIDES (acting).

RAILWAYS

In 2005 there were 153,956 km (95,664 miles) of Class I freight railroads, 24,765 km of regional freight railroads and 46,988 km of local freight railroads. In addition, there were 37,015 km of Amtrak passenger railroads.

Federal Railroad Administration: Dept of Transportation, 1200 New Jersey Ave, SE, Washington, DC 20005; tel. (202) 493-6000; fax (202) 493-6013; e-mail webmaster@fra.dot.gov; internet www.fra.dot.gov; f. 1966; part of the Dept of Transportation; formulates federal railway policies and administers and enforces safety regulations; Admin. JOSEPH C. SZABO.

Principal Companies

Alaska Railroad Corpn: 327 West Ship Creek Ave, Anchorage, AK 99510; tel. (907) 265-2695; fax (907) 265-2312; e-mail thompsont@akrr.com; internet www.akrr.com; f. 1912; independent corpn owned by the State of Alaska; year-round freight service and summer passenger service; operates 845 km of track; Pres. and CEO PATRICK GAMBLE.

Amtrak (National Railroad Passenger Corpn): 60 Massachusetts Ave, NE, Washington, DC 20002; tel. (202) 906-3860; fax (202) 906-3306; internet www.amtrak.com; f. 1970; govt-funded private corpn operating inter-city passenger services over 33,796 track-km in 46 states; Chair. THOMAS C. CARPER; Pres. and CEO JOSEPH H. BOARDMAN.

BNSF Railway: 2650 Lou Menk Dr., Fort Worth, TX 76131-2830; tel. (913) 551-4479; fax (913) 551-4285; e-mail steven.forsberg@bnsf.com; internet www.bnsf.com; fmrly Burlington Northern Santa Fe Corpn; freight services; 51,498 track-km; Pres., Chair. and CEO MATTHEW K. ROSE.

Consolidated Rail Corpn (Conrail): 2001 Market St, Philadelphia, PA 19103; tel. (215) 209-2000; e-mail info@conrail.com; internet www.conrail.com; f. 1976 by fed. govt merger of six bankrupt freight carriers; jtly owned by CSX (42%) and Norfolk Southern (58%); switching and terminal railroad operating in three locations: Northern New Jersey, Southern New Jersey/Philadelphia, and Detroit, MI; Pres. and COO RONALD L. BATORY.

CSX Transportation, Inc (Rail Transport): 500 Water St, Jacksonville, FL 32202; tel. (904) 359-3100; internet www.csx.com; f. 1980 by merger; operates 34,371 km of track (2005); Chair., Pres. and CEO MICHAEL J. WARD.

Kansas City Southern Railway Co: 427 West 12th St, Kansas City, MO 64105; tel. (816) 983-1303; internet www.kcsouthern.com; Chair. and CEO MICHAEL R. HAVERTY; Pres. and COO DAVID L. STARLING; operates 4,989 km of track.

Long Island Rail Road Co: Jamaica Station, Jamaica, NY 11435-4380; tel. (718) 558-7400; internet www.mta.info/lirr; f. 1834; operates 3,291 km of track (Dec. 2007); operated by the Metropolitan Transportation Authority—State of New York; Chair. H. DALE HEMMERDINGER; Exec. Dir and CEO ELLIOT G. SANDER.

Norfolk Southern Corpn: NS Tower, 3 Commercial Pl., Norfolk, VA 23510; tel. (757) 629-2600; fax (757) 664-5117; e-mail contactus@nscorp.com; internet www.nscorp.com; f. 1988; operates 37,600 miles of track (2008); Pres., Chair. and CEO C. WICK MOORMAN.

Pan Am Railways: 1700 Iron Horse Park, North Billerica, MA 01862; tel. (978) 663-1130; e-mail customerservice@panamrailways.com; internet www.guilfordrail.com; frmly Guilford Rail System; name changed as above in 2006; Pres. DAVID FINK.

THE UNITED STATES OF AMERICA

Union Pacific Railroad Co: 1400 Douglas St, Omaha, NE 68179; tel. (402) 544-5000; fax (402) 350-7362; internet www.uprr.com; f. 1897; division of Union Pacific Corpn; operates 52,143 km of track in 23 states; Pres. and CEO JAMES R. YOUNG.

Associations

American Short Line and Regional Railroad Association: 50 F St, NW, Suite 7020, Washington, DC 20001; tel. (202) 628-4500; fax (202) 628-6430; e-mail aslrra@aslrra.org; internet www.aslrra.org; f. 1913; 418 mems; operates and maintains 29% of US rail mileage; Pres. and Treas. RICHARD F. TIMMONS.

Association of American Railroads: 50 F St, NW, Washington, DC 20001-1564; tel. (202) 639-2100; fax (202) 639-2286; e-mail preilly@aar.org; internet www.aar.org; f. 1934; membership represents virtually all major railroads in the USA, Canada and Mexico, as well as rail industry products and services; oversees 173,000 miles of track; Pres. and CEO EDWARD R. HAMBERGER.

ROADS

In 2005 there were 75,432 km (46,871 miles) of interstate highway, 185,882 km of other national highway system roads and 6,194,782 km of other roads. Road network kilometres in that year totalled 6,429,154, of which some 64.5% was classified as paved.

Federal Highway Administration (FHWA): 1200 New Jersey Ave, SE, Washington, DC 20590; tel. (202) 366-0604; fax (202) 366-3244; internet www.fhwa.dot.gov; part of the Dept of Transportation; implements federal highway policy and promotes road safety; Admin. THOMAS J. MADISON, Jr.

INLAND WATERWAYS

In 2005 there were some 41,840 km (26,000 miles) of navigable channels in the USA.

St Lawrence Seaway Development Corpn: US Dept of Transportation, 400 Seventh St, SW, Suite 5424, Washington, DC 20590; tel. (202) 366-0091; fax (202) 366-7147; e-mail tim.downey@sls.dot.gov; internet www.seaway.dot.gov; responsible for the operations and maintenance of sections of the St Lawrence Seaway within the territorial limits of the USA; Admin. COLLISTER JOHNSON, Jr.

Principal Companies

American Commercial Lines, Inc: 1701 East Market St, Jeffersonville, IN 47130; tel. (812) 288-0100; e-mail aclinfo@aclines.com; internet www.aclines.com; f. 1915; operates barge services along c. 24,000 km of the Mississippi and Ohio rivers and tributaries to the Gulf Intracoastal Waterway; fleet of 3,375 barges and 120 towboats; Pres. and CEO MICHAEL P. RYAN.

Great Lakes Dredge & Dock Corpn: 2122 York Rd, Oak Brook, IL 60523; tel. (630) 574-3000; fax (630) 574-2909; internet www.gldd.com; f. 1890; dredging, marine construction and reclamation; operates tugboats, drillboats, carfloats, barges and dredges; 180 vessels; Pres. and CEO DOUGLAS B. MACKIE.

Great Lakes Fleet, Inc: 212 South 37th Ave, Suite 200, Duluth, MN 55807; tel. (218) 723-2420; fax (218) 723-2455; internet www.cn.ca/specialized/great_lakes/en_KFGreatLakes.shtml; Gen. Man. CHARLES PATTERSON, III; 8 vessels.

Associations

American Waterways Operators: 801 North Quincy St, Suite 200, Arlington, VA 22203; tel. (703) 841-9300; fax (703) 841-0389; internet www.americanwaterways.com; f. 1944; over 400 mems; Pres. THOMAS A. ALLEGRETTI.

Lake Carriers' Association: 20325 Center Ridge Rd, Suite 720, Rocky River, OH 44116; tel. (440) 333-4444; fax (440) 333-9993; e-mail info@lcaships.com; internet www.lcaships.com; f. 1892; 18 mem. cos; Pres. JAMES H. I. WEAKLEY.

National Waterways Conference, Inc: 4650 Washington Blvd, Suite 608, Arlington, VA 22201; tel. (703) 243-4090; fax (866) 371-1390; e-mail info@waterways.org; internet www.waterways.org; f. 1960; 200 mems; Chair. GARY LAGRANGE; Pres. AMY W. LARSON.

OCEAN SHIPPING

At 31 December 2007 a merchant fleet of 6,486 vessels, with a total displacement of 11,411,335 grt, was registered in the USA.

Federal Maritime Commission: 800 North Capitol St, NW, Washington, DC 20573; tel. (202) 523-5725; fax (202) 523-0014; e-mail secretary@fmc.gov; internet www.fmc.gov; f. 1961 to regulate the water-borne foreign commerce of the USA; comprises 5 Commrs; Chair. (vacant).

Maritime Administration: 1200 New Jersey Ave, SE, Washington, DC 20590; tel. (202) 366-5807; e-mail pao.marad@dot.gov; internet www.marad.dot.gov; concerned with promoting the US Merchant Marine; also administers subsidy programmes to ship operators; Administrator JAMES E. CAPONITI (acting).

Principal Ports

The three largest ports in the USA, in terms of traffic handled, are the Port of South Louisiana, handling 243m. tons in 2005, Houston (200m. tons in 2005) and New York (84.8m. tons in 2005). Many other large ports serve each coast, 24 of them handling between 25m. and 85m. tons of traffic annually. The deepening of channels and locks on the St Lawrence–Great Lakes Waterway, allowing the passage of large ocean-going vessels, has increased the importance of the Great Lakes ports, of which the largest, Duluth-Superior, handled an average annual 40m. tons.

Principal Companies

Alcoa Steamship Co, Inc: 201 Isabella St, Pittsburgh, PA 15212-5858; tel. (412) 553-4545; fax (412) 553-2624; bulk services worldwide; 5 vessels; Pres. R. S. HOSPODAR.

American President Lines Ltd (APL): 1111 Broadway, Oakland, CA 94607-5500; tel. (510) 272-8000; e-mail paul_barrett@nol.com.sg; internet www.apl.com; f. 1938; serves east and west coasts of North America, Mexico, Caribbean Basin, Middle East and Far East; wholly owned subsidiary of Neptune Orient Lines (Singapore); 100 vessels; CEO ENG AIK MENG.

Central Gulf Lines, Inc: 11 North Water St, Suite 18290, Mobile, AL 36602; tel. (251) 243-9228; e-mail wildkm@intship.com; internet www.intship.com/cgl.htm; Vice-Pres. KEVIN M. WILD.

Chevron Shipping Co: 6001 Bollinger Canyon Rd, San Ramon, CA 94583-5177; tel. (925) 842-1000; e-mail comment@chevron.com; internet www.chevron.com; f. 1895; subsidiary of Chevron Corpn; world-wide tanker sevices; regional offices in Houston, London, United Kingdom, and Singapore; 39 tankers; Chair. and CEO DAVID J. O'REILLY.

Colonial Marine Industries, Inc: Hamilton House, 26 East Bryan St, POB 9981, Savannah, GA 31412; tel. (912) 233-7000; fax (912) 232-8216; e-mail colonial@colonialmarine.com; internet www.colonialmarine.com; 5 vessels; Exec. Vice-Pres. RICHARD C. WIGGER.

Coscol Marine Corpn: 9 Greenway Plaza, Houston, TX 77046; tel. (713) 877-3370; fax (713) 877-3433; e-mail edward.knutsen@coastalcorp.com; subsidiary of the Coastal Corpn; 4 tankers; Pres. EDWARD W. KNUTSEN.

Crowley Maritime Corpn: 555 12th St, Suite 2130, Oakland, CA 94607; tel. (510) 251-7500; fax (510) 251-7510; internet www.crowley.com; f. 1892; 280 vessels; Pres., Chair. and CEO THOMAS B. CROWLEY, Jr.

Energy Transportation Group, Inc: 654 Madison Ave, New York, NY 10022; tel. (212) 813-9360; fax (212) 813-6390; e-mail info@etgglobal.com; internet www.etgglobal.com; 8 vessels; Chair. and CEO KIMBALL C. CHEN; Pres. and COO ALEX W. EVANS.

ExxonMobil Corpn: 3225 Gallows Rd, Fairfax, VA 22037; tel. (703) 846-3000; 32 vessels; Chair. and CEO REX W. TILLERSON.

Horizon Lines: 4064 Colony Rd, Suite 200, Charlotte, NC; tel. (704) 973-7000; e-mail customercare@horizonlines.com; internet www.horizon-lines.com; f. 2001; Chair., Pres. and CEO CHARLES G. RAYMOND; 21 vessels.

Lykes Lines Ltd: 401 East Jackson St, Suite 3300, POB 31244, Tampa, FL 33631-3244; tel. (813) 276-4600; fax (813) 276-4873; f. 1997; routes from US Gulf and Atlantic ports to United Kingdom and northern Europe, Mediterranean and Africa.

Maritime Overseas Corpn: 511 Fifth Ave, New York, NY 10017; tel. (212) 953-4100; fax (212) 536-3735; manages c. 60 tankers and dry bulk carriers.

Matson Navigation Co: 555 12th St, Suite 700, Oakland, CA 94607; tel. (510) 628-4000; e-mail general_info@matson.com; internet www.matson.com; f. 1901; container and other freight services between US west coast and Hawaii; container leasing world-wide; subsidiary of Alexander & Baldwin, Inc; 17 vessels; Chair. W. ALLEN DOANE; Pres. and CEO JAMES S. ANDRASICK.

OMI Corpn: 1 Station Pl., Stamford, CT 06902; tel. (203) 602-6700; fax (203) 602-6701; e-mail info@omicorp.com; internet www.omicorp.com; acquired by Teekay Corpn and A/S Dampkibsselskabet TORM in June 2007; 43 vessels; Chair. and CEO CRAIG H. STEVENSON, Jr; Pres. and COO ROBERT BUGBEE.

Stolt-Nielsen Transportation Group, Inc: 800 Connecticut Ave, 4th Floor, East Norwalk, CT 06854; tel. (203) 838-7100; fax (203) 299-0067; internet www.stolt-nielsen.com; over 130 tankers; Chair. JACOB STOLT-NIELSEN; CEO NIELS G. STOLT-NIELSEN.

Waterman Steamship Corpn: 1 Whitehall St, New York, NY 10004; tel. (212) 747-8550; fax (212) 747-8588; e-mail waterman@intship.com; internet www.waterman-steamship.com; f. 1919; owned by International Shipholding Corpn; services between the USA and the Middle East.

THE UNITED STATES OF AMERICA

Associations

American Bureau of Shipping: 16855 Northchase Dr., Houston, TX 77060; tel. (281) 877-5800; fax (281) 877-5803; e-mail abs-worldhq@eagle.org; internet www.eagle.org; f. 1862; 814 mems; Chair. ROBERT D. SOMMERVILLE; Pres. CHRISTOPHER WIERNICKI.

American Maritime Congress: Hall of the States, Suite G-50, 400 North Capitol St, NW, Washington, DC 20001; tel. (202) 347-8020; fax (202) 347-1550; internet www.americanmaritime.org; f. 1977 as Joint Maritime Congress; adopted current name 1989; mems represent major US-flag ship operating cos; Chair. DON KEEFE.

Chamber of Shipping of America (CSA): 1730 M St, NW, Suite 407, Washington, DC 20036-4517; tel. (202) 775-4399; fax (202) 659-3795; e-mail omoore@knowships.org; internet www.knowships.org; fmrly American Institute of Merchant Shipping; 31 mem. cos; Pres. and CEO JOSEPH J. COX.

CIVIL AVIATION

Federal Aviation Administration: 800 Independence Ave, SW, Washington, DC 20591; tel. (202) 366-4000; internet www.faa.gov; f. 1958; part of the Dept of Transportation; promotes safety in the air, regulates air commerce and assists in development of an effective national airport system; Administrator ROBERT A. STURGELL (acting).

Principal Scheduled Companies

In 2006 there were 5,233 public-use airports in the USA. In 2003 there were 80 registered air carriers operating in the USA; of these, 14 companies were classified as major carriers.

Alaska Airlines: 19300 International Blvd, POB 68900, Seattle, WA 98188; tel. (206) 433-3200; fax (206) 392-7750; e-mail reservations@alaskaair.com; internet www.alaskaair.com; f. 1932; scheduled passenger services to 70 destinations in the USA, Canada and Mexico; Pres., Chair. and CEO WILLIAM S. AYER.

Horizon Air: 19521 Pacific Hwy South, Seattle, WA 98188; tel. (206) 431-3647; e-mail support@horizonair.com; internet www.horizonair.com; f. 1981; scheduled cargo services; Pres. and CEO JEFFERY D. PINNEO.

American Airlines, Inc: POB 619612, Dallas/Fort Worth Airport, TX 75261-9612; tel. (817) 967-1234; fax (817) 962-4162; internet www.aa.com; f. 1934; coast-to-coast domestic routes, and services to Canada, Hawaii, Mexico, the Caribbean, South America, Europe and the Far East; acquired Trans World Airlines in 2001; Pres., Chair. and CEO GERARD J. ARPEY.

Continental Airlines, Inc: POB 4607, Houston, TX 77210-4607; 1600 Smith St, Houston, TX 77002; tel. (713) 324-5152; fax (713) 324-2637; e-mail geninfo@coair.com; internet www.continental.com; f. 1934; serves 154 US destinations and 138 international destinations; Pres. JEFF SMISEK.

Delta Air Lines, Inc: 1030 Delta Blvd, POB 20706, Atlanta, GA 30320-6001; tel. (770) 715-2600; internet www.delta.com; f. 1928; merged with Northwest Airlines in 2008; domestic and international services to 368 destinations in 66 countries; CEO RICHARD H. ANDERSON.

Hawaiian Airlines, Inc: 3375 Koapaka St, G-350, Honolulu, HI 96819; tel. (808) 835-3700; fax (808) 835-3690; internet www.hawaiianair.com; f. 1929 as Inter-Island Airways Ltd; inter-island, US mainland and South Pacific services; Pres. and CEO MARK B. DUNKERLEY.

Southwest Airlines: POB 36647, Dallas, TX 75235-1647; tel. (214) 792-4223; internet www.southwest.com; f. 1971; scheduled services to 64 cities in 32 states; Pres. COLLEEN BARRETT; Chair. and CEO GARY KELLY.

United Airlines Corpn: POB 66100, Chicago, IL 60666; tel. (847) 700-9838; fax (847) 700-4081; internet www.united.com; f. 1931; domestic and international services to over 200 destinations; Pres., Chair. and CEO GLENN F. TILTON, Jr.

US Airways, Inc: 4000 East Sky Harbor Blvd, Phoenix, AZ 85034; tel. (480) 693-0800; fax (480) 693-2300; internet www.usairways.com; f. 1939 as All-American Airways; merged with America West Airlines in 2005; scheduled passenger services to 237 destinations world-wide; Chair. and CEO DOUG PARKER; Pres. SCOTT KIRBY.

Associations

Air Transport Association of America, Inc: 1301 Pennsylvania Ave, NW, Suite 1100, Washington, DC 20004-1707; tel. (202) 626-4000; fax (202) 626-4181; e-mail ata@airlines.org; internet www.airlines.org; f. 1936; 18 US airlines mems, 3 non-US assoc. mems; Pres. and CEO JAMES C. MAY.

National Air Carrier Association: 1000 Wilson Blvd, Suite 1700, Arlington, VA 22209; tel. (703) 358-8060; e-mail eheffernan@naca.cc; internet www.naca.cc; f. 1962; 16 mems; Pres. TOM ZOELLER.

National Air Transportation Association: 4226 King St, Alexandria, VA 22302; tel. (703) 845-9000; fax (703) 845-8176; internet www.nata.aero; f. 1940; approx. 2,000 mems; Pres. JAMES K. COYNE.

Regional Airline Association: 2025 M St, NW, Suite 800, Washington, DC 20036-3309; tel. (202) 367-1170; fax (202) 367-2170; e-mail raa@raa.org; internet www.raa.org; f. 1975; 42 mems; Pres. ROGER COHEN.

Tourism

American Society of Travel Agents: 1101 King St, Alexandria, VA 22314; tel. (703) 739-2782; fax (703) 684-8319; e-mail askasta@asta.com; internet www.asta.org; f. 1931; Pres. and CEO CHERYL HUDAK; Exec. Vice-Pres. and COO WILLIAM A. MALONEY; over 20,000 mems.

Office of Travel and Tourism Industries: International Trade Administration, US Department of Commerce, 14th and Constitution Ave, NW, Rm 1003, Washington, DC 20230; tel. (202) 482-0140; fax (202) 482-2887; e-mail tinet_info@ita.doc.gov; internet tinet.ita.doc.gov; f. 1996; fed. govt agency; collects and analyses data and develops US tourism policy; Dir HELEN MARANO; Dep. Asst Sec. for Services ANA GUEVARA.

United States Travel Association: 1100 New York Ave, NW, Suite 450, Washington, DC 20005-3934; tel. (202) 408-8422; fax (202) 408-1225; internet www.ustravel.org; f. 2009 after merger between Travel Industry Association (f. 1941) and the Travel Business Roundtable; Pres. and CEO ROGER DOW; Chair. CAROLINE BETETA.

UNITED STATES COMMONWEALTH TERRITORIES

There are two US Commonwealth Territories, the Northern Mariana Islands, in the Pacific Ocean, and Puerto Rico, in the Caribbean Sea. A Commonwealth is a self-governing incorporated territory that is an integral part of, and in full political union with, the USA.

THE NORTHERN MARIANA ISLANDS

Introductory Survey

Location, Climate, Language, Religion, Flag, Capital

The Commonwealth of the Northern Mariana Islands comprises 14 islands (all the Marianas except Guam) in the western Pacific Ocean, about 5,300 km (3,300 miles) west of Honolulu (Hawaii). The temperature normally ranges between 24°C (75°F) and 30°C (86°F) in June–November, but is generally cooler and drier from December to May. The average annual rainfall is about 2,120 mm (84 ins). English, Chamorro and Carolinian are the official languages. The population is predominantly Christian, mainly Roman Catholic. The national flag of the United States of America (q.v.) is used by the Northern Mariana Islands. Six islands, including the three largest (Saipan, Tinian and Rota), are inhabited; the principal settlement and the administrative centre are on Saipan.

Recent History

The islands that comprise the Territory of the Northern Mariana Islands were first sighted by Europeans during the 1520s, and were claimed for Spain in 1565. They were sold to Germany in 1899, but control was transferred to Japan, which had taken the islands from Germany in 1914, by the League of Nations in 1921. During the Second World War the USA captured Saipan and Tinian from the Japanese, after fierce fighting in 1944, and the Northern Mariana Islands became a part of the Trust Territory of the Pacific Islands in 1947 (see the chapter on the Marshall Islands).

In June 1975 the Northern Mariana Islands voted for separate status as a US Commonwealth Territory, and in March 1976 President Gerald Ford of the USA signed the Northern Marianas Commonwealth Covenant. In October 1977 US President Jimmy Carter approved the Constitution of the Northern Mariana Islands, which provided for the former Marianas District to be internally self-governing from January 1978. In December 1977 elections took place for a bicameral legislature, a Governor and a Lieutenant-Governor. The gubernatorial election was won by Carlos Camacho of the Democratic Party, who took office in January 1978. The islanders also elected a Resident Representative (known as the 'Washington Representative') to promote their interests in the federal legislature in Washington, DC. In early 1982, following his defeat in the election held in late 1981, Camacho was replaced by Pedro (Pete) Tenorio of the Republican Party. The Northern Marianas were formally admitted to US Commonwealth status in November 1986, after the ending of the Trusteeship in the Territory. At the same time a proclamation issued by US President Ronald Reagan conferred US citizenship on the islands' residents.

At elections in late 1989 Republicans retained control of the governorship of the Northern Marianas and ousted a Democrat from the position of the islands' Resident Representative in Washington, DC. Lorenzo (Larry) De Leon Guerrero was elected Governor, following Pedro Tenorio's decision to resign. However, candidates of the Democratic Party won a majority of seats in the islands' House of Representatives.

Guerrero took office in January 1990. In December the UN Security Council voted to end the Trusteeship of the Northern Marianas, as well as that of two other Pacific Trust Territories. Although the decision to terminate the relationship had been taken in 1986, voting had been delayed. However, Governor Guerrero opposed the termination on the grounds that the new relationship would leave the islands subject to US law while remaining unrepresented in the US Congress.

At elections conducted in late 1991 Republicans regained a majority in the islands' House of Representatives (which had been enlarged by three seats), and in the Senate the Republican Party increased the number of its representatives to eight. Republicans retained their majority at elections to the House of Representatives in 1993. However, in the gubernatorial election a Democrat, Froilan Tenorio, was successful; Jesús Borja was elected as Lieutenant-Governor. Juan N. Babauta remained as the Northern Marianas' Resident Representative in Washington, DC.

The Territory's reputation was marred in April 1995 when the Government of the Philippines introduced a ban on its nationals accepting unskilled employment in the islands, owing to persistent reports of abuse and exploitation of immigrant workers. Meanwhile, the US Congress announced that it was to allocate US $7m. towards the enforcement of the islands' labour and immigration laws, following the publication of a report in late 1994 that alleged the repeated violations of these regulations, as well as widespread corruption among immigration officials and business leaders.

In May 1997 US President Bill Clinton informed Governor Tenorio of his intention to apply US immigration and minimum wage laws to the Territory, stating that labour practices in the islands were inconsistent with US values. In the previous month Democratic Congressman George Miller had proposed legislation (the Insular Fair Wage and Human Rights Act) in the US House of Representatives that would equalize the minimum wage level in the islands with that of the US mainland by 1999. The Territory's Government, which denied many of the claims of exploitation of immigrant workers, responded to the proposed legislation by successfully lobbying the Republican majority in the US House of Representatives to oppose the bill.

In January 1999 the Office of Insular Affairs (OIA) of the US Department of the Interior published a report in which it concluded that the Government's attempts to eradicate abuses of labour and immigration laws had been unsuccessful. In particular, the islands' administration was deemed to have failed to reduce the Territory's reliance on alien workers, to enforce US minimum wage laws and to curb evasions of trade legislation governing the export of garments to the USA. In the same month former employees of 18 US clothing retailers initiated legal action against the companies, which were accused of failing to comply with US labour laws in Saipan. In April 2000 a settlement was reached with the garment manufacturers, providing some US $8m. in compensation for the workers. The companies also agreed to conform to regulations established by an independent monitoring system in Saipan.

At the islands' legislative elections in November 1997 Republican candidates won 13 of the 18 seats in the House of Representatives and eight of the nine seats in the Senate. At the gubernatorial election, held concurrently, the incumbent Pedro Tenorio was successful, securing 46% of total votes. However, opponents of Tenorio subsequently initiated an unsuccessful legal challenge to his re-election on the grounds that his return to office constituted his third term as Governor, thereby violating the Constitution: this stated that a maximum of two gubernatorial terms could be served by any one individual, although the Constitution had been amended to include this provision only during the course of Tenorio's second term of office. Following legislative elections in November 1999, Democratic candidates held six of the 18 seats in the House of Representatives and two of the nine seats in the Senate.

In February 2000 the US Senate approved a bill granting permanent residency in the Northern Marianas to some 40,000 immigrant workers. However, the bill also included provisions for limiting the stay of all future guest workers. In December 2000 Governor Tenorio announced that he was to oppose the decision by the US Government to bring the Northern Marianas' labour and immigration laws under federal control; Tenorio argued that this would have a negative impact on the Northern Marianas' economy. In May 2001, following intense lobbying by the Northern Marianas Government, the US Congress abandoned the bill. The issue of permanent residency for qualified immigrant workers re-emerged in 2007 with the introduction of minimum wage legislation (see below).

Legislative elections were held in November 2001, at which the Republican Party secured 12 seats in the House of Representatives, the Democratic Party won five and the Covenant Party took one. The Republican Party won six seats in the Senate, the Democratic Party two and the Covenant Party one. At the concurrent gubernatorial election Juan Babauta, the Republican Party candidate and former Washington Representative won a convincing victory, securing 42.8% of the votes cast. Benigno R. Fitial, of the Covenant Party, received 24.4%. Babauta was inaugurated as Governor in January

2002, while Diego Benavente, the former Speaker of the House of Representatives, became Lieutenant-Governor.

In January 2002 the Supreme Court suspended deportation proceedings against an immigrant labourer working illegally in the Northern Marianas, after he appealed to the office of the UN High Commissioner for Refugees. The Court warned the Government that it might not be able to order the deportation of up to 10,000 of the Chinese, Sri Lankan and Bangladeshi workers in the Northern Marianas. In late 2002 the Government successfully resisted an attempt by the US Administration to place the Northern Mariana Islands' immigration and labour legislation under direct federal control. In September 2003 the Northern Mariana Islands announced the conclusion of a new immigration co-operation agreement with the US Department of the Interior, which removed the right of overseas political refugees in the territory to seek asylum in the USA.

In May 2002 the issue of the Northern Marianas' working conditions was raised again by US Senator Edward Kennedy, who proposed a bill that would incrementally increase the minimum wage. In September seven further major US clothing retailers agreed to pay US $11.25m. in compensation to employees alleged to have suffered intolerable working conditions and poor rates of pay. The funds also included sponsorship of independent monitoring of labour conditions in the islands. The case was finally settled in April 2003, when a total of $20m. in compensation was ordered to be paid to the claimants. The Garment Oversight Board was constituted in June, with the authority to withdraw certification of working conditions in garment factories supplying major US clothing companies. In March 2004 the Board decertified one of the 26 participating garment manufacturers. In April more than 400 garment workers were referred to the Division of Immigration for probable deportation as a result of their non-co-operation with a Fair Labor Standards Act civil action against garment manufacturers. Nevertheless, a delegate from the US Commission on Civil Rights concluded in May of that year that the situation of garment workers on Saipan appeared to be improving. However, owing to unfavourable external circumstances (see Economic Affairs), in 2005 about a dozen garment factories had ceased operations or reduced their work-force. In early April the repatriation of migrant workers no longer in employment began. In mid-2005 the minimum hourly wage in the Northern Marianas stood at $3.05, some 40% less than the rate prevailing on the US mainland. Legislation seeking to harmonize the minimum wage in the Northern Marianas with that of the USA was introduced in the US Senate in May. The legislation was criticized by the Speaker of the islands' House of Representatives, Benigno Fitial, who believed that the resultant rise in the minimum wage would place the Northern Marianas at a disadvantage with regional competitors. In July 2005, after further lobbying from the Government and the Saipan Chamber of Commerce, the Northern Marianas were excluded from minimum wage legislation that would have ensured equivalence with the US wage increase to $7.25 an hour. In late January 2007 the Northern Marianas were finally included in the new legislation, while various tax concessions were provisionally approved to ease any losses incurred by small businesses as a result of the increase. The legislation, which was yet to be ratified, also sought to allow qualified immigrant workers to apply for permanent residency. However, within the Northern Marianas strong opposition to the federal legislation continued, as more garment factories risked closure. In early 2008 the islands' once thriving garment industry faced further decline, with the number of operating factories having dwindled to fewer than 10.

In May 2002 the Government 'froze' the assets of the Bank of Saipan, pending auditing of its accounts, after the institution's former Chairman was arrested for allegedly attempting to defraud the bank of more than US $6.6m. The bank, which was reported to hold substantial uninsured US government deposits, was placed in receivership and remained closed for 11 months. Following the bank's reopening in April 2003 with assets of some $12m., customers were permitted to retrieve a limited monthly quota of savings deposits. Four defendants were convicted in relation to the case in June.

In September 2002 Governor Babauta proposed reforms to reduce government expenditure. In November the Government announced plans for a US $40m. bond issue to cover the cost of compensating traditional landowners for the loss of property expropriated for government use, and in April 2003 draft legislation was proposed that would substantially reduce government personnel costs. However, in August credit ratings agencies expressed concerns that the Government's other outstanding debts, in particular those to the Northern Mariana Islands' Retirement Fund, would prevent full repayment of the bonds.

At the islands' legislative elections of 1 November 2003 the Covenant Party gained a majority in the House of Representatives, winning nine of the 18 seats. The Republican Party secured seven seats, the Democrat Party took one seat and an independent candidate won one seat. The Covenant Party won three seats in the Senate, the Republican Party took two and the Democratic Party won one; three independent candidates were also elected.

Several instances of corruption in public office were reported in 2003; in April Senator Ricardo S. Atalig was found guilty of illegally employing relatives of another Senator, José M. de la Cruz (who was suspended from office following his own conviction in July). In August 2004 the Superior Court convicted the chief financial officer of Tinian municipality, Romeo Atalig Diaz, in the first public corruption case lodged by the new anti-corruption unit of the Attorney-General's Office. However, the sentence imposed (fines totalling only US $2,800) was considered derisory by the local press.

At legislative elections held on 5 November 2005 the Covenant Party won eight seats in the House of Representatives, the Republican Party seven seats, the Democratic Party two seats and an independent candidate one seat. Following the election, the Covenant Party and the Republican Party each held three seats in the Senate, the Democratic Party had two seats and there was one independent senator. At the concurrent gubernatorial election Benigno Fitial of the Covenant Party and Timothy P. Villagomez, hitherto Vice-Speaker of the House, were elected Governor and Lieutenant-Governor, respectively, winning 3,809 votes (equivalent to 28.0% of valid votes cast). Independent Republican Heinz S. Hofschneider and his vice-gubernatorial candidate, David M. Apatang, received 3,710 votes (27.3%), while incumbent Governor Babauta and Lieutenant-Governor Diego Benavente garnered 3,610 votes (26.7%). The new Governor and Vice-Governor took office in January 2006.

In March 2006 Jack Abramoff, who was involved, along with other lobbyists and government officials, in transforming and impeding congressional action relating to the Northern Marianas (particularly with regard to the issue of the federal minimum wage—see above), was sentenced to five years and 10 months in prison on fraud and conspiracy charges, and ordered to pay restitution of more than US $21m. Abramoff and his law firm had reportedly received large sums of money from the Northern Marianas Government between 1995 and 2001.

Legislative elections were held on 3 November 2007, with the number of seats in the islands' House of Representative having been increased to 20. The Republican Party regained a majority in the House of Representatives, securing 12 seats, while the Covenant Party won four seats, the Democratic Party one seat and independent candidates three seats. In the mid-term Senate elections, three incumbents (two independent candidates and one Covenant Party candidate) were re-elected to the three contested seats. The electorate also voted on several municipal and judicial posts, along with issues such as gaming. In January 2008 the House of Representatives elected Arnold I. Palacios as its Speaker.

In August 2008 Lieutenant-Governor Timothy Villagomez was indicted for conspiracy, wire fraud and theft, along with Tony Guerrero, former executive director of the Commonwealth Utilities Corporation (CUC). Also indicted were the Lieutenant-Governor's sister, Joaquina V. Santos, and James Santos, his brother-in-law and the islands' Secretary of Commerce. It was alleged in the indictment that Lieutenant-Governor Villagomez had presided over a scheme to misappropriate federal funds by exaggerating the cost of financial transactions with the CUC pertaining to the purchase of chemicals. Shortly after the indictment James Santos resigned from office, although Villagomez retained his position pending a trial, which commenced in March 2009.

In September 2008 Governor Benigno Fitial filed legal proceedings against the US Government to prevent the implementation, scheduled for June 2009, in the Northern Marianas of the federalization law. Fitial submitted a request to the US District Court for a permanent injunction against the US Administration on the basis that the federalization law, introducing new restrictions on immigration policy, violated aspects of the islands' right to self-government.

In April 2009 Timothy Villagomez resigned as Lieutenant-Governor after being convicted on corruption charges. Governor Fitial appointed Eloy Inos as the new Lieutenant-Governor following consultations with the Senate in May.

Unlike other US territories such as American Samoa and Guam, the Northern Marianas continued to be represented in the federal legislature by the islands' Resident Representative in Washington, DC. However, in early 2004 the Northern Marianas requested provision for the appointment of a non-voting delegate to the US Congress from the islands. In May four members of the original team of Covenant negotiators gave public consideration to the possibility of the Northern Marianas becoming the 51st state of the USA. Upon the US House of Representatives' approval of the Northern Mariana Islands Immigration, Security, and Labor Act in December 2007, the bill was transferred to the US Senate, which returned it to the House of Representatives with amendments in April 2008. In May US President George W. Bush approved the legislation, which brought the Northern Marianas under federal immigration laws and created a delegate seat for the Territory in the US House of Representatives. In November 2008 the congressional election was held to select the Northern Marianas' first delegate to represent the Territory in Washington. Gregorio Sablan, a former Democratic member of the islands' House of Representatives standing as an independent candidate, won the election with 2,474 votes, defeating his Republican rival Pete Tenorio, who received 2,117 votes. Sablan vowed to improve relations with the federal Government and was sworn into office in January 2009.

Government

Legislative authority is vested in the Northern Marianas Commonwealth Legislature, a bicameral body consisting of the Senate and the House of Representatives. There are nine senators, elected for four-year terms, and 20 members of the House of Representatives, elected for two-year terms. Executive authority is vested in the Governor, who is elected by popular vote for a four-year term. The islands are represented in the federal legislature by their Resident Representative ('Washington Representative'). The Northern Marianas' first non-voting delegate was elected in November 2008.

Defence

The USA is responsible for the defence of the Northern Marianas.

Economic Affairs

The Commonwealth of the Northern Mariana Islands' gross national income (GNI) was estimated by the Bank of Hawaii (BOH) to be US $696.3m. in 1999. GNI per head was estimated at $8,582. According to the UN's 2006 revision of population prospects, the population of the Northern Marianas increased at an estimated annual rate of some 2.7% during 2000–08. According to estimates by the Secretariat of the Pacific Community, the territory's gross domestic product (GDP) totalled $948.7m. in 2005, equivalent to $12,638 per head. Total reported business gross revenue (BGR—a measure of total revenues generated by business transactions which provides an indicator of economic performance in the absence of gross domestic product data, which the Government does not publish) was recorded at $1,689m. in 2008.

Agriculture is concentrated in smallholdings, important crops being taro, sweet potatoes, coconuts, breadfruit, bananas and melons. Cattle-ranching is practised on Tinian. Vegetables, beef and pork are produced for export. There is little commercial fishing in the islands (the total catch was 183 metric tons in 2006), although there is a major transshipment facility at Tinian harbour. Agriculture (including forestry, fishing and mining) engaged 1.5% of the employed labour force, according to the census of 2000, and its commercial value as a sector is minimal, although FAO estimated that almost 25% of the total labour force was engaged in the sector, largely at subsistence level, in 2005. In 2002 the sector accounted for only 0.1% of BGR.

Industry (including manufacturing and construction) engaged 47.2% of the employed labour force in 2000. Manufacturing alone engaged 31.4% of payroll workers according to a US economic survey of island areas conducted in 2007. The principal manufacturing activity has been the garment industry, which grew rapidly after its establishment in the mid-1980s to become the islands' leading export sector. Manufacturers benefited from US regulations that permitted duty-free and quota-free imports from the Commonwealth. Garment manufacturing accounted for 23.6% of BGR in 2002, and overall exports of garments were worth US $1,017m. in 2000. However, following the liberalization of trade regulations in January 2005, which allowed developing countries to export garments to the USA, about 13 garment factories closed down. By 2008 the value of exports of garments was estimated to have dwindled to just $98.2m. In February 2009 Saipan's two remaining garment factories were closed down, signalling an end to production on the islands. Other small-scale manufacturing activities include handicrafts and the processing of fish and copra. Construction is very closely related to the tourist industry and demand for additional hotel capacity.

Service industries dominate the economy, particularly tourism. In 2000 services (including utilities) engaged 51.3% of the employed labour force, and accounted for 29.2% of BGR. According to the 2007 US economic census of island areas, some 21% of payroll workers were employed in hotels and restaurants. However, tourism receipts declined from an estimated US $430m. in 2001 to $225m. in 2002, and visitor numbers decreased from almost 600,000 in 2004 to some 400,000 in 2008. Japan provided the majority (51%) of the islands' visitors in 2008. Other significant sources of tourists were the Republic of Korea, Guam, the USA and the People's Republic of China. In 1995 a US company opened the Territory's first casino on Tinian (gambling being prohibited on other islands). The Northern Marianas were expected to receive some $12m. annually in revenue from this casino, and further large leisure industry developments were announced for Tinian in 2005.

The Northern Marianas are dependent on imports, the value of which totalled US $267.2m. in 2000. The principal imports in that year were clothing (which accounted for 27.6% of the total), beverages (2.8%), construction materials (2.8%) and automobiles and parts (2.2%). In 1991 there was a trade deficit of $126.9m. In 2008 remittances from overseas workers and investments were valued at $76.8m.

The annual rate of inflation averaged 1.6% in 2000–07. Consumer prices increased by 4.9% in 2006, and by 6.9% in 2007.

Under the Covenant between the Commonwealth of the Northern Mariana Islands and the USA, the islands receive substantial annual development grants. Loans from the Commonwealth Development Authority totalled more than US $0.5m. in 2001.

The Territory is a member of the Pacific Community (see p. 391) and an associate member of the UN Economic and Social Commission for Asia and the Pacific (ESCAP, see p. 36).

Continued economic problems in the Territory have been largely attributed to the substantial increase in the Northern Marianas' population. The main constraints on development have included the inadequacy of the islands' infrastructure, labour shortages and the dependence on foreign workers, Filipino nationals in particular. However, owing to the large numbers of immigrant workers, wages remained relatively low, amid widespread complaints of poor working conditions, which led to legal action (see Recent History). The cessation of garment manufacturing (see above) was estimated to have precipitated a 35.6% decline in employment during 2004–08. None the less, the Northern Mariana Islands have long benefited from their political association with the USA; US federal funding and development assistance totalled some US $13m. in 2001/02, and in January 2004 an agreement was signed whereby the Northern Mariana Islands were to receive some US $5.1m. in federal funding in order to offset the impact of migration, under the Compact of Free Association, to the Territory from the Marshall Islands, the Federated States of Micronesia, and Palau. In 2002 the Government introduced tax incentives for new businesses and developers. Despite improved expenditure controls, the continued recession in the islands led to a deterioration in the Government's fiscal position and an increase in public debt. Adverse conditions resulting from the international financial crisis in the latter part of 2008 were likely to lead to a further decline in tourist arrivals, particularly given the onset of a recession in Japan. Owing to the closure of the garment industry (see above), tourism had become the main source of income on the islands. The tourism sector was further threatened by difficulties in the airline industry: a merger between Delta Airlines and Northwest Airlines led to the announcement, in January 2009, that services between Japan and the Northern Mariana Islands were to be significantly reduced. Furthermore, the application of US immigration law to the territory (scheduled to take effect from 1 June 2009) was to deprive citizens of China and Russia the right to special visitor permits, thereby requiring tourists from these countries to apply for US visas prior to arrival. In April 2009 the islands received more than $90m. in federal stimulus funding.

Education

School attendance is compulsory from six to 16 years of age. In 2002/03 there were 12 state primary schools, with a total of 5,849 pupils enrolled, and there were nine state secondary schools, with a total enrolment of 4,705 pupils. There was a total of 18 private schools, with a total enrolment of 2,326 pupils. There was one college of further education, with 1,641 students in 2000/01. Budgetary expenditure on education totalled US $49.6m. in 2000, equivalent to 22.0% of total government expenditure.

Public Holidays

2009: 9 January (Commonwealth Day), 19 January (Martin Luther King Day), 16 February (Presidents' Day), 24 March (Covenant Friday), 10 April (Good Friday), 25 May (Memorial Day), 3 July (for Liberation Day), 7 September (Labor Day), 12 October (Commonwealth Cultural Day), 4 November (Citizenship Day), 11 November (Veterans' Day), 27 November (Thanksgiving Day), 9 December (Constitution Day), 25 December (Christmas Day).

2010: 9 January (Commonwealth Day), 20 January (Martin Luther King Day), 15 February (Presidents' Day), 23 March (Covenant Day), 2 April (Good Friday), 25 May (Memorial Day), 5 July (for Liberation Day), 6 September (Labor Day), 11 October (Commonwealth Cultural Day), 4 November (Citizenship Day), 11 November (Veterans' Day), 25 November (Thanksgiving Day), 9 December (Constitution Day), 25 December (Christmas Day).

Weights and Measures

With certain exceptions, the imperial system is in force. One US cwt equals 100 lb; one long ton equals 2,240 lb; one short ton equals 2,000 lb. A policy of gradual voluntary conversion to the metric system is being encouraged by the Federal Government.

Statistical Survey

Source: (unless otherwise stated): Department of Commerce, Central Statistics Division, POB 10007, Saipan, MP 96950; tel. 664-3000; fax 664-3001; internet www.commerce.gov.mp.

UNITED STATES COMMONWEALTH TERRITORIES

The Northern Mariana Islands

AREA AND POPULATION

Area: 457 sq km (176.5 sq miles). *By Island*: Saipan 120 sq km; Tinian 102 sq km; Rota 85 sq km; Pagan 48 sq km; Anatahan 32 sq km; Agrihan 30 sq km; Alamagan 11 sq km; Asuncion 7 sq km; Aguijan (Goat Is) 7 sq km; Sarigan 5 sq km; Guguan 4 sq km; Farallon de Pajaros 3 sq km; Maug 2 sq km; Farallon de Medinilla 1 sq km.

Population: 43,345 at census of 1 April 1990; 69,221 (males 31,984, females 37,237) at census of 1 April 2000. *By Island* (2000 census): Saipan 62,392; Rota 3,283; Tinian (with Aguijan) 3,540; Northern Islands 6. *2002* (estimates): Saipan 67,011; Total 74,151. *Mid-2008* (UN estimate): 85,430 (Source: UN, *Population Prospects: The 2006 Revision*).

Density (2007): 183.5 per sq km.

Ethnic Groups (2000 census): Filipino 18,141; Chinese 15,311; Chamorro 14,749; part-Chamorro 4,383; Total (incl. others) 69,221.

Principal Towns (population at 2000 census): San Antonio 4,741; Garapan (capital) 3,588; Koblerville 3,543; San Vincente 3,494; Tanapag 3,318; Chalan Kanoa 3,108; Kagman 3,026. Source: Thomas Brinkhoff, *City Population* (internet www.citypopulation.de).

Births and Deaths (2002): Registered live births 1,289 (birth rate 17.4 per 1,000); Registered deaths 164 (death rate 2.2 per 1,000).*2005* (estimates); Live Births 1,335, Deaths 189 (Source: UN, *Population and Vital Statistics Report*).

Employment (2000 census, persons aged 16 years and over): Agriculture, forestry, fisheries and mining 623; Manufacturing 17,398; Construction 2,785; Transport, communication and utilities 1,449; Trade, restaurants and hotels 9,570; Financing, insurance and real estate 1,013; Community, social and personal services 9,915; Total employed 42,753 (males 19,485, females 23,268); Unemployed 1,712 (males 888, females 824); Total labour force 44,465 (males 20,373, females 24,092). *Mid-2005* (estimates): Agriculture, etc. 9,000; Total labour force 38,000 (Source: FAO. *2007* (US economic census, paid employment only, excl. public administration): Total employed 22,622 (Manufacturing 7,094; Wholesale and retail 3,642, Hotels and restaurants 4,772).

HEALTH AND WELFARE
Key Indicators

Access to Water (% of persons, 2006): 98.

Access to Sanitation (% of persons, 2006): 94.

For sources and definitions, see explanatory note on p. vi.

AGRICULTURE, ETC.

Principal Crops (crops harvested for sale, '000 lb, 2007): Cassava 30.3; Taro 221.6; Yams 67.7; Sweet potatoes 352.3; Beans, yard long 40.2; Chinese cabbage 38.2; Cucumbers 93.8; Aubergines (Eggplant) 47.3; Pumpkins and squash 68.0; Watermelons 150.2; Bananas 146.9; Breadfruits 4.8; Papayas 50.7; Betel nuts 88.3; Coconuts 42.9; Ginger 1.5.

Livestock (2007): Cattle 1,395; Pigs 1,483; Goats 276; Poultry birds 12,390.

Livestock Products (sales of dozens, 2007): Hen eggs 195,510.

Fishing (metric tons, live weight, 2006): Total catch 183 (Skipjack tuna 95; Yellowfin tuna 15; Common dolphinfish 6). Source: FAO.

FINANCE

Currency and Exchange Rates: United States currency is used: 100 cents = 1 United States dollar (US $). *Sterling and Euro Equivalents* (31 December 2008): £1 sterling = US $1.4578; €1 = US $1.3917; US $100 = £68.60 = €71.85.

Federal Direct Expenditures (US $ million, year ending September 2007): Retirement and disability 28.1; Total (incl. others) 130.0 (Source: US Census Bureau, *Consolidated Federal Funds Report*).

Budget (US $ million, 2008): General fund revenue 162.8 (Taxes 125.9, Fees, charges and other revenues 33.2; Net transfers from other funds 3.7); Total expenditure 172.2.

Cost of Living (Consumer Price Index for Saipan; base: 2000 = 100): All items 99.8 in 2005; 104.7 in 2006; 111.9 in 2007. Source: ILO.

Gross Domestic Product (US $ million in current prices, estimate): 557.0 in 2002. Source: Bank of Hawaii, *Commonwealth of the Northern Mariana Islands Economic Report* (October 2003).

EXTERNAL TRADE

Principal Commodities (US $ million): *Imports* (1997): Beverages 12.8; Tobacco 5.4; Automobiles (incl. parts) 42.1; Clothing 309.2; Total (incl. others) 836.2. *Exports* (2000): Total 1,000. *Value of Garment Exports* (US $ million): 486.5 in 2006; 307.6 in 2007; 98.2 in 2008.

Principal Trading Partners (US $ million, 1997): *Imports*: Guam 298.0; Hong Kong 200.5; Japan 118.3; Korea, Republic 80.6; USA 63.3; Total (incl. others) 836.2.

Sources: partly UN, *Statistical Yearbook for Asia and the Pacific* and *Statistical Yearbook*.

TRANSPORT

Road Traffic (registered motor vehicles, 2001): 17,900.

Shipping: *Registered Fleet* (2001): 1,029 vessels (791 fishing vessels); *Traffic* ('000 short tons, 1997): Goods loaded 184.1; Goods unloaded 425.9.

Civil Aviation (Saipan Int. Airport, year ending September 1999): 23,853 aircraft landings; 562,364 boarding passengers. *2006:* Passenger arrivals 511,720, Passenger departures 516,366. Source: Commonwealth Ports Authority.

TOURISM

Visitor Arrivals: 435,494 in 2006; 389,261 in 2007; 396,410 in 2008.

Visitor Arrivals by Country (2008): China, People's Republic (incl. Hong Kong) 31,095; Japan 201,982; Korea, Republic 116,710; USA (incl. Guam) 32,199; Total (incl. others) 396,410.

Tourism Receipts (US $ million): 407 in 1999; 430 in 2000; 225 in 2002 (approximate figure). Source: Bank of Hawaii, *Commonwealth of the Northern Mariana Islands Economic Report* (October 2003).

COMMUNICATIONS MEDIA

Radio Receivers (households with access, census of 2000): 10,684.

Television Receivers (estimate, 1995): 15,460 in use.

Telephones (main lines in use, 2008): 30,458.

Mobile Cellular Telephones (2004): 20,500 subscribers*.

Facsimile Machines (1996): 1,200 in use†.

*Source: International Telecommunication Union.
†Source: UN, *Statistical Yearbook*.

EDUCATION

Pre-primary (2002/03, state schools, Headstart programme): 12 schools; 98 teachers; 606 pupils.

Primary (2002/03, state schools): 12 schools; 283 teachers; 5,849 students.

Secondary (2002/03, state schools): 9 schools; 248 teachers; 4,705 students.

Higher (2000/01): 1 college; 1,641 students (full- and part-time students).

Private Schools (2002/03): 18 schools; 186 teachers; 2,326 students.

Directory

The Constitution

The Northern Mariana Islands became part of the US-administered UN Trust Territory of the Pacific Islands in 1947. In 1975 the Northern Mariana Islands voted for separate status as a US Commonwealth Territory; the Covenant to Establish a Commonwealth of the Northern Mariana Islands (CNMI) in Political Union with the United States was approved by the US Congress in 1976 and took effect fully in 1986. According to the Covenant, CNMI comes under federal law, with certain exceptions including customs. In 1977 the Government of the CNMI adopted a new Constitution, and in the following year the Territory became self-governing. Under the terms of the Constitution, executive authority is vested in the Governor, who is elected by popular vote for a four-year term. Legislative authority is vested in the bicameral Legislature, comprising the nine-member Senate and the 20-member House of Representatives. The Constitution also provides for a Lieutenant-Governor and a judicial system including a Superior Court and a Supreme Court. The Northern Mariana Islands elect a Resident Representative to the federal legislature.

UNITED STATES COMMONWEALTH TERRITORIES

The Northern Mariana Islands

The Government
(May 2009)

Governor: BENIGNO R. FITIAL (took office 9 January 2006).
Lieutenant-Governor: ELOY S. INOS.

DEPARTMENT SECRETARIES

Secretary of the Department of Finance: ROBERT SCHRACK (acting).
Secretary of the Department of Community and Cultural Affairs: MELVIN FAISAO (acting).
Secretary of the Department of Labor: GIL M. SAN NICOLAS.
Secretary of the Department of Lands and Natural Resources: IGNACIO DELA CRUZ.
Secretary of the Department of Public lands: JOHN S. DEL ROSARIO, Jr.
Secretary of the Department of Public Works: JOSE S. DEMAPAN.
Secretary of the Department of Commerce: MICHAEL ADA.
Commissioner of the Department of Public Safety: REBECCA WARFIELD.
Secretary of the Department of Public Health: JOSEPH KEVIN P. VILLAGOMEZ.

GOVERNMENT OFFICES

Office of the Governor: Caller Box 10007, Capitol Hill, Saipan, MP 96950; tel. 664-2276; fax 664-2290; e-mail gov.frosario@saipan.com; internet www.gov.mp.
Office of the Resident Representative to the USA, Commonwealth of the Northern Mariana Islands: 2121 R St, NW, Washington, DC 20008, USA; tel. (202) 673-5869; fax (202) 673-5873; e-mail rep@resrep.gov.mp; the Commonwealth Govt also has liaison offices in Hawaii and Guam.
Department of the Interior, Office of Insular Affairs (OIA): Field Office of the OIA, Dept of the Interior, POB 502622, Saipan, MP 96950; tel. 234-8861; fax 234-8814; e-mail jeff.schorr@pticom.com; internet www.doi.gov/oia/Islandpages/cnmipage.htm; OIA representation in the Commonwealth; Field Representative JEFFREY SCHORR.
Department of Commerce: Capitol Hill, Saipan, MP 96950; tel. 664-3003; fax 664-3067; e-mail commercedept@pticom.com; internet www.commerce.gov.mp.
Department of Community and Cultural Affairs: Capitol Hill, Saipan, MP 96950; tel. 664-2576; fax 664-2570; e-mail dccaoos@pticom.com; internet www.dcca.gov.mp.
Department of Finance: Capitol Hill, Saipan, MP 96950; tel. 664-1100; fax 664-1115; e-mail procurement@gtepacifica.net; internet www.dof.gov.mp.
Department of Labor: POB 10007, Saipan, MP 96950; tel. 236-0900; fax 236-0991; e-mail webmaster@marianaslabor.net; internet marianaslabor.net.
Department of Lands and Natural Resources: Capitol Hill, Saipan, MP 96950; tel. 322-9830; fax 322-2633.
Department of Public Health: Capitol Hill, Saipan, MP 96950; tel. 234-8950; fax 236-8390; e-mail fbraig@cnmidph.net; internet www.dphsaipan.com.
Department of Public Lands: Capitol Hill, Saipan, MP 96950; tel. 234-2751; fax 234-3755.
Department of Public Safety: Jose M. Sablan Bldg, Saipan, MP 96950; tel. 664-9022; fax 664-9027; internet www.dps.gov.mp.
Department of Public Works: Capitol Hill, Saipan, MP 96950; tel. 235-5827; fax 235-6346.

Legislature

NORTHERN MARIANAS COMMONWEALTH LEGISLATURE

Legislative authority is vested in the Northern Marianas Commonwealth Legislature, a bicameral body consisting of the Senate and the House of Representatives. There are nine senators, elected for four-year terms, and 20 members of the House of Representatives, elected for two-year terms. The most recent legislative election was held on 3 November 2007. The Republican Party won 12 seats in the House of Representatives, the Covenant Party four seats, the Democratic Party one seat and independent candidates three seats. Meanwhile, two independent candidates and one Covenant Party candidate were re-elected to the three Senate seats being contested.

Senate President: PETE P. REYES.
Speaker of the House: ARNOLD I. PALACIOS.
Commonwealth Legislature: Capitol Hill, Saipan, MP 96950; tel. 664-7757; fax 322-6344.

CONGRESS

Since 2008 the Northern Mariana Islands have been able to elect a non-voting Delegate to the US House of Representatives. The first election for this position was held on 4 November 2008.
Delegate of the Northern Mariana Islands: GREGORIO C. SABLAN.

Election Commission

Commonwealth Election Commission: POB 500470, Saipan, MP 96950-0470; tel. 664-8683; fax 664-8689; e-mail executivedirector@votecnmi.gov.mp; internet www.votecnmi.gov.mp; Exec. Dir JULITA A. VILLAGOMEZ (acting).

Political Organizations

Covenant Party: c/o Commonwealth Legislature, Capitol Hill, Saipan, MP 96950; Leader BENIGNO R. FITIAL; Chair. ELOY INOS.
Democratic Party of the Commonwealth of the Northern Mariana Islands, Inc: Saipan, MP 96950; tel. 234-7497; fax 233-0641; Pres. Dr CARLOS S. CAMACHO; Chair. LORENZO CABRERA.
Republican Party of the Northern Marianas: POB 500777, Saipan, MP 96950; tel. 233-1288; fax 233-1288; e-mail dpwpio@vzpacifica.net; State Chair. TOM PANGELINAN; Exec. Dir (vacant).

Judicial System

The judicial system in the Commonwealth of the Northern Mariana Islands (CNMI) consists of the Superior Court, the Commonwealth Supreme Court (which considers appeals from the Superior Court) and the Federal District Court. Under the Covenant, federal law applies in the Commonwealth, with some exceptions: for example, the CNMI is not part of the US Customs Territory, and it may enact its own taxation laws.

Chief Justice of the Commonwealth Supreme Court: MIGUEL S. DEMAPAN.
Presiding Judge of the Superior Court: ROBERT C. NARAJA.
Attorney-General: GREGORY BAKA.
Public Defender: ADAM HARDWICKE.

Religion

The population is predominantly Christian, mainly Roman Catholic. There are small communities of Episcopalians (Anglicans—under the jurisdiction of the Bishop of Hawaii, in the USA) and Protestants.

CHRISTIANITY

The Roman Catholic Church

The Northern Mariana Islands comprise the single diocese of Chalan Kanoa, suffragan to the archdiocese of Agaña (Guam). The Bishop participates in the Catholic Bishops' Conference of the Pacific, based in Suva, Fiji. At 31 December 2006 there were 43,000 adherents, including temporary residents, in the Northern Mariana Islands.

Bishop of Chalan Kanoa: Most Rev. TOMAS AGUON CAMACHO, Bishop's House, Chalan Kanoa, POB 500745, Saipan, MP 96950; tel. 234-3000; fax 235-3002; e-mail diocese@pticom.com.

The Press

The weekly *Focus on the Commonwealth* is published in Guam, but distributed solely in the Northern Mariana Islands.

Marianas Observer: POB 502119, Saipan, MP 96950; tel. 233-3955; fax 233-7040; weekly; Publr JOHN VABLAN; Man. Editor ZALDY DANDAN; circ. 2,000.
Marianas Review: POB 501074, Saipan, MP 96950; tel. and fax 234-7160; f. 1979 as *The Commonwealth Examiner*; weekly; English and Chamorro; independent; Publr LUIS BENAVENTE; Editor RUTH L. TIGHE; circ. 1,700.
Marianas Variety: POB 6338, Tamuning 96931; tel. 234-6341; fax 234-9271; e-mail mvariety@pticom.com; internet www.mvarietynews.com; Mon.–Fri.; English and Chamorro; independent; f. 1972; Publrs ABED E. YOUNIS, PAZ C. YOUNIS; circ. 8,000.
North Star: Chalan Kanoa, POB 500745, Saipan, MP 96950; tel. 234-3000; fax 234-2531; e-mail north.star@saipan.com; weekly; English and Chamorro; Roman Catholic; f. 1976; Publr BISHOP TOMAS A. CAMACHO; Man. Editor RUY VALENTE M. POLISTICO.
Pacific Daily News (Saipan bureau): POB 500822, Saipan, MP 96950; tel. 234-6423; fax 234-5986; Publr LEE WEBBER; circ. 5,000.

UNITED STATES COMMONWEALTH TERRITORIES
The Northern Mariana Islands

Pacific Star: POB 505815 CHRB, Saipan, MP 96950; tel. 288-0746; fax 288-0747; weekly; Operational Man. NICK LEGASPI; circ. 3,000.

Pacifica: POB 502143, Saipan, MP 96950; monthly; Editor MIKE MALONE.

Saipan Tribune: POB 10001, PMB 34, Saipan, MP 96950-8901; tel. 235-6397; fax 235-3740; e-mail editor.tribune@saipan.com; internet www.saipantribune.com; 2 a week; Publr LYNN KNIGHT; Editor JAYVEE L. VALLEJERA; circ. 3,500.

Broadcasting and Communications

TELECOMMUNICATIONS

Pacific Telecom Inc: POB 500306 CK, Saipan, MP 96950; tel. 682-1060; fax 682-4555; internet www.pticom.com.

SAIPANCELL Communications: Gualo Rai Commercial Center, Main Bldg, Gualo Rai, Middle Rd, Saipan; tel. 483-2273; fax 235-7640; e-mail service@guamcell.net; internet www.saipancell.com; fmrly Saipan Cellular & Paging; cellular services; Pres. JAY SHEDD.

BROADCASTING
Radio

Far East Broadcasting Co, Inc: POB 500209, Saipan, MP 96950; tel. 322-9088; fax 322-3060; e-mail saipan@febc.org; internet www.febc.org; f. 1946; non-commercial religious broadcasts; Pres. GREGG HARRIS; Field Dir ROBERT L. HARRIS.

KSAI-AM: tel. 234-6520; fax 234-3428; e-mail ksai@febc.org; f. 1978; local service; mainly religious broadcasts; Station Man. CHRIS SLABAUGH.

KFBS-SW: POB 500209, Saipan, MP 96950; tel. 322-9088; fax 322-3060; e-mail saipan@febc.org; internet www.febc.org; f. 1946; international broadcasts in Chinese, Indonesian, Russian and Vietnamese; owned by Far East Broadcasting Co, Inc; Exec. Dir ROBERT SPRINGER.

Inter-Island Communications, Inc: POB 500914, Saipan, MP 96950; tel. 234-7239; fax 234-0447; f. 1984; commercial; station KCNM-AM, or KZMI-FM in stereo; Gen. Man. HANS W. MICKELSON; Programme Dir KEN WARNICK; CEO ANGEL OCAMPO.

KRNM: POB 501250, Saipan, MP 96950; tel. 234-5498; fax 235-0915; internet www.krnm.org; f. 1994; public station based on Northern Marianas Coll. campus; Gen. Man. CARL POGUE.

Magic 100.3: Magic Studio, 1st Floor, Naru Bldg, Susupe; fax 234-2262; e-mail Kwaw100.3@Magic100Radio.com; internet www.magic100radio.com.

Power 99: POB 10000, Saipan, MP 96950; tel. 235-7996; fax 235-7998; e-mail tpalacios@spbguam.com; Station Man. TINA PALACIOS; Gen. Man. CURTIS DANCOE.

The Rock 97.9: POB 10000 Saipan, MP 96950; tel. 235-7996; fax 235-7998; e-mail cdancoe@spbguam.com; Man. ALBERT JUAN.

Television

KMCV-TV: POB 501298, Saipan, MP 96950; tel. 235-6365; fax 235-0965; f. 1992; 52-channel commercial station, with 8 pay channels, broadcasting 24 hours a day; US programmes and local and international news; 5,650 subscribers; Gen. Man. WAYNE GAMBLIN.

Marianas CableVision: Nauru Bldg, 2°, Susupe, Saipan, MP 96950; tel. 235-4628; fax 235-0965; e-mail mcv.service@saipan.com; internet www.mcvcnmi.com; 55-channel cable service provider, broadcasting US and Pacific Rim programmes; Pres. JOHN CRUIKSHANK; Gen. Man. MARK BIRMINGHAM.

Finance

BANKING

Bank of Guam (USA): POB 500678, Saipan, MP 96950; tel. 233-5000; fax 233-5003; internet www.bankofguam.com; Gen. Man. MARCIE TOMOKANE; 5 brs.

Bank of Hawaii: Bank of Hawaii Bldg, El Monte Ave, Garapan, POB 500566, Saipan, MP 96950; tel. 236-8450; fax 235-3913; internet www.boh.com; Man. JOHN SHEATHER; 2 brs.

Bank of Saipan: POB 500690, Saipan, MP 96950; tel. 234-6260; fax 235-1802; e-mail bankofsaipan@gtepacifica.net; internet www.bankofsaipan.com; dep. US $23m. (Dec. 2004); Pres. JON BARGFREDE; 4 brs.

City Trust Bank: Gualo Rai, POB 501867, Saipan, MP 96950; tel. 235-7701; fax 234-8664; e-mail citytrustbank@ctbsaipan.com; Asst Vice-Pres. and Acting Man. MARIA LOURDES JOHNSON.

First Hawaiian Bank: Gualo Rai Commercial Center, Middle Rd, Gualo Rai, Saipan MP 96950; tel. 235-3090; fax 236-8936; internet www.fhb.com; Area Man. JUAN LIZAMA.

Guam Savings and Loan Bank: POB 503201, Saipan, MP 96950; tel. 233-2265; fax 233-2227; Gen. Man. GLEN PEREZ.

INSURANCE

Allied Insurance/Takagi and Associates, Inc: PPP 602 Box 10000 Saipan, MP 96950; tel. 233-2554; fax 670-2553; Gen. Man. PETER SIBLY.

Aon Insurance: Aon Insurance Micronesia (Saipan) Inc, POB 502177, Saipan, MP 96950; tel. 234-2811; fax 234-5462; e-mail rod.rankin@aon.com.au; internet www.aon.com; Communications Officer RODNEY RANKIN.

Associated Insurance Underwriters of the Pacific, Inc: POB 501369, Saipan, MP 96950; tel. 234-7222; fax 234-5367; e-mail aiup@pticom.com; Gen. Man. MAGGIE GEORGE.

Calvo's Insurance Underwriters, Inc.: Oleai Shopping Center, Saipan, MP 96950; tel. 234-5690; fax 234-5693; e-mail calvospc@vzpacifica.net; internet www.calvosinsurance.com; Man. ELI C. BUENAVENTURA.

Century Insurance (Tan Holdings Corpn): Century Insurance PMB 193, POB 10000, Saipan, MP 96950; tel. 234-0609; fax 234-1845; e-mail nel_matanguihan@cicspn.com; internet www.cicspn.com; Gen. Man. NEL MATANGUIHAN.

General Accident Insurance Asia Ltd (Microl Insurance): POB 502177, Saipan, MP 96950; tel. 234-2811; fax 234-5462; Man. Dir MICHAEL W. GOURLAY.

Marianas Insurance Co Ltd: POB 502505, Saipan, MP 96950-2505; tel. 234-5091; fax 234-5093; e-mail admin@marianasinsurance.com; internet www.marianasinsurance.com; Gen. Man. ROSALIA S. CABRERA.

Midland Insurance Underwriters, Inc.: PMB 219, POB 10000, Capitol Hill, Saipan, MP 96950; tel. 235-3598; fax 235-3597; e-mail midland@vzpacifica.net.

Moylan's Insurance Underwriters (Int.), Inc: POB 500658, Saipan, MP 96950; tel. 234-6571; fax 632-3788; e-mail saipan@moylans.net; internet www.moylansinsurance.com; Branch Man. TAMARA HUNTER.

Nichido Insurance: Oleai Central Bldg, San Jose, Saipan, MP 96950; tel. 234-5690; fax 234-5693.

Pacifica Insurance Underwriters, Inc: POB 500168, Saipan, MP 96950; tel. 234-6267; fax 234-5880; e-mail piui@pacificains.com; internet www.pacificains.com; f. 1972; Pres. NORMAN T. TENORIO.

Primerica Financial Services: POB 500964, Saipan, MP 96950; tel. 235-2912; fax 235-7910; Gen. Man. JOHN SABLAN.

Royal Crown Insurance: Royal Crown Bldg, Beach Road, Chalan LauLau, POB 10001, Saipan, MP 96950; tel. 234-2256; fax 234-2258.

Staywell: POB 502050, Saipan, MP 96950; tel. 323-4260; fax 323-4263; e-mail stwspn@ite.net; Man. FRANNY PANGELINAN.

Trade and Industry

GOVERNMENT AGENCIES

Commonwealth Development Authority: POB 502149, Wakins Bldg, Gualo Rai, Saipan, MP 96950; tel. 234-6245; fax 235-7147; e-mail administration@cda.gov.mp; internet www.cda.gov.mp; govt lending institution; funds capital improvement projects and private enterprises; offers tax incentives to qualified investors; Chair. PEDRO I. ITIBUS (acting); CEO OSCAR C. CAMACHO (acting).

Marianas Public Lands Authority: POB 500380, Saipan, MP 96950; tel. 234-3751; fax 234-3755; manages public land, which constitutes 82% of total land area in the Commonwealth (14% on Saipan).

CHAMBER OF COMMERCE

Saipan Chamber of Commerce: Chalan Kanoa, POB 500806 CK, Saipan, MP 96950; tel. 233-7150; fax 233-7151; e-mail saipanchamber@saipan.com; internet www.saipanchamber.com; Pres. JIM ARENOVSKI; Exec. Dir DOUGLAS BRENNAN.

EMPLOYERS' ASSOCIATIONS

Association of Commonwealth Teachers (ACT): POB 5071, Saipan, MP 96950; tel. and fax 256-7567; e-mail cnmiteachers@netscape.net; supports the teaching profession and aims to improve education in state schools.

Saipan Garment Manufacturers' Association (SGMA): POB 10001, Saipan, MP 96950; tel. 235-7699; fax 235-7899; e-mail sgmaemy@vzpacifica.net; internet www.sgma-saipan.org; Exec. Dir (vacant).

UTILITIES

Commonwealth Utilities Corporation (CUC): POB 501220, Saipan, MP 96950; tel. 235-7025; fax 235-6145; e-mail cucedp@gtepacifica.net; internet www.cuccnmi.com; Exec. Dir ANTONIO MUNA.

TRADE UNION AND CO-OPERATIVES

International Brotherhood of Electrical Workers: c/o Micronesian Telecommunications Corpn, Saipan, MP 96950; Local 1357 of Hawaii branch of US trade union based in Washington, DC.

The Mariana Islands Co-operative Association, Rota Producers and Tinian Producers Associations operate on the islands.

Transport

RAILWAYS

There have been no railways operating in the islands since the Japanese sugar industry railway, on Saipan, ceased operations in the Second World War.

ROADS

In 1991 there were 494 km (307 miles) of roads on the islands, 320 km (199 miles) of which are on Saipan. First grade roads constitute 135 km (84 miles) of the total, 99 km (62 miles) being on Saipan. There is no public transport, apart from a school bus system.

SHIPPING

The main harbour of the Northern Mariana Islands is the Port of Saipan, which underwent extensive renovation in the mid-1990s. There are also two major harbours on Rota and one on Tinian. Several shipping lines link Saipan, direct or via Guam, with ports in Japan, Asia, the Philippines, the USA and other territories in the Pacific.

Commonwealth Ports Authority (CPA): POB 501055, Saipan, MP 96950; tel. 664-3500; fax 234-5962; e-mail cpa.admin@saipan.com; internet net.saipan.com/cftemplates/cpa/index.cfm; Exec. Dir LEE CABRERA (acting).

Mariana Express Lines: POB 501937, CTS Bldg, Saipan, MP 96950; tel. 322-1690; fax 323-6355; e-mail desmond_aw@mariana-express.com; internet www.mariana-express.com; services between Saipan, Guam, Japan and Hong Kong; Man. DESMOND AW.

Saipan Shipping Co Inc (Saiship): Saiship Bldg, Charlie Dock, POB 500008, Saipan, MP 96950; tel. 322-9706; fax 322-3183; e-mail darlene_cabrera@saipanshipping.com; f. 1956; weekly barge service between Guam, Saipan and Tinian; monthly services to Japan and Micronesia; Gen. Man. DARLENE CABRERA.

Westpac Freight: POB 2048, Puerto Rico, Saipan, MP 96950; tel. 322-8798; fax 322-5536; e-mail westpac@gtepacifica.net; services between Saipan, Guam and the USA; Man. MICHIE CAMACHO.

CIVIL AVIATION

Air services are centred on the main international airport, Isley Field, on Saipan. There are also airports on Rota and Tinian.

Continental Micronesia: POB 508778, A.B. Won Pat International Airport, Tamuning, GU 96911; tel. 647-6595; fax 649-6588; internet www.continental.com; f. 1968, as Air Micronesia, by Continental Airlines (USA); name changed 1992; subsidiary of Continental Airlines; hub operations in Saipan and Guam; services throughout the region and to destinations in the Far East and the mainland USA; Pres. MARK ERWIN.

Freedom Air: POB 500239 CK, Saipan, MP 96950; tel. 234-8328; e-mail freedom@ite.net; internet www.freedomairguam.com; scheduled internal flights.

Tourism

Tourism is one of the most important industries in the Northern Mariana Islands, earning some US $225m. in 2002. In that year there were 4,313 hotel rooms. Most of the islands' hotels are Japanese-owned, and in 2008 more than 50% of tourists came from Japan. The Republic of Korea, the People's Republic of China and the USA are also important sources of tourists. The islands received a total of 396,410 visitors in 2008. The islands of Asuncion, Guguan, Maug, Managaha, Sariguan and Uracas (Farallon de Pajaros) are maintained as uninhabited reserves. Visitors are mainly attracted by the white, sandy beaches and the excellent diving conditions. There is also interest in the *Latte* or *Taga* stones (mainly on Tinian), pillars carved from the rock by the ancient Chamorros and relics from the Second World War.

Hotel Association of the Northern Mariana Islands: POB 5075 CHRB, Saipan, MP 96950; tel. 233-6964; fax 233-1424; e-mail lynn_knight@tanholdings.com; internet www.saipanhotels.org; f. 1983; Chair. LYNN KNIGHT.

Marianas Visitors Authority (MVA): POB 500861 CK, Saipan, MP 96950; tel. 664-3200; fax 664-3237; e-mail mva@mymarianas.com; internet www.mymarianas.com; f. 1976; responsible for the promotion and development of tourism in the Northern Mariana Islands; Chair. JERRY TAN; Man. Dir PERRY TENORIO.

PUERTO RICO

Introductory Survey

Location, Climate, Language, Religion, Flag, Capital

The Commonwealth of Puerto Rico comprises the main island of Puerto Rico, together with the small offshore islands of Vieques and Culebra and numerous smaller islets, lying about 80 km (50 miles) east of Hispaniola (Haiti and the Dominican Republic) in the Caribbean Sea. The climate is maritime-tropical, with an average annual temperature of 24°C (75°F) and a normal range between 17°C (63°F) and 36°C (97°F). The official languages are Spanish and English. Christianity is the dominant religion, and about 73% of the population are Roman Catholics. The flag (proportions 3 by 5) has five alternating red and white horizontal stripes of equal width, with a blue triangle, in the centre of which is a five-pointed white star, at the hoist. The capital is San Juan.

Recent History

Puerto Rico, also known as Borinquen (after the original Arawak Indian name Boriquen), was ruled by Spain from 1509 until 1898, when it was ceded to the USA at the conclusion of the Spanish–American war, and administered as an 'unincorporated territory' of the USA. In 1917 Puerto Ricans were granted US citizenship, and in 1947 Puerto Rico obtained the right to elect its own Governor. A Constitution, promulgated in 1952, assigned Puerto Rico the status of a self-governing 'Commonwealth', or 'Estado Libre Asociado', in its relation to the USA.

The Partido Popular Democrático (PPD) held a majority in both chambers of the legislature from 1944 until 1968, when, following a split within the party, the Partido Nuevo Progresista (PNP), an advocate of statehood, won the governorship and legislative control. This followed a plebiscite in 1967, when 61% of voters had ratified a continuation of Commonwealth status in preference to independence (1%) or incorporation as a State of the USA (39%). In the general election of 1972 the PPD, under the leadership of Rafael Hernández Colón, regained the governorship and legislative control from the PNP, only to lose them again in 1976. The victorious PNP was led by Carlos Romero Barceló, who became Governor in January 1977.

Romero Barceló, who had promised a referendum on statehood if re-elected for a further term in 1980, abandoned this plan following the election, in which he narrowly defeated former Governor Hernández Colón. The PPD, however, gained control of the legislature. The 1984 gubernatorial election, which was contested mainly on economic issues, was won by Hernández Colón by only 50,000 votes, with the PPD retaining substantial majorities in both legislative chambers. In September 1985 Romero Barceló was succeeded as leader of the PNP by Baltasar Corrada del Río.

A gubernatorial election, held in November 1988, resulted in the re-election of Hernández Colón. Electoral participation was unusually high, at almost 90%.

The question of eventual independence for Puerto Rico has been a politically sensitive issue for over 50 years. With the PPD supporting the continuation and enhancement of Commonwealth status and the PNP advocating Puerto Rico's inclusion as a state of the USA, mainstream party encouragement of independence aims has come mainly from the Partido Independentista Puertorriqueño (PIP) and other left-wing groups. There are two small, and occasionally violent, terrorist factions, the Ejército Popular Boricua (Los Macheteros), which operates in Puerto Rico, and the Fuerzas Armadas de Liberación Nacional (FALN), functioning principally on the US mainland.

In the 1988 election campaign, Corrada del Río, whose campaign was endorsed by the successful US presidential candidate, George

Bush, advocated the admission of Puerto Rico as the 51st state of the USA, while Hernández Colón reiterated the traditional PPD policy of 'maximum autonomy' for Puerto Rico 'within a permanent union with the USA'. President Bush's open support of the statehood option was criticized by Hernández Colón and the PPD. In January 1989 Hernández Colón promised that a further plebiscite would be held. Although it was initially planned to hold this referendum in June 1991, in February the proposed legislation to make its result binding on the US Government failed to obtain sufficient support in the US Senate to allow it to proceed to full consideration by the US Congress.

In December 1991 the PPD Government organized a referendum on a proposal to adopt a charter of 'democratic rights', which included guarantees of US citizenship regardless of future change in Puerto Rico's constitutional status, and the maintenance of Spanish as the official language. The proposed charter was rejected by a margin of 53% to 45%. This result was widely interpreted as an indication that the majority of voters wished to retain Puerto Rico's Commonwealth status. Hernández Colón announced in January 1992 that he would not seek re-election in the gubernatorial election in November, and in the following month resigned as leader of the PPD. His successor as party leader, Victoria Muñoz Mendoza, was defeated in the election by the PNP candidate, Pedro Rosselló. The leadership of the PPD subsequently passed to Héctor Luis Acevedo.

Rosselló, who took office in January 1993, announced that a further referendum on Puerto Rico's future constitutional status would be held during the year. The Government proceeded with legislation rescinding the removal, in 1991, of English as an official language of the island. The referendum, which took place in November 1993, resulted in a 48% vote favouring the retention of Commonwealth status, with 46% of voters supporting accession to statehood and 4% advocating full independence.

In July 1996 a committee of the US House of Representatives unanimously recommended that Puerto Rican voters be given an opportunity, before 1998, to choose whether to retain the island's present status, or to proceed to statehood or full self-government. A preference for change would be followed by a 10-year 'Transition Plan' based on the result, during which time ballots would be held periodically to confirm the direction of the Plan. These proposals, however, were opposed by the Resident Commissioner representing the Puerto Rican Government in the House of Representatives, and were withdrawn in late 1996.

At elections held in November 1996 Rosselló was re-elected as Governor. The PNP retained control of both chambers of the legislature. During the campaign, the levels of minimum wages on the island, together with the recent abolition by US President Bill Clinton of federal tax exemptions for US companies establishing plants in Puerto Rico, formed the main political issues.

In March 1998, by a majority of only one vote, the US House of Representatives passed legislation providing for a referendum to determine the island's future status. Under the referendum plan, a vote in favour of statehood would oblige the US Congress to legislate for a 51st state during 1999, with Puerto Rico's admission to the union following within a 10-year period. In December 1998, however, the Puerto Rican electorate rejected the statehood proposal by a margin of 50% to 47%; 71% of eligible voters participated in the referendum. Rosselló proceeded to describe the result as a reflection of the PNP Government's decline in popularity over domestic issues, and indicated that he was to petition the US Congress to implement measures to facilitate the island's transition to statehood. In June 1999, however, Rosselló unexpectedly announced that he would not seek re-election in the gubernatorial election scheduled to take place in November 2000. In July 2001 the new Governor, Sila María Calderón, voiced support for a further referendum on the island's status during 2002. In July 2002 Calderón announced the creation of a 'Status Committee' to resolve the issue; the Committee was to consist of representatives of the PPD, PNP and PIP, including Colón and Barceló.

An extended period of public protest followed the accidental death, in April 1999, of a civilian security guard during routine US military exercises on the small offshore island of Vieques, the eastern section of which, covering a coastline of 32 km, was used by the US Navy as an ammunition testing range. With support from the PIP, groups of protesters promptly established camps on the firing range, compelling the US Navy temporarily to suspend these operations. Following extended negotiations between the Puerto Rican and US Governments, in January 2000 Rosselló and President Clinton announced a compromise plan to end the protesters' occupation by undertaking that, in return for the resumption of naval exercises in which only dummy ammunition would be used, the US Administration would provide immediate development aid to Vieques of $40m. This figure would rise to $90m. if residents of the island would agree in a referendum (provisionally scheduled for November 2001 but subsequently cancelled—see below) to allow the US Navy to resume live ammunition testing, in which event the Navy would undertake to leave Vieques permanently by 2003. In May 2000, prior to a proposed unilateral resumption of naval exercises (using dummy ammunition), protests on Vieques intensified, and several hundred federal government agents were sent to remove the protesters forcibly. The US Navy subsequently declared a 5-km land and sea 'security area' around the island.

Gubernatorial and legislative elections were held on 7 November 2000. Sila María Calderón of the PPD was elected Governor, narrowly defeating Carlos Pesquera of the PNP. The PPD also secured a majority in both the Senate and the House of Representatives (albeit by a narrow majority in the latter).

Upon taking office, Calderón announced her administration's repudiation of the agreement on military activity on Vieques signed in January 2000 by Clinton and Rosselló. Military exercises on the island were resumed in April 2001, despite legal challenges and protests. In June the new US President, George W. Bush, announced that the US Navy would end military activity on the island by May 2003. Meanwhile, Calderón announced plans for a referendum on US military activity on Vieques to be held in July 2001; it was postponed until November, but was subsequently cancelled by the US Congress, which ordered the US military to remain on Vieques until an alternative location was found. The US Congress claimed that ongoing tests were necessary as part of the US-led 'war on terror' following the terrorist attacks on Washington, DC, and New York in September. (A non-binding referendum had been held in July, in which 68% of voters were in favour of the immediate departure from the island of the US Navy.) Tests resumed in April 2002, amid protests from members of the PIP. In mid-2002 the PIP threatened to call a general strike and instigate a campaign of civil disobedience if the US Navy failed to leave the island by May 2003. The final scheduled bombing exercises took place in February 2003, and the US Navy withdrew from the island on 1 May. The firing range was to become a wildlife reserve. The last remaining base, at Ceiba, was closed on 31 March 2004. In 2006 environmental concerns were raised over underwater detonations carried out by the US Navy as part of its ongoing clean-up operations.

In 2002 several prominent PNP officials who had served in the Rosselló administration went on trial on charges of corruption and in December former education secretary Victor Fajardo was sentenced to 12 years' imprisonment after being convicted of diverting state funds to the PNP. In January 2003 the former Speaker of the House of Representatives under the Rosselló administration, Edison Misla Aldorano, was found guilty of extortion, money-laundering and perverting the course of justice; in the same month a former member of Rosselló's staff was sentenced to 18 months' imprisonment. In March 2004 a legislative ethics committee found Oscar Ramos, a PNP deputy, guilty of bribery charges. However, the party voted not to expel Ramos, prompting the PPD to claim that the PNP was not taking seriously the fight against corruption in public office.

Legislative and gubernatorial elections were held on 2 November 2004. Initial results showed that Aníbal Acevedo Vilá of the ruling PPD won the gubernatorial election by just 3,880 votes, a margin of only 0.2%. Under electoral law a victory by a margin of 0.5% or less was subject to a recount. In December it was announced that, with 99.9% of the votes recounted, Acevedo Vilá had won 48.4% of the ballot, while the PNP's candidate, former Governor Rosselló, attracted 48.2% of the votes cast. The third placed candidate, Rubén Berríos Martínez, representing the PIP, won 2.7%. Acevedo Vilá was duly sworn in as Governor on 2 January 2005. In the concurrently held legislative election, the PNP gained control of both houses from the PPD, winning a majority of seats in both the Senate and the House of Representatives. Voter turn-out was 81.6%.

In March 2005 both houses of the legislature unanimously approved legislation providing for a referendum in July on whether to petition the US Congress and President Bush to agree to honour the results of a further referendum on how the island's future status should be decided, to be held before the end of 2006. However, the following month, Governor Acevedo Vilá vetoed the legislation on the grounds that it did not make sufficient provision for the option of a constituent assembly, instead of a popular, binding referendum, to decide on the eventual status of the island.

Also in March 2005, there was widespread opposition to the decision by the US Territorial District Court of Puerto Rico to impose the death sentence on two convicted murderers. Capital punishment had been banned in the Territory in 1930, a decision that had been upheld in 2000 by a ruling of the Supreme Court of Puerto Rico that it violated the island's Constitution. However, the ruling was subsequently overturned by the US Court of Appeals, which found that Puerto Rico was subject to US federal law and that the death penalty was applicable in certain cases; this decision was upheld by the US Supreme Court. In early April Acevedo Vilá wrote to the US Attorney-General requesting that the death penalty should not apply to residents of Puerto Rico. In May the jury serving on the trial moved to sentence the two men to life imprisonment.

In May 2005, at the PNP's general assembly, a majority of party members voted that Pedro Rosselló should replace fellow party member Kenneth McClintock Hernández as President of the Senate. McClintock announced that he would refuse to stand down. He received the support of five PNP senators who were consequently suspended from the party, and finally expelled in March 2006, as was

UNITED STATES COMMONWEALTH TERRITORIES

Puerto Rico

McClintock. McClintock continued to serve as President of the Senate and stated that he still considered himself a PNP politician.

In July 2005 Acevedo Vilá vetoed the proposed budget on the grounds that expenses were greater than income and that it was therefore unconstitutional. The Government continued to operate using the previous year's budget. However, in April 2006 Acevedo Vilá announced that the budget was insufficient to provide for the Government's operating expenses until the end of the financial year (30 June) and that non-essential public sector services would be suspended from 1 May unless the legislature approved an emergency loan, to fund the shortfall of US $740m., and the introduction of a 7% sales tax, to finance the loan repayments. The announcement prompted a protest march through San Juan in which more than 45,000 people participated. None the less, it was reported that 45 government agencies closed on 1 May, together with some 1,600 public schools, affecting an estimated 500,000 pupils and rendering some 95,760 workers temporarily unemployed. At a series of demonstrations in the capital, public sector employees demanded an early resolution to the impasse between the executive and the legislature. However, discussions between Acevedo Vilá and José Aponte Hernández, Speaker of the PNP-controlled House of Representatives, foundered on the proposed rate of tax. An emergency commission was established in May, composed of the Governor, members of the House of Representatives and banking agents, and mediated by the Archbishop of San Juan, Roberto Octavio González Nieves. The initiative resulted in an agreement to secure a loan and to replace excise tax with a general sales and use tax of 5.5%, with revenue to be divided between federal and local government. However, owing to inaccurate phrasing, the legislation that was enacted on 13 May authorized a combined sales tax of 7.0%. A petition filed by PNP deputies in early November requesting the Supreme Court to uphold the intended rate of tax was rejected and the law took effect later that month. In early February 2008 Acevedo Vilá suggested proposals to reduce the sales tax to 2.5% and introduce a new excise tax of 4.5% in order to stimulate the economy, but faced criticism from members of the legislature for failing to reduce government spending.

In December 2005 a US presidential task force on the status of Puerto Rico, commissioned by President Bush in December 2003, delivered its findings. It recommended that Congress approve legislation for a two-stage plebiscite to be held in Puerto Rico within a year. In the first stage, the people of Puerto Rico would be given the option to continue as part of the Commonwealth or to seek a change in status. In the event that they chose the latter, a second vote would be held on whether to be incorporated as a state within the USA or become an independent country. Irrespective of the outcome, any decision would have to be approved mutually by the US Congress and the Government of Puerto Rico. While the PNP and the PIP welcomed the report, it was criticized by Governor Acevedo Vilá and the PPD because it omitted autonomy as an option. In January 2006 both houses of the Puerto Rican legislature approved legislation calling on Congress to act on the recommendations of the task force. A series of proposed laws consistent with the findings of the task force was submitted to Congress throughout 2006, while a bill supported by Acevedo Vilá and the PPD was submitted in March 2007. The latter advocated that a constitutional convention choose one of three options: statehood, independence or a new or modified commonwealth status. The proposal provided for a referendum to be held on the recommended option, prior to its submission for debate in Congress.

Acevedo Vilá was the subject of corruption allegations in 2008 when an investigation by the FBI revealed details of improper campaign financing and tax fraud between 1999 and 2004. On 28 March the Governor was charged on 19 criminal counts relating to the use of illegally obtained donations to eliminate campaign debts and to pay for family holidays and other personal expenses. Among a further 12 associates also indicted were four businessmen from Philadelphia, Pennsylvania (USA), and a Puerto Rican business owner, who were accused of obtaining government contracts in return for making campaign donations. Acevedo Vilá pleaded not guilty to the charges and stated his intention to remain in office—and, indeed, stand for re-election in the November gubernatorial election—despite calls from opposition parties for his resignation. Following a federal court trial, Acevedo Vilá was cleared of all charges on 24 March 2009.

Gubernatorial and legislative elections were held on 4 November 2008. In the gubernatorial ballot Luis Fortuño of the PNP defeated the incumbent Acevedo Vilá, attracting 52.8% of the votes cast. The beleaguered Acevedo Vilá (see above) attracted 41.3% of the ballot. The PNP also increased its representation in the Legislative Assembly at the expense of the PPD, securing a majority in both the Senate and the House of Representatives (22 of 27 senate seats and 37 of 51 lower-house seats). Voter turn-out stood at 78%. Fortuño was sworn in as Governor on 5 January 2009. His new cabinet included former Senate President Kenneth McClintock Hernández as Secretary of State. Fortuño's running mate, Pedro Pierluisi Urrutia, succeeded him as Resident Commissioner in Washington, DC.

Government

Executive power is vested in the Governor, elected for a four-year term by universal adult suffrage. The Governor is assisted by an appointed Cabinet. Legislative power is held by the bicameral Legislative Assembly, comprising the Senate (with 27 members) and the House of Representatives (51 members). Additional members may be assigned in each chamber to ensure adequate representation of minority parties. The members of both chambers are elected by direct vote for four-year terms. The Resident Commissioner, also elected for a four-year term, represents Puerto Rico in the US House of Representatives, but is permitted to vote only in committees of the House. Puerto Ricans are citizens of the USA, but those resident in Puerto Rico, while eligible to participate in national party primary elections, may not vote in presidential elections.

Defence

The USA is responsible for the defence of Puerto Rico. Puerto Rico has a paramilitary National Guard numbering about 11,000, which is funded mainly by the US Department of Defense.

Economic Affairs

In the fiscal year ending 30 June 2007, according to official estimates, Puerto Rico's gross national income (GNI) was US $58,712m., equivalent to approximately $14,900 per head. During 2000–07, it was estimated the population increased at an average annual rate of 0.5%. Gross domestic product (GDP) per head increased, in real terms, by an average of 1.6% per year during 1998–2007, while GDP increased, in real terms, by an average of 2.1% per year over the same period. According to government estimates, GDP increased by 0.9% in 2006 but declined by 1.6% in 2007.

Agriculture, forestry and fishing contributed an estimated 0.4% of GDP in the fiscal year ending 30 June 2008, according to preliminary figures, and employed an average of 1.2% of the working population in the same period, according to preliminary official figures. Dairy produce and other livestock products are the mainstays of the agricultural sector. The principal crops are fruits (principally plantains, bananas and oranges) and coffee. Cocoa cultivation has been successfully introduced, and measures to improve agricultural land use have included the replanting of some sugar-growing areas with rice and the cultivation of plantain trees over large areas of unproductive hill land. Commercial fishing is practised on a small scale. The GDP of the agricultural sector increased, in real terms, at an average rate of 2.1% per year between 1980/81 and 1990/91. Agricultural GDP rose by approximately 1.5% in 1993/94.

According to preliminary official figures, industry (including manufacturing, construction and mining) provided an estimated 43.6% of GDP and employed 17.4% of the working population in 2007/08. Industrial GDP increased, in real terms, at an average annual rate of 2.9% between 1980/81 and 1990/91. It rose by 3.3% in 1993/94.

Mining and construction was estimated to provide about 2.1% of GDP in 2007/08 and construction alone employed 6.7% of the working population in the same fiscal year. Otherwise, Puerto Rico has no commercially exploitable mineral resources, although deposits of copper and nickel have been identified.

Manufacturing is a significant source of income, accounting for an estimated 41.5% of GDP and employing 10.6% of the working population in 2007/08. The principal branch of manufacturing in 2002/03, based on the value of output, was chemical products (accounting for 72.4% of the total sector), mainly drugs and medicines. Other important products were computers, electronic and electrical products (12.6%) and food products (6.0%). The GDP of the manufacturing sector increased, in real terms, by 2.9% per year between 1980/81 and 1990/91. The rate of advance was 3.5% in 1993/94. In 2007 total electricity production stood at 25,081m. kWh.

Services (including electricity, gas and water) provided an estimated 55.9% of GDP and engaged 81.4% of the employed labour force in 2007/08 (including 22.9% employed by the Government). In real terms, the GDP of all service sectors increased at an average rate of 4.9% per year between 1980/81 and 1990/91, and by 4.4% in 1993/94. Tourism is of increasing importance; in 2006/07 tourist arrivals were estimated at 5.1m. visitors (including 1.4m. excursionists), generating revenue totalling US $3,413.9m. Visitors from the US mainland comprised more than 75% of the total number of visitors (excluding excursionists) in 2006/07. The Government planned to add some 6,000 hotel rooms by 2009.

In 2006/07 there was a visible trade surplus of US $14,742.6m. but there was a deficit of $4,861m. on the current account of the balance of payments. In 2006/07 the principal source of imports was the USA (responsible for 50.1% of the total value of imports), which was also the principal market for exports (77.2% of the total). Other important trading partners included Belgium, Germany, Ireland, Japan and the US Virgin Islands. The principal imports in that year were chemicals and related manufactures (particularly pharmaceuticals and medicines, which accounted for 36.4% of the total value of imports), petroleum and coal products and manufactured food products. The principal exports were manufactured chemical products (pharmaceuticals and medicines accounted for 60.9% of total value of exports), medical equipment and supplies and computer and electronic products.

In 2006/07 there was a budget deficit of US $2,169.4m. (excluding other government fund financing), equivalent to 2.4% of GDP in that fiscal year. Puerto Rico's gross public debt at the end of the fiscal year to 30 June 2007 was an estimated $42,818.3m. The annual inflation rate averaged 9.7% in 2000–07. Consumer prices increased by an average of 6.8% in 2007. Puerto Rico is very densely populated, and unemployment has been a persistent problem, although, assisted by the growth in the tourism industry, the jobless rate declined during the 1990s. The average rate of unemployment was estimated at 10.4% in 2006/07.

Puerto Rico holds associate status in the UN Economic Commission for Latin America and the Caribbean (ECLAC, see p. 40) and has observer status in the Caribbean Community and Common Market (CARICOM, see p. 206). Puerto Rico declined to accept associate status in the Association of Caribbean States (ACS), formed in 1994, on the grounds of opposition by the US Government to the inclusion of Cuba. In July 2001 Puerto Rico applied for associate membership of CARICOM; the USA criticized the move, emphasizing that it had authority over the island's foreign policy as long as Puerto Rico held Commonwealth status.

US federal aid programmes are of central importance to the Puerto Rican economy, and the island has also received disaster relief in respect of hurricanes that widely disrupt the Puerto Rican economy intermittently. Economic growth has been inhibited by the lack of an adequate infrastructure. Government programmes of industrial and taxation incentives, aimed at attracting US and foreign investors and encouraging domestic reinvestment of profits and long-term capital investment, have generated growth in the manufacturing and services sectors. However, from 1996 the US Government progressively withdrew a number of important tax exemptions (collectively known as Section 936) enjoyed by US and foreign investors; the last vestiges of Section 936 were ended on 31 December 2006. The Government of Puerto Rico attempted to counteract the economic impact of their removal by seeking to establish the island as a centre for the finishing of Latin American manufactured goods destined for member states of the North American Free Trade Agreement (NAFTA, see p. 350). Following the closure of the US naval base at Ceiba in March 2004 (see Recent History), the former base became the site of the US $6,700m. Portal del Futuro development. The development was expected to create 20,000 direct jobs and a further 50,000 jobs indirectly over the following 30 years. Problems associated with years of local government financial mismanagement crystallized in 2006 when a calamitous budget shortfall precipitated a major political and economic crisis (see Recent History), resulting in a period of economic recession out of step with the region. The introduction of major revisions to the tax system produced some positive results in reducing the fiscal deficit, but with it came a fall in consumer and business confidence. In early 2009 the incoming Governor, Luis Fortuño, inherited an economy that was suffering its third consecutive year of decline. Worsening global economic conditions, together with the already poor investment climate, were expected to precipitate further economic decline in 2008/09–2010/11. Puerto Rico's close relationship with the USA made it particularly vulnerable to downturns in that nation's economy and Puerto Rico's financial institutions accrued heavy losses during the international banking crisis (which ensued from September 2008), as a result of their exposure to US 'sub-prime' loans. Many of the Commonwealth's banks were reported to have requested assistance under the US Treasury's Trouble Asset Relief Plan (TARP) in 2009. Upon taking office, Fortuño declared a state of fiscal emergency, introducing measures to reduce the fiscal deficit. However, the deterioration of the global economy during the second half of 2008 placed considerable strain on the budget for 2008/09, owing, in part, to higher and unemployment and a concomitant decline in receipts from income tax. He announced reductions in public sector employment, as well as freezes on salaries and social security benefits and tax increases. A fiscal stimulus programme was also introduced, in the hope of boosting investor confidence. GDP was estimated to have declined by 2.5% in 2008, with a further contraction, of 4.2%, forecast for 2009.

Education

The public education system is centrally administered by the Department of Education. Education is compulsory for children between six and 16 years of age. In 2005 there were an estimated 563,490 pupils attending public day schools and in 2007/08 an estimated 114,627 pupils attending private schools. The 12-year curriculum, beginning at five years of age, is subdivided into six grades of elementary school, three years at junior high school and three years at senior high school. Vocational schools at the high-school level and kindergartens also form part of the public education system. Instruction is conducted in Spanish, but English is a required subject at all levels. In 2004 there were five universities. The State University system consists of three principal campuses and six regional colleges. In 2005 there were some 101,453 students enrolled in higher education at public institutes. An estimated 31,227 students were enrolled at private institutes of higher education in 2007/08. In 2006/07 US $4,400.3m. of general government expenditure was allocated to education (equivalent to 25.6% of total expenditure).

Public Holidays

2009: 1 January (New Year), 6 January (Epiphany), 12 January (Birthday of Eugenio María de Hostos), 19 January (Martin Luther King Day), 16 February (Presidents' Day), 22 March (Emancipation of the Slaves), 10 April (Good Friday), 20 April (Birthday of José de Diego), 25 May (Memorial Day), 24 June (Feast of St John the Baptist), 4 July (US Independence Day), 20 July (Birthday of Luis Muñoz Rivera), 25 July (Constitution Day), 27 July (Birthday of José Celso Barbosa), 7 September (Labor Day), 12 October (Columbus Day), 11 November (Veterans' Day), 19 November (Discovery of Puerto Rico Day), 26 November (US Thanksgiving Day), 25 December (Christmas Day).

2010: 1 January (New Year), 6 January (Epiphany), 11 January (Birthday of Eugenio María de Hostos), 18 January (Martin Luther King Day), 15 February (Presidents' Day), 22 March (Emancipation of the Slaves), 2 April (Good Friday), 19 April (Birthday of José de Diego), 24 May (Memorial Day), 24 June (Feast of St John the Baptist), 4 July (US Independence Day), 20 July (Birthday of Luis Muñoz Rivera), 25 July (Constitution Day), 27 July (Birthday of José Celso Barbosa), 7 September (Labor Day), 12 October (Columbus Day), 11 November (Veterans' Day), 19 November (Discovery of Puerto Rico Day), 26 November (US Thanksgiving Day), 25 December (Christmas Day).

Weights and Measures

The US system is officially in force. Some old Spanish weights and measures, as well as the metric system, are used in local commerce.

Statistical Survey

Source (unless otherwise stated): Puerto Rico Planning Board, POB 41119, San Juan, 00940-1119; tel. (787) 723-6200; internet www.jp.gobierno.pr.

Area and Population

AREA, POPULATION AND DENSITY

Area (sq km)	8,959*
Population (census results)	
1 April 1990	3,522,037
1 April 2000	
Males	1,833,577
Females	1,975,033
Total	3,808,610
Population (estimates at mid-year)†	
2006	3,926,698
2007	3,941,160
2008	3,954,037
Density (per sq km) at mid-2008	441.3

* 3,459 sq miles.
† Source: Population Division, US Census Bureau.

PRINCIPAL TOWNS
(population estimates at mid-2008)

San Juan (capital)	422,665	Caguas	143,176
Bayamón	219,740	Guaynabo	102,956
Carolina	187,438	Arecibo	102,645
Ponce	179,353		

Source: Population Division, US Census Bureau.

UNITED STATES COMMONWEALTH TERRITORIES

Puerto Rico

BIRTHS, MARRIAGES AND DEATHS

	Registered live births Number	Rate (per 1,000)	Registered marriages Number	Rate (per 1,000)*	Registered deaths Number	Rate (per 1,000)
2000	59,460	15.5	25,980	8.9	28,550	7.6
2001	55,983	14.6	28,598	7.4	28,794	7.5
2002	52,871	13.7	25,645	6.6	28,098	7.3

* Rates calculated using estimates of population aged 15 years and over.
Source: Department of Health, Commonwealth of Puerto Rico.

2003 (rounded figures): Births 51,000 (birth rate 13.1 per 1,000); Deaths 28,000 (death rate 7.3 per 1,000).

2004 (rounded figures): Births 51,000 (birth rate 13.2 per 1,000); Deaths 29,000 (death rate 7.5 per 1,000).

2005 (rounded figures): Births 51,000 (birth rate 13.0 per 1,000); Deaths 30,000 (death rate 7.6 per 1,000).

2006 (rounded figures): Births 49,000 (birth rate 12.4 per 1,000); Deaths 28,000 (death rate 7.2 per 1,000).

2007 (rounded figures, preliminary): Births 50,000 (birth rate 12.7 per 1,000); Deaths 29,000 (death rate 7.4 per 1,000).

Source: mainly Population Division, US Census Bureau; Department of Health, Commonwealth of Puerto Rico; Puerto Rico Planning Board, Office of the Census.

Life expectancy (years at birth): 78.9 (males 74.9; females 82.8) in 2008 (Source: Pan American Health Organization).

ECONOMICALLY ACTIVE POPULATION
('000 persons aged 16 years and over)

	2005/06	2006/07	2007/08*
Agriculture, forestry and fishing	22	16	15
Mining	0	1	1
Manufacturing	136	135	129
Construction	88	94	82
Trade	271	260	257
Transportation	26	23	23
Communication	16	16	16
Finance, insurance and real estate	46	45	43
Other public utilities	16	14	15
Services	355	364	359
Government	280	296	279
Total employed	1,256	1,263	1,218
Unemployed	166	147	151
Total labour force	1,422	1,409	1,368

* Preliminary figures.

Health and Welfare

KEY INDICATORS

Total fertility rate (children per woman, 2008)	1.8
Under-5 mortality rate (per 1,000 live births, 2007)	8.9
Physicians (per 1,000 head, c. 2007)	2.2
Hospital beds (per 1,000 head, 2006)	3.0
Health expenditure (public, 2004): % of GDP	3.5

Source: mainly Pan American Health Organization.

For other sources and definitions see explanatory note on p. vi.

Agriculture

PRINCIPAL CROPS
('000 metric tons)

	2005	2006*	2007*
Tomatoes	18.7	18.7	18.8
Pumpkins, squash and gourds	14.3	14.3	14.3
Bananas	52.2	52.3	53.5
Plantains	76.4	77.0	80.0
Oranges	18.8	18.9	19.5
Guavas, mangoes and mangosteens	12.9	13.1	13.5
Pineapples	15.3	15.6	17.0
Coffee, green	7.9	8.0	8.1

* FAO estimates.

Aggregate production (may include official, semi-official or estimated data): Total fruits (excl. melons) 193.4 in 2005, 190.0 in 2006, 197.1 in 2007; Total roots and tubers 10.8 in 2005, 10.9 in 2006, 11.3 in 2007; Total vegetables (incl. melons) 45.5 in 2005, 45.5 in 2006, 45.8 in 2007.

Source: FAO.

LIVESTOCK
('000 head, year ending September)

	2005	2006*	2007*
Asses	4.5*	n.a.	n.a.
Cattle	376.9	378.0	380.0
Sheep	6.1	6.1	6.2
Goats	3.1	3.2	3.2
Pigs	48.7	48.7	50.0
Horses	6.4	6.5	6.5
Chickens	12,376	12,500	13,000

* FAO estimate(s).
Source: FAO.

LIVESTOCK PRODUCTS
('000 metric tons)

	2004	2005	2006*
Cattle meat	12.6	9.8	9.8
Pig meat	11.9	10.7	11.0
Chicken meat	49.8	49.6	50.0
Cows' milk	349.6	338.6	350.1
Hen eggs	11.4	11.2	11.2

* FAO estimates.

2007: Hen eggs 11,500 metric tons. Production of other commodities assumed to be unchanged from 2006 (FAO estimates).

Source: FAO.

Fishing

(metric tons, live weight)

	2004	2005	2006
Capture	2,428	2,551	2,042
Groupers	65	53	44
Snappers and jobfishes	404	498	370
Seerfishes	54	70	53
Other marine fishes	524	422	394
Caribbean spiny lobster	158	157	148
Stromboid conchs	1,203	1,329	1,005
Aquaculture	417	311	266
Tilapias	158	20	12
Penaeus shrimps	166	258	237
Total catch	2,845	2,862	2,308

Source: FAO.

UNITED STATES COMMONWEALTH TERRITORIES   Puerto Rico

Industry

SELECTED PRODUCTS
(year ending 30 June)

	1995/96	1996/97	1997/98*
Distilled spirits ('000 proof gallons)	25,343	36,292	33,471

*Preliminary.

Electric energy (million kWh): 24,500.2 in 2005; 24,870.0 in 2006; 25,080.6 in 2007 (Source: Government Development Bank for Puerto Rico, *Puerto Rico in Figures*).

Cement ('000 94–lb sacks): 37,173 in 2004; 36,847 in 2005; 36,910 in 2006 (Source: US Geological Survey).

Beer ('000 hectolitres): 317 in 1997; 263 in 1998; 259 in 1999 (Source: UN, *Industrial Commodity Statistics Yearbook*).

Finance

CURRENCY AND EXCHANGE RATES

Monetary Units
United States currency: 100 cents = 1 US dollar (US $).

Sterling and Euro Equivalents (31 December 2008)
£1 sterling = US $1.458;
€1 = US $1.392;
US $100 = £68.60 = €71.85.

BUDGET
(US $ '000, general government operations, year ending 30 June)

Revenue	2004/05	2005/06	2006/07
Income tax	5,564,673	6,181,995	6,389,973
Excise tax	2,101,216	2,013,998	1,475,311
Sales and use tax	—	—	583,639
Other taxes	7,128	15,145	4,663
Charges for services	702,691	828,993	757,724
Intergovernmental transfers	4,319,977	4,663,422	5,166,604
Interest	116,686	117,080	176,674
Other revenue	869,338	334,591	434,024
Total	13,681,709	14,155,224	14,988,612

Expenditure	2004/05	2005/06	2006/07
General government services	1,675,428	2,489,093	2,537,999
Public safety	2,409,668	2,108,152	1,864,256
Health	2,344,522	1,429,888	1,948,201
Public housing and welfare	3,320,849	3,130,373	3,048,585
Education	4,177,664	4,101,980	4,400,321
Economic development	706,066	516,444	533,253
Intergovernmental transfers	—	409,727	593,247
Capital outlays	665,630	502,348	512,824
Principal on debt servicing	391,554	446,281	904,604
Interest	733,931	822,234	814,723
Total	16,425,312	15,956,520	17,158,013

*Excluding net financing (US $ '000): 2,107,107 in 2004/05; 1,819,389 in 2005/06; 1,865,572 in 2006/07.

Source: Department of the Treasury, Commonwealth of Puerto Rico.

COST OF LIVING
(Consumer Price Index; base: 2000 = 100)

	2005	2006	2007
Food (incl. beverages)	212.1	257.1	281.0
Fuel and light	136.5	157.2	171.8
Rent	109.0	110.9	114.0
Clothing (incl. footwear)	95.1	95.5	100.7
All items (incl. others)	156.1	178.9	191.1

Source: ILO.

NATIONAL ACCOUNTS
(US $ million at current prices, year ending 30 June)

Expenditure on the Gross Domestic Product

	2005/06	2006/07	2007/08*
Government final consumption expenditure	10,329.6	10,512.4	10,320.7
Private final consumption expenditure	49,660.0	52,009.0	54,354.3
Gross domestic investment	12,211.2	11,980.5	11,380.5
Net sales to the rest of the world	–15,468.5	–15,938.9	–15,268.3
Gross national product	56,732.3	58563.1	60,787.2
Exports of goods and services			
Less Imports of goods and services	29,425.2	30,339.2	32,475.7
GDP in purchasers' values	86,157.5	88,902.3	93,262.9

*Preliminary.

Gross Domestic Product by Economic Activity

	2005/06	2006/07	2007/08*
Agriculture	394.1	417.6	385.9
Manufacturing	35,638.4	36,309.0	38,457.7
Construction and mining†	1,788.2	1,928.9	1,991.4
Transportation and public utilities‡	5,906.5	6,111.4	6,019.5
Trade	10,674.8	11,109.5	11,810.8
Finance, insurance and real estate	14,833.0	15,927.0	16,391.1
Services	8,277.0	8,571.8	8,866.5
Government	8,424.2	8,584.9	8,762.2
Sub-total	85,936.2	88,960.1	92,685.1
Statistical discrepancy	221.4	–58.1	577.7
Total	86,157.5	88,902.3	93,262.9

*Preliminary.
† Mining includes only quarries.
‡ Includes radio and television broadcasting.

BALANCE OF PAYMENTS
(US $ million, year ending 30 June)

	2004/05	2005/06	2006/07*
Merchandise exports	59,900.5	64,999.2	66,077.1
Merchandise imports	–45,998.9	–50,138.0	–51,334.5
Trade balance	13,901.6	14,861.2	14,742.6
Exports of services	6,346.3	6,199.4	6,788.2
Imports of services	–5,205.3	–4,950.5	–5,164.3
Balance on goods and services	15,042.6	16,110.1	16,366.5
Other income received	2,000.3	2,455.6	1,998.6
Other income paid	–32,140.0	–33,702.1	–34,013.8
Balance on goods, services and income	–15,097.4	–15,136.4	–15,648.7
Net transfers and interest	9,296.6	10,040.6	10,787.6
Current balance	–5,800.4	–5,095.9	–4,861.0
Net capital movements	5,631.4	–64.4	4,078.6
Overall balance	–169.0	–5,160.3	–782.4

*Preliminary.

4898
www.europaworld.com

UNITED STATES COMMONWEALTH TERRITORIES   *Puerto Rico*

External Trade

PRINCIPAL COMMODITIES
(US $ million, year ending 30 June)

Imports	2004/05	2005/06	2006/07
Mining products	1,347.4	1,231.0	1,510.0
Manufacturing products	35,921.3	39,808.4	42,259.4
Food	2,162.7	2,380.4	2,440.6
Products of petroleum and coal	2,924.5	3,962.1	4,152.8
Chemical products	17,086.8	19,089.0	21,675.9
Basic chemicals	3,211.2	3,543.1	4,150.3
Pharmaceuticals and medicines	12,967.6	14,467.3	16,494.7
Machinery, except electrical	1,111.2	1,267.8	1,266.0
Computer and electronic products	2,833.8	2,707.5	2,932.8
Transport equipment	2,786.2	2,674.3	1,922.3
Motor vehicles	2,454.8	2,325.0	1,608.7
Miscellaneous manufacturing	1,456.0	1,627.5	1,617.9
Total (incl. others)	38,905.2	42,630.2	45,265.8

Exports	2004/05	2005/06	2006/07
Manufacturing products	56,022.9	59,542.1	59,378.1
Food	3,626.0	3,956.2	3,751.5
Chemicals	37,191.0	38,618.9	39,587.8
Pharmaceuticals and medicines	34,712.2	35,970.3	36,567.9
Computer and electronic products	7,090.9	7,452.1	6,885.0
Computers and peripheral equipment	4,144.8	3,838.6	4,023.0
Electrical equipment, appliances and components	1,123.3	1,362.6	1,281.4
Miscellaneous manufacturing	4,010.7	5,164.4	4,788.6
Medical equipment and supplies	3,913.2	4,993.8	4,675.2
Total (incl. others)	56,543.2	60,118.7	60,010.8

PRINCIPAL TRADING PARTNERS
(US $ million, year ending 30 June)

Imports	2004/05	2005/06	2006/07
Brazil	689.9	676.4	672.9
China, People's Republic	n.a.	566.7	644.9
Dominican Republic	643.9	596.4	485.7
Germany	828.0	903.0	871.9
Ireland	7,716.8	7,950.2	9,492.6
Japan	1,554.8	1,834.9	1,661.3
Nigeria	n.a.	n.a.	903.4
Singapore	956.7	592.7	612.2
United Kingdom	524.5	513.4	n.a.
USA	19,133.7	21,502.9	22,662.4
US Virgin Islands	1,264.7	1,486.1	1,377.5
Total (incl. others)	38,905.2	42,629.5	45,265.8

Exports	2004/05	2005/06	2006/07
Belgium	1,335.5	1,464.1	2,013.9
Dominican Republic	845.2	887.0	987.6
France	693.5	410.2	358.8
Germany	544.5	635.5	2,046.3
Italy	414.9	216.3	n.a.
Japan	n.a.	458.3	526.6
Netherlands	1,800.6	2,356.7	2,763.8
Singapore	608.0	849.7	1,119.2
Spain	n.a.	n.a.	353.6
United Kingdom	749.2	693.8	935.0
USA	46,703.0	49,651.8	46,324.0
Total (incl. others)	56,543.2	60,118.7	60,010.8

Transport

ROAD TRAFFIC
(motor vehicles registered at 31 December)

	2004	2006*	2007
Passenger cars	2,210,998	2,341,820	2,421,055
Buses and coaches	3,308	3,503	3,698
Lorries (trucks) and vans	36,063†	100,841	106,446
Motorcycles	31,770	91,082	115,865

* Data for 2005 were not available.
† Privately-owned vehicles only.

Source: Federal Highway Administration, US Department of Transportation, *Highway Statistics*.

SHIPPING
(Port of San Juan, year ending 30 June)

	2005/06	2006/07	2007/08
Cruise passenger movements	1,299,323	1,374,379	1,496,853
Cruise-ship calls	550	563	581
Cargo movements ('000 short tons)	9,707.3	9,609.5	9,395.9

Source: Puerto Rico Ports Authority.

CIVIL AVIATION
(year ending 30 June)

	2005/06	2006/07	2007/08
Luis Muñoz Marín International Airport			
Passenger movements ('000)	10,680.8	10,321.2	n.a.
Freight (million lbs)	541.0	521.4	n.a.
Regional airports			
Passenger movements ('000)	1,008.1	1,129.5	1,294.7
Freight (million lbs)	266.3	255.5	243.2

Source: Puerto Rico Ports Authority.

Tourism

(year ending 30 June)

	2004/05	2005/06	2006/07*
Total visitors ('000)	3,685.9	3,722.0	3,687.0
From USA	2,828.6	2,910.7	2,867.3
From US Virgin Islands	18.8	19.2	19.4
From elsewhere	838.5	792.1	800.3
Excursionists (incl cruise passengers)	1,386.9	1,300.9	1,375.4
Expenditure ($ million)	3,238.6	3,369.3	3,413.9

* Preliminary figures.

Communications Media

	2003	2004	2005
Telephones ('000 main lines in use)	1,212.8	1,111.9	1,037.7
Mobile cellular telephones ('000 subscribers)	1,860.0	2,682.0	3,353.8
Internet users ('000)	764.0	862.0	915.6
Broadband subscribers ('000)	54.3	86.3	118.3

2006: Internet users 1,000,000.

Television receivers ('000 in use): 1,270 in 1999.

Radio receivers ('000 in use): 2,840 in 1997.

Facsimile machines ('000 in use): 543 in 1993.

Daily newspapers (1996): 3; average circulation ('000 copies) 475.

Non-daily newspapers (1988 estimates): 4; average circulation ('000 copies) 106.

Sources: UNESCO, *Statistical Yearbook*; UN, *Statistical Yearbook*; International Telecommunication Union.

Education

(public education at fall 2005, unless otherwise indicated)

	Institutes	Teachers	Enrolment
Elementary and secondary	1,523*	42,036	563,490
Post-secondary†	17‡	14,557§	67,990

* 2005/06.
† Excluding adult (enrolment 33,463 in 2005) and vocational education.
‡ 2006/07.
§ Four-year full-time equivalent teaching staff.

Adult and vocational education: 80 institutes (private only); 33,463 students enrolled (public only).

Source: National Center for Education Statistics, US Department of Education.

Private education (accredited private institutions, 2007/08 unless otherwise indicated): Institutes 145 (2003/04); Pre-primary enrolment 26,534; Elementary and secondary enrolment 114,627; Post-secondary enrolment 31,227 (Source: Consejo General de Educacíon, San Juan).

Adult literacy rate (UNESCO estimates): 94.1% (males 93.9%; females 94.4%) in 2002 (Source: UNESCO Institute for Statistics).

Directory

The Constitution

RELATIONSHIP WITH THE USA

On 3 July 1950 the Congress of the United States of America adopted Public Law No. 600, which was to allow 'the people of Puerto Rico to organize a government pursuant to a constitution of their own adoption'. This Law was submitted to the voters of Puerto Rico in a referendum and was accepted in the summer of 1951. A new Constitution was drafted in which Puerto Rico was styled as a Commonwealth, or estado libre asociado, 'a state which is free of superior authority in the management of its own local affairs', though it remained in association with the USA. This Constitution, with its amendments and resolutions, was ratified by the people of Puerto Rico on 3 March 1952, and by the Congress of the USA on 3 July 1952; and the Commonwealth of Puerto Rico was established on 25 July 1952.

Under the terms of the political and economic union between the USA and Puerto Rico, US citizens in Puerto Rico enjoy the same privileges and immunities as if Puerto Rico were a member state of the Union. Puerto Rican citizens are citizens of the USA and may freely enter and leave that country.

The Congress of the USA has no control of, and may not intervene in, the internal affairs of Puerto Rico.

Puerto Rico is exempted from the tax laws of the USA, although most other federal legislation does apply to the island. Puerto Rico is represented in the US House of Representatives by a non-voting delegate, the Resident Commissioner, who is directly elected for a four-year term. The island has no representation in the US Senate.

There are no customs duties between the USA and Puerto Rico. Foreign products entering Puerto Rico—with the single exception of coffee, which is subject to customs duty in Puerto Rico, but not in the USA—incur the same customs duties as would be paid on their entry into the USA.

The US social security system is extended to Puerto Rico, except for unemployment insurance provisions. Laws providing for economic co-operation between the Federal Government and the States of the Union for the construction of roads, schools, public health services and similar purposes are extended to Puerto Rico. Such joint programmes are administered by the Commonwealth Government.

Amendments to the Constitution are not subject to approval by the US Congress, provided that they are consistent with the US federal Constitution, the Federal Relations Act defining federal relations with Puerto Rico and Public Law No. 600. Subject to these limitations, the Constitution may be amended by a two-thirds' vote of the Puerto Rican Legislature and by the subsequent majority approval of the electorate.

BILL OF RIGHTS

No discrimination shall be made on account of race, colour, sex, birth, social origin or condition, or political or religious ideas. Suffrage shall be direct, equal and universal for all over the age of 18. Public property and funds shall not be used to support schools other than State schools. The death penalty shall not exist. The rights of the individual, of the family and of property are guaranteed. The Constitution establishes trial by jury in all cases of felony, as well as the right of habeas corpus. Every person is to receive free elementary and secondary education. Social protection is to be afforded to the old, the disabled, the sick and the unemployed.

THE LEGISLATURE

The Legislative Assembly consists of two chambers, the members of which are elected by direct vote for a four-year term. The Senate is composed of 27 members, who must be over 30 years of age. The House of Representatives is composed of 51 members, of whom 40 are elected on a constituency basis, and a further 11 are at large members, elected by proportional representation. Representatives must be over 25 years of age. The Constitution guarantees the minority parties additional representation in the Senate and the House of Representatives, which may fluctuate from one quarter to one third of the seats in each House.

The Senate elects a President and the House of Representatives a Speaker from their respective members. The sessions of each house are public. A majority of the total number of members of each house constitutes a quorum. Either house can initiate legislation, although bills for raising revenue must originate in the House of Representatives. Once passed by both Houses, a bill is submitted to the Governor, who can either sign it into law or return it, with his reasons for refusal, within 10 days. If it is returned, the Houses may pass it again by a two-thirds' majority, in which case the Governor must accept it.

The House of Representatives, or the Senate, can impeach one of its members for treason, bribery, other felonies and 'misdemeanours involving moral turpitude'. A two-thirds' majority is necessary before an indictment may be brought. The cases are tried by the Senate. If a Representative or Senator is declared guilty, he is deprived of his office and becomes punishable by law.

THE EXECUTIVE

The Governor, who must be at least 35 years of age, is elected by direct suffrage and serves for four years. Responsible for the execution of laws, the Governor is Commander-in-Chief of the militia and has the power to proclaim martial law. At the beginning of every regular session of the Assembly, in January, the Governor presents a report on the state of the treasury, and on proposed expenditure. The Governor chooses the Secretaries of Departments, subject to the approval of the Legislative Assembly. These are led by the Secretary of State, who replaces the Governor at need.

LOCAL GOVERNMENT

The island is divided into 78 municipal districts for the purposes of local administration. The municipalities comprise both urban areas and the surrounding neighbourhood. They are governed by a mayor and a municipal assembly, both elected for a four-year term.

The Government

EXECUTIVE
(April 2009)

Governor: LUIS FORTUÑO (took office 2 January 2009).
Secretary of State: KENNETH D. MCCLINTOCK HERNÁNDEZ.
Secretary of the Interior: JUAN CARLOS BLANCO.

UNITED STATES COMMONWEALTH TERRITORIES

Puerto Rico

Secretary of Justice: Antonio M. Sagardía.
Secretary of the Treasury: Juan Carlos Puig.
Secretary of Education: Carlos E. Chardón.
Secretary of the Family: Wilfredo J. Maldonado García.
Secretary of Labour and Human Resources: Miguel Romero.
Secretary of Transportation and Public Works: Rubén A. Hernández Gregorat.
Secretary of Health: Dr Jaime Rivera Dueño.
Secretary of Agriculture: Javier Rivera Aquino.
Secretary of Housing: Yesef Y. Cordero.
Secretary of Natural and Environmental Resources: Daniel Galán.
Secretary of Consumer Affairs: Luis Geraldo Rivera Marín.
Secretary of Recreation and Sports: Henry Newmann.
Secretary of Economic Development and Commerce: José R. Pérez Riera.
Secretary of Correction and Rehabilitation: Carlos Molina Rodríguez.
Secretary of Organization and Public Policy: Alejandro J. Figueroa.
Attorney-General: Irene S. Soroeta Kodesh.
Resident Commissioner in Washington: Pedro Pierluisi Urrutia.

GOVERNMENT OFFICES

Office of the Governor: La Fortaleza, POB 9020082, PR 00902-0082; tel. (787) 721-7000; fax (787) 724-1472; e-mail secretariomail@fortaleza.gobierno.pr; internet www.fortaleza.gobierno.pr.

Department of Agriculture: POB 10163, Santurce, PR 00908-1163; tel. (787) 721-2120; fax (787) 723-8512; e-mail webmaster@agricultura.pr; internet www.agricultura.gobierno.pr.

Department of Consumer Affairs: POB 41059, Minillas Station, San Juan, PR 00940-1059; tel. (787) 722-7555; fax (787) 726-0077; e-mail webmaster@daco.gobierno.pr; internet www.daco.gobierno.pr.

Department of Correction and Rehabilitation: Edif. Metropolitan Professional Park, Carretera 21, Km 4.2, Bo. Monacillos, San Juan, PR 00971; POB 71308, San Juan, PR 00936; tel. (787) 273-6464; fax (787) 792-7677; internet www.ac.gobierno.pr.

Department of Economic Development and Commerce: 355 Avda Roosevelt, Suite 401, Hato Rey, PR 00918; internet www.ddecpr.com; tel. (787) 765-2900; fax (787) 753-6874.

Department of Education: Avda Teniente César González, esq. Calle Juan Calaf, Urb. Industrial Tres Monjitas, San Juan, PR 00919-0759; POB 190759, Hato Rey, PR 00917; tel. (787) 759-2000; fax (787) 250-0275.

Department of the Family: POB 11398, Santurce, San Juan, PR 00910-1398; tel. (787) 294-4900; fax (787) 294-0732; internet www.familia.gobierno.pr.

Department of Health: POB 70184, San Juan, PR 00936-8184; tel. (787) 274-7676; e-mail webmaster@salud.gov.pr; internet www.salud.gov.pr.

Department of Housing: 606 Avda Barbosa, Juan C. Cordero, San Juan, PR 00928-1365; Apdo 21365, Rio Piedras, PR 00928; tel. (787) 274-2527; fax (787) 758-9263; e-mail mcardona@vivienda.gobierno.pr; internet www.vivienda.gobierno.pr.

Department of Justice: POB 9020192, San Juan, PR 00902-0192; tel. (787) 721-2900; fax (787) 724-4770; e-mail aalamo@justicia.gobierno.pr; internet www.justicia.gobierno.pr; incl. the Office of the Attorney-General.

Department of Labour and Human Resources: Edif. Prudencio Rivera Martínez, 505 Avda Muñoz Rivera, Hato Rey, PR 00918; tel. (787) 754-5353; fax (787) 753-4201; e-mail lortiz@dtrh.gobierno.pr; internet www.dtrh.gobierno.pr.

Department of Natural and Environmental Resources: Carretera 8838, Km 6.3, Sector El Cinco, Río Piedras, POB 366147, San Juan, PR 00936; tel. (787) 999-2200; fax (787) 723-4255; e-mail webmaster@drna.gobierno.pr; internet www.drna.gobierno.pr.

Department of Recreation and Sports: 1611 Antiguo Edif. del Fondo del Seguro del Estado, Avda Fernández Juncos, esq. Calle Bolívar, San Juan, PR 00902-3207; POB 9023207, Rio Piedras, PR 00909; tel. (787) 721-2800; fax (787) 728-0736; e-mail mraffaele@drd.gobierno.pr; internet www.drd.gobierno.pr.

Department of State: Apdo 9023271, San Juan, PR 00902-3271; tel. (787) 721-1768; fax (787) 723-3304; e-mail estado@gobierno.pr; internet www.estado.gobierno.pr.

Department of Transportation and Public Works: POB 41269, San Juan, PR 00940; tel. (787) 722-2929; fax (787) 728-8963; e-mail servciud@act.dtop.gov.pr; internet www.dtop.gov.pr.

Department of the Treasury: POB 9024140, San Juan, PR 00902-4140; tel. (787) 723-7085; e-mail infoserv@hacienda.gobierno.pr; internet www.hacienda.gobierno.pr.

Gubernatorial Election, 4 November 2008

Candidate	Votes	%
Luis G. Fortuño Burset (PNP)	1,025,945	52.84
Aníbal Acevedo Vilá (PPD)	801,053	41.26
Rogelio Figueroa García (PPR)	53,690	2.77
Edwin Irizarry Mora (PIP)	39,590	2.04
Total (incl. others)*	1,941,663	100.00

*Including 13,215 votes for write-in candidates, 3,282 blank votes and 4,888 invalid votes.

Legislature

LEGISLATIVE ASSEMBLY

Senate

President of the Senate: Thomas Rivera Schatz.

Election, 4 November 2008

Party	Seats
PNP	22
PPD	5
Total	27

House of Representatives

Speaker of the House: Jenniffer González Colón.

Election, 4 November 2008

Party	Seats
PNP	37
PPD	14
Total	51

Election Commission

Comisión Estatal de Elecciones de Puerto Rico (CEE): Avda Arterial B 500, Hato Rey, San Juan, PR 00919; POB 195552, San Juan, PR 00919-5552; tel. (787) 294-1190; e-mail hava@cee.gobierno.pr; internet www.ceepur.org; f. 1977; independent; Pres. Ramón E. Gómez-Colón; Dir Yvonne Rivera Picorelli.

Political Organizations

Frente Socialista: 103 Américo Miranda, POB 70359, San Juan, PR 00936; e-mail informacion@frentesocialista.org; internet members.tripod.com/frentesocialistapr; f. 2001; mem. orgs incl. the Partido Revolucionario de los Trabajadores Puertorriqueños (PRTP—Los Macheteros) and Movimiento Socialista de Trabajadores

Movimiento Socialista de Trabajadores (MST): Apdo 22699, Estación UPR, San Juan, PR 00931-2699; e-mail info@bandera.org; internet www.bandera.org; f. 1982 by merger of the Movimiento Socialista Popular and Partido Socialista Revolucionario; pro-independence; mainly composed of workers and university students.

Movimiento Independentista Nacional Hostosiano (MINH): f. 2004 by merger of the Congreso Nacional Hostosiano and Nuevo Movimiento Independentista (fmr mems of the Partido Socialista Puertorriqueño); pro-independence; Co-Pres Julio Muriente Pérez, Noel Colón Martínez.

Partido Independentista Puertorriqueño (PIP) (Puerto Rican Independence Party): 963 F. D. Roosevelt Ave, Hato Rey, San Juan PR 00920-2901; e-mail wjrb@independencia.net; internet www.independencia.net; f. 1946; advocates full independence for Puerto Rico as a socialist-democratic republic; Leader Rubén Berríos Martínez; Exec. Pres. Fernando Martín; Sec.-Gen. Juan Dalmau Ramírez; c. 6,000 mems.

Partido Nuevo Progresista (PNP) (New Progressive Party): POB 1992, Fernández Zuncos Station, San Juan 00910-1992; tel. (787) 289-2000; e-mail dannyls@caribe.net; internet www.pnp.org; f. 1967; advocates eventual admission of Puerto Rico as a federated state of the USA; Pres. Luis G. Fortuño Burset; c. 225,000 mems.

Partido Popular Democrático (PPD) (Popular Democratic Party): Comité Central PPD, Puerta de Tierra, POB 9065788, San

Juan, PR 00906-5788; tel. (787) 721-2001; e-mail lherrero@ppdpr.net; internet ppdpr.net; f. 1938; supports continuation and improvement of the present Commonwealth status of Puerto Rico; Pres. and Leader HÉCTOR J. FERRER RÍOS; c. 950,000 mems.

Partido Puertorriqueños por Puerto Rico (Puerto Ricans for Puerto Rico—PPR): POB 9858, San Juan, PR 00908; tel. (787) 622-0002; fax (787) 725-0001; e-mail contacto@popuertorico.com; internet www.porpuertorico.com; f. 2003 as an ecological ('green') party; formally registered as political party in 2007; promotes citizen participation, sustainable devt and quality of life; Pres. ROGELIO FIGUEROA.

Puerto Rican Republican Party: Suite 203, 1629 Avda Piñero, San Juan, PR 00920; tel. (787) 793-8084; e-mail cchardon@goppr.org; internet www.goppr.org; Chair. Dr TIODY DE JESÚS DE FERRÉ; Exec. Dir ANNIE J. MAYOL.

Puerto Rico Democratic Party: POB 19328, San Juan, PR 00910-3939; tel. (787) 274-2921; fax (787) 759-9075.

Refundación Comunista Puerto Rico: Organización RC, POB 13362, San Juan, PR 00908-3362; e-mail refundacionpcp@yahoo.es; internet www.refundacioncomunistapr.com; f. 2001; Marxist-Leninist; pro-independence; maintains close relations with the Frente Socialista; Contact ABALLARDE ROJO.

Judicial System

The Judiciary is vested in the Supreme Court and other courts as may be established by law. The Supreme Court comprises a Chief Justice and up to six Associate Justices, appointed by the Governor with the consent of the Senate. The lower Judiciary consists of Superior and District Courts and Municipal Justices equally appointed.

There is also a US Federal District Court, whose judges are appointed by the President of the USA. Judges of the US Territorial District Court are appointed by the Governor.

Supreme Court of Puerto Rico

POB 2392, Puerta de Tierra, San Juan, PR 00902-2392; tel. (787) 724-3551; fax (787) 725-4910; e-mail buzon@tribunales.gobierno.pr; internet www.tribunalpr.org.
Chief Justice: FEDERICO HERNÁNDEZ DENTON.
Justices: FEDERICO HERNÁNDEZ DENTON, EFRAÍN E. RIVERA PÉREZ, LIANA FIOL MATTA, ANABELLE RODRÍGUEZ RODRÍGUEZ, ERICK V. KOLTHOFF CARABALLO, MILDRED G. PABÓN CHARNECO, RAFAEL L. MARTÍNEZ TORRES.

US Territorial District Court for Puerto Rico

Clemente Ruiz-Nazario US Courthouse & Federico Degetau Federal Bldg, 150 Carlos Chardón St, Hato Rey, PR 00918; tel. (787) 772-3011; fax (787) 766-5693; internet www.prd.uscourts.gov.
Judges: JOSÉ A. FUSTÉ, CARMEN C. CEREZO, DANIEL R. DOMÍNGUEZ, JAY A. GARCÍA-GREGORY, AIDA M. DELGADO-COLÓN, GUSTAVO A. GELPÍ, FRANCISCO A. BESOSA, JUAN M. PÉREZ GIMÉNEZ, JAIME PIERAS, Jr, RAYMOND L. ACOSTA, SALVADOR E. CASELLAS.

Religion

About 73% of the population belonged to the Roman Catholic Church at the end of 2006. The Protestant churches active in Puerto Rico include the Episcopalian, Baptist, Presbyterian, Methodist, Seventh-day Adventist, Lutheran, Mennonite, Salvation Army and Christian Science. There is a small Jewish community numbering around 2,500 adherents.

CHRISTIANITY

The Roman Catholic Church

Puerto Rico comprises one archdiocese and four dioceses. At 31 December 2006 there were 2,873,860 adherents.

Bishops' Conference of Puerto Rico

POB 40682, San Juan, PR 00940-0682; tel. (787) 728-1650; fax (787) 728-1654; e-mail ceppr@coqui.net.
f. 1960; Pres. Rt Rev. ROBERTO OCTAVIO GONZÁLEZ NIEVES (Archbishop of San Juan de Puerto Rico).

Archbishop of San Juan de Puerto Rico: Rt Rev. ROBERTO OCTAVIO GONZÁLEZ NIEVES, Arzobispado, Calle San Jorge 201, Santurce, POB 00902-1967; tel. (787) 725-4975; fax (787) 723-4040; e-mail cancilleria@arqsj.org.

Other Christian Churches

Episcopal Church of Puerto Rico: POB 902, St Just, PR 00978; tel. (787) 761-9800; fax (787) 761-0320; e-mail iep@episcopalpr.org; internet www.episcopalpr.org; f. 1872; diocese of the Episcopal Church in the USA, part of the Anglican Communion; Leader Bishop Rt Rev. DAVID ANDRÉS ALVAREZ; 42,000 baptized mems.

Puerto Rico Council of Churches: Calle El Roble 54, Apdo 21343, Río Piedras, San Juan, PR 00928; tel. (787) 765-6030; fax (787) 765-5977; f. 1954 as the Evangelical Council of Puerto Rico; Pres. Rev. HÉCTOR SOTO; Exec. Sec. Rev. CRUZ A. NEGRÓN TORRES; 8 mem. churches.

BAHÁ'Í FAITH

National Spiritual Assembly: POB 11603, San Juan, PR 00910-2703; tel. (787) 763-0982; fax (787) 753-4449; e-mail bahaipr@prtc.net; internet www.bahaipr.org.

JUDAISM

Sha'are Zedek Synagogue-Community Center: 903 Avda Ponce de León, Santurce, San Juan, PR 00907; tel. (809) 724-4157; fax (809) 722-4157; f. 1942; Conservative congregation with 250 families Rabbi GABRIEL FRYDMAN.

There is also a reform congregation with 60 families.

The Press

Puerto Rico has high readership figures for its few newspapers and magazines, as well as for mainland US periodicals. Several newspapers have a large additional readership among the immigrant communities in New York.

DAILIES

(m = morning; s = Sunday)

El Nuevo Día: Parque Industrial Amelia, Carretera 165, Guaynabo; POB 9067512, San Juan, PR 00906-7512; tel. (787) 641-8000; fax (787) 641-3924; e-mail laferre@elnuevodia.com; internet www.elnuevodia.com; f. 1970; Chair. and Editor MARÍA LUISA FERRÉ RANGEL; Pres. MARÍA EUGENIA FERRÉ RANGEL; Dir LUIS ALBERTO FERRÉ RANGEL; circ. 202,212 (m), 254,769 (s).

Primera Hora: Parque Industrial Amelia, Calle Diana Lote 18, Guaynabo, PR 00966; POB 2009, Cataño, PR 00963-2009; tel. (787) 641-5454; fax (787) 641-4472; e-mail servicios@primerahora.com; internet www.primerahora.com; Pres. and Editor ANTONIO LUIS FERRÉ; Dir JORGE CABEZAS; Gen. Man. JUAN MARIO ALVAREZ CARTAÑA; circ. 133,483 (m), 92,584 (Sat.).

The San Juan Star: POB 364187, San Juan, PR 00936-4187; tel. (787) 782-4200; fax (787) 783-5788; internet www.thesanjuanstar.com; f. 1959; English; Pres. and Publr GERRY ANGULO; Gen. Man. SALVADOR HASBÚN; circ. 50,000.

El Vocero de Puerto Rico: Apdo 7515, San Juan, PR 00906-7515; tel. (787) 721-2300; fax (787) 722-0131; e-mail opinion@vocero.com; internet www.vocero.com; f. 1974; Publr and Editor GASPAR ROCA; circ 143,150 (m), 123,869 (Sat.).

PERIODICALS

BuenaVIDA: 1700 Fernández Juncos Ave, San Juan, PR 00909; tel. (787) 728-7325; f. 1990 as Buena Salud; monthly; health and fitness; Editor IVONNE LONGUEIRA; circ. 61,000.

Caribbean Business: 1700 Fernández Juncos Ave, San Juan, PR 00909-2938; POB 12130, San Juan, PR 00914-0130; tel. (787) 728-9300; fax (787) 726-1626; e-mail cbeditor@casiano.com; internet www.casiano.com/html/cb.html; f. 1973; weekly; business and finance; Man. Editor RAQUEL ROMÁN; circ. 45,000.

Educación: c/o Dept of Education, POB 190759, Hato Rey Station, San Juan, PR 00919; f. 1960; 2 a year; Spanish; Editor JOSÉ GALARZA RODRÍGUEZ; circ. 28,000.

La Estrella de Puerto Rico: 140 Roosevelt Bldg, Ave F. D. Roosevelt, Hato Rey, PR 00917; tel. (787) 754-4440; fax (787) 754-4457; e-mail myrna.lopez@periodicolaestrella.com; internet www.periodicolaestrella.com; f. 1983; weekly; Spanish and English; Editor-in-Chief FRANK GAUD; circ. 123,500.

Imagen: 1700 Fernández Juncos Ave, Stop 25, San Juan, PR 00909-2999; tel. (787) 728-4545; fax (787) 728-7325; e-mail imagen@casiano.com; internet www.casiano.com/html/imagen.html; f. 1986; monthly; women's interest; Editor ANNETTE OLIVERAS; circ. 80,000.

Qué Pasa: Loiza St Station, POB 6338, San Juan, PR 00914; tel. (787) 728-3000; fax (787) 728-1075; e-mail manoly@casiano.com; internet www.casiano.com/html/quepasa.html; f. 1948; quarterly; English; publ. by Puerto Rico Tourism Co; official tourist guide; Editor RONALD FLORES; circ. 120,000.

Resonancias: Instituto de Cultura Puertorriqueña, Oficina de Publicaciones, Ventas y Mercadeo. POB 9024184, San Juan, PR 00902-4184; tel. (787) 724-4215; fax (787) 723-0168; e-mail revista@icp.gobierno.pr; internet www.icp.gobierno.pr; f. 2000; 2 a year; Spanish; Puerto Rican and general culture and music; Editor GLORIA TAPIA; circ. 3,000.

Revista Colegio de Abogados de Puerto Rico: POB 9021900, San Juan, PR 00902-1900; tel. (787) 721-3358; fax (787) 725-0330;

e-mail carlosgil@prtc.net; f. 1914; quarterly; Spanish; law; Editor Lic. CARLOS GIL AYALA; circ. 10,000.

Revista del Instituto de Cultura Puertorriqueña: Oficina de Publicaciones, Ventas y Mercadeo, POB 9024184, San Juan, PR 00902-4184; tel. (787) 721-0901; e-mail revista@icp.gobierno.pr; internet www.icp.gobierno.pr; f. 1958; 2 a year; Spanish; arts, literature, history, theatre, Puerto Rican culture; Editor GLORIA TAPIA; circ. 3,000.

La Semana: Calle Cristóbal Colón, esq. Ponce de León, Casilla 6537, Caguas 00726-6537; tel. (787) 743-6537; e-mail gerentegeneral@lasemana.com; internet www.lasemana.com; weekly; f. 1963; Spanish; regional interest; Gen. Man. MARJORIE M. RIVERA RIVERA.

TeVe Guía: San Juan, PR; weekly; TV listings; circ. 470,000 (monthly).

La Torre: POB 23322, UPR Station, San Juan, PR 00931-3322; tel. (787) 758-0148; fax (787) 753-9116; e-mail ydef@hotmail.com; f. 1953; publ. by University of Puerto Rico; quarterly; literary criticism, linguistics, humanities; Editor YUDIT DE FERDINANDY; circ. 1,000.

Vea: POB 190240, San Juan, PR 00919-0240; tel. (787) 721-0095; fax (787) 725-1940; f. 1969; weekly; Spanish; TV, films and celebrities; Editor ENRIQUE PIZZI; circ. 92,000.

Vida Actual: 1700 Fernández Juncos Ave, San Juan, PR 00909; tel. (787) 728-3000; fax (787) 268-0135; internet www.casiano.com/html/vida_actual.html; f. 2000; fortnightly; family and general information; Editor ELSA FERNÁNDEZ MIRALLES; circ. 120,000.

El Visitante: POB 41305, San Juan, PR 00940-1305; tel. (787) 728-3710; fax (787) 268-1748; e-mail director@elvisitante.biz; internet www.elvisitante.net; f. 1975; weekly; Roman Catholic; Dir JOSÉ R. ORTIZ VALLADARES; Editor Rev. EFRAÍN ZABALA; circ. 59,000.

Publishers

Ediciones Huracán Inc: 874 Baldorioty de Castro, San Juan, PR 00925; tel. (787) 763-7407; fax (787) 753-1486; e-mail edhucan@caribe.net; f. 1975; textbooks, literature, social studies, history; Pres. CARMEN RIVERA-IZCOA.

Editorial Académica, Inc: 67 Santa Anastacia St, El Vigía, Río Piedras, PR 00926; tel. (787) 760-3879; f. 1988; regional history, politics, government, educational materials, fiction; Dir FIDELIO CALDERÓN.

Editorial Cordillera, Inc: 1500 Ponce de León Local 2, El Cinco, POB 3148, San Juan, PR 00926; tel. (787) 767-6188; fax (787) 767-8646; e-mail info@editorialcordillera.com; internet www.editorialcordillera.com; f. 1962; Puerto Rican history, culture and literature, educational, trade; Pres. PATRICIA GUTIÉRREZ; Sec. and Treas. ADOLFO R. LÓPEZ.

Editorial Cultural Inc: POB 21056, Río Piedras, San Juan, PR 00928; tel. (787) 765-9767; f. 1949; general literature and political science; Dir FRANCISCO M. VÁZQUEZ.

Instituto de Cultura Puertorriqueña: Oficina de Publicaciones, Ventas y Mercadeo, POB 9024184, San Juan, PR 00902-4184; tel. (787) 724-0700; fax (787) 723-0168; e-mail revista@icp.gobierno.pr; internet www.icp.gobierno.pr; f. 1955; literature, history, poetry, music, textbooks, arts and crafts; Dir GLORIA TAPIA.

University of Puerto Rico Press (EDUPR): POB 23322, UPR Station, Río Piedras, San Juan, PR 00931-3322; tel. (787) 250-0435; fax (787) 753-9116; e-mail edupr@upr.edu; internet www.laeditorialupr.com; f. 1947; general literature, children's literature, Caribbean studies, law, philosophy, science, educational; Exec. Dir MANUEL G. SANDOVAL BAÉZ.

Broadcasting and Communications

TELECOMMUNICATIONS

Junta Reglamentadora de Telecomunicaciones de Puerto Rico: Edif. Capital Center II, 235 Avda Arterial Hostos, Suite 1001, San Juan, PR 00918-1453; tel. (787) 756-0804; fax (787) 756-0814; e-mail correspondencia@jrtpr.gobierno.pr; internet www.jrtpr.gobierno.pr; telecommunications regulator; Pres. MIGUEL REYES DÁVILA.

Puerto Rico Telephone Co (PRTC): POB 360998, San Juan, PR 00936-0998; tel. (787) 782-8282; fax (787) 774-0037; internet www.telefonicapr.com; provides all telecommunications services in Puerto Rico; fmrly state-owned; acquired by America Móvil in 2007; Pres. and CEO ENRIQUE ORTIZ DE MONTELLANO RANGEL.

BROADCASTING

There were 120 radio stations and 15 television stations operating in 2002. The only non-commercial stations are the radio station and the two television stations operated by the Puerto Rico Department of Education. The US Armed Forces also operate a radio station and three television channels.

Asociación de Radiodifusores de Puerto Rico (Puerto Rican Radio Broadcasters' Asscn): Caparra Terrace, Delta 1305, San Juan, PR 00920; tel. (787) 783-8810; fax (787) 781-7647; e-mail prbroadcasters@centennialpr.net; f. 1947; Pres. MANUEL SANTIAGO SANTOS; Exec. Dir JOSÉ A. RIBAS DOMINICCI; 102 mems.

Finance

(cap. = capital; res = reserves; dep. = deposits; brs = branches; amounts in US dollars)

BANKING

Government Bank

Government Development Bank for Puerto Rico (Banco Gubernamental de Fomento para Puerto Rico—BGF): POB 42001, San Juan, PR 00940-2001; tel. (787) 722-2525; fax (787) 721-1443; e-mail gdbpr@bgf.gobierno.pr; internet www.gdb-pur.com; f. 1942; independent govt agency; acts as fiscal (borrowing) agent to the Commonwealth Govt and its public corpns and provides long- and medium-term loans to private businesses; equity 2,096.4, dep. 10,409.5m. (June 2006); Pres. CARLOS M. GARCÍA; Chair. RAFAEL F. MARTÍNEZ MARGARIDA.

Autoridad para el Financiamiento de la Vivienda de Puerto Rico: Edif. Capital Center, Arterial Hostos 235, Torre Norte, 11° y 12°, Of. 1201, Hato Rey, PR 00918; tel. (787) 765-7577; fax (787) 754-1440; f. 1961; fmrly Banco y Agencia de Financiamiento de la Vivienda de Puerto Rico; present name adopted in 2001; subsidiary of the Government Development Bank for Puerto Rico; finance agency; helps low-income families to purchase houses; Exec. Dir FERNANDO BERIO MUÑIZ.

Commercial Banks

Banco Bilbao Vizcaya Argentaria Puerto Rico: 15th Floor, Torre BBVA, 258 Muñoz Rivera Ave, San Juan 00918; POB 364745, San Juan, PR 00936-4745; tel. (787) 777-2000; fax (787) 777-2999; internet www.bbvapr.com; f. 1967 as Banco de Mayagüez; taken over by Banco Occidental in 1979; merged with Banco Bilbao Vizcaya, S.A. in 1988; named changed from BBV Puerto Rico in 2000; cap. 138.7m., res, surplus and profits 381.0m., dep. 5,598.9m. (Dec. 2006); Pres. ANTONIO UGUINA; 65 brs.

Banco Popular de Puerto Rico: POB 362708, San Juan, PR 00936-2708; tel. (787) 724-3659; e-mail internet@bppr.com; internet www.bppr.com; f. 1893; cap. 7.0m., res, surplus and profits 1,684.0m., dep. 22,448.0m. (Dec. 2006); Chair. and CEO RICHARD L. CARRIÓN; Pres. DAVID H. CHAFEY, Jr; 195 brs.

Banco Santander Puerto Rico: 207 Ponce de León Ave, Hato Rey, PR 00919; POB 362589, San Juan, PR 00936-0062; tel. (787) 759-7070; fax (787) 767-7913; e-mail jdiaz@bspr.com; internet www.santanderpr.com; f. 1976; cap. 101.2m., res, surplus and profits 486.9m., dep. 7,405.1m. (Dec. 2006); Pres. and CEO JUAN MORENO BLANCO; Chair. GONZALO DE LAS HERAS; 67 brs.

Citibank NA: Ochoa Bldg, 500 Tanca St, San Juan, PR 00901; tel. (787) 721-0108; 14 brs.

Doral Bank: Galería Paseos Mall, Grand Blvd Paseos, Suite 107, San Juan, PR 00926; tel. (787) 725-6060; fax (787) 725-6062; e-mail dbcw@doralbank.com; internet www.doralbank.com; cap. 400m., dep. 2,730m., assets 6,726m. (Dec. 2003); subsidiary of local bank-holding co, Doral Financial Corpn, which completed buyout negotiations with financial group, led by Bear Stearn Cos Inc (USA), in July 2007; 90% investor-owned, through Doral Holdings Delaware, LLC, since July 2007; CEO GLEN R. WAKEMAN; Chair. CALIXTO GARCÍA VELEZ; 37 brs.

Scotiabank de Puerto Rico: Plaza Scotiabank, 273 Ponce de León Ave, esq. Calle Méjico, Hato Rey, PR 00918; POB 362230, San Juan PR 00936-2230; tel. (787) 758-8989; fax (787) 766-7879; internet www.scotiabankpr.com; f. 1910; cap. 23.2m., res, surplus and profits 146.2m., dep. 1,333.8m. (Dec. 2006); Chair. PETER CARDINAL; Pres. and CEO TROY K. WRIGHT; 19 brs.

Savings Banks

First BanCorp: First Federal Bldg, 1519 Ponce de León Ave, POB 9146, Santurce, PR 00908-0146; tel. (787) 729-8200; fax (787) 729-8139; internet www.firstbankpr.com; f. 1948, adopted current name in 1998; operates FirstBank Puerto Rico; cap. and res 368.3m., dep. 3,363.0m. (Dec. 2000); Chair. LUIS M. BEAUCHAMP; 45 brs.

Oriental Bank and Trust: Ave Fagot, esq. Obispado M-26, Ponce; tel. (787) 259-0000; fax (787) 259-0700; e-mail ofg@anreder.com; internet www.orientalonline.com; total assets 2,039m. (June 2001); Pres. and CEO JOSÉ ENRIQUE FERNÁNDEZ; Chair. JOSÉ J. GIL DE LAMADRID.

Ponce Federal Bank, FSB: Villa esq. Concordia, POB 1024, Ponce, PR 00733; tel. (787) 844-8100; fax (787) 848-5380; f. 1958; Pres. and CEO HANS H. HERTELL; 19 brs.

UNITED STATES COMMONWEALTH TERRITORIES

Puerto Rico

R & G Corporation: POB 2510, Guaynabo, PR 00970; tel. (787) 766-6677; fax (787) 766-8175; internet www.rgonline.com; total assets 4,676m. (Dec. 2001); Pres. and CEO ROLANDO RODRÍGUEZ; Chair. JUAN AGOSTO-ALICEA.

SAVINGS AND LOAN ASSOCIATIONS

Westernbank Puerto Rico: 19 West McKinley St, Mayagüez, PR 00680; tel. (787) 834-8000; fax (787) 831-5958; internet www.wbpr.com; cap. and res 250.6m., dep. 2,610.4m. (Dec. 2000); Chair. and CEO FRANK C. STIPES; 31 brs.

Banking Organization

Puerto Rico Bankers' Association: 208 Ponce de León Ave, Suite 1014, San Juan, PR 00918-1002; tel. (787) 753-8630; fax (787) 754-6022; e-mail info@abpr.com; internet www.abpr.com; Pres. RAFAEL BLANCO; Vice-Pres. JOSÉ DÍAZ.

INSURANCE

Atlantic Southern Insurance Co: POB 362889, San Juan, PR 00936-2889; tel. (787) 767-9750; fax (787) 764-4707; internet www.atlanticsouthern.com; f. 1945; Chair. DIANE BEAN SCHWARTZ; Pres. RAMÓN L. GALANES.

Caribbean American Life Assurance Co: 273 Ponce de León Ave, Suite 1300, Scotiabank Plaza, San Juan, PR 00917; tel. (787) 250-1199; fax (787) 250-7680; internet www.calac.com; Pres. IVÁN C. LOPÉZ.

Cooperativa de Seguros Multiples de Puerto Rico: POB 363846, San Juan, PR 00936-3846; internet www.segurosmultiples.coop; general insurance; Pres. RENÉ A. CAMPOS CARBONELL.

La Cruz Azul de Puerto Rico: Carretera Estatal 1, Km 17.3, Río Piedras, San Juan, PR 00927; POB 366068, San Juan, PR 00936-6068; tel. (787) 272-9898; fax (787) 272-7867; e-mail scliente@cruzazul.com; internet www.cruzazul.com; Exec. Dir MARKS VIDAL.

FirstBank Insurance Agency, Inc: Las Vistas Shopping Village, Suite 11, 300 Felisa Rincón de Gautier, POB 9146, San Juan, PR 00908-0146; tel. (787) 292-4380; fax (787) 292-4355; internet www.firstbankpr.com; owned by First BanCorp.

Great American Life Assurance Co of Puerto Rico: POB 363786, San Juan, PR 00936-3786; tel. (787) 758-4888; fax (787) 766-1985; e-mail galifepr@galifepr.com; known as General Accident Life Assurance Co until 1998; Pres. ARTURA CARIÓN; Sr Vice-Pres. EDGARDO DIAZ.

National Insurance Co: POB 366107, San Juan, PR 00936-6107; tel. (787) 758-0909; fax (787) 756-7360; internet www.nicpr.com; f. 1961; subsidiary of National Financial Group; Chair., Pres. and CEO CARLOS M. BENÍTEZ, Jr.

Pan American Life Insurance Co: POB 364865, San Juan, PR 00936-4865; tel. (787) 620-1414; fax (787) 999-1250; e-mail jortega@panamericanlife.com; internet www.panamericanlife.com; Regional Pres. JUAN A. ORTEGA; Gen. Man. MAITE MUÑOZGUREN.

Puerto Rican-American Insurance Co: POB 70333, San Juan, PR 00936-8333; tel. (787) 250-5214; fax (787) 250-5371; f. 1920; total assets 119.9m. (1993); Chair. and CEO RAFAEL A. ROCA; Pres. RODOLFO E. CRISCUOLO.

Security National Life Insurance Co: POB 193309, Hato Rey, PR 00919; tel. (787) 753-6161; fax (787) 758-7409; Pres. CARLOS FERNÁNDEZ.

Universal Insurance Group: Calle 1, Lote 10, 3°, Metro Office Park, Guaynabo; POB 2145, San Juan, PR 00922-2145; tel. (787) 793-7202; fax (787) 782-0692; internet www.universalpr.com; f. 1972; comprises Universal Insurance Co, Eastern America Insurance Agency and Caribbean Alliance Insurance Co; Chair. and CEO LUIS MIRANDA CASAÑAS.

There are numerous agents, representing Puerto Rican, US and foreign companies.

Trade and Industry

DEVELOPMENT ORGANIZATION

Puerto Rico Industrial Development Co (PRIDCO): POB 362350, San Juan, PR 00936-2350; 355 Roosevelt Ave, Hato Rey, San Juan, PR 00918; tel. (787) 758-4747; fax (787) 764-1415; internet www.pridco.com; public agency responsible for the govt-sponsored industrial devt programme; Exec. Dir JAVIER VASQUÉZ MORALES.

CHAMBERS OF COMMERCE

Chamber of Commerce of Puerto Rico: 100 Calle Tetuán, POB 9024033, San Juan, PR 00902-4033; tel. (787) 721-6060; fax (787) 723-1891; e-mail ebigas@camarapr.net; internet www.camarapr.org; f. 1913; Pres. JOSÉ JULIÁN ALVAREZ-MALDONADO; Exec. Vice-Pres. EDGARDO BIGAS VALLADARES; 1,800 mems.

Chamber of Commerce of the South of Puerto Rico: 65 Calle Isabel, POB 7455, Ponce, PR 00732-7455; tel. (787) 844-4400; fax (787) 844-4705; e-mail camarasur@prtc.net; internet www.camarasur.org; f. 1885; Pres. ROLANDO EMMANUELLI JIMÉNEZ; 550 mems.

Chamber of Commerce of the West of Puerto Rico Inc: Edif. Doral Bank, Suite 905, 101 Calle Méndez Vigo Oeste, POB 9, Mayagüez, PR 00680; tel. (787) 832-3749; fax (787) 832-4287; e-mail info@ccopr.com; internet www.ccopr.com; f. 1962; Pres. NELSON ALBINO; 300 mems.

Puerto Rico/United Kingdom Chamber of Commerce: 102 San Justo, San Juan, PR 00901; tel. (877) 594-7354; fax (787) 721-7333; e-mail iancourt@bivapr.net; internet users.bivapr.net/iancourt; Chair. Dr IAN COURT; 120 mems.

INDUSTRIAL AND TRADE ASSOCIATIONS

Home Builders' Association of Puerto Rico: 1605 Ponce de León Ave, Condominium San Martín, Santurce, San Juan, PR 00909; tel. (787) 723-0279; Exec. Dir MARÍA ELENA CRISTY; 150 mems.

Pharmaceutical Industry Association of Puerto Rico (PIA-PR): City View Plaza, Suite 407, Guaynabo, PR 00968; tel. (787) 622-0500; fax (787) 622-0503; e-mail contact@piapr.com; internet www.piapr.com; Chair. DANERIS FERNÁNDEZ; 19 mem. cos.

Puerto Rico Farm Bureau: 1605 Ponce de León Ave, Suite 403, Condominium San Martín, San Juan, PR 00909-1895; tel. (787) 721-5970; fax (787) 724-6932; f. 1925; Pres. ANTONIO ALVAREZ; over 1,500 mems.

Puerto Rico Manufacturers' Association (PRMA): POB 195477, San Juan, PR 00919-5477; tel. (787) 759-9445; fax (787) 756-7670; e-mail williamriefkohl@prma.com; internet www.prma.com; Pres. JOSEN ROSSI; Exec. Vice-Pres. WILLIAM RIEFKOHL.

Puerto Rico United Retailers Center: POB 190127, San Juan, PR 00919-0127; tel. (787) 641-8405; fax (787) 641-8406; e-mail cud@centrounido.com; internet www.centrounido.org; f. 1891; represents small and medium-sized businesses; Pres. PEDRO L. MALAVE; 20,000 mems.

UTILITIES

Electricity

Autoridad de Energía Eléctrica (AEE): POB 364267, San Juan, PR 00936-4267; tel. (787) 289-3434; fax (787) 289-4690; e-mail director@prepa.com; internet www.aeepr.com; govt-owned electricity corpn, opened to private co-generators in the mid-1990s; installed capacity of 4,389 MW; Exec. Dir MIGUEL CORDERO LÓPEZ.

TRADE UNIONS

American Federation of Labor–Congress of Industrial Organizations (AFL–CIO): San Juan; internet www.afl-cio.org; Regional Dir AGUSTÍN BENÍTEZ; c. 60,000 mems.

Central Puertorriqueña de Trabajadores (CPT): POB 364084, San Juan, PR 00936-4084; tel. (787) 781-6649; fax (787) 277-9290; f. 1982; Pres. FEDERICO TORRES MONTALVO.

Confederación General de Trabajadores de Puerto Rico: 620 San Antonio St, San Juan, PR 00907; f. 1939; Pres. FRANCISCO COLÓN GORDIANY; 35,000 mems.

Federación del Trabajo de Puerto Rico (AFL–CIO): POB S-1648, San Juan, PR 00903; tel. (787) 722-4012; f. 1952; Pres. HIPÓLITO MARCANO; Sec.-Treas. CLIFFORD W. DEPIN; 200,000 mems.

Puerto Rico Industrial Workers' Union, Inc: POB 22014, UPR Station, San Juan, PR 00931; Pres. DAVID MUÑOZ HERNÁNDEZ.

Sindicato Empleados de Equipo Pesado, Construcción y Ramas Anexas de Puerto Rico, Inc (Construction and Allied Trades Union): Calle Hicaco 95, Urb. Milaville, Río Piedras, San Juan, PR 00926; f. 1954; Pres. JESÚS M. AGOSTO; 950 mems.

Sindicato de Obreros Unidos del Sur de Puerto Rico (United Workers' Union of South Puerto Rico): POB 106, Salinas, PR 00751; f. 1961; Pres. JOSÉ CARABALLO; 52,000 mems.

Unión General de Trabajadores de Puerto Rico: Apdo 29247, Estación de Infantería, Río Piedras, San Juan, PR 00929; tel. (787) 751-5350; fax (787) 751-7604; f. 1965; Pres. JUAN G. ELIZA-COLÓN; Sec.-Treas. OSVALDO ROMERO-PIZARRO.

Unión de Trabajadores de la Industria Eléctrica y Riego de Puerto Rico (UTIER): POB 13068, Santurce, San Juan, PR 00908; tel. (787) 721-1700; e-mail utier@coqui.net; internet www.utier.org; Pres. RICARDO SANTOS RAMOS; 6,000 mems.

Transport

RAILWAYS

In January 2004 a 17-km urban railway (Tren Urbano), capable of carrying some 300,000 passengers per day, was inaugurated in greater San Juan. The railway took eight years to build and cost some US $2,150m. In 2007 plans were announced for a light-rail line to connect the urban area of Caguas with the Tren Urbano system, at a cost of US $450m. As of May 2009 construction was yet to begin.

Alternativa de Transporte Integrado (ATI) (Integrated Transportation Alternative): San Juan; internet www.ati.gobierno.pr; govt agency; operates the Tren Urbano railway system.

Ponce and Guayama Railway: Aguirre, PR 00608; tel. (787) 853-3810; owned by the Corporación Azucarera de Puerto Rico; transports sugar cane over 96 km of track route; Exec. Dir A. MARTÍNEZ; Gen. Supt J. RODRÍGUEZ.

ROADS

The road network totalled 24,431 km (15,181 miles) in 2003, of which some 94% was paved. A modern highway system links all cities and towns along the coast and cross-country. A highways authority oversees the design and construction of roads, highways and bridges. In April 2002 it was announced that some US $585.6m. was to be invested in projects to improve or expand the road network.

Autoridad de Carreteras: Centro Gobierno Roberto Sanchez Vilella, Edif. Sur Avda de Diego 328, POB 42007, Santurce, San Juan, PR 00940-2007; tel. (787) 721-8787; fax (787) 727-5456; internet www.dtop.gov.pr/act; Exec. Dir LUIS TRINIDAD GARAY.

SHIPPING

There are 11 major ports on the island, the principal ones being San Juan, Ponce and Mayagüez. Other ports include Guayama, Guayanilla, Guánica, Yabucoa, Aguirre, Aguadilla, Fajardo, Arecibo, Humacao and Arroyo. San Juan, one of the finest and longest all-weather natural harbours in the Caribbean, is the main port of entry for foodstuffs and raw materials and for shipping finished industrial products. In 2005 it handled more than 10.0m. metric tons of cargo. Under US cabotage laws all maritime freight traffic between the USA and Puerto Rico must be conducted using US-registered vessels. Passenger traffic is limited to tourist cruise vessels. Work on the US $700m. Las Américas 'megaport' was ongoing in 2009. In April 2005 a high-speed ferry service was launched, connecting San Juan to the islands of Vieques and Culebra.

Autoridad de los Puertos (Puerto Rico Ports Authority): Calle Lindbergh, 64 Antigua Base Naval Miramar, San Juan, PR 00907; POB 362829, San Juan, PR 00936-2829; tel. (787) 723-2260; fax (787) 722-7867; e-mail webmaster@prpa.gobierno.pr; internet www.prpa.gobierno.pr; f. 1942 as the Autoridad de Transporte de Puerto Rico; present name adopted in 1955; manages and administers all ports and airports; Exec. Dir FERNANDO J. BONILLA.

CIVIL AVIATION

There are two international airports on the island (Luis Muñoz Marín at Carolina, San Juan, and Rafael Hernández at Aguadilla) and nine regional airports. There are also six heliports.

Tourism

An estimated 3.7m. tourists visited Puerto Rico in 2006/07, when revenue from this source was estimated at US $3,414m. Almost 78% of all tourist visitors were from the US mainland. In 2004 there were approximately 12,864 hotel rooms. The Government planned to add a further 6,000 rooms by 2009.

Compañía de Turismo (Puerto Rico Tourism Co): Edif. La Princesa, 2 Paseo La Princesa, POB 9023960, San Juan, PR 00902-3960; tel. (787) 721-2400; fax (787) 722-6238; e-mail drodriguez2@prtourism.com; internet www.gotopuertorico.com; f. 1970; Exec. Dir TERESTELLA GONZÁLEZ DENTON.

UNITED STATES EXTERNAL TERRITORIES

The External or Unincorporated Territories of the USA comprise the Pacific Territories of American Samoa and Guam, the Caribbean Territory of the US Virgin Islands, and a number of smaller islands.

AMERICAN SAMOA

Introductory Survey

Location, Climate, Language, Religion, Flag, Capital

American Samoa comprises the seven islands of Tutuila, Ta'u, Olosega, Ofu, Aunu'u, Rose and Swains. They lie in the southern central Pacific Ocean, along latitude 14°S at about longitude 170°W, about 3,700 km (2,300 miles) south-west of Hawaii. The temperature normally ranges between 21°C (70°F) and 32°C (90°F), and the average annual rainfall is 5,000 mm (197 ins), the greatest precipitation occurring between December and March. English and Samoan, a Polynesian language, are spoken. The population is largely Christian, more than 50% being members of the Christian Congregational Church. The flag has a dark blue field, on which is superimposed a red-edged white triangle (with its apex at the hoist and its base at the outer edge of the flag), containing an eagle, representing the USA, grasping in its talons a yellow *fue* (staff) and *uatogi* (club), Samoan symbols of sovereignty. The capital is Pago Pago, on Tutuila (the officially designated seat of government is the village of Fagatogo).

Recent History

The Samoan islands were first visited by Europeans in the 1700s, but it was not until 1830 that missionaries from the London Missionary Society settled there. In 1878 the Kingdom of Samoa, then an independent state, gave the USA the right to establish a naval base at Pago Pago. The islands were also of interest to the United Kingdom and Germany, but the former withdrew in 1899, leaving the western islands for Germany to govern. The chiefs of the eastern islands ceded their lands to the USA in 1904, and the islands officially became an Unincorporated Territory of the USA in 1922.

Until 1978 American Samoa was administered by a Governor, appointed by the US Government, with a legislature comprising the Senate and the House of Representatives. In November 1977 American Samoa's first gubernatorial election took place, and in January 1978 Peter Tali Coleman of the Republican Party, who had previously served in the position between 1956 and 1961, was inaugurated as the islands' first directly elected Governor. He was re-elected for a further term in November 1980, after three years in office instead of the prescribed four, in order to allow synchronization with mainland US elections in 1980. At the gubernatorial election of November 1984 A. P. Lutali of the Democratic Party was elected Governor and Eni Hunkin (who subsequently adopted the use of his chiefly name, Faleomavaega) became Lieutenant-Governor. The High Court of American Samoa had previously ruled that Coleman was ineligible to stand for election to a third successive term as Governor, as legislation restricted tenure by any individual to two successive terms. In October 1986 a constitutional convention completed a comprehensive redrafting of the American Samoan Constitution. However, the draft revision had yet to be submitted to the US Congress in the early 21st century. In April 2004 it was announced that the Political Status Study Commission was to examine the territory's situation and submit its recommendations prior to the holding of another constitutional convention.

Meanwhile, American Samoa continued to be represented in the federal legislature by a non-voting delegate, the first election for this post having been held in 1981. The islands' Delegate was permitted to vote in committee but not on the floor of the US House of Representatives. In July 1988 the Territory's Delegate in Washington, DC, Fofo Sunia, announced that he would not seek re-election, as he was under official investigation for alleged financial mismanagement. In October he received a prison sentence for fraud. Eni Faleomavaega replaced Sunia as American Samoa's Delegate to the US House of Representatives in November. At the gubernatorial election held in November 1988 Republican Peter Coleman was returned to office for a third term as Governor, and Galea'i Poumele replaced Faleomavaega as Lieutenant-Governor. However, at the next gubernatorial election conducted in November 1992 Peter Coleman was defeated by A. P. Lutali. At elections to the House of Representatives in November 1994 about one-third of those members seeking re-election were defeated. Faleomavaega was re-elected as non-voting Delegate.

Gubernatorial and legislative elections took place in November 1996. An estimated 87% of eligible voters participated in the election, at which only eight of the 18 members seeking re-election to the Fono were successful. At a second round of voting the incumbent Lieutenant-Governor, the Democrat Tauese Sunia, was elected Governor with 51.3% of the votes cast, defeating Lealaifuaneva Peter Reid, Jr, who secured 48.7% of votes. Eni Faleomavaega was re-elected as Delegate to the US House of Representatives, winning 56.5% of the votes cast, defeating Gus Hannemann, who won 43.5% of votes.

The decision in July 1997 by the Government of neighbouring Western Samoa to change the country's name to simply Samoa caused some controversy. Legislation approved in March 1998 by the Territory's House of Representatives stated that American Samoa should not recognize the new name, which was viewed by many islanders as serving to undermine their own Samoan identity. Also in response to the change of name, legislation prohibiting citizens of the former Western Samoa from owning land in American Samoa was approved. Nevertheless, some rapprochement followed. In August 2004 plans were announced for greater economic co-operation, and in November a twice-weekly air link commenced operations. However, concerns were expressed at the decision of the Samoan Government in March 2005 to require of American Samoan citizens travelling to Samoa a permit and a passport. In April a bilateral meeting was held in the Samoan capital, and leaders began negotiations on the issue of travel requirements. Meanwhile, in late March the Samoan Government announced plans to open a consulate in American Samoa.

In November 1998 Eni Faleomavaega was re-elected as the islands' Delegate to the US House of Representatives. In the same month, following a dispute lasting several years, five leading US tobacco companies reached a legal settlement with most of the individual states of the USA and several of its territories, including American Samoa. It was agreed that between 1998 and 2025 American Samoa was to receive a total of some US $29m. in compensation for the harmful effects of cigarette-smoking suffered by its inhabitants.

At elections held on 7 November 2000 Democrat Tauese Sunia was narrowly re-elected as Governor, receiving 50.7% of the votes cast, compared with 47.9% for the independent candidate, Senator Lealaifuaneva. However, following the Chief Electoral Officer's refusal to allow a recount, as requested by Lealaifuaneva (who claimed that absentee ballots had not been properly handled), Lealaifuaneva filed a lawsuit against the Government; this was dismissed by the High Court in early December. At the US congressional elections, held concurrently, no candidate received the necessary 50% majority, Eni Faleomavaega winning 45.7% of votes cast, compared with 30.3% for Gus Hannemann. A second round of polling took place on 21 November, when Faleomavaega was reported to have won 61.1% of the votes.

The issue of US jurisdiction in the Territory was raised again in September 2001, when the islands' Senate approved a resolution urging discussion with the US Government with regard to the conferral of limited federal jurisdiction to the High Court of American Samoa, the only US territory without a sitting federal judge. A congressional public survey, conducted in the same month, registered wide popular support for a Federal Court and Public Prosecutor. At a meeting of the UN General Assembly in January 2002, the UN accepted American Samoa's proposal of May 2001 to be removed from the list of colonized territories. The Governor had sent a resolution to the UN Committee on Decolonization affirming American Samoa's wish to remain a US territory.

In September 2002 the Territory's immigration procedures were amended to give the Attorney-General, rather than the Immigration Board, the ultimate authority to grant permanent residency status to aliens. The House of Representatives of American Samoa also approved a resolution to repeal legislation automatically conferring US citizenship in the Territory to foreign parents. In the same month the Territory's intelligence agencies claimed that the Speaker of the House of Representatives, Tuanaitau Tuia, had used public funds to purchase a car and to finance private travel for his wife. Meanwhile, in June a former president of the Amerika Samoa Bank (now ANZ Amerika Samoa Bank) was convicted of fraud for his involvement in a scheme that had misappropriated US $75m. of investors' money.

Further allegations of corruption in the banking sector followed in 2004. The government-owned Development Bank of American Samoa was being investigated in April of that year by an anti-corruption committee of the Senate, after records suggested favouritism in the approval of loans.

In elections for American Samoa's Delegate to the US House of Representatives on 6 November 2002, Eni Faleomavaega won 41.3% of the votes cast, Fagafaga Daniel Langkilde secured 32.1% and Aumua Amata Coleman won 26.6%. Since none of the candidates received the requisite 50% of votes, Faleomavaega and Langkilde entered a second round of voting on 19 November, at which Faleomavaega secured an eighth term in office. In March 2003 Governor Tauese Sunia died while en route to Hawaii for medical treatment; Lieutenant-Governor Togiola Tulafono replaced him and appointed Ipulasi Aitofele Sunia, late Governor's younger brother, as his deputy.

In December 2002 legislation was introduced that prohibited nationals of 23 countries deemed to present a terrorist threat from entering the Territory, unless they were granted special permission. Opposition groups in Fiji expressed their displeasure at the inclusion of their country on the list, owing to its large Muslim population.

In January 2003 the Senate approved a motion to begin expulsion hearings against Senator Faamausili Pola. Members of the chamber had already voted to remove him in September 2002, when it was alleged that he had not been elected according to Samoan tradition. In March 2003 it was reported that the South Korean owner of the Daewoosa Samoa clothing factory, Kil Soo Lee, had been convicted by a US court of trafficking in humans. (In June 2005 Lee was sentenced to 40 years' imprisonment; Lee subsequently announced his intention to appeal against the verdict.) The mainly Vietnamese and Chinese factory employees had reportedly received very low wages and worked in appalling conditions. The American Samoan High Court had previously ordered Daewoosa to pay workers US $3.5m. in compensation and fined the company an additional $290,000 in April 2002. In March 2004 Governor Tulafono announced plans for legislation that would allow prosecution of human-trafficking offences in the territory. In July it was announced that a US senate committee would hold a hearing on human-trafficking at the site of the closed garment factory.

During 2003 several allegations of official corruption were made against American Samoan government officials. In September an employee of the Territory's Office of Procurement was allowed to return to work despite a recent conviction in an insurance fraud case. In the same month the Senate ordered an official investigation into contracts awarded by Tafua Faau Seumanutafa, the Chief Procurement Officer, and senior officials from the Department of Health and Social Security and the Department of Education. In May 2004 Seumanutafa pleaded guilty in the Hawaii Federal District Court to one count of conspiracy to defraud the US Government, in a case that also implicated senior officials from the Department of Health and Social Security and the Department of Education. Also in May the Senate Select Investigative Committee issued subpoenas to several senators to testify in relation to alleged corruption in the allocation of government contracts. In early September the Committee recommended that, while under investigation for alleged corruption, Lieutenant-Governor Ipulasi Aitofele Sunia be placed on leave and have his name removed from the list of candidates for the forthcoming gubernatorial election. Governor Tulafono claimed that the charges were politically motivated.

At the gubernatorial election held on 2 November 2004 incumbent Governor Togiola Tulafono of the Democratic Party received 48.4% of the votes cast in the first round of polling, while Afoa Moega Lutu obtained 39.4%. At the second round of voting, conducted on 16 November, Tulafono was re-elected, having secured 55.7% of the votes; Moega Lutu received 44.3%.

In October 2006 the minimum hourly wage for five industry categories was increased by between seven and nine cents. However, plans to raise the hourly rate for the cannery sector encountered strong opposition from the business community and from the Government itself, which argued that the decision would adversely affect companies' cost effectiveness. The tuna-canning industry, as the greatest source of revenue for the islands, was consequently able to exert significant pressure on wage levels. However, supporters of the decision pressed for a greater increase in order to attract and retain employees. Minimum-wage legislation was brought under federal control in 2007, when it was envisaged that the minimum wage in the Territory would increase to US $7.25 per hour by 2014. This rise was to be implemented in phases, with variations among industries. In early 2008, however, the US Senate was investigating proposed legislation to restrict further increases in view of their consequences for the territorial economy.

Eni Faleomavaega, the incumbent Delegate to the US House of Representatives, was re-elected for an unprecedented 10th two-year term in office in November 2006, defeating his closest rival, Amata Aumua Coleman, by just 702 votes of the total of 11,033 cast. In February 2008 the Territory's House of Representatives endorsed an amendment to the Constitution that sought to confer ultimate legislative authority to the Fono in the event of the Governor's use of the veto.

The first stage of the gubernatorial election was held on 4 November 2008, when none of the four candidates obtained the requisite 50% of the votes cast to secure office. The second stage of the election therefore took place on 18 November and resulted in the re-election of incumbent Governor Togiola Tulafono, who received 6,590 votes, in comparison with the 5,084 votes received by rival candidate Utu Abe Malae. In the concurrent legislative election conducted on 4 November eight incumbents were re-elected to the Fono, including Speaker Savali Tavalou, while the islands' only two female legislators lost their seats. Also held on 4 November was the election to determine American Samoa's Congressional Delegate to the US House of Representatives. Eni Faleomavega was re-elected for an 11th consecutive term. American Samoan voters also participated in a referendum, coinciding with the elections of 4 November, on the issue of an amendment to the Constitution proposing to empower the Fono to overrule the Governor's power of veto; however, this was defeated by a narrow margin of only 22 votes.

Concerns regarding the issue of official corruption continued. In February 2004 the US Federal Bureau of Investigation (FBI) began an investigation into the alleged misuse of US government funds. In March 2005 the FBI effected an unannounced search of the government offices in Pago Pago, forbidding entry to the Governor, Lieutenant-Governor and Attorney-General for the duration of the operation. In mid-March the Government announced its intention to challenge the legality of the search warrants. In October Dr Sili K. Sataua and Patolo Mageo, the former Directors of the Education and Human Resources Departments, respectively, were sentenced in a federal court in Honolulu, Hawaii, to custodial sentences following their conviction on corruption charges. In September 2007 Lieutenant-Governor Ipulasi Aitofele Sunia and Senator Tulifua Tini Lam Yuen were detained on federal charges of fraud, bribery and obstruction in relation to business transactions involving the Department of Education. Their trial was scheduled to commence in June 2009.

Meanwhile, the islands remained vulnerable to adverse weather phenomena. In May 2003 severe flooding and landslides led to the deaths of five people, and in the following month US President George W. Bush declared the Territory a federal disaster area. In January 2004 a state of emergency was declared when a cyclone damaged the islands. The USA allocated US $12.5m. towards the relief effort. In February 2005 Cyclone Olaf caused extensive damage to the territory's Manu'a islands, destroying numerous buildings and interrupting electricity supplies. An estimated 70 homes were destroyed in Manu'a, while some 200 houses suffered major damage. The islands' Governor subsequently declared a state of emergency.

Government

Executive power is vested in the Governor, who is elected by popular vote and has authority that extends to all operations within the Territory of American Samoa. The Governor has the power of veto with respect to legislation approved by the Fono (Legislature). The Fono comprises the Senate and the House of Representatives, with a President and a Speaker presiding over their respective divisions. The Senate is composed of 18 members, elected, according to Samoan custom, from local chiefs, or Matai, for a term of four years. The House of Representatives consists of 20 members who are elected by popular vote for a term of two years, and a non-voting delegate from Swains Island. The Fono meets twice a year, in January and July, for not more than 45 days, and at such special sessions as the Governor may call. The Governor, who serves a four-year term, has the authority to appoint heads of government departments with the approval of the Fono. The islands' non-voting Delegate to the US House of Representatives is elected every two years.

Defence

The USA is responsible for the defence of American Samoa.

Economic Affairs

In 2000, according to estimates by the American Samoa National Income and Product Accounts Task Force, American Samoa's gross national income (GNI), measured at constant 1999 prices, was about US $348.6m., equivalent to some $6,332 per head. Between 1973 and 1985, it was estimated, GNI increased, in real terms, at an average rate of 1.7% per year, with real GNI per head rising by only 0.1% per year. Gross domestic product (GDP) was estimated (at constant 1999 prices and allowing for statistical discrepancy) in 1999 at $444.2m. and in 2000 at $437.9m. In 2005, according to estimates by the Secretariat of the Pacific Community, American Samoa's GDP was $558.8m., equivalent to $9,041 per head. In 2001–07 the population increased by an average of 2.3% per year. An estimated 91,000 American Samoans live on the US mainland or Hawaii.

Agriculture, hunting, forestry, fishing engaged 32.0% of the total labour force in 2005, according to FAO estimates, and the sector (excluding fish processing), according to estimates by the American Samoa National Income and Product Accounts Task Force, accounted for 11.3% of GDP in 2002. Agricultural production provides little surplus for export. Major crops are coconuts, bananas, taro, pineapples, yams and breadfruit. Local fisheries are at subsistence level, but tuna-canning plants at Pago Pago process fish from US, Taiwanese and South Korean vessels. Canned tuna constituted some 98.4% of export revenue in 2005/06, when earnings reached US $431.5m.

Within the industrial sector, manufacturing activities engaged 35.3% of the employed labour force in 2000. Fish-canning is the dominant industry; in 2001 some 70% of those employed in these factories were guest workers from Samoa (formerly Western Samoa). According to official estimates, basic employment in fish-processing increased from 1,300 workers in 1975 to 4,546 in 2005. According to estimates by the American Samoa National Income and Product Accounts Task Force, fish processing accounted for 22.3% of GDP in 2002. Other manufacturing activities include garment-manufacturing, meat-canning, handicrafts, dairy-farming, orchid-farming and the production of soap, perfume, paper products and alcoholic beverages. Exports of textiles and garments were valued at US $7.3m. in 2000/01, accounting for 3.2% of total exports. The construction sector engaged 6.4% of the employed labour force in 2000.

Service industries engage a majority of the employed labour force in American Samoa (55.2% in 2000), and the sector contributed an estimated 51.5% of GDP in 2002, according to estimates by American Samoa National Income and Product Accounts Task Force. The Government, supported by federal government grants, engaged almost 20% of all employed workers in 2005, according to official estimates. The tourist industry is developing slowly, and earned some US $10m. in 1998, although the number of tourist arrivals declined from 44,158 in 2000 to 24,496 in 2005. Of those 46.0% were from Samoa, while 27.6% originated from the USA and 12.8% from New Zealand. The total number of tourist arrivals increased marginally, to 25,347, in 2006.

In 2005/06 American Samoa recorded a visible trade deficit of US $140.7m. Most of American Samoa's trade is conducted with the USA. Other trading partners in 2005/06 included New Zealand, which supplied 9.1% of total imports (excluding items imported by the Government and goods by the fish-canning sector), and Singapore (8.0%).

A fiscal deficit of US $10,484m. was recorded in the year to September 2006. The Government's proposed budget for 2008/09 budget represented an increase of 12% in comparison with the previous year's expenditure. The annual rate of inflation averaged 3.9% in 2000–07. Consumer prices increased by an average of 2.9% in 2006. An estimated 10.5% of the total labour force were unemployed in 2003.

American Samoa is a member of the Pacific Community (see p. 391), and is an associate member of the UN Economic and Social Commission for Asia and the Pacific (ESCAP, see p. 36).

Economic development has been hindered by the islands' remote location, the limited infrastructure and lack of skilled workers. American Samoa's financial problems have been compounded by the high demand for government services from an increasing population and by the limited economic and tax base, as well as by natural disasters. A controversial minimum wage structure, in which American Samoa's minimum hourly rates of pay were considerably lower than the rest of the USA, was largely attributed to the presence of the two tuna-canning plants on the islands. These two operations provided employment for almost one-half of the labour force and consequently exerted substantial influence over the setting of wage levels. However, the remit of US minimum wage legislation was extended to American Samoa from 2007; with annual increases of US $0.50 per hour scheduled until such time that wages complied with terms delineated under the Fair Labour Standards Act. The closure of one plant, scheduled for September 2009, and retrenchment at the other led to concerns that the yearly increases in wages had placed too much pressure on employers, whose difficulties had been compounded by the decline in global economic activity. In early 2009 the islands' Governor requested that the US authorities postpone the increase in the minimum wage. Attempts to achieve a greater measure of financial security for American Samoa have included substantial reductions in the number of public-sector employees and increased fees for government services. Various initiatives to diversify the economy through the promotion of tourism, expansion of manufacturing activity and introduction of business outsourcing services have also been considered; plans for the establishment of a new call centre were under way in early 2009. In April 2008 the US Treasury agreed to allocate to the Government the sum of $20.4m. to be redistributed to those among the population eligible for a personal tax rebate. In March 2009 it was announced that American Samoa was to receive $19m. in federal economic stimulus funding, most of which was to be used to promote the conservation of energy in the islands.

Education

Education is officially compulsory for 12 years between six and 18 years of age. Primary education begins at six years of age and lasts for eight years. Secondary education, beginning at the age of 14, lasts for a further four years. In 20064 there were 40 pre-primary schools, 35 primary schools and 12 secondary schools. There was also a community college of further education, with 1,607 students. In the same year there were 11,100 pupils enrolled at primary schools and 5,074 at secondary schools. Expenditure on education and culture in 2004/05 was US $65.8m., or 34.2% of total government expenditure.

Public Holidays

2009: 1 January (New Year's Day), 19 January (Martin Luther King Day), 16 February (Presidents' Day), 17 April (Flag Day, commemorating the first raising of the US flag in American Samoa), 25 May (Memorial Day), 3 July (for Independence Day), 7 September (Labor Day), 12 October (Columbus Day), 11 November (Veterans' Day), 26 November (Thanksgiving Day), 25 December (Christmas Day).

2010: 1 January (New Year's Day), 18 January (Martin Luther King Day), 15 February (Presidents' Day), 17 April (Flag Day, commemorating the first raising of the US flag in American Samoa), 31 May (Memorial Day), 5 July (for Independence Day), 6 September (Labor Day), 11 October (Columbus Day), 11 November (Veterans' Day), 25 November (Thanksgiving Day), 25 December (Christmas Day).

Weights and Measures

With certain exceptions, the imperial system is in force. One US cwt equals 100 lb; one long ton equals 2,240 lb; one short ton equals 2,000 lb. A policy of gradual voluntary conversion to the metric system is being encouraged by the Federal Government.

Statistical Survey

Source (unless otherwise indicated): Statistics Division, Department of Commerce, Pago Pago, AS 96799; tel. 633-5155; fax 633-4195; internet www.asdoc.info/index.htm.

AREA AND POPULATION

Area: 201 sq km (77.6 sq miles); *By Island* (sq km): Tutuila 137; Ta'u 46; Ofu 7; Olosega 5; Swains Island (Olohenga) 3; Aunu'u 2; Rose 1.

Population: 46,773 at census of 1 April 1990; 57,291 (males 29,264, females 28,027) at census of 1 April 2000. *Mid-2007* (official estimate): 68,200. *By Island* (2000): Tutuila 55,400; Manu'a District (Ta'u, Olosega and Ofu islands) 1,378; Aunu'u 476; Swains Island (Olohenga) 37.

Density (mid-2007): 339.3 per sq km.

Ethnic Groups (2000 census): Samoan 50,545; part-Samoan 1,991; Asian 1,631; Tongan 1,598; Total (incl. others) 57,291.

Principal Towns (population at 2000 census): Tafuna 8,409; Nu'uuli 5,154; Pago Pago (capital) 4,278; Leone 3,568; Ili'ili 2,513.

Births, Marriages and Deaths (2006): Registered live births 1,442 (birth rate 21.6 per 1,000); Registered marriages 171; Registered deaths 267 (death rate 4.0 per 1,000). *2007:* Live birth rate 21.6 per 1,000, Death rate 4.0 per 1,000.

Life Expectancy (years at birth, 2006): Males 68.5; Females 76.2.

Economically Active Population (persons aged 16 years and over, 2000 census): Agriculture, hunting, forestry, fishing and mining 517; Manufacturing 5,900; Construction 1,066; Trade, restaurants and hotels 2,414; Transport, storage, communications and utilities 1,036; Financing, insurance, real estate and business services 311; Community, social and personal services 5,474; *Total employed* 16,718 (males 9,804, females 6,914); Unemployed 909 (males 494, females 415); *Total labour force* 17,627 (males 10,298, females 7,329) (Source: US Department of Commerce, *2000 Census of Population and Housing*). *2003* (estimates): Total employed 14,319; Unemployed 1,681; Total labour force 16,000 (Source: US Department of State). *2005* (official estimates): Basic employment 8,428 (Fish processing 4,546, Government employment—supported by federal grants 3,282, Other 600); Non-basic employment 8,916; Total employment 17,344. *Mid-2005* (estimates): Agriculture, etc. 8,000; Total labour force 25,000 (Source: FAO).

AGRICULTURE, ETC.

Principal Crops ('000 metric tons, 2007, FAO estimates): Coconuts 4.7; Taro 9.0; Bananas 0.8.

Livestock (year ending September 2007, FAO estimates): Pigs 10,500; Cattle 100; Chickens 40,000.

Livestock Products (metric tons, 2007, FAO estimates): Pig meat 315; Chicken meat 25; Cows' milk 22; Hen eggs 30.

Fishing (metric tons, live weight, 2006): Total catch 5,421 (Albacore 4,176; Yellowfin tuna 496; Wahoo 278).

Source: FAO.

INDUSTRY

Production (2005): Electric energy 189 million kWh. Source: UN, *Industrial Commodity Statistics Yearbook*.

FINANCE

Currency and Exchange Rates: United States currency is used: 100 cents = 1 United States dollar (US $). Sterling and Euro Equivalents (31 December 2008): £1 sterling = US $1.4578; €1 = US $1.3917; US $100 = £68.60 = €71.85.

Federal Direct Expenditures (US $ million, year ending September 2007): Retirement and disability payments 51; Grants 128; Total (incl. others) 213 (Source: US Census Bureau, *Consolidated Federal Funds Report*).

Budget (US $ '000, year ending September 2005): *Revenue:* Taxes 50,397; Licences and permits 1,160; Intergovernmental 111,783; Charges for services 8,438; Fines and fees 1,869; Total (incl. others) 182,015. *Expenditure:* General government 45,555; Public safety 11,827; Public works 5,801; Health and recreation 31,952; Education and culture 65,881; Economic development 20,083; Capital projects 7,411; Debt-servicing 3,989; Total 192,499.

Cost of Living (Consumer Price Index; base: 2000 = 100): All items (excl. rent) 116.1 in 2004; 122.1 in 2005; 125.7 in 2006. Source: ILO.

Expenditure on the Gross Domestic Product (US $ million at current prices, 2002): Personal consumption expenditure 331.5; Private investment 43.7; American Samoa government expenditures 62.4; Federal government expenditures 126.8; Exports 449.0; *Less* Imports 532.0; *Gross domestic product* 481.4. Note: Recorded accounts are not available; figures represent the findings of the American Samoa National Income and Product Accounts Task Force, established to produce reliable economic statistics for the territory.

Gross Domestic Product by Economic Activity (US $ million at current prices, 2002): Agriculture and fishing (excl. fish processing) 54.3; Fish processing 107.3; Wholesale and retail trade 36.6; Government services 100.0; Other services 111.3; Other non-services 71.9; *Total* 481.4. Note: Recorded accounts are not available; figures represent the findings of the American Samoa National Income and Product Accounts Task Force, established to produce reliable economic statistics for the territory.

EXTERNAL TRADE

Principal Commodities (US $ million): *Imports* (excl. government purchases and cannery goods, year ending September 2006): Food 141.3 (Fish 74.4); Fuel and oil 35.8 (Diesel fuel 14.4); Textiles and clothing 6.6; Machinery and transport equipment 21.8 (Road motor vehicles and parts 13.7); Miscellaneous manufactured articles 113.7 (Tin plates 48.0); Construction materials 17.5; Total (incl. others) 341.5. *Exports:* Total exports 438.5 (Canned tuna 431.5; Pet food 7).

Principal Trading Partners (US $ million, year ending September 2006): *Imports* (excl. government purchases and cannery goods): Australia 8.4; Fiji 22.5; Japan 2.0; Korea, Republic 21.2; New Zealand 31.1; Samoa 17.0; Singapore 27.2; USA 133.4; Total (incl. others) 341.5. *Exports:* Total 438.5 (almost entirely to the USA).

TRANSPORT

Road Traffic ('000 registered motor vehicles, year ending September 2006): Passenger cars 7.8; Total 9.2.

International Sea-borne Shipping (freight traffic, '000 metric tons, year ending September 2006): Goods loaded 148; Goods unloaded 400.

Civil Aviation (Pago Pago Int. Airport, year ending September 2006): Flights 4,344; Passengers (excl. transit) 157,023 (Boarding 81,907, Disembarking 75,116); Transit 385; Freight and mail ('000 lb): Loaded 3,893, Unloaded 3,939.

TOURISM

Tourist Arrivals by Country (2006): Australia 950; China, People's Republic 439; Fiji 345; New Zealand 3,224; Philippines 230; Samoa 11,313; Tonga 450; United Kingdom 148; USA 7,037; Total (incl. others) 25,347.

Tourism Receipts (US $ million): 9 in 1996; 10 in 1997; 10 in 1998.

Source: World Tourism Organization.

COMMUNICATIONS MEDIA

Daily Newspapers (1996): 2; estimated circulation 5,000*.

Non-daily Newspapers (1996): 1; estimated circulation 3,000*.

Radio Receivers (1997): 57,000* in use.

Television Receivers (1999): 15,000* in use.

Telephones (2006): 10,737 main lines in use.

Facsimile Machines (2006): 686 subscribers.

Mobile Cellular Telephones (2006): 8,525 subscribers.

*Sources: UNESCO, *Statistical Yearbook*; American Samoa Telecommunications Authority.

EDUCATION

Pre-primary (2006): 40 schools ; 140 teachers; 2,038 pupils.

Primary (2006): 35 schools ; 450 teachers; 11,100 pupils.

Secondary (2006): 12 high schools; 213 teachers; 5,074 pupils.

Higher (2006): American Samoa Community College 1,607 students.

Sources: American Samoa Department of Education.

Directory

The Constitution

American Samoa is an Unincorporated Territory of the USA. Therefore, not all the provisions of the US Constitution apply. As an unorganized territory it has not been provided with an organic act by Congress. Instead the US Secretary of the Interior, on behalf of the President, has plenary authority over the Territory and enabled the people of American Samoa to draft their own Constitution.

According to the 1967 Constitution, executive power is vested in the Governor, whose authority extends to all operations within the Territory of American Samoa. The Governor has veto power with respect to legislation passed by the Fono (Legislature). The Fono consists of the Senate and the House of Representatives, with a President and a Speaker presiding over their respective divisions. The Senate is composed of 18 members, elected, according to Samoan custom, from local chiefs, or Matai, for a term of four years. The House of Representatives consists of 20 members who are elected by popular vote for a term of two years, and a non-voting delegate from Swains Island. The Fono meets twice a year, in January and July, for not more than 45 days and at such special sessions as the Governor may call. The Governor has the authority to appoint heads of government departments with the approval of the Fono. Local government is carried out by indigenous officials. In August 1976 a referendum on the popular election of a Governor and a Lieutenant-Governor resulted in an affirmative vote. The first gubernatorial elections took place on 8 November 1977 and the second was held in November 1980; subsequent elections were to take place every four years.

American Samoa sends one non-voting Delegate to the US House of Representatives, who is popularly elected every two years.

The Government
(April 2009)

Governor: TOGIOLA TULAFONO; (took office March 2003, re-elected 16 November 2004 and 18 November 2008).

Lieutenant-Governor: IPULASI AITOFELE SUNIA.

GOVERNMENT OFFICES

Governor's Office: Executive Office Bdg, Third Floor, Utulei, Pago Pago, AS 96799; tel. 633-4116; fax 633-2269; e-mail governorsoffice@asg-gov.net; internet americansamoa.gov/gov_office/gov_office.htm.

Department of the Interior, Office of Insular Affairs (OIA): Field Office of the OIA, Dept of the Interior, POB 1725, Pago Pago, AS 96799; tel. 633-2800; fax 633-2415; internet www.doi.gov/oia/Islandpages/asgpage; Field Representative LYDIA FALEAFINE NOMURA.

Office of the Representative to the Government of American Samoa: Amerika Samoa Office, 1427 Dillingham Blvd, Suite 210, Honolulu HI 96817, USA; tel. (808) 847-1998; fax (808) 847-3420; e-mail hawaiioff@aol.com; Representative SOLOALI'I FA'ALEPO, Jr.

Department of Administrative Services: American Samoa Government, Executive Office Bldg, Utulei, Pago Pago, AS 96799; tel. 633-4158; fax 633-1841; internet americansamoa.gov/departments/depts/admin.htm; Dir NU'UTAI SONNY THOMPSON.

Department of Agriculture: American Samoa Government, Executive Office Building, Utulei, Pago Pago, AS 96799; tel. 699-1497; fax 699-4031; internet americansamoa.gov/departments/depts/agriculture.htm; Dir APEFA'I TAIFANE.

Department of Commerce: American Samoa Government, Executive Office Bldg, 2nd Floor, POB 1147, Utulei, Pago Pago, AS 96799;

tel. 633-5155; fax 633-4195; internet www.asdoc.info/IndexCSSDOC.htm; Dir FALESEU ELIU PAOPAO.

Department of Education: American Samoa Government, Executive Office Bldg, Utulei, Pago Pago, AS 96799; tel. 633-4256; fax 633-4240; e-mail webmaster@doe.as; internet www.doe.as; Dir Dr CLAIR POUMELE.

Department of Health: American Samoa Government, Pago Pago, AS 96799; tel. 633-4606; fax 633-5379; internet americansamoa.gov/departments/depts/health.htm; Dir UTO'OFILI ASOFA'AFETAI MAGA.

Department of Homeland Security: tel. 633-2827; fax 633-2979; e-mail mrsala@americansamoa.gov; internet americansamoa.gov/departments/depts/dhs.htm; Dir MICHAEL SALA.

Department of Human Resources: American Samoa Government, Executive Office Bldg, Utulei, Pago Pago, AS 96799; tel. 633-4485; fax 633-1139; internet americansamoa.gov/departments/depts/human_resources.htm; Dir EVELYN LANGFORD.

Department of Human and Social Services: American Samoa Government, Pago Pago, AS 96799; tel. 633-1187; fax 633-7449; internet americansamoa.gov/departments/depts/hss.htm; Dir LEILUA STEVENSON.

Department of Legal Affairs: American Samoa Government, Executive Office Bldg, Utulei, Pago Pago, AS 96799; tel. 633-4163; fax 633-1838; internet americansamoa.gov/departments/depts/legal.htm; Dir Attorney-General FEPULEA'I AFA RIPLEY, Jr.

Department of Local Government (Office of Samoan Affairs): American Samoa Government, Pago Pago, AS 96799; tel. 633-5201; fax 633-5590; internet americansamoa.gov/departments/depts/local.htm; Dir MAUGA TASI ASUEGA.

Department of Marine and Wildlife Resources: American Samoa Government, Executive Office Bldg, Utulei, Pago Pago, AS 96799; tel. 633-4456; fax 633-5590; e-mail ray@americansamoa.gov; internet americansamoa.gov/departments/depts/mwr.htm; Dir UFAGAFA RAY TULAFONO.

Department of Parks and Recreation: American Samoa Government, Pago Pago, AS 96799; tel. 699-9614; fax 699-4427; internet americansamoa.gov/departments/depts/parks.htm; Dir TA'AMUVAIGAFA IAKOPO.

Department of Planning and Budget: tel. 633-4201; fax 633-1148; internet americansamoa.gov/departments/depts/budget.htm; Dir MAGALEI LOGOVI'I.

Department of Port Administration: American Samoa Government, Pago Pago, AS 96799; tel. 633-4251; fax 633-5281; internet americansamoa.gov/departments/depts/port.htm; Dir MATAGI MAILO RAY MCMOORE.

Department of Procurement: tel. 699-1170; fax 699-2387; internet americansamoa.gov/departments/depts/procurement.htm; Dir LA'AU M. SEUI.

Department of Public Information: American Samoa Government, Pago Pago, AS 96799; tel. 633-4191; fax 633-1044; internet americansamoa.gov/departments/depts/information.htm; Dir PAOLO SIVIA SIVIA.

Department of Public Safety: American Samoa Government, Pago Pago, AS 96799; tel. 633-1111; fax 633-7296; internet americansamoa.gov/departments/depts/safety.htm; Dir SOTOA M. SAVALI.

Department of Public Works: American Samoa Government, Executive Office Bldg, Utulei, Pago Pago, AS 96799; tel. 633-4141; fax 633-5958; internet americansamoa.gov/departments/depts/works.htm; Dir PUNAOFO TILEI.

Department of Treasury: American Samoa Government, Executive Office Bldg, Utulei, Pago Pago, AS 96799; tel. 633-4155; fax 633-4100; internet americansamoa.gov/departments/depts/treasury.htm; Dir AITOFELE SUNIA.

Department of Youth and Women's Affairs: American Samoa Government, Executive Office Bldg, Utulei, Pago Pago, AS 96799; tel. 633-2836; fax 633-2875; Dir Leiataua Dr LEUGA TURNER.

Environmental Protection Agency: American Samoa Government, Office of the Governor, Pago Pago, AS 96799; tel. 633-2304; fax 633-5801; e-mail tv5551@yahoo.com; internet americansamoa.gov/departments/agencies/epa.htm; Dir Dr TOA'FA VAIAGA'E.

Legislature

FONO

Senate

The Senate has 18 members, elected, according to Samoan custom, from local chiefs, or Matai, for a term of four years.

President: GAOTEOTE PALAIE GAOTEOTE.

House of Representatives

The House has 20 members who are elected by popular vote for a term of two years, and a non-voting delegate from Swains Island.

Speaker: SAVALI TALAVOU ALE.

CONGRESS

Since 1980 American Samoa has been able to elect, for a two-year term, a Delegate to the Federal Congress, who may vote in committee but not on the floor of the House of Representatives. At the election to the post in November 2008 incumbent Congressman Eni F. Hunkin Faleomavaega was re-elected for a record 11th two-year term.

Delegate of American Samoa: ENI F. HUNKIN FALEOMAVAEGA, US House of Representatives, 2422 Rayburn House Office Bldg, Washington, DC 20515, USA; tel. (202) 225-8577; fax (202) 225-8757; e-mail faleomavaega@mail.house.gov; internet www.house.gov/faleomavaega.

Judicial System

The judicial system of American Samoa consists of the High Court, presided over by the Chief Justice and assisted by Associate Justices (all appointed by the Secretary of the Interior), and a local judiciary in the District and Village Courts. The judges for these local courts are appointed by the Governor, subject to confirmation by the Senate of the Fono. The High Court consists of three Divisions: Appellate, Trial, and Land and Titles. The Appellate Division has limited original jurisdiction and hears appeals from the Trial Division, the Land and Titles Division and from the District Court when it has operated as a court of record. The Trial Division has general jurisdiction over all cases. The Land and Titles Division hears cases involving land or Matai titles.

The District Court hears preliminary felony proceedings, misdemeanours, infractions (traffic and health), civil claims less than US $3,000, small claims, Uniform Reciprocal Enforcement of Support cases, and *de novo* trials from Village Courts. The Village Courts hear matters arising under village regulations and local customs.

Chief Justice: MICHAEL KRUSE.
Associate Justice: LYLE L. RICHMOND.
Attorney-General: FEPULEAI AFA RIPLEY.

High Court

Office of the Chief Justice, High Court, Pago Pago, AS 96799; tel. 633-1261; fax 633-1318; e-mail hcourt@samoatelco.com.

Judge of the District Court: JOHN L. WARD II, POB 427, Pago Pago, AS 96799; tel. 633-1101.

Judge of the Village Court: FAISIOTA TAUANU'U, Pago Pago, AS 96799; tel. 633-1102.

Religion

The population is largely Christian, more than 50% being members of the Congregational Christian Church and about 20% being Roman Catholics.

CHRISTIANITY

American Samoa Council of Christian Churches: c/o CCCAS Offices, POB 1637, Pago Pago, AS 96799; f. 1985; six mem. churches; Pres. (vacant); Gen. Sec. Rev. ENOKA L. ALESANA (Congregational Christian Church in American Samoa).

The Roman Catholic Church

American Samoa comprises the single diocese of Samoa-Pago Pago, suffragan to the archdiocese of Samoa-Apia and Tokelau. At 31 December 2006 there were 14,000 adherents in the islands. The Bishop participates in the Catholic Bishops' Conference of the Pacific, based in Suva, Fiji.

Bishop of Samoa-Pago Pago: Rev. JOHN QUINN WEITZEL, Diocesan Pastoral Center, POB 596, Fatuoaiga, Pago Pago, AS 96799; tel. 699-1402; fax 699-1459; e-mail quinn@samoatelco.com.

The Anglican Communion

American Samoa is within the diocese of Polynesia, part of the Church of the Province of New Zealand. The Bishop of Polynesia is resident in Fiji.

Protestant Churches

Congregational Christian Church in American Samoa (CCCAS): POB 1537, Pago Pago, AS 96799; tel. 699-9810; fax 699-1898; e-mail cccasgs@samoatelco.com; internet www.efkas.org; f. 1980; Gen. Sec. Rev SAMUEL TIALAVEA; 40,000 mems (incl. congregations in New Zealand, Australia and USA) in 2004.

2008–12 at almost US $130m. In early 2008 the proposed legislation had yet to be debated in the US Senate.

In May 2004, meanwhile, the US State Department's Radiation Exposure Compensation Program declared Guam eligible for compensation for the effects of nuclear tests carried out in the Pacific region during the 'Cold War' (the long period of mutual hostility between the USA and the Soviet Union). In April 2005 the US Congressional Committee to Assess the Scientific Information for the Radiation Exposure Screening and Education Program published a report recommending, in accordance with the wishes of the Guam delegation, that scientific criteria (including radiation measurements and analyses of public health data) be used for assessing eligibility for compensation, rather than geographical proximity to nuclear testing, which had determined eligibility hitherto. The report concluded that although Guam had been exposed to radiation through wind-borne particles, this exposure had not significantly increased the incidence of cancers and other radiation-related illnesses. Future claims for compensation were therefore thought unlikely to succeed.

At the legislative election held on 2 November 2004 the Republican party secured a majority, winning nine of the 15 seats in the island's legislature; five Democrat incumbents were deposed. At a concurrently held plebiscite, a proposal to legalize casinos on the island was rejected. Later in the month a group of campaigners for the proposal filed an appeal in the Superior Court against the result of the election, alleging electoral malpractice.

Meanwhile, numerous investigations into allegations of official corruption were conducted. In April 2003 a former Republican Senator and gubernatorial candidate, Tommy Tanaka, pleaded guilty to charges of misprision of felony, which related to his alleged involvement in a fraudulent government contract. In the same month Joseph Mafnas, a former chief of the Guam police department, was indicted on forgery charges. However, the case against him foundered in September 2004 owing to the absence from the island of the key witness for the prosecution. In March 2004 former Governor Carl Gutierrez was tried for his involvement in a private property development scheme, which allegedly involved the misappropriation of public funds. All but two minor charges against him were dismissed by a Superior Court judge in April. Although in August charges ranging from theft by deception to official misconduct were filed against the former Governor, these were dismissed in early September. Gutierrez stood trial in June 2005 for alleged improper dealings relating to the island's retirement fund; he was acquitted of all charges in the following month, and in August announced his intention to contest the next gubernatorial election, scheduled for November 2006. However, in December 2005 new corruption charges connected to the retirement fund were filed against Gutierrez and others responsible for its operation. In January 2006 further charges were brought against the former Governor relating to his administration of the Guam Memorial Hospital. Meanwhile, in October 2005 Gutierrez's former Chief of Staff, Gil Shinohara, was convicted of conspiracy to commit fraud.

In an important decision in January 2006 the US House of Representatives approved an amendment to grant limited voting rights to the Delegate from Guam. Although the Delegate would be unable to vote on the final passage of legislation, the ruling would permit the island's envoy to cast a vote in the 'Committee of the Whole House on the State of the Union', a means by which the House expedites consideration of certain legislation, particularly amendments. The decision was expected to allow for more effective lobbying on the part of Guam's Delegate to Washington, DC, and the promotion of the islanders' views on a number of important issues within the federal system.

Legislative and gubernatorial elections took place on 7 November 2006. Felix P. Camacho secured a second term as Governor, defeating Robert Underwood, who later filed an unsuccessful appeal at the US Supreme Court seeking clarification of the results, in a dispute over the exclusion of 'crossover' ballots from the valid votes. Michael W. Cruz was elected Lieutenant-Governor, replacing Kaleo Moylan. Madeleine Bordallo secured a third term as Delegate to the US House of Representatives. The Republicans retained control of the legislature, albeit with a decreased majority, winning eight seats, compared with the Democrats' seven; the incumbent Speaker, Republican Mark Forbes, was re-elected.

On 4 November 2008 legislative elections were held at which the Democrats won 10 of the 15 seats in the Guam Legislature. Three incumbent Republicans, including Speaker Mark Forbes, lost their seats. Judith Won Pat was subsequently appointed as the chamber's Speaker. The Democrats' increased majority was largely attributed to the party's opposition to the legalization of gambling in Tamuning, an initiative that appeared to be widely unpopular with the electorate. At a concurrent poll, Madeleine Bordallo won a fourth term as Delegate to the US House of Representatives.

Guam remains of vital strategic importance to the USA. However, during his visit to the island in 1998 US President Clinton approved the transfer of some 1,300 ha of federal land to the local administration and undertook to accelerate the transfer of a further 2,020 ha of former US air force and navy land. In August 2001 the US Army announced plans to move some combat weaponry and equipment from Europe to storage bases in Guam, as well as in Taiwan and Hawaii. During 2004/05 the US Air Force stationed several of its B-52 and B-2 bombers on Guam, following the construction of a new hangar on the island. In May 2005 the US Government announced plans substantially to increase military spending in 2005/06 in Guam, with some US $162m. allocated for new construction projects. Notwithstanding the concerns of some anti-war and Chamorro rights activists, the increased military presence on Guam was widely welcomed as a source of new investment and employment. Rights activists continued to express their opposition after plans were revealed to relocate 8,000 US marines and their families from their base on the Japanese island of Okinawa to Guam, as part of a broader agreement on the redeployment of US forces. While Japan was likely to bear much of the financial burden, US President George W. Bush submitted a proposed budget for 2008 that included $345m. for military construction projects, including the relocation costs of the marines and their dependants. A final agreement on the relocation of troops to Guam was concluded in May 2006. Legislation authorizing funding of some $6,000m. for the relocation had been approved by both chambers of the Japanese legislature by May 2007. The US Government had committed funding of $4,000m. for the realignment, which would also involve a reorganization of US troops within Japan. During a visit to the Territory in February 2007, US Vice-President Richard Cheney emphasized the strategic importance of Guam, while reports suggested that the inflow of funds related to the increased military presence might reach $15,000m. The relocation of troops was expected to begin in 2010, with a target completion date of 2014 As many as 15,000 skilled workers would be required to implement the move. However, some islanders remained sceptical about the benefits of the relocation, fearing that the influx might lead to an increase in violent crimes and other social and environmental disturbance. In March 2009 the US Government announced that Guam was to receive US $45m. in funding for the modernization and maintenance of its military bases, as part of a federal plan of economic stimulus (see Economic Affairs). The US Government's proposed budget for 2010, submitted in May 2009, envisaged an allocation of $787m. towards military construction projects on Guam. A new naval hospital was to be built at a projected cost of $259m.

In March 1998, meanwhile, delegates from several Pacific island nations and territories met in Hawaii to discuss methods of controlling the increasing population of brown tree snakes in Guam. The venomous reptile, which was accidentally introduced to the island from New Guinea after the Second World War, had been responsible for frequent power cuts, as they were able to ascend electricity poles and short-circuit the lines, as well as for major environmental problems (including the decimation of native bird, rodent and reptile populations). The US Geological Survey estimated the density of tree snakes on Guam to be roughly 13,000 per sq mile (33,670 per sq km) of forested land. By 2004 a team of 25 full-time snake-trappers and nine dog-handlers was capturing an estimated 6,000 tree snakes annually at Guam's five main ports (air and sea), but in September of that year plans were announced to reduce funding to this programme by nearly one-half. Also in September the US House of Representatives approved a bill allocating US $104m. of federal funds towards the eradication of Guam's tree snake population. In October, furthermore, the US Senate authorized expenditure of $77m., to be divided among Guam, Hawaii and other islands, for the purposes of snake-eradication programmes.

The island remained vulnerable to the impact of extreme weather formations. President George W. Bush declared the island a federal disaster area following Typhoon Chata'an in July 2002 and Super-typhoon Pongsona in December 2002. Some 35,000 islanders were homeless in early 2003, and the US Government granted US $10m. towards the recovery effort. In July, in response to the high costs incurred by the recovery programme, the island's Delegate to the US House of Representatives, Madeleine Bordallo, introduced a bill to amend the Organic Act of Guam. The legislation attempted to empower the US Secretary of the Interior to waive Guam's outstanding federal debt, in order to offset social costs caused by migration to Guam from Compact of Free Association countries (see the chapter on the Marshall Islands). The measure was defeated, although the amended Compact of Free Association signed in December approved some $14m. to offset Guam's migration costs and erased $157m. of debt owed to the US federal Government. In February 2006 Governor Camacho announced his intention to restart negotiations on some $60.5m. of debt relief for Guam. Also in that month, legislation seeking to amend the Organic Act of Guam, in order to grant the Territory greater autonomy from the US federal Government, was submitted to the island's legislature.

Government

Guam is governed under the Organic Act of Guam of 1950, which gave the island statutory local power of self-government. Its inhabitants are citizens of the USA, although they are not permitted to vote in national elections. Guam's non-voting Delegate to the US House of

Representatives is elected every two years. Executive power is vested in the Governor, who is elected by popular vote every four years. The heads of the executive departments are appointed by the Governor, with the consent of the Guam Legislature. The Legislature comprises 15 members, known as Senators, who are elected by popular vote every two years. It is empowered to enact legislation on local matters, including taxation and fiscal appropriations.

Defence

Guam is an important strategic military base for the USA, with 1,791 members of the Air Force and 1,093 naval personnel stationed there, as assessed at November 2008. Substantial numbers of US military personnel are to be relocated from Japan to Guam (see Recent History).

Economic Affairs

In 2000, according to estimates by the Bank of Hawaii (BOH), Guam's gross national income (GNI), at current prices, was US $2,772.8m., equivalent to $16,575 per head. Between 1988 and 1993, it was estimated, GNI increased, in real terms, at an average rate of some 10% per year. GNI increased by 3.9% in 1994. Official estimates of gross island product (GIP—the official measure of the Territory's economic performance) were estimated at some $3,700m. in 2005, equivalent to almost $22,700 per head. In 2000–07, according to World Bank figures, the population increased at an average annual rate of 1.6%.

Agriculture (including forestry, fishing and mining) engaged only an estimated 0.6% of the labour force in paid employment in June 2008, according to official payroll records. The principal crops cultivated on the island include watermelons, coconuts, cucumbers, gherkins, bananas, runner beans, aubergines (eggplants), squash, tomatoes and papaya. Livestock reared includes pigs, goats and poultry. The fishing catch totalled an estimated 729 metric tons in 2006, according to FAO.

The industrial sector accounted for some 15% of gross domestic product (GDP) in 1993. According to official payroll records, construction and manufacturing engaged an estimated 12.3% of the labour force in paid employment in June 2008. Construction, which alone engaged 9.6% of the employed labour force in June 2008, is the dominant industrial activity, and is closely related to the tourist industry. According to official figures, in 1995 construction contributed 12.6% of GIP. Manufacturing industries, including textile and garment production and boat-building, engaged an estimated 2.7% of the labour force in paid employment in June 2008.

Service industries dominate the economy, engaging 87.0% of the labour force in paid employment in June 2008, according to payroll records. The federal and territorial Governments together employed 24.5% of workers at that time. According to official estimates, the services sector contributed 69.2% of GIP in 1995. Tourism is Guam's most important industry; the sector provided 18% of GDP and engaged an estimated 21.4% of the employed labour force in 1994. In 2007 some 1,225,000 tourists visited the island (of whom 79% were from Japan).

The Territory consistently records a visible trade deficit, and in 2008 this amounted to US $120m. Major imports in 2008 included motor cars (17.8% of the total value of imports), luggage items (8.6%), clothing, perfumes and toilet water, beef, beer, sugared water, jewellery and watches. Exports in 2008 were dominated by motor cars (45.9% of the total value of exports) and fish (18.3%). Singapore supplied 39.1% of total imports in 2002. Japan purchased 21.8% of the island's exports in 2008. Other important trading partners included the People's Republic of China, Germany, Hong Kong, the Republic of Korea, Philippines and Singapore. Guam is a low-duty port, and is an important distribution point for goods destined for Micronesia. Re-exports constitute a high proportion of Guam's exports, major commodities being petroleum and petroleum products, iron and steel scrap, and eggs.

In the year ending September 2007 there was a surplus of US $119.6m. on the general fund budget. In May 2005 the Office of the Public Auditor reported that some $26m. of public money had been lost in 2004 either through fraud or inefficiency. US federal Government expenditure in Guam totalled $1,479.0m. in 2006/07. The Government's total debt stood at $326.7m. at the end of the financial year 2003/04. According to official figures, the average annual rate of inflation was 5.0% in 2000–08. Consumer prices increased by 6.2% in 2008. Guam's unemployment rate stood at 8.3% in March 2007.

Guam is a member of the Pacific Community (see p. 391) and an associate member of the UN's Economic and Social Commission for Asia and the Pacific (ESCAP, see p. 36). In early 1996 Guam joined representatives of the other countries and territories of Micronesia at a meeting in Hawaii, at which a new regional organization, the Council of Micronesian Government Executives, was established. The body aimed to facilitate discussion of economic developments in the region and to examine possibilities for reducing the considerable cost of shipping essential goods between the islands.

Guam continues to receive considerable financial support from the USA, particularly in the area of defence (federal expenditure on defence in Guam reached US $738.6m. in 2005/06, but declined to $507.1m. in 2006/07). The privatization of the Guam Telephone Authority was finalized in December 2004, and in February 2005 Governor Camacho announced his intention to privatize the Guam Waterworks Authority. An agreement worth $72,000m. to sell a number of Guam-based telecommunications companies to a Japanese cellular telephone services provider, was formally approved in November 2006 by the Federal Communications Commission. The construction sector continued to strengthen; the value of building permits increased by 36%, to $167.6m., between 2004 and 2005. The planned relocation of US marines and their families from the Japanese island of Okinawa to Guam (see Recent History), and a further US military proposal to station a Global Strike Task Force at Andersen air force base on Guam (the projected cost of which was $2,000m.), were crucial to the island's strategic planning. Indeed, the significant increase in Guam's population resulting from the new troop deployments compelled government agencies to commit the sum of $25m. towards the establishment of a mass transit system. Furthermore, in mid-2009 the USA pledged $1,000m. to fund a new road between northern and southern Guam. However, as a result of the decline in global economic activity, the island's economy was expected to perform poorly in 2009. In particular, deteriorating economic conditions in Japan, the Republic of Korea and the USA, important sources of visitors, were expected to deter potential tourists from travelling. Variations in exchange rates, notably the relative weakness of the South Korean currency, also affected the tourism industry in 2008. The exclusion of Chinese citizens from a federal visa waiver programme was expected to impede Guam's plans to attract more visitors from China; the island's Government requested a postponement of its imposition. In early 2009 the US Government allocated more than $140m. of its economic stimulus plan towards rebuilding military infrastructure and other projects in Guam. The modernization of the island's port was to be accorded priority. A job training programme was to commence in June 2009.

Education

School attendance is compulsory from six to 16 years of age. There were 26 public elementary schools, seven junior high and four senior high schools, as well as a number of private schools operating on the island in 2003. Total secondary enrolment in public schools in 2005/06 was 12,048 students. Some 3,034 students were enrolled at the university of Guam in that year. In 2000 the rate of adult illiteracy was estimated at 1.0%. Government expenditure on education was US $2,000m. in 2003/04 (equivalent to 29% of total expenditure).

Public Holidays

2009: 1 January (New Year's Day), 19 January (Martin Luther King Day), 16 February (Presidents' Day), 2 March (Guam Discovery Day), 10 April (Good Friday), 25 May (Memorial Day), 3 July (for US Independence Day), 21 July (Liberation Day), 7 September (Labor Day), 12 October (Columbus Day), 2 November (All Souls' Day), 11 November (Veterans' Day), 26 November (Thanksgiving Day), 8 December (Immaculate Conception), 25 December (Christmas Day).

2010: 1 January (New Year's Day), 18 January (Martin Luther King Day), 15 February (Presidents' Day), 1 March (Guam Discovery Day), 2 April (Good Friday), 26 May (Memorial Day), 5 July (for US Independence Day), 21 July (Liberation Day), 1 September (Labor Day), 11 October (Columbus Day), 2 November (All Souls' Day), 11 November (Veterans' Day), 25 November (Thanksgiving Day), 8 December (Immaculate Conception), 25 December (Christmas Day).

Weights and Measures

With certain exceptions, the imperial system is in force. One US cwt equals 100 lb; one long ton equals 2,240 lb; one short ton equals 2,000 lb. A policy of gradual voluntary conversion to the metric system is being encouraged by the Federal Government.

Statistical Survey

Sources (unless otherwise stated): Guam Bureau of Statistics and Plans, PO Box 2950, Hagåtña; tel. 472-4201; fax 477-1812; internet www.bsp.guam.gov.

AREA AND POPULATION

Area: 549 sq km (212 sq miles).

Population: 133,152 at census of 1 April 1990; 154,805 (males 79,181, females 75,624) at census of 1 April 2000. *Mid-2008* (official estimate): 175,877.

Density (mid-2008): 320.4 per sq km.

Ethnic Groups (2000 census): Chamorro 57,297; Filipino 40,729; White 10,509; Other Asian 9,600; part-Chamorro 7,946; Chuukese 6,229; Total (incl. others) 154,805.

Regions (population at 2000 census): North 80,466; Central 45,382; South 28,957.

Principal Towns (population at 2000 census): Tamuning 10,833; Mangilao 7,794; Yigo 6,391; Astumbo 5,207; Barrigada 4,417; Hagåtña (capital) 1,122.

Births, Marriages and Deaths (2007, unless otherwise indicated): Registered live births 3,501 (birth rate 20.2 per 1,000); Registered marriages (2004) 1,561; Registered deaths 786 (death rate 4.5 per 1,000). Sources: mostly UN, *Population and Vital Statistics Report*; Office of Insular Affairs, *2005 Guam Statistical Yearbook*.

Life Expectancy (years at birth, estimates): 79.1 (males 76.7; females 81.2) in 2008.

Economically Active Population (persons aged 16 years and over, excl. armed forces, 2002 estimates): Agriculture, forestry, fishing and mining 290; Manufacturing 1,570; Construction 3,420; Transport, storage and utilities 4,590; Wholesale and retail trade 12,690; Finance, insurance and real estate 2,450; Public administration 16,500; Education, health and social services 14,510; *Total employed* 56,020; Unemployed 7,070; *Total labour force* 63,090. *2007* (persons aged 16 years and over, excl. armed forces, at March): Total employed 58,290; Unemployed 5,310; Total labour force 63,600. *2008* (payroll data at June): Agriculture, forestry, fishing and mining 370; Manufacturing 1,580; Construction 5,610; Transport, storage and utilities 4,720; Wholesale and retail trade 13,380; Finance, insurance and real estate 2,390; Public administration 14,260; Education, health and social services 16,000; Total employed 58,310 (Source: Guam Department of Labor).

AGRICULTURE, ETC.

Principal Crops (metric tons, 2007, FAO estimates): Coconuts 53,200; Roots and tubers 2,500; Cucumbers and gherkins 400; Watermelons 2,500; Other melons 370; Bananas 350.

Livestock (head, year ending September 2007, FAO estimates): Chickens 210,000; Ducks 5,000; Pigs 5,200; Goats 700.

Livestock Products (metric tons, 2007, FAO estimates): Chicken meat 45; Hen eggs 750; Pig meat 150.

Fishing (metric tons, live weight, 2006): Common dolphinfish 67; Wahoo 37; Skipjack tuna 73; Total capture (incl. others) 729.

Source: FAO.

INDUSTRY

Electric Energy (million kWh, estimates): 1,777 in 2003; 1,877 in 2004; 1,897 in 2005. Source: UN, *Industrial Commodity Statistics Yearbook*.

FINANCE

Currency and Exchange Rates: US currency is used. For details, see section on the Northern Mariana Islands.

Federal Direct Expenditures (US $ million, year ending September): 1,412.8 (Defence 711.7) in 2005; 1,380.4 (Defence 738.6) in 2006; 1,479.0 (Defence 507.1) in 2007. Source: US Census Bureau, *Consolidated Federal Funds Report*.

General Fund Budget (US $ million, year ending September 2007): *Revenue:* Taxes 426.3 (Income tax 250.8, Gross receipts 172.7, Other 2.7); Licences, fees and permits 4.3; Use of money and property 0.3; Federal contributions 74.7; Other 8.8; Total 514.4. *Expenditure:* General government 44.0; Public order 72.8; Public health 10.0; Community services 5.6; Recreation 3.6; Individual and collective rights 11.8; Public education 180.4; Economic development 3.5; Debt service 12.8; Total (incl. others) 394.8.

Cost of Living (Consumer Price Index; annual averages, base: October–December 2007 = 100): All items 92.0 in 2006; 98.2 in 2007; 104.3 in 2008.

Gross Island Product (US $ million at current prices, estimate): 3,700 in 2005.

Gross Island Product by Economic Activity (US $ million, 1995): Construction 379.02; Trade 622.86; Public administration 965.97; Other services 486.94; Other non-services 544.61; Total 2,999.40.

EXTERNAL TRADE

Principal Commodities (US $ million, 2008): *Imports f.o.b.:* Food and non-alcoholic beverages 66.5 (Meat and edible offal of beef 5.9; Meat and edible offal of poultry 4.7; Bread and bakery products 3.8; Water, containing sugar 8.2); Alcoholic beverages 8.5 (Malt beer 6.0); Home appliances, equipment, etc. 5.3; Transportation and parts 52.1 (Motor cars 40.0); Construction materials 14.4 (Structures of iron and steel 3.4); Men's and women's apparel 12.5; Plastics, leather and paper 28.9 (Travel goods, handbags, etc. 19.4); Miscellaneous manufactured imports 36.6 (Perfumes and toilet waters 8.0; Articles of jewellery 3.5; Watches 4.9); Total 224.9. *Exports (incl. re-exports) f.o.b.:* Food and non-alcoholic beverages 20.6 (Fish—fresh, chilled, frozen and preserved 19.2); Transportation and parts 49.8 (Motor cars 48.1); Construction materials 9.3 (Iron and steel 3.4; Aluminium waste, scraps, tubes and fittings 3.2); Plastics, leather and paper 5.0 (Travel goods, handbags, etc. 3.6); Miscellaneous manufactured imports 18.1 (Perfumes and toilet waters 3.8; Articles of jewellery 8.5; Watches 2.1); Total (incl. others) 104.9.

Principal Trading Partners: *Imports* (US $ '000, 2002): Australia 9,770; Hong Kong 36,240; Japan 96,450; Korea, Republic 9,688; New Zealand 5,520; Philippines 1,437; Singapore 180,076; Total (incl. others) 527,000 (Source: UN, *Statistical Yearbook for Asia and the Pacific*). *Exports* (US $ million, 2008): China, People's Republic 7.7; Finland 5.7; Germany 20.1; Hong Kong 15.1; Japan 22.9; Micronesia, Federated States 6.5; Philippines 6.0; Singapore 6.5; Total (incl. others) 104.9.

TRANSPORT

Road Traffic (registered motor vehicles, 2005): Private cars 63,631; Taxis 348; Buses 644; Goods vehicles 24,971; Motorcycles 1,273; Total (incl. others) 96,112. Source: Department of Revenue and Taxation, Government of Guam.

International Sea-borne Shipping (estimated freight traffic, '000 revenue tons, 2005): Goods loaded 246.7; Goods unloaded 1,170.2; Goods transshipped 624.8. *Merchant Fleet* (total displacement, '000 grt at 31 December 1992): 1 (Source: Lloyd's Register-Fairplay, *World Fleet Statistics*).

Civil Aviation (Guam International Airport): *Passengers* (year ending May 2008): Arrivals 933,364; Departures 934,263; Transit 285,762. *Cargo* (metric tons, 2005): Unloaded 17,917; Loaded 14,099. *Mail* (metric tons, 2005): Incoming 3,996; Outgoing 1,668. *Aircraft Movements* (year ending May 2008): 14,093. Source: Guam International Airport Authority.

TOURISM

Foreign Tourist Arrivals ('000): 1,227.6 in 2005; 1,211.7 in 2006; 1,225.0 in 2007.

Tourist Arrivals by Country of Residence ('000, 2006): Japan 955.7; Korea, Republic 117.0; Philippines 8.1; Taiwan 16.7; USA 44.2; Total (incl. others) 1,211.7.

Tourism Receipts (US $ million): 2,361 in 1998; 1,908 in 1999.

Source: World Tourism Organization.

COMMUNICATIONS MEDIA

Radio Receivers (1997): 221,000 in use.

Television Receivers (1999): 110,000 in use.

Telephones (2007): 65,500 main lines in use.

Mobile Cellular Telephones (2007, estimate): 98,000 subscribers*.

Internet Users (2005): 65,000*.

Broadband Subscribers (2007): 2,700.

Daily Newspapers (1997): 1 (circulation 24,457).

Non-daily Newspapers (1988): 4 (estimated circulation 26,000).

*Sources: International Telecommunication Union; UN, *Statistical Yearbook for Asia and the Pacific*.

EDUCATION

Institutions (2005/06): Primary (incl. kindergarten, grades 1–8) 42 (public 27, private 15); Secondary (grades 9–12) 9 (public 4, private 5); Guam Community College; University of Guam.

Teachers (2005/06): Primary 1,917 (public 1,405, private 512); Secondary 1,108 (public 470, private 638).

Enrolment (2005/06): Kindergarten (grades 1–5) 18,842 (public 14,555, private 4,287); Primary (grades 6–8) 8,893 (public 6,852, private 2,041); Secondary (grades 9–12) 12,048 (public 9,371, private 2,677); High school (graduates) 1,735 (public 1,218, private 517); Guam Community College 10,268; University of Guam 3,034.

Sources: Department of Education, Guam Community College, Office of Insular Affairs, *2005 Guam Statistical Yearbook*; University of Guam.

Directory

The Constitution

Guam is governed under the Organic Act of Guam of 1950, which gave the island statutory local power of self-government and made its inhabitants citizens of the United States, although they cannot vote in presidential elections. Their Delegate to the US House of Representatives is elected every two years. Executive power is vested in the civilian Governor and the Lieutenant-Governor, first elected, by popular vote, in 1970. Elections for the governorship occur every four years. The Government has 48 executive departments, whose heads are appointed by the Governor with the consent of the Guam Legislature. The Legislature consists of 15 members elected by popular vote every two years (members are known as Senators). It is empowered to pass laws on local matters, including taxation and fiscal appropriations.

The Government
(April 2009)

Governor: FELIX CAMACHO (Republican—took office January 2003; re-elected 7 November 2006).
Lieutenant-Governor: Dr MICHAEL W. CRUZ.

GOVERNMENT OFFICES

Government offices are located throughout the island.

Office of the Governor: POB 2950, Hagåtña, GU 96932; tel. 472-8931; fax 477-4826; e-mail governor@mail.gov.gu; internet governor.guam.gov.

Department of the Interior, Office of Insular Affairs (OIA): Hagåtña, GU 96910; tel. 472-7279; fax 472-7309; Field Representative KEITH A. PARSKY.

Customs and Quarantine Agency: 13–16A Mariner Ave, Tiyan, Barrigada, GU 96913; tel. 475-6202; fax 475-6227; internet www.cqa.guam.gov; Dir ROBERT D. CAMACHO.

Department of Administration: POB 884, Hagåtña, GU 96932; tel. 475-1110; fax 475-6788; e-mail doadir@mail.gov.gu; internet www.doa.guam.gov; Dir LOURDES M. PEREZ.

Department of Agriculture: 192 Dairy Rd, Mangilao, GU 96913; tel. 734-3942; fax 734-6569; e-mail guamagriculture@yahoo.com; internet www.agriculture.guam.gov; Dir PAUL BASSLER.

Department of Chamorro Affairs: tel. 475-4278; fax 475-4227; e-mail dcapres1@chamorroaffairs.org; internet www.chamorroaffairs.org; Pres. SYLVIA FLORES.

Department of Commerce: 102 M St, Tiyan, GU 96913; tel. 475-0321; fax 477-9031; e-mail commerce@mail.gov.gu.

Department of Corrections: POB 3236, Hagåtña, GU 96932; tel. 734-4668; fax 734-4990; internet www.doc.guam.gov; Dir JOSÉ PALACIOS (acting).

Environmental Protection Agency: 17-3304 Mariner Ave, Tiyan, GU 96913; tel. 475-1658; fax 477-9402; e-mail mmann@guamepa.govguam.net; internet www.guamepa.govguam.net; Administrator LORILEE T. CRISOSTOMO.

Housing and Urban Renewal Authority: 117 Bien Venida Ave, Sinajana, GU 96910; tel. 472-3910; fax 472-7565; e-mail rdeguzman@netpci.com; internet www.ghura.org; Exec. Dir BENNY PILAUNA.

Department of Integrated Services for Individuals with Disabilities: Suite 703, 238 Archbishop F. C. Flores St, Pacific News Bldg, Hagåtña, GU 96910; tel. 475-4645; fax 477-2892; Dir ROSEANNE ADA.

Department of Labor: 414 West Soledad Ave, GCIC Bldg, Hagåtña, GU 96910; tel. 475-7000; fax 475-7045; e-mail connent@ite.net; internet www.guamdol.net; Dir MARIA CONNELLEY.

Department of Land Management: 590 South Marine Corps Dr., Route 1, Tamuning, GU 96913; tel. 649-5390; fax 649-5383; internet dlm.guam.gov; Dir TEREZO R. MORTERO.

Department of Law: Suite 2-200E, Judicial Center Bldg, 120 West O'Brien Drive, Hagåtña, GU 96910; tel. 475-3324; fax 475-2493; e-mail law@ns.gov.gu; internet www.justice.gov.gu/dol.

Department of Mental Health and Substance Abuse: e-mail info@guamdmhsa.com; internet dmhsa.guam.gov; Dir ANDREA M. LEITHEISER (acting).

Department of Military Affairs: 430 Army Dr., Bldg 300, Barrigada; tel. 735-0406; fax 649-8775; internet dma.guam.gov.

Department of Parks and Recreation: 490 Chalan Palasyo, Agaña Heights, GU 96910; tel. 475-6296; fax 477-0997; e-mail parks@ns.gov.gu; internet www.dpr.guam.gov; Dir JOSEPH W. DUENAS.

Department of Public Health and Social Services: 123 Chalan Kareta, Route 10, Mangilao, GU 96923; tel. 735-7102; fax 734-5910; internet dphss.guam.gov; Dir PETER JOHN D. CAMACHO (acting).

Public School System: POB DE, Hagåtña, GU 96932; tel. 475-0457; fax 472-5003; internet www.gdoe.net; fmrly known as Department of Education.

Department of Public Works: 542 North Marine Drive, Tamuning, GU 96911; tel. 646-3131; fax 646-3233; internet www.dpw.guam.gov; Dir LAWRENCE P. PEREZ.

Department of Revenue and Taxation: 1240 Route 16, Barrigada, GU 96913; tel. 635-1817; fax 633-2643; e-mail pinadm@revtax.gov.gu; internet www.guamtax.com; Dir ARTEMIO ILAGAN.

Department of the Treasury: PDN Bldg, Suite 404, 238 Archbishop Flores St, Hagåtña, GU 96910.

Department of Youth Affairs: POB 23672, Guam Main Facility, GU 96921; tel. 735-5010; fax 734-7536; e-mail ddell@ns.gov.gu; internet guamyouth.org; Dir CHRISTOPHER M. DUENAS.

Office of Civil Defense (Guam Homeland Security): 221-B Chalan Palasyo, Agana Heights, GU 96910; tel. 475-9600; fax 477-3727; internet www.guamhs.org; f. 1999; Administrator CHARLES H. ADA, II (acting).

Legislature

GUAM LEGISLATURE

The Guam Legislature has 15 members, known as Senators, who are directly elected by popular vote for a two-year term. Elections took place on 4 November 2008, when the Democratic Party secured a majority of seats.

Speaker: JUDITH WON PAT.

CONGRESS

Guam elects a non-voting Delegate to the US House of Representatives. An election was held on 4 November 2008, when the Democratic candidate, Madeleine Z. Bordallo, was re-elected for a fourth term as Delegate.

Delegate of Guam: MADELEINE Z. BORDALLO, Cannon House Office Bldg, 427, Washington, DC 20515-5301, USA; tel. (202) 225-1188; fax (202) 226-0341; e-mail madeleine.bordallo@mail.house.gov; internet www.house.gov/bordallo.

Election Commission

Guam Election Commission: Guam Capital Investment Corpn Bldg, 414 West Soledad Ave, Suite 200, Hagåtña 96910; tel. 477-9791; fax 477-1895; e-mail gec@kuentos.guam.net; internet www.guamelection.org; Chair. FREDERICK J. HORECKY; Exec. Dir JOHN BLAS.

Judicial System

Attorney-General: ALICIA LIMTIACO.
US Attorney: LEONARDO M. RAPADAS.

Supreme Court of Guam: Suite 300, Guam Judicial Center, 120 West O'Brien Drive, Hagåtña, GU 96910; tel. 475-3162; fax 475-3140; e-mail justice@guamsupremecourt.com; internet www.guamsupremecourt.com; Chief Justice ROBERT J. TORRES, Jr.

District Court of Guam

4th Floor, US Courthouse, 520 West Soledad Ave, Hagåtña, GU 96910; tel. 473-9180; fax 473-9118; e-mail judith_hattori@gud.uscourts.gov; internet www.gud.uscourts.gov.

Judge appointed by the President of the USA. The court has the jurisdiction of a Federal district court and of a bankruptcy court of the United States in all cases arising under the laws of the United States. Appeals may be made to the Court of Appeals for the Ninth Circuit and to the Supreme Court of the United States.

Magistrate Judge: JOAQUIN V. E. MANIBUSAN, Jr.

Superior Court of Guam

120 West O'Brien Drive, Hagåtña, GU 96910; tel. 475-3250; internet www.justice.gov.gu/superior.html.

Judges are appointed by the Governor of Guam for an initial eight-year term and are thereafter retained by popular vote. The Superior Court has jurisdiction over cases arising in Guam other than those heard in the District Court.

Presiding Judge: ALBERTO C. LAMORENA, III.

There are also Probate, Traffic, Domestic, Juvenile and Small Claims Courts.

UNITED STATES EXTERNAL TERRITORIES   Guam

Religion

The majority of the population are Roman Catholic, but there are also members of the Episcopal (Anglican) Church, the Baptist churches and the Seventh-day Adventist Church. There are small communities of Muslims, Buddhists and Jews.

CHRISTIANITY

The Roman Catholic Church

Guam comprises the single archdiocese of Agaña. The Archbishop participates in the Catholic Bishops' Conference of the Pacific, based in Suva, Fiji, and the Federation of Catholic Bishops' Conferences of Oceania, based in Wellington, New Zealand.

At 31 December 2006 there were 141,177 adherents in Guam.

Archbishop of Agaña: Most Rev. ANTHONY SABLAN APURON, Chancery Office, Cuesta San Ramón 96910B, Hagåtña, GU 96910; tel. 472-6116; fax 477-3519; e-mail archbishop@mail.archdioceseofguam.com; internet www.archdioceseofagana.com.

BAHÁ'Í FAITH

National Spiritual Assembly: POB Box BA, Hagåtña, GU 96931; tel. 472-9100; fax 472-9101; e-mail nsamar@ite.net; mems resident in 19 localities in Guam and 10 localities in the Northern Mariana Islands.

The Press

NEWSPAPERS AND PERIODICALS

Bonita: POB 11468, Tumon, GU 96931; tel. 632-4543; fax 637-6720; f. 1998; monthly; Publr IMELDA SANTOS; circ. 3,000.

Directions: POB 27290, Barrigada, GU 96921; tel. 635-7501; fax 635-7520; f. 1996; monthly; Publr JERRY ROBERTS; circ. 3,800.

Hospitality Guahan: POB 8565, Tamuning, GU 96931; tel. 649-1447; fax 649-8565; e-mail info@ghra.org; internet www.ghra.org; f. 1996; quarterly; circ. 3,000.

Marianas Business Journal: POB 3191, Hagåtña, GU 96932; tel. 649-0883; fax 649-8883; e-mail glimpses@glimpsesofguam.com; internet www.mbjguam.net; f. 2003; fortnightly; Publr MAUREEN N. MARATITA; Editor PATRICIA SHOOK; circ. 3,000.

Pacific Daily News and Sunday News: POB DN, Hagåtña, GU 96932; tel. 477-1736; fax 472-1512; e-mail cblas@guampdn.com; internet www.guampdn.com; f. 1944; Publr RINDRATY LIMTIACO; Man. Editor DAVID CRISOSTOMO; circ. 28,520 (weekdays), 26,237 (Sunday).

The Pacific Voice: POB 2553, Hagåtña, GU 96932; tel. 472-6427; fax 477-5224; f. 1950; Sunday; Roman Catholic; Gen. Man. TEREZO MORTERA; Editor Rev. Fr HERMES LOSBANES; circ. 6,500.

TV Guam Magazine: 237 Mamis St, Tamuning, GU 96911; tel. 646-4030; fax 646-7445; f. 1973; weekly; Publr DINA GRANT; Man. Editor EMILY UNTALAN; circ. 15,000.

NEWS AGENCY

United Press International (UPI) (USA): POB 1617, Hagåtña, GU 96910; tel. 632-1138; Correspondent DICK WILLIAMS.

Broadcasting and Communications

TELECOMMUNICATIONS

Guam Educational Telecommunication Corporation (KGTF): POB 21449, Guam Main Facility, Barrigada, GU 96921; tel. 734-2207; fax 734-3476; e-mail kgtfl2@ite.net; internet www.kgtf.org.

Guam Telephone Authority: 624 North Marines Corps Dr., POB 9008, Tamuning, GU 96913; tel. 644-4482; fax 649-4821; e-mail ask@gta.net; internet www.gta.net; acquired by TeleGuam Holdings LLC in Dec. 2004; CEO and Pres. DAN MOFFAT.

BROADCASTING

Radio

K-Stereo: POB 20249, Guam Main Facility, Barrigada, GU 96921; tel. 477-9448; fax 477-6411; operates on FM 24 hours a day; Pres. EDWARD H. POPPE; Gen. Man. FRANCES W. POPPE.

KOKU-FM: 424 West O'Brien Drive, Julale Center, Hagåtña, GU 96910; tel. 477-5658; fax 472-7663; e-mail marketing@hitradio100.com; operates on FM 24 hours a day; Pres. KURT S. MOYLAN; Marketing and Sales Man. VINCE LIMUACO.

KPRG FM: KPRG, UoG Station Mangilao, GU 96923; tel. 734-8930; fax 734-2958; e-mail kprg@kprg.org; internet www.kprg.org; operated by the University of Guam; news and music; Chair. MARIE MESA-KERLIN; Chairs TOD THOMPSON, NICK CAPTAIN; Gen. Man. CHRIS HARTIG (acting).

Radio Guam (KUAM): 600 Harman Loop, Dededo, GU 96912; tel. 637-5826; fax 637-9865; e-mail generalmanager@kuam.com; internet www.kuam.com; f. 1954; operates on AM and FM 24 hours a day; Pres. PAUL M. CALVO; Gen. Man. JOEY CALVO.

Sorensen Media Group: Suite 800, 111 Chalan Santo Papa, Hagåtña, GU 96910; tel. 477-5700; fax 477-3982; e-mail rex@spbguam.com; internet www.sorensenmediagroup.com; f. 1981; Chair. and CEO REX SORENSEN.

Trans World Radio Pacific (TWR): POB CC, Hagåtña, GU 96932; tel. 477-9701; fax 477-2838; e-mail ktwr@twr.org; internet www.guam.net/home/twr; f. 1975; broadcasts Christian programmes on KTWR and one medium-wave station, KTWG, covering Guam and nearby islands, and operates five short-wave transmitters reaching most of Asia, Africa and the Pacific; Chair. THOMAS J. LOWELL; Pres. Dr DAVID G. TUCKER; Station Dir MICHAEL DAVIS.

Television

KGTF—TV: POB 21449 Guam Main Facility, Barrigada, GU 96921; tel. 734-3476; fax 734-5483; e-mail kgtfl2@kgtf.org; internet www.kgtf.org; f. 1970; cultural, public service and educational programmes; Gen. Man. SHIRLEY M. SUOZA (acting); Operations Man. BENNY T. FLORES.

KTGM—TV: 692 Marine Dr., Tamuning 96911; tel. 649-8814; fax 649-0371.

KUAM—TV: 600 Harmon Loop, Dededo, Hagåtña, GU 96912; tel. 637-5826; fax 637-9865; e-mail generalmanager@kuam.com; internet www.kuam.com; f. 1956; operates channels 8 and 11; News Dir SABRINA SALAS.

Finance

(cap. = capital; res = reserves; = dep. = deposits; m. = million; brs = branches; amounts in US dollars)

BANKING

Commercial Banks

Allied Banking Corpn (Philippines): Suite 104, Bejess Commercial Bldg, 719 South Marine Drive, Tamuning, GU 96913; tel. 649-5001; fax 649-5002; e-mail abcguam@kuentos.guam.net; Asst Vice-Pres. MARIO R. PALISOC; 1 br.

Bank of Guam: POB BW, 111 Chalan Santo Papa, Hagåtña, GU 96932; tel. 472-5300; fax 477-8687; e-mail customerservice@bankofguam.com; internet www.bankofguam.com; f. 1972; total assets $704.6m. (2003); Chair. LOURDES A. LEON GUERRERO; Exec. Vice-Pres. WILLIAM D. LEON GUERRERO; 19 brs.

Bank of Hawaii (USA): POB BH, Hagåtña, GU 96932; tel. 479-3500; fax 479-3777; Vice-Pres. RODNEY KIMURA; 3 brs.

BankPacific, Ltd: 151 Aspinall Ave, Hagåtña, GU 96910; tel. 472-6704; fax 477-1483; e-mail philipf@bankpacific.com; internet www.bankpacific.com; f. 1954; Pres. and CEO PHILIP J. FLORES; Exec. Vice-Pres. MARK O. FISH; 4 brs in Guam; 1 br. in Palau; 1 br. in Northern Mariana Islands.

Citibank NA (USA): 402 East Marine Drive, POB FF, Hagåtña, GU 96932; tel. 477-2484; fax 477-9441; internet www.citibank.com/guam; Vice-Pres. RASHID HABIB; 2 brs.

Citizens Security Bank (Guam) Inc: Suite 112, 424 West O'Brien Dr., Julale Shopping Center, Hagåtña, GU 96932; tel. 479-9000; fax 479-9090; internet csb.com.gu; mem. of ANZ Group; Pres. and CEO DANIEL L. WEBB; 4 brs.

First Commercial Bank (Taiwan): POB 2461, Hagåtña, GU 96932; tel. 472-6864; fax 477-8921; e-mail fcbgu@ite.net; Gen. Man. JENN-HWA WANG; 1 br.

First Hawaiian Bank (USA): Compadres Mall 562, Harmon Loop Rd, Dededo, GU 96912; tel. 475-7900; fax 637-9686; internet www.fhb.com; Regional Man. LAURA-LYNN DACANAY; 3 brs.

HSBC Ltd: POB 27C, Hagåtña, GU 96932; tel. 647-8588; fax 646-3767; CEO GUY N. DE B. PRIESTLEY; 2 brs.

Metropolitan Bank and Trust Co: 665 South Marine Drive, Tamuning, GU 96911; tel. 649-9555; fax 649-9558; e-mail mbguam@metrobank.com.ph; f. 1975; Sen. Man. JOSEPHINE M. PAPELERA.

Union Bank of California (USA): 194 Hernan Cortes Ave, POB 7809, Hagåtña, GU 96910; tel. 477-8811; fax 472-3284; Man. KINJI SUZUKI; 2 brs.

INSURANCE

American National Insurance Co: POB 3340, Hagåtña, GU 96910; tel. 477-9600.

Chung Kuo Insurance Co: GCIC Bldg, Suite 707, 414 West Soledad Ave, Hagåtña, GU 96910; tel. 477-7696; fax 477-4788; e-mail chungkuo@ite.net; internet www.cki.com.tw.

Midland National Life Insurance Co: Winner Bldg, Suite 20N, Tamuning, GU 96911; tel. 649-0330; internet www.mnlife.com; f. 1906 as Dakota Mutual Life Insurance Company; name changed as above in 1925.

Moylan's Insurance Underwriters, Inc: Suite 102 Julale Shopping Center, 424 West O'Brien Dr., Hagåtña, GU 96910; tel. 477-8613; fax 477-1837; e-mail agana@moylansinsurance.com; internet www.moylansinsurance.com; Pres. KURT S. MOYLAN; Admin. Man CECILIA ANAS.

Nanbo Insurance: POB 2980, Hagåtña, GU 96910; tel. 477-9754; internet www.nanbo.com.

Pioneer Pacific Financial Services, Inc of Guam: POB EM, Hagåtña, GU 96910; tel. 477-6400.

Trade and Industry

DEVELOPMENT ORGANIZATION

Guam Economic Development and Commerce Authority (GEDCA): Guam International Trade Center Bldg, Suite 511, 590 South Marine Dr., Tamuning, GU 96911; tel. 647-4332; fax 649-4146; e-mail help@investguam.com; internet www.investguam.com; f. 1965; Admin. ANTHONY BLAZ.

CHAMBER OF COMMERCE

Guam Chamber of Commerce: Ada Plaza Center, Suite 101, 173 Aspinall Ave, POB 283, Hagåtña, GU 96932; tel. 472-6311; fax 472-6202; e-mail gchamber@guamchamber.com; internet www.guamchamber.com.gu; f. 1924; Chair. LAURA-LYNN DACANAY; Pres. REINA A. LEDDY.

EMPLOYERS' ORGANIZATION

The Employers' Council: 718 North Marine Drive, Suite 201, East-West Business Center, Upper Tumon, GU 96913; tel. 649-6616; fax 649-3030; e-mail tecinc@ite.net; internet www.ecouncil.org; f. 1966; private, non-profit asscn providing management development training and advice on personnel law and labour relations; Exec. Dir E. L. GIBSON.

UTILITIES

Electricity

Guam Energy Office: 548 North Marine Corps Dr., Tamuning, GU 96913; tel. 646-4361; fax 649-1215; e-mail lucybk@teleguam.net; internet www.guamenergy.com; Dir J. LAWRENCE M. CRUZ.

Guam Power Authority: POB 2977, Hagåtña, GU 96932; tel. 648-3225; fax 649-3290; internet www.guampowerauthority.com; f. 1968; autonomous government agency; supplies electricity throughout the island; Gen. Man. JOHN BENAVENTE.

Water

Guam Waterworks Authority: 578 North Marine Corps Drive, Tamuning, GU 96913; tel. 647-2603; fax 646-2335; e-mail heidi@guamwaterworks.org; internet www.guamwaterworks.org; CEO JOHN BENAVENTE.

TRADE UNIONS

Many workers belong to trade unions based in the USA such as the American Federation of Government Employees and the American Postal Workers' Union.

Guam Federation of Teachers (GFT): Local 1581, POB 2301, Hagåtña, GU 96932; tel. 735-4390; fax 734-8085; e-mail webmaster@gftunion.com; internet www.gftunion.com; f. 1965; affiliate of American Federation of Teachers; Pres. MATT RECTOR; 2,000 mems.

Guam Hotel and Restaurant Association: POB 8565, Tamuning, GU 96931; tel. 649-1447; fax 649-8565; e-mail president@ghra.org; internet www.ghra.org; 37 mem. restaurants and hotels; Pres. MARY P. TORRE.

Guam Landowners' Association: Hagåtña; Sec. RONALD TEEHAN.

Transport

ROADS

There are 885 km (550 miles) of public roads, of which some 675 km (420 miles) are paved. A further 685 km (425 miles) of roads are classified as non-public, and include roads located on federal government installations. In September 2008 the Government announced that the sum of US $25m. was to be allocated to the creation of a mass transit network on the island, to accommodate the projected rise in the population that would result from the relocation of thousands of US marines to Guam. In February 2009 a $140m. project to upgrade the island's road system was announced. In the same month the US Government announced that it was committing $1,000m. to fund a new road to link US military facilities in northern and southern Guam. The works were expected to be completed by 2014.

SHIPPING

Apra, on the central western side of the island, is one of the largest protected deep-water harbours in the Pacific. Plans for the modernization of the port were under way in 2009.

Port Authority of Guam: 1026 Cabras Highway, Suite 201, Piti, GU 96925; tel. 477-5931; fax 477-2689; e-mail webmaster@portofguam.com; internet www.portofguam.com; f. 1975; government-operated port facilities; Gen. Man. GLEN LEON GUERRERO; Chair. MONTE MESA.

Ambyth, Shipping and Trading, Inc: 1026 Cabras Highway, Piti, GU 96915; tel. 477-7250; fax 472-1264; e-mail ops@ambyth.guam.net; internet www.ambyth.com; agents for all types of vessels and charter brokers; Pres. ALFRED LAM; Gen. Man. ANDREW MILLER.

Atkins, Kroll, Inc: 443 South Marine Dr., Tamuning, GU 96913; tel. 649-6410; fax 646-9592; e-mail atkins_kroll@akguam.com; internet www.akguam.com; f. 1914; vehicle distribution; Pres. DAN CAMACHO.

COAM Trading Co Ltd: PAG Bldg, Suite 110, 1026 Cabas Highway, Piti, GU 96925; tel. 477-1737; fax 472-3386.

Dewitt Moving and Storage: Suite 100, 165-1, Guerrero St, Tamuning, GU 96913; tel. 648-1800; fax 648-0034; e-mail ezdewitt@dewittguam.com; internet www.dewittguam.com; Pres. JOHN BURROWS.

Guam Shipping Agency: POB GD, Hagåtña, GU 96932; tel. 477-7381; fax 477-7553; Gen. Man. H. KO.

Interbulk Shipping (Guam) Inc: Bank of Guam Bldg, Suite 502, 111 Chalan Santo Papa, Hagåtña, GU 96910; Man. S. GYSTAD.

Maritime Agencies of the Pacific Ltd: Piti, GU 96925; tel. 477-8500; fax 477-5726; e-mail rehmapship@kuentos.guam.net; f. 1976; agents for fishing vessels, cargo, dry products and construction materials; Pres. ROBERT E. HAHN.

Pacific Navigation System: POB 7, Hagåtña, GU 96910; f. 1946; Pres. KENNETH T. JONES, Jr.

Seabridge Micronesian, Inc: 1026 Cabras Highway, Suite 114, Piti, Guam 96925; tel. 477-7345; fax 477-6206; Gen. Man. PAUL L. BLAS.

Sea-Land Service, Inc: POB 8897, Tamuning, GU 96931; tel. 475-8100; internet www.horizon-lines.com; CEO CHARLES RAYMOND.

Tucor Services: 180 Guerrero St, Harmon Industrial Park, POB 6128, Tamuning, GU 96911; tel. 646-6947; fax 646-6945; e-mail boll@tucor.com; general agents for numerous dry cargo, passenger and steamship cos; Pres. MICHELLE BOLL.

CIVIL AVIATION

Guam is served by A. B. Won Pat International Airport.

Guam International Airport Authority: POB 8770, Tamuning, GU 96931; tel. 646-0300; fax 646-8823; e-mail lizb@guamairport.net; internet www.guamairport.com; Chair. MARTIN GERBER; Exec. Man. CARLOS H. SALAS (acting).

Asia Pacific Airlines (APA): POB 24858, Guam Main Facility, Barrigada, Guam 96921; fax 647-8440; e-mail info@flyapa.com; internet www.flyapa.com; f. 1999; affiliate of Tan Holdings Corpn. (Commonwealth of the Northern Mariana Islands); cargo; serving Guam, Hawaii, Hong Kong, Marshall Islands, Federated States of Micronesia, Palau and the Philippines.

Continental Micronesia Airlines: POB 8778, Tamuning, GU 96931; tel. 649-6594; fax 649-6588; internet www.continental.com; f. 1968, as Air Micronesia, by Continental Airlines (USA); hub operations in Guam and Saipan (Northern Mariana Islands); services throughout the region and to destinations in the Far East and the mainland USA; Pres. and CEO LARRY KELLNER.

Freedom Air: POB 1578, Hagåtña, GU 96932; tel. 647-8359; fax 646-7488; e-mail freedom@ite.net; internet www.freedomairguam.com; f. 1974; Man. Dir JOAQUIN L. FLORES, Jr.

Tourism

Tourism is the most important industry on Guam. In 2006 there were 1,211,674 visitor arrivals. In that year some 78.6% of arrivals were visitors from Japan; 9.7% were from the Republic of Korea, and 3.6% from the USA. In 2007 the number of tourist arrivals reached 1,223,290. Most of Guam's hotels are situated in, or near to, Tumon, where amenities for entertainment are well-developed. Numerous sunken wrecks of aircraft and ships from Second World War battles provide interesting sites for divers. There were 7,561 hotel rooms on Guam in 2004. A total of US $16.2m. was collected in hotel occupancy taxes in 2002. The industry as a whole earned some $1,908m. in 1999.

Guam Visitors Bureau: 401 Pale San Vitores Rd, Tumon, GU 96913; tel. 646-5278; fax 646-8861; e-mail guaminfo@visitguam.org; internet www.visitguam.org; Chair. DAVID B. TYDINGCO; Gen. Man. GERALD S. A. PEREZ.

THE UNITED STATES VIRGIN ISLANDS

Introductory Survey

Location, Climate, Language, Religion, Flag, Capital

The United States Virgin Islands consists of three main inhabited islands (St Croix, St Thomas and St John) and about 50 smaller islands, mostly uninhabited. They are situated at the eastern end of the Greater Antilles, about 64 km (40 miles) east of Puerto Rico in the Caribbean Sea. The climate is tropical, although tempered by the prevailing easterly trade winds. The temperature averages 26°C (79°F), with little variation between winter and summer. The humidity is low for the tropics. English is the official language, but Spanish and Creole are also widely used. The people of the US Virgin Islands are predominantly of African descent. There is a strong religious tradition, and most of the inhabitants are Christians, mainly Protestants. The flag (proportions 2 by 3) is white, with a modified version of the US coat of arms (an eagle holding an olive branch in one foot and a sheaf of arrows in the other, with a shield, comprising a small horizontal blue panel above vertical red and white stripes, superimposed), between the letters V and I, in the centre. The capital is Charlotte Amalie, on the island of St Thomas.

Recent History

The Virgin Islands, originally inhabited by Carib and Arawak Indians, were discovered by Europeans in 1493. The group subsequently passed through English, French, and Dutch control, before the western islands of St Thomas and St John, colonized by Denmark after 1670, and St Croix, purchased from France in 1733, became the Danish West Indies. In 1917 these islands, which are strategically placed in relation to the Panama Canal, were sold for US $25m. by Denmark to the USA. They now form an unincorporated territory of the USA. Residents of the US Virgin Islands are US citizens, but cannot vote in presidential elections, if resident in the islands. The US Virgin Islands is represented in the US House of Representatives by one popularly elected Delegate, who is permitted to vote only in committees of the House.

The inhabitants of the islands were granted a measure of self-government by the Organic Act, as revised in 1954, which created the elected 15-member Senate. Since 1970, executive authority has been vested in the elected Governor and Lieutenant-Governor. In the first gubernatorial election, in 1970, the Republican incumbent, Melvin Evans, retained office. In 1974 Cyril E. King, leader of the Independent Citizens Movement (a breakaway faction of the Democratic Party), was elected Governor. On King's death in 1978, the former Lieutenant-Governor, Juan Luis, was elected Governor. He was returned to power in the 1982 election. The governorship passed to the Democratic Party with the election of Alexander Farrelly in 1986. Farrelly was re-elected Governor in 1990, and in the 1994 elections was succeeded by an Independent, Dr Roy Schneider. The governorship was regained by a Democrat, Charles Turnbull, in the 1998 elections. Turnbull was re-elected to the post in 2000 and 2002.

Since 1954 there have been five attempts to redraft the Constitution to give the US Virgin Islands greater autonomy. Each draft has, however, been rejected by a referendum. The US Government has expressed the view that it would welcome reform, if approved by the residents, as long as it was economically feasible and did not affect US national security. A non-binding referendum on the islands' future status, which was to take place in November 1989, was postponed following the disruption caused by 'Hurricane Hugo'. Voting, which eventually took place in October 1993, produced support of 80% for retaining the islands' existing status, with 14% favouring full integration with the USA and 5% advocating the termination of US sovereignty. The result of the referendum was, however, invalidated by the low turn-out: only 27% of registered voters took part, falling short of the 50% participation required for the referendum to be valid. Subsequent legislation to create a constitutional convention was presented to the US Virgin Islands Senate, and in May 2000 a committee of the US House of Representatives began consideration of a range of measures to enlarge the scope of local self-government in the territory. In November 2004 Governor Turnbull approved legislation allowing the creation of a further constituent assembly to redraft the Constitution.

In February 2005 a 7,000-signature petition was submitted to the US Congress by residents of St Croix, in support of making the island a separate US External Territory from St Thomas and St John. Organizers of the petition claimed that such a move would generate more federal funding for the island, which was affected by a higher unemployment rate than the other two islands, despite being the location for one of the world's largest petroleum refineries. In May the Territorial Government brought a court case against the owners of the Hovensa LLC oil refinery (see Economic Affairs) and the defunct St Croix Alumina plant for contaminating the sole groundwater supply on St Croix. Both companies had reached an agreement with the US Environmental Protection Agency (EPA) in 2001 to clean up petroleum spillages; according to the EPA some 2m. gallons of petroleum leaked into the local aquifer between 1978 and 1991.

At a gubernatorial election to the US Virgin Islands' Senate on 7 November 2006 neither of the two leading candidates for the governorship managed to secure a requisite 50% share of the vote. As a result, a run-off election was held on 21 November: John deJongh, representing the Democratic Party of the Virgin Islands, defeated independent candidate Kenneth Mapp by 16,644 votes to 12,402. DeJongh was sworn into office, together with Lieutenant-Governor Gregory Francis, on 1 January 2007. Outgoing Governor Turnbull had been constitutionally precluded from contesting the office, having already served two consecutive four-year terms. The territory's Delegate to Congress, Donna M. Christensen, formally commenced a sixth consecutive term of office on 4 January during a ceremony in Washington, DC, USA. Appointments to the new cabinet were announced from mid-January and the 13 members of the new Executive were officially inaugurated in early May in St Thomas and St Croix, respectively. Notable appointments included Beverly Nicholson-Doty—former President of the US Virgin Islands Hotel and Tourism Association—as Commissioner of Tourism, James H. McCall as Commissioner of Police, and Robert S. Mathes as Commissioner of Planning and Natural Resources. Attorney-General Vincent Frazer was also re-elected and his appointment formalized on 4 May.

In November 2006 the US Virgin Islands Government exercised its right to establish a territorial appellate court, conferred by a US Congress amendment to the Revised Organic Act in 1984 and signed into law by Governor Turnbull in October 2004, becoming the last US sovereign jurisdiction to do so. A Supreme Court would, from 1 January 2007, administer all appeals transferred from the Superior Court without the need for recourse to the federal judiciary, in accordance with the Islands' state and territorial counterparts. In December the first judicial officers were officially sworn in, with Rhys Hodge, formerly a presiding judge of the Superior Court, appointed Chief Justice of the new judicial body.

Progress towards formulating a new constitution for the territory was furthered in April 2007 when the availability of petitions for prospective delegate candidates to participate in the fifth Constitutional Convention was announced. A special election was held on 12 June to determine the composition of a constitutional development committee; the resultant constitutional development process would facilitate the territory's transition from a US Constitution- and Organic Act-governed state to one enjoying greater autonomy. It was also hoped that a new constitution would precipitate greater distinction between the legislative, executive and judicial branches of government. The Fifth Constitutional Convention was assembled on 23 July 2007 to commence work upon the drafting of a new constitution. A final draft document would require the approval of two-thirds of all convention delegates before being put to a referendum for approval. The Convention began its work in October 2007 and was scheduled to deliver a proposed constitution in 2009.

In March 2002 the islands were removed from the Organisation for Economic Co-operation and Development's list of tax havens, after pledging to improve the transparency of its financial services sector by the end of 2005. In May 2007 Christensen presented legislation for the institution of a Chief Financial Officer (CFO) in the territory to function as an independent arbiter upon government fiscal policy. Although a similar law had been earlier approved, Christensen proposed a number of amendments to it, including provision for the chairman of the CFO appointment commission, to be elected by a majority vote of the panel (where the Chief Judge of the Superior Court had previously been designated chairman). It was hoped that the new legislation would encourage greater co-operation between the Governor and Legislative Assembly towards reducing the fiscal deficit, and would facilitate and enhance the transparency of financial policy. A number of financial scandals earlier in the year had foregrounded the necessity of financial services regulatory reform: in June 2006 former director of the US Virgin Islands Department of Planning and Natural Resources Division of Environmental Protection, Hollis L. Griffin, was accused, together with two other islanders, of conspiring to defraud the islands' Government of US $1.4m. Hollis and his two co-defendants were given custodial sentences at the federal court in Atlanta, Georgia, in early May. Furthermore, an economic development programme, implemented by the Territorial Government and permitting firms operating in the islands to reduce their tax payments by up to 90%, was discovered to have been exploited in March 2007 when four individuals, including one islander, were charged with tax evasions amounting to £74m. Following initial reports in 2003 that the programme was being used as a means of tax evasion, the US Federal Government had imposed restrictions on the tax incentive scheme in 2004. Since that time, 23 of 49 registered hedge funds established within the territory had withdrawn or suspended operations. In February 2007 the US Inland Revenue Service announced that the financial affairs of 8,500 high-salaried residents of the US Virgin Islands would be subjected to increased scrutiny. In April Alric Simmonds, Deputy Chief of Staff to erstwhile Governor Turnbull, was indicted on charges of embezzlement, conversion of government property and grand larceny. He was sentenced to eight years' imprisonment in June 2008.

An election was held on 4 November 2008 to decide the islands' delegate to the US House of Representatives, at which Donna M. Christensen was elected unopposed for a fourth term. She was sworn in on 6 January 2009.

Combating crime and terrorism was a stated objective of Governor deJongh's administration. An anti-crime initiative was announced in February 2007; measures included an increase in the size of the police force and establishment of a forensic facility. Specialized police professionals from external US police jurisdictions were also to be drafted in to support and instruct existing personnel. A previous scheme, the Blue Lightning Marine unit (based on St Thomas), was to be reinstated to address the problem of guns- and drugs-trafficking and illegal immigrant incursions through coastal patrols. Governor deJongh had expressed dismay at his predecessor's decision to grant 26 pardons and 11 sentence commutations in December 2006, several of which related to violent crimes. Despite the enhanced crime prevention measures, according to local news sources a record number of murders, 46, took place in 2007 while the number of incidents involving a firearm increased by 40 from levels in 2006, to 171 cases. In his State of the Territory Address in January 2008 deJongh reiterated his commitment to reducing the crime level, and focused particularly on increasing the effectiveness of law-enforcement. To that end, in March he submitted legislation to abolish the Drug Enforcement Bureau and to redirect funding to the police department, which had proved to be more successful in targeting drugs-trafficking, having seized 20,000 kg of marijuana plants and 20 kg of cocaine in 2007.

Economic Affairs

According to estimates by the Territorial Government, the islands' gross national income (GNI) in 1989 was US $1,344m., equivalent to about $13,100 per head. Average personal income in 2007 was $19,787 per head, or about 54.2% of the US mainland average. GNI increased, in real terms, at an average rate of 2.5% per year during 1980–89. In 2000–07 the population increased by an annual average of 0.5%.

Most of the land is unsuitable for large-scale cultivation, but tax incentives have encouraged the growing of vegetables, fruit and cereals, which are produced for local consumption. According to the 2000 census figures, 0.7% of the economically active population were engaged in agriculture, forestry, fishing and mining. According to FAO estimates, however, the sector engaged around 21.6% of the labour force in mid-2005.

The islands are heavily dependent on links with the US mainland. There are no known natural resources, and, because of limited land space and other factors, the islands are unable to produce sufficient food to satisfy local consumption. Most goods are imported, mainly from the mainland USA.

Industry (including construction and mining) engaged some 12.0% of the non-agricultural labour force in 2002, according to official figures. The manufacturing sector employed 5.0% of the employed labour force in 2007. The main branch of manufacturing is petroleum-refining.

Services (including public administration) employed some 88.0% of the non-agricultural labour force in 2002, according to official figures, of which about 33% was employed in public administration. Tourism, which is estimated to account for more than 60% of gross domestic product (GDP), is the mainstay of the islands' income and employment, and provides the major source of direct and indirect revenue for other service sectors (including trade and transport). The emphasis is on the visiting cruise-ship business and the advantages of duty-free products for tourist visitors. In 2008 visitor arrivals (including excursionists and cruise passengers) totalled 2.4m.; in 2007 expenditures amounted to US $1,433.0m. In late 2005 an agreement was signed to build a $500m. casino and resort on St Croix; construction was scheduled for completion by 2022. In 2009 work was ongoing on a number of construction projects related to the tourism industry, including a $63m. recreation centre on St Thomas and the addition of a cruise-ship dock at St Croix harbour. Construction of a $47m. marina facility at Gallows Bay was scheduled to commence in that year. A $150m. hotel and marina complex was completed on St Thomas in late 2006; the Yacht Haven Grande facility, equipped to accommodate the largest cruise ships, accepted its first 'mega-yacht' in November of that year, while the complex was officially inaugurated in March 2007.

St Croix has the world's second largest petroleum refinery, Hovensa LLC (a joint venture between the US oil company Amerada Hess and Petróleos de Venezuela, SA) which produced some 484,000 barrels per day (b/d) in 2004. In that year Hovensa exported refined petroleum products to the USA worth US $6,193m. while, in 2005, shipments of refined petroleum products reached 488,747 barrels, representing almost double the volume (253,560 barrels) exported in the previous year. In response to stricter environmental controls, in September 2005 the company began work on a $400m. desulphurization unit. An Energy Efficiency and Renewable Energy Rebate Progam, launched by the US Virgin Islands Energy Office in October 2006, originally was intended to run for a limited number of months, but was extended until September the following year. It sought to promote awareness of and participation in alternative, renewable energy practices in an attempt to reduce utility costs. In January 2007 four solar power sites on St Thomas, constructed by residents with government funding, were certified by the Energy Office as suitable power generation units from which the Water and Power Authority might purchase energy that was surplus to the residents' requirements. Efforts have been made to introduce labour-intensive and non-polluting manufacturing industries. Rum is an important product; the industry, however, was expected to encounter increased competition from Mexico as a result of the North American Free Trade Agreement (NAFTA, see p. 350), which entered into operation in January 1994. In 2003 the industry was based around a single company, Virgin Islands Rum Industries Ltd, which, in that year alone, exported some 5,973.3m. gallons of rum to the USA. Federal excise taxes collected on rum exports to the USA returned $86.7m. of revenue in 2007.

The population increased dramatically from the 1960s. This inflow included people from neighbouring Caribbean countries, together with wealthy white settlers from the US mainland, attracted by the climate and the low taxes. At the 2000 census 31% of the population originated from other Caribbean islands and 14.5% from the mainland USA.

Throughout the 1990s the budget deficit of the Territorial Government increased. By December 1999 the deficit was estimated to have risen to US $305m., and in that year the Territorial Government introduced a Five-Year Strategic and Financial Operating Plan to reduce government expenditure and enhance the effectiveness of procedures for revenue collection. By 2003/04 the budget deficit had been reduced to $4.6m. In 2005/06 the islands' debt amounted to some $1,150m., equivalent to $10,272 per head. The average rate of unemployment stood at to 5.9% in 2007. The islands were expected, in the foreseeable future, to continue to receive grants and other remittances from the US Government, although greater efforts towards achieving enhanced financial accountability were demanded.

In 2007 the islands recorded a trade surplus of US $710.8m. In that year the USA provided 10.3% of imports and took 94.0% of exports. Venezuela was also a major source of imports. Of total exports to the USA in 2007 some 92.3% were refined petroleum products. Crude petroleum accounted for 77.3% of the islands' total imports in that year.

Owing to the islands' heavy reliance on imported goods, local prices and inflation are higher than on the mainland, and the islands' economy, in contrast to that of the USA, remained in recession for most of the 1990s. It was hoped that amendments to the Western Hemisphere Travel Initiative, ratified by US Congress in October 2006 and requiring all US citizens and foreign nationals travelling to and from the Caribbean to hold a valid passport from 2007, would confer an advantage on US territories in the Caribbean. In October 2004 the US Congress approved legislation to reform corporate tax in the US Virgin Islands. There were concerns that the measures would deter companies from using the territory as a tax haven, at a cost to the local economy of up to US $63m. in lost revenue and as many as 600 jobs. In 2006 US Treasury Regulations, effecting a relaxation of the residency requirements for companies and individuals in the islands, were implemented in an attempt to assuage such concerns and encourage greater confidence in the beleaguered Economic Development Commission programme. (The financial services sector had experienced a period of stagnation since early 2005 following the introduction of the 2004 law.) In December 2006 legislation confirming the right of the US Virgin Islands Government to formulate its own tax policy was approved by the US House of Representatives.

UNITED STATES EXTERNAL TERRITORIES

The United States Virgin Islands

While concern had been expressed by the US General Accounting Office and Department of the Interior in December that the governments of US insular territories—including the Virgin Islands—represented 'high-risk' investments for federal funding, owing to their reliance on a narrow range of volatile key industries and scarce natural resources, some limited progress had been made towards diversification and economic independence by that time. The threat of a prolonged recession in the USA was likely to reduce tourist arrivals in 2009, and this decrease, as well as lower tax receipts, meant that growth was forecast to slow to 1.0% in that year. Furthermore, higher levels of unemployment increased the volume of people claiming benefits, which was likely to stretch government finances. The construction of a US $162m. rum refinery, begun in April 2009, was expected to not only provide employment and increase investment, but also to allow the Government to borrow against the predicted revenues. Under the $787,000m. economic stimulus programme, announced by the incoming federal Government in early 2009, the US Virgin Islands was to receive approximately $248m. in additional funding. In 2007 the territory recorded GDP growth of 2.4%, with growth in 2008 estimated at 2.8%.

The territory is an associate member of the UN Economic Commission for Latin America and the Caribbean (ECLAC, see p. 40).

Education

Education is compulsory up to the age of 16 years. It generally comprises eight years at primary school and four years at secondary school. In 2005 there were 21,772 students enrolled at elementary and secondary schools. The University of the Virgin Islands, with campuses on St Thomas and St Croix, had 2,610 students in 2004. The territorial education system is comprised of a State Education Agency and two Local Education Agencies covering the St Thomas/St John District and the St Croix District. The Department of Education was allocated US $38.2m. in the federal budget for 2007.

Public Holidays

2009: 1 January (New Year's Day), 6 January (Three Kings' Day), 19 January (Martin Luther King Day), 16 February (Presidents' Day), 27 March (Transfer Day), 10–13 April (Easter), 25 May (Memorial Day), 15 June (Organic Act Day), 3 July (Danish West Indies Emancipation Day), 4 July (US Independence Day), 27 July (Hurricane Supplication Day), 7 September (Labor Day), 12 October (Columbus Day/Puerto Rico Friendship Day), 19 October (Virgin Islands Thanksgiving Day), 1 November (Liberty Day), 11 November (Veterans' Day), 26 November (US Thanksgiving Day), 25–26 December (Christmas).

2010: 1 January (New Year's Day), 6 January (Three Kings' Day), 18 January (Martin Luther King Day), 15 February (Presidents' Day), 27 March (Transfer Day), 2–5 April (Easter), 24 May (Memorial Day), 14 June (Organic Act Day), 3 July (Danish West Indies Emancipation Day), 4 July (US Independence Day), 26 July (Hurricane Supplication Day), 6 September (Labor Day), 11 October (for Columbus Day/Puerto Rico Friendship Day), 18 October (Virgin Islands Thanksgiving Day), 1 November (Liberty Day), 11 November (Veterans' Day), 25 November (US Thanksgiving Day), 25–26 December (Christmas).

Statistical Survey

Sources (unless otherwise stated): Office of Public Relations, Office of the Governor, Charlotte Amalie, VI 00802; tel. (340) 774-0294; fax (340) 774-4988; Bureau of Economic Research, Dept of Economic Development and Agriculture, 1050 Norre Gade No. 5, Suite 301, Charlotte Amalie, VI 00802; POB 6400, Charlotte Amalie, VI 00804; tel. (340) 774-8784; e-mail dhazell@usviber.org; internet www.usviber.org.

AREA AND POPULATION

Area: 347.1 sq km (134 sq miles): St Croix 215 sq km (83 sq miles); St Thomas 80.3 sq km (31 sq miles); St John 51.8 sq km (20 sq miles).

Population: 101,809 at census of 1 April 1990; 108,612 (males 51,684, females 56,748) at census of 1 April 2000. *By Island* (2000 census): St Croix 53,234, St Thomas 51,181, St John 4,197. Source: US Bureau of the Census. *2004* (official figures): St Croix 54,629; St Thomas 52,523; St John 4,307; Total 111,459. *2007* (resident population, estimates): St Croix 55,293; St Thomas 53,160; St John 4,359; Total 112,812.

Density (2007, estimate): 325.0 per sq km.

Principal Towns (population at census of 1 April 2000): Charlotte Amalie (capital) 11,004; Christiansted 2,637; Frederiksted 732. Source: Thomas Brinkhoff, *City Population* (internet www.citypopulation.de).

Births and Deaths (2006, preliminary): Registered live births 1,431 (birth rate 13.2 per 1,000); Registered deaths 629 (death rate 5.8 per 1,000) (Source: US National Center for Health Statistics). *2008:* Birth rate 13.4 per 1,000; Death rate 6.8 per 1,000 (Source: Pan American Health Organization).

Life Expectancy (years at birth, estimates): 79.5 (males 75.6; females 83.4) in 2008. Source: Pan American Health Organization.

Economically Active Population (persons aged 16 years and over, 2000 census): Agriculture, forestry, fishing, hunting and mining 324; Manufacturing 2,754; Construction 4,900; Wholesale trade 912; Retail trade 6,476; Transportation, warehousing and utilities 3,321; Information 931; Finance, insurance, real estate, rental and leasing 2,330; Professional, scientific, management, administrative and waste management services 3,058; Educational, health, and social services 6,742; Arts, entertainment, recreation, accommodation and food services 7,351; Public administration 4,931; Other services 2,535; *Total employed* 46,565 (Source: US Bureau of the Census). *2007* (number of waged and salaried jobs, official figures): Construction and mining 3,470; Manufacturing 2,318; Transportation, warehouse and utilities 1,625; Wholesale and retail trade 7,013; Financial activities 2,459; Leisure and hospitality 7,469; Information 803; Other services 9,400; Federal government 946; Territorial government 11,752.

HEALTH AND WELFARE

Total Fertility Rate (children per woman, 2007): 2.1.

Under-5 Mortality Rate (per 1,000 live births, 2006): 9.8.

Physicians (per 1,000 head, 2003): 1.47.

Hospital Beds (per 1,000 head, 1996): 18.7.

Source: Pan American Health Organization.

For definitions, see explanatory note on p. vi.

AGRICULTURE, ETC.

Livestock (2007, FAO estimates): Cattle 8,100; Sheep 3,250; Pigs 2,650; Goats 4,100; Chickens 40,000.

Fishing (metric tons, live weight, 2006): Total catch (all capture) 1,614 (Groupers 47; Snappers, jobfishes, etc. 149; Grunts, sweetlips, etc. 41; Parrotfishes 206; Surgeonfishes 39; Triggerfishes, durgons, etc. 45; Caribbean spiny lobster 124; Stromboid conchs 787).

Source: FAO.

INDUSTRY

Production ('000 metric tons unless otherwise indicated, 2002, estimates): Jet fuels 1,745; Motor spirit (petrol) 2,654; Kerosene 91; Gas-diesel (distillate fuel) oil 5,725; Residual fuel oils 3,550; Liquefied petroleum gas 164; Electric energy (2005) 1,060 million kWh. Source: UN, *Industrial Commodity Statistics Yearbook*.

FINANCE

Currency and Exchange Rates: 100 cents = 1 United States dollar (US $). *Sterling and Euro Equivalents* (31 December 2008): £1 sterling = US $1.458; €1 = US $1.392; US $100 = £68.60 = €71.85.

Budget (US $ million, year ending 30 September 2007): Operating budget 842.8 (Net revenues from taxes, duties and other sources 734.6); Rum excise taxes (Federal remittance) 86.7; Direct Federal expenditures 649.

Cost of Living (Consumer Price Index; base: 2001 = 100): All items 114.2 in 2005; 117.6 in 2006; 123.3 in 2007.

EXTERNAL TRADE

Total Trade (US $ million): *Imports:* 10,243.3 in 2005; 11,614.8 in 2006; 12,251.0 in 2007. *Exports:* 10,476.3 in 2005; 11,626.6 in 2006; 12,961.8 in 2007. Note: The main import is crude petroleum ($9,465.7m. in 2007), while the principal exports are refined petroleum products ($11,242.1 m. in 2007).

Trade with the USA (US $ million): *Imports:* 1,153.6 in 2005; 1,321.4 in 2006; 1,261.0 in 2007. *Exports:* 9,954.1 in 2005; 11,047.4 in 2006; 12,182.1 in 2007.

TRANSPORT

Road Traffic (registered motor vehicles, 2007): 73,353.

Shipping: *Freight Imports* ('000 metric tons) 1,056 in 2002; 879 in 2003; 979 in 2004. *Cruise-ship Arrivals:* 782 in 2006; 752 in 2007; 687 in 2008. *Passenger Arrivals:* 1,903,533 in 2006; 1,917,878 in 2007; 1,757,067 in 2008.

Civil Aviation (visitor arrivals): 671,361 in 2006; 693,373 in 2007; 678,905 in 2008.

UNITED STATES EXTERNAL TERRITORIES

TOURISM

Visitor Arrivals ('000): 2,574.9 (arrivals by air 670.7, cruise-ship passengers 1,903.5) in 2006; 2,611.3 (arrivals by air 693.4, cruise-ship passengers 1,917.9) in 2007; 2,436.0 in 2008 (arrivals by air 679.0, cruise-ship passengers 1,757.1).

Visitor Receipts (US $ million, 2007): Total receipts 1,433.0 (tourists 829.4, excursionists 603.5).

COMMUNICATIONS MEDIA

Radio Receivers (1997): 107,100 in use.
Television Receivers (1999): 71,000 in use.
Telephones (2007): 62,566 main lines in use.
Mobile Cellular Telephones (2005): 80,300 subscribers.
Internet Users (2007): 30,000.
Broadband Subscribers (2005): 3,000.
Daily Newspapers (1996): 3 titles; average circulation 42,000 copies.
Non-daily Newspapers (1988, estimates): 2; average circulation 4,000 copies.

Sources: UNESCO, *Statistical Yearbook*; International Telecommunication Union.

EDUCATION

Pre-primary (1992/93, unless otherwise indicated): 62 schools; 121 teachers; 4,714 students (2000).
Elementary (1992/93, unless otherwise indicated): 62 schools; 790 teachers (public schools only); 11,728 students (2005).
Secondary: 541 teachers (public schools only, 1990); 5,022 students (2005).
Higher Education: 266 teachers (2003/04); 2,610 students (2004).

Sources: UNESCO, *Statistical Yearbook*; US Bureau of the Census.

Directory

The Constitution

The Government of the US Virgin Islands is organized under the provisions of the Organic Act of the Virgin Islands, passed by the Congress of the United States in 1936 and revised in 1954 and 1984. Subsequent amendments provided for the popular election of the Governor and Lieutenant-Governor of the Virgin Islands in 1970 and, since 1973, for representation in the US House of Representatives by a popularly elected Delegate. The Delegate has voting powers only in committees of the House. Executive power is vested in the Governor, who is elected for a term of four years by universal adult suffrage and who appoints, with the advice and consent of the legislature, the heads of the executive departments. The Governor may also appoint administrative assistants as his representatives on St John and St Croix. Legislative power is vested in the legislature of the Virgin Islands, a unicameral body comprising 15 Senators, elected for a two-year term by popular vote. Legislation is subject to the approval of the Governor, whose veto can be overridden by a two-thirds vote of the Legislature. All residents of the islands who are citizens of the USA and at least 18 years of age have the right to vote in local elections, but not in national elections. In 1976 the Virgin Islands were granted the right to draft their own constitution, subject to the approval of the US President and Congress. A constitution permitting a degree of autonomy was drawn up in 1978 and gained the necessary approval, but was then rejected by the people of the Virgin Islands in a referendum in March 1979. A fourth draft, providing for greater autonomy than the 1978 draft, was rejected in a referendum in November 1981. At a further attempt, in October 1993, the referendum was invalidated by the insufficient turn-out of registered voters. In November 2004 legislation was approved to allow the creation of a constituent assembly to redraft the Constitution. A constitutional convention, composed of 30 publicly elected delegates, was convened in October 2007 with a view to drafting a new constitution during 2009.

The Government

EXECUTIVE
(April 2009)

Governor: JOHN DEJONGH, Jr.
Lieutenant-Governor: GREGORY FRANCIS.

The United States Virgin Islands

Commissioner of Agriculture: LOUIS E. PETERSON, Jr.
Commissioner of Education: Dr LAVERNE TERRY.
Commissioner of Finance: CLAUDETTE J. WATSON-ANDERSON.
Commissioner of Health: VIVIAN EBBESEN-FLUDD.
Commissioner of Housing, Parks and Recreation: ST CLAIRE N. WILLIAMS.
Commissioner of Human Services: CHRISTOPHER FINCH.
Commissioner of Labor: ALBERT BRYAN, Jr.
Commissioner of Licensing and Consumer Affairs: KENRICK ROBERTSON.
Commissioner of Planning and Natural Resources: ROBERT S. MATHES.
Commissioner of Police: JAMES H. MCCALL.
Commissioner of Property and Procurement: LYNN A. MILLIN.
Commissioner of Public Works: DARRYL SMALLS.
Commissioner of Tourism: BEVERLY NICHOLSON-DOTY.
Attorney-General: VINCENT FRAZER.
US Virgin Islands Delegate to the US Congress: DONNA M. CHRISTENSEN.

GOVERNMENT OFFICES

Office of the Governor: Government House, 21–22 Kongens Gade, Charlotte Amalie, VI 00802; tel. (340) 774-0001; fax (340) 693-4374; e-mail contact@governordejongh.com; internet www.governordejongh.com.

Office of the Lieutenant-Governor: Government Hill, 18 Kongens Gade, Charlotte Amalie, VI 00802; tel. (340) 774-2991; fax (340) 774-6953; e-mail celeste.lawrence@lgo-vi.gov; internet www.ltg.gov.vi.

Department of Agriculture: Estate Lower Love, Kingshill, St Croix, VI 00850; tel. (340) 774-0991; fax (340) 774-1823.

Department of Education: 1834 Kongens Gade, Charlotte Amalie, VI 00802-6746; tel. (340) 774-0100; fax (340) 779-7153; e-mail llarsen@sttj.k12.vi; internet www.doe.vi.

Department of Finance: GERS Bldg, 2nd Floor, 76 Kronprindsens Gade, Charlotte Amalie, VI 00802; tel. (340) 774-4750; fax (340) 776-4028; e-mail candercpa@msn.com.

Department of Health: 1303 Hospital Ground Suite 10, Charlotte Amalie, St Thomas, VI 00802; tel. (340) 774-0117; fax (340) 777-4001; internet www.healthvi.org.

Department of Housing, Parks and Recreation: Property & Procurement Bldg No. 1, Sub Base, 2nd Floor, Rm 206, Charlotte Amalie, VI 00802; tel. (340) 774-0255; fax (340) 774-4600.

Department of Human Services: Knud Hansen Complex Bldg A 1303, Hospital Ground, Charlotte Amalie, VI 00802; tel. (340) 774-0930; fax (340) 774-3466; internet www.dhs.gov.vi.

Department of Justice: GERS Bldg, 2nd Floor, 48B–50C Kronprindsens Gade, Charlotte Amalie, VI 00802; tel. (340) 774-5666; fax (340) 774-9710; e-mail vfrazer@doj.vi.gov.

Department of Labor: St Thomas: POB 302608, St Thomas, VI 00803-2608; St Croix: 2203 Church St, St Croix, VI 00820-4612; tel. (340) 776-3700; fax (340) 774-5908; e-mail customersupport@vidol.gov; internet www.vidol.gov.

Department of Licensing and Consumer Affairs: Property & Procurement Bldg, 1 Sub Base, Rm 205, Charlotte Amalie, St Thomas VI 00802; tel. (340) 774-3130; fax (340) 776-0675; e-mail dlcacommissioner@dlca.gov.vi; internet www.dlca.gov.vi.

Department of Planning and Natural Resources: Terminal Bldg, 2nd Floor, Suite 6, 8100 Lindberg Bay, St Thomas VI 00802; tel. (340) 774-3320; fax (340) 775-5706; internet www.dpnr.gov.vi.

Department of Police: Alexander Farrelly Criminal Justice Center, Charlotte Amalie, St Thomas, VI 00802; tel. (340) 774-2211; fax (340) 715-5517; e-mail police.commissioner@vipd.gov.vi; internet www.vipd.gov.vi.

Department of Property and Procurement: Property & Procurement Bldg No. 1, 3rd Floor, Sub Base, Charlotte Amalie, VI 00802; tel. (340) 774-0828; fax (340) 777-9587; e-mail lnibbs@pnpvi.org; internet www.pnpvi.org.

Department of Public Works: Bldg No. 8, Sub Base, Charlotte Amalie, VI 00802; tel. (340) 776-4844; fax (340) 774-5869; e-mail darryl.smalls@dpw.vi.gov.

Department of Tourism: POB 6400, St Thomas, VI 00804; tel. (340) 774-8784; fax (340) 774-4390; e-mail info@usvitourism.vi; internet www.usvitourism.vi.

UNITED STATES EXTERNAL TERRITORIES

Legislature

LEGISLATIVE ASSEMBLY

Senate
(15 members)

President of the Senate: USIE RICHARDS.

Election, 4 November 2008

Party	Seats
Democrats	10
Independent Citizens' Movement	2
Independent	3
Total	15

Political Organizations

Democratic Party of the Virgin Islands: POB 2033, St Thomas Democratic District, VI 00803; affiliated to the Democratic Party of the USA; Chair. CECIL R. BENJAMIN, Jr.

Independent Citizens' Movement (The ICM Party, VI): POB 305188, St Thomas, VI 00803-5188; tel. (340) 774-0880; Chair. Sen. TERRENCE NELSON.

Republican Party of the Virgin Islands: 6067 Questa Verde, Christiansted, St Croix, VI 00820-4485; tel. (340) 332-2579; e-mail info@virepublicanwomen.com; internet www.vigop.com; f. 1948; affiliated to the Republican Party of the USA since 1952; Chair. HERB SCHOENBOHM; Pres. TRACY PARDO DE ZELA; Sec. MITSOOKO KING; Exec. Dir JIM OLIVER.

Judicial System

Supreme Court of the Virgin Islands: 1000 Blackbeards Hill, 3rd Floor, Suite 10, St Thomas, VI 00802; tel. (340) 777-4935; fax (340) 774-2258; internet www.visupremecourt.org; f. Jan. 2007, pursuant to legislation passed in Oct. 2004; assumed jurisdiction for all appeals formerly administered by the Superior Court; highest local appellate body, established to administer justice independently of the US federal justice system; judges are appointed by the Governor.

Judges: RHYS S. HODGE (Chief Judge), IVE ARLINGTON SWAN, MARIA M. CABRET.

Superior Court of the Virgin Islands: Alexander A. Farrelly Justice Center, 5400 Veteran's Dr., St Thomas, VI 00802; tel. (340) 774-6680; fax (340) 776-9889; e-mail court.administrator@visuperiorcourt.org; internet www.visuperiorcourt.org; f. 1976 as the Territorial Court of the Virgin Islands; name officially changed in 2004; jurisdiction over all local civil actions and criminal matters; court in St Croix also; judges are appointed by the Governor.

Judges: DARRYL DEAN DONOHUE (Presiding), ISHMAEL A. MEYERS, BRENDA J. HOLLAR, AUDREY L. THOMAS, LEON A. KENDALL, PATRICIA D. STEELE, JULIO A. BRADY, JAMES S. CARROLL, MICHAEL C. DUNSTON; 1 vacancy.

US Federal District Court of the Virgin Islands: Division of St Thomas/St John: 5500 Veteran's Dr., Charlotte Amalie, St Thomas, VI 00802-6424; Division of St Croix: 3013 Estate Golden Rock, Christiansted, St Croix, VI 00820-4355; tel. (340) 774-0640; fax (340) 774-1293; internet www.vid.uscourts.gov; jurisdiction in civil, criminal and federal actions; judges are appointed by the President of the USA with the advice and consent of the Senate.

Judges: CURTIS V. GOMEZ (Chief Judge), RAYMOND L. FINCH.

Religion

The population is mainly Christian. The main churches with followings in the islands are Baptist, Roman Catholic, Episcopalian, Lutheran, Methodist, Moravian and Seventh-day Adventist. There is also a small Jewish community, numbering around 900 adherents.

CHRISTIANITY

The Roman Catholic Church

The US Virgin Islands comprises a single diocese, suffragan to the archdiocese of Washington, DC, USA. At 31 December 2006 there were an estimated 30,221 adherents in the territory (27.7% of the population).

Bishop of St Thomas: Most Rev. GEORGE V. MURRY, Bishop's Residence, 29A Princesse Gade, POB 301825, Charlotte Amalie, VI 00803-1825; tel. (340) 774-3166; fax (340) 774-5816; e-mail chancery@islands.vi; internet www.catholicvi.com.

The Anglican Communion

Episcopal Church of the Virgin Islands: Bishop: Rt Rev. AMBROSE GUMBS, 13 Commandant Gade, Charlotte Amalie, POB 10437, St Thomas, VI 00801; tel. (340) 776-1797; fax (340) 777-8485; e-mail episcopal@vipowernet.net; internet www.episcopaldioceseofthevirginislands.com.

The Press

Pride Magazine: 22A Norre Gade, POB 7908, Charlotte Amalie, VI 00801; tel. (340) 776-4106; f. 1983; monthly; Editor JUDITH WILLIAMS; circ. 4,000.

St Croix Avis: La Grande Princesse, Christiansted, St Croix, VI 00820; tel. (340) 773-2300; f. 1944; morning; Editor RENA BROADHURST-KNIGHT; circ. 10,000.

St John Tradewinds: The Marketplace, Office Suites II, Office 104, POB 1500, Cruz Bay, St John, VI 00831; tel. (340) 776-6496; fax (340) 693-8885; e-mail editor@tradewinds.vi; internet www.stjohnnews.com; f. 1972; weekly; Publr MALINDA NELSON; circ. 2,500.

Virgin Islands Daily News: 9155 Estate Thomas, VI 00802; tel. (340) 774-8772; fax (340) 776-0740; e-mail dailynews@vipowernet.net; internet www.virginislandsdailynews.com; f. 1930; acquired from Innovative Communication Corpn by Times-Shamrock Communications, USA in 2008; morning; CEO and Exec. Editor JASON ROBBINS; circ. 15,000.

Virgin Islands Source: St Thomas; tel. (340) 777-8144; fax (340) 777-8136; e-mail source@viaccess.net; internet www.visource.com; f. 1998; comprises the *St Thomas Source*, *St Croix Source* and *St John Source*; daily; digital; Publr SHAUN A. PENNINGTON.

Broadcasting and Communications

TELECOMMUNICATIONS

Innovative Telephone: Bjerget House, POB 1730, St Croix, VI 00821; tel. (340) 777-7700; fax (340) 777-7701; e-mail info@iccvi.com; internet www.iccvi.com; f. 1959 as Virgin Islands Telephone Corpn (Vitelco); acquired by Innovative Communication Corpn in 1987; present name adopted in 2001; provides telephone services throughout the islands; launched internet service, Innovative PowerNet, in 1999; Pres. and CEO CLARKE GARNETT (acting).

Innovative Wireless: 4006 Estate Diamond, Christiansted, St Croix, VI 00820; fax (340) 778-6011; internet www.vitelcellular.com; f. 1989 as VitelCellular; subsidiary of Innovative Communication Corpn; mobile cellular telecommunications; Man. Dir BEULAH JONIS (acting).

RADIO

WDHP 1620 AM, WRRA 1290 AM, WAXJ 103.5 FM: 79A Castle Coakley, Christiansted, St Croix, VI 00820; tel. (340) 719-1620; fax (340) 778-1686; e-mail info@reefbroadcasting.com; internet www.reefbroadcasting.com; operated by Reef Broadcasting, Inc; commercial; English and Spanish; broadcasts to the US and British Virgin Islands, Puerto Rico and the Eastern Caribbean; Owner and Gen. Man. HUGH PEMBERTON.

WEVI (Power 101.7 WeVi-FM): 2C Hogensborg, Frederiksted, St Croix, VI 00840; POB 892, Christiansted, VI 00821; tel. (340) 719-9384; e-mail aw@frontlinemissions.org; internet www.wevifm.net; operated by FrontLine Missions International, Inc; non-commercial; Christian programming; English, Spanish and Créole/Patois.

WGOD: Crown Mountain, POB 5012, Charlotte Amalie, VI 00803; tel. (340) 774-4498; fax (340) 776-0877; operated by Moody Broadcasting Network, USA; commercial; Christian religious programming; Pres. Rev. REYNOLD CHARLES.

WIUJ: c/o WTJX-TV (PBS), Mountain Top, Estate Solberg, St Thomas; POB 2477, St Thomas, VI 00803; e-mail information@wiuj.com; internet www.wiuj.com; operated by V. I. Youth Development Radio, Inc; non-commercial; educational and public service programmes; Gen. Man. LEO MORONE.

WJKC (Isle 95-FM), WMNG (Mongoose), WVIQ (Sunny): 5020 Anchor Way, POB 25680, Christiansted, St Croix, VI 00824; tel. (340) 773-0995; e-mail jkc@viradio.com; internet www.isle95.com; f. 1982; commercial; Gen. Man. JONATHAN K. COHEN.

WSTA (Lucky 13): 121 Sub Base, POB 1340, St Thomas, VI 00804; tel. (340) 774-1340; fax (340) 776-1316; e-mail addie@wsta.com; internet www.wsta.com; f. 1950; acquired by Ottley Communications Corpn in 1984; commercial; Owner and Gen. Man. ATHNIEL C. OTTLEY.

WVGN: Nisky Mall Center, PMB 105, St Thomas, VI 00802; e-mail info@wvgn.org; internet www.wvgn.org; f. 2002; operated by Caribbean Community Broadcasting Co; non-commercial; news and public affairs programming; affiliated to NBC, USA; CEO KEITH BASS; Gen. Man. LORRAINE BAA-ELISHA.

WVWI (Radio One), WVJZ (Jamz), WWKS (Kiss), WIVI (Pirate Radio) (Ackley Media Group Stations): 13 Crown Bay Fill, St Thomas, VI 00802; tel. (340) 776-1000; fax (340) 776-5357; e-mail support@ackleycomm.com; internet www.amg.vi; f. 1962; acquired from Knight Quality Stations by Ackley Media Group in 2006; commercial; Pres. and CEO GORDON P. ACKLEY.

WZIN (Buzzrocks): Nisky Mall Center, PMB 357, St Thomas 00802; tel. (340) 776-1043; fax (340) 775-446; e-mail cristy@buzrocks.com; internet www.buzzrocks.com; operated by Pan Caribbean Broadcasting, Inc; commercial; Gen. Man. ALAN FRIEDMAN.

Other radio stations include: WIVH, WMYP (Latino 98.3 FM), WSTX (Magic 97X), and WYAC (Voice of the Virgin Islands).

TELEVISION

Innovative Cable Television (St Croix, St Thomas, St John): 4006 Estate Diamond, Christiansted, St Croix, VI 00820; fax (340) 778-6011; e-mail info@iccvi.com; internet www.innovativecable.com; f. 1997 following acquisition of St Croix Cable TV (f. 1981); subsidiary of Innovative Communication Corpn; acquired Caribbean Communication Corpn in 1998; comprises TV2 (f. 2000); broadcasts to seven Caribbean islands and France; Pres. and Gen. Man. JENNIFER MATARANGAS-KING.

WSVI-TV8 (Channel 8): Sunny Isle Shopping Center, POB 6000, Christiansted, St Croix, VI 00823; tel. (340) 778-5008; fax (340) 778-5011; e-mail channel8@wsvitv.com; internet www.wsvi.tv; f. 1965; operated by Alpha Broadcasting Corpn; affiliated to ABC; one satellite channel and one analogue translator.

WTJX-TV (Public Television Service): Barbel Plaza, POB 7879, Charlotte Amalie, VI 00801; tel. (340) 774-6255; fax (340) 774-7092; e-mail pphipps@wtjxtv.org; internet www.wtjxtv.org; f. 1968; educational and public service programmes; affiliated to PBS; broadcasts on one terrestrial and four digital (cable) channels; broadcasts to the US and British Virgin Islands and Puerto Rico; Chair. ROAN CREQUE; Exec. Dir OSBERT POTTER.

Finance

BANKING

Banco Popular of the Virgin Islands: 193 Altona and Welgunst, Charlotte Amalie, VI 00802; tel. (340) 693-2702; fax (340) 693-2782; e-mail internet@bppr.com; internet www.bancopopular.com; Chair. RICHARD L. CARRIÓN; 8 brs.

Bank of Nova Scotia (Scotiabank): 214C Altona and Welgunst, POB 420, Charlotte Amalie, VI 00804; tel. (340) 774-0037; fax (340) 693-5994; e-mail lawrence.aqui@scotiabank.com; internet www.usvi.scotiabank.com; Vice-Pres. LAWRENCE AQUI; Man. ALLAN TOBIN; 10 brs.

Bank of St Croix: POB 24240, Gallows Bay, St Croix 00824; tel. (340) 773-8500; fax (340) 773-8508; e-mail info@bankofstcroix.com; internet www.bankofstcroix.com; f. 1994; CEO JAMES BRISBOIS; 1 br.

FirstBank of Puerto Rico: POB 3126, St Thomas, VI 00803; tel. (340) 774-2022; fax (340) 776-1313; acquired First Virgin Islands Federal Savings Bank in 2000 and Virgin Islands Community Bank in January 2008; Pres. and CEO JAMES E. CRITES; 4 brs.

Virgin Islands Community Bank: 12–13 King St, Christiansted, St Croix, VI 00820; tel. (340) 773-0440; fax (340) 773-4028; internet www.vibank.org/vicbank.html; acquired by FirstBank of Puerto Rico in Jan. 2008; Pres. and CEO MICHAEL J. DOW; 3 brs.

INSURANCE

A number of mainland US companies have agencies in the Virgin Islands.

Trade and Industry

GOVERNMENT AGENCY

US Virgin Islands Economic Development Authority: Government Development Bank Bldg, 1050 Norre Gade, POB 305038, St Thomas, VI 00803; tel. (340) 774-8104; e-mail edc@usvieda.org; internet www.usvieda.org; semi-autonomous body comprising Government Devt Bank, Economic Devt Commission, Industrial Park Devt Corpn, Small Business Devt Agency and the Enterprise Zone program; offices in St Thomas and St Croix; Exec. Dir PERCIVAL CLOUDEN.

CHAMBERS OF COMMERCE

St Croix Chamber of Commerce: 3009 Orange Grove, Suite 12, Christiansted, St Croix, VI 00820; tel. (340) 773-1435; fax (340) 773-8172; e-mail info@stxchamber.net; internet www.stxchamber.net; f. 1924; Pres. OMER ERSELCUK; Exec. Dir MICHAEL DEMBECK; 250 mems.

St Thomas-St John Chamber of Commerce: 6–7 Dronningens Gade, POB 324, Charlotte Amalie, VI 00804; tel. (340) 776-0100; fax (340) 776-0588; e-mail chamber@islands.vi; internet www.usvichamber.com; Pres. THADDEUS BAST; Exec. Dir JOSEPH S. AUBAIN; c. 700 mems.

UTILITIES

Regulatory Authority

Virgin Islands Energy Office: 45 Estate Mars Hill, Frederiksted, St Croix, VI 00840; tel. (340) 773-1082; fax 772-0063; e-mail dbuchanan@vienergy.org; internet www.vienergy.org; Dir BEVAN R. SMITH, Jr.

Electricity and Water

Virgin Islands Water and Power Authority (WAPA): POB 1450, Charlotte Amalie, VI 00804-1450; tel. (340) 774-3552; fax (340) 774-3422; internet www.viwapa.vi; f. 1964; public corpn; manufactures and distributes electric power and desalinated sea water; Chair. CHERYL BOYNES-JACKSON; Exec. Dir and CEO HUGO HODGE, Jr; c. 50,000 customers.

Transport

ROADS

The islands' road network totals approximately 855.5 km (531.6 miles). Throughout 2004 the Department of Public Works implemented a programme, valued at US $17.5m., to repair roads damaged in storms in November 2003.

SHIPPING

The US Virgin Islands are a popular port of call for cruise ships. The bulk of cargo traffic is handled at a container port on St Croix. A passenger and freight ferry service provides frequent daily connections between St Thomas and St John and between St Thomas and Tortola (British Virgin Islands). In June 2004 the Port Authority approved a US $9.3m. project to expand freight, vehicle and passenger facilities at Red Hook. A $150m. marina restoration project on St Thomas, completed in October 2006, included provision for 'mega-yacht' docking facilities in addition to conventional moorings which, it was hoped, would invigorate the cruise ship industry.

Virgin Islands Port Authority: POB 301707, Charlotte Amalie, VI 00803-1707; tel. (340) 774-1629; fax (340) 774-0025; e-mail info@viport.com; internet www.viport.com; f. 1968; semi-autonomous govt agency; maintains, operates and develops marine and airport facilities; Exec. Dir KENN HOBSON (acting).

CIVIL AVIATION

There are airports on St Thomas and St Croix, and an airfield on St John. Seaplane services link the three islands. The runways at Cyril E. King Airport, St Thomas, and Alexander Hamilton Airport, St Croix, can accommodate intercontinental flights.

Tourism

The islands have a well-developed tourism infrastructure, offering excellent facilities for fishing, yachting and other aquatic sports. A National Park covers about two-thirds of St John. There were 4,757 guest rooms in 2007. In 2008 there were some 2.4m. visitors to the islands, of whom 679,000 were tourists and 1.8m. were cruise-ship passengers. Visitors from the USA comprised 80.1% of hotel guests in 2007. Tourism expenditure stood at US $1,433.0m. in that year.

St Croix Hotel Association: POB 24238, St Croix, VI 00824; tel. (340) 773-7117; fax (340) 773-5883.

US Virgin Islands Hotel and Tourism Association: POB 2300, Charlotte Amalie, St Thomas, VI 00803; tel. (340) 774-6835; fax (340) 774-4993; e-mail stsjhta@vipowernet.net; internet www.virgin-islands-hotels.com; Pres. LISA HAMILTON.

OTHER UNITED STATES TERRITORIES

Baker and Howland Islands

The Baker and Howland Islands lie in the Central Pacific Ocean, about 2,575 km (1,600 miles) south-west of Honolulu, Hawaii; they comprise two low-lying coral atolls without lagoons, and are uninhabited. Both islands were mined for guano in the late 19th century. Settlements, known as Meyerton (on Baker) and Itascatown (on Howland), were established by the USA in 1935, but were evacuated during the Second World War, owing to Japanese air attacks. The islands are National Wildlife Refuges, and since 1974 have been administered by the US Fish and Wildlife Service. In 1990 legislation before Congress proposed that the islands be included within the boundaries of the State of Hawaii. In January 2009 President George W. Bush established by proclamation the Pacific Remote Islands Marine National Monument, which included Baker and Howland Islands. The islands are administered by the US Department of the Interior, US Fish and Wildlife Service, Refuge Complex Office, POB 50167, Honolulu, Hawaii 96850; internet www.fws.gov.

Jarvis Island

Jarvis Island lies in the Central Pacific Ocean, about 2,090 km (1,300 miles) south of Hawaii. It is a low-lying coral island and is uninhabited. The island was mined for guano in the late 19th century. A settlement, known as Millersville, including a weather station for the benefit of trans-Pacific aviation, was established by the USA in 1935, but was evacuated during the Second World War. Legislation before Congress in 1990 proposed that the island be included within the State of Hawaii. In January 2009 Jarvis Island became part of the Pacific Remote Islands Marine National Monument (see above). The island is a National Wildlife Refuge and is administered by the US Department of the Interior, US Fish and Wildlife Service (details as above, under Baker and Howland Islands).

Johnston Atoll

Johnston Atoll lies in the Pacific Ocean, about 1,319 km (820 miles) west-south-west of Honolulu, Hawaii. It comprises Johnston Island, Sand Island (uninhabited) and two man-made islands, North (Akua) and East (Hikina); area 2.6 sq km (1 sq mile). Johnston Atoll was designated a Naval Defense Sea Area and Airspace Reservation in 1941, and is closed to public access. In 1985 construction of a chemical weapons disposal facility began on the atoll, and by 1990 it was fully operational. In 1989 the US Government agreed to remove artillery shells containing more than 400 metric tons of nerve gas from the Federal Republic of Germany, and destroy them on Johnston Island. In late 1991, following expressions of protest to the US Government by the nations of the South Pacific Forum (now Pacific Islands Forum, see p. 393), together with many environmental groups, a team of scientists visited the chemical disposal facility to monitor the safety and environmental impact of its activities. In May 1996 it was reported that all nerve gases stored on the atoll had been destroyed. However, 1,000 tons of chemical agents remained contained in landmines, bombs and missiles at the site. In December 2000 it was announced that the destruction of the remaining stock of chemical weapons had been completed (the original deadline for the destruction of 40,000 weapons stored on the island had been August 1995). The closure and decontamination of the facility was completed in 2004 and, in June of that year, all military personnel left and control of the Atoll was transferred to the US Fish and Wildlife Service, which has reported its intention eventually to create a nature reserve on the atoll. In March 2005 the Department of Defense announced the termination of the Air Force mission in Johnston Atoll. A facility capable of performing atmospheric tests of nuclear weapons remains operational on the atoll. The atoll had an estimated population of 173 in 1990, although this increased to approximately 1,000, mainly military, personnel during weapons disposal operations in previous years. In January 2009 Johnston Atoll became part of the Pacific Remote Islands Marine National Monument (see above, under Baker and Howland Islands). Johnston Atoll falls under the jurisdiction of the Department of the Interior, US Fish and Wildlife Service (details as above, under Baker and Howland Islands). Operational control is the responsibility of the US Air Force. Permission to land on Johnston Island must be obtained from the US Air Force. The residing military commander of Johnston Island acts as the agent for the DTRA.

Kingman Reef

Kingman Reef lies in the Pacific Ocean, about 1,500 km (925 miles) south-west of Hawaii, and comprises a reef and shoal measuring about 8 km (5 miles) by 15 km (9.5 miles). In 2000 administrative control was transferred from the US Navy to the Department of the Interior. In 2001 the waters around the reef were designated a National Wildlife Refuge, under the jurisdiction of the US Fish and Wildlife Service (details as above, under Baker and Howland Islands). In January 2009 Kingman Reef became part of the Pacific Remote Islands Marine National Monument (see above, under Baker and Howland Islands).

Midway Atoll

Midway Atoll lies in the northern Pacific Ocean, about 1,850 km (1,150 miles) north-west of Hawaii. A coral atoll, it comprises Sand Island, Eastern Island and several small islets within the reef, has a total area of about 5 sq km (2 sq miles). The islands had a population of 2,200 in 1983, but by 1990 this had declined to 13. Since the transfer of the islands' administration from the US Department of Defense to the Department of the Interior in October 1996, limited tourism is permitted. There is a National Wildlife Refuge on the Territory, which is home to many species of birds. Legislation before Congress in 1990 proposed the inclusion of the Territory within the State of Hawaii. The islands are administered by the US Department of the Interior, US Fish and Wildlife Service (details as above, under Baker and Howland Islands).

Navassa Island

Navassa Island lies in the Caribbean Sea, about 160 km (100 miles) south of Guantánamo Bay, Cuba, and 65 km (40 miles) west of Haiti. It is a raised coral island with a limestone plateau and has an area of 5.2 sq km (2 sq miles). The island is uninhabited. Navassa became a US Insular Area in 1857, and was mined throughout the late 19th century, under the Navassa Phosphate Co. All mining activities were terminated in 1898. In 1996 the US Coast Guard ceased operations of the island's lighthouse, and in January 1997 the Office of Insular Affairs (under the control of the US Department of the Interior) assumed control of the island. A research expedition undertaken in mid-1998 revealed the presence of numerous undiscovered plant and animal species, many of which were thought to be unique to the island. Visits to the island and its surrounding waters were subsequently prohibited, pending further assessment of the island's environment. In December 1999 administrative responsibility for Navassa passed wholly to the US Department of the Interior, US Fish and Wildlife Service (details as above, under Baker and Howland Islands); however, control over political matters was retained by the Office of Insular Affairs.

Palmyra

Palmyra lies in the Pacific Ocean, about 1,600 km (1,000 miles) south of Honolulu, Hawaii. It comprises some 50 low-lying islets, has a total area of 100 ha, is uninhabited and is privately owned. Since 1961 the Territory has been administered by the US Department of the Interior. In 1990 legislation before Congress proposed the inclusion of Palmyra within the boundaries of the State of Hawaii. In mid-1996 it was announced that the owners (the Fullard-Leo family in Hawaii) were to sell the atoll to a US company, which, it was believed, planned to establish a nuclear waste storage facility in the Territory. The Government of neighbouring Kiribati expressed alarm at the proposal, and reiterated its intention to seek the reinclusion of the atoll within its own national boundaries. However, in June one of the Hawaiian Representatives to the US Congress proposed legislation in the US House of Representatives to prevent the establishment of such a facility, and a US government official subsequently announced that the atoll would almost certainly not be used for that purpose. Palmyra was purchased by The Nature Conservancy (internet www.tnc.org) in December 2000. Designated a National Wildlife Refuge, the lagoons and surrounding waters within the 12 nautical mile zone of US territorial seas were transferred to the US

UNITED STATES EXTERNAL TERRITORIES

Fish and Wildlife Service (details as above, under Baker and Howland Islands) in January 2001; the US Fish and Wildlife Service subsequently undertook negotiations to purchase part of the 680 acres of emergent lands owned by The Nature Conservancy. In November 2005 an international team of scientists joined with The Nature Conservancy to establish a new station on the Palmyra Atoll in order to undertake environmental research. In January 2009 Palmyra became part of the Pacific Remote Islands Marine National Monument (see above, under Baker and Howland Islands).

Wake Island

Wake Island lies in the Pacific Ocean, about 2,060 km (1,280 miles) east of Guam. It is a coral atoll comprising the three islets of Wake, Wilkes and Peale, with an area less than 8 sq km (3 sq miles) and a population estimated to be almost 2,000 in 1988. Legislation before Congress in 1990 proposed the inclusion of the islands within the Territory of Guam. However, the Republic of the Marshall Islands, some 500 km (310 miles) south of Wake, exerted its own claim to the atoll (called Enenkio by the Micronesians), which is a site of great importance for the islands' traditional chiefly rituals. Plans by a US company, announced in 1998, to establish a large-scale nuclear waste storage facility on the atoll were condemned by environmentalists and politicians in the region. In August 2006 Hurricane Loke severely damaged much of the island's infrastructure. The US Air Force had previously evacuated all 188 residents. In January 2009 Wake Island became part of the Pacific Remote Islands Marine National Monument (see above, under Baker and Howland Islands). Since 1972 the group has been administered by the US Department of Defense, Department of the Air Force (Pacific/East Asia Division), The Pentagon, Washington, DC 20330; tel. (202) 694-6061; fax (703) 696-7273; internet www.af.mil.

URUGUAY

Introductory Survey

Location, Climate, Language, Religion, Flag, Capital

The Eastern Republic of Uruguay lies on the south-east coast of South America, with Brazil to the north and Argentina to the west. The climate is temperate, with an average temperature of 14°C–16°C (57°F–61°F) in winter and 21°C–28°C (70°F–82°F) in summer. The language is Spanish. There is no state religion but Roman Catholicism is predominant. The national flag (proportions 2 by 3) has nine horizontal stripes (five white and four blue, alternating), with a square white canton, containing a yellow sun with 16 alternating straight and wavy rays, in the upper hoist. The capital is Montevideo.

Recent History

After independence, gained in 1825, domestic politics in Uruguay became dominated by two parties: the Colorados ('reds' or Liberals) and the Blancos ('whites' or Conservatives, subsequently also known as the Partido Nacional). Their rivalry resulted in frequent outbreaks of civil war in the 19th century: the names derive from the flags of the 1836 civil war. From 1880 to 1958 the governing Partido Colorado was led by the Batlle family. Owing to the progressive policies of José Batlle y Ordóñez, Colorado President in 1903–07 and in 1911–15, Uruguay became the first welfare state in Latin America. During 1951–66 the presidency was in abeyance, being replaced by a collective leadership.

In December 1967 Jorge Pacheco Areco assumed the presidency. His period in office was notable for massive increases in the cost of living, labour unrest and the spectacular exploits of the Tupamaro urban guerrilla movement. In March 1972 Pacheco was succeeded by Juan María Bordaberry Arocena, a Colorado, who won the presidential election in November 1971. The army took complete control of the campaign against the Tupamaros, and by late 1973 had suppressed the movement. Military intervention in civilian affairs led, in 1973, to the closure of the Congreso (Congress) and its replacement by an appointed 25-member Council of State (subsequently increased to 35 members). The Partido Comunista and other left-wing groups were banned; repressive measures, including strict press censorship, continued. In September 1974 army officers were placed in control of the major state-owned enterprises.

President Bordaberry was deposed by the army in June 1976 because of his refusal to countenance any return, however gradual, to constitutional rule. In July the recently formed Council of the Nation elected Aparicio Méndez Manfredini to the presidency for five years. Despite the Government's announcement that there would be a return to democracy, persecution of opponents continued; some 6,000 political prisoners were thought to be in detention in 1976.

President Méndez introduced constitutional amendments, known as Institutional Acts, to consolidate the internal situation and to create a 'new order'. By 1980 severe economic problems made the army anxious to return executive responsibility to civilian politicians. A new constitution, under which the armed forces would continue to be involved in all matters of national security, was drafted and submitted to a plebiscite in November 1980, but was rejected by 58% of voters. The military leadership was therefore forced to amend the draft document in consultation with leaders of the recognized political parties, and in September 1981 a retired army general, Gregorio Alvarez Armellino, was appointed by the Joint Council of the Armed Forces to serve as President during the transition period to full civilian government.

The Government's reluctance to permit greater public freedom and to improve observance of human rights caused serious unrest throughout 1983. Popular discontent was further aroused by the rapid deterioration of the economy and by the effect of events in Argentina. In August the authorities suspended all public political activity and reserved the right to impose a new constitution without consultation, insisting, however, that the original electoral timetable would be maintained. The political opposition responded by threatening to boycott the elections and by uniting with proscribed groups to hold a national day of protest. In September the first organized labour protest for 10 years was supported by 500,000 workers.

Political agitation increased during 1984, and the Government threatened to postpone the elections, planned for 25 November, unless the political parties agreed to its proposals for constitutional reform. Tensions increased in June, following the return from exile and the subsequent arrest of Ferreira Aldunate, the proposed presidential candidate of the Partido Nacional. Talks between the Government, the Partido Colorado and the Unión Cívica (a Christian democratic party) resumed in July; the parties obtained several important concessions, including the right to engage in political activity. In August, encouraged by the Government's commitment to the restoration of the democratic process, the parties (with the exception of the Partido Nacional) agreed to the Government's proposals. The Government confirmed that elections would take place, and all restrictions on political activity were withdrawn.

At elections in November 1984 the Partido Colorado, led by Dr Julio María Sanguinetti Cairolo, secured a narrow victory over the opposition. In February 1985 the military regime relinquished power, one month earlier than originally planned. President Sanguinetti was inaugurated on 1 March, as was a Government of national unity, incorporating representatives of the other parties. Concurrently, various outlawed organizations, including the Partido Comunista, were legalized. All political prisoners were released under an amnesty law later in the month.

The new Government announced its commitment to reversing the economic recession; however, its efforts to address the crisis were hampered by frequent industrial stoppages. Discussions between the administration and trade union and business leaders began in August 1985. Although the Government suspended negotiations following another series of strikes, discussions resumed in September.

A major political issue in 1986 was the investigation into alleged violations of human rights by the armed forces during the military dictatorship. In August the Government proposed legislation that would offer an amnesty for all military and police personnel accused of this type of crime, in accordance with a pact made with the armed forces that human rights trials would not take place. In October the draft legislation was rejected by opposition parties, but in December a revised law (the Ley de Caducidad, or Statute of Limitations Law) was approved, which brought an end to current military trials and made the President responsible for any further investigations. The law was widely opposed and in February 1987 a campaign was initiated to organize a petition containing the signatures of at least 25% of the registered electorate, as required by the Constitution, in order to force a referendum on the issue. The campaign was supported principally by human rights groups, trade unions and the centre-left coalition, the Frente Amplio (FA). A referendum duly took place in April 1989, at which a total of 53% of the votes were cast in favour of maintaining the amnesty law.

The presidential and legislative elections in November 1989 resulted in victory (for the first time since 1962) for the Partido Nacional. In the presidential election, Luis Alberto Lacalle, the party's main candidate (the electoral code permitted each party to present more than one candidate), received 37% of the votes, while his closest rival, Jorge Batlle Ibáñez of the Partido Colorado, won 30%. However, the Partido Nacional failed to obtain an overall majority in the Congreso, thus compelling the President-elect to seek support from a wider political base. Immediately before taking office, in March 1990, he announced the conclusion of an agreement, the 'coincidencia nacional', between the two principal parties, whereby the Partido Colorado undertook to support proposed legislation on economic reform, in return for the appointment of four of its members to the Council of Ministers.

Labour unrest intensified during the early 1990s. The trade union confederation, the Plenario Intersindical de Trabajadores—Convención Nacional de Trabajadores (PIT—CNT), organized a series of general strikes in support of demands for wage increases and in opposition to government austerity measures and privatization plans. Opposition from within the ruling coalition to the planned sale of state enterprises became apparent in May 1991, when former President Sanguinetti, the leader of the Partido Colorado's Foro Batllista faction, withdrew his support from the Government, thus forcing the resignation of the Minister of Public Health, the faction's sole representative in the Council of Ministers. Reservations were also expressed by elements of the Partido Nacional. In September, none the less, the privatization legislation was narrowly approved by the Congreso. In response, the opposition FA, with the support of another political organization, Nuevo Espacio, and the trade unions, began a campaign to overrule the legislature by way of a referendum. In October 1992, in a special poll, some 30% of the electorate voted for a full referendum to be held on the partial amendment of the Government's privatization legislation. At the referendum, held in December, 72% of voters supported the proposal for a partial repeal of the legislation. The vote was also widely recognized as a vote of censure against the President's economic policy, and in particular his determination to keep public sector wage increases to a minimum. While the result of the referendum did not affect all planned divestments, it was considered to be a serious reverse and served to undermine confidence in government economic policy.

Industrial unrest in the public sector intensified in 1992, owing primarily to the Government's refusal to grant wage increases in line with inflation. In November, following a four-day strike by the police, the Government was forced to concede wage increases of up to 50% to the security forces. Encouraged by this concession, transport and public health workers initiated strikes in support of demands for wage increases.

The presidential and legislative elections in November 1994 were notable for the emergence of a third political force to rival the traditional powers of the Partido Nacional and the Partido Colorado. The Encuentro Progresista (EP)—a predominantly left-wing alliance principally comprising the parties of the FA, as well as dissidents of the Partido Nacional and other minor parties—secured 31% of the votes in the presidential poll, as did the Partido Nacional, while the Partido Colorado won a narrow victory, with 33% of the vote. Sanguinetti, the leading presidential candidate of the Partido Colorado, was pronounced President-elect; he indicated his intention to appoint a broadly based Council of Ministers in order to ensure legislative support for his administration.

In early 1995, following talks with opposition parties, the Partido Colorado established a 'governability pact' with the Partido Nacional, providing for a coalition Government. The Council of Ministers contained six members of the Partido Colorado, four from the Partido Nacional, one Unión Cívica member, and one representative from the Partido por el Gobierno del Pueblo (Lista 99), which had contested the elections in alliance with Sanguinetti's Foro Batllista faction of the Partido Colorado, and whose leader, Hugo Batalla, had been elected as Sanguinetti's Vice-President.

In July 1995 the Government and the legislative opposition reached an agreement providing for the reform of the electoral system. Under the existing system, known as the Ley de Lemas, parties were permitted to present more than one presidential candidate, with the leading candidate in each party assuming the total number of votes for candidates in that party. According to the proposed reform, each party would present one candidate, selected by means of an internal election, and, in the event of no candidate securing an absolute majority, a second round of voting would be conducted. In October 1996 President Sanguinetti finally secured the necessary two-thirds' support for the reform in the legislature, notwithstanding a degree of opposition from elements of the FA. Besides abolishing the Ley de Lemas and introducing provision for second-round presidential elections, the reform also accorded greater autonomy to municipal administrations and established a framework for environmental protection. The amendments were approved by 51% of voters in a plebiscite held in December, and came into effect in January 1997.

In May 1997 some 20,000 civilians staged a rally in the capital to demand that the Government and the armed forces provide information on the whereabouts of as many as 140 people who had 'disappeared' during the military dictatorship. In December President Sanguinetti issued a decree that granted an amnesty to 41 former army officers who had been dismissed from service during the dictatorship, owing to their political beliefs. Lt-Gen. Raúl Mermot, the Commander-in-Chief of the Armed Forces, resigned from his post one month ahead of schedule, in protest at the decision. In May 1999 some 15,000 people participated in a further march in support of demands that the authorities account for the disappearance of friends and relatives during the military dictatorship.

In late April 1999, in the first primary elections to be held in Uruguay, Lacalle, Batlle and Tabaré Ramón Vázquez Rosas were selected as the presidential candidates for the Partido Nacional, the Partido Colorado and the EP (subsequently known as Encuentro Progresista—Frente Amplio, EP—FA), respectively. Vázquez, a former Mayor of Montevideo, won a particularly convincing victory, securing 82% of the votes of his party's supporters, while Batlle defeated Sanguinetti's favoured candidate, Luis Hierro López, who was later nominated as the Partido Colorado's candidate for the vice-presidency.

The presidential and legislative elections of October 1999 confirmed the end of the traditional dominance of the Partido Colorado and the Partido Nacional. The EP—FA became the largest single party in both the Cámara de Representantes (Chamber of Representatives) and the Cámara de Senadores (Senate), winning 40 and 12 seats, respectively. The Partido Colorado largely maintained its representation, securing 33 and 10 seats, while support for the Partido Nacional declined considerably, with the party winning only 22 seats in the lower house and seven in the Cámara de Senadores, having held a combined total of 41 seats in the outgoing legislature. Vázquez won 39% of the vote, compared with 31% for Batlle and 21% for Lacalle. Despite the convincing success of the EP—FA in the first round, Batlle defeated Vázquez in a second round of voting on 28 November, with 52% of the vote, aided by the support of the Partido Nacional (under a formal accord). Following his inauguration on 1 March 2000, President Batlle appointed a new Council of Ministers, allocating eight portfolios to the Partido Colorado and five to the Partido Nacional.

In early 2000 Batlle held several meetings with Vázquez, in an apparent attempt to achieve a degree of rapprochement with the left, and also committed himself to resolving the issue of the 'disappeared', in marked contrast to his predecessor, Sanguinetti, who had consistently resisted pressure to investigate their fate. In April 2000 Batlle dismissed Gen. Manuel Fernández, one of the country's most senior army officials, after he sought to justify the military repression of the 1970s. In August Batlle announced the formation of a commission, composed of representatives from the Government, the opposition, the Church and the victims' families, to investigate the fate of 164 people who 'disappeared' during the military dictatorship. The unexpected dismissal in January 2001 of Gen. Juan Geymonat, Commander-in-Chief of the Armed Forces, was interpreted as a first step in a military reform programme advocated by Batlle. In October 2002 the Commission reported its preliminary findings that 26 of the 33 'disappeared' Uruguayan citizens under its investigation had been murdered by Argentine and Uruguayan military officers.

Against a background of ongoing economic recession, the Batlle administration encountered opposition to its policies from organized labour groups from 1999. In June 2000 a general strike was organized by the PIT—CNT to demand increased action on unemployment and more finance for education and health care, as well as to protest against emergency legislation, approved that month, which would allow the partial privatization of some public services, including the railways and the ports. A more widespread strike was held in December to protest at the same issues. However, an attempt by the EP—FA to force a referendum on the controversial law in February 2001 failed, owing to a lack of public support.

The financial crisis in neighbouring Argentina of December 2001–January 2002 caused additional economic hardship in Uruguay, with continued rural unrest and political and trade-union opposition to the austerity measures introduced by the Government. There was an unprecedented rise in street violence and organized crime, along with accelerated rates of emigration. In May the Argentine Government's imposition of severe restrictions on bank withdrawals prompted many Argentine citizens holding assets in Uruguay to access their funds, precipitating a crisis in Uruguay's financial system. In late June the Government was forced to abandon exchange rate controls in order to maintain the peso uruguayo's competitiveness against the devalued Argentine and Brazilian currencies. However, by late July, following a 30% decline in the peso's value in relation to the US dollar, and amid rising concerns over the viability and transparency of the banking sector, substantial numbers of Uruguayans also began to withdraw their deposits. In an attempt to avert a financial collapse, the Government instructed all banking institutions in Uruguay to close for a period of four days and introduced emergency economic measures, which included an increase in taxation on salaries and pensions. Three state-owned banks were placed under direct government administration, and restrictions were imposed on their customers' access to long-term foreign exchange deposits. The Government successfully sought an immediate loan of US $1,500m. from the USA to prevent a severe deterioration in international reserves and in November agreement was reached with the IMF on stand-by loans totalling some $2,800m., to be disbursed in 2002 and 2003. Nevertheless, as a result of the financial crisis, in late July Alberto Bensión, the Minister of Economy and Finance, was forced to resign, having lost the support of the Partido Nacional. He was succeeded by Alejandro Atchugarry, a prominent member of the Partido Colorado.

As well as fomenting popular resentment towards the Government's economic strategy and unprecedentedly high levels of unemployment in mid-2002, the financial crisis led to a greater willingness within the Partido Nacional to reconsider its association with the Partido Colorado. In November the Partido Nacional terminated discussions on a new 'governability pact' between the two parties, removed its five ministers from the Government and withdrew from the ruling coalition, leaving the FA as the largest political bloc in the Congreso. President Batlle subsequently appointed non-partisan ministers to the vacant posts and a limited rationalization of ministries was effected.

In November 2002 it was announced that the three suspended state-run banks were to be merged into one: in March 2003 the Nuevo Banco Comercial began operations. The incorporation of the new bank coincided with the resumption of IMF disbursements, suspended in November owing to the Government's perceived lack of progress on the restructuring of the banking sector. (In January 2005 the International Court of Arbitration of the International Chamber of Commerce (ICC, see p. 323) ruled that Uruguay must pay US $100m., in addition to legal expenses and accrued interest, to foreign investors in the liquidated Banco Comercial.)

In August 2003 a series of strikes was held by public sector workers to protest at the Government's reform programme, in particular at plans to increase private sector participation in the economy. In June the EP—FA succeeded in gaining parliamentary approval for a referendum to be held on the proposed partial privatization of the state-run fuel, cement and alcohol monopoly, the Administración Nacional de Combustible, Alcohol y Portland (ANCAP). In the referendum held in December some 62% voted to repeal the controversial legislation; the high level of opposition was widely interpreted as a further expression of public dissatisfaction with the Batlle administration. The EP—FA pledged to maintain state control of public utilities if successful in the 2004 presidential and legislative elections.

At the presidential election in October 2004 Tabaré Vázquez, the candidate of the EP—FA—Nueva Mayoría (as the grouping became known until late 2005), won the presidency in the first round of voting, with 50.7% of the ballot. His nearest rival, Jorge Larrañaga, the Partido Nacional candidate, obtained some 34.1% of the votes, while the Partido Colorado's nominee, Guillermo Stirling, attracted 10.3% of the votes cast. The EP—FA—Nueva Mayoría coalition also made gains in the concurrent legislative elections, winning a majority in both chambers of the legislature, with 16 of the 30 seats of the Cámara de Senadores and 52 of the 99 seats of the Cámara de Representantes. The Partido Colorado's legislative representation fell sharply (from 33 to 10 seats in the lower house, and from 10 to just three seats in the upper), while the Partido Nacional became the second largest party in both chambers, winning 35 seats in the Cámara de Representantes and 11 seats in the Cámara de Senadores. The EP—FA—Nueva Mayoría's electoral campaign had centred on pledges to increase social spending dramatically, to effect a radical reform of the tax and pension systems, and to retain state control over utilities and services.

Concurrently with the presidential election, a referendum was held on a proposal that the water industry remain under state control. The proposal was supported by the EP—FA—Nueva Mayoría, but opposed by the incumbent Colorado administration. In the poll, 64.5% of those voting were in favour of the water sector remaining under state control. However, following the result of the ballot, the outgoing Colorado Government propounded that all private sector contracts in the water industry be rescinded in order to achieve full nationalization, a proposal that was opposed by President-elect Vázquez.

In November 2004 Larrañaga (who was also the leader of the Alianza Nacional faction of the Partido Nacional) and Sanguinetti, leader of the Foro Batllista tendency within the Partido Colorado, indicated that neither the Partido Nacional nor the Partido Colorado would participate in the incoming Government; however, in February 2005 it was announced that the new administration would receive cross-party support for its economic policies (in addition to the support already pledged for its policies on education and foreign affairs). President Vázquez, who took office on 1 March, notably appointed Danilo Astori of the Asamblea Uruguay as Minister of Economy and Finance. The appointment of Astori, an orthodox economist on the right wing of the EP—FA—Nueva Mayoría (renamed the FA in late 2005), was widely interpreted as an attempt to strengthen investor confidence in a broadly left-wing administration. In mid-March both opposition parties withdrew their support for the Government's economic policies in protest at their allocation of positions on the governing bodies of state banks, companies and quasi-autonomous agencies, which, they considered, fell short of the number traditionally allocated to members of the opposition.

An immediate priority of the new Government was to eradicate poverty; to this end, in March 2005 President Vázquez announced the Plan de Atención Nacional de Emergencia Social, a programme of social spending, expected to total some US $200m. over two years. The following day the new Minister of National Defence, Azucena Berruti (a former human rights lawyer), announced that the Government had begun investigations into the 'disappearances' that occurred during the years of military rule. In August the heads of Uruguay's armed forces submitted to the President a report admitting the kidnap, torture and murder of political dissidents, and purportedly detailing the whereabouts of their remains. Information in the report led to the exhumation in November of the bodies of two dissidents murdered by members of the air force. Earlier that month Vázquez had proposed legislation seeking to amend the Ley de Caducidad of 1986 in order to facilitate prosecution of members of the military for human rights abuses committed during military rule. In December 35 unidentified corpses were exhumed from a cemetery in a town near the Brazilian border.

The investigation of human rights abuses allegedly committed during the military dictatorship continued during 2006 and 2007. In May 2006 six former Uruguayan military officers were arrested in connection with the 'disappearance' and presumed murder in 1976 of María Claudia García, the daughter of the Argentine poet Juan Gelman, following an extradition request from Argentina. The arrests represented the first occasion on which any individuals had faced legal action for their alleged role in the torture and murder of dissidents during the period of military repression in the 1970s. In November 2006 former President Bordaberry and his then foreign minister, Juan Carlos Blanco, were charged with the abduction and murder of four opponents of the authorities in 1976. Furthermore, in February 2007 a former officer of senior rank in the Uruguayan military was arrested in Brazil, and his extradition to Uruguay sought, on charges relating to the murders of three dissidents in 1976, as well as the 'disappearance' of García. In December former President Alvarez was arrested and charged, along with two army captains, with the forced disappearance of up to 40 dissidents in 1978, during which time he was Commander-in-Chief of the Army. Alvarez's arrest was facilitated by legislation, adopted in September 2006, which established that acts of forced disappearance were considered to be ongoing, and were therefore not excluded from prosecution by the Ley de Caducidad.

President Vázquez announced an extensive government reorganization in February 2008, involving six cabinet posts. Notably, the Minister of Foreign Affairs, Reinaldo Gargano, who had reportedly maintained a tense relationship with Vázquez and other members of the Government, was replaced by Dr Gonzalo Fernández, while Jorge Bayardi succeeded Berrutti as Minister of National Defence. The changes were reportedly in order to enable the outgoing ministers to concentrate on party political activities ahead of the presidential and legislative elections due in October 2009.

In November 2008 a law to allow abortion without restriction in the first 12 weeks of pregnancy was approved by the Cámara de Senadores, despite vociferous opposition from the Roman Catholic Church. However, Vázquez promptly vetoed the legislation (to which he was ethically opposed), leading the Partido Socialista del Uruguay (PS) to criticize the President for placing his personal beliefs before the will of the party. Vázquez subsequently resigned from the PS. Vázquez also suffered a reverse in

November when the FA party delegation nominated the outspoken and flamboyant José (Pepe) Mujica (a senator and erstwhile Tupamaro guerrilla), of the Movimiento de Participación Nacional, as the coalition's official candidate for the presidential election due in October 2009. Vázquez openly favoured Danilo Astori (the former Minister of Economy and Finance) as his successor; however, in early 2009 opinion polls indicated that Mujica remained the most likely candidate to win the FA primary elections, scheduled to be held in June. (A third candidate, Marcos Carámbula, a doctor and mayor of Canelones, was also to contest the FA primaries.) Although there were concerns that the open rivalry between Astori and Mujica might prove detrimental to the coalition, the Partido Nacional also remained divided, with Luis Alberto Lacalle and Jorge Larrañaga fiercely competing for the party's nomination. Opinion polls in April suggested that the FA had the support of some 42% of voters, followed by the Partido Nacional (37%) and the Partido Colorado (8%).

In April 2009 the legislature approved plans to hold a referendum (in October, concurrently with presidential and legislative elections) to reform the Constitution in order to allow Uruguayan emigrants to vote in elections from 2014. It was estimated that as many as 600,000 Uruguayans lived abroad; critics of the proposed reform noted that of these, the majority were believed to be supporters of the FA. A referendum to consider whether to repeal the Ley de Caducidad was also to be held concurrently, following the presentation of some 325,000 signatures (far exceeding the requisite 250,000) to the Congreso in April. (In March the FA had won a non-binding vote in the Congreso declaring the Ley de Caducidad unconstitutional; however, it remained for the Supreme Court to decide on its constitutionality.)

Following a summit conference in Paraguay in March 1991, the Governments of Argentina, Brazil, Paraguay and Uruguay agreed to create a common market of the 'Southern Cone' countries, the Mercado Común del Sur (Mercosur, see p. 405). The Treaty of Asunción allowed for the dismantling of trade barriers between the four countries, and entered full operation in 1995. However, in February 2002, following the drastic reduction in exports to other Mercosur member states as a result of the devaluation of the Argentine peso at the beginning of that year, President Batlle declared that Uruguay would begin bilateral free trade negotiations with the USA. In January 2007 the two countries signed a trade and investment framework, which was regarded as a step towards eventual free trade agreement negotiations. In August 2008, during a visit to Uruguay by Paraguay's Minister of Foreign Affairs, the two countries agreed to assist one another within Mercosur to increase their authority within the organization, while the possibility of re-establishing an association agreement between Uruguay, Paraguay and Bolivia was also discussed.

In April 2002 Uruguay severed diplomatic relations with Cuba, citing insults by the Cuban Government after Uruguay sponsored a motion, which was adopted by the UN Human Rights Commission, calling on Cuba to improve its civil and political rights record. Diplomatic relations were restored, however, following the inauguration of the Vázquez administration in March 2005.

Relations with Argentina were strained from April 2005, when a Finnish company began construction of a cellulose plant in the Uruguayan city of Fray Bentos near the River Uruguay, which separates the two countries. The Argentine Government expressed concerns over the environmental impact of this plant and of a further mill scheduled to be built nearby. The two plants were expected to generate some US $1,800m. of investment in Uruguay. (Construction of the second plant was cancelled in 2006 as a result of the dispute, although the company responsible later announced that it would build the mill at a different location.) In January 2006 Argentine demonstrators blocked passage across the three bridges spanning the river in protests that were tolerated by the Argentine authorities, drawing condemnation from the Uruguayan Government. Furthermore, in March reports appeared in Argentine media suggesting that Uruguayan officials had been bribed to approve the plants' construction; the Government denied the accusations. Demonstrations, attended by some 10,000 people claiming that the project would cause serious environmental damage, continued in the Argentine city of Gualeguaychú. The dispute escalated in May when the Argentine Government initiated proceedings at the International Court of Justice (ICJ) on the grounds that the project would contravene the Statute of the River Uruguay treaty, signed by the two countries in 1975. The ICJ declined to order the suspension of construction of the mills in July, but in January 2007 also rejected a request by the Government of Uruguay to order Argentina to end the ongoing blockade of major roads and bridges between the two countries. Uruguay had claimed that Argentina's protests were resulting in economic hardship for Uruguay and had caused a loss of revenue of some $800m., much of this in the form of lost earnings from tourism. Bilateral relations improved slightly in April following mediation by Spain, as a result of which both countries declared their willingness to reach a resolution to the impasse. None the less, in November President Vázquez authorized the recently inaugurated mill to begin production, provoking condemnation from Argentina, and temporarily closed the border between the countries in anticipation of violent protests. Argentine demonstrations continued to impede cross-border traffic in early 2008, prompting an official complaint from Uruguay regarding the damage caused to its economy. In July Uruguay made its final written presentation to the ICJ regarding its alleged infringement of the Statute of the River Uruguay treaty; a final ruling was anticipated in late 2009. Meanwhile, in October 2008 Uruguay had vetoed the nomination of former Argentine President Néstor Kirchner as a candidate for the first permanent secretary of the newly created Union of South American Nations (Unión de Naciones Suramericanas—UNASUR).

Government

Uruguay is a republic comprising 19 departments. Under the 1966 Constitution, executive power is held by the President, who is directly elected by universal adult suffrage for a five-year term. The President is assisted by the Vice-President and the appointed Council of Ministers. Legislative power is vested in the bicameral Congreso, comprising the Cámara de Senadores (Senate) and the Cámara de Representantes (Chamber of Representatives), also directly elected for five years. The President, the Vice-President, the Senators (who number 31, including the Vice-President, who is automatically allocated a seat as President of the Cámara de Senadores) and the 99 Deputies are elected nationally.

Defence

As assessed at November 2008, Uruguay's active armed forces totalled 25,382, comprising an army of 16,891, a navy of 5,491 and an air force of 3,000. Paramilitary forces numbered 920. Defence expenditure in 2007 was budgeted at some 6,990m. pesos uruguayos.

Economic Affairs

In 2007, according to estimates by the World Bank, Uruguay's gross national income (GNI), measured at average 2005–07 prices, was US $21,186m., equivalent to $6,380 per head (or $11,040 per head on an international purchasing-power parity basis). During 2000–07, it was estimated, the population increased at an average annual rate of 0.1%, while gross domestic product (GDP) per head increased, in real terms, by an average 2.6% per year. According to official figures, overall GDP increased, in real terms, at an average annual rate of 2.7% in 2000–07; GDP increased by 7.0% in 2006 and by 7.4% in 2007.

Agriculture (including forestry and fishing) contributed 10.1% of GDP in 2007. Some 4.5% of the active labour force was employed in the sector in 2003. The principal crops are rice, sugar cane, wheat, barley, potatoes, sorghum and maize. Livestock-rearing, particularly sheep and cattle, is traditionally Uruguay's major economic activity. Food and live animals provided 46.7% of export revenues in 2007, while exports of leather provided a further 7.0% in the same year. Agricultural GDP increased at an average annual rate of 4.8% per year in 2000–07. Agricultural GDP increased by 2.5% in 2007.

Industry (including mining, manufacturing, construction and power) contributed 31.8% of GDP in 2007, and employed 21.5% of the working population in 2003. Industrial GDP increased at an average annual rate of 2.7% in 2000–07; industrial GDP increased by 7.9% in 2007.

Uruguay has few mineral resources and no proven hydrocarbon reserves. Accordingly, mining and quarrying only contributed 0.3% of GDP in 2007, and employed 0.1% of the working population in 2003. Apart from the small-scale extraction of building materials, industrial minerals and semi-precious stones, there has been little mining activity, although gold deposits are currently being developed. The GDP of the mining sector declined at an average annual rate of 1.8% in 2000–07; mining GDP rose by 15.0% in 2006 and by 1.1% in 2007.

Manufacturing contributed 22.6% of GDP in 2007 and employed 14.6% of the working population in 2003. The principal branches of manufacturing were food products, beverages and tobacco, chemicals, metal products, machinery and equipment, and textiles, clothing and leather products. Manufacturing GDP increased at an average annual rate of 3.8% in 2000–07. Manufacturing GDP increased by 8.0% in 2007.

Energy is derived principally from hydroelectric power (87.0% of total electricity production in 2005). The first natural gas pipeline between Uruguay and Argentina, with an operating capacity of 4.9m. cu ft per day, began operating in late 1998. A second natural gas pipeline between Uruguay and Argentina, the Gasoducto Cruz del Sur (GCDS—Southern Cross pipeline), with a transportation capacity of 180m. cu ft per day, was completed in 2002. Plans were under consideration for a possible extension of the GCDS to reach Porto Alegre, Brazil. Imports of mineral fuels and lubricants comprised 22.1% of the value of total imports in 2007. In August 2005 the Venezuelan President, Lt-Col (retd) Hugo Rafael Chávez Frías, agreed to supply Uruguay with petroleum on preferential terms for the next 25 years.

The services sector contributed 58.1% of GDP in 2007, and engaged 73.9% of the working population in 2003. Tourism is a significant source of foreign exchange, earning US $597m. in 2006. The GDP of the services sector increased at an average annual rate of 1.4% in 2000–07, according to preliminary figures. The GDP of the services sector increased by 5.9% in 2007.

In 2007 Uruguay recorded an estimated visible trade deficit of US $491.3m., and there was a deficit of $185.7m. on the current account of the balance of payments. In 2007 the principal source of imports was Brazil (23.2%); other major suppliers were Argentina, Venezuela and the People's Republic of China. Brazil was also the principal market for exports (16.2%) in that year; other major recipients were the USA and Argentina. The main exports in 2007 were food and live animals, and basic manufactures. The principal imports in that year were machinery and transport equipment, mineral fuels and chemicals and related products.

In 2007 there was a budgetary deficit of 6,797m. pesos uruguayos, equivalent to some 1.3% of GDP. At the end of 2006 Uruguay's total external debt was US $9,804m., of which $7,211m. was long-term public debt. In that year the cost of debt-servicing was equivalent to 87.8% of the value of exports of goods and services. The average annual rate of inflation was 9.3% in 2000–07. Consumer prices increased by 6.4% in 2006 and by a further 8.1% in 2007. According to the International Labour Organization (ILO), 10.1% of the labour force was unemployed in 2007.

Uruguay is a member of the Inter-American Development Bank (IDB, see p. 318), the Asociación Latinoamericana de Integración (ALADI, see p. 342), the Sistema Económico Latinoamericano (SELA, see p. 427) and the Mercado Común del Sur (Mercosur, see p. 405). In December 2004 Uruguay was one of 12 countries that were signatories to the agreement, signed in Cusco, Peru, creating the South American Community of Nations (Comunidad Sudamericana de Naciones), intended to promote greater regional economic integration. It had been anticipated that the new entity would become operational by 2007; however, by 2009 implementation of the necessary legal frameworks remained incomplete. A treaty for the community—referred to as the Union of South American Nations (Unión de Naciones Suramericanas—UNASUR) since its reinvention in April 2007—was initialled in May 2008, with full functionality of economic union tentatively scheduled for 2019.

The 1999–2002 recession in Uruguay was largely precipitated by the economic crises in Argentina and Brazil, the devaluation of the Brazilian currency in early 1999 and low world prices for Uruguay's principal export products. In 2002 the Government announced a plan to reduce the fiscal deficit by tax increases and privatization, while in 2003 new bonds were issued to restructure the country's short-term external debt. The World Bank disbursed loans to finance infrastructure and social welfare projects; additional assistance was provided by the IDB, among others. Economic growth resumed in 2003, continuing into 2008, owing primarily to improved export prices, banking sector reforms and increased industrial output. The Government of Tabaré Vázquez, which took office in March 2005, announced a dramatic rise in social welfare expenditure, partly to be funded by sustained economic growth and increased foreign investment, as well as by radical tax reforms. In June of that year the IMF approved a new stand-by arrangement, worth some US $1,110m.; positive reviews of the Government's economic policy led to subsequent disbursements. GDP rates of growth of 7.0% and 7.4% were recorded in 2006 and 2007, respectively, rising to an estimated 11.5% in 2008. Foreign investment in the country grew by some 25% in 2008, and foreign reserves reached $6,200m., double the pre-crisis figure. Between 2004 and 2008 indigence halved, while the level of poverty fell from 31.9% to 21.7%. Receipts from tourism in 2008 exceeded $1,000m. for the first time, and exports in that year surged, partly as a result of operations commencing at the Botnia paper mill (whose controversial location near the River Uruguay adversely affected bilateral trade and tourism with Argentina—see Recent History). However, inflation rose to 8.1% in 2007 (from less than 4% in late 2005), not least because of higher international commodity prices. In addition, record poor rainfall meant that fossil fuel power generation had to be employed to supplement hydroelectric energy. Although it initially seemed that Uruguay was faring well in the wake of the international financial crisis, exports fell markedly in early 2009 owing to depressed global demand, and the IMF forecast GDP growth of just 1.3% for the year. As part of the Government's strategy to encourage foreign direct investment and diversify the country's export markets (thereby lessening dependence on Brazil and Argentina), Vázquez visited the People's Republic of China in March 2009.

Education

All education, including university tuition, is provided free of charge. Education is officially compulsory for six years between six and 14 years of age. Primary education begins at the age of six and lasts for six years. Secondary education, beginning at 12 years of age, lasts for a further six years, comprising two cycles of three years each. In 1996 the total enrolment at primary and secondary schools was equivalent to 97% of the school-age population. In that year primary enrolment included 93% of children in the relevant age-group (males 92%; females 93%), while secondary enrolment was equivalent to 85% of the population in the appropriate age-group (males 77%; females 92%). Primary enrolment in 2006 included 99.7% of children in the relevant age-group, while total enrolment ratio at primary, secondary and tertiary levels in 2004 was equivalent to 88.9% of the population in the relevant age-group. The programmes of instruction are the same in both public and private schools, and private schools are subject to certain state controls. There were six universities in 2005. Central government expenditure on education in 2006 was 14,392m. pesos uruguayos (12.3% of central government spending).

Public Holidays

2009: 1 January (New Year's Day), 6 January (Epiphany), 23–24 February (Carnival), 6–10 April (Holy Week), 19 April (Landing of the 33 Patriots), 1 May (Labour Day), 18 May (Battle of Las Piedras), 19 June (Birth of José Artigas), 18 July (Constitution Day), 25 August (National Independence Day), 12 October (Discovery of America and Battle of Sarandí), 2 November (All Souls' Day), 25 December (Christmas Day).

2010: 1 January (New Year's Day), 6 January (Epiphany), 16–17 February (Carnival), 29 March–2 April (Holy Week), 19 April (Landing of the 33 Patriots), 1 May (Labour Day), 17 May (for Battle of Las Piedras), 19 June (Birth of José Artigas), 18 July (Constitution Day), 25 August (National Independence Day), 11 October (for Discovery of America and Battle of Sarandí), 2 November (All Souls' Day), 25 December (Christmas Day).

Many businesses close for the entirety of Carnival week (23–27 February 2009 and 15–19 February 2010).

Weights and Measures

The metric system is in force.

URUGUAY

Statistical Survey

Sources (unless otherwise stated): Instituto Nacional de Estadística, Río Negro 1520, 11100 Montevideo; tel. (2) 9027303; internet www.ine.gub.uy; Banco Central del Uruguay, Avda Juan P. Fabini, esq. Florida 777, Casilla 1467, 11100 Montevideo; tel. (2) 9085629; fax (2) 9021634; e-mail info@bcu.gub.uy; internet www.bcu.gub.uy; Cámara Nacional de Comercio y Servicios del Uruguay, Edif. Bolsa de Comercio, Rincón 454, 2°, Casilla 1000, 11000 Montevideo; tel. (2) 9161277; fax (2) 9161243; e-mail info@cncs.com.uy; internet www.cncs.com.uy.

Area and Population

AREA, POPULATION AND DENSITY

Area (sq km)	
Land area	175,016
Inland water	1,199
Total	176,215*
Population (census results)†	
22 May 1996	3,163,763
May–July 2004	
Males	1,565,533
Females	1,675,470
Total	3,241,003
Population (official estimates at mid-year)	
2006	3,314,466
2007	3,323,906
2008	3,334,052
Density (per sq km) at mid-2008	19.0

* 68,037 sq miles.
† Excluding adjustment for underenumeration.

DEPARTMENTS
(population estimates at mid-2008)

	Area (sq km)	Population	Density (per sq km)	Capital
Artigas	11,928	79,297	6.6	Artigas
Canelones	4,536	514,616	113.5	Canelones
Cerro Largo	13,648	89,871	6.6	Melo
Colonia	6,106	120,842	19.8	Colonia del Sacramento
Durazno	11,643	61,321	5.3	Durazno
Flores	5,144	25,648	5.0	Trinidad
Florida	10,417	70,235	6.7	Florida
Lavalleja	10,016	61,910	6.2	Minas
Maldonado	4,793	149,071	31.1	Maldonado
Montevideo	530	1,340,273	2,528.8	Montevideo
Paysandú	13,922	115,854	8.3	Paysandú
Río Negro	9,282	55,934	6.0	Fray Bentos
Rivera	9,370	110,180	11.8	Rivera
Rocha	10,551	70,515	6.7	Rocha
Salto	14,163	127,345	9.0	Salto
San José	4,992	108,649	21.8	San José de Mayo
Soriano	9,008	87,508	9.7	Mercedes
Tacuarembó	15,438	95,313	6.2	Tacuarembó
Treinta y Tres	9,529	49,670	5.2	Treinta y Tres
Total	**175,016***	**3,334,052**	**19.0**	

* Land area only.

PRINCIPAL TOWNS
(population at 22 May 1996 census)

Montevideo (capital)	1,378,707	Mercedes	50,800
Salto	93,420	Maldonado	50,420
Paysandú	84,160	Melo	47,160
Las Piedras	66,100	Tacuarembó	42,580
Rivera	63,370		

Mid-2007 ('000, incl. suburbs, UN estimate): Montevideo 1,513 (Source: UN, *World Urbanization Prospects: The 2007 Revision*).

BIRTHS, MARRIAGES AND DEATHS*

	Registered live births		Registered marriages		Registered deaths	
	Number	Rate (per 1,000)	Number	Rate (per 1,000)	Number	Rate (per 1,000)
2001	51,959	15.7	13,988	4.2	31,228	9.4
2002	51,953	15.7	14,073	4.3	31,628	9.6
2003	50,631	15.3	14,147	4.3	32,587	9.9
2004	50,052	15.2	13,123	4.0	32,222	9.8
2005	46,944†	14.2†	13,075	4.0	32,319†	9.8†
2006	47,410†	14.2†	12,415	3.7	31,056†	9.4†
2007	47,373	14.3	12,771	3.8	33,706†	10.3†

* Data are tabulated by year of registration rather than by year of occurrence and have not been adjusted to take account of the most recent census.
† Preliminary.

Life expectancy (years at birth, WHO estimates): 75.3 (males 71.6; females 79.0) in 2006 (Source: WHO, *World Health Statistics*).

ECONOMICALLY ACTIVE POPULATION
(ISIC major divisions, '000 persons aged 14 years and over, urban areas)

	2001	2002	2003
Agriculture, hunting, forestry and fishing	45.4	43.7	46.9
Mining and quarrying	1.3	1.2	1.2
Manufacturing (incl. electricity, gas and water)	167.1	154.2	151.1
Construction	87.9	77.4	69.6
Trade, restaurants, hotels and repair of vehicles and household goods	240.8	228.9	225.4
Transport, storage and communications	66.8	62.4	61.1
Financing, insurance, real estate and business services	97.4	96.5	91.0
Public administration and defence, compulsory social security	85.1	86.9	91.2
Education	57.2	62.2	61.6
Health and social work	72.5	76.7	76.7
Community, social and personal services	56.2	52.2	54.8
Private households with employed persons	98.5	96.0	100.9
Activities not adequately defined	—	—	0.3
Total employed	**1,076.2**	**1,038.3**	**1,032.0**
Males	617.7	597.9	589.7
Females	458.5	440.4	442.3
Unemployed	193.2	211.3	208.5
Total labour force	**1,269.4**	**1,250.1**	**1,240.5**

Source: ILO.

2006 ('000 persons aged 14 years and over, estimates): Total employed 1,413; Unemployed 167; Total labour force 1,580 (males 892, females 688).

URUGUAY

Health and Welfare

KEY INDICATORS

Total fertility rate (children per woman, 2006)	2.1
Under-5 mortality rate (per 1,000 live births, 2006)	15
HIV/AIDS (% of persons aged 15–49, 2007)	0.6
Physicians (per 1,000 head, 2002)	3.7
Hospital beds (per 1,000 head, 2006)	2.9
Health expenditure (2006): US $ per head (PPP)	989
Health expenditure (2006): % of GDP	8.2
Health expenditure (2006): public (% of total)	43.5
Human Development Index (2006): ranking	47
Human Development Index (2006): value	0.859

For sources and definitions, see explanatory note on p. vi.

Agriculture

PRINCIPAL CROPS
('000 metric tons)

	2005	2006	2007
Wheat	387.5	611.2	620.0*
Rice, paddy	1,214.5	1,145.7	1,200.0*
Barley	225.0	432.1	435.0*
Maize	251.0	205.0	210.0*
Oats*	27.0	27.5	27.0
Sorghum	84.7	61.3	70.0*
Potatoes	157.6	148.0	150.0*
Sweet potatoes*	60.0	30.0	30.0
Sugar cane	177.3	177.5*	190.0*
Sunflower seed	150.5	80.6	60.0†
Tomatoes	47.5	47.5*	45.0*
Onions, dry	35.0	35.0*	38.0*
Carrots and turnips	27.2	32.0*	34.0*
Oranges	176.5	138.3	140.0*
Tangerines, mandarins, clementines and satsumas	94.4	88.2	90.0*
Lemons and limes	46.0	42.9	43.0*
Apples	77.3	61.3	66.9
Pears	18.4	17.7	18.7
Peaches and nectarines	15.9	17.3	17.6
Grapes	124.3	130.2	130.0*

* FAO estimate(s).
† Unofficial figure.

Aggregate production ('000 metric tons, may include official, semi-official or estimated data): Total cereals 2,192.3 in 2005, 2,485.4 in 2006, 2,564.6 in 2007; Total fruits (excl. melons) 576.7 in 2005, 513.5 in 2006, 523.5 in 2007; Total vegetables (incl. melons) 188.4 in 2005, 183.6 in 2006, 187.0 in 2007.

Source: FAO.

LIVESTOCK
('000 head, year ending September)

	2005	2006	2007*
Cattle	11,956	11,709	12,000
Sheep	10,836	11,086	11,000
Pigs	255	240	255
Horses	432	525	550
Chickens*	14,000	14,000	14,000

* FAO estimates.
Source: FAO.

Statistical Survey

LIVESTOCK PRODUCTS
('000 metric tons)

	2005	2006	2007
Cattle meat	600.0*	560.0†	570.0†
Sheep meat†	34.0	31.0	32.0
Pig meat	19.8	18.5	19.0†
Chicken meat†	45.0	45.0	45.0
Cows' milk	1,619.0	1,620.0	1,650.0†
Hen eggs†	41.6	42.3	43.0
Wool, greasy	42.0	46.7	50.0†

* Unofficial figure.
† FAO estimate(s).
Source: FAO.

Forestry

ROUNDWOOD REMOVALS
('000 cubic metres, excl. bark)

	2005	2006	2007
Sawlogs and veneer logs	580	734	1,168
Pulpwood	3,128	3,497	3,929
Other industrial wood	21	23	14
Fuel wood	1,973	2,111	2,062
Total	**5,702**	**6,365**	**7,173**

* FAO estimate.
Source: FAO.

SAWNWOOD PRODUCTION
('000 cubic metres, incl. railway sleepers)

	2005	2006	2007
Coniferous (softwood)	91	104	109
Broadleaved (hardwood)	177	189	199
Total	**268**	**293**	**308**

Source: FAO.

Fishing

('000 metric tons, live weight)

	2004	2005	2006
Capture	123.0	125.9	134.1
Argentine hake	41.7	41.5	31.2
Striped weakfish	11.0	8.6	10.0
Whitemouth croaker	29.4	27.8	28.9
Patagonian toothfish	2.1	0.8	1.5
Argentine shortfin squid	4.7	7.7	16.3
Red crab	2.7	2.7	1.8
Aquaculture	0.0	0.0	0.0
Total catch	**123.0**	**126.0**	**134.1**

Source: FAO.

Mining

('000 metric tons, unless otherwise indicated)

	2005	2006	2007
Gold (kg)	3,151	3,000	2,820
Gypsum*	1,130	1,150	1,150
Feldspar (metric tons)	2,150	2,470	2,500

* Estimates.
Source: US Geological Survey.

Industry

SELECTED PRODUCTS
('000 metric tons, unless otherwise indicated)

	2002	2003	2004
Raw sugar*	6.7	6.3	n.a.
Wine	71.4	81.8	112.6
Cigarettes (million)	8,449	5,718	n.a.
Motor spirit (petrol) ('000 barrels)†	2,200	2,200	1,793
Kerosene ('000 barrels)†	500	500	75
Distillate fuel oils ('000 barrels)†	4,100	4,200	8,810
Residual fuel oils ('000 barrels)†	3,600	3,650	3,650
Cement (hydraulic)	1,000†	1,050†	1,050
Electric energy (million kWh)	9,605	8,578	5,936

* Unofficial figures.
† US Geological Survey estimate(s).

Sources: FAO; US Geological Survey; UN, *Industrial Commodity Statistics Yearbook*.

2005 ('000 barrels, unless otherwise indicated): Motor spirit (petrol) 1,830; Kerosene 67; Distillate fuel oil 8,476; Residual fuel oil 3,650; Cement (hydraulic) 1,050,000 metric tons (estimate) (Source: US Geological Survey).

2006 ('000 barrels, unless otherwise indicated): Motor spirit (petrol) 1,850; Kerosene 100; Distillate fuel oil 8,500; Residual fuel oils 3,650; Cement (hydraulic) 1,050,000 metric tons (estimate) (Source: US Geological Survey).

2007 ('000 barrels, unless otherwise indicated): Motor spirit (petrol) 1,850; Kerosene 100; Distillate fuel oil 8,500; Residual fuel oils 3,650; Cement (hydraulic) 1,050,000 metric tons (estimate) (Source: US Geological Survey).

Finance

CURRENCY AND EXCHANGE RATES

Monetary Units
100 centésimos = 1 peso uruguayo.

Sterling, Dollar and Euro Equivalents (31 December 2008)
£1 sterling = 35.497 pesos;
US $1 = 24.350 pesos;
€1 = 33.888 pesos;
1,000 pesos uruguayos = £28.17 = $41.07 = €29.51.

Average Exchange Rate (pesos per US $)
2006 24.073
2007 23.471
2008 20.949

Note: On 1 March 1993 a new currency, the peso uruguayo (equivalent to 1,000 former new pesos), was introduced.

BUDGET*
(million pesos uruguayos)

Revenue	2005	2006	2007
Tax revenue	72,819	100,293	113,947
Taxes on income, profits, etc.	16,377	20,448	22,724
Individual taxes	4,665	6,235	9,638
Corporate taxes	11,271	13,694	11,952
Taxes on property	8,030	7,951	8,276
Domestic taxes on goods and services	43,174	65,804	75,868
General sales, take-over or value-added tax	31,411	51,749	61,119
Taxes on international trade and transactions	2,194	2,524	3,275
Taxes on leisure activities	31	50	52
Other taxes and rates	3,013	3,516	3,752
Non-tax revenue	7,097	7,462	8,347
Transfers	3,832	3,318	3,700
Other income	611	248	938
Total	84,359	111,321	126,932

Expenditure	2004	2005	2006
General public services	23,204	25,519	28,230
Government administration	13,444	15,058	16,290
Defence	4,376	4,660	5,187
Public order and safety	5,385	5,801	6,753
Special and community services	37,148	38,747	58,271
Education	11,873	12,573	14,392
Health	6,521	7,135	8,654
Social security and welfare	16,817	17,109	32,375
Housing and community amenities	1,259	1,371	2,029
Recreational, cultural and religious affairs	679	559	821
Economic affairs and services	3,353	5,931	6,435
Fuel and energy	186	179	194
Agriculture, fishing, forestry and hunting	1,421	2,033	1,584
Mining and mineral resources	253	273	275
Transport and communications	2,530	2,728	3,725
Other economic services	964	718	657
Debt-servicing and governmental transfers	22,805	20,322	24,289
Total	88,510	90,519	117,225

* Figures represent the consolidated accounts of the central Government, which include social security revenue and expenditure.

2007: Total expenditure 133,729.

INTERNATIONAL RESERVES
(US $ million at 31 December)

	2006	2007	2008
Gold	5	7	7
IMF special drawing rights	1	—	4
Foreign exchange	3,084	4,114	6,317
Total	3,090	4,121	6,328

Source: IMF, *International Financial Statistics*.

MONEY SUPPLY
(million pesos uruguayos at 31 December)

	2005	2006	2007
Currency outside banks	13,315.1	16,130.7	18,892.5
Demand deposits at commercial banks	15,440.9	19,317.9	27,006.5
Total money (incl. others)	29,680.1	35,633.2	46,136.7

Source: IMF, *International Financial Statistics*.

COST OF LIVING
(Consumer Price Index for Montevideo; base: March 1997 = 100)

	2005	2006	2007
Food and beverages	210.1	223.2	256.9
Housing	213.5	230.8	251.2
Clothing and footwear	154.5	158.4	161.5
Transport and communications	237.3	251.5	252.4
All items (incl. others)	207.3	220.6	238.5

URUGUAY

NATIONAL ACCOUNTS
(million pesos uruguayos at current prices)

Expenditure on the Gross Domestic Product

	2005	2006	2007
Government final consumption expenditure	44,902.9	51,232.5	60,384.8
Private final consumption expenditure	300,314.8	347,131.2	403,617.8
Increase in stocks	152.5	2,251.2	6,232.4
Gross fixed capital formation	50,849.5	67,539.7	75,344.7
Total domestic expenditure	396,219.7	468,154.6	545,579.7
Exports of goods and services	126,286.5	139,604.2	158,247.5
Less Imports of goods and services	115,800.9	142,956.9	161,958.7
GDP in purchasers' values	406,705.4	464,801.9	541,868.4
GDP at constant 1983 prices	300.1	321.1	344.9

Gross Domestic Product by Economic Activity

	2005	2006	2007
Agriculture	36,023.2	40,879.2	53,458.7
Fishing	1,411.1	1,773.6	1,488.8
Mining and quarrying	1,004.1	1,317.5	1,490.6
Manufacturing	91,539.6	107,944.7	123,411.0
Electricity, gas and water	20,128.9	21,698.9	26,084.1
Construction	15,606.5	19,701.0	22,361.9
Trade, restaurants and hotels	52,948.6	60,992.1	73,094.3
Transport, storage and communications	39,392.9	44,953.6	49,616.1
Finance and insurance	32,726.3	35,478.7	37,421.7
Real estate and business services	49,648.2	55,045.9	63,629.6
General government services	34,227.7	38,671.1	45,579.3
Other community, social and personal services	37,863.7	42,085.1	47,814.8
Sub-total	412,520.7	470,541.4	545,451.1
Import duties	21,929.2	24,343.6	28,205.4
Less Imputed bank service charge	27,744.5	30,083.1	31,787.8
GDP in purchasers' values	406,705.4	464,801.9	541,868.4

BALANCE OF PAYMENTS
(US $ million)

	2005	2006	2007
Exports of goods f.o.b.	3,774.1	4,407.1	5,063.0
Imports of goods f.o.b.	−3,753.3	−4,867.0	−5,554.3
Trade balance	20.8	−459.9	−491.3
Exports of services	1,311.3	1,392.2	1,761.8
Imports of services	−939.5	−986.7	−1,248.9
Balance on goods and services	392.6	−54.3	21.6
Other income received	563.1	734.0	878.5
Other income paid	−1,057.3	−1,175.2	−1,220.0
Balance on goods, services and income	−101.5	−495.5	−319.9
Current transfers received	143.1	150.0	159.4
Current transfers paid	−17.3	−23.7	−25.1
Current balance	24.3	−369.2	−185.7
Capital account (net)	3.8	6.5	3.7
Direct investment abroad	−36.3	1.0	−3.6
Direct investment from abroad	847.4	1,398.8	879.2
Portfolio investment assets	577.7	−97.2	176.7
Portfolio investment liabilities	228.2	1,783.5	995.3
Other investment assets	−1,112.7	1,414.9	−1,853.1
Other investment liabilities	419.4	−1,660.7	1,031.5
Net errors and omissions	−173.4	−110.3	−38.7
Overall balance	778.4	2,367.4	1,005.4

Source: IMF, *International Financial Statistics*.

External Trade

PRINCIPAL COMMODITIES
(US $ million)

Imports c.i.f.	2005	2006	2007
Food and live animals	252.5	324.8	394.6
Mineral fuels and lubricants	941.4	1,312.6	1,234.6
Petroleum and petroleum products	827.1	1,129.4	1,120.2
Petroleum oils and oils obtained from bituminous minerals, crude	736.5	864.6	708.8
Chemicals and related products	752.9	833.7	1,121.5
Medicinal and pharmaceutical products	96.2	107.2	122.6
Plastics in primary forms	176.6	192.7	237.7
Basic manufactures	536.5	620.4	712.0
Paper, paperboard and related articles	88.1	96.6	110.1
Textile yarn, fabrics, made-up articles and related products	99.9	105.8	122.3
Iron and steel	92.4	126.0	138.2
Machinery and transport equipment	900.1	1,118.0	1,420.4
Machinery specialized for particular industries	130.8	124.8	196.0
General industrial machinery and equipment	126.2	153.4	210.7
Telecommunications, sound recording and reproducing equipment	160.0	179.7	223.1
Electrical machinery, apparatus, appliances and electrical parts	133.0	143.7	178.5
Miscellaneous manufactured articles	280.9	337.5	428.3
Total (incl. others)	3,878.9	4,774.9	5,588.6

Exports f.o.b.	2005	2006	2007
Food and live animals	1,669.7	1,967.8	2,098.9
Meat and meat preparations	840.8	1,057.5	927.8
Dairy products and birds' eggs	244.6	256.6	333.8
Fish, crustaceans, molluscs and preparations thereof	139.0	148.1	172.7
Cereals and cereal preparations	295.2	331.2	444.6
Rice	199.8	218.6	280.6
Crude materials, inedible, except fuels	454.9	547.5	705.5
Mineral fuels and lubricants	162.3	139.6	185.0
Chemicals and related products	198.5	226.4	299.7
Basic manufactures	490.9	584.1	640.9
Leather	243.8	296.1	298.6
Machinery and transport equipment	98.6	147.4	167.7
Road vehicles	63.2	105.0	116.2
Miscellaneous manufactured articles	234.6	226.3	249.8
Total (incl. others)	3,404.5	3,952.3	4,496.0

PRINCIPAL TRADING PARTNERS
(US $ million)

Imports c.i.f.	2005	2006	2007
Argentina	785.7	1,078.5	1,235.3
Brazil	824.7	1,077.9	1,295.1
Canada	21.6	18.3	19.3
Chile	69.6	71.2	77.3
China, People's Republic	242.3	350.9	540.2
Equatorial Guinea	20.6	142.3	0.0
France (incl. Monaco)	67.8	82.2	83.7
Germany	87.8	99.3	112.0
India	37.3	34.9	49.4
Iran	0.7	130.2	1.1
Italy	75.7	81.9	94.0

URUGUAY

Imports c.i.f.—continued	2005	2006	2007
Japan	42.9	50.4	60.9
Korea, Republic	48.9	55.8	59.8
Mexico	50.9	60.6	83.8
Nigeria	227.9	0.0	0.0
Russia	308.6	43.5	195.6
Spain	48.1	56.0	71.5
United Kingdom	34.1	45.7	42.9
USA	260.8	327.8	415.9
Venezuela	244.7	599.5	637.6
Total (incl. others)	3,878.9	4,774.9	5,588.6

Exports f.o.b.	2005	2006	2007
Argentina	266.9	301.5	441.2
Brazil	458.2	582.5	728.4
Canada	87.1	44.6	72.3
Chile	83.1	165.3	108.0
China, People's Republic	119.6	159.5	161.5
France (incl. Monaco)	31.0	33.3	35.7
Germany	143.3	164.6	205.6
Iran	80.7	51.2	29.6
Israel	25.9	55.5	44.9
Italy	92.6	112.4	101.1
Japan	32.1	42.8	32.5
Mexico	139.4	133.9	207.3
Netherlands	46.9	67.4	94.1
Paraguay	55.8	58.1	76.9
Russia	37.8	224.2	113.3
Spain	130.8	119.7	147.4
Thailand	44.7	56.2	47.8
United Kingdom	84.7	95.4	120.4
USA	788.9	536.6	505.2
Venezuela	33.5	78.2	98.6
Total (incl. others)	3,404.5	3,952.3	4,496.0

Transport

RAILWAYS
(traffic)

	2002	2003	2004
Passenger-km (million)	8	11	11
Net ton-km (million)	178	188	297

Source: UN, *Statistical Yearbook*.

ROAD TRAFFIC
(motor vehicles in use at 31 December)

	1995	1996	1997
Passenger cars	464,547	485,109	516,889
Buses and coaches	4,409	4,752	4,984
Lorries and vans	41,417	43,656	45,280
Road tractors	12,511	14,628	15,514
Motorcycles and mopeds	300,850	328,406	359,824

Source: International Road Federation, *World Road Statistics*.

2003: Passenger cars and vans 526,236; Coaches and minibuses 6,681; Lorries and road tractors 53,615; Motorcycles and mopeds 427,286; Taxis and hire cars 5,447.

SHIPPING
Merchant Fleet
(registered at 31 December)

	2005	2006	2007
Number of vessels	120	123	127
Total displacement ('000 grt)	95.2	97.4	111.5

Source: Lloyd's Register-Fairplay, *World Fleet Statistics*.

CIVIL AVIATION
(traffic on scheduled services)

	2004	2005	2006
Kilometres flown (million)	9.3	7.7	7.6
Passenger-km (million)	1,075.9	979.6	940.4
Total ton-km (million)	4.5	4.3	4.2

Source: UN Economic Commission for Latin America and the Caribbean, *Statistical Yearbook*.

Tourism

ARRIVALS BY NATIONALITY*
('000)

	2004	2005	2006
Argentina	1,108.6	1,107.5	975.0
Brazil	187.7	197.7	228.4
Total (incl. others)	1,870.9	1,917.0	1,824.3

* Figures refer to arrivals at frontiers of visitors from abroad, including Uruguayan nationals permanently resident elsewhere.

Tourism receipts (US $ million): 493.9 in 2004; 593.5 in 2005; 596.6 in 2006.
Source: mainly World Tourism Organization.

Communications Media

	2005	2006	2007
Telephones ('000 main lines in use)	1,006.0	986.9	965.2
Mobile cellular telephones ('000 subscribers)	1,154.9	2,330.0	3,004.3
Internet users ('000)	668	850	968
Broadband subscribers ('000)	61.2	106.6	164.9

Television receivers (2000): 1,770,000 in use.
Radio receivers (1997): 1,970,000 in use.
Book production (1996): 934 titles.
Daily newspapers (1996): 36 (estimated average circulation 950,000).
Facsimile machines (1995): 11,000 in use.

Sources: UNESCO, *Statistical Yearbook*; UN, *Statistical Yearbook*; International Telecommunication Union.

Education

(2006, unless otherwise indicated)

	Institutions	Teachers	Students
Pre-primary	1,302	3,973	106,636
Primary	2,400	17,111	353,528
Secondary: general	436	25,168*†	218,816
Secondary: vocational	124‡	n.a.	69,896
University and equivalent institutions*‡	6	7,723	72,100

* Public education only.
† 2003.
‡ 2005.

Adult literacy rate (UNESCO estimates): 98.0% (males 97.6%; females 98.3%) in 2007 (Source: UNESCO Institute for Statistics).

Directory

The Constitution

The Constitution of Uruguay was ratified by plebiscite, on 27 November 1966, when the country voted to return to the presidential form of government after 15 years of 'collegiate' government. The main points of the Constitution, as amended in January 1997, are as follows:

GENERAL PROVISIONS

Uruguay shall have a democratic republican form of government, sovereignty being exercised directly by the Electoral Body in cases of election, by initiative or by referendum, and indirectly by representative powers established by the Constitution, according to the rules set out therein.

There shall be freedom of religion; there is no state religion; property shall be inviolable; there shall be freedom of thought. Anyone may enter Uruguay. There are two forms of citizenship: natural, being persons born in Uruguay or of Uruguayan parents, and legal, being people established in Uruguay with at least three years' residence in the case of those with family, and five years' for those without family. Every citizen has the right and obligation to vote.

LEGISLATURE

Legislative power is vested in the Congreso (Congress or General Assembly), comprising two houses, which may act separately or together according to the dispositions of the Constitution. It elects in joint session the members of the Supreme Court of Justice, of the Electoral Court, Tribunals, Administrative Litigation and the Accounts Tribunal.

Elections for both houses, the President and the Vice-President shall take place every five years on the last Sunday in October; sessions of the Assembly begin on 1 March each year and last until 15 December (15 September in election years, in which case the new Congress takes office on 15 February). Extraordinary sessions can be convened only in case of extreme urgency.

CHAMBER OF REPRESENTATIVES

The Chamber of Representatives has 99 members elected by direct suffrage according to the system of proportional representation, with at least two representatives for each Department. The number of representatives can be altered by law by a two-thirds' majority in both houses. Their term of office is five years and they must be over 25 years of age and be natural citizens or legal citizens with five years' exercise of their citizenship. Representatives have the right to bring accusations against any member of the Government or judiciary for violation of the Constitution or any other serious offence.

SENATE

The Senate comprises 31 members, including the Vice-President, who sits as President of the Senate, and 30 members elected directly by proportional representation on the same lists as the representatives, for a term of five years. They must be natural citizens or legal citizens with seven years' exercise of their rights, and be over 30 years of age. The Senate is responsible for hearing cases brought by the representatives and can deprive a guilty person of a post by a two-thirds' majority.

THE EXECUTIVE

Executive power is exercised by the President and the Council of Ministers. There is a Vice-President, who is also President of the Congress and of the Senate. The President and Vice-President are directly elected by absolute majority, and remain in office for five years. They must be over 35 years of age and be natural citizens.

The Council of Ministers comprises the office holders in the ministries or their deputies, and is responsible for all acts of government and administration. It is presided over by the President of the Republic, who has a vote.

THE JUDICIARY

Judicial power is exercised by the five-member Supreme Court of Justice and by Tribunals and local courts; members of the Supreme Court must be over 40 years of age and be natural citizens, or legal citizens with 10 years' exercise and 25 years' residence, and must be lawyers of 10 years' standing, eight of them in public or fiscal ministry or judicature. Members serve for 10 years and can be re-elected after a break of five years. The Court nominates all other judges and judicial officials.

The Government

HEAD OF STATE

President: Dr Tabaré Ramón Vázquez Rosas (took office 1 March 2005).
Vice-President: Rodolfo Nin Novoa (AP).

COUNCIL OF MINISTERS
(April 2009)

Minister of the Interior: Daisy Tourné (PS).
Minister of Foreign Affairs: Dr Gonzalo Fernández (PS).
Minister of National Defence: Dr José Bayardi (VA).
Minister of Social Development: Marina Arismendi (PCU).
Minister of Economy and Finance: Alvaro Garcia (PS).
Minister of Industry, Energy and Mining: Daniel Martínez (PS).
Minister of Livestock, Agriculture and Fishing: Ernesto Agazzi (MPP).
Minister of Tourism and Sport: Dr Héctor Lescano (AP).
Minister of Transport and Public Works: Víctor Rossi (AP).
Minister of Labour and Social Security: Eduardo Bonomi (MPP).
Minister of Education and Culture: María Simón (Ind.).
Minister of Public Health: Dra María Julia Muñoz (VA).
Minister of Housing, Territorial Regulation and the Environment: Carlos Colacce (Ind.).
Director of the Planning and Budget Office: Enrique Rubio (VA).

MINISTRIES

Office of the President: Casa de Gobierno, Edif. Libertad, Avda Luis Alberto de Herrera 3350, Montevideo; tel. (2) 4872110; fax (2) 4809397; e-mail sepredi@presidencia.gub.uy; internet www.presidencia.gub.uy.

Ministry of Economy and Finance: Colonia 1089, 3°, 11100 Montevideo; tel. (2) 7122910; fax (2) 7122919; e-mail seprimef@mef.gub.uy; internet www.mef.gub.uy.

Ministry of Education and Culture: Reconquista 535, 9°, 11000 Montevideo; tel. (2) 9161174; fax (2) 9161048; e-mail webmaster@mec.gub.uy; internet www.mec.gub.uy.

Ministry of Foreign Affairs: Avda 18 de Julio 1205, 11100 Montevideo; tel. (2) 9022132; fax (2) 9021349; e-mail webmaster@mrree.gub.uy; internet www.mrree.gub.uy.

Ministry of Housing, Territorial Regulation and the Environment: Zabala 1432, 11000 Montevideo; tel. (2) 9163989; fax (2) 9163914; e-mail ministro@mvotma.gub.uy; internet www.mvotma.gub.uy.

Ministry of Industry, Energy and Mining: Paysandú esq. Libertador Brig. Gral Lavalleja 4°, Montevideo; tel. (2) 9009939; fax (2) 9021245; internet www.miem.gub.uy.

Ministry of the Interior: Mercedes 953, 11100 Montevideo; tel. (2) 9021665; fax (2) 9023142; e-mail webmaster@minterior.gub.uy; internet www.minterior.gub.uy.

Ministry of Labour and Social Security: Juncal 1511, 4°, 11000 Montevideo; tel. (2) 9162681; fax (2) 9162708; internet www.mtss.gub.uy.

Ministry of Livestock, Agriculture and Fishing: Avda Constituyente 1476, 11200 Montevideo; tel. (2) 4126326; fax (2) 4184051; e-mail webmaster@mgap.gub.uy; internet www.mgap.gub.uy.

Ministry of National Defence: Edif. General Artigas, Avda 8 de Octubre 2628, Montevideo; tel. (2) 4872828; fax (2) 4809397; e-mail rrpp.secretaria@mdn.gub.uy; internet www.mdn.gub.uy.

Ministry of Public Health: Avda 18 de Julio 1892, 11100 Montevideo; tel. (2) 4001086; fax (2) 4085360; e-mail msp@msp.gub.uy; internet www.msp.gub.uy.

Ministry of Social Development: Avda 18 de Julio 1453, 11200 Montevideo; tel. and fax (2) 4000302; e-mail dirgeneral@mides.gub.uy; internet www.mides.gub.uy.

Ministry of Tourism and Sport: Rambla 25 de Agosto 1825, esq. Yacaré, Montevideo; tel. (2) 1885100; fax (2) 9162487; e-mail difusion@mtop.gub.uy; internet www.turismo.gub.uy.

Ministry of Transport and Public Works: Rincón 561, 11000 Montevideo; tel. (2) 9160509; fax (2) 9165044; e-mail direcciongeneral@mtop.gub.uy; internet www.mtop.gub.uy.

URUGUAY

Planning and Budget Office: Edif. Libertad, Luis A. de Herrera 3350, Montevideo; tel. (2) 4872110; fax (2) 2099730; e-mail direccion@opp.gub.uy; internet www.opp.gub.uy.

President and Legislature

PRESIDENT

Election, 31 October 2004

Candidate	% of vote
Tabaré Ramón Vázquez Rosas (Encuentro Progresista—Frente Amplio—Nueva Mayoría)	50.70
Jorge Larrañaga (Partido Nacional)	34.06
Guillermo Stirling (Partido Colorado)	10.32
Others	2.53
Invalid votes	2.39
Total	100.00

CONGRESO

Cámara de Senadores
(Senate)

Election, 31 October 2004

Party	Seats
Encuentro Progresista—Frente Amplio—Nueva Mayoría	16
Partido Nacional	11
Partido Colorado	3
Total*	30

* An additional seat is reserved for the Vice-President, who sits as President of the Senate.

Cámara de Representantes
(Chamber of Representatives)

President: ROQUE ARREGUI.

Election, 31 October 2004

Party	Seats
Encuentro Progresista—Frente Amplio—Nueva Mayoría	52
Partido Nacional	35
Partido Colorado	10
Other parties	2
Total	99

Election Commission

Corte Electoral: Ituzaingó 1474, Montevideo; tel. (2) 9159626; fax (2) 9155087; e-mail corelect@adinet.com.uy; internet www.corteelectoral.gub.uy; f. 1967; Pres. CARLOS A. URRUTY NAVATTA.

Political Organizations

Alianza Libertadora Nacionalista: Montevideo; extreme right-wing; Leader OSVALDO MARTÍNEZ JAUME.

Asamblea Popular: Montevideo; f. 2008; extreme left-wing; mems include:

    Movimiento de Defensa de los Jubilados: Leader HÉCTOR MORALES.

    Movimiento 26 de Marzo: Durazno 1118, 11200 Montevideo; tel. (2) 9011584; f. 1971; socialist; Pres. EDUARDO RUBIO; Sec.-Gen. FERNANDO VÁZQUEZ.

    Partido Comunista Revolucionario: internet pcr.org.uy.

    Partido Humanista: Leader DANIEL ROCA.

Frente Amplio (FA): Colonia 1367, 2°, 11100 Montevideo; tel. (2) 9022176; e-mail comunicacion@frenteamplio.org.uy; internet www.frenteamplio.org.uy; f. 1971; left-wing grouping; contested 2004 legislative and presidential elections as Encuentro Progresista—Frente Amplio—Nueva Mayoría; Pres. JORGE BROVETTO; mems include:

    Alianza Progresista 738 (AP): Colonia 1831, Montevideo; tel. and fax (2) 4016365; e-mail a738@adinet.com.uy; internet www.alianza738.org.uy; left-wing; Leader RODOLFO NIN NOVOA.

    Asamblea Uruguay (AU): Carlos Quijano 1271, Montevideo; tel. (2) 9032121; fax (2) 9241147; e-mail jmahia@parlamento.gub.uy; internet www.asamblea.org.uy; f. 1994; centre-left; Leader DANILO ASTORI.

    Frente Izquierda de Liberación (FIDEL): Mercedes 1244, Montevideo; tel. (2) 9087530; e-mail dibarra@parlamento.gub.uy; f. 1962; socialist; Leader ADOLFO AGUIRRE GONZÁLEZ.

    Movimiento de Acción Nacionalista (MAN): Montevideo; left-wing nationalist org.; Leader JOSÉ DURÁN MATOS.

    Movimiento Blanco Popular y Progresista (MBPP): Montevideo; moderate left-wing; Leader A. FRANCISCO RODRÍGUEZ CAMUSSO.

    Movimiento de Participación Popular (MPP): Germán Barbato 1491, Montevideo; tel. (2) 9086948; e-mail correos@mppuruguay.org; internet www.mppuruguay.org; f. 1989; grouping of left-wing parties incl. MLN—Tupamaros (see below); Leader JOSÉ (PEPE) MUJICA.

    Movimiento de Liberación Nacional (MLN)—Tupamaros: Tristán Narvaja 1578, 11200 Montevideo; tel. (2) 4092298; fax (2) 4099957; e-mail mln@chasque.apc.org; internet www.chasque.net/mlnweb; f. 1962; radical socialist; during 1962–73 the MLN, operating under its popular name of the Tupamaros, conducted a campaign of urban guerrilla warfare until it was defeated by the Armed Forces in late 1973; following the return to civilian rule, in 1985, the MLN announced its decision to abandon its armed struggle; legally recognized in May 1989; Sec.-Gen. JOSÉ (PEPE) MUJICA.

    Nuevo Espacio: Eduardo Acevedo 1615, 11200 Montevideo; tel. (2) 4026990; fax (2) 4026989; e-mail internacionales@nuevoespacio.org.uy; internet www.nuevoespacio.org.uy; f. 1994; social-democratic; allied to the FA since Dec. 2002; moderate left-wing; Leader RAFAEL MICHELINI; Sec. EDGARDO CARVALHO.

    Partido Comunista de Uruguay (PCU): Río Negro 1525, 11100 Montevideo; tel. (2) 9017171; fax (2) 9011050; e-mail comitecentral@webpcu.org; internet www.webpcu.org; f. 1920; Sec.-Gen. MARINA ARISMENDI; c. 42,000 mems.

    Partido de Democracia Avanzada: Montevideo; Communist.

    Partido Socialista del Uruguay (PS): Casa del Pueblo, Soriano 1218, 11100 Montevideo; tel. (2) 9013344; fax (2) 9082548; e-mail info@ps.org.uy; internet www.ps.org.uy; f. 1910; Pres. REINALDO GARGANO; Sec.-Gen. EDUARDO (LALO) FERNÁNDEZ.

    Partido por la Victoria del Pueblo (PVP): Mercedes 1551, esq. Tacuarembó, Montevideo; tel. (2) 4020370; e-mail amvera@pvp.org.uy; internet www.pvp.org.uy; f. 1975 in Buenos Aires, Argentina; left-wing; Sec.-Gen. (vacant); Spokesman ANGEL VERA.

    Vertiente Artiguista (VA): San José 1191, 11200 Montevideo; tel. (2) 9000177; e-mail vertiente@vertiente.org.uy; internet www.vertiente.org.uy; f. 1989; left-wing; Leader MARCELO MANO.

Partido Azul (PA): Paul Harris 1722, Montevideo; tel. and fax (2) 6016327; e-mail hablacon@partidoazul.s5.com; internet www.partidoazul.s5.com; liberal; f. 1993; Leader Dr ROBERTO CANESSA; Gen. Sec. Ing. ARMANDO VAL.

Partido Colorado: Andrés Martínez Trueba 1271, 11100 Montevideo; tel. (2) 4090180; f. 1836; Sec.-Gen. JORGE LUIS BATLLE IBÁÑEZ; factions include:

    Foro Batllista: Col. 1243, 11100 Montevideo; tel. (2) 9030154; e-mail info@forobatllista.com; internet www.forobatllista.com; Leader Dr JULIO MARÍA SANGUINETTI CAIROLO.

    Lista 15: Leader JORGE LUIS BATLLE IBÁÑEZ.

    Unión Colorada y Batllista (Pachequista): Buenos Aires 594, 11000 Montevideo; tel. (2) 9164648; right-wing.

    Vanguardia Batllista: Casa de Vanguardia, Paysandú 1333, entre Ejido y Curiales, Montevideo; tel. (2) 9027779; e-mail albertoscavarelli@yahoo.com; internet www.scavarelli.com; f. 1999; Leader Dr ALBERTO SCAVARELLI.

Partido Demócrata Cristiano (PDC): Aquiles Lanza 1318 bis, Montevideo; tel. and fax (2) 9030704; e-mail pdc@chasque.apc.org; internet www.chasque.apc.org/pdc; f. 1962; fmrly Unión Cívica del Uruguay; allied to the Alianza Progresista since 1999; Pres. Dr HÉCTOR LESCANO; Sec.-Gen. FRANCISCO OTTONELLI.

Partido Justiciero: Montevideo; extreme right-wing; Leader BOLÍVAR ESPÍNDOLA.

Partido Nacional (Blanco): Juan Carlos Gómez 1384, Montevideo; tel. (2) 9163831; fax (2) 9163758; e-mail partidonacional@partidonacional.com.uy; internet www.partidonacional.com.uy; f. 1836; Exec. Pres. LUIS ALBERTO LACALLE; Sec.-Gen. ALBERTO ZUMARÁN; tendencies within the party include:

    Alianza Nacional: Leader JORGE LARRAÑAGA.

URUGUAY

Consejo Nacional Herrerista: Leader LUIS ALBERTO LACALLE.
Desafío Nacional: Leader JUAN ANDRÉS RAMÍREZ.
Línea Nacional de Florida: Leader ARTURO HEBER.
Manos a la Obra: Plaza Cagancha 1145, 3°, 11100 Montevideo; tel. and fax (2) 9011921; e-mail alberto.volonte@gmail.com; Leader ALBERTO VOLONTÉ.
Movimiento Nacional de Rocha—Corriente Popular Nacionalista: Avda Uruguay 1324, Montevideo; tel. (2) 9027502; Leader CARLOS JULIO PEREYRA.
Partido del Sol: Peatonal Yi 1385, 11000 Montevideo; tel. (2) 9001616; fax (2) 9006739; e-mail partidodelsol@adinet.com.uy; internet www.partidodelsoluruguay.org; ecologist, federal, pacifist; Leader HOMERO MIERES.
Partido de los Trabajadores: Convención 1196, 11100 Montevideo; tel. (2) 9082624; f. 1980; extreme left-wing; Leader JUAN VITAL ANDRADE.
Unión Cívica: Montevideo; tel. (2) 9005535; e-mail info@unioncivica.org; internet www.dreamsmaker.com.uy/trabajos/union-civica; f. 1912; recognized Christian Democrat faction, split from the Partido Demócrata Cristiano in 1980; Leader W. GERARDO AZAMBUYA.

Diplomatic Representation

EMBASSIES IN URUGUAY

Argentina: Cuareim 1470, 11800 Montevideo; tel. (2) 9028166; fax (2) 9028172; e-mail emargrou@adinet.com.uy; internet emb-uruguay.mrecic.gov.ar; Ambassador HERNÁN MARÍA PATIÑO MAYER.
Bolivia: Dr Prudencio de Peña 2469, 11300 Montevideo; tel. (2) 7083573; fax (2) 7080066; e-mail embouy@adinet.com; Ambassador MARCELO JANKO ALVAREZ.
Brazil: Blvr Artigas 1328, 11300 Montevideo; tel. (2) 7072119; fax (2) 7072086; e-mail montevideu@brasemb.org.uy; internet www.brasil.org.uy; Ambassador JOSÉ EDUARDO FELÍCIO.
Canada: Plaza Independencia 749, Of. 102, 11100 Montevideo; tel. (2) 9022030; fax (2) 9022029; e-mail mvdeo@international.gc.ca; internet www.dfait-maeci.gc.ca/uruguay; Ambassador ALAIN LATULIPPE.
Chile: 25 de Mayo 575, Montevideo; tel. (2) 9164090; fax (2) 9153804; e-mail echileuy@netgate.com.uy; Ambassador EDUARDO ARAYA ALEMPARTE.
China, People's Republic: Miraflores 1508, Carrasco, Casilla 18966, Montevideo; tel. (2) 6016126; fax (2) 6018508; e-mail embchina@adinet.com.uy; internet uy.china-embassy.org; Ambassador LI ZHONGLIANG.
Colombia: Edif. Tupí, Juncal 1305, 18°, 11000 Montevideo; tel. (2) 9161592; fax (2) 9161594; e-mail embajada@colombia.com.uy; internet www.colombia.com.uy; Ambassador CLAUDIA TURBAY QUINTERO.
Costa Rica: Casilla 12242, Montevideo; tel. (2) 7083645; fax (2) 7089727; e-mail embarica@adinet.com.uy; Ambassador MARCO VINICIO VARGAS PEREIRA.
Cuba: Echevarriarza 3471, Montevideo; tel. (2) 6232803; fax (2) 6232805; e-mail cancilleria@netgate.com.uy; Ambassador MARIELENA RUIZ CAPOTE.
Dominican Republic: Tomás de Tezanos 1186, 11300 Montevideo; tel. (2) 6287766; fax (2) 6289655; e-mail embajadomuruguay@hotmail.com; Chargé d'affaires a.i. RAFAEL EMILIO REYES PINEDA.
Ecuador: Pedro Berro 1217, entre Guayaquí y Pereira, Montevideo; tel. (2) 7076463; fax (2) 7076465; e-mail embajadaecuador@netgate.com.uy; Ambassador EDMUNDO VERA MANZO.
Egypt: Avda Brasil 2663, 11300 Montevideo; tel. (2) 7096412; fax (2) 7080977; e-mail boustanemontevideo@easymail.com.uy; Ambassador MOHAMED ABOU ELDAHAB.
El Salvador: Melitón González 1157, Apto 501, Montevideo 11300; tel. (2) 6222005; fax (2) 6226842; e-mail embasauy@dedicado.net.uy; Ambassador VLADIMIRO PVILLALTA.
France: Avda Uruguay 853, Casilla 290, 11100 Montevideo; tel. (2) 9020077; fax (2) 9023711; e-mail ambafranceuruguay@gmail.com; internet www.ambafranceuruguay.org; Ambassador JEAN-CLAUDE MOYRET.
Germany: La Cumparsita 1417/1435, Casilla 20014, 11200 Montevideo; tel. (2) 9025222; fax (2) 9023422; e-mail info@montevideo.diplo.de; internet www.montevideo.diplo.de; Ambassador BERNHARD GRAF VON WALDERSEE.
Greece: Edif. Artigas, Rincón 487, 2°, 11100 Montevideo; tel. (2) 9165191; fax (2) 9150795; e-mail gremb.mvd@mfa.gr; Ambassador NICOLAOS DICTAKIS.

Guatemala: Costa Rica 1538, Carrasco, Montevideo; tel. and fax (2) 6012225; fax (2) 6014057; e-mail embajadaguatemala@netgate.com.uy; Ambassador JUAN JOSÉ BARRIOS TARACENA.
Holy See: Blvr Artigas 1270, Casilla 1503, Montevideo (Apostolic Nunciature); tel. (2) 7072016; fax (2) 7072209; Apostolic Nuncio Most Rev. ANSELMO GUIDO PECORARI (Titular Archbishop of Populonia).
Iran: Blvr Artigas 531, Montevideo; tel. (2) 7116657; fax (2) 7116659; e-mail embajada.iran@adinet.com.uy; Ambassador MORTEZA TAFRISHI.
Israel: Blvr Artigas 1585, 11200 Montevideo; tel. (2) 4004164; fax (2) 4095821; e-mail info@montevideo.mfa.gov.il; internet montevideo.mfa.gov.il; Ambassador YOEL BARNEA.
Italy: José Benito Lamas 2857, Casilla 268, 11300 Montevideo; tel. (2) 7084916; fax (2) 7084148; e-mail ambasciata.montevideo@esteri.it; internet www.ambmontevideo.esteri.it; Ambassador GUIDO SCALICI.
Japan: Blvr Artigas 953, 11300 Montevideo; tel. (2) 4187645; fax (2) 4187980; e-mail embjapon@adinet.com.uy; internet www.uy.emb-japan.go.jp; Ambassador MASAMI TAKEMOTO.
Korea, Republic: Edif. World Trade Center, Avda Luis Alberto de Herrera 1248, Torre 2, 10°, Montevideo; tel. (2) 6289374; fax (2) 6289376; e-mail ecorea@adinet.com.uy; Ambassador TAE-SHIN JAN.
Lebanon: Avda General Rivera 2278, Montevideo; tel. (2) 4086640; fax (2) 4086365; e-mail embliban@adinet.com.uy; Ambassador VICTOR GEORGES BITAR GHANEM.
Mexico: 25 de Mayo 512/514 esq. Treinta y Tres, 11100 Montevideo; tel. (2) 9166034; fax (2) 9166098; e-mail embajada-mexico@techtelnet.com.uy; internet www.sre.gob.mx/uruguay; Ambassador CASSIO MANUEL LUISELLI FERNÁNDEZ.
Netherlands: Leyenda Patria 2880, Of. 202, 2°, Casilla 1519, 11300 Montevideo; tel. (2) 7112956; fax (2) 7113301; e-mail mtv@minbuza.nl; internet www.holanda.org.uy; Ambassador H. E. C. M. (RASHA) TER BRAACK.
Panama: Juan Benito Blanco 3388, Montevideo; tel. (2) 6230301; fax (2) 6230300; e-mail empanuru@netgate.com.uy; Ambassador ELVIRA BARRIOS ICAZA.
Paraguay: Blvr Artigas 1256, Montevideo; tel. (2) 7072138; fax (2) 7083682; e-mail embapur@netgate.com.uy; internet www.geocities.com/embapur; Chargé d'affaires a.i. CARLOS SCAVONE GODOY.
Peru: Obligado 1384, 11300 Montevideo; tel. (2) 7076862; fax (2) 7077793; e-mail emba8@embaperu.com.uy; internet www.angelfire.com/country/embaperu; Ambassador MAX DE LA FUENTE PREM.
Poland: Jorge Canning 2389, Casilla 1538, 11600 Montevideo; tel. (2) 4801313; fax (2) 4873389; e-mail ambmonte@netgate.com.uy; internet www.embajadapoloniauruguay.com; Ambassador LECH ZBIGNIEW KUBIAK.
Portugal: Avda Dr Francisco Soca 1128, Casilla 701, 11300 Montevideo; tel. (2) 7084061; fax (2) 7096456; e-mail embport@montevideu.dgaccp.pt; Ambassador LUISA BASTOS DE ALMEIDA.
Romania: Echevarriarza 3452, Casilla 12040, 11000 Montevideo; tel. (2) 6220876; fax (2) 6220135; e-mail bcemontevideo@adinet.com.uy; Ambassador GHEORGHE PETRE.
Russia: Blvr España 2741, 11300 Montevideo; tel. (2) 7081884; fax (2) 7086597; e-mail embaru@montevideo.com.uy; internet www.uruguay.mid.ru; Ambassador SERGUEY N. KOSHKIN.
South Africa: Echevarriarza 3335, Casilla 498, 11000 Montevideo; tel. (2) 6230161; fax (2) 6230066; e-mail safem@netgate.com.uy; Ambassador PETER GOOSEN (resident in Argentina).
Spain: Avda Libertad 2738, 11300 Montevideo; tel. (2) 7086010; fax (2) 7083291; e-mail embespuy@correo.mae.es; internet www.maec.es/embajadas/montevideo; Ambassador AURORA DÍAZ-RATO REVUELTA.
Switzerland: Ing. Federico Abadie 2936/40, 11°, Casilla 12261, 11300 Montevideo; tel. (2) 7115545; fax (2) 7115031; e-mail vertretung@mtv.rep.admin.ch; internet www.eda.admin.ch/montevideo; Ambassador MICHEL COQUOZ.
United Kingdom: Marco Bruto 1073, Casilla 16024, 11300 Montevideo; tel. (2) 6223630; fax (2) 6227815; e-mail ukinuruguay@gmail.com; internet www.britishembassy.org.uy; Ambassador PATRICK MULLEE.
USA: Lauro Muller 1776, 11200 Montevideo; tel. (2) 4187777; fax (2) 4188611; e-mail webmastermvd@state.gov; internet uruguay.usembassy.gov; Chargé d'affaires a.i. ROBIN MATTHEWMAN.
Venezuela: Iturriaga 3589, esq. Tomás de Tezanos, Puerto Buceo, Montevideo; tel. (2) 6221262; fax (2) 6282530; e-mail embaven@adinet.com.uy; internet www.repbolvenezuela.com.uy; Ambassador FRANKLIN GONZÁLEZ.

URUGUAY

Judicial System

The Supreme Court of Justice comprises five members appointed at the suggestion of the executive, for a period of five years. It has original jurisdiction in constitutional, international and admiralty cases, and hears appeals from the appellate courts, of which there are seven, each with three judges.

Cases involving the functioning of the state administration are heard in the ordinary Administrative Courts and in the Supreme Administrative Court, which consists of five members appointed in the same way as members of the Supreme Court of Justice.

In Montevideo there are 19 civil courts, 10 criminal and correctional courts, 19 courts presided over by justices of the peace, three juvenile courts, three labour courts and courts for government and other cases. Each departmental capital, and some other cities, have a departmental court; each of the 224 judicial divisions has a justice of the peace.

The administration of justice became free of charge in 1980, with the placing of attorneys-at-law in all courts to assist those unable to pay for the services of a lawyer.

Supreme Court of Justice

H. Gutiérrez Ruiz 1310, Montevideo; tel. (2) 9001041; fax (2) 902350; e-mail secparga@poderjudicial.gub.uy; internet www.poderjudicial.gub.uy.

President of the Supreme Court of Justice: Dr DANIEL GUTIÉRREZ.

Supreme Administrative Court: Mercedes 961, 11100 Montevideo; tel. (2) 9008047; fax (2) 9080539.

Religion

Under the Constitution, the Church and the State are declared separate and toleration for all forms of worship was proclaimed. Roman Catholicism predominates.

CHRISTIANITY

Federación de Iglesias Evangélicas del Uruguay: Avda 8 de Octubre 3324, 11600 Montevideo; tel. and fax (2) 4875907; e-mail fieu@dcd.com.uy; internet www.chasque.net/obra/skontakt.htm; f. 1956; eight mem. churches; Pres. OSCAR BOLIOLI; Sec. OBED BODYAJIAN.

The Roman Catholic Church

Uruguay comprises one archdiocese and nine dioceses. At 31 December 2006 there were an estimated 2,294,900 adherents in the country, representing about 71% of the total population.

Bishops' Conference

Conferencia Episcopal Uruguaya, Avda Uruguay 1319, 11100 Montevideo; tel. (2) 9002642; fax (2) 9011802; e-mail ceusecre@adinet.com.uy; internet www.iglesiauruguaya.com.

f. 1972; Pres. Rt Rev CARLOS MARÍA COLLAZZI IRAZÁBAL (Bishop of Mercedes).

Archbishop of Montevideo: Most Rev. NICOLÁS COTUGNO FANIZZI, Arzobispado, Treinta y Tres 1368, Casilla 356, 11000 Montevideo; tel. (2) 9158127; fax (2) 9158926; e-mail info@arquidiocesis.net; internet www.arquidiocesis.net.

The Anglican Communion

Uruguay constitutes a diocese in the Province of the Southern Cone of America. The presiding Bishop of the Iglesia Anglicana del Cono Sur de América is the Bishop of Northern Argentina.

Bishop of Uruguay: Rt Rev. MIGUEL TAMAYO ZALDÍVAR, Centro Diocesano, Reconquista 522, Casilla 6108, 11000 Montevideo; tel. (2) 9159627; fax (2) 9162519; e-mail mtamayo@netgate.com.uy; internet www.uruguay.anglican.org.

Other Churches

Baptist Evangelical Convention of Uruguay: Mercedes 1487, 11100 Montevideo; tel. and fax (2) 2167012; e-mail suspasos@adinet.com.uy; f. 1948; 4,500 mems; Pres. Dr JUAN CARLOS OTORMÍN.

Iglesia Adventista (Adventist Church): Castro 167, Montevideo; f. 1901; 4,000 mems; Principal Officers Dr GUILLERMO DURÁN, Dr ALEXIS PIRO.

Iglesia Evangélica Metodista en el Uruguay (Evangelical Methodist Church in Uruguay): San José 1457, 11200 Montevideo; tel. (2) 4136552; fax (2) 4136554; e-mail iemu@adinet.com.uy; internet www.gbgm-umc.org/iemu; f. 1878; 1,193 mems (1997); Pres. Rev. OSCAR BOLIOLI.

Iglesia Evangélica Valdense (Waldensian Evangelical Church): Avda 8 de Octubre 3039, 11600 Montevideo; tel. and fax (2) 4879406;

Directory

e-mail ievm@internet.com.uy; f. 1952; 15,000 mems; Pastor ALVARO MICHELIN SALOMÓN.

Iglesia Pentecostal Unida Internacional en Uruguay (United Pentecostal Church International in Uruguay): Helvecia 4032, Piedras Blancas, 12200 Montevideo; tel. (2) 5133618; e-mail lrodrigu@montevideo.com.uy; internet members.tripod.com/~lrodrigu; Pastor LUIS RODRÍGUEZ.

Primera Iglesia Bautista (First Baptist Church): Avda Daniel Fernández Crespo 1741, Casilla 5051, 11200 Montevideo; tel. (2) 4098744; fax (2) 4094356; e-mail piebu@adinet.com.uy; f. 1911; 314 mems; Pastor LEMUEL J. LARROSA.

Other denominations active in Uruguay include the Iglesia Evangélica del Río de la Plata and the Iglesia Evangélica Menonita (Evangelical Mennonite Church).

BAHÁ'Í FAITH

National Spiritual Assembly of the Bahá'ís: Blvr Artigas 2440, 11600 Montevideo; tel. (2) 4875890; fax (2) 4802165; e-mail bahai@multi.com.uy; f. 1938; mems resident in 140 localities.

The Press

DAILIES

Montevideo

El Diario Español: Cerrito 551–555, Casilla 899, 11000 Montevideo; tel. (2) 9159481; fax (2) 9157389; f. 1905; morning (except Monday); newspaper of the Spanish community; Editor MARCELO REINANTE; circ. 20,000.

Diario Oficial: Avda 18 de Julio 1373, Montevideo; tel. (2) 9085042; fax (2) 9023098; e-mail impo@impo.com.uy; internet www.impo.com.uy; f. 1905; biweekly; publishes laws, official decrees, parliamentary debates, judicial decisions and legal transactions; Dir ALVARO PÉREZ MONZA.

La Mañana: Casilla 5005, Suc. 2, 11100 Montevideo; tel. (2) 9029055; fax (2) 9021326; f. 1917; supports the Partido Colorado; Editor Dr SALVADOR ALABÁN DEMARE; circ. 50,000.

El Observador: Cuareim 2052, 11800 Montevideo; tel. (2) 9247000; fax (2) 9248698; e-mail elobservador@observador.com.uy; internet www.observador.com.uy; f. 1991; morning; circ. 26,000.

El País: Zelmar Michelini 1287, 4°, 11100 Montevideo; tel. (2) 9020115; fax (2) 9020464; e-mail cartas@elpais.com.uy; internet www.elpais.com.uy; f. 1918; morning; supports the Partido Nacional; Editor MARTÍN AGUIRRE; circ. 106,000.

La República: Avda Gral Garibaldi 2579, 11600 Montevideo; tel. (2) 4873565; fax (2) 4873824; e-mail ffasano@chasque.net; internet www.larepublica.com.uy; f. 1988; morning; Editor FEDERICO FASANO MERTENS; Gen. Man. PABLO FASANO MÁRQUEZ; circ. 25,000.

Ultimas Noticias: Paysandú 1179, 11100 Montevideo; tel. (2) 9020452; fax (2) 9024669; e-mail avisos@ultimasnoticias.com.uy; internet www.ultimasnoticias.com.uy; f. 1981; evening (except Saturday); owned by Impresora Polo; Publr Dr ALPHONSE EMANUILOFF-MAX; circ. 25,000.

Florida

El Heraldo: Independencia 824, 94000 Florida; tel. (35) 22229; fax (35) 24546; e-mail elheraldo@elheraldo.com.uy; internet www.elheraldo.com.uy; f. 1919; morning; independent; Dir ALVARO RIVA REY; circ. 20,000.

Maldonado

Correo de Punta del Este: Zelmar Michelini 815 bis, 20000 Maldonado; tel. and fax (42) 35633; e-mail gallardo@adinet.com.uy; internet www.diariocorreo.com; f. 1993; morning; Editor MARCELO GALLARDO; circ. 2,500.

Minas

La Unión: Florencio Sánchez 569, Minas; tel. (442) 2065; fax (442) 4011; e-mail union@chasque.apc.org; f. 1877; evening (except Sunday); Dir LAURA PUCHET MARTÍNEZ; Editor ALEJANDRO MAYA SOSA; circ. 2,600.

Paysandú

El Telégrafo: 18 de Julio 1027, 60000 Paysandú; tel. (722) 3141; fax (722) 7999; e-mail correo@eltelegrafo.com; internet www.eltelegrafo.com; f. 1910; morning; independent; Dir FERNANDO A. BACCARO; circ. 8,500.

URUGUAY

Salto

El Pueblo: 18 de Julio 15, Salto; tel. (733) 4133; e-mail dipueblo@adinet.com.uy; internet www.diarioelpueblo.com.uy; morning; Dir ADRIANA MARTÍNEZ.

Tribuna Salteña: Joaquín Suárez 71, Salto; f. 1906; morning; Dir MODESTO LLANTADA FABINI; circ. 3,000.

PERIODICALS
Montevideo

Aquí: Zabala 1322, Of. 102, 11000 Montevideo; weekly; supports the Frente Amplio; Dir FRANCISCO JOSÉ O'HONELLI.

Brecha: Avda Uruguay 844, 11100 Montevideo; tel. (2) 9008777; fax (2) 9020388; e-mail brecha@brecha.com.uy; internet www.brecha.com.uy; f. 1985; weekly; politics, current affairs; Dir GABRIEL PAPA; Editor-in-Chief ROBERTO LÓPEZ BELLOSO; circ. 8,500.

Búsqueda: Avda Uruguay 1146, 11100 Montevideo; tel. (2) 9021300; fax (2) 9022036; e-mail busqueda@adinet.com.uy; f. 1972; weekly; independent; politics and economics; Dir DANILO ARBILLA FRACHIA; circ. 25,000.

Charoná: Gutiérrez Ruiz 1276, Of. 201, Montevideo; tel. (2) 9086665; internet www.charona.com; f. 1968; fortnightly; children's; Dir SERGIO BOFFANO; circ. 25,000.

Colorín Colorado: Dalmiro Costa 4482, Montevideo; f. 1980; monthly; children's; Dir SARA MINSTER DE MURNINKAS; circ. 3,000.

Crónicas Económicas: Avda Libertador Brig.-Gen. Lavalleja 1532, Montevideo; tel. (2) 9004790; fax (2) 9020759; e-mail cronicas@netgate.com.uy; internet www.cronicas.com.uy; f. 1981; weekly; independent; business and economics; Dirs JULIO ARIEL FRANCO, WALTER HUGO PAGÉS, JORGE ESTELLANO.

La Gaceta Militar Naval: Montevideo; monthly.

Guambia: Rimac 1576, 11400 Montevideo; tel. and fax (2) 6132703; e-mail info@guambia.com.uy; internet www.guambia.com.uy; f. 1983; monthly; satirical; Dir and Editor ANTONIO DABEZIES.

Indice Industrial-Anuario de la Industria Uruguaya: Sarandí 456, 11000 Montevideo; tel. (2) 9151963; f. 1957; annual; Dir W. M. TRIAS; circ. 6,000.

La Justicia Uruguaya: 25 de Mayo 555, 11000 Montevideo; tel. (2) 9157587; fax (2) 9159721; e-mail lajusticiauruguaya@lju.com.uy; internet www.lajusticiauruguaya.com.uy; f. 1940; bimonthly; jurisprudence; Dirs EDUARDO ALBANELL, ADOLFO ALBANELL; circ. 3,000.

La Juventud: 18 de Julio 1357, Of. 202, Montevideo; tel. (2) 9030305; e-mail weblajuve@yahoo.com.ar; internet www.chasque.apc.org/juventud; weekly; supports the Movimiento 26 de Marzo; Dir GUILLERMO FERNÁNDEZ; Editor JOSÉ L. BORGES.

Marketing Directo: Guaná 2237 bis, 11200 Montevideo; tel. (2) 4012174; fax (2) 4087221; e-mail consumo@adinet.com.uy; internet www.ciecc.org; f. 1988; monthly; Dir EDGARDO MARTÍNEZ ZIMARIOFF; circ. 9,500.

Mate Amargo: Tristán Narvaja 1578 bis, Montevideo; f. 1986; organ of the Movimiento de Liberación Nacional; circ. 22,500.

Opción: J. Barrios Amorín 1531, Casilla 102, 11100 Montevideo; f. 1981; weekly; Dir FRANCISCO JOSÉ OTTONELLI; circ. 15,000.

Patatín y Patatán: Montevideo; f. 1977; weekly; children's; Dir JUAN JOSÉ RAVAIOLI; circ. 3,000.

Patria: Montevideo; internet www.patria.com.uy; weekly; organ of the Partido Nacional; right-wing; Dir LUIS A. HEBER; Editor Dr JOSÉ LUIS BELLANI.

Revista Naval: Soriano 1117, 11100 Montevideo; tel. (2) 9087884; f. 1988; 3 a year; military; Editor GUSTAVO VANZINI; circ. 1,000.

PRESS ASSOCIATIONS

Asociación de Diarios del Uruguay: Río Negro 1308, 6°, 11100 Montevideo; f. 1922; Pres. BATLLE T. BARBATO.

Asociación de la Prensa Uruguaya: San José 1330, Montevideo; tel. and fax (2) 9013695; e-mail apu@adinet.com.uy; internet www.apu.org.uy; f. 1944; Pres. VÍCTOR ABELANDO.

Publishers

Autores Uruguayos: Paysandú 1561, 11200 Montevideo; e-mail mensajes@autoresuruguayos.com.uy; internet www.autoresuruguayos.com; publishes works by Uruguayan authors; Man. ADRIANA DOS SANTOS.

Editorial Arca: Ana Monterroso 2231, Montevideo; tel. (2) 4099796; fax (2) 4099788; f. 1963; general literature, social science and history; Man. Dir ENRIQUE PIQUÉ.

Directory

Ediciones de la Banda Oriental: Gaboto 1582, 11200 Montevideo; tel. (2) 4083206; fax (2) 4098138; e-mail ebo@chasque.net; general literature; Man. Dir HEBER RAVIOLO.

CENCI—Uruguay (Centro de Estadísticas Nacionales y Comercio Internacional): Juncal 1327D, Of. 1603, Casilla 1510, 11000 Montevideo; tel. (2) 9152930; fax (2) 9154578; e-mail cenci@cenci.com.uy; internet www.cenci.com.uy; f. 1956; economics, statistics; Dir KENNETH BRUNNER.

Editorial y Librería Jurídica Amalio M. Fernández SRL: 25 de Mayo 589, 11000 Montevideo; tel. and fax (2) 9151782; e-mail amflibrosjurid@movinet.com.uy; f. 1951; law and sociology; Man. Dir CARLOS W. DEAMESTOY.

Editorial La Flor del Itapebí: Luis Piera 1917/401, Montevideo; tel. and fax (2) 7109267; internet www.itapebi.com.uy; f. 1991; cultural, technical, educational.

Fundación de Cultura Universitaria: 25 de Mayo 568, Casilla 1155, 11000 Montevideo; tel. (2) 9152532; fax (2) 9152549; e-mail ventas@fcu.com.uy; internet www.fcu.com.uy; f. 1968; law and social sciences; Pres. Dr PABLO DONNÁNGELO.

Hemisferio Sur: Buenos Aires 335, Casilla 1755, 11000 Montevideo; tel. (2) 9164515; fax (2) 9164520; e-mail editorial@hemisferiosur.com; internet www.hemisferiosur.com; f. 1951; agronomy and veterinary science.

Editorial Idea: Misiones 1424, 5°, 11000 Montevideo; tel. (2) 9165456; fax (2) 9150868; e-mail vescovi@fastlink.com.uy; law; Dir Dr GUILLERMO VESCOVI.

Librería Linardi y Risso: Juan C. Gómez 1435, 11000 Montevideo; tel. (2) 9157129; fax (2) 9157431; e-mail lyrbooks@linardiyrisso.com.uy; internet www.linardiyrisso.com.uy; f. 1944; general; Man. Dirs ALVARO RISSO, ANDRÉS LINARDI.

Editorial Medina SRL: Gaboto 1521, Montevideo; tel. (2) 4085800; f. 1933; general; Pres. MARCOS MEDINA VIDAL.

A. Monteverde & Cía, SA: Treinta y Tres 1475, Casilla 371, 11000 Montevideo; tel. (2) 9152939; fax (2) 9152012; f. 1879; educational; Man. Dir LILIANA MUSSINI.

Mosca Hermanos SA: Avda 18 de Julio 1578, 11300 Montevideo; tel. (2) 4093141; fax (2) 4088059; e-mail mosca@attmail.com.uy; f. 1888; general; Pres. Lic. ZSOLT AGARDY.

Librería Selecta Editorial: Guayabo 1865, 11200 Montevideo; tel. (2) 4086989; fax (2) 4086831; f. 1950; academic books; Dir FERNANDO MASA.

Ediciones Trilce: Durazno 1888, 11200 Montevideo; tel. (2) 4127662; fax (2) 4127722; e-mail trilce@trilce.com.uy; internet www.trilce.com.uy; f. 1985; science, politics, history.

Vintén Editor: Hocquart 1771, 11804 Montevideo; tel. (2) 2090223; internet vinten-uy.com; poetry, theatre, history, art, literature.

PUBLISHERS' ASSOCIATION

Cámara Uruguaya del Libro: Juan D. Jackson 1118, 11200 Montevideo; tel. (2) 4015732; fax (2) 4011860; e-mail camurlib@adinet.com.uy; f. 1944; Pres. ERNESTO SANJINÉS; Man. ANA CRISTINA RODRÍGUEZ.

Broadcasting and Communications
TELECOMMUNICATIONS

Administración Nacional de Telecomunicaciones (ANTEL): Complejo Torre de las Telecomunicaciones, Guatemala 1075, Montevideo; e-mail antel@antel.com.uy; internet www.antel.com.uy; f. 1974; state-owned; Pres. EDGARDO CARVALHO; Gen. Man. JOSÉ LUIS SALDÍAS.

  ANCEL: Pablo Galarza 3537, Montevideo; internet www.ancel.com.uy; f. 1974; state-owned mobile telephone co.

CTI Móvil: Montevideo; internet www.cti.com.uy; owned by América Móvil, SA de CV (Mexico); mobile cellular telephone services; launched wireless services in Dec. 2004.

Movistar Uruguay: Avda Constituyente, Edif. Torre el Gaucho, 1467 Montevideo; tel. (2) 4087502; internet www.movistar.com.uy; owned by Telefónica Móviles, SA (Spain); mobile telephone services.

Unidad Reguladora de Servicios de Comunicaciones (URSEC): Uruguay 988, Casilla 11100, Montevideo; tel. (2) 9028082; fax (2) 9005708; e-mail webmaster@ursec.gub.uy; internet www.ursec.gub.uy; regulates telecommunications and postal sectors; Pres. JAIME IGORRA.

BROADCASTING
Regulatory Authority

Asociación Nacional de Broadcasters Uruguayos (ANDEBU): Carlos Quijano 1264, 11100 Montevideo; tel. (2) 9021525; fax (2)

… URUGUAY — Directory

9021540; e-mail andebu@internet.com.uy; internet www.andebu.com.uy; f. 1933; 101 mems; Pres. CARLOS FALCO; Vice-Pres. Dr WALTER C. ROMAY.

Radio

El Espectador: Río Branco 1481, 11100 Montevideo; tel. (2) 9023531; fax (2) 9083192; e-mail ventas@espectador.com.uy; internet www.espectador.com; f. 1923; commercial; Gen. Man. ESTELA BARTOLIC.

Radio Carve: Mercedes 973, 11100 Montevideo; tel. (2) 9026162; fax (2) 9020126; e-mail carve@sadrep.com.uy; internet www.carve850.com.uy; f. 1928; commercial; Dir HÉCTOR CARLOS VERA.

Radio Montecarlo: Avda 18 de Julio 1224, 1°, 11100 Montevideo; tel. (2) 9030703; fax (2) 9017762; f. 1928; commercial; Dir DANIEL ROMAY.

Radio Sarandí: Enriqueta Compte y Riqué 1250, 11800 Montevideo; tel. (2) 2082612; fax (2) 2036906; e-mail direccion@sarandi690.com.uy; internet www.radiosarandi.com.uy; f. 1931; commercial; Pres. RAMIRO RODRÍGUEZ VALLAMIL RIVIERE.

Radio del Sol: tel. (2) 6283314; e-mail comoestamos@fmdelsol.com; internet www.comoestamos.com.uy.

Radio Universal: Avda 18 de Julio 1220, 3°, 11100 Montevideo; tel. (2) 9026022; fax (2) 9026050; e-mail info@22universal.com; internet www.22universal.com; f. 1929; commercial; Pres. OSCAR IMPERIO.

Radiodifusión Nacional SODRE: Sarandí 430, 11000 Montevideo; tel. (2) 957865; fax (2) 9161933; f. 1929; state-owned; Pres. JULIO CÉSAR OCAMPOS.

In 2002 there were some 16 AM and six FM radio stations in the Montevideo area. In addition, there were approximately 41 AM and 56 FM radio stations outside the capital.

Television

The Uruguayan Government holds a 10% stake in the regional television channel Telesur (q.v.), which began operations in May 2005 and is based in Caracas, Venezuela.

Canal 4 Monte Carlo: Paraguay 2253, 11800 Montevideo; tel. (2) 9244444; fax (2) 9247929; e-mail secretarias@montecarlotv.com.uy; internet www.canal4.com.uy; f. 1961; Dir HUGO ROMAY SALVO.

SAETA TV—Canal 10: Dr Lorenzo Carnelli 1234, 11200 Montevideo; tel. (2) 4102120; fax (2) 4009771; internet www.canal10.com.uy; f. 1956; Pres. JORGE DE FEO.

SODRE (Servicio Oficial de Difusión Radiotelevisión y Espectáculos): Blvr Artigas 2552, 11600 Montevideo; tel. (2) 4806448; fax (2) 4808515; e-mail direccion@tveo.uy; internet www.sodre.gub.uy; f. 1963; Pres. Dra NELLY GOITIÑO.

Teledoce Televisora Color—Canal 12: Enriqueta Compte y Riqué 1276, 11800 Montevideo; tel. (2) 2083555; fax (2) 2037623; e-mail latele@teledoce.com; internet www.teledoce.com; f. 1962; Gen. Man. HORACIO SCHECK.

TV Ciudad: Javier Barrios Amorín 1460, Montevideo; tel. (2) 4021908; fax (2) 4001908; e-mail griselda.diaz@imm.gub.uy; internet www.montevideo.gub.uy/teveciudad; f. 1996; state-owned; Ge. Dir GRISELDA DÍAZ.

In 1999 there were 21 television stations outside the capital.

Finance

BANKING

(cap. = capital; res = reserves; dep. = deposits; m. = million; brs = branches; amounts in pesos uruguayos unless otherwise indicated)

State Banks

Banco Central del Uruguay: Avda Juan P. Fabini 777, Casilla 1467, 11100 Montevideo; tel. (2) 9085629; fax (2) 9021634; e-mail info@bcu.gub.uy; internet www.bcu.gub.uy; f. 1967; note-issuing bank, also controls private banking; cap. 1,547.7m., res –13,844.4m., dep. 103,138.6m. (Dec. 2005); Pres. WALTER CANCELA; Dir ALVARO CORREA.

Banco Hipotecario del Uruguay (BHU): Avda Daniel Fernández Crespo 1508, Montevideo; tel. (2) 4090000; fax (2) 4090782; e-mail info@bhu.net; internet www.bhu.net; f. 1892; state mortgage bank; in 1977 assumed responsibility for housing projects in Uruguay; Pres. MIGUEL PIPERNO.

Banco de la República Oriental del Uruguay (BROU): Cerrito y Zabala 351, 11000 Montevideo; tel. (2) 9150157; fax (2) 9162064; e-mail broupte@adinet.com.uy; internet www.brounet.com.uy; f. 1896; cap. 12,517.6m., res 2,825.1m., dep. 124,856.8m. (Dec. 2006); Pres. FERNANDO CALLOIA RAFFO; Gen. Man. FERNANDO JORAJURÍA; 117 brs.

Principal Commercial Banks

ABN AMRO Bank Uruguay NV: Julio Herrera y Obes 1365, Casilla 888, 11100 Montevideo; tel. (2) 9031073; fax (2) 9025011; internet www.abnamro.com.uy; f. 1952; owned by ABN AMRO Bank NV (Netherlands); Country Rep. FRANCISCO DI ROBERTO, Jr; 24 brs.

Banco Bilbao Vizcaya Argentaria Uruguay SA (BBVA): 25 de Mayo 401, esq. Zabala, 11000 Montevideo; tel. (2) 9161444; fax (2) 9162821; internet www.bbvabanco.com.uy; f. 1968; fmrly Unión de Bancos del Uruguay, and later Banesto Banco Uruguay, SA and Banco Francés Uruguay, SA; adopted current name in 2000 following merger with Banco Exterior de América, SA; cap. 883.0m., res 674.1m., dep. 10,336.3m. (Dec. 2004); Pres. TOMÁS DEANE; Vice-Pres. and Gen. Man. ANGEL SORIA; 14 brs.

Banco Galicia Uruguay, SA: Edif. World Trade Center, Luis A. Herrera 1248, 22°, Montevideo; tel. 6281230; e-mail contactenos@bancogalicia.com.uy; internet www.bancogalicia.com.uy; f. 1999.

Banco Surinvest SA: Rincón 530, 11000 Montevideo; tel. (2) 9160177; fax (2) 9160241; e-mail bancosurinvest@surinvest.com.uy; internet www.surinvest.com.uy; f. 1981 as Surinvest Casa Bancaria; name changed as above 1991; cap. 249.3m., res 71.4m., dep. 2,351.2m. (Dec. 2004); Gen. Man. ALBERTO A. MELLO.

Crédit Uruguay Banco SA: Rincón 500, 11000 Montevideo; tel. (2) 9150095; fax (2) 9164282; internet www.credituruguay.com.uy; f. 1998 as Banco Acac SA; adopted current name 2004; owned by Crédit Agricole (France); cap. 413.4m., res 18.4m., dep. 11,616.1m. (Dec. 2005); Pres. GERMÁN VILLAR; Gen. Man. MARCELO OTEN.

Discount Bank (Latin America), SA: Rincón 390, 11000 Montevideo; tel. (2) 9164848; fax (2) 9160890; e-mail mensajes@discbank.com.uy; internet www.discbank.com.uy; f. 1978; owned by Israel Discount Bank of New York (USA); cap. US $12.8m., res $0.62m., dep. $179.3m. (Dec. 2002); Pres. and Chair. REUVEN SPIEGEL; Dir and Gen. Man. VALENTIN D. MALACHOWSKI; 4 brs.

HSBC Bank (Uruguay), SA: Ituzaingó 1389, 11000 Montevideo; tel. (2) 9153395; fax (2) 9153396; f. 1995; owned by HSBC Bank PLC (United Kingdom); CEO ALAN WILKINSON.

Nuevo Banco Comercial, SA (NBC): Misiones 1399, CP 11000 Montevideo; tel. (2) 1401300; fax (2) 1401185; e-mail servicioalcliente@nbc.com.uy; internet www.nbc.com.uy; f. 2003 by merger of Banco Comercial, Banco La Caja Obrera and Banco de Montevideo; fmrly state-owned, privatized in June 2006; dep. US $923m., total assets $1,153m. (July 2006); Pres. ERNEST BACHRACH; Gen. Man. JOSÉ FUENTES; 46 brs.

Credit Co-operative

There are several credit co-operatives, which permit members to secure small business loans at preferential rates.

Federación Uruguaya de Cooperativas de Ahorro y Crédito (FUCAC): Blvr Artigas 1472, Montevideo; tel. and fax (2) 7088888; e-mail info@fucac.com.uy; internet www.fucac.com.uy; f. 1972; Pres. CARLOS ALBERTO ICASURIAGA SAMANO; Gen. Man. JAVIER HUMBERTO PI LEÓN.

Development Bank

Banco Bandes Uruguay: Sarandí 402, CP 111000, Montevideo; tel. (2) 9160100; internet www.cofac.com.uy; owned by the Banco de Desarrollo Económico y Social (BANDES) of Venezuela.

Bankers' Association

Asociación de Bancarios del Uruguay (Bankers' Association of Uruguay—AEBU): Camacuá 575, Montevideo; tel. (2) 9161060; e-mail secprensa@aebu.org.uy; internet www.aebu.org.uy; f. 1945; 7 mem. banks; Dir OSCAR JORGE VISSANI.

STOCK EXCHANGE

Bolsa de Valores de Montevideo: Edif. Bolsa de Comercio, Misiones 1400, 11000 Montevideo; tel. (2) 9165051; fax (2) 9161900; e-mail info@bolsademontevideo.com.uy; internet www.bolsademontevideo.com.uy; f. 1867; 75 mems; Pres. IGNACIO ROSPIDE.

INSURANCE

From mid-1994, following the introduction of legislation ending the state monopoly of most types of insurance, the Banco de Seguros del Estado lost its monopoly on all insurance except life, sea transport and fire risks, which have been traditionally open to private underwriters.

AIG Uruguay Compañía de Seguros, SA (USA): Colonia 993, 1°, Montevideo; tel. (2) 9000330; fax (2) 9084552; e-mail aig.uruguay@aig.com; internet www.aig.com; f. 1996; all classes; Gen. Man. JORGE FERRANTE.

Alico Compañía de Seguros de Vida, SA (USA): 18 de Julio 1738, Montevideo; tel. (2) 4033939; fax (2) 4033938; e-mail alico@alico.com

URUGUAY

Directory

.uy; internet www.alico.com; f. 1996; life; Gen. Man. JUAN ETCHEVERRY.

Banco de Seguros del Estado: Avda Libertador 1465, Montevideo; tel. (2) 9089303; fax (2) 9017030; e-mail directorio@bse.com.uy; internet www.bse.com.uy; f. 1912; state insurance org.; all risks; Pres. ENRIQUE ROIG CURBELO; Gen. Man. CARLOS VALDÉS.

Compañía de Seguros Aliança da Bahia Uruguay, SA (Brazil): Río Negro 1394, 7°, Montevideo; tel. (2) 9021086; fax (2) 9021087; e-mail avivo@netgate.com.uy; f. 1995; transport; Gen. Man. BERNARDO VIVO.

Mapfre Compañía de Seguros, SA (Spain): Blvr Artigas 459, Montevideo; tel. and fax (2) 7116595; e-mail info@mapfre.com.uy; internet www.mapfre.com.uy; f. 1994; general; Gen. Man. DIEGO SOBRINI.

Porto Seguro, Seguros del Uruguay SA (Brazil): Blvr Artigas 2025; tel. (2) 4028000; fax (2) 4030097; e-mail admin@portoseguro.com.uy; internet www.portoseguro.com.uy; f. 1995; property; Pres. LEANDRO SUÁREZ.

Real Uruguaya de Seguros SA (Netherlands): Avda 18 de Julio 988, Montevideo; tel. (2) 9025858; fax (2) 9024515; e-mail realseguros@abnamro.com; internet www.realseguros.com.uy; f. 1900; life and property; part of the ABN AMRO Group; Gen. Man. JOSÉ LUIZ TOMAZINI.

Royal & SunAlliance Seguros, SA (United Kingdom): Peatonal Sarandí 620, Montevideo; tel. (2) 9170505; fax (2) 9170490; internet www.royalsunalliance.com.uy; f. 1997; life and property; Dir Dr JUAN QUARTINO.

Surco, Compañía Cooperativa de Seguros: Blvr Artigas 1320, Montevideo; tel. (2) 7090089; fax (2) 7077313; e-mail surco@surco.com.uy; internet www.surco.com.uy; f. 1995; insurance co-operative; all classes; Gen. Man. ANDRÉS ELOLA.

L'UNION de Paris Compañía Uruguaya de Seguros, SA (France): Misiones 1549, Montevideo; tel. (2) 9160850; fax (2) 9160847; e-mail gabriel.penna@axa-seguros.com.uy; internet www.axa-seguros.com.uy; f. 1897 as L'Union IARD; present name adopted 2004; general; Gen. Man. GABRIEL PENNA.

INSURANCE ASSOCIATION

Asociación Uruguaya de Empresas Aseguradoras (AUDEA): Juncal 1305, Of. 1901, 11000 Montevideo; tel. (2) 9161465; fax (2) 9165991; e-mail audea@adinet.com.uy; Pres. MANUEL RODRÍGUEZ; Gen. Man. MAURICIO CASTELLANOS.

Trade and Industry

GOVERNMENT AGENCIES

Administración Nacional de Combustibles, Alcohol y Portland (ANCAP): Paraguay 1598, 11100 Montevideo; tel. (2) 9020608; fax (2) 9021136; e-mail webmaster@ancap.com.uy; internet www.ancap.com.uy; f. 1931; deals with transport, refining and sale of petroleum products, and the manufacture of alcohol, spirit and cement; tanker services, also river transport; Pres. RAÚL SENDIC; Gen. Man. SERGIO LATTANZIO; Sec.-Gen. JORGE URRUTIA.

Oficina de Planeamiento y Presupuesto de la Presidencia de la República: Edif. Libertad, Luis A. de Herrera 3350, Montevideo; tel. (2) 4872110; fax (2) 2099730; e-mail direccion@opp.gub.uy; internet www.opp.gub.uy; f. 1976; responsible for the implementation of devt plans; co-ordinates the policies of the various ministries; advises on the preparation of the budget of public enterprises; Dir Prof. ENRIQUE RUBIO; Sub-Dir Dr CONRADO RAMOS.

Uruguay XXI (Instituto de Promoción de Inversiones y Exportaciones de Bienes y Servicios): Yaguarón 1407, Of. 1103, 11100 Montevideo; tel. (2) 9002912; fax (2) 9008298; e-mail info@uruguayxxi.gub.uy; internet www.uruguayxxi.gub.uy; f. 1996; govt agency to promote economic investment and export; Exec. Dir CARLOS VIERA.

DEVELOPMENT ORGANIZATIONS

Corporación Nacional para el Desarrollo (CND): Rincón 528, 7°, Casilla 977, 11000 Montevideo; tel. (2) 9162800; fax (2) 9159662; e-mail cnd@cnd.org.uy; internet www.cnd.org.uy; f. 1985; national devt corpn; mixed-capital org.; obtains 60% of funding from state; Vice-Pres. JUAN ARTURO ECHEVARRÍA; Dir TOMÁS ALONZO BASTRERI; Gen. Man. MARTÍN J. DIBARBOURE ROSSINI.

Asociación Nacional de Micro y Pequeños Empresarios (ANMYPE): Miguelete 1584, Montevideo; tel. (2) 9241010; e-mail info@anmype.org.uy; internet www.anmype.org.uy; promotes small businesses; f. 1988; Pres. PABLO VILLAR.

Asociación Nacional de Organizaciones No Gubernamentales Orientadas al Desarrollo: Avda del Libertador 1985 esq. 202, Montevideo; tel. and fax (2) 9240812; e-mail anong@anong.com.uy; internet www.anong.org.uy; f. 1992; umbrella grouping of devt NGOs; Pres. MARÍA ELENA MARTÍNEZ.

Centro Interdisciplinario de Estudios sobre el Desarrollo, Uruguay (CIEDUR): 18 de Julio 1645-7, 11200 Montevideo; tel. and fax (2) 4084520; e-mail ciedur@ciedur.org.uy; internet www.ciedur.org.uy; f. 1977; devt studies and training; Pres. JAIME BEHAR; Exec. Sec. CARLOS PÉREZ ARRARTE.

Fundación Uruguaya de Cooperación y Desarrollo Solidario (FUNDASOL) (Uruguayan Foundation for Supportive Co-operation and Development): Blvr Artigas 1119, esq. Maldonado, 11200 Montevideo; tel. (2) 4002020; fax (2) 4081485; e-mail consultas@fundasol.org.uy; internet www.fundasol.org.uy; f. 1979; Pres. EDUARDO PIETRA; Gen. Man. JORGE NAYA.

CHAMBERS OF COMMERCE

Cámara de Industrias del Uruguay (Chamber of Industries): Avda Italia 6101, 11500 Montevideo; tel. (2) 6040464; fax (2) 6040501; e-mail ciu@ciu.com.uy; internet www.ciu.com.uy; f. 1898; Pres. DIEGO BALESTRA.

Cámara Nacional de Comercio y Servicios del Uruguay (National Chamber of Commerce): Edif. Bolsa de Comercio, Rincón 454, 2°, Casilla 1000, 11000 Montevideo; tel. (2) 9161277; fax (2) 9161243; e-mail info@cncs.com.uy; internet www.cncs.com.uy; f. 1867; 1,500 mems; Pres. JULIO LACARTE MURÓ; Man. Dr CLAUDIO PIACENZA.

Cámara Mercantil de Productos del País (Chamber of Commerce for Local Products): Avda General Rondeau 1908, 1°, 11800 Montevideo; tel. (2) 9240644; fax (2) 9240673; e-mail info@camaramercantil.com.uy; internet www.camaramercantil.com.uy; f. 1891; 180 mems; Pres. RICARDO SEIZER; Gen. Man. GONZALO GONZÁLEZ PIEDRAS.

EMPLOYERS' ORGANIZATIONS

Asociación de Importadores y Mayoristas de Almacén (Importers' and Wholesalers' Asscn): Edif. Bolsa de Comercio, Of. 317/319, Rincón 454, 11000 Montevideo; tel. (2) 9156103; fax (2) 9160796; e-mail fmelissari@nidera.com.uy; f. 1926; 52 mems; Pres. FERNANDO MELISSARI.

Asociación Rural del Uruguay (ARU): Avda Uruguay 864, 11100 Montevideo; tel. (2) 9020484; fax (2) 9020489; e-mail consultas@aru.com.uy; internet www.aru.com.uy; f. 1871; 1,800 mems; Pres. GUZMÁN TELLECHEA OTERO; Vice-Pres. Dr JUAN GARCÍA REQUENA.

Federación Rural: Avda 18 de Julio 965, 1°, Montevideo; tel. (2) 9005583; fax (2) 9004791; e-mail fedrural@gmail.com; internet www.federacionrural.org; f. 1915; 2,000 mems; Pres. RODRIGO HERRERO.

Unión de Exportadores del Uruguay (Uruguayan Exporters' Asscn): Edif. Nacional de Aduanas, Yacaré s/n, 11000 Montevideo; tel. (2) 9170105; fax (2) 9165967; e-mail info@uruguayexporta.com; internet www.uruguayexporta.com; Pres. RODOLFO MERZARIO; Exec. Sec. ALEJANDRO BZUROVSKI.

UTILITIES

Electricity

Administración Nacional de Usinas y Transmisiones Eléctricas (UTE): Paraguay 2431, 10°, 11100 Montevideo; tel. (2) 2003424; fax (2) 2037082; e-mail ute@ute.com.uy; internet www.ute.com.uy; f. 1912; autonomous state body; sole purveyor of electricity until 1997; Pres. BENO RUCHANSKY; Gen. Man. ALEJANDRO PERRONI.

Gas

Conecta: Sanlúcar 1631, esq. Avda Rivera, Montevideo; tel. (2) 6008400; fax (2) 6006732; internet www.conecta.com.uy; gas distribution; Dir FRANCISCO LLANO.

MontevideoGas: 25 de Mayo 702, 11000 Montevideo; tel. (2) 9017454; e-mail mlcoitino@montevideogas.com.uy; internet www.montevideogas.com.uy; gas producers and service providers.

Water

Aguas de la Costa: Calle 1 y 20, La Barra, Maldonado; tel. (42) 771930; fax (42) 771932; e-mail adlcosta@adinet.com.uy; subsidiary of Aguas de Barcelona (Spain); operating in Uruguay since 1994, contract due to expire in 2019; management of water supply in Maldonado Dept.

Obras Sanitarias del Estado (OSE): Carlos Roxlo 1275, 11200 Montevideo; tel. (2) 4001151; fax (2) 4088069; e-mail oserou@adinet.com.uy; internet www.ose.com.uy; f. 1962; processing and distribution of drinking water, sinking wells, supplying industrial zones of the country; Pres. MARTÍN PONCE DE LEÓN.

TRADE UNION

Plenario Intersindical de Trabajadores—Convención Nacional de Trabajadores (PIT—CNT): Avda 18 de Julio 2190, Montevideo; tel. (2) 4096680; fax (2) 4004160; e-mail pitcnt@adinet.com.uy; f. 1966; org. comprising 83 trade unions, 17 labour federations; 320,000 mems; Pres. JORGE CASTRO; Exec. Sec. JUAN CASTILLO.

Transport

Dirección Nacional de Transporte: Rincón 575, 5°, 11000 Montevideo; tel. (2) 9163122; fax (2) 9163122; e-mail pitcnt@adinet.com.uy; internet www.dnt.gub.uy; co-ordinates national and international transport services.

RAILWAYS

Administración de los Ferrocarriles del Estado (AFE): Avda del Libertador 1672, Montevideo; tel. (2) 9033030; e-mail rrpp-afe@adinet.com.uy; internet www.afe.com.uy; f. 1952; state org.; 3,002 km of track connecting all parts of the country; there are connections with the Argentine and Brazilian networks; passenger services ceased in 1988; passenger services linking Montevideo with Florida and Canelones were resumed in mid-1993; Pres. ANTONIO GALLICCHIO QUEIROLO.

ROADS

In 2006 Uruguay had an estimated 8,730 km of motorways (forming the most dense motorway network in South America), connecting Montevideo with the main towns of the interior and the Argentine and Brazilian frontiers. There was also a network of approximately 40,000 km of paved roads under departmental control.

Corporación Vial del Uruguay, SA: Rincón 528, 5°, 11000 Montevideo; tel. (2) 9261680; fax (2) 9170114; e-mail cvu@cnd.org.uy; internet www.cvu.com.uy; road construction agency; 100% owned by the Corporación Nacional para el Desarrollo; Pres. ALVARO GARCÍA; Gen. Man. ANDRÉS PEREYRA.

INLAND WATERWAYS

There are about 1,250 km of navigable waterways, which provide an important means of transport.

Nobleza Naviera, SA: Avda General Rondeau 2257, Montevideo; tel. (2) 9243222; fax (2) 9243218; e-mail nobleza@netgate.com.uy; operates cargo services on the River Plate, and the Uruguay and Paraná rivers; Chair. AMÉRICO DEAMBROSI; Man. Dir DORIS FERRARI.

SHIPPING

Administración Nacional de Puertos (ANP): Rambla 25 de Agosto de 1825 160, Montevideo; tel. (2) 9151441; fax (2) 9161704; e-mail presidencia@anp.com.uy; internet www.anp.com.uy; f. 1916; national ports admin; Pres. FERNANDO PUNTIGLIANO; Gen. Man. ALBERTO DÍAZ.

Prefectura Nacional Naval: Edif. Comando General de la Armada, 4°, Rambla 25 de Agosto de 1825 s/n, esq. Maciel, Montevideo; tel. (2) 9155500; fax (2) 9156786; internet www.armada.gub.uy/Prena; f. 1829; maritime supervisory body, responsible for rescue services, protection of sea against pollution, etc.; Prefect Rear-Adm. OSCAR DEBALI DE PALLEJA.

Navegación Atlántida, SA: Río Branco 1373, 11100 Montevideo; tel. (2) 9084449; f. 1967; ferry services for passengers and vehicles between Argentina and Uruguay; Pres. H. C. PIETRANERA.

Transportadora Marítima de Combustibles, SA (TRAMACO, SA): Rincón 540, Puerta Baja, 11000 Montevideo; tel. (2) 9165754; fax (2) 9165755; e-mail tramaco@tramaco.com.uy; owned by the Christopherson Group; Pres. JORGE FERNÁNDEZ BAUBETA.

CIVIL AVIATION

Civil aviation is controlled by the Dirección General de Aviación Civil and the Dirección General de Infraestructura Aeronáutica. The main airport is at Carrasco, 21 km from Montevideo, and there are also airports at Paysandú, Rivera, Salto, Melo, Artigas, Punta del Este and Durazno.

Primeras Líneas Uruguayas de Navegación Aérea (PLUNA): Colonia 1013, 11000 Montevideo; tel. (2) 9030273; fax (2) 9023916; e-mail info@pluna.com.uy; internet www.pluna.aero; f. 1936; nationalized 1951; partially privatized in 1994; 49% stake acquired by Aerolíneas Argentinas in 2004; operates international services to Argentina, Brazil, Chile, El Salvador, Paraguay, Spain and the USA; Pres. CARLOS BOUZAS.

Aeromás, SA: Avda de las Americas 5120, Montevideo; tel. (2) 6046359; e-mail aeromas@aeromas.com; internet www.aeromas.com; private hire, cargo, and air ambulance flights; internal mass transit services to Salto, Paysandú, Rivera, Tacuarembó and Artigas; f. 1983; Dir DANIEL DALMÁS.

Tourism

The sandy beaches and woodlands on the coast and the grasslands of the interior, with their variety of fauna and flora, provide the main tourist attractions. About 52% of tourists came from Argentina, and a further 15% from Brazil in 2008. Uruguay received 2.0m. visitors in that year, while tourism revenues totalled US $1,029m.

Asociación Uruguaya de Agencias de Viajes (AUDAVI): Río Branco 1407, Of. 205, 11100 Montevideo; tel. (2) 9012326; fax (2) 9021972; e-mail audavi@netgate.com.uy; internet www.audavi.com.uy; f. 1951; 100 mems; Pres. GIORGIO VALENTI; Man. LEDO SILVA.

Cámara Uruguaya de Turismo: San José 942, 2°, Of. 4, 11200 Montevideo; tel. and fax (2) 9000453; internet camtur.com.uy; Pres. LUIS BORSARI.

Uruguay Natural: Rambla 25 de Agosto de 1825, esq. Yacaré, Montevideo; tel. (2) 1885100; e-mail webmaster@mintur.gub.uy; internet www.uruguaynatural.com; f. 2003; state-run tourism promotion agency; Dir-Gen. Dr ANTONIO CARÁMBULA.

UZBEKISTAN

Introductory Survey

Location, Climate, Language, Religion, Flag, Capital

The Republic of Uzbekistan is located in Central Asia. It is bordered by Kazakhstan to the north, Turkmenistan to the south-west, Kyrgyzstan to the east, Tajikistan to the south-east and Afghanistan to the south. The climate is marked by extreme temperatures and low levels of precipitation. Summers are long and hot with average temperatures in July of 32°C (90°F); daytime temperatures often exceed 40°C (104°F). During the short winter there are frequent severe frosts, and temperatures can fall as low as −38°C (−36°F). The official language is Uzbek. Islam is the predominant religion. Most Uzbeks are Sunni Muslims, principally of the Hanafi school, although there are small communities of Salafis; Sufism is relatively well established in southern Uzbekistan. There are also Orthodox Christians among the Slavic communities. The national flag (proportions 1 by 2) consists of five unequal horizontal stripes of (from top to bottom) light blue, red, white, red and light green, with a white crescent and 12 white stars near the hoist on the top stripe. The capital is Tashkent (Toshkent).

Recent History

Soviet power was first established in parts of Uzbekistan in November 1917. In April 1918 the Turkestan Autonomous Soviet Socialist Republic (ASSR), a vast region in Central Asia including Uzbekistan, was proclaimed, but Soviet forces withdrew against opposition from the nationalist *basmachi* movement, the White Army and a British expeditionary force. Soviet power was re-established in September 1919, although armed opposition continued until the early 1920s. The khanates of Buxoro (Bukhara) and Xiva (Khiva) became nominally independent Soviet republics in 1920, but by 1924 had been incorporated into the Turkestan ASSR. On 27 October 1924 the Uzbek Soviet Socialist Republic (SSR) was established (including, until 1929, the Tajik ASSR). In May 1925 the Uzbek SSR became a constituent republic of the Union of Soviet Socialist Republics (USSR, which had been established in December 1922). In 1936 Qoraqalpog'iston (Karakalpakstan) was transferred from the Russian Federation to the Uzbek SSR, retaining its status as a nominally autonomous viloyat (oblast or region).

The National Delimitation of the Central Asian republics of 1924–25 established an Uzbek nation-state for the first time. Its formation was accompanied by the development of a new literary language. Literacy rose from 3.8% at the 1926 census to 52.5% in 1932, and there was an increase in the provision of educational facilities, which played a crucial role in the policy of secularization. Muslim schools, courts and mosques were closed, and Muslim clergy were persecuted.

There had been little industrial development in Central Asia under the tsarist regime, other than the extraction of raw materials. Under the first two Five-Year Plans (1928–33 and 1933–38), however, there was considerable economic growth, aided by the immigration of skilled workers from other republics of the USSR. Although economic expansion continued at a significant rate after the Second World War (during which Uzbekistan's industrial base was enlarged by the transfer of industries from the war-zone), most Uzbeks continued to lead a traditional rural life-style, affected only by the huge increase in the amount of cotton grown in the republic.

There was a greater measure of freedom of the press in the late 1980s, facilitated by the policies of the Soviet leader, Mikhail Gorbachev, which allowed discussion of previously unexamined aspects of Uzbek history and contemporary ecological and economic concerns. The over-irrigation of land to feed the vast cotton-fields had caused both salination of the soil and, most importantly, the desiccation of the Aral Sea, a vital element in the ecology of the entire region.

Environmental problems and the status of the Uzbek language were among the concerns on which Uzbekistan's first major non-communist political movement, Unity (Birlik), campaigned. Formed in 1988, it rapidly became the main challenger to the ruling Communist Party of the Uzbek SSR (CPU). However, the movement remained unregistered and was unsuccessful in the 1989 elections to the USSR's Congress of People's Deputies; nevertheless, its campaign led to the adoption of legislation declaring Uzbek to be the official language of the republic in October of that year.

On 18 February 1990 elections were held to the 500-seat Uzbekistani Supreme Soviet (Supreme Council—legislature), which came to be dominated by the CPU (members of Unity were not permitted to stand). The new Supreme Soviet convened in March and elected Islam Karimov, the First Secretary (leader) of the CPU, to the newly created post of executive President.

In April 1991 Uzbekistan agreed, together with eight other Soviet republics, to sign a new Union Treaty to redefine the state structure of the USSR. However, on 19 August, the day before the signing was to take place, there was an attempt to stage a coup by conservative communists in Moscow, the Russian and Soviet capital. President Karimov only expressed his opposition to the coup once it became clear that it had failed. On 31 August an extraordinary session of the Supreme Soviet voted to declare the republic independent, as the Republic of Uzbekistan. The CPU voted to dissociate itself from the Communist Party of the Soviet Union, and in November the party was restructured as the People's Democratic Party of Uzbekistan (PDPU), under Karimov's leadership.

On 21 December 1991 Karimov agreed, together with 10 other republican leaders, to dissolve the USSR and formally establish the Commonwealth of Independent States (CIS, see p. 225). On 29 December a direct presidential election was held for the first time in Uzbekistan, which was won by Karimov, with a reported 86% of the total votes cast. His sole rival (winning 12% of the votes) was the poet Muhammad Salih, the leader of the Freedom (Erk) party, which had been established as an offshoot of Unity in 1990. A referendum was held concurrently, in which 98.2% of participants endorsed Uzbekistan's independence.

Under Karimov's leadership, there was widespread repression of opposition and Islamist groups. Uzbekistan's new Constitution, adopted on 8 December 1992, firmly enshrined the concept of state secularism, although the formal provisions for a democratic multi-party system, freedom of expression and the observance of human rights were largely ignored, in practice. It also provided for a new, smaller legislature, the 250-member Oly Majlis (Supreme Assembly), to take effect from elections due to be held in late 1994. On the day of the adoption of the new Constitution three leading opposition members were seized by Uzbekistani security police in the Kyrgyzstani capital, Bishkek, on charges of sedition. On the following day Unity was banned. Restriction of the media also intensified: in mid-1993 the Government instructed all newspapers and periodicals to be re-registered with the State Committee for the Press; only organs of state and government were permitted official registration.

Only the PDPU and its ally, Progress of the Fatherland (PF), were permitted to register for the elections to the Oly Majlis in 1994. At the elections, held on 25 December (with a second round of voting in January 1995), the PDPU won 69 of the 250 seats, and the PF secured 14. The remaining 167 deputies elected had been nominated by local councils rather than by political parties; however, the majority of these deputies (some 120) were members of the PDPU, and thus the party's domination of the Majlis was retained. Some 94% of eligible voters were reported to have participated in the election.

In January 1995 Karimov announced that the Government would permit the formation of blocs in the Oly Majlis, and in February a new political party, the Justice (Adolat) Social Democratic Party of Uzbekistan, was registered; it immediately declared its intention to establish such a parliamentary faction. A referendum held in March produced a 99.6% vote in favour of extending Karimov's presidential term, originally scheduled to end in 1997, until 2000, in which year parliamentary elections were due to be held. In May two new political formations emerged: the National Revival (Milliy Tiklanish) Democratic Party and the People's Unity (Xalq Birligi) Movement. Both were reported to be pro-Government, and were officially registered in June. In December 1995 O'tkir Sultonov, hitherto the Minister of Foreign Economic Relations, replaced Abdulkhashim Mutalov as Prime Minister. In June 1996 Karimov resigned from his position as Chairman of the PDPU.

During 1996 Karimov began to advocate the creation of a political opposition to the PDPU, and in December a new law on political parties was approved by the Oly Majlis. The legislation prohibited the organization of parties on a religious or ethnic basis and compelled prospective parties to provide evidence of some 5,000 members drawn from a majority of Uzbekistan's administrative regions.

In late 1997 there was an upsurge of violence in eastern Uzbekistan, particularly in the densely populated Farg'ona (Fergana) valley, which was attributed to groups of Islamist activists. In November the deputy head of the local administration of Namangan Viloyat (region) was assassinated, and in the following month four police officers were killed; government troops were dispatched to the area, whereupon they arrested hundreds of suspects. The Government's campaign against Islamist militancy intensified in early 1998. In February the Ministry of Foreign Affairs appealed to the Pakistani Government to extirpate military training camps in that country, where Uzbeks were allegedly being trained in dissident activities. (Pakistan denied the existence of any such camps.) In May the Oly Majlis adopted legislation that severely limited the activities of religious organizations in Uzbekistan and Karimov declared to the Majlis that he would be prepared personally to execute members of Islamist groups found guilty of terrorism. In May–July several suspected militant Islamists were sentenced to terms of imprisonment, and a member of an Islamist organization was sentenced to death following his conviction for the murder of five people and for his role in the training of militants in Afghanistan. In January 1999 five men allegedly linked with a former *imam* of a mosque in Tashkent, who had been in hiding since early 1998, were found guilty of attempting to overthrow the Government and establish an Islamist state. Meanwhile, in June 1998 new legislation was adopted banning the purchase, sale or exchange of land.

In February 1999 a series of bombs exploded in the centre of Tashkent, killing an estimated 15 people. Government officials claimed that the explosions had been carried out in an attempt to assassinate President Karimov and destabilize the country. Following the trial, in June, of 22 people suspected of involvement in the bomb attacks, six of the accused were sentenced to death, and the other defendants received lengthy prison sentences. In August six members of the banned Freedom party were also given prison sentences of between eight and 15 years for their alleged involvement in the bombings. In November the Tashkent region was infiltrated by a group of about 15 armed militants, resulting in the shooting of three police officers and three civilians. (It was alleged that the group, who were subsequently killed by security forces, had been trained in the separatist Chechen Republic, Russia, and had entered Uzbekistan from Kyrgyzstan.) Following the violence, Karimov demanded increased security in the capital and appealed to the Organization for Security and Co-operation in Europe (OSCE, see p. 366) to assist Uzbekistan in combating international terrorism.

At elections to the Oly Majlis, held on 5 and 19 December 1999, the PDPU secured the largest representation of any single party in the legislature, winning 48 seats, but non-partisan local council nominees obtained a combined total of 110 seats. Of the 250 seats, only 184 were filled at the first round, on 5 December, which necessitated a second round of voting on 19 December, at which all but one deputy was elected. The rate of voter participation at the first round was reported to be some 93.5%. The OSCE had sent only a limited number of observers to the elections, since all of the parties participating were pro-Government, two opposition parties having been prevented from contesting.

President Karimov reportedly secured 91.9% of the votes cast at the presidential election held on 9 January 2000, compared with only 4.2% for his sole opponent, the leader of the PDPU, Abdulkhafiz Jalolov. He was duly inaugurated for another five-year term on 22 January. A reported 95% of the registered electorate participated in the poll. However, both the OSCE and the US Government criticized the election as undemocratic, as opposition parties had been barred from nominating candidates.

The trial of 12 defendants accused of involvement in the bomb attacks of February 1999 opened in October 2000. In November the spiritual leader of the banned militant group the Islamic Movement of Uzbekistan (IMU), Takhir Yoldoshev, and his field commander, Jumaboy Khojiyev (known as Juma Namangoniy), were sentenced to death, *in absentia*. The remaining 10 defendants (including, *in absentia*, Salih) were sentenced to between 12 and 20 years' imprisonment. In June 2001 10 further Islamist militants were reported to have received prison sentences for attempting to overthrow the Government. In December it was reported that Karimov had requested the extradition of Salih from the Czech capital, Prague. However, Salih was released by a Czech court later that month.

The Government's repression of minority groups continued in 2001. During March, in the towns of Samarqand and Buxoro, books in the Tajik language were removed from libraries and schools. In April allegations emerged that the Ministry of Education had commanded the destruction of books in Tajik elsewhere in the country.

The perceived threat of militant Islamist movements intensified in the latter half of 2001, following the suicide attacks in the USA on 11 September (see below), and Uzbekistan's decision to co-operate with the USA in its attempts to form an international coalition to combat the al-Qa'ida (Base) organization (elements of the leadership of which were harboured by the de facto ruling Taliban militia in Afghanistan). It was widely believed that Karimov expected to secure strategic benefits from such co-operation, notably the suppression of the IMU and the moderation of international criticism of his Government's position on economic reforms and human rights. In the mean time, further restrictions were placed on the media in an attempt to limit public reprisals against the country's co-operation with the USA. There were frequent allegations of the torture and arrest of suspected members of the IMU and Hizb-ut-Tahrir al-Islami (Hizb-ut-Tahrir—the Party of Islamic Liberation), a clandestine, transnational organization, which sought to re-establish a caliphate, apparently solely through peaceful means, and which was alleged to enjoy significant support in Uzbekistan and neighbouring countries, particularly in the Farg'ona valley region. In October an estimated 5,000–7,000 members of the IMU (which both the UN and the USA identified as a terrorist organization) were reported to be fighting alongside Taliban forces in Afghanistan.

On 27 January 2002 a referendum took place to seek approval for proposed constitutional amendments, which would extend the President's term of office for a further two years and change the legislative structure. Some 91.6% of the electorate participated, of whom 93.7% approved the establishment of a bicameral legislature and 91.8% endorsed the extension of the presidential term to seven years. In April the Oly Majlis approved a resolution delaying the next presidential election by two years, until 2007. (The amendments also prescribed that elections to all offices of state were henceforth to be held in the third week of December in the year in which the term of office expired, effectively awarding President Karimov constitutional legitimacy to extend his mandate for a further 11 months, until December 2007.)

In December 2002 the Oly Majlis approved legislation on the formation of the new, bicameral legislature; Karimov announced that the upper chamber, the Senat (Senate), would assume some of the duties formerly performed by the President. In April 2003 the Oly Majlis approved constitutional amendments permitting the redistribution of authority within the Government, with effect from the next legislative elections. Most notably, the amendments prohibited the same person from serving simultaneously as President and Prime Minister, with the latter leading the Cabinet of Ministers. In addition, a law granting former presidents lifelong immunity from prosecution and permanent membership of the Senat was endorsed, and the judiciary was restructured.

On 11 December 2003 the Oly Majlis confirmed the appointment by Karimov of a new Prime Minister, Shavkat Mirziyoyev, who had substantial experience in the agricultural sector; Sultonov became a Deputy Prime Minister, with responsibility for the energy, petroleum and chemicals sectors. In March 2004 the Deputy Prime Minister and Minister of the Economy, Rustam Azimov, revealed plans to improve the efficiency of the Government, which was reorganized to comprise 13 ministries and 11 state committees.

On 28–29 March 2004 three police officers were reportedly killed in two separate shooting incidents in Tashkent; on 29 March two apparent suicide bomb attacks in the city's Chorsu market resulted in further casualties. It was also reported that 10 people had been killed and 26 injured after bombs exploded in an apartment block in Buxoro, which police alleged was being used to manufacture explosives. On 30 March security forces carried out a raid in Tashkent, during which at least 16 suspected militants and three police officers were reported to have been killed. Karimov attributed the violence to militant Islamist organizations, and at the end of the month the Uzbekistani authorities began to make numerous arrests. A further bomb attack on 1 April killed one person and prompted the Government temporarily to close its land borders. By July some 85 people suspected of involvement in the attacks had been arrested. In August 15 of the accused were sentenced to between six and 18 years' imprisonment; in October a further 23 Islamist militants were sentenced to between three and 18 years' imprisonment; and in July 2005 another 20 men were given gaol sentences for their involvement in the attacks.

Meanwhile, in July 2004 seven people were killed as a result of suicide bomb attacks in Tashkent outside the Israeli and US embassies and outside the Office of the Prosecutor-General. President Karimov rejected allegations of IMU involvement in the attacks and accused Hizb-ut-Tahrir of bearing primary responsibility. In December the Office of the Prosecutor-General declared that all three of the suicide bombers had been Kazakhstani citizens.

Further civil unrest broke out in November 2004, with riots in Qoqand in the Farg'ona valley, where some 5,000–10,000 people protested against the introduction of new laws affecting market traders; the protests spread to markets in other towns in Uzbekistan, including Buxoro and Margilan. In December human rights groups and opposition parties gathered outside the US embassy, urging the USA to encourage the Uzbekistani Government to promote democracy and respect for human rights in Uzbekistan, after three opposition parties (Unity, Freedom and the Free Peasants' Party) were refused permission to put forward candidates for the legislative elections scheduled for the end of the month.

Elections to the Qoqunchilik palatasi Kengashi (Legislative Chamber), as the lower chamber of the new 120-member bicameral legislature was designated, were held on 26 December 2004, with a second round of voting on 9 January 2005 in the 58 constituencies in which no candidate had obtained an absolute majority of votes cast. All five of the parties permitted to participate in the elections supported the Karimov regime. A party established in late 1993 led by Muhammadjon Ahmadjonov, the Movement of Entrepreneurs and Businessmen—Liberal Democratic Party of Uzbekistan, obtained 41 seats, securing the largest representation of any single party in the legislature. The PDPU obtained 28 seats, the Self-Sacrificers' National Democratic Party 18, the National Revival Democratic Party 11 and the Justice Social Democratic Party 10. The rate of voter participation at the first round was estimated to be 85.1%. A number of ministerial changes were effected in late 2004 and early 2005. On 14 January 2005 President Karimov announced the appointment of 16 members of the Senat; regional council members elected a further 84 senators on 17–20 January. The Senat's inaugural session took place on 27 January.

There were reports of heightened political tensions in early 2005, particularly in the Farg'ona valley, which were attributed to a number of factors, including dissatisfaction at widespread poverty, the influence of the political upheaval in neighbouring Kyrgyzstan in March (see the chapter on Kyrgyzstan), and discontent at restrictions on trade and on the freedom of association. From February daily peaceful protests, some of which were apparently attended by up to 1,000 people, were reported outside a court in Andijon, where 23 local business executives had been brought to trial on charges of belonging to a prohibited Islamist organization, referred to by the authorities as Akramiya, and which was alleged to have broken away from Hizb-ut-Tahrir. All 23 denied the charges brought against them. In the early hours of 13 May, several days before the trial of the alleged Islamists was due to conclude, a group of armed men stormed the gaol in Andijon, and released as many as 2,000 prisoners, including the 23 people charged with belonging to Akramiya. Armed rebels were reported to have taken control of the regional administration building in the city later that day, and several thousand people gathered in the main city square, apparently to protest against both the trial of the alleged militants and economic difficulties. Heavily armed state security forces, including troops in tanks, entered the city and opened fire on the demonstrators. The exact number of people killed was disputed, in part because of the strict restrictions placed on media coverage and on access to the region by foreign diplomatic representatives or members of non-governmental organizations (NGOs). Protests continued in Andijon later in the month, and unrest was reported in Qorasuv, south-east of Andijon, on the border with Kyrgyzstan, where local Islamist rebels seized control of the local administration and reopened a border crossing with Kyrgyzstan that had been closed since 2000. State forces subsequently recaptured the town. Meanwhile, Kyrgyzstan reported that it had registered more than 500 Uzbekistani refugees in the immediate aftermath of the violence in Andijon (see below).

President Karimov rejected requests by the international community for an independent investigation into the events in Andijon. In July 2005 the Prosecutor of Andijon Viloyat announced that 187 people had been killed as a result of the violence, including 94 terrorists, 57 civilians, 20 law-enforcement officials and 11 soldiers; in contrast, independent reports claimed that as many as 1,000 people, mainly civilians, had been killed. In September a report released by the Office of the Prosecutor-General stated that foreign-based Islamists had staged the violence. The report also claimed that in January–April instructors in Kyrgyzstan had trained some 70 Islamist fundamentalists in terrorist techniques. In August Karimov approved a decree abolishing capital punishment (with effect from 1 January 2008).

In September 2005 The First Deputy Prosecutor-General suggested that 'external forces' had instructed Western journalists to publish false information about the events in Andijon in the foreign media. Meanwhile, individuals and organizations providing accounts that undermined the credibility of the Government's version of events were subject to official harassment, and many were expelled from the country or imprisoned. In October the European Union (EU, see p. 255) imposed sanctions on Uzbekistan (including a ban on travel to EU states by officials suspected of involvement in the shooting of civilians in Andijon, and an embargo on the export of weapons and other related equipment), owing to the Government's refusal either to permit an international investigation into events at Andijon or to bring those who had perpetrated the killings to trial. (These sanctions were extended in November 2006 and again in May 2007.) By December more than 150 people had been sentenced to terms of imprisonment for their involvement in the protests in Andijon; in November the USA and the Office of the UN High Commissioner for Human Rights expressed concern that defendants were being convicted without being permitted a fair trial. There were also allegations of the use of torture to extract confessions. In February 2006 the Government approved a resolution that made journalists deemed to be interfering in internal affairs or insulting Uzbekistani citizens liable to prosecution. In March the authorities requested that the UN High Commission for Refugees vacate its offices in Uzbekistan, asserting that it was no longer required in the country.

Meanwhile, frequent government and security personnel changes continued to be effected in 2005–06. In June 2005 the First Deputy Head of the Military Intelligence Directorate, Lt-Col Sanjar Ismoilov, was arrested on suspicion of spying for Russia and, following his conviction, was sentenced to 20 years' imprisonment in January 2006. Ismoilov appealed against his sentence, but this was rejected by the Supreme Court in February. In November 2005 Karimov dismissed the Minister of Defence, Qodir G'ulomov, who was subsequently succeeded by Ruslan Mirzayev. (G'ulomov was given a five-year suspended prison sentence in July 2006 for offences committed during his term of office.) Later in November 2005 Rustam Azimov was appointed as Minister of Finance; Azimov, hitherto the Minister of Foreign Economic Relations, Investment and Trade, was replaced in that position by Alisher Shayxov. In December the Minister of Internal Affairs, Zokirjon Almatov (whom the EU held responsible for overseeing the violent repression of the protests in Andijon), resigned from his post, citing ill health. In January 2006 he was succeeded by Bahodir Matlyubov. In February Murat Shafirkhodjaev resigned as Speaker of the Senat, apparently for reasons of ill health; he was succeeded by Ilgizar Sobirov. In April Vyacheslav Golishev was dismissed from the position of Deputy Prime Minister, responsible for the Economic Sector and Foreign Economic Relations, and Minister of the Economy. Azimov, the Minister of Finance, replaced Golishev in the former post, and Botir Hojayev was appointed Minister of the Economy. In June Lt-Col Erkin Musayev, former head of the Ministry of Defence Directorate for International Military Co-operation, was sentenced to 15 years' imprisonment after being convicted of negligence, dereliction of duty and divulging secret information to the North Atlantic Treaty Organization (NATO). Elyor G'aniyev was replaced as Minister of Foreign Affairs by Vladimir Norov in July, although he retained a post in the Cabinet as Minister of Foreign Economic Relations,

UZBEKISTAN

Investment and Trade. In late 2006 several Hokims (regional governors) were replaced.

The arrest of human rights activists and political dissidents, and the closure of foreign-funded NGOs, continued unabated in 2006–07. The operations in Uzbekistan of several NGOs were terminated at the behest of a Tashkent court, ostensibly owing to alleged financial offences, engagement in improper activities and dissemination of false information against the republic. In August 2006 the trial commenced in Tashkent of a popular musician and songwriter, Dodokhon Hasan, who was accused of defaming the President. In mid-September Jamshid Karimov, formerly a reporter for the United Kingdom-based NGO the Institute for War and Peace Reporting (IWPR) and a nephew of President Karimov, was reported to have disappeared; it was subsequently announced that he had been detained at a psychiatric hospital in Samarqand. Another former reporter for the IWPR, Ulughbek Haydarov, was convicted on charges of extortion in October and sentenced to six years' imprisonment. A human rights activist, Umida Niyazova, was convicted on charges of illegal cross-border smuggling and sentenced to seven years' imprisonment in May 2007, although this was subsequently commuted to a three-year suspended sentence. In June the six-year prison sentence of another human rights activist, Gulbahor Turayeva, convicted in April by an Andijon court for distributing press material that threatened public order, was also reduced on appeal to a three-year suspended sentence.

In September 2007 the Central Election Commission announced that a presidential election was to take place on 23 December, following the expiry of Karimov's seven-year term in the previous January (in accordance with a constitutional stipulation that the election be held in December of the year in which the presidential term of office ended). Karimov subsequently confirmed that he would contest the election, despite a constitutional provision restricting the President to two consecutive terms in office; the authorities maintained that the extension of the presidential term to seven years from 2002 effectively meant that Karimov's previous terms in office would not be taken into account for the purposes of this restriction. In October EU foreign ministers, while extending the embargo on the export of armaments to Uzbekistan for a further year, adopted a decision to suspend for a period of six months the travel restrictions on senior Uzbekistani officials, including the Minister of Defence, with the stated aim of encouraging the authorities to improve the human rights situation in the country. Prior to the poll, a number of human rights activists were summarily arrested.

On 23 December 2007 Karimov was re-elected, receiving some 88.1% of votes cast at the presidential election (the other three candidates permitted to contest the election were all considered to be loyal to Karimov); voter turnout was officially recorded at 90.6%. An observer mission from the Office for Democratic Institutions and Human Rights of the OSCE stated that the poll had failed to meet democratic standards. At the end of December Karimov appointed Azimov (who retained the finance portfolio) as First Deputy Prime Minister, responsible for the Economic Sector and Foreign Economic Relations; new appointments were made to the posts of Minister of Justice and Minister of Higher and Secondary Specialized Education. A presidential decree abolishing the death penalty (issued by Karimov in August 2005) officially entered into effect on 1 January 2008. In January, following the removal of the Speaker of the lower legislative chamber, Erkin Halilov, for misuse of office, Dilorom Tashmuhamedova (who had contested the presidential election as a candidate of Adolat) was elected to the post. In April the EU extended for a further six months the suspension of the travel sanctions on Uzbekistani officials. In the same month a prominent poet and human rights activist, Yusuf Juma, was sentenced to five years' imprisonment for resisting arrest (after staging a protest at the detention of one of his sons). In June Ahmadjon Odilov, a former opposition figure who had been imprisoned in 1984 on charges of corruption in the cotton industry and was believed to be the longest-serving political prisoner in the country, was released. In the same month a prominent human rights activist was granted early release. In September Karimov dismissed Ruslan Mirzayev as Minister of Defence, he was succeeded by Qobul Berdiyev. In October a summit meeting of EU ministers of foreign affairs issued a declaration stating that the travel ban on Uzbekistani officials would officially end in the following month (while the embargo on the export of armaments remained in place), citing improvements in the human rights situation in Uzbekistan; however,

continued concern was expressed over custodial sentences frequently imposed on human rights activists (including a 10-year term of imprisonment on an independent journalist in that month).

Uzbekistan's closest relations are with the neighbouring Central Asian republics—Kazakhstan, Kyrgyzstan, Tajikistan and Turkmenistan. In September 1997 a Central Asian peace-keeping battalion participated, with troops from the USA and other countries, in military manoeuvres, which were held in Uzbekistan and elsewhere in the region under the auspices of NATO's 'Partnership for Peace' (see p. 353) programme of military co-operation. (Uzbekistan had joined the programme in 1994.) In January 2006 Uzbekistan acceded to membership of the Eurasian Economic Community (EURASEC, see p. 426); hitherto Uzbekistan had been the sole member of the Central Asian Co-operation Organization (CACO—which organization was thereby absorbed into EURASEC) that did not also belong to the former organization. In November 2008 EURASEC officially confirmed that it had been informed of Uzbekistan's decision to suspend its membership of the organization; the decision was widely perceived as an indication of the country's realignment towards closer co-operation with Western states, following the removal of EU travel sanctions against state officials (see above).

In April 1999 Uzbekistan joined the GUAM grouping, comprising Azerbaijan, Georgia, Moldova and Ukraine, which envisaged implementing joint economic and transportation initiatives and establishing a sub-regional free trade zone; the organization was therefore renamed GUUAM. However, Uzbekistan was not an active participant in the group, and in early May 2005 announced its intention to withdraw. In March 2006 President Karimov approved legislation adopted by the Oly Majlis earlier in the year, which completed Uzbekistan's withdrawal from the organization (which was renamed the Organization for Democracy and Economic Development—GUAM, see p. 440—later in the year).

Uzbekistan was a member, alongside the People's Republic of China, Kazakhstan, Kyrgyzstan, Russia and Tajikistan, of the Shanghai Five, founded in 1996 to address border disputes, and acceded to that organization's successor, the Shanghai Co-operation Organization (SCO, see p. 440), signing the Shanghai Convention on Combating Terrorism, Separatism and Extremism. The organization subsequently established a regional anti-terrorism centre, located in Tashkent.

In June 2006 it was announced that Uzbekistan had commenced participation in the Collective Security Treaty Organization (CSTO, see p. 438), the successor organization to the CIS Collective Security Treaty (from which Uzbekistan had withdrawn in March 1999). In March 2008 the Oly Majlis officially approved Uzbekistan's full membership of the CSTO (which also comprised Armenia, Belarus, Kazakhstan, Kyrgyzstan, Russia and Tajikistan).

In October 1998 Uzbekistan and Kazakhstan signed a Treaty of Eternal Friendship and agreed on a seven-year programme of bilateral economic co-operation. In November 2001 Uzbekistan and Kazakhstan signed a treaty demarcating most of their border. However, the demarcation of certain areas, including the villages of Bagys and Turkestanets, remained unresolved. The majority of citizens in Bagys were ethnic Kazakhs, and it had been hoped that the land, hitherto leased to Uzbekistan, would be returned to Kazakhstan following independence. In December residents declared an 'Independent Kazakh Republic of Bagys', and elected a president and legislature. The Uzbekistani security forces subsequently arrested a number of activists, and in April 2002 it was reported that troops had barricaded the villages. In September a new agreement delimiting the Kazakhstani–Uzbekistani border was signed by the countries' Presidents. However, at the end of 2002 Uzbekistan closed its border with Kazakhstan, following the introduction of new import taxes. The creation of a working group to finalize the demarcation of the border between the two countries was announced in August 2003. However, there was a reported increase in violent confrontations on the border between Uzbekistan and Kazakhstan following the arrests of Kazakhstani citizens in connection with a series of bombings in Uzbekistan in mid-2004 (see above), and in January 2005 representatives from the Uzbekistani Ministry of Defence reportedly announced that they considered Kazakhstan to be a potential military adversary and a base for armed groups opposed to the Uzbekistani regime. In the same month the Uzbekistani authorities announced proposals for the demolition of settlements along the border, apparently in response to cross-border smuggling. Demonstrations in February by residents demanding compensation for the destruction of their homes were met with a promise from the Hokim (Governor) of Tashkent Viloyat that an assessment of property values in the village would be conducted with the view of providing the residents with compensation. In March President Karimov and the President of Kazakhstan, Nursultan Nazarbayev, agreed to establish a working group to create a future free trade zone.

Relations with Kyrgyzstan worsened in September 2000, when Uzbekistani government forces planted land-mines along the Kyrgyzstani–Uzbekistani border, apparently without having informed Kyrgyzstani border guards, in order to prevent insurgents from entering Uzbekistan. Although it was announced in June 2001 that the mines were to be removed, there were claims in September that the laying of mines was continuing. As a result, the Kyrgyzstani legislature refused to ratify an agreement with Uzbekistan on arms supplies. Relations were again strained in mid-2005, when the Kyrgyzstani Government refused to return a large number of refugees, who had fled there from Uzbekistan following the violence in Andijon in May (see above). In July more than 400 refugees were deported from Kyrgyzstan to Romania, which Uzbekistan condemned as a violation of international law. There were subsequent reports that refugees repatriated to Uzbekistan had been tortured, and in August 2005 Uzbekistan annulled a bilateral agreement to supply natural gas to Kyrgyzstan. In the following month Uzbekistan issued a report accusing Kyrgyzstan of having permitted extremist Islamists to use bases in that country to foment unrest in Andijon. In August 2006 Kyrgyzstan deported to Uzbekistan refugees from Andijon. In early 2007 a bilateral agreement providing for visa-free travel between the two countries took effect.

In September 2000 Turkmenistan and Uzbekistan signed a treaty demarcating their 1,867-km border. Tighter control of the border, however, exacerbated tension (see the Turkmenistan chapter). In December 2002 Turkmenistani special forces entered the Uzbekistani embassy in the Turkmenistani capital, Aşgabat, purportedly in order to investigate reports that it was harbouring Boris Shikhmuradov, whom the Turkmenistani authorities blamed for an assassination attempt against that country's President, Saparmyrat Niyazov. Uzbekistan's ambassador to Turkmenistan was subsequently declared *persona non grata*, on the grounds that he had offered support to Shikhmuradov. The Uzbekistani authorities denied the allegations and reacted with hostility; open confrontation rapidly led to the deployment of troops from both countries along their mutual border, and an associated increase in border security. However, in November 2004 Presidents Karimov and Niyazov met for their first presidential summit in more than four years, in Buxoro, where they signed three bilateral agreements, pertaining to: friendship, mutual trust, and co-operation; simplifying regulations concerning cross-border travel for residents of border zones (where cross-border smuggling and related shooting incidents had become a problem in recent years); and a framework for sharing regional water resources. The Presidents declared that all bilateral issues had been resolved, and in January 2005 Uzbekistan appointed a new ambassador to Turkmenistan. President Karimov made an official visit to Turkmenistan in October 2007, meeting the President of Turkmenistan installed earlier in that year, Gurbanguly Berdymuhamedov.

Uzbekistan dispatched troops to Tajikistan in 1992, as part of a CIS peace-keeping contingent, and it tightened border controls with Tajikistan in an attempt to prevent the civil conflict in that country from extending into Uzbekistan (see the chapter on Tajikistan). In August 1997 Uzbekistan agreed to act as one of the guarantors of a peace accord reached between the Tajikistani Government and opposition forces two months earlier. During a visit to Uzbekistan in January 1998 President Imamali Rakhmonov (later Rakhmon) of Tajikistan met Karimov, and the two leaders expressed their opposition to religious extremism. In the following month an intergovernmental agreement on restructuring Tajikistan's debt to Uzbekistan was agreed. In February 1999 Uzbekistan announced its intention to withdraw from the CIS Collective Security Treaty, owing to its opposition to Russia's attempts at closer integration within the CIS and, in particular, Russia's military presence in Tajikistan. In August the Uzbekistani Government accused Tajikistan of allowing militant groups to operate from its territory. From August 2000 armed Islamist militants made a series of incursions into the section of the Farg'ona valley in Uzbekistan from Tajikistan, leading to armed conflict with government forces. By September, however, the remaining militants were reported to have been killed by government troops. In the mean time, Uzbekistan, which had begun laying land-mines along its border with Tajikistan from mid-2000, in an effort to prevent cross-border incursions by Islamist insurgents, officially informed Tajikistan of its actions only in May 2001. However, relations between the two countries subsequently improved. President Rakhmonov met President Karimov in Uzbekistan in December; although no border agreement was reached, it was announced that the crossing between the Penjakent district in Tajikistan and Samarqand Viloyat, in Uzbekistan, was to reopen. The leaders also agreed to collaborate to combat terrorism, crime and the illegal drugs trade. At a meeting of the Tajikistani and Uzbekistani Prime Ministers in February 2002, an agreement on border-crossing procedures was reached. The continued influx of illegal drugs from Tajikistan also threatened relations. Later in the year the Presidents of the two countries agreed on the demarcation of more than 85% of the two countries' shared borders.

Tajikistani-Uzbekistani relations, which had become increasingly strained, deteriorated sharply following the suspension at the beginning of 2009 of Turkmenistan's electricity exports to Tajikistan, resulting from the continued failure of the Tajikistani and Uzbekistani authorities to agree a transit rate. Tajikistan accused Uzbekistan state utility Uzbekenergo of interrupting deliveries of Turkmenistani electricity, and threatened to limit the amount of water flowing downstream to Uzbekistan, in order to maintain levels in its reservoirs (Tajikistan is a principal supplier of water to Uzbekistan). An additional matter of contention between the two countries was the planned construction of a hydroelectric plant at Roghun, in central Tajikistan, which was strongly opposed by Uzbekistan, owing to concerns regarding the potential impact of the project on its own water supplies. Later in January Karimov and Russian President Dmitrii Medvedev issued a joint declaration, stating that any hydroengineering projects with transboundary implications were required to meet international laws and standards. However, in February Karimov unexpectedly announced that Uzbekistan was prepared to reconsider its opposition to the project, provided that international auditors verified its viability. On 19 February First Deputy Prime Minister Azimov visited Tajikistan to attend the first bilateral high-level commission meeting in seven years; it was reported that negotiations resulted in agreement on a debt repayment schedule, and on a protocol regarding a reservoir in northern Tajikistan; however, a number of the fundamental issues remained unresolved. In March an agreement was reached between the national airlines of Uzbekistan and Tajikistan on the resumption of direct flights between Tashkent and the Tajikistani capital, Dushanbe (which had been suspended in 1992).

Relations with Russia, the most influential member state of the CIS, have been intermittently strained by concerns regarding Uzbekistan's ethnic Russian population (which comprised an estimated 5.5% of the population in 1996, according to official figures). Uzbekistan has repeatedly refused to grant dual citizenship to its Russian minority, and since independence many thousands of these Russians have emigrated (Russians had comprised 8.3% of the population in 1989, according to census figures). In October 1998 Russia, Uzbekistan and Tajikistan signed a pact offering mutual military assistance, especially against 'the threat of religious extremism'; at the same time Russia and Uzbekistan signed a number of inter-governmental agreements. Russia supported the Uzbekistani Government's official report on the events in Andijon in May 2005. Uzbekistan forged closer relations with Russia in 2005, as relations of both Uzbekistan and Russia with Western countries notably worsened, and in November Karimov and the Russian President, Vladimir Putin, signed a bilateral agreement, which provided for co-operation in: trade and security; the use of military facilities; and efforts to combat drugs-trafficking and terrorism. Notably, the two countries agreed to provide mutual support in the event that one of them came under attack. In January 2009 Russian President Dmitrii Medvedev (who had succeeded Putin in May 2008) undertook a state visit to Uzbekistan to discuss issues of bilateral co-operation. Uzbekistan provided assurances that it would only export gas by way of Russia, and offered to increase the volume of gas to be allocated for purchase by Russia to an annual quota of 31,000m. cu m, after Russia agreed that the purchases would be made at market rates; additionally, the Russian energy company LUKoil was to invest some US $5,000m. in Uzbekistan's gas sector over the following seven years.

Uzbekistan's concerns for the security of the Central Asian region, and the threat to stability caused by Islamist extremism, were augmented by the long-standing civil war in Afghanistan. In the early 1990s President Burhanuddin Rabbani of Afghanistan claimed that Uzbekistan was providing military and financial assistance to the Afghan (and ethnic Uzbek) militia leader Gen. Abdul Rashid Dostam, whose forces controlled parts of northern Afghanistan. In 1994 the Uzbekistani Government denied any military involvement in Afghanistan and declared that only humanitarian aid had been given. At a summit meeting attended by representatives of Russia and the Central Asian republics in October 1996, Karimov confirmed that no military assistance would be accorded to Gen. Dostam, but declared that Dostam's forces provided the only defence for the Central Asian republics against the Taliban militant Islamist grouping. Following the defeat of Dostam's forces in May 1997, increased numbers of troops were deployed on the Uzbekistani–Afghan border. In late 1997 the Uzbekistani Government denied having facilitated the return of Gen. Dostam to Afghanistan from exile in Turkey. In October 2000 Gen. Dostam rejected allegations that his troops fought alongside Uzbekistani government forces in August–September to repel incursions by Islamist militants. Relations with the de facto ruling Taliban regime in Afghanistan deteriorated after they granted political asylum to Khojiyev, the field commander of the IMU. Relations worsened further following reports in the Pakistani press in August 2001 that Khojiyev had been appointed the deputy Commander-in-Chief of the Taliban forces.

The Islamist militant threat intensified following the suicide attacks on the USA of 11 September 2001 (see the chapter on the USA). At the same time, Uzbekistan's relationship with the USA became closer. (Relations had already improved noticeably in the latter half of the 1990s, and during a visit to Tashkent in April 2000 the US Secretary of State had affirmed the USA's willingness to assist Uzbekistan in combating the spread of Islamist extremism.) Uzbekistan's decision to support the US-led 'coalition against global terrorism' was of great strategic importance to the USA, which hoped to benefit from access to the country's transportation facilities. On 23 September the Uzbekistani Government confirmed that US military aircraft had landed at an airfield near Tashkent. On 7 October Uzbekistan and the USA signed a co-operation agreement, whereby Uzbekistan agreed to make its airbases available for use in humanitarian and 'search-and-rescue' operations during the US-led aerial bombardment of Taliban and terrorist bases in Afghanistan. The USA also agreed to enter into urgent negotiations, should Uzbekistan's security be threatened. In October 2001 Uzbekistan commenced the deployment of its troops on the Uzbekistani–Afghan border. The Uzbekistani Government was reluctant to accept refugees from Afghanistan, even though 1.5m. of them were ethnic Uzbeks, citing security concerns. Initially, the Government also refused to open the border to allow humanitarian aid to reach Afghanistan. However, following the military successes of the anti-Taliban forces in November, the Government was persuaded to open the 'Friendship Bridge', the only transit point into Afghanistan, in the following month. Khojiyev was reported to have been killed during the US-led military action in Afghanistan. At an official summit of the heads of the Central Asian states in Tashkent in December 2001 (at which Turkmenistan was not represented), the leaders declared their support for the new Afghan Interim Administration, which was established following the defeat of the Taliban regime. In March 2002 the leaders of Uzbekistan and Afghanistan pledged jointly to combat terrorism and the drugs trade; the IMU, for example, continued to be a threat to both countries.

Meanwhile, in November 2001 Uzbekistan and the USA signed a number of agreements pledging to improve bilateral relations and to increase economic co-operation. The USA agreed to donate more than US $150m. in aid towards improving Uzbekistan's security and economic development. Further bilateral agreements on political, economic and military co-operation were signed in January and March 2002, and Karimov visited the USA in March. Disagreements over Uzbekistan's pace of democratization, however, persisted, and in July 2004 Uzbekistan's lack of progress in democratic reform and human rights practices led the USA to reduce its aid programme by $18m. In October the US Drug Enforcement Agency and Uzbekistan's Ministry of Internal Affairs, together with Azerbaijan, Georgia, Kazakhstan, Kyrgyzstan, Moldova, Russia, Tajikistan and Ukraine, initiated an operation to control the flow of illegal drugs.

Following the violence in Andijon in May 2005, the USA urged Uzbekistan to allow an international inquiry to be undertaken. In June a spokesman from the US Department of State stated that witnesses had reported the killing of hundreds of civilians by Uzbekistani government forces. Uzbekistan subsequently imposed restrictions on the USA's use of the Qarshi-Khanabad ('K-2') military base, which had been used by the USA since October 2001 to support military and other operations in Afghanistan (see above); Uzbekistan also proposed that the USA withdraw from the airbase. Uzbekistan denied allegations that its decision to impose restrictions on the USA's use of the base was prompted by that country's stance on the events in Andijon. However, in July 2005 the SCO issued a statement demanding that deadlines be imposed on the use of military bases in Central Asia by Western countries for operations in Afghanistan. Later in the month, following discussions with the USA, Uzbekistan renounced the agreement under which the USA was permitted to use the Qarshi-Khanabad airbase, and demanded that it vacate the base within six months. The last US military aircraft left the Qarshi-Khanabad base in November. After Kyrgyzstan announced the closure of the US airbase on its territory that had been used by forces operating in Afghanistan in February 2009, it was reported that US and Uzbekistani officials were engaged in negotiations on an arrangement to allow US forces to return to the Qarshi-Khanabad base. In early April Uzbekistan signed an agreement with the USA allowing the use of Uzbekistani territory for the transit of non-military supplies to Afghanistan.

Relations with the People's Republic of China improved in the 1990s, and in July 1996 Jiang Zemin became the first Chinese President to visit Uzbekistan; a joint declaration on bilateral relations and co-operation was signed. China and Uzbekistan signed further co-operation agreements in November 1999, including a joint communiqué on the development of bilateral relations. In October 2000 the two countries signed an agreement on combating terrorism. In May 2005 China praised Uzbekistan's management of the outbreak of violence in Andijon earlier that month.

Government

Under the terms of the Constitution of 8 December 1992, Uzbekistan is a secular, democratic presidential republic. The directly elected President is Head of State and also holds supreme executive power. In April 2002 the Oly Majlis adopted a resolution extending the presidential term from five to seven years, with immediate effect. The Government (Cabinet of Ministers) is subordinate to the President, who appoints the Prime Minister, Deputy Prime Ministers and Ministers (subject to the approval of the legislature). The highest legislative body is the bicameral Oly Majlis (Supreme Assembly). The Majlis may be dissolved by the President (with the approval of the Constitutional Court). The Oly Majlis comprises the 120-member lower chamber, the Qoqunchilik palatasi Kengashi (Legislative Chamber), whose members are directly elected for a five-year term. The upper chamber, the Senat (Senate), is composed of 84 members indirectly elected by regional Council members and 16 citizens appointed by the President. Uzbekistan is divided into 12 Viloyats (regions), the city of Toshkent (Tashkent), and one sovereign republic (Qoraqalpog'iston—Karakalpakstan).

Defence

The establishment of Uzbekistani national armed forces was initiated in 1992. As assessed at November 2008, active armed forces numbered some 67,000, comprising an army of 50,000 and an air force of some 17,000. There were also paramilitary forces numbering up to 20,000 (comprising a 1,000-strong National Guard attached to the Ministry of Defence and up to 19,000 troops attached to the Ministry of Internal Affairs). Compulsory military service lasts for 12 months. The budget for 2007 allocated an estimated 120,000m. sum to defence. In July 1994 Uzbekistan joined the North Atlantic Treaty Organization's (NATO) 'Partnership for Peace' (see p. 353) programme of military co-operation. In April 1999 Uzbekistan withdrew its membership of the Collective Security Treaty of the Commonwealth of Independent States (CIS, see p. 225).

Economic Affairs

In 2007, according to the World Bank, Uzbekistan's gross national income (GNI), measured at average 2005–07 prices, was US $19,721m., equivalent to $730 per head (or $2,430 per head on an international purchasing-power parity basis). During 2000–07, it was estimated, the population increased by an annual average of 1.2%, while gross domestic product (GDP) per head increased, in real terms, at an average annual rate of 5.0%. Overall GDP increased, in real terms, by an average of 6.3% per year in 2000–07. According to the Asian Development Bank (ADB, see p. 191), growth was 9.5% in 2007 and 8.5% in 2008.

In 2007, according to the ADB, agriculture (including forestry) contributed 24.0% of GDP; the agricultural sector employed 29.1% of the working population in 2005. Some 60% of the country's land is covered by desert and steppe, while the remainder comprises fertile valleys watered by two major river systems. The massive irrigation of arid areas has greatly increased production of the major crop, cotton, but has caused devastating environmental problems (most urgently the desiccation of the Aral Sea). Uzbekistan is among the five largest producers of cotton in the world, and the crop accounted for 27.5% of the value of total exports in 2000. Other major crops include grain, rice, vegetables and fruit. Since independence the Government has striven to reduce the area under cultivation for cotton in order to produce more grain. Private farming was legalized in 1992, and by 1996 more than 98% of agricultural production originated in the non-state sector. According to World Bank figures, during 2000–07 agricultural GDP increased, in real terms, by an annual average of 6.6%. Agricultural GDP increased by 6.1% in 2007 and by 4.0% in 2008, according to the ADB.

According to the ADB, industry (including mining, manufacturing, utilities and construction) contributed 32.6% of GDP in 2007. It provided 13.2% of total employment in 2005. According to World Bank figures, during 2000–07 industrial GDP increased by an average of 5.0% annually, in real terms. GDP in the sector increased by 8.3% in 2007 and by 12.0% in 2008, according to the ADB.

Uzbekistan is well endowed with mineral deposits, in particular gold, natural gas, petroleum and coal. At the end of 2007 Uzbekistan had sufficient proven recoverable reserves of natural gas to maintain output at 2007 levels for almost 30 years, and enough petroleum for over 14 years. There are large reserves of silver, copper, lead, zinc and tungsten, and Uzbekistan is one of the world's largest producers of uranium and gold. In 2005 2,712 metric tons of uranium ore was produced; all uranium mined is exported. The Murantau mine, in the Kyzyl-kum desert, was reportedly the world's largest single open-cast gold mine, and produced a reported 74% of Uzbekistan's estimated output in 2003. In 2004 Oxus Gold (of the United Kingdom) and the Uzbekistani Government officially opened a further gold-mining complex in Amantaytau, 30 km from the Murantau mine. Each party had a 50% share in the mine, which had estimated reserves of some 1,400 tons, and was expected to produce some 14 tons of gold per year by 2007.

The manufacturing sector contributed 9.9% of GDP in 2007, according to the World Bank. Significant investment has been directed to the expansion of the raw-materials processing industry. According to the World Bank, manufacturing GDP grew at an average of 2.5% per year in 2000–07. GDP for the sector increased by 5.0% in 2007.

Uzbekistan is self-sufficient in natural gas, crude petroleum and coal, and became a net exporter of crude petroleum in 1995. Energy products accounted for 4.2% of the value of imports in 2000. The opening of two petroleum refineries, which had a total refining capacity of 173,000 barrels per day (b/d), significantly increased Uzbekistan's hydrocarbons capacity. In 2005 68.8% of electricity was generated by natural gas, 13.6% by petroleum and 12.8% by hydroelectric power.

According to the ADB, the services sector contributed 43.4% of GDP in 2007. It employed 57.7% of the working population in 2005. According to World Bank figures, during 2000–07 the GDP of the services sector increased, in real terms, by an average of 6.9% annually. Services GDP increased by 17.4% in 2007 and by 13.5% in 2008, according to the ADB.

In 2007, according to the IMF, Uzbekistan recorded a visible trade surplus of an estimated US $2,296m., and there was a surplus of $4,267m. on the current account of the balance of payments. In 2007 the principal source of imports was Russia (accounting for 26.0% of the total value of imports). Other major suppliers were the People's Republic of China, the Republic of Korea, Germany and Kazakhstan. Russia was also the main market for exports in that year (accounting for 24.5% of the total value of exports); other important purchasers were Poland, Turkey, Hungary, Kazakhstan and China. The principal exports in 2000 were cotton fibre, energy products, metals and food products. The main imports in that year were machinery and equipment, chemicals and plastics, food products and metals. By 2000 trade with republics of the former USSR represented only about 35% of Uzbekistan's total trade, compared with some 83% in 1990.

In 2007, according to preliminary figures, Uzbekistan's overall budget surplus (including extrabudgetary operations) was an estimated 419,000m. sum (equivalent to 1.5% of GDP). At the end of 2006 Uzbekistan's total external debt was US $3,892m., of which $3,322m. was long-term public debt. The annual average rate of inflation declined from 1,568% in 1994 to 26.6% in 2001. According to ADB figures, inflation amounted to 6.8% in 2007. In 2007 some 23,000 people (0.2% of the economically active population) were registered as unemployed, although the actual level was believed to be considerably higher.

In 1992 Uzbekistan became a member of the IMF and the World Bank, also joining the European Bank for Reconstruction and Development (EBRD, see p. 251) as a 'Country of Operations'. In the same year Uzbekistan was admitted to the Economic Co-operation Organization (ECO, see p. 249). Uzbekistan became a member of the ADB in 1995, and in 2003 it joined the Islamic Development Bank (see p. 340). In January 2006 Uzbekistan became a member of the Eurasian Economic Community (EURASEC), a customs union founded in 2000 by the Presidents of Russia, Belarus, Kazakhstan, Kyrgyzstan, and Tajikistan. In November 2008, however, EURASEC officially confirmed that it had been informed of Uzbekistan's decision to suspend its membership of the organization. Uzbekistan is pursuing membership of the World Trade Organization (WTO, see p. 410).

Following the collapse of the USSR in 1991, GDP declined sharply and inflation increased rapidly. In April 2004 the EBRD announced that it was to limit its activities in Uzbekistan, owing to the Government's failure to implement reform; in July 2005, following the violence in the city of Andijon in May, the EBRD announced that it would not participate in any further public sector projects in Uzbekistan. Meanwhile, in 2004 the Russian state-controlled natural gas company Gazprom and the Uzbekistani company Uzbekneftgazkurilish agreed a 15-year production-sharing agreement at the Shakhpakhty gas and condensate field in Uzbekistan, where annual production was expected to reach 500m. cu m by 2010. In December 2004 a consortium of three companies from Iran, Ukraine and the United Kingdom won a tender to increase liquefied gas production at Uzbekneftgazkurilish's Shurtan gas complex; this, together with other planned projects, was expected to increase annual output of liquefied gas to 615,000 metric tons by 2010, compared with 119,000 tons in 2002. In January 2006 Uzbekistan signed a production-sharing agreement with Gazprom for three further natural gas fields, and an agreement was also signed on joint exploration of the region for further resources. In January 2009, moreover, it was announced that the Russian energy company LUKoil was to invest some US $5,000m. in Uzbekistan's gas sector over the following seven years. Output of natural gas increased by 5.6% in 2007. In early 2008 the Government introduced tax reforms, in particular the lowering of the unified tax rate for micro- and small-business and the lowering of the corporate income tax rate for banks. However, progress in the planned privatization of large enterprises continued to be limited. According to the ADB, GDP growth slowed in 2008, largely owing to a relatively subdued expansion in the services sector compared with the previous year. None the less, overall GDP growth remained high, driven by significantly increased export receipts resulting from high international fuel prices. Exports grew by some 25% in that year, while trade restrictions contributed to lower growth in imports, of just 15%. Remittances from nationals living in Russia provided an estimated 13% of GDP in 2008. However, in late 2008, in light of the global economic downturn, many Uzbekistani migrant workers were reportedly returning home, having lost their jobs. A budget surplus equivalent to an estimated 2.0% of GDP in 2008 was attributed mainly to high commodity and fuel prices. The ADB forecast more moderate GDP growth of 7.0% in 2009, as recessionary conditions in Uzbekistan's main trading partners weakened demand for the country's exports.

Education

Primary education, beginning at seven years of age, lasts for four years. Secondary education, beginning at 11 years of age, lasts for seven years, comprising a first cycle of five years and a second cycle of two years. In 2006/07, according to UNESCO, gross enrolment at primary schools was equivalent to 95.5% of children in the relevant age-group. In 2002 the comparable ratio for secondary education was 97% of males and 94% of females. In 2004 some 6.2m. pupils were enrolled in general secondary

UZBEKISTAN

schools. Higher education was provided in 63 institutes in that year, with a total enrolment of 263,600 students. Legislation adopted in May 1993 banned private educational establishments in Uzbekistan. In 1999 the Tashkent Islamic University was established by presidential decree. The 2006 budget allocated some 1,285,078.5m. sum to education (29.8% of total budgetary expenditure).

Public Holidays

2009: 1 January (New Year's Day), 8 March (International Women's Day), 21 March (Navruz Bairam, Spring Holiday), 9 May (Victory Day), 1 September (Independence Day), 20 September* (Ruza Hayit, Id al-Fitr or end of Ramadan), 1 October (Teachers' and Instructors' Day), 27 November* (Kurban Hayit, Id al-Adha or Feast of the Sacrifice), 8 December (Constitution Day).

2010: 1 January (New Year's Day), 8 March (International Women's Day), 21 March (Navruz Bairam, Spring Holiday), 9 May (Victory Day), 1 September (Independence Day), 10 September* (Ruza Hayit, Id al-Fitr or end of Ramadan), 1 October (Teachers' and Instructors' Day), 16 November* (Kurban Hayit, Id al-Adha or Feast of the Sacrifice), 8 December (Constitution Day).

* These holidays are dependent on the Islamic lunar calendar and may vary by one or two days from the dates given.

Weights and Measures

The metric system is in force.

Statistical Survey

Area and Population

AREA, POPULATION AND DENSITY

Area (sq km)	447,400*
Population (census results)†	
17 January 1979	15,389,307
12 January 1989	
Males	9,784,156
Females	10,025,921
Total	19,810,077
Population (UN estimates at mid-year)‡	
2006	26,611,000
2007	26,900,000
2008	27,191,000
Density (per sq km) at mid-2008	60.8

* 172,740 sq miles.
† Figures refer to *de jure* population. The *de facto* total at the 1989 census was 19,905,158.
‡ Source: UN, *World Population Prospects: The 2008 Revision*.

POPULATION BY ETHNIC GROUP
(1996, rounded estimates)

	%
Uzbek	80.0
Russian	5.5
Tajik	5.0
Kazakh	3.0
Kara-Kalpak	2.5
Tatar	1.5
Others	2.5
Total	**100.0**

Source: Ministry of Health, Tashkent.

ADMINISTRATIVE DIVISIONS
(1996, rounded figures, official estimates)

	Area (sq km)	Population	Density (per sq km)	Capital city (with population)
Sovereign Republic:				
Qoraqalpog'iston	165,600	1,400,000	8.5	Nukus (236,700)
Viloyats				
Andijon	4,200	1,899,000	452.1	Andijon (303,000)
Buxoro	39,400	1,384,700	35.2	Buxoro (263,400)
Farg'ona	6,800	2,597,000	381.9	Farg'ona (214,000)
Jizzax	20,500	910,500	44.4	Jizzax (127,200)
Namangan	7,900	1,862,000	235.7	Namangan (341,000)
Navoiy	110,800	767,500	6.9	Navoiy (128,000)
Qashqadaryo	28,400	2,029,000	71.4	Qarshi (177,000)
Samarqand	16,400	2,322,000	141.6	Samarqand (366,000)
Sirdaryo	5,100	648,100	127.1	Guliston (54,000)
Surxondaryo	20,800	1,676,000	80.6	Termiz (95,000)
Tashkent*	15,300	4,450,000	290.9	Tashkent (2,100,000)
Xorazm	6,300	1,200,000	190.5	Urgench (135,000)
Total	**447,400**	**23,145,800**	**51.7**	

* Including Tashkent City, which subsequently assumed a separate administrative status.

Source: Government of Uzbekistan.

PRINCIPAL TOWNS
(estimated population at 1 January 2001)

Toshkent (Tashkent, the capital)	2,137,218	Farg'ona	183,037
Namangan	391,297	Margilan	149,646
Samarqand	361,339	Chirchik	141,742
Andijon	338,366	Urgench	138,609
Buxoro	237,361	Navoiy	138,082
Nukus	212,012	Jizzax	131,512
Qarshi	204,690	Termiz	116,467
Qoqand	197,450	Olmaliq	113,114

Source: UN, *Demographic Yearbook*.

Mid-2007 ('000, incl. suburbs, UN estimate): Toshkent (Tashkent) 2,184 (Source: UN, *World Urbanization Prospects: The 2007 Revision*).

UZBEKISTAN

BIRTHS, MARRIAGES AND DEATHS

	Registered live births Number	Rate (per 1,000)	Registered marriages Number	Rate (per 1,000)	Registered deaths Number	Rate (per 1,000)
1994	657,725	29.5	176,287	7.9	148,423	6.7
1995	677,999	29.9	170,828	7.5	145,439	6.4
1996	634,842	27.4	171,662	7.4	144,829	6.3
1997	602,694	25.6	181,126	7.7	137,331	5.8
1999*	553,745	23.1	170,525	7.1	140,526	5.9
2000	527,580	21.4	168,908	6.9	135,598	5.5
2001	512,950	20.5	170,101	6.8	132,542	5.3

* Figures for 1998 are not available.

Source: UN, *Demographic Yearbook*.

Registered live births: 553,700 in 1998; 532,500 in 2002; 508,400 in 2003; 540,400 in 2004 (Source: UNDP Country Office and Center for Economic Research, Tashkent, *Uzbekistan in Figures*).

2005: Birth rate 20.9 per 1,000; Death rate 5.0 per 1,000 (Source: Ministry of Health, Tashkent).

Life expectancy (years at birth, WHO estimates): 67.8 (males 65.1; females 70.5) in 2006 (Source: WHO, *World Health Statistics*).

EMPLOYMENT
(annual averages, '000 persons)

	1998	1999	2000
Agriculture*	3,467	3,213	3,083
Industry†	1,114	1,124	1,145
Construction	573	640	676
Transport and communications	362	370	382
Trade and catering‡	717	735	754
Other services	1,976	2,042	2,042
Housing, public utilities and personal services	235	240	246
Health care, social security, physical culture and sports	502	538	567
Education, culture and art	1,073	1,094	1,120
Banking and insurance	50	48	51
General administration	111	122	126
Information and computer services	5	—	—
Total (incl. others)	**8,800**	**8,885**	**8,983**

* Including forestry.
† Comprising manufacturing (except printing and publishing), mining and quarrying, electricity, gas, water, logging and fishing.
‡ Including material and technical supply.

Source: Centre for Economic Research, Tashkent, *Uzbek Economic Trends*.

2001 ('000 persons): Total employed 9,136 (Agriculture 3,062, Industry 1,160, Other 4,914) (Source: Asian Development Bank).

2002 ('000 persons): Total employed 9,333 (Agriculture 3,046, Industry 1,186, Other 5,101) (Source: Asian Development Bank).

2003 ('000 persons): Total employed 9,589 (Agriculture 3,063, Industry 1,223, Other 5,303) (Source: Asian Development Bank).

2004 ('000 persons): Total employed 9,911 (Agriculture 3,068, Industry 1,284, Other 5,559) (Source: Asian Development Bank).

2005 ('000 persons): Total employed 10,196 (Agriculture 2,970, Industry 1,348, Other 5,879) (Source: Asian Development Bank).

2006 ('000 persons): Total employed 10,467 (Source: Asian Development Bank).

2007 ('000 persons): Total employed 10,735 (Source: Asian Development Bank).

Unemployed ('000 persons registered): 38 in 2001; 35 in 2002; 32 in 2003; 35 in 2004; 28 in 2005; 26 in 2006; 23 in 2007 (Source: Asian Development Bank).

Statistical Survey

Health and Welfare

KEY INDICATORS

Total fertility rate (children per woman, 2006)	2.6
Under-5 mortality rate (per 1,000 live births, 2006)	44
HIV/AIDS (% of persons aged 15–49, 2007)	0.1
Physicians (per 1,000 head, 2005)	2.7
Hospital beds (per 1,000 head, 2005)	5.2
Health expenditure (2006): US $ per head (PPP)	177
Health expenditure (2006): % of GDP	4.7
Health expenditure (2006): public (% of total)	50.2
Access to water (% of persons, 2006)	88
Access to sanitation (% of persons, 2006)	96
Human Development Index (2006): ranking	119
Human Development Index (2006): value	0.701

For sources and definitions, see explanatory note on p. vi.

Agriculture

PRINCIPAL CROPS
('000 metric tons)

	2005	2006	2007*
Wheat	6,057	5,996	5,900
Rice, paddy	172	220	169
Barley	109	73	110
Maize	164	194	165
Sorghum*	7	4	4
Potatoes	924	1,021	890
Broad beans, horse beans, dry	4†	4*	5
Sunflower seed	10	9	11
Safflower seed	7	3	4
Sesame seed*	18	20	18
Seed cotton*	3,728	3,600	3,300
Cabbages and other brassicas	287	369	276
Tomatoes	1,317	1,584	1,327
Cucumbers and gherkins	200	259	195
Onions, dry	546	591	536
Garlic	32	38	30
Carrots and turnips	506	745	366
Watermelons	615	744	599
Apples	402†	514	447
Pears	36†	54	35
Apricots	170†	236	155
Sweet cherries	17†	54	53
Peaches and nectarines	56†	67	53
Plums and sloes	64†	57	60
Grapes	642	804	590
Tobacco, unmanufactured*	20	20	19
Jute*	20	20	20

* FAO estimate(s).
† Unofficial figure.

Aggregate production ('000 metric tons, may include official, semi-official or estimated data): Total cereals 6,531 in 2005, 6,511 in 2006, 6,372 in 2007; Total roots and tubers 924 in 2005, 1,021 in 2006, 890 in 2007; Total vegetables (incl. melons) 4,133 in 2005, 5,001 in 2006, 4,068 in 2007; Total fruits (excl. melons) 1,596 in 2005, 1,988 in 2006, 1,539 in 2007.

Source: FAO.

LIVESTOCK
('000 head at 1 January)

	2005	2006	2007
Horses	158	162	162*
Cattle	6,571	7,045	7,043
Camels	17	17	17*
Pigs	87	93	92
Sheep	9,555	10,034	10,450*
Goats	1,797	1,973	1,974
Chickens	20,540	24,188	24,220
Turkeys*	350	350	360

* FAO estimate(s).

Source: FAO.

UZBEKISTAN

LIVESTOCK PRODUCTS
('000 metric tons)

	2005	2006	2007*
Cattle meat	518.1	551.6	586.3
Sheep meat	73.6	83.6	88.9
Pig meat	16.0	18.1	19.2
Chicken meat	21.3	23.4	24.9
Cows' milk	4,447.2	4,821.4	5,121.0
Sheep's milk*	450.0	500.0	500.0
Goats' milk	107.5	34.2	36.3
Hen eggs	107.8†	116.5*	37.5
Other poultry eggs	3.2	3.1	3.2
Honey	2.1	2.0	2.2
Wool, greasy	20.1	21.4	22.6

* FAO estimate(s).
† Unofficial figure.

Source: FAO.

Fishing

(metric tons, live weight)

	2004	2005*	2006
Capture	1,230	2,000	3,400
Common carp	238	550	1,140
Crucian carp	191	190	188
Roach	234	230	223
Silver carp	106	140	180
Aquaculture	3,093	3,800	3,800
Common carp	574	700	266
Crucian carp	145	200	19
Grass carp (White amur)	249	300	190
Silver carp	1,189	2,400	3,268
Bighead carp	936	200	57
Total catch	4,323	5,800	7,200

* FAO estimates.

Source: FAO.

Mining

(metric tons, unless otherwise indicated)

	2003	2004	2005
Coal ('000 metric tons)*	1,913	2,699	3,033
Crude petroleum ('000 metric tons)†	7,169	6,617	5,449
Natural gas ('000 million cu metres)	58	59	60
Copper ore‡§	80,000	95,000	100,000
Molybdenum ore‡§	500	500	500
Silver ore (kilograms)‡§	80,000	80,000	83,000
Gold (kilograms)‡§	90,000	93,000	90,000
Kaolin ('000 metic tons)§	5,500	5,500	5,500
Feldspar§	4,300	4,300	4,300
Uranium ore (metric tons)‡	1,874	2,377	2,712

* Including lignite and brown coal.
† Including gas condensate.
‡ Figures refer to the metal content of ores.
§ Estimated production.

2006 ('000 metric tons): Crude petroleum 5,384.

2007 ('000 metric tons): Crude petroleum 4,937.

Sources: Asian Development Bank and US Geological Survey.

Industry

SELECTED PRODUCTS
('000 metric tons, unless otherwise indicated)

	1998	1999	2000
Beer ('000 hectolitres)	569	422	609
Cigarettes (million)	7,582	10,668	7,766
Wool yarn (pure and mixed)	2	3	3
Cotton yarn (pure and mixed)	105	105	135
Woven cotton fabrics (million sq m)	314	333	360
Sulphuric acid	856	897	823
Nitrogenous fertilizers (a)*	755	707	717
Phosphate fertilizers (b)*	141	169	117
Motor spirit (petrol)	1,603	1,638	1,709
Gas-diesel (distillate fuel) oils	2,227	2,220	1,900
Residual fuel oils	1,977	1,750	1,700
Lubricating oils	229	223	238
Cement	3,331	3,284	3,722
Domestic refrigerators ('000)	16	2	1
Domestic washing machines ('000)	5	—	—
Television receivers ('000)	192	50	26
Electric energy (million kWh)†	54,790	55,581	56,401

* Production in terms of (a) nitrogen; (b) phosphoric acid.
† Source: Asian Development Bank, *Key Indicators of Developing Asian and Pacific Countries*.

Source (unless otherwise indicated): UN, *Industrial Commodity Statistics Yearbook*.

2001: Cement ('000 metric tons) 3,722; Electric energy (million kWh) 47,961 (Source: Asian Development Bank).

2002: Cement ('000 metric tons) 3,927; Electric energy (million kWh) 49,398 (Source: Asian Development Bank).

2003: Cement ('000 metric tons) 4,062 (Source: Asian Development Bank).

2004: Cement ('000 metric tons) 4,805 (Source: Asian Development Bank).

2005: Cement ('000 metric tons) 5,058; Electric energy (million kWh) 47,706 (Source: Asian Development Bank).

2006: Cement ('000 metric tons) 5,583; Electric energy (million kWh) 49,300 (Source: Asian Development Bank).

2007: Cement ('000 metric tons) 6,043; Electric energy (million kWh) 48,950 (Source: Asian Development Bank).

Finance

CURRENCY AND EXCHANGE RATES

Monetary Units
100 teen = 1 sum.

Sterling, Dollar and Euro Equivalents (28 November 2008)
£1 sterling = 2,036.6 sum;
US $1 = 1,328 sum;
€1 = 1,690.1 sum;
10,000 sum = £4.91 = $7.53 = €5.92.

Average Exchange Rate (sum per US $)
2000 236.61
2001 423.31
2002 769.50

Note: Prior to the introduction of the sum (see below), Uzbekistan used a transitional currency, the sum-coupon. This had been introduced in November 1993 to circulate alongside (and initially at par with) the Russian (formerly Soviet) rouble. Following the dissolution of the USSR in December 1991, Russia and several other former Soviet republics retained the rouble as their monetary unit. The Russian rouble ceased to be legal tender in Uzbekistan from 15 April 1994.

On 1 July 1994 a permanent currency, the sum, was introduced to replace the sum-coupon at 1 sum per 1,000 coupons. The initial exchange rate was set at US $1 = 7.00 sum. Sum-coupons continued to circulate, but from 15 October 1994 the sum became the sole legal tender. On 15 October 2003 the sum became fully convertible.

UZBEKISTAN

Statistical Survey

CONSOLIDATED BUDGET
('000 million sum)

Revenue	2006	2007*	2008†
Tax revenue	4,365	5,870	6,791
Taxes on incomes and profits	1,293	1,758	2,002
Taxes on property	276	349	438
Taxes on goods and services	2,623	3,470	4,104
VAT	1,142	1,682	2,001
Excises	881	1,017	1,170
Customs duties	173	293	248
Other budget revenue	333	522	317
Social security contributions	1,253	1,761	2,650
Road fund and other extra-budgetary revenue	273	355	412
Education development tax	233	365	431
Grants	62	50	30
Total	6,519	8,922	10,632

Expenditure‡	2006	2007*	2008†
Socio-cultural expenditure	2,169	2,906	3,910
Social safety net	1,735	2,283	3,400
Low income support	366	397	620
Pension and employment fund	1,369	1,886	2,780
Pension fund	1,335	1,841	2,726
Employment fund	35	45	54
Economy	594	678	915
Public authorities and administration	124	176	243
Public investment	532	627	847
Interest expenditure	74	172	103
Other expenditure in the budget	879	1,138	1,078
Road fund	204	270	349
Extra-budgetary expenditure financed by grants	62	50	30
Statistical discrepancy	—	155	—
Total	6,374	8,455	10,875

* Preliminary.
† Projected.
‡ Excluding net lending ('000 million): 40 in 2006; 48 in 2007 (preliminary); –90 in 2008 (projected).

Source: IMF, *Republic of Uzbekistan: 2008 Article IV Consultation-Staff Report; Public Information Notice on the Executive Board Discussion; and Statement by the Executive Director for the Republic of Uzbekistan* (July 2008).

INTERNATIONAL RESERVES
(US $ million at 31 December)

	2002	2003	2004
Gold (national valuation)	505.8	558.0	418.5
IMF special drawing rights	1.1	0.1	0.0
Foreign exchange	709.8	1,101.2	1,728.0
Total	1,215.0	1,659.3	2,146.5

Total reserves (US $ million at 31 December): 2,895.0 in 2005; 4,604.0 in 2006.

Source: Asian Development Bank, *Key Indicators of Developing Asian and Pacific Countries*.

MONEY SUPPLY
(million sum at 31 December)

	2002	2003	2004
Currency outside banks	273,347	404,928	590,199
Demand deposits at deposit money banks	194,839	170,036	214,596
Total money	468,186	574,964	804,795

Source: Asian Development Bank, *Key Indicators of Developing Asian and Pacific Countries*.

COST OF LIVING
(Consumer Price Index; base: previous year = 100)

	2005	2006	2007
Food	106.7	103.9	103.3
Other goods	106.9	108.0	108.4
All items	107.8	106.8	106.8

Source: Asian Development Bank.

NATIONAL ACCOUNTS
('000 million sum at current prices)

Expenditure on the Gross Domestic Product

	2003	2004	2005
Final consumption expenditure	7,192.2	8,387.3	10,231.7
Households			
Non-profit institutions serving households	5,474.8	6,305.8	7,736.3
General government	1,717.4	2,081.5	2,495.4
Gross capital formation	2,042.8	2,913.1	3,499.5
Gross fixed capital formation	2,069.1	2,694.5	3,518.4
Acquisitions, less disposals, of valuables	−26.3	218.6	−18.9
Changes in inventories			
Total domestic expenditure	9,235.0	11,300.4	13,731.2
Exports of goods and services (net)	602.9	889.0	1,479.3
GDP in market prices	9,837.8	12,189.5	15,210.4

Gross Domestic Product by Economic Activity

	2005	2006	2007
Agriculture and forestry	3,802.6	5,003.0	6,116.4
Mining and quarrying			
Manufacturing	3,148.6	4,587.8	6,764.7
Electricity, gas and water			
Construction	745.3	1,058.7	1,550.2
Trade	1,399.4	1,972.1	2,649.5
Transport and communications	1,718.8	2,366.6	3,128.7
Finance			
Public administration	2,722.7	3,861.2	5,299.0
Other services			
GDP at factor cost	13,537.4	18,849.4	25,508.5
Indirect taxes	1,673.1	1,909.9	2,677.7
Less Subsidies			
GDP in purchasers' values	15,210.4	20,759.3	28,186.2

Source: Asian Development Bank.

UZBEKISTAN

BALANCE OF PAYMENTS
(US $ million)

	2005	2006	2007*
Exports of goods f.o.b.	4,757	5,615	8,026
Imports of goods f.o.b.	−3,310	−3,841	−5,730
Trade balance	1,446	1,774	2,296
Export of services	659	775	965
Import of services	−790	−828	−1,007
Balance on goods and services	1,315	1,721	2,254
Income (net)	−24	41	62
Current transfers (net)	658	1,171	1,951
Current balance	1,949	2,933	4,267
Capital account (net)	31	−116	−104
Foreign direct and portfolio investment (net)	88	195	739
Existing public and publicly-guaranteed debt (net)	−241	−347	−213
Commercial non-guaranteed debt (net)	34	43	273
Foreign assets of commercial banks (net)	—	−290	−433
Other capital and statistical discrepancy	−1,093	−854	−2,430
Adjustment	—	—	56
Overall balance	768	1,564	2,155

*Preliminary.

Source: IMF, *Republic of Uzbekistan: 2008 Article IV Consultation-Staff Report; Public Information Notice on the Executive Board Discussion; and Statement by the Executive Director for the Republic of Uzbekistan* (July 2008).

External Trade

PRINCIPAL COMMODITIES
(US $ million)

Imports f.o.b.	1998	1999	2000
Chemicals and plastics	407.2	363.0	399.5
Metals	303.6	245.4	253.5
Machinery and equipment	1,553.7	1,393.5	1,044.1
Food products	512.2	408.1	361.1
Energy products	16.3	66.6	112.7
Total (incl. others)	3,288.7	3,110.7	2,696.4

Exports f.o.b.	1998	1999	2000
Cotton fibre	1,361.0	883.7	897.1
Chemicals and plastics	51.7	101.8	93.4
Metals	180.7	138.9	216.7
Machinery and equipment	146.6	103.2	111.8
Food products	111.9	206.7	176.4
Energy products	277.8	371.5	335.2
Total (incl. others)	3,528.2	3,235.8	3,264.7

Source: Center for Economic Research, Tashkent, *Uzbek Economic Trends*.

PRINCIPAL TRADING PARTNERS
(US $ million)

Imports	2005	2006	2007
China, People's Republic	253.2	446.7	790.9
Germany	313.4	306.5	395.9
Italy	68.2	44.8	74.1
Kazakhstan	253.5	313.3	373.9
Korea, Republic	542.4	652.0	778.2
Russia	946.6	1,194.9	1,475.3
Tajikistan	73.2	74.2	88.5
Turkey	166.2	193.6	247.6
Ukraine	165.7	204.8	244.4
USA	80.9	59.3	97.6
Total (incl. others)	3,551.6	4,290.9	5,678.5

Exports	2005	2006	2007
Bangladesh	163.1	214.6	256.1
China, People's Republic	410.0	514.4	333.5
Hungary	17.0	140.6	358.6
Japan	113.0	161.7	131.7
Kazakhstan	236.4	292.2	348.8
Poland	243.3	575.6	633.9
Russia	820.0	1,172.4	1,445.8
Tajikistan	139.0	160.3	191.4
Turkey	235.9	377.9	558.0
Ukraine	186.7	230.7	275.3
Total (incl. others)	3,467.5	4,944.3	5,912.5

Note: Data reflect the IMF's direction of trade methodology and, as a result, the totals may not be equal to those presented for trade in commodities.

Source: Asian Development Bank.

Transport

RAILWAYS
(traffic)

	2002	2003	2004
Passenger-km (million)	2	2	2
Freight ton-km (million)	18	19	18

Source: UN, *Statistical Yearbook*.

CIVIL AVIATION
(estimated traffic on scheduled services)

	2002	2003	2004
Kilometres flown (million)	39	40	44
Passengers carried ('000)	1,451	1,466	1,588
Passenger-km (million)	3,835	3,889	4,454
Total ton-km (million)	417	424	486

Source: UN, *Statistical Yearbook*.

Tourism

FOREIGN VISITOR ARRIVALS
('000, incl. excursionists)

Region of origin	2002	2003	2004
Africa	1.0	1.0	1.0
Americas	4.1	2.0	12.0
East Asia and the Pacific	195.1	145.0	140.0
Europe	99.8	51.0	68.6
Middle East	23.5	24.0	30.0
South Asia	8.0	8.0	10.0
Total	331.5	231.0	261.6

Tourism receipts (US $ million, excl. passenger transport): 28 in 2004; 28 in 2005; 43 in 2006.

Source: World Tourism Organization.

Communications Media

	2003	2004	2005
Telephones ('000 main lines in use)	1,717.1	1,750.4	1,793.5
Mobile cellular telephones ('000 subscribers)	320.8	544.1	720.0
Internet users ('000)	492.0	675.0	880.0
Broadband subscribers ('000)	2.8	5.5	8.3

Source: International Telecommunication Union.

2006: Mobile cellular telephones ('000 subscribers) 2,500.0; Internet users ('000) 1,100.0 (Source: International Telecommunication Union).

2007: Internet users ('000) 1,200.0 (Source: International Telecommunication Union).

Book production: 1,003 titles and 30,914,000 copies in 1996 (Source: UNESCO, *Statistical Yearbook*).

Daily newspapers: 3 titles and 75,000 copies (average circulation) in 1996; 5 titles in 2004 (Sources: UNESCO, *Statistical Yearbook*; UNESCO Institute for Statistics).

Non-daily newspapers: 350 titles and 1,404,000 copies (average circulation) in 1996 (Source: UNESCO, *Statistical Yearbook*).

Other periodicals: 81 titles and 684,000 copies (average circulation) in 1996 (Source: UNESCO, *Statistical Yearbook*).

Radio receivers ('000 in use): 10,800 in 1997 (Source: UNESCO, *Statistical Yearbook*).

Television receivers ('000 in use): 7,000 in 2001 (Source: International Telecommunication Union).

Facsimile machines (number in use): 3,325 in 2001 (Source: International Telecommunication Union).

Education

(2006, unless otherwise indicated)

	Schools	Teachers	Students
Pre-primary	6,413	96,100*	562,200
Primary			1,905,693*
Secondary:	9,816†	463,100	
general			5,715,100
teacher training	n.a.	2,464‡	35,411‡
vocational	1,052	7,900*	214,500*
Higher	63§	18,400*	263,600§
Universities	20*	n.a.	131,100*

* 1994/95.
† Including 20 evening schools.
‡ 1993.
§ 2004.

Sources: UNESCO, *Statistical Yearbook* and Center for Economic Research, Tashkent.

Adult literacy rate (UNESCO estimates): 99.3% (males 99.6%; females 98.9%) in 2002 (Source: UN Development Programme, *Human Development Report*).

Directory

The Constitution

A new Constitution was adopted by the Supreme Council on 8 December 1992. It declares Uzbekistan to be a secular, democratic and presidential republic. Basic human rights are guaranteed. The principal features of the Constitution, as subsequently revised, are as follows:

THE OLY MAJLIS

The highest legislative body is the Oly Majlis (Supreme Assembly). The Oly Majlis comprises two chambers: the Qoqunchilik palatasi Kengashi (Legislative Chamber); and the Senat (Senate). The 120 deputies of the Qoqunchilik palatasi Kengashi are elected for a term of five years. Of the 100 members of the Senat, 84 members are indirectly elected by regional Council members, and 16 are appointed by the President of the Republic. The Oly Majlis may be dissolved by the President, with the agreement of the Constitutional Court. The Oly Majlis enacts legislation and constitutional legislation, and elects its own officials, the judges of the higher courts and the Chairman of the State Committee for Environmental Protection. It confirms the President's appointments to ministerial office, the procuracy-general and the governorship of the Central Bank. It must ratify international treaties, changes to borders and presidential decrees on emergency situations. Legislation may be initiated by the deputies, by the President, by the higher courts, by the Procurator-General and by the Autonomous Republic of Qoraqalpog'iston.

PRESIDENT OF THE REPUBLIC

The President of the Republic, who is directly elected by the people for a seven-year term, is Head of State and holds supreme executive power. (The term of office was extended, with immediate effect, from five to seven years in April 2002.) An individual may be elected President for a maximum of two consecutive terms*. The President is required to form and supervise the Cabinet of Ministers, appointing the Prime Minister and Ministers, subject to confirmation by the Oly Majlis. The President also nominates the candidates for appointment to the higher courts and certain offices of state, subject to confirmation by the Oly Majlis. The President appoints the judges of the lower courts and the hokims (governors) of the regions. Legislation may be initiated, reviewed and returned to the Oly Majlis by the President, who must promulgate all laws. The President may dissolve the Oly Majlis. The President is also Commander-in-Chief of the Armed Forces and may declare a state of emergency or a state of war, subject to confirmation by the Oly Majlis within three days.

* Despite this constitutional restriction, ISLAM KARIMOV was elected to a third consecutive term of office in December 2007, his second term having formally ended in January of that year.

THE CABINET OF MINISTERS

The Cabinet of Ministers is the Government of the republic; it is subordinate to the President, who appoints its Prime Minister, Deputy Prime Ministers and Ministers, subject to the approval of the legislature. Local government is carried out by elected councils and appointed hokims, the latter having significant personal authority and responsibility.

JUDICATURE

The exercise of judicial power is independent of government. The higher courts, of which the judges are nominated by the President and confirmed by the Oly Majlis, consist of the Constitutional Court, the Supreme Court and the High Economic Court. There is also a Supreme Court of the Sovereign Republic of Qoraqalpog'iston. Lower courts, including economic courts, are based in the regions, districts and towns. The Procurator-General's office is responsible for supervising the observance of the law.

The Government

HEAD OF STATE

President of the Republic: ISLAM A. KARIMOV (elected by Supreme Soviet 24 March 1990; term of office extended by popular referendum 26 March 1995; re-elected 9 January 2000 and 23 December 2007; inaugurated 16 January 2008).

CABINET OF MINISTERS
(April 2009)

Prime Minister: SHAVKAT M. MIRZIYOYEV.

First Deputy Prime Minister, responsible for the Economic Sector and Foreign Economic Relations, and Minister of Finance: RUSTAM S. AZIMOV.

UZBEKISTAN

Deputy Prime Minister, responsible for Communal Services, Transport, Capital Works and Construction: Nodirxon M. Xanov.

Deputy Prime Minister, responsible for Geology, the Fuel-Energy Complex, and the Chemical and Petroleum Industries and Metallurgy: Ergash R. Shoismatov.

Deputy Prime Minister, responsible for the Development of Machine-construction, Electrical Technology, the Aviation Industry and Standardization of Production, Chairman of the Board of O'zavtosanoat Company: Ulugbek U. Rozukulov.

Deputy Prime Minister, responsible for Information Systems and Telecommunications, Director-General of the Communications and Information Agency of Uzbekistan: Abdulla N. Aripov.

Deputy Prime Minister, responsible for Education, Health and Social Welfare: Rustam S. Qosimov.

Deputy Prime Minister, Chairman of the Committee of Women of Uzbekistan: Farida Sh. Akbarova.

Minister of the Economy: Batir A. Xodjayev.

Minister of Foreign Economic Relations, Investment and Trade: Elyor M. G'aniyev.

Minister of Labour and Social Protection: Aktam A. Xaitov (acting).

Minister of Culture and Sports: Rustam J. Qurbonov.

Minister of Internal Affairs: Bahodir A. Matlyubov.

Minister of Foreign Affairs: Vladimir I. Norov.

Minister of Defence: Qobul R. Berdiyev.

Minister of National Education: G'ayrat B. Shoumarov.

Minister of Higher and Secondary Specialized Education: Azimjon P. Parpiev.

Minister of Agriculture and Water Resources: Sayfiddin U. Ismoilov.

Minister of Justice: Ravshan A. Muxitdinov.

Minister of Health: Feruz G. Nazirov.

Minister of Emergency Situations: Bakhtiyor Subanov.

Note: The Constitution provides for the Chairman of the Council of Ministers of the Republic of Qoraqalpog'iston to serve as an ex officio member of the Council of Ministers of the Republic of Uzbekistan. Since March 2006 this position has been held by Baxodir Yangiboyev. The following are also members of the Council of Ministers: the Chairman of the Central Bank and chairmen of state committees and agencies.

MINISTRIES

Office of the President: 100163 Tashkent, O'zbekiston shoh ko'ch. 43; tel. (71) 239-54-04; fax (71) 239-53-25; e-mail presidents_office@press-service.uz; internet www.press-service.uz.

Office of the Cabinet of Ministers: 100078 Tashkent, Mustaqillik maydoni 5; tel. (71) 239-82-95; fax (71) 239-84-63; internet www.gov.uz.

Ministry of Agriculture and Water Resources: 100004 Tashkent, A. Navoiy ko'ch. 4; tel. (71) 244-21-30; fax (71) 232-21-59; e-mail qshv@intal.uz; internet www.agro.uz.

Ministry of Culture and Sport: 100159 Tashkent, Mustaqillik maydoni 5; tel. (71) 239-46-11; fax (71) 239-45-52; e-mail madaniyat@sport.uz; internet www.madaniyat.sport.uz.

Ministry of Defence: 100000 Tashkent, Ak. Abdullaev ko'ch. 100; tel. (71) 269-82-43; fax (71) 269-82-28.

Ministry of the Economy: 100003 Tashkent, O'zbekiston shoh ko'ch. 45A; tel. (71) 232-63-20; fax (71) 232-63-72; e-mail mineconomy@mmes.gov.uz; internet www.mineconomy.uz.

Ministry for Emergency Situations: 100084 Tashkent, Yunusobodn tumani, Kichik xalka yo'li–4; tel. (71) 239-16-85; fax (71) 239-44-14; e-mail it@mchs.uz; internet www.mchs.uz.

Ministry of Finance: 100008 Tashkent, Mustaqillik maydoni 5; tel. (71) 233-70-73; fax (71) 244-56-43; e-mail info@mf.uz; internet www.mf.uz.

Ministry of Foreign Affairs: 100029 Tashkent, O'zbekiston shoh ko'ch. 9; tel. (71) 233-64-75; fax (71) 239-15-17; e-mail rnews@mfa.uz; internet www.mfa.uz.

Ministry of Foreign Economic Relations, Investment and Trade: 100029 Tashkent, Shevchenko ko'ch. 1; tel. (71) 238-50-00; fax (71) 238-51-00; e-mail secretary@mfer.uz; internet www.mfer.uz.

Ministry of Health: 100011 Tashkent, A. Navoiy ko'ch. 12; tel. (71) 239-48-08; fax (71) 244-10-33; e-mail minzdrav@med.uz; internet www.minzdr.uz.

Ministry of Higher and Specialized Secondary Education: 100095 Tashkent, 2-Chimboy ko'ch. 96; tel. and fax (71) 246-01-95; e-mail mhsse@edu.uz; internet www.edu.uz.

Ministry of Internal Affairs: 100029 Tashkent, Yu. Rajaby ko'ch. 1; tel. and fax (71) 233-38-82; e-mail info@mvd.uz; internet www.mvd.uz.

Ministry of Justice: 100047 Tashkent, Sayilgoh ko'ch. 5; tel. (71) 233-13-05; fax (71) 233-51-76; e-mail info@minjust.gov.uz; internet www.minjust.uz.

Ministry of Labour and Social Security: 100100 Tashkent, A. Avloniy ko'ch. 20A; tel. and fax (71) 239-41-12; e-mail axborot@mintrud.uz; internet www.mintrud.uz.

Ministry of National Education: 100078 Tashkent, Mustaqillik maydoni 5; tel. (71) 239-13-10; fax (71) 239-19-34; e-mail info@uzedu.uz; internet www.uzedu.uz.

President

Presidential Election, 23 December 2007

Candidate	Votes	%
Islam Karimov (Liberal Democratic Party of Uzbekistan)	13,008,357	88.10
Asliddin Rustamov (People's Democratic Party of Uzbekistan)	468,064	3.17
Dilorom Tashmuhamedova (Justice Social Democratic Party of Uzbekistan)	434,111	2.94
Akmal Saidov (Independent)	420,815	2.85
Total*	**14,765,444**	**100.00**

* Including 434,097 invalid votes (2.94% of the total).

Legislature

The Oly Majlis (Supreme Assembly) is a bicameral legislative body, comprising the 100-member upper chamber, the Senat (Senate), and the 120-member lower chamber, the Qoqunchilik palatasi Kengashi (Legislative Chamber).

Qoqunchilik palatasi Kengashi (Legislative Chamber)

100008 Tashkent, Xalqlar Do'stligi shoh ko'ch. 1; tel. (71) 239-87-07; fax (71) 239-41-51; internet www.parliament.gov.uz.

Speaker: Dilorom H. Tashmuhamedova.

General Election, 26 December 2004 and 9 January 2005

Parties, etc.	Seats
Movement of Entrepreneurs and Businessmen—Liberal Democratic Party of Uzbekistan	41
People's Democratic Party of Uzbekistan	28
Self-Sacrificers' National Democratic Party (Fidokorlar)	18
National Revival Democratic Party of Uzbekistan (Milliy Tiklanish)	11
Justice Social Democratic Party of Uzbekistan (Adolat)	10
Citizens' groups	12
Total	**120**

Senat (Senate)

100029 Tashkent, Mustaqillik maydoni 6; tel. (71) 238-26-66; fax (71) 238-29-01; e-mail info@senat.uz; internet www.senat.gov.uz.

Of the 100 members of the chamber, 84 members are indirectly elected by regional Council members and 16 are appointed by the President of the Republic. The first presidential appointees to the Senat were announced on 14 January 2005, while the first indirect elections of senators were held on 17–20 January 2005. The inaugural session of the chamber convened on 27 January.

Speaker: Ilgizar M. Sobirov.

Election Commission

Central Election Commission (O'zbekiston Respublikasi Markaziy Saylov Kommissiyasi): 100000 Tashkent; tel. (71) 239-15-72; fax (71) 239-43-91; internet www.elections.uz; mems approved by the Oly Majlis; Chair. Mirzo-Ulug'bek E. Abdusalomov.

Political Organizations

Following Uzbekistan's independence (achieved in August 1991), the ruling People's Democratic Party of Uzbekistan (PDPU—the successor to the Communist Party of the Uzbek SSR) took increasingly repressive measures against opposition and Islamist parties. A new law on political parties was approved in 1996; among other provisions, the law prohibited the establishment of parties on a religious or ethnic basis and stipulated a minimum membership, per party, of 5,000 people (with stipulation that membership be distributed across the country's regions). From February 2004 the minimum membership requirement was increased to 20,000 people. Since independence a number of opposition elements have been based abroad, particularly in Russia.

Free Peasants' Party (Ozod Dehqonlar partiyasi—Ozod Dehqonlar): 100000 Tashkent; f. 2003; denied registration; Exec. Sec. of Political Council NIGORA HIDOYATOVA; Ideological Leader BABUR MALIKOV (in USA).

Freedom Democratic Party of Uzbekistan (O'zbekiston Erk Demokratik Partiyasi—Erk): 100055 Tashkent, Ipakchi ko'ch. 38; tel. (71) 220-65-30; e-mail erkparty@yahoo.com; f. 1990; banned in 1993; Chair. MUHAMMAD SALIH (based in Norway).

Justice Social Democratic Party of Uzbekistan ('Adolat' Sotsial Demokratik Partiyasi—Adolat): 100047 Tashkent, Musahanov ko'ch. 103; tel. (71) 233-26-75; f. 1995; advocates respect of human rights, improvement of social justice and consolidation of democratic reform; supports President Karimov; First Sec. TURG'UNPO'LAT O. DAMINOV; 50,000 mems (2003).

Liberal Democratic Party of Uzbekistan (O'zbekiston Liberal Demokratik Partiyasi—O'zlidep): 100015 Tashkent, Mirobod tumani, Nukus ko'ch. 73A; tel. (71) 252-16-04; fax (71) 252-52-84; e-mail info@uzlidep.uz; internet www.uzlidep.uz; f. 2003; supports President Karimov; Chair. MUXAMMADYUSUF M. TESHABAEV; 142,000 members (Dec. 2004).

National Revival Democratic Party of Uzbekistan (O'zbekiston Milliy Tiklanish Demokratik Partiyasi—Milliy Tiklanish): 100000 Tashkent, Navoiy ko'ch. 30; tel. (71) 244-81-28; f. 1995; supports President Karimov; merged with Self-Sacrificers' National Democratic Party 2008; Leader AXTAM S. TURSUNOV.

People's Democratic Party of Uzbekistan (O'zbekiston Xalq demokratik partiyasi): 100029 Tashkent, Mustaqillik maydoni 5/1; tel. (71) 239-83-11; fax (71) 233-59-34; f. 1991; successor of Communist Party of the Uzbek SSR; Leader ASLIDDIN A. RUSTAMOV; c. 580,000 mems (2003).

Unity People's Movement Party ('Birlik' Xalq Harakati Partiyasi—Birlik): c/o Union of Writers of Uzbekistan, 100000 Tashkent, Neru ko'ch. 1; tel. (71) 233-63-74; e-mail webmaster@birlik.net; internet www.birlik.net; f. 1988; leading opposition group, banned in 1992; registered as a social movement; refused registration as a political party 2004; Chair. Prof. ABDURAKHIM PULAT; Sec.-Gen. VASILA INOYATOVA.

The militant Islamist group **Islamic Movement of Uzbekistan (IMU)** was founded in 1999. It was banned by the Uzbek Government in 1999 and its leaders sentenced to death *in absentia* in 2000. The IMU's activities were believed to have been seriously curtailed after the death of one its leaders during the US-led military campaign in Afghanistan that commenced in late 2001. The transnational militant Islamist **Hizb-ut-Tahrir al-Islami (Party of Islamic Liberation)** was believed to operate in Uzbekistan. As in neighbouring states, the organization was proscribed in Uzbekistan. A related organization, **Akramiya**, also banned, was founded in 1996 by AKRAM YULDOSHEV, who received a 17-year sentence of imprisonment in 1999 for involvement in terrorist activity.

Diplomatic Representation

EMBASSIES IN UZBEKISTAN

Afghanistan: 100000 Tashkent, Kichik Beshyog ko'ch. 79; tel. (71) 134-84-32; fax (71) 234-84-65; e-mail afgemuz@mail.tps.uz; Chargé d'affaires a.i. MESBAH MOHAMMED ESSA.

Algeria: 100000 Tashkent, Beshog'aynilar ko'ch. 46; tel. (71) 235-52-99; fax (71) 235-21-99; Ambassador BERRAH MOHAMED.

Azerbaijan: 100000 Tashkent, Sharq Tongi ko'ch. 25; tel. (71) 273-61-67; fax (71) 273-26-58; e-mail sefir@tsk.sarkor.uz; Ambassador NAMIQ ABBASOV.

Bangladesh: 100000 Tashkent, Vasit Vaxidov ko'ch. 33; tel. (71) 281-43-21; fax (71) 150-21-18; e-mail bdoot.tas@online.ru; Ambassador HASIB MOHAMMED AZIZ.

Belarus: 100047 Tashkent, Ya. G'ulomov ko'ch. 75; tel. (71) 120-75-11; fax (71) 120-72-53; e-mail uzbekistan@belembassy.org; internet www.uzbekistan.belembassy.org; Ambassador IGOR S. SOKOL.

Bulgaria: 100000 Tashkent, Rakatboshi ko'ch. 52; tel. (71) 258-48-88; fax (71) 252-39-52; e-mail misiyabg@bcc.com.uz; internet www.mfa.bg/tashkent; Chargé d'affaires a.i. ILKO D. SLAVCHEV.

China, People's Republic: 100047 Tashkent, Ya. G'ulomov ko'ch. 79; tel. (71) 233-80-88; fax (71) 233-47-35; e-mail chinaemb@bcc.com.uz; internet uz.china-embassy.org; Ambassador YU HONGJUN.

Czech Republic: 100041 Tashkent, Navnixol ko'ch. 6; tel. (71) 120-74-95; fax (71) 120-60-75; e-mail tashkent@embassy.mzv.cz; internet www.mzv.cz/tashkent; Ambassador ROBERT KOPECKÝ.

Egypt: 100115 Tashkent, Chilonzor ko'ch. 53A; tel. (71) 120-50-08; fax (71) 120-64-52; Ambassador NADIA IBRAHIM KFAFI.

France: 100041 Tashkent, Oxunboboev ko'ch. 25; tel. (71) 233-53-82; fax (71) 233-51-97; e-mail presse@ambafrance-uz.org; internet www.ambafrance-uz.org; Ambassador HUGUES PERNET.

Georgia: 100170 Tashkent, Polkovnik A. Muxitdinov ko'ch. 6; tel. (71) 262-62-43; fax (71) 262-91-39; e-mail gruzemb@geo-embassy.co.uz; Ambassador GIORGI KUBLASHVILI.

Germany: 100017 Tashkent, Sh. Rashidov ko'ch. 15, POB 4337; tel. (71) 120-84-40; fax (71) 120-66-93; e-mail info@taschkent.diplo.de; internet www.taschkent.diplo.de; Ambassador MATTHIAS MEYER.

Holy See: 100000 Tashkent, Rakatboshi ko'ch. 52; tel. and fax (71) 233-70-25; Apostolic Nuncio ANTONIO MENNINI (Titular Archbishop of Ferentium) (resident in Moscow, Russia).

India: 100000 Tashkent, Qarabuloq ko'ch. 15–16; tel. (71) 140-09-83; fax (71) 140-09-99; e-mail indhoc@buzton.com; internet www.indembassy.uz; Ambassador SYED MANAL SHAH AL QUADRI.

Indonesia: 100000 Tashkent, Ya. G'ulomov ko'ch. 73; tel. (71) 232-02-36; fax (71) 220-65-40; e-mail tashkent@indonesia.embassy.uz; internet www.indonesia.embassy.uz; Ambassador SJAHRIL SABARUDIN.

Iran: 100007 Tashkent, Parkent ko'ch. 20; tel. (71) 268-69-68; fax (71) 220-67-61; e-mail iriemuz@hotmail.com; Ambassador MOHAMMAD GHOLAMALI KESHAVARZZADEH.

Israel: 100000 Tashkent, A. Qaxxor ko'ch. 3; tel. (71) 120-58-09; fax (71) 120-58-12; e-mail info@tashkent.mfa.gov.il; internet tashkent.mfa.gov.il; Ambassador HILLEL NEUMAN.

Italy: 100031 Tashkent, Yusuf Xos Xojib ko'ch. 40; tel. (71) 252-11-19; fax (71) 220-66-06; e-mail segreteria.tashkent@esteri.it; internet www.ambtashkent.esteri.it; Ambassador GIOVANNI RICCIULLI.

Japan: 100047 Tashkent, S. Azimov ko'ch., 1-tor 28; tel. (71) 120-80-60; fax (71) 120-80-77; internet www.uz.emb-japan.go.jp; Ambassador TSYTOMU HIRAOKA.

Jordan: 100000 Tashkent, Dipvilla, Farxod ko'ch. 9; tel. (71) 274-24-79; fax (71) 120-66-44; e-mail jordanembuzb@mail.ru; Chargé d'affaires a.i. MUHAMMAD NOUR OTHMAN YOUSEF BALKAR.

Kazakhstan: 100015 Tashkent, Chexov ko'ch. 23; tel. (71) 252-16-54; fax (71) 252-16-50; e-mail kazembassy@kaz.uz; Ambassador ZAUTBEK K. TURISBEKOV.

Korea, Democratic People's Republic: 100000 Tashkent, Usmon Nosir ko'ch. 95A; tel. (71) 250-59-44; fax (71) 250-27-99; Ambassador LEE DON-PAL.

Korea, Republic: 100000 Tashkent, Afrosiyob ko'ch. 7; tel. (71) 252-31-51; fax (71) 120-62-48; e-mail admin1@korea.anet.uz; internet uzb.mofat.go.kr; Ambassador KYUN JEA MIN.

Kuwait: 100000 Tashkent, Batumskaya ko'ch. 2; tel. (71) 120-58-88; fax (71) 120-84-96; Ambassador MOHAMED A. H. HAYAT.

Kyrgyzstan: 100000 Tashkent, X. Samatova ko'ch. 30; tel. (71) 237-47-94; fax (71) 220-72-94; e-mail erkindik@sarkor.uz; Ambassador AZIZBEK M. MADMAROV.

Latvia: 100000 Tashkent, A. Lashkarbegi ko'ch. 16A; tel. (71) 237-22-15; fax (71) 120-70-36; e-mail embassy.uzbekistan@mfa.gov.lv; Ambassador IGORS APOKINS.

Malaysia: 100031 Tashkent, M. Yaqubova ko'ch. 30; tel. (71) 256-30-27; fax (71) 252-30-71; e-mail mwtskent@rol.uz; Ambassador ABDUL AZIZ BIN HARUN.

Pakistan: 100115 Tashkent, Kichik Xalqa Yo'li ko'ch. 15; tel. (71) 248-86-49; fax (71) 120-49-21; e-mail parepuzb@online.ru; Ambassador SAJJAD KAMRAN.

Poland: 100084 Tashkent, Firdavsiy ko'ch. 66; tel. (71) 120-86-50; fax (71) 120-86-51; e-mail ambasada@bcc.com.uz; internet www.taszkent.polemb.net; Chargé d'affaires a.i. JERZY STANKIEWICZ.

Romania: 100000 Tashkent, Rejametov ko'ch. 44A; tel. (71) 252-63-55; fax (71) 120-75-67; e-mail romanian_embassy@sarkor.uz; Ambassador CONSTANTIN ALEXA.

Russia: 100015 Tashkent, Nukus ko'ch. 83; tel. (71) 120-35-02; fax (71) 120-35-09; e-mail embassy@russia.uz; internet www.russia.uz; Chargé d'affaires a.i. VAZYKH I. SERAZEV.

Saudi Arabia: 100000 Tashkent, Bobur ko'ch. 3 A; tel. (71) 281-51-01; fax (71) 281-51-06; Ambassador IBRAHIM MANSOUR AL-MANSOUR.

UZBEKISTAN

Slovakia: 100070 Tashkent, Yakkasaroy ko'ch. 18; tel. (71) 120-68-52; fax (71) 120-68-51; e-mail slovakia@buzton.com; internet www.tashkent.mfa.sk; Ambassador JOSEF MAČISÁK.

Switzerland: 100070 Tashkent, U. Nosir ko'ch., tupik 1/4; tel. (71) 120-67-38; fax (71) 120-62-59; e-mail tas.vertretung@eda.admin.ch; internet www.eda.admin.ch/tashkent; Ambassador ANNE BAUTY.

Tajikistan: 100000 Tashkent, A. Kaxxor ko'ch., 6-chi tor, 61; tel. (71) 254-99-66; fax (71) 254-89-69; e-mail tajembuz@yandex.ru; Ambassador BOBOKHON MAHMADOV.

Turkey: 100000 Tashkent, Ya. G'ulomov ko'ch. 87; tel. (71) 113-03-00; fax (71) 113-03-33; e-mail turemb@bcc.com.uz; Ambassador ASYA KEMAL.

Turkmenistan: 100000 Tashkent, 1-chi Katta Mirobod ko'ch. 10; tel. (71) 120-52-78; fax (71) 120-52-81; Ambassador SOLTAN PIRMUHAMEDOV.

Ukraine: 100000 Tashkent, Ya. G'ulomov ko'ch. 68; tel. (71) 236-08-12; fax (71) 233-10-89; e-mail emb_uz@mfa.gov.ua; internet www.ukraine.uz; Ambassador VYACHESLAV V. POKHVALSKY.

United Kingdom: 100000 Tashkent, ul. Ya. G'ulomov ko'ch. 67; tel. (71) 120-78-52; fax (71) 120-65-49; e-mail brit@emb.uz; internet ukinuzbekistan.fco.gov.uk; Ambassador IAIN KELLY.

USA: 100093 Tashkent, Moyqurg'on ko'ch. 3, Yunusobod District; tel. (71) 120-54-50; fax (71) 120-63-35; e-mail consulartashkent@state.gov; internet uzbekistan.usembassy.gov; Ambassador RICHARD B. NORLAND.

Viet Nam: 100000 Tashkent, Sh. Rashidov ko'ch. 100; tel. (71) 234-03-93; fax (71) 120-62-65; e-mail dsqvntas@online.ru; Ambassador LE VAN TOAN.

Judicial System

Supreme Court of the Republic of Uzbekistan
(O'zbekiston Respublikasi Oliy sud)
100000 Tashkent, A. Qodiriy ko'ch. 1; tel. and fax (71) 244-62-93.
Chairman: FARUHA F. MUHITDINOVA.

Office of the Prosecutor-General: 100000 Tashkent, Ya. G'ulomov ko'ch. 66; tel. (71) 233-20-66; Prosecutor-Gen. RASHIDJON H. QODIROV.

Constitutional Court (Konstitutsiyaviy sud): 100000 Tashkent, Mustaqillik maydoni 6; tel. (71) 239-80-20; fax (71) 239-86-36; e-mail interconcourt@sarkor.uz; Chair. (vacant); Dep. Chair. BAKHTIYAR MIRBABAEV.

Supreme Economic Court (Oliy Xo'jalik Sudi): 100097 Tashkent, Cho'ponota ko'ch. 6; tel. (71) 267-36-18; fax (71) 273-84-78; e-mail economical-court@sarkor.uz; internet www.economical-court.uz; Chair. DILMURAD A. MIRZAKARIMOV.

Religion

The Constitution of 8 December 1992 stipulates that, while there is freedom of worship and expression, there may be no state religion or ideology. A new law on religion was adopted in May 1998, which severely restricted the activities of religious organizations.

The most widespread religion in Uzbekistan is Islam; the majority of ethnic Uzbeks are Sunni Muslims (Hanafi school), but the number of Salafi communities is increasing. At 1 October 2002 there were 1,965 Islamic organizations registered in Uzbekistan, including 11 educational institutions. Most ethnic Slavs in Uzbekistan are adherents of Orthodox Christianity; there were 36 Russian Orthodox organizations registered in Uzbekistan at October 2002. At the end of 1993 there were some 32,000 Jews in Uzbekistan; many Jews have since emigrated to Israel.

State Committee for Religious Affairs: 100017 Tashkent, Mustaqillik 5; tel. and fax (71) 239-17-63; e-mail info@religions.uz; Chair. ARTIKBEK YUSUPOV (acting).

ISLAM

Muslim Board of Central Asia: 100002 Tashkent, Zarkainar ko'ch. 103, Madrese 'Barakhan'; tel. (71) 240-39-33; fax (71) 240-08-31; f. 1943 as state body with 'official' spiritual jurisdiction over Muslims in the Kyrgyz, Tajik, Turkmen and Uzbek SSRs; Chair. USMON OLIMOV (Chief Mufti of Mowarounnahr—Central Asia).

CHRISTIANITY

Roman Catholic Church

The Church is represented in Uzbekistan by an Apostolic Administration, established in January 2005. There were an estimated 4,000 adherents at 31 December 2006.

Apostolic Administrator: Most Rev. JERZY MACULEWICZ, 100047 Tashkent, Musahanov ko'ch. 80/1; tel. (71) 233-70-25; fax (71) 233-70-35; e-mail adm.ap@agnuz.info.

Russian Orthodox Church (Moscow Patriarchate)

Eparchy of Tashkent and Central Asia (Moscow Patriarchate)—Orthodox Church of Central Asia: 100047 Tashkent, S. Azimov ko'ch. 22/3D; tel. (71) 233-33-21; fax (71) 236-79-39; e-mail church@albatros.uz; internet www.pravoslavie.uz; Metropolitan of Tashkent and Central Asia VLADIMIR (IKIM); has jurisdiction over Kyrgyzstan, Tajikistan and Uzbekistan.

JUDAISM

Chief Rabbi: Rabbi DAVID GUREVICH, 100100 Tashkent, Shohzahon ko'ch. 30; tel. (71) 252-59-78; fax (71) 220-64-31; e-mail jewish@jewish.uz; internet www.jewish.uz.

The Press

The publications listed below are in Uzbek, unless otherwise stated.

REGULATORY AUTHORITY

Uzbek Agency for Press and Information (O'zAAA) (O'zbekiston Aloqa Va Axborotlashtirash Agentligi): 100129 Tashkent, Navoiy ko'ch. 28A; tel. (71) 238-41-07; fax (71) 239-87-82; e-mail info@aci.uz; internet aci.uz; f. 2002; Gen. Dir ABDULLA N. ARIPOV.

PRINCIPAL NEWSPAPERS

XXI ASR (21st Century): 100000 Tashkent, Nukus ko'ch. 73A; tel. and fax (371) 281-33-80; e-mail axborotXXIasr@yahoo.com; internet www.21asr.com; f. 2003; in Uzbek; weekly; Chief Editor MIRODIL ABDURAHMONOV.

Adolat (Justice): 100000 Tashkent, Matbuotchilar ko'ch. 32; tel. (71) 233-41-89; f. 1995; organ of the Justice Social Democratic Party of Uzbekistan (Adolat); weekly; Editor TOHTAMUROD TOSHEV; circ. 5,900.

Biznes-vestnik Vostoka (Business Bulletin of the East): 100000 Tashkent, Matbuotchilar ko'ch. 32; tel. (71) 132-27-30; fax (71) 136-00-55; e-mail bvv-info@mail.ru; f. 1991; 3 a week; in Russian; economic and financial news; also weekly English edition, *BVV Business Report*; Editor-in-Chief RALIF NIGMATULLIN (acting); circ. 8,000.

Ekonomicheskoye Obozreniye (Economic Survey): 100070 Tashkent, Usman Nosir ko'ch., 1 tupik, 5; tel. (71) 150-02-02; fax (71) 361-45-48; e-mail review@cer.uz; weekly; economics, politics, civil society, finance.

Inson va Qonun (Person and Law): 100047 Tashkent, Sayilgoh ko'ch. 5; internet www.minjust.uz/uz/group.scm?groupId=4146; weekly; organ of the Ministry of Justice; Editor-in-Chief SHODIQUL HAMROEV.

Ma'rifat (Enlightenment): 100000 Tashkent, Matbuotchilar ko'ch. 32; tel. (71) 233-50-55; e-mail mariat@ars-inform.uz; internet www.marifat.uz; f. 1931; 2 a week; in Uzbek and Russian; Editor KHALIM SAIDOV; circ. 33,000 (2006).

Mulkdor (The Proprietor): 100083 Tashkent, Buyuk Turon ko'ch. 41; tel. (71) 239-21-96; f. 1994; weekly; Editor-in-Chief MIRODIL ABDURAKHMANOV; circ. 10,000.

Novyi Vek (New Age): 100060 Tashkent, Movarounnaxr ko'ch. 19; tel. (71) 233-48-55; fax (71) 233-76-84; f. 1992; fmrly *Kommercheskii Vestnik* (Commerical Herald); in Russian; weekly; Editor VALERII NIYAZMATOV; circ. 22,000.

O'zbekiston Adabiyoti va San'ati (Literature and Art of Uzbekistan): 100000 Tashkent, Matbuotchilar ko'ch. 32; tel. (71) 233-52-91; internet www.uzas.uz; f. 1956; weekly; organ of the Union of Writers of Uzbekistan; Editor AKHMAJON MELIBOYEV; circ. 10,300.

O'zbekiston ovozi/Golos Uzbekistana (Voice of Uzbekistan): 100000 Tashkent, Matbuotchilar ko'ch. 32; tel. (71) 236-55-15; fax (71) 233-65-45; e-mail info@uzbekistonovozi.uz; internet www.uzbekistonovozi.uz; f. 1918; Uzbek and Russian edns; organ of the People's Democratic Party of Uzbekistan; Editor-in-Chief SAFAR OSTONOV.

Postda/Na postu: 100029 Tashkent, Yu. Rajaby ko'ch. 1; f. 1930; in Uzbek and Russian; military; weekly; Editor Z. ATAYEV.

Pravda Vostoka (Truth of the East): 100000 Tashkent, Matbuotchilar ko'ch. 32; tel. (71) 233-56-33; fax (71) 233-70-98; e-mail pvbox@mail.ru; internet www.pv.uz; f. 1917; 5 a week; in Russian; organ of the Cabinet of Ministers; Editor ABBASKHAN USMANOV; circ. 12,000 (2008).

UZBEKISTAN

Savdogar (The Trader): 100000 Tashkent, Buyuk Turon ko'ch. 41; tel. (71) 233-34-55; f. 1992; Editor MUHAMMAD ORAZMETOV; circ. 17,000.

Sport: 100000 Tashkent, O'zbekiston shoh ko'ch. 98 A; tel. (71) 244-07-52; f. 1932; Editor HAYDAR AKBAROV; circ. 8,490.

Toshkent Haqiqati/Tashkentskaya Pravda (Tashkent Truth): 100000 Tashkent, Matbuotchilar ko'ch. 32; tel. (71) 233-64-95; fax (71) 233-58-85; internet www.th.uz; f. 1954; 2 a week; Uzbek and Russian edns; Editor FATKHIDDIN MUKHITDINOV; circ. 19,000 (Uzbek edn), 6,400 (Russian edn).

Turkiston (Turkestan): 100000 Tashkent, Matbuotchilar ko'ch. 32; tel. (71) 236-56-58; f. 1925 as *Yash Leninchy* (Young Leninist), renamed as above 1992; 2 a week; organ of the Kamolot Asscn of Youth of Uzbekistan; Editor GAFAR KHATOMOV; circ. 12,580.

UzReport: 100000 Tashkent, Buxoro ko'ch. 26; tel. (71) 232-27-29; fax (71) 232-27-30; e-mail info@corp.uzreport.com; internet www.uzreport.com; online only; in Uzbek, Russian and English; business, economics; f. 1999.

Vatanparvar (The Patriot): 100000 Tashkent, Ak. Abdullaev ko'ch. 100; tel. (71) 269-82-43; fax (71) 269-82-28; fmrly *Frunzevets* (Supporter of Frunze); publ. by Ministry of Defence; weekly.

Xalk Suzi/ Narodnoye Slovo (People's Word): 100000 Tashkent, Matbuotchilar ko'ch. 32; tel. (71) 233-15-22; e-mail info@narodnoeslovo.uz; internet www.narodnoeslovo.uz; f. 1991; Uzbek and Russian edns; 5 a week (Uzbek), weekly (Russian); organ of the Oly Majlis and the Cabinet of Ministers; Editor ABBASKHON USMANOV; circ. 41,580 (Uzbek edn), 12,750 (Russian edn).

Xamkor/ Delovoi Partner/ Business Partner: 100084 Tashkent, Amir Temir ko'ch. 107A; tel. (71) 138-59-77; fax (71) 138-58-23; e-mail info@dp.uz; internet www.dp.uz; f. 1990; weekly; Uzbek, Russian and English edns; circ. 4,735.

Xurriiat (Freedom): 100000 Tashkent; tel. (71) 244-25-06; fax (71) 244-36-16; e-mail amir@uzpac.uz; f. 1996; weekly; independent; circ. 5,000.

PRINCIPAL PERIODICALS

Monthly, unless otherwise indicated.

Erk (Freedom): 100055 Tashkent, Ipakchi ko'ch. 38; tel. (71) 220-65-30; e-mail erkgazetasi@yahoo.com; internet www.erkgazetasi.org; organ of Freedom Democratic Party of Uzbekistan (Erk); f. 1991; four a month; Uzbek and Russian edns; circ. 5,300 (2007).

Fan va turmush/Nauka i Zhizn Uzbekistana (Science and Life): 100052 Tashkent, Ya. G'ulomov ko'ch. 70; tel. (71) 233-50-33; fax (71) 236-00-37; e-mail shuhrat@astrin.uzsci.net; internet fvat.uz; f. 1933 as *Sosialistik ilm va Texnika* (Socialist Science and Technology); every 2 months; Uzbek and Russian edns; publ. by the Fan (Science) Publishing House; popular scientific; Editor Prof. SHUXRAT A. EGAMBERDIEV; circ. 28,000.

Guliston: 100000 Tashkent, Buyuk Turon ko'ch. 41; tel. (71) 236-78-90; f. 1925; present name adopted 1967; every 2 months; sociopolitical, literary; Editor-in-Chief AZIM SUYUN; circ. 4,000.

Gulxan (Bonfire): 100000 Tashkent, Buyuk Turon ko'ch. 41; tel. (71) 236-78-85; f. 1929; monthly; illustrated juvenile fiction; Editor SAFAR BARNOYEV; circ. 26,000.

Guncha (Small Bud): 100000 Tashkent, Buyuk Turon ko'ch. 41; tel. (71) 236-78-80; f. 1958; illustrated; for pre-school-age children; Editor ERKIN MALIKOV; circ. 35,000.

Ijtimoij fikr/Obshchestvennoe mneniye. Prava Cheloveka (Public Opinion. Human Rights): 100029 Tashkent, Mustaqilliq maidoni 5/3; tel. (71) 239-46-55; fax (71) 239-85-48; e-mail if@tkt.uz; internet www.ijtimoiy-fikr.uz; f. 1998; 4 a year; in Uzbek, Russian and English; publ. by the Republican Centre for the Study of Public Opinion; Editor MARIANNA YU. PALNOVA.

Jahon Adabiyoti (World Literature): 100129 Tashkent, A. Navoiy ko'ch. 30; tel. (71) 244-41-60; fax (71) 244-41-61; f. 1997; Editor MUPRIYRAT MUPZAEB; circ. 2,000.

Mushtum (The Fist): 100000 Tashkent, Buyuk Turon ko'ch. 41; tel. (71) 233-99-72; f. 1923; every two months; satirical; Editor ASHURALI JURAYEV; circ. 10,650.

Oila va zhamiiat (Family and Society): 100000 Tashkent, A. Navoiy k'och. 30; tel. (71) 139-40-42; fax (71) 139-40-12; e-mail womancomitet@mail.ru; f. 1991; weekly; publ. by Women's Committee of Uzbekistan; in Uzbek.

O'zbekiston Iktisoij Axborotnomasi/ Ekonomicheskii Vestnik Uzbekistana (The Uzbekistan Economic Herald): 100000 Tashkent, Suleymanov ko'ch. 29; six a year; Uzbek and Russian edns.

San'at (Art): 100029 Tashkent, Mustaqilliq maidoni 2; tel. (71) 239-44-51; fax (71) 239-46-86; e-mail bientash@globalnet.uz; internet sanat.orexca.com; f. 1997; 4 a year; publ. by Academy of the Arts of Uzbekistan; Uzbek, Russian and English edns; illustrated journal about the arts and crafts.

Saodat (Happiness): 100083 Tashkent, Buyuk Turon ko'ch. 41; tel. (71) 233-68-10; internet www.saodat.uz; f. 1925; 8 a year; women's popular; Editor OIDIN KHAJIYEVA; circ. 70,000.

Sharq Yulduzi/Zvezda Vostoka (Star of the East): 100000 Tashkent, Buyuk Turon ko'ch. 41; tel. (71) 233-09-18; f. 1932; journal of the Union of Writers of Uzbekistan; fiction; Uzbek and Russian edns; Editor (Uzbek edn) UTKUR KHASHIMOV; Editor (Russian edn) NIKOLAI KRASILNIKOV; circ. 10,000 (Uzbek edn), 3,000 (Russian edn).

Sikhat Salomatlik (Health): 100000 Tashkent, Parkent ko'ch. 51; tel. (71) 268-17-54; f. 1990; every 2 months; Editor DAMIN A. ASADOV; circ. 36,000.

Tafakkur (Contemplation): 100000 Tashkent, Movaraunnakhr ko'ch.; f. 1994; 4 a year; literary; organ of the (state-controlled) Republican Committee for Spirituality and Enlightenment; Editor-in-Chief ERKIN A'ZAM.

NEWS AGENCIES

Jahon (World) Information Agency: 100029 Tashkent, O'zbekiston shoh ko'ch. 9; tel. (71) 233-65-91; fax (71) 220-64-43; e-mail aajahon@mfa.uz; internet jahon.mfa.uz; information agency of Ministry of Foreign Affairs; Dir ABROR GULYAMOV.

Press-UZ.info: Tashkent; e-mail admin@press-uz.info; internet www.press-uz.info; f. 2005; independent; news from Uzbekistan, Central Asia and Russia, in Uzbek, Russian and English.

Uzbekistan National News Agency (UzA): 100047 Tashkent, Musahanov ko'ch. 38; tel. (71) 233-16-22; fax (71) 233-24-45; internet www.uza.uz; Dir MAMATSKUL KHAZRATSKULOV.

Publishers

Uzbek Agency for Press and Information: 100129 Tashkent, A. Navoiy ko'ch. 30; tel. (71) 244-32-87; fax (71) 244-14-84; e-mail ozmaa@uzpak.uz; internet www.uzapi.gov.uz; f. 2002; mass media, press and information exchange; printing, publishing and distribution of periodicals; Gen. Dir BABUR ALIMOV.

Chulpon (Morning Star) Publishers: 100129 Tashkent, A. Navoiy ko'ch. 30; tel. (71) 239-13-75; fax (71) 244-22-52; e-mail chulpan@sarkor.uz; internet www.chulpon.uz; Dir R. ZAPAROV.

Fan (Science) Publishers: 100047 Tashkent, Ya. G'ulomov ko'ch. 70/102; tel. (71) 233-69-61; scientific books and journals; Dir N. T. KHATAMOV.

Gafur Gulom Publishing House: 100129 Tashkent, A. Navoiy ko'ch. 30; tel. (71) 244-22-53; fax (71) 241-35-47; f. 1957; fiction, the arts; books in Uzbek, Russian and English; Dir MIZROB M. BURONOV; Editor-in-Chief NAZIRA J. JURAYEVNA.

Mekhnat (Labour) Publishers: 100129 Tashkent, A. Navoiy ko'ch. 30; tel. (71) 244-22-27; f. 1985; Dir RUSTAM A. MIRZAYEV.

O'qituvchi (Teacher) Publishing-Printing and Creative House: 100129 Tashkent, A. Navoiy ko'ch. 30; tel. and fax (71) 244-26-89; f. 1936; literary textbooks, education manuals, popular science, juvenile; Dir R. O. MIRZAYEV.

O'zbekiston Milliy Entsiklopediyasi (Uzbekistan National Encyclopedias): 100129 Tashkent, A. Navoiy ko'ch. 30; tel. (71) 244-34-38; fax (71) 244-24-91; e-mail ume2@yandex.ru; internet www.ensiklopediya.uz; f. 1997; encyclopedias, dictionaries and reference books; Dir N. TUKHLIYEV.

O'zbekiston (Uzbekistan) Publishing and Printing Creative House: 100129 Tashkent, A. Navoiy ko'ch. 30; tel. (71) 244-34-01; fax (71) 244-38-10; e-mail aptpk@ars-inform.uz; f. 2004; politics, economics, law, history, art, illustrated, manuals and textbooks for schools and higher educational institutes; Dir ZAIR T. ISADJANOV; Editor-in-Chief SHOMUXITDIN SH. MANSUROV.

Yozuvchi (Writer) Publishers: 100129 Tashkent, A. Navoiy ko'ch. 30; tel. (71) 244-29-97; f. 1990; Dir M. U. TOICHIYEV.

Broadcasting and Communications

TELECOMMUNICATIONS

Communications and Information Agency of Uzbekistan (O'zbekistol Aloqa Va Axborotlashtirish Agentligi): 100011 Tashkent, A. Navoiy ko'ch. 28A; tel. (71) 233-65-03; fax (71) 239-87-82; e-mail info@aci.uz; internet www.aci.uz; Dir-Gen. ABDULLA N. ARIPOV.

Service Providers

Coscom: 100031 Tashkent, V. Vaxidov ko'ch. 118; tel. (71) 252-15-51; fax (71) 220-72-65; e-mail inform@coscom.uz; internet www

UZBEKISTAN

.coscom.uz; f. 1996; Uzbekistani–US jt venture; mobile cellular telecommunications.

Unitel (Beeline): 100000 Tashkent, Buxoro ko'ch. 1; tel. (71) 233-33-30; fax (71) 232-12-22; internet www.beeline.uz; f. 1996; fmrly Daewoo Unitel; subsidiary of VympelKom-Bilain (Russia); mobile cellular telecommunications; more than 1m. subscribers (2007).

Uzbektelecom: 100000 Tashkent, Amir Temur ko'ch. 24; tel. (71) 233-42-59; fax (71) 236-01-88; e-mail uztelecom@intal.uz; internet www.uztelecom.uz; f. 2000; provides local, regional and international telecommunications services; partial privatization pending; Gen. Dir KH. A. MUKHITDINOV.

Uzdunrobita: 100000 Tashkent, Amir Temur ko'ch. 24; tel. (97) 130-01-01; fax (97) 130-01-05; e-mail office@uzdunrobita.com.uz; internet www.uzdunrobita.uz; f. 1991; mobile cellular telecommunications; 74% owned by Mobile Telesystems (Russia); Gen. Dir BEKHZOD AKHMEDOV.

BROADCASTING

State Television and Radio Broadcasting Company of Uzbekistan (UZTELERADIO): 100011 Tashkent, A. Navoiy ko'ch. 69; tel. (71) 233-81-06; fax (71) 244-16-60; e-mail uztele@tkt.uz; local broadcasts, as well as relays from Egypt, France, India, Japan, Russia and Turkey; Chair. ALISHER KHUJAYEV.

Television

Kamalak Television: 100084 Tashkent, Amir Temur ko'ch. 109; tel. (71) 237-51-77; fax (71) 220-62-28; e-mail kam.tv@kamalak.co.uz; f. 1992; jt venture between State Television and Radio Broadcasting Company and a US company; satellite broadcasts; relays from France, Germany, India, Russia, the United Kingdom and the USA; Gen. Dir PULAT UMAROV.

Uzbekistan Television and Radio Company (Uzteleradio): 100011 Tashkent, A. Navoiy ko'ch. 69; tel. (71) 233-81-06; fax (71) 244-16-60; e-mail uztcint@hotmail.com; four local programmes as well as relays from Russia, Kazakhstan, Egypt, India and Turkey; Chair. ALISHER KHADJAYEV.

Finance

(cap. = capital; res = reserves; dep. = deposits; m. = million; amounts in Uzbek sum, unless otherwise stated; brs = branches)

BANKING

A reform of the banking sector was begun in 1994. A two-tier system was introduced, consisting of the Central Bank and about 30 commercial banks. An association of commercial banks was established in 1995 to co-ordinate the role of commercial banks in the national economy. At the end of 2002 there were reported to be 35 banks in Uzbekistan, of which 13 were under private ownership.

Central Bank

Central Bank of the Republic of Uzbekistan: 100001 Tashkent, O'zbekiston shoh ko'ch. 6; tel. (71) 212-61-94; fax (71) 233-00-44; e-mail webmaster@cbu.st.uz; internet www.cbu.uz; f. 1991; Chair. of Bd FAIZULLA M. MULLAJONOV.

State Commercial Bank

National Bank for Foreign Economic Activity of the Republic of Uzbekistan (NBU) (O'zbekiston Respublikasi Tashqi Iqtisodiy Faoliyat Milliy Banki): 100047 Tashkent, Oxunbabaev ko'ch. 23; tel. (71) 233-62-87; fax (71) 232-01-72; e-mail webmaster@central.nbu.com; internet eng.nbu.com; f. 1991; cap. 22,386m., res 434,316m., dep. 2,343,991m. (Dec. 2006); Chair. SAIDAKHMAT B. RAKHIMOV; 95 brs.

State Joint-Stock Commercial Banks

Asaka—Specialized State Joint-Stock Commercial Bank: 100015 Tashkent, Nukus ko'ch. 67; tel. (71) 120-81-11; fax (71) 120-86-91; e-mail contact@asakabank.com; internet www.asakabank.com; f. 1995; cap. US $150m., dep. $678.4m., total assets $1,000m. (Dec. 2007); 98.3% owned by Ministry of Finance; Chair. KAHRAMON T. ARIPOV; 27 brs.

Ipoteka Commercial Mortgage Bank: 100000 Tashkent, Pushkin ko'ch. 17; tel. (71) 233-11-22; fax (71) 232-13-23; e-mail info@ipotekabank.uz; internet www.ipotekabank.uz; f. 2005 by merger of UzJilSberBank and Zaminbank; cap. 30,417.7m., res 22,571.0m., dep. 402,897.4m. (Dec. 2007); Chair. of Bd ABDURASUL ABDULLAYEV; 38 brs.

Other Banks

Aloqabank: 100015 Tashkent, Tolstoy ko'ch. 1A; tel. (71) 252-78-74; fax (71) 252-78-03; e-mail alokauz@uzpak.uz; internet www.alokabank.uz; f. 1995; cap. 12,574.8m., dep. 21,190.2m., total assets 102,090.7m. (Dec. 2007); Chair. ABDULLA N. ARIPOV; 12 brs, 28 sub-brs (2007).

HamkorBank: 170111 Andijon, Babura ko'ch. 85; tel. and fax (74) 24-70-39; e-mail hamkorbank@mail.ru; internet www.hamkorbank.uz; f. 1991; Chair. IKRAM IBRAHIMOV; 15 brs.

Ipak Yuli Bank (Silk Road Bank): 100135 Tashkent, Farkod ko'ch. 12A; tel. (71) 220-00-09; fax (71) 220-38-86; e-mail info@ipakyulibank.com; internet www.ipakyulibank.com; f. 2000; Chair. of Bd ALISHER H. MUMINOV; Gen. Man. RUSTAMBEK R. RAHIMBEKOV.

O'zsanoatkurilishbank (Uzpromstroibank) (Uzbek Industrial Construction Bank): 100000 Tashkent, Shaxrisab ko'ch. 3; tel. (71) 233-24-88; fax (71) 232-06-14; e-mail cor_bank@uzpsb.com; internet www.uzpsb.com; f. 1922; cap. 23,843.7m., res 10,871.4m., dep. 485,679.6m. (Dec. 2005); Chair. KIYOMIDDIN K. RUSTAMOV; 47 brs, 79 sub-brs.

Paxta Bank (Pakhta Bank): 100096 Tashkent, Mukimi ko'ch. 43; tel. (71) 278-12-96; fax (71) 220-88-18; e-mail headoffice@pakhtabank.com; internet www.pakhtabank.com; f. 1995; cap. 65,625.0m., res 2,649.3m., dep. 468,049.0m. (Dec. 2007); renaming and restructuring as Agrobank pending in 2009; Chair. ABDURAXMAT BOYMURATOV; 187 brs.

Qishloq Qurilish Bank (Rural Construction Bank): 100060 Tashkent, Lahuti ko'ch. 38; tel. and fax (71) 133-42-25; f. 2009 on basis of Galla Bank.

Savdogarbank: 100060 Tashkent, S. Barak ko'ch. 76; tel. (71) 254-19-91; fax (71) 256-56-71; internet www.savdogarbank.uz; Chair. MURSURMON N. NURMAMATOV.

Tadbirkor Bank: 100047 Tashkent, S. Azimov ko'ch. 52; tel. (71) 233-18-75; fax (71) 236-88-32; f. 2006; micro-credit bank; Chair. MUZAFFARBEK SABIROV.

Trustbank: 100038 Tashkent, A. Navoiy ko'ch. 7; tel. (71) 244-76-21; fax (71) 244-76-61; e-mail info@trustbank.uz; internet www.trustbank.uz; f. 1994; cap. 6,411.7m., res −99.3m., dep. 148,112.4m. (Dec. 2007); Chair. ILHOM F. SOLIYEV; 2 brs.

Turonbank: 100011 Tashkent, Abay 4A; tel. (71) 700-55-55; fax (71) 244-25-81; e-mail info@turonbank.uz; internet www.turonbank.uz; f. 1990; cap. US $8m., res $1.7m., dep. $10.7m. (Jan. 2008); Chair. of Bd DANIYOR B. ARIFJANOV; 18 brs.

Uzbekistan-Turkish UT Bank: 100043 Tashkent, Xalqlar Do'stligi ko'ch. 15B; tel. (71) 273-83-25; fax (71) 220-63-62; e-mail utbank@utbk.com; internet www.utbk.com; f. 1993; 50% owned by Paxta Bank, 50% owned by Türkiye Cumhuriyeti Ziraat Bankası (Agricultural Bank of the Turkish Republic); cap. 2,608.8m., res 252.0m., dep. 17,037.0m. (Dec. 2006); Chair. AZIM TANGIRBERDIYEV.

INSURANCE

Ark Sug'urta: 100000 Tashkent, Pushkin ko'ch. 88; tel. (71) 240-03-69; fax (71) 267-70-28; e-mail info@arksugurta.uz; internet www.arksugurta.uz; f. 1991; life and non-life; Dir-Gen. ZAFAR O. TURSUNOV.

Ishonch: 100027 Tashkent, Xojaev ko'ch. 1A; tel. and fax (71) 238-69-65; e-mail info@ishonch-iic.uz; internet www.ishonch-iic.uz; f. 1996; life and non-life; Dir-Gen. MIRSHAMSIDDIN M. XIKMATILLAEV.

Kalofat: 100000 Tashkent, Mustaqillik maydoni 5, 9th floor; tel. (71) 233-26-98; fax (71) 233-38-49; internet www.kalofatdask.uz; f. 1997; life and non-life; Dir-Gen. SHERALI B. IMAMOV.

O'zbekinvest (Uzbekinvest) National Export–Import Insurance Co: 100017 Tashkent, Istiqlol ko'ch. 49; tel. (71) 233-05-56; fax (71) 233-07-04; e-mail office@uzbekinvest.uz; internet www.insurance.uz; f. 1994, restructured 1997; jt venture with American International Group (AIG—USA); cap. US $60m.; Dir-Gen. FAKHRITDIN SAIDAKHMEDOV.

Standard Insurance Group: 100015 Tashkent, Kunaev ko'ch. 25; tel. (71) 250-99-99; fax (71) 220-31-13; e-mail office@sig-insurance.uz; internet www.sig-insurance.uz; f. 2005; non-life; Dir-Gen. UMUD U. KAMILOV.

Temir Yo'llari Sug'urta: 100060 Tashkent, Shevchenko ko'ch. 7; tel. (71) 238-86-27; fax (71) 238-85-97; e-mail tys_KDilshod@mail.ru; internet www.tysugurta.sk.uz; f. 2002; non-life; Chair. of Bd YOKUBZHON MUHAMMEDOV; Dir-Gen. DILSHOD KADYROV.

COMMODITY EXCHANGE

Tashkent Republican Commodity and Raw Materials Exchange: 100003 Tashkent, O'zbekiston shoh ko'ch. 53; tel. (71) 239-83-77; fax (71) 239-83-92; Chair. of Bd NABIHON S. SAMATOV.

STOCK EXCHANGE

Tashkent Republican Stock Exchange (UZSE) (Respublika Fond Birjasi 'Toshkent'): 100047 Tashkent, Buxoro koʻch. 10; tel. (71) 236-76-13; fax (71) 233-32-31; e-mail gairat@uzse.uz; internet www.uzse.uz; f. 1994; Chair. BAKHTIYOR I. KHUDOYAROV.

Trade and Industry

GOVERNMENT AGENCIES

Foreign Investment Agency: 100077 Tashkent, Buyuyk Ipak Yulli koʻch. 75; tel. (71) 268-77-05; fax (71) 267-07-52; e-mail afi@mail.uznet.net; Gen. Dir SHAZIYATOV S. SHOAZIZ.

State Committee for De-monopolization and the Development of Competition (Oʻzbekiston Respublikasi Monopoliadan Chiqarish va Raqobatni Rivojlantirish Davlat Qoʻmitasi): 100011 Tashkent, A. Navoiy koʻch. 18A; tel. (71) 239-15-42; e-mail devonhona@antimon.uz; internet www.antimon.uz; Chair. BAIMUROD S. ULASHOV (acting).

State Committee for the Management of State Property (State Property Committee): 100003 Tashkent, Oʻzbekiston shoh koʻch. 55; tel. (71) 239-44-46; fax (71) 259-20-37; e-mail ves@gki.uz; internet www.gki.uz; f. 1994; Chair. DILSHOD O. MUSAEV.

CHAMBER OF COMMERCE

Chamber of Commerce and Industry of Uzbekistan (Oʻzbekiston Respublikasi Savdo-Sanoat Palatasi): 100047 Tashkent, Buxoro koʻch. 6; tel. (71) 150-60-00; fax (71) 150-60-09; e-mail info@chamber.uz; internet www.chamber.uz; f. 1996 as Chamber of Commodity Producers and Entrepreneurs of Uzbekistan; re-established and renamed as above by presidential decree 2004; provides assistance, consultancy and support for businesses; Chair. ALISHER SHAIHOV.

STATE HYDROCARBONS COMPANY

Uzbekneftegaz (Uzbekistani Petroleum and Natural Gas Co): 100047 Tashkent, Akhunbabayev koʻch. 21; tel. (71) 233-57-57; fax (71) 236-77-71; e-mail nhk@uzneftegaz.uz; internet www.uzneftegaz.uz; f. 1999; national petroleum and gas corpn; Chair. of Bd NURMUHAMMAD A. AHMETOV.

TRADE UNIONS

Federation of Trade Unions of Uzbekistan: 100000 Tashkent; Chair. of Council KHULKAR JAMALOV.

Transport

RAILWAYS

Uzbekistan's railway network is connected to those of the neighbouring republics of Kazakhstan, Kyrgyzstan, Tajikistan and Turkmenistan, and to that of Russia. There were 3,645 km of track in 2007.

Oʻzbekiston Temir Yoʻllari (Uzbekistan State Railway Co): 100060 Tashkent, T. Shevchenko koʻch. 7; tel. (71) 238-80-00; fax (71) 233-45-49; e-mail uzrailway@uzpak.uz; internet www.uzrailway.uz; f. 1994; state-owned joint-stock co; Chair. of Bd ACHILBAY ZH. RAMATOV.

Toshkent metropoliteni (Tashkent Metro): 100027 Tashkent, Oʻzbekiston shoh koʻch. 93A; tel. (71) 232-38-52; fax (71) 233-66-81; e-mail metro@sarkor.uz; f. 1977; three lines with total length of 36 km, and fourth line due to open by 2010; Chair. M. A. ODILOV.

ROADS

In 1999 the total length of the road network was estimated at 81,600 km, of which 87.3% was paved.

INLAND WATERWAYS

The extensive use of the waters of the Amu Dar'ya and Syr Dar'ya for irrigation lessened the flow of these rivers and caused the desiccation of the Aral Sea. This reduced a valuable transport asset. However, the Amu Dar'ya Steamship Co still operates important river traffic.

CIVIL AVIATION

There is an international airport at Tashkent. From 1996 the airports at Samarqand, Urgench and Buxoro were upgraded to stimulate tourism.

Uzbekistan Airways (Uzbekiston Havo Yollari): 100061 Tashkent, A. Timur koʻch. 41; tel. and fax (71) 140-46-23; e-mail info@uzairways.com; internet www.uzairways.com; f. 1992; operates flights between Uzbekistan and destinations in Central Asia, South-East Asia, the USA, the Middle East and Europe; Dir-Gen. VALERIY TYAN.

Tourism

Since independence, Uzbekistan has sought to promote tourism as an important source of revenue. The republic has more than 4,000 historical monuments, many of which are associated with the ancient 'Silk Route', particularly in the cities of Samarqand (Timur—Tamerlane's capital), Xiva (Khiva) and Buxoro (Bukhara), as well as other historic sites. Infrastructure limitations, however, have constrained development. In 2004 Uzbekistan received an estimated 261,600 foreign visitors (including excursionists). In that year tourism receipts totalled some US $57m.

Uzbektourism: 100047 Tashkent, Xorazm koʻch. 47; tel. (71) 233-54-14; fax (71) 233-80-68; e-mail info@uzbektourism.uz; internet www.uzbektourism.uz; f. 1992; Chair. ZAHID L. XAKIMOV.

VANUATU

Introductory Survey

Location, Climate, Language, Religion, Flag, Capital

The Republic of Vanuatu comprises an irregular archipelago of 83 islands in the south-west Pacific Ocean, lying about 1,000 km (600 miles) west of Fiji and 400 km (250 miles) north-east of New Caledonia. The group extends over a distance of about 1,300 km (808 miles) from north to south. The islands have an oceanic tropical climate, with a season of south-east trade winds between May and October. Winds are variable, with occasional cyclones for the rest of the year, and annual rainfall varies between 2,300 mm (90 ins) in the south and 3,900 mm (154 ins) in the north. In Port Vila, in the centre of the group, mean temperatures vary between 22°C (72°F) and 27°C (81°F). The national language is Bislama, ni-Vanuatu pidgin. There are many Melanesian languages and dialects. English, French and Bislama are the official languages. Most of the inhabitants (about 80%) profess Christianity, of which a number of denominations are represented. The national flag (proportions 3 by 5) consists of two equal horizontal stripes, red above green, on which are superimposed a black-edged yellow horizontal 'Y' (with its base in the fly) and, at the hoist, a black triangle containing two crossed yellow mele leaves encircled by a curled yellow boar's tusk. The capital is Port Vila, on the island of Efate.

Recent History

During the 19th century the New Hebrides (now Vanuatu) were settled by British and French missionaries, planters and traders. The United Kingdom and France established a Joint Naval Commission for the islands in 1887. The two countries later agreed on a joint civil administration, and in 1906 the territory became the Anglo-French Condominium of the New Hebrides (Nouvelles-Hébrides). Under this arrangement, there were three elements in the structure of administration: the British National Service, the French National Service and the Condominium (Joint) Departments. Each power was responsible for its own citizens and other non-New Hebrideans who chose to be 'ressortissants' of either power. Indigenous New Hebrideans were not permitted to claim either British or French citizenship. This resulted in two official languages, two police forces, three public services, three courts of law, three currencies, three national budgets, two resident commissioners in Port Vila (the capital) and two district commissioners in each of the four Districts.

Local political initiatives began after the Second World War, originating in New Hebridean concern over the alienation of native land. More than 36% of the New Hebrides was owned by foreigners. Na-Griamel, one of the first political groups to emerge, had its source in cult-like activities. In 1971 the leaders of Na-Griamel petitioned the UN to prevent further sales of land at a time when areas were being sold to US interests for development as tropical tourist resorts. In 1972 the New Hebrides National Party was formed, with support from Protestant missions and covert support from British interests. In response, French interests formed the Union des Communautés Néo-Hébridaises in 1974. Discussions in the United Kingdom in 1974 resulted in the replacement of the Advisory Council, established in 1957, by a Representative Assembly of 42 members, of whom 29 were directly elected in November 1975. The Assembly did not hold its first full working session until November 1976, and it was dissolved in early 1977, following a boycott by the National Party, which had changed its name to the Vanuaaku Pati (VP) in 1976. However, the VP reached an agreement with the Condominium powers on new elections for the Representative Assembly, based on universal suffrage for all seats.

In 1977, at a conference in France involving British, French and New Hebridean representatives, it was announced that the islands would become independent in 1980, following a referendum and elections. The VP boycotted this conference, as it demanded immediate independence. The VP also boycotted the elections in November 1977, and declared a 'People's Provisional Government'. Nevertheless, a reduced Assembly of 39 members was elected, and a measure of self-government was introduced in early 1978. A Council of Ministers and the office of Chief Minister (occupied by Georges Kalsakau) were created, and the French, British and Condominium Services began to be replaced by a single New Hebrides Public Service. In December a Government of National Unity was formed, with Fr Gérard Leymang as Chief Minister and Fr Walter Lini (the VP President) as Deputy Chief Minister.

At elections in November 1979 the VP won 26 of the 39 seats in the Assembly. The outcome of the election led to rioting by supporters of Na-Griamel on the island of Espiritu Santo, who threatened non-Santo 'foreigners'. However, the new Assembly elected Lini as Chief Minister.

In June 1980 Jimmy Stevens, the leader of Na-Griamel, declared Espiritu Santo independent of the rest of the New Hebrides, styling it the 'Independent State of Vemarana'. Members of his movement, allegedly assisted by French *colons* and supported by private US business interests, moved to the coast and imprisoned government officers and police, who were later released together with other European and indigenous public servants. British Royal Marines were deployed as a peacekeeping force, prompting strong criticism by the French authorities, which would not permit Britain's unilateral use of force on Espiritu Santo.

However, in mid-July 1980 agreement was reached between the two Condominium powers and Lini, and the New Hebrides became independent within the Commonwealth, under the name of Vanuatu, as planned, on 30 July. The first President was the former Deputy Chief Minister, George Kalkoa, who adopted the surname Sokomanu ('leader of thousands'), although the post was largely ceremonial. Lini became Prime Minister. The Republic of Vanuatu signed a defence pact with Papua New Guinea, and in August units of the Papua New Guinea Defence Force replaced the British and French troops on Espiritu Santo and arrested the Na-Griamel rebels.

At a general election in November 1983 the VP retained a majority in Parliament, taking 24 of the 39 seats. Sokomanu remained as President and Lini as Prime Minister. In February 1984 Sokomanu resigned as President, after pleading guilty in court to the late payment of road taxes, but he was re-elected in the following month. In October 1987 the Government expelled the French ambassador (see below). The envoy was alleged to have provided 'substantial financial assistance' to the opposition Union of Moderate Parties (UMP). Parliament was expanded to 46 seats for the general election held in December. Of these, the VP won 26 seats, the UMP 19 and the Fren Melanesia Pati one. Lini retained the premiership. Following the election, the Secretary-General of the VP, Barak Sope, unsuccessfully challenged Lini for the party presidency, but later accepted a portfolio in the Council of Ministers.

In May 1988 a government decision to abolish a local land corporation, which had been a principal source of patronage for Sope, prompted a demonstration in Port Vila by Sope's supporters. Serious rioting ensued, in which one person was killed and several others injured. Lini accused Sope of being instrumental in provoking the riots, and subsequently dismissed him from the Council of Ministers. In July Sope and four colleagues resigned from the VP, and were subsequently dismissed from Parliament at Lini's behest. In addition, 18 members of the UMP were dismissed after they had boycotted successive parliamentary sittings in protest at the expulsions. In September Sope and his colleagues announced the formation of a new political party, the Melanesian Progressive Pati (MPP), and in October the VP expelled 128 of its own members for allegedly supporting the new party. In October the Court of Appeal ruled as unconstitutional the dismissal from Parliament of Sope and his colleagues, and reinstated them, but upheld the expulsion of the 18 members of the UMP. In November Sope resigned from Parliament, citing loss of confidence in its Speaker. In December President Sokomanu dissolved Parliament and announced that Sope would act as interim Prime Minister, pending a general election scheduled for February 1989. Lini immediately denounced Sokomanu's actions, and the Governments of Australia, New Zealand and Papua New Guinea refused to recognize the interim Government. The islands' police force remained loyal to Lini, and later in December Sokomanu, Sope and other members of the interim Government were arrested and charged with treason. In 1989

Sokomanu was sentenced to six years' imprisonment, and Sope and the then leader of the parliamentary opposition, Maxime Carlot Korman, were jailed for five-year terms, for seditious conspiracy and incitement to mutiny. However, representatives of the International Commission of Jurists, who had been present at the trials, criticized the rulings, and in April the Court of Appeal overruled the original judgment, citing insufficient evidence for the convictions. Fred Timakata, the former Minister of Health, replaced Sokomanu as President in January 1989.

Diminishing support for Lini's leadership led to the approval in August 1991 of a motion of no confidence in Lini as party leader at the VP's congress. Donald Kalpokas, the Secretary-General of the VP, was unanimously elected to replace Lini as President of the party. In September a motion of no confidence in the premiership of Lini was narrowly approved in Parliament, and Kalpokas was elected Prime Minister. Subsequently, Lini, with the support of a substantial number of defectors from the VP, formed the National United Party (NUP). At a general election in December the UMP secured 19 seats, while the VP and NUP each won 10 seats, the MPP four and Tan Union, Fren Melanesia and Na-Griamel one each. The leader of the UMP, Maxime Carlot Korman, was appointed Prime Minister, and a coalition Government was formed between the UMP and the NUP.

At a presidential election in February 1994 neither the UMP's candidate, Fr Luc Dini, nor Fr John Bani, who was supported by the opposition, attained the requisite two-thirds of total votes cast. The election was rescheduled for March. The VP subsequently agreed to vote with the ruling UMP, in return for a guaranteed role in a future coalition government. As a result of this agreement, the UMP's candidate, Jean-Marie Leye, was elected to the presidency with 41 votes. The VP subsequently withdrew its support for the UMP when Carlot refused to offer the party more than one ministerial post; the VP had requested three.

In May 1994 the 'breakaway' members of the NUP who had remained in their ministerial posts, Sethy Regenvanu, Edward Tabisari and Cecil Sinker, were expelled from the party. They subsequently formed a new grouping, the People's Democratic Party (PDP), and later that month signed an agreement with the UMP to form a new coalition Government, the third since the election of December 1991. The UMP-PDP coalition held a total of 26 legislative seats.

In October 1994 the Supreme Court granted the Government a restraining order against further actions by the President, pending the hearing of an application to the Supreme Court to overrule several of the President's recent decisions. Members of the Government and judiciary had become increasingly alarmed by Leye's exercise of his presidential powers, which had included orders to free 26 criminals (many of whom had been convicted on extremely serious offences) and to appoint a convicted criminal to the position of Police Commissioner (on the recommendation of the Prime Minister).

In April 1995 Carlot attracted severe criticism from the Vanuatu-based regional news agency, Pacnews, when he dismissed two senior government officials for making comments critical of the Government; moreover, the journalists who reported the comments were threatened with dismissal. The Prime Minister's increasing reputation for intolerance of criticism was compounded by allegations that, as part of his Government's policy of reducing the number of employees in the public service, civil servants believed to be opposition sympathizers were among the first to lose their jobs.

At a general election held in November 1995, 20 of the 50 seats in the newly enlarged Parliament were won by the Unity Front coalition, the anglophone grouping led by Donald Kalpokas, which incorporated the VP, the MPP, the Tan Union and the NUP. The UMP secured 17 seats. A period of intense political manoeuvring followed the election, as the two main parties sought to form coalitions with other members in an attempt to secure a parliamentary majority. The situation was compounded by the emergence of two factions within the UMP, one comprising the supporters of Carlot and another led by Serge Vohor (the party's President). The Carlot faction of the UMP and the Unity Front both sought the political allegiance of the NUP. The latter's decision to accept the offer of a coalition with the UMP effectively excluded the Unity Front (the grouping with the largest number of seats) from Government, and, in protest, its members boycotted the opening of Parliament in December, thus preventing a vote on the formation of a new government taking place. At a subsequent parliamentary session Vohor was elected as Prime Minister, despite continuing allegations of irregularities in the election of senior members of Government.

In early February 1996 seven dissident UMP members of Parliament proposed a motion of no confidence in Vohor, supported by 22 other opposition members. However, Vohor announced his resignation as Prime Minister, thus preventing the vote from taking place. A parliamentary session to elect a new premier was abandoned as a result of a boycott by supporters of Vohor, who was reported to have retracted his resignation. However, at a further sitting, Carlot was elected Prime Minister.

In July 1996 a report published by the national ombudsman revealed a serious financial scandal, involving the issuing of 10 bank guarantees with a total value of US $100m. The Minister of Finance, Barak Sope, who had issued the guarantees in April, had been persuaded by an Australian financial adviser, Peter Swanson, that the scheme could earn the country significant revenue. Swanson, who left Vanuatu after securing the guarantees, was subsequently traced and charged with criminal offences relating to his dealings with Sope. (In February 1998 the Supreme Court found Swanson guilty on seven charges arising from the scandal, sentencing him to 18 months' imprisonment.) Carlot, meanwhile, rejected demands for his resignation for his compliance with the scheme and resisted considerable pressure to dismiss Sope and the Governor of the Reserve Bank of Vanuatu. In the following month, however, Sope was dismissed following his defection to the opposition.

In an attempt to restore a measure of political stability, Carlot appealed for reconciliation among the various political groups in the country in August 1996 and invited members of the opposition to join the Government. The opposition responded by reiterating its demand for Carlot's resignation, and in September a motion of no confidence in the Government was approved and Vohor was elected Prime Minister. Vohor's coalition Government comprised the pro-Vohor faction of the UMP, the NUP, the MPP, Tan Union and Fren Melanesia. A new Council of Ministers, in which Sope was appointed Deputy Prime Minister, was announced in mid-October.

A dispute over unpaid allowances, dating from 1993, led members of the 300-strong Vanuatu Mobile Force (VMF—the country's paramilitary force) briefly to abduct the President and Deputy Prime Minister to demand a settlement. Both Leye and Sope expressed sympathy for the VMF members. Sope was replaced as Deputy Prime Minister by Donald Kalpokas, and Fr Walter Lini was appointed Minister of Justice. Following a further incident in November in connection with the pay dispute, in which an official from the Department of Finance was abducted and allegedly assaulted, Lini ordered the arrest of more than half of the members of the VMF. About 30 members were detained and charged with criminal offences. In June 1999 18 VMF members were charged with the alleged kidnapping of a number of government officers in 1996. One was found guilty and was to be referred to a court martial for sentencing.

In March 1997 a memorandum of agreement was signed between the VP, the NUP and the UMP, the three parties of the newly formed governing coalition. However, the defection in May of five NUP members of Parliament, including two cabinet ministers, to the VP led to the party's expulsion from the Government. As a result, a new coalition, comprising the UMP, the MPP, Tan Union and Fren Melanesia, was formed. The subsequent designation of a new Cabinet was controversial for the appointment of Sope to the position of Deputy Prime Minister and Minister of Commerce, Trade and Industry. Sope had been described in January by the national ombudsman, Marie-Noëlle Ferrieux-Patterson (in a further report on the financial scandal of the previous year), as unfit for public office. Ferrieux-Patterson also criticized the recent appointment of Willie Jimmy as Minister of Finance.

In July 1997 legal action was initiated to recover the estimated US $300,000 of public funds paid in 1993 by Jimmy, together with Carlot, as compensation to the 23 members dismissed from Parliament following their boycott of the legislature in 1988. In the same month it was reported that the Government was preparing to amend legislation governing the powers of the ombudsman, in an attempt to contain her increasingly vociferous criticism of certain public figures.

In September 1997 Vohor dismissed Jimmy from his position as Minister of Finance, apparently owing to a dispute between Jimmy and the Prime Minister over the latter's decision to remove several areas of responsibility from the Finance portfolio. Meanwhile, further allegations of financial impropriety were published by the ombudsman, this time concerning the illegal sale of ni-Vanuatu passports to foreign nationals. In September the Prime Minister ordered an investigation into the matter. With both Vohor and Jimmy alleging the involvement of the other, the dispute intensified the disunity within the UMP, which had now come to comprise three factions, led respectively by Vohor, Carlot and Jimmy.

In November 1997 Parliament approved legislation to repeal the Ombudsman Act and the Government announced that it was to establish a commission of inquiry to determine if the ombudsman had exceeded her constitutional powers. However, President Leye refused to promulgate the new law on the grounds that it was unconstitutional, and he referred it to the Supreme Court. Later in the month Carlot filed a motion of no confidence in Vohor's Government. When Vohor attempted to withdraw all proposed legislation in order to prevent debate on the motion, Leye announced the dissolution of Parliament. However, the Supreme Court revived the parliamentary session in December. The matter was referred to the Court of Appeal, and Vohor and Carlot agreed to co-operate temporarily pending its judgment, which was eventually delivered in January 1998 and which once again ordered the immediate dissolution of Parliament. Following Leye's announcement of a forthcoming general election, Carlot announced the formation of the Vanuatu Republikan Pati (VRP). Meanwhile, Ferrieux-Patterson released a report in December 1997 in which she recommended that Vohor be investigated for offences relating to the illegal sale of ni-Vanuatu passports. The release of outspoken reports by the ombudsman continued into early 1998 and was widely believed to have contributed significantly to the domination of the election campaign by allegations of government corruption.

At a general election held on 6 March 1998, the VP won 18 of the 52 seats in the newly enlarged Parliament, the UMP secured 12, the NUP won 11, the MPP obtained six, the John Frum Movement secured two, the VRP obtained one, and independent candidates won two seats. In mid-March the VP and the NUP agreed to form a coalition Government, with the support of Carlot (the VRP's sole representative) and one independent member. At the end of the month Donald Kalpokas was elected Prime Minister with 35 parliamentary votes, defeating Vohor (who secured 17). Kalpokas also assumed three ministerial portfolios, including that for Foreign Affairs, while Lini, who was appointed to the revived post of Deputy Prime Minister, also became Minister of Justice and Internal Affairs.

In June 1998, despite strong opposition, notably from the UMP, Parliament approved a new 'leadership code'. Regarded as a crucial element in ensuring greater accountability and transparency in public life, the code defined clear guide-lines for the conduct of state officials (including a requirement that all public figures submit an annual declaration of assets to Parliament), and laid down strict penalties for those convicted of corruption. Shortly before, the Supreme Court upheld the repeal of the Ombudsman Act, as approved by Parliament in November 1997. The Kalpokas Government emphasized its commitment to strengthening the role of the ombudsman, stating that new legislation governing the office would be prepared. Although the ombudsman was to continue to function in the mean time, in early August 1998 Ferrieux-Patterson issued a statement in which she expressed concern that her powers of jurisdiction had been diminished.

In October 1998 Kalpokas expelled the NUP from the governing coalition, following reports that Lini (who died in February 1999), the party's leader, had organized a series of meetings with prominent members of the opposition, with the aim of forming a new coalition government which would exclude the VP. NUP ministers were largely replaced by members of the UMP faction led by Jimmy, which included the Deputy President of the party, Vincent Boulekone, and its Secretary-General, Henri Taga; one ministerial post was allocated to the John Frum Movement. In March 1999 Fr John Bani was chosen by the electoral college to succeed Jean-Marie Leye as President of Vanuatu.

The issue of press freedom returned to the fore in May 1999 when the Pacific Islands News Association expressed concern at the alleged assault on a local newspaper publisher by an associate of the Deputy Prime Minister, Willie Jimmy. Jimmy was reportedly displeased with the newspaper's coverage of an election campaign. The news association urged the Government to act against the increasing number of cases of media intimidation on the island.

The governing coalition was threatened in August 1999 by a decision by the National Council of the UMP to oppose participation in the Government. The Council issued a directive to the 17 members of Jimmy's faction to resign from the Kalpokas administration. Following their refusal to comply with the directive, the National Council acted to suspend the members in October. However, later that month the suspensions were overruled by the Supreme Court. The two factions of the UMP had previously attempted reunification but negotiations had stalled over the demands of Vohor's faction for two of the four ministerial positions held by Jimmy's faction. (The UMP achieved reunification in November 2000.)

At the end of August 1999 four by-elections took place, three of which were won by opposition parties, thus eliminating the Government's majority in Parliament. In November the Government staged a boycott of Parliament to avoid a proposed vote of no confidence by opposition parties against the Kalpokas administration. However, the subsequent defection to the opposition of an independent representative, followed by that of the Minister of Health, forced the resignation of Kalpokas prior to a no confidence motion on 25 November. The Speaker, Edward Natapei, announced his resignation shortly afterwards and Paul Ren Tari of the NUP was elected as his replacement. The leader of the MPP, Barak Sope, was elected to lead a new Government the same day; he secured 28 votes compared with the 24 votes gained by Natapei as the newly appointed President of the VP. Sope formed a five-party coalition Government, comprising the MPP, the NUP, the Vohor faction of the UMP, the VRP and the John Frum Movement. The composition of the new Council of Ministers was swiftly announced; it included Vohor as Minister of Foreign Affairs and Carlot as Minister of Lands and Mineral Resources, both of whom, with Sope, had been the subject of critical reports by the ombudsman. The new Government pledged to reduce the country's dependence on foreign advisers, review the recently introduced value-added tax and ensure that adequate services were delivered to rural communities.

In May 2000 Parliament approved controversial legislation (the Public Services Amendment Bill and the Government Amendment Bill) giving the Government direct power to appoint and dismiss public servants. The opposition criticized the changes, claiming that they contravened the principles of the Comprehensive Reform Programme (a range of economic measures supported by the Asian Development Bank—ADB, see p. 191). President John Bani subsequently referred both pieces of legislation to the Supreme Court, which, in August, ordered that he approve them. The ADB reacted strongly to the development, arguing that it allowed for political bias in the public sector, and threatened to withhold further funds from Vanuatu. The bank's stance served to perpetuate an ongoing dispute between the organization and the Vanuatu Government, which had often expressed the view that the bank imposed harsh conditions in return for its finance.

An incident in August 2000 in which the Deputy Prime Minister, Reginald Stanley, was allegedly involved in the serious assault of two people and in causing criminal damage to property while under the influence of alcohol, led to Stanley's dismissal from the post. He was replaced by the Minister of Trade Development, James Bule.

In September 2000 the opposition leader, Edward Natapei, invited the Vohor faction of the UMP to join the opposition and form a new government. Vohor declined the offer, saying that his priority was the stability of the current Government. The resignation of a VP member in October prevented the success of a motion of no confidence in the Prime Minister. Also in October the Government was forced to defend a controversial plan, which allowed a Thai company, Apex, to pay off a portion of government debt, allegedly in return for 'tax-haven' privileges. The President of Apex, Amarendra Nath Ghosh, was also Vanuatu's recently appointed honorary consul to Thailand. In January 2001 the Government deported Mark Neil-Jones, the publisher of the independent newspaper, Trading Post, on the grounds of instigating instability in the country. (The Trading Post had recently published several critical articles about the Government, including reports on the Government's financial dealings with Nath Ghosh.) However, the Supreme Court reversed the decision, declaring that the deportation order was illegal, and Neil-Jones was allowed to return to the country. An investigation was subsequently launched into the circumstances of the deportation.

In late January 2001 three members of the UMP resigned from the party, further reducing the Government's majority. The Government's problems intensified in March after the withdrawal of the UMP from the ruling coalition. Opposition attempts to vote on a motion of no confidence were delayed as

Sope initiated legal action against the motion, and the Speaker, Paul Ren Tari, refused to allow the vote while legal action was pending. The Chief Justice, however, ordered the vote to proceed, and after further postponements by the Speaker, the Sope Government was voted out of office in mid-April. A new Government, led by Edward Natapei of the VP, was elected. The incoming administration, a coalition of the VP and UMP, was duly sworn in, and pledged to continue the reform programme and to restore investor confidence. One of the Government's first acts was to remove Nath Ghosh from his diplomatic position. Vohor was appointed Deputy Prime Minister. In early May Parliament held an extraordinary session to debate a motion to remove Ren Tari as Speaker because of his conduct during the political crisis. Ren Tari responded by suspending Natapei, along with five other Members of Parliament who held cabinet posts, for breaching parliamentary procedure. Despite an order by the Chief Justice that they be allowed to return to Parliament to continue the extraordinary session, Ren Tari refused to open the legislature while he appealed to the Supreme Court against the order. In response, Ren Tari and his two deputies were arrested and charged with sedition. A new Speaker, Donald Kalpokas, President of the UMP, was elected, thus reducing Natapei's majority in Parliament to one. In September 2001 opposition leader Sope tabled a motion of no confidence against the ruling coalition but was defeated.

In November 2001 Sope was ordered to appear in court to answer charges that he had forged two government-supported Letters of Guarantee, worth US $23m., while he was Prime Minister. It was reported that police were also investigating the activities of the former Minister of Finance, Morkin Steven, whose signature appeared on the documents. Meanwhile, Sope was under investigation for possible involvement in the illegal issuing of diplomatic passports and in connection with allegations of bribery. The preliminary hearing of the forgery charges was postponed until February 2002, enabling Sope to contest the general election due to take place later in that year.

In March 2002 Parliament was dissolved after the Supreme Court ruled that its four-year term had expired. Prime Minister Natapei remained in charge of an interim Government until the general election, scheduled for early May. Also in March it was announced that the newly established People's Progressive Party (PPP) and Fren Melanesia were to form a coalition with the ruling NUP to contest the forthcoming election. It was reported that the general election was to be monitored by an independent group of observers. The future of the Comprehensive Reform Programme was widely perceived to be the main issue in the electoral campaign.

The general election was held on 2 May 2002. A total of 327 candidates contested the 52 seats available in Parliament. A record 138 candidates stood as independents, prompting Natapei to comment prior to the election that for Vanuatu to attain political stability the electoral constituency should vote only for party candidates. After some initial uncertainty, it was announced that the UMP had won 15 seats in the new Parliament and that the VP had secured 14. However, in accordance with the terms of the coalition agreement, the VP was permitted to nominate the next Prime Minister. The new Government was formed in early June, with Natapei duly re-elected Prime Minister.

In July 2002 former Prime Minister Barak Sope was convicted of fraud by the Supreme Court and sentenced to three years' imprisonment. It was alleged soon afterwards that New Zealand had interfered in Vanuatu's internal affairs by funding the investigation that had led to Sope's conviction. In early August, following the controversial appointment of Mael Apisai as Vanuatu's new Police Commissioner, disaffected police officers staged a raid during which they arrested Apisai, Attorney-General Hamilton Bulu and 14 other senior civil servants on charges of seditious conspiracy. Following an investigation, the charges were abandoned owing to a lack of evidence. Prime Minister Natapei subsequently assumed the police and VMF portfolios from the Minister of Internal Affairs, Joe Natuman, in what was thought to be an attempt to distance Natuman from some members of the police force, with whom he had reportedly become too closely involved. Later in the month members of the VMF surrounded the police headquarters in Port Vila to serve arrest warrants on 27 of those who had been involved in the raid, including the acting police commissioner, Holis Simon, and the commander of the VMF, Api Jack Marikembo. Shortly afterwards, in an attempt to bring an end to hostilities, the Government signed an agreement with representatives from the police department and the VMF during a traditional Melanesian reconciliation ceremony. The police officers involved, who had been suspended from their posts, were reinstated, the police and the VMF pledged to make no further arrests and it was agreed that Apisai's appointment would be reviewed by a newly appointed police services commission. At the same time it was decided that the allegations of conspiracy that had been brought against the 15 officials initially arrested would be considered by the judicial authorities. A new acting police commissioner, Lt-Gen. Arthur Coulton, was then appointed. In early October 2002 it was announced that the charges against 18 of those arrested in connection with the August raid would be abandoned, leaving eight senior officers to face trial on charges of mutiny and incitement to mutiny. In early December four of these police officers were found guilty by the Supreme Court on charges of mutiny, incitement to mutiny, kidnapping and false imprisonment and were given suspended two-year prison sentences. In the same month police intervened to prevent former Prime Minister Barak Sope from reclaiming his seat in Parliament, claiming that this was nullified by his conviction for fraud in July, despite receiving a pardon in November from President Bani. The pardon, which Bani stated he had made on the grounds of Sope's poor health, provoked widespread public opposition and led the Government to announce the appointment of a commission of inquiry to investigate the President's decision. However, in November 2003, at a by-election to the seat vacated by his conviction for fraud, Barak Sope was re-elected.

In April 2003 the election of Ham Lini (brother of Walter Lini, the late founder of the NUP) as President of the NUP led to the signing of a memorandum of understanding inviting that party to join the coalition Government. The NUP was expected to assume three ministerial portfolios (including finance) in a development which observers believed might lead to the reunification of the NUP with the VP (which had been a single political organization until the split of 1991). However, in late April the NUP rejected the VP's offer and announced its intention to remove the Government in a motion of no confidence. A further attempt to propose a motion of no confidence in the Government led Natapei to remove the UMP from the ruling coalition in a reorganization of cabinet portfolios in November. The party was replaced in the coalition by members of the NUP, the PPP, the Green Confederation Party and independents. Continued instability within the governing coalition prompted three further cabinet reorganizations during the first three months of 2004.

In April 2004 former Speaker Alfred Maseng Nalo was sworn in as Vanuatu's new President following a lengthy and closely contested election. Maseng defeated 31 other candidates during a total of four rounds of voting. However, the validity of the election was questioned when it was revealed that Maseng was serving a suspended prison sentence, having been convicted of misappropriation and receiving property dishonestly. In May, only four weeks after his appointment to the presidency, the Supreme Court ruled that Maseng should be removed from office; in August Kalkot Mataskelekele was elected as President. The likelihood that the Government, which held a minority of seats in Parliament, would be removed in an imminent vote of no confidence led to a decision by the Council of Ministers to dissolve Parliament in June.

A general election was held on 6 July 2004, at which no single party won an overall majority and 25 new members were elected, including many independent candidates. However, the validity of the election was jeopardized by an incident on Tanna in which ballot boxes *en route* to Port Vila for processing were ambushed and burnt. More than 40 people were arrested in connection with the incident, including the acting Minister of Finance, Jimmy Nickelim of the VP. In late July Serge Vohor was elected Prime Minister, defeating Ham Lini by 28 votes to 24. A Council of Ministers composed of five political groups and several independents was appointed shortly afterwards. However, the stability of the new administration was threatened by rumours of shifting allegiances and reports that several members were being persuaded to cross the floor of Parliament. Despite these suggestions, an opposition motion of no confidence in the new Government, proposed in September, was defeated, with Vohor's administration securing the support of 31 of the 52 members. Further doubts over Vohor's ability to continue as Prime Minister were cast when the country's police commissioner attempted to arrest him on charges of contempt, following comments made in Parliament accusing the Chief Justice, Vincent Lunabeck, of being unduly influenced by a desire to please foreign interests in the country. The Supreme Court, however, dismissed the charges against Vohor during an appeal in late September.

The Prime Minister became the focus of further serious controversy in November 2004 when he announced the establishment of diplomatic relations with Taiwan. The announcement, which Vohor defended by claiming that Taiwan's assistance was necessary to cover the budgetary deficit, was made only weeks after the Prime Minister had made an official visit to the People's Republic of China during which he had reiterated Vanuatu's allegiance to that country. The Council of Ministers, which had not given the necessary approval of the agreement with Taiwan, responded by demanding that Vohor renounce recognition of Taiwan or dismiss the entire cabinet. Controversy increased following reports that Vohor had assaulted the Chinese ambassador when questioned over the legitimacy of the Taiwanese flag flying in Port Vila. A parliamentary vote of no confidence in Vohor took place in early December, despite the Prime Minister's attempts to prevent the motion by means of a legal challenge, and was approved by 35 votes to 14. Ham Lini was elected Prime Minister and subsequently appointed a cabinet that included five former ministers who had crossed the floor of the legislature to vote against Vohor.

Lini's Government reversed the policy of the previous administration regarding Taiwan, and in July 2005 the Minister for Home Affairs made an official visit to China to sign a co-operation agreement providing for technical, logistical and financial support for the Vanuatu Police Force. Lini effected a cabinet reorganization in the same month. Further changes to the Council of Ministers reflected the decision of five opposition members to join the Green Confederation Party led by the Minister of Finance, Moana Carcasses Kalosil. Their defection resulted in the Green Confederation Party becoming Lini's most significant partner in the governing coalition. In November 2005, in a cabinet reorganization, Moana Carcasses was replaced as Minister of Finance by Willie Jimmy, hitherto Minister of Lands, Geology and Mines. In a further reallocation of portfolios announced in March 2006, Dunstan Hilton replaced Barak Sope as Minister of Agriculture, following reports that the former Prime Minister had been conducting negotiations aimed at attempting to oust the incumbent, Ham Lini, from office. In the same month the Prime Minister defeated by 30 parliamentary votes to 20 a motion of no confidence, which had been presented by the opposition partly as a result of criticism of the Government's handling of the ban on the import of Fijian biscuits, which had been imposed in retaliation for Fiji's ban on kava from Vanuatu.

As part of a programme of judicial reform, in early 2006 a new building accommodating a magistrate's court was opened in Port Vila. New court buildings were also to be constructed on three other islands, thus improving the population's access to the justice system. In June 2007 the Supreme Court building in Port Vila was destroyed in a fire. Two men were charged with arson in early July and, after pleading guilty to the charge, were sentenced to six years' imprisonment in December 2008. In late 2006 activists of the Vete association, which comprised inhabitants of Tongoa, vandalized unoccupied government buildings in Port Vila to publicize their campaign for land ownership rights. Vete claimed that prior to the declaration of areas of the capital as public land, no custom owner had been named. In December it was reported that members of Vete were occupying several empty government buildings, prompting police to warn of prosecution. In March 2007 allegations of witchcraft, following the death of a woman, led to civil unrest in outlying areas of Port Vila, with migrants from two islands engaging in violence that resulted in three fatalities and some 150 arrests. A two-week state of emergency, forbidding public gatherings and providing security forces with special powers, was declared. Nine people were later charged in relation to the violence, which was estimated to have displaced approximately 150 people. The unrest provoked renewed public debate about internal migration in Vanuatu.

In May 2007 the Minister of Agriculture, Forestry and Fisheries, Marcellino Pipite, was dismissed, having been accused of disloyalty to the Government ; he was replaced by Donna Brounie in the same month. Following further cabinet changes in June, the VP was removed from the governing coalition and replaced by the UMP, whose President, Serge Vohor, was appointed Minister of Infrastructure and Public Utilities. The VP had reportedly allied itself with the UMP in the latter's attempt to oust the Government in a motion of no confidence, but the UMP subsequently retracted the motion. Vohor himself was dismissed in July, allegedly having been involved in an altercation with a government official. At the same time, the Deputy Prime Minister and Minister for Foreign Affairs, Sato Kilman, and the Minister of Youth and Sports, Dunstan Hilton, both of the PPP, were removed from office owing to allegations of fraud (in August Hilton was reported to have been charged in a fraud case involving funds misappropriated from the National Bank of Vanuatu). The VP rejoined the Government in order to ensure its retention of a majority and its members were allocated important portfolios including that of home affairs. Former Prime Minister and VP President Edward Natapei assumed the role of Deputy Prime Minister and returned to the infrastructure and public utilities portfolio. However, in April 2008 speculation arose about the strength of the coalition after it was reported that plans for another motion of no confidence had been discussed. In mid-August Maxime Carlot Korman, the Minister for Lands, was obliged to answer a bribery charge relating to a land lease in Lelepa; however, he was cleared of the charge on the grounds of lack of evidence.

Parliamentary elections took place on 2 September 2008, when more than 300 candidates contested the 52 seats. About one-third of the incumbent members of Parliament were reported to have lost their seats at the poll, including Barak Sope, the former Prime Minister, and Willie Jimmy, hitherto the Minister of Finance. The VP won 11 seats, thus obtaining the largest representation in Parliament, followed by the NUP with eight seats, the UMP with seven and the VRP, also with seven. The failure of any single party to win a sufficient number of parliamentary seats led to a brief period of uncertainty; both Edward Natapei, leader of the VP, and Maxime Carlot Korman, leader of the VRP, claimed to have enough support to form a government. On 22 September Napatei was elected Prime Minister after obtaining 27 parliamentary votes, while Carlot received 25. The former Minister of Foreign Affairs, George Andre Wells, was elected Speaker of Parliament. Napatei appointed outgoing Prime Minister Ham Lini as his Deputy Prime Minister. Within days of its formation Carlot led a motion of no confidence against the Natapei administration. However, before the motion could be presented to Parliament, in early October the Prime Minister effected a cabinet reorganization, in order to accommodate members of the UMP, which was allocated three portfolios. The new appointments were those of Serge Vohor as Minister of Public Utilities, Charlod Saluwai as Minister of Education and Rafael Vorvor as Minister of Lands, Geology and Mines. The Natapei Government was thus able to defeat the subsequent motion of no confidence by 31 votes to 20. In March 2009 the former Deputy Prime Minister, Sato Kilman, replaced Carlot as Leader of the Opposition. It was announced that a by-election was to be held in the constituency of Tanna, following the conviction on bribery charges of an independent member of Parliament, Judah Issac, and his campaign team. A date for the poll was to be set later in the year.

In late December 2008 30 prisoners in Vanuatu's high-risk detention centre burned down the prison and escaped, following weeks of protests against allegedly inhumane conditions in the centre. By the end of the week the escaped prisoners had been recaptured; two politicians, including former Minister of Finance Moana Carcasses Kalosil, were charged with aiding the prisoners, after they allegedly harboured a number of escaped inmates and tried to negotiate their return with the police.

In foreign affairs, Vanuatu has had an uneasy relationship with France. In 1981 the French ambassador to Vanuatu was expelled following the deportation from New Caledonia of the VP Secretary-General, who had been due to attend an assembly of the New Caledonian Independence Front. France immediately withdrew aid to Vanuatu, but this was subsequently restored and a new ambassador was appointed. However, the French ambassador was expelled again in 1987, for allegedly providing 'substantial financial assistance' to Vanuatu's opposition parties. In response to the expulsion, the French Government again announced that it would withdraw aid to Vanuatu. Maxime Carlot Korman, Vanuatu's first francophone Prime Minister, made an official visit to France in May 1992, and the two countries fully restored diplomatic relations in October. In July, however, the Carlot Government reaffirmed its support for the Kanak independence movement on the French Territory of New Caledonia, following threats by Walter Lini to withdraw from the Government unless Carlot's pro-French policies were modified. Improved relations with France were confirmed in

1993 with the signing of a bilateral co-operation agreement. In mid-1995 the Carlot Government was virtually alone in the region in failing to condemn France's resumption of nuclear tests in French Polynesia. The opposition criticized the Government's stance as not reflecting the views of the vast majority of ni-Vanuatu. France provided food and other items for the relief effort in Port Vila following the communal violence of March 2007.

In March 1988 Vanuatu signed an agreement with Papua New Guinea and Solomon Islands to form the Melanesian Spearhead Group, which aimed to preserve Melanesian cultural traditions and to lobby for independence for New Caledonia. In 1994 the Melanesian Spearhead Group concluded an agreement providing for the gradual establishment of a free trade area encompassing the three countries. Fiji joined the group in 1996. In March 2006 the Melanesian Spearhead Group met in Port Vila to discuss several issues concerning regional trade and security. Vanuatu had been accused of breaching the group's agreement by restricting its markets through the imposition of export licences for the sale of kava and other commodities. Negotiations were also taking place regarding the construction in Vanuatu of a permanent headquarters for the Melanesian Spearhead Group Secretariat. In August it was reported that a Chinese team was creating the designs for the new Port Vila headquarters. In March 2007 the members of the Melanesian Spearhead Group signed a constitution at a meeting in Vanuatu.

In August 2005 it was announced that discussions had taken place between the Prime Ministers of Vanuatu and Solomon Islands on the possibility of establishing an agreement governing border control and a patrol system. The issues were discussed amid concerns regarding drug- and people-trafficking, money-laundering and other border-related crime. It was hoped that a system of mutual co-operation similar to that operating between Solomon Islands and Papua New Guinea might be established. In December 2006 approximately 10 ni-Vanuatu police officers joined international peace-keeping forces in Timor-Leste. In April 2009 the Australian Minister for Trade, Simon Crean, visited Vanuatu for discussions with the Government regarding the negotiation of a free trade agreement by Australia, New Zealand and the Pacific islands. The Vanuatu Government was reported to be supportive of the proposed agreement. Later in that month, the Minister of Foreign Affairs and External Trade, Bakoa Kaltonga, was reported to have announced the decision to create three new Vanuatu diplomatic missions. The proposed establishment of High Commissions in Malaysia, New Zealand and Fiji formed part of the Government's plans to strengthen relations with the countries of the Asia-Pacific region. In May Vanuatu reaffirmed its support for dialogue on the issue of the desire for independence of the Indonesian province of Papua (see the chapter on Indonesia).

In February 2009 a government delegation travelled to New York for a meeting of the UN Economic and Social Council (ECOSOC, see p. 20) to present a case against recommendations that Vanuatu's status be raised from that of Least Developed Country (LDC) to Developing Country. The change in status, to be decided by ECOSOC in late May, would lead to the loss of a number of economic privileges, including special treatment in areas such as trade and foreign aid. In March of that year the Government re-entered negotiations on its accession to the World Trade Organization (WTO, see p. 410), initiated in 1995 but subsequently suspended; however, the benefits of membership were questioned by some local non-government organizations.

Government

Vanuatu is a republic. Legislative power is vested in the unicameral Parliament, with 52 members who are elected by universal adult suffrage for four years. The Head of State is the President, elected for a five-year term by an electoral college consisting of Parliament and the Presidents of the Regional Councils. Executive power is vested in the Council of Ministers, appointed by the Prime Minister and responsible to Parliament. The Prime Minister is elected by and from members of Parliament. Legislation enacted in 1994 resulted in the replacement of the 11 local government councils by six provincial bodies, with greater executive powers. The six provincial authorities are Malampa, Penama, Sanma, Shefa, Tafea and Torba.

Defence

Vanuatu signed a defence agreement with Papua New Guinea in 1980. The Vanuatu Mobile Force comprises 300 paramilitaries. In 2002 the Government allocated 766m. vatu for defence, equivalent to 7.4% of total recurrent budgetary expenditure.

Economic Affairs

In 2007, according to estimates by the World Bank, Vanuatu's gross national income (GNI), measured at average 2005–07 prices, was US $417m., equivalent to $1,840 per head (or $3,410 per head on an international purchasing-power parity basis). During 2000–07, it was estimated, the population increased at an average annual rate of 2.5%, while gross domestic product (GDP) per head decreased, in real terms, by an average of 0.2% per year. Overall GDP increased, in real terms, at an average annual rate of 2.6% in 2000–07. According to the Asian Development Bank (ADB), GDP increased by 6.8% in 2007 and by 6.3% in 2008.

The agricultural sector (including forestry and fishing) contributed 13.6% of GDP in 2007, compared with some 40% in the early 1980s. According to official sources, the GDP of the agricultural sector was estimated to have increased by an average annual rate of 1.0% in 2000–07. The sector's GDP increased by 2.4% in 2006 and by 2.2% in 2007. About 34% of the employed labour force were engaged in agricultural activities in 2005, according to FAO estimates. Coconuts, cocoa and coffee are grown largely for export (copra being the most important agricultural exports), while yams, taro, cassava, breadfruit and vegetables are cultivated for subsistence purposes. Cattle, pigs, goats and poultry are the country's principal livestock, and beef is a significant export commodity. The forestry industry is also important, with timber having become a major export item. The Government derives substantial revenue from the sale of fishing rights to foreign fleets. In October 2005 the Government and the People's Republic of China signed an agreement that provided for the financing of the establishment of a new fish-processing plant near Port Vila. The facility would also be available for processing other products for export, such as beef.

The industrial sector (including manufacturing, utilities and construction) contributed about 8.3% of GDP in 2007, although only 3.5% of the employed labour force were engaged in the sector in 1989. In 2000–07 the GDP of the industrial sector was estimated to have increased at an average annual rate of 3.1%. Compared with the previous year, industrial GDP increased by 7.0% in 2006 and by 10.4% in 2007. Construction activity alone contributed 3.5% of GDP in 2007.

Manufacturing, which contributed about 2.9% of GDP in 2007, is mainly concerned with the processing of agricultural products. In 2000–07, however, the GDP of the manufacturing sector decreased by an average annual rate of 0.9%. The country's first kava extraction plant (for the manufacture of alcoholic beverages) was opened in 1998. However, in 2001 a ban was imposed on kava imports by several countries in Europe, owing to health concerns.

Various mineral deposits have been identified. These include manganese on the island of Efate, and there are reserves of gold, copper and petroleum around the islands of Malekula and Espiritu Santo. In March 2006 an agreement was signed by the Vanuatu Government to allow a Swiss-US company to extract manganese and to export the commodity.

Electricity generation is largely thermal. Long-term plans focus on the potential of renewable resources. Imports of mineral fuels comprised 16.7% of the value of total imports in 2008.

The economy depends heavily on the services sector, which accounted for 78.0% of GDP in 2007. In 2000–07 the GDP of the services sector was estimated to have increased at an average annual rate of 3.0%. The GDP of the services sector increased by 8.7% in 2006 and by 7.4% in 2007. Tourism, 'offshore' banking facilities and a shipping registry, providing a 'flag of convenience' to foreign-owned vessels, make a significant contribution to the country's income. In 2008 a total of 90,521 foreign tourists (mainly from Australia) visited Vanuatu by air, compared with 81,345 in the previous year. According to official sources, the number of tourist arrivals by cruise-ship decreased slightly, from 85,922 in 2006 to 85,737 in 2007, before increasing to 106,138 in 2008. Revenue from tourism was estimated to have increased from US $93m. in 2004 to $104m. in 2005 and to $109m. in 2006.

In 2007 Vanuatu recorded a visible trade deficit of US $142.93m., and there was a deficit of $53.78m. on the current account of the balance of payments. In 2008 the principal sources of imports were Australia (28.1%), New Zealand (13.3%) and Fiji (10.4%), while New Caledonia was the principal market for exports (accounting for 9.8% of the total). The principal imports in 2008 were machinery and transport equipment (30.9% of total imports), mineral fuels and lubricants (16.7%) and food and live animals (15.4%). Copra (which provided 30.3% of total export earnings), coconut oil (20.3%) and kava (13.7%) were the main export commodities in 2008.

Budget estimates for 2008 projected a deficit of 2,657m. vatu, excluding grants from abroad in that year totalling 3,975m. vatu. Australia, New Zealand, France, the United Kingdom and Japan are significant sources of development assistance. In 2008/09 Australia budgeted for aid of some $A51.8m., and in the same year development assistance from New Zealand was projected at $NZ17.0m. Vanuatu's total external debt reached US $86m. at the end of 2006. In that year the cost of debt-servicing was estimated to be equivalent to 1.7% of the value of exports of goods and services. The annual rate of inflation averaged 2.5% in 2000–07. Consumer prices increased by 5.8% in 2008, according to the ADB.

Vanuatu is a member of the Pacific Community (see p. 391), the Pacific Islands Forum (see p. 393), the Asian Development Bank (ADB, see p. 191) and the UN Economic and Social Commission for Asia and the Pacific (ESCAP, see p. 36). The country is a signatory of the South Pacific Regional Trade and Economic Agreement (SPARTECA, see p. 395) and of the Lomé Conventions and the successor Cotonou Agreement (see p. 311) with the EU. Vanuatu is also a member of the Melanesian Spearhead Group, along with Fiji, Papua New Guinea and Solomon Islands; a free trade agreement concluded by members grants most-favoured nation status for all trading transactions.

Vanuatu's economic development has been curtailed by its weak infrastructure, dependence on the agricultural sector, which is vulnerable to adverse weather conditions, and by the relatively high rate of population growth, which (despite the continuation of robust overall GDP growth in 2008) has impeded any significant rise in GDP in terms of per caput income. In the early 21st century the country's GDP per head was estimated to be below the level of the mid-1980s. A major challenge for the Government is the problem of rural hardship. In contrast to the situation in other Pacific islands, opportunities for emigration and for engagement in overseas employment have been limited. However, it was hoped that the establishment in 2008 of a scheme whereby Pacific islanders were able to travel to Australia and work in the horticulture industry on a seasonal basis, would provide wider employment opportunities for ni-Vanuatu; in April 2009 the first six workers arrived in the country. In March 2006 Vanuatu and the US Millennium Challenge Corporation signed an agreement providing the country with a grant of US $65.9m., to be disbursed between 2007 and 2011, for the purpose of financing various infrastructural projects. The authorities hoped to develop an effective regulatory framework for the utilities sector, in an effort to improve efficiency and to reduce costs in the fields of electricity, telecommunications and water supply. In rural areas access to such services had remained extremely limited. The continued GDP growth of 2008 was sustained by strong performance in the tourism and property sectors, although the effect of the deterioration in global economic conditions on Australia (the leading source of visitors) was expected to have a detrimental impact on tourist arrivals in 2009. Despite a 47% increase in the value of Vanuatu's merchandise exports, dominated by sales of coconut oil and copra, in 2008 the cost of imports rose by 31%; imports were reported to have reached a level seven times greater than that of exports, thus resulting in a substantial increase in the trade deficit. GDP growth was forecast to decline to 3.5% in 2009, as foreign investment decreased and as global commodity prices for Vanuatu's main exports remained weak.

Education

The abolition of nominal fees for primary education following independence resulted in a significant increase in enrolment at that level. Thus, at the beginning of the 1990s it was estimated that about 85% of children between the ages of six and 11 were enrolled at state-controlled primary institutions. Secondary education begins at 12 years of age, and comprises a preliminary cycle of four years and a second cycle of three years. In 2000/01 enrolment at pre-primary schools included 41% of pupils from the relevant age-group. In 2004/05 enrolment at primary schools included 93.9% of pupils in the relevant age-group, while in 2003/04 enrolment in secondary schools included 39.3% of pupils. Vocational education and teacher-training are also available. The relatively low level of secondary enrolment has been a cause of some concern to the Government, and a major programme for the expansion of the education system was inaugurated in 1989. Low literacy rates have been another cause of concern.

An extension centre of the University of the South Pacific was opened in Port Vila in 1989. Students from Vanuatu can also receive higher education at the principal faculties of that university (in Suva, Fiji), in Papua New Guinea or in France.

The 2002 budget allocated an estimated 2,062m. vatu to education (20.1% of total recurrent expenditure by the central Government).

Public Holidays

2009: 1 January (New Year's Day), 21 February (Father Walter Lini Day), 5 March (Custom Chief's Day), 10–13 April (Easter), 1 May (Labour Day), 21 May (Ascension Day), 24 July (Children's Day), 30 July (Independence Day), 15 August (Assumption), 5 October (Constitution Day), 30 November (Unity Day), 25 December (Christmas Day), 26 December (Family Day).

2010: 1 January (New Year's Day), 21 February (Father Walter Lini Day), 5 March (Custom Chief's Day), April (Easter), 1 May (Labour Day), 13 May (Ascension Day), 24 July (Children's Day), 30 July (Independence Day), 15 August (Assumption), 5 October (Constitution Day), 29 November (Unity Day), 25 December (Christmas Day), 26 December (Family Day).

Weights and Measures

The metric system is in force.

Statistical Survey

Source (unless otherwise indicated): National Statistics Office, Ministry of Finance and Economic Management, PMB 9019, Port Vila; tel. (678) 22110; fax (678) 24583; e-mail stats@vanuatu.com.vu; internet www.spc.int/prism/country/vu/stats .

AREA AND POPULATION

Area: 12,190 sq km (4,707 sq miles); *By Island* (sq km): Espiritu Santo 4,010; Malekula 2,024; Efate 887; Erromango 887; Ambrym 666; Tanna 561; Pentecost 499; Epi 444; Ambae 399; Vanua Lava 343; Gaua 315; Maewo 300.

Population: 142,419 at census of 16 May 1989; 186,678 (males 95,682, females 90,996) at census of 16 November 1999. *Mid-2008* (estimate): 233,026. *By Island* (mid-1999, official estimates): Espiritu Santo 31,811; Malekula 19,766; Efate 43,295; Erromango 1,554; Ambrym 7,613; Tanna 26,306; Pentecost 14,837; Epi 4,706; Ambae 10,692; Vanua Lava 2,074; Gaua 1,924; Maewo 3,385.

Density (mid-2008): 19.1 per sq km.

Principal Towns (population at 1999 census): Port Vila (capital) 29,356; Luganville (Santo) 10,738. *Mid-2007* (incl. suburbs, UN estimate) Port Vila (capital) 40,000 (Source: UN, *World Urbanization Prospects: The 2007 Revision*).

Births and Deaths (annual averages, 2000–05, UN estimates): Birth rate 32.1 per 1,000; Death rate 5.7 per 1,000. Source: UN, *World Population Prospects: The 2008 Revision*.

Life Expectancy (years at birth, WHO estimates): 68.6 (males 67.2; females 70.1) in 2006. Source: WHO, *World Health Statistics*.

Economically Active Population (census of May 1989): Agriculture, forestry, hunting and fishing 40,889; Mining and quarrying 1; Manufacturing 891; Electricity, gas and water 109; Construction 1,302; Trade, restaurants and hotels 2,712; Transport, storage and communications 1,030; Financing, insurance, real estate and business services 646; Community, social and personal services 7,891; Activities not adequately defined 11,126; *Total labour force* 66,597 (males 35,692, females 30,905). *1999 Census* (persons aged 15 to 64 years): Subsistence farmers 51,309; Total employed (incl. others) 75,110; Unemployed (seeking work) 1,260; Total labour force 76,370 (males 42,072, females 34,298). *Mid-2005* (estimates): Agriculture, etc. 32,000; Total labour force 95,000 (Source: FAO).

VANUATU

HEALTH AND WELFARE
Key Indicators

Total Fertility Rate (children per woman, 2006): 3.9.
Under-5 Mortality Rate (per 1,000 live births, 2006): 36.
Physicians (per 1,000 head, 2004): 0.1.
Hospital Beds (per 1,000 head, 2005): 4.1.
Health Expenditure (2006): US $ per head (PPP): 139.
Health Expenditure (2006): % of GDP: 4.2.
Health Expenditure (2006): public (% of total): 64.7.
Access to Water (% of persons, 2004): 60.
Access to Sanitation (% of persons, 2004): 50.
Human Development Index (2006): ranking: 123.
Human Development Index (2006): value: 0.686.

For sources and definitions, see explanatory note on p. vi.

AGRICULTURE, ETC.

Principal Crops ('000 metric tons, 2007, FAO estimates): Coconuts 322; Roots and tubers 43.0; Vegetables and melons 11.5; Bananas 14.5; Groundnuts, with shell 2.6; Maize 0.8; Cocoa beans 1.4.
Livestock ('000 head, year ending September 2007, FAO estimates): Cattle 156; Pigs 63; Goats 12; Horses 3; Chickens 360.
Livestock Products (metric tons, 2007, FAO estimates): Cattle meat 2,750; Pig meat 2,850; Chicken meat 550; Cows' milk 3,200; Hen eggs 370.
Forestry ('000 cu m, 2001): *Roundwood Removals* (excl. bark): Sawlogs and veneer logs 28; Fuel wood 91; Total 119. *Sawnwood Production* (all broadleaved, incl. railway sleepers): Total 28. *2002–07:* Annual output as in 2001 (FAO estimates).
Fishing ('000 metric tons, live weight, 2006): Marine fishes 102.3 (Skipjack tuna 60.2; Yellowfin tuna 8.4; Bigeye tuna 3.9; Albacore 13.3); Marine crustaceans 250.0; Total catch (incl. others) 88.2.

Source: FAO.

FINANCE

Currency and Exchange Rates: Currency is the vatu. *Sterling, Dollar and Euro Equivalents* (31 December 2008): £1 sterling = 164.177 vatu; US $1 = 112.620 vatu; €1 = 156.733 vatu; 1,000 vatu = £6.09 = $8.80 = €6.38. *Average Exchange Rate* (vatu per US $): 110.64 in 2006; 102.44 in 2007; 101.33 in 2008.
Budget (million vatu, 2008): *Revenue:* Tax revenue 11,444; Other current revenue 1,191; Capital assets 13; Total 12,648, excluding grants from abroad (3,975). *Expenditure:* Current expenditure 11,104; Transfers to government bodies 1,209; Capital expenditure 2,489; Total (incl. others) 15,305.
International Reserves (US $ million at 31 December 2008): IMF special drawing rights 2.00; Reserve position in IMF 3.84; Foreign exchange 109.39; *Total* 115.23. Source: IMF, *International Financial Statistics.*
Money Supply (million vatu at 31 December 2007): Currency outside banks 3,570; Demand deposits at banks 7,211; *Total money* 10,781. Source: IMF, *International Financial Statistics.*
Cost of Living (Consumer Price Index for Port Vila and Luganville, average of quarterly figures; base: 2000 = 100): All items 111.7 in 2005; 114.0 in 2006; 118.5 in 2007. Source: IMF, *International Financial Statistics.*
Gross Domestic Product (million vatu at constant 1983 prices): 17,906 in 2005; 19,236 in 2006; 20,550 in 2007.
Expenditure on the Gross Domestic Product (million vatu at current prices, 2006): Government final consumption expenditure 8,562; Private final consumption expenditure 26,414; Gross fixed capital formation 10,412; Increase in stocks 573; Statistical discrepancy 6,201; *Total domestic expenditure* 52,163; Exports of goods and services 20,254; *Less* Imports of goods and services 26,516; *GDP in purchasers' values* 45,901. Source: Asian Development Bank.
Gross Domestic Product by Economic Activity (million vatu at current prices, 2007): Agriculture, forestry and fishing 7,480; Manufacturing 1,605; Electricity, gas and water 1,037; Construction 1,941; Wholesale and retail trade 16,076; Hotels and restaurants 3,462; Transport, storage and communications 6,677; Finance and insurance 4,511; Real estate and business services 3,473; Government services 7,601; Others 1,087; *Sub-total* 54,950; *Less* Imputed bank service charge 2,970; *GDP in purchasers' values* 51,980.
Balance of Payments (US $ million, 2007): Exports of goods f.o.b. 33.55; Imports of goods f.o.b. –176.48; *Trade balance* –142.93; Exports of services 185.94; Imports of services –75.68; *Balance on goods and services* –32.67; Other income received 36.26; Other income paid –61.01; *Balance on goods, services and income* –57.41; Current transfers received 6.65; Current transfers paid –3.02; *Current balance* –53.78; Capital account (net) 29.96; Direct investment abroad –0.63; Direct investment from abroad 34.16; Portfolio investment assets 1.68; Other investment assets 51.25; Other investment liabilities –71.48; Net errors and omissions –4.31; *Overall balance* –13.16. Source: IMF, *International Financial Statistics.*

EXTERNAL TRADE

Principal Commodities (million vatu, 2008): *Imports c.i.f.* (excl. imports for re-export): Food and live animals 4,452; Beverages and tobacco 806; Mineral fuels, lubricants, etc. 4,818; Chemicals 2,033; Basic manufactures 4,162; Machinery and transport equipment 8,924; Miscellaneous manufactured articles 2,484; Total (incl. others) 28,850. *Exports f.o.b.* (excl. re-exports): Cocoa 241; Copra 1,079; Beef 385; Timber 80; Coconut oil 727; Shells 43; Kava 487; Total (incl. others) 3,566.
Principal Trading Partners (million vatu, 2008): *Imports c.i.f.* (excl. imports for re-export): Australia 8,099; Fiji 3,005; France 1,320; Japan 1,348; New Zealand 3,830; Singapore 1,492; Total (incl. others) 28,850. *Exports f.o.b.* (excl. re-exports): Australia 126; European Union countries 783; Japan 241; New Caledonia 350; New Zealand 194; Total (incl. others) 3,566.

TRANSPORT

Road Traffic ('000 motor vehicles in use, 2001, estimates): Passenger cars 2.6; Commercial vehicles 4.4. Source: UN, *Statistical Yearbook.*
Shipping: *Merchant Fleet* (registered at 31 December 2007): Vessels 433; Total displacement ('000 grt) 1,955.4 (Source: Lloyd's Register-Fairplay, *World Fleet Statistics*). *International Sea-borne Freight Traffic* ('000 metric tons, 1990, estimates): Goods loaded 80; Goods unloaded 55 (Source: UN, *Monthly Bulletin of Statistics*).
Civil Aviation (traffic on scheduled services, 2004): Kilometres flown (million) 3; Passengers carried ('000) 104; Passenger-km (million) 217; Total ton-km (million) 21. Source: UN, *Statistical Yearbook.*

TOURISM

Foreign Tourist Arrivals: 68,179 in 2006; 81,345 in 2007; 90,521 in 2008. Note: Figures refer to arrivals by air only; arrivals from cruise-ships were: 85,922 in 2006; 85,737 in 2007; 106,138 in 2008.
Tourist Arrivals by Country of Residence (2008): Australia 53,249; New Caledonia 9,531; New Zealand 13,917; Other Pacific 3,757; Europe 4,868; North America 2,579; Total (incl. others) 90,521.
Tourism Receipts (US $ million, incl. passenger transport): 93 in 2004; 104 in 2005; 109 in 2006.

Source: World Tourism Organization.

COMMUNICATIONS MEDIA

Radio Receivers (1997): 62,000 in use*.
Television Receivers (1999): 2,000 in use†.
Telephones (2007): 8,800 main lines in use‡.
Facsimile Machines (1996): 600 in use†.
Mobile Cellular Telephones (2007): 26,000 subscribers‡.
Internet Users (2007): 17,000‡.
Broadband Subscribers (2007): 1,000‡.
Personal Computers (2004): 3,000 in use‡.
Non-daily Newspapers (1996): 2 (estimated circulation 4,000)*.

* Source: UNESCO, *Statistical Yearbook.*
† Source: UN, *Statistical Yearbook.*
‡ Source: International Telecommunication Union.

EDUCATION

Pre-primary (1992, unless otherwise indicated): 252 schools; 49 teachers (1980); 5,178 pupils.
Primary (2007, unless otherwise indicated): 374 schools (1995); 1,614 teachers (2002); 38,026 pupils.
Secondary (2007, unless otherwise indicated): 27 schools (1995); 591 teachers (2002); 15,132 students.
Tertiary (2002): 2,124 students.
Secondary (Teacher Training): 1 college (1989); 13 teachers (1983); 124 students (1991).

Directory

The Constitution

A new Constitution came into effect at independence on 30 July 1980. The main provisions are as follows:

The Republic of Vanuatu is a sovereign democratic state, of which the Constitution is the supreme law. Bislama is the national language and the official languages are Bislama, English and French. The Constitution guarantees protection of all fundamental rights and freedoms and provides for the determination of citizenship.

The President, as head of the Republic, symbolizes the unity of the Republic and is elected for a five-year term of office by secret ballot by an electoral college consisting of Parliament and the Presidents of the Regional Councils.

Legislative power resides in the single-chamber Parliament, consisting of 39 members (amended to 46 members in 1987, to 50 in 1995 and further to 52 in 1998) elected for four years on the basis of universal franchise through an electoral system that includes an element of proportional representation to ensure fair representation of different political groups and opinions. Parliament is presided over by the Speaker elected by the members. Executive power is vested in the Council of Ministers which consists of the Prime Minister (elected by Parliament from among its members) and other ministers (appointed by the Prime Minister from among the members of Parliament). The number of ministers, including the Prime Minister, may not exceed a quarter of the number of members of Parliament.

Special attention is paid to custom law and to decentralization. The Constitution states that all land in the Republic belongs to the indigenous custom owners and their descendants. There is a National Council of Chiefs, composed of custom chiefs elected by their peers sitting in District Councils of Chiefs. It may discuss all matters relating to custom and tradition and may make recommendations to Parliament for the preservation and promotion of the culture and languages of Vanuatu. The Council may be consulted on any question in connection with any bill before Parliament. Each region may elect a regional council and the Constitution lays particular emphasis on the representation of custom chiefs within each one. (A reorganization of local government was initiated in May 1994, and resulted in September of that year in the replacement of 11 local councils with six provincial governments.)

The Constitution also makes provision for public finance, the Public Service, the Ombudsman, a leadership code and the judiciary (see Judicial System).

The Government

HEAD OF STATE

President: Kalkot Mataskelekele (appointed 16 August 2004).

COUNCIL OF MINISTERS
(April 2009)

In September 2008 a coalition Government was appointed, comprising members of the Vanuaaku Pati (VP), the National United Party (NUP), the Vanuatu Labour Party, the Melanesian Progressive Pati (MPP) and Na-Griamel, along with one independent (Ind.). Members of the Union of Moderate Parties (UMP) joined the Council of Ministers in October.

Prime Minister and Minister for Media Services: Edward Natapei (VP).
Deputy Prime Minister: Ham Lini (NUP).
Minister of Foreign Affairs and External Trade: Bakoa Kaltonga (VP).
Minister of Internal Affairs: Patrick Crowby Manarewo (NUP).
Minister of Agriculture, Quarantine, Livestock, Forestry and Fisheries: Havo Molisale (Na-Griamel).
Minister of Trade and Commerce: James Bule (NUP).
Minister of Health: Toto Sambo (NUP).
Minister of Education: Charlod Saluwai (UMP).
Minister of Finance and Economic Management: Sela Molisa (VP).
Minister of Public Utilities: Serge Vohor (UMP).
Minister of Justice and Social Welfare: Joshua Kalsakau (Vanuatu Labour Party).
Minister of Lands, Geology and Mines: Rafael Vorvor (UMP).
Minister of Ni-Vanuatu Business: Esmon Saimon (MPP).
Minister of Youth Department and Training: Don Ken (Ind.).

MINISTRIES AND DEPARTMENTS

Prime Minister's Office: PMB 053, Port Vila; tel. 22413; fax 22863; internet www.vanuatugovernment.gov.vu.
Deputy Prime Minister's Office: PMB 057, Port Vila; tel. 22750; fax 27714.
Ministry of Agriculture, Livestock, Forestry and Fisheries: PMB 39, Port Vila; tel. 23406; fax 26498.
Ministry of Civil Aviation, Public Works and Transport: PMB 057, Port Vila; tel. 22790; fax 27214.
Ministry of the Comprehensive Reform Programme: POB 110, Port Vila.
Ministry of Culture, Home Affairs and Justice: PMB 036, Port Vila; tel. 22252; fax 27064.
Ministry of Education, Youth and Sports: PMB 028, Port Vila; tel. 22309; fax 24569.
Ministry of Energy, Lands, Mines and Rural Water Supply: PMB 007, Port Vila; tel. 27833; fax 25165.
Ministry of Finance: PMB 058, Port Vila; tel. 23032; fax 27937.
Ministry of Foreign Affairs: PMB 051, Port Vila; tel. 27750; fax 27832.
Ministry of Health: PMB 042, Port Vila; tel. 22545; fax 26113.
Ministry of Meteorology, Postal Services and Telecommunications: PMB 011, Port Vila; tel. 22790; fax 27714.
Ministry of Trade, Industry, Co-operatives and Commerce: PMB 056, Port Vila; tel. 25674; fax 25677.
Ministry of Women's Affairs: PMB 091, Port Vila; tel. 25099; fax 26353; e-mail emorris@vanuatu.gov.vu.

Legislature

PARLIAMENT

Speaker: George Wells.
General Election, 2 September 2008

	Seats
Vanuaaku Pati	11
National United Party	8
Union of Moderate Parties	7
Vanuatu Republikan Pati	7
People's Progressive Party	4
Green Confederation Party	2
Others	9
Independents	4
Total	**52**

Election Commission

Vanuatu Electoral Commission: PMB 033, Port Vila; tel. 23914; fax 26681; Principal Electoral Officer Martin Tete.

Political Organizations

Efate Laketu Party: Port Vila; f. 1982; regional party, based on the island of Efate.
Green Confederation Party: POB 538, Port Vila; tel. 7778069; e-mail moanakalosil6@gmail.com; f. 2001; est. by breakaway group of the UMP; Leader Moana Carcasses Kalosil.
Melanesian Progressive Pati (MPP): POB 39, Port Vila; tel. 23485; fax 23315; f. 1988; est. by breakaway group from the VP; Chair. Barak Sope; Sec.-Gen. Georges Calo.
National Democratic Party (NDP): Port Vila; f. 1986; advocates strengthening of links with France and the UK; Leader John Naupa.
National United Party (NUP): Port Vila; f. 1991; est. by supporters of Walter Lini, following his removal as leader of the VP; Pres. Ham Lini; Sec.-Gen. Willie Titongoa.
People's Democratic Party (PDP): Port Vila; f. 1994; est. by breakaway faction of the NUP.
People's Progressive Party (PPP): Port Vila; f. 2001; formed coalition with National United Party (NUP) and Fren Melanesia to contest 2002 elections; Pres. Sato Kilman.

VANUATU

Directory

Tu Vanuatu Kominiti: Port Vila; f. 1996; espouses traditional Melanesian and Christian values; Leader HILDA LINI.

Union of Moderate Parties (UMP): POB 698, Port Vila; f. 1980; Pres. SERGE VOHOR; the UMP is divided into two factions, one led by SERGE VOHOR and the other by WILLIE JIMMY.

Vanuaaku Pati (VP) (Our Land Party): POB 472, Port Vila; tel. 22584; f. 1971; est. as the New Hebrides National Party; advocates 'Melanesian socialism'; Pres. EDWARD NATAPEI; First Vice-Pres. IOLU ABBIL; Sec.-Gen. SELA MOLISA.

Vanuatu Independent Alliance Party (VIAP): Port Vila; f. 1982; supports free enterprise; Leaders THOMAS SERU, GEORGE WOREK, KALMER VOCOR.

Vanuatu Independent Movement: Port Vila; f. 2002; Pres. WILLIE TASSO.

Vanuatu Labour Party: Port Vila; f. 1986; trade-union based; Leader JOSHUA KALSAKU.

Vanuatu Republikan Pati (VRP): Port Vila; f. 1998; est. by breakaway faction of the UMP; Leader MAXIME CARLOT KORMAN.

The Na-Griamel (Leader FRANKLEY STEVENS), Namaki Aute, Tan Union (Leader VINCENT BULEKONE) and Fren Melanesia (Leader ALBERT RAVUTIA) represent rural interests on the islands of Espiritu Santo and Malekula. The John Frum Movement represents interests on the island of Tanna.

Diplomatic Representation

EMBASSIES AND HIGH COMMISSIONS IN VANUATU

Australia: Winston Churchill Ave, Port Vila; tel. 22777; fax 23948; e-mail australia_vanuatu@dfat.gov.au; internet www.vanuatu.embassy.gov.au; High Commissioner PABLO KANG.

China, People's Republic: PMB 071, Rue d'Auvergne, Nambatu, Port Vila; tel. 23598; fax 24877; e-mail publicinfo@chinese-embassy.com.vu; Ambassador CHENG SHUPING.

France: Kumul Highway, POB 60, Port Vila; tel. 22353; fax 22695; e-mail ambafra@vanuatu.com.vu; internet www.ambafrance-vu.org; Ambassador FRANÇOISE MAYLIÉ.

New Zealand: La Casa d'Andrea e Luciano, Rue Pierre Lamy St, Port Vila; tel. 22933; fax 22518; e-mail kiwi@vanuatu.com.vu; High Commissioner JEFF LANGLEY.

Judicial System

The Supreme Court has unlimited jurisdiction to hear and determine any civil or criminal proceedings. It consists of the Chief Justice, appointed by the President of the Republic after consultation with the Prime Minister and the leader of the opposition, and three other judges, who are appointed by the President of the Republic on the advice of the Judicial Service Commission.

The Court of Appeal is constituted by two or more judges of the Supreme Court sitting together. The Supreme Court is the court of first instance in constitutional matters and is composed of a single judge.

Magistrates' Courts have limited jurisdiction to hear and determine any civil or criminal proceedings. Island Courts have been established in several local government regions, and are constituted when three justices are sitting together to exercise civil or criminal jurisdiction, as defined in the warrant establishing the court. A magistrate nominated by the Chief Justice acts as Chairman. The Island Courts are competent to rule on land disputes.

In late 2001 legislation was introduced to establish a new Land Tribunal which was intended to expedite the hearing of land disputes. The tribunal was to have three levels, and no cases were to go beyond the tribunal and enter either the Supreme Court or the Island Courts. The tribunal was to be funded by the disputing parties.

In 1986 Papua New Guinea and Vanuatu signed a memorandum of understanding, under which Papua New Guinea Supreme Court judges were to conduct court hearings in Vanuatu, chiefly in the Court of Appeal.

Supreme Court of Vanuatu

PMB 041, rue de Querios, Port Vila; tel. 22420; fax 22692.

Attorney-General: ISHMAEL KALSAKAU.

Chief Justice: VINCENT LUNABEK.

Chief Prosecutor: HEATHER LINI LEO.

Religion

Most of Vanuatu's inhabitants profess Christianity. Presbyterians form the largest Christian group (with about one-half of the population being adherents), followed by Anglicans and Roman Catholics.

CHRISTIANITY

Vanuatu Christian Council: POB 13, Luganville, Santo; tel. 03232; f. 1967; est. as New Hebrides Christian Council; five mem. churches, two observers; Chair. (vacant); Sec. Rev. JOHN LIU.

The Roman Catholic Church

Vanuatu forms the single diocese of Port Vila, suffragan to the archdiocese of Nouméa (New Caledonia). At 31 December 2006 there were an estimated 32,500 adherents in the country. The Bishop participates in the Catholic Bishops' Conference of the Pacific, based in Fiji.

Bishop of Port Vila: (vacant), Evêché, POB 59, Port Vila; tel. 22640; fax 25342; e-mail catholik@vanuatu.com.vu.

The Anglican Communion

Anglicans in Vanuatu are adherents of the Church of the Province of Melanesia, comprising eight dioceses: Vanuatu (which also includes New Caledonia), Banks and Torres and six dioceses in Solomon Islands. The Archbishop of the Province is the Bishop of Central Melanesia, resident in Honiara, Solomon Islands. In 1985 the Church had an estimated 16,000 adherents in Vanuatu.

Bishop of Vanuatu: Fr JAMES LIGO, Bishop's House, POB 238, Luganville, Santo; tel. 37065; fax 36026.

Bishop of Banks and Torres: Rt Rev. NATHAN TOME, Bishop's House, POB 19, Toutamwat, Torba Province.

Protestant Churches

Presbyterian Church of Vanuatu (Presbitirin Jyos long Vanuatu): POB 150, Port Vila; tel. 27184; fax 23650; f. 1948; 56,000 mems (1995); Moderator Pastor BANI KALSINGER; Assembly Clerk Pastor FAMA RAKAU.

Other denominations active in the country include the Apostolic Church, the Assemblies of God, the Churches of Christ in Vanuatu and the Seventh-day Adventist Church.

BAHÁ'Í FAITH

National Spiritual Assembly of the Bahá'ís of Vanuatu: POB 1017, Port Vila; tel. 22419; e-mail nsavanuatu@vanuatu.com.vu; f. 1953; Sec. CHARLES PIERCE; mems resident in 216 localities.

The Press

Hapi Tumas Long Vanuatu: POB 1292, Port Vila; tel. 23642; fax 23343; quarterly tourist information; English; Publr MARC NEIL-JONES; circ. 12,000.

Pacific Island Profile: Port Vila; f. 1990; monthly; general interest; English and French; Editor HILDA LINI.

Port Vila Presse: 1st Floor, Raffea House, POB 637, Port Vila; tel. 22200; fax 27999; e-mail marke@presse.com.vu; internet www.presse.com.vu; f. 2000; daily; English and French; Publr MARKE LOWEN; Editor RICKY BINIHI.

Vanuatu Daily Post: POB 1292, Port Vila; tel. 23111; fax 24111; e-mail tpost@vanuatu.com.vu; internet www.dailypost.vu; daily; English; Publr MARC NEIL-JONES; Editor LEN GARAE; circ. 2,000.

Vanuatu Weekly: PMB 049, Port Vila; tel. 22999; fax 22026; f. 1980; weekly; govt-owned; Bislama, English and French; circ. 1,700.

Vanuatu Wikli Post: f. 2008; weekly; Bislama; Editor RICKY BINIHI.

Viewpoints: Port Vila; weekly; newsletter of Vanuaaku Pati; Editor PETER TAURAKOTO.

Wantok Niuspepa: POB 1292, Port Vila; tel. 23642; fax 23343.

Broadcasting and Communications

TELECOMMUNICATIONS

Digicel Vanuatu: PMB 9103, Ellouk Plateau, Port Vila; tel. 27692; fax 26404; e-mail customercare.vanuatu@digicelgroup.com; internet www.digicelvanuatu.com; Gen. Man. TANYA MENZIES.

Telecom Vanuatu Ltd (TVL): POB 146, Port Vila; tel. 22185; fax 22628; e-mail sales@tvl.net.vu; internet www.tvl.vu; f. 1989; national and international telecommunications services; Man. Dir MICHEL DUPUIS.

BROADCASTING
Radio

Vanuatu Broadcasting and Television Corpn (VBTC): PMB 049, Port Vila; tel. 22999; fax 22026; internet www.vbtc.com.vu; fmrly Government Media Services, name changed in 1992; Gen. Man. FRED VUROBARAVU; Chair. GODWIN LIGO; Dir of Programmes A. THOMPSON.

> **Radio Vanuatu:** PMB 049, Port Vila; tel. 22999; fax 22026; f. 1966; govt-owned; broadcasts in English, French and Bislama; Dir JOE BOMAL CARLO.

Television

Vanuatu Broadcasting and Television Corpn (VBTC): see Radio

> **Television Blong Vanuatu:** PMB 049, Port Vila; f. 1993; govt-owned; French-funded; broadcasts for four hours daily in French and English; Gen. Man. CLAUDE CASTELLY; Programme Man. GAEL LE DANTEC.

Finance

(cap. = capital; res = reserves; dep. = deposits; amounts in vatu unless otherwise indicated)

Vanuatu has no personal income tax nor tax on company profits and is therefore attractive as a financial centre and tax haven.

BANKING
Central Bank

Reserve Bank of Vanuatu: PMB 9062, Port Vila; tel. 23333; fax 24231; e-mail enquiries@rbv.gov.vu; internet www.rbv.gov.vu; f. 1981; est. as Central Bank of Vanuatu; name changed as above in 1989; govt-owned; cap. 100.0m., res 613.6m., dep. 7,722.1m. (Dec. 2006); Gov. ODO TEVI.

Development Bank

Development Bank of Vanuatu: Rue de Paris, POB 241, Port Vila; tel. 22181; fax 24591; f. 1979; govt-owned; Man. Dir AUGUSTINE GARAE.

National Bank

National Bank of Vanuatu: POB 249, Rue de Paris, Port Vila; tel. 22201; fax 27227; e-mail nationalbank@vanuatu.com.vu; internet www.nbv.com.vu; f. 1991; est. upon assumption of control of Vanuatu Co-operative Savings Bank; govt-owned; cap. 600m., dep. 7,187.3m. (Dec. 2007); Chair. JOHN ARUHURI; Man. Dir BOB HUGHES; 19 brs.

Foreign Banks

ANZ Bank (Vanuatu) Ltd: PMB 9003, Port Vila; tel. 26355; fax 22814; e-mail vanuatu@anz.com; internet www.anz.com/vanuatu; f. 1971; cap. 3.7m., res 317.7m., dep. 24,734.2m. (Sept. 2003); Man. MARILYN KALANGIS; brs in Port Vila and Luganville.

European Bank Ltd (USA): International Bldg, Fr Walter Lini Highway, POB 65, Port Vila; tel. 27700; fax 22884; e-mail info@europeanbank.net; 'offshore' and private banking; cap. US $0.7m., res US $1.2m., dep. US $34.3m. (Dec. 2007); Chair. THOMAS MONTGOMERY BAYER; Pres. ROBERT MURRAY BOHN.

Westpac Banking Corporation (Australia): Lini Highway, Port Vila; tel. 22084; fax 24773; e-mail westpacvanuatu@westpac.com.au; internet www.westpac.vu; Man. R. B. WRIGHT; 2 brs.

Financial Institutions

The Financial Centre Association: POB 1128, Port Vila; tel. 24619; fax 26008; f. 1980; group of banking, legal, accounting and trust companies administering 'offshore' banking and investment; Chair. JIM BATTY; Sec. CHARLES KLEIMAN.

Vanuatu Financial Services Commission (VFSC): Bougainville St, PMB 023, Port Vila; tel. 22247; fax 22242; e-mail info@vfsc.vu; internet www.vfsc.vu; f. 1993; regulation and supervision of non-banking financial services; Commr GEORGE ANDREWS.

INSURANCE

Pacific Insurance Brokers: POB 229, Port Vila; tel. 23863; fax 23089.

QBE Insurance (Vanuatu) Ltd: La Casa D'Andrea Bldg, POB 186, Port Vila; tel. 22299; fax 23298; e-mail info.van@qbe.com; Gen. Man. GEOFFREY R. CUTTING.

Trade and Industry
GOVERNMENT AGENCY

Vanuatu Investment Promotion Authority: 1st Floor, Pilioko House, Port Vila; tel. 24096; fax 25216; e-mail ataritambe@vanuatu.gov.vu; internet www.investinvanuatu.com; fmrly the Vanuatu Investment Board, name changed as above in 2000; CEO SMITH TEBU.

CHAMBER OF COMMERCE

Chamber of Commerce and Industry of Vanuatu: POB 189, Port Vila; tel. 27543; fax 27542; e-mail vancci@vanuatu.com.vu; internet www.vanuatuchamber.com; Pres. JOSEPH JACOBE.

MARKETING BOARD

Vanuatu Commodities Marketing Board: POB 268, Luganville, Santo; f. 1982; sole exporter of major commodities, including copra, kava and cocoa; Gen. Man. GEORGE CALO.

UTILITIES
Electricity

Union Electrique du Vanuatu (Unelco Vanuatu Ltd): POB 26, rue Winston Churchill, Port Vila; tel. 22211; fax 25011; e-mail unelco@unelco.com.vu; private organization contracted for the generation and supply of electricity in Port Vila, Luganville, Tanna and Malekula, and for the supply of water in Port Vila; Dir-Gen. JEAN FRANÇOIS BARBEAU.

Village generators provide electricity in rural areas. The Government provides recirculated water supplies to about 85% of urban and 30% of rural households.

TRADE UNIONS

Vanuatu Council of Trade Unions (VCTU): PMB 89, Port Vila; tel. 24517; fax 23679; Pres. OBED MASINGIOW; Sec.-Gen. EPHRAIM KALSAKAU.

National Union of Labour: Port Vila.

The principal trade unions include:

Oil and Gas Workers' Union: Port Vila; f. 1984.

Vanuatu Airline Workers' Union: Port Vila; f. 1984.

Vanuatu Public Service Association: Port Vila.

Vanuatu Teachers' Union: Port Vila; Gen. Sec. CHARLES KALO; Pres. OBED MASSING.

Vanuatu Waterside, Maritime and Allied Workers' Union: Port Vila.

Transport
ROADS

There are about 1,070 km of roads, of which 54 km, mostly on Efate Island, are sealed.

SHIPPING

The principal ports are Port Vila and Luganville. At the end of 2007 the merchant fleet comprised 433 vessels, with a total displacement of 1,955,413 grt. A shipping registry, based in Singapore, provides a 'flag of convenience' to foreign-owned vessels.

Vanuatu Maritime Authority: POB 320, Marine Quay, Port Vila; tel. 23128; fax 22949; e-mail iantchichine@vma.com.vu; domestic and international ship registry, maritime safety regulator; Commissioner of Maritime Affairs JOHN T. ROOSEN; Chair. LENNOX VUTI.

Ports and Harbour Department: PMB 9046, Port Vila; tel. 22339; fax 22475; e-mail nhamish@vanet.com; Harbour Master Capt. LUKE BEANDI; Dir NORRIS HAMISH.

Burns Philp (Vanuatu) Ltd: POB 27, Port Vila.

Ifira Shipping Agencies Ltd: POB 68, Port Vila; tel. 22929; fax 22052; f. 1986; Man. Dir CLAUDE BOUDIER.

Sami Ltd: Kumul Highway, POB 301, Port Vila; tel. 24106; fax 23405.

South Sea Shipping: POB 84, Port Vila; tel. 22205; fax 23304.

Vanua Navigation Ltd: POB 44, Port Vila; tel. 22027; f. 1977; by the Co-operative Federation and Sofrana Unilines; Chief Exec. GEOFFREY J. CLARKE.

The following services call regularly at Vanuatu: Compagnie Générale Maritime, Kyowa Shipping Co, Pacific Forum Line, Papua New Guinea Shipping Corpn, Sofrana-Unilines, Bank Line, Columbus Line and Bali Hai Shipping. Royal Viking Line, Sitmar and P & O cruises also call at Vanuatu.

CIVIL AVIATION

The principal airports are Bauerfield (Efate, for Port Vila) and Pekoa (Espiritu Santo, for Luganville). There are airstrips on all Vanuatu's principal islands, and an international airport at White Grass on Tanna was completed in 1998. In early 2000 it was announced that a further three airports were to be built on the islands of Pentecost, Malekula and Tanna. Major improvements providing for the accommodation of larger aircraft at both Bauerfield and Pekoa airports began in 2000. Moreover, in September 2000 plans for a new international airport at Teouma (Efate) were announced, with finance from a private Thai investor. In late 2003 plans for the construction of an international air terminal at Pekoa (Espiritu Santo) costing US $1.6m. were announced.

Civil Aviation Authority: POB 131, Port Vila; tel. 25111; fax 25532.

Air Vanuatu: 3rd Floor, Air Vanuatu House, Rue de Paris, Port Vila; tel. 23838; fax 23250; e-mail sales@airvanuatu.com.vu; internet www.airvanuatu.com; f. 1981; govt-owned national carrier since 1987; regular services between Port Vila and Sydney, Brisbane and Melbourne (Australia), Nadi (Fiji), Nouméa (New Caledonia), Auckland (New Zealand) and Honiara (Solomon Islands); the frequency of flights from Auckland, Sydney, Brisbane and Honiara to Port Vila was increased in mid-2004; CEO HOLLINGSWORTH ALA NGWELE.

Dovair: Port Vila; privately owned; operates domestic services.

Tourism

Tourism is an important source of revenue for the Government of Vanuatu. Visitors are attracted by the islands' unspoilt landscape and rich local customs. There were some 120 hotels and guest houses in 2003, providing more than 1,300 rooms. In 2008 foreign visitor arrivals in Vanuatu totalled an estimated 90,521, compared with 81,345 in 2007. In 2007 some 58% of visitors were from Australia and 17% were from New Zealand. Receipts from tourism totalled some US $109m. in 2006. The development of the tourist industry has hitherto been concentrated on the islands of Efate, Espiritu Santo and Tanna; however, other islands are also being promoted as tourist centres.

Vanuatu Hotel and Resorts Association: POB 215, Port Vila; tel. 22040; fax 27579; Pres. JOHN GROCOCK.

Vanuatu Tourism Office: Lini Highway, POB 209, Port Vila; tel. 22685; fax 23889; e-mail tourism@vanuatu.com.vu; internet www.vanuatutourism.com; Gen. Man. ANNIE NIATU; Chair. BEN TARI.

THE VATICAN CITY
(THE HOLY SEE)

Introductory Survey

Location, Climate, Language, Religion, Flag

The State of the Vatican City is situated entirely within the Italian capital, Rome, on the right bank of the Tiber river. It covers an area of 0.44 sq km (0.17 sq mile). The climate is Mediterranean, with warm summers and mild winters (see Italy). Italian and Latin are the official languages. Roman Catholicism is the official religion. The state flag, which is square, consists of two vertical stripes of yellow and white, with the papal coat of arms superimposed on the white stripe.

History

For a period of nearly 1,000 years, dating roughly from the time of Charlemagne to the year 1870, the Popes ruled much of the central Italian peninsula, including the city of Rome. During the process of unification, the Kingdom of Italy gradually absorbed these States of the Church, the process being completed by the entry into Rome of King Victor Emmanuel's troops in September 1870. From 1860 to 1870 many attempts had been made to induce the Pope, Pius IX, to surrender his temporal possessions. Since, however, he regarded them as a sacred trust from a higher Power, to be guarded on behalf of the Church, he refused to do so. After the entry of the Royal Army into Rome, he retired to the Vatican from where no Pope emerged again until the ratification of the Lateran Treaty of 11 February 1929. By the Law of Guarantees of May 1871, Italy attempted to stabilize the position of the Papacy by recognizing the Pope's claim to use of the Palaces of the Lateran and the Vatican, the Papal villa of Castelgandolfo, and their gardens and annexes, and to certain privileges customary to sovereignty. This unilateral arrangement was not accepted by Pius IX, and his protest against it was repeated constantly by his successors.

In 1929 two agreements were made with the Italian Government—the Lateran Treaty and the Concordat. By the terms of the Lateran Treaty, the Holy See was given exclusive power and sovereign jurisdiction over the State of the Vatican City, which was declared neutral and inviolable territory. Financial compensation was also given for the earlier losses. Under the Concordat, Roman Catholicism became the state religion of Italy, with special privileges defined by law. The new Italian Constitution of 1947 reaffirmed adherence to the Lateran Treaty. In December 1978 the two sides agreed on a draft plan for a new Concordat, under which Catholicism would cease to be the official Italian state religion and most of the Catholic Church's special privileges in Italy would be removed. The revised version was signed in February 1984.

In 1917 the first legal code, the Code of Canon Law (Codex Iuris Canonici), was devised for the Catholic Church. In 1963 a pontifical commission was inaugurated to investigate possible reforms to the law, and in 1981 the Pope received more than 70 cardinals and bishops who had prepared the new code's 1,752 rules. Revisions included a reduction in the number of cases meriting excommunication and a general relaxing of penalties, with increased emphasis on the importance of the laity within the church. The code was ratified in January 1983, and came into force in November.

In October 1978 Cardinal Karol Wojtyła (then Archbishop of Kraków, Poland) became the first non-Italian Pope since the 16th century, taking the name John Paul II. Security surrounding the Pontiff was tightened considerably after an attempt on his life in May 1981 and another in May 1982. An Italian parliamentary inquiry, which published its findings in March 2006, concluded that the 1981 attempt was orchestrated by the former USSR.

In April 1984 Pope John Paul II announced a major reshuffle of offices in the Roman Curia, which included the delegation of most of his responsibility for the routine administration of the Vatican to the Secretariat of State. In July 1988 a number of reforms to the Curia were introduced. These consolidated the power of the Secretariat of State, as well as reorganizing some of the Congregations and Pontifical Commissions.

In February 1987 Italian judges issued a warrant for the arrest of Archbishop Paul Marcinkus, the Chairman of the Istituto per le Opere di Religione ('Vatican Bank'), and two other bank officials for alleged involvement in the fraudulent bankruptcy of the Banco Ambrosiano in Milan, which collapsed in 1982. In July 1987, however, the Italian Supreme Court cancelled the warrants for the arrest of the three bank officials, stating that the Vatican stood outside Italian jurisdiction and that, according to the Lateran Treaty, Italy did not have the right to interfere in the affairs of the central organs of the Roman Catholic Church. In May 1988, following an appeal, the Archbishop's immunity was endorsed by the Constitutional Court. In March 1989 the Vatican announced a wide-ranging reorganization of the Istituto per le Opere di Religione, by abolishing the post of Chairman, held by Marcinkus, and appointing a commission of five cardinals, nominated by the Pope, to preside over the bank, assisted by a committee of financial experts. Archbishop Marcinkus retired from papal service in October 1990 and died in February 2006.

In March 1998 the Vatican released its long-awaited 'definitive statement' condemning anti-Semitism and anti-Judaism, and repenting for Roman Catholic passivity during the Nazi Holocaust. However, a number of high-ranking Jewish officials expressed disappointment in the document and demanded an explicit apology for the attitude of Pope Pius XII and the Roman Catholic Church's failure to speak out, at the time, against Nazi atrocities. In March 2000, during a service in St Peter's Basilica in Rome, despite misgivings expressed by some theologians that such a statement would undermine the Church's authority, the Pope made a comprehensive and unprecedented plea for forgiveness for the 'past sins of the Church', including racial and ethnic discrimination and Christian mistreatment of minorities, women and native peoples. However, in July 2001 a panel of Catholic and Jewish historians was forced to halt its study of the Church's role in the Holocaust when the Vatican refused it access to files on Pope Pius XII, prompting allegations that the Vatican was seeking to conceal potentially damaging evidence. Following further pressure, however, archives covering the years 1922–39 were released in February 2003.

In February 2001 it was announced that the Constitution, dating back to the Lateran Treaty of 1929, was to be replaced by a new Basic Law incorporating a number of constitutional amendments made over the years. The Basic Law clarified the distinction between the legislative, executive and judicial branches.

In November 2001 Pope John Paul II issued an apology to victims of sexual abuse perpetrated by members of the Catholic clergy. Furthermore, in January 2002 new regulations were published by the Vatican, outlining the appropriate method of dealing with cases of alleged sexual abuse, notably against children, by members of the clergy. However, in mid-2002, in the most significant scandal to affect the Roman Catholic Church in many years, it was revealed that Cardinal Bernard Law, the Archbishop of Boston, Massachusetts, USA, had protected a number of priests who faced accusations of sexual misconduct against children. Hundreds of priests in the USA resigned or were subsequently suspended or sued in the wake of more than 200 allegations of sexual abuse involving members of the clergy in the Boston area. In April the Pope summoned 13 US cardinals to the Vatican to discuss the crisis. A 'zero tolerance' policy adopted by the US Conference of Catholic Bishops in June was subsequently rejected by the Vatican; a somewhat altered charter, which provided for the eventual dismissal of any priests found guilty of sexual abuse in a church tribunal, was accepted by the Vatican in December. Victims' groups were disappointed with the revisions, however, which reintroduced a 10-year statute of limitation on accusations. Following the filing of 450 lawsuits against Cardinal Law's archdiocese and the petition of 58 Boston priests, Law resigned in December 2002.

The publication in March 2003 of a *Lexicon On Ambiguous and Colloquial Terms About Family Life and Ethical Questions* caused controversy by its reaffirmation of the Catholic Church's uncompromising stance regarding birth control and homosexuality. In July a document was circulated to all bishops confirming the Vatican's opposition to the legalization of same-sex unions. Further controversy arose in October following claims by certain Vatican officials that the AIDS virus could be transferred through condoms, provoking much criticism from the World Health Organization (WHO, see p. 153). Of the 30 new cardinals elected at the ninth consistory of John Paul II's papacy, which took place in October, only six were Italian, while the representation from Africa and Latin America was increased. An additional cardinal was elevated *in pectore* (i.e. his name was not publicly divulged).

In August 2004, in an open letter to the bishops entitled 'On the collaboration of men and women in the Church and the World', the Pope criticized radical feminism for having created a culture of enmity between the sexes. In October the *Compendium of the Social Doctrine of the Church*, published by the Pontifical Council for Justice and Peace, called on Catholics to include their faith in the life and legislation of the State and reiterated the Church's oppositional stance on homosexuality and birth control.

Following a long period of ill health, Pope John Paul II died on 2 April 2005 at the age of 84. Only St Peter and Pius IX, in the mid-19th century, had enjoyed longer papacies. More than 3m. people visited the Vatican City in the period between the death of John Paul II and his funeral, which took place on 8 April and was attended by around 200 world leaders. By the time of his death, John Paul II had canonized 482 saints (more than all his predecessors combined since the 16th century), performed 1,338 beatifications and created 232 cardinals.

The conclave to elect a new Pope began on 18 April 2005 and was attended by 115 of the 117 cardinals of voting age (under 80 years old). On 19 April Cardinal Joseph Ratzinger was elected as the Supreme Pontiff, and took the name Benedict XVI. Ratzinger, who was aged 78 years, was hitherto the Dean of the College of Cardinals, the Prefect of the Congregation for the Doctrine of the Faith and President of the International Theological Commission and of the Pontifical Biblical Commission. The new Pope's inauguration as the 265th Roman pontiff took place on 24 April. Benedict XVI subsequently reappointed the officials of the Roman Curia, who had, according to custom, ceased to hold their offices on the death of John Paul II. In May Benedict announced the commencement of the process of beatification of John Paul II, waiving the five-year delay normally required after a person's death. In his first addresses as Pope, Benedict pledged to continue his predecessor's attempts to improve ties with other religions and branches of Christianity. In October the first synod of Benedict XVI's papacy took place, at which the celibacy of the priesthood was reaffirmed.

In early 2006 it was reported that the Pope had decided to stop using one of his nine official titles, that of Patriarch of the West; this was regarded as a gesture of reconciliation towards the Orthodox churches. Pope Benedict's first encyclical, *Deus Caritas Est*, on the nature of love, was published in January. On 24 March Benedict appointed 15 new cardinals. Notable among the appointees was Joseph Zen Ze-kiun, Bishop of Hong Kong and an outspoken critic of the Chinese Government.

In September 2006 Cardinal Angelo Sodano retired as Secretary of State and was replaced by Cardinal Tarcisio Bertone, hitherto Archbishop of Genoa, Italy, while Cardinal Edmund Szoka was replaced as President of the Pontifical Commission for the Vatican City State and of the Governorate of the Vatican City State by Most Rev. Giovanni Lajolo, who had been Secretary of State for Relations with States—in effect the foreign minister. Most Rev. Dominique Mamberti was appointed Secretary of State for Relations with States.

In November 2007 Pope Benedict appointed 23 new cardinals, of whom 18 were of voting age, thus bringing the number of cardinals eligible to vote in the conclave to elect a new pontiff to 121.

In January 2009 it was announced that, with effect from 1 January, the Vatican would examine legislation passed in Italy on an individual basis prior to adoption. A Vatican spokesman stated that the decision had been motivated by the number and instability of Italian laws, as well as their increasing 'contrast with the inviolable principles of the Church'. Under the terms of the Lateran Treaty, all laws promulgated in Italy had, hitherto, been incorporated automatically into Vatican law.

Later in January 2009 the decision of Pope Benedict XVI to rehabilitate four bishops who had been excommunicated in 1988 provoked severe criticism from world leaders and jeopardized efforts to improve relations with Israel. Days before the announcement, one of the bishops, Richard Williamson, had given an interview to a Swedish television channel in which he denied the existence of gas chambers at the Nazi concentration camps during the Second World War. In early February the German Federal Chancellor, Angela Merkel, criticized the decision and demanded that the Pope 'clarify unambiguously that there can be no denial (of the Nazi Holocaust)'. Following the criticism, the Vatican published a statement in which it claimed that Benedict XVI had not been aware of Williamson's views, and demanded that he recant them before taking up his appointment as a bishop in the Roman Catholic Church. Williamson later apologized for causing offence, but did not retract his remarks over the Holocaust; the Vatican demanded further action on his part before the process of rehabilitation could be completed.

Pope Benedict XVI provoked further controversy in March 2009, following remarks made to journalists during a tour of Africa in which he appeared to claim that the use of condoms aggravated the spread of the AIDS virus. The comments prompted much criticism from government officials across Europe, as well as from WHO. However, the Vatican subsequently clarified the remarks, reiterating the Roman Catholic Church's commitment to combating AIDS through fidelity, abstinence and monogamy and claiming that the Pope had said that condoms 'risked' aggravating the problem.

The Vatican's prominence in international affairs increased from the late 1980s. In July 1989 diplomatic relations with Poland, severed in 1945, were restored. The Vatican had hitherto maintained no diplomatic relations with eastern European governments under communist rule, except for Yugoslavia. During the early 1990s diplomatic relations were restored or established with many former communist states, including with the USSR in 1990. In 1992 full diplomatic relations were restored, after more than 120 years of discord, between the Vatican and Mexico. In December 1993 the Vatican and Israel signed a mutual-recognition agreement, which led to the establishment of full diplomatic ties and the exchange of ambassadors in September 1994. Meanwhile, in February 1994 the Vatican established diplomatic relations with Jordan, in an apparent move to strengthen links with the Arab world to counterbalance its recent recognition of Israel. Similarly, in October of that year the Vatican instituted 'official relations' with the Palestine Liberation Organization.

Diplomatic relations between the Vatican and the People's Republic of China had been severed in 1951 following the communists' accession to power in Beijing. In August 1999 China vetoed plans for Pope John Paul II to visit Hong Kong later that year, owing to the Vatican's diplomatic ties with Taiwan. Any hope of a reconciliation between China and the Vatican looked increasingly unlikely in January 2000, when the state-controlled Patriotic Church in Beijing ordained five bishops in a ceremony timed to upstage official papal ordinations in the Vatican City. Relations further deteriorated following the Pope's announcement in September 2000 that he was to canonize 120 western and Chinese Catholics killed in China between 1648 and 1930. The controversy was exacerbated by the decision to hold the ceremony on China's National Day, the anniversary of the accession to power of the Chinese Communist Party (although the Vatican insisted that the date was merely coincidental). However, in October 2001 Pope John Paul II issued an apology to China for the sins committed by Christians against the country; an appeal was also made for diplomatic relations between the two states to be restored. Informal talks recommenced in early 2003, but were adversely affected by the outspoken anti-Government stance of Hong Kong's Bishop (later Cardinal), Joseph Zen Ze-kiun. Following the accession of Benedict XVI, there appeared to be a growing emphasis on the need to improve Sino-Vatican relations. However, the ordination of a series of bishops by the Patriotic Church in April and May 2006 provoked criticism from the Pope. Attempts to improve relations continued in 2007. In July an open letter addressed to Chinese Catholics on behalf of the Pope called for 'respectful and constructive' relations. In September the Vatican approved the ordination of a bishop by the Patriotic Church, allaying fears that efforts toward reconciliation would be undermined by the death earlier that month of a Vatican-appointed bishop, John Han Dingxiang, while in detention by the Chinese authorities.

In February 2000 the Vatican and the Palestinian (National) Authority signed an historic agreement on joint interests, which appealed for a peaceful solution, through dialogue, to the Israeli-Palestinian conflict, and called for an internationally guaranteed special statute for the city of Jerusalem that safeguarded freedom of religion and conscience. The Israeli Government criticized the accord as representing unwelcome 'interference' by the Vatican in the ongoing Middle East peace talks. In early 2000 the Pope undertook a millennial pilgrimage to some of the principal biblical sites of the Middle East, visiting Egypt in February (the first visit by a pontiff to that country) and Israel, Jordan and the West Bank in March. Pope John Paul II's six-day visit to the politically volatile Holy Land constituted the first papal visit to that region for 36 years. In 2002 an agreement was signed by the Vatican and the Turkish Government, promoting religious dialogue between Muslims and Christians.

In mid-2001 Pope John Paul II undertook visits to Greece and Syria, the first by a Roman pontiff since the division of Christianity into eastern and western churches. During his visit to Greece, the Pope attempted to heal the historic rift between the Roman Catholic and Orthodox churches by presenting an apology to the Orthodox community for wrongs committed over the centuries by the Roman Catholic Church. The Pope, despite not being granted the consent of the Russian Orthodox Patriarch, also visited Ukraine, where he called for an end to the 1,000-year schism between Roman Catholicism and the Orthodox Church in Ukraine and, by extension, the Russian Orthodox Church. The leaders of the Orthodox Church in Ukraine refused to meet the Pope, although his visit attracted much popular support.

Tensions between the Roman Catholic Church and the Russian Orthodox Church increased in February 2002 when the Vatican announced that the four apostolic administrations in Russia (officially considered to be temporary) had become dioceses. This move was interpreted by representatives of the Russian Orthodox Church as the establishment of an alternative church within the country, and a few days later a visit to Russia by the Head of the Pontifical Council for the Promotion of Christian Unity, Cardinal Walter Kasper, was cancelled by the Russian Orthodox Church.

In November 2002 John Paul II became the first pontiff to address the Italian Parliament, symbolically closing the Vatican's territorial dispute with Italy. His speech advocated institutional recognition by the European Union (EU, see p. 255) of Europe's Christian heritage. This followed an ultimately unsuccessful call in October for Christianity to be enshrined in the proposed EU constitution. In June 2004 John Paul II publicly criticized the lack of reference to Christianity in the approved text of the EU constitutional treaty, and in early 2005 the Vatican again criticized the increasing secularization of the EU. In 2007 Pope Benedict XVI also criticized the Italian Government for its plans to give homosexual and unmarried couples equal legal status with married couples.

During late 2002 and early 2003 Pope John Paul II was prominent in opposing the prospect of US-led military intervention to remove the regime of Saddam Hussain in Iraq; he denounced the planned conflict as a 'defeat for humanity', and urged a diplomatic resolution to the crisis. During February and March the Pope granted a series of private audiences to important international figures, including the Deputy Prime Minister of Iraq, Tareq Aziz, the Secretary-General of the UN, Kofi Annan, the British Prime Minister, Tony Blair, and the Italian Prime Minister, Silvio Berlusconi. Papal envoys were also sent to Baghdad and Washington, DC. This was followed in March by an historic five-day meeting with a delegation from Israel's Chief Rabbinate. Later in the year the Pope received the Iranian and Israeli ministers responsible for foreign affairs and the Palestinian Prime Minister, Ahmad Quray.

While the number of foreign visits undertaken by John Paul II was reduced in 2003 owing to his increasing frailty, he continued to receive foreign leaders in the Vatican, including President Vladimir Putin of Russia in November. The Pope maintained his engagement with former Soviet bloc countries, visiting Slovakia in September and receiving the Prime Ministers of the former Yugoslav republic of Macedonia and Croatia. In September talks on an accord between Croatia and the Vatican stalled owing to differences of opinion over the Catholic Church's presence in the largely Orthodox country. The Dalai Lama, the head of the Tibetan Buddhist hierarchy, had a private audience with the Pope in November. In total, John Paul II made 104 journeys outside Italy during his papacy, making him by far the most widely travelled pontiff.

Pope John Paul II visited Switzerland in June 2004, where it was announced that diplomatic relations, which had been severed in 1873, were to be restored. In mid-2004 the Pope continued his policy of engagement with the Orthodox churches, which included the return of a copy of the icon 'Our Lady of Kazan' to Moscow. On 1 July the Pope issued a joint statement with Patriarch Bartholomew I of Constantinople, the Orthodox Patriarch in İstanbul, Turkey, confirming their commitment to dialogue between the Roman Catholic and Orthodox churches.

Pope Benedict XVI's first major foreign visit as pontiff was to his native Germany in August 2005, during which he made a symbolic visit to a synagogue. In May 2006 the Pope made a trip to Poland, where he visited the Nazi concentration camp at Auschwitz.

Tensions between the Vatican and the Muslim world increased in September 2006 after Benedict XVI delivered a lecture at the University of Regensburg, Germany, in the course of which he quoted a medieval Byzantine emperor as saying that the Prophet Muhammad had contributed only 'evil and inhuman' things to the world. The Pope's remarks provoked widespread protest in Muslim countries. Benedict later apologized for causing offence, stating that the quotation did not reflect his personal belief. In November Benedict visited Turkey, where he was praised by Muslims for facing Mecca while praying in the Blue Mosque in İstanbul. He also held a joint service with Patriarch Bartholomew I, a gesture that was regarded as an attempt to heal the divisions between the Roman Catholic and Greek Orthodox churches.

Relations between Israel and the Vatican were strained in April 2007, when the Apostolic Nuncio to Israel, Archbishop Antonio Franco, announced his intention to boycott the Holocaust Memorial Day commemoration at the Yad Vashem Holocaust museum in protest at a caption the museum had attached to a photograph of Pope Pius XII, which condemned the late Pope's attitude to the extermination of the Jews. Franco later reversed his decision not to attend. Later that month it was announced that negotiations between the Vatican and Israel over tax and judicial matters would resume after five years of stalemate.

Following the controversy over a speech given by Pope Benedict XVI in September 2006 (see above), efforts to establish good relations between the Roman Catholic Church and the Muslim world intensified. In May 2007 it was announced that the Pontifical Council for Inter-Religious Dialogue was to be restored, thereby reversing a decision in March 2006 to place it under the direction of the Pontifical Council for Culture. (The decision to downgrade the Council, which had previously been led by an expert on Islamic affairs, had been criticized by Muslim leaders.) King Abdullah of Saudi Arabia visited the Vatican in November 2007 for talks with the Pope, representing the first meeting between a Saudi monarch and a pontiff. It was subsequently revealed that the discussions had focused on inter-faith relations and the 'necessity of finding a just solution' to the Israeli–Palestinian conflict. In March 2008 Benedict XVI received a delegation of Muslim religious leaders at the Vatican. The talks were organized after the publication in October 2007 of an open letter to the Pope, in which 138 Muslim leaders had urged increased co-operation between Roman Catholic and Muslim religious leaders. In an attempt to further inter-faith relations, in November 2008 the Vatican hosted a three-day conference of Roman Catholic and Muslim scholars, at which the Pope urged political and religious leaders to co-operate in efforts to protect the freedom of conscience and of worship.

Pope Benedict XVI made a six-day trip to the USA in April 2008. During the visit the Pope gave an address to the UN General Assembly in New York, in which he urged greater efforts on the part of UN members to protect human rights. In June the US President, George W. Bush, visited the Vatican as part of a series of meetings with European leaders.

Efforts to improve relations with Israel continued in 2009. In early May Pope Benedict XVI spent five days in Israel and the West Bank. In a speech in Tel Aviv, the Pope condemned anti-Semitism as 'totally unacceptable' and, during a visit to the Yad Vashem Holocaust museum in Jerusalem, he repudiated denial of the Nazi Holocaust. The Pope reiterated those views in his farewell speech, while also appealing for an end to conflict in the region. However, Benedict XVI attracted some criticism, having also expressed support for the creation of a Palestinian state.

The population of the Vatican City was 805 at October 2007, comprising 556 citizens of the Vatican City and 249 resident non-citizens. Its inhabitants are of many nationalities, representing the presence of the Roman Catholic Church throughout the world. The papal guards, who numbered 98 in 2007, are of Swiss nationality.

THE VATICAN CITY

Finance

The Vatican has three main sources of income: the Istituto per le Opere di Religione (see Directory), voluntary contributions to the Church, known as 'Peter's Pence' (Obolo di San Pietro), and interest on financial investments, managed by the Administration of the Patrimony of the Holy See. The euro is used as currency. The Vatican first revealed budget figures for the Holy See in 1979, when it disclosed a deficit of US $20.1m. This was incurred through the normal operating expenses of the Vatican bureaucracy, including the newspaper and radio services and overseas diplomatic missions. The alleged mismanagement of investments, banking scandals and the decline in the value of the US dollar contributed to a deficit of $56.7m. in 1986, when annual income reached $57.0m. The deficit was met by the receipt of $32.0m. from the 'Peter's Pence' levy, and by the withdrawal of $24.7m. from the 'Peter's Pence' reserve fund. In March 1988 the Vatican published an independently audited annual balance sheet, thereby, for the first time in its history, revealing the church's financial affairs to public scrutiny. During 1988–1990 the budget deficit continued to grow, and in April 1991 more than 100 representatives of bishops' conferences from around the world attended an unprecedented meeting held in the Vatican City, at which they discussed ways of making local dioceses systematically share the burden of the Vatican's annual budgetary deficit. In that year, however, the budgetary deficit reached a peak of $87.5m. The establishment of new diplomatic missions in the late 1980s and early 1990s (see History) entailed considerable capital expenditure for the papacy. However, in 1992 the deficit fell substantially and in 1993, after 23 years of budgetary deficits, a modest surplus, of $1.5m., was recorded. A small annual budgetary surplus was maintained throughout the 1990s, cumulating in a surplus of $8.5m. in 2000, a 70% rise compared with 1999, which reflected the greater receipts generated by activities associated with the jubilee year. The budget for 2001, in contrast, showed the first deficit since 1993, of $3.1m., as a result of a general slowdown in the global economy following the terrorist attacks in the USA on 11 September 2001. In 2002 another budget deficit, of $21.0m., was recorded. The considerable increase in the deficit was largely attributed to losses in investments of $18.5m., compared with profits of $37.0m. from investments in 2001. 'Peter's Pence' contributions, however, rose by almost 86%, compared with the previous year, to $96.6m. in 2002. Another budget deficit, of $22.5m., was recorded in 2003. In 2004 a budget surplus of $3.7m. was recorded, the first since 2000, due in part to the sale of properties outside the Vatican. In 2005 the budget surplus increased to $12.3m., largely as a result of a seven-fold increase in returns on investments, assisted by favourable exchange rates. The surplus was achieved despite the costs incurred in conducting the funeral of John Paul II and the election of Benedict XVI. In 2006 a budget surplus of $3.2m. was recorded, despite a decline in the value of the Vatican's financial investments precipitated by a fall in the value of the US dollar against that of the euro. A large increase in 'Peter's Pence' contributions was recorded in that year, with donations totalling $101.9m. However, in 2007 contributions totalled just $94.1m. The Vatican recorded a budget deficit of some $14.3m. in that year, owing largely to the continued decline of the US dollar against the euro and the poor performance of stocks.

Directory

Government

The State of the Vatican City came into existence with the Lateran Treaty of 1929. The Holy See (a term designating the papacy, i.e. the office of the Pope, and thus the central governing body of the Roman Catholic Church) is a distinct, pre-existing entity. Both entities are subjects of international law. Ambassadors and Ministers are accredited to the Holy See, which sends diplomatic representatives (nuncios and pro-nuncios) to more than 120 states, as well as having delegates or observers at the UN and other international organizations. The Vatican City is also a member of certain international organizations, including specialized agencies of the UN.

Both entities are indissolubly united in the person of the Pope, the Bishop of Rome, who is simultaneously ruler of the State and visible head of the Roman Catholic Church.

On 1 February 2001 a new Basic Law replaced the former Constitution dating back to the 1929 Lateran Treaty.

THE GOVERNMENT OF THE VATICAN CITY STATE

The Vatican City State is under the temporal jurisdiction of the Pope, the Supreme Pontiff elected for life by a conclave comprising members of the Sacred College of Cardinals. The Pope holds all legislative, executive and judicial power. Legislative power is vested in the Pontifical Commission for the Vatican State, which comprises a Cardinal President and six other cardinals, nominated by the Pope for a five-year period. Executive power is vested in the President of the Pontifical Commission (who is also the President of the Governorate of the Vatican City State), who is assisted by a Secretary-General. The State Councillors, including one General Councillor and eight other Councillors, are nominated by the Pope for a five-year period, and assist in the drawing-up of laws and report to the Pontifical Commission. Judiciary power is vested in a number of Tribunals and the Apostolic Penitentiary, who exercise their judicial authority in the name of the Pope. The Pontiff exclusively retains the right to grant pardons and amnesties.

Head of State

His Holiness Pope BENEDICT XVI (elected 19 April 2005).

Pontifical Commission for the Vatican City State

Most Rev. GIOVANNI LAJOLO (President).
Cardinal GIOVANNI BATTISTA RE.
Cardinal JOSÉ SARAIVA MARTINS.
Cardinal JEAN-LOUIS PIERRE TAURAN.
Cardinal RENATO RAFFAELE MARTINO.
Cardinal ATTILIO NICORA.
Cardinal LEONARDO SANDRI.

State Councillors

Prof. CESARE MIRABELLI (General Councillor).
There are 10 additional councillors.

Governorate of the Vatican City State

President: Most Rev. GIOVANNI LAJOLO.
Secretary-General: Rt Rev. RENATO BOCCARDO (Titular Bishop of Aquipendium).
Vice Secretary-General: Rev. GIORGIO CORBELLINI.

THE SUPREME PONTIFF

His Holiness Pope Benedict XVI (Joseph Ratzinger), Bishop of Rome, Vicar of Christ, Successor of the Prince of the Apostles, Supreme Pontiff of the Universal Church, Primate of Italy, Archbishop and Metropolitan of the Province of Rome, Sovereign of the Vatican City State, Servant of the Servants of God, acceded on 19 April 2005 as the 265th Roman pontiff.

THE SACRED COLLEGE OF CARDINALS AND THE ROMAN CURIA

Members of the Sacred College of Cardinals are created by the Pope. The cardinals are divided into three orders: Bishops, Priests and Deacons. Under the decree of November 1970, *Ingravescentem Aetatem*, only cardinals under 80 years of age have the right to enter the conclave for the election of the Pope. Cardinals who reside in Rome, Italy, as the Pope's immediate advisers are styled Cardinals 'in Curia'. The Roman Curia acts as the Papal court and the principal administrative body of the Church. The College of Cardinals derives from the Church's earliest days. In March 1973 Pope Paul VI announced that the number of cardinals permitted to participate in the conclave would be limited to 120. This was increased to 135 by Pope John Paul II in February 2001. At 18 April 2005, as the conclave to elect John Paul II's successor began, there were 183 cardinals, of whom 117 were under the age of 80; 115 cardinals participated in the conclave. Following Benedict XVI's second consistory on 24 November 2007 there were 201 cardinals, of whom 121 were of voting age. There are usually six Cardinal Bishops, who are in titular charge of suburban sees of Rome. The order of Cardinal Bishops also includes

THE VATICAN CITY

the Cardinals of Patriarchal Sees of Oriental Rites. Cardinal Priests occupy titular churches in Rome, Italy, founded soon after Christianity originated. The administration of the Church's affairs is undertaken through the Secretariat of State and the Council for the Public Affairs of the Church, under the Cardinal Secretary of State, and through a number of Congregations, each under the direction of a cardinal or senior member of the Church, as well as through Tribunals, Offices, Commissions and Secretariats for special purposes.

The 'Apostolic Constitution' (*Regimini Ecclesiae Universae*), published in August 1967 and effective from 1 March 1968, reformed the Roman Curia. Among the changes were the creation of new organs and the restructuring of the Secretariat of State. In 1969 the Congregation of Rites was divided into two Congregations—one for Divine Worship and the other for the Causes of Saints. The Congregation for the Discipline of the Sacraments and the Congregation for Divine Worship were amalgamated in 1975, but separated again in 1984.

In July 1988 further reforms of the Curia were introduced. The Secretariat of State was divided into two sections: the first section dealing with 'General Affairs' and the second 'Relations with States'. The Congregation for Divine Worship was again amalgamated with the Congregation for the Discipline of the Sacraments.

Members in order of precedence:

Cardinal Bishops

ANGELO SODANO (Italy—Titular Bishop of Albano and of Ostia and Dean of the College of Cardinals).

ROGER ETCHEGARAY (France—Titular Bishop of Porto-Santa Rufina and Vice-Dean of the College of Cardinals).

GIOVANNI BATTISTA RE (Italy—Titular Bishop of Sabina-Poggio Mirteto, Prefect of the Congregation for the Bishops and President of the Pontifical Commission for Latin America).

FRANCIS A. ARINZE (Nigeria—Titular Bishop of Velletri-Segni, Prefect of the Congregation for Divine Worship and the Discipline of the Sacraments).

TARCISIO BERTONE (Italy—Titular Bishop of Frascati, Secretary of the Secretariat of State and Chamberlain of the Apostolic Chamber).

Cardinals of Patriarchal Sees of Oriental Rites

NASRALLAH PIERRE SFEIR (Lebanon—Maronite Patriarch of Antioch).

IGNACE MOUSSA I DAOUD (Syria—Prefect Emeritus of the Congregation for the Eastern Churches).

EMMANUEL III DELLY (Iraq—Chaldean Patriarch of Babylon).

Cardinal Priests

EUGÊNIO DE ARAÚJO SALES (Brazil).
LUIS APONTE MARTÍNEZ (Puerto Rico).
PAULO EVARISTO ARNS (Brazil).
WILLIAM WAKEFIELD BAUM (USA).
MARCO CÉ (Italy).
FRANCISZEK MACHARSKI (Poland).
MICHAEL MICHAI KITBUNCHU (Thailand—Archbishop of Bangkok).
ALEXANDRE DO NASCIMENTO (Angola).
GODFRIED DANNEELS (Belgium—Archbishop of Mechelen-Brussels).
THOMAS STAFFORD WILLIAMS (New Zealand).
CARLO MARIA MARTINI (Italy).
JÓZEF GLEMP (Poland).
JOACHIM MEISNER (Germany—Archbishop of Cologne).
DURAISAMY SIMON LOURDUSAMY (India).
MIGUEL OBANDO BRAVO (Nicaragua).
PAUL AUGUSTIN MAYER (Germany).
RICARDO JAMIN VIDAL (Philippines—Archbishop of Cebu).
HENRYK ROMAN GULBINOWICZ (Poland).
JOZEF TOMKO (Slovakia).
ANDRZEJ MARIA DESKUR (Poland).
PAUL JOSEPH JEAN POUPARD (France).
FRIEDRICH WETTER (Germany).
SILVANO PIOVANELLI (Italy).
ADRIANUS JOHANNES SIMONIS (Netherlands).
BERNARD FRANCIS LAW (USA—Archpriest of the Patriarchal Liberian Basilica of Santa Maria Maggiore).
GIACOMO BIFFI (Italy).
EDUARDO MARTÍNEZ SOMALO (Spain).
ACHILLE SILVESTRINI (Italy).
JOSÉ FREIRE FALCÃO (Brazil).
MICHELE GIORDANO (Italy).
ALEXANDRE JOSÉ MARIA DOS SANTOS (Mozambique).
GIOVANNI CANESTRI (Italy).
SIMON IGNATIUS PIMENTA (India).
EDWARD BEDE CLANCY (Australia).
EDMUND CASIMIR SZOKA (USA).
LÁSZLÓ PASKAI (Hungary).
CHRISTIAN WIYGHAN TUMI (Cameroon—Archbishop of Douala).
JEAN MARGÉOT (Mauritius).
EDWARD IDRIS CASSIDY (Australia).
NICOLÁS DE JESÚS LÓPEZ RODRÍGUEZ (Dominican Republic—Archbishop of Santo Domingo).
JOSÉ TOMÁS SÁNCHEZ (Philippines).
VIRGILIO NOÈ (Italy).
FIORENZO ANGELINI (Italy).
ROGER MICHAEL MAHONY (USA—Archbishop of Los Angeles).
ANTHONY JOSEPH BEVILACQUA (USA).
GIOVANNI SALDARINI (Italy).
CAHAL BRENDAN DALY (Ireland).
CAMILLO RUINI (Italy).
JÁN CHRYZOSTOM KOREC (Slovakia).
HENRI SCHWÉRY (Switzerland).
GEORG MAXIMILIAN STERZINSKY (Germany—Archbishop of Berlin).
MILOSLAV VLK (Czech Republic—Archbishop of Prague).
LUIGI POGGI (Italy).
PETER SEIICHI SHIRAYANAGI (Japan).
CARLO FURNO (Italy).
JULIUS RIYADI DARMAATMADJA (Indonesia—Archbishop of Jakarta).
JAIME LUCAS ORTEGA Y ALAMINO (Cuba—Archbishop of San Cristóbal de la Habana).
GILBERTO AGUSTONI (Italy).
EMMANUEL WAMALA (Uganda).
WILLIAM HENRY KEELER (USA).
JEAN-CLAUDE TURCOTTE (Canada—Archbishop of Montreal).
RICARDO MARÍA CARLES GORDÓ (Spain).
ADAM JOSEPH MAIDA (USA—Superior of the Cayman Islands).
VINKO PULJIĆ (Bosnia and Herzegovina—Archbishop of Vrhbosna).
ARMAND GAÉTAN RAZAFINDRATANDRA (Madagascar).
JUAN SANDOVAL IÑIGUEZ (Mexico—Archbishop of Guadalajara).
KAZIMIERZ ŚWIĄTEK (Belarus).
ERSILIO TONINI (Italy).
JORGE ARTURO AUGUSTIN MEDINA ESTÉVEZ (Chile).
DARÍO CASTRILLÓN HOYOS (Colombia—President of the Pontifical Commission 'Ecclesia Dei').
LORENZO ANTONETTI (Italy—Pontifical Delegate for the Patriarchal Basilica of St Francis in Assisi).
JAMES FRANCIS STAFFORD (USA—Major Penitentiary of the Apostolic Penitentiary).
SALVATORE DE GIORGI (Italy).
SERAFIM FERNANDES DE ARAÚJO (Brazil).
ANTONIO MARÍA ROUCO VARELA (Spain—Archbishop of Madrid).
ALOYSIUS MATTHEW AMBROZIC (Canada).
DIONIGI TETTAMANZI (Italy—Archbishop of Milan).
POLYCARP PENGO (Tanzania—Archbishop of Dar-es-Salaam).
CHRISTOPH SCHÖNBORN (Austria—Archbishop of Vienna).
NORBERTO RIVERA CARRERA (Mexico—Archbishop of Mexico City).
FRANCIS EUGENE GEORGE (USA—Archbishop of Chicago).
PAUL SHAN KUO-HSI (Taiwan).
GIOVANNI CHELI (Italy).
MARIAN JAWORSKI (Ukraine).
JĀNIS PUJATS (Latvia—Archbishop of Rīga).
IVAN DIAS (India—Prefect of the Congregation for the Evangelization of Peoples).
GERALDO MAJELLA AGNELO (Brazil—Archbishop of São Salvador de Bahia).
PEDRO RUBIANO SÁENZ (Colombia—Archbishop of Santafé de Bogotá).
THEODORE EDGAR MCCARRICK (USA).
DESMOND CONNELL (Ireland).
AUDRYS JUOZAS BAČKIS (Lithuania—Archbishop of Vilnius).
FRANCISCO JAVIER ERRÁZURIZ OSSA (Chile—Archbishop of Santiago de Chile).

THE VATICAN CITY

Julio Terrazas Sandoval (Bolivia—Archbishop of Santa Cruz de la Sierra).
Wilfrid Fox Napier (South Africa—Archbishop of Durban).
Óscar Andrés Rodríguez Maradiaga (Honduras—Archbishop of Tegucigalpa).
Bernard Agré (Côte d'Ivoire).
Juan Luis Cipriani Thorne (Peru—Archbishop of Lima).
Francisco Alvarez Martínez (Spain).
Cláudio Hummes (Brazil—Prefect of the Congregation for the Clergy).
Varkey Vithayathil (India—Major Archbishop of Ernakulam-Angamaly).
Jorge Mario Bergoglio (Argentina—Archbishop of Buenos Aires).
José da Cruz Policarpo (Portugal—Patriarch of Lisbon).
Severino Poletto (Italy—Archbishop of Turin).
Cormac Murphy-O'Connor (United Kingdom).
Edward Michael Egan (USA).
Lubomyr Husar (Ukraine—Archbishop-Major of Kyiv-Halyč, Byzantine Ukrainian Rite).
Karl Lehmann (Germany—Bishop of Mainz).
Jean Marcel Honoré (France).
Crescenzio Sepe (Italy—Archbishop of Naples).
Angelo Scola (Italy—Patriarch of Venice).
Anthony Olubunmi Okogie (Nigeria—Archbishop of Lagos).
Bernard Louis Auguste Panafieu (France).
Gabriel Zubeir Wako (Sudan—Archbishop of Khartoum).
Carlos Amigo Vallejo (Spain—Archbishop of Seville).
Justin Francis Rigali (USA—Archbishop of Philadelphia).
Keith Michael Patrick O'Brien (United Kingdom—Archbishop of St Andrews and Edinburgh).
Eusébio Oscar Scheid (Brazil).
Ennio Antonelli (Italy—President of the Pontifical Council for the Family).
Peter Kodwo Appiah Turkson (Ghana—Archbishop of Cape Coast).
Telesphore Placidus Toppo (India—Archbishop of Ranchi).
George Pell (Australia—Archbishop of Sydney).
Josip Bozanić (Croatia—Archbishop of Zagreb).
Jean-Baptiste Pham Minh Mân (Viet Nam—Archbishop of Ho Chi Minh City).
Rodolfo Quezada Toruño (Guatemala—Archbishop of Guatemala City).
Philippe Xavier Ignace Barbarin (France—Archbishop of Lyon).
Péter Erdő (Hungary—Archbishop of Esztergom-Budapest).
Marc Ouellet (Canada—Archbishop of Québec).
Agostino Vallini (Italy—Vicar-General of His Holiness for the Diocese of Rome and Archpriest of the Lateran Patriarchal Archbasilica).
Jorge Liberato Urosa Savino (Venezuela—Archbishop of Caracas—Santiago de Venezuela).
Gaudencio Borbon Rosales (Philippines—Archbishop of Manila).
Jean-Pierre Bernard Ricard (France—Archbishop of Bordeaux).
Antonio Cañizares Llovera (Spain—Prefect of the Congregation for Divine Worship and the Discipline of the Sacraments).
Nicholas Cheong Jin-Suk (Republic of Korea—Archbishop of Seoul).
Sean Patrick O'Malley (USA—Archbishop of Boston).
Stanisław Dziwisz (Poland—Archbishop of Kraków).
Carlo Caffarra (Italy—Archbishop of Bologna).
Joseph Zen Ze-kiun (Hong Kong).
Agustín García-Gasco y Vicente (Spain).
Seán Baptist Brady (Ireland—Archbishop of Armagh).
Lluís Martínez Sistach (Spain—Archbishop of Barcelona).
André Armand Vingt-Trois (France—Archbishop of Paris).
Angelo Bagnasco (Italy—Archbishop of Genoa).
Théodore-Adrien Sarr (Senegal—Archbishop of Dakar).
Oswald Gracias (India—Archbishop of Mumbai).
Francisco Robles Ortega (Mexico—Archbishop of Monterrey).
Daniel Nicholas DiNardo (USA—Archbishop of Galveston-Houston).
Odilo Pedro Scherer (Brazil—Archbishop of São Paulo).
John Njue (Kenya—Archbishop of Nairobi).
Estanislao Esteban Karlic (Argentina).

Cardinal Deacons

Agostino Cacciavillan (Italy).
Sergio Sebastiani (Italy).
Zenon Grocholewski (Poland—Prefect of the Congregation for Catholic Education and Grand Chancellor of the Università Gregoriana).
Jorge María Mejía (Argentina).
Walter Kasper (Germany—President of the Pontifical Council for the Promotion of Christian Unity).
Roberto Tucci (Italy).
Jean-Louis Pierre Tauran (France—Titular Archbishop of Thelepte and President of the Pontifical Council for Inter-Religious Dialogue).
Renato Raffaele Martino (Italy—Titular Bishop of Segerme, President of the Pontifical Council for Justice and Peace).
Francesco Marchisano (Italy—President of the Labour Office of the Apostolic See).
Julián Herranz Casado (Spain—Titular Archbishop of Vertara, President of the Disciplinary Commission of the Roman Curia).
Javier Lozano Barragán (Mexico).
Attilio Nicora (Italy—President of the Administration of the Patrimony of the Holy See).
Georges Marie Martin Cottier (Switzerland).
Thomáš Špidlík (Czech Republic).
Stanisław Kazimierz Nagy (Poland).
William Joseph Levada (USA—Prefect of the Congregation for the Doctrine of the Faith, Prefect of the Pontifical Biblical Commission, Prefect of the International Theological Commission).
Franc Rodé (Slovenia—Prefect of the Congregation for Institutes of Consecrated Life and for Societies of Apostolic Life).
Andrea Cordero Lanza di Montezemolo (Italy).
Albert Vanhoye (France).
Leonardo Sandri (Argentina—Prefect of the Congregation for the Oriental Churches).
John Patrick Foley (USA—Pro Grand Master of the Equestrian Order of the Holy Sepulchure of Jerusalem).
Giovanni Lajolo (Italy—President of the Governorate of the Vatican City State).
Paul Josef Cordes (Germany—President of the Pontifical Council 'Cor Unum').
Angelo Comastri (Italy—President of the Fabric of St Peter).
Stanisław Ryłko (Poland—President of the Pontifical Council for the Laity).
Raffaele Farina (Italy—Archivist of the Vatican Secret Archives).
Giovanni Coppa (Italy).
Urbano Navarrete Cortés (Spain).

THE ROMAN CURIA

Secretariat of State: Palazzo Apostolico Vaticano, 00120 Città del Vaticano; tel. (06) 69883913; fax (06) 69885255; e-mail vati026@relstat-segstat.va; Sec. of State Cardinal Tarcisio Bertone.

First Section—General Affairs: Segreteria di Stato, 00120 Città del Vaticano; tel. (06) 69883438; fax (06) 69885088; e-mail vati023@genaff-segstat.va; Asst Sec. of State Most Rev. Fernando Filoni (Titular Archbishop of Volturnum).

Second Section—Relations with States: Segreteria di Stato, 00120 Città del Vaticano; tel. (06) 69883014; fax (06) 69885364; e-mail vati032@relstat-segstat.va; Sec. Most Rev. Dominique Mamberti (Titular Archbishop of Sagona).

Congregations

Congregation for the Doctrine of the Faith: Piazza del S. Uffizio 11, 00120 Città del Vaticano; tel. (06) 69883357; fax (06) 69883409; e-mail cdf@cfaith.va; concerned with questions of doctrine and morals; examines doctrines and gives a judgement on them; Prefect Cardinal William Joseph Levada; Sec. Most Rev. Luis Francisco Ladaria Ferrer (Titular Archbishop of Thibica).

Congregation for the Oriental Churches: Palazzo del Bramante, Via della Conciliazione 34, 00193 Rome, Italy; tel. (06) 69884281; fax (06) 69884300; e-mail cco@orientchurch.va; f. 1862; exercises jurisdiction over all persons and things pertaining to the Oriental Rites; Prefect Cardinal Leonardo Sandri; Sec. Most Rev. Antonio Cyril Vasil (Titular Archbishop of Ptolemais in Libya).

Congregation for Divine Worship and the Discipline of the Sacraments: Palazzo delle Congregazioni, Piazza Pio XII 10, 00193 Rome, Italy; tel. (06) 69884316; fax (06) 69883499; considers all questions relating to divine worship, liturgy and the sacraments; Prefect Cardinal Antonio Cañizares Llovera; Sec. Most Rev. Albert

THE VATICAN CITY

MALCOLM RANJITH PATABENDIGE DON (Titular Archbishop of Umbriatico).

Congregation for the Causes of Saints: Palazzo delle Congregazioni, Piazza Pio XII 10, 00193 Rome, Italy; tel. (06) 69884247; fax (06) 69881935; e-mail vati335@csaints.va; concerned with proceedings relating to beatification and canonization; Prefect Most Rev. ANGELO AMATO (Titular Archbishop of Sila); Sec. Most Rev. MICHELE DI RUBERTO (Titular Archbishop of Biccari).

Congregation for the Bishops: Palazzo delle Congregazioni, Piazza Pio XII 10, 00193 Rome, Italy; tel. (06) 69884217; fax (06) 69885303; e-mail vati076@cbishops.va; designed for the preparation of matters for the erection and division of dioceses and the election of Bishops and for dealing with Apostolic Visitations; Prefect Cardinal GIOVANNI BATTISTA RE; Sec. Most Rev. FRANCESCO MONTERISI (Titular Archbishop of Alba Maritima).

Congregation for the Evangelization of Peoples: Palazzo di Propaganda Fide, Piazza di Spagna 48, 00187 Rome, Italy; tel. (06) 69879299; fax (06) 69880118; e-mail cepsegreteria@evangel.va; exercises ecclesiastical jurisdiction over missionary countries; Prefect Cardinal IVAN DIAS; Sec. Most Rev. ROBERT SARAH.

Congregation for the Clergy: Palazzo delle Congregazioni, Piazza Pio XII 3, 00193 Rome, Italy; tel. (06) 69884151; fax (06) 69884845; e-mail clero@cclergy.va; internet www.clerus.org; has jurisdiction over the life and discipline of the clergy and its permanent formation; parishes, chapters, pastoral and presbyteral councils; promotes catechesis and the preaching of the Word of God; deals with economic questions related to the compensation of the clergy and the patrimony of the Church; Prefect Cardinal CLÁUDIO HUMMES; Sec. Most Rev. MAURO PIACENZA (Titular Archbishop of Victoriana).

Congregation for Institutes of Consecrated Life and for Societies of Apostolic Life: Palazzo delle Congregazioni, Piazza Pio XII 3, 00193 Rome, Italy; tel. (06) 69884128; fax (06) 69884526; e-mail civcsva@religiosi.va; promotes and supervises practice of evangelical counsels, according to approved forms of consecrated life, and activities of societies of apostolic life; Prefect Cardinal FRANC RODÉ; Sec. Most Rev. GIANFRANCO AGOSTINO GARDIN (Titular Archbishop of Torcello).

Congregation for Catholic Education: Palazzo delle Congregazioni, Piazza Pio XII 3, 00193 Rome, Italy; tel. (06) 69884167; fax (06) 69884172; e-mail cec@cec.va; f. 1588; concerned with the direction, temporal administration and studies of Catholic universities, seminaries, schools and colleges; Prefect Cardinal ZENON GROCHOLEWSKI; Sec. Most Rev. JEAN-LOUIS BRUGUÈS.

Tribunals

Apostolic Penitentiary: Palazzo della Cancelleria, Piazza della Cancelleria 1, 00186 Rome, Italy; tel. (06) 69887526; fax (06) 69887557; e-mail regente@apostpnt.va; internet www.penitenzieria.va; Major Penitentiary Cardinal JAMES FRANCIS STAFFORD; Regent Rt Rev. GIANFRANCO GIROTTI (Titular Bishop of Meta).

Supreme Tribunal of the Apostolic Signature: Palazzo della Cancelleria, Piazza della Cancelleria 1, 00186 Rome, Italy; tel. (06) 69887520; fax (06) 69887553; Prefect Most Rev. RAYMOND LEO BURKE; Sec. Rt Rev. FRANS DANEELS (Titular Bishop of Bita).

Tribunal of the Roman Rota: Palazzo della Cancelleria, Piazza della Cancelleria 1, 00186 Rome, Italy; tel. (06) 69887502; fax (06) 69887554; Dean Rt Rev. ANTONI STANKIEWICZ (Titular Bishop of Nova Petra).

Pontifical Councils

Pontifical Council for the Laity: Piazza S. Calisto 16, 00153 Rome, Italy; tel. (06) 69887396; fax (06) 69887214; e-mail pcpl@laity.va; advises and conducts research, on lay apostolic initiatives; Pres. Cardinal STANISŁAW RYŁKO (Titular Archbishop of Novica); Sec. Rt Rev. JOSEF CLEMENS (Titular Bishop of Segerme).

Pontifical Council for Promoting Christian Unity: Via della Conciliazione 5, 00193 Rome, Italy; tel. (06) 69884083; fax (06) 69885365; e-mail office1@chrstuni.va; f. 1964; Pres. Cardinal WALTER KASPER; Sec. Rt Rev. BRIAN FARRELL (Titular Bishop of Abitinae).

Pontifical Council for the Family: Piazza S. Calisto 16, 00153 Rome, Italy; tel. (06) 69887243; fax (06) 69887272; e-mail pcf@family.va; Pres. Cardinal ENNIO ANTONELLI; Sec. (vacant).

Pontifical Council for Justice and Peace: Piazza S. Calisto 16, 00153 Rome, Italy; tel. (06) 69879911; fax (06) 69887205; e-mail pcjustpax@justpeace.va; promotes social justice, human rights, peace and development in needy areas; Pres. Cardinal RENATO RAFFAELE MARTINO; Sec. Rt Rev. GIAMPAOLO CREPALDI (Titular Bishop of Bisarcio).

Pontifical Council 'Cor Unum': Cor Unum, Via della Conciliazione 5, 00193 Rome, Italy; tel. (06) 69889411; fax (06) 69887301; e-mail corunum@corunum.va; f. 1971; cares for the needy, promotes human fellowship; Pres. Cardinal PAUL JOSEF CORDES (Titular Archbishop of Naissus).

Pontifical Council for the Pastoral Care of Migrants and Itinerant People: Piazza S. Calisto 16, 00153 Rome, Italy; tel. (06) 69887131; fax (06) 69887111; e-mail office@migrants.va; f. 1970; Pres. Most Rev. ANTONIO MARIA VEGLIÒ (Titular Archbishop of Eclano); Sec. Most Rev. AGOSTINO MARCHETTO (Titular Archbishop of Astigi).

Pontifical Council for Health Pastoral Care: Via della Conciliazione 3, 00193 Rome, Italy; tel. (06) 69883138; fax (06) 69883139; e-mail opersanit@hlthwork.va; internet www.healthpastoral.org; Pres. Most Rev. ZIGMUNT ZIMOWSKI; Sec. Rt Rev. JOSÉ LUIS REDRADO MARCHITE (Titular Bishop of Ofena).

Pontifical Council for Legislative Texts: Palazzo delle Congregazioni, Piazza Pio XII 10, 00193 Rome, Italy; tel. (06) 69884008; fax (06) 69884710; e-mail vati100@legtxt.va; f. 1984; publishes *Communicationes* journal twice yearly; Pres. Most Rev. FRANCESCO COCCOPALMERIO (Titular Archbishop of Celiana); Vice-Pres. Most Rev. BRUNO BERTAGNA (Titular Archbishop of Drivasto); Sec. Rt Rev. JUAN IGNACIO ARRIETA OCHOA DE CHINCHETRU (Titular Bishop of Civitate).

Pontifical Council for Inter-Religious Dialogue: Via della Conciliazione 5, 00193 Rome, Italy; tel. (06) 69884321; fax (06) 69884494; e-mail dialogo@interrel.va; f. 1964; Pres. Cardinal JEAN-LOUIS PIERRE TAURAN; Sec. Most Rev. PIER LUIGI CELATA (Titular Archbishop of Doclea).

Pontifical Council for Culture: Via della Conciliazione 5, 00193 Rome, Italy; tel. (06) 69893811; fax (06) 69887368; e-mail cultura@cultura.va; merged with Pontifical Council for Dialogue with Non-Believers in 1993; promotes understanding and dialogue between the Church, people from the field of learning, artists and non-believers; Pres. Most Rev. GIANFRANCO RAVASI.

Pontifical Council for Social Communications: Palazzo S. Carlo, 00120 Città del Vaticano; tel. (06) 69883197; fax (06) 69885373; e-mail pccs@pccs.va; f. 1948; examines the relationship between the media and religious affairs; manages radio, TV, film and photographic work in the Vatican; Pres. Most Rev. CLAUDIO MARIA CELLI (Titular Archbishop of Cluentum).

Pontifical Commissions and Committees

Pontifical Commission for the Cultural Patrimony of the Church: Via della Conciliazione 5, 00193 Rome, Italy; tel. (06) 69885640; fax (06) 69884621; e-mail beniculturali@beniculturali.va; f. 1988; Pres. Most Rev. GIANFRANCO RAVASI (Titular Archbishop of Villamagna in Proconsulari).

Pontifical Biblical Commission: Palazzo della Congregazione per la Dottrina della Fede, Piazza del S. Uffizio 11, 00193 Rome, Italy; tel. (06) 69884682; e-mail pcombiblica@cfaith.va; Prefect Cardinal WILLIAM JOSEPH LEVADA.

Pontifical Commission of Sacred Archaeology: Palazzo del Pontificio Istituto di Archeologia Cristiana, Via Napoleone III 1, 00185 Rome, Italy; tel. (06) 4465610; fax (06) 4467625; e-mail pcas@arcsacra.va; Pres. Most Rev. GIANFRANCO RAVASI.

Pontifical Commission 'Ecclesia Dei': Palazzo della Congregazione per la Dottrina della Fede, Piazza del S. Uffizio 11, 00120 Città del Vaticano; tel. (06) 69885213; fax (06) 69883412; e-mail eccdei@ecclsdei.va; Pres. Cardinal DARÍO CASTRILLÓN HOYOS.

Pontifical Commission for Latin America: Palazzo di San Paolo, Via della Conciliazione 1, 00193 Rome, Italy; tel. (06) 69883131; fax (06) 69884260; e-mail pcal@latinamer.va; Pres. Cardinal GIOVANNI BATTISTA RE; Vice-Pres. Most Rev. JOSÉ OCTAVIO RUIZ ARENAS (Archbishop of Villavicencio).

International Theological Commission: Palazzo della Congregazione per la Dottrina della Fede, Piazza del S. Uffizio 11, 00193 Rome, Italy; tel. (06) 69884727; Prefect Cardinal WILLIAM JOSEPH LEVADA; Sec.-Gen. Fr LUIS LADARIA.

Pontifical Committee for International Eucharistic Congresses: Palazzo S. Calisto 16, 00120 Città del Vaticano; tel. (06) 69887366; fax (06) 6987154; e-mail eucharistcongress@org.va; Pres. Most Rev. PIERO MARINI (Titular Archbishop of Martirano).

Pontifical Committee of Historical Sciences: Palazzo delle Congregazioni, Piazza Pio XII 3, 00193 Rome, Italy; tel. (06) 69884618; fax (06) 69873014; e-mail semeraro@unisal.it; Pres. Mgr WALTER BRANDMÜLLER; Sec. Rev. Prof. COSIMO SEMERARO.

Archives of the Second Vatican Council: c/o Archivio Segreto Vaticano, 00120 Città del Vaticano; tel. (06) 69883314; fax (06) 69885574; e-mail asv@asv.va; Dir Rt Rev. SERGIO PAGANO (Titular Bishop of Celene).

Commission for Lawyers: Palazzo della Cancelleria, Piazza della Cancelleria 1, 00186 Rome, Italy; tel. (06) 69887523; fax (06) 698887557; f. 1988; Pres. Most Rev. RAYMOND LEO BURKE.

THE VATICAN CITY

Disciplinary Commission of the Roman Curia: Palazzo delle Congregazioni, Piazza Pio XII 10, 00120 Città del Vaticano; tel. (06) 69884008; fax (06) 69884710; e-mail vati494@legtxt.va; Pres. Cardinal JULIÁN HERRANZ CASADO.

Offices

Apostolic Chamber: Palazzo Apostolico, 00120 Città del Vaticano; tel. (06) 69883554; Chamberlain of the Holy Roman Church Cardinal TARCISIO BERTONE; Vice-Chamberlain Most Rev. PAOLO SARDI (Titular Archbishop of Sutri).

Administration of the Patrimony of the Holy See: Palazzo Apostolico, 00120 Città del Vaticano; tel. (06) 69893403; fax (06) 69883141; e-mail apsa-ss@apsa.va; f. 1967; Pres. Cardinal ATTILIO NICORA; Sec. Most Rev. DOMENICO CALCAGNO.

Labour Office of the Apostolic See: Via della Conciliazione 1, 00193 Rome, Italy; tel. (06) 69884449; fax (06) 69883800; e-mail ulsa1@ulsa.va; Pres. Cardinal FRANCESCO MARCHISANO.

Prefecture for the Economic Affairs of the Holy See: Palazzo delle Congregazioni, Largo del Colonnato 3, 00193 Rome, Italy; tel. (06) 69884263; fax (06) 69885011; e-mail rmpaess@econaffr.va; f. 1967; Pres. Most Rev. VELASIO DE PAOLIS; Sec. Rt Rev. VINCENZO DI MAURO (Titular Bishop of Arpi).

Prefecture of the Papal Household: 00120 Città del Vaticano; tel. (06) 69883114; fax (06) 69885863; f. 1967; responsible for domestic administration and organization; Prefect Most Rev. JAMES MICHAEL HARVEY (Titular Archbishop of Memphis).

Office of the Liturgical Celebrations of the Supreme Pontiff: Palazzo Apostolico, 00120 Città del Vaticano; tel. (06) 69883253; fax (06) 69885412; Master Mgr GUIDO MARINI.

Central Statistical Office of the Church: Palazzo Apostolico, 00120 Città del Vaticano; tel. (06) 69883493; fax (06) 69883816; e-mail vformenti@statistica.va; Dir Mgr VITTORIO FORMENTI.

Holy See Press Office: Via della Conciliazione 54, 00120 Città del Vaticano; tel. (06) 698921; fax (06) 69885178; internet www.vatican.va; Dir Fr FEDERICO LOMBARDI; Vice-Dir Fr CIRO BENEDETTINI.

Pontifical Administration of the Patriarchal Basilica of San Paolo Fuori-le-Mura: 00120 Città del Vaticano; tel. (06) 5409374; fax (06) 54074049; e-mail spbasilica@org.va; Archpriest Cardinal ANDREA DI MONTEZEMOLO.

Diplomatic Representation

DIPLOMATIC MISSIONS IN ROME ACCREDITED TO THE HOLY SEE

Albania: Via Silla 7/1, 00192 Rome, Italy; tel. (06) 39754085; fax (06) 39733150; e-mail embassy.vatican@mfa.gov.al; Ambassador RROK LOGU.

Angola: Palazzo Odeschalchi, Piazza SS. Apostoli 81, 00166 Rome, Italy; tel. (06) 69190650; fax (06) 69788483; Ambassador ARMINDO FERNANDES DO ESPÍRITO SANTO VIEIRA.

Argentina: Via del Banco di Santo Spirito 42, 00186 Rome, Italy; tel. (06) 68801701; fax (06) 6879021; e-mail emba.argentina@flashnet.it; Ambassador JUAN PABLO CAFIERO.

Australia: Via Paola 24/10, 00186 Rome, Italy; tel. (06) 6877688; fax (06) 6896255; e-mail holysee.embassy@dfat.gov.au; internet www.holysee.embassy.gov.au; Ambassador TIM FISCHER.

Austria: Via Reno 9, 00198 Rome, Italy; tel. (06) 853725; fax (06) 8543058; e-mail vatikan-ob@bmeia.gv.at; Ambassador Dr MARTIN BOLLDORF.

Belgium: Via Giuseppe de Notaris 6A, 00197 Rome, Italy; tel. (06) 3224740; fax (06) 3226042; e-mail vatican@diplobel.fed.be; internet www.diplomatie.be/vaticanfr; Ambassador FRANK DE CONINCK.

Bolivia: Via di Porta Angelica 15/2, 00193 Rome, Italy; tel. (06) 6874191; fax (06) 6874193; e-mail embolivat@rdn.it; Ambassador CARLOS FEDERICO DE LA RIVA GUERRA.

Bosnia and Herzegovina: Piazzale le Clodio 12, 00195 Rome, Italy; tel. (06) 39742411; fax (06) 39742484; e-mail embvavat@tin.it; Ambassador JASNA KRIVOŠIĆ PRPIĆ.

Brazil: Via della Conciliazione 22, 00193 Rome, Italy; tel. (06) 6875252; fax (06) 6872540; e-mail embaixada@vatemb.it; internet www.vatemb.it; Ambassador LUIZ FELIPE DE SAIXAS CORRÊA.

Bulgaria: Via di Porta Angelica 63, 00193 Roma, Italia; tel. (06) 6875717; fax (06) 6865233; e-mail ambulvat@yahoo.it; internet www.mfa.bg/vatican; Ambassador VALENTIN VASSILEV BOZHILOV.

Canada: Palazzo Pio, Via della Conciliazione 4D, 00193 Rome, Italy; tel. (06) 68307316; fax (06) 68806283; e-mail vatcn@international.gc.ca; internet geo.international.gc.ca/canada-europa/holysee; Ambassador ANNE LEAHY.

Chile: Piazza Risorgimento 55, 00192 Rome, Italy; tel. (06) 6861232; fax (06) 6874992; e-mail echileva@uni.net; Ambassador PEDRO PABLO CABRERA GAETE.

China (Taiwan): Via della Conciliazione 4D, 00193 Rome, Italy; tel. (06) 68136206; fax (06) 68136199; e-mail taiwan@embroc.it; internet www.taiwanembassy.org/va; Ambassador WANG LARRY YOU-YUAN.

Colombia: Via Cola di Rienzo 285/4B, 00192 Rome, Italy; tel. (06) 3211681; fax (06) 3211703; e-mail estasede@minrelext.gov.co; Ambassador JUAN PABLO MARÍA GÓMEZ MARTÍNEZ.

Congo, Democratic Republic: Via del Castro Pretorio 28/2, 00185 Rome, Italy; tel. (06) 45447860; Chargé d'affaires a.i. EDOUARD KAMBEMBO NGUNZA.

Congo, Republic: Rome, Italy; Ambassador PIERRE-CLAVER AKOUALA.

Costa Rica: Via G.B. Benedetti 3, 00197 Rome, Italy; tel. and fax (06) 80660390; e-mail embcr.vaticano@iol.it; Ambassador LUIS PARÍS CHAVERRI.

Côte d'Ivoire: Via Sforza Pallavicini 11, 00193 Rome, Italy; tel. (06) 6877503; fax (06) 6867925; e-mail ambco.va@flashnet.it; Ambassador KOUAMÉ BENJAMIN KONAN.

Croatia: Via della Conciliazione 44, 00193 Rome, Italy; tel. (06) 6877000; fax (06) 6877003; e-mail velrhvat@tin.it; internet va.mfa.hr; Ambassador Prof. EMILIO MARIN.

Cuba: Via Aurelia 137/5A, 00165 Rome, Italy; tel. (06) 39366680; fax (06) 636685; e-mail embajada@cubassede.com; Ambassador RAÚL ROA KOURÍ.

Czech Republic: Via Crescenzio 91/1B, 00193 Rome, Italy; tel. (06) 6874696; fax (06) 6879731; e-mail vatican@embassy.mzv.cz; internet www.mzv.cz/vatican; Ambassador PAVEL VOŠALÍK.

Dominican Republic: Lungotevere Marzio 3, 00186 Rome, Italy; tel. and fax (06) 6864084; e-mail embajadardss@tiscali.it; Ambassador VICTOR GRIMALDI CÉSPEDES.

Ecuador: Via di Porta Angelica 64, 00193 Rome, Italy; tel. (06) 6897179; fax (06) 68892786; e-mail mecuadorsantasede@ecuaemss.it; Ambassador FAUSTO CÓRDOVEZ CHIRIBOGA.

Egypt: Piazza della Città Leonina 9, 00193 Rome, Italy; tel. (06) 6865878; fax (06) 6832335; e-mail ambegyptvatican@tiscali.it; Ambassador LAMIA ALI HAMADA MEKHEMAR.

El Salvador: Via Panama 22/2, 00198 Rome, Italy; tel. (06) 8540538; fax (06) 85301131; e-mail embasalssede@iol.it; Ambassador FRANCISCO SOLER.

France: Villa Bonaparte, Via Piave 23, 00186 Rome, Italy; tel. (06) 42030900; fax (06) 42030968; e-mail ambfrssg@tin.it; internet www.france-vatican.org; Ambassador STANISLAS LEFEBVRE DE LABOULAYE.

Gabon: Piazzale Clodio 12, 00195 Rome, Italy; tel. (06) 39721584; fax (06) 39724847; Ambassador FIRMIN MBOUTSOU.

Georgia: Via Emilia 25, 00187 Rome, Italy; tel. and fax (06) 42010664; e-mail georgiasantasede@gmail.com; Ambassador KETEVAN BAGRATION-MUKHRANBATONI.

Germany: Via di Villa Sacchetti 4–6, 00197 Rome, Italy; tel. (06) 809511; fax (06) 80951227; internet www.vatikan.diplo.de; Ambassador HANS-HENNING HORSTMANN.

Greece: Via Giuseppe Mercalli 6, 00197 Rome, Italy; tel. (06) 8070786; fax (06) 8079862; e-mail grembassyvat@grembassyvat.191.it; Ambassador MILTIADIS HISKAKIS.

Guatemala: Piazzale Gregorio VII 65A, 00165 Rome, Italy; tel. (06) 6381632; fax (06) 39376981; e-mail embsantasede@minex.gob.gt; Ambassador ACISCLO VALLADARES MOLINA.

Haiti: Via de Villa Patrizi 5B, 00161 Roma, Italy; tel. (06) 44242749; fax (06) 44236637; Chargé d'affaires a.i. PATRICK SAINT-HILAIRE.

Honduras: Via Boezio 45, 00192 Rome, Italy; tel. and fax (06) 6876051; e-mail honvati@fastwebnet.it; Ambassador ALEJANDRO EMILIO VALLADARES LANZA.

Hungary: Piazza Girolamo Fabrizio 2, 00161 Rome, Italy; tel. (06) 4402167; fax (06) 4402312; e-mail mission.vat@kum.hu; Ambassador JÁNOS BALASSA.

Indonesia: Piazzale Roberto Ardigò 42, 00142 Rome, Italy; tel. (06) 5940441; fax (06) 5417934; e-mail indonesia.vat@agora.stm.it; Ambassador SUPRAPTO MARTOSEMOTO.

Iran: Via Bruxelles 57, 00198 Rome, Italy; tel. (06) 8552494; e-mail chalac@libero.it; Chargé d'affaires a.i. MUHAMMAD HOSSEIN CHALAK-SARAEI.

Iraq: Via della Camilluccia 355, 00135 Rome, Italy; tel. (06) 3014508; fax (06) 35506416; e-mail ftkemb@iraqmofamail.net; Ambassador ALBERT EDWARD ISMAIL YELDA.

Ireland: Villa Spada, Via Giacomo Medici 1, 00153 Rome, Italy; tel. (06) 5810777; fax (06) 5895709; internet www.embassyofirelandholysee.it; Ambassador NOEL FAHEY.

Israel: Via Michele Mercati 12, 00197 Rome, Italy; tel. (06) 36198690; fax (06) 36198626; e-mail info-vat@holysee.mfa.gov.il; internet vatican.mfa.gov.il; Ambassador MORDECHAY LEWY.

Italy: Palazzo Borromeo, Viale delle Belle Arti 2, 00196 Rome, Italy; tel. (06) 3264881; fax (06) 3201801; e-mail amb.scv@esteri.it; Ambassador ANTONIO ZANARDI LANDI.

Japan: Via Virgilio 30, 00193 Rome, Italy; tel. (06) 6875828; fax (06) 68807543; Ambassador KAGEFUMI UENO.

Lebanon: Via di Porta Angelica 15, 00193 Rome, Italy; tel. (06) 6833512; fax (06) 6833507; Ambassador GEORGES CHAKIB AL-KHOURI.

Libya: Via Orazio 31B, 00193 Rome, Italy; tel. (06) 97605051; fax (06) 45433476; Sec. of the People's Bureau ABD AL-HAFID GADDUR.

Lithuania: Corso Vittorio Emanuele II 308, 00186 Rome, Italy; tel. (06) 68192858; fax (06) 68809596; e-mail amb.va@urm.lt; internet va.mfa.lt; Ambassador VYTAUTAS ALIŠAUSKAS.

Luxembourg: Via Casale di S. Pio V 20, 00165 Rome, Italy; tel. (06) 660560; fax (06) 66056309; Ambassador PAUL DÜHR.

Macedonia, former Yugoslav Republic: Via di Porta Cavalleggeri 143, 00165 Rome, Italy; tel. (06) 635878; fax (06) 634826; e-mail vatican@mfa.gov.mk; Ambassador BARTOLOMEJ KAJTAZI.

Mexico: Via Ezio 49, 00192 Rome, Italy; tel. (06) 3230360; fax (06) 3230361; e-mail embamex-s.sede@mclink.it; internet portal.sre.gob.mx/vaticano; Ambassador LUIS FELIPE BRAVO MENA.

Monaco: Largo Nicola Spinelli 5, 00198 Rome, Italy; tel. (06) 8414357; fax (06) 8414507; e-mail ambmonacovat@alice.it; Ambassador JEAN-CLAUDE MICHEL.

Montenegro: Via Crescenzio 97/II, 00193 Rome, Italy; tel. (06) 68134897; fax (06) 68130569; e-mail ambmont.vat@hotmail.it; Ambassador ANTUN SBUTEGA.

Morocco: Via delle Fornaci 203, 00165 Rome, Italy; tel. (06) 39388398; fax (06) 6374459; e-mail sifamavat@marocco.191.it; Ambassador ALI ACHOUR.

Netherlands: Piazza della Città Leonina 9, 00193 Rome, Italy; tel. (06) 6868044; fax (06) 6879593; e-mail vat@minbuza.nl; Ambassador MONIQUE P. A. FRANK.

Nicaragua: Via Luigi Luciani 42/1, 00197 Rome, Italy; tel. (06) 32600265; fax (06) 3207249; e-mail embanicsantasede@tin.it; Ambassador JOSÉ CUADRA CHAMORRO.

Panama: Largo di Torre Argentina 11/28, 00186 Rome, Italy; tel. (06) 68809764; fax (06) 68809812; e-mail embapass@tiscalinet.it; Chargé d'affaires a.i. JAVIER FRANCISCO TORRES GONZÁLEZ.

Paraguay: Via Alpinismo 24, 4° int. 1, Rome, Italy; tel. (06) 39751368; fax (06) 39745063; e-mail pyssede@mclink.it; Ambassador GERÓNIMO NARVÁEZ TORRES.

Peru: Via di Porta Angelica 63, 00193 Rome, Italy; tel. (06) 68308535; fax (06) 6896059; e-mail embaperuva@tin.it; Ambassador ALFONSO DÁMASO ANTONIO RIVERO MONSALVE.

Philippines: Via Paolo VI 29, 00193 Rome, Italy; tel. (06) 68308020; fax (06) 6834076; e-mail vaticanpe@philamsee.mysam.it; Ambassador CRISTINA CASTAÑER-PONCE ENRILE.

Poland: Via dei Delfini 16/3, 00186 Rome, Italy; tel. (06) 6990958; fax (06) 6990978; e-mail polamb.wat@agora.it; Ambassador HANNA SUCHOCKA.

Portugal: Villa Lusa, Via S. Valentino 9, 00197 Rome, Italy; tel. (06) 8091581; fax (06) 8077585; e-mail embportugalvatican@tiscalinet.it; Ambassador JOÃO ALBERTO BACELAR DA ROCHA PÁRIS.

Romania: Via Panama 92, 00198 Rome, Italy; tel. (06) 8541802; fax (06) 8554067; e-mail ambasciata@vatican.mae.ro; internet vatican.mae.ro; Ambassador MARIUS GABRIEL LAZURCA.

Russia: Via della Conciliazione 10, 00193 Rome, Italy; tel. (06) 6877078; fax (06) 6877168; Ambassador NIKOLAY SADCHIKOV.

San Marino: Piazza G. Winckelmann 14, 00162 Rome, Italy; tel. (06) 86321798; fax (06) 8610814; e-mail amb-sanmarino@libero.it; Ambassador SANTE CANDUCCI.

Senegal: Via dei Monti Parioli 51, 00197 Rome, Italy; tel. (06) 3218892; fax (06) 3203624; e-mail senvat@iol.it; Ambassador FÉLIX OUDIANE.

Serbia: Via dei Monti Parioli 20, 00197 Rome, Italy; tel. (06) 3200099; fax (06) 3204530; e-mail amb.serbia.vatican@ambroma.com; Ambassador VLADETA JANKOVIĆ.

Slovakia: Via dei Colli della Farnesina 144, 00194 Rome, Italy; tel. (06) 36715234; fax (06) 36715237; e-mail emb.vatican@mzv.sk; internet www.mzv.sk/vatikan; Ambassador JOZEF DRAVECKÝ.

Slovenia: Via della Conciliazione 10, 00193 Rome, Italy; tel. (06) 6833009; fax (06) 68307942; e-mail vva@gov.si; Ambassador IVAN REBERNIK.

Spain: Palazzo di Spagna, Piazza di Spagna 57, 00187 Rome, Italy; tel. (06) 6784351; fax (06) 6784355; e-mail emb.santasede@mae.es; internet www.maec.es/embajadas/santasede; Ambassador FRANCISCO VÁZQUEZ Y VÁZQUEZ.

Turkey: Via Lovanio 24/1, 00198 Rome, Italy; tel. (06) 85508601; fax (06) 85508660; e-mail vatibe@libero.it; Ambassador MUAMMER DOGAN AKDUR.

Ukraine: Via A. G. Barrili 68A, Int. 5, 00152 Rome, Italy; tel. (06) 39378800; fax (06) 45439216; e-mail emb_va@mfa.gov.ua; Ambassador TETIANA IZHEVSKA.

United Kingdom: Via XX Settembre 80A, 00187 Rome, Italy; tel. (06) 42204000; fax (06) 42204205; e-mail holysee@fco.gov.uk; internet www.ukinholysee.fco.gov.uk; Ambassador FRANCIS MARTIN-XAVIER CAMPBELL.

USA: Villa Domiziana, Via delle Terme Deciane 26, 00153 Rome, Italy; tel. (06) 46743428; fax (06) 5758346; e-mail vaticaninfo@mail.usembassy.it; internet vatican.usembassy.gov; Chargé d'affaires a.i. JULIETA VALLS NOYES.

Uruguay: Via Antonio Gramsci 9/14, 00197 Rome, Italy; tel. (06) 3218904; fax (06) 3613249; e-mail uruvati@tin.it; Ambassador MARIO JUAN BOSCO CAYOTA ZAPPETTINI.

Venezuela: Via Antonio Gramsci 14, 00197 Rome, Italy; tel. (06) 3225868; fax (06) 36001505; e-mail evidano@iol.it; Ambassador IVÁN GUILLERMO RINCÓN URDANETA.

Ecclesiastical Organization

The organization of the Church consists of:

(1) Patriarchs, Archbishops and Bishops in countries under the common law of the Church.

(2) Abbots and Prelates 'nullius dioceseos'.

(3) Vicars Apostolic and Prefects Apostolic in countries classified as Missionary and under Propaganda, the former having Episcopal dignity.

The population of the world adhering to the Roman Catholic faith, according to official estimates, was 1,131m. at 31 December 2006. Around 50% of adherents live in the Americas, 26% in Europe and 14% in Africa.

Among the Pope's official titles until early 2006, when Pope Benedict XVI decided no longer to use it, was that of Patriarch of the West. There are five other Patriarchates of the Latin Rite—Jerusalem, the West Indies, the East Indies, Lisbon and Venice. The Eastern Catholic Churches each have Patriarchs: Alexandria for the Coptic Rite, Babylon for the Chaldean Rite, Cilicia for the Armenian Rite, and Antioch for the Syrian, Maronite and Melkite Rites.

At 31 December 2007 there were 2,789 residential sees—13 patriarchates, four senior archbishoprics, 536 metropolitan archbishoprics, 75 archbishoprics and 2,161 bishoprics. Of the 2,062 titular sees (92 metropolitan archbishoprics, 91 archbishoprics and 1,879 bishoprics), 1,067 are filled by bishops who have been given these titles, but exercise no territorial jurisdiction. Other territorial divisions of the Church include 49 prelacies, 11 territorial abbacies, 25 exarchates of the Eastern Church, 35 military orders, 79 apostolic vicariates, 45 apostolic prefectures, nine apostolic administrations and nine missions 'sui iuris'.

The Press

Acta Apostolicae Sedis: Periodical Dept, Libreria Editrice Vaticana, 00120 Città del Vaticano; tel. (06) 69883529; fax (06) 39884716; e-mail mariasic2@publish.va; internet www.libreriaeditricevaticana.com; f. 1909; official bulletin issued by the Holy See; monthly, with special editions on special occasions; the record of Encyclicals and other Papal pronouncements, Acts of the Congregations and Offices, nominations, etc.; circ. 6,000.

Annuario Pontificio: Libreria Editrice Vaticana, Via del Tipografia, 00120 Città del Vaticano; tel. (06) 69883493; fax (06) 69885088; e-mail segreteria.lev@lev.va; official year book edited by Central Statistical Office; Dir Mgr VITTORIO FORMENTI.

L'Osservatore Romano: Tipografica Vaticana, Via del Pellegrino, 00120 Città del Vaticano; tel. (06) 69883461; fax (06) 69883675; e-mail ornet@ossrom.va; internet www.vatican.va/news_services/or/home_ita.html; f. 1861; an authoritative daily newspaper in Italian; its special columns devoted to the affairs of the Holy See may be described as semi-official; the news service covers religious matters and, in a limited measure, general affairs; weekly editions in English, French, German, Italian, Polish, Portuguese and Spanish; Editor-in-Chief GIOVANNI MARIA VIAN; Man. Editor CARLO DE LUCIA; circ. (Italian daily) 20,000.

Pro Dialogo: Via della Conciliazione 5, 00193 Rome, Italy; tel. (06) 69884321; fax (06) 69884494; e-mail dialogo@interrel.va; three per year; publ. by the Pontifical Council for Inter-Religious Dialogue.

Statistical Yearbook of the Church: Central Statistical Office of the Church, Palazzo Apostolico, 00120 Città del Vaticano; tel. (06)

69883493; fax (06) 69883816; e-mail vformenti@statistica.va; Dir Mgr VITTORIO FORMENTI.

NEWS AGENCY

Agenzia Internazionale FIDES: Palazzo de 'Propaganda Fide', Via di Propaganda 1C, 00187 Rome, Italy; tel. (06) 69880115; fax (06) 69880107; e-mail fides@fides.va; internet www.fides.org; f. 1926; handles news of missions throughout the world and publishes a weekly bulletin in six languages (circ. 3,000), provides a daily news service by e-mail; Dir LUCA DE MATA.

Publishers

Biblioteca Apostolica Vaticana: Cortile del Belvedere, 00120 Città del Vaticano; tel. (06) 69879402; fax (06) 69884795; e-mail bav@vatlib.it; internet www.vaticanlibrary.va; f. 1451; philology, classics, history, catalogues; Librarian of the Holy Roman Church Cardinal RAFFAELE FARINA.

Libreria Editrice Vaticana: Via della Posta, 00120 Città del Vaticano; tel. (06) 69884834; fax 69884716; e-mail lev@publish.va; internet www.libreriaeditricevaticana.com; f. 1926; religion, philosophy, literature, art, Latin philology, history; Pres. Mgr GUISEPPE SCOTTI; Dir Rev. GIUSEPPE COSTA.

Tipografia Vaticana (Vatican Press): Via della Tipografia, 00120 Città del Vaticano; tel. (06) 69883506; fax (06) 69884570; e-mail tipvat@tipografia.va; f. 1587; religion, theology, education, juveniles, natural and social sciences; prints *Acta Apostolicae Sedis* and *L'Osservatore Romano*; Dir-Gen. Rev. ELIO TORRIGIANI.

Broadcasting and Communications

RADIO

Radio Vaticana was founded in 1931 and is situated within the Vatican City. A transmitting centre, inaugurated by Pius XII in 1957, is located at Santa Maria di Galeria, about 20 km north-west of the Vatican. Under a special treaty between the Holy See and Italy, the site of this centre, which covers 420 ha, enjoys the same extraterritorial privileges as are recognized by international law for the diplomatic headquarters of foreign states.

The station operates an all-day service, normally in 40 languages, but with facilities for broadcasting liturgical and other religious services in additional languages, including Latin.

The purpose of the Vatican Radio is to broadcast papal teaching, to provide information on important events in the Roman Catholic Church, to express the Catholic point of view on problems affecting religion and morality, and, above all, to form a continuous link between the Holy See and Roman Catholics throughout the world.

Radio Vaticana: Palazzo Pio, Piazza Pia 3, 00193 Rome, Italy; tel. (06) 69883551; fax (06) 69883237; e-mail dirgen@vatiradio.org; internet www.vaticanradio.org; f. 1931; Dir-Gen. Rev. Fr FEDERICO LOMBARDI (SJ); Tech. Dir SANDRO PIERVENAZI; Administrative Dir ALBERTO GASBARRI; Dir of Programmes Rev. Fr ANDREJ KOPROWSKI (SJ).

TELEVISION

Centro Televisivo Vaticano (CTV) (Vatican Television Centre): Via del Pellegrino, 00120 Città del Vaticano; tel. (06) 69885467; fax (06) 69885192; e-mail ctv@ctv.va; f. 1983; produces and distributes programmes about the Pope and the Vatican City; Pres. Dott. EMILIO ROSSI; Dir-Gen. Rev. Fr FEDERICO LOMBARDI.

Finance

Istituto per le Opere di Religione (IOR): 00120 Città del Vaticano; tel. (06) 69883354; fax (06) 69883809; e-mail dige@sistonet.org; f. 1887; renamed in 1942; oversees the distribution of capital designated for religious works; it takes deposits from religious bodies and Vatican residents; governed by a Board of Superintendence comprising 5 financial experts, overseen by a commission of 5 cardinals; Pres. Prof. ANGELO CALOIA; Dir-Gen. PAOLO CIPRIANI; Commission mems Cardinals TARCISIO BERTONE, ATTILIO NICORA, JEAN-LOUIS PIERRE TAURAN, TELESPHORE PLACIDUS TOPPO, ODILO PEDRO SCHERER.

Lay Employees' Association

In 1989 Pope John Paul II agreed to establish a Labour Council to settle any disputes between the Holy See and its lay employees.

Associazione Dipendenti Laici Vaticani (Association of Vatican Lay Workers): Via della Posta, 00120 Città del Vaticano; tel. (06) 69885343; fax (06) 69884400; f. 1979; aims to safeguard the professional, legal, economic and moral interests of its members; Sec.-Gen. ALESSANDRO CANDI; 320 mems.

Transport

There is a small railway (863 m) which runs from the Vatican into Italy. It began operating in 1934 and now carries supplies and goods. There is also a heliport used by visiting heads of state and Vatican officials.

VENEZUELA

Introductory Survey

Location, Climate, Language, Religion, Flag, Capital

The Bolivarian Republic of Venezuela lies on the north coast of South America, bordered by Colombia to the west, Guyana to the east and Brazil to the south. The climate varies with altitude from tropical to temperate; the average temperature in Caracas is 21°C (69°F). The language is Spanish. There is no state religion, but some 85% of the population is Roman Catholic. The national flag (proportions 2 by 3) has three horizontal stripes of yellow, blue and red, with eight five-pointed white stars, arranged in an arc, in the centre of the blue stripe. The state flag has, in addition, the national coat of arms (a shield bearing a gold wheat sheaf in the first division, a panoply of swords, an indigenous bow and arrow quiver, a machete, flags and a lance in the second, and a white running horse in the base, flanked by branches of laurel and palm and with two cornucopias at the crest) in the top left-hand corner. The capital is Caracas.

Recent History

Venezuela was a Spanish colony from 1499 until 1821 and, under the leadership of Simón Bolívar, achieved independence in 1830. The country was governed principally by dictators until 1945, when a military-civilian coup replaced Isaías Medina Angarita with Rómulo Betancourt as head of a revolutionary junta. Col (later Gen.) Marcos Pérez Jiménez seized power in December 1952 and took office as President in 1953. He remained in office until 1958, when he was overthrown by a military junta under Adm. Wolfgang Larrazábal. Betancourt was elected President in the same year.

A new Constitution was promulgated in 1961. Three years later President Betancourt became the first Venezuelan President to complete his term of office. Dr Raúl Leoni was elected President in December 1963. Supporters of former President Pérez staged an abortive military uprising in 1966. Dr Rafael Caldera Rodríguez became Venezuela's first Christian Democratic President in March 1969. He achieved some success in stabilizing the country politically and economically, although political assassinations and abductions committed by underground organizations continued into 1974. At elections in December 1973 Carlos Andrés Pérez Rodríguez, candidate of Acción Democrática (AD), the main opposition party, was chosen to succeed President Caldera. The new Government invested heavily in agriculture and industrial development, creating a more balanced economy, and also undertook to nationalize important sectors. The presidential election of December 1978 was won by the leader of the Partido Social-Cristiano (Comité de Organización Política Electoral Independiente—COPEI), Dr Luis Herrera Campíns, who took office in March 1979.

In 1981 a deteriorating economic situation provoked social unrest and a succession of guerrilla attacks. At a presidential election conducted in December 1983, Dr Jaime Lusinchi, the candidate of the AD, was elected with 57% of the votes cast. The AD also won the majority of seats in the Congreso Nacional; Lusinchi assumed power in February 1984.

At presidential and legislative elections conducted in December 1988, AD candidate Carlos Andrés Pérez Rodríguez became the first former President to be re-elected (he previously held office in 1974–79). However, the AD lost its overall majority in the Congreso Nacional. Following his inauguration in February 1989 President Pérez implemented a series of adjustments designed to halt Venezuela's economic decline. These measures, which included increases in the prices of petrol and public transport, provoked rioting throughout the country in late February. The Government introduced a curfew and suspended various constitutional rights in order to quell the disturbances, but it was estimated that some 246 people had died during the protests. In early March the curfew was revoked, and all constitutional rights were restored, after wages had been increased and the prices of some basic goods were frozen.

In May 1989 popular opposition to the Government's austerity programme became co-ordinated by the country's largest trade union, the Confederación de Trabajadores de Venezuela (CTV), which organized a 24-hour general strike (the first for 31 years) in favour of the introduction of pro-labour reforms. However, in July, despite its growing dissatisfaction with the stabilization plan then in progress, the CTV signed an agreement with the Government and the business sector to promote national harmony and to support the continuation of economic adjustment policies that had been agreed with the IMF in June.

In May 1991 a controversial new labour law came into effect, providing for a severance benefit scheme and a social security system. In the second half of that year a series of widespread demonstrations and strikes were staged to protest against monthly increases in the price of petrol, or to demand, *inter alia*, wage increases, the reintroduction of price controls on basic goods, and the suspension of planned public sector redundancies. The protesters often clashed with security forces and there were several fatalities.

On 4 February 1992 an attempt to overthrow the President by rebel army units was defeated by armed forces loyal to the Government. The rebels, identified as members of the 'Movimiento Bolivariano Revolucionario 200' (MBR-200), attempted to occupy the President's office, the Miraflores palace, and his official residence, but were forced to capitulate. Simultaneous rebel action in the cities of Maracay, Valencia and Maracaibo ended when one of the leaders of the coup, Lt-Col Hugo Rafael Chávez Frías, broadcast an appeal for their surrender. More than 1,000 soldiers were arrested, and 33 officers were subsequently charged. A number of constitutional guarantees were immediately suspended, and press and television censorship was imposed to exclude coverage of Chávez, who had received considerable passive popular support. The rebels' stated primary reasons for staging the insurrection were the increasing social divisions and uneven distribution of wealth resulting from government economic policy, and widespread corruption in public life. In what was widely perceived as an attempt to appease disaffected sectors of society, immediately following the attempted coup Pérez authorized a 50% increase in the minimum wage and a 30% increase in the pay of middle-ranking officers of the armed forces. He also announced plans to bring forward a US $4,000m. social project, aimed at improving health care, social welfare and education.

In March 1992 Pérez announced a series of proposed political and economic reforms, including the introduction of legislation for immediate reform of the Constitution. In addition, the President announced the suspension of increases in the price of petrol and electricity, and the reintroduction of price controls on a number of basic foodstuffs and on medicine. In that month, in an effort to broaden the base of support for his Government, Pérez appointed two members of COPEI to the Council of Ministers. Full constitutional rights were finally restored in April. Nevertheless, widespread protests against government austerity measures and alleged official corruption continued in September and October. A series of bomb attacks, attributed to the rebel movements Los Justicieros de Venezuela and the Fuerzas Bolivarianos de Liberación (an organization claiming to have links with MBR-200), were directed at the residences of allegedly corrupt senior politicians.

On 27 November 1992 a further attempt by rebel members of the armed forces to overthrow the President was suppressed by forces loyal to the Government. The attempted coup, led by senior air force and navy officers, was reported to have been instigated by members of MBR-200. A videotaped statement by the imprisoned Lt-Col Chávez, transmitted from a captured government-owned television station, urged Venezuelans to stage public demonstrations in support of the rebels. Principal air force bases were seized, and rebel aircraft attacked the presidential palace and other strategically important installations. The Government introduced a state of emergency and suspended the Constitution. Sporadic fighting continued into the following day, but by 29 November order had been restored and some 1,300 rebel members of the armed forces had been arrested. President Pérez rejected demands from the press and opposition parties for his resignation. The curfew imposed during the coup was ended at the beginning of December, and further constitutional rights were restored later in the month.

Popular discontent with the Government was reflected further in regional and municipal elections held in December 1992, which resulted in significant gains for COPEI as well as revealing increasing support for the left-wing Movimiento al Socialismo (MAS) and La Causa Radical (La Causa R), whose candidate, Aristóbulo Istúriz, was elected mayor of Caracas. In March 1993 the Supreme Court annulled the rulings of an extraordinary summary court martial, which had been established by presidential decree to try those implicated in the attempted coup of November 1992, on the grounds that the court was unconstitutional. Those sentenced by the court were to be retried by an ordinary court martial.

In May 1993 an extraordinary joint session of the Congreso Nacional voted to endorse a Supreme Court ruling that sufficient evidence existed for Pérez to be prosecuted on corruption charges. The charges concerned allegations that Pérez, and two former government ministers, had, in 1989, embezzled US $17m. from a secret government fund. Pérez was subsequently suspended from office and, in accordance with the terms of the Constitution, replaced by the President of the Senado, Octavio Lepage, pending the election by the Congreso Nacional of an interim President who would assume control until the expiry of the presidential term in February 1994, should Pérez be found guilty. On 5 June the Congreso Nacional elected Ramón José Velásquez, an independent senator, as interim President. Velásquez immediately undertook a broad-ranging reorganization of the Council of Ministers. In August the Congreso Nacional approved legislation enabling Velásquez to introduce urgent economic and financial measures by decree in order to address the growing economic crisis. In late August a special session of the Congreso Nacional voted in favour of the permanent suspension from office of Pérez, regardless of the outcome of the legal proceedings being conducted against him. (In May 1994 Pérez was arrested and imprisoned, pending trial by the Supreme Court on charges of corruption.)

The presidential and legislative elections of December 1993 proceeded peacefully. Dr Rafael Caldera Rodríguez, the candidate of a newly formed party, the Convergencia Nacional (CN), was elected President (having previously held office in 1969–74). However, the CN and its electoral ally, the MAS, secured only minority representation in the Congreso Nacional. Caldera took office in February 1994. In that month the AD and COPEI established a legislative pact using their combined majority representation in the Congreso Nacional in order to gain control of the major legislative committees. In response, Caldera warned that he would dissolve the legislature and organize elections to a Constituent Assembly should the government programme encounter obstructions in the Congreso Nacional. Also in February, in an attempt to consolidate relations with the armed forces, Caldera initiated proceedings providing for the release and pardon of all those charged with involvement in the coup attempts of February and November 1992.

In June 1994 the Government announced that it was to assume extraordinary powers, in view of the deepening economic crisis and the virtual collapse of the banking sector. Six articles of the Constitution were suspended concerning guarantees including freedom of movement, freedom from arbitrary arrest, and the right to own property and to engage in legal economic activity. The Government also announced the introduction of price controls and a single fixed exchange rate, in order to address the problems of a rapidly depreciating currency and depleted foreign exchange reserves. Later that month Caldera issued a decree placing the financial system under government control. Of those banks affected by the crisis, 10 were closed permanently; the majority of those still operational were to be returned to private control. In July the Congreso Nacional voted to restore five of the six suspended constitutional guarantees. Despite protest, the Government promptly reintroduced the suspensions. Later that month, however, the legislative opposition, with the exception of La Causa R, which withdrew from the legislature in protest, endorsed emergency financial measures, including an extension of price controls and the strengthening of finance sector regulation, which were presented by the Government as a precursor to the restoration of full constitutional guarantees.

In March 1995 the arrest of some 500 alleged subversives (including activists of the MBR-200) by the security forces prompted demonstrations in the capital in support of demands for the release of those detained and in opposition to the deployment of the National Guard to patrol Venezuela's cities. In July the constitutional guarantees were restored, except in border areas with Brazil, in light of continued criminal activity there. In September 1997 the Congreso Nacional approved an 'enabling law' ('ley habilitante') that conferred extraordinary powers on President Caldera to enact legislation by decree, in order to facilitate the implementation of emergency economic measures designed to reduce the huge fiscal deficit and to accelerate social security reforms.

In May 1996 former President Pérez was found guilty by the Supreme Court of misuse of public funds, although he was acquitted of charges of embezzlement. He was sentenced to two years and four months under house arrest, of which he had already served two years. In July the Senado voted to deny Pérez the seat-for-life in that chamber to which former Presidents of the country were normally entitled. In April 1998 Pérez was charged with misappropriation of public funds during his time in office, and was placed under house arrest pending full investigation of the charges. At legislative elections conducted in November (see below), however, he was successfully elected to the Senado, and was therefore entitled to parliamentary immunity from prosecution.

The legislative elections of 8 November 1998 were won by the Polo Patriótico, an alliance of small, mainly left-wing parties led by the Movimiento V República (MVR). The MVR had been founded in the previous year by the leader of the attempted coup of February 1992, Lt-Col (retd) Chávez; its electoral success was widely considered to reflect the popular rejection of apparent corruption in the country's major political parties. Proyecto Venezuela, the party created to support the presidential candidacy of the independent Henrique Salas Römer, also performed well.

In the light of the MVR's success in the legislative poll, prior to the presidential election the AD and COPEI withdrew their support for their respective candidates and united in support of Salas Römer, hoping to forestall the loss of their long-standing political predominance. However, Chávez, who had styled himself as a radical left-wing populist, promising social revolution and constitutional reform, was elected President on 6 December 1998, with 56% of the votes cast, ahead of Salas Römer, who received the support of some 40% of voters.

Chávez immediately announced plans for elections to a Constituent Assembly to draft a new constitution, and asked the Congreso to pass an enabling law to allow him to implement an extensive restructuring of public administration and a comprehensive economic recovery programme. Chávez was inaugurated as President on 2 February 1999 and a new Council of Ministers was installed. At the end of February Chávez announced details of an ambitious emergency social improvement plan (the Plan Bolívar 2000) to rehabilitate public property and land through voluntary civil and military action. Such pledges (together with a promise that the armed forces would not be used against the civilian population) prompted a series of rural and urban public land occupations, none of which was forcibly ended.

In April 1999, following prolonged negotiation and compromise, the Congreso approved Chávez's proposed enabling law. On 25 April a national referendum, organized to ascertain levels of popular support for the convening of a Constituent Assembly and the regulations governing the election of such a body, demonstrated 82% support for the Assembly and 80% support for Chávez's proposals for electoral procedures. (The successful endorsement of the proposals was, however, qualified by the 60% rate of voter abstention.) Elections to the National Constituent Assembly (ANC) in late July resulted in an outright victory for the Polo Patriótico, which won 120 out of the 131 seats. The leadership of COPEI and of the AD subsequently resigned. The ANC was formally inaugurated on 3 August and by late August had assumed most functions of the opposition-controlled Congreso Nacional; the Congreso itself was put into recess indefinitely. In response, the opposition accused the Government of establishing a de facto dictatorship. Chávez justified the control of the legislature, executive and judiciary as necessary in order to eradicate corruption and implement social reforms. A Judicial Emergency Commission was appointed in August with the task of investigating the notoriously corrupt judicial system. (By November 1999 200 judges had been dismissed or suspended.) In response, the Supreme Court President resigned. In September the ANC and the Congreso Nacional signed an agreement of political coexistence that guaranteed the full functioning of the legislative branch from 2 October until a new constitution entered into force. However, relations between the Government and the Congreso Nacional were further strained when Chávez ignored congressional objections to the 2000 budget proposal and asked the ANC to approve it instead.

The draft of the new Constitution was signed by the ANC on 19 November 1999 and was approved by 71% of the popular vote in a referendum held on 15 December. The low rate of voter participation (only 46%) was largely blamed on torrential rain in much of the country (which resulted in the deaths of 30,000 and left a further 200,000 homeless in the central state of Vargas). The 350-article Constitution, which renamed the country the Bolivarian Republic of Venezuela, was promulgated on 30 December. It extended the President's term from five to six years, eliminated the Senate, permitted more state intervention in the economy, reduced civilian supervisory powers over the military, guaranteed the Government's oil monopoly and strengthened minority rights. The Government's political opponents challenged the Constitution because of its centralization of power in the executive branch. The Constitution also promoted public participation by giving the electorate the right to remove elected officials from office by referendum and to annul all but a handful of key laws with an absolute majority. The monitoring of such election processes was to be carried out by an independent National Electoral Council (Consejo Nacional Electoral—CNE). The Constitution also granted social security and labour benefits, including the reduction of the working week to 44 hours, which was strongly opposed by business leaders. The Congreso Nacional was officially dissolved on 4 January 2000. A new post of executive Vice-President was created, and on 24 January Chávez appointed Isaías Rodríguez (ANC Vice-President) to the position.

New elections for the President, governors, legislators and mayors, as stipulated under the new Constitution, were scheduled for May 2000. The ANC was dissolved in January after it formally delegated its powers to a newly created 21-member Legislative Commission, which was designated as an interim body until the formation of a new Asamblea Nacional. On 25 May, three days before voting was scheduled to take place, the Tribunal Supremo de Justicia suspended the elections, citing technical faults with the electronic voting system. Elections for the President, national legislators and governors were eventually held on 30 July, separate from the local elections, which were postponed until December. Despite the weak economic situation, popular support for the President, especially from the poorest sections of society, remained strong: Chávez won 59.7% of the valid votes cast in the presidential poll, compared with the 37.5% of the ballot polled by Francisco Arias Cárdenas, Governor of the state of Zulia and one of the four commanders who had led the abortive coup against President Pérez. At the concurrent election to the new, 165-seat Asamblea Nacional, the ruling MVR secured a majority of 93 seats, short of the three-fifths' majority required to appoint members of the judiciary and the Attorney-General and Comptroller-General.

In November 2000 Chávez's powers were further enhanced when the Asamblea Nacional approved a new enabling law, allowing the President to decree, without legislative debate, a wide range of laws (in areas including public finance and land reform) for one year. In the same month the legislature passed controversial legislation that assigned the power to appoint important government posts, such as Attorney-General, Ombudsman (Defensor del Pueblo) and senior judges, to a 15-member congressional committee that was dominated by members of the ruling party.

In May 2001 thousands of petroleum and steel workers went on strike to demand recognition of trade union rights. By late November the Chávez administration had antagonized both the labour and business sectors sufficiently for them to find common cause. The opposition-controlled CTV allied itself with the country's largest business association, Fedecámaras (Federación Venezolana de Cámaras y Asociaciones de Comercio y Producción), to demand a nation-wide general strike. Fedecámaras was protesting against a recently decreed series of 49 laws (passed using the enabling law, thereby bypassing legislative scrutiny); these measures included land reform legislation allowing the Government to expropriate land it deemed unproductive, and a hydrocarbons law, which increased royalties on the petroleum industry. The CTV leaders objected to the hydrocarbons law, claiming that it threatened foreign investment and jobs. In the same month thousands of AD supporters marched on the Asamblea Nacional to demand the resignation of the President. A one-day general strike paralysed the country on 11 December and garnered support from a broad range of sectors.

In January 2002 Chávez replaced his Vice-President, Adina Bastidas, with his conspirator in the 1992 military coup attempt, Diosdado Cabello. Another participant in the 1992 coup attempt, Rámon Rodríguez Chacín, was appointed Minister of the Interior and Justice, while later in the month another former army colleague, Francisco Usón, was named Minister of Finance. The cabinet reorganization was interpreted by many as a move to the left that would increase political instability in the country. Also in February, four military officials, in separate statements, publicly demanded that Chávez resign, leading to further anti-Government protests and counter-demonstrations in support of the Government. In the same month, in the face of increasing economic uncertainty, the Government abandoned the fixed currency exchange regime and allowed the bolívar to float freely, in an attempt to halt mass capital flight. The bolívar subsequently lost nearly 19% of its value against the US dollar.

In early March 2002 business leaders, trade union leaders and representatives of the Catholic Church signed a pact calling for the installation of a government of national unity, and more transparency in government, as well as action against poverty and corruption. At the same time, industrial unrest continued to escalate. Following the appointment of a new management board of the state petroleum company Petróleos de Venezuela, SA (PDVSA), several thousand PDVSA managers marched through Caracas in protest; the managers claimed that the appointments were politically motivated. The demonstrators were supported by Fedepetrol, the petroleum workers' trade union, as well as by Fedecámaras. On 9 April a 48-hour general strike was organized by the CTV and Fedecámaras. It was subsequently announced that the strike would continue indefinitely, and on 11 April more than 150,000 people marched on the presidential palace to demand Chávez's resignation. In the subsequent clashes outside the Miraflores palace between protesters, government supporters and the security forces, 20 people were killed and more than 100 injured.

On 12 April 2002 a group of senior military officers announced that President Chávez had resigned amid allegations that pro-Government loyalists had fired on opposition protesters. It later emerged that Chávez had, in fact, refused to resign and that, in effect, a military coup had taken place. The military conspirators appointed Pedro Carmona, the President of Fedecámaras, interim President, while Chávez was held incommunicado. On assuming power, Carmona immediately dissolved the Asamblea Nacional and the Tribunal Supremo de Justicia and pronounced Chávez's Bolivarian Constitution to be null and void. The removal from office by the military of an elected head of state was immediately condemned by many Governments in the region; however, in contrast, the US Administration of George W. Bush blamed the crisis on Chávez and refused to call his ousting from power a coup (see below). Thousands of pro-Chávez and pro-democracy supporters immediately took to the streets to demand Chávez's reinstatement, while many senior military officers also expressed their continued loyalty to the deposed President. In the face of threats by officers loyal to Chávez to attack the presidential palace, Carmona immediately resigned; Vice-President Cabello was sworn in as interim President on 13 April. Chávez returned to the Miraflores palace within hours and, in a televised ceremony, resumed his presidential powers, less than two days after his ouster.

On reassuming the presidency, as a gesture of reconciliation, Chávez announced the resignation of the disputed PDVSA board of directors. He also declared that there would be no persecution of those who had supported his removal from office. Nevertheless, Carmona and 100 military personnel were arrested. (Carmona escaped from house arrest and was subsequently granted asylum in Colombia.) In late April 2002 the Asamblea Nacional approved the establishment of a Truth Commission to investigate the events surrounding the coup attempt. (In mid-October 2004 eight people, including workers, business leaders and students, were convicted and sentenced to prison terms of between three and six years for their roles in the uprising.)

The country's political and economic situation continued to deteriorate in mid-2002. In August the Supreme Court ruled that there was insufficient evidence to prosecute four senior members of the military who had participated in the failed coup attempt in April. (However, this ruling was overturned in March 2005.) In late October the opposition and its allies in the CTV labour union and Fedecámaras called a one-day strike, intended to force President Chávez to accept early presidential and legislative elections. The strike brought much of Venezuela to a halt, although the country's important oil industry was not seriously affected. On 23 October a group of 14 senior military officers declared themselves in rebellion against the Chávez Government. The men, many of whom had been involved in April's failed coup, occupied a square in eastern Caracas, where they were joined by hundreds of opposition activists. More than 100 junior officers later also expressed their rejection of Chávez's policies and joined the protest. All of the officers involved were subsequently dismissed from the armed forces. In an attempt to find a constitutional solution to the ongoing political crisis, 12 representatives of the opposition and the Government began roundtable discussions in early November. The negotiations were chaired by the Secretary-General of the Organization of American States (OAS, see p. 373), César Gaviria Trujillo, and were also attended by representatives of the US-based Carter Center. The talks failed to make any immediate progress, however, and in late November the opposition, the CTV and Fedecámaras announced that a general strike would be held from 2 December to force President Chávez to call fresh elections or submit to a referendum. The general strike lasted a further nine weeks. The majority of large businesses and international companies observed the stoppage, although small shopkeepers and public transport continued to operate throughout. The strike had a particularly severe impact on the oil industry. The majority of managers and administrative staff at PDVSA observed the strike, and the company was obliged to declare *force majeure* on its exports of crude petroleum and petroleum products. The President of PDVSA, Alí Rodríguez Araque, sought to restart the industry by replacing the strikers with new staff, contract workers and retired employees. He eventually dismissed 18,000 of PDVSA's previous 33,000 full-time work-force for observing the strike, and production reportedly recovered to pre-strike levels by late March 2003. The strike caused enormous difficulties for the Government, which saw oil revenues collapse, while ordinary Venezuelans suffered from severe shortages of food and other basic products.

In January 2003 President Chávez suspended trading in the national currency, the bolívar, in response to the economic crisis. Early the following month it was announced that the bolívar was to be pegged to the US dollar, and that price controls were to be introduced on basic food items. None the less, the Government refused to negotiate on the issue of early elections, although discussions between the two sides, suspended at the start of the strike, began once more in late January. In early February the opposition parties, the CTV and Fedecámaras announced an end to the two-month general strike after failing to secure any concessions from the Government. The opposition, which had combined under the Coordinadora Democrática (CD) grouping, presented an estimated 4m. signatures in support of early elections. The Government did not respond to the petition, and several days later it announced new exchange rate rules, which critics alleged were designed to punish companies that had participated in the recent strike. In mid-February the Government and opposition representatives at the OAS-sponsored negotiations signed an agreement to seek to reduce political tension in Venezuela. The pact was immediately thrown into question, however, when the following day police arrested the President of Fedecámaras, Carlos Fernández Pérez, on charges including treason, relating to his role in organizing the recent general strike. A warrant was also issued for his fellow strike leader, the President of the CTV, Carlos Ortega, who went into hiding and later obtained political asylum in Costa Rica. (Ortega was expelled from that country in March 2004, and in December 2005 was found guilty of insurrection, incitement and use of false documents and sentenced to 15 years' imprisonment.) The opposition immediately accused President Chávez of authoritarianism and observers expressed fears that a further deterioration in the political situation was likely. In March an appeals court ordered the release without charge of Fernández Pérez, ruling that there was no evidence against him.

In April 2003, following further OAS-sponsored negotiations, the Government and opposition agreed in principle that a referendum on the Chávez Government could be held if the opposition succeeded in collecting 2.4m. signatures in support of a vote. The agreement was finalized in the following month. The signatures collected by the opposition were to be verified by the CNE. However, since the Asamblea Nacional was unable to agree on appointments to the electoral body, responsibility passed, as stipulated by the Constitution, to the Tribunal Supremo de Justicia, which appointed, in August, a new head of the electoral authority, as well as four other board members. One week earlier opposition parties had submitted a 2.4m.- signature petition to the CNE demanding a recall referendum. However, in early September the new board of the electoral authority ruled that the petition was not valid, as some of the signatures had been collected more than six months before the date on which a referendum could be held. Furthermore, in late September the CNE issued a new and more stringent set of referendum guidelines, which stipulated that, in the case of a binding presidential recall referendum, a President would then only be removed from office if a greater proportion of the electorate voted against him than had supported him in the most recent election (in the case of Chávez in the 2000 ballot, this would be greater than 59.7% of the votes). Also, if there were insufficient valid signatures collected (20% of the electorate, equivalent to some 2.4m. voters), no further recall petitions would be permitted during that President's term of office.

In October 2003 the CD presented a new recall referendum request to the CNE. In response, the MVR announced that it intended to compile more than 40 recall petitions on opposition deputies and state governors. The CNE ruled that any recall referendums would be restricted to members of the Asamblea Nacional and federal Government. It subsequently announced that signature-gathering for the recall of 37 opposition politicians would take place on 21–24 November, while that for the presidential recall (plus those of 33 MVR deputies) would be held one week later.

The CNE was scheduled to announce the validity of both sets of petitions by the end of December 2003. However, a series of technical problems and doubts over the validity of some petitions led to delays, provoking civil unrest in which eight protesters were killed in February 2004. Finally, following further delays in order to revalidate signatures, in June the CNE ruled that the number of valid signatures collected was sufficient to force a presidential recall referendum. The Government accepted this ruling, and the poll was duly held on 15 August. The motion to recall the President was defeated, with 59% of valid votes cast against Chávez's removal from office. The rate of participation was 70% of the electorate. Despite assertions by the Carter Center, the OAS and other international observers that the ballot had been conducted fairly, the CD disputed the result, claiming that large-scale electoral fraud had been perpetrated by the Government. In late September the CNE rejected the CD's appeal against the referendum result, citing a lack of evidence.

In November 2004 state prosecutor Danilo Anderson, who had been investigating the failed coup of April 2002, with a view to bringing charges against those involved, was assassinated in Caracas. In late November a former police commissioner of Caracas, Iván Simonovis, was arrested on suspicion of involvement with the murder; two other suspects were killed by police while allegedly resisting arrest. In October 2005 Attorney-General Isaías Rodríguez Díaz accused the US and Colombian intelligence services and Colombian paramilitaries of colluding in Anderson's assassination; both countries denied the accusation and cited a lack of supporting evidence. In November Patricia Poleo and three others were named in connection with the case.

In January 2005 President Chávez signed a decree initiating a 90-day review process into both the level of productivity on privately owned land and into the validity of its ownership. Local authorities were granted powers to expropriate estates deemed unproductive by the review for redistribution to landless farmers. The number of 'unproductive' estates was estimated at over 500, according to a preliminary government survey published earlier that month. In September President Chávez vowed to accelerate the process of land expropriations. In January 2006 the Government took control of 32 oilfields under private operation, in accordance with its policy of revising all private sector contracts for hydrocarbon exploitation in order to give the government-owned PDVSA a majority stake.

At elections to the Asamblea Nacional on 4 December 2005 the ruling MVR secured 114 of a total 167 seats; the pro-Chávez party Por la Democracia Social (PODEMOS) took 15 seats, with the remaining seats won by other parties allied to the Government. The overwhelming government victory was primarily owing to the boycott of the ballot by the main opposition parties (including the AD, Primero Justicia and Proyecto Venezuela), which claimed that the electronic voting system could not guarantee voters' anonymity. As a result, voter participation was estimated at just 25%. However, observers from the European Union (EU, see p. 255) and the OAS declared the elections to be free and transparent; a report published by the EU observer group in March 2006 stated that the principal discernible problem in the elections had been a lack of confidence among some voters in the electoral process. (In late 2007 PODEMOS abandoned its support for the Government, thus becoming the sole opposition party in the legislature.)

The Government announced further measures under its so-called Bolivarian social reform programme in early 2006. In March it was stated that 150,000 new homes were to be built during the year to begin to address the housing crisis among impoverished sectors of society. In April a programme costing US $24m. to extend basic services to some 77,000 people living in rural areas was announced. Moreover, in November new measures aimed at extending access to higher education and at providing dental care for the poor were introduced. The Government's ongoing revision of its hydrocarbons operations also continued during 2006. In April the state assumed control of seven oilfields operated by foreign petroleum companies, five of which were relinquished under legislation introduced in 2001 and two of which were retaken without the agreement of the companies currently operating the sites. Further amendments to the hydrocarbon laws, approved in May 2006, provided for an increase in royalties required from foreign companies operating Venezuelan oilfields from one-sixth to one-third.

At the presidential election held on 3 December 2006 Chávez was decisively re-elected with 62.9% of the vote. The opposition's unity candidate, Manuel Rosales Guerrero, the Governor of Zulia, secured 36.9% of votes cast. Observers from the EU declared themselves to be generally satisfied with the conduct of the election and praised the high rate of electoral participation in the poll (some 75% of registered voters took part). The victory was seen as a strong endorsement of the Government's Bolivarian programme of social reform, and of Chávez himself, as a charismatic and popular national leader. Shortly after the election it was announced that the MVR was to be dissolved and replaced by a new political organization, the Partido Socialista Unido de Venezuela (PSUV), which was intended to unite the various left-wing parties allied to the Government. In January 2007 the Asamblea Nacional approved a wide-ranging enabling law granting the President powers to legislate by decree for a period of 18 months in 11 areas, including the reform of state institutions and public services. The law was intended, in particular, to facilitate one of the stated priorities of the new administration, the return to state ownership of privatized industries (particularly in the telecommunications, electricity and hydrocarbons sectors). To this end, in February the Government agreed the terms of the purchase of shares in Electricidad de Caracas, and in May it bought a majority share in the telecommunications concern Compañía Anónima Nacional Telefónos de Venezuela. In June PDVSA gained control of petroleum operations in the Orinoco Belt, a large reserve of heavy crude petroleum, by acquiring majority stakes in four joint ventures with foreign companies. Two further companies refused to renegotiate their contracts with PDVSA, and the projects in which they were involved came under full state ownership.

The Government was widely criticized for its attitude towards civil liberties following an announcement in December 2006 that it would not renew the broadcasting licence of Radio Caracas Televisión (RCTV), Venezuela's oldest television station, upon its expiry in May 2007. Chávez cited the station's support for the brief coup of 2002 and the anti-Government bias of its news reporting as reasons for the decision, which was condemned by numerous international media organizations. The station duly ceased broadcasting in May and was replaced by a state-owned channel, Televisora Venezolana Social; however, RCTV recommenced broadcasting via cable in July by means of its US-based subsidiary, RCTV International.

In August 2007 Chávez presented the Asamblea Nacional with a proposal to amend 33 articles of the 1999 Constitution. The most significant of the amendments would have removed the restriction limiting the President to two consecutive terms in office—allowing him to be re-elected indefinitely—and increased the presidential term from six to seven years. The revised Constitution would, inter alia, have abolished the autonomy of the central bank and placed the country's international reserves under government control, defined a political role for the armed forces, and reduced the maximum working day from eight to six hours. In November the Asamblea Nacional approved Chávez's proposed amendments, along with a further 36 proposed by the legislature. A referendum was held on 2 December on the two sets of amendments, both of which were rejected by some 51% of valid votes cast. Only 56% of the electorate participated in the referendum, leading observers to attribute the result, which represented Chávez's first defeat in a nation-wide popular vote since he won the 1998 presidential election, to the abstention of many of the President's supporters. Gen. Raúl Isaías Baduel, a former close ally of Chávez who had retired as Minister of National Defence in July, had been prominent in his opposition to the reform, claiming that it would have amounted to a coup.

Chávez carried out an extensive cabinet reorganization in January 2008. Notably, Vice-President Jorge Rodríguez Gómez was dismissed and replaced by Ramón Alonso Carrizalez Rengifo, hitherto Minister of Housing, who was in turn replaced by Col (retd) Jorge Isaac Pérez Prado; Ramón Rodríguez Chacín substituted Pedro Carreño as Minister of the Interior and Justice (a position he had previously held in 2001–02); and Rafael Isea replaced Rodrigo Cabezas as Minister of Finance. The appointment of more moderate figures to the Council of Ministers was seen as a response to the Government's defeat in the referendum of December 2007. (However, several of the new ministers were themselves replaced in the subsequent months: in March Pérez Prado was dismissed and replaced by Edith Gómez; in June Isea resigned in order to stand in the forthcoming regional elections and was substituted by Alí Rodríguez Araque, the erstwhile President of PDVSA and Minister of Foreign Affairs from 2004–06; and in September Rodríguez Chacín also resigned, Tarek El Aissami being appointed in his stead.) Meanwhile, in April Chávez announced that the Government would take control of the cement industry in Venezuela, in order to guarantee supplies for state housing construction programmes. Majority stakes in two of the three main cement companies were purchased in August; however, in the same month, following its failure to negotiate a take-over of the Venezuelan operations of the Mexican firm Cemex, the Government seized and expropriated the firm's plants and offices by force.

In late May 2008 Chávez used his powers under the enabling law of January 2007 to enact a law on intelligence and counter-intelligence by decree. The new legislation was widely criticized by the opposition and human rights organizations, in particular for an article that established prison terms of up to four years for any person who refused to co-operate with the intelligence services. In response to the controversy, in early June the President conceded that mistakes had been made in the drafting of the law, and shortly afterwards he announced that it had been repealed. On 31 July Chávez made further use of the enabling law—just before it was scheduled to expire—to promulgate 26 decrees, many of which introduced measures that had been included in the proposed constitutional reforms rejected in 2007. Several of the new laws increased state control over the economy, notably in the area of food security; among the other decrees was one that established a National Bolivarian Militia, directly responsible to the President and incorporated into the armed forces.

Municipal and gubernatorial elections on 23 November 2008 were participated in by more than 65% of registered voters, representing the highest turn-out ever recorded in local elections. Although PSUV candidates were elected Governor in 17 of the 22 contested states (including four in which the incumbent Governors had broken away from Chávez's new party and campaigned against it), the opposition's gain of three of the most populous states, in addition to the two it already held, was seen as a significant challenge to the pro-Chávez hegemony across the country. Equally significantly, opposition candidates took the mayoralty of the metropolitan district of Caracas and four of the capital's five municipalities, including one of its most impoverished neighbourhoods; in addition, former presidential candidate Manuel Rosales was elected Mayor of Maracaibo, the second-largest city.

In December 2008 Chávez initiated another attempt to remove the restriction on presidential re-election, asking PSUV members to gather signatures in support of the necessary constitutional amendment. In an effort to widen support for the initiative, in early January 2009 the President proposed that term limits should be abolished for all popularly elected offices, including governors, mayors and deputies. Later in that month the Asamblea Nacional approved, subject to referendum, Chávez's proposed amendments to five articles of the Constitution that would enable re-election to all posts. A referendum was duly held on 15 February, at which the amendments were approved by 55% of valid votes cast. Some 70% of the electorate participated in the poll. Immediately after the result was announced, Chávez confirmed his intention to stand in the presidential election due in 2012.

The Government made further moves to increase its control over the economy and public administration in the months following the referendum. In late February 2009 Chávez ordered the National Guard to take control of all rice-processing plants, in order to ensure that they complied with government regulations requiring 60% of their output to be basic rice sold at fixed prices. Shortly afterwards, in early March, the Government established more stringent regulations on food production, increasing to 80% the proportion of rice that producers were to sell at regulated prices and setting similar quotas on other basic foodstuffs; on the following day Chávez announced the expropriation of a rice mill belonging to the US multinational corporation Cargill, accusing it of failing to meet production quotas, and threatened other food producers with nationalization if they similarly contravened the regulations. In mid-March the Asamblea Nacional approved legislation allowing the President to reassume the administration of strategic infrastructure, including ports, airports and roads, from state governments (to which control had been devolved in 1999). Chávez subsequently ordered the armed forces to take control of three major ports—Puerto Cabello, Guamache and Maracaibo—and an airport, all in states governed by the opposition. Furthermore, in April the Asamblea Nacional approved a law allowing the President to appoint a Head of Government of the Capital District (comprising the largest of Caracas's five municipalities), to whom most of the budget hitherto assigned to the metropolitan authority would be transferred. The new arrangements were widely regarded as being intended to diminish the authority of the recently elected opposition Mayor of the metropolitan district, Antonio Ledezma. In May the Government began the nationalization of all companies providing services to the petroleum and gas industry, taking control of terminals and boats on Lake Maracaibo.

Meanwhile, Chávez effected another government reorganization in early March 2009, merging several ministries in an effort to reduce costs. Among other appointments, former Vice-President Diosdado Cabello (who had been ousted as Governor of Miranda in the regional election of November 2008 and appointed Minister of Infrastructure in December) was designated to head a new Ministry of Public Works and Housing, replacing the Ministries of Infrastructure and of Housing, while Gen. Gustavo Rangel Briceño was dismissed as Minister of Defence and replaced in an acting capacity by Vice-President Carrizalez.

Also in March 2009, following an investigation begun in October 2008 at Chávez's request, the Attorney-General issued an arrest order against Rosales, who was accused of having embezzled public funds while he was Governor of Zulia. The opposition leader denied the charges, which he denounced as politically motivated, and went into hiding. In the following month he fled to Peru, claiming that the Venezuelan judicial system would not afford him a fair trial; the Peruvian Government swiftly granted him political asylum, prompting Venezuela to recall its ambassador to that country in protest.

In 1982 Venezuela refused to renew the 1970 Port of Spain Protocol, which declared a 12-year moratorium on the issue of Venezuela's claim to a large area of Guyana to the west of the Essequibo river. Venezuela's border garrisons were strengthened and border violations were reported. In 1985 Venezuela and Guyana requested UN mediation in an attempt to resolve their dispute over the Essequibo region. A UN mediator was appointed in late 1989; however, negotiations remained deadlocked. The dispute resurfaced in 1999 when Guyana granted offshore oil concessions in the disputed waters to foreign oil firms, and in October of that year President Chávez renewed Venezuela's claim to the Essequibo region. The tension escalated in March 2000 when Guyana gave preliminary approval to the installation of a US satellite-launching facility in the disputed area. In March 2004 Chávez met his Guyanese counterpart, Bharrat Jagdeo; although no progress was made on resolving the dispute, the Venezuelan Government indicated its willingness to 'authorize' Guyanese mineral exploration in the Essequibo region. In mid-2005 Guyana signed the PetroCaribe energy accord with Venezuela, granting Guyana preferential terms for purchasing Venezuelan petroleum.

Venezuela also has a claim to some islands in the Netherlands Antilles, and a territorial dispute with Colombia concerning maritime boundaries in the Gulf of Venezuela. In March 1989 an agreement was reached with Colombia on the establishment of a border commission to negotiate a settlement for the territorial dispute. In March 1990 President Virgilio Barco of Colombia and President Pérez signed the 'San Pedro Alejandrino' document, by which they pledged to implement the commission's proposals. At a meeting of the Presidents of Colombia and Venezuela in Caracas in January 1992, Pérez publicly recognized that Colombia had legitimate territorial rights in the Gulf of Venezuela.

Periodic incursions into Venezuelan territory by Colombian combatants and criminal elements continually strained relations with Colombia. Despite agreements signed by both countries in 1997 and 2000 to increase co-operation in policing the border area, clashes between the Venezuelan military and Colombian guerrillas were frequent. Tensions were exacerbated in 2000, owing to Chávez's public opposition to the military component of 'Plan Colombia' (Colombia's US-supported anti-drugs strategy) and accusations by Colombia that Venezuela was covertly aiding the guerrilla forces. In November 2000 Colombia briefly recalled its ambassador to Venezuela after a representative of the Fuerzas Armadas Revolucionarias de Colombia—Ejército del Pueblo (FARC) was allowed to speak in the Venezuelan Asamblea Nacional. In March 2001 Venezuela refused to extradite to Colombia a member of a guerrilla group accused of hijacking an aircraft in 1999. Although the right-wing Government of Alvaro Uribe Vélez repeatedly criticized President Chávez for failing to classify the FARC as a terrorist organization, in November there were indications of rapprochement following a meeting between the two Presidents to promote bilateral trade and security co-operation. However, the Venezuelan Government continued to demand improvements to border security arrangements, following confrontations with armed Colombian groups in December 2003 and September 2004 that resulted in the deaths of several Venezuelan soldiers. In a public demonstration of amity, Presidents Uribe and Chávez met in Cartagena, Colombia, in November 2004 to discuss border security and economic co-operation. However, relations were severely strained in December following the arrest by the Colombian authorities of Rodrigo Granda Escobar, the supposed international spokesperson of the FARC. It was subsequently alleged by the Venezuelan Government that Granda, although ultimately arrested in Cúcuta, Colombia, was first kidnapped in Caracas by Venezuelan and Colombian agents in the pay of the Colombian Government and with the collusion of US intelligence services; the Uribe and US Governments denied any involvement. In consequence, the Venezuelan ambassador to Colombia was recalled in January 2005 and restrictions on trade and passage between the two countries were imposed by the Chávez Government. Following an expression of regret by the Colombian Government in January and a visit to Caracas by President Uribe in February, relations between the two countries were normalized. Relations were strengthened in September following the Colombian authorities' refusal of political asylum to seven Venezuelan military officials and one diplomat accused of participating in the failed coup attempt of April 2002. However, in 2005 and early 2006 the Colombian and US Governments repeatedly expressed concern over Venezuela's rapid military expansion, which, it was argued, would upset the military balance of the region. In August 2007 Uribe engaged Chávez in negotiating with FARC leaders in respect of the release of hostages held by the guerrilla group. Relations between the two countries deteriorated significantly in November after Uribe abruptly cancelled Chávez's mediation attempt, accusing him of making contact with senior Colombian military officers against his orders; nevertheless, the Venezuelan President's subsequent role in securing the release of two of the hostages in January 2008 led to a slight improvement in relations. Chávez strongly condemned Uribe following Colombia's incursion into Ecuadorean territory in early March, during which time a senior FARC commander was killed; in response to the incident Chávez ordered the closure of the Venezuelan embassy in the Colombian capital, Bogotá, and sent troops to the Colombian border. Uribe subsequently alleged that evidence gathered during the raid indicated that Chávez had aided the FARC, and threatened to prosecute him in the International Criminal Court. However, formal diplomatic relations were swiftly restored a few days later after Chávez mediated a rapprochement between Uribe and the Ecuadorean President, Rafael Correa Delgado, at a Rio Group summit in the Dominican Republic. In June, in a reversal of his previous declarations in support of the rebels, Chávez publicly urged the FARC to end its armed struggle and release all its remaining hostages. The personal animosity between Chávez and Uribe was put aside in the following month when the two Presidents held a cordial meeting in Venezuela.

VENEZUELA

Following his election in December 1998, President Chávez announced that his administration would seek greater integration in large regional organizations such as the Caribbean Community and Common Market (CARICOM, see p. 206) and the Southern Common Market (Mercosur, see p. 405). In September 2005 Chávez launched PetroCaribe, an initiative to promote energy integration and offer preferential prices for petroleum in the Caribbean region. Venezuela was admitted to Mercosur in July 2006, but its entry was subject to ratification by the group's existing members; by May 2009 Venezuela's accession had yet to be ratified by the legislatures of Brazil and Paraguay.

President Chávez made closer relations with Cuba a priority, and in October 2000 Chávez and the Cuban Head of State Fidel Castro Ruz signed a co-operation agreement allowing the export of oil to Cuba on the same preferential terms enjoyed by a number of Central American and Caribbean countries. In 2003–04 improved relations between the two countries led to increased Cuban assistance for the Government's social-welfare programmes, and Venezuela continued to support Cuba's integration into regional trade associations.

Venezuela's relations with Mexico deteriorated in November 2005 at the Summit of the Americas in Mar del Plata, Argentina, owing to President Chávez's strident denunciation of an initiative promoted by Mexican President Vicente Fox Quesada for a free trade area of the Americas. The Venezuelan ambassador to Mexico was recalled later that month, as was the Mexican ambassador to Venezuela. Meanwhile, from early 2005 the Mexican authorities accused Venezuela with increasing frequency of failing to police adequately its sea and air ports in order to prevent the transshipment of illegal narcotics, primarily from Colombia, to Mexico. In April 2006 Mexican officials reportedly discovered 5.5 metric tons of cocaine on an aircraft that had arrived from Venezuela; the ultimate destination of the drugs was believed to be the USA. Relations with Mexico improved after Felipe Calderón Hinojosa took office as President of that country in late 2006, and in August 2007 an exchange of ambassadors marked the restoration of full diplomatic relations.

Relations between Venezuela and the USA (the main purchaser of Venezuelan crude petroleum) deteriorated markedly following the election of Chávez. In 2000 Chávez refused to authorize US drugs-surveillance flights over Venezuela. Furthermore, the President's close relationship with Fidel Castro led to further estrangement from the USA. Bilateral relations further deteriorated after the US Administration of George W. Bush refused to condemn the short-lived military ouster of Chávez in April 2002. Relations with the USA remained hostile during the mid-2000s, owing in large part to Chávez's sustained personal criticism of President Bush and his outspoken rhetoric against US 'imperialism'. In April 2005 Venezuela suspended its military exchange programmes with the USA. In August of that year Chávez suspended co-operation with the US Drug Enforcement Agency (DEA), following its repeated criticism of Venezuela's counter-narcotics policies. Chávez accused DEA agents of spying on Venezuela and the US Government responded by 'decertifying' Venezuela for non-compliance in fulfilling its obligations to combat the trade in illegal drugs. None the less, in January 2006 Venezuela agreed to renew some co-operation with the DEA, although US agents from the organization were not to be allowed on Venezuelan territory. In the same month the US Department of State intervened to prevent the sale to Venezuela of Spanish military aircraft worth some US $2,000m., ostensibly on the grounds that the aircraft contained US-built components requiring an export licence. However, in February it was announced that the sale would proceed despite US opposition. Later that month Venezuela expelled a US naval attaché in Venezuela, Capt. John Correa, accusing him of espionage. The following day the USA expelled a Venezuelan diplomat in response. Meanwhile, throughout 2005 and 2006 members of the Government, including President Chávez, repeatedly alleged that the USA was planning to invade Venezuela in order to secure its supply of petroleum and that the country's armed forces were being strengthened in preparation for this; the USA dismissed the allegation as unsubstantiated and accused Chávez of seeking to destabilize the region by expanding its military capability so significantly. During 2006 the Venezuelan Government continued to strengthen its armed forces, purchasing military aircraft from Russia as well as 100,000 assault rifles. In March the US authorities announced an embargo on all commercial arms sales to Venezuela. The US Government continued to express concern regarding Venezuela's close relations with countries including Cuba, Libya and Iran, with whose Government Chávez publicly stated his commitment to co-operate in the field of nuclear energy. In September 2008 Venezuela expelled the US ambassador, Patrick Duddy, and recalled its own ambassador from the USA, in solidarity with Bolivia, which had just carried out a similar action as part of an ongoing dispute.

Venezuela continued to strengthen its alliance with Russia in 2008. Chávez visited Russia in July to sign co-operation agreements in the fields of energy and defence. Russian President Dmitrii Medvedev paid a return visit to Venezuela in November (the first by a Russian leader) as part of a wider tour of Latin America, and promised Russian assistance to enable Venezuela to build its first nuclear power plant. Coinciding with Medvedev's visit, a Russian naval squadron visited Venezuelan waters and participated in joint exercises with the Venezuelan navy.

Venezuela is a member of the Non-aligned Movement (see p. 439).

Government

Venezuela is a federal republic comprising 23 states, a Capital District and 72 Federal Dependencies. Under the 1999 Constitution, legislative power is held by the unicameral Asamblea Nacional (National Assembly). Executive authority rests with the President. The President is elected for six years by universal adult suffrage. The President has extensive powers, and is assisted by a Council of Ministers. Each state has a directly elected executive governor and an elected legislature.

Defence

Military service is selective for two years and six months between 18 and 45 years of age. As assessed at November 2008, the armed forces numbered an estimated 115,000: an army of 63,000, a navy of 17,500 (including 7,000 marines), an air force of 11,500 and a National Guard of 23,000. There was an army reserve numbering 8,000. The defence budget for 2008 was 7,120,000m. bolívares.

Economic Affairs

In 2007, according to estimates by the World Bank, Venezuela's gross national income (GNI), measured at average 2005–07 prices, was US $201,146m., equivalent to $7,320 per head (or $11,920 per head on an international purchasing-power parity basis). During 2000–07, it was estimated, the population increased by an annual average of 1.8%, while gross domestic product (GDP) per head decreased, in real terms, at an average of 2.7% per year. Overall GDP increased, in real terms, by an average annual rate of 4.5% in 2000–07; according to World Bank estimates, GDP grew by 8.4% in 2007.

According to the World Bank, agriculture (including hunting, forestry and fishing) contributed an estimated 4.0% of GDP in 2004 and engaged 8.7% of the employed labour force in 2007. The principal crops are sugar cane, bananas, maize, rice, plantains, oranges, sorghum and cassava. Cattle are the principal livestock, but the practice of smuggling cattle across Venezuela's border into Colombia has had a severe effect on the livestock sector. According to the World Bank, agricultural GDP increased by an estimated annual average of 3.3% during 2000–06. The sector's GDP decreased, in real terms, by 8.1% in 2006.

Industry (including mining, manufacturing, petroleum-related activities, construction and power) contributed a preliminary 39.7% of GDP in 2008 and engaged 23.3% of the employed labour force in 2007. According to official estimates, industrial GDP rose by an annual average of 2.1% during 2000–07. Sectoral GDP increased, in real terms, by a preliminary 2.5% in 2008.

Mining and quarrying (including petroleum and petroleum-related activities) contributed a preliminary 13.5% of GDP in 2008. However, in 2007 mining and quarrying engaged only 0.9% of the employed labour force. Petroleum and petroleum-related products provided 92.2% of export revenues in 2006. At the end of 2007 proven reserves totalled 87,000m. barrels, although if heavy and extra-heavy crude petroleum reserves were included, Venezuela's total reserves were estimated to be considerably higher. Production averaged 2.6m. barrels per day in 2007. As well as large reserves of petroleum, Venezuela has substantial deposits of natural gas, coal, diamonds, gold, zinc, copper, lead, silver, phosphates, manganese and titanium. The GDP of the mining sector declined by an estimated average of 1.3% per year in 2000–07; the sector rose, in real terms, by a preliminary 2.7% in 2008.

Manufacturing contributed a preliminary 17.1% of GDP in 2008 and engaged approximately 12.3% of the employed labour force in 2007. The most important sectors were food products,

VENEZUELA
Introductory Survey

transport equipment, industrial chemicals and iron and steel. According to official estimates, manufacturing GDP increased by an annual average of 4.2% during 2000–07. The sector's GDP increased, in real terms, by a preliminary 1.4% in 2008.

Energy is derived principally from domestic supplies of petroleum and coal, and from hydroelectric power. Hydroelectric power provided 75.0% of electricity production in 2006, according to the US Energy Information Administration, with thermal generation supplying the remainder. Imports of mineral fuels comprised 0.4% of the total value of merchandise imports in 2007.

The services sector (excluding hotels and restaurants) contributed a preliminary 59.7% of GDP in 2008 and engaged some 67.9% of the employed labour force in 2007. The sector increased by an annual average of 5.2% in 2000–07. Sectoral GDP increased, in real terms, by a preliminary 16.4% in 2008.

In 2008 Venezuela recorded a visible trade surplus of US $45,447m., and there was a surplus of $39,202m. on the current account of the balance of payments. In 2007 the principal source of imports (20.2%) was the USA; other major suppliers were Colombia, Brazil, Panama and Mexico. The USA was also the principal market for exports (50.9%) in 2006; other major purchasers were the Netherlands Antilles, Spain, Brazil and the Netherlands. The principal exports in 2006 were petroleum and related products (92.2%), steel, aluminium and chemical products. The principal imports in 2007 were machinery and transport equipment (38.7%), basic manufactures, and chemicals.

There was a budgetary deficit of 12,967,600m. bolívares in 2007. Venezuela's total external debt was US $44,635m. at the end of 2006, of which $27,180m. was long-term public debt. In that year the cost of servicing the debt was equivalent to 13.3% of the value of exports of goods and services. The average annual rate of inflation was 19.3% in 2000–07. Consumer prices increased by an annual average of 18.7% in 2007. An estimated 10.3% of the labour force were unemployed in March 2007.

Venezuela is a member of the Inter-American Development Bank (IDB, see p. 318), the Latin American Integration Association (Asociación Latinoamericana de Integración—ALADI, see p. 342), the Organization of the Petroleum Exporting Countries (OPEC, see p. 386), the Latin American Economic System (Sistema Económico Latinoamericano—SELA, see p. 427) and the Group of Three (G3, see p. 426). In July 2004 Venezuela became an associate member of Mercosur (see p. 405), and in July 2006 the country was admitted to full membership (although this remained subject to ratification by Brazil and Paraguay at mid-2009). In November 2005, at the Summit of the Americas in Mar del Plata, Argentina, President Chávez discounted the possibility of Venezuela joining the proposed Free Trade Area of the Americas (FTAA), advanced by the USA. In April 2006 President Chávez withdrew Venezuela from the Andean Community of Nations (see p. 178). In the same month Chávez, and the Cuban and Bolivian heads of state, Fidel Castro Ruz and Evo Morales Aima, respectively, signed a trade agreement, the Bolivarian Alternative for the Americas (Alternativa Bolivariana para las Américas—ALBA), intended to be an alternative to the stalled FTAA. In December 2004 Venezuela was one of 12 countries that were signatories to the agreement, signed in Cusco, Peru, creating the South American Community of Nations (Comunidad Sudamericana de Naciones), intended to promote greater regional economic integration, due to become operational by 2007. In May 2007 Chávez announced that Venezuela was to withdraw from the IMF and the World Bank, but reversed the decision later that year.

Venezuela's economy is largely dependent on the petroleum sector and is therefore particularly vulnerable to fluctuations in global oil prices. Unlike previous governments, the Chávez administration, inaugurated in 1999, has done little to diversify the economy away from oil, and in the first nine months of 2008 oil accounted for 92% of export revenues. The failure of the coup against President Chávez in April 2002, and of the opposition's attempt to unseat Chávez in a recall referendum in mid-2004, allowed the Government to consolidate its policy of increased state intervention. The Chávez Government increased petroleum taxes and royalties and in January 2006 appropriated 32 privately operated oilfields. Following his re-election in the previous December, in early 2007 Chávez signalled his intent further to advance his Bolivarian socialism project, with the nationalization of parts of the telecommunications and electricity sectors. In April 2008 Chávez announced that the cement industry was to be nationalized in an attempt to deal with severe housing shortages. The Chávez administration was also able to continue with its regional integration project, offering, *inter alia*, discounted petroleum to Caribbean and Latin American nations. Nevertheless, this economic largesse only remained possible while the price of oil remained high and from mid-2008 international oil prices suffered serious decreases, from a high of US $147 per barrel in July to under $40 in February 2009. As a result, Chávez was forced in March to revise the 2009 budget, which was based on oil prices of $60 a barrel. It was announced that value added tax was to be increased from 9% to 12% and budgeted spending was to be decreased by 6.7%. However, the budget deficit remained at over $10m., which, it was announced, was to be decreased through extra domestic borrowing. While foreign exchange reserves had been built up in the boom years, analysts feared these would run dry by the end of 2009. Furthermore, the Government's policy of heightened state intervention continued to deter investment, as did the increasingly hostile relationship between Venezuela and the USA. Inflation increased from 17.0% in 2006 to 31.9% in 2008. Consumer prices were forecast to rise further, to some 36% over 2009, owing in part to continuing high food prices; the country imports some two-thirds of its food. The IMF predicted that GDP would decline by 2.2% in 2009, compared with growth of 8.4% in 2007 and 4.9% in 2008.

Education

Education is officially compulsory for 10 years, to be undertaken between six and 15 years of age. Primary education, which is available free of charge, begins at six years of age and lasts for nine years. Secondary education, beginning at the age of 15, lasts for a further two years. In 2006/07 enrolment at primary schools included 92.2% of children in the relevant age-group, while secondary enrolment included 68.4% of the relevant age-group (males 64.1%; females 72.9%). In 2003/04 there were 48 universities. Expenditure by the central Government on education and sport was an estimated 29,601.6m. bolívares in 2004.

Public Holidays

2009: 1 January (New Year's Day), 23–24 February (Carnival), 9 April (Maundy Thursday), 10 April (Good Friday), 19 April (Declaration of Independence), 1 May (Labour Day), 24 June (Battle of Carabobo), 5 July (Independence Day), 24 July (Birth of Simón Bolívar and Battle of Lago de Maracaibo), 12 October (Day of Indigenous Resistance), 25 December (Christmas).

2010: 1 January (New Year's Day), 15–16 February (Carnival), 1 April (Maundy Thursday), 2 April (Good Friday), 19 April (Declaration of Independence), 1 May (Labour Day), 24 June (Battle of Carabobo), 5 July (Independence Day), 24 July (Birth of Simón Bolívar and Battle of Lago de Maracaibo), 12 October (Day of Indigenous Resistance), 25 December (Christmas).

Banks and insurance companies also close on: 6 January (Epiphany), 19 March (St Joseph), Ascension Day (21 May 2009, 13 May 2010), 29 June (SS Peter and Paul) and 8 December (Immaculate Conception).

Weights and Measures

The metric system is in force.

VENEZUELA

Statistical Survey

Sources (unless otherwise stated): Instituto Nacional de Estadística (formerly Oficina Central de Estadística e Informática), Edif. Fundación La Salle, Avda Boyacá, Caracas 1050; tel. (212) 782-1133; fax (212) 782-2243; e-mail ocei@platino.gov.ve; internet www.ine.gov.ve; Banco Central de Venezuela, Avda Urdaneta, esq. de las Carmelitas, Caracas 1010; tel. (212) 801-5111; fax (212) 861-0048; e-mail mbatista@bcv.org.ve; internet www.bcv.org.ve.

Area and Population

AREA, POPULATION AND DENSITY

Area (sq km)	916,445*
Population (census results)	
20 October 1990†	18,105,265
30 October 2001‡	
Males	11,402,869
Females	11,651,341
Total	23,054,210
Population (official postcensal estimates at mid-year)§	
2006	27,030,656
2007	27,483,208
2008	27,934,783
Density (per sq km) at mid-2008	30.5

* 353,841 sq miles.
† Excluding Indian jungle population and adjustment for underenumeration, estimated at 6.7%.
‡ Excluding Indian jungle population, enumerated at 183,143 in a separate census of indigenous communities in 2001. Also excluding adjustment for underenumeration, estimated at 6.7%.
§ Based on results of 2001 census, including Indian jungle population and adjustment for underenumeration.

ADMINISTRATIVE DIVISIONS
(official postcensal estimates at mid-2008)

	Area (sq km)	Population	Density (per sq km)	Capital
Capital District	433	2,091,452	4,830.1	Caracas
Amazonas	177,617	146,029	0.8	Puerto Ayacucho
Anzoátegui	43,300	1,502,197	34.7	Barcelona
Apure	76,500	485,470	6.3	San Fernando
Aragua	7,014	1,689,056	240.8	Maracay
Barinas	35,200	772,734	22.0	Barinas
Bolívar	240,528	1,563,600	6.5	Ciudad Bolívar
Carabobo	4,650	2,262,070	486.5	Valencia
Cojedes	14,800	306,273	20.7	San Carlos
Delta Amacuro	40,200	156,233	3.9	Tucupita
Falcón	24,800	917,696	37.0	Coro
Guárico	64,986	759,508	11.7	San Juan de los Morros
Lara	19,800	1,824,087	92.1	Barquisimeto
Mérida	11,300	859,924	76.1	Mérida
Miranda	7,950	2,902,235	365.1	Los Teques
Monagas	28,900	872,996	30.2	Maturín
Nueva Esparta	1,150	443,648	385.8	La Asunción
Portuguesa	15,200	890,503	58.6	Guanare
Sucre	11,800	930,989	78.9	Cumaná
Táchira	11,100	1,198,892	108.0	San Cristóbal
Trujillo	7,400	724,839	98.0	Trujillo
Vargas	1,497	335,368	224.0	La Guaira
Yaracuy	7,100	609,861	85.9	San Felipe
Zulia	63,100	3,687,332	58.4	Maracaibo
Federal Dependencies	120	1,791	14.9	—
Total	916,445	27,934,783	30.5	—

PRINCIPAL TOWNS
(city proper, estimated population at 1 July 2000)

Caracas (capital)	1,975,787	Mérida	230,101
Maracaibo	1,764,038	Barinas	228,598
Valencia	1,338,833	Turmero	226,084
Barquisimeto	875,790	Cabimas	214,000
Ciudad Guayana	704,168	Baruta	213,373
Petare	520,982	Puerto la Cruz	205,635
Maracay	459,007	Los Teques	183,142
Ciudad Bolívar	312,691	Guarenas	170,204
Barcelona	311,475	Puerto Cabello	169,959
San Cristóbal	307,184	Acarigua	166,720
Maturín	283,318	Coro	158,763
Cumaná	269,428		

Mid-2007 ('000, incl. suburbs, UN estimates): Caracas 2,985; Maracaibo 2,072; Valencia 1,770; Barquisimeto 1,116; Maracay 1,007 (Source: UN, *World Urbanization Prospects: The 2007 Revision*).

BIRTHS, MARRIAGES AND DEATHS*

	Registered live births		Registered marriages		Registered deaths	
	Number	Rate (per 1,000)	Number	Rate (per 1,000)	Number	Rate (per 1,000)
2001	529,552	23.2	81,516	3.3	107,867	5.0
2002	492,678	22.9	73,163	2.9	105,388	5.0
2003	555,614	22.6	74,562	2.9	118,562	5.0
2004	637,792	22.3	74,103	2.8	110,946	5.0
2005	665,997	22.0	86,093	3.2	110,301	5.0
2006	646,225	21.8	89,772	3.2	115,348	5.1
2007	615,371	21.5	93,003	3.4	118,594	5.1

* Figures for numbers of births and deaths exclude adjustment for underenumeration. Rates are calculated using adjusted data.

Life expectancy (years at birth, WHO estimates): 74 (males 71; females 78) in 2006 (Source: WHO, *World Health Statistics*).

ECONOMICALLY ACTIVE POPULATION
(labour force survey, '000 persons aged 15 years and over, 2007)*

	Males	Females	Total
Agriculture, hunting, forestry and fishing	924.0	77.9	1,001.9
Mining and quarrying	86.2	16.5	102.7
Manufacturing	966.2	452.2	1,418.4
Electricity, gas and water	39.2	12.3	51.5
Construction	1,059.2	50.5	1,109.7
Wholesale and retail trade, restaurants and hotels	1,308.2	1,395.5	2,703.8
Transport, storage and communications	898.4	96.0	994.4
Financing, insurance, real estate business services	366.4	223.2	589.6
Community, social and personal services	1,409.0	2,085.9	3,494.8
Activities not adequately defined	16.3	8.8	25.2
Total employed	7,073.0	4,418.9	11,491.9
Unemployed	536.7	391.5	928.2
Total labour force	7,609.7	4,810.5	12,420.2

* Figures exclude members of the armed forces.
Source: ILO.

VENEZUELA

Health and Welfare

KEY INDICATORS

Total fertility rate (children per woman, 2006)	2.6
Under-5 mortality rate (per 1,000 live births, 2006)	21
HIV/AIDS (% of persons aged 15–49, 2005)	0.7
Physicians (per 1,000 head, 2001)	1.94
Hospital beds (per 1,000 head, 2003)	0.9
Health expenditure (2006): US $ per head (PPP)	396
Health expenditure (2006): % of GDP	5.1
Health expenditure (2006): public (% of total)	49.5
Access to water (% of persons, 2004)	83
Access to sanitation (% of persons, 2004)	68
Human Development Index (2006): ranking	61
Human Development Index (2006): value	0.826

For sources and definitions, see explanatory note on p. vi.

Agriculture

PRINCIPAL CROPS
('000 metric tons)

	2005	2006	2007*
Rice, paddy	1,004.5	1,122.9	800.0
Maize	2,193.5	2,336.8	2,104.0
Sorghum	385.4	584.4	498.0
Potatoes	443.1	454.1	454.0
Cassava (Manioc)	531.3	489.0	490.0
Yautia (Cocoyam)	59.2	86.0	86.0
Yams	76.9	87.2	87.5
Sugar cane	9,654.4	9,322.9	9,300.0
Coconuts	176.8*	173.4	174.0
Oil palm fruit	304.5	307.4	307.5
Cabbages and other brassicas	92.6	101.4	101.0
Tomatoes	211.7	195.9	196.0
Chillies and peppers, green	110.3	122.0	123.0
Onions, dry	265.4	255.0	255.0
Carrots and turnips	185.0	211.6	211.6
Watermelons	285.7	150.7	151.0
Cantaloupes and other melons	293.6	131.6	132.0
Bananas	529.7	509.0	523.0
Plantains	492.0	335.3	337.0
Oranges	374.4	377.9	378.0
Tangerines, mandarins, etc.	95.7	93.0	93.0
Lemons and limes	65.5	49.6	50.0
Guavas, mangoes and mangosteens	74.9	74.4	75.0
Avocados	63.1	58.7	58.7
Pineapples	349.2	356.9	360.0
Papayas	118.1	151.4	151.4
Coffee, green	64.5	74.3	75.0

* FAO estimate(s).

Aggregate production ('000 metric tons, may include official, semi-official or estimated data): Total cereals 3,584 in 2005, 4,044 in 2006, 3,402 in 2007; Total roots and tubers 1,165 in 2005, 1,175 in 2006, 1,176 in 2007; Total vegetables (incl. melons) 1,751 in 2005, 1,412 in 2006, 1,413 in 2007; Total fruits (excl. melons) 2,370 in 2005, 2,071 in 2006, 2,081 in 2007.

Source: FAO.

LIVESTOCK
('000 head, year ending September)

	2005	2006	2007*
Horses*	500	500	510
Asses, mules or hinnies*	512	n.a.	n.a.
Cattle	16,615	16,700	16,700
Pigs	3,264	3,303	3,305
Sheep	525	536	536
Goats	1,342	1,362	1,360
Chickens*	110,000	110,000	120,000

* FAO estimates.
Source: FAO.

LIVESTOCK PRODUCTS
('000 metric tons)

	2005	2006	2007*
Cattle meat	424.7	489.9	430.0
Pig meat	126.2	137.5	138.0
Chicken meat	739.4	707.2	740.0
Cows' milk	1,347.7	1,388.1	1,390.0
Hen eggs*	173.6	160.5	160.0

* FAO estimates.
Source: FAO.

Forestry

ROUNDWOOD REMOVALS
('000 cubic metres, excl. bark)

	2005	2006	2007
Sawlogs, veneer logs and logs for sleepers	1,027	1,051	1,289
Pulpwood	416	622	847
Fuel wood*	3,843	3,884	3,925
Total	5,286	5,557	6,061

* FAO estimates.
Source: FAO.

SAWNWOOD PRODUCTION
('000 cubic metres, incl. railway sleepers)

	2005	2006	2007
Coniferous (softwood)	371	538	598
Broadleaved (hardwood)	191	300	250
Total	562	838	848

Source: FAO.

Fishing

('000 metric tons, live weight)

	2004	2005	2006
Capture*	487.0	470.0	460.0
Round sardinella*	141.9	141.9	141.9
Yellowfin tuna	62.1	48.6	24.9
Ark clams*	45.9	45.9	45.9
Aquaculture	22.2	22.2*	22.2*
Total catch*	509.2	492.2	482.2

* FAO estimate(s).

Note: Figures exclude crocodiles, recorded by number rather than by weight. The number of spectacled caimans caught was: 63,902 in 2004; 65,915 in 2005; 60,864 in 2006.

Source: FAO.

VENEZUELA
Statistical Survey

Mining

('000 metric tons, unless otherwise indicated)

	2004	2005	2006
Hard coal	8,107	7,195	7,459
Crude petroleum ('000 barrels)	933,305	936,225	916,515
Natural gas (million cu metres)†	57,398	67,000*	56,000*
Iron ore: gross weight	19,196	20,000*	23,000*
Iron ore: metal content	12,669	13,000*	15,200*
Nickel ore (metric tons)‡	20,468	20,000*	20,000*
Bauxite	5,842	5,900*	5,928
Gold (kilograms)‡	9,666	10,000*	12,400*
Phosphate rock	300	392	400*
Salt (evaporated)*	350	350	350
Diamonds (carats): Gem*	40,000	46,000	45,000
Diamonds (carats): Industrial*	60,000	69,000	70,000

* Estimated production.
† Figures refer to the gross volume of output: marketed production (in million cu metres) was: 31,687 in 2004, 34,000 in 2005 (estimate) and 28,500 in 2006 (estimate).
‡ Figures refer to the metal content of ores and concentrates.

Source: US Geological Survey.

Crude petroleum ('000 metric tons): 151,000 in 2005; 144,200 in 2006; 133,900 in 2007 (Source: BP, *Statistical Review of World Energy*).

Natural gas (million cu metres, excl. flared or recycled): 28,100 in 2005; 27,900 in 2006; 28,500 in 2007 (Source: BP, *Statistical Review of World Energy*).

Industry

PETROLEUM PRODUCTS
('000 barrels)

	2004	2005*	2006*
Motor spirit (petrol)	139,929	75,000	85,000
Kerosene	179	120	120
Jet fuel	29,412	32,000	32,000
Distillate fuel oils	109,555	109,000	109,000
Residual fuel oils	101,481	90,000	90,000

* Estimated production.

Source: US Geological Survey.

SELECTED OTHER PRODUCTS
('000 metric tons, unless otherwise indicated)

	2003	2004	2005
Raw sugar*	736†	n.a.	n.a.
Fertilizers*‡	572	751	745
Cement§†	7,700	9,000	10,000
Crude steel§	3,930	4,575	4,907
Aluminium§	601	624	615
Electric energy (million kWh)‖	85,708	96,431	104,092

* FAO figures.
† Estimate(s).
‡ Including phosphatic, nitrogenous and potassic fertilizers, year beginning 1 July.
§ Data from US Geological Survey.
‖ Source: Ministerio del Poder Popular para la Energía y Petróleo, Caracas.

2006 ('000 metric tons, estimates): Cement 11,000; Crude steel 4,900; Aluminium 610.

Finance

CURRENCY AND EXCHANGE RATES

Monetary Units
100 céntimos = 1 bolívar fuerte.

Sterling, Dollar and Euro Equivalents (30 September 2008)
£1 sterling = 3.864 bolívares fuertes;
US $1 = 2.147 bolívares fuertes;
€1 = 3.071 bolívares fuertes;
10 bolívares fuertes = £2.59 = $4.66 = €3.26.

Average Exchange Rate (bolívares fuertes per US dollar)
2005   2.090
2006   2.147
2007   2.147

Note: Venezuela adopted a new currency, the bolívar fuerte, equivalent to 1,000 of the former currency, on 1 January 2008; this was to become the sole legal tender from the end of June of the same year. Most of the relevant historical data in this survey continue to be presented in terms of Venezuelan bolívares.

BUDGET
('000 million bolívares, preliminary figures)

Revenue	2005	2006	2007
Current revenue	114,385.3	147,865.9	161,881.8
Tax revenue	36,756.2	49,056.5	62,670.2
Taxes on income	7,086.1	12,155.5	17,208.8
Social security contributions	1,889.9	2,743.4	4,217.6
Other	27,780.2	34,157.5	41,243.8
Non-tax revenue	77,599.7	98,801.6	99,211.6
State petroleum company surplus	53,181.0	64,725.6	74,902.5
Transfers	29.3	7.8	—
Capital revenue	27.5	0.5	—
Total revenue	**114,412.8**	**147,866.5**	**161,881.8**

Expenditure*	2005	2006	2007
Current expenditure	64,842.6	94,617.7	109,721.8
Operating expenditure	16,779.6	27,759.0	31,000.2
Wages and salaries	11,594.3	16,270.5	20,852.9
Interest and commission on public debt	9,046.1	8,223.0	8,036.7
Transfers	38,463.3	57,420.5	69,852.0
Other current expenditure	553.7	1,215.2	832.9
Capital expenditure	34,867.9	55,935.9	63,153.9
Acquisition of fixed capital	11,967.9	17,666.9	24,550.9
Capital transfers	22,900.0	38,269.0	38,603.0
Extrabudgetary expenditure	1,415.7	1,894.4	518.6
Total expenditure	**101,126.1**	**152,448.0**	**173,394.4**

* Excluding net lending (preliminary figures): 835.0 in 2005; 1,275.6 in 2006; 1,455.0 in 2007.

CENTRAL BANK RESERVES
(US $ million at 31 December)

	2006	2007	2008
Gold (national valuation)	7,255	9,281	9,201
IMF special drawing rights	—	1	21
Reserve position in IMF	484	509	496
Foreign exchange	28,933	23,686	32,581
Total	**36,672**	**33,477**	**42,299**

Source: IMF, *International Financial Statistics*.

MONEY SUPPLY
('000 million bolívares at 31 December)

	2003	2004	2005
Currency outside banks	4,778	6,506	8,926
Demand deposits at commercial banks	13,651	20,037	32,394
Total (incl. others)	**19,056**	**27,927**	**42,922**

Source: IMF, *International Financial Statistics*.

VENEZUELA

COST OF LIVING
(Consumer Price Index for Caracas; Base: 2000 = 100)

	2005	2006	2007
Food	332.5	399.3	506.3
Clothing and footwear	187.2	203.3	232.5
Rent	180.3	192.5	205.1
All items (incl. others)	255.0	289.8	343.9

Source: ILO.

NATIONAL ACCOUNTS
('000 million bolívares at constant 1997 prices, preliminary)

Expenditure on the Gross Domestic Product

	2006	2007	2008
Final consumption expenditure	41,505.9	48,194.4	51,492.6
Households }			
Non-profit institutions serving households }	33,627.2	39,912.2	42,738.9
General government	7,878.7	8,282.2	8,753.7
Gross capital formation	18,352.8	23,226.1	23,891.1
Gross fixed capital formation }			
Acquisitions, less disposals, of valuables }	15,000.3	18,805.8	18,363.6
Changes in inventories*	3,352.5	4,420.3	5,527.5
Total domestic expenditure	59,858.7	71,420.5	75,383.7
Exports of goods and services	11,196.6	10,572.6	10,280.7
Less Imports of goods and services	19,717.8	26,343.0	27,332.0
GDP in market prices	51,337.6	55,650.1	58,332.5

* Including statistical discrepancy.

Gross Domestic Product by Economic Activity

	2006	2007	2008
Petroleum-related activities	7,103.4	6,802.1	7,018.0
Non-petroleum activities	41,326.6	45,402.9	47,371.4
Mining and quarrying	347.1	354.1	334.2
Manufacturing	8,574.3	9,192.6	9,318.1
Electricity and water	1,201.9	1,230.4	1,286.1
Construction	3,367.8	3,815.3	3,975.2
Wholesale and retail trade; repair of motor vehicles, motorcycles and personal and household goods	5,231.7	6,115.1	6,401.8
Transport and storage	1,796.8	2,040.1	2,121.1
Communications	1,977.5	2,373.4	2,801.1
Financial intermediation and insurance	2,254.9	2,637.8	2,594.2
Real estate, renting and business activities	5,037.7	5,369.6	5,503.2
Community, social and personal services	2,628.3	2,914.7	3,181.7
Government services	5,851.3	6,145.9	6,461.8
Others*	3,057.3	3,213.9	3,392.9
Sub-total	48,430.0	52,205.0	54,389.4
Less Financial intermediation services indirectly measured	2,563.1	2,952.4	2,745.1
Gross value added in basic prices	45,866.9	49,252.6	51,644.3
Taxes on products }			
Less Subsidies on products }	5,470.7	6,397.6	6,688.3
GDP in market prices	51,337.6	55,650.1	58,332.5

* Including agriculture and hotels and restaurants.

BALANCE OF PAYMENTS
(US $ million)

	2006	2007	2008
Exports of goods f.o.b.	65,210	69,165	93,542
Imports of goods f.o.b.	−32,498	−45,463	−48,095
Trade balance	32,712	23,702	45,447
Exports of services	1,572	1,673	1,867
Imports of services	−6,005	−7,524	−8,264
Balance on goods and services	28,279	17,851	39,050
Other income received	7,934	10,114	7,892
Other income paid	−9,026	−7,549	−7,185
Balance on goods, services and income	27,187	20,416	39,757
Current transfers received	296	285	338
Current transfers paid	−334	−700	−893
Current balance	27,149	20,001	39,202
Direct investment abroad	−2,076	−2,237	−2,757
Direct investment from abroad	−590	646	1,716
Portfolio investment assets	−5,382	−37	2,006
Portfolio investment liabilities	−3,982	4,129	429
Other investment assets	−7,020	−30,029	−28,823
Other investment liabilities	−194	4,609	1,430
Net errors and omissions	−2,828	−2,439	−3,751
Overall balance	5,077	−5,357	9,452

Source: IMF, *International Financial Statistics*.

External Trade

PRINCIPAL COMMODITIES
(US $ million)

Imports f.o.b.	2005	2006	2007
Food and live animals	1,757.8	1,813.1	2,441.8
Cereals and cereal preparations	463.8	467.8	590.5
Mineral fuels	176.6	152.2	166.5
Petroleum and products	158.2	140.4	155.6
Animal and vegetable oils, fats and waxes	220.6	274.6	326.8
Chemicals and related products	2,941.5	3,348.4	3,572.6
Organic chemicals	452.8	752.6	556.9
Medicinal and pharmaceutical products	833.6	931.8	1,184.2
Medicaments (incl. veterinary)	646.2	730.6	890.0
Basic manufactures	3,182.1	3,164.5	3,972.8
Iron and steel	787.0	682.7	787.2
Machinery and transport equipment	10,654.0	12,668.2	16,206.8
Power generating equipment and machinery	681.4	602.1	587.3
Machinery specialized for particular industries	1,009.4	1,089.3	1,437.0
General industrial machinery equipment and parts	1,671.7	1,681.8	2,108.2
Heating and cooling equipment and parts	383.6	369.2	528.7
Telecommunications and sound recording and reproducing equipment	1,756.6	2,399.4	2,999.6
Telecommunications equipment parts and accessories	1,285.8	1,761.1	1,850.1
Other electrical machinery, apparatus, etc.	1,071.4	1,261.0	1,608.4
Road vehicles	3,056.5	3,696.1	5,258.6
Passenger motor vehicles (except buses)	1,702.1	1,976.0	2,874.7
Other transport equipment	534.2	841.5	797.3
Ships, boats and floating structures	385.8	711.3	376.3
Miscellaneous manufactured articles	2,404.6	2,379.9	3,542.8
Total (incl. others)	21,848.1	30,559.0	41,911.0

VENEZUELA

Exports f.o.b.	2004	2005	2006
Mineral fuels, lubricants and related materials	32,829.4	47,763.5	56,818.4
Petroleum, petroleum products and related materials	32,670.7	47,410.5	56,617.7
Crude petroleum	32,636.9	47,094.8	56,228.5
Chemicals and related products	939.2	1,256.6	691.3
Basic manufactures	3,457.0	3,908.0	2,983.6
Iron and steel	1,978.2	2,339.9	1,691.7
Aluminium	917.9	1,004.1	1,056.8
Total (incl. others)	38,748.0	54,510.1	61,385.2

Source: UN, *International Trade Statistics Yearbook*.

PRINCIPAL TRADING PARTNERS
(US $ million)

Imports f.o.b.	2005	2006	2007
Argentina	518.4	505.1	966.7
Bolivia	12.7	251.6	22.5
Brazil	1,988.7	2,456.6	3,003.4
Canada	363.0	430.1	373.2
Chile	338.9	405.3	619.8
China, People's Republic	808.4	1,652.6	2,076.3
Colombia	2,409.2	2,420.7	3,729.5
France (incl. Monaco)	274.4	360.0	376.3
Germany	610.6	702.2	701.2
Italy	496.1	587.3	707.5
Japan	712.1	843.9	874.6
Korea, Republic	372.0	512.3	608.5
Mexico	1,514.8	1,638.3	1,569.7
Netherlands	254.7	163.1	264.6
Panama	847.6	548.0	1,617.9
Spain	504.3	465.8	686.1
Switzerland-Liechtenstein	169.4	190.7	300.3
United Kingdom	256.0	266.9	281.8
USA	6,897.5	7,393.3	8,462.2
Total (incl. others)	21,848.1	30,559.0	41,911.0

Exports f.o.b.	2004	2005	2006
Brazil	131.1	1,044.5	1,410.5
Canada	1,160.3	834.0	631.9
Colombia	984.9	1,030.2	585.6
Cuba	85.1	95.5	70.0
Ecuador	281.3	304.7	191.0
Mexico	407.0	478.2	595.0
Netherlands	256.7	613.7	1,211.9
Netherlands Antilles	120.6	2,765.1	3,516.8
Peru	106.5	163.6	103.6
Spain	335.6	491.4	1,914.2
Trinidad and Tobago	49.4	141.5	67.0
United Kingdom	600.8	791.8	776.7
USA	23,555.1	28,463.7	31,268.7
Total (incl. others)	38,748.0	54,510.1	61,385.2

Source: UN, *International Trade Statistics Yearbook*.

Transport

RAILWAYS
(traffic)

	1994	1995	1996
Passenger-kilometres (million)	31.4	12.5	0.1
Net ton-kilometres (million)	46.8	53.3	45.7

Net ton-kilometres (million): 54 in 1997; 79 in 1998; 54 in 1999; 59 in 2000; 81 in 2001; 32 in 2002; 12 in 2003; 22 in 2004.

Source: UN, *Statistical Yearbook*.

ROAD TRAFFIC
('000 motor vehicles in use)

	2002	2003	2004
Passenger cars	2,092	2,173	2,466
Commercial vehicles	615	630	677

Source: UN, *Statistical Yearbook*.

SHIPPING
Merchant Fleet
(registered at 31 December)

	2005	2006	2007
Number of vessels	305	321	327
Total displacement ('000 grt)	1,078.9	1,034.0	1,068.8

Source: Lloyd's Register-Fairplay, *World Fleet Statistics*.

CIVIL AVIATION
(traffic on scheduled services)

	2004	2005	2006
Kilometres flown (million)	57.4	59.4	61.2
Passenger-km (million)	2,468.9	2,578.7	2,635.0
Freight ton-km (million)	0.6	2.1	2.1

Source: UN Economic Commission for Latin America and the Caribbean.

Tourism

ARRIVALS BY NATIONALITY

	2004	2005	2006
Argentina	18,708	26,596	26,287
Belgium	12,130	3,171	3,594
Brazil	13,404	18,574	45,438
Canada	31,794	25,527	28,014
Chile	8,402	15,872	15,020
Colombia	32,030	74,497	84,293
France	21,041	25,464	23,487
Germany	65,733	38,797	37,089
Italy	27,867	56,521	53,177
Mexico	10,344	16,514	18,011
Netherlands	56,521	16,892	18,129
Peru	3,847	28,202	27,671
Portugal	4,174	19,351	19,561
Spain	16,429	66,181	65,894
Trinidad and Tobago	6,120	15,534	18,682
United Kingdom	24,399	25,990	24,057
USA	76,202	89,701	88,825
Total (incl. others)	486,401	706,103	747,930

Tourism receipts (US $ million, incl. passenger transport): 554 in 2004; 722 in 2005; 843 in 2006.

Source: World Tourism Organization.

VENEZUELA

Communications Media

	2005	2006	2007
Telephones ('000 main lines in use)	3,605.5	4,216.8	5,082.2
Mobile cellular telephones ('000 subscribers)	12,495.7	18,789.5	23,820.1
Internet users ('000)	3,354.9	4,139.8	5,719.7
Broadband subscribers ('000)	356.3	537.5	858.0

Personal computers ('000 in use, 2004): 2,145.

Facsimile machines ('000 in use, 1997): 70.

Radio receivers ('000 in use, 1997, estimate): 10,750.

Television receivers ('000 in use, 2001): 10,750.

Book production (titles, 1997): 3,851*.

Daily newspapers (1996): 86 (estimated average circulation 4,600,000).

* First editions only.

Sources: UNESCO Institute for Statistics; UN, *Statistical Yearbook*; International Telecommunication Union.

Education

(2003/04)

	Institutions	Teachers	Students*
Pre-school	14,857†	59,178	984,224
Basic education:			
grades 1–6	17,521†	172,322	3,449,579
grades 7–9	4,667†	109,437	1,383,891
Further education:			
general	} 3,362† {	56,458	501,243
professional		8,844	68,372
Adult education	2,402	43,660	506,301
Special needs	1,999	8,723	317,687
Universities	48	51,459	626,837
Other higher	120‡	30,664	447,513‡

* Excluding students in out-of-school education: 720,726 in 2003/04.
† Data may be duplicated for institutions where education is offered at more than one level. The total number of pre-school, basic and further educational establishments in 2003/04 was 24,634.
‡ Estimate.

Sources: Ministry of Education, Caracas; National Council of Universities, Caracas.

Adult literacy rate (UNESCO estimates): 93.0% (males 93.3%; females 92.7%) in 2001 (Source: UNESCO Institute for Statistics).

Directory

The Constitution

The Bolivarian Constitution of Venezuela was promulgated on 30 December 1999.

The Bolivarian Republic of Venezuela is divided into States, a Capital District and Federal Dependencies. The States are autonomous but must comply with the laws and Constitution of the Republic.

LEGISLATURE

Legislative power is exercised by the unicameral National Assembly (Asamblea Nacional). This replaced the bicameral Congreso Nacional (National Congress) following the introduction of the 1999 Constitution.

Deputies are elected by direct universal and secret suffrage, the number representing each State being determined by population size on a proportional basis. A deputy must be of Venezuelan nationality and be over 21 years of age. Indigenous minorities have the right to select three representatives. Ordinary sessions of the Asamblea Nacional begin on the fifth day of January of each year and continue until the fifteenth day of the following August; thereafter, sessions are renewed from the fifteenth day of September to the fifteenth day of December, both dates inclusive. The Asamblea is empowered to initiate legislation. The Asamblea also elects a Comptroller-General to preside over the Audit Office (Contraloría General de la República), which investigates Treasury income and expenditure, and the finances of the autonomous institutes.

GOVERNMENT

Executive power is vested in a President of the Republic, elected by universal suffrage for a term of six years. (In February 2009 a constitutional amendment removed any limit on the number of terms a President may serve.) The President is empowered to discharge the Constitution and the laws, to nominate or remove Ministers, to take supreme command of the Armed Forces, to direct foreign relations of the State, to declare a state of emergency and withdraw the civil guarantees laid down in the Constitution, to convene extraordinary sessions of the Asamblea Nacional and to administer national finance.

JUDICIARY

Judicial power is exercised by the Supreme Tribunal of Justice (Tribunal Supremo de Justicia) and by the other tribunals. The Supreme Tribunal forms the highest court of the Republic and the Magistrates of the Supreme Tribunal are appointed by the Asamblea Nacional following recommendations from the Committee for Judicial Postulations, which consults with civil society groups. Magistrates serve a maximum of 12 years.

The 1999 Constitution created two new elements of power. The Moral Republican Council (Consejo Moral Republicano) is comprised of the Comptroller-General, the Attorney-General and the Peoples' Defender (or ombudsman). Its principal duty is to uphold the Constitution. The National Electoral Council (Consejo Nacional Electoral) administers and supervises elections.

The Government

HEAD OF STATE

President of the Republic: Lt-Col (retd) Hugo Rafael Chávez Frías (took office 2 February 1999; re-elected 30 July 2000 and 3 December 2006).

COUNCIL OF MINISTERS
(May 2009)

Vice-President and Acting Minister of Defence: Ramón Alonso Carrizalez Rengifo.

Minister of the Economy and Finance: Alí Rodríguez Araque.

Minister of the Interior and Justice: Tarek El Aissami.

Minister of Basic Industry and Mining: Rodolfo Sanz.

Minister of Trade: Eduardo Samán.

Minister of Energy and Petroleum: Rafael Darío Ramírez Carreño.

Minister of Foreign Affairs: Nicolás Maduro Moros.

Minister of Labour and Social Security: María Cristina Iglesias.

Minister of Food: Félix Osorio Guzmán.

Minister of Education: Héctor Augusto Navarro Díaz.

Minister of Tourism: Pedro Morejón Carrillo.

Minister of Health and Social Protection: Lt-Col Jesús María Mantilla Oliveros.

Minister of Higher Education: Luis Augusto Acuña Cedeño.

Minister of Public Works and Housing: Diosdado Cabello.

Minister of the Environment: Yuvirí del Carmen Ortega Lovera.

Minister of Agriculture and Lands: Elías Jaua Milano.

Minister of Planning and Development: Jorge A. Giordani.

Minister of Science, Technology and Intermediate Industries: Jesse Chacón Escamillo.

Minister of Communes: Erika Farías.

Minister of Communications and Information: Blanca Eekhout.

VENEZUELA

Minister of Sport: Victoria Mata.
Minister of Culture: Héctor Soto Castellanos.
Minister for Indigenous Peoples: Nicia Marina Maldonado.
Minister of Women's Affairs: María León.
Minister of the Presidency: Luis Reyes Reyes.

MINISTRIES

Ministry of Agriculture and Lands: Avda Urdaneta, entre esq. Platanal a Candilito, a media cuadra de la Plaza la Candelaria, Caracas; tel. (212) 509-0405; e-mail pda2007@mat.gob.ve; internet www.mat.gob.ve.

Ministry of Basic Industry and Mining: Torre Las Mercedes, 9°, Avda La Estancia, Chuao, Caracas; e-mail webmaster@mibam.gob.ve; tel. (212) 950-0311; fax (212) 906-4576; internet www.mibam.gob.ve.

Ministry of Communes: Edif. INCE, Avda Nueva Granada, Caracas; tel. (212) 603-2396; e-mail visitantes@minep.gov.ve; internet www.minec.gob.ve.

Ministry of Communications and Information: Torre MCT, 10°, Avda Universidad, esq. el Chorro, Caracas 1010; tel. (212) 505-3207; e-mail contactenos@mci.gob.ve; internet www.mci.gob.ve.

Ministry of Culture: Edif. Archivo General de la Nación, Avda Panteón, Foro Libertador, Caracas; tel. (212) 509-5600; e-mail mcu@ministeriodelacultura.gob.ve; internet www.ministeriodelacultura.gob.ve.

Ministry of Defence: Edif. 17 de Diciembre, planta baja, Base Aérea Francisco de Miranda, La Carlota, Caracas; tel. (212) 908-1264; fax (212) 237-4974; e-mail prensamd@mindefensa.gov.ve; internet www.mindefensa.gob.ve.

Ministry of the Economy and Finance: Edif. Ministerio de Finanzas, esq. Carmelitas, Avda Urdaneta, Caracas 1010; tel. (212) 802-1000; e-mail web@mf.gov.ve; internet www.mf.gov.ve.

Ministry of Education: Edif. Ministerio de Educación, Mezzanina, esq. de Salas, Parroquia Altagracia, Caracas 1010; tel. (212) 506-8999; e-mail atencionsocial@me.gob.ve; internet www.me.gob.ve.

Ministry of Energy and Petroleum: Edif. Petróleos de Venezuela, Torre Oeste, Avda Libertador con Avda Empalme, La Campiña, Porroquia El Recreo, Caracas; tel. (212) 708-7581; fax (212) 708-7598; internet www.menpet.gob.ve.

Ministry of the Environment: Torre Sur, 25°, Centro Simón Bolívar, Caracas 1010; tel. (212) 408-1111; internet www.minamb.gob.ve.

Ministry of Food: Edif. Las Fundaciones, Avda Andrés Bello, Caracas; tel. (212) 395-7474; e-mail oirp@minal.gob.ve; internet www.minal.gob.ve.

Ministry of Foreign Affairs: Torre MRE, esq. Carmelitas, Avda Urdaneta, Caracas 1010; tel. (212) 806-1411; fax (212) 861-2505; e-mail web.master@mre.gov.ve; internet www.mre.gov.ve.

Ministry of Health and Social Protection: Torre Sur, 9°, Centro Simón Bolívar, El Silencio, Caracas 1010; tel. (212) 408-0000; e-mail mpps@mpps.gob.ve; internet www.mpps.gob.ve.

Ministry of Higher Education: Torre MCT, 6°, Avda Universidad, esq. el Chorro, Caracas 1010; tel. (212) 596-5270; fax (212) 569-5261; e-mail lacuna@mes.gob.ve; internet www.mes.gob.ve.

Ministry for Indigenous Peoples: Edif. Sudeban, Avda Universidad Antiguo 8°, Caracas; tel. (212) 543-1599; fax (212) 543-3100; e-mail atencionlindigena@minpi.gob.ve; internet www.minpi.gob.ve.

Ministry of the Interior and Justice: Edif. Ministerio del Interior y Justicia, esq. de Platanal, Avda Urdaneta, Caracas 1010; tel. (212) 506-1101; fax (212) 506-1559; e-mail webmaster@mij.gov.ve; internet www.mpprij.gob.ve.

Ministry of Labour and Social Security: Torre Sur, 5°, Centro Simón Bolívar, Caracas 1010; tel. (212) 481-1368; fax (212) 483-8914; internet www.mintra.gov.ve.

Ministry of Planning and Development: Torre Oeste, 22°, Avda Lecuna, Parque Central, Caracas 1010; tel. (212) 507-0811; fax (212) 573-3076; e-mail haiman2@gmail.com; internet www.mpd.gov.ve.

Ministry of the Presidency: Palacio de Miraflores, final Avda Urdaneta, esq. de Bolero, Caracas; tel. (212) 806-3111; fax (212) 806-3229; e-mail mdpcomunicaciones@venezuela.gob.ve; internet www.venezuela.gob.ve.

Ministry of Public Works and Housing: Torre Este, 50°, Parque Central, Caracas 1010; tel. (212) 201-5551; e-mail atencionalciudadano@infraestructura.gob.ve; internet www.infraestructura.gob.ve.

Ministry of Science, Technology and Intermediate Industries: Torre MCT, Avda Universidad, esq. El Chorro, Caracas; tel. (212) 210-3410; fax (212) 210-3504; e-mail mct@mct.gob.ve; internet www.mct.gob.ve.

Ministry of Sport: Sede del IND, Velódromo Teo Capriles, Avda Teherán (antigua prolongación La Vega), Caracas; tel. (212) 472-2376; internet www.ind.gob.ve.

Ministry of Tourism: Edif. Mintur, Avda Francisco de Miranda con Avda Principal de la Floresta, Municipio Chacao, Caracas; tel. (212) 208-4511; e-mail auditoria@mintur.gob.ve; internet www.mintur.gob.ve.

Ministry of Trade: Torre Este, 18°, Avda Lecuna, Parque Central, Caracas 1010; tel. (212) 509-0445; fax (212) 574-2432; e-mail ministro@milco.gob.ve; internet www.milco.gob.ve.

Ministry of Women's Affairs: Caracas.

State Agencies

Consejo de Defensa de la Nación (Codena): Edif. 2, 2°, Fuerte Tiuna, Caracas; tel. (212) 690-3222; e-mail secodena@codena.gob.ve; internet www.codena.gob.ve; national defence council.

Contraloría General de la República (CGR): Edif. Contraloría, Avda Andrés Bello, Guaicaipuro, Caracas 1050; tel. (212) 508-3111; e-mail atencionciudadano@cgr.gov.ve; internet www.cgr.gov.ve; national audit office for Treasury income and expenditure, and for the finances of the autonomous institutes; Comptroller-Gen. Clodosbaldo Russián Uzcátegui.

Defensoría del Pueblo: Edif. Defensoría del Pueblo, Plaza Morelos, Los Caobos, Caracas; tel. and fax (212) 578-3862; e-mail prensadefensoria@hotmail.com; internet www.defensoria.gob.ve; acts as an ombudsman and investigates complaints between citizens and the authorities; Ombudsman Gabriela Ramírez Pérez.

Procuraduría General de la República: Paseo Los Ilustres con Avda Lazo Martí, Santa Mónica, Caracas; tel. (212) 597-3300; e-mail webmaster@pgr.gov.ve; internet www.pgr.gob.ve; Procurator-Gen. Gladys María Gutiérrez Alvarado.

President

Presidential Election, 3 December 2006

Candidates	Votes	% of total
Lt-Col (retd) Hugo Rafael Chávez Frías (MVR)	7,309,080	62.84
Manuel Antonio Rosales Guerrero (UNT)	4,292,466	36.91
Others	28,606	0.25
Total*	11,630,152	100.00

* In addition, there were 160,245 blank or spoiled ballots.

Legislature

ASAMBLEA NACIONAL
(National Assembly)

President: Cilia A. Flores.
First Vice-President: Saúl Ortega.
Second Vice-President: José Albornoz.

Election, 4 December 2005*

Party	Seats
Movimiento V República (MVR)†	114
Por la Democracia Social (PODEMOS)	15
Patria para Todos (PPT)	11
Movimiento Electoral del Pueblo (MEP)‡	11
Partido Comunista de Venezuela (PCV)	8
Unidad Popular Venezolana (UPV)‡	8
Total	167

* The election was boycotted by opposition parties.
† Dissolved in December 2006 and replaced by the Partido Socialista Unido de Venezuela (PSUV).
‡ Merged into the PSUV in 2007–08.

Election Commission

Consejo Nacional Electoral (CNE): Edif. 3, Sucursal de BAMPRO, esq. San Francisco, Frente a la Asamblea Nacional, Caracas; tel. (212) 542-2244; fax (212) 542-3317; internet www.cne.gov.ve; f. 2002; Pres. Tibisay Lucena Ramírez.

VENEZUELA

Political Organizations

Acción Democrática (AD): Casa Nacional Acción Democrática, Calle Los Cedros, La Florida, Caracas 1050; internet www.acciondemocratica.org.ve; f. 1936 as Partido Democrático Nacional; adopted present name and obtained legal recognition in 1941; social democratic; Sec-Gen. HENRY RAMOS ALLUP; Pres. JESÚS MÉNDEZ QUIJADA.

Alianza Bravo Pueblo: Caracas; e-mail alianzabravopueblo@gmail.com; internet www.bravopueblo.com.ve; oppositionist; Pres. ANTONIO LEDEZMA.

La Causa Radical (La Causa R): Santa Teresa a Cipreses, Residencias Santa Teresa, 2°, Ofs 21 y 22, Caracas; tel. (212) 545-7002; internet www.lacausar.org.ve; f. 1971; radical democratic; Leader ANDRÉS VELÁSQUEZ.

Convergencia Nacional (CN): Edif. Tajamar, 2°, Of. 215, Parque Central, Avda Lecuna, El Conde, Caracas 1010; tel. (212) 578-1177; fax (212) 578-0363; e-mail jjcaldera@convergencia.org.ve; internet www.convergencia.org.ve; f. 1993; Leader Dr RAFAEL CALDERA RODRÍGUEZ; Gen. Co-ordinator JUAN JOSÉ CALDERA.

Movimiento Demócrata Liberal: Quinta El Encuentro, 1°, Avda de Santa Eduvigis, entre 5a y 6a transversal, Caracas; e-mail mpolesel@cantv.net; internet www.democrataliberales.org; liberal opposition party; Political Dir MARCO POLESEL.

Movimiento Republicano (MR): Reynaldo Hahn 1606, Urb. Santa Mónica, Caracas; tel. (212) 693-2937; e-mail movimientorepublicano@gmail.com; internet movimientorepublicano.blogspot.com; f. 1997; Pres. CARLOS PANDILLA; Sec.-Gen. MANUAL RIVAS.

Movimiento al Socialismo (MAS): Quinta Alemar, Avda Valencia, Las Palmas, Caracas 1050; tel. (212) 793-7800; fax (212) 761-9297; e-mail asamblea07@cantv.net; f. 1971 by PCV dissidents; opposition democratic-socialist party; split in 1997 over issue of support for presidential campaign of Lt-Col (retd) Hugo Rafael Chávez Frías; Pres. FELIPE MUJICA; Sec.-Gen. LEOPOLDO PUCHI.

Partido Comunista de Venezuela (PCV): Edif. Cantaclaro, esq. San Pedro, Apdo 20428, San Juan, Caracas; tel. (212) 484-0061; fax (212) 481-9737; internet www.pcv-venezuela.org; f. 1931; Pres. JERÓNIMO CARRERA; Sec. CAROLUS WIMMER.

Partido Social-Cristiano (Comité de Organización Política Electoral Independiente) (COPEI): El Bosque, Avda Principal El Bosque con Avda Gloria Quinta Cujicito, Chacao, Caracas; tel. (212) 731-4746; fax (212) 731-4953; internet www.partidocopei.org.ve; f. 1946; Christian democratic; Pres. LUIS IGNACIO PLANAS; Sec.-Gen. LUIS CARLOS SOLÓRZANO.

Partido Socialista Unido de Venezuela (PSUV): Calle Lima, cruce con Avda Libertador, Los Caobos, Caracas; tel. (212) 782-3808; fax (212) 782-9720; e-mail salapsuv2007@gmail.com; internet www.psuv.org.ve; f. 2007; successor party to the Movimiento V República (dissolved Dec. 2006); promotes Bolivarian revolution; Pres. Lt-Col (retd) HUGO RAFAEL CHÁVEZ FRÍAS.

Patria Para Todos (PPT): Caracas; tel. (212) 577-3098; fax (212) 577-4545; e-mail partidoppt@gmail.com; internet www.ppt.org.ve; f. 1997; breakaway faction of La Causa Radical; revolutionary humanist party; Nat. Sec.-Gen. JOSÉ ALBORNOZ.

Por la Democracia Social (PODEMOS): Caracas; f. 2001 by dissident mems of MAS (q.v.); abandoned support for the Govt in 2007; Leader ISMAEL GARCÍA.

Primero Justicia: Centro Comercial Chacaíto, Nivel sótano, local 26, Caracas; tel. (212) 952-9733; e-mail pjelhaltillo@cantv.net; internet www.primerojusticia.org.ve; f. 2000; opposition party; Nat. Co-ordinator JULIO BORGES; Nat. Sec. MÁXIMO SÁNCHEZ.

Proyecto Venezuela (PRVZL): e-mail administrador@vpvonline.com; internet www.proyectovenezuela.org.ve; f. 1998; humanist party; ended alliance with Govt in Jan. 2002; Leader JORGE SUCRE.

Un Nuevo Tiempo (UNT): Maracaibo; internet www.unnuevotiempo.org.ve; f. 2005; opposes Pres. Chávez; Pres. OMAR BARBOZA.

OTHER ORGANIZATIONS

Asociación Civil Queremos Elegir: Edif. Industrial, 4°, Avda Sucre, Los Dos Caminos, Municipio Sucre, Caracas; tel. (212) 286-9785; e-mail info@queremoselegir.org; internet www.queremoselegir.org; f. 1991; opposition grouping promoting citizens' rights; mem. of Alianza Cívica de la Sociedad Venezolana; Principal Co-ordinator ELÍAS SANTANA.

Comité de Familiares Víctimas de los Sucesos de Febrero y Marzo de 1989 (COFAVIC): Edif. El Candil, 1°, Of. 1-A, Avda Urdaneta, esq. El Candilito, Apdo 16150, La Candelaria, Caracas 1011-A; tel. (212) 572-9631; fax (212) 572-9908; e-mail cofavic@cofavic.org.ve; internet www.cofavic.org.ve; f. 1989 as asscn of relatives of those who had died in demonstrations of Feb.–March; promotes human rights; Exec. Dir L. ORTEGA.

Movimiento 1011: tel. (414) 304-0432; e-mail contacto@movimiento1011.com; internet www.movimiento1011.com; civil asscn promoting educational reform; mem. of Alianza Cívica de la Sociedad Venezolana.

Rumbo Propio para Zulia: Edif. Boyscouts de Venezuela, planta baja, Avda 3E con Calle 73, Maracaibo; tel. (414) 638-1657; e-mail rumbopropio@hotmail.com; internet rumbopropio.org.ve; f. 2005; right-wing autonomist grouping; Pres. NÉSTOR SUÁREZ.

Súmate: Caracas; e-mail info@sumate.org; internet www.sumate.org; f. 2002; opposition grouping promoting citizens' rights; Leader MARÍA CORINA MACHADO.

Diplomatic Representation

EMBASSIES IN VENEZUELA

Algeria: 8a Transversal con 3a Avda, Quinta Azahar, Urb. Altamira, Caracas 1062; tel. (212) 263-2092; fax (212) 261-4254; e-mail ambalgcar@cantv.net; Ambassador RACHID BLADEHANE.

Argentina: Edif. Fedecámaras, 3°, Avda El Empalme, El Bosque, Apdo 569, Caracas; tel. (212) 731-3311; fax (212) 731-2659; e-mail evene@cancilleria.gov.ar; internet www.venezuela.embajada-argentina.gov.ar; Ambassador ALICIA AMALIA CASTRO.

Austria: Avda Orinoco, entre Mucuchíes y Perijá, Torre D&D, Piso PT, Of. PT-NO, Urb. Las Mercedes, Apdo 61381, Caracas 1060-A; tel. (212) 991-1211; fax (212) 993-2753; e-mail caracas-ob@bmeia.gv.at; internet www.aussenministerium.at/caracas; Ambassador THOMAS SCHULLER-GÖTZBURG.

Barbados: Edif. Los Frailes, 5°, Of. 501, Avda Principal con Calle La Guairita, Chuao, Caracas 1060; tel. (212) 992-0545; fax (212) 991-0333; e-mail caracas@foreign.gov.bb; Ambassador Maj. CHARLES I. W. BRAITHWAITE.

Belarus: Quinta Campanera, 3a Transversal (Calle Aveledo) con Avda 7, Urb. Los Chorros, Municipio Sucre, Caracas; tel. (212) 239-2760; fax (212) 239-0419; e-mail venezuela@belembassy.org; Chargé d'affaires a.i. VLADIMIR GRUSHEVICH.

Belgium: 10a Transversal con 9a Transversal, Apdo del Este 61550, Altamira, Caracas 1060; tel. (212) 263-3334; fax (212) 261-1333; e-mail caracas@diplobel.fed.be; internet www.diplomatie.be/caracas; Ambassador LÉOPOLD CARREWYN.

Bolivia: Avda Luis Roche con 6a Transversal, Altamira, Caracas; tel. (212) 263-3015; fax (212) 261-3386; e-mail embaboliviaven@hotmail.com; Chargé d'affaires a.i. JORGE ALVARADO RIVAS.

Brazil: Avda Mohedano con Calle Los Chaguaramos, Centro Gerencial Mohedano, 6°, La Castellana, Caracas; tel. (212) 261-5505; fax (212) 261-9601; e-mail brasembcaracas@cantv.net; internet www.embajadabrasil.org.ve; Ambassador ANTONIO FERREIRA SIMÕES.

Bulgaria: Quinta Sofía, Calle Las Lomas, Urb. Las Mercedes, Apdo 68389, Caracas; tel. (212) 993-2714; fax (212) 993-4839; e-mail embulven@cantv.net; internet www.mfa.bg/caracas; Ambassador KIRIL GEORGIEV KOTSALIEV.

Canada: Edif. Embajada de Canadá, Avda Francisco de Miranda con Avda Sur, Altamira, Apdo 62302, Caracas 1060-A; tel. (212) 600-3101; fax (212) 261-8741; e-mail crcas@international.gc.ca; internet www.caracas.gc.ca; Ambassador PERRY CALDERWOOD.

Chile: Edif. Torre La Noria, 10°, Calle Paseo Enrique Eraso, Las Mercedes, Caracas; tel. (212) 992-3378; fax (212) 992-0614; e-mail echileve@cantv.net; internet www.embachileve.org; Ambassador ROLANDO DRAGO RODRÍGUEZ.

China, People's Republic: Avda El Paseo, Quinta El Oriente, Prados del Este, Caracas; tel. (212) 977-4949; fax (212) 978-0876; e-mail embcnven@cantv.net; internet ve.chineseembassy.org; Ambassador ZHANG TUO.

Colombia: Torre Credival, 11°, 2A Calle de Campo Alegre con Avda Francisco de Miranda, Apdo 60887, Caracas; tel. (212) 261-6596; fax (212) 261-1358; e-mail ecaracas@minrelext.gov.co; Ambassador MARÍA LUISA CHIAPPE.

Costa Rica: Edif. For You P.H., Avda San Juan Bosco, entre 1a y 2a Transversal, Altamira, Apdo 62239, Caracas; tel. (212) 267-1104; fax (212) 265-4660; e-mail embaricavene@yahoo.com.mx; Ambassador VLADIMIR DE LA CRUZ DE LEMOS.

Cuba: Calle Roraima e Rio de Janeiro y Choroni, Chuao, Caracas 1060; tel. (212) 991-6611; fax (212) 993-5695; e-mail embacubavzla@cantv.net; Ambassador GERMÁN SÁNCHEZ OTERO.

Czech Republic: Calle Los Cedros, Quinta Isabel, Urb. Country Club, Altamira, Caracas 1060; tel. (212) 261-8528; fax (212) 266-3987; e-mail caracas@embassy.mzv.cz; internet www.mfa.cz/caracas; Ambassador STANISLAV SLAVICKÝ.

VENEZUELA

Dominican Republic: Edif. Argentum, Ofs 1 y 2, 2a Transversal, entre 1a Avda y Avda Andrés Bello, Los Palos Grandes, Caracas 1060; tel. (212) 283-3709; fax (212) 283-3965; e-mail embajadominicana@cantv.net; Ambassador JAIME DURÁN HERNÁNDEZ.

Ecuador: Centro Andrés Bello, Torre Oeste, 13°, Avda Andrés Bello, Maripérez, Apdo 62124, Caracas 1060; tel. (212) 265-0801; fax (212) 264-6917; e-mail embajadaecuador@cantv.net; Ambassador Gen. (retd) RENÉ VARGAS PAZOS.

Egypt: Calle Caucagua con Calle Guaicaipuro, Quinta Maribel, Urb. San Román, Apdo 490007, Caracas; tel. (212) 992-6259; fax (212) 993-1555; e-mail egyptianembassy@cantv.net; Ambassador ESSAM SALEH AWAD MOUSTAFA.

El Salvador: Centro Comercial Ciudad Tamanaco (CCCT), Torre C, 4°, Of. 406, Chuao, Caracas; tel. (212) 959-0817; fax (212) 959-3920; e-mail embasalve@cantv.net; Chargé d'affaires a.i. RAFAEL HERNÁNDEZ GUTIÉRREZ.

Finland: Edif. Atrium, 1°, Calle Sorocaima, El Rosal, Caracas; tel. (212) 952-4111; fax (212) 952-7536; e-mail sanomat.car@formin.fi; internet www.finland.org.ve; Ambassador MIKKO PYHÄLÄ.

France: Calle Madrid con Avda Trinidad, Las Mercedes, Apdo 60385, Caracas 1060; tel. (212) 909-6500; fax (212) 909-6630; e-mail infos@francia.org.ve; internet www.francia.org.ve; Ambassador HADELIN DE LA TOUR-DU-PIN.

The Gambia: 4a Avda con 8a Transversal, Quinta La Paz, Urb. Los Palos Grandes, Chacao, Caracas; tel. (212) 285-2554; fax (212) 285-6250; Ambassador BALA GARBA JAHUMPA.

Germany: Torre La Castellana, 10°, Avda Eugenio Mendoza, cruce con Avda José Angel Lamas, La Castellana, Caracas 1010-A; tel. (212) 219-2500; fax (212) 261-0641; e-mail info@caracas.diplo.de; internet www.caracas.diplo.de; Ambassador GEORG-CLEMENS DICK.

Greece: Quinta Maryland, Avda Principal del Avila, Alta Florida, Caracas 1050; tel. (212) 730-3833; fax (212) 731-0429; e-mail gremb.car@mfa.gr; Ambassador EFSTATHIOS DARAS.

Grenada: Avda Norte 2, Quinta 330, Los Naranjos del Cafetal, Caracas; tel. (212) 985-5461; fax (212) 985-6391; e-mail mcphail@spiceisle.com; internet www.grenadaembassycaracas.org; Ambassador RICHARD PAUL MCPHAIL.

Guatemala: Avda de Francisco de Miranda, Torre Dozsa, 1°, Urb. El Rosal, Caracas; tel. (212) 952-5247; fax (212) 954-0051; e-mail embaguat@cantv.net; Ambassador ERICK MOLINA.

Guyana: Quinta 'Roraima', Avda El Paseo, Prados del Este, Apdo 51054, Caracas 1050; tel. (212) 977-1158; fax (212) 976-3765; e-mail embaguy@cantv.net; Ambassador ODEEN ISHMAEL.

Haiti: Quinta Flor 59, Avda Las Rosas, La Florida, Caracas; tel. (212) 730-7220; fax (212) 730-4605; Chargé d'affaires a.i. ANTOINE ELIACIN.

Holy See: Avda La Salle, Los Caobos, Apdo 29, Caracas 1010-A (Apostolic Nunciature); tel. (212) 781-8939; fax (212) 793-2403; e-mail nunapos@cantv.net; Apostolic Nuncio Most Rev. GIACINTO BERLOCO (Titular Archbishop of Fidene).

Honduras: Edif. Banco de Lara, 8°, Of. B2, Avda Principal de la Castellana con 1a Transversal de Altamira, La Castellana, Apdo 68259, Caracas; tel. (212) 264-0606; fax (212) 263-4379; e-mail honduven@cantv.net; Chargé d'affaires a.i. FERNANDO SUÁREZ LOVO.

India: Quinta Tagore, No. 12, Avda San Carlos, La Floresta, Caracas; tel. (212) 285-7887; fax (212) 286-5131; e-mail info@embindia.org; internet www.embindia.org; Ambassador YASHVARDHAN KUMAR SINHA.

Indonesia: Quinta La Trinidad, Avda El Paseo, Prados del Este, Apdo 80807, Caracas 1080; tel. (212) 976-2725; fax (212) 976-0550; e-mail kbri@telcel.net.ve; Ambassador ALFRED T. PALEMBANGAN.

Iran: Quinta Ommat, Calle Kemal Atatürk, Valle Arriba, Apdo 68460, Caracas; tel. (212) 992-3575; fax (212) 992-9989; e-mail embairanve@cantv.net; Ambassador ABDOLLAH ZIFAN.

Iraq: Quinta Babilonia, Avda Nicolás Copérnico con Calle Los Malabares, Valle Arriba, Caracas; tel. (212) 991-1627; fax (212) 992-0268.

Italy: Edif. Atrium, Calle Sorocaima, entre Avdas Tamanaco y Venezuela, El Rosal, Apdo 3995, Caracas; tel. (212) 952-7311; fax (212) 952-4960; e-mail ambcaracas@esteri.it; internet www.ambcaracas.esteri.it; Ambassador LUIGI MACCOTTA.

Jamaica: Edif. Los Frailes, 5°, Calle La Guairita, Urb. Chuao, Caracas 1062; tel. (212) 991-6741; fax (212) 991-5708; e-mail embjaven@cantv.net; Ambassador AUDLEY RODRÍQUEZ.

Japan: Edif. Bancaracas, 10°, Avda San Felipe con 2a Transversal, La Castellana, Caracas; tel. (212) 261-8333; fax (212) 261-6780; e-mail ajapon@genesisbci.net; internet www.ve.emb-japan.go.jp; Ambassador SHUJI SHIMOKOJI.

Korea, Republic: Avda Francisco de Miranda, Centro Lido, Torre B, 9°, Ofs 91-B y 92-B, El Rosal, Caracas; tel. (212) 954-1270; fax (212) 954-0619; e-mail venembajada@cantv.net; internet ven.mofat.go.kr; Ambassador CHOI WON SUN.

Kuwait: Quinta El-Kuwait, Avda Las Magnolias con Calle Los Olivos, Los Chorros, Caracas; tel. (212) 239-4234; fax (212) 238-3878; Ambassador YOUSEF HUSSAIN AL-GABANDI.

Lebanon: Edif. Embajada del Líbano, Prolongación Avda Parima, Colinas de Bello Monte, Calle Motatán, Caracas 1050; tel. (212) 751-5943; fax (212) 753-0726; e-mail emblibano@telcel.net.ve; Ambassador CHARBEL WEHBI.

Malaysia: Centro Profesional Eurobuilding, 6°, Ofs 6D-G, Calle La Guairita, Apdo 65107, Chuao, Caracas 1060; tel. (212) 992-1011; fax (212) 992-1277; e-mail malcaracas@kln.gov.my; internet www.embajadamalasia.com; Ambassador RAMLAN KIMIN.

Mexico: Edif. Forum, Calle Guaicaipuro con Principal de las Mercedes, 5°, El Rosal, Apdo 61371, Caracas; tel. (212) 952-5777; fax (212) 952-3003; e-mail mexico@embamex.com.ve; internet www.embamex.com.ve; Ambassador JESÚS MARIO CHACÓN CARRILLO.

Netherlands: Edif. San Juan Bosco, 9°, San Juan Bosco con 2a Transversal de Altamira, Caracas; tel. (212) 276-9300; fax (212) 276-9311; e-mail car@minbuza.nl; internet www.mfa.nl/car; Ambassador HINKINUS NIJENHUIS.

Nicaragua: Avda El Paseo, Quinta Doña Dilia, Prados del Este, Caracas; tel. (212) 977-3289; fax (212) 977-3973; e-mail spoveda@cancilleria.gob.ni; Ambassador RAMÓN ENRIQUE LEETS CASTILLO.

Nigeria: Calle Chivacoa cruce con Calle Taría, Quinta Leticia, Urb. San Román, Apdo 62062, Chacao, Caracas 1060-A; tel. (212) 993-1520; fax (212) 993-7648; e-mail embnig@cantv.net; Ambassador FELIX OBORO.

Norway: Centro Lido, Torre A-92A, Avda Francisco de Miranda, El Rosal, Apdo 60532, Caracas 1060-A; tel. (212) 953-0269; fax (212) 953-6877; e-mail emb.caracas@mfa.no; internet www.noruega.org.ve; Chargé d'affaires a.i. ELISABETH SLÅTTUM.

Panama: Edif. Los Frailes, 6°, Calle La Guairita, Chuao, Apdo 1989, Caracas; tel. (212) 992-9093; fax (212) 992-8107; e-mail empanve@cantv.net; Ambassador ELIXSANDRO A. BALLESTEROS RODRÍGUEZ.

Paraguay: Quinta Helechales, 4a Avda, entre 7a y 8a Transversal, Urb. Altamira, Chacao, Caracas; tel. and fax (212) 267-5543; e-mail embaparven@cantv.net; Ambassador FEDERICO GONZÁLEZ FRANCO.

Peru: Edif. San Juan, 5°, Avda San Juan Bosco con 2a Transversal, Altamira, Caracas; tel. (212) 264-1483; fax (212) 265-7592; e-mail leprucaracas@cantv.net; Ambassador Dr LUIS SANTA MARÍA CALDERÓN.

Philippines: 5a Transversal de Altamira, Quinta Filipinas, Altamira, Caracas 1060; tel. (212) 266-4725; fax (212) 266-6443; e-mail caracas@embassyph.com; Chargé d'affaires a.i. JOSÉ ARTHUR P. AMPESO.

Poland: Quinta Ambar, Final Avda Nicolás Copérnico, Sector Los Naranjos, Las Mercedes, Apdo 62293, Caracas; tel. (212) 991-1461; fax (212) 992-2164; e-mail ambcarac@cantv.net; internet www.caracas.polemb.net; Ambassador KRZYSZTOF JACEK HINZ.

Portugal: Torre La Castellana, 3°, Avda Eugénio Mendoza, cruce con José Angel Lamas, La Castellana, Caracas 1062; tel. (212) 263-2529; fax (212) 266-4908; e-mail embajadaportugal@cantv.net; Ambassador JOÃO JOSÉ GOMES CAETANO DA SILVA.

Qatar: Avda Principal Lomas El Mirador, Alto Claro, Municipio Baruta, Caracas; tel. (212) 909-7800; fax (212) 993-2917; e-mail qatarven@cantv.net; Ambassador RASHID MUBARAK AL-KUWARI.

Romania: 4a Avda entre 8a y 9a Transversales, Quinta Guardatinajas 94-14, Altamira, Caracas; tel. (212) 261-9480; fax (212) 263-7161; e-mail ambasadaccs@cantv.net; Ambassador MARINEL IOANA.

Russia: Quinta Soyuz, Calle Las Lomas, Las Mercedes, Caracas; tel. (212) 993-4395; fax (212) 993-6526; e-mail rusemb@cantv.net; internet www.venezuela.mid.ru; Ambassador MIKHAIL I. ORLOVETS.

Saudi Arabia: Calle Andrés Pietri, Quinta Makkah, Los Chorros, Caracas 1071; tel. (212) 239-0290; fax (212) 239-6494; e-mail saudiembassycaracas@cantv.net; Ambassador JUDIYA AL-HATHAL.

South Africa: Edif. Atrium PH-A, Sorocaima con Avda Venezuela, El Rosal, Chacoa, Apdo 2613, Caracas 1064; tel. (212) 952-0026; fax (212) 951-3613; e-mail embajador.caracas@foreign.gov.za; Ambassador (vacant).

Spain: Avda Mohedano entre 1a y 2a Transversal, La Castellana, Caracas; tel. (212) 263-2855; fax (212) 261-0892; internet www.maec.es/embajadas/caracas; Ambassador DÁMASO DE LARIO RAMÍREZ.

Suriname: 4a Avda entre 7a y 8a Transversal, Quinta 41, Altamira, Caracas; Apdo 61140, Chacao, Caracas; tel. (212) 261-2724; fax (212) 263-9006; e-mail emsurl@cantv.net; Ambassador SAMUEL PAWIRONADI.

Switzerland: Centro Letonia, Torre Ing-Bank, 15°, La Castellana, Apdo 62555, Chacao, Caracas 1060-A; tel. (212) 267-9585; fax (212) 267-7745; e-mail car.vertretung@eda.admin.ch; internet www.eda.admin.ch/caracas; Ambassador ARMIN RITZ.

VENEZUELA

Syria: Avda Casiquiare, Quinta Damasco, Colinas de Bello Monte, Caracas; tel. (212) 753-5375; fax (212) 751-6146; Ambassador MOHAMMAD SALEH KHAFIF.

Trinidad and Tobago: Quinta Serrana, 4a Avda entre 7 y 8 Transversales, Altamira, Caracas; tel. (212) 261-5796; fax (212) 261-9801; e-mail embassytt@cantv.net; Ambassador RAZIA ALI.

Turkey: Calle Kemal Atatürk, Quinta Turquesa 6, Valle Arriba, Apdo 62078, Caracas 1060-A; tel. (212) 991-0075; fax (212) 992-0442; e-mail turkishemb@cantv.net; Ambassador NIHAT AKYOL.

United Kingdom: Torre La Castellana, 11°, Avda Principal La Castellana, Caracas 1061; tel. (212) 263-8411; fax (212) 267-1275; e-mail britishembassy@internet.ve; internet ukinvenezuela.fgo.gov.uk; Ambassador CATHERINE ROYLE.

USA: Calle Suapure con Calle F, Colinas de Valle Arriba, Caracas; tel. (212) 975-6411; fax (212) 975-6710; e-mail embajada@state.gov; internet caracas.usembassy.gov; Chargé d'affaires a.i. JOHN CAULFIELD.

Uruguay: Torre Seguros Altamira, 4°, Of. D y E, 4a. Avenida de los Palos Grandes, Apdo 60366, Caracas 1060-A; tel. (212) 285-3549; fax (212) 286-6777; e-mail uruvene@cantv.net; Ambassador GERÓNIMO CARDOZO CHARQUERO.

Viet Nam: 6a Avda, entre 8a y 9a Transversal, Quinta El Cigarral, Urb. Altamira, Caracas; tel. (212) 261-0074; fax (212) 264-7324; internet www.vietnamembassy-venezuela.org; Ambassador TRAN THANH HUAN.

Judicial System

The judicature is headed by the Supreme Tribunal of Justice, which replaced the Supreme Court of Justice after the promulgation of the December 1999 Constitution. The judges are divided into penal and civil and mercantile judges; there are military, juvenile, labour, administrative litigation, finance and agrarian tribunals. In each state there is a superior court and several secondary courts which act on civil and criminal cases. A number of reforms to the judicial system were introduced under the Organic Criminal Trial Code of March 1998. The Code replaced the inquisitorial system, based on the Napoleonic code, with an adversarial system in July 1999. In addition, citizen participation as lay judges and trial by jury was introduced, with training financed by the World Bank.

SUPREME TRIBUNAL OF JUSTICE

The Supreme Tribunal comprises 32 judges appointed by the Asamblea Nacional for 12 years. It is divided into six courts, each with three judges: political-administrative, civil, constitutional, electoral, social and criminal. When these act together the court is in full session. It has the power to abrogate any laws, regulations or other acts of the executive or legislative branches conflicting with the Constitution. It hears accusations against members of the Government and high public officials, cases involving diplomatic representatives and certain civil actions arising between the State and individuals.

Tribunal Supremo de Justicia

Final Avda Baralt, esq. Dos Pilitas, Foro Libertador, Caracas 1010; tel. (212) 801-9178; fax (212) 564-8596; e-mail cperez@tsj.gov.ve; internet www.tsj.gov.ve.

President: LUISA ESTELLA MORALES LAMUÑO.

President of the Constitutional Court: LUISA ESTELLA MORALES LAMUÑO.

President of the Political-Administrative Court: EVELYN MARGARITA MARRERO ORTÍZ.

President of the Court of Civil Cassation: YRIS ARMENIA PEÑA ESPINOZA.

President of the Court of Penal Cassation: ELADIO RAMÓN APONTE APONTE.

President of the Court of Social Cassation: OMAR ALFREDO MORA DÍAZ.

President of the Electoral Court: LUIS ALFREDO SUCRE CUBA.

Attorney-General: LUISA ORTEGA DÍAZ.

Religion

Roman Catholicism is the religion of the majority of the population, but there is complete freedom of worship.

CHRISTIANITY

The Roman Catholic Church

For ecclesiastical purposes, Venezuela comprises nine archdioceses, 23 dioceses and four Apostolic Vicariates. There are also apostolic exarchates for the Melkite and Syrian Rites. At 31 December 2006 adherents represented an estimated 87.7% of the total population.

Latin Rite

Bishops' Conference

Conferencia Episcopal de Venezuela, Prolongación Avda Páez, Montalbán, Apdo 4897, Caracas 1010; tel. (212) 471-6284; fax (212) 472-7029; e-mail prensa@cev.org.ve; internet www.cev.org.ve.

f. 1985; statutes approved in 2000; Pres. Most Rev. BALTAZAR ENRIQUE PORRAS CARDOZO (Archbishop of Mérida).

Archbishop of Barquisimeto: Most Rev. ANTONIO JOSÉ LÓPEZ CASTILLO, Arzobispado, Venezuela con Calle 29 y 30 Santa Iglesia Catedral, Nivel Sótano, Barquisimeto 3001; tel. (251) 231-3446; fax (251) 231-3724; e-mail arquidiocesisdebarquisimeto@hotmail.com.

Archbishop of Calabozo: MANUEL FELIPE DÍAZ SÁNCHEZ, Arzobispado, Calle 4, No 11–82, Apdo 954, Calabozo 2312; tel. (246) 871-0483; fax (246) 871-2097; e-mail el.real@telcel.net.ve.

Archbishop of Caracas (Santiago de Venezuela): Most Rev. JORGE LIBERATO UROSA SAVINO, Arzobispado, Plaza Bolívar, Apdo 954, Caracas 1010-A; tel. (212) 542-1611; fax (212) 542-0297; e-mail arzobispado@cantv.net.

Archbishop of Ciudad Bolívar: Most Rev. MEDARDO LUIS LUZARDO ROMERO, Arzobispado, Avda Andrés Eloy Blanco con Calle Naiguatá, Apdo 43, Ciudad Bolívar 8001; tel. (285) 654-4960; fax (285) 654-0821; e-mail arzcb@cantv.net.ve.

Archbishop of Coro: Most Rev. ROBERTO LÜCKERT LEÓN, Arzobispado, Calle Federación esq. Palmasola, Apdo 7342, Coro; tel. (268) 251-7024; fax (268) 251-1636; e-mail dioceco@reaccium.ve.

Archbishop of Cumaná: Most Rev. DIEGO RAFAEL PADRÓN SÁNCHEZ, Arzobispado, Calle Bolívar 34 con Catedral, Apdo 134, Cumaná 6101-A; tel. (293) 431-4131; fax (293) 433-3413; e-mail dipa@cantv.net.

Archbishop of Maracaibo: Most Rev. UBALDO RAMÓN SANTANA SEQUERA, Arzobispado, Calle 95, entre Avdas 2 y 3, Apdo 439, Maracaibo; tel. (261) 722-5351; fax (261) 721-0805; e-mail ubrasan@hotmail.com.

Archbishop of Mérida: Most Rev. BALTAZAR ENRIQUE PORRAS CARDOZO, Arzobispado, Avda 4, Plaza Bolívar, Apdo 26, Mérida 5101-A; tel. (274) 252-5786; fax (274) 252-1238; e-mail arquimer@latinmail.com.

Archbishop of Valencia: Most Rev. REINALDO DEL PRETTE LISSOT, Arzobispado, Avda Urdaneta 100-54, Apdo 32, Valencia 2001-A; tel. (241) 858-5865; fax (241) 857-8061; e-mail arqui_valencia@cantv.net.

Melkite Rite

Apostolic Exarch: Rt Rev. GEORGES KAHHALÉ ZOUHAÏRATY, Iglesia San Jorge, Final 3a Urb. Montalbán II, Apdo 20120, Caracas; tel. (212) 472-5367; fax (212) 443-0131; e-mail georgeskhhale@cantv.net.

Syrian Rite

Apostolic Exarch: IWANNIS LOUIS AWAD, Parroquia Nuestra Señora de la Asunción, 1A Calle San Jacinto, Apdo 11, Maracay; tel. (243) 235-0821; fax (243) 235-7213.

The Anglican Communion

Anglicans in Venezuela are adherents of the Episcopal Church in the USA, in which the country forms a single, extra-provincial diocese attached to Province IX.

Bishop of Venezuela: Rt Rev. ORLANDO DE JESÚS GUERRERO, Avda Caroní 100, Apdo 49-143, Colinas de Bello Monte, Caracas 1042-A; tel. (212) 753-0723; fax (212) 751-3180; e-mail iglanglicanavzla@cantv.net.

Protestant Churches

Convención Nacional Bautista de Venezuela: Avda Santiago de Chile 12–14, Urb. Los Caobos, Caracas 1050; Apdo 61152, Chacao, Caracas 1060-A; tel. (212) 782-2308; fax (212) 781-9043; e-mail cnbv@telcel.net.ve; internet www.cnbv.org.ve; f. 1951; Pres. Rev. IVÁN MARTÍNEZ; Dir-Gen. Rev. ALEXANDER MONTERO.

Iglesia Evangélica Luterana en Venezuela: Apdo 68738, Caracas 1062-A; tel. and fax (212) 264-1868; e-mail iglesia_ielv@cantv.net; internet ielv.tripod.com; Pres. AKOS V. PUKY; 4,000 mems.

VENEZUELA

JUDAISM

Confederación de Asociaciones Israelitas de Venezuela: Avda Washington, al lado del Hotel Avila, San Bernardino, Caracas; tel. (212) 551-0368; fax (212) 551-0377; internet www.caiv.org; f. 1966; federation of five Jewish orgs; Pres. ABRAHAM LEVY BENSHIMOL.

ISLAM

Mezquita Sheikh Ibrahim bin-Abdulaziz bin-Ibrahim: Calle Real de Quebrada Honda, Los Caobos, Caracas; tel. (212) 577-7382; f. 1994; Leader OMAR KADWA.

BAHÁ'Í FAITH

National Spiritual Assembly of the Bahá'ís: Colinas de Bello Monte, Apdo 49133, Caracas; tel. and fax (212) 751-7669; e-mail aenbaven@telcel.net.ve; internet www.bci.org/venezuela; f. 1961; mems resident in 954 localities.

The Press

PRINCIPAL DAILIES

Caracas

Abril: Edif. Bloque DeArmas, final Avda San Martín cruce con Avda La Paz, Caracas; tel. (212) 406-4376; fax (212) 443-1575; e-mail ldelosreyes@dearmas.com; internet www.abril.com.ve; f. 1997; independent; morning; Mon. to Sat.; Pres. ANDRÉS DE ARMAS S.; Vice-Pres. MARTÍN DE ARMAS S.

Así es la Noticia: Maderero a Puente Nuevo, Caracas; tel. (212) 408-3444; fax (212) 408-3911; e-mail ipacheco@el-nacional.com; f. 1996; morning; Editor ERNESTINA HERRERA.

The Daily Journal: Avda Principal de Boleíta Norte, Apdo 76478, Caracas 1070-A; tel. (212) 237-6441; fax (212) 232-6831; e-mail redaccion@dj.com.ve; internet www.dj.com.ve; f. 1945; morning; English; Chief Editor RUSSELL M. DALLEN, Jr.

Diario 2001: Edif. Bloque DeArmas, 2°, final Avda San Martín cruce con Avda La Paz, Caracas; tel. (212) 406-4111; fax 443-4961; e-mail contacto@dearmas.com; internet www.2001.com.ve; f. 1973; Pres. ANDRÉS DE ARMAS S.; Dir ISRAEL MÁRQUEZ.

El Diario de Caracas: Calle Los Laboratorios, Torre B, 1°, Of. 101, Los Ruices, Caracas 1070; tel. (212) 238-0386; e-mail editor@eldiariodecaracas.net; internet www.eldiariodecaracas.net; f. 2003; Editor JULIO AUGUSTO LÓPEZ.

El Globo: Avda Principal de Maripérez, Transversal Colón con Avda Libertador, Apdo 16415, Caracas 1010-A; tel. (2) 576-4111; fax (212) 576-1730; f. 1990; Dir ANÍBAL J. LATUFF.

Meridiano: Edif. Bloque DeArmas, final Avda San Martín cruce con Avda La Paz, Caracas 1010; tel. (212) 406-4040; fax (212) 442-5836; e-mail meridian@dearmas.com; internet www.meridiano.com.ve; f. 1969; morning; sport; Dir ANDRÉS DE ARMAS S.; Vice-Pres. MARTÍN DE ARMAS S.

El Mundo: Torre de la Prensa, 4°, Plaza del Panteón, Apdo 1192, Caracas; tel. (212) 596-1911; fax (212) 596-1478; e-mail dgomez@la-cadena.com; internet www.elmundo.com.ve; f. 1958; evening; independent; Pres. MIGUEL ANGEL CAPRILES LÓPEZ; Dir ENRIQUE RONDÓN.

El Nacional: Edif. El Nacional, Puente Nuevo a Puerto Escondido, El Silencio, Apdo 209, Caracas; tel. (212) 408-3111; fax (212) 408-3169; e-mail contactenos@el-nacional.com; internet www.el-nacional.com; f. 1943; morning; right-wing; independent; Pres. and Editor MIGUEL HENRIQUE OTERO; Asst Editor YELITZA LINARES; circ. 12,000.

El Nuevo País: Pinto a Santa Rosalía 44, Caracas; tel. (212) 541-5211; fax (212) 545-9675; e-mail enpais1@telcel.net.ve; f. 1988; Dir and Editor RAFAEL POLEA.

Puerto: Avda Soublette, Maiquetia, Caracas; tel. (212) 331-2275; fax (212) 331-0886; e-mail diariopuerto@telcel.net.ve; f. 1975; Pres. CARLOS PARMIGIANI.

La Religión: Edif. Juan XXIII, Torre a Madrices, Caracas; tel. (212) 563-0600; fax (212) 563-5583; e-mail religion@cantv.ve; internet www.iglesia.org.ve; f. 1890; morning; independent; Dir ENNIO TORRES.

Reporte (Diario de la Economía): Torre Británica, 12°, Of. B, Avda Luis Roche, Altamira Sur, Caracas; tel. (212) 264-0591; fax (212) 264-6023; e-mail info@reporte.com.ve; internet www.diarioreportedelaeconomia.com; f. 1988; Pres. TANNOUS GERGES; Editor JOSÉ PALMAR.

TalCual: Edif. Menegrande, 5°, Of. 51, Avda Francisco de Miranda, Caracas; tel. (212) 286-7446; fax (212) 232-7446; e-mail tpetkoff@talcualdigital.com; internet www.talcualdigital.com; f. 2000; evening; right-wing; Pres. TEODORO PETKOFF; Editor-in-Chief MAYE PRIMERA.

Ultimas Noticias: Torre de la Prensa, 3°, Plaza del Panteón, Apdo 1192, Caracas; tel. (212) 596-1911; fax (212) 596-1433; e-mail edrangel@cadena-capriles.com; internet www.ultimasnoticias.com.ve; f. 1941; morning; independent; Pres. MIGUEL ANGEL CAPRILES LÓPEZ; Dir ELEAZAR DÍAZ RANGEL.

El Universal: Edif. El Universal, Avda Urdaneta, esq. de Animas, Apdo 1909, Caracas; tel. (212) 505-2314; fax (212) 505-3710; e-mail consejoeditorial@eluniversal.com; internet www.eluniversal.com; f. 1909; morning; Dir ANDRÉS MATA OSORIO; Chief Editor ELIDES ROJAS.

Vea: Edif. San Martín, Sótano Uno, Parque Central, Caracas 1010; tel. (212) 516-1004; fax (212) 578-3031; e-mail webmaster@diariovea.com.ve; internet www.diariovea.com.ve; f. 2003; morning; left-wing; Editor and Dir GUILLERMO GARCÍA PONCE; Asst Editor MANUEL PÉREZ RODRÍGUEZ.

La Voz: C. C. Nueva Guarenas, Mezzanina, Urb. Trapichito, Sector 2, Caracas; tel. (212) 362-9702; fax (212) 362-0851; e-mail diariolavoz@cantv.net; internet www.diariolavoz.net; morning; right-wing; Exec. Dir FREDDY BLANCO; Editor ALEXIS CASTRO BLANDÍN.

Barcelona

El Norte: Avda Intercomunal Andrés Bello, Sector Colinas del Neverí, Barcelona; tel. (281) 682-5694; fax (281) 286-2884; e-mail administrac@elnorte.com.ve; internet www.elnorte.com.ve; f. 1989; morning; Exec. Dir MARIELA DÁVILA; circ. 133,000.

Barquisimeto

El Impulso: Avda Los Comuneros, entre Avda República y Calle 1a, Urb. El Parque, Apdo 602, Barquisimeto; tel. (251) 250-2222; fax (251) 250-2129; e-mail reaccion@elimpulso.com; internet www.elimpulso.com; f. 1904; morning; independent; Dir and Editor JUAN MANUEL CARMONA PERERA.

El Informador: Edif. El Informador, Carrera 21, esq. Calle 23, Barquisimeto; tel. (251) 231-1811; fax (251) 231-0624; e-mail mauriciogomez@elinformador.com.ve; internet www.elinformador.com.ve; f. 1968; morning; Dir-Gen. MAURICIO GÓMEZ.

Ciudad Bolívar

El Bolivarense: Calle Igualdad 26, Apdo 91, Ciudad Bolívar; tel. (414) 893-4443; fax (285) 632-5667; e-mail publicidad@elbolivarense.com; internet www.elbolivarense.com; f. 1957; morning; independent; Dir ALVARO NATERA.

El Expreso: Paseo Gáspari con Calle Democracia, Ciudad Bolívar; tel. and fax (285) 632-0334; e-mail webmaster@diarioelexpreso.com.ve; internet www.diarioelexpreso.com.ve; f. 1969; morning; independent; Dir LUIS ALBERTO GUZMÁN.

Maracaibo

Panorama: Avda 15, No 95–60, Apdo 425, Maracaibo; tel. (261) 725-6888; fax (261) 725-6911; e-mail editor@panodi.com; internet www.panodi.com; f. 1914; morning; independent; Pres. ESTEBAN PINEDA BELLOSO; Editorial Dir LUIS CAÑÓN; circ. 16,000.

Maracay

El Aragueño: Calle 3a Oeste con Avda 1 Oeste, Urb. Ind. San Jacinto, Maracay; tel. (243) 235-9018; fax (243) 235-7866; e-mail el-aragueno@cantv.net; internet www.el-aragueno.com.ve; f. 1972; morning; Editor EVERT GARCÍA.

El Periodiquito: Calle Páez Este 178, Maracay; tel. (243) 321-422; fax (243) 336-987; e-mail farandula@elperiodiquito.com; internet www.elperiodiquito.com; f. 1986; Editorial Co-ordinator PACO FRANK; circ. 45,000.

El Siglo: Edif. 'El Siglo', Avda Bolívar Oeste 244, La Romana, Maracay; tel. (243) 554-9521; fax (243) 554-5154; e-mail direccion@elsiglo.com.ve; internet www.elsiglo.com.ve; f. 1973; morning; independent; Editor TULIO CAPRILES.

Puerto la Cruz

El Tiempo: Edif. Diario El Tiempo, Avda Municipal 153, Puerto La Cruz; tel. (281) 260-0600; fax (281) 260-0660; e-mail buzon@eltiempo.com.ve; internet www.eltiempo.com.ve; f. 1958; independent; Dir JESÚS MÁRQUEZ; Editorial Dir GIOCONDA DE MÁRQUEZ.

San Cristóbal

Diario Católico: Carrera 4a, No 3–41, San Cristóbal; tel. (276) 343-2819; fax (276) 343-4683; e-mail catolico@truevision.net; internet www.diariocatolico.com.ve; f. 1924; morning; Catholic; Man. Dir Mgr NELSON ARELLANO.

VENEZUELA   *Directory*

Diario La Nación: Edif. La Nación, Calle 4 con Carrera 6 bis, La Concordia, Apdo 651, San Cristóbal; tel. (276) 346-4263; fax (276) 346-5051; e-mail lanacion@lanacion.com.ve; internet www.lanacion.com.ve; f. 1968; morning; independent; Editor José Rafael Cortez.

El Tigre

Antorcha: Edif. Antorcha, Avda Francisco de Miranda, El Tigre; tel. (283) 235-2383; fax (283) 235-3923; e-mail yurbina@diarioantorcha.com; internet www.diarioantorcha.com; f. 1954; morning; independent; Pres. and Editor Antonio Briceño Amparán.

Valencia

El Carabobeño: Edif. El Carabobeño, Avda Universidad, Urb. La Granja, Naguanagua, Valencia; tel. (241) 867-2918; fax (241) 867-3450; e-mail website@el-carabobeno.com; internet www.el-carabobeno.com; f. 1933; morning; Dir Eduardo Alemán Pérez.

Notitarde: Avda Boyacá entre Navas Spínola y Flores, Valencia; tel. (241) 850-1666; fax (241) 850-1534; e-mail lauodr@notitarde.com; internet www.notitarde.com; evening; Dir Laurentzi Odriozola Echegaray.

SELECTED PERIODICALS

Ambiente: Edif. Sur, Nivel Plaza Caracas, Local 9, Centro Simón Bolívar, Caracas; tel. (212) 408-1549; fax (212) 408-1546; e-mail fundamb@cantv.net; environmental issues; Gen. Man. Avra Marina Sánchez.

Artesanía y Folklore de Venezuela: C. C. Vista Mar, Local 20, Urbaneja, Lecherías, Estado Anzoátegui; tel. and fax (212) 286-2857; e-mail ismandacorrea@cantv.net; handicrafts and folklore; Dir Ismanda Correa.

Automóvil de Venezuela: Avda Caurimare, Quinta Expo, Colinas de Bello Monte, Caracas 1041; tel. (212) 751-1355; fax (212) 751-1122; e-mail ortizauto@cantv.net; internet www.automovildevenezuela.com; f. 1961; monthly; automotive trade; circ. 6,000; Editor María A. Ortiz.

Barriles: Centro Parque Carabobo, Torre B, 20°, Of. 2003, Avda Universidad, La Candelaria, Caracas; e-mail informaciones@camarapetrolera.org; publ. of the Cámara Petrolera de Venezuela; Editor Haydée Reyes.

Bohemia: Edif. Bloque DeArmas, final Avda San Martín cruce con Avda La Paz, Apdo 575, Caracas; tel. (212) 406-4040; fax (212) 451-0762; e-mail bohemia@dearmas.com; f. 1966; weekly; general interest; Dir Pedro Ramón Romera.

Business Venezuela: Torre Credival, Avda de Campo Alegre, Apdo 5181, Caracas 1010-A; tel. (212) 263-0833; fax (212) 263-2060; e-mail publicaciones@venamcham.org; internet www.bvonline.com.ve; every 2 months; business and economics journal in English; published by the Venezuelan-American Chamber of Commerce and Industry; Gen. Man. Antonio Herrera.

Computer World: Edif. Marystella, Avda Carabobo, El Rosal, Caracas; tel. (212) 952-7427; fax (212) 953-3950; e-mail cernic@cwv.com.ve; Editor Clelia Santambrogio.

Contrapunto: Edif. Unión, 1°, Of. 2, Avda El Parque, Las Acacias Sur, Caracas; tel. (212) 690-0431; Dir Víctor Vera Morales.

Convenciones: Torre Nonza, 4°, Plaza Venezuela, Caracas; tel. (212) 793-1962; e-mail redacta@tutopia.com; Dir Mario Ernesto Arbeláez.

El Corresponsal: Conj. Residencial El Naranjal, Torre D, 8°, No 82-D, Urb. Los Samanes, Caracas; tel. and fax (212) 941-0409; Editor Domingo García Pérez.

Dinero: Edif. Aco, Entrada A, 7°, Avda Principal Las Mercedes, Caracas; tel. (212) 993-5011; fax (212) 991-3132; e-mail lomonaco@gep.com.ve; internet www.dinero.com.ve; business and finance; Dir Salvatore Lomonaco.

Exceso: Edif. Karam, Avda Urdaneta, 5°, Caracas; tel. (212) 564-1702; fax (212) 564-6760; e-mail baf-exceso@cantv.net; internet www.exceso.net; lifestyle; Dir Ben Amí Fihman; Editor Armando Coll.

Gerente Venezuela: Avda Orinoco 3819, entre Muchuchies y Monterrey, Las Mercedes, Caracas 1060; tel. (212) 267-3733; fax (212) 267-6583; business and management; Editor Luis Rodán; circ. 15,000.

El Mirador: Edif. Pascal, Torre A, 1°, Of. 12-A, Avda Rómulo Gallegos, Santa Eduvigis, Caracas; tel. (212) 286-1661; fax (212) 283-5823; e-mail diarioelmirador@cantv.net; Dir Jesús Couto.

Mujer-Mujer: Centro Banaven, Nivel Sótano, No 13-A, Avda La Estancia, Chuao, Caracas; tel. (212) 959-5393; fax (212) 959-7864; e-mail ceciliapicon@hotmail.com.ve; women's interest; Dir and Editor Cecilia Picón de Torres.

Nueva Sociedad: Edif. IASA, 6°, Of. 606, Plaza La Castellana, Apdo 61712, Caracas; tel. (212) 265-9975; fax (212) 267-3397; e-mail nusoven@nuevasoc.org.ve; internet www.nuevasoc.org.ve; f. 1972; Latin American affairs; Editor Dietmar Dirmoser.

Primicia: Edif. El Nacional, 4°, Puente Nuevo a Puerto Escondido, Caracas; tel. (212) 408-3434; fax (212) 408-3485; e-mail primicia@el-nacional.com; current affairs and business; Editor Franchesca Cordido.

Quinto Día: Avda Principal de Los Ruices con Avda Rómulo Gallegos, Residencia Los Almendros, nivel mezzanina, Of. 5, Los Ruices, Caracas; tel. (212) 237-9809; fax (212) 239-2955; e-mail acarrera@quintodia.com; internet www.quintodia.com; weekly; current affairs; Dir Carlos Croes.

La Razón: Edif. Valores, Sótano 'A', Avda Urdaneta, esq. de Urapal, Apdo 16362, La Candelaria, Caracas; tel. (212) 578-3143; fax (212) 578-2397; e-mail larazon@internet.ve; internet www.razon.com; weekly, on Sun.; independent; Dir Pablo López Ulacio.

La Red: Urb. Vista Alegre, Calle 7, Quinta Luisa Amelia, Caracas; tel. (212) 472-0703; fax (212) 471-7749; e-mail ldavila@lared.com.ve; internet www.lared.com.ve; f. 1996; information technology; Editor Luis Manuel Dávila.

Reporte Petrolero: Torre Británica, 12°, Of. B, Altamira Sur, Caracas; tel. (212) 264-6023; fax (212) 266-9991; e-mail reporte2002@hotmail.com; journal of the petroleum industry; Dir Enrique Romai; Editor Miguel López Trocelt.

Sic: Edif. Centro de Valores, esq. de Luneta, Centro Gumilla, Caracas; tel. (212) 564-9803; fax (212) 564-7557; e-mail sic@gumilla.org.ve; internet www.gumilla.org.ve/sic.htm; f. 1938; monthly; liberal Jesuit publ; Dir Jesús María Aguirre.

Variedades: Edif. Bloque DeArmas, final Avda San Martín cruce con Avda La Paz, Caracas 1020; tel. (212) 406-4390; fax (212) 451-0762; e-mail mgonzalez@dearmas.com; women's weekly; Dir Gloria Fuentes de Valladares.

VenEconomía: Edif. Gran Sabana, 1°, Avda Abraham Lincoln 174, Blvr de Sabana Grande, Caracas; tel. (212) 761-8121; fax (212) 762-8160; e-mail editor@veneconomia.com; internet www.veneconomia.com; f. 1982; monthly; Spanish and English; business and economic issues; Editor Toby Bottome.

Venezuela Gráfica: Torre de la Prensa, Plaza del Panteón, Apdo 2976, Caracas 101; tel. (212) 781-4931; f. 1951; weekly; illustrated news magazine, especially entertainment; Dir Diego Fortunato; Editor Miguel Angel Capriles.

Zeta: Pinto a Santa Rosalía 44, Apdo 14067, Santa Rosalía, Caracas; tel. (212) 541-5211; fax (212) 545-9675; e-mail enpaiscolumna@hotmail.com; f. 1974; weekly; politics and current affairs; Dir Jurate Rosales; Editor Rafael Poleo.

Zulia Deportivo: Torre Luali, 5°, Of. 3, Piñango a Muñoz, Avda Baralt, Maracaibo; tel. (261) 787-2809; sports; Dir Manuel Colina Hidalgo.

PRESS ASSOCIATIONS

Asociación de Prensa Extranjera en Venezuela (APEX): Hotel Caracas Hilton, Torre Sur, 3°, Of. 301, Avda México, Caracas; tel. (212) 503-5301; fax (212) 576-9284; e-mail caracashilton@hotmail.com; Pres. Philip Gunson.

Bloque de Prensa Venezolano (BEV): Edif. El Universal, 5°, Of. C, Avda Urdaneta, Caracas; tel. (212) 561-7704; fax (212) 561-9409; e-mail luichi@telcel.net.ve; asscn of newspaper owners; Pres. Miguel Angel Martínez.

Colegio Nacional de Periodistas (CNP): Casa Nacional del Periodista, 2°, Avda Andrés Bello, Caracas; tel. and fax (212) 781-7601; e-mail cnpjdn@cantv.net; journalists' asscn; Pres. Levy Benshimol; Sec.-Gen. Noel Molina.

STATE PRESS AGENCY

Agencia Bolivariana de Noticias: Avda Bolívar, Torre Oeste, 16°, Parque Central, Caracas; tel. (212) 572-6543; fax (212) 571-0563; internet www.abn.info.ve; fmrly Venpress; Pres. Freddy Fernández Torres.

Publishers

Alfadil Ediciones: Calle Las Flores con Calle Paraíso, Sábana Grande, Apdo 50304, Caracas 1020-A; tel. (212) 762-3036; fax (212) 762-0210; f. 1980; general; Pres. Leonardo Milla A.

Armitano Editores, CA: Centro Industrial Boleita Sur, 4a Transversal de Boleita, Apdo 50853, Caracas 1070; tel. (212) 234-2565; fax (212) 234-1647; e-mail armiedit@telcel.net.ve; internet www.alfagrupo.com; art, architecture, ecology, botany, anthropology, history, geography; Pres. Ernesto Armitano.

VENEZUELA

Ediciones La Casa Bello: Mercedes a Luneta, Apdo 134, Caracas 1010; tel. (212) 562-7100; f. 1973; literature, history; Pres. Oscar Sambrano Urdaneta.

Editorial El Ateneo, CA: Complejo Cultural, Plaza Morelos, Los Caobos, Apdo 662, Caracas; tel. (212) 573-4622; f. 1931; school-books and reference; Pres. María Teresa Castillo; Dir Antonio Polo.

Editorial Cincel Kapelusz Venezolana, SA: Avda Cajigal, Quinta K No 29, entre Avdas Panteón y Roraima, San Bernardino, Apdo 14234, Caracas 1011-A; f. 1963; school-books; Pres. Dante Toni; Man. Mayela Morgado.

Colegial Bolivariana, CA: Edif. COBO, 1°, Avda Diego Cisneros (Principal), Los Ruices, Apdo 70324, Caracas 1071-A; tel. (212) 239-1433; internet www.co-bo.com; f. 1961; Dir Antonio Juzgado Arias.

Ediciones Ekaré: Edif. Banco del Libro, final Avda Luis Roche, Altamira Sur, Apdo 68284, Caracas 1062; tel. (212) 264-7615; fax (212) 263-3291; e-mail editorial@ekare.com.ve; internet www.ekare.com; f. 1978; children's; Pres. Carmen Diana Dearden; Exec. Dir María Francisca Mayobre.

Editora Ferga, CA: Torre Bazar Bolívar, 5°, Of. 501, Avda Francisco de Miranda, El Marqués, Apdo 16044, Caracas 1011-A; tel. (212) 239-1564; fax (212) 234-1008; e-mail ddex1@ibm.net; internet www.ddex.com; f. 1971; Venezuelan Exporters' Directory; Dir Nelson Sánchez Martínez.

Fundación Biblioteca Ayacucho: Centro Financiero Latino, 12°, Ofs 1, 2 y 3, Avda Urdaneta, Animas a Plaza España, Apdo 14413, Caracas 1010; tel. (212) 561-6691; fax (212) 564-5643; e-mail biblioayacucho@cantv.net; internet www.bibliotecayacucho.gob.ve/fba; f. 1974; literature; Pres. Stefania Mosca.

Fundación Bigott: Casa 10-11, Calle El Vigia, Plaza Sucre, Centro Histórico de Petare, Caracas 1010-A; tel. (212) 272-2020; fax (212) 272-5942; e-mail contacto@fundacionbigott.com; internet www.fundacionbigott.com; f. 1936; Venezuelan traditions, environment, agriculture; Admin. Co-ordinator Nelson Reyes.

Fundación Editorial Salesiana: Paradero a Salesianos 6, Apdo 369, Caracas; tel. (212) 571-6109; fax (212) 574-9451; e-mail administracion@salesiana.com.ve; internet www.salesiana.com.ve; f. 1960; education; Gen. Man. Jaime García.

Fundarte: Edif. Tajamar P. H., Avda Lecuna, Parque Central, Apdo 17559, Caracas 1015-A; tel. (212) 573-1719; fax (212) 574-2794; internet www.fundarte.gob.ve; f. 1975; literature, history; Pres. Alfredo Gosen; Dir Roberto Lovera de Sola.

Editorial González Porto: Sociedad a Traposos 8, Avda Universidad, Caracas; Pres. Dr Pablo Perales.

Ediciones IESA: Edif. IESA, 3°, Final Avda IESA, San Bernardino, Apdo 1640, Caracas 1010-A; tel. (212) 555-4298; e-mail ediesa@iesa.edu.ve; internet www.iesa.edu.ve/publicaciones/ediciones; f. 1984; economics, business; Pres. Ramón Piñango.

Ediciones María Di Mase: Caracas; f. 1979; children's books; Pres. María di Mase; Gen. Man. Ana Rodríguez.

Monte Avila Editores Latinoamericana, CA: Avda Principal La Castellana, Quinta Cristina, Apdo 70712, Caracas 1070; tel. (212) 265-6020; fax (212) 263-8783; e-mail maelca@telcel.net.ve; internet www.monteavila.gob.ve; f. 1968; general; Pres. Mariela Sánchez Urdaneta.

Nueva Sociedad: Edif. IASA, 6°, Of. 606, Plaza La Castellana, Apdo 61712, Chacao, Caracas 1060-A; tel. (212) 265-0593; fax (212) 267-3397; e-mail nuso@nuevasoc.org.ve; internet www.nuevasoc.org.ve; f. 1972; social sciences; Dir Dietmar Dirmoser.

Ediciones Panamericanas EP, SRL: Edif. Freites, 2°, Avda Libertador cruce con Santiago de Chile, Apdo 14054, Caracas; tel. (212) 782-9891; Man. Jaime Salgado Palacio.

Oscar Todtmann Editores: Avda Libertador, Centro Comercial El Bosque, Local 4, Caracas 1050; tel. (212) 763-0881; fax (212) 762-5244; science, literature, photography; Dir Carsten Todtmann.

Vadell Hermanos Editores, CA: Edif. Golden, Avda Sur 15, esq. Peligro a Pele el Ojo, Caracas; tel. (212) 572-3108; fax (212) 572-5243; e-mail edvadell1@cantv.net.ve; internet www.vadellhermanos.com; f. 1973; science, social science; Gen. Man. Manuel Vadell Graterol.

Ediciones Vega, SRL.: Edif. Odeon, Plaza Las Tres Gracias, Los Chaguaramos, Caracas 1050-A; tel. (212) 662-2092; fax (212) 662-1397; f. 1965; educational; Man. Dir Fernando Vega Alonso.

PUBLISHERS' ASSOCIATION

Cámara Venezolana del Libro: Centro Andrés Bello, Torre Oeste, 11°, Of. 112-0, Avda Andrés Bello, Caracas 1050-A; tel. (212) 793-1347; fax (212) 793-1368; f. 1969; Pres. Hans Schnell; Sec. Isidoro Duarte.

Broadcasting and Communications

TELECOMMUNICATIONS
Regulatory Authority

Comisión Nacional de Telecomunicaciones (CONATEL): Avda Veracruz con Cali, Edif. Conatel, 6°, Las Mercedes, Municipio Baruta, Caracas; tel. (212) 909-0510; fax (212) 993-6122; e-mail conatel@conatel.gov.ve; internet www.conatel.gov.ve; regulatory body for telecommunications; Dir-Gen. Elda Rodríguez Fernández.

Major Service Providers

AT&T Venezuela: Edif. Centro Banaven, Avda La Estancia A, Chuao, Caracas 1060; internet www.att.com.

Compañía Anónima Nacional Teléfonos de Venezuela (CANTV): Edif. NEA, 20, Avda Libertador, Caracas 1010-A; tel. (212) 500-3016; fax (212) 500-3512; e-mail amora@cantv.com.ve; internet www.cantv.net; privatized in 1991; renationalized in 2007; Pres. Socorro Hernández.

Movilnet: Edif. NEA, 20, Avda Libertador, Caracas 1010-A; tel. (202) 705-7901; e-mail info@movilnet.com.ve; internet www.movilnet.com.ve; f. 1992; mobile cellular telephone operator; owned by CANTV; 6.3m. subscribers (June 2006); Pres. Jacqueline Faría.

Digicel, CA: Caracas; internet www.digicel.com.ve; owned by Banco Santander Central Hispano of Spain; fixed-line telecommunications; 110,200 subscribers (June 2006).

Digitel TIM: Caracas; e-mail 0412empres@digitel.com.ve; internet www.digitel.com.ve; f. 2000; mobile cellular telephone operator; owned by Telecom Italia, Italy; 2.4m. subscribers (June 2006).

Intercable: Avda La Pedregosa Sur, cruce con Avda Los Próceres, Tapias; e-mail jguerrero@multimedios.net; internet www.intercable.net/default.asp; cable, internet and telecommunications services; Dir Juan Gerardo Guerrero.

Movistar: Edif. Parque Cristal, Torre Oeste, Avda Francisco Miranda, 14°, Los Palos Grandes, Caracas 1062; tel. (582) 201-8200; internet www.movistar.com.ve; f. 2005; subsidiary of Telefónica Móviles (Spain); 6.5m. subscribers (June 2006); Pres. Luis Malvido.

NetUno: Edif. Insenica II, planta baja, Calle 7, La Urbina, Caracas; tel. (212) 710-0404; e-mail atccaracas@netuno.net; internet www.netuno.net; f. 1995; voice, data and video transmission services; Pres. Gilbert Minionis.

Telecom Venezuela: Puerto Ordaz; tel. (212) 393-1912; e-mail eauverana@cvgtelecom.com.ve; internet www.cvgtelecom.com.ve; f. 2004 as CVG Telecomunicaciones, CA; present name adopted Aug. 2007; state-owned telecommunications co; Pres. Carmen Leonor Márquez; Man. Evelyn Auverana.

Telecomunicaciones Gran Caribe: Caracas; f. 2007; owned by Telecom Venezuela (60%) and Transbit of Cuba (40%); construction and operation of 1,550 km fibre-optic cable connecting La Guaira (Venezuela) and Siboney (Cuba).

BROADCASTING

In 2007 there were 99 television stations, of which seven were state-owned, and 796 radio stations, of which 36 were run by the state.

Regulatory Authorities

Cámara Venezolana de la Industria de Radiodifusión: Avda Antonio José Istúriz entre Mohedano y Country Club, La Castellana, Caracas; tel. (212) 263-2228; fax (212) 261-4783; e-mail camradio@camradio.org.ve; internet www.camradio.org; Pres. Ciro García.

Cámara Venezolana de Televisión por Suscripción: Edif. Venevisión, 4°, Colinas de Los Caobos, Caracas; tel. (212) 708-9223; fax (212) 708-9146; e-mail cavetesu@cavetesu.org.ve; internet www.cavetesu.org.ve; regulatory body for private stations; Man. Evelyn González.

Radio

Radio Nacional de Venezuela (RNV): Final Calle Las Marías, entre Chapellín y Country Club, La Florida, Caracas 1050; tel. (212) 730-6022; fax (212) 731-1457; e-mail rnv@rnv.gov.ve; internet www.rnv.gov.ve; f. 1936; state broadcasting org.; 15 stations; Gen. Man. Helena Salcedo.

There are also 20 cultural and some 500 commercial stations.

Television
Government Stations

Telesur (Televisora del Sur): Edif. Anexo VTV, 4°, Avda Principal Los Ruices, Caracas; tel. (212) 237-6365; e-mail contactenos@telesurtv.net; internet www.telesurtv.net; f. 2005; jtly owned by Govts of Venezuela (51%), Argentina (20%), Cuba (19%) and

VENEZUELA

Uruguay (10%); regional current affairs and general interest; Pres. Lt (retd) ANDRÉS IZARRA; Vice-Pres. ARAM AHARONIAN.

Televisora Venezolana Social—Canal 2 (TVes): Quinta Thaizza, Avda Principal Augusto César Sandino con 10a Transversal, Maripérez, Municipio Libertador, Caracas; tel. (212) 781-8069; e-mail info@tves.com.ve; internet tves.org.ve; f. May 2007 to replace private channel RCTV (q.v.); govt-owned; Pres. LIL RODRÍGUEZ.

Venezolana de Televisión (VTV)—Canal 8: Edif. VTV, Avda Principal Los Ruices, Caracas; tel. (212) 239-4870; fax (212) 239-8102; internet www.vtv.gob.ve; f. 1964; 26 relay stations; Pres. JESÚS ROMERO ANSELMI.

ViVe TV (Visión Venezuela): Edif. Biblioteca Nacional, AP-4, Final Avda Panteón, Foro Libertador, Altagracia, Caracas; tel. (212) 505-1611; e-mail dmercadeo@vive.gov.ve; internet www.vive.gob.ve; f. 2003; govt-run cultural channel; Pres. BLANCA EEKHOUT.

Private Stations

Corporación Venezolana de Televisión (Venevisión)—Canal 4: Edif. Venevisión, final Avda La Salle, Colinas de los Caobos, Apdo 6674, Caracas; tel. (212) 708-9224; fax (212) 708-9535; e-mail mponce@venevision.com.ve; internet www.venevision.net; f. 1961; privately owned; Pres. GUSTAVO CISNEROS.

Globovisión—Canal 33: Quinta Globovisión, Avda Los Pinos, Urb. Alta Florida, Caracas; tel. (212) 730-2290; fax (212) 731-4380; e-mail info@globovision.com; internet www.globovision.com; f. 1994; 24-hour news and current affairs channel; Pres. GUILLERMO ZULOAGA; Dir-Gen. ALBERTO RAVELL.

Meridiano Televisión: Caracas; e-mail opina@dearmas.com; f. 1982; sports programming; Pres. MARTÍN DE ARMAS; Dir-Gen. JUAN ANDRÉS DAZA.

Radio Caracas Televisión (RCTV): Edif. RCTV, Dolores a Puente Soublette, Quinta Crespo, Caracas; tel. (212) 401-2222; fax (212) 401-2647; e-mail marriaga@rctv.net; internet www.rctv.net; f. 1953; frmly broadcast on terrestrial channel as Radio Caracas Televisión—Canal 2; ceased broadcasting in May 2007; subsidiary RCTV International (based in Miami, FL, USA) recommenced broadcasting in Venezuela via cable in July 2007; Pres. MARCEL GRANIER.

Televén—Canal 10 (Televisión de Venezuela): Edif. Televén, 4a Transversal con Avda Rómulo Gallegos, Urb. Horizonte, Apdo 1070, Caracas; tel. (212) 280-0011; fax (212) 280-0204; e-mail aferro@televen.com; internet www.televen.com; f. 1988; privately owned; Pres. OMAR CAMERO ZAMORA.

Televisora Andina de Mérida (TAM)—Canal 6: Edif. Imperador, Entrada Independiente, Avda 6 y 7, Calle 23, Mérida 5101; tel. and fax (274) 251-0660; f. 1982; regional channel; Pres. Most Rev. BALTAZAR ENRIQUE PORRAS CARDOZO.

VALE TV (Valores Educativos Televisión)—Canal 5: Quinta VALE TV, final Avda La Salle, Colinas de los Caobos, Caracas 1050; tel. (212) 793-9215; fax (212) 708-9743; e-mail webmaster@valetv.com; internet www.valetv.com; f. 1998; Pres. JORGE CARDENAL L. UROSA SAVINO; Man. MARÍA ISABEL ROJAS.

Zuliana de Televisión—Canal 30: Edif. 95.5 América, Avda 11 (Veritas), Maracaibo; tel. (261) 641-0355; fax (261) 641-0565; e-mail elregionalredac@iamnet.com; Pres. GILBERTO URDANETA FIDOL.

Zuvisión: Maracaibo; f. 2007; regional channel for the state of Zulia; Pres. RAFAEL URDANETA.

Finance

(cap. = capital; res = reserves; dep. = deposits; m. = million; brs = branches; amounts in bolívares unless otherwise indicated)

BANKING

Regulatory Authority

Superintendencia de Bancos (SUDEBAN): Edif. Centro Empresarial Parque del Este, Avda Francisco de Miranda, Urb. La Carlota, Municipio Sucre del Estado Miranda, Apdo 6761, Caracas; tel. (212) 505-0933; e-mail sudeban@sudeban.gov.ve; internet www.sudeban.gov.ve; regulates banking sector; Supt TRINO A. DÍAZ.

Central Bank

Banco Central de Venezuela: Avda Urdaneta, esq. de Carmelitas, Caracas 1010; tel. (212) 801-5111; fax (212) 861-0048; e-mail info@bcv.org.ve; internet www.bcv.org.ve; f. 1940; bank of issue and clearing house for commercial banks; granted autonomy 1992; controls international reserves, interest rates and exchange rates; cap. 10m., res 8,171,432m., dep. 71,972,619m. (Dec. 2006); Pres. and Chair. NELSON JOSÉ MERENTES DÍAZ; 2 brs.

Commercial Banks

Banco del Caribe, CA: Edif. Banco del Caribe, 1°, Dr Paúl a esq. Salvador de León, Apdo 6704, Carmelitas, Caracas 1010; tel. (212) 505-5103; fax (212) 562-0460; e-mail producto@bancaribe.com.ve; internet www.bancaribe.com.ve; f. 1954; cap. 101,547m., res 90,052m., dep. 3,543,328m. (Dec. 2006); Founding Pres. JUAN CARLOS DAO; Pres. MIGUEL IGNACIO PURROY; 70 brs and agencies.

Banco Caroní: Edif. Multicentro Banco Caroní, Vía Venezuela, Puerto Ordaz, Estado Bolívar; tel. (286) 23-2230; fax (286) 22-0995; e-mail carupsis@telcel.net.ve; internet www.bancocaroni.com.ve; Pres. ARÍSTIDES MAZA TIRADO.

Banco de Comercio Exterior (Bancoex): Central Gerencial Mohedano, 1°, Calle Los Chaguaramos, La Castellana, Caracas 1060; tel. (212) 265-1433; fax (212) 265-6722; e-mail exports@bancoex.com; internet www.bancoex.com; f. 1997 principally to promote non-traditional exports; state-owned; cap. US $200m.; Pres. VÍCTOR ALVAREZ.

Banco Confederado: Edif. Centro Financiero Confederado, Blvr Gómez cruce con Calle Marcano, Porlamar, Estado Nuevo Esparta; tel. (95) 65-4230; fax (95) 63-7033; e-mail dbanel002@bancoconfederado.com; internet www.bancoconfederado.com; Pres. HASSAN SALEH SALEH.

Banco Exterior, CA—Banco Universal: Edif. Banco Exterior, 1°, Avda Urdaneta, esq. Urapal a Río, Candelaria, Apdo 14278, Caracas 1011-A; tel. (212) 501-0211; fax (212) 501-0745; e-mail lperez@bancoexterior.com; internet www.bancoexterior.com; f. 1958; cap. 85,050m., res 70,794m., dep. 4,902,286m. (Dec. 2007); Chair. JOSÉ LORETO ARISMENDI; Pres. RAÚL BALTAR ESTÉVEZ; 70 brs.

Banco Federal, CA: Avda Manaure, cruce con Avda Ruiz Pineda, Coro, Falcón; tel. (268) 51-4011; e-mail masterbf@bancofederal.com; internet www.bancofederal.com; f. 1982; Pres. NELSON MEZERHANE; Exec. Pres. ROGELIO TRUJILLO.

Banco de Fomento Regional Los Andes, CA: Avda 8, La Concordia con Calle 4, San Cristóbal, Táchira; tel. (276) 43-1269; f. 1951; Pres. EDGAR A. HERNÁNDEZ; Exec. Vice-Pres. PEDRO ROA SÁNCHEZ.

Banco de Fomento Regional Coro, CA: Avda Manaure, entre Calles Falcón y Zamora, Coro, Falcón; tel. (268) 51-4421; f. 1950; transferred to private ownership in 1994; Pres. ABRAHAM NAÍN SENIOR URBINA.

Banco Guayana, CA: Edif. Los Bancos, Avda Guayana con Calle Caura, Puerto Ordaz, Bolívar; internet www.bancoguayana.net; f. 1955; state-owned; Pres. OSCAR EUSEBIO JIMÉNEZ AYESA.

Banco Industrial de Venezuela, CA: Torre Financiera BIV, Avda Las Delicias de Sabana Grande, cruce con Avda Francisco Solano López, Caracas 1010; tel. (212) 952-4051; fax (212) 952-6282; e-mail webmaster@biv.com.ve; internet www.biv.com.ve; f. 1937; 98% state-owned; cap. 9,840m., res 278,645m., dep. 8,600,674m. (Dec. 2006); Pres. LUIS QUIARO; 60 brs.

Banco Occidental de Descuento Banco Universal, CA: Calle 77, esq. Avda 17, Maracaibo 4001, Apdo 695, Zulia; tel. (261) 759-3011; fax (261) 594-9811; e-mail atclient@bodinternet.com; internet www.bodinternet.com; f. 1957; transferred to private ownership in 1991; cap. 169,675m., res 228,827m., dep. 6,948,220m. (Dec. 2006); Pres. VÍCTOR VARGAS IRAUSQUIN; Dir-Gen. CÁNDIDO RODRÍGUEZ LOSADA; 17 brs.

Banco Standard Chartered: Edif. Banaven, Torre D, 5°, Avda la Estancia A, Chuao, Caracas 1060; tel. (212) 993-3293; fax (212) 993-3130; internet www.standardchartered.com; f. 1980 as Banco Exterior de los Andes y de España; current name adopted in 1998 following acquisition by Standard Chartered Bank (United Kingdom); representative office only; CEO DAVID LORETTA; 3 brs.

Banco de los Trabajadores de Venezuela (BTV), CA: Edif. BTV, Avda Universidad, esq. Colón a esq. Dr Díaz, Caracas; tel. (212) 541-7322; f. 1968 to channel workers' savings for the financing of artisans and small industrial firms; came under state control in 1982; Pres. JOSÉ SÁNCHEZ PIÑA; Man. SILVERIO ANTONIO NARVÁEZ; 11 agencies.

Banco de Venezuela, SA (Grupo Santander): Torre Banco de Venezuela, 16°, Avda Universidad, esq. Sociedad a Traposos, Apdo 6268, Caracas 1010-A; tel. (212) 501-3333; fax (212) 501-2570; e-mail bancodevenezuela@banvenez.com; internet www.bancodevenezuela.com; f. 1890; frmly Banco de Venezuela CA; 93.38% share purchased by Banco Santander (Spain) in Dec. 1996; adopted current name in 1998; nationalization pending in mid-2009; cap. 40,524m., res 496,464m., dep. 16,837,805m. (Dec. 2006); Exec. Pres. and Dir MICHEL J. GOGUIKIAN; 242 brs.

Banesco Banco Universal, CA: Edif. Banesco, 12°, Avda Guaicaipura con Avda Principal de Las Mercedes, Caracas; tel. (212) 952-4972; fax (212) 952-7124; e-mail atclient@banesco.com; internet www.banesco.com; cap. 554,373.0m., res 321,830.8m., dep. 16,405,178.4m. (Dec. 2006); Chair. JUAN CARLOS ESCOTET RODRÍGUEZ; Exec. Pres. LUIS XAVIER LUJÁN PUIGBÓ.

VENEZUELA

BBVA Banco Provincial, SA: Centro Financiero Provincial, 27°, Avda Vollmer con Avda Este O, San Bernadino, Apdo 1269, Caracas 1011; tel. (212) 504-5098; fax (212) 574-9408; e-mail calidad@provincial.com; internet www.provincial.com; f. 1952; 55.14% owned by Banco Bilbao Vizcaya Argentaria, 26.27% owned by Grupo Polar; cap. 165,301.5m., res 1,176,358.1m., dep. 13,678,404.1m. (Dec. 2006); Pres. HERNÁN ANZOLA GIMÉNEZ; Exec. Pres. JOSÉ CARLOS PLA ROYO.

Corp Banca, CA Banco Universal: Torre Corp Banca, Plaza la Castellana, Chacao, Caracas 1060; tel. (212) 206-3333; fax (212) 206-4950; e-mail calidad@corpbanca.com.ve; internet www.corpbanca.com.ve; f. 1969; fmrly Banco Consolidado, current name adopted in 1997; cap. 40,000m., res 47,740m., dep. 2,754,500m. (Dec. 2006); Chair. JORGE SELUME ZAROR; CEO MARIO CHAMORRO; 116 brs.

Mercantil CA Banco Universal: Edif. Mercantil, 35°, Avda Andrés Bello 1, San Bernardino, Apdo 789, Caracas 1010-A; tel. (212) 503-1111; fax (212) 503-1075; e-mail mercan24@bancomercantil.com; internet www.bancomercantil.com; f. 1925; cap. 134,112m., res 143,623m., dep. 14,697,042m. (Dec. 2006); Chair. and CEO Dr GUSTAVO A. MARTURET; 309 brs.

Unibanca Banco Universal, CA: Torre Grupo Unión, Avda Universidad, esq. El Chorro, Apdo 2044, Caracas; tel. (212) 501-7031; fax (212) 563-0986; internet www.unibanca.com.ve; f. 2001 by merger of Banco Unión (f. 1943) and Caja Familia; Pres. Dr IGNACIO SALVATIERRA; Vice-Pres. JOSÉ Q. SALVATIERRA; 174 brs.

Venezolano de Crédito, SA—Banco Universal: Edif. Banco Venezolano de Crédito, Avda Alameda, San Bernadino, Caracas 1011; tel. (212) 806-6111; fax (212) 541-2757; e-mail jurbano@venezolano.com; internet www.venezolano.com; f. 1925 as Banco Venezolano de Crédito, SACA; name changed as above in 2001; cap. 9,888m., res 100,499m., dep. 3,260,957m. (Dec. 2006); Pres. Dr OSCAR GARCÍA MENDOZA; 95 brs in Venezuela and abroad.

Mortgage and Credit Institutions

Banco Hipotecario Unido, SA: Edif. Banco Hipotecario Unido, Avda Este 2, No 201, Los Caobos, Apdo 1896, Caracas 1010; tel. (212) 575-1111; fax (212) 571-1075; f. 1961; cap. 230m., res 143m., dep. 8,075m. (May 1990); Pres. ARTURO J. BRILLEMBOURG; Gen. Man. ALFONSO ESPINOSA M.

Banco Hipotecario de la Vivienda Popular, SA: Intersección Avda Roosevelt y Avda Los Ilustres, frente a la Plaza Los Símbolos, Caracas; tel. (212) 62-9971; f. 1961; cap. 100m., res 68.2m., dep. 259.3m. (Dec. 1987); Pres. HELY MALARET M.; First Vice-Pres. ALFREDO ESQUIVAR.

Banco Hipotecario del Zulia, CA: Avda 2, El Milagro con Calle 84, Maracaibo, Zulia; tel. (261) 91-6055; f. 1963; cap. 120m., res 133.5m., dep. 671.5m. (Nov. 1986); Pres. ALBERTO LÓPEZ BRACHO.

Development Banks

Banco de Desarrollo Económico y Social de Venezuela (BANDES): Torre Bandes, Avda Universidad, Traposos a Colón, Caracas 1010; tel. (212) 505-8010; fax (212) 505-8030; e-mail apublicos@bandes.gov.ve; internet www.bandes.gov.ve; state-owned; Pres. EDGAR HERNÁNDEZ BEHRENS.

Banco de Desarrollo de la Mujer (BANMUJER): Edif. Sudameris, planta baja, Avda Urdaneta, entre Plaza España y esq. de Animas, Caracas 1010; tel. (212) 564-3015; fax (212) 564-4087; e-mail banmujer@cantv.net; internet www.banmujer.gov.ve; f. 2001; state-owned bank offering loans to women; Pres. NORA CASTAÑEDA.

Banco del Pueblo Soberano, CA: Edif. El Gallo de Oro, Gradillas a San Jacinto Parroquia Catedral, Caracas; tel. (212) 505-2800; fax (212) 505-2995; e-mail abarrera@bancodelpueblo.com.ve; internet www.bancodelpueblo.com.ve; f. 1999; microfinance; Pres. HUMBERTO ORTEGA DÍAZ; Dir JORGE GONZÁLEZ.

Banco del Sur: Caracas; f. 2007 by Govts of Argentina, Bolivia, Brazil, Ecuador, Paraguay, Uruguay and Venezuela; regional devt bank; brs in Buenos Aires (Argentina) and La Paz (Bolivia).

Fondo de Desarrollo Microfinanciero (FONDEMI): Edif. Sudameras, 2°, Avda Urdaneta, esq. Fuerzas Armadas, Caracas 1030; tel. (212) 564-4327; fax (212) 564-0170; e-mail promocion@fondemi.gov.ve; internet www.fondemi.gov.ve; f. 2001; microfinancing devt fund; Pres. ISA MERCEDES SIERRA FLORES.

Banking Association

Asociación Bancaria de Venezuela: Torre Asociación Bancaria de Venezuela, 1°, Avda Venezuela, El Rosal, Caracas; tel. (212) 951-4711; fax (212) 951-3696; e-mail abvinfo@asobanca.com.ve; internet www.asobanca.com.ve; f. 1959; 49 mems; Pres. ARÍSTIDES MAZA TIRADO.

STOCK EXCHANGE

Bolsa de Valores de Caracas, CA: Edif. Atrium, Nivel C-1, Calle Sorocaima entre Avdas Tamanaco y Venezuela, Urb. El Rosal, Apdo 62724-A, Caracas 1060-A; tel. (212) 905-5511; fax (212) 952-2640; e-mail bvc@bolsadecaracas.com; internet www.bolsadecaracas.com; f. 1947; 65 mems; Pres. NELSON ORTIZ CUSNIER.

INSURANCE

Supervisory Board

Superintendencia de Seguros: Edif. Torre del Desarollo P.H., Avda Venezuela, El Rosal, Chacao, Caracas 1060; tel. (212) 905-1611; fax (212) 953-8615; e-mail sudeseg@sudeseg.gov.ve; internet www.sudeseg.gov.ve; Supt LUDMILA SOTO.

Principal Insurance Companies

Adriática, CA de Seguros: Edif. Adriática de Seguros, Avda Andrés Bello, esq. de Salesianos, Caracas; tel. (212) 571-5702; fax (212) 571-0812; e-mail adriatica@adriatica.com.ve; internet www.adriatica.com.ve; f. 1952; Pres. FRANÇOIS THOMAZEAU; Exec. Vice-Pres. GHISLAIN FABRE.

Avila, CA de Seguros: Edif. Centro Seguros La Paz, 7°, Avda Francisco de Miranda, Caracas; tel. (212) 239-7911; fax (212) 238-2470; f. 1936; Pres. RAMÓN RODRÍGUEZ; Vice-Pres. JUAN LUIS CASAÑAS.

Carabobo, CA de Seguros: Edif. Centro Empresarial Sábana Grande, 12°, Ofs 1 y 2, Calle Negrín, entre Avda Francisco Solano y Blvd de Sábana Grande, El Recreo, Caracas; tel. (212) 761-8514; fax (212) 761-5727; f. 1955; Pres. PAUL FRAYND; Gen. Man. ENRIQUE ABREU.

La Occidental, CA de Seguros: Edif. Seguros Occidental, Avda 4 (Bella Vista) esq. con Calle 71, No 10126, Maracaibo, Zulia; tel. (261) 798-4780; fax (261) 797-5422; e-mail relaciones@laoccidental.com; internet www.laoccidental.com; f. 1956; Pres. TOBÍAS CARRERO NÁCAR; Dir CARLOS MONÍZ ROCHA.

La Oriental, CA de Seguros: Avda Venezuela, cruce con Avda Sojo, Urb. El Rosal, Chacao, Caracas 1060; tel. (212) 905-9924; fax (212) 905-9652; internet www.laoriental.com; f. 1975; Pres. GONZALO LAURÍA ALCALÁ.

Seguros Los Andes, CA: Edif. Seguros Los Andes, Avda Las Pilas, Santa Inés, San Cristóbal, Táchira; tel. (276) 340-2611; fax (276) 340-2596; Pres. RAMÓN RODRÍGUEZ.

Seguros Caracas de Liberty Mutual, CAV: Torre Seguros Caracas C-4, Centro Comercial El Parque, Avda Francisco de Miranda, Los Palos Grandes, Caracas; tel. (212) 209-9111; fax (212) 209-9556; f. 1943; Pres. ROBERTO SALAS.

Seguros Catatumbo, CA: Edif. Seguros Catatumbo, Avda 4 (Bella Vista), No 77–55, Apdo 1083, Maracaibo; tel. (261) 700-5555; fax (261) 216-0037; e-mail mercado@seguroscatatumbo.com; internet www.seguroscatatumbo.com; f. 1957; cap. 9,300m. (2003); Pres. ATENÁGORAS VERGEL RIVERA.

Seguros Mapfre La Seguridad, CA: Calle 3A, Frente a La Torre Express, La Urbina Sur, Apdo 473, Caracas 1010; tel. (212) 204-8000; fax (212) 204-8751; f. 1943; owned by Seguros Mapfre (Spain); Pres. ARISTÓBULO BAUSELA.

Seguros Mercantil, CA: Edif. Seguros Mercantil, Avda Libertador con calle Andrés Galarraga, Chacao, Caracas; tel. (212) 276-2000; fax (212) 276-2596; e-mail rcubillan@segurosmercantil.com; internet www.segurosmercantil.com; f. 1988; acquired Seguros Orinoco in 2002; Pres. ALBERTO BENSHIMOL; Gen. Man. RAFAEL CUBILLÁN.

Seguros Nuevo Mundo, SA: Edif. Seguros Nuevo Mundo, Avda Luis Roche con 3a Transversal, Altamira, Apdo 2062, Caracas; tel. (212) 201-1111; fax (212) 263-1435; internet www.nmbc.com.ve; f. 1856; cap. 100m. (2003); Pres. RAFAEL PEÑA ALVAREZ; Exec. Vice-Pres. RAFAEL VALENTINO.

Seguros La Previsora, CNA: Torre La Previsora, Avda Abraham Lincoln, Sábana Grande, Caracas; tel. (212) 709-1555; fax (212) 709-1976; internet www.previsora.com; f. 1914; Pres. ALBERTO QUINTANA; Exec. Vice-Pres. JUAN CARLOS MALDONADO.

Seguros Venezuela, CA: Edif. Seguros Venezuela, 8° y 9°, Avda Francisco de Miranda, Urb. Campo Alegre, Caracas; tel. (212) 901-7111; fax (212) 901-7218; e-mail carmen.guillen@segurosvenezuela.com; internet www.segurosvenezuela.com; part of American International group; Exec. Pres. ENRIQUE BANCHIERI ORTIZ.

Universitas de Seguros, CA: Edif. Impres Médico, 2°, Avda Tamanaco, El Rosal, Caracas; tel. (212) 951-6711; fax (212) 901-7506; e-mail tbarrera@universitasdeseguros.com; internet www.universitasdeseguros.com; cap. 6,500m; Pres. ANA TERESA FERRINI.

Insurance Association

Cámara de Aseguradores de Venezuela: Torre Taeca, 2°, Avda Guaicaipuro, El Rosal, Apdo 3460, Caracas 1010-A; tel. (212) 952-4411; fax (212) 951-3268; e-mail rrpp@camaraseg.org; internet www

VENEZUELA
Directory

.camaraseg.org; f. 1951; 42 mems; Pres. Carlos Luengo; Exec. Pres. Juan B. Blanco-Uribe.

Trade and Industry

GOVERNMENT AGENCIES

Comisión de Administración de Divisas (CADIVI): Antiguo Edif. PDVSA Servicios, 6°, Avda Leonardo Da Vinci, Los Chaguaramos, Caracas; tel. (212) 606-3904; fax (212) 606-3026; e-mail info@cadivi.gov.ve; internet www.cadivi.gov.ve; f. 2003; regulates access to foreign currency; Pres. Manuel Antonio Barroso.

Corporación Venezolana de Guayana (CVG): Edif. General, 2°, Avda La Estancia, Apdo 7000, Chuao, Caracas; tel. (212) 992-9764; fax (212) 993-0554; e-mail presidenciaccs@cvg.com; internet www.cvg.com; f. 1960 to organize devt of Guayana area, particularly its metal ore and hydroelectric resources; Pres. Rodolfo Sanz (Minister of Basic Industry and Mining).

Fondo Intergubermental para la Decentralización (FIDES): Avda Las Acacias, cruce con Avda Casanova, Torre Banhorient, Sábana Grande, Caracas; tel. (212) 708-0000; fax (212) 708-3642; e-mail info@fides.gov.ve; internet www.fides.gov.ve; f. 1993; part of the Ministry of Planning and Development; co-ordinates investment; Pres. José Julián Villalba.

Instituto Nacional de Tierras (INTI): Quinta La Barranca, Calle San Carlos, Urb. Vista Alegre, Caracas; tel. (212) 574-8554; fax (212) 576-2201; internet www.inti.gob.ve; f. 1945 as Instituto Agrario Nacional (IAN); present name adopted in 2001; established under Agrarian Law to assure ownership of the land to those who worked on it; now authorized to expropriate and redistribute idle or unproductive lands; Pres. Juan Carlos Loyo.

Instituto Nacional de la Vivienda: Torre Inavi, Avda Francisco de Miranda entre Guaicaipuro y San Ignacio de Loyola, Chacao, Caracas; tel. (212) 206-9279; e-mail comunica@inavi.gov.ve; internet www.inavi.gov.ve; f. 1975; administers govt housing projects; Pres. Alfredo Bozo Pinto.

Mercal, CA: Edif. Torres Seguros Orinoco, Avda Fuerzas Armadas, esq. Socarras, Caracas; tel. (212) 564-3856; e-mail fosorio@correo.mercal.gob.ve; internet www.mercal.gob.ve; responsible for marketing agricultural products; fmrly Corporación de Mercadeo Agrícola; Pres. Lt-Col Félix Osorio Guzmán.

Superintendencia de Inversiones Extranjeras (SIEX): Edif. La Perla, Bolsa a Mercaderes, 3°, Apdo 213, Caracas 1010; tel. (212) 483-6666; fax (212) 484-4368; e-mail siexdespacho@cantv.net; internet www.siex.gov.ve; f. 1974; supervises foreign investment in Venezuela; Supt Miriam Beatriz Aguilera de Blanco.

DEVELOPMENT ORGANIZATIONS

Fondo de Desarrollo Agropecuario, Pesquero, Forestal y Afines (FONDAFA): Edif. FONDAFA, esq. Salvador de León a Socarras, La Hoyada, Caracas; tel. (212) 542-3570; fax (212) 542-5887; e-mail fondafa@fondafa.gov.ve; internet www.fondafa.gov.ve; f. 1974; devt of agriculture, fishing and forestry; Pres. Alirio Rondón.

Fondo de Desarrollo Microfinanciero (FONDEMI): see Finance—Development Banks.

Instituto de Desarrollo de la Pequeña y Mediana Industria (INAPYMI): Torre Británica, 14°, 15°, 16° y planta baja, Avda José Felix Sosa, Altamira Sur, Caracas; tel. (212) 276-9511; internet www.inapymi.gob.ve; f. 2001; govt agency; promotes the devt of small and medium-sized industries; Pres. Patricia Febles Montes; Exec. Dir Zaida María Carrillo.

CHAMBERS OF COMMERCE AND INDUSTRY

Federación Venezolana de Cámaras y Asociaciones de Comercio y Producción (Fedecámaras): Edif. Fedecámaras, Avda El Empalme, Urb. El Bosque, Apdo 2568, Caracas; tel. (212) 731-1711; fax (212) 730-2097; e-mail presidencia@fedecamaras.org.ve; internet www.fedecamaras.org.ve; f. 1944; 307 mems; Pres. José Manuel González de Tovar; Gen. Man. Gilberto Delgado G.

Cámara de Comercio, Industria y Servicios de Caracas: Edif. Cámara de Comercio de Caracas, 8°, Avda Andrés Eloy Blanco 215, Los Caobos, Caracas; tel. (212) 571-3222; fax (212) 571-0050; e-mail administración@lacamaradecaracas.org.ve; internet www.lacamaradecaracas.org.ve; f. 1893; 650 mems; Pres. Dr Diana Mayoral; Exec. Dir Víctor Maldonado.

Cámara Venezolano-Americana de Industria y Comercio (Venamcham): Torre Credival, 10°, Of. A, 2a Avda Campo Alegre, Apdo 5181, Caracas 1010-A; tel. (212) 263-0833; fax (212) 263-2060; e-mail venam@venamcham.org; internet www.venamcham.org; f. 1950; Pres. Edmund Saade; Gen. Man. Carlos Tejera.

There are chambers of commerce and industry in all major provincial centres.

EMPLOYERS' ORGANIZATIONS
Caracas

Asociación Nacional de Industriales Metalúrgicos y de Minería de Venezuela (AIMM): Centro Empresarial Senderos, 3°, Ofs 302 y 303a, Avda Principal Los Cortijos de Lourdes, 2a Transversal, Caracas 1071; tel. and fax (212) 237-5169; e-mail aimmv@cantv.net; internet www.aimm-ven.org; metallurgy and mining; Pres. Eduardo Garmendia; Exec. Dir María Graciela Ferreira.

Asociación Textil Venezolana: Edif. Textilera Gran Colombia, Calle el Club 8, Los Cortijos de Lourdes, Caracas; tel. (212) 238-1744; fax (212) 239-4089; f. 1957; textiles; Pres. David Fihman; 68 mems.

Asociación Venezolana de Exportadores (AVEX): Centro Comercial Coneresa, Redoma de Prados del Este 435, 2°, Prados del Este, Caracas; tel. (212) 979-5042; fax (212) 979-4542; e-mail directorejecutivo@avex.com.ve; internet www.avex.com.ve; Pres. Francisco Mendoza.

Cámara Petrolera: Torre Domus, 3°, Of. 3-A, Avda Abraham Lincoln con Calle Olimpo, Sábana Grande, Caracas; tel. (212) 794-1222; fax (212) 793-8529; e-mail informacion@camarapetrolera.org; internet www.camarapetrolera.org; f. 1978; asscn of petroleum-sector cos; Pres. Antonio Vincentelli.

Confederación Venezolana de Industriales (CONINDUSTRIA): Edif. CIEMI, Avda Principal de Chuao, Caracas 1061; tel. (212) 991-2116; fax (212) 991-7737; e-mail comunicaciones@conindustria.org; internet www.conindustria.org; asscn of industrialists; Pres. Eduardo Gómez Sigala; Exec. Pres. Ismael Pérez Vigil.

Confederación Nacional de Asociaciones de Productores Agropecuarios (FEDEAGRO): Edif. Casa de Italia, planta baja, Avda La Industria, San Bernardino, Caracas 1010; tel. (212) 571-4035; fax (212) 573-4423; e-mail fedeagro@fedeagro.org; internet www.fedeagro.org; f. 1960; agricultural producers; 133 affiliated asscns; Pres. Gustavo Moreno Lleras.

Federación Nacional de Ganaderos de Venezuela (FEDENAGA): Avda Urdaneta, Centro Financiero Latino, 18°, Ofs 18-2 y 18-4, La Candelaria, Caracas; tel. (212) 563-2153; fax (212) 564-7273; e-mail fedenagat@cantv.net; internet www.fedenaga.org; f. 1962; cattle owners; Pres. Genaro A. Méndez Contreras.

Unión Patronal Venezolana del Comercio: Edif. General Urdaneta, 2°, Marrón a Pelota, Apdo 6578, Caracas; tel. (582) 561-7025; fax (582) 561-4321; trade; Sec. H. Espinoza Banders.

Other Towns

Asociación de Comerciantes e Industriales del Zulia (ACIZ): Edif. Los Cerros, 3°, Calle 77 con Avda 3c, Apdo 91, Maracaibo, Zulia; tel. (261) 91-7174; fax (261) 91-2570; e-mail info@aciz.org; f. 1941; traders and industrialists; Pres. Jorge Avila.

Asociación Nacional de Cultivadores de Algodón (ANCA) (National Cotton Growers' Association): Edif. Portuguesa, Avda Los Pioneros, Sector Aspiga-Acarigua; tel. (255) 621-5111; fax (255) 621-4368; Sec. Concepción Quijada G.

Asociación Nacional de Empresarios y Trabajadores de la Pesca: Cumaná; fishermen's org.

Unión Nacional de Cultivadores de Tabaco: Urb. Industrial La Hamaca, Avda Hustaf Dalen, Maracay; tobacco growers.

STATE HYDROCARBONS COMPANIES

Corporación Petroquímica de Venezuela (CPV): Torre Pequiven, Avda Francisco de Miranda, Chacao, Apdo 2066, Caracas 1010-A; tel. (212) 201-4011; fax (212) 201-3189; e-mail webmaster@pdvsa.com; internet www.pequiven.com; f. 1956 as Instituto Venezolano de Petroquímica; became Pequiven in 1977; name changed as above in 2005 following independence from PDVSA; involved in many joint ventures with foreign and private Venezuelan interests for expanding petrochemical industry; active in regional economic integration; an affiliate of PDVSA from 1978 until 2005; Pres. Saúl Ameliach.

Petróleos de Venezuela, SA (PDVSA): Edif. Petróleos de Venezuela, Torre Este, Avda Libertador, La Campiña, Apdo 169, Caracas 1010-A; tel. (212) 708-4743; fax (212) 708-4661; e-mail saladeprensa@pdvsa.com; internet www.pdvsa.com; f. 1975; holding co for national petroleum industry; responsible for petrochemical sector since 1978 and for devt of coal resources in western Venezuela since 1985; Pres. Rafael Darío Ramírez Carreño (Minister of Energy and Petroleum); Vice-Pres. of Exploration and Production Luis Vierma; Vice-Pres. of Refining Alejandro Granado; the following are subsidiaries of PDVSA:

Bariven, SA: Edif. PDVSA Los Chaguaramos, 6°, Avda Leonardo Da Vinci, Urb. Los Chaguaramos, Apdo 1889, Caracas 1010-A; tel. (212) 606-4060; fax (212) 606-2741; handles the petroleum, petrochemical and hydrocarbons industries' overseas purchases of equipment and materials.

Bitúmenes Orinoco, SA (PDVSA-BITOR): Edif. PDVSA Exploración, Producción y Mejoramiento, 9°, Avda Ernesto Blohm, La Estancia, Chuao, Apdo 3470, Caracas 1010-A; tel. (212) 908-2811; fax (212) 908-3982; e-mail abreuew@pdvsa.com; plans, develops and markets the bitumen resources of the Orinoco belt; produces Venezuela's trademark boiler fuel, Orimulsion.

Corporación Venezolana del Petróleo (CVP): Edif. Pawa, Calle Cali con Avda Veracruz, Las Mercedes, Caracas; internet www.pdvsa.com/index2.html; f. 1960, reformed 2003; responsible for PDVSA's negotiations with other petroleum cos.

Deltaven, SA: Edif. PDVSA Deltaven, Avda Principal de La Floresta, La Floresta, Caracas 1060; tel. (212) 208-1111; internet www.pdvsa.com/index2.html; f. 1997; markets PDVSA products and services within Venezuela.

INTERVEN Venezuela, SA: Edif. Chacofi II, planta baja, entrepiso y 2°, Avda del Libertador 602, Buenos Aires, Argentina; tel. (11) 4813-9652; f. 1986; manages PDVSA's interests in South America.

Intevep, SA: Centro de Investigación y Apoyo Tecnológico, Edif. Sede Central, Urb. Santa Rosa, Sector El Tambor, Los Teques, Apdo 76343, Caracas 1070-A; tel. (212) 330-6011; fax (212) 330-6448; internet www.intevep.pdvsa.com/index2.html; f. 1973 as Fundación para la Investigación de Hidrocarburos y Petroquímica; present name adopted in 1979; research and devt br. of PDVSA; undertakes applied research and devt in new products and processes and provides specialized technical services for the petroleum and petrochemical industries.

Palmaven: Edif. PDVSA La Floresta, Torre Palmaven, 7°, Avda Principal, Urb. La Floresta, Caracas; tel. (212) 204-4511; internet www.pdvsa.com/index2.html; sustainable devt agency of PDVSA; Man. Dir EDDIE RAMÍREZ.

PDV Marina: Edif. Petróleos de Venezuela Refinación, Suministro y Comercio, Torre Oeste, 9°, Avda Libertador, La Campiña, Apdo 2103, Caracas 1010-A; tel. (212) 708-1111; fax (212) 708-2200; internet www.pdvsa.com/index2.html; f. 1990; responsible for the distribution, by ship, of PDVSA products; Pres. FERNANDO CAMEJO ARENAS.

PDVSA Gas: Edif. Sucre, Avda Francisco de Miranda, La Floresta, Caracas; tel. (212) 208-6212; fax (212) 208-6288; e-mail messina@pdvsa.com; internet www.pdvsa.com/index2.html; f. 1998; gas exploration and extraction; Pres. NELSON MARTÍNEZ; Dir-Gen. JUAN JOSÉ GARCÍA.

UTILITIES
Electricity

CADAFE (Compañía de Administración y Fomento Eléctrico): Edif. Cadafe, 14°, Avda Sanz, El Marqués, Caracas; tel. (212) 280-8583; fax (212) 280-8667; e-mail dirgestion@cadafe.com.ve; internet www.cadafe.com.ve; f. 1958; electricity transmission; Pres. MARÍA GABRIELA GONZÁLEZ; six subsidiaries:

CADELA (Compañía Anónima Electricidad de los Andes): San Cristóbal; tel. (276) 341-6128; fax (276) 300-3066; e-mail webmaster@cadela.gov.ve; internet www.cadela.gov.ve; f. 1991; electricity transmission in Táchira, Mérida, Barinas and Trujillo; Pres. JHONNY CASTRO; Dir-Gen. CARLOS ESTEBAN SÁNCHEZ.

DESURCA (Desarrollo Uribante Caparo Compañía Anónima): Centro Comercial El Pinar, nivel sótano, Urb. Las Acacias, San Cristóbal; tel. (276) 347-1404; fax (276) 347-4428; internet www.cadafe.gov.ve/ns/desurca; f. 1990; oversees construction of the Uribante-Caparo hydroelectric complex.

ELECENTRO (Compañía Anónima Electricidad del Centro): Avda Rómulo Gallegos, frente a Domesa, Puerto Ayacucho; tel. (248) 521-1584; internet www.elecentro.gov.ve; f. 1991; electricity transmission in Aragua, Miranda, Guárico, Apure and Amazonas.

ELEOCCIDENTE (Compañía Anónima Electricidad de Occidente): Edif. Centro Profesional MASCOLO, Calle 28, entre Avdas 30 y 31, Acarigua; tel. (255) 600-2026; fax (255) 600-2071; internet eleoccidente.gob.ve; f. 1991; electricity transmission in Falcón, Lara, Yaracuy, Carabobo, Cojedes and Portuguesa; Dir KHALED ORTÍZ VILLEGAS.

ELEORIENTE (Compañía Anónima Electricidad de Oriente): Edif. Eleoriente, Avda Universidad, Cumana; tel. (293) 400-1177; fax (293) 400-1188; internet www.eleoriente.com.ve; f. 1991; electricity transmission in Anzoátegui, Bolívar and Sucre.

Semda (Sistema Eléctrico de Monagas y Delta Amacuro): Edif. Nicamale, Calle Mariño con Piar, Maturín; tel. (291) 641-3654; fax (291) 641-3613; f. 1998; generation and transmission of electricity in Monagas and Delta Amacuro.

La Electricidad de Caracas (EDC): Edif. La Electricidad de Caracas, Avda Vollmer, San Bernadino, Caracas; tel. (212) 502-2111; e-mail info@edc-ven.com; internet www.laedc.com.ve; supplies electricity to Caracas; state-owned; Pres. JAVIER ALVARADO.

Electrificación del Caroní, CA (Edelca): Edif. General, planta baja, Avda La Estancia, Chuao, Caracas; tel. (212) 950-2111; fax (212) 950-2808; e-mail wriera@edelca.com.ve; internet www.edelca.com.ve; affiliate of Corporación Venezolana de Guayana; supplies some 70% of the country's electricity; Pres. HIPÓLITO IZQUIERDO.

Enelco (Energía Eléctrica de la Costa Oriental): tel. (264) 370-5555; e-mail atencionalcliente@enelco.com.ve; internet www.enelco.com.ve; electricity services to the eastern coast of the Lago de Maracaibo region.

Sistema Eléctrico de Nueva Esparta (Seneca): Caracas; tel. (295) 260-1412; fax (295) 260-1419; e-mail seneca@seneca.com.ve; internet www.seneca.com.ve; electricity co; privatized in Oct. 1998.

Gas

ENAGAS (Ente Nacional del Gas): Edif. PDVSA, Torre Sur, 9° y 10°, Avda Libertador, Caracas; tel. (212) 706-6654; fax (212) 706-6471; e-mail webmaster@enagas.gov.ve; internet www.enagas.gov.ve; f. 1999; autonomous agency attached to the Ministry of Energy and Petroleum; regulatory body.

Water

Hidroven: Edif. Hidroven, Avda Augusto César Sandino con 9a Transversal, Maripérez, Caracas; tel. (212) 781-4778; fax (212) 781-6424; e-mail hvenpres@cantv.net; internet www.hidroven.gov.ve; national water co; owns Hidroandes, Hidrocapital, Hidrocaribe, Hidrofalcon, Hidrolago, Hidrollanos, Hidropaez, Hidrosuroeste, Aguas de Monagas, Aguas de Ejido, Hidrolara, Aguas de Anaco, Aguas de Cojedes, Aguas de Mérida, Aguas de Apure, Aguas de Yaracuy, Aguas de Portuguesa; Pres. CRISTÓBAL FRANCISCO ORTIZ; Vice-Pres. FRANCISCO DURÁN.

Compañía Anónima Hidrológica de la Región Capital (Hidrocapital): Edif. Hidroven, Avda Augusto César Sandino con 9a Transversal, Maripérez, Caracas; tel. (212) 793-1638; fax (212) 793-6794; internet www.hidrocapital.com.ve; f. 1992; owned by Hidroven; operates water supply in Federal District and states of Miranda and Vargas; Pres. ALEJANDRO HITCHER.

TRADE UNIONS

About one-quarter of the labour force in Venezuela belongs to a trade union. Most unions in Venezuela are legally recognized. The country's union movement is strongest in the public sector.

Confederación de Trabajadores de Venezuela (CTV) (Confederation of Venezuelan Workers): Edif. José Vargas, 17°, Avda Este 2, Los Caobos, Caracas; tel. (212) 574-1049; e-mail ctv@ctv.org.ve; internet www.ctv.org.ve; f. 1936; largest trade union confederation; principally active in public sector; Chávez Govt disputes legitimacy of election of CTV leadership; Pres. CARLOS ALFONSO ORTEGA CARVAJAL; Sec.-Gen. MANUEL JOSÉ COVA FERMÍN; 26 regional and 57 industrial feds.

Fedepetrol: union of petroleum workers; Pres. RAFAEL ROSALES.

Federación Campesina (FC): peasant union; CTV affiliate; Leader RUBÉN LANZ.

Fetrametal: union of metal workers; Leader JOSÉ MOLLEGAS.

Fuerza Bolivariana de Trabajadores (FBT): f. 2000; pro-Govt union.

Unión Nacional de Trabajadores (UNT): f. 2003; pro-Govt federation; Nat. Co-ordinators STALIN PÉREZ BORGES, ORLANDO CHIRINO.

Other trade union federations include the Alianza Sindical Independiente (ASI), the Central Unitaria de Trabajadores de Venezuela (CUTV), the Confederación de Sindicatos Autónomos de Venezuela (CODESA) and the Confederación General de Trabajadores de Venezuela (CGT).

Transport
RAILWAYS

In 1999 work began on lines linking Acarigua and Turén (45 km) and Morón and Riecito (100 km). Construction of the first section (Caracas–Cúa) of a line linking the capital to the existing network at Puerto Cabello (219 km in total) was also begun. Services on the Caracas underground system began in 1983 on a two-line system: east to west from Palos Verdes to Propatria; north to south from Capitolio/El Silencio to Zoológico. A southern extension from Plaza Venezuela to El Valle opened in 1995. Further extensions to the lines were under way in 2009.

CVG Ferrominera Orinoco, CA: Vía Caracas, Puerto Ordaz, Apdo 399, Bolívar; tel. (286) 930-3775; fax (286) 930-3783; e-mail contacto@ferrominera.com; internet www.ferrominera.com; f. 1976; part of

VENEZUELA

state-owned Corporación Venezolana de Guayana (see Trade and Industry—Government Agencies); operates two lines, San Isidro mine–Puerto Ordaz (316 km) and El Pao–Palua (55 km), for transporting iron ore; Pres. RADWAN SABBAGH (acting).

Ferrocarril de CVG Bauxilum—Operadora de Bauxita: Avda Fuerzas Armadas, Zona Industrial Matanzas, Ciudad Guayana, Bolívar; tel. (286) 950-6271; fax (286) 950-6270; internet www.bauxilum.com; f. 1989; state-owned; operates line linking Los Pijiguaos with river Orinoco port of Gumilla (52 km) for transporting bauxite; Pres. JESÚS CALDO.

Instituto Autónomo de Ferrocarriles del Estado (IAFE): Edif. Torre Británica de Seguros, 7° y 8°, Avda José Félix Sosa, Urb. Altamira, Chacao, Caracas 1062-A; tel. (212) 201-8736; fax (212) 201-6902; e-mail info@iafe.gov.ve; state co; operates 336 km of track; Pres. ANGEL GARCÍA ONTIVEROS.

CA Metro de Caracas: Multicentro Empresarial del Este, Edif. Miranda, Torre B, 7°, Avda Francisco de Miranda, Apdo 61036, Caracas; tel. (212) 206-7111; fax (212) 266-3346; internet www.metrodecaracas.com.ve; f. 1976 to supervise the construction and use of the underground railway system; state-owned; Pres. CLAUDIO ROMÁN FARÍAS ARIAS.

ROADS

In 2004 there were an estimated 96,200 km of roads, of which 32,300 km were paved.

Of the three great highways, the first (960 km) runs from Caracas to Ciudad Bolívar. The second, the Pan-American Highway (1,290 km), runs from Caracas to the Colombian frontier and is continued as far as Cúcuta. A branch runs from Valencia to Puerto Cabello. The third highway runs southwards from Coro to La Ceiba, on Lake Maracaibo.

A new 'marginal highway' was under construction along the western fringe of the Amazon Basin in Venezuela, Colombia, Ecuador, Peru, Bolivia and Paraguay. The Venezuelan section now runs for over 440 km and is fully paved.

INLAND WATERWAYS

Instituto Nacional de Canalizaciones: Edif. INC, Calle Caracas, al lado de la Torre Diamen, Chuao, Caracas; tel. (212) 908-5106; fax (212) 959-6906; e-mail rrpp@incanal.gov.ve; internet www.incanal.gov.ve; f. 1952; semi-autonomous institution connected with the Ministry of Infrastructure; Pres. JUAN CARLOS FERRER SÁNCHEZ; Vice-Pres. SEGUNDO RAMÓN JUSTO PINTO.

Compañía Anónima La Translacustre: Maracaibo; freight and passenger service serving Lake Maracaibo, principally from Maracaibo to the road terminal from Caracas at Palmarejo.

SHIPPING

There are 13 major ports, 34 petroleum and mineral ports and five fishing ports. Formerly the main port for imports, La Guaira, the port for Caracas, was affected by mudslides caused by heavy rains in November 1999. Venezuela's main port is now Puerto Cabello, which handles raw materials for the industrial region around Valencia. Maracaibo is the chief port for the petroleum industry. Puerto Ordaz, on the Orinoco River, was also developed to deal with the shipments of iron from Cerro Bolívar.

Consolidada de Ferrys, CA (CONFERRY): Torre Banhorient, 3°, Avda Las Acacias y Avda Casanova, Apdo 87, Sabana Grande, Caracas 1010-A; tel. (212) 781-9711; fax (212) 781-8739; f. 1970; Dir RAFAEL MATA.

Consorcio Naviero Venezolano (Conavén): Torre Uno, 4°, Avda Orinoco, Las Mercedes, Caracas; tel. (212) 993-2922; fax (212) 993-1636; e-mail conavent@conaven.com.

Corpoven, SA: Edif. Petróleos de Venezuela, Avda Libertador, La Campiña, Apdo 61373, Caracas 1060-A; tel. (212) 708-1111; fax (212) 708-1833; Pres. Dr ROBERTO MANDINI; Vice-Pres. JUAN CARLOS GÓMEZ; 2 oil tankers.

Lagoven, SA: Edif. Lagovén, Avda Leonardo da Vinci, Los Chaguaramos, Apdo 889, Caracas; tel. (212) 606-3311; fax (212) 606-3637; f. 1978 as a result of the nationalization of the petroleum industry; fmrly Creole Petroleum Group; transports crude petroleum and by-products between Maracaibo, Aniba and other ports in the area; Pres. B. R. NATERA; Marine Man. P. D. CAREZIS; 10 tankers.

Tacarigua Marina, CA: Torre Lincoln 7A-B, Avda Lincoln, Apdo 51107, Sábana Grande, Caracas 1050-A; tel. (212) 781-1315; Pres. R. BELLIZZI.

Transpapel, CA: Edif. Centro, 11°, Of. 111, Centro Parque Boyaca, Avda Sucre, Los Dos Caminos, Apdo 61316, Caracas 1071; tel. (212) 283-8366; fax (212) 285-7749; e-mail nmaldonado@cantv.net; f. 1985; Chair. GUILLERMO ESPINOSA F.; Man. Dir Capt. NELSON MALDONADO.

Transporte Industrial, SA: Edif. Anzoátegui, Planta Vencemos, Pertigalete, Carretera Guanta, Km 5, Apdo 4356, Puerto la Cruz; tel. (281) 68-5607; fax (281) 68-5683; f. 1955; bulk handling and cement bulk carrier; Chair. VÍCTOR ROMO; Man. Dir RAFAEL ANEE.

CIVIL AVIATION

There are two adjacent airports 13 km from Caracas: Maiquetía for domestic and Simón Bolívar for international services. There are 61 commercial airports, 11 of which are international airports.

National Airlines

Instituto Nacional de Aeronáutica Civil: Torre Británica, Urb. Altamira Sur, Avda José Félix Sosa, Chacao, Caracas 1060; tel. (212) 277-4411; e-mail contacto@inac.gov.ve; internet www.inac.gov.ve; f. 2005; regulatory authority; Pres. JOSÉ LUIS MARTÍNEZ BRAVO.

Aeropostal (Alas de Venezuela): Torre Polar Oeste, 22°, Plaza Venezuela, Los Caobos, Caracas 1051; tel. (212) 708-6211; fax (212) 782-6323; internet www.aeropostal.com; f. 1933; transferred to private ownership in Sept. 1996, acquired by Venezuelan/US consortium Corporación Alas de Venezuela; domestic services and flights to destinations in the Caribbean, South America and the USA; Pres. and CEO NELSON RAMIZ.

Aerovías Venezolanas, SA (AVENSA): Torre Humboldt, 1°, Avda Rio Caura, Prados del Este, Caracas; tel. (212) 976-5240; fax (212) 563-0225; e-mail info@avensa.com.ve; internet www.avensa.com.ve; f. 1943; provides domestic services from Caracas and services to Europe and the USA; govt-owned; Pres. WILMAR CASTRO SOTELDO.

Aserca Airlines: Torre Exterior, 8°, Avda Bolívar Norte, Valencia, Carabobo 2002; tel. (241) 237-111; fax (241) 220-210; e-mail rsv@asercaairlines.com; internet www.asercaairlines.com; f. 1968; domestic services and flights to Caribbean destinations; Pres. SIMEÓN GARCÍA.

Consorcio Venezolano de Industrias Aeronáutica y Servicios Aéreos, SA (CONVIASA): Avda Lecuna, Parque Central, Torre Oeste, 49°, Caracas; e-mail mercadeo@conviasa.aero; internet www.conviasa.aero; f. 2004; state-owned; Pres. FRANKLIN FERNÁNDEZ MARTÍNEZ.

LASER (Línea Aérea de Servicio Ejecutivo Regional): Torre Bazar Bolívar, 8°, Avda Francisco de Miranda, El Marqués, Caracas; tel. (212) 202-0100; fax (212) 235-8359; internet www.laser.com.ve; f. 1994; scheduled and charter passenger and cargo services to domestic and international destinations; Pres. INOCENCIO ALVAREZ; Gen. Man. JORGE ANDRADE HIDALGO.

Línea Turística Aereotuy, CA: Edif. Gran Sábana, 5°, Blvd de Sábana Grande, Apdo 2923, Carmelitas, Caracas 1050; tel. (212) 761-6231; fax (212) 762-5254; e-mail tuysales@etheron.net; internet www.tuy.com; f. 1982; operates on domestic and international routes; Pres. PETER BOTTOME; Gen. Man. JUAN C. MÁRQUEZ.

Santa Barbara Airlines: Avda 3H, No 78-51, Res. República, Local 01, Maracaibo; tel. (261) 922-090; fax (261) 927-977; internet www.sbairlines.com; f. 1996; domestic and international services; Pres. FRANCISCO GONZÁLEZ YANES.

Tourism

In 2006 Venezuela received 747,930 tourists. Receipts from tourism in that year amounted to US $843m. Venezuela's high crime levels, political instability and high prices relative to regional competitors have deterred tour operators. An estimated 90% of tourists visit the island of Margarita, while only 20% of tourists visit the mainland.

Asociación Venezolana de Agencias de Viajes y Turismo (AVAVIT): Caracas; e-mail turvspecialtours@cantv.net; internet www.avavit.com; Pres. ELIAS M. RAJBE S.

Instituto Nacional de Turismo (INATUR): Hotel Caracas Hilton, Torre Sur, 4°, Of. 424, Caracas; tel. (212) 576-4193; fax (212) 576-5138; e-mail inatur@inatur.gob.ve; internet www.inatur.gob.ve; f. 2001; govt tourism devt agency; Pres. YEAN LUIS DURÁN; Exec. Dir ANTONIO SALVUCHI.

Venezolana de Turismo, SA (VENETUR): Edif. Mintur, Avda Francisco de Miranda con Avda Principal de La Floresta, Torre Norte, 3°, Municipio Chacao, Caracas; tel. (212) 208-4812; fax (212) 208-8160; e-mail informacion@venetur.gob.ve; internet www.venetur.gob.ve; govt tourism promotion agency; Dir JORGE GONZÁLEZ VÁSQUEZ.

VIET NAM

Introductory Survey

Location, Climate, Language, Religion, Flag, Capital

The Socialist Republic of Viet Nam is situated in South-East Asia, bordered to the north by the People's Republic of China, to the west by Laos and Cambodia, and to the east by the South China Sea. The climate is humid during both the hot summer and the relatively cold winter, and there are monsoon rains in both seasons. Temperatures in Hanoi are generally between 13°C (55°F) and 33°C (91°F). The language is Vietnamese. The principal religion is Buddhism. There are also Daoist, Confucian, Hoa Hao, Caodaist and Christian (mainly Roman Catholic) minorities. The national flag (proportions 2 by 3) is red, with a large five-pointed yellow star in the centre. The capital is Hanoi.

Recent History

Cochin-China (the southernmost part of Viet Nam) became a French colony in 1867. Annam and Tonkin (central and northern Viet Nam) were proclaimed French protectorates in 1883. Later all three were merged with Cambodia and Laos to form French Indo-China. Throughout the French colonial period, but especially after 1920, nationalist and revolutionary groups operated in Viet Nam. The best-organized was the Vietnamese Revolutionary Youth League, founded by Ho Chi Minh. The League was succeeded in 1930 by the Communist Party of Indo-China, also led by Ho Chi Minh.

In September 1940 Japanese forces began to occupy Viet Nam, although (Vichy) France retained administrative authority, and in June 1941 the nationalists formed the Viet Nam Doc Lap Dong Minh Hoi (Revolutionary League for the Independence of Viet Nam), or Viet Minh. In March 1945 French control was ended by a Japanese coup. Following Japan's surrender in August, Viet Minh forces entered Hanoi, and on 2 September the new regime proclaimed independence as the Democratic Republic of Viet Nam (DRV), with Ho Chi Minh as President. The Communist Party, formally dissolved in 1945, continued to be the dominant group within the Viet Minh Government. In March 1946, after French forces re-entered Viet Nam, an agreement between France and the DRV recognized Viet Nam as a 'free' state within the French Union. However, the DRV Government continued to seek complete independence. Negotiations with France broke down, and full-scale hostilities began in December 1946.

In March 1949 the French established the State of Viet Nam in the South. Meanwhile, in the North the Viet Minh was dissolved in 1951, and the Communists formed the Dang Lao Dong Viet Nam (Viet Nam Workers' Party), with Ho Chi Minh as Chairman of the Central Committee. After the defeat of French forces at Dien Bien Phu in May 1954, terms for a cease-fire were settled in Geneva, Switzerland. Agreements signed in July provided for the provisional partition of Viet Nam into two military zones, with French forces south of latitude 17°N and DRV forces in the north. Later in 1954 the French withdrew from South Viet Nam. Ngo Dinh Diem became Prime Minister of the State of Viet Nam, and in 1955, following a referendum, proclaimed himself President of the Republic of Viet Nam. He thereby deposed Bao Dai, Emperor of Viet Nam from 1932 until his forced abdication in 1945, who had become Head of the State of Viet Nam in 1949. (The former Emperor died in exile in France in 1997.) Ngo Dinh Diem refused to participate in elections envisaged by the Geneva agreement. In the DRV Ho Chi Minh was succeeded as Prime Minister by Pham Van Dong in 1955, but remained Head of State and party Chairman.

The anti-communist regime in the South was opposed by former members of the Viet Minh, who became known as the Viet Cong. Ngo Dinh Diem was overthrown by a coup in November 1963, and a series of short-lived military regimes held power until June 1965, when some stability was restored by the National Leadership Committee, with Lt-Gen. Nguyen Van Thieu as Chairman and Air Vice-Marshal Nguyen Cao Ky as Prime Minister. In 1967 Gen. Nguyen Van Thieu was elected President, with Marshal Nguyen Cao Ky as Vice-President; in 1971, after a division with the latter, the President was re-elected unopposed.

From 1959 the DRV actively assisted the insurgent movement in South Viet Nam, supporting the establishment there of the communist-dominated National Liberation Front (NLF) in December 1960. In 1961 the USA joined the war on the side of the anti-communist regime in the South, later bombing the North extensively from 1965 to 1968. In November 1968 peace talks between the four participants in the Viet Nam war began in Paris, France, but remained deadlocked as the fighting continued. In June 1969 the NLF formed the Provisional Revolutionary Government (PRG) in the South. Ho Chi Minh died in September 1969: he was succeeded as Head of State by Ton Duc Thang, while political leadership passed to Le Duan, First Secretary of the Viet Nam Workers' Party since 1960.

In 1972 PRG and North Vietnamese forces launched a major offensive in South Viet Nam, and US bombing of the North was renewed with greater intensity. In January 1973 a peace agreement was finally signed in Paris, providing for a cease-fire in the South, the withdrawal of US forces, the eventual peaceful reunification of the whole country, and US aid to the Government in the North to assist in reconstruction. US troops withdrew, and in December 1974 combined PRG and North Vietnamese forces began a final offensive, taking the southern capital, Saigon, in April 1975. By May the new regime was in complete control of the South.

While South Viet Nam, under the PRG, remained technically separate from the DRV, effective control of the whole country passed to Hanoi. In July 1976 the country's reunification was proclaimed under the name of the Socialist Republic of Viet Nam, and Saigon was renamed Ho Chi Minh City. A new Government was appointed, dominated by members of the former Government of the DRV but including some members of the PRG. In December Le Duan was appointed General Secretary of the Communist Party of Viet Nam (formerly the Viet Nam Workers' Party). President Ton Duc Thang died in March 1980. A new Constitution was adopted in December of that year. Truong Chinh was appointed President of the Council of State (Head of State) in July 1981, but real power remained with Le Duan.

Le Duan died in July 1986, and was succeeded as General Secretary of the Communist Party by Truong Chinh. At the Sixth Party Congress, held in December, the country's three most senior leaders, Truong Chinh, Pham Van Dong and Le Duc Tho, announced their retirement from the party Political Bureau (Politburo). However, they continued to attend politburo meetings in an advisory capacity. Truong Chinh and Pham Van Dong retained their respective posts as President of the Council of State and Chairman of the Council of Ministers (Prime Minister) until 1987, and Le Duc Tho continued to wield considerable political influence until his death in October 1990. The Congress appointed Nguyen Van Linh, a long-standing party official, as General Secretary of the Party.

In February 1987 an extensive government reorganization involved the dismissal of 12 ministers, as well as the merger or restructuring of several ministries, apparently with a view to the implementation of economic reforms. An election to the National Assembly took place in April. There were 829 candidates for the 496 seats (compared with 613 candidates at the previous election). In June the new Assembly elected Vo Chi Cong and Pham Hung, both former Vice-Chairmen of the Council of Ministers, to the posts of President of the Council of State and Chairman of the Council of Ministers respectively. Although a veteran of the struggle with the South, and reputedly a strict conservative, Pham Hung gave his support to the programme of economic reform, referred to as *doi moi* (renovation), initiated by Nguyen Van Linh. The new liberalism of the regime was demonstrated by the release in September of 480 political prisoners from 're-education' camps, as part of an amnesty for more than 6,600 prisoners on the anniversary of independence from France in 1945. In February 1988 more than 1,000 political prisoners were released. In March Pham Hung died. The Council of State appointed Vo Van Kiet, a Vice-Chairman of the Council of Ministers and the Chairman of the State Commission for Planning, as acting Chairman of the Council of Ministers.

At the meeting of the National Assembly in June, members from the south took the unprecedented step of nominating the reformist Vo Van Kiet to oppose the Central Committee's more conservative candidate, Do Muoi (ranked third in the Politburo), in the election for the chairmanship of the Council of Ministers. Do Muoi was elected to the position, but Vo Van Kiet received unexpectedly strong support. Despite his reputation, Do Muoi declared his commitment to the advancement of reform. Widespread dissatisfaction with the condition of the economy led to the removal of hundreds of cadres from government posts in a 'purification' of the party. In an attempt to improve international relations, and thus secure much-needed Western aid, Viet Nam amended its Constitution in December, removing derogatory references to the USA, the People's Republic of China, France and Japan. In March 1989 a reorganization of senior economic ministers adjusted the balance further towards reform and strengthened the position of Nguyen Van Linh.

In August 1989 68 members of a US-based exiles' movement, the National Front for the Liberation of Viet Nam, were arrested while crossing from Thailand into Laos. Viet Nam formally protested to Thailand for supporting the group, which had allegedly attempted to incite a rebellion in southern Viet Nam, although the Thai Government denied involvement. In January 1990 38 suspected rebels were extradited to Viet Nam; in October they were sentenced to long terms of imprisonment.

Municipal elections to provincial and district councils took place in November 1989. Under new legislation, candidates who were not members of the Communist Party were allowed to participate for the first time. In December the National Assembly approved legislation imposing new restrictions on the press: the appointment of editors became subject to government approval, and journalists were required to reveal sources of information on request. Open dissension towards Communist Party policy also became a criminal offence. In late 1989 progress towards political reform under *doi moi* was adversely affected by government concern regarding the demise of socialism in Eastern Europe. At a meeting of the Central Committee in March 1990, disagreement on the issue of political pluralism resulted in the dismissal of a member of the Politburo, Tran Xuan Bach, who had openly advocated reform.

In the second half of 1990 the Government dismissed or brought charges against more than 18,000 officials, in an attempt to eradicate corruption. In December the Central Committee produced draft political and economic reports, reaffirming the party's commitment to socialism and to the process of economic liberalization, which were to be submitted to the next Party Congress. In the same month Bui Tin, the deputy editor of the official organ of the Communist Party, *Nhan Dan*, criticized government policy. He was subsequently expelled from the Politburo and dismissed as deputy editor. Following a request by the Central Committee for public comment on the reports, in early 1991 the party journal, *Tap Chi Cong San* (Communist Review), published articles by prominent intellectuals that severely criticized the reports and questioned the effectiveness of the socialist system. The Communist Party subsequently increased surveillance of dissidents and instructed the press to publish retaliatory articles condemning party critics. In June the Communist Party Congress approved the reports. It elected Do Muoi to replace Nguyen Van Linh as General Secretary of the Party; seven members of the Politburo were removed from their posts, including Nguyen Van Linh, although he, together with Pham Van Dong and the President of the Council of State, Vo Chi Cong, remained in the Central Committee in an advisory capacity. At a session of the National Assembly held in late July and early August, the reformist Vo Van Kiet was elected to replace Do Muoi as Chairman of the Council of Ministers. In addition, the National Assembly studied proposals, made by a constitutional commission, for amendments to the Constitution.

A new draft Constitution was published in December 1991 and, after being reviewed in public discussions, was adopted by the National Assembly in April 1992. Like the previous (1980) Constitution, it emphasized the central role of the Communist Party; however, the new document stipulated that the party must be subject to the law. While affirming adherence to a state-regulated socialist economy, the new Constitution guaranteed protection for foreign investment in Viet Nam, and permitted foreign travel and overseas investment for Vietnamese. Land was to remain the property of the State, although the right was granted to procure long-term leases, which could be inherited or sold. The National Assembly was to be reduced in number, but was to have greater power. The Council of State was to be replaced by a single President as Head of State, to be responsible for appointing (subject to the approval of the National Assembly) a Prime Minister and senior members of the judiciary. The new Constitution was to enter into effect after the July 1992 general election.

In July 1992 a total of 601 candidates contested 395 seats in the National Assembly. Almost 90% were members of the Communist Party: although independent candidates (i.e. not endorsed by the Viet Nam Fatherland Front—the grouping of mass organizations, such as trade unions, affiliated to the Communist Party) were for the first time permitted to seek election, in the event only two were deemed to qualify, and neither was elected.

At the first session of the new National Assembly, in September 1992, the conservative Gen. Le Duc Anh (a member of the Politburo and a former Minister of Defence) was elected to the new post of executive President. Vo Van Kiet was appointed Prime Minister (the equivalent of his former post) by the Assembly in October. Only four ministers, all of whom had been implicated in corruption scandals, were not reappointed. During 1993 the Government emphasized its determination to continue progress towards a market-led economy and to encourage foreign investment. However, there was no tolerance of political dissent. In August 14 people were sentenced to terms of imprisonment, after having been convicted of conspiring to overthrow the Government, and in November several Buddhist monks were imprisoned for allegedly inciting anti-Government demonstrations. In January 1994 four new members were appointed to the Politburo, including the Minister of Foreign Affairs, Nguyen Manh Cam, and 20 new members (all under the age of 55) were elected to the Communist Party's Central Committee. In June the National Assembly approved a labour law that guaranteed the right to strike (providing that the 'social life of the community' was not adversely affected). Strikes followed in some southern provinces, and in August the first incident of industrial action in Hanoi was reported. At the fourth Congress of the Fatherland Front, in August, a new, 200-member Central Committee was elected. Elections to provincial and district councils took place during December 1994.

In February 1995 a prominent human rights organization, Amnesty International, protested to the Vietnamese Government about the recent detention of members of the anti-Government Unified Buddhist Church of Viet Nam. In August the People's Court of Ho Chi Minh City sentenced nine political activists, who had attempted to organize pro-democracy conferences, to terms of imprisonment. (Two of those sentenced, who held joint US-Vietnamese nationality, were released in November following a request from the US Government.) In October the National Assembly adopted an extensive civil code (drafted over a period of 10 years), guaranteeing the rights of the individual and enshrining existing rights concerning land usage and inheritance of property. In November two former prominent members of the Communist Party, Do Trung Hieu and Hoang Minh Chinh, were sentenced to custodial terms on charges of damaging national security: The former had been involved with an organization demanding political pluralism, while the latter had published articles urging the restoration of senior party officials removed in the 1960s.

In April 1996 the Central Committee of the Communist Party released draft reports on political and economic policy, which were to be submitted to the Eighth Communist Party Congress at the end of June, indicating that the party intended to maintain state control of the economy (while remaining committed to economic growth) and to continue to reject political pluralism. Also in April the Vice-Chairman of the National Assembly was dismissed from the Politburo and from the Communist Party; it was reported that he had been accused of treason in connection with the Viet Nam war. In June the Congress elected a new, 170-member Central Committee and an expanded (19-member) Politburo. A five-member Standing Board, which included Do Muoi, Le Duc Anh and Vo Van Kiet, was created. In November 12 ministers were dismissed in an extensive cabinet reorganization. Later in the month Le Duc Anh withdrew temporarily from politics, owing to ill health: this prompted considerable speculation regarding the eventual leadership succession. In subsequent months Lt-Gen. Le Kha Phieu, a member of the new Standing Board, came to the fore as a likely successor to Do Muoi as General Secretary of the Communist Party. Widely seen as a conservative, Le Kha Phieu was expected to seek an increased political role for the military. Le Duc Anh returned to active politics in April 1997.

In December 1996 the Politburo issued a directive requiring the establishment of Communist Party cells in all foreign-invested enterprises. In January 1997 an unprecedentedly high-profile corruption case was brought to trial: the case involved former senior officials of Tamexco (an import-export company owned by the Communist Party), along with officials from Vietcombank (the state foreign trade bank) and the financial sector. The 20 defendants were accused of a range of financial crimes, principally embezzlement of socialist property. In late January four death sentences were pronounced, together with one sentence of life imprisonment, two suspended sentences and a combined total of 103 years' imprisonment for the remaining defendants. In February 1997 a judge of the Supreme People's Court was sentenced to two years' imprisonment, having been found to have abused a position of influence for personal gain, and was thus the first member of Viet Nam's judiciary to be convicted of corruption.

In May 1997 substantial amendments to the criminal code were approved by the National Assembly in respect of corruption, bribery, child abuse and drugs-trafficking. The acceptance of bribes in excess of 50m. dông, and possession of 5 kg of opium or 100 grams of heroin, became crimes punishable by death or life imprisonment; increased penalties were introduced for first-time offenders in cases of corruption. In the same month a group of 22 people, including police, customs and border officials, stood trial for drugs-trafficking: all were convicted, with eight sentenced to death and eight to life imprisonment. In July two people were sentenced to death, and three others to life imprisonment, following what was reported as Viet Nam's first terrorism trial, having been convicted of involvement in a bomb attack in Ho Chi Minh City in October 1994. Official reports stated that the defendants were members of the National Resistance Front for the Restoration of Viet Nam, which was alleged to have issued death threats to foreign nationals who had established businesses in Viet Nam.

Elections to the 10th National Assembly took place on 20 July 1997. A record 663 candidates contested 450 seats (expanded from 395 seats). Under a modified selection process, 112 non-Communist Party members registered as potential candidates. However, following rigorous screening procedures, only 11 independent ('self-nominated') candidates qualified to contest the elections, of whom three secured seats in the Assembly. Do Muoi was among senior figures who did not seek re-election, and, in total, fewer than one-third of the members of the outgoing Assembly returned to office. At the first session of the new National Assembly in late September, Tran Duc Luong, hitherto a Deputy Prime Minister, was elected as President in succession to Le Duc Anh, who, owing to continued ill health, did not seek re-election. The Assembly subsequently endorsed the appointment of Nguyen Thi Binh as Vice-President, Nong Duc Manh as Chairman of the National Assembly Standing Committee, and Phan Van Khai as Prime Minister. (Vo Van Kiet had also stepped down.) A reorganization of the Cabinet was approved at the end of September: the new Cabinet included an increased number of Deputy Prime Ministers, each of whom held a wide portfolio of responsibilities. In October Do Que Luong was appointed acting Governor of the State Bank of Viet Nam (a cabinet post), following the refusal of the National Assembly to re-elect the incumbent Cao Si Kiem, deemed responsible for recent corruption scandals in the banking sector.

Reports emerged during September 1997 of violent unrest in the northern province of Thai Binh. The unrest, which had begun in May and intensified in June as hundreds of farmers protested against taxes and local corruption, had remained largely unreported earlier in the year as the province had been closed to foreign journalists. There was violence in November in the predominantly Roman Catholic province of Dong Nai, in southern Viet Nam, as thousands of protesters demonstrated against corruption in local government and attempts to confiscate church land. At the end of November the Government pledged to provide financial aid to Thai Binh province, and in February 1998 President Luong made an official tour of the province. In July 1998 more than 30 people were sentenced to terms of imprisonment for their involvement in the previous year's violent unrest in Thai Binh.

In December 1997 Le Kha Phieu was elected to succeed Do Muoi as General Secretary of the Central Committee of the Communist Party. At the same time Do Muoi, Le Duch Anh and Vo Van Kiet resigned from the Politburo; all three were subsequently appointed as advisers to the Central Committee. Four new members were elected to the Politburo, and in January 1998 the election by the Politburo of a new Standing Board, comprising Le Kha Phieu, Tran Duc Luong, Phan Van Khai, Nong Duc Manh and Pham The Duyet, was announced. The new appointments were widely perceived to reflect the consolidation of the conservative tendency within the leadership, to the detriment of reformists, among them the Prime Minister. In March, in an illustration of the Government's commitment to countering corruption, the Communist Party announced that in 1997 it had disciplined and expelled some 18,000 members, and sentenced 469 to terms of imprisonment. Further members of the party were reported to have been disciplined over corruption-related offences in July.

In a general amnesty announced by the Government to mark Viet Nam's National Day on 2 September 1998, more than 5,000 prisoners, including four of the country's most prominent dissidents—Doan Viet Hoat, Nguyen Dan Que, Thich Quang Do and Thich Tue Sy—were released from detention; however, the release of at least two of the dissidents was reported to be dependent upon their immediate exile from Viet Nam. In October amnesty was granted to a further 2,630 prisoners. Also in October, the former editor-in-chief of *Doanh Nghiep*, Nguyen Hoang Linh, was convicted of 'abusing freedom and democratic rights to violate the interests of the State', following the publication in his newspaper of articles detailing alleged government corruption; Nguyen Hoang Linh was sentenced to more than 12 months' imprisonment, but was released almost immediately as his sentence represented the exact time he had served in detention while awaiting trial. In October the Special Rapporteur on religious intolerance of the UN Commission on Human Rights, Abdelfattah Amor, visited Viet Nam to investigate assertions made by the Vietnamese authorities that greater freedom of religious expression was being afforded in the country. However, at the end of his visit, Amor stated that his investigation had been obstructed by government officials and that he had been prevented from meeting key religious dissidents.

In January 1999 the leadership of the Communist Party announced that it had expelled Gen. (retd) Tran Do from the party in response to his explicit criticism of the establishment. His expulsion caused renewed speculation about party divisions, and also set the precedent for the continued suppression of political dissent. In March the prominent writer and geophysicist, Nguyen Thanh Giang, whose critiques of the Communist Party were reported to have been widely disseminated both within Viet Nam and abroad, was arrested on the grounds of 'propagandizing against the socialist regime'; he was released in May, but reportedly remained under house arrest. In September the trial opened of 24 members of the dissident People's Action Party, charged with 'exiting the country illegally for the purpose of undermining the people's administration'; all 24 defendants were subsequently convicted and sentenced to terms of imprisonment ranging from two to 20 years. Prior to the trial Le Kha Phieu, speaking at the Seventh Plenum of the Eighth Party Central Committee in August, had emphasized the Communist Party's opposition to political pluralism.

In 1999 the issue of corruption remained a major source of concern for the Communist Party. The trial of 74 people accused of smuggling (more than one-half of whom were reported to be former government officials) opened in March, with two of the defendants being subsequently sentenced to death, and the remainder to terms of imprisonment. In May 77 businessmen, bankers and government officials appeared in court charged with the fraudulent procurement of state loans; in August six of the defendants were sentenced to death (although two of these subsequently had their sentences commuted to life imprisonment), and the remainder to various terms of imprisonment. In December, in a further demonstration of the efforts of the Communist Party to address corruption, Deputy Prime Minister Ngo Xuan Loc was dismissed from the Cabinet following his implication in a corrupt land deal related to a private-sector project. However, in April 2000 he was reinstated to a government post and resumed responsibility for the sectors connected to the initial accusations against him, thus attracting speculation as to the extent of the Government's attempts to eliminate corruption. In September 2001 eight officials were tried on charges of fraud in Hanoi in connection with the land deal. One businessman received a 20-year prison sentence; the remaining defendants were either released or sentenced to prison terms of nine months or less.

In October 2000 the Politburo issued orders to develop the country's information technology (IT) capabilities and raise them to a level comparable to other countries in the region by 2010. The order emphasized the application of IT for the development of economics, culture and society, along with defence and security. Also in October the Ministry of Public Security announced a nation-wide campaign against the use of illicit drugs. In November Communist Party documents divulged to the US-based human rights group Freedom House emphasized the leadership's level of concern regarding the increasing number of ethnic minorities converting to Christianity, and the fear that religion would be used by the USA and other countries to undermine communism in Viet Nam. In December the Minister of National Defence, Lt-Gen. Pham Van Tra, instructed the army not to become depoliticized, and to remain vigilant and safeguard the Communist Party and the socialist system.

Ethnic violence broke out in the Central Highland provinces of Gia Lai and Dak Lak in February 2001, as local hill minorities (known as Montagnards) protested against perceived injustices caused by the migration of ethnic Vietnamese from the densely populated coastal regions and by the deforestation resulting from the establishment of coffee plantations. Some 5,000 protesters in the provincial capitals of Pleiku and Buon Ma Thuot respectively attacked state offices and blocked roads. The Vietnamese authorities deployed troops, riot police, water cannon and helicopters to quell the unrest, and injuries were reported on both sides. Some 20 people were arrested in connection with instigating the violence, which was attributed to 'extremists' seeking to use religion to foment unrest. The protesters had demanded autonomy, freedom to practise their Protestant religion, the return of ancestral lands confiscated for use as coffee plantations and the right to preserve their traditional way of life. The Ministry of Public Security accused the US-based Montagnard Foundation of organizing the violence, stating that several of those arrested were former members of the United Front for the Liberation of Oppressed Races (FULRO), a guerrilla unit that had close links to the US military and Central Intelligence Agency (CIA) during the Viet Nam war. The Vietnamese authorities also stated that during 2000 there had been several incursions into the country by agents of Free Viet Nam, a movement based in Thailand. The unrest coincided with a climate of increasing repression of religion, and it was feared that 'hardliners' in the Communist Party might use the incident to strengthen their position and to delay economic and political reforms. In March the authorities denounced a Catholic priest, Nguyen Van Ly, for writing to the US Congress and urging it not to ratify a bilateral trade agreement, owing to human rights abuses in Viet Nam. In October Nguyen Van Ly was sentenced to 15 years in prison after a court convicted him of undermining national unity and contravening a detention order. (His sentence was reduced by five years in July 2003 and by a further five years in June 2004, and in February 2005 he was released from prison, having been granted amnesty. However, he was imprisoned again in March 2007—see below.) Exiled Vietnamese Buddhist leaders also claimed that their followers in Viet Nam were routinely harassed. In September 2001 Ho Tan Anh, leader of the Buddhist Youth Movement, burnt himself to death in protest at the restrictions that had been imposed upon his organization.

The Ninth Party Congress was held in April 2001, and resulted in the election of a new 150-member Central Committee, 15-member Politburo and nine-member Secretariat. Nong Duc Manh was appointed General Secretary, replacing Le Kha Phieu, who was accused of using military intelligence against party members and of slowing the pace of reforms. Phieu had agreed to step down under pressure from the Central Committee. Nong Duc Manh, who was rumoured to be the illegitimate son of Ho Chi Minh, was the first ethnic Tay to attain such a senior position. Some 84 members of the previous Central Committee were re-elected. President Tran Duc Luong and Prime Minister Phan Van Khai retained their party posts, but former President Le Duc Anh, former Prime Minister Vo Van Kiet and former General Secretary Do Muoi lost their positions as senior advisers to the Central Committee upon the abolition of the posts. Manh was believed to favour economic reforms and greater democracy, the latter a major theme at the Congress. However, the Congress reiterated its commitment to socialism as a means to national industrialization and modernization. In June 2001 Nguyen Van An, a member of the Politburo, was elected to the chairmanship of the National Assembly, succeeding Nong Duc Manh.

In September 2001 14 Montagnards received sentences of between six and 12 years' imprisonment for participating in the protests of February of that year. In October a further six men were convicted of distributing propaganda and inciting ethnic unrest in the city of Buon Ma Thuot during the disturbances. A critical report issued by the international organization Human Rights Watch in April 2002 warned of further violence in the Central Highlands if the Government continued to implement its repressive policies towards ethnic minorities. In November 2002 it was alleged that the Government had executed three Montagnards in the previous month, reportedly owing to their involvement in the violence of February 2001. In December a further eight people were convicted of charges of undermining national unity, having allegedly aided people attempting to leave the region following the violence. In January 2003, according to Human Rights Watch, 70 Montagnards were known to be imprisoned in Viet Nam owing to their political or religious beliefs. In April a report issued by Human Rights Watch claimed that government persecution of the Montagnards had escalated since January. In May 15 Montagnards were convicted of causing social disorder during the protests of February 2001 and sentenced to lengthy prison terms. In April 2004 Human Rights Watch again accused the Vietnamese Government of repression, following reports that a rally held by Montagnards in that month in Dak Lak province, in protest against land confiscation and religious persecution, had been violently suppressed by government officials. Human Rights Watch claimed that at least 10 Montagnards had been killed, although the Vietnamese Government insisted that only two people had died. In May Human Rights Watch reported that the Vietnamese authorities had arrested a number of Montagnard church leaders, as well as Montagnards with relatives in the USA. In August nine Montagnards, who were alleged to be former members of the FULRO, were convicted of fomenting disorder and undermining national unity during the demonstrations of February 2001 and thereafter. They were sentenced to prison terms of between five and 12 years.

In December 2001 the National Assembly gave its approval to several constitutional amendments, including one allowing politicians to instigate mid-term votes of no confidence if they considered any minister to be performing unsatisfactorily. The amendments were intended to encourage the development of Viet Nam's market economy and improve democracy, thus facilitating the country's further integration into the international community.

It was reported in January 2002 that the Communist Party had approved a decree authorizing the police to engage in the destruction of publications that had not been approved by the party. Books written by several leading dissidents, including Gen. Tran Do, had subsequently been destroyed. In March the Politburo was reported to have established a special investigation into allegations that more than 50 government officials had colluded in organized crime. Several of those accused were reported to have accepted bribes to protect a gang whose alleged leader, Truong Van Cam, also known as Nam Cam, was undergoing investigation on murder charges. As the investigation continued, more than 100 government officials and an estimated 50 police officers were implicated; two members of the Central Committee (the Director-General of the state radio station Voice of Viet Nam, Tran Mai Hanh, and Pham Sy Chien) were expelled from the Communist Party in July owing to their involvement. In November the Deputy Minister of Public Security, Maj.-Gen. Haong Ngoc Nhat, was dismissed from his position and demoted in rank, owing to his alleged complicity. In January 2003 the director of the Economic Commission of the Politburo, Truong Tan San, became the most senior member of the Communist Party to be punished in relation to the investigation; he was formally reprimanded for 'dereliction of duty' during his tenure as secretary of the party in Ho Chi Minh City in 1996–2000.

Meanwhile, in March 2002 the Communist Party decided that it would formally permit its members to engage in private business, indicating the Government's desire to encourage the expansion of the role of the private sector within the economy. In April 59 people went on trial in Ho Chi Minh City charged with embezzling state assets and violating commercial law in connection with the Chinese-owned Viet Hoa bank. In the following month all those tried were found guilty of the charges against them; 43 were sentenced to prison terms of varying lengths, while those remaining were given suspended sentences. The trial was widely perceived to constitute a further attempt on the part of the Government to take firm action against corruption.

Elections to the 11th National Assembly took place on 19 May 2002. The 498 seats available were contested by 759 candidates, only 13 of whom were independent. Non-Communist Party candidates won 51 seats and independents two, the remainder being secured by party members. In July and August the newly elected National Assembly held its first session, during which significant reorganizations of both the Standing Committee and the Cabinet were approved. Three new ministries were created during the extensive reorganization, in which Vu Khoan, the former Minister of Trade, was promoted to the position of Deputy Prime Minister. President Tran Duc Luong, Prime Minister Phan Van Khai and the Chairman of the National Assembly, Nguyen Van An, were all formally re-elected to their posts, while Truong My Hoa succeeded Nguyen Thi Binh as Vice-President.

In November 2002 Le Chi Quang, a lawyer, was convicted of committing 'acts of propaganda' against the State, after allegedly publishing material critical of the Government on the internet. He was sentenced to a four-year prison term (but was released early, in June 2004, to serve a three-year term of house arrest). In December 2002 another dissident, Nguyen Khac Toan, was sentenced to 12 years in prison, having been convicted of using the internet for espionage purposes; he was subsequently granted amnesty and released in January 2006. In March 2003 the dissident Nguyen Dan Que, who had spent over 18 years in prison for campaigning for improved democracy and human rights in Viet Nam and had been freed five years previously, was arrested again after publishing an essay on the internet concerning Viet Nam's control of the media. In July 2004 he was sentenced to a 30-month prison term, but was granted amnesty and released in February 2005, one of an estimated 12 political or religious prisoners to be granted early release during the course of that year. Meanwhile, at the Seventh Plenum of the Central Committee of the Communist Party held in January 2003, a resolution intended to increase the Party's control over religious affairs was approved. At the Plenum Nguyen Van Chi was appointed to the Party Secretariat.

In February 2003 the trial of Nam Cam and 154 other defendants on a number of charges, including murder, organized gambling, bribery, drugs-trafficking and extortion, began in Ho Chi Minh City. Among the defendants were 21 former state and government officials. The hearings constituted Viet Nam's largest corruption trial to date. In June Nam Cam was convicted of all the charges against him and sentenced to death. In the same month many more defendants in the trial were convicted of the charges against them, including Tran Mai Hanh, who received a 10-year prison term, and Pham Sy Chien, who was to serve a six-year sentence. Five other defendants were given death sentences. In June 2004 Nam Cam and four of his co-defendants were executed by firing squad, the death sentence of the fifth having been commuted to life imprisonment.

In April 2003 Prime Minister Phan Van Khai held talks with Thich Huyen Quang, leader of the anti-Government Unified Buddhist Church of Viet Nam, who had been held under house arrest since the group was proscribed almost 20 years previously. While the meeting was welcomed by international diplomats, there was speculation that the Communist Party might use it to respond to continued criticism of its human rights record, while avoiding making any more substantial reforms. In May Thich Huyen Quang was permitted to meet with his deputy, Thich Quang Do, for only the third time in 21 years. In June Thich Quang Do was released from house arrest, two months before the end of his two-year sentence. In the same month, however, Pham Hong Son, a doctor, was sentenced to a 13-year prison term, to be followed by three years of house arrest, having been found guilty of charges of espionage and disseminating false information about the State on the internet. The Government later reduced the length of his prison sentence to five years. In October a one-day 'stand-off' was reported to have taken place in Binh Dinh province between government security forces and supporters of the Unified Buddhist Church of Viet Nam, following an attempt by Thich Huyen Quang and Thich Quang Do to depart for Ho Chi Minh City. In November both the US House of Representatives and the European Parliament approved resolutions condemning the continuing official repression of non-recognized religious organizations in Viet Nam and calling for the release of Thich Huyen Quang.

In November 2003 the trial opened in Hanoi of two former junior agriculture ministers, Nguyen Thien Luan and Nguyen Quang Ha, together with La Thi Kim Oanh, the former director of a company controlled by the Ministry of Agriculture and Rural Development, and five other officials, on embezzlement charges. The opening of the trial was televised as part of the Government's ongoing campaign to combat corruption. In December all those tried were found guilty of the charges against them. La Thi Kim Oanh was sentenced to death, while the remaining defendants received prison sentences of various lengths. Meanwhile, in the same month former journalist Nguyen Vu Binh was sentenced to a seven-year prison term, having been convicted of espionage charges. (Nguyen Vu Binh was granted a presidential amnesty in June 2007, shortly before a visit by the Vietnamese President to the USA, which had pressed for the dissident's release.) In June 2004 the National Assembly approved the dismissal of the Minister of Agriculture and Development, Le Huy Ngo, on the grounds that he had failed adequately to monitor his subordinates and organizations under his administration in connection with the embezzlement case; he was replaced by Cao Duc Phat.

In March 2004 police arrested four members of the Mennonite Church, which was not officially recognized by the Government, after scuffles broke out when a number of Mennonites attempted to photograph police officers who were posted outside the headquarters of the Church. In June Nguyen Hong Quang, the Secretary-General of the Mennonite Church in Viet Nam, was also arrested for his involvement in the incident, and a sixth church member was detained the following month. In November Quang was sentenced to three years' imprisonment for preventing officials from carrying out their duties, while the five other defendants received custodial sentences of between nine months and two years.

Two veteran dissidents, Tran Van Khue, a retired academic, and Pham Que Duong, a military historian, were sentenced to 19 months' imprisonment in July 2004, having been convicted of abusing democratic freedoms to undermine the interests of the State. Both men had posted articles critical of the Government on the internet. However, they were released at the end of the month, as they had been in detention since December 2002. In late July 2004 the Minister of Posts and Telecommunications, Do Trung Ta, issued new regulations aimed at controlling access to the internet by allowing internet service providers to suspend contracts with cafés that allowed customers to view pornographic websites or those deemed to threaten national security. In the following month a special police unit was established to combat internet crime and prevent the spread of banned materials.

Also in July 2004 the President promulgated an Ordinance on Beliefs and Religions, which came into effect in November. A coalition of non-recognized Protestant churches condemned the new law, which, while upholding the right of citizens to freedom of religious belief, decreed that only state-authorized clergy be entitled to preach and only within defined territorial jurisdictions. The ordinance also provided for the suspension of religious activities that were deemed to jeopardize national security, public order or national unity. In February 2005 it was reported that the Government had issued a decree allowing outlawed Protestant churches to operate if they renounced connections to the FULRO.

Details emerged in September 2004 of a major corruption scandal in which local textile companies had been allegedly obliged to pay large bribes to trade officials in order to secure export quotas to the USA. Some 19 people were subsequently arrested in connection with the case; the most prominent of these was Deputy Minister of Trade Mai Van Dau, who was charged with abuse of power and dismissed from the Government in November. Mai Van Dau's trial was conducted in March 2007: the former Deputy Minister of Trade was convicted of receiving bribes and sentenced to 14 years' imprisonment, while 12 other defendants received sentences ranging from one year to 17 years; Mai Van Dau's sentence was reduced to 12 years in June. Meanwhile, in October 2004 Prime Minister Phan Van Khai announced plans to establish an anti-corruption agency. In November the National Assembly approved new legislation on national security, which stipulated the principles of security policy and the powers and responsibilities of the agencies in charge of national security.

In December 2004 two retired state physicists, Tran Van Luong and Nguyen Thi Minh Hoan, were sentenced, respectively, to 21 months' and eight months' imprisonment for sending to state agencies documents and petitions that were critical of the Government and the Communist Party. In January 2005 the Government announced that 8,323 prisoners, including six political dissidents and 33 foreigners, were to be released in an amnesty to mark Tet (the lunar New Year). In March the Government issued a decree aimed at tightening control over demonstrations and banning unauthorized gatherings. It was reported that the decree required the approval in advance of all gatherings not organized by the Communist Party or state organs.

It was reported in June 2005 that, according to the Ministry of Public Security, 176,534 economic crimes had been exposed in the 12 previous years; 9,960 of those were said to be related to corruption. In November the National Assembly ratified a long-awaited Anti-Corruption Law, the terms of which required all officials, and their close relatives, to disclose fully their assets. There was considerable scepticism as to how effectively this would be enforced, especially in view of the protection given to the authorities by state control of the media. In the previous month the deputy head of the State Inspectorate's department of economic inspection, Luong Cao Khai, was arrested amid claims that he had accepted bribes and had abused his position to provide relatives with employment; in November 2007 he was convicted of the charges against him and sentenced to 21 years' imprisonment, while two other former senior officials from the State Inspectorate received shorter custodial terms for accepting bribes.

In April 2006 the Minister of Transport and Communications, Dao Dinh Binh, tendered his resignation from the Cabinet, following allegations concerning an apparent misappropriation of state funds by staff members within his ministry. It was claimed that officials had stolen money allocated to construction projects and had accepted numerous bribes. Binh announced that he would accept full responsibility for the actions of those employed in his ministry. The Deputy Minister of Transport and Communications, Nguyen Viet Tien, was arrested in connection with the embezzlement of state funds. In August 2007 eight people were sentenced to between seven and 13 years' imprisonment for their involvement in the scandal, while a ninth defendant received a suspended two-year term. Criminal charges against Nguyen Viet Tien were withdrawn in March 2008.

The 10th Communist Party Congress was held in late April 2006, during which elections were held for a new 160-member Central Committee, 14-member Politburo and eight-member Secretariat. Nong Duc Manh was retained as General Secretary of the Party; five other members of the previous Politburo also secured re-election. President Tran Duc Luong, Prime Minister Phan Van Khai and Chairman of the National Assembly Standing Committee, Nguyen Van An, all announced that they were to resign, thus preparing the way for a younger generation of officials to assume prominent positions within the party leadership. The Congress reaffirmed its commitment to socialism, announced its aim of Viet Nam achieving the status of a developed country by 2020 and adopted the Report and Five-Year Plan of Action on Socio-economic Development Goals for 2006–10; the issue of corruption within the party was also given considerable focus, with General Secretary Manh vowing in his opening speech to 'intensify' the fight against it. In June 2006, at its annual session, the National Assembly formally approved the resignations of Tran Duc Luong, Phan Van Khai and Nguyen Van An. Phan Van Kai's nominee, Nguyen Tan Dung, was confirmed as Prime Minister, while Nguyen Minh Triet succeeded Tran Duc Luong as President. Nguyen Phu Trong was elected Chairman of the National Assembly Standing Committee. Soon after, a cabinet reorganization was approved: Minister of Finance Nguyen Sinh Hung, who had been promoted to the position of Deputy Prime Minister, was replaced by Vu Van Ninh, while another Deputy Prime Minister, Pham Gia Khiem, took additional charge of the foreign affairs portfolio. Among the new appointees were Truong Vinh Trong as Deputy Prime Minister and Lt-Gen. Phung Quang Thanh as Minister of National Defence (to replace Lt-Gen. Pham Van Tra following his retirement); however, several other ministers retained their portfolios. Vu Khoan, who had retired from the post of Deputy Prime Minister, was later appointed as the Prime Minister's special envoy for foreign affairs.

At the end of June 2006 the new Prime Minister's decision to waive possible disciplinary action against the retiring former Minister of Transport and Communications, Dao Dinh Binh, encountered significant, although unsuccessful, opposition within the National Assembly. In October it appeared that the campaign against corruption was progressing, with the establishment of the Central Steering Committee for Corruption Prevention and Control, chaired by Nguyen Tan Dung. The committee, which was created to oversee and co-ordinate national anti-corruption operations, would have the power to suspend government officials for unlawful practices. In the following month the Government was reported to have established a department to address the issue of corruption, as part of the General Directorate of Police, with links to the Ministry of Public Security. In late January 2007 a Communist Party Central Committee plan for partial privatization was announced, with the military and the party projected to relinquish ownership of several businesses; however, the details of the programme were yet to be revealed. Earlier in the month a list of state companies due to sell shares to the public (with the Government remaining majority shareholder) by 2010, including Viet Nam Airlines, had been authorized by the Prime Minister.

Meanwhile, in August 2006 Pham Hong Son (see above) was one of thousands of prisoners freed under an amnesty to commemorate National Day in the following month. In November seven people, three of them US nationals, were convicted on terrorism charges and sentenced to 15 months' imprisonment. In the same month the USA's decision to remove Viet Nam from its list of 'countries of particular concern' in relation to religious freedom provoked criticism from Thich Quang Do. Although the decision recognized the country's progress towards greater religious freedom, reports of cases against dissidents continued: in March 2007 a Catholic priest, Father Nguyen Van Ly, was convicted of disseminating information against the State and sentenced to eight years' imprisonment. None the less, relations between the Vietnamese Government and the Roman Catholic Church were improving. In January 2007 Nguyen Tan Dung became the first Vietnamese Prime Minister to visit the Vatican, where he held talks with Pope Benedict XVI, and in March a delegation from the Vatican visited Viet Nam to discuss the possibility of establishing full diplomatic relations. Moreover, during 2007 the Government's Committee for Religious Affairs granted operating licences to several additional religions, including the Mennonite Church, the Baptist Church and the Bahá'í faith.

Elections to the 12th National Assembly held on 20 May 2007 were contested by 875 candidates, including 30 independents. Of the 493 deputies elected, only one was an independent, while a further 42 were non-Communist Party members. A high turnout, of 99.6%, was recorded. Earlier that month several political dissidents were convicted of spreading propaganda intended to undermine the State. Le Nguyen Sang, Nguyen Bac Truyen, Huynh Nguyen Dao and Tran Quoc Hien received prison terms ranging from three to five years in Ho Chi Minh City, while the Hanoi People's Court sentenced two human rights lawyers, Nguyen Van Dai and Le Thi Cong Nhan, to terms of five years and four years, respectively.

The first session of the newly elected National Assembly commenced in July 2007. Nguyen Minh Triet, Nguyen Tan Dung and Nguyen Phu Trong were all re-elected to their respective positions as President, Prime Minister and Chairman of the National Assembly Standing Committee, while Nguyen Thi Doan succeeded Truong My Hoa as Vice-President. In early August the National Assembly endorsed a cabinet reorganization, which included a reduction in the number of ministries from 26 to 22 and the appointment of Hoang Trung Hai and Nguyen Thien Nhan, both relatively young and with economic backgrounds, as additional Deputy Prime Ministers (joining Nguyen Sinh Hung, Pham Gia Khiem and Truong Vinh Trong), with Nguyen Thien Nhan also remaining Minister of Education and Training. The incumbent Ministers of National Defence, Public Security, Finance and Foreign Affairs all remained in the Cabinet, while new appointees were allocated responsibility for some of the less strategic portfolios. A reduction in the term of the 12th National Assembly from five years to four years was also approved. Meanwhile, hundreds of peasant farmers from the Mekong River Delta protested in Ho Chi Minh City in July against the seizure of their land and alleged abuse of legislation on land usage by local government officials; a smaller demonstration also took place in Hanoi. Deputy Prime Minister Truong Vinh Trong urged local leaders to conduct a swift investigation into the farmers' complaints.

Six political activists, including one French, one Thai and two US nationals, were arrested in Ho Chi Minh City in November 2007, reportedly after participating in pro-democracy discussions. The US and French citizens were members of the US-based Viet Tan (Vietnam Reform Party), which stated that its aim was to promote democratic reform in Viet Nam through peaceful means, although it was described as a terrorist organization by the Vietnamese state media. Six days later two other US nationals were detained for allegedly attempting to enter Viet Nam with a firearm; Viet Tan denied any link to them. They were freed in mid-December, as were the French citizen and one of the two US members of Viet Tan, following international demands for their release, although the others remained in detention. Meanwhile, rising inflation provoked labour unrest in late 2007 and early 2008, with large increases in food prices being of particular concern.

In July 2008 thousands of people attended the funeral of Thich Huyen Quang, the leader of the outlawed Unified Buddhist

Church of Viet Nam. The authorities, under international pressure, had permitted the ceremony to proceed despite having earlier condemned the dissident's supporters as 'extremist elements disguised as Buddhist monks'. In late September it was reported that the Government had threatened to take legal action against the Archbishop of Hanoi, Joseph Ngo Quang Kiet, and four other senior Roman Catholic priests in a dispute over two pieces of land in the capital that the Church claimed to own. Church officials asserted that the State had illegally confiscated the land in 1954 after independence from France and that they had documentation proving continuing church ownership of the land; for its part, the Government stated that the land had been officially signed over to the city authorities in 1962 and that the disputed areas were now public parks. In late March 2009 seven Roman Catholics, who had taken part in demonstrations in Hanoi in August and September in the previous year to protest against the Government's alleged confiscation of the land, received suspended prison sentences of between 12 and 15 months on charges of public order offences and damage to public property.

In mid-October 2008 a respected investigative journalist, Nguyen Viet Chien, who worked for the daily newspaper *Thanh Nien*, was sentenced to two years' imprisonment after being found guilty of 'abusing freedom and democratic rights' during his investigation into the 2006 government corruption case involving the Ministry of Transport and Communications. Another journalist, Nguyen Van Hai of the daily *Tuoi Tre*, having pleaded guilty, was sentenced to two years' re-education without detention on the same charges. Although the Vietnamese press remained generally deferential to the authorities, the Government's treatment of the two journalists prompted unprecedented criticism from the Vietnamese media on the grounds that it would discourage further action against corruption. The issue of government corruption came to the fore again in January 2009 when the former Deputy Chief of the Government Office, Vu Dinh Thuan, was charged with embezzlement and abuse of power. Thuan had been in charge of so-called Project 112, a flawed plan to computerize Viet Nam's administrative system that had been abandoned in April 2007, and, together with the project secretary, Luong Cao Son, was alleged to have misappropriated some 1,000m. dông of allocated funds.

By the end of 1976, meanwhile, Viet Nam had established diplomatic relations with many countries, including all of its South-East Asian neighbours. However, tension arose over the growing number of Vietnamese refugees (particularly ethnic Chinese) arriving in Thailand and other nearby countries. In 1979 more than 200,000 fled Viet Nam, and in July an international conference was convened in Geneva to discuss the situation. The Orderly Departure Programme, sponsored by the office of the UN High Commissioner for Refugees (UNHCR, see p. 69), whereby Viet Nam agreed to legal departures, was negotiated, and by the end of 1988 about 140,000 people had left the country in this way. However, illegal departures continued, and the increasing reluctance of Western countries to provide resettlement opportunities led to a meeting in Malaysia in March 1989, at which representatives of 30 nations were present and a comprehensive programme of action was drafted. Members of the Association of South East Asian Nations (ASEAN, see p. 194) subsequently ceased to accept refugees for automatic resettlement and planned to institute a screening procedure to distinguish genuine refugees from economic migrants. A similar procedure had been in effect since June 1988 in Hong Kong, and an agreement had been signed in November, whereby Viet Nam agreed to accept voluntary repatriation of refugees from Hong Kong, funded by UNHCR and the United Kingdom, with UN supervision to protect the returning refugees from punitive measures by the Vietnamese Government.

In June 1989 a UN-sponsored conference adopted the so-called Comprehensive Action Plan that had been drafted in March, introducing the desired screening procedures to distinguish political refugees from economic migrants (who might be forcibly repatriated if efforts to secure their voluntary return proved unsuccessful). In December the United Kingdom forcibly repatriated a group of 51 Vietnamese from Hong Kong, provoking international criticism; this policy was abandoned as a result both of opposition by the USA and of Viet Nam's refusal to accept further deportations. However, in July 1990 the USA accepted in principle the 'involuntary' repatriation of refugees classed as economic migrants who did not actively oppose deportation. In September the United Kingdom, Viet Nam and UNHCR reached an agreement whereby the Vietnamese Government would no longer refuse refugees who had been repatriated 'involuntarily'. In May 1992 the United Kingdom and Viet Nam signed an agreement providing for the compulsory repatriation of all economic migrants from Hong Kong. In 1991–95 some 66,132 Vietnamese were voluntarily repatriated, while an additional 1,562 were forcibly returned. In January 1996 ASEAN member states, including Viet Nam (see below), agreed that all Vietnamese residing in South-East Asian refugee camps (apart from those in Hong Kong) would be repatriated by the end of June of that year. (China had already indicated that all Vietnamese refugees in Hong Kong should be returned prior to the transfer of the territory to Chinese sovereignty in June 1997.) In March 1996 UNHCR announced that it would suspend funding of Vietnamese refugee camps from the end of June. In April a new initiative, proposed by the US Government in an effort to accelerate the repatriation programme, whereby refugees who returned to Viet Nam would be eligible to apply for settlement in the USA under a new screening process, was received with caution by the Vietnamese authorities. By February 1997 Malaysia, Singapore, Indonesia and Thailand had closed their camps, following the repatriation of all Vietnamese refugees from those countries, leaving Hong Kong as the only South-East Asian country with a significant number (12,000 in November 1996). In December 1996 repatriates were prohibited from engaging in any type of political activity, and from January 1997 anti-communist activists and critics of the Government were banned from returning to Viet Nam. In mid-June the main Vietnamese detention centre in Hong Kong was closed. However, the scheduled repatriation of all remaining Vietnamese (estimated at some 1,600 people qualifying as refugees and 700 non-refugees) before the end of the month was not achieved. In July 1999 Hong Kong announced that the Vietnamese who remained in the territory—estimated to number around 1,400, some classed as refugees, others as 'stateless' persons—would be given permanent residency in Hong Kong; the last remaining camp for Vietnamese refugees in Hong Kong was closed in May 2000.

Following the unrest in the Central Highlands in February 2001 (see above), many Montagnards fled over the border into Cambodia, where they were accommodated in two camps situated in the provinces of Mondol Kiri and Rotanak Kiri. By December the camps housed 805 refugees, who sought a supervised return to the Highlands, accompanied by a guarantee that they would be given permission to reoccupy their ancestral lands. In January 2002 Viet Nam and Cambodia signed a joint repatriation agreement with UNHCR, and in February 15 refugees left the camps to return to their home in Kon Tum province. Later in the same month the Vietnamese Government criticized UNHCR for the delay in the repatriation of the refugees (of whom there were now more than 1,000). It had imposed a deadline of 30 April 2002 for the completion of the repatriation process. The programme was later suspended, as UNHCR claimed that by imposing the deadline the Government was undermining the voluntary nature of returns. In March 2002 UNHCR announced its withdrawal from the agreement, owing to the frequent intimidation of both refugees and UN staff at the camps. Its decision was precipitated by an incident in which more than 400 Vietnamese had crossed the border with Cambodia and threatened inmates and staff at the Mondol Kiri camp. Following the termination of the agreement, the US Government stated that it was prepared to offer asylum to the refugees who remained in Cambodia. The Cambodian Government announced in April that, while it would authorize the resettlement of the Montagnard refugees in the USA, it planned to close down the camps housing the refugees and cease its provision of asylum within one month. In April 2003 the Cambodian Government also announced its intention to shut the refugee transit centre operated by UNHCR in Phnom-Penh as soon as the remaining refugees housed there had been resettled. Following the repression of a protest rally in the Central Highland province of Dak Lak in April 2004 (see above), there was a further influx of Montagnards into Cambodia. In January 2005 UNHCR and the Governments of Cambodia and Viet Nam signed an agreement on the resettlement to third countries or the repatriation to Viet Nam of some 750 Montagnards in Cambodia. The Vietnamese Government guaranteed that returnees would not be punished, discriminated against or prosecuted for their departure. In March the first group of 43 Montagnards who had opted for repatriation returned to Viet Nam; by that time a further 297 had decided to accept resettlement in third countries, including the USA, Finland and Canada. The Cambodian Government insisted that it would not allow the Montagnards to stay in

Cambodia. However, according to UNHCR, in October 2008 about 300 Montagnards, who had been granted refugee or asylum-seeker status, remained in Cambodia.

Relations with Kampuchea (known as Cambodia until 1976 and again from 1989) deteriorated during 1977, and in December Viet Nam launched a major offensive into eastern Kampuchea. Sporadic fighting continued, and in December 1978 Viet Nam invaded Kampuchea in support of elements opposed to the regime of the Khmers Rouges (see the chapter on Cambodia). By January 1979 the Government of Pol Pot had been overthrown and a pro-Vietnamese regime was installed. The invasion prompted much international criticism, and in February 1979 Chinese forces launched a punitive attack across the border into Viet Nam. Peace talks began in April but made little progress, and in March 1980 they were suspended by China. In March 1983 Viet Nam rejected a five-point peace plan, proposed by China, aimed at resolving the dispute over Kampuchea. In 1984 Chinese and Vietnamese troops engaged in heavy fighting, accusing each other of persistent border violations. China refused to normalize relations with Viet Nam until the withdrawal of Vietnamese troops from Kampuchea. Throughout 1986 and 1987 further armed clashes between Vietnamese and Chinese soldiers occurred on the Sino-Vietnamese border. Both sides denied responsibility for initiating the attacks. In early 1988 the tension between the two countries was exacerbated by the re-emergence of conflict over the Spratly Islands in the South China Sea, when the Vietnamese Government alleged that China had dispatched warships to the islands. (For many years the sovereignty of the islands had been contested, not only by Viet Nam and China, which engaged in military conflict over the issue in 1974, but also by the neighbouring states of Brunei, Malaysia, the Philippines and Taiwan.)

In March 1984 Viet Nam agreed in principle that it would eventually withdraw its troops from Kampuchea, and in August 1985 it was announced that all Vietnamese troops would be withdrawn by 1990. An eight-point peace plan, proposed by Kampuchean resistance leaders in March 1986 (involving the installation of a quadripartite government in Kampuchea, to be followed by UN-supervised elections), was rejected by Viet Nam. Viet Nam's urgent need of Western aid, together with increasing pressure from the USSR, prompted an announcement in May 1988 that Viet Nam would withdraw 50,000 (of an estimated total of 100,000) troops from Kampuchea by the end of the year. The Vietnamese military high command left Kampuchea in June, placing the remainder of the Vietnamese forces under Kampuchean control.

In April 1989 the Vietnamese Government and the Heng Samrin regime in Kampuchea declared that Vietnamese troops would withdraw by September even if a political settlement had not been reached, on condition that military assistance to the three other Kampuchean factions also ceased by that date. China responded that it would halt military aid to the Khmers Rouges only after a complete withdrawal of Vietnamese troops had been verified. The Vietnamese Government claimed that the withdrawal of troops had been completed by the end of September. However, the absence of a UN commission to verify the troops' departure led to claims by the Government-in-exile of Democratic Kampuchea that a number of troops remained in the country, while China, the ASEAN countries and the USA initially refused to recognize the alleged withdrawal. In July 1990 the USA finally acknowledged that all troops had been withdrawn.

In September 1990 secret negotiations took place between Viet Nam and China, during which the Vietnamese endorsed a new UN Security Council agreement to resolve the conflict in Cambodia (q.v.). It was widely believed that the Chinese had promised an improvement in Sino-Vietnamese relations in exchange for Vietnamese support for the UN plan. In October 1991 Viet Nam was a signatory to a peace agreement whereby an interim Supreme National Council was established in Cambodia, representing all four factions there, as a prelude to the holding of UN-supervised elections. The agreement allowed immediate progress towards ending Viet Nam's diplomatic and economic isolation (see below). During 1992–93 there were several massacres of civilians of Vietnamese origin living in Cambodia. In January 1995 the First Prime Minister of Cambodia, Prince Norodom Ranariddh, visited Viet Nam for discussions. In November of that year Viet Nam accused the Cambodian Government of supporting a dissident Vietnamese movement, based in Phnom-Penh. In January 1996 it was reported that Cambodian troops had opened fire in a southern border area; Cambodia subsequently claimed that Vietnamese forces had made incursions into Cambodian territory. Discussions between Vietnamese and Cambodian government officials on the border issue took place in April and May. In March 1997 Viet Nam and Cambodia signed an agreement on bilateral co-operation in combating crime and, during 2000, security officials from the two countries signed a number of agreements aimed at combating drugs-trafficking and strengthening border controls. In November 2005 Viet Nam and Cambodia signed a supplementary border treaty to an existing one concluded in 1985; under the new agreement, the demarcation of the border between the two countries was to be finalized by the end of 2008. However, owing to technical problems, such as unclear maps drawn up during colonial times, and to flooding, work on demarcation progressed slowly and the projected date for its completion was postponed until 2012. In May 2008 a new body, the Vietnam-Laos-Cambodia Economic Cooperation and Development Association, was established in Hanoi; its initial membership of 500 organizations, individuals and enterprises was expected to double by 2012.

From the mid-1970s Viet Nam developed closer relations with the USSR, and became increasingly dependent on its support. In 1990–91 the USSR substantially reduced financial assistance to Viet Nam. After the dissolution of the USSR, the Vietnamese Government pursued close relations with its successor states. In June 1994 Vo Van Kiet visited Ukraine, Kazakhstan and Russia to discuss economic and defence co-operation issues. During a visit by the Russian Minister of Foreign Affairs in July 1995, it was agreed that Russian vessels would continue to use the former Soviet naval base at Cam Ranh Bay, in central Viet Nam. In February 1997 Russia announced plans further to develop its defence links with Viet Nam, and in November of that year the Russian Prime Minister, Viktor Chernomyrdin, paid an official visit to Viet Nam; Tran Duc Luong made a reciprocal visit to Russia in August 1998. The Russian Deputy Prime Minister, Viktor Khristenko, visited Viet Nam in July 2000 to discuss Russian involvement in oil and gas development, and Viet Nam's outstanding 11,000m. rouble Soviet-era debt. Agreement on the latter was reached in September, when it was arranged that Viet Nam would repay Russia US $1,700m. over 23 years, mostly in the form of business concessions. A major concern for Russia was its continued use of the naval base at Cam Ranh Bay. Under a 1978 agreement, Russia was to have access to the facilities until 2004. In February–March 2001 the Russian President, Vladimir Putin, became the first Russian (or Soviet) Head of State to visit Viet Nam. The two countries agreed to strengthen co-operation in economic, energy, and military and defence matters, and proclaimed a new 'strategic partnership'. In May 2002 control of the naval base at Cam Ranh Bay was formally transferred to the Vietnamese Government, two years ahead of the agreed date. President Tran Duc Luong visited Ukraine in April 2000 and pledged to increase bilateral economic and political co-operation. Viet Nam also signed a military co-operation agreement with Ukraine in May. In May 2004 President Tran Duc Luong visited Russia and held talks with President Putin on bilateral relations, focusing particularly on expanding economic co-operation. Both leaders confirmed their commitment to the 'strategic partnership'. In April 2007 Russia and Viet Nam reached agreement in principle on reducing barriers to bilateral trade, and in June the two countries initialled a memorandum of understanding on Russia's bid for accession to the World Trade Organization (WTO, see p. 410), which Viet Nam had joined in January. Trade and investment were also the main areas of discussion during visits by Prime Minister Nguyen Tan Dung to Russia, the Czech Republic and Poland in September. During a state visit to Russia in October 2008, President Nguyen Minh Triet stressed that Viet Nam wished to increase co-operation with Russia in all areas, including the media, the oil and gas sectors and education; Nguyen's proposal to establish a joint Vietnamese-Russian university was welcomed by his Russian counterpart.

The collapse of communism in Eastern Europe prompted renewed efforts by Viet Nam to restore political and economic links with China. Relations between Viet Nam and China improved significantly in the second half of 1990, owing to the co-operation of the Vietnamese Government concerning Cambodia. After the conclusion of the Cambodian peace agreement in October 1991, Vo Van Kiet and Do Muoi paid an official visit to China in November, during which normal diplomatic relations were restored and agreements were concluded on trade and on border affairs, while in March 1992 further agreements were signed on the resumption of transport and communications links (severed in 1979), and on the reopening of border posts. In May

1992 Viet Nam protested to China when the latter unilaterally granted exploration rights to a US petroleum company in an area of the South China Sea regarded by Viet Nam as part of its continental shelf. Several more protests were lodged later in the year over the presence of Chinese vessels in disputed areas. In November the Chinese Premier, Li Peng, made an official visit to Viet Nam (the first visit by a Chinese head of government since 1971): new agreements on economic, scientific and cultural co-operation were signed, and the two Governments agreed to accelerate negotiations on disputed territory that had begun in the previous month. In October 1993 Viet Nam and China concluded an agreement to avoid the use of force when resolving territorial disputes. In November 1994 the two countries agreed to co-operate in seeking an early resolution to all border disputes. During an official visit by Do Muoi to China in November 1995, it was agreed that rail links between the two countries would be restored (they were subsequently reopened in February 1996). In April 1996 the state-owned petroleum company, Petrovietnam, signed a joint exploration contract with a US enterprise that covered part of the South China Sea where the Chinese Government had granted exploration rights in May 1992. In May 1996 China agreed to abide by the UN Convention on the Law of the Sea, which provided for international arbitration, but at the same time announced a new delineation of its sea border, attracting criticism from Viet Nam and other nations in the region.

In March 1997 Chinese vessels entered Vietnamese waters around the disputed Spratly Islands and were believed to be carrying out exploratory activities. China defended its actions, declaring a legitimate claim to the territory. In April China agreed to hold talks with Viet Nam over the issue; however, China withdrew the vessels before the discussions took place, stating that its operation in the area had been completed. In May China ratified the opening to traffic of a sea route between northeastern Viet Nam and China. In July Do Muoi visited China and met with President Jiang Zemin to discuss the development of bilateral relations. In October 1998 Phan Van Khai made an official visit to China, during which it was agreed that Viet Nam and China would increase efforts to reach a settlement on their various border disputes; in November, however, Viet Nam reiterated its territorial claim to the disputed Spratly Islands. In February 1999 Le Kha Phieu paid an official visit to China, and in December the Chinese Premier, Zhu Rongji, visited Viet Nam. Also in December a formal border treaty was signed by Viet Nam and China. Vietnamese leaders travelled to China in June 2000 to attend an ideological symposium on methods of introducing market reforms without incurring any loss of political control. The visit was regarded as a major improvement in bilateral relations, and was followed by a second symposium in Hanoi in November. The two countries also made further progress in delineating their mutual land border, which took effect from July 2000, and finalized their border in the Gulf of Tonkin in late December, the latter agreement demarcating their economic and fishing zones. Chinese military delegations visited Viet Nam in July 2000 and February 2001 to enhance military co-operation, and President Tran Duc Luong visited China in December 2000 and 2001. In February 2002 Chinese President Jiang Zemin paid an official visit to Viet Nam, his second since the restoration of normal bilateral relations in 1991. His visit coincided with campaigns mounted by several dissidents expressing concern over the agreements that had been signed to demarcate the Sino-Vietnamese border. An ongoing dispute over fishing rights in the Gulf of Tonkin prevented the ratification of any agreement to delineate the shared maritime boundary. During the Chinese President's visit modest agreements on technical and economic co-operation were signed, and the framework was agreed for a Chinese loan of US $12m. to Viet Nam. In April 2002 it was reported that the two countries had begun demarcating their land border. In November of that year, following an ASEAN summit meeting attended by China, a declaration was issued outlining a code of conduct to be observed by those countries contesting the Spratly Islands. It was hoped that the agreement would end Viet Nam's dispute with China over the issue. However, China strongly opposed Viet Nam's decision, in March 2004, to allow tourists to visit the Spratly Islands, claiming that the tours infringed its territorial sovereignty.

Viet Nam and China accelerated efforts to delineate their border in early 2005, and an 11th round of talks was held on the issue in Hanoi in February and March. In October Viet Nam and China agreed to conduct joint military patrols of the Gulf of Tonkin. Later that month Chinese President Hu Jintao made a three-day state visit to Viet Nam, during which he met with President Tran Duc Luong and General Secretary of the Central Committee of the Communist Party Nong Duc Manh. Bilateral relations were discussed, as were issues of regional and international concern, and both countries pledged to work together to promote mutual trust and encourage further bilateral co-operation. President Nguyen Minh Triet visited China in May 2007, holding talks with Hu Jintao and Premier Wen Jiabao. Several agreements on co-operation were signed during the visit, including nine economic accords. Notably, a joint working group was established to formulate a five-year plan for the further development of economic and trade co-operation between Viet Nam and China. Border issues were also addressed, with Presidents Nguyen and Hu pledging to complete the demarcation of the 1,350-km land border in 2008 and to accelerate negotiations on the delineation of boundaries in the Gulf of Tonkin. However, the territorial dispute in the South China Sea continued to provoke tensions, and in July 2007 a Chinese naval vessel fired on Vietnamese fishing boats near the Spratly Islands, sinking one boat; one fisherman died in the incident and several others were injured. In late November, moreover, Viet Nam protested after China conducted naval exercises near the Paracel Islands, and in the following month Vietnamese students demonstrated outside China's embassy in Hanoi and its consulate in Ho Chi Minh City, following reports that China was to create a new municipality incorporating the Spratly and Paracel Islands. In July 2008 Viet Nam announced that it intended to continue with a joint petroleum exploration project with ExxonMobil in disputed waters in the South China Sea, despite a warning from China to the US energy company to cancel the agreement. At the end of December it was reported that the Chinese and Vietnamese Governments, following four days of negotiations in Hanoi, had completed the demarcation of the land border as scheduled.

In the late 1990s Viet Nam developed closer links with India, ostensibly because of mutual concerns about China. The Indian Minister of Defence visited Viet Nam in March 2000 and signed a wide-ranging defence agreement that would allow Viet Nam to train the Indian army in jungle warfare and counter-insurgency methods, and India to assist in the modernization of the Vietnamese military. The two countries also agreed to take action to combat piracy in the South China Sea. The Indian Minister of External Affairs, Jaswant Singh, and Prime Minister Atal Bihari Vajpayee made separate visits to Viet Nam in November 2000 and January 2001 respectively and agreed to co-ordinate their positions in the Non-Aligned Movement (NAM), South-South Co-operation and regional forums. India's Oil and Natural Gas Company became an investor in Viet Nam's Nam Con Son gas field in 2000, and India pledged some US $238m. of investment in the Vietnamese petroleum and gas industries. In September 2001 the Minister of Foreign Affairs, Nguyen Dy Nien, visited India, and in March 2002 Vice-President Nguyen Thi Binh also visited the country to discuss the possibility of closer bilateral co-operation. Relations were further strengthened in July 2007 by a state visit to India by Prime Minister Nguyen Tan Dung, during which a joint declaration was signed on the establishment of a 'strategic partnership' between India and Viet Nam, covering bilateral co-operation in the areas of politics, the economy, security, defence, culture, science and technology. In March 2008 the Vietnamese Minister of Public Security, Le Hong Anh, and the Indian Minister of Home Affairs, Shivraj Patil, signed a memorandum of understanding on bilateral co-operation in combating international terrorism and drugs-trafficking. The Indian President, Pratibha Devisingh Patil, held talks with President Nguyen regarding the expansion of economic relations between the two countries in November 2008 during her first official visit to Viet Nam.

From 1984 Viet Nam indicated that it would welcome a return to normal diplomatic relations with the USA, but the latter rejected any re-establishment of relations until agreements were made concerning the return to the USA of the remains of US soldiers 'missing in action' (MIA) from Viet Nam, and the proposed resettlement in the USA of some 10,000 Vietnamese 'political prisoners'. A number of senior US officials visited Hanoi during 1985 and 1986 for discussions about missing soldiers (estimated to total 1,797), and Viet Nam arranged for the return of some of the remains. In September 1987 the Vietnamese Government agreed to investigate the fate of some 70 soldiers who were believed to have been captured alive, while the US Government, in turn, agreed to facilitate humanitarian aid for Viet Nam from US charities and private groups, which had hitherto been illegal. In July 1988 Viet Nam agreed in principle to the resettlement of former political detainees in the USA or elsewhere. In early 1991 a US representative was stationed in Hanoi to supervise inquiries into MIA, the first official US presence in Viet Nam since 1975. In April 1991 the USA proposed a four-stage programme for the resumption of normal diplomatic relations with Viet Nam, conditional on Vietnamese co-operation in reaching a diplomatic settlement in Cambodia and in accounting for the remaining MIA. Following the conclusion of the peace agreement on Cambodia in October, Viet Nam made a plea for the removal of the US economic embargo, and in November discussions on the establishment of normal trade relations began. In early 1992 the US Government agreed to provide humanitarian aid for Viet Nam, but refused to end the economic embargo, reiterating that relations would not fully return to normal until after the UN-supervised elections in Cambodia, due to take place in early 1993. The embargo was renewed for another year in September 1992, although in December the US Government announced that US companies would now be allowed to open offices and sign contracts in Viet Nam, in anticipation of a future removal of the embargo. In July 1993 the new administration of President Bill Clinton revoked the US veto on assistance from the IMF and the World Bank for Viet Nam. In September the USA permitted US companies to take part in projects in Viet Nam that were financed by international aid agencies. The trade embargo was finally removed in February 1994.

In January 1995 Viet Nam and the USA signed an agreement that permitted the two countries to establish liaison offices in each other's capitals (these were opened immediately), and which resolved a long-standing dispute concerning former US diplomatic properties seized by the Vietnamese authorities in 1975. The establishment of full diplomatic relations was announced in July 1995. In May 1996 Clinton formally ended Viet Nam's official classification as a combat zone. In March 1997 military relations were established between the two countries. In April Douglas Peterson was appointed as the first US ambassador to Viet Nam, and in May Le Van Bang was formally appointed the first Vietnamese ambassador to the USA. In June Madeleine Albright became the first US Secretary of State to visit the country since the end of the Viet Nam war. During a visit to Washington, DC, by the Vietnamese Minister of Planning and Investment, an agreement was signed to promote greater economic co-operation. This was facilitated in March 1998, when Clinton signed a waiver to the 'Jackson-Vanik amendment' to 1974 US trade legislation, which restricted trade with communist countries. (In August 1999 the US House of Representatives voted in favour of an extension of the waiver of the amendment for Viet Nam.) In September 1998 the Vietnamese Deputy Prime Minister and Minister of Foreign Affairs, Nguyen Manh Cam, made an official visit to the USA. In July 1999 Viet Nam and the USA reached agreement in principle on the establishment of normal trade relations. Madeleine Albright made another official visit to Viet Nam in September. In March 2000 the US Secretary of Defense, William Cohen, made the first visit to Viet Nam by a US Secretary of Defense since the end of the Viet Nam war.

Although in early 2000 the US Government continued to refuse to acknowledge the responsibility of the chemical defoliant Agent Orange, sprayed in large quantities over areas of Viet Nam by the USA during the Viet Nam war, for widespread health problems (including birth defects) among the Vietnamese, Cohen, during his visit in March, reportedly indicated that the US Government would be willing to conduct joint research with the Vietnamese Government into the effects of the chemical. In May the US House of Representatives approved a resolution calling for the release of all political and religious prisoners in Viet Nam, a motion that was criticized as 'impudent interference' by Viet Nam. A landmark bilateral trade agreement between the USA and Viet Nam was signed in Washington, DC, in July 2000, paving the way for an increase in exports to, and investment from, the USA. The agreement was subject to an annual review by the US Congress. US President Bill Clinton made a highly significant visit to Viet Nam in November, the first since a brief stop-over by Richard Nixon in 1969. Although warmly received by the Vietnamese people, Clinton's calls for greater freedoms were rebuffed by General Secretary Le Kha Phieu, who defended the socialist system. In March 2001 Viet Nam accused US-based groups of fomenting the recent unrest in the Central Highlands (see above). In April a helicopter carrying nine Vietnamese and seven US citizens, searching for the remains of MIA, crashed in the highlands, killing all on board. Some 1,498 US servicemen and 300,000 Vietnamese remained unaccounted for in Viet Nam.

Following the September 2001 attacks on the USA (see the chapter on the USA) the Vietnamese Government expressed its support for the US-led 'war on terror'. In October the severe penalty imposed on the dissident Roman Catholic priest Father Nguyen Van Ly (see above) accelerated the passage of the Viet Nam Human Rights Act through the US House of Representatives. The act was intended to make US non-humanitarian aid to Viet Nam conditional upon the improvement of its human rights record, thus antagonizing the Vietnamese Government, but was subsequently blocked and never voted on in the Senate. (The act was reintroduced and approved again by the US House of Representatives in July 2004, but subsequently stalled in the Senate. The House of Representatives adopted another version of the act in September 2007.) In November 2001 the National Assembly finally ratified the bilateral trade agreement, marking the complete restoration of normal relations between the two countries. In March 2002 Vietnamese and US scientists attended an unprecedented joint conference in Hanoi, at which the effects of Agent Orange were discussed. As a result, the two countries formally agreed to conduct joint research into the effects of the defoliant. However, relations with the USA threatened to deteriorate once more when the US Government expressed its concern for the safety of refugees returning to the Central Highlands from Cambodia. In March 2002, following the collapse of Viet Nam's agreement with UNHCR, the USA offered asylum to those refugees who remained in Cambodia. In the same month relations were further strained when the US Government issued a critical report on Viet Nam's human rights record.

In early 2003 the Vietnamese Government condemned the US-led campaign to oust the regime of Saddam Hussain in Iraq. However, in November relations improved when Minister of National Defence Lt-Gen. Pham Can Tra visited Washington, DC, and held talks with US Secretary of Defense Donald Rumsfeld. In the same month a US frigate spent four days in the port of Ho Chi Minh City, the first visit to Viet Nam by a US warship since the end of the Viet Nam war in 1975. In December 2003 an aviation agreement was signed with the USA, enabling direct flights between the two countries for the first time; the first US flight arrived in Ho Chi Minh City in December 2004. In February 2004, during a visit to the country, Adm. Thomas Fargo, head of the US Pacific Command, reportedly became the first foreign official to visit the naval base at Da Nang. Meanwhile, an independent organization, the Vietnam Association for Victims of Agent Orange, submitted a lawsuit to the US Federal Court, on behalf of three Vietnamese people who had been affected by the defoliant, against the US companies that were responsible for its manufacture. The lawsuit was the first of its kind to have been filed. In March 2005, however, the US Federal Court dismissed the lawsuit, ruling that there was no legal basis for the claims of the plaintiffs. In February 2008 an appeal against the judgment was rejected. The Vietnam Association for Victims of Agent Orange condemned the decision and announced its intention to file an appeal with the US Supreme Court.

In September 2004 the US Secretary of State designated Viet Nam as a 'country of particular concern' under the International Religious Freedom Act for particularly severe violations of religious freedom. (Viet Nam was removed from the list in November 2006.) The Department of State again urged the Vietnamese Government to release prisoners detained for their religious beliefs and to reopen churches closed in the Central Highlands. The designation was denounced by the Vietnamese Government, which lodged an official protest with the US Government. In June 2005 Prime Minister Phan Van Khai, accompanied by a delegation of government officials, made an official state visit to the USA. He thus became the most senior Vietnamese official to visit the USA since the end of the Viet Nam war three decades previously. During his visit, he met with US President George W. Bush. Among the issues discussed were Viet Nam's application to join the WTO, human rights, religious freedom and corporate development. In May 2006 the two countries signed a bilateral trade agreement, marking the final stage of Viet Nam's accession to the WTO. US Secretary of Defense Rumsfeld's visit to Viet Nam in June was followed by a visit from President Bush in November. In December the US Congress approved legislation permitting 'permanent normal trade relations' with Viet Nam. It appeared that progress was being made with regard to the ongoing Agent Orange issue when the Bush Administration approved funding of US $400,000 towards a $1m. study into the decontamination of its former base in Da Nang in February 2007. In June Nguyen Minh Triet became the first Vietnamese Head of State to visit the USA since the end of the Viet Nam war. Nguyen held talks with President Bush during the visit, and several bilateral economic agreements were signed, including a Trade and Investment Framework Agreement (TIFA). However, while the two Presidents were meeting, hundreds of protesters, including many Vietnamese exiles, demanded the release of Vietnamese political prisoners. The first ministerial-level meeting on the TIFA took place in Washington, DC, in December, focusing on Viet Nam's implementation of its WTO commitments, following its accession to that organization in January, as well as measures to expand bilateral trade and investment ties. Bilateral trade between Viet Nam and the USA exceeded $12,000m. in 2007, an increase of 30% over the previous year. In June 2008 Prime Minister Nguyen Tan Dung visited the USA, where he had discussions with President Bush in the fourth bilateral meeting between Vietnamese and US leaders in as many years.

In October 1990 the European Community (now the European Union—EU, see p. 255) announced the restoration of diplomatic relations with Viet Nam. In October 1991 a group of industrialized countries, led by France, agreed to assist Viet Nam in paying its arrears to the IMF, thereby enabling it to qualify for future IMF loans (which nevertheless remained dependent on the approval of the USA, as the IMF's principal vote-holder). In February 1993 President Mitterrand of France made an official visit to Viet Nam (the first Western Head of State to do so since the country's reunification). France's Geopetrol oil company formed part of a consortium to develop Vietnamese offshore oil and gas deposits. In October 2002 President Tran Duc Luong paid the first visit to France by a Vietnamese leader since the establishment of diplomatic relations with France in 1973. President Jacques Chirac of France made an official visit to Viet Nam in early October 2004, attending the fifth biennial Asia-Europe Meeting, which took place in Hanoi. Several agreements on bilateral co-operation were signed during the visit, and President Chirac pledged his country's support for Viet Nam's bid to join the WTO. Prime Minister Nguyen Tan Dung visited Germany, Ireland and the United Kingdom in March 2008, agreeing with his counterparts in the three countries to strengthen bilateral co-operation in a range of areas. In June the first session of negotiations on a Partnership and Co-operation Agreement (PCA) between Viet Nam and the EU took place in Brussels. The PCA was a comprehensive agreement covering a broad range of areas for dialogue and co-operation in the political, economic, development, social and cultural fields.

In January 1992 a Japanese government mission visited Viet Nam to negotiate the repayment of Vietnamese debts, and in November Japan (which—although a principal trading partner—had hitherto imposed a ban on official economic co-operation) began to provide financial assistance to Viet Nam. In March 1999 Prime Minister Phan Van Khai made an official visit to Japan. During 2000 Viet Nam and Japan also strengthened their defence links, with the aim of promoting regional security. In June 2001 Phan Van Khai paid a further visit to Japan. In May 2008 Japan signed an agreement to help Viet Nam to build its first nuclear power plant; construction work was expected to commence in 2015.

The Cambodian peace agreement of 1991 allowed Viet Nam to initiate closer relations with ASEAN member states: Vo Van Kiet visited Indonesia, Thailand and Singapore in October and November 1991 and Malaysia, Brunei and the Philippines in early 1992; agreements on economic co-operation were concluded with these countries, including guarantees of protection for future investment by them in Viet Nam. In July 1992 Viet Nam signed the ASEAN agreement (of 1976) on regional amity and co-operation, and in July 1995 became a full member of the organization. In September 1992 an agreement was signed with Singapore on the mutual provision of 'most-favoured nation' trading status. In April 1995 Viet Nam, Thailand, Laos and Cambodia signed an agreement providing for the establishment of the Mekong River Commission (see p. 427), which was to co-ordinate the sustainable development of the resources of the Lower Mekong River basin. In October 1997 Viet Nam and Thailand reached an agreement to demarcate their maritime boundary, following a series of incidents between Vietnamese and Thai fishing vessels. In December 1998 Viet Nam hosted the sixth summit meeting of the heads of state and government of the ASEAN grouping of countries. During 2000 Viet Nam reaffirmed sovereignty over the Spratly and Paracel Islands, but reassured ASEAN that it was committed to a peaceful solution to the territorial dispute through multilateral negotiations. It was hoped that the declaration of November 2002, which established a code of conduct to be adhered to by the claimants of the islands, would provide such a solution. Vietnamese and Laotian officials held several meetings during the course of 2000, and Viet Nam provided assistance to Laos in its fight against ethnic Hmong rebels. In November 2001 President Tran Duc Long held talks with President Gloria Macapagal Arroyo while on an official visit to the Philippines. The two countries agreed to the enhancement of economic relations and to co-operation in trade, investment and tourism. In February 2002 the Prime Minister met with the Prime Ministers of Cambodia and of Laos in Ho Chi Minh City. The three countries agreed to promote co-operation in the development of tourism and infrastructure within the 'development triangle'. In February 2004 the first joint meeting of the Cabinets of Viet Nam and Thailand took place. During the meeting, several co-operation agreements were signed concerning various social and economic issues. Prime Minister Phan Van Khai paid a four-day visit to Singapore (the largest foreign investor in Viet Nam) in March, during which a comprehensive co-operation framework document was signed. Following the announcement also in March that Viet Nam intended to allow tourists to begin visiting the Spratly Islands, the first tour took place in April, despite opposition from other claimants to the disputed islands. In May Viet Nam announced that it was renovating a disused runway on one of the islands to further its tourism plans. As part of efforts to strengthen relations with other ASEAN member states, particularly in the area of economic co-operation, Vietnamese Prime Minister Nguyen Tan Dung visited Brunei, Indonesia, Myanmar, the Philippines and Singapore in August 2007. In February 2008 Viet Nam, Cambodia and Laos concluded a draft agreement on defining the intersection point of their borders. In the following month Viet Nam ratified the new ASEAN Charter, which codified the principles and purposes of the Association and had been signed in November 2007 at the 13th summit meeting in Singapore. Viet Nam initially opposed the inclusion of a human rights mechanism in the Charter, but later agreed to the provision.

In mid-November 1997 Viet Nam hosted the seventh summit meeting of francophone states (La Francophonie), which was attended by representatives of 49 countries. In April 2000 President Tran Duc Luong attended the Group of 77 (G-77) South Summit meeting of developing countries, held in Havana, Cuba.

Viet Nam has sought to expand its participation in international organizations in recent years. Two significant achievements were made in this regard in 2007: accession to the WTO in January; and in October election as a non-permanent member of the UN Security Council for 2008–09.

Government

The 1992 Constitution declares the supremacy of the Communist Party. Legislative power is vested in the National Assembly, which is elected for a four-year term by universal adult suffrage and, from 2007, had 493 members. The President, elected by the National Assembly from among its members, is the Head of State and Commander-in-Chief of the armed forces. The President appoints a Prime Minister (from among the members of the National Assembly, and subject to their approval), who forms a government (again, subject to ratification by the National Assembly). The country is divided into provinces and municipalities, which are subordinate to the central government. Local government is entrusted to locally elected People's Councils.

Defence

As assessed at November 2008, the active ('Main Force') armed forces of Viet Nam had an estimated total strength of 455,000: an estimated 412,000 in the army, an estimated 13,000 in the navy, and 30,000 in the air and air defence forces. Military service is compulsory and usually lasts for two years. Paramilitary forces number in excess of 40,000 and include the urban People's Self-Defence Force and the rural People's Militia. The defence budget for 2007 was estimated at US $3,730m.

Economic Affairs

In 2007, according to estimates by the World Bank, Viet Nam's gross national income (GNI), measured at average 2005–07 prices, was US $67,236m., equivalent to $790 per head (or $2,550 per head on an international purchasing-power parity basis). During 2000–07, it was estimated, the population increased at an average annual rate of 1.3%, while gross domestic product (GDP) per head increased, in real terms, by an average of 6.3% per year. Overall GDP increased, in real terms, at an average annual rate of 7.7% in 2000–07. According to the Asian Development Bank (ADB), GDP grew by 8.5% in 2007 and by 6.2% in 2008.

Agriculture (including forestry and fishing) contributed an estimated 22.1% of GDP in 2008 and engaged 52.6% of the employed labour force in the same year. The staple crop is rice, which also provided 3.3% of total export earnings in 2007. In addition, Viet Nam is a major producer of coffee; this commodity accounted for 4.2% of export revenue in 2007. Other important cash crops include sugar cane, groundnuts, cashew nuts, rubber, tea and cotton. According to the ADB, exports of wood and wood products increased from US $1,943m. in 2006 to $2,404m. in 2007, when they accounted for 5.3% of total export earnings. Livestock-rearing and fishing are also important. In 2007 marine products accounted for some 8.3% of export revenues. According to figures from the ADB, agricultural GDP increased at an average annual rate of 3.7% in 2000–07; the sector's GDP expanded by 3.8% in 2008.

In 2008 industry (comprising manufacturing, mining and quarrying, construction and utilities) contributed an estimated 39.7% of GDP. In the same year, the industrial sector engaged an estimated 20.8% of the labour force. According to figures from the ADB, industrial GDP increased at an average annual rate of 10.3% in 2000–07. The sector's GDP expanded by 6.3% in 2008.

In 2007 mining and quarrying contributed an estimated 9.8% of GDP. In 2008 the mining sector engaged an estimated 1.0% of the labour force. Viet Nam's principal mineral exports are petroleum and coal. Tin, zinc, iron, antimony, chromium, natural phosphates, bauxite and gold are also mined. Significant reserves of offshore natural gas were discovered in 1993. In 2006 exports of crude petroleum accounted for 24.4% of total merchandise exports. According to figures from the ADB, mining GDP increased at an average annual rate of 2.9% in 2000–07. However, mining GDP fell by 2.0% in 2007.

Manufacturing contributed an estimated 21.4% of GDP in 2007, and, according to preliminary figures, accounted for 14.0% of employment in 2008. The main manufacturing sectors in 2000, measured by gross value of output, included food-processing, cigarettes and tobacco, textiles, chemicals and electrical goods. According to the ADB, the value of textile exports reached US $7,750m. in 2007, when they accounted for 16.0% of total export revenue. Manufacturing GDP increased at an average annual rate of 11.9% in 2000–07. The sector's GDP expanded by 12.8% in 2007.

Energy is derived principally from hydroelectric power, which in 2005 accounted for 40.1% of the total electricity produced, natural gas (38.5%), coal (16.7%) and petroleum (4.6%). In 2006 fuel imports accounted for 14.5% of the value of total merchandise imports. Imports of mineral fuels accounted for 14.9% of total imports in 2006. In February 2009 Viet Nam's first petroleum refinery at Dung Quat became operational and was expected to reach full capacity by August of that year. Viet Nam operates a 500-kW nuclear research reactor at Da Lat, in the Central Highlands, with Russian assistance. In February 2006 the Government announced its intention to construct a 2,000-MW nuclear power plant by 2020.

The services sector contributed an estimated 38.2% of GDP in 2008 and employed 26.5% of the labour force. Tourism is an important source of foreign exchange; receipts from tourism totalled US $3,200m. in 2006. In 2007 around 4.2m. foreign tourists visited Viet Nam. According to figures from the ADB, the GDP of the services sector increased by an average of 7.4% per year in 2000–07. The sector's GDP rose by 7.2% in 2008.

In 2007 Viet Nam recorded a visible trade deficit of US $10,360m. The deficit on the current account of the balance of payments in that year was an estimated $6,992m. In 2007, according to the ADB, the People's Republic of China was Viet Nam's principal source of imports, supplying 20.4% of total imports; other major sources were Singapore (11.8%), Japan (9.6%) and the Republic of Korea (7.7%). The principal market for exports in that year was the USA (22.8%); other important purchasers were Japan (11.4%) and China (7.5%). The principal exports in 2006 were mineral fuels (24.4%), food and live animals and machinery and transport equipment. In 2006 the principal imports were basic manufactures (27.1%), machinery and transport equipment, and mineral fuels.

In 2006 the budgetary deficit was recorded at 3,400,000m. dông. In 2007 the budgetary deficit was forecast at some 38,800,000m. dông. The fiscal deficit was projected to be equivalent to 7.9% of GDP in that year. Viet Nam's total external debt was estimated by the ADB at US $27,240m. in 2008. In that year the cost of servicing the debt was equivalent to 6.5% of the value of exports of goods and services. The annual rate of inflation averaged 5.5% in 2000–07. According to the ADB, the rate of inflation reached 23.0% in 2008. In that year an estimated 4.7% of the labour force were unemployed.

Viet Nam is a member of the Asian Development Bank (ADB, see p. 191), the Association of South East Asian Nations (ASEAN, see p. 194), the Asia-Pacific Economic Co-operation (APEC, see p. 185), the UN Economic and Social Commission for Asia and the Pacific (ESCAP, see p. 36) and the Mekong River Commission (see p. 427). Viet Nam also joined the ASEAN Free Trade Area (AFTA) in 1996 and was granted until 2003 to comply with the requisite tariff reductions (to between 0% and 5%). The area was formally established on 1 January 2002. Viet Nam joined the World Trade Organization (WTO, see p. 410) in January 2007.

From 1990 the process of *doi moi* (renovation) aimed to transform Viet Nam's centralized economy to a market-orientated system. Agricultural production was stimulated by the removal of price controls, by a new system of land tenure and by the relaxation of the state monopoly on rice exports; by the mid-1990s Viet Nam had become one of the world's principal rice exporters. During 2001–05 about 3,590 of a total of 5,655 state enterprises were restructured, 2,347 of which were subject to 'equitization' (privatization). The 2006–11 socio-economic development plan, which envisaged average annual GDP growth of 7.5%–8.0%, included measures to stimulate the private sector. Limits on foreign ownership in firms were to be relaxed. Viet Nam's accession to the WTO in January 2007 further improved the country's investment potential. Foreign direct investment was estimated to have risen from US $6,550m. in 2007 to about $8,000m. in 2008. The ADB forecast GDP growth of 4.5% in 2009. Moreover, the imposition in January 2008 of a new labour law in the People's Republic of China (enforcing a higher minimum wage in that country) was expected to improve the competitiveness of Viet Nam's export sectors, where lower salaries prevailed. Mounting inflation during the first half of 2008, together with the onset of the international banking crisis in September, constrained growth during that year. Inflationary pressures eased with the sharp decline in global commodity prices in the latter half of 2008. However, the deterioration of economic conditions in Viet Nam's major external markets was likely to curb growth in 2009. Various measures to stimulate domestic consumption and maintain links between businesses and credit markets were implemented. In early 2008, with the aim of bolstering export-orientated industries, the exchange rate was realigned, thereby allowing for the depreciation of the dông. While growing international turmoil presented the Vietnamese economy with a number of obstacles, the country's long-term prospects were favourable, owing partly to the Government's strong commitment to continue with its programme of privatization.

Education

Primary education, which is compulsory, begins at six years of age and lasts for five years. Secondary education, beginning at the age of 11, lasts for seven years, comprising a first cycle of four years and a second cycle of three years. In 2004/05 total pre-primary enrolment included 61% of children in the relevant age-group. In the same year enrolment within primary education included 93% of children in the relevant age-group (males 96%; females 90%), while secondary enrolment included 75% of the relevant age-group (males 76%, females 94%). In 2007/08 there were 10,822 pre-primary institutions, 15,441 primary schools and 12,098 secondary schools, as well as 322 higher education institutions at which over 1.5m. students were enrolled. In 1989 Viet Nam's first private college since 1954 was opened in Hanoi; Thang Long College was to cater for university students. Of total planned budgetary expenditure by the central Government in 2007, 38,100,000m. dông (11.9%) was allocated to education.

Public Holidays

2009: 1 January (New Year's Day), 26–27 January* (Tet, lunar new year), 3 February (Founding of the Communist Party), 30 April (Liberation of Saigon), 1 May (May Day), 2 September (National Day).

2010: 1 January (New Year's Day), 3 February (Founding of the Communist Party), 7–9 February* (Tet, lunar new year), 30 April (Liberation of Saigon), 1 May (May Day), 2 September (National Day).

*Varies according to the lunar calendar.

Weights and Measures

The metric system is in force.

VIET NAM

Statistical Survey

Statistical Survey

Sources (unless otherwise stated): General Statistics Office of Viet Nam, 2 Hoang Van Thu, Ba Dinh District, Hanoi; tel. (4) 7332997; e-mail banbientap@gso.gov.vn; internet www.gso.gov.vn; Communist Party of Viet Nam, 1 Hoang Van Thu, Hanoi; e-mail cpv@hn.vnn.vn; internet www.cpv.org.vn.

Area and Population

AREA, POPULATION AND DENSITY

Area (sq km)	331,212*
Population (census results)	
1 April 1989	64,411,713
1 April 1999	
Males	37,469,117
Females	38,854,056
Total	76,323,173
Population (official estimates of annual averages)	
2006	84,136,800
2007	85,171,700
2008	86,210,800†
Density (per sq km) at 2008	260.3

* 127,881 sq miles.
† Preliminary.

ADMINISTRATIVE DIVISIONS
(2008, annual averages, preliminary figures)

	Area (sq km)	Population ('000)	Density (per sq km)
Red River Delta	14,950.3	18,545.2	934
Hanoi	3,349.2	6,116.2	1,826
Vinh Phuc	1,231.6	1,014.5	824
Bac Ninh	823.1	1,022.5	1,242
Hai Duong	1,652.8	1,745.3	1,056
Haiphong	1,520.7	1,845.9	1,214
Hung Yen	923.5	1,167.1	1,264
Thai Binh	1,546.5	1,872.9	1,211
Ha Nam	859.7	834.1	970
Nam Dinh	1,650.8	1,990.4	1,206
Ninh Binh	1,392.4	936.3	672
North East	64,025.2	9,652.3	151
Ha Giang	7,945.8	705.1	89
Cao Bang	6,724.6	528.1	79
Bac Kan	4,868.4	308.9	63
Tuyen Quang	5,870.4	746.9	127
Lao Cai	6,383.9	602.3	94
Yen Bai	6,899.5	750.2	109
Thai Nguyen	3,546.6	1,149.1	324
Lang Son	8,331.2	759.0	91
Quang Ninh	6,099.0	1,109.6	182
Bac Giang	3,827.4	1,628.4	425
Phu Tho	3,528.4	1,364.7	387
North West	37,446.0	2,665.1	71
Dien Bien	9,562.9	475.6	50
Lai Chau	9,112.3	335.3	37
Son La	14,174.4	1,036.5	73
Hoa Binh	4,596.4	817.7	178
North Central Coast	51,551.9	10,795.1	209
Thanh Hoa	11,136.3	3,712.5	333
Nghe An	16,498.5	3,131.0	190
Ha Tinh	6,026.5	1,307.3	217
Quand Binh	8,065.2	857.8	106
Quang Tri	4,760.1	635.7	134
Thua Thien-Hué	5,065.3	1,150.8	227
South Central Coast	33,166.1	7,253.2	219
Da Nang	1,257.3	818.3	651
Quang Nam	10,438.3	1,492.1	143
Quang Ngai	5,152.7	1,302.6	253
Binh Dinh	6,039.6	1,592.6	264
Phu Yen	5,060.6	885.5	175
Khanh Hoa	5,217.6	1,162.1	223
Central Highlands	54,659.6	5,004.2	92
Kon Tum	9,690.5	401.5	41
Gia Lai	15,536.9	1,188.5	76
Dak Lak	13,139.2	1,777.0	135
Dak Nong	6,516.9	431.0	66
Lam Dong	9,776.1	1,206.2	123
South East	34,807.8	14,600.7	419
Ninh Thuan	3,363.1	583.4	173
Binh Thuan	7,836.9	1,188.5	152
Binh Phuoc	6,883.5	835.3	121

—continued	Area (sq km)	Population ('000)	Density (per sq km)
Tay Ninh	4,035.9	1,058.5	262
Binh Duong	2,696.2	1,072.0	398
Dong Nai	5,903.9	2,290.2	388
Ba Ria-Vung Tau	1,989.6	961.2	483
Ho Chi Minh City	2,098.7	6,611.6	3,150
Mekong River Delta	40,604.7	17,695.0	436
Long An	4,493.8	1,438.8	320
Tien Giang	2,484.2	1,742.1	701
Ben Tre	2,360.2	1,360.3	576
Tra Vinh	2,295.1	1,062.0	463
Vinh Long	1,479.1	1,069.1	723
Dong Thap	3,376.4	1,682.7	498
An Giang	3,536.8	2,250.6	636
Kien Giang	6,348.3	1,727.6	272
Can Tho	1,401.6	1,171.1	836
Hau Giang	1,601.1	808.5	505
Soc Trang	3,312.3	1,301.7	393
Bac Lieu	2,584.1	829.3	321
Ca Mau	5,331.7	1,251.2	235
Total	**331,211.6**	**86,210.8**	**260**

PRINCIPAL TOWNS
(excl. suburbs, estimated population at mid-1992)

Ho Chi Minh City (formerly Saigon)	3,015,743*	Nam Dinh		171,699
Hanoi (capital)	1,073,760	Qui Nhon		163,385
Haiphong	783,133	Vung Tau		145,145
Da Nang	382,674	Rach Gia		141,132
Buon Ma Thuot	282,095	Long Xuyen		132,681
Nha Trang	221,331	Thai Nguyen		127,643
Hué	219,149	Hong Gai		127,484
Can Tho	215,587	Vinh		112,455
Cam Pha	209,086			

* Including Cholon.

Source: UN, *Demographic Yearbook*.

Mid-2007 ('000, incl. suburbs, UN estimates): Ho Chi Minh City 5,723; Hanoi 4,378; Haiphong 2,129 (Source: UN, *World Urbanization Prospects: The 2007 Revision*).

BIRTHS AND DEATHS
(annual averages, UN estimates)

	1990–95	1995–2000	2000–05
Birth rate (per 1,000)	28.5	21.3	19.1
Death rate (per 1,000)	6.8	5.7	5.3

Source: UN, *World Population Prospects: The 2008 Revision*.

Life expectancy (years at birth, WHO estimates): 71.9 (males 69.4; females 74.7) in 2006 (Source: WHO, *World Health Statistics*).

VIET NAM

EMPLOYMENT
('000 persons aged 15 years and over, averages at mid-year)

	2006	2007	2008*
Agriculture, hunting and forestry	22,439.3	22,177.4	21,950.4
Fishing	1,555.5	1,634.5	1,684.3
Mining and quarrying	370.0	397.5	431.2
Manufacturing	5,655.8	5,963.4	6,306.2
Power and utilities	173.4	197.0	224.6
Construction	2,136.5	2,267.8	2,394.0
Wholesale and retail trade; repair of motor vehicles, motor cycles and personal and household goods	5,114.0	5,291.9	5,371.9
Hotels and restaurants	783.3	813.9	830.9
Transport, storage and communications	1,213.8	1,217.4	1,221.7
Financial intermediation	182.8	209.9	220.1
Scientific activities and technology	26.0	26.9	26.9
Real estate, renting and business activities	178.7	216.0	251.5
Public administration and defence; compulsory social security	716.9	793.2	866.9
Education and training	1,300.2	1,356.7	1,401.4
Health and social work	372.7	384.3	399.8
Recreational, cultural and sporting activities	134.3	136.4	134.7
Activities of the Communist Party and of membership organizations	171.5	192.9	220.1
Community, social and personal service activities and private household with employed persons	814.2	896.7	979.2
Total employed	43,338.9	44,173.8	44,915.8

* Preliminary figures.

Unemployed (million persons): 1.1 in 2005; 1.0 in 2006; 0.9 in 2007 (Source: Asian Development Bank).

Health and Welfare

KEY INDICATORS

Total fertility rate (children per woman, 2006)	2.2
Under-5 mortality rate (per 1,000 live births, 2006)	17
HIV/AIDS (% of persons aged 15–49, 2007)	0.5
Physicians (per 1,000 head, 2002)	0.6
Hospital beds (per 1,000 head, 2005)	2.6
Health expenditure (2006): US $ per head (PPP)	264
Health expenditure (2006): % of GDP	6.6
Health expenditure (2006): public (% of total)	32.4
Access to water (% of persons, 2006)	92
Access to sanitation (% of persons, 2006)	65
Human Development Index (2006): ranking	114
Human Development Index (2006): value	0.717

For sources and definitions, see explanatory note on p. vi.

Agriculture

PRINCIPAL CROPS
('000 metric tons)

	2005	2006	2007
Rice, paddy	35,791	35,827	35,567*
Maize	3,756	3,819	4,313†
Potatoes*	370	370	370
Sweet potatoes	1,461	1,455	1,450*
Cassava (Manioc)	6,646	7,714	8,900*
Sugar cane	14,949	15,679	16,000*
Beans, dry*	158	158	158
Cashew nuts, with shell	961	942	961*
Soybeans (Soya beans)	293	258	410†
Groundnuts, with shell	489	465	490*
Coconuts	977	982	962*
Cabbages and other brassicas*	700	700	700

—continued	2005	2006	2007
Onions, dry*	225	225	225
Watermelons*	420	420	420
Bananas	1,344	1,350*	1,355*
Oranges	601	601*	601*
Guavas, mangoes and mangosteens	368	370*	370*
Pineapples	470	470*	470*
Coffee, green	752	854	1,060†
Tea	133	142	153*
Tobacco, unmanufactured	26	43	43*
Natural rubber	482	546	550*

* FAO estimate(s).
† Unofficial figure.

Aggregate production ('000 metric tons, may include official, semi-official or estimated data): Total cereals 39,549 in 2005, 39,648 in 2006, 39,881 in 2007; Total roots and tubers 8,477 in 2005, 9,539 in 2006, 10,720 in 2007; Total vegetables (incl. melons) 7,991 in 2005, 7,991 in 2006, 7,991 in 2007; Total fruits (excl. melons) 5,707 in 2005, 2,843 in 2006; 2,848 in 2007.

Source: FAO.

LIVESTOCK
('000 head, year ending September)

	2005	2006	2007
Horses	110.5	87.3	87.0*
Cattle	5,540.7†	6,510.8	6,840.0*
Buffaloes	2,922.2	2,921.0	2,921.1*
Pigs	27,434.9	26,855.3	26,500.0*
Goats	1,314.1	1,525.3	1,641.0†
Chickens	153,937	150,220	150,000*
Ducks	65,973	64,380	62,800*

* FAO estimate.
† Unofficial figure.

Source: FAO.

LIVESTOCK PRODUCTS
('000 metric tons)

	2005	2006	2007
Cattle meat	142.2	159.5	166.0*
Buffalo meat*	103.2	103.2	103.2
Pig meat	2,288.3	2,505.1	2,500.0
Chicken meat	321.9	344.4*	344.0*
Duck meat*	88.2	86.0	84.0
Cows' milk	197.7	216.0	243.0†
Buffaloes' milk*	31.0	31.0	31.0
Hen eggs*	197.0	225.0	225.0
Silk-worm cocoons*	3.0	3.0	3.0

* FAO estimate(s).
† Unofficial figure.

Source: FAO.

Forestry

ROUNDWOOD REMOVALS
('000 cubic metres, excl. bark)

	2005	2006	2007
Sawlogs, veneer logs and logs for sleepers*	2,737	2,200	2,270
Pulpwood	1,067	1,291	1,291
Other industrial wood	950	1,380	650
Fuel wood*	26,350	26,151	29,956
Total	31,104	31,022	34,167

* FAO estimates.

Source: FAO.

VIET NAM

SAWNWOOD PRODUCTION
('000 cubic metres, incl. railway sleepers)

	2005	2006	2007
Total (all broadleaved)	3,232	3,000	3,150

Source: FAO.

Fishing

('000 metric tons, live weight)

	2004	2005	2006
Capture*	1,879.5	1,929.9	1,959.9
Freshwater fishes	134.1	130.4	136.2
Marine fishes	1,315.8	1,349.0	1,377.5
Prawns and shrimps*	107.1	107.9	97.9
Cephalopods*	185.0	197.0	200.0
Aquaculture*	1,198.6	1,437.3	1,657.7
Freshwater fishes*	761.6	961.1	1,157.0
Giant tiger prawns*	185.6	177.2	150.0
Marine molluscs	155.2	143.8	146.2
Total catch*	3,078.1	3,367.2	3,617.6

* FAO estimates.

Note: Figures exclude aquatic plants ('000 metric tons, all aquaculture): 30 in 2004–06 (FAO estimates).

Source: FAO.

Mining

('000 metric tons)

	2004	2005	2006*
Crude petroleum ('000 barrels)	141,930	131,003	119,300
Natural gas (million cubic metres)†	6,266	6,342	6,766
Coal (anthracite)	27,349	34,100	38,900
Chromium ore—gross weight	82	89	90
Ilmenite—gross weight	145	150	150
Gold (kilograms)	2,065	2,138	2,500
Kaolin*	650	650	650
Barite (metric tons)	120,000	130,000*	130,000
Phosphate rock:			
gross weight	902	1,066	1,220
P_2O_5 content	271*	320*	366
Salt (unrefined)	906	925	950

* Estimate(s).
† Gross production.

Source: US Geological Survey.

Industry

SELECTED PRODUCTS
('000 metric tons, unless otherwise indicated)

	2006	2007	2008*
Raw sugar	1,465.1	1,671.1	1,164.9
Beer (million litres)	1,547.2	1,655.3	1,849.9
Cigarettes ('000 million packets)	3.9	4.5	4.4
Fabrics (million metres)	570.3	700.4	770.5
Chemical fertilizers	2,182.6	2,499.6	2,524.0
Insecticides	53.1	59.5	65.4
Soap	531.1	408.6	452.4
Cement	32,700	33,300	36,500
Crude steel	3,800	4,600	5,100
Paint	220.3	204.4	200.5
Footwear (million pairs)	234.2	213.2	234.6
Ready-made clothes (million pieces)	1,155.5	1,936.1	2,323.3

* Preliminary figures.

Electric energy (million kWh): 52,072 in 2005; 59,050 in 2006; 66,800 in 2007 (Source: Asian Development Bank).

Finance

CURRENCY AND EXCHANGE RATES

Monetary Units
100 xu = 1 new dông.

Sterling, Dollar and Euro Equivalents (31 December 2008)
£1 sterling = 24,749.1 dông;
US $1 = 16,977.0 dông;
€1 = 23,626.9 dông;
100,000 new dông = £4.04 = $5.89 = €4.23.

Average Exchange Rate (new dông per US $)
2006   15,994.3
2007   16,179.0
2008   16,302.3

Note: The new dông, equivalent to 10 former dông, was introduced in September 1985.

BUDGET
('000,000 million dông)

Revenue (incl. grants)	2005	2006	2007*
Tax revenue	166.2	210.3	231.4
Corporate income tax	71.7	100.8	99.0
Individual income tax	4.2	5.2	6.1
Tax on the transfer of properties	2.8	3.4	3.8
Value-added tax (VAT)	45.7	54.8	78.9
Excises	15.7	17.1	17.1
Taxes on international trade	23.6	26.3	23.8
Other taxes	2.3	2.8	2.7
Non-tax and capital revenue	48.5	50.3	47.5
Fees and charges	21.0	23.1	23.1
Income from natural resources	21.9	20.2	19.9
Capital revenues	0.9	1.5	0.8
Grants	2.3	3.6	3.0
Total	217.1	264.2	281.9

VIET NAM

Statistical Survey

Expenditure (cash basis)†	2005	2006	2007*
Current expenditure	155.0	181.5	221.3
General administrative services	16.8	19.0	24.8
Economic services	12.8	15.0	16.3
Social services	77.3	91.4	97.3
Education	29.1	33.8	38.1
Health	10.7	12.7	14.7
Social subsidies	23.6	28.7	26.8
Other services (incl. defence)	13.8	16.3	17.8
Interest on public debt	7.0	8.9	11.7
Capital expenditure	72.0	86.1	99.5
Total	226.9	267.6	320.7

* Forecasts.
† Excluding off-budget investment expenditure ('000,000 million dông): 39.4 in 2005; 33.7 in 2006; 39.4 in 2007 (forecast).

Source: IMF, *Vietnam: Statistical Appendix* (December 2007).

INTERNATIONAL RESERVES
(US $ million at 31 December)

	2005	2006	2007
Gold (market valuation)	165.9	206.9	268.3
IMF special drawing rights	0.9	1.6	7.6
Foreign exchange	9,049.7	13,382.5	23,471.8
Total	9,216.5	13,591.0	23,747.7

Source: IMF, *International Financial Statistics*.

MONEY SUPPLY
('000 million dông at 31 December)

	2005	2006	2007
Currency outside banks	131,179	158,809	220,514
Demand deposits at banks	110,823	133,405	214,653
Total money	242,002	292,215	435,168

Source: IMF, *International Financial Statistics*.

COST OF LIVING
(Consumer Price Index; base: December of previous year = 100)

	2006	2007	2008
Food	107.9	118.9	131.9
Beverages and tobacco	105.2	106.8	113.1
Clothing (incl. footwear)	105.8	106.7	112.9
Household goods	106.2	105.2	112.7
Housing and construction	105.9	117.1	108.5
Transport and communications	104.0	107.3	106.6
Education	103.6	102.0	106.9
All items (incl. others)	106.6	112.6	119.9

NATIONAL ACCOUNTS
('000 million dông at current prices)

Expenditure on the Gross Domestic Product

	2005	2006	2007
Government final consumption expenditure	51,652	58,734	69,397
Private final consumption expenditure	533,141	617,182	741,924
Increase in stocks	22,702	33,680	51,598
Gross fixed capital formation	275,841	324,949	424,852
Total domestic expenditure	883,336	1,034,545	1,287,771
Exports of goods and services	582,069	716,652	878,473
Less Imports of goods and services	617,157	765,827	1,032,158
Sub-total	848,248	985,370	1,134,086
Statistical discrepancy	–9,037	–11,104	9,928
GDP in purchasers' values	839,211	974,266	1,144,015
GDP at constant 1994 prices	393,030	425,373	461,466

Gross Domestic Product by Economic Activity

	2005	2006	2007
Agriculture, forestry and fishing	175,984	198,798	232,188
Mining and quarrying	88,897	99,702	111,664
Manufacturing	173,122	207,027	244,537
Electricity, gas and water	28,929	33,464	39,862
Construction	53,276	64,503	79,617
Trade	113,768	132,794	156,286
Transport, storage and communications	36,629	43,825	50,769
Finance	15,072	17,607	20,752
Public administration	66,556	82,224	94,565
Other community, social and personal services	86,978	94,321	113,774
Total	839,211	974,266	1,144,015

Source: Asian Development Bank.

2008 ('000,000 million dông at current prices, preliminary): Agriculture, forestry and fishing 326.5; Industry 587.2; Services 564.0; *Gross domestic product* 1,477.7.

BALANCE OF PAYMENTS
(US $ million)

	2005	2006	2007
Exports of goods f.o.b.	32,447	39,826	48,561
Imports of goods f.o.b.	–34,886	–42,602	–58,921
Trade balance	–2,439	–2,776	–10,360
Other goods, services and income (net)	–1,501	–1,437	–3,062
Balance on goods, services and income	–3,940	–4,213	–13,422
Unrequited transfers	3,380	4,049	6,430
Current balance	–560	–164	–6,992
Direct investment (net)	1,889	2,315	6,550
Portfolio investment (net)	865	1,313	6,243
Other long-term capital	921	1,025	2,045
Other short-term capital	46	–30	79
Money and deposits	–634	–1,535	2,623
Net errors and omissions	–396	1,398	–349
Overall balance	2,131	4,322	10,199

Source: Asian Development Bank.

External Trade

SELECTED COMMODITIES
(distribution by SITC, US $ million)

Imports c.i.f.	2004	2005	2006
Food and live animals	1,495	1,955	2,299
Beverages and tobacco	163	176	145
Crude materials (inedible) except fuels	1,454	1,623	2,084
Mineral fuels, etc.	3,982	5,366	6,699
Animal and vegetable fats, and oils	224	188	254
Chemicals and related products	4,694	5,310	6,317
Basic manufactures	8,859	10,172	12,164
Machinery and transport equipment	8,737	9,252	10,806
Miscellaneous manufactured goods	1,795	1,899	2,244
Total (incl. others)	31,969	36,761	44,891

VIET NAM

Exports f.o.b.	2004	2005	2006
Food and live animals	5,278	6,346	7,509
Crude materials (inedible) except fuels	831	1,229	1,845
Mineral fuels, etc.	6,233	8,358	9,709
Basic manufactures	1,890	1,165	2,926
Machinery and transport equipment	2,562	3,145	4,195
Total (incl. others)	26,485	32,447	39,826

2007: Total imports c.i.f. 62,682; Total exports f.o.b. 48,561 (Textile products 7,750; Marine products 3,763; Rice 1,489; Coffee 1,911; Wood and wood products 2,404; Rubber 1,393; Coal 1,000).

Source: Asian Development Bank.

PRINCIPAL TRADING PARTNERS
(US $ million)

Imports c.i.f.	2005	2006	2007
China, People's Republic	5,900	8,215	12,384
Germany	662	979	1,860
Hong Kong	1,235	1,661	2,399
Indonesia	700	880	1,002
Japan	4,074	4,554	5,844
Korea, Republic	3,594	3,920	4,679
Malaysia	1,257	1,934	2,475
Singapore	4,482	6,005	7,169
Thailand	2,374	3,403	4,183
USA	863	1,210	2,093
Total (incl. others)	36,761	46,120	60,790

Exports f.o.b.	2005	2006	2007
Australia	2,723	3,728	3,399
China, People's Republic	3,228	2,260	2,850
France	653	873	957
Germany	1,086	1,790	2,342
Japan	4,340	4,871	5,206
Malaysia	1,028	1,287	1,660
Singapore	1,917	1,500	1,946
Thailand	863	826	1,020
United Kingdom	1,016	1,357	1,558
USA	5,924	8,423	10,387
Total (incl. others)	32,447	38,350	45,498

Note: Data reflect the IMF's direction of trade methodology and, as a result, the totals may not be equal to those presented for trade in commodities.

Source: Asian Development Bank.

Transport

RAILWAYS
(traffic)

	2006	2007	2008*
Passengers carried (million)	11.6	11.6	11.3
Passenger-km ('000 million)	4.3	4.7	4.6
Freight carried (million metric tons)	9.2	9.1	8.4
Freight ton-km ('000 million)	3.4	3.9	4.0

* Preliminary figures.

ROAD TRAFFIC

	2005	2006	2007*
Passengers carried (million)	1,011.5	1,148.3	1,273.7
Passenger-km ('000 million)	38.4	46.4	50.6
Freight carried (million metric tons)	212.3	237.3	259.7
Freight ton-km ('000 million)	11.5	12.6	13.8

* Preliminary figures.

Commercial vehicles ('000 in use): 49.4 in 1998; 57.8 in 1999; 69.9 in 2000 (Source: UN, *Statistical Yearbook*).

INLAND WATERWAYS

	2006	2007	2008*
Passengers carried (million)	143.2	144.5	160.5
Passenger-km ('000 million)	3.2	3.2	3.3
Freight carried (million metric tons)	123.0	135.3	137.1
Freight ton-km ('000 million)	18.8	22.2	22.7

* Preliminary figures.

SHIPPING
Merchant Fleet
(registered at 31 December)

	2005	2006	2007
Number of vessels	883	1,191	1,235
Total displacement ('000 grt)	1,677.9	2,053.8	2,529.6

Source: Lloyd's Register-Fairplay, *World Fleet Statistics*.

International Sea-Borne Shipping
(freight traffic)

	2006	2007	2008*
Freight carried (million metric tons)	42.7	49.0	59.7
Freight ton-km ('000 million)	70.5	83.8	125.7

* Preliminary figures.

CIVIL AVIATION
(traffic on scheduled services)

	2003	2004	2005*
Domestic:			
Passengers carried ('000)	2,688.0	3,120.0	3,932.0
Passenger-km (million)	2,688.0	2,565.0	3,730.8
Freight carried ('000 metric tons)	48.2	51.8	58.7
Freight ton-km (million)	53.8	59.6	62.7
International:			
Passengers carried ('000)	1,831.0	2,411.0	2,907.0
Passenger-km (million)	5,028.2	6,811.0	8,228.9
Freight carried ('000 metric tons)	41.5	46.4	46.4
Freight ton-km (million)	156.9	176.2	180.4

* Preliminary figures.

Tourism

TOURIST ARRIVALS BY COUNTRY OF RESIDENCE

Country	2005	2006	2007
Australia	145,359	172,519	227,300
Cambodia	186,543	154,956	150,655
China, People's Republic	752,576	516,286	558,719
France	126,402	132,304	182,501
Japan	320,605	383,896	411,557
Korea, Republic	317,213	421,741	475,535
Laos	44,462	33,980	31,374
Malaysia	76,755	105,558	145,535
Singapore	77,676	104,947	127,040
Taiwan	286,324	274,663	314,026
Thailand	84,100	123,804	160,747
United Kingdom	80,884	84,264	105,918
USA	333,566	385,654	412,301
Total (incl. others)	3,467,757	3,583,486	4,171,564

Source: Viet Nam National Administration of Tourism.

Tourism receipts (US $ million): 1,700 in 2004; 1,880 in 2005; 3,200 in 2006. Source: World Tourism Organization.

Communications Media

	2005	2006	2007
Telephones ('000 main lines in use)	15,845.0	27,505.4	28,529.3
Mobile cellular telephones ('000 subscribers)	9,593.2	15,505.4	23,730.2
Internet users ('000)	10,711	14,684	17,872
Broadband subscribers ('000)	210.0	516.6	1,294.1

Personal computers ('000 in use): 1,044 in 2004.

Facsimile machines ('000 in use): 31 in 1999.

Radio receivers ('000 in use): 8,200 in 1997.

Television receivers ('000 in use): 14,750 in 2000.

Book production: 11,455 titles (166,500,000 copies) in 2001.

Daily newspapers: 5 (with estimated circulation of 450,000 copies) in 1999.

Sources: partly International Telecommunication Union; UN, *Statistical Yearbook*; UNESCO, *Statistical Yearbook*.

Education

(2007/08, preliminary)

	Institutions	Teachers ('000)	Students (million)
Pre-primary	10,822	119.7	2.4
Primary	15,441	346.7	6.9
Lower secondary	9,841	313.8	5.9
Upper secondary	2,257	125.2	3.1
Universities and colleges	322	53.5	1.5

Adult literacy rate (UNESCO estimates): 90.3% (males 93.9%; females 86.9%) in 1999 (Source: UNESCO Institute for Statistics).

Directory

In October 2008 telephone numbers in many regions were expanded by one digit; however, full details of the changes were not immediately available.

The Constitution

On 15 April 1992 the National Assembly adopted a new Constitution, a revised version of that adopted in December 1980 (which in turn replaced the 1959 Constitution of the Democratic Republic of Viet Nam). The National Assembly approved amendments to 24 articles of the Constitution on 12 December 2001. The main provisions of the Constitution (which originally entered into force after elections in July 1992) are summarized as follows:

POLITICAL SYSTEM

All state power belongs to the people. The Communist Party of Viet Nam is a leading force of the state and society. All party organizations operate within the framework of the Constitution and the law. The people exercise power through the National Assembly and the People's Councils.

ECONOMIC SYSTEM

The State develops a multi-sectoral economy, in accordance with a market mechanism based on state management and socialist orientations. All lands are under state management. The State allots land to organizations and individuals for use on a stabilized and long-term basis: they may transfer the right to the use of land allotted to them. Individuals may establish businesses with no restrictions on size or means of production, and the State shall encourage foreign investment. Legal property of individuals and organizations, and business enterprises with foreign invested capital, shall not be subjected to nationalization.

THE NATIONAL ASSEMBLY

The National Assembly is the people's highest representative agency, and the highest organ of state power, exercising its supreme right of supervision over all operations of the State. It elects the President and Vice-President, the Prime Minister and senior judicial officers, and ratifies the Prime Minister's proposals for appointing members of the Government. It decides the country's socio-economic development plans, national financial and monetary policies, and foreign policy. The term of each legislature is five years. The National Assembly Standing Committee supervises the enforcement of laws and the activities of the Government. Amendments to the Constitution may only be made by a majority vote of at least two-thirds of the Assembly's members.

THE PRESIDENT OF THE STATE

The President, as Head of State, represents Viet Nam in domestic and foreign affairs. The President is elected by the National Assembly from among its deputies, and is responsible to the National Assembly. The President's term of office is the same as that of the National Assembly. He or she is Commander-in-Chief of the people's armed forces, and chairs the National Defence and Security Council. The President asks the National Assembly to appoint or dismiss the Vice-President, the Prime Minister, the Chief Justice of the Supreme People's Court and the Chief Procurator of the Supreme People's Organ of Control. According to resolutions of the National Assembly or of its Standing Committee, the President appoints or dismisses members of the Government, and declares war or a state of emergency.

THE GOVERNMENT

The Government comprises the Prime Minister, the Vice-Prime Ministers, ministers and other members. Apart from the Prime Minister, ministers do not have to be members of the National Assembly. The Prime Minister is responsible to the National Assembly, and the term of office of any Government is the same as that of the National Assembly, which ratifies the appointment or dismissal of members of the Government.

LOCAL GOVERNMENT

The country is divided into provinces and municipalities, which are subordinate to the central Government; municipalities are divided into districts, precincts and cities, and districts are divided into villages and townships. People's Councils are elected by the local people.

JUDICIAL SYSTEM

The judicial system comprises the Supreme People's Court, local People's Courts, military tribunals and other courts. The term of office of the presiding judge of the Supreme People's Court corresponds to the term of the National Assembly, and he or she is responsible to the National Assembly. The Supreme People's Organ of Control ensures the observance of the law and exercises the right of public prosecution. Its Chief Procurator is responsible to the National Assembly. There are local People's Organs of Control and Military Organs of Control.

The Government

HEAD OF STATE

President: NGUYEN MINH TRIET (appointment approved by the 11th National Assembly on 27 June 2006; re-elected 25 July 2007).
Vice-President: NGUYEN THI DOAN.

CABINET
(April 2009)

Prime Minister: NGUYEN TAN DUNG.
Standing Deputy Prime Minister: NGUYEN SINH HUNG.
Deputy Prime Minister and Minister of Foreign Affairs: PHAM GIA KHIEM.
Deputy Prime Minister and Minister of Education and Training: NGUYEN THIEN NHAN.
Deputy Prime Ministers: TRUONG VINH TRONG, HOANG TRUNG HAI.
Minister of National Defence: Gen. PHUNG QUANG THANH.

VIET NAM

Minister of Public Security: LE HONG ANH.
Minister of Justice: HA HUNG CUONG.
Minister of Finance: VU VAN NINH.
Minister of Labour, War Invalids and Social Affairs: NGUYEN THI KIM NGAN.
Minister of Health: NGUYEN QUOC TRIEU.
Minister of Culture, Sports and Tourism: HOANG TUAN ANH.
Minister of Construction: NGUYEN HONG QUAN.
Minister of Transportation: HO NGHIA DUNG.
Minister of Internal Services: TRAN VAN TUAN.
Minister of Agriculture and Rural Development: CAO DUC PHAT.
Minister of Industry and Trade: VU HUY HOANG.
Minister of Planning and Investment: VO HONG PHUC.
Minister of Sciences and Technology: HOANG VAN PHONG.
Minister of Natural Resources and the Environment: PHAM KHOI NGUYEN.
Minister of Information and Communication: LE DOAN HOP.
Chief Government Inspector: TRAN VAN TRUYEN.
Minister, Chairman of Ethnic Minorities Committee: GIANG SEO PHU.
Minister, Chairman of the Government Office: NGUYEN XUAN PHUC.

MINISTRIES AND COMMISSIONS

Ministry of Agriculture and Rural Development: 2 Ngoc Ha, Ba Dinh District, Hanoi; tel. (4) 8468160; fax (4) 8454319; e-mail icard@agroviet.gov.vn; internet www.agroviet.gov.vn.

Ministry of Construction: 37 Le Dai Hanh, Hai Ba Trung District, Hanoi; tel. (4) 9760271; fax (4) 9762153; e-mail bxd-vp@hn.vnn.vn; internet www.moc.gov.vn.

Ministry of Culture and Information: 51–53 Ngo Quyen, Hoan Kiem District, Hanoi; tel. (4) 9438231; fax (4) 9439009; internet www.cinet.gov.vn.

Ministry of Education and Training: 49 Dai Co Viet, Hai Ba Trung District, Hanoi; tel. (4) 8694904; fax (4) 8694085; e-mail intlaff@iupui.edu; internet www.edu.net.vn.

Ministry of Finance: 28 Tran Hung Dao, Hoan Kiem District, Hanoi; tel. (4) 2202828; fax (4) 2208129; e-mail support@mof.gov.vn; internet www.mof.gov.vn.

Ministry of Fisheries: 10 Nguyen Cong Hoan, Hanoi; tel. (4) 7716396; fax (4) 7716702; e-mail mofi@mofi.gov.vn; internet www.mofi.gov.vn.

Ministry of Foreign Affairs: 1 Ton That Dam, Ba Dinh District, Hanoi; tel. (4) 8452980; fax (4) 82318725; e-mail banbientap@mofa.gov.vn; internet www.mofa.gov.vn.

Ministry of Health: 138A Giang Vo, Ba Dinh District, Hanoi; tel. (4) 8464416; fax (4) 8464051; internet www.moh.gov.vn.

Ministry of Industry: 54 Hai Ba Trung, Hoan Kiem District, Hanoi; tel. (4) 8258311; fax (4) 8265303; e-mail webmaster@moi.gov.vn; internet www.moi.gov.vn.

Ministry of Internal Services: 137A Nguyen Binh Khiem, Hai Ba Trung District, Hanoi; tel. (4) 9760370; fax (4) 9781005; e-mail ngoc-hien@hn.vnn.vn.

Ministry of Justice: 60 Tran Phu, Ba Dinh District, Hanoi; tel. (4) 8438847; fax (4) 8431431; e-mail vpb@moj.gov.vn; internet www.moj.gov.vn.

Ministry of Labour, War Invalids and Social Affairs: 12 Ngo Quyen, Hoan Kiem District, Hanoi; tel. (4) 8269557; fax (4) 8248036; e-mail tapchildxh@molisa.gov.vn; internet www.molisa.gov.vn.

Ministry of National Defence: 1A Hoang Dieu, Ba Dinh District, Hanoi; tel. (4) 069 882041; fax (4) 069 532090.

Ministry of Natural Resources and the Environment: 83 Nguyen Chi Thanh, Dong Da District, Hanoi; tel. (4) 8343911; fax (4) 8359221; e-mail webmaster@monroe.gov.vn; internet www.monre.gov.vn.

Ministry of Planning and Investment: 2 Hoang Van Thu, Ba Dinh District, Hanoi; tel. (4) 8453027; fax (4) 8234453; internet www.mpi.gov.vn.

Ministry of Information and Communication: 18 Nguyen Du, Hanoi; tel. (4) 39430204; fax (4) 38226590; e-mail dic@mic.gov.vn; internet mic.gov.vn.

Ministry of Public Security: 44 Yet Kieu, Hoan Kiem District, Hanoi; tel. (4) 8226602; fax (4) 9420223.

Ministry of Science and Technology: 39 Tran Hung Dao, Hoan Kiem District, Hanoi; tel. (4) 9439057; fax (4) 8252733; e-mail ttth@most.gov.vn; internet www.most.gov.vn.

Ministry of Trade: 21 Ngo Quyen, Hanoi; tel. (4) 8262522; fax (4) 8264696; e-mail bitec@mot.gov.vn; internet www.mot.gov.vn.

Ministry of Transport: 80 Tran Hung Dao, Hoan Kiem District, Hanoi; tel. (4) 9424015; fax (4) 8267291; internet www.mt.gov.vn.

National Commission for Population, Family and Children: 33 Tran Phu, Ba Dinh District, Hanoi; tel. (4) 7473851; fax (4) 8237983; e-mail banbientap@vcfpc.gov.vn; internet www.vcpfc.gov.vn.

Government Inspection Committee: 220 Doi Can, Ba Dinh District, Hanoi; tel. (4) 8325558; fax (4) 8325786; e-mail ttcp@thanhtra.gov.vn; internet www.thanhtra.gov.vn.

NATIONAL DEFENCE AND SECURITY COUNCIL

President: NGUYEN MINH TRIET.
Vice-President: NGUYEN TAN DUNG.
Members: NGUYEN PHU TRONG, PHAM GIA KHIEM, PHUNG QUANG THANH, LE HONG ANH.

Legislature

QUOC HOI
(National Assembly)

Elections to the 12th National Assembly were held on 20 May 2007. The new Assembly comprised 493 members (compared with 498 in the previous legislature), elected from among 875 candidates; 42 non-party candidates and one independent were elected.

Standing Committee

Chairman: NGUYEN PHU TRONG.
Vice-Chairmen: NGUYEN DUC KHIEN, UONG CHU LUU, TONG THI PHONG, HUYNH NGOC SON.

Political Organizations

COMMUNIST PARTY

Dang Cong San Viet Nam (Communist Party of Viet Nam): 1 Hoang Van Thu, Hanoi; e-mail dangcongsan@cpv.org.vn; internet www.cpv.org.vn; f. 1976; ruling party; fmrly the Viet Nam Workers' Party, f. 1951 as the successor to the Communist Party of Indo-China, f. 1930; c. 3.1m. mems (2006); Gen. Sec. of Cen. Cttee NONG DUC MANH.

Political Bureau (Politburo)

Members: NONG DUC MANH, LE HONG ANH, NGUYEN MINH TRIET, NGUYEN TAN DUNG, TRUONG TAN SANG, NGUYEN PHU TRONG, PHAM GIA KHIEM, PHAM QUANG NGHI, NGUYEN SINH HUNG, NGUYEN VAN CHI, HO DUC VIET, Sr Lt-Gen. PHUNG QUANG THANH, TRUONG VINH TRONG, LE THANH HAI.

Secretariat

Members: NONG DUC MANH, TRUONG TAN SANG, TRUONG VINH TRONG, NGUYEN VAN CHI, PHAM QUANG NGHI, Sr Lt-Gen. LE VAN DUNG, TONG THI PHONG, TO HUY RUA.

OTHER POLITICAL ORGANIZATIONS

Ho Chi Minh Communist Youth Union: 60 Ba Trieu, Hanoi; tel. (4) 9435709; fax (4) 9348439; e-mail cydeco@hn.vnn.vn; f. 1931; 4m. mems; First Sec. VO VAN THUONG.

People's Action Party (PAP): POB 4752, San Jose, CA 95150-4752, USA; e-mail dang@ndhd.net; internet www.dndhd.org; Chair. NGUYEN SI BINH.

Viet Nam Fatherland Front: 46 Trang Thi, Hanoi; e-mail pttmattran@hn.vnn.vn; internet www.mattran.org.vn; f. 1930; replaced the Lien Viet (Viet Nam National League), the successor to Viet Nam Doc Lap Dong Minh Hoi (Revolutionary League for the Independence of Viet Nam) or Viet Minh; in 1977 the original org. merged with the National Front for the Liberation of South Viet Nam and the Alliance of National, Democratic and Peace Forces in South Viet Nam to form a single front; 200-member Cen. Cttee; Pres. Presidium of Cen. Cttee HUYNH DAM; Gen. Sec. VU TRONG KIM.

Vietnam Women's Union (VWU): 39 Hang Chuoi, Hanoi; tel. (4) 9713436; fax (4) 9713143; internet hoilhpn.org.vn; f. 1930; 11m. mems; Pres. HA THI KHIET.

VIET NAM

Diplomatic Representation

EMBASSIES IN VIET NAM

Algeria: 13 Phan Chu Trinh, Hanoi; tel. (4) 8253865; fax (4) 8260830; e-mail ambalghanoi@ambalgvn.org.vn; internet www.ambalgvn.org.vn; Ambassador NACEUR BOUCHERIT.

Argentina: 8th Floor, Office Tower, Daeha Business Centre, 360 Kim Ma, Ba Dinh District, Hanoi; tel. (4) 8315262; fax (4) 8315577; e-mail embarg@hn.vnn.vn; internet www.embargentina.org.vn; Ambassador TOMÁS FERRARI.

Australia: 8 Dao Tan, Ba Dinh District, Hanoi; tel. (4) 8317755; fax (4) 8317711; e-mail austemb@fpt.vn; internet www.vietnam.embassy.gov.au; Ambassador ALLASTAR COX.

Austria: Prime Centre, 8th Floor, 53 Quang Trung, Hai Ba Trung District, Hanoi; tel. (4) 9433050; fax (4) 9433055; e-mail hanoi-ob@bmeia.gv.at; internet www.aussenministerium.at/hanoi; Ambassador Dr JOHANNES PETERLIK.

Bangladesh: 7th Floor, Daeha Business Centre, 360 Kim Ma, Ba Dinh District, Hanoi; tel. (4) 7716625; fax (4) 7716628; Ambassador MOHD ENAMUL KABIR.

Belarus: 11th Floor, 44b Ly Thuong Kiet, Hanoi; tel. (4) 9344416; fax (4) 9344417; e-mail check@hn.vnn.vn; Ambassador ALYAKSANDR KUTSALAY.

Belgium: 9th Floor, Hanoi Towers, 49 Hai Ba Trung, Hanoi; tel. (4) 9346179; fax (4) 9346183; e-mail hanoi@diplobel.be; internet www.diplomatie.be/hanoi; Ambassador HUBERT COOREMAN.

Brazil: 14 Thuy Khue, T72 Hanoi; tel. (4) 8430817; fax (4) 8432542; e-mail vetbrem@netnam.org.vn; internet www.brazil.org.vn; Ambassador JOÃO DE MENDONÇA LIMA NETO.

Brunei: Villa No. 8 & 9, Van Phuc Diplomatic Quarter, 44/8 Van Bao, Ba Dinh District, Hanoi; tel. (4) 7262001; fax (4) 7262010; e-mail bruemviet@hn.vnn.vn; Ambassador Dato Paduka Haji MAHADI BIN WASLI.

Bulgaria: Van Phuc Quarter, 5 Nui Truc, Hanoi; tel. (4) 8452095; fax (4) 8460856; e-mail bgremb@fpt.vn; internet www.mfa.bg/hanoi; Ambassador GEORGI VASSILIEV.

Cambodia: 71 Tran Hung Dao, Hanoi; tel. (4) 8253788; fax (4) 9423225; e-mail arch@fpt.vn; Ambassador (vacant).

Canada: 31 Hung Vuong, Hanoi; tel. (4) 7345000; fax (4) 7345049; e-mail hanoi@international.gc.ca; internet www.dfait-maeci.gc.ca/vietnam; Ambassador DEANNA HORTON.

Chile: Suite 1201–1203, 12th Floor, 2 Ngo Quyen, Tung Shing Sq. Bldg, Hoan Kiem District, Hanoi; tel. (4) 9351147; fax (4) 9351150; e-mail embajada1@chile.org.vn; Ambassador JORGE CANELAS UGALDE.

China, People's Republic: 46 Hoang Dieu, Hanoi; tel. (4) 8453736; fax (4) 8232826; e-mail eossc@hn.vnn.vn; internet vn.chineseembassy.org; Ambassador SUN GUOXIANG.

Cuba: 65A Ly Thuong Kiet, Hanoi; tel. (4) 9424775; fax (4) 9422426; e-mail embacuba@netnam.org.vn; internet embacuba.cubaminrex.cu/vietnaming; Ambassador JESÚS AISE SOTOLONGO.

Czech Republic: 13 Chu Van An, Hanoi; tel. (4) 8454131; fax (4) 8233996; internet www.mfa.cz/hanoi; Ambassador MICHAL KRAL.

Denmark: 19 Dien Bien Phu, Hanoi; tel. (4) 8231888; fax (4) 8231999; e-mail hanamb@um.dk; internet www.ambhanoi.um.dk; Ambassador PETER LYSHOLT HANSEN.

Egypt: 63 To Ngoc Van, Quang An, Tay Ho District, Hanoi; tel. (4) 8294999; fax (4) 8294997; e-mail arabegypt@ftp.vn; Ambassador MUHAMMAD ALAA EL-DEIN SAAD EL-LEISI.

Finland: Suite 63, 6th Floor, Central Bldg, 31 Hai Ba Trung, Hanoi; tel. (4) 8266788; fax (4) 8266766; e-mail sanomat.han@formin.fi; internet www.finland.org.vn; Ambassador PEKKA HYVÖNEN.

France: 57 Tran Hung Dao, Hanoi; tel. (4) 9437719; fax (4) 9437236; internet www.ambafrance-vn.org; Ambassador HERVÉ BOLOT.

Germany: 29 Tran Phu, Hanoi; tel. (4) 8453836; fax (4) 8453838; e-mail germanemb.hanoi@fpt.vn; internet www.hanoi.diplo.de; Ambassador ROLF SCHULZE.

Hungary: Daeha Business Centre, 12th Floor, 360 Kim Ma, Ba Dinh District, Hanoi; tel. (4) 7715714; fax (4) 7715716; e-mail hoi.missions@kum.hu; internet www.mfa.gov.hu/emb/hanoi; Ambassador LÁSZLÓ VIZI.

India: 58–60 Tran Hung Dao, Hanoi; tel. (4) 8244990; fax (4) 8244998; e-mail india@netnam.org.vn; internet www.indembassy.com.vn; Ambassador N. RAVI.

Indonesia: 50 Ngo Quyen, Hanoi; tel. (4) 8253353; fax (4) 8259274; e-mail komhan@hn.vnn.vn; internet www.indonesia-hanoi.org.vn; Ambassador ARTAULI RATNA MENARA PANGGABEAN TOBING.

Iran: 54 Tran Phu, Ba Dinh District, Hanoi; tel. (4) 8232068; fax (4) 8232120; e-mail iriemb@fpt.vn; Ambassador JAVAD GHAVAM SHAHIDI.

Iraq: 66 Tran Hung Dao, Hanoi; tel. (4) 9424141; fax (4) 9424055; e-mail hanemb@iraqmofamail.net; Ambassador AMAL ABOOD FAIROOZ.

Ireland: Vincom City Towers, 8th Floor, 191 Ba Trieu, Hai Ba Trung District, Hanoi; tel. (4) 9743291; fax (4) 9743295; e-mail irishembassyhanoi@dfanet.ie; Ambassador MAEVE COLLINS.

Israel: 68 Nguyen Thai Hoc, Dong Da, Hanoi; tel. (4) 8433141; fax (4) 8435760; e-mail info@hanoi.mfa.gov.il; internet hanoi.mfa.gov.il; Ambassador AMNON EFRAT (designate).

Italy: 9 Le Phung Hieu, Hoan Kiem District, Hanoi; tel. (4) 8256256; fax (4) 8267602; e-mail ambasciata.hanoi@esteri.it; internet www.ambhanoi.esteri.it; Ambassador ANDREA PERUGINI.

Japan: 27 Lieu Giai, Ba Dinh District, Hanoi; tel. (4) 8463000; fax (4) 8463043; e-mail soumuhan@vnn.vn; internet www.vn.emb-japan.go.jp; Ambassador MITSUO SAKABA.

Korea, Democratic People's Republic: 25 Cao Ba Quat, Hanoi; tel. (4) 8453008; fax (4) 8231221; e-mail emb.dprk@hn.vnn.vn; Ambassador MA CHOL SU.

Korea, Republic: 4th Floor, Daeha Business Centre, 360 Kim Ma, Ba Dinh District, Hanoi; tel. (4) 8315111; fax (4) 8315117; e-mail korembviet@mofat.go.kr; internet vnm-hanoi.mofat.go.kr; Ambassador IM HONG-JAE.

Laos: 22 Tran Binh Trong, Hanoi; tel. (4) 9424576; fax (4) 8228414; Ambassador SOUNTHONE SAYACHAK.

Libya: A3 Van Phuc Residential Quarter, Hanoi; tel. (4) 8453379; fax (4) 8454977; e-mail libpbha@yahoo.com; Secretary SALEM ALI SALEM DANNAH.

Malaysia: 43-45 Dien Bien Phu, Ba Dinh District, Hanoi; tel. (4) 7343836; fax (4) 7343832; e-mail mwhanoi@hn.vnn.vn; internet www.kln.gov.my/perwakilan/hanoi; Ambassador LIM KIM ENG.

Mexico: 14 Thuy Khue, T-11, Hanoi; tel. (4) 8470948; fax (4) 8470949; e-mail embvietnam@sre.gob.mx; Ambassador RICARDO CÁMARA SÁNCHEZ.

Mongolia: Villa 5, Van Phuc Diplomatic Quarter, Hanoi; tel. (4) 8453009; fax (4) 8454954; e-mail mongembhanoi@hn.vnn.vn; Ambassador PALAMYN SÜNDEV.

Morocco: Sofitel Plaza, 1 Thanh Nien, Hanoi; tel. (4) 7345586; fax (4) 7345589; e-mail embamaroc-hanoi@vnn.vn; Ambassador EL HOUCINE FARDANI.

Myanmar: A-3 (101–104), Van Phuc Diplomatic Quarter, Kim Ma, Hanoi; tel. (4) 8453369; fax (4) 8452404; e-mail myan.emb@fpt.vn; Ambassador U KHIN AUNG.

Netherlands: Daeha Office Tower, 6th Floor, 360 Kim Ma, Ba Dinh District, Hanoi; tel. (4) 8315650; fax (4) 8315655; e-mail han@minbuza.nl; internet www.netherlands-embassy.org.vn; Ambassador ANDRÉ HASPELS.

New Zealand: Level 5, 63 Ly Thai To, Hanoi; tel. (4) 8241481; fax (4) 8241480; e-mail nzembhan@fpt.vn; Ambassador HEATHER RIDDELL.

Norway: 10th Floor, Block B, Vincom City Towers, 191 Ba Trieu, Hanoi; tel. (4) 9742930; fax (4) 9743301; e-mail emb.hanoi@mfa.no; internet www.norway.org.vn; Ambassador KJELL STORLØKKEN.

Pakistan: 44/2 Van Bao, Van Phuc Diplomatic Quarter, Hanoi; tel. (4) 7262251; fax (4) 7262253; e-mail parep-hanoi@hn.vnn.vn; Ambassador GHULAM RASOOL BALUCH.

Panama: 18th Floor, 44th St, Ly Thuong Kiet, Hanoi; tel. (4) 9365213; Ambassador LIZIA LU.

Philippines: 27B Tran Hung Dao, Hanoi; tel. (4) 9437873; fax (4) 9435760; e-mail hanoipe@dfa.gov.ph; Ambassador ESTRELLA BERENGUEL.

Poland: 3 Chua Mot Cot, Hanoi; tel. (4) 8452027; fax (4) 8236914; e-mail polamb@hn.vnn.vn; Ambassador MIROSŁAW GAJEWSKI.

Romania: 5 Le Hong Phong, Hanoi; tel. (4) 8452014; fax (4) 8430922; e-mail romambhan@fpt.vn; Ambassador DUMITRU OLARU.

Russia: 191 La Thanh, Hanoi; tel. (4) 8336991; fax (4) 8336995; e-mail moscow.vietnam@hn.vnn.vn; Ambassador VADIM VIKTOROVICH SERAFIMOV.

Singapore: Pacific Place, Unit V804–808, 8th Floor, 83B, Ly Thuong Kiet, Hanoi; tel. (4) 9460808; fax (4) 9460821; e-mail singemb_hanoi@sgmfa.gov.sg; internet www.mfa.gov.sg/hanoi; Ambassador SIMON WONG WIE KUEN.

South Africa: 3rd Floor, Central Bldg, 31 Hai Ba Trung, Hanoi; tel. (4) 9362000; fax (4) 9361991; e-mail hanoi@foreign.gov.za; Ambassador RATUBATSI SUPER MOLOI.

Spain: 15th Floor, Daeha Business Centre, 360 Kim Ma, Ba Dinh District, Hanoi; tel. (4) 7715207; fax (4) 7715206; e-mail embespvn@fpt.vn; Ambassador MARÍA SOLEDAD FUENTES GÓMEZ.

Sri Lanka: 55B Tran Phu, Ba Dinh District, Hanoi; tel. (4) 7341894; fax (4) 7341897; e-mail slembvn@fpt.vn; internet www.slembvn.org; Ambassador A. L. RATNAPALA.

VIET NAM *Directory*

Sweden: 2 Nui Truc, Ba Dinh District, Hanoi; tel. (4) 7260400; fax (4) 8232195; e-mail ambassaden.hanoi@foreign.ministry.se; internet www.swedenabroad.com/hanoi; Ambassador ROLF BERGMAN.

Switzerland: 44B Ly Thuong Kiet, 15th Floor, Hanoi; tel. (4) 9346589; fax (4) 9346591; e-mail vertretung@han.rep.admin.ch; internet www.eda.admin.ch/hanoi; Ambassador JEAN HUBERT LEBET.

Thailand: 63–65 Hoang Dieu, Hanoi; tel. (4) 8235092; fax (4) 8235088; e-mail thaiemhn@netnam.org.vn; internet www.thaiembassy.org.vn; Ambassador KITTIPHONG NA RANONG.

Turkey: 4th Floor, North Star Bldg, 4 Da Truong, Hanoi; tel. (4) 8222460; fax (4) 8222458; e-mail turkeyhn@fpt.vn; Ambassador (vacant).

Ukraine: 6B Le Hong Phong, Hanoi; tel. (4) 7344484; fax (4) 7344497; e-mail emb_vn@mfa.gov.ua; internet www.mfa.gov.ua/vietnam; Ambassador IVAN DOVGANYCH.

United Kingdom: Central Bldg, 4th Floor, 31 Hai Ba Trung, Hanoi; tel. (4) 9360500; fax (4) 9360561; e-mail behanoi@hn.vnn.vn; internet ukinvietnam.fco.gov.uk; Ambassador MARK ANDREW GEOFFREY KENT.

USA: 7 Lang Ha, Ba Dinh District, Hanoi; tel. (4) 8505000; fax (4) 8505010; e-mail irchanoi@state.gov; internet vietnam.usembassy.gov; Ambassador MICHAEL W. MICHALAK.

Venezuela: 368 Lac Long Quan, Tay Ho District, Hanoi; tel. (4) 7588891; fax (4) 7588893; e-mail embavenezhanoi@yahoo.com; Ambassador JORGE JOSÉ RONDÓN UZCÁTEGUI.

Judicial System

SUPREME PEOPLE'S COURT
48 Ly Thuong Kiet, Hanoi.

The Supreme People's Court in Hanoi is the highest court and exercises civil and criminal jurisdiction over all lower courts. The Supreme Court may also conduct trials of the first instance in certain cases. There are People's Courts in each province and city which exercise jurisdiction in the first and second instance. Military courts hear cases involving members of the People's Army and cases involving national security. In 1993 legislation was adopted on the establishment of economic courts to consider business disputes. The observance of the law by ministries, government offices and all citizens is the concern of the People's Organs of Control, under a Supreme People's Organ of Control. The Chief Justice of the Supreme People's Court and the Chief Procurator of the Supreme People's Organ of Control are elected by the National Assembly, on the recommendation of the President.

Chief Justice of the Supreme People's Court: TRUONG HOA BINH.

Chief Procurator of the Supreme People's Organ of Control: TRAN QUOC VUONG.

Religion

Traditional Vietnamese religion included elements of Indian and all three Chinese religions: Mahayana Buddhism, Daoism and Confucianism. Its most widespread feature was the cult of ancestors, practised in individual households and clan temples. Various Buddhist sects belong to the 'new' religions of Caodaism and Hoa Hao. The Protestant and Roman Catholic Churches are also represented. In 2007 operating licences were granted to several additional religions, including the Mennonite Church, the Baptist Church and the Bahá'í faith.

BUDDHISM

In the North a Buddhist organization, grouping Buddhists loyal to the Democratic Republic of Viet Nam, was formed in 1954. In the South the United Buddhist Church was formed in 1964, incorporating several disparate groups, including the 'militant' An-Quang group (mainly natives of central Viet Nam), the group of Thich Tam Chau (mainly northern emigrés in Saigon) and the southern Buddhists of the Xa Loi temple. In 1982 most of the Buddhist sects were amalgamated into the state-approved Viet Nam Buddhist Church (which comes under the authority of the Viet Nam Fatherland Front). The number of adherents was estimated at 10m. in 2005, approximately 12% of the total population. The Unified Buddhist Church of Viet Nam is an anti-Government organization.

Viet Nam Buddhist Church: Pres. Exec. Council Most Ven. THICH TRI TINH; Gen. Sec. THICH MING CHAU.

Unified Buddhist Church of Viet Nam: Leader Patriarch THICH QUANG DO.

CAODAISM

Formally inaugurated in 1926, this is a syncretic religion based on spiritualist seances with a predominantly ethical content, but sometimes with political overtones. There are 13 different sects, of which the most politically involved (1940–75) was that of Tay Ninh. Another sect, the Tien Thien, was represented in the National Liberation Front from its inception. There were an estimated 2.4m. adherents in 2005, resident mainly in the South.

Leader: Cardinal THAI HUU THANH.

CHRISTIANITY

In 2005 the number of Christian adherents represented an estimated 7.2% of the total population.

The Roman Catholic Church

The Roman Catholic Church has been active in Viet Nam since the 17th century, and since 1933 has been led mainly by Vietnamese priests. Many Roman Catholics moved from North to South Viet Nam in 1954–55, but some remained in the North. The total number of adherents was estimated at 5,990,355 in December 2006, representing 6.8% of the population. For ecclesiastical purposes, Viet Nam comprises three archdioceses and 23 dioceses.

Bishops' Conference
Conférence Episcopale du Viet Nam, 22 Tran Phu, Khank Hoa, Nha Trang; tel. (58) 822842; fax (58) 815494; e-mail vangia@dng.vnn.vn. f. 1980; Pres. Most Rev. PIERRE NGUYEN VAN NHON (Bishop of Da Lat).

Archbishop of Hanoi: Most Rev. JOSEPH NGO QUANG KIET, Archevêché, 40 Pho Nha Chung, Hanoi; tel. (4) 8254424; fax (4) 9285073; e-mail ttgmhn@hn.vnn.vn.

Archbishop of Ho Chi Minh City: Cardinal JEAN-BAPTISTE PHAM MINH MÂN, Archevêché, 180 Nguyen Dinh Chieu, Ho Chi Minh City 3; tel. (8) 9303828; fax (8) 9300598.

Archbishop of Hué: Most Rev. ETIENNE NGUYEN NHU THE, Archevêché, 6 Nguyen Truong To, Hué; tel. (54) 824937; fax (54) 833656; e-mail tgmhue@dng.vnn.vn.

Committee for Solidarity of Patriotic Vietnamese Catholics: 59 Trang Thi, Hanoi; Pres. Rev. VUONG DINH AI.

The Protestant Church

Introduced in 1920 with 500 adherents; the total number was estimated at 500,000 in 2005.

HOA HAO

A new manifestation of an older religion called Buu Son Ky Huong, the Hoa Hao sect was founded by Nguyen Phu So in 1939. There were an estimated 1.6m. adherents in 2005.

ISLAM

The number of Muslims was estimated at 65,000 in 2005.

The Press

The Ministry of Culture and Information supervises the activities of newspapers, news agencies and periodicals.

DAILIES

Hanoi

Le Courrier du Viet Nam: 33 Le Thanh Tong, Hanoi; tel. (4) 9334587; fax (4) 8258368; e-mail courrier@vnagency.com.vn; internet lecourrier.vnagency.com.vn; French; publ. by the Viet Nam News Agency; Editor-in-Chief TRAN SON MACH.

Dan Tri (Intellectual People's Standard): 2/48 Giang Vo, Dong Da District, Hanoi; tel. (4) 7366491; fax (4) 7366490; e-mail info@dantri.com.vn; internet www.dantri.com.vn; f. 1982, fmrly known as *Tin Tuc* (News); publ. by the Viet Nam News Agency; afternoon; Vietnamese; Editor-in-Chief HUY HOAN PHAM.

Hanoi Moi (New Hanoi): 44 Le Thai To, Hoan Kiem District, Hanoi; tel. (4) 8253067; fax (4) 8248054; e-mail toasoan@hanoimoi.com.vn; internet www.hanoimoi.com.vn; f. 1976; organ of Hanoi Cttee of the Communist Party of Viet Nam; Editor HO QUANG LOI; circ. 35,000.

Lao Dong (Labour): 15/167 Tay Son, Dong Da District, Hanoi; tel. (4) 5330305; fax (4) 5370141; e-mail webmaster@laodong.com.vn; internet www.laodong.com.vn; f. 1929; organ of the Viet Nam General Confederation of Labour; Editor-in-Chief VUONG VAN VIET; circ. 80,000.

Nhan Dan (The People): 71 Hang Trong, Hoan Kiem District, Hanoi; tel. (4) 8254231; fax (4) 8255593; e-mail toasoan@nhandan.org.vn; internet www.nhandan.org.vn; f. 1946; official organ of the Communist Party of Viet Nam; Editor-in-Chief DINH THE HUYNH; circ. 180,000.

Quan Doi Nhan Dan (People's Army): 7 Phan Dinh Phung, Hanoi; tel. (4) 7471748; fax (4) 7474913; e-mail bqdnd@yahoo.com; internet www.qdnd.vn; f. 1950; organ of the armed forces; Editor LE PHUC NGUYEN; circ. 80,000.

Thanh Nien: 248 Cong Quynh St, District 1, Hanoi; tel. (8) 8394046; fax (8) 8322025; internet www.thanhniennews.com; f. 1986; flagship publication of the Viet Nam National Youth Federation; Chief Editor NGUYEN CONG KHE.

Viet Nam Economic Times: 96 Hoang Quoc Viet, Cau Giay District, Hanoi; tel. (4) 7552060; fax (4) 7552046; e-mail vet@hn.vnn.vn; internet www.vneconomy.com.vn; f. 1994; in Vietnamese (with monthly edn in English); Editor-in-Chief Prof. DAO NGUYEN CAT; Dep. Editor-in-Chief NGUYEN THI VAN ANH; circ 38,900.

Viet Nam News: 11 Tran Hung Dao, Hanoi; tel. (4) 9332314; fax 9332311; e-mail vnnews@vnagency.com.vn; internet vietnamnews .vnanet.vn; f. 1991; English; publ. by the Viet Nam News Agency; Editor-in-Chief TRAN MAI HUONG; circ. 60,000.

Ho Chi Minh City

Sai Gon Giai Phong (Liberated Saigon): 432–438 Nguyen Thi Minh Khai, District 3, Ho Chi Minh City; tel. (8) 8395942; fax (8) 8324958; internet www.sggp.org.vn; f. 1975; organ of Ho Chi Minh City Cttee of the Communist Party of Viet Nam; Editor-in-Chief TRAN THE TUYEN; circ. 100,000.

Saigon Times: 35 Nam Ky Khoi Nghia, District 1, Ho Chi Minh City; tel. (8) 8295936; fax (8) 8294294; e-mail sgt@thesaigontimes.vn; internet www.saigontimes.com.vn; f. 1991; Vietnamese and English; business issues; Editor-in-Chief TRAN THI NGOC HUE.

PERIODICALS

Dai Doan Ket (Great Unity): 66 Ba Trieu, Hanoi; tel. (4) 8262420; internet www.mattran.org.vn/Daidoanket; f. 1977; weekly; organ of the Viet Nam Fatherland Front; Editor NGUYEN QUANG CANH.

Dau Tu: 175 Nguyen Thai Hoc, Hanoi; tel. (4) 8450537; fax (4) 8457937; e-mail vir@hn.vnn.vn; internet www.vir.com.vn/Client/ dautu/default.asp; 3 a week; business newspaper publ. in Vietnamese; Editor-in-Chief Dr NGUYEN ANH TUAN; circ. 40,000.

Dau Tu Chung Khoan: 175 Nguyen Thai Hoc, Hanoi; tel. (4) 8450537; fax (4) 8457937; e-mail vir@hn.vnn.vn; internet www.vir .com.vn/CLIENT/DautuChungkhoan/default.asp; weekly; stock market news publ. in Vietnamese; Editor-in-Chief Dr NGUYEN ANH TUAN; circ. 50,000.

Giao Duc Thoi Dai (People's Teacher): 29B Ngo Quyen, Hoan Kiem District, Hanoi; tel. (4) 8241781; fax (4) 9345611; e-mail gdtd@fpt.vn; internet www.gdtd.com.vn; f. 1959; weekly; organ of the Ministry of Education and Training; Editor TRAN DANG THAO.

Giao Thong-Van Tai (Communications and Transport): 1 Nha Tho, Hanoi; tel. (4) 9286763; fax (4) 8255387; e-mail baogiaothong@jpt.vn; internet www.giaothongvantai.com; f. 1962; weekly; Thursday; organ of the Ministry of Transport; Editor NGUYEN VAN LUU; circ. 30,000.

Hoa Hoc Tro (Pupils' Flowers): 5 Hoa Ma, Hanoi; tel. (4) 8211065; internet www.hoahoctro.com; weekly; Editor NGUYEN PHONG DOANH; circ. 150,000.

Khoa Hoc Ky Thuat Kinh Te The Gioi (World Science, Technology and Economy): 5 Ly Thuong Kiet, Hanoi; tel. (4) 8252931; f. 1982; weekly.

Khoa Hoc va Doi Song (Science and Life): 70 Tran Hung Dao, Hanoi; tel. (4) 8253427; f. 1959; weekly; Editor-in-Chief TRAN CU; circ. 30,000.

Nghe Thuat Dien Anh (Cinematography): 65 Tran Hung Dao, Hanoi; tel. (4) 8262473; f. 1984; fortnightly; Editor DANG NHAT MINH.

Nguoi Cong Giao Viet Nam (Vietnamese Catholic): 59 Trang Thi, Hanoi; tel. (4) 8256242; f. 1984; weekly; organ of the Cttee for Solidarity of Patriotic Vietnamese Catholics; Editor-in-Chief SO CHI.

Nguoi Dai Bieu Nhan Dan (People's Deputy): 35 Ngo Quyen, Hanoi; tel. (4) 08046231; fax (4) 08046659; e-mail ndbnd@hn.vnn.vn; f. 1988; bi-weekly; disseminates resolutions of the National Assembly and People's Council; Editor-in-Chief HO ANH TAI (acting); circ. 2m.

Nguoi Hanoi (The Hanoian): 19 Hang Buom, Hanoi; tel. (4) 8255662; f. 1984; Editor VU QUAN PHUONG.

Nha Bao Va Cong Luan (The Journalist and Public Opinion): 59 Ly Thai To, Hanoi; tel. (4) 8253609; fax (4) 8250797; f. 1985; monthly review; organ of the Viet Nam Journalists' Asscn; Editor-in-Chief PHAN DUOC TOAN; circ. 40,000.

Nong Nghiep Viet Nam (Viet Nam Agriculture): 14 Ngo Quyen, Hanoi; tel. (4) 8256492; fax (4) 8252923; f. 1987; weekly; Editor LE NAM SON.

Outlook: 11 Tran Hung Dao, Hanoi; tel. (4) 8222884; fax (4) 9424908; e-mail vnnews@vnagency.com.vn; internet vietnamnews .vnanet.com.vn; f. 2002; monthly news magazine; Editor-in-Chief TRAN MAI HUONG; circ. 6,000.

Phu Nu (Woman): Vietnam Women's Union, International Relations Dept, 39 Hang Chuoi, Hanoi; e-mail VWUnion@netnam.org.vn; f. 1997; fortnightly; women's magazine; circ. 100,000.

Phu Nu Thu Do (Capital Women): 72 Quan Su, Hanoi; tel. (4) 8247228; fax (4) 8223989; f. 1987; weekly; magazine of the Hanoi Women's Union; Editor-in-Chief MAI THUC.

Phu Nu Viet Nam (Vietnamese Women): 39 Hang Chuoi, Hanoi; tel. (4) 8253500; weekly; magazine of the Vietnam Women's Union; Editor-in-Chief PHUONG MINH.

Suc Khoe Va Doi Song (Health and Life): 138A Giang Vo, Hanoi; tel. (4) 8443144; weekly; published by the Ministry of Public Health; Editor LE THAU; circ. 20,000.

Tap Chi Cong San (Communist Review): 28 Tran Binh Trong Thanh, Hanoi; tel. (4) 9429753; fax (4) 9429754; e-mail bbttccs@hn .vnn.vn; internet www.tapchicongsan.org.vn; f. 1955 as *Hoc Tap*; fortnightly; political and theoretical organ of the Communist Party of Viet Nam; Editor-in-Chief TA NGOC TAN; circ. 50,000.

Tap Chi Nghiên Cuu Van Hoc (Literature Research Magazine): 20 Ly Thai To, Hanoi; tel. (4) 8252895; e-mail tcvapmail@vnn.vn; monthly; published by the Institute of Literature; Editor-in-Chief PHAN TRONG THUONG.

Tap Chi San Khau (Theatre Magazine): 51 Tran Hung Dao, Hanoi; tel. (4) 9434423; fax (4) 9434293; e-mail trongkhoi@hn.vnn.vn; f. 1973; monthly; Editor NGO THAO.

Tap Chi Tac Pham Van Hoc: 65 Nguyen Du, Hanoi; tel. (4) 8252442; f. 1987; monthly; organ of the Viet Nam Writers' Asscn; Editor-in-Chief NGUYEN DINH THI; circ. 15,000.

Tap Chi Tu Tuong Van Hoa (Ideology and Culture Review): Hanoi; f. 1990; organ of the Central Committee Department of Ideology and Culture; Editor PHAM HUY VAN.

The Thao Van Hoa (Sports and Culture): 5 Ly Thuong Kiet, Hanoi; tel. (4) 8267043; fax (4) 8264901; f. 1982; weekly; Editor-in-Chief NGUYEN HUU VINH; circ. 100,000.

The Thao Viet Nam (Viet Nam Sports): 5 Trinh Hoai Duc, Hanoi; tel. (4) 35625457; fax (4) 35625455; e-mail baottvn@yahoo.com; internet www.thethaovietnam.com.vn; f. 1968; weekly; Editor HOANG DUR.

Thieu Nhi Dan Toc (The Ethnic Young): 5 Hoa Ma, Hanoi; tel. (4) 9317133; bi-monthly; Editor PHAM THANH LONG; circ. 60,000.

Thieu Nien Tien Phong (Young Pioneers): 5 Hoa Ma, Hanoi; tel. (4) 9713133; fax (4) 8215710; e-mail toasoan@tntp.org.vn; internet www .tntp.org.vn; 3 a week; Editor PHAM THANH LONG; circ. 210,000.

Thoi Bao Kinh Te Viet Nam: 175 Nguyen Thai Hoc, Hanoi; tel. (4) 8452411; fax (4) 8432755; f. 1993; 2 a week; Editor-in-Chief PAVEF DAONGUYENCAT; circ. 37,000.

Thoi Trang Tre (New Fashion): 12 Ho Xuan Huong, Hanoi; tel. (4) 8254032; fax (4) 8226002; f. 1993; monthly; Editor VU QUANG VINH; circ. 80,000.

Thuong Mai (Commerce): 100 Lo Duc, Hanoi; tel. (4) 8263150; f. 1990; weekly; organ of the Ministry of Trade; Editor TRAN NAM VINH.

Tien Phong (Vanguard): 15 Ho Xuan Huong, Hanoi; tel. (4) 8264031; fax (4) 8225032; f. 1953; four a week; organ of the Ho Chi Minh Communist Youth Union and of the Forum of Vietnamese Youth; Editor DUONG XUAN NAM; circ. 165,000.

Van Hoa (Culture and Arts): 26 Dien Bien Phu, Hanoi; tel. (4) 8257781; f. 1957; fortnightly; Editor PHI VAN TUONG.

Van Nghe (Arts and Letters): 17 Tran Quoc Toan, Hanoi; tel. (4) 8264430; f. 1949; weekly; organ of the Vietnamese Writers' Union; Editor HUU THINH; circ. 40,000.

Van Nghe Quan Doi (Army Literature and Arts): 4 Ly Nam De, Hanoi; tel. (4) 8254370; f. 1957; monthly; Editor NGUYEN TRI HUAN; circ. 50,000.

Viet Nam Business Forum: 9 Dao Duy Anh, 4th Floor, Dong Da District, Hanoi; tel. (4) 35771365; fax (4) 35771563; e-mail vbfhn@hn .vnn.vn; internet vibforum.vcci.com.vn; f. 1995; weekly magazine in English; publ. by the Viet Nam Chamber of Commerce and Industry; Editor-in-Chief DOAN DUY KHUONG.

Viet Nam Courier: 5 Ly Thuong Kiet, Hanoi; tel. (4) 8261847; fax (4) 8242317; weekly; English; publ. by the Viet Nam News Agency; Editor-in-Chief NGUYEN DUC GIAP.

Viet Nam Cultural Window: 46 Tran Hung Dao, Hanoi; tel. (4) 8253841; fax (4) 8269578; e-mail vncw@hn.vnn.vn; f. 1998; every 2 months; English; Dir TRAN DOAN LAM.

Viet Nam Investment Review (VIR): 175 Nguyen Thai Hoc, Hanoi; tel. (4) 8450537; fax (4) 8235281; e-mail vir@hn.vnn.vn; internet www.vir.com.vn/Client/VIR/Default.asp; f. 1990; weekly;

business newspaper publ. in English; Editor-in-Chief Dr NGUYEN PHU KY; circ 40,000.

Vietnam Pictorial: 11 Tran Hung Dao, Hanoi; tel. (4) 9332303; fax (4) 9332291; e-mail vietnampictorial@vnanet.vn; f. 1954; monthly online, in Vietnamese, English, French, Chinese, Japanese, Spanish and Russian; fmrly Viet Nam Review; Editor-in-Chief NGUYEN VINH QUANG; circ. 138,000.

Viet Nam Renovation: Hanoi; f. 1994; quarterly magazine on reform of the agricultural sector; in Vietnamese, Chinese and English.

Viet Nam Social Sciences: 27 Tran Xuan Soan, Hanoi; tel. (4) 9784578; fax (4) 9783869; e-mail 21.6.tapchikxh@fpt.vn; f. 1984; every 2 months; publ. in English and Vietnamese; organ of Viet Nam Social Academy; Editor-in-Chief Dr LE DINH CUC.

Vietnamese Studies: 46 Tran Hung Dao, Hanoi; tel. (4) 8253841; fax (4) 8269578; e-mail thegioi@hn.vnn.vn; internet www.thegioipublishers.com.vn; f. 1964; quarterly; English and French edns; Dir and Chief Editor Dr TRAN DOAN LAM.

NEWS AGENCY

Viet Nam News Agency (VNA): 5 Ly Thuong Kiet, Hoan Kiem District, Hanoi; tel. (4) 8252931; fax (4) 8252984; e-mail btk@vnanet.vn; internet www.vnanet.vn; f. 1945; mem. of Organization of Asian and Pacific News Agencies; Gen. Dir NGUYEN QUOC UY.

PRESS ASSOCIATION

Viet Nam Journalists' Association (VJA): 59 Ly Thai To, Hanoi; tel. (4) 39386270; fax (4) 38250797; e-mail sumocon@gmail.com; internet www.vja.org.vn; f. 1950; asscn of editors, reporters and photographers working in the press, radio, television and news agencies; 16,000 mems (2006); Pres. DINH THE HUYNH; Vice-Pres. LE QUOC TRUNG.

Publishers

Am Nhac Dia Hat (Music) Publishing House: 61 Ly Thai To, Hoan Kiem District, Hanoi; tel. (4) 8256208; f. 1986; produces cassettes, videocassettes, books and printed music; Dir PHAM DUC LOC.

Cong An Nhan Dan (People's Public Security) Publishing House: 167 Mai Hac De, Hai Ba Trung District, Hanoi; tel. (4) 8260910; f. 1981; cultural and artistic information, public order and security; Dir PHAM VAN THAM.

Giao Thong Van Tai (Communications and Transport) Publishing House: 80B Tran Hung Dao, Hanoi; tel. (4) 8255620; fax (4) 8224784; f. 1983; managed by the Ministry of Transport and Communications; 350 titles annually; Dir LE TU GIANG.

Khoa Hoc Va Ky Thuat (Science and Technology) Publishing House: 70 Tran Hung Dao, Hanoi; tel. (4) 9424786; fax (4) 8220658; e-mail nxbkhkt@hn.vnn.vn; internet www.nxbkhkt.com.vn; f. 1960; scientific and technical works, guide books, dictionaries, popular and management books; Dir Prof. Dr TO DANG HAI.

Khoa Hoc Xa Hoi (Social Sciences) Publishing House: 61 Phan Chu Trinh, Hanoi; tel. (4) 8255428; f. 1967; managed by the Institute of Social Science; Dir Dr NGUYEN DUC ZIEU.

Kim Dong Publishing House: 55 Quang Trung, Hanoi; tel. (4) 9434730; fax (4) 8229085; e-mail kimdong@hn.vnn.vn; internet www.nxbkimdong.com.vn; f. 1957; children's; managed by the Ho Chi Minh Communist Youth Union; Dir PHAM QUANG VINH; Editor-in-Chief LE THI DAT.

Lao Dong (Labour) Publishing House: 54 Giang Vo, Hanoi; tel. (4) 8515380; f. 1945; translations and political works; managed by the Viet Nam General Confederation of Labour; Dir LE THANH TONG.

My Thuat (Fine Arts) Publishing House: 44B Hamlong, Hanoi; tel. (4) 8253036; f. 1987; managed by the Plastic Arts Workers' Association; Dir TRUONG HANH.

Nha Xuat Ban Giao Duc (Education) Publishing House: 81 Tran Hung Dao, Hanoi; tel. (4) 8220801; fax (4) 9422010; e-mail vanphong@nxbgd.vn; internet www.nxbgd.com.vn; f. 1957; managed by the Ministry of Education and Training; Dir NGO TRAN AI; Editor-in-Chief NGUYEN QUY THAO.

Nha Xuat Ban Hoi Nha Van (Writers' Association) Publishing House: 65 Nguyen Du, Hoan Kiem District, Hanoi; tel. and fax (4) 8222135; f. 1957; managed by the Vietnamese Writers' Association; Editor-in-Chief and Dir (acting) NGO VAN PHU.

Nong Nghiep (Agriculture) Publishing House: DH 14, Phoung Mai Ward, Dong Da District, Hanoi; tel. (4) 8523887; f. 1976; managed by the Ministry of Agriculture and Rural Development; Dir DUONG QUANG DIEU.

Phu Nu (Women) Publishing House: 16 Alexandre De Rhodes, Hanoi; tel. (4) 8294459; f. 1957; managed by the Vietnamese Women's Union; Dir TRAN THU HUONG.

Quan Doi Nhan Dan (People's Army) Publishing House: 25 Ly Nam De, Hanoi; tel. (4) 8255766; managed by the Ministry of National Defence; Dir DOAN CHUONG.

San Khau (Theatre) Publishing House: 51 Tran Hung Dao, Hanoi; tel. (4) 8264423; f. 1986; managed by the Stage Artists' Association.

Su That (Truth) Publishing House: 24 Quang Trung, Hanoi; tel. (4) 8252008; fax (4) 8251881; f. 1945; managed by the Communist Party of Viet Nam; Marxist-Leninist classics, politics and philosophy; Dir TRAN NHAM.

Thanh Nien (Youth) Publishing House: 270 Nguyen Dinh Chieu, District 3, Hanoi; tel. and fax (4) 8222612; f. 1954; managed by the Ho Chi Minh Communist Youth Union; Dir BUI VAN NGOI.

The Duc The Thao (Physical Education and Sports) Publishing House: 7 Trinh Hoai Duc, Hanoi; tel. (4) 8256155; f. 1974; managed by the Ministry of Culture and Information; Dir NGUYEN HIEU.

The Gioi Publishers: 46 Tran Hung Dao, Hanoi; tel. (4) 8253841; fax (4) 8269578; e-mail thegioi@hn.vnn.vn; internet www.thegioipublishers.com.vn; f. 1957; foreign language publications; managed by the Ministry of Culture and Information; Dir and Chief Editor Dr TRAN DOAN LAM.

Thong Ke (Statistics) Publishing House: 96 Thuy Khe, Hanoi; tel. (4) 8257814; f. 1980; managed by the Gen. Statistics Office; Dir NGUYEN DAO.

Van Hoa (Culture) Publishing House: 43 Lo Duc, Hanoi; tel. (4) 8253517; f. 1971; managed by the Ministry of Culture and Information; Dir QUANG HUY.

Van Hoc (Literature) Publishing House: 19 Nguyen Truong To, Ba Dinh, Hanoi; tel. (4) 8294783; fax (4) 8294781; f. 1948; managed by the Ministry of Culture and Information; Dir NGUYEN VAN CU.

Xay Dung (Building) Publishing House: 37 Le Dai Hanh, Hanoi; tel. (4) 8268271; fax (4) 8215369; f. 1976; managed by the Ministry of Construction; Dir NGUYEN LUONG BICH.

Y Hoc (Medicine) Publishing House: 4 Le Thanh Ton, Phan Chu Trinh, Hoan Kiem District, Hanoi; tel. (4) 8255281; e-mail xuatbanyhoc@netnam.vn; managed by the Ministry of Public Health; Dir HOANG TRONG QUANG.

Broadcasting and Communications

TELECOMMUNICATIONS

Directorate General for Posts and Telecommunications (DGPT): Department of Science-Technology and International Cooperation, 18 Nguyen Du, Hanoi; tel. (4) 8226580; fax (4) 8226590; industry regulator; Sec.-Gen. Dr MAI LIEM TRUC.

Board of the Technical and Economic Programme on Information Technology: 39 Tran Hung Dao, Hanoi; e-mail nyenet@itnet.gov.vn; Gen. Dir Dr DO VAN LOC.

Electricity of Viet Nam Telecommunications Co (EVN Telecom): 18 Tran Nguyen Han, Hanoi; tel. (4) 8249508; fax (4) 8249461; internet www.evntelecom.com; provides fixed and cellular telephone services, as well as broadband internet services.

Hanoi Telecommunications Co (Hanoi Telecom): 149C Truong Dinh, District 3, Ho Chi Minh City; tel. (3) 5729833; fax (4) 5729834; e-mail info@hanoitelecom.com; internet www.hanoitelecom.com; f. 2005; cellular telephone service provider.

Saigon Post and Telecommunications Service Corpn: 45 Le Duan, District 1, Ho Chi Minh City; tel. (8) 4040608; fax (8) 4040609; e-mail saigonpostel@saigonpostel.com.vn; internet www.saigonpostel.com.vn; f. 1995; partially owned by the State; nationwide post and telecommunications services; Chair. TRAN THI NGOC BINH; Pres. PHAM NGOC TUAN.

Viet Nam Military Electronics and Telecommunications Corpn (Viettel): 16 Phao Dai Lang, Dong Da District, Hanoi; tel. (4) 2556789; fax (4) 2996789; internet www.viettel.com.vn; f. 1998; offers range of post and telecommunication services, including cellular telephone and broadband internet services; Dir HOANG ANG XUAN.

Viet Nam Posts and Telecommunications Corpn (VNPT): 18 Nguyen Du, Hai Ba Trung District, Hanoi; tel. (3) 5775104; fax (3) 5775851; e-mail vnpt_website@vnpt.com.vn; internet www.vnpt.com.vn; f. 1995; state-owned communications co; Chair. PHAM LONG TRAN (acting); Pres. and CEO VU TUAN HUNG.

Viet Nam Mobile Telecommunication Services Co (MobiFone): Hanoi; internet www.mobifone.com.vn; f. 1993; mobile cellular telephone service provider.

VIET NAM

Viet Nam Telecommunication Services Co (VinaPhone): 57A Huynh Thuc Khang, Dong Da District, Hanoi; tel. (4) 8358816; fax (4) 7731745; internet www.vinaphone.com.vn; f. 1996; provides mobile cellular telephone services; Dir HOANG TRUNG HAI.

Vietnam Power Telecommunications Co (VP Telecom): Hanoi; f. 2004; cellular telephone service provider.

RADIO

Voice of Viet Nam (VOV): 58 Quan Su, Hanoi; tel. (4) 9344231; fax (4) 9344230; e-mail english@vovnews.vn; internet www.vov.org.vn; f. 1945; four domestic channels in Vietnamese; two foreign service channels in English, Japanese, French, Khmer, Laotian, Spanish, Thai, Cantonese, Mandarin, Indonesian, Vietnamese and Russian; Dir-Gen. Dr VU VAN HIEN.

TELEVISION

Viet Nam Television (VTV): 43 Nguyen Chi Thanh, Hanoi; tel. (4) 8354992; fax (4) 8350882; e-mail webmaster@vtv.org.vn; internet www.vtv.org.vn; television was introduced in South Viet Nam in 1966 and in North Viet Nam in 1970; broadcasts from Hanoi (via satellite) to the whole country, the Asia region, Western Europe and North America; Vietnamese, French, English; Dir-Gen. Dr VU VAN HIEN.

Vietnam Multimedia Corpn (Vietnam Television Corpn—VTC): internet www.vtc.com.vn.

Finance

(cap. = capital; p.u. = paid up; res = reserves; dep. = deposits; m. = million; brs = branches; amounts in new dông unless otherwise indicated)

BANKING

In 2002 the Vietnamese banking system comprised five state-owned commercial banks, one policy bank, five joint-venture banks, 26 foreign bank branches, 36 joint-stock commercial banks and approximately 900 People's Credit Funds. From March 2006 foreign banks were for the first time allowed to offer a full range of banking services.

Central Bank

State Bank of Viet Nam: 47–49 Ly Thai To, Hanoi; tel. (4) 8242479; fax (4) 8268765; e-mail nhnn@sbv.gov.vn; internet www.sbv.gov.vn; f. 1951; central bank of issue; provides a national network of banking services and supervises the operation of the state banking system; Gov. NGUYEN VAN GIAU; 61 brs and sub-brs.

State Banks

Bank for Agriculture and Rural Development: 2 Lang Ha, Ba Dinh District, Hanoi; tel. (4) 8313694; fax (4) 8313717; e-mail webmaster@vbard.com; internet www.vbard.com; f. 1988; cap. 10,734,214m., res 3,039,786m., dep. 251,489,365m. (Dec. 2007); Chair. NGOC DO TAT; Gen. Dir VAN SO LE; 1,291 brs.

Bank for Foreign Trade of Viet Nam (Vietcombank): 198 Tran Quang Khai, Hanoi; tel. (4) 8251322; fax (4) 8269067; e-mail webmaster@vietcombank.com.vn; internet www.vietcombank.com .vn; f. 1963; authorized to deal in foreign currencies and all other international banking business; undergoing equitization in mid-2005; cap. (p.u.) 5,537,564m., res 5,331,561m., dep. 136,247,226m. (Dec. 2006); Chair. NGUYEN HOA BINH; Dir-Gen. VU VIET NGOAN; 23 brs.

Bank for Investment and Development of Vietnam (Vietinde Bank): Vincom City Tower, Block A, 191 Ba Trieu, Hai Ba Trung District, Hanoi; tel. (4) 2200422; fax (4) 2200399; e-mail fi@bidv.com .vn; internet www.bidv.com.vn; cap. 4,077,401m., res 3,437,687m., dep. 149,352,743m. (Dec. 2006); Chair. VU QUOC SAU; Gen. Dir TRAN BAC HA.

Saigon Bank for Industry and Trade: 2C Pho Duc Chinh, District 1, Ho Chi Minh City; tel. (8) 9143183; fax (8) 9143193; internet www .saigonbank.com.vn; cap. 400,000m., res 98,294m., dep. 3,475,260m. (Dec. 2005); specializes in trade and industry activities; Chair. NGUYEN PHUC MINH; Dir-Gen. TRAN THI VIET ANH; 11 brs and 7 sub-brs.

Vietnam Bank for Industry and Trade (VietinBank): 108 Tran Hung Dao, Hanoi; tel. (4) 9421030; fax (4) 9421032; e-mail webteam@ icbv.com; internet www.icb.com.vn; f. 1987; fmrly Industrial and Commercial Bank of Viet Nam (Incombank); state-owned; authorized to receive personal savings, extend loans, issue stocks and invest in export-orientated cos and jt ventures with foreign interests; cap. 3,405,705m., res 1,262,749m., dep. 100,571,938m. (Dec. 2005); Chair. PHAM HUY HUNG; Gen. Dir PHAM XUAN LAP; 131 brs.

Vietnam Export-Import Commercial Joint-Stock Bank (Vietnam Eximbank): 7 Le Thi Hong Gam, District 1, Ho Chi Minh City; tel. (8) 8210055; fax (8) 8296063; internet www.eximbank.com.vn; f. 1989 as Vietnam Export Import Bank, name changed as above 1992; authorized to undertake banking transactions for the production and processing of export products and export-import operations; cap. 1,688,273m., res 56,903m., dep. 15,636,201m. (Dec. 2006); Chair. NGUYEN THANH LONG; Dir-Gen. NGUYEN GIA DINH; 5 brs.

Viet Nam Technological and Commercial Joint-Stock Bank (Techcombank): 15 Dao Duy Tu, Hoan Kiem District, Hanoi; tel. (4) 8243941; fax (4) 8250545; internet www.techcombank.com.vn; cap. 2,521,308m., res 623,472m., dep. 34,845,195m. (Dec. 2007); Chair. HO HUNG AHN; Pres. and CEO NGUYEN DUC VINH.

Joint-Stock and Other Banks

CBD (Codo Rural Share Commercial Bank): Co Do, Thoi Dong, O Mon, Can Tho Province; tel. (71) 61642; Dir TRAN NGOC HA.

DS Bank (Dongthap Commercial Joint-Stock Bank): 48 Rad 30/4, Cao Lanh Town, Dong Thap Province; tel. (67) 51441; fax (67) 51878; Dir HOANG VAN TU.

Ficombank (Denhat Joint-Stock Commercial Bank): 67A Le Quang Sung, District 6, Ho Chi Minh City; tel. (8) 8556066; fax (8) 8557093; Dir VAN DUONG.

Indovina Bank Ltd: 39 Ham Nghi, District 1, Ho Chi Minh City; tel. (8) 8224995; fax (8) 8230131; internet www.indovinabank.com.vn; f. 1990; jt venture of the Cathay United Bank (Taiwan) and the Industrial and Commercial Bank of Viet Nam; also has brs in Hanoi, Haiphong, Binh Duong, Can Tho and Dong Nai; cap. US $25m., res $3.4m., dep. $151m. (Dec. 2004); Chair. ROGER MING HSIEN LEE; Gen. Dir JAN YEI FONG; 5 brs.

Maritime Bank: 5A Nguyen Tri Phuong, Haiphong; tel. (3) 7718989; fax (3) 7718899; internet www.msb.com.vn; f. 1991; cap. 109,310m. (2003); Pres. TRAN BA VINH; 9 brs.

Phuong Nam Commercial Joint-Stock Bank (Southern Bank): 279 Ly Thuong Kiet, District 11, Ho Chi Minh City; tel. (8) 8663890; fax (8) 8663904; internet www.southernbank.com.vn; f. 1993; Chair. TRUONG TY.

Quedo Joint-Stock Bank: 1-3-5 Can Giuoc, District 8, Ho Chi Minh City; tel. (8) 8562418; fax (8) 8553596; Dir BAO LAN.

Sacombank (Saigon Thuong Tin Commercial Joint-Stock Bank): 278 Nam Ky Khoi Nghia St, District 3, Ho Chi Minh City; tel. (8) 9320420; fax (8) 9320424; e-mail sacombank@vnn.vn; internet www .sacombank.com.vn; f. 1991; became the first bank to list on the Securities Trading Centre in July 2006; Chair. DANG VAN THANH; CEO TRAN XUAN HUY.

Shinhanvina Bank: 3-5 Ho Tung Mau, District 1, Ho Chi Minh City; tel. (8) 8291581; fax (8) 8291583; e-mail hcmc.fvb@hcm.vnn.vn; f. 1993; jt venture between the Bank for Foreign Trade of Viet Nam and Korea First Bank; fmrly known as Chohung Vina Bank; cap. US $30.0m., res $3.3m., dep. $181.5m. (Dec. 2007); Chair. PHU THAI VU; Dir-Gen. SUNG HO NOH.

VID Public Bank: Ground Floor, Hanoi Tungshing Square, 2 Ngo Quyen, Hanoi; tel. (4) 8268307; fax (4) 8268228; e-mail vpb.han@hn .vnn.vn; internet www.vidpublicbank.com.vn; f. 1992; jt venture between the Bank for Investment and Development of Viet Nam and the Public Bank Berhad (Malaysia); commercial bank; cap. US $20m. (2001); Chair. TRAN ANH TUAN (acting); Gen. Dir TAY HONG HENG; 5 brs.

VinaSiam Bank: 2 Pho Duc Chinh, District 1, Ho Chi Minh City; tel. (8) 8210557; fax (8) 8210585; internet www.vinasiambank.com; f. 1995; jt venture between Bank for Agriculture and Rural Development, Siam Commercial Bank (Thailand) and Charoen Pokphand Group (Thailand); cap. US $20.0m., res. $1.1m., dep. $37.2m. (Dec. 2005); Chair. LE VAN SO; Gen. Man. VIROJ THANAPITAK.

VP Bank (Viet Nam Commercial Joint-Stock Bank for Private Enterprises): 18B Le Thanh Tong, Hanoi; tel. (4) 8245246; fax (4) 8260182; internet www.vpb.com.vn; Chair. LAM HOANG LOC.

STOCK EXCHANGE

Ho Chi Minh Stock Exchange: 45–47 Ben Chuong Duong, Nguyen Thai Binh District, Ho Chi Minh City; tel. (8) 8217713; fax (8) 8217452; internet www.vse.org.vn; f. 2000 by the State Securities Commission (see Development Organization); fmrly Securities Trading Centre; name changed as above in 2007; Chair. NGUYEN DOAN HUNG.

INSURANCE

In September 2006 there were 22 insurance companies operating in the country.

Aon Vietnam Ltd: Suites 1403/6/7, 14th Floor, Vietcombank Tower, 198 Tran Quang Khai, Hoan Kiem District, Hanoi; tel. (4) 8260832;

fax (4) 8243983; e-mail vu_my_lan@aon-asia.com; f. 1993; fmrly Inchibrok Insurance; Man. Dir Vu My Lan.

Bao Long (Nha Rong Joint-Stock Insurance Co): 185 Dien Bien Phu, District 1, Ho Chi Minh City; tel. (8) 8239219; fax (8) 8239223; internet www.nharong.com; Dir Tran Van Binh.

Bao Minh Insurance Co (Ho Chi Minh City Insurance Co): 26 Ton That Dam, District 1, Ho Chi Minh City; tel. (8) 8294180; fax (8) 8294185; e-mail baominh@baominh.com.vn; internet www.baominh .com.vn; f. 1994; non-life; Chair. and CEO Vinh Duc Tran.

Baoviet (Viet Nam Insurance Co): 35 Hai Ba Trung, Hoan Kiem District, Hanoi; tel. (4) 8262632; fax (4) 8262614; internet www .baoviet.com.vn; f. 1965; property and casualty, personal accident, liability and life insurance; total assets 8,817,000m. dông (2004); CEO Nguyen Thi Phuc Lam; Chair. Le Quang Binh.

Dai-ichi Life Insurance Co of Vietnam Ltd: 3rd Floor, Saigon Riverside Office Center, 2A–4A, Ton Duc Thang, District 1, Ho Chi Minh City; tel. (8) 8291919; fax (8) 8293131; e-mail info@dai-ichi-life .com.vn; internet www.dai-ichi-life.com.vn; f. 2007.

Manulife (Vietnam) Ltd: Manulife Plaza, 75 Hoang Van Thai, Tan Phu Ward, District 7, Ho Chi Minh City; tel. (8) 4166888; fax (8) 4161818; e-mail manulifevn_info@manulife.com; internet www .manulife.com.vn; f. 1999; fmrly Chinfon-Manulife Life Insurance Co Ltd; first wholly foreign-owned life insurance co to operate in Viet Nam; Gen. Dir David Wong.

Petrolimex Joint-Stock Insurance Co (PJICO Insurance): 532 Lang Ha, Dong Da District, Hanoi; tel. (4) 7760865; fax (4) 7760868; e-mail pjico@petrolimex.com.vn; internet www.pjico.com.vn; f. 1995; non-life insurance; Chair. Bui Ngoc Bao; CEO Nguyen Anh Dung.

PetroVietnam Insurance Joint Stock Corpn (PVI): 154 Nguyen Thai Hoc, Ba Dinh District, Hanoi; tel. (4) 7335588; fax (4) 7336284; e-mail contact@pvi.com.vn; internet www.pvi.com.vn; f. 1996; non-life insurance; Man. Dir Le Van Hung.

Viet Nam International Assurance Co (VIA): 3rd Floor, Petro-Vietnam Tower, 1–5 Le Duan, District 1, Ho Chi Minh City; tel. (8) 8221340; fax (8) 8221338; e-mail hcm@via.com.vn; internet www.via .com.vn; f. 1996; jt-venture co, 51% owned by Baoviet, 49% owned by Tokyo Marine and Fire Insurance Co (Japan); non-life insurance and reinsurance for foreign cos; Marketing Man. Peter Huy.

INSURANCE ASSOCIATION

Association of Vietnamese Insurers: 8th Floor, 141 Le Duan, Hanoi; tel. (4) 9428106; fax (4) 9422601; internet www.avi.org.vn; Chair. Trinh Quang Tuyen.

Trade and Industry

GOVERNMENT AGENCIES

State Financial and Monetary Council (SFMC): f. 1998; established to supervise, review and resolve matters relating to national financial and monetary policy.

Vietrade (Viet Nam Trade Promotion Agency): 20 Ly Thuong Kiet, Hanoi; tel. (4) 9347628; fax (4) 9344260; e-mail xttm@vietrade.gov .vn; internet www.vietrade.gov.vn; part of the Ministry of Trade; responsible for state management, co-ordination and implementation of trade and trade-related investment promotion and development activities; Dir-Gen. Do Thang Hai.

Vinacontrol (The Viet Nam Superintendence and Inspection Joint Stock Co): 54 Tran Nhan Tong, Hanoi; tel. (4) 9436011; fax (4) 9433844; e-mail vinacontrolvn@hn.vnn.vn; internet www .vinacontrol.com.vn; f. 1957; brs in all main Vietnamese ports and trade centres; controls quality and volume of exports and imports and transit of goods, and conducts inspections of deliveries and production processes; price, assets and enterprise valuation, marine survey, damage survey, claim settling and adjustment; Chair. Bui Duy Chinh; Gen. Dir Mai Tien Dung; 600 employees.

DEVELOPMENT ORGANIZATION

State Securities Commission: 164 Tran Quang Khai, Hanoi; tel. (4) 9340750; fax (4) 9340739; e-mail banbientap@ssc.gov.vn; internet www.ssc.gov.vn; f. 1997; responsible for developing the capital markets, incl. the establishment of a stock exchange; 14 mems; Chair. Bang Vu.

CHAMBER OF COMMERCE

VCCI (Viet Nam Chamber of Commerce and Industry): 9 Dao Duy Anh, 4th Floor, Hanoi; tel. (4) 5743985; fax (4) 5743063; e-mail vcci@ fmail.vnn.vn; internet www.vcci.com.vn; f. 1963; offices in Ho Chi Minh City, Da Nang, Haiphong, Can Tho, Vung Tau, Nha Trang, Nghe An, Thanh Hoa and Vinh; promotes business and investment between foreign and Vietnamese cos; protects interests of businesses; organizes training activities, exhbns and fairs in Viet Nam and abroad; provides information about and consultancy in Viet Nam's trade and industry; represents foreign applicants for patents and trade mark registration; issues certificates of origin and other documentation; helps domestic and foreign businesses to settle disputes by negotiation or arbitration; in 1993 foreign businesses operating in Viet Nam and Vietnamese businesses operating abroad were permitted to become assoc. mems; Pres. and Chair. Dr Vu Tien Loc; Sec.-Gen. Pham Gia Tuc; associated organizations: Viet Nam International Arbitration Centre, Viet Nam General Average Adjustment Committee, Advisory Board.

Viet Nam International Arbitration Centre (VIAC): 9 Dao Duy Anh, 6th Floor, Dong Da District, Hanoi; tel. (4) 5742021; fax (4) 5743001; e-mail viac-vcci@hn.vnn.vn; internet www.viac.org .vn; f. 1993; adjudicates in disputes concerning both domestic and international economic relations.

INDUSTRIAL AND TRADE ORGANIZATIONS

Agrex Saigon (Agricultural Products and Foodstuffs Export Co): 58 Vo Van Tan, District 3, Ho Chi Minh City; tel. (8) 9303186; fax (8) 9303451; e-mail tt-agr@hcm.fpt.vn; internet www.agrexsaigon.com .vn; f. 1976; exports agricultural produce, coffee, frozen foods and aquatic products; imports agricultural and industrial materials, machinery and equipment, and consumer goods; Gen. Dir Duong Ky Hung; 1,200 employees.

Agrimex (Viet Nam National Agricultural Products Corpn): 173 Hai Ba Trung, District 3, Ho Chi Minh City; tel. (8) 8241049; fax (8) 8291349; e-mail agrimex@hcm.fpt.vn; f. 1956; imports and exports agricultural products; Gen. Dir Nguyen Bach Tuyet.

Airimex (General Civil Aviation Import-Export and Forwarding Co): 100 Nguyen Van Cu, Gia Lam, Long Bien District, Hanoi; tel. (4) 8271939; fax (4) 8271925; e-mail airimex@fpt.vn; f. 1989; imports and exports aircraft, spare parts and accessories for aircraft and air communications; Gen. Dir Pham Doa Hong.

An Giang Afiex Co (An Giang Agriculture and Foods Import and Export Co): 34–36 Hai Ba Trung, Long Xuyen Town, An Giang Province; tel. (76) 841021; fax (76) 843199; e-mail xnknstpagg@hcm .vnn.net; f. 1992; mfr and sale of agricultural products, also beverages; Dir Pham Van Bay.

Artexport–Hanoi (Viet Nam Handicrafts and Art Articles Export-Import Corpn): 31–33 Ngo Quyen, Hanoi; tel. (4) 8252760; fax (4) 8259275; e-mail artexport.hn@fpt.vn; internet www.artexport.com .vn; f. 1964; deals in craft products and art articles; Gen. Dir Do Van Khoi.

Barotex (Viet Nam National Bamboo and Rattan Export-Import Co): 100 Thai Thinh, Dong Da District, Hanoi; tel. (4) 8573428; fax (4) 8573036; e-mail info@barotex.com.vn; internet www.barotex.com .vn; f. 1971; specializes in art and handicrafts made from natural materials, sports shoes, ceramic and lacquer wares, gifts and other housewares, fibres, agricultural and forest products; Gen. Dir Ta Quoc Toan.

Bimson Cement Co: Badinh, Bimson Town, Thanh Hoa Province; tel. (37) 824242; fax (37) 824046; e-mail ktkh_bs@yahoo.com; internet www.ximangbimson.com.vn; mfr of cement; Dir Le Van Chung.

Binh Tay Import-Export Joint Stock Co (BITEX): 110–112 Hau Giang, District 6, Ho Chi Minh City; tel. (8) 9604325; fax (8) 9602478; e-mail bitexvn@bitexvn.com; internet www.bitexvn.com; trade in miscellaneous goods; Dir Nguyen Van Thien.

B12 Petroleum Co: Cai Lan, Bay Chay Sub-District, Ha Long City, Quang Ninh Province; tel. (33) 846360; fax (33) 846349; internet www.b12petroleum.com.vn; distribution of petroleum products; Dir Vu Ngoc Hai.

Centrimex (Viet Nam National General Import-Export Corpn): 247 Giang Vo, Dong Da District, Hanoi; tel. (58) 8512986; fax (58) 8512974; e-mail centrimexhn@fpt.vn; internet www.centrimexhn .com.vn; f. 1986; exports and imports goods for five provinces in the south-central region of Viet Nam; Gen. Dir Hoang Dinh Dung.

Coalimex (Vinacoal Import-Export Joint Stock Co): 33 Trang Thi, Hanoi; tel. (4) 9723845; fax (4) 9723846; e-mail coalimexhn@vnn.vn; internet www.coalimex.com.vn; f. 1982; exports coal, imports mining machinery and equipment; Gen. Dir Pham Hong Khanh.

Cocenex (Central Production Import-Export Corpn): 80 Hang Gai, Hanoi; tel. (4) 8254535; fax (4) 8294306; f. 1988; Gen. Dir Bui Thi Thu Huong.

Coffee Supply, Processing and Materials Co: 38B Nguyen Bieu, Nha Trang City, Khanh Hoa Province; tel. (58) 21176; coffee producer.

Cokyvina (Post and Telecommunication Equipment Import-Export Service Corpn): 178 Trieu Viet Vuong, Hanoi; tel. (4) 9782362; fax (4) 9782368; e-mail cokyvina@hn.vnn.vn; f. 1987; imports and exports telecom equipment, provides technical advice on related subjects, undertakes authorized imports, jt ventures, jt co-ordination and co-

VIET NAM
Directory

operation on investment with foreign and domestic economic organizations; Dir Nguyen Kim Ky.

Constrexim (Viet Nam Construction Investment and Export-Import Holdings Corpn): 39 Nguyen Dinh Chieu, Hanoi; tel. (4) 9744836; fax (4) 9742701; e-mail constrexim@fpt.vn; internet www.constrexim.com.vn; f. 1982; exports and imports building materials, equipment and machinery; undertakes construction projects in Viet Nam and abroad, and production of building materials with foreign partners; also involved in investment promotion and projects management, real estate development, and human resources development and training; Gen. Dir Ly Ngoc Tuan.

Culturimex (State Enterprise for the Export and Import of Works of Art and other Cultural Commodities): 22B Hai Ba Trung, Hanoi; tel. (4) 8252226; fax (4) 8259224; e-mail namson@fpt.vn; f. 1988; exports cultural items and imports materials for the cultural industry; Gen. Dir Nguyen Lai.

Dau Tieng Rubber Corpn: Dau Tieng Townlet, Dau Tieng District, Binh Duong Province; tel. (650) 561847; fax (650) 561488; e-mail vanphong@caosudautieng.com.vn; internet www.caosudautieng.com.vn; f. 1981; planting, processing and export of natural rubber; Man. Dir Le Van Khoa.

Epco Ltd (Export Import and Tourism Co Ltd): 1 Nyuyen Thuong Hien, District 3, Ho Chi Minh City; tel. (8) 8324392; fax (8) 8324744; f. 1986; processes seafood; tourism and hotel business; Gen. Dir Nguyen Loc Ri.

Foocosa (Food Co Ho Chi Min City): 57 Nguyen Thi Minh Khai, District 1, Ho Chi Minh City; tel. (8) 9309070; fax (8) 9304552; e-mail foocosa@hcm.vnn.vn; internet www.foocosa.com; mfr and distributor of food products (rice, instant noodles, porridge, sauces, biscuits); Dir Ngo Van Tan; 3,500 employees.

Forexco Quang Nam (Quang Nam Forest Products Export Joint Stock Co): Dien Ngoc Village, Dien Ban District, Quangnam Province; tel. (510) 843595; fax (510) 843619; e-mail forexcoqnam@dng.vnn.vn; internet www.forexco.com.vn; f. 1986; mfr and exporter of furniture and other wood products; Gen. Dir Pham Phu Tong.

Garmex Saigon (Saigon Garment Manufacturing Import-Export Co): 213 An Duong Vuong, District 5, Ho Chi Minh City; tel. (8) 8557166; fax (8) 8557299; e-mail gmsg@hcm.fpt.vn; f. 1993; garment production and export; Gen. Dir Le Quang Hung.

Genecofov (General Co of Foods and Services): 64 Ba Huyen Thanh Quan, District 3, Ho Chi Minh City; tel. (8) 9325366; fax (8) 9325428; e-mail gecofov@hcm.fpt.vn; f. 1956; import and export of food products, handicrafts and ceramics, garage services, vehicle trading; under the Ministry of Trade; Dir To Van Phat.

Generalexim (Viet Nam National General Export-Import Corpn): 46 Ngo Quyen, Hoan Kiem, Hanoi; tel. (4) 8264009; fax (4) 8259894; e-mail gexim@generalexim.com.vn; f. 1981; export and import on behalf of production and trading organizations, also garment processing for export and manufacture of toys; Gen. Dir Hoang Tuan Khai.

Generalimex (General II Import-Export Joint Stock Co): 216/4 Dien Bien Phu, Ward 7, District 3, Ho Chi Minh City; tel. (8) 2907517; fax (8) 2907518; e-mail generalimex@hcm.fpt.vn; internet www.generalimex.com.vn; exports of agricultural products and spices, imports of machinery, vehicles, chemicals and fertilizers; Gen. Dir Nguyen Van Hoang.

Geruco (Viet Nam General Rubber Corpn): 236 Nam Ky Khoi Nghia, District 3, Ho Chi Minh City; tel. (8) 9327857; fax (8) 9327341; e-mail grc@vngeruco.com; internet www.vngeruco.com; merged with Rubexim (rubber export-import corpn) in 1991; manages and controls the Vietnamese rubber industry, including the planting, processing and trading of natural rubber and rubber wood products; also imports chemicals, machinery and spare parts for the industry; Chair. Tran Ngoc Thanh; Dir-Gen. Le Quang Thung.

Haprosimex (Hanoi General Production and Import-Export Company): Km 11, National Highway 1A, Van Dien, Hanoi; tel. (4) 8618341; fax (4) 8615390; e-mail business@hapro.com.vn; internet www.hapro.com.vn; specializes in handicrafts, textiles, clothing and agricultural and forestry products; Gen. Dir Nguyen Minh Tuan.

Hatien 1 Cement Joint Stock Co: Km 8 Highway Hanoi, Thu Duc, Ho Chi Minh City; tel. (8) 8966608; fax (8) 8967635; e-mail hatien1@hatien1.com.vn; internet www.hatien1.com.vn; mfr of cement; Dir Nguyen Ngoc Anh.

Hatien Cement Co No 2: Kien Luong Town, Ha Tien, Kien Giang Province; tel. (77) 53004; fax (77) 53005; e-mail xmht2@vnn.vn; internet www.xmht2.com; mfr of cement; Dir Nguyen Manh.

Haugiang Petrolimex (Haugiang Petrol and Oil Co): 21 Cach Mang Thang 8, Can Tho City, Can Tho Province; tel. (71) 21657; fax (71) 12746; distributor of fuel; Dir Trinh Mang Thang.

Hoang Thach Cement Co: Minh Tan Hamlet, Kim Mon, Hai Hung Province; tel. (32) 821092; fax (32) 821098; sale of construction materials; Dir Nguyen Duc Hoan.

Intimex Import-Export Corpn: 96 Tran Hung Dao, Hanoi; tel. (4) 9423240; fax (4) 9424250; e-mail intimex@hn.vnn.vn; internet www.intimexco.com; f. 1979; exports mainly agricultural products and processed items; imports mainly consumer goods, motorcycles and raw materials, machinery and equipment for the construction industry; Gen. Dir Vu Anh.

Lefaso (Viet Nam Leather and Footwear Asscn): Rm 120–2, Block 9, 7 Dao Duy Anh, Hanoi; tel. (4) 7281560; fax (4) 7281561; e-mail hhdg@hn.vnn.vn; internet www.lefaso.org.vn; f. 1990 to promote external trade relations, to provide technical support and technological training and to disseminate market information; Chair. Nguyen Gia Thao; Gen. Sec. Nguyen Thi Tong.

Machinoimport (Viet Nam Machinery and Spare Parts Co): 8 Trang Thi, Hoan Kiem, Hanoi; tel. (4) 8253703; fax (4) 8254050; e-mail machinokhdt@hn.vnn.vn; internet www.machinoimport.com.vn; f. 1956 as Vietnam National Machinery Export-Import Corpn; reorganized in 2003; now controlled by Ministry of Trade; imports and exports machinery, spare parts and tools; consultancy, investment, jt-venture, and manufacturing services; comprises 12 cos; Chair. Nguyen Tran Dat; Gen. Dir Tran Duc Truong.

Marine Supply (Marine Technical Materials Import-Export and Supplies): 276A Da Nang, Ngo Quyen, Haiphong; tel. (31) 847308; fax (31) 845159; f. 1985; imports and exports technical materials for marine transportation industry; Dir Phan Trang Chan.

Mecanimex (Viet Nam National Mechanical Products Export-Import Co): 37 Trang Thi, Hoan Kiem District, Hanoi; tel. (4) 8257459; fax (4) 9349904; e-mail mecahn@fpt.vn; internet mecanimex.com.vn; exports and imports mechanical products and hand tools; Gen. Dir Tran Bao Gioc.

Nafobird (Viet Nam Forest and Native Birds, Animals and Ornamental Plants Export-Import Enterprises): 64 Truong Dinh, District 3, Ho Chi Minh City; tel. (8) 8290211; fax (8) 8293735; f. 1987; exports native birds, animals and plants, and imports materials for forestry; Dir Vo Ha An.

Naforimex (Hanoi Forest Products Export-Import and Production Corpn): 19 Ba Trieu, Hoan Kiem District, Hanoi; tel. (4) 8261255; fax (4) 8259264; e-mail naforimexhanoi@fpt.vn; f. 1960; imports chemicals, machinery and spare parts for the forestry industry and water supply network; exports oils, forest products, gum benzoin and resin; CEO Nguyen Ba Hung.

Nitagrex (Ninh Thuan Agricultural Products Import-Export Co): 158 Bac Ai, Do Vinh Ward, Phan Rang Thap Cham, Ninh Thuan Province; tel. (68) 888779; fax (68) 888842; e-mail nitagrex@hcm.vnn.vn; internet www.nitagrex.com.vn; f. 1999; production and export of agricultural products; import of consumer goods, transport vehicles and agricultural materials and equipment; Gen. Dir Dao Van Chan.

Packexport (Viet Nam National Packaging Technology and Import-Export Co): 31 Hang Thung, Hanoi; tel. (4) 8262792; fax (4) 8269227; e-mail packexport-vn@vnn.vn; f. 1976; manufactures packaging for domestic and export demand, and imports materials for the packaging industry; Gen. Dir Trinh Le Kieu.

Petec Trading and Investment Corpn: 194 Nam Ky Khoi Nghia, District 3, Ho Chi Minh City; tel. (8) 9303633; fax (8) 9305686; e-mail petectonghop@hcm.vnn.vn; internet www.petec.com.vn; f. 1981; imports equipment and technology for oil drilling, exploration and oil production; exports crude petroleum, rice, coffee and agricultural products; invests in silk, coffee, financial and transport sectors; Gen. Dir Tran Huu Lac.

Petrol and Oil Co (Zone 1): Duc Gliang Town, Gia Lam, Hanoi; tel. (4) 8271400; fax (4) 8272432; sales of oil and gas; Dir Phan Van Du.

Petrolimex (Viet Nam National Petroleum Corpn): 1 Kham Thien, Dong Da District, Hanoi; tel. (4) 8512603; fax (4) 8519203; e-mail xttm@petrolimex.com.vn; internet www.petrolimex.com.vn; f. 1956; import, export and distribution of petroleum products and liquefied petroleum gas; Chair. Nguyen Manh Tien; Dir-Gen. Tran Van Duc.

Petrolimex Saigon Petroleum Co (Zone 2): 15 Le Duan, District 1, Ho Chi Minh City; tel. (8) 8292081; fax (8) 8222082; sales of petroleum products; Dir Tran Van Thang.

Petrovietnam (The Viet Nam Oil and Gas Corpn): 22 Ngo Quyen, Hoan Kiem District, Hanoi; tel. (4) 8252526; fax (4) 8265942; e-mail webmaster@hn.pv.com.vn; internet www.petrovietnam.com.vn; f. 1975; exploration and production of petroleum and gas; Chair. Dr Pham Quang Du; Pres. and CEO Dr Tran Ngoc Canh.

Saigon Beer Alcohol Beverage Corpn (Sabeco): 6 Hai Ba Trung, Ben Nghe District, Ho Chi Minh City; tel. (8) 8294081; fax (8) 8296856; e-mail biasaigon@sabeco.com.vn; internet www.sabeco.com.vn; producer of beer; Pres. Nguyen Anh Dzung.

Seaco (Sundries Electric Appliances Co): 64 Pho Duc Chinh, District 1, Ho Chi Minh City; tel. (8) 8210961; fax (8) 8210974; deals in miscellaneous electrical goods; Dir Mai Minh Cuong.

Seaprodex Hanoi (Hanoi Sea Products Export-Import Co): 20 Lang Ha, Hanoi; tel. (4) 8344437; fax (4) 8354125; e-mail seahn@

seaprodexhanoi.com.vn; internet www.seaprodexhanoi.com.vn; Dir DANG DINH BAO.

Seaprodex Saigon (Ho Chi Minh City Sea Products Import-Export Corpn): 87 Ham Nghi, District 1, Ho Chi Minh City; tel. (8) 8293669; fax (8) 9142236; e-mail seasaigon@hcm.vnn.vn; internet www.seaprodexsg.com; f. 1978; exports frozen and processed sea products; imports machinery and materials for fishing and processing; Gen. Dir PHUNG QUOC MAN.

SJC (Saigon Jewellery Co): 115 Nguyen Cong Tru, District 1, Ho Chi Minh City; tel. (8) 9144056; fax (8) 9144057; e-mail sjc@hcm.vnn.vn; f. 1998; manufacturing, processing and trading of gold, gemstones, silver and jewellery; Man. Dir NGUYEN THANH LONG.

Technimex JSC (Technology Import-Export Joint Stock Company): 70 Tran Hung Dao, Hanoi; tel. (4) 9423751; fax (4) 8220377; e-mail technimex@hn.vnn.vn; internet www.technimexvn.com; f. 1982 under the name Viet Nam Technology Import-Export Corpn; name changed as above in 2001; exports and imports machines, equipment, instruments, etc.; Dir NGUYEN HUY BINH.

Technoimport (Viet Nam National Complete Equipment and Technics Import-Export Corpn): 16–18 Trang Thi, Hanoi; tel. (4) 8254974; fax (4) 8254059; e-mail technohn@netnam.vn; f. 1959; imports and exports equipment, machinery, transport equipment, spare parts, materials and various consumer commodities; exports products by co-investment and jt-venture enterprises; provides consulting services for trade and investment, transport and forwarding services; acts as import-export brokering and trading agents; Gen. Dir VU CHU HIEN.

Terraprodex (Corpn for Processing and Export-Import of Rare Earth and Other Specialities): 35 Dien Bien Phu, Hanoi; tel. (4) 8232010; fax (4) 8256446; f. 1989; processing and export of rare earth products and other minerals; Dir TRAN DUC HIEP.

Thanglong Minerals and Metals Co Ltd: 127 Khuat Duy Tien, Hanoi; tel. (4) 5535218; fax (4) 5532669; e-mail thanglongmetal@fpt.vn; internet www.thanglongcastiron.com; fmrly Viet Nam National Minerals Export Import Corpn; exports cast iron products; imports pig iron and crude steel; Gen. Dir LE THI MINH.

Tocontap Saigon (Saigon Sundries Export-Import Joint Stock Co): 35 Le Quy Don, District 3, Ho Chi Minh City; tel. (8) 9325687; fax (8) 9325963; e-mail tocontapsaigon@hcm.vnn.vn; internet www.tocontapsaigon.com; f. 1956; imports and exports apparel, agricultural products, art and handicrafts and sundries; Gen. Dir LE THI THANH HUONG.

Tracimexco (Transport Investment Co-operation and Import-Export Corpn): 22 Nguyen Van Troi, Phu Nhuan District, Ho Chi Minh City; tel. (8) 9433954; fax (8) 9433947; e-mail tralico@hn.vnn.vn; internet www.tracimexco.vnn.vn; fmrly Vietranscimex; exports and imports specialized equipment and materials for transportation and communication; Gen. Dir PHAM QUANG VINH.

Vama (Viet Nam Automobile Manufacturers' Association): 13 Quang Trung, Go Vap District, Ho Chi Minh City; tel. (8) 5536893; fax (8) 5536841; e-mail vama.office@gmail.com; internet www.vama.org.vn; f. 2000; 17 mems; Chair. AKITO TACHIBANA.

Vasep (Viet Nam Asscn of Seafood Exporters and Producers): 10–12 Nguyen Cong Hoan, Ba Dinh District, Hanoi; tel. (4) 7715055; fax (4) 7715084; e-mail vasep@hn.vnn.vn; internet www.vasep.com.vn; f. 1998; exports seafood products; provides essential market information to Viet Nam's seafood industry; organizes and implements activities designed to develop and promote the industry; Chair. TRAN THIEN HAI.

Vegetexco (Viet Nam National Vegetables and Fruit Export-Import Corpn): 2 Pham Ngoc Thach, Dong Da District, Hanoi; tel. (4) 5740779; fax (4) 8523926; e-mail vegetexcovn@fpt.vn; internet vegetexcovn.tripod.com; f. 1971; exports fresh and processed vegetables and fruit, spices and flowers, and other agricultural products; imports vegetable seeds and processing materials; Gen. Dir LE VAN ANH.

Viet Nam Dairy Products JS Company (VINAMILK): 184–188 Nguyen Dinh Chieu, Ward 6, District 3, Ho Chi Minh City; tel. (8) 9304860; fax (8) 9304880; e-mail vthieu@vinamilk.com.vn; internet www.vinamilk.com.vn; f. 1976; producer of dairy products; Dir MAI KIEU LIEN.

Vietrans (Viet Nam National Foreign Trade Forwarding and Warehousing Corpn): 13 Ly Nam De, Hoan Kiem District, Hanoi; tel. (4) 8457417; fax (4) 8455829; e-mail vietrans@hn.vnn.vn; internet www.vietrans.com.vn; f. 1970; agent for forwarding and transport of exports and imports, diplomatic cargoes and other goods, warehousing, shipping and insurance; Gen. Dir THAI DUY LONG.

Viettronimex (Viet Nam Electronics Import-Export Corpn): 74–76 Nguyen Hue, District 1, Ho Chi Minh City; tel. (8) 8298201; fax (8) 8294873; e-mail vtr@hcm.vnn.vn; f. 1981; imports and exports electronic goods; Dir NGUYEN HUU THINH.

Vigecam (Viet Nam General Corpn of Agricultural Materials): 16 Ngo Tat To, Dong Da District, Hanoi; tel. (4) 8231972; fax (4) 7474647; exports and imports agricultural products; Gen. Dir TRAN VAN KANH.

Viglacera (Viet Nam Glass and Ceramics Corpn): 628 Hoang Hoa Tham, Ba Dinh District, Hanoi; tel. (4) 5536665; fax (4) 5536671; e-mail vgc@hn.vnn.vn; internet www.viglacera.com.vn; f. 1974; mfr of building materials; Gen. Dir NGUYEN AHN TUAN.

Vimedimex II (Vimedimex Medi-Pharma Joint Stock Co): 246 Cong Quynh, District 1, Ho Chi Minh City; tel. (8) 8990164; fax (8) 8990165; e-mail info@vietpharm.com; internet www.vietpharm.com.vn; f. 1984; exports and imports medicinal and pharmaceutical materials and products, medical instruments; Gen. Dir NGUYEN TIEN HUNG.

Vimico (Viet Nam National Minerals Corpn): 562 Nguyen Van Cu, Gia Lam District, Hanoi; tel. (4) 8770010; fax (4) 8770006; e-mail vimico@hn.vnn.vn; internet www.vimicovn.com; Chair. VU XUAN KHOAT; Gen. Dir NGO VAN TROI.

Vinacafe (Viet Nam National Coffee Import-Export Corpn): 240 Nguyen Dinh Chinh, 11 Ward, Phu Nuan District, Ho Chi Minh City; tel. (8) 4495514; fax (8) 4495513; e-mail vinacafe@hn.vnn.vn; internet www.vinacafe.com.vn; f. 1995; state-owned; exports coffee, and imports equipment and chemicals for coffee production; Pres. and CEO DO VAN NAM.

Vinachem (Viet Nam National Chemical Corpn): 1A Trang Tien, Hoan Kiem District, Hanoi; tel. (4) 8240551; fax (4) 8252995; e-mail vinachem@hn.vnn.vn; internet www.vinachem.com.vn; production, import and export of chemicals and fertilizers; Chair. NGUYEN QUOC TUAN; Pres. and CEO DO DUY PHI.

Vinachimex (Viet Nam National Chemicals Import-Export Corpn): 4 Pham Ngu Lao, Hanoi; tel. (4) 8256377; fax (4) 8257727; f. 1969; exports and imports chemical products, minerals, rubber, fertilizers, machinery and spare parts; Dir NGUYEN VAN SON.

Vinafilm (Viet Nam Film Import, Export and Film Service Corpn): 73 Nguyen Trai, Dong Da District, Hanoi; tel. (4) 8244566; f. 1987; export and import of films and video tapes; film distribution; organization of film shows and participation of Vietnamese films in international film festivals; Gen. Man. NGO MANH LAN.

Vinafimex (Viet Nam National Agricultural Produce and Foodstuffs Import and Export Corpn): 58 Ly Thai To, Hanoi; tel. (4) 8255768; fax (4) 8255476; e-mail fime@hn.vnn.vn; internet www.vinafimex.com.vn; f. 1984; exports cashews, peanuts, coffee, rubber and other agricultural products, and garments; imports malt, fertilizer, insecticide, seeds, machinery and equipment, etc.; Pres. NGUYEN TOAN THANG; Gen. Dir NGUYEN VAN THANG.

Vinafood Hanoi (Hanoi Food Import-Export Co): 6 Ngo Quyen, Hoan Kiem District, Hanoi; tel. (4) 8256771; fax (4) 8258528; f. 1988; exports rice, maize, tapioca; imports fertilizers, insecticides, wheat and wheat flour; Dir NGUYEN DUC HY.

Vinalivesco (Vietnam National Livestock Corpn): 519 Minh Khai, Hanoi; tel. (4) 8626763; fax (4) 8623645; f. 1996; imports and exports animal and poultry products, animal feeds and other agro-products, and foodstuffs; Gen. Dir NGUYEN VAN KHAC.

Vinapimex (Viet Nam Paper Corpn): 25A Ly Thuong Kiet, Hanoi; tel. (4) 8260143; fax (4) 8260381; f. 1995; production and marketing of paper; Pres. and CEO VO SY DONG.

Vinaplast (Viet Nam Plastics Corpn): 92–94 Ly Tu Trong, District 1, Ho Chi Minh City; tel. (8) 8238011; fax (8) 8237956; e-mail vnplast@hcm.vnn.vn; internet www.vinaplast.com.vn; f. 1976; import and export of products for plastic processing industry; production and trade of plastic products; Gen. Dir NGUYEN KHAC LONG.

Vinasteel (Viet Nam National Steel Corpn): D2 Ton That Tung, Dong Da District, Hanoi; tel. (4) 8525537; fax (4) 8262657; distributor of metal products; Dir NGO HUY PHAN.

Vinataba (Viet Nam National Tobacco Corpn): 25A Ly Thuong Kiet, Hoan Kiem District, Hanoi; tel. (4) 8265778; fax (4) 8265777; internet www.vinataba.com.vn; mfr of tobacco products; Chair. NGUYEN THAI SINH; Gen. Dir NGUYEN NAM HAI.

Vinatea (Viet Nam National Tea Development Investment and Export-Import Co): 92 Vo Thi Sau, Hanoi; tel. (4) 6226990; fax (4) 6226991; e-mail info@vinatea.com.vn; internet www.vinatea.com.vn; exports tea, imports tea-processing materials; Gen. Dir NGUYEN THIEN TOAN.

Vinatex (Viet Nam National Textile and Garment Corpn): 25 Ba Trieu, Hoan Kiem District, Hanoi; tel. (4) 8257700; fax (4) 8262269; e-mail vinatexhn@vinatex.com.vn; internet www.vinatex.com; f. 1995; imports raw material, textile and sewing machinery, spare parts, accessories, dyestuffs; exports textiles, ready-made garments, carpets, jute, silk; Gen. Dir VU DUC GIANG.

Vitas (Viet Nam Tea Association): 92 Vo Thu Sau, Hai Ba Trung District, Hanoi; tel. (4) 6250908; fax (4) 6251801; e-mail vitas@fpt.vn; internet www.vitas.org.vn; f. 1988; promotes the trading and marketing of tea products; offers advice and information, both to the Govt and to farmers, regarding development schemes and policies; Chair. and Pres. NGUYEN KIM PHONG.

VNCC (Viet Nam Cement Industry Corpn—Vinacement): 228 Le Duan, Dong Da District, Hanoi; tel. (4) 8510593; fax (4) 8512778; e-mail banbt@vinacement.com.vn; internet www.vinacement.com.vn; f. 1980; manufactures and exports cement and clinker; Chair. LE VAN CHUNG; Gen. Dir NGUYEN NGOC ANH.

Vocarimex (National Co for Vegetable Oils, Aromas, and Cosmetics of Viet Nam): 58 Nguyen Binh Khiem, District 1, Ho Chi Minh City; tel. (8) 8294513; fax (8) 8290586; e-mail vocar@hcm.vnn.vn; internet www.vocarimex.com; f. 1976; producing and trading vegetable oils, oil-based products and special industry machinery; packaging; operating port facilities; Gen. Dir DO NGOC KAI.

Xunhasaba (Viet Nam State Corpn for Export and Import of Books, Periodicals and other Cultural Commodities): 32 Hai Ba Trung, Hanoi; tel. (4) 8262989; fax (4) 8252860; e-mail xunhasaba@hn.vnn.vn; internet www.xunhasaba.com.vn; f. 1957; exports and imports books, periodicals, postage stamps, greetings cards, calendars and paintings; Dir HA TRIEU KIEN.

UTILITIES

Electricity

Electricity of Viet Nam (EVN): 18 Tran Nguyen Han, Hanoi; tel. (4) 8249508; fax (4) 8249461; e-mail vp@evn.com.vn; internet www.evn.com.vn; produces, transmits and distributes electrical power; Chair. DAO VAN HUNG; Pres. and CEO PHAM LE TANH.

Power Co No 1 (PC1): 20 Tran Nguyen Han, Hoan Kiem, Hanoi; tel. (4) 8255074; fax (4) 8244033; e-mail anhdn@pc1.com.vn; manages the generation, transmission and distribution of electrical power in northern Viet Nam; Dir DO VAN LOC.

Power Co No 2 (PC2): 72 Hai Ba Trung, District 1, Ho Chi Minh City; tel. (8) 8231303; fax (8) 8299680; manages the distribution of electrical power in southern Viet Nam; Dir NGUYEN THANH DUY.

Power Co No 3 (PC3): 315 Trung Nu Vuong, Hai Chau District, Da Nang; tel. (511) 621028; fax (511) 625071; f. 1975; manages the generation, transmission and distribution of electrical power in central Viet Nam; Gen. Dir TA CANH.

Water

Hanoi Water Business Co: 44 Yen Phu, Hanoi; tel. (4) 8293179; fax (4) 8294069; f. 1954; responsible for the supply of water to Hanoi and its five urban and two suburban districts; Dir-Gen. NHU HAI NGUYEN.

Saigon Water Corpn (SAWACO): 1 Cong Truong Quoc Te, District 3, Ho Chi Minh City; tel. (8) 8291974; fax (8) 8241644; e-mail hcmcwater@hcm.vnn.vn; f. 1966; manages the water services and water construction works of Ho Chi Minh City; Gen. Dir DINH PHU TRAN.

CO-OPERATIVES

Viet Nam Co-operative Alliance (VCA): 77 Nguyen Thai Hoc, Ba Dinh District, Hanoi; tel. (4) 8431689; fax (4) 8431883; e-mail admin@vca.org.vn; internet www.vca.org.vn; f. 1993; fmrly Viet Nam Co-operatives Council; Pres. Dr NGUYEN TIEN QUAN.

TRADE UNIONS

Tong Lien doan Lao dong Viet Nam (Viet Nam General Confederation of Labour): 82 Tran Hung Dao, POB 627, Hanoi; tel. (4) 9421794; fax (4) 9423781; e-mail doingoaitld@hn.vnn.vn; internet www.congdoanvn.org.vn; f. 1929; merged in 1976 with the South Viet Nam Trade Union Fed. for Liberation; 6,000,000 mems; 20 affiliated unions; Pres. DANG NGOC TUNG; Vice-Pres. NGUYEN HOA BINH.

Cong Doan Nong Nghiep Cong Nghiep Thu Pham Viet Nam (Viet Nam Agriculture and Food Industry Trade Union): Hanoi; f. 1987; 550,000 mems.

National Union of Building Workers: 12 Cua Dong, Hoan Kiem, Hanoi; tel. (4) 8253781; fax (4) 8281407; f. 1957; Pres. NGUYEN VIET HAI.

Vietnam National Union of Industrial Workers: 54 Hai Ba Trung, Hanoi; tel. (4) 9344426; fax (4) 8245306; f. 1997; Pres. VU TIEN SAU.

Vietnam National Union of Post and Telecoms Workers: 30 Hang Chuoi, Hai Ba Trung, Hanoi; tel. (4) 9713514; fax (4) 9720236; f. 1947; Chair. HOANG DUY CAN.

Transport

RAILWAYS

In 2007 the Government approved plans to construct a new rail link between Hanoi and Ho Chi Minh City, which would reduce the journey time from 29 hours to 10 hours. Construction was expected to take six years. In 2008 construction commenced of a metro system in Ho Chi Minh City. The 19.7 km route was due for completion in 2014.

Duong Sat Viet Nam (DSVN) (Viet Nam Railways): 118 Le Duan, Hanoi; tel. (4) 8220537; fax (4) 9424998; e-mail vr.hn.irstd@fpt.vn; internet www.vr.com.vn; 2,600 km of main lines (1996); lines in operation are: Hanoi–Ho Chi Minh City (1,726 km), Hanoi–Haiphong (102 km), Hanoi–Dong Dang (167 km), Hanoi–Lao Cai (296 km), Hanoi–Thai Nguyen (75 km), Thai Nguyen–Kep–Bai Chay (106 km); Chair. and Gen. Dir Dr NGUYEN HUU BANG.

ROADS

In 2004 there were an estimated 137,359 km of roads, of which 53,610 km were asphalted and 6,681 km were stone-paved. In 1995 the Government announced plans to upgrade 430 km of the national highway, which runs from Hanoi in the north to Ho Chi Minh City in the south. In 1997 the Government announced plans to build a new 1,880-km north–south highway in the east of the country. In 2001 the Government also announced plans to upgrade the section of the national highway that runs between the northern provinces of Hoa Binh and Son La. In 2006 an upgrade of National Highway No. 2, linking An Giang province in Viet Nam to Takeo province in Cambodia, was completed; 95% of the funding of US $13m. was provided by Japan. In the following year the Government announced plans to upgrade the section of National Highway No. 1 in the central province of Thua Thien-Hué; construction was scheduled for completion in 2010.

SHIPPING

The principal port facilities are at Haiphong, Da Nang and Ho Chi Minh City. At the end of 2007 the Vietnamese merchant fleet (1,235 vessels) had a combined displacement totalling 2,529,619 grt.

Vietnam Ocean Shipping Agency Corporation (VOSA Corpn): Unit 1003, 10th Floor, Harbour View Tower, 35 Nguyen Hue, District 1, Ho Chi Minh City; tel. (8) 9141490; fax (8) 9140422; e-mail vosagroup@hcm.vnn.vn; internet www.vosagroup.com; f. 1957; fmrly the Viet Nam Ocean Shipping Agency; controlled by the Viet Nam National Shipping Lines (VINALINES); in charge of merchant shipping; arranges ship repairs, salvage, passenger services, air and sea freight forwarding services; main br. offices in Haiphong, Quang Ninh, Hanoi, Ben Thuy, Da Nang, Qui Nhon, Nha Trang, Ho Chi Minh City, Vung Tau and Can Tho; brs in Mong Cai, Cua Ong, Cam Pha, Vung Ang, Dung Quat, Chan May, Van Phong, Ca Mau and Kien Giang; Dir-Gen. TRAN DUNG KHANG (acting).

Cong Ty Van Tai Duong Bien Viet Nam (VOSCO) (Viet Nam Ocean Shipping Joint Stock Co): 215 Tran Quoc Toan, Ngo Quyen District, Haiphong; tel. (31) 731090; fax (31) 731007; e-mail pid@vosco.vn; drycargo.vosco.vn; internet www.vosco.com.vn; controlled by the Viet Nam Gen. Dept of Marine Transport; Gen. Dir VU HUU CHINH.

Transport and Chartering Corpn (Vietfracht): 74 Nguyen Du, Hai Ba Trung, Hanoi; tel. (4) 8228915; fax (4) 8228916; e-mail vfhan@hn.vnn.vn; internet www.vietfracht.com.vn; f. 1963; ship broking, chartering, ship management, shipping agency, international freight forwarding; logistic and consultancy services, import-export services; Chair. NGUYEN QUANG THOAI; CEO TRAN VAN QUY.

Viet Nam Sea Transport and Chartering Co (Vitranschart): 428–432 Nguyen Tat Thanh, District 4, Ho Chi Minh City; tel. (8) 9404271; fax (8) 9404711; e-mail vtc-hcm@vitranschart.com.vn; internet www.vitranschart.com.vn; Dir VO PHUNG LONG.

CIVIL AVIATION

Viet Nam's principal airports are Tan Son Nhat International Airport (Ho Chi Minh City) and Noi Bai International Airport (Hanoi), which cater for both overseas and domestic traffic. There is a third international airport at Da Nang. In 1997 it was announced that numerous abandoned wartime airstrips were to be repaired and returned to service under a programme scheduled for completion in 2010, by which time the Government also aimed to expand the annual capacity of Tan Son Nhat to 30m. passengers and 1m. metric tons of freight. In January 2004 plans were announced for the construction of a new international airport at Long Thang, in Dong Nai province; work on the project was expected to commence in 2010. The airport, with a projected passenger capacity of 20m. a year, was to have four runways and four terminals, the first of which were scheduled to become operational in 2015. Five new airports to handle domestic traffic were opened in 2004, at Ca Mau, Can Tho, Con Son, Chu Lai and Nha Trang. As of late 2006 there were 20 domestic airports in Viet Nam.

Jetstar Pacific Airlines: 112 Hong Ha, Tan Binh District, Ho Chi Minh City; tel. (8) 8487145; fax (8) 8450085; internet www.jetstar.com/ve; f. 1991; fmrly Pacific Airlines; name changed as above in 2008; 18% owned by Qantas (Australia); operates low-cost domestic flights; Chair. PHAM VU HIEN; CEO LUONG HOAI NAM.

VIET NAM

Viet Nam Airlines: Gialem Airport, Hanoi; tel. (4) 8731484; fax (4) 8272291; internet www.vietnamairlines.com; fmrly the Gen. Civil Aviation Admin. of Viet Nam, then Hang Khong Viet Nam; remained wholly state-owned in 2006, with plans for transfer to private sector; operates domestic passenger services from Hanoi and from Ho Chi Minh City to the principal Vietnamese cities, and international services to 18 countries; Pres. and CEO PHAM NGOC MINH; Chair. NGUYEN SY HUNG.

Tourism

According to the Viet Nam National Administration of Tourism, approximately 4.2m. tourists visited the country in 2007, of whom the largest proportion were from the People's Republic of China (13%), followed by the Republic of Korea (11%), the USA and Japan (about 10% each). In 2006 revenue from tourism totalled US $3,200m.

Viet Nam National Administration of Tourism (VNAT): 80 Quan Su, Hanoi; tel. (4) 9423998; fax (4) 9424115; e-mail titc@vietnamtourism-info.com; internet www.vietnamtourism.com; f. 1960; Gen. Dir NGO HUY PHUONG.

Hanoi Tourism Service Co (HANOI TOSERCO): 273 Kim Ma, Hanoi; tel. (4) 7262626; fax (4) 7262571; e-mail hanoitoserco@hn.vnn.vn; internet www.tosercohanoi.com; f. 1988; manages the development of tourism, hotels and restaurants in the capital and other services including staff training; Dir TRAN TIEN HUNG.

Tong Cong ty Du lich Saigon (Saigon Tourist Holding Co): 23 Le Loi, District 1, Ho Chi Minh City; tel. (8) 8225887; fax (8) 8291026; e-mail saigontourist@sgtourist.com.vn; internet www.saigon-tourist.com; f. 1975; holding co controlling 11 tour operators, 56 hotels, 10 resorts and 24 restaurants; Gen. Dir NGUYEN HUU THO.

YEMEN

Introductory Survey

Location, Climate, Language, Religion, Flag, Capital

The Republic of Yemen is situated in the south of the Arabian peninsula, bounded to the north by Saudi Arabia, to the east by Oman, to the south by the Gulf of Aden, and to the west by the Red Sea. The islands of Perim and Kamaran at the southern end of the Red Sea, the island of Socotra, at the entrance to the Gulf of Aden, and the Kuria Muria islands, near the coast of Oman, are also part of the Republic. The climate in the semi-desert coastal strip is hot, with high humidity and temperatures rising to more than 38°C (100°F); inland, the climate is somewhat milder, with cool winters and relatively heavy rainfall in the highlands. The eastern plateau slopes into desert. The language is Arabic. The population is almost entirely Muslim, and mainly of the Sunni Shafi'a sect. The national flag (proportions 2 by 3) has three equal horizontal stripes, of red, white and black. The capital is San'a.

Recent History

The Republic of Yemen was formed in May 1990 by the amalgamation of the Yemen Arab Republic (YAR) and the People's Democratic Republic of Yemen (PDRY). The YAR (from 1967 also known as North Yemen) had formerly been a kingdom. When Turkey's Ottoman Empire was dissolved in 1918, the Imam Yahya, leader of the Zaidi community, was left in control. In 1948 Yahya was assassinated in a palace coup, when power was seized by forces opposed to his feudal rule. However, Yahya's son, Ahmad, defeated the rebel forces to become Imam. In 1958 Yemen and the United Arab Republic (Egypt and Syria) formed a federation called the United Arab States, though this was dissolved in 1961. The Imam Ahmad died in September 1962 and was succeeded by his son, Muhammad. Less than a week later army officers, led by Col (later Marshal) Abdullah as-Sallal, removed the Imam and proclaimed the YAR. Civil war ensued between royalist forces, supported by Saudi Arabia, and republicans, aided by Egyptian troops. The republicans prevailed and Egyptian forces withdrew in 1967. In November President Sallal was deposed by a Republican Council.

The People's Republic of Southern Yemen, comprising Aden and the former Protectorate of South Arabia, was formed on 30 November 1967. Aden had been under British rule since 1839 and the Protectorate was developed by a series of treaties between the United Kingdom and local leaders. Prior to the British withdrawal, two rival factions, the National Liberation Front (NLF) and the Front for the Liberation of Occupied South Yemen, fought for control. The Marxist NLF eventually prevailed and assumed power as the National Front (NF). The country's first President, Qahtan ash-Sha'abi, was forced out of office in June 1969, when a Presidential Council, led by Salem Rubayi Ali, took power. Muhammad Ali Haitham became Prime Minister. In November 1970, on the third anniversary of independence, the country was renamed the PDRY. In May 1971 a provisional Supreme People's Council (SPC) was established as the national legislature. In August Haitham was replaced as Prime Minister by Ali Nasser Muhammad. Following the introduction of repressive measures against dissidents by the Government after independence, more than 300,000 Southern Yemenis fled to the YAR. Backed by Saudi Arabia and Libya, many of the refugees joined mercenary organizations, aimed at the overthrow of the Marxist regime in Southern Yemen, and conducted cross-border raids.

Intermittent fighting, beginning in early 1971, flared into open warfare between the two Yemens in October 1972, with the YAR receiving aid from Saudi Arabia and the PDRY being supplied with Soviet arms. A cease-fire was arranged in the same month, under the auspices of the League of Arab States (Arab League, see p. 344), and soon afterwards both sides agreed to the union of the two Yemens within 18 months. The union was not, however, implemented.

On 13 June 1974 a 10-member Military Command Council (MCC) seized power in the YAR, under the leadership of the pro-Saudi Lt-Col Ibrahim al-Hamadi. Mohsin al-Aini was appointed Prime Minister, but was replaced by Abd al-Aziz Abd al-Ghani in January 1975. An unsuccessful pro-royalist coup was reported in August. Al-Hamadi subsequently attempted to reduce the influence of the USSR, and endeavoured to re-equip the army with US weapons, making use of financial assistance from Saudi Arabia. In October 1977, however, al-Hamadi was killed by unknown assassins in San'a. Another member of the MCC, Lt-Col Ahmad bin Hussain al-Ghashmi, took over as Chairman, and martial law was imposed. In February 1978 the MCC appointed a Constituent People's Assembly, and in April the Assembly elected al-Ghashmi President of the Republic. The MCC was then dissolved.

In June 1978 the proposed union of the two Yemens was seriously hampered when President al-Ghashmi of the YAR was assassinated by a bomb carried in the suitcase of a PDRY envoy. In the following month the Constituent People's Assembly elected a senior military officer, Lt-Col (later Gen., and subsequently Field Marshal) Ali Abdullah Saleh, as President of the YAR. During recriminations that followed the assassination, President Rubayi Ali of the PDRY was deposed and executed by opponents within the ruling party, which had been known as the United Political Organization—National Front (UPO—NF) since its merger with two smaller parties in October 1975. The Prime Minister, Ali Nasser Muhammad, became interim Head of State. Two days after the overthrow of Rubayi Ali, it was announced that the UPO—NF had agreed to form a Marxist-Leninist 'vanguard' party. At the constituent congress of this Yemen Socialist Party (YSP), held in October 1978, Abd al-Fattah Ismail, who favoured uncompromising Marxist policies, became Secretary-General. A new SPC was elected in December and appointed Ismail to be Head of State. In April 1980 Ali Nasser Muhammad replaced Ismail as Head of State, Chairman of the Presidium of the SPC and Secretary-General of the YSP, while retaining the post of Prime Minister; his posts were confirmed at an extraordinary congress of the YSP in October.

Renewed fighting broke out between the YAR and the PDRY in February and March 1979, when the National Democratic Front (NDF), an alliance of disaffected YAR politicians, won the support of the PDRY and began a revolt. Later in the same month, however, at a meeting between the North and South Yemeni Heads of State in Kuwait, arranged by the Arab League, an agreement was signed pledging unification of the two states. Following a series of meetings, in December 1981 the two sides signed a draft Constitution for a unified state and established a joint YAR/PDRY Yemen Council to monitor progress towards unification. NDF forces rebelled again in 1982, but they were defeated and forced over the border into the PDRY.

Abd al-Aziz Abd al-Ghani was replaced as Prime Minister of the YAR in October 1980, but was reappointed in November 1983. Meanwhile, in May 1983 President Saleh submitted his resignation at an extraordinary meeting of the Constituent People's Assembly, declaring his intention to nominate himself for a presidential election. His five-year term of office was due to end in July. However, he was nominated and unanimously re-elected by the Assembly for a further five-year term. Elections to the Assembly itself, scheduled for early 1983, were postponed.

In the PDRY, President Muhammad relinquished the post of Prime Minister in February 1985, nominating the Minister of Construction, Haidar Abu Bakr al-Attas, as his successor (while retaining his other senior posts). The former President, Abd al-Fattah Ismail, returned from exile in the USSR in the same month, and was reappointed to the Secretariat of the YSP's Central Committee. At the party's third General Congress, in October, President Muhammad was re-elected to the posts of Secretary-General of the YSP and of its Political Bureau for a further five years. However, his control over the party was weakened by the enlargement of the Political Bureau from 13 members to 16 (including his rival, Ismail), and by an increase in membership of the Central Committee from 47 to 77, to incorporate a number of his critics.

On 13 January 1986 President Muhammad attempted to eliminate his opponents in the Political Bureau: his personal guard opened fire on six members who had assembled for a meeting with the President. Three were killed, and three escaped, including Ismail (who was, however, officially declared to have been killed in subsequent fighting). Muhammad was reported to have left Aden for his tribal stronghold in Abyan province, to the east of the city. In Aden itself, rival elements of the armed forces fought for control, causing widespread destruction, and the conflict quickly spread to the rest of the country, despite diplomatic efforts by the USSR. Apparently prompted by reports of massacres by President Muhammad's supporters, the army intervened decisively, turning back pro-Muhammad tribesmen from Abyan who were advancing on Aden. On 24 January al-Attas, the Prime Minister, who had been abroad when the troubles began, was named by the YSP Central Committee as head of an interim administration in Aden, and Muhammad was stripped of all his party and state posts; he reportedly fled to Ethiopia. An estimated 5,000 people died in the conflict. A new Government of the PDRY was formed in February. Al-Attas was confirmed as President, Chairman of the Presidium of the SPC and Secretary-General of the YSP Political Bureau. The former Deputy Prime Minister and Minister of Fisheries, Dr Yasin Said Numan, was named as Prime Minister. The new Council of Ministers contained only three members of the previous Government. In March a general amnesty was proclaimed, inviting supporters of Muhammad to return from the YAR, where some 10,000 of them had sought refuge. In October a general election took place for a 111-member SPC. Al-Attas was unanimously elected Chairman of the YSP. In December the Supreme Court sentenced Muhammad to death, *in absentia*, for treason; 34 other men received the same sentence, although it was only carried out in five cases.

In July 1988 the first general election took place in the YAR for 128 seats in the new 159-member Consultative Council, which replaced the non-elected Constituent People's Assembly. The remaining 31 seats were filled by presidential decree. More than 1m. people registered to vote and more than 1,200 candidates contested the poll. Approximately 25% of the elective seats were won by candidates sympathetic to the Muslim Brotherhood, a militant Islamist organization. Later in the month President Saleh was re-elected by the Consultative Council for a third five-year term, winning 96% of the votes, while the Vice-President, Abd al-Karim al-Arashi, was elected as Speaker of the Consultative Council. Al-Ghani was reappointed Prime Minister.

The first session of the joint YAR/PDRY Yemen Council (which had been established in 1981) was held in San'a in August 1983 and discussed the state of progress towards unification. These sessions were scheduled to take place every six months and to alternate between San'a and Aden. A joint committee on foreign policy met for the first time in March 1984 in Aden. In July 1986 Presidents Saleh of the YAR and al-Attas of the PDRY met for the first time in Libya to discuss unification. In early 1987 Kuwait acted as a mediator between the two Yemens in an effort to solve the problem of the thousands of refugees from the PDRY who had recently sought refuge in the north. In July it was reported that more than 50% of these refugees had returned to the PDRY.

In May 1988 the Governments of the YAR and the PDRY agreed to withdraw troops from their mutual border and to create a demilitarized zone, covering an area of 2,200 sq km, between Marib and Shabwah, where they intended to carry out joint projects involving exploration for petroleum. The movement of citizens between the two states was also to be facilitated. In July a programme of wide-ranging political and economic reforms was introduced in the PDRY, indicating the country's intention to create a free-market economy. In November President Saleh and the Secretary-General of the Central Committee of the YSP, Ali Salim al-Baid, signed an agreement to unify the two states. On 1 December a draft Constitution for the unified state was published: it was to be ratified by both countries within six months, and was subsequently to be approved by a referendum. At the end of December the Governments of the YAR and the PDRY agreed to release all political prisoners in their respective countries.

The first joint meeting of the two Councils of Ministers was held in San'a in January 1990 and resulted in restrictions on travel between the two countries being rescinded. In February President Saleh held talks with King Fahd of Saudi Arabia, who pledged his official support for the unification of the YAR and the PDRY. However, opposition to unification developed in the YAR in early 1990. The Muslim Brotherhood, which believed that *Shari'a* (Islamic) law should be enshrined in the Constitution of the unified state (as in the YAR Constitution), condemned the draft Constitution, which was based principally, but not solely, on *Shari'a* law, and advocated a boycott of the referendum on the Constitution. In the PDRY, meanwhile, there were demonstrations by women, who feared that the increasing influence of Islamist militancy might jeopardize their freedom, and demanded that their existing rights in the secular Republic be guaranteed in the new Constitution.

In May 1990 the armed forces of the YAR and the PDRY were declared to be technically dissolved, prior to their unification, and it was announced that they were to be withdrawn from their respective capitals to designated military zones. In the same month a draft law embodying the freedom of the press was signed. The unification of the YAR and the PDRY was proclaimed on 22 May, six months ahead of the agreed deadline, apparently in order to counter the threat to the unification process posed by disruption in the north of the YAR. The unification agreement had been ratified on the previous day by both countries' legislatures. The new country was to be known as the Republic of Yemen, with San'a as its political capital and Aden its economic and commercial centre. President Saleh of the YAR became President of the new state, while al-Baid was elected Vice-President. The President of the PDRY, al-Attas, became Prime Minister, leading a transitional coalition Council of Ministers with 39 members, of whom 20 were from the YAR (members of the General People's Congress—GPC—a broad grouping of supporters of President Saleh) and 19 from the PDRY (all members of the YSP, under the continued leadership of al-Baid). A five-member Presidential Council (chaired by Saleh) was formed, together with a 45-member advisory council. The two legislatures were amalgamated to form the House of Representatives, pending elections to be held after a 30-month transitional period; an additional 31 members, including opponents of the YAR and PDRY governments, were nominated by President Saleh. In September it was reported that more than 30 new political parties had been formed since unification. The Yemeni Congregation for Reform (al-Islah), an Islamic grouping with considerable support in the House of Representatives, was regarded as the most influential of the new parties.

In May 1991 the people of Yemen voted in a referendum on the Constitution for the unified state. Religious fundamentalists and sympathizers, including al-Islah members, had urged a boycott of the referendum, owing to the proposed role of Islam. Those who participated in the referendum approved the new Constitution by a large majority, although less than 50% of the electorate registered to vote. Members of al-Islah and other opposition groups claimed that irregularities in the voting procedure had invalidated the result.

During late 1991 and early 1992 the deteriorating economic situation prompted domestic unrest. A shooting incident in San'a in October 1991 led to two days of rioting, in which nine people were believed to have died. In March 1992 workers in some parts of the country held a one-day strike, in support of demands for salary increases and the establishment of a job creation programme for the estimated 850,000 returnees from Saudi Arabia (see below). In December at least 15 people were killed in riots in several towns, apparently caused by a sharp rise in consumer prices.

At legislative elections held on 27 April 1993, an estimated 4,730 candidates contested the 301 elective seats in the House of Representatives, of whom approximately 30% were affiliated to political parties. International observers were largely satisfied with the conduct of the elections. The GPC secured 123 of the 300 seats for which results were announced. Al-Islah won 62 seats, and the YSP 56, with independents securing 47 of the remaining seats. In May the two former ruling parties, the GPC and YSP, agreed to merge, thereby creating a single political group with an overall majority in the new House of Representatives. The subsequent election of al-Islah's leader, Sheikh Abdullah bin Hussain al-Ahmar, as Speaker of the House was regarded as a concession to his party, whose influence had been weakened by the merger. At the end of the month, however, a 31-member coalition Government was announced, including representatives of all three leading parties. Al-Attas was reappointed Prime Minister.

In August 1993 the YSP leader, al-Baid, ceased to participate in the political process and withdrew from San'a to Aden. This followed a visit to the USA, apparently without the approval of President Saleh, for talks with the US Vice-President, Al Gore. Al-Baid claimed that Saleh had made no attempt to halt the numerous armed attacks by northern officials on southerners, and claimed that as many as 150 YSP members had been assassinated since unification. He also protested at what he perceived to be the increasing marginalization of the south, particularly with regard to the distribution of petroleum revenues. In October the House of Representatives elected a new five-member Presidential Council, and later in the month the Council, in the absence of al-Baid, re-elected Saleh as its Chairman, and, accordingly, as President of the Republic of Yemen, for a further four-year term. Al-Baid was unanimously re-elected as Vice-President, but was not sworn in.

The political deadlock persisted into November 1993. Reports emerged that the armed forces of the former YAR and the PDRY (which had failed to integrate since unification) were being deployed along the former frontier. In September al-Baid, who remained in Aden, had submitted an 18-point programme of conditions for his return to San'a. Although President Saleh accepted the programme in December, there was no indication of any improvement in the political situation. In January 1994, following Jordanian mediation, representatives of the main political parties signed a 'Document of Pledge and Agreement' designed to resolve the crisis. In February Saleh and al-Baid signed the document, which contained certain security guarantees, as well as providing for a degree of decentralization, and for a review of the Constitution and of the country's economic policies. Nevertheless, both leaders remained active in mustering support for their positions throughout the region. At the same time there were reports of clashes between rival army units.

In March 1994 Saleh and al-Baid held talks in Oman, but at the end of the month al-Baid, together with Salim Salih Muhammad, refused to attend a meeting of the Presidential Council, which he had boycotted since August 1993. At the end of April 1994 the First Deputy Prime Minister, Hassan Muhammad Makki, was wounded during an assassination attempt in San'a. A series of pitched battles followed between battalions stationed in the territory of their former neighbour. On 5 May President Saleh declared a 30-day state of emergency, and dismissed al-Baid from his position as Vice-President, together with four other southern members of the Government, including Salim Muhammad. On the same day missile attacks were launched against economic and military targets, including San'a, Aden and other main airports. On 9 May Saleh announced that al-Attas had been replaced as Prime Minister by the Minister of Industry, Muhammad Said al-Attar, and that the Minister of Petroleum and Minerals had also been replaced. By this time fighting had become concentrated around Aden, and along the former north–south frontier. Several thousand southern reservists were mobilized, as the forces of the former YAR attempted to isolate and capture Aden. Meanwhile, President Saleh rejected appeals for a negotiated settlement to the civil war, and demanded that al-Baid surrender.

On 21 May 1994, the fourth anniversary of the unification of Yemen, al-Baid, in a televised address, declared the independence of a new Democratic Republic of Yemen (DRY), with Aden as its capital. He also announced the formation of a Presidential Council, with himself as President and Abd ar-Rahman al-Jifri, the leader of the League of the Sons of Yemen (LSY), as Vice-President. The composition of the Council reflected al-Baid's need to achieve a consensus of the different political and tribal groups of the former PDRY. Saleh denounced the secession as illegitimate, and offered an amnesty to all in the PDRY who rejected it, with the exception of 16 YSP leaders (including al-Baid).

At the beginning of June 1994, with the northern army attacking Aden on three fronts to the north and east of the city, the UN Security Council adopted Resolution 924, demanding a cease-fire and the resumption of dialogue in Yemen, and ordering the dispatch of a UN commission of inquiry to the region. Although welcomed by the authorities in Aden, the resolution was initially rejected by the Government in San'a, which urged the Arab League to support the unity of Yemen. Subsequently, however, the San'a Government declared itself positively disposed towards the resolution.

On 1 June 1994 the House of Representatives voted to extend the state of emergency for a further 30 days. On the following day al-Baid announced the composition of a DRY Government, in which al-Attas was to be Prime Minister and Minister of Finance. Although most of the ministers were from the YSP, the Government contained a range of religious, political and tribal representatives. As northern forces made further territorial gains around Aden, it was reported that al-Baid had transferred his centre of operations to Mukalla, east of Aden. On 7 July Aden came under the control of Saleh's troops. Many of the southern secessionist leaders fled to neighbouring Arab states, and it was officially announced that the civil war had ended. Al-Baid was believed to have requested political asylum in Oman. In March 1998 al-Baid, al-Attas and three other rebel leaders were sentenced to death in absentia.

According to official sources, 931 civilians and soldiers were killed, and 5,000 wounded, in the civil war, although this was generally regarded as a conservative estimate. President Saleh immediately undertook measures to consolidate his position and bring stability to the country, ending the state of emergency and reiterating the general amnesty; by August 1994, when the amnesty expired, more than 5,000 Yemenis had returned to the country. In the same month, in an attempt to undermine the strength of southern military units loyal to the YSP, President Saleh announced that party membership would no longer be permitted within the armed forces. In September, moreover, Saleh introduced amendments to the Constitution intended to strengthen his position further: the Presidential Council was abolished, and in future the President would be elected by universal suffrage. Shari'a would also serve as the basis of all legislation. On 1 October Saleh was re-elected President; he appointed Abd ar-Rabbur Mansur Hadi as his deputy, and Abd al-Aziz Abd al-Ghani (hitherto a member of the Presidential Council) as Prime Minister. In the new Council of Ministers members of the GPC retained the key portfolios, the YSP was denied representation and al-Islah was rewarded for its allegiance during the civil war by the allocation of nine ministerial posts. In a reorganization of the Council of Ministers in June 1995, the GPC increased its share of portfolios at the expense of independents, leading to a Government composed entirely of GPC and al-Islah members. Also in June President Saleh was re-elected Chairman of the GPC at the party's first general assembly since 1988.

In July 1994 UN-sponsored negotiations between the Yemeni leadership and the secessionists proved inconclusive. President Saleh announced that any further discussions would have to be conducted in Yemen, effectively terminating dialogue, as the YSP leaders remained in exile. In August a faction of the YSP in Yemen declared itself the new party leadership. In October, nevertheless, exiled leaders of the YSP announced the formation of a coalition, the National Opposition Front, which included former Prime Minister al-Attas and Abd ar-Rahman al-Jifri, leader of the LSY. The role of the YSP in Yemeni politics subsequently diminished considerably. In February 1995 another opposition grouping, the Democratic Coalition of Opposition, was formed, embracing 13 political parties and organizations, including a faction of the YSP and the LSY.

The economic repercussions of the civil war on the population were significant, particularly in the south. During March and April 1994, following the devaluation of the riyal (YR) and the doubling of the price of fuel, demonstrators clashed with police in Aden, San'a and Dhamar, resulting in three deaths and more than 50 arrests. The activities of militant Islamists, meanwhile, posed an additional threat to internal stability. In September some 20 people were reportedly killed in clashes with the security forces in Abyan province, following the destruction of three Muslim saints' shrines by Islamists who deemed them idolatrous. In September 1995 security forces arrested six alleged members of the Islamic Jihad group for their apparent involvement in acts of terrorism in Aden.

The results of elections, conducted on 27 April 1997, demonstrated a decisive victory for the GPC, which increased its parliamentary representation from 123 to 187 seats. Al-Islah secured 53 seats (compared with 62 in 1993), and independent candidates won 54 seats. The remaining seats were shared between Nasserite and Baathist parties. The GPC's position was further consolidated by the stated intention of 39 newly elected independent deputies to demonstrate parliamentary allegiance to the GPC.

Al-Ghani presented his Government's resignation in May 1997. Two days later Faraj Said bin Ghanim, a political independent, was appointed Prime Minister. All but four of the new ministers were GPC members. In April 1998 bin Ghanim resigned; the Deputy Prime Minister and Minister of Foreign Affairs, Abd al-Karim al-Iryani, was appointed Prime Minister, announcing his new Government in May. A substantial increase in the price of petrol and basic foodstuffs in June led to public demonstrations in which more than 50 people died. In September a series of explosions in Yemen was attributed by the Government to 'foreign elements'.

The suppression of lawlessness, which had been exacerbated by the widespread ownership of weapons dating from the period of internal unrest, was a persistent domestic problem in the late 1990s. A number of armed kidnappings, frequently of tourists, attracted international attention during 1997–98, and in December 1998 16 foreign tourists were taken hostage; four were later killed during an attempt to release them. Yemen was criticized for failing to warn foreign embassies of an increased terrorist threat to tourists and for its precipitate use of force to free the hostages. In May 1999 three of the kidnappers, who belonged to the Islamic Aden-Abyan Army, a small extremist Islamist movement, were sentenced to death, a fourth defendant received a 20-year prison sentence and the remainder were acquitted. Two of the death sentences were later commuted to life imprisonment, and in October the leader of the Islamic Aden-Abyan Army, Ziene al-Abidine al-Mihdar, was executed. His was the first execution under legislation, enacted in August 1998, providing for the use of capital punishment in kidnapping cases. In August 1999 eight British citizens and two Algerians, who were reported to have links to the Islamic Aden-Abyan Army, were found guilty of plotting terrorist attacks on British targets in Aden, receiving sentences of up to seven years' imprisonment. (In October 2002 the Islamic Aden-Abyan Army attacked a French supertanker, the *Limburg*, off the coast of Yemen. A spokesman for the group declared the attack, which killed a crew member, to be revenge for the execution of al-Mihdar.)

On 23 September 1999 the first direct presidential elections were held in Yemen. Saleh was re-elected, winning 96.3% of the votes; his only opponent was Najib Qahtan ash-Sha'bi, a member of the GPC who stood as an independent. The elections, which were boycotted by the YSP, were criticized for their lack of a credible candidate to oppose President Saleh.

Some internal instability was reported in 1999, with a number of bomb explosions in San'a. In March 2000 a demonstration was held in ad-Dali governorate, north of Aden, in protest at the detention of two YSP officials; in April 15 YSP officials were arrested in Abyan governorate and the Secretary-General was arrested at San'a airport on his return to the country. Kidnappings continued throughout 1999 and early 2000, involving hostages from a number of Western nations; all were released unharmed. However, in June a Norwegian diplomat was killed during a police operation to release him and his son from kidnappers in San'a. In October Hatim Muhsin bin Farid, the alleged new leader of the Islamic Aden-Abyan Army, was sentenced to a seven-year term of imprisonment, having been convicted of kidnapping charges. Owing to a lack of evidence, he was cleared of charges relating to his leadership of the movement and to the possession of heavy weapons.

In mid-October 2000 a suicide bomb attack on a US destroyer, the USS *Cole*, in Aden harbour, as a result of which 17 US naval personnel were killed, was linked by many commentators to the escalating crisis in the Middle East. The Yemeni authorities responded by arresting several Islamist militants, including leading members of Islamic Jihad from Yemen, Egypt, Algeria and other Arab states. The USA blamed agents of Osama bin Laden, the Saudi-born fundamentalist Islamist believed at that time to be based in Afghanistan, for the attack, and claimed to have evidence that the two suicide bombers were Saudi nationals. Only days after the USS *Cole* bombing, the British embassy in San'a was the target of an attack, although it was unclear as to whether the two incidents were linked. (In July 2001 four Yemenis were found guilty of plotting and orchestrating the embassy bombing, and sentenced to between four and 15 years' imprisonment.)

In November 2000 Yemen and the USA signed an anti-terrorism agreement whereby the Yemeni authorities agreed to allow the US Federal Bureau of Investigation to assist in investigations into the USS *Cole* explosion, and to extradite any persons accused of involvement in terrorism against foreign targets. It was announced in the following month that investigations into the bombing had been completed and that six Yemeni nationals would stand trial in early 2001. In January, however, the Yemeni Government agreed to a postponement of the trial, following a request by US officials for more time to gather additional evidence. A further two Yemenis entering the country from Afghanistan were detained in February; another three suspects were reportedly arrested in April. In November a Yemeni newspaper published claims that the individual suspected of planning the attack had subsequently sought refuge in Afghanistan. The man was named as Muhammad Omar al-Harazi, and was also believed to have been one of the principal organizers of the 1998 attacks on the US embassies in Kenya and Tanzania. In February 2002 it was reported that the trial of eight of the suspects in the bombing of the USS *Cole* had been postponed at the request of the US authorities because of the possibility that new information about the case would be obtained during interrogation of al-Qa'ida (see below) and Taliban prisoners captured by US military forces in Afghanistan in late 2001. Two senior al-Qa'ida operatives believed to have been responsible for planning the attack on USS *Cole* were arrested by US forces and Pakistani police in November 2002 and April 2003, respectively. In April 2003 10 of the Yemenis accused of involvement in the USS *Cole* attack escaped from a high security prison; two of the fugitives were captured in May, and charged with the murder of US military personnel. The remaining eight, in addition to one further suspect, were reportedly captured in March 2004. In September two men (a Yemeni and a Saudi) were sentenced to death for their role in the attack. Four other Yemeni nationals received prison sentences of between five and 10 years. In February 2005 an appeal court ruling upheld one of the death sentences, but commuted the other to 15 years in prison and reduced the sentence of one of the other men from eight to five years.

In January 2001 the formation of a new opposition grouping, the Opposition Co-ordination Council, was announced in Yemen. The bloc, which included the YSP, was created in anticipation of the forthcoming municipal elections, Yemen's first since unification, which were held on 20 February. A national referendum was held concurrently on proposed amendments to the Constitution that would extend the President's term of office from five to seven years and the mandate of the House of Representatives from four to six years, abolish the right of the President to issue decree laws when parliament is not in session and provide for the creation of a 111-member Consultative Council. According to official sources, 77.5% of voters endorsed the constitutional changes. There were claims of electoral irregularities and harassment of opposition candidates, and violent clashes were reported (principally between supporters of the GPC and those of al-Islah) in which, according to certain sources, up to 45 people were killed. The elections were boycotted by some opposition parties and were criticized by human rights groups, which claimed that the President and the GPC were seeking to consolidate their dominant position at the expense of further democratization.

In March 2001 President Saleh dismissed Prime Minister Abd al-Karim al-Iryani and declared the formation of a new Government, to be led by the former Deputy Prime Minister and Minister of Foreign Affairs, Abd al-Qadir Bajammal. The new Council of Ministers was composed exclusively of GPC members and included Yemen's first female minister). Commentators believed that al-Iryani's dismissal was an attempt to hasten the country's reform programme. In April the President elected a new Consultative Council, which for the first time included three female politicians.

In early 2003 22 political parties were registered for a parliamentary election, which was held on 27 April. The GPC recorded another decisive victory, winning 228 of the 301 seats, while al-Islah secured 47 seats, independents 14 and the YSP seven. (Final results were published following three by-elections held in July.) Voter turn-out was a reported 76% of the electorate. The European Union (EU, see p. 255) expressed its satisfaction with the elections, but the US-based National Democratic Institute for International Affairs claimed that the electoral process was flawed, citing instances of under-age voting, ballot-buying and inappropriate behaviour by security forces. Opposition parties threatened to boycott the new Parliament after widespread claims of ballot-rigging, fraud and intimidation. None the less, on 10 May the President re-appointed Bajammal as Prime Minister. Bajammal's new Council of Ministers included 17 new appointees, among them a Minister of Human Rights, Amat al-Alim as-Susua, although the key portfolios of defence, the interior, petroleum and mineral resources, and foreign affairs remained unchanged.

Meanwhile, also in May 2003 President Saleh declared an amnesty for five exiled southern secessionist leaders who had been sentenced to death *in absentia* in 1998. In June 2003 the House of Representatives endorsed a government proposal that Yemen's counter-terrorism organization should become a separate department overseen by the Ministry of the Interior; the resources allocated to the unit were also increased. In July security forces killed six suspected Islamist militants during an operation in Abyan province, where alleged members of the Islamic Aden-Abyan Army had taken refuge after attacking a military detachment. The Government had previously maintained that the Islamic Aden-Abyan Army had ceased to exist following the execution of its leader in 1999.

In August 2003 it was reported that the Government was determined to remove imams suspected of affiliation to al-Islah; a senior official accused al-Islah of seeking to dominate the mosques. Later, the Minister of Religious Endowments and Guidance announced that the Government had formulated a programme to train imams to promote moderation and tolerance and was determined to prevent the preaching of *jihad* against the West or Israel. In June 2004 the Director of the Ministry of Religious Endowments and Guidance stated that the authorities would not allow Islamist parties to share control over state-controlled mosques and use them as platforms to preach extremism. Firm measures would be taken against imams who preached opposition to the Government and incited worshippers to violence. Later that month the Council of Ministers ordered the closure of all unlicensed religious schools in an effort to combat extremism, and stated that an extensive review of religious education in public schools was urgently needed to ensure that teaching about Islam advocated moderation.

As part of efforts to combat violence and extremism, the Government stated in 2003 that it had spent over US $32m. since 2002 purchasing weapons on sale on the open market and seeking to persuade ordinary citizens to sell their weapons to the authorities. (According to the Government, 60m.–80m. guns were owned by the country's population, which numbered some 19m.) Officials indicated that they had approached the USA for financial assistance to continue the scheme. An initiative endorsed by President Saleh to prevent the public from carrying firearms resulted in riots in February 2005, in which five people died in northern Yemen. Saudi Arabia had recently complained to Yemen over reports of the smuggling of arms into the kingdom, and in 2004 began the construction of a 'separation wall' along the Saudi–Yemeni border (see below).

In June 2004 violent clashes took place in the mountainous north-western province of Saada between the security forces and supporters of a militant Zaidi cleric, Hussain al-Houthi, leader of Ash-Shabab al-Mo'men (Believing Youth). The authorities alleged that al-Houthi's movement had formed its own militia near the border with Saudi Arabia and had launched attacks against government buildings and mosques in Saada. Although the group appeared to be motivated by opposition to the USA and Israel and to have a militant Islamist agenda, it was not thought to have links to al-Qa'ida. Reports estimated that al-Houthi had some 3,000 armed supporters, of whom some 200–300 had been killed since the conflict began, with hundreds of rebels wounded or arrested. In September al-Houthi was killed by members of the security forces; the Government declared this development to have effectively ended the uprising. However, renewed fighting broke out with followers of the cleric in April 2005; five Yemeni soldiers and eight members of Ash-Shabab al-Mo'men were understood to have been killed. On 12 April it was reported that the conflict had decreased in intensity and that government forces were seeking al-Houthi's relatives, in particular his brother, Abd al-Malik al-Houthi, and his father, Badr ad-Din al-Houthi, who were believed to have acceded to the leadership of the movement. After several months of relative peace, fighting broke out again in November when two days of conflict reportedly left 16 rebels and eight government soldiers dead. Further violent clashes occurred in February 2006.

In 2005 and early 2006 the President faced political pressure from the USA over the Chairman of al-Islah's Shura Council, Sheikh Abd al-Majid az-Zindani. Az-Zindani was described as a 'financier of terrorism' by the UN Security Council and as a 'global terrorist' by the USA; it was understood that the latter might increase the pressure on the Yemeni Government to arrest or extradite az-Zindani. Despite having announced in July 2005 that he would not seek re-election to the presidency in September 2006, President Saleh was re-elected as Chairman of the GPC in December 2005, prompting speculation that he would in fact continue in office.

In late 2005 and 2006 a series of kidnappings further undermined Yemen's image abroad. Meanwhile, in July 2005 at least 39 people were killed in severe riots in San'a, Aden and several other towns in protest at the Government's decision to remove subsidies on fuel and the consequent doubling in the price of petroleum products. The GPC accused opposition parties of instigating the riots after they publicly criticized the price increases. The opposition denied the allegations and condemned the killing of civilians by security forces. At the end of July the Government announced a partial reduction in fuel prices.

President Saleh effected a comprehensive reorganization of the Council of Ministers, which was increased in size, to 34 members (including two new female ministers), in February 2006. The ministers in charge of the key portfolios of defence, oil, finance and planning were all removed from their posts; however, the Minister of the Interior, Maj.-Gen. Dr Rashad Muhammad al-Alimi, who had been under pressure following the escape of 23 suspected al-Qa'ida sympathizers (including Jamal al-Badawi, who had been convicted for the bombing of USS *Cole* in 2000—see above) from a San'a prison earlier in the month, was promoted to Deputy Prime Minister. The President claimed that the changes would add new impetus to the process of economic and political reform, although the opposition suggested that the reorganization was targeted at strengthening the regime before the forthcoming presidential and municipal elections.

Also in February 2006 the authorities charged three journalists (from separate publications) with denigrating Islam after they reprinted cartoons regarded as extremely offensive to Muslims that had been originally published in Denmark in late 2005. The arrests came amid complaints that the freedom of the press was being reduced ahead of the 2006 presidential election. (In November 2006 the editor of *Ar-Ra'i al-'Am*, Kamal Alufi, was convicted and sentenced to one year's imprisonment. Muhammad al-Asaadi, editor-in-chief of the *Yemen Observer*, was convicted in December and fined YR 500,000. In the same month *Al-Huriya* was ordered to cease publication for one month, and its editor, Abd al-Halim Akram Sabra, and a senior reporter were both sentenced to four months' imprisonment.)

The presidential election was held on 20 September 2006, with turn-out estimated at approximately 65% of the 9.2m. registered voters. As widely predicted, Saleh, who had rescinded his statement that he would not seek re-election, was chosen to serve another seven-year term, attracting 77.17% of the total ballot, according to official results published by the Supreme Commission for Elections and Referendums (SCER). Saleh's primary opponent, Faisal bin Shamlan of the Joint Meeting Parties (JMP—a recently formed opposition bloc comprising five Islamist and leftist parties, including the YSP, al-Islah and the al-Haq party), garnered 21.82% of the ballot, although Shamlan's supporters rejected the results, claiming that he had received at least 40% of all votes; three other candidates each won less than 0.5% of the total number of votes cast. The SCER acknowledged that tens of thousands of votes had had to be discounted due to 'voter error'; however, the Minister of Foreign Affairs, Abu Bakr al-Kurbi, denied claims of electoral fraud. (One week prior to the polls at least 51 people died, and more than 230 were injured, during a stampede at an election campaign rally for the incumbent Saleh.) EU election observers reported that the presidential and municipal elections had been conducted in a reasonably free and fair manner, but identified a number of problems, particularly with regard to voter registration and the use of state resources to promote the ruling party. The JMP agreed to accept the election results on the condition that the Government enter into negotiations on electoral reform.

In September 2006 the Ministry of the Interior announced that security forces had foiled two co-ordinated suicide attacks intended to destroy oil facilities in Marib and Hadramout. Security guards identified vehicles laden with explosives at both locations, and destroyed the vehicles before they reached their intended targets, killing all four assailants and one security guard. In October it was reported that security forces had killed two of the 23 suspected al-Qa'ida sympathizers who had escaped from prison in February during a gun battle on the outskirts of San'a. In November a militant Islamist group calling itself 'al-Qa'ida in Yemen' issued a statement via the internet in which it claimed responsibility for the attempted bombing of oil facilities.

Renewed violence broke out in the province of Saada in early 2007, with a series of clashes between insurgents led by Abd al-Malik al-Houthi and government forces. President Saleh issued an ultimatum warning of a full military campaign against the rebels if they did not surrender their weapons, and thousands of additional troops were subsequently deployed to the region. Following an escalation of the violence in late February, in early March it was reported that more than 500 people, including more than 400 troops, had died in the fighting since the beginning of the year.

A presidential decree was issued at the end of March 2007 appointing Ali Muhammad Mujawar, hitherto Minister of Electricity, as Prime Minister, to replace Bajammal, whose dismissal was reported to be the result of weak anti-corruption policies. A new Council of Ministers was formed in early April. Key portfolios remained unchanged, with the Ministers of Foreign Affairs, Defence, the Interior, Information, and Oil and Minerals all being retained. The Ministry of Expatriate Affairs was reintroduced, to be headed by Saleh Hassan Sumi'e, and there were 11 other new appointments, including those of Noman Taher as-Souhaibi as Minister of Finance and Abd al-Qader Ali Hilal as Minister of Local Administration. Addressing the new cabinet for the first time, President Saleh urged ministers to: adopt a tougher stance against corruption; abandon nepotism; tackle rising inflation; and improve living standards.

President Saleh dismissed Yahya ash-Shami, the Governor of Saada province, in mid-April 2007, as confrontations between the al-Houthi rebels and the security forces continued, causing further fatalities on both sides, and appointed Maj.-Gen. Mutahar Rashad al-Masri, hitherto Deputy Minister of the Interior, in his place. In mid-May it was reported that government forces had succeeded in regaining control of the as-Saifi district of Saada, hitherto a significant al-Houthi stronghold, following fierce fighting in the area. Following mediation by Qatar, in mid-June 2007 the Government and the leaders of the al-Houthi rebellion reached a cease-fire agreement, which required the rebels to relinquish their weapons and the Government to release imprisoned rebels, fund reconstruction efforts in areas affected by the fighting and facilitate the return to their homes of displaced people (estimated at more than 50,000 by the International Committee of the Red Cross—ICRC); in addition, Abd al-Malik al-Houthi, two of his brothers and another rebel leader were to move to the Qatari capital, Doha, for an unspecified period of exile. A committee was established to monitor the implementation of the agreement. However, later that month it was reported that the rebel leaders remained in Saada and that insurgents were continuing to attack government troops in the province, amid some dissent within the al-Houthi movement regarding the accord with the Government. The rebels had apparently issued a new set of demands, most notably the return of the body of Hussain al-Houthi (who had been killed by the security forces in 2004—see above). Also in June Reporters sans frontières, an international non-governmental organization (NGO) concerned with press freedom, criticized the Yemeni Government for banning services that distributed news to mobile telephones and blocking access to opposition websites. The Government was also accused of attempting to prevent journalists from covering the conflict in Saada. At the end of the month a new anti-corruption body was established, its 11 members being elected by the legislature.

The threat to national security posed by purported Islamist militants also increased in 2007. A suicide bomber drove an explosives-laden car into a convoy of tourist vehicles in Marib in early July, killing eight Spanish tourists and two local drivers. Several arrests were made in connection with the attack, for which the Government held al-Qa'ida responsible By this time a total of nine of the 23 suspected al-Qa'ida sympathizers who had escaped from prison in February 2006 had apparently surrendered to the authorities; five had been killed in various clashes with the Yemeni security forces; one had been killed by US forces in Somalia; one was under arrest in Kenya; and seven—including Nasir al-Wuhayshi (reported to be the new leader of al-Qa'ida in Yemen), Kassem ar-Raimi (who, together with al-Wuhayshi, was believed to have been involved in the July 2007 attack) and Jamal al-Badawi—remained at large. In August three al-Qa'ida militants were killed by Yemeni security forces. Al-Badawi surrendered to the Yemeni authorities in October; initial reports that he had been placed under house arrest, after declaring his allegiance to President Saleh, and was effectively at liberty prompted criticism from the USA, although in December a statement from the Ministry of the Interior insisted that he remained in custody. In November 32 people were found guilty of planning the attacks on oil facilities in Marib and Hadramout in September 2006 and sentenced to prison terms of between two and 15 years; six of those convicted, including ar-Raimi and al-Wuhayshi, had been tried *in absentia*, while four other defendants were acquitted owing to a lack of evidence.

Thousands of military and security officers who had been forced to retire after the civil war in 1994 demonstrated in Aden in July 2007, demanding to be allowed to return to work and to be paid wages for the intervening years. A few days earlier President Saleh had ordered the return to service of more than 600 officers, but this was regarded as inadequate by the protesters, some of whom advocated the redivision of Yemen. Unrest persisted in the south of the country in the following months, provoked not only by the issue of the military retirees, but also by economic concerns. In mid-August sit-ins were staged outside local government buildings in several towns in protest against water shortages, increases in consumer prices, unemployment, poverty and corruption; it was reported that more than 10,000 people participated in Taiz. Further demonstrations took place in Aden and Mukalla, the capital of Hadramout, in early September, during which 40 protesters were reportedly arrested on suspicion of treason for chanting secessionist slogans. Six people were believed to have been killed in clashes between the security forces and protesters in Aden and Lahij in mid-October. Meanwhile, in a renewed effort to improve security and reassure foreign investors and tourists, in late August the Ministry of the Interior decided to enforce a ban on carrying firearms in San'a and provincial capitals, noting that some 5,000 people had been killed and 18,500 others injured in gun-related incidents during the previous three years. (By late April 2008 more than 100,000 weapons had been confiscated under the initiative.)

The cease-fire between government forces and al-Houthi insurgents in Saada was breached in mid-October 2007, when at least three armed rebels and one soldier were killed in clashes resulting from the rebels' refusal to surrender their weapons. Four soldiers died in further fighting later that month after al-Houthi supporters reportedly attacked a police station. Insecurity was not confined to Saada in late 2007. Six civilians and 10 soldiers were killed in the south-eastern province of Shabwa in November when violence erupted between tribesmen and troops protecting employees of a Ukrainian oil company. In December, furthermore, it was reported that two bomb explosions at military posts in Hadramout had resulted in the deaths of two security officials, while three soldiers were killed in attacks in Taiz.

Sheikh Abdullah bin Hussain al-Ahmar, Speaker of the House of Representatives since 1993 and Chairman of al-Islah, died in December 2007. Yahya Ali ar-Ra'ei, of the GPC, was elected to succeed al-Ahmar as Speaker in February 2008, while Sheikh Muhammad Ali al-Yadoumi became Chairman of al-Islah, initially in an acting capacity.

Clashes between government forces and al-Houthi rebels continued in Saada in early 2008, resulting in deaths on both sides, while further demonstrations against the perceived marginalization of the south took place in Aden and other southern towns. At the same time a series of attacks and bomb explosions, mainly targeting Western interests, exacerbated tensions. In mid-January 2008 two Belgian tourists and their Yemeni driver were killed in Hadramout by gunmen who ambushed their convoy. Another al-Qa'ida-affiliated group, calling itself Jund al-Yaman (Soldiers of Yemen), later claimed responsibility for the attack, as well as that perpetrated against Spanish tourists in July 2007. A grenade attack believed to have been aimed at the US embassy in San'a wounded 13 pupils at a neighbouring school, as well as several soldiers, in March 2008. In early April three explosions took place at a residential compound housing Western workers in the capital, but no injuries were reported. Two days later the US embassy announced that it was evacuating non-essential personnel from Yemen. In mid-April three police officers were killed in a bomb attack in Marib, and later that month there were two explosions in San'a near the Italian embassy.

Public unrest in the south of the country intensified in late March 2008, as large demonstrations degenerated into rioting in the provinces of Aden, Lahij and ad-Dali. The protesters had various demands, ranging from an improvement in living standards to the secession of south Yemen, while youths claimed that the authorities had reneged on promises to offer them employment in the army. In response, the Government heightened security in the region and arrested those believed to be organizing the rallies. The Prime Minister stated that 283 people had been detained in connection with the disturbances between 30 March and 9 April, but that 161 had been released. Several members of the YSP were reported to be among those arrested.

Meanwhile, with the security situation in Saada deteriorating further, the Qatari Government renewed its efforts to mediate between the Yemeni Government and the al-Houthi insurgents, and at the beginning of February 2008 a document was signed outlining measures for the implementation of the initial agreement reached in June 2007; the full details of the new accord were not disclosed. Some progress in restoring stability in Saada was achieved in the following weeks. In mid-February 2008 it was reported that hostilities had ceased and that the rebels had freed two military commanders who had been captured in January. Furthermore, by early March the Government had released 376 detainees arrested in connection with the rebellion.

However, the Government subsequently accused the rebels of violating the cease-fire agreement and of killing a detainee whom they had recently abducted, and sporadic violence resumed. Two soldiers were reportedly killed and six al-Houthi rebels wounded in clashes in the district of Hidan in mid-March. Fighting broke out between al-Houthi followers and al-Bakhtan tribesmen in Saada in early April, after the pro-Government tribe accused the rebels of killing one of its members two months previously; more than 20 people died in the confrontations. In mid-April a GPC member of the House of Representatives, Saleh al-Hindi Daghsan, was killed, together with his son and a bodyguard, in an ambush carried out by unknown gunmen in Saada. Later that month Abd al-Malik al-Houthi asserted that efforts to implement the peace agreement had failed, owing to the Government's refusal to withdraw its forces from the areas in which they were deployed during the conflict with the rebels. A few days later further clashes resulted in the deaths of eight al-Houthi insurgents and three soldiers. In early May at least 15 people were killed and up to 60 injured in a bombing at a mosque frequented by military personnel in Saada. Abd al-Malik al-Houthi denied claims of his followers' involvement in the incident.

Gubernatorial elections were held for the first time on 17 May 2008, governors having hitherto been appointed by the President. The electorate consisted of almost 7,500 elected members of local councils in the 20 governorates and the capital, and the Ministry of Local Administration reporting a turn-out of 87%. With the JMP opting to boycott the elections, the GPC secured the mayoralty of San'a and all governorships except three that were won by independent candidates, in al-Baida, Marib and al-Jawf. However, the election result in al-Jawf was subsequently overturned by the Government, amid allegations that the successful candidate had links to al-Houthi militants; an alternative Governor, selected by the Government, was appointed in June.

Immediately following the gubernatorial elections, President Saleh effected a reorganization of the Council of Ministers, in which Rashad al-Alimi, hitherto Deputy Prime Minister and Minister of the Interior, was allocated the newly expanded post of Deputy Prime Minister for Defence and Security Affairs. Mutahar al-Masri, Governor of Saada, was appointed Minister of the Interior, and there were changes to a further seven cabinet posts. The local administration portfolio was added to al-Alimi's responsibilities in November, following the resignation of Abd al-Qader Ali Hilal. Hilal, who had been responsible for the post-conflict reconstruction programme in Saada (see below), was under investigation for alleged close links with both al-Houthi followers and al-Islah.

The failure of the Government and the opposition to reach agreement on electoral reform led to an escalating political crisis in 2008. The opposition, dissatisfied with the Government's apparent reluctance to introduce promised revisions, refused to participate in the appointment of new commissioners to the SCER, which was due to review voter registration lists, prompting fears that the legislative elections scheduled for April 2009 might be delayed. Despite lengthy negotiations throughout 2007–08, in August 2008 an electoral reform bill was rejected by the GPC-dominated House of Representatives; the Government blamed the JMP's refusal to participate in the SCER for the rejection. A new SCER, formed without opposition involvement, appointed 35,000 teachers to sub-committees tasked with undertaking a comprehensive revision of the voter registry, beginning in November. However, as opposition parties appealed for a boycott of the registration process, which they claimed was illegitimate, sub-committees were hindered in their activities by protests in most governorates, and there were reports of attacks on committee members. Violent clashes between police and protesters intensified throughout November, and numerous opposition activists were reportedly arrested. In late November the House of Representatives voted to delay the forthcoming municipal elections, which had been due to be held in April 2009. Meanwhile, the Government continued to insist that the legislative polls would proceed as scheduled, urging the opposition parties to participate. However, in late February 2009, after negotiations between the Government and the JMP, the House of Representatives voted overwhelmingly to postpone the elections for two years, during which time, it was hoped, agreement could be reached on the reform of the electoral system.

Meanwhile, in July 2008 President Saleh announced that the conflict with the al-Houthi militants had ended, adding that the combatants were engaged in constructive dialogue. Despite this pronouncement, there were continued reports of sporadic violence in the region. In early August Abd al-Malik al-Houthi was reported to have accepted the President's 10-point proposal for a final settlement of the conflict, which was believed to encompass most of the terms of the Qatari-mediated agreement of 2007. In September 2008 the Government established a Saada Reconstruction Fund and announced a four-year strategy to rehabilitate the war-ravaged province. The cost of the reconstruction plan was estimated at US $500m., and the authorities appealed for international donors to contribute a significant proportion. According to the Ministry of Local Administration, more than 6,000 houses, 900 farms, 80 schools and 90 mosques had been destroyed or damaged during the four-year conflict. In addition to the hundreds of fatalities caused by the fighting, thousands of people had been displaced, many of whom were living in poor conditions in makeshift refugee camps. Several international NGOs, including the ICRC and Médecins sans frontières, endeavoured to bring medical and other humanitarian aid into affected areas, although all reported severe difficulties in delivering aid, mainly due to ongoing instability. By November there were complaints from al-Houthi representatives that the Government was sending military reinforcements into the area. Also in November delegates at a convention organized by the Yemeni NGO Arab Sisters Forum for Human Rights, including human rights activists and opposition politicians, urged the Government to release detainees imprisoned for alleged links to the al-Houthi rebellion; to desist from the arbitrary arrest of civilians; and to guarantee the legal and human rights of all prisoners. By April 2009 the truce appeared increasingly fragile, as both government and al-Houthi sources released reports of clashes between the two sides.

In November 2008 a new secessionist movement, the Southern Liberation Council, was formed in southern Yemen, and appealed for a boycott of the legislative elections, due to take place in April 2009 (and subsequently postponed—see above). There were further disturbances in Aden, Lahij and ad-Dali in January 2009, as demonstrations organized by supporters of the so-called Southern Movement (an increasingly separatist group led by former military officers) once again escalated into violent clashes with security forces. Rioting followed a demonstration in Mukalla, in Hadramout, in late April, leading to the arrests of at least 50 protesters. After the provincial authorities established additional military checkpoints in Lahij, apparently in violation of a prior agreement, armed confrontation between separatist militants and security forces erupted in early May. After five days of fighting in the Radfan region, in which up to eight people, including several soldiers, were killed, a truce was arranged and a mediation committee was charged with resolving the crisis. Meanwhile, in April the Ministry of the Interior initiated proceedings to remove the immunity from prosecution of two parliamentary deputies, most notably Nasser al-Khabji, a YSP deputy and alleged leader of the Southern Movement in Lahij, whom it accused of violating the Constitution. In an effort to suppress media coverage of the conflict in the south, the Ministry of Information issued a directive in early May banning the publication of any material deemed harmful to national unity. Seven newspapers were ordered to suspend operations, and existing copies of their publications were seized by the authorities. The offices of the independent daily *Al-Ayyam* were reportedly surrounded by security forces, preventing distribution of the newspaper.

There was growing domestic and international concern about the rise in militant Islamist activity in Yemen during 2008 and early 2009. Observers speculated that successful counter-terrorism operations in neighbouring Saudi Arabia were resulting in the migration of al-Qa'ida-affiliated groups into Yemen. A security officer was killed in Sayoun, in Hadramout, in a suicide bombing in July 2008, for which al-Qa'ida claimed responsibility. In August, also in Hadramout, two government troops and five suspected al-Qa'ida militants were killed in a confrontation in Tarim. Later in August security officials arrested 30 alleged al-Qa'ida members in the same governorate, and at the end of the month the arrest was announced of Khalid Abd an-Nabi, reported to be the leader of the Islamic Aden-Abyan Army. On 17 September a car bomb was detonated outside the US embassy in San'a and armed militants attacked the heavily fortified building from a second car. Responsibility for the attack, in which at least 16 people were killed, including all six militants as well as security guards and civilian bystanders, was initially claimed by an organization calling itself Islamic Jihad in Yemen. Six men were arrested in October on suspicion of membership of the terrorist cell responsible for the US embassy bombing and the subsequent issuing of threats to attack other embassies in San'a.

The Yemeni authorities also accused the suspects of collaborating with the Israeli intelligence service; the Israeli Government strongly denied any involvement. Of the six suspects detained, three were released, while the remaining three were found guilty of offences including espionage and fraud in March 2009; two of those convicted were sentenced to three and five years' imprisonment, respectively, the third receiving the death penalty. Meanwhile, unconfirmed reports suggested that Kassem ar-Raimi, one of the three remaining fugitives from the prison escape in February 2006, had been killed in the embassy attack.

The first detainee at the US military detention camp at Guantánamo Bay, Cuba, to be convicted by a US military court was a Yemeni citizen. Salim Hamdan, who had worked as a driver for Osama bin Laden, was found guilty in August 2008 of providing material support for terrorism and sentenced to five-and-a-half years' imprisonment. Having been in US custody since 2001, Hamdan was transferred to a prison in Yemen in November 2008 and released in January 2009. Another Yemeni detainee at the camp, Ali Hamza Ahmad al-Bahlul, was sentenced to life imprisonment on terrorism charges in November 2008. The strategic importance of Yemen as a base for jihadist activity in the region was underlined in late January 2009, when, in video footage posted on the internet, al-Qa'ida announced the merger of its Saudi Arabian and Yemeni operations. The authorities in Yemen responded by strengthening their counter-terrorism operations and increasing security co-operation with Saudi Arabia. In March a list of 154 wanted militants, including many who were also sought by Saudi Arabia, was issued by the Yemeni Ministry of the Interior. In the same month the trial began of 16 suspected members of Jund al-Yaman who were accused of perpetrating the attacks against Spanish and Belgian tourists in July 2007 and January 2008, as well as several other attacks on foreign interests in San'a. Four South Korean tourists and a Yemeni guide were killed in a suicide bombing at a popular tourist site at Shibam, in Hadramout, in mid-March 2009. A second attack, a few days later, targeted a delegation of South Korean government officials and bereaved relatives of the tourists killed at Shibam; none of the group, which reportedly included the South Korean ambassador, was injured.

An agreement on the long-disputed former PDRY–Omani border was signed in San'a in October 1992 and ratified in December. Demarcation was completed in June 1995. Oman withdrew an estimated 15,000 troops from the last of the disputed territories on the Yemeni border in July 1996, in accordance with the 1992 agreement. In May 1997 officials from both countries signed the demarcation maps at a ceremony in Muscat, Oman. In January 2004 the two countries signed an agreement on their sea border during wider discussions over the establishment of a joint free trade zone.

The Iraqi invasion of Kuwait in August 1990 proved problematic for the Yemeni Government, as the economy was heavily dependent on trade with, and aid from, Iraq, and also on aid from Saudi Arabia, which was host to a considerable number of Yemeni expatriate workers. In December Yemen assumed the chair of the UN Security Council (which rotates on a monthly basis), and the Government increased its efforts to mediate in the Gulf crisis. It was, however, unable to prevent the outbreak of war, despite a peace plan, presented in January 1991, and further diplomatic initiatives. Yemen condemned the US-led military offensive against Iraq, and large demonstrations were held in support of Iraq. Later in January it was confirmed that US aid to Yemen was to be suspended indefinitely, apparently as a result of Yemen's policy towards Iraq, although reduced US economic aid was resumed in August. Yemen continued to support Iraq and in December 1998 it requested an Arab League summit on Iraq and called for an end to the sanctions. The Yemeni Government expressed its concerns regarding the US-led military operations against Iraqi air defence targets in 1999–2002.

Following the suicide attacks apparently perpetrated by Osama bin Laden's al-Qa'ida network against New York and Washington, DC, USA on 11 September 2001, the Yemeni Government arrested a number of suspected Islamist militants and froze the assets of individuals and organizations deemed to have links with al-Qa'ida. In December up to 30 people (including about 19 soldiers) were reportedly killed during clashes in the central Marib governorate, when local residents apparently fought to prevent the Yemeni security forces from arresting a group of alleged militants. (President Saleh had, during a visit to Washington in November, been presented with a list of suspected al-Qa'ida members residing in Yemen.) Meanwhile, at least 100 foreign students enrolled at the country's Islamic institutes were said to have been arrested on charges of violating residency requirements. In January 2002 the US embassy in San'a was closed amid fears of an imminent terrorist attack; two grenades were thrown at the building in March, although no injuries were reported. There were reports in March that the US Administration was considering the deployment of several hundred US troops to Yemen to assist the authorities in their struggle against militant Islamist organizations. In April an explosion was reported close to the home of a leading security official involved in the search for al-Qa'ida militants; a previously unknown group styled the al-Qa'ida Sympathizers was suspected of having carried out the bombing. Despite increasing popular resentment towards US activities in the Middle East among Yemenis, President Saleh continued to co-operate with the USA over anti-terrorism initiatives, and in November an unmanned US aircraft killed six men in northern Yemen believed to have links with al-Qa'ida. In December three US missionaries were murdered by a Yemeni who confessed to having links with bin Laden's network.

In February 2002 President Saleh was reported to have warned the US Government that a US-led attack on the regime of Saddam Hussain in Iraq, as part of its 'war on terror', would jeopardize the continued support of its traditional allies in the Arab region. However, Saleh was careful to emphasize his own ongoing efforts to persuade the Iraqi authorities to accept the return of UN weapons inspectors. When the US-led military campaign commenced in Iraq in March 2003, some 30,000 protesters, some of them armed, marched on the US embassy in San'a. Public resentment also continued to increase towards President Saleh's regime, as a result of its perceived co-operation with the USA. In June, however, the Director of the US Federal Bureau of Investigation, Robert Mueller, met Saleh in Aden to discuss further co-operation on security and intelligence. In September the human rights organization Amnesty International released a report claiming that the authorities were holding some 200 people without trial in an effort to assuage US concerns that Yemen was not co-operating fully with the 'war on terror'. In November Muhammad Hamdi al-Ahdal, who, according to the USA, had been among the 20 most significant al-Qa'ida members still at large, was captured by security forces; al-Ahdal was suspected of having organized the bombings of the USS *Cole* in 2000 and the French petroleum tanker, the *Limburg*, in 2002 (see above). Another reported senior al-Qa'ida operative, who had apparently survived a US attempt to assassinate him in 2002, was arrested by security forces in March 2004.

In March 2004 Yemen welcomed the signing of an interim constitution in Iraq, describing it as a step towards Iraq recovering its sovereignty, but continued to press for the USA and its allies to withdraw their forces from the country. In August the Minister of Foreign Affairs confirmed that Yemen was preparing a peace-keeping force for Iraq under mandates from the Arab League and the UN, but would only send the troops should the US-led coalition forces withdraw from Iraq. In December 2006 the US embassy in San'a was again closed after a man bearing a semi-automatic rifle had opened fire at the compound. Security guards on site returned fire, incapacitating the gunman and allowing him to be arrested; no embassy staff were injured in the incident and the embassy was reopened on the following day. Discussions held between Saleh and US President George W. Bush in May 2007, during a visit by the Yemeni President to Washington, focused on efforts to combat terrorism and developments in the Middle East, as well as bilateral relations. In November Saleh al-Ammari was convicted of shooting at the embassy in December 2006 and sentenced to five years' imprisonment; an appeals court reduced his sentence to three years in May 2008. In September 2008 the US embassy in San'a was the target of another violent attack (see above), in which at least 16 people were killed, although no embassy staff were reported to have been injured in the incident.

Relations with Saudi Arabia deteriorated as a result of Yemen's initially strong opposition to the presence of foreign armed forces in the Gulf and to the ambiguous stance it had subsequently adopted in this respect. In September 1990, apparently in retaliation, Saudi Arabia announced that it had withdrawn the privileges that Yemeni workers had previously enjoyed. This resulted in an exodus from Saudi Arabia of some 850,000 Yemeni workers during October and November, which caused widespread economic and social disruption. The expulsion and consequent return to Yemen of the workers not only caused a reduction in the country's income from remittances, but also led to a serious increase in unemployment. During 1995, at negotiations proceeding from the February 1995 memorandum of understanding—see below—it was reported that the Saudi authorities had agreed to allow Yemenis sponsored by Saudi nationals to seek employment in the kingdom. In 1998 Saudi Arabia began issuing visas to Yemeni workers.

The Governments of Yemen and Saudi Arabia held negotiations concerning the demarcation of their common border during 1992–94; however, in December 1994 Yemen accused Saudi Arabia of trespassing on Yemeni territory and alleged that three of its soldiers had been killed during clashes earlier in that month. Further clashes were reported in January 1995 following the failure of the two countries to renew the 1934 Ta'if agreement (renewable every 20 years), which delineated their existing frontier. Intense mediation by Syria culminated in a joint statement in mid-January 1995, in which Yemen and Saudi Arabia pledged to cease all military activity in the border area. It was subsequently announced that the demarcation of the disputed border would be undertaken by a joint committee. In February the Yemeni and Saudi Governments signed a memorandum of understanding that reaffirmed their commitment to the Ta'if agreement and provided for the establishment of six joint committees to delineate the land and sea borders and develop economic and commercial ties. In June President Saleh led a high-ranking delegation to Saudi Arabia, constituting the first official visit to that country since February 1990. The two Governments expressed their satisfaction with the memorandum of understanding and, in addition, pledged their commitment to strengthening economic, commercial and cultural co-operation.

In July 1996 Yemen and Saudi Arabia signed a bilateral security agreement which included provisions intended to counter the cross-border trafficking of illicit drugs. Friction over border claims, however, was revived in 1997, and in May 1998 it was reported that Saudi Arabia had occupied an uninhabited island in the Red Sea regarded by Yemen as within its national boundaries. In the same month Saudi Arabia sent a memorandum to the UN stating that it did not recognize the 1992 border agreement between Yemen and Oman and claiming that parts of the area involved were Saudi Arabian territory. The Saudi objection to the accord was widely believed to be related to its attempts to gain land access to the Arabian Sea, via a corridor between Yemen and Oman, which it had thus far been denied in its negotiations with Yemen. In July 1998 Yemen submitted a memorandum to the Arab League refuting the Saudi claim to the land, and stating that the Saudi protests contravened the Ta'if agreement signed by that country. In the same month three Yemeni troops were killed during fighting with a Saudi border patrol on the disputed island of Duwaima in the Red Sea; Saudi Arabia claimed its actions on the island were in self-defence and that, under the Ta'if agreement, three-quarters of the island belonged to Saudi Arabia. Meanwhile, bilateral discussions continued and the Saudi Minister of Foreign Affairs visited Yemen at the end of July. The Yemeni Prime Minister cancelled a planned visit to Saudi Arabia in October 1999, reportedly owing to the failure of the two Governments to agree on the issues to be discussed.

Despite reported clashes in the border area during 1999, however, relations continued to improve. In June 2000, at a ceremony in Riyadh, Saudi Arabia, the Saudi Arabian and Yemeni ministers responsible for foreign affairs signed a final border treaty demarcating their joint land and sea border. The treaty incorporated both the 1934 Ta'if agreement and the 1995 memorandum of understanding, although it failed to define the eastern section of the Saudi–Yemeni land frontier. The two countries also agreed to further economic, commercial and cultural ties, and each pledged not to permit its territory to be used as a base for political or military aggression against the other. In the months following the signing of the treaty, however, clashes were reported between rival tribal groups near the border. In December 2000 a meeting was held of the Saudi-Yemeni Co-operation Council (the first since before the Gulf conflict), at which Saudi officials pledged financial assistance to Yemen for development projects. However, talks concerning the proposed construction of a petroleum pipeline between the two countries had reportedly been unsuccessful. In April 2001 Yemen and Saudi Arabia were said to have agreed on the location of four crossing-points on their joint border. At the same time reports suggested that the withdrawal of Yemeni and Saudi troops from their respective sides of the border was almost complete. Renewed tensions surfaced in early 2004 after the Saudi Government began construction of a 'separation wall' along the border that some considered to be in violation of the treaty of June 2000 on border demarcation. The construction of the wall reflected unease on the part of the Saudis regarding the capacity of the Yemeni authorities to maintain their own border security. In June 2006 the Saudi and Yemeni ministers responsible for internal affairs signed an agreement on the final demarcation of their shared border.

In November 1995 there were reports that Eritrean troops had attempted to land on the Red Sea island of Greater Hanish, one of three islands (the others being Lesser Hanish and Zuqar) claimed by both Yemen and Eritrea. The attempted invasion had apparently been prompted by Yemen's announced intention to develop Greater Hanish as a tourist resort, and its subsequent refusal to comply with an Eritrean demand that the island be evacuated. Negotiations in Yemen and Eritrea failed to defuse the crisis, and on 15 December fighting broke out between the two sides, resulting in the deaths of six Eritrean and three Yemeni soldiers. On 17 December Yemen and Eritrea agreed to a cease-fire. None the less, fighting was renewed the following day and Eritrean forces succeeded in occupying Greater Hanish. The cease-fire was adhered to thenceforth, and some 180 Yemeni soldiers (captured during the fighting) were released at the end of the month.

In May 1996, following French mediation, it was announced that Yemen and Eritrea would sign an arbitration agreement, whereby both countries would renounce the use of force and submit their dispute to an international tribunal. France subsequently undertook to observe and supervise military movements in the area around the disputed islands. Eritrean troops occupied Lesser Hanish in mid-August, but were withdrawn later in the month after representations by France and a UN Security Council edict to evacuate the island forthwith. At a meeting held in Paris, France, in October, representatives of Eritrea and Yemen confirmed that they would submit the dispute to an international tribunal. In October 1998 the tribunal ruled that Yemen had sovereignty over Greater and Lesser Hanish, and all islands to their north-west, while Eritrea had sovereignty over the Mohabaka islands. The court recommended that the fishing traditions around the islands be maintained, thereby granting access to the Hanish islands to Eritrean and Yemeni fishermen. Both countries accepted the ruling, and shortly afterwards they agreed to establish a joint committee to strengthen bilateral co-operation. In May 1999 the Presidents of Eritrea and Yemen held talks to discuss bilateral relations. A final ruling on the Hanish islands, issued by the tribunal in December, delineated the joint maritime border as the median line between their mainland coastlines. This was welcomed by both countries, and in January 2000 the Yemeni Vice-President made an official visit to Eritrea for talks with President Afewerki. In March Eritrea denied reports that it had appealed against the tribunal's decision on the islands. In June 2003 a number of Yemeni fishing boats and 133 crew members were arrested by Eritrean naval patrols in the area around the Hanish islands. Although the men were released in July, this latest development was an indication of increased tension between the countries since the decision of the tribunal.

Since the mid-1990s President Saleh has increasingly sought to widen the range of Yemen's international contacts, particularly in relation to aid and co-operation agreements. In November 1997, on an official visit to the United Kingdom (during which a co-operation agreement was signed with the EU), President Saleh made a formal application for Yemen to join the Commonwealth (see p. 217). Saleh made a state visit to the People's Republic of China in February 1998, during which extensive agreements were negotiated for Yemen to receive technical and economic assistance. In early 2000 Saleh made official visits to Canada, the USA, Italy and Iran; at the same time Yemen repeatedly denied reports that it had had secret contacts with Israel and that it was seeking to normalize relations with that country. In December 2003 Yemen consolidated its improved relations with two of its neighbours to the west, Sudan and Ethiopia, with the establishment of the Tripartite San'a Co-operation Forum. Eritrea, however, accused the group of collaborating against it. In December 2005 Yemen offered to mediate between Ethiopia and Eritrea over the two countries' border demarcation dispute. At a meeting held in London, United Kingdom, in November 2006, international donors pledged some US $5,000m. in development assistance for Yemen. In August 2007 Yemen signed a 10-year development partnership agreement with the United Kingdom.

YEMEN

Introductory Survey

In September 2005 Yemen signed a security agreement with Bahrain; the two states agreed to co-operate on training, combating crime and terrorism, and exchanging intelligence. Furthermore, in November 2008 the Bahraini authorities announced their intention to establish an embassy in Yemen in the near future. Meanwhile, in May 2007 the staging of a demonstration intended to protest against perceived Iranian and Libyan interference in Yemeni domestic affairs was prevented by the Ministry of the Interior, provoking outrage among, in particular, many in Saada, who were angered by alleged Iranian and Libyan support for those rebels loyal to al-Houthi who were thought to be responsible for much of the violence in that region. A few days previously Yemen had recalled its ambassadors from both countries. The Iranian and Libyan Governments both denied any involvement in the rebellion in Saada and sought to ease tensions with Yemen. Later in May the Libyan leader dispatched an envoy to San'a to deliver a letter to President Saleh expressing support for the Yemeni Government's efforts to quash the insurgency, and in July Muhammad Reza Baqeri, the Iranian Deputy Foreign Minister for Arab and African Affairs, visited Yemen in an effort to improve bilateral relations. However, in November 2008 Rashad al-Alimi, Yemen's Deputy Prime Minister for Defence and Security Affairs, alleged that al-Houthi militants were receiving training and support from Iran. Two Yemeni citizens were convicted in April 2009 of spying for Iran and sentenced to death.

President Saleh sought to mediate in the dispute that arose between rival Palestinian political factions the Islamic Resistance Movement (Hamas) and Fatah after Hamas had seized control of the Gaza Strip in June 2007. In March 2008 the Yemeni President brokered a reconciliation agreement, the San'a Declaration, which was signed by the two organizations (see the chapter on the Palestinian Autonomous Areas). The launch of Israel's military offensive against Hamas targets in the Gaza Strip in late December 2008 led to angry demonstrations throughout Yemen. Protesters angered by Egypt's perceived support for Israel stormed the Egyptian consulate in Aden, causing serious damage. President Saleh attended the Arab Economic, Social and Development Summit in Kuwait in January 2009, at which he presented proposals for the formation of a union of Arab states.

Government

Legislative power is vested in the House of Representatives, with 301 members directly elected by universal adult suffrage. Under the revised Constitution, the President of the Republic (Head of State) is to be elected directly by voters for a period of seven years, renewable once. The President appoints a Council of Ministers, headed by a Prime Minister.

Defence

As assessed at November 2008, the armed forces of the Republic of Yemen totalled 66,700: army 60,000; navy 1,700; air force 3,000; air defence 2,000. There was a paramilitary force with a strength in excess of 71,200, comprising the 50,000-strong Ministry of the Interior Forces and tribal levies numbering at least 20,000. Military conscription was ended in May 2001, and in 2004 a voluntary programme of military service was introduced. The defence budget for 2007 was forecast at YR 179,000m.

Economic Affairs

In 2007, according to estimates by the World Bank, Yemen's gross national income (GNI), measured at average 2005–07 prices, was US $19,421m., equivalent to $870 per head (or $2,200 per head on an international purchasing-power parity basis). During 2000–07, it was estimated, the population increased at an average annual rate of 3.0%, while gross domestic product (GDP) per head increased, in real terms, by an average of 0.9% per year. Overall GDP increased, in real terms, at an average annual rate of 4.0% in 2000–07; GDP growth in 2007 was 4.7%.

Agriculture (including forestry and fishing) contributed an estimated 8.9% of GDP in 2007, and the sector engaged 31.0% of the working population at the 2004 census. According to FAO estimates, however, the sector engaged 45.3% of the total labour force in mid-2005. The principal cash crops are coffee, cotton and fruits. Subsistence crops include sorghum, wheat, barley and potatoes. However, cultivation of the amphetamine-like narcotic qat has displaced other crops in many areas. Livestock-rearing (particularly in the east and north) and fishing are also important activities. Estimates indicated growth in the agricultural sector averaging 2.4% annually in 2000–07. Real agricultural GDP declined by 0.4% in 2007, according to provisional estimates.

Industry (including mining, manufacturing, construction and power) contributed an estimated 42.5% of GDP in 2007, and 16.3% of the working population were employed in the sector at the 2004 census. According to estimates, industrial GDP decreased at an average annual rate of 2.3% in 2000–07. Real industrial GDP was provisionally estimated to have declined by 7.4% in 2007.

Mining and quarrying contributed an estimated 27.0% of GDP in 2007, and employed 0.5% of the working population at the 2004 census. Yemen's proven petroleum reserves totalled 2,800m. barrels at the end of 2007, sufficient to maintain production at that year's levels for almost 23 years. Petroleum production averaged 336,000 barrels per day (b/d) during 2007. The value of exports of petroleum and petroleum products accounted for 90.4% of the value of total exports in 2007. There are also significant reserves of natural gas: proven reserves at the end of 2007 were 490,000m. cu m. Salt and gypsum are also exploited on a large scale. It was announced in late 2008 that the country's first gold mine was to be established at Haddah, on the border with Saudi Arabia. In addition, there are deposits of copper, lead, zinc, sulphur and molybdenum. The GDP of the mining sector decreased at an estimated average annual rate of 3.7% in 2000–07; real mining GDP contracted by 4.2% in 2007, according to provisional estimates.

The manufacturing sector contributed an estimated 8.9% of GDP in 2007; at the 2004 census 5.9% of the working population were employed in the sector. The most important branches of manufacturing are food-processing, petroleum refining, construction materials (particularly cement and iron and steel), paper and paper products and traditional light industries (including textiles, leather goods and jewellery). Production of liquefied natural gas (LNG) was expected to commence by the second half of 2009. Real growth in manufacturing GDP was estimated at an average of 3.7% annually in 2000–07; according to provisional estimates, the sector's real GDP increased by 9.2% in 2007.

Some domestic energy requirements are served by locally produced petroleum, but the country is somewhat reliant on fuel imports (particularly petroleum from other producers in the region). Imports of fuel and energy comprised 22.0% of the value of total imports in 2007. The northern and southern electricity grids were linked in 1997.

The services sector contributed an estimated 48.7% of GDP in 2007, and employed 52.7% of the working population at the 2004 census. A free trade zone at Aden was inaugurated in May 1991. Security concerns have undermined Yemen's attractiveness as a destination for tourists and investment. The real GDP of the services sector increased at an estimated average annual rate of 10.2% in 2009–07. Real services GDP expanded by 15.0% in 2007, according to provisional estimates.

In 2007 Yemen recorded a visible trade deficit of US $81.3m., and there was a deficit of $1,327.7m. on the current account of the balance of payments. In 2007 the principal source of imports (20.0%) was the United Arab Emirates (UAE); other major suppliers were Saudi Arabia, the People's Republic of China and Switzerland-Liechtenstein. In that year China was the main export destination (21.0%). Other important export markets were Thailand, India, the UAE and Switzerland-Liechtenstein. The principal exports in 2007 were petroleum and petroleum products (90.4%). The main imports in that year were food and live animals (especially cereals and cereal preparations), machinery and transport equipment, and basic manufactures.

A preliminary budget deficit of YR 341,900m. was recorded in 2007. Total external debt at the end of 2006 was estimated to be US $5,563m., of which $5,000m. was long-term public debt. In that year the cost of debt-servicing was equivalent to 2.4% of the value of exports of goods and services. The annual rate of inflation averaged 12.8% in 2000–07; consumer prices increased by 10.0% in 2007. The rate of unemployment is estimated to be as high as 25% of the labour force.

Yemen is a member of the Arab Fund for Economic and Social Development (AFESD, see p. 183) and the Council of Arab Economic Unity (see p. 233). Yemen is pursuing membership of the Co-operation Council for the Arab States of the Gulf (the Gulf Co-operation Council—GCC, see p. 229)

In view of the near-exhaustion of Yemen's petroleum reserves, diversification of the economy remains a priority if Yemen's high level of poverty and the needs of a rapidly expanding population are to be addressed. The commencement of output by a new LNG plant in 2009 was expected to present a significant new source of revenue, but this would be insufficient to offset an eventual loss of oil income. Beyond the hydrocarbons sector, planned promotion of the tourist industry requires substantial investment in infrastructure, as well as effective efforts to alleviate security concerns. In the fisheries sector, meanwhile, the Government planned to introduce measures to address diminishing stocks. Security concerns also remain to be resolved in the maritime sector, and have notably been a disincentive to offshore exploration for hydrocarbons. Severe shortages of water have impeded diversification in the agriculture sector: some 95% of the water supply is used for agriculture, although much of this is taken up by qat production. Severe flooding in Hadramout and Mahrah provinces in October 2008 caused considerable damage to agricultural land and infrastructure, and also adversely affected the tourist sector. In an assessment of the economy published in early 2009, the IMF forecast that the commencement of LNG production in that year would provide a substantial but temporary boost to the economy: overall GDP in 2009 was projected to increase by 7.7%, reflecting a 44.5% increase in hydrocarbons GDP, compared with projected overall growth of 3.9% and a decline of 5.4% in hydrocarbons GDP in 2008. The IMF emphasized the need for futher measures to widen the tax base, following the partial implementation of a general services tax in 2007. Meanwhile, high international prices for oil for much of 2008 resulted in a narrowing in the external current account deficit in that year to a projected 2.0% of GDP, from 7% in 2007 (the latter figure reflecting in large part expenditure related to the LNG project). However, the sharp decline in oil prices from late 2008 required adjustments to the budget for 2009: non-priority spending was to be reduced, and selected investment projects deferred. The projected fiscal and external current account deficits for 2009 were 6.1% and 2.8%, respectively. Inflation was expected to ease somewhat in 2009, following a sharp increase in 2008 as a result of high food prices, although it remained an issue of concern.

Education

Primary education, between the ages of six and 15, is compulsory. Secondary education, beginning at 15, lasts for a further three years. In 2004/05 enrolment at primary schools included 75% of children in the relevant age-group (85% of boys; 65% of girls); in 2006/07 the total number of students in primary education was 4,270,086. Enrolment at secondary schools in 2004/05, according to UNESCO estimates, included 37% of students (48% of boys; 26% of girls) in the appropriate age-group; in 2006/07 the total number of students in secondary education was 581,029. In 2006/07 233,903 students were enrolled at universities; a further 18,309 students were enrolled at vocational training centres. In 2007 public expenditure on education amounted to an estimated YR 229,861m., equivalent to 14.4% of total government spending (excluding loan repayments). A Basic Education Development project aimed to improve the quality of education and to increase enrolment at primary schools to 85% over 40 years; the World Bank approved the project in September 2004 and provided a loan of US $65m. to assist with its implementation.

Public Holidays

2009: 1 January (New Year's Day), 7 January*† (Ashoura), 8 March (International Women's Day), 9 March* (Mouloud, Birth of the Prophet), 1 May (Labour Day), 13 June (Corrective Movement Anniversary), 19 July* (Leilat al-Meiraj, Ascension of the Prophet), 22 August* (Ramadan begins), 20 September* (Id al-Fitr, end of Ramadan), 14 October (National Day), 27 November* (Id al-Adha, Feast of the Sacrifice), 18 December* (Muharram, Islamic New Year), 27 December*† (Ashoura).

2010: 1 January (New Year's Day), 26 February* (Mouloud, Birth of the Prophet), 8 March (International Women's Day), 1 May (Labour Day), 13 June (Corrective Movement Anniversary), 8 July* (Leilat al-Meiraj, Ascension of the Prophet), 11 August* (Ramadan begins), 10 September* (Id al-Fitr, end of Ramadan), 14 October (National Day), 16 November* (Id al-Adha, Feast of the Sacrifice), 7 December* (Muharram, Islamic New Year), 16 December* (Ashoura).

* These holidays are dependent on the Islamic lunar calendar and may vary by one or two days from the dates given.

† This festival occurs twice (in the Islamic years AH 1430 and 1431) within the same Gregorian year.

Weights and Measures

Local weights and measures are used, and vary according to location.

Statistical Survey

Sources (unless otherwise indicated): Republic of Yemen Central Statistical Organization, POB 13434, San'a; tel. (1) 250619; fax (1) 250664; e-mail csoi@y.net.ye; internet www.cso-yemen.org; Central Bank of Yemen, POB 59, Ali Abd al-Mughni St, San'a; tel. (1) 274314; fax (1) 274360; e-mail info@centralbank.gov.ye; internet www.centralbank.gov.ye.

Area and Population

AREA, POPULATION AND DENSITY

Area (sq km)	536,869*
Population (census results)	
16 December 1994†	14,587,807
16 December 2004‡	
Males	10,036,953
Females	9,648,208
Total	19,685,161
Population (UN estimates at mid-year)§	
2006	21,638,000
2007	22,269,000
2008	22,917,000
Density (per sq km) at mid-2008	42.7

* 207,286 sq miles.
† Excluding adjustment for underenumeration.
‡ Population is *de jure*.
§ Source: UN, *World Population Prospects: The 2008 Revision*.

PRINCIPAL TOWNS
(population at 1994 census)

San'a (capital)	954,448	Hodeida	298,452
Aden	398,294	Mukalla	122,359
Taiz	317,571	Ibb	103,312

Source: UN, *Demographic Yearbook*.

Mid-2007 ('000, incl. suburbs, UN estimate): San'a 2,008 (Source: UN, *World Urbanization Prospects: The 2007 Revision*).

BIRTHS, MARRIAGES AND DEATHS
(annual averages, UN estimates)

	1990–95	1995–2000	2000–05
Birth rate (per 1,000)	48.6	42.9	38.6
Death rate (per 1,000)	11.9	10.1	8.6

Source: UN, *World Population Prospects: The 2008 Revision*.

Registered births: 153,945 in 2004; 152,792 in 2005.

Registered deaths: 22,255 in 2004; 19,653 in 2005.

Marriages (2002, estimate): 10,934 (Source: UN, *Demographic Yearbook*).

Life expectancy (years at birth, WHO estimates): 60.7 (males 59.1; females 62.4) in 2006 (Source: WHO, *World Health Statistics*).

YEMEN

EMPLOYMENT
('000 persons aged 15 years and over, 2004 census results)

	Males	Females	Total
Agriculture, forestry and fishing	973	130	1,103
Mining and quarrying	17	1	18
Manufacturing	185	25	210
Electricity, gas and water	16	1	17
Construction	331	2	333
Trade, restaurants and hotels	736	20	756
Transport, storage and communications	188	4	192
Finance, insurance and real estate	39	5	44
Education	217	70	287
Health and social welfare	33	17	50
Personal and social services	49	4	53
Public administration and defence	444	25	469
Private households with employed persons	13	6	19
Extra-territorial organizations	3	1	4
Total	**3,244**	**311**	**3,555**

Mid-2005 (estimates in '000): Agriculture, etc. 3,091; Total labour force 6,820 (Source: FAO).

Health and Welfare

KEY INDICATORS

Total fertility rate (children per woman, 2006)	5.6
Under-5 mortality rate (per 1,000 live births, 2006)	100
HIV/AIDS (% of persons aged 15–49, 2003)	0.1
Physicians (per 1,000 head, 2004)	0.3
Hospital beds (per 1,000 head, 2006)	0.7
Health expenditure (2006): US $ per head (PPP)	82
Health expenditure (2006): % of GDP	4.6
Health expenditure (2006): public (% of total)	46.4
Access to water (% of persons, 2004)	66
Access to sanitation (% of persons, 2004)	46
Human Development Index (2006): ranking	138
Human Development Index (2006): value	0.567

For sources and definitions, see explanatory note on p. vi.

Agriculture

PRINCIPAL CROPS
('000 metric tons)

	2005	2006	2007
Wheat	113	149	157
Barley	21	28	30
Maize	31	66	70
Millet	67	82	88
Sorghum	264	402	430
Potatoes	218	226	231
Chick-peas	37	54	54*
Sesame seed	19	22	22*
Seed cotton	21	22	24*
Tomatoes	204	212	212*
Cucumbers and gherkins	10	13	13*
Chillies and peppers, green	17	17	17*
Onions, dry	173	174	174*
Garlic	8*	3	4*
Beans, green	12*	3	3*
Carrots and turnips	12	13	13*
Okra	18	18	19*
Watermelons	144	148	148*

—continued	2005	2006	2007
Cantaloupes and other melons	28	27	27*
Bananas	90	112	113*
Oranges	84	101	101*
Tangerines, mandarins, etc.	13	20	20*
Grapes	108	118	120*
Mangoes, mangosteens and guavas	345	349	350*
Dates	30	50	50*
Papayas	21	22	22*
Coffee, green	11	17	n.a.
Tobacco, unmanufactured	18	20	20

* FAO estimate.

Aggregate production ('000 metric tons, may include official, semi-official or estimated data): Total cereals 496 in 2005, 727 in 2006, 774 in 2007; Total roots and tubers 218 in 2005, 227 in 2006, 232 in 2007; Total vegetables (incl. melons) 702 in 2005, 711 in 2006, 712 in 2007; Total fruits (excl. melons) 754 in 2005, 822 in 2006, 826 in 2007.

Source: FAO.

LIVESTOCK
('000 head, year ending September)

	2005	2006	2007*
Horses*	3	3	3
Asses*	500	n.a.	n.a.
Cattle	1,447	1,464	1,480
Camels	357	359	361
Sheep	7,980	8,197	8,420
Goats	7,864	8,042	8,220
Chickens (million)*	47,500	49,300	51,000

* FAO estimates.
Source: FAO.

LIVESTOCK PRODUCTS
('000 metric tons)

	2005	2006	2007*
Cattle meat	72.6	72.8	73.0
Sheep meat*	31.9	32.2	33.0
Goat meat*	31.6	26.2	26.8
Chicken meat	113.2	117.7	122.6
Camels' milk*	17.7	17.9	18.1
Cows' milk	216.6	224.2	232.2
Sheep's milk*	27.2	27.9	28.6
Goats' milk*	37.5	38.4	39.2
Hen eggs*	48.4	50.8	51.6
Wool (greasy)*	6.5	6.8	7.0

* FAO estimates.
Source: FAO.

Forestry

ROUNDWOOD REMOVALS
('000 cubic metres, excl. bark, estimates)

	2005	2006	2007
Total (all fuel wood)	367	381	395

Source: FAO.

Fishing

('000 metric tons, live weight of capture)

	2004	2005	2006
Demersal percomorphs*	12.4	12.7	12.7
Indian oil sardine*	10.7	11.0	11.0
Yellowfin tuna	31.3	26.4	19.2
Pelagic percomorphs*	119.5	127.7	121.0
Sharks, rays and skates, etc.*	12.5	12.8	12.8
Cuttlefish and bobtail squids	12.8*	13.2*	13.2
Total catch (incl. others)*	256.3	263.0	250.0

* FAO estimate(s).
Source: FAO.

Mining

('000 metric tons, unless otherwise indicated)

	2005	2006	2007
Crude petroleum ('000 barrels)	146,090	133,330	118,000
Natural gas (million cu m)*	29,500	28,100	25,000
Salt	90	100	100
Gypsum (crude)	38	44	44

* Gross production.
Source: US Geological Survey.

Industry

SELECTED PRODUCTS
('000 barrels, unless otherwise indicated)

	2003	2004	2005
Mineral water (million litres)	146	153	n.a.
Soft drinks (million litres)	105*	127	154
Cigarettes (million packets)	298*	90	109
Liquefied petroleum gas	1,100	800	900
Benzene	7,400	8,100	8,100
Kerosene	3,510	3,100	1,700
Distillate fuel oils	16,000	16,900	18,200
Residual fuel oils	10,000	9,000	6,800
Cement ('000 metric tons)	1,541	1,546	1,550
Paints ('000 litres)	15,564	15,664	n.a.
Plastic bags ('000 metric tons)	10,891	10,993	n.a.
Electric energy (million kWh)	4,094*	4,366	4,767

* Provisional figure.

2006 ('000 barrels, unless otherwise indicated): Kerosene 1,700; Distillate fuel oil 18,000; Residual fuel oil 6,800; Cement ('000 metric tons) 1,470.

2007 ('000 barrels, unless otherwise indicated): Kerosene 1,600; Distillate fuel oil 19,000; Residual fuel oil 7,000; Cement ('000 metric tons) 1,728.

Source: partly US Geological Survey.

Finance

CURRENCY AND EXCHANGE RATES

Monetary Units
100 fils = 1 Yemeni riyal (YR).

Sterling, Dollar and Euro Equivalents (31 October 2008)
£1 sterling = YR 323.25;
US $1 = YR 199.86;
€1 = YR 254.96;
YR 1,000 = £3.09 = $5.00 = €3.92.

Average Exchange Rate (YR per US $)
2005   191.509
2006   197.049
2007   198.953

Note: The exchange rate of US $1 = YR 9.76, established in the YAR in 1988, remained in force until February 1990, when a new rate of $1 = YR 12.01 was introduced. Following the merger of the two Yemens in May 1990, the YAR's currency was adopted as the currency of the unified country. In March 1995 the official exchange rate was amended from YR 12.01 to YR 50.04 per US dollar. The rate has since been adjusted. From mid-1996 data refer to a market-determined exchange rate, applicable to most private transactions

CENTRAL GOVERNMENT BUDGET
(YR '000 million)

Revenue*	2005	2006	2007†
Oil and gas	752.7	1,059.8	972.5
Exports	481.8	611.8	510.4
Domestic revenues	270.9	448.0	462.1
Non-oil revenues	354.9	374.9	427.7
Tax revenues	234.9	266.4	307.4
Non-tax revenues	120.0	108.5	120.3
Total	1,107.6	1,434.7	1,400.2

Expenditure	2005	2006	2007†
Current expenditure	890.7	1,107.7	1,379.2
Civil wages and salaries	195.9	386.9	487.6
Materials and services	78.2	206.5	246.7
Interest	69.1	87.0	99.8
Domestic	60.1	76.4	87.3
Foreign	9.0	10.6	12.5
Transfers and subsidies	372.8	404.8	520.1
Current transfers	86.5	95.5	112.4
Subsidies	286.3	309.3	407.7
Other current expenditure	18.5	22.5	25.0
Capital development expenditure	225.7	228.4	308.9
Net lending	62.9	67.0	60.2
Total	1,179.3	1,404.0	1,748.3

* Excluding grants received (YR '000 million): 13.7 in 2005; 15.0 in 2006; 6.2 in 2007 (preliminary).
† Preliminary figures.

INTERNATIONAL RESERVES
(US $ million at 31 December)

	2006	2007	2008
Gold (national valuation)	32.9	44.2	46.1
IMF special drawing rights	7.1	—	0.4
Foreign exchange	7,504.4	7,715.4	8,111.0
Total	7,544.7	7,759.6	8,157.5

Source: IMF, *International Financial Statistics*.

MONEY SUPPLY
(YR million at 31 December)

	2006	2007	2008
Currency outside banks	412,520	425,840	472,667
Demand deposits at commercial banks	99,625	130,417	151,636
Total money (incl. others)	558,461	613,748	680,600

Source: IMF, *International Financial Statistics*.

YEMEN

Statistical Survey

COST OF LIVING
(Consumer Price Index; base: 2000 = 100)

	2005	2006	2007
Food	199.9	269.5	317.9
Rent	139.7	146.8	n.a.
Clothing	121.9	120.0	n.a.
All items (incl. others)	174.5	211.6	232.8

Source: ILO.

NATIONAL ACCOUNTS
(YR million at current prices)

National Income and Product

	2005	2006*	2007†
Domestic factor incomes	3,341,549	4,097,441	4,819,371
Consumption of fixed capital	210,683	272,055	322,058
Gross domestic product (GDP) at factor cost	3,552,232	4,369,496	5,141,429
Indirect taxes, *less* subsidies	−160,970	−172,706	−217,742
GDP in purchasers' values	3,391,262	4,196,790	4,923,687
Factor income from abroad (net)	−295,678	−229,847	−215,059
Gross national product (GNP)	3,095,584	3,966,943	4,708,628
Less Consumption of fixed capital	210,683	272,055	322,058
National income in purchasers' values	2,884,901	3,694,888	4,386,570
Other transfers from abroad (net)	255,689	253,862	261,837
National disposable income	3,140,590	3,948,750	4,648,407

Expenditure on the Gross Domestic Product

	2005	2006*	2007†
Government final consumption expenditure	392,941	545,699	625,553
Private final consumption expenditure	2,061,174	2,372,027	2,642,120
Changes in stocks	168,252	542,786	1,069,448
Gross fixed capital formation	606,395	721,167	897,201
Total domestic expenditure	3,228,762	4,181,679	5,234,322
Exports of goods and services	1,311,034	1,549,130	1,544,461
Less Imports of goods and services	1,148,534	1,534,019	1,855,096
GDP in purchasers' values	3,391,262	4,196,790	4,923,687
GDP at constant 2000 prices	1,957,483	2,045,530	2,141,712

Gross Domestic Product by Economic Activity

	2005	2006*	2007†
Agriculture, hunting, forestry and fishing‡	343,951	390,897	450,427
Mining and quarrying	1,153,724	1,322,108	1,367,199
Manufacturing	231,461	330,297	472,384
Electricity, gas and water	24,558	30,230	34,136
Construction	172,717	210,269	275,756
Trade, restaurants and hotels	428,560	610,148	806,861
Transport, storage and communications	385,579	514,144	578,451
Finance, insurance, real estate and business services	328,700	417,146	518,211
Government services	307,032	408,850	485,372
Other community, social and personal services	42,839	55,255	69,646
Private non-profit services and services to households	3,478	4,181	4,706
Sub-total	3,422,599	4,293,525	5,063,149
Import duties	51,945	36,135	42,283
Less Imputed bank service charge	83,282	132,870	181,745
GDP in purchasers' values	3,391,262	4,196,790	4,923,687

* Provisional.
† Preliminary estimates.
‡ Including production of qat.

BALANCE OF PAYMENTS
(US $ million)

	2005	2006	2007
Exports of goods f.o.b.	6,413.2	7,316.4	7,131.0
Imports of goods f.o.b.	−4,712.9	−5,926.1	−7,212.3
Trade balance	1,700.3	1,390.3	−81.3
Exports of services	372.1	548.8	643.1
Imports of services	−1,241.4	−1,855.0	−2,124.6
Balance on goods and services	830.9	84.0	−1,562.8
Other income received	178.2	316.2	384.9
Other income paid	−1,790.7	−1,550.5	−1,536.9
Balance on goods, services and income	−781.5	−1,150.3	−2,714.7
Current transfers received	1,458.4	1,401.7	1,435.6
Current transfers paid	−52.8	−45.7	−48.6
Current balance	624.1	205.7	−1,327.7
Capital account (net)	202.3	94.4	94.2
Direct investment from abroad	−302.1	1,121.0	917.3
Portfolio investment assets	−14.2	−34.0	−8.5
Other investment assets	−81.6	−387.1	−87.8
Other investment liabilities	−208.0	−68.2	−73.7
Net errors and omissions	213.3	179.8	132.4
Overall balance	433.8	1,111.7	−353.7

Source: IMF, *International Financial Statistics*.

External Trade

PRINCIPAL COMMODITIES
(distribution by SITC, US $ million)

Imports c.i.f.	2005	2006	2007
Food and live animals	991.6	873.3	1,881.5
Meat and meat preparations	120.8	87.0	137.5
Dairy products and bird eggs	142.8	148.3	211.1
Cereal and cereal preparations	321.4	221.9	942.8
Sugars, sugar preparations and honey	154.3	155.7	224.5
Beverages and tobacco	71.7	76.3	87.5
Mineral fuels and lubricants	1,039.7	1,081.7	1,824.3
Petroleum and petroleum products	1,039.7	1,081.6	1,824.2
Animal and vegetable oils and fats	76.0	82.6	132.6
Chemicals and related products	392.5	431.5	609.2
Medicinal and pharmaceutical products	132.2	160.0	227.9
Basic manufactures	788.1	928.7	1,233.9
Non-metallic mineral manufactures	129.0	150.3	172.8
Iron and steel	293.9	399.9	499.6
Machinery and transport equipment	1,094.9	1,155.2	1,936.8
Power-generating machinery and equipment	157.3	93.9	238.5
Machinery specialized for particular industries	184.8	238.9	379.9
General industrial machinery, equipment and parts	189.9	178.5	213.3
Telecommunications, sound recording and reproducing equipment	60.9	74.1	197.9
Electrical machinery, apparatus and appliances	152.5	115.0	196.0
Road vehicles	308.6	394.1	627.4
Passenger motor vehicles (excl. buses)	161.2	229.2	355.8
Miscellaneous manufactured articles	335.4	235.4	506.8
Total (incl. others)	4,862.7	4,935.1	8,299.0

YEMEN

Exports f.o.b.	2005	2006	2007
Food and live animals	218.3	237.1	295.8
Mineral fuels and lubricants	5,166.6	5,747.4	5,653.1
Petroleum and petroleum products	5,144.2	5,737.9	5,653.0
Petroleum oils and oils obtained from bituminous minerals, crude	4,744.3	5,375.7	4,940.2
Basic manufactures	18.1	34.0	33.9
Machinery and transport equipment	103.7	143.5	131.6
Road vehicles	56.2	47.1	52.7
Total (incl. others)	5,608.9	6,264.0	6,253.2

Source: UN, *International Trade Statistics Yearbook*.

PRINCIPAL TRADING PARTNERS
(distribution by SITC, US $ million)

Imports c.i.f.	2005	2006	2007
Argentina	83.4	55.6	50.8
Australia	33.5	109.5	68.6
Brazil	150.0	140.5	172.6
China, People's Republic	295.1	388.8	668.3
Egypt	111.0	93.5	125.7
France (incl. Monaco)	105.6	108.9	142.1
Germany	137.4	135.6	342.1
India	136.3	167.2	330.1
Indonesia	32.4	37.2	116.0
Italy	68.2	56.1	68.7
Japan	96.1	204.0	186.4
Korea, Republic	59.7	60.6	92.7
Kuwait	319.3	251.6	425.5
Malaysia	97.1	103.7	131.4
Netherlands	48.2	36.8	88.3
Oman	65.2	63.4	140.4
Saudi Arabia	427.3	502.4	683.5
Singapore	46.2	48.6	116.9
Somalia	57.2	55.7	74.2
Switzerland-Liechtenstein	410.4	413.3	623.5
Thailand	37.7	44.3	112.6
Turkey	148.7	129.4	186.2
United Arab Emirates	905.2	1,017.9	1,659.8
United Kingdom	133.9	132.4	157.0
USA	216.1	129.2	467.4
Total (incl. others)	4,835.1	4,935.1	8,299.0

Exports f.o.b.	2005	2006	2007
Australia	35.7	41.1	0.2
China, People's Republic	1,978.2	1,417.8	1,315.3
Egypt	22.4	30.3	51.6
France (incl. Monaco)	3.7	45.8	51.6
India	910.3	1,560.8	1,015.0
Iraq	21.2	24.6	24.1
Italy	—	—	—
Japan	354.8	114.0	368.5
Korea, Democratic People's Rep.	0.0	216.4	0.4
Korea, Republic	352.5	173.2	224.5
Kuwait	117.1	77.3	127.7
Malaysia	26.3	12.2	39.0
New Zealand	64.3	25.1	0.0
Saudi Arabia	128.3	129.3	138.9
Singapore	40.0	43.0	73.4
Somalia	29.1	26.2	38.3
South Africa	2.9	42.7	260.7
Switzerland-Liechtenstein	307.1	129.4	401.1
Thailand	666.1	892.8	1,233.5
United Arab Emirates	212.7	170.8	446.4
United Kingdom	6.0	394.1	3.4
USA	182.4	380.6	197.1
Total (incl. others)	5,608.9	6,264.0	6,253.2

Source: UN, *International Trade Statistics Yearbook*.

Transport

ROAD TRAFFIC
(vehicles in use at 31 December)

	1994	1995	1996
Passenger cars	227,854	229,084	240,567
Buses and coaches	2,712	2,835	3,437
Goods vehicles	279,154	279,780	291,149

2004: Private cars 285,335; Taxi cars 36,371; Buses 22,214; Lorries 127,213; Motorcycles 64,845.

Source: IRF, *World Road Statistics*.

SHIPPING

Merchant Fleet
(registered at 31 December)

	2005	2006	2007
Number of vessels	48	47	47
Total displacement ('000 grt)	33.6	29.2	29.2

Source: Lloyd's Register-Fairplay, *World Fleet Statistics*.

International Sea-borne Freight Traffic
('000 metric tons unless otherwise indicated, excluding dhows)

	2004	2005	2006
Vessels called (number)	2,828	3,089	3,177
Dry cargo:*			
goods loaded	308	309	400
goods unloaded	6,800	7,917	7,473
Oil products:			
goods loaded	4,560	4,615	4,610
goods unloaded	8,537	9,158	9,516

*Excluding livestock and vehicles.

CIVIL AVIATION
(traffic on scheduled services)

	2002	2003	2004
Kilometres flown (million)	16	18	22
Passengers carried ('000)	869	844	1,022
Passenger-km (million)	1,598	1,956	2,473
Total ton-km (million)	180	225	282

Source: UN, *Statistical Yearbook*.

Tourism

TOURISM ARRIVALS

	2004	2005	2006
Africa	7,798	10,449	10,204
Sudan	3,055	2,179	2,821
Americas	17,099	18,253	18,771
Europe	28,608	26,456	32,788
France	3,101	3,078	5,465
Germany	2,757	2,975	2,705
Italy	2,332	3,054	2,436
United Kingdom	7,061	4,348	9,230
Middle East	178,734	240,703	281,206
Egypt	8,464	6,947	10,915
Iraq	3,945	1,687	3,464
Jordan	5,129	3,483	6,060
Saudi Arabia	123,799	162,160	178,670
Syria	7,307	7,622	11,044
Total (incl. others)	273,732	335,870	382,332

Tourism receipts (US $ million, incl. passenger transport): 139 in 2004; 181 in 2005; 181 in 2006.

Source: partly World Tourism Organization.

YEMEN

Communications Media

	2004	2005	2006
Telephones ('000 main lines in use)	798.1	901.4	968.3
Mobile cellular telephones ('000 subscribers)	1,072.0	2,277.6	2,977.8
Personal computers ('000 in use)	300	300	n.a.
Internet users ('000)	180.0	220.5	270.0

2007: Internet users ('000) 320.0.

Source: International Telecommunication Union.

Radio receivers ('000 in use): 1,050 in 1997.

Television receivers ('000 in use): 5,200 in 2000.

Facsimile machines ('000 in use, estimate): 2,784 in 1995.

Daily newspapers: 6 titles (total circulation 83,300 copies) in 2004.

Sources: UN, *Statistical Yearbook*; UNESCO, *Statistical Yearbook*; UNESCO Institute for Statistics.

Education

(2004/05)

	Schools	Teachers	Males	Females	Total
Pre-primary	63	615	4,911	4,272	9,183
Primary	11,045	99,839	2,450,272	1,622,022	4,072,294
Secondary	307	6,217	409,896	185,218	595,114
Higher	16	6,164	138,039	50,085	188,124

Adult literacy rate (UNESCO estimates): 58.9% (males 77.0%; females 40.5%) in 2007 (Source: UNESCO Institute for Statistics).

Directory

The Constitution

A draft Constitution for the united Republic of Yemen, based on that endorsed by the Yemen Arab Republic (YAR) and the People's Democratic Republic of Yemen (PDRY) in December 1981, was published in December 1989; it was approved by a popular referendum on 15–16 May 1991.

On 29 September 1994 52 articles were amended, 29 added and one cancelled, leaving a total of 159 articles in the Constitution. Further amendments to the Constitution were adopted by the House of Representatives in late November 2000 and approved in a national referendum on 20 February 2001.

The Constitution defines the Yemeni Republic as an independent and sovereign Arab and Islamic country. The document states that the Republic 'is an indivisible whole, and it is impermissible to concede any part of it. The Yemeni people are part of the Arab and Islamic nation'. The Islamic *Shari'a* is identified as the basis of all laws.

The revised Constitution provides for the election, by direct universal suffrage, of the President of the Republic; the President is elected for a seven-year term (increased from five years by the amendments approved in 2001). The President is empowered to appoint a Vice-President. The President of the Republic is, ex officio, Supreme Commander of the Armed Forces. The Constitution as amended in 2001 requires presidential candidates to obtain the endorsement of 5% of a combined vote of the appointed Consultative Council and the elected House of Representatives (in place of 10% of the latter chamber alone).

Legislative authority is vested in the 301-member House of Representatives, which is elected, by universal suffrage, for a six-year term (increased from four years by amendment in 2001). The role of the House of Representatives is defined as to 'monitor' the executive. The President is empowered to dissolve the legislature and call new elections within a period of 60 days.

The upper house of the legislature, the Consultative Council, has 111 members (increased from 59 by amendment in 2001), nominated by the President.

The President of the Republic appoints the Prime Minister and other members of the Government on the advice of the Prime Minister.

The Constitution delineates the separation of the powers of the organs of State, and guarantees the independence of the judiciary. The existence of a multi-party political system is confirmed. Serving members of the police and armed forces are banned from political activity.

The Government

HEAD OF STATE

President: Field Marshal ALI ABDULLAH SALEH (took office 24 May 1990; re-elected 1 October 1994, 23 September 1999 and 20 September 2006).

Vice-President: Maj.-Gen. ABD AR-RABBUH MANSUR AL-HADI.

COUNCIL OF MINISTERS
(April 2009)

Prime Minister: ALI MUHAMMAD MUJAWAR.

Deputy Prime Minister for Defence and Security Affairs and Minister of Local Administration: Maj.-Gen. Dr RASHAD MUHAMMAD AL-ALIMI.

Deputy Prime Minister for Economic Affairs and Minister of Planning and International Co-operation: ABD AL-KARIM ISMAIL AL-ARHABI.

Deputy Prime Minister for Local Authority Affairs: SADIQ AHMIN ABU RAS.

Minister of the Interior: Maj.-Gen. MUTAHAR RASHAD AL-MASRI.

Minister of Finance: NOMAN TAHER AS-SOUHAIBI.

Minister of Oil and Minerals: AMIR SALIM AL-AIDAROUS.

Minister of Social Affairs and Labour: AMAT AR-RAZZAK ALI HAMAD.

Minister of Human Rights: HUDA ABD AL-LATIF AL-BAN.

Minister of Transport: KHALID IBRAHIM AL-WAZIR.

Minister of Information: HASSAN AHMAD AL-LAWZI.

Minister of Foreign Affairs: ABU BAKR AL-KURBI.

Minister of Expatriate Affairs: AHMAD MUSAEAD HUSSEIN.

Minister of Electricity and Energy: AWADH SA'AD AS-SUQATRI.

Minister of Legal Affairs: RASHAD AHMAD AR-RASSAS.

Minister of Religious Endowments and Guidance: HAMOUD ABD AL-HAMID AL-HITAR.

Minister of Culture: MUHAMMAD ABU BAKR AL-MAFLAHI.

Minister of Agriculture and Irrigation: MANSOUR AHMAD AL-HOUSHABI.

Minister of Industry and Trade: YAHYA AL-MUTAWAKEL.

Minister of Public Health and Population: ABD AL-KARIM RAS'E.

Minister of Education: ABD AS-SALAM AL-JAWFI.

Minister of Fisheries: MUHAMMAD SALEH SHAMLAN.

Minister of Justice: GHAZI SHAYEF AL-AGHBARI.

Minister of Higher Education and Scientific Research: SALEH ALI BASORRA.

Minister of Technical Education and Vocational Training: IBRAHIM OMAR HAJRI.

Minister of Tourism: NABIL HASSAN AL-FAQIH.

Minister of the Civil Service and Social Security: Dr YAHYA ASH-SHUAIBI.

Minister of Communications and Information Technology: KAMAL HUSSEIN AL-JABRI.

Minister of Defence: Brig.-Gen. MUHAMMAD NASSER AHMAD ALI.

Minister of Public Works and Highways: OMAR ABDULLAH AL-KURSHUMI.

Minister of Water and the Environment: ABD AR-RAHMAN AL-IRYANI.

Minister of Youth and Sports: HAMOUD MUHAMMAD UBAD.

YEMEN

Minister of State for Parliament and Shoura Council Affairs: AHMAD MUHAMMAD AL-KUHLANI.

Minister of State and Mayor of San'a: ABD AR-RAHMAN AL-AQWA.

Minister of State: ABD AR-RAHMAN TARMOUM.

MINISTRIES

All ministries are in San'a.

Ministry of Agriculture and Irrigation: POB 2805, San'a; tel. (1) 282962; fax (1) 289509; e-mail info@mai-yemen.org; internet www.mai-yemen.org.

Ministry of Communications and Information Technology: POB 17045, San'a; tel. (1) 331469; fax (1) 333420; e-mail mtit@mtit.gov.ye; internet www.mtit.gov.ye.

Ministry of Culture: San'a; tel. (1) 235461; fax (1) 251557; e-mail moc@y.net.ye.

Ministry of Defence: POB 1399, San'a; tel. (1) 252374; fax (1) 252378.

Ministry of Education: San'a; tel. (1) 274548; fax (1) 274555; e-mail moetele@yemen.net.ye; internet www.moe.gov.ye.

Ministry of Electricity and Energy: POB 11422, San'a; tel. (1) 326191; fax (1) 326214; e-mail yempec@y.net.ye.

Ministry of Expatriate Affairs: San'a; tel. (1) 402643; fax (1) 400710.

Ministry of Finance: POB 190, San'a; tel. (1) 260365; fax (1) 263040; internet www.mof.gov.ye.

Ministry of Fisheries: San'a; tel. (1) 268583; fax (1) 263182.

Ministry of Foreign Affairs: POB 1994, San'a; tel. (1) 276612; fax (1) 286618; e-mail mofa1@mofa.gov.ye.

Ministry of Industry and Trade: POB 22210, San'a; tel. (1) 252345; fax (1) 252337; e-mail info@moitye.net; internet www.moitye.net.

Ministry of Information: POB 3040, San'a; tel. (1) 274011; fax (1) 282004; e-mail yemen-info@y.net.ye; internet www.infoyemen.net.

Ministry of the Interior: POB 4991, San'a; tel. (1) 274147; fax (1) 332511; internet www.moi.gov.ye.

Ministry of Legal Affairs: POB 1192, San'a; tel. (1) 402743; fax (1) 402695; e-mail legal@y.net.ye; internet www.legalaffairs.gov.ye.

Ministry of Local Administration: POB 2198, San'a; tel. (1) 252532; fax (1) 251513; internet www.molayemen.com.

Ministry of Oil and Minerals: POB 81, San'a; tel. (1) 202306; fax (1) 202314; e-mail mom@y.net.ye; internet www.mom.gov.ye.

Ministry of Planning and International Co-operation: POB 175, San'a; tel. (1) 250101; fax (1) 251665; internet www.mpic-yemen.org.

Ministry of Public Health and Population: POB 274160, San'a; tel. (1) 252193; fax (1) 252247; e-mail his@moh.gov.ye; internet www.mophp-ye.org.

Ministry of Public Works and Highways: San'a; tel. (1) 262602; fax (1) 262609; e-mail info@mpwh-ye.net; internet www.mpwh-ye.net.

Ministry of Social Affairs and Labour: San'a; tel. (1) 274921; fax (1) 262806.

Ministry of Tourism: POB 5607, San'a; tel. (1) 251033; fax (1) 251034; e-mail tourism@yementourism.com; internet www.yementourism.com/gov.

Ministry of Transportation: POB 2781, San'a; tel. (1) 260903; fax (1) 260901; internet wadi.transport-hadhramaut.info.

Ministry of Water and the Environment: San'a; tel. (1) 418290; fax (1) 418282; internet www.mweye.org.

President and Legislature

PRESIDENT

Presidential Election, 20 September 2006

Candidates	Valid votes cast	% of valid votes
Field Marshal Ali Abdullah Saleh	4,149,673	77.17
Faisal bin Shamlan	1,173,025	21.81
Fathi al-Azab	24,524	0.46
Yassin Abdo Said	21,642	0.40
Ahmad al-Majidi	8,324	0.15
Total	**5,377,188***	**100.00**

* Excluding 648,580 invalid votes.

HOUSE OF REPRESENTATIVES

Speaker: YAHYA ALI AR-RA'EI.

General Election, 27 April 2003

Party	Seats*
General People's Congress (GPC)	228
Yemeni Congregation for Reform (al-Islah)	47
Independents	14
Yemeni Socialist Party (YSP)	7
Nasserite Unionist Popular Organization	3
Arab Socialist Baath Party	2
Total	**301**

* Includes the results of three by-elections held in July 2003.

Election Commission

Supreme Commission for Elections and Referendums (SCER): San'a; tel. (1) 202325; e-mail scer@y.net.ye; internet www.scer.org.ye; f. 2001; Chair. KHALED A. ASH-SHARIF.

Political Organizations

In the former PDRY the Yemen Socialist Party (YSP) was the only legal political party until December 1989, when the formation of opposition parties was legalized. There were no political parties in the former YAR. The two leading parties that emerged in the unified Yemen were the General People's Congress and the YSP. During 1990 an estimated 30–40 further political parties were reported to have been formed, and in 1991 a law was passed regulating the formation of political parties. Following the civil war from May to July 1994, President Saleh excluded the YSP from the new Government formed in October. There were 22 registered political parties in April 2003.

General People's Congress (GPC): San'a; e-mail gpc@y.net.ye; internet www.almotamar.net; f. 1982; a broad grouping of supporters of President Saleh; Chair. Field Marshal ALI ABDULLAH SALEH; Vice-Chair. Maj.-Gen. ABD AR-RABBUH MANSUR HADI; Sec.-Gen. Dr ABD AL-QADIR BAJAMMAL.

Al-Haq: San'a; f. 1995; conservative Islamic party; operates within the JMP opposition coalition; Sec.-Gen. HASSAN MUHAMMAD ZAID.

Joint Meeting Parties (JMP): San'a; f. 2006 as a coalition of five parties including al-Haq, al-Islah and the YSP; a sixth party, the Arab Socialist Baath Party, joined in 2008; Chair. SULTAN AL-ATWANI.

League of the Sons of Yemen (Rabitat Abna' al-Yemen—RAY): Aden; e-mail services@ray-party.org; internet www.ray-party.org; f. 1951; represents interests of southern tribes; Chair. OMAR ABDULLAH AL-JIFRI; Sec.-Gen. MOHSEN BIN FARID MUHAMMAD ABU BAKR.

Nasserite Unionist Popular Organization: Aden; tel. (1) 536497; e-mail alwahdawinet@hotmail.com; internet www.alwahdawi.net; f. 1989 as a legal party; operates within the JMP opposition coalition; Sec.-Gen. SULTAN AL-ATWANI.

National Opposition Council: San'a; a coalition of eight small opposition parties.

Yemen Socialist Party (YSP): San'a; f. 1978 to succeed the United Political Organization—National Front (UPO—NF); fmrly Marxist-Leninist 'vanguard' party based on 'scientific socialism'; has Political Bureau and Cen. Cttee; mem. of the JMP opposition coalition; Leader ALI AS-SARARI.

Yemeni Congregation for Reform (al-Islah): POB 23090, San'a; tel. (1) 213281; fax (1) 213311; e-mail an84a@hotmail.com; internet www.al-islah.net; f. 1990 by mems of the legislature, other political figures and tribal leaders; seeks constitutional reform based on Islamic law; a leading mem. of the JMP opposition coalition; Chair. Sheikh MUHAMMAD ALI AL-YADOUMI; Sec.-Gen. ABD AL-WAHAB AL-ANISI.

Other parties in Yemen include the **Arab Socialist Baath Party**; the **Federation of Popular Forces**; the **Liberation Front Party**; the **Nasserite Democratic Party**; the **National Democratic Front**; the **National Social Party**; the **Popular Nasserite Reformation Party**; the **Social Green Party**; the **Yemen League**; the **Yemeni Unionist Congregation Party** and the **Yemeni Unionist Rally Party**.

YEMEN

Diplomatic Representation

EMBASSIES IN YEMEN

Algeria: POB 509, 67 Amman St, San'a; tel. (1) 206350; fax (1) 209688; Ambassador BEN SAAD BIN AL-ABED.

Bulgaria: POB 1518, Asr, St 4, Residence 5, San'a; tel. (1) 208469; fax (1) 207924; e-mail bgemb_yem@y.net.ye; internet www.mfa.bg/sanaa; Chargé d'affaires BORIS BORISOV.

China, People's Republic: POB 482, az-Zubairy St, San'a; tel. (1) 275337; fax (1) 275341; e-mail chinaem@y.net.ye; internet ye.chineseembassy.org; Ambassador LUO XIAOGUANG.

Cuba: POB 15256, St 6B, Block 9, House 3, Safia Zone, nr Amman St, San'a; tel. (1) 442321; fax (1) 442322; e-mail embacubayemen@y.net.ye; Ambassador BUENAVENTURA REYES ACOSTA.

Czech Republic: POB 2501, Safiya Janoobia, St 16, House 6, San'a; tel. (1) 440946; fax (1) 440762; e-mail sanaa@embassy.mzv.cz; internet www.mzv.cz/sanaa; Ambassador JOZEF VRABEC.

Djibouti: POB 3322, 6 Amman St, San'a; tel. (1) 445236; fax (1) 445237; e-mail youssouf@y.net.ye; Ambassador SAHAL ISMAIL NAUR.

Egypt: POB 1134, Gamal Abd an-Nasser St, San'a; tel. (1) 275948; fax (1) 274196; Ambassador MUHAMMAD MORSY MUHAMMAD AWAD.

Eritrea: POB 11040, Western Safia Bldg, San'a; tel. (1) 209422; fax (1) 214088; Ambassador MOUSA YASSIN SHEIKH ALDDIN.

Ethiopia: POB 234, Al-Hamadani St, San'a; tel. (1) 208833; fax (1) 213780; e-mail ethoembs@y.net.ye; Ambassador TOFIKI ABDULAHI.

France: POB 1286, cnr Sts 2 and 21, San'a; tel. (1) 268888; fax (1) 269160; e-mail ambaf@y.net.ye; internet www.ambafrance-ye.org; Ambassador GILLES GAUTHIER.

Germany: POB 2562, Hadda, San'a; tel. (1) 413174; fax (1) 413179; e-mail info@sanaa.diplo.de; internet www.sanaa.diplo.de; Ambassador MICHAEL KLOR-BERCHTOLD.

India: POB 1154, Bldg 12, Djibouti St, San'a; tel. (1) 441251; fax (1) 441257; e-mail indiaemb@y.net.ye; internet www.eoisanaa.com.ye; Ambassador PRAVEEN VERMA (designate).

Indonesia: POB 19873, Bldg 16, Beirut St, Haddah, San'a; tel. (1) 414633; fax (1) 412956; e-mail indosan@y.net.ye; Ambassador NOUR AL-AULIA'A.

Iran: POB 1437, Haddah St, San'a; tel. (1) 413552; fax (1) 414139; e-mail iriranemb@y.net.ye; Ambassador MAHMOUD HASSAN ALI.

Iraq: POB 498, South Airport Rd, San'a; tel. (1) 440184; fax (1) 440187; e-mail snaemb@iraqmofamail.net; Ambassador TALAL JAMEEL SALEH AL-OBAYDI.

Italy: POB 1152, Haddah St No. 131, San'a; tel. (1) 269164; fax (1) 266137; e-mail ambasciata.sanaa@esteri.it; internet www.ambsanaa.esteri.it; Ambassador MARIO BOFFO.

Japan: POB 817, Haddah Area, San'a; tel. (1) 423700; fax (1) 417850; internet www.ye.emb-japan.go.jp; Ambassador MASAKAZU TOSHIKAGE.

Jordan: POB 2152, Hadat Damascus St, San'a; tel. (1) 413276; fax (1) 414516; e-mail sanaa@fm.gov.jo; Ambassador AHMAD ALI JARADAT.

Korea, Democratic People's Republic: POB 1209, al-Hasaba, Mazda Rd, San'a; tel. (1) 232340; CHANG MYONG SON.

Korea, Republic: POB 5005, San'a; tel. (1) 431801; fax (1) 431806; e-mail yemen@mofat.go.kr; internet yem.mofat.go.kr/eng/af/yem/main; Ambassador KWAK WON-HO.

Kuwait: POB 3746, South Ring Rd, San'a; tel. (1) 268876; fax (1) 268875; Ambassador SALEM GHOSAB AZ-ZAMANAN.

Lebanon: POB 38, St 3, San'a; tel. (1) 203959; fax (1) 201120; e-mail lebem@y.net.ye; Ambassador HASSAN FOUAD ABI ASKAR.

Libya: POB 1506, Ring Rd, St No. 8, House No. 145, San'a; Secretary of Libyan Brotherhood Office MUSTAFA HWAIDI.

Malaysia: POB 16157, San'a; tel. (1) 415605; fax (1) 416181; e-mail malsanaa@kln.gov.my; internet www.kln.gov.my/perwakilan/yemen; Ambassador Dato' ABD-ASSAMD BIN OTHMAN.

Mauritania: POB 19383, No. 6, Algeria St, San'a; tel. (1) 264188; fax (1) 215926; Ambassador MOHAMED AL-AMEEN AS-SALIM OULD AD-DAH.

Morocco: Faj Attan, Hay Assormi, ave Beyrouth, San'a; tel. (1) 426628; fax (1) 426627; e-mail sifama_yemen@hotmail.com; Ambassador MUHAMMAD HAMMA.

Netherlands: POB 463, off 14th October St, San'a; tel. (1) 421800; fax 421035; e-mail saa@minbuza.nl; internet www.holland.com.ye; Ambassador R. H. BUIKEMA.

Oman: POB 6163, 14th October St, al-Gala Quarter, Bldg 2, Khormaskar, San'a; tel. (1) 208874; fax (1) 204586; e-mail omanembassy@y.net.ye; Ambassador ABDULLAH BIN HAMAD AL-BADI.

Pakistan: POB 2848, Ring Rd, off Haddah St, San'a; tel. (1) 248814; fax (1) 248866; e-mail pakembassy@yemen.net.ye; Ambassador (vacant).

Qatar: POB 19717, San'a; tel. (1) 304640; fax (1) 304645; e-mail sanaa@mofa.gov.qa; Ambassador JASIM BIN ABD AL-AZIZ AL-BUENINE.

Russia: POB 1087, 26 September St, San'a; tel. (1) 278719; fax (1) 283142; e-mail remb@y.net.ye; internet www.rusemb-ye.org; Ambassador VLADIMIR TROFIMOV.

Saudi Arabia: POB 1184, Zuhara House, Hadda Rd, San'a; tel. (1) 240429; Ambassador ALI BIN MUHAMMAD AL-HAMDAN.

Somalia: San'a; tel. (1) 208864; Ambassador MUHAMMAD DAWARE.

Spain: POB 7108, San'a; tel. (1) 429899; fax (1) 429893; e-mail emb.sanaa@maec.es; Ambassador MARCOS VEGA GÓMEZ.

Sudan: POB 2561, 82 Abou al-Hassan al-Hamadani St, San'a; tel. (1) 265231; fax (1) 265234; Ambassador MOHAMMED ISMAEL.

Syria: POB 494, Hadda Rd, Damascus St 1, San'a; tel. (1) 414891; Ambassador ABD AL-GHAFOUR SABOUNI.

Tunisia: POB 2561, Diplomatic area, St No. 22, San'a; tel. (1) 240458; Ambassador TAWFIQ JABER.

Turkey: POB 18371, as-Safiya, San'a; tel. and fax (1) 430480; fax (1) 430484; e-mail turkbe@yemen.net.ye; Ambassador MUHAMMAD DONAMAZ.

United Arab Emirates: POB 2250, Ring Rd, San'a; tel. (1) 248777; Ambassador ABDULLAH MATAR AL-MAZROUEI.

United Kingdom: POB 1287, 938 Thaher Himiyar St, East Ring Rd, San'a; tel. (1) 308100; fax (1) 302454; e-mail BritishEmbassySanaa@fco.gov.uk; internet ukinyemen.fco.gov.uk; Ambassador TIM TORLOT.

USA: POB 22347, Sa'awan St, Sheraton Hotel District, San'a; tel. (1) 7552000; fax (1) 303182; e-mail passanaa@state.gov; internet yemen.usembassy.gov; Ambassador STEPHEN A. SECHE.

Judicial System

Yemen's Constitution guarantees the independence of the judiciary and identifies Islamic law (*Shari'a*) as the basis of all laws.

Yemen is divided into 20 governorates in addition to the Capital Secretariat of San'a (a municipality), each of which is further divided into districts. Each district has a Court of First Instance in which all cases are heard by a single magistrate. Appeals against decisions of the Courts of First Instance are referred to a Court of Appeal. Each governorate has a Court of Appeal with four divisions: Civil, Criminal, Matrimonial and Commercial, each of which consists of three judges.

The Supreme Court of the Republic, which sits in San'a, rules on matters concerning the Constitution, appeals against decisions of the Courts of Appeal and cases brought against members of the Legislature. The Supreme Court has eight divisions, each of which consists of five judges.

The Supreme Judicial Council supervises the proper function of the courts and its Chairman is the President of the Republic.

Religion

ISLAM

The majority of the population are Muslims. Most are Sunni Muslims of the Shafi'a sect, except in the north-west of the country, where Zaidism (a moderate sect of the Shi'a order) is the dominant persuasion.

CHRISTIANITY

The Roman Catholic Church

Apostolic Vicariate of Arabia: POB 54, Abu Dhabi, United Arab Emirates; tel. (2) 4461895; fax (2) 4465177; e-mail vicapar@emirates.net.ae; f. 1889; responsible for a territory comprising most of the Arabian peninsula (including Saudi Arabia, the UAE, Oman, Qatar, Bahrain and Yemen), containing an estimated 1,950,000 Roman Catholics (31 December 2007); Vicar Apostolic PAUL FRIDOLIN HINDER (Titular Bishop of Macon, Georgia, resident in the UAE); Vicar Delegate for Yemen Rev. GEORGE PUDUSSERY.

The Anglican Communion

Within the Episcopal Church in Jerusalem and the Middle East, Yemen forms part of the diocese of Cyprus and the Gulf. The Anglican congregations in San'a and Aden are entirely expatriate; the Bishop in Cyprus and the Gulf is resident in Cyprus, while the Archdeacon in the Gulf is resident in Bahrain.

HINDUISM

There is a small Hindu community.

The Press

Legislation embodying the freedom of the press in the unified Republic of Yemen was enacted in May 1990. The lists below include publications that appeared in the YAR and the PDRY prior to their unification in May 1990.

DAILIES

Al-Ayyam: POB 648, al-Khalij al-Imami, Crater, Aden; tel. (2) 255170; fax (2) 255692; e-mail editor@al-ayyam-yemen.com; internet www.al-ayyam.info; f. 1958; Editor HISHAM BASHRAHEEL.

Al-Jumhuriya: Taiz Information Office, Taiz; tel. (4) 216748; Arabic; Deputy Editor ZAID MUHAMMAD AL-GHABIRI; circ. 100,000.

Ar-Rabi' 'Ashar Min Uktubar (14 October): POB 4227, Crater, Aden; f. 1968; not publ. on Sat; Arabic; Editorial Dir FAROUQ MUSTAFA RIFAT; Chief Editor MUHAMMAD HUSSAIN MUHAMMAD; circ. 20,000.

Ash-Sharara (The Spark): 14 October Corpn for Printing, Publishing, Distribution and Advertising, POB 4227, Crater, Aden; Arabic; circ. 6,000.

Ath-Thawra (The Revolution): POB 2195, San'a; tel. (1) 262626; fax (1) 274139; e-mail contact@althawranews.net; internet www.althawranews.net; Arabic; govt-owned; Editor MUHAMMAD AZ-ZORKAH; circ. 110,000.

WEEKLIES AND OTHERS

Almotamar Net: San'a; tel. (1) 208934; fax (1) 402983; e-mail editing@almotamar.net; internet www.almotamar.net; online news organ of the General People's Congress; Editor-in-Chief ABD AL-MALIK AL-FUAIDI.

Attijarah (Trade): POB 3370, Hodeida; tel. (3) 213784; fax (3) 211528; e-mail hodcci@y.net.ye; monthly; Arabic; publ. by Hodeida Chamber of Commerce.

Al-Balagh: San'a; tel. (1) 280581; fax (1) 280584; internet www.al-balagh.net; Arabic; weekly; Editor ABDULLAH IBRAHIM.

Al-Bilad (The Country): POB 1438, San'a; weekly; Arabic; centre-right; Editor-in-Chief ABD AL-MALIK AL-FAISHANI.

Dar as-Salam (Peace): POB 1790, San'a; tel. (1) 272946; f. 1948; weekly; Arabic; political, economic and general essays; Editor ABDULLAH MUKBOOL AS-SICGUL.

Al-Fanoon: Ministry of Culture and Tourism, POB 1187, Tawahi 102, Aden; tel. (2) 23831; f. 1980; Arabic; monthly arts review; Editor FAISAL SOFY; circ. 15,500.

Al-Gundi (The Soldier): Ministry of Defence, Madinat ash-Sha'ab; fortnightly; Arabic; circ. 8,500.

Al-Hares: Aden; fortnightly; Arabic; publ. by Ministry of the Interior; circ. 8,000.

Al-Hikma (Wisdom): POB 4227, Crater, Aden; monthly; Arabic; publ. by the Writers' Union; circ. 5,000.

Al-Ma'in (Spring): Ministry of Information, San'a; monthly; general interest.

Majallat al-Jaish (Army Magazine): POB 2182, San'a; tel. (1) 231181; monthly; publ. by Ministry of Defence.

Al-Maseerah (Journey): Ministry of Information, POB 2182, San'a; tel. (1) 231181; monthly; general interest.

Al-Mithaq (The Charter): San'a; weekly; organ of the General People's Congress.

Ar-Ra'i al-'Am (Public Opinion): POB 293, San'a; tel. (1) 253785; fax (1) 223378; e-mail alraialaam2002@yahoo.com; internet www.alraialaam.com.ye; weekly; independent; Editor KAMAL ALUFI.

Ray: Aden; tel. (1) 400532; internet www.ray-yem.com; Arabic; organ of League of the Sons of Yemen.

Ar-Risalah: POB 55777, 26 September St, Taiz; tel. (4) 214215; fax (4) 221164; e-mail alaws@y.net.ye; f. 1968; weekly; Arabic; publ. by Assalam Trading Houses.

As-Sahwa (Awakening): POB 11126, Hadda Road, San'a; tel. (1) 247892; fax (1) 269218; e-mail aa230317@yahoo.com; internet www.alsahwa-yemen.net; weekly; publ. by Yemeni Congregation for Reform (al-Islah); Editor-in-Chief MUHAMMAD YOUSUFI.

As-Salam (Peace): POB 181, San'a; tel. (1) 272946; weekly.

San'a: POB 193, San'a; fortnightly; Arabic; left-wing.

Sawt al-'Ummal (The Workers' Voice): POB 4227, Crater, Aden; weekly; Arabic.

Sawt al-Yemen (Voice of Yemen): POB 302, San'a; weekly; Arabic.

Ash-Shoura: POB 15114, San'a; tel. (1) 251106; fax (1) 251104; e-mail info@al-shoura.net ; internet www.al-shora.net; circ. 15,000.

At-Ta'awun (Co-operation): at-Ta'awun Bldg, az-Zubayry St, San'a; weekly; Arabic; supports co-operative societies.

Ath-Thawri (The Revolutionary): POB 4227, Crater, Aden; internet www.althawry.org; weekly, on Sat.; Arabic; organ of Cen. Cttee of Yemen Socialist Party.

26 September: 26 September Publishing, POB 17, San'a; tel. (1) 262626; fax (1) 274139; e-mail 26sept@yemen.net.ye; internet www.26september.info; armed forces weekly; Editor-in-Chief ALI ASH-SHATIR; circ. 25,000.

Al-Wahda al-Watani (National Unity): Al-Baath Printing House, POB 193, San'a; tel. (1) 77511; f. 1982; fmrly Al-Omal; monthly; Editor MUHAMMAD SALEM ALI; circ. 40,000.

Al-Yemen: Yemen Printing and Publishing Co, POB 1081, San'a; tel. (1) 72376; f. 1971; weekly; Arabic; centre-right; Editor MUHAMMAD AHMAD AS-SABAGH.

Yemen Observer: POB 19183, 38 Algeria St, San'a; tel. (1) 203393; fax (1) 207239; e-mail info@yobserver.com; internet www.yobserver.com; f. 1996; twice-weekly; English; independent; Editor-in-Chief ZAID AL-ALYA'A.

Yemen Post: POB 15531, San'a; tel. (1) 450262; fax (1) 450262; e-mail editor@yemenpost.net; internet www.yemenpost.net; f. 2007; English; weekly; Editor-in-Chief HAKIM AL-MASMARI.

The Yemen Times: POB 2579, Hadda St, San'a; tel. (1) 268661; fax (1) 268276; e-mail editor@yementimes.com; internet www.yementimes.com; f. 1991; privately owned; Mon. and Thur.; English; Editor-in-Chief NADIA AS-SAQQAF; circ. 30,000.

Yemeni Women: POB 4227, Crater, Aden; monthly; circ. 5,000.

NEWS AGENCY

Yemen News Agency (SABA): Five Story Office Bldg and Printing Plant, al-Jama'ah al-Arabia St, al-Hasaba, San'a; tel. (1) 252944; fax (1) 251586; e-mail info@sabanews.net; internet www.sabanews.net; f. 1990 by merger of Saba News Agency and Aden News Agency following reunification of Yemen; mem. of the Federation of Arab News Agencies and of the Non-Aligned News Agencies; Editor-in-Chief NASR TAHA MUSTAFA.

Publishers

Armed Forces Printing Press: POB 17, San'a; tel. (1) 274240.

14 October Corpn for Printing, Publishing, Distribution and Advertising: POB 4227, Crater, Aden; under control of the Ministry of Information; Chair. AHMAD AL-HUBAISHI.

26 September Publishing: POB 17, San'a; tel. (1) 274240.

Ath-Thawrah Corpn: POB 2195, San'a; fax (1) 251505; Chair. M. R. AZ-ZURKAH.

Yemen Printing and Publishing Co: POB 1081, San'a; Chair. AHMAD MUHAMMAD HADI.

PUBLISHERS' ASSOCIATION

Yemeni Publishers' Association: f. 2008; Man. Dr NABIL ABADI.

Broadcasting and Communications

TELECOMMUNICATIONS

Public Telecommunications Corpn: POB 17045, Airport Rd, al-Jiraf, San'a; tel. (1) 331109; fax (1) 331150; e-mail ptc@yemen.net.ye; internet www.ptc.gov.ye; state-owned; Dir-Gen. MUHAMMAD AL-KASSOUS.

Yemen International Telecommunications Co (TeleYemen): az-Zubairy St, San'a; tel. (1) 7523331; fax (1) 481522; e-mail teleyemen@y.net.ye; internet www.teleyemen.com.ye; f. 1990 as a jt venture with Cable and Wireless PLC (United Kingdom); wholly owned by Public Telecommunications Corpn since 2003; provides fixed-line, mobile and internet services; CEO PHILLIPPE BAUDIN.

Yemen Mobile Co: San'a; internet www.yemenmobile.com.ye; f. 2004 as a subsidiary of Yemen International Telecommunications Co (TeleYemen); initial public offering of 45% of shares in 2006; provides mobile services; Chair. ALI NAJI NASRI; CEO SADEK MUHAMMAD MOUSLEH; 1.9m. subscribers (2009).

MTN Yemen: POB 4562, San'a; e-mail customer_service@mtn.com.ye; internet www.mtn.com.ye; f. 2000 as Spacetel Yemen; renamed as above in 2006, following merger of MTN Group Ltd with Investcom LLC; provides mobile services; CEO RAED AHMAD.

Yemen Co for Mobile Telephony (SabaFon): POB 18550, San'a; e-mail website@sabafon.com; internet www.sabafon.com; f. 2001; shareholders include Al-Ahmar Group For Trade and Batelco (Bahrain); provides mobile services; Chair. Sheikh HAMID AL-AHMAR; CEO TARIK AL-HAIDARY.

YEMEN

BROADCASTING

Yemen Radio and Television Corpn: POB 2182, San'a; tel. (1) 230654; fax (1) 230761; e-mail info@yemenradio.net; internet www.yemenradio.net; state-controlled; operates two television channels and eight regional radio stations for San'a, Taiz, Mukalla, Aden, Lahij, Sayoun, Hodeida and Abyan; Chair. ABDULLAH AZ-ZALAB; Gen. Man. AHMAD T. SHAYANY.

Finance

(cap. = capital; res = reserves; dep. = deposits; m. = million; brs = branches; amounts in Yemeni riyals unless otherwise indicated)

BANKING

Central Bank

Central Bank of Yemen: POB 59, Ali Abd al-Mughni St, San'a; tel. (1) 274314; fax (1) 274360; e-mail cbyh@y.net.ye; internet www.centralbank.gov.ye; f. 1971; merged with Bank of Yemen in 1990; cap. 6,000.0m., res 235,299.8m., dep. 759,657.9m. (Dec. 2006); Gov. AHMAD ABD AR-RAHMAN AS-SAMAWI; Dep. Gov. MUHAMMAD AWAD BIN HUMAM; 20 brs.

Principal Banks

Co-operative and Agricultural Credit Bank: POB 2015, Banks Complex, az-Zubairy St, San'a; tel. (1) 220090; fax (1) 220088; internet www.cacbank.com.ye; f. 1976; cap. 6,000.0m., res 452.4m., total assets 125,867.0m. (Dec. 2007); Chair. Dr HAFID FAKHER MAYAD; Dir-Gen. YAHIA AS-SABRI; 27 brs.

International Bank of Yemen YSC: POB 4444, 106 az-Zubairy St, San'a; tel. (1) 407000; fax (1) 407020; e-mail info@ibyemen.com; internet www.ibyemen.com; f. 1980; commercial bank; 75% private Yemeni interests; 25% foreign shareholders; cap. 3,400.0m., res 347.7m., dep. 116,441.8m. (Dec. 2007); Chair. HAYEL A. HAQ BESHER; Gen. Man. AHMAD T. N. AL-ABSI; 11 brs.

Islamic Bank of Yemen for Finance and Investment: POB 18452, Mareb Yemen Insurance Co Bldg, az-Zubairy St, San'a; tel. (1) 206117; fax (1) 206116; internet www.islbank.com; f. 1996; savings, commercial, investment and retail banking; cap. 2,011.2m., res 142.6m., dep. 13,220.1m. (Dec. 2006); Chair. ABD AL-KAREM AL-ASWADI; Gen. Man. ABD AL-MALIK THABET.

National Bank of Yemen: POB 5, Arwa Rd, Crater, Aden; tel. (2) 253753; fax (2) 252325; e-mail nby.ho@y.net.ye; internet www.nbyemen.com; f. 1970 as National Bank of South Yemen; reorg. 1971; 100% state-owned; cap. 7,500.0m., res 2,220.9m., dep. 81,534.0m. (Dec. 2007); Chair. and Gen. Man. ABD AR-RAHMAN MUHAMMAD AL-KUHALI; 27 brs.

Shamil Bank of Yemen and Bahrain: POB 19382, Haddah St, San'a; tel. (1) 264702; fax (1) 264703; e-mail shamilbank@y.net.ye; internet www.sbyb.net; f. 2002; cap. and res 2,000.0m., dep. 9,163.8m. (Dec. 2004); Chair. AHMAD ABUBAKER OMER BAZARA; Gen. Man. MUHAMMAD NAJIB AHMAD SAAD.

Tadhamon International Islamic Bank: POB 2411, as-Saeed Commercial Bldg, az-Zubairy St, San'a; e-mail tib@y.net.ye; internet www.tiib.com; f. 1995 as Yemen Bank for Investment and Development; became Tadhamon Islamic Bank in 1996; name changed as above in 2002; cap. 9,101.3m., res 6,233.0m., dep. 46,261.5m. (Dec. 2006); Chair. ABD AL-GABBAR HAYEL SAID; Gen. Man. AMER M. TAWQAN; 21 brs.

Yemen Bank for Reconstruction and Development (YBRD): POB 541, 26 September St, San'a; tel. (1) 270483; fax (1) 271684; e-mail ybrdho@y.net.ye; internet www.ybrd.com.ye; f. 1962; 51% state; 49% public shareholders; cap. 6,000.0m., res 3,462.0m., dep. 79,812.5m. (Dec. 2007); Chair. ABDULLAH SALIM AL-GIFRI; Gen. Man. HUSSAIN FADHLE MUHAMMAD; 41 brs.

Yemen Commercial Bank: POB 19845, ar-Rowaishan Bldg, az-Zubairy St, San'a; tel. (1) 277224; fax (1) 277291; e-mail info@ycb.com.ye; internet www.ycb.com.ye; f. 1993; cap. 3,650.2m., res 250.4m., dep. 34,946.6m. (Dec. 2006); Chair. Sheikh MUHAMMAD BIN YAHYA AR-ROWAISHAN; Chief Exec. and Gen. Man. AYED AL-MASHNI; 8 brs.

INSURANCE

Aman Insurance Co (YSC): POB 1133, az-Zubairy St, San'a; tel. (1) 202106; fax (1) 209452; e-mail aman-ins@y.net.ye; internet www.y.net.ye/amaninsurance; all classes of insurance; Chair. MUHAMMAD ABDULLAH AS-SUNIDAR; Man. Dir AKIL AS-SAKKAF.

Mareb Yemen Insurance Co: POB 2284, az-Zubairy St, San'a; tel. (1) 206111; fax (1) 206118; e-mail maryinsco74@y.net.ye; internet www.marebinsurance.com.ye; f. 1974; all classes of insurance; cap. 150m.; Chair. and CEO ALI MUHAMMAD HASHIM; Gen. Man. ALI ABD AR-RASHID.

Directory

Saba Yemen Insurance Co: POB 19214, Ishaq Bldg, az-Zubairy St, San'a; tel. (1) 240908; fax (1) 240943; e-mail info@saba-insurance.com; internet www.saba-insurance.com; f. 1990; all classes of insurance; cap. 400m. (Jan. 2006); Chair. Sheikh MUHAMMAD BIN YAHIAH AR-ROWAISHAN; Man. Dir MUHAMMAD HUSSEIN ZAWIYAH.

Trust Yemen Insurance and Reinsurance Co: POB 18392, San'a; tel. (1) 425007; fax (1) 412570; e-mail trust-yemen@y.net.ye; internet www.trustgroup.net/Main; f. 1995; all classes of insurance; Chair. ALI DHIB; Gen. Man. HUSSAIN AYYOUB.

United Insurance Co: POB 1883, as-Saeed Commercial Bldg, 2nd Floor, az-Zubairy St, San'a; tel. (1) 555555; fax (1) 214012; e-mail uuicyemen@uicyemen.com; internet www.uicyemen.com; f. 1981; general and life insurance; cap. 400m. (2005); Chair. AHMAD SAID; Gen. Man. TAREK A. HAYEL SAID.

Al-Watania Insurance Co (YSC): POB 15497, al-Kasr St, San'a; tel. (1) 272874; fax (1) 272924; e-mail alwatania-ins@y.net.ye; f. 1993; all classes of insurance; cap. 100m. (2005); Exec. Chair. YOUSUF ABD AL-WADUD.

Yemen General Insurance Co (SYC): POB 2709, YGI Bldg, 25 Algiers St, San'a; tel. (1) 442489; fax (1) 442492; e-mail ygi-san@y.net.ye; internet www.yginsurance.com; f. 1977; all classes of insurance; cap. 500m. (2005); Chair. ABD AL-GABBAR THABET; Gen. Man. BAKIR AL-MUNSHI.

Yemen Insuryards Co: POB 8437, San'a; tel. (1) 272806; fax (1) 274177; e-mail sanaa@yemenins.com; internet yemenins.com; f. 1990; all classes of insurance; cap. 100m.; Chair. MUHAMMAD MUBARAK ADHBAN; Gen. Man. KHALID BASHIR TAHIR.

Yemen Insurance and Reinsurance Co: POB 456, Aden; tel. (2) 54286; fax (2) 57336; e-mail yireico@y.net.ye; f. 1969; Lloyd's Agents; cap. 5m.; Gen. Man. HUSSAIN AL-HADDAD.

Trade and Industry

GOVERNMENT AGENCIES

General Corpn for Foreign Trade and Grains: POB 710, San'a; tel. (1) 202361; fax (1) 209511; f. 1976; Dir-Gen. ABD AR-RAHMAN AL-MADWAHI.

General Corpn for Manufacturing and Marketing of Cement: POB 1920, San'a; tel. (1) 215691; fax (1) 263168; Chair. AMIN ABD AL-WAHID AHMAD.

General Investment Authority (GIAY): POB 19022, al-Quds St, San'a; tel. (1) 262962; fax (1) 262964; e-mail info@giay.org; internet www.giay.org; f. 1992; Pres. SALEH MUHAMMAD SAID AL-ATTAR.

National Co for Foreign Trade: POB 90, Crater, Aden; tel. (2) 42793; fax (2) 42631; f. 1969; incorporates main foreign trading businesses (nationalized in 1970) and arranges their supply to the National Co for Home Trade; Gen. Man. AHMAD MUHAMMAD SALEH (acting).

National Co for Home Trade: POB 90, Crater, Aden; tel. (2) 41483; fax (2) 41226; f. 1969; marketing of general consumer goods, building materials, electrical goods, motor cars and spare parts, agricultural machinery, etc.; Man. Dir ABD AR-RAHMAN AS-SAILANI.

National Dockyards Co: POB 1244, Hedjuff, Aden; tel. (2) 244503; fax (2) 241681; f. 1969; Man. Dir ABDULLAH ALI MUHAMMAD.

Public Corpn for Maritime Affairs (PCMA): POB 19396, San'a; tel. (1) 414412; fax (1) 414645; e-mail pcm@y.net.ye; f. 1990; protection of the marine environment; registration of ships; implementation of international maritime conventions; Chair. SAID YAFAI.

Yemen Co for Industry and Commerce Ltd (YCIC): POB 5423, Taiz; tel. (4) 218058; fax (4) 218054; e-mail ycic@ycic.com; internet www.ycic.com; f. 1970; manufacture of confectionery products; Chair. ALI MUHAMMAD SAID.

Yemen Drug Co for Industry and Commerce (YEDCO): POB 40, San'a; tel. (1) 370210; fax (1) 370209; e-mail yedco@y.net.ye; import, maufacture and distribution of pharmaceutical products, chemicals, medical supplies, baby foods and scientific instruments; Chair. MUHAMMAD AL-KOHLANI; Gen. Man. MUHAMMAD ALI AL-KADIR.

Yemen Economic Corpn: POB 1207, San'a; tel. (1) 262501; fax (1) 262508; e-mail yeco@yeco.biz; internet www.yeco.biz; f. 1973; promotes and facilitates investment and development across various sectors of the economy; Gen. Man. ALI MUHAMMAD AL-KUHLANI.

Yemen Trading and Construction Co: POB 1092, San'a; tel. (1) 264005; fax (1) 240624; e-mail ytcc@y.net.ye; f. 1979; initial cap. YR 100m.

DEVELOPMENT ORGANIZATIONS

Agricultural Research and Extension Authority: POB 87148, Dhamar; tel. (6) 423913; fax (6) 423914; e-mail area@yemen.net.ye; internet www.area.gov.ye; Chair. Dr ISMAIL A. MUHARRAM.

YEMEN

Social Fund for Development (SFD): POB 15485, Fij Attan, San'a; tel. (1) 449669; fax (1) 449670; e-mail sfd@sfd-yemen.org; internet www.sfd-yemen.org; f. 1997; autonomous devt agency, governed by a bd of dirs representing the Govt, non-governmental orgs and the private sector, chaired by the Prime Minister.

Tihama Development Authority: POB 3792, Doreihemy Rd, Hodeida; e-mail arcechodeida@y.net.ye; agricultural devt agency under the supervision of the Ministry of Agriculture and Irrigation; Chair. MUHAMMAD YAHIA AL-GASHAM.

Yemen Free Zone Public Authority: POB 5842, Aden; tel. (2) 241210; fax (2) 221237; e-mail yfzpa@y.net.ye; internet www.yemenfreezone.com; f. 1991; supervises creation of a free zone for industrial investment; Vice-Chair. ABD AL-GALIL SHAIF ASH-SHAIBI.

CHAMBERS OF COMMERCE

Chamber of Commerce and Industry—Aden: POB 473, Crater 101, Aden; tel. (2) 251104; fax (2) 255446; e-mail info@adenchamber.org; internet www.adenchamber.org; f. 1886; 7,708 mems (July 2006); Chair. MUHAMMAD OMER BAMASHMUS; Dir-Gen. G. AHMAD HADI SALEM.

Federation of Chambers of Commerce: POB 16992, San'a; tel. (1) 232445; fax (1) 221765; e-mail moh-saeed@fycci.org; internet www.fycci.org; Chair. MUHAMMAD ABDO SAID AN'AM; Dir-Gen. MUHAMMAD AL-MAITAMI.

Hadramout Chamber of Commerce and Industry: POB 8302, Main St, Mukalla City, Hadramout; tel. (5) 353258; fax (5) 303437; e-mail hdramoutchamber@y.net.ye; Chair. OMER A. R. BAJARASH.

Hodeida Chamber of Commerce: POB 3370, 20 az-Zubairy St, Hodeida; tel. (3) 217401; fax (3) 211528; e-mail hodcci@y.net.ye; f. 1960; 6,500 mems; cap. YR 10m.; Dir NABIL AL-WAGEEH.

Ibb Chamber of Commerce and Industry: POB 70004, Ibb; tel. (4) 404868; fax (4) 403893.

Saadah Chamber of Commerce and Industry: POB 3754-2566, Saadah; tel. (7) 521524; fax (7) 513671; Chair. MUHAMMAD R. JARMAN.

San'a Chamber of Commerce and Industry: Airport Rd, al-Hasabah St, POB 195, San'a; tel. (1) 232361; fax (1) 232412; e-mail sanaacomyemen@y.net.ye; f. 1963; over 15,000 mems; Pres. Al-Haj HUSSAIN AL-WATARI; Gen. Man. ABDULLAH H. AR-RUBAIDI.

Taiz Chamber of Commerce and Industry: POB 5029, Chamber St, Taiz; tel. (4) 210580; fax (4) 212335; e-mail taizchamber@y.net.ye; internet www.taizchamber.com; f. 1962; 5,600 mems; Chair. AHMED HAYEL SAID; Dir MOFID A. SAIF.

Thamar Chamber of Commerce and Industry: POB 87010, Thamar; tel. (5) 502200; fax (6) 501191.

STATE HYDROCARBONS COMPANIES

General Corpn for Oil and Mineral Resources: San'a; f. 1990; state petroleum co; Pres. AHMAD BARAKAT.

Ministry of Oil and Minerals: POB 81, San'a; tel. (1) 202306; fax (1) 202314; e-mail mom@y.net.ye; internet www.mom.gov.ye; responsible for the refining and marketing of petroleum products, and for prospecting and exploitation of indigenous hydrocarbons and other minerals; subsidiaries include:

Aden Refinery Co: POB 3003, Aden 110; tel. (2) 376214; fax (2) 376600; e-mail info@arc-ye.com; internet www.arc-ye.com; f. 1952; operates petroleum refinery; capacity 8.6m. metric tons per year; operates one oil tanker; Exec. Dir FATHI SALEM ALI; Refinery Man. MUHAMMAD YESLAM.

Petroleum Exploration and Production Authority (PEPA): POB 7196, Haddah St, San'a; tel. (1) 442630; fax (1) 442632; e-mail pepa-expo.com@y.net.ye; internet www.pepa.com.ye; f. 1990; manages petroleum concessions; Chair. AHMED ALI ABDULLAH.

Yemen General Oil and Gas Corporation: POB 19137, San'a; tel. (1) 446857; fax (1) 446417; e-mail info@yogc.com.ye; internet www.yogc.com.ye; f. 1996; ABD AL-KADER SHAEA.

Yemen National Oil Co: POB 5050, Ma'alla, Aden; importer and distributor of petroleum products; Gen. Man. MUHAMMAD ABD HUSSEIN.

Yemen Petroleum Company: tel. (1) 444046; fax (1) 447691; internet www.ypcye.com; f. 1961; responsible for marketing of oil in domestic market; Exec. Dir OMAR MUHAMMAD ISMAIL AL-ARHABI.

Yemen Gas Co: Al-Raqas St, San'a; internet www.yemengasco.com; f. 1993 as General Gas Corpn; renamed as above 1996; 100% govt-owned; production and distribution of LPG; Deputy Dir NAJEEB AL-OUD.

Yemen LNG Co Ltd: POB 15347, San'a; tel. (1) 438000; fax (1) 428042; e-mail pr@yemenlng.com; internet www.yemenlng.com; f. 2005; shareholders include Total SA, France (39.62%), Hunt Oil, USA (17.22%), Yemen Gas Co (16.73%), SK Corpn, Repub. of Korea (9.55%); operates a two-train LNG plant in Marib region; Chair. AMIR SALIM AL-AIDAROUS (Minister of Oil and Minerals); Gen. Man. JOEL FORT.

UTILITIES

Electricity

Public Electricity Corpn: POB 178, Airport Rd, San'a; tel. (1) 328141; fax (1) 328150; e-mail ypecnt@y.net.ye; Man. Dir ABD AL-MONIM MUTAHAR.

Water

General Authority for Rural Water Supply Projects (GARWSP): San'a; govt agency responsible for water supply in rural areas.

National Water Resources Authority (NWRA): POB 8944, Amran St, Al-Hassaba, San'a; tel. (1) 231733; e-mail info@nwra-yemen.org; internet www.nwra-yemen.org; govt agency responsible for management of water resources; Chair. SALEM HASSAN BASHUEB.

National Water and Sewerage Authority (NWSA): POB 104, San'a; tel. (1) 250158; fax (1) 251536; e-mail NWSA@y.net.ye; govt agency responsible for water supply in urban areas.

TRADE UNIONS

Agricultural Co-operatives Union: POB 649, San'a; tel. (1) 270685; fax (1) 274125.

General Confederation of Workers: POB 1162, Ma'alla, Aden; f. 1956; affiliated to WFTU; 35,000 mems; Pres. RAJEH SALEH NAJI; Gen. Sec. ABD AR-RAZAK SHAIF.

Trade Union Federation: San'a; Pres. ALI SAIF MUQBIL.

Transport

RAILWAYS

There are no railways in Yemen.

ROADS

In 1996 Yemen had a total road network of 64,725 km, including 5,234 km of main roads and 2,474 km of secondary roads. In 2006 there were an estimated 73,200 km of roads, of which 13.7% was paved.

General Corpn for Roads and Bridges: POB 1185, az-Zubairy St, Asir Rd, San'a; tel. (1) 202278; fax (1) 209571; e-mail gcrb@y.net.ye; responsible for maintenance and construction.

Yemen Land Transport Co: POB 279, Taiz St, San'a; tel. (1) 262108; fax (1) 263117; f. 1961; incorporates fmr Yemen Bus Co and all other public transport of the fmr PDRY; oversees provision of public transport; scheduled for privatization; Chair. YAHYA AHMED AL-KOHLANI; Gen. Man. SALEH ABDULLAH ABD AL-WALI.

SHIPPING

Aden is the main port. Aden Main Harbour has 28 first-class berths. In addition there is ample room to accommodate vessels of light draught at anchor in the 18-ft dredged area. There is also 800 ft of cargo wharf accommodating vessels of 300 ft length and 18 ft draught. Aden Oil Harbour accommodates four tankers of 57,000 metric tons and up to 40 ft draught. In 1999 work was completed on a US $580m. programme to expand container handling facilities at Aden, with the aim of establishing the port as a major transshipment centre. A long-term concession to operate Aden Container Terminal and nearby Ma'alla Container Terminal, in partnership with the Gulf of Aden Port Corporation, was signed by Dubai Ports World, of the United Arab Emirates, in late 2005 and came into effect in November 2008, incorporating an estimated $220m. upgrade programme; this was expected to increase the annual capacity from 700,000 containers in 2007 to 1.5m. containers by 2012. Hodeida port, on the Red Sea, also handles a considerable amount of traffic. The port of Bal Haf has been developed to accommodate natural gas liquefaction and export facilities: shipments from Bal Haf were expected to commence by the second half of 2009.

At 31 December 2007 Yemen's merchant fleet comprised 47 vessels, with a combined displacement of 29,169 grt.

Yemen Ports Authority: POB 1316, Steamer Point, Tawahi, Aden; tel. (2) 202666; fax (2) 203521; e-mail info@portofaden.com; internet www.portofaden.com; f. 1888; Chair. MUHAMMAD A. MUBARAK BIN AEFAN; Port Officer Capt. BARAKAT ALI DERWISH.

Principal Shipping Companies

Aden Refinery Co: POB 3003, Aden 110; tel. (2) 430743; fax (2) 376600; e-mail aden-refinery@y.net.ye; internet www.arc-ye.com;

f. 1952; two general tankers and one chemical tanker; Exec. Dir FATHI SALEM ALI.

Arabian Gulf Navigation Co (Yemen) Ltd: POB 3740, Hodeida; tel. (3) 2442; one general cargo vessel.

Elkirshi Shipping and Stevedoring Co: POB 3813, al-Hamdi St, Hodeida; tel. (3) 204448; fax (3) 241199; operates at ports of Hodeida, Mocha and Salif; Contact FATHI ALI MUHAMMAD.

Hodeida Shipping and Transport Co Ltd: POB 3337, Hodeida; tel. (3) 228543; fax (3) 228533; e-mail hodship_1969@y.net.ye; internet www.hodship.aden.com.ye; f. 1969; shipping agents, stevedoring, Lloyd's agents; clearance, haulage, land transportation, cargo and vessel surveys; Chair. MUHAMMAD ABDO THABET.

Al-Katiri Shipping Corpn: POB 716, Aden; tel. (2) 255538; fax (2) 251152; one general cargo vessel.

Middle East Shipping Co Ltd (Mideast): POB 3700, Hayel Saeed Bldg, at-Tahreer St, Hodeida; tel. (3) 203977; fax (3) 203910; e-mail mideast@mideastshipping.com; internet www.mideastshipping.com; f. 1962; Chair. ABD AL-WASA HAYEL SAID; Gen. Man. AHMAD GAZEM SAID; brs in Mocha, Aden, Taiz, Mukalla, San'a, Salif, Ras Isa, ash-Shihr.

National Shipping Co: POB 1228, Steamer Point, Aden; tel. (2) 204861; fax (2) 202644; e-mail natship@y.net.ye; shipping, bunkering, clearing and forwarding, and travel agents; Dir-Gen. MOHSEN SALEM BIN BREIK.

Yemen Navigation Line: POB 4190, Aden; tel. (2) 24861; fleet of three general cargo vessels.

Yemen Shipping Development Co Ltd: POB 3686, Hodeida; tel. (3) 224103; fax (3) 211584; one general cargo vessel; Shipping Man. FAHDLE A. KARIM.

Yeslam Salem Alshagga: POB 778, Aden; one general cargo vessel.

CIVIL AVIATION

There are six international airports—San'a International (13 km from the city), Aden Civil Airport (at Khormaksar, 11 km from the port of Aden), al-Ganad (at Taiz), Mukalla (Riyan), Seyoun and Hodeida Airport. A US $500m. expansion of San'a international airport was scheduled for completion in 2009.

Civil Aviation and Meteorology Authority: POB 1042, San'a; tel. (1) 274717; fax (1) 274718; e-mail hasconst@cama.gov.ye; internet www.cama.gov.ye; supervisory body for civil aviation and meteorology affairs; Chair. HAMED AHMAD FARAG.

Yemen Airways (Yemenia): POB 1183, Airport Rd, San'a; tel. (1) 232400; fax (1) 252991; e-mail info@yemenia.com; internet www.yemenia.com; f. 1961 as Yemen Airlines; nationalized as Yemen Airways Corpn 1972; present name adopted 1978; merged with airlines of fmr PDRY in 1996; owned 51% by Yemeni Govt and 49% by Govt of Saudi Arabia; scheduled for privatization; supervised by a ministerial cttee under the Ministry of Transportation; internal services and external services to more than 30 destinations in the Middle East, Asia, Africa, Europe and the USA; Chair. and CEO ABD AL-KALEK S. AL-KADI.

Tourism

The former YAR formed a joint tourism company with the PDRY in 1980. Yemen boasts areas of beautiful scenery, a favourable climate and towns of historic and architectural importance. UNESCO has named San'a, Shibam and Zabid as World Heritage sites because of their cultural significance; in 2008 the Socotra Archipelago was added to the list of World Heritage sites as a natural landmark. However, the growth of tourism has, in recent years, been hampered by political instability, with a number of foreign tourists being victims of fatal attacks and kidnappings. In 2006 some 382,332 tourists visited Yemen; tourism receipts totalled US $181m. in that year.

Association of Yemen Tourism and Travel Agencies: San'a; e-mail ysaleh@y.net.ye; internet www.aytta.org.ye; f. 1996; Chair. YAHYA M. A. SALEH.

General Authority of Tourism: POB 129, San'a; tel. (1) 252319; fax (1) 252317; e-mail gtda@gtda.gov.ye; internet www.gtda.gov.ye; Chair. MUTAHAR TAQI.

Yemen Tourism Promotion Board: POB 5607, 48 Amman St, San'a; tel. (1) 251033; fax (1) 251034; e-mail ytpb@yementourism.com; internet www.yementourism.com; f. 1999; Exec. Dir AHMAD AL-BIEL.

ZAMBIA

Introductory Survey

Location, Climate, Language, Religion, Flag, Capital

The Republic of Zambia is a land-locked state in southern central Africa, bordered to the north by Tanzania and the Democratic Republic of the Congo, to the east by Malawi and Mozambique, to the south by Zimbabwe, Botswana and Namibia, and to the west by Angola. The climate is tropical, modified by altitude, with average temperatures from 18°C to 24°C (65°F–75°F). The official language is English. The principal African languages are Nyanja, Bemba, Tonga, Lozi, Lunda and Luvale. Christians comprise an estimated 50% of the population and are roughly divided between Protestants and Roman Catholics. A sizeable proportion of the population follow traditional animist beliefs. Most Asians are Muslims, although some are Hindus. The national flag (proportions 2 by 3) is green, with equal red, black and orange vertical stripes in the lower fly corner, and an orange eagle in flight in the upper fly corner. The capital is Lusaka.

Recent History

In 1924 control of Northern Rhodesia was transferred from the British South Africa Company to the Government of the United Kingdom. In 1953 the protectorate united with Southern Rhodesia (now Zimbabwe) and Nyasaland (now Malawi) to form the Federation of Rhodesia and Nyasaland. In 1962, following a campaign of civil disobedience organized by the United National Independence Party (UNIP), in support of demands that Northern Rhodesia be granted independence, the British Government introduced a new Constitution, which provided for a limited African franchise. In December 1963 the Federation was formally dissolved. Northern Rhodesia, which was henceforth known as Zambia, became an independent republic within the Commonwealth on 24 October 1964, with the leader of UNIP, Dr Kenneth Kaunda, as the country's first President.

Following its accession to power, the Kaunda administration supported African liberation groups operating in Southern Rhodesia (then known as Rhodesia) and Mozambique; repeated clashes along the border with both countries were reported, while incidents of internal political violence, particularly in the Copperbelt region, also occurred. In December 1972 Zambia was declared a one-party state. In January 1973 the Rhodesian administration closed the border with Zambia. Kaunda, the sole candidate, was re-elected to the presidency in 1978, 1983 and 1988.

In May 1990 Kaunda announced that a popular referendum on the subject of multi-party politics would take place in October of that year, and that supporters of such a system (which Kaunda and UNIP opposed) would be permitted to campaign and hold public meetings. Accordingly, in July the Movement for Multi-party Democracy (MMD), an unofficial alliance of political opponents of the Government, was formed. The MMD, which was led by a former government minister, Arthur Wina, and the Chairman of the Zambian Congress of Trade Unions (ZCTU), Frederick Chiluba, swiftly gained widespread public support. Later in July Kaunda announced that the referendum was to be postponed until August 1991, to facilitate the registration of a large section of the electorate. In September 1990, however, following the recommendation by Kaunda that a multi-party political system be reintroduced, that multi-party elections be organized by October 1991, that the national referendum be abandoned, and that a commission be appointed to revise the Constitution, the National Council of UNIP endorsed proposals for multi-party legislative and presidential elections, and accepted the recommendations of a parliamentary committee regarding the restructuring of the party.

In December 1990 constitutional amendments were adopted that permitted the formation of other political associations to contest the forthcoming elections. The MMD was subsequently granted official recognition. In early 1991 several prominent members of UNIP resigned from the party and declared their support for the MMD, while the ZCTU officially transferred allegiance to the MMD. Several other opposition movements were also established.

In June 1991 the constitutional commission presented a series of recommendations, including the creation of the post of Vice-President, the expansion of the National Assembly to 150 members and the establishment of a constitutional court. Kaunda accepted the majority of the proposed constitutional amendments, which were subsequently submitted for approval by the National Assembly. The MMD, however, rejected the draft, and announced that it would boycott the forthcoming elections if the National Assembly accepted the proposals. In July, following discussions between Kaunda, Chiluba and delegates from seven other political associations, Kaunda agreed to suspend the review of the draft Constitution in the National Assembly pending further negotiations. Subsequent discussions between the MMD and UNIP resulted in the establishment of a joint commission to revise the draft Constitution. In late July Kaunda conceded to opposition demands that ministers be appointed only from the National Assembly and that proposals for a constitutional court be abandoned. A provision granting the President the power to impose martial law was also rescinded.

On 2 August 1991 the National Assembly formally adopted the new Constitution. At the UNIP congress in the same month Kaunda was unanimously re-elected as President of the party. Kaunda also announced the dissociation of the armed forces from UNIP; senior officers in the armed forces were subsequently obliged to retire from the party's Central Committee. In September Kaunda officially dissociated UNIP from the State; workers in the public sector were henceforth prohibited from engaging in political activity.

On 31 October 1991 Chiluba, with 75.8% of votes cast, defeated Kaunda in the presidential election. In the concurrent legislative elections, contested by 330 candidates representing six political parties, the MMD secured 125 seats in the National Assembly, while UNIP won the remaining 25 seats; only four members of the previous Government were returned to the National Assembly. Kaunda's failure to secure re-election was attributed to widespread perceptions of economic mismanagement by his administration. On 2 November Chiluba was inaugurated as President. He appointed Levy Mwanawasa, a constitutional lawyer, as Vice-President and Leader of the National Assembly, and formed a new Cabinet. Chiluba subsequently initiated a major restructuring of the civil service and of parastatal organizations, as part of efforts to reverse the country's significant economic decline and eradicate widespread corruption among officials.

In March 1993 Chiluba declared a state of emergency, following the discovery of UNIP documents that allegedly revealed details of a conspiracy to destabilize the Government. Several prominent members of UNIP, including Kaunda's three sons, were subsequently arrested. Kaunda claimed that the conspiracy had been fabricated by Zambian security forces, with the assistance of US intelligence services, in an attempt to undermine the opposition.

Divisions within the MMD became apparent in August 1993, when 15 prominent members (11 of whom held seats in the National Assembly) resigned from the party: they accused the Government of protecting corrupt cabinet ministers and of failing to respond to numerous reports linking senior party officials with the illegal drugs trade. Their opposition to the Government was consolidated later in the month by the formation of a new political group, the National Party (NP). In November Chiluba appointed a 22-member commission to revise the Constitution; it was announced that the draft document was to be submitted for approval by a Constituent Assembly, and subsequently by a national referendum. At partial elections for 10 of the 11 vacated seats in the National Assembly, which took place in November 1993 and April 1994, the MMD regained five seats, while the NP secured four and UNIP took one. The remaining seat was secured by UNIP at a by-election in December.

Meanwhile, in July 1994 Mwanawasa resigned as Vice-President, citing long-standing differences with Chiluba, and was subsequently replaced by Brig.-Gen. Godfrey Miyanda. Also in July Kaunda stated that he intended to contest the presidential election due in 1996; however, UNIP officials indicated that he would only be allowed to resume the leadership of the party if he were officially elected by members.

In June 1995 some members of the Constitutional Review Commission rejected a final draft of the Constitution, objecting, in particular, to restrictions on the independent press, and on public gatherings and demonstrations; they claimed that the four members of the Commission who had prepared the draft had taken payments from the Government, and accused the Chairman of complicity with the authorities. Later that month, however, the draft Constitution was submitted for approval. At the end of June Kaunda was elected President of UNIP and reiterated his intention of seeking re-election to the state presidency, despite provisions in the draft Constitution that effectively debarred his candidature. At by-elections in 13 constituencies in September–October 1995, the MMD secured seven seats, and UNIP six. In October the Minister for Legal Affairs announced that Kaunda had not officially relinquished Malawian citizenship until 1970 (and had therefore governed illegally for six years), and that he had not obtained Zambian citizenship through the correct procedures. However, following widespread reports that the authorities intended to deport Kaunda, the Government ordered security forces to suspend investigations into the former President's citizenship (apparently owing to fears of civil unrest).

In January 1996 seven opposition parties, including UNIP and the NP, established an informal alliance to campaign in favour of democratic elections and the establishment of a Constituent Assembly to approve the draft Constitution by a process of national consensus. Opposition parties subsequently demanded that the Government abandon the draft Constitution and negotiate with them regarding electoral reform. Later that month UNIP deputies withdrew from a parliamentary debate on the draft, which was subsequently approved by a large majority in the National Assembly. On 28 May the Constitution was officially adopted by Chiluba. In early June Western donor Governments suspended aid to Zambia, in protest at the constitutional provisions that effectively precluded Kaunda from contesting the presidency, while Kaunda announced that he intended to defy the ban.

In August 1996 Chiluba and Kaunda met for discussions, as part of a programme of dialogue between the Government and opposition parties. Following Kaunda's decision to boycott a scheduled second round of discussions in September, the Government made minor concessions regarding the conduct of forthcoming elections, including assurances that votes would be counted at polling stations and that the Electoral Commission (appointed by Chiluba) would be independent; UNIP's request that the elections be conducted according to the 1991 Constitution was rejected. In mid-October 1996 Chiluba dissolved the National Assembly and announced that presidential and legislative elections would take place on 18 November. UNIP, still dissatisfied with the electoral system, announced its intention to boycott the elections and organize a campaign of civil disobedience; by early November a further six political parties had also decided to boycott the elections. There was widespread criticism of the voter registration process, in which fewer than one-half of the estimated 4.6m. eligible voters had been listed.

Despite appeals for a postponement, the elections were held as planned, and Chiluba and the MMD were returned to power by a large majority. In the presidential election Chiluba defeated the four other candidates with 72.5% of the valid votes cast. His nearest rival (with only 12.5%) was Dean Mung'omba of the Zambia Democratic Congress (ZADECO), an erstwhile opponent of Chiluba within the MMD. The MMD secured 131 of the 150 seats in the National Assembly. Of the eight other parties that contested the elections, only the NP (five seats), ZADECO (two seats) and Agenda for Zambia (AZ—two seats) won parliamentary representation, with independent candidates taking the remaining 10 seats.

Chiluba was inaugurated for a second presidential term on 21 November 1996. Amid demands for his resignation and for fresh elections to be held, Chiluba dissolved the Cabinet and placed the military on alert at the end of the month. In early December a new Government was appointed, although the main portfolios remained largely unchanged.

Political tension increased in the second half of 1997. In response to reports in June claiming that Kaunda and Roger Chongwe, the leader of the Liberal Progressive Front, were appealing for international assistance to overcome a political crisis in Zambia, the MMD denied that any such crisis existed. Chongwe insisted that the opposition would welcome dialogue, but only if the 1996 elections were annulled and the Constitution repealed. Meanwhile, the opposition's campaign of civil disobedience continued. In August 1997 Kaunda and Chongwe were shot and wounded (Chongwe seriously) when the security forces opened fire on an opposition gathering in Kabwe, north of Lusaka. Kaunda's subsequent allegation that the shooting was an assassination attempt organized by the Government was strongly denied by Chiluba.

On 28 October 1997 rebel army officers briefly captured the national television and radio station from where they proclaimed the formation of a military regime. The attempted coup was swiftly suppressed by regular military units; 15 people were arrested during the operation. Allegations by Kaunda that the Government had orchestrated the coup in order to be in a position to detain prominent members of the opposition were repeated by other opposition figures after Chiluba declared a state of emergency on 29 October, providing for the detention for 28 days without trial of people suspected of involvement in the attempted coup.

Chiluba carried out an extensive cabinet reshuffle in early December 1997. Observers interpreted the transfer to lesser cabinet posts of Miyanda and of Benjamin Mwila, hitherto the Minister of Defence, as an attempt to forestall the emergence of potential rivals to Chiluba within the MMD. Lt-Gen. Christon Tembo, hitherto the Minister of Mines and Mineral Development, replaced Miyanda as Vice-President.

On 25 December 1997 Kaunda was arrested under emergency powers and imprisoned, shortly after his return to Zambia from more than two months abroad. Numerous regional and international Governments expressed serious concern at the detention of Kaunda. On the following day Kaunda was placed under house arrest at his home in Lusaka. He was arraigned in court in January 1998, and in mid-February he was formally notified that he was to stand trial for 'misprision of treason', on the grounds that he had failed to report in advance to the authorities details allegedly known to him of the attempted coup of October 1997. Meanwhile, in late January 1998 the National Assembly voted to extend the state of emergency for a further three months; Chiluba eventually revoked the state of emergency on 17 March, following pressure from external donors. Also in March, Chiluba effected a minor cabinet reshuffle, most notably dismissing the Minister of Finance and Economic Development, Ronald Penza. In April 80 people who were being detained in connection with the attempted coup, including Kaunda and Mung'omba, were committed to summary trial in the High Court. Kaunda was released from detention in June, after charges against him were withdrawn, apparently owing to lack of evidence.

In November 1998 Penza was murdered at his home by a gang of masked men. Shortly afterwards five of the six suspects were shot dead by police-officers, who claimed the motive for Penza's murder was robbery, although it was reported that nothing had been stolen. The police action, and Chiluba's subsequent approval of legislation providing for Zambia's intelligence service to be armed, were of considerable concern to human rights organizations. In December Mung'omba was granted bail, as no witnesses had provided evidence against him since his detention on charges of treason following the failed coup attempt of October 1997.

At the end of March 1999 the High Court delivered its judgment in a case concerning Kaunda's citizenship, declaring him to be a stateless person. The following day Kaunda appealed to the Supreme Court against the ruling, and later that day he escaped a reported assassination attempt, when a group of armed men opened fire on his car. In April five opposition parties, including the AZ and ZADECO, formed a new alliance, the Zambia Alliance for Progress (ZAP). However, the authorities refused to register the ZAP on the grounds that its constituent parties had not been dissolved. The ZAP initially disputed the ruling and announced its intention to appeal to the High Court, but in August ZADECO formally announced its dissolution, thus effectively losing its parliamentary seat.

In September 1999 59 soldiers were sentenced to death for their part in the failed coup against the Chiluba administration in October 1997. A further soldier was sentenced to 21 years' imprisonment for concealing information regarding the coup attempt from the authorities, while another eight soldiers were acquitted of charges of treason, owing to lack of evidence. In October 1999 55 of the soldiers sentenced to death launched an appeal against the convictions.

In March 2000 Kaunda announced his resignation as President of UNIP and his retirement from active politics. At an extraordinary congress, which was convened in Ndola in May, Francis Nkhoma, a former governor of the Bank of Zambia, was elected to replace Kaunda as President of UNIP, while Kaunda's son, Tilyenji, became the party's new Secretary-General.

In May 2000 the Minister of the Environment and Natural Resources and MMD National Treasurer, Benjamin Mwila, announced that he intended to stand in the presidential election scheduled for 2001; Chiluba had previously prohibited members of his Cabinet from publicly discussing their potential candidacy for the presidency upon the expiry of the two terms permitted to him by the Constitution. Mwila was subsequently dismissed from the Government and expelled from the MMD. In July Mwila and a number of other MMD members formed a new political movement, the Republican Party (RP); Mwila reiterated his intention to seek election to the presidency. The RP merged with the ZAP in February 2001, Mwila becoming leader of the new movement, known as the Zambia Republican Party (ZRP).

In early 2001 a number of prominent figures in the MMD publicly advocated Chiluba's election to a third presidential term, despite such an event being prohibited by the Constitution. Chiluba, while declining to reveal his intentions, was reported to have expressed a willingness to listen to the outcome of any public debate on the issue. Opposition parties and some leading MMD members (including Tembo) demanded that Chiluba announce that he would not seek re-election. In April, amid increasing controversy, a convention of the MMD approved a motion removing the stipulation that the party's President should serve a maximum of two five-year terms. Tembo, Miyanda and seven other ministers expressed their opposition to the convention's decision and were expelled from the party; their supporters subsequently alleged that intimidation by supporters of Chiluba had caused some who opposed the motion not to attend the conference. Several Western donor governments also expressed their opposition to Chiluba's re-election. In April Tilyenji Kaunda was adopted as the President of UNIP.

In May 2001 a motion to impeach Chiluba for misconduct, proposed by two MMD deputies, was signed by more than one-third of the members of the National Assembly. The following day Chiluba announced that he would not seek re-election and dissolved the Cabinet. A new Cabinet was appointed some days later, with the ministers who had opposed Chiluba all being replaced—Tembo was succeeded as Vice-President by Kavindele, the Vice-President of the MMD and hitherto Minister of Health. In July the FDD won a by-election in Lusaka, occasioned by the resignation of Tembo after his expulsion from the MMD; violent confrontations between rival supporters from the MMD and FDD were reported. Tembo was elected President of the FDD in October. Meanwhile, Miyanda had established a further opposition party, the Heritage Party (HP).

The MMD adopted former Vice-President Mwanawasa as its presidential candidate in August 2001. Later that month seven opposition parties, including UNIP and the recently established Forum for Democracy and Development (FDD), agreed to form a government of national unity following the forthcoming legislative elections, in order to provide effective opposition in the event of the MMD securing the presidency. In September Michael Sata resigned as Minister without Portfolio and as National Secretary of the MMD, in protest at the nomination of Mwanawasa as presidential candidate. He subsequently formed a new political party, the Patriotic Front (PF). In October Tembo was elected as the FDD's presidential candidate.

The presidential and legislative elections took place on 27 December 2001. On 1 January 2002 (the scheduled date for the announcement of the election results) violent confrontations took place between anti-Government demonstrators and the security forces in Lusaka and Kitwe, amid allegations that the MMD had engaged in electoral fraud and voter intimidation. Mwanawasa was officially declared President the following day, with 29.2% of the valid votes cast, narrowly defeating Anderson Mazoka, the leader of the United Party for National Development (UPND, established in 1998), who secured 27.2%, while Tembo won 13.2% and Tilyenji Kaunda 10.1%. The High Court had rejected a petition for the further postponement of the declaration of the results by opposition parties, which were demanding an investigation into their allegations. The MMD secured 69 of the 150 elective seats in the National Assembly (and subsequently all eight of the seats nominated by the President); the UPND became the second largest party in the National Assembly, with 49 seats. Other parties to gain legislative representation were UNIP (with 13 seats), the FDD (12 seats), the HP (four seats), and the PF and the ZRP (one seat each); one independent candidate was also elected.

Although the MMD held only 77 of the 158 seats in the National Assembly, Mwanawasa refused to form a coalition with any of the opposition parties to ensure a working majority, and appointed a new Cabinet in early January, retaining many ministers from the previous administration. Kavindele remained Vice-President, and Kalumba was appointed as Minister of Foreign Affairs, while Mwanawasa assumed the defence portfolio himself.

In July 2002 the Minister of Foreign Affairs and the Chief Justice resigned, apparently in response to pressure from Mwanawasa, exerted in what was regarded as an attempt to rid the administration of corrupt officials. Later that month the National Assembly voted to remove Chiluba's immunity from prosecution, pending a review by the High Court, in order to allow his trial on charges of corruption against him to proceed. Mwanawasa offered Chiluba a full pardon, on condition that he return the assets he was alleged to have embezzled. The decision to remove his immunity was upheld by the High Court in August. In February 2003 the Supreme Court ruled that Chiluba's immunity could not be restored, and a few days later he was arrested and charged with stealing more than US $2m. of public funds while President.

In August 2003 Chiluba, who had been released on bail following his arrest in February, was rearrested and charged with the theft of US $29.7m. while in office. In October, amid an intensification of demands for political reform, President Mwanawasa convened a four-day national conference. The principal opposition parties and reformist civil organizations refused to participate in the conference, however. In December two concurrent trials of Chiluba commenced. The former President was reportedly arraigned on 264 charges of stealing a total of some $40m., in collaboration, in some instances, with other former government officials. In March 2004 Vice-President Mumba announced that about 150 former government officials and businessmen linked to Chiluba's administration were under investigation in connection with the theft of public funds. By January 2005 the charges against Chiluba had been reduced to six counts of theft of some $488,000. In November 2006 a magistrates' court ruled that Chiluba was not fit to stand trial because of a chronic heart condition. The court ordered the release of his passport so that he could undergo medical treatment in South Africa.

In early August 2004 the National Assembly approved legislation postponing local elections—scheduled to take place in November—until 2006, when they were to be held concurrent with legislative and presidential elections. The legislation also extended the terms of office for mayors and councillors from three to five years. In late September the Constitutional Review Commission (CRC) made recommendations that included, the appointment of a non-executive President and the adoption of an electoral process based on proportional representation. In October President Mwanawasa announced that the Constitution could only be amended with the support of at least two-thirds of the National Assembly. In late June 2006 the CRC published its report and a draft constitution, which included, *inter alia*, an updated bill of rights, the requirement for a presidential candidate to win more than 50% of the vote and certain limitations on the President's statutory powers. After considering the draft, in mid-January 2006 it was reported that Mwanawasa was prepared to accept the recommendations and implement constitutional reform prior to that year's elections. However, in early February he announced that the elections would be held under the terms of the existing Constitution and that a referendum and a national census were necessary before a new constitution could be enacted. Meanwhile, minor government reorganizations were effected in August and October 2005, and in March 2006. Concerns over Mwanawasa's health surfaced in April after he suffered a stroke. He resumed light duties after some weeks and subsequently declared himself fit to stand for re-election to the presidency.

During the presidential election campaign Mwanawasa focused on his Government's economic reforms and anti-corruption drive that had elicited international praise. His main challenger for the presidency was Sata, the candidate for the PF, who made poverty his main campaign theme, and threatened to deport Chinese, Indian and Lebanese businessmen who he accused of exploiting Zambian workers. While this enhanced his populist credentials among the electorate, it damaged his reputation internationally, and led the Chinese Government to warn that it would consider the suspension of diplomatic ties with Zambia if Sata was elected. Sata, who commanded the support of Chiluba, increased his populist rhetoric by praising Zimbabwean President Robert Mugabe's policy of seizing white-owned land.

In the event, Mwanawasa secured a second presidential term on 28 September 2006, with 43.0% of the votes cast. Sata took 29.4%, while Hakainde Hichilema of the opposition United Democratic Alliance (UDA) coalition, won 25.3%. Voter turn-out was estimated at 70.8%. Sata alleged electoral fraud, claiming that as many as 400,000 votes appeared not to have been counted in areas where he had expected to win support. Clashes between PF supporters and the security forces broke out in Lusaka when the Electoral Commission of Zambia (ECZ) announced that Sata had fallen from first place to third in interim vote counts. Protesters threw stones at police who responded with tear gas and by firing live ammunition into the air. The subsequent violence, which lasted two days, and allegations of irregularities contrasted with the voting on election day, which international observers proclaimed took place in a generally efficient and transparent manner. In concurrently held parliamentary elections, the MMD took 72 seats, the PF won 43 and the UDA secured 26. Voting in two constituencies was postponed until 26 October, owing to the deaths of candidates.

Mwanawasa was in sworn in as President on 3 October 2006 and a new Cabinet was announced a few days later: Rupiah Banda was named as Vice-President, while Mundia Sikatana and George Mpombo were appointed to the foreign affairs and defence portfolios, respectively. In December Sata was arrested for allegedly making a false declaration of his assets before the presidential elections; however, the charges were dropped later that month.

Meanwhile, in October 2006 Zambia announced its first discoveries of oil and gas reserves in the Chavuma and Zambezi districts, close to the border with Angola. Mwanawasa announced that the Government would appoint a special cabinet committee to select foreign petroleum firms to conduct comprehensive exploration. In February 2007 Chinese President Hu Jintao announced new investment worth US $800m. in Zambia after talks in Lusaka with Mwanawasa. The two leaders stated that a special economic zone would be created in Zambia's copper-mining area in Chambishi, north of Lusaka, where Chinese firms could operate without paying import or value-added taxes. Part of Zambia's bilateral debt to the People's Republic of China was also written off. Later in February a High Court judge ruled that Zambia must pay a substantial sum to a so-called 'vulture fund' (companies which buy up the debt of poor nations cheaply when it is about to be written off, then sue for the full value of the debt plus interest). British Virgin Islands-based Donegal International paid less than $4m. for a debt Zambia owed, but sued Zambia for a $42m. repayment. There were concerns that such funds were eradicating the benefits that international debt relief was envisaged to bring to poor countries.

In March 2007 police demolished some 250 houses in Lusaka which the authorities maintained were built without official approval. The Government announced that it was the beginning of a campaign to eradicate corruption in the way land plots were distributed. Earlier that month the Minister of Lands, Gladys Nyirongo, was dismissed for allocating plots of land to family members; in April Minister of Information and Broadcasting Services Vernon Mwaanga was removed from office. In May a further governmental reorganization was effected in which Minister of Health Angela Chifire was replaced by Brig.-Gen. Brian Chituwo, hitherto Minister of Science, Technology and Vocational Training. In August Minister of Foreign Affairs Mundia Sikatana was replaced by Kabinga Pande in another cabinet reshuffle. Pande was succeeded at the Ministry of Tourism, the Environment and Natural Resources by Michael Kaingu.

In late June 2008 President Mwanawasa suffered a stroke prior to the African Union (AU, see p. 172) summit in Egypt and was transferred to a hospital in Paris, France, for treatment. However, in mid-August his condition deteriorated suddenly and on 19 August 2008 Mwanawasa's death was announced. Vice-President Banda replaced him as acting head of state, as stipulated in the Constitution, and was subsequently selected by the MMD to contest the presidential election which was to be held on 30 October. (The successful candidate would serve the remainder of Mwanawasa's presidential term, which was to expire in October 2011.) At the election, which took place as scheduled, Banda narrowly defeated Sata, again representating the PF, winning 40.63% of the votes to Sata's 38.64%; Hichilema took third place in the ballot with 19.96% of the votes cast. AU monitors declared the election to be free and fair, but Sata refused to accept the result, alleging vote-rigging, and petitioned the Supreme Court for a recount; he withdrew this request in March 2009. On 1 November police used tear gas to suppress a demonstration in Lusaka, where Sata's supporters marched through deprived areas of the capital and set fire to market stalls. In mid-November 38 people were arrested when violent protests broke out in the city of Kitwe; demonstrators attacked a police station and set cars alight, apparently in response to the arrest of Frank Bwalya, a priest and manager of a Catholic radio station which had been critical of Banda's Government.

Meanwhile, Banda was sworn in as President on 2 November 2008 and later that month he appointed a new Cabinet in which George Kunda, Minister of Justice since 2001, was appointed to the vice-presidency while retaining responsibility for the justice portfolio. There were several new additions to the Government; most notably Dr Situmbeko Musokotwane, a former senior central bank official, was appointed as Minister of Finance and National Planning, and Kapemmbwa Simbao was named as Minister of Health, replacing Chituwo who became Minister of Agriculture and Co-operatives. Banda pledged that his administration would prioritize the elimination of poverty and would take steps to improve performance in the agricultural, mining, energy and tourism sectors. In a minor government reshuffle in March 2009 Banda appointed Peter Daka as Minister of Lands, replacing Ronald Muykuma who was named as Minister of Presidential Affairs. Gabriel Namulambe succeeded Daka as Minister of Science, Technology and Vocational Training.

In 1986 South African troops launched attacks on alleged bases of the African National Congress of South Africa (ANC) in Zambia; a number of foreigners and Zambian citizens were subsequently arrested in Zambia on suspicion of spying for South Africa. In August of that year Zambia undertook to impose economic sanctions against South Africa, and the South African Government retaliated by temporarily enforcing trade restrictions on Zambia. Further attacks on ANC targets took place during 1987–89. During the 1980s President Kaunda's support for the Governments of Angola and Mozambique resulted in attacks on Zambian civilians by Angolan rebels (with assistance from the Governments of South Africa and the USA) and by Mozambican rebels (also allegedly supported by South Africa). In September 1992 the Governments of Zambia and Angola signed a security agreement providing for common border controls. In early 1996 Zambia contributed some 1,000 troops to the UN Angola Verification Mission. Zambia consistently denied allegations, made by the Angolan Government in 1997–98, that it was providing military and logistical support to the Angolan rebel movement, União Nacional para a Independência Total de Angola (UNITA).

In early 1999, however, tension between the two countries intensified as the accusations resurfaced and a bomb severely damaged the Angolan embassy in Lusaka (see above). In March the Angolan Government delivered a letter to the UN explaining its accusations against Zambia. The Zambian Government again refuted all allegations against it. In April, however, relations appeared to have improved, when both countries were reported to have signed an agreement aimed at resolving their differences, under the mediation of Swaziland's King Mswati III. In June the Zambian and Angolan Governments signed a further agreement, which provided for the reactivation of the joint permanent commission on defence and security and the organization of a summit between Chiluba and the Angolan President, José Eduardo dos Santos. In December it was reported that Angolan jets had bombed Zambian territory in pursuit of UNITA rebels, and in January 2000 it was announced that some 21,000 Angolan refugees had entered Zambia since October 1999. During January–February 2000 UNITA rebels carried out a series of raids on Zambian villages, which prompted Chiluba to announce that he would not permit UNITA troops to operate from Zambia. In February, following the convention of the joint permanent commission on defence and security to discuss the security situation along the common border, both sides resolved to strengthen measures against UNITA forces operating in the common border area. In September the Zambian Government declined a request from the Angolan Government for its forces to be allowed to use Zambian territory to attack UNITA positions near the frontier.

In February 2001 the Governments of Zambia, Angola and Namibia agreed to establish a tripartite mechanism for political and security co-operation in an attempt to improve security on their joint borders. However, armed Angolans raided three Zambian villages close to the border in November, reportedly abducting some 100 Zambians and subsequently killing seven of them; Zambian forces claimed to have killed 10 Angolans in retaliation. Reports in the Zambian press attributed the attacks on the villages to the Angolan armed forces, which admitted occupying UNITA bases in the area, but claimed to have observed UNITA rebels crossing the border shortly before the attacks. At the end of 2002 there were 188,436 Angolan refugees in Zambia, compared with 218,154 at the beginning of the year, and by the end of 2007, according to the office of the UN High Commissioner for Refugees (UNHCR) that figure had been reduced to 40,757.

In early March 1997 the Zambian Government appealed for international assistance in coping with the influx of refugees fleeing the civil conflict in Zaire (now the Democratic Republic of the Congo—DRC); by March some 6,000 Zairean refugees had arrived in Zambia. In January 1998 Zambia and the DRC agreed to establish a joint permanent commission on defence and security. During late 1998 and early 1999 the Zambian Government was involved in regional efforts to find a political solution to the conflict in the DRC, after a rebellion was mounted against the Government in August 1998; President Chiluba was appointed to co-ordinate peace initiatives on the crisis by the Southern African Development Community (SADC, see p. 400) and the Organization of African Unity (OAU, now the AU, see p. 172). Meanwhile, thousands of Congolese entered Zambia, fleeing the renewed fighting, prompting the Government to appeal to the international community for immediate assistance to cope with the refugees, which, by then, reportedly numbered more than 30,000. In addition, several hundred DRC soldiers crossed into Zambia seeking refuge, but were subsequently repatriated. At a summit held in Lusaka during June–July 1999 a cease-fire document was formulated, providing for the withdrawal of foreign forces from the DRC and for political reform in the country. The accord was signed by the President of the DRC and the leaders of the five other countries involved in the conflict in July, and by rebel leaders in August. Nevertheless, progress with its implementation was slow. Zambia's involvement in mediation efforts aimed at achieving a definitive end to the conflict in the DRC diminished in the early 2000s, although a number of regional summit meetings were held in Lusaka. In March 2004 it was reported that more than 1,000 DRC nationals had entered Zambia, fleeing renewed fighting between government and rebel forces in south-eastern DRC. At the end of 2006 there were more than 64,000 refugees living in UNHCR refugee camps in Zambia, of whom 43,788 were from the DRC. In addition, UNHCR estimated that a further 75,000 refugees (including 49,000 Angolans) had settled among the Zambian population. In July 2007 some 100 Angolan refugees refused to be repatriated until the Zambian Government paid wages due for construction work carried out in 2003. The refugees had been employed on a casual basis by a government agency that had since been dissolved. Other refugees had returned to Angola in late 2006 without receiving their wages, despite being assured that they would receive payment. According to the UNHCR over 7,000 refugees from the DRC were repatriated between May and December 2007, and almost 10,000 were returned home in 2008; the UNHCR planned to repatriate over 18,000 refugees in 2009. In October 2008 Zambia closed its border to refugees arriving from the DRC, due to heavy fighting in the east of the country.

Relations with Zimbabwe deteriorated following the disputed presidential election in that country in March 2008. Mwanawasa, in his capacity as Chairman of SADC, had been highly critical of the conduct of Mugabe's ZANU—PF and had proposed the postponement of the second round of polling in view of the worsening situation in Zimbabwe. Mwananwasa also denounced the outcome of the run-off as undemocratic and unacceptable; however his forthright stance was not endorsed by most other SADC leaders. The installation of a power-sharing government in Zimbabwe in February 2009 resulted in an improvement in relations and in May Banda pledged his support for Zimbabwe's economic recovery plan during a four-day visit to that country.

Government

Under the provisions of the Constitution, which was formally adopted in May 1996, Zambia is a multi-party state. Executive power is vested in the President, who is the constitutional Head of State. Legislative power is vested in a National Assembly, which comprises 158 members, of whom 150 are elected by universal adult suffrage, and eight nominated by the President. The President and the National Assembly are elected simultaneously by universal adult suffrage for a five-year term. The maximum duration of the President's tenure of office is limited to two five-year terms. The President governs with the assistance of a Vice-President and a Cabinet, whom he appoints from members of the National Assembly. The Constitution also provides for a 27-member House of Chiefs, which represents traditional tribal authorities. Each of Zambia's nine provinces has a minister, who is appointed by the President.

Defence

The total strength of armed forces, as assessed at November 2008, was 15,100, with 13,500 in the army and 1,600 in the air force. Paramilitary forces numbered 1,400. Military service is voluntary. There is also a National Defence Force responsible to the Government. The defence budget for 2007 was estimated at K933,000m.

Economic Affairs

In 2007, according to estimates by the World Bank, Zambia's gross national income (GNI), measured at average 2005–07 prices, was US $9,479m., equivalent to $800 per head (or $1,220 per head on an international purchasing-power parity basis). During 2000–07, it was estimated, the population increased at an average annual rate of 1.9%, while gross domestic product (GDP) per head increased, in real terms, by an average of 3.2% per year. Overall GDP increased, in real terms, at an average annual rate of 5.2% in 2000–07; growth in 2007 was 6.0%.

Agriculture (including forestry and fishing) contributed 20.4% of GDP in 2007. According to the 2000 census, 71.6% of those employed were engaged in the sector. However, in 2006 only 11.7% of those in paid employment were engaged in agriculture. The principal crops are sugar cane, maize, cassava, cotton, wheat, sweet potatoes and groundnuts. Millet, rice, sorghum, tobacco, sunflower seeds and horticultural produce are also cultivated. Cattle-rearing remains important. During 2000–07, according to the World Bank, agricultural GDP increased by an average of 1.9% per year. Agricultural GDP increased by 7.2% in 2007.

Industry (including mining, manufacturing, construction and power) contributed 33.6% of GDP in 2007, and engaged 22.7% of all those in paid employment in 2006. According to the World Bank, industrial GDP grew at an average annual rate of 9.4% in 2000–07. Industrial GDP increased by 9.0% in 2007.

In 2006 mining and quarrying contributed 4.1% of GDP, according to official figures, and engaged 5.5% of those in paid employment. According to the UN, exports of copper contributed 71.1% of the value of total exports in 2007. Output of copper ore increased from 426,900 metric tons in 2004 to 514,000 tons in 2006. Cobalt is also an important export, while coal, gold, emeralds, amethyst, limestone and selenium are also mined. The issuing of licences for the mining of uranium was expected to commence in mid-2009. In addition, Zambia has reserves of phosphates, fluorspar and iron ore. During 2002–06, according to the IMF, mining GDP increased by an estimated average of 8.1% per year. Mining GDP increased by 7.3% in 2006.

Manufacturing contributed 10.0% of GDP in 2007, and engaged 11.6% of those in paid employment in 2006. The principal manufacturing activities are food-processing, the smelting and refining of copper and other metals, vehicle assembly, petroleum-refining, and the production of fertilizers, explosives, textiles, bottles, batteries, bricks and copper wire. During 2000–07, according to the World Bank, manufacturing GDP increased at an average annual rate of 5.3%. Manufacturing GDP increased by 6.3% in 2007.

Energy is derived principally from hydroelectric power (99.4% in 2005), in which Zambia is self-sufficient. Imports of mineral fuels accounted for 12.3% of the value of merchandise imports in 2007. In an effort to address the problem of power shortages and expand availability of electricity, construction was planned of three new hydroelectric plants during 2009–15, for which a financing requirement of some US $1,200m. was anticipated.

In 2007 the services sector contributed 46.0% of GDP, and engaged 65.6% of those in paid employment in 2006. According to the World Bank, the GDP of the services sector increased by an average of 6.6% per year in 2000–07. Services GDP increased by 12.5% in 2007.

In 2007 Zambia recorded a trade surplus of US $983.1m., but there was a deficit of $780.3m. on the current account of the balance of payments. In 2007 the principal source of imports (47.4%) was South Africa; other major suppliers were the United

Arab Emirates and the People's Republic of China. The principal market for exports in 2007 was Switzerland-Liechtenstein (accounting for 41.8% of the total); other significant purchasers were South Africa, Thailand, the Democratic Republic of the Congo and Egypt. The principal exports in 2007 was copper, which accounted for 71.1% of the total; metalliferous ore and metal scrap and food and live animals were also important exports. The principal imports in that year were machinery and transport equipment, petroleum, chemicals and related products, and iron and steel.

In 2008 there was an overall budgetary deficit of K573,000m., equivalent to 1.3% of GDP. Zambia's total external debt was US $2,325m. at the end of 2006, of which $1,003m. was long-term public debt. In 2000–08 the average annual rate of inflation was 16.6%. Consumer prices increased by 12.5% in 2008.

Zambia is a member of the Southern African Development Community (see p. 400) and the Common Market for Eastern and Southern Africa (see p. 215).

In the mid-2000s Zambia experienced a period of robust economic growth, attributable principally to the impact of high international prices for its major export, copper, in conjunction with extensive debt relief and the consolidation of economic restructuring under the supervision of the IMF and World Bank. Inflation had been brought beneath 10% by the end of 2006, and was held at this level in 2007, even accounting for the strong upward pressure of world petroleum prices. By mid-2009, however, and despite attempts by the Zambian authorities to diversify the economy away from its dependence on copper, the global economic slowdown had begun to effect Zambia as a result of falling international prices for that commodity, which declined from some US $9,000 per metric ton in July 2008 to $2,900 in December. Mines were forced to cut production levels and job losses in the sector were estimated at 8,200 between December 2008 and March 2009. The downturn in the mining sector and the consequent reduction in inflows of foreign exchange also had a drastic effect on the Zambian currency, the kwacha, which depreciated steeply against the US dollar in early 2009. In the assessment of the IMF, under consultations which resulted in agreement of a new Poverty Reduction and Growth Facility (PRGF) in support of Zambia's Fifth National Development Plan (2006–10)—the previous PRGF having expired in September 2007—real annual GDP growth of 6.5% was expected in 2008–09, while year-end inflation was expected to slow to 7%, with a further contraction to 5% achievable by 2010. These estimates were however amended by the Fund in early 2009 in view of the worsening global economic conditions, with inflation expected to reach 12.2% in 2009 and GDP to grow by only 4%. Under the plan, the Government aimed to increase expenditure on poverty-reduction programmes and infrastructural investment, while promoting diversification notably through creating an economic environment attractive to the private sector. Infrastructural developments in the mining sector were to be accompanied by progress towards participation in the international Extractive Industries Transparency Initiative. Policy in the agricultural sector was to focus on increased productivity and food security. Meanwhile, a principal obstacle to further economic diversification, and thus a reduction in dependence on the copper sector, remained infrastructural inadequacies, particularly in the energy sector. To accompany efforts to rehabilitate and expand capacity for electricity generation, the IMF emphasized the necessity of improving the governance and efficiency of the state power monopoly, ZESCO Ltd, notably to include the negotiation of a new pricing structure for mining companies hitherto guaranteed priority supply at below-cost prices.

Education

Between 1964 and 1979 enrolment in schools increased by more than 260%. Primary education, which is compulsory, begins at seven years of age and lasts for seven years. Secondary education, beginning at the age of 14, lasts for a further five years, comprising a first cycle of two years and a second of three years. According to UNESCO estimates, in 2006/07 94.0% of children (93.7% of boys; 94.4% of girls) in the relevant age-group attended primary schools, while enrolment at secondary schools included 40.9% of children (43.7% of boys; 38.1% of girls) in the relevant age-group. There are two universities: the University of Zambia at Lusaka, and the Copperbelt University at Kitwe (which is to be transferred to Ndola). There are 14 teacher training colleges. In 2005 expenditure on education was K1,062.0m. The 2006 budgetary allocation for education was K1,647.0m., some 26.9% of the overall budget. The Government recruited an additional 8,000 teachers in 2005 and planned to recruit a further 4,500 in 2006.

Public Holidays

2009: 1 January (New Year's Day), 8 March (International Women's Day), 11 March (Youth Day), 10–13 April (Easter), 1 May (Labour Day), 25 May (African Freedom Day, anniversary of OAU's foundation), 6 July (Heroes' Day), 7 July (Unity Day), 3 August (Farmers' Day), 24 October (Independence Day), 25 December (Christmas Day).

2010: 1 January (New Year's Day), 8 March (International Women's Day), 11 March (Youth Day), 2–5 April (Easter), 1 May (Labour Day), 25 May (African Freedom Day, anniversary of OAU's foundation), 5 July (Heroes' Day), 6 July (Unity Day), 2 August (Farmers' Day), 24 October (Independence Day), 25 December (Christmas Day).

Weights and Measures

The metric system is in use.

Statistical Survey

Source (unless otherwise indicated): Central Statistical Office, POB 31908, Lusaka; tel. (21) 1211231; internet www.zamstats.gov.zm.

Area and Population

AREA, POPULATION AND DENSITY

Area (sq km)	752,612*
Population (census results)	
20 August 1990	7,383,097
25 October 2000	
Males	4,946,298
Females	4,939,293
Total	9,885,591
Population (UN estimates at mid-year)†	
2006	11,738,000
2007	12,314,000
2008	12,620,000
Density (per sq km) at mid-2008	16.8

* 290,585 sq miles.
† Source: UN, *World Population Prospects: The 2008 Revision*.

PROVINCES
(2000 census)

	Area	Population	Density
Central	94,394	1,012,257	10.7
Copperbelt	31,328	1,581,221	50.5
Eastern	69,106	1,306,173	18.9
Luapula	50,567	775,353	15.3
Lusaka	21,896	1,391,329	63.5
Northern	147,826	1,258,696	8.5
North-Western	125,826	583,350	4.6
Southern	85,283	1,212,124	14.2
Western	126,386	765,088	6.1
Total	**752,612**	**9,885,591**	**13.1**

ZAMBIA

PRINCIPAL TOWNS
(population at 2000 census)

Lusaka (capital)	1,084,703	Lundazi	236,833
Kitwe	376,124	Petauke	235,879
Ndola	374,757	Choma	204,898
Chipata	367,539	Solwezi	203,797
Chibombo	241,612	Mazabuka	203,219

Mid-2007 ('000, incl. suburbs, UN estimate): Lusaka 1,328 (Source: UN, *World Urbanization Prospects: The 2007 Revision*).

BIRTHS AND DEATHS
(annual averages, UN estimates)

	1990–95	1995–2000	2000–05
Birth rate (per 1,000)	44.0	45.1	44.6
Death rate (per 1,000)	15.6	19.0	20.2

Source: UN, *World Population Prospects: The 2008 Revision*.

Life expectancy (years at birth, WHO estimates): 42.9 (males 42.2; females 43.5) in 2006 (Source: WHO, *World Health Statistics*).

EMPLOYMENT
(Usually active population aged 12 years and over at 2000 census)

Agriculture, hunting, forestry and fishing	2,014,028
Mining and quarrying	36,463
Manufacturing	77,515
Electricity, gas and water	11,016
Construction	36,790
Wholesale and retail trade; restaurants and hotels	190,354
Transport, storage and communication	53,736
Financial, insurance, real estate and business services	29,151
Community, social and personal services	363,375
Total	**2,812,428**

Source: ILO.

2006 (persons in paid employment, labour force survey, January): Agriculture, forestry and fishing 56,139; Mining and quarrying 26,253; Manufacturing 55,709; Electricity and water 12,399; Construction 14,343; Wholesale and retail trade 65,012; Transport and communication 19,378; Finance and insurance 54,032; Public administration 176,062; *Total* 479,327 (Source: IMF, *Zambia: Statistical Appendix* (January 2008).

Health and Welfare

KEY INDICATORS

Total fertility rate (children per woman, 2006)	5.6
Under-5 mortality rate (per 1,000 live births, 2006)	182
HIV/AIDS (% of persons aged 15–49, 2007)	15.2
Physicians (per 1,000 head, 2004)	0.1
Hospital beds (per 1,000 head, 2004)	0.2
Health expenditure (2006): US $ per head (PPP)	62
Health expenditure (2006): % of GDP	5.2
Health expenditure (2006): public (% of total)	46.8
Access to water (% of persons, 2006)	58
Access to sanitation (% of persons, 2006)	52
Human Development Index (2006): ranking	163
Human Development Index (2006): value	0.453

For sources and definitions, see explanatory note on p. vi.

Agriculture

PRINCIPAL CROPS
('000 metric tons)

	2005	2006	2007
Wheat	137	94*	116
Rice, paddy	13	15*	18
Maize	866.2	1,424.4*	1,366.2
Millet	29.6	48.2*	21.7
Sorghum	18.7	21.0*	12.8
Potatoes	14	14*	15*
Sweet potatoes	67	67*	68*
Cassava (Manioc)	1,056	950*	940*
Sugar cane*	2,500	2,500	2,500
Soybeans (Soya beans)†	12	12	13
Groundnuts, with shell†	40	40	41
Sunflower seed†	8	8	8
Seed cotton	142	156*	160*
Onions, dry*	31	27	27
Tomatoes*	27	25	25
Tobacco, unmanufactured	58.2	4.8*	4.8*

* FAO estimate(s).
† Unofficial figures.

Aggregate production ('000 metric tons, may include official, semi-official or estimated data): Total cereals 1,063 in 2005, 1,599 in 2006, 1,531 in 2007; Total pulses 23 in 2005, 23 in 2006, 24 in 2007; Total roots and tubers 1,137 in 2005, 1,031 in 2006, 1,022 in 2007; Total vegetables (incl. melons) 298 in 2005, 267 in 2006, 267 in 2007; Total fruits (excl. melons) 105.5 in 2005, 4.2 in 2006, 4.2 in 2007.

Source: FAO.

LIVESTOCK
('000 head, year ending September, FAO estimates)

	2005	2006	2007
Cattle	2,900	2,600	2,610
Sheep	190	150	152
Goats	1,950	1,270	1,275
Pigs	345	340	340
Chickens	32,000	30,000	30,000

Source: FAO.

LIVESTOCK PRODUCTS
('000 metric tons, FAO estimates)

	2005	2006	2007
Cattle meat	59.2	41.6	42.4
Pig meat	11.2	11.0	11.0
Chicken meat	39.0	36.5	36.5
Cows' milk	84.0	64.5	65.2
Hen eggs	46.8	46.4	46.9
Cattle hides	7.8	n.a.	n.a.

Source: FAO.

Forestry

ROUNDWOOD REMOVALS
('000 cubic metres, FAO estimates)

	2005	2006	2007
Sawlogs, veneer logs and logs for sleepers	245	245	245
Other industrial wood	752	1,080	1,080
Fuel wood	8,798	8,798	8,705
Total	**9,795**	**10,123**	**10,030**

Source: FAO.

ZAMBIA

SAWNWOOD PRODUCTION
('000 cubic metres, incl. railway sleepers, FAO estimates)

	1995	1996	1997
Coniferous (softwood)	300	230	145
Broadleaved (hardwood)	20	15	12
Total	320	245	157

1998–2007: Figures assumed to be unchanged from 1997 (FAO estimates).
Source: FAO.

Fishing

('000 metric tons, live weight)

	2004	2005*	2006*
Capture	65.0*	65.0	65.0
Dagaas	8.5*	8.5	8.5
Other freshwater fishes	56.5*	56.5	56.5
Aquaculture	5.1	5.1	5.1
Three-spotted tilapia	2.0	2.0	2.0
Total catch*	70.1	70.1	70.1

* FAO estimate(s).

Note: Figures exclude aquatic animals, recorded by number rather than weight. The number of Nile crocodiles caught was: 26,353 in 2004; 28,490 in 2005; 39,604 in 2006.

Source: FAO.

Mining
(estimates)

	2004	2005	2006
Coal ('000 metric tons)	240.0	240.0	100.0
Copper ore ('000 metric tons)*	426.9	447.0	514.0
Cobalt ore (metric tons)*	10,000	9,300	8,000
Amethysts ('000 kilograms)	1,100	1,100	1,200

* Figures refer to the metal content of ore.

Source: US Geological Survey.

Industry

SELECTED PRODUCTS
('000 metric tons, unless otherwise indicated, estimates)

	2004	2005	2006
Cement	390	435	650
Copper (unwrought): smelter	280	270	290
Copper (unwrought): refined	410	399	460
Cobalt (refined, metric tons)	5,791	5,422	4,665

Raw sugar ('000 metric tons): 189 in 2000; 279 in 2001; 232 in 2002.

Electric energy (million kWh): 8,448 in 2004; 8,255 in 2005; 8,906 in 2006.

Sources: FAO; US Geological Survey; UN, *Industrial Commodity Statistics Yearbook*; IMF, *Zambia: Statistical Appendix* (January 2008).

Finance

CURRENCY AND EXCHANGE RATES

Monetary Units
100 ngwee = 1 Zambian kwacha (K).

Sterling, Dollar and Euro Equivalents (31 December 2008)
£1 sterling = 7,044.5 kwacha;
US $1 = 4,832.3 kwacha;
€1 = 6,725.1 kwacha;
10,000 Zambian kwacha = £1.42 = $2.07 = €1.49.

Average Exchange Rate (Zambian kwacha per US $)
2006 3,603.07
2007 4,002.52
2008 3,745.66

CENTRAL GOVERNMENT BUDGET
(K '000 million)*

Revenue	2006	2007	2008‡
Tax revenue	6,317	8,184	10,051
Income tax	2,960	3,832	5,162
Excise taxes	821	1,205	1,345
Value-added tax (VAT)	1,792	2,231	2,397
Customs duty	744	916	1,147
Non-tax revenue	301	338	695
Total†	6,618	8,522	10,746

Expenditure	2006	2007	2008‡
Current expenditure	7,203	9,045	10,575
Wages and salaries	2,833	3,531	4,256
Goods and services	1,779	2,437	2,830
Interest payments	749	776	698
Other current expenditure	1,842	2,302	2,791
Capital expenditure	1,601	1,842	2,662
Domestic arrears payments	247	322	669
Total	9,051	11,209	13,906

* The budgetary out-turn includes a statistical discrepancy; a negative value indicates overfinancing (K '000 million): –483 in 2006; 474 in 2007; –111 in 2008.
† Excluding grants received (K '000 million): 10,207 in 2006; 2,104 in 2007; 2,698 in 2008.
‡ Projections.

Source: IMF, *Zambia: Request for a Three-Year Arrangement Under the Poverty Reduction and Growth Facility - Staff Report; Staff Statement; Press Release on the Executive Board Discussion; and Statement by the Executive Director for Zambia* (June 2008).

INTERNATIONAL RESERVES
(US $ million at 31 December)

	2006	2007	2008
IMF special drawing rights	13.3	9.7	10.6
Foreign exchange	706.4	1,080.2	1,085.0
Total	719.7	1,089.9	1,095.6

Source: IMF, *International Financial Statistics*.

MONEY SUPPLY
(K '000 million at 31 December)

	2005	2006	2007
Currency outside banks	818.9	1,066.4	1,299.8
Demand deposits at commercial banks	1,338.3	2,264.8	2,511.8
Total money (incl. others)	2,168.2	3,340.1	3,828.9

Source: IMF, *International Financial Statistics*.

ZAMBIA

COST OF LIVING
(Consumer Price Index; low-income group; base: 2000 = 100)

	2001	2002	2003
Food (incl. alcohol and tobacco)	118.9	151.1	184.5
Clothing and footwear	120.5	139.4	168.8
Fuel and rent	121.4	145.1	176.5
All items (incl. others)	121.4	148.4	180.1

Food (incl. alcohol and tobacco): 214.7 in 2004; 254.5 in 2005; 267.1 in 2006; 281.1 in 2007; 319.9 in 2008.
All items: 212.5 in 2004; 251.4 in 2005; 274.1 in 2006; 303.3 in 2007; 341.1 in 2008.

Source: ILO.

NATIONAL ACCOUNTS
Expenditure on the Gross Domestic Product
(US $ million at current prices)

	2005	2006	2007
Final consumption expenditure	5,709.36	7,150.24	7,858.43
Households	4,245.31	4,946.16	6,671.74
General government	1,464.05	2,204.08	1,186.69
Gross fixed capital formation	1,781.71	2,762.17	2,637.35
Total domestic expenditure	7,491.07	9,912.41	10,495.78
Exports of goods and services	2,449.35	4,119.49	4,806.59
Less Imports of goods and services	2,668.94	3,167.85	3,885.26
GDP in purchasers' values	7,271.48	10,864.06	11,417.11

Source: African Development Bank.

Gross Domestic Product by Economic Activity
(K '000 million at current prices)

	2004	2005	2006
Agriculture, forestry and fishing	5,568	6,724	7,800
Mining and quarrying	810	1,031	1,613
Manufacturing	2,828	3,430	4,016
Electricity, gas and water	695	923	1,166
Construction	2,402	3,728	5,463
Wholesale and retail trade, restaurants and hotels	4,844	5,869	6,525
Transport and communications	1,252	1,396	1,629
Finance and insurance	2,283	2,772	3,247
Real estate and business services	1,692	1,979	2,296
Restaurants and hotels	671	894	1,120
Community, social and personal services*	2,047	2,710	3,366
Other services	907	1,001	983
Sub-total	25,997	32,456	39,223
Import duties	2,219	2,594	2,849
Less imputed bank service charge	1,312	1,593	1,866
GDP in purchasers' values	26,904	33,457	40,207

*Includes public administration, defence, sanitary services, education, health, recreation, and personal services.

Source: IMF, *Zambia: Statistical Appendix* (January 2008).

2007 (US $ million): Agriculture, hunting, forestry and fishing 2,317; Mining, manufacturing and utilities 2,025 (Manufacturing 1,138); Construction 1,800; Wholesale, retail trade, restaurants and hotels 2,180; Transport, storage and communications 465; Other services 2,588; *Total, all industries* 11,375 (Source: UN Statistics Division, National Accounts Main Aggregates Database).

BALANCE OF PAYMENTS
(US $ million)

	2005	2006	2007
Exports of goods f.o.b.	2,246.8	3,928.9	4,593.7
Imports of goods f.o.b.	-2,160.8	-2,635.8	-3,610.6
Trade balance	86.1	1,293.1	983.1
Export of services	273.3	228.1	278.6
Import of services	-470.8	-586.9	-913.9
Balance on goods and services	-111.4	934.3	347.9
Other income received	12.6	18.4	35.2
Other income paid	-607.8	-1,186.7	-1,418.6
Balance on goods, services and income	-706.6	-234.0	-1,035.5
Current transfers received	52.9	248.2	351.1
Current transfers paid	-77.0	-92.7	-95.9
Current account	-730.7	-78.5	-780.3
Capital account (net)	287.0	197.0	222.8
Direct investment from abroad	357.0	615.8	983.9
Portfolio investment liabilities	122.4	50.4	41.8
Other investment assets	-225.6	-508.0	-647.7
Other investment liabilities	-1,821.1	-1,764.2	350.9
Net errors and omissions	-75.1	-303.2	-139.8
Overall balance	-2,086.1	-1,790.6	31.5

Source: IMF, *International Financial Statistics*.

External Trade

PRINCIPAL COMMODITIES
(US $ million)

Imports c.i.f.	2005	2006	2007
Food and live animals	110.8	172.2	125.3
Crude materials except fuels	88.2	84.6	191.1
Mineral fuels and lubricants	267.6	465.7	487.3
Petroleum and petroleum products	252.1	432.2	467.3
Petroleum oils and oils obtained from bituminous minerals, crude	101.3	232.2	228.6
Chemicals and related products	452.2	448.8	540.1
Medicinal and pharmaceutical products	69.8	71.5	98.2
Basic manufactures	380.2	434.1	632.1
Iron and steel	95.4	132.5	200.0
Machinery and transport equipment	806.4	1,234.6	1,685.1
Machinery specialized for particular industries	170.9	386.6	552.4
General industrial machinery, equipment and machine parts	173.3	176.8	310.6
Electrical machinery, apparatus, appliances and electrical parts	89.6	137.5	202.8
Road vehicles	199.7	308.5	369.8
Miscellaneous manufactured articles	374.7	174.1	179.6
Total (incl. others)	2,558.0	3,074.3	3,971.1

ZAMBIA

Exports f.o.b.	2005	2006	2007
Food and live animals	167.7	141.5	253.0
Beverages and tobacco	65.3	76.9	64.8
Crude materials except fuels	238.9	548.8	371.2
Metalliferous ore and metal scrap	92.3	435.5	296.5
Chemicals and related products	15.3	24.0	80.8
Basic manufactures	1,227.4	2,839.2	3,643.9
Non-ferrous metals	1,004.0	2,615.2	3,286.7
Copper	1,003.6	2,610.4	3,283.3
Machinery and transport equipment	24.0	105.5	105.9
Miscellaneous manufactured articles	57.2	10.6	33.7
Total (incl. others)	1,809.8	3,770.4	4,618.6

Source: UN, *International Trade Statistics Yearbook*.

PRINCIPAL TRADING PARTNERS
(US $ million)

Imports c.i.f.	2005	2006	2007
China, People's Repub.	85.5	83.8	234.0
Congo, Democratic Repub.	21.8	31.4	129.2
Finland	12.3	12.9	55.1
France (incl. Monaco)	89.8	23.0	116.7
Germany	36.1	43.9	80.9
India	79.8	85.9	162.7
Japan	41.6	47.4	51.6
Kenya	37.5	56.4	78.1
Netherlands	29.9	45.6	75.8
Norway	1.5	123.6	2.4
South Africa	1,216.5	1,446.4	1,883.1
Sweden	36.4	57.6	88.4
Tanzania	65.5	53.3	23.5
United Arab Emirates	94.1	320.3	255.8
United Kingdom	321.7	112.8	159.4
USA	41.2	58.3	65.3
Zimbabwe	110.1	175.7	111.0
Total (incl. others)	2,558.0	3,074.3	3,971.1

Exports f.o.b.	2005	2006	2007
Belgium	31.4	9.5	45.7
Botswana	41.4	6.1	19.3
China, People's Repub.	38.4	256.5	188.3
Congo, Democratic Repub.	97.4	134.4	245.7
Egypt	0.1	159.4	232.9
France-Monaco	45.4	16.8	54.1
India	25.4	134.0	52.5
Japan	29.8	3.5	37.1
Korea, Repub.	0.0	41.3	93.6
Malawi	62.3	56.3	31.3
Malaysia	0.0	78.7	53.8
Netherlands	45.8	43.0	50.2
Pakistan	0.0	50.7	49.2
Saudi Arabia	0.0	87.9	216.3
South Africa	336.9	415.2	553.8
Switzerland-Liechtenstein	519.4	1,502.0	1,930.1
Tanzania	92.8	17.5	95.2
Thailand	0.1	288.8	273.4
United Arab Emirates	0.3	85.5	51.3
United Kingdom	261.3	102.6	56.3
Zimbabwe	74.9	53.4	82.0
Total (incl. others)	1,809.8	3,770.4	4,618.6

Source: UN, *International Trade Statistics Yearbook*.

Transport

ROAD TRAFFIC
(estimates, '000 motor vehicles in use at 31 December)

	1994	1995	1996
Passenger cars	123	142	157
Lorries and vans	68	74	81

Source: IRF, *World Road Statistics*.

CIVIL AVIATION
(traffic on scheduled services)

	2002	2003	2004
Kilometres flown (million)	2	2	2
Passengers carried ('000)	47	45	50
Passenger-km (million)	16	14	16
Total ton-km (million)	1	1	1

Source: UN, *Statistical Yearbook*.

Tourism

VISITOR ARRIVALS BY NATIONALITY
(provisional figures)

	2004	2005	2006
Australia	7,490	16,336	14,617
South Africa	110,710	110,272	100,286
Tanzania	33,502	65,881	74,039
United Kingdom	37,520	44,369	57,119
USA	20,547	23,895	38,800
Zimbabwe	123,573	148,436	194,639
Total (incl. others)	515,000	668,862	756,860

Tourism receipts (US $ million, excl. passenger transport): 92 in 2004; 98 in 2005; 110 in 2007.

Source: World Tourism Organization.

Communications Media

	2005	2006	2007
Telephones ('000 main lines in use)	94.7	93.4	91.8
Mobile cellular telephones ('000 subscribers)	949.6	1,663.3	2,639.0
Internet users ('000)	334.8	500.0	500.0
Broadband subscribers ('000)	0.2	2.3	n.a.

Personal computers ('000 in use): 113 in 2005.

Radio receivers ('000 in use): 1,436 in 1999.

Television receivers ('000 in use): 540 in 2001.

Facsimile machines (number in use): 1,005 (estimate) in year ending 31 March 1999.

Daily newspapers: 3 (average circulation 114,000 copies) in 1996; 3 in 2004.

Sources: UNESCO, *Statistical Yearbook*; UNESCO Institute for Statistics; UN, *Statistical Yearbook*; International Telecommunication Union.

Education

(2005/06 unless otherwise indicated)

	Institutions	Teachers	Students
Primary	4,221*	52,323	2,678,610
Secondary	n.a.	33,964†	408,971‡
Tertiary	n.a.	n.a.	24,553§

* 1998 figure.
† 2002/03 estimate.
‡ 2004/05 figure.
§ 1999/2000 estimate.

Source: UNESCO Institute for Statistics.

Adult literacy rate (UNESCO estimates): 68.0% (males 76.3%; females 59.8%) in 1999 (Source: UNESCO Institute for Statistics).

Directory

The Constitution

The Constitution for the Republic of Zambia, which was formally adopted on 28 May 1996 (amending the Constitution of 1991), provides for a multi-party form of government. The Head of State is the President of the Republic, who is elected by popular vote at the same time as elections to the National Assembly. The President's tenure of office is limited to two five-year terms. Foreign nationals and those with foreign parentage are prohibited from contesting the presidency. The legislature comprises a National Assembly of 158 members: 150 are elected by universal adult suffrage, while the remaining eight are nominated by the President. The President appoints a Vice-President and a Cabinet from members of the National Assembly.

The Constitution also provides for a House of Chiefs numbering 27: four from each of the Northern, Western, Southern and Eastern Provinces, three each from the North-Western, Luapula and Central Provinces and two from the Copperbelt Province. It may submit resolutions to be debated by the Assembly and consider those matters referred to it by the President.

The Supreme Court of Zambia is the final Court of Appeal. The Chief Justice and other judges are appointed by the President. Subsidiary to the Supreme Court is the High Court, which has unlimited jurisdiction to hear and determine any civil or criminal proceedings under any Zambian law.

The Government

HEAD OF STATE

President: RUPIAH BANDA (took office 2 November 2008).

THE CABINET
(April 2009)

President: RUPIAH BANDA.
Vice-President and Minister of Justice: GEORGE KUNDA.
Minister of Home Affairs: KALOMBO MWANSA.
Minister of Foreign Affairs: KABINGA PANDE.
Minister of Defence: GEORGE MPOMBO.
Minister of Finance and National Planning: Dr SITUMBEKO MUSOKOTWANE.
Minister of Commerce, Trade and Industry: FELIX MUTATI.
Minister of Agriculture and Co-operatives: Brig.-Gen. BRIAN CHITUWO.
Minister of Communications and Transport: (vacant).
Minister of Energy and Water Development: KENNETH KONGA.
Minister of Tourism, the Environment and Natural Resources: CATHERINE NAMUGALA.
Minister of Education: GEOFFREY LUNGWANGWA.
Minister of Science, Technology and Vocational Training: GABRIEL NAMULAMBE.
Minister of Health: KAPEMMBWA SIMBAO.
Minister of Local Government and Housing: BENNIE TETAMASHIMBA.
Minister of Works and Supply: MIKE MULONGOTI.
Minister of Community Development and Social Services: MICHAEL KAINGU.
Minister of Sport, Youth and Child Development: KENNETH CHIPUNGU.
Minister of Lands: PETER DAKA.
Minister of Labour and Social Security: AUSTIN LIATO.
Minister of Mines and Mineral Development: MAWELL MWALE.
Minister of Information and Broadcasting Services: RONNIE SHIKAPWASHA.
Minister of Gender and Development: SARAH SAYIFWANDA.
Minister of Presidential Affairs: RONALD MUYKUMA.
There are, in addition, 26 Deputy Ministers.

MINISTRIES

Office of the President: POB 30135, Lusaka; tel. (21) 1266147; fax (21) 1266092; internet www.statehouse.gov.zm.
Ministry of Agriculture and Co-operatives: Mulungushi House, Independence Ave, Nationalist Rd, POB RW50291, Lusaka; tel. (21) 1213551.
Ministry of Commerce, Trade and Industry: 9th and 10th Floor, Nasser Rd, POB 31968, Lusaka; tel. (21) 1228301; fax (21) 1226984; internet www.mcti.gov.zm.
Ministry of Communications and Transport: Fairley Rd, POB 50065, Lusaka; tel. (21) 151444; fax (21) 151795; internet www.mct.gov.zm.
Ministry of Community Development and Social Welfare: Fidelity House, POB 31958, Lusaka; tel. (21) 1228321; fax (21) 1225327.
Ministry of Defence: POB 31931, Lusaka; tel. (21) 1252366.
Ministry of Education: 15102 Ridgeway, POB RW50093, Lusaka; tel. (21) 1227636; fax (21) 1222396; internet www.education.gov.zm.
Ministry of Energy and Water Development: Mulungushi House, Independence Ave, Nationalist Rd, POB 36079, Lusaka; tel. and fax (21) 1252589; internet www.mewd.gov.zm.
Ministry of Finance and National Planning: Finance Bldg, POB 50062, Lusaka; tel. (21) 1252121; fax (21) 1251078; e-mail info@mofnp.gov.zm; internet www.mofnp.gov.zm.
Ministry of Foreign Affairs: POB RW50069, Lusaka; tel. (21) 1213822; fax (21) 1222440.
Ministry of Gender and Development: Lusaka.
Ministry of Health: Ndeke House, POB 30205, Lusaka; tel. (21) 1253040; fax (21) 1253344; internet www.moh.gov.zm.
Ministry of Home Affairs: POB 32862, Lusaka; tel. (21) 1213505.
Ministry of Information and Broadcasting Services: Independence Ave, POB 32245, Lusaka; tel. (21) 1228202; fax (21) 1253457; internet www.mibs.gov.zm.
Ministry of Justice: Fairley Rd, POB 50106, 15101, Ridgeway, Lusaka; tel. (21) 1228522.
Ministry of Labour and Social Security: Lechwe House, Freedom Way, POB 32186, Lusaka; tel. (21) 1212020; internet www.mlss.gov.zm.
Ministry of Lands: POB 50694, Lusaka; tel. (21) 1252288; fax (21) 1250120; internet www.ministryoflands.gov.zm.
Ministry of Local Government and Housing: Church Rd, POB 50027, Lusaka; tel. (21) 1250528; fax (21) 1252680; e-mail ps@mlgh.gov.zm; internet www.mlgh.gov.zm.
Ministry of Mines and Mineral Development: Chilufya Mulenga Rd, POB 31969, 10101 Lusaka; tel. (21) 1235323; fax (21) 1235346.
Ministry of Science, Technology and Vocational Training: Los Angeles Blvd, Lusaka; tel. (21) 1252911; fax (21) 1252951; e-mail psmstvt@mstvt.gov.zm; internet www.mstvt.gov.zm.
Ministry of Sport, Youth and Child Development: Memaco House, POB 50195, Lusaka; tel. (21) 1227158; fax (21) 1223996.
Ministry of Tourism, the Environment and Natural Resources: 3rd Floor, Kwacha House, Cairo Rd, Lusaka; tel. (21) 1227645; fax (21) 1222189; internet www.mtenr.gov.zm.
Ministry of Works and Supply: POB 50003, Lusaka; tel. (21) 1253088; fax (21) 1253404.

President and Legislature

PRESIDENT

Presidential Election, 30 October 2008

Candidate	Votes	% of votes
Rupiah Banda (MMD)	718,359	40.63
Michael Sata (PF)	683,150	38.64
Hakainde Hichilema (UDA)	353,018	19.96
Brig.-Gen. Godfrey Miyanda (HP)	13,683	0.77
Total	**1,768,210**	**100.00**

NATIONAL ASSEMBLY

Speaker: AMUSAA KATUNDA MWANAMWAMBWA.

ZAMBIA

General Election, 28 September 2006*

Party	Seats
Movement for Multi-party Democracy (MMD)	75
Patriotic Front (PF)	43
United Democratic Alliance (UDA)†	26
Independents	3
United Liberal Party (ULP)	2
National Democratic Focus (NDF)	1
Total	**150**

* Includes the results of voting in two constituencies where the elections were postponed until 26 October 2006, owing to the deaths of candidates.
† Coalition of the Forum for Democracy and Development (FDD), the United National Independence Party (UNIP) and the United Party for National Development (UPND).

House of Chiefs

The House of Chiefs is an advisory body which may submit resolutions for debate by the National Assembly. There are 27 Chiefs, four each from the Northern, Western, Southern and Eastern Provinces, three each from the North-Western, Luapula and Central Provinces, and two from the Copperbelt Province.

Election Commission

Electoral Commission of Zambia (ECZ): Elections House, Haile Selassie Ave, POB 50274, Longacres, Lusaka; tel. (21) 1253155; fax (21) 1253884; e-mail elections@electcom.org.zm; internet www.elections.org.zm; f. 1996; independent; Chair. FLORENCE MUMBA; Dir DAN KALALE.

Political Organizations

Citizens Democratic Party (CDP): POB 37277, Lusaka; tel. 968347292; e-mail citizens@thecitizensdemocraticparty.com; internet www.thecitizensdemocraticparty.com.

Agenda for Change (AfC): POB 37119, Lusaka; e-mail genda@zambia.co.zm; internet www.agenda123.com; f. 1995; Pres. Prof. HENRY KYAMBALESA; Nat. Chair. DARROH P. CHOONGA.

Democratic Party (DP): Plot C4, President Ave (North), POB 71628, Ndola; f. 1991; Pres. EMMANUEL MWAMBA.

Heritage Party (HP): POB 51055, Lusaka; f. 2001 by expelled mems of the MMD; Pres. Brig.-Gen. GODFREY MIYANDA.

Liberal Progressive Front (LPF): POB 31190, Lusaka; f. 1993; Pres. Dr RODGER CHONGWE.

Movement for Multi-party Democracy (MMD): POB 30708, Lusaka; tel. (21) 1250177; fax (21) 1252329; e-mail mmd@zamtel.zm; internet www.mmdzam.org; f. 1990; governing party since Nov. 1991; Pres. RUPIAH BANDA; Nat. Sec. KATELE KALUMBA.

National Democratic Front: Lusaka; f. 2006 to contest the presidential election; Acting Chair. NEVERS MUMBA (RP).

Comprising:

All Peoples' Congress Party (APC): Lusaka; f. 2005 by fmr mems of the FDD; Pres. WINRIGHT K. NGONDO.

Party for Unity, Democracy and Development (PUDD): Lusaka; f. 2004 by fmr mems of the MMD; Pres. CHITALU SAMPA.

Reform Party: Lusaka; f. 2005 by fmr mems of the MMD; Pres. NEVERS MUMBA; Nat. Chair. EVA SANDERSON; Sec.-Gen. CLEMENT MICHELO.

Zambia Democratic Conference (ZADECO): Lusaka; f. 1998 as the Zambia Democratic Congress Popular Front by fmr mems of the Zambia Democratic Congress; disbanded in 1999; reformed after 2001 election by fmr mems of the ZAP; Pres. Rev. Dr DAN PULE.

Zambia Republican Party (ZRP): Lusaka; f. 2001 by merger of the Republican Party (f. 2000) and the Zambia Alliance for Progress (f. 1999); Gen. Sec. SILVIA MASEBO; Nat. Chair. BEN KAPITA.

National Leadership for Development (NLD): POB 34161, Lusaka; f. 2000; Pres. Dr YOBERT K. SHAMAPANDE.

National Party (NP): POB 37840, Lusaka 10101; tel. (21) 1849431; e-mail nationalparty1993@yahoo.com; f. 1993; by fmr mems of MMD; promotes human rights; Pres. Rev. RICHARD KAMBULU; Sec.-Gen. NDANISO BANDA.

Patriotic Front (PF): internet www.michaelsata.co.zm; f. 2001 by expelled mems of the MMD; Pres. MICHAEL SATA; Sec.-Gen. GUY SCOTT.

United Democratic Alliance (UDA): Kenneth Kaunda House, Cairo Rd, Lusaka; f. 2006 to contest that year's elections; Nat. Chair. TILYENJI KAUNDA (FDD).

Comprising:

Forum for Democracy and Development (FDD): POB 35868, Lusaka; f. 2001 by expelled mems of the MMD; Pres. EDITH NAWAKWI; Chair. SIMON ZUKAS.

United National Independence Party (UNIP): POB 30302, Lusaka; tel. (21) 1221197; fax (21) 1221327; f. 1959; sole legal party 1972–90; Pres. TILYENJI KAUNDA; Nat. Chair. KEN KAIRA.

United Party for National Development (UPND): POB 33199, Lusaka; internet www.upnd.org; f. 1998; incl. fmr mems of the Progressive People's Party and Zambia Dem. Party; Pres. HAKAINDE HICHILEMA.

Unity Party for Democrats (UPD): POB RW28, Ridgeway, Lusaka; f. 1997; Pres. MATHEW PIKITI.

Zambia Alliance for Progress (ZAP): Lusaka; f. 1999; re-registered as ZAP in 2001 after splitting from Zambia Republican Party; Pres. (vacant).

Diplomatic Representation

EMBASSIES AND HIGH COMMISSIONS IN ZAMBIA

Angola: Plot 108, Great East Rd, Northmead, POB 31595, 10101 Lusaka; tel. (21) 1134764; fax (21) 1221210; Ambassador PEDRO DE MORAIS NETO.

Botswana: 5201 Pandit Nehru Rd, Diplomatic Triangle, POB 31910, 10101 Lusaka; tel. (21) 1250555; fax (21) 1250804; High Commissioner T. DITLHABI-OLIPHANT.

Brazil: 74 Anglo American Bldg, Independence Ave, POB 33300; tel. (21) 1250400; fax (21) 1251652; e-mail brasemblusaca@iconnect.zm; Ambassador JOSAL LUIZ PELLEGRINO.

Canada: Plot 5199, United Nations Ave, POB 31313, 10101 Lusaka; tel. (21) 1250833; fax (21) 1254176; e-mail lsaka@international.gc.ca; High Commissioner PIERRE-PAUL PERRON.

China, People's Republic: Plot 7430, United Nations Ave, Longacres, POB 31975, 10101 Lusaka; tel. (21) 1251169; fax (21) 1251157; e-mail chinaemb_zm@mfa.gov.cn; Ambassador LI QIANGMIN.

Congo, Democratic Republic: Plot 1124, Parirenyatwa Rd, POB 31287, 10101 Lusaka; tel. and fax (21) 1235679; Ambassador JOHNSON WA BINANA.

Cuba: 5574 Mogoye Rd, Kalundu, POB 33132, 10101 Lusaka; tel. (21) 1291308; fax (21) 1291586; e-mail ambassador@iconnect.zm; Ambassador FRANCISCO CORREA.

Denmark: 5219 Haile Selassie Ave, POB 50299, Lusaka; tel. (21) 1254277; fax (21) 1254618; e-mail lunamb@um.dk; internet www.amblusaka.um.dk/en; Ambassador THOMAS NEWHOUSE TRIGG SCHJERBECK.

Egypt: Plot 5206, United Nations Ave, Longacres, POB 32428, Lusaka 10101; tel. (21) 1250229; fax (21) 1252213; Ambassador SHERIF MOHAMED KAMAL ED-DEIN SHAHIN.

Finland: Haile Selassie Ave, opp. Ndeke House, Longacres, POB 50819, 15101 Lusaka; tel. (21) 1251988; fax (21) 1253783; e-mail sanomat.lus@formin.fi; internet www.finland.org.zm; Ambassador SINIKKA ANTILA.

France: Mpile Bldg, 74 Independence Ave, POB 30062, 10101 Lusaka; tel. (21) 1251322; fax (21) 1254475; e-mail france@ambafrance-zm.org; internet www.ambafrance-zm.org; Ambassador FRANÇOISE LE BIHAN.

Germany: Plot 5209, United Nations Ave, POB 50120, 15101 Ridgeway, Lusaka; tel. (21) 1250644; fax (21) 1254014; e-mail info@lusaka.diplo.de; internet www.lusaka.diplo.de; Ambassador Dr IRENE HINRICHSEN.

Holy See: 283 Los Angeles Blvd, POB 31445, 10101 Lusaka; tel. (21) 1251033; fax (21) 1250601; e-mail nuntius@coppernet.zm; Apostolic Nuncio Most Rev. NICOLA GIRASOLI (Titular Archbishop of Egnazia Appula).

India: 1 Pandit Nehru Rd, POB 32111, 10101 Lusaka; tel. (21) 1253159; fax (21) 1254118; e-mail chancery@india.zm; High Commissioner YOGESH K. GUPTA.

Ireland: 6663 Katima Mulilo Rd, Olympia Park, POB 34923, 10101 Lusaka; tel. (21) 1290650; fax (21) 1290482; e-mail iremb@zamnet.zm; Ambassador BILL NOLAN.

Italy: Plot 5211, Embassy Park, Diplomatic Triangle, POB 50497, Lusaka; tel. (21) 1250781; fax (21) 1254929; e-mail ambasciata

ZAMBIA

.lusaka@esteri.it; internet www.amblusaka.esteri.it; Ambassador Dr GIOVANNI CERUTI.

Japan: Plot 5218, Haile Selassie Ave, POB 34190, 10101 Lusaka; tel. (21) 1251555; fax (21) 1254425; e-mail jez@zamtel.zm; internet www.zm.emb-japan.go.jp; Ambassador HIDETO MITAMURA.

Kenya: 5207 United Nations Ave, POB 50298, 10101 Lusaka; tel. (21) 1250722; fax (21) 1253829; e-mail kenhigh@zamnet.zm; High Commissioner LAZARUS O. AMAYO.

Libya: 251 Ngwee Rd, off United Nations Ave, Longacres, POB 35319, 10101 Lusaka; tel. (21) 1253055; fax (21) 1251239; Ambassador KHALIFA OMER SWIEXI.

Malawi: 31 Bishops Rd, Kabulonga, POB 50425, Lusaka; tel. (21) 1213750; fax (21) 1265764; e-mail mhcomm@zamtel.zm; High Commissioner Dr CHRISSIE MUGHOGHO.

Mozambique: Kacha Rd, Plot 9592, POB 34877, 10101 Lusaka; tel. (21) 1220333; fax (21) 1220345; e-mail embamoc.zambia@minec.gov.mz; High Commissioner MARIA LEOCÁDIA TIVANE MATE.

Namibia: 30B Mutende Rd, Woodlands, POB 30577, 10101 Lusaka; tel. (21) 1260407; fax (21) 1263858; e-mail namibia@coppernet.zm; High Commissioner MARTIN SHALLI.

Netherlands: 5208 United Nations Ave, POB 31905, 10101 Lusaka; tel. (21) 1253819; fax (21) 1253733; e-mail lus@minbuza.nl; internet www.netherlandsembassy.org.zm; Ambassador EDUARD J. M. MIDDELDORP.

Nigeria: 17 Broads Rd, Fairview, POB 32598, Lusaka; tel. (21) 1229860; fax (21) 1223791; High Commissioner Chief IBIRONKE O. VAUGHAN-ADEFOPE.

Norway: cnr Birdcage Walk and Haile Selassie Ave, Longacres, POB 34570, 10101 Lusaka; tel. (21) 1252188; fax (21) 1253915; e-mail emb.lusaka@mfa.no; internet www.norway.org.zm; Ambassador TORE GJØS.

Russia: Plot 6407, Diplomatic Triangle, POB 32355, 10101 Lusaka; tel. (21) 1252120; fax (21) 1253582; internet www.russianembassy.biz/zambia-lusaka.htm; Ambassador ANVAR AZIMOV.

Saudi Arabia: 27BC Leopards Hill Rd, Kabulonga, POB 34411, 10101 Lusaka; tel. (21) 1266861; fax (21) 1266863; e-mail saudiemb@uudial.zm; Ambassador TALAT SALEM RADWAN.

Serbia: Independence Ave 5216, POB 33379, 10101 Lusaka; tel. (21) 1250235; fax (21) 1253889; e-mail serbianemba@zamnet.zm; Chargé d'affaires a.i. MIRKO MANOJLOVIC.

Somalia: G3/377A Kabulonga Rd, POB 34051, Lusaka; tel. (21) 1262119; Ambassador Dr OMAN UMAL.

South Africa: D26, Cheetah Rd, Kabulonga, Private Bag W369, Lusaka; tel. (21) 1260999; fax (21) 1263001; e-mail sahcadmin@samnet.zm; High Commissioner MOSES MABOKELA CHIKANE.

Sudan: 31 Ng'umbo Rd, Longacres, POB RW179X, 15200 Lusaka; tel. (21) 1215570; Ambassador ABDALLAH KHIDIR BASHIR.

Sweden: Haile Selassie Ave, POB 50264, 10101 Lusaka; tel. (21) 1251711; fax (21) 1254049; e-mail ambassaden.lusaka@foreign.ministry.se; internet www.swedenabroad.com/lusaka; Ambassador LARS RONNÅS.

Tanzania: Ujamaa House, Plot 5200, United Nations Ave, POB 31219, 10101 Lusaka; tel. (21) 1253222; fax (21) 1254861; e-mail tzreplsk@zamnet.zm; High Commissioner GEORGE MWANJABALA.

United Kingdom: Plot 5201, Independence Ave, POB 50050, 15101 Ridgeway, Lusaka; tel. (21) 1251133; fax (21) 1253798; Jt High Commissioner CAROLYN DAVIDSON, THOMAS CARTER.

USA: cnr Independence and United Nations Aves, POB 31617, Lusaka; tel. (21) 1250955; fax (21) 1252225; internet zambia.usembassy.gov; Ambassador DONALD E. BOOTH.

Zimbabwe: 11058, Haile Selassie Ave, Longacres, POB 33491, 10101 Lusaka; tel. (21) 1254012; fax (21) 1227474; Ambassador LOVEMORE MAZEMO.

Judicial System

The judicial system of Zambia comprises a Supreme Court, composed of a Chief Justice, a Deputy Chief Justice and five Justices; a High Court comprising the Chief Justice and 30 Judges; Senior Resident and Resident Magistrates' Courts, which sit at various centres; and Local Courts, which deal principally with customary law, but which also have limited criminal jurisdiction.

Supreme Court of Zambia
Independence Ave, POB 50067, Ridgeway, Lusaka; tel. (21) 1251330; fax (21) 1251743.
Chief Justice: ERNEST SAKALA.
Deputy Chief Justice: IREEN MAMBILIMA.
Supreme Court Judges: LOMBE CHIBESAKUNDA, DENNIS CHIRWA, PETER CHITENGI, FLORENCE MUMBA, SANDSON SILOMBA.

Religion

CHRISTIANITY

Council of Churches in Zambia: Church House, Cairo Rd, POB 30315, Lusaka; tel. (21) 1229551; fax (21) 1224308; e-mail info@ccz.org.zm; f. 1945; Chair. Rt Rev. THUMA HAMUKANG'ANDU (Brethren in Christ Church); Gen. Sec. JAPHET NDHLOVU; 22 mem. churches and 18 affiliate mem. orgs.

The Anglican Communion

Anglicans are adherents of the Church of the Province of Central Africa, covering Botswana, Malawi, Zambia and Zimbabwe. The Church comprises 15 dioceses, including five in Zambia. The Archbishop of the Province is the Bishop of Upper Shire in Malawi. There are an estimated 80,000 adherents in Zambia.

Bishop of Central Zambia: Rt Rev. DEREK G. KAMUKWAMBA, POB 70172, Ndola; tel. (21) 2612431; fax (21) 2615954; e-mail adcznla@zamnet.zm.

Bishop of Eastern Zambia: Rt Rev. WILLIAM MUCHOMBO, POB 510154, Chipata; tel. and fax (21) 6221294; e-mail dioeastzm@zamnet.zm.

Bishop of Luapula: Rt Rev. ROBERT MUMBI, POB 710210, Mansa, Luapula.

Bishop of Lusaka: Rt Rev. DAVID NJOVU, Bishop's Lodge, POB 30183, Lusaka; tel. (21) 1264515; fax (21) 1262379; e-mail angdiolu@zamnet.zm.

Bishop of Northern Zambia: Rt Rev. ALBERT CHAMA, POB 20798, Kitwe; tel. (21) 2223264; fax (21) 2224778; e-mail dionorth@zamnet.zm.

Protestant Churches

At mid-2000 there were an estimated 2.7m. Protestants.

African Methodist Episcopal Church: Carousel Bldg, Lumumba Rd, POB 36628, Lusaka; tel. 955708031; fax (21) 1225067; Presiding Elder Rev. PAUL KAWIMBE; 440 congregations, 880,000 mems.

Baptist Church: Lubu Rd, POB 30636, Lusaka; tel. (21) 1253620.

Baptist Mission of Zambia: Baptist Bldg, 3062 Great East Rd, POB 50599, 15101 Ridgeway, Lusaka; tel. (21) 1222492; fax (21) 1227520; internet bmoz.org.

Brethren in Christ Church: POB 630115, Choma; tel. (21) 3320228; fax (21) 3320127; e-mail biccz@zamtel.zm; internet www.bic.org; f. 1906; Bishop Rev. T. HAMUKANG'ANDU; 180 congregations, 19,526 mems.

Evangelical Lutheran Church in Zambia: POB 37701, Mpezeni Rd, 10101 Lusaka; tel. 97787584; fax (21) 1224023; e-mail elcza_head@yahoo.com; Leader Rev. RABSON MWANZA; 5,683 mems (2009).

Reformed Church in Zambia: POB 38255, Lusaka; tel. (21) 1295369; e-mail info@rczsynod.co.zm; internet www.rczsynod.co.zm; f. 1899; African successor to the Dutch Reformed Church mission; Gen. Sec. Rev. WILLIAM ZULU (acting); 147 congregations, 400,000 mems.

Seventh-day Adventist Church: Plot 9221, cnr Burma Rd and Independence Ave, POB 36010, Lusaka; tel. and fax (21) 1254036; e-mail lcsdac@zamnet.zm; internet www.lcsdac.net.zm; f. 1905; Pres. Dr CORNELIUS MULENGA MATANDIKO; Sec. HARRINGTON SIMUI AKOMBWA; 534,126 mems.

United Church of Zambia: Synod Headquarters, Nationalist Rd at Burma Rd, POB 50122, Lusaka; tel. (21) 1250641; fax (21) 1252198; e-mail uczsynod@zamnet.zm; f. 1965; Synod Bishop Rev. MUTALE MULUMBWA (Interim Synod Bishop); Gen. Sec. Rev. Prof. TEDDY KALONGO; c. 3m. mems.

Other denominations active in Zambia include the Assemblies of God, the Church of Christ, the Church of the Nazarene, the Evangelical Fellowship of Zambia, the Kimbanguist Church, the Presbyterian Church of Southern Africa, the Religious Society of Friends (Quakers) and the United Pentecostal Church. At mid-2000 there were an estimated 2m. adherents professing other forms of Christianity.

The Roman Catholic Church

Zambia comprises two archdioceses and eight dioceses. At 31 December 2006 there were an estimated 3,794,016 adherents in the country, equivalent to 29.7% of the total population.

Bishops' Conference

Catholic Secretariat, Unity House, cnr Freedom Way and Katunjila Rd, POB 31965, 20201 Lusaka; tel. (21) 1212070; fax (21) 1220996.

f. 1984; Pres. Rt Rev. TELESPHORE GEORGE MPUNDU (Archbishop of Lusaka).

Archbishop of Kasama: Most Rev. JAMES SPAITA, Archbishop's House, POB 410143, Kasama; tel. (21) 4221248; fax (21) 4222202; e-mail archkasa@zamtel.zm.

Archbishop of Lusaka: Most Rev. TELESPHORE GEORGE MPUNDU, 41 Wamulwa Rd, POB 32754, 10101 Lusaka; tel. (21) 1255973; fax (21) 1255975; e-mail adl@zamnet.zm.

ISLAM

There are about 10,000 members of the Muslim Association in Zambia.

BAHÁ'Í FAITH

National Spiritual Assembly: Sekou Touré Rd, Plot 4371, Private Bag RW227X, Ridgeway 15102, Lusaka; tel. and fax (21) 1254505; f. 1952; Sec.-Gen. MARGARET K. LENGWE; mems resident in 1,456 localities.

The Press

DAILIES

The Post: 36 Bwinjimfumu Rd, Rhodespark, Private Bag E352, Lusaka; tel. (21) 1231092; fax (21) 1229271; e-mail post@post.co.zm; internet www.postzambia.com; f. 1991; privately owned; Editor-in-Chief FRED M'MEMBE; circ. 29,000.

The Times of Zambia: Kabelenga Ave, POB 70069, Ndola; tel. and fax (21) 2614469; e-mail times@zamtel.zm; internet www.times.co.zm; f. 1943; govt-owned; English; Deputy Editor-in-Chief DAVEY SAKALA; circ. 25,000.

Zambia Daily Mail: Zambia Publishing Company, POB 31421, Lusaka; tel. (21) 1225131; fax (21) 1225881; internet www.daily-mail.co.zm; f. 1968; govt-owned; English; Man. Editor EMMANUEL NYIRENDA; circ. 40,000.

PERIODICALS

African Social Research: Institute of Economic and Social Research, University of Zambia, POB 32379, Lusaka; tel. (21) 1294131; fax (21) 1253952; f. 1944; two a year; Editor MUBANGA E. KASHOKI; circ. 1,000.

The Challenge: Mission Press, Chifubu Rd, POB 71581, Ndola; tel. (21) 2680456; fax (21) 2680484; e-mail info@missionpress.org; internet www.missionpress.org; f. 1999; quarterly; English; social, educational and religious; Roman Catholic; edited by Franciscan friars; Dir Fr MIHA DREVENSEK; circ. 7,000.

Chipembele Magazine: POB 30255, Lusaka; tel. (21) 1254226; six a year; publ. by Wildlife Conservation Soc. of Zambia; circ. 20,000.

Farming in Zambia: POB 50197, Lusaka; tel. (21) 1213551; f. 1965; quarterly; publ. by Ministry of Agriculture, Food and Fisheries; Editor L. P. CHIRWA; circ. 3,000.

Imbila: POB RW20, Lusaka; tel. (21) 1217254; f. 1953; monthly; publ. by Zambia Information Services; Bemba; Editor D. MUKAKA; circ. 20,000.

Intanda: POB RW20, Lusaka; tel. (21) 1219675; f. 1958; monthly; publ. by Zambia Information Services; Tonga; Editor J. SIKAULU; circ. 6,000.

Konkola: Zambia Consolidated Copper Mines Ltd, PR Dept, POB 71505, Ndola; tel. (21) 2640142; f. 1973 as *Mining Mirror*; monthly; English; Editor G. MUKUWA; circ. 30,000.

Leisure Magazine: Farmers House, Cairo Rd, POB 8138, Woodlands, Lusaka; monthly; general interest.

The Lowdown: Lusaka; internet www.lowdown.co.zm; f. 1995; monthly; English; Editor HEATHER CHALCRAFT.

Lukanga News: POB 919, Kabwe; tel. (21) 5217254; publ. by Zambia Information Services; Lenje; Editor J. H. N. NKOMANGA; circ. 5,500.

National Mirror: Multimedia Zambia, 15701 Woodlands, POB 320199, Lusaka; tel. (21) 1263864; fax (21) 1263050; f. 1972; fortnightly; news, current affairs and foreign affairs; publ. by Multimedia Zambia; Editor SIMON MWANZA; circ. 40,000.

Ngoma: POB RW20, Lusaka; tel. (21) 1219675; monthly; Lunda, Kaonde and Luvale; publ. by Zambia Information Services; Editor B. A. LUHILA; circ. 3,000.

Outlook: TBM Publicity Enterprises Ltd, POB 40, Kitwe; f. 1971; monthly; general interest.

Speak Out!: POB 70244, Ndola; tel. (21) 2612241; fax (21) 2620630; e-mail speakout@zamnet.zm; f. 1984; six a year; Christian; aimed at youth readership up to 35 years; Man. Editor CONSTANTIA TREPPE; circ. 25,000.

The Sportsman: POB 31762, Lusaka; tel. (21) 1214250; f. 1980; monthly; Man. Editor SAM SIKAZWE; circ. 18,000.

Sunday Express: Lusaka; f. 1991; weekly; Man. Editor JOHN MUKELA.

Sunday Times of Zambia: Kabelenga Ave, POB 70069, Ndola; tel. (21) 1614469; fax (21) 2617096; e-mail times@zamtel.zm; internet www.times.co.zm/sunday; f. 1965; owned by UNIP; English; Man. Editor ARTHUR SIMUCHOBA; circ. 78,000.

Tsopano: POB RW20, Lusaka; tel. (21) 1217254; f. 1958; monthly; publ. by Zambia Information Services; Nyanja; Editor S. S. BANDA; circ. 9,000.

Workers' Voice: POB 20652, Kitwe; tel. (21) 2211999; f. 1972; fortnightly; publ. by Zambia Congress of Trade Unions.

Youth: POB 30302, Lusaka; tel. (21) 1211411; f. 1974; quarterly; publ. by UNIP Youth League; Editor-in-Chief N. ANAMELA; circ. 20,000.

Zambia Government Gazette: POB 30136, Lusaka; tel. (21) 1228724; fax (21) 1224486; f. 1911; weekly; English; official notices.

NEWS AGENCY

Zambia News Agency (ZANA): Mass Media Complex, 2nd Floor, Alick Nkhata Rd, POB 30007, Lusaka; tel. (21) 1219673; fax (21) 1251631; e-mail zana@zamnet.zm; internet www.zana.gov.zm; f. 1969; Dir LEWIS MWANANGOMBE; Editor-in-Chief VILLIE LOMBANYA; headquarters in Lusaka and nine regional offices.

PRESS ASSOCIATION

Press Association of Zambia (PAZA): Bishops Rd, Multi-Media Centre, POB 37065, Lusaka; tel. (21) 1263595; fax (21) 1263110; f. 1983; Pres. ANDREW SAKALA; Vice-Pres. AMOS CHANDA.

Publishers

Africa: Literature Centre, POB 21319, Kitwe; tel. (21) 2210765; fax (21) 2210716; general, educational, religious; Dir JACKSON MBEWE.

African Social Research: Institute of Economic and Social Research, University of Zambia, POB 32379, Lusaka; tel. (21) 1294131; fax (21) 1253952; social research in Africa; Editor MUBANGA E. KASHOKI.

Bookworld Ltd: Plot 10442, off Lumumba Rd, POB 31838, Lusaka; tel. (21) 1230606; fax (21) 1230614; e-mail bookworld@realtime.zm.

Daystar Publications Ltd: POB 32211, Lusaka; f. 1966; religious; Man. Dir S. E. M. PHEKO.

Directory Publishers of Zambia Ltd: Mabalenga Rd, POB 30963, Lusaka; tel. (21) 1257133; fax (21) 1257137; e-mail dpz@coppernet.zm; f. 1958; trade directories; Gen. Man. W. D. WRATTEN.

Multimedia Zambia: Woodlands, POB 320199, Lusaka; tel. and fax (21) 1261193; f. 1971; religious and educational books, audio-visual materials; Exec. Dir EDDY MUPESO.

University of Zambia Press (UNZA Press): POB 32379, 10101 Lusaka; tel. (21) 1292269; fax (21) 1253952; f. 1938; academic books, papers and journals.

Zambia Educational Publishing House: Chishango Rd, POB 32708, 10101 Lusaka; tel. (21) 1222324; fax (21) 1225073; f. 1967; educational and general; Man. Dir BENIKO E. MULOTA.

Zambia Printing Co Ltd: POB 34798, 10101 Lusaka; tel. (21) 1227673; fax (21) 1225026; Gen. Man. BERNARD LUBUMBASHI.

GOVERNMENT PUBLISHING HOUSES

Government Printer: POB 30136, Lusaka; tel. (21) 1228724; fax (21) 1224486; official documents and statistical bulletins.

Zambia Information Services: POB 50020, Lusaka; tel. (21) 1219673; state-controlled; Dir BENSON SIANGA.

PUBLISHERS' ASSOCIATION

Booksellers' and Publishers' Association of Zambia: POB 31838, Lusaka; tel. (21) 1222647; fax (21) 1225195; Chair. RAY MUNAMWIMBU; Sec. BASIL MBEWE.

Broadcasting and Communications

REGULATORY AUTHORITY

Zambian Communications Authority: Plot 3141, cnr Lumumba and Buyantanshi Rds, POB 36871, Lusaka; tel. (21) 1241236; fax (21) 1246701; e-mail info@caz.zm; internet www.caz.zm; f. 1994; Acting CEO RICHARD MWANZA.

TELECOMMUNICATIONS

MTN (Zambia) Ltd: 5033 Longolongo Rd, POB 35464, Lusaka; tel. 966750750; fax 966761234; e-mail mtn@mtnzambia.co.zm; internet www.mtnzambia.co.zm; f. 1997 as Telecel (Zambia) Ltd; acquired by MTN Group, South Africa, in 2005; mobile cellular telecommunications provider; CEO PER ERIKSSON; 152,000 subscribers (2006).

Zain Zambia Ltd: POB 320001, Nyerere Rd, Woodlands, Lusaka; tel. (21) 1250707; e-mail customerservice.zm@zain.com; internet www.zm.zain.com; f. 1997 as ZamCell Ltd; fmrly Celtel Zambia; mobile cellular telephone operator; Man. Dir DAVID HOLLIDAY; c. 500,000 subscribers.

Zambia Telecommunications Co Ltd (ZAMTEL): Provident House, Buteko Ave, POB 71660, Ndola; tel. (21) 2611111; fax (21) 2615855; e-mail zamtel@zamtel.zm; internet www.zamtel.zm; transfer to private sector abandoned in 2005; commercialization pending; operates Cell-Z cellular network (f. 1995); Chair. BASIL SICHALI; Man. Dir SIMON TEMBO.

BROADCASTING

Zambia National Broadcasting Corpn: Mass Media Complex, Alick Nkhata Rd, POB 50015, Lusaka; tel. (21) 1252005; fax (21) 1254013; e-mail lukundosa@yahoo.com; internet www.znbc.co.zm; f. 1961; state-owned; two national radio stations (Radio 1 and Radio 2) and one line-of-rail station (Radio 4); television broadcasts along the line of rail, from Livingstone to Chililabombwe; services in English and seven Zambian languages; Dir-Gen. EDDY MUPESO.

Radio

Breeze FM: POB 511178, Chipata; tel. (21) 6221175; fax (21) 6221823; e-mail breezefm@zamtel.zm; internet www.breezefm.com; f. 2003; Nyanja and English; community based commercial radio; broadcasts to the Eastern Province; signal is also received in parts of north-west Malawi and border areas of Tete Province in Mozambique; Man. Dir MIKE DAKA.

Educational Broadcasting Services: Headquarters: POB 50231, Lusaka; tel. (21) 1251724; radio broadcasts from Lusaka; audiovisual aids service from POB 50295, Lusaka; Controller MICHAEL MULOMBE.

Radio Maria Zambia: POB 510307, Chipata; tel. and fax (21) 6221154; e-mail info.zam@radiomaria.org; internet www.radiomaria.org; f. 1999; part of The World Family of Radio Maria, Italy; Roman Catholic religious programming; broadcasts to Eastern Province; Dir MWANZA GABRIEL KWAKU.

Radio Phoenix: Private Bag E702, Lusaka; tel. (21) 1223581; fax (21) 1226839; e-mail rphoenix@zamnet.zm; commercial radio station; Chair. ERROL T. HICKEY.

Yatsani Radio: Leopards Hill Rd, Bauleni Catholic Church, POB 320147, Lusaka; tel. (21) 1261082; fax (21) 1265842; internet yatsani.com; f. 1999; owned by the Archdiocese of Lusaka; Roman Catholic religious community; broadcasts to Lusaka; Dir Most Rev. MEDARDO JOSEPH MAZOMBWE (Archbishop of Lusaka).

Television

Educational Broadcasting Services: (see Radio).

Muvi Television: Plot No. 17734, Nangwenya Rd, POB 33932, Lusaka; tel. (21) 1254766; fax (21) 1257351; e-mail frontoffice@muvitv.com; internet www.muvitv.com.

Finance

(cap. = capital; auth. = authorized; res = reserves; dep. = deposits; m. = million; br(s). = branch(es); amounts in kwacha)

BANKING

From 30 June 1996 all banks operating in Zambia were required to have capital of not less than K2,000m. in order to receive a banking licence or to continue to function.

Central Bank

Bank of Zambia: Bank Sq., Cairo Rd, POB 30080, 10101 Lusaka; tel. (21) 1228888; fax (21) 1225652; internet www.boz.zm; f. 1964; bank of issue; cap. 10,020m., res 440,332m., dep. 3,275,524m. (Dec. 2006); Gov. and Chair. Dr CALEB M. FUNDANGA; br. in Ndola.

Commercial Banks

Finance Bank Zambia Ltd: 2101 Chanik House, Cairo Rd, POB 37102, 10101 Lusaka; tel. (21) 1229733; fax (21) 1227290; e-mail fbz@financebank.co.zm; internet www.financebank.co.zm; f. 1986 as Leasing Finance Bank Ltd; name changed as above 1988; cap. 3,630m., res 9,320m., dep. 823,894m. (Dec. 2006); Chair. Dr R. L. MAHTANI; Man. Dir DICK KING; 33 brs and 10 agencies.

National Savings and Credit Bank of Zambia: Plot 248B, Cairo Rd, POB 39568, Lusaka; tel. (21) 1232333; fax (21) 1223296; internet www.natsave.co.zm; f. 1972; total assets 6,598m. (Dec. 1998); Man. Dir LEONARD Z. MWANZA.

New Capital Bank PLC: Anchor House, Mezzanine Floor, Sapele Rd, POB 36452, Lusaka; tel. (21) 1229508; fax (21) 1224055; f. 1992; cap. and res 4,510m., total assets 18,538m. (Dec. 2001); Chair. WILA D. MUNG'OMBA; CEO and Gen. Man. GODFREY P. MSISKA.

ZANACO (ZNCB): POB 33611, Plot 33454 Cairo Rd, Lusaka; tel. (21) 1228979; fax (21) 1223106; e-mail support@zanaco.co.zm; e-mail zncbidf@zamnet.zm; internet www.zanaco.co.zm; f. 1969; fmrly Zambia National Commercial Bank PLC, name changed as above in 2008; 50.8% govt-owned; cap. and res 63,370m., total assets 584,667m. (Dec. 2000); Chair. Dr MUTUMBA BULL LAWANIKA; Man. Dir LIKOLO NDALAMEI; 41 brs.

Foreign Banks

Bank of China (Zambia) Ltd (China): Amandra House, Ben Bella Rd, POB 34550, Lusaka; tel. (21) 1235349; fax (21) 1235350; e-mail service_zm@bank-of-china.com; f. 1997; cap. and res 5,731m., total assets 73,237m. (Dec. 2001); Chair. PING YUE; Gen. Man. HONG XINSHENG.

Barclays Bank Zambia PLC (United Kingdom): Kafue House, Cairo Rd, POB 31936, Lusaka; tel. (21) 1228858; fax (21) 1226185; e-mail barclays.zambia@barclays.com; internet www.africa.barclays.com; f. 1971; cap. 101,327m., res 10,852m., dep. 1,667,873m. (Dec. 2006); Chair. JACOB SIKAZWE; Man. Dir ZAFAR MASUD; 5 brs.

Citibank Zambia Ltd (USA): Citibank House, Cha Cha Cha Rd, POB 30037, Southend, Lusaka; tel. (21) 1229025; fax (21) 1226264; internet www.citibank.co.zm; f. 1979; cap. 1,000.0m., res 18,411.4m., dep. 754,605.0m. (Dec. 2006); Man. Dir SAVIOR CHIBIYA; 1 br.

Indo-Zambia Bank (IZB): Plot 6907, Cairo Rd, POB 35411, Lusaka; tel. (21) 1224653; fax (21) 1225090; e-mail izb@zamnet.zm; internet www.izb.co.zm; f. 1984; cap. 10,000.0m., res 12,126.4m., dep. 487,168.4m. (March 2007); Chair. ORLENE Y. MOYO; Man. Dir CYRIL PATRO; 9 brs.

Stanbic Bank Zambia Ltd: Woodgate House, 6th Floor, Cairo Rd, POB 32111, Lusaka; tel. (21) 1229285; fax (21) 1225380; e-mail stanbic@zamnet.zm; internet www.stanbicbank.co.zm; f. 1971; wholly owned by Standard Bank Investment Corpn; cap. 7,700m., res 10,568m., dep. 945,055m. (Dec. 2005); Chair. V. CHITALU; Man. Dir L. F. KALALA; 7 brs.

Standard Chartered Bank Zambia PLC: Standard House, Cairo Rd, POB 32238, Lusaka; tel. (21) 1229242; fax (21) 1225337; internet www.standardchartered.com/zm; f. 1971; 90% owned by Standard Chartered Holdings (Africa) BV, Amsterdam; 10% state-owned; cap. 2,048m., res 14,420m., dep. 1,484,681m. (Dec. 2006); Chair. GEORGE SOKOTA; Man. Dir MIZINGA MELU; 16 brs.

Development Banks

Development Bank of Zambia: Development House, Katondo Rd, POB 33955, Lusaka; tel. (21) 1228576; fax (21) 1222821; e-mail projects@dbz.co.zm; internet www.dbz.co.zm; f. 1973; 99% state-owned; provides medium- and long-term loans and administers special funds placed at its disposal; cap. and res 7,580.0m., total assets 145,976.6m. (March 1998); Chair. NAMUKULO MUKUTU; Man. Dir RICHARD PHIRI (acting); 2 brs.

Zambia Agricultural Development Bank: Society House, Cairo Rd, POB 30847, Lusaka; tel. (21) 1219251; f. 1982; loan finance for devt of agriculture and fishing; auth. cap. 75m.; Chair. K. MAKASA; Man. Dir AMON CHIBIYA.

Zambia Export and Import Bank Ltd: Society House, Cairo Rd, POB 33046, Lusaka; tel. (21) 1229486; fax (21) 1222313; f. 1987; Man. Dir LIKANDO NAWA.

STOCK EXCHANGE

Lusaka Stock Exchange (LuSE): Exchange Bldg, 3rd Floor, Central Park, Cairo Rd, POB 34523, Lusaka; tel. (21) 1228391; fax (21) 1225969; e-mail info@luse.co.zm; internet www.luse.co.zm; f. 1994; Chair. FRIDAY NDHLOVU; Gen. Man. BEATRICE NKANZA.

INSURANCE

African Life Assurance Zambia: Mukuba Pension House, 4th Floor, Dedan Kimathi Rd, POB 31991; tel. (21) 1225452; fax (21) 1225435; e-mail customercare@african-life.com.zm; f. 2002; life insurance; CEO STEVE WILLIAMS.

Cavmont Capital Insurance Corpn Ltd: Anchor House, Mezzanine Floor, POB 38474, Lusaka; tel. (21) 1224280; fax (21) 1221643; e-mail info@cavmont.com.zm; internet www.cavmont.com.zm; f. 2003; subsidiary of Cavmont Capital Holdings Ltd; Dir PAUL CAVE.

Goldman Insurance Ltd: Zambia National Savings and Credit Bank Bldg, 2nd Floor, Cairo Rd, Private Bag W395, Lusaka; tel. (21) 1235234; fax (21) 1227262; f. 1992; Chair. BWALYA CHITI.

Madison Insurance Co Ltd: Plot 255, Kaleya Rd, Roma, POB 37013, Lusaka; tel. (21) 1295311; fax (21) 1295320; internet www .madisonzambia.com; f. 1992; general and micro-insurance; Chair. DAVID A. R. PHIRI; Man. Dir LAWRENCE S. SIKUTWA.

NICO Insurance Zambia Ltd (NIZA): 1131 Parirenyatwa Rd, Fairview, POB 32825, Lusaka; tel. (21) 1222862; fax (21) 1222863; e-mail nicozam@zamnet.zm; internet www.nicomw.com/zambia; f. 1997; subsidiary of NICO Group, Malawi; general insurance; Chair. JOHN MWANAKATWE; Gen. Man. TITUS KALENGA.

Professional Insurance Corpn Zambia Ltd (PICZ): Finsbury Park, Kabwe Roundabout, POB 34264, Lusaka; tel. (21) 1227509; fax (21) 1222151; e-mail customerservice@picz.co.zm; internet www.picz .co.zm; f. 1992; Chair. R. L. MATHANI; Man. Dir ASHOK CHAWLA.

Zambia State Insurance Corpn Ltd: Premium House, Independence Ave, POB 30894, Lusaka; tel. (21) 1229343; fax (21) 1222263; e-mail zsic@zsic.co.zm; internet www.zsic.co.zm; f. 1968; sole authorized insurance provider in Zambia 1971–92; transfer to private sector pending; Chair. ALBERT WOOD; Man. Dir IRENE MUYENGA.

ZIGI Insurance Co Ltd: Mukuba Pension House, 5th Floor, POB 37782, Lusaka; tel. (21) 1226835; fax (21) 1231564; e-mail zigi@ zamnet.zm; f. 1998; Chair. and CEO SAVIOUR H. KONIE.

Trade and Industry

GOVERNMENT AGENCY

Zambia Development Agency: Privatisation House, Nasser Rd, POB 30819, Lusaka; tel. (21) 1220177; fax (21) 1225270; e-mail zda@ zda.org.zm; internet www.zda.org.zm; f. 2006 by merger of the Zambia Privatisation Agency, the Zambia Investment Centre, the Export Board of Zambia, the Zambia Export Processing Zones Authority and the Small Enterprises Development Board; operational in July 2007; 262 cos privatized by mid-2006, 22 privatizations pending; Dir-Gen. and CEO ANDREW CHIPWENDE.

DEVELOPMENT ORGANIZATIONS

Industrial Development Corpn of Zambia Ltd (INDECO): Indeco House, Buteko Place, POB 31935, Lusaka; tel. (21) 1228026; fax (21) 1228868; f. 1960; auth. cap. K300m.; taken over by the Nat. Housing Authority in May 2005; Chair. R. L. BWALYA; Man. Dir S. K. TAMELÉ.

Mpongwe Development Company: Block 4450, Mpongwe, POB 90599, Luanshya; tel. (21) 2510584; fax (21) 2511713; promotes the production of crops for domestic and regional markets; CEO HENK MARMELSTEIN.

CHAMBERS OF COMMERCE

Zambia Association of Chambers of Commerce and Industry: Great East Rd, Showgrounds, POB 30844, Lusaka; tel. (21) 1252483; fax (21) 1253020; e-mail secretariat@zacci.co.zm; internet www.zacci .org.zm; f. 1938; Chair. HANSON SINDOWE; CEO JUSTIN M. CHISULO; 10 district chambers, 8 trade assocs, 35 corporate mems.

Member chambers and associations include:

Chamber of Mines of Zambia: POB 22100, Kitwe; tel. (21) 2214122; f. 1941 as Northern Rhodesia Chamber of Mines; replaced by the Copper Industry Service Bureau 1965–2000; represents mining employers; 19 mems; Pres. NATHAN CHISHIMBA; Gen. Man. FREDERICK BANTUBONSE.

Zambia Association of Manufacturers: POB 30036, Lusaka; tel. (21) 1242780; fax (21) 1222912; e-mail babbar@zamnet.zm; f. 1985; Chair. D. BABBAR; 180 mems.

Chamber of Small and Medium Business Associations.

INDUSTRIAL AND TRADE ASSOCIATIONS

Tobacco Board of Zambia (TBZ): POB 31963, Lusaka; tel. (21) 1288995; fax (21) 1287118; e-mail tbz@zamnet.zm; promotes, monitors and controls tobacco production; Sec. JONATHAN M. CHIZUNI.

Zambia Farm Employers' Association (ZFEA): Farmers' Village, Lusaka Agricultural and Commercial Showgrounds, POB 30395, Lusaka; tel. (21) 1252649; fax (21) 1252648; e-mail znfu@ zamnet.zm; Chair. R. DENLY; 350 mems.

Other associations include: the Bankers Asscn of Zambia; the Cotton Asscn of Zambia; the Environmental Conservation Asscn of Zambia; the Insurance Brokers Asscn of Zambia; the Kapenta Fishermen Asscn; the National Aquaculture Asscn of Zambia; the National Council for Construction; the Poultry Asscn of Zambia; the Tobacco Asscn of Zambia; the Wildlife Producers Asscn of Zambia; the Young Farmers Clubs of Zambia; the Zambia Asscn of Clearing and Forwarding; the Zambia Asscn of Manufacturers; the Zambia Coffee Growers Asscn; the Zambia Export Growers Asscn; and the Zambian Women in Agriculture.

UTILITIES

Electricity

ZESCO (Zambia Electricity Supply Corpn) Ltd: Stand 6949, Great East Rd, POB 33304, Lusaka; tel. (21) 1226084; fax (21) 1222753; e-mail mchisela@zesco.co.zm; internet www.zesco.co.zm; f. 1970; state-owned; Man. Dir RHODNIE P. SISALA.

Copperbelt Energy Corpn PLC (CEC): Private Bag E835, Postnet No. 145, Chindo Rd, Kabulonga, Lusaka; tel. (21) 1261647; fax (21) 1261640; e-mail info@cec.com.zm; internet www .copperbeltenergy.com; f. 1997 upon privatization of the power div. of Zambia Consolidated Copper Mines; privately owned co supplying power generated by ZESCO to mining cos in the Copperbelt; Exec. Chair HANSON SINDOWE.

CO-OPERATIVE

Zambia Co-operative Federation Ltd: Co-operative House, Cha Cha Cha Rd, POB 33579, Lusaka; tel. 2220157; fax 2222516; f. 1973; agricultural marketing; supply of agricultural chemicals and implements; cargo haulage; insurance; agricultural credit; auditing and accounting; property and co-operative devt; Chair. B. TETAMASHIMBA; Man. Dir G. Z. SIBALE.

TRADE UNIONS

Zambia Congress of Trade Unions (ZCTU): Solidarity House, Oxford Rd, POB 20652, Kitwe; tel. (21) 2211999; fax (21) 2228284; e-mail zctu@microlink.zm; f. 1965; Pres. LEONARD HIKAUMBA; Sec.-Gen. SYLVESTER TEMBO; c. 350,000 mems (2007).

Affiliated Unions

Airways and Allied Workers' Union of Zambia: Lusaka International Airport, 2nd Floor, Terminal Bldg, POB 30175, 10101 Lusaka; affiliated to the Int. Transport Workers' Fed.; Pres. F. MULENGA; Gen. Sec. B. CHINYANTA.

Civil Servants' & Allied Workers Union of Zambia (CSAWUZ): Plot 5045A, Mumbwa Rd, POB 50160, Lusaka; tel. and fax (21) 1287106; e-mail csuz@zamnet.zm; f. 1975; Chair. L. C. HIKAUMBA; Gen. Sec. DARISON CHAALA; 35,000 mems.

Guards Union of Zambia (GUZ): POB 21882, Kitwe; tel. (21) 2216189; e-mail uni-africa@union-network.org; f. 1972; affiliated to the Union Network Int.; Chair. D. N. S. SILUNGWE; Gen. Sec. MICHAEL S. SIMFUKWE; 13,500 mems.

Hotel Catering Workers' Union of Zambia: POB 35693, Lusaka; affiliated to the Int. Union of Food, Agricultural, Hotel, Restaurant, Catering, Tobacco and Allied Workers' Asscns; Chair. IAN MKANDAWIRE; Gen. Sec. STOIC KAPUTU; 9,000 mems.

Mineworkers' Union of Zambia (MUZ): POB 20448, Kitwe; tel. (21) 2214022; affiliated to the Int. Fed. of Chemical, Energy, Mine and Gen. Workers' Unions; Pres. RAYFORD MBULU; Sec.-Gen. OSWELL MUNYENYEMBE; 50,000 mems.

National Union of Building, Engineering and General Workers (NUBEGW): City Sq., Millers Bldg, Plot No. 1094, POB 21515, Kitwe; tel. (21) 2224468; fax (21) 2661119; e-mail nubegw@zamtel .zm; affiliated to the Building and Wood Workers Int. and the Int. Metalworkers' Fed.; Chair. LUCIANO MUTALE (acting); Gen. Sec. P. N. NZIMA; 18,000 mems.

National Union of Commercial and Industrial Workers (NUCIW): 17 Obote Ave, POB 21735, Kitwe; tel. (21) 2228607; fax (21) 2225211; e-mail nuciw@zamtel.zm; f. 1982; affiliated to the Int. Fed. of Chemical, Energy, Mine and Gen. Workers' Unions, the Int. Textile, Garment and Leather Workers' Fed., the Int. Union of Food, Agricultural, Hotel, Restaurant, Catering, Tobacco and Allied Workers' Asscns and the Union Network Int.; Chair. I. M. KASUMBU; Gen. Sec. JOHN M. BWALYA; 16,000 mems.

National Union of Communication Workers: POB 70751, 92 Broadway, Ndola; tel. (21) 2611345; fax (21) 2614679; e-mail nucw@ zamtel.zm; affiliated to the Union Network Int.; Pres. PATRICK KAONGA; Gen. Sec. CLEMENT KASONDE; 4,700 mems.

National Union of Plantation and Agricultural Workers: POB 80529, Kabwe; tel. (21) 5224548; e-mail nupawhq@yahoo.com; affiliated to the Int. Union of Food, Agricultural, Hotel, Restaurant, Catering, Tobacco and Allied Workers' Asscns; Pres. MUDENDA RISHER; Gen. Sec. MULENGA MUKUKA; 15,155 mems.

National Union of Public Services' Workers (NUPSW): POB 32523, Lusaka; tel. (21) 1227451; fax (21) 1287105; e-mail znslib@ zamtel.zm; affiliated to the Public Services Int.; Gen. Sec. DAVIS J. CHINGONI.

ZAMBIA

National Union of Transport and Allied Workers (NUTAW): Cha Cha Cha House, Rm 4, 1st Floor, POB 30068, Cario Rd, Lusaka; tel. (21) 1214756; e-mail sapphiri2005@yahoo.com; Pres. Patrick C. Chanda; Gen. Sec. Sam A. P. Phiri.

Railway Workers' Union of Zambia: POB 80302, Kabwe; tel. (21) 5224006; affiliated to the Int. Transport Workers' Fed.; Chair. H. K. Ndamana; Gen. Sec. Benson L. Ngula; 10,228 mems.

University of Zambia and Allied Workers' Union: POB 32379, Lusaka; tel. (21) 1213221; f. 1968; Chair. Beriate Sunkutu; Gen. Sec. Saini Phiri.

Zambia Electricity Workers' Union: POB 70859, Ndola; f. 1972; Chair. Cosmas Mpampi; Gen. Sec. Adam Kaluba; 3,000 mems.

Zambia National Farmers' Union: ZNFU Head Office, Tiyende Pamodzi Rd, opp. Polo Grounds, Farmers' Village, Zambia Agricultural and Commercial Showgrounds, POB 30395, Lusaka; tel. (21) 1252649; fax (21) 1252648; e-mail znfu@zamnet.zm; internet www.znfu.org.zm; Exec. Dir Songowayo Zyambo.

Zambia National Union of Teachers: POB 31914, Lusaka; tel. (21) 1214623; fax (21) 1214624; e-mail znut@microlink.zm; affiliated to Education Int.; Chair. Richard M. Liywalii; Gen. Sec. Roy Mwaba; 2,120 mems.

Zambia Graphical and Allied Workers' Union (ZAGRAWU): POB 290346, Ndola; tel. and fax (21) 2614457; e-mail zatawu@yahoo.com; affiliated to the Union Network Int.; Gen. Sec. David S. Mwaba.

Zambia Union of Journalists: POB 30394, Lusaka; tel. (21) 1227348; fax (21) 1221695; e-mail zuj.zambia@yahoo.com; Vice-Pres. Morgan Chonya; Gen. Sec. Nigel Mulenga.

Zambia Union of Local Government Officers: f. 1997; Pres. Isaac Mwanza.

Zambia United Local Authorities Workers' Union (ZULAWU): Mugala House, POB 70575, Ndola; tel. (21) 2615022; affiliated to the Public Services Int.; Chair. Abraham M. Mutakila; Gen. Sec. Amon Daka (acting).

Principal Non-Affiliated Union

Zambian African Mining Union: Kitwe; f. 1967; 40,000 mems.

Transport

RAILWAYS

Total length of railways in Zambia was 2,162 km (including 891 km of the Tanzania–Zambia railway) in 2000. There are two major railway networks: the Zambia Railways network, which traverses the country from the Copperbelt in northern Zambia and links with the National Railways of Zimbabwe to provide access to South African ports, and the Tanzania–Zambia Railway (Tazara) network, linking New Kapiri-Mposhi in Zambia with Dar es Salaam in Tanzania. The Tazara railway line increased its capacity from 1976, in order to reduce the dependence of southern African countries on trade routes through South Africa. In April 1987 the Governments of Zambia, Angola and Zaire (now the Democratic Republic of the Congo) declared their intention to reopen the Benguela railway, linking Zambian copper mines with the Angolan port of Lobito, following its closure to international traffic in 1975 as a result of the guerrilla insurgency in Angola. In 1997 a programme of repairs was begun, and plans were announced in June 2002 to rebuild the Benguela railway. It was announced in 2003 that a line would be built linking the Zambian port of Mpulungu to the Tazara network. In April 2005 Northwest Railways undertook to develop a new line between Chingola, in the Copperbelt Province, and Lumwana, in the North-Western Province. It was anticipated that the line could eventually be linked to the Benguela railway.

Tanzania–Zambia Railway Authority (Tazara): POB T01, Mpika; Head Office: POB 2834, Dar es Salaam, Tanzania; tel. (21) 4370684; fax (21) 4370228; f. 1975; operates passenger and freight services linking New Kapiri-Mposhi, north of Lusaka, with Dar es Salaam in Tanzania, a distance of 1,860 km, of which 891 km is in Zambia; jtly owned and administered by the Govts of Tanzania and Zambia; Chair. Salim H. Msoma; Man. Dir Clement Mwiya.

Zambia Railways Ltd: cnr Buntungwa St and Ghana Ave, POB 80935, Kabwe; tel. (21) 5222201; fax (21) 5224411; f. 1967; management assumed in 1998 by consortium of Hifab Int. AB, Sweden, and DE Consult, Germany; concession of assets and operations to consortium of New Limpopo Bridge Project Investments Ltd and Transnet Freight Rail, South Africa, agreed in early 2003; Chair. B. Nonde; Man. Dir Göran Malmberg.

ROADS

In 2001 there was a total road network of 91,440 km, including 4,222 km of main roads and 8,948 km of secondary roads. The main arterial roads run from Beitbridge (Zimbabwe) to Tunduma (the Great North Road), through the copper-mining area to Chingola and Chililabombwe (hitherto the Zaire Border Road), from Livingstone to the junction of the Kafue river and the Great North Road, and from Lusaka to the Malawi border (the Great East Road). In 1984 the 300-km BotZam highway linking Kazungula with Nata, in Botswana, was formally opened. A 1,930-km main road (the TanZam highway) links Zambia and Tanzania. In 1998 the Government initiated a 10-year Road Sector Investment Programme with funding from the World Bank, and in its second phase the European Union.

Road Development Agency: POB 50003, Lusaka; tel. (21) 1253801; fax (21) 1253404; e-mail rda_hq@roads.gov.zm; internet www.rda.org.zm; f. 2002; fmrly Dept of Roads; CEO Watson Ng'ambi.

CIVIL AVIATION

In 1984 there were 127 airports, aerodromes and air strips. An international airport, 22.5 km from Lusaka, was opened in 1967.

National Airports Corpn Ltd (NACL): Airport Rd, 10101 Lusaka; tel. (21) 1271313; fax (21) 1271048; e-mail nacl@zamnet.zm; internet www.lun.aero; f. 1973; air cargo services; Man. Dir Robinson Misitala (acting).

Zambia Skyways (Eastern Air): Plot 6, Addis Ababa Rd, POB 32661, Lusaka; tel. (21) 1250987; fax (21) 1250767; e-mail yzumla@zambiaskyways.aero; internet www.zambiaskyways.aero; f. 1995; operates scheduled passenger services to domestic destinations and South Africa; Chair. Yoosuf Zumla.

Zambian Airways: Lusaka International Airport, POB 34777, Lusaka; tel. (21) 1271230; fax (21) 1271054; e-mail reservations@zambiaairways.com; internet www.zambiaairways.com; f. 1988 as Roan Air; present name adopted in 1999; operates domestic and regional routes; CEO Donald MacDonald.

Tourism

Zambia's main tourist attractions, in addition to the Victoria Falls, are its wildlife, unspoilt scenery and diverse cultural heritage; there are 19 national parks and 36 game management areas. In 2006 756,860 tourists visited Zambia, up from 668,862 in the previous year; tourism receipts totalled US $110m. in 2007.

Tourism Council of Zambia: 55–56 Mulungushi International Conference Centre, POB 36561, Lusaka; tel. and fax (21) 1290436; e-mail secretariat.tcz@iconnect.zm; internet www.zambiatourism.com/travel/localnews/tcz.htm; Exec. Dir Josephine Mahl.

Zambia National Tourist Board: Century House, Lusaka Sq., POB 30017, Lusaka; tel. (21) 1229087; fax (21) 1225174; e-mail zntb@zambiatourism.org.zm; internet www.zambiatourism.com; Chair. Errol Hickey; Man. Dir Chanda Charity Lumpa.

ZIMBABWE

Introductory Survey

Location, Climate, Language, Religion, Flag, Capital

The Republic of Zimbabwe is a land-locked state in southern Africa, with Mozambique to the east, Zambia to the north-west, Botswana to the south-west and South Africa to the south. The climate is tropical, modified considerably by altitude. Average monthly temperatures range from 13°C (55°F) to 22°C (72°F) on the Highveld, and from 20°C (68°F) to 30°C (86°F) in the low-lying valley of the Zambezi river. The rainy season is from November to March. The official languages are English, ChiShona and SiNdebele. About 55% of the population are Christians. A large number of the African population follow traditional beliefs, while the Asian minority comprises both Muslims and Hindus. The national flag (proportions 1 by 2) has seven equal horizontal stripes, of green, gold, red, black, red, gold and green, with a white triangle, bearing a red five-pointed star on which a gold 'Great Zimbabwe bird' is superimposed, at the hoist. The capital is Harare.

Recent History

In 1923 responsibility for Southern Rhodesia (now Zimbabwe) was transferred from the British South Africa Company to the Government of the United Kingdom, and the territory became a British colony. It had full self-government (except for African interests and some other matters) under an administration controlled by European settlers. African voting rights were restricted.

In 1953 the colony united with two British protectorates, Northern Rhodesia (now Zambia) and Nyasaland (now Malawi), to form the Federation of Rhodesia and Nyasaland. A new Constitution, which ended most of the United Kingdom's legal controls and provided for a limited African franchise, came into effect in November 1962. At elections in December the Prime Minister, Sir Edgar Whitehead, lost power to the Rhodesian Front (RF), a coalition of white opposition groups committed to maintaining racial segregation. The leader of the RF, Winston Field, became Prime Minister.

As a result of pressure from African nationalist movements in Northern Rhodesia and Nyasaland, the Federation was dissolved in December 1963. African nationalists were also active in Southern Rhodesia. The African National Congress, founded in 1934, was revived in 1957, with Joshua Nkomo as President. Following the banning of the Congress in February 1959, some of its members formed the National Democratic Party (NDP) in January 1960. Nkomo, although in exile, was elected President of the NDP in October. When the NDP was banned in December 1961, Nkomo formed the Zimbabwe African People's Union (ZAPU), which was declared an unlawful organization in September 1962. ZAPU split in July 1963, and a breakaway group, led by the Rev. Ndabaningi Sithole, formed the Zimbabwe African National Union (ZANU) in August. Robert Mugabe became Secretary-General of ZANU.

In April 1964 Field was succeeded as Prime Minister of Southern Rhodesia by his deputy, Ian Smith. The new regime rejected British conditions for independence, including acceptance by the whole Rhodesian population and unimpeded progress to majority rule. In August ZANU was banned. After Northern Rhodesia became independent as Zambia in October, Southern Rhodesia became generally (although not officially) known as Rhodesia. On 5 November 1965 a state of emergency (to be renewed annually) was declared, and on 11 November Smith made a unilateral declaration of independence (UDI) and proclaimed a new Constitution, naming the country Rhodesia. The British Government regarded Rhodesia's independence as unconstitutional and illegal, and no other country formally recognized it. The United Kingdom terminated all relations with Rhodesia, while the UN applied economic sanctions. Both ZAPU and ZANU took up arms against the RF regime.

Following a referendum in June 1969, Rhodesia was declared a republic in March 1970. The 1969 Constitution provided for a bicameral Legislative Assembly, comprising a 23-member Senate and a 66-member House of Assembly (50 Europeans and 16 Africans). The President had only formal powers, and Smith remained Prime Minister. The RF won all 50 European seats in the House of Assembly in 1970, 1974 and 1977.

In November 1971 the British and Rhodesian Governments agreed on draft proposals for a constitutional settlement, subject to their acceptability to the Rhodesian people 'as a whole'. In December the African National Council (ANC), led by Bishop Abel Muzorewa, was formed to co-ordinate opposition to the plan. In December 1974, however, the Rhodesian Government and leaders of four nationalist organizations (including ZAPU, ZANU and the ANC) agreed the terms of a cease-fire, conditional on the release of African political detainees and on the convening of a constitutional conference in 1975. The African organizations agreed to unite within the ANC, with Muzorewa as President. Mugabe opposed the incorporation of ZANU into the ANC, and in mid-1975 left Rhodesia for neighbouring Mozambique, where he took control of ZANU's external wing, and challenged Sithole's leadership of the party. In September the ANC split into rival factions, led by Muzorewa and Nkomo. Constitutional talks between the Government and the Nkomo faction began in December 1975, but were abandoned in March 1976. In September, under pressure from South Africa, Smith announced his Government's acceptance of proposals leading to majority rule within two years. In late 1976 representatives of the RF, the African nationalists and the British Government met to discuss the transition to majority rule. The nationalists were led by Muzorewa, Sithole, Nkomo and Mugabe (by then the recognized leader of ZANU). Nkomo and Mugabe adopted a joint position as the Patriotic Front (PF).

In January 1977 Angola, Botswana, Mozambique, Tanzania and Zambia (the 'front-line' states) declared their support for the PF. Smith rejected British proposals for an interim administration, and received a mandate from the RF to repeal racially discriminatory laws and to seek agreement with such African factions as he chose. In November Smith accepted the principle of universal adult suffrage, and talks on an internal settlement were initiated with Muzorewa's United African National Council (UANC), Sithole's faction of the ANC and the Zimbabwe United People's Organization, led by Chief Jeremiah Chirau. These talks led to the signing of an internal settlement on 3 March 1978, providing for an interim power-sharing administration to prepare for independence on 31 December. The proposals were rejected by the PF and by the UN Security Council. In May 1978 the newly created Executive Council, consisting of Smith, Sithole, Muzorewa and Chirau, ordered the release of all political detainees in an attempt to bring about a cease-fire.

In January 1979 a 'majority rule' Constitution, with entrenched safeguards for the white minority, was approved by the House of Assembly and endorsed by a referendum of European voters. In April elections to the new House of Assembly (the first by universal adult suffrage) were held in two stages: for 20 directly elected European members (chosen by non-African voters only) and then for 72 African members (chosen by the whole electorate). The elections were boycotted by the PF. The UANC emerged as the majority party, with 51 seats, while the RF won all 20 seats for whites. In May the new Parliament elected Josiah Gumede as President. Muzorewa became Prime Minister of the country (renamed Zimbabwe Rhodesia) in June. In accordance with the Constitution, Muzorewa formed a government of national unity, including European members (Smith became Minister without Portfolio). However, international recognition was not forthcoming, and UN sanctions remained in force.

New impetus for a lasting and internationally recognized settlement followed the Commonwealth Conference in Zambia in August 1979. In September a Rhodesian Constitutional Conference in London, United Kingdom, was attended by delegations under Muzorewa and the joint leaders of the PF. The PF reluctantly agreed to special representation for the whites under the proposed new Constitution, which was eventually accepted by both parties; complete agreement was reached on transitional arrangements in November, and a cease-fire between the guerrillas of the PF and the Rhodesian security forces was finalized the following month. On 11 December the Zimbabwe Rhodesia

ZIMBABWE

Parliament voted to renounce independence and to revert to the status of a British colony, as Southern Rhodesia. Illegal rule ended on the following day, when Parliament was dissolved, the President, Prime Minister and Cabinet resigned, and the British-appointed Governor, Lord Soames, was vested with full executive and legislative authority for the duration of the transition to legal independence. The United Kingdom immediately revoked economic sanctions.

Lord Soames ended the ban on the two wings of the PF (ZAPU and ZANU) and ordered the release of most of the detainees who were held under the 'emergency powers' laws. Elections to a new House of Assembly proceeded in February 1980 (again in two stages) under the supervision of a British Electoral Commissioner. Mugabe's ZANU—PF emerged as the largest single party, winning 57 of the 80 African seats; Nkomo's PF—ZAPU took 20 seats and the UANC only three. In a separate poll of white voters, the RF secured all 20 reserved seats. The new state of Zimbabwe became legally independent, within the Commonwealth, on 18 April, with Rev. Canaan Banana as President (with largely ceremonial duties) and Mugabe as Prime Minister, at the head of a coalition Government.

Relations within the Government were strained, particularly between Mugabe and Nkomo. The latter was removed from the Cabinet, with two PF colleagues, in February 1982, under suspicion of plotting against Mugabe. By May 1984 the RF, now restyled the Republican Front, retained only seven of the 20 seats reserved for whites, the remaining 13 being held by independents. In July the RF was renamed the Conservative Alliance of Zimbabwe (CAZ), and opened its membership to all races.

There were several outbreaks of violence prior to a general election in June–July 1985. ZANU—PF was returned to power with an increased majority, winning 63 of the 79 'common roll' seats in the House of Assembly (and an additional seat at a by-election in August). ZAPU won 15 seats, retaining its traditional hold over Matabeleland, and ZANU—Sithole took a single seat. The UANC failed to gain representation. Of the 20 seats reserved for whites, 15 were secured by the CAZ. However, the CAZ was not represented in the new Cabinet.

During mid-1985 a large number of ZAPU officials were detained for questioning about dissident activity in Matabeleland. The failure, in August 1987, of talks aimed at uniting ZANU and ZAPU led to renewed rebel activity, whereupon the Government took steps to prevent ZAPU from functioning effectively. Furthermore, ZANU declined to endorse seven ZAPU-nominated candidates for the parliamentary seats made vacant in September by the abolition of seats reserved for whites (see below). In December Mugabe and Nkomo finally signed an agreement of unity, which was ratified by both parties in April 1988 and implemented in December 1989 (see below). In January 1988 Nkomo was appointed as one of the Senior Ministers in the President's Office, and two other ZAPU officials were given government posts. Following the unity agreement there was a significant improvement in the security situation in Matabeleland. However, the state of emergency remained in force, owing to incursions into eastern Zimbabwe by the Mozambican rebel movement, the Resistência Nacional Moçambicana (Renamo, see below).

Two major constitutional reforms were enacted during 1987. In September the reservation for whites of 20 seats in the House of Assembly and 10 seats in the Senate was abolished, as permitted by the Constitution, subject to a majority vote in the House. In October the 80 remaining members of the House of Assembly elected 20 candidates, who were nominated by ZANU, including 11 whites, to fill the vacant seats in the House of Assembly until the next general election. In the same month Parliament approved the replacement of the ceremonial presidency by an executive presidency. The post of Prime Minister was to be incorporated into the presidency. President Banana (who, as the only candidate, had been sworn in for a second term of office as President in April 1986) retired in December 1987, and at the end of that month Mugabe (the sole candidate) was inaugurated as Zimbabwe's first executive President.

In April 1989 Edgar Tekere, a former Secretary-General of ZANU, founded the Zimbabwe Unity Movement (ZUM), intending to challenge ZANU at the next general election. In December ZANU and ZAPU merged to form a single party, named the Zimbabwe African National Union—Patriotic Front (ZANU—PF). The united party aimed to establish a one-party state with a Marxist-Leninist doctrine. Mugabe was appointed President of ZANU—PF, while Nkomo became one of its two Vice-Presidents.

Presidential and parliamentary elections were held concurrently in March 1990; at these elections legislation approved in late 1989 came into effect, abolishing the Senate and increasing the number of seats in the House of Assembly from 100 to 150 (of which 120 were to be directly elected; 12 were to be allocated to presidential nominees, 10 to traditional Chiefs and eight to provincial governors). Mugabe won nearly 80% of all votes cast at the presidential election and at the parliamentary elections ZANU—PF secured 117 of the 120 elective seats in the House of Assembly. Although ZANU—PF won an outright victory, only 54% of the electorate voted, and representatives of the ruling party were accused of intimidating voters. Following the elections Nkomo was appointed as one of two Vice-Presidents (the other being Simon Muzenda, also a Vice-President of ZANU—PF), and remained one of the Senior Ministers in the President's Office. In August 1990 the state of emergency was finally revoked.

In March 1992 the House of Assembly approved legislation (the Land Acquisition Act) that permitted the compulsory acquisition of land by the Government; this was intended to facilitate the redistribution of land ownership from Europeans (who owned about one-third of farming land in early 1992) to Africans. In May 1993 the Government published a list of properties allotted for transfer to the State under the Act, provoking a strong protest from the white-dominated Commercial Farmers' Union (CFU). The High Court subsequently ruled against three white farmers who had attempted to prove that the confiscation of their land was unconstitutional. A lack of available funds impeded the progress of the Government's land resettlement programme.

ZANU—PF won an overwhelming victory at legislative elections in April 1995, receiving more than 82% of the votes cast and securing 118 of the 120 elective seats in the House of Assembly (55 of which were uncontested). The remaining two elective seats were taken by ZANU—Ndonga (formerly ZANU—Sithole). Following the allocation of nominated and reserved seats, ZANU—PF controlled 148 of the total 150 seats. However, only 54% of the electorate voted, and the elections were boycotted by eight opposition groups, including the ZUM. In mid-April Mugabe appointed a reorganized and enlarged Cabinet; Nkomo and Muzenda remained as Vice-Presidents.

Mugabe retained the presidency at an election in March 1996, winning 92.7% of the votes cast. Turn-out was, however, low. In late March Mugabe was sworn in for a third term as President. Between August and November there were a number of national strikes by public-sector workers demanding pay increases. In October it was announced that ZANU—PF was abandoning Marxism-Leninism as its guiding principle. In August the Government announced that the independence war veterans (an increasingly powerful lobby) were to be awarded a number of substantial, unbudgeted benefits.

In October 1997 Mugabe announced that the pace of the land resettlement programme would be accelerated, declaring that the constitutional right of white commercial farmers to receive full and fair compensation for confiscated land would not be honoured and (unsuccessfully) challenging the United Kingdom, in its role as former colonial power, to take responsibility for assisting them. A list of 1,503 properties to be reallocated forthwith was published in November. In January 1998, however, the IMF stipulated on an assurance from the Mugabe administration that it would respect the Constitution during the land resettlement procedure as a condition for the release of financial assistance; such an assurance was eventually given in March, when it was announced that 120 farms would be acquired in the near future in exchange for full and fair compensation. In August Mugabe introduced the second phase of the programme, to resettle 150,000 families on 1m. ha of land each year for the next seven years. Under pressure from Western donors, the Government agreed to reduce its plans, and was restricted to using 118 farms that it had already been offered. In November, however, 841 white-owned farms were ordered to be confiscated by the state: compensation was to be deferred. Pressure exerted by the IMF in light of a forthcoming release of aid brought an assurance from Mugabe that his administration would not break agreements for a gradual land reform programme; however, at the end of March 1999 the President contravened the agreement when he announced a new plan to acquire a further 529 white-owned farms. Mugabe accused the USA and the United Kingdom of 'destabilizing' Zimbabwe through their alleged control over the IMF, which was delaying financial assistance to the country. In May the Government agreed a plan that aimed to resettle 77,700 black families on 1m. ha by 2001. Some of this land was to come from the 118 farms that had already been offered. The remainder would be the result of uncontested acquisitions under the Government's reduced list of 800 farms for compulsory purchase. The plan was to be partially funded by the World Bank, and was broadly accepted by the white landowners' association.

Meanwhile, labour unrest escalated in December 1997, when a general strike was organized by the Zimbabwe Congress of Trade Unions (ZCTU), in protest at the imposition by the Government of three unpopular new taxes in order to finance the provision of benefits to war veterans (see above); the authorities capitulated, withdrawing two of the taxes immediately. Shortly after the demonstrations had subsided, Morgan Tsvangirai, the Secretary-General of ZCTU, was attacked in his office by unknown assailants. The weak Zimbabwe currency and soaring food prices aggravated the nation-wide mood of discontent. In January 1998 riots erupted in most of the country's urban areas in protest at rises in the price of maize meal, the staple food. In response Mugabe agreed to withdraw the most recent price increase. However, the army was deployed to suppress the disturbances and was authorized to open fire on protesters; nine people were reportedly killed and some 800 rioters were arrested. The ZCTU organized a further two-day strike in March, to protest against the continuing rise in living costs.

In September 1998 threats for a five-day stoppage in support of demands for tax cuts resulted in government concessions. Meanwhile, further consumer price increases were followed by renewed rioting. A series of one-day strikes over pay were called by unions, and action took place until banned by Mugabe. In February 1999, however, the ban was ruled to be illegal. In that month growing unrest followed an address to the nation by Mugabe in which he attacked the judiciary, the independent media and 'British agents'. He also accused whites of 'fomenting unrest' and disturbances continued throughout 1999.

Meanwhile, in October 1998 the Government discussed potential amendments to Zimbabwe's Constitution with an opposition grouping, known as the National Constitutional Assembly (NCA). In March 1999 Mugabe appointed a commission of inquiry to make recommendations for a new constitution. The NCA refused to participate, owing to the alleged high risk of presidential manipulation.

An international constitutional conference was held in November 1999, but several experts suspected that the draft constitution had already been written, and that they had been invited primarily to give the process global credibility. In late November a document bearing no relation to that prepared by the 400-member constitutional commission, a drafting committee overseen by ZANU—PF having deleted crucial clauses (particularly relating to the reduction of the President's powers and the introduction of a parliamentary system), was declared to have been 'adopted by acclamation', despite vigorous protests. In January 2000 Mugabe announced that a referendum on the new constitution would take place on 12–13 February. Confusion before the polls over such issues as eligibility to vote and the location of polling stations was believed by the opposition to have been orchestrated by ZANU—PF to maximize Mugabe's chances of victory. Despite fears that a lack of supervision of the ballot had led to widespread irregularities on ZANU—PF's part, 54.6% of the 26% of the electorate who participated in the polls voted to reject the draft constitution. The level of participation was highest in urban areas where support for the recently formed opposition party, the Movement for Democratic Change (MDC), led by Tsvangirai, was strong.

The Government embarked on a campaign to restore its popularity prior to the legislative elections, which, it was announced in March 2000, were to be held in May rather than April. Illegal occupations of white-owned farms by black 'war veterans' (many of whom, too young to have taken part in the war of independence, were suspected of having been paid to participate), which began in late February, were rumoured to have been organized by the Government in an attempt to regain support through the land issue. The security forces refused to act against the occupiers, declaring that the 'political issue' lay outside their jurisdiction. Occupations increased, and the police also failed to take steps to evict the protesters, following a ruling by the High Court in mid-March in favour of the white farmers (which was ignored by the veterans). Mugabe repeatedly denied that his administration was behind the occupations, but made no secret of his support for them. The invasions became increasingly violent, and two farmers were killed in April. The international community condemned the Government's increasingly militant stance, which also extended to the treatment of the opposition, in particular the MDC, which was subjected to a campaign of intimidation and aggression. A constitutional amendment approved in April stated that white farmers dispossessed of their land would have to apply to the 'former colonial power', the United Kingdom, for compensation (see below). Many farmers were aggrieved, as their land had been purchased under Zimbabwean law. In May Mugabe met with war veterans and white farmers and announced the creation of a land commission to redistribute farmland. Shortly afterwards, however, he signed a law allowing the seizure of 841 white-owned farms without compensation. Violence continued unabated throughout the month. In June a list was published of 804 farms that were to be confiscated. Farmers were to be granted approximately one month to contest the list.

Prior to legislative elections, which took place on 24–25 June 2000, there were reports of violence towards observers, and a UN team, sent to co-ordinate the polls, was recalled following obstruction by the Government. The authorities also refused to permit the accreditation of some 200 foreign monitors. ZANU—PF secured 48.6% of the votes cast and 62 of the 120 elective seats in the House of Assembly, the MDC won 47.0% of the ballot and 57 seats, while ZANU—Ndonga received one seat. Morgan Tsvangirai failed to win his constituency, as did the Ministers of Justice and Home Affairs. There were reports of widespread irregularities in the polls, which international observers declared not to have been free and fair. The MDC announced that it was to submit 10 dossiers listing alleged incidents of electoral fraud to the High Court. In total, the MDC challenged the results in 37 constituencies. In April 2001 the Court announced that results in two constituencies, including that contested by Tsvangirai, were to be nullified and new elections held; the MDC had previously abandoned proceedings relating to two other constituencies, and had been defeated in its challenge to the result in another. In June one further result was nullified, and one upheld.

Shortly after the legislative elections, Mugabe announced that some 500 additional white-owned farms would be appropriated for resettlement. In December 2000 a court ruling upheld previous opinions that declared the appropriation of white-owned farms without compensation payments to be unlawful, and urged the Government to produce a feasible land-reform programme by June 2001; Mugabe announced that sufficient white-owned land had been appropriated for resettlement, but repeated his assertion that he would not accept court-imposed impediments to any further land-reform measures. Negotiations between the Government and farmers' representatives resumed in January 2001.

In March 2001 the Commonwealth announced that it would send a delegation comprising the foreign ministers of Australia, Barbados and Nigeria to Zimbabwe for discussions with the Government. Mugabe refused to meet the delegation, however, claiming that the decision had been inspired by the United Kingdom. Similar criticisms were made of an attempt by the European Union (EU, see p. 255) to establish a dialogue with Zimbabwe regarding its record on human rights. In April Mugabe dismissed speculation that he would resign and arrange a presidential election for July, by stating that he intended to contest the election at its scheduled time in 2002. In early June Mugabe urged war veterans to intensify the occupation of white-owned farms, and in the following days attacks against such farms throughout the country were reported to have increased, causing the death of at least one farm worker. The Zimbabwean Government criticized US and British media coverage of the events, and in mid-June it imposed severe restrictions on journalists visiting the country. Later that month the Government listed a further 2,030 farms for compulsory acquisition, and in early August Joseph Made, the Minister of Lands, Agriculture and Rural Development announced the Government's intention to appropriate 8.3m. ha of commercial farmland. Further unrest occurred later that month in the north of the country, where approximately 100 white-owned farms were reported to have been evacuated following attacks by war veterans.

In early September 2001 a meeting of Commonwealth ministers was convened in Abuja, Nigeria, to discuss Mugabe's land resettlement programme; it was agreed that illegal farm seizures would cease and that international donors would compensate white farmers for the distribution of their land to landless black families. The agreement was broadly supported by both ZANU—PF and the MDC. By the end of September, however, more than 20 new farm invasions were reported to have taken place, resulting in several deaths, and talks between the Government and the CFU collapsed. Mugabe's intention to disregard the terms of the Abuja agreement became apparent in early October, when he ordered the Supreme Court to recognize the land reform programme as legal, reversing the ruling of December 2000; widespread criticism was directed at the Government for its manipulation of the judiciary. Commonwealth ministers and officials visited Zimbabwe later in October 2001 to monitor the Government's adherence to the Abuja agreement, but failed to persuade the Government to comply with its terms. Government repression intensified in November, when it amended the Land Act by decree. According to the revised legislation, any farm issued with a 'notice of acquisition' would become the property of the state with immediate effect; previously, a farm owner had been served 90 days' notice.

In November 2001 the Government ordered *The Daily News* to close its offices, alleging financial irregularities; it was widely believed, however, that the measure was taken to suppress criticism of the Government. The editor of that newspaper was charged with false reporting and undermining the Government in October 2002, under the Public Order and Security Act (see below), and resigned in December. In December 2001 Mugabe was nominated as the presidential candidate of ZANU—PF and announced that the election would take place in March 2002.

International concern about the situation in Zimbabwe intensified at the end of 2001. South African President Thabo Mbeki expressed doubts about whether conditions were suitable for a free and fair election, and the Commonwealth Ministerial Action Group on the Harare Declaration, meeting in London, United Kingdom, in late December, warned the Zimbabwean Government that it risked suspension from the organization unless it ended violent land seizures and political intimidation of the media and opposition groups. Despite Zimbabwe's growing isolation in the international community, in January 2002 further controversial legislation, aimed at suppressing opposition to Mugabe, was introduced: the Public Order and Security Bill prohibited the publication of documents that incited public disorder or undermined the security services, and banned public gatherings that incited rioting; the General Laws Amendment Bill prohibited foreign and independent missions from monitoring the elections, and forbade voter education (the Bill was repealed by the Supreme Court in February, following a challenge from the MDC); and the Access to Information Bill made it an offence for foreign news services to report from Zimbabwe unless authorized by the Zimbabwean Government. The EU finally imposed so-called 'smart' sanctions on Zimbabwe in mid-February, after the leader of its electoral observer mission was expelled from the country. The sanctions included an embargo on the sale of arms to Zimbabwe, the suspension of €128m. of aid scheduled to be disbursed during 2002–07, and the freezing of the assets of 19 Zimbabwean officials, including Mugabe, who were also prohibited from visiting any EU state; the USA imposed similar measures several days later. In July the EU applied the sanctions to a further 53 people, including all cabinet members. The EU extended sanctions for a further 12 months in February 2003, although Mugabe attended the Franco-African summit in Paris, France, later that month. The USA also extended its sanctions to more than 70 senior officials in March 2003.

The presidential election took place on 9–10 March 2002, but voting was extended to 11 March by the High Court, in response to a request from the MDC, which had claimed that the number of polling stations in areas with strong MDC support was inadequate, and that certain stations had closed on 10 March before many people had been able to vote. Mugabe was declared the winner on 13 March, with 56.2% of the valid votes cast; Tsvangirai secured 42.0%. Independent observers were divided in their judgement of whether the election was free and fair; most observers from African countries declared the election result legitimate, while the Norwegian delegation (the only European representatives) and independent Zimbabwean observers condemned the result and reported widespread electoral fraud and intimidation of the electorate and of observers by members of ZANU—PF. The MDC claimed that a number of its agents had been abducted from certain polling stations and detained by the police. Tsvangirai mounted a legal challenge to have the results declared null and void; however, after a protracted case, the High Court eventually ruled against him in 2005 and the Supreme Court dismissed his application in February 2006.

Prior to the presidential election the Commonwealth had nominated the Nigerian President, Olusegun Obasanjo, President Mbeki and the Australian Prime Minister, John Howard, to consider the conduct of the election and to formulate the organization's response. Mbeki and Obasanjo visited Zimbabwe following the election and urged Mugabe and the MDC to form a government of national unity; however, the MDC refused to co-operate unless the election was held again. The Commonwealth suspended Zimbabwe from meetings of the organization for one year in mid-March, stating that the election result had been undermined by politically motivated violence and that conditions did not permit the free will of the electorate to be expressed. (The suspension was extended for a further nine months in March 2003.) Immediately after the election the Government enacted the Access to Information and Protection of Privacy Act, which required all journalists reporting in Zimbabwe to be approved by the state; seven journalists had been detained under the Act by early May. In April the NCA organized demonstrations in support of demands for a new constitution and a rerun of the presidential election, at which more than 80 demonstrators were arrested. Violence directed at supporters of the MDC intensified following the election, allegedly committed by ZANU—PF supporters, and more than 50 people were reported to have been killed between the election and the end of April.

Land seizures also escalated, and in late March 2002 the Government listed almost 400 white-owned farms for compulsory acquisition, bringing the area scheduled for redistribution to the black population to around 85% of total commercial farmland. In June Mugabe issued an order listing some 2,900 white-owned farms for seizure; farmers were obliged to cease working their land on 25 June, or face up to two years' imprisonment, and to leave their properties by early August. Some 860 farmers had vacated their properties by the deadline, while 1,700 refused to leave. (Some 300 had left their farms temporarily to avoid confrontation.) In a speech in August Mugabe stated that white farmers who were 'loyal' to the Government had the option of staying, although later that month it was reported that almost 200 farmers had been arrested for refusing to leave their properties, while others had gone into hiding. In September the Land Acquisition Act was amended to allow the eviction of white farmers within seven days, as opposed to the 90 days previously required.

In April 2002 ZANU—PF and the MDC engaged in talks in an effort to end the political crisis, but negotiations collapsed in the following month when ZANU—PF withdrew, citing the MDC's petition to the High Court, seeking to overturn the election results, which ZANU—PF regarded as unlawful. In August Mugabe dissolved his Cabinet and appointed a new Government a few days later, retaining several ministers from the previous administration. In February 2003, following their arrest the previous year, the trial of Tsvangirai and two other senior MDC officials for allegedly plotting to assassinate Mugabe began in Harare, but was adjourned until May. In March the MDC led a 'mass action' against the Government, aimed at forcing it to repeal what the party called repressive legislation and to release political prisoners; the Government claimed that the MDC had detonated bombs in Kadoma, south-west of Harare, and it was reported that up to 500 members of the opposition had been arrested and many more driven from their homes and beaten. In early June Tsvangirai was arrested at the conclusion of further demonstrations against the Government organized by the MDC, reportedly in connection with statements he had made in May; he was released on bail in late June.

In September 2003 the closure of *The Daily News*, owing to the failure of its publisher to register with the Government's Media and Information Commission (MIC), provoked international condemnation. A court ruling that the newspaper should be allowed to resume publication pending the result of an application that it had made to register with the MIC was initially disregarded by the police. Publication of *The Daily News* did subsequently resume, despite the refusal of the MIC to grant it a licence, but was suspended again in February 2004 when the Supreme Court confirmed that its unlicensed appearance was illegal. (By early 2005 four newspapers had been closed under the Act: *The Daily News*, the *Daily News on Sunday*, *The Tribune* and *The Weekly Times*.)

The death, in September 2003, of Simon Muzenda, one of Zimbabwe's two Vice-Presidents, reignited speculation regarding an eventual successor to President Mugabe. It was reported in December that leading ZANU—PF officials had persuaded Mugabe to retire before the expiry of his term of office in 2008, but the annual conference of the party, held in December, elicited no indication of the President's intentions in this respect. Nor was there any confirmation of speculation that ZANU—PF was willing to engage in dialogue with the MDC in order to resolve Zimbabwe's political crisis.

From October 2003 increased concern was expressed at divisions within the Commonwealth over the political crisis in Zimbabwe. The decision, taken at a meeting of Commonwealth Heads of Government held in Abuja, Nigeria, in December, to extend Zimbabwe's suspension from the organization indefinitely, until the country had restored democracy and the rule of law, confirmed the existence of a rift between African Commonwealth members and their Western counterparts. The 12 members from southern Africa criticized the decision, and Mbeki claimed that other Commonwealth members had failed to understand the question of land ownership in Zimbabwe and that they were mistaken in their belief that the presidential election held in Zimbabwe in 2002 had been unfair. Zimbabwe, for its part, announced its decision to withdraw from the Commonwealth shortly before the conclusion of the Heads of Government meeting.

In January 2004, giving evidence for the first time in his trial for treason, Tsvangirai denied that he had ever plotted to assassinate President Mugabe or to overthrow the Government. Tsvangirai was acquitted of the assassination charges in mid-October 2004; the outstanding treason charge was finally dropped in August 2005. In February 2004 a cabinet reorganization was effected in which, among other changes, Herbert Murerwa was replaced as Minister of Finance and Economic Development by Chris Kuruneri. In late April, however, Kuruneri was arrested on charges of illegally trading foreign currency; his arrest was stated by the authorities to be part of an anti-corruption campaign inaugurated earlier in the year; Murerwa, who was now serving as the Minister of Higher Education and Technology, was subsequently appointed to replace Kuruneri on an acting basis. (Kuruneri's trial began in May 2005. The Governor of the Reserve Bank of Zimbabwe, Gideon Gono, gave evidence that the currency in question had been legitimately obtained by Kuruneri. Kuruneri was granted bail in late July but placed under house arrest.) Meanwhile, in February 2004 the EU renewed sanctions imposed upon the Mugabe regime, extending the travel ban and assets freeze to cover a total of 95 Zimbabwean officials, and in March the USA imposed a further series of sanctions on Zimbabwe, notably targeting government-owned enterprises.

In late 2004 a power struggle developed within ZANU—PF. There was speculation that Mugabe was actively assigning key posts in the administration to members of his own Zezuru clan, replacing members of the majority Karanga clan. In December 2004 the country's voting constituencies were redrawn, reportedly increasing the number of seats available in traditional ZANU—PF strongholds, while reducing those available in areas where the MDC commanded popular support.

According to provisional results of the legislative elections held on 31 March 2005, Mugabe's ruling ZANU—PF party won 78 out of the 120 seats available, taking 56.4% of the vote. The opposition MDC took 41 seats with 42.1% of the votes cast. Under the Constitution the President could allocate 12 seats in the House of Assembly to candidates of his choosing and appoint the eight provincial governors; a further 10 seats were reserved for tribal chiefs, also loyal to Mugabe. The overall result therefore gave ZANU—PF a two-thirds majority in the Assembly which would allow Mugabe to amend the Constitution. International observers from the African Union (AU, see p. 172) and the Southern African Development Community (SADC, see p. 400) endorsed the results; observers from the Commonwealth, the EU and the USA were not invited owing to their perceived hostility towards the Mugabe Government. The Governments of Malawi, Mozambique, South Africa and Zambia were among those who accepted the elections as free and fair; however, the results were dismissed by Australia, the EU and the USA. (The observers from the AU later reversed their opinion and called for investigations into allegations of electoral fraud.) The MDC contested the results citing electoral irregularities in 76 out of the 120 constituencies, and claimed that it should, in fact, have won 94 seats. In mid-April the MDC released a report alleging that some 134,000 people had been turned away from polling stations and that ballot boxes had been filled with votes for ZANU—PF after the polls had closed. The MDC filed petitions at the Electoral Court challenging the results in 13 constituencies. Meanwhile, the outgoing Minister responsible for Land Reform and Resettlement, John Nkomo, announced that white farmers who had lost their farms during the resettlement programme would be compensated for the value of assets and improvements but not for the land itself, which the Government maintained was the responsibility of the United Kingdom. It was estimated that the white population in Zimbabwe had fallen from 200,000 in 2000 to around 25,000 at March 2005; of these some 500 were farmers.

The EU renewed its sanctions against Zimbabwe in February 2005, but in early April Italy was obliged to allow Mugabe to travel through the country to the Vatican City in order to attend the funeral of the Supreme Pontiff of the Roman Catholic Church, Pope John Paul II. The Zimbabwe Government exploited international treaties which obliged countries to allow foreign government officials to travel to international organizations hosted within those countries. In July 2005 Gono and Murerwa both attended a meeting of the IMF in New York, USA, despite sanctions which otherwise would have prevented them travelling to that country, while in October Mugabe attended a conference of the Food and Agriculture Organization in Rome, Italy.

In April 2005 Mugabe announced his new Government, which he described as a 'development Cabinet': the former Zimbabwean ambassador to the United Kingdom, Simbarashe Mumbengegwi, was appointed Minister of Foreign Affairs replacing Stanislaus Mudenge, who moved to head the Ministry of Higher and Tertiary Education; Murerwa was confirmed as Minister of Finance. Sixteen ministers retained their portfolios, including Patrick Chinamasa as Minister of Justice, Legal and Parliamentary Affairs. Didymus Mutasa was appointed Minister of State for National Security and head of the Central Intelligence Organization, and in mid-May also assumed overall responsibility for the land redistribution programme.

In late May 2005 the Government launched Operation Murambatsvina ('Sweep Away the Rubbish'), which targeted black market trading—principally in foreign currency and fuel—and 'general lawlessness'. The MDC claimed that it was a punitive action against the urban poor who had voted against ZANU—PF in the elections in March. Shanty towns were razed to the ground in Harare and other major cities, including Bulawayo and Gweru. The operation attracted widespread international condemnation and, according to a report by UN-Habitat published in late July, some 700,000 people were made homeless; however, the Government refused offers of humanitarian aid. In late June President Mugabe announced that some Z.$3,000,000m. was to be spent on new housing and commercial premises under a three-year redevelopment programme entitled Operation Garikai/Hlalani Kuhle. (In September 2006 the human rights organization Amnesty International reported that the Government had not met its housing obligations as just 3,325 new homes had been built, while 92,460 had been demolished.) In late 2005 Vice-President Mujuru announced the official end of Operation Murambatsvina and appealed for humanitarian aid; nevertheless the Government reaffirmed that it would not make an official appeal to the UN for food aid.

In late August 2005 the House of Assembly approved a bill which provided for a number of changes to the Constitution. The bill also included legislation designed to conclude the land redistribution programme: courts would no longer be able to hear appeals on land acquisition and once listed for appropriation land would immediately become state property. (However, in early 2006 banks were still refusing to extend loans to resettled farmers because they were not in possession of the title deeds to the land.) Under the bill it became a criminal offence for Zimbabweans to endorse sanctions or military action against their country, and the Zimbabwe Electoral Commission (ZEC) was established in place of the Electoral Supervisory Commission. In addition, the bill provided for the reintroduction of a 66-member Senate (abolished in 1990) as the second chamber of the legislature; senatorial elections were held in late November 2005. The MDC was deeply divided over the issue of participating in the elections. Tsvangirai opposed electoral participation, advocating mass protests and 'democratic resistance'; however, a faction led by the party's Secretary-General, Welshman Ncube, fielded 26 candidates. ZANU—PF won 43 of the 50 elected seats, receiving 73.7% of the vote; MDC candidates took the remaining seven seats with 20.3% of the vote. The MDC effectively split in two, a 'pro-Senate' faction electing Arthur Mutumbara as its leader in February 2006. The rump of the party re-elected Tsvangirai as its President in late March at a conference reportedly attended by some 15,000 supporters.

In July 2006 five senior members of the MDC were injured in an attack as they left the Harare suburb of Mabvuku. A statement from the pro-Senate faction blamed the attack on Tsvangirai. However, Tsvangirai's spokesman suggested that the attack was the work of government agents attempting to sow division within the party. In late December Lovemore Madhuku, the Chairman of the NCA, was the victim of an arson attack on his home; the NCA alleged that it was the third attempt on Madhuku's life in four years and the attack occurred as the organization was mobilizing supporters to resist a proposed extension of Mugabe's term in office until 2010. An alliance of 23 opposition parties, church and civic groups had agreed to unite under the 'Save Zimbabwe' banner to campaign against any such extension.

Meanwhile, in March 2006 the IMF postponed a decision to expel Zimbabwe after it repaid US $120m. of its debt to the fund and pledged to clear its remaining obligations by November. In December the IMF recommended sharp reductions in public spending to lower inflation (the annual rate was recorded as 1,594% in January 2007) as well as the reform of exchange rates, the liberalization of price controls, the removal of restrictions on current account payments and the strengthening of private property rights. In August 2006 the Reserve Bank of Zimbabwe unexpectedly devalued the Zimbabwe dollar by 59.3%, and removed three zeros from the currency in an attempt to stem both corruption and hyperinflation. New banknotes were introduced later that month, which led to the seizure of more than $50m. worth of old banknotes at roadblocks and border posts in a crackdown on money launderers. In June the People's Republic of China had signed an agreement worth $1,300m. with Zimbabwe to help relieve an acute shortage of energy. In exchange for chrome from Zimbabwe, Chinese companies agreed to build new coal mines and three thermal power stations in the Zambezi valley on the Zambian border. In December Zimbabwe opened talks with China regarding a US $2,000m. loan in an attempt to secure much needed funding to boost its rapidly deteriorating economy.

In February 2007 President Mugabe dismissed Murerwa, and made a number of other changes to the Cabinet. Murerwa had been involved in a prolonged public disagreement with Gono over economic policies, in particular over the latter's refusal further to devalue the national currency, and had also been subjected to sustained criticism with regard to the subsidizing of the prices of grain, fuel and electricity; Mugabe had also denounced a number of Murerwa's decisions as 'disastrous'.

Between November 2006 and February 2007 more than 31,000 people were arrested in a major police crackdown, known as Operation Chikorokoza Chapera ('The End of Illegal Gold Dealings'). With the rate of unemployment reportedly standing at more than 80%, many Zimbabweans turned to gold- or diamond-prospecting following the collapse of commercial agriculture. Earlier in February the Government had announced that the last white farmers, numbering some 400, could remain on their land long enough to harvest their crops, even though the deadline to leave had passed. In the previous month the US-based Famine Early Warning System warned that Zimbabwe was likely to record a shortfall in maize of some 850,000 metric tons in 2007.

In mid-February 2007 police used tear gas and water cannons to prevent an MDC rally from proceeding in Harare, despite the organization obtaining a High Court order allowing the rally to take place. In late February anti-Government protesters took control of Budiriro township in Harare for several hours, setting up roadblocks of boulders and burning tyres. Political tensions intensified further when Tsvangirai was arrested in mid-March along with five other members of the MDC after riot police violently dispersed a 'Save Zimbabwe' prayer meeting in Harare's Highfield township. One activist was killed by the police and Tsvangirai suffered severe injuries while in police custody. The Government stated that the rally breached a recently introduced three-month ban on political gatherings. The incident provoked widespread international condemnation and demands for the release of those detained. Following an SADC summit in Dar es Salaam, Tanzania, in late March, it was announced that Mbeki had agreed to mediate between the MDC and the Zimbabwean Government; however, there were further reports of the mistreatment of MDC activists in police custody, provoking renewed opposition protests and repeated calls for Mugabe to relinquish the presidency. Nevertheless, in early April ZANU—PF declared that Mugabe would stand as the party's candidate in the 2008 presidential election. In mid-May Zimbabwe was elected to lead the UN Commission on Sustainable Development, prompting widespread objections from EU and US officials, who had opposed Zimbabwe's candidacy and questioned the nation's ability to assume such a role.

In early June 2007 constitutional amendments were proposed that would allow the legislative elections to be brought forward to coincide with the presidential election in 2008, harmonizing the presidential and parliamentary terms of office. The proposals also contained provisions for amendments to the structure of the House of Assembly and the Senate. The MDC opposed the proposals, which would, *inter alia*, allow the House of Assembly to nominate a new President should the incumbent stand down; under the existing structure, new elections would be required if the presidency were vacated. The MDC continued to be weakened by divisions between party members and in July it was announced that the two factions planned to field separate candidates in the presidential and legislative elections. Meanwhile, South African-led mediation between the MDC and ZANU—PF faltered amid worsening political and economic conditions; however, Mbeki denied that negotiations would collapse.

On 30 October 2007 a number of changes to the Constitution were officially adopted. With effect from the 2008 elections, the House of Assembly was to be enlarged to comprise 210 directly elected members, while the total number of members of the Senate was to be increased to 93. Of these, 60 were to be directly elected, five were to be nominated by the President and 10 seats were reserved for provincial governors; the remaining 18 were to include the President and the Deputy President of the Council of Chiefs and 16 traditional Chiefs. The presidential term was reduced to five years. However, talks between ZANU—PF and the opposition failed to produce any agreement on electoral procedures and negotiations continued. ZANU—PF representatives insisted that further negotiations, expected to continue throughout November, would not delay the March 2008 elections.

In January 2008 Mugabe confirmed that presidential and legislative elections would be held concurrently on 29 March, resulting in complaints from the opposition which continued to demand further electoral and constitutional reforms. The MDC announced that it was to organize a mass protest against the Government's decision not to delay elections, claiming that Mugabe had reneged on agreements reached during the earlier talks mediated by Mbeki. In February Simba Makoni, a senior member of ZANU—PF who had served as Minister of Finance and Economic Development in 2000–02, announced his intention to challenge Mugabe for the presidency; Makoni was later expelled from the ruling party.

Presidential and legislative elections took place as scheduled on 29 March 2008. According to results released by the ZEC, the faction of the MDC led by Tsvangirai secured 99 of the 210 seats in the House of Assembly, while ZANU—PF took 97 seats; the MDC faction led by Mutambara secured 10 seats. However, no immediate announcement was made regarding the outcome of the presidential poll. Widespread irregularities were reported and observers expressed concern that the delay in releasing official results was allowing the ruling party to manipulate ballot papers. A recount of the legislative votes in 23 constituencies—the majority of which had been awarded to the MDC after the first count—commenced in mid-April. Following completion of the recount, the ZEC confirmed that the original results remained unchanged. It was subsequently announced that the two MDC factions intended to reunite, consolidating that party's legislative majority. In mid-May it was reported that ZANU—PF party had filed legal petitions challenging the results in 53 constituencies, while the MDC had challenged the election of 52 deputies. Provisional results of the senatorial elections indicated that ZANU—PF had secured 30 of the 60 directly elected seats in the upper chamber; Tsvangirai's faction of the MDC (MDC—T) took 24 seats, while the Mutambara-led faction (MDC—M) won six.

On 2 May 2008 the ZEC released results of the disputed presidential election, according to which Tsvangirai secured 47.9% of the votes cast, while Mugabe took 43.2%. Makoni was placed third with 8.3%. As no candidate secured the requisite 50% of the votes, a second round of voting was to be conducted. Following an alleged campaign of violent intimidation of MDC supporters by ZANU—PF loyalists, Tsvangirai refused to confirm his participation in the run-off. On 10 May, however, Tsvangirai, who had temporarily relocated to South Africa, announced that he would take part in the second round. Nevertheless, the Chairman of the ZEC expressed doubt that the run-off would take place within three weeks of the declaration of the election results, as stipulated by the Electoral Law, and in mid-May it was announced that the second round would take place on 27 June. Tsvangirai withdrew his candidacy shortly before the election, claiming he was unwilling to ask his supporters to vote amid the increasing violence in which some 80 MDC members were reported to have been killed. On 23 June the UN Security Council issued a statement condemning the actions of ZANU—PF and ruled that a free and fair ballot would be 'impossible'. The UN Secretary-General, Ban Ki-Moon, expressed his support for the postponement of the second round; however, the run-off proceeded as scheduled with Mugabe as the sole candidate. On 29 June the ZEC announced that Mugabe had secured 85.5% of votes cast in the second round of voting and he was sworn in for a sixth term as President. However, turn-out was low and the MDC claimed that ZANU—PF had been coercing people to vote; Tsvangirai appealed to the international community to denounce the results.

Following an AU summit held in Sharm esh-Sheikh, Egypt, on 29 June–1 July 2008 African leaders failed to condemn the result of the presidential election, instead appealing to Mugabe and Tsvangirai to enter into negotiations to establish a government of national unity; by contrast, Western observers insisted that Mugabe should be removed from power and that financial assistance to Zimbabwe would be dependent on the formation of a government led by Tsvangirai. The AU's stance also appeared divided as it later emerged that several members, including Nigeria and Senegal, were keen to see a government formed on the basis of the results of the first round of the election, won by Tsvangirai. In August Lovemore Moyo of the MDC was elected Speaker of the House of Assembly, strengthening that party's position. However, following protracted negotiations involving SADC mediation, a power-sharing agreement was concluded in September. Under the terms of the so-called Interparty Political Agreement (IPA), Mugabe was to remain as President with executive authority and would chair the 31-member Cabinet (which would evaluate and adopt all government policies and approve all international agreements) and the National Security Council, while Tsvangirai would be appointed Prime Minister, also with executive authority, and would chair the Council of Ministers, which was to consist of all Cabinet ministers and would 'ensure that the Prime Minister properly discharges his responsibility to oversee the implementation of the work of government and assesses the implementation of Cabinet decisions'. The IPA also stipulated that there would be no reversal of the land redistribution policy. Meanwhile, in mid-March 2008 Mugabe had signed a controversial nationalization law requiring 51% of all companies operating in Zimbabwe to be owned by black Zimbabweans. The legislation also banned mergers and restructuring of businesses unless the majority share was owned by black interests.

Further lengthy negotiations regarding the composition of the Cabinet followed, again mediated by Mbeki and SADC, and in early February 2009 the House of Assembly and the Senate approved a number of transitional amendments to the Constitution. These confirmed the arrangements agreed under the IPA and also stipulated the division of senior roles among the three signature parties. Mugabe and/or ZANU—PF was to nominate two Vice-Presidents, while provision was made for the appointment of two Deputy Prime Ministers, one from the MDC—T and one from the MDC—M. On 11 February Tsvangirai was inaugurated as Prime Minister and Thokozani Khupe and Arthur Mutambara were sworn in as First and Second Deputy Prime Ministers, respectively. The installation of the Cabinet was delayed slightly owing to late changes to the list of appointments and the MDC—T questioning a number of nominations by ZANU—PF. The original agreement, providing for a 31-member cabinet, was amended to allow ZANU—PF and the MDC—T to share responsibility for the Ministry of Home Affairs. Kembo Mohadi was nominated for ZANU—PF while Giles Mutsekwa represented the MDC—T in that ministry. Eventually 35 ministers were sworn in on 13 February 2009 with ZANU—PF allocated a total of 17 ministers in the new Cabinet, including Mumbengegwi, who retained the foreign affairs portfolio, and Chinamasa who remained as Minister of Justice. Emmerson Mnangwagwa was named Minister of Defence. The MDC—T had 15 representatives in the Government, most notably Tendai Biti as Minister of Finance and Elton Mangoma as Minister of Economic Planning and Development. The MDC—M held three portfolios. Shortly before the inauguration ceremony, the designated Deputy Minister of Agriculture, Roy Bennett, of the MDC—T, was arrested and charged with treason. His detention delayed proceedings and threatened to undermine the projected image of unity within the Government, which was already viewed by many analysts with extreme suspicion.

In early March 2009 Tsvangirai was involved in a car accident in which his wife died. Despite rumours of ZANU—PF involvement in the incident, Tsvangirai insisted later that he suspected no foul play and Mugabe attended the funeral, offering his condolences and declaring his intention to co-operate in the power-sharing Government. However, in April Mugabe's commitment was called into question when he unilaterally announced that the ZANU—PF-controlled Ministry of Transport would absorb the functions hitherto carried out by the Minister for Information and Communications Technology, Nelson Chamisa of the MDC—T. Earlier that month the Government adopted a 100-day renewal plan aimed at improving ties with Western nations, in particular the USA and the United Kingdom. The Government also pledged to restore human rights, address security concerns, stabilize the economy and confirmed that it intended to introduce a new constitution before Parliament by February 2010. Furthermore, the Government announced that it would review the media legislation which currently prevented independent local and international media from operating freely within Zimbabwe.

Zimbabwe severed diplomatic relations with South Africa in September 1980 and subsequently played an important role in international attempts to stabilize southern Africa and to end apartheid in South Africa. In July 1987 the Cabinet rejected a proposal by Mugabe to impose sanctions against South Africa, and the Government opted instead for less stringent economic measures. South Africa is believed to have been responsible for intermittent attacks during the 1980s against the then banned African National Congress of South Africa (ANC) in Zimbabwe. A meeting between President Mugabe and a South African government official in April 1991 (following the implementation of a programme of political reforms by President F. W. de Klerk of South Africa in February 1990) constituted the first direct contact between the Zimbabwean and South African Governments since 1980. The two countries re-established diplomatic relations following the holding of the first democratic elections in South Africa in April 1994, and in March 1997 a mutual defence co-operation agreement was concluded. Relations deteriorated in 1998 owing to South Africa's opposition to Zimbabwe's military intervention in the civil war in the DRC (see below). Relations were also strained from 1999, owing to Zimbabwe's increasingly negative economic and political circumstances (see above). In February 2000 South Africa denied reports that it had offered a substantial loan to Zimbabwe to help the country to resolve its financial crisis. However, President Mbeki offered to negotiate on Zimbabwe's behalf with the IMF and the World Bank for emergency aid to prevent the collapse of the economy. By May the increasingly turbulent land reform situation in Zimbabwe had adversely affected South Africa's economy, prompting Mbeki to appeal to foreign donors to fund the transfer of white-owned land to black farmers.

During the 1980s and early 1990s Zimbabwe provided support to the Mozambican Government against Renamo rebels; in late 1992–early 1993, under the terms of the peace agreement in Mozambique (q.v.), Zimbabwean troops, who had been stationed in Mozambique since 1982, were withdrawn. During the mid-1990s a group of armed Zimbabwean dissidents, known as the Chimwenjes, were reportedly active in western Mozambique (see above). In January 1996 the Mozambican Government announced its intention to expel the rebels, and in January 1997 an accord was signed by representatives of Mozambique and Zimbabwe on the co-ordination of activities against the rebels. Plans for the repatriation of some 145,000 Mozambican refugees were announced in March 1993; this scheme, co-ordinated by the office of the UN High Commissioner for Refugees, was completed by May 1995.

Following an SADC summit in Harare in August 1998, the Zimbabwean Government dispatched troops and arms to the DRC to support the regime of President Laurent-Désiré Kabila against advancing rebel forces. Despite repeated summits attempting to find a peaceful solution to the conflict, by May 1999 it was reported that Zimbabwe had spent at least $500m. on the continuing unpopular military action. A cease-fire agreement was signed at Lusaka, Zambia, on 10 July and troop withdrawals were to follow within the next few months. However, a few days later, both the rebels and the allies of the DRC were accused of violating the accord. The Zimbabwe and DRC Governments unveiled a plan in September to establish a joint diamond and gold marketing venture to finance the war. Nevertheless, in early 2000 the Zimbabwean Government was reportedly unable to pay allowances to its troops fighting in the region

Statistical Survey

Source (unless otherwise stated): Central Statistical Office, Ministry of Finance and Economic Development, Blocks B, E and G, Composite Bldg, cnr Samora Machel Ave and Fourth St, Private Bag 7705, Causeway, Harare; tel. (4) 706681; fax (4) 728529; internet www.mofed.gov.zw.

Area and Population

AREA, POPULATION AND DENSITY

Area (sq km)	390,757*
Population (census results)	
18 August 1997	11,789,274
17 August 2002†	
Males	5,634,180
Females	5,997,477
Total	11,631,657
Population (UN estimates at mid-year)‡	
2006	12,459,000
2007	12,449,000
2008	12,463,000
Density (per sq km) at mid-2008	31.9

* 150,872 sq miles.
† Source: UN, *Population and Vital Statistics Report*.
‡ Source: UN, *World Population Prospects: The 2008 Revision*.

PRINCIPAL TOWNS
(population at census of August 1992)

Harare (capital)	1,189,103	Masvingo	51,743
Bulawayo	621,742	Chinhoyi (Sinoia)	43,054
Chitungwiza	274,912	Hwange (Wankie)	42,581
Mutare (Umtali)	131,367	Marondera (Marandellas)	39,384
Gweru (Gwelo)	128,037	Zvishavane (Shabani)	32,984
Kwekwe (Que Que)	75,425	Redcliff	29,959
Kadoma (Gatooma)	67,750		

Mid-2007 ('000, incl. suburbs, UN estimate): Harare 1,572 (Source: UN, *World Urbanization Prospects: The 2007 Revision*).

BIRTHS AND DEATHS
(annual averages, UN estimates)

	1990–95	1995–2000	2000–05
Birth rate (per 1,000)	35.6	32.0	30.3
Death rate (per 1,000)	9.5	14.8	18.7

Source: UN, *World Population Prospects: The 2008 Revision*.

2006: Birth rate 28.1 per 1,000; Death rate 18.4 per 1,000 (Source: African Development Bank).

2007: Birth rate 27.9 per 1,000; Death rate 17.9 per 1,000 (Source: African Development Bank).

Life expectancy (years at birth, WHO estimates): 43.4 (males 43.9; females 42.7) in 2006 (Source: WHO, *World Health Statistics*).

ECONOMICALLY ACTIVE POPULATION
(sample survey, persons aged 15 years and over, 1999)

	Males	Females	Total
Agriculture, hunting, forestry and fishing	1,215,661	1,584,839	2,800,500
Mining and quarrying	46,946	3,367	50,313
Manufacturing	283,090	94,667	377,757
Electricity, gas and water	10,158	n.a.	10,158
Construction	98,908	6,659	105,567
Trade, restaurants and hotels	154,198	178,341	332,539
Transport, storage and communications	93,289	8,288	101,577
Financing, insurance, real estate and business services	100,425	20,749	121,174
Community, social and personal services	320,020	258,505	578,525
Activities not adequately defined	63,052	124,286	187,338
Total employed	2,385,747	2,279,701	4,665,448
Unemployed	187,142	110,669	297,811
Total labour force	2,572,889	2,390,370	4,963,259

2004 ('000 employees, annual average): Agriculture, hunting, forestry and fishing 154; Mining and quarrying 50; Manufacturing 136; Electricity, gas and water 11; Construction 25; Trade, restaurants and hotels 114; Transport, storage and communications 38; Financing, insurance, real estate and business services 38; Public administration 68; Education 151; Health 26; Domestic 102; Other services 88; *Total employed* 999 (Source: IMF, *Zimbabwe: Selected Issues and Statistical Appendix*—October 2005).

Mid-2005 (estimates in '000): Agriculture, etc. 3,688; Total labour force 6,180 (Source: FAO).

Health and Welfare

KEY INDICATORS

Total fertility rate (children per woman, 2006)	3.3
Under-5 mortality rate (per 1,000 live births, 2006)	85
HIV/AIDS (% of persons aged 15–49, 2007)	15.3
Physicians (per 1,000 head, 2004)	0.2
Hospital beds (per 1,000 head, 2006)	3.0
Health expenditure (2006): US $ per head (PPP)	147
Health expenditure (2006): % of GDP	8.4
Health expenditure (2006): public (% of total)	52.6
Access to water (% of persons, 2006)	81
Access to sanitation (% of persons, 2006)	46
Human Development Index (2005): ranking	151
Human Development Index (2005): value	0.513

For sources and definitions, see explanatory note on p. vi.

ZIMBABWE

Agriculture

PRINCIPAL CROPS
('000 metric tons)

	2005	2006	2007
Wheat	134	144	128
Barley	43	54	48
Maize	915	1,485	953
Millet	28	63	44
Sorghum	38	101	76
Potatoes*	40	35	36
Cassava (Manioc)*	190	190	192
Beans, dry*	21	30	30
Sugar cane	3,290†	3,600*	3,600*
Soybeans (Soya beans)	60	71	112
Groundnuts, with shell	58	83	125
Sunflower seed	7	17	26
Oranges*	95	93	93
Bananas*	95	85	85
Coffee, green	4†	5†	5*
Tea*	22	22	22
Tobacco, unmanufactured	83.2	44.5	79.0

* FAO estimate(s).
† Unofficial figure.

Aggregate production ('000 metric tons, may include official, semi-official or estimated data): Total cereals 1,162 in 2005, 1,849 in 2006, 1,251 in 2007; Total roots and tubers 233 in 2005, 228 in 2006, 231 in 2007; Total vegetables (incl. melons) 181 in 2005, 161 in 2006, 162 in 2007; Total fruits (excl. melons) 244 in 2005, 222 in 2006, 222 in 2007.

Source: FAO.

LIVESTOCK
('000 head, year ending September, FAO estimates)

	2005	2006	2007
Horses	28.0	28.0	28.0
Asses	112	n.a.	n.a.
Cattle	5,300	5,400	5,400
Sheep	500	610	610
Pigs	630	625	630
Goats	2,960	3,000	3,000
Chickens	28,000	23,000	23,000

Source: FAO.

LIVESTOCK PRODUCTS
('000 metric tons, FAO estimates)

	2004	2005	2006
Cattle meat	94.5	94.5	97.0
Goat meat	13.3	13.2	13.0
Pig meat	30.0	30.4	27.5
Chicken meat	46.1	52.9	40.0
Cows' milk	242	242	250
Hen eggs	25	27	22

2007: Production assumed to be unchanged from 2006 (FAO estimates).
Source: FAO.

Forestry

ROUNDWOOD REMOVALS
('000 cubic metres, excl. bark)

	2005	2006	2007*
Sawlogs, veneer logs and logs for sleepers	632	578	578
Pulpwood*	83	81	81
Other industrial wood*	112	112	112
Fuel wood*	8,115	8,380	8,461
Total*	8,942	9,151	9,232

* FAO estimates.
Source: FAO.

SAWNWOOD PRODUCTION
('000 cubic metres, incl. railway sleepers)

	2004*	2005	2006
Coniferous (softwood)	354	594	533
Broadleaved (hardwood)	43	22	32
Total	397	617	565

* FAO estimates.
2007: Production assumed to be unchanged from 2006 (FAO estimates).
Source: FAO.

Fishing

('000 metric tons, live weight, FAO estimates)

	2003	2004	2005
Capture	13.0	13.0	13.0
Tilapias	0.8	0.8	0.8
Other freshwater fishes	1.8	1.8	1.8
Dagaas	10.4	10.4	10.4
Aquaculture	2.6	3.0	2.5
Total catch	15.6	16.0	15.5

2006: Catch assumed to be unchanged from 2005 (FAO estimates).

Note: Figures exclude aquatic animals, recorded by number rather than weight. The number of Nile crocodiles caught was: 73,707 in 2003; 60,185 in 2004; 69,374 in 2005; 75,961 in 2006.

Source: FAO.

Mining

('000 metric tons, unless otherwise indicated)

	2005	2006	2007*
Asbestos	122	97	100
Chromium ore	614.7	700.0	650.0
Coal	2,891	2,107	2,400
Cobalt ore (metric tons)†	281	26	50
Copper ore‡	2.6	2.6	3.0
Gold (kilograms)	14,024	11,354	6,750
Iron ore	377	104	110
Limestone	84	50*	50
Magnesite (metric tons)	893	939	2,000
Nickel ore (metric tons)	8,556	8,825	7,100
Phosphate rock	45.7	65.8	30.0
Silver (kilograms)	187	500*	250

* Estimated figure(s).
† Figures include metal content of compounds and salts and may include cobalt recovered from nickel-copper matte.
‡ Figures refer to the metal content of ores and concentrates.

Source: US Geological Survey.

ZIMBABWE

Industry

SELECTED PRODUCTS
('000 metric tons, unless otherwise indicated)

	2005	2006	2007*
Coke (metallurgical)	200	160	400
Cement	600	700	700
Pig-iron	129	25*	50
Ferro-chromium	218.1	200.7	200.0
Crude steel	107	24	100
Refined copper—unwrought (metric tons)*	2,570	2,581	3,000
Refined nickel—unwrought (metric tons)	13,200	14,500	14,000

* Estimated figure(s).

Source: US Geological Survey.

Raw sugar ('000 metric tons): 585 in 2000; 639 in 2001; 554 in 2002; 208 in 2003 (Source: UN, *Industrial Commodity Statistics Yearbook*).

Electric energy (net production, million kWh): 8,587 in 2002; 8,789 in 2003; 9,908 in 2004; 10,269 in 2005 (Source: UN, *Industrial Commodity Statistics Yearbook*).

Finance

CURRENCY AND EXCHANGE RATES

Monetary Units
100 cents = 1 Zimbabwe dollar (Z.$).

Sterling, US Dollar and Euro Equivalents (30 April 2008)
£1 sterling = Z.$59,004.01;
US $1 = Z.$30,000.00;
€1 = Z.$46,619.97;
Z.$1,000 = £0.02 = US $0.03 = €0.02.

Average Exchange Rate (Z.$ per US dollar)
2005   22,363.60
2006   164,361.00
2007   9,675,780.00

Note: On 1 August 2008 a redenomination of the Zimbabwe dollar was introduced whereby 10,000m. of the former currency was revalued at 1 dollar. In January 2009, in order to address the diminishing value of the national currency, a number of foreign currencies (including the US dollar, the euro, the British pound sterling, the South African rand and the Botswana pula), were also declared legal tender in Zimbabwe. A further massive redenomination of the Zimbabwe dollar was announced in February (whereby 1,000,000m. of the former currency was to be revalued at 1 dollar), but in April of the same year it was announced that legal use of the national currency was to be suspended for at least one year

BUDGET
(US $ million)

Revenue	2006	2007	2008*
Tax revenue	504	193	128
Personal income tax	122	56	22
Corporate income tax	88	33	18
Other direct taxes	50	17	3
Customs	68	12	45
Excise	17	8	6
Value-added tax	147	62	32
Other taxes	12	5	2
Non-tax revenue	17	9	5
Total	**520**	**202**	**133**

Expenditure†	2006	2007	2008*
Current expenditure	572	305	241
Salaries and wages	211	89	52
Interest payments	178	125	139
Foreign	114	122	138
Domestic	64	3	1
Grants and transfers	74	49	18
Other current expenditure	68	29	32
Capital expenditure	121	70	14
Total	**694**	**375**	**255**

* Estimates.
† Excluding net lending (US $ million): 2 in 2006; 9 in 2007; 3 in 2008 (estimate).

Source: IMF, *Zimbabwe: 2009 Article IV Consultation-Staff Report; Public Information Notice on the Executive Board Discussion; and Statement by the Executive Director for Zimbabwe* (May 2009).

INTERNATIONAL RESERVES
(US $ million at 31 December)

	2000	2001	2002
Gold*	45.4	27.5	22.7
IMF special drawing rights	0.2	—	—
Reserve position in IMF	0.4	0.4	0.4
Foreign exchange	192.5	64.3	82.9
Total	**238.5**	**92.2**	**106.0**

* Valued at a market-related price which is determined each month.

2003–08 (US $ million at 31 December): Reserve position in IMF 0.5.

Source: IMF, *International Financial Statistics*.

MONEY SUPPLY
(Z.$ '000 million at 31 December)

	2005	2006	2007
Currency outside banks	9,876	228,064	73,074,687
Demand deposits at deposit money banks	34,048	404,965	350,998,729
Total money (incl. others)	**44,746**	**636,799**	**425,445,154**

Note: The value of the Zimbabwe dollar has not been adjusted retrospectively to reflect subsequent redenominations.

Source: IMF, *International Financial Statistics*.

COST OF LIVING
(Consumer Price Index; base: 2000 = 100)

	2005	2006	2007
Food	35,321	420,485	123,813,058
All items (incl. others)	34,700	415,100	101,748,800

Source: ILO.

NATIONAL ACCOUNTS

Expenditure on the Gross National Product
(US $ million at current prices, estimates)

	2005	2006	2007
Government final consumption expenditure	142.52	215.94	204.67
Private final consumption expenditure	3,503.53	4,173.46	3,746.44
Gross capital formation	150.47	683.86	826.06
Total domestic expenditure	**3,796.52**	**5,073.26**	**4,777.17**
Exports of goods and services	1,458.18	1,715.97	1,370.60
Less Imports of goods and services	1,836.60	1,845.95	1,416.00
GDP in purchasers' values	**3,418.09**	**4,943.28**	**4,731.77**

Source: African Development Bank.

ZIMBABWE

Gross Domestic Product by Economic Activity
(Z.$ million, at factor cost)

	1997	1998	1999
Agriculture, hunting, forestry and fishing	17,042	27,135	35,812
Mining and quarrying	1,400	2,400	3,380
Manufacturing	16,208	20,708	30,538
Electricity and water	2,849	3,139	5,171
Construction	2,544	3,640	5,132
Trade, restaurants and hotels	17,163	22,652	36,261
Transport, storage and communications	5,192	6,712	11,373
Finance, insurance and real estate	9,797	15,679	26,917
Government services	13,640	16,916	22,913
Other services	5,320	6,806	8,273
Sub-total	91,155	125,762	185,770
Less Imputed bank service charges	1,149	1,242	1,357
Total	90,006	124,540	184,413

Note: The value of the Zimbabwe dollar has not been adjusted retrospectively to reflect subsequent devaluations and redenominations.

2007 (US $ million): Agriculture, hunting, forestry and fishing 264; Mining, manufacturing and utilities 350 (Manufacturing 217); Construction 23; Wholesale, retail trade, restaurants and hotels 202; Transport, storage and communications 131; Other services 629; *Total, all industries* 1,599 (Source: UN Statistics Division, National Accounts Main Aggregates Database).

BALANCE OF PAYMENTS
(US $ million, estimates)

	2007	2008
Exports of goods f.o.b.	1,804	1,651
Imports of goods f.o.b.	−2,113	−2,630
Trade balance	−310	−979
Non-factor services (net)	−144	−194
Balance on goods and services	−453	−1,173
Investment income (net)	−370	−369
Balance on goods, services and income	−823	−1,542
Private transfers (net)	440	637
Current balance	−383	−906
Official transfers (net)	42	73
Direct investment (net)	66	44
Portfolio investment (net)	−27	—
Long-term capital (net)	26	−173
Short-term capital (net)	−213	521
Net errors and omissions	−158	−171
Overall balance	−647	−612

Source: IMF, *Zimbabwe: 2009 Article IV Consultation-Staff Report; Public Information Notice on the Executive Board Discussion; and Statement by the Executive Director for Zimbabwe* (May 2009).

External Trade

PRINCIPAL COMMODITIES
(US $ million)

Imports f.o.b.	2005	2006	2007
Food and live animals	101.8	198.5	283.8
Cereals and preparations thereof	51.6	149.6	223.1
Maize, unmilled	30.6	94.6	150.3
Crude materials (inedible) except fuels	266.3	203.9	337.5
Metalliferous ore and metal scrap	202.5	160.2	168.9
Mineral fuels and related materials	313.3	572.6	646.5
Petroleum and related products	119.7	534.7	564.1
Chemicals and related products	145.0	360.3	453.2
Medicinal and pharmaceutical products	27.8	41.3	75.5
Fertilizers	13.0	42.8	65.6
Basic manufactures	769.8	292.9	376.0
Non-ferrous metals	586.9	23.5	26.5
Copper	458.6	17.1	19.7
Machinery and transport equipment	329.8	583.3	1,052.7
Road vehicles	100.5	218.6	335.0
Miscellaneous manufactured articles	53.7	98.0	101.4
Total (incl. others)	2,072.3	2,576.6	3,594.4

Exports	2005	2006	2007
Food and live animals	136.7	635.5	284.6
Vegetables and fruit	40.9	509.1	154.7
Beverages and tobacco	219.8	293.5	278.7
Crude materials (inedible) except fuels	307.6	1,273.7	808.2
Textile fibres	52.5	132.1	132.2
Cotton	50.3	89.8	94.9
Mineral fuels and related materials	3.8	2,432.8	21.3
Coal, coke and briquettes	2.5	2,432.5	16.7
Chemicals and related products	26.7	296.9	48.0
Dyeing, colouring and tanning materials	0.4	263.5	2.7
Basic manufactures	324.2	659.4	805.8
Iron and steel	188.3	349.2	417.9
Non-ferrous metals	65.6	115.3	205.8
Nickel	62.0	110.8	196.1
Machinery and transport equipment	27.9	227.6	355.7
Road vehicles	6.2	17.3	179.0
Miscellaneous manufactured articles	138.9	455.4	569.8
Commodities and transactions not classified elsewhere	207.9	151.9	137.5
Total (incl. others)	1,393.6	6,427.4	3,310.2

Source: UN, *International Trade Statistics Yearbook*.

/ ZIMBABWE

PRINCIPAL TRADING PARTNERS
(US $ million)

Imports f.o.b.	2005	2006	2007
Botswana	104.6	212.1	409.0
China, People's Repub.	50.6	105.5	206.5
Congo, Democratic Repub.	77.7	1.6	7.1
Germany	46.7	60.7	49.1
India	35.1	31.4	40.8
Japan	27.5	19.0	31.8
Kuwait	83.2	97.1	167.9
Malawi	2.9	17.9	171.6
Mozambique	204.5	198.3	172.2
South Africa	310.1	1,172.1	1,537.9
Switzerland (incl. Liechtenstein)	12.0	57.3	19.7
United Arab Emirates	27.5	24.3	29.9
United Kingdom	34.4	91.6	106.7
USA	29.4	240.7	123.3
Zambia	846.8	45.3	110.5
Total (incl. others)	2,072.3	2,576.6	2,594.4

Exports f.o.b.	2005	2006	2007
Belgium	33.9	53.7	28.4
Botswana	29.6	290.4	200.9
China, People's Repub.	70.7	56.0	63.8
Congo, Democratic Repub.	7.2	948.3	84.0
France (incl. Monaco)	8.0	91.5	9.3
Germany	28.7	83.9	39.0
Italy	17.7	25.9	26.6
Malawi	25.8	43.9	57.7
Mozambique	39.2	366.5	431.4
Netherlands	41.2	900.5	153.1
Russia	16.5	10.6	48.6
South Africa	578.2	1,109.3	1,238.9
Switzerland (incl. Liechtenstein)	89.1	61.1	133.5
United Kingdom	73.4	266.4	245.3
USA	96.6	187.0	78.0
Zambia	77.4	1,649.0	124.3
Total (incl. others)	1,393.6	6,427.4	3,310.2

Source: UN, *International Trade Statistics Yearbook*.

Transport

RAIL TRAFFIC
(National Railways of Zimbabwe, including operations in Botswana)

	1998	1999	2000
Total number of passengers ('000)	1,787	1,896	1,614
Revenue-earning metric tons hauled ('000)	12,421	12,028	9,422
Gross metric ton-km (million)	9,248	8,962	6,953
Net metric ton-km (million)	4,549	4,375	3,326

ROAD TRAFFIC
('000 motor vehicles in use, estimates)

	1998	1999	2000
Passenger cars	540	555	573
Commercial vehicles	37	38	39

2002: Passenger cars 570,866; Lorries and vans 84,456; Motorcycles 45.

CIVIL AVIATION
(traffic on scheduled services)

	2002	2003	2004
Kilometres flown (million)	8	6	6
Passengers carried ('000)	251	201	225
Passenger-km (million)	674	437	500
Total ton-km (million)	87	58	67

Source: UN, *Statistical Yearbook*.

Tourism

VISITOR ARRIVALS BY NATIONALITY

	2004	2005	2006
Australia and New Zealand	28,540	13,369	20,023
Botswana	135,860	189,751	86,117
Canada and USA	60,093	39,779	36,855
Malawi	81,247	55,965	78,039
Mozambique	299,122	183,792	114,988
South Africa	653,352	626,677	1,516,135
United Kingdom	42,260	42,525	22,045
Zambia	220,060	194,311	146,143
Total (incl. others)	1,854,488	1,558,501	2,286,572

Tourism receipts (US $ million, incl. passenger transport): 194 in 2004; 99 in 2005; 338 in 2006.

Source: World Tourism Organization.

Communications Media

	2005	2006	2007
Telephones ('000 main lines in use)	328.0	335.6	344.5
Mobile cellular telephones ('000 subscribers)	647.1	849.1	1,225.7
Internet users ('000)	1,000	1,220	1,351.0
Broadband subscribers ('000)	10.2	10.2	15.2

Personal computers ('000 in use): 1,200 in 2005.

Radio receivers ('000 in use): 4,488 in 1999.

Television receivers ('000 in use): 410 in 2000.

Facsimile machines: 4,100 in use in year ending 30 June 1995.

Daily newspapers: 2 (average circulation 209,000 copies) in 1996; 3 in 2004.

Sources: UNESCO, *Statistical Yearbook*; UNESCO Institute for Statistics; UN, *Statistical Yearbook*; Inter-national Telecommunication Union.

Education

(2002/03, unless otherwise indicated)

	Institutions*	Teachers	Students
Pre-primary	n.a.	19,588	448,124
Primary	4,699	64,001†	2,445,520†
Secondary	1,539	33,964	831,488†
Tertiary	n.a.	n.a.	55,689

* 1998 figures.
† 2005/06.

Source: mainly UNESCO Institute for Statistics.

Adult literacy rate (UNESCO estimates): 91.2% (males 94.1%; females 88.3%) in 2007 (Source: UNESCO Institute for Statistics).

Directory

The Constitution

The Constitution of the Republic of Zimbabwe took effect at independence on 18 April 1980. Amendments to the Constitution must have the approval of two-thirds of the members of both the House of Assembly and the Senate. The provisions of the 1980 Constitution (with subsequent amendments) are summarized below. Amendments pertaining to the transitional period were approved in February 2009. These amendments are summarized at the foot of this section.

THE REPUBLIC

Zimbabwe is a sovereign republic and the Constitution is the supreme law.

DECLARATION OF RIGHTS

The declaration of rights guarantees the fundamental rights and freedoms of the individual, regardless of race, tribe, place of origin, political opinions, colour, creed or sex.

THE PRESIDENT

Executive power is vested in the President, and may be exercised by him/her directly or through the Cabinet, a Vice-President, a Minister or a Deputy Minister. The President is Head of State, Head of Government and Commander-in-Chief of the Defence Forces. The President appoints no more than two Vice-Presidents and other Ministers and Deputy Ministers, to be members of the Cabinet. The President holds office for five years and is eligible for re-election.

PARLIAMENT

Legislative power is vested in the Legislature, which consists of the President and a bicameral Parliament, comprising the Senate and the House of Assembly. The Senate comprises 93 members, of whom 60 are directly elected by universal adult suffrage (six are elected in each of the 10 provinces by voters registered in the 60 senatorial constituencies), five are nominated by the President, 10 are provincial governors, two are the President and the Deputy President of the Council of Chiefs and 16 are traditional Chiefs. The life of the Senate is ordinarily to be five years. The House of Assembly comprises 210 members, all of whom are directly elected by universal adult suffrage. The life of the House of Assembly is ordinarily to be five years.

OTHER PROVISIONS

A Public Protector shall be appointed by the President, acting on the advice of the Judicial Service Commission, to investigate complaints against actions taken by employees of the Government or of a local authority.

Chiefs shall be appointed by the President, and shall form a Council of Chiefs from their number in accordance with customary principles of succession.

Other provisions relate to the Judicature, Defence and Police Forces, public service and finance.

TRANSITIONAL AMENDMENTS AND PROVISIONS

Following the unanimous approval of the Zimbabwe Amendment (No. 19) Bill by the House of Assembly and the Senate on 5 February 2009, certain transitional amendments to the Constitution, pertaining to the Interparty Political Agreement signed on 15 September 2008, were adopted. These stated that the President, the Prime Minister and the Cabinet shall all exercise executive authority. The Office of the President shall continue to be occupied by Robert Gabriel Mugabe, who chairs the Cabinet and the National Security Council and formally appoints the Vice-Presidents, the Prime Minister, the Deputy Prime Ministers, ministers and deputy ministers. Following consultation with the Vice-Presidents, the Prime Minister and the Deputy Prime Ministers, he also allocates ministerial portfolios. The Office of the Prime Minister shall be occupied by Morgan Tsvangirai, who chairs the Council of Ministers and is Deputy Chairperson of the Cabinet. There shall be two Vice-Presidents nominated by the President and/or the Zimbabwe African National Union—Patriotic Front (ZANU—PF). There shall be two Deputy Prime Ministers, one from the Movement for Democratic Change—Tsvangirai (MDC—T) and one from the Movement for Democratic Change—Mutambara (MDC—M). Provision is made for the nomination of ministers and deputy ministers by ZANU—PF, the MDC—T and the MDC—M. The President shall, at his discretion, appoint five persons to the existing positions of presidential senatorial appointments. An additional six appointed senatorial posts shall be created and filled by persons appointed by the President, four of whom shall be nominated by MDC—T and two by the MDC—M. The Cabinet, *inter alia*, evaluates and adopts all government policies and the consequential programmes and approves all international agreements. The Council of Ministers, which consists of all Cabinet ministers, ensures that the Prime Minister properly discharges his responsibility to oversee the implementation of the work of government and assesses the implementation of Cabinet decisions.

The Government

HEAD OF STATE

President: ROBERT GABRIEL MUGABE (took office 31 December 1987; re-elected March 1990, 16–17 March 1996, 9–11 March 2002 and 27 June 2008).

THE CABINET
(April 2009)

The Cabinet comprises representatives of the Zimbabwe African National Union—Patriotic Front (ZANU—PF), the Movement for Democratic Change—Tsvangirai (MDC—T) and the Movement for Democratic Change—Mutambara (MDC—M).

Vice-President (ZANU—PF): JOSEPH MSIKA.
Vice-President (ZANU—PF): JOYCE MUJURU.
Prime Minister (MDC—T): MORGAN TSVANGIRAI.
First Deputy Prime Minister (MDC—T): THOKOZANI KHUPE.
Second Deputy Prime Minister (MDC—M): ARTHUR MUTAMBARA.
Minister of Agriculture (ZANU—PF): JOSEPH MADE.
Minister of Constitutional and Parliamentary Affairs (MDC—T): ERIC MATINENGA.
Minister of Defence (ZANU—PF): EMMERSON MNANGWAGWA.
Minister of Economic Planning and Development (MDC—T): ELTON MANGOMA.
Minister of Education (MDC—M): DAVID COLTART.
Minister of Energy and Power Development (MDC—T): ELIAS MUDZURI.
Minister of the Environment (ZANU—PF): FRANCIS NHEMA.
Minister of Finance (MDC—T): TENDAI BITI.
Minister of Foreign Affairs (ZANU—PF): SIMBARASHE MUMBENGEGWI.
Minister of Health (MDC—T): HENRY MADZORERA.
Minister of Higher Education (ZANU—PF): I. STANISLAUS GORERAZVO MUDENGE.
Minister of Home Affairs (ZANU—PF): KEMBO MOHADI.
Minister of Home Affairs (MDC—T): GILES MUTSEKWA.
Minister of Industry and Commerce (MDC—M): WELSHMAN NCUBE.
Minister of Information and Publicity (ZANU—PF): WEBSTER SHAMU.
Minister for Information and Communications Technology (MDC—T): NELSON CHAMISA.
Minister of Justice (ZANU—PF): PATRICK ANTHONY CHINAMASA.
Minister of Labour (MDC—T): PAULINE MPARIWA.
Minister of Lands and Land Resettlement (ZANU—PF): HERBERT MURERWA.
Minister of Local Government (ZANU—PF): Dr IGNATIUS MORGAN CHIMINYA CHOMBO.
Minister of Mines (ZANU—PF): OBERT MPOFU.
Minister of National Housing (MDC—T): FIDELIS MHASHU.
Minister of Public Service (MDC—T): ELPHAS MUKONOWESHURO.
Minister of Public Works (MDC—T): THERESA MAKONE.
Minister of Regional Integration and International Trade (MDC—M): PRISCILLA MISIHAIRABWI.
Minister of Science and Technology (MDC—T): HENERI DZINOTYIWEI.
Minister of State Enterprises (MDC—T): SAMUEL SIPEPA NKOMO.
Minister of State for National Security in the President's Office (ZANU—PF): SYDNEY SEKERAMAYI.
Minister of State for Presidential Affairs (ZANU—PF): DIDYMUS MUTASA.
Minister of State in the Prime Minister's Office (MDC—T): GORDON MOYO.
Minister of Tourism (ZANU—PF): WALTER MZEMBI.
Minister of Transport (ZANU—PF): NICHOLAS GOCHE.

ZIMBABWE

Minister of Water Resources (MDC—T): JOEL GABBUZA.
Minister of Women's Affairs (ZANU—PF): OLIVIA MUCHENA.
Minister of Youth Development (ZANU—PF): SAVIOR KASUKUWERE.

In addition, there are 15 deputy ministers, eight from ZANU—PF, six from the MDC—T and one from the MDC—M.

The Constitution provides for the Attorney-General to serve as an ex officio member of the Cabinet.

MINISTRIES

Office of the President: Munhumutapa Bldg, Samora Machel Ave, Private Bag 7700, Causeway, Harare; tel. (4) 707091.
Office of the Vice-Presidents: Munhumutapa Bldg, Samora Machel Ave, Private Bag 7700, Causeway, Harare; tel. (4) 707091.
Ministry of Agriculture and Rural Resettlement: Ngungunyana Bldg, Private Bag 7701, Causeway, Harare; tel. (4) 700596; fax (4) 734646; internet www.moa.gov.zw.
Ministry of Defence: Defence House, cnr Kwame Nkuruma and 3rd Sts, Harare; tel. (4) 700155; fax (4) 727501; internet www.mod.gov.zw.
Ministry of Economic Development: New Complex Bldg, Government Composite Offices, cnr 3rd St and Samora Machel Ave, Harare; e-mail moed@gta.gov.zw; internet www.mofed.gov.zw.
Ministry of Education, Sports and Culture: Ambassador House, Union Ave, POB CY121, Causeway, Harare; tel. (4) 734051; fax (4) 707599; internet www.moesc.gov.zw.
Ministry of Energy and Power Development: Chaminuka Bldg, Private Bag 7758, Causeway, Harare; tel. (4) 791760; fax (4) 797956; e-mail energy@gta.gov.zw; internet www.energy.gov.zw.
Ministry of the Environment and Tourism: Kaguvi Bldg, 12th Floor, cnr 4th St and Central Ave, Private Bag 7753, Causeway, Harare; tel. (4) 701681; fax (4) 252673; e-mail metlib@zarnet.ac.zw; internet www.met.gov.zw.
Ministry of Finance: Blocks B, E and G, Composite Bldg, cnr Samora Machel Ave and Fourth St, Private Bag 7705, Causeway, Harare; tel. (4) 738603; fax (4) 792750; internet www.mofed.gov.zw.
Ministry of Foreign Affairs: Munhumutapa Bldg, Samora Machel Ave, POB 4240, Causeway, Harare; tel. (4) 727005; fax (4) 705161; internet www.zimfa.gov.zw.
Ministry of Health and Child Welfare: Kaguvi Bldg, Fourth St, POB CY198, Causeway, Harare; tel. (4) 730011; fax (4) 729154; internet www.mohcw.gov.zw.
Ministry of Higher Education and Technology: Government Composite Bldg, cnr Fourth St and Samora Machel Ave, Union Ave, POB UA275, Harare; tel. (4) 796440; fax (4) 790923; e-mail thesecretary@mhet.ac.zw; internet www.mhet.ac.zw.
Ministry of Home Affairs: Mukwati Bldg, Private Bag 7703, Causeway, Harare; tel. (4) 703641; fax (4) 707231; e-mail moha@gvt.co.zw; internet www.moha.gov.zw.
Ministry of Indigenization and Empowerment: Harare.
Ministry of Industry and International Trade: Mukwati Bldg, Fourth St, Private Bag 7708, Causeway, Harare; tel. (4) 702731; fax (4) 729311; internet www.miit.gov.zw.
Ministry of Information and Publicity: Linquenda House, Baker Ave, POB CY825, Causeway, Harare; tel. (4) 703894; fax (4) 707213.
Ministry of Justice, Legal and Parliamentary Affairs: Corner House, cnr Samora Machel Ave and Leopold Takawira St, Private Bag 7751, Causeway, Harare; tel. (4) 774620; fax (4) 772999; internet www.justice.gov.zw.
Ministry of Local Government, Public Works and National Housing: Mukwati Bldg, Fourth St, Private Bag 7755, Causeway, Harare; tel. (4) 7282019; fax (4) 708493; internet www.mlgpwud.gov.zw.
Ministry of Mines and Mining Development: ZIMRE Centre, 6th Floor, cnr Leopold Takawira St and Kwame Nkrumah Ave, Private Bag 7709, Causeway, Harare; tel. (4) 777022; fax (4) 777044; e-mail minsec@technopark.co.zw; internet www.mines.gov.zw.
Ministry of National Security: Chaminuka Bldg, POB 2278, Harare; tel. (4) 700501; fax (4) 732660.
Ministry of Policy Implementation: Harare.
Ministry of Public Service, Labour and Social Welfare: Compensation House, cnr Central Ave and Fourth St, Private Bag 7707, Causeway, Harare; tel. (4) 790871; fax (4) 794568; e-mail mpslsw@gta.gov.zw; internet www.pslsw.gov.zw.
Ministry of Transport and Communications: Kaguvi Bldg, 4th Central Ave, POB 595, Causeway, Harare; tel. (4) 252396; fax (4) 726661; e-mail angiekaronga@yahoo.co.uk; internet www.transcom.gov.zw.
Ministry of Water Resources, Infrastructural Development, and Small and Medium Enterprises: Kurima House, cnr Nelson Madela Ave and Fourth St, Private Bag CY 7767, Harare; tel. (4) 700596; fax (4) 738165; internet www.water.gov.zw.
Ministry of Youth Development, Gender and Employment Creation: ZANU—PF Bldg, Private Bag 7762, Causeway, Harare; tel. (4) 734691; fax (4) 732709; e-mail mydgec@zarnet.ac.zw; internet www.mydgec.gov.zw.

PROVINCIAL GOVERNORS
(February 2009)

Bulawayo: CAIN MATHEMA.
Harare: DAVID KARIMANZIRA.
Manicaland: CHRISTOPHER MUSHOHWE.
Mashonaland Central: MARTIN DINHA.
Mashonaland East: AENEAS CHIGWEDERE.
Mashonaland West: FABER CHIDARIKIRE.
Masvingo: TITUS MALULEKE.
Matabeleland North: THOKOZILE MATHUTHU.
Matabeleland South: ANGELINA MASUKU.
Midlands: JAISON MACHAYA.

President and Legislature

PRESIDENT

Presidential Election, First Round, 29 March 2008

Candidate	Votes	% of valid votes
Morgan Tsvangirai	1,195,562	47.87
Robert Gabriel Mugabe	1,079,730	43.24
Simba Herbert Makoni	207,470	8.31
Langton Towungana	14,503	0.58
Total	**2,497,265**	**100.00**

Presidential Election, Second Round, 27 June 2008, provisional results

Candidate	Votes	% of valid votes
Robert Gabriel Mugabe	2,150,269	90.21
Morgan Tsvangirai*	233,000	9.78
Total†	**2,383,629**	**100.00**

*Tsvangirai announced his withdrawal from the second round of voting on 22 June; however, the Zimbabwe Election Commission stated that the Constitution necessitated that the run-off take place and Tsvangirai's name remained on the ballot papers.
† Excludes 131,481 spoilt ballots.

HOUSE OF ASSEMBLY

Speaker: LOVEMORE MOYO.

General Election, 29 March 2008, provisional results

Party	Votes	% of votes	Seats
MDC—Tsvangirai	1,041,176	42.99	99
ZANU—PF	1,110,649	45.86	97
MDC—Mutambara	202,259	8.35	10
Independents	54,254	2.24	1
Others	13,635	0.56	—
Total	**2,421,973**	**100.00**	**207***

*Voting was postponed in three constituencies, owing to the deaths of candidates.

SENATE

Speaker: EDNA MADZONGWE.

General Election, 29 March 2008, provisional results

Party	Seats
ZANU—PF	30
MDC—Tsvangirai	24
MDC—Mutambara	6
Total	**60***

*In addition to the 60 directly elective seats, five are held by nominees of the President, 10 by provincial governors, two by the President and the Deputy President of the Council of Chiefs and 16 by traditional Chiefs.

ZIMBABWE

Election Commission

Zimbabwe Electoral Commission (ZEC): Century House East, Private Bag 7782, Causeway, Harare; tel. (4) 759130; fax (4) 781903; e-mail zecpr@gta.gov.zw; internet www.zimbabweelectoralcommission.org; f. 2005; the President appoints eight members, four of whom must be women, and also the Chair. in consultation with the Judicial Service Commission and the Committee on Standing Rules and Orders for a six-year term; superseded and replaced the Electoral Supervisory Commission (abolished Aug. 2005); responsible for establishing constituency boundaries, voter registration and conducting elections; Chair. GEORGE CHIWESHE.

Political Organizations

Christian Democratic Party: Leader WILLIAM GWATA.

Committee for a Democratic Society (CODESO): f. 1993; Karanga-supported grouping, based in Matabeleland; Leader SOUL NDLOVU.

Federal Democratic Union: f. 2008; Leader PAUL SIWELA.

Forum Party of Zimbabwe (FPZ): POB 74, Bulawayo; f. 1993; conservative; Pres. WASHINGTON SANSOLE.

General Conference of Patriots: Harare; f. 1998; opposes the Govt; aims to organize and direct dissent; Leader OBEY MUDZINGWA.

Movement for Democratic Change—Mutambara (MDC—M): Harare; e-mail a.mutambara@mdczim.com; internet www.mdczim.com; f. 2005; Pres. Prof. ARTHUR MUTAMBARA; Sec.-Gen. Prof. WELSHMAN NCUBE.

Movement for Democratic Change—Tsvangirai (MDC—T): Harvest House, 6th Floor, cnr Angwa St and Nelson Mandela Ave, Harare; internet www.mdc.co.zw; f. 1999; split into two factions in 2005; allied to Zimbabwe Congress of Trade Unions; Pres. MORGAN TSVANGIRAI; Sec.-Gen. TENDAI BITI.

National Progressive Alliance: f. 1991; Chair. CANCIWELL NZIRAMASANGA.

United National Federal Party (UNFP): Harare; f. 1978; conservative; seeks a federation of Mashonaland and Matabeleland; Leader Chief KAYISA NDIWENI.

United People's Party (UPP): f. 2006; Leader DANIEL SHUMBA.

Zimbabwe Active People's Unity Party: Bulawayo; f. 1989; Leader NEWMAN MATUTU NDELA.

Zimbabwe African National Union—Ndonga (ZANU—Ndonga): POB UA525, Union Ave, Harare; tel. and fax (4) 481180; f. 1977; breakaway faction from ZANU, also includes fmr mems of United African Nat. Council; supports free market economy; Pres. (vacant); Sec.-Gen. EDWIN C. NGUWA.

Zimbabwe African National Union—Patriotic Front (ZANU—PF): cnr Rotten Row and Samora Machel Ave, POB 4530, Harare; tel. (4) 753329; fax (4) 774146; f. 1989 by merger of PF—ZAPU and ZANU—PF; Pres. ROBERT GABRIEL MUGABE; Vice-Pres SIMON VENGAYI MUZENDA, JOSEPH W. MSIKA; Nat. Chair. JOHN LANDAU NKOMO.

Zimbabwe Congress Party: Harare; f. 1994; Pres. KENNETH MANO.

Zimbabwe Development Party: Harare; Leader KISINOTI MUKWAZHE.

Zimbabwe Federal Party (ZFPO): Stand 214, Nketa 6, P.O. Nkulumane, Bulawayo; f. 1994; aims to create national federation of five provinces; Leader RICHARD NCUBE.

Zimbabwe Integrated Programme: f. 1999; seeks economic reforms; Pres. Prof. HENEDI DZINOCHIKIWEYI.

Zimbabwe People's Democratic Party: POB 4001, Harare; e-mail mail@zpdp.org; internet www.zpdp.org; f. 1991; Chair. ISABEL SHANANGURAI MADANGURE; Sec.-Gen. DUDLEY GURA.

Zimbabwe Progressive People's Democratic Party: Harare; Leader TAFIRENYIKA MUDAVANHU.

Zimbabwe Unity Movement (ZUM): f. 1989 by a breakaway faction from ZANU—PF; merged with United African National Council in 1994; Leader EDGAR TEKERE.

Zimbabwe Youth in Alliance: Leader MOSES MUTYASIRA.

Diplomatic Representation

EMBASSIES IN ZIMBABWE

Angola: 26 Speke Ave, POB 3590, Harare; tel. (4) 770075; fax (4) 770077; Ambassador FILIPE MONIMAMBU.

Australia: 1 Green Close, Borrowdale, Harare; POB 4541, Harare; tel. (4) 852471; fax (4) 870566; e-mail zimbabwe.embassy@dfat.gov.au; internet www.zimbabwe.embassy.gov.au; Ambassador JOHN COURTNEY.

Austria: 13 Duthie Rd, Alexandra Park, POB 4120, Harare; tel. (4) 702921; fax (4) 705877; e-mail harare-ob@bmeia.gv.at; Ambassador Dr GERHARD ZIEGLER.

Bangladesh: 9 Birchenough Rd, POB 3040, Harare; tel. (4) 727004; Ambassador NASIMA HAIDER.

Botswana: 22 Phillips Ave, Belgravia, POB 563, Harare; tel. (4) 729551; fax (4) 721360; Ambassador PELOKGALE SELOMA.

Brazil: Old Mutual Centre, 9th Floor, Jason Moyo Ave, POB 2530, Harare; tel. (4) 790740; fax (4) 790754; e-mail brasemb@ecoweb.co.zw; Ambassador RAUL DE TAUNAY.

Bulgaria: 15 Maasdorp Ave, Alexandra Park, POB 1809, Harare; tel. (4) 730509; fax (4) 732504; e-mail bgembhre@ecoweb.co.zw; Ambassador CHRISTO TEPAVITCHAROV.

Canada: 45 Baines Ave, POB 1430, Harare; tel. (4) 252181; fax (4) 252186; e-mail hrare@international.gc.ca; internet www.harare.gc.ca; Ambassador BARBARA RICHARDSON.

China, People's Republic: 30 Baines Ave, POB 4749, Harare; tel. and fax (4) 794155; e-mail chinaemb_zw@mfa.gov.cn; internet www.chinaembassy.org.zw; Ambassador NANSHENG YUAN.

Congo, Democratic Republic: 5 Pevensey Rd, Highlands, POB 2446, Harare; tel. (4) 481172; fax (4) 796421; Ambassador MAWAMPANGA MWANA NANGA.

Cuba: 5 Phillips Ave, Belgravia, POB 4139, Harare; tel. (4) 720256; Ambassador COSME TORRES ESPINOSA.

Czech Republic: 4 Sandringham Dr., Alexandra Park, GPO 4474, Harare; tel. (4) 700636; fax (4) 720930; e-mail harare@embassy.mzv.cz; internet www.mzv.cz/harare; Ambassador VÁCLAV JÍLEK.

Egypt: 7 Aberdeen Rd, Avondale, POB A433, Harare; tel. (4) 303445; fax (4) 303115; Ambassador GAMEEL SAEED FAYED.

Ethiopia: 14 Lanark Rd, Belgravia, POB 2745, Harare; tel. (4) 701514; fax (4) 701516; e-mail emb@ecoweb.co.zw; Ambassador ADBI DALAL MOHAMMED.

France: Bank Chambers, 11th Floor, 74–76 Samora Machel Ave, POB 1378, Harare; tel. (4) 703216; fax (4) 730078; internet www.ambafrance-zw.org; Ambassador LAURENT CONTINI.

Germany: 30 Ceres Rd, Avondale, Harare; tel. (4) 308655; fax (4) 303455; e-mail botschaft_harare@gmx.de; Ambassador Dr ALBRECHT CONZE.

Ghana: 11 Downie Ave, Belgravia, POB 4445, Harare; tel. (4) 700982; fax (4) 701014; e-mail ghcom25@africaonline.co.zw; Ambassador JOHN K. GBENAH.

Greece: 8 Deary Ave, Belgravia, POB 4809, Harare; tel. (4) 793208; fax (4) 703662; e-mail grembha@ecoweb.co.zw; Ambassador MICHAEL KOUKAKIS.

Holy See: 5 St Kilda Rd, Mount Pleasant, POB MP191, Harare (Apostolic Nunciature); tel. (4) 744547; fax (4) 744412; e-mail nunzim@zol.co.zw; Apostolic Nuncio Most Rev. GEORGE KOCHERRY (Titular Archbishop of Othona).

India: 12 Natal Rd, Belgravia, POB 4620, Harare; tel. (4) 795955; fax (4) 722324; e-mail ambassador@embindia.org.zw; Ambassador V. ASHOK.

Indonesia: 3 Duthie Ave, Belgravia, POB CY 69, Causeway, Harare; tel. (4) 251799; fax (4) 796587; e-mail indohar@ecoweb.co.zw; internet www.indonesia-harare.org; Ambassador HUPUDIO SUPARDI.

Iran: 8 Allan Wilson Ave, Avondale, POB A293, Harare; tel. (4) 726942; Ambassador RASOUL MOMENI.

Italy: 7 Bartholomew Close, Greendale North, POB 1062, Harare; tel. (4) 498190; fax (4) 498199; e-mail ambasciata.zimbabwe@esteri.it; internet www.ambharare.esteri.it; Chargé d'affaires a.i. FERNANDO PALLINI ONETO DI SAN LORENZO.

Japan: Social Security Centre, 4th Floor, cnr Julius Nyerere Way and Sam Nujoma St, POB 2710, Harare; tel. (4) 250025; fax (4) 250111; internet www.zw.emb-japan.go.jp; Ambassador MORITO KOICHI.

Kenya: 95 Park Lane, POB 4069, Harare; tel. (4) 704820; fax (4) 723042; Ambassador Prof. JOHN ABDUBA.

Korea, Democratic People's Republic: 102 Josiah Chinamano Ave, Greenwood, POB 4754, Harare; tel. (4) 724052; Ambassador RI MYONG CHOL.

Kuwait: 1 Bath Rd, Avondale, POB A485, Harare; Ambassador SAUD FAISAL AL-DAWESS.

Libya: 124 Harare St, POB 4310, Harare; tel. (4) 728381; Ambassador MAHMOUD YOUSEF AZZABI.

Malawi: 9–11 Duthie Rd, Alexandra Park, POB 321, Harare; tel. (4) 798584; fax (4) 799006; e-mail malahigh@africaonline.co.zw; Ambassador Dr BENSON M. TEMBO.

ZIMBABWE

Malaysia: 40 Downie Ave, Avondale, POB 5570, Harare; tel. (4) 334413; fax (4) 334415; e-mail malharare@kln.gov.my; Ambassador CHEAH CHOONG KIT.

Mozambique: 152 cnr Herbert Chitepo Ave and Leopold Takawira St, POB 4608, Harare; tel. (4) 253871; fax (4) 253875; e-mail emba@embamoc.org.zw; Ambassador VICENTE MEBUNIA VELOSO.

Netherlands: 2 Arden Rd, Highlands, POB HG601, Harare; tel. (4) 776701; fax (4) 776700; e-mail har@minbuza.nl; Ambassador JOSEPH WETERINGS.

Nigeria: 36 Samora Machel Ave, POB 4742, Harare; tel. (4) 253900; Ambassador ADEKUNLE ADEYANJU.

Norway: 5 Lanark Rd, Belgravia, POB A510, Avondale, Harare; tel. (4) 252426; fax (4) 252430; e-mail emb.harare@mfa.no; internet www.norway.org.zw; Ambassador GUNNAR FØRELAND.

Pakistan: 314 Pipendale Rd, Barrowadalf, Harare; tel. (4) 762018; fax (4) 794264; e-mail pahichar@yahoo.com; Ambassador RIFFAT IQBAL.

Poland: 16 Cork Rd, Belgravia, POB 3932, Harare; tel. (4) 253442; fax (4) 253710; Ambassador MARCIN KUBIAK.

Portugal: 12 Harvey Brown Ave, Milton Park, Harare; tel. (4) 253023; fax (4) 253637; e-mail embport@harare.dgaccp.pt; Ambassador JOÃO DA CÂMARA.

Romania: 105 Fourth St, POB 4797, Harare; tel. (4) 700853; fax (4) 725493; e-mail romemb@cybersatafrica.com; Chargé d'affaires a.i. FLORICĂ BARBU.

Russia: 70 Fife Ave, POB 4250, Harare; tel. (4) 701957; fax (4) 700534; e-mail russianembassy@zol.co.zw; internet www.zimbabwe.mid.ru; Ambassador SERGEI KRYUKOV.

South Africa: 7 Elcombe Rd, Belgravia, POB A1654, Harare; tel. (4) 753147; fax (4) 749657; e-mail admin@saembassy.co.zw; Ambassador MLUNGISI MAKALIMA.

Spain: 16 Phillips Ave, Belgravia, POB 3300, Harare; tel. (4) 250740; fax (4) 795261; e-mail emb.harare@mae.es; Ambassador PILAR FUERTES FERRAGUT.

Sudan: 4 Pascoe Ave, Harare; tel. (4) 700111; fax (4) 703450; e-mail sudan@africaonline.co.zw; internet www.sudaniharare.org.zw; Ambassador HASSAN AHMED FAGEERI.

Sweden: 32 Aberdeen Rd, Avondale, POB 4110, Harare; tel. (4) 302636; fax (4) 302236; e-mail ambassaden.harare@foreign.ministry.se; internet www.swedenabroad.com/harare; Ambassador STEN RYLANDER.

Switzerland: 15 Fleetwood Rd, Alexandra Park, POB 3440, Harare; tel. (4) 745682; fax (4) 745465; e-mail har.vertretung@eda.admin.ch; internet www.eda.admin.ch/harare; Ambassador MARCEL STUTZ.

Tanzania: Ujamaa House, 23 Baines Ave, POB 4841, Harare; tel. (4) 792714; fax (4) 792747; e-mail tanrep@icon.co.zw; Ambassador ADADI RAJABU.

United Kingdom: Corner House, cnr Samora Machel Ave and Leopold Takawira St, POB 4490, Harare; tel. (4) 772990; fax (4) 774617; e-mail consular.harare@fco.gov.uk; internet ukinzimbabwe.fco.gov.uk/en; Ambassador Dr ANDREW POCOCK.

USA: 172 Herbert Chitepo Ave, POB 3340, Harare; tel. (4) 758803; fax (4) 796488; e-mail hararepas@state.gov; internet harare.usembassy.gov; Ambassador JAMES D. MCGEE.

Zambia: Zambia House, cnr Union and Julius Nyerere Aves, POB 4698, Harare; tel. (4) 773777; fax (4) 773782; Ambassador SIPULA KABANJE.

Judicial System

The legal system is Roman-Dutch, based on the system which was in force in the Cape of Good Hope on 10 June 1891, as modified by subsequent legislation.

The Supreme Court has original jurisdiction in matters in which an infringement of Chapter III of the Constitution defining fundamental rights is alleged. In all other matters it has appellate jurisdiction only. It consists of the Chief Justice, a Deputy Chief Justice and such other judges of the Supreme Court, being not less than two, as the President may deem necessary.

The High Court consists of the Chief Justice, the Judge President, and such other judges of the High Court as may from time to time be appointed. Below the High Court are Regional Courts and Magistrates' Courts with both civil and criminal jurisdiction presided over by full-time professional magistrates.

The Customary Law and Local Courts Act, adopted in 1990, abolished the village and community courts and replaced them with customary law and local courts, presided over by chiefs and headmen; in the case of chiefs, jurisdiction to try customary law cases is limited to those where the monetary values concerned do not exceed Z.$1,000 and in the case of a headman's court Z.$500. Appeals from the Chiefs' Courts are heard in Magistrates' Courts and, ultimately, the Supreme Court. All magistrates now have jurisdiction to try cases determinable by customary law.

Chief Justice: GODFREY CHIDYAUSIKU.
Judges of Appeal: W. SANDURA, ANELE MATIKA, TADIUS KARWI, SUSAN MAVANGIRA, LAVENDER MAKONI.
Judge President: PADDINGTON GARWE.
Attorney-General: JOHANNES TOMANA.

Religion

AFRICAN RELIGIONS

Many Zimbabweans follow traditional beliefs.

CHRISTIANITY

About 55% of the population are Christians.

Zimbabwe Council of Churches: 128 Mbuya Nehanda St, POB 3566, Harare; tel. (4) 772043; fax (4) 773650; e-mail zcc@africaonline.co.zw; f. 1964; Pres. Rt Rev. Dr WILSON SITSHEBO; Gen. Sec. DENSEN MAFIYANI; 24 mem. churches, nine assoc. mems.

The Anglican Communion

Anglicans are adherents of the Church of the Province of Central Africa, covering Botswana, Malawi, Zambia and Zimbabwe. The Church comprises 15 dioceses, including five in Zimbabwe. The current Archbishop of the Province is the Bishop of Upper Shire, Malawi. The Church had an estimated 320,000 members at mid-2000.

Bishop of Central Zimbabwe: Rt Rev. ISHMAEL MUKUWANDA, POB 25, Gweru; tel. (54) 21030; fax (54) 21097; e-mail diocent@telconet.co.zw.

Bishop of Harare: Rt Rev. SEBASTIAN BAKARE, Bishopsmount Close, POB UA7, Harare; tel. (4) 702253; fax (4) 700419; e-mail angbishophre@mango.zw.

Bishop of Manicaland: PETER HATENDI (acting), 113 Herbert Chitepo St, Mutare; tel. (20) 64194; fax (20) 63076; e-mail diomani@syscom.co.zw; internet www.anglicandioceseofmanicaland.co.zw.

Bishop of Masvingo: Rt Rev. GODFREY TOANEZVI, POB 1421, Masvingo; tel. (39) 362536; e-mail anglicandiomsv@comone.co.zw.

Bishop of Matabeleland: Rt Rev. CLEOPHAS LUNGA, POB 2422, Bulawayo; tel. (9) 61370; fax (9) 68353; e-mail angdiomat@telconet.co.zw.

The Roman Catholic Church

For ecclesiastical purposes, Zimbabwe comprises two archdioceses and six dioceses. At 31 December 2006 there were some 1.4m. adherents, equivalent to an estimated 9.0% of the total population.

Zimbabwe Catholic Bishops' Conference (ZCBC)
Catholic Secretariat, Causeway, 29 Selous Ave, POB 8135, Harare; tel. (4) 705368; fax (4) 705369; internet www.zcbc.co.zw.
f. 1969; Pres. Most Rev. ROBERT C. NDLOVU (Archbishop of Harare).

Archbishop of Bulawayo: Most Rev. MARTIN SCARP, cnr Lobengula St and 9th Ave, POB 837, Bulawayo; tel. (9) 63590; fax (9) 60359; e-mail archdbyo@mweb.co.zw.

Archbishop of Harare: Most Rev. ROBERT C. NDLOVU, Archbishop's House, 66 Fifth St, POB CY330, Causeway, Harare; tel. (4) 727386; fax (4) 721598; e-mail hrearch@zol.co.zw.

Other Christian Churches

At mid-2000 there were an estimated 4.8m. adherents professing other forms of Christianity.

Dutch Reformed Church in Zimbabwe (Nederduitse Gereformeerde Kerk): 35 Samora Machel Ave, POB 503, Harare; tel. (4) 774738; fax (4) 774739; e-mail pvanvuuren@mango.zw; f. 1895; 10 congregations in Zimbabwe and two in Zambia; Chair. Rev. PIET F. J. VAN VUUREN; Sec. Rev. J. HAASBROEK; 100,000 mems.

Evangelical Lutheran Church: 7 Lawley Rd, POB 2175, Bulawayo; tel. (9) 254991; fax (9) 254993; e-mail elczhead@mweb.co.zw; f. 1903; Sec. Rt Rev. L. M. DUBE; 150,000 mems (2009).

Greek Orthodox Church: POB 2832, Harare; tel. (4) 744991; fax (4) 744928; e-mail zimbabwe@greekorthodox-zimbabwe.org; internet www.greekorthodox-zimbabwe.org; Archbishop GEORGE.

Methodist Church in Zimbabwe: POB CY71, Causeway, Harare; tel. (4) 250523; fax (4) 723709; e-mail methodistconn@zol.co.zw; f. 1891; Presiding Bishop Rev. SIMBARASHE SITHOLE; Sec. of Conference Rev. AMOS NDHLUMBI.

United Congregational Church of Southern Africa: 40 Jason Moyo St, POB 2451, Bulawayo; tel. (9) 63686; internet www.uccsa

ZIMBABWE

.org.za/zimbabwe-synod; Chair. Rev. B. MATHEMA (acting); Sec. Rev. MAJAHA NTHLIZIYO.

United Methodist Church: POB 3408, Harare; tel. (4) 704127; f. 1890; Bishop of Zimbabwe ABEL TENDEKAYI MUZOREWA; 45,000 mems.

Among other denominations active in Zimbabwe are the African Methodist Church, the African Methodist Episcopal Church, the African Reformed Church, the Christian Marching Church, the Church of Christ in Zimbabwe, the Independent African Church, the Presbyterian Church (and the City Presbyterian Church), the United Church of Christ, the Zimbabwe Assemblies of God and the Ziwezano Church.

JUDAISM

The Jewish community numbered 897 members at 31 December 1997; by 2006 that number had fallen to around 300.

Zimbabwe Jewish Board of Deputies: POB 1954, Harare; tel. (4) 702507; fax (4) 702506; Pres. P. STERNBERG; Sec. E. ALHADEFF.

BAHÁ'Í FAITH

National Spiritual Assembly: POB GD380, Greendale, Harare; tel. (4) 495945; fax (4) 744611; internet www.bahai.co.zw; Nat. Sec. DEREK SITHOLE; f. 1970; mems resident in 57 clusters.

The Press

DAILIES

The Chronicle: 9th Ave and George Silundika St, POB 585, Bulawayo; tel. (9) 888871; fax (9) 888884; e-mail editor@chronicle.co.zw; internet www.chronicle.co.zw; f. 1894; publ. by govt-controlled co Zimpapers; circulates throughout south-west Zimbabwe; English; Editor MAKUWERERE BWITITI; circ. 25,000 (2004).

Daily Mirror (Zim Mirror): Charter House, 70 Samora Machel Ave, Harare; tel. (4) 725251; fax (4) 729607; internet www.zimmirror.co.zw; f. 2002; publ. by Zimbabwe Mirror Newspapers Group; also publ. *Sunday Mirror* (f. 1997 as *The Zimbabwe Mirror Weekly*, circ. c. 15,000); English; CEO and Editor-in-Chief IBBO MANDAZA.

The Daily News: 18 Sam Nujoma St and cnr Speke Ave, Harare; tel. (4) 753027; fax (4) 753024; publ. by Associated Newspapers of Zimbabwe; English; publ. suspended Sept. 2003; Editor NQOBILE NYATHI; CEO SAM SIPEPA NKOMO; Chair. STRIVE MASIYIWA; circ. c. 80,000 (2003).

The Herald: POB 396, Harare; tel. (4) 795771; fax (4) 700305; internet www.herald.co.zw; f. 1891; publ. by govt-controlled co Zimpapers; English; Editor PIKIRAYI DEKETEKE; circ. c. 60,000 (2006).

WEEKLIES

Financial Gazette: Coal House, 5th Floor, cnr Nelson Mandela Ave and Leopold Takawira St, Harare; tel. (4) 781571; fax (4) 781578; e-mail schamunorwa@fingaz.co.zw; internet www.fingaz.co.zw; f. 1969; publ. by ZimInd Publrs (Pvt) Ltd; affiliated to the ZANU—PF party; Editor-in-Chief SUNSLEEY CHAMUNORWA; Gen. Man. JACOB CHISESE; circ. c. 40,000 (2004).

Indonsakusa/Ilanga: c/o CNG, POB 6520, Harare; tel. (4) 796855; fax (4) 703873; publ. by Community Newspaper Group (Mass Media Trust); distributed in north and south Matabeleland; circ. c. 10,000.

Kwayedza: POB 396, Harare; tel. (4) 795771; fax (4) 791311; internet www.kwayedza.co.zw; publ. by govt-controlled co Zimpapers; f. 1985; ChiShona; Editor GERVASE M. CHITEWE; circ. c. 15,000 (2003).

Manica Post: POB 960, Mutare; tel. (20) 61212; fax (20) 61149; internet www.manicapost.com; f. 1893; publ. by govt-controlled co Zimpapers; English; Editor PAUL MAMBO; circ. 15,000 (2004).

Mashonaland Guardian/Telegraph: c/o CNG, POB 6520, Harare; tel. (4) 796855; fax (4) 703873; publ. by Community Newspaper Group (Mass Media Trust); distributed in Mashonaland; circ. c. 10,000.

Masvingo Mirror: POB 1214, Masvingo; tel. (39) 64372; fax (39) 64484; independent; Editor NORNA EDWARDS.

Masvingo Star: 2–3 New Market Centre, R. Tangwena Ave, POB 138, Masvingo; tel. and fax (39) 63978; publ. by Community Newspaper Group (Mass Media Trust); English; distributed in Masvingo province; Editor (vacant); circ. c. 10,000.

Midlands Observer: POB 533, Kwekwe; tel. (55) 22248; fax (55) 23985; e-mail nelson_mashiri@yahoo.com; f. 1953; weekly; English; Editor R. JARIJARI; circ. 20,000.

North Midlands Gazette: POB 222, Kadoma; tel. and fax (68) 3731; f. 1912; Editor C. B. KIDIA.

Directory

The Standard: 1st Block, 3rd Floor, Ernst and Young Bldg, 1 Kwame Nkrumah Ave, POB 661730, Kopje, Harare; tel. (4) 773930; fax (4) 798897; internet www.thestandard.co.zw; f. 1997; publ. by ZimInd Publrs (Pvt) Ltd; Sun.; Exec. Chair. and CEO TREVOR NCUBE; circ. 42,000 (2004).

Sunday Mail: POB 396, Harare; tel. (4) 795771; fax (4) 700305; internet www.sundaymail.co.zw; f. 1935; publ. by govt-controlled co Zimpapers; English; Chair. THOMAS SITHOLE; Editor WILLIAM CHIKOTO; circ. 110,000 (2004).

Sunday News: POB 585, Bulawayo; tel. (9) 540071; fax (9) 540084; f. 1930; publ. by govt-controlled co Zimpapers; English; Editor BREZHNEV MALABA; circ. 30,000 (2004).

The Times: c/o CNG, POB 6520, Harare; tel. (4) 796855; fax (4) 703873; f. 1897; fmrly *The Gweru Times*; publ. by Community Newspaper Group (Mass Media Trust); distributed in Mashonaland; English; circ. c. 5,000.

uMthunywa (The Messenger): 9th Ave and George Silundika St, POB 585 Bulawayo; tel. (9) 880888; fax (9) 888884; e-mail advertising@chronicle.co.zw; internet www.umthunywa.co.zw; f. 2004; SiNdebele; publ. by govt-controlled co Zimpapers; Editor BHEKITHEMBA J. NCUBE.

The Vanguard: Zimbabwe National Students' Union, 21 Wembley Cres., Eastlea, Harare; tel. (4) 788135; e-mail zinasu@gmail.com; internet www.zinasu.org/vanguards/latest.html; publ. by the Zimbabwe Nat. Students' Union.

The Zimbabwean: POB 248, Hythe, SO45 4WX, United Kingdom; tel. (23) 8084-8694; e-mail feedback@thezimbabwean.co.uk; internet www.thezimbabwean.co.uk; f. 2005; independent; publ. in the United Kingdom and South Africa; focus on news in Zimbabwe and life in exile; Publr and Editor WILF MBANGA.

Zimbabwe Independent: Zimind Publishers (Pvt) Ltd, Suites 23/24, 1 Union Ave, POB BE1165, Belvedere, Harare; e-mail trevorn@mg.co.za; internet www.theindependent.co.zw; f. 1996; publ. by ZimInd Publrs (Pvt) Ltd; English; Publr TREVOR NCUBE; Editor VINCENT KAHIYA; circ. 30,500 (2005).

Zimbabwean Government Gazette: POB 8062, Causeway, Harare; official notices; Editor L. TAKAWIRA.

PERIODICALS

The Agenda: Information Department, 348 Herbert Chitepo Ave, Harare; tel. (4) 736338; fax (4) 721146; e-mail info@nca.org.zw; internet www.nca.org.zw; f. 1997; publ. by the Nat. Constitutional Assembly; quarterly; civil rights issues.

Chamber of Mines Journal: Stewart House, North Wing, 4 Central Ave, POB 712, Harare; tel. (4) 702841; fax (4) 707983; publ. by Thomson Publs; monthly.

Chaminuka News: POB 650, Marondera; f. 1988; publ. by Community Newspaper Group (Mass Media Trust); fortnightly; English and ChiShona; distributed in Manicaland and Mashonaland North provinces; Editor M. MUGABE; circ. c. 10,000.

Indonsakusa: Hwange; f. 1988; monthly; English and SiNdebele; Editor D. NTABENI; circ. 10,000.

The Insider: Insider Publications, POB FM 415, Famona, Bulawayo; tel. (11) 789-739; e-mail charlesrukuni@insiderzim.com; internet www.insiderzim.com; f. 1990; monthly; digital newsletter; news and current affairs; Editor and Publr CHARLES RUKUNI.

JASSA: Journal of Applied Science in Southern Africa: University of Zimbabwe Publications, POB MP203, Mount Pleasant, Harare; tel. (4) 303211; fax (4) 333407; e-mail uzpub@admin.uz.ac.zw; internet www.uz.ac.zw/publications; applied science journal of the Univ. of Zimbabwe; 2 a year; Editor-in-Chief Prof. C. F. B. NHACHI.

Mahogany: POB UA589, Harare; tel. (4) 752063; fax (4) 752062; f. 1980; 6 a year; English; women's interest; Editor TENDAI DONDO; circ. 240,000.

Masiye Pambili (Let Us Go Forward): POB 591, Bulawayo; tel. (9) 75011; fax (9) 69701; f. 1964; 2 a year; English; Editor M. N. NDLOVU; circ. 25,000.

Moto (Fire): POB 890, Gweru; tel. (54) 24886; fax (54) 28194; e-mail mot@hnetzim.wn.apc.org; f. 1959; monthly; publ. by govt-controlled co Zimpapers; banned in 1974; relaunched in 1980 as a weekly newspaper, then in magazine format in 1982; Roman Catholic; Editor SYDNEY SHOKO; circ. 22,000.

Mukai-Vukani Jesuit Journal for Zimbabwe: Jesuit Communications, 1 Churchill Ave, Alexandra Park, POB ST194, Southerton, Harare; tel. (4) 744571; fax (4) 744284; e-mail owermter@zol.co.zw; internet www.jescom.co.zw; 4–6 a year; Catholic; Editor Fr OSKAR WERMTER; circ. 2,000.

New Farmer: Herald House, cnr George Sikundika and Sam Nujoma Sts, POB 55, Harare; tel. (4) 708296; fax (4) 702400; e-mail advertising@chronicle.co.zw; internet www.newfarmer.co.zw; f. 2002; publ. by govt-controlled co Zimpapers; weekly; English; Editor GEORGE CHISOKO.

ZIMBABWE

The Outpost: POB HG106, Highlands; tel. (4) 724571; fax (4) 703631; e-mail theoutpostmag@yahoo.com; f. 1911; publ. of the Zimbabwe Republic Police; monthly; English; Editor MOSES MOYO; circ. c. 27,000 (2005).

Railroader: National Railways of Zimbabwe, cnr Fife St and 10th Ave, POB 596, Bulawayo; tel. (9) 363716; fax (9) 363502; f. 1952; publ. by Nat. Railways of Zimbabwe; monthly; Editor M. GUMEDE; circ. 10,000.

Southern African Political and Economic Monthly (SAPEM): Southern Africa Political Economy Series Trust, 2–6 Deary Ave, Belgravia, POB MP111, Mt Pleasant, Harare; tel. (4) 252962; fax (4) 252964; f. 1987; monthly; publ. by the SAPES Trust; incorporating *Southern African Economist*; Editor-in-Chief KHABELE MATLOSA; circ. 16,000.

Trends: 9th Ave and George Silundika St, POB 585 Bulawayo; tel. (09) 880888; fax (09) 888884; e-mail advertising@chronicle.co.zw; internet www.zimtrends.co.zw; f. 2003; publ. by govt-controlled co Zimpapers; monthly; English; leisure and entertainment; Editor EDWIN DUBE.

The Worker: ZCTU, Chester House, 9th Floor, Speke Ave and Third St, POB 3549, Harare; tel. (4) 794742; fax (4) 728484; e-mail info@zctu.co.zw; publ. by the Zimbabwe Congress of Trade Unions; News Editor BRIGHT CHIBVURI.

Zambezia: University of Zimbabwe Publications, POB MP203, Mount Pleasant, Harare; tel. (4) 303211; fax (4) 333407; e-mail uzpub@admin.uz.ac.zw; internet www.uz.ac.zw/publications; publ. by the Univ. of Zimbabwe; 2 a year; humanities and general interest; Editor Dr ZIFIKILE MGUNI-GAMBAHAYA.

Zimbabwe Agricultural Journal: Dept of Research and Specialist Services, 5th St, Extension, POB CY594, Causeway, Harare; tel. (4) 704531; fax (4) 728317; f. 1903; 6 a year; Editor R. J. FENNER; circ. 2,000.

Zimbabwean Travel: Herald House, cnr George Sikundika and Sam Nujoma Sts, POB 55, Harare; tel. (4) 708296; fax (4) 702400; e-mail advertising@chronicle.co.zw; internet www.zimtravel.com; f. 2003; publ. by govt-controlled co Zimpapers; monthly; English; Editor NOMSA NKALA.

Zimbabwe National Army Magazine: Ministry of Defence, Defence House, cnr Kwame Nkuruma Ave and 3rd St, Harare; tel. (4) 700316; f. 1982; 4 a year; Dir of Communications Col LIVINGSTONE CHINEKA; circ. 5,000.

The Zimbabwe Farmer: POB 1683, Harare; tel. (4) 736836; fax (4) 749803; monthly; fmrly *Tobacco News*; present name adopted in 2003; publ. by Thomson Publs; Editor D. MILLER; circ. 2,000.

NEWS AGENCY

NewZiana (Pvt) Ltd: Mass Media House, 19 Selous Ave, POB CY511, Causeway, Harare; tel. (4) 251754; fax (4) 794336; internet www.newziana.co.zw; f. 1981 as Zimbabwe Inter-Africa News Agency; present name adopted in 2003; owned by govt-controlled co Multimedia Investment Trust (fmrly Zimbabwe Mass Media Trust); operates 10 community newspapers; CEO MUNYARADZI MATANYAIRE.

Publishers

Academic Books (Pvt) Ltd: POB 567, Harare; tel. (4) 755408; fax (4) 781913; educational; Editorial Dir IRENE STAUNTON.

Amalgamated Publications (Pvt) Ltd: POB 1683, Harare; tel. (4) 736835; fax (4) 749803; f. 1949; trade journals.

Anvil Press: POB 4209, Harare; tel. (4) 751202; fax (4) 739681; f. 1988; general; Man. Dir PAUL BRICKHILL.

The Argosy Press: POB 2677, Harare; tel. (4) 755084; magazine publrs; Gen. Man. A. W. HARVEY.

Baobab Books (Pvt) Ltd: POB 567, Harare; tel. (4) 665187; fax (4) 665155; general, literature, children's.

The Bulletin: POB 1595, Bulawayo; tel. (9) 78831; fax (9) 78835; fmrly Directory Publrs Ltd; educational; CEO BRUCE BEALE.

College Press Publishers (Pvt) Ltd: 15 Douglas Rd, POB 3041, Workington, Harare; tel. (4) 754145; fax (4) 754256; f. 1968; educational and general; Man. Dir B. B. MUGABE.

Harare Publishing House: Chiremba Rd, Hatfield, Harare; tel. (4) 570342; f. 1982; Dir Dr T. M. SAMKANGE.

HarperCollins Publishers Zimbabwe (Pvt) Ltd: Union Ave, POB UA201, Harare; tel. (4) 721413; fax (4) 732436; Man. S. D. MCMILLAN.

Longman Zimbabwe (Pvt) Ltd: POB ST125, Southerton, Harare; tel. (4) 62711; fax (4) 62716; f. 1964; general and educational; Man. Dir N. L. DLODLO.

Mambo Press: Senga Rd, POB 779, Gweru; tel. (54) 24017; fax (54) 21991; f. 1958; religious, educational and fiction in English and African languages.

Modus Publications (Pvt) Ltd: Modus House, 27–29 Charter Rd, POB 66070, Kopje, Harare; tel. (4) 738722; Man. Dir ELIAS RUSIKE.

Munn Publishing (Pvt) Ltd: POB UA460, Union Ave, Harare; tel. (4) 481048; fax (4) 7481081; Man. Dir I. D. MUNN.

Standard Publications (Pvt) Ltd: POB 3745, Harare; Dir G. F. BOOT.

Southern African Printing and Publishing House (SAPPHO): 109 Coventry Rd, Workington, POB MP1005, Mount Pleasant, Harare; tel. (4) 621681; fax (4) 666061; internet www.zimmirror.co.zw; Editor-in-Chief Dr IBBO MANDAZA.

University of Zimbabwe Publications: University of Zimbabwe, POB MP203, Mount Pleasant, Harare; tel. (4) 303211; fax (4) 333407; e-mail uzpub@admin.uz.ac.zw; internet www.uz.ac.zw/publications; f. 1969; Dir MUNANI SAM MTETWA.

Zimbabwe Newspapers (1980) Ltd (Zimpapers): POB 55, Harare; tel. (4) 704088; fax (4) 702400; e-mail theherald@zimpapers.co.zw; internet www.herald.co.zw; f. 1981; 51% state-owned; publ. the newspapers *The Herald, The Sunday Mail, The Manica Post, The Chronicle, The Sunday News, Kwayedza, Umthunywa* and *The Southern Times* (based in Namibia); and magazines incl. *The Zimbabwean Travel, Trends Magazine* and *New Farmer Magazine*; Chair. HERBERT NKALA; Group CEO JUSTIN MUTASA.

ZPH Publishers (Pvt) Ltd: 183 Arcturus Rd, Kamfinsa, GD510, Greendale, Harare; tel. (4) 497548; fax (4) 497554; e-mail tafi@zph.co.zw; f. 1982 as Zimbabwe Publishing House Ltd; Chair. BLAZIO G. TAFIREYI.

Broadcasting and Communications

TELECOMMUNICATIONS

Econet Wireless Zimbabwe: Econet Park, No. 2 Old Mutare Rd, Msasa, POB BE1298, Belvedere, Harare; tel. (4) 486121; fax (4) 486120; e-mail enquiry@econet.co.zw; internet www.econet.co.zw; f. 1998; mobile cellular telecommunications operator; Chair. TAWANDA NYAMBIRAI; CEO DOUGLAS MBOWENI.

Net.One Ltd: POB CY579, Causeway, Harare; tel. (4) 707138; e-mail marketing@netone.co.zw; internet www.netone.co.zw; f. 1998; state-owned; mobile cellular telecommunications operator; Chair. CALLISTUS NDLOVU; CEO REWARD KANGAI.

Posts and Telecommunication Regulatory Authority (POTRAZ): Block A, Emerald Park, 30 The Chase, Mt Pleasant, POB MP 843, Harare; tel. (4) 333032; fax (4) 333041; e-mail the.regulator@potraz.gov.zw; internet www.potraz.gov.zw; fmrly Post and Telecommunications Corpn; Chair. Prof. FRED ZINDI; Dir GIDEON MAGODO.

Telecel Zimbabwe: 148 Seke Rd, Graniteside, POB CY232, Causeway, Harare; tel. (4) 748321; fax (4) 748328; e-mail info@telecelzim.co.zw; internet www.telecel.co.zw; f. 1998; 60% owned by Telecel Int. and 40% owned by Empowerment Corpn; mobile cellular telecommunications operator; Chair. JAMES MAKAMBA; Man. Dir REX JOHN CHIBESA.

TelOne: Runhare House, 107 K. Nkrumah Ave, POB CY331, Causeway, Harare; tel. (4) 798111; e-mail webmaster@telone.co.zw; internet www.telone.co.zw; state-owned; sole fixed-line telecommunications operator.

BROADCASTING

There are four govt-controlled radio stations (National FM, Power FM, Radio Zimbabwe and Spot FM) and one television station. Radio Voice of the People was established as an alternative to state broadcasting. An independent radio station, SW Radio Africa, broadcasts to Zimbabwe from London, United Kingdom. Since 2003 Voice of America has broadcast a weekday news and entertainment programme (Studio 7) from the USA in ChiShona, English and SiNdebele.

Radio

Voice of the People (VOP): POB 5750, Harare; tel. (4) 707123; e-mail voxpop@ecoweb.co.zw; internet www.vopradio.co.zw; f. 2000 by fmr ZBC staff; broadcasts one hour per day; relayed by Radio Netherlands transmitters in Madagascar; news and information in ChiShona, SiNdebele and English; Chair. DAVID MASUNDA; Exec. Dir JOHN MASUKU.

Zimbabwe Broadcasting Corpn: Broadcasting Center, Pocket Hill, POB HG444, Highlands, Harare; tel. and fax (4) 498940; e-mail zbc@zbc.co.zw; internet www.zbc.co.zw; f. 1957; programmes in English, ChiShona, SiNdebele and 14 minority languages, incl. Chichewa, Venda and Xhosa; broadcasts a general service (mainly in

ZIMBABWE

English), vernacular languages service, light entertainment, and educational programmes; Editor-in-Chief CHRISTINA TARUVINGA.

Television

Zimbabwe Broadcasting Corpn: (see Radio).
The main broadcasting centre is in Harare, with a second studio in Bulawayo; broadcasts ZBC-TV 24 hours per day.

Finance

(cap. = capital; res = reserves; dep. = deposits; m. = million; br(s). = branch(es); amounts in Zimbabwe dollars)

BANKING

Central Bank

Reserve Bank of Zimbabwe: 80 Samora Machel Ave, POB 1283, Harare; tel. (4) 703000; fax (4) 707800; e-mail rbzmail@rbz.co.zw; internet www.rbz.co.zw; f. 1964 as Reserve Bank of Rhodesia; bank of issue; cap. 2m., res 6m., dep. 11,734,195m. (Dec. 2004); Gov. Dr GIDEON GONO.

Commercial Banks

Barclays Bank of Zimbabwe Ltd: Barclays House, cnr First St and Jason Moyo Ave, POB 1279, Harare; tel. (4) 758281; fax (4) 752913; e-mail barmkt@africaonline.co.zw; internet www.barclays.com/africa/zimbabwe; f. 1912; commercial and merchant banking; cap. 1,000m., res 18,123m., dep. 125,836m. (Dec. 2004); Chair. Dr ROBBIE MATONGO MUPAWOSE; 44 brs.

CBZ Bank Ltd (CBZ): Union House, 60 Kwame Nkrumah Ave, POB 3313, Harare; tel. (4) 748050; e-mail info@cbz.co.zw; internet www.cbz.co.zw; state-owned; f. 1980 as Bank of Credit and Commerce Zimbabwe Ltd; renamed Commercial Bank of Zimbabwe Ltd in 1991; present name adopted 2005; cap. and res 2,551m., total assets 36,057m. (Dec. 2001); Chair. RICHARD V. WILDE; CEO N. J. MAKUVISE; 27 brs.

Kingdom Bank Ltd: 6th Floor, Karigamombe Centre, 53 Samora Machel Ave, Harare; tel. (4) 749400; fax (4) 781580; e-mail kmb@kingdom.co.zw; internet www.kingdom.co.zw; f. 1997; cap. 0.1m., res 2,743m., dep. 40,256m.; Man. Dir MARK WOOD.

Stanbic Bank Zimbabwe Ltd: Stanbic Centre, 1st Floor, 59 Samora Machel Ave, POB 300, Harare; tel. (4) 759471; fax (4) 751324; e-mail zimbabweinfo@stanbic.com; internet www.stanbicbank.co.zw; f. 1990 as ANZ Grindlays Bank; acquired by Standard Bank Investment Corpn in 1992; cap. 1,000m., res 1,761,842m., dep. 7,386,055m. (Dec. 2005); Chair. S. MOYO; Man. Dir JOSHUA TAPAMBGWA; 16 brs.

Standard Chartered Bank Zimbabwe Ltd: Mutual Centre, 2nd Floor, POB 373, Harare; tel. (4) 52852; fax (4) 752609; internet www.standardchartered.com/zw/; f. 1983; cap. and res 3,422.7m., total assets 558,124m. (2003); Chair. H. P. MKUSHI; CEO WASHINGTON MATSAIRA; 28 brs.

Trade and Investment Bank Ltd: Cabs Centre, 10th Floor, 74 Jason Moyo Ave, POB CY1064, Causeway, Harare; tel. (4) 703791; fax (4) 705491; f. 1997; cap. and res 32m., total assets 421m. (Dec. 1997); Chair. Dr BERNARD THOMAS CHIDZERO; CEO Dr KOMBO JAMES MOYANA.

Zimbabwe Banking Corpn Ltd (Zimbank): Zimbank House, Speke Ave and First St, POB 3198, Harare; tel. (4) 757471; fax (4) 757497; e-mail finhold@finhold.co.zw; internet www.finhold.co.zw; f. 1951; state-owned; cap. 102m., res 178,293m., dep. 821,214m. (Sept. 2004); Chair. RICHARD CHEMIST HOVE; Group CEO ELISHA N. MUSHAYAKARARA; 35 brs.

Development Banks

African Export-Import Bank (Afreximbank): Eastgate Bldg, 3rd Floor, Gold Bridge (North Wing), Second St, POB 1600, Causeway, Harare; tel. (4) 729751; fax (4) 729756; e-mail info@afreximbank.com; internet www.afreximbank.com; Pres. and Chair. J. L. EKRA.

Infrastructure Development Bank of Zimbabwe (IDBZ): 99 Rotten Row, Harare; tel. (4) 774226; fax (4) 774225; e-mail enquiries@zdb.co.zw; internet www.zdb.co.zw; f. 2005.

Zimbabwe Development Bank (ZDB): ZDB House, 99 Rotten Row, POB 1720, Harare; tel. (4) 774226; fax (4) 774225; e-mail enquiries@zdb.co.zw; internet www.zdb.co.zw; f. 1985; 33.3% state-owned; cap. and res 355m., total assets 2,317m. (Dec. 2001); Chair. Dr T. MASAYA; Man. Dir CORNELIUS MARADZA; 3 brs.

Merchant Banks

African Banking Corpn of Zimbabwe Ltd (ABC): ABC House, 1 Endeavour Cres., Mount Pleasant Business Park, Mount Pleasant, POB 2786, Harare; tel. (4) 369260; fax (4) 369939; e-mail abcz@africanbankingcorp.com; internet www.africanbankingcorp.com; f. 1956 as Rhodesian Acceptances Ltd; name changed to First Merchant Bank of Zimbabwe Ltd in 1990; merged with Heritage Investment Bank in 1997; present name adopted in 2002; subsidiary of ABC Holdings Ltd, Botswana; cap. and res 36.8m., total assets 475.6m. (Dec. 2001); Chair. O. M. CHIDAWU; Man. Dir F. M. DZANYA; 1 br.

MBCA Bank Ltd: Old Mutual Centre, 14th Floor, cnr Third St and Jason Moyo Ave, POB 3200, Harare; tel. (4) 701636; fax (4) 708005; e-mail mbcabank@mbca.co.zw; internet www.mbca.co.zw; f. 1956; cap. 0.5m., res 13,952.9m., dep. 50,468.7m. (Dec. 2006); Chair. V. W. ZIREVA; Man. Dir MBERIKWAZVO C. CHITAMBO.

NMB Bank Ltd: Unity Court, 4th Floor, cnr Union Ave and First St, POB 2564, Harare; tel. (4) 759651; fax (4) 759648; e-mail enquiries@nmbz.co.zw; internet www.nmbz.co.zw; f. 1993; fmrly Nat. Merchant Bank of Zimbabwe; cap. 0.3m., res 8,017m., dep. 51,128m. (Dec. 2006); Chair. Dr GIBSON MANYOWA MANDISHONA; CEO Dr DAVID T. HATENDI; 10 brs.

Standard Chartered Merchant Bank Zimbabwe Ltd: Standard Chartered Bank Bldg, cnr Second St and Nelson Mandela Ave, POB 60, Harare; tel. (4) 708585; fax (4) 725667; f. 1971; cap. and res 78m., dep. 83m. (Dec. 1998); Chair. BARRY HAMILTON; Man. Dir EBBY ESSOKA.

Discount Houses

African Banking Corpn Securities Ltd: 69 Samora Machel Ave, POB 3321, Harare; tel. (4) 752756; fax (4) 790641; cap. and res 68m. (Dec. 1999); fmrly Bard Discount House Ltd; Chair. N. KUDENGA; Man. Dir D. DUBE.

The Discount Co of Zimbabwe (DCZ): 70 Park Lane, POB 3424, Harare; tel. (4) 705414; fax (4) 731670; cap. and res 8.9m., total assets 377.4m. (Feb. 1995); Man. Dir PETER MUKUNGA.

Intermarket Discount House: Unity Court, 5th Floor, Union Ave, POB 3290, Harare.

National Discount House Ltd: MIPF House, 5th Floor, Central Ave, Harare; tel. (4) 700771; fax (4) 792927; internet www.ndh.co.zw; cap. and res 168.4m., total assets 2,365.2m. (Dec. 2000); Chair. EDWIN MANIKAI; Man. Dir LAWRENCE TAMAYI.

Banking Organizations

Bankers' Association of Zimbabwe (BAZ): Kuwana House, 4th Floor, Union Ave and First St, POB UA550, Harare; tel. (4) 728646; Pres. PINDIE NYANDORO; Dir FRANK READ.

Institute of Bankers of Zimbabwe: Centre Block, Second Floor, Suite 13, 1 Union Ave, POB UA521, Harare; tel. (4) 752474; fax (4) 750281; e-mail info@iobz.co.zw; internet www.iobz.co.zw; f. 1973; Chair. S. MALABA; Pres. STEVE GWASIRA; Dir T. BIYAM; 7,000 mems.

STOCK EXCHANGE

Zimbabwe Stock Exchange: Chiyedza House, 5th Floor, cnr First St and Kwame Nkrumah Ave, POB UA234, Harare; tel. (4) 736861; fax (4) 791045; e-mail zse@econet.co.zw; internet www.zse.co.zw; f. 1946; Chair. G. MHLANGA; CEO EMMANUEL MUNYUKWI.

INSURANCE

Export Credit Guarantee Corpn of Zimbabwe (Pvt): 6 Earles Rd, Alexandra Park, POB CY2995, Causeway, Harare; tel. and fax (4) 744644; e-mail ecgc@telco.co.zw; internet www.ecgc.co.zw; f. 1999 as national export credit insurance agency; also provides export finance guarantee facilities; 100% owned by Reserve Bank of Zimbabwe; Chair. J. A. L. CARTER; Man. Dir RAPHAEL G. NYADZAYO.

Credit Insurance Zimbabwe (Credsure): Credsure House, 69 Sam Nujoma St, POB CY1584, Causeway, Harare; tel. (4) 706101; fax (4) 706105; e-mail headoffice@credsure.co.zw; export credit insurance; Man. Dir BRIAN HILLEN-MOORE.

Fidelity Life Assurance of Zimbabwe (Pvt) Ltd: 66 Julius Nyerere Way, POB 435, Harare; tel. (4) 750927; fax (4) 751723; f. 1977; 52% owned by Zimre Holdings Ltd; pensions and life assurance; Chair. J. P. MKUSHI; Man. Dir SIMON B. CHAPAREKA.

NICOZ Diamond: Insurance Centre, 30 Samora Machel and Leopold Takawira Ave, POB 1256, Harare; tel. (4) 704911; fax (4) 704134; e-mail enquiries@nicozdiamond.co.zw; internet www.nicozdiamond.co.zw; f. 2003 by merger of National Insurance Co of Zimbabwe and Diamond Insurance of Zimbabwe; Chair. PHINEAS S. CHINGONO; Man. Dir GRACE MURADZIKWA.

Old Mutual PLC: POB 70, Highlands, Harare; tel. (4) 308400; fax (4) 308467; e-mail info@oldmutual.co.zw; internet www.oldmutual.co.zw; f. 1845; life and general insurance, asset management and banking services; Chair. M. J. LEVETT; CEO J. H. SUTCLIFFE.

ZB Life Assurance Ltd: Harare; tel. (4) 757535; fax (4) 757141; e-mail info@zb.co.zw; internet www.zb.co.zw; f. 1964 as Intermarket

ZIMBABWE

Life Assurance; subsidiary of ZB Financial Holdings Ltd; Man. Dir AMBROSE G. CHINEMBIRI.

Zimnat Lion Insurance Co Ltd: Zimnat House, cnr Nelson Mandela Ave and Third St, POB CY1155, Causeway, Harare; tel. (4) 707581; fax (4) 793441; e-mail enquiries@zimnatlion.co.zw; internet www.zimnatlion.co.zw; f. 1998 by merger of Zimnat Insurance Co Ltd and Lion of Zimbabwe Insurance; merged with AIG Zimbabwe in 2005; short-term insurance; Chair. SHINGAI MUTASA; Man. Dir ELISHA K. MOYO.

Trade and Industry

GOVERNMENT AGENCIES

Industrial Development Corpn of Zimbabwe (IDC): 93 Park Lane, POB CY1431, Causeway, Harare; tel. (4) 706971; fax (4) 250385; e-mail pr@idc.co.zw; internet www.idc.co.zw; f. 1963; state investment agency; Gen. Man. MIKE NDUDZO.

State Enterprises Restructuring Agency (SERA): Cecil House, 1st Floor, cnr Jason Moyo Ave and Third St, Private Bag 7728, Causeway, Harare; tel. (4) 729164; fax (4) 726317; e-mail communications@sera.co.zw; internet www.sera.co.zw; f. 1999 as Privatisation Agency of Zimbabwe; named changed as above in 2005; CEO ANDREW N. BVUMBE.

Zimbabwe Investment Authority (ZIA): Investment House, 109 Rotten Row, POB 5950, Harare; tel. (4) 757931; fax (4) 773843; e-mail info@zia.co.zw; internet www.zia.co.zw; f. 2007 by merger of Zimbabwe Investment Centre and the Export Processing Zones Authority; promotes domestic and foreign investment; CEO RICHARD MBAIWA.

ZimTrade: 904 Premium Close, Mt Pleasant Business Park, POB 2738, Harare; tel. (4) 369330; fax (4) 369244; e-mail info@zimtrade.co.zw; internet www.zimtrade.co.zw; f. 1991; national export promotion org.; Chair. J. D. CHIGARU; CEO HERBERT CHAKANYUKA.

DEVELOPMENT ORGANIZATIONS

Alternative Business Association (ABA): Stand No. 15295, cnr First St and Eighth Cres., Sunningdale, Harare; tel. (4) 589625; fax (4) 799600; f. 1999 to address urban and rural poverty; programme areas include: agriculture, micro-mining, cross-border trade, microenterprise devt and micro-finance; Dir ISRAEL MABHOU.

Indigenous Business Development Centre (IBDC): Pocket Bldg, 1st Floor, Jason Moyo Ave, POB 3331, Causeway, Harare; tel. (4) 748345; f. 1990; Pres. BEN MUCHECHE; Sec.-Gen. ENOCH KAMUSHINDA.

Indigenous Business Women's Organisation (IBWO): 73B Central Ave, POB 3710, Harare; tel. (4) 702076; fax (4) 614012; Pres. JANE MUTASA.

Zidco Holdings: 88 Robert Mugabe Rd, POB 1275, Harare; tel. (4) 253682; fax (4) 704391; f. 1981; fmrly Zimbabwe Devt Corpn; privatized in 2001; CEO (vacant).

Zimbabwe Human Rights NGO Forum: Blue Bridge, 8th Floor, Eastgate, POB 9077, Harare; tel. (4) 250511; fax (4) 250494; e-mail admin@hrforum.co.zw; internet www.hrforumzim.com; f. 1998; provides legal and 'psycho-social' assistance to the victims of organized violence; comprises 16 mem. orgs.

Zimbabwe Women's Bureau: 43 Hillside Rd, POB CR 120, Cranborne, Harare; tel. (4) 747809; fax (4) 707905; e-mail zwbtc@africaonline.co.zw; f. 1978; promotes entrepreneurial and rural community devt; Dir BERTHA MSORA.

CHAMBERS OF COMMERCE

Manicaland Chamber of Industries: 91 Third St, POB 92, Mutare; tel. (20) 61718; f. 1945; Pres. KUMBIRAI KATSANDE; 60 mems.

Mashonaland Chamber of Industries: POB 3794, Harare; tel. (4) 772763; fax (4) 750953; f. 1922; Pres. CHESTER MHENDE; 729 mems.

Matabeleland Chamber of Industries: 104 Parirenyatwa St, POB 2317, Bulawayo; tel. (9) 60642; fax (9) 60814; f. 1931; Pres. FELIX TSHUMA; 75 mems (2003).

Midlands Chamber of Industries: POB 213, Gweru; tel. (54) 2812; Pres. Dr BILL MOORE; 50 mems.

Zimbabwe National Chamber of Commerce (ZNCC): ZNCC Business House, 42 Harare St, POB 1934, Harare; tel. (4) 749335; fax (4) 750375; e-mail info@zncchq.co.zw; internet www.zncc.co.zw; f. 1983; represents small and medium businesses; Pres. LUXON ZEMBE; CEO CAIN MPOFU (acting); 2,500 mems; 8 brs.

INDUSTRIAL AND TRADE ASSOCIATIONS

Chamber of Mines of Zimbabwe: Stewart House, North Wing, 4 Central Ave, POB 712, Harare; tel. (4) 702841; fax (4) 707983; internet www.chamines.co.zw; f. 1939 by merger of the Rhodesian Chamber of Mines (Bulawayo) and Salisbury Chamber of Mines; Pres. Dr JACK MUREHWA; Chief Exec. and Sec. DAVID E. H. MURANGARI.

Confederation of Zimbabwe Industries (CZI): 31 Josiah Chinamano Ave, POB 3794, Harare; tel. (4) 251490; fax (4) 252424; e-mail cmsileya@czi.co.zw; internet www.czi.org.zw; f. 1957; Pres. CALLISTO M. JOKONYA; CEO CLIFFORD M. SILEYA.

Specialized affiliate trade associations include:

CropLife Zimbabwe: POB MP712, Mount Pleasant, Harare; tel. (4) 487211; fax (4) 487242; e-mail graeme.reid@bayer.co.zw; internet www.croplifeafrica.org; fmrly Agricultural Chemical Industry Asscn; Chair. MAX MAKUVISE.

Furniture Manufacturers' Association: c/o CZI, 31 Josiah Chinamano Ave, POB 3794, Harare; Pres. MATT SNYMAN.

Zimbabwe Association of Packaging: 17 Coventry Rd, Workington, Harare; tel. (4) 753800; fax (4) 882020.

Construction Industry Federation of Zimbabwe: Conquenar House, 256 Samora Machel Ave East, POB 1502, Harare; tel. (4) 746661; fax (4) 746937; e-mail cifoz@comone.co.zw; Pres. GILBERT MATIKA; CEO MARTIN CHINGAIRA; c. 460 mems.

Grain Marketing Board (GMB): Dura Bldg, 179–187 Samora Machel Ave, POB CY77, Harare; tel. (4) 701870; fax (4) 251294; e-mail marketing@gmbdura.co.zw; internet www.gmbdura.co.zw; f. 1931; responsible for maintaining national grain reserves and ensuring food security; CEO SAMUEL MUVUTI (acting).

Indigenous Petroleum Group of Zimbabwe (IPGZ): Harare; f. 2004 following split from Petroleum Marketers' Asscn of Zimbabwe; Chair. HUBERT NYAMBUYA; represents 68 importers.

Minerals Marketing Corpn of Zimbabwe (MMCZ): 90 Mutare Rd, Msasa, POB 2628, Harare; tel. (4) 487200; fax (4) 487161; e-mail administrator@mmcz.co.zw; internet www.mmcz.co.zw; f. 1982; sole authority for marketing of mineral production (except gold); Chair. MERCY MKUSHI (acting); Gen. Man. and CEO ONESIMO MAZAI MOYO.

Petroleum Marketers' Association of Zimbabwe (PMAZ): 142 Samora Machel Ave, Harare; tel. (4) 797556; represents private importers of petroleum-based products; Chair. GORDON MUSARIRA.

Timber Council of Zimbabwe: Conquenar House, 256 Samora Machel Ave, POB 3645, Harare; tel. (4) 746645; fax (4) 746013; Exec. Dir MARTIN DAVIDSON.

Tobacco Growers' Trust (TGT): POB AY331, Harare; tel. (4) 781167; fax (4) 781722; f. 2001; manages 20% of tobacco industry foreign exchange earnings on behalf of Reserve Bank of Zimbabwe; affiliated orgs include Zimbabwe Tobacco Asscn and Zimbabwe Farmers' Union; Chair. WILFANOS MASHINGAIDZE; Gen. Man. ALBERT JAURE.

Tobacco Industry and Marketing Board: POB 10214, Harare; tel. (4) 613310; fax (4) 613264; internet www.timb.co.zw; f. 1936; Chair. NJODZI MACHIRORI; CEO STANLEY MUTEPFA.

Tobacco Trade Association: c/o 4–12 Paisley Rd, POB ST180, Southerton, Harare; tel. (4) 773858; fax (4) 773859; e-mail tta@zol.co.zw; f. 1948; represents manufacturers and merchants.

Zimbabwe National Traditional Healers' Association (ZINATHA): Red Cross House, 2nd Floor, Rm 202, 98 Cameron St, POB 1116, Harare; tel. and fax (11) 606771; f. 1980; certifies and oversees traditional healers and practitioners of herbal medicine through the Traditional Medical Practitioners Council; promotes indigenous methods of prevention and treatment of HIV/AIDS; Pres. Prof. GORDON CHAVUNDUKA; 55,000 mems (2004).

Zimbabwe Tobacco Association (ZTA): 108 Prince Edward St, POB 1781, Harare; tel. (4) 796931; fax (4) 791855; e-mail fctobacco@zta.co.zw; internet www.zta.co.zw; f. 1928; represents growers; Pres. ANDREW FERREIRA; CEO RODNEY AMBROSE; c. 5,500 mems.

EMPLOYERS' ASSOCIATIONS

Commercial Farmers' Union (CFU): Agriculture House, cnr Adylinn Rd and Marlborough Dr., Marlborough; POB WGT390, Westgate, Harare; tel. (4) 309800; fax (4) 309849; e-mail aisd3@cfu.co.zw; internet www.cfu.co.zw; f. 1942; Pres. DOUGLAS TAYLOR-FREEME; Dir HENDRIK W. OLIVIER; 1,200 mems.

Cattle Producers' Association (CPA): Agriculture House, cnr Adylinn Rd and Marlborough Dr., Marlborough; POB WGT390, Westgate, Harare; tel. and fax (4) 309837; e-mail cpa@cfu.co.zw; Chair. MARYNA ERASMUS.

Coffee Growers' Association: Agriculture House, cnr Adylinn Rd and Marlborough Dr., Marlborough; POB WGT390, Westgate, Harare; tel. and fax (4) 750238; e-mail pres@cfu.co.zw; f. 1961; Chair. T. GIFFORD; Dir H. OLIVIER.

Commercial Cotton Growers' Association: Agriculture House, cnr Adylinn Rd and Marlborough Dr., Marlborough; POB WGT390, Westgate, Harare; tel. (4) 309800; fax (4) 309849; f. 1951; Chair. NEVILLE BROWN.

ZIMBABWE

Crops Association: Agriculture House, cnr Adylinn Rd and Marlborough Dr., Marlborough; POB WGT390, Westgate, Harare; tel. (4) 309843; fax (4) 309850; e-mail copa@cfu.co.zw; comprises the Commercial Oilseeds Producers' Asscn (COPA), the Zimbabwe Cereal Producers' Asscn (ZCPA) and the Zimbabwe Grain Producers' Asscn (ZGPA); Chair. DENNIS LAPHAM; Man. (Crops) GEORGE HUTCHISON; represents c. 800 producers.

National Association of Dairy Farmers: Agriculture House, cnr Adylinn Rd and Marlborough Dr., Marlborough; POB WGT390, Westgate, Harare; tel. (4) 309800; fax (4) 309837; e-mail nadf@cfu.co.zw; f. 1953; CEO ROB J. VAN VUUREN; 174 mems.

Ostrich Producers' Association of Zimbabwe (TOPAZ): Agriculture House, cnr Adylinn Rd and Marlborough Dr., Marlborough; POB WGT390, Westgate, Harare; tel. (4) 309800; fax (4) 309862; Chair. CEDRIC WILDE; Exec. Dir CLARE DAVIES.

Zimbabwe Association of Tobacco Growers (ZATG): Agriculture House, cnr Adylinn Rd and Marlborough Dr., Marlborough; POB WGT390, Westgate, Harare; f. 2001; Pres. JULIUS NGORIMA; CEO CANAAN RUSHIZHA; 1,500 mems.

Zimbabwe Poultry Association (Commercial Poultry Producers' Association): Agriculture House, cnr Adylinn Rd and Marlborough Dr., Marlborough; POB WGT390, Westgate, Harare; tel. (4) 309800; fax (4) 309849; Chair. PETER DRUMMOND; represents c. 200 producers.

Employers' Confederation of Zimbabwe (EMCOZ): Stewart House, 4 Central Ave, 2nd Floor, POB 158, Harare; tel. (4) 739647; fax (4) 739630; e-mail emcoz@emcoz.co.zw; Pres. DAVID GOVERE; Exec. Dir JOHN W. MUFUKARE.

Horticultural Promotion Council (HPC): 12 Maasdorp Ave, Alexandra Park; POB WGT290, Westgate, Harare; tel. (4) 745492; fax (4) 745480; Chief Exec. BASILIO SANDAMU; represents c. 1,000 producers.

Export Flower Growers' Association of Zimbabwe (EFGAZ): 12 Maasdorp Ave, Alexandra Park; POB WGT290, Westgate, Harare; tel. (4) 725130; fax (4) 795303; e-mail exflower@icon.co.zw; Dir MARY DUNPHY; c. 300 mems.

National Employment Council for the Construction Industry of Zimbabwe: St Barbara House, Nelson Mandela Ave and Leopold Takawira St, POB 2995, Harare; tel. (4) 773966; fax (4) 773967; CEO STANLEY R. MAKONI; represents over 19,000 mem. cos (2002).

National Employment Council for the Engineering and Iron and Steel Industry: Adven House, 5th Floor, cnr Inez Terrace and Speke Ave, POB 1922, Harare; tel. (4) 775144; fax (4) 775918; f. 1943; Gen. Sec. E. E. SHARPE.

Zimbabwe Association of Consulting Engineers (ZACE): 16 Murandy Sq. East, POB HG836, Highlands, Harare; tel. (4) 746010; fax (4) 746010; e-mail zace@mango.zw.

Zimbabwe Building Contractors' Association: Caspi House, Block C, 4 Harare St, Harare; tel. (4) 780411; represents small-scale building contractors; CEO CONCORDIA MUKODZI.

Zimbabwe Commercial Farmers' Union (ZCFU): 53 Third St, Mutare; tel. (20) 67163; fmrly Indigenous Commercial Farmers' Union; Pres. TREVOR GIFFORD; Dir JOHN MAUTSA; represents c. 11,000 black farmers (2003).

Zimbabwe Farmers' Union (ZFU): POB 3755, Harare; tel. (4) 704763; fax (4) 700829; Pres. SILAS HUNGWE; Exec. Dir KWENDA DZAVIRA; represents c. 200,000 small-scale black farmers (2002).

UTILITIES

Electricity

Rural Electrification Agency (REA): Office 720, 7th Floor, Megawatt House, 44 Samora Machel Ave, Harare; tel. (4) 770666; fax (4) 101661; e-mail emidzi@zesa.co.zw; f. 2002; manages the Rural Electrification Fund to expand and accelerate the electrification of rural areas; Chair. Dr SYDNEY GATA; CEO EMMANUEL MIDZI.

ZESA Holdings (Pvt) Ltd: 25 Samora Machel Ave, POB 377TA, Harare; tel. (4) 774508; fax (4) 774542; e-mail pr@zesa.net; internet www.zesa.co.zw; f. 2002 following restructure of Zimbabwe Electricity Supply Authority; operates one hydroelectric and four thermal power stations; CEO BEN RAFEMOYO; dependable generation capacity of 1,700 MW.

Zimbabwe Electricity Transmission Co (ZETCO): Electricity Centre, 8th Floor, 25 Samora Machel Ave, POB 1760, Harare; tel. (4) 774508; fax (4) 756179; e-mail zetconews@zetco.co.zw; internet www.zetco.org; f. 2002; develops, operates and maintains transmission infrastructure; Man. Dir (vacant).

Zimbabwe Electricity Regulatory Commission (ZERC): Century Towers, 14th Floor, 45 Samora Machel Ave, POB CY2585, Causeway, Harare; tel. (4) 780010; fax (4) 250696; e-mail admin@zerc.co.zw; internet www.zerc.co.zw; f. 2004 to oversee the unbundling from ZESA of the Zimbabwe Power Co, the Zimbabwe Electricity Transmission Co and the Zimbabwe Electricity Distribution Co; Dir-Gen. MAVIS CHIDZONGA.

Oil

National Oil Company of Zimbabwe (Pvt) Ltd (NOCZIM): NOCZIM House, 100 Leopold Takawira St, POB CY223, Causeway, Harare; tel. (4) 748543; fax (4) 748525; responsible for importing liquid fuels; Chair. CHARLES CHIPATO; Man. Dir ZVINECHIMWE CHURA.

Water

Zimbabwe National Water Authority (ZINWA): POB CY1215, Causeway, Harare; tel. and fax (4) 793139; e-mail mtetwa@utande.co.zw; f. 2001; fmrly Dept of Water, privatized in 2001; construction of dams, water supply, resources planning and protection; Chief Exec. ALBERT MUYAMBO.

TRADE UNIONS

Zimbabwe Congress of Trade Unions (ZCTU): Chester House, 9th Floor, Speke Ave and Third St, POB 3549, Harare; tel. (4) 794742; fax (4) 728484; internet www.zctu.co.zw; f. 1981 by merger of the African Trade Union Congress, the Nat. African Trade Union Congress, the Trade Union Congress of Zimbabwe, the United Trade Unions of Zimbabwe, the Zimbabwe Fed. of Labour and the Zimbabwe Trade Union Congress; affiliated to the Int. Trade Union Confed., the Org. of African Trade Union Unity and the Southern African Trade Union Co-ordination Council; co-ordinating org. for trade unions; Pres. LOVEMORE MATOMBO; Sec.-Gen. WELLINGTON CHIBEBE; c. 70,000 mems (2007).

In 2005 there were 35 affiliated unions. Affiliates with over 3,000 mems include:

Associated Mineworkers of Zimbabwe (AMWZ): St. Andrew's House, 4th Floor, Leopold Takawira St and Samora Machel Ave, POB 384, Harare; tel. (4) 700287; fax (4) 706543; e-mail amwz@mweb.co.zw; affiliated to the Int. Fed. of Chemical, Energy, Mine and Gen. Workers' Unions; Nat. Pres. TINAGO EDMUND RUZIVE; 10,000 mems (2002).

Commercial Workers' Union of Zimbabwe (CWUZ): CWUZ House, 15 Sixth Ave, Parktown; POB 3922 Harare; tel. (4) 664701; Pres. TAITUS MAGAYA; Gen. Sec. LOVEMORE MUSHONGA (acting); 22,000 mems (2003).

Communication and Allied Services Workers' Union of Zimbabwe (CASWUZ): Morgan House, 4th Floor, G. Silundika Ave, POB 739, Harare; tel. (4) 794763; e-mail caswuz@africaonline.co.zw; fmrly the Zimbabwe Post and Telecommunication Workers' Union; present name adopted 2002; Gen. Sec. REWARD S. MUSIWOKUWAYA; 5,700 mems (2002).

Federation of Food and Allied Workers' Union of Zimbabwe (FFAWUZ): c/o ZCTU, Chester House, 9th Floor, Speke Ave and Third St, POB 3549, Harare; tel. (4) 74150; f. 1962; affiliated to the Int. Union of Food, Agricultural, Hotel, Restaurant, Catering, Tobacco and Allied Workers' Asscns; Gen. Sec. LEONARD KUZONDISHAYA; 3,000 mems (2002).

General Agricultural and Plantation Workers' Union (GAPWUZ): POB 1952, Harare; tel. (4) 734141; fax (4) 797918; e-mail alb@cfu.co.zw; affiliated to the Building and Wood Workers' Int. and the Int. Union of Food, Agricultural, Hotel, Restaurant, Catering, Tobacco and Allied Workers' Asscns; Gen. Sec. GERTRUDE HAMBIRA; 5,000 mems (2002).

National Engineering Workers' Union (NEWU): St Barbara House, cnr Nelson Mandela Ave and Leopold Takawira St, Harare; tel. (4) 759597; fax (4) 759598; e-mail information@newu.org.zw; affiliated to the Int. Metalworkers' Fed.; Pres. ISAAC MATONGO; Gen. Sec. JAPHET MOYO; 9,000 mems (2002).

National Union of Clothing Industry Workers (NUCI): Union House, 139A Lobengula St with 13th Ave, POB RY28, Raylton, Bulawayo; tel. (9) 64432; fax (9) 71089; affiliated to the Int. Textile, Garment and Leather Workers' Fed.; Gen. Sec. FRED MPOFU; 4,500 mems (2002).

Progressive Teachers' Union of Zimbabwe (PTUZ): 14 McLaren Rd, Milton Park, Harare; POB CR620, Cranborne, Harare; tel. (4) 757746; fax (4) 741937; e-mail ptuz@mweb.co.zw; f. 1997; Pres. TAKAVAFIREI ZHOU; Sec.-Gen. RAYMOND MAJONGWE; 12,000 mems (2002).

Public Service Association: PSA House, 9 Livingstone Ave, POB 179, Harare; tel. (4) 726506; fax (4) 704971; e-mail psahq@mweb.co.zw; f. 1919; affiliated to the Public Services Int.; Pres. CECILIA ALEXANDER-KHOWA; Gen. Sec. MAXWELL KAITANO; 20,689 mems (2003).

Civil Service Employees' Association (CSEA): PSA House, 3rd floor, 9 Livingstone Ave, POB CY202, Causeway, Harare; tel. (4) 701123; fax (4) 707208; e-mail civilsea@africaonline.co

.zw; f. 1966; represents public sector employees; Pres. MASIMBA KADZIMU; Gen. Sec. GEORGE NASHO WILSON; 5,000 mems (2006).

Zimbabwe Amalgamated Railway Workers' Union (ZARU): Unity House, 13th Ave, Herbert Chitepo St, POB 556, Bulawayo 10; tel. (9) 60948; affiliated to the Int. Transport Workers' Fed.; Gen. Sec. GIDEON P. SHOKO; 7,000 mems (2002).

Zimbabwe Banks and Allied Workers' Union (ZIBAWU): 1 Meredith Dr., Eastlea, POB 966, Harare; tel. (4) 703744; e-mail bankunion@zol.co.zw; Pres. GEORGE KAWENDA; Gen. Sec. COLLEN GWIYO; 4,560 mems (2002).

Zimbabwe Catering and Hotel Workers' Union (ZCHWU): Nialis Bldg, 1st Floor, Manyika, POB 3913, Harare; tel. (4) 753338; affiliated to the Int. Union of Food, Agricultural, Hotel, Restaurant, Catering, Tobacco and Allied Workers' Asscns; 8,500 mems (2002).

Zimbabwe Chemical, Plastics and Allied Workers' Union (ZCPAWU): St Andrew's House, 2nd Floor, Leopold Takawira St and Samora Machel Ave, POB 4810, Harare; tel. (4) 796533; Gen. Sec. F. P. GOMBEDZA; 3,723 mems (2002).

Zimbabwe Construction and Allied Trades Workers' Union (ZCAWU): St Barbara House, Office 306, cnr Nelson Mandela Ave and Leopold Takawira St, POB 1291, Harare; tel. (4) 750159; fax (4) 773967; affiliated to the Building and Wood Workers' Int.; Gen. Sec. CHARLES GUMBO; 3,000 mems (2002).

Zimbabwe Electricity and Energy Workers' Union (ZEEWU): Crossroads House, 43 Julius Nyere Way, POB 5537, Harare; tel. and fax (4) 724430; e-mail zeewu@comone.co.zw; affiliated to the Int. Fed. of Chemical, Energy, Mine and Gen. Workers' Unions and the Building and Wood Workers' Int.; Pres. ANGELINE CHITAMBO; 3,075 mems (2002).

Zimbabwe Furniture, Timber and Allied Trades Union (ZFTATU): St Andrew's House, 4th Floor, Samora Machel Ave, POB 4793, Harare; tel. (4) 728056; fax (4) 737686; e-mail invioftbb@yahoo.com; affiliated to the Building and Wood Workers' Int.; Gen. Sec. L. CHISHAKWE; 3,500 mems (2002).

Zimbabwe Graphical Workers' Union (ZGWU): 6 Harare St, POB 494, Harare; tel. (4) 775627; fax (4) 775727; represents employees in the printing and packaging industries; Gen. Sec. MADZIVO CHIMHUKA; 5,000 mems (2005).

Zimbabwe Leather Shoe and Allied Workers' Union (ZLSAWU): POB 4450, Harare; tel. (4) 727925; fax (4) 727926; affiliated to the Int. Textile, Garment and Leather Workers' Fed.; Gen. Sec. ISIDORE MANHANDO ZINDOGA; 6,745 mems (2002).

Zimbabwe Textile Workers' Union (ZTWU): 50 Jason Moyo Ave, Pockets Bldg, 2nd Floor, South Wing, Hillside, POB 10245, Harare; tel. (4) 770226; fax (4) 758233; e-mail ztwu@mweb.co.zw; affiliated to the Int. Textile, Garment and Leather Workers' Fed.; Gen. Sec. SILAS KUVEYA; 11,636 mems (2004).

Zimbabwe Tobacco Industry Workers' Union (ZTIWU): St Andrew's House, 2nd Floor, Samora Machel Ave, POB 2757, Harare; tel. (4) 702339; Gen. Sec. ESTEVAO CUMBULANE; 3,000 mems (2002).

Zimbabwe Urban Councils Workers' Union (ZUCWU): POB CY 1859, Causeway, Harare; tel. (4) 729412; f. 1990; represents workers in engineering, housing and community services, health and emergency services, and clerical and treasury services; affiliated to the Public Services Int.; Pres. SIMON TAYALI; Gen. Sec. MOSES TSHIMKENI-MAHLANGU; 10,200 mems (2003).

Zimbabwe Federation of Trade Unions (ZFTU): Makombe Complex, Causeway, Harare; f. 1996 as alternative to ZCTU; 23 affiliated unions (2006); Gen. Sec. ADAMS VERENGA.

Affiliated unions include:

Zimbabwe Teachers' Union (ZITU): POB GV1, Glen View, Harare; tel. (4) 692454; fax (4) 708929; f. 2002; Gen. Sec. SIMPLISIO K. MATUMBA.

Non-affiliated Unions

Zimbabwe National Students' Union (ZINASU): 53 Hebert Chitepo Ave, Harare; tel. (4) 788135; fax (4) 793246; e-mail zinasu@gmail.com; internet www.zinasu.org; represents students in more than 43 tertiary institutions; Pres. CLEVER BERE; Nat. Co-ordinator BENJAMIN NYANDORO; c. 260,000 mems (2006).

Zimbabwe Nurses' Association (ZINA): 47 Livingstone Ave, POB 2610, Harare; tel. and fax (4) 700479; e-mail zimnurse@mweb.co.zw; f. 1980; affiliated to the Public Services Int.; Pres. DOREEN CHORUMA; 4,500 mems (2003).

Zimbabwe Teachers' Association (ZIMTA): POB 1440, Harare; tel. (4) 728438; fax (4) 791042; e-mail zimta@telco.co.zw; affiliated to Education Int.; Pres. TENDAI CHIKOWORE; Sec.-Gen. RICHARD GUNDANI (acting); 55,000 mems (2004).

Transport

RAILWAYS

In 1998 the rail network totalled 2,592 km, of which 313 km was electrified. Trunk lines run from Bulawayo south to the border with Botswana, connecting with the Botswana railways system, which, in turn, connects with the South African railways system; north-west to the Victoria Falls, where there is a connection with Zambia Railways; and north-east to Harare and Mutare connecting with the Mozambique Railways' line from Beira. From a point near Gweru, a line runs to the south-east, making a connection with the Mozambique Railways' Limpopo line and with the Mozambican port of Maputo. A connection runs from Rutenga to the South African Railways system at Beitbridge. A 320-km line from Beitbridge to Bulawayo was opened in 1999.

National Railways of Zimbabwe (NRZ): cnr Fife St and 10th Ave, POB 596, Bulawayo; tel. (9) 363716; fax (9) 363502; internet www.nrz.co.zw; f. 1899; reorg. 1967; privatization under way; Chair. Brig. DOUGLAS NYIKAYARAMBA; Gen. Man. Air Commodore MIKE TICHAFA KARAKADZAI.

ROADS

In 2002 the road system in Zimbabwe totalled an estimated 97,267 km; some 18,481 km of the total network was paved. In December 2005 tollgates were introduced at the borders to raise funds to maintain the road network.

CIVIL AVIATION

AirZim operates an effective monopoly over air travel and transport within Zimbabwe. International and domestic air services connect most of the larger towns.

Civil Aviation Authority of Zimbabwe (CAAZ): Harare Int. Airport Terminal, Level 3, Private Bag CY7716, Causeway, Harare; tel. (4) 585073; fax (4) 585112; e-mail ais@caaz.co.zw; internet www.caaz.co.zw; f. 1999; operates eight airports incl. Harare Int. Airport and Joshua Mqabuko Nkomo Int. Airport (fmrly Bulawayo Airport); CEO DAVID CHAWOTA.

Air Zimbabwe (Pvt) Ltd (AirZim): POB AP1, Harare Airport, Harare; tel. (4) 575111; fax (4) 575068; internet www.airzimbabwe.com; f. 1967; scheduled domestic and international passenger and cargo services to Africa, Australia and Europe; plans were announced in April 2006 to separate operations, creating the new cos Air Zimbabwe Technical, Air Zimbabwe Cargo, Nat. Handling Services and Galileo Zimbabwe, in addition to Air Zimbabwe; Chair. MIKE BIMHA; CEO Dr PETER CHIKUMBA.

Tourism

The principal tourist attractions are the Victoria Falls, the Kariba Dam and the Hwange Game Reserve and National Park. Zimbabwe Ruins, near Fort Victoria, and World's View, in the Matapos Hills, are also of interest. There is climbing and trout-fishing in the Eastern Districts, around Umtali. In 2006 2,286,572 tourists visited Zimbabwe; revenue from tourism in that year totalled US $338m. in 2006.

Zimbabwe Tourism Authority (ZTA): Samora Machel Ave, POB CY286, Causeway, Harare; tel. (4) 752570; fax (4) 758826; e-mail info@ztazim.co.zw; internet www.zimbabwetourism.co.zw; f. 1984; promotes tourism domestically and from abroad; Chair. EMMANUEL FUNDIRA.

Associations licensed by the ZTA include:

Safari Operators Association of Zimbabwe (SOAZ): 18 Walter Hill Ave, Eastlea, Harare; tel. (4) 702402; fax (4) 707306; e-mail enquiries@soaz.net; internet www.soaz.net; Chair. JACOB MUDENDA.

INDEX OF TERRITORIES IN VOLUMES I AND II

	Page
Abu Dhabi	4640
Afghanistan	491
Ajman	4640
Åland Islands	1790
Albania	517
Alderney	4737
Algeria	537
American Samoa	4906
Andorra	564
Angola	572
Anguilla	4746
Antarctic Territory, Australian	694
Antarctic Territory, British	4760
Antarctica	591
Antigua and Barbuda	593
Argentina	603
Armenia	632
Aruba	3345
Ascension	4803
Ashmore Islands	694
Australia	650
Australian Antarctic Territory	694
Austria	696
Azad Kashmir	3565
Azerbaijan	725
Bahamas	744
Bahrain	755
Baker Island	4925
Bangladesh	775
Barbados	801
Barbuda	593
Belarus	811
Belau (see Palau)	
Belgium	831
Belize	860
Benin	871
Bermuda	4753
Bhutan	888
Bolivia	905
Bosnia and Herzegovina	926
Botswana	951
Bouvetøya	3499
Brazil	966
Brecqhou	4737
British Antarctic Territory	4760
British Indian Ocean Territory	4761
British Virgin Islands	4762
Brunei	1000
Bulgaria	1012
Burkina Faso	1032
Burma (see Myanmar)	
Burundi	1049
Caicos Islands	4805
Cambodia	1068
Cameroon	1090
Canada	1108
Cape Verde	1149
Cartier Island	694
Cayman Islands	4769
Central African Republic	1158
Ceuta	4203
Chad	1173
Channel Islands	4734
Chile	1191
China, People's Republic	1217
China (Taiwan)	1305
Christmas Island	686

	Page
Cocos Islands	689
Colombia	1339
Comoros	1364
Congo, Democratic Republic	1376
Congo, Republic	1396
Cook Islands	3394
Coral Sea Islands Territory	695
Costa Rica	1412
Côte d'Ivoire	1429
Croatia	1452
Cuba	1472
Cyprus	1496
Czech Republic	1522
Democratic People's Republic of Korea	2649
Democratic Republic of the Congo	1376
Denmark	1542
Djibouti	1579
Dominica	1588
Dominican Republic	1597
Dronning Maud Land	3499
Dubai	4640
East Timor (see Timor-Leste)	
Ecuador	1615
Egypt	1638
El Salvador	1670
Equatorial Guinea	1687
Eritrea	1697
Estonia	1710
Ethiopia	1729
Falkland Islands	4777
Faroe Islands	1567
Federated States of Micronesia	3128
Fiji	1750
Finland	1766
Former Yugoslav republic of Macedonia	2920
France	1794
French Guiana	1850
French Polynesia	1880
French Southern and Antarctic Territories	1908
Fujairah	4640
Futuna Islands	1902
Gabon	1921
Gambia	1937
Georgia	1951
Germany	1975
Ghana	2025
Gibraltar	4783
Great Britain	4660
Greece	2044
Greenland	1573
Grenada	2065
Grenadines	3896
Guadeloupe	1857
Guam	4912
Guatemala	2075
Guernsey	4734
Guinea	2095
Guinea-Bissau	2112
Guyana	2126
Haiti	2139
Heard Island	695
Herm	4737

INDEX OF TERRITORIES IN VOLUMES I AND II

	Page
Herzegovina	926
Holy See	4976
Honduras	2160
Hong Kong	1269
Howland Island	4925
Hungary	2176
Iceland	2196
India	2210
Indian Ocean Territory, British	4761
Indonesia	2270
Iran	2310
Iraq	2344
Ireland	2380
Isle of Man	4741
Israel	2406
Italy	2450
Ivory Coast (see Côte d'Ivoire)	
Jamaica	2488
Jan Mayen	3499
Japan	2504
Jarvis Island	4927
Jersey	4738
Jethou	4737
Johnston Atoll	4925
Jordan	2555
Kazakhstan	2597
Keeling Islands	689
Kenya	2617
Kingman Reef	4925
Kiribati	2640
Korea, Democratic People's Republic	2649
Korea, Republic	2679
Kosovo	2714
Kuwait	2726
Kyrgyzstan	2747
Laos	2765
Latvia	2781
Lebanon	2799
Lesotho	2830
Liberia	2843
Libya	2860
Liechtenstein	2880
Lihou	4737
Lithuania	2888
Luxembourg	2908
Macao	1291
Macedonia, former Yugoslav republic	2920
Madagascar	2939
Malawi	2957
Malaysia	2974
Maldives	3013
Mali	3027
Malta	3044
Man, Isle of	4741
Marshall Islands	3056
Martinique	1865
Mauritania	3065
Mauritius	3081
Mayotte	1892
McDonald Islands	695
Melilla	4208
Mexico	3097
Micronesia, Federated States	3128
Midway Atoll	4925
Miquelon	1898
Moldova	3136
Monaco	3155
Mongolia	3162

	Page
Montenegro	3186
Montserrat	4791
Morocco	3195
Mozambique	3220
Myanmar	3239
Namibia	3266
Nauru	3284
Navassa Island	4925
Nepal	3292
Netherlands	3319
Netherlands Antilles	3352
Nevis	3875
New Caledonia	1909
New Zealand	3364
Nicaragua	3408
Niger	3428
Nigeria	3446
Niue	3401
Norfolk Island	690
North Korea	2649
Northern Areas (Pakistan)	3565
Northern Ireland	4660
Northern Mariana Islands	4887
Norway	3472
Oman	3500
Pakistan	3516
Palau	3566
Palestinian Autonomous Areas	3574
Palmyra	4925
Panama	3601
Papua New Guinea	3620
Paraguay	3641
People's Republic of China	1217
Peru	3659
Peter I Øy	3499
Philippines	3683
Pitcairn Islands	4798
Poland	3722
Portugal	3747
Príncipe	3922
Puerto Rico	4893
Qatar	3774
Ras al-Khaimah	4640
Republic of China (Taiwan)	1305
Republic of the Congo	1396
Republic of Korea	2679
Réunion	1872
Romania	3792
Ross Dependency	3389
Russian Federation	3816
Rwanda	3857
Saint-Barthélemy	1897
Saint Christopher and Nevis	3875
Saint Helena	4800
Saint Lucia	3885
Saint-Martin	1897
Saint Pierre and Miquelon	1898
Saint Vincent and the Grenadines	3896
Samoa	3906
San Marino	3915
São Tomé and Príncipe	3922
Sark	4737
Saudi Arabia	3932
Senegal	3957
Serbia	3981
Seychelles	4006
Sharjah	4640

5105

www.europaworld.com

INDEX OF TERRITORIES IN VOLUMES I AND II

	Page		Page
Sierra Leone	4014	Turkey	4530
Singapore	4030	'Turkish Republic of Northern Cyprus'	1496
Slovakia	4056	Turkmenistan	4568
Slovenia	4076	Turks and Caicos Islands	4805
Solomon Islands	4093	Tuvalu	4585
Somalia	4106		
South Africa	4125		
South Georgia	4805	Uganda	4592
South Korea	2679	Ukraine	4610
South Sandwich Islands	4805	Umm al-Qaiwain	4640
Spain	4160	United Arab Emirates	4640
Spanish North Africa	4203	United Kingdom	4660
Sri Lanka	4213	United States of America	4812
St Kitts (Saint Christopher)	3875	United States Virgin Islands	4919
Sudan	4242	Uruguay	4927
Suriname	4267	Uzbekistan	4945
Svalbard	3497		
Swaziland	4280		
Sweden	4294	Vanuatu	4964
Switzerland	4320	Vatican City	4976
Syria	4347	Venezuela	4986
		Viet Nam	5012
Taiwan	1305	Virgin Islands, British	4762
Tajikistan	4373	Virgin Islands, US	4919
Tanzania	4392		
Thailand	4412	Wake Island	4926
Timor-Leste	4445	Wallis and Futuna Islands	1902
Tobago	4493	Western Samoa (see Samoa)	
Togo	4464		
Tokelau	3389	Yemen	5041
Tonga	4482		
Trinidad and Tobago	4493	Zambia	5063
Tristan da Cunha	4804	Zimbabwe	5080
Tunisia	4511		